S0-BBY-936

THE GENEVA BIBLE

THE GENEVA BIBLE

A facsimile of the 1560 edition

With an introduction by Lloyd E. Berry

The University of Wisconsin Press
Madison, Milwaukee, and London

1969

Published by
The University of Wisconsin Press
Box 1379, *Madison, Wisconsin* 53701

The University of Wisconsin Press, Ltd.
27-29 *Whitfield Street, London, W.* 1

Printed in the United States of America by
The Meriden Gravure Co., Meriden, Connecticut

SBN 299-05251-6 *cloth,* 299-05259-1 *morocco; LC* 75-81318

Preface

There is no question that the publication of the Geneva Bible in 1560 was a landmark in the history of the English Bible. This Bible is second in importance only to the Authorized Version of 1611, and its influence in sixteenth- and seventeenth-century England, Scotland, and New England was considerable.

Even after the publication of the Authorized Version, the Geneva Bible continued to be printed until 1644, the date of the last known edition. The only reprints since that time are of the 1557 Whittingham New Testament in Bagster's *Hexapla* (London, 1841) and the 1560 New Testament in Weigle's *Octapla* (London, 1962). To reproduce only the text, however, would be to ignore one of the most important features of the Geneva Bible—the marginal notes. A facsimile reproduction is thus the only practicable means of reprinting the complete Geneva Bible at a less than exorbitant cost.

My introduction reviews briefly the earlier English translations of the Bible, the historical context of the Geneva Bible's preparation, the scholarship of its translators, and the publication and subsequent history and influence of this Bible, closing with a location guide to copies of the 1560 edition in North America and Great Britain. In other words, the purpose of the introduction has been to aid the general reader who may not be familiar with the history of the Geneva Bible. A brief bibliography of secondary materials has been appended.

I would suggest that much remains to be done by way of scholarship: the Geneva Bible's influence on individual literary authors and preachers of the sixteenth and seventeenth centuries, the theology of the Bible itself, a more comprehensive study of the marginal notes than has yet been done—these are just a few of the projects that come to mind. But, as scholars who were consulted about this facsimile have said, the primary purpose in publishing such an edition is to make a valuable tool readily accessible.

I would like to acknowledge my deepest gratitude to Mr. William Scheide and to Dr. H. Richard Archer, Custodian of the Chapin Library at Williams College, who permitted the use of their copies of the 1560 Geneva Bible for this edition. I have seen twenty-one of the twenty-four copies of this edition located in the United States and Canada, and the Scheide and Chapin copies are the only two that are suitable for a facsimile edition. Other copies either lacked various leaves, or were badly stained or foxed or underlined, or were so closely cropped that many of the running titles had been shaved.

Mr. John Peckham of the Meriden Gravure Company has been very helpful to me in explaining the technical aspects of the photographic method used in this facsimile. Dr. J. David Alexander very kindly lent me a copy of his thesis on the Geneva Bible; he and Professors Madeleine Doran, Roland Mushat Frye, William Haller, and Robert M. Kingdon have been kind enough to read and comment on my introduction. It goes without saying, however, that I alone am responsible for faults that remain.

To my wife I owe more than I can adequately express, for her encouragement in this undertaking as in all previous ones.

LLOYD E. BERRY

Urbana, Illinois
August 1, 1968

Introduction to the Facsimile Edition

From early Anglo-Saxon times to the present there have been translations of the Bible, or of parts of it, into English; and almost without exception each translation has met with opposition.

In the Anglo-Saxon period there were translations of the Hexateuch, the Psalms, and the New Testament into Old English, mainly in the time of Ælfric. In the Middle English period the translation of the entire Bible into English was accomplished by Wycliffe and his followers (ca. 1382), and for the next two and one-half centuries the so-called Purvey Revision of the Wycliffe Bible (ca. 1388) was *the* English Bible. The survival of over two hundred manuscripts of this version indicates that there was indeed a demand for an English version despite the action of the Provincial Council at Oxford in 1408 prohibiting English translations of the Bible on pain of excommunication and trial for heresy.[1]

The Old and Middle English translations were based on the Latin Vulgate text of the Bible. Perhaps the most important advance in the translations of the Bible in the sixteenth century was that, beginning with Tyndale, all translators except Coverdale returned to the Greek and Hebrew originals.

William Tyndale, a graduate of Oxford (B.A. 1512, M.A. 1515) and afterwards a student at Cambridge, began his career as a tutor to the children of Sir John Walsh in Old Sodbury in Gloucestershire, where he translated Erasmus' *Enchiridion Militis Christiani* (*The Christian Soldier's Handbook*). One of the principal themes of this book is that Christians have individual responsibility to study the New Testament and to count it the final authority for matters of life and doctrine. No doubt it was during his time as tutor that Tyndale conceived of translating the Bible, for he is reported to have said then to a learned man: "If God spare my life, ere many years I will cause a boy that driveth the plough should know more of the scripture than thou dost." However, the prohibition of the Council at Oxford was still in effect, and only by the permission of a bishop could a translation be prepared. So in 1523 Tyndale went to London

1. Alfred W. Pollard, ed., *Records of the English Bible* (London, 1911), pp. 79–81.

to seek the patronage of Cuthbert Tunstall, the Bishop of London. Tunstall refused to support the project, but a wealthy merchant, Humphrey Monmouth, agreed to do so. Tyndale soon became convinced, however, that England was not a safe place to work; as he recorded in his preface to his translation of the Pentateuch, printed in 1530, he "understode at the laste not only that there was no rowme in my lorde of londons palace to translate the new testament, but also that there was no place to do it in all englonde, as experience doth now openly declare."

In 1524 Tyndale left England, settled for a time in Hamburg and in Wittenberg, and the next year moved to Cologne, where he finished his translation of the New Testament and where its printing was undertaken at the press of Peter Quentell. The Senate of Cologne learned of the work and forbade its production, with the consequence that only one copy survives.[2] Tyndale fled to Worms, where in 1526 an octavo edition of his New Testament was printed. His translation of the Pentateuch appeared in 1530, followed by the Book of Jonah in 1531 and the revised New Testament in 1534. He had completed the translation of the historical books of the Old Testament from Joshua to II Chronicles before his martyrdom in 1536.

Tyndale encountered opposition not so much because his work was unauthorized as because his prefaces, notes, and choice of ecclesiastical words (e.g., *repent* for *penance*, *congregation* for *church*) were simply unacceptable to the Church of England, and because he was reluctant to compromise on these matters. The excellence of his translation rested upon his style and idiom no less than upon his scholarship; and the importance of his work in the history of the English Bible is common knowledge: all subsequent translations of the Bible into English show Tyndale's influence.[3]

In December 1534, the Synod of Canterbury, under the leadership of Archbishop Thomas Cranmer, petitioned Henry VIII "to decree that the holy scripture shall be translated into the vulgar English tongue by certain upright and learned men to be named by the said most illustrious king."[4] Encouraged by Cranmer and Thomas Cromwell, Miles Coverdale translated the entire Bible and published it

2. See the facsimile edition with an introduction by Alfred W. Pollard (Oxford, 1926).

3. For further information on Tyndale, see John F. Mozley, *William Tyndale* (London, 1937); S. L. Greenslade, ed., *The Cambridge History of the Bible* (Cambridge, England, 1963), pp. 141–147; F. F. Bruce, *The English Bible* (New York, 1961), pp. 28–52; H. Wheeler Robinson, ed., *The Bible in Its Ancient and English Versions* (Oxford, 1940), pp. 149–167.

4. Pollard, *Records*, p. 177.

without formal authority in 1535. Coverdale was not the scholar that Tyndale was and did not translate directly from the Hebrew and Greek but instead, as he himself states in his preface, used the Vulgate, Pagninus' Latin version of 1528, Luther's translation, the Zurich Bible of 1531 and 1534, and the translations of Tyndale. The Coverdale Bible was reprinted, with some revision, in 1537 in England by James Nicholson of Southwark, thus becoming the first complete Bible to be printed in England. It furthermore claimed to have the king's license. Coverdale's Bible was the first to introduce chapter summaries and to separate the books of the Apocrypha from the canonical Old Testament and to place them at the end of the Old Testament.

Also in 1537, there appeared a Bible "truly and purely translated into English by Thomas Matthew." It is generally accepted that the editor was Tyndale's friend John Rogers, the first of the Marian martyrs. This Bible, "set forth with the King's most gracious licence" no doubt through the efforts of Archbishop Cranmer and Thomas Cromwell, was based on Tyndale, printing for the first time his translation of Joshua through II Chronicles and making use of a revision of the Coverdale Bible for the rest of the Old Testament. More important than the text were the "aids," which included a church calendar, an exhortation to the study of the Bible, a summary of the chief doctrines of the Bible, and a concordance—all clearly the influence of Lefèvre's French Bible, 1534, and Olivetan's French Bible, 1535. There were notes to help in understanding the Bible, taken principally from Tyndale, Lefèvre, and Olivetan.

By the end of 1537 there were thus two Bibles with the king's license, and the Bible now circulated without hindrance. But neither the Coverdale nor the Matthew translation was totally satisfactory —the Coverdale because it was not translated from the originals, and the Matthew because of the controversiality of its notes and prologues. Possibly on Cromwell's order, Coverdale revised the Matthew Bible, using Münster's annotated Hebrew-Latin Bible of 1535 to correct the Old Testament and Erasmus' Greek New Testament to correct the New Testament. Coverdale promised "to avoid any private opinion or contentious words," and the "Great Bible" was printed without notes or the other "aids" of the Matthew Bible. The printing was undertaken in Paris in 1538, but after the Inquisitor-General of France ordered confiscation of the sheets, the printers—with type, presses, and as many sheets as they could rescue—returned to England, where the Bible was published in 1539 by Grafton and Whitchurch and the patent for printing was given to Cromwell for five years. In April 1540, a revised edition of the Great Bible appeared, with a preface by Archbishop Cranmer and with the words "This is the Bible appointed to the use of the churches" on the title page. This Bible became the official Bible of the English Church and remained so until the Bishops' Bible of 1568 appeared.

In May 1541, Henry VIII issued a proclamation that "in al and synguler paryshe churches, there shuld be prouyded by a certen day nowe expyred, at the costes of the curates and paryshioners, Bybles conteynynge the olde and newe Testament, in the Englyshe tounge, to be fyxed and set vp openlye in euery of the sayd paryshe churches."[5] However, from 1541 until Henry's death in 1547, the more conservative elements of the church attempted to limit the use of the English Bible, and their efforts were partly successful, for in 1546 Henry prohibited the use of Tyndale or any other annotated Bible in English.

In the first year of his reign, Edward VI renewed the injunction that a Bible in English should be placed in each church, with the result that there were many new editions of the Great Bible. Furthermore, in 1549, the Book of Common Prayer was published in English, and thus for the first time the entire worship of the church was conducted in English. A revised edition of the Book of Common Prayer was issued in 1552, the year before Edward's death.

II

With the accession of Mary in 1553, the Protestants in England found themselves in perilous condition. John Rogers and Thomas Cranmer were imprisoned in the first year of her reign and subsequently executed; Miles Coverdale and others fled for safety to the Continent. Before the end of Queen Mary's reign between 700 and 1,000 Englishmen had settled in Europe, mainly in Germany and Switzerland. The fact that such a relatively small number preferred exile to conformity belies the significance of the exiles on two counts: (1) theologically this group represented the most liberal faction of English Protestantism, although they disagreed as to how much the Church of England should be reformed, and (2) from this group came many of the political and religious leaders of Queen Elizabeth's reign.[6]

The colonies of English exiles in Germany and Switzerland differed one from another in composition and in their experiences during exile. The Englishmen at Emden, for instance, seem to have made it a center for printing and distributing Protestant propaganda to the

5. Pollard, *Records*, p. 262.

6. Christina Hallowell Garrett, *The Marian Exiles* (Cambridge, England, 1938), and Charles Martin, *Les Protestants anglais* (Geneva, 1915), are particularly useful books on the subject of the exiles.

faithful in England. The settlement at Strasbourg, one of the most stable, was important for the prominence of several of its members in Court and Church circles in England both before and after the exile. The Zurich group were all students, mostly from Cambridge or Oxford, and included William Cole, who later assisted in the Geneva Bible translation.

Basel attracted a number of exiles who matriculated at its university—among them the Geneva Bible translators Anthony Gilby and Christopher Goodman. It was at Basel that John Foxe wrote his *Book of Martyrs* and John Bale his *Scriptores Illustrium Catalogus*. With such vocal members as John Bale, the English church at Basel came to be noted for its disputes over ritual and ceremony. However, these controversies found their fullest expression not in Basel but in Frankfurt. Because of its influence upon the leaders of the group that produced the Geneva Bible, the English church at Frankfurt, as well as the one at Geneva, deserves some detailed attention here.[7]

The Marian exiles who settled in Frankfurt arrived there in June 1554, led by William Whittingham, Edmund Sutton, and Thomas Wood. Having petitioned for and received permission to reside in Frankfurt, they were further given leave to worship in the Church of the White Virgins; they shared the use of this church with a group of French Huguenots who had arrived several months earlier. The Englishmen elected deacons and ministers (including John Knox) and agreed upon using the second prayer book of Edward VI (1552) in their worship (*Brief Discourse*, pp. 24–25).

On August 2 Whittingham and others wrote a general letter to the various English congregations in Germany and Switzerland "to persuade them . . . to repair thither, that they might all together . . . both lament their former wickedness, and also be thankful to their merciful Father that had given them such a Church in a strange land wherein they might hear God's Word truly preached, the Sacraments rightly ministered, and Discipline used; which in their own country could never be obtained" (*ibid.*, p. 25). The tone and wording of this letter initiated the long controversy between the group led by Whittingham at Frankfurt and the leaders of the other churches, but particularly those of Strasbourg. The controversy deepened over the order of service. Some of the Frankfurt congregation objected to parts of the English prayer book and preferred

7. The main source of information about the English church at Frankfurt is *A Brief Discourse of the Troubles at Frankfort* (1575), cited hereafter in the text; page references are to the edition published in London, 1907, ed. Edward Arber. William Whittingham has generally been assumed to be the author; however, Patrick Collinson in "The Authorship of *A Brieff Discours off the Troubles Begonne at Franckford*," *Journal of Ecclesiastical History*, IX (1958), 188–208, argues for Thomas Wood, one of the original Frankfurt exiles.

the Genevan order of Calvin. Knox would not use the Genevan order unless Strasbourg and Zurich would give their consent and approval, nor would he use the English Book of Common Prayer, which he thought contained errors. Knox, Whittingham, and others drew up an outline of the English prayer book and sent it to Calvin for his comments (*ibid.*, pp. 44–49). Calvin responded on January 20, 1555: "In the Liturgy of England, I see that there were many tolerable foolish things. By these words I mean, that there was not that purity which was to be desired.... I cannot tell what they mean which so greatly delight in the leavings of Popish dregs" (*ibid.*, p. 51). No solution seemed possible, until the congregation appointed a committee led by Knox and Whittingham to draw up a compromise order of service. This was done and approved by the congregation on February 6, with the understanding that, should contention arise, the matter would be submitted to Calvin, Musculus, Martyr, Bullinger, and Viret, whose decision would be binding (*ibid.*, pp. 52–53).

The harmony thus achieved lasted only until the arrival from England of a group led by Dr. Richard Cox, who had aided in preparing both of the Edwardian prayer books. The ensuing dissension forced Knox to leave Frankfurt, after having been, in Calvin's words, "neither godly nor brotherly dealt withal" (*ibid.*, p. 79). Thereupon, the group that supported Knox decided to leave also and seek another place to worship; on August 27, 1554, William Williams, William Whittingham, Anthony Gilby, Christopher Goodman, Thomas Cole, John Foxe, William Kethe, and a number of others informed the congregation of their decision (*ibid.*, p. 81). John Foxe and a few others settled in Basel, but the greater number went to Geneva, where they were cordially received.

The English group settled in Geneva on October 13 and immediately requested permission to organize a church. Some difficulty was encountered, but Calvin interceded, and on November 11 the council of Geneva granted them the use of the Church of Marie la Neuve.[8] According to the records of the English church in Geneva, John Knox was elected pastor and Anthony Gilby and Christopher Goodman were appointed to preach the Word of God and administer the sacraments in the absence of John Knox.[9] William Williams and William Whittingham were elected seniors, or elders, of the congregation.

The choice of Geneva was a natural one for this particular group, whose members were in sympathy with the prevailing theological Protestantism of the city. Knox, Whittingham, and the other lead-

8. Martin, pp. 39–40.

9. Martin, p. 334.

ers of the Frankfurt church had already made it clear they preferred Calvin's order of service to the English prayer book; and they were influenced not only by Calvin but also by others in Calvin's academy, such as Theodore Beza. In his address to the reader in his 1557 translation of the New Testament, Whittingham called Geneva "the place where God hath appointed vs to dwel" and spoke of "the store of heauenly learning & judgement, which so abundeth in this Citie of Geneua, that iustely it may be called the patron and mirrour of true religion and godlynes."

Geneva in the 1550's was a center for biblical textual scholarship which resulted in new editions of the Greek and Hebrew texts (such as Estienne's Greek New Testament of 1551, which divided the text into verses for the first time), Estienne and Badius' edition of the Vulgate in 1555, Estienne's edition of 1556–57 which included Old Testament versions of the Vulgate, and Pagninus and Beza's version of the New Testament. Translations of the Scripture into Italian and Spanish were also published in Geneva in 1555 and 1556, respectively. There were at least twenty-two editions of French Bibles published in Geneva in the 1550's by such distinguished scholar-printers as Robert Estienne, Conrad Badius, Jean Crespin, Jean Girard, Nicholas Barbier, Thomas Courteau, and Jean Rivery.

So it is not surprising to find that the leaders of the English church in Geneva soon turned their attention to the study of the text of the Bible. Their great contribution was the production of the English Bible of 1560, more commonly known as the Geneva Bible.

III

In the introduction "To our beloved in the Lord," the translators of the Geneva Bible said that they were motivated to prepare a new translation because it behooved Christians to walk in the fear and love of God and this could be best done when one had knowledge of the Word of God. Therefore, they said, "we thoght that we colde bestowe our labours & studie in nothing which colde be more acceptable to God and comfortable to his Churche then in the translating of the holy Scriptures into our natiue tongue." Having decided to prepare the translation and having been greatly encouraged by the members of the church, they were with "feare and trembling . . . for the space of two yeres and more day and night occupied herein."

Who were these men who worked so diligently—and with remarkable speed—to produce the Bible? The translators do not identify themselves anywhere in the Bible, and Westcott is probably right in suggesting "they were several and perhaps not the same during the whole time."[10] William Whittingham has always been considered to have been the general editor, and the author of a contemporary life of Whittingham states that Miles Coverdale, Christopher Goodman, Anthony Gilby, Thomas Sampson, and William Cole were associated with Whittingham in the project.[11] Others have been added to this list by various scholars: John Knox, William Kethe, Rowland Hall, John Pullain, John Bodley, John Baron, and William Williams.[12]

A pertinent consideration is the time during which the translating was being done, since not all of these men were in Geneva during the "two yeres and more" devoted to the preparation of the Geneva Bible. In *The Boke of Psalmes* (published in 1559) the translators commented in the dedicatory epistle to Queen Elizabeth, dated February 10, 1559, that the entire Bible was "Praysed be God . . . in good readines."[13] This would indicate that most of the work on the Bible was done in 1558, and thus would limit the participation of Coverdale, Goodman, and Pullain, who were in Geneva for only a part of 1558. Another point is that many of the Englishmen returned to England in 1559 after Elizabeth's accession on November 17, 1558. A letter from Miles Coverdale to William Cole in Geneva, dated February 22, 1560, indicates that Gilby, Cole, Kethe, Baron, and Williams had remained with Whittingham to finish the work on the Bible and to see it through the press.[14] In all probability, then, Whittingham was the general editor and was responsible for the New Testament. It is also probable that Anthony Gilby, known for his ability in Hebrew and for his commentaries on various Old Testament books, was responsible for the Old Testament. Cole, Kethe, and Baron no doubt participated actively; and Goodman, Pullain, Coverdale, and Sampson may have participated from time to time while they were in Geneva. John Knox probably did not have much to do with the actual work, since in addition to his position as minister of the English church in Geneva, he also traveled in France and elsewhere encouraging Protestant groups.

William Williams and John Bodley, both members of the English congregation, engaged in printing while in Geneva and may have assisted Rowland Hall, also a member of the congregation, in the

10. Brooke F. Westcott, *A General View of the History of the English Bible* (New York, 1927), p. 91.

11. *The Life of Mr. William Whittingham*, ed. Mary A. E. Green (London, 1870), pp. 9–10.

12. For biographical accounts of these persons, see Garrett; see also the *Dictionary of National Biography*.

13. See John David Alexander, "The Genevan Version of the English Bible" (unpublished D.Phil. thesis, Oxford University, 1956), p. 85.

14. John F. Mozley, *Coverdale and His Bibles* (London, 1953), p. 316.

printing of the Bible.[15] On his return to England in 1560 Bodley petitioned for and received the sole printing rights to the Geneva Bible for seven years, and in 1565 Archbishop Parker and Bishop Grindal recommended that his privilege be extended for another twelve years.[16]

The Geneva Bible was thus the culmination of the work of the English scholars who had begun as early as 1556 to devote themselves to translating the Scriptures into English. The congregation at Geneva already had the English version of Calvin's liturgy, but needed translations of the New Testament and Psalms suitable for their worship. Two books published in 1557 seemed the logical and first steps toward producing a complete Bible:

(1) On June 10, 1557, there appeared a New Testament in English: "The Newe Testament of our Lord Iesus Christ. Conferred diligently with the Greke, and best approued translations. With the arguments, aswel before the chapters, as for euery Boke & Epistle, also diuersities of readings, and moste proffitable annotations of all harde places: whereunto is added a copious Table. . . . At Geneva. Printed by Conrad Badius M.D.LVII." The text is in roman type, not black letter; the Scripture is divided into verses; and, as the title page indicates, there are ample explanatory and textual notes. In addition, italic type is used to indicate words supplied by the translators that were not in the original. The Greek texts referred to were no doubt Stephanus' (Estienne's) Greek New Testament of 1551 and Beza's of 1556. The English text most heavily relied on was Tyndale's New Testament, most likely the edition published by Richard Jugge in 1552.

This was the only English translation to appear during the reign of Queen Mary, and although the preface is not signed, most scholars agree that the translator and reviser was William Whittingham. As has been mentioned earlier, Whittingham was one of the leaders of the English congregation in Geneva from its inception: in 1556 and 1557 he served as elder of the church; in 1559 he became deacon. It is reasonable to assume that Whittingham's experience in translating the New Testament led him to request that the church not elect him to a responsible position of leadership for the year 1558, when presumably he was most fully occupied in preparing the text of the Geneva Bible.

(2) There also appeared in 1557 a translation of the Psalms into English: "The Psalmes of David Translated Accordying to the veritie and truth of th' Ebrue, wyth annotacions moste profitable." The

15. E. H. Gaullieur, "Etudes sur la typographie genevoise," *Bulletin de l'Institut National Genevois*, II (1855), 130.

16. Pollard, *Records*, pp. 284–286.

only known copy of this edition is in the Bodleian Library and was discovered by Dr. Alexander, who has in considerable detail studied its contents and its relationship to the Geneva Bible of 1560.[17] His conclusions are that *The Psalmes* was printed by Conrad Badius in 1557, and that in all probability Anthony Gilby, the most competent Hebraist of the Englishmen in Geneva, was the editor and probably the translator and reviser of *The Psalmes*. The work owes a great deal to the Sternhold and Hopkins *One and Fiftie Psalmes of Dauid* (Geneva, 1556) for those psalms that are common to both editions, in that there is a great dependency of *The Psalmes* upon the *One and Fiftie Psalmes* for the arguments or summaries of each psalm. For other psalms, the translator relied heavily upon John Calvin's *Commentaries upon the Psalms,* which appeared in July 1557. Like the New Testament of 1557, the Scripture was divided into verses and was printed in roman type, with basically the same format.

The Geneva group was now convinced that biblical textual scholarship had advanced to such a stage that there was significant need to prepare a new English translation of the complete Bible: "... diuers heretofore haue indeuored to atchieue [the translating of Scripture into English]," they wrote in the preface to the Geneva Bible, "yet considering the infancie of those tymes and imperfect knollage of the tongues, in respect of this ripe age and cleare light which God hath now reueiled, the translations required greatly to be perused and reformed."

The English versions prior to the Geneva Bible have been discussed above; the versions of particular significance for the translators were the Great Bible and, to a lesser extent, the Coverdale and Matthew Bibles. Coverdale's Diglot, which prints Jerome's Vulgate and a revised translation of his own work, was probably used in revising the New Testament. But the "cleare light which God hath now reueiled" refers not so much to the work of any Englishman as to the work of various Continental scholars.

The translators of the Geneva Bible were certainly familiar with the French Bible of Pierre Robert Olivetan, Calvin's cousin. This first appeared in 1535 and was revised on several occasions; the translators most probably used the 1553 edition published by Estienne with the New Testament corrected by Calvin and Beza and with the Scripture divided into verses. The translators also used the greatly revised edition of Estienne's own Bible published in Geneva in 1557 in three folio volumes with complete concordances included.[18] For the Old Testament, Estienne himself revised the work of the He-

17. See "The Genevan Version," pp. 59–82.

18. Elizabeth Armstrong, *Robert Estienne* (Cambridge, England, 1954), p. 232.

brew scholar, Pagninus; and for the Apocrypha and the New Testament, he commissioned new translations from the two most noted Greek scholars in Geneva, Claude Baduel and Theodore Beza. There is also evidence that the translators of the Geneva Bible knew the Hebrew-Latin Bible of Sebastian Münster (1534–35) and the Latin version of the Old Testament by the Hebraist Leo Juda. Juda's Old Testament, together with Cholin's Apocrypha and Gualther's revision of Erasmus' New Testament, was published in 1544.

Although the English translators clearly utilized the work of these scholars, it must be emphasized that Whittingham and Gilby were among the most competent of the English linguists of the time. As David Daiches points out:

> The Hebrew scholarship of the Geneva Bible translators is attested by . . . the clear fact that in many instances they restored the literal meaning of the Hebrew text which had been obscured . . . in all the earlier English versions. . . . Further, there is strong evidence for concluding that the Geneva Bible translators were the first of the English translators to make considerable use at first hand of the Hebrew commentary of David Kimchi. A large number of the A[uthorized] V[ersion] renderings which agree with Kimchi against most other interpretations follow the Geneva Bible.[19]

In the New Testament the English translators obviously made use of the most recent textual studies of Beza, so that although they probably used the Great Bible as the foundation of their text, all scholarly investigation indicates they were quite accurate in claiming that they had "translated according to the Ebrue and Greke, and conferred with the best translations in diuers langages," as the 1560 title page states.[20]

In February 1559, or a little more than a year after beginning their work, the translators published an edition of the Psalms to honor Queen Elizabeth upon her accession to the throne. The edition was published in Geneva and printed by Rowland Hall, who was to be the printer of the complete Bible a year later. In the "Dedicatorie Epistle," the translators say:

> . . . with moste ioyful mindes and great diligence we indeuored ourselues to set forth and dedicate this moste excellent boke of the Psalmes vnto your grace, as a special token of our seruice and good wil, til the rest of the Bible, which, praised be God, is in good readines, may be accomplished and presented.

19. *The King James Version of the English Bible* (Chicago, 1941), pp. 179, 180.

20. The most detailed study of the methods of translation of the translators is in Dr. Alexander's thesis, especially Chapter 4, "The Methods of Revision," pp. 100–175. Daiches, pp. 178–208, and Westcott, pp. 212–228, are also useful.

In both notes and text this edition is identical with the Psalms as published in the 1560 Bible, thus reinforcing the statement that most of the work was "in good readines." This text is printed in roman type with italic type for words not in the original Hebrew, and marks are placed over the accented syllables in Hebrew proper names—practices that would be followed in the Geneva Bible.

IV

The Geneva Bible appeared in 1560, some time between April 10, the date of the preface, and May 30, the date Whittingham left Geneva to return to England. The timing could scarcely have been more auspicious. The translators began their work while Mary was still Queen of England; indeed, in the preface the translators commented "the tyme then was moste dangerous and the persecution sharpe and furious." No English Bible was published during her reign (except for Whittingham's New Testament), and the reading of Scripture by the laity was strongly discouraged. However, on Elizabeth's accession in November 1558, the Catholic bishops were deprived of their sees, the Church of England was restored, and the injunction of Edward VI that a Bible should be placed in each church was renewed. The official Bible—the one that would be found in the churches and read from the pulpit—was still the Great Bible. A need remained, however, to provide a Bible for the people, and it was to the people that the translators of the Geneva Bible addressed themselves: "For God is our witnes that we haue by all meanes indeuored to set forthe the puritie of the worde and right sense of the holy Gost for the edifying of the brethren in faith and charitie."

The Geneva Bible had a number of new features designed for the convenience and edification of "the brethren." Instead of the large unwieldy folio volumes that had been common, the new Bible was a handy quarto. It was the first English Bible to be printed in roman type rather than black letter. Another important innovation was the division of the Scripture into verses: "Which thing as it is moste profitable for memorie: so doeth it agre with the best translations, & is moste easie to finde out both by the best Concordances, and also by the cotations which we haue dilygently herein perused." Words interpolated into the text were printed in italic type; proper names were accented and spelled to conform as nearly as possible with their originals. To further aid the reader, the translators provided marginal commentary, both textual and explanatory, "vpon all the hard places."

In addition the Geneva Bible contains twenty-six woodcuts, located in the Pentateuch, Kings, and Ezekiel, to elucidate passages "so darke that by no description thei colde be made easie to the simple reader." There are five maps "which necessarely serue for the perfect vnderstanding and memorie of diuers places and countreys, partely described, and partely by occasion touched, bothe in the olde and newe Testament." Arguments precede each book and each chapter of the Bible. At the head of each page the translators have set "some notable worde or sentence which may greatly further aswel for memorie, as for the chief point of the page." The Bible also has a "Table of the interpretation of the propre names which are chiefly founde in the olde Testament," a "Table of the principal things that are conteined in the Bible," a "Perfite svppvtation of the yeres and times from Adam vnto Christ," and "The order of the yeres from Pauls conuersion."

Tyndale had written prefaces and notes for the parts of the Bible he had translated; however, he was martyred before he had completed his translation of the Bible, and the opposition of the clergy and government to his notes and ecclesiastical words, together with the prevalent attitude that the Bible should not be given to the people, prevented the acceptance of his work. Now for the first time, the English people had a Bible, scholarly in its translation, but also designed for use by the laity; and it is quite evident that the "aids" the translators provided accounted for its extraordinary popularity among the people. Equally significant, however, was the acceptance of the Geneva Bible by the clergy. In supporting John Bodley's request for an extension of his patent for printing the Geneva Bible, Archbishop Parker in 1565 said:

> So it is that we thinke so well of the first impression, and reviewe of those whiche have sithens travailed therin, that we wishe it wold please you [Queen Elizabeth] to be a meane that twelve yeres longer tearme maye be . . . graunted him. . . . For thoughe one other speciall bible for the churches be meant by vs to be set forthe as convenient tyme and leysor hereafter will permytte: yet shall it nothing hindre but rather do moche good to have diversitie of translacions and readinges.[21]

In the five years before this letter was written, the Geneva Bible had firmly established itself as the most popular Bible in England, without, however, supplanting the Great Bible in official use. Parker's recognition of the inadequacies of the Great Bible prompted him to plan the "speciall bible" mentioned above. Under his and Bishop Richard Cox's leadership the Anglican bishops prepared this new translation, which was published in 1568 and became known as the Bishops' Bible. Though supporting in theory the notion of "diversi-

21. Pollard, *Records*, pp. 285, 286.

tie of translacions," Parker in fact used his position to secure for the Bishops' Bible official use, objecting to the "bitter" notes of the Geneva Bible.

First the Great Bible and then the Bishops' Bible were the Bibles to be used in churches; and no new edition of the Geneva Bible was printed in England until shortly after the death of Parker in 1575, despite the printing privilege granted to Bodley in 1565. There is no doubt that having to import copies of the Bible from Geneva did hinder somewhat its circulation; but the Geneva Bible had become so popular by 1575 that Parker's death simply opened the floodgates. Indeed, from 1575 until 1618 at least one new edition of the Geneva Bible appeared each year. It was printed in folio, quarto, octavo, duodecimo, and even sextodecimo. It is illuminating to compare the number of editions of the various English Bibles published from 1560 to 1611, when the King James version was published.

Tyndale's New Testament	5
Great Bible	7
Bishops' Bible	22
Geneva Bible	over 120

No doubt the fact that Edmund Grindal succeeded Parker as Archbishop of Canterbury had a great deal to do with promoting the popularity of the Geneva Bible, for as Patrick Collinson has remarked, "Grindal was an archbishop for thoroughgoing protestants, one of the very few Elizabethan bishops who enjoyed the full approval of the protestant governing class and the equal confidence of all but a small embittered minority of the godly preaching ministers."[22] Among his strong supporters was Sir Francis Walsingham, who in 1575 secured for his friend Christopher Barker the printing rights of the Geneva Bible. Grindal's preference is further evidenced by the fact that no edition of the Bishops' Bible appeared during his term as archbishop—nor indeed until 1584, a year after John Whitgift had succeeded him. By that time it was evident that the Bishops' Bible was no match for the Geneva Bible. Even the appearance of the King James version in 1611 did not immediately eclipse the popularity of the Geneva Bible. Archbishop William Laud exerted his influence to prevent the printing of the Geneva Bible in England, and after 1616 it was printed in Amsterdam. The extraordinary fact, however, is that over sixty editions (some, of the New Testament only) appeared after the Authorized Version.[23]

The Geneva Bible of 1560 underwent several changes during its

22. *The Elizabethan Puritan Movement* (Berkeley and Los Angeles, 1967), p. 159.

23. See Charles Eason, *The Genevan Bible: Notes on Its Production and Distribution* (Dublin, 1937), pp. 1–12.

long history, some of which should be noted. In 1576, the Puritan Lawrence Tomson, scholar, member of Parliament, and aide to Sir Francis Walsingham, brought out an edition of the Genevan New Testament. Although there were some revisions in the text, mainly from Beza's later work, the substantial changes were in the marginal notes, which were based on those of Beza and Camerarius in the 1573 edition of the Greek Testament edited by Pierre Loisseleur de Villiers. In 1587 a quarto edition of the Geneva Bible was brought out with Tomson's New Testament and notes substituted for those in the 1560 edition, and from this time on some editions had the Tomson and some the original notes. Another important addition was the commentary of Franciscus Junius on the book of Revelation, translated in 1592 from Latin into English. These notes, extremely anti-Catholic, were first appended to Tomson's New Testament, then to some editions of the Geneva Bible, and from 1599 on replaced the original notes on Revelation in the Geneva Bible. Various editions of the Geneva Bible included other elements, such as the metrical psalms of Sternhold and Hopkins, a poem entitled "Of the Incomparable Treasure of the Holy Scriptures, with a prayer for the true use of the same,"[24] and a diagram showing the reader "How to take profite in reading of the Holy Scriptures." Calvin's Catechism was printed in the Geneva Bible of 1568–70; and in most editions from 1579 on, the catechism "Certain Questions and Answers Touching the Doctrine of Predestination, the Use of God's Word and Sacraments" was appended.[25]

The single most important feature of the Geneva Bible, to both the laity and the clergy, consisted in the marginal notes. Almost from the first appearance of the Geneva Bible in 1560, these notes provoked critical response. In a memorandum to the translators of the Bishops' Bible, Archbishop Parker said: "Item to make no bitter notis vppon any text, or yet to set downe any determinacion in places of controversie."[26] At the Hampton Court Conference in 1604, King James is reported to have given orders for the Authorized Version that reflected adversely upon the Geneva Bible:

Marry, withall, hee gaue this caueat (vpon a word cast out by my Lord of London) that no marginall notes should be added, hauing found in them which are annexed to the *Geneua* translation (which he sawe in a Bible giuen him by an English Lady) some notes very partiall, vntrue, seditious, and sauouring too much of daungerous, and trayterous conceites. As for example, *Exod.* 1,19, where the marginal note alloweth

24. See Alexander, pp. 194–195.

25. For a more detailed account of the history of the various editions of the Geneva Bible, see Eason and see the Nicholas Pocock entry in the Bibliography below.

26. Pollard, *Records,* p. 297.

disobedience to Kings. And *2. Chron.* 15,16, the note taxeth *Asa* for deposing his mother, *onely*, and *not killing her*.[27]

More recent critics have echoed this notion—J. Isaacs, for example: "The popularity of the Geneva Bible, and above all of its controversial notes from the extreme Protestant point of view, was distasteful to the Bishops."[28] Perhaps the most just evaluation of the notes is by Bishop Westcott (p. 93): "A marginal commentary also was added, pure and vigorous in style, and, if slightly tinged with Calvinistic doctrine, yet on the whole neither unjust nor illiberal." One must remember that by the end of the sixteenth century the Geneva Bible had become far different from the 1560 edition. Tomson's notes on the New Testament in 1576, the two Calvinistic catechisms added in 1568 and 1579, and the Junius notes to Revelation that appeared in editions from 1599 on—all reinforced the Calvinistic tone of the Geneva Bible. However, the notes of the 1560 edition are by and large exegetical and not argumentative. Obviously many examples could be given to demonstrate the changes that took place: compare these two notes for Romans 9:15 ("For he saith to Moses, I wil haue mercie on him, to whome I wil shewe mercie: and wil haue compassion on him, on whome I wil haue compassion"); the first is from the 1560 Geneva Bible; the second, from Tomson's 1576 New Testament:

> As the onelie wil & purpose of God is the chief cause of election & reprobacion: so his fre mercie in Christ is an inferior cause of saluacion, & the hardening of the heart, an inferior cause of damnacion.

> He answereth first touching them which are chosen to salvation, in chusing of whom he denieth that God may seeme uniust, although he chuse and predestinate to saluation, them that are not yet borne, without any respect of worthinesse: because he bringeth not the chosen to the appointed end, but by the meanes of his mercie, which is a cause next vnder predestination. Now mercy presupposeth miserie, and againe miserie presupposeth sinne or voluntarie corruption of mankind, and corruption presupposeth a pure and perfect creation. Moreover mercy is shewed by her degrees: to wit, by calling, by faith, by iustification and sanctification, so that at length we come to glorification, as the Apostle will shew afterward. Nowe all these things, orderly following the purpose of God, doe clearely prooue that he can by no meanes seeme vniust in louing and sauing his.

The changes in Revelation are even more startling; here is the 1560 Geneva Bible's brief note on "two & fortie moneths" in Revelation 11:2:

27. Pollard, *Records*, p. 46.
28. Quoted from Robinson, p. 186.

Meaning, a certeine time: for God hathe limited the times of Antichrists tyranie.

Compare the Tomson-Junius annotation on the same phrase:

Or a thousand, two hundred and threescore dayes, as is sayd in the next verse: that is a thousand two hundred and threescore yeeres, a day for a yeere, as often in Ezechiel & Daniel, which thing I noted before 2,10. The beginning of these thousand two hundred and threescore yeeres wee account from the passion of Christ, whereby (the partition wall being broken downe) wee were made of two one, Ephes. 2,14. I say one flocke vnder one Shepheard, Iohn, 10,16, and the end of these yeeres precisely falleth into the Popedome of Boniface the eight who a little before the end of ye yeere of Christ a thousand two hundreth ninetie foure, enterd the Popedome of Rome, in the feast of S. Lucie (as *Bergomensis* saith) hauing put in prison his predecessor *Coelestinus*, whom by fraud, vnder colour of oracle, he deceived: for which cause, there was well said of him, *Intrauit vt vulpes, regnauit vt leo, moriuus est vt canis.* That is, he enterd like a foxe, raigned like a lyon, and died like a dogge. For if from a thousand two hundred ninetie foure yeeres thou shalt take the age of Christ which he liued on the earth, thou shalt finde there remaineth iust 1260 yeeres, which are mentioned in this place and many others.[29]

V

From what has been said thus far, it is clear that the Geneva Bible had immense influence on English culture and mentality; but before the more general influence is discussed, it would be well to consider for a moment the literary influence of the Geneva Bible on the King James version. As C. C. Butterworth has said:

In the lineage of the King James Bible this volume [the Geneva Bible] is by all means the most important single volume. Only in the New Testament and the Pentateuch is its contribution overshadowed by the work of William Tyndale. In the Historical Books it matches the contribution of the Matthew Bible; in the Poetical Books it matches the contribution of the Coverdale Bible; while in the Books of the Prophets it is supreme, challenging even the contribution of the King James Bible itself. Even in the Apocrypha, where the King James version was pretty much a law unto itself, the Geneva Bible makes its influence felt.[30]

Compare the rendering of Psalm 23, verses 1–3, in the Coverdale (1535), Great (1539), Geneva (1560), and King James (1611) Bibles:

29. As I suggested in my preface, it seems to me much remains to be done in analyzing the theological and historical implications of the marginal notes. Alexander (pp. 213–238) devotes a chapter to the doctrine of the notes, and Hardin Craig, Jr., has written an article on their political significance, "The Geneva Bible as a Political Document," *Pacific Historical Review*, VII (1938), 40–49.

30. *The Literary Lineage of the King James Bible* (Philadelphia, 1941), p. 163.

The Lorde is my shepherde, I can wante nothinge. He fedeth me in a grene pasture, and ledeth me to a fresh water. He quickeneth my soule, and bringeth me forth in the waye of rightuousnes for his names sake.

The Lord is my shepeherd: therfore can I lack nothing. He shal fede me in a greene pasture, and leade me forth besyde the waters of comforte. He shal conuert my soule, and bring me forth in the pathes of ryghteousnesse for his names sake.

The Lord is my shepherd, I shal not want. He maketh me to rest in grene pasture, and leadeth me by the stil waters. He restoreth my soule, and leadeth me in the paths of righteousnes for his Names sake.

The Lord is my shepheard, I shall not want. He maketh me to lie downe in greene pastures: he leadeth mee beside the still waters. He restoreth my soule: he leadeth me in the pathes of righteousnes, for his names sake.[31]

In statistical terms, Butterworth estimates the amount of material from earlier versions incorporated in the King James version; the figures represent percentages of the finished text of the King James Bible:

Wycliffe versions, including English Sermons	4%
Tyndale's work, including the Matthew Bible	18
Coverdale's work, including Great Bibles	13
Geneva Bible and Geneva New Testament	19
Bishops' Bible and its revision	4
All other versions before 1611	3
TOTAL	61%
King James Bible, new material	39%
TOTAL	100%

In the reigns of Edward VI and Elizabeth, royal injunctions required clergy with insufficient formal training to train themselves in biblical study. Commonly these ministers would come to the market town on an appointed day for "exercise" or biblical exegesis. The practice gradually developed of permitting the laity to listen to the discussion. Usually a panel of preachers, presided over by a moderator, would preach the day's text that they had reached in the course of the systematic exegesis of some book of the Bible. Each would explain a part of the text, and the last speaker concluded with the practical uses of the doctrine. After the speakers had finished, the moderator would ask any learned man to confirm or confute the doctrine delivered. In Puritan and Scottish circles, the laity was permitted to take part in the proceedings at this point. The whole exercise was known as "prophesyings" and became extremely popular

31. For further examples, see Butterworth, pp. 253–353.

until Elizabeth, for fear of sedition and distaste for dissent, ordered the suppression of such activities, in 1576. Meanwhile the Geneva Bible had provided a basic tool for biblical exegesis; there is much evidence that both the unlettered clergy and the laity relied on its notes for proper interpretation of Scripture.

One of the most remarkable aspects of Elizabethan and Jacobean religion was the great vogue of the sermon; and it is in the sermon that we can see much influence of the Geneva Bible. It is not surprising to find that the majority of the Marian exiles used the Geneva Bible in their sermons; nor is it surprising that others of Puritan persuasion—and even the separatists—also used it. Indeed, one of the most famous of Elizabethan preachers, Henry Smith (called for his eloquence "silver tongued Smith"), generally used the Geneva Bible in his sermons. But it is surprising to discover men like Bishop Lancelot Andrewes, Bishop William Laud (before he became Archbishop of Canterbury), Bishop Carleton, and Bishop Joseph Hall using the Geneva Bible in sermons, especially so since these sermons were preached between 1611 and 1630. Randall T. Davidson, who examined more than fifty sermons preached between 1611 and 1630, states: "In twenty-seven of these sermons the preacher takes his text from the Genevan Version, and in five from the Bishops' Bible. Of the remainder, only about one half quote from the Authorised Version, the texts of eleven sermons being apparently translated or adapted by the preacher himself."[32]

Closely allied to the sermon literature are the commentaries on Scripture and polemical treatises. John Knox's *Answer to a Great Number of Blasphemous Cavillations . . . Adversarie to God's Eternal Predestination* (Geneva, 1560) was the first work which quotes the Geneva Bible. English translations of the commentaries of Luther and Calvin more often than not used the Geneva Bible.[33]

It is only logical to suppose that the influence of the Geneva Bible would make itself felt in the popular literature of the sixteenth and seventeenth centuries. Puritan writers such as John Stubbs, whose right hand was struck off by order of Queen Elizabeth, for his "lewd and seditious book," *The Discovery of a Gaping Gulf*, generally used no other version of the Bible. A good case has been made for Thomas Dekker's preference for the Geneva Bible; for example,

32. "The Authorisation of the English Bible," *Macmillan's Magazine*, XLIV (1881), 441. See also William Haller, *The Rise of Puritanism* (New York, 1938), pp. 3–48; and Louis B. Wright, *Middle-Class Culture in Elizabethan England* (Chapel Hill, 1935), pp. 269–292.

33. E.g., Luther's *Commentary on Galatians* (London, 1575); Calvin's *Commentaries upon the Prophet Daniel* (London, 1578), *Sermons on the Decalogue* (London, 1579), *A Commentary upon the Epistle to the Galacians* (London, 1581), *A Commentary upon Romans* (London, 1583), *A Commentary on Hebrews* (London, 1605). See Alexander, pp. 249–251.

in the *Second Part of the Honest Whore*, Lodovico says: "This is the Blackamore that by washing was turned white" (I.i.89). This is an allusion to Jeremiah 13:23: "Can the black Moor change his skin?" The Bishops' Bible reads "man of Inde" for "black Moor."[34] Shakespeare no doubt is representative of a much larger group of writers. In the earlier plays it is clear that Shakespeare used the Bishops' Bible, but from about 1596 on, he more or less consistently used the Genevan version.[35] Edmund Spenser more often than not used the Geneva Bible, but there is good evidence that he also used the Great Bible and the Bishops' Bible.[36] Many examples could be given from these and other writers to prove the widespread use of the Geneva Bible; to do so, however, would be to labor the obvious.

Not only the text itself but also the marginal notes influenced the writers. This can be seen in Stubbs's *The Discovery of a Gaping Gulf*, where he presents many examples from Scripture to dissuade Queen Elizabeth from marrying Francis, Duke of Alençon.[37] More significant, however, is the influence of the theology of the marginal notes on Milton as seen in *Paradise Lost* and *Samson Agonistes*. Of *Paradise Lost*, George W. Whiting writes that "in the statement of God's relationship to man, in some fundamental points of theology, in some significant minor details, Milton's interpretation of Scripture and that of the commentary agree."[38] Mr. Whiting's comments on the relationship of the Geneva Bible and Milton's *Samson Agonistes* are especially important:

> The Samson of the Geneva Bible and of *Samson Agonistes*, quite unlike the crafty strong man of Hebrew legend, is, on the whole, the chosen and dedicated servant of God, definitely conscious of his vocation, animated by faith and zeal, invincible against the idolatrous enemies of Israel, undone by his folly which forfeits God's favor, and in the end signally triumphant by repentance and reconciliation with God. (p. 218)

In Scotland, the Geneva Bible was from the beginning the version appointed to be read in churches. In May 1559, John Knox returned to Scotland to lead the reformers against the Catholic regent Mary of Lorraine, widow of James V. And with his return the reformation

34. See Fordyce Judson Bennett, "The Use of the Bible in the Dramatic Works of George Chapman, Thomas Dekker, John Marston, Cyril Tourneur, and John Webster" (unpublished Ph.D. thesis, University of Illinois, 1964), pp. 34–38.

35. See Richmond Noble, *Shakespeare's Biblical Knowledge* (London, 1935), pp. 75–76.

36. See Grace Warren Landrum, "Spenser's Use of the Bible and His Alleged Puritanism," *PMLA*, XLI (1926), 517–544.

37. Lloyd E. Berry, ed., *John Stubbs's "Gaping Gulf" with Letters and Other Relevant Documents* (Charlottesville, 1968), pp. 6–21.

38. *Milton and This Pendant World* (Austin, 1958), p. 130. Professor Roy Flannagan has kindly sent me the typescript of his article, "Milton's Eve and the Geneva Bible," which reinforces Whiting's arguments.

of the church in Scotland had begun. Although it would be many years before any settlement was reached, from 1560 when the Parliament gave its sanction to the basic tenets of the reformed church, the church in Scotland was staunchly Protestant.[39] This Parliament gave its approval to the *Scots Confession* and to the *Book of Common Order*, but it was not until April 14, 1568, that the Geneva Bible was officially licensed to be printed in Scotland. The licensee, Robert Lekprevik, never exercised his rights; therefore, in 1575, Thomas Bassandyne, a printer, and Alexander Arbuthnot, a burgess of Edinburgh, presented to the General Assembly of the Kirk of Scotland certain articles for printing of the English Bible. These were approved by the Assembly, and on June 30, 1576, a license was granted to them by the Privy Council for ten years for the printing of English Bibles in Scotland. Bassandyne and Arbuthnot immediately began their work; the New Testament was completed in 1576 and the Old Testament in 1579. The Bassandyne Bible, as it was known, was a reprint of the second edition of the Geneva Bible, the folio of 1561, and contained a dedication praising James VI (later James I of England) for having authorized its publication:

> Truth it is, that the godly men of the nation of England, for the most part banished from their country for the Gospels cause, and conveened at Geneva, who did faithfully and learnedly translate this book out of the pure fountains of the Hebrew and Chaldaick and Greek tongues, ought to have their own praise for their labours bestowed to the common weale of them that speak our language; yet forsameekle as things once well begunne crave and require great diligence to preserve them from decay, after that with great labours they have been brought to perfection; and great part of the honour of advancing this work pertaineth unto you, be whose authority it was of a certain tyme bypast ordained, That this holy book of God should be set forth, and printed of new within your own realme, to the end that in every parish kirk there should be at least one thereof keeped, to be called the Common Book of the Kirk.[40]

An Act of Parliament, passed soon after the publication of the Bible, made it mandatory that every householder worth 300 marks of yearly rent and every yeoman and burgess worth £500 stock should have a Bible and Psalm Book, in the vulgar tongue, in their homes, under a penalty of ten pounds; and there is evidence that this Act was enforced.

Although there is considerable evidence that the Geneva Bible

39. See Gordon Donaldson, *The Scottish Reformation* (Cambridge, England, 1960), and J. H. S. Burleigh, *A Church History of Scotland* (London, 1960).

40. *Acts and Proceedings of the General Assemblies of the Kirk of Scotland*, II (Edinburgh, 1840), 443.

and the Bassandyne Bible were the versions in use in the churches and in the homes, no further edition of a Bible was printed in Scotland until 1610, when Andro Hart, a printer of Edinburgh, issued a Bible in folio which used the Geneva version of the Old Testament and the Tomson New Testament. The only conclusion that can be reached, therefore, is that copies of the Geneva Bible were imported from England and, after 1616, from the Continent. Interestingly, the last known edition of the Geneva Bible, that printed in Amsterdam in 1644, stated, correctly, that it conformed to Hart's Bible of 1610.

The King James Bible did not make much headway in Scotland until the issuance of the "Canons and Constitutions Ecclesiastical" in 1636 which stipulated that each parish should possess a Bible "of the translation of King James." In spite of this injunction, many of the leading ministers in Scotland continued to use the Geneva Bible.[41]

Not only was the Geneva Bible popular in England and Scotland, but also it was the favored Bible of the Plymouth and Virginia settlements in America. It is highly probable that the Geneva Bible was first brought to America in 1607 and used in the Jamestown settlement. William Strachey, secretary of the Virginia Company, used the Geneva Bible in writing his history of Virginia in 1609, and William Whitaker, who was one of the most influential ministers of the colony, used the Geneva Bible in his sermons.

The Pilgrims brought the Geneva Bible with them on the *Mayflower* to Plymouth in 1620. In fact, the religious writings and sermons published by the members of the Plymouth colony suggest that the Geneva Bible was used exclusively by them in the colony's early days.[42]

It is interesting to note that the Geneva Bible, a version prepared by exiles when persecution was "sharpe and furious," would ultimately become a major influence on the religious life of the people of three countries and would prove to be the major reason for the publication of the King James Bible. As John Eadie has said:

> The vitality of the Genevan Bible was wonderful. It had commended itself to general acceptance, for it had been made by earnest and scholarly men, driven by persecution out of England; made in a city revered as the home and metropolis of the popular theology; and it was also a better translation than any of its rivals. It did not die under episcopal frown, nor was its circulation promoted to any extent by episcopal patronage. The people loved it for itself and its history. It was a con-

41. See Duncan Anderson, *The Bible in Seventeenth-Century Scottish Life and Literature* (London, 1936), pp. 10–13.

42. P. Marion Simms, *The Bible in America* (New York, 1936), pp. 75–78, 89–93.

temporary of the Great Bible for nine years, and outlived it; and of the Bishops' for nigh forty years, and outlived it too for more than a quarter of a century. ... Though King James had scornfully depreciated the Genevan notes at the Hampton Court Conference, the people relished them greatly, and, according to Fuller, when the version was disappearing, they complained that they "could not see into the sense of Scripture for lack of the spectacles of those Genevan annotations." The Genevan Bible having done its work at length passed away, making room for another version in so many respects its superior.[43]

VII

The Geneva Bible was printed in Geneva by Rowland Hall in 1560. It is in quarto and collates ***^{4}, a–z^4, A–Z^4, Aa-Zz^4, &^{6}, Aaa–Zzz^4, Aaaa–Zzzz^4, Aaaaa–Bbbbb^4, AA–ZZ^4, AAa–LLl^4; 614 folios (misnumbering folio 94 of the New Testament as 84). The text is in roman type, double columns. There are twenty-six engravings in the text and five maps: (1) the wanderings of the Israelites (Numbers); (2) the division of the land of Canaan (Joshua); (3) the Temple and Jerusalem restored (Ezekiel); (4) the Holy Land (Matthew); (5) countries and places mentioned in Acts (Acts).

In the United States and Canada copies of the 1560 edition can be found in the following libraries: Boston Public Library; Chapin Library, Williams College; Columbia University (Plimpton Collection); Folger Shakespeare Library; General Theological Seminary, New York; Georgetown University; Harvard University; Henry E. Huntington Library; Library of Congress; McGill University; Newberry Library; New York Public Library (3 copies); Pierpont Morgan Library; Princeton University; Scheide Library, Princeton University; St. John's Seminary, Carmarilla, California; University of Chicago; University of Pennsylvania (2 copies); Wesleyan University; Yale University; Zion Research Library, Boston University.

In the United Kingdom copies can be found in the following libraries: Aberdeen University; Bodleian Library, Oxford; Bristol University; British and Foreign Bible Society, London; British Museum; Cambridge University; Glasgow University; King's College, Newcastle; Lambeth Palace Library, London; Leicester University; Manchester University; Norwich Public Library.

In preparing this facsimile edition the Scheide Library copy was used for the vast majority of pages; however, the Chapin Library copy has been used for those pages in the Scheide copy that were badly stained, had wormholes, or proved to be unsatisfactory for any other reason. The following pages are from the Chapin Library copy:

43. *The English Bible*, II (London, 1876), 51–52.

title	78r	138r	238r	275r	323r	379v	437r	33r	103v
2v	81r	144r	241r	276r	324r	380r	438r	36v	105v
6v	88r	146r	242r	277v	329r	382r	439r	40r	107r
18r	92r	150r	244r	278r	332r	384r	442r	41v	107v
24v	92v	158r	251r	281v	334r	385r	442v	43v	109r
27r	97r	165v	254r	284r	345v	386r	453v	46r	110v
27v	98r	174r	255r	286r	349r	398r	454r	55r	116v
30r	99v	174v	257r	296r	350r	405v	456v	58r	117v
41v	100r	178r	262r	298r	353r	407v	462v	58v	119v
43v	106r	195v	262v	299r	353v	408r	467r	59v	122r
52r	107r	199r	265r	300r	355v	409r	470r	63v	[sigs.]
53v	111r	199v	265v	301r	357r	413r		71v	KKkiiv
61v	112r	207v	266r	302r	363r	415r	12v	79r	LLlir
62v	114r	208v	267r	304r	367r	416r	18r	81r	LLliv
63r	120r	216r	269v	304v	370r	416v	21v	86v	LLliir
63v	130r	222r	270r	312r	372r	417r	24r	94r	LLliiv
65v	135r	226r	271r	313r	376r	435r	26r	96r	
75r	136r	229r	272r	313v	378r	436r	30v	96v	

This facsimile was produced by fine-line photography. This method does not distinguish between some fox marks, blemishes in the paper, or show-through; however, this has not been a serious problem since both the Scheide and Chapin copies are exceptionally clean. No retouching has been done other than to remove the few handwritten notes in the margin of the Scheide copy, but this has in no way affected the text or printed notes. The area outside the type area has been masked.

In the 1560 edition each of the five maps was tipped onto a stub page. In this facsimile each map appears at the same place as in the original but is turned broadside. It was necessary to reduce the size of the map of the Temple to about four-fifths of the original; no other reduction of any page has been made.

Bibliography

The following list is not exhaustive, its purpose being to direct interested persons to more detailed information on matters discussed in the introduction.

The English Bible

Bagster, Samuel, ed. *T[illegible]lish Hexapla*. London, 1841.
Bruce, F. F. *The En*[illegible]ew York, 1961.
Butterworth, Charles [illegible]*terary Lineage of the King James Bible*. Philadelphia, 1941.
Daiches, David. *The King James Version of the English Bible*. Chicago, 1941.
Eadie, John. *The English Bible*. 2 vols. London, 1876.
Edgar, Andrew. *The Bibles of England*. London, 1889.
Greenlaw, H. J. C. *The English Bible*. London, 1947.
Greenslade, S. L. *The Cambridge History of the Bible*. Cambridge, England, 1963.
Heaton, W. J. *The Puritan Bible*. London, 1913.
Mozley, John F. *Coverdale and His Bibles*. London, 1953.
———. *William Tyndale*. London, 1937.
Paine, Gustavus S. *The Learned Men*. New York, 1959.
Pollard, Alfred W., ed. *The New Testament Translated by William Tyndale, 1525*. Oxford, 1926.
———. *Records of the English Bible*. London, 1911.
Robinson, H. Wheeler, ed. *The Bible in Its Ancient and English Versions*. Oxford, 1940.
Weigle, Luther A., ed. *The New Testament Octapla*. New York, 1962.
Westcott, Brooke F. *A General View of the History of the English Bible*. 3d ed., revised by William Aldis Wright. New York, 1927.
Whitley, W. T. *The English Bible under the Tudor Sovereigns*. London, n.d.
Willoughby, Edwin Elliott. *The Making of the King James Bible*. Los Angeles, 1956.

The Geneva Bible

Alexander, John David. "The Genevan Version of the English Bible." Unpublished D.Phil. thesis, Oxford University, 1956.

Craig, Hardin, Jr. "The Geneva Bible as a Political Document," *Pacific Historical Review*, VII (1938), 40–49.

Darlow, T. H., and H. F. Moule. *Historical Catalogue of the Printed Editions of the Holy Scripture*. 2 vols. London, 1903–1911.

Davidson, Randall T. "The Authorisation of the English Bible," *Macmillan's Magazine*, XLIV (1881), 436–444.

Eason, Charles. *The Genevan Bible: Notes on Its Production and Distribution*. Dublin, 1937.

Green, Mary Anne Everett, ed. *The Life of Mr. William Whittingham*. London, 1870.

Hall, Basil. *The Genevan Version of the English Bible*. London, 1957.

Lee, John. *Memorial for the Bible Societies in Scotland*. Edinburgh, 1824.

Lupton, Lewis. *A History of the Gen[illegible]e*. London, 1966.

Morison, Stanley. *The Geneva Bible*. [illegible], 1955.

Pocock, Nicholas. "Some Notices of the [illegible]van Bible," *The Bibliographer*, II (1882), 40–44, 97–100, 160–163; III (1882–1883), 28–31, 103–106; IV (1883), 34–38; V (1883–1884), 76–79; VI (1884), 105–107.

The Marian Exiles

Arber, Edward, ed. *A Brief Discourse of the Troubles at Frankfort*. London, 1907.

Armstrong, Elizabeth. *Robert Estienne*. Cambridge, England, 1954.

Collinson, Patrick. "The Authorship of *A Brieff Discours off the Troubles Begonne at Franckford*," *Journal of Ecclesiastical History*, IX (1958), 188–208.

Garrett, Christina Hallowell. *The Marian Exiles*. Cambridge, England, 1938.

Geisendorf, Paul F. *Bibliographie raisonnée de l'histoire de Genève, des origines à 1798*. Geneva, 1966.

Isaac, F. S. *Egidius van der Erve and His English Printed Books*. London, 1931.

Kingdon, Robert M. *Geneva and the Coming of the Wars of Religion in France*. Geneva, 1956.

Martin, Charles. *Les Protestants anglais*. Geneva, 1915.

Moeckli, Gustave. *Les Livres imprimés à Genève de 1550 à 1600*. Revised ed. Geneva, 1966.

Robinson, Hastings, ed. *Original Letters Relative to the English Reformation*. 2 vols. Cambridge, England, 1846–1847.

———. *The Zurich Letters.* 2 vols. Cambridge, England, 1842-1845.

Southgate, W. M. "The Marian Exiles and the Influence of John Calvin," *History*, XXVII (1942), 148–152.

Wilson, James Robert, Jr. "Marian Exiles and Elizabethan Nonconformity." Unpublished Master's thesis, University of Illinois, 1956.

Sixteenth- and Seventeenth-Century England

Bennett, Fordyce Judson. "The Use of the Bible in the Dramatic Works of George Chapman, Thomas Dekker, John Marston, Cyril Tourneur, and John Webster." Unpublished Ph.D. thesis, University of Illinois, 1964.

Berry, Lloyd E., ed. *John Stubbs's "Gaping Gulf" with Letters and Other Relevant Documents.* Folger Documents of Tudor and Stuart Civilization. Charlottesville, 1968.

Collinson, Patrick. *The Elizabethan Puritan Movement.* Berkeley and Los Angeles, 1967.

Haller, William. *The Elect Nation: The Meaning and Relevance of Foxe's "Book of Martyrs."* New York, 1964.

———. *The Rise of Puritanism.* New York, 1938.

Knappen, Marshall M. *Tudor Puritanism.* Chicago, 1939.

Landrum, Grace Warren. "Spenser's Use of the Bible and His Alleged Puritanism," *PMLA*, XLI (1926), 517–544.

Maclure, Millar. *The Paul's Cross Sermons, 1534–1642.* Toronto, 1958.

New, John F. H. *Anglican and Puritan.* Stanford, 1964.

Noble, Richmond. *Shakespeare's Biblical Knowledge.* London, 1935.

Pearson, A. F. Scott. *Church and State: Political Aspects of Sixteenth-Century Puritanism.* Cambridge, England, 1928.

———. *Thomas Cartwright and Elizabethan Puritanism.* Cambridge, England, 1925.

Thompson, Craig R. *The English Church in the Sixteenth Century.* Ithaca, 1958.

Thompson, E. N. S. *The Controversy Between the Puritans and the Stage.* New York, 1903.

Whiting, George W. *Milton and This Pendant World.* Austin, 1958.

Wright, Louis B. *Middle-Class Culture in Elizabethan England.* Chapel Hill, 1935.

Sixteenth- and Seventeenth-Century Scotland

Acts and Proceedings of the General Assemblies of the Kirk of Scotland. 2 vols. Edinburgh, 1839–1840.

Anderson, Duncan. *The Bible in Seventeenth-Century Scottish Life and Literature.* London, 1936.
Brown, P. Hume. *John Knox.* 2 vols. London, 1895.
Burleigh, J. H. S. *A Church History of Scotland.* London, 1960.
Dickinson, William C., ed. *John Knox's History of the Reformation.* 2 vols. New York, 1950.
Dobson, William T. *History of the Bassandyne Bible.* Edinburgh, 1887.
Donaldson, Gordon. *The Scottish Reformation.* Cambridge, England, 1960.
Ridley, Jasper. *John Knox.* Oxford, 1968.

Seventeenth-Century America

Morison, Samuel Eliot. *The Puritan Pronaos.* New York, 1936.
Simms, P. Marion. *The Bible in America.* New York, 1936.
Wright, Thomas Goddard. *Literary Culture in Early New England.* New Haven, 1920.

THE GENEVA BIBLE

THE BIBLE

AND

HOLY SCRIPTVRES

CONTEYNED IN

THE OLDE AND NEWE Testament.

TRANSLATED ACCORding to the Ebrue and Greke, and conferred With the best translations in diuers langages.

WITH MOSTE PROFITABLE ANNOTAtions vpon all the hard places, and other things of great importance as may appeare in the Epistle to the Reader.

FEARE YE NOT, STAND STIL, AND BEHOLDE the saluacion of the Lord, which he wil shewe to you this day. Exod. 14,13.

Great are the troubles of the rightcous:

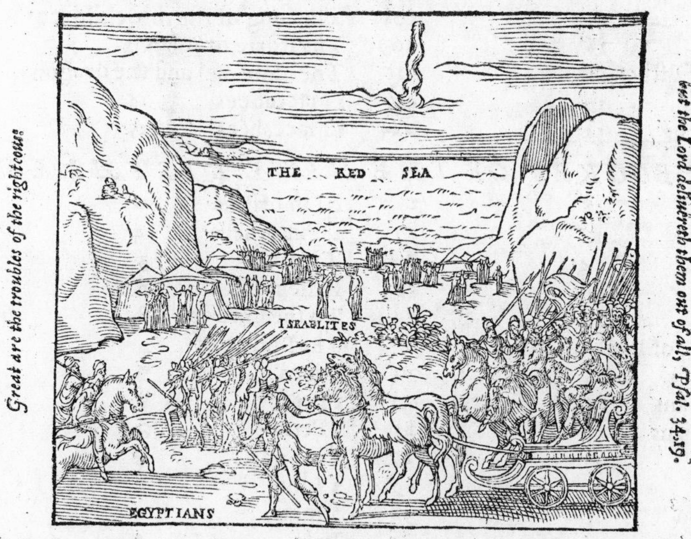

but the Lord deliuereth them out of all, Psal. 34,19.

THE LORD SHAL FIGHT FOR YOU: THEREFORE holde you your peace, Exod. 14, vers. 14.

AT GENEVA

PRINTED BY ROVLAND HALL.

M. D. L X.

THE NAMES AND ORDER OF ALL THE BOokes of the olde and newe Testamēt with the nombre of their chapters, and the leafe where thei begyn.

Booke	chapters	leafe
Genesis chapters	50	leafe 1
Exodus	40	24
Leuiticus	27	45
Nombres	36	59
Deuteronomie	34	80
Ioshua	24	96
Iudges	21	108
Ruth	4	119
1 Samuel	31	121
2 Samuel	24	136
1 Kings	22	148
2 Kings	25	164
1 Chronicles	29	178
2 Chronicles	36	191
The prayer of Manasseh, apocryphe		207
Ezra	10	207
Nehemiah	13	212
Ester	10	219
Iob	42	222
Psalmes	150	235
Prouerbes chap.	31	leafe 267
Ecclesiastes	12	277
The song of Salomon	8	280
Isaiah	66	285
Ieremiah	52	306
Lamentations	5	331
Ezekiel	48	333
Daniel	12	357
Hosea	14	365
Ioel	3	368
Amos	9	370
Obadiah	1	372
Ionah	4	373
Micah	7	374
Nahum	3	376
Habakkuk	3	377
Zephaniah	3	378
Haggai	2	379
Zechariah	14	380
Malachi	4	384

THE BOOKES CALLED APOCRYPHA.

Booke	chapters	leafe
1 Esdras	9	386
2 Esdras	16	393
Tobit	14	405
Iudeth	16	409
The rest of Esther	6	416
Wisdome	19	417
Ecclesiasticus	51	424
Baruc with the epistle of Ieremiah	6	444
The song of the thre children		447
The storie of Susanna		448
The idole Bel and the dragon		449
1 Maccabees	16	450
2 Maccabees	15	464

THE BOOKES OF THE NEWE TESTAMENT.

Booke	chapters	leafe
Matthewe	28	2
Marke	16	17
Luke	24	26
Iohn	21	42
The Actes	28	54
The Epistle of Paul to the Romains	16	70
1 Corinthians	16	76
2 Corinthians	13	83
Galatians	6	87
Ephesians	6	89
Philippians	4	92
Colossians	4	93
1 Thessalonians	5	95
2 Thessalonians	3	96
1 Timotheus	6	97
2 Timotheus	4	99
Titus	3	100
Philemon	1	101
To the Ebrewes	13	102
The Epistle of Iames	5	107
1 Peter	5	108
2 Peter	3	110
1 Iohn	5	111
2 Iohn	1	113
3 Iohn	1	113
Iude	1	114
Reuelation	22	114

TO THE MOSTE VERTVOVS AND NOBLE QVENE ELISABET, Quene of England, France, ād Ireland, &c. Your humble subiects of the English Churche at Geneua, wish grace and peace from God the Father through Christ Iesus our Lord.

* * *

HOW hard a thing it is, and what great impedimentes let, to enterprise any worthie act, not only dailie experience sufficiently sheweth (moste noble and vertuous Quene) but also that notable prouerbe doeth cōfirme the same, which admonisheth vs, that all thīgs are hard which are faire and excellēt. And what enterprise can there be of greater importance, and more acceptable vnto God, or more worthie of singuler commendation, then the
building of the Lords ‖ Temple, the ‖ house of God, the ‖ Church of Christ, where- 1.Cor.3.17. 1.Tim.3.14.
of the ‖ Sonne of God is the head and perfection? Ephes.1.22.

When Zerubbabel went about to builde the material Temple, according to the Ebr.3.6.
commandement of the Lord, what difficulties and stayes ‖ daily arose to hinder his
worthy indeuours, ẏ bookes of Ezra & Esdras playnely witnesse: how that not on Ezra, 4.
ly he and the people of God were sore molested with ‖ foreyn aduersaries, (whereof 1.Esdr.2.16
some maliciously ‖ warred against them, and corrupted the Kings officers: and o-
thers craftely practised vnder ‖ pretence of religion) but also at home with dome- Ezra 4.7 Ezra 4.2
stical enemies, as ‖ false Prophetes, ‖ craftie worldlings, faint hearted soldiers, and Nehem.6.10
‖ oppressors of their brethren, who aswel by false doctrine and lyes, as by subtil Nehem.6.18
counsel, cowardies, and extortion, discouraged the heartes almoste of all: so that Nehem.5.1.
the Lords worke was not only interrupted and left of for ‖ a long tyme, but scarcely Ioh.2.20
at the length with great labour and danger after a ‖ sort broght to passe. Ezra 3.12

Which thing when we weigh aright, and consider earnestly how muche greater charge God hath laid vpon you in making you a builder of his spiritual Temple, we can not but partely feare, ‖ knowing the crafte and force of Satan our spi- 2.Cor.2.11
ritual enemie, and the weakenes and vnabilitie of this our nature: and partely be feruent in our prayers toward God that he wolde bring to perfection this noble worke which he hath begon by you: and therefore we indeuour our selues by all meanes to ayde, & to bestowe our whole force vnder your graces stādard, whome God hath made as our Zerubbabel for the erecting of this moste excellent Temple, and to plant and maynteyn his holy worde to the aduancement of his glorie,
for your owne honour and saluatiō of your soule, and for the singuler comfort of Ebr.13.20
that great flocke which Christ Iesus the ‖ great shepherd hath boght with his ‖ pre- 1.Pet.1.19
cious blood, and committed vnto your charge to be fed both in body and soule. The enemies ẇ labour to stay religion.

Considering therefore how many enemies there are, which by one meanes or o-
ther, as the ‖ aduersaries of Iudah and Beniamin went about to stay the building of Ezra 4.1
that Temple, so labour to hinder the course of this building (whereof some are Pa- 2.Tim.4.10
pistes, who vnder pretence of fauoring Gods worde, traiterously seke to erect ido- Amos 7.12
latrie and to destroy your maiestie: some are worldlings, who as ‖ Demas haue for 3.Iohn 9
sakē Christ for the loue of this worlde: others are ambicious prelats, who as ‖ Ama- Act.19.24
siah & ‖ Diotrephes can abide none but them selues: and as ‖ Demetrius many practise sedition to maynteyne their errors) we persuaded our selues that there was no
way so expedient and necessarie for the preseruation of the one, and destruction of The necessitie of gods worde for ẏ reformīg of religion.

the other, as to present vnto your Maiestie the holy Scriptures faithfully and playnely translated according to the langages wherein thei were first written by the holy Gost. For the worde of God is an euident token of Gods ‖ loue and our assurance of his defence, wheresoeuer it is obediently receyued: it is the trial of the ‖ spirits: and as the Prophet saieth, ‖ It is as a fyre and hammer to breake the stonie heartes of them that resist Gods mercies offred by the preaching of the same. Yea it is ‖ sharper then any two edged sworde to examine the very thoghtes and to iudge the affections of the heart, and to discouer whatsoeuer lyeth hid vnder hypocrisie and wolde be secret from the face of God and his Churche. So that this must be the first fundacion and groundworke, according whereunto the good stones of this building must be framed, and the euil tried out and reiected.

Iohn 14.23 · *1. Iohn 4.1* · *Ier. 23.29* · *Ebr. 4.12* · The grounde of true religion.

Now as he that goeth about to lay a fundacion surely, first taketh away suche impedimentes, as might iustely ether hurt, let or disforme the worke: so is it necessarie that your graces zeale appeare herein, that nether the craftie persuasion of man, nether worldly policie, or natural feare dissuade you to roote out, cut downe and destroy these wedes and impedimentes which do not only deface your building, but vtterly indeuour, yea & threaten the ruine thereof. For when the noble ‖ Iosias entreprised the like kinde of worke, among other notable and many things he destroyed, not only with vtter confusion the idoles with their appertinances, but also burnt (in signe of detestatiō) the idolatrous priests bones vpon their altars, and put to ‖ death the false prophetes and sorcerers, to performe ‖ the wordes of the Lawe of God: and therefore the Lord gaue him good successe & blessed him wonderfully, so long as he made ‖ Gods worde his line and rule to followe, and enterprised nothing before he had inquired at the mouth of the Lord.

All impedimētes must be taken away. · *2. King. 23.16* · *2. chro. 34.5* · Iosias zeale and true obediēce to God. · *Deu. 13.5* · *Leu. 20.6* · *deu. 18.11* · *2. Chro. 35.22*

And if these zealous begynnings seme dangerous and to brede disquietnes in your dominions, yet by the storie of King ‖ Asa it is manifest, that the quietnes and ‖ peace of kingdomes standeth in the vtter abolishing of idolatrie, and in aduancing of true religion: for in his dayes Iudah lyued in rest and quietnes for the space of fyue and thirtie yere, til at length he began to be colde in the zeale of the Lord, feared the power of man, imprisoned the Prophet of God, and oppressed the people: then the Lord sent him warres, & at length toke him away by death.

2. Chro. 14.5. & 15.15 · Wherein standeth ẏ quietnes of kingdomes. · *2. Chro. 12.8*

Wherefore great wisdome, not worldelie, but heauenly is here required, which your grace must earnestly craue of the Lord, as did ‖ Salomon, to whome God gaue an vnderstanding heart to iudge his people aright, and to discerne betwene good and bad. For if God for the furnishing of the olde temple gaue the Spirit of wisdome & vnderstanding to them that shulde be the workemen thereof, as to ‖ Bezaleel, Aholiab, and ‖ Hiram: how muche more wil he indewe your grace and other godly princes and chefe gouernours with a principal Spirit, that you may procure and commande things necessarie for this moste holy Temple, forese and take hede of things that might hinder it, and abolish and destroy whatsoeuer might impere and ouerthrowe the same?

What wisdome is requisite for the establishing of religion and the meanes to obteyne it. · *1. King. 3.9* · *2. chro. 1.10* · *Exod. 31.1* · *1. King. 7.14*

Moreouer the maruelous diligence and zeale of Iehoshaphat, Iosiah, and Hezekiah are by the singuler prouidence of God left as an example to all godly rulers to reforme their countreys and to establish the worde of God with all spede, lest the ‖ wrath of the Lord fall vpon them for the neglecting thereof. For these excellent Kings did not onely imbrace the worde promptely and ioyfully, but also procured earnestly and commanded the same to be taught, preached and mayntevned through all their countreys and dominions, ‖ bynding them and all their subiectes bothe great and smale with solemne protestations and couenantes before God to obey the worde, and to walke after the waies of the Lord. Yea and in the daies of

Diligence and zeale are necessarie to builde it spedely. · *2. Chro. 34.21* · *2. Chro. 34.31* · A solemne othe for ẏ mayntenāce of Gods worde.

of Kyng‖ Asa it was enacted that whosoeuer wolde not seke the Lord God of Israel, shulde be slayne, whether he were smale or great, man or woman. And for the establishing hereof and performance of this solemne othe, aswel‖ Priests as Iudges were appointed and placed through all the cities of Iudah to instruct the people in the true knollage and feare of God, and to minister iustice according to the worde, knowing that, except God by his worde dyd reigne in ‖the heartes and soules, all mans diligence and indeuors were of none effect: for without this worde we can not discerne betwene iustice, and iniurie, protection and oppresion, wisdome and foolishnes, knollage and ignorance, good and euil. Therefore the Lord, who is the chefe gouernour of his Church, willeth that nothing be attempted before we haue inquired thereof at his mouth. For seing he is our God, of duetie we must giue him this preeminence, that of our selues we entreprise nothing, but that which he hath appointed, who only knoweth all things, and gouerneth them as may best serue to his glorie and our saluation. We oght not therefore to preuent him, or do any thing without his worde,‖ but assone as he hath reueiled his wil, immediately to put it in execution.

2.Chro.15.13 An act against them that obeied not Gods worde. 2.Chro.17.7. & 19.5 What policie must be vsed for the plāting of religio. Deut.6.6.& 11.18 Gods worde must go before, or els we builde in vaine. We must first cōsult with God. Isa.30.2

Now as concerning the maner of this building, it is not according to man, nor after the wisdome of the flesh, but of the Spirit, & according to the worde of God, whose‖ wais are diuers from mans wais. For if it was not lawful for Moses to builde the material Tabernacle after any other sorte then God had shewed him by a ‖patern, nether to prescribe any other ‖ ceremonies & lawes then suche as the Lord had expresly cōmāded: how can it be lawful to procede in this spiritual building any other waies, then Iesus Christ the Sonne of God, who is bothe the fundacion, head and chief corner stone thereof, hath commanded by his worde? And for asmuche as he hath established and left an order in his Churche for the building vp of his body,‖ appointing some to be Apostles, some Prophetes, others Euangelistes, some pastors, and teachers, he signifieth that euery one according as he is placed in this body which is the Church, oght to inquire of his ministres concerning the wil of the Lord, which is reueiled in his worde. For thei are, saieth ‖ Ieremiah, as the mouth of the Lord: yea he ‖ promiseth to be with their mouth, & that their‖ lippes shal kepe knollage, & that the trueth & the law shalbe in their mouth. For it is their office chefely to vnderstand the Scriptures & teache them. For this cause the people of Israel in matters of difficultie vsed to‖ aske the Lord ether by the‖ Prophets, or by the meanes of the hie ‖ Priest, who bare Vrim & Thummim, which were tokens of light & knollage, of holines & perfectiō which shulde be in the hie Priest. Therefore when Iehoshaphat toke this order in the Church of Israel, he appointed Amariah to be the chief concerning the worde of God, because he was moste expert in the law of the Lord, and colde gyue cōusel and gouerne according vnto the same. Els there is no degre or office which may haue that autoritie and priuiledge to decise concerning Gods worde, except withall he hath the Spirit of God, and sufficient knollage and iudgement to define according thereunto. And as euery one is indued of God with greater giftes, so oght he to be herein chefely heard, or at least that without the expresse worde none be heard: for he that hathe not the worde, ‖speaketh not by the mouthe of the Lord. Agayne, what danger it is to do any thing, seme it neuer so godly or necessarie, without consulting with Gods mouth, the examples of the Israelites, ‖ deceiued hereby through the Gibeonites: and of ‖Saul, whose intention semed good and necessarie: and of‖ Iosiah also, who for great considerations was moued for the defence of true religion & his people, to fight against Pharaoh Necho King of Egypt, may sufficiently admonish vs.

The maner of building is as God hathe prescribed by his worde. Isa.55.8 Exod.25.4 act.7.44 ebr.8.5 Deut.5.32 Ephes.4.11 Of whome we must inquire concerning the wil of the Lord and knollage of his worde. Ier.15.19 Exod.4.12 Mal.2.7. Iudg.1.1.& 20.1 1.Sam.10.22 1.Sam.9.9 2.king.22.13 Exod.28.30 What is requisite in them that must giue counsel by Gods worde. Ier.23.16 Iosh.9.14 1.Sam.13.11 2.Chro.35.20

Last of all (moste gracious Quene) for the aduancement of this building

The setting vp of the building.

and rearing vp of the worke, two things are necessarie, First, that we haue a lyuely
Ephes.3.17 & stedfast faith in Christ Iesus, who must ‖ dwel in our heartes, as the only meanes
Gen.28.12 and assurance of our saluation: for he is the ‖ ladder that reacheth from the earth to
Iohn.1.15 heauen: he lifteth vp his Churche and setteth it in the heauenly places: he maketh
vs ‖ lyuely stones and buildeth vs vpon him selfe: he ioyneth vs to him selfe as the mē-
1.Pet.2.5 2.Cor 12.12 bres and body to the head: yea he maketh him selfe and his Churche one ‖ Christ,
The next is, that our faith bring forthe good fruites, so that our godly conuersa-
2.Pet.1.10 tion may serue vs as a witnes to ‖ confirme our election, and be an example to all
Ephes.4.1 others to ‖ walke as apperteyneth to the vocation whereunto thei are called: lest
the worde of God be ‖ euil spoken of, and this building be stayed to growe vp to a
Rom.2.12 iust height, which cā not be without the great prouocatiō of Gods iuste vengeance
and discouraging of many thousandes through all the worlde, if thei shulde se that
our life were not holy and agreable to our profession. For the eyes of all that feare
2.Thess.1.7 God in all places beholde your countreyes as an ‖ example to all that beleue, and the
prayers of all the godly at all tymes are directed to God for the preseruatiō of your
maiestie. For considering Gods wonderful mercies toward you at all seasons, who
2.Tim.3.15 hath pulled you out of the mouthe of the lyons, and how that from your ‖ youth
you haue bene broght vp in the holy Scriptures, the hope of all men is so increased,
that thei cā not but looke that God shulde bring to passe some wōderful worke by
your grace to the vniuersal comfort of his Churche. Therefore euen aboue strēgth
you must shewe your selfe strong and bolde in Gods matters: and thogh Satan lay
all his power and craft together to hurt and hinder the Lordes building: yet be you
Reuel.12.9 assured that God wil fight from heauen against this great ‖ dragon, the ancient serpent, which is called the deuil and Satan, til he haue accomplished the whole wor-
Ephes.4.27 ke and made his Churche ‖ glorious to him selfe, without spot or wrincle. For albeit all other kingdomes and monarchies, as the Babylonians, Persians, Grecians &
Romains haue fallen & taken end: yet the Churche of Christ euen vnder the Crosse
hath from the begynning of the worlde bene victorious, and shalbe euerlastingly. Trueth it is, that sometyme it semeth to be shadowed with a cloude, or driuen
with a stormie persecution, yet suddenly the beames of Christ the sunne of iustice
shine and bring it to light and libertie. If for a tyme it lie couered with ashes, yet it
is quickely kindeled agayne by the wynde of Gods Spirit: thogh it seme drowned
in the sea, or parched and pyned in the wildernes, yet God giueth euer good successe. for he punisheth the enemies, and deliuereth his, nourisheth them and stil preserueth thē vnder his wyngs. This Lord of lordes & King of kings who hath euer
defended his, strengthē, cōfort and preserue your maiestie, that you may be able to
builde vp the ruines of Gods house to his glorie, the discharge of your conscience,
and to the comfort of all them that loue the comming of Christ Iesus our Lord.
From Geneua. 10. April. 1560.

TO OVR BELOVED IN THE LORD THE BRETHREN OF England, Scotland, Ireland, &c. Grace, mercie and peace, through Christ Iesus.

BEsides the manifolde and continual benefites which almightie God bestoweth vpon vs, bothe corporal and spiritual, we are especially bounde (deare brethren) to giue him thankes without ceasing for his great grace and vnspeakable mercies, in that it hath pleased him to call vs vnto this meruelous light of his Gospel, & mercifully to regarde vs after so horrible backesliding and falling away from Christ to Antichrist, from light to darcknes, from the liuing God to dumme and dead idoles, & that after so cruel murther of Gods Saintes, as alas, hathe bene among vs, we are not altogether cast of, as were the Israelites, and many others for the like, or not so manifest wickednes, but receyued agayne to grace with moste euident signes and tokens of Gods especial loue and fauour. To the intent therefore that we may not be vnmyndeful of these great mercies, but seke by all meanes (according to our duetie) to be thankeful for the same, it behoueth vs so to walke in his feare and loue, that all the daies of our life we may procure the glorie of his holy name. Now forasmuche as this thing chefely is atteyned by the knollage and practising of the worde of God (which is the light to our paths, the keye of the kingdome of heauen, our comfort in affliction, our shielde and sworde against Satan, the schoole of all wisdome, the glasse wherein we beholde Gods face, the testimonie of his fauour, and the only foode and nourishment of our soules) we thoght that we colde bestowe our labours & studie in nothing which colde be more acceptable to God and comfortable to his Churche then in the translating of the holy Scriptures into our natiue tongue: the which thing, albeit that diuers heretofore haue indeuored to atchieue: yet considering the infancie of those tymes and imperfect knollage of the tongues, in respect of this ripe age and cleare light which God hath now reueiled, the translations required greatly to be perused and reformed. Not that we vendicat any thing to our selues aboue the least of our brethren (for God knoweth with what feare and trembling we haue bene now, for the space of two yeres and more day and night occupied herein) but being earnestly desired, and by diuers, whose learning and godlynes we reuerence, exhorted, and also incouraged by the ready willes of suche, whose heartes God likewise touched, not to spare any charges for the fortherance of suche a benefite and fauour of God toward his Churche (thogh the tyme then was moste dangerous and the persecution sharpe and furious) we submitted our selues at length to their godly iudgementes, and seing the great oportunitie and occasions, which God presented vnto vs in this Churche, by reason of so many godly and learned men: and suche diuersities of translations in diuers tongues, we vndertoke this great and wonderful worke (with all reuerence, as in the presence of God, as intreating the worde of God, whereunto we thinke our selues vnsufficient) which now God according to his diuine prouidence and mercie hath directed to a moste prosperous end. And this we may with good conscience protest, that we haue in euery point and worde, according to the measure of that knollage which it pleased al mightie God to giue vs, faithfully rendred the text, and in all hard places moste syncerely expounded the same. For God is our witnes that we haue by all meanes indeuored to set forthe the puritie of the worde and right sense of the holy Gost for the edifying of the brethren in faith and charitie.

Now as we haue chiefely obserued the sense, and laboured alwaies to restore it to all integritie: so haue we moste reuerently kept the proprietie of the wordes, considering that the Apostles who spake and wrote to the Gentiles in the Greke tongue, rather constrayned them to the liuely phrase of the Ebrewe, then entreprised farre by mollifying their langage to speake as the Gentils did. And for this and other causes we haue in many places reserued the Ebrewe phrases, notwithstanding that thei may seme somewhat hard in their eares that are not wel practised and also delite in the swete sounding phrases of the holy Scriptures. Yet lest ether the simple shulde be discouraged, or the malicious haue any occasion of iust cauillation, seing some translations read after one sort, and some after another, whereas all may serue to good purpose and edification, we haue in the margent noted that diuersitie of speache or reading which may also seme agreable to the mynde of the holy Gost and propre for our langage with this marke ".

Agayne where as the Ebrewe speache semed hardly to agre with ours, we haue noted it in the margent after this sort", vsing that which was more intelligible. And albeit that many of the Ebrewe names be altered from the olde text, and restored to the true writing and first original, whereof thei haue their signification, yet in the vsual names litle is changed for feare of troubling the simple readers. Moreouer whereas the necessitie of the sentence required any thing to be added (for suche is the grace and proprietie of the Ebrewe and Greke tongues, that it can not but ether by circumlocution, or by adding the verbe or some worde be vnderstand of them that are not wel practised therein) we haue put it in the text with another kynde of lettre, that it may easely be discerned from the common lettre. As touching the diuision of the verses, we haue followed the Ebrewe examples, which haue so euen from the begynning distinct them. Which thing as it is moste profitable for memorie: so doeth it agre with the best translations, & is moste easie to finde out both by the best Concordances, and also by the cotations which we haue dilygently herein perused and set forthe by this starre *. Besides this the principal matters are noted and distincted by this marke ¶. Yea and the argumentes bothe for the booke and for the chapters with the nombre of the verse are added, that by all meanes the reader might be holpen. For the which cause also we haue set ouer the head of euery page some notable worde or sentence which may greatly further aswel for memorie, as for the chief point of the page. And considering how hard a thing it is to vnderstand the holy Scriptures, and what errors, sectes and heresies growe dailie for lacke of the true knollage thereof, and how many are discouraged (as thei pretend) because thei can not atteine to the true and simple meaning of the same, we haue also indeuored bothe by the diligent reading of the best commentaries, and also by the conference with the godly and learned brethren, to gather brief annotations vpon all the hard places, aswel for the vnderstanding of suche wordes as are obscure, and for the declaratiō of the text, as for the application of the same as may moste apperteine to Gods glorie and the edification of his Churche. Forthermore whereas certeyne places in the bookes of Moses, of the Kings and Ezekiel semed so darke that by no description thei colde be made easie to the simple reader, we haue so set them forthe with figures and notes for the ful declaration thereof, that thei which can not by iudgement, being holpen by the annotations noted by the lettres a b c. &c. atteyn thereunto, yet by the perspectiue, and as it were by the eye may sufficiently knowe the true meaning of all suche places. Whereunto also we haue added certeyne mappes of Cosmographie which necessarely serue for the perfect vnderstanding and memorie of diuers places and countreys, partely described, and partely by occasion touched, bothe in the olde and newe Testament. Finally that nothing might lacke which might be boght by labors, for the increase of knowlage and fortherance of Gods glorie, we haue adioyned two moste profitable tables, the one seruing for the interpretation of the Ebrewe names: and the other conteyning all the chefe and principal matters of the whole Bible: so that nothing (as we trust) that any colde iustely desire, is omitted. Therefore, as brethren that are partakers of the same hope and saluation with vs, we beseche you, that this riche perle and inestimable treasure may not be offred in vayne, but as sent from God to the people of God, for the increase of his kingdome, the comfort of his Churche, and discharge of our conscience, whome it hath pleased him to raise vp for this purpose, so you wolde willingly receyue the worde of God, earnestly studie it and in all your life practise it, that you may now appeare in dede to be the people of God, not walking any more according to this worlde, but in the frutes of the Spirit; that God in vs may be fully glorified through Christ Iesus our Lord, who lyueth and reigneth for euer. Amen. From Geneua, 10. April. 1560.

THE FIRST BOKE OF Mosés, called [*] Genesis.

[*] This worde signifieth the beginning and generacion of the creatures.

THE ARGVMENT.

MOSES in effect declareth the things, which are here chiefly to be considered: First, that the worlde & all things therein were created by God, & that man being placed in this great tabernacle of the worlde to beholde Gods wonderful workes, & to praise his Name for the infinite graces, wherewith he had endued him, fel willingly from God through disobedience: who yet for his owne mercies sake restored him to life, & confirmed him in the same by his promes of Christ to come, by whome he shulde overcome Satan, death and hel. Secondely, that the wicked, vnmindeful of Gods moste excellent benefites, remained stil in their wickednes, & so falling moste horribly from sinne to sinne, prouoked God (who by his preachers called them continually to repentance) at length to destroye the whole worlde. Thirdly, he assureth vs by the examples of Abrahám, Izhák, Iaakób & the rest of the Patriarkes, that his mercies neuer faile them, whome he chuseth to be his Church, and to professe his Name in earth, but in all their afflictions and persecutions he euer assisteth them, sendeth comforte, & deliuereth them. And because the beginning, increase, preseruacion and successe thereof might be onely attributed to God, Mosés sheweth by the examples of Káin, Ishmaél, Esáu and others, which were noble in mans iudgement, that this Church dependeth not on the estimacion and nobilitie of the worlde: and also by the fewenes of them, which haue at all times worshiped him purely according to his worde, that it standeth not in the multitude, but in the poore and despised, in the smale flocke and litle nomber, that man in his wisdome might be confounded, & the Name of God euer more praised.

CHAP. I.

1 God created the heauen & the earth, 3 The light & the darkenes, 8 The firmamēt. 9 He separateth the water from the earth 16 He createth the sunne, the moone, & the starres 21 He createth the fish, birdes, beastes 26 He createth man and giueth him rule ouer all creatures, 29 And prouideth nourriture for man and beast.

1 IN THE [a] beginning
[*] God created ẏ hea-
uen and the earth.
2 And the earth was [b]
without forme & voy-
de, and [c] darkenes *was*
vpon the depe, & the
Spirit of God [d] moued
vpon the waters.
3 Then God said, [*] Let there be light: and
there was [e] light.
4 And God sawe ẏ light that it was good,
and God separated the light from the
darkenes.
5 And God called the light, Day, and the
darkenes, he called Night. ‖ So the euenīg
and the morning were the first day.
6 ¶ Againe God said, [*] Let there be a [″] firmament in the middes of the waters: and
let it separate the waters from the waters.
7 Then God made the firmament, & parted the waters, which were [f] vnder the
firmament, from the waters which were
[*] aboue the firmament. and it was so.
8 And God called the firmament, [g] Heauen. ‖ So the euening and the morning
were the seconde day.
9 ¶ God said againe, [*] Let the waters vnder the heauē be gathered into one place,
& let the drye land appeare. and it was so.
10 And God called the drye land, Earth, &
he called ẏ gathering together of the waters, Seas: & God sawe that it was good.
11 Then God said, [h] Let the earth budde
forthe the budde of the herbe, that sedeth
sede, the fruteful tre, ẇ beareth frute according to his kinde, which *maie haue* his
sede in it self vpon the earth. & it was so.
12 And the earth broght forthe the budde
of the herbe, that sedeth sede accordīg to
his kinde, also the tre that yeldeth frute, ẇ
hathe his sede in it selfe according to his
kinde: & God [i] sawe that it was good.
13 ‖ So the euening and the morning were
the third daie.
14 ¶ And God said, [*] Let there be [k] lightes
in the firmament of the heauen, to [l] separate the daie from the night, & let them be
for [m] signes, and for seasons, and for daies
and yeres.
15 And let them be for lightes in the firmament of the heauen to giue light vpō the
earth. and it was so.
16 God then made two [n] great lightes: the
greater light [o] to rule the daie, & the lesse
light to rule ẏ night: he *made* also ẏ starres.
17 And God set them in the firmament of
the heauen, to shine vpon the earth,
18 And to [*] rule in the daie, & in the night,
and to separate the light from the darkenes: and God sawe that it was good.
19 ‖ So the euening and the morning were
the fourth daie.
20 Afterwarde God said, Let the waters
bring forthe in abundāce *euerie* [p] creping
thing that hathe [″] life: & let the foule flie
vpon the earth in the [″] open firmament of
the heauen.
21 Then God created the great whales, &
euerie thing liuing & mouing, ẇ the [q] waters broght forthe in abundance, accordīg
to their kinde, & euerie fethered foule according to his kinde: & God sawe that it
was good.

a First of all, & before that anie creature was, God made heauen and earth of nothing.
Psal 33.6. & 136.5 eccles. 18.1. act. 14.15 & 17.24.
b As a rude lumpe & without anie creature in it: for the waters couered all.
c Darkenes couered ẏ depe waters: for as yet ẏ light was not created.
d He mainteined this cōfuse heape by his secret power.
Ebr. 11.3.
e The light was made before ether sunne or moone was created: therefore we must not attribute that to ẏ creatures that are Gods instruments, ẇ onely apperteineth to God.
‖ The 1. day.
Psal. 33.6. & 136.5. iere. 10.12. & 51.15.
″ *Or, spreading ouer, & ayre.*
f As the sea & riuers, from those waters that are in the cloudes, which are vpholden by Gods power, lest they shulde ouerwhelme the worlde.
Psal. 148.4.
g That is, the region of the ayre, and all ẏ is aboue vs.
‖ The 2. day.
Psal. 33.7. & 89.12.
h So that we se it is the onely power of Gods worde that maketh ẏ earth fruteful, which els naturally is baren.

i This sentence is so oft repeated, to signifie ẏ God made all his creatures to serue to his glorie, & to the profit of man: but for sinne thei were acursed, yet to ẏ elect, by Christ they are restored & serue to their welth.
‖ The 3. day.
Psal 136.7. deut. 4.19.
k By ẏ lightes he meaneth ẏ sunne, the moone and the starres.
l Which is ẏ artificial day, frō the sunne rising to the going downe.
m Of things apperteining to natural and political ordres and seasons.
n To wit, the sunne and the moone: & here he speaketh as man iudgeth by his eye: for els the moone is lesse thē the planete Saturnus.
o To giue it sufficiēt light, as instruments appointed for ẏ same, to serue to mās vse.
Iére. 31.35.
‖ The 4. day.
p As fish and wormes which slide, swimme or crepe.
″ *Ebr. the soule of life.*
″ *Ebr. face of the firmament.*
q The fish & foules had bothe one beginning, wherein we se that nature giueth place to Gods wil, forasmuche as the one sorte is made to flie aboue in the ayre, & the other to swimme beneth in the water.

22 Then God [r] blessed them, saying,
Bring forthe frute and multiplie, and fil
the waters in the seas, & let the foule multiplie in the earth.
23 ‖So the euening & the morning were the
fifte day.
24 ¶ Moreouer God said, Let the earth
bring forthe the "liuing thing according
to his kinde, cattel, & that which crepeth,
& the beast of the earth, according to his
kinde. and it was so.
25 And God made ẏ beast of the earth according to his kinde, and the cattel according to his kinde, & euerie creping thing
of ẏ earth according to his kinde: & God
sawe that it was good.
26 Furthermore God said, *[f] Let vs make
man in our [t] image according to our lickenes, and let them rule ouer the fish of
the sea, and ouer the foule of the heauen,
and ouer the beastes, & ouer all the earth,
and ouer euerie thing that crepeth & moueth on the earth.
27 *Thus God created the man in his image: in the image of God created he him:
he created them* male and female.
28 And God [u] blessed them, and God said
to them, *Bring forthe frute and multiplie, and fil the earth, and subdue it, and
rule ouer the fish of the sea and ouer the
foule of the heauen, & ouer euerie beast
that moueth vpon the earth.
29 And God said, Beholde, I haue giuen
vnto you [x] euerie herbe bearīg sede, which
is vpon all the earth, & euerie tre, wherein is the frute of a tre bearing sede: * *that*
shalbe to you for meat.
30 Likewise to euerie beast of the earth, and
to euerie foule of the heauen, & to euerie
thing that moueth vpon the earth, which
hathe life in it selfe, euerie grene herbe
shalbe for meat. and it was so.
31 * And God sawe all that he had made, &
lo, it was very good. ‖So the euening and
the morning were the sixt day.

CHAP. II

2 God resteth the seuenth day, and sanctifieth it. 15 He setteth man in the garden. 22 He createth the womā. 29 Mariage is ordeined.

1 Thus the heauens and the earth were
finished, & all the [a] hoste of them.
2 For in the seuenth day God ended his
worke which he had made, * & the seuenth
daye he [b] rested from all his worke, which
he had made.
3 So God blessed the seuenth day, & [c] sanctified it, because that in it he had rested
from all his worke, which God had created and made.
4 ¶ These are the "generacions of the heauens & of the earth, when thei were created, in the day that the Lord God made
the earth and the heauens,

[r] That is, by the vertue of his worde he gaue power to his creatures to ingendre.
‖The 5 day.
"Ebr. *soule of life.*
Chap.5,5. & 9,6. 1.cor.11,7 colos.3,10.
[f] God cōmanded the water and the earth, to brig forthe other creatures: but of man he saith, Let vs make: signifying ẏ God taketh counsel with his wisdome & vertue, purposing to make an excellent worke aboue all the rest of his creacion.
[t] This image and licknes of God in man is expounded Ephes 4,24: where it is writē, ẏ man was created after God in righteousnes & true holines, meaning by these two wordes all perfection, as wisdome, trueth, innocencie, power, &c.
Wisdo.2,23. eccles.17,1.
Matt.19,4.
[u] The propagacion of man is the blessing of God, Psal. 128.
Chap.8,17. & 9,1.
[x] Gods great liberalitie to man taketh away all excuse of his ingratitude.
Chap.9,3.
Exod.3,17. eccles.39,21. mar.7,37.
‖The 6 day.
[a] That is, the innumerable abundance of creatures in heauē & earth.
Exod.20,11. & 31,17. ebr.4,4.
[b] For he had now finished his creacion, but his prouidence stil watcheth ouer his creatures, and gouerneth thē.
[c] Appointed it to be kept holy, that man might therein consider ẏ excellencie of his workes & Gods goodnes towards him.
"*Or, the original & begining.*

5 And euerie "plant of the field, before it
was in the earth, and euerie herbe of the
field, before it grewe: for the Lord God
had not caused it to [d] raine vpō the earth,
nether *was there* a man to til the grounde,
6 But a myst went vp from the earth, and
watred all the earth.
7 ¶ The Lord God also made the mā [e] of
the dust of the grounde, and breathed in
his face breath of life, and the man was a
liuing soule.
8 And the Lord God plāted a garden Eastwarde in [f] Eden, and there he put the man
whome he had made.
9 (For out of the grounde made the Lord
God to growe euerie tre pleasant to the
sight, and good for meat: the [g] tre of life
also in the middes of the garden, [h] and the
tre of knowledge of good and of euil.
10 And out of Eden went a riuer to water
the garden, and from thence it was deuided, and became into foure heades.
11 The name of one *is* * Pishón: the same
compasseth the whole land [i] of Hauiláh, where *is* golde.
12 And the golde of that land is good: there *is* also "bdelium, and the onix stone.
13 And the name of the secōde riuer *is* Gihón: the same compasseth the whole land
of "Cush.
14 The name also of ẏ third riuer *is* "Hiddékel: this goeth towarde the Eastside of
"Asshúr: and the fourth riuer is "Peráth)
15 ¶ Then the Lord God toke the man, and
put him into the garden of Eden, that he
might [k] dresse it and kepe it.
16 And the Lord God [l] commanded the
man, saying, Thou shalt eat frely of euerie tre of the garden,
17 But as touching the tre of knowledge
of good and euil, thou shalt not eat of it:
for "whensoeuer thou eatest thereof,
thou shalt dye the [m] death.
18 Also the Lord God said, It is not good
that the man shulde be him selfe alone: I
wil make him an helpe "mete for him.
19 So the Lord God formed of the earth
euerie beast of the field, and euerie foule of
the heauen, & broght *them* vnto the [n] mā
to se how he wolde call *thē*: for howsoeuer
the man named the liuing creature, so was
the name thereof.
20 The man therefore gaue names vnto all
cattel, and to the foule of the heauen, and
to euerie beast of the field: but for Adám
founde he not an helpe mete for him.
21 ¶ Therefore the Lord God caused an
heauie slepe to fall vpon the man: & whiles he slept, he toke one of his rybbes, and
closed vp the flesh in steade thereof.
22 And the rybbe which the Lord God had
taken from the man, "made he a [o] woman,
and broght her to the man.

"*Or, tre, as Chap.21,15.*
[d] God onely openeth the heauens and shutteth thē, he sendeth drought and raine according to his good pleasure.
[e] He sheweth whereof mans bodye was created, to the intent that mā shulde not glorie in the excellēcie of his owne nature.
[f] This was the name of a place, as some thike, in Mesopotamia, moste pleasant & abundant in all things.
[g] Which was a signe of the life receaued of God.
[h] That is, of miserable experiēce, which came by disobeying God.
Eccle.24,35.
[i] Which Hauiláh is a coūtrey ioyning to Persia Estwarde & enclineth towarde the West.
"*Or, precious stone, or perle. Plinie sayth it is the name of a tre.*
"*Or, Ethiopia.*
"*Or, Tygris.*
"*Or, Assyria.*
"*Or, Euphrates.*
[k] God wolde not haue man ydle, though as yet there was no nede to labour.
[l] So that man might knowe there was a soueraigne Lord, to whome he owed obediēce.
"*Ebr. in the day*
[m] By this death he meaneth the separacion of man frō God, who is our life and chief felicitie: and also that our disobediēce is the cause thereof.
"*Ebr. before him.*
[n] By mouing them to come & submit thē selues to Adám.
"*Ebr. buylt.*
[o] Signifying, that mankinde was perfit, when ẏ womā was created, ẇ before was like an vnperfit buylding.

23 Then

1.Cor.11,8.
23 Then the man said,* This now is bone
of my bones, and flesh of my flesh. She
shalbe called ״woman, because she was taken out of man.
24 *Therefore shal man leaue p his father
and his mother, and shal cleaue to his wife,
and they shalbe one flesh.
25 And they were bothe naked, the man &
his wife, and were not q ashamed.

״*Or, Manner, because she cometh of man: for in Ebr. Ish, is man, and Ishah the woman.*

Mat.19,5. mar.10,7. 1.cor.6,16. ephes.5,31.

p So that mariage requireth a greater duetie of vs towarde ye wiues, then otherwise we are bounde to shewe to our parents.

q For before sinne entred, all things were honest and comely.

THE SITVACION OF THE GARDEN OF EDEN.

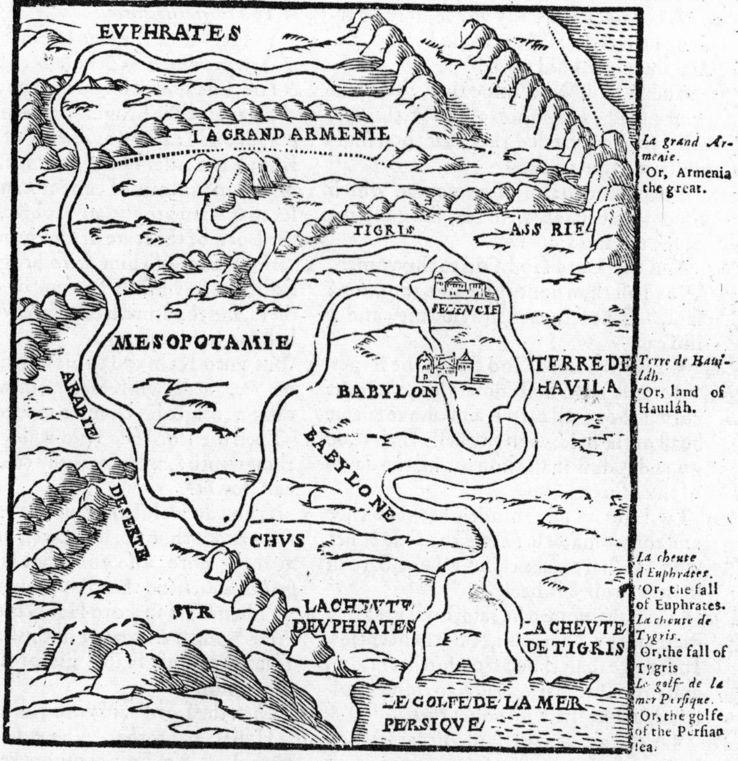

La grand Armenie. ״Or, Armenia the great.

Terre de Hauiláh. ״Or, land of Hauiláh.

La cheute d Euphrates. ״Or, the fall of Euphrates.

La cheute de Tygris. ״Or, the fall of Tygris

Le golfe de la mer Persique. ״Or, the golfe of the Persian sea.

Because mencion is made in the tenth verse of this seconde chapter of the riuer that watered the garden, we muste note that Euphrates and Tygris called in Ebrewe, Peráth and Hiddékel, were called but one riuer where they ioyned together, els they had foure heades: that is, two at their springs, & two where they fel into the Persian sea. In this countrey and moste plentiful land Adám dwelt, and this was called Paradise: that is, a garden of pleasure, because of the frutefulnes and abundance thereof. And whereas it is said that Pishón compasseth the land of Hauiláh, it is meant of Tygris, which in some place, as it passed by diuers places, was called by sundry names, as some time Diglitto, in other places Pasitygris, & of some Phasin or Pishón. Likewise Euphrates towarde the countrey of Cush or Ethiopia, or Arabia was called Gihon. So that Tygris and Euphrates (which were but two riuers, and some time when they ioyned together, were called after one name) were according to diuers places called by these foure names, so that they might seme to haue bene foure diuers riuers.

CHAP. III.

1 The womã seduced by the serpẽt, 6 Entiseth her housbãd to sinne. 14 They thre are punished. 15 Christ is promised. 19 Man is dust. 22 Man is cast out of paradise.

1 NOw*the serpent was more a subtil
then anie beast of the field, which ye
Lord God had made: and he b said to the
woman, Yea, hathe God in dede said, Ye
shal not eat of euerie tre of the garden?
2 And the woman said vnto the serpẽt, We
eat of the frute of the trees of the garden,
3 But of the frute of the tre, which is in the
middes of the garden, God hathe said, Ye
shal not eat of it, nether shal ye touche it,
c lest ye dye.
4 Then*the serpent said to the woman, Ye
shal not d dye at all,
5 But God doeth knowe, that when ye shal
eat thereof, your eyes shalbe opened, & ye
shalbe as gods, e knowing good and euil.
6 So the woman (seing that the tre was
good for meat, and that it was pleasant to
the eyes, & a tre to be desired to get knowledge) toke of the frute thereof, and did
* eat, and gaue also to her housband with
her, and he f did eat.
7 Then the eyes of them bothe were opened, & they g knewe that they were naked,
and they sewed figtre leaues together, and
made them selues ״breeches.
8 ¶Afterwarde they heard the voyce of

Wisdo.2,25.

a As Satan cã change him selfe into an Angel of light, so did he abuse the wisdome of the serpent to deceaue man.

b God suffered Satan to make the serpent his instrument and to speake in him.

c In douting of Gods threatnĩg, she yelded to Satan.

2.Cor.11,3.

d This is Satans chiefest subtiltie, to cause vs not to feare Gods threatenings.

e As thogh he shulde say, God doeth not forbid you to eat of the frute, saue that he knoweth that if you shulde eat thereof, you shulde be like to him.

Eccles.25,33. 1.tim.2,14.

f Not so muche to please his wife, as moued by ambicion at her persuasion.

g They began to fele their miserie, but they soght not to God for remedie.

״*Ebr. things to girde about them to hide their priuities.*

the Lord God walking in the garden in
the "coole of the day, and the man and his
wife [h] hid them selues from the presence
of the Lord God among the trees of the
garden.
9 But the Lord God called to the man, and
said vnto him, Where art thou?
10 Who said, I heard thy voyce in the garden, and was afraied: because I was [i] naked, therefore I hid my self.
11 And he said, Who tolde thee, that thou
wast naked? Hast thou eaten of the tre,
whereof I cōmanded thee that thou shuldest not eat in no case?
12 Then the man said, The woman which
thou [k] gauest *to be* with me, she gaue me
of the tre, and I did eat.
13 And the Lord God said to the woman,
Why hast thou done this? And the womā
said, [l] The serpent beguyled me, and I
did eat.
14 ¶ Then the Lord God said to the serpēt,
[m] Because thou hast done this, thou art
cursed aboue all cattel, and aboue euerie
beast of the field: vpon thy belly shalt thou
go, and [n] dust shalt thou eat all the dayes
of thy life.
15 I wil also [o] put enimitie betwene thee
and the womā, & betwene thy sede & her
sede. He shal breake thine [p] head, & thou
shalt [q] bruise his heele.
16 ¶ Vnto the woman he said, I wil greately
increase thy [r] sorowes, & thy conceptiōs.
In sorowe shalt thou bring forthe childrē,
and thy desire *shal be subiect* to thine housband, and he shal * rule ouer thee.
17 ¶ Also to Adám he said, Because thou
hast obeied the voyce of thy wife, and hast
eaten of the tre (whereof I cōmāded thee,
saying, Thou shalt not eat of it) [s] cursed
is the earth for thy sake: in sorowe shalt
thou eat of it all the dayes of thy life.
18 [t] Thornes also, and thystles shal it bring
forthe to thee, and thou shalt eat the herbe of the field.
19 In the sweat of thy face shalt thou eat
bread, til thou returne to the earth: for
out of it wast thou taken, because thou art
dust, and to dust shalt thou returne.
20 (And the man called his wiues name
Heuáh, because she was the mother of all
liuing)
21 Vnto Adám also and to his wife did the
Lord God [u] make coates of skinnes, and
clothed them.
22 ¶ And the Lord God said, [x] Beholde,
the man is become as one of vs, to knowe
good and euil. And now lest he put forthe
his hand, and [y] take also of the tre of life
and eat and liue for euer,
23 Therefore ẏ Lord God sent him forthe
from the garden of Eden, to til the earth,
whencé he was taken.
24 Thus he cast out man, and at the Eastside of the garden of Eden he set the Cherubíms, and the blade of a sworde shaken,
to kepe the waye of the tre of life.

'Or, winde.
h The sinful cōsciēce fleeth Gods presence.
i His hypocrisie appeareth in that he hid ẏ cause of his nakednes, ẇ was the transgresion of Gods commādement.
k His wickednes & lacke of true repentāce appeareth in this ẏ he burdeneth God ẇ his faute, because he had giuē hī a wife.
l In stead of confessing her sinne, she increaseth it by accusing the serpent.
m He asked ẏ reason of Adā and his wife, because he wolde bring them to repentance, but he asketh not the serpēt, because he wolde shewe him no mercie.
n As a vile & contemptible beast, Isa. 65, 25.
o He chiefly meaneth Satā, by whose motion & craft ẏ serpent deceiued ẏ woman.
p That is, the power of sinne and death.
q Satan shal sting Christ & his members, but not ouercome them.
r The Lord comforteth Adám by the promes of the blessed sede, & also punisheth ẏ body for the sinne, which ẏ soule shulde haue bene punished for, ẏ the spirit hauing conceiued hope of forgiuenes, might liue by faith.
1.Cor. 14,34.
s The transgressiō of Gods cōmandement was the cause ẏ bothe mankinde and all other creatures were subiect to the curse.
t These are not ẏ natural frutes of the earth, but procede of ẏ corruption of sinne.
u Or gaue thē knowledge to make thē selues coates.
x By this derision he reprocheth Adās miserie, whereinto he was fallen by ambition. y Adám depriued of life lost also the signe thereof.

CHAP. IIII.

1 The generation of mankinde. 8 Káin killeth Hábel. 23 Lámech a tyrant encourageth his feareful wiues. 26 True religion is restored.

1 After warde the man knewe Heuáh his
wife, which [a] cōceiued & bare Káin,
& said, I haue obteined a man [b] by ẏ Lord.
2 And againe she broght forthe his brother
Hábel, and Hábel was a keper of shepe, &
Káin was a tiller of the grounde.
3 ¶ And in processe of time it came to passe, that Káin broght an [c] oblacion vnto
the Lord of the frute of the grounde.
4 And Hábel also him selfe broght of the
first frutes of his shepe, and of the fat of
them, and the Lord had respect vnto * Hábel, and to his offring,
5 But vnto Káin and to his offring he had
no [d] regarde: wherefore Káin was exceding wroth, & his countenance fel downe.
6 Then the Lord said vnto Káin, Why art
thou wroth? and why is thy countenance
cast downe?
7 If thou do wel, shalt thou not be [e] accepted? and if thou doest not wel, sinne lieth
at the [f] dore: also vnto thee his [g] desire
shal be subiect, and thou shalt rule ouer him.
8 ¶ Then Káin spake to Hábel his brother.
And * when they were in the field, Káin
rose vp against Hábel his brother, and
slewe him.
9 Then the Lord said vnto Káin, Where
is Hábel thy brother? Who answered, I cā
not tel. [h] Am I my brothers keper?
10 Againe he said, What hast thou done? the
[i] voyce of thy brothers blood cryeth vnto me from the grounde.
11 Now therefore thou art cursed [k] frō the
earth, ẇ hathe opened her mouth to receiue thy brothers blood from thine hand.
12 When thou shalt til the grounde, it
shal not henceforthe yelde vnto thee her
strength: a [l] vagabonde and a rennegate
shalt thou be in the earth.
13 Then Káin said to the Lord, [m] 'My punishment is greater, then I can beare.
14 Beholde, thou hast cast me out this day
from the earth, and from thy face shal I
be hid, and shalbe a vagabonde and a rennegate in the earth, & whosoeuer findeth
me, shal slaye me.
15 Then the Lord said vnto him, Douteles
whosoeuer slayeth Káin, he shalbe [n] punished seuen folde. And ẏ Lord set a [o] marke vpon Káin, lest anie man finding him
shulde kil him.
16 Then Káin went out from the presence
of the Lord and dwelt in the land of Nod
towarde the Eastside of Eden.

a Mans nature, the state of mariage, & Gods blessing were not vtterly abolished through sinne, but the qualitie or conditiō thereof was changed.
b That is, according to the Lords promes, as chap. 3, 15: some read, To the Lord, as reioycing for ẏ sonne, ẇ she hadborne, who me she wolde offer to ẏ Lord as the first frutes of her birth.
c This declareth that the father instructed his childrē in ẏ knowledge of God, and also how God gaue thē sacrifices to signifie their saluatiō: albeit they were destitute of the sacrament of the tre of life.
Ebr. 11,4.
d Because he was an hypocrite and offred onely for an outwarde shew without sinceritie of heart.
e Bothe thou and thy sacrifice shalbe acceptable to me.
f Sinne shal stil tormēt thy conscience.
g The dignitie of ẏ first borne is giuen to Káin ouer Hábel.
Wisd. 10,3. mat. 23,35. 1.ioh. 3,12. iud. 11.
h This is the nature of the reprobate whē thei are reproued of their hypocrisie, euē to neglect God and despite him.
i God reuengeth ẏ wrōgs of his Saints, thogh none cōplaine: for the iniquitie it selfe cryeth for vengeance.
k The earth shalbe a witnes agaīst thee which mercifully receiued that blood, ẇ thou moste cruelly shed.
l Thou shalt neuer haue rest: for thine heart shalbe in continual feare & care.
m He burdeneth God as a cruel iudge, because he did punish him so sharpely. 'Or, my sinne is greater then can be pardoned. n Not for the loue he bare to Káin, but to suppresse murther. o A visible signe of Gods iudgement that others shulde feare.

17 Káin also knewe his wife, which cóceiued and bare Henóch: and he buylt a [p] citie and called the name of the citie by the name of his sonne, Henóch.
18 And to Henóch was borne Irád, and Irád begate Mehuiaél, and Mehuiaél begate Methushaél, and Methushaél begate Lámech.
19 ¶ And Lámech toke to him [q] two wiues: the name of the one *was* Adáh, and the name of the other Zilláh.
20 And Adáh bare Iabál, who was the [″] father of suche as dwel in the tentes, and of suche as haue cattel.
21 And his brothers name *was* Iubál, who was the father of all that playe on the harpe and [″] organes.
22 And Zilláh also bare Tubal-káin, who wroght cunningly euerie crafte of brasse and of yron: and the sister of Tubal-káin *was* Naamáh.
23 Then Lámech said vnto his wiues Adáh and Zilláh, Heare my voyce, *ye* wiues of Lámech: hearken vnto my speche: [r] for I wolde slaye a man in my woúde, & a yong man in mine hurt.
24 If Káin shalbe auenged seuen folde, truely Lámech, [s] seuentie times seuen folde.
25 ¶ And Adám knewe his wife againe, and she bare a sonne, and she called his name Sheth: for God, *said she*, hathe appointed me another sede for Hábel, because Káin slewe him.
26 And to the same Sheth also there was borne a sonne, and he called his name Enósh. Then began men to [t] call vpon the Name of the Lord.

p Thinking thereby to be sure & to haue lesse occasion to feare Gods iudgements against him.

q The lawful institucion of mariage, which is that two shulde be one flesh, was first corrupt in the house of Káin by Lámech.

″ Or, first inuenter.

″ Or, flutes and pipes.

r His wiues seing that all mé hated him for his crueltie, were afraied: therefore he braggeth that there is none so lusty that were able to risist, althogh he were already wounded.

s He mocked at Gods sufferáce in Káin, iestig as thogh God wolde suffre none to punish him, & yet giue him licéce to murther others.

t In these dayes God began to moue the hearts of the godlie to restore religion, which a long time by the wicked had bene suppressed.

CHAP. V.

1 The genealogie. 5 Age and deathe of Adám. 6 His succession vnto Nóah and his children.

1 This is the [″] boke of the generacions of Adám. In the day that God created Adám, in the [a] lickenes of God made he him,
2 Male and female created he thé, & blessed them, and called their name [b] Adám in the day that they were created.
3 ¶ Now Adám liued an húdreth and thirtie yeres and begate a childe in his owne [c] lickenes after his image, and called his name Sheth.
4 *And the dayes of Adám, after he had begotten Sheth, were eight hundreth yeres, and he begate sonnes and daughters.
5 So all the dayes that Adám liued, were nine hundreth and thirtie yeres: and he dyed.
6 And [d] Sheth liued an hundreth, and fyue yeres, and begate Enósh.
7 And Sheth liued, after he begate Enósh, eight hundreth and seuen yeres, and begate sonnes and daughters.

″ Or, rehearsal of the stocke.

a Read Chap. 1,26.

b By giuing them bothe one name, he noteth the inseparable cóiunction of mã and wife.

c Aswel concerning his creation, as his corruption.

* 1. Chro. 1,1.

d He proueth Adams generation by thé, which came of Sheth, to shewe which is the true Church, and also what care God had ouer the same from the beginning, in that he continued euer his graces toward it by a continual succeision.

8 So all the dayes of Sheth were [e] nine húdreth and twelue yeres: & he dyed.
9 ¶ Also Enósh liued ninety yeres & begate Kenán.
10 And Enósh liued, after he begate Kenán, eight hundreth and fiftene yeres, and begate sonnes and daughters.
11 So all the daies of Enósh were nine hundreth and fiue yeres: and he dyed.
12 ¶ Likewise Kenán liued seuentie yeres, and begate Mahalaleél.
13 And Kenán liued, after he begate Mahalaleél, eight hundreth and fourty yeres, & begate sonnes and daughters.
14 So all the dayes of Kenán were nine húdreth and ten yeres: and he dyed.
15 ¶ Mahalaleél also liued sixty & fiue yeres and begate Iéred.
16 Also Mahalaleél liued, after he begate Iéred, eight hundreth and thirty yeres, & begate sonnes and daughters.
17 So all the dayes of Mahalaleél were eight hundreth ninety and fiue yeres: and he dyed.
18 ¶ And Iéred liued an hundreth sixty and two yeres, and begate Henóch.
19 Then Iéred liued, after he begate Henóch, eight hundreth yeres, and begate sonnes and daughters.
20 So all the dayes of Iéred were nine hundreth sixty and two yeres: & he dyed.
21 ¶ * Also Henóch liued sixty and fiue yeres, and begate Methushélah.
22 And Henóch [f] walked with God, after he begate Methushélah, thre hundreth yeres, and begate sonnes and daughters.
23 So all the daies of Henóch were thre húdreth sixty and fiue yeres.
24 And Henóch walked with God, and he was no more *sene*: for [g] God toke him away.
25 Methushélah also liued an hundreth eighty and seuen yeres, and begate Lámech.
26 And Methushélah liued, after he begate Lámech, seuen hundreth eighty and two yeres, and begate sonnes and daughters.
27 So all the dayes of Methushélah were nine hundreth sixty and nine yeres: and he dyed.
28 ¶ Then Lámech liued an húdreth eighty and two yeres, and begate a sonne,
29 And called his name Nóah, saying, This same shal [h] comforte vs concerning our worke and sorowe of our hands, as touching the earth, which the Lord hathe cursed.
30 And Lámech liued, after he begate Nóáh, fiue hundreth ninety and fiue yeres, and begate sonnes and daughters.
31 So all the dayes of Lámech were seué hundreth seuenty and seuen yeres: and he dyed.

e The chief cause of long life in the first age was the multiplicatió of mankinde that accordig to Gods commandement at the beginning the worlde might be increased with people, which might vniuersally praise his Name.

* Eccl. 44,15. ebr. 11,5.

f That is, he led an vpright & godlie life.

g To shewe that there was a better life prepared, & to be a testimonie of the immortalitie of soules & bodies. As to inquire where he became, is mere curiositie.

h Lámech had respect to the promes, Chap. 3,15, and desired to se the deliuerer, which shulde be sent, & yet sawe but a figure thereof. he also spake this by the Spirit of prophecie, because Nóah deliuered the Church, and preserued it by his obedience.

32 And Nóah was fiue hundreth yere olde. And Nóah begate Shem, Ham and
Iápheth.

CHAP. VI.

3 God threateneth to bring the flood. 5 Man is altogether corrupt 18 Nóah is preserued in the Arke, which he was commanded to make.

1 SO when men began to be multiplied
vpon the earth, and there were daughters borne vnto them,
2 Then the [a] sonnes of God sawe the
daughters [b] of men that they were [c] faire, and they toke them wiues of all that
they liked.
3 Therefore the Lord said, My Spirit shal
not alway [d] striue with man, because he
is but flesh, & his dayes shal be an [e] hundreth and twentie yeres.
4 There were "gyantes in the earth in those dayes: yea, and after that the sonnes of
God came vnto the daughters of mē, and
they had borne them children, these were
mightie men, which in olde time were men
of [f] renoume.
5 ¶When the Lord sawe that the wickednes of man was great in the earth, and all
the imaginacions of the thoghts of his
*heart *were* onely euil continually,
6 Then it [g] repéted the Lord, that he had
made man in the earth, and he was sorie in
his heart.
7 Therefore the Lord said, I wil destroye
from the earth the man, whome I haue
created, from man [h] to beast, to the creping thing, & to the foule of the heauen:
for I repent that I haue made them.
8 But Nóah [i] founde grace in the eyes of
the Lord.
9 ¶These are the "generacions of Nóah.
Nóah was a iuste and vpright man in his
time, *and* walked with God.
10 And Nóah begate thre sonnes, Shem,
Ham and Iápheth.
11 The earth also was corrupt before God:
for the earth was filled with [k] crueltie.
12 Then God loked vpō the earth, and beholde, it was corrupt: for all flesh had corrupt his way vpon the earth.
13 And God said vnto Nóah, "An end of
all flesh is come before me: for the earth is
filled with "crueltie through them: and beholde, I wil destroye them with the earth.
14 ¶Make thee an Arke of "pine trees: thou
shalt make "cabines in the Arke, and shalt
pytch it within and without with pytch.
15 And "thus shalt thou make it: The lēgth
of the Arke shalbe thre hundreth cubites,
the breadth of it fiftie cubites, and the
height of it thirtie cubites.
16 A windowe shalt thou make in the Arke,
and in a cubite shalt thou finish it aboue,
and the dore of the Arke shalt thou set in
the side thereof: thou shalt make it with
the [l] lowe, seconde and third *roume.*
17 And I, beholde, I wil bring a flood of waters vpon the earth to destroye all flesh,
wherein is ỷ breath of life vnder the heauen: all that is in the earth shal perish.
18 But with thee wil I [m] establish my couenant, & thou shalt go into the Arke, thou,
and thy sonnes, and thy wife, and thy sonnes wiues with thee.
19 And of euerie liuing thing, of all flesh
two of euerie sorte shalt thou cause to come into the Arke, to kepe *them* aliue with
thee: they shalbe male and female.
20 Of the foules after their kinde, and of
the cattel after their kinde, of euerie creping thing of the earth after his kinde,
two of euerie sorte shal come vnto thee,
that thou maiest kepe *them* aliue.
21 And take thou with thee of all meat
that is eatē: & thou shalt gather it to thee,
that it may be meat for thee & for them.
22 *Nóah therefore did according vnto
all, that God commanded him: *euen* [n] so
did he.

a The childrē of the godlie, which begā to degenerate.
b Those that came of wicked parents as of Káin.
c Hauing more respect to their beautie, & to worldely consideratiōs, then to their maners, and godlines.
d Because mā colde not be wōne by Gods lenitie and lōg sufferāce, whereby he stroue to ouercome him, he wolde no longer stay his vengeāce.
e Which terme God gaue man to repent before he wolde destroy the earth, 1 Pet. 3, 20.
"Or, tyrants.
f Which vsurped autoritie ouer others & did degenerate from ỷ simplicitie, wherein their fathers liued.
Chap. 8, 21. mat. 15, 19.
g God doeth neuer repent, but he speaketh after our capacitie, because he did destroy him, & in that, as it were, did disauowe him to be his creature.
h God declareth how muche he detesteth sinne, seing the punishment thereof extēdeth to the brute beastes.
i God was merciful vnto him
"Or, historie.

k Meaning ỷ all were giuen to the contēpt of God and oppression of their neighbours.
"Or, I wil destroy mankinde.
"Or, oppression & wickednes.
"Ebr. Gopher.
"Ebr. nestes.
"Or, of this measure.
l That is, of thre heightes, as appeareth in this figure.
m To the intēt that in this great enterprise & mockings of the whole worlde thou maist be confirmed, that thy faith faile not.
Ebr. 11, 7.
n That is, he obeyd Gods cōmandement in all points.

A. B. The length thre hūdreth cubites.
A C. The breadth fifty.
D. E. The height thirty.
E. The windowe a cubite long.
F. The dore.
G. H. I. The thre heightes.

CHAP. VII.

1 Nóah and his entre into the Arke. 20 The flood destroyeth all the rest vpon the earth.

1 AND the Lord said vnto Nóah, Entre
thou and all thine house into the Arke: for thee haue I sene* [a] righteous before me in this age.
2 Of euerie [b] cleane beast thou shalt take
to thee by seuens, the male and his female:
but of vncleane beastes by couples, ȳ male
and his female.
3 Of the foules also of the heauen by seuens, male and female, to kepe sede aliue
vpon the whole earth.
4 For seuen dayes hence I wil cause it raine vpon the earth fourty dayes & fourty
nights, and all the substance that I haue
made, wil I destroye from of the earth.
5 *Nóah therefore did according vnto all
that the Lord commanded him.
6 And Nóah *was* six hundreth yeres olde,
when the flood of waters was vpon the
earth.
7 ¶ So Nóah entred and his sonnes, & his
wife, and his sonnes wiues with him into the Arke, because of the waters of the
flood.
8 Of the cleane beastes, and of the vncleane beastes, and of the foules, & of all that
crepeth vpon the earth,
9 There [c] came two & two vnto Nóah into
the Arke, male & female, as God had commanded Nóah.
10 And so after seuen dayes the waters of
the flood were vpon the earth.
11 ¶ In the six hundreth yere of Noahs life
in the [d] seconde moneth, the seuententh
day of the moneth, in the same day were
all the [e] fountaines of the great depe broken vp, and the windowes of heauen were
opened,
12 And the raine was vpon the earth fourty dayes and fourty nights.
13 In the selfe same day entred Nóah with
Shem, & Ham and Iápheth, the sonnes of
Nóah, and Noahs wife, and the thre wiues of his sonnes with thē into the Arke.
14 They and euerie beast after his kinde, &
all cattel after their kinde, & euerie thing
that crepeth and moueth vpon the earth
after his kinde, & euerie foule after his
kinde, *euen* euerie birde of euerie fether.
15 For they came to Nóah into the Arke,
two and two, [f] of all flesh wherein is the
breath of life.
16 And they entring in, came male & female of all flesh, as God had cōmanded him:
and the Lord [g] shut him in.
17 Then the flood was fourty dayes vpon
the earth, and the waters were increased, &
bare vp ȳ Arke, which was lifte vp aboue
the earth.
18 The waters also waxed strong, and were

2.Pet.2,5.
a In respect of the rest of the worlde, & because he had a desire to serue God and liue vprightly.
b Which might be offred in sacrifice, whereof six were for breed and the seuēth for sacrifice.
Mat.24,37. luk.17,26. 1.pet.3,20.
c God compelled them to presēt thē selues to Nóah, as they did before to Adám, when he gaue them names, Chap.2,19.
d Which was about the beginning of Maie, when all things did moste florish.
e Bothe ȳ waters in ȳ earth did ouerflowe, and also the cloudes powred downe.
f Euerie liuīg thīg that God wolde haue to be preserued on earth, came into the Arke to Nóah.
g So ȳ Gods secret power defended him against the rage of ȳ mightie waters.

increased excedingly vpon the earth, and
the Arke went vpon the waters.
19 The waters ″preuailed so excedingly
vpon the earth, that all the high mountaines, that are vnder the whole heauen, were
couered.
20 Fiftene cubites vpwarde did the waters
preuaile, when the mountaines were couered.
21 *Then all flesh perished that moued vpon the earth, bothe foule and cattel and
beast, & euerie thing that crepeth & moueth vpon the earth, and euerie man.
22 Euerie thing in whose nostrels the spirit
of life did breathe, whatsoeuer they were
in the drye land, they dyed.
23 So [h] he destroyed euerie thing that was
vpon the earth, from man to beast, to the
creping thing, and to the foule of the heauen: they were euen destroyed from the
earth. and Nóah onely [i] remained, & they
that were with him in the Arke.
24 And the waters preuailed vpon the earth
an hundreth and fiftie dayes.

″Ebr. waxed very mightie.
Wisd.10,4. eccles.39,28.
h That is, God.
i Learne what it is to obey God onely, & to forsake the multitude, 1.Pet.3,20.

CHAP. VIII.

13 The flood ceaseth 16 Nóah is commanded to come forthe of the Arke with his. 20 He sacrificeth to the Lord. 22 God promiseth that all things shal continue in their first ordre.

1 NOw God [a] remembred Nóah & [b] e-
uerie beast, & all the cattel that was
with him in the Arke: therefore God made
a winde to passe vpon the earth, and the
waters ceased.
2 The fountaines also of the depe & the
windowes of heauen were stopped & the
raine from heauen was restrained,
3 And the waters returned from aboue the
earth, going and returning: and after the
end of the hundreth and fiftieth day the
waters abated.
4 And in the [c] seuenth moneth, in the seuententh day of the moneth, the Arke ″ rested vpon the mountaines of ″ Ararát.
5 And the waters were going & decreasing
vntil the [d] tenth moneth: in the tenth moneth, & in the first day of the moneth were the toppes of the mountaines sene.
6 ¶ So ″after fourty dayes, Nóah opened ȳ
windowe of the Arke, which he had
made,
7 And sent forthe a ‖ rauen, which went out
going forthe and returning, vntil the waters were dryed vp vpon the earth.
8 Againe he sent a ‖ doue from him, that he
might se if the waters were diminished
from of the earth.
9 But the doue founde no rest for the sole
of her foote: therefore she returned vnto
him into the Arke (for the waters *were* vpon the whole earth) & he [e] put forthe his
hand, & toke her, and pulled her to him
into the Arke.

a Not that God forgetteth his at any time, but when he sendeth succour, then he sheweth that he remēbreth them.
b If God remēber euerie brute beast, what oght to be the assurāce of his childrē?
c Which conteined parte of September & parte of October.
″Or, stayed.
″Or, Armenia.
d Which was the moneth of December.
″Ebr at the end of fourty dayes.
‖The rauen is sent forthe & returneth.
‖He sendeth the doue.
e It is like, ȳ the rauen did flie to and fro, resting on the Arke, but came not in to it, as the doue that was taken in.

10 And he abode yet other seuen dayes,
and againe he sent forthe the doue out of
the Arke.
11 And the doue came to him in the eueniḡ,
& lo, in her "mouthe *was* an f oliue leafe
that she had pluct: whereby Nóah knewe
that ẏ waters were abated from of ẏ earth.
12 Notwithstanding he waited yet other
seuen dayes,& sent forthe the doue,which
returned not againe vnto him any more.
13 ¶And in the six hundreth and one yere,
in the first *daie* of the g first moneth the
waters were dryed vp from of the earth:&
Nóah remoued the couering of the Arke
& loked,& beholde,the vpper parte of the
grounde was drye.
14 And in the seconde moneth,in the seuen
and twentieth day of the moneth was the
earth drye.
15 ¶Then God spake to Nóah,saying,
16 h Go forthe of ẏ Arke, thou & thy wife,
& thy sonnes & thy sonnes wiues w̄ thee.
17 Bring forthe with thee euerie beast that
is with thee , of all flesh, *bothe* foule and
cattel,& euerie thing that crepeth & moueth vpon the earth , that thei maie brede
abundantly in the earth,* & bring forthe
frute and increase vpon the earth.
18 So Nóah came forthe,and his sonnes, &
his wife,and his sonnes wiues with him.
19 Euerie beast,euerie creping thing, & e-
uerie foule,all that moueth vpō the earth
after their kindes went out of the Arke.
20 ¶Then Nóah i buylt an altar to ẏ Lord
and toke of euerie cleane beast, & of euerie cleane foule, and offred burnt offrings
vpon the altar.
21 And the Lord smelled a "k sauour of rest,&
ẏ Lord said in his heart,I wil henceforthe
curse the ground no more for mās cause:
for the imaginacion of mans *heart *is* euil,
euen frō his youth: nether wil I smite anie
more all things liuing,as I haue done.
22 Hereafter l sede time & haruest,& colde
& heate,& sommer and winter, & daie &
night shal not cease,so long as the earth remaineth.

"Or, bil.
f Which was a signe that ẏ waters were muche diminished: for the oliues growe not on the hie mountaines.
g Called in Ebrewe Abib, cōteining part of Marche & parte of April.
h. Nóah declareth his obedience in ẏ he wolde not departe out of the Arke without Gods expresse cōmādement, as he did not entre in without the same.
Chap.1,22. & 9,1.
i. For sacrifices,which were as an exercise of their faith,whereby thei vsed to giue thankes to God for his benefites
"*Or, a swete sauour.*
k That is,thereby he shewed him selfe appeased, and his angre to rest.
Chap.6,5. mat 15,19.
l The ordre of nature destroyed by the flood is restored by Gods promes.

CHAP. IX.

1 The confirmatiō of mariage. 3 Permissiō of meates. 6 The power of the sworde. 14 The rainebowe is the signe of Gods promes. 21 Nóah is drunken & mocked of his sonne, whome he curseth. 29 The age & death of Nóah.

1 AND God a blessed Nóah & his sōnes,
and said to them , Bring forthe frute,
and multiplie,and replenish the earth.
2 Also the b feare of you, and the dread of
you shalbe vpon euerie beast of the earth,
and vpon euerie foule of the heauen , vpon all that moueth on the earth,& vpō all
the fishes of the sea : into your hand are
thei deliuered.
3 Euerie c thing that moueth & liueth,shal-
be meat for you:as ẏ * grene herbe,haue I
giuen you all things.
4 *d But flesh with the life thereof, *I meane,*
with the blood thereof,shal ye not eat.
5 e For surely I wil require your blood,
wherein your liues *are*:at the hand of euerie beast wil I require it : and at the hand
of man,*euen* at the hand of a mās "brother
wil I require the life of man.
6 Whoso * shedeth mans blood, f by man
shal his blood be shed: for in the g image
of God hathe he made man.
7 But bring ye forthe frute and multiplie:
growe plētifully in the earth,and increase
therein.
8 ¶God spake also to Nóah & to his sonnes with him,saying,
9 Beholde,I,euen I establish my h couenāt
with you,and with your i sede after you,
10 And with euerie liuing creature that is
with you,with the foule,with the cattel,&
with euerie beast of the earth with you,
from all that go out of the Arke , vnto e-
uerie beast of the earth.
11 *And my couenant wil I establish with
you , that from henceforthe all flesh shal
not be rooted out by the waters of the flood,nether shal there be a flood to destroye
the earth any more.
12 Then God said,This is the token of the
couenant which I make betwene me and
you,& betwene euerie liuing thing,that is
with you vnto perpetual generacions.
13 I haue set my k bowe in the cloude,and it
shalbe for a signe of the couenāt betwene
me and the earth.
14 And when *I shal couer the earth with a
cloude, and the bowe shal be sene in the
cloude,
15 Then wil I remēber my l couenāt,which
is betwene me and you,& betwene euerie
liuing thing in all flesh,& there shalbe no
more waters of a flood to destroy all flesh.
16 Therefore ẏ bowe shalbe in the cloude,ẏ
I may se it, & remember the euerlasting
couenant betwene God,and euerie liuing
thing in all flesh that is vpon the earth.
17 God said yet to Nóah, m This is the signe of the couenant, which I haue established betwene me and all flesh that is vpon
the earth.
18 ¶Now the sonnes of Nóah going forthe of the Arke,were Shem & Ham & Iápheth. And Ham is the father of Canáan.
19 These are the thre sonnes of Nóah , and
of them was the n whole earth ouerspred.
20 "Nóah also began *to be* an housband mā
and planted a vineyarde.
21 And he drōke of ẏ wine & was o dronkē,
& was vncouered in ẏ middes of his tent.
22 And when Ham the father p of Canáan
sawe the nakednes of his father, q he tolde
his two brethren without.
23 Then toke Shem and Iápheth a garmēt,
and

a God increased them with frute,& declared vnto them his counsel as touching ẏ replenishing of the earth.
b By the vertue of this cōmandement beastes rage not so muche against man as they wolde, yea and many serue to his vse thereby.
c By this permission man may with a good conscience vse ẏ creatures of God for his necessitie.
Chap.1,29.

Leu.17,14.
d That is, liuing creatures & the flesh of beastes that are strāgled: & hereby all crueltie is forbidden.
e That is, I wil take vengeāce for your blood
"*Or, neighbour*
Mat.26,52. reuel.13,10.
f Not onely by the magistrate, but oft times God raiseth vp one murtherer to kil another.
g Therefore to kil man is to deface Gods image, and so iniurie is not onely done to man , but to God.
h To assure you that the worlde shalbe no more destroyed by a flood.
i The childrē which are not yet borne, are comprehēded in Gods couenant made w̄ their fathers.
Isa.54,9.
k Hereby we se that signes or sacraments oght not to be separate from the worde.
Eccles 43,12.
l When men shal se my bowe in ẏ heauen, thei shal knowe that I haue not forgotten my couenant with them.
m God doeth repeat this the oftener to confirme Noahs faith so muche more
n This declareth what was the vertue of Gods blessing, when he said, Increase and bring forthe, Chap.1,28.
"*Or, Nóah begā againe.*
o. This is set before our eies to shewe what an horrible thing drōkennes is.
p Of whome came the Canaanites that wicked natiō, who were also cursed of God.
q In derisiō & contempt of his father.

and put it vpon bothe their shulders and
wẽt backward,and couered the nakednes
of their father with their faces backwarde : so thei sawe not their fathers nakednes.
24 Then Nóah awoke from his wine, and
knewe what his yonger sonne had done
vnto him,
25 And said,[r] Cursed *be* Canáan:a [s] seruant
of seruantes shal he be vnto his brethren.
26 He said moreouer, Blessed *be* the Lord
God of Shem, and let Canáan be his
seruant.
27 God [″] [t] persuade Iápheth, that he may
dwel in the tentes of Shem, and let Canáan be his seruant.
28 ¶And Nóah liued after ẏ flood thre hũdreth and fifty yeres.
29 So all the dayes of Nóah were nine hũdreth and fifty yeres:and he dyed.

r He pronoũceth as a Prophet the curse of God against all thẽ, that honour not their parents:for Ham and his posteritie were accursed.
s That is, a moste vile slaue.
″Or, enlarge, or, cause to returne.
t He declareth that the Gentiles,which came of Iápheth & were separated from the Church, shulde be ioyned to the same by the persuasion of Gods Spirit and preaching of the Gospel.

CHAP. X.

1 The increase of mankinde by Nóah and his sonnes. 10 The beginning of cities,contreis and nations.

1 NOw these are the [a] generacions of ẏ
sonnes of Nóah,Shem,Ham & Iá-
pheth:vnto whome sonnes were borne after the flood.
2 The sonnes of Iápheth *were* Gómer and
Magóg,and [b] Madái, and Iauán,and Tubál and Méshech,and Tirás.
3 And the sonnes of Gómer,Ashkenáz,and
Ripháth and Togarmáh.
4 Also ẏ sonnes of Iauán,Elisháh and Tarshísh,Kittím,and Dodaním.
5 Of these were the [c] yles of the Gentiles
deuided in their landes, euerie man after
his tongue, *and* after their families in
their nacions.
6 ¶Moreouer ẏ sõnes of Ham *were* [d] Cush,
and Mizráim,and Put,and Canáan.
7 And the sonnes of Cush, Sebá and Hauiláh, and Sabtáh, and Raamáh, and Sab-
techá: also the sonnes of Raamáh *were*
Shebá and Dedán.
8 And Cush begate Nimród, who began
to be [e] mighty in the earth.
9 He was a mighty hũter before the Lord.
wherfore it is said, [f] As Nimród ẏ mighty hunter before the Lord.
10 And the beginning of his kingdome was
Babél,and Erech,and Accád,and Calnéh,
in the land [g] of Shinár.
11 Out of that land came Asshúr, & buylded Niniuéh, and the [″] citie Rehobóth,
and Cálah:
12 Résen also betwene Niniuéh and Cálah:
this is a great citie.
13 And Mizráim begate [h] Ludím,and Ana-
mím,and Lehabím,and Naphtuhím.
14 Pathrusím also, and Casluhim (out of
whome came the Philistíms)and [″] Caphtoríms.
15 ¶Also Canáan begate Zidón his first

a These generatiõs are here recited partely to declare the maruelous increase in so smale a time, and also to set forthe their great for getfulnes of Gods graces toward their fathers.
b Of Madái, & Iauán came the Medes and Grekes.
c The Iewes so call all cõtreis ẘ are separated frõ thẽ by sea, as Grecia, Italie, &c. ẘ were giuen to the childrẽ of Iapheth, of whome came the Gentiles.
d Of Cush & Mizráim came the Ethiopiãs & Egyptians.
e Meaning, a cruel oppressor & tyrant.
f His tyrannie came into a prouerbe as hated bothe of God and man: for he passed not to commit crueltie euẽ in Gods presẽce.
g For there was an other citie in Egypt called also Babél.
″Or, the stretes of the citie.
h Of Lud came the Lydians.
″Or, the Cappadocians.

borne,and Heth,
16 And Iebusí,and Emorí,and Girgashí,
17 And Hiuí,and Arkí,and Siní,
18 And Aruadí,and Zemarí,& Hamathí:&
afterwarde were the families of ẏ Canaanites spred abroad.
19 Then the border of the Canaanites was
from Zidón, as thou commest to Gerár
vntil Azzáh,& as thou goest vnto Sodóm,
and Gomoráh,and Admáh, & Zeboiím,
euen vnto Lásha.
20 These are ẏ sonnes of Ham according
to their families, according to their tongues in their coũtries *and* in their naciõs.
21 ¶Vnto [i] Shem also the father of all the
sonnes [k] of Eber,and elder brother of Iápheth were children borne.
22 *The sonnes of Shem *were* Elám and Asshúr,and Arpachshád,and Lud,and Arám.
23 And the sonnes of Arám,Vz & Hul, and
Gether and Mash.
24 Also Arpachshád begate Shélah, and
Shélah begate Eber.
25 Vnto Eber also were borne two sonnes:
the name of the one *was* Péleg: for in his
dayes was the earth [l] diuided: & his brothers name *was* Ioktán.
26 Then Ioktán begate Almodád and Shéleph,& Hazarmáueth,and Iérah,
27 And Hadorám,& Vzál,and Dickláh,
28 And Obál,& Abimaél,and Shebá,
29 And Ophír,and Hauiláh,and Iobáb.all
these *were* the sonnes of Ioktán.
30 And their dwelling was from Meshá,
as thou goest vnto Sephár a mount of the
East.
31 These are ẏ sonnes of Shem according
to their families,according to their tongues,in their countreis and nacions.
32 These are the families of the sonnes of
Nóah,after their generacions amõg their
people:and [″] out of these were the nacions
diuided in the earth after the flood.

i In his stock the Church was preserued therfore Moses leaueth of speaking of Iápheth and Ham, and intreateth of Shem more at large.
k Of whome came the Ebrewes or Iewes.
1. Chro. 1,17.
l This diuision came by the diuersitie of languages, as appeareth, chap. 11,9.
″Or, of these came diuers nacions.

CHAP. XI.

6 The buylding of Babél was the cause of the confusion of tongues. 10 The age and generacion of Shem vnto Abram. 31 Abrams departure from Vr with his father Térah, Sarai & Lot. 32 The age and death of Térah.

1 THen the whole earth was of one *lan
guage and one speache.
2 And [a] as [b] they went from the [c] East, they
founde a plaine in the land of [d] Shinár,&
there they abode.
3 And they said one to an other, Come let
vs make brycke,and burne it in the fire. So
thei had brycke for stone, and slyme had
they in steade of morter.
4 Also they said, Go to,let vs [e] buylde vs a
citie and a tower, whose toppe *may reach*
vnto the heauen, that we may get vs a name,lest we be scatred vpon ẏ whole earth.
5 But the Lord [f] came downe, to se the citie
& tower,which ẏ sonnes of men buylded.

Wisd. 10,5.
a In the yere an hundreth and thirtie after the flood.
b To wit, Nimród and his companie.
c That is, frõ Armenia, where the Arke staied.
d Which was afterward called Caldea.
e They were moued ẘ pride and ambition, thinking to preferre their own glorie to Gods honour.
f Meaning, ẏ he declared by effect that he knewe their wicked entreprise:for Gods power is euerie where.

6 And the Lord said, [g] Beholde, the people
is one, & thei all haue one language, & this
thei beginne to do, nether can thei now be
stopped from whatsoeuer thei haue imagined to do.
7 Come on, [h] let vs go downe, and [i] there
confounde their language, that euerie one
perceiue not an others speache.
8 So the Lord scatred them from thence
vpon all the earth, and they left of to
buylde the citie.
9 Therfore the name of it was called "Babél,
because the Lord did there confounde
the language of all the earth: frõ thence
then did the Lord scater them vpon all
the earth.
10 ¶ * These are the generacions [k] of Shem:
Shem *was* an hũdreth yere olde, and begate
Arpachshád two yere after the flood.
11 And Shẽ liued, after he begate Arpachshád,
fiue hundreth yeres, and begate sonnes
and daughters.
12 Also Arpachshád liued fiue and thirty
yeres, and begate Shélah.
13 And Arpachshád liued, after he begate
Shélah, foure hundreth and thre yeres, and
begate sonnes and daughters.
14 And Shélah liued thirty yeres, and begate
Eber.
15 So Shélah liued, after he begate Eber,
foure hundreth and thre yeres, and begate
sonnes and daughters.
16 Likewise Eber liued foure and thirty yeres,
and begate Péleg.
17 So Eber liued, after he begate Péleg, foure
hundreth and thirty yeres, and begate
sonnes and daughters.
18 And Péleg liued thirty yeres, and begate
Reú.
19 * And Péleg liued, after he begate Reú,
two hundreth and nine yeres, and begate
sonnes and daughters.
20 Also Reú liued two and thirty yeres, &
begate Serúg.
21 So Reú liued, after he begate Serúg, two
hundreth and seuen yeres, and begate sonnes
and daughters.
22 Moreouer Serúg liued thirty yeres, and
begate Nahór.
23 And Serúg liued, after he begate Nahór,
two hundreth yeres, and begate sonnes &
daughters.
24 And Nahór liued nine & twenty yeres,
and begate Térah.
25 So Nahór liued, after he begate Térah,
an hũdreth and ninetene yeres, and begate
sonnes and daughters.
26 * So Térah liued seuentie yeres, & begate
Abrám, Nahór, and Harán.
27 ¶ Now these are ÿ generaciõs of Térah:
Térah begate [l] Abrám, Nahór, & Harán:
and Harán begate Lot.
28 Then Harán dyed before Térah his father
in the land of his natiuitie, in Vr of
"the Caldees.
29 So Abrám and Nahór toke them wiues.
the name of Abrams wife *was* Sarái, and
the name of Nahors wife Milcáh, the
daughter of Harán, the father of Milcáh,
and the father of [m] Iscáh.
30 But Sarái was barren, *and* had no childe.
31 Then [n] Térah toke Abrám his sonne, &
Lot the sonne of Harán, his sonnes sonne,
and Sarái his daughter in lawe, his sonne
Abrams wife: and they departed together
from Vr of the Caldees, to * go into the
land of Canáan, and thei came to [o] Harán,
and dwelt there.
32 So the dayes of Térah were two hundreth
and fiue yeres, and Térah dyed in
Harán.

g God speketh this in derisiõ because of their foolish persuasion & enterprise.
h He speketh, as thogh he toke coũsel with his owne wisdome and power: to wit, with the Sõne and holy Gost: signifying the greatnes and certeintie of ÿ punishement.
i By this great plague of the confusion of tõgues, appeareth Gods horrible iudgemẽt against mans pride and vaine glorie.
"Or, confusion.
1.Chro.1,17.
k He returneth to ÿ genealogie of Shem, to come to the historie of Abrám, wherein the Church of God is described, which is Moses principal purpose.
1.Chro.1,29.
1.Chro.1,26.
iosh.24,2.
l He maketh mẽciõ first of Abrám, not because he was the first borne, but for the historie, which properly perteineth vnto him.
"Ebr. Casdim.
m Some thinke that this Iscáh was Sarái.
n Albeit the oracle of God came to Abrám, yet the honour is giuen to Térah, because he was ÿ father.
Iosh.24,2.
nehe.9,7.
iudi.5,6.
act.7,4.
o Which was a citie of Mesopotamia.

CHAP. XII.

1 Abrám by Gods commandement goeth to Canáan. 3 Christ is promised. 7 Abram buyldeth altars for exercise and declaration of his faith among the infidelles. 10 Because of the derthe he goeth into Egypt. 15 Pharaóh taketh his wife, and is punished.

1 FOr the Lord had said vnto Abrám,
* [a] Get thee out of thy countrei, and
frõ thy kindred, and frõ thy fathers house
vnto [b] the land that I wil shewe thee.
2 And I wil make of thee a great nacion,
and wil blesse thee, and make thy name
great, and thou shalt be [c] a blessing.
3 I wil also blesse them that blesse thee, &
curse them that curse thee, & in thee shal
all families of the earth be blessed.
4 So Abrám departed, euen as the Lord
spake vnto him, and Lot went with him.
(And Abrám was seuenty and fiue yere
olde, when he departed out of Harán)
5 Then Abrám toke Sarái his wife, & Lot
his brothers sonne, and all their substance
that thei possessed, & the [d] soules that thei
had gotten in Harán, and they departed,
to go to the land of Canáan: and to the
land of Canáan they came.
6 ¶ So Abrám [e] passed through ÿ land vnto
ÿ place of Shechém, and vnto the "plaine
of Moréh (and the [f] Canaanite *was* then in
the land)
7 And the Lord appeared vnto Abrám,
and said, Vnto thy sede wil I giue this
lãd. And there buylded he an [g] altar vnto
the Lord, which appeared vnto him.
8 Afterward remouing [h] thence vnto a
mountaine Eastward from Beth-él, he pitched
his tent hauing Beth-él on the Westside,
& Haái on ÿ East: and there he buylt
an [i] altar vnto the Lord, and called on the
name of the Lord.
9 [k] Againe Abrám wẽt forth going & iourneing
towarde the South.
10 ¶ Then there came a [l] famine in the lãd:
therfore Abrám went downe into Egypt,
to soiourne there: for there was a great
famine

Act.7,3.
a From the flood to this time were thre hundreth thre score and thre yere.
b In appointing him no certeine place he proueth so muche more his faith & obedience.
c The worlde shal recouer by thy sede, ẘ is Christ, the blessĩg ẘ thei lost in Adám.
d Meaning, aswel seruãts as cattel.
e He wandred to and fro in ÿ lãd before he colde finde a settling place: thus God exerciseth the faith of his children.
"Or, oke groue.
f Which was a cruel and rebellious natiõ, by whome God kept his in a continual exercise.
g It was not ynough for hĩ to worship God in his heart, but it was expedient to declare by outward profession his faith before men, whereof this altar was a signe,
h Because of the troubles that he had amõg that wicked people.
i And so serued ÿ true God & renoũced all idolatrie
k Thus ÿ children of God may loke for no rest in this worlde, but must waite for ÿ heauẽlie rest and quietnes.
l This was a newe trial of Abrams faith: wherby we se that the end of one afflictiõ is ÿ beginning of an other.

famine in the land.
11 And when he drewe nere to entre into
Egypt, he said to Sarái his wife, Beholde
now, I knowe that thou art a faire woman
to loke vpon:
12 Therfore it wil come to passe, that whẽ
the Egyptians se thee, they wil say, She
is his wife: so wil thei kil me, but they
wil kepe thee aliue.
13 Say, I pray thee, yͭ thou art my [m] sister,
that I may fare wel for thy sake, and that
my [''] life may be preserued by thee.
14 ¶ Now, when Abrám was come into E-
gypt, the Egyptians beheld the woman:
for she was very faire.
15 And the princes of Pharaóh sawe her,
and commended her vnto Pharaóh: so
the woman was [n] taken into Pharaohs
house:
16 Who intreated Abrám wel for her sake,
and he had shepe, and beues, and he asses,
and men seruantes and maide seruantes,
and she asses, and camelles.
17 But the Lord [o] plagued Pharaóh and
his house with great plagues, because of
Sarái Abrams wife.
18 Then Pharaóh called Abrám and said,
Why hast yͧ done this vnto me? Wherfore didest thou not tel me, that she was
thy wife?
19 Why saidest thou, She is my sister, that I
shulde take her to be my wife? Now therfore beholde thy wife, take *her* and go
thy way.
20 And Pharaóh gaue men [p] commandemẽt concerning him: and they conueied
him forthe, and his wife, and all yͭ he had.

m By this we maie learne not to vse vnlauful meanes, nor to put others in danger to saue our selues. read verse twentie albeit it maie appeare yͭ Abrã feared not somuch death, as that, if he shuld die without issue, Gods promes shulde not haue takẽ place: wherein appeared a weake faith.
'' *Ebr. that my soule maie liue.*
n To be his wife.
o The Lord toke yͤ defence of this poore stranger agaist a mightie Kig: and as he is euer careful ouer his, so did he preserue Sarái.
p To the entẽt yͭ none shulde hurt him ether in his persone or goods.

CHAP. XIII.

1 Abrám departeth out of Egypt. 11 Lot departeth from him. 13 The wickednes of the Sodomites. 14 The promes made to Abrám is renued. 18 Abrám buyldeth an altar to the Lord.

1 THen [a] Abrám went vp from Egypt,
he, and his wife, and all that he had, &
Lot with him towarde the South.
2 And Abrám *was* very riche in cattel, in
siluer and in golde.
3 And he wẽt on his iourney frõ the South
toward [b] Beth-él, to the place where his
tent had bene at the beginning, betwene
Beth-él and Haái,
4 Vnto yͤ place of the * altar, which he had
made there at the first: and there Abrám
called on the Name of the Lord.
5 ¶ Lot also, who wẽt with Abrám, had shepe cattel and tentes,
6 So that the land colde not [c] beare them,
that they might dwel together: for their
* substance was great, so that they colde
not dwel together.
7 Also there was debate betwene the herdmen of Abrams cattel, & the herdmen of
Lots cattel. (and the [d] Canaanites & the
Perizzites dwelled at that time in yͤ lãd)
8 Then said Abrám vnto Lot, Let there be
no [e] strife, I pray thee, betwene thee & me,
nether betwene mine herdmen and thine
herdmen: for we be brethren.
9 Is not the whole lãd before thee? departe I pray thee frõ me: if thou wilt [f] take yͤ
left hand, then I wil go to the right: or if
thou go to the right hand, then I wil take
the left.
10 So when Lot lifted vp his eies, he sawe yͤ
all the plaine of Iordén was watered euerie where: (*for* before the Lord destroyed
Sodóm and Gomoráh, *it was* as the [g] garden of the Lord, like the land of Egypt, as
thou goest vnto Zóar)
11 Thẽ Lot chose vnto him all yͤ plaine of
Iordén and toke his iourney frõ the East:
& they departed the [h] one from yͤ other.
12 Abrám dwelled in the land of Canáan,
and Lot abode in the cities of the plaine,
and pitched his tent euen to Sodóm.
13 Now the men of Sodóm *were* wicked &
exceading [i] sinners against the Lord.
14 ¶ Thẽ yͤ Lord said vnto [k] Abrám, (after
that Lot was departed from him) Lift vp
thine eies now, and loke from the place,
where yͧ art, Northward, and Southward,
and Eastward, and Westward:
15 For all * the land, which thou seest, wil I
giue vnto thee and to thy sede for [l] euer,
16 And I wil make thy sede, as the dust of yͤ
earth: so that if a man can nomber yͤ dust
of the earth, then shal thy sede be nõbred.
17 Arise, walke through the land, in the
length thereof, and bredth thereof: for I
wil giue it vnto thee.
18 Then Abrám remoued his tent, and came and dwelled in the plaine of Mamré,
which is in Hebrón, & buylded there an
altar vnto the Lord.

a His great riches gotte in Egypt hindred him not to folowe his vocation.
b He calleth yͤ place by that name, which was after giuẽ vnto it. chap. 28,19.
Chap. 12,7.
c This incõmoditie came by their riches, wͨ brake friendeship, and as it were, the bond of nature.
Chap. 36,7.
d Who seing their cõtẽciõ might blaspheme God and destroie them.
e He cutteth of the occasion of contẽcion: therfore the euil ceaseth.
f Abrám resigneth his owne right to bie peace.
g Which was yͤ Edẽ, chap. 2,10
h This was done by Gods guidence, that onely Abrám and his sede might dwel in the lãd of Canáan.
i Lot thinking to get paradise found hel.
k The Lord cõforted him, lest he shulde haue taken thoght for the departure of his nepheu.
Chap. 12,7. & 15,1. & 26,4. deu 34,4.
l Meanig, a lõg time, and til yͤ comming of Christ, as Exo. 21,6. deu. 15,17. ier. 2,20. and spiritually this is referred to the true children of Abrám, borne according to yͤ promes & not according to yͤ flesh, which are heires of the true land of Canáan.

CHAP. XIIII.

12 In the ouerthrowe of Sodóm Lot is taken prisoner. 16 Abrám deliuereth him. 18 Melchi-zédek commeth to mete him. 23 Abrã wolde not be enriched by the King of Sodóm.

AND in the daies of Amraphél King of
[a] Shinár, Arióch King of Ellasár, Chedor-laómer King of Elám, and Tidál
King of the [b] nacions:
2 *These men* made warre with Berá King of
Sodóm, & with Birshá King of Gomoráh, Shináb King of Admáh, and Sheme-
bér King of Zeboiím, and the King of
Belá, which is Zóar.
3 All these [c] ioyned together in the vale of
'' Siddím, which is the [d] salte Sea.
4 Twelue yeres were they subiect to Chedor-laómer, but in yͤ thirtenthe yere they
rebelled.
5 And in the fourtenth yere came Chedor-
laómer, & the Kings that were with him,
& smote the Rephaims in Ashteróth kar-

a That is, of Babilon: by Kings here meaning thẽ, that were gouernors of cities.
b Of a people gathered of diuers cõutries.
c Ambicion is the chief cause of warres among princes.
'' *Or, of the labored fieldes.*
d Called also yͤ dead Sea, or yͤ lake Asphaltites nere vnto Sodóm and Gomoráh.

náim, and the Zuzíms in Ham, and the E-
"Or, plaine.
míms in" Shauéh Kiriatháim.
6 And the Horites in their mount Seír, vnto the plaine of Parán, wͨ is by yͤ wildernes.
7 And thei returned and came to En-mish-
"Or, destroied.
pát, which is Kadésh, and" smote all yͤ cou̅-
trie of the Amalekites, and also the Amorites that dwelled in Hazezon-tamár.
8 Then went out the King of Sodóm, & the
King of Gomoráh, & yͤ King of Admáh &
yͤ King of Zeboiím, & the King of Béla, wͨ
is Zóar: and thei ioyned battel with them
in the vale of Siddím:
9 *To wit,* with Cheder-laómer King of Elám,
and Tidál King of nacions, and Amraphél
King of Shinár, and Arióh King of Ellasár:
foure Kings against fiue.
10 Now the [e] vale of Siddím was ful of sly-
e And afterward was ouer whelmed with water and so was called the salt Sea.
me pittes, and yͤ Kings of Sodóm and Go-
moráh fled" & fel there: and yͤ residue fled
"Or, were discōfited.
to the mountaine.
11 Then thei toke all the substance of Sodóm
and Gomoráh, and all their vitailes and
went their waie.
12 Thei [f] toke Lot also Abrams brothers
f The godlie are plagued manie times with the wicked: therfore their companie is dangerous.
sonne, and his substance (for he dwelt at
Sodóm) and departed.
13 ¶ Then came one that had escaped, and
tolde Abrám the Ebrewe, which dwelt in yͤ
plaine of Mamré the Amorite, brother of
Eshcól, and brother of Anér, which were
[g] confederat with Abrám.
14 When Abrám heard that his brother was
g God moued them to ioyne with Abrám, and preserued him frō their idolatrie and superstitions.
taken," he broght forthe of them that were
"Or, armed.
borne and broght vp in his house, thre hu̅-
dreth & eightene, & pursued the̅ vnto Dan.
15 The̅ he, & his seruantes diuided them selues against the̅ by night, & smote them and
pursued them vnto Hobáh, which is on the
left side of " Damascus,
"Ebr. Dámmések.
16 And he recouered all the substance, and
also broght againe his brother Lot, and
his goods, & the women also and yͤ people.
17 ¶ After that he returned frō the slaughter
of Chedor-laómer and of the Kings that
were with him, came the King of Sodóm
forthe to mete him in the valley of Shauéh,
which is the *Kings dale.
2.Sam.18,18.
18 And * Melchi-zédek King of Shalém
Ebr.7,3.
[h] broght forthe bread and wine: & he was
h For Abrám and his soldiors refection, & not to offer sacrifice.
a Priest of the moste high God.
19 Therfore he [i] blessed him, saying, Blessed
i In that Melchi-zédek fed Abrám, he declared him selfe to represent a King: & in yͤ he blessed him, the high Priest.
art thou, Abrám, of God moste high pos-
sessor of heauen and earth,
20 And blessed *be* the moste high God, wͨ
hathe deliuered thine ennemies into thine
hand.* And *Abrám* gaue him tithe of all.
Ebr.7,8.
21 Then the King of Sodóm said to Abrám,
Giue me the " personnes, and take yͤ goods
"Ebr. soules.
to thy selfe.
22 And Abrám said to the King of Sodóm,
" I haue lift vp mine hand vnto the Lord
"Or, I haue sworne.
the moste high God possessor of heauen
and earth,
23 "That I wil not take of all that is thine,
"Ebr. If I take frō thee a threde &c read 1 Sam. 14, 44
so muche as a threde or shoulachet, lest yͧ
shuldest saie, I haue made Abrám riche,
24 [k] Saue onely that, which the yong men
k He wolde not yͭ his liberalitie shuld be hurtful vnto others.
haue eaten, and the partes of the men wͨ
we̅t with me, Anér, Eshcól, and Mamré: let
them take their partes.

CHAP. XV.

1 The Lord is Abrams defence and rewarde. 6 He is iustified by faith. 13 The seruitude and deliuerance out of Egypt is declared. 18 The land of Canáan is promised the fourth time.

1 After these things, yͤ" worde of yͤ Lord
"Or, the Lord spake to Abrám
came vnto Abrám in a *visiō, saying,
Rom.12,6.
Feare not, Abrám, I am thy buckler, *and*
thine exceading *great rewarde.
Psal 16,6.
2 And Abrám said, [a] O Lord God, what
a His feare was not onely lest he shulde not haue children, but lest the promes of the blessed sede shulde not be accomplished in him.
wilt thou giue me, seing I go childeles,
and the stuarde of mine house *is* this Eliézer of Damascus?
3 Againe Abrám said, Beholde, to me thou
hast giuen no sede: wherfore lo, a seruant
of mine house shalbe mine heire.
4 Then beholde, the worde of yͤ Lord came
vnto him, saying, He shal not be thine heire, but one that shal come out of thine
owne bowelles, he shalbe thine heire.
5 Moreouer he broght him forthe and said,
*Loke vp now vnto heauen, & tel the star-
Rom.4,18.
res, if thou be able to nombre them: and
Rom.4,3. iam.2,2 gal.3,6.
he said vnto him, So shal thy sede be.
6 And *Abrám** beleued the Lord, and he
counted that to him for righteousnes.
Chap.11,28.
7 Againe he said vnto him, I am the Lord,
that broght thee out of * Vr of the Caldees, to giue thee this land to inherit it.
8 And he said, O Lord God, [b] whereby
b This is a particular mocion of Gods Spirit, which is not lawful for all to follow in asking signes: but was permitted to some by a peculiar mocion, as to Gideón, and Ezechiáh.
shal I knowe that I shal inherit it?
9 Then he said vnto him, Take me an hey-
fer of thre yeres olde, and a she goate of
thre yeres olde, and a ramme of thre yeres
olde, a turtel doue also and a pigion.
10 So he toke all these vnto him, & [c] diuided
c This was yͤ olde custome in making coue̅nāts, Ierem. 34, 18: to the which God added these condicions, yͭ Abrams posteritie shulde be as torne in peces, but after thei shulde be coupled together: also that it shulde be assalted, but yet deliuered.
them in the middes, and laied euerie pece
one against an other: but the birdes diuided he not.
11 Then foules fel on the carkases, and A-
brám droue them awaie.
12 And when the sunne went downe, there
fel an heauie slepe vpon Abrám: & lo, " a
"Ebr. a feare of great darcknes.
verie feareful darcknes fel vpon him.
13 Then he said to Abrám, *Knowe this of
Act.7,6.
a suretie, that thy sede shal be a stranger in
a land, that is not theirs, [d] foure hundreth
d Counting frō the birthe of Izhák to their departure out of Egypt which declareth that God wil suffer his to be afflicted in this worlde.
yeres, and shal serue them: and thei shal
entreate them euil.
14 Notwithstanding the nacion, whome
thei shal serue, wil I iudge: and afterward
shal thei come out with great substance.
15 But yͧ shalt go vnto thy fathers in peace, *and* shalt be buryed in a good age.
16 And in the " fourthe generaciō thei shal
"Or, after foure hundreth yeres.
come

e Thogh God suffre the wicked for a time, yet his végeance falleth vpõ them, whẽ the measure of their wickednes is ful.

come hether againe: for the [e] wickednes
of the Amorites is not yet ful.
17 Also when the sunne went downe, there
was a darckenes: & beholde, a smoking fur
nace, and a firebrãde, which went betwene
those peces.
18 * In that same day the Lord made a couenant with Abrám, saying, Vnto thy sede
haue I giuen this land, * from the riuer of
Egypt vnto the great riuer, the riuer " Euphrátes.
19 The Kenites, & the Kenizites, & ý Kad-
mõnites,
20 And the Hittites, and the Perizzites, &
the Rephaíms,
21 The Amorites also, & the Canaanites &
the Girgashites, and the Iebusites.

Cha. 12,7.13, 15:26,4.deut. 4,4.
1.King.4,21. 2 chrõ.9,26.
" Ebr. Perath.

CHAP. XVI.

1 Sarái being barren, giueth Hagár to Abrám. 4 Which cõceiueth & despiseth her dame: 6 And being il hande led fleeth. 7 The Angel comforteth her. 11, 12 The name and maners of her sonne. 13 She calleth vpon the Lord, whome she findeth true.

a It semeth that she had respect to Gods promes, which colde not be accomplished without issue.
b She faileth in binding Gods power to the commõ ordre of nature, as thogh God colde not giue her children in her olde age.
" Ebr. be buylded by her.

1 NOw [a] Sarái Abrams wife bare him
no children, and she had a maide an
Egyptian, Hagár by name.
2 And Sarái said vnto Abrám, Beholde
now, the Lord hathe [b] restrayned me from
childe bearing. I pray thee go in vnto my
maide: it may be ý I shal " receiue a childe
by her. And Abrám obeied the voice of
Sarái.
3 Then Sarái Abrams wife toke Hagár her
maide the Egyptian, after Abrám had
dwelled ten yere in the land of Canáan,
and gaue her to her housband Abrám for
his wife.
4 ¶ And he wẽt in vnto Hagár, & she conceiued. and when she sawe ý she had conceiued, her dame was [c] despised in her eies.
5 Then Sarái said to Abrám, " Thou doest
me wrõg. I haue giuen my maide into thy
bosome, and she seeth that she hathe cõcei
ued, and I am despised in her eies: ý Lord
iudge betwene me and thee.
6 Then Abrám said to Sarái, Beholde, thy
maide *is* in thine " hand: do with her as it
pleaseth thee. Thẽ Sarái delt roughly with
her: wherfore she fled from her.
7 ¶ But the [d] Angel of the Lord founde her
beside a fountayne of water in the wildernes by the fountaine in the way to Shur,
8 And he said, Hagár Sarais maide, whence
comest thou? and whether wilt thou go?
And she said, I flee from my dame Sarái.
9 Thẽ the Angel of ý Lord said to her, [e] Re
turne to thy dame, and humble thy selfe
vnder her handes.
10 Againe the Angel of the Lord said vnto her, I wil so greatly encrease thy sede,
that it shal not be nõbred for multitude.
11 Also the Angel of the Lord said vnto
her, Se, thou art with childe, and shalt bea-

c This punishmẽt declareth what thei gaine that attẽpt any thing agaist the worde of God.
" Ebr. mine iniurie is vpon thee.
" Or, power.
d Which was Christ, as appeareth verse 10. & chap. 18, 13.
e God reiecteth none estate of people in their miseries, but sendeth them cõfort.

re a sonne, and shalt call his name Ishmaél: for the Lord hathe heard thy tribulation.
12 And he shal be a " wilde man: his hand
shalbe against euerie man, and euerie mãs
hãd against him. * and [f] he shal dwel in the
presence of all his brethren.
13 Then she called the name of the Lord,
that spake vnto her, Thou God lokest on
me: for she said, [g] Haue I not also here loked after him that seeth me?
14 * Wherfore the well was called, " Beér-la
hái-roi. lo, *it is* betwene Kadésh & Béred.
15 ¶ And Hagár bare Abrám a sonne, and A-
brám called his sonnes name, which Hagár bare, Ishmaél.
16 And Abrám *was* foure score and sixe yere olde, when Hagár bare him Ishmaél.

" Or, fearce and cruel, or, as a wilde asse.
Chap. 25,17.
f That is, the Ishmaelites shalbe a peculiar people by them selues & not a portion of an other people.
g She rebuketh her owne dulnes and acknowledgeth Gods graces, who was present with her euery where.
Chap. 24, 62.
" Or, the well of the liuing and seing me.

CHAP. XVII.

1 Abrams name is changed to confirme him in the promes. 8 The land of Canáan is the fist time promised. 12 Circũcision is instituted. 15 Sarái is named Saráh. 18 Abrahã prayeth for Ishmaél. 19 Izhák is promised.

1 WHen Abrám was ninety yere olde and nine, the Lord appeared
to Abrám, and said vnto him, I am God
" all sufficient. * walke before me, and be
thou " vpright,
2 And I wil make my couenant betwene
me and thee, and I wil multiply thee exceadingly.
3 Then Abrám fel on his face, and God
talked with him, saying,
4 Beholde, I *make* my couenant with thee,
& thou shalt be a [a] father of manie naciõs,
5 Nether shal thy name anie more be called Abrám, but thy name shalbe [b] Abrahám: * for a father of manie nacions haue
I made thee.
6 Also I wil make thee exceading fruteful,
and wil make naciõs of thee: yea, Kings
shal procede of thee.
7 Moreouer I wil establish my couenant
betwene me and thee, and thy sede after
thee in their generacions, for an * euerlasting couenant, to be God vnto thee and
to thy sede after thee.
8 And I wil giue thee and thy sede after
thee the land, wherin thou art a stranger,
euen all the lãd of Canáan, for an euerlasting possession, and I wil be their God.
9 ¶ Againe God said vnto Abrahám, Thou
also shalt kepe my couenant, thou, and
thy sede after thee in their generacions.
10 [c] This is my couenant, which ye shal kepe betwene me and you, and thy sede after
thee, * Let euerie man childe among you
be circumcised:
11 That is, ye shal circumcise the [d] foreskin
of your flesh, and it shal be a * signe of
the couenant betwene me and you.
12 And euerie mã childe of eight daies olde among you, shalbe circucised in your

" Or, almightie.
Chap. 5,22.
" Or, with out hypocrisie.
a Not only according to ý fleshe, but of a farre greater multitude by faith, ro. 4,17.
b The changing of his name is a seale to confirme Gods promes vnto him.
Rom. 4,37.
Chap. 13,11.
c Circumcisiõ is called the couenãt, because it signifieth the couenãt & hathe the promes of grace ioyned to it: which phrase is commune to all sacraments.
Act. 7,8.
d That priuie parte is circũcised to shewe that all that is begotten of mã is corrupt and must be mortified
Rom. 4,11.

generaciós,aswel he that is borne in *thi-*
ne house,as he that is boght with money
of any stranger,which is not of thy sede.
13 He that is borne in thine house, and he
that is boght with thy money, must nedes
be circumcised: so my couenant shal be
in your flesh for an euerlasting couenant.
14 But the vncircumcised [e] man childe, in
whose flesh the foreskinne is not circumcised, euen that personne shal be cut of
fro his people, *because* he hathe broke my
couenant.
15 ¶ Afterward God said vnto Abrahám,
Sarái thy wife shalt thou not call Sarái,
but ″ Saráh *shalbe* her name.
16 And I wil blesse her,& wil also giue thee
a sonne of her, yea,I wil blesse her & she
shalbe *the mother* of nations: Kings *also* of
people shal come of her.
17 The Abrahám fel vpó his face,& [f] laughed, & said in his heart, Shal a childe be
borne vnto him,that is an hundreth yere
olde? and shal Saráh that is ninety yere
olde beare?
18 And Abrahám said vnto God,*Oh,that
Ishmaél might liue in thy sight.
19 The God said, Saráh thy wife shal beare
thee a sonne in dede,& thou shalt call his
name Izhák: & I wil establish my couenát with him for an [g] euerlasting couenát,
and with his sede after him.
20 And as cócerning Ishmaél,I haue heard
thee: lo, I haue blessed him, and wil make him fruteful,and wil multiplie him″ex
ceadingly: twelue princes shal he beget,
and I wil make a great nacion of him.
21 But my couenant wil I establish with
Izhák,which Saráh shal beare vnto thee, ÿ
next* yere at this season.
22 And he left of talking with him, and
God went vp from Abrahám.
23 ¶ Then Abrahám toke Ishmaél his sonne and all that were borne in his house,
& all that was boght with his money, *that*
is,euerie man childe among the men of A-
brahams house, and [h] he circumcised the
foreskinne of their flesh in that self same
day,as God had commanded him.
24 Abrahám also him selfe was ninety yere olde & nine, when the foreskinne of his
flesh was circumcised.
25 And Ishmaél his sonne was thirtene yere olde,when the foreskinne of his flesh
was circuncised.
26 The selfe same day was Abrahám circumcised,and Ishmaél his sonne:
27 And all the men of his house, *bothe* borne in his house,and boght with money of
the stráger, were circumcised with him.

e Albeit wome were not circumcised, yet were they partakers of Gods promes: for vnder the mankinde all was consecrated. & here is declared, that whosoeuer cótemneth ÿ signe, despiseth also the promes.

″*Or, dame, or, princesse.*

f Which proceded of a soden ioye, and not of infidelitie.

Chap 18,10. and,21,2.

g The euerlasting couenant is made with the childre of the Spirit: and with the childre of the fleshe is made ÿ temporal promes, as was promised to Ishmaél

″*Ebr. greatly greatly*

Chap.21,2.

h Thei were wel instructed which obeied to be circumcised without resistance: ŵ thig declareth ÿ masters in their houses oght to be as preachers to their families, that from the hiest to ÿ lowest they may obey the wil of God.

CHAP. XVIII.

1 Abrahám receiueth thre Angels into his house.
10 Izhák is promised againe. 12 Saráh laugheth.
18 Christ is promised to all nations. 19 Abraham
taught his familie to knowe God. 21 The destruction
of Sodom is declared vnto Abrahám. 23 Abrahám
prayeth for them.

1 Againe the Lord*appeared vnto him
in the″plaine of Mamré,as he sate in
his tent dore about the heate of the day.
2 And he lift vp his eies,and loked: and lo,
thre [a] men stode by him,and when he sawe *them*,he ran to mete them from the tent
dore,& bowed him selfe to the grounde.
3 And he said,[b] Lord, if I haue now found
fauour in thy sight, go not, I praie thee,
from thy seruant.
4 Let a litle water,I pray you, be broght,
and [c] wash your fete,and rest your selues
vnder the tre.
5 And I wil bring a morsel of bread, that
you may cófort your heartes, afterwarde
ye shal go your waies: for therfore are ye
[d] come to your seruant. And they said,Do
euen as thou hast said.
6 Then Abrahám made haste into the tét
vnto Saráh, and said, Make ready at once
thre″measures of fine meale: knede it,and
make cakes vpon the herthe.
7 And Abrahám ran to ÿ beastes, & toke a
tender and good calfe, and gaue it to the
seruant,who hasted to make it ready.
8 And he toke butter & milke, and the calfe,which he had prepared,and set before
them,and stode him selfe by them vnder
the tre,and [e] thei did eat.
9 ¶ The thei said to him,Where is Saráh
thy wife?And he answered, Beholde, *she is*
in the tent.
10 And he said,* I wil certeinly come agai
ne vnto thee according to ÿ time [f] of li-
fe:and lo,Saráh thy wife shal haue a son-
ne.and Saráh heard in the tét dore, which
was behinde him.
11 (Now Abrahám and Saráh *were* olde &
stryken in age,*and* it ceased to be with Saráh after the maner of women)
12 Therfore Saráh [g] laughed within her sel
fe,saying, After I am waxed olde, * & my
lord also,shal I haue lust?
13 And ÿ Lord said vnto Abrahám, Wherfore did Saráh thus laugh, saying, Shal I
certeinly beare a childe,which am olde?
14 (Shal anie thig be″hard to the Lord?at
ÿ time appointed wil I returne vnto thee,
euen according to the time of life,and Saráh shal haue a sonne.)
15 But Saráh denied,saying,I laughed not:
for she was afraied. And he said, It is not
so:for thou laughedst.
16 ¶ Afterward ÿ mé did rise vp fró théce
& loked toward Sodóm: and Abrahám
wét with them to bring them on ÿ waie.
17 And the [h] Lord said, Shal I hide from
Abrahám that thing which I do,
18 Seig ÿ Abrahám shalbe in dede a great
and a mightie nacion,&*all the naciós of
the

Ebr.13,2.

″*Or, oke groue.*

a That is,thre Angels in mans shape.

b Speaking to one of them, in whome appeared to be most maiestie: for he thoght thei had bene men

c For men vsed because of the great heat to go bare foted in those parties

d As sent of God, that I shulde do my duetie to you.

″*Ebr. Seim.*

e For as God gaue them bodies for a time,so gaue he the ÿ faculties thereof, to walke, to eat and drincke, & suche like.

Chap.17,19. and 21,2.ro. 9,9.

f That is,whé she shalbe deliuered, or whé the childe shal come into this life.

g For she rather had respect to the ordre of nature, then beleued the promes of God.

1.Pet.3,6.

″*Or, hid.*

h Iehouáh the Ebrewe worde, which we call Lord,sheweth that this Angel was Christ: for this worde is onely applied to God.

Chap.12,13. and.22,17.

the earth shal be blessed in him?

i He sheweth that fathers oght bothe to knowe Gods iudgements & to declare them to their children.

19 For I knowe him [i] ŷ he wil commande
his sonnes and his housholde after him,
that thei kepe the waie of the Lord, to do
righteousnes and iudgement, that the
Lord maie bring vpon Abrahám that he
hathe spoken vnto him.
20 Then the Lord said, Because the crie
of Sodóm and Gomoráh is great, and because their sinne is exceading grieuous,

k God speaketh after the facion of mē: that is, I wil entre into iudgement with good aduis.
l For our sins crie for vengeance thogh none accuse vs.

21 I wil [k] go downe now, and se whether
thei haue done altogether according to ŷ
[l] crie, which is come vnto me: and if not,
that I maie knowe.
22 And ŷ men turned thence & went toward Sodóm: but Abrahám stode yet before the Lord.
23 Thē Abrahám drewe nere, & said, Wilt
ŷ also destroie ŷ righteous with ŷ wicked?
24 If there be fiftie righteous within the citie, wilt thou destroie & not spare the place for ŷ fiftie righteous that are therein?
25 Be it farre frō thee frō doing this thing,
to slay the righteous with the wicked: &
that the righteous shulde be euen as the
wicked, be it farre from thee. shal not the
judge of all the worlde " do right?

" Ebr do iudgement?

m God declareth that his iudgements were done ŵ great mercie, forasmuche as all were so corrupt, that not onely fiftie, but ten righteous men colde not be founde there: and also that the wicked are spared for the righteous sake.

26 And the Lord answered, If I shal finde
in Sodóm [m] fifty righteous within ŷ citie,
thē wil I spare all the place for their sakes.
27 Then Abrahám answered and said, Beholde now, I haue begonne to speake vnto
my Lord, and I am [n] but dust and asshes.
28 If there shal lacke fiue of fiftie righteous,
wilt ŷ destroie all the citie for fiue? And
he said, If I finde there fiue and fourty, I
wil not destroie it.
29 And he yet spake to him againe, and
said, What if there shalbe founde fourtie?
Then he answered, I wil not do it for four
ties sake.

n Hereby we learne, that ŷ nerer we aproche vnto God, the more doeth our miserable estate appeare, and the more are we humbled.

30 Againe he said, Let not my Lord now be
angry ŷ I speake, What if thirtie be foūde there? Then he said, I wil not do it, if I
finde thirtie there.
31 Moreouer he said, Beholde, now I haue
begōne to speake vnto my Lord, What if
twentie be founde there? And he āswered,
I wil not destroie it for twenties sake.

o If God refused not the praier for the wicked Sodomites, euen to ŷ sixt request, how muche more wil he grante the praiers of the godlie for ŷ afflicted Church?

32 Then he said, Let not my Lord be now
angrie, & I wil speak but this [o] once, What
if ten be founde there? And he answered, I
wil not destroie it for tens sake.
33 ¶ And ŷ Lord went his waie when he had
left communing with Abrahám, & Abrahám returned vnto his place.

CHAP. XIX

¶ 3 Lot receiueth two Angels into his house, 4 The filthy lustes of the Sodomites. 16 Lot is deliuered 24. Sodō is destroied 26. Lots wife is made a piller of salt. 33. Lots daughters lye with their father, of whome come Moab and Ammón.

a Wherein we se Gods prouident care in preseruing his: albeit he reueileth not him selfe to all a like: for Lot had but two Angels and Abrahám thre.

AND in ŷ euening their came two [a] Angels to Sodóm: and Lot sate at the gate
of Sodóm, & Lot sawe *them*, & rose vp to
mete them, and he bowed him selfe with
his face to the grownd:
2 And he said, Se my Lords, I praie you
turne in now into your seruants house, &
tarie all night, and * wash your fete, and
ye shal rise vp early and go your waies.
Who said, Naie, but we wil abide in the
strete all night.

Chap. 18. 4.

b That is, he praied them so instantly.
c Not for ŷ thei had necessitie, but because ŷ time was not yet come that thei wolde reueile them selues.
d Nothing is more dangerous, then to dwel where sinne reigneth: for it corrupteth all.

3 Then [b] he preased vpon them earnestly,
and thei turned into him, and came to his
house, and he made them a feast, and did
bake vnleauened bread, and thei [c] did eat.
4 But before thei went to bed, the men of
the citie, *euen* the men of Sodóm compassed the house round about from the yong
to the olde, [d] all the people from *all* quarters.
5 Who cryīg vnto Lot said to him, Where
are ŷ men, which came to thee this night?
bring them out vnto vs that we maie
knowe them.
6 Then Lot went out at ŷ dore vnto them,
and shut the dore after him,
7 And said, I praie you, my brethren, do
not *so* wickedly.

e He deserueth praise in defending his guestes, but he is to be blamed in seking vnlauful meanes.
f That I shulde preserue them from all iniurie.

8 Beholde now, I haue two [e] daughters, ŵ
haue not knowen man: thē wil I bring out
now vnto you, and do to them as semeth
you good: onely vnto these men do nothing. [f] for therfore are thei come vnder
the shadowe of my rofe.
9 Then thei said, Awaie hence. and thei
said, He is come alone as a stranger, & shal
he iudge and rule? we wil now deale worse
with thee then with them. So thei preased
sore vpon Lot * him selfe, & came to breake
ŷ dore.

2 Pet. 2, 7.

10 But the men put forthe their hand & pulled Lot into the house to them and shut
to the dore.
11 * Then thei smote the men that were at
the dore of ŷ house with blindenes bothe
smale and great, so that thei were wearie
in " seking the dore.

Wisdo. 19, 16.

" Ebr. finding.

12 ¶ Then the men said vnto Lot, Whome
hast thou yet here? ether sonne in lawe or
thy sonnes, or thy daughters, or what soeuer thou hast in the citie, bring it out of
this place.

g This proueth that the Angels are ministers, aswel to execute Gods wrath, as to declare his fauour

13 For we [g] wil destroie this place, because
the * crie of them is great before ŷ Lord,
and the Lord hathe sent vs to destroie it.
14 Then Lot went out and spake vnto his
sonnes in lawe, which " maried his daughters, & said, Arise, get you out of this place:
for the Lord wil destroie the citie: but he
semed to his sonnes in lawe as thogh he
had mocked.

Chap. 18. 20.

" Or, shulde marie.

15 ¶ And when ŷ morning arose, the Angels
hasted Lot, saying, Arise, take thy wife and
thy two daughters " which are here, lest ŷ
be destroied in the punishmēt of the citie.

" Ebr. which are founde.

h The mercie of God striueth to ouercome mans slownes in following Gods calling.
Wisd.10,6.

16 And *as* he [h] prolonged the time, * the
men caught bothe him & his wife, and
his two daughters by the handes (ÿ Lord
being merciful vnto him) & they broght
him forthe, & set him without the citie.
17 ¶ And when they had broght thẽ out, *the
Angel* said: escape for thy life: [i] loke not
behinde thee, nether tarie thou in all the
plaine: escape into the mountaine, lest
thou be destroied.
18 And Lot said vnto them, Not so, I praie
thee, my Lord.
19 Beholde now, thy seruant hathe founde
grace in thy sight, and thou hast magnified thy mercie, which thou hast shewed
vnto me in sauing my life: and I can not
escape in the mountaine, lest *some* euil take me, and I die.
20 Se now this citie hereby to flee vnto,
which is a litle one: Oh let me escape thi
ther: is it not a [k] litle one, & my soule shal
liue?
21 Then he said vnto him, Beholde, I haue
receiued "thy request also cõcerning this
thing, that I wil not ouerthrowe this citie, for the which thou hast spoken.
22 Haste thee, saue thee there: for I cã do
[l] nothĩg til thou be come thether. Therfore ÿ name of ÿ citie was called [m] Zóar.
23 ¶ The sunne did rise vpon the earth, whẽ
Lot entred into Zóar.
24 Then the Lord * rained vpon Sodóm
and vpon Gomoráh brimstone, and fire
from the Lord out of heauen,
25 And ouerthrewe those cities and all the
plaine, & all the inhabitãts of the cities,
and that that grewe vpon the earth.
26 ¶ Now his wife behĩde him loked backe,
and was turned in to a [n] piller of salt.
27 ¶ And Abrahám rising vp early in ÿ mor
nig *went* to ÿ place, where he had stand before the Lord, and loking toward Sodóm
and Gomoráh and toward all the land of
the plaine:
28 Beholde, he sawe the smoke of the land
mounting vp as the smoke of a fornace.
29 ¶ But yet when God destroied the cities
of the plaine, God thoght vpon Abrahã,
and sent Lot out from the middes of the
destructiõ, whẽ he ouerthrewe the cities,
wherein Lot dwelled.
30 ¶ Then Lot went vp frõ Zóar, and dwelt
in the mountaine with his two daughters:
for he [o] feared to tarie in Zóar, but dwelt
in a caue, he, and his two daughters.
31 And the elder said vnto ÿ yonger, Our fa
ther is olde, and there is not a man in the
[p] earth to come in vnto vs after the maner
of all the earth.
32 Come, we wil make our father [q] drinke
wine, and lye with him, that we maie preserue sede of our father.
33 So thei made their father drinke wine ÿ
night, and the elder went and laie with her
father: but he perceiued not, nether when
she laie downe, nether when she rose vp.
34 And on the morow the elder said to the
yonger, Beholde, yester night laie I with
my father: let vs make him drinke wine
this night also, and go thou *and* lye with
him, ÿ we maie "preserue sede of õ father.
35 So thei made their father drinke wine ÿ
night also, and the yonger arose, and laie
with him, but he perceiued not, when she
laie downe, nether when she rose vp.
36 Thus were [r] bothe the daughters of Lot
with childe by their father.
37 And the elder bare a sonne, & she called
his name Moáb: the same is the father of ÿ
[s] Moabites vnto this daie.
38 And the yonger bare a sonne also, and
she called his name [t] Ben-ammi: the same
is ÿ father of ÿ Ammonites vnto this daie.

i He willed hĩ to flee from Gods iudgementes, and not to be sorie to depart from ÿ riche countrei and ful of vaine pleasures.

k Thogh it be litle, yet it is great ynough to saue my life: wherĩ he offendeth in chosing another place then the Angel had appointed him.
" *Ebr. thy face.*
l Because Gods commandemẽt was to destroie the citie and to saue Lot.
m Which before was called Beláh, cha.14,2.
Deu.29,23. isai 13,19. ierem.50,40. ezech.16,49. oze.11,8. amo.4,11. luk.17,29. iude 7.
n As touching the bodie onely: & this was a notable monumẽt of Gods vengeance to all them that passed that way.

o Hauing before felt Gods mercies he durst not prouoke him againe by continuing among the wicked.
p Meaning, in the countrei, which ÿ Lord had now destroied.
q For except he had bene ouercome wt wine, he wolde neuer haue done ÿ abominable act.

" *Ebr. kepe aliue.*
r Thus God permitted him to fall moste horribly in ÿ solitarie mountaynes, whome the wickednes of Sodóm colde not ouercome.
s Who as they were borne in moste horrible incest, so were they and their posteritie vile and wicked.
t That is, sone of my people: signifying, that thei rather reioyced ĩ their sinne, then repented for the same.

CHAP. XX.

1 Abrahám dwelleth as a stranger in the land of Gerár. 2 Abimélech taketh awaie his wife. 3 God reproueth the King, 9 And the King, Abrahã. 11 Saráh is restored with great giftes. 17 Abrahám praieth, and the King and his are healed.

1 Afterwarde Abrahám departed thence
toward the South countrie and dwelled betwene Cadésh & [a] Shur, and soiourned in Gerár.
2 And Abrahám said of Saráh his wife,
[b] She is my sister. Thẽ Abimélech King of
Gerár sent and toke Saráh.
3 But God came to Abimélech in a dreame
by night and said to him, Beholde, [c] thou
art but dead, because of the womã, which
thou hast taken: for she is a mans wife.
4 (Notwithstanding Abimélech had not
yet come nere her) And he said, Lord, wilt
thou slaie euen [d] the righteous nacion?
5 Said not he vnto me, She is my sister? yea,
and she her selfe said, He is my brother: wt
an vpright [e] minde, and [f] innocẽt hãds haue I done this.
6 And God said vnto him by a dreame, I
knowe ÿ thou didest this euen with an vpright minde, & I [g] kept thee also that thou
shuldest not sinne against me: therfore suffred I thee not to touche her.
7 Now then deliuer ÿ man his wife againe: for he is a [h] Prophet, & he [i] shal praye
for thee ÿ thou mayest liue: but if thou deliuer her not againe, be sure ÿ thou shalt
die the death, thou, & all that thou hast.
8 Then Abimélech rising vp early in the
morning called all his seruãtes, and tolde
all these things "vnto them, and the men
were sore afraide.
9 Afterward Abimélech called Abrahám,
and said vnto him, What hast thou done
vnto vs? and what haue I offended thee,
that thou hast broght on me and on my
[k] kingdome *this* great sinne? thou hast done
things vnto me that oght not to be done.

a Which was toward Egypt.
b Abrahám had now twise fallẽ into this faute: suche is mans frailtie.
c So greatly God detesteth the breache of mariage.
d The infideles confessed that God wold not punish but for iust occasion: therfore when soeuer he punisheth, ÿ occasion is iust.
e As one failing by ignorance, and not doing euil of purpose.
f Not thinkĩg to do any man harme.
g God by his holie Spirit reteineth thẽ that offend by ignorãce, that thei fall not into greater inconueniẽce.
h That is, one, to whome God reueileth him self familiarly.
i For ÿ prayer of ÿ godlie is of force towards God.
" *Ebr in their eares.*
k The wickednes of the King bringeth Gods wrath vpon ÿ whole realme.

10 So

10 So Abimélech said vnto Abrahám,
What sawest yͧ that yͧ hast done this thĩg?
11 Then Abrahám answered, Because I
thoght *thus*, Surely yͤ [l] feare of God *is* not
in this place, and they wil slay me for my
wiues sake.

l He sheweth that no honestie can be hoped for, where the feare of God is not.

12 Yet in very dede she is my [m] sister: for she
is the daughter of my father, but not the
daughter of my mother, & she is my wife.

m By sister, he meaneth his cosingermain, & by daughter, Abrahams nece: for so the Ebrewes vse these wordes.

13 Now when God caused me to wandre
out of my fathers house, I said thẽ to her,
This is thy kindenes that yͧ shalt shewe vn
to me in all places where we come, * Say
thou of me, He is my brother.

Chap. 12, 13.

14 Then toke Abimélech shepe & beues, &
men seruantes, and women seruantes, and
gaue them vnto Abrahám, and restored
him Saráh his wife.
15 And Abimélech said, Behold, my land *is*
" before thee: dwel where it pleaseth thee.

" *Or, is at thy commandemẽt.*

16 Likewise to Saráh he said, Beholde, I ha
ue giuen thy brother a thousand peces of
siluer: beholde, he is yͤ [n] vaile of thine eies
to all that are with thee, and to all *others*:
and she was [o] thus reproued.

n Such an head, as with whome thou maist be preserued from all dangers.
o God caused this heathen King to reproue her, because she dissembled, since God had giuen her a housband, as her vaile and defense.

17 ¶ Then Abrahám praied vnto God, &
God healed Abimélech, and his wife, and
his maid seruants: and they bare children.
18 For yͤ Lord [p] had shut vp euerie wõbe of yͤ
house of Abimélech, because of Saráh A-
brahams wife.

p Had taken away frõ the the gift of conceiuing.

CHAP. XXI.

2 Izhák is borne. 9 Ishmaél mocketh Izhák. 14 Hagár is cast out with her sonne. 17 The Angel comforteth Hagár. 22 The couenãt betwene Abimélech & Abrahã.

1 NOw yͤ Lord visited Saráh, as he had
said, and did vnto her * according
as he had promised.
2 For * Saráh conceiued, & bare Abrahám
a sonne in his [a] olde age, at the same season
that God tolde him.

Chap 17, 19. & 18, 10. Act. 7, 8. gal. 4, 23. ebr. 11, 11.
a Therefore yͤ miracle was greater.

3 And Abrahám called his sonnes name
that was borne vnto him, which Saráh bare him, Izhák.
4 Then Abrahám circumcised Izhák his
sonne, when he was eight daies olde, * as
God had commanded him.

Chap. 17, 12.

5 So Abrahám was an hundreth yere olde,
whẽ his sonne Izhák was borne vnto him.
6 ¶ Thẽ Saráh said, God hathe made me to
reioyce: all that heare wil reioyce wͭ me.
7 Againe she said, [b] Who wolde haue said
to Abrahám, that Saráh shulde haue giuen
children sucke? for I haue borne him a
sonne in his olde age.

b She accuseth her selfe of ingratitude that she did not beleue the Angel.

8 Then the childe grewe & was weaned: &
Abrahám made a great feast the same day
that Izhák was weaned.
9 ¶ And Saráh sawe yͤ sonne of Hagár the
Egyptiã (which she had borne vnto Abra
hám) [c] mocking.

c He derided Gods promes made to Izhák, which yͤ Apostle calleth persecutiõ. Gal. 4, 29.

10 Wherefore she said vnto Abrahám, Cast
out this bond woman and her sonne: for
the sonne of this bond woman shal not be
heire with my sonne Izhák.
11 And this thing was very grieuous in A-
brahams sight, because of his sonne.
12 ¶ But God said vnto Abrahám, Let it not
be grieuous in thy sight for the childe,
and for thy bond womã: in all that Saráh
shal saie vnto thee, heare her voice: for in
Izhák shal thy sede be [d] called.
13 As for yͤ sonne of yͤ bond womã, I wil ma
ke hĩ [e] a naciõ also, because he is thy sede.
14 So Abrahám arose vp early in the morning, and toke bread, and a bottel of water, and gaue it vnto Hagár, putting it on
her shulder and the childe *also*, and [f] sent
her away: who departing wandred in the
wildernes of Beer-shéba.

d The promised sede shal be coũted frõ Izhák and not from Ishmaél. Rom 9, 7. ebr. 11, 18.
e The Ishmaelites shal come of him.
f True faith renoũceth all natural affectiõs to obey Gods cõmandemẽt.

15 And when the water of the bottel was
spẽt, she cast yͤ childe vnder a certeine tre.
16 Then she went and sate her ouer against
him a farre of about a bowe shote: for she
said, I wil not se the death of the childe.
and she sate downe ouer against *him*, and
lift vp her voyce and wept.
17 Then God [g] heard the voyce of the chil
de, and the Angel of God called to Hagár from heauen, and said vnto her, What
aileth thee, Hagár? feare not, for God
hathe heard yͤ voyce of the childe where
he is.

g For his promes sake made to Abrahám, and not because yͤ childe had discretion and iudgemẽt to pray.

18 Arise, take vp yͤ childe, and holde him in
thine hand: for I wil make of him a great
people.
19 And God [h] opened her eies, & she sawe
a well of water. so she went and filled the
bottel with water, & gaue yͤ boye drinke.
20 So God was [i] with the childe & he grewe and dwelt in the wildernes, and was an
" archer.

h Except God open our eies, we can nether se, nor vse the meanes which are before vs.
i As touching outwarde thĩgs God caused him to prosper.
" *Or, shot in the bowe and was an hunter.*

21 And he dwelt in the wildernes of Parán,
and his mother toke him a wife out of the
land of Egypt.
22 ¶ And at that same time Abimélech and
Phichól his chief captaine spake vnto A-
brahám, saying, God *is* with thee in all yͭ
thou doest.
23 Now therefore sweare vnto me here by
God, that thou wilt not " hurt me, nor my
children, nor my childrens children: thou
shalt deale with me, and with yͤ countrie,
where thou hast bene a strãger, according
vnto the kĩdenes that I haue shewed thee.

" *Ebr. deale falsly with me, or lye.*

24 Then Abrahám said, I wil [k] sweare.
25 And Abrahám rebuked Abimélech for a
well of water, wͨ Abimelechs seruants had
violently taken away.
26 And Abimélech said, [l] I knowe not who
hathe done this thing: also thou toldest
me not, nether heard I *of it* but this daie.
27 Then Abrahám toke shepe, and beues,
and gaue them vnto Abimélech: and they
two made a couenant.
28 And Abrahám set seuen lambes of the

k So yͭ it is a lauful thĩg to take an othe i matters of importance, for to iustifie the trueth and to assure others of our sinceritie.
l Wicked seruants do many euils vnknowẽ to their masters.

flocke by them selues.
29 Then Abimélech said vnto Abrahám,
What meane these seuen lambes, which
thou hast set by them selues?
30 And he answered, Because thou shalt receiue of mine hand *these* seuen lambes, ỳ it
may be a witnes vnto me, that I haue dig
ged this well.
31 Wherefore the place is called "Beer-shé
ba, because there thei bothe sware.
32 Thus made they a [m] couenant at Beer-
shéba: afterward Abimélech & Phichól
his chief captaine rose vp, & turned againe
vnto the land of the Philistíms.
33 ¶ And Abrahám planted a groue in Beer-
shéba, and [n] called there on the Name of
the Lord, the euerlasting God.
34 And Abrahám was a stranger in the Phi
listíms land a long season.

"Or, well of the othe, or, of seuē, meaning lābes.
m Thus we se that ỳ godlie, as touchīg out warde things, may make peace with ỳ wicked ỳ knowe not the true God.
n That is, he worshiped God in all points of true religion.

CHAP. XXII.

2.2. The faith of Abrahám is proued in offring his sonne Izhák. 8 Izhák is a figure of Christ. 20 The generacion of Nahór Abrahams brother, of whome cometh Rebekáh.

Ebr. 11,17.

1 AND after these thīgs God did *proue
Abrahám, & said vnto hī, Abrahám.
Who answered, "Here am I.
2 And he said, Take now thine onely sonne
Izhák whome thou louest, & get thee vnto the lande of [a] Moriáh, and [b] offre him
there for a burnt offring vpon one of the
mountaines, which I wil shewe thee.
3 Then Abrahám rose vp early in the mor
ning, and sadled his asse, and toke two of
his seruants with him, and Izhák his sonne, and cloue wood for the burnt offring,
and rose vp and went to the place, which
God had tolde him.
4 ¶ Then ỳ third day Abrahám lift vp his
eies, and sawe the place a farre of,
5 And said vnto his seruants, Abide you here ẘ the asse: for I & the childe wil go yō-
der & worship, & [c] come againe vnto you.
6 Then Abrahám toke the wood of ỳ burnt
offring, & laied it vpon Izhák his sonne,
& he toke the fire in his hand, & the knife:
and they went bothe together.
7 Then spake Izhák vnto Abrahám his father, & said, My father. And he answered,
Here am I, my sonne. And he said, Beholde the fire & the wood, but where is the
lambe for the burnt offring?
8 Thē Abrahám answered, My sonne, God
wil [d] prouide him a lambe for a burnt offring: so they went bothe together.
9 Whē they came to ỳ place ẘ God had she
wed hī, Abrahám buylded an altar there,
& couched ỳ wood, & [e] boūd Izhák his sō
ne *& laied him on ỳ altar vpon ỳ wood.
10 And Abrahám stretching forthe his
hand, toke the knife to kil his sonne.
11 But ỳ Angel of the Lord called vnto him
from heauē, saying, Abrahám, Abrahám.

"Ebr. Lo, I.
a Which signifieth the feare of God, in the which place he was honored: and Salomō afterward buylt the temple.
b Herein stode ỳ chiefest point of his tētation, seing he was commanded to offre vp him in whome God had promised to blesse all the nations of the worlde.
c He douted not, but God wolde accomplish his promes thogh he shulde sacrifice his sonne.
d The onely way to ouercome all tentations is to rest vpō Gods prouidence.
e For it is like ỳ his father had declared to him Gods cōmandement whereunto he shewed him self obedient.
Iam. 2,21.

And he answered, Here am I.
12 Then he said, Lay not thine hand vpon
the childe, nether do anie thing vnto him:
for now I [f] knowe that thou fearest God,
seing for my sake "thou hast not spared
thine onely sonne.
13 And Abrahám lifting vp his eies, loked:
& beholde, there was a ram behinde *him*
caught by ỳ hornes in a bushe. then Abrā
hám wēt & toke the ram & offred him vp
for a burnt offring in ỳ stede of his sonne.
14 And Abrahám called the name of that
place, "Iehouáh-iireh. as it is said this day,
In the mount wil the Lord [g] be sene.
15 ¶ And the Angel of the Lord cryed vnto
Abrahám from heauen the seconde time,
16 And said, By [h] my selfe haue I sworne
(saith ỳ Lord) because thou hast done this
thīg, & hast not spared thine onely sonne,
17 Therefore wil I surely blesse thee, and
wil greatly multiplie thy sede, as ỳ starres
of the heauen, and as ỳ sande which is vpon the seashore, and thy sede shal possesse the "gate of his ennemies.
18 *And in thy sede shal all ỳ naciōs of the
earth be blessed, because thou hast obeied
my voyce.
19 Then turned Abrahám againe vnto his
seruants, and they rose vp and went together to Beer-shéba: and Abrahám dwelt
at Beer-shéba.
20 ¶ And after these thīgs one tolde Abrahám, sayīg, Beholde Milcáh, she hathe also
borne children vnto thy brother Nahór:
21 *To wit*, Vz his eldest sonne, & Buz his bro
ther, & Kemuél the father of "Arám,
22 And Chésed and Hazó, & Pildásh, & Iid
láph, and Bethuél.
23 And Bethuél begate Rebekáh: these
eight did Milcáh beare to Nahór Abrahams brother.
24 And his [i] cōcubine called Reumáh, she
bare also Tébah, & Gáhan & Tháhash &
Maacháh.

f That is, by thy true obedience thou hast declared thy liuelie faith.
"Or, and hast not withholden thine onelie sonne from me.
"Or, The Lord wil se, or prouide.
g The name is changed, to shewe ỳ God dothe both se & prouide secretly for his, and also euidently is sene and felt in time couenient.
h Signifiing, that there is no greater then he.
"Or, holder.
Chap. 12,3, & 18,18. eccles. 44,25. act. 3,25. gal. 3,8.
"Or, of the Syrians.
i Concubine is oftentimes taken in the good parte for those women which were inferior to the wiues.

CHAP. XXIII.

2. Abrahám lamenteth the death of Saráh. 4 He bieth a field, to bury her, of the Hittites. 13 The equitie of Abrahám. 19 Saráh is buryed in Machpeláh.

1 WHen Saráh was an hūdreth twenty and seuen yere olde ("so long
liued she)
2 Then Saráh dyed in Kiriath-arbá: the
same is Hebrón in the land of Canáan. &
Abrahám came to mourne for Saráh and
to wepe for her.
3 ¶ Then Abrahám [a] rose vp frō ỳ sight of
his corps, & talked ẘ the "Hittites, saying,
4 I am a stranger, & a foriner among you,
giue me a possesion of buryal with you,
that I may bury my dead out of my sight.
5 Then the Hittites answered Abrahám,
saying vnto him,
6 Heare vs, my Lord: thou art a prince [b] of
God among vs: in the chiefest of our sepul
chres

"Ebr. the yeres of the life of Sarah.
a That is whē he had mourned: so ỳ godlie may mourne, if thei passe not measure: and ỳ natural affection is cōmendable.
"Ebr. sonnes of Hethe.
b That is, godlie or excellēt: for ỳ Ebrewes so speake of all things that are notable, because all excellencie cometh of God.

chres bury thy dead: none of vs shal forbid thee his sepulchre, but thou maiest
bury thy dead *therein*.
7 Then Abrahám stode vp, & bowed him
selfe before the people of the land of the
Hittites.
8 And he communed with them, saying, If
it be "your minde, yͭ I shal bury my dead
out of my sight, heare me, and intreat for
me to Ephrón the sonne of Zóhar,
9 That he wolde giue me yͤ caue "of Machpe
láh, which he hathe in the end of his field:
yͭ he wolde giue it me for as muche "money as it is worthe, for a possession to bury in among you.
10 (For Ephrón dwelt among yͤ Hittites)
Then Ephrón the Hittite answered Abra
hám in the audience of all the Hittites yͭ
[c] went in at the gates of his citie, saying,
11 No, my lord, heare me: the field giue I
thee, and the caue, that therein is, I giue it
thee: *euen* in the presence of the sonnes of
my people giue I it thee, to bury thy dead.
12 Then Abrahám [d] bowed him self before the people of the land,
13 And spake vnto Ephrón in the audience
of the people of the coūtrey, saying, Seing
yͧ *wilt giue it*, I praye thee, heare me, I wil
giue yͤ price of the field: receiue it of me,
and I wil bury my dead there.
14 Ephrón then answered Abrahám, saying
vnto him,
15 My Lord, harkē vnto me: yͤ land *is worthe*
four hūdreth [e] shekels of siluer: what *is* yͭ be
twene me & thee? bury therefore thy dead.
16 So Abrahám hearkened vnto Ephrón,
& Abrahám weyed to Ephrón the siluer,
which he had named, in the audience of
the Hittites, *euen* foure hūdreth siluer shekels of currant money among marchātes.
17 ¶ So yͤ field of Ephrón *which was* in Mach
peláh, & ouer against Mamré, *euen* yͤ field
& the caue yͭ was therein, and all the trees
yͭ were in the field, which were in all the
borders roundabout, was made sure
18 Vnto Abrahám for a possession, in the
sight of the Hittites, *euen* of all that "went
in at the gates of his citie.
19 And after this, Abrahám buryed Saráh
his wife in the caue of the field of Machpe
láh ouer against Mamré: the same is Hebrón in the land of Canáan.
20 Thus bothe the field and the caue, yͭ is
therein, was made sure vnto Abrahám for
a possession of buryal [f] by the Hittites.

"*Ebr. in your soule.*
"*Or, double caue, because one was within an other.*
"*Ebr. in ful siluer.*
c Meaning, all the citizens & inhabitants.
d To shewe yͭ he had them in good estima tion and reuerence.
e The commē shekel is about 20 pēce, so thē 400 shekels mount to 33 li. 6. shill. & 8 pence, after 5. shill. sterl. the once.
"*Or, citizens.*
f That is, all the people cōfirmed yͤ sale.

CHAP. XXIIII.

2 *Abrahám causeth his seruant to sweare to take a wife for Izhák in his owne kinred. 12 The seruant prayeth to God. 34 His fidelitie towarde his master. 50 The friends of Rebekáh commit the matter to God. 58 They aske her consent and she agreeth. 67 And is maryed to Izhák.*

1 NOw Abrahám was olde, *and* "striken
in yeres, and the Lord had blessed
Abrahám in all things.
2 Therefore Abrahám said vnto his eldest
seruant of his house, which had the rule ō-
uer all that he had, * [a] Put now thine hand
vnder my thigh,
3 And I wil make thee [b] sweare by the Lord
God of yͤ heauen, & God of yͤ earth, that
thou shalt not take a wife vnto my sonne
of the daughters of the Canaanites amōg
whome I dwel.
4 But thou shalt go vnto my [c] countrie, &
to my kinred, & take a wife vnto my son
ne Izhák.
5 And the seruant said to him, What if the
woman wil not come wͭ me to this land?
shal I bring thy sonne againe vnto the lād
from whence thou camest?
6 To whome Abrahám answered, Beware
yͭ yͧ bring not my sonne [d] thether againe.
7 ¶ The Lord God of heauen, who toke me
from my fathers house, & from yͤ lād whe
re I was borne, and that spake vnto me,
& that sware vnto me, saying, * Vnto thy
sede wil I giue this land, he shal send his
Angel before thee, and thou shalt take a
wife vnto my sonne from thence.
8 Neuertheles if the womā wil not followe
thee, then shalt thou be "discharged of this
mine othe: onely bring not my sonne thether againe.
9 Then the seruant put his hand vnder the
thigh of Abrahám his master, & sware to
him for this matter.
10 ¶ So the seruant toke ten camels of the
camels of his master, and departed: for he
had all his masters goods in his hād, & so
he arose, and went to "Arám Naharáim, vn
to the [e] citie of Nahór.
11 And he made his camels to "lie downe
without the citie by a well of water, at e-
uen about the time that women come out
to drawe water.
12 And he said, O [f] Lord God of my master Abrahám, I beseche thee, "send me good spede this day, and shewe mercie vnto
my master Abrahám.
13 Lo, I stand by the well of water, whiles
the mēs daughters of this citie come out
to drawe water.
14 [g] Grant that yͤ maide, to whome I saie,
Bowe downe thy pitcher, I pray thee, that
I may drinke: if she say, Drinke, and I wil
giue thy camels drinke also: may be she yͭ
thou hast ordeined for thy seruant Izhák:
& thereby shal I knowe yͭ thou hast shewed mercie on my master.
15 ¶ Now yer he had left speaking, beholde,
[h] Rebekáh came out, the daughter of Bethuél, sonne of Milcáh the wife of Nahór
Abrahams brother, and her pitcher vpon
her shuldre.
16 (And the maide was very faire to loke
vpon, a virgine and vnknowen of man) &

"*Ebr. come into dayes.*
Chap. 47.29.
a Which ceremonie declared yͤ seruants obedience towards his master, and yͤ masters power ouer the seruāt.
b This sheweth that an othe may be required in a lawful cause.
c He wolde not yͭ his sonne shulde mary out of the godlie familie: for the inconuenients yͭ come by marying with the vngodlie are set forthe in sondrie places of the Scriptures.
d Lest he shulde lose the inheritance promised.
Cha. 12,7. & 13,15. & 15, 18, & 26,4.
"*Ebr. innocent.*
"*Or, Mesopotamia, or, Syria of the two floods: to wit, of Tygris and Euphrates.*
e That is, to Charán.
"*Ebr. to bowe their knees.*
f He groūdeth his prayer vpō Gods promes made to his master.
"*Or, cause me to mete.*
g The seruant moued by Gods Spirit desired to be assured by a signe, whether God prospered his iourney or no.
h God giueth good successe to all things yͭ are vndertaken for the glorie of his Name and according to his worde.

i Here is declared ẏ God euer heareth the praiers of his, and granteth their requestes.

she [i] went downe to the well, and filled her
pitcher, and came vp.
17 Then the seruant ran to mete her, and
said, Let me drincke, I praye thee a litle
water of thy pitcher.

"Ebr. my lord.

18 And she said, Drinke" syr: and she hasted,
& let downe her pitcher vpon her hand &
gaue him drinke.
19 And when she had giuen him drinke, she
said, I wil drawe water for thy camels also vntil thei" haue dronken ynough.

" Ebr. haue made an end of drinking.

20 And she poured out her pitcher into the
trogh spedely, and ranne againe vnto the
well to drawe water, and she drewe for all
his camels.
21 So the man wondred at her, and helde
his peace, to wit, whether the Lord had
made his iourney prosperous or not.
22 And when the camels had left drinking,
the man toke a golden" [k] abillement of
[l] halfe a *shekel* weight, & two bracelettes
for her hãds, of tẽ shekels weight of golde:
23 And he said, Whose daughter art thou?
tel me, I praie thee, Is there roume in thy
fathers house for vs to lodge in?
24 Then she said to him, I am ẏ daughter
of Bethuél the sonne of Milcáh whome
she bare vnto Nahór.

"Or, earing.
k God permitted manie things both in apparel and other things ẇ are nowe forbid: specially when thei apperteine not to our mortificacion.
l The golden shekel is here ment and not that of siluer.

25 Moreouer she said vnto him, We haue
lytter also and prouander ynough, and
roume to lodge in.
26 And the man bowed him selfe and worshipped the Lord,
27 And said, Blessed *be* the Lord God of
my master Abrahám, ẇ hathe not withdrawen his mercie [m] and his trueth from
my master: *for* whẽ I was in ẏ waie, ẏ Lord
broght me to my masters brethrẽs house.
28 And the maide ran & tolde them of her
mothers house according to these wordes.
29 ¶ Now Rebekáh had a brother called Labán, & Labán ran vnto ẏ mã to the well.

m He boasteth not his good fortune (as do the wicked) but acknollageth that God hath dealt mercifully with his master in kepĩg promes.

30 For when he had sene the earings & the
bracelettes in his sisters hands, & when he
heard the wordes of Rebekáh his sister,
saying, Thus said the man vnto me, then
he went to the man, & lo [n] he stode by
the camels at the well.
31 And he said, Come in ẏ blessed of ẏ Lord:
wherfore standest ẏ without, seing I haue
prepared the house, & roume for ẏ camels?
32 ¶ Then ẏ man came into ẏ house, and [o] he
vnsadeled the [p] camels and broght lytter
& prouander for the camels, and water to
washe his fete, & the mens fete that were
with him.
33 Afterward the meat was set before him:
but he said, I [q] wil not eat, vntil I haue
said my message: And he said, Speake on.
34 Then he said, I am Abrahams seruant,
35 And the Lord hathe [r] blessed my master
wonderfully, that he is become great: for
he hathe giuen him shepe, and beues, & sil-

n For he waited on Gods hand, who had now heard his praier.
o To wit, Labã.
p The gentle interteinemẽt of strangers vsed among the godlie fathers.
q The fidelitie that seruants owe to their masters, causeth them to preferre their masters busines to their owne necessitie.
r To blesse, signifieth here to enriche, or encrease with substance, as ẏ text in ẏ same verse declareth.

uer, and golde, and men, seruantes, & maide
seruantes, and camels, and asses.
36 And Saráh my masters wife hathe borne
a sonne to my master, whẽ she was olde, &
vnto him hathe he giuẽ all that he hathe.
37 Now my master made me sweare, saying,
Thou shalt not take a wife to my sonne
of the daughters of the [s] Canaanites, in
whose land I dwel:
38 But thou shalt go vnto my [t] fathers house and to my kinred, and take a wife vnto
my sonne.
39 Then I said vnto my master, What if the
woman wil not followe me?

s The Canaanites were accursed & therfore the godlie colde not ioine with the in mariage.
t Meaning among his kinsfolkes, as vers. 40.

40 Who answered me, The Lord, before
whome I walke, wil send his Angel with
thee, and prosper thy iourney, and thou
shalt take a wife for my sonne of my kĩd-
red and my fathers house.
41 Then shalt ẏ be discharged of [u] mine
othe, when thou commest to my kinred:
and if thei giue thee not one, thou shalt be
fre from mine othe.

u Which by mine autoritie I caused thee to make.

42 So I came this daie to the well, and said,
O Lord, the God of my master Abrahám,
if ẏ now prosper my" iourney which I go,
43 Beholde, * I stand by the well of water:
when a virgine commeth forthe to drawe
water, & I saie to her, Giue me, I praie
thee, a litle water of thy pitcher to drinke,
44 And she saie to me, Drinke ẏ, and I wil
also drawe for thy camels, let her be the
wife, which the Lord hathe" prepared for
my masters sonne.

"Or, waie.
Verse 13.
"Or, shewed.

45 And before I had made an end of speakĩg
in mine [x] heart, beholde, Rebekáh came
forthe, and her pitcher on her shuldre, &
she went downe vnto the well, and drewe
water. Thẽ I said vnto her, Giue me drĩke,
I praie thee.

x Signifyng ẏ this praier was not spokẽ by the mouth, but onely meditate in his heart.

46 And she made haste, and toke downe her
pitcher from her *shulder*, and said, Drinke,
& I wil giue thy camels drinke also. So I
dranke, & she gaue the camels drinke also.
47 Then I asked her, & said, Whose daughter art ẏ? And she answered, The daughter of Bethuél Nahors sonne, whome Milcáh bare vnto him. Then I put the abillement vpon her face, and the bracelettes
vpon her handes:
48 [y] And I bowed downe & worshipped ẏ
Lord, and blessed the Lord God of my
master Abrahám, which had broght me ẏ
" right waie to take my masters brothers
daughter vnto his sonne.
49 Now therefore, if ye wil deale [z] mercifully and truely with my master, tel me: and
if not, tel me that I maie turne me to the
[a] right hand or to the left.
50 Then answered Labán and Bethuél, &
said, [b] This thing is proceded of the Lord:
we can not therefore saie vnto thee, *nether*
euil nor good.

y He sheweth what is our ductie, when we haue receiued anie benefite of the Lord.
"Ebr. in the waie of trueth.
z Yf you wil frely & faithfully giue your daughter to my masters sonne.
a That is, ẏ I maie prouide ells where.
b So sone as thei perceiue that it is Gods ordinance thei yelde.

Or, at thy com mandement.
Or, ordeined.

51 Beholde, Rebekáh *is* "before thee. take *her*
& go, that she maie be thy masters sonnes
wife, euen as the Lord hathe "said.
52 And when Abrahams seruant heard their
wordes, he bowed him selfe towarde the
earth vnto the Lord.
53 Then the seruãt toke forthe iewels of siluer, & iewels of golde, & raiment, & gaue
to Rebekáh: also vnto her brother and to
her mother he gaue giftes.
54 Afterwarde they did eat & drinke, *bothe*
he, and the men that were with him, and
taried all night. and when they rose vp in
the morning, he said, *Let me departe vnto my master.

Ver. 56, & 59.

55 Then her brother and her mother answered, Let the maide abide with vs, at
the least "ten dayes: then shal she go.

"Ebr. dayes, or ten.

56 But he said vnto thẽ, Hidre you me not,
seig ỹ Lord hathe prospered my iourney:
send me away, ỹ I may go to my master.
57 Then they said, We wil call the maide,
and aske [c] her "consent.
58 And they called Rebekáh, and said vnto
her, Wilt thou go with this man? And she
answered, I wil go.
59 So they let Rebekáh their sister go, and
her nourse, with Abrahams seruant and
his men.

c This sheweth that parents haue not autoritie to mary their childrẽ without consent of the parties.
"Ebr. her mouthe.

60 And thei blessed Rebekáh, and said vnto her, Thou art our sister, growe into
thousand thousandes, and thy sede possesse the [d] gate of his ennemies.
61 ¶ Then Rebekáh arose, and her maides,
& rode vpon the camels, and followed ỹ
mã. & ỹ seruãt toke Rebekáh, & departed.
62 Now Izhák came from the way of * Beér-lahai-roí, (for he dwelt in the South
countrey)

d That is, let it be victorious ouer his ennemies: w^t blessĩg is fully accomplisshed in Iesus Christ.
Chap. 16, 14. and 25, 10.

63 And Izhák went out to [e] pray in the field
toward the euening: who lift vp his eies
and loked, and beholde, the camels came.
64 Also Rebekáh lift vp her eies, and when
she sawe Izhák, she lighted downe from
the camel.

e This was ỹ exercise of ỹ godlie fathers to meditate Gods promisses & to pray for the accõplishmẽt thereof.

65 (For she had said to the seruant, Who is
yonder man, that commeth in the field to
mete vs? And the seruãt had said, It is my
master) So she toke [f] a vaile and couered her.
66 And the seruant tolde Izhák all things,
that he had done.
67 Afterward Izhák broght her into the tẽt
of Saráh his mother, & he toke Rebekáh,
& she was his wife, & he loued her: so Izhák was "cõforted after his mothers *death.*

f The custome was, that the spouse was broght to her housband, her head beig couered, in tokẽ of shamefastnes & chastitie.
"Or, had left mourning for his mother.

CHAP. XXV.

1 Abrahám taketh Keturáh to wife, and getteth many children. 6 Abrahám giueth all his goods to Izhák. 12 The genealogie of Ishmaél. 25 The birth of Iaakób and Esau. 30 Esau selleth his birth right for a messe of potage.

1 NOw Abrahám had taken [a] him another wife called Keturáh,

a Whiles Saráh was yet aliue.

2 Which bare him Zimrán, & Iokshán, &
Medán, & Mideán, & Ishbák, and Shúah.
3 And Iokshán begate Shebá & Dedán:
* And the sonnes of Dedán were Asshu-
rím, & Letushím, and Leummím.

1. Chro. 1. 32.

4 Also the sonnes of Mideán *were* Epháh,
& Ephér, & Hanóch, & Abidá, and Eldá-
ah. all these were the sonnes of Keturáh.
5 ¶ And Abrahám gaue " all his goods to
Izhák,

"Ebr. all that he had.

6 But vnto the [b] sonnes of the [c] concubines,
which Abrahám had, Abrahám [d] gaue gif
tes, and sent them away from Izhák his
sonne (while he yet liued) Eastward to the
East countrey.
7 And this is the age of Abrahams life,
which he liued, an hundreth seuenty and
fiue yere.
8 Thẽ Abrahám yelded the spirit, & dyed
in a good age, an olde man, and of great
yeres, and was [e] gathered to his people.

b For by the vertue of Gods worde he had not onely Izhák, but begate mauy mo.
c Reade, chap. 22, 24.
d To auoyde the dissension that els might haue come because of the heritage.

9 And his sonnes, Izhák and Ishmaél
buryed him in the caue of Machpeláh in
the field of Ephrón sonne of Zóhar the
Hittite, before Mamré.
10 Which field Abrahám boght of the
Hittites, where Abrahám was buryed w^t
Saráh his wife.
11 ¶ And after the death of Abrahám God
blessed Izhák his sonne, * and Izhák dwelt
by Beér-lahai-roí.

e Hereby the Anciens signified that man by death perished not wholy: but as the soules of the godlie liued after in ꝑpetual ioye, so the soules of the wicked in perpetual peine.
Chap. 16, 14. and 24, 62.

12 ¶ Now these are the generacions of Ishmaél Abrahams sonne, whome Hagár the
Egyptian Sarahs handmaide bare vnto A-
braham.
13 * And these are ỹ names of the sonnes of
Ishmaél, name by name, accordĩg to their
kinreds: the " eldest sonne of Ishmaél
was Nebaióth, then Kedár, & Adbeél, &
Mibsám,

1. Chro. 1. 29.
"Ebr first borne.

14 And Mishmá, & Dumáh, & Massá,
15 Hadár, & Temá, Ietúr, Naphish, & Kédemah.
16 These are the sonnes of Ishmaél, and these are their names, by their townes and by
their castels *to wit*, twelue princes of their
nations.
17 (And these are ỹ yeres of the life of Ishmaél, an hundreth thirty and seuen yere,
and he yelded the spirit, and dyed, & was
gathered vnto his [f] people)
18 And they dwelt frõ Hauiláh vnto Shur,
that is towardes Egypt, as thou goest to
Asshúr. *Ishmaél* dwelt " [g] in the presence of
all his brethren.

f Which dwelt among the Arabians, and were separat from the blessed sede.
"Or, his lot fel.
g He meaneth that his lot fel to dwel among his brethren, as the Angel promised. chap. 16, 12.

19 ¶ Likewise these are the generacions of
Izhák Abrahams sonne. Abrahám begate
Izhák,
20 And Izhák was fourty yere olde, when
he toke Rebekáh to wife, the daughter of
Bethuél the "Aramite of Padán Arám, *and*
sister to Labán the Aramite.

"Or, Syrian of Mesopotamia.

21 And Izhák prayed vnto the Lord for his

c. iii.

wife,because she was baren: and the Lord
was intreated of him, and Rebekáh his
wife conceiued,
22 But the children "stroue together within
her:therefore she said,Seig *it is* so,why am
[h] I thus? wherefore she wẽt [i] to aske ẏ Lord.
23 And the Lord said to her, two nations
are in thy wombe, and two maner of people shalbe deuided out of thy bowels,and
the one people shalbe mightier then the
other,and the * elder shal serue ẏ yonger.
24 ¶ Therefore when her time of deliuerãce was fulfilled, beholde, twinnes *were* in
her wombe.
25 So he that came out first was red, and he
was all ouer as a rough garment,and they
called his name Esáu.
26 * And afterwarde came his brother out,
and his hand held Esáu by the hele:there-
fore his name was called Iaakób. Now
Izhák was thre score yere olde when *Rebekáh* bare them.
27 And the boyes grewe,& Esáu *was* a cunning hunter,& " liued in ẏ fields:but Iaakób was a "plaine man,and dwelt in tẽtes.
28 And Izhák loued Esáu, for "venison *was*
his meat,but Rebekáh loued Iaakób.
29 Now Iaakób sodde pottage,& Esáu came from the field and was wearie.
30 Then Esáu said to Iaakób,"Let me eat,I
pray thee,of ẏ *pottage* so red,for I am weary. Therefore was his name called Edóm.
31 And Iaakób said, Sel me euen now thy
birthright.
32 And Esáu said, Lo, I am almost dead,
what *is* then this [k] birthright to me?
33 Iaakób then said, Sweare to me euẽ now.
And he sware to him,*& [l] solde his birthright vnto Iaakób.
34 Then Iaakób gaue Esáu bread and pottage of lentiles:and he did eat and drinke
and rose vp,& went his way: So Esáu cõtemned *his* birthright.

"Or,hurt one an other.
h That is, ẇ childe, seing one shal destroye another.
i For that is the onely refuge in all our miseries.
Rom 9,10.
Gen.25,3. Mat.1,2.
"Ebr. a man of the field.
"Or, simple and innocent.
"Ebr. venison in his mouthe.
"Or, fede me quickely.
k The reprobat esteme not Gods benefits except they fele them presently,& therfore they preferre present pleasures.
Ebr 12,16.
l Thus ẏ wicked preferre their worldelie cõmodities to Gods spiritual graces: but ẏ childrẽ of God do the contrary.

CHAP. XXVI.

1 God prouideth for Izhák in the famine. 3 He renueth his promes. 9 The king blameth him for denying his wife. 14 The Philistíms hate him for his riches, 15 Stoppe his welles, 16 And driue him away. 24 God comforteth him. 31 He maketh alliance with Abimélech.

1 AND there was a famine in the [a] land
besides the first famine that was in
the dayes of Abrahám. wherefore Izhák
went to Abimélech King of the Philistíms vnto Gerár.
2 For the Lord appeared vnto him,& said,
[b] Go not downe into Egypt, *but* abide in
the land which I shal shewe vnto thee.
3 Dwel in this land, & I wil be with thee,
and wil blesse thee:for to thee, and to thy
sede I wil giue all these *countreis:and I
wil performe the othe which I sware vnto Abrahám thy father.
4 Also I wil cause thy sede to multiplie as
the starres of heauen, and wil giue vnto

a In the land of Canáan.
b Gods prouidẽce alwaies watcheth to direct ẏ waies of his childrẽ.
Chap.13,15. & 15,18.

thy sede all these countreis: & in thy sede
shal all the naciõs of the earth be*blessed,
5 Because that Abrahám [c] obeied my voyce and kept mine " ordinance, my com-
mandemẽtes,my statutes,and my Lawes.
6 ¶ So Izhák dwelt in Gerár.
7 And the men of the place asked *him* of
his wife,& he said,She is my sister:for he
[d] feared to say, She is my wife, lest,*said he*,
the men of the place shulde kil me, because of Rebekáh: for she was beautiful
to the eie.
8 So after he had bene there long time, A-
bimélech King of the Philistíms loked
out at a windowe, and lo, he sawe Izhák
[e] sporting with Rebekáh his wife.
9 Then Abimélech called Izhák, and said,
Lo, she is of a suretie thy wife,& why saidest ẏ, She is my sister? To whome Izhák
answered,Because I thoght *this*,It maie be
that I shal die for her.
10 Then Abimélech said, Why hast thou
done this vnto vs? one of the people had
almost lien by thy wife, so shuldest thou
haue broght [f] sinne vpon vs.
11 Thẽ Abimélech charged all his people,
saying,He that toucheth this man, or his
wife,shal die the death.
12 Afterward Izhák sowed in that land,and
founde in the same yere an " hũdreth folde
by estimacion:and so ẏ Lord blessed him.
13 And the man waxed mightie, and " stil
increased,til he was exceading great,
14 For he had flockes of shepe,and herdes of
cattel,and a mightie housholde: therefore
the Philistíms had [g] enuie at him,
15 In so muche that ẏ Philistíms stopped &
filled vp with earth all the wells which his
fathers seruants digged in his father Abrahams time.
16 Then Abimélech said vnto Izhák, Get
thee from vs,for thou art mightier thẽ we
a great deale.
17 ¶ Therefore Izhák departed thẽce & pit
ched his tent in the [h] vallei of Gerár, and
dwelt there.
18 And Izhák returning, digged the welles of water,which thei had digged in the
dayes of Abrahám his father: for the Philistíms had stopped them after the death
of Abrahám, & he gaue thẽ the same names,which his father gaue them.
19 Izhaks seruants then digged in the vallei,& found there a well of " liuing water.
20 But the herd men of Gerár did striue ẇ
Izhaks herd mẽ sayĩg,The water is ours:
therefore called he the name of the well
"Esek,because thei were at strief ẇ him.
21 Afterward thei digged another well,and
stroue for that also, and he called the name of it "Sitnáh.
22 Then he remoued thence, & digged an
other well,for the ẇ thei stroue not:there-

Chap.12,37. and 15,18. & 22,19.and 23. 14.
c He commendeth Abrahãs obedience because Izhák shulde be the more readie to follow ẏ like: for as God made this ꝓmes of his fre mercie,so doeth ẏ confirmation thereof ꝓcede of the same fountaine.
"Ebr. my keping.
d Whereby we se ẏ feare and distrust is found in ẏ mo ste faithful.
e Or shewing some familiar signe of loue, whereby it might be knowen that she was his wife.
f In all ages men were persuaded ẏ Gods vẽgeãce shulde light vpon wedloke breakers.
"Or,an hũdreth measures.
"Ebr. he went forthe going & increasing.
g The malicious enuie alwaies the graces of God in others.
h The Ebrewe worde signifieth a flood, or vallei, where water at any time runneth.
"Or,springing.
"Or,Contention, strife.
"Or,hatred.

"Or, largenes, roume.

fore called he the name of it " Rehobóth,
& said, Because ỹ Lord hathe now made
vs roume, we shal encrease vpon ỹ earth.
23 So he went vp thence to Beer-shéba.
24 And the Lord appeared vnto him the
same night, and said, I am the God[i] of A-
brahám thy father: feare not, for I am with
thee, and wil blesse thee and multiplie thy
sede for my seruant Abrahams sake.
25 Thẽ he buylt an [k] altar there, and called
vpon the name of the Lord, & there spred
his tent: where also Izhaks seruants digged a well.
26 ¶ Then came Abimélech to him frõ Gerár, and Ahuzzáth *one* of his friends, and
Phichól the captaine of his armie.
27 To whome Izhák said, Wherefore come ye to me, seing ye hate me and haue
put me awaie from you?
28 Who answered, We sawe certeinly that
the Lord was with thee, and we thoght
thus, Let there be now an othe betwene vs,
euen betwene vs and thee, and let vs make
a couenant with thee.
29 Thou [l] shalt do vs no hurt, as we haue
not touched thee, and as we haue done vn
to thee nothing but good, and sent thee
awaie in peace: thou now, the blessed of
the Lord, *do this*.
30 Then he made them a feast, & thei did
eat and drinke.
31 And thei rose vp betimes in the morning, and sware one to an other: then Izhák let them go, and thei departed from
him in peace.
32 And that same daye Izhaks seruants came & tolde him of a well, which thei had
digged, & said vnto him, We haue found
water.
33 So he called it " Shibáh: therefore the name of the citie is called " Beer-shéba vnto this daye.
34 ¶ Now when Esáu was fourtie yere olde,
he toke to wife Iudíth, the daughter of
Beerí an Hittite, & Bashemáth ỹ daughter of Elón an Hittite *also*.
35 And thei * were " a grief of minde to Izhák and to Rebekáh.

i God assureth Izhák against all feare by rehersing the promes made to Abrahám.

k To signifie that he wolde serue none other God, but the God of his father Abrahám.

l The Ebrewes in swearing begin comonly wᵗ If, & vnderstand ỹ rest: ỹ is that God shal punishe him that breaketh the othe: here the wicked shewe that thei are afraied lest ỹ come to them wᶜ thei wolde do to other.

"Or, othe.

"Or, the well of the othe.

Chap. 27. 46.

" Or, disobedie͂t and rebellious.

CHAP. XXVII.

8 Iaakób getteth the blessing from Esáu by his mothers counsel. 38 Esáu by weping moueth his father to pitie him. 41 Esáu hateth Iaakób and threateneth his death. 43 Rebekáh sendeth Iaakób awaie.

1 AND when Izhák was olde, & his eies
were dimme (so that he colde not se)
he called Esáu his eldest sonne, and said
vnto him, My sonne. And he answered
him, "I am here.
2 Then he said, Beholde, I am now olde
and knowe not the daie of my death:
3 Wherefore now, I praie thee take thine
instruments, thy quiuer and thy bowe, &
get thee to the field, that thou maiest
"take me some venison.
4 Then make me sauourie meat, such as I
loue, and bring it me that I maie eat, *and*
ỹ my [a] soule maie blesse thee, before I dye.
5 (Now Rebekáh heard, when Izhák spake
to Esáu his sonne) and Esáu went into the
field to hunt for venison, and to bring it.
6 ¶ Then Rebekáh spake vnto Iaakób her
sonne, saying, Beholde, I haue heard thy
father talking wᵗ Esáu thy brother, saying,
7 Bring me venison, and make me sauourie meat, that I maie eat and blesse thee
before the Lord, afore my death.
8 Now therefore, my sonne, heare my voyce in that which I commande thee.
9 [b] Get thee now to the flocke, & bring me
thence two good kyds of the goates, that
I maie make pleasant meat of them for
thy father, such as he loueth.
10 Then thou shalt bring it to thy father,
and he shal eat, to the intent that he maie
blesse thee before his death.
11 But Iaakób said to Rebekáh his mother,
Beholde, Esáu my brother *is* rough, and I
am smothe.
12 My father maie possibly fele me, and I
shal seme " to him to be a " mocker: so shal
I bring a curse vpon me, and not a blessing.
13 But his mother said vnto him, " [c] Vpõ me
be thy curse, my sonne: onely heare my
voyce, and go and bring me *them*.
14 So he went and fet *them*, and broght *them*
to his mother: and his mother made pleasant meat, such as his father loued.
15 And Rebekáh toke faire clothes of her
elder sonne Esáu, which were in her house, and clothed Iaakób her yonger sonne:
16 And she couered his hands and the smothe of his necke with the skinnes of the
kyds of the goates.
17 Afterwarde she put the pleasant meat
and bread, which she had prepared, in the
hand of her sonne Iaakób.
18 ¶ And whẽ he came to his father, he said,
My father. Who answered, I am here:
who art thou, my sonne?
19 And Iaakób said to his father, [d] I am E-
sáu thy first borne, I haue done as ỹ badest
me, arise, I praie thee: sit vp and eat of my
venison, that thy soule maie blesse me.
20 Then Izhák said vnto his sonne, How
hast thou founde it so quickly my sonne?
Who said, Because the Lord thy God
broght it to mine hand.
21 Againe said Izhák vnto Iaakób, Come
nere now, that I maie fele thee, my sonne,
whether thou be that my sonne Esáu or
not.
22 Then Iaakób came nere to Izhák his
father, and he felt him and said, The
[e] voyce *is* Iaakobs voyce, but the hãds *are*
the handes of Esáu.

"Ebr. lo, I.

" Ebr. hunt.

a The carnal affectiõ, which he bare to his sonne, made him forget ỹ which God spake to his wife. Chap. 25, 23.

b This subtilitie is blameworthie because she shulde haue taried til God had performed his promes.

"Ebr. before his eies.

" Or, as thogh I wolde deceiue him

"Or, I wil take the danger on me.

c The assurance of Gods decre made her bolde.

d Althogh Iaakób was assured of this blessing by faith: yet he did euil to seke it by lies and the more because he abuseth Gods Name therunto.

e This declareth that he suspected something, yet God wolde not haue his decre altered.

23 (For he knewe him not, because his handes were rough as his brother Esaus handes: wherefore he blessed him)
24 Again he said, Art thou that my sonne
Esáu? Who answered, "Yea.
25 Then said he, Bring it me hether, and I
wil eat of my sonnes venisõ, that my soule may blesse thee. And he broght it to hĩ
and he ate: also he broght him wine, and
he dranke.
26 Afterwarde his father Izhák said vnto
him, Come nere now, and kisse me, my
sonne.
27 And he came nere and kissed him. Then
he smelled the sauour of his garments, &
blessed him, and said, Beholde, the smel of
my sonne *is* as the smel of a field, which ẏ
Lord hathe blessed.
28 * God giue thee therefore of the dewe
of heauen, and the fatnes of the earth, and
plentie of wheat and wine.
29 Let people be thy seruants, and nacions
bowe vnto thee: be lord ouer thy brethrẽ,
and let thy mothers childrẽ honour thee.
cursed *be he* that curseth thee, and blessed
be he that blesseth thee.
30 ¶ And when Izhák had made an end of
blessing Iaakób, and Iaakób was scace
gone out from the presence of Izhák his
father, then came Esáu his brother from
his hunting,
31 And he also prepared sauourie meat and
broght it to his father, and said vnto his
father, Let my father arise, and eat of his
sonnes venison, that thy soule may blesse me.
32 But his father Izhák said vnto him, Who
art thou? And he answered, I am thy sõne,
euen thy first borne Esáu.
33 Then Izhák was [f] stricken with a meruelous great feare, & said, Who *and* where *is*
he *that* hunted venison, and broght it me,
and I haue eat "of all before thou camest?
and I haue blessed him, therefore he shal
be blessed.
34 When Esáu heard the wordes of his father, he cryed out with a great crye and
bitter, out of measure, and said vnto his
father, Blesse me, *euen* me also, my father.
35 Who answered, Thy brother came with
subtiltie, and hathe taken away thy blessing.
36 Then he said, Was he not iustely called
[g] Iaakób? for he hathe deceiued me these
two times: he toke my birthright, and lo,
now hathe he taken my blessing. Also he
said, Hast thou not reserued a blessing
for me?
37 Then Izhák answered, and said vnto E-
sáu, Beholde, I haue made him [h] thy lord,
and all his brethren haue I made his seruantes: also with wheat and wine haue I
furnished him, and vnto thee now what
shal I do, my sonne?
38 Thẽ Esáu said vnto his father, Hast thou
but one blessing my father? blesse me, "*euen*
me also, my father: and Esáu lifted vp his
voyce, and * wept.
39 Then Izhák his father answered, and said
vnto him, Beholde, the fatnes of the earth
shalbe thy dwelling place, and *thou shalt
haue* of the dewe of heauen from aboue.
40 And [i] by thy sworde shalt thou liue, and
shalt be thy brothers [k] seruant. But it shal
come to passe, whẽ thou shalt get the mastrie, that thou shalt breake his yoke from
thy necke.
41 ¶ Therefore Esáu hated Iaakób, because
of ẏ blessing, wherewith his father blessed
him. And Esáu thoght in his minde, * The
dayes of mourning for my father wil come shortely, [l] then I wil slay my brother
Iaakób.
42 And it was tolde to Rebekáh of ẏ wordes
of Esáu her elder sonne, and she sent and
called Iaakób her yonger sonne, and said
vnto him, Beholde, thy brother Esáu [m] is
comforted against thee, *meaning* to kil
thee:
43 Now therefore my sõne, heare my voyce: arise, and flee thou to Harán to my
brother Labán,
44 And tary with him a while vntil thy
brothers fearcenes be swaged,
45 And til thy brothers wrath turne away
from thee, and he forget the things, which
thou hast done to him: then wil I send and
take thee from thence: why shulde I be
[n] depriued of you bothe in one day?
46 Also Rebekáh said to Izhák, * I am weary
of my life, for the [o] daughters of Heth.
If Iaakób take a wife of the daughters of
Heth like these of the daughters of the
land, [p] what auaileth it me to liue?

CHAP. XXVIII.

*1 Izhák forbiddeth Iaakób to take a wife of the Canaa-
nites. 6 Esáu taketh a wife of the daughters of Ishmaél
against his fathers wil. 12 Iaakób in the way to Harán
seeth a ladder reaching to heauen. 14 Christ is promised. 20 Iaakób asketh of God onely meat and clothing.*

1 THen Izhák called Iaakób and [a] blessed him, and charged him, and said
vnto him, Take not a wife of the daughters of Canáan.
2 Arise, * get thee to * Padán Arám to the
house of Bethuél thy mothers father, and
thence take thee a wife of the daughters of
Labán thy mothers brother.
3 And God "all sufficiẽt blesse thee, & make thee to encrease, & multiplie thee, that
thou maiest be a multitude of people,
4 And giue thee the blessing of Abrahám, *euen* to thee & to thy sede with thee,
that thou maiest inherit the lãd (wherein
thou art a [b] strãger) which God gaue vnto
Abrahám.

5 Thus

"Ebr. I am.

Ebr.11,20.

f In perceiuĩg his errour, by appointing his heyre against Gods sentence pronoũced before.

"*Or, sufficiently.*

g In the chap. 25. he was so called because he helde his brother by ẏ hele, as thogh he wolde ouerthrowe hĩ: & therfore he is here called an ouerthrower, or deceyuer.

h For Izhák did this as he was the minister and Prophet of God.

"*Or, I am also (thy sonne)*

Ebr.12,16.

i Because thine ennemies shalbe rounde about thee.

k Which was fulfilled in his posteritie the Idumeãs: who were tributaries for a time to Israél, and after came to libertie.

Abd.1,10.

l Hypocrites onely absteine from doing euil for feare of men.

m He hathe good hope to recouer his birthright by killing thee.

n For ẏ wicked sonne wil kil the godlie: & ẏ plague of God wil afterward light on ẏ wicked sõne.

Chap.26,35.

o Which were Esaus wiues.

p Hereby she persuaded Izhák to agre to Iaakobs departing.

a This secõde blessing was to cõfirme Iaakobs faith, lest he shuld thinke ẏ his father had giuen it without Gods motion.

Oze.12,12.

Chap.24,10.

"*Or, all mightie.*

b The godlie fathers were put in minde continually, ẏ they were but strãgers ĩ this worlde: to thẽtẽt thei shulde lift vp their eyes to ẏ heauẽs where they shulde haue a sure dwellĩg.

5 Thus Izhák ſent forthe Iaakób, and he
went to Padán Arám vnto Labán ſonne
of Bethuél the Aramite, brother to Rebekáh,Iaakobs and Eſaus mother.
6 ¶ Whẽ Eſáu ſawe that Izhák had bleſſed
Iaakób, and ſent him to Padán Arám, to
fet him a wife thence, and giuen him a
charge when he bleſſed him,ſaying, Thou
ſhalt not take a wife of the daughters of
Canáan,
7 And *that* Iaakób had obeied his father &
his mother,& was gone to Padán Arám:
8 Alſo Eſáu ſeing ȳ the daughters of Canáan diſpleaſed Izhák his father,
9 Then went Eſáu to Iſhmaél,& toke "vnto
ȳ wiues, *which he had*,Mahaláth the daughter of [c] Iſhmaél Abrahams ſonne, the ſiſter of Nabaióth,to be his wife.
10 ¶ Now Iaakób departed frõ Beer-ſhéba,and went to Harán,
11 And he came vnto a *certeine* place, & taried there all night, becauſe ȳ ſonne was
downe, and toke of the ſtones of the place and laied vnder his head and ſlept in
the ſame place.
12 Then he dreamed, and beholde, there
ſtode a [d] ladder vpon the earth and the
top of it reached vp to heauen:and lo,the
Angels of God went vp and downe by it.
13 *And beholde, the Lord ſtode aboue it,
and ſaid,I am the Lord God of Abrahám
thy father,& the God of Izhák: the land,
vpon the which thou ſlepeſt, [e] wil I giue
thee and thy ſede.
14 And thy ſede ſhal be as the duſt of the
earth,and thou ſhalt ſpreade abrode*to ȳ
Weſt, and to the Eaſt,and to the North,
and to the South, and in thee and in thy
ſede ſhal all the * families of the earth be
bleſſed.
15 And lo, I am with thee,& wil kepe thee
whitherſoeuer thou goeſt, and wil bring
thee againe into this land: for I wil not
forſake thee vntil I haue performed that,
that I haue promiſed thee.
16 ¶ Then Iaakób awoke out of his ſlepe,
and ſaid, Surely the Lord is in this place,
and I was not aware.
17 And he was [f] afraid and ſaid,How fearful is this place! this is none other but the
houſe of God,and this is the gate of heauen.
18 Then Iaakób roſe vp early in the morning, and toke the ſtone that he had laied
vnder his head, and [g] ſet it vp *as* a piller,
and powred oyle vpon the top of it.
19 And he called the name of that place
"Beth-él: notwithſtãding the name of the
citie was at the firſt called Luz.
20 Then Iaakób vowed a vowe,ſaying,If
[h] God wil be with me, and wil kepe me in
this iourney which I go, and wil giue me
bread to eat,and clothes to put on:

" Or, beſide his wiues.

c Thinkĩg hereby to haue reconciled hĩ ſelfe to his father, but all in vaine: for he taketh not awaie the cauſe of the euil.

d Chriſt is the ladder whereby God and mã are ioyned together, and by whome the Angels miniſtre vnto vs: all graces by him are giuen vnto vs, & we by him aſcende into heauẽ.

Chap.35,1. and 48,3.

e He felt the force of this promes onely by faith: for all his life time he was but a ſtranger in this land.

Deut.12, 20. and 19,14.

Chap.13, 35. and 18,18. & 22,18.and 26,4.

f He was touched with a godlie feare & reuerence.

g To be a remembrance onely of ȳ viſiõ ſhewed vnto him.

" Or, houſe of God.

h He bindeth not God vnder this condition but acknollageth his infirmitie,and promiſeth to be thankeful.

21 So that I come againe vnto my fathers
houſe in ſafety, then ſhal the Lord be my
God.
22 And this ſtone, ŵ I haue ſet vp *as* a piller,ſhalbe Gods houſe:& of all that ȳ ſhalt
giue me,wil I giue the tenth vnto thee.

CHAP. XXIX.

13 Iaakób commeth to Labán and ſerueth ſeuen yere for Rahél. 23 Leáh broght to his bed in ſtede of Rahél. 27 He ſerueth ſeuen yere more for Rahél. 32 Leáh conceiueth and beareth foure ſonnes.

1 THen Iaakób [a] lift vp his fete and came into the "Eaſt countrei.
2 And as he loked about,beholde there was
a well in the field, [b] and lo,thre flockes of
ſhepe lay thereby (for at that well were ȳ
flockes watered)and there was a great ſtone vpon the welles mouthe.
3 And thither were all ȳ flockes gathered,
and they rolled the ſtone from the welles
mouthe, and watered the ſhepe, and put
the ſtone againe vpon the welles mouthe
in his place.
4 And Iaakób ſaid vnto them, My [c] brethren,whence be ye? And they anſwered,
We are of Harán.
5 Then he ſaid vnto them, Knowe ye Labán the ſonne of Nahór? Who ſaid, We
knowe him.
6 Againe he ſaid vnto them,[d] Is he ĩ good
helth? And they anſwered, *He is* in good
helth, and beholde, his daughter Rahél
commeth with the ſhepe.
7 Thẽ he ſaid,Lo,*it is* yet hie day, nether *is*
it time ȳ the cattel ſhulde be gathered together: watter ye the ſhepe & go fede *thẽ*.
8 But they ſaid,We may not vntil all the
flockes be broght together, & til *that men*
rolle the ſtone frõ thẽ welles mouth, that
we may watter the ſhepe.
9 ¶ While he talked with them, Rahél alſo
came ŵ her fathers ſhepe,for ſhe kept thẽ.
10 And aſſone as Iaakób ſawe Rahél the
daughter of Labán his mothers brother,
and the ſhepe of Labán his mothers brother,thẽ came Iaakób nere,and rolled the
ſtone from the welles mouth,and watered
the flocke of Labán his mothers brother.
11 And Iaakób kiſſed Rahél,and lift vp his
voyce and wept.
12 (For Iaakób tolde Rahél,that he was her
fathers "brother,& that he was Rebekahs
ſonne) then ſhe ran and tolde her father.
13 And whẽ Labán heard tel of Iaakób his
ſiſters ſonne,he ran to mete him,and em-
braſed him and kiſſed him,& broght him
to his houſe:and he tolde Labán [e] all theſe things.
14 To whome Labán ſaid, Wel, thou art
my [f] bone and my fleſh.and he abode with
him the ſpace of a moneth.
15 ¶ For Labán ſaid vnto Iaakób, Thogh
thou be my brother, ſhuldeſt thou there-

a That is, he wẽt forthe on his iourney.

" Ebr.to the lãd of the children of the Eaſt.

b Thus he was directed by ȳ onely prouidẽce of God who broght hĩ alſo to Labãs houſe.

c It ſemeth ȳ in thoſe daies ȳ custome was to call euẽ ſtrãgers brethren.

d Or, is he in peace? by the ŵ worde the Ebrewes ſignifie all proſperitie.

" Or, nephew.

e That is, the cauſe why he departed from his fathers houſe,& what he ſawe in ȳ way.

f That is, of my blood and kinred.

fore serue me for noght? tel me, what *shal be* thy wages?
16 Now Labán had two daughters, the elder called Leáh, & ẏ yonger called Rahél.
17 And Leáh was ″ tender eyed, but Rahél was beautiful and faire.
18 And Iaakób loued Rahél, and said, I wil serue thee seuen yeres for Rahél thy yonger daughter.
19 Then Labán answered, It is better that I giue her thee, then that I shulde giue her to another man: abide with me.
20 And Iaakób serued seuen yeres for Rahél, and they semed vnto him but a [g] fewe daies, because he loued her.
21 ¶ Then Iaakób said to Labán, Giue *me* my wife that I maie go in to her: for my ″terme is ended.
22 Wherefore Labán gathered together all the men of the place, and made a feast.
23 But [h] whē the euening was come, he toke Leáh his daughter and broght her to him, and he went in vnto her.
24 And Labán gaue his maide Zilpáh to his daughter Leáh, *to be* her seruant.
25 But when the morning was come, beholde, it was Leáh. Then said he to Labán, Wherefore hast thou done thus to me? did not I serue thee for Rahél? wherefore then hast thou beguiled me?
26 And Labán answered, It is not the [i] maner of this place, to giue the yonger before the elder.
27 Fulfil seuen yeres for her, and we wil also giue thee this for the seruice, which thou shalt serue me yet seuen yeres more.
28 Thē Iaakób did so, & fulfilled her seuen yeres, so he gaue him Rahél his daughter to *be* his wife.
29 Labán also gaue to Rahél his daughter Bilháh his maide *to be* her seruant.
30 So entred he in to Rahél also, and loued also Rahél more then Leáh, and serued him yet seuen yeres mo.
31 ¶ When ẏ Lord sawe that Leáh was despised, he ″ made her [k] fruteful: but Rahél *was* baren.
32 And Leáh conceiued and bare a sonne, and she called his name Reubén: for she said, Because the [l] Lord hathe loked vpon my tribulacion, now therefore mine housband wil [m] loue me.
33 And she conceiued againe and bare a sonne, and said, Because the Lord heard that I was hated, he hathe therefore giuen me this *sonne* also, and she called his name Simeón.
34 And she conceiued againe and bare a sonne, and said, Now at this time wil my housbād kepe me companie, because I haue borne him thre sonnes: therefore was his name called Leuí.
35 Moreouer she conceiued againe and bare a sonne, saying, Now wil I ″ praise the Lord: * therefore she called his name Iudáh, and ″ left bearing.

″ Or, bleare eied.

g Meaning, after that the yeres were accomplished.

″ Hebr. my daies are ful.

h The cause why Iaakób was deceiued was, that in olde time the wife was coue red with a vaile, when she was broght to her housband in signe of chastitie & shamefastnes.

i He estemed more the profit that he had of Iaakobs seruice thē ether his promes or the maner of the countrie, thogh he alleged custome for his excuse.

″ Hebr. opened her wombe.

k This declareth, that oft times thei, ẏ are despised of men, are fauored of God.

l Hereby appeareth, that she had recours to God in her affliction.

m For children are a great cause of mutual loue betwene man and wife.

″ Or, confesse.

Mat. 1, 2.

″ Ebr. stode from bearing.

CHAP. XXX.

4. 9. *Rahél and Leáh being bothe baren giue their maides vnto their housband, and they beare him children. 15 Leáh giueth mādrakes to Rahél that Iaakób might lie with her. 27 Labán is enriched for Iaakobs sake. 43 Iaakób is made very riche.*

1 And when Rahél sawe that she bare Iaakób no children, Rahél enuied her sister, and said vnto Iaakób, Giue me children, or els I dye.
2 Thē Iaakobs angre was kindeled against Rahél, and he said, Am I in [a] Gods stede, which hathe withholden frō thee the frute of the wombe?
3 And she said, Beholde my maide Bilháh, go in to her, and she shal beare vpon my [b] knees, & ″ I shal haue childrē also by her.
4 Then she gaue him Bilháh her maide to wife, and Iaakób went in to her.
5 So Bilháh conceiued and bare Iaakób a sonne.
6 Thē said Rahél, God hathe giuen sentēce on my side, & hathe also heard my voyce, and hathe giuen me a sonne: therefore called she his name, Dan.
7 And Bilháh Rahels maide conceiued againe, and bare Iaakób the seconde sonne.
8 Then Rahél said, With ″ [c] excellēt wrestlings haue I wrestled with my sister and haue gotten the vpper hand: and she called his name, Naphtalí.
9 And when Leáh sawe that she had left bearing, she toke Zilpáh her maide, and gaue her Iaakób to wife.
10 And Zilpáh Leahs maide bare Iaakób a sonne.
11 Then said Leáh, [d] A companie cometh: and she called his name, Gad.
12 Againe Zilpáh Leahs maide bare Iaakób another sonne.
13 Then said Leáh, Ah, blessed am I, for the daughters wil blesse me. and she called his name, Ashér.
14 ¶ Now Reubén went in the dayes of the wheat haruest and found [e] mandrakes in the field & broght them vnto his mother Leáh. Then said Rahél to Leáh, Giue me, I pray thee, of thy sonnes mandrakes.
15 But she answered her, Is it a smale matter for thee to take mine housbād, except thou take my sonnes mādrakes also? Thē said Rahél, Therefore he shal slepe with thee this night for thy sonnes mandrakes.
16 And Iaakób came from the field in the euening, and Leáh went out to mete him, & said, Come in to me, for I haue ″ boght and payed for thee with my sonnes mandrakes: and he slept with her that night.
17 And God heard Leáh and she cōceiued, and bare vnto Iaakób the fift sonne.

a It is onely God that maketh barē and fruteful, and therfore I am not in faute.

b I wil receiue her childrē on my lappe, as thogh they were mine owne.

″ Ebr. I shalbe buylded.

″ Ebr. wrestlings of God.

c The arrogācie of mās nature appeareth in that she cōtemneth her sister, after she hath receiued this benefit of God to beare children.

d That is, God doeth increase me ẇ a multitude of children: for so Iaakób doeth expounde this name Gad, chap. 49, 9.

e Which is a kinde of herbe whose rote hath a certeine likenes of ẏ figure of a man.

″ Ebr. bying I haue boght.

18 Then

18 Thē said Leáh, God hathe giuen *me* my
rewarde, because I gaue my [f] maide to my
housband, & she called his name Issachár.

f In stede of acknolledgig her faute, she boasteth as if God had rewarded her therefore.

19 After, Leáh conceiued againe, and bare
Iaakób the sixt sonne.
20 Thē Leáh said, God hathe endued me
w̄ a good dowrie: now wil mine housbād
dwel with me, because I haue borne him
six sōnes: & she called his name Zebulún.
21 After that, she bare a daughter, and she
called her name Dináh.
22 ¶ And God remembred Rahél, and God
heard her, "and opened her wombe.

" Or, made her fruteful.

23 So she conceiued and bare a sonne, and
said, God hathe taken away my [g] rebuke.

g Because frutefulnes came of Gods blessing, who said, Increase and multiplie: barenes was counted as a curse.

24 And she called his name Ioséph, saying,
The Lord wil giue me yet another sonne.
25 ¶ And assone as Rahél had borne Ioséph, Iaakób said to Labán, Sēd me away
that I may go vnto my place and to my
countrey.
26 Giue *me* my wiues and my children, for
whome I haue serued thee, and let me go:
for thou knowest what seruice I haue done thee.
27 To whome Labán answered, If I haue
now founde fauour in thy sight, *tarie*: I haue " perceiued that the Lord hathe blessed
me for thy sake.

" Or, tried by experience.

28 Also he said, Appoint vnto me thy wages, and I wil giue it *thee*.
29 But he said vnto hī, Thou knowest, what
seruice I haue done thee, and in what taking thy cattel hathe bene "vnder me.

" Or, with me.

30 For the litle, that thou haddest before I
came, is increased into a multitude: and
the Lord hathe blessed thee "by my comming: but now whē shal [h] I trauel for mine owne house also?

" Ebr. at my fote.

h The ordre of nature requireth that euerie one prouide for his owne familie.

31 Then he said, What shal I giue thee? And
Iaakób answered, Thou shalt giue me nothing at all: if thou wilt do this thing for
me, I wil returne, fede, *and* kepe thy shepe.
32 I wil passe through all thy flockes this
day, *and* " separat from them all the shepe
with litle spottes and great spottes, & all
"blacke lambes among the shepe, and the
great spotted, and litle spotted amōg the
goates: [i] and it shalbe my wages.

" Or, separat thou.

" Or, red.

i That which shal hereafter be thus spotted.

33 So shal my [k] righteousnes answere for
me hereafter, when it shal come for my
rewarde before thy face, & euerie one that
hathe not litle or great spottes among
the goates, and blacke among the shepe,
the same shalbe "theft with me.

k God shal testifie for my righteous dealing by rewarding my labours.

" Or, counted theft.

34 Then Labán said, Go to, wolde God it
might be according to thy saying.
35 Therefore "he toke out the same day the
he goates that were party coloured and
with great spottes, and all the she goates
with litle and great spottes, *and* all ȳ had
white in thē, and all the " blacke among ȳ
shepe, & put thē in ȳ keping of his sonnes.

" Or, Labán.

" Or, red, or, browne.

36 And he set thre daies iourney betwene
him selfe and Iaakób. & Iaakób kept the
rest of Labans shepe.
37 ¶ Then Iaakób [l] toke roddes of grene
popular, and of hasel, and of the chesnut
tre, and pilled white strakes in them, and
made the white appeare in the roddes.

l Iaakób herein vsed no deceit: for it was Gods commādement as he declareth in ȳ next chapter, ver. 9. and 11.

38 Then he put ȳ roddes, which he had pilled, in the gutters *and* watering troghes,
when the shepe came to drinke, before
ȳ shepe: (for thei were in heate, when thei
came to drinke)
39 And the shepe "were in heate before the
roddes, & *afterward* broght forthe yong of
party colour, and with smale & great
spottes.

" Or, conceiued.

40 And Iaakób parted these lambes, and
turned the faces of the flocke towards
these lambes party coloured and all maner
of blacke, among the shepe of Labán: so
he put his owne flockes by them selues, &
put them not with Labans flocke.
41 And in euerie ramming tyme of the
[m] stronger shepe, Iaakób laied the roddes
before the eies of the shepe in the gutters
ȳ thei might conceiue before the roddes.

m As they ẘ toke ȳ ram about Septēbre, & broght forthe about marche: so the febler in marche, & lambde in Septembre.

42 But when the shepe were feble, he put
them not in: and so ȳ febler were Labans,
and the stronger Iaakobs.
43 So the man encreased excedingly, and
had manie flockes, and maide seruāts, and
men seruants, and camels and asses.

CHAP. XXXI.

1 Labans children murmure against Iaakób. 3 God commandeth him to returne to his countrey. 14 The care of God for Iaakób. 19 Rahél stealeth her fathers idoles. 23 Labán followeth Iaakób. 44 The couenant betwene Labán and Iaakób.

1 NOw he heard the [a] wordes of Labās
sonnes, saying, Iaakób hathe takē a-
way all that was our fathers, and of our fathers goods hathe he gottē all this honour.

a The childrē vttered in wordes that ẘ the father dissembled in heart. for ȳ couetous think ȳ whatsoeuer thei cā not snatche, is pluct frō thē.

2 Also Iaakób behelde the countenance
of Labán, "that it was not towards him as
in times past:

" Ebr. and lo, not he with him, as yesterday & yer yesterday.

3 And the Lord had said vnto Iaakób, Turne againe into the land of thy fathers, and
to thy kinred, and I wil be with thee.
4 Therefore Iaakób sent and called Rahél
and Leáh to the field vnto his flocke.
5 Thē said he vnto them, I se your fathers
countenance, that it is not towarde me as
it was wonte, and the [b] God of my father
hathe bene with me.

b The God whome my father worshipped.

6 And ye knowe that I haue serued your
father with all my might.
7 But your father hathe deceiued me, and
changed my wages "ten times: but God
suffred him not to hurt me.

" Or, many times.

8 If he thus said, The spotted shalbe thy wages, thē all the shepe bare spotted: & if he
said thus, The partie coloured shal be thy
reward, thē bare all ȳ shepe particoloured.

9 Thus hathe c God taken awaie your fathers" substance, and giuen it me.
10 ¶ For in ramming time I lifted vp mine
eies and sawe in a dreame, and beholde, the
he goates leaped vpō the she goates, that
were partie coloured with litle and great
spottes spotted.
11 And the Angel of God said to me in a
dreame, Iaakób. And I answered, Lo, I am
here.
12 And he said, lift vp now thine eies, and
se all the he goates leaping vpon the she
goates that are partie coloured, spotted
with litle & great spottes: for I haue sene
all that Labán doeth vnto thee.
13 d I am the God of Beth-él, where thou
* anointedst ẏ piller, where thou vowedst
a vowe vnto me. Now arise, get thee out
of this countrei & returne vnto the land
where thou wast borne.
14 Then answered Rahél and Leáh, and
said vnto him, Haue we anie more porcion and enheritance in our fathers house?
15 Doeth not he count vs as strangers? for
he hathe e solde vs, and hathe eaten vp &
consumed our monie.
16 Therefore all ẏ riches, which God hathe
taken from our father, is ours and our
childrēs: now then whatsoeuer God hathe
said vnto thee do it.
17 ¶ Thē Iaakób rose vp, and set his sonnes
and his wiues vpon camels.
18 And he caried awaie all his flockes, and
all his substance which he had gotten, *to
wit*, his riches, which he had gotten in
Padán Arám, for to go to Izhák his father vnto the land of Canáan.
19 When Labán was gone to shere his shepe, then Rahél stale her fathers f idoles.
20 Thus Iaakób "stale awaie the heart of
Labán the Aramite: for he tolde him not
that he fled.
21 So fled he with all that he had, & he rose
vp, and passed the" riuer, and set his face
toward mount Gileád.
22 The third day after was it tolde Labán,
that Iaakób fled.
23 Then he toke his" brethren with him, &
followed after him seuen dayes iourney,
and" ouertoke him at mount Gileád.
24 And God came to Labán the Aramite
in a dreame by night, and said vnto him,
Take hede that thou speake not to Iaakób
"oght saue good.
25 ¶ Then Labán ouertoke Iaakób, & Iaakób had pitched his tent in the mount: &
Labán also with his brethren pitched vpon mount Gileád.
26 Then Labán said to Iaakób, What hast
thou done? " thou hast euen stollen away
mine heart & caried away my daughters
as thogh they had bene taken captiues ẘ
the sworde.

c This declareth that the thing, which Iaakób did before, was by Gods cōmandement, & not through deceite.
" Or, cattel.
d This Angel was Christ ẘ appeared to Iaakób in Bethel: & hereby appeareth he had taught his wiues ẏ feare of God: for he talketh as thogh they knewe this thing.
Chap. 28, 18.
e For they were giuen to Iaakób in recompence of his seruice: ẘ was a kinde of sale.
f For so the worde here signifieth, becau se Labán calleth thē gods, vers. 30.
" Or, went a way priuely from Laban.
" Or, Euphrates.
" Or, kinsfolkes & friends.
" Or, ioyned with him.
" Ebr. from good to euil.
" Or, conueighed thy selfe away priuely.

27 Wherefore diddest thou flee so secretly
& steale away from me, & diddest not tel
me, that I might haue sent thee forthe
with mirth & with songs, with timbrel &
with harpe?
28 But thou hast not suffered me to kisse
my sonnes and my daughters: now thou
hast done foolishly in doing so.
29 I am "able to do you euil: but the g God
of your father spake vnto me yester night,
saying, Take hede that thou speake not to
Iaakób oght saue good.
30 Now thogh thou wentest thy way, because thou greatly longedst after thy fathers house: *yet* wherefore hast thou stollē
my gods?
31 Thē Iaakób answered, & said to Labán,
Because I was afraid, & thoght that thou
woldest haue taken thy daughters from
me.
32 *But* with whome thou findest thy gods,
"let him not liue. Serche thou before our
brethren what I haue *of thine*, and take it
to thee (but Iaakób wist not that Rahél
had stollen them)
33 Then came Labán into Iaakobs tent, &
into Leahs tent, and into the two maides
tentes, but founde *them* not. so he wēt out
of Leahs tent, & entred into Rahels tent.
34 (Now Rahél had takē the idoles & put
them in the camels" litter & sate downe
vpon them) & Labán serched all the tent,
but founde *them* not.
35 Then said she to her father, "My lord, be
not angry that I can not rise vp before
thee: for the custome of womē *is* vpon me:
so he serched, but found not the idoles.
36 ¶ Thē Iaakób was wroth, & chode with
Labán: Iaakób also answered and said to
Labán, What haue I trespaced? what haue
I offended, that thou hast pursued after
me?
37 Seing thou hast serched all my stuffe,
what hast ẏ founde of all thine housholde
stuffe? put it here before my brethren and
thy brethren, that they may iudge betwene vs bothe.
38 This twēty yere I haue bene with thee:
thine ewes and thy goates haue not " cast
their yong, & the rams of thy flocke haue
I not eaten.
39 "Whatsoeuer was torne *of beastes*, I broght
it not vnto thee, *but* made it good my selfe: *of mine hāde diddest thou require it,
were it stollen by day or stollen by night.
40 I was in the day consumed with heat,
and with frost in the night, and my" slepe
departed from mine eies.
41 Thus haue I bene twenty yere in thine
house, and serued thee fourtēth yeres for
thy two daughters, and six yeres for thy
shepe, and thou hast changed my wages
ten times.

" Ebr. power is in mine hand.
g He was an idolater, and therfore wold not acknollage the God of Iaakób for his God.
" Or, let him dye.
" Or, strawe, or, saddle.
" Ebr. let not angre be in the eyes of my Lord.
" Or, bene barren.
" Ebr. the torne or takē by pray.
Exod. 22, 12.
" Or, I slept not.

42 Except

42 Except the God of my father, the God of
Abrahám, & the [h] feare of Izhák had bene
with me, surely thou haddest sent me a-
way now empty: *but* God behelde my tribulacion, & the labour of mine handes, &
rebuked *thee* yester night.

h That is, the God whome Izhák did feare & reuerēce.

43 Then Labán answered, & said vnto Iaakób, These daughters are my daughters,
and these sonnes are my sonnes, and these
shepe are my shepe, and all that thou seest,
is mine, and what can I do this day vnto
these my daughters, or to their sonnes
which they haue borne?
44 Now therefore [i] come and let vs make a
couenant, I and thou, which may be a witnes betwene me and thee.

i His cōsciēce reproued him of his misbehauiour toward Iaakób and therefore moued hī to seke peace.

45 Then toke Iaakób a stone, and set it vp
as a piller:
46 And Iaakób said vnto his brethren, Gather stones: who broght stones, and made
an heape, and they did eat there vpon the
heape.
47 And Labán called it *Iegár-sahaduthá,
and Iaakób called it [k] Galeéd.
48 For Labán said, This heape is witnes
betwene me & thee this day: therefore he
called the name of it Galeéd. Also *he called it*
49 *Mizpáh, because he said, The Lord [l] loke betwene me & thee, when we shalbe departed one from another,

*Or, The heape of witnes.
k The one nameth the place in the Syrian tongue, & the other in the Ebrewe tongue.
*Or, watch towr.
l To punishe the trespacer.

50 If ye shalt uexe my daughters, or shalt
take [m] wiues beside my daughters: *there is*
no man with vs, beholde, God *is* witnes betwene me and thee.

m Nature cōpelleth him to cōdemne that vice, wherunto through couetousnes he forced Iaakób.

51 Moreouer Labán said to Iaakób, Beholde this heape, & beholde, the piller, which
I haue set betwene me and thee,
52 This heape *shalbe* witnes, and the piller
shalbe witnes, yt I wil not come ouer this he
ape to thee, and that yu shalt not passe ouer
this heape & this piller vnto me for euil.
53 The God of Abrahám, & the God of
[n] Nahór, & ye God of their father be iudge betwene vs: but Iaakób sware by the
[o] feare of his father Izhák.
54 Then Iaakób did offre a sacrifice vpon
the mount, and called his brethren to eat
*bread. and they did eat bread, & taried all
night in the mount.

n Beholde, how the idolaters mingle the true God with their fayned gods.
o Meaning, by the true God whome Izhák worshipped.
*Or, meat.

55 And early in the morning Labán rose vp
and kissed his sonnes & his daughters, &
[p] blessed them, and Labán departing, went
vnto his place againe.

p We se that there is euer some sede of ye knollage of God in ye heartes of the wicked.

CHAP. XXXII.

*1 God cōforteth Iaakób by his Angels. 9.10 He praieth vn
to God confessing his Vnworthines. 13 He sendeth presentes vnto Esáu. 24.28 He wrestled with the Angel
who nameth him Israél.*

1 NOw Iaakób wēt forthe on his iourney & the Angels of God met him.
2 And when Iaakób sawe them, he said,
[a] This is Gods host, & called the name of
the same place *Mahanáim.

a He acknollageth Gods benefits: who for the preseruation of his sendeth hostes of Angels.
*Or, Tentes.

3 Then Iaakób sent messengers before
him to Esáu his brother, vnto the land of
Seír into the countrey of Edóm:
4 To whome he gaue commandemēt, saying, Thus shal ye speake to my [b] lord E-
sáu: Thy seruant Iaakób saith thus, I haue
bene a stranger with Labán & taried vnto this time.

b He reuerenced his brother in worldlie things, because he chiefely loked to be preferred to ye spiritual promes.

5 I haue beues also & asses, shepe, & men
seruantes, and women seruantes, and haue
sent to shewe my lord, that I may finde
grace in thy sight.
6 ¶ So the messengers came againe to Iaakób, saying, We came vnto thy brother
Esáu, and he also commeth against thee
and foure hundreth men with him.
7 Then Iaakób was [c] greatly afraid, and
was sore troubled, & deuided the people
that was with him, and the shepe, and the
beues, and the camels into two cōpanies.

c Albeit he was cōforted by the Angels, yet the infirmitie of ye fleshe doeth appeare.

8 For he said, if Esáu come to the one companie and smite it, the other companie
shal escape.
¶ Moreouer Iaakób said, O God of my
father Abrahám, and God of my father
Izhák: Lord, which saidest vnto me, Returne vnto thy countrei & to thy kinred,
and I wil do thee good,
10 I am not *worthie of the least of all the
mercies & all the trueth, which thou hast
shewed vnto thy seruant: For wt my [d] staffe came I ouer this Iordén, and now haue I gotten two bandes.

*Ebr. I am lesse then all thy mercies.
d That is, poore, & without all prouision.

11 I pray thee, Deliuer me from the hand
of my brother, from the hand of Esáu: for
I feare him, lest he wil come and smite
me, & the [e] mother vpon the children.
12 For yu saidest, I wil surely do thee good,
and make thy sede as the sand of the sea,
which can not be nōbred for multitude.
13 ¶ And he taried there the same night, &
toke of that which came to hand, a [f] pre-
sente for Esáu his brother:

e Meaning, he wil put all to death: this prouerbe commeth of them which kille the birde together with her yong ones.
f Not distrusting Gods assistance, but vsing such meanes as God had giuē him.

14 Two hūdreth she goates and twenty he
goates, two hundreth ewes and twentie
rammes:
15 Thirty milche camels with their coltes,
fourtie kine, & ten bullockes, twētie she asses and ten foles.
16 So he deliuered them into the hand of
his ser uātes, euerie droue by them selues,
& said vnto his seruants, Passe before me,
and put a space betwene droue & droue.
17 And he commanded the formest, saying,
If Esáu my brother mete thee, and aske
thee, saying, Whose *seruant* art thou? &
whither goest thou? and whose are these
before thee?
18 Then thou shalt say, *they be* thy seruant
Iaakobs: it is a present sent vnto my lord
Esáu: and beholde, he him selfe also is behinde vs.

19 So likewise commanded he the seconde
& the third, & all that followed the dro-
ues, saying, After this maner, ye shal speake vnto Esáu, when ye finde him.
20 And ye shal say moreouer, Beholde, thy
seruant Iaakób *commeth* after vs (for he
thoght, I [g] wil appease his wrath with the
present that goeth before me, and afterward I wil se his face: it may be that he
wil " accept me)
21 So went the present before him: but he
taried that night with the companie.
22 And he rose vp the same night, and toke
his two wiues, and his two maides, and
his eleuē children, & went ouer the forde
Iabbók.
23 And he toke them, & sent them ouer the
riuer, & sent ouer that he had.
24 ¶ Whē Iaakób was left him selfe alone,
there wrestled a [h] man with him vnto the
breaking of the day.
25 And he sawe that he colde not [i] preuaile
against him: therefore he touched ye holow of his thigh, & the holow of Iaakobs
thigh was losed, as he wrestled with him.
26 And he said, Let me go, for ye morning
appeareth. Who answered, *I wil not let
thee go except thou blesse me.
27 Then said he vnto him, What is thy name? And he said, Iaakób.
28 Then said he, *Thy name shal be called
Iaakób no more, but Israél: because thou
hast had [k] power with God, thou shalt
also preuaile with men.
29 Then Iaakób demāded, saying, Tel me,
I pray thee, thy name. And he said, Wherefore now doest thou aske my name? And
he blessed him there.
30 And Iaakób called the name of the place, Peniél: for, *said he*, I haue sene God face to face, and my "life is preserued.
31 And the sunne rose to him as he passed
Peniél, and he [l] halted vpon his thigh.
32 Therefore the children of Israél eat not
of the sinew that shranke in the holow of
the thigh, vnto this day: because he touched the sinew that shranke in the holow
of Iaakobs thigh.

g He thoght it no losse to departe wt these goods, to the intēt he might follow the vocatiō wherūto God called him.

"Ebr. receiue my face.

h That is, God in forme of man.

i For God assaileth his wt the one hand, & vpholdeth them with the other.

Oze.12,4.

Chap.35,10.

k God gaue Iaakób bothe power to ouercome & also ye praise of the victorie.

"Or, soule.

l The faithful so ouercome their tētatiōs, that thei fele the smart thereof, to the intēt that thei shulde not glorie, but ī their humilitie.

CHAP. XXXIII.

4. Esáu and Iaakób mete and are agreed. 11. Esáu receiueth his gifts. 19. Iaakob byeth a possession, 20. And buyldeth an altar.

1 AND as Iaakób lift vp his eies, and
loked, beholde, Esáu came, and with
him foure hundreth men: and he [a] deuided the children to Leáh, and to Rahél,
and to the two maides.
2 And he put the maides, & their children
formost, and Leáh and her children after,
and Rahél, and Ioseph hindermost.
3 So he went before thē and [b] bowed him
selfe to the grounde seuen times, vntil he
came nere to his brother.

a That if the one part were assailed, the other might escape.

b By this gesture he partly did reuerence to his brother, & partely praied to God to mitigate Esaus wrath.

4 Then Esáu ran to mete him and embraced him, and fel on his necke and kissed
him, and thei wept.
5 And he lift vp his eies, and sawe the women, and the children, and said, Who are
these with thee? And he answered, *Thei are*
ye childrē whome God of his grace hathe
giuen thy seruant.
6 Then came ye maides nere, thei, and their
children, and [c] bowed them selues.
7 Leáh also with her children came nere
and made obeisance: and after Ioseph &
Rahél drewe nere and did reuerence.
8 Then he said, What meanest thou by all
this droue, which I met? Who answered,
I haue sent it, that I maie finde fauour in ye
sight of my lord.
9 And Esáu said, I haue ynough, my brother: kepe that thou hast to thy selfe.
10 But Iaakób answered, Nay, I pray thee:
if I haue founde grace now in thy sight,
then receiue my present at mine hand: for
[d] I haue sene thy face, as thogh I had sene
the face of God, because thou hast accepted me.
11 I praie thee take my "blessing, that is
broght thee: for God hathe had mercie
on me, & therefore I haue all things: so he
[e] compelled him, and he toke it.
12 And he said, Let vs take our iourney &
go, and I wil go before thee.
13 Then he answered him, My lord knoweth, that the children *are* tendre, and the
ewes & kine with yong vnder mine hād:
& if thei shulde ouerdriue them one day,
all the flocke wolde dye.
14 Let now my lord go before his seruāt,
and I wil driue softly, according to the
passe of the cattel, which is before me, and
as the children be able to endure, vntil
[f] I come to my lord vnto Seír.
15 Then Esáu said, I wil leaue thē some of
my folke with thee. And he answered,
What *nedeth* this? let me finde grace in
the sight of my lord.
16 ¶ So Esáu returned, *and went* his way
that same day vnto Seír.
17 And Iaakób went forwarde towarde
Succóth, & buylt him an house, and made
boothes for his cattel: therefore he called
the name of the place "Succóth.
18 ¶ Afterwarde, Iaakób came safe to Shechém a citie, which is in the land of Canáan, when he came from " Padán Arám,
and pitched before the citie.
19 And there he boght a parcel of groūde,
where he pitched his tent, at the hand of
the sonnes of Hamór Shechems father,
for an hundreth " pieces of money.
20 And he set vp there an altar, and called
[g] it, The mightie God of Israél.

c Iaakób and his familie are the image of ye Church vnder the yoke of tyrants, wc for feare are broght to subiection.

d In that that his brother imbraced him so louingly, cōtrary to his expectation, he accepted it as a plaine signe of Gods presence.

"Or, gift.

e By earnest intreatie.

f He promised that wc (as semeth) his minde was not to performe.

"Or, tentes.

"Or, Mesopotamia.

"Or, lambes, or, money so marked.

g He calleth the signe the thing, which it signifieth, in token ye God had mightely deliuered him.

CHAP. XXXIIII.

2 Dináh is rauished. 8 Hamór asketh her in mariage

for

for his sonne. 22 The Shechemites are circumcised at
the request of Iaakobs sonnes, and the persuasion of
Hamór. 25 The whoredome is reuenged. 28 Iaakob
reproueth his sonnes.

1 THen Dináh the daughter of Leáh,
which she bare vnto Iaakób, [a] wẽt out
to se the daughters of that countrey.
2 Whome when Shechém the sonne of Ha
mór the Hiuite lord of that coũtrie sawe,
he toke her, and lay w^t her, & " defiled her.
3 So his heart claue vnto Dináh ye daughter of Iaakób: and he loued the maide, &
" spake kindely vnto the maide.
4 Thẽ said Shechém to his father Hamór,
saying, [b] Get me this maide to wife.
5 (Now Iaakób heard that he had defiled
Dináh his daughter, and his sonnes were
with his cattel in ye field: therefore Iaakób
helde his peace, vntil they were come)
6 ¶ Then Hamór the father of Shechém
went out vnto Iaakób to commune with
him.

a This example teacheth that to muche libertie is not to be giuen to youthe.

" *Ebr. humbled her.*

" *Ebr. spake to the heart of the maide.*

b This proueth that the consent of parẽts is requisite in mariage, seing the very infideles did also obserue it as a thing necessarie.

7 And when the sonnes of Iaakób were come out of the field and heard it, it grieued the men, & they were very angrie, because he had wroght " vilennie in Israél,
in that he had liẽ with Iaakobs daughter:
" which thing oght not to be done.
8 And Hamór cõmuned with them, saying,
The soule of my sonne Shechém longeth
for your daughter: giue her him to wife,
I pray you.
9 So make " affinitie w^t vs: giue your daughters vnto vs, and take our daughters vnto you,
10 And ye shal dwel with vs, and the land
shal be before you: dwel, and do your busines in it, and haue your possessions therein.
11 Shechém also said vnto her father and
vnto her brethren, " Let me finde fauour in
your eies, and I wil giue whatsoeuer ye
shal appoint me.
12 " Aske of me abundantly bothe dowrie
and giftes, & I wil giue as ye appoint me,
so that ye giue me the maide to wife.
13 Thẽ the sonnes of Iaakób answered She
chém and Hamór his father, talking a-
mong them selues deceitfully, because he
had defiled Dináh their sister,
14 And they said vnto them, [c] We can not
do this thing, to giue our sister to an vncircumcised man: for that were a [d] reprofe vnto vs.
15 But in this wil we consent vnto you, if
ye wil be as we *are*, that euerie mã childe
among you be [e] circumcised:
16 Then wil we giue our daughters to you,
and we wil take your daughters to vs, and
wil dwel with you, and be one people.
17 But if ye wil not hearken vnto vs to be cir
cumcised, then wil we take our daughter
& departe.

" *Or, follie.*

" *Ebr. and it shal not be so done.*

" *Or, mariages.*

" *Or, grant my request.*

" *Ebr. multiply greatly the dowry.*

c They made the holy ordinance of God a meane to cõpasse their wicked purpose.

d As it is abomination for them that are baptized to ioine with infidels.

e Their faute is the greater, in that they make religion a cloke for their craft.

18 Now their wordes pleased Hamór, and
Shechém Hamors sonne.
19 And the yong man deferde not to do the
thĩg because he loued Iaakobs daughter:
he was also the moste set by of all his fathers house.
20 ¶ Then Hamór and Shechém his sonne
went vnto the [f] gate of their citie, & communed with the men of their citie, saying,
21 These men are [g] peaceable with vs: &
y^t they may dwel in the land, and do their
affaires therein (for beholde, the land
hathe roume ynough for them) let vs take
their daughters to wiues, and giue them
our daughters.
22 Onely herein wil ye men consent vnto vs
for to dwel with vs, and to be one people,
if all the men children among vs be circũcised as they are circumcised.
23 Shal not [h] their flockes and their substãce and all their cattel be ours? onely let vs
consent *herein* vnto thẽ, and they wil dwel
with vs.
24 And vnto Hamór, & Shechém his sonne hearkened all that went out of the gate
of his citie: and all the men children were
circumcised, *euen* all that went out of the
gate of his citie.

f For the people vsed to assemble there, and iustice was also ministred.

g Thus many pretẽd to speke for a publike profit, whẽ they only speke for their owne priuate gaine and commoditie.

h Thus they lacke no kinde of persuasion, which preferre their owne cõmodities before the common welth.

25 And on the third day (when thei were
sore) two of the sonnes of Iaakób, [i] Simeón and Leuí, Dinahs brethren toke e-
ther of them his sworde & went into the
citie boldely, and * slewe [k] euerie male.
26 Thei slewe also Hamór and Shechém
his sonne with the " edge of the sworde, &
toke Dináh out of Shechems house, and
went their way.
27 *Againe* the *other* sonnes of Iaakób came
vpon the dead, and spoiled the citie, because they had defiled their sister.
28 Thei toke their shepe, and their beues,
and their asses, and whatsoeuer was in the
citie, and in the fields.
29 Also they caried away captiue and spoiled all their goods, and all their children
and their wiues, and all that was in the
houses.
30 Then Iaakób said to Simeón and Leuí,
Ye haue troubled me, & made me " stinke
among the inhabitants of the land, *aswel*
the Canaanites, as the Perizzites, and I
being fewe in nombre, they shal gather
them selues together against me, and slay
me, *and* so shal I, and my house be destroied.
31 And they answered, Shulde he abuse our
sister as a whore?

i For they were the chief of the cõpanie.

Chap. 49,6.

k The people are punished with their wicked princes.

" *Ebr. mouthe of the sworde.*

" *Or, to be abhorred.*

CHAP. XXXV.

1 Iaakób at Gods commãdement goeth vp to Beth-el.
2 He reformeth his housholde. 8 Deborah dyeth. 12 The
land of Canáan is promised him. 18 Rahél dyeth in la-
bour. 22 Reubén lieth with his fathers cõcubine. 30 The
death of Izhák.

a God is euer at hand to succour his in their troubles.

Chap.28,13.

1 THen a God said to Iaakób, Arise, go
vp to Beth-él & dwel there, & make
there an altar vnto God, that appeared vn
to thee,* whẽ thou fleddest from Esáu thy
brother.

b That by this outwarde act they shuld shewe their inwarde repentance.

2 Then said Iaakób vnto his housholde &
to all that were with him, Put away the
strãge gods that are among you, & b clense
your selues, and change your garments:
3 For we wil rise and go vp to Beth-él, and
I wil make an altar there vnto God, which
heard me in the day of my tribulacion, &
was with me in the way which I went.

c For therein was some signe of superstition as in tablets & Agnus deis.

4 And they gaue vnto Iaakób all the strange gods, which *were* in their hands, and all
their c earings which were in their eares,
and Iaakób hid them vnder an oke, which
was by Shechém.

d Thus, notwithstanding ÿ inconuenience ÿ came before, God deliuered Iaakób.

5 Then they went on their iourney, and
the d feare of God was vpon the cities, that
were round about them: so that thei did
not followe after the sonnes of Iaakób.
6 ¶ So came Iaakób to Luz, which is in the
land of Canáan: (the same is Beth-él) he
and all the people that was with him.

Chap.28,19.

7 And he buylt there an altar, & * had called the place, The God of Beth-él, because that God appeared vnto him there, whẽ
he fled from his brother.

‖ Or, oke of lamentation.

8 Then Deboráh Rebekahs nourse dyed,
and was buryed beneth Beth-él vnder an
oke: and he called the name of it ‖ Allón
bachúth.
9 ¶ Againe God appeared vnto Iaakób, af
ter he came out of Padán Arám, and blessed him.

Chap.32,28.

10 Moreouer God said vnto him, Thy name
is Iaakób: thy name shal be no more called
Iaakób, but * Israél shalbe thy name: and
he called his name Israél.

‖ Or, almightie.

11 Againe God said vnto him, I am God
‖ all sufficiẽt. growe, & multiplie: a nation
& a multitude of natiõs shal sprĩg of thee,
and Kings shal come out of thy loynes.
12 Also I wil giue ÿ land, which I gaue to A
brahám and Izhák, vnto thee: & vnto thy
sede after thee wil I giue that land.

e As God is said to descend, when he sheweth some signe of his presence: so he is said to ascẽde, when ÿ vision is ended.

13 So God e ascended from him in the place where he had talked with him.
14 And Iaakób set vp a piller in the place where he talked with him, a piller of sto
ne, and powred drinke offring thereon: also he powred oyle thereon.
15 And Iaakób called the name of the place, where God spake with him, Beth-él.

f The Ebrewe worde signifieth as muche grounde as one may go frõ bayte to bayte, ÿ is takẽ for halfe a days iourney.

16 ¶ Then they departed from Beth-él, &
whẽ there was f about halfe a daies iourney
of grounde to come to Ephráth, Rahél
trauailed, and in trauailing she was in
peril.
17 And when she was in peines of her labour, the midwife said vnto her, Feare
not: for thou *shalt haue* this sonne also.
18 Then as she was about to yelde vp the
goste (for she dyed) she called his name
Ben-oní, but his father called him Beniamín.
19 Thus dyed Rahél, & was buryed in the
way to Ephráth, which is Beth-léhem.

g The ancient fathers vsed this ceremonie to testifie their hope of the resurrection to come, which was not generally reuealed.

20 And Iaakób set a piller vpon her graue: This is the piller of Rahels graue vnto
this day.
21 ¶ Thẽ Israél went forwarde, & pitched
his tent beyonde Migdal-éder.

h This teacheth that the fathers were not chosen for their merites, but by Gods onely mercies, whose electiõ by their fautes was not changed.

Chap.48,7.

22 Now, when Israél dwelt in that land,
Reubén went, and h laye * with Bilháh his
fathers concubine, and it came to Israels
eare. And Iaakób had twelue sonnes.
23 The sonnes of Leáh: Reubén Iaakobs el
dest sonne, and Simeón, & Leuí, & Iudáh,
& Issachár, & Zebulún.
24 The sonnes of Rahél: Ioséph and Beniamín.
25 And ÿ sonnes of Bilháh Rahels maide:
Dan and Naphtalí.
26 And the sonnes of Zilpáh Leahs maide:
Gad and Ashér. these are the sonnes of
Iaakób, which were borne him in Padán
Arám.
27 ¶ Then Iaakób came vnto Izhák his fa
ther to Mamré a citie of Arbáh: this is
Hebrón, where Abrahám and Izhák were
strangers.
28 And the dayes of Izhák were an hundreth and foure score yeres.

Chap.25,8.

29 And Izhák gaue vp the goste and dyed,
and was * gathered vnto his people, being
olde and ful of daies: & his sonnes Esáu
and Iaakób buryed him.

CHAP. XXXVI.

2 The wiues of Esáu. 7 Iaakób and Esáu are riche. 9 The genealogie of Esáu. 24 The finding of mules.

a This genealogie declareth that Esáu was blessed temporally, & that his fathers blessing toke place in worldlie things.

b Besides those wiues wherof is spoken, chap. 26,34.

1.Chro.1,35.

1 NOw these are the a generations of
Esáu, which is Edóm.
2 Esáu toke his wiues of the b daughters of
Canáan: Adáh the daughter of Elón an
Hittite, and Aholibamáh the daughter of
Anáh, the daughter of Zibeón an Hiuite,
3 And *toke* Basemáth Ishmaels daughter,
sister of Nebaióth.
4 And * Adáh bare vnto Esáu, Eliphāz: &
Basemáth bare Reuél.
5 Also Aholibamáh bare Ieúsh, & Iaalám,
and Kórah: these are the sonnes of Esáu
which were borne to him in the land of
Canáan.

c Herein appeareth Gods prouidence, which causeth the wicked to giue place to the godlie ÿ Iaakób might enioye Canáã according to Gods promes.

6 So Esáu toke his wiues and his sonnes, &
his daughters, & all the soules of his house, and his flockes, and all his cattel, and
all his substance, which he had gotten in
the land of Canáan, & c went into *an other*
countrei from his brother Iaakób.
7 For their riches were so great that they
colde not dwel together, & the land, wherein they were strangers, colde not receiue them because of their flockes.

8 There-

Iosh.24,4.
8 *Therefore dwelt Esáu in mout Seír:this
Esáu is Edóm.
9 ¶So these are the generaciōs of Esáu father of "Edóm in mount Seír.
10 These are the names of Esaus sonnes:
*Elipház, the sonne of Adáh, the wife of
Esáu, & Reuél the sonne of Bashemáth,
the wife of Esáu.
11 And the sonnes of Elipház were Temán,
Omár, Zephó, and Gatám, and Kenáz.
12 And Timná was concubine to Elipház
Esaus sonne, & bare vnto Elipház, Amalék: these be the sonnes of Adáh Esaus
wife.
13 ¶And these are ỹ "sonnes of Reuél: Náhath, and Zérah, Shammáh, and Mizzáh:
these were the sonnes of Bashemáth Esaus
wife.
14 ¶And these were ỹ sonnes of Aholibamáh the daughter of Anáh, "daughter of
Zibeón Esaus wife: for she bare vnto E-
sáu, Ieúsh, and Iaalám, and Kórah.
15 ¶These were" d Dukes of the sonnes of
Esáu: the sonnes of Elipház, the first borne of Esáu: duke Temán, duke Omár,
duke Zephó, duke Kenáz,
16 Duke Kórah, duke Gatám, duke Amalék: these are ỹ dukes *that came* of Elipház
in the land of Edóm: these were the" sonnes of Adáh.
17 ¶And these are the sonnes of Reuél E-
saus sonne: duke Náhath, duke Zérah, duke Shammáh, duke Mizzáh: these are the
dukes *that came* of Reuél in the land of E-
dóm: these are the "sonnes of Bashemáth
Esaus wife.
18 ¶Likewise these were the sonnes of A-
holibamáh Esaus wife: Duke Ieúsh, duke
Iaalám, duke Kórah: these dukes *came* of
Aholibamáh, the daughter of Anáh Esaus
wife.
19 These are the children of Esáu, & these
are the dukes of thē: This *Esáu* is Edóm.
20 ¶*These are the sonnes of Seír the Horite, which e inhabited the land *before*, Lotán, and Shobál, and Zibeón, and Anáh.
21 And Dishón, and Ezer, and Dishán: these are the dukes of the Horites, the sonnes of Seír in the land of Edóm.
22 And the sonnes of Lotan were, Horí
& Hemám, and Lotans sister *was* Timná.
23 And the sonnes of Shobál were these:
Aluán, and Manáhath, and Ebál, Shephó,
And Onám.
24 And these are the sonnes of Zibeón:
bothe Aiáh, & Anáh: this was Anáh that
founde f mules in the wildernes, as he fed
his father Zibeons asses.
25 And the children of Anáh were these:
Dishón & Aholibamáh, the daughter of
Anáh.
26 Also these are the sonnes of Dishán:
Hemdán, & Eshbán, & Ithrán, & Cherán.

"Or, the Edomites.
1.Chro.1,35.
"Or, nephewes.
"Or, nece.
"Or, chief men.
d If Gods promes be so sure towardes thē, which are not of his houshol de, how muche more wil he performe the same to vs?
"Or, nephewes.
"Or, nephewes.
1.Chro.1,38.
e Before that Esáu did there inhabit.
f Who not cōtented with those kides of beastes, which God had created, found out the mōstruous generacion of mules betwene the asse and the mare.

27 The sonnes of Ezer are these: Bilhán, &
Zaauán, and Akán.
28 The sonnes of Dishán are these: Vz, and
Arán.
29 These are the dukes of the Horites: duke Lotán, duke Shobál, duke Zibeón, duke
Anáh,
30 Duke Dishón, duke Ezer, duke Dishán:
these be the dukes of the Horites, after
their dukedomes in the land of Seír.
31 ¶And these are ỹ g Kings that reigned
in the lād of Edóm, before there reigned
any King ouer the childrēn of Israél.
32 Thē Béla the sonne of Beór reigned in
Edóm, and the name of his citie *was* Dinhábah.
33 And when Béla dyed, Iobáb the sonne of
Zérah of Bozrá reigned in his stede.
34 When Iobáb also was dead, Hushám
of the lād of Temaní reigned in his stede.
35 And after the death of Hushám, Hadád
the sonne of Bedád, which slewe Midián
in the field of Moáb, reigned in his stede,
and the name of his citie *was* Auíth.
36 When Hadád was dead, then Samláh of
Masrekáh reigned in his stede.
37 When Samláh was dead, Shaúl of h Rehobóth by the riuer, reigned in his stede.
38 When Shaúl dyed, Baal-hanán the sonne of Achbór reigned in his stede.
39 And after the death of Baal-hanán the
sonne of Achbór, Hadád reigned in his
stede, and the name of his citie *was* Páu:
& his wiues name Mehetabél the daughter of Matréd, the "daughter of Mezaháb.
40 Then these are the names of the dukes
of Esáu according to their families, their
places *and* by their names: duke Timná,
duke Aluáh, duke Iethéth,
41 Duke Aholibamáh, duke Eláh, duke Pinón,
42 Duke Kenáz, duke Temán, duke Mibzár,
43 Duke Magdiél, duke Irám: these be the
dukes of Edóm, according to their habitacions, in the land of their inheritance.
This Esáu is the father of i Edóm.

CHAP. XXXVII.

2 Ioséph accuseth his brethren. 5 He dreameth and is hated of his brethren. 28 They sel him to the Ishmaelites. 34 Iaakób bewaileth Ioséph.

1 IAakób now dwelt in the land, wherein
his father was a stranger, in the lād of
Canáan.
2 These are the a generacions of Iaakób,
when Ioséph was seuenteen yere olde: he
kept shepe with his brethrē, & the childe
was with the sonnes of Bilháh, and with
the sonnes of Zilpáh, his fathers wiues.
And Ioséph broght vnto their father
their euil" b saying.
3 Now Israél loued Ioséph more then all
his sonnes, because he begate him in his

g The wicked rise vp sodēly to honour, and perish as quickely: but the inheritance of the childrē of God cōtinueth euer. psal 105, 28.
h Which citie is by the riuer Euphrátes.
"Or, nece.
i Of Edóm came the Idumeans.
a That is, the storie of suche thīgs as came to him and his familie, as chap.5,1.
"Or, slander.
b He cōplained of the euil wordes & iniuries, which thei spake & did against hī.

olde age,and he made him a coate of many "colours.
4 So when his brethren sawe that their father loued him more then all his brethrẽ,
then thei hated him,and colde not speake
peaceably vnto him.
5 ¶ And Ioséph [c] dreamed a dreame, and
tolde his brethren, who hated him so
muche the more.
6 For he said vnto thẽ,Heare, I pray you,
this dreame which I haue dreamed.
7 Beholde now,we were binding sheues in
ẏ middes of the field:& lo,my shefe arose
and also stode vpright, & beholde, your
sheues compassed rounde about, and did
reuerence to my shefe.
8 Then his brethren said to him, What,
shalt thou reigne ouer vs,and rule vs? or
shalt thou haue altogether dominiõ ouer
vs? And thei [d] hated him so muche the
more, for his dreames, & for his wordes.
9 ¶ Againe he dreamed an other dreame,
& tolde it his brethren,& said,Beholde,I
haue had one dreame more, and beholde,
the sunne and the moone and eleuen starres did reuerence to me.
10 Then he tolde it vnto his father & to his
brethren,and his father [e] rebuked him, &
saidvnto him,What is this dreame,which
thou hast dreamed? shal I,& thy mother,
and thy brethren come in dede and fall
on the grounde before thee?
11 And his brethren enuied him,but his father" [f] noted the saying.
12 ¶ Then his brethren went to kepe their
fathers shepe in Shechém.
13 And Israél said vnto Ioséph,Do not thy
brethren kepe in Shechém? come & I wil
send thee to them.
14 And he answered him,I am here. Then
he said vnto him,Go now,se whether it be
wel with thy brethren, and how the flockes prosper, and bring me worde againe.
so he sent him from the vale of Hebrón,
and he came to Shechém.
15 ¶ Then a man founde him:for lo,he was
wandring in the field, and the man asked
him,saying,What sekest thou?
16 And he answered,I seke my brethren: tel
me,I pray thee, where they kepe *shepe*.
17 And the man said, Thei are departed
hence:for I heard them say,Let vs go vnto Dothán. Then went Ioséph after his
brethren,and found them in Dothán.
18 And when thei saw him a far of, euen
before he came at them, thei [g] conspired
against him for to slaie him.
19 For thei said one to an other, Beholde,
this "dreamer commeth.
20 Come now therefore,& let vs slaie him,
and cast him into some pit, & we wil say,
A wicked beast hathe deuoured him: thẽ
we shal se,what wil come of his dreames.

"Or,pieces.

c God reueiled to him by a dreame, what shulde come to passe.

d The more ẏ God sheweth him selfe fauorable to his, ẏ more doeth the malice of ẏ wicked rage against them.

e Not despising the vision, but seking to appease his brethren.

"Or,kept diligently.

f He knewe that God was autor of the dreame,but he vnderstode not the meaning.

g The holy Gost couereth not mens fautes, as do vaine writers ẇ make vice vertue.

"Or,master of dreames.

21 *But whẽ Reubén heard *that*,he deliuered him out of their hands, & said, " Let
vs not kil him.
22 Also Reubén said vnto them, Shed not
blood, *but* cast him into this pit that is in
the wildernes, & lay no hand vpon him.
Thus he said,that he might deliuer him out
of their hand, and restore him to his father againe.
23 ¶ Now when Ioséph was come vnto his
brethrẽ,thei stript Ioséph out of his coat,
his particoloured coate ẏ was vpon him.
24 And thei toke him,&cast [h] hĩ into a pit,
& the pit *was* empty, without water in it.
25 Then thei sat them downe to eat bread:
and thei lift vp their eies and loked, and
beholde,there came a company of Ishmeelites from Gileád, and their camels ladẽ
with spicerie,and rosen, and myrrhe, and
were going to carie it downe into Egypt.
26 Thẽ Iudáh said vnto his brethrẽ,What
auaileth it,if we slaie our brother,thogh
we kepe his blood secret?
27 Come and let vs sel him to the Ishmeelites, and let not our hands be vpon him:
for he is our brother & our flesh: and his
brethren obeied.
28 Thẽ the * Midianites marchãt men passed by,and thei drewe forthe,and lift Ioséph out of the pit,and solde Ioséph vnto
the [i] Ishmeelites for twentie *pieces* of siluer: who broght Ioséph into Egypt.
29 ¶ Afterward Reubén returned to ẏ pit,
and beholde,Ioséph *was* not in the pit:thẽ
he rent his clothes,
30 And returned to his brethrẽ,& said, The
childe is not *yóder*, & I,whether shal I go?
31 And thei toke Iosephs coate, and killed
a kid of the goates, and depped the coate
in the blood.
32 So thei sent that particoloured coate,
[k] and thei broght it vnto their father, &
said, This haue we fouñde: se now,whether
it be thy sonnes coate,or no.
33 Then he knew it and said, *It is* my sonnes coat: a wicked beast hathe * deuoured
him: Ioséph is surely torne in pieces.
34 And Iaakób rẽt his clothes, & put sackcloth about his loynes, & sorowed for his
sonne a long season.
35 Then all his sonnes & all his daughters
rose vp to cõforte him, but he wolde not
be comforted, but said, " Surely I wil go
downe into ẏ graue vnto my sõne mourning: so his father wept for him.
36 And the Midianites solde him into E-
gypt vnto Potiphár [l] an Eunuche of Pharaohs,*and* his " chief stuarde.

Chap.42,22.

"Ebr.let vs not smite his life.

h Their hypocrisie appeareth in this ẏ thei feared mã more then God:& thoght it was not murther, if thei shed not his blood: or els had an excuse to couer their faute.

Wisd.10,13. psal.105,17.

i Moses writing accordig to the opinion of thẽ, which toke the Midianites and Ishmeelites to be bothe one, doeth here cõ founde their names: as also appeareth vers. 36. and chap.39,1. or els he was first offred to ẏ Midianites, but solde to the Ishmeelites.

k To wit, the messengers ẇ were sent.

Chap 44,28.

"Or,I wil mourne for him so lõg as I liue.

l Which worde doeth not alwaie signifie him, ẏ is gelded, but also him that is ĩ some high dignitie.

"Or, captaine of the garde.

CHAP. XXXVIII.

2 The mariage of Iudáh. 29 The trespasse of Er and Onán,and the vengeance of God that came thereupõ. 18 Iudáh lyeth with his daughter in lawe Tamár. 29.30 The birth of Thárez and Zárah.

And

a Moses describeth ỹ genealogie of Iudáh because the Messias shuld come of him.

1 AND at that time [a] Iudáh went downe from his brethren, and turned in
to a man called Hiráh an Adullamite.
2 And Iudáh sawe there the daughter of a
man called * Shuáh a [b] Canaanite: and he
toke her *to wife*, and went in vnto her.

1.Chro.2,3.
b Which affinitie notwithstanding was condemned of God.

3 So she conceiued and bare a sonne, & he
called his name Er.

Nom.26,9.

4 * And she conceiued againe, and bare a
sonne, and she called his name Onán.
5 Moreouer she bare yet a sonne, whome
she called Sheláh: and *Iudáh* was at Che-
zíb when she bare him.
6 Thē Iudáh toke a wife to Er his first borne *sonne* whose name *was* Tamár.

Nom. 26,19.

7 *Now Er ỹ first borne of Iudáh was wicked in the sight of the Lord: therefore the
Lord slewe him.
8 Then Iudáh said to Onán, Go in vnto
thy brothers wife, and do the office of a
kinsman vnto her, & raise [c] vp sede vnto
thy brother.

c This ordre was for ỹ preseruation of ỹ stocke, that ỹ childe begotten by the seconde brother shulde haue ỹ name and inheritance of ỹ first. Which is in the new Testament abolished.

9 And Onán knewe ỹ the sede shulde not
be his: therefore when he wēt in vnto his
brothers wife, he spilled it on the groūde,
lest he shulde giue sede vnto his brother.
10 And it was wicked in the eies of ỹ Lord,
which he did: wherefore he slewe hī also.
11 Then said Iudáh to Tamár his daughter in lawe, [d] Remaine a widowe in thy
fathers house, til Sheláh my sonne growe
vp (for he thoght *thus*, Lest he die aswel
as his brethren) So Tamár went & dwelt
in her fathers house.

d For she colde not mary in any other familie so long as Iudáh wolde reteine her in his.

12 ¶ And in processe of time also the daugh
ter of Shuáh Iudahs wife dyed. Then Iudáh, when he "had left mourning, went vp
to his shepe sherers to Timnáh, he, and
his neighbour Hiráh the Adullamite.

"Ebr, was comforted.

13 And it was tolde Tamár, saying, Beholde, thy father in lawe goeth vp to Timnáh, to shere his shepe.
14 Then she put her widowes garmentes of from her, & couered *her* with a vaile, and wrapped her selfe, & sate downe in
"Petháh-enaim, ẘ is by the way to Timnáh, because she sawe ỹ Sheláh was grow-
en, & she was not giuē vnto him to wife.

"Or, in the dore of the fonteines: or, where were two waies.

15 When Iudáh sawe her, he iudged her a
whore: for she had couered her face.
16 And he turned to the way, towards her,
& said, Come, I pray thee, let me lye with
thee. (for he [e] knewe not that she was his
daughter in lawe) And she answered,
What wilt thou giue me for to lie ẘ me?

e God had wonderfully blinded him ỹ he colde not knowe her by her talke.

17 Then said he, I wil send thee a kid of ỹ
goates from the flocke. & she said, *Wel*, if
thou wilt giue me a pledge, til ỹ send it.
18 Then he said, What is the pledge that
I shal giue thee? And she answered, Thy
signet, & thy "cloke, and thy staffe that is
in thine hand. So he gaue it her, and lay by
her, and she was with childe by him.

"Or, tyre of thine head.

19 Then she rose, and went & put her vaile frō her & put on her widowes raymēt.
20 Afterward Iudáh sent a kid of the goates by the hād of his [f] neighbour ỹ Adullamite, for to receiue his pledge from the
womans hand: but he founde her not.

f That his wickednes might not be knowē to others.

21 Then asked he the mē of that place, saying, Where is ỹ whore, *that sate* in Enáim
by ỹ way side? And they answered, There was no whore here.
22 He came therefore to Iudáh againe, &
said, I cā not finde her, & also the mē of ỹ
place said, There was no whore there.
23 Then Iudáh said, Let her take it to her,
lest we be "[g] shamed: beholde, I sent this
kid, and thou hast not founde her.

"Ebr. in contēpt.
g He feareth man more thē God.

24 ¶ Now after thre moneths, one tolde Iudáh, saying, Tamár thy daughter in lawe
hathe played the whore, and lo, with
playing the whore, she is great with childe. Then Iudáh said, Bring ye her forthe
and let her be [h] burnt.

h We se that ỹ lawe, which was writen in mans heart, taught them that whoredome shulde be punished with death: albeit no lawe as yet was giuen.

25 When she was broght forthe, she sent to
her father in law, saying, By the man, vnto
whome these thīgs *perteine*, am I with chil
de: & said also, Loke, I praye thee, whose
these are, the seale, & ỹ cloke, and ỹ staffe.
26 Then Iudáh knewe *them*, and said, She is
[i] more righteous thē I: for *she hath done it*
because I gaue her not to Sheláh my sonne. So he laye with her [k] no more.

i That is, she oght rather to accuse me thē I her.
k For ỹ horrour of ỹ sinne cōdēned him.

27 ¶ Now, whē the time was come that she
shulde be deliuered, beholde, there *were*
twinnes in her wombe.
28 And when she was in trauel, *the one* put
out his hand: & the midwife toke and bounde a red *threde* about his hand, saying,
This is come out first.
29 But when he [l] plucked his hād backe againe, lo, his brother came out, & *the midwife*
said, How hast [m] thou broken the breache
vpō thee? & his name was called *Phárez.
30 And afterwarde came out his brother ỹ
had the red *threde* about his hand, and his
name was called Zárah.

l Their hainous sinne was signified by this monstruous birth.
m Or the separation betwene thee & thy brother.
1.Chro.2,4.
mat.1,3.

CHAP. XXXIX.

1 Ioséph is solde to Potiphár. 2 God prospereth him. 7 Potiphars wife tempteth him. 13, 20 He is accused & cast in prison. 21 God sheweth him fauour.

1 NOw Ioséph was broght downe into Egypt: & Potiphár [a] an Eunuche
of Pharaohs (*and his* chief stuard an Egyptian) boght him at the hand of the Ishmeelites, which had broght him thether.

a Read chap. 37,36.

2 And the Lord [b] was with Ioséph, and he
was a man that prospered and was in the
house of his master the Egyptian.

b The fauour of God is the founteine of all prosperitie.

3 And his master sawe that the Lord *was*
with him, and that the Lord made all that
he did to prosper in his hand.
4 So Ioséph founde fauour in his sight, &
serued him: and he made him [c] ruler of his
house, and put all that he had in his hand.

c Because God prospered his and so he made religion to serue his profite.

5 And frō that time that he had made him
ruler ouer his house & ouer all that he
had,the Lord [d] blessed the Egyptiās house for Iosephs sake : & the blessing of the
Lord was vpon all that he had in ŷ house,
and in the field.

d The wicked are blessed by ŷ companie of the godlie.

6 Therefore he left all ŷ he had in Iosephs
hād,[e] & toke accompte of nothīg, *that was*
ŵ him, saue onely of the bread,which he
did eat. And Ioséph was a faire personne,
and wel fauoured.

e For he was assured ŷ all things shulde prosper wel: therforehe ate and dranke & toke no care.

7 ¶ Now therefore after these thīgs,his ma
sters wife cast her eyes vpon Ioseph, and
said, [f] Lye with me.

f In this word he declareth ŷ somme whe reunto all her flatteries did tend.

8 But he refused & said to his masters wife, Beholde,my master knoweth not what
he hathe in the house with me,but hathe cō
mitted all that he hathe to mine hand.
9 There is no man greater in this house
then I:nether hathe he kept any thing frō
me,but only thee,because thou art his wi-
fe:how then can I do this great wickednes
& *so* sinne against [g] God?

g The feare of God preserued him against her continual tētatiōs.

10 And albeit she spake to Ioséph day by
day,yet he hearkened not vnto her, to lye
with her, *or* to be in her companie.
11 Then on a certeine day *Ioseph* entred into the house,to do his busines: & there was
no man of the housholde in the house:
12 Therefore she caught him by his garment,sayīg, Slepe ŵ me:but he left his gar
ment in her hand and fled,& got him out.
13 Now when she sawe that he had left his
garment in her hand,and was fled out,
14 She called vnto the men of her house,
and tolde them, saying, Beholde,he hathe
broght ī an Ebrewe vnto vs" to mocke vs:
who came into me for to haue slept with
me:but I [h] cryed with a loude voyce.

"Or, to do vs vilenie and shame.

h This declareth that where incontinencie is, thereunto is ioyned extreme impudencie and craft.

15 And when he heard ŷ I lift vp my voyce
and cryed,he left his garment with me,&
fled away,and got him out.
16 So she layed vp his garment by her,vntil
her lord came home.
17 Then she tolde him "according to these wordes,saying, The Ebrewe seruant, ŵ
thou hast brogt vnto vs, came into me to
mocke me.

"Or, after this maner.

18 But assone as I lift vp my voyce and
cryed,he left his garmēt ŵ me,& fled out.
19 Then when his master heard the wordes
of his wife, which she tolde him, saying,
After this maner did thy seruāt to me,his
angre was kindled.
20 And Iosephs master toke him and put
him in" [i] prison, in the place, where the
Kings prisoners lay bounde: and there he
was in prison.

"Ebr. in the prison house.

i His euil intreatement in the prison may be gathered of the psal 105,18.

21 ¶ But ŷ Lord was with Ioséph,&"shewed him mercie, and got him fauour in the
sight of the" master of the prison.

"Ebr. inclined mercie vnto him.

"Or, lord.

22 And the keper of the prison committed
to Iosephs hād all the prisoners that were
in the prison, and [k] whatsoeuer they did
there,that did he.

k That is,nothing was done without his cōmandemēts.

23 And the keper of the prison loked vnto
nothing that was vnder his hand, seing
that the Lord *was* with him: for whatsoeuer he did,the Lord made it to prosper.

CHAP. XL.

8 The interpretation of dreames is of God. 12. 19. Ioséph expoundeth the dreames of the two prisoners. 23 The ingratitude of the butler.

1 And after these thīgs,the butler of ŷ
King of Egypt and his baker offended their lord the king of Egypt.
2 And Pharaóh was angry against his two
"officers, against the chief butler, and a-
gainst the chief baker.

"Or, eunuches. the worde signifieth them that were in high estate, or, them that were gelded.

3 Therefore he put them in warde in his
chief stuardes house,in the prison *and* place where [a] Ioséph was bounde.

a God worked many wonderful meanes to deliuer his.

4 And the chief stuarde gaue Ioséph charge ouer them,& he serued them : and they
continued a season in warde:
5 ¶ And they bothe dreamed a dreame,ether
of thē his dreame in one night, [b] eche one
according to ŷ interpretation of his drea
me, *bothe* ŷ butler & the baker of the King
of Egypt, ŵ were bounde in the prison.

b That is, euerie dreame had his interpretation, as the thing afterward declared.

6 And when Ioséph came in vnto them in
the morning,and loked vpon them,behol-
de,they were sad.
7 And he asked Pharaohs officers , that
were with him in his masters warde, saying,Wherefore "loke ye so sadly to day?

"Ebr. why are your faces euil?

8 Who answered him, We haue dreamed,
eche one a dreame,& there is none to interpret the same. Then Ioséph said vnto thē,
[c] Are not interpretations of God? tel them
me now.

c Can not God raise vp suche as shal interpret suche things?

9 So the chief butler tolde his dreame to
Ioséph,and said vnto him,In my dreame,
beholde,a vine *was* before me,
10 And in the vine *were* thre branches , and
as it budded,her floure came forthe: & the
clusters of grapes waxed ripe.
11 And *I had* Pharaohs cup in mine hand,&
I toke the grapes, and wrong them into
Pharaohs cup, and I gaue the cup into
Pharaohs hand.
12 Then Ioséph said vnto him, This [d] is the
interpretation of it: The thre branches a-
re thre dayes.

d He was assured by the Spirit of God ŷ his interpretation was true.

13 Within thre dayes shal Pharaóh lift vp
thine head, & restore thee vnto thine "office,and thou shalt giue Pharaohs cup into his hand after the olde maner,when ŷ
wast his butler.

"Ebr. place.

14 But haue me in remembrāce with thee,
when thou art in good case,& shewe mercie,I pray thee , vnto me, and [e] make mēcion of me to Pharaóh, that thou maiest
bring me out of this house.

e He refused not the meanes to be deliuered, which he thoght God had appoited.

15 For I was stollen away by theft out of ŷ
land of the Ebrewes, & here also haue I
done

done nothing, wherefore they shulde put
me "in the dungeon.

"Or, in the pit.

16 And when the chief baker sawe that the
interpretaciō was good, he said vnto Iosēph, Also me thoght in my dreame that I
had thre [f] white baskets on mine head.

f That is, made of white twigges, or, as some read, baskets ful of holes.

17 And in the vppermost basket there *was*
of all maner bakē meates for Pharaóh: &
the birdes did eat them out of the basket
vpon mine head.
18 Then Iosēph answered, & said, [g] This is
the interpretacion thereof: The thre baskets are thre dayes:

g He sheweth that the ministers of God oght not to cōceile that, w God reueileth vnto them.

19 Within thre daies shal Pharaóh take thine head from thee, & shal hang thee on a
tre, and the birdes shal eat thy flesh from
of thee.
20 ¶ And so the third day, *which was* Pharaohs [h] birthday, he made a feast vnto all
his seruantes: and he lifted vp the head of
the chief butler, and the head of the chief
baker among his seruantes.

h Which was an occasion to appoint his officers and so to examine thē that were in prison.

21 And he restored the chief butler vnto
his butlership, who gaue the cup in to
Pharaohs hand,
22 But he hanged the chief baker, as Iosēph
had interpreted vnto them.
23 Yet the chief butler did not remembre
Iosēph, but forgat him.

CHAP. XLI.

26 Pharaohs dreames are expounded by Iosēph. 40 He is made ruler ouer all Egypt. 51 He hathe two sonnes: Manasseh and Ephraim. 54 The famine beginneth throughout the worlde.

1 AND" two yeres after, Pharaóh also
[a] dreamed, and beholde, he stode by
a riuer,

"Eb. at the end of two yeres of daies.
a This dreame was not so muche for Pharaóh, as to be a meane to deliuer Iosēph, and to prouide for his Church.
"Or, flaggy places.

2 And lo, there came out of the riuer seuen
goodlie kine and fatfleshed, and thei fed
in a "medow:
3 And lo, seuen other kine came vp after
them out of the riuer, euilfauoured and
leane fleshed, and stode by the *other* kine
vpon the brinke of the riuer.
4 And the euilfauoured and leane fleshed
kine did eat vp the seuen welfauoured &
fat kine: so Pharaóh awoke.
5 Againe he slept, and dreamed the [b] seconde time: and beholde, seuen eares of
corne grewe vpon one stalke, ranke and
goodlie.

b All these meanes God vsed to deliuer his seruant, & to bring him in to fauour and autoritie.

6 And lo, seuē thinne eares, & blasted with
the East winde, sprang vp after them:
7 And the thinne eares deuoured the seuē
ranke and ful eares. then Pharaóh awaked, and lo, *it was* a dreame.
8 Now when the morning came, his spiri-
te was [c] troubled: therefore he sent and
called all the sothesaiers of Egypt, & all
the wise men thereof, and Pharaóh tolde
them his dreames: but [d] none colde interpret them to Pharaóh.

c This feare was ynough to teache him, that this vision was sent of God.
d The wise of the worlde vnderstand not Gods secrets, but to his seruants his wil is reueiled.
e He cōfesseth his faute against ẏ King, before he speake of Iosēph.

9 Then spake the chief butler vnto Pharaóh, saying, I [e] call to minde my fautes
this day.
10 Pharaóh being angry with his seruantes, put me in warde in the chief stuardes
house, *bothe* me and the chief baker.
11 Thē we dreamed a dreame in one night,
bothe I, and he: we dreamed eche man according to the interpretacion of his dreame.
12 And there *was* with vs a yong man, an
Ebrewe, seruant vnto the chief stuarde,
whome when we tolde, he declared our
dreames to "vs, to euerie one he declared
according to his dreame.

" Read Chapter. 40, 5.

13 And as he declared vnto vs, so it came
to passe: *for* he restored me to mine office, and hanged him.
14 *Then sent Pharaóh, and [f] called Iosēph, and they broght him hastely out of
prison, and he shaued him, and changed
his raiment, and came to Pharaóh.

*Psal. 105, 20.
f The wicked seke to ẏ Prophets of God in their necessitie, whome in their prosperitie they abhorre.

15 Then Pharaóh said to Iosēph, I haue
dreamed a dreame, and no man can interpret it, and I haue heard say of thee, *that*
when thou hearest a dreame, thou canst
interpret it.
16 And Iosēph answered Pharaóh, saying,
[g] Without me God shal " answer for
the welth of Pharaóh.

g As thogh he wolde say, If I interpret thy dreame, it cometh of God & not of me.
"Ebr. answer peace.

17 And Pharaóh said vnto Iosēph, In my
dreame, beholde, I stode by the banke of
the riuer:
18 And lo, there came vp out of ẏ riuer seuē
fatfleshed, and welfauoured kine, and thei
fed in the medow.
19 Also lo, seuen other kine came vp after
them, poore and very "euilfauoured, and
leanefleshed: I neuer sawe the like in all
the land of Egypt, for euilfauoured.

"Ebr. naught.

20 And the leane and euilfauoured kine
did eat vp the first seuen fat kine.
21 And when they " had eaten them vp, it
colde not be knowen that they had eaten
them, but they were stil as euilfauoured,
as they were at the beginning: so did I
awake.

"Ebr. were gone into theire inwarde partes.

22 Moreouer I sawe in my dreame, and beholde, seuen eares sprang out of one stalke, ful and faire.
23 And lo, seuen eares, withered, thinne, *and*
blasted with the East winde, sprang vp
after them.
24 And the thinne eares deuoured the seuen good eares. Now I haue tolde the
sothesaiers, and none can declare it vnto
me.
25 ¶ Then Iosēph answered Pharaóh, *Bo-*
the Pharaohs dreames are one. [h] God hathe
shewed Pharaóh, what he is about to do.

h Bothe his dreames tend to one end.

26 The seuen good kine are seuen yeres, &
the seuen good eares are seuen yeres: this
is one dreame.
27 Likewise the seuen thinne and euil fauoured kine, that came out after them, are
seuen yeres: and the seuen emptie eares

blasted with the East winde are seuen
yeres of famine.
28 This is the thing, which I haue said vnto Pharaóh, that God hathe shewed vnto
Pharaóh, what he is aboute to do.
29 Beholde, there come seuen yeres of great" plentie in all the land of Egypt.

"Or, abundance and saturitie.

30 Againe, there shal arise after them seuen yeres of famine, so that all the plentie
shalbe forgotten in the land of Egypt, and
the famine shal consume the land:
31 Nether shal the plentie "be knowē in the
land, by reason of this famine that *shal come* after: for it shalbe exceading great.

"Or, they shal remembre no more the plētie.

32 And therefore the dreame was doubled
vnto Pharaóh the second time, because
the thing is established by God, & God
hasteth to performe it.
33 Now therefore let Pharaóh [l] prouide for
a man of vnderstanding and wisdome, &
set him ouer the land of Egypt.

l The office of a true Prophet is not onely to shewe ẏ euils to come, but also the remedies for the same.

34 Let Pharaóh make and appoint officers
ouer the lād, and take vp the fifte parte of
ẏ lād of Egypt in ẏ seuen plenteous yeres.
35 Also let them gather all the fode of these good yeres that come, and lay vp corne vnder the hand of Pharaóh for fode, in
the cities, and let them kepe *it*.
36 So the fode shalbe for the prouision of
the land, against the seuen yeres of famine, which shalbe in the land of Egypt, that
the land perish not by famine.
37 ¶ And ẏ saying pleased Pharaóh and all
his seruantes.
38 Then said Pharaóh vnto his seruantes,
Can we finde *suche* a man as this, in whome
is the [k] Spirit of God?

k None shuld be preferred to honour ẏ haue not gifts of God mete for the same.

39 Thē Pharaóh said to Ioséph, For as muche
as God hathe shewed thee all this, there is
no man of vnderstanding, or of wisdome
like vnto thee.
40 *Thou shalt be ouer mine house, & at thy
" [l] worde shal all my people be armed, only in ẏ Kings throne wil I be aboue thee.

*Psal.105,21. 1.mac.2,53. act.7,10.
"Ebr. mouthe.
l Some read, The people shal kisse thy mouthe: that is, shal obey thee in all things.

41 Moreouer Pharaóh said to Ioséph, Beholde, I haue set thee ouer all the land of
Egypt.
42 And Pharaóh toke of his" ring from his
hand, and put it vpon Iosephs hand, and
araied him in garments of fine linen and
put a golden cheine about his necke.

"Or, his signet.

43 So he set him vpon the " best charet that
he had, saue one: & they cryed before him,
[m] Abréch, and placed him ouer all the land
of Egypt.

"Ebr. seconde charet.
m In signe of honour: which worde some expound, tender father, or father of the King, or knele downe.

44 Againe Pharaóh said vnto Ioséph, I am
Pharaóh, & without thee shal no man lift
vp his hand or his fote in all the land of
Egypt.
45 And Pharaóh called Iosephs name" Zaph
náth-paaneáh: and he gaue him to wife
Asnáth ẏ daughter of Poti-phéraḣ" prince of On. then went Ioséph abroad in the
land of Egypt.

"Or, the expounder of secrets.
"Or, priest.

46 ¶ And Ioséph *was* [n] thirty yere olde whē
he stode before Pharaóh King of Egypt:
and Ioséph departing from the presence
of Pharaóh, went through out all the land
of Egypt.

n His age is mencioned both to shewe that his autoritie came of God, and also that he suffred imprisonment & exile twelue yeres and mo.

47 And in the seuen plenteous yeres the
earth " broght forthe store.

"Ebr. made for gatherings.

48 And he gathered vp all the fode of the
seuen plenteous yeres, which were in the
land of Egypt, and layed vp fode in the
cities: the fode of the field, that was roúd
about *euery* citie, layed he vp in the same.
49 So Ioséph gathered wheat, like vnto the
sand of ẏ sea in multitude out of measure, vntil he left nombring: for *it was* without nombre.
50 Now vnto Ioséph were borne* two sons
nes (before the yeres of famine came) ẇ
Asenáth the daughter of Poti-phérah prīce of On bare vnto him.

*Chap. 46,20. & 48,5.

51 And Ioséph called the name of the first
borne Manasséh: for God, *said he*, hathe
made me forget all my labour & all my
[o] fathers housholde.

o Notwithstanding that his fathers house was the true Church of God: yet ẏ companie of the wicked & prosperitie caused him to forget it.

52 Also he called the name of the seconde Ephráim: for God, *said he*, hathe made
me fruteful in the land of mine afflictiō.
53 ¶ So the seuen yeres of the plentie that
was in the land of Egypt were ended.
54 *Thē began the seuen yeres of famine
to come, according as Ioséph had said: &
the famine was in all landes, but in all the
land of Egypt was" bread.

*Psal.105,16.
"Or, fode.

55 At the length all the land of Egypt was
affamished and the people cryed to Pharaóh for bread. And Pharaóh said vnto
all the Egyptians, Go to Ioséph: what he
saith to you, do ye.
56 When the famine was vpon all the lād,
Ioséph opened all *places*, wherein *the store
was* and solde vnto the Egyptians: for the
famine waxed sore in the land of Egypt.
57 And all countreis" came to Egypt to bye
corne of Ioséph, because the famine was
sore in all landes.

"Or, came to Egypt to Ioséph.

CHAP. XLII.

3 Iosephs brethren come into Egypt to bye corne. 7 He knoweth them, and tryeth them. 24, 25. Simeón is put in prison. 26 The other returne to their father to fet Beniamin.

1 Then [a] Iaakób sawe that there was fode in Egypt, & Iaakób said vnto his
sonnes, Why [b] gaze ye one vpō another?
2 And he said, Beholde, I haue heard that
there is fode in Egypt, * Get you downe
thether & bye vs fode thence, that we may
liue, and not die.

a This storie sheweth plainely that all things are gouerned by Gods prouidence for the profite of his Church.
b As men destitute of counsel.
*Act.7,12.

3 ¶ So went Iosephs ten brethrē downe to
bye corne of the Egyptians.
4 But Béiamín Iosephs brother wolde not
Iaakób send with his brethrē: for he said,
Lest death shulde " befall him.

"Ebr. shulde mete him.

5 And the sonnes of Israél came to bye
fode amōg them that came: for there was
famine in the land of Canáan.
6 Now Ioséph was gouerner of the land
who solde to all the people of the lād: thē
Iosephs brethren came, and bowed their
face to the grounde before him.
7 And whē Ioséph sawe his brethrē, he knewe them, and [c] made him selfe strange
toward them, and spake to them roughly,
& said vnto them, Whēce come ye? Who
answered, Out of the land of Canáan, to
bye vitaile.

c This dissembling is not to be followed, nor any particular facts of ȳ fathers not approued by Gods worde.

8 (Now Ioséph knewe his brethren, but
they knewe not him.
9 And Ioséph remembred the * dreames,
which he dreamed of them) and he said
vnto them, Ye are spies, *and* are come to
se the " weakenes of the land.

Chap. 37, 5.

" Ebr. nakednes, or, filthines.

10 But they said vnto him, Nay, my lord,
but to bye vitaile thy seruātes are come.
11 We are all one mans sonnes: we meane
truely, and thy seruantes are no spies.
12 But he said vnto them, Nay, but ye are
come to se the weakenes of the land.
13 And they said, We thy seruantes are
twelue brethren, the sonnes of one man in
the land of Canáan: and beholde, the yōgest *is* this day with our father, and one
" is not.

" Or, is dead.

14 Againe Ioséph said vnto thē, This is it
that I spake vnto you, sayīg, Ye are spies.
15 Hereby ye shalbe proued: [d] *by* the life of
Pharaóh, ye shal not go hēce, except your
yongest brother come hether.
16 Sēd one of you which may fet your brother, and ye shal be kept in prison, that
your wordes may be proued, whether there be trueth in you: or els *by* the life of
Pharaóh ye are but spies.

d The Egyptians, which were idolaters, vsed to sweare by their kings life: but God forbiddeth to sweare by any but him: yet Ioséph dwelling among ȳ wicked smelleth of their corruptions.

17 So he put them in warde thre dayes.
18 Then Ioséph said vnto them the third
day, This do, and liue: *for* I [e] feare God.

e And therefore am true and iust.

19 If ye be true men, let one of your brethren be bounde in your prison house, &
go ye, carie fode *for* the famine of your
houses:
20 * But bring your yonger brother vnto
me, that your wordes may be tried, and ȳ
ye die not: and they did so.

Chap. 43, 5.

21 ¶ And thei said one to an other, [f] We haue verely sinned against our brother, in ȳ
we sawe the anguish of his soule, when he
besoght vs, and we wolde not heare *him*:
therefore is this trouble come vpon vs.

f Affliction maketh men to acknowledge their fautes w otherwise thei wolde dissemble.

22 And Reubén answered them, saying,
Warned I not you, saying, * Sinne not a-
gainst the childe, and ye wolde not heare?
and lo, his [g] blood is now required.

Chap. 37, 21.
g God wil take vengeance vpō vs, & measure vs w our owne measure.

23 (And they were not aware that Ioséph
vnderstode them: for he " spake vnto them
by an interpreter)

" Ebr. an interpreter betwene them.

24 Then he turned from them, and [h] wept,
and turned to them againe, and communed with them, and toke Simeón from
amōg them, and bounde him before their
eyes.

h Thogh he shewed him selfe rigorous, yet his brotherlie affectiō remained.

25 ¶ So Ioséph commanded that thei shulde fille their sackes with wheat, and put
euerie mans money againe in his sacke, &
giue them vitaile for the iourney: and
thus did he vnto them.
26 And they laied their vitaile vpon their
asses, and departed thence.
27 And as one of them opened his sacke for
to giue his asse prouandre in the ynne,
he espied his money: for lo, it was in his
sackes mouthe.
28 Then he said vnto his brethren, My money is restored: for lo, it is euen in my sacke. And their heart " failed them, & they
were [i] astonnished, and said one to an o-
ther, What is this, *that* God hathe done
vnto vs?

" Ebr. went out.
i Because their conscience accused them of their sinne, they thoght God wolde haue broght thē to trouble by this money.

29 ¶ And they came vnto Iaakób their father vnto the land of Canáan, and tolde
him all that had befallen them, saying,
30 The man, *who is* lord of the land, spake
roughly to vs, and put vs *in prison* as spies
of the countrei.
31 And we said vnto him, We are true mē,
and are no spies.
32 We be twelue brethren, sonnes of our
father: one is " not, and the yongest *is* this
day with our father in the lād of Canáan.

" Or, can not be founde.

33 Then the lord of the countrei said vnto
vs, Hereby shal I knowe if ye be true mē:
Leaue one of your brethren with me, and
take *fode* for the famine of your houses &
departe,
34 And bring your yongest brother vnto
me, that I may knowe that ye are no spies,
but true mē: *so* wil I deliuer you your brother, and ye shal occupie in the land.
35 ¶ And as they empted their sackes, beholde, euerie mans bundel of money was
in his sacke: and when they and their father sawe the būdels of their money, they
were afraied.
36 Then Iaakób their father said to them,
Ye haue robbed me of my childrē: Ioséph
is not, and Simeón is not, and ye wil take
Béiamín: all these thīgs " are against [k] me.

" Or, light vpon me.
k For they semed not to be touched w any loue towarde their brethrē, w increased his sorowe: & partely as appeareth he suspected them for Ioséph.

37 Then Reubén answered his father, saying, Slay my two sōnes, if I brīg him not
to thee againe: deliuer him to mine hand,
and I wil bring him to thee againe.
38 But he said, My sōne shal not go downe
w you: for his brother is dead, & he is left
alone: if death come vnto him by ȳ way,
which ye go, then ye shal bring my graie
head with sorowe vnto the graue.

CHAP. XLIII.

13 Iaakób suffreth Beniamin to departe with his childrē. 23 Simeón is deliuered out of prison. 30 Ioséph goeth aside and wepeth. 32 They feast together.

a This was a great tentatiō to Iaakób to suffre so great famine in that lād, where God had promised to blesse him.

1 NOw great [a] famine *was* in the land.
2 And when they had eaten vp the
vitaile, which they had broght from E-
gypt, their father said vnto them, Turne
againe, *and* bye vs a litle fode.
3 And Iudáh answered him, saying, The
man charged vs by an othe, saying, * Neuer se my face, except your brother *be*
with you.
4 If thou wilt send our brother with vs, we
wil go downe, and by thee fode:
5 But if thou wilt not send *him*, we wil not
go downe: for the man said vnto vs, * Loke
me not in the face, except your brother
be with you.
6 And Israél said, Wherefore delt ye so euil
with me, as to tel the man, whether ye had
yet a brother or no?
7 And they answered, The man asked
straitly of ″ our selues and of our kinred,
sayīg, Is your father yet aliue? haue ye *any*
brother? And we tolde him ″according to
these wordes: colde we knowe certeinly ẏ
he wolde say, Bring your brother downe?
8 Then said Iudáh to Israél his father,
Sēd the boye with me, that we may rise &
go, and that we may liue and not dye, bothe we, and thou, and our children.
9 I wil be suretie for him: of mine hand
shalt thou require him. * If I bring him
not to thee, & set him before thee, ″ then
let me beare the blame for euer.
10 For except we had made this tarying,
doutles by this we had returned the seconde time.
11 Then their father Israél said vnto them,
If *it must nedes be* so nowe, do thus: take
of the best frutes of the land in your vessels, and bring the man a present, a litle
rosen, and a litle honie, ″spices and myrre, nuttes, and almondes:
12 And take [b] double money in your hand,
and the money, that was broght againe in
your sackes mouthes: carie it againe in
your hand, lest it were some ouer sight.
13 Take also your brother and arise, *and* go
againe to the man.
14 And [c] God almightie giue you mercie
in the sight of the man, that he maie deliuer you your other brother, and Beniamín: but I shalbe [d] robbed of my childe,
as I haue bene.
15 ¶ Thus ẏ men toke this present, and toke
twise so muche money in their hand with
Beniamín, and rose vp, and went downe to
Egypt and stode before Ioséph.
16 And when Ioséph sawe Beniamín ẘ thē,
he said to ″his stuard, Bring these men
home and kil meat and make readie: for
the men shal eat with me at noone.
17 And ẏ man did as Ioséph bad, & broght
the men vnto Iosephs house.
18 Now when the mē were broght into Iosephs house, thei were [e] afraied, and said,
Because of the money, that came in our
sackes mouthes at the first time, are we
broght, that he maie ″pike a quarel agaīst
vs, and ″ laie some thing to our charge,
and bring vs in bondage and our asses.
19 Therefore came thei to Iosephs stuard, and communed with him at the dore
of the house.
20 And said, Oh syr, * we came ī dede downe hether at the first time to bye fode,
21 And as we came to an ynne and opened
our sackes, behold, euerie mans money
was in his sackes mouth, *euen* our money
in ful weight, but we haue broght it againe in our hands.
22 Also other money haue we broght in ō
handes to bye fode, *but* we cā not tel, who
put our money in our sackes.
23 And he said, ″Peace be vnto you, feare not:
[f] your God and the God of your father
hathe giuen you that treasure in your sackes, I had your money: and he broght forthe Simeón to them.
24 So the man led thē in to Iosephs house,
and gaue them water to wash their fete,
and gaue their asses prouander.
25 And thei made redy their presēt against
Ioséph came at none, (for thei heard saie,
that thei shulde eat bread there)
26 When Ioséph came home, thei broght
the present into the house to him, which
was in their hands, and bowed downe to
the grounde before him.
27 And he asked them of *their* ″prosperitie,
and said, Is your father the olde man, of
whome ye tolde me, in good health? is he
yet aliue?
28 Who answered, Thy seruāt our father is
in good helth, he is yet aliue: and they
bowed downe, and made obeisance.
29 And he lifting vp his eies, behelde his
brother Beniamín his [g] mothers sonne, &
said, Is this your yonger brother, of whome ye tolde me? And he said, God be merciful vnto thee, my sonne.
30 And Ioséph made haste (for his ″ affection was inflamed toward his brother,
and soght *where* to wepe) and entred into
his chambre, and wept there.
31 Afterward he washed his face, and came out, and refrained him selfe, and said,
Set on ″meat.
32 And they [h] prepared for him by him
selfe, and for them by them selues, and
for ẏ Egyptians, which did eat with him,
by them selues, because the Egyptians
might not eat bread with ẏ Ebrewes: for
that was an [i] abominacion vnto the E-
gyptians.
33 So they sate before him: the eldest according vnto his age, and the yongest according vnto his youthe. and the men
marueiled

Chap. 42, 20.

Chap. 42, 20.

″Or, of our estate and condition.

″Ebr. to the mouthe of these wordes: that is, that thing which he asked vs.

Chap. 44, 32.

″Ebr. I wil sinne to thee.

″Or, swete smelles.

b Whē we are in necessitie or danger God forbiddeth not to vse all honest meanes to better ō estate and condition.

c Our chief trust oght to be in God and not in worldelie meanes.

d He speaketh these wordes not so much of despaire, as to make his sonnes more careful to bring againe their brother.

″Or, to the ruler of his house.

e So the iudgement of God pressed their conscience.

″Ebr. role him selfe vpon vs.

″Ebr cast him selfe vpon vs.

Chap. 42, 3.

″Or, you are wel.

f Notwithstāding the corruptions of Egypt, yet Ioseph taught his familie to feare God.

″Ebr peace.

g For they two onely were borne of Rahél.

″Ebr. bowels.

″Ebr bread.

h To signifie his dignitie.

i The nature of the superstitious is to cōdemne all other in respect of thē selues.

marueiled among them selues.
34 And thei toke meases frõ before him,&
sent to thẽ: but Beniamins mease was fiue
times so muche as anie of theirs: & thei
dronke[k] & had of the best drinke w̃ him.

k Sometime this worde signifieth to be dronken, but here it is mẽt, that thei had ynough, and dronke of the best wine.

CHAP. XLIIII.

15 *Iosěph accuseth his brother of theft. 33 Iudáh offreth him selfe to be seruant for Beniamin.*

1 AFterwarde he cõmanded his stuard,
saying, Fil the mens sackes with
fode,as muche as thei can cary,and put e-
uerie mans money in his sackes mouthe.
2 And [a] put my cup, *I meane* the siluer cup,
in the sackes mouthe of the yongest, and
his corne money. And he did according
to the commandement that Iosěph gaue
him.

a We may not by this example vse any vnlawful practises, seing God hathe cõmãded vs to walke in simplicitie.

3 And in the "morning the men were sent
away,thei,and their asses.

"Ebr. the morning shone.

4 And when thei went out of the citie not
farre of, Iosěph said to his stuard, Vp,
followe after the men: & whẽ thou doest
ouertake them,say vnto them,Wherefore
haue ye rewarded euil for good?
5 Is that not *the cup*,wherein my lord drinketh?[b] and in the which he doeth deuine
and prophecie? ye haue done euil in so
doing.

b Because the people thoght he colde deuine, he attributeth to him selfe ŷ knowledge: or els he faineth that he consulted w̃ sothesaiers for it: which simulation is worthy to be reproued.

6 ¶And whẽ he ouertoke thẽ,he said those
wordes vnto them.
7 And thei answered him,Wherefore saieth my lord suche wordes? God forbid
that thy seruants shulde do suche a thing.
8 Beholde, the money which we found in
our sackes mouthes, we broght againe to
thee out of the land of Canáan: how then
shulde we steale out of thy lordes house
siluer,or golde?
9 With whomesoeuer of thy seruants it
be founde, let him dye,and we also wil be
my lords bondmen.
10 And he said, Now then let it be according vnto your wordes: he with whome
it is founde,shalbe my seruant, & ye shal
be" blameles.

"Ebr. innocent.

11 Then at once euerie mã toke downe his
sacke to the grounde,and euerie one opened his sacke.
12 And he searched,and began at the eldest
and left at the yongest: and the cup was
founde in Beniamins sacke.
13 Then thei[c] rent their clothes, and laded
euerie man his asse, and went againe into
the citie.

c To signifie how greatly the thing displeased them, and how sory thei were for it.

14 ¶So Iudáh & his brethren came to Iosephs house(for he *was* yet there)and thei
fel before him on the grounde.
15 Thẽ Iosěph said vnto thẽ,What acte is
this,which ye haue done? Knowe ye not
that suche a man as I, can deuine & prophecie?
16 Then said Iudáh, What shal we say vnto my lord? what shal we speake? & how
can we iustifie our selues? [d] God hathe
founde out the wickednes of thy seruantes: beholde we *are* seruants to my lord,
bothe we,and he, with whome the cup is
founde.

d If we se no euident cause of our afflictiõ,let vs loke to the secret cõusel of God, who punisheth vs iustly for our sinnes.

17 But he answered, God forbid,ŷ I shulde
do so, *but* the man, with whome the cup is
founde, he shalbe my seruant, & go ye in
peace vnto your father.
18 ¶Thẽ Iudáh drewe nere vnto him, and
said, Oh my lord, let thy seruant now
speake a worde in my lords eares, and let
not thy wrath be kindled against thy ser-
uant:for thou art euen[e] as Pharaóh.

e Equal in autoritie: or, next vnto the King.

19 My lord asked his seruãts,saying,*Haue
ye a father,or a brother?

Chap.42,13.

20 And we answered my lord, We haue a
father that is olde, and a yong "childe,
which he begate in his age: and his brother
is dead, & he alone is left of his mother,
and his father loueth him.

"Ebr. childe of his olde age.

21 Now ŷ saidest vnto thy seruants, Bring
him vnto me,that I may "set mine eie vpon him.

"Or, that I may se him.

22 And we answered my lord, The childe
can not departe from his father: for if he
leaue his father,*his father* wolde dye.
23 Then saidest thou vnto thy seruãts,*Except your yonger brother come downe
with you,loke in my face no more.

Chap.43,5.

24 So when we came vnto thy seruant our
father,and shewed him what my lord had
said,
25 And our father said vnto vs, Go againe,
bye vs a litle fode,
26 Thẽ we answered,We can not go dowe-
ne: *but* if our yongest brother "go with vs,
then wil we go downe:for we may not se
the mãs face, except our yongest brother
be with vs.

"Ebr. be with vs.

27 Then thy seruant my father said vnto
vs,Ye knowe that my[f] wife bare me two
sonnes,

f Rahél bare to Iaakób Iosěph and Beniamín.

28 And the one went out from me, and I
said,Of a surety he is torne in pieces,and
I sawe him not since.
29 Now ye take this also away from me:
if death take him,then[g] ye shal bring my
gray head in sorowe to the graue.

g Ye shal cause me to dye for sorowe.

30 Now therefore, whẽ I come to thy seruant my father,and the childe *be* not with
vs (seing that his "life dependeth on the
childes life)

"Ebr. his soule is bonde to his soule.

31 Then when he shal se that the childe *is*
not *come*, he wil dye: so shal thy seruants
bring the gray head of thy seruant our
father with sorowe to the graue.
32 Doutles thy seruant became suretie for
the childe to my father, and said, * If I
bring him not vnto thee againe, thẽ I wil
beare the blame vnto my father for euer.

Chap.43,9.

33 Now therefore,I pray thee,let *me* thy ser
uant bide for the childe, *as* a seruant to

my lord, and let the childe go vp with
his brethren.

h Meaning, he had rather remaine there prisoner, then to returne and se his father in heauines.

34 For h how can I go vp to my father, if
the childe *be* not with me, onles I wolde
se the euil that shal come on my father?

CHAP. XLV.

1 Ioséph maketh him selfe knowen to his brethren. 8 He sheweth that all was done by Gods prouidēce. 18 Pharaóh commandeth him to send for his father. 24 Ioséph exhorteth his brethren to cōcorde. 27 Iaakób reioyceth.

Then Ioséph colde not refraine him
selfe before all that stode by him,
but he cryed, a Haue forthe euerie mã frõ
me. And there taried not one with him,
while Ioséph vttered him selfe vnto his
brethren.

a Not that he was ashamed of his kinred, but that he wolde couer his brethrens faute.

2 And he wept & cryed, so that the Egyptiãs heard: ẏ house of Pharaóh heard also.
3 Then Ioséph said to his brethren, I am
Ioséph: doeth my father yet liue? But his
brethren colde not answer him, for thei
were astonished at his presence.
4 Againe Ioséph said to his brethren, Come nere, I pray you, to me. And thei came
nere. And he said, * I am Ioséph your brother, whome ye solde into Egypt.

Act. 7,13.

5 Now therefore be not b sad, nether grieued with your selues, that ye solde me
hether: *for God did send me before you
for *your* preseruation.

b This exãple teacheth, that we must by all meanes cõfort thẽ, which are truely hũbled & wounded for their sinnes.

Chap. 50,20.

6 For now two yeres of famine *haue bene*
through the land, and fiue yeres *are* behinde, wherein nether *shal be* earing nor
haruest.
7 Wherefore God sent me before you to
preserue your posteritie in this land, and
to saue you aliue by a great deliuerance.
8 Now then you sent not me hether, but
c God, who hathe made me a father vnto
Pharaóh, and lord of all his house, and
ruler through out all the land of Egypt.

c Albeit God detest sinne, yet he turneth mans wickednes to serue to his glorie.

9 Haste you and go vp to my father, and
tel him, Thus saieth thy sonne Ioséph,
God hathe made me lord of all Egypt:
come downe to me, tary not.
10 And thou shalt dwel in the land of Góshen, and shalt be nere me, thou and thy
children, & thy childrens childrẽ, & thy
shepe, & thy beastes, & all that thou hast.
11 Also I wil nourish thee there (for yet *remaine* fiue yeres of famine) lest thou perish through pouertie, thou & thy housholde, and all that thou hast.
12 And beholde, your eies do se, & the eies
of my brother Beniamín, ẏ d my mouth
speaketh to you.

d That is, that I speake in your owne lãgage, and haue none interpreter.

13 Therefore tel my father of all mine honour in Egypt, & of all that ye haue sene,
& make haste, & bring my father hether.
14 Then he fel on his brother Beniamins
necke, and wept, & Beniamín wept on his
necke.
15 Moreouer he kissed all his brethren, and
wept vpon them: and afterwarde his brethren talked with him.
16 ¶ And the "tydings came vnto Pharaohs
house, so that thei said, Iosephs brethren
are come: and it pleased Pharaóh wel, &
his seruants.

"Ebr. voice

17 Then Pharaóh said vnto Ioséph, Say
to thy brethren, This do ye, lade your
beastes & departe, go to ẏ lãd of Canáan,
18 And take your father, and your housholdes, and come to me, and I wil giue
you the e best of the land of Egypt, and
ye shal eat of the f fat of the land.

e The moste plẽtiful groũde.
f The chiefest frutes & commodities.

19 And I commande thee, Thus do ye,
take you charets out of the land of E-
gypt for your children, and for your wiues, and bring your father and come.
20 Also " regard not your stuffe: for the
best of all the land of Egypt is yours.

"Ebr. let not your eie spare your vessels.

21 And the children of Israél did so: and
Ioséph gaue them charets according to
the commãdement of Pharaóh: he gaue
them vitaile also for the iourney.
22 He gaue thẽ all, none except, change of
raiment: but vnto Beniamín he gaue thre
hundreth pieces of siluer, & fiue sutes of
rayment.
23 And vnto his father "likewise he sent ten
he asses laden with the best things of E-
gypt, and ten she asses ladẽ with wheat, &
bread, & meat for his father by the way.

"Or, he sent asmuch to wit, siluer, as vers. 22. & ten asses.

24 So sent he his brethren away, and thei
departed: and he said vnto them, g Fall
not out by the way.

g Seing he had remitted the faute done toward him, he wolde not ẏ thei shulde accuse one another.

25 ¶ Then thei wẽt vp from Egypt, & came
vnto the land of Canáan vnto Iaakób
their father,
26 And tolde him, saying, Ioséph *is* yet a-
liue, and he also is gouerner ouer all the
lãd of Egypt, and *Iaakobs* heart h failed:
for he beleued them not.

h As one betwene hope & feare.

27 And thei tolde him all the wordes of
Ioséph, which he had said vnto them: but
when he sawe the charets, which Ioséph
had sent to cary him, then the spirit of
Iaakób their father reuiued.
28 And Israél said, *I haue* ynough: Ioséph
my sonne *is* yet aliue: I wil go and se him
yer I dye.

CHAP. XLVI.

1 God assureth Iaakób of his iourney into Egypt. 27 The nombre of his familie when he went into Egypt. 29 Ioséph meteth his father. 34 He teacheth his brethren what to answer to Pharaóh.

1 Then Israél toke his iourney with all
that he had, & came to Beer-shéba,
and a offred sacrifice vnto the God of his
father Izhák.

a Whereby he both signified, that he worshipped ẏ true God, and also that he kept in his heart ẏ possession of that land, frõ whẽce present necessitie droue him.

2 And God spake vnto Israél in a vision by
night, saying, Iaakób, Iaakób. Who answered, I am here.
3 Then he said, I am God, the God of thy
father, feare not to go downe into Egypt:
for

for I wil there make of thee a great nation.

b Conducting thee by my power.
c In thy posteritie.
d Shal shut thine eies when thou diest: w apperteined to him that was moste dearest or chief of the kinred.

4 I wil [b] go downe with thee into Egypt,
and I wil also [c] bring thee vp againe, and
Ioséph shal [d] put his hād vpō thine eies.
5 Then Iaakób rose vp from Beer-shéba:
and the sonnes of Israél caried Iaakób
their father, and their children, and their
wiues in the charets, which Pharaóh had
sent to cary him.
6 And thei toke their cattel & their goods,
which they had gotten in the land of Canáan, and came into Egypt, *bothe* * Iaakób
and all his sede with him,

Iosh.24,4. psal.105,23. isa.52,4.

7 His sonnes and his sonnes sonnes with
him, his daughters and his sonnes daughters, and all his sede broght he with him
into Egypt.
8 ¶ And these are the names of the children of Israél, which came into Egypt,
euen Iaakób & his sonnes: * Reubén, Iaakobs first borne.

Exod.1,2.and 6,14. nom.26,5. 1.chro.5,1.

9 And the sonnes of Reubén: Hanóch, and
Phallú, and Hezrón and Carmí.
10 ¶ And the sōnes of * Simeón: Iemuél, &
Iamín, and Ohad, and Iachín, & Zóhar,
& Shaúl ỹ sonne of a Canaanitish womā.

Exod.6,15. 1.chro.4,24.

11 ¶ Also ỹ sonnes of * Leuí: Gershón, Koháth and Merarí.

1.Chro.6,1.

12 ¶ Also the sonnes of * Iudáh: Er, and O-
nán, and Sheláh, and Phárez, and Zérah:
(but Er, and Onán dyed in ỹ land of Canáan) And the sonnes of Phárez *were*
Hezrón and Hamúl.

1.Chro.2,3. & 4,21. chap.38,3.

13 ¶ Also the sonnes of * Issachár: Tolá, &
Phuuáh, and Iob, and Shimrón.

1.Chro.7,1.

14 ¶ Also the sonnes of Zebulún: Séred, &
Elón, and Iahleél.
15 These be the sonnes of Leáh, which she
bare vnto Iaakób in Padán Arám, with
his daughter Dináh. All the " soules of his
sōnes & his daughters *were* thirty & thre.

" Or, persons.

16 ¶ Also the sonnes of Gad: Ziphión, and
Haggí, Shuní, and Ezbón, Erí, and Aro-
dí, and Arelí.
17 ¶ Also the sonnes of * Ashér: Iimnáh, &
Ishuáh and Isuí, and Beriáh, and Sérah
their sister. And the sonnes of Beriáh:
Héber, and Malchiél.

1.Chro.7,30.

18 These are ỹ childrē of Zilpáh, whome
Labán gaue to Leáh his daughter: & these she bare vnto Iaakób, *euē* sixtene soules.
19 The sonnes of Rahél Iaakobs wife *were* Ioséph, and Beniamín.
20 ¶ And vnto Ioséph in the lād of Egypt
were borne Manasséh, & Ephráim, which
* Asenáth the daughter of Poti-phérah
prince of On bare vnto him.

Chap.41,50.

21 ¶ Also ỹ sonnes of * Beniamín: Bélah, &
Bécher, & Ashbél, Gerá, and Naamán,
Ehí, & Rosh, Muppím, & Huppím, & Ard.

1.Chro.7,6. and 8,1.

22 These are the sonnes of Rahél, w were
borne vnto Iaakób, fourtene soules in all.
23 ¶ Also the sonnes of Dan: Hushím.
24 ¶ Also the sōnes of Nephtalí: Iahzeél,
and Guní, and Iézer, and Shillém.
25 These are the sonnes of Bilháh, ẇ Labán gaue vnto Rahél his daughter, & she
bare these to Iaakób, in all, seuē soules.
26 All the * soules, that came with Iaakób
into Egypt, which came out of his " loynes (beside Iaakobs sonnes wiues) *were* in
the whole, thre score and sixe soules.

Deut.10,22.
" Ebr. thighes.

27 Also the sonnes of Ioséph, which were
borne him ī Egypt, *were* two soules: *so that*
all the soules of ỹ house of Iaakób, which
came into Egypt, *are* seuentie.
28 ¶ Then he sent Iudáh before him vnto
Ioséph, to " direct his way vnto Góshen,
and they came into the land of Góshen.

" Or, to prepare him a place.

29 Then Ioséph " made ready his charet &
went vp to Góshen to mete Israél his father, and presented him selfe vnto him, &
fel on his necke, and wept vpon his necke
a " good while.

" Ebr. bounde his charet.
" Eb. yet, or still.

30 And Israél said vnto Ioséph, Now let
me dye, since I haue sene thy face, *and*
that thou art yet aliue.
31 Then Ioséph said to his brethren, and to
his fathers house, I wil go vp and shewe
Pharaóh, and tel him, My brethren and
my fathers house, which were in the land
of Canáan, are come vnto me,
32 And the men *are* [e] shepherdes, & because they are shepherdes, they haue broght
their shepe & their cattel, & all ỹ thei haue.

e He was not ashamed of his father and kinred, thogh thei were of basse cōdition.

33 And if Pharaóh call you, and aske you,
What is your trade?
34 Thē ye shal say, Thy seruants are men
occupied about cattel, frō our childhode
euen vnto this time, bothe we and our fathers: that ye may dwel in the lād of Góshen: for euerie shepekeper is an [f] abominacion vnto the Egyptians.

f God suffreth the worlde to hate his, that they may forsake the filth of ỹ worlde & cleaue to him.

CHAP. XLVII.

7 Iaakób commeth before Pharaóh, and telleth him his age 11 The land of Góshen is giuen him. 22 The idolatrous priests haue liuing of the King. 28 Iaakobs age, when he dyeth. 30 Ioséph sweareth to bury him with his fathers.

1 THen came Ioséph and tolde Pharaóh,
and said, My father, & my brethrē, &
their shepe, & their cattel, and all ỹ they
haue, are come out of the land of Canáan,
& beholde, they are in ỹ land of Góshen.
2 And Ioséph toke parte of his brethrē, *euē*
[a] fiue men, & presented thē vnto Pharaóh.
3 Thē Pharaóh said vnto his brethrē, What
is your trade? And thei answered Pharaóh,
Thy seruants *are* shepherdes, bothe we
and our fathers.

a That ỹ King might be assured they were come, and se what maner of people they were.

4 Thei said moreouer vnto Pharaóh, For
to soiourne in ỹ land are we come: for thy
seruāts haue no pasture for *their* shepe, so
sore is the famine in the land of Canáan.
Now therefore, we pray thee, let thy seruants dwel in the land of Góshen.

5 Then ſpake Pharaóh to Ioséph, ſaying,
Thy father and thy brethrẽ are come vnto thee.

b Iosephs great modeſtie appeareth in ỹ he wolde enterpriſe nothing without the Kings cõmandement.

6 The [b] land of Egypt is before thee: in ỹ
beſt place of the land make thy father and
thy brethren dwel: let them dwel in the
land of Góshen: and if thou knoweſt that
there be men of actiuitie among them,
make them rulers ouer my cattel.

"Ebr. bleſſed.

7 Ioséph alſo broght Iaakób his father, &
ſet him before Pharaóh. And Iaakób "ſaluted Pharaóh.

"Ebr. how many daies are the yeres of thy life?

8 Then Pharaóh ſaid vnto Iaakób," How
olde art thou?

Ebr. 11,9.

9 And Iaakób ſaid vnto Pharaóh, The whole time of my*pilgrimage *is* an hũdreth &
thirty yeres: fewe and euil haue the dayes
of my life bene, & I haue not atteined vnto the yeres of the life of my fathers, in ỹ
dayes of their pilgrimages.

"Ebr. bleſſed.

10 And Iaakób "toke leaue of Pharaóh,
& departed from ỹ preſence of Pharaóh.
11 ¶ And Ioséph placed his father, and his
brethren, and gaue them poſſeſsion in the
land of Egypt, in the beſt of the land, *e-
uen* in the land of [c] Rameſés, as Pharaóh
had commanded.

c Which was a citie in the contrey of Góſhẽ. Exod 1,11.

12 And Ioséph nouriſhed his father, and
his brethren, and all his fathers houſholde with bread, euen [d] to the yong children.

d Some read, that he fed thẽ as litle babes, becauſe they colde not prouide for them ſelues againſt that famine.

13 ¶ Now there was no bread in all the lãd:
for the famine *was* exceading ſore: ſo that
the land of Egypt & the land of Canáan
were famiſhed by the reaſon of ỹ famine.
14 And Ioséph gathered all the money, that
was foũde in the lãd of Egypt, and in the
land of Canáan, for the corne which they
boght, & [e] Ioséph laied vp the money in
Pharaohs houſe.

e Wherein he bothe declareth his fidelitie toward the King, and his minde fre frõ couetouſnes.

15 So when money failed in the land of E-
gypt, and in the land of Canáan, then all
the Egyptiãs came vnto Ioséph, and ſaid,
Giue vs bread: for why ſhulde we dye
before thee? for *our* money is ſpent.
16 Then ſaid Ioséph, Bring your cattel, &
I wil giue you for your cattel, if *your* money be ſpent.
17 So they broght their cattel vnto Ioséph,
& Ioséph gaue them bread for the horſes,
and for the flockes of ſhepe, and for the
herdes of cattel, and for the aſſes: ſo he fed
them with bread for all their cattel that
yere.
18 But when the yere was ended, they came
vnto him the next yere, & ſaid vnto him,
We wil not hide from my lord, that ſince
our money is ſpent, & my lord hathe the
herdes of the cattel, there is nothing left
in the ſight of my lord, but our bodies &
our grounde.

f For except the groũde be tilled & ſowẽ, it periſheth & is, as it were dead.

19 Why ſhal we periſh in thy ſight, bothe
we, and our [f] land? bye vs and our lãd for
bread, and we and our land wil be bonde
to Pharaóh: therefore giue vs ſede, ỹ we
may liue and not dye, and that the land go
not to waſte.
20 So Ioséph boght all the lãd of Egypt for
Pharaóh: for ỹ Egyptians ſolde euerie mã
his grounde becauſe the famine was ſore
vpon them: ſo the land became Pharaohs.
21 And he [g] remoued the people vnto the
cities," from one ſide of Egypt euen to
the other.

g By this chãging they ſignified ỹ they had nothing of their owne, but receiued all of the Kings liberalitie

"Ebr. ende of the border.

22 Onely the land of the Prieſtes boght
he not: for the Prieſtes had an ordinarie
of Pharaóh, and they did eat their ordinarie, which Pharaóh gaue thẽ: wherefore they ſolde not their grounde.
23 Then Ioséph ſaid vnto the people, Beholde, I haue boght you this day and your
land for Pharaóh: lo, *here is* ſede for you:
ſowe therefore the grounde.
24 And of the encreaſe ye ſhal giue the fift
parte vnto Pharaóh, and foure partes ſhal
be yours for the ſede of the field, and for
your meat, and for them of your houſholdes, and for your children to eat.
25 Then they anſwered, Thou haſt ſaued
our liues: let vs finde grace in the ſight
of my lord, & we wil be Pharaohs ſeruãts.
26 Then Ioséph made it a lawe ouer the
land of Egypt vnto this day, that Pharaóh
ſhulde haue the fift *parte*, [h] except the land
of the Prieſtes onely, ẇ was not Pharaohs.

h Pharaóh in prouiding for idolatrous prieſts, ſhalbe a condemnation to all them ẇ neglect ỹ true miniſters of Gods worde.

27 ¶ And Iſraél dwelt in the lãd of Egypt,
in the countrey of Góshen: and they had
their poſſeſsions therein, and grewe and
multiplied exceadingly.
28 Moreouer, Iaakób liued in the land of
Egypt ſeuentene yeres, ſo that the whole
age of Iaakób *was* an hundreth fourtie &
ſeuen yere.
29 Now when the time drewe nere ỹ Iſraél
muſt dye, he called his ſonne Ioséph, and
ſaid vnto him, If I haue now foũde grace
in thy ſight, put thine hãd vnder my
thigh, and deale mercifully and truely ẇ
me: bury me not, I pray thee, in Egypt,
30 But when I ſhal [i] ſlepe with my fathers,
thou ſhalt cary me out of Egypt, and bury me in their burial. And he anſwered, I
wil do as thou haſt ſaid.
31 Then he ſaid, Sweare vnto me. And he
ſware vnto him. And Iſráel [k] worſhipped
toward the beds head.

i Hereby he proteſted ỹ he died in ỹ faith of his fathers, teaching his childrẽ to hope for the promiſed land.

k He reioyced ỹ Ioséph had promiſed him, & ſetting him ſelfe vp vpon his pillowe, praiſed God, read 1. Chro. 29.10.

CHAP. XLVIII.

1 Ioséph with his two ſonnes viſiteth his ſicke father. 3. Iaakób rehearſeth Gods promes. 5 He receiueth Ioſéphs ſonnes as his. 19 He preferreth the yonger. 21 He prophecieth their returne to Canáan.

1 AGaine after this, one ſaid to Ioséph,
Lo, thy father is ſicke: then he toke ẇ
hĩ his [a] two ſonnes, Manaſſéh & Ephráim.
2 Alſo one tolde Iaakób, & ſaid, Beholde,
thy ſonne Ioséph is come to thee, and Iſraél

a Ioséph more eſtemeth ỹ his childrẽ ſhulde be receiued into Iaakobs familie ẇ was ỹ Church of God, then to enioye all the treaſors of Egypt.

raél toke his ſtrength vnto him and ſate
vpon the bed.
3 Then Iaakób ſaid vnto Ioséph, God"almightie appeared vnto me at *Luz in the
land of Canáan,and bleſſed me.

"Or, all ſufficiẽt.

Chap.28,13.

4 And he ſaid vnto me,Beholde,I wil make thee fruteful,and wil multiplie thee,&
wil make a great *nombre of people of
thee,and wil giue this land vnto thy ſede
after thee for an [b] euerlaſting poſſeſsion.

Chap.41,50. ioſh.13,7.

b Which is true in ẏ carnal Iſraél vnto the cōming of Chriſt, and in the ſpiritual for euer.

5 ¶And now thy two ſonnes, Manaſſéh &
Ephráim, which are borne vnto thee in ẏ
land of Egypt,before I came to thee into
Egypt,ſhalbe mine, as Reubén and Simeón are mine.
6 But thy lignage, which thou haſt begotten after them, ſhalbe thine: they ſhalbe
called after the names of their brethrẽ in
their enheritance.
7 Now whẽ I came frõ Padán, Rahél*dyed
vpon mine hãd in the land of Canáan, by
the way when *there was* but halfe a daies
iourney of grounde to come to Ephráth:
and I buryed her there in the way to E-
phráth: the ſame *is* Beth-léhem.

Chap.35,19.

8 Then Iſraél behelde Iosephs ſonnes and
ſaid, Whoſe are theſe?
9 And Ioséph ſaid vnto his father, Thei are
my ſõnes,which [c] God hathe giuẽ me here. then he ſaid,I pray thee,bring them to
me, that I may bleſſe them:

c The faithful acknowledge all benefits to come of Gods fre mercies.

10 (For the eies of Iſraél were dim for age,
ſo that he colde not *wel* ſe) Then he cauſed
them to come to him,and he kiſſed them
and embraced them.
11 And Iſraél ſaid vnto Ioséph, I had not
thoght to haue ſene thy face: yet lo, God
hathe ſhewed me alſo thy ſede.
12 And Ioséph toke thẽ away frõ his knees,
and did reuerence"downe to the ground.

"Ebr. his face to the grounde.

13 Then toke Ioséph them bothe, Ephraim
in his right hand toward Iſraels left hãd,
and Manaſſéh in his left hand toward Iſraels right hãd, ſo he broght *thẽ* vnto hĩ.
14 But Iſraél ſtretched out his right hand,
and laid it on [d] Ephraims head,which was
the yonger, and his left hand vpon Manaſſehs head (directing his hands of purpoſe) for Manaſſéh *was* the elder.

d Gods iudgement is oft times contrary to mans, & he preferreth ẏ, which man deſpiſeth.

Ebr.11,21.

15 ¶*Alſo he bleſſed Ioséph and ſaid, The
God, before whome my fathers Abrahám
and Izhák did walke, the God, which hathe fed me all my life long vnto this day,
bleſſe thee.
16 The [e] Angel,which hathe deliuered me
from all euil, bleſſe the children,and let
my [f] name be named vpon them, and the
name of my fathers Abrahám and Izhák,
that they may growe as fiſh into a multitude in the middes of the earth.

e This Angel muſt be vnderſtãd of Chriſt, as chap.31,13. & 32,1.

f Let them be taken as my children.

17 But whẽ Ioséph ſawe that his father laid
his right hãd vpõ the head of Ephráim, it
[g] diſpleaſed him: and he ſtayed his fathers
hand to remoue it from Ephraims head
to Manaſſehs head.

g Ioséph faileth in bindĩg Gods grace to the ordre of nature.

18 And Ioséph ſaid vnto his father, Not ſo
my father, for this is ẏ eldeſt: put thy right
hand vpon his head.
19 But his father refuſed, and ſaid, I knowe
wel, my ſonne, I knowe wel: he ſhalbe alſo
a people, & he ſhalbe great likewiſe: but
his yonger brother ſhalbe greater thẽ he,
and his ſede ſhalbe ful of nations.
20 So he bleſſed them that day, and ſaid, In
thee Iſraél ſhal bleſſe, and ſay, God make
thee as [h] Ephráim and as Manaſſéh. & he
ſet Ephráim before Manaſſéh.

h In whome Gods graces ſhulde manifeſtly appeare.

21 Then Iſraél ſaid vnto Ioséph, Beholde,
I dye, and God ſhalbe with you, & bring
you againe vnto the land of [i] your fathers.
22 Moreouer, I haue giuen vnto thee one
porcion aboue thy brethrẽ, which [k] I gate
out of the hand of the Amorite by my
ſworde & by my bowe.

i Which they had by faith in the promes.

k By my children, whome God ſpared for my ſake.

CHAP. XLIX.

1 Iaakób bleſſeth all his ſonnes by name, and ſheweth them what is to come. 29 He wil be buryed with his fathers. 33 He dyeth.

1 THen Iaakób called his ſonnes, & ſaid,
Gather your ſelues together, that I
may tel you what ſhal come to you in the
[a] laſt daies.

a When God ſhal bring you out of Egypt.

2 Gather your ſelues together, & heare, ye
ſonnes of Iaakób, & hearken vnto Iſraél
your father.
3 ¶Reubén mine eldeſt ſonne, thou art my
[b] might, & the beginning of my ſtrength,
[c] the excellencie of dignitie, & the excellencie of power.

b Begotten in my youthe.

c If thou hadeſt not loſt thy birthright by thine offence.

4 *Thou waſt* light as water: thou ſhalt not
be excellent, becauſe thou wenteſt vp to
thy fathers bed: then dideſt thou defile
my bed, *thy dignitie* is gone.
5 ¶Simeón and Leuí, brethrẽ *in euil*, the"inſtrumẽts of crueltie are in their habitaciõs.

"Or, their ſwerdes were inſtrumẽts of violẽce.

6 Into their ſecret let not my ſoule come: my [d] glorie, be not thou ioyned with
their aſſemblie: for in their wrath they
ſlewe a [e] man, and in their ſelfewil they
digged downe a wall.

d Or tongue: meaning that he nether conſented to thẽ in worde nor thoght.

e The Sheche mites. chap. 34.26.

7 Curſed be their wrath, for it was fearce,
& their rage, for it was cruel: I wil [f] diuide them in Iaakób, & ſcater thẽ in Iſraél.

f For Leuí had no parte, & Simeón was vnder Iudáh. Ioſ. 19,1, til God gaue them the place of the Amalechites. 1.Chro.4,43.

8 ¶Thou Iudáh, thy brethren ſhal praiſe
thee: thine hãd *ſhalbe* in ẏ necke of thine
ennemies: thy fathers ſonnes ſhal [g] bowe
downe vnto thee.

g As was verified in Dauid and Chriſt.

9 Iudáh, *as* a lions whelpe ſhalt thou come
vp from the ſpoile, my ſonne. He ſhal lie
downe *&* couche as a lion, & as a lioneſſe.
[h] Who ſhal ſter him vp?

h His ennemies ſhal ſo feare him.

10 The"ſceptre ſhal not departe from Iudáh, nor a lawgiuer from betwene his fete, vntil [i] Shilóh come, and the people *ſhal*
be gathered vnto him.

"Or, Kingdome.

i Which is Chriſt the Meſſias, the geuer of all proſperitie: who ſhal call the Gentiles to ſaluation.

11 He ſhal binde his aſſe fole vnto the

k A cōtrey moste abundant with vines and pastures is promised him.

[k] vine, & his asses colte vnto the best vine.
he shal wash his garment in wine, and his
cloke in the blood of grapes.
12 His eies *shalbe* red with wine, and his tethe white with milke.
13 ¶ Zebulún shal dwel by the sea side, & he
shalbe an hauen for shippes: his border *shal*
be vnto Zidón.

"Ebr. As asse of great bones.
l His force shalbe great, but he shal want courage to resist his enemies.

14 Issachár *shalbe* " [l] a strong asse, couching
downe betwene two burdens:
15 And he shal se that rest is good, and that
the land is pleasant, and he shal bowe his
shulder to beare, and shalbe subiect vnto
tribute.

m Shal haue ye honour of a tribe.
n That is, ful of subteltie.

16 ¶ Dan [m] shal iudge his people as one of
the tribes of Israél.
17 Dan shalbe a [n] serpēt by the way, an adder by the path, byting the horse heles, so
that his ryder shal fall backwarde.

o Seing ye miseries that his posteritie shulde fall into, he brasteth out in praier to God to remedie it.
p He shal abūde in corne & pleasāt frutes.
q Ouercomig more by faire wordes then by force.
"Ebr. a sonne of increase.
"Ebr. daughters
r As his brethren, Potiphár, and others.

18 [o] O Lord, I haue waited for thy saluacion.
19 ¶ Gad, an host of mē shal ouercome him,
but he shal ouercome at the last.
20 Cōcerning Ashér, his [p] bread *shalbe* fat,
and he shal giue pleasures for a King.
21 ¶ Naphtalí *shalbe* a hinde let go, giuing
[q] goodlie wordes.
22 ¶ Ioséph *shalbe* " a fruteful bough, *euen* a
fruteful bough by the well side: the " smale
boughes shal runne vpon the wall.
23 [r] And the archers grieued him, and shot
against him, and hated him.
24 But his bowe abode strong, and the hādes of his armes were strengthened, by
the hāds of the mightie *God* of Iaakób, of
whome *was* the feeder *appointed by* the [f] sto
ne of Israél,

f That is, God.

25 *Euen* by the God of thy father, who shal
helpe thee, & by the almightie, who shal
blesse thee with heauenlie blessings frō
aboue, with blessings of ye depe, that lieth
beneath, with blessings of the brests, & of
the wombe.

t In as muche as he was more nere to ye accomplishment of the promes, & it had bene more often cōfirmed.
u Ether in dignitie, or whē he was solde from his brethren.

26 The blessings of thy father shalbe [t] strē-
ger thē the blessings of mine elders: vnto
the end of the hilles of the worlde they
shalbe on the head of Ioséph, and on the
toppe of the head of him that was [u] separ-
rat from his brethren.
27 ¶ Beniamín shal rauine *as* a wolfe: in the
morning he shal deuoure the praie, and
at night he shal diuide the spoile.
28 ¶ All these are the twelue tribes of Israél, and thus their father spake vnto thē,
and blessed them: euerie one of them blessed he with a seueral blessing.
29 And he charged them & said vnto thē, I
am ready to be gathered vnto my people:
*bury me with my fathers in the caue that
is in the field of Ephrón the Hittite,

Chap. 47, 30.

30 In the caue that is in the field of Machpeláh besides Mamré in the land of Canáan: which *caue* Abrahám boght wt the
field of Ephrón the Hittite for a possession to bury in.
31 There thei buryed Abrahám and Saráh
his wife: there thei buryed Izhák & Rebekáh his wife: and there I buryed Leáh.
32 The purchase of the field & the caue yt
is therein, *was boght* of ye childrē of Heth.
33 Thus Iaakób made an end of giuing
charge to his sonnes, and [x] plucked vp his
fete into the bed and gaue vp the gost, &
was gathered to his people.

x Whereby is signified how quietly he dyed.

CHAP. L.

12 Iaakób is buryed. 19 Ioséph forgiueth his brethren. 23 He seeth his childrens children. 25 He dyeth.

1 THen Ioséph fel vpon his fathers face
and wept vpon him, and kissed him.
2 And Ioséph commanded his seruantes
the [a] phisicions, to enbaume his father, &
the phisicions enbaumed Israél.

a He meaneth thē ye enbaumed the dead & buryed thē.

3 So fourty daies were accōplished (for so
long did the daies of them that were enbaumed last) and the Egyptiās bewailed
him [b] seuenty daies.
4 And when the daies of his mourning
were past, Ioséph spake to the house of
Pharaóh, saying, If I haue now founde
fauour in your eies, speak, I pray you, in ye
eares of Pharaóh, and say,

b They were more excessiue in lamēting thē ye faithful.

5 My father made me * sweare, saying, Lo,
I dye, bury me in my graue, which I haue
made me in the lād of Canáan: now therefore let me go, I praie thee, & bury my
father and I wil come againe.

Chap. 47, 29.

6 Thē Pharaóh said, Go vp and bury thy
father, [c] as he made thee to sweare.
7 ¶ So Ioséph went vp to bury his father,
and with him went all the seruantes of
Pharaóh, *bothe* the elders of his house and
all the elders of the land of Egypt.

c The very infideles wolde haue othes performed.

8 Likewise all the house of Ioséph, and his
brethren, and his fathers house: onely
their children, and their shepe, and their
cattel left they in the land of Góshen.
9 And there went vp with him bothe charets and horsemen: and they were an exceading great companie.
10 And they came to " Góren Atád, which
is beyonde Iordén, and there they made
a great and exceading sore lamentacion:
and he mourned for his father seuē daies.

"Or, the corne floore of Atad.

11 And whē the Canaanites the inhabitāts
of the land sawe the mourning in Góren
Atád, they said, This is a great mourning
vnto the Egyptians: wherefore the name
thereof was called " Abél Mizráim, which
is beyonde Iordén.

"Or, the lamentation of the Egyptians.

12 So his sonnes did vnto him according
as he had commanded them:
13 *For his sonnes caried him into the land
of Canáan, & buryed him in the caue of
the field of Machpeláh, wc *caue* * Abrahám
boght with ye field, to be " a place to bury
in, of Ephrón ye Hittite besides Mamré.

Act. 7, 16.
Chap. 23, 16.
"Or, a possession.

14 ¶ Then

14 ¶ Then Iosēph returned into Egypt, he
and his brethren, & all that went vp with
him to bury his father, after that he had
buryed his father.
15 And whē Iosephs brethrē sawe that their
father was dead, they said, [d] It may be yͭ
Iosēph wil hate vs, and wil paye vs againe
all the euil, which we did vnto him.
16 Therefore they sent vnto Iosēph, sayīg,
Thy father commanded before his death,
saying,
17 Thus shal ye say vnto Iosēph, Forgiue
now, I pray thee, yͤ trespace of thy brethrē,
and their sinne: for they rewarded thee e-
uil. And now, we pray thee, forgiue yͤ trespace of the seruants of thy fathers [e] God.
And Iosēph wept, when "they spake vnto him.
18 Also his brethrē came vnto him, and fel
downe before his face, & said, Beholde, we
be thy seruantes.
19 To whome Iosēph said, Feare not: for am
not I vnder [f] God?
20 When ye thoght euil against me, God

d An euil conscience is neuer fully at rest.

e Meaning, yͭ they which haue one God, shulde be ioyned in moste sure loue.

"Or, *the messengers.*

f Who by the good successe semeth to remit it, & therefore it oght not to be reuēged by me.

disposed it to good, that he might bring
to passe, as it is this day, and saue muche
people aliue.
21 Feare not now therefore, I wil nourish
you, and your children: and he comforted
them, and spake "kindely vnto them.
22 ¶ So Iosēph dwelt in Egypt, he, and his
fathers house: and Iosēph liued an [g] hundreth and ten yere.
23 And Iosēph sawe Ephraims children,
euen vnto the third generacion: also the
sonnes of Machír the sonne of Manasséh
were broght vp on Iosephs knees.
24 And Iosēph said vnto his brethrē, *I am
ready to dye, & God wil surely viset you,
and bring you out of this land vnto the
land, which he sware vnto Abrahám, vnto
Izhák, and vnto Iaakób.
25 And Iosēph toke an othe of the childrē
of Israél, saying, [h] God wil surely viset
you, and ye shal cary my bones hence.
26 So Iosēph dyed, when he was an hundreth and ten yere olde: and they enbaumed him & put him in a chest in Egypt.

"*Ebr. to their heart.*

g Who, notwithstādīg he bare rule in Egypt about foure score yeres, yet was ioyned with yͤ Church of God in faith and religion.

Ebr.11,22.

h He speaketh this by the spirit of prophecie, exhorting his brethren, to haue ful trust in Gods promes for their deliuerauce.

THE SECONDE BOKE of Mosés, called Exodus.

THE ARGUMENT.

AFTER *that Iaakób by Gods commandemēt Gen. 46,3. had broght his familie into Egypt, where they remained for the space of foure hundreth yeres, and of seuenty persones grewe to an infinite nombre, so that the King and the countrey grudged and endeuored bothe by tyrannie and cruel slauery to suppresse them: the Lord according to his promes Gen. 15,14. had compassion of his Church & deliuered them, but plagued their ennemies in moste strāge and sondry sortes. And the more that the tyrānie of the wicked enraged against his Church, the more did his heauy iudgements increase against them, til Pharaóh & his armie were drowned in the same Sea, which gaue an entrie and passage to the childrē of God. But as the ingratitude of man is great, so did they immediatly forget Gods wōderful benefites: & albeit he had giuen them the Passeouer to be a signe & memorial of the same, yet they fel to distrust, & tempted God with sondry murmurings and grudgings against him and his ministers: sometime moued with ambitiō, sometime for lacke of drincke or meate to cōtent their lustes, sometime by idolatrie, or suche like. Wherfore God visited them with sharpe roddes and plagues that by his corrections they might seke to him for remedy against his scourges & earnestly repent them for their rebelliōs & wickednes. And because God loueth thē to the end, whome he hathe once begōne to loue, he punished thē not according to their desertes, but dealt with them in great mercies, and euer with newe benefites labored to ouercome their malice: for he stil gouerned them and gaue thē his worde & Law, bothe cōcerning the maner of seruing him, & also the forme of iudgements and ciuil policie: to the intent that thei shoulde not serue God after their owne inuentions, but according to that ordre, which his heauenlie wisdome had appointed.*

CHAP. I.

2 The childrē of Iaakób that came into Egypt. 8 The newe Pharaóh oppresseth them. 12 The prouidence of God towarde them. 15 The Kings cōmandemēt to the midwiues. 22 The sonnes of the Ebrewes are commanded to be cast into the riuer.

1 NOw [a] these are yͤ names
of yͤ childrē of Israél, wͨ
came ī to Egypt (euerie
man and his housholde
came *thither* wͭ Iaakób)
2 Reubén, Simeón, Leuí,
and Iudáh,
3 Issachár, Zebulún, and Beniamín,

a Moses describeth the wonderful ordre that God obserueth in performing his promes to Abrahám, Gen. 15, 14.

4 Dan, & Naphthalí, Gad, & Ashér.
5 So all yͤ "soules, that came out of yͤ loynes of Iaakób, were *seuētie soules: Iosēph
was in Egypt already.
6 Now Iosēph dyed and all his brethrē, &
that whole generacion.
7 ¶ And the *children of Israél broght
forthe frute and encreased in abundance,
& were multiplied, and were exceading
mightie, so that the [b] lād was ful of them.
8 Then there rose vp a newe King in E-
gypt, who [c] knewe not Iosēph.
9 And he said vnto his people, Beholde, the

"*Or, persones.*

Gen. 46,28. deu. 10,22.

Act. 7,17.

b He meaneth the coūtrey of Góshen.

c He considered not how God had preserued Egypt for Iosephs sake.

people of the children of Iſraél *are* greater and mightier then we.
10 Come,let vs worke wiſely with thẽ, leſt
they multiplie,and it come to paſſe,that if
there be warre,they ioyne them ſelues alſo vnto our ennemies , & fight againſt vs,
and [d] get them out of the land.

d In to Canáan, and ſo we ſhal loſe our commoditie.

11 Therefore did they ſet taſkemaſters o-
uer them, to kepe them vnder with burdens : and they buylt the cities Pithóm &
Raamſés for the "treaſures of Pharaóh.

Or, corne and prouiſion.

12 But the more they vexed them, the more they multiplied and grewe : therefore
[e] they were more grieued againſt the children of Iſraél.

e The more that God bleſſeth his, the more doeth ẏ wicked inuie them.

13 Wherefore the Egyptians by crueltie
cauſed the children of Iſraél to ſerue.
14 Thus they made them weary of their liues by ſore labour in claye and in bricke,
and in all worke in the field , with all maner of bondage," which they laied vpon
them moſte cruelly.

"Ebr wherwith thei ſerued thẽ ſelues of them by crueltie.

15 ¶Moreouer the King of Egypt cõmanded the midwiues of the Ebrewe women,
(of which the ones name was [f] Shiphráh,
and the name of the other Puáh)

f Theſe ſeme to haue bene the chief of ẏ reſt.

16 And ſaid , When ye do the office of a
midwife to the women of the Ebrewes &
ſe them on their "ſtolles , if it be a ſonne,
thẽ ye ſhal kil him:but if it be a daughter,
then let her liue.

"Or, ſeates wher vpon they ſate in trauel.

17 Notwithſtanding the midwiues feared
God,& did not as the King of Egypt cõmanded them, but preſerued aliue the mẽ
children.
18 Then the King of Egypt called for the
midwiues,& ſaid vnto thẽ, Why haue ye
done thus , and haue preſerued aliue the
men children?
19 And the midwiues anſwered Pharaóh,
Becauſe the Ebrewe [g] womẽ *are* not as the
women of Egypt:for they are liuelie,and
are deliuered yer ẏ midwife come at thẽ.

g Their diſobediẽce herein was lawful, but their diſſembling euil.

20 God therefore proſpered the midwiues,
and the people multiplied & were very
mightie.
21 And becauſe the midwiues feared God,
therefore he [h] made them houſes.

h That is,God increaſed the families of ẏ Iſraelites by their meanes.

22 Then Pharaóh charged all his people,
ſaying , Euerie man childe that is borne,
[i] caſt ye into the riuer, but reſerue euerie
maidchilde aliue.

i When tyrãts can not preuaile by craft, thei braſt forthe into open rage.

CHAP. II.

2 Moſes is borne and caſt into the flagges. 5 He is taken vp of Pharaohs daughter & kept. 12 He killeth the Egyptian. 15 He fleeth and marieth a wife. 23 The Iſraelites crye vnto the Lord.

1 THen there went a [a] man of the houſe
of Leuí,& toke *to wife* a daughter of
Leuí,

a This Leuite was called Amrám , who maried Iochabéd,cha.6,20.

2 And the woman conceiued & bare a ſonne:& whẽ ſhe ſawe that he was faire, * ſhe
hid him thre moneths.

Act 7,20. hebr.11,23.

3 But when ſhe colde no longer hide him,
ſhe toke for him an arke *made* of rede,and
daubed it ẇ ſlime & with pitch, & [b] laid
the childe therein,& put *it* among ẏ bulruſhes by the riuer brinke.

b Committing hĩ to ẏ prouidence of God, whome ſhe colde not kepe from the rage of ẏ tyrãt.

4 Now his ſiſter ſtode a far of,to wit what
wolde come of him.
5 ¶Then the daughter of Pharaóh came
downe to waſh her in the riuer , and her
maidens walked by the riuers ſide: & whẽ
ſhe ſawe the arke among the bulruſhes,
ſhe ſent her maid to fet it.
7 Then ſhe opened it , and ſawe it was a
childe:and beholde,the babe wept : ſo ſhe
had compaſsion on it,and ſaid, This is one
of the Ebrewes children.
7 Thẽ ſaid his ſiſter vnto Pharaohs daughter, Shal I go & call vnto thee a nurce of
the Ebrewe womẽ to nurce thee ẏ childe?
8 And Pharaohs daughter ſaid to her, Go.
So the maid went and called the [c] childes
mother.

c Mans cõſel cã not hindre that , which God hathe determined ſhal come to paſſe.

9 To whome Pharaohs daughter ſaid, Take this childe away , and nurce it for me,
& I wil rewarde thee. Thẽ the woman toke the childe and nurced him.
10 Now the childe grewe, and ſhe broght
him vnto Pharaohs daughter , & he was
as her ſonne, and ſhe called his name Moſés,becauſe, ſaid ſhe, I drewe him out of
the water.
11 ¶And in thoſe dayes , when Moſés was
[d] growẽ, he went forthe vnto his brethrẽ,
and loked on their burdens : alſo he ſawe
an Egyptiã ſmiting an Ebrewe one of his
brethren.

d That is,was fourtie yere olde , Act.7,23.

12 And he loked " rounde about, & whẽ he
ſawe no man,he [e] ſlew the Egyptian , and
hid him in the ſand.

"Ebr. thus & thus.

e Beĩg aſſured that God had appoĩted him to deliuer the Iſraelites, Act.7,25.

13 Againe he came forthe the ſeconde day,
and beholde, two Ebrewes ſtroue:and he
ſaid vnto him that did the wrõg, Wherefore ſmiteſt thou thy felowe?
14 And he anſwered, Who made thee a mã
of autoritie & a iudge ouer vs ? Thinkeſt
thou to kil me, as thou killedſt the Egyptian? Then Moſés [f] feared and ſaid, Cer-
tenly this thing is knowen.

f Thogh by his feare he ſhewed his infirmitie, yet faith couered it.Ebr.11,27.

15 Now Pharaóh heard this matter , and
ſoght to ſlay Moſés:therefore Moſés fled
from Pharaóh , & dwelt in the lãd of Midián,and he ſate downe by a well.
16 And ẏ "Prieſt of Midiã had ſeuẽ daughters,which came and drewe *water*, and filled the troghes, for to watter their fathers ſhepe.

"Or, prince.

17 Then the ſhepherdes came and droue
them away: but Moſés roſe vp & "defended them,and wattered their ſhepe.

"Ebr ſaued thẽ.

18 And when they came to Reuél their "father,he ſaid , How are ye come ſo ſone to
day?

"Or, grande father.

19 And they ſaid, A man of Egypt deliuered

red vs from the hand of the shepherdes,
& also drewe vs water ynough, and wattered the shepe.
20 Then he said vnto his daughters, And
where is he? why haue ye so left the man?
[g] call him that he may eat bread.
21 And Mosés agreed to dwel with the
mã: who gaue vnto Mosés Zipporáh his
daughter:
22 And she bare a sonne, * whose name he
called Gershóm: for he said, I haue bene a
stranger in a strange land.
23 ¶ Then in processe of time, the King of
Egypt dyed, & the childrẽ of Israél sighed for the bondage and [h] cryed: & their
crye for the bondage came vp vnto God.
24 Then God heard their mone, and God
remembred his couenant with Abrahám,
Izhák, and Iaakób.
25 So God loked vpon the children of Israél, and God [i] had respect vnto them.

g Wherein he declared a thankful minde, ȳ wolde recompence ȳ benefite done vnto his.

Chap. 18,3.

h God humbleth his by afflictiõs, that thei shulde crye vnto hĩ, & receiue the frute of his promes.

i He iudged their cause: or, acknowledged thẽ to be his.

CHAP. III.

1 Mosés kepeth shepe, and God appeareth vnto him in a bushe. 10 He sendeth him to deliuer the children of Israél. 14 The name of God. 16 God teacheth him what to do.

1 WHen Mosés kept the shepe of Iethró his father in lawe, Priest of
Midian, & droue the flocke to the" backe
side of the desert, and came to the [a] Mountaine of God, [b] Horéb,
2 Then the Angel of the Lord appeared
vnto him in a flame of fyre, out of the
middes of a [c] bushe: & he loked, & beholde, the bushe burned with fyre, and the
bushe was not consumed.
3 Therefore Mosés said, I wil turne aside
now, & se this great sight, why the bushe
burneth not.
4 And when the [d] Lord saw that he turned
aside to se, God called vnto him out of
the middes of the bushe, and said, Mosés,
Mosés. And he answered, I am here.
5 Then he said, Come not hither, [e] put thy
shooes of thy fete: for the place whereon
thou standest is [f] holy grounde.
6 Moreouer he said, * I am the God of thy
father, the God of Abrahám, the God of
Izhák, & the God of Iaakób. Then Mosés hid his face: for he was [g] afraied to loke vpon God.
7 ¶ Then the Lord said, I haue surely sene
the trouble of my people, which are in
Egypt, & haue heard their crye, because
of their [h] taskemasters: for I knowe their
sorowes.
8 Therefore I am come downe to deliuer
them out of the hand of the Egyptians,
and to bring them out of that land into a
good lãd & a large, into a lãd that [i] floweth with milke & hony, *euen* into the place of the Canaanites, and the Hittites, &
the Amorites, and the Perizzites, and the

"Or, far with in the desert.

a It was so called after ȳ Lawe was giuẽ

b Called also Sinái.

c This signifieth that the Church is not consumed by ȳ fier of afflictiõs, because God is in the middes therof.

d Whome he called the Angel, vers 2.

e Resigne thy selfe vp to me, Ruth. 4,7. iosh. 5,15.

f Because of my presence.

Mat. 22,32. act. 7,32.

g For sinne causeth man to feare Gods iustice.

h Whose crueltie was intollerable.

i Moste plentiful of all things.

Hiuites, and the Iebusites.
9 [k] And now lo, the crye of the children
of Israél is come vnto me, and I haue also
sene the oppresion, wherewith the Egyptians oppresse them.
10 Come now therefore, and I wil send
thee vnto Pharaóh, that thou maiest brĩg
my people the children of Israél out of
Egypt.
11 ¶ But Mosés said vnto God, Who am [l] I,
that I shulde go vnto Pharaóh, and that
I shulde bring the children of Israél out
of Egypt?
12 And he answered, [m] Certeinly I wil be
with thee: & this shalbe a tokẽ vnto thee,
that I haue sét thee, After that thou haste
broght the people out of Egypt, ye shal
serue God vpon this Mountaine.
13 Then Mosés said vnto God, Beholde,
when I shal come vnto the children of Israél, and shal say vnto them, The God of
your fathers hathe sent me vnto you: if
thei say vnto me, What is his Name? what
answere shal I giue them?
14 And God answered Mosés, I [n] AM
THAT I AM. Also he said, Thus
shalt thou say vnto the children of Isaaél,
I AM hathe sent me vnto you.
15 And God spake further vnto Mosés,
Thus shalt thou say vnto the children of
Israél, The Lord God of your fathers,
the God of Abrahám, the God of Izhák,
and the God of Iaakób hathe sent me vnto you: this is my Name for euer, & this
is my memorial vnto all ages.
16 Go and gather the Elders of Israél together, & thou shalt say vnto them, The
Lord God of your fathers, ȳ God of A-
brahám, Izhák, & Iaakób appeared vnto
me, & said," I haue surely remẽbred you,
& that which is done to you in Egypt.
17 Therefore I did say, I wil bring you
out of the affliction of Egypt vnto the
land of the Canaanites, and the Hittites,
and the Amorites, and the Perizzites, &
the Hiuites, and the Iebusites, vnto a land
that floweth with milke and hony.
18 Then shal thei obeie thy voyce, & thou
and the Elders of Israél shal go vnto the
King of Egypt, and saie vnto him, The
Lord God of the Ebrewes hathe" met w
vs: we pray thee now therefore, let vs go
thre dayes iourney in the wildernes, that
we may [o] sacrifice vnto ȳ Lord our God.
19 ¶ But I knowe, that the King of Egypt
wil not let you go, but by strong hand.
20 Therefore wil I stretch out mine hãd
and smite Egypt with all my wonders, ȳ
I wil do in the middes thereof: and after
that shal he let you go.
21 And I wil make this people to be fauored of the Egyptians: so that when ye go,
ye shal not go emptie.

k He heard before, but now he wolde reuenge it.

l He doeth not fully disobey God, but acknowledgeth his owne weakenes.

m Nether feare thine owne weakenes, nor Pharaohs tyrannie.

n The God ȳ haue euer bene, am & shalbe: ȳ God almightie, by whome all things haue their being, & ȳ God of mercie mindeful of my promes, Reuel 1,4.

"Ebr. in visiting haue visited.

"Or, appeared vnto vs.

o Because Egypt was ful of idolatrie, God wolde appoint them a place where they shulde serue him purely.

p This exãple may not be followed generally: though at Gods cõmandemẽt thei did it iustly, receiuing some recompence of their labours.
" Or, in whose house she soiourneth.

22 p For euerie woman shal aske of her
neighbour, and of her " that soiourneth in
her house, iewels of siluer and iewels of
golde & raiment, & ye shal put them on
your sonnes, and on your daughters, and
shal spoile the Egyptians.

CHAP. IIII.

3 *Mosés rod is turned into a serpẽt. 6 His hand is leprous.*
9 The water of the riuer is turned into blood. 14 Aa-
rón is giuen to helpe Mosés. 21 God hardeneth Pha-
raóh. 25 His wife circũciseth her sonne. 27 Aarón me-
teth with Mosés, and thei come to the Israelites and
are beleued.

a God beareth with Mosés doutĩg, because he was not al together without faith.

1 THen Mosés answered, and said, a But
lo, thei wil not beleue me, nor hearken vnto my voyce: for thei wil say, The
Lord hathe not appeared vnto thee.
2 And the Lord said vnto him, What is
ỹ in thine hãd? And he answered, A rod.
3 Then said he, Cast it on the grounde. So
he cast it on the grounde, and it was *turned*
into a serpent: and Mosés fled from it.
4 Againe the Lord said vnto Mosés, Put
forthe thine hãd, and take it by the taile.
Then he put forthe his hand and caught
it, and it was *turned* into a rod in his hand.

b This power to worke miracles was to confirme his doctrine, & to assure him of his vocation.

5 *Do this* b that thei may beleue, that the
Lord God of their fathers, the God of
Abrahám, the God of Izhák, & the God
of Iaakób hathe appeared vnto thee.
6 ¶ And the Lord said furthermore vnto
him, Thrust now thine hand into thy bosome. And he thrust his hand into his bosome, and when he toke it out *againe*, beholde, his hand was " leprous as snowe.

" Or, white as snowe.

7 Moreouer he said, Put thine hand into
thy bosome againe. So he put his hãd into
his bosome againe, & pluckt it out of his
bosome, and beholde, it was turned againe as his *other* flesh.
8 So shal it be, if thei wil not beleue thee,
nether obey " the voyce of the first signe,
yet shal thei beleue for the voyce of the
seconde signe.

" Or, the wordes confirmed by the first signe.

9 But if thei wil not yet beleue these two
signes, nether obey vnto thy voyce, then
shalt thou take of the c water of the riuer, and powre it vpon the drye land: so
the water which thou shalt take out of
the riuer, shalbe *turned* to blood vpon the
drye land.

c Because these thre signes shulde be sufficient witnesses to proue ỹ Mosés shulde deliuer Gods people.

10 ¶ But Mosés said vnto the Lord, Oh
my Lord, I am not eloquent, " nether at
any time *haue bene*, nor yet since thou
haste spoken vnto thy seruant: but I am
" slow of speache and slow of tongue.

" Ebr. from yesterday, & yet yesterday.
" Ebr. heauie of mouthe.

11 Then the Lord said vnto him, Who hathe giuen the mouth to man? or who hathe made the dõme, or the deafe, or him ỹ
seeth, or the blinde? haue not I the Lord?
12 Therefore go now, and * I wil be with
thy mouth, & wil teache thee what thou
shalt say.

Mat. 10, 19. & 21, 13.

13 But he said, Oh my Lord, send, I pray
thee, by the " hand *of him*, whome ỹ d shuldest send.

" Or, ministerie.
d That is, of the Mesias: or some other, that is more mete then I.

14 Then the Lord was e very angry with
Mosés, and said, Do not I knowe Aarón
thy brother the Leuite, that he him selfe
shal speake? for lo, he cõmeth also forthe
to mete thee, and when he seeth thee, he
wilbe glad in his heart.

e Thogh we prouoke God iustly to angre, yet he wil neuer reiect his.

15 Therefore thou shalt speake vnto him,
& f put these wordes in his mouth, and I
wilbe with thy mouth, and ẘ his mouth,
and wil teache you what ye oght to do.

f Thou shalt instruct him what to say.

16 And he shalbe thy spokesman vnto the
people: he shalbe, *euen* he shalbe as thy
mouth, & thou shalt be to him as g God.
17 Moreouer ỹ shalt take this rod in thine
hand, wherewith thou shalt do miracles.

g Meaning as a wise coũsellor and ful of Gods Spirit.

18 ¶ Therefore Mosés went and returned
to Iethró his father in lawe, & said vnto
him, I pray thee, let me go, and returne
to my " brethren, which are in Egypt, and
se whether thei be yet aliue. Then Iethró
said to Mosés, Go in peace.

" Or, kinsfolke, & linage.

19 (For the Lord had said vnto Mosés in
Midián, Go, returne to Egypt: for thei
are all dead which went about to kil thee)
20 Then Mosés toke his wife, and his sonnes, and " put them on an asse, and returned towarde the land of Egypt, & Mosés
toke the h rod of God in his hand.

" Ebr. caused them to ride.
h Whereby he wroght the miracles.

21 And the Lord said vnto Mosés, When
thou art entred and come into Egypt a-
gaine, se that thou do all the wonders before Pharaóh, which I haue put in thine
hand: but I wil i harden his heart, and he
shal not let the people go.

i By reteining my spirit and deliuerĩg him vnto Satan to increase his malice.

22 Then thou shalt say to Pharaóh, Thus
saith the Lord, Israél *is* my sonne, *euẽ* my
k first borne.

k Meaning, moste dere vnto him.

23 Wherefore I say to thee, Let my sonne
go, that he may serue me: if thou refuse to
let him go, beholde, I wil slay thy sonne,
euen thy first borne.
24 ¶ And as he was by the way in the ynne,
the Lord met him, and l wolde haue killed him.

l God punished him with sickenes for neglecting his Sacrament.

25 Then Zipporáh toke a sharpe knife, and
m cut away the fore skinne of her sonne,
and cast it at his fete, and said, Thou *art* in
dede a bloodie housband vnto me.
26 So " he departed frõ him. Then she said,
O bloodie housband (because of the circumcision)

m This acte was extraordinarie: for Mosés was sore sicke, and God euen the required it.
" Or, the Angel.

27 ¶ Then the Lord said vnto Aarón, Go
mete Mosés in the wildernes. And he wẽt
and met him in the " Mount of God, and
kissed him.

" Or, Horéb.

28 Then Mosés tolde Aarón all the wordes
of the Lord, who had sent him, and all
the signes wherewith he had charged him.
29 ¶ So went Mosés and Aarón, & gathered
all the Elders of the children of Israél.
30 And Aarón tolde all the wordes, which
the

the Lord had spoken vnto Mosés, and he
did the miracles in the sight of the people,
31 And the [n] people beleued, and when they
heard that the Lord had visited ẏ children
of Israél, and had loked vpon their tribu
lació, they bowed downe, & worshipped.

n So that Mosés had now experience of Gods promes that he shulde haue good successe.

CHAP. V.

1 Mosés and Aarón do their message to Pharaóh, who letteth not the people of Israél departe but oppresseth them more and more. 20 They crye out vpon Mosés & Aarón therefore, and Mosés complaineth to God.

1 THen afterward Mosés & Aarón went
& said to [a] Pharaóh, Thus saith the
Lord God of Israél, Let my people go,
that they maie [b] celebrate a feast vnto me
in the wildernes.
2 And Pharaóh said, Who is the Lord, ẏ
I shulde heare his voyce, & let Israél go?
I knowe not the Lord, nether wil I let Israél go.
3 And they said, "We worship the God of ẏ
Ebrewes: we pray thee, suffre vs to go thre
daies iournei in the desert and to sacrifice
vnto the Lord our God, lest " he bring
vpon vs the pestilence or sworde.
4 Thẽ said the King of Egypt vnto them,
Mosés and Aarón, why cause ye the people to cease from their workes? get you to
your burdens.
5 Pharaóh said furthermore, Beholde, muche people *is* now in the land, & ye [c] make
them leaue their burdens.
6 Therefore Pharaóh gaue cõmãdemẽt
the same day vnto the taskemasters of the
people, and to their [d] officers, saying,
7 Ye shal giue the people no more strawe,
to make bricke (as in time past) *but* let
them go and gather them straw them selues:
8 Notwithstanding lay vpon them the nõ
bre of bricke, which they made in time
past, diminish nothing thereof: for they
be idle, therefore thei crye, saying, Let vs
go to offre sacrifice vnto our God.
9 [e] Lay more worke vpon the men, and cause them to do it, and let them not regarde
[f] vaine wordes.
10 ¶ Then went the taskemasters of ẏ people & their officers out, and tolde the peo
ple, saying, Thus saith Pharaóh, I wil giue you no more straw.
11 Go your selues, get you straw where ye
can finde it, yet shal nothing of your labour be diminished.
12 Then were the people scatred abrode
throughout all the land of Egypt, for to
gather stubble in stede of straw.
13 And the taskemasters hasted thẽ, saying,
Finish your dayes worke " euerie dayes
taske, as *ye did* when ye had straw.
14 And the officers of the children of Israél, which Pharaohs taskemasters had set

a Faith ouercommeth feare, and maketh men bolde in their vocatiõ.
b And offre sacrifice.
"Or, God hathe met vs.
"Ebr. lest he mete vs with pestilence.
c As though ye wolde rebel.
d Which were of the Israelites and had charge to se them do their worke.
e The more cruelly that tyrãts rage, ẏ nerer is Gods helpe.
f Of Mosés & Aarón.
"Ebr. the worke of a day in his day.

ouer them, were beaten, and demanded,
Wherfore haue ye not fulfilled your taske
in making bricke yesterday and to day, as
in times past?
15 ¶ Thẽ the officers of the childrẽ of Israél came, & cryed vnto Pharaóh, sayĩg,
Wherefore dealest thou thus with thy ser
uants?
16 There is no straw giuen to thy seruants,
and they say vnto vs, Make bricke: and lo,
thy seruants are beaten, and "thy people is
blamed.
17 But he said, " Ye are to muche idle: therefore ye say, Let vs go to offre sacrifice to
the Lord.
18 Go therefore now *&* worke: for there
shal no straw be giuen you, yet shal ye deliuer the whole tale of bricke.
19 Then the officers of the children of Israél "sawe thẽ selues in an euil case, because
it was said, Ye shal diminish nothing of
your bricke, *nor* of euerie daies taske,
20 ¶ And they met Mosés & Aarón, which
stode in their way as they came out from
Pharaóh,
21 To whome they said, The Lord loke vpon you and iudge: for ye haue made our
sauour to * stincke before Pharaóh & before his seruants, in that ye haue [g] put a
sworde in their hand to slay vs.
22 Wherefore Mosés returned to ẏ Lord,
and said, Lord, why hast thou afflicted
this people? wherefore hast thou thus sent
me?
23 For since I came to Pharaóh to speake
in thy Name, he hathe vexed this people,
and yet thou hast not deliuered thy people.

"Or, thy people the Egyptians are in the faut.
"Ebr. idle, ye are idle.
"Or, loked sad on them, which said.
Read. Gen. 34,30.
g It is agrieuous thing to the seruants of God to be accused of euil, specially of their brethren, when they do as their duetie requireth.

CHAP. VI.

3 God renueth his promes of the deliuerance of the Israelites. 9 Mosés speaketh to the Israelites, but they beleue him not. 10 Mosés and Aarón are sent againe to Pharaóh. 14 The genealogie of Reubén, Simeón, and Leui, of whome came Mosés and Aarón.

1 THẽ the Lord said vnto Mosés, Now
shalt thou se, what I wil do vnto Pha
raóh: for by a strong hand shal he let them
go, and euen "be constreined to driue thẽ
out of his land.
2 Moreouer God spake vnto Mosés, and
said vnto him, I am the Lord,
3 And I appeared vnto Abrahám, to Izhák,
and to Iaakób by *the Name of* "Almightie
God: but by my Name [a] Iehouáh was I
not knowen vnto them.
4 Furthermore as I made my couenãt with
them to giue them the land of Canáan,
the lãd of their pilgremage, wherein they
were strangers:
5 So I haue also heard the groning of the
children of Israél, whome the Egyptians
kepe in bondage, & haue remembred my
couenant.

"Ebr. in a strõg hand.
"Or, all sufficient.
a Wherby he signifieth that he wil performe in dede ẏ, which he promised to their fathers: for this Name declareth ẏ he is constant & wil performe his promes.

6 Wherefore say thou vnto the childrẽ of
Israél, I am the Lord, and I wil bring you
out from the burdens of the Egyptians,
and wil deliuer you out of their bondage,
and wil redeme you in a stretched out arme, and in great "iudgementes.
7 Also I wil [b] take you for my people, and
wil be your God: then ye shal knowe ẏ I
the Lord your God bring you out from ẏ
burdens of the Egyptians.
8 And I wil bring you into the land which
I " sware that I wolde giue to Abrahám,
to Izhák and to Iaakób, and I wil giue it
vnto you for a possession: I am the Lord.
9 ¶ So Mosés tolde the children of Israél
thus: but thei hearkened [c] not vnto Mosés,
for anguish of spirit & for cruel bõdage.
10 Then the Lord spake vnto Mosés,
saying,
11 Go speake to Pharaóh King of Egypt,
that he let the children of Israél go out of
his land.
12 But Mosés spake before ẏ Lord, saying,
Beholde, the children of Israél hearken
not vnto me, how then shal Pharaóh heare
me, which am of [d] vncircumcised lippes?
13 Then the Lord spake vnto Mosés and vn
to Aarón, & charged them *to go* to the chil
dren of Israél and to Pharaóh King of E-
gypt, to bring the children of Israél out
of the land of Egypt.
14 ¶ These be the [e] heades of their fathers
houses: the sonnes of Reubén the first borne of Israél *are* Hanóch and Pallú, Hezrón and Carmí: these are the families of
Reubén.
15 Also the sonnes of Simeón: Iemuél &
Iamín, & Ohád, and Iachín, & Zóar, and
Shaúl the sonne of a Canaanitish womã:
these are the families of Simeón.
16 ¶ These also are the names of the sonnes
of Leuí in their generacions: Gershón &
Koháth and Merarí (and the yeres of the
life of Leuí *were* an hundreth [f] thirty and
seuen yere)
17 The sonnes of Gershón *were* Libní &
Shimí by their families.
18 And the sonnes of Koháth, Amrám and
Izhár, & Hebrón and Vzziél. (& Koháth
liued an hundreth thirty and thre yere)
19 Also the sonnes of Merarí *were* Mahalí
and Mushí: these are the families of Leuí
by their kinreds.
20 And Amrám toke Iochébed his [g] fathers
sister to his wife, and she bare him Aarón
and Mosés (and Amrám liued and hundreth thirty and seuen yere)
21 ¶ Also the sonnes of Izhár: [h] Kórah, &
Népheg, and Zichrí.
22 And the sonnes of Vzziél: Mishaél, and
Elzaphán, and Sithrí.
23 And Aarón toke Elishéba daughter of
[i] Amminadáb, sister of Nahashón to his
wife, which bare him Nadáb, and Abihú,
Eleazár and Ithamár.
24 Also the sonnes of Kórah: Asír, & Elkanáh, & Abiasáph: these are the families
of the Korhites.
25 And Eleazár Aarons sonne toke him *one*
of the daughters of Putiél to his wife,
which bare him * Phinehás: these are the
principal fathers of the Leuites through
out their families.
26 These are Aarón and Mosés to whome
the Lord said, Bring the childrẽ of Israél
out of the land of Egypt, according to
their [k] armies.
27 These are ẏ Mosés & Aarón, ẇ spake to
Pharaóh King of Egypt, that they might
bring the childrẽ of Israél out of Egypt.
28 ¶ And at that time when the Lord spake
vnto Mosés in the land of Egypt,
29 When the Lord, *I say*, spake vnto Mosés,
saying, I am the Lord, speake thou vnto
Pharaóh the King of Egypt all that I say
vnto thee,
30 Then Mosés said before the Lord, Beholde, I am of [l] vncircumcised lippes, and
how shal Pharaóh heare me?

"Or, plagues.
b He meaneth, as touchĩg the outward vocatiõ: for election to life euerlastĩg is immutable.
" Ebr. lift vp mine hand.
c So hard a thing it is to shewe true obedience vnder the crosse.
d Or, barbarous and rude in speache. & by this worde (vncircumcised) is signified the whole corruption of mans nature.
e This genealogie sheweth of whome Mosés and Aarón came.
f For he was 42. yere olde, when he came ĩto Egypt, and there liued 94.
g Which kinde of mariage was after in ẏ lawe forbidden, Leuit 18, 12.
h Mosés and he were brethrẽs childrẽ, whose rebellion was punished, Nomb. 16,1.
i Who was a Prince of Iudáh, Nom. 2,3.
* Nom. 25,10.
k For their families were so great, ẏ they might be compared to armies.
l The disobedience both of Mosés and of ẏ people sheweth ẏ their deliuerance came onely of Gods fre mercie.

CHAP. VII.

3 God hardeneth Pharaohs heart. 10 Mosés and Aarón do the miracles of the serpent, and the blood: and Pharaohs sorcerers do the like.

1 THẽ the Lord said to Mosés, Beholde,
I haue made thee Pharaohs [a] God, &
Aarón thy brother shal "be thy Prophet.
2 Thou shalt speake all that I commanded
thee: and Aarón thy brother shal speake
vnto Pharaóh, that he suffre the children
of Israél to go out of his land.
3 But I wil harden Pharaohs heart, and
multiplie my miracles and my wondres in
the land of Egypt.
4 And Pharaóh shal not hearkẽ vnto you,
that I may lay mine hand vpon Egypt, &
bring out mine armies, *eue͂* my people, the
childrẽ of Israél out of the lãd of Egypt,
by great [b] iudgements.
5 Then the Egyptians shal know that I am
ẏ Lord, when I stretch forthe mine hand
vpon Egypt, and bring out the children
of Israél from among them.
6 So Mosés and Aarón did as the Lord
commanded them, *euen* so did they.
7 (Now Mosés was [c] foure score yere olde,
& Aarón foure score and thre, when thei
spake vnto Pharaóh)
8 ¶ And the Lord had spoken vnto Mosés
and Aarón, saying,
9 If Pharaóh speake vnto you, saying,
Shewe a miracle for you, then ẏ shalt say
vnto Aarón, Take thy rod & cast it before
Pharaóh, *and* it shal be *turned* ĩto a "serpẽt.
10 ¶ Then went Mosés and Aarón vnto
Pharaóh, and did euen as the Lord had
commanded: and Aarón caste forthe his
rod

a I haue giuẽ thee power & autoritie to speake in my name and to execute my iudgemẽts vpon him.
"Or, shal speake for thee (before Pharaóh)
b To strengthẽ Mosés faith, God promiseth againe to punishe moste sharpely the oppression of his Church.
c Mosés liued in affliction & bannishement 40 yere before he enioyed his office to deliuer. Gods people.
"Or, dragon.

rod before Pharaóh and before his seruants,and it was *turned* into a serpent.
11 Then Pharaóh called also for the wise
men and [d] sorcerers: and those charmers
also of Egypt did in like maner with their
enchantements.
12 For they cast downe euerie man his rod,
and thei were *turned* into serpents:but Aarons rod deuoured their rods.
13 So Pharaohs heart was hardened, & he
hearkned not to thẽ, as the Lord had said.
14 ¶ The Lord then said vnto Mosés, Pharaohs heart is "obstinat, he refuseth to let
the people go.
15 Go vnto Pharaóh in the morning, (lo,
he wil come vnto the water) & thou shalt
stand & mete him by [e] the riuers brinke,
and the rod,which was turned into a serpent,shalt thou take in thine hand.
16 And thou shalt say vnto him, The Lord
God of ẏ Ebrews hath sent me vnto thee,
saying,Let my people go, that they may
serue me in the wildernes : & beholde,hi-
therto thou woldest not heare.
17 Thus saith the Lord, In this thou shalt
knowe that I am the Lord: beholde, I wil
smite with the rod that is in mine hãd vpon ẏ water that is in the riuer, & it shalbe
turned to blood.
18 And the fish that is in the riuer shal dye,
and the riuer shal stinke,& it shal "greue ẏ
Egyptiãs to drinke of ẏ water of ẏ riuer.
19 ¶ The Lord then spake to Mosés, Say vn
to Aarón, Take thy rod,&stretch out thine hand ouer the waters of Egypt, ouer
their streames,ouer their riuers, and ouer
their pondes, and ouer all pooles of their
waters,and they shalbe ‖ blood, and there
shalbe blood through out all ẏ land of E-
gypt, bothe in *vessels* of wood,& of stone.
20 So Mosés and Aarón did euẽ as the Lord
commanded: * and he lift vp the rod, and
smote the water that was in the riuer in ẏ
sight of Pharaóh , and in the sight of his
seruants: and all the water that was in the
riuer, was turned into blood.
21 And the [f] fish that was in the riuer dyed,
and the riuer stanke: so that the Egyptiãs
colde not drinke of the water of the riuer:
and there was blood through out all the
land of Egypt.
22 And the enchanters of Egypt did [g] like
wise ẇ their sorceries:& the heart of Pha
raóh was hardened : so ẏ he did not hearken vnto them,as the Lord had said.
23 Then Pharaóh returned , & wẽt againe
into his house , " nether did this yet entre
into his heart.
24 All ẏ Egyptiãs thẽ digged round about
ẏ riuer *for* waters to drinke : for they colde not drinke of the water of the riuer.
25 And *this* cõtinued fully seuẽ daies after
the Lord had smitten the riuer.

d It semeth that these were Iannes and Iambres, read 2. Tim. 3,8: so euer the wicked maliciously resist the trueth of God.

"Or, *heauy and dul.*

e To wit, the riuer Nilus.

"Or, *they shalbe weary , and ab horre to drinke.*

‖ The first plague.

Chap. 17, 5.

f To signifie that it was a true miracle, and that God plagued them in that, which was moste necessarie for ẏ preseruatiõ of life.

g In outward appearance, & after that the 7. daies were ended.

" *Ebr he set not his heart at all thereunto.*

CHAP. VIII.

6 Frogges are sent. 13 Mosés praieth and they dye. 17 Lyce are sẽt, whereby the sorcerers acknowledge Gods power. 24 Egypt is plagued with noysom flies. 30 Mosés praieth againe: 32 But Pharaohs heart is hardened.

1 AFterwarde the Lord said vnto Mosés,Go vnto Pharaóh, and tel him,
Thus saith the Lord,Let my people go,ẏ
they may serue me:
2 And if thou wilt not let them go, beholde,I wil smite all thy cõutrey with [a] frogges:
3 And the riuer shal scrall ful of frogges,
which shal go vp and come into thine
house: and into thy chambre, where thou
slepest,and vpon thy bed, & into the house of thy seruants , and vpon thy people,
and into thine ouens,and " into thy knea-
ding troghes.
4 Yea , the frogges shal climbe vp vpon
thee,and on thy people, and vpon all thy
seruants.
5 ¶ Also the Lord said vnto Mosés , Say
thou vnto Aarón, Stretch thine hand with
thy rod vpon the streames , vpon the riuers,and vpon the põdes,and cause frogges to come vp vpon the land of Egypt.
6 Then Aarón stretched his hãd vpon the
waters of Egypt, and the ‖ frogges came
vp,and couered the land of [b] Egypt.
7 And ẏ sorcerers did likewise with their
sorceries,and broght frogges vp vpõ the
land of Egypt.
8 Then Pharaóh called for Mosés & Aarón, & said, [c] Pray ye vnto the Lord that
he may take away the frogges from me,
and from my people, & I wil let the people go , that they may do sacrifice vnto
the Lord.
9 And Mosés said vnto Pharaóh," As concerning me,euen commande when I shal
praye for thee, and for thy seruants , and
for thy people , to destroye the frogges
frõ thee and from thine houses,that they
may remaine in the riuer onely.
10 Thẽ he said, To morowe.And he answered,Be it " as ẏ hast said,that thou maiest
knowe, that there is none like vnto the
Lord our God.
11 So the frogges shal departe frõ thee, &
from thine houses,and from thy seruants,
and from thy people : onely they shal remayne in the riuer.
12 Then Mosés and Aarón went out from
Pharaóh:and Mosés cryed vnto the Lord
cõcerning the frogges,which he had "sent
vnto Pharaóh.
13 And the Lord did according to the saying of Mosés : so the frogges [d] dyed in
the houses,in the townes,& in the fields.
14 And they gathered them togither by
heapes,and the land stanke *of them.*
15 But whẽ Pharaóh sawe that he had rest

a There is nothing so weake , that God cã not cause to ouercome the greatest power of man.

"Or, *vpon thy dogh. or, into thine ambries.*

‖ The seconde plague.

b But Góshen, where Gods people dwelt, was excepted.

c Not loue, but feare causeth the very infideles to seke vnto God.

" *Ebr. Haue this honour ouer me.*

" *Ebr. according to thy worde.*

"Or, *laid vpon.*

d In things of this life God oft times heareth the praiers of the iust for the vngodly.

giuen him, he hardened his heart, and
hearkened not vnto them, as the Lord
had said.
16 ¶ Againe the Lord said vnto Mosés,
Say vnto Aarón, Stretche out thy rod, &
smite the dust of the earth, that it may be
turned to ‖ lyce throughout all the land of
Egypt.
17 And they did so: for Aarón stretched
out his hand with his rod, and smote the
dust of the earth: and lyce came vpõ man
& vpon beast: all the dust of the earth was
lyce throughout all the land of Egypt.
18 Now yͤ enchãters assaied likewise with
their enchantments to bring forthe lyce,
but they [e] colde not. so the lyce were vpõ
man and vpon beast.
19 Then said yͤ enchanters vnto Pharaóh,
This is [f] the finger of God. But Pharaohs
heart remained obstinat, and he hearcke-
ned not vnto them, as the Lord had said.
20 ¶ Moreouer the Lord said to Mosés,
Rise vp early in yͤ morning, and stand before Pharaóh (lo, he wil come forthe vnto the water) & say vnto him, Thus saith
yͤ Lord, Let my people go, that they may
serue me.
21 Els, if yͧ wilt not let my people go, beholde, I wil send ″ swarmes of flies bothe
vpon thee, & vpon thy seruants, and vpon
thy people, & into thine houses: and the
houses of the Egyptiãs shalbe ful of swarmes of flies, and the grounde also whereon they are.
22 But the land of Gó shen, where my people are, wil I cause to be ″ wonderful in
that day, so that no swarmes of flies shal
be there, yͭ thou maiest knowe that I am
the Lord in the middes of the ″ earth.
23 And I wil make a deliuerãce of my people from thy people: to morowe shal this
miracle be.
24 And the Lord did so: for there came
‖ great swarmes of flies into the house of
Pharaóh, and *into* his seruants houses, so
that through all the land of Egypt the
earth was corrupt by the swarmes of flies.
25 Then Pharaóh called for Mosés and
Aarón, & said, Go, do sacrifice vnto your
God in this land.
26 But Mosés answered, It is not mete to
do so: for *then* we shulde offre vnto the
Lord our God *that, which is* an [g] abominacion vnto the Egyptians. Lo, can we sacrifice the abominacion of the Egyptians
before their eies, and they not stone vs?
27 Let vs go thre daies iourney in the desert, & sacrifice vnto the Lord our God,
as he hathe commanded vs.
28 And Pharaóh said, I wil let you go, yͭ
ye may sacrifice vnto the Lord your God
in the wildernes: but [h] go not farre away,
pray for me.

‖ The third plague.

e God confoũded their wisdome & autoritie in a thing moste vile.

f They acknowledged yͭ this was done by Gods power and not by sorcerie.

″ Or, a multitude of venimous beastes, as serpents, &c.

″ Or, I wil seperat.

″ Or, land of Egypt.

‖ The fourthe plague.

g For the Egyptians worshipped diuers beasts, as the oxe, the shepe & suche like, wͨ the Israelites offred in sacrifice.

h So yͤ wicked prescribe vnto Gods messengers how farre they shal go.

29 And Mosés said, Beholde, I wil go out
from thee, and pray vnto the Lord, that
yͤ swarmes of flies may departe frõ Pharaóh, from his seruants, and from his people tomorowe: but let Pharaóh frõ henceforthe [i] deceiue no more, in not suffring yͤ
people to sacrifice vnto the Lord.
30 So Mosés went out from Pharaóh and
prayed vnto the Lord.
31 And the Lord did according to yͤ saying
of Mosés, and the swarmes of flies departed from Pharaóh, from his seruants, and
frõ his people, & there remained not one.
32 Yet Pharaóh [k] hardened his heart euen
then also, & did not let the people go.

CHAP. IX.

1 The moraine of beastes. 10 The plague of botches & sores. 23 The horrible haile, thundre, and the lightening. 26 The land of Góshen euer is excepted. 27 Pharaóh cõfesseth his wickednes. 33 Mosés praieth for him, 35 Yet is he obstinat.

1 THen the Lord said vnto Mosés, Go
to Pharaóh, and tel him, Thus saith yͤ
Lord God of the Ebrewes, Let my people
go, that they may serue me.
2 But if thou refuse to let *them* go, & wilt
yet holde them stil,
3 Beholde, the hand of the Lord is vpõ thy
flocke which is in the field: *for* vpon yͤ horses, vpon the asses, vpon the camels, vpon
the cattel, & vpõ the shepe *shalbe* a ‖ mighty great moraine.
4 And the Lord shal do [a] wonderfully betwene the beastes of Isráel, and the beastes
of Egypt: so that there shal nothing dye
of all, yͭ *perteineth* to the childrẽ of Isráel.
5 And the Lord appointed a time, saying,
Tomorowe the Lord shal finish this thing
in this land.
6 So the Lord did it on the morowe, & all
the cattel of Egypt dyed: but of the cattel
of the children of Isráel dyed not one.
7 Then Pharaóh [b] sent, and beholde, there
was not one of the cattel of the Israelites
dead: and the heart of Pharaóh was obstinat, and he did not let the people go.
8 ¶ And the Lord said to Mosés & to Aarón, Take your handful of ″ asshes of the
fornace, and Mosés shal sprinkle them towarde the heauen in the sight of Pharaóh,
9 And they shalbe *turned* to dust in all the
land of Egypt: & it shalbe as a scab breaking out into blisters vpon man and vpon
beast throughout all the land of Egypt.
10 Then they toke asshes of the fornace,
and stode before Pharaóh: and Mosés
sprinkled them towarde the heauen, and
there came ‖ a scab breaking out into blisters vpon man, and vpon beast.
11 And the sorcerers colde not stãd before
Mosés, because of yͤ scab: for the scab was
vpon the enchanters, & vpon all the E-

i He colde not iudge his heart, but yet he charged hĩ to do this vnfainedly.

k Where God giueth not faith, no miracles can preuaile.

‖ The fift plague.

a He shal declare his heauie iudgement against his ennemies, & his fauour toward his children.

b In to the lãd of Góshẽ, where the Israelites dwelled.

″ Or, imbers.

‖ The sixt plague.

gyptians.
12 And the Lord hardened the heart of
Pharaóh, and he hearkened not vnto thẽ,
*as the Lord had said vnto Mosés.
13 ¶Also the Lord said vnto Mosés, Rise
vp earely in the morning, and stand before Pharaóh, and tel him, Thus saith the
Lord God of ẏ Ebrewes, Let my people
go, that they may serue me.
14 For I wil at this time send all my plagues vpon [c] thine heart, and vpon thy seruants, & vpon thy people, that thou maiest know that there is none like me in all
the earth.
15 For now I wil stretche out mine hand,
that I may smite thee & thy people with
the pestilence: & thou shalt perish from
the earth.
16 And in dede, *for this cause haue ″I appointed thee, to ″shewe my power in thee,
& to declare my [d] Name throughout all
the world.
17 Yet thou exaltest thy selfe against my
people, and lettest them not go.
18 Beholde, tomorowe this time I wil cause to raine a mightie great haile, suche as
was not in Egypt since the fundatiõ thereof was laid vnto this time.
19 Send therefore now, *and* [e] gather thy
cattel, and all that thou hast in the field:
for vpon all the men, & the beastes, which
are founde in the field, and not broght
home, the haile shal fall vpon them and
they shal dye.
20 Suche *then* as feared the worde of the
Lord among the seruantes of Pharaóh,
made his seruants & his cattel flee into
the houses:
21 But suche as ″regarded not the [f] worde
of the Lord, left his seruants, and his cattel in the field.
22 ¶And the Lord said to Mosés, Stretche
forthe thine hãd toward heauen, that there may be haile in all the land of Egypt,
vpon man and vpon beast, and vpon all ẏ
herbes of the field in the land of Egypt.
23 Then Mosés stretched out his rod toward heauen, and the Lord sent thundre &
‖haile, and ″lightening vpon the grounde: and the Lord caused haile to raine vpon the land of Egypt.
24 So there was haile, & fire mingled with
the haile, so grieuous, as there was none
throughout all the land of Egypt, since
″it was a nation.
25 And the haile smote throughout all the
lãd of Egypt all that was in ẏ field, bothe
man and beast: also the haile smote all ẏ
herbes of the field, and brake to pieces all
the trees of the field.
26 Onely in the land of Góshen (where
the children of Israél were) was no haile.
27 Then Pharaóh sent and called for Mosés and Aarón, and said vnto them, I [g] haue now sinned: the Lord is righteous, but
I and my people are wicked.
28 Pray ye vnto ẏ Lord (for it is ynough)
that there be no more ″mightie thunders
& haile, and I wil let you go, and ye shal
tary no longer.
29 Then Mosés said vnto him, Assone as I
am out of ẏ citie, I wil spreade mine handes vnto the Lord, *and* the thunder shal
cease, nether shal there be any more haile, that thou maiest know that the earth is
the Lords.
30 Now I knowe that thou, and thy seruãtes feare the Lord God, [h] before I pray.
31 (And the flaxe, and the barly were smitten: for the barly was eared, and the flaxe
was bolled.
32 But the wheat & the rye were not smitten, for they were ″hid in the grounde)
33 Then Mosés went out of the citie from
Pharaóh & spred his hands to the Lord,
and the thundre and the haile ceased, nether rained it vpon the earth.
34 And when Pharaóh saw that the raine
and the haile and the thundre were ceased, he sinned againe, and hardened his
heart *bothe* he, and his seruants.
35 So the heart of Pharaóh was hardened:
nether wolde he let the children of Israél
go, as the Lord had said ″by Mosés.

Chap. 4,21.

c So that thine owne conscience shal cõdemne thee of ingratitude & malice.

Rom. 9,17. ″Or, set thee vp. ″Or, to shewe thee.

d That is, ẏ all the world may magnifie my power in ouercõming thee.

e Here we se, though Gods wrath be kindeled, yet there is a certein mercie shewed euen to his enemies.

″Ebr. set not his heart to.

f The worde of the minister is called the worde of God.

‖The seuenth plague. ″Ebr. fire walked.

″Or, since it was inhabited.

g The wicked confesse their sinnes to their condemnation, but they can not beleue to obteine remission.

″Ebr. voices of God.

h Meaning, ẏ whẽ they haue their request, they are neuer the better.

″Or, late sowen.

″Eb. by the hãd of Mosés.

CHAP. X.

7 Pharaohs seruants counsel him to let the Israelites departe. 13 Greshoppers destroye the coũtrey. 16 Pharaóh confesseth his sinne. 22 Darkenes is sent. 28 Pharaóh forbiddeth Mosés to come any more in his presence.

1 AGain the Lord said vnto Mosés, Go
to Pharaóh: for * I haue hardened
his heart, & the heart of his seruants, that
I might worke these my miracles ″in the
middes of his *realme*.
2 And that thou maiest declare in the [a] eares of thy sonne, and of thy sonnes sonne,
what things I haue done in Egypt, & my
miracles, which I haue done among
them: that ye may know that I am the
Lord.
3 Then Mosés and Aarón came vnto Pharaóh, and said vnto him, Thus saith the
Lord God of the Ebrewes, How lõg wilt
thou refuse [b] to humble thy selfe before
me? Let my people go, that they may serue me.
4 But if thou refuse to let my people go,
beholde, tomorowe wil I bring ″gresshop-
pers into thy coastes.
5 And they shal couer the face of the earth,
that a man can not se the earth: and they
shal eat the residue which remaineth vnto
you, and hathe escaped from the haile: &
they shal eat all your trees that bud in
the field.

Chap. 4,24.

″Or, in his presence.

a The miracles shulde be so great, ẏ they shuld be spokẽ of for euer. where also we se ẏ duetie of parẽts toward their childrẽ.

b The end of afflictions is, to humble our selues wt true repentãce vnder the hand of God.

″Or, locustes.

6 And they shal fil thine houses, & all thy
seruants houses, and the houses of all the
Egyptians, as nether thy fathers, nor thy
fathers fathers haue sene, since the time
they were vpon the earth vnto this day.
So he returned, and went out from Pharaóh.
7 Then Pharaohs seruants said vnto him,
How lōg shal he be ʺ an [c] offence vnto vs?
let the men go, that they may serue the
Lord their God: wilt thou first knowe ỳ
Egypt is destroyed?
8 So Mosés and Aarón were broght againe vnto Pharaóh, & he said to them, Go,
serue the Lord your God, but who are
they that shal go?

ʺOr, snare.
c Meaning, the occasion of all these euils: so are the godlie euer charged, as Elias was by Achâb.

9 And Mosés answered, We wil go with ō
yong and with our olde, with our sonnes and with our daughters, with our
shepe and with our cattel wil we go: for
we *must celebrate* a feast vnto the Lord.
10 And he said vnto them, Let [d] the Lord
so be with you, as I wil let you go and
your children: beholde, for [e] euil is before your face.
11 *It shal* not *be* so: now go ye *that are* mē,
and serue the Lord: for that was your
desire. Then they were thrust out from
Pharaohs presence.

d That is, I wolde ỳ Lord were no more affectioned toward you, thē I am minded to let you go.
e Punishemēt is prepared for you. Some read, Ye entend some mischief.

12 ¶ After, ỳ Lord said vnto Mosés, Stretch
out thine hand vpon the land of Egypt
for the greshoppers, that they may come
vpon the land of Egypt, and eat all the
herbes of the land, *euen* all that the haile
hathe left.
13 Then Mosés stretched forthe his rod
vpon the land of Egypt: and the Lord
broght an East winde vpon the land all
that day, and all that night: and in the
morning, ỳ East winde broght the ‖ greshoppers.
14 So the greshoppers went vp vpō all the
land of Egypt, and ʺ remained in all quarters of Egypt: so grieuous greshoppers,
like to these were neuer before, nether
after them shalbe suche.

‖ The eight plague.
ʺOr, he caused thē to remaine.

15 For they couered all the face of ỳ earth,
so that the land was darcke: and they did
eat all the herbes of the land, and all the
frutes of the trees, which ỳ haile had left,
so ỳ there was no grene thing left vpon
the trees, nor among ỳ herbes of the field
throughout all the land of Egypt.
16 Therefore Pharaóh called for [f] Mosés
and Aarón in haste, and said, I haue sinned against the Lord your God, and a-
gainst you.
17 And nowe forgiue me my sinne onely
this once, and pray vnto the Lord your
God, that he may take away from me
this death onely.
18 *Mosés* then went out from Pharaóh, and
praied vnto the Lord.

f The wicked in their miserie seke to Gods ministers for helpe, albeit they hate & detest thē.

19 And the Lord turned a mightie strong
West winde, and toke away the greshoppers, and violently cast thē into the [g] red
Sea, *so that* there remained not one greshopper in all the coast of Egypt.
20 But the Lord hardened Pharaohs heart, and he did not let the children of Israél go.

g The water semeth red because the sand or grauel is red: ỳ Ebrewes call it ỳ Sea of bulrusshes.

21 ¶ Againe the Lord said vnto Mosés,
Stretch out thine hand toward heauen, ỳ
there may be vpon ỳ lād of Egypt darcknes, euen darcknes that may be [h] felt.
22 Then Mosés stretched forthe his hand
toward heauen, and there was a ‖ blacke
* darcknes in all the land of Egypt thre
dayes.
23 No man saw an other, nether rose vp frō
the place where he was *for* thre dayes: *but
all the children of Israél had light where
they dwelt.

h Because it was so thicke.
‖ The ninthe plague.
Wisd.17,2.
Wisd.18,1.

24 Then Pharaóh called for Mosés and
said, Go, serue the Lord: onely your shepe
and your cattel shal abide, and your children shal go with you.
25 And Mosés said, Thou must giue vs also
sacrifices, and burnt offrings that we may
do *sacrifice* vnto the Lord our God.
26 Therefore our cattel also shal go ẘ vs:
there shal not an [i] hoofe be left, for thereof must we take to serue the Lord our
God: nether do we knowe [k] how we shal
serue the Lord, vntil we come thither.
27 (But ỳ Lord hardened Pharaohs heart,
and he wolde not let them go)
28 And Pharaóh said vnto him, Get thee
frō me: loke thou se my face no more: for
whensoeuer thou commest in my sight,
thou shalt [l] dye.
29 Then Mosés said, Thou hast said wel:
from henceforthe wil I se thy face nomore.

i The ministers of God oght not to yelde one iote to the wicked, as touching their charge.
k That is, with what beastes or how many.
l Thogh before he cōfessed Mosés iust, yet agaist his owne conscience he threateneth to put him to death.

CHAP. XI.

1 God promiseth their departure. 2 He willeth them to borrow their neighbours iewels. 3 Mosés was estemed of all saue Pharaóh. 5 He signifieth the death of the first borne.

1 NOw (the Lord had said vnto Mosés, Yet wil I bring one plague more vpon Pharaóh, and vpon Egypt: after
that he wil let you go hence: when he
letteth you go, he shal [a] at once chase you
hence.
2 Speake thou now to the people, that euerie man ʺ require of his neighbour, and e-
uerie woman of her neighbour * iewels
of siluer and iewels of golde.
3 And the Lord gaue the people fauour in
the sight of the Egyptians: also * Mosés
was verie great in the land of Egypt, in
the sight of Pharaohs seruants, and in the
sight of the people)
4 Also Mosés said, Thus saith ỳ Lord, *A-
bout midnight wil I go out into ỳ middes

a Without any condition, but with haste and violence.
ʺOr, borrowe.
Chap.3,22.
Ecc.45,1.

des of Egypt.
5 And all the first borne in the land of E-
gypt ſhal dye, frō the firſtborne of Pharaóh that ſitteth on his throne, vnto the
firſtborne of the maid ſeruant, that is at
[b] the mille, & all the firſt borne of beaſtes.
6 Then there ſhal be a great crye throughout all the land of Egypt, ſuche as was
neuer none like, nor ſhalbe.
7 But againſt none of the children of Iſraél ſhal a dog moue his tongue, nether a-
gainſt man nor beaſt, that ye may knowe
that the Lord putteth a difference betwene the Egyptians and Iſraél.
8 And all theſe thy ſeruantes ſhal come
downe vnto me, and fall before me, ſaying, Get thee out, and all the people that
[c] are at thy fete, & after this wil I depart.
So he wēt out from Pharaóh very angry.
9 And the Lord ſaid vnto Moſés, Pharaóh
ſhal not heare you, [d] that my wonders
may be multiplied in the land of Egypt.
10 So Moſés and Aarón did all theſe wonders before Pharaóh: but the Lord hardened Pharaohs heart, and he ſuffred
not the children of Iſraél to go out of his
land.

b From the hieſt to the loweſt.

c That is, vnder thy power and gouernement.

d God hardeneth the heartes of ẏ reprobat, that his glorie thereby might be the more ſet forthe, rom. 9, 17.

CHAP. XII.

1 The Lord inſtituteth the Paſſeouer. 26 The fathers muſt teache their children the myſterie thereof. 29 The firſt borne are ſlaine. 31 The Iſraelites are driuen out of the land. 35 The Egyptians are ſpoiled. 37 The nombre that departeth out of Egypt. 40 How long thei were in Egypt.

1 THen the Lord ſpake to Moſés and to
Aarón in the land of Egypt, ſaying,
2 This [a] moneth *ſhal be* vnto you the beginning of moneths: it *ſhalbe* to you the
firſt [b] moneth of the yere.
3 Speake ye vnto all the Congregacion of
Iſraél, ſaying, In the tenth of this moneth
let euerie man take vnto him a lambe according to the houſe of the [c] fathers, a lābe for an houſe.
4 If the houſholde be to litle for the lambe, he ſhal take his neighbour, which is
next vnto his houſe, according to the
nōbre of the perſones: euerie one of you,
according to his [d] eating ſhal make your
compt for the lambe.
5 Your lambe ſhalbe without blemiſh, a
male of a yere olde: ye ſhal take it of the
lambes, or of the kiddes.
6 And ye ſhal kepe *it* vntil the fourtenth
day of this moneth: then [e] all the multitude of the Congregacion of Iſraél ſhal
kil it "at euen.
7 After thei ſhal take of the blood & ſtrike
it on the two poſtes, and on the vpper
doore poſt of the houſes where thei ſhal
eat it.
8 And thei ſhal eat the fleſh ẏ ſame night,
roſte with fyre, & vnleauened bread: with
ſower *herbes* thei ſhal eat it.

a Called Niſān, conteinig parte of Marche & parte of April.

b As touching the obſeruatiō of feaſtes: as for other policies, thei rekoned from Septembre.

c As ẏ fathers of ẏ houſholde had great or ſmale families.

d He ſhal take ſo many as are ſufficient to eat the lambe.

e Euerie one in his houſe.

"*Ebr. betwene the two euenings, or twielight.*

9 Eat not thereof rawe, boiled nor ſoddē in
water, but roſte with fyre, both his [f] head,
his fete, and his purtenance.
10 And ye ſhal reſerue nothing of it vnto
the morning: but that, which remaineth
of it vnto the morowe, ſhal ye burne with
fyre.
11 ¶ And thus ſhal ye eat it, Your loynes
girded, your ſhoes on your fete, & your
ſtaues in your hands, and ye ſhal eat it in
haſte: *for* [g] it is the Lords Paſſeouer.
12 For I wil paſſe through the land of E-
gypt the ſame night, and wil ſmite all the
firſt borne in the land of Egypt, bothe mā
and beaſt, and I wil execute iudgement
vpō all the "gods of Egypt. I *am* the Lord.
13 And the blood ſhalbe a token for you
vpon the houſes where ye are: ſo when I
ſe the blood, I wil paſſe ouer you, and the
plague ſhal not be vpon you to deſtruction, when I ſmite the land of Egypt.
14 And this day ſhalbe vnto you a [h] remēbrance: and ye ſhal kepe it an holy feaſt
vnto the Lord, throughout your generacions: ye ſhal kepe it holy by an ordinance [i] for euer.
15 Seuē daies ſhal ye eat vnleauened bread,
& in any caſe ye ſhal put away leauen the
firſt day out of your houſes: for whoſoeuer eateth leauened bread from the firſt
day vntil the ſeuenth day, that perſone
ſhal be cut of from Iſraél.
16 And in the firſt day *ſhalbe* an holy "aſſemblie: alſo in the ſeuenth day ſhal be an holy aſſemblie vnto you: no worke ſhalbe
done in them, ſaue about that which euerie man muſt eat: that onely may ye do.
17 Ye ſhal kepe alſo *the feaſt* of vnleauened
bread: for that ſame day I wil bring your
armies out of the land of Egypt: therefore ye ſhal obſerue this day, throughout
your poſteritie, by an ordinance for euer.
18 ¶ In the firſt *moneth* and the fourtenth
day of the moneth at [k] euen, ye ſhal eat
vnleauened bread vnto the one and twentieth day of the moneth at euen.
19 Seuen dayes ſhal no leauen be founde in
your houſes: for whoſoeuer eateth leauened bread, that perſone ſhalbe cut of frō
the Congregacion of Iſraél: whether he
be a ſtranger, or borne in the land.
20 Ye ſhal eat no leauened bread: *but* in all
your habitacions ſhal ye eat vnleauened
bread.
21 ¶ Thē Moſés called all the Elders of Iſraél, and ſaid vnto them, Choſe out and
take you for *euerie* of your houſholdes
a lambe, and kil the Paſſeouer.
22 And take a * bunche of hyſſope, and
dip it in the blood that is in the baſſen, &
ſtrike the "lintel, and the "dore chekes with
the blood that is in the baſſen, & let none
of you go out at the dore of his houſe, vn-

f That is, all that may be eaten.

g The lambe was not the Paſſeouer, but ſignified it: as ſacramēts are not the thing it ſelfe, which thei do repreſent, but ſignifie it.

"*Or, princes, or, idoles.*

h Of the benefite receiued for your deliuerance.

i That is, vntil Chriſts comming: for then ceremonies had an end.

"*Or, calling together of the people to ſerue God.*

k For in olde time ſo thei cōpted, beginnig the day at ſunne ſet til ẏ next day at ẏ ſame time.

Ebr. 11, 28.

"*Or, tranſome, or, vpper dore poſte.*

"*Or, two ſide poſtes.*

til the morning.
23 For the Lord wil passe by to smite the
Egyptians: and when he seeth the blood
vpon the lintel & on the two dore chekes,
the Lord wil passe ouer the dore, & wil
not suffre the [l] destroyer to come into
your houses to plague *you*.

l The Angel sent of God to kil the first borne.

24 Therefore shal ye obserue this thing
as an ordinance *bothe* for thee and thy sonnes for euer.
25 And when ye shal come into the [m] land,
which the Lord wil giue you, as he hathe
promised, then ye shal kepe this [*] seruice.

m The land of Canáan.

* Or, ceremonie.

Iosh.4,6.

26 *And whē your children aske you, What
seruice is this ye *kepe?*
27 Then ye shal say, It is the sacrifice of
the Lords Passeouer, which passed ouer
the houses of the children of Israél in E-
gypt, when he smote the Egyptians, and
preserued our houses. Then the people
[n] bowed them selues, and worshipped.

n Thei gaue God thankes for so great a benefite.

28 So the children of Israél went, and did
as the Lord had commanded Mosés and
Aarón: so did thei.
29 ¶ Now at * midnight, the Lord ‖ smote
all the firstborne in the lād of Egypt, frō
the firstborne of Pharaóh that sate on his
throne, vnto the * firstborne of the captiue
that was in prison, and all the firstborne
of beastes.

Chap.11,4. ‖ The tenth plague.

Wisd.18,5.

30 And Pharaóh rose vp in the night, he,
and all his seruants & all the Egyptians:
and there was a great crye in Egypt: for
there *was* [o] no house where there *was* not
one dead.

o Of these houses, wherin any firstborne was ether of mē or beastes.

31 And he called to Mosés and to Aarón
by night, & said, Rise vp, get you out frō
among my people, bothe ye, and the children of Israél, and go serue the Lord as
ye haue said.
32 Take also your shepe and your cattel as
ye haue said, and departe, and [p] blesse me
also.

p Pray for me.

33 And the Egyptiās did force the people,
because thei wolde send them out of the
land in haste: for thei said, We dye all.
34 Therefore the people toke their dowe
before it was leauened, *euen* their dowe
bounde in clothes vpon their shulders.
35 And the children of Israél did according to the saying of Mosés, and thei asked of the Egyptians * iewels of siluer &
iewels of golde, and raiment.

Chap.3,22. & 11,2. Wisd.10,17.

36 And the Lord gaue the people fauour in
the sight of the Egyptians: and thei [*] grāted their request: so thei spoiled the E-
gyptians.

* Or, lent them.

37 Then the * children of Israél toke their
iourney from [q] Ramesés to Succóth a-
bout six hundreth thousand men of fote,
beside children.

Nomb.33,3.

q Which was a citie in Góshen, Gen.47, 11.

38 And [r] a great multitude of sundry sortes of people went out with them, and
shepe, and beues, & cattel in great abundance.

r Which were strangers, and not borne of the Israelites.

39 And thei baked the dowe which thei
broght out of Egypt, & *made* vnleauened
cakes: for it was not leauened, because thei
were thrust out of Egypt, nether colde
thei tary, nor yet prepare them selues vitailes.
40 ¶ So the dwelling of the childrē of Israél, while thei dwelled in Egypt, *was* * foure hundreth and thirty yeres.

Gen.15,13. act.7,6. gala.3,17.

41 And when the [s] foure hundreth & thirty
yeres were expired, euen the selfe same
day departed all the hostes of the Lord
out of the land of Egypt.

s Frō Abrahās departing frō Vr in Chaldea vnto ẏ departing of ẏ children of Israél from Egypt, are 430 yere.

42 It *is* a night to be kept *holy* to the Lord,
because he broght them out of the land
of Egypt: this is that night of the Lord,
which all the childrē of Israél musti kepe
throughout their generacions.
43 Also the Lord said vnto Mosés and Aarón, This is the lawe of the Passeouer:
[t] no stranger shal eat thereof.

t Except he be circūcised & onely professe your religion.

44 But euerie seruāt that is boght for money, when thou hast circūcised him, then
shal he eat thereof.
45 A stranger or an hyred seruant shal not
eat thereof.
46 *In one house shal it be eatē: thou shalt
cary none of the flesh out of the house,
*nether shal ye breake a bone thereof.

Nombr.9,12. Iohn.19,36.

47 All the Cōgregacion of Israél shal obserue it.
48 But if a stranger dwel with thee, & wil
obserue the Passeouer of ẏ Lord, let him
circumcise all the males, that belong vnto
him, and then let him come and obserue
it, and he shalbe as one that is borne in
the land: for none vncircumcised persone
shal eat thereof.
49 One [u] law shalbe to him that is borne
in the land, & to the stranger that dwelleth among you.

u Thei that are of ẏ housholde of God, must be all ioyned in one faith and religion.

50 Then all the children of Israél did as
the Lord commanded Mosés and Aarón:
so did thei.
51 And the selfe same day did the Lord
bring the children of Israél out of the
land of Egypt by their armies.

CHAP. XIII.

1 *The firstborne are offred to God. 3 The memorial of their deliuerance. 8.14 An exhortacion to teache their children to remembre this deliuerance. 17 Why thei are led by the wildernes. 19 The bones of Ioséph. 21 The piller of the cloude and of the fire.*

1 AND the Lord spake vnto Mosés,
saying,
2 *Sanctifie vnto me all the firstborne: *that
is*, euerie one that *first* openeth the wombe
among the children of Israél, as wel of
man as of beast: *for* it is mine.

Chap.22,29. & 34,19. leu.27,26. nom.3,13. & 8,16. luk.2,23.

3 ¶ Then Mosés said vnto the people, *Remembre this day in the which ye came
out of

Exod.23,13.

"Ebr. house of seruants.
a Where thei were in moste cruel slauerie.
b To signifie that thei had not leasure to leauin their bread.
c Conteining parte of Marche & parte of April, when corne begã to ripe in that countrey.

out of Egypt, out of the "house of [a] bondage: for by a mightie hand the Lord
broght you out from thence: therefore no
leauened bread shalbe [b] eaten.
4 This day come ye out in the moneth of
[c] Abib.
5 ¶ Now whẽ the Lord hathe broght thee
into the land of the Canaanites, and Hittites, and Amorites, and Hiuites, and Iebusites (which he sware vnto thy fathers,
that he wolde giue thee, a land flowing
with milke and hony) thẽ thou shalt kepe
this seruice in this moneth.
6 Seuen daies shalt thou eat vnleauened
bread, & the [d] seuenth day *shalbe* the feast
of the Lord.

d Bothe the seuenth & the first day were holy, as chap. 12,16.

7 Vnleauened bread shalbe eaten seuen
daies, & there shal no leauened bread be
sene with thee, nor yet leauẽ be sene with
thee in all thy quarters.

e When thou doest celebrat the feast of vnleauened bread.

8 ¶ And thou shalt shewe thy sonne [e] in
ŷ day, saying, *This is done*, because of that
which the Lord did vnto me, whẽ I came
out of Egypt.

f Thou shalt haue continual remembrance thereof, as ŷ woldest of a thing that is in thine hand or before thine eies.

9 And it shal be a signe vnto thee [f] vpon
thine hand, & for a remẽbrance betwene
thine eies, that the Lawe of the Lord may
be in thy mouth: for by a strong hand the
Lord broght thee out of Egypt.
10 Kepe therefore this ordinance in his
season appointed from yere to yere.
11 ¶ And when the Lord shal bring thee
into the land of the Canaanites, as he
sware vnto thee and to thy fathers, & shal
giue it thee,

Chap. 22,29. & 34,19. ezech. 44,30.

12 *Then ŷ shalt set a parte vnto the Lord
all that *first* openeth the wombe: also euerie thing that *first* doeth opẽ *the wombe*, &
commeth forthe of thy beast: the males
shalbe the Lords.

g This is also vnderstand of the horse and other beastes, which were not offred in sacrifice.
h By offring a cleane beast in sacrifice, Leui. 12,6.
"Or, here afterwardes.

13 But euerie first fole of an [g] asse, ŷ shalt
redeme with a lambe: and if thou redeme him not, then thou shalt breake his
necke: likewise all the first borne of man
among thy sonnes shalt thou [h] bye out.
14 ¶ And when thy sonne shal aske thee
"tomorowe, saying, What is this? thou
shalt then say vnto him, With a mightie
hand the Lord broght vs out of Egypt,
out of the house of bondage.
15 For when Pharaóh was hard hearted against our departing, the Lord thẽ slewe
all the firstborne in the lãd of Egypt: frõ
the firstborne of man euẽ to the firstborne
of beast: therefore I sacrifice vnto ŷ Lord
all the males that *first* open the wõbe, but
all the firstborne of my sonnes I redeme.

"Or, signes of remembrance.

16 And it shalbe as a token vpon thine
hand, & as "frõtelets betwene thine eies,
that the Lord broght vs out of Egypt by
a mightie hand.
17 ¶ Now whẽ Pharaóh had let the people
go, God caried thẽ not by the way of the
Philistíms countrey, "thogh it *were* nerer:
(for God said, Lest ŷ people repent whẽ
thei se [i] warre, & turne againe to Egypt)

"Or, because.
i Which the Philistims wolde haue made against them by stopping them the passage.
k That is, not priuely, but openly, and as the worde doeth signifie, set in ordre by fiue and fiue.

18 But God made the people to go about
by ŷ way of the wildernes of the red Sea:
and the children of Israél went vp [k] armed out of the land of Egypt.

Gen. 50,25. iosh. 24,32.

19 (And Mosés toke the bones of Iosépḥ
with him: for he had made the childrẽ of
Israél sweare, saying, *God wil surely visite you, and ye shal take my bones away
hence with you)
20 ¶ So thei toke their iourney from Succóth, and camped in Ethám in the edge
of the wildernes.

Nom. 14,14. deut. 1,13. psal. 78,14. 1. cor. 10,1.
l To defend them from the heat of the sunne.
Nehe. 9,19.

21 *And the Lord went before thẽ by day
in a piller of a [l] cloude to leade them the
way, & by night in a piller of fyre to giue
them light, that thei might go bothe by
day and by night.
22 *He toke not away the piller of the cloude by day, nor the piller of fyre by night
from before the people.

CHAP. XIIII.

4.8 Pharaohs heart is hardened, and pursueth the Israelites. 11 The Israelites striken with feare murmure against Mosés. 21 He deuideth the Sea. 23.27 The Egyptians followe and are drowned.

1 THen the Lord spake vnto Mosés,
saying,

a Frõ towarde the countrey of the Philistims.
b So the Sea was before thẽ, mouñteines on ether side, and the ennemie at their backe: yet thei obeyed God and were deliuered.
c By punishĩg his obstinat rebellion.

2 Speake to the children of Israél, that thei
[a] returne & campe before [b] Pi-hahiróth,
betwene Migdól and ŷ Sea, ouer against
*Baal-zephón: about it shal ye campe by
the Sea.
3 For Pharaóh wil say of the children of
Israél, Thei are tangled in the land: the
wildernes hathe shut them in.
4 And I wil harden Pharaohs heart that
he shal follow after you: so I wil [c] get me
honour vpon Pharaóh, and vpon all his
hoste: the Egyptians also shal knowe that
I am the Lord: and thei did so.
5 ¶ Then it was tolde the King of Egypt,
that the people fled: & the heart of Pharaóh & of his seruants was turned against
the people, and they said, Why haue we
this done, & haue let Israél go out of our
seruice?
6 And he made ready his charets, & toke
his people with him,

d Iosephus writeth ŷ besides these charets there were 50000. horsemen, and 200000. fotemen.
e With great ioye & boldenes.
Iosh. 24,6. 1. mac. 4,9.

7 And toke six hundreth chosen charets, &
[d] all the charets of Egypt, and captaines
ouer euerie one of them.
8 (For the Lord had hardened the heart of
Pharaóh King of Egypt, and he followed
after the children of Israél: but the children of Israél went out with an [e] hye hãd)
9 *And the Egyptians pursued after thẽ, &
all the horses *and* charets of Pharaóh, &
his horsemen & his hoste ouertoke them
camping by the Sea, beside Pi-hahiróth,
before Baal-zephón.

10 And when Pharaóh drewe nie, the children of Iſraél lift vp their eies, and beholde, the Egyptians marched after thé,
and they were ſore [f] afraied: wherefore the children of Iſraél cryed vnto the
Lord.

f Thei, which a litle before in their deliuerance reioyced, being now in danger are afraied & murmure.

In this figure foure chief points are to be conſidered. first that the Church of God is euer ſubiect in this worlde to the Croſſe & to be afflicted after one ſort or other. The ſecond, that the miniſters of God following their vocation ſhalbe euil ſpoken of, and murmured againſt, euen of them that pretend the ſame cauſe and religion that thei do. The third, that God deliuereth not his Church incontinently out of dangers, but to exerciſe their faith and pacience continueth their troubles, yea and often tymes augmẽteth them as the Iſraelites were now in leſſe hope of their liues then when thei were in Egypt. The fourth point is, that when the dangers are moſte great, then Gods helpe is moſte ready to ſuccour: for the Iſraelites had on ether ſide thẽ, huge rockes & mountaines, before them the Sea, behinde them moſte cruel ennemies, ſo that there was no way left to eſcape to mans iudgement.

11 And thei ſaid vnto Moſés, Haſt thou
broght vs to dye in the wildernes, becauſe
there were no graues in Egypt? wherefore
haſt thou ſerued vs thus, to cary vs out of
Egypt?
12 Did not we tel thee this thing in Egypt,
ſaying, Let [g] vs be in reſt, that we may
ſerue the Egyptians? for it had bene better for vs to ſerue the Egyptians, thẽ that
we ſhulde dye in the wildernes.
13 Then Moſés ſaid to the people, Feare ye
not, ſtand ſtil, and beholde *the ſaluacion
of the Lord which he wil ſhewe to you
this day. For the Egyptians, whome ye
haue ſene this day, ye ſhal neuer ſe them
againe.
14 The Lord ſhal fight for you: therefore
[h] holde you your peace.
15 ¶ And the Lord ſaid vnto Moſés, Wherefore [i] cryeſt thou vnto me? ſpeake vnto
the children of Iſraél that thei go forwarde:
16 And lift thou vp thy rod, & ſtretch out
thine hand vpon the Sea & deuide it, and
let the childrẽ of Iſraél go on drye groũde through the middes of the Sea.
17 And I, beholde I wil harden the heart of
the Egyptians that thei may followe thẽ,
and I wil get me honour vpon Pharaóh,
& vpon all his hoſte, vpon his charets, &
vpon his horſemen.
18 Then the Egyptians ſhal knowe that I
am the Lord, when I haue gotten me honour vpon Pharaóh, vpon his charets, &
vpon his horſemen.
19 (And the Angel of God, which went before the hoſte of Iſraél, remoued & went
behinde them: alſo the piller of the cloude went from before them, and ſtode behinde them,
20 And came betwene the campe of the E-
gyptians and the campe of Iſraél: it was
bothe a cloude and darckenes, yet gaue it
[k] light by night, ſo that all the night lõg
the one came not at the other)
21 And Moſés ſtretched forthe his hãd vpon the Sea, and the Lord cauſed the Sea
to runne backe by a ſtrong Eaſt winde all
the night, and made the Sea drye land:
for the waters were* deuided.
22 Thẽ the *children of Iſraél wẽt through
the middes of the Sea vpon the drye
grounde, and the waters *were* a wall vnto
them on the right hand, and on their left
hand.
23 And the Egyptians purſued and went
after them to the middes of the Sea, *euen*
all Pharaohs horſes, his charets, and his
horſemen.
24 Now in the morning [l] watche, whẽ the
Lord loked vnto the hoſte of the Egyptians, out of the firy and cloudy piller, he
ſtroke the hoſte of the Egyptians with
feare.
25 For he toke of their charet wheles, and
thei draue them with *muche a do: ſo that
the Egyptiãs *euerie* one ſaid, I wil flee frõ
the face of Iſraél: for the Lord fighteth
for them againſt the Egyptians.
26 ¶ Then the Lord ſaid to Moſés, Stretch
thine hand vpon the Sea, that the waters
may returne vpon the Egyptians, vpon
their charets and vpon their horſemen.
27 Then Moſés ſtretched forthe his hand
vpon

g Suche is the impaciencie of the fleſh, that it can not abide Gods appointed time.

*Or, deliuerãce.

h Onely put your truſt in God without grudging or douting.

i Thus in tentations faith fighteth agaiſt the fleſh, and cryeth with inwarde gronings to the Lord.

k The cloude ſheweth light to the Iſraelites, but to the Egyptians it was darcknes, ſo that their two hoſtes colde not ioyne together.

Ioſh.4,23. pſal.114,3.

Pſal.78,13. 1 cor.10,1. ebr.11,29.

l Which was about the thre laſt houres of the night.

*Or, heauely.

vpon the Sea, and the Sea returned to his
force early in the morning, & the Egyptians fled against it: but the Lord [m] ouerthrewe the Egyptiās in the middes of the
Sea.
28 So the water returned & couered ỳ charets and the horsemen, *euen* all the hoste of
Pharaóh that came into the Sea after thé:
there remained not one of them.
29 But the children of Israél walked vpon
drye land through the middes of the Sea,
and the waters *were* a wall vnto them on
their right hand, & on their left.
30 Thus ỳ Lord saued Israél the same day
out of the hand of the Egyptians & Israél sawe ỳ Egyptiās dead vpō ỳ Sea backe.
31 And Israél sawe ỳ mighty "power, which
the Lord shewed vpon the Egyptians: so
the people feared the Lord and beleued ỳ
Lord, and his [n] seruant Mosés.

m So the Lord by the water saued his, and by the water drowned his ennemies.

"Ebr. hand.

n That is, the doctrine ẘ he taught them in the Name of the Lord.

CHAP. XV.

1.20. Mosés with the men and women sing praises vnto God for their deliuerance. 23 The people murmure. 25 At the praier of Mosés the bitter waters are swete. 26 God teacheth the people obedience.

1 THē [a] sang *Mosés & the childrē of Israél this song vnto the Lord, and said
in this maner, I wil sing vnto the Lord:
for he hathe triūphed gloriously: ỳ horse
and him that rode vpō him hathe he ouerthrowen in the Sea.
2 The Lord *is* my strength and "praise, and
he is become my saluaciō. He is my God,
and I wil [b] prepare him a tabernacle. *he is*
my fathers God, and I wil exalt him.
3 The Lord *is* a [c] man of warre, his [d] Name
is Iehouáh.
4 Pharaohs charets & his hoste hath he cast
into the Sea: his chosen captaines also were drowned in the red Sea.
5 The depths haue couered thē, they sancke to the bothome as a stone.
6 Thy "right hād, Lord, is glorious in power: thy right hand, Lord, hathe bruised the
ennemie.
7 And in thy great glorie thou hast ouer-
throwē them that rose against [e] thee: thou
sentest forthe thy wrath, *which* consumed
them as the stubble.
8 And by ỳ blast of thy nostrels the waters
were gathered, the floods stode stil as an
heape, the depths congeled together in
the "heart of the Sea.
9 The ennemie said, I wil pursue, I wil o-
uertake *them*, I wil deuide the spoile, my
lust shalbe satisfied vpō them, I wil drawe
my sworde, mine hand shal destroy them.
10 Thou blewest with thy winde, the Sea
couered them, they sancke as lead in the
mightie waters.
11 Who is like vnto thee, ô Lord, among
the [f] gods! who is like thee *so* glorio⁹ in holines, [g] fearful in praises, shewing wōders!

a Praising God for the ouerthrowe of his ennemies and their deliuerance.

Wisd.10,24.

"Or, the occasion of my song of praise.

b To worship him therein.

c In battel he ouercommeth euer.

d Euer constāt in his promes.

"Or, power.

e Those, that are ennemies to Gods people, are his ennemies.

"Or, in the depth of the Sea.

f For so, oftentimes ỳ Scripture calleth the mightie men of the worlde.

g Which oght to be praised with all feare & reuerence.

12 Thou stretchedst out thy right hād, the
earth swalowed them.
13 Thou wilt by thy mercie carye this peo
ple, *which* thou deliueredst: thou wil bring
them in thy strength vnto thine holy [h] habi
tacion.
14 The people shal heare & be afraied: sorowe shal come vpon the inhabitants of
Palestina.
15 Then the dukes of Edóm shalbe amased,
and trembling shal come vpon the great
men of Moáb: all the inhabitants of Canáan shal waxe faint hearted.
16 *Feare & dread shal fall vpon them: because of the "greatnes of thine arme, they
shalbe stil as a stone, til thy people passe, ô
Lord: til this people passe, *which* thou hast
purchased.
17 Thou shalt bring them in, and plant
them in the mountaine of thine [i] inheritāce, *which is* the place *that* thou hast prepared, ô Lord, for to dwel in, *euē* the sanctuarie, ô Lord, *which* thine hāds shal establish.
18 The Lord shal reigne for euer and euer.
19 For Pharaohs horses went with his charets and horsmen into the Sea, and the
Lord broght the waters of the Sea vpon
them: but the children of Israél went on
drye land in the middes of the Sea.
20 ¶And Miriám the prophetesse sister of
Aarón toke a timbrel in her hand, and all
the women came out after her ẘ timbrels
and [k] daunces.
21 And Miriám [l] answered the men, Sing ye
vnto the Lord: for he hathe triūphed gloriously: the horse and his rider hathe he o-
uerthrowen in the Sea.
22 Then Mosés broght Israél from the red
Sea, and they went out into the wildernes
of Shur: and they went thre dayes in the
wildernes, & founde no waters.
23 And whē they came to Maráh, they colde not drinke of the waters of Maráh,
for they were bitter: therefore ỳ name of
the place was called "Maráh.
24 Thē the people murmured against Mo
sés, saying, What shal we drinke?
25 And he cryed vnto the Lord, & ỳ Lord
shewed him a * tre, *which* when he had cast
into ỳ waters, the waters were swete: there
he made them an ordinance & a lawe, and
there he [m] proued them,
26 And said, If thou wilt diligently hearkē,
o Israel, vnto the voyce of the Lord thy
God, and wilt do that, which is [n] right in
his sight, and wilt giue eare vnto his com
mandements, and kepe all his ordinances,
then wil I put none of these diseases vpō
thee, which I broght vpon the Egyptians:
for I *am* the Lord that healeth thee.
27 ¶*And they came to Elim, where *were*
twelue founteines of water & seuētie "palme trees, & they cāped there by ỳ waters.

h That is, into the lād of Canáan: or into mount Zión.

Deut.2,25. iosh.2,9.

"Or, for thy great power.

i Which was mount Zión, where afterward the Temple was buylt.

k Signifiing their great ioye, which custome the Iewes obserued in certein solēnities. Iud.11,34.& 21,21: but it oght not to be a cloke to couer our wanten dāces.

l By singing ỳ like song of thākes giuig.

"Or, Bitternes.

Eccle.38,5.

m That is, God, or, Mosés in Gods name.

n Which is, to do that onely that God commandeth.

Nom.33,9.

"Or, date trees.

CHAP. XVI.

The Israelites come to the desert of Sin, and murmure against Mosés and Aarón. 13 The Lord sendeth quailes and Māna. 27 The seuēth day Mamna colde not be foūde. 32 It is kept for a remembrance to the posteritie.

1 AFterward all the Cōgregacion of ẏ
children of Israél departed from E-
lím, and came to the wildernes of [a] Sin,
(which is betwene Elím and Sinái) the
fifteenth day of the seconde moneth after
their departing out of the land of Egypt.
2 And the whole Cōgregaciō of the children of Israél murmured against Mosés
and against Aarón in the wildernes.
3 For the children of Israél said to them,
Oh ẏ we had dyed by the hand of ẏ Lord
in the land of Egypt, when we sate by ẏ
flesh [b] pottes, when we ate bread *our* bellies ful: for ye haue broght vs out into
this wildernes, to kil this whole companie with famine.
4 ¶ Then said the Lord vnto Mosés, Beholde, I wil cause bread to raine frō heauen to you, and the people shal go out, &
gather that ẏ is sufficient for euerie [c] day,
that I may proue them, whether they wil
walke in my Lawe or no.
5 But the sixt day they shal prepare that,
which they shal bring *home*, and it shalbe
twise as muche as they gather daiely.
6 Then Mosés and Aarón said vnto all the
children of Israél, At euen ye shal knowe,
that the Lord broght you out of the land
of Egypt:
7 And in the morning ye shal se the glorie
of ẏ Lord: [d] for he hathe heard your grud
gings against the Lord: and what are we ẏ
ye haue murmured against vs?
8 Againe Mosés said, At euē shal the Lord
giue you flesh to eat, and in the morning
your fil of bread: for ẏ Lord hathe heard
your murmurings, which ye murmure a-
gaīst him: for what are we? your murmurings *are* not against vs, but against the
[e] Lord.
9 ¶ And Mosés said to Aarón, Say vnto
all the Cōgregacion of the childrē of Israél, Drawe nere before ẏ Lord: for he hathe heard your murmurings.
10 Now as Aarón spake vnto the whole Cō
gregacion of the children of Israél, they
loked toward the wildernes, and beholde,
ẏ glorie of the Lord appeared * ī a cloude.
11 (For the Lord had spoken vnto Mosés,
saying,
12 * I haue heard ẏ murmurings of the chil
dren of Israél: tel them *therefore*, & say, "At
euen ye shal eat flesh, and in the morning
ye shalbe filled with bread, and ye shal
knowe that I am the Lord your God)
13 And so at euē the * quailes came & couered the campe: & in the morning ẏ dewe
laye rounde about the hoste.

a This is the eight place wherein they had camped: there is an other place called Zin, which was the 33 place, wherī they camped: and is also called Kadésh. Nom. 33, 36.

b So hard a thing it is to the flesh not to murmure against God, when the belly is pinched.

c To signifie, ẏ they shulde patiently depēd vpō Gods prouidēce frō day to day.

d He gaue thē not Manna because they murmured, but for his promes sake.

e He that contemneth Gods ministers contemneth God him self.

Chap. 13, 21.

Eccle. 45, 4.

"Or, in the twie light.

Nom. 11, 31.

14 * And when the dewe that was fallē was
ascended, beholde, a smale rounde thing
was vpon the face of the wildernes, smale
as the hore frost on the earth.
15 And when the children of Israél sawe it,
they said one to another, It is [f] MAN, for
they wist not what it was. And Mosés said
vnto them, * This is the bread which the
Lord hathe giuen you to eat.
16 ¶ This is the thing which ẏ Lord hathe
commanded: gather of it euerie man according to his eating [g] an Omer for "a mā
according to the nombre of your persones:
euerie man shal take for thē which are in
his tent.
17 And the children of Israél did so, & gathered, some more, some lesse.
18 And when they did measure it with an
Omer, * he that had gathered muche, had
nothing ouer, & he that had gathered litle, had no [h] lacke: *so* euerie man gathered
according to his eating.
19 Mosés then said vnto them, Let no man
reserue thereof til morning.
20 Notwithstāding thei obeid not Mosés:
but some of them reserued of it til morning, and it was ful of wormes, & [i] stanke:
therefore Mosés was angry with them.
21 And they gathered it euerie morning,
euerie mā accordīg to his eating: for whē
the heat of the sunne came, it was melted.
22 ¶ And the sixt day they gathered [k] twise
so muche bread, two Omers for one man:
then all the rulers of the Congregacion
came and tolde Mosés.
23 And he answered thē, This is that, which
ẏ Lord hathe said, To morowe *is* the rest
of the holy Sabbath vnto the Lord: bake
that *to daie* which ye wil bake, and sethe ẏ
which ye wil sethe, and all that remaineth,
lay it vp to be kept til ẏ mornīg for you.
24 And they laied it vp til the morning, as
Mosés bade, and it stanke not, nether was
there any worme therein.
25 Then Mosés said, Eat that to day: for to
day *is* the Sabbath vnto the Lord: to day
ye shal not [l] finde it in the field.
26 Six dayes shal ye gather it, but in ẏ seuēth day *is* the Sabbath: in it there shalbe
none.
27 ¶ Notwithstanding, there [m] went out
some of the people in the seuenth day for
to gather, and they founde none.
28 And the Lord said vnto Mosés, How lōg
refuse ye to kepe my commandements, &
my lawes?
29 Beholde, how the Lord hathe giuē you
the Sabbath: therefore he giueth you the
sixt day bread for two dayes: tary *therefore* euerie man in his place: let no man go
out of his place the seuenth day.
30 So the people rested the seuenth day.
31 And the house of Israél called the name
of it

Nomb. 11, 7. psal. 78, 24. wisd. 16, 20.

f Which signifieth a parte, portiō, or gift: also meat prepared.

Ioh. 6, 31. 1. cor. 10, 3.

g Which conteineth about a pottle of our measure.

"Ebr. for an head.

2. Cor. 8, 15.

h God is a riche feder of all, & none cā iustely cōplaine.

i No creature is so pure, but being abused, it turneth to our destructiō.

k Which portiō shulde serue for the Sabbath and the day before.

l God toke away the occasiō from their labour, to signifie how he wolde haue the Sabbath kept.

m Their infidelitie was so great, that thei did expresly against Gods commandemēt.

n In forme & figure, but not in colour. Nom. 11,7.

of it, MAN. and it was like n to coriandre
sede, *but* white: and the taste of it was like
vnto wafers *made* with hony.
31 And Mosés said, This is that which the
Lord hathe commanded, Fil an Omer
of it, to kepe it for your posteritie: that
they may se ỹ bread wherewith I haue fed
you in wildernes, when I broght you out
of the land of Egypt.
33 Mosés also said to Aarón, Take a o pot
and put an Omer ful of MAN therein, &
set it before the Lord to be kept for your
posteritie.
34 As the Lord commanded Mosés: so Aarón laied it vp before the p Testimonie to
be kept.
35 And the children of Israél did eat MAN
* fourty yeres, vntil they came vnto a lād
inhabited: they did eat MAN vntil they
came to the borders of the land of Canáan.
36 The Omer *is* the tenth part of the q E-
pháh.

o Of this vessel read, Ebr. 9.4.

p That is, the Arke of ỹ couenant: to wit, after that the Arke was made.

Iosh. 5,12. nehe. 9,35. iudith. 5,15.

q Which measure conteined about ten pottels.

CHAP. XVII.

1 The Israélites come into Rephidim and grudge for water. 6 Water is giuen them out of the rocke. 11 Mosés holdeth vp his hands, & thei ouercome the Amalekites.

1 AND all the Congregaciō of the chil
dren of Israél departed from the wil
dernes of Sin, by their iourneis at the '' cō
mandemēt of the Lord, & camped in a Re
phidím, where *was* no water for the people to drinke.
2 * Wherefore the people contended with
Mosés, and said, Giue vs water that we
may drinke. And Mosés said vnto them,
Why contend ye with me? wherefore do
ye b tempt the Lord?
3 So the people thirsted there for water, &
the people murmured against Mosés, and
said, Wherefore hast thou thus broght vs
out of Egypt to kil vs and our children &
our cattel with thirst?
4 And Mosés cryed to the Lord, saying,
What shal I do to this people? for they be
almost ready to c stone me.
5 And ỹ Lord answered to Mosés, Go before the people, and take with thee of the
Elders of Israél: and thy rod, wherewith
thou * smotest the riuer, take in thine hād,
and go:
6 * Beholde, I wil stād there before thee vpon the rocke in Horéb, & thou shalt smite
on the rocke & water shal come out of it,
that the people may drinke. And Mosés did so in the sight of the Elders of
Israél.
7 And he called the name of the place, '' Mas
sáh and '' Meribáh, because of the contention of the children of Israél, and because
they had tempted the Lord, saying, Is the

'' Ebr. at the mouthe.

a Mosés here noteth not euerie place, where they camped, as Nom. 33. but onely those places where some notable thing was done.

Nom. 20,4.

b Why distrust you God? why loke you not for succour of him without murmuring against vs?

c How readie the people are for their owne matters to slay ỹ true prophets, and how slow thei are to reuenge Gods cause against his enemies and false prophets?

Chap. 7,20. Nomb. 20,9. wisd. 11,4. psal. 78,15. & 105,41. 1. cor. 10,4.

'' Or, Tentacion. '' Or, Strife.

d Lord among vs, or no?
8 ¶ * Then came e Amalék and foght with
Israél in Rephidím.
9 And Mosés said to Ioshúa, Chuse vs out
men, and go fight ẃ Amalék: tomorowe
I wil stand on the top of the f hil with
the rod of God in mine hand.
10 So Ioshúa did as Mosés bade hī, & foght
with Amalék: & Mosés, Aarón, and Hur,
went vp to the top of the hil.
11 And when Mosés held vp his hand, Israél preuailed: but when he let his hand
g downe, Amalék preuailed.
12 Now Mosés hāds were heauy: therefore
they toke a stone and put it vnder him, &
he sate vpon it: and Aarón & Hur staied
vp his hands, the one on the one side, and
the other on the other side: so his hands
were steady vntil the going downe of the
sunne.
13 And Ioshúa discomfited Amalék and his
people with the edge of the sworde.
14 ¶ And ỹ Lord said to Mosés, Write this
for a remembrance h in the boke, and '' re
hearse it to Ioshúa: for * I wil vtterly put
out the remembrance of Amalék from
vnder heauen.
15 (And Mosés buylte an altar and called
the name of it, i Iehouáh-nissi)
16 Also he said, '' The Lord hathe sworne,
that he wil haue warre with Amalék from
generacion to generacion.

d When in aduersitie we thinke God to be absent, we neglect his promes & make him a lier.

Deut. 25,17. wisd. 11,3.

e Who came of Elipház, sonne of Esáu, Gen. 36,12.

f That is, Horéb, which is also called Sinái.

g So that we se how dāgerous a thing it is to fainte in prayer.

h In the boke of ỹ lawe.

'' Ebr. put it in the eares of Ioshua.

Nom. 24, 20. 1. sam. 15,3.

i That is, the Lord is my bāner: as he declared by holding vp his rod and his hands.

'' Ebr. The hand of the Lord vpō the throne.

CHAP. XVIII.

1 Iethró commeth to se Mosés his sonne in lawe. 8 Mosés telleth him of the wonders of Egypt. 9 Iethró reioyceth and offreth sacrifice to God. 24 Mosés obeieth his counsel in appointing officers.

1 WHen Iethró the * Priest of Midián Mosés father in lawe heard
all that God had done for Mosés, and for
Israél his people, & how the Lord had
broght Israél out of Egypt,
2 Then Iethró the father in lawe of Mosés
toke Zipporáh Mosés wife, (after he had
a sent her away)
3 And her two sonnes, (whereof ỹ one was
called Gershóm: for he said, I haue bene
an aliant in a strange land:
4 And the name of the other *was* Eliézer:
for the God of my father, *said he, was* mine helpe, and deliuered me from the
sworde of Pharaóh)
5 And Iethró Mosés father in lawe came
with his two sonnes, & his wife vnto Mosés into the wildernes, where he camped
by the b mount of God.
6 And he c said to Mosés, I thy father in
lawe Iethró am come to thee, & thy wife
and her two sonnes with her.
7 ¶ And Mosés wēt out to mete his father
in lawe, and did obeisance and kissed
him, and eche asked other of his '' welfare:

Chap. 2,16.

a It may seme ỹ he sent her backe to her father for her impaciencie, lest she shulde be a let to his vocation, ẃ was so dangerous. chap. 4,25.

b Horéb is called ỹ mouñt of God, because God wroght many miracles there.

c That is, he sent messengers to say vnto him.

'' Ebr. of peace.

and they came into the tent.
8 Then Mosés tolde his father in law all
that the Lord had done vnto Pharaóh, &
to the Egyptians for Iſraels ſake, *and* all
the trauaile that had come vnto them by
the way, and *how* the Lord deliuered thē.
9 And Iethró reioyced at all the goodnes,
which the Lord had ſhewed to Iſraél, *and*
becauſe he had deliuered them out of the
hand of the Egyptians.
10 Therefore Iethró ſaid, [d] Bleſſed *be* the
Lord who hathe deliuered you out of the
hãd of ỹ Egyptians, and out of ỹ hand of
Pharaóh: who hathe *alſo* deliuered the peo
ple from vnder the hãd of the Egyptiãs.
11 Now I knowe that the Lord is greater
then all the gods: * for as they haue dealt
proudely with them, *ſo are they* [e] *recompenſed*.
12 Then Iethró Mosés father in law toke
burnt offringes and ſacrifices *to offre* vnto
God. And Aarón and all the Elders of Iſraél came to eat bread with Mosés father
in law [f] before God.
13 ¶ Now on the morowe, when Mosés ſate
to iudge the people, the people ſtode a-
boute Mosés from morning vnto euen.
14 And when Mosés father in lawe ſawe all
that he did to the people, he ſaid, What is
this that thou doeſt to the people? why ſitteſt thou thy ſelfe alone, and all the people ſtand about thee from morning vnto
euen?
15 And Mosés ſaid vnto his father in lawe,
Becauſe the people come vnto me to ſeke
[g] God.
16 Whē they haue a matter, they come vnto me, and I iudge betwene one and an o-
ther, and declare the ordinances of God,
and his lawes.
17 But Mosés father in law ſaid vnto him,
The thing, which thou doeſt, is not wel.
18 Thou bothe " weariest thy ſelfe greatly,
& this people that is ẇ thee: for the thing
is to heauie for thee: thou art not able to
do it thy ſelfe alone.
19 * Heare now my " voyce, (I wil giue
thee counſel, and God ſhalbe with thee)
be thou for the people to [h] Godwarde, &
reporte thou the cauſes vnto God,
20 And admoniſh them of the ordinances,
and of the lawes, & ſhewe them the way,
wherein they muſt walke, & the worke ỹ
they muſt do.
21 Moreouer prouide thou among all the
people [i] men of courage, fearing God,
men dealing truely, hating couetouſnes:
and appoint *ſuche* ouer them *to be* rulers o-
uer thouſandes, rulers ouer hundreths, rulers ouer fifties, and rulers ouer tens.
22 And let them iudge the people at all ſeaſons: but euerie great matter let thē bring
vnto thee, & let them iudge all ſmale cau-

d Wherby it is euident that he worſhiped the true God, and therefore Mosés refuſed not to mary his daughter.

Chap.1.10. alſo ver 16,22. chap.5,7. chap.14,18.

e For they, ỹ drowned the children of ỹ Iſraelites, periſhed them ſelues by water.

f They ate in ỹ place, where the ſacrifice was offred: for parte was burnt and the reſt eaten.

g That is, to knowe Gods wil, and to haue iuſtice executed.

" *Ebr. thou wilt faint and fall.*

Deu.1,9.
" *Or, counſel.*

h Iudge thou in harde cauſes, which can not be decided but by conſulting with God.

i What maner of men oght to be choſen to beare office.

ſes: ſo ſhal it be eaſier for thee, when they
ſhal beare *the burden* with thee.
23 If thou do this thing, (and God *ſo* commãde thee) bothe thou ſhalt be able to endure, & all this people ſhal alſo go quietly to their place.
24 So Mosés [k] obeied ỹ voyce of his father
in lawe, and did all that he had ſaid:
25 And Mosés choſe men of courage out of
all Iſraél, and made them heades ouer the
people, rulers ouer thouſandes, rulers ouer
hundreths, rulers ouer fifties, and rulers
ouer tens.
26 And they iudged the people at all ſeaſons, *but* they broght the hard cauſes vnto
Mosés: for they iudged all ſmale matters
them ſelues.
27 Afterward Mosés [l] let his father in lawe
departe, and he went into his contrey.

k Godlie counſel oght euer to be obeied, thogh it come of our inferiors: for to ſuche God oftē times giueth wiſdome to humble them that are exalted.

l Read the occaſion, Nomb. 10,29.

CHAP. XIX.

1 The Iſraelites come to Sinái. 5 Iſraél is choſen from among all other nations. 8 The people promes to obey God. 12 He that toucheth the hil dyeth. 16 God appeareth vnto Mosés vpon the mount in thunder and lightening.

1 IN the [a] third moneth, after the childrē
of Iſraél were gone out of the land of
Egypt, the ſame [b] day came they into the
wildernes of Sinái.
2 For they departed from Rephidím, and
came to ỹ deſert of Sinái, & cãped in the
wildernes: euen there Iſraél camped before the mount.
3 *But Mosés wēt vp vnto God, for ỹ Lord
had called out of the mount vnto him,
ſaying, Thus ſhalt thou ſay to the houſe of
[c] Iaakób, and tel the children of Iſraél,
4 *Ye haue ſene what I did vnto the Egyptians, and *how* I caryed you vpon [d] egles
wings, and haue broght you vnto me.
5 Now therefore *if ye wil heare my voyce
in dede, & kepe my couenãt, thē ye ſhalbe
my chief treaſure aboue all people, *thogh
all the earth be mine.
6 Ye ſhalbe vnto me alſo a kingdome of
* Prieſtes, and an holy nation. Theſe *are*
the wordes which thou ſhalt ſpeake vnto
the children of Iſraél.
7 ¶ Mosés then came & called for the Elders of the people, and propoſed vnto thē
all theſe things, which the Lord commanded him.
8 And the people anſwered altogether, &
ſaid, *All that the Lord hathe commãded,
we wil do. And Mosés reported the wordes of the people vnto the Lord.
9 And ỹ Lord ſaid vnto Mosés, Lo, I come
vnto thee in a thicke cloude, that the people may heare, whiles I talke with thee, &
that they may alſo beleue thee for euer.
(for Mosés had tolde the wordes of the
people vnto the Lord)
10 Moreouer the Lord ſaid vnto Mosés,
Go

a Which was in ỹ begining of the monthe Siuán, conteining parte of May and parte of Iune.

b That they departed from Rephidím.

Act.7,38.

c God called Iaakób Iſraél: therefore the houſe of Iaakób, and the people of Iſraél ſignifie onely Gods people.

Deut.29,2.

d For the egle by flying hie, is out of danger, and in carying her birdes rather on her wings thē in her talants declareth her loue.

Deu.5,2.
Deu.10,14. pſa.24,1.
1.Pet.2,9. reu.1,6.
Chap.24,3. deu.5,27. and,26,17. ioſh.24,16.

e Teache thē to be pure in heart, as they shewe thē selues outwardly cleane by washing.

Go to the people, and e sanctifie them to
daie and to morowe, and let them wash
their clothes.
11 And let thē be ready on the third daie:
for the third daie the Lord wil come
downe in the sight of all the people vpon
mount Sinái:
12 And thou shalt set markes vnto the people rounde about, saying, Take hede to
your selues that ye go not vp to the moūt,
nor touche the bordre of it: whosoeuer
toucheth the * mount, shal surely dye.

Ebr.12,20.

13 No hand shal touche it, but he shal be
stoned to death, or stricken through with
dartes: whether it be beast or man, he shal
not liue: when the ″ horne bloweth long,
thei shal come vp ″ into the mountaine.

″Or, trumpet.

″Or, towarde.

14 ¶ Then Mosés went downe from the
mount vnto the people, & sanctified the
people, and thei washed their clothes.
15 And he said vnto the people, Be ready
on the third daie, *and* come not at *your*
f wiues.

f But giue your selues to prayer and abstinēce, that you may at this time attēd only vpon the Lord. 1.Cor. 7,5.

16 And the third daie, whē it was morning,
there was thūders & lightnings, & a thicke cloude vpon the mount, & the sound of
the trumpet exceding loude, so that all
the people, that was in the campe, was
afraid.
17 Then Mosés broght the people out of
the tents to mete with God, & thei stode
in the nether part of the mount.
18 * And mount Sinái *was* all on smoke, because the Lord came downe vpon it in
fire, and the smoke thereof ascended, as
the smoke of a fornace, and all the mount
g trembled excedingly.

Deu.4,11.

g God vsed these fearful signes that his Lawe shuld be had in greater reuerence, and his maiestie ỳ more feared.

19 And when the sound of the trūpet blewe
long, and waxed louder and louder, Mosés spake, and God answered him by
h voyce.

h He gaue autoritie to Mosés by plaine wordes, that ỳ people might vnderstand hī.

20 (For the Lord came downe vpon moūt
Sinái on the top of the mount) and whē
the Lord called Mosés vp into the top of
the mount, Mosés went vp.
21 Then the Lord said vnto Mosés, Go
downe, charge ỳ people, that thei breake
not *their boūdes, to go vp* to the Lord to gaze,
lest manie of them perish.
22 And let the ″ Priests also which come to
the Lord be sanctified, lest the Lord ″ destroye them.

″Or, rulers.

″Or, breake out vpon them.

23 And Mosés said vnto the Lord, The
people can not come vp into the mount
Sinái: for thou hast charged vs, saying, Set
markes on the mountaine, & sanctifie it.
24 And the Lord said vnto him, Go, get
thee downe, and come vp, thou, & Aarón
with thee: but let not the i Priestes & the
people breake *their boūdes* to come vp vnto the Lord, lest he destroye them.
25 So Mosés went downe vnto the people,
and tolde them.

i Nether dignitie nor multitude haue autoritie to passe ỳ boūdes, that Gods worde prescribeth.

CHAP. XX.

2 The commandements of the first table. 12. The commādements of the seconde. 18. The people afraid are cōforted by Mosés. 23. Gods of siluer and golde are againe forbiden. 24. Of what sort the altar oght to be.

1 THen God a spake all these wordes,
saying,
2 * I am the Lord thy God, which haue
broght thee out of the land of Egypt, out
of the house of ″ bondage.
3 Thou shalt haue none other gods b before me.

a Whē Mosés and Aarón were gone vp, or had passed the boundes of the people, God spake thus out of ỳ mount Horéb, ỳ all the people heard.

Deu.5,6.

psal.81,11.

″Or, seruants.

b To whose eies all thigs are open.

4 * Thou shalt make thee no grauē image,
nether anie similitude *of things* that are
in heauen aboue, nether that are in the
earth beneth, nor that are in the waters
vnder the earth.

Leu.26,1.

psal.97,7.

5 Thou shalt not c bowe downe to them,
nether serue them: for I am the Lord thy
God, a d ielouse God, visiting the iniquitie of the fathers vpon the children, vpon
the third *generacion* and vpon the fourth
of them that hate me:
6 And shewing mercie vnto e thousandes
to them that loue me and kepe my commandements.

c By this outwarde gesture all kinde of seruice & worship to idoles is forbidden.

d And wil be reuenged of ỳ contemners of mine honour.

e So ready is he rather to shewe mercie then to punish.

7 * Thou shalt not take the Name of the
Lord thy God in f vaine: for the Lord wil
not holde him giltles that taketh his Name in vaine.

Leu.19,12.

deu.5,12.

mat.5,28.

f Ether by swearing falsely or rashly or contēning.

8 Remembre the Sabbath daie, g to kepe
it holy.
9 * Six daies shalt thou labour, and do all
thy worke,
10 But the seuenth daie *is* the Sabbath of ỳ
Lord thy God: *in it* thou shalt not do anie
worke, thou, nor thy sóne, nor thy daughter, thy man seruant, nor thy maid, nor
thy beast, nor thy stranger that is within
thy ″ gates.

g Which is, by meditating the spiritual rest, by hearing Gods worde, and resting frō worldelie trauailes.

Chap.23,12.

ezek.20,12.

″Or, citie.

11 * For in six daies the Lord made the heauen and the earth, the sea, and all that in
them is, & rested the seuenth daie: therefore the Lord blessed the Sabbath daie,
and hallowed it.

Gen.2,2.

Deu.5,16.

mat.15,4.

ephe.6,2.

h By ỳ which is mēt all that haue autoritie ouer vs.

12 ¶ * Honour thy h father and thy mother,
that thy daies maie be prolonged vpon ỳ
land, ẇ the Lord thy God giueth thee.
13 * Thou shalt not i kil.
14 Thou shalt not k commit adulterie.
15 Thou shalt not l steale.
16 Thou shalt not beare false m witnes a-
gainst thy neighbour.

Mat.5,16.

i But loue and preserue thy brothers life.

k But be pure in heart, word and dede.

l But studie to saue his goods

m But further his good name, and speake trueth.

17 * Thou shalt not n couet thy neighbours
house, nether shalt thou couet thy neighbours wife, nor his man seruant, nor his
maid, nor his oxe, nor his asse, nether any
thing that is thy neighbours.

Rom.7,7.

n Thou maiest not so muche as wishe his hinderance in anie thing.

18 ¶ And all the people ″ sawe the thunders,
and the ″ lightenings, and the sound of
the trumpet, and the mountaine smoking.
and when the people sawe it thei fled and
stode afarre of,

″Or, heard.

″Ebr. fire brāds.

Deut.5,24. & 18,16 ebr. 12,18.

19 And said vnto Mosés,*Talke thou with
vs,and we wil heare: but let not God talke with vs, lest we dye.
20 Then Mosés said vnto the people, Feare not: for God is come to o proue you,
and that his feare may be before you,that
ye sinne not.

o Whether you wil obey his precepts as you promi-sed,chap.19,8.

21 So the people stode a far of, but Mosés
drewe nere vnto the darcknes where God
was.
22 ¶And the Lord said vnto Mosés, Thus
thou shalt say vnto the children of Israél, Ye haue sene that I haue talked with
you from heauen.
23 Ye shal not make *therefore* with me gods
of siluer,nor gods of golde:you shal make you none.
24 *An altar of earth ỹ shalt make vnto me,
& thereon shalt offre thy burnt offrings,
& thy* peace offrings,thy shepe,& thine
oxen:in all places,where I shal put the remembrance of my Name,I wil come vnto thee,and blesse thee.

Chap.27 8. & 38,7. Leui.3,1.

25 *But if thou wilt make me an altar of
stone, thou shalt not buylde it of hewen
stones: for *if* thou lift vp thy tole vpon
them,thou hast polluted "them.
26 Nether shalt thou go vp by steppes vnto mine altar, that thy p filthines be not
discouered thereon.

Deut.27,5. iosh.8,31.

"Ebr.it,that is, the stone.

p Which might be by his stouping, or flyĩg abroad of his clothes.

CHAP. XXI.

Temporal and ciuile ordinances, appointed by God, touching seruitude, murthers, and wronges: the obseruatiõ whereof doeth not iustifie a man, but are giuen to bridel our corrupt nature, which els wolde breake out into all mischief and crueltie.

1 NOw these are the lawes,which thou
shalt set before them:
2 *If thou bye an Ebrewe seruant, he shal
serue six yeres, and in the seuenth he shal
go out fre, a for nothing.
3 If he came b him selfe alone, he shal go
out him selfe alone:if he *were* maried,thẽ
his wife shal go out with him.

Leui.25,39. deut.15,12. ierem.34,14.

a Paying no money for his libertie.

b Not hauing wife nor children.

4 If his master hathe giuen him a wife, &
she hathe borne him sonnes or daughters,
the wife and her children shalbe her c masters,but he shal go out him self alone.
5 But if the seruant say thus, I loue my
master, my wife and my children, I wil
not go out fre,

c Til her time of seruitude was expired, which might be the seuenth yere or the fiftieth.

6 Then his master shal bring him vnto
the "Iudges, and set him to the d dore, or
to the poste, and his master shal bore his
eare through with a nawle,& he shal serue him for e euer.

"Ebr gods.

d Where the Iudges sate.

e That is,to ỹ yere of Iubile, which was euerie fiftieth yere.

7 ¶Likewise if a man f sel his daughter to
be a seruant,she shal not go out as the mẽ
seruants do.
8 If she please not her master, who hathe
betrothed her to him selfe, then shal g he
cause to bye her:he shal haue no power to
sel her to a strange people,seing he "despised her.

f Constreined ether by pouertie,or els,ỹ ỹ master shuld mary her.

g By giuing another money to bye her of him.

"Or, deflowred her.

9 But if he hathe betrothed her vnto his
sonne, he shal deale with her h according
to the custome of the daughters.
10 If he take i him an other *wife*,he shal not
diminish her fode, her rayment, and recompence of her virginitie.

h That is, he shal giue her dowrie.

i For his sonne.

11 And if he do not these k thre vnto her,
thẽ shal she go out fre,paying no money.
12 ¶*He that smiteth a man, and he dye,
shal dye the death.
13 And if a man hathe not laied waite, but
l God hathe offred *him* into his hãd, *then
I wil appoĩte thee a place whither he shal
flee.

k Nether mary her him selfe, nor giue an other money to bye her, nor bestowe her vpõ his sonne.

Leui.24,17.

l Though a mã be killed at vnwares,yet it is Gods prouidẽce, that it shulde so be.

14 But if a man come presumpteously vpon his neighbour to slaie him with guile,
thou shalt take him from mine m altar,
that he may dye.

Deut.19,2.

m The holines of the place oght not to defẽd the murther.

15 ¶Also he that smiteth his father or his
mother, shal dye the death.
16 ¶And he that stealeth a man, & selleth
him, if it be founde with him, shal dye
the death.
17 ¶*And he that curseth his father or
his mother,shal dye the death.
18 ¶When men also striue together,& one
smite another with a n stone, or with the
fist,& he dye not,but lieth in bed,

n Ether far of him or nere.

19 If he rise againe and walke without vpon his staffe, then shal he that smote him
go o quite, saue onely he shal beare his
charges" for his resting, and shal pay for
his healing.

o By the ciuile iustice.

"Or, lesing of his time.

20 ¶And if a man smite his seruant, or
his mayd with a rod, & he dye vnder his
hand,he shal be surely punished.
21 But if he continue a day, or two daies,
he shal not p be punished: for he *is* his
money.

p By the ciuile Magistrate, but before God he is a murtherer.

22 ¶Also if men striue and hurt a woman
with childe,so that her childe departe frõ
her, & q death followe not, he shal be surely punished according as the womans
housband shal appoint him,or he shal pay
as the "Iudgés determine.

q Of the mother,or childe.

"Or, arbiters.

23 But if death followe, thẽ thou shalt paye
life for life,
24 *r Eie for eie, tothe for tothe, hand for
hand,fote for fote,
25 Burning for burning, wonde for wõde,
stripe for stripe.

Leui.24,20. deut.19,20. matt.5,33.

r The executiõ of this lawe onely belõged to the Magistrat,mat.5,33.

26 ¶And if a man smite his seruant in the
eie, or his maid in the eie, and hathe perished it,he shal let him go fre for his eie.
27 Also if he smite f out his seruants tothe,
or his maydes tothe, he shal let him go
out fre for his tothe.

f So God reuẽgeth crueltie in moste least things.

28 ¶If an oxe gore a man or a woman,that
he dye,the* oxe shalbe t stoned to death,
and his flesh shal not be eaten,but the owner of the oxe *shal* go quite.
29 If the oxe were wonte to push in times
past

Gen.9,5.

t If the beast be punished, muche more shal the murtherer.

"Or, testified to him.

past, & it hathe bene " tolde his master, &
he hathe not kept him, and after he killeth
a man or a woman, the oxe shal be stoned
and his owner shal dye also.

u By the next of the kinred of him that is so slayne.

30 If there be set to him a [u] summe of money, then he shal pay the rãsom of his life,
whatsoeuer shalbe laied vpon him.
31 Whether he hathe gored a sonne, or gored a daughter, he shal be iudged after the
same maner.
32 If the oxe gore a seruant or a mayd, he
shal giue vnto their master thirty [x] she-
kles of siluer, and the oxe shalbe stoned.

x Read Gen. 23,15.

33 ¶ And when a man shal open a well, or
when he shal dig a pit and couer it not,
& an oxe or an asse fall therein,
34 The owner of the pit shal [y] make it
good, *and* giue money to the owners thereof, but the dead *beast* shalbe his.

y This lawe forbiddeth not onely not to hurt, but to beware lest any be hurt.

35 ¶ And if a mans oxe hurt his neighbours
oxe that he dye, then thei shal sel the liue
oxe, & deuide the money thereof, & the
dead *oxe* also thei shal deuide.
36 Or if it be knowen that the oxe hathe
vsed to push in times past, and his master hathe not kept him, he shal pay oxe
for oxe, but the dead shalbe his owne.

CHAP. XXII.

*1 Of theft. 5 Dommage. 7 Lending. 14 Borrowing.
16 Intising of maides. 18 Witchcraft. 20 Idolatrie.
21 Support of strangers, widows, and fatherles. 25 V-
surie. 28 Reuerence to Magistrates.*

a Ether great beast of the herd, or a smale beast of the flocke.

1 IF a man steale an [a] oxe or a shepe,
and kil it or sel it, he shal restore fiue
oxen for the oxe, * & foure shepe for the
shepe.

2.Sam.12,6.

2 ¶ If a thefe be founde [b] breaking vp, &
be smitten that he dye, no blood *shalbe
shed* for him.

b Breaking an house to entre in, or vndermining.

"Ebr. when the sunne riseth vpon him.
c He shalbe put to death.

3 But if it be" in the day light, [c] blood *shalbe
shed* for him: *for* he shulde make ful restitutiõ: if he had not *wherewith*, then shulde
he be solde for his theft.

"Ebr. in his hand.

4 If the theft be founde" with him, aliue,
(whether it be oxe, asse, or shepe) he shal
restore the double.
5 ¶ If a man do hurt field, or vineyarde,
and put in his beast to fede in another
mãs field, he shal recompence of the best
of his owne field, & of the best of his owne vineyarde.
6 ¶ If fyre breake out, and catche in the
thornes, and the stackes of corne, or the
standing corne, or the field be cõsumed,
he that kindeled the fire shal make ful restitution.
7 ¶ If a man deliuer his neighbour money or stuffe to kepe, and it be stollen out
of his house, if the thefe be found, he
shal paye the double.

"Ebr. gods.
d That is, whether he hathe stollen.

8 If the thefe be not founde, then the master of the house shal be broght vnto the
" Iudges *to sweare*, whether he hathe [d] put
his hãd vnto his neighbours good, or no.
9 In all maner of trespasse, whether it be
for oxen, for asse, for shepe, for rayment,
or for any maner of lost thing, which an
other chalengeth to be his, the cause of
bothe *parties* shal come before the Iudges,
& whome the Iudges condemne, he shal
pay the double vnto his neighbour.
10 If a man deliuer vnto his neighbour
to kepe asse, or oxe, or shepe, or any beast,
and it dye, or be " hurt, or taken away by
ennemies, & no man se it,

"Ebr. broken.

11 [e] An othe of the Lord shalbe betwene
them twaine, that he hathe not put his
hand vnto his neighbours good, and the
owner of it shal take *the othe*, & he shal not
make it good:

e Thei shulde sweare by the Name of the Lord.

12 * But if it be stollen from him, he shal
make restitutiõ vnto the owner thereof.

Gen.31,39.

13 If it be torne in pieces, he shal bring
[f] recorde, & shal not make that good, *which
is* deuoured.

f He shal shewe some parte of the beast.

14 ¶ And if a mã borowe *oght* of his neighbour, and it be hurt, or els dye, the owner
thereof not being by, he shal surely make
it good.
15 If the owner thereof be by, he shal not
make it good: *for* if it *be* an hired thing, it
[g] came for his hire.

g He that hyred it shalbe fre by paying the hire.

16 ¶ * And if a mã entise a mayd that is not
betrothed, & lye with her, he shal endowe
her, and take her to his wife.

Deut.22,28.

17 If her father refuse to giue her to him,
he shal pay money, according to the dowrie of virgines.
18 ¶ Thou shalt not suffre a witche to liue.
19 ¶ Whosoeuer lieth with a beast, shal dye
the death.
20 ¶ * He that offreth vnto *any* gods, saue
vnto the Lord onely, shalbe slaine.

Deut.13,13. 1.mac.2,24.

21 ¶ * Moreouer thou shalt not do iniurie
to a stranger, nether oppresse him: for ye
were strangers in the land of Egypt.

Leui.19,33.

22 ¶ * Ye shal not trouble any widowe, nor
fatherles childe.

Zach.7,10.

23 If thou vexe or trouble suche, and so he
call and crye vnto me, I wil surely heare
his crye.
24 Then shal my wrath be kindeled, and I
wil kil you with the sworde, & your [h] wiues shal be widowes, and your children
fatherles.

h The iust plague of God vpon y oppressers.

25 ¶ * If thou lend money to my people,
that is, to the poore with thee, thou shalt
not be as an vsurer vnto him: ye shal not
oppresse him with vsurie.

Leui.25,37. deut.23,19. psal.15,5.

26 If thou take thy neighbours rayment to
pledge, thou shalt restore it vnto him before the sunne go downe:
27 For that is his couering onely, & this is
his garment for his skin: wherein shal he
slepe? therefore when he [i] cryeth vnto me,
I wil heare him: for I am merciful.

i For colde & necessitie.

Act.23,5. 28 ¶ *Thou shalt not raile vpõ the Iudges,
nether speake euil of the ruler of thy
people.

k Thine abundãce of thy corne, oyle & wine.
29 ¶ Thine[k] abundance & thy licour shalt
thou not kepe backe. *The firstborne of
thy sonnes shalt thou giue me.

Chap.13,2. & 34,19.
30 Likewise shalt thou do with thine oxen
and with thy shepe: seuen dayes it shalbe
with his damme, & the eight day thou
shalt giue it me.

Leui.22,8. ezek.44,31.
31 ¶ Ye shalbe an holy people vnto me, *nether shal ye eat any flesh that is torne *of
beastes* in the field: ye shal cast it [l] to the
dog.

l And so haue nothing to do with it.

CHAP. XXIII.

2 *Not to followe the multitude. 13 Not to make mention of the strange gods. 14 The thre solemne feastes.
20.23 The Angel is promised to leade the people.
25 What God promiseth, if thei obey him. 29 God wil
cast out the Canaanites by litle and litle, and why.*

Or, reporte a false tale. *Or, cruel.*
1 THou shalt not "receiue a false tale,
nether shalt thou put thine hãd with
the wicked, to be a" false witnes.

Ebr. answer. a Do that ŷ is godlie though few do fauour it.
2 ¶ Thou shalt not followe a multitude to
do euil, nether "agre in a controuersie [a] to
decline after many & ouerthrow *the trueth.*
3 ¶ Thou shalt not esteme a poore man in
his cause.

b If we be bõde to do good to our enemies beast, muche more to our enemie him selfe, Mat.5, 44.
4 ¶ If thou mete thine enemies oxe, or
his asse going a straye, thou shalt [b] bring
him to him againe.
5 If thou se thine enemies [c] asse lying
vnder his burden, wilt thou cease to helpe him? thou shalt helpe him vp againe
with it.

c If God commãde to helpe vp our enemies asse vnder his burden, wil he suffre vs to cast downe our brethren with heauie burdens?
6 ¶ Thou shalt not ouerthrowe the right
of thy poore in his sute.
7 Thou shalt kepe thee farre from a false
matter, and shalt not slay the [d] innocent
and the righteous: for I wil not iustifie a
wicked man.

d Whether ŷ be magistrate: or art commãded by the magistrate.
Deut.16,19. eccl.20,32.
8 ¶ *Thou shalt take no gift: for the gift
blindeth the" wise, & peruerteth ŷ wordes
of the righteous.

Ebr. seing. e For in that ŷ he is a strãger, his heart is sorful ynough.
9 ¶ Thou shalt not oppresse a stranger: for
ye knowe the [e] heart of a stranger, seing
ye were strangers in the land of Egypt.

Leui.25,3.& 26,43. deut. 15,1.
10 *Moreouer, six yeres thou shalt sowe thy
land, and gather the frutes thereof,
11 But the seuẽth yere thou shalt let it rest
and lye stil, that the poore of thy people
may eat, and what thei leaue, the beastes
of the field shal eat. In like maner thou
shalt do with thy vineyarde, & with thine oliue trees.

Chap.20,8. deut.5,12.
12 *Six daies thou shalt do thy worke, and
in the seuẽth day thou shalt rest, that thine oxe, and thine asse may rest, & the sonne of thy maid and the stranger may be
refreshed.

f Nether by swearing by thẽ, nor speaking of them, Psal.16,4. eph. 5,3.
13 And ye shal take hede to all things that
I haue said vnto you: and ye shal make
[f] no mencion of the name of other gods,
nether shal it be heard out of thy mouth.
14 ¶ Thre times thou shalt kepe a feast vnto me in the yere.

g That is, Easter, in remembrãce that the Angel passed ouer & spared the Israelites, when he slewe the firstborne of the Egyptians.
15 Thou shalt kepe the feast [g] of vnleaue-
ned bread: thou shalt eat vnleauened
bread seuen daies, as I cõmanded thee, in
the season of the moneth of Abib: for in
it thou camest out of Egypt: & none shal
appeare before me emptie:

h Which is, Witsontide, in token that the Law was giuẽ 50. daies after they departed from Egypt.
16 The[h] feast also of the haruest of the
first frutes of thy labours, which thou hast
sowen in the field: and the [i] feast of gathering *frutes* in the end of the yere, when
thou hast gathered in thy labours out of
the field.

i This is, the feast of tabernacles, signifiing that thei dwelled 40. yere vnder the tents or the tabernacles in wildernes.
17 *These* thre times in the yere shal all thy
men children appeare before the Lord
Iehouah.

k No leauened bread shalbe then in thine house.
18 Thou shalt not offre the blood of my
sacrifice with [k] leauened bread: nether
shal the fat of my sacrifice remaine vntil
the morning.
19 The first of the first frutes of thy land
thou shalt bring into ŷ house of the Lord
thy God: *yet* shalt thou not seeth a kid in
his [l] mothers milke.

l Meanĩg that no frutes shulde be takẽ before iust time: & hereby are brideled all cruel & wantõ appetites.
20 ¶ Beholde, I send an Angel before thee,
to kepe thee in the way, and to bring thee
to the place which I haue prepared.
21 Beware of him, and heare his voyce, &
puoke him not: for he wil not spare your
misdedes, because my [m] Name is in him.

m I wil giue him mine autoritie, and he shal gouerne you in my Name.
22 But if thou hearken vnto his voyce, and
do all that I speake, then I wil be an enemie vnto thine enemies, and wil afflict
them that afflict thee.

Chap.33.2. deut.7,21. iosh.24,11.
23 For mine Angel * shal go before thee,
and bring thee vnto the Amorites, & the
Hittites, and the Perizzites, and the Canaanites, the Hiuites, and the Iebusites,
and I wil destroye them.

n God commãdeth his not onely not to worship idoles, but to destroye them.
24 Thou shalt not bowe downe to their
gods, nether serue them, nor do after the
workes of thẽ: but [n] vtterly ouerthrowe
them, and breake in pieces their images.

o That is, all things necessarie for this present life.
25 For ye shal serue the Lord your God, &
he shal blesse thy [o] bread and thy water, &
I wil take all sickenes away frõ the middes of thee.

Deut.7,14.
26 ¶ *There shal none cast their frute nor
be barren in thy land: the nombre of thy
dayes wil I fulfil.

p I wil make them afraid at thy comming.
27 I wil send my [p] feare before thee, & wil
destroy all the people amõg whome thou
shalt go: and I wil make all thine enemies
turne their backes vnto thee:
28 And I wil send hornets before thee,
which shal driue out the Hiuites, the Canaanites, and the Hittites from thy face.
29 I wil not cast them out from thy face in
one yere, lest the land growe to a wildernes: and the beastes of the field multiplie
against thee.

30 By

30 By litle and litle I wil driue them out
from thy face vntil thou encrease, and inherite the land.
31 And I wil make thy coastes frō the red
Sea vnto the sea [q] of the Philistíms, and
from the [r] desert vnto the [s] Riuer: for I wil
deliuer the inhabitants of the land into
your hand, and thou shalt driue them out
from thy face.
32 *Thou shalt make no couenant with thē,
nor with their gods:
33 Nether shal they dwel in thy land, lest
they make thee sinne against me: for if ye
serue their gods, surely it shal be thy "destruction.

q Called the sea of Syria.
r Of Arabia called deserta.
s To wit, Euphrátes.
Chap.34,15. deu.7,2.
" Ebr. offence, or snare.

CHAP. XXIIII.

3 The people promis to obey God. 4 Mosés writeth the ciuile lawes. 9,13. Mosés returneth into the mountaine. 14 Aarón and Hur haue the charge of the people. 18 Mosés was. 40 daies & 40 nights in the mountaine.

1 NOw he had [a] said vnto Mosés, Come vp to the Lord, thou, and Aarón,
Nadáb, & Abihú, and seuenty of the Elders of Israél, & ye shal worship a far of.
2 And Mosés hīselfe alone shal come nere
to the Lord, but they shal not come nere,
nether shal the people go vp with him.
3 ¶ [b] Afterward Mosés came and tolde the
people all the wordes of the Lord and all
the "lawes: and all the people answered
with one voyce, and said, *All the things
which the Lord hathe said, wil we do.
4 And Mosés wrote all the wordes of the
Lord, and rose vp early, and set vp an *altar " vnder the mountaine, and twelue pillers according to the twelue tribes of Israél.
5 And he sent yong [c] men of the children
of Israél, which offered burnt offrings of
beues, & sacrificed peace offrings vnto the
Lord.
6 Thē Mosés toke halfe of the blood, and
put it in basens, and halfe of the blood he
sprinkled on the altar.
7 After he toke the " boke of the couenant,
and read it in the audience of the people:
who said, All that the Lord hathe said, we
wil do, and be obedient.
8 Then Mosés toke the * blood, and sprinkled it on the people, & said, Beholde, the
[d] blood of the couenant, which the Lord
hathe made with you concerning all these things.
9 ¶ Then went vp Mosés and Aarón, Nadáb and Abihú, and seuenty of the Elders
of Israél.
10 And they [e] sawe the God of Israél, and
vnder his fete was as it were a " worke of
a Saphir stone, & as the verie heauen whē
it is cleare.
11 And vpon the nobles of the children of
Israél he [f] laid not his hand: also they sawe
God, and [g] did eat & drinke.

a When he called him vp to the moūtaine to giue him ye lawes, beginning at the 20. chap. hitherto.
b Whē he had receiued these lawes i mount Sinái.
" Ebr. iudgements.
Chap.19,8.
Chap.20,24.
" Or, at the fete of the moūtaine.
c For as yet the priesthode was not giuen to Leui.
" Or, of the boke of the Lawe.
1.Pet.1,2. ebr.9,20.
d Which blood signifieth that the couenant broken can not be satisfied with out blood shedding.
e As perfectly as their infirmities colde beholde his maiestie.
" Ebr. bricke worke
f He made thē not afraid, nor punished them.
g That is, reioyced.

12 ¶ And the Lord [h] said vnto Mosés, Come
vp to me into the mountaine, & be there,
and I wil giue thee [i] tables of stone, and the
Lawe & the commandement, which I ha-
ue written, for to teache [k] them.
13 Then Mosés rose vp & his minister Ioshúa, & Mosés went vp into the mountaine of God,
14 And said vnto the Elders, Tarie vs here,
vntil we come againe vnto you: & beholde, Aarón, and Hur are wt you: whosoeuer
hathe anie matters, let him come to them.
15 Then Mosés went vp to the mount, and
the cloude couered the mountaine,
16 And the glorie of the Lord abode vpon
mount Sinái, & the cloude couered " it six
daies: and the seuenth day he called vnto
Mosés out of the middes of the cloude.
17 And the sight of the glorie of the Lord
was like [l] consuming fire on the top of the
mountaine, in the eies of the children of
Israél.
18 And Mosés entred into the middes of
the cloude, & went vp to the mountaine:
& Mosés was in the * mount fourty dayes
and fourty nightes.

h The secōde time.
i Signifiing the hardenes of our hearts, except God do write his lawes therin by his Spirit. Iere.31,33. ezek.11,19. 2.cor.3,3. ebr.8,10. & 10,16.
k To wit, the people.
" Or, him.
l The Lord appeareth like deuouring fire to carnal men: but to them that he draweth with his Spirit, he is like pleasant Saphir.
Chap.34,28. deu.9,9.

CHAP. XXV.

2 The voluntarie gifts for the making of the Tabernacle. 10 The forme of the Arke. 17 The Merciseat. 23 The Table. 31 The Cādelstick. 40 All must be done according to the patern.

1 THen the Lord spake vnto Mosés,
saying,
2 [a] Speake vnto the children of Israél, that
they receiue an offring for me: of * euerie
mā, whose heart giueth it frely, ye shal take
the offring for me.
3 And this is ye offring which ye shal [b] take
of them, golde, and siluer, and brasse,
4 "And blewe silke, and purple, and skarlet,
and fine linen, and goates heere.
5 And ramme skins coulored red, and the
skins of badgers, and the wood [c] Shittím,
6 Oyle for the light, spices for [d] anointing
oyle, & for the perfume of swete sauour,
7 Onix stones, and stones to be set in the
*Ephod, and in the * brest plate.
8 Also they shal make me a [e] Sanctuarie, that
I may dwel among them.
9 According to all that I shewe thee, euen
so shal ye make the forme of the Tabernacle, and the facion of all the instruments
thereof.
10 ¶ They shal make also an * Arke of Shittím wood, two cubites and an halfe long,
& a cubite and an halfe broad, & a cubite
and an halfe hie.
11 And thou shalt ouerlaie it with pure golde: within & without shalt thou ouerlaie
it, and shalt make vpō it a " crowne of golde rounde about.
12 And thou shalt cast foure rings of golde
for it, and put them in the foure " corners

a After the moral and iudicial lawe he giueth them ye ceremonial lawe, that nothing shuld be left to mans inuention.
Chap.35,5.
b For the buylding and vse of the Tabernacle.
" Or, yelow.
c Which is thoght to be a kinde of cedar, which wil not rot.
d Ordeined for the Priests.
Chap.28,4.
Chap.28,15.
e A place bothe to offre sacrifice and to heare the Lawe.
Chap.37,1.
" Or, a circle or a bordre.
" Or, fete.

thereof: that is, two rings *shalbe* on ẏ one
side of it, and two rings on the other side thereof.
13 And thou shalt make barres of Shittím
wood, and couer them with golde.
14 Then thou shalt put the barres in the
rings by the sides of the Arke, to beare ẏ
Arke with them.

THE ARKE OF THE TESTIMONIE.

A B The length, two cubites and an halfe.
B C. The breadth a cubite and an halfe.
A D The height a cubite and an halfe.
E E The goldē crowne aboue the Arke.
F The foure rings of golde in the foure corners.
G The barres couered ẇ golde to putthrough the rings to cary the Arke.
H The inner parte of the Arke where the Testimonie was put.
I The Mercie seate, ẇ was the couering of the Arke: where were thetwo Cherubíms, & whence ẏ oracle came.

15 The barres shal be in the rings of the Arke: they shal not be taken away from it.
16 So thou shalt put in the Arke the [f] Testimonie which I shal giue thee.
17 Also thou shalt make a ″ [g] Merciseat of
pure golde, two cubites and an halfe lōg,
and a cubite and an halfe broad.
18 And thou shalt make two Cherubíms of
golde: of worke beaten out with the hammer shalt thou make them at ẏ two endes
of the Merciseat.
19 And the one Cherúb shalt thou make at
the one end, & the other Cherúb at ẏ o-
ther end: of *the matter* of the Merciseat shal
ye make the Cherubíms, on the two endes
thereof.
20 And the Cherubíms shal stretch their
wings on hie, couering the Merciseat with
their wings, & their faces one to an other:
to the Merciseat ward shal the faces of ẏ
Cherubíms be.
21 And thou shalt put the Merciseat aboue
vpon the Arke, and in the Arke thou shalt
put ẏ Testimonie, which I wil giue thee,
22 And there I wil ″ declare my selfe vnto
thee, and from aboue the Merciseat * betwene the two Cherubíms, which are vpō
the Arke of the Testimonie, I wil tel thee
all things which I wil giue thee in cōmandement vnto the children of Israél.

f The stone tables, the rod of Aarón and Manna, which were a testimonie of Gods presēce.

″ Or, couering: or, propitiatorie.

g There God appeared mercifully vnto them: and this was a figure of Christ.

″ Or, wil appeine with thee.

* Nom. 7, 89.

THE TABLE OF THE SHEWE BREAD.

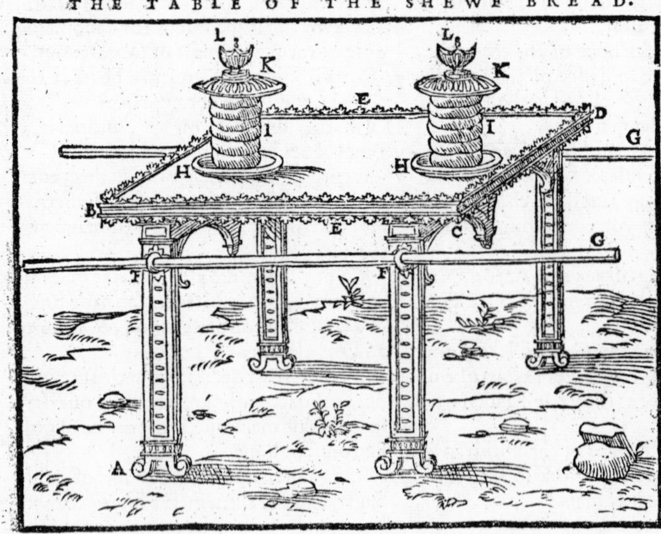

A B The height a cubite and an halfe.
B C The length two cubites.
C D The breadth a cubite.
E A crowne of golde aboue & beneth separated the one frō the other by a border of an hand breadth thicke, ẇ declareth that the table was an hand breadth thicke.
F The foure rings.
G The barres to cary the table, which were put through ẏ rings.
H Dishes wherein ẏ shewe bread was put.
I The twelue cakes or loaues called the shewe bread.
K The goblets or couerings.
L The incense cuppes.

Chap. 37,10.
23 ¶ * Thou ſhalt alſo make a table of Shittím wood, of two cubites long, & one cubite broad, and a cubite and an half hie:
24 And thou ſhalt couer it ẇ pure golde,
and make thereto a crowne of golde rounde about.
25 Thou ſhalt alſo make vnto it a border
of [g] foure fingers rounde about: and thou
ſhalt make a golden crowne rounde about
the border thereof.

g Or, an hand bread.

26 After, thou ſhalt make for it foure rings
of golde, & ſhalt put the rings in ẏ foure
corners that are in the foure fete thereof.
27 Ouer againſt the border ſhal the rings
be for places for barres, to beare the Table.
28 And thou ſhalt make the barres of Shittím wood, and ſhalt ouerlay them with
golde, that ẏ Table may be borne with
them.
29 Thou ſhalt make alſo [h] diſhes for it, and
incens cups for it and couerings for it, and
goblets, wherewith it ſhalbe couered, *eue*
of fine golde ſhalt thou make them.
30 And thou ſhalt ſet vpō the Table ſhewbread before me continually.

h To ſet the bread vpon.

THE CANDELSTICKE.

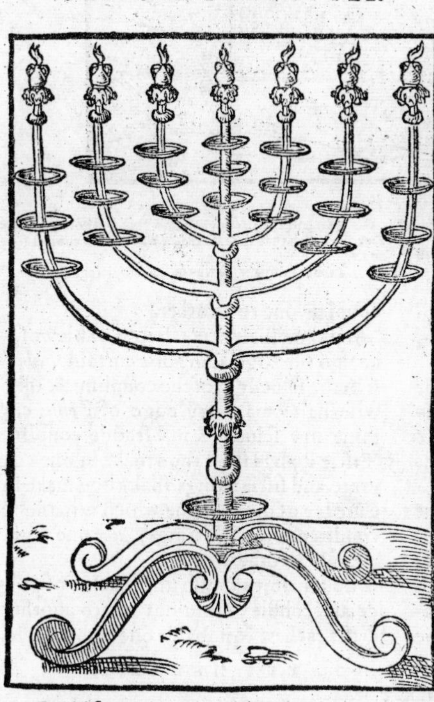

Because the facion of the candelſtick is ſo plaine & euidēt, it nedeth not to deſcribe the particular partes thereof according to the ordre of lettres. Onely where as it is ſaid in the 34 verſe, that there ſhalbe foure bowles or cuppes in the cādelſticke, it muſt be vnderſtād of the ſhaft or ſhāke: for there are but thre for euerie one of the other branches. Alſo the knoppes of the cādelſtick are thoſe which are vnder the brāches as thei iſſue out of the ſhaft on ether ſide.

Chap. 37,17.
31 ¶ * Alſo thou ſhalt make a Candelſticke
of pure golde: of [i] worke beaten out ẇ the
hāmer ſhal the Cādelſticke be made, his
ſhaft, & his brāches, his bolles, his knops:
and his floures ſhal be of the ſame.

i It ſhal not be molton, but beaten out of the lumpe of golde with ẏ hammer.

32 Six branches alſo ſhal come out of the
ſides of it: thre branches of the Candelſticke out of the one ſide of it, and thre
branches of the Candelſticke out of the o-
ther ſide of it.
33 Thre bolles like vnto almondes, one
knop and *one* floure in one branche: and
thre bolles like almondes in the *other* brāche, one knop and *one* floure: ſo through
out the ſix branches that come out of the
Candelſticke.
34 And in the *ſhaft* of ẏ Candelſticke *ſhalbe*
foure bolles like vnto almōdes, his knops
& his floures.
35 And *there ſhalbe* a knop vnder two branches *made* thereof: & a knop vnder two brā
ches *made* thereof: and a knop vnder two
brāches *made* thereof according to the ſix
branches comming out of the Candelſticke.
36 Their knops and their branches ſhalbe
thereof. all this ſhalbe one beatē worke of
pure golde.
37 And ẏ ſhalt make the ſeuen lāpes thereof, & ẏ lāpes thereof ſhalt ẏ put theron,
to giue light toward that that is before it.
38 Alſo the ſnoffers & ſnoffediſhes thereof
ſhal be of pure golde.
39 Of [k] a talēt of fine golde ſhalt thou make
it with all theſe inſtruments.
40 * Loke therefore that thou make *them*
after their facion, that was ſhewed thee
in the mountaine.

k This was ẏ talent weight of the temple & waied 120 pounde.
Ebr. 8,9.
act. 7,44.

THE FIRST COVERING OF THE TABERNACLE.

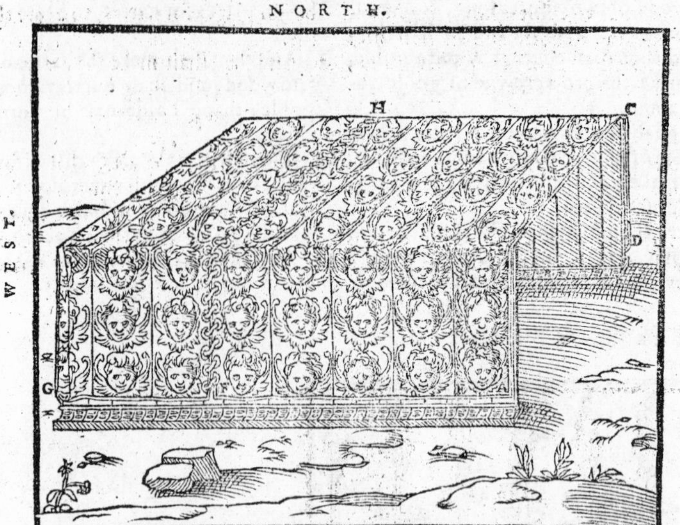

A B C D The ten curtaines, which were eight and twentie cubites long of Cherubin worke.
A E The breadth of a curtaine was foure cubites, and so the ten were fourtie cubites broad.
F G Two curtaines & an halfe: so that ẏ whole laid together declareth that the tabernacle was thirtie cubites long and twelue broad.
F H Taches or hokes to tie the curtaines together.

CHAP. XXVI.

1. The forme of the Tabernacle and the appertinances, 33 The place of the Arke, of the Merciseat, of the Table, and of the Candelsticke.

1 AFterward thou shalt make the Taber
nacle with ten curtaines of fine twined linen, and blewe silke, and purple, &
skarlet: & in thē thou shalt make Cherubims of [a] broidred worke.
2 The length of one curtaine *shalbe* eight
and twentie cubites, & the breadth of o-
ne curtaine, foure cubites: euerie one of ẏ
curtaines shal haue one measure.
3 Fiue curtaines shalbe coupled one to a-
nother: and the *other* fiue curtains shalbe
coupled one to an other.
4 And thou shalt make strings of blewe silke vpō the edge of the one curtaine, *which*
is in the seluedge [b] of the coupling: & likewise shalt ẏ make in ẏ edge of ẏ *other* cur
taine in ẏ seluedge, in ẏ secōde couplīg.
5 Fiftie strings shalt thou make in one cur
taine, and fiftie strings shalt thou make in
the edge of the curtaine, which is in the [c] se
conde coupling: ẏ strings *shalbe* one right
against an other.
6 Thou shalt make also fiftie [*] taches of golde, and couple ẏ curtaines one to another
ẇ the taches, & it shalbe one [*] tabernacle.

a That is, of moste conning or fine worke.

b On the side that the curtaines might be tied together.

c In tying together bothe the sides.

*Or, hokes.

*Or, partition.

THE CVRTAINES OF GOATES HEERE.

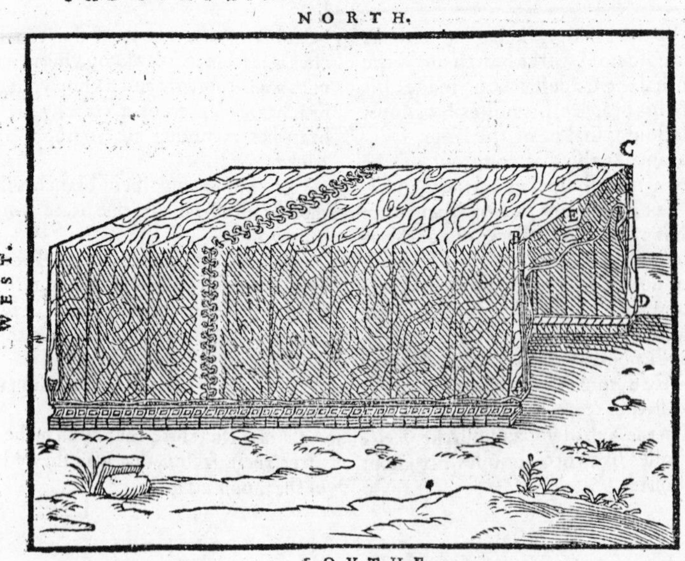

These eleuen curtaines of goates heere were put aboue the other ten, and the eleuenth hanged before the entrie of the Tabernacle, loke E. These also were 30. cubites long and the other but eight and twenty, and therefore on the Southe side thei were a cubite longer then the other, loke A. and also another on the North side, that the boardes might be couered.

7 ¶ Also ỹ shalt make curtaines of goates *heere*, to be a [d] couering vpon the Tabernacle: thou shalt make them *to the nomber* of eleuen curtaines.

d Lest raine and wether shulde marre it.

8 The length of a curtaine *shalbe* thirtie cubites, & the breadth of a curtaine foure cubites: the eleuen curtaines *shalbe* of one measure.

9 And thou shalt couple fiue curtaines by them selues, and the six curtaines by them selues: but thou shalt double the [e] sixt curtaine vpon the fore fronte of the couering.

e That is, fiue on ỹ one side, & fiue on the other, and the sixt shulde hang ouer the dore of ỹ Tabernacle.

10 And thou shalt make fifty strings in the edge of one curtaine in the seluedge of the coupling, and fifty strings in the edge of the *other* curtaine in the seconde coupling.

11 Likewise thou shalt make fifty ″taches of brasse, and fasten them on the strings, & shalt couple the couering together, that it may be one.

″Or, hokes.

12 And the [f] renant that resteth in the curtaines of the couering, *euen* the halfe curtaine that resteth, shalbe left at the backe side of the Tabernacle,

f For these curtaines were two cubites longer the the curtaines of ỹ Tabernacle: so that thei were sider by a cubite on bothe sides.

13 That the cubite on the one side, and the cubite on the other side of that which is left in the length of the curtaines of the couering, may remaine on ether side of the Tabernacle to couer it.

14 Moreouer for that couering thou shalt make a [g] couering of rams skins died red, & a couering [h] of badgers skins aboue.

g To be put vpon the couering, ỹ was made of goates heere.

h This was ỹ thirde couering for the Tabernacle.

15 ¶ Also thou shalt make boardes for the Tabernacle of Shittím wood to stand vp.

THE TABERNACLE.

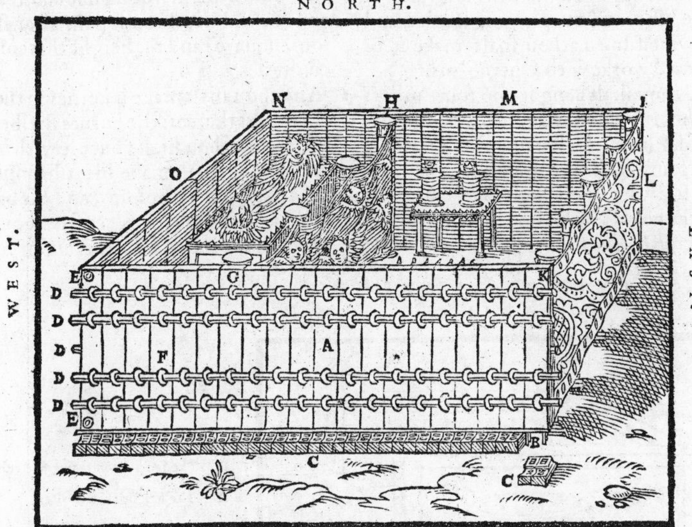

A M Twentie boardes on the Southe side and twentie on the North side.
B K The length of euerie one ten cubites, & the breadth a cubite and an halfe.
E K & N I Declare that all the boardes ioyned together made thirtie cubites, which was the length of the Tabernacle. Iosephus writeth that euerie boarde was an handful thicke.

16 Ten cubites *shalbe* the length of a boarde, and a cubite and an halfe cubite the breadth of one boarde.

17 Two tenons *shalbe* in one boarde set in ordre as the fete of a ladder, one against an other: thus shalt thou make for all the boardes of the Tabernacle.

18 And thou shalt make boardes for the Tabernacle, *euen* twentie boardes on the Southe side, euen ful Southe.

19 And thou shalt make fourtie ″ sockets of siluer vnder the twentie boardes, two sockets vnder one boarde for his two tenõs,

″Or, basse pieces, wherin were the mortaises for the tenons.

& two sockets vnder an other boarde for his two tenons.

20 In like maner on the other side of the Tabernacle towarde the North side *shalbe* twentie boardes,

21 And their fourtie sockets of siluer, two sockets vnder one boarde, and two sockets vnder a nother boarde.

22 And on the side of the Tabernacle, toward the West shalt thou make six boardes.

23 Also two boardes shalt thou make in the corners of the Tabernacle in ỹ two sides.

24 Also thei shalbe [i] ioyned beneth, & like-

i The Ebrewe worde signifieth twinnes: declaring that thei shulde be so perfect and wel ioyned as were possible.

wise thei shalbe ioyned aboue to a ring:
thus shal it be for them two: thei shalbe
for the two corners.
25 So thei shalbe eight boardes hauing sockets of siluer, *euē* sixtene sockets, *that is,* two
sockets vnder one boarde, & two sockets
vnder an other boarde.
26 ¶ Then thou shalt make fiue barres of
Shittim wood for the boardes of one side
of the Tabernacle,
27 And fiue barres for the boardes of the
other side of the Tabernacle: also fiue
barres for the boardes of the side of the
Tabernacle towarde the Westside.
28 And the midle barre shal go through the
middes of the boardes, from end to end.
29 And thou shalt couer the boardes with
golde, and make their rings of golde, for
places for the barres, and thou shalt couer
the barres with golde.
30 So thou shalt rere vp the Tabernacle
* according to the facion thereof, which
was shewed thee in the mount.
31 ¶ Moreouer thou shalt make a vaile of
blewe silke, and purple, and skarlet, and
fine twined linen: thou shalt make it of
broydred worke with Cherubims.
32 And thou shalt hang it vpō foure pillers
of Shittim wood couered with golde,
(whose [k] hokes shalbe of golde) *standing*
vpon foure sockets of siluer.
33 ¶ Afterward thou shalt hang the vaile
" on the hokes, that thou maiest bring in
thither, *that is* (within ỷ vaile) the Arke of

Chap 25,9. & 40. ebr. 8,5. act. 7,44.

[k] Some read, heades of the pillers.

" *Ebr. vnder the hokes: meaning that it shulde hang downe-ward from the hokes.*

the Testimonie: and the vaile shal make
you a separacion betwene the Holy place
and the [l] moste Holy place.
34 Also thou shalt put the Merciseat vpon
the Arke of the Testimonie in the moste
Holy place.
35 And thou shalt set the Table [m] without
the vaile, & the Candelsticke ouer against
the Table on ỷ Southside of the Tabernacle, and thou shalt set the Table on the
Northside.
36 Also thou shalt make an [n] hanging for
the dore of the Tabernacle of blewe silke, and purple, and skarlet, and fine twined
linen wroght with nedle.
37 And thou shalt make for the hanging
fiue pillers of Shittim, and couer thē with
golde: their heades *shalbe* of golde, & thou
shalt cast fiue sockets of brasse for them.

[l] Whereunto the hie Priest onely entred once a yere.

[m] Meaning in ỷ holy place.

[n] This hangĩg or vaile was betwene the holy place & there where ỷ people were.

CHAP XXVII.

1 The altar of the burnt offring. 2 The courte of the Tabernacle. 10 The lampes continually burning.

1 MOreouer thou shalt make ỷ [a] altar
of Shittim wood, fiue cubites long
and fiue cubites broade (the altar shalbe
foure square) and the height thereof thre
cubites.
2 And thou shalt make it hornes in the foure corners thereof: the hornes shalbe of it
[b] selfe, and thou shalt couer it with brasse.
3 Also thou shalt make his asshpannes for
his asshes and his besoms, and his basens,
and his fleshokes, & his " censers: thou shalt
make all the instrumēts thereof of brasse.

[a] For ỷ burnt offring.

[b] Of the same wood & matter, not fastened vnto it.

" *Or, fire pānes.*

THE ALTAR OF BVRNT OFFRING.

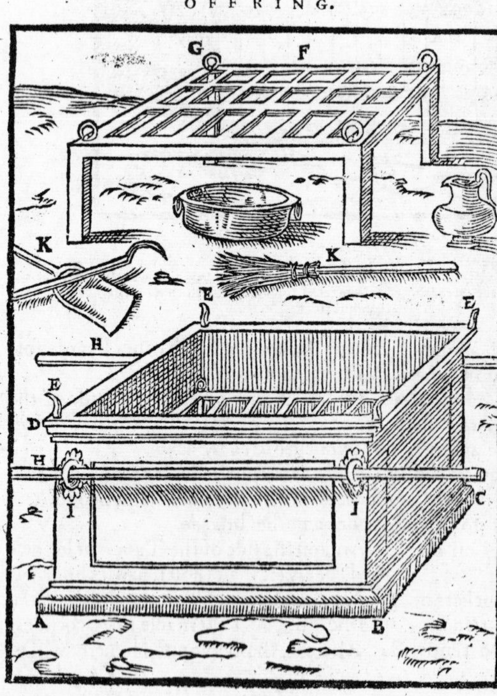

A B The length, conteining fiue cubites.
A D The height thre cubites.
B C The breadth asmuche.
E The foure hornes or foure corners.
F The grate, which was put within the altar, and whereupon the sacrifice was burnt.
G Foure rings to lift vp the grate by, when thei auoided the asshes.
H The barres to cary the altar.
I The rings through the which the barres were put.
K Asshpans, besoms, fleshokes, basens & suche instruments apparteining to the altar.

4 And thou ſhalt make vnto it a grate *like*
networke of braſſe: alſo vpon that "grate
ſhalt thou make foure braſen rings vpon
the foure corners thereof.
5 And thou ſhalt put it vnder the cōpaſſe
of the altar beneth, that the grate may be
in the middes of the altar.
6 Alſo thou ſhalt make barres for the altar, barres, *I ſay*, of Shittim wood, & ſhalt
couer them with braſſe.
7 And the barres thereof ſhalbe put in the
rings, the which barres ſhalbe vpō the two
ſides of the altar to beare it.
8 Thou ſhalt make ẏ *altar* holowe *betwene*
the boardes: as *God* ſhewed thee in the
mount, ſo ſhal they make it.
9 ¶ Alſo thou ſhalt make the [c] courte of ẏ
Tabernacle in the Southſide, euen ful
Southe: the courte ſhal haue curtaines of
fine twined linen, of an hundreth cubites
long, for one ſide,
10 And it ſhal haue twentie pillers, with
their twentie ſockets of braſſe: the heades
of the pillers, & their [d] filets *ſhalbe* ſiluer.
11 Likewiſe on the Northſide in length
there ſhalbe hangings of an hundreth *cubites*
long, & the twētie pillers thereof ẇ their
twentie ſockets of braſſe: the heades of ẏ
pillers and the filets *ſhalbe* ſiluer.
12 ¶ And the breadth of the courte on the
Weſtſide *ſhal haue* curtaines of fiftie cubites, *with* their ten pillers & their ten ſockets.
13 And the breadth of the courte, Eaſtward
ful Eaſt *ſhal haue* [e] fiftie cubites.
14 Alſo hangings of fiftene cubites *ſhalbe*
on the *one* [f] ſide *with* their thre pillers and
their thre ſockets.
15 Likewiſe on the other ſide *ſhalbe* hangings of fiftene cubites, *with* their thre pillers, and their thre ſockets.
16 ¶ And in the gate of the courte *ſhalbe* a
vaile of twentie cubites, of blewe ſilke, &
purple, and ſkarlet, and fine twined linen
wroght with nedle, *with* the foure pillers
thereof and their foure ſockets.
17 All the pillers of the courte ſhal haue filets of ſiluer rounde about, *with* their heades of ſiluer, and their ſockets of braſſe.
18 ¶ The length of the court *ſhalbe* an hundreth cubites, and the breadth fiftie "at e-
ther end, and the height fiue cubites, *and
the hangings* of fine twined linen, & their
ſockets of braſſe.
19 All the veſſels of the Tabernacle for
all maner ſeruice thereof, & all the [g] pins
thereof, & all the pins of the courte *ſhalbe*
braſſe.
20 ¶ And thou ſhalt commande the childrē
of Iſraél, that they bring vnto thee pure
oyle oliue [h] beaten for the light, that the
lampes may alwaye "burne.
21 In the Tabernacle of the Congregaciō

"Ebr. net.

c This was ẏ firſt entrie into the Tabernacle, where ẏ people abode.

d They were certein hopes or circles for to beautifie ẏ piller.

e Meaning curtaines of fifty cubites.

f Of the dore of the courte.

" Ebr. fifty in fifty.

g Or ſtakes, wherewith ẏ curtaines were faſtened to the grounde.

h Suche as cōmeth from ẏ oliue, when it is firſt preſſed or beaten.

" Or, aſcēde vp.

without the vaile, which is before the Teſtimonie, ſhal Aarón and his ſonnes dreſ-
ſe them from euening to morning before
the Lord, for a ſtatute for euer vnto their
generacions *to be obſerued* by the children
of Iſraél.

CHAP. XXVIII.

1 The Lord calleth Aarón & his ſonnes to the Prieſthode. 4 Their garmēts 12.29 Aarón entreth in to the Sāctuarie in the name of the children of Iſraél. 30 Vrim and Thummim. 38 Aarón beareth the iniquitie of the Iſraelites offrings.

1 AND cauſe thou thy brother Aarón
to come vnto thee and his ſonnes ẇ
him, from among the children of Iſraél,
that he may ſerue me in the Prieſts office:
I meane Aarón, Nadáb, and Abihú, Eleazár, and Ithamár Aarons ſonnes.
2 Alſo ẏͧ ſhalt make holy garments for Aarón thy brother, [a] glorious & beautiful.
3 Therefore thou ſhalt ſpeake vnto all "cō
ning mē, whome I haue filled with the ſpi
rite of wiſdome, that they make Aarons
garments to [b] conſecrate him, that he may
ſerue me in the Prieſtes office.

a Whereby his office may be knowen to be glorious & excellent.

" Ebr. wiſe in heart.

b Which is, to ſeparat him from the reſt.

THE GARMENTS OF THE HIGH PRIEST.

A The Ephod, or vpmoſt coate, which was like cloth of golde and was girded vnto him, wherein was the breſt plate with the twelue ſtones, which was tied aboue with two cheines to two onix ſtones and beneth with two laces.

B The robe ẇ was next vnder the Ephod, whereunto were ioined the pomegranates and belles of golde.

C The tunicle or broydred coate, which was vnder ẏ robe and longer then it, and was alſo with out ſleues.

4 Now theſe ſhalbe ẏ garmēts, ẇ thei ſhal
make, a breſt plate, & ā [c] Ephod, & a robe, &

c A ſhort and ſtreict coate without ſleeues put vpmoſt vpon his garments to kepe thē cloſe vnto him.

a broydred coat, a mitre, & a girdle. ſo *the*
ſe holy garmẽts ſhal they make for Aarón
thy brother, & for his ſonnes, that he may
ſerue me in the Prieſts office.
5 Therefore they ſhal take golde, & blewe
ſilke, and purple, and ſkarlet, & fine linen,
6 ¶ And they ſhal make the Ephod of golde,
blewe ſilke, and purple, ſkarlet, & fine twined linen of broydred worke.
7 The two ſhulders thereof ſhalbe ioyned
together by their two edges: ſo ſhal it be
cloſed.
8 And ẏ [d] embroydred garde of the ſame
Ephod, which ſhalbe vpõ him, ſhalbe of ẏ
ſelfe ſame worke and ſtuffe, *euen* of golde,
blewe ſilke, and purple, and ſkarlet, and fine twined linen.
9 And thou ſhalt take two onix ſtones, and
graue vpon them the names of the children of Iſraél:
10 Six names of thẽ vpon the one ſtone, &
the ſix names that remaine, vpõ the ſecõde ſtone, according to [e] their generaciõs.
11 Thou ſhalt cauſe to graue ẏ two ſtones
accordĩg to the names of ẏ childrẽ of Iſ
raél by a grauer of ſignets, ẏ worketh and
graueth in ſtone, and ſhalt make them to
be ſet and emboſſed in golde.
12 And thou ſhalt put the two ſtones vpon
the ſhulders of the Ephod, *as* ſtones of [f] re
mẽbrance of ẏ children of Iſraél: for Aarón ſhal beare their names before ẏ Lord
vpõ his two ſhulders for a remẽbrance.
13 So thou ſhalt make boſſes of golde,
14 ¶ And two cheines of fine golde [g] at
the ende, of wrethed worke ſhalt yͧ make
them, & ſhalt faſten the wrethed cheines
vpon the boſſes.
15 ¶ Alſo thou ſhalt make the breſt plate of
[h] iudgemẽt with broydred worke: like the
worke of the Ephod ſhalt thou make it:
of golde, blewe ſilke, and purple, and ſkarlet, & fine twined linen ſhalt yͧ make it.
16 [i] Foure ſquare it ſhalbe *and* double, an
hand bred long and an hand bred broad.
17 Then thou ſhalt ſet it ful of places for
ſtones, *euen* foure rowes of ſtones: ẏ ordre
ſhalbe this, a ‖ ruby, a topaze, and a ‖ carbũcle in the firſt rowe.
18 And in the ſeconde rowe *thou ſhalt ſet* an
‖ emeraude, a ſaphir, and a ‖ diamond.
19 And in ẏ third rowe a turkeis, an achate,
and an hematite.
20 And in the fourte rowe a ‖ chryſolite, an
onix, and a iaſper: and they ſhalbe ſet in
golde in their emboſſements.
21 And the ſtones ſhalbe according to the
names of the childrẽ of Iſraél, twelue, according to their names, grauen as ſignets,
euerie one after his name, & they ſhalbe
for the twelue tribes.
22 ¶ Then thou ſhalt make vpon the breſt
plate two cheines at the endes of wrethen

d Which wẽt about his vpmoſt coat.
e As they were in age, ſo ſhulde thei be grauen in ordre.
f That Aarón might remembre the Iſraelites to God warde.
g Of the boſſes.
h It was ſo called, becauſe ẏ hie Prieſt colde norgiue ſentence in iudgement without that on his breaſt.
i The deſcription of the breſt plate.
‖ Or, ſardine.
‖ Or, emeraude.
‖ Or, carbuncle.
‖ Or, iaſper.
‖ Ebr. tarſhiſh.

worke of pure golde.
23 Thou ſhalt make alſo vpõ the breſt plate
two rings of golde, and put the two rings
on [k] the two endes of the breſt plate.
24 And thou ſhalt put the two wrethẽ cheines of golde in the two rings in the endes
of the breſt plate.
25 And the *other* two endes of the two wrethen *cheines*, thou ſhalt faſten in the two
emboſſements, and ſhalt put *them* vpõ the
ſhulders of the Ephod on ẏ foreſide of it.
26 ¶ Alſo thou ſhalt make two rings of
golde, which thou ſhalt put in the [l] two *o-*
ther endes of the breſt plate, vpon the border thereof, toward ẏ inſide of ẏ Ephod.
27 And two *other* rings of golde thou ſhalt
make, & put them on the two ſides of the
Ephod, beneth in the fore parte of it ouer
againſt the coupling of it vpon the broydred garde of the Ephod.
28 Thus they ſhal binde the breſt plate by
his rings vnto the rings of the Ephod, ẇ
a lace of blewe ſilke, that it may be *faſt* vpon the broydred garde of the Ephod, & ẏ
the breſt plate be not loſed frõ ẏ Ephod.
29 So Aarón ſhal [m] beare the names of the
childrẽ of Iſraél in the breſt plate of iudgement vpon his heart, when he goeth into the holy place, for a remembrance continually before the Lord.
30 ¶ Alſo thou ſhalt put in the breſt plate of
iudgement the [n] Vrím & the Thúmím,
ẇ ſhalbe vpõ Aarons heart, whẽ he goeth
in before the Lord: and Aarón ſhal beare
the iudgemẽt of the children of Iſraél vpon his heart before the Lord continually.
31 ¶ And thou ſhalt make the robe of the E-
phod altogether of blewe ſilke.
32 And the hole for his heade ſhalbe in the
middes of it, hauĩg an edge of wouẽ worke rounde about ẏ coller of it: ſo it ſhalbe
as ẏ coller of an habergeõ that it rẽt not.
33 ¶ And beneth vpon the ſkirtes thereof yͧ
ſhalt make pomgranates of blewe ſilke, &
purple, & ſkarlet, round about the ſkirtes
thereof and belles of golde betwene them
round about:
34 *That is,* * a golden bel and a pomgranate,
a golden bel and a pomgranate rounde a-
bout vpon the ſkirtes of the robe.
35 So it ſhalbe vpon Aarón, when he miniſtreth, and his ſound ſhalbe heard, when
he goeth into the holy place before the
Lord, and when he commeth out, and he
ſhal not dye.
36 ¶ Alſo thou ſhalt make a plate of pure
golde, & graue therõ, as ſignets are grauẽ,
[o] HOLINES TO THE LORD,
37 And yͧ ſhalt put it on a blewe ſilke lace,
and it ſhalbe vpon the mitre: *euen* vpon ẏ
fore fronte of the mitre ſhal it be.
38 So it ſhalbe vpon Aarons forehead, that
Aarón may [p] beare the iniquitie of ẏ offrings

k Which are vpmoſt toward the ſhulder.
l Which are beneth.
m Aarón ſhal not entre into the holy place in his owne name, but in the name of all the children of Iſrael.
n Vrím ſignifieth light, and Thúmím perfection: declaring that the ſtones of the breſt plate were moſte cleare, and of perfect beautie: by Vrím alſo is mẽt knolage, and Thũmim holynes, ſhewing what vertues are required in the Prieſts.
* Ecclec. 45,10.
o Holines apperteineth to the Lord: for he is moſte holy, and nothĩg vnholy may appeare before him.
p Their offrĩgs colde not be ſo perfect, but ſome faute wolde be therein: ẇ ſinne the hie Prieſt bare and pacified God.

frings, which the childrẽ of Iſraél ſhal offre in all their holy offrĩgs: & it ſhalbe alwaies vpon his forehead, to make them acceptable before the Lord.
39 Likewiſe thou ſhalt embroydre the fine
linen coat, and thou ſhalt make a mitre
of fine linen, but thou ſhalt make a girdel of nedle worke.
40 Alſo thou ſhalt make for Aarons ſonnes coates, & thou ſhalt make thẽ girdels,
& bonets ſhalt thou make them for glorie
and comelines.
41 And thou ſhalt put them vpon Aarón
thy brother, & on his ſonnes with him, &
ſhalt anoynt them, and [q] fil their hands,
and ſanctifie them, ẏ they may miniſtre
vnto me in the Prieſts office.
42 Thou ſhalt alſo make them linen breches to couer their priuities: frõ the loynes vnto the thighs ſhal they reache.
43 And they ſhalbe for Aarón and his ſonnes when they come into the Tabernacle
"of the Cõgregacion, or when they come
vnto the altar to miniſter in ẏ holy place,
that they [r] cõmit not iniquitie, & ſo dye.
This ſhalbe a lawe for euer vnto him and to
his ſede after him.

q That is, conſecrat thẽ, by giuing them things to offre, and therby admit them to their office.

"Or, of Witnes.

r In not hiding their nakednes.

CHAP. XXIX.

1 The maner of conſecrating the Prieſts. 38 The continual ſacrifice. 45 The Lord promiſeth to dwel among the children of Iſraél.

1 THis thing alſo ſhalt thou do vnto thẽ
when thou cõſecrateſt them to be my
Prieſtes,* Take a yong calf, and two rams
without blemiſh,
2 And vnleauened bread & cakes vnleauened tempered with oyle, & wafers vnleauened anointed with oyle: (of fine wheat
flower ſhalt thou make them)
3 Thẽ ẏ ſhalt put thẽ in one baſket, & [a] pre
ſent them in the baſket with the calf and
the two rams,
4 And ſhalt bring Aarón and his ſonnes
vnto the dore of the Tabernacle of ẏ Cõ
gregacion, and waſh them with water.
5 Alſo thou ſhalt take the garments, & put
vpon Aarón the tunicle, and the robe of
the [b] Ephod, and the Ephod, and the breſt
plate, and ſhalt cloſe *them* to him with the
broydred garde of the Ephod.
6 Then thou ſhalt put the mitre vpon his
head, and ſhalt put the holy *crowne vpon
the mitre.
7 And thou ſhalt take the anointing *oyle, and ſhalt powre vpon his head, and
anoint him.
8 And thou ſhalt bring his ſonnes, and put
coates vpon them,
9 And ſhalt girde them with girdels, *bothe*
Aarón & his ſonnes: and ſhalt put the bonets on them, and the Prieſtes office ſhalbe theirs for a perpetual lawe: thou * ſhalt
alſo "fil the hands of Aarón, and the hãds
of his ſonnes.

Leu. 9, 2.

a To offre thẽ in ſacrifice.

b Which was next vnder the Ephod.

Chap. 28, 36.

Chap. 30, 23.

Chap. 28, 41.

"Or, conſecrat them.

10 After, thou ſhalt preſent the calf before
the Tabernacle of the Cõgregacion, *and
Aarón and his ſonnes ſhal [c] put their hãds
vpon the head of the calf.
11 So thou ſhalt kil the calf before ẏ Lord,
at the dore of the Tabernacle of the Con
gregacion.
12 Then thou ſhalt take of ẏ blood of the
calf, and put it vpon the hornes of the altar with thy finger, and ſhalt powre all *the
reſt* of the blood at the fote of the altar.
13 *Alſo thou ſhalt take all the fat that couereth the inwardes, and the kall, *that is*
on the liuer, and the two kidneis, and the
fat that is vpon thẽ, and ſhalt burne them
vpon the altar.
14 But the fleſh of the calf, and his ſkin, and
his doũg ſhalt thou burne with fire with
out the hoſte: it is a "ſinne offring.
15 ¶ Thou ſhalt alſo take one ram, and Aarón and his ſonnes ſhal put their hands
vpon the head of the ram.
16 Then thou ſhalt kil the ram, and take his
blood, and ſprinkle it round about vpon
the altar,
17 And thou ſhalt cut the ram in pieces, and
waſh ẏ inwardes of him and his legges, &
ſhalt put them vpõ the pieces thereof, and
vpon his head.
18 So thou ſhalt burne the whole ram vpon
the altar: *for* it is a burnt offring vnto the
Lord [d] for a ſwete ſauour: it is an offring
made by fire vnto the Lord.
19 ¶ And thou ſhalt take the other ram, and
Aarón and his ſonnes ſhal put their hands
vpon the head of the ram.
20 Then ſhalt thou kil the ram, and take of
his blood & put it [e] vpon the lap of Aarõs
eare, and vpon the lap of the right eare of
his ſonnes, and vpon the thumbe of their
right hand, & vpon the great toe of their
right fote, and ſhalt ſprinkle the blood
vpon the altar round about.
21 And thou ſhalt take of the blood that is
[f] vpon the altar, and of the anointing oyle,
and ſhalt ſprinkle it vpon Aarón, and vpõ
his garments, and vpon his ſonnes, and vpon the garments of his ſonnes with him:
ſo he ſhalbe halowed, and his clothes, and
his ſonnes, and the garments of his ſonnes with him.
22 Alſo thou ſhalt take of the rams ẏ fat &
the rompe, euen the fat that couereth the
inwardes, and the kall of the liuer, and the
two kidneis, and the fat that is vpon them,
and the right ſhulder, (for it is the [g] ram
of conſecration)
23 And one loaf of bread, and one cake of
bread *tempered* with oyle, & one wafer, out
of ẏ baſket of the vnleauened *bread* that
is before the Lord.
24 And thou ſhalt put all this in the hãds of
Aarón, and in the hãds of his ſonnes, and

Leuit. 1, 3.

c Signifiing that the ſacrifice was alſo offred for them, and that they did approue it.

Leuit. 3, 3.

"Ebr. ſinne. 2. cor. 5, 21.

d Or a ſauour of reſt, which cauſeth the wrath of God to ceaſe.

e Meaning the ſoft & nether parte of the eare.

f Wherewith the altar muſt be ſprinkled.

g Which is offred for the cõſecration of ẏ hie Prieſt.

shalt shake them to and fro before ẏ Lord.
25 Againe, thou shalt receiue them of their
hands, and burne them vpon the altar besides the burnt offring for a swete sauour
before the Lord: *for* this is an offring made by fire vnto the Lord.
26 Likewise thou shalt take the brest of the
ram of the consecracion, which is for Aarón, and shalt shake it to [h] and fro before
the Lord, and it shalbe thy parte.
27 And thou shalt sanctifie the brest of the
shaken offring, & the shulder of the [i] heaue offring, which was shaken to and fro,
& which was heaued vp of the ram of the
consecracion, which *was* for Aarón, and
which *was* for his sonnes.
28 And Aarón and his sonnes shal haue it
by a statute for euer, of the children of Israél: for it is an heaue offring, and it shalbe an heaue offring of the children of Israél, of their [k] peace offrings, *euen* their heaue offring to the Lord.
29 ¶ And the holy garmẽts, which *appertey-
ne* to Aarón, shalbe his sonnes after him,
to be anointed therein, and to be cõsecrat
therein.
30 That sonne that shalbe Priest in his stede, shal put them on seuen dayes, when he
cometh into the Tabernacle of the Congregacion to minister in the holy place.
31 ¶ So thou shalt take the ram of ẏ cõsecra
cion, and sethe his flesh in the holy place.
32 *And Aarón and his sonnes shal eat the
flesh of the ram, and the bread that is in ẏ
basket, at the dore of the Tabernacle of ẏ
Congregacion.
33 So they shal eat these things, [l] whereby
their atonemẽt was made, to cõsecrat thẽ,
and to sanctifie thẽ: but a stranger shal not
eate *thereof*, because they are holy things.
34 Now if oght of ẏ flesh of the cõsecraciõ,
or of ẏ bread remaine vnto the morning,
then thou shalt burne the rest with fire: it
shal not be eatẽ, because it is an holy thĩg.
35 Therefore shalt thou do thus vnto Aarón and vnto his sonnes, according to all
things, which I haue commanded thee: seuen daies shalt thou " consecrat them,
36 And shalt offer euerie day a calf or a sinne offring, for [m] reconciliation: and thou
shalt clense ẏ altar, when thou hast offred
vpon it for reconciliation, & shalt anoint
it, to sanctifie it.
37 Seuen daies shalt thou clense the altar,
and sanctifie it, so the altar shalbe moste
holy: *and* whatsoeuer toucheth the altar,
shalbe holy.
38 ¶ *Now this is ẏ which thou shalt present vpon the altar: *euen* two lãbes of one
yere olde, day by day continually.
39 The one lambe thou shalt present in the
morning, and the other lambe thou shalt
present at euen.
40 And with ẏ one lãbe, a [n] tenth parte of fi
ne floure mingled wᵗ the fourte parte of an
[o] Hin of beaten oile, and the fourte parte
of an Hin of wine, for a drinke offring.
41 And the other lambe ẏ shalt present at
euen: thou shalt do thereto according to
the offring of the morning, & according
to the drinke offring thereof, *to be* a burnt
offring for a swete sauoure vnto the Lord.
42 *This shal be* a continual burnt offring in
your generatiõs at the dore of the Tabernacle of the Cõgregacion before ẏ Lord,
where I wil " make appointment with you,
to speake there vnto thee.
43 There I wil appoint with the children
of Israél, and *the place* shalbe sanctified by
my [p] glorie.
44 And I wil sanctifie the Tabernacle of ẏ
Cõgregacion & the altar: I wil sanctifie
also Aarón & his sonnes to be my Priests,
45 And I wil *dwel among the children of
Israél, and wil be their God.
46 Then shal they knowe that I am ẏ Lord
their God, that broght them out of ẏ land
of Egypt, that I might dwel among them:
[q] I am the Lord their God.

h This sacrifice the Priest did moue toward the East, West, North and South.

i So called, because it was not onely shakẽ to and fro, but also lifted vp.

k Which were offrigs of thãkes giuing to God for his benefites.

*Leu.8,31, & 20,9.mat.12,4.

l That is, by the sacrifices.

" Ebr. fil their handes.

m To appease Gods wrath ẏ sinne may be pardonned.

*Num.28,3.

n That is, an Omer. read chap.16,16.

o Which is about a pinte.

" Or, declare my selfe to you.

p Because of my glorious presence.

*Leu.26,12 2.cor.6,16

q It is I the Lord, that am their God.

CHAP. XXX.

1 The Altar of incense. 13 The summe that the Israelites shulde pay to the Tabernacle. 16 The brasen Lauer. 23 The anointing Oyle. 34 The making of the perfume.

1 FVrthermore thou shalt make an altar
[a] for swete perfume, of Shittim wood
thou shalt make it.
2 The length therof a cubite & ẏ breadth
thereof a cubite (it shalbe foure square)
and the height thereof two cubites: the
hornes thereof *shalbe* [b] of the same,
3 And ẏ shalt ouerlaie it with fine golde,
bothe ẏ top thereof & ẏ sides thereof roũd
about, and his hornes: also thou shalt make vnto it " a crowne of gold roũde about.

a Vpon the which the swete perfume was burnt. vers.34.

b Of the same wood & matter.

" Or, a circle & bordre.

THE ALTAR OF SWETE PERFUME.

This altar was one cubite long, and one cubite broad, and in height was two cubites: the rest may be vnderstãd by the former figures.

4 Besides this thou shalt make vnder this
crowne two golden rings on ether side:
euen on euerie side shalt thou make *them*,
that thei may be as places for the barres
to beare it with all.
5 The ŵ barres thou shalt make of Shittím wood, and shalt couer them ŵ golde.
6 After thou shalt set it [c] before the vaile,
that is nere the Arke of Testimonie, before the Merciseat that is vpon the Testimonie, where I wil appoint with thee.

c That is, in ŷ Sanctuarie, and not in the Holiest of all.

7 And Aarón shal burne thereon swete incense euerie morning: when he [d] dresseth
the lampes thereof, shal he burne it.
8 Likewise at euen, when Aarón setteth
vp the lápes thereof, he shal burne incése:
this perfume *shalbe* perpetually before the
Lord, throughout your generations.

d Meaning whē he trimmeth them, & refresheth the oyle.

9 Ye shal offre no [e] strange incense thereon,
nor burnt sacrifice, nor offring, nether powre anie drinke offring [f] thereon.

e Otherwise made thē this, which is described.

f But it must onely serue to burne perfume

10 And Aarón shal make recóciliation vpō
ŷ hornes of it once in a yere ŵ the blood
of the sinne offring *in the day* of recóciliation: once in the yere shal he make reconciliation vpon it throughout your genera
tions: this is moste holy vnto the Lord.
11 ¶ Afterward the Lord spake vnto Mosés, saying,
12 *When thou takest the summe of ŷ children of Israél after their nōbre, then they
shal giue euerie man [g] a redemption of his
life vnto the Lord, whē thou tellest them,
that there be no plague among them whē
thou countest them.

Nom.1,2,5.

g Wherby he testified ŷ he redemed his life which he had forfait, as is declared by Dauid, 2.Sam. 24,1.

13 This shal euerie mā giue, that goeth into
the nombre, half a shekel, after the [h] shekel of the Sanctuarie: (* a shekel *is* twenty
geráhs) the halfe shekel *shalbe* an offring
to the Lord.

h This shekel valued two cōmune shekels: & ŷ geráh valued about 2. pence after 5. shill. sterl. the once of siluer.

Leu.27,25. nom.3,47. ezek.45,12.

14 All that are nōbred frō twenty yere olde
and aboue, shal giue an offring to ŷ Lord.
15 The riche shal not passe, and the poore
shal not diminish from halfe a shekel,
whé ye shal giue an offring vnto ŷ Lord,
[i] for the redemption of your liues.

i That God shuld be merciful vnto you.

16 So thou shalt take the money of ŷ redép
tion of the children of Israél, and shalt
put it vnto the vse of the Tabernacle of ŷ
Cōgregacion, that it may be a memorial
vnto the children of Israél before ŷ Lord
for the redemption of your liues.

THE LAVER OF BRASSE.

A The fundation or fote of the Lauer.
B The Lauer. Because Mosés describeth not the maner of this Lauer, this figure is made after the facion of Salomons, ŵ semeth to be moste agreable to this, 1.King. 7,38. saue in stede of wheles are put barres to beare it, as in the other figures also appeareth.

17 ¶ Also ŷ Lord spake vnto Mosés, saying,
18 Thou shalt also make a lauer of brasse,
& his fote of brasse to wash, and shalt put
it betwene ŷ Tabernacle of ŷ Congregaciō & the altar, & shalt put water therein.
19 For Aarón and his sonnes shal [k] wash
their hands and their fete thereat.

k Signifiing ŷ he that commeth to God, must be washed from all sinne and corruption.

20 When they go into the Tabernacle of
the Congregacion, or when they go vnto
the altar to minister & to make ŷ perfume
of the burnt offring to the Lord, they shal
wash thē selues with water, lest they dye.
21 So they shal wash their hāds & their fete
ŷ they dye not: & *this* shalbe to thē an ordi
nance [l] for euer, *bothe* vnto him and to his
sede throughout their generacions.

l So long as ŷ priesthode shal last.

22 ¶ Also ŷ Lord spake vnto Mosés, saying,
23 Take thou also vnto thee, principal spices of ŷ moste pure myrrhe fiue hūdreth
[m] *shekels*, of swete cinamō halfe so muche,
that is, two hundreth & fiftie, and of swete
[n] calamus, two hundreth, and fiftie:

m Waying so muche.

n It is a kinde of reede of a very swete sauour within, & is vsed in poudres & odours.

24 Also of cassia fiue hundreth, after the
shekel of the Sanctuarie, and of oile oliue
an *Hin.

Chap.29,40.

25 So thou shalt make of it the oile of holy
ointement, *euen* a moste precious ointement after the arte of the apotecarie: this

ſhalbe the oile of holy ointement.
26 And thou ſhalt anoint yͤ [o] Tabernacle of
the Congregacion therewith, & the Arke of the Teſtimonie:

o All things which apparteine to the Tabernacle.

27 Alſo the Table, and all the inſtruments
therof, and the Candelſticke, with all yͤ inſtruments thereof, & the altar of incenſe:
28 Alſo the altar of burnt offring with all
his inſtruments, and the lauer & his fote.
29 So thou ſhalt ſanctifie them, and they
ſhalbe moſte holy: all yͭ ſhal touche them,
ſhalbe holy.
30 Thou ſhalt alſo anoint Aarón and his
ſonnes, and ſhalt conſecrat them, that they
may miniſtre vnto me in the Prieſts office.
31 Moreouer thou ſhalt ſpeake vnto yͤ children of Iſraél, ſaying, This ſhal be an holy ointing oyle vnto me, throughout your
generacions.
32 None ſhal anoint [p] mãs fleſh therewith,
nether ſhal ye make any compoſition like
vnto it: *for* it is holy, *and* ſhalbe holy vnto
you.

p Nether at their burialls nor other wiſe.

33 Whoſoeuer ſhal make yͤ like ointemẽt, or
whoſoeuer ſhal put any of it vpon [q] a ſtrãger, euẽ he ſhalbe cut of from his people.
34 And the Lord ſaid vnto Moſés, Take vn
to thee *theſe* ſpices, pure myrrhe & [r] cleare
gũme and galbanum, *theſe* odoures with
pure frankincenſe, of eche like weight:

q Ether a ſtrãger, or an Iſraelite, ſaue onely the Prieſts.

r In Ebrewe, Shehéleth: wͨ is a ſwete kinde of gumme and ſhineth as the naile.

35 Then thou ſhalt make of them perfume
compoſed after the arte of the apotecary,
mingled together, pure & holy.
36 And thou ſhalt beate it to pouder, and
ſhalt put of it before *the Arke* of yͤ Teſtimonie in the Tabernacle of the Congregacion, where I wil make appointement
with thee: it ſhalbe vnto you moſte holy.
37 And ye ſhal not make vnto you any cõ-
poſition like this perfume, which thou
ſhalt make: it ſhalbe vnto thee holy for
the [ſ] Lord.
38 Whoſoeuer ſhal make like vnto that
to ſmel thereto, euẽ he ſhal be cut of from
his people.

ſ Onely dedicat to the vſe of the Tabernacle.

CHAP. XXXI.

2 God maketh Bezaleél & Aholiáb mete for his worke. 13 The Sabbath day is the ſigne of our ſanctification. 18 The tables written by the finger of God.

1 AND yͤ Lord ſpake vnto Moſés, ſayĩg,
2 Beholde, I [a] haue called by name,
Bezaleél, the ſonne of Vri, the ſonne of
Hur of the tribe of Iudáh,

a I haue choſen and made mete. Chap. 35, 30.

3 Whome I haue filled with the Spirit of
God, in wiſdome, & in vnderſtanding &
in knowledge & in all [b] workemanſhip:
4 To finde out curious workes to worke in
golde, & in ſiluer, and in braſſe,
5 Alſo in the art to ſet ſtones, and to carue
in timber, *and* to worke in all maner of
workemanſhip.
6 And beholde, I haue ioyned with hĩ Aholiáb the ſonne of Ahiſamáh of the tribe of
Dan, & in the heartes of all that are [c] wiſe
hearted, haue I put wiſdome to make all yͭ
I haue commanded thee:

b This ſheweth that hãdy crafts are the gifts of Gods Spirit, & therefore oght to be eſtemed.

c I haue inſtructed them, and increaſed their knowledge.

7 *That is*, yͤ Tabernacle of yͤ Congregaciõ,
and the Arke of the Teſtimonie, and the
Merciſeat that ſhalbe thereupon, with all
inſtruments of the Tabernacle:
8 Alſo the Table and the inſtruments thereof, and the [d] pure Candelſticke with all
his inſtruments, and the Altar of perfume:
9 Likewiſe the Altar of burnt offring with
all his inſtrumẽts, and the Lauer with his
fote:

d So called, becauſe of the conning and arteyſed therein, or becauſe the whole was beaten out of one piece.

10 Alſo the garmentes of the miniſtration,
and the holy garmẽts for Aarón yͤ Prieſt,
and the garmẽts of his ſonnes, to miniſter
in the Prieſts office,
11 And the [e] anointing oyle, and ſwete perfume for the Sanctuarie: according to all
that I haue cõmãded thee, ſhal they do.
12 ¶ Afterward the Lord ſpake vnto Moſés,
ſaying,

e Which onely was to annoint the Prieſts & yͤ inſtruments of the Tabernacle, and not to burne.

13 Speake thou alſo vnto the children of Iſraél, & ſay, [f] Notwithſtãding kepe ye my
Sabbaths: for it is a ſigne betwene me and
you in your generations, that ye may knowe that I the Lord do ſanctifie you.
14 *Ye ſhal therefore kepe yͤ [g] Sabbath: for
it is holy vnto you: he that defileth it, ſhal
dye yͤ death: therfore whoſoeuer worketh
therein, the ſame perſone ſhalbe euen cut
of from among his people.
15 Six dayes ſhal men worke, but in the ſeuenth day *is* the Sabbath of the holy reſt
to the Lord: whoſoeuer doeth any worke
in the Sabbath day, ſhal dye the death.
16 Wherefore the childrẽ of Iſraél ſhal kepe the Sabbath, that they may obſerue the
[*] reſt through out their generations for an
euerlaſting couenant.

f Thogh I cõmande theſe workes to be done, yet wil I not that you breake my Sabbath daies.

Chap. 20, 8. ezek. 20, 12.

g God repeteth this point becauſe the whole keping of the Lawe ſtandeth in the true vſe of the Sabbath, wͨ is to ceaſe from our workes, & to obey the wil of God.

*Or, Sabbath.

17 It is a ſigne betwene me and the children of Iſraél for euer: *for in ſix dayes yͤ
Lord made the heauen and the earth, and
in the ſeuenth day [h] he ceaſed, and reſted.
18 Thus (when the Lord had made an end
of cõmuning with Moſés vpon mount Sinái) *he gaue him two Tables [i] of the Teſtimonie, *euen* tables of ſtone, written with
the finger of God.

Gen. 1, 31. & 2, 2.

h From creating his creatures, but not frõ gouernig & preſeruing them.

Deut. 9, 10.

i Whereby he declared his wil to his people.

CHAP. XXXII.

4 The Iſraelites impute their deliuerance to the calf. 14 God is appaiſed by Moſés prayer. 19 Moſés breaketh the Tables. 27 He ſlayeth the idolaters. 32 Moſés zeale for the people.

1 BVt when the people ſawe, that Moſés
taried lõg or he came downe from yͤ
mõutaine, the people gathered thẽ ſelues
together againſt Aarón, & ſaid vnto him,
Vp, [a] make vs gods to go before vs: for of
this Moſés (the man that broght vs out of
the land of Egypt) we knowe not what is
become of him.
2 And Aarón ſaid vnto them, [b] Plucke of
the

a The rote of idolatrie is, whẽ mẽ thinke yͭ God is not at hand, except they ſe him carnally.

b Thinking yͭ they wolde rather forgo idolatrie, thẽ to reſigne their moſte precious iewels.

the golden earings,which are in the eares
of your wiues,of your sonnes,and of your
daughters,and bring them vnto me.
3 Then all the people pluckte from thẽ
[c] selues the golden earings, which were in
their eares,and they broght *them* vnto Aarón.

c Suche is the rage of idolaters,that they spare no cost to satisfie their wicked desires.

4 *Who receiued them at their hands,and
facioned it with the grauing tole, & made of it a [d] molten calf: then they said,
* These be thy gods, ô Israél,ẇ broght
thee out of the land of Egypt.

Psal.106,19.
d Thei smelled of their leuẽ of Egypt, where thei sawe calues, oxẽ,& serpẽts worshipped
1.King.12,28.

5 When Aarón sawe *that*, he made an altar
before it: and Aarón proclaimed, saying,
To morowe *shalbe* the holy day of the
Lord.
6 So they rose vp the next day in the morning,and offred burnt offrings, & broght
peace offrings: also *the people sate them
downe to eat and drinke, and rose vp to
playe.

1.Cor.10,7.

7 ¶Then the Lord said vnto Mosés,* Go,
get the downe:for thy people which thou
hast broght out of the lãd of Egypt,hathe
corrupted *their waies.*
8 Thei [e] are sone turned out of the way,
which I commanded them: *for* thei haue
made them a moltẽ calf,& haue worshipped it,& haue offred thereto, sayĩg,*These be thy gods,ô Israél,which haue broght
thee out of the land of Egypt.

e Whereby we se what necessitie we haue to pray earnestly to God, to kepe vs in his true obedience and to send vs good guides.
1.King.12,28

9 Againe the Lord said vnto Mosés,* I
haue sene this people, and beholde,it is a
stifnecked people.

Chap.33.3. deut.9,13.

10 Nowe [f] therefore let me alone,that my
wrath may waxe hote against them, for I
wil consume them:but I wil make of thee
a mightie people.

f God sheweth ẏ the praiers of the godly stay his punishment.

11 *But Mosés praied vnto ẏ Lord his God,
and said, O Lord, why doeth thy wrath
waxe hote against thy people,which thou
hast broght out of the lãd of Egypt, with
great power and with a mightie hand?

Psal 106,23.

12 *Wherefore shal the Egyptians "speake,
and say, He hathe broght them out maliciously for to slay them in the moũtaines,
and to consume them from the earth? turne from thy fearce wrath,and "change thy
minde from this euil toward thy people.

Nomb.14,13
"Or, blaspheme.
"Or, repent.

13 Remembre [g] Abrahám, Izhák, & Israél
thy seruants, to whome thou swarest by
thine owne selfe,and saidest vnto them,*I
wil multiplie your sede, as the starres of
the heauen, and all this land, that I haue
spoken of, wil I giue vnto your sede, and
thei shal inherit it for euer.

g That is, thy promes made to Abrahám.
Gen.12,7. & 15,7.& 48,16

14 Then the Lord changed his minde from
the euil, which he threatened to do vnto
his people.
15 So Mosés returned and went downe
from the mountaine with the two Tables
of the Testimonie in his hãd: the Tables
were writtẽ on bothe their sides,euen on ẏ
one side & on the other were thei written.
16 And these Tables were the worke of
God, and [h] this writing was the writing
of God grauen in the Tables.

h All these petitiõs shewe how excellent a thĩg thei defrauded them selues of by their idolatrie

17 And whẽ Iosshúa heard the noise of the
people,as thei showted, he said vnto Mosés, *There is* a noise of warre in the hoste.
18 Who answered,It is not the noise of thẽ
that haue the victorie,nor the noise of thẽ
that are ouercome: *but* I do heare the noise of singing.
19 Nowe, assone as he came nere vnto the
hoste,he sawe the calf and the dancing: so
Mosés wrath waxed hote, and he cast the
Tables out of his hands, and brake them
in pieces beneth the mountaine.
20 *After,he toke the calf, which they had
made, & burned it in the fire, and ground
it vnto powder, and strowed it vpon the
water,& made the childrẽ of Israél [i] drinke of it.

Deut.9,21.
i Partely to despite them of their idolatrie,& partely ẏ thei shulde haue none occasiõ to remẽber it afterwardo.

21 Also Mosés said vnto Aarón, What did
this people vnto thee, ẏ thou hast broght
so great a sinne vpon them?
22 Thẽ Aarón answered, Let not the wrath
of my lord waxe fearce:thou knowest this
people,that thei are *euen set* on mischief.
23 And thei said vnto me, Make vs gods to
go before vs: for we knowe not what is
become of this Mosés (the man ẏ broght
vs out of the land of Egypt.)
24 Thẽ I said to them, Ye that haue golde,
plucke it of: and thei broght it me, and I
did cast it into the fire, and *thereof* came
this calf.
25 Mosés therefore sawe that the people
were [k] naked(for Aarón had made them
naked vnto *their* shame among their enemies)

k Bothe destitute of Gods fauour,& an occasion to their enemies to speake euil of their God.

26 And Mosés stode in the gate of the cãp,
and said, Who *perteineth* to the Lord? *let
him come* to me. And all the sonnes of Leuí
gathered them selues vnto him.
27 Then he said vnto them, Thus saith the
Lord God of Israél, Put euerie man his
sworde by his side: go to and fro,frõ gate
to gate,through the hoste,and [l] slay euerie man his brother, and euerie man his
companion,& euerie man his neighbour.
28 So the children of Leuí did as Mosés
had commanded:and there fel of the people the same day about thre thousand mẽ.

l This fact did so please God, that he turned the curse of Iaakób against Leuí,to a blessing,Deut 33,9

29 (For Mosés had said, Consecrat your
hands vnto the Lord this day,euen euerie
man vpon his [m] sonne, and vpon his brother, that there may be giuen you a blessing this day)

m In reuenging Gods glorie we must haue no respect to persone, but put of all carnal affection.

30 And whẽ the morning came,Mosés said
vnto the people, Ye haue cõmitted a grieuous crime: but now I wil go vp to the
Lord, if I may pacifie *him* for your sinne.
31 Mosés therefore went againe vnto the
Lord,and said, Oh, this people haue sin-

ned a great sinne and haue made thẽ gods
of golde.
32 Therefore now if thou pardone their
sinne, *thy mercie shal appeare*: but if thou
wilt not, I pray thee, rase me [n] out of thy
boke, which thou hast written.

n So muche he estemed ÿ glorie of God, ÿ he preferred it eue to his owne saluacion.

33 Then the Lord said to Mosés, Whosoeuer hathe sinned against me, I wil put him
out of my [o] boke.

o I wil make it knowẽ that he was neuer predestinate in mine eternal cõũsel to life euerlasting.

34 Go now therefore, bring the people vnto the place which I commanded thee: beholde, mine Angel shal go before thee,
but yet in the day of my visitacion I wil
[p] viset their sinne vpon them.
35 So the Lord plagued the people, because
thei caused Aarón *to make* the calf which
he made.

p This declareth how grieuous a sinne idolatrie is, seing that at Mosés praier God wolde not fully remitte it.

CHAP. XXXIII.

2 The Lord promiseth to send an Angel before his people. 4 Thei are sad because the Lord denieth to go vp with them. 9 Mosés talketh familiarely with God. 13 He praieth for the people. 18 And desireth to se the glorie of the Lord.

1 AFterwarde the Lord said vnto Mosés, Departe, [a] go vp frõ hence, thou,
and the people (which thou hast broght
vp out of the land of Egypt) vnto the lãd
ẇ I sware vnto Abrahám, to Izhák and to
Iaakób, sayĩg, *Vnto thy sede wil I giue it.
2 And * I wil send an Angel before thee &
wil cast out the Canaanites, ÿ Amorites,
and the Hittites, and the Perizzites, the
Hiuites, and the Iebusites:
3 To a lãd, *I say*, that floweth with milke &
hony: for I wil not go vp with thee, *because thou art a stifnecked people, lest I
consume thee in the way.

a The land of Canaan was compassed ẇ hilles: so thei, that entred into it, must passe vp by the hilles.

Gen.12,7. exod.23,27. iosh.24,11. Deu.7,21.

Chap.32,9. deut.9,13.

4 And when the people heard this euil tidings, they sorowed, & no man put on his
best rayment.
5 (For the Lord had said to Mosés, Say vnto the children of Israél, Ye are a stifnecked people, I wil come sodenly vpon thee,
and consume thee: therefore now put thy
costly rayment frõ thee, that I may knowe
[b] what to do vnto thee)
6 So the childrẽ of Israél laied their good
rayment from them, *after Mosés came downe*
from the mount Horéb.

b That ether may shewe mercie, if thou repent, or els punish thy rebellion.

7 Then Mosés toke *his* tabernacle, & pitched it without the hoste far of from the
hoste, and called it [c] Ohel-moéd. And
when anie did seke to the Lord, he wẽt out
vnto the Tabernacle of the Congregacion, which was without the hoste.
8 And when Mosés went out vnto the Tabernacle, all the people rose vp, and stode
euerie man at his tent dore, and loked after Mosés, vntil he was gone into the Tabernacle.
9 And assone as Mosés was entred into the
Tabernacle, the cloudy piller descended
and stode at the dore of the Tabernacle,
and *the Lord* talked with Mosés.

c That is, the Tabernacle of the Cõgregaciõ: so called, because the people resorted thether, when they shulde be instructed of the Lords wil.

10 Now when all the people sawe the cloudy piller stand at the Tabernacle dore,
all the people rose vp, & worshipped euerie man in his tent dore.
11 And the Lord spake vnto Mosés, [d] face to
face, as a man speaketh vnto his friend.
After he turned againe into the hoste, but
his seruant Ioshúa the sonne of Nun a
yong man, departed not out of the Tabernacle.

d Moste plainely & familiarely of all others, Nomb. 12,7.

12 ¶ Then Mosés said vnto the Lord, Se,
ÿ saiest vnto me, Lead this people fourth,
& thou hast not shewed me whome thou
wilt send with me: thou hast said moreouer, I knowe thee by [e] name, & thou hast
also founde grace in my sight.

e I care for thee and wil preserue thee in this thy vocation.

13 Now therefore, I pray thee, if I haue founde fauour in thy sight, shewe me now
thy way, that I may knowe thee, *and* that
I may finde grace in thy sight: consider also that this nacion *is* thy people.
14 And he answered, My " [f] presence shal go
with thee, and I wil giue thee rest.
15 Then he said vnto him, If thy presence
go not *with vs*, cary vs not hence.
16 And wherein now shal it be knowẽ, that
I and thy people haue founde fauour in
thy sight? shal it not be when thou goest
with vs? so I, & thy people shal haue preeminence before all the people that are
vpon the earth.

" Ebr. face.

f Signifying ÿ the Israelites shulde excel through Gods fauour all other people, vers.16.

17 And the Lord said vnto Mosés, I wil do
this also that thou hast said: for thou hast
founde grace in my sight, and I knowe
thee by name.
18 Againe he said, I beseche thee, shewe me
thy [g] glorie.
19 And he answered, I wil make all my
[h] good go before thee, and I wil [i] proclaime the Name of the Lord before thee:
* for I wil shewe [k] mercie to whome I
wil shewe mercie, & wil haue compassion
on whome I wil haue compassion.
20 Furthermore he said, Thou cãst not se
my face, for there shal no man se me, and
[l] liue.
21 Also the Lord said, Beholde, *there is* a
place by [m] me, and thou shalt stãde vpon
the rocke:
22 And while my glorie passeth by, I wil put
thee in a cleft of the rocke, and wil couer
thee with mine hand whiles I passe by.
23 After I wil take away mine hand, & thou
shalt se my [n] backe partes: but my face
shal not be sene.

g Thy face, thy substance, and thy maiestie.

h My mercie, & fatherlie care.

i Read chap. 34, vers.6,7.

Rom.9,15.

k For finding nothing in mã that cã deserue mercie, he wil frely saue his.

l For Mosés sawe not his face in ful maiestie, but as mans weakenes colde beare.

m In mount Horéb.

n So muche of my glorie as in this mortal life thou art able to se.

CHAP. XXXIIII.

1 The Tables are renued. 6 The description of God. 12 All felowship with idolaters is forbidden. 18 The thre feasts. 28 Mosés is 40. daies in the mount. 30 His face shineth, and he couereth it with a vaile.

1 ANd ÿ Lord said vnto Mosés, *Hewe
thee two Tables of stone, like vnto ẏ
first

Deut.10,1.

first, and I wil write vpon the Tables the
wordes that were in ẏ first Tables, which
thou brakest in pieces.
2 And be ready in the morning, that thou
maiest come vp early vnto the moũt of Sinái, and "waite there for me in the top of
the mount.
3 But let no man come vp with thee, nether
let anie man be sene throughout all the
mount, nether let the shepe nor cattel fede
before this mount.
4 ¶ Thẽ Mosés "hewed two Tables of stone like vnto the first, and rose vp early in ẏ
morning, and went vp vnto the mount of
Sinái, as the Lord had cõmanded him, &
toke in his hand two Tables of stone.
5 And the Lord descended in the cloude,
and stode with him there, and proclaimed
the Name of the Lord.
6 So the Lord passed before his face, and
[a] cryed, The Lord, ẏ Lord, strong, merciful, and gracious, slow to angre, & abundant in goodnes and trueth,
7 Reseruing mercie for thousands, forgiuing iniquitie, & transgression and sinne, and not "making *the wicked* innocent,
*visiting the iniquitie of the fathers vpon
the children, and vpon childrens childrẽ,
vnto the third and fourth *generation*.
8 Then Mosés made haste and bowed him
self to the earth, and worshipped,
9 And said, ô Lord, I praye thee, if I haue
founde grace in thy sight, that the Lord
wolde now go wᵗ vs (ᵇ for it is a stifnecked
people) and pardone our iniquitie & our
sinne, and take vs for thine enheritance.
10 And he answered, Beholde, * I wil make
a couenant before all thy people, *and* wil
do meruels, suche as haue not bene done
in all the world, nether in all nations: and
all the people amõg whome thou art, shal
se the worke of ẏ Lord: for it is a terrible
thing that I wil do with thee.
11 Kepe diligently that which I commande thee this day: beholde, I wil cast out
before thee the Amorites, and the Canaanites, and the Hittites, & the Perizzites,
and the Hiuites, and the Iebusites.
12 *Take hede to thy self, that thou make
no compact with the inhabitants of the
land whither ẏ goest, lest thei be the cause
of [c] ruine among you:
13 But ye shal ouerthrowe their altars, and
breake their images in pieces, and cut downe their [d] groues,
14 (For thou shalt bowe downe to none o-
ther god, because the Lord, whose Name
is *Ielous, is a ielous God)
15 Lest thou make a * compact with the inhabitants of the land, and when they go
a whoring after their gods, and do sacrifice vnto their gods, *some man* call thee, and
thou * eat of his sacrifice:

"Ebr. stand to me.

"Or, polished.

a This oght to be referred to the Lord & not to Mosés proclaiming: as chap. 33. vers. 19.

"Ebr. not making innocent.
Deut. 5,9.
iere. 32,18.

b Seing ẏ people are thus of nature, ẏ rulers haue nede to call vpõ God, that he wolde alwais be present with his Spirit.

Deu. 5,2.

Deu. 7,12.

c If thou followe their wickednes, and pollute thy selfe wᵗ their idolatrie.
d Which pleasãt places thei chosed for their idoles.
Chap. 20,5.
Chap. 23,32.
deu. 7,2.
1. Cor. 8,10.

16 And *lest* thou take of their * daughtets
vnto thy sonnes, and their daughters go a
whoring after their gods, and make thy
sonnes go a whoring after their gods.
17 Thou shalt make thee no gods of [e] metal.
18 ¶ The feast of vnleauened bread shalt ẏ"
kepe: seuẽ dayes shalt thou eat vnleauened
bread, as I commanded thee, in the time
of the * moneth of Abíb: for in the moneth of Abíb thou camest out of Egypt.
19 *Euerie *male*, that *first* openeth ẏ wombe
shalbe mine: also all the first borne of thy
flocke shalbe reconed *mine, bothe* of beues
and shepe.
20 But the first of the asse thou shalt bye
out with a lambe: and if thou redeme *him*
not, then thou shalt breake his necke: all
the first borne of thy sonnes shalt thou redeme, and none shal appeare before me
[f] empty.
21 ¶ Six dayes thou shalt worke, and in the
seuẽth day thou shalt rest: bothe in earing
time, and in the haruest thou shalt rest.
22 ¶ *Thou shalt also obserue the feast of
wekes *in the time* of ẏ first frutes of wheat
haruest, and the feast of gathering *frutes* in
[g] the end of the yere.
23 ¶ Thrise in a yere shal all your mẽ childrẽ appeare before ẏ Lord Iehouah God
of Israél.
24 For I wil cast out the nacions before
thee, and enlarge thy coastes, so that no
man shal [h] desire thy land, whẽ thou shalt
come vp to appeare before the Lord thy
God thrise in the yere.
25 Thou shalt not offer the blood of my sacrifice with leauen, nether shal oght of
the sacrifice of the feast of Passeouer be
left vnto the morning.
26 The first ripe frutes of thy land thou
shalt bring vnto the house of the Lord
thy God: *yet* shalt thou not [i] sethe a kid
in his mothers milke.
27 And the Lord said vnto Mosés, Write
thou these wordes: for after the tenoure
of * these wordes I haue made a couenant
with thee and with Israél.
28 So he was there with the Lord [k] fourtie
daies and fourtie nights, *and* did nether
eat bread nor drinke water: and he wrote
in the Tables *the wordes of ẏ couenant,
euen the ten "commandements.
29 ¶ So when Mosés came downe frõ moũt
Sinái, the two Tables of the Testimonie
were in Mosés hand, as he descended from
the mount: (now Mosés wist not that
ẏ skin of his face shone bright, after that
God had talked with him)
30 And Aarón and all the childrẽ of Israél
loked vpon Mosés, and beholde, the skin
of his face shone bright, and they were
[l] afraide to come nere him.

1. King 11,2.

e As golde, siluer, brasse, or any thing that is molten.

Chap. 13,4.

Chap. 13,3. & 22,29. ezek. 44,30.

f With out offring some thing.

Chap. 23,16.

g Which was in September, when ẏ sunne declined, which in the counte of political things thei called ẏ ende of ẏ yere.

h God promiseth to defend them & theirs, which obey his commandement.

i Read chap. 23,19. deu. 14, 21.

Chap. 24,18. deu. 9,9.

k This miracle was to cõfirme the autoritie of the Lawe, and oght no more to be followed then other miracles.

Deu. 4,13.
"Or, wordes.

l Read 2 Cor. 3,7.

31 But Mosés called them: and Aarón and
all the chief of the Congregacion returned vnto him: and Mosés talked with
them.
32 And afterward all the childrẽ of Israél
came nere, and he charged them with all
that the Lord had said vnto him in mout
Sinái.
33 So Mosés made an end of communing
with them, * and had put a couering vpon
his face.

2.Cor.3.13.

34 But, when Mosés came [m] before ỷ Lord
to speake with him, he toke of the couering vntil he came out: then he came out,
and spake vnto the children of Israél that
which he was commanded.

m Which was in the Tabernacle of the Cõgregacion.

35 And the children of Israél sawe the face
of Mosés, how the skin of Mosés face
shone bright: therefore Mosés put the couering vpõ his face, vntil he went to speake with God.

CHAP. XXXV.

2 The Sabbath. 5 The fre gifts are required. 21 The readines of the people to offer. 30 Bezaleél & Aholiáb are praised of Mosés.

1 THen Mosés assembled all the Congre
gacion of the children of Israél, and
said vnto thẽ, These are the wordes which
the Lord hathe commãded, that ye shulde
do them:
2 *Six dayes thou shalt worke, but the seuẽth day shal be vnto you the holy [a] Sabbath of rest vnto ỷ Lord: whosoeuer doeth *anie* worke therein, shal dye.

Chap.20.8. *a Wherein ye shal rest from all bodelie worke.*

3 Ye shal kindle no fire throughout all
your habitations vpon the Sabbath day.
4 ¶ Againe, Mosés spake vnto all the Congregacion of ỷ children of Israél, saying,
This is the thing which the Lord commandeth, saying,
5 Take from among you an offring vnto
the Lord: whosoeuer is of a * willing heart, let him bring this offring to the Lord,
namely golde, and siluer, and brasse:

Chap.25,2.

6 Also blewe silke, and purple, and skarlet,
and fine linen, and goates *heere*,
7 And rams skins died red, and badgers
skins with Shittím wood:
8 Also oyle for light, & spices for the anointing oyle, and for the swete incense,
9 And onix stones, and stones to be set in
the Ephód, and in the brest plate.
10 And all the wise [b] hearted among you,
shal come & make all that the Lord hathe
commanded:

b Read Chap. 28,3.

11 *That is*, the * Tabernacle, the pauillion thereof, & his couering, & his taches & his bo
ardes, his barres, his pillers & his sockets,

Chap.26,31.

12 The Arke, and the barres thereof: the
Merciseat, & the vaile that [c] couereth *it*,

c Which hanged before the Merciseat that it colde not be sene.

13 The Table, and the barres of it, and all
the instrumẽts thereof, & the shewe bread:
14 Also the Cãdelsticke of light and his instruments and his lampes with the oyle
for the light:
15 * Likewise the Altar of perfume and his
barres, and the anointing oyle, and the
swete incense, and the vaile of the dore at
the entring in of the Tabernacle,

Chap.30,1.

16 The * Altar of burnt offring with his
brasen grate, his barres and all his instruments, the Lauer and his fote,

Chap.27,1.

17 The hãgings of the courte, his pillers &
his sockets, and the vaile of ỷ gate of the
courte,
18 The pins of the Tabernacle, and ỷ pins
of the courte with their cordes,
19 The [d] ministring garments to ministre
in the holy place, *and* the holy garments
for Aarón the Priest, and the garments
of his sonnes, that they may ministre in
the Priestes office.

d Suche as apperteine to ỷ seruice of the Tabernacle.

20 ¶ Then all the Congregacion of ỷ children of Israél departed from the presence of Mosés.
21 And euerie one, whose hearts" encouraged him, & euerie one, whose spirit made
him willing, came *and* broght an offring
to ỷ Lord, for the worke of the Tabernà-
cle of the Congregacion, and for all his
vses, and for the holy garments.

"Ebr. lifted him vp.

22 Bothe men & women, as many as were
fre hearted, came *and* broght " taches and
earings, and rings, and bracelets, all *were*
iewels of golde: and euerie one that offred
an offring of golde vnto the Lord:

"Or, hokes.

23 Euerie man also, which had blewe silke,
and purple, & skarlet, and fine linen, and
goats *heere*, and rams skins died red, and
badgers skins, broght *them*.
24 All that offred an oblatiõ of siluer & of
brasse, broght ỷ offring vnto the Lord: &
euerie one, ỷ "had Shittím wood for anie
maner worke of ỷ ministraciõ, broght *it*.

"Ebr. With whome was founde.

25 And all the womẽ that were [e] wise hearted, did spin with their hãdes, and broght
the spun worke, *euen* the blewe silke, and
the purple, the skarlet, and the fine linen.

e Which were witty and expert.

26 Likewise all the women, [f] whose heartes
were moued with knowledge, spun goates *heere*.

f That is, ỷ were good spinners.

27 And the rulers broght onix stones, and
stones to be set in the Ephód, and in the
brest plate:
28 Also spice, and oyle for light, and for
the * anointing oyle, and for the swete perfume.

Chap.30,23.

29 Euerie man and woman of the childrẽ of
Israél, whose hearts moued thẽ willingly
to bring for all the worke which the Lord
had commãded thẽ to make [g] by the hãd
of Mosés, broght a fre offring to ỷ Lord.

g Vsing Mosés as a minister thereof.

30 ¶ Then Mosés said vnto the childrẽ of
Israél, Beholde, * ỷ Lord hathe called by
name Bezaleél the sonne of Vrí, the sonne
of Hur of the tribe of Iudáh,

Chap.31,2.

"Or, with the Spirit of God.

31 And hathe filled him "with an excellent
spirit of wisdome, of vnderstanding, and
of knowledge, and in all maner worke,
32 To finde out curious workes, to worke in
golde, and in siluer, and in brasse,
33 And in grauing stones to set thẽ, and in
karuing of wood, *euen* to make anie maner
of fine worke.
34 And he hathe put in his heart that he
may teache *other*: bothe he, and Aholiáb ỹ
sonne of Ahisamách of the tribe of Dan:
35 Them hathe he filled with wisdome of
heart to worke all maner [h] of conning *&
broydred, & nedle worke: in blewe silke,
and in purple, in skarlet, and in fine linen
& weauing, *euen* to do all maner of worke and subtile inuentions.

h Perteining to grauing, or karuing, or suche like.
Chap. 26, 1.

CHAP. XXXVI.

5 The great readines of the people, insomuche that he cõmanded thẽ to cease. 8 The curtaines made. 19 The couerings. 20 The boardes. 31 The barres, 35 And the vaile.

1 THen wroght Bezaleél, and Aholiáb,
and all "conning men, to whome the
Lord gaue wisdome, and vnderstanding,
to knowe how to worke all maner worke
for the seruice of the [a] Sanctuarie, according to all that the Lord had cõmanded.
2 For Mosés had called Bezaleél, & Aholiáb, and all the wise hearted men, in whose hearts the Lord had giuẽ wisdome, *euen*
as manie as their heartes encouraged to
come vnto that worke to worke it.
3 And they receiued of Mosés all ỹ offring
which the children of Isráel had broght
for the worke of the seruice of the Sanctua
rie, to make it: also [b] they broght stil vnto him fre gifts euerie morning.
4 So all the wise men, that wroght all the
holy worke, came euerie man frõ his wor
ke which they wroght,
5 And spake to Mosés, saying, The people
bring to [c] muche, *and* more then ynough
for the vse of the worke, which the Lord
hathe commanded to be made.
6 Then Mosés gaue a commandemẽt, and
they caused it to be proclaimed throughout the hoste, saying, Let nether man nor
woman prepare anie more worke for the
oblacion of the Sanctuarie. So the people
were stayed from offring.
7 For the stuffe they had, was sufficient for
all the worke to make it, and to muche.
8 *All the conning men therefore among
the workemen, made *for* the Tabernacle ten curtaines of fine twined linen, and
of blewe silke, and purple, and skarlet:
[d] Cherubíms of broydred worke made
they *vpon* them.
9 The length of one curtaine *was* twenty
and eight cubites, and the breadth of one
curtaine foure cubitis: *and* the curtaines
were all of one cise.

"Ebr. wise in heart.
a By the Sanctuarie he meaneth here all ỹ Tabernacle.
b Meaning ỹ Israelites.
c A rare exãple & notable to se the people so ready to serue God with their goods.
Chap. 26, 4.
d Which were litle pictures with wingges in the forme of children.

10 And he coupled fiue curtaines together,
and other fiue coupled he together.
11 And he made strings of blewe silke by ỹ
edge of one curtaine, in the seluedge of ỹ
coupling: likewise he made on the side of
the *other* curtaine in the seluedge in the
seconde coupling.
12 *Fiftie strings made he in the one curtaine, and fiftie strings made he in the edge
of the *other* curtaine, which was in the seconde coupling: the strings were set one
against an other.
13 After, he made fiftie "taches of golde, &
coupled the curtaines one to an other ẇ
the taches: *so* was it one Tabernacle.
14 ¶ Also he made curtaines of goates *heere*
for the "couering vpon the Tabernacle:
he made them *to the nomber* of eleuen curtaines.
15 The length of one curtaine *had* thirty
cubites, and the breadth of one curtaine
foure cubites: the eleuen curtaines *were*
of one cise.
16 And he coupled fiue curtaines by them
selues, and six curtaines by them selues:
17 Also he made fiftie strings vpon the edge of *one* curtaine in ỹ seluedge in the cou
pling, and fiftie strings made he vpon the
edge of the *other* curtaine in the seconde
coupling.
18 He made also fiftie taches of brasse to
couple the couering that it might be one.
19 And he made a [e] couering vpon the pauillion of rams skins died red, & a couering of badgers skins aboue.
20 ¶ Likewise he made the boardes for the
Tabernacle of Shittím [f] wood to stãd vp.
21 The length of a boarde *was* ten cubites,
& the breadth of one boarde *was* a cubite, and an halfe.
22 One boarde had two tenons, set in ordre
as the fete of a ladder, one against an o-
ther: thus made he for all the boardes of ỹ
Tabernacle.
23 So he made twẽtie boardes for ỹ Southside of the Tabernacle, euen ful South.
24 And fourtie sockets of siluer made he vn
der the twẽtie boardes, two sockets vnder
one boarde for his two tenõs, & two sockets vnder another boarde for his two tenons.
25 Also for the other side of the Tabernacle towarde the North, he made twentie
boardes,
26 And their fourtie sockets of siluer, two
sockets vnder one boarde, & two sockets
vnder an other boarde.
27 Likewise towarde [g] the Westside of the
Tabernacle he made six boardes.
28 And two boardes made he in the corners
of the Tabernacle, for ether side,
29 And they were *ioyned beneth, and likewise were made sure aboue with a ring:

Chap. 26, 10.
"Or, hokes.
"Or, pauillion.
e These two were aboue ỹ couering of goates heere.
f And to beare vp the curtaines of the Tabernacle.
g Or towarde the sea, ẇ was the sea called mediterraneũ westward frõ Ierusalem.
Chap. 26, 24.

thus he did to bothe in bothe corners.
30 So there were eight boardes and their
sixtene sockets of siluer, vnder euerie boarde two sockets.
Chap.25,27. & 30,4. 31 ¶ After, he made *barres of Shittím wood,
fiue for the boardes in the one side of the
Tabernacle,
32 And fiue barres for the boardes in the o-
ther side of the Tabernacle, and fiue barres for the boardes of the Tabernacle on
the side towarde the West.
33 And he made the middest barre to shote
through the boardes, from the one end
to the other.
34 He ouerlaied also the boardes with golde, and made their rings of golde for places for the barres, and couered the barres
with golde.
h Which was betwene ẏ Sãctuarie and ẏ Moliest of all. 35 ¶ Moreouer he made a [h] vaile of blewe
silke, and purple, and of skarlet, and of fi-
ne twined linen: with Cherubims of broy
dred worke made he it:
36 And made thereunto foure pillers of
Shittím, and ouerlaied them with golde:
Or, heades. whose "hokes *were also* of golde, and he cast
for them foure sockets of siluer.
i which was betwene the court and the Sanctuarie. 37 And he made an [i] hanging for the Taber
nacle dore, of blewe silke, and purple, and
skarlet, and fine twined linen, *and* nedle
worke,
38 And the fiue pillers of it with their hokes, and ouerlaied their chapiters & their
Or, grauen borders. "filets with golde, but their fiue sockets
were of brasse.

CHAP. XXXVII.

1 The Arke. 6 The Merciseat. 10 The Table. 17 The Candelsticke. 25 The Altar of incense.

Chap.25,10 1 AFter this, Bezaleél made the *Arke of
Shittím wood, two cubites and an
halfe long, and a cubite and an halfe broade, and a cubite and an halfe hie:
2 And ouerlaied it with fine golde within
a Like battelments. and without, and made a [a] crowne of golde to it round about,
3 And cast for it foure rings of golde for ẏ
foure corners of it: that is, two rings for ẏ
one side of it, and two rings for the other
side thereof.
4 Also he made barres of Shittím wood, &
couered them with golde,
5 And put the barres in the rings by the sides of the Arke, to beare the Arke.
Chap.25,17. 6 ¶ And he made the * Merciseat of pure
golde: two cubites and an halfe *was* the
length thereof, and one cubite and an halfe the breadth thereof.
7 And he made two Cherubíms of golde,
vpon the two ends of the Merciseat: *euen*
of worke beaten with the hammer made
he them.
8 One Cherúb on ẏ one end, and an other
b Of the self same matter ẏ the Merciseat was. Cherúb on the other end: [b] of the Merciseat made he the Cherubíms, at the two
ends thereof.
9 And ẏ Cherubíms spred out their wings
on hie, and couered the Merciseat wͭ their
wings, and their faces *were* one towardes
an other: toward the Merciseat were the
faces of the Cherubíms.
10 ¶ Also he made the Table of Shittím
wood: two cubites *was* the lẽgth thereof,
and a cubite the breadth thereof, and a
cubite and an halfe the height of it.
11 And he ouerlaied it with fine golde, and
made thereto a crowne of golde round a-
bout.
12 Also he made thereto a border of an "hãd Or, foure fingers.
breadth round about, and made vpon
ẏ border a crowne of golde round about.
13 And he cast for it foure rings of golde,
and put the rings in the foure corners that
were in the foure fete thereof.
14 Against the border were the rings, as
places for the barres to beare the Table.
15 And he made the barres of Shittím wood, and couered them with golde to beare
the Table.
16 * Also he made the instruments for the Chap.25,29.
Table of pure golde: dishes for it, & incẽs
cups for it, and goblets for it, & couerings
for it, wherewith it shulde be couered.
17 ¶ Likewise he made the Candelsticke
of pure golde: of worke beaten out with
the hammer made he the Candelsticke:
and his shaft, & his branche, his bolles, his
knops, and his floures were of one piece.
18 And six branches came out of the sides
thereof: thre branches of the Cãdelsticke
out of the one side of it, and thre branches
of the Candelsticke out of the other side of it.
19 In one branche thre bolles made like almondes, a knop and a floure: and in an o-
ther branche thre bolles made like al-
mõdes, a knop & a floure: *and* so throughout the six branches that proceded out of
the Candelsticke.
20 And vpon the Candelsticke *were* foure
bolles after the facion of almondes, the
knops thereof and the floures thereof:
21 That is, vnder euerie two branches a
knop *made* thereof, and a knop vnder the
secõde branche thereof, and a knop vnder
the third branche thereof, according to
the six branches comming out of it.
22 Their knops and their branches were of
the same: it was all one * beaten worke of Chap.25,31.
pure golde.
23 And he made for it seuen lampes with ẏ
snuffers, & snufdishes thereof of pure gold.
24 Of a [c] talent of pure golde made he it c Read chap. 25,39.
with all the instruments thereof.
25 Furthermore he made the * perfume Chap.30,34.
altar of Shittím wood: the length of it *was*
a cubite, and the breadth of it a cubite (it
was square) and two cubites hie, *and* the
hornes

hornes thereof was of the same.
26 And he couered it with pure golde, bothe the top and the sides thereof round a-
bout, and the hornes of it, and made vnto
it a crowne of golde round about.
27 And he made two rings of golde for it,
vnder the crowne thereof in the two corners of the two sides thereof, to put barres
in for to beare it therewith.
28 Also he made the barres of Shittím wood, and ouerlaied them with golde.
29 And he made the holy * anointing oyle,
& the swete pure incense after the apote-
caries arte.

Chap.30,35.

CHAP. XXXVIII.

1 The Altar of burnt offrings. 8 The brasen Lauer. 9 The Courte. 24 The summe of that the people offred.

1 ALso he made the altar of the burnt
offring * of Shittím wood: fiue cubites *was* the length thereof, and fiue cubi
tes the breadth thereof: *it was* square and
thre cubites hie.
2 And he made vnto it hornes in the foure
corners thereof: the hornes thereof were
of the same, & he ouerlaied it with brasse.
3 Also he made all the instruments of the
Altar: ŷ * asshpans, & the besomes, and the
basins, ŷ fleshokes, & the "censers: all the
instruments thereof made he of brasse.
4 Moreouer he made a brasé grate wroght
like a net to the Altar, vnder the compas
of it beneth in the a middes of it,
5 And cast foure rings of brasse for ŷ foure ends of the grate to put barres in.
6 And he made the barres of Shittím wood, and couered them with brasse.
7 The which barres he put into the rings
on the sides of the altar to beare it withall, and made it holowe *within* ŷ boardes.
8 ¶ Also he made the Lauer of brasse, and
the fote of it of brasse of the b glasses of ŷ
women that did assemble and came together at the dore of the Tabernacle of the
Congregacion.
9 ¶ Finally he made ŷ courte on the Southside ful Southe: the hangings of the courte *were* of fine twined linen, hauing an
hundreth cubites.
10 Their pillers *were* twentie, & their bra
sen sockets twentie: the hokes of the pillers, and their filets *were* of siluer.
11 And on the Northside *the hangings*
were an hundreth cubites: their pillers
twentie, & their sockets of brasse twētie,
ŷ hokes of ŷ pillers & their filets of siluer.
12 On the Westside also *were* hangings of
fiftie cubites, their ten pillers with their
ten sockets: ŷ hokes of the pillers and their
filets of siluer.
13 And toward the Eastside, ful East, *were*
hangings of fiftie cubites.
14 The hangings of the one side *were* fiftene cubites, their thre pillers, and their

Chap.27,1.

Chap.27,3. "Or, fyre panns.

a So ŷ the grid yron or grate was halfe so hie as ŷ altar, & stode within it.

b R. Kimhi saith, that the women broght their loking glasses, which were of brasse or fine metal and offred them frely vnto the vse of the Tabernacle: ŵ was a bright thing & of great maiestie.

thre sockets:
15 * And of the other side of the courte gate on bothe sides *were* hangings of fiftene
cubites, *with* their thre pillers and their
thre sockets.
16 All the hangings of the courte round a-
bout *were* of fine twined linen:
17 But the sockets of the pillers *were* of
brasse: the hokes of the pillers and their
filets of siluer, and the couering of their
chapiters of siluer: and all the pillers of
the courte were hooped about with siluer.
18 *He made* also the hanging of the gate of
the courte of nedle worke, blewe silke, and
purple, and skarlet, and fine twined linen
euen twentie cubites long, and fiue cubites in height & breadth, "like the hāgings
of the courte.
19 And their pillers *were* foure with their
foure sockets of brasse: their hokes of siluer, and the couering of their chapiters,
and their filets of siluer.
20 But all the * pins of the Tabernacle and
of the courte round about *were* of brasse.
21 ¶ These are the partes of the Tabernacle, *I meane*, of the Tabernacle of the Testimonie, which was appointed by the com
mandement of Mosés for the office of ŷ
c Leuites by the hand of Ithamár sonne
to Aarón the Priest.
22 So Bezaleél the sonne of Vrí the sonne
of Hur of the tribe of Iudáh, made all ŷ
the Lord commanded Mosés.
23 And with him Aholiáb sonne of Ahisamách of the tribe of Dan, a d cūning workeman and an embroyderer and a worker
of nedle worke in blewe silke, and in purple, and in skarlet, and in fine linen.
24 All the golde that was occupied in all ŷ
worke wroght for the holy place (which
was the golde of the offring) was nine
& twentie talents, and seuen hundreth and
thirtie shekels, according to the shekel of
the Sanctuarie.
25 But the siluer of them that were nombred in the Cōgregacion, *was* an hūdreth
talēts, and a thousand seuen hundreth seuentie and fiue shekels, after the shekel of
the Sanctuarie.
26 A "portion for a man, *that is*, halfe a shekel after the shekel of the Sanctuarie, for
all them that were nombred from twentie yere olde and aboue, among six hundreth thousand, and thre thousand, & fiue
hundreth and fiftie men.
27 Moreouer there were an hundreth talents of siluer, to cast the sockets of the
Sanctuarie, and the sockets of the vaile: an
hundreth sockets of an hundreth talents, a
talent for a socket.
28 But he made the hokes for the pillers of
a thousand seuen hundreth and seuētie &
fiue *shekels*, and ouerlaied their chapiters,

Chap.27,14.

"Ebr. ouer against.

Chap.27,19.

c That the Leuites might haue the charge therof, and minister in the same, as did Eleazér and Ithamár, Nōb. 3,4.

d As a grauer or carpenter, chap.31,4.

"Or, halfe a shekel.

and made filets about them.
29 Also the brasse of the offring *was* seuentie [e] talents, and two thousand, and foure
hundreth shekels.

e Read the weight of a talent, Chap. 25,39.

30 Whereof he made ỹ sockets to the dore
of the Tabernacle of the Congregacion
and the brasen Altar, & the brasen grate
which was for it, with all the instruments
of the Altar,
31 And the sockets of the courte roũd about,
and the sockets for the courte gate, & all
the * pins of the Tabernacle, and all the
pins of the courte round about.

Chap. 27,19.

CHAP. XXXIX.

1 The apparel of Aarón and his sonnes. 32 All that the Lord commanded, was made, and finished. 43 Mosés blesseth the people.

a As couerings for the Arke, ỹ Cãdelsticke, the Altars & suche like.
Chap. 31,10. & 35,19.

1 MOreouer they made [a] garments of
ministration to ministre in the San
ctuarie of blewe silke, and purple, & skarlet: thei * made also the holy garments for
Aarón, as the Lord had commanded Mosés.
2 So he made the Ephód of golde, blewe
silke, and purple, and skarlet, and fine twined linen.
3 And they did beate the golde into thin
plates, and cut it into wiers, to worke it in
the blewe silke & in the purple, and in the
skarlet, & in the fine linen, with broydred
worke.
4 For the which thei made shulders to cou
ple together: *for* it was closed by the two
edges thereof.
5 And the broydred garde of his Ephód
that was vpon him, was of the same stuffe,
and of like worke: *euen* of golde, of blewe
silke, and purple, and skarlet, and fine twined linen, as the Lord had commanded
Mosés.

Chap. 28,9.
b That is, of very fine and curious workmanship.

6 ¶ And they wroght * *two* onix stones closed
in ouches of golde, and graued, as [b] signets are grauen, with the names of the
children of Israél,
7 And put thẽ on the shulders of ỹ Ephód,
as stones for a * remembrance of the children of Israél, as the Lord had commanded Mosés.

Chap. 28,12.

8 ¶ Also he made the brest plate of broydred worke like the worke of the Ephód:
to wit, of golde, blewe silke, and purple, &
skarlet, and fine twined linen.
9 They made the brest plate double, and it
was square, an hand breadth long, and
an hand breadth broad: *it was also* double.
10 And they filled it with foure rowes of
stones. The ordre *was thus*, a ruby, a topaze, and a carbuncle in the first rowe.

c Or a ligure, which stone autors write that it commeth of the vrine of the beast called Lynx.

11 And in the seconde rowe, an emeraude,
a saphir, and a diamond:
12 Also in the third rowe, [c] a turkeis, an a-
chate, and an hematite:
13 Likewise in the fourte rowe, a chrysolite,
an onix, and a iasper: closed and set in ouches of golde.
14 So the stones *were* according to the names of the children of Israél, *euen* twelue
[d] after their names, grauen like signets e-
uerie one after his name according to the
twelue tribes.

d That is, euerie tribe had his name writ ten in a stone.

15 After, they made vpon the brest plate
cheines at the endes, of wrethen worke
& pure golde.
16 They made also two bosses of golde, &
two golde rings, and put the two rings in
the two corners of the brest plate.
17 And they put the two wrethen cheines
of golde in the two rings, in the corners
of the brest plate.
18 Also the two *other* endes of the two wrethen cheines they fastened in the two bosses, and put them on the shulders of the
Ephód vpon the fore fronte of it.
19 Likewise they made two rings of golde,
and put them in the two *other* corners of
the brest plate vpon the edge of it, which
was on the inside of the Ephód.
20 They made also two *other* golden rings,
and put them on the two sides of the E-
phód, beneth on the foreside of it and o-
uer against his coupling aboue the broydred garde of the Ephód.
21 Then they fastened the brest plate by his
rings vnto the rings of the Ephód, with
a lace of blewe silke, that it might be *fast*
vpon the broydred garde of the Ephód,
and that the brest plate shulde not be losed from the Ephód, as the Lord had cõmanded Mosés.
22 ¶ Moreouer he made the robe of the
[e] Ephód of wouen worke, altogether of
blewe silke.

e Which was next vnder the Ephód.

23 And [f] the hole of the robe *was* in the
middes of it, as ỹ coller of an habergeon,
with an edge about the coller, that it shulde not rent.

f Where he shulde put through his head.

24 And they made vpon the skirtes of the
robe pomegranates, of blewe silke, & purple, and skarlet, and *fine linen* twined.
25 They made also * belles of pure golde,
& put the belles betwene the pomegranates vpon the skirtes of the robe rounde a-
bout betwene the pomegranates.

Chap. 28,33.

26 A bel & a pomegranate, a bel & a pomegranate round about the skirtes of the robe to minister in, as the Lord had cõmanded Mosés.
27 ¶ After, they made coates of fine linẽ, of
wouẽ worke for Aarón & for his sonnes.
28 And the mitre of fine linen, and goodlie
bonnets of fine linen, and linen * breches
of fine twined linen,

Chap. 28,42.

29 ¶ And the girdel of fine twined linen,
& of blewe silke, & purple, & skarlet, *euen*
of nedle worke, as the Lord had commanded Mosés.

30 Final-

30 ¶ Finally thei made the plate for the
holy crowne of fine golde, and wrote vpon it a superscription *like* to the grauing
of a signet,* HOLINES TO THE
LORD.

Chap.28,36.

31 And thei tied vnto it a lace of blewe silke to fasten it on hye vpon the mitre, as
the Lord had commanded Mosés.
32 ¶ Thus was all the worke of the Tabernacle, *euen* of the* Tabernacle of the Cōgregacion finished: & the children of Israél did according to all that the Lord
had commanded Mosés: so did thei.

Chap 27,21.

33 ¶ Afterwarde thei broght the Tabernacle vnto Mosés, the Tabernacle & all his
instruments, his taches, his boardes, his
barres, and his pillers, and his sockets,
34 And the couering of rāmes skins died
red, & the couerings of badgers skinnes,
and the [g] couering vaile.
35 The Arke of the Testimonie, and the
barres thereof, and the Merciseat,
36 The Table, with all the instruments
thereof, and the shewe bread,
37 The pure Candelsticke, the lampes thereof, *euen* the lampes [h] set in ordre, and all
the instruments thereof, and the oyle for
light:
38 Also the golden Altar & the anointing
oyle, and the swete incens, and the hāging
of the Tabernacle dore,
39 The brasen Altar with his grate of brasse, his barres and all his instruments, the
Lauer and his fote.
40 The curtaines of the court with his pillers, and his sockets, & the hanging to the
courte gate, & his cordes, and his pinnes,
and all the instruments of the seruice of
the Tabernacle, *called* the Tabernacle
of the Congregacion.
41 *Finally*, the ministring garments to serue in the Sanctuarie, & the holy garmēts
for Aarón the Priest, and his sonnes garments to minister in the Priests office.
42 According to euerie point that the Lord
had [i] commanded Mosés, so the children
of Israél made all the worke.
43 And Mosés beholde all the worke, and
beholde, thei had done it as the Lord had
commanded: so had thei done: and Mosés
[k] blessed them.

g So called, because it hāged before ẏ merciseat & couered it frō sight chap.35,12.

h Or, which Aarón dressed and refreshed with oyle euerie mornīg, chap.30,7.

i Signifiyng ẏ in Gods matters man may nether adde nor diminish.

k Praised God for ẏ peoples diligence and praied for thē.

CHAP. XL.

1 *The Tabernacle with the appertinances is reared vp.*
34 The glorie of the Lord appeareth in the cloude couering the Tabernacle.

1 THen the Lord spake vnto Mosés, saying,
2 In the [a] *first* day of the first moneth in the
very first *of the same* moneth shalt thou set
vp the Tabernacle, *called* the Tabernacle
of the Congregacion:
3 And thou shalt put therein the Arke of
the Testimonie, and couer the Arke with
the vaile.

a After ẏ Mosés had bene 40. daies and 40 nights in ẏ mount, that is, frō the beginning of August to the 10. of Sept. he came downe, & caused this worke to be done: which being finished, was set vp in Abíb, which moneth cōteineth halfe Marche and halfe April.

4 Also thou shalt bring in the* Table, and
set it in ordre as it doeth require: thou
shalt also bring in the Candelsticke, and
light his lampes,

Read chap. 26,35.

5 And thou shalt set the incense Altar [b] of
golde before the Arke of the Testimonie,
and put the [c] hanging at the dore of the
Tabernacle.

b That is, the altar of perfume, or to burne incense on.

c This hāging or vaile was betwene the Sanctuarie and the courte.

6 Moreouer thou shalt set the burnt offrīg
Altar before the dore of the Tabernacle,
called the Tabernacle of the Congregacion.
7 And thou shalt set the Lauer betwene
the Tabernacle of the Congregacion &
the Altar, and put water therein.
8 Then thou shalt appoint the courte roūd
about, and hang vp the hanging at the
courte gate.
9 After, thou shalt take the anointing oyle,
and anoint the Tabernacle, and all that
is therein, and halowe it with all the instruments thereof, that it may be holye.
10 And thou shalt anoint the Altar of the
burnt offring, and all his instruments, and
shalt sanctifie the Altar, that it may be an
altar moste holy.
11 Also thou shalt anoint the Lauer and
his fote, and shalt sanctifie it.
12 Then thou shalt bring Aarón and his
sonnes vnto the dore of the Tabernacle
of the Congregacion, & wash them with
water.
13 And thou shalt put vpon Aarón the holy garments, and shalt anoint him, & sanctifie him that he may minister vnto me
in the Priests office.
14 Thou shalt also bring his sonnes, and
clothe them with garments,
15 And shalt anoint them as thou diddest
anoint their father, that thei may minister vnto me in the Priests office: for their
anointing shal be *a signe*, that ẏ priesthode
[d] shalbe euerlasting vnto thē throughout
their generacions.
16 So Mosés did according to all that the
Lord had commanded him: so did he.

d Til bothe ẏ priesthode and ẏ ceremonies shulde ende, wc was at Christs comming.

17 ¶* Thus was the Tabernacle reared vp
the first day of the first moneth in [e] the seconde yere.

Nomb.7,1.

e After thei came out of Egypt, Nomb. 7,1.

18 Then Mosés reared vp the Tabernacle,
and fastened his sockets, and set vp the boardes thereof, and put in the barres of it,
and reared vp his pillers.
19 And he spred the couering ouer the
Tabernacle, and put the couering of that
couering on hie aboue it, as the Lord had
commanded Mosés.
20 ¶ And he toke and put the [f] Testimonie
in the Arke, and put the barres in *the rings*
of the Arke, and set the Merciseat on hie
vpon the Arke.

f That is, the tables of the Lawe, chap. 31,18.& 34,29.

21 He broght also the Arke into the Tabernacle, and hanged vp the* couering vaile,

Chap.35,12.

and couered the Arke of the Testimonie,
as the Lord had commanded Mosés,
22 ¶ Furthermore he put the Table in the
Tabernacle of the Congregacion in the
Northside of the Tabernacle, without
the vaile,
23 And set the bread in ordre before the
Lord, as the Lord had commanded Mosés.
24 ¶ Also he put the Candelsticke in the
Tabernacle of the Congregacion ouer a-
gainst the Table towarde the Southside
of the Tabernacle.
25 And he f lighted the lampes before the
Lord, as the Lord had commanded Mosés.
26 ¶ Moreouer he set the golden Altar in
the Tabernacle of the Congregacion before the vaile,
27 And burnt swete incése thereon, as the
Lord had commanded Mosés.
28 ¶ Also he häged vp the vaile at the g dore of the Tabernacle.
29 After, he set the burnt offring Altar *without* the dore of the Tabernacle, *called* the
Tabernacle of the Congregacion, & offred the burnt offring and the sacrifice
thereon, as the Lord had cōmäded Mosés.
30 ¶ Likewise he set the Lauer betwene
the Tabernacle of the Congregacion &
the Altar, and powred water therein to
wash with.
31 So Mosés, and Aarón, and his sonnes,
washed their hands & their fete thereat.
32 When thei went into the Tabernacle
of the Congregacion, and when thei approched to the Altar, thei washed, as the
Lord had commanded Mosés.
33 Finally he reared vp the courte round
about the Tabernacle and the Altar, and
hanged vp the vaile at the courte gate: so
Mosés finished the worke.
34 ¶ *Then the cloude couered the Tabernacle of the Congregacion, and the glorie of the Lord filled the Tabernacle.
35 So Mosés colde not entre into the Tabernacle of the Congregacion, because
the cloude abode thereon, and the glorie
of the Lord filled the Tabernacle.
36 Now when the cloude ascéded vp from
the Tabernacle, the children of Israél
went forwarde in all their iourneis.
37 But if the cloude ascended not, then thei
iourneied not til the day that it ascended.
38 For h the cloude of the Lord *was* vpon
the Tabernacle by day, and fire was in it
by night, in the sight of all the house of
Israél, throughout all their iorneies.

f Or, set vp.

g Betwene the Sanctuarie and the courte.

Nomb. 9, 15. 1. king. 8, 10.

h Thus the presence of God preserued & guided the night and day til thei came to the land promised.

THE THIRD BOKE OF
Mosés, called * Leuiticus.

* Because in this boke is chiefly intreated of ÿ Leuites, and of things perteining to their office.

THE ARGUMENT.

As God daily by moste singular benefites declared him selfe to be mindeful of his Church: so he wolde not that thei shulde haue anie occasion to trust ether in them selues, or to depend vpon others for lacke of temporal things, or oght that belonged to his diuine seruice and religion. Therefore he ordeined diuers kindes of oblations and sacrifices, to assure them of forgiuenes of their offenses. (if thei offred them in true faith and obedience) Also he appointed their Priests and Leuites, their apparel, offices, conuersation and portion: he shewed what feastes thei shulde obserue, and in what times. Moreouer he declared by these sacrifices & ceremonies that the reward of sinne is death, and that without the blood of Christ the innocent Lambe there can be no forgiuenes of sinnes. And because thei shulde giue no place to their owne inuentions (which thing God moste detesteth as appeareth by the terrible example of Nadáb and Abihú) he prescribed euen to the least things, what thei shulde do, as what beastes thei shulde offre and eat: what diseases were contagious and to be auoyded: what ordre thei shulde take for all maner of filthines and pollution: whose companie thei shulde flee: what mariages were lawful: and what politike lawes were profitable. Which things declared, he promised fauour and blessing to them that kept his Lawes, and threatened his curse to them that transgressed them.

CHAP. I.

2 Of burnt offrings for particular persons. 3. 10. & 14 The maner to offre burnt offrings aswel of bulloks, as of shepe and birdes.

1 Now the a Lord called
Mosés, and spake vnto
him out of the Taber-
nacle of the Cōgrega-
cion, saying,
2 Speake vnto the chil-
dré of Israél, & thou shalt say vnto thē, If
anie of you offer a sacrifice vnto the Lord,
ye shal offer your sacrifice of b cattel, *as* of
beues and of the shepe.
3 *If his sacrifice *be* a burnt offring of the
herde, he shal offer a male without blemish, presenting him of his owne volun-
tary wil at the dore of the c Tabernacle
of the Congregacion before the Lord.

a Hereby Mosés declareth that he taught nothing to the people but ÿ, which he receiued of God

b So thei colde offre of none other sort, but of those which were commanded.

Exod. 29, 10.

c Meaning within ÿ court of the Tabernacle.

4 And he shal put his hand vpon the head
of the burnt offring and it shalbe accepted
"to *the Lord*, to be his atonement.
5 And [d] he shal kil the bullocke before the
Lord, and the Priestes Aarons sonnes shal
offer the blood, and shal sprinkle it round
about vpon the [e] altar, that is by the dore
of the Tabernacle of the Congregacion.
6 Then shal he fley the burnt offring and
cut it in pieces.
7 So the sonnes of Aarón the Priest shal
put fire vpon the altar, and lay the wood
in ordre vpon the fire.
8 Then the Priestes Aarons sonnes shal lay
the partes in ordre, the head and the "kall
vpon the wood that is in the fire which is
vpon the altar.
9 But the inwardes thereof and the legs
thereof he shal wash in water, and the
Priest shal burne all on the altar: *for* it is a
burnt offring, an oblatiõ made by fire, for
a swete sauour [f] vnto the Lord.
10 ¶ And if his sacrifice for ỹ burnt offrĩg *be*
of the flockes (*as* of the shepe, or of ỹ goates) he shal offer a male without blemish,
11 [g] And he shal kil it on the Northside of
the altar [h] before the Lord, & the Priestes
Aarons sonnes shal sprinkle the blood thereof round about vpon the Altar.
12 And he shal cut it in "pieces, *separating*
his head and his "kall, and the Priest shal
lay them inordre vpõ the wood that *lieth*
in the fire which is on the altar:
13 But he shal wash the inwardes, and the
legs with water, and the Priest shal offer
the whole & burne it vpon the altar: *for* it
is a burnt offring, an oblatiõ made by fire
for a swete sauoure vnto the Lord.
14 ¶ And if his sacrifice *be* a burnt offring
to the Lord of the foules, thẽ he shal offer
his sacrifice of the turtle doues, or of the
yong pigeons.
15 And the Priest shal bring it vnto the altar, and [i] wring the necke of it a sunder,
and burne it on the altar: and the blood
thereof shal be "shed vpon the side of the
altar.
16 And he shal plucke out his mawe ẘ his
fethers, and cast them beside the altar on
the [k] Eastparte in the place of the ashes.
17 And he shal cleaue it with his wings,
but not deuide it a sundre: and the Priest
shal burne it vpon the altar vpon the wood that is in ỹ fire: *for* it is a burnt offring,
an oblatiõ made by fire for a swete sauour
vnto the Lord.

"Ebr. to him.
d The Priest or Leuite.
e Of the burnt offring, Exod. 27,1
"Or, the body of the beast or the fat.
f Or a sauour of rest, which pacifieth the angre of the Lord.
g Read vers.5.
h Before the altar of the Lord.
"Ebr. into his pieces.
"Or, fat.
i The Ebrewe worde signifieth to pinch of with the nayle.
"Or, strained, or pressed.
k On the side of the courte gate in ỹ pãnes, which stode with ashes, Exod.27,3.

CHAP. II.

1 The meat offring is after thre sortes: of fine floure vnbaken, 4 Of bread baken, 14 And of corne in the eare.

1 And whẽ anie wil offer a [a] meat offrĩg
vnto the Lord, his offring shalbe of
fine floure, and he shal poure oyle vpõ it,
and put incense thereon,

a Because the burnt offring colde not be without the meat offring.

2 And shal bring it vnto Aarons sonnes the
Priests, and [b] he shal take thence his handful of the floure, and of the oyle with all
the incense, and the Priest shal burne it
for a [c] memorial vpon the altar: *for* it is an
offring made by fire for a swete sauour
vnto the Lord.
3 *But the remnant of the meat offring *shal
be* Aarõs and his sonnes: *for* it is [d] moste ho
ly of the Lords offrings made by fire.
4 ¶ If thou bring also a meat offring baken in the ouẽ, *it shalbe* an vnleauened cake of fine floure mingled with oyle, or an
vnleauened wafer anointed with oyle.
5 ¶ But if thy [e] meat offring *be* an oblatiõ
of the friyng pan, it shalbe of fine floure
vnleauened, mingled with oyle.
6 And thou shalt parte it in pieces, and powre oyle thereon: *for* it is a meat offring.
7 ¶ And if thy meat offring *be* an oblation
made in the caudron, it shalbe made of fine floure with oyle.
8 After, thou shalt bring the meat offring
(ỹ is made of these things) vnto ỹ Lord,
& shalt present it vnto the Priest, and he
shal bring it to the altar,
9 And the Priest shal take from the meat
offring a * memorial of it, and shal burne
it vpon the altar: *for* it is an oblation * made by fire for a swete sauour vnto the
Lord.
10 But ỹ which is left of the meat offring,
shalbe Aarons and his sonnes: *for it is* moste
holy of the offrings of the Lord made by
fire.
11 All the meat offrings which ye shal offer
vnto ỹ Lord, shalbe made without leauẽ:
for ye shal nether burne leauen nor hony
in any offring of the Lord made by fire.
12 ¶ *In* the oblation of the first frutes ye
shal offer [f] them vnto the Lord, but they
shal not be burnt [g] vpõ the altar for a swete sauour.
13 (All the meat offrings also shalt thou
season with * salt, nether shalt thou suffre
the salt of the [h] couenant of thy God to
be lacking from thy meat offring, *but* vpon all thine oblations thou shalt offer
salt)
14 If then thou offer a meat offring of thy
first frutes vnto the Lord, thou shalt offer
for thy meat offring of thy first frutes * eares of corne dried by the fire, and wheat
beaten out of "the grene eares.
15 After, thou shalt put oyle vpon it, and
laie incense thereon: *for* it is a meat offring.
16 And the Priest shal burne the memorial
of it, *euen* of that that is beaten and of the
oyle of it with all the incense thereof: *for*
it is an offring vnto the Lord made by
fire.

b The Priest.
c To signifie that God remẽbreth him that offreth.
Eccle.7,34.
d Therefore none colde eat of it but the Priests.
e Which is a gift offred to God to pacifie him.
Vers.2.
Exod.29,18.
f That is, frutes, which are swete as hony, ye may offer.
g But reserued for ỹ Priests.
Mar.9,49.
h Which thei werebound (as by a couenãt) to vse in all sacrifices, Nõb. 18, 19. ezek. 43, 24: or it meaneth a sure and pure couenant.
Chap.23,14.
"*Or, ful eares: for the worde signifieth a fruteful field.*

CHAP. III.

1 The maner of peace offrings, and beasts for the same. 17 The Israelites may nether eat fat, nor blood.

1 ALso if his oblation *be* a [a] peace offring, if he wil offer of ye droue (whether it be male or female) he shal offer suche as is without blemish, before ye Lord,
2 And shal put his hand vpon the head of
his offring, and kil it at the dore of the
Tabernacle of the Congregacion: & Aarons sonnes the Priests shal sprinckle the
blood vpon the altar round about.
3 So he shal offer [b] *parte* of the peace offrĩgs
as a sacrifice made by fire vnto the Lord,
euen the * fat that couereth the inwardes,
and all the fat that is vpon the inwardes.
4 He shal also take away the two kidneis,
and the fat that is on them, and vpon ″ the
flanks, and the kall on the liuer with the
kidneis.
5 And Aarons sonnes shal burne it on the
altar with the burnt offring, which is vpõ
the wood, that is on the fire: *this is* a sacrifice made by fire for a swete sauour vnto
the Lord.
6 ¶ Also if his oblation *be* a peace offring
vnto the Lord out of the flocke, whether
it be [c] male or female, he shal offer it without blemish.
7 If he offer a lambe for his oblation, then
he shal bring it before the Lord,
8 And lay his hand vpon the head of his
offring, and shal kil it before the Tabernacle of the Congregacion, and Aarons
sonnes shal sprinkle ye blood thereof roũd
about vpon the altar.
9 After, of the peace offrings he shal offer
[d] an offring made by fire vnto ye Lord: he
shal take away the fat thereof, & the rumpe altogether, hard by the backe bone, &
the fat that couereth the inwardes, and
all the fat that is vpon the inwardes.
10 Also he shal take away the two kidneis,
with the fat that is vpon them, and vpon
the * flanks, & the kall vpon the liuer with
the kidneis.
11 Thẽ the Priest shal burne it vpon the altar, *as* the meat of an offring made by fire
vnto the Lord.
12 ¶ Also if his offring *be* a goat, then shal
he offer it before the Lord,
13 And shal put his hand vpon the head of
it, and kil it before [e] the Tabernacle of
the Cõgregacion, & the sonnes of Aarõ
shal sprinkle the blood thereof vpõ the altar round about.
14 Thẽ he shal offer thereof his offring, *euẽ*
an offring made by fire vnto the Lord, the
fat that couereth the inwardes, and all the
fat that is vpon the inwardes.
15 Also he shal take away the two kidneis,
& the fat that is vpon them, and vpon the
flanks & the kall vpon the liuer with the
kidneis.
16 So the Priest shal burne them vpon the
altar, *as* ye meat of an offring made by fire
for a swete sauour: * all ye fat *is* the Lords.
17 *This shalbe* a perpetual ordinãce for your
generacions, through out all your dwellings, *so that* ye shal eat nether [f] fat nor
* blood.

a A sacrifice of thankesgiuing offred for peace & prosperitie, ether generally or particularly.

b One parte was burnt, an other was to the Priests, & the third to hĩ that offred.

Exod.29,29.

″ *Or, the which kidneis are nere the flanks.*

c In the peace offring it was indifferent to offre ether male or female, but in ye burnt offring onely the male: so here can be offred no birdes, but in the burnt offring thei might: all there was consumed with fire, and in the peace offring but a parte.

d The burnt offring was wholy consumed, and of ye offring made by fire onely the inwardes &c, were burnt: ye shulder & breast, with the two chawes and ye mawe were ye Priests, & the rest his that offred.

Vers.4.

e Meaning at the Northside of the altar, chap.1,11.

Chap.7,25.

f By eating fat, was meant to be carnal, and by blood eating, was signified cruelte.

Gene.9,4. chap.2,23.

CHAP. IIII.

1 The offring for sinnes done of ignorãce, 3 For the Priest, 13 The Congregation, 22 The ruler, 27 And the priuate man.

1 MOreouer the Lord spake vnto Moses, saying,
2 Speake vnto the children of Israél, saying, If ″ anie shal sinne through [a] ignorãce,
in anie of the commandements of ye Lord
(which oght not to be done) but shal do
contrarie to anie of them,
3 If the [b] Priest that is anointed do sinne
(according to the sinne of the people) thẽ
shal he offer, for his sinne which he hathe
sinned, a yong bullocke without blemish
vnto the Lord for a sinne offring,
4 And he shal bring the bullocke vnto the
dore of the Tabernacle of the Cõgregacion before the Lord, & shal put his hãd
vpon the bullocks head, and [c] kil the bullocke before the Lord.
5 And the Priest that is anointed shal take
of the bullocks blood, and bring it into ye
Tabernacle of the Congregacion.
6 Then the Priest shal dip his finger in the
blood, and sprinkle of the blood seuen times before the Lord, before the vaile of
the [d] Sanctuarie.
7 The Priest also shal put *some* of the blood
before the Lord, vpõ the hornes of ye altar
of swete incẽs, which is in ye [e] Tabernacle
of the Congregacion, then shal he powre
* all *the rest* of the blood of the bullocke at
the fote of ye altar of burnt offring, which
is at the dore of the Tabernacle of the
Congregacion.
8 And he shal take away all the fat of the
bullocke for the sinne offring: *to wit*, ye fat
that couereth the inwardes, and all the fat
that is about the inwardes.
9 He shal take away also the two kidneis,
and the fat that is vpon them, and vpon
the flanks, & the kall vpon the liuer with
the kidneis,
10 As it was taken away from the bullocke
of the peace offrings, and the Priest shal
burne thẽ vpon the altar of burnt offring.
11 * But the skin of the bullocke, and all his
flesh, with his head, and his legs, & his inwardes, and his doung *shal be beare out*.
12 So he shal cary the whole bullocke out
of the * hoste vnto a cleane place, where ye
ashes are powred, & shal burne him on ye
wood in the fire: where the ashes are cast
out, shal he be burnt.
13 ¶ And if the [f] whole Congregacion of
Israél

″ *Ebr. a soule.*

a That is, of negligẽce or ignorance, specially of the ceremonial lawe: for otherwise the punishements for crimes are apointed according to the transgression. Nomb.15,22.

b Meaning the hie Priest.

c Hereby cõfessing that he deserued the same punishment which ye beast suffred.

d Which was betwene the Holiest of all & ye Sãctuarie.

e Which was in the courte meanig by the Tabernacle ye Sanctuarie: & in the end of this verse it is taken for the courte.

Chap.5,8.

Exod.29,19. nomb.19,5.

Ebr.13,11.

f The multitude excuseth not the sinne.

Chap.5,2.

Iſraél ſhal ſinne through ignorance, and
the thing be * hid from the eies of the
multitude, and haue done *againſt* anie of ẏ
cõmandements of the Lord which ſhulde
not be done, and haue offended:
14 When the ſinne which they haue cõmitted ſhalbe knowen, then the Congregaciõ
ſhal offre a yong bullocke for the ſinne,
and bring him before the Tabernacle of
the Congregacion,
15 And the g Elders of the Congregacion
ſhal put their hands vpon the head of the
bullocke before the Lord, and " he ſhal kil
the bullocke before the Lord,
16 Then the Prieſt that is anointed, ſhal
bring of the bullocks blood into the Tabernacle of the Congregacion,
17 And the Prieſt ſhall dip his finger in the
blood, and ſprinkle it ſeuen times before
the Lord, *euen* before the vaile.
18 Alſo he ſhal put *ſome* of the blood vpon
the hornes of the altar, which is before the
Lord, ẏ is in the Tabernacle of the Congregacion: then ſhal he powre all the *reſt*
of ẏ blood at ẏ fote of the altar of burnt
offring, which is at the dore of the Taber
nacle of the Congregacion,
19 And he ſhal take all his fat from him, &
" burne it vpon the altar.
20 And *the Prieſt* ſhal do with this bullocke,
as he did with the bullocke for *his* ſinne:
ſo ſhal he do ẇ this: ſo the Prieſt ſhal make an atonement for them, and it ſhalbe
forgiuen them.
21 For he ſhal carie the bullocke without ẏ
hoſte, and burne him as he burned the firſt
bullocke: *for* it is an offring for the ſinne
of the Congregacion.
22 ¶ When a ruler ſhal ſinne, & do through
ignorance *againſt* anie of the cõmãde-
ments of the Lord his God, which ſhulde
not be done and ſhal offende,
23 If one ſhewe vnto him his ſinne which
he hathe cõmitted, then ſhal he bring for
his offring an " he goat without blemiſh,
24 And ſhal lay his hand vpon the head of
the he goat, & kil it in h the place where
he ſhulde kil the burnt offring before the
Lord: *for* it is a ſinne offring,
25 Then the Prieſt ſhal take of the blood
of the ſinne offring with his finger, & put
it vpon the hornes of the burnt offring altar, and ſhal powre *the reſt* of his blood at
the fote of the burnt offring altar,
26 And ſhal burne all his fat vpõ the altar,
as the fat of the peace offring: ſo ẏ Prieſt
ſhal make an i atonement for him, concer
ning his ſinne, and it ſhal be forgiuẽ him.
27 ¶ Likewiſe if anie of the " people of the
land ſhal ſinne through ignorance in doing *againſt* anie of the commandements
of the Lord, which ſhulde not be done, &
ſhal offend,

g For all the people colde not lay on their hands: therefore it was ſufficient that the Anciens of the people did it in ẏ name of all the Cõgregacion.
" *Or, the Prieſt.*
" *Or, make a perfume with it.*
" *Or, the male goat of the folde.*
h That is, the Prieſt ſhal kil it: for it was not lawful for anie out of ẏ office to kil ẏ beaſt.
i Wherein he repreſented Ieſus Chriſt.
" *Or, priuate perſone.*

28 If one ſhewe him his ſinne which he hathe cõmitted, then he ſhal bring for his offring " a ſhe goat without blemiſh for his
ſinne which he hathe committed,
29 k And he ſhal lay his hand vpon the head
of the ſinne offring, and ſlay the ſinne offring in the place of burnt offring.
30 Then the Prieſt ſhal take of the blood
thereof with his finger, and put it vpõ the
hornes of the burnt offring altar, & powre
all *the reſt* of the blood thereof at the fote
of the altar.
31 And ſhal take away all his fat, as the fat
of the peace offrings is taken away, and
the Prieſt ſhal burne it vpõ the altar for a
* ſwete ſauour vnto the Lord, & the Prieſt
ſhal make an atonement for him, and it
ſhalbe forgiuen him.
32 And if he bring a lambe for his ſinne offrĩg, he ſhal brĩg a female without blemiſh,
33 And ſhal lay his l hand vpon the head of
the ſinne offring, and he ſhal ſlay it for a
ſinne offring in the place where he ſhulde
kil the burnt offring.
34 Then the Prieſt ſhal take of the blood
of the ſinne offring with his finger, and put
it vpon the hornes of the burnt offring altar, & ſhal powre all *the reſt* of the blood
thereof at the fote of the altar.
35 And he ſhal take away all ẏ fat thereof,
as the fat of the lambe of ẏ peace offrings
is taken away: then the Prieſt ſhal burne it
vpon the altar m with the oblatiõs of the
Lord made by fire, & the Prieſt ſhal make
an atonement for him cõcerning his ſinne that he hathe committed, and it ſhalbe
forgiuen him.

" *Or, the female of the goates.*
k Read verſ. 24
Exod. 29, 18.
l Meaning ẏ ẏ puniſhmẽt of his ſinne ſhulde be laid vpon that beaſt, or, that he had receiued all things of God, and offred this willingly.
m Or, beſides ẏ burnt offrings, which were daily offred to the Lord.

CHAP. V.

1 Of him that teſtifieth not the trueth, if he heare another ſweare falſely. 4 Of him that voweth raſhely. 15 Of him that by ignorance withdraweth anie thing dedicate to the Lord.

1 ALſo if " anie haue ſinned, *that is,* if " he
haue heard ẏ voyce of an othe, & he
can be a witnes, whether he hathe ſene or
a knowen of it, if he do not vtter it, he ſhal
beare his iniquitie:
2 Ether if one touche anie vncleane thing,
whether it be a cariõ of an vncleane beaſt,
or a carion of vncleane cattel, or a carion
of vncleane creping things, & is not ware
of it, yet he is vncleane, & hathe offended:
3 Ether if he touche anie vnclennes of mã
(what ſoeuer vnclennes it be, that he is defiled with) and is not ware of it, and after
commeth to the knowledge of it, he hathe ſinned:
4 Ether if anie b ſweare, and pronounce ẇ
his lippes to do euil, or to do good (whatſoeuer it be that a man ſhal pronoũce ẇ an
othe & it be hid frõ him, & after knoweth
ẏ he hathe offended in one of theſe *points,*
5 When he hathe ſinned in anie of theſe
c things, then he ſhal cõfeſſe that he hathe

" *Ebr. a ſoule.*
" *Or, if the iudge hathe taken an othe of anie other.*
a Whereby it is cõmãded to beare witnes to the trueth and diſcloſe ẏ iniquitie of ẏ vngodly.
b Or vowe raſhely without iuſt examinatiõ of the circũſtãces, & not knowing what ſhalbe ẏ iſſue of the ſame.
c Which haue bene mẽcioned before in this chapter.

sinned therein.
6 Therefore shal he bring his trespasse offring vnto the Lord for his sinne which
he hathe cōmitted, *euen* a female from ẏ
flocke, *be it* a lambe or a she goat for a sinne offring, and the Priest shal make an atonement for him, concerning his sinne.
7 But "if he be not able to bring a shepe,
he shal bring for his trespasse which he
hathe committed, two turtle doues, or two
yōg pigeōs vnto the Lord, one for a sinne
offring, and the other for a burnt offring.
8 So he shal bring them vnto the Priest,
who shal offer the sinne offring first, and
*wring ẏ necke of it a sundre, but not plu-
cke it cleane of.
9 After he shal sprinkle of the blood of the
sinne offring vpon the side of the altar, &
the rest of the blood shal "be shed at the
fote of the altar: *for* it is a sinne offring.
10 Also he shal offer the secōde for a burnt
offring "as the maner is: so shal the Priest
[d] make an atonement for him (for his sinne which he hathe committed) and it shalbe forgiuen him.
11 ¶ But if he * be not able to bring two
turtle doues, or two yong pigeōs, then he
ẏ hathe sinned, shal bring for his offring,
the tēth parte of an [e] Ephah of fine floure
for a sinne offring, he shal put none [f] oyle
thereto, nether put anie incēse thereon: for
it is a sinne offring.
12 Then shal he bring it to the Priest and
ẏ Priest shal take his hādeful of it for the
*remēbrance thereof, and burne it vpon
the altar * with the offrings of the Lord
made by fire: *for* it is a sinne offring.
13 So the Priest shal make an atonemēt for
him, as touching his sinne that he hathe cō
mitted in one of these *points*, and it shal be
forgiuen him: and *the remnant* shalbe the
Priests, as the meat offring.
14 ¶ And the Lord spake vnto Mosés, saying,
15 If anie persone transgresse and sinne
through ignorāce [g] *by taking awaie* things
consecrated vnto the Lord, he shal then
brīg for his trespasse offring vnto ẏ Lord
a ram without blemish out of the flocke,
worthe two shekels of siluer [h] by thy estima
tion after the shekel of the Sāctuarie, for
a trespasse offring.
16 So he shal restore ẏ wherein he hathe offended, *in taking awaie* of the holy thing,
and shal put the fift parte more thereto, &
giue it vnto the Priest: so the Priest shal
make an atonement for him with the ram
of the trespasse offring, and it shalbe forgiuen him.
17 ¶ Also if anie sinne & * do *against* anie of
the commandements of the Lord, which
oght not to be done, & knowe not & [i] sinne and beare his iniquitie,

"Ebr. if his hand can not touche, meaning for his pouertie.
Chap. 1,15.
"Or, powred.
"Or, according to the lawe.
d Or declare him to be purged of that sinne.
Vers. 7.
e Which is about a pottel.
f As in the meatoffring. Chap. 2,1.
Chap. 2,2.
Chap. 4,35.
g As touching the first frutes or tithes, due to the Priests and Leuites.
h By the estimation of the Priest, chap. 27,12.
Chap. 4,2.
i That is, afterward remembreth that he hathe sinned when his conscience doeth accuse him.

18 Then shal he bring a ram without blemish out of the flocke, in thy estimation
worth * *two shekels* for a trespasse offring vnto
ẏ Priest: and the Priest shal make an atonemēt for him concerning his [k] ignorance
wherein he erred, and was not ware: so it
shal be forgiuen him.
19 This is the trespasse offring for the trespasse committed against the Lord.

CHAP. VI.

6 The offring for sinnes which are done willingly. 9 The lawe of the burnt offrings. 13 The fire must abide euermore vpon the altar. 14 The lawe of the meat offring. 20 The offrings of Aarón, and his sonnes.

1 AND ẏ Lord spake vnto Mosés, sayīg,
2 If anie sinne and commit a trespasse
against the Lord, & denie vnto his neighbour that, which was taken him to kepe, or
ẏ which was put to him [a] of trust, or doeth
by [b] robberie, or by violence oppresse his
neighbour,
3 Or hathe found that which was lost, and
denieth it, and sweareth falsely, * for anie
of *these* things that a man doeth, [c] wherein
he sinneth:
4 Whē, I say, he thus sinneth & trespasseth,
he shal then restore the robbery that he
robbed, or the thing taken by violence ẇ
he toke by force, or the thing which was
deliuered him to kepe, or the lost thing
which he founde,
5 Or for whatsoeuer he hathe sworne falsely, he shal bothe restore it in the whole
*summe, & shal adde the fift parte more
thereto, *and* giue it vnto him to whome it
perteineth, the same day that he offreth
for his trespasse.
6 Also he shal bring for his trespasse vnto
the Lord, a ram without blemish out of
the * flocke in thy estimation *worthe two shekels* for a trespasse offring vnto the Priest.
7 And the Priest shal make an atonement
for him before the Lord, & it shal be forgiuen him, whatsoeuer thing he hathe done, and trespassed therein.
8 ¶ Then ẏ Lord spake vnto Mosés, sayīg,
9 Cōmāde Aarón and his sonnes, saying,
This is the [d] lawe of the burnt offring, (it
is the burnt offring because it burneth vpō
the altar all the night vnto the morning,
and the fire burneth on the altar)
10 And the Priest shal put on his linnē garment, and shal put on his linnen breches
vpon [e] his flesh, and take away the ashes
when the fire hathe consumed the burnt
offring vpō the altar, and he shal put them
beside the [f] altar.
11 After he shal put of his garments, & put
on other raiment, & cary the ashes forthe
without the hoste vnto a cleane place.
12 But ẏ fire vpon ẏ altar shal burne thereō
and neuer be put out: wherefore the Priest
shal burne wood on it euerie mornīg, & lay
ẏ

Exod. 30,13.
k Els if his sinne against God come of malice he must die, Nomb. 15,30.
a To bestowe & occupie for the vse of him that gaue it.
b By anie guile or vnlauful meanes.
Nomb. 5,6.
c Wherein he can not but sinne: or, wherein a mā accustometh to sinne by periurie or such like thīg.
Nomb. 5,7.
Chap. 5,15.
d That is, the ceremonies ẇ oght to be obserued therin.
e Vpon his secret partes, Exod. 28,43.
f In the ashpānes appointed for that vse.

ÿ burnt offring in ordre vpon it, & he shal
burne thereon the fat of ÿ peace offrings.
13 The fire shal euer burne vpon the altar,
and neuer go out.
14 ¶*Also this is the lawe of ÿ meat offring,
which Aarõs sonnes shal offer in the presence of the Lord, before the altar.
15 He shal euen take thence his handful of
fine floure of the meat offring and of the
oyle, and all the incens which *is* vpon the
meat offring & shal burne it vpõ the altar
for a swete sauour, *as* a * memorial therefore vnto the Lord:
16 But the rest thereof shal Aarón and his
sonnes eat: it shal be eaten without leauen
in ÿ holy place: in ÿ courte of the Tabernacle of the Congregaciõ they shal eat it.
17 It shal not be [g] bake with leauen: I haue
giuen it for their porciõ of mine offrings
made by fire: *for* it is as the sinne offring
and as the trespasse offring.
18 All the males among the children of Aa
rón shal eat of it: It *shalbe* a statute for e-
uer in your generacions concerning the
offrings of the Lord, made by fire:* whatsoeuer toucheth them shalbe holy.
19 ¶Againe the Lord spake vnto Mosés,
saying,
20 This is ÿ offring of Aarón and his sonnes, which they shal offer vnto the Lord in
the day whẽ he is anointed: the tẽth parte
of an*Ephah of fine floure, for a meat offring [h] perpetual: halfe of it in the morning, and halfe thereof at night.
21 In the friyng pan it shalbe made with oyle: thou shalt bring it fried, *and* shalt offer
the "baken pieces of the meat offring for
a swete sauour vnto the Lord.
22 And the Priest that is [i] anointed in his
stede, among his sonnes shal offer it: *it is* ÿ
Lords ordinance for euer, it shal be burnt
altogether.
23 For euerie meat offring of ÿ Priest shal
be *burnt* altogether, it shal not be eaten.
24 ¶Furthermore the Lord spake vnto Mo
ses, saying,
25 Speake vnto Aarón, and vnto his sonnes,
and say, This is the lawe of the sin offring,
In the place where the burnt offring is killed, shal the sin offring be killed before the
Lord, *for* it is moste holy.
26 The Priest that offreth this sin offring,
shal eat it: in the holy place shal it be eaten, in the courte of the Tabernacle of the
Congregacion.
27 Whatsoeuer shal touche ÿ flesh thereof
shalbe holy: & when there droppeth of ÿ
blood thereof vpõ a [k] garmẽt, ÿ shalt wash
ÿ whereon it droppeth in the holy place.
28 Also the earthẽ pot that it is sodden in,
shalbe broken, but if it be soddẽ in a brasen pot, it shal bothe be scoured & washed
with [l] water.

Chap.2,1. nomb.15,4.
Chap.2,9.
g Or kned with leauen and after baken.
Exod.29,37.
Exod.16,36.
h So oft as the hie Priest shal be elected and anointed.
"Or, fried.
i His sonne that shal succede him.
k Meaning the garment of ÿ Priest.
l Which was in the lauer, Exod.30,16.

29 All the males among the Priests shal eat
thereof, *for* it is moste holy.
30 *But no sin offrĩg, whose blood is broght
in to the Tabernacle of ÿ Cõgregacion to
make recõciliacion in the holy place, shal
be eaten, *but* shal be burnt in the [m] fire.

CHAP. VII.

1 The lawe of the trespasse offring. 11 Also of the peace offrings. 23 The fat & the blood may not be eaten.

1 Likwise this is the lawe of the [a] trespasse offring, it is moste holy.
2 In the place [b] where they kil the burnt
offring, shal they kil the trespasse offring,
& the blood thereof shal he sprinkle roũd
about vpon the altar.
3 All the fat thereof also shal [c] he offer, the
rũpe & the fat that couereth the inwards.
4 After he shal take away ÿ two kidneis,
ŵ the fat that is on thẽ & vpon the flãks,
and the kall on the liuer with the kidneis.
5 Then the Priest shal burne them vpõ the
altar, for an offring made by fire vnto the
Lord: this is a trespasse offring.
6 All the males among the Priests shal eat
thereof, it shalbe eaten in the holy place,
for it is moste holy.
7 As the sin offring *is*, so *is* ÿ trespasse offrĩg,
one [d] lawe serueth for both, [e] ÿ wherewith
the Priest shal make atonemẽt, shalbe his.
8 Also the Priest that offreth anie mans
burnt offring, shal haue the skin of the
burnt offring which he hathe offred.
9 And all the meat offring that is baken in
the ouen, and that is dressed in ÿ pan, & in
ÿ friyng pan, shalbe ÿ Priests ÿ offreth it.
10 And euerie meat offring mingled with
oyle, and that is [f] drie, shal perteine vnto
all the sonnes of Aarón, to all alike.
11 Furthermore this is ÿ lawe of the peace
offrĩgs, which he shal offer vnto the Lord.
12 If he offer it to [g] giue thãkes, thẽ he shal
offer for his thankes offring, vnleauened
cakes mingled with oyle, and vnleauened
wafers anointed with oyle, and fine floure
fried *with* the cakes mingled with oyle.
13 He shal offre *also* his offring with cakes
of leauened bread, for his peace offrings,
to giue thankes.
14 And of all the sacrifice he shal offre one
cake for an heaue offring vnto the Lord, &
it shalbe the Priests that sprinkleth ÿ blood
of the peace offrings.
15 Also the flesh of his peace offrings, for
thankes giuing, shalbe eaten the same day
that it is offred: he shal leaue nothing
thereof vntil the morning.
16 But if the sacrifice of his offring *be* a
[h] vowe, or a fre offring, it shalbe eaten ÿ
same day that he offreth his sacrifice: & so
in ÿ morning ÿ residue thereof shalbe eatẽ.
17 But asmuch of ÿ offred flesh as remaineth
vnto the third day, shalbe burnt with fire.
18 For if anie of ÿ flesh of his peace offrings

Chap.4,5. ebr.13,11.
m Out of the campe.
a Which is for the smaler sinnes, & such as are cõmitted by ignorance.
b At the courte gate.
c The Priest.
d The same ceremonies: notwithstanding that this worde trespasse signifieth lesse then sinne.
e Meaning the rest which is left and not burnt.
f Because it had no oyle nor licour.
g Peace offrĩgs conteine a cõfession and thanks giuing for a benefite receiued, and also a vowe, & fre offring to receiue a benefite.
h If he make a vowe to offre: for els the flesh of the peace offrings must be eaten the same day.

be eaten in ỷ third day;he shal not be accepted that offreth it,nether shal it be reckoned vnto him, *but* shalbe an abomina-
nacion: therefore the persone that eateth
of it shal [i] beare his iniquitie.

i The sinne, wherefore he offred shal remaine.

19 The flesh also that toucheth anie vnclea
ne [k] thing, shal not be eatẽ,*but* burnt with
fire:but [l] of this flesh all that be cleane
shal eat thereof.

k After it be sacrificed.
l Of the peace offring, that is cleane.

20 But if anie eat of the flesh of the peace
offrings that perteineth to ỷ Lord,hauing
his * vnclennes vpon him, euen the same
persone shal be cut of from his people.

Chap.15,3.

21 Moreouer when anie toucheth anie vncleane thing, as the vnclennes of man, or
of an vncleane beast,or of anie filthie abominacion, and eat of the flesh of the
peace offrings,which perteineth vnto the
Lord,euẽ that persone shal be cut of from
his people.

22 ¶ Againe the Lord spake vnto Mosés,
saying, Speake vnto the children of Israél,and say, *Ye shal eat no fat of beues,
nor of shepe,nor of goates:

Chap.3,17.

24 Yet the fat of the dead beast,and the fat
of that, which is torne *with beastes*,shalbe
occupied to anie vse, but ye shal not eat
of it.

25 For whosoeuer eateth the fat of ỷ beast,
of the which he shal offer an offring made
by fire to the Lord, euen the persone that
eateth,shal be cut of from his people.

26 Nether*shal ye eat anie blood,ether of
foule,or of beast in all your dwellings.

Gen.9,4.
chap.17,14.

27 Euerie persone that eateth anie blood,
euẽ the same persone shalbe cut of from
his people.

28 ¶ And ỷ Lord talked ẘ Mosés,saying,

29 Speake vnto the children of Israél,and
say,He that offreth his peace offrings vnto the Lord, shal bring his gift vnto the
Lord of his peace offrings:

30 His [m] hands shal bring the offrings of
the Lord made by fire: *euen* the fat with
the breast shal he bring, that the breast
may be * shaken to and fro before the
Lord.

m And shulde not send it by another.

Exod,29,24.

31 Then the Priest shal burne the fat vpon
the altar,and the breast shal be Aarons &
his sonnes.

32 And the right shulder shal ye giue vnto
the Priest for an heaue offring, of your
peace offrings.

33 The same that offreth the blood of the
peace offrings,and the fat,among the sonnes of Aarón, shal haue the right shulder for his parte.

34 For the breast shaken to and fro,and the
shulder lifted vp, haue I takẽ of the childrẽ of Israél,*euen* of their peace offrings,
and haue giuẽ them vnto Aarón ỷ Priest
and vnto his sonnes by a statute for euer
from among the children of Israél.

35 ¶ This is the [n] anointing of Aarón,and
the anointing of his sonnes, concerning
the offrings of the Lord made by fire, in
the day when he presented them to serue
in the Priests office vnto the Lord.

n That is, his priuiledge, rewarde and portion.

36 The which *portions* the Lord cõmãded
to giue them in the day that he anointed
them from among the children of Israél,
by a statute for euer in their generacions.

37 This is *also* the lawe of ỷ burnt offring,
of the meat offring,and of ỷ sinne offring,
& of the trespasse offring,and of the [o] cõ-
secrations,and of the peace offrings,

o Which sacrifice was offred whẽ ỷ Priests were consecrated, Exod. 29,22.

38 Which the Lord commanded Mosés in
the mount Sinái, when he cõmanded the
children of Israél to offer their gifts vnto
the Lord in the wildernes of Sinái.

CHAP. VIII.

*The anointing of Aarón, and his sonnes, with the sa-
crifice concerning the same.*

1 AFterwarde the Lord spake vnto Mosés,saying,

2 *Take Aarón and his sonnes with him,&
the garments and the * anointing oyle,
and a bullocke for the sin offring,and two
rams,and a basket of vnleauened bread,

Exod.28.4.
Exod.30,24.

3 And assemble all the companie at the dore of the Tabernacle of the Congregaciõ.

4 So Mosés did as the Lord had commanded him,and the companie was assembled
at the dore of the Tabernacle of the Cõgregacion.

5 Then Mosés said vnto the companie,
*This is the thing which the Lord hathe
commanded to do.

Exod.29,4.

6 And Mosés broght Aarón and his sonnes,and washed them with water,

7 And put vpõ him ỷ coat, & girded him
with a girdel, and clothed him with the
robe,and put the Ephód on him,which he
girded with the broydred garde of the
Ephód, & bonde it vnto him therewith.

8 After he put the brest plate thereon, and
put in the brest plate * the Vrím and the
Thummím.

Exod.28,30.

9 Also he put the mitre vpon his head,and
put vpon the mitre on the fore fronte the
golden plate, *and* the [a] holy crowne,as the
Lord had commanded Mosés.

a So called because this superscriptiõ, Holines to the Lord, was grauen in it.

10 (Now Mosés had taken the anointing
oyle,& anointed the [b] Tabernacle,and all
that was therein,and sanctified them,

b That is, the Holiest of all, the Sanctuarie and the court.

11 And sprinkled thereof vpon the altar
seuen times, & anointed the altar and all
his instruments, and the lauer,and his fote,to sanctifie them)

12 *And he powred of the anointing oyle
vpon Aarons head, and anointed him, to
sanctifie him.

Ecclus.45,18.
Psal.133,2.

13 After,Mosés broght Aarons sonnes,and
put coates vpon them, and girded them
with girdels, and put bonets vpon their
heades,as the Lord had cõmanded Mosés.

Exod.29,1.
14 *Then he broght the bullocke for the
sin offring, & Aarón & his sonnes put their
hands vpon the head of the bullocke for
the sinne offring.
15 And Mosés slewe him, & toke the blood,
which he put vpon the hornes of the [c] Altar round about with his finger, and purified the Altar, and powred *the rest* of the
blood at the fote of the Altar: so he sanctified [d] it, to make reconciliation vpon it.
16 Then he toke all the fat that was vpon
the inwardes, and the kall of the liuer and
the two kidneis, with their fat, which Mosés burned vpon the Altar.
17 But the bullocke and his [e] hide, and his
flesh, and his doung, he burnt with fire
without the hoste as the Lord had commanded Mosés.
18 ¶Also he broght the ram for the burnt
offring, and Aarón & his sonnes put their
hands vpon the head of the ram.
19 So Mosés killed it, and sprinkled the
blood vpon the Altar round about,
20 And Mosés cut ỹ ram in pieces, & burnt
the head with the pieces, and the fat,
21 And washed the inwardes and the legs
in water: so Mosés burnt the ram euerie
whit vpon the Altar: *for* it was a burnt offring for a swete sauour, which was made
by fire vnto the Lord, as the Lord had cõmanded Mosés.

Exod.29,31.
22 ¶*After, he broght ỹ other ram, the ram
of consecracions, and Aarón and his sonnes laied their hãds vpon the head of the
ram,
23 Which Mosés [f] slewe, and toke of the
blood of it, and put it vpon the lap of Aarons right eare, and vpon the thombe of
his right hand, and vpon the great toe of
his right fote.
24 Then Mosés broght Aarons sonnes, &
put of the blood on the lap of their right
eares, & vpon the thumbes of their right
hãds, & vpon the great toes of their right
fete, and Mosés sprinkled *the rest* of the
blood vpon the Altar round about.
25 And he toke the fat and the rumpe, and
all the fat that was vpon the inwardes, &
the kall of the liuer, and the two kidneis
with their fat, and the right shulder.
26 Also he toke of the basket of the vnleauened bread that was before the Lord,
one vnleauened cake and a cake of oyled
bread, and one wafer, and put them on the
fat, and vpon the right shulder.

Exod.29,24.
27 So he put * all in Aarons hands, and in
his sonnes hands, and shoke it to and fro
before the Lord.
28 After, Mosés toke thẽ out of their hãds,
and burnt thẽ vpon the Altar for a burnt
offring: *for* these were consecracions for a
swete sauour which were made by fire vnto the Lord.

c Of the burnt offring.

d To offre for the sinnes of the people.

e In other burnt offrings, which are not of consecracion, or offring for him selfe, ỹ Priest hathe the skinne, Chap.7,8.

f Mosés did this because ỹ ỹ Priests were not yet established i their office.

29 Likewise Mosés toke the breast of the
ram of consecracions and shoke it to and
fro before the Lord: *for* it was Mosés *portion, as the Lord had commanded Mosés.
30 Also Mosés toke of the anointing oyle,
and of the blood which was vpon the Altar, and sprinkled it vpon Aarón, vpon his
garments, and vpon his sonnes, and on his
sonnes garmẽts with him: so he sanctified
Aarón, his garments, and his sonnes, and
his sonnes garments with him.
31 ¶Afterward Mosés said vnto Aarón &
his sonnes, Sethe the flesh at the dore of
the [g] Tabernacle of the Congregacion,
and there * eat it with the bread that is in
the basket of cõsecracions, as I commanded, saying, Aarón and his sonnes shal
eat it,
32 But that which remaineth of the flesh &
of the bread, shal ye burne with fire.
33 And ye shal not departe from the dore
of the Tabernacle of the Congregacion
seuen daies, vntil the daies of your consecracions be at an end: * for seuen daies,
said the Lord, shal he "consecrate you,
34 As "he hathe done this day: *so* the Lord
hathe commanded to do, to make an atonement for you.
35 Therefore shal ye abide at the dore of
the Tabernacle of the Cõgregacion day
and night, seuen daies, and shal kepe the
watch of the Lord, that ye dye not: for so
I am commanded.
36 So Aarón and his sonnes did all things
which the Lord had commanded by the
[h] hand of Mosés.

Exod.29,26.

g At the dore of the courte.
Exod.29,32.
chap.28,9.

Exod.29,35.
"Ebr. fil your hands
"Or, as I haue done.

h By cõmissiõ giuẽ to Mosés.

CHAP. IX.

8 *The first offrings of Aarón. 22 Aarón blesseth the people. 23 The glorie of the Lord is shewed. 24 The fire commeth from the Lord.*

1 AND in the [a] eight day Mosés called
Aarón and his sonnes, and the Elders of Israél:
2 *Then he said vnto Aarón, Take thee a
yong calf for a [b] sinne offring, & a ram
for a burnt offring, *bothe* without blemish,
and bring *them* before the Lord.
3 And vnto the childrẽ of Israél thou shalt
speake, saying, Take ye an he goate for a
sinne offring, and a calf, & a lambe bothe
of a yere olde, without blemish for a burnt
offring:
4 Also a bullocke, and a ram for peace offrings, to offer before the Lord, & a meat
offring mingled with oyle: for to day the
Lord wil appeare vnto you.
5 ¶Then thei broght that which Mosés
cõmãded, before the Tabernacle of the
Congregacion, & all the assemblie drewe
nere and stode before the [c] Lord.
6 (For Mosés had said, This is the thing,
which the Lord commanded that ye shulde do, and the glorie of the Lord shal ap-

a After their cõsecraciõ: for the seuen daies before, the Priests were consecrate.
Exod.29,1.
b Aarón entreth into the possessiõ of ỹ priesthode & offreth the foure principal sacrifices: the burnt offring, the sin offring, ỹ peace offrings, & ỹ meat offrig.

c Before the altar, where his glorie appeared.

peare vnto you)
7 Then Mosés said vnto Aarón, Drawe
nere to the Altar, & offer thy sin offring,
and thy burnt offring, and make an atonement for [d] thee and for the people: offer
also the offring of the people, and make
an atonemēt for them, as the Lord hathe
commanded.
8 ¶ Aarón therefore went vnto the Altar,
& killed the calf of the sin offring, which
was for him self.
9 And the sonnes of Aarón broght the
blood vnto him, and he dipt his finger in
the blood, and put it vpon the hornes of
the Altar, & powred *the rest* of the blood
at the fote of the Altar.
10 But the fat and the kidneis and the kall
of the liuer of the sin offring, he [e] burnt
vpon the Altar, as the Lord had commanded Mosés.
11 The flesh also and the hyde he burnt
with fire without the hoste.
12 After, he slewe the burnt offring, & Aarons sonnes broght vnto him the blood,
which he sprinkled round about vpon the
Altar.
13 Also thei broght the burnt offring vnto
him with the pieces thereof, and the head,
and he burnt *them* vpon the Altar.
14 Likewise he did wash the inwardes and
the legs, and [f] burnt *them* vpon the burnt
offring on the Altar.
15 ¶ Then he offred the peoples offring,
& toke a goat, which was the sin offring
for the people, and slewe it, and offred it
for sinne, as the first:
16 So he offred the burnt offring, & prepared it, according to the maner.
17 He presented also the meat offring, and
filled his hand thereof, and * beside the
burnt sacrifice of the morning he burnt
this vpon the Altar.
18 He slewe also the bullocke, and the ram
for the peace offrīgs, that was for the people, and Aarons sonnes broght vnto him
the blood, which he sprinkled vpō the Altar round about,
19 With the fat of the bullocke, and of the
ram, the rumpe, and that which coureth
the inwardes and the kidneis, and the kall
of the liuer.
20 So thei laied the fat vpon the breasts,
and he burnt the fat vpon the Altar.
21 But the [g] breasts and the right shulder
Aarón shoke to and fro before the Lord,
as the Lord had commanded Mosés.
22 So Aarón lift vp his hand towarde the
people, and blessed them, & [h] came downe
from offring of the sinne offring, and the
burnt offring, and the peace offrings.
23 After, Mosés and Aarón went into the
Tabernacle of the Congregacion and
came out, and [i] blessed the people, * & the

d Read for the vnderstanding of this place, Ebr 5,3. & 7, 27.

e That is, he laied them in ordre, and so thei were burnt whē the Lord sēt downe fire.

f All this must be vnderstand of the preparacion of the sacrifices which were burnt after, vers. 24.

Exod. 29, 38.

g Of the bullocke and the ram.

h Because the altar was nere the Sanctuarie which was ȳ vpper end, therefore he is said to come downe.

i Or praied for ȳ people.

2. Mac. 2, 11.

glorie of the Lord appeared to all the
people.
24 *And there came a fire out frō the Lord
and consumed vpon the Altar the burnt
offring and the fat: ȳ when all the people
sawe, thei "gaue thākes, & fel on their faces.

CHAP. X.

2 Nadáb & Abihu are burnt. 6 Israél murneth for thē, but the Priests might not. 9 The Priests are forbidden wine.

1 BVt *Nadáb and Abihú, the sonnes of
Aarón, toke ether of them his cēsor,
and put fire therein, and put incens thereupon, and offred [a] strange fire before the
Lord, which he had not commādded them.
2 Therefore a fire wēt out from the Lord,
& deuoured them: so thei dyed before the
Lord.
3 Then Mosés said vnto Aarón, This is it
that the Lord spake, saying, I wil be [b] sanctified in them that come nere me, & before all the people I wil be glorified: but
Aarón helde his peace.
4 And Mosés called Mishaél and Elzaphán
the sonnes of Vzziél, the vncle of Aarón,
and said vnto them, Come nere, cary your
"brethren from before the Sanctuarie out
of the hoste.
5 Then thei went, & caryed them in their
coates out of the hoste, as Mosés had cōmanded.
6 After, Mosés said vnto Aarón and vnto
Eleazár and Ithamár his sonnes, [c] Vncouer not your heades, nether rent your
clothes, lest ye dye, and lest wrath come vpon all the people: but let your brethren, all the house of Israél bewaile the
burning which the Lord hathe [d] kindled.
7 And go not ye out from the dore of the
Tabernacle of the Congregacion, lest ye
dye: for the anointing oyle of the Lord *is*
vpon you: and thei did according to Mosés commandement.
8 ¶ And ȳ Lord spake vnto Aarón, saying,
9 Thou shalt not drinke wine nor " strong
drinke, thou, nor thy sonnes with thee, whē
ye come into the Tabernacle of the Cōgregacion, lest ye dye: *this is* an ordinance
for euer throughout your generacions,
10 That ye may put difference betwene
the holy and the vnholy, and betwene the
cleane and the vncleane,
11 And that ye may teache the children of
Israél all the statutes which the Lord hathe cōmanded thē by the "hand of Mosés.
12 ¶ Then Mosés said vnto Aarón & vnto
Eleazár and to Ithamár his sonnes that
were left, Take the meat offring that remaineth of the offrings of the Lord, made
by fire, & eat it without leauen beside the
altar: for it is moste holy:
13 And ye shal eat it in the holy place, because it is thy duetie & thy sonnes duetie
of

Gen. 4, 4. 1. king. 18, 38. 2 chro. 7, 1. 2. mac. 2, 11.

"Or, gaue a shoute for ioye.

Nomb. 3, 4. & 26. 62. 1. chro. 24, 2.

a Not taken of the altar ȳ was sent from heauen, & endured til the captiuitie of Babylon.

b I wil punish thē that serue me otherwise thē I haue cōmāded not sparing the chief, that ȳ people may feare and praise my iudgements.

"Or, cosins.

c As thogh ye lamented for them, preferring your carnal affection to Gods iust iudgement, Deut. 14, 1, & 33, 9.

d In destroyīg Nadáb and Abihú ȳ chief, and menacing the rest except thei repent.

"Or, drinke that maketh dronke.

"Or, commission.

Exod.29,24.
"Or, where is no vnclenes.
e For ẏ breast and shulders of the peace offrings might be broght to their families so ẏ their daughters might eat of them, as also of the offrings of first frutes, the first borne, and the Easter lambe, read chap.22, 12.
"Or, right, or portion.

of the offrings of the Lord made by fire:
for so I am commanded.
14 Also * the shaken breast and the heaue
shulder shal ye eat in" a cleane place: thou,
and thy sonnes, and thy [e] daughters with
thee: for thei are giuen as thy" duetie and
thy sonnes duetie, of the peace offrings of
the children of Israél.
15 The heaue shulder, and the shakē breast
shal they bring with the offrings made
by fire of the fat, to shake *it* to and fro before the Lord, and it shalbe thine and thy
sonnes with thee by a lawe for euer, as
the Lord hathe commanded.

2.Mac.2,11.
f And not consumed as Nadáb, & Abihú.

16 ¶ * And Mosés soght ẏ goat that was offred for sinne, and lo, it was burnt: therefore he was angry with Eleazár and Ithamár the sonnes of Aarón, which were [f] left
aliue, saying,
17 Wherefore haue ye not eaten the sin
offring in the holy place, seing it is moste
holy? and *God* hathe giuen it you, to beare
the iniquitie of the Cōgregaciō, to make
an atonement for them before the Lord.
18 Beholde, the blood of it was not broght
within the holy place: ye shulde haue eaten *it* in the holy place, * as I cōmāded.

Chap.6,26.
g That is, Nadáb, & Abihú.
h Mosés bare with his infirmitie considerig his great sorow, but dothe not leaue an example to forgiue them ẏ maliciously transgresse the commādement of God.

19 And Aarón said vnto Mosés, Beholde,
this day [g] haue they offred their sin offring and their burnt offring before the
Lord, and suche things *as thou knowest* are
come vnto me: if I had eaten the sin offring to day, shulde it haue bene accepted
in the sight of the Lord?
20 So when Mosés heard *it*, he was [h] cōtēt.

CHAP. XI.

1 *Of beastes, fishes and birdes, which be cleane, and which be vncleane.*

Gene 7,2. deu.14,4. act.10,14.
a Or, whereof ye may eat.
b He noteth foure sortes of beastes: some chewe the cud onely, and some haue onely the fote cleft: others nether chewe the cud nor haue the hoofe cleft: ẏ fourthe bothe chewe the cud and haue the hoofe deuided which may be eaten.

1 After, the Lord spake vnto Mosés &
to Aarón, saying vnto them,
2 Speake vnto the children of Israél, and
say, * These are the beastes which ye [a] shal
eat, among all the beastes that are on the
earth.
3 Whatsoeuer parteth the [b] hoofe, and is
clouen foted, and chaweth the cud among
the beastes, that shal ye eat.
4 But of them that chewe the cud, or deuide the hoofe onely, of them ye shal not
eat: as the camel, because he cheweth the
cud, and deuideth not the hoofe, he shalbe vncleane vnto you.
5 Likewise the conie, because he cheweth
the cud & deuideth not ẏ hoofe, he shalbe vncleane to you.
6 Also the hare, because he cheweth the
cud, & deuideth not the hoofe, he shalbe
vncleane to you.

2.Mac.6,18.
c God wolde that herby for a time thei shulde be discerned as his people from ẏ Gentiles.

7 * And the swine, because he parteth the
hoofe and is clouen foted, but cheweth
not the cud, he shalbe vncleane to you.
8 Of their [c] flesh shal ye not eat, and their
carkeis shal ye not touche: *for* thei shalbe
vncleane to you.
9 ¶ These shal ye eat, of all that are in the
waters: whatsoeuer hathe finnes & skales
in the waters, in the seas, or in the riuers,
them shal ye eat.

d As litle fish ingendred of the slime.
e As thei were come of generation.

10 But all that haue not fins nor skales in
the seas, or in ẏ riuers, of all that [d] moueth
in the waters & of all [e] liuing things that
are in the waters, thei shalbe an abominacion vnto you.
11 Thei, I say, shalbe an abominacion to
you: ye shal not eat of their flesh, but shal
abhorre their carkeis.
12 Whatsoeuer hathe not fins nor skales
in the waters, that shalbe abominacion
vnto you.

"Or, gryphin, as is in the greke.

13 ¶ These shal ye haue also in abominaciō
amōg the foules, thei shal not be eaten: *for*
thei are an abominacion, the egle, and the
"goshauke, and the osprey:
14 Also the vultur, and the kite after his
kinde,
15 And all rauens after their kinde:

"Or, cookow.

16 The ostriche also, and the night crowe,
and the "seamcawe, and the hauke after his
kinde:
17 The litle owle also, and the cormorant,
and the great owle.

"Or, porphyrie.

18 Also the "redshāke and the pelicane, and
the swanne:
19 The storke also, the heron after his kinde, and the lapwing, and the backe:
20 Also euerie foule that crepeth *and* goeth
vpon all foure, suche shalbe an abominacion vnto you.

"Or, haue no bowings on their fete.
f These were certeine kindes of grashoppers, which are not now proprely knowen.

21 Yet these shal ye eat: of euerie foule that
crepeth, *and* goeth vpon all foure which
"haue their fete and leggs all of one to leape withall vpon the earth,
22 Of them ye shal eat these, the grashoper
after his kinde, and the [f] solean after his
kinde, the hargol after his kinde, and the
hagab after his kinde.
23 But all *other* foules ẏ crepe *&* haue foure fete, thei *shalbe* abominacion vnto you.
24 For by suche ye shalbe polluted: whosoeuer toucheth their carkeis, shalbe vncleane vnto the euening.

g Out of the campe.

25 Whosoeuer also [g] beareth of their carkeis, shal wash his clothes, and be vncleane vntil euen.

"Or, hathe not his fote clouen in two.

26 Euerie beast that hathe clawes deuided,
and is "not clouen foted, nor cheweth the
cud, suche shalbe vncleane vnto you: euerie one ẏ toucheth thē, shalbe vncleane.
27 And whatsoeuer goeth vpon his pawes
among all maner beastes that goeth on all
foure, suche shalbe vncleane vnto you:
whoso doeth touche their carkeis shalbe
vncleane vntil the euen.
28 And he that beareth their carkeis, shal
wash his clothes, and be vncleane vntil the
euen: *for* suche shalbe vncleane vnto you.

29 ¶Also these shalbe vncleane to you a-
mõg the things that crepe and moue vpon
the earth, the weasel, and the mouse, and
the h " frog, after his kinde:

h The grene frog that sitteth on the busshes. "Or, crocodile.

30 Also the rat, and the lizard, and the cha-
meleon, and the stellio, and the molle.
31 These shalbe vncleane to you amõg all ẏ
crepe: whosoeuer doeth touche thẽ when
thei be dead, shalbe vncleane vntil the euẽ.
32 Also whatsoeuer anie of the dead carkeises of them doeth fall vpon, shalbe vncleane, whether it be vessel of wood, or rai
ment, or i skin, or sacke: whatsoeuer vessel
it be that is occupied, it shalbe put in the
water as vncleane vntil the euen, and *so*
be purified.

i As a bottel or bag.

33 But euerie earthẽ vessel, whereinto anie
of them falleth, whatsoeuer is with in it
shal be vncleane, and *ye shal breake it.

Chap.6,28.

34 All meat also that shalbe eaten, if anie
suche water come vpon it, shalbe vncleane:
and all drinke that shalbe dronke in all *suche* vessels shalbe vncleane.
35 And euerie thing that their carkeis fall
vpon, shalbe vncleane: the fornais or the
pot shalbe broken: *for* thei are vncleane,
and shalbe vncleane vnto you.
36 Yet the fountaines & welles where there is plentie of water shal be cleane: but
that which k toucheth their carkeises shal
be vncleane.

k So muche of the water as toucheth it.

37 And if there fall of their dead carkeis
vpon anie sede, which vseth to be sowen,
it shal be cleane.
38 But if anie l water be powred vpon the
sede, and there fall of their dead carkeis
thereon, it shalbe vncleane vnto you.

l He speaketh of sede, that is layed to stepe before it be sowen.

39 If also anie beast, whereof ye may eat,
dye, he that toucheth the carkeis thereof
shalbe vncleane vntil the euen.
40 And he that eateth of the carkeis of it,
shal wash his clothes and be vncleane vntil the euen: he also that beareth the carkeis of it, shal wash his clothes, and be vncleane vntil the euen.
41 Euerie creping thing therefore that crepeth vpon the earth shalbe an abominacion, *and* not be eaten.
42 Whatsoeuer goeth vpon the breast, and
whatsoeuer goeth vpon all foure, or that
hathe manie fete amõg all creping things
that crepe vpon the earth, ye shal not eat
of them, for thei shalbe abominacion.
43 Ye shal not pollute your selues with anie
thing ẏ crepeth, nether make your selues
vncleane ẇ them, nether defile your selues
thereby: ye shal not, I say, be defiled by thẽ,
44 For I am the Lord your God: be sancti
fied therefore, and be m holy, for I am holy, and defile not your selues with anie cre
ping thing, that crepeth vpon the earth.

m He sheweth why God did chuse them to be his people, 1.Pet.1.15.

45 For I am the Lord that broght you out
of the land of Egypt, to be your God, and
that you shulde be holy, for I am holy.
46 This is the lawe of beastes, & of foules,
and of euerie liuing thing that moueth
in the waters, and of euerie thing that crepeth vpon the earth:
47 That there may be a difference betwene
the vncleane and cleane, and betwene the
beast that may be eaten, & the beast that
oght not to be eaten.

CHAP. XII.

2 *A lawe how women shulde be purged after their deliuerance.*

1 AND the Lord spake vnto Mosés, saying,
2 Speake vnto the children of Israél, and
say, When a woman hathe broght forthe
sede, and borne a manchilde, she shal be
vncleane a seuẽ daies, like as she is vncleane whẽ she is put a parte for her "*disease.

a So that her housband for that time colde not resorte to her. "Or, flowres. *Chap.15,19.*

3 (*And in the eight day the foreskin of
the *childes* flesh shalbe circumcised)

Luk.2,21. ioh.7,22.

4 And she shal continue in the blood of
her purifiyng thre b and thirty daies: she
shal touche no c halowed thing, nor come
in to the d Sanctuarie, vntil the time of her
purifiyng be out.

b. Besides the first seuen daies. c As sacrifice or suche like. d That is, into the courte gate, til after fourtie daies.

5 But if she beare a maide childe, then she
shalbe vncleane two e wekes, as when she
hathe her disease: and she shal continue
in the blood of her purifiyng thre score
and six daies.

e Twise so lõg as if she bare a man childe.

6 Now when the daies of her purifiyng
are out, (whether it be for a sonne or for
a daughter) she shal bring to the Priest a
lambe of one yere olde for a burnt offring, and a yong pigeon or a turtle doue
for a sin offring, vnto ẏ dore of the f Tabernacle of the Congregacion,

f Where the burnt offrings were wonte to be offred.

7 Who shal offer it before the Lord, and
make an atonement for her: so she shalbe
purged of the issue of her blood. this is ẏ la
we for her ẏ hathe borne a male or female.
8 But if she "be not able to bring a lãbe, she
shal bring two *turtles, or two yong pigeons: the one for a burnt offring, and
the other for a sin offring: and the Priest
shal make an atonement for her: so she
shalbe cleane.

"Ebr. if her hãd finde not the worthe of a lãbe. *Luk.2,24.*

CHAP. XIII.

2 *What consideracions the Priest oght to obserue in iudging the leprosie.* 29 *The blacke spot or skab,* 47 *and the leprie of the garment.*

1 MOreouer the Lord spake vnto Mosés, and to Aarón, saying,
2 The man that shal haue in the skin of his
flesh a swelling or a skab, or a white spot,
so that in the skin of his flesh a it be like ẏ
plague of leprosie, then he shalbe broght
vnto Aarón the Priest, or vnto one of his
sonnes the Priests,

a That it may be suspected to be the leprie.

3 And the Priest shal loke on the sore in
the skin of *his* flesh: if the heere in the sore be turned into white, and the sore seme

b That is, ſhronke in, & be lower then the reſt of the ſkin.
"Ebr. ſhal pol-lute him.

me to be b lower thẽ the ſkin of his fleſh,
it is a plague of leproſie: therefore the
Prieſt ſhal loke on him, and "pronounce
him vncleane:
4 But if the white ſpot be in ỹ ſkin of his
fleſh, and ſeme not to be lower then the
ſkin, nor the heere thereof be turned vnto white, then the Prieſt ſhal ſhut vp *him
that hathe* the plague, ſeuen daies.
5 After, the Prieſt ſhal loke vpon him the
ſeuenth day: & if the plague ſeme "to him
to abide ſtil, and the plague growe not in
the ſkin, the Prieſt ſhal ſhut him vp yet ſeuen daies more.
6 Then the Prieſt ſhal loke on him againe the ſeuenth day, and if the plague c be
darcke, and the ſore growe not in the ſkin,
then the Prieſt ſhal "pronoũce him cleane, *for* it is a ſkab: therefore he ſhal waſh
his clothes, and be cleane.
7 But if the ſkab growe more in the ſkin,
after that he is ſene of the Prieſt, for to be
purged, he ſhalbe ſene of the Prieſt yet
againe.
8 Then the Prieſt ſhal conſider, and if the
ſkab "growe in the ſkin, then the Prieſt
ſhal pronounce him d vncleane: *for* it is
leproſie.
9 ¶ When the plague of leproſie is in a
man, he ſhalbe broght vnto the Prieſt,
10 And the Prieſt ſhal ſe *him*: & if the ſwel
ling *be* white in the ſkin, & haue made ỹ
heere white, & there be rawe fleſh in the
ſwelling,
11 It is an olde leproſie in the ſkin of his
fleſh: and the Prieſt ſhal pronounce him
vncleane, and ſhal not ſhut him vp, for he
is vncleane.
12 Alſo if the leproſie "breake out in the
ſkin, and the leproſie couer all the ſkin of
the plague, from his head euen to his fete,
whereſoeuer the Prieſt loketh,
13 Then the Prieſt ſhal conſider: and if the
leproſie couer all his fleſh, he ſhal pronoũ
ce ỹ plague to be e cleane, becauſe it is all
turned into whitenes: *ſo* he ſhalbe cleane.
14 But if *there be* rawe fleſh on him when
he is ſene, he ſhalbe vncleane.
15 For the Prieſt ſhal ſe the rawe fleſh, and
declare him to be vncleane: *for* the rawe
fleſh is f vncleane, *therefore* it is the leproſie.
16 Or if the rawe fleſh change and be turned into white, then he ſhal come to the
Prieſt,
17 And the Prieſt ſhal beholde him: and if
the ſore be changed into white, then the
Prieſt ſhal pronoũce the plague cleane, *for*
it is cleane.
18 ¶ The fleſh alſo in whoſe ſkin there is "a
bile and is healed,
19 And in the place of the bile there be a
white ſwelling, or a white ſpot ſome what

"Ebr. in his eies
c As hauing ỹ ſkin drawen together, or blackiſh.
"Ebr. ſhal clean-ſe him.
"Or, be ſpred abroade.
d As touching his bodely diſeaſe: for his diſeaſe was not imputed to him for ſin before God, though it were the puniſhement of ſinne.
"Or, bud.
e For it is not that cõtagious leprie that infecteth, but a kinde of ſkirfe, which hathe not ỹ fleſh rawe as the leproſie.
f That is, declareth that ỹ fleſh is not ſounde, but is in danger to be leprous.
"Or, impoſtume.

reddiſh, it ſhalbe ſene of the Prieſt.
20 And whẽ the Prieſt ſeeth it, if it appeare
lower then the ſkin, and the heere thereof
be changed into white, the Prieſt thẽ ſhal
pronounce him g vncleane: *for* it is a plague of leproſie, broken out in the bile.
21 But if the Prieſt loke on it and there be
no white heeres therein, & if it be not lower then the ſkin, but be darcker, then the
Prieſt ſhal ſhut him vp ſeuen daies.
22 And if it ſpread abroade in the fleſh, the
Prieſt ſhal pronounce him vncleane; *for* it
is a ſore.
23 But if the ſpot continue in his place, &
growe not, it is a burning bile: therefore
the Prieſt ſhal declare him to be cleane.
24 ¶ If there be anie fleſh, in whoſe ſkin
there is an hote burning, and the quicke
fleſh of the burning haue a h white ſpot,
ſomewhat reddiſh or pale,
25 Then the Prieſt ſhal loke vpon it: and if
the heere in that ſpot be chãged into white, and it appeare lower then the ſkin, it is
a leproſie broke out in the burning: therefore the Prieſt ſhal pronoũce him vncleane: *for* it is the plague of leproſie.
26 But if the Prieſt loke on it, and there be
no white heere in the ſpot, and be no lower thẽ the *other* ſkin, but be darcker, then
the Prieſt ſhal ſhut him vp ſeuen daies.
27 After, the Prieſt ſhal loke on him the ſeuenth day: if it be growen abroade in the
ſkinne, then the Prieſt ſhal pronoũce him
vncleane: *for* it is the plague of leproſie.
28 And if the ſpot abide in his place, not
growing in the ſkin, but is darcke, it is a "ri
ſing of the burning: the Prieſt ſhal therefore declare him cleane, for it is the drying vp of the burning.
29 ¶ If alſo a man or woman hathe a ſore
on the head or in the beard,
30 Then the Prieſt ſhal ſe the ſore: and if it
appeare lower then the ſkin, and there be
in it a ſmale yelowe i heere, then the Prieſt
ſhal pronounce him vncleane: *for* it is a
blacke ſpot, and leproſie of the head or
of the beard.
31 And if the Prieſt loke on the ſore of the
blacke ſpot, and if it ſeme not lower then
ỹ ſkin nor haue anie blacke heere in it, thẽ
the Prieſt ſhal ſhut *vp him, that hathe* the
ſore of the blacke ſpot, ſeuen daies.
32 After, in the ſeuenth day the Prieſt ſhal
loke on the ſore: and if ỹ blacke ſpot growe not, & there be in it no yelowe heere,
and the blacke ſpot ſeme not lower then
the ſkin,
33 Then he ſhalbe ſhauen, but *the place* of ỹ
blacke ſpot ſhal he not ſhaue: but ỹ Prieſt
ſhal ſhut vp *him, that hathe* the blacke ſpot,
ſeuen daies more.
34 And the ſeuenth day the Prieſt ſhal loke
on the blacke ſpot: and if the blacke ſpot

g None were exempted, but if the Prieſt pronõced him vncleane, he was put out from among ỹ people: as appeareth by Marie the propheteſſe, Nõb. 12, 14, and by King Ozias. 2. Chro. 26, 20.
h If he haue a white ſpot in that place, where the burning was, and was after healed.
"Or, ſwelling.
i Which was not wont to be there, or els ſmaler then in any other parte of the body.

growe not in the ſkin, nor ſeme lower thē
the *other* ſkin, then ẏ Prieſt ſhal clēſe him,
& he ſhal waſh his clothes, and be cleane.
35 But if the blacke ſpot growe abroade in
the fleſh after his clenſing,
36 Then the Prieſt ſhal loke on it : and if
the blacke ſpot growe in the ſkin, ẏ Prieſt
ſhal not [k] ſeke for the yelowe heere: *for* he
is vncleane.

k He ſhal not care whether the yelowe heere be there, or no.

37 But if the blacke ſpot ſeme to him to a-
bide, and that blacke heere growe therein,
the blacke ſpot is healed, he *is* cleane, and
the Prieſt ſhal declare him to be cleane.
38 ¶ Furthermore if there be manie white
ſpots in ẏ ſkin of ẏ fleſh of man or womā,
39 Then the Prieſt ſhal cōſider: and if the
ſpots in the ſkin of their fleſh be ſomewhat darcke and white withall, it is but a
white ſpot broken out in the ſkin : *therefore* he is cleane.
40 And the man whoſe heere is fallen of
his head *and* is balde, is cleane.
41 And if his head loſe the [l] heere on the
fore parte, & be balde before, he is cleane.

l By ſickenes, or anie other inconuenience.

42 But if there be in the balde head, or in
the balde fore heade a white reddiſh ſore,
it is a leproſie ſpringīg in his balde head,
or in his balde forehead.
43 Therefore the Prieſt ſhal loke vpon it,
and if the riſing of the ſore be white reddiſh in his balde head, or in his balde fore head, appearing like leproſie in the ſkin
of the fleſh,
44 He is a leper and vncleane: *therefore* the
Prieſt ſhal pronounce him altogether vncleane: *for* the ſore *is* in his head.
45 The leper alſo in whome the plague is,
ſhal haue his clothes [m] rent, and his head
bare, and ſhal put a couering vpō his [n] lippes, and ſhal crye, *I am* vncleane, *I am* vncleane.

m In ſigne of ſorowe and lamentacion.
n Ether in token of mourning, or for feare of infecting others.

46 As long as the diſeaſe *ſhalbe* vpon him,
he ſhalbe polluted, *for* he is vncleane : he
ſhal dwel alone, * without the campe *ſhal*
his habitacion *be*.

Nomb.5,2.
2.kin. 15.5.

47 ¶ Alſo the garmēt that the plague of leproſie is in, whether it be a wollen garment or a linen garment,
48 Whether it be in the warpe or in the
woofe of linen or of wollen, ether in a
ſkin or in anie thing made of ſkin,
49 And if the ſore be grene or ſomewhat
reddiſh in the garment or in the ſkin, or
in the warpe, or in the woofe, or in anie
thīg that is made of [o] ſkin, it is a plague of
leproſie & ſhalbe ſhewed vnto the Prieſt.

o Whether it be garment, veſſel, or inſtrument.

50 Then the Prieſt ſhal ſe the plague, and
ſhut vp *it that hathe* the plague, ſeuē daies,
51 And ſhal loke on the plague the ſeuenth
day: if the plague growe in the garment
or in the warpe, or in the woofe, or in the
ſkin or in anie thing that is made of ſkin,
that plague *is* a freating leproſie and vncleane.
52 And he ſhal burne the garment, or the
warpe, or the woofe, whether it be wollen
or linen, or anie thing that is made of
ſkin, wherein the plague is: for it is a freating leproſie, *therefore* it ſhalbe burnt in
the fire.
53 If the Prieſt yet ſe that the plague [p] growe not in the garment, or in the woofe,
or in whatſoeuer thing of ſkin it be,

p But abide ſtil in one place, as verſ.37.

54 Then the Prieſt ſhal cōmāde them to
waſh the thing wherein the plague is, &
he ſhal ſhut it vp ſeuen dayes more.
55 Againe the Prieſt ſhal loke on the plague, after it is waſhed : and if the plague
haue not changed his [q] colour, thogh the
plague ſpred no further, it is vncleane:
thou ſhalt burne it in ẏ fire, *for* it is a freat
inwarde, [r] whether *the ſpot* be in the bare
place of the whole, or in parte thereof.

q But remaine as it did before.
r Or whether it be in anie bare place before or behinde.

56 And if the Prieſt ſe that the plague be
darcker, after that it is waſhed, he ſhal cut
it out of the garment, or out of the ſkin,
or out of the warpe, or out of the woofe.
57 And if it appeare ſtil in the garment or
in the warpe, or in the woofe, or in anie
thing made of ſkin, it is a ſpreading *leprie*:
thou ſhalt burne the thing wherein the
plague is, in the fire.
58 If thou haſt waſhed the garment or the
warpe, or ẏ woofe, or whatſoeuer thing of
ſkin it be, if the plague be departed therefrom, then ſhal it be waſhed [ſ] the ſeconde
time, and be cleane.
59 This is the lawe of the plague of leproſie in a garment of wollen or linen, or in
the warpe, or in the woofe, or in anie thing
of ſkin, to make it cleane or vncleane.

ſ To the intēt he might be ſure that the leproſie was departed and that all occaſion of infection might be takē away.

CHAP. XIIII.

3 The clenſing of the leper, 34 And of the houſe that he is in.

1 AND the Lord ſpake vnto Moſes,
ſaying,
2 * This is the [a] lawe of the leper in the day
of his clenſing : that is, he ſhalbe broght
vnto the Prieſt,
3 And the Prieſt ſhal go out of the campe,
and the Prieſt ſhal conſider *him*: and if the
plague of leproſie be healed in the leper,

Mat.8,2. mar.1,40. luk.5,12.
a Or the ceremonie which ſhalbe vſed in his purgation.

4 Then ſhal the Prieſt commande to take
for *him* that is clenſed, two ″ ſparowes aliue and [b] cleane, and ceder wood and a
ſkarlet *lace*, and hyſſope.
5 And the Prieſt ſhal commande to kil
one of the birdes ouer [c] pure water in an
earthen veſſel.

″ *Or, litle birdes.*
b Of birdes which were permitted to be eaten.
c Running water, or of ẏ fountaine.

6 After, he ſhal take the liue ſparowe with
the cedar wood, and the ſkarlet *lace*, and
the hyſſope, and ſhal dip them and the liuing ſparowe in the blood of the ſparowe
ſlaine, ouer the pure water,
7 And he ſhal ſprinkle vpon him, that muſt
be clenſed of his leproſie, ſeuen times, and
clenſe

d Signifing ẏ he that was made cleane, was set at libertie, and restored to the companie of others.

clense him, and shal [d] let go the liue sparowe into the broade field.
8 Then he that shalbe clensed, shal wash
his clothes, and shaue of all his heere, and
wash him selfe in water, so he shalbe cleane: after that shal he come into the hoste,
but shal tarie without his tent seuē dayes.
9 So in the seuenth day he shal shaue of all
his heere, *bothe* his head, and his beard, &
his eie browes: euen all his heere shal he
shaue, & shal wash his clothes & shal wash
his flesh in water: so he shalbe cleane.
10 Then in the eight day he shal take two
he lambes without [e] blemish, and an ewe
lambe of an yere olde without blemish,
and thre tenth deales of fine floure for a
meat offring, mingled with oyle, [f] and a
pinte of oyle.

e Which hath no imperfection in anie member.

f This measure ī Ebrewe is called, log, and conteineth six eggs in measure.

11 And the Priest that maketh him cleane
shal bring the man which is to be made
cleane, and those things, before the Lord,
at the dore of the Tabernacle of the Cōgregacion.
12 Then the Priest shal take one lambe, &
offer him for a trespasse offring, and the
pinte of oyle, and * shake them to and fro
before the Lord.

Exod. 29,24.

13 And he shal kil the lambe in the place
where the sinne offring and the burnt offring are slaine, *euen* in the holy place: for
as the * sin offring is the Priests, *so* is the
trespasse offring: *for* it is moste holy.

Chap. 7,1.

14 So the Priest shal take of the blood of
the trespasse offring, and put it vpon the
lap of the right eare of him that shalbe clensed, and vpon the thumbe of his
right hand, and vpon the great toe of his
right fote.
15 The Priest shal also take of the pinte of
oyle, and powre it into the palme of his
left hand,
16 And the Priest shal dip his "right finger
in the oyle that is in his left hād, & sprinkle of the oyle with his finger seuen times
before the Lord.

"Ebr. the finger of his right hand.

17 And of the rest of the oyle that is in his
hand, shal the Priest put vpon the lap of
the right eare of him that is to be clensed, & vpon the thumbe of his right hand,
and vpon the great toe of his right fote,
" where the blood of the trespas offring
was put.

"Ebr. vpon the blood of the trespas offring.

18 But the remnant of the oyle that is in
the Priestes hand, he shal powre vpon the
head of him that is to be clensed: so the
Priest shal make an atonemēt for him before the Lord.
19 And the Priest shal offer the sin offring
and make an atonement for him that is to
be clensed of his vnclennes: thē after shal
he kil the burnt offring.
20 So the Priest shal offer the burnt offring
& the meat offring vpon the altar: and the
Priest shal make an atonement for him: so
he shalbe cleane.
21 But if he be poore, & " not able, then he
shal bring one lābe for a trespas offring to
be shakē, for his recōciliation, & a [g] tenth
deale of fine floure mingled with oyle, for
a meat offring, with a pinte of oyle.

"Ebr. his hand can not take it.

g Which is an omer, read Exod. 16,16.

22 Also two turtle doues, or two yong pigeons, as he is able, whereof the one shalbe a sin offring, and the other a burnt offring,
23 And he shal bring them the eight day
for his clensing vnto the Priest at the dore of the Tabernacle of the Congregacion before the Lord.
24 Then the Priest shal take the lambe of
the trespas offring, and the pinte of oyle,
and the Priest shal [h] shake them to and
fro before the Lord.

h Or shal offre them as ẏ offring that is shaken to and fro.

25 And he shal kil the lambe of the trespas
offring, & the Priest shal take of ẏ blood
of the trespas offring, and put it vpon the
lap of his right eare that is to be clensed,
and vpon the thumbe of his right hand, &
vpon the great toe of his right fote.
26 Also the Priest shal powre of the oyle
into the palme of his owne "left hand.
27 So the Priest shal with his right finger
sprinkle of the oyle that is in his left
hand, seuen times before the Lord.

"Ebr. in to the palme of the Priests left hand.

28 Then the Priest shal put of the oyle
that is in his hand, vpon the lap of the
right eare of him that is to be clensed, and
vpon the thumbe of his right hand, and
vpon the great toe of his right fote: vpon
the place "of the blood of the trespas offring.

"Or, where the blood of the trespas offring was put, as ver. 17.

29 But ẏ rest of the oyle that is in ẏ Priests
hād, he shal put vpon the head of him that
is to be clensed, to make an atonement for
him before the Lord.
30 Also he shal present one of the turtle
doues, or of the yong pigeons, [i] as he is
able:

i Whether of them he can get.

31 Suche, I say, as he is able, the one for a sin
offring, and the other for a burnt offring
"with the meat offring: so the Priest shal
make an atonement for him that is to be
clensed before the Lord.

"Or, besides the meat offring.

32 This is the [k] lawe of him which hathe ẏ
plague of leprosie, who is not able in his
clensing *to offre the whole.*

k This ordre is appointed for the poore man.

33 ¶ The Lord also spake vnto Mosés and
to Aarón, saying,
34 When ye be come vnto the land of Canáan which I giue you in possession, if I
[l] send the plague of leprosie in an house
of the land of your possession,
35 Then he that oweth the house, shal come and tel the Priest, saying, Me thinke there is like a plague *of leprosie* in the
house.
36 Then the Priest shal commande thē to

l This declareth that no plague nor punishement cōmeth to man without gods prouidence & his sending.

empty the house before the Priest go into it to se the plague, that all that is in
the house be not made vncleane, and then
shal the Priest go in to se the house,
37 And he shal marke the plague: and if the
plague *be* in the walles of the house, and
that there be ″ depe spots, grenish or red-
dish, which seme to be lower thē the wall,

″Or, blackner. or hollow strakes.

38 Then the Priest shal go out of the house to the dore of the house, and shal cause
to shut vp the house seuen daies.
39 So ẏ Priest shal come againe the seuēth
day: and if he se that the plague be increased in the walles of the house,
40 Then the Priest shal commande them
to take away ẏ stones wherein the plague
is, and they shal cast them into a ″ foule place without the citie.

″Or, polluted.

41 Also he shal cause to scrape the house
within round about, and powre the dust,
that they haue pared of, without the citie
in [m] an vncleane place.
42 And they shal take other stones, and put
thē in ẏ places of those stones, & shal take
other mortar, to plaister the house with.

m Where carions were cast, and other filth that the people might not be there with infected.

43 But if the plague come againe and breake out in the house, after that he hathe taken away the stones, and after ẏ he hathe
scraped and plaistred the house,
44 Then the Priest shal come and see: and
if the plague growe in the house, it is a
freating leprosie in the house: it is *therefore*
vncleane.
45 And he shal [n] breake downe the house,
with the stones of it, and the timber thereof, and all the ″ mortar of the house, and
he shal carie them out of the citie vnto an
vncleane place.

n That is, he shal commande it to be pulled downe, as ver. 40.
″Or, dust.

46 Moreouer he that goeth into the house
all ẏ while that it is shut vp, he shalbe vncleane vntil the euen.
47 He also that slepeth in the house shal
wash his clothes: he likewise that eateth
in the house, shal wash his clothes.
48 But if the Priest shal come and se, that
the plague hathe spred no further in the
house, after the house be plaistered, the
Priest shal pronounce that house cleane,
for the plague is healed.
49 Then shal he take to purifie the house,
two sparowes, and cedar wood, [o] & skarlet *lace*, and hyssope.
50 And he shal kil one sparowe ouer pure
water in an earthen vessel,
51 And shal take the cedar wood, and the
hyssope, and the skarlet *lace* with the liue
sparowe, and dip them in the blood of the
slaine sparowe, and in the pure water, and
sprinkle the house seuen times:
52 So shal he clense the house ẇ the blood
of the sparowe and with the pure water,
and with the liue sparowe, & with the cedar wood, and with the hyssope, and with
the skarlet *lace*.

o It semeth ẏ this was a lace or string to binde ẏ hyssope to ẏ wood, & so was made a sprinkle: the Apostle to the Ebrewes calleth it skarlet wolle, Ebr. 9, 19.

53 Afterwarde he shal let go ẏ liue sparowe
out of the ″ towne into ẏ ″ broade fieldes:
so shal he make atonement for the house,
and it shalbe cleane.

″Ebr. citie.
″Ebr. on the face of the field.

54 This is the lawe for euerie plague of leprosie and *blacke spot, Chap. 13. 30.
55 And of the leprosie of the garment, and
of the house,
56 And of the ″ swelling, and of the skab, &
of the white spot.

″Or, rising.

57 This is the lawe of ẏ leprosie to teache
″ when *a thing* is vncleane, and when it is
cleane.

″Ebr. in the day of the vncleane, and in the day of the cleane.

CHAP. XV.

2. 19 The maner of purging the vncleane issues bothe of
mē and women. 31 The children of Israél must be sepa-
rate from all vnclennes.

1 Moreouer the Lord spake vnto Moses, and to Aarón, saying,
2 Speake vnto the children of Israél, and
say vnto them, Whosoeuer hathe an issue
from his [a] flesh, is vncleane, *because* of his
issue.
3 And this shalbe his vnclēnes in his issue:
when his flesh auoideth his issue, or if his
flesh be stopped from his issue, this is his
[b] vnclennes.

a Whose sede ether in sleping, or els of weakenes of nature issueth at his secret parte.

b Or ẏ thing wherefore he shalbe vncleane.

4 Euerie bed whereon he lieth that hathe ẏ
issue, shalbe vncleane, & euerie thing whereon he sitteth, shalbe vncleane.
5 Whosoeuer also toucheth his bed, shal
wash his clothes, and wash him selfe in water, and shalbe vncleane vntil the euen.
6 And he ẏ sitteth on anie thing, whereon
he sate that hathe the issue, shal wash his
clothes, & wash him selfe in water, & shal
be vnclēane vntil the euen.
7 Also he that toucheth the flesh of him
that hathe the issue, shal wash his clothes,
& wash him selfe in water, and shalbe vncleane vntil the euen.
8 If he also, ẏ hathe the issue, spit vpō him
that is cleane, [c] he shal wash his clothes, &
wash him selfe in water, & shal be vncleane vntil the euen.

c On whome the vncleane man spat.

9 And what [d] saddle soeuer he rideth vpon,
that hathe the issue, shalbe vncleane,

d The worde signifieth euerie thing wheron a man rideth.

10 And whosoeuer toucheth anie thing that
was vnder him, shalbe vncleane vnto the
euen: and he that beareth those *things*,
shal wash his clothes, and wash him selfe
in water, and shal be vncleane vntil the
euen.
11 Likewise whomesoeuer he toucheth ẏ
hathe the issue (and hathe not washed his
hands in water) shal wash his clothes &
wash him selfe in water, & shal be vncleane vntil the euen.
12 *And the vessel of earth that he toucheth, Chap. 6, 28.
which hathe the issue, shalbe broken: and
euerie vessel of wood shalbe rinsed in water.

e That is, be restored to his olde state, and be healed thereof.

13 But if he that hathe an issue, be e clensed of his issue, then shal he count him
seuen daies for his clensing, and wash his
clothes, and wash his flesh in pure water:
so shal he be cleane.
14 Then the eight day he shal take vnto
him two turtle doues or two yong pigeōs,
and come before the Lord at the dore of
the Tabernacle of the Congregacion, &
shal giue them vnto the Priest.
15 And the Priest shal make of the one of
them a sinne offring, and of the other a
burnt offring: so the Priest shal make an
atonement for him before the Lord, for
his issue.
16 Also if anie mans issue of sede departe
from him, he shal wash all his f flesh in
water, and be vncleane vntil the euen.

f Meaning all his bodie.

17 And euerie garment, and euerie skin
whereupō shalbe issue of sede, shalbe euen
washed with water, & be vncleane vnto
the euen.
18 If he that hathe an issue of sede, do lie
with a woman, thei shal bothe wash them
selues with water, and be vncleane vntil
the euen.
19 ¶ Also when a woman shal haue an issue,
and her issue in her ʺ flesh shalbe blood,
she shalbe put aparte seuen daies: & whosoeuer toucheth her, shalbe vncleane vnto
the euen.

ʺOr, secret parte.

20 And whatsoeuer she lieth vpon in g her
separacion, shalbe vncleane, and euerie
thing ŷ she sitteth vpon, shalbe vncleane.
21 Whosoeuer also toucheth her bed, shal
wash his clothes, and wash him selfe with
water, & shal be vncleane vnto the euen.

g That is, whē she hathe her floures, whereby she is separat frō her housband, from the tabernacle and from touching of anie holy thing.

22 And whosoeuer toucheth anie thīg that
she sate vpō, shal wash his clothes, & wash
him selfe in water, and shalbe vncleane
vnto the euen:
23 So that whether he touche her bed, or a-
nie thing whereon she hathe sit, he shalbe
vncleane vnto the euen.
24 And if a man lie with her, and *the floures*
of her separacion h touche him, he shal be
vncleane seuen daies, & all the whole bed
whereon he lieth, shalbe vncleane.
25 Also when a womans issue of blood runneth long time besides the time of her
ʺfloures, or when she hathe an issue, lōger
then her floures, all the daies of the issue
of her vnclennes she shalbe vncleane, as
in the time of her floures.

h If anie of her vnclennes did onely touche him in the bed: for els the man that companyed with suche a womā shulde dye, Chap 20,18.

ʺEbr separaciō.

26 Euerie bed whereon she lieth (as long
as her issue lasteth) shalbe to her as her
i bed of her separacion: and whatsoeuer
she sitteth vpon, shalbe vncleane, as her
vnclennes when she is put aparte.
27 And whosoeuer toucheth these *things*,
shalbe vncleane, & shal wash his clothes,
and wash him selfe in water, & shalbe vncleane vnto the euen.

i Shalbe vncleane as the bed whereon she lay when she had her natural disease.

28 But if she be clensed of her issue, then
she shal k counte her seuen daies, & after,
she shalbe cleane.

k After the time that she is recouered.

29 And in the eight day she shal take vnto
her two turtles or two yong pigeons, and
bring them vnto the Priest at the dore of
the Tabernacle of the Congregacion.
30 And the Priest shal make of the one a
sinne offring, and of the other a burnt offring, & the Priest shal make an atonemēt
for her before the Lord, for the issue of
her vnclennes.
31 Thus shal ye l separate the children of
Israél from their vnclennes, that thei dye
not in their vnclennes, if thei defile my
Tabernacle that is among them.

l Seing ŷ God requireth of his, puritie & clennes: we cā not be his, except our filth and sinnes be purged with the blood of Iesus Christ.

32 This is the lawe of him that hathe an issue, & of him from whome goeth an issue
of sede whereby he his defiled:
33 Also of her that is sicke of her floures,
& of him that hathe a running issue, whether it be man or woman, and of him that
lieth with her which is vncleane.

CHAP. XVI.

2 The Priest might not at all times come into the moste holy place. 8 The scape goat. 14 The purging of the Sanctuarie. 17 The clensing of the Tabernacle. 21 The Priest confesseth the sinnes of the people. 29 The feast of clensing sinnes.

1 FVrthermore the Lord spake vnto
Mosés, * after the death of the two
sonnes of Aarón, when thei came *to offer*
before the Lord, and dyed:

Chap.10,1.

2 And the Lord said vnto Mosés, Speake
vnto Aarón thy brother, * that he come
not at a all times in to the Holy place
within the vaile, before the Merciseat,
which is vpon the Arke, that he dye not:
for I wil appeare in the cloude vpon the
Merciseat.

Exod.30,10. ebr.9,7.

a The hie Priest entred into the Holiest of all but once a yere, euen in ŷ moneth of Septēber.

3 After this *sort* shal Aarón come into the
Holy place: *euen* with a yong bullocke
for a sinne offring, and a ram for a burnt
offring.
4 He shal put on the holy linen coat, and
shal haue linen breches vpon his ʺ flesh,
and shalbe girded with a linen girdel, and
shal couer his head with a linen mitre:
these are the holy garments: therefore
shal he wash his flesh in water, when he
doeth put them on.

ʺOr, priuities.

5 And he shal take of the Congregacion
of the children of Israél, two he goates
for a sinne offring, and a ram for a burnt
offring.
6 Then Aarón shal offer the bullocke for
his sinne offring, * & make an atonement
for him selfe, and for his house.

Ebr.9,7.

7 And he shal take the two he goates, and
present them before the Lord at the dore
of the Tabernacle of the Congregacion.
8 Then Aarón shal cast lots ouer the two

O.i.

b In Ebrewe it is called Azazél, which some say is a mountaine nere Sinái whether this goat was sét: but rather it is called the scape goat because he was not offred, but sent into the desert, as vers. 21.

he goates: one lot for the Lord, and the o-
ther for the b Scape goat.
9 And Aarón shal offer the goat, vpon
which the Lords lot shal fall, and make
him a sinne offring.
10 But the goat, on which the lot shal fall
to be the Scape goat, shalbe presented a-
liue before the Lord, to make reconciliacion by him, & to let him go (as a Scape
goat) into the wildernes.
11 Thus Aarón shal offer the bullocke for
his sinne offring, & make a reconciliacion
for him selfe, and for his house, and shal
kil the bullocke for his sinne offring.
12 And he shal take a censer ful of burning
coles from of the Altar before the Lord,
& his hādful of swete incens beatē small,
and bring *it* within the c vaile,

c The Holiest of all.

13 And shal put the incens vpon the fire before the Lord, that the "cloude of the incens may couer the Merciseat that is vpon" the Testimonie: so he shal not dye.

"Or, the smoke.

"Or, Arke.

14 And he shal* take of the blood of the
bullocke,* and sprinkle it with his finger
vpon the Merciseat d Eastward: and before the Merciseat shal he sprinkle of the
blood with his finger seuen times.

Ebr. 1, 13. & 10, 4.

Chap. 4, 6.

d That is, on the side which was toward ỳ people: for the head of the Sāctuarie stode Westward.

15 ¶ Then shal he kil the goat that is the
peoples sinne offring, & bring his blood
within the vaile, and do with that blood,
as he did with the blood of the bullocke,
& sprinkle it vpon the Merciseat, and before the Merciseat.
16 So he shal purge the Holy place from
the vnclennes of the children of Israél, &
from their trespasses of all their sinnes: so
shal he do also for the Tabernacle of the
Congregacion e placed with them, in the
middes of their vnclennes.

e Placed amōg them which are vncleane.

Luk. 1, 10, 17.

17 *And there shal be no man in the Tabernacle of the Congregacion, when he
goeth in to make an atonemēt in the Holy
place, vntil he come out, & haue made an
atonement for him selfe, & for his housholde, and for all the Congregacion of
Israél.
18 After, he shal go out vnto the f Altar
that is before the Lord, & make a reconciliacion vpon it, & shal take of the blood
of the bullocke, and of the blood of the
goat, and put it vpon the hornes of the
Altar round about:

f Wherevpon ỳ swete incēse & perfume was offred.

19 So shal he sprinkle of the blood vpon it
with his finger seuen times, and clense it,
and halowe it from the vnclennes of the
children of Israél.
20 ¶ Whē he hathe made an ēd of purging
the Holy place, & the Tabernacle of the
Congregacion, and the altar, then he shal
bring the liue goat:
21 And Aarón shal put bothe his hands vpō
the head of the liue goat, and confesse
ouer him all the iniquities of the childrē
of Israél, & all their trespasses, in all their
sinnes, putting thē g vpō the head of the
goat, and shal send *him* away (by the hand
of a man appointed) into the wildernes.

g Herein this goat is a true figure of Iesus Christ, who beareth the sinnes of the people, Isa. 53, 4.

22 So the goat shal beare vpon him all their
iniquities into " the land that is not inhabited, and he shal let the goat go into the
wildernes.

"Ebr. the land of separacion.

23 After, Aarón shal come into the Tabernacle of the Congregacion, and put of
the linen clothes, which he put on whē he
went into ỳ Holy place, & leaue thē there.
24 He shal wash also his flesh with water in
h the Holy place, and put on his owne raiment, and come out, and make his burnt
offring, and the burnt offring of the people, and make an atonement for him self,
and for the people.

h In the court where was ỳ Lauer, Exod. 30, 18.

25 Also the fat of the sinne offring shal he
burne vpon the Altar.
26 And he that caryed forthe the goat, *called* the Scape goat, shal wash his clothes,
and wash his flesh in water, and after that
shal come into the hoste.
27 Also the bullocke for the sinne offring,
and the goat for the sinne offring (whose
blood was broght to make a recōciliaciō
in ỳ Holy place) shal one * cary out without the hoste to be burnt in the fire, with
their skins, and with their flesh, and with
their doung.

Chap. 6, 30. ebr. 13, 11.

28 And he that burneth them shal wash his
clothes, and wash his flesh in water, and
afterwarde come into the hoste.
29 ¶ So this shalbe an ordinance for euer
vnto you: the tenth *day* of the i seuenth
moneth, ye shal k humble your soules, and
do no worke at all, whether it be one of ỳ
same countrey or a stranger that soiourneth among you.

i Which was Tisri, & answereth to parte of Septēber & parte of October.

k Meaning by abstinence and fasting.

30 For ỳ* day shal the Priest make an atonemēt for you to clēse you: ye shal be cleane
from all your sinnes before the Lord.

Chap. 23, 7.

31 This shalbe a l Sabbath of rest vnto you,
and ye shal humble your soules, by an ordinance for euer.

l Or a rest ỳ ye shal kepe moste diligētly.

32 And the Priest m whome he shal anoint,
and whome he shal cōsecrate (to minister
in his fathers stede) shal make the atonement, and shal put on the linen clothes &
holy vestments,

m Whome the Priest shal anoint by Gods commaundemēt to succede in his fathers rowme.

33 And shal purge the holy Sanctuarie and
the Tabernacle of the Congregacion, &
shal clense the Altar, & make an atonemēt
for the Priests and for all the people of
the Congregacion.
34 And this shalbe an euerlasting ordināce
vnto you, to make an atonement for the
childrē of Israél for all their sinnes* once
a yere: and as the Lord cōmanded Mosés,
he did.

Exod. 30, 10. ebr. 9, 7.

CHAP. XVII.

4 *All sacrifices muste be broght to the dore of the Tabernacle*

bernacle. 7 To deuils may they not offer. 10 They may not eat blood.

1 AND the Lord spake vnto Moses, saying,
2 Speake vnto Aarón, and to his sonnes, &
to all the children of Israél, and say vnto
them, This is the thing which the Lord
hathe [a] commanded, saying,
3 Whosoeuer *he be* of the house of Israél
that [b] killeth a bullocke, or lãbe, or goat in
ẏ hoste, or that killeth it out of the hoste,
4 And bringeth it not vnto the dore of the
Tabernacle of the Congregacion to offer
an offring vnto the Lord before the Tabernacle of the Lord, [c] blood shalbe imputed vnto that man: he hathe shed blood,
wherefore that man shalbe cut of from a-
mong his people.

a Lest they shulde practise that idolatrie, ẇ they had learned among the Egyptians.
b To make a sacrifice or offring thereof.
c I do asmuch abhorre it as thogh he had killed a man, as Isa. 66,3.

5 Therefore the children of Israél shal
bring their offrings, which they wolde offer [d] abroad in the field, and present them
vnto the Lord at ẏ dore of the Tabernacle of the Congregacion by the Priest, &
offer thẽ for peace offrings vnto ẏ Lord.
6 Then the Priest shal sprinkle the blood
vpon the altar of the Lord before the dore of the Tabernacle of the Congregacion, and burne the fat for a *swete sauour
vnto the Lord.

d Wheresoeuer they were moued with folish deuotiõ to offre it.
Exod. 29,18. chap. 4,31.

7 And thei shal no more offer their offrĩgs
vnto [e] deuils, after whome they haue gone
a [f] whoring: this shalbe an ordinance for
euer vnto them in their generacions.
8 ¶ Also thou shalt say vnto them, Whosoeuer *he be* of the house of Israél, or of the
strangers which soiourne among them,
that offreth a burnt offring or sacrifice,
9 And bringeth it not vnto the dore of the
Tabernacle of the Congregacion to offer it vnto the Lord, euẽ that man shal be
cut of from his people.

e Meaning whatsoeuer is not the true God, 1 Cor. 10 20. psal 95,5.
f For idolatrie is spiritual whordome, because faith toward God is broken.

10 ¶ Likewise whosoeuer *he be* of the house of Israél, or of the strãgers that soiourne among them, that eateth anie blood, I
wil euen set [g] my face against that persone
that eateth blood, & wil cut him of from
among his people:
11 For the life of the flesh is in the blood, &
I haue giuen it vnto you *to offer* vpon the
altar, to make an atonement for your soules: for this blood shal make an atonement
for the soule.
12 Therefore I said vnto the childrẽ of Israél, None of you shal eat blood: nether
the stranger that soiourneth among you,
shal eat blood.
13 Moreouer whosoeuer *he be* of the children of Israél, or of the strangers that
soiourne among them, which by hunting
taketh anie beast or foule that maie be
[h] eatẽ, he shal powre out ẏ blood thereof,
and couer it with dust:
14 For the life of all flesh is his blood, it is
ioyned with his life: therefore I said vnto
the children of Israél, *Ye shal eat the
blood of no "flesh: for the life of all flesh
is the blood thereof: whosoeuer eateth
it, shal be cut of.
15 And euerie persone that eateth it which
dyeth *alone*, or that which is torne *with beastes*, whether it be one of the same cõtrey
or a stranger, he shal bothe wash his clothes, & washe him selfe in water, & be vncleane vnto ẏ euen: after he shalbe "cleane.
16 But if he wash *them* not, nor wash his
"flesh, then he shal beare "his iniquitie.

g I wil declare my wrath by taking vengeãce on him, as Chap. 20,3.
h Which the Lawe permitteth to be eaten, because it is cleane.
Gen. 9,5.
"Or, liuing creature.
"Or, counted cleane.
"Or, him selfe.
"Or, the punishmẽt of his sinne.

CHAP. XVIII.

3 The Israelites oght not to follow the maners of the Egyptians and Canaanites. 6 The mariages that are vnlawful.

1 AND the Lord spake vnto Moses, saying,
2 Speake vnto the children of Israél, and
say vnto them, I am the Lord your God.
3 After the [a] doings of the land of Egypt,
wherein ye dwelt, shal ye not do: & after
the maner of the land of Canáan, whither
I wil bring you, shal ye not do, nether walke in their ordinances,
4 But do after my iudgements, & kepe mine ordinances, to walke therein: I am the
Lord your God.
5 Ye shal kepe therefore my statutes, and
my iudgements, *which if a man do, he
shal then liue in them: [b] I am the Lord.
6 ¶ None shal come nere to anie of ẏ kinred of his flesh to [c] vncouer *her* shame: I
am the Lord.
7 Thou shalt not vncouer the shame of
thy father, nor the shame of thy mother:
for she is thy mother, thou shalt not discouer her shame.
8 *The shame of thy fathers [d] wife shalt
ẙ not discouer: *for* it is thy fathers shame.
9 Thou shalt not discouer the shame of
thy [e] sister the daughter of thy father, or
the daughter of thy mother, whether she
be borne at home, or borne without: thou
shalt not discouer their shame.

a Ye shal preserue your selues from these abominations following, ẇ the Egyptians and Canaanites vse.
Ezek. 20,11. rom. 10,5. gala. 3,12.
b And therefore ye oght to serue me alone, as my people.
c That is, to lie with her, thogh it be vnder title of mariage.
Chap. 20,11.
d Which is thy stepmother.
e Ether by father or mother, borne in mariage or otherwise.

10 The shame of thy sonnes daughter, or
of thy daughters daughter, thou shalt not,
I say, vncouer their shame: for it is thy
[f] shame.
11 The shame of thy fathers wiues daughter, begotten of thy father (*for* she is thy
sister) ẙ shalt not, *I say*, discouer her shame.
12 *Thou shalt not vncouer the "shame of
thy fathers sister: *for* she is thy fathers kinsewoman.
13 Thou shalt not discouer the shame of
thy mothers sister: for she is thy mothers
kinsewoman.
14 *Thou shalt not vncouer the shame of
thy [g] fathers brother: *that is*, thou shalt
not go into his wife, *for* she is thine" ante.
15 * Thou shalt not discouer the shame

f Thei are her children whose shame thou hast vncouered.
Chap. 20,19.
"Or, secrets.
Chap. 20,20.
g Which thine vncle doeth discouer.
"Ebr. thy fathers brothers wife.
Chap. 20,21.

of thy daughter in lawe: *for* she is thy sonnes wife: *therefore* shalt thou not vncouer her shame.

Chap.20,21. 16 *Thou shal not discouer ye shame of thy
h brothers wife: *for* it is thy brothers shame.
17 Thou shalt not discouer the shame of ye
wife & of her daughter, nether shalt thou take her sonnes daughter, nor her daughters daughter, to vncouer her shame: *for* they are *thy* kinsfolkes, & it were wickednes.
18 Also thou shalt not take a wife with her sister, during her life, to i vexe *her*, in vncouering her shame vpon her.
19 *Thou shalt not also go vnto a woman to vncouer her shame, as long as she is put
k aparte for her disease.
20 Moreouer, thou shalt not giue *thy* selfe to thy neighbours wife by carnal copulatiō, to be defiled with her.
21 *Also thou shalt not giue thy " children to " offer *them* vnto l Mólech, nether shalt thou defile the Name of thy God: *for* I am the Lord.
22 Thou shalt not lie with the male as one lieth with a woman: *for* it is abominacion.
23 *Thou shalt not also lie with anie beast to be defiled therewith, nether shal anie woman stand before a beast, to lie downe thereto: *for* it is " abominacion.
24 Ye shal not defile your selues in anie of these things: for in all these the nacions are defiled, which I wil cast out before you:
25 And the land is defiled: therefore I wil
m visit the wickednes thereof vpon it, and the land n shal vomet out her inhabitants.
26 Ye shal kepe therefore mine ordinances, and my iudgements, and commit none of these abominacions, *aswel* he that is of the same countrey, as the strāger that soiourneth among you.
27 (For all these abominacions haue the men of the land done, which were before you, and the land is defiled:
28 And shal not the land spue you out if ye defile it, as it o spued out the people yt were before you?)
29 For whosoeuer shal commit anie of these abominacions, the persones that do *so*, shal p be cut of from among their people.
30 Therefore shal ye kepe mine ordinances that ye do not anie of the abominable customes, which haue bene done before you, and that ye defile not your selues therein: *for* I am the Lord your God.

h Because the idolaters, among whome Gods people had dwelt & shulde dwel, were giuen to these horrible incests, God chargeth his to beware of the same.
i By seig thine affection more bent to her sister the to her.
Chap.20,18.
k Or whiles she hathe her floures.
Chap.20,2. 2.kin.23,10.
" Ebr. of thy sede.
" Or, to make the passe
l Which was an idole of ye Ammonites, vnto whome they burned and sacrificed their childrē, 2 King.23,10.
Chap. 20, 15.
" Or, cōfusion.
m I wil punishe the land where such incestuous mariages & pollutions are suffred.
n He compareth the wicked to euil humours and surfeting, which corrupt ye stomacke and oppresse nature, and therefore muste be cast out by vomet.
o Bothe for their wicked mariages, vnnatural copulations, idolatrie or spiritual whoredome with Mólech, and suche like abominacions.
p Ether by ye ciuile sworde, or by some plague that God wil send vpon suche.

CHAP. XIX.

1 *A repeticion of sondrie lawes and ordinances.*

1 AND the Lord spake vnto Mosés, saying,
2 Speake vnto all the Congregacion of the children of Israél, and say vnto them, *Ye shal be a holy, for I the Lord your God *am* holy.
3 ¶ Ye shal feare euerie man his mother & his father, and shal kepe my Sabbaths: *for* I am the Lord your God.
4 ¶ Ye shal not turne vnto idoles, nor make you molten gods: I am the Lord your God.
5 ¶ And when ye shal offer a peace offring vnto the Lord, ye shal offer it b frely.
6 *It shalbe eaten the day ye offer it, or on the morowe: & that which remaineth vntil the third day, shal be burnt in the fire.
7 For if it be eaten the third day, it shalbe vncleane, it shal not be c accepted.
8 Therefore he that eateth it, shal beare his iniquitie, because he hathe defiled the halowed thing of the Lord, and that persone shal be cut of from his people.
9 ¶ *When ye reape ye haruest of your land, ye shal not reape euerie corner of your field, nether shalt thou gather the " glainings of thy haruest.
10 Thou shalt not gather the grapes of thy vineyarde *cleane*, nether gather euery grape of thy vineyarde, *but* thou shalt leaue them for the poore and for the stranger: I am the Lord your God.
11 ¶ Ye shal not steale, nether d deale falsely, nether lie one to another.
12 ¶ *Also ye shal not sweare by my Name falsely, nether shalt thou defile the Name of thy God: I am the Lord.
13 ¶ Thou shalt not do thy neighbour " wrōg, nether robbe *him*. *The worckemās hire shal not abide with thee vntil the morning.
14 ¶ Thou shalt not curse the deafe, *nether put a stumbling blocke before the blinde, but shalt feare thy God: I am the Lord.
15 ¶ Ye shal not do vniustely in iudgement. *Thou shalt not fauour the persone of the poore, nor honour the persone of the mighty, *but* yu shalt iudge thy neighbour iustly.
16 ¶ Thou shalt not e walke *about* with tales among thy people. Thou shalt not f stād against the blood of thy neighbour: I am the Lord.
17 ¶ Thou shalt not hate thy brother in thine heart, *but* thou shalt plainely rebuke thy neighbour, " and suffre him not to sinne.
18 ¶ Thou shalt not auenge, nor be mindeful *of wrong* against the childrē of thy people, *but shalt loue thy neighbour as thy selfe: I am the Lord.
19 ¶ Ye shal kepe mine ordinances. Thou shalt not let thy cattel gendre with g o*thers* of diuers kīdes. Thou shalt not sowe thy field with mingled *sede*, nether shal a garment of diuers things, *as* of linen and wollen come vpon thee.
20 ¶ Whosoeuer also lieth and medleth with a woman that is a bonde maid, afianced to a housband, and not redemed,

Chap.11,44. & 20,7. 1 pet. 1,16.
a That is, voide of all pollution, idolatrie, and superstition bothe of soule and body.
b Of your owne accorde.
Chap.7,16.
c To wit, of God.
Chap. 23,22.
" Or, gatherings & leasings.
d In that wc is committed to your credit.
Exod.20,7. deut.5,11. mat.5,34.
" Or, oppresse him by violēce.
Deu. 24, 14. tob.4,15.
Deut.27,18.
Exod.23,3. deut.1,17. & 16,16. prou.24,23. iam.2,2.
e As a slanderer, backbiter or quarelpiker.
f By consenting to his death, or conspiring with the wicked
" Ebr. suffre not sinne vpon him.
Mat.5,43. rom.13,9. gal.5,14. iam.2,8.
g As a horse to leape an asse, or a mule a mare.

nor

" Ebr. a beating shalbe. Some rede they shalbe beaten.

nor fredome giuen her,"she shalbe scourged, *but* they shal not dye, because she is
not made fre.
21 And he shal bring for his trespas offring
vnto the Lord, at the dore of the Tabernacle of the Congregacion, a ram for a
trespas offring.
22 Then the Priest shal make an atonemēt
for him with the ram of the trespas offring before the Lord, cōcerning his sinne which he hath done, and pardon shalbe giuen him for his sinne which he hathe
committed.
23 ¶ Also when ye shal come into the land,
and haue planted euerie tre for meat, ye
[h] shal counte the frute thereof as vncircūcised: thre yere shal it be vncircumcised vnto you, it shal not be eaten:

h It shal be vncleane, as ẏ thing which is not circumcised.

24 But in the fourth yere all the frute
thereof shal be holy to the praise of the
Lord.
25 And in the fift yere shal ye eat of the
frute of it that it may"yelde to you the encrease thereof: I am the Lord your God.

"Or, that God may multiplie.

26 ¶ Ye shal not eat *the flesh* with the blood,
ye shal not vse witch craft, nor [i] obserue
times.

i To measure luckie or vnluckie daies.

27 *Ye shal not [k] cut round the corners of
your heades, nether shalt thou" marre the
tuftes of thy beard.

Chap.21,5.
k As did the Gentiles in signe of mourning.
"*Or, cut, or teare*

28 *Ye shal not cut your flesh for the"dead,
nor make anie printe of a [l] marke vpon
you: I am the Lord.

Deut.14,1.
" *Ebr. soule, or persone.*
l By whipping your bodies or burning markes therī.

29 ¶ Thou shalt not make thy daughter
commen, to cause her to be a [m] whore, lest
the land also fall to whoredome and the
land be ful of wickednes.

m As did the Cyprians, and Locrenses.

30 ¶ Ye shal kepe my Sabbaths and reuerence my Sanctuarie: I am the Lord.
31 ¶ Ye shal not regarde them that worke
ẇ spirits, *nether sothesaiers: ye shal not
seke *to them* to be defiled by them: I am the
Lord your God.

1.Sam.28,8.

32 ¶ Thou shalt [n] rise vp before the hore-
hed, and honour the persone of the olde
man, and dread thy God: I am the Lord.

n In token of reuerence.

33 ¶ And if a stranger soiourne with thee
in your land, ye shal not"vexe him.
34 * *But* the strāger that dwelleth with you,
shalbe as one of your selues, & thou shalt
loue him as thy selfe: for ye were strangers
in the land of Egypt: I am the Lord your
God.

"*Or, do him wrong.*
Exod.22,21.

35 ¶ Ye shal not do vniustly in iudgement,
in [o] line, in weight, or in measure.
36 *You shal haue iuste balances, true weightes, a true [p] Ephāh, and a true Hin. I
am ẏ Lord your God, which haue broght
you out of the land of Egypt.
37 Therefore shal ye obserue all mine ordinances, and all my iudgements, and do
them: I am the Lord.

o As in measuring the grounde.
Prou.11,1.& 16,11.& 20,10
p By these two measures he meaneth all other, of Ephāh, read Exod.16,36, & of Hin Exod.29,40.

CHAP. XX.

2 They that giue of their sede to Mólech, must dye.
6 They that haue recours to sorcerers. 10 The man
that committeth adulterie. 11 Incest, or fornicacion
with the kinred or affinitie. 24 Israél a peculiar peo-
ple to the Lord.

1 AND the Lord spake vnto Mosés,
saying,
2 Thou shalt say also to the children of Israél, *Whosoeuer *he be* of the children of
Israél, or of the strāgers that dwel in Israél, that giueth his children vnto [a] Mólech, he shal dye the death, the people of
the land shal stone him to death.

Chap.18,21.
a By Mólech he meaneth anie kinde of idole, Chap.18, 21.

3 And I [b] wil set my face against that man
and cut him of from among his people, because he hathe giuen his childrē vnto Mó
lech, for to defile my Sanctuarie, and to
pollute mine holy Name.

b Read Chap. 18,21.

4 And if the [c] people of the land hide their
eyes, *and* winke at that man when he giueth his children vnto Mólech, and kil
him not,
5 Then wil I set my face against that man,
and against his familie, & wil cut him of,
and all that go a whoring after him to
commit whoredome with Mólech, from
among their people.

c Thogh the people be negligent to do their duetie & defend Gods right, yet he wil not suffre wickednes to go vnpunished

6 ¶ If anie turne after suche as worke with
spirits, & after sothesaiers, to go a [d] whoring after them, then wil I set my face a-
gainst that persone, and wil cut him of
from among his people.

d To esteme sorcerers or cōiurers is spiritual whoredome, or idolatrie.

7 ¶ Sanctifie your selues therefore, *and be
holy, for I am the Lord your God.

Chap.11,44.
1.pet.1,16.

8 Kepe ye therefore mine ordinances, and
do them. I am the Lord which doeth sanctifie you.
9 ¶ *If *there be* anie that curseth his father or
his mother, he shal dye the death: *seing* he
hathe cursed his father & his mother, [e] his
blood *shal be* vpon him.

Exod.21,17.
pro.20,20.
mat.15,4.
e He is worthy to dye.

10 ¶ *And the man that committeth adulterie with another mans wife, because he
hathe committed adulterie with his neighbours wife, the adulterer and the adul-
teres shal dye the death.

Deu.22,22.
ioh.8,4.

11 And the man that lieth with his fathers
wife, *because* he hathe vncouered his fathers *shame, thei shal bothe dye: their blood *shal be* vpon them.

Chap.18,8.

12 Also the man that lieth with his daughter in lawe, they bothe shal dye the death,
they haue wroght" abominacion, their
blood *shal be* vpon them.

"*Or, confusion.*

13 *The mā also that lieth with the male, as
one lieth with a woman, they haue bothe
committed abominacion: they shal dye
the death, their blood *shal be* vpon them.

Chap.18,22.

14 Likewise he that taketh a wife and her
mother, [f] committeth wickednes: thei
shal burne him and them with fire, that
there be no wickednes among you.

f It is an execrable and detestable thing.

Chap.18,9. 15 *Also the man that lieth with a beast,shal
dye the death,and ye shal slay the beast.
16 And if a woman come to anie beast, and
lie therewith, then thou shalt kil the womã and the beast:they shal dye the death,
their blood *shal be* vpon them.
17 Also the mã that taketh his sister,his fathers daughter, or his mothers daughter,
and seeth her shame & she seeth his shame, it is vilennie: therefore they shalbe
cut of in the sight "of their people, *because* he hathe vncouered his sisters shame,
he shal beare his iniquitie.
18 *The man also that lieth with a woman
hauing her" disease,& vncouereth her shame, & openeth her fountaine,and she opẽ
the fountaine of her blood,thei shalbe euẽ
bothe cut of from among their people.
19 Moreouer thou shalt not vncouer ỹ shame of thy mothers sister, * nor of thy fathers sister,because he hathe vncouered his
"kin:they shal beare their iniquitie.
20 Likewise the man that lieth with his fathers brothers wife,& vncouereth his vncles shame:they shal beare their iniquitie,
& shal dye g childles.
21 So the man that taketh his brothers wife,cõmitteth filthines, *because* he hathe vncouered his brothers h shame:they shal be
childles.
22 ¶ Ye shal kepe therefore all mine *ordinances & all my iudgements, and do thẽ,
that the land,whither I bring you to dwel
therein,*spue you not out.
23 Wherefore ye shal not walke in the maners of this nacion which I cast out before you:for they haue committed all these
things,*therefore I abhorred them.
24 But I haue said vnto you,ye shal inherit
their land, and I wil giue it vnto you to
possesse it, *euen* a land that i floweth with
milke & honie:I am the Lord your God,
ṽ haue separated you from *other* people.
25 *Therefore shal ye put differẽce betwene cleane beastes and vncleane,and betwene vncleane foules and cleane:nether shal
ye k defile your selues with beastes & foules,nor with anie *creping thing*, that ỹ grouͣ-
de brĩgeth forthe,which I haue separated
from you as vncleane.
26 Therefore shal ye be *holie vnto me:for
I the Lord am holie,and I haue separated
you frõ *other* people,ỹ ye shulde be mine.
27 ¶*And if a man or woman haue a spirit
of diuinaciõ,or sothesaying in them,they
shal dye the death: they shal stone thẽ to
death,their blood *shalbe* vpon them.

"Ebr. In the eies of the children of their people.

Chap.18,19. "Or,flowres.

"Ebr.flesh.

g They shalbe cut of from their people, & their children shal be taken as bastards:and not counted amõg the Israelites.

h Read Chap. 18,16.

Chap. 18, 26.

Chap. 18, 25.

Deut.9,5.

i Ful of abundance of all things.

Chap.11,3. deut.14,4.

k By eating them contrarie to my commandement.

Ver.7.

Deut.18,7. 1.Sam.28,7.

CHAP. XXI.

1 *For whome the Priests may lament. 6 How pure the Priests oght to be,bothe in them selues and in their familie.*

1 AND the Lord said vnto Mosés, Speake vnto the Priestes the sonnes of
Aarón, and say vnto them, Let none be
a defiled by the dead among his people,
2 But by his kinsemã that is nere vnto him:
to wit, by his mother, or by his father, or
by his sonne,or by his daughter,or by his
brother,
3 Or by his sister a b maid,that is nere vnto
him,which hathe not had a housband:for
her " he may lament.
4 He shal not lament for the c prince a-
mong his people,to pollute him selfe.
5 Thei shal not make * balde partes vpon their head, nor shaue of the lockes of
their beard,nor make anie cuttigs in their
flesh.
6 They shal be holy vnto their God, and
not pollute the Name of their God: for
the sacrifices of ỹ Lord made by fire, *and*
the bread of their God thei do offer:there
fore they shalbe holy.
7 Thei shal not take to wife an whore, or
d one polluted,nether shal thei marie a woman diuorced from her housband:for suche one *is* holy vnto his God.
8 Thou shalt e sanctifie him therefore, for
he offreth the f bread of thy God: he shal
be holy vnto thee:for I the Lord,which
sanctifie you, am holy.
9 ¶ If a Priests daughter fall to playe the
whore, she polluteth her father: *therefore*
shal she be burnt with fire.
10 ¶ Also ỹ hie Priest among his brethren,
(vpon whose head the anointing oyle was
powred, and hathe consecrated his hand
to put on the garments)shal not g vncouer his head,nor rent his clothes,
11 Nether shal he go to anie " dead body,
nor make him selfe vncleane by his father or by his mother,
12 Nether shal he go out of the h Sanctuarie,nor pollute the holy place of his God:
for the i croune of the anointing oyle of
his God *is* vpon him:I am the Lord.
13 Also he shal take a maid vnto his wife:
14 *But* a widowe, or a diuorced woman,or a
polluted, *or* an harlot, these shal he not
mary, but shal take a maid of his owne
k people to wife:
15 Nether shal he defile his l sede amõg his
people:for I am the Lord ṽ sanctifie him.
16 ¶ And ỹ Lord spake vnto Mosés, saying,
17 Speake vnto Aarón, and say, Whosoeuer of thy sede in their generacions hathe
anie blemishes,shal not preace to offer the
bread of his God:
18 For whosoeuer hathe anie blemish, shal
not come nere: *as* a man blinde or lame, or
that hathe m a flat nose, or that hathe anie
n misshapen *membre*,
19 Or a man that hathe a broken fote, or a
broken hand,
20 Or *is* croke backt,or bleare eied, o or hathe a blemish in his eie, or be skiruie, or
skabbed

a By touching the dead,lamenting, or being at their burial.

b For being maried she semed to be cut of from his familie.

"Ebr.he may be defiled.

c Onely the Priest was permitted to mourne for his next kinred.

Chap.19,27.

d Which haue an euil name or is defamed.

e Thou shalt counte them holy and reuerence them.

f The shewe bread.

g He shal vse no suche ceremonies as the mourners obserued.

"Or,to the houses of the dead.

h To go to the dead.

i For by his annointing he was preferred to the other Priests,& therefore colde not lament the dead, lest he shuld haue polluted his holy ointing.

k Not onely of his tribe but of all Israél.

l By maryng anie vnchaste or defamed woman.

m Which is deformed or bruised.

n As not of equal proporciõ, or hauing in nombre more or lesse.

o Or that hathe a web,or perle.

ſkabbed,or haue *his* ſtones broken.
21 None of the ſede of Aarón the Prieſt ẏ
hathe a blemiſh, ſhal come nere to offer ẏ
ſacrifices of the Lord made by fire,hauing
a blemiſh: he ſhal not preace to offer the
[p] bread of his God.
22 The bread of his God,*euen* of the [q] moſte holy,and [r] of the holy ſhal he eat:
23 But he ſhal not go in vnto the [ſ] vaile,nor
come nere the altar,becauſe he hathe a ble
miſh,leſt he pollute my Sanctuaries:for I
am the Lord that ſanctifie them.
24 Thus ſpake Moſés vnto Aarón, and to
his ſonnes,and to all the childrẽ of Iſraél.

p As the ſhewe bread, and meat offrings.
q As of ſacrifice for ſinne.
r As of the tenthes & firſt frutes.
ſ In to the Sãctuarie.

CHAP. XXII.

3 Who oght to abſtaine from eating the things that were offred. 19 What oblacions ſhulde be offred.

1 AND the Lord ſpake vnto Moſes,ſay-
ing,
2 Speake vnto Aarón, and to his ſonnes,
that they be [a] ſeparated from the holy
things of the children of Iſrael, and that
they pollute not mine holy Name in thoſe
things, which they halowe vnto me:I am
the Lord.
3 Say vnto them, Whoſoeuer *he be* of all
your ſede among your generacions after
you,that [b] toucheth the holy things which
the childrẽ of Iſraél halowe vnto ẏ Lord,
hauing his vnclennes vpon him, euẽ that
perſone ſhal be cut of from my ſight: I
the Lord.
4 *Whoſoeuer alſo of ẏ ſede of Aarón is
a leper,or hathe a rũning iſſue,he ſhal not
eat of the holy things vntil he be cleane:
and whoſo toucheth anie that is [c] vncleane *by reaſon* of the dead,or a man whoſe
iſſue of ſede runneth from him,
5 Or the man that toucheth anie creping
thing,whereby he may be made vncleane,
or a man, by whome he may take vnclennes, "whatſoeuer vnclennes he hathe,
6 The perſone that hathe touched ſuche,
ſhal therefore be vncleane vntil the euen,
and ſhal not eat of the holy things," except he haue waſhed his fleſh with water.
7 But when the ſunne is downe, he ſhal be
cleane, and ſhal afterward eat of the holy
things:for it is his "fode.
8 *Of a beaſt that dyeth, or is rent *with
beaſts*,whereby he may be defiled,he ſhal
not eat:I am the Lord.
9 Let them kepe therefore mine ordinance,leſt they beare *their* ſinne for it,and
dye for it,if they defile it: I the Lord ſanctifie them.
10 There ſhal no [d] ſtranger alſo eat of the
holy thing,nether [e] the geſt of the Prieſt,
nether ſhal an hired ſeruant eat of the holy thing:
11 But if the Prieſt bie anie with money,he
ſhal eat of it, alſo he that is borne in his
houſe: they ſhal eat of his meat.

a Meaning ẏ the Prieſts abſteine from eating,ſo long as they are polluted.
b To eat thereof.
Chap.15,2.
c By touching anie dead thĩg or being at burial of ẏ dead.
"Ebr.according to all his vncleanes.
"Or,vntil.
"Or,bread.
Exod.22,31. ezek.44,31.
d Which is not of the tribe of Leui.
e Some read,ẏ ſeruant which had his eare bored and wolde not go fre,Exod.21,6.

12 If the Prieſts daughter alſo be maried
vnto a [f] ſtranger,ſhe may not eat of the
holy offrings.
13 Notwihſtanding if the Prieſts daughter
be a widow or diuorced,and haue no childe,but is returned vnto her fathers houſe,
ſhe ſhal eat of her fathers bread,as ſhe did
in her* youth: but there ſhal no ſtranger
eat thereof.
14 ¶If a man eat of the holy thing vnwittingly, he ſhal put the [g] fifte parte thereunto, and giue it vnto the Prieſt with the
halowed thing.
15 So they ſhal not defile the holy things of
the children of Iſraél,which thei offer vnto the Lord.
16 Nether cauſe the *people* to beare the iniquitie *of their* [h] treſpas,while they eat their
holy thing:for I ẏ Lord do halow them.
17 ¶And ẏ Lord ſpake vnto Moſés,ſaying,
18 Speake vnto Aarón, and to his ſonnes,
and to all the children of Iſraél, and ſay
vnto them,Whoſoeuer *he be* of the houſe
of Iſraél,or of the ſtrangers in Iſraél,that
wil offer his ſacrifice for all their vowes,
and for all their fre offrings,ẇ they vſe to
offer vnto the Lord for a burnt offring,
19 *Ye ſhal offer* of your fre minde a male
without blemiſh of the beues, of the ſhepe,or of the goates.
20 Ye ſhal not offer anie thing ẏ hath a ble-
miſh:for ẏ ſhal not be acceptable for you.
21 *And whoſoeuer brĩgeth a peace offring
vnto the Lord to accompliſh his vow, or
for a fre offring, of the beues, or of ẏ ſhepe, his fre offring ſhal be perfect, no blemiſh ſhalbe in it.
22 Blinde,or broken,or maimed,or hauing
a "wenne,or ſkiruie,or ſkabbed:theſe ſhal
ye not offer vnto the Lord nor make an
offring by fire of theſe vpon the altar of
the Lord.
23 Yet a bullocke,or a ſhepe that hathe *anie*
*mẽbre ſuperfluous, or lackĩg,ſuche maieſt
thou preſent for a fre offring, but for a
vowe it ſhal not be accepted.
24 Ye ſhal not offer vnto ẏ Lord that which
is bruiſed or cruſhed, or broken, or cut
away,nether ſhal ye make *an offring thereof*
in your land,
25 Nether [i] of the hand of a ſtrãger ſhal ye
offer the bread of your God of anie of theſe, becauſe their corrupcion *is* in them,
there is a blemiſh in thẽ:*therefore* ſhal they
not be accepted for you.
26 ¶And ẏ Lord ſpake vnto Moſés,ſaying,
27 Whẽ a bullocke,or a ſhepe,or a goat ſhal
be broght forthe, it ſhalbe euẽ ſeuẽ daies
vnder his damme: and from the eight day
forthe, it ſhalbe accepted for a ſacrifice
made by fire vnto the Lord.
28 As for the cowe or the ewe,ye ſhal not
*kil her, and her yong *bothe* in one day.

f Who is not of the Prieſts kinred.
Chap.10,14.
g He ſhal giue that and a fift parte ouer.
h For if they did not offer for their errour,the people by their exãple might commit the like offence.
Deut.15,21. eccleſ.35,14.
"Or,warte.
Chap.21,18.
i Ye ſhal not receiue anie vnperfect thĩg of a ſtranger, to make it the Lords offring: which he calleth the bread of the Lord.
Deut.22,6.

29 So when ye wil offer a thanke offring vnto the Lord,ye ſhal offer willingly.
30 The ſame day it ſhal be eaten,ye ſhal
leaue* none of it vntil the morowe: I am
the Lord.

Chap.7,15.

31 Therefore ſhal ye kepe my commandements and do them:*for* I am the Lord.
32 Nether ſhal ye [k] pollute mine holy Name,but I wil be halowed among the children of Iſraél.I the Lord ſanctifie you,
33 Which haue broght you out of the land
of Egypt,to be your God:I am the Lord.

k For whoſoeuer doeth otherwiſe then God commandeth,polluteth his name.

CHAP. XXIII.

*2 The feaſts of the Lord. 3 The Sabbath. 5 The paſ-
ſeouer. 6 The feaſt of vnleauened bread. 10 The
feaſt of firſt frutes. 16 Witſontide. 24 The feaſt
of blowing trompets. 34 The feaſt of tabernacles.*

1 AND the Lord ſpake vnto Moſés,
ſaying,
2 Speake vnto the children of Iſraél, and
ſay vnto them, The feaſts of the Lord
which ye ſhal call the holy " aſſemblies,
euen theſe are my feaſts.

"Or,conuocatiõs.

3 *Six daies " ſhal worke be done,but in the
ſeuenth day *ſhalbe* the Sabbath of reſt, an
holy " conuocacion: ye ſhal do no worke
therein,it is the Sabbath of the Lord,in all
your dwellings.

Exod.20,9.
"Or,ye may worke.
"Or,aſſemblie.

4 ¶ Theſe are ý feaſts of the Lord, *and* holy conuocacions , which ye ſhal proclame
in their [a] ſeaſons.
5 In the firſt moneth, *and* in the fourtenth
day of the moneth at euening *ſhalbe* the
Paſſeouer of the Lord.
6 And on the fiftenth day of this moneth
ſhalbe the feaſt * of vnleauened bread vnto
the Lord:ſeuen daies ye ſhal eat vnleauened bread.

a For the Sabbath was kept euerie weke,& theſe other were but kept once euerie yere.

Exod.12,15.
nom.28,17.

7 In the firſt day ye ſhal haue an holy conuocacion: ye ſhal do no [b] ſeruile worke
therein.
8 Alſo ye ſhal offer ſacrifice made by fire
vnto the Lord ſeuen daies, *and* in the [c] ſeuenth day *ſhalbe* an holy conuocacion : ye
ſhal do no ſeruile worke *therein.*
9 ¶ And ý Lord ſpake vnto Moſés,ſaying,
10 Speake vnto the children of Iſraél , and
ſay vnto thẽ, When ye be come into the
land,which I giue vnto you,and reape the
harueſt thereof,thẽ ye ſhal bring "a ſheafe
of the firſt frutes of your harueſt vnto the
Prieſt,
11 And he ſhal ſhake the ſheafe before
the Lord , that it may be acceptable for
you:the morowe after the [d] Sabbath, the
Prieſt ſhal ſhake it.
12 And that day when ye ſhake the ſheafe,
ſhal ye prepare a lambe without blemiſh
of a yere olde,for a burnt offring vnto the
Lord:
13 And the meat offring thereof *ſhalbe* two
[e] tenth deales of fine floure mingled with
oyle,for a ſacrifice made by fire vnto the

b Or bodelie labour , ſaue about that ý one muſte eat, Exod.12,16.

c The firſt day of the feaſt & ý ſeuenth were kept holy: in the reſt thei might worke, except anie feaſt were entermedeled, as ý feaſt of vnleauened bread ý fifteth day, & the feaſt of ſheaues the ſixtenth day.

"Or, an omer: reade Deut.24, 19. ruth. 2,15. pſal.129,7.

d That is, the ſeconde Sabbath of ý Paſſeouer.

e Which is,ý fift parte of an Ephah or two omers. read Exod.16,16.

Lord of ſwete ſauour : and the drinke offring thereof the fourth part [f] of an Hin
of wine.
14 And ye ſhal eat nether bread nor parched corne, nor " grene eares vntil the ſelfe ſame day that ye haue broght an offring vnto your God:*this ſhal be* a lawe for
euer in your generacions and in all your
dwellings.

f Read Exod. 29,40.

"Or,ful eares.

15 ¶ Ye ſhal count alſo to you from the morowe after the [g] Sabbath , *euen* from the
day that ye ſhal bring the ſheafe of the
ſhake offring,ſeuen " Sabbaths, thei ſhalbe
complete.
16 Vnto the morowe after the ſeuenth Sab
bath ſhal ye nombre fifty daies: then ye
ſhal bring a newe meat offring vnto the
Lord.

g That is, the ſeuẽth day after the firſt Sabbath of the Paſſeouer.

"Or,wekes.

17 Ye ſhal bring out of your habitacions
bread for the ſhake offring : thei ſhalbe
two *loaues* of two tenth deales of fine
floure , *which* ſhalbe baken with [h] leauen
for firſt frutes vnto the Lord.
18 Alſo ye ſhal offer with the bread ſeuen
lambes without blemiſh of one yere olde, and a yong bullocke and two rams:
thei ſhal be for a burnt offring vnto the
Lord, with their meat offrings and their
drinke offrings,for a ſacrifice made by fire of a ſwete ſauour vnto the Lord.

h Becauſe the Prieſt ſhulde eat them, as chap.7,13, and they ſhulde not be offred to ý Lord vpon the altar.

19 Then ye ſhal prepare an he goat for a
ſin offring,and two lambes of one yere olde for peace offrings.
20 And the Prieſt ſhal ſhake them to and
fro with the bread of the firſt frutes before the Lord , *and* with the two lambes:
thei ſhalbe holy to the Lord , for the
[i] Prieſt.
21 So ye ſhal proclame the ſame day, *that* it
may be an holy conuocacion vnto you:
ye ſhal do no ſeruile worke *therein*: *it ſhal
be* an ordinance for euer in all your dwellings,throughout your generacions.

i That is, offred to the Lord , and the reſt ſhuld be for ý Prieſts.

22 ¶ *And when you reape the harueſt of
your land,thou ſhalt not rid cleane ý corners of thy fielde when thou reapeſt , nether ſhalt thou make anie aftergathering
of thy harueſt,*but* ſhalt leaue them vnto
the poore and to the ſtranger : I am the
Lord your God.

Chap.19,9.
deu.24,19.

23 ¶ And ý Lord ſpake vnto Moſés,ſaying,
24 Speake vnto the children of Iſraél, and
ſay, In the [k] ſeuẽth moneth, *and* in the firſt
day of the moneth ſhal ye [l] haue a Sabbath,for the remembrance of [m] blowing
the trompets,an holy conuocacion.
25 Ye ſhal do no ſeruile worke *therein*,but
offer ſacrifice made by fire vnto the Lord.
26 ¶ And the Lord ſpake vnto Moſés,
ſaying,
27 The*tenth alſo of this ſeuenth moneth
ſhalbe a day of recõciliation:it ſhal be an
holy conuocacion vnto you, and ye ſhal
humble

k That is,about the end of September.

l Or an holyday to ý Lord.

m Which blowing was to put them in remẽbrance of the manifolde feaſts ý were in ý monethe,and of the Iubile.

Chap.16.30.
nom.29,7.

n By fasting.

n humble your soules,& offer sacrifice made by fire vnto the Lord.
28 And ye shal do no worke that same day:
for it is a day of reconciliacion,to make an
atonement for you before the Lord your
God.
29 For euerie persone that humbleth not
him selfe that same day, shal euen be cut
of from his people.
30 And euerie persone that shal do anie
worke that same day, the same persone
also wil I destroye from amõg his people.
31 Ye shal do no maner worke *therefore*: *this*
shalbe a lawe for euer in your generacions,
throughout all your dwellings.
32 This shalbe vnto you a Sabbath of rest,
and ye shal hũble your soules:in the ninth
day of the moneth at euen, from o euen
to euen shal ye" celebrate your Sabbath.
33 ¶And ẏ Lord spake vnto Mosés,saying,
34 Speake vnto the children of Israél, and
say,*In the fiftiẽth day of this seuẽth moneth *shalbe* for seuen daies the feast of Tabernacles vnto the Lord.
35 In the first day *shalbe* an holy conuoca-
cion:ye shal do no seruile worke *therein*.
36 Seuen daies ye shal offer* sacrifice made
by fire vnto the Lord,*and* in the eight day
shalbe an holy conuocacion vnto you,and
ye shal offer sacrifices made by fire vnto
the Lord: it is the p solemne assemblie,
ye shal do no seruile worke *therein*.
37 These are ẏ feastes of the Lord(which
ye shal call holy conuocacions)to offer sacrifice made by fire vnto ẏ Lord, *as* burnt
offring, and meat offring, q sacrifice,and
drinke offrings,euerie one vpon his day,
38 Beside the Sabbaths of the Lord, & beside your gifts,and beside all your vowes,
and beside all your fre offrings, which ye
shal giue vnto the Lord.
39 But in the fiftienth day of the seuenth
moneth, whẽ ye haue gathered in the frute of the land, ye shal kepe an holy feast
vnto the Lord seuen daies: in the first day
shalbe a r Sabbath: likewise in the eight
day *shalbe* a Sabbath.
40 And ye shal take you in the first day the
frute of goodlie trees, branches of palme
trees,and the boughes of " thicke trees, &
willowes of the broke, and shal reioyce
before the Lord your God seuen daies.
41 So ye shal kepe this feast vnto the Lord
seuen daies in the yere,by a perpetual ordinance through your generacions:in the
seuenth moneth shal you kepe it.
42 Ye shal dwel in boothes seuen daies:all
that are Israelites borne, shal dwel in boothes,
43 That your posteritie may knowe that I
haue made the children of Israél to dwel
in f boothes, when I broght them out of
the lãd of Egypt:I am ẏ Lord your God.

o Which cõteineth a night and a day: yet thei toke it but for their natural day.
" Ebr. rest your Sabbath.
Nomb.29,12.
Iohn.7,37.
Exod.29,18.
p Or a day wherein the people are stayed from all worke.
q Or peace offring
r Or a solẽne feast.
" Or, of bowes thicke with leaues.
f In the wildernes, forasmuche as thei wolde not credit Iosúa and Caléb, when thei returned from spying the land of Canáan.

44 So Mosés declared vnto the children of
Israél the feastes of the Lord.

CHAP. XXIIII.

2 The oyle for the lampes. 5 The Shewebread. 14 The blasphemer shalbe stoned. 17 He that killeth shalbe killed.

1 AND the Lord spake vnto Mosés,
saying,
2 a Commande the children of Israél that
thei bring vnto thee pure oyle oliue beaten, for the light, to cause the lampes to
burne continually.
3 Without the vaile b of the Testimonie,
in the Tabernacle of the Congregacion,
shal Aarón dresse them, bothe euen and
morning before the Lord alwaies:*this shal-*
be a lawe for euer through your generacions.
4 He shal dresse the lampes vpon the* pure Candelsticke before the Lord perpetually.
5 ¶Also thou shalt take fine floure,& bake
twelue* cakes thereof:two c tenth deales
shal be in one cake.
6 And thou shalt set them in two rowes,six
in a rowe vpon the pure table before the
Lord.
7 Thou shalt also put pure incense vpõ the
rowes, that d in stede of the bread it may
be for a remembrance,*and* an offring made by fire to the Lord.
8 Euerie Sabbath he shal put thẽ in rowes
before the Lord euermore, *receauing them*
of the childrẽ of Israél for an euerlasting
couenant.
9 *And the *bread* shalbe Aarons & his sonnes, and thei shal eat it in the holy place:
for it is moste holy vnto him of the offrings of the Lord made by fire by a perpetual ordinance.
10 ¶And there went e out among the children of Israél the sonne of an Israelitish
woman,whose father was an Egyptian: &
this sonne of the Israelitish woman, and
a man of Israél stroue together in the
hoste.
11 So the Israelitish womans sonne f blasphemed the Name *of the Lord*,and cursed,
and thei broght him vnto Mosés(his mothers name also was Shelomíth, ẏ daughter of Dibrí,of the tribe of Dan)
12 And thei * put him in warde,til he tolde
them the minde of the Lord.
13 Then the Lord spake vnto Mosés, saying,
14 Bring the blasphemer without the hoste, and let all that heard him,* put their
hands vpon his head, and let all the Congregacion stone him.
15 And thou shalt speake vnto the children
of Israél, saying, Whosoeuer curseth his
God,shal g beare his sinne.
16 And he that blasphemeth the Name of

a Read Exod.27,20.
b Which vaile separated ẏ Holiest of all, where was ẏ Arke of the testimonie,frõ the Sãctuarie.
Exod.31,8.
Exod.25,30.
c That is,two Omers: read Exod 16,16.
d For it was burnt euerie Sabbath when the bread was taken away.
Exod.29,33.
chap.8,31.
mat.12,4.
e Out of his tente.
f By swearing or dispiting God.
Nomb.15,34
Deu.13,9.
& 17,7.
g Shalbe punished.

the Lord, shal be put to death: all the Cõgregacion shal stone him to death: aswel
the stranger, as he that is borne in the lãd:
when he blasphemeth the Name *of the*
Lord, let him be slaine.

Exod.21,12. deut.19,4.
"*Ebr. smiteth the soule of anie man.*
"*Ebr. soule for soule.*

17 ¶ * He also that " killeth anie man, he
shalbe put to death.
18 And he that killeth a beast, he shal restore it," beast for beast.
19 Also if a man cause *anie* blemish in his
neighbour: as he hathe done, so shal it be
done to him:

Exod.21,24. deut.19,21. mat.5,24.

20 * Breache for breache, eie for eie, tothe for tothe: suche a blemish as he hathe
made in anie, suche shalbe repaied to him.
21 And he that killeth a beast shal restore it:
but he that killeth a man shalbe slaine.

Exod.12,49.

22 Ye shal haue* one lawe: it shalbe aswel
for the stranger as for one borne in the
countrey: for I am the Lord your God.

h Because the punishment was not yet appointed by the Lawe for the blasphemer, Mosés consulted with the Lord, & tolde ỹ people what God commanded.

23 ¶ Then [h] Mosés tolde the children of
Israél, and thei broght the blasphemer
out of the hoste, and stoned him with stones: so the children of Israél did as the
Lord had commanded Mosés.

CHAP. XXV.

2 The Sabbath of the seuenth yere. 8 The Iubile in the fiftieth yere. 14 Not to oppresse their brethren. 23 The sale, and redeming of lands, houses and persones.

1 AND the Lord spake vnto Mosés in
mount Sinái, saying,
2 Speake vnto the children of Israél, and
say vnto them, When ye shal come into
the land which I giue you, the * land shal
"kepe Sabbath vnto the Lord.

Exod.23,10.
"*Ebr. shal rest a rest.*
a The Iewes begã the cõut of this yere in September: for then all the frutes were gathered.

3 [a] Six yeres thou shalt sowe thy field, and
six yeres thou shalt cut thy vineyard, and
gather the frute thereof.
4 But the seuenth yere shalbe a Sabbath of
rest vnto the land: *it shalbe* the Lords Sabbath: thou shalt nether sowe thy field, nor
cut thy vineyarde.

b By reason of the corne ỹ fel out of the eares the yere past.
c Or, which thou hast separated from thy selfe, and consecrated to God for the poore.
d That which ỹ lãd bringeth forthe in her rest.

5 That which groweth of it [b] owne accorde of thy haruest, thou shalt not reape,
nether gather the grapes that thou haste
[c] left vnlaboured: *for* it shalbe a yere of
rest vnto the land.
6 And the [d] rest of the lãd shalbe meat for
you, *euen* for thee, & for thy seruant, & for
thy maid, & for thy hyred seruant, and for
the stranger that soiourneth with thee:
7 And for thy cattel, and for the beastes
that are in thy land shal all the increase
thereof be meat.

"*Or, weekes.*
e In the beginning of the 50. yere was the Iubile, so called, because the ioyful tidings of libertie was publikely proclaimed by the sounde of a cornet.

8 ¶ Also thou shalt nomber seuen "Sabbaths
of yeres vnto thee, *euen* seuẽn times seuen
yere: and the space of the seuen Sabbaths
of yeres wil be vnto thee nine and fourty
yere.
9 [e] Then thou shalt cause to blowe the
trumpet of the Iubile in the tenth *day* of
the seuenth moneth: euen in the day of
the reconciliacion shal ye make the trumpet blowe, through out all your land.
10 And ye shal halowe that yere, *euen* the
fiftieth yere, and proclaime libertie in the
land to all the [f] inhabitants thereof: it
shal be the Iubile vnto you, and ye shal
returne euerie man vnto his [g] possession,
and euerie man shal returne vnto his familie.

f Which were in bondage.
g Because the tribes shulde nether haue their possessions, or families diminished nor cõfonded.

11 This fiftieth yere shalbe a yere of Iubile vnto you: ye shal not sowe, nether reape
that which groweth of it selfe, nether gather *the grapes* thereof, that are left vnlaboured.
12 For it is the Iubile, it shal be holy vnto
you: ye shal eat of the increase thereof
out of the field.
13 In the yere of this Iubile, ye shal returne euerie man vnto his possession.
14 And whẽ thou sellest oght to thy neighbour, or byest at thy neighbours hand, ye
shal [h] not oppresse one another:
15 *But* according to the nomber of [i] yeres
after the Iubile thou shalt bye of thy
neighbour: *also* according to the nomber
of the yeres of the reuenues, he shal sel
vnto thee.

h By deceit or otherwise.
i If the Iubile to come be nere, thou shalt sel better cheape: if it be farre of, dearer.

16 According to the multitude of yeres,
thou shalt encrease the price thereof, and
according to the fewnes of yeres, thou
shalt abate the price of it: for the nomber
of [k] frutes doeth he sel vnto thee.

k And not the ful possession of the land.

17 Oppresse not ye therefore anie man his
neighbour, but thou shalt feare thy God:
for I am the Lord your God.
18 ¶ Wherefore ye shal obey mine ordinãces, and kepe my lawes, and do them, and
ye shal dwel in the land " in saftie.

"*Or, boldely without feare.*

19 And the land shal giue her frute, and
ye shal eat your fil, and dwel therein in
saftie.
20 And if ye shal say, What shal we eat the
seuenth yere, for we shal not sowe, nor ga-
therin our increase?
21 I wil "send my blessing vpon you in the
sixt yere, and it shal bring forthe frute for
thre yeres.

"*Ebr. I wil commande.*

22 And ye shal sowe the eight yere, and eat
of the olde frute vntil the ninth yere: vntil
the frute thereof come, ye shal eat the
olde.
23 ¶ Also the land shal not be solde to be
[l] cut of *from the familie*: for the land is mine, *and* ye be but strangers and soiourners
with me.
24 Therefore in all the land of your possession ye shal [m] grante a redempcion for
the land.

l It colde not be solde for euer, but must returne to the familie in the Iubile.
m Ye shal sel it on condiciõ that it may be redemed.

25 ¶ If thy brother be impouerished, & sel
his possession, thẽ his redemer shal come,
euen his nere kinsman, and bye out that
which his "brother solde.

"*Or, kinsman.*

26 And if he haue no redemer, but " hathe
gotten and founde to bye it out,

"*Ebr. his hand hathe gotten.*

27 Then

n Abating the money of the yeres past, and paying for the rest of the yeres to come.

27 Then shal he n counte the yeres of his
sale, and restore the ouerplus to the man,
to whome he solde it: so shal he returne
to his possession.
28 But if he can not get sufficient to restore
to him, then that which is solde, shal remaine in the hād of him that hathe boght
it, vntil the yere of the Iubile: and in the
Iubile it shal come o out, and he shal returne vnto his possession.

o Frō his hādes that boght it.

29 Likewise if a man sel a dwelling house
in a walled citie, he may bye it out againe
within a whole yere after it is solde: within a yere may he bye it out.
30 But if it be not boght out within the space of a ful yere, then the house that is in
the walled citie, shalbe stablished, p as cut
of *from the familie*, to him that boght it,
throughout his generacions: it shal not go
out in the Iubile.

p That is, for euer. read ver. 23.

31 But the houses of villages, which haue
no walles rounde about them, shalbe estemed as the field of the countrie: they may
be boght out againe, and shal " go out in
the Iubile.

" Or, returne.

32 Notwithstanding, the cities of the Leuites, *and* the houses of the cities of their
possession, may the Leuites redeme" at all
seasons.

" Ebr for euer.

33 And if a mā purchase of the Leuites, the
house that was solde, and the citie of their
possession shal go out in the Iubile: for yͤ
houses of the cities of yͤ Leuites are their
possession among the children of Israél.
34 But the field of the q suburbes of their cities, shal not be solde: for it is their perpetual possession.

q Where the Leuites kept their cattel.

35 ¶Moreouer if thy brother be impouе-
rished, and r fallen in decay with thee,
thou shalt releue him, and *as* a strāger and
soiourner, so shal he liue with thee.
36 *Thou shalt take no vsurie of him, nor
vantage, but thou shalt feare thy God,
that thy brother may liue with thee.
37 Thou shalt not giue him thy money to
vsurie, nor lend him thy vitailes for increase.

r In ebr. it is, if his hād shake: meaning if he stretch forthe his hand for helpe as one in miserie.
Exod 22,25. deu 23,19. prouer.28,8. ezek.18,8. & 22,12.

38 I am the Lord your God, which haue
broght you out of the lād of Egypt, to giue you the land of Canáan, *and* to be your
God.
39 ¶*If thy brother also *that dwelleth* by
thee, be impouerished, and be solde vnto
thee, thou shalt not compel him to serue
as a bonde seruant,

Exod.21,2. deu.15,12. ier.34,14.

40 *But* as an hyred seruant, and as a soiourner he shal be with thee: he shal serue
thee vnto the yere of the Iubile.
41 Thē shal he departe from thee, *bothe* he,
and his children with him, and shal returne vnto his familie, and vnto the possession of his fathers shal he returne:
42 For they are my seruants, whome I
broght out of the land of Egypt: they shal
not s be solde as bonde men are solde.

s Vnto perpetual seruitude.

43 *Thou shalt not rule ouer him cruelly,
but shalt feare thy God.

Eph.6,9. col.4,1.

44 Thy bonde seruant also, and thy bonde
maid, which thou shalt haue, *shal be* of the
heathen that are roūde about you: of thē
shal ye bye seruants and maids.
45 And moreouer of the children of the
strangers, that are soiourners among you,
of them shal ye bye, and of their families
that are with you, which they begate in
your land: these shalbe your t possession.

t For thei shal not be boght out at the Iubile.

46 So ye shal take them as inheritance for
your children after you, to possesse them
by inheritance, ye shal vse their labours
for euer: but ouer your brethren the children of Israél ye shal not rule one ouer a-
nother with crueltie.
47 ¶If a " soiourner or a stranger *dwelling*
by thee get *riches*, and thy brother by him
be impouerished, and sel him selfe vnto
the stranger or soiourner *dwelling* by thee,
or to the stocke of the strangers familie,

" Ebr. If his hād take holde.

48 After that he is solde, he may be boght
out: one of his brethren may bye him out,
49 Or his vncle, or his vncles sōne may bye
him out, or *anie* of the kinred of his flesh
among his familie, may redeme him: e-
ther if he can u get *so muche*, he may bye
him selfe out.

u If he be able.

50 Then he shal reken with his byer from
the yere that he was solde to him, vnto the
yere of Iubile: and the money of his sale
shalbe according to the nomber of x yeres: according to the time of an hyred
seruant shal he be with him.

x Which remaine yet to yͤ Iubile.

51 If there be manie yeres behinde, according to them he shal giue againe for his
deliuerance, of the money that he was
boght for.
52 If there remaine but fewe yeres vnto the
yere of Iubile, thē he shal coūte with him,
and according to his yeres giue againe
for his redemption.
53 He shalbe with him yere by yere as an
hyred seruāt: he shal not rule cruelly ouer
him in thy y sight.
54 And if he be not redemed thus, he shal
go out in the yere of Iubile, he, and his
children with him.

y Thou shalt not suffre him to intreat him rigorously, if yͤ knowe it.

55 For vnto me the children of Israél *are*
seruants: they are my seruants, whome
I haue broght out of the land of Egypt: I
am the Lord your God.

CHAP. XXVI.

1 Idolatrie forbidden. 3 A blessing to them that kepe the cōmandemēts. 14 The curse to those that breake them. 42 God promiseth to remembre his couenant.

1 YE shal make you none idoles nor
grauen image, nether reare you vp
anie *piller, nether shal ye set" anie image
of stone in your lād to bowe downe to it: for

Exod.20,4. deu.5,8. psal 97,7.
" Or, stone hauing anie imagerie.

I am the Lord your God.
Chap.19,30.
2 Ye shal kepe my Sabbaths, and *reuerence my Sanctuarie: I am the Lord.
Deu.28,1.
3 ¶*If ye walke in mine ordinances, and
kepe my commandements, and do them,
a By promesing abundance of earthly things he stirreth the mindes to consider the riche treasures of ÿ spiritual blessings.
4 I wil then send you [a] raine in due season,
and the land shal yelde her increase, and
the trees of the field shal giue their frute.
5 And your threshing shal reache vnto the
vintage, and the vintage shal reache vnto
sowing time, and you shal eat your bread
Iob 11,19.
in plenteousnes, and* dwel in your land
safely.
6 And I wil send peace in the land, and ye
shal slepe and none shal make you afraied:
"Ebr. I wil cause the euil beast to cease.
b Ye shal haue no warre.
also I "wil rid euil beasts out of the land,
and the [b] sworde shal not go through your
land.
7 Also ye shal chase your enemies, and they
shal fall before you vpon the sworde.
Iosh 23,10.
8 *And fiue of you shal chase an hundreth,
and an hundreth of you shal put ten thousand to flight, and your enemies shal fall
before you vpon the sworde.
"Ebr I wil turne vnto you.
c Perfourme that which I haue promised.
9 For" I wil haue respect vnto you, & make you encrease, & multiplie you, and [c] e-
stablish my couenant with you.
10 Ye shal eat also olde store, and cary out
olde because of the newe.
Ezek.37,26.
2.cor.6,16.
d I wil be daily present with you.
11 *And I wil set my [d] Tabernacle among
you, and my soule shal not lothe you.
12 Also I wil walke among you, and I wil
be your God, and ye shal be my people.
13 I am the Lord your God which haue
broght you out of the land of Egypt, that
ye shulde not be their bondmen, and I ha-
e I haue set you at ful libertie, where as before ye were as beasts tied in bãdes.
ue broken the [e] bondes of your yoke, and
made you go vpright.
14 ¶*But if ye wil not obey me, nor do all
these commandements,
Deu.28,15.
lament.2,17.
mal.2,2.
15 And if ye shal despise mine ordinances,
ether if your soule abhorre my Lawes, so
that ye wil not do all my commãdemẽts,
but breake my [f] couenant,
f Which I made with you in chosing you to be my people.
"Or, an hasty plague.
16 Then wil I also do this vnto you, I
wil appoint ouer you" fearfulnes, a consumption, and the burning ague to consume the eies, and make the heart heauie, and you shal sowe your sede in vaine:
for your enemies shal eat it:
g Read Chap. 17,10.
17 And I wil set [g] my face against you, and
ye shal fall before your enemies, and they
Prouer.28,1.
that hate you, shal reigne ouer you,* and
ye shal flee when none pursueth you.
18 And if ye wil not for these *things* obey
h That is, more extremely.
me, then wil I punish you [h] seuen times
more, according to your sinnes,
19 And I wil breake the pride of your power, and I wil make your heauen as [i] yrõ,
i Ye shal haue drought & barennes, Agge 1,10.
"Or, labour.
& your earth as brasse:
20 And your "strẽgth shalbe spent in vaine:
nether shal your land giue her increase,
nether shal the trees of the land giue
their frute.
21 ¶And if ye walke [k] stubbernely against
k Or, as some read, by fortune, imputing my plagues to chãce and fortune.
me, and wil not obey me, I wil then bring
seuen times mo plagues vpon you, according to your sinnes.
22 I wil also send wilde beastes vpon you,
l Of your children. 2. King. 17,25.
which shal [l] spoile you, and destroy your
cattel, and make you fewe in nomber: so
m Because none dare passe thereby for feare of beastes.
your hye [m] wayes shalbe desolate.
23 Yet if by these ye wil not be reformed
by me, but walke stubbernely against me,
24 Then wil I also walke *stubbernely a-
2.Sam.22,27.
psal.17,26.
gainst you, and I wil smite you yet seuen
times for your sinnes:
25 And I wil send a sworde vpon you, that
shal auenge ỹ quarel of my couenãt: and
when ye are gathered in your cities, I wil
send ỹ pestilence among you, and ye shalbe deliuered into the hand of the enemie.
26 When I shal breake the [n] staffe of your
n That is, ỹ strẽgth, wherby the life is susteined, Ezek. 4, 16. & 5,16.
bread, then ten womẽ shal bake your bread
in one [o] ouen, and they shal deliuer your
bread againe by weight, and ye shal eat,
but not be satisfied.
o One ouen shalbe sufficient for ten families.
27 Yet if ye wil not for this obey me, but
walke against me stubbernely,
28 Thẽ wil I walke stubbernely in *mine* angre against you, & I wil also chastice you
seuẽ times *more* according to your sinnes.
29 And ye shal eat the flesh of your sonnes,
and the flesh of your daughters shal ye
deuoure.
30 I wil also destroye your hie places, and
2.Chro.34,7.
*cut away your images, and cast your car-
"Or, carions.
keises vpon the "bodies of your idoles, &
my soule shal abhorre you.
31 And I wil make your cities desolate, and
bring your Sanctuarie vnto noght, and
p I wil not accept your sacrifices.
[p] wil not smel the sauour of your swete
odoures.
32 I wil also bring the land vnto a wildernes, & your enemies, which dwel therein,
shal be astonished thereat.
33 Also I wil scatter you among the heathẽ,
q Signifyng that none enemie can come without Gods sending.
and [q] wil drawe out a sworde after you,
and your land shalbe waste, and your cities shalbe desolate.
34 Then shal the lãd enioye her *Sabbaths,
Chap.25,8.
as long as it lieth voyde, and ye shalbe in
your enemies land: then shal the land rest,
and enioye her Sabbaths.
35 All the daies that it lieth voyde, it shal
r Which I cõmãded you to kepe.
rest, because it did not rest in your [r] Sabbaths, when ye dwelt vpon it.
36 And vpon them that are left of you, I wil
"Or, cowardnes.
send euen a" faintenes into their hearts in
the land of their enemies, & the sounde of
a leafe shaken shal chase them, and they
s As if their enemies did chase them.
shal [s] flee as fleing from a sworde, & they
shal fall, no man pursuing them.
37 They shal fall also one vpon an other,
as before a sworde, thogh none pursue
them, and ye shal not be able to stand be-

fore your enemies:
38 And ye shal perish among ẏ heathen, &
the land of your enemies shal eat you vp.
39 And they that are left of you, shal pine
away for their iniquitie, in your enemies
lãds, & for the iniquities of their fathers
shal they pine away with [t] them also.

t Forasmuche-as they are culpable of their fathers fautes, they shalbe punished aswel as their fathers.

40 Then thei shal confesse their iniquitie,
and ẏ wickednes of their fathers for their
trespas, which they haue trespased against
me, and also because thei haue walked
stubbernely against me.
41 Therefore I wil walke stubbernely against thẽ, and bring them into the land of
their enemies: so thẽ their vncircumcised
hearts shal be humbled, and thẽ they shal
"willingly beare *the punishmẽt of* their iniquitie.

"Or praye for their sinne.

42 Then I wil remembre my couenant
with Iaakób, and my couenant also with
Izhák, and also my couenant with Abrahám wil I remember, and wil remember
the land.
43 [u] The land also *in the meane season* shalbe
left of them, & shal enioye her Sabbaths
while she lieth waste without them, but
they shal willingly suffre *the punishment* of
their iniquitie, because thei dispised my
lawes, & because their soule abhorred mine ordinances.

u Whiles they are captiues, and without repentance.

44 Yet notwithstanding this, when they
shal be in the land of their enemies, *I
wil not cast them away, nether wil I abhorre them, to destroy them vtterly, *nor* to
breake my couenant with them: for I am
the Lord their God:

Deu.4,31. rom.11,29.

45 But I wil remembre for them the [x] coue
nant of olde when I broght them out of
ẏ land of Egypt in the sight of the heathẽ
that I might be their God: I am the Lord.

x Made to their forefathers.

46 These are the ordinances, & the iudgements, & the lawes, which the Lord made
betwene him, and the children of Israél
in mount [y] Sinái, by the hand of Mosés.

y Fifty daies after they came out of Egypt.

CHAP. XXVII.

2 Of diuers vowes, and the redemption of the same.
28 A thing separate from the vse of man can not be
solde, nor redemed, but remaineth to the Lord.

1 MOreouer the Lord spake vnto Mosés, saying,
2 Speake vnto ẏ childrẽ of Israél, & say vnto thẽ, If anie mã shal make a [a] vowe of a
persone vnto ẏ Lord, by [b] thy estimaciõ,
3 Then thy estimacion shalbe *thus*: a male
frõ twenty yere olde vnto sixty yere olde
shalbe by thy estimacion euẽ fifty [c] shekels
of siluer, after the shekel of the Sãctuarie.
4 But if it be a female, then thy valuacion
shalbe thirty shekels.
5 And from fiue yere olde to twenty yere
olde thy valuacion shalbe for the male
twẽty shekels, & for ẏ female ten shekels.
6 But from a [d] moneth olde vnto fiue yere
olde, thy price of the male shalbe fiue shekels of siluer, and thy price of the female,
thre shekels of siluer.

a As of his sonne or his daughter.
b Which art the Priest.
c Read the value of the shekel, Exod.30,13.
d He speaketh of those vowes whereby ẏ fathers dedicated their children to God, which were not of suche force, but thei might be redemed from thẽ.

7 And from sixty yere olde and aboue, if
he be a male, then thy price shal be fiftene
shekels, and for the female ten shekels.
8 But if he be poorer [e] then thou hast estemed *him*, thẽ shal he present him selfe before the Priest, & the Priest shal value him,
according to the abilitie of him ẏ vowed, *so* shal the Priest value him.

e If he be not able to pay after thy valuation.

9 And if *it be* a [f] beast, whereof men bring
an offring vnto the Lord, all that one giueth of suche vnto the Lord, shal be holy.

f Which is cleane, Chap.11,2.

10 He shal not alter it nor chãge it, a good
for a bad, nor a bad for a good: and if he
change beast for beast, then *bothe* this and
ẏ, which was chãged for it, shalbe [g] holy.

g That is, consecrate to the Lord.

11 And if *it be* anie vncleane beast, of ẇ mẽ
do not offer a sacrifice vnto ẏ Lord, he shal
then present the beast before the Priest.
12 And the Priest shal value it, whether it be
good or bad: *and* as thou valuest it, *which
art* the Priest, so shal it be.
13 But if he wil bie it againe, then he shal
giue the fift parte of it more, aboue thy
valuacion.
14 ¶ Also whẽ a man shal dedicate his house
to be holy vnto ẏ Lord, thẽ the Priest shal
value it, whether it be good or bad, & as
ẏ Priest shal prise it, "so shal the value be.

"Ebr. so shal it stand.

15 But if he that sanctified it, wil redeme
his house, then he shal giue thereto the
fift parte of money more then thy estimacion, and it shalbe his.
16 If also a man dedicate to the Lord anie
groũde of his inheritance, then shalt thou
esteme it according to the [h] sede thereof:
an [i] Homer of barlie sede *shalbe* at fiftie
shekels of siluer.
17 If he dedicate his field *immediately* frõ
ẏ yere of Iubile, it shal be worthe as thou
doest esteme it.

h Valuing the price thereof, according to the sede that is sowen, or by the sede ẏ it doeth yelde.
i Homer is a measure conteining 10 Epháhs: read of Epháh Exod.16,16.

18 But if he dedicate his field after ẏ Iubile, thẽ the Priest shal rekẽ him the money
according to the yeres that remaine vnto
the yere of Iubile, and it shalbe abated by
thy estimacion.
19 And if he that dedicateth it, wil redeme
the field, then he shal put the fift parte of
the price, that thou estemedst it at, thereunto, and it shal remaine his.
20 And if he wil not redeme the field, but
the Priest [k] sel the field to another man, it
shalbe redemed nomore.

k For their owne necessitie or godlie vses.

21 But the field shalbe holie to the Lord,
when it goeth out in the Iubile, as a field
[l] separate from commune vses: the possession thereof shalbe the Priestes.

l That is, ẇ is dedicate to the Lord ẇ a curse to him that doeth turne it to his priuate vse Nõ.21,2. deut.13,17. iosh.6,17.

22 If a man also dedicate vnto the Lord a
field which he hathe boght, which is not
of the grounde of his inheritance,
23 Thẽ the Priest shal set the price to him,

Vers 12. m The Priests valuacion.

as*thou estemest it, vnto the yere of Iubile, and he shal giue m thy price the same
day, *as a thing* holy vnto the Lord.
24 *But* in the yere of Iubile, the field shal returne vnto him, of whome it was boght:
to him, *I say*, whose inheritāce ȳ land was.
25 And all thy valuacion shalbe according
to the skekel of.* the Sanctuarie : a shekel
conteineth twenty gerahs.
26 ¶*Notwithstanding the first borne of
ȳ beastes, because it is the Lords first borne, none shal dedicate suche, be it bullocke, or shepe: *for* it is the n Lords.
27 But if it be an vncleane beast, then he
shal redeme it by thy valuacion, and giue
the fift parte more thereto: & if it be not
redemed, then it shal be solde, according
to thy estimacion.
28 *Notwithstādīng, nothing separate frō
the cōmune vse that a man doeth separate
vnto the Lord of all that he hathe (whether it be man or beast, or land of his inheritance) may be solde nor redemed: *for* e-
uerie thing seperate from the cōmune vse
is moste holy vnto the Lord.
29 Nothing separate from the cōmune vse,
which shalbe separate frō man, shal be redemed, *but* o dye the death.
30 Also all the tithe of the land *bothe* of the
sede of the ground, *and* of the frute of the
trees is the Lords: *it is* holy to the Lord.
31 But if a man wil redeme *anie* of his tithe,
he shal adde the p fift parte thereto.
32 And euerie tithe of bullocke, and of shepe, *and* of all that goeth vnder the q rod,
the tenth shalbe holy vnto the Lord.
33 He shal not loke if it be good or bad, nether shal he change it: els if he change it,
bothe it, and that it was changed withall,
shalbe holy, *and* it shal not be redemed.
34 These are the cōmandements which the
Lord commāded by Mosés vnto the children of Israél in mount Sinái.

Exod.30,13. nom.3,47. ezek.45,12.
Exod.13,2.& 22,29. nom. 3,13.
n It was the Lords already
Iosh.6,19.
o It shal remaine without redemption.
p Besides the value of the thing it selfe.
q All that ẇ is nombred: that is, euerie teth, as he falleth by tale without acception or respect.

THE FOVRTHE BOKE OF Mosés, called* Nombers.

*So called because of the diuersitie and multitude of nombrings ẇ are here chiefly conteined.

THE ARGVMENT.

FOrasmuche as God hathe appointed that his Church in this worlde shalbe vnder the crosse, bothe because they shulde learne not to put their trust in worldely things, and also fele his comforte, when all other helpe faileth: he did not straight way bring his people, after their departure out of Egypt, into the land which he promised them: but led them to and fro for the space of fourtie yeres, and kept them in continual exercises before they enioyed it, to trye their faith, and to teache thē to forget the worlde and to depend on him. Which tryal did greately profit to discerne the wicked and the hypocrites from the faithful and true seruants of God, who serued him with pure heart, where as the other preferring their carnal affections to Gods glorie, and making religion to serue their purpose, murmured when they lacked to content their lustes, and despised them whome God had appointed rulers ouer them. By reason whereof they prouoked Gods terrible iudgements against them, and are set forthe as a moste notable example for all ages to beware how they abuse Gods worde, preferre their owne lustes to his wil, or despise his ministers. Notwithstanding God is euer true in his promes, and gouerneth his, by his holy Spirit, that ether they fall not to suche inconueniences, or els returne to him quickely by true repentance: and therefore he continueth his graces toward them, he giueth them ordinances and instructions, aswel for religion as outward policie: he preserueth them against all craft and conspiracie, and giueth them manifolde victories against their enemies. And to auoyd all controuersies that might arise, he taketh away the occasiōs, by diuiding among all the tribes, bothe the land, which they had wonne, & that also which he had promised, as semed best to his godlie wisdome.

CHAP. I.

2 Mosés and Aarón with the twelue princes of the tribes are commanded of the Lord to nomber them that are able to go to warre. 49 The Leuites are exempted for the seruice of the Lord.

1 THe Lord spake againe
vnto Mosés in ȳ wilder-
nes of a Sinái, in the Tabernacle of the Congre-
gaciō, in the first *day* of ȳ
b seconde moneth, in the
seconde yere after they were come out of
the land of Egypt, saying,
2 *Take ye the summe of all the Congregacion of the children of Israél, after their
families, *and* housholdes of their fathers
with the nomber of their names: *to wit*, all
the males, "man by man:
3 From twentie yere olde and aboue, all
that go forthe to the warre in Israél, thou
and Aarón shal nomber them, throughout their armies.
4 And with you shalbe c men of euerie tribe, suche *as are* the heads of the house of
their fathers.
5 And these are the names of the men
that

a In that place of the wildernes ȳ was nere to mount Sinái
b Which conteineth part of April, & parte of Maie.
Exod.30,12.
"*Ebr. by their heades.*
c That is, the chiefest mā of euerie tribe.

d And assist you when ye nōber the people.

that shal[d] stād with you, of *the tribe of* Reubén, Elizúr, the sonne of Shedeúr:
6 Of Simeón, Shelumiél the sonne of Zurishaddái:
7 Of Iudáh, Nahshón the sonne of Amminadáb:
8 Of Issachár, Nethaneél, the sonne of
Zuár:
9 Of Zebulún, Eliáb, the sonne of Helón:
10 Of the children of Ioséph: of Ephráim, Elishamá the sonne of Ammihúd: of
Manasséh, Gamliél, the sonne of Pedah-
zúr:
11 Of Beniamín, Abidán the sonne of Gideoní:
12 Of Dan, Ahiézer, the sonne of Ammishaddái:
13 Of Ashér, Pagiél, the sonne of Ocrán:
14 Of Gad, Eliasáph the sonne of Deuél:
15 Of Naphtalí, Ahirá the sonne of Enán.
16 These were famous in the Congregacion, [e] princes of the tribes of their fathers, & heades ouer thousands in Israél.

e Or captaines, & gouernors.

17 ¶ Thē Mosés and Aarón toke these men
which are expressed by *their* names.
18 And they called all the Congregacion
together, in the first *day* of the secōde moneth, who declared [f] their kinreds by their
families, & by the houses of their fathers,
according to the nomber of *their* names,
from twentie yere olde and aboue, man by
man.

f In shewing euerie mā his tribe, & his ancesters.

19 As the Lord had commanded Mosés, so
he nombred them in the wildernes of Sinái.
20 So were the sonnes of ‖ Reubén Israels
eldest sonne by their generacions, by
their families, & by the houses of their fa
thers, according to the nomber of *their*
names, man by man, euerie male from twē
tie yere olde and aboue, as many as ʹ went
forthe to warre:

‖ These are § names of the twelue tribes, as first of Reubén.

ʹ Or, *as were able to beare weapons.*

21 The nomber of them, *I say*, of the tribe
of Reubén, *was* six & fourtie thousand, &
fiue hundreth.
22 Of the sonnes of ‖ Simeón by their generacions, by their families, & by the houses of their fathers, the summe thereof
by the nomber of *their* names, man by mā,
euerie male from twentie yere olde and
aboue, all that went forthe to warre:

‖ Simeón.

23 The summe of them, *I say*, of the tribe
of Simeón *was* nine and fiftie thousand, &
thre hundreth.
24 ¶ Of the sonnes of ‖ Gad by their generacions, by their families, & by the houses
of their fathers, according to the nomber
of *their* names, from twentie yere olde and
aboue, all that went forthe to warre:

‖ Gad.

25 The nomber of them, *I say*, of the tribe
of Gad *was* fiue and fourtie thousand, and
six hundreth and fiftie.
26 ¶ Of the sonnes of ‖ Iudáh by their generaciōs, by their families, & by the houses of their fathers, according to the nomber of *their* names, from twentie yere olde
and aboue, all that went forthe to warre:

‖ Iudáh.

27 The nomber of them, *I say*, of the tribe
of Iudáh *was* threscore & fourtene thousand, and six hundreth.
28 ¶ Of the sonnes ‖ of Issachár by their
generacions, by their families, & by the
houses of their fathers, according to the
nomber of *their* names, from twentie yere
olde & aboue, all that wēt forthe to warre:

‖ Issachár.

29 The nomber of them *also* of the tribe
of Issachár *was* foure and fiftie thousand
and foure hundreth.
30 ¶ Of the sonnes of ‖ Zebulún, by their
generacions, by their families, & by the
houses of their fathers, according to the
nomber of *their* names, from twentie yere
olde and aboue, all that went forthe to
warre:

‖ Zebulún.

31 The nomber of them *also* of the tribe of
Zebulún *was* seuen and fiftie thousand &
foure hundreth.
32 ¶ Of the sonnes of Ioséph, *namely* of
the sonnes of ‖ Ephráim by their generacions, by their families, & by the houses
of their fathers, according to the nomber
of *their* names, from twentie yere olde &
aboue, all that went forthe to warre:

‖ Ephráim.

33 The nomber of them *also* of the tribe of
Ephráim *was* fourtie thousand and fiue
hundreth.
34 ¶ Of the sonnes of ‖ Manasséh by their
generacions, by their families, & by the
houses of their fathers, according to the
nomber of *their* names, from twentie yere
olde and aboue, all that went forthe to
warre:

‖ Manasséh.

35 The nomber of them *also* of the tribe
of Manasséh *was* two & thirtie thousand
and two hundreth.
36 Of the sonnes of ‖ Beniamín by their
generacions, by their families, & by the
houses of their fathers, according to the
nōber of *their* names, frō twentie yere olde & aboue, all that wēt forthe to warre:

‖ Beniamín.

37 The nomber of them *also* of the tribe
of Beniamín *was* fiue and thirtie thousand and foure hundreth.
38 Of the sonnes of ‖ Dan by their genera
cions, by their families, & by the houses
of their fathers, according to the nomber of *their* names, from twentie yere olde & aboue, all that went forthe to warre:

‖ Dan.

39 The nomber of them *also* of the tribe
of Dan *was* threscore and two thousand
and seuen hundreth.
40 ¶ Of the sonnes of ‖ Ashér by their generaciōs, by their families, & by the houses of their fathers, according to the nōber of *their* names, from twentie yere olde
and aboue, all that went forthe to warre:

‖ Ashér.

41 The nombre of them *also* of the tribe of
Ashér *was* one and fourtie thousand and
fiue hundreth.

‖Naphtalí.

42 ¶ Of the childrẽ of ‖Naphtalí, by their
generacions, by their families, & by the
houses of their fathers " according to the
nomber of *their* names, from twentie yere
olde and aboue, all that went to the warre.
43 The nomber of them *also* of the tribe of
Naphtalí, *was* thre and fiftie thousand, &
foure hundreth.

"Or, *the* counte.

44 These are the "summes which Mosés, &
Aarón nombred, and the Princes of Israél: the twelue men, *which* were euerie one
for the house of their fathers.
45 So *this* was all the summe of the sonnes of
Israél, by the houses of their fathers, from
twentie yere olde and aboue, all that wẽt
to the warre in Israél,
46 And all they were in nõber six hũdreth
& thre thousand, fiue hundreth and fiftie.
47 But the Leuites, after the tribes of their
fathers were not nombred among g them.
48 For the Lord had spoken vnto Mosés,
and said,
49 Onely thou shalt not nomber the tribe
of Leuí, nether take the summe of them
among the children of Israél:
50 But thou shalt appoint the Leuites o-
uer the Tabernacle of the Testimonie,
and ouer all the instruments thereof, and
ouer all things that belong to it: they shal
beare the Tabernacle, and all the instruments thereof, and shal minister in it,
and shal " dwel round about the Tabernacle.

g Which were warriers, but were appoited to the vse of ỹ Tabernacle.

"Ebr. campe.

THE FIGVRE OF THE TABERNACLE ERECTED, AND OF THE TENTES PITCHED ROVNDE ABOVT IT.

A B The lẽgth of the court, of an hundreth cubites on the Southe side, which in this figure is called midi: in the ẇ space were twẽtie pillers of fiue cubites high, to ỹ ẇ were tied ỹ curtaines, to shut and close vp ỹ court: ỹ North side called Septentrion was all alike.
C D The Westside called Occident, was fiftie cubites broad, wherein were ten pillers of like height with the other, whereunto were fastened the curtaines to close that side. The Eastside also called Orient was fiftie cubites broad. A B.
Thus the court was fiftie cubites longer then it was broad. Thei entred into the court on ỹ Eastside and before the gate was an hanging of twentie cubites long. F G fastened on foure pillers, and on the sides thereof to make it close, were curtaines of fiftene cubites long, E F & G H, which on euerie side were fastened on thre pillers, as this figure sufficiẽtly declareth.

51 And when the Tabernacle goeth forthe,
the Leuites shal take it downe: and when
the Tabernacle is to be pitched, the Leuites shal set it vp: for the [h] stranger that
cometh nere, shal be slaine.

h Whosoeuer is not of the tribe of Leui.

52 Also the children of Israél shal pitch
their tents, euerie man in his campe, and
euerie man vnder his stáderd throughout
their armies.
53 But the Leuites shal pitch round about
the Tabernacle of the Testimonie, lest
vengeance [i] come vpon the Congregacion of the children of Israél, & the Leuites shal take the charge of the Tabernacle of the Testimonie.

i By not hauing due regard to ẏ Tabernacle of the Lord.

54 So the children of Israél did according
to all that the Lord had commanded Mosés: so did thei.

CHAP. II.

2 *The ordre of the tents, and the names of the captaines of the Israelites.*

1 AND the Lord spake vnto Mosés, &
to Aarón, saying,
2 [a] Euerie man of the childrẽ of Israél shal
campe by his standerd, *and* vnder the ensigne of their fathers house: farre of about
the Tabernacle of the Congregaciõ shal
thei pitch.

a In the twelue tribes were foure principal standerds, so that euerie thre tribes had their standerd.

3 On the Eastside towarde the rising of the
sunne, shal thei of the standerd of the hoste of Iudáh pitch according to their armies: & Nahshón the sonne of Amminadáb *shalbe* ["] captaine of the sonnes of
Iudáh.

" Or, prince.

4 And his hoste and the nomber of them
were seuenty and foure thousand and six
hundreth.
5 Next vnto him shal thei of the tribe [b] of
Issachár pitch, and Nethaneél the sonne
of Zuár *shalbe* the captaine of the sonnes
of Issachár:

b Iudáh, Issachár & Zebulún the sones of Leáh were of the first stáderd.

6 And his hoste, and the nomber thereof
were foure and fiftie thousand, and foure
hundreth.
7 *Then* the tribe of Zebulún, and Eliáb the
sonne of Helón, captaine ouer the sonnes
of Zebulún:
8 And his hoste, and the nomber thereof
seuen and fiftie thousand and foure hundreth:
9 The whole nomber of the [c] hoste of Iudáh *are* an hundreth foure score and six
thousand, & foure hundreth according to
their armies: thei shal first set forthe.

c Of them ẇ were cõteined vnder that name.

10 ¶ On the Southside *shalbe* the stáderd of
the hoste [d] of Reubén according to their
armies, & the captaine ouer the sonnes of
Reubén *shalbe* Elizúr the sonne of Shedeúr.

d Reubén and Simeón ẏ sonnes of Leáh, & Gad the sonne of Zilpáh her maid, were of the seconde standerd.

11 And his hoste, and the nomber thereof
six and fourtie thousand & fiue hundreth.
12 And by him shal the tribe of Simeón
pitch, and the captaine ouer the sonnes of
Simeón *shalbe* Shelumiél the sonne of
Zurishaddái:
13 And his hoste, and the nomber of them,
nine and fiftie thousand & thre hundreth.
14 And the tribe of Gad, and the captaine
ouer the sonnes of Gad *shalbe* Eliasáph
the sonne of ["] Deuél:

" Or, Reuél.

15 And his hoste and the nomber of them
were fiue and fourtie thousand, six hũdreth
and fiftie.
16 All the nomber of the campe of Reubén *were* an hundreth and one and fiftie
thousand, & foure hundreth and fiftie according to their armies, and thei shal set
forthe in the seconde place.
17 ¶ Then the Tabernacle of the Congregacion shal go *with* the hoste of ẏ Leuites,
in the [e] middes of the campe as thei haue
pitched, so shal thei go forwarde, euerie
man in his ordre according to their standerds.

e Because it might be in equal distance from echeone, and all indifferently haue recours thereunto.

18 ¶ [f] The stáderd of the cãpe of Ephráim
shalbe toward the West accordĩg to their
armies: and the captaine ouer the sonnes
of Ephráim *shalbe* Elishamá the sonne of
Ammihúd:
19 And his hoste and the nomber of them
were fourtie thousand and fiue hundreth.
20 And by him *shalbe* the tribe of Manasséh, and the captaine ouer the sonnes of
Manasséh *shalbe* Gamliél the sonne of
Pedahzúr:

f Because Ephráim & Manasséh supplied ẏ place of Ioséph their father, thei are taken to be Rahels children: so thei & Beniamín make the third standerd.

21 And his hoste and the nomber of them
were two & thirtie thousand & two hundreth.
22 And the tribe of Beniamín, & the captaine ouer the sonnes of Beniamín *shalbe*
Abidán the sonne of Gideoní:
23 And his hoste, and the nomber of them
were fiue and thirtie thousand and foure
hundreth.
24 All the nomber of the campe of Ephráim *were* an hundreth and eight thousand
and one hundreth according to their armies, and thei shal go in the third place.
25 ¶ The standerd of the hoste of [g] Dan
shalbe toward the North according to
their armies: and the captaine ouer the
children of Dan *shalbe* Ahiézer the sonne
of Ammishaddái:

g Dan & Naphtalí the sonnes of Bilhá Raels maid, with Ashér the sonne of Zilpáh make ẏ fourth standerd.

26 And his hoste and the nomber of them
were two & thre score thousand and seuen
hundreth.
27 And by him shal ẏ tribe of Ashér pitch,
and the captaine ouer the sonnes of A-
shér *shalbe* Pagiél the sonne of Ocrán.
28 And his hoste and the nomber of them
were one and fourtie thousand and fiue
hundreth:
29 ¶ Thẽ the tribe of Naphtalí, & the captaine ouer the children of Naphtalí *shalbe* Ahirá the sonne of Enán:
30 And his hoste & the nomber of them

were thre and fiftie thousand and foure
hundreth.
31 All the nomber of the hoste of Dan *was*
an hundreth and seuen and fiftie thousand
and six hundreth: thei shal go hinmoste
with their standerds.

h Which were of twentie yeres and aboue.

32 ¶ These are the [h] summes of the childrẽ
of Israél by the houses of their fathers,
all the nomber of the hoste, according to
their armies, six hundreth and thre thousand, fiue hundreth and fiftie.
33 But the Leuites were not nombred amõg
the children of Israél, as the Lord had
commanded Mosés.
34 And the children of Israél did according to all that the Lord had commanded
Mosés: so thei pitched according to their
[i] standerds, and so thei iourneyed euerie
one with his families, according to the
houses of their fathers.

i For vnder euerie one of the foure pricipal stãderds were diuers signes to kepe euerie bande in ordre.

CHAP. III.

6 The charge and office of the Leuites. 12.35. Why the Lord separated the Leuites for him self. 16 Their nomber, families and captaines. 40 The firstborne of Israél is redemed by the Leuites. 47 The ouerplus is redemed by money.

a Or, families & kinreds.

1 These also were the [a] generacions of
Aarón & Mosés, in the day that the
Lord spake with Mosés in mount Sinái.
2 So these are the names of the sonnes of
Aarón, * Nadáb the firstborne, & Abihú,
Eleazár, and Ithamár.

Exod. 6, 23.

3 These are the names of the sonnes of Aarón the anointed Priests, whome *Mosés* did
* consecrate to minister in the Priests office.

Exod. 27, 3.

4 * And Nadáb and Abihú dyed [b] before
the Lord, when thei offred * strange fire
before the Lord in the wildernes of Sinái, and had no children: but Eleazár and
Ithamár serued in the Priests office in the
[c] sight of Aarón their father.

Leui. 10, 1. chap. 26, 61. 1. chro. 24, 2.
b Or, before the Altar.
Leui. 9, 24.
c Whiles their father liued.

5 Thẽ the Lord spake vnto Mosés, saying,
6 Bring the tribe of Leuí, and [d] set them
before Aarón the Priest that thei may serue him,

d Offer them vnto Aarón for the vse of the Tabernacle.

7 And take the charge with him, euen the
charge of the whole Congregacion [e] before the Tabernacle of the Congregacion to do the seruice of the Tabernacle.
8 Thei shal also kepe all the instrumẽts of
the Tabernacle of the Congregacion, &
haue the charge of the children of Israél
to do the seruice of the Tabernacle.

e Which apperteined to ẏ executig of ẏ hie Priests cõmaundement, to the ouer sight of the people, & to the seruice of the Tabernacle.

9 And thou shalt giue the Leuites vnto A-
arón & to his [f] sonnes: *for* thei are giuen
him frely from among the children of Israél.
10 And thou shalt appoint Aarón and his
sonnes to execute their Priests office: and
the [g] stranger that commeth nere, shal
be slaine.
11 ¶ Also the Lord spake vnto Mosés, saying,

f Aarons sonnes the Priests serued in the Sanctuarie in praying for ẏ people & offring sacrifice: ẏ Leuites serued for the inferior vses of the same.
g Anie that wolde minister, not being a Leuite.

12 Beholde, I haue euẽ taken ẏ Leuites frõ
among the children of Israél for all the
firstborne, that openeth the matrice amõg
the children of Israél, & the Leuites shalbe mine,
13 Because all the firstborne are mine: for
the same day, that I smote all the firstborne in the land of Egypt, * I sanctified vnto me all the firstborne in Israél, bothe
man and beast: mine thei shalbe: I am the
Lord.

Exod. 13, 1. & 34, 19. leui. 27, 26. chap. 8, 16. luk. 2, 23.

14 ¶ Moreouer the Lord spake vnto Mosés
in the wildernes of Sinái, saying,
15 Nomber the children of Leuí after the
houses of their fathers, in their families:
euerie male from a moneth olde & aboue
shalt thou nomber.
16 * Then Mosés nombred them according
to the worde of the Lord, as he was commanded.

Exod. 6, 17. chap. 26, 57. 1. chro. 6, 11. & 23, 6.

17 And these were the sonnes of Leuí by
their names, * Gershón, and Koháth, and
Merarí.

Gen. 46, 11.

18 Also these are the names of the sonnes
of Gershón by their families: Libní and
Shimeí.
19 The sonnes also of Koháth by their families: Amrám, and Izehár, Hebrón, and
Vzziél.
20 And the sonnes of Merarí by their families: Mahlí and Mushí. These are the
families of Leuí, according to the houses
of their fathers.
21 Of Gershón *came* the familie of the
Libnites & the familie of the Shimeites:
these are the families of the Gershonites.
22 The summe whereof ([h] after the nõber
of all the males from a moneth olde and
aboue) was counted seuen thousand and
fiue hundreth.

h Onelie nõbring the male children.

23 ¶ The families of the Gershonites shal
pitch behinde ẏ Tabernacle Westwarde.
24 The captaine and [*] ancient of the house of the Gershonites *shalbe* Eliasaph the
sonne of Laél.

* Or, father.

25 And the charge of the sonnes of Gershón in the Tabernacle of the Congregaciõ *shalbe* the [i] Tabernacle, & the pauillion, the couering thereof, & the vaile of
the dore of the Tabernacle of the Congregacion,

i Their charge was to cary ẏ couerigs & hangings of ẏ Tabernacle.

26 And the hanging of the courte, & the
vaile of the dore of the courte, which is
nere the Tabernacle, and nere the Altar
round about, and the cordes of it for all
the seruice thereof.
27 ¶ And of Koháth *came* the familie of the
Amramites, & the familie of the Izehari-
tes, and the familie of the Hebronites, and
the familie of the Vzzielites: these are
the families of the Kohathites.
28 The nomber of all the males from a
moneth olde & aboue *was* eight thousand

and

k Doing euerie one his duetie in the Sanctuarie.

and six hundreth, hauing the [k] charge of ye
Sanctuarie.
29 The families of the sonnes of Koháth
shal pitch on the Southside of the Tabernacle.
30 The captaine and ancient of the house,
and families of the Kohathites *shalbe* Elizaphán the sonne of Vzziél:
31 And their charge *shalbe* the [l] Arke, and
the table, and the candelsticke, and the altars, and the instruments of the Sanctuarie
that they minister with, and the vaile, and
all that serueth thereto.
32 And Eleazár the sonne of Aarón the
Priest *shalbe* [*] chief captaine of the Leuites, *hauing* the ouersight of them that haue the charge of the Sanctuarie.
33 ¶ Of Merarí *came* the familie of the
Mahlites, and the familie of the Mushites: these are the families of Merarí.
34 And the summe of them, according to
the nōber of all the males, from a moneth
olde and aboue *was* six thousand and two
hundreth.
35 The captaine and the anciēt of the house of the families of Merarí *shalbe* Zuriél
the sonne of Abihaíl: thei shal pitch on
the Northside of the Tabernacle.
36 And in the charge & custodie of the sonnes of Merarí *shalbe* [m] the boardes of the
Tabernacle, and the barres thereof, & his
pillers, & his sockets, & all the instrumēts
thereof, and all that serueth thereto,
37 With the pillers of the court round a-
bout, with their sockets, and their pins &
their cordes.
38 ¶ Also on the forefront of the Tabernacle toward the East, before the Tabernacle, *I say*, of the Cōgregacion Eastwarde shal Mosés and Aarón and his sonnes
pitch, hauing the charge of the Sanctuarie, [n] and the charge of the children of Israél: but the stranger that commeth nere,
shalbe slaine.
39 The whole summe of the Leuites, wc Mosés & Aarón nombred at the commandement of the Lord throughout their families, *euen* all the males from a moneth olde
& aboue, *was* two and twentie [o] thousand.
40 ¶ And the Lord said vnto Mosés, Nom
ber all the first borne that are males amōg
the children of Israél, from a moneth olde
and aboue, and take the nomber of their
names.
41 And thou shalt take the Leuites to me
[p] for all the first borne of the childrē of Israél (I *am* the Lord) and the cattel of the
Leuites for all the first borne of the cattel of the children of Israél.
42 And Mosés nombred, as the Lord commãded him, all the first borne of the children of Israél.
43 And all ye first borne males rehearsed by

l The chief things within the Sanctuarie were committed to the Kohathites.

*Or, prince of princes.

m The woodworke & ye rest of the instruments were cōmitted to their charge.

n That none shulde entre into the Tabernacle contrarie to Gods appointemēt.

o So that ye first borne of the children of Israél were mo by 273.

p So that now the Leuites shulde satisfie vnto the Lord for the first borne of Israél, saue for the 273, which were mo then the Leuites, for whome they payed money.

name (from a moneth olde and aboue, according to their nōber were two & twētie
thousand, two hundreth seuentie & thre.
44 ¶ And the Lord spake vnto Mosés, sayĩg,
45 Take the Leuites for all the first borne
of the children of Israél, and the cattel
of the Leuites for their cattel, & the Leuites shalbe mine, (I am the Lord)
46 And for the redeming of the two hundreth seuentie and thre, which are mo thē
the Leuites of the first borne of the children of Israél)
47 Thou shalt also take fiue shekels for e-
uerie persone: after the weight of the Sãctuarie shalt thou take it: * the shekel *con-*
teineth twentie gerahs.
48 And yu shalt giue the money, wherewith
the odde nomber of them is redemed, vnto Aarón and to his sonnes.
49 Thus Mosés toke the redempcion of
them that were redemed, being mo then
the Leuites:
50 Of the [q] firstborne of the children of
Israél toke he the money: *euen* a thousand
thre hundreth thre score and fiue *shekels* after the shekel of the Sanctuarie.
51 And Mosés gaue the money of thē that
were redemed, vnto Aarón & to his sōnes
according to the worde of the Lord, as the
Lord had commanded Mosés.

Exod.30,13. leu.27,25. chap.18,16. ezek.45,12.

q Of the two hundreth seuētie & thre, wc were more thē the Leuites.

CHAP. IIII.

5 The offices of the Leuites, when the hoste remoued. 46 The nōber of the thre families of Koháth, Gershón, and Merari.

1 AND the Lord spake vnto Mosés, and
to Aarón, saying,
2 Take the summe of the sonnes of Koháth frō among the sonnes of Leuí, after
their families, & houses of their fathers,
3 Frō [a] thirtie yere olde & aboue euen vntil
fiftie yere olde, all that entre into the assemblie to do the worke in the Tabernacle of the Congregacion.
4 This shalbe the office of the sonnes of
Koháth in the Tabernacle of the Cōgregacion *about* the Holiest of all.
5 ¶ When the hoste remoueth, then Aarón
& his sōnes shal come & take downe [b] the
couering vaile, & shal couer the Arke of
the Testimonie therewith.
6 And they shal put thereon a couering
of badgers skins, and shal spread vpon it a
cloth altogether of blewe silke, and put to
[c] the barres thereof:
7 And vpon the * table of shewe *bread* they
shal spread a cloth of blewe silke, and put
thereon the dishes, & ye *incens* cups, & goblets, & couerings to couer it [d] with, & the
bread shalbe thereon continually:
8 And they shal spread vpon them a couering of skarlet, and couer the same with a
couering of badgers skins, and put to, the
barres thereof.

a The Leuites were nombred after thre sorts: first at a moneth olde whē thei were consecrate to the Lord, next at 25 yere olde whē they were apoited to serue in ye Tabernacle, & at 30 yere olde to beare the burthēs of the Tabernacle.

b Which deuided the Sanctuarie from ye Holiest of all.

c That is, put thē vpon their shulders to carie it: for the barres of the Arke colde neuer be remoued, Exod. 25, 15.

Exod.25,30.

d Meaning to couer ye bread.

Exod.25,14. Exod.25,38.

9 Then they shal take a cloth of blewe silke, and couer the * candelsticke of light
with his lampes and his snoffers, * and his
snoffedishes, and all the oyle vessels thereof, which they occupie about it.
10 So they shal put it, and all the instrumēts
thereof in a couering of badgers skins,
and put it vpon the e barres.
11 Also vpon the golden f altar they shal
spreade a cloth of blewe silke, and couer
it with a couering of badgers skins, & put
to the barres thereof.
12 And they shal take all the instruments of
the ministerie wherewith they minister in
the Sanctuarie, and put *them* in a cloth of
blewe silke, and couer them with a couering of badgers skins, & put them on the
barres.

e The Ebrewe worde signifieth an instrument made of two staues or barres.
f Which was to burne incens: read Exod. 30,1.

13 Also they shal take away the ashes from
the g altar, & spread a purple cloth vpō it,
14 And shal put vpon it all the instruments
thereof, which they occupie about it: the
censers, the fleshhokes & the besomes, and
the basens, *euen* all the instruments of the
altar: & they shal spread vpō it a couering
of badgers skins, & put to the barres of it.
15 And whē Aarón & his sonnes haue made
an end of couering the h Sanctuarie, and
all the instruments of the Sanctuarie, at
the remouing of the hoste, afterwarde the
sonnes of Koháth shal come to beare it,
but they shal not i touche *anie* holy thing
lest thei dye. This is the charge of the sonnes of Koháth in the Tabernacle of the
Congregacion.

g Of the burnt offring.
h That is, in folding vp the things of the Sanctuarie, as the Arke, &c.
i Before it be couered.

16 ¶ And to the office of Eleazár the sonne
of Aarón the Priest *perteineth* the oyle for
the light, and the * swete incens and the
k dailie meat offring, and the * anointing
oyle, *with* the ouersight of all the Tabernacle, and of all that therein is, *bothe* in the
Sāctuarie & in all the instrumēts thereof.
17 ¶ And the Lord spake vnto Mosés and to
Aarón, saying,
18 Ye shal not l cut of the tribe of ŷ families
of ŷ Kohathites from among ŷ Leuites:
19 But thus do vnto them, that they may liue & not dye, when they come nere to the
moste holy things: let Aarón and his sonnes come and appoint m them, euerie one
to his office, and to his charge.
20 But let them not go in, to se when the
Sanctuarie is folden vp, lest they dye.
21 ¶ And ŷ Lord spake vnto Mosés, saying,
22 Take also the summe of the sonnes of
Gershón, euerie one by ŷ houses of their
fathers throughout their families:
23 From thirtie yere olde and aboue, vntil
fiftie yere olde shalt thou nōbre them, all
that n entre into ŷ assemblie for to do seruice in ŷ Tabernacle of ŷ Congregacion.
24 This shalbe the seruice of the families
of the Gershonites, to serue and to beare.

Exod. 30,34.
k Which was offred at morning and euening.
Exod.30,23.
l Committing by your negligence that the holy things be not wel wrapped, and so they by touching thereof perish.
m Shewing what part euerie man shal beare.
n Which were receiued into the companie of them that ministred in the Tabernacle of the Congregaciō.

25 They shal beare ŷ curtaines of the Tabernacle, & the Tabernacle of the Cōgregacion, his couering, and the couering of
badgers skins, that is on hie vpon it, and
ŷ vaile of the o dore of the Tabernacle of
the Congregacion:
20 The curtaines also of the court, and the
vaile of the entring in of the gate of the
court, p which is nere the Tabernacle &
nere the altar round about, with their cordes, and all the instrumentes for their seruice, and all that is made for them: so shal
they serue.

o Which vaile hāged betwene ŷ Sāctuarie and the court.
p Which court cōpassed bothe the Tabernacle of the Cōgregacion & ŷ altar of burnt offring.

27 At the commandement of Aarón and
his sonnes shal all the seruice of the sonnes of ŷ Gershonites be done, in all their
charges and in all their seruice, & ye shal
appoint them to kepe all their charges.
28 This is the seruice of the families of ŷ
sonnes of the Gershonites in the Tabernacle of the Congregacion, & their watch
shalbe vnder the q hand of Ithamár the
sonne of Aarón the Priest.
29 ¶ Thou shalt nomber the sonnes of Merarí by their families, & by the houses of
their fathers:
30 From thirtie yere olde & aboue, euen vnto fiftie yere olde, shalt thou nōber them,
all that entre into the assemblie, to do the
seruice of the Tabernacle of the Cōgregacion.
31 And this is their office & charge according to all their seruice in the Tabernacle of the Congregacion: the * boardes of
the Tabernacle with the barres thereof,
and his pillers, and his sockets.
32 And the pillers round about the court,
with their sockets and their pins, and their
cordes, ŵ all their instrumentes, euen for
all their seruice, & by r name ye shal rekē
the instruments of their office & charge.
33 This is the seruice of the families of the
sonnes of Merarí, according to all their
seruice in the Tabernacle of the Congregaciō vnder the hād of Ithamár the sonne of Aarón the Priest.

q Vnder the charge and ouersight.
Exod.26,15.
r Ye shal make an inuentorie of all the things, ŵ ye cōmit to their charge.

34 ¶ Then Mosés and Aarón and the princes of the Congregacion nombred the
sonnes of ŷ Kohathites, by their families
and by the houses of their fathers,
35 Frō thirtie yere olde & aboue, euen vnto
fiftie yere olde, all that entre into the assemblie for the seruice of the Tabernacle
of the Congregacion.
36 So the " nombers of them throughout
their families were two thousand, seuen
hundreth and fiftie.
37 These are the nombers of the families
of the Kohathites, all that serue in the
Tabernacle of the Congregacion, which
Mosés and Aarón did nomber according
to the commandemēt of the Lord by the
s hand of Mosés.

" Ebr. The nombred of them.
s God appointing Mosés to be ŷ minister & executer thereof.

38 Also

38 Also the nombers of the sonnes of Gershón throughout their families and houses of their fathers,
39 From thirtie yere olde and vpward, euen
vnto fiftie yere olde: all that entre into
the assemblie for the seruice of the Tabernacle of the Congregacion.
40 So the nombers of them by their families, & by the houses of their fathers
were two thousand six hũdreth & thirtie.
41 These are the nõbers of ỹ families of ỹ
sõnes of Gershón: of all that [t] did seruice
in the Tabernacle of the Congregacion,
whome Mosés & Aarón did nõber according to the commandement of the Lord.

t Which were of competent age to serue therein, that is, betwene 30. and 50.

42 ¶ The nõbers also of the families of the
sonnes of Merarí by their families, & by
the houses of their fathers,
43 Frõ thirtie yere olde & vpward, euẽ vnto
fiftie yere olde: all that entre into ỹ assemblie for the seruice of the Tabernacle of
the Congregacion.
44 So the nombers of them by their families were thre thousand, & two hundreth.
45 These are ỹ summes of ỹ families of the
sonnes of Merarí, whome Mosés & Aarón
nõbred according to the commandemẽt
of the Lord, by the hand of Mosés.
46 *So* all the nombers of the Leuites, which
Mosés, & Aarón, & the princes of Israél
nombred, by their families & by the houses of their fathers,
47 Frõ thirtie yere olde & vpward, euen to
fiftie yere olde, euerie one that came to do
[u] his duetie, office, seruice and charge in
the Tabernacle of the Congregacion.
48 So the nombers of them were eight
thousand fiue hundreth and foure score.
49 According to the "cõmandement of ỹ
Lord by ỹ hãd of Mosés did *Aarón* nõber
thẽ, euerie one according to his seruice, &
according to his charge. Thus *were* thei of
that tribe nõbred, as the Lord commãded
[x] Mosés.

u Whosoeuer of the Leuites that had any maner of charge in the Tabernacle.
"*Ebr. Accordĩg to the mouthe, or worde.*
x So that Mosés nether added nor diminished from that which ỹ Lord commanded him.

CHAP. V.

2 *The Leprous & the polluted shalbe cast forthe. 6 The purging of sinne 15 The tryal of the suspect wife.*

1 AND ỹ Lord spake vnto Mosés, sayĩg,
2 Commande the children of Israél ỹ
they *put out of the hoste euerie leper, and
euerie one ỹ hathe * an issue, & whosoeuer
is defiled by * the dead.
3 Bothe male and female shal ye put out:
"out of ỹ hoste shal ye put thẽ, that they de
file not their [a] tẽtes amõg whome I dwel.
4 And the children of Israél did so, and put
thẽ out of ỹ hoste, euen as ỹ Lord had cõ
manded Mosés, so did ỹ childrẽ of Israél.
5 ¶ And ỹ Lord spake vnto Mosés, saying,
6 Speake vnto the childrẽ of Israél, *Whẽ
a man or woman shal commit anie sinne
[b] that men commit, and trãsgresse against
the Lord, when that persone shal trespas,
7 Then they shal cõfesse their sinne which

Leuit.13,3.
Leu.15,2.
Leu.21,1.
"*Or, in a place out of the hoste.*
a There were thre maner tẽtes, of ỹ Lord, of ỹ Leuites, & of the Israelites.
Leu.6,3.
b Cõmit anie faute willigly.

thei haue done, and shal restore the dommage thereof * with his principal, and put
the fift parte of it more thereto, and shal
giue it vnto him, against whome he hathe
trespassed.
8 But if the [c] man haue no kinsman, to
whome he shulde restore the dommage,
the dommage shalbe restored to the Lord
for the Priests vse, besides the ram of the
atonement, whereby he shal make atonement for him.
9 And euerie offring of all the [d] holy things
of the childrẽ of Israél, which they bring
vnto the Priest, shalbe *his.
10 And euerie mans halowed things shal be
his: *that is*, whatsoeuer anie man giueth the
Priest, it shalbe his.

Leui.6,5.
c If he be dead, to whome the wrong is done, and also haue no kinsman.
d Or, things offred to the Lord, as first-frutes, &c.
Leu.10,12.

11 ¶ And ỹ Lord spake vnto Mosés, saying,
12 Speake vnto the children of Israél, and
say vnto them, If anie mãs [e] wife turne to
euil, and commit a trespas against him,
13 So that another man lie with her fleshly,
and it be hid frõ the eies of her housbãd,
and kept close, and yet she be defiled, and
there be no witnes against her, nether she
taken with the maner,
14 "If he be moued with a ielous minde, so
that he is ielous ouer his wife, which is
defiled, or if he haue a ielous minde, so
that he is ielous ouer his wife, which is
not defiled,
15 Then shal the man bring his wife to the
Priest, and bring her offring with her, the
tenth parte of an Epháh of barly meale,
but he shal not powre [f] oyle vpon it, nor
put incens thereon: for it is an offring of
ielousie, an offring for a remembrãce, calling the sinne to [g] minde:
16 And the Priest shal bring her, & set her
before the Lord.
17 Then the Priest shal take [h] the holy water in an earthẽ vessel, and of the dust that
is in the floore of the Tabernacle, *euen*
the Priest shal take it and put it into the
water.

e By breaking the band of mariage, and playing the harlot.
"*Ebr. If the spirit of ielousie come vpon him.*
f Onely in the sinne offring, & this offring of ielousie were nether oyle nor incense offred.
g Or making the sinne knowen, and not purging it.
h Which also is called the water of purification or sprinkeling, read Chap. 19, 9.

18 After, the Priest shal set the woman before the Lord, and vncouer the womans
head, and put the offring of the memorial
in her hands: it is the ielousie offring, and
the Priest shal haue bitter *and* [i] cursed water in his hand,
19 And the Priest shal charge her by an
othe, and say vnto the woman, If no man
haue lien with thee, nether thou hast turned to vnclennes from thine housband, be
fre from this bitter *and* cursed water.
20 But if thou hast turned from thine housband, and so art defiled, and some man hathe lien with thee beside thine housband,
21 (Then the Priest shal charge the womã
with an othe of cursing, and the Priest
shal say vnto the woman) The Lord make
thee to be [k] accursed, and detestable for

i It was so called by the effect, because it declared the woman to be accursed and turned to her destructiõ.
k Bothe because she had committed so hainous a faut, and forsware her selfe in denying the same.

the othe amōg thy people, & ỳ Lord cause thy thigh to "rott, and thy belly to swel:
22 And that this cursed water maie go into
thy bowels, to cause thy belly to swel, and
thy thigh to rott. Thē the woman shal answer, [l] Amen, Amen.
23 After, the Priest shal write these curses
in a boke, and shal [m] blot them out with
the bitter water,
24 And shal cause the woman to drinke
the bitter and cursed water, and the cursed water, *turned* into bitternes, shal entre
into her.
25 Thē the Priest shal take the ielousie offring out of the womans hand, & shal shake the offring before the Lord, and offer it
vpon the altar.
26 And the Priest shal take *an handful* of the
offring for a "memorial thereof, and burne
it vpon the [n] altar, and afterward make ỳ
woman drinke the water.
27 When he hathe made her drinke the water, (if she be defiled and haue trespassed
against her housbād) then shal the cursed
water, *turned* into bitternes, entre into her,
and her belly shal swel, and her thigh shal
rott, & the woman shalbe accursed amōg
her people.
28 But if the woman be not defiled, but be
"cleane, she shal be fre and shal cōceiue &
beare.
29 This is the lawe of ielousie, when a wife turneth frō her housband & is defiled,
30 Or when a man is moued with a ielous
minde being ielous ouer his wife, then
shal he bring the woman before ỳ Lord,
and the Priest shal do to her according to
all this lawe,
31 And the man shalbe [o] fre from sinne, but
this woman shal beare her iniquitie.

"Ebr. to falle.

l That is, be it so, as thou wisshest, as psa. 41,14. deu. 27, 14.

m Shal wash the curses, ẘ are writen, in to the water in the vessel.

"Or, perfume.

n Where the incēse was offred.

"Or, innocent.

o The man might accuse his wife and not be reproued.

CHAP. VI.

2 The lawe of the consecraciō of the Nazarites. 24 The maner to blesse the people.

1 AND the Lord spake vnto Mosés, saying,
2 Speake vnto the children of Israél, and
say vnto them, When a man or a woman
doeth separate thē selues to vowe a vowe
of a [a] Nazarite to separate *him selfe* vnto
the Lord,
3 He shal absteine frō wine & strōg drinke, and shal drinke no sowre wine nor sowre drinke, nor shal drinke anie licour of
grapes, nether shal eat fresh grapes nor
dried.
4 As long as his abstinence endureth, shal
he eat nothing ỳ is made of the wine of ỳ
vine, nether the kernels, nor the huske.
5 While he is separate by his vowe, the *ra-
sure shal not come vpō his head, vntil the
dayes be out, in the which he separateth
him selfe vnto the Lord, he shalbe holie,
and shal let the lockes of the heere of his
head growe.
6 During the time that he separateth him
selfe vnto the Lord, he shal come at no
[b] dead body:
7 He shal not make him selfe vncleane at
the death of his father, or mother, brother,
or sister: for the consecracion of his God
is vpon [c] his head.
8 All the dayes of his separacion he shalbe
holy to the Lord.
9 And if anie dye sodēly by him, or he beware, then the [d] head of his consecracion
shalbe defiled, and he shal shaue his head
in the day of his clensing: in the seuenth
day he shal shaue it.
10 And in the eight day he shal bring two
turtles, or two yong pigeōs to the Priest,
at the dore of the Tabernacle of the Cōgregacion.
11 Then the Priest shal prepare the one for
a sin offring, and the other for a burnt offring, & shal make an atonemēt for him,
because he sinned by [e] the dead: so shal he
halowe his head the same day,
12 And he shal [f] consecrate vnto the Lord
the daies of his separacion, and shal bring
a lambe of a yere olde for a trespas offrig,
and the first [g] daies shalbe voyde: for his
consecracion was defiled.
13 ¶ This then is the lawe of the Nazarite:
When the time of his consecracion is out,
he shal come to the dore of the Tabernacle of the Congregacion,
14 And he shal bring his offring vnto the
Lord, an he lambe of a yere olde without
blemish for a burnt offring, and a she lābe
of a yere olde without blemish for a sin
offring, and a ram without blemish for
peace offrings,
15 And a basket of vnleauened bread, of *cakes of fine floure, mingled with oyle, and
wafers of vnleauened bread anoited with
oyle, with their meat offring, and their
drinke offrings:
16 The which the Priest shal bring before
the Lord, and make his sin offring and his
burnt offring.
17 He shal prepare also the ram for a peace
offring vnto the Lord, with the basket of
vnleauened bread, and the Priest shal make his meat offring, and his drinke offring.
18 And *ỳ Nazarite shal shaue the head [h] of
his consecraciō at the dore of the Tabernacle of the Congregacion, and shal take
the heere of the head of his consecracion,
and [i] put it in the fire, which is vnder the
peace offring.
19 Then the Priest shal take the sodē shulder of the ram, and an vnleauened cake
out of the basket, & a wafer vnleauened,
and put them vpon the hands of the Nazarite, after he hathe shauē his cōsecraciō.
20 And the Priest shal * shake them to and
fro

a Which separated them selues from the world, & dedicated them selues to God: ẘ figure was accomplished in Christ.

Iudg. 13, 5. 1. sam. 1, 11.

b As at burials, or mournings.

c In that he suffred his heere to growe, he signified ỳ he was consecrate to God.

d Which lōg heere is a signe that he is dedicate to God.

e By being present, where the dead was.

f Beginning at the eight day, when he is purified.

g So that he shal beginne his vowe anewe.

Leu. 2, 15.

Act. 21, 24.

h In token ỳ his vowe is ended.

i For the heere, which was consecrat to ỳ Lord, might not be cast in to anie prophane place.

Exod. 29, 27.

fro before the Lord: this is an holy thing
*Or, with the breast.
for the Priest *besides the shaken breast,
& besides the heaue shulder: so afterward
the Nazarite may drinke wine.
21 This is the lawe of the Nazarite, which
he hathe vowed, *and* of his offring vnto
k At the least he shal do this, if he be able to offre no more.
the Lord for his consecracion, [k] besides
that that he is able to bring: according to
the vowe which he vowed, so shal he do
after the lawe of his consecracion.
22 ¶ And ŷ Lord spake vnto Mosés, saying,
23 Speake vnto Aarón and to his sonnes,
l That is, pray for them, Eccl.36,19.
saying, Thus shal ye [l] blesse the children
of Israél, and say vnto them,
24 The Lord blesse thee, an kepe thee,
25 The Lord make his face shine vpō thee,
and be merciful vnto thee,
26 The Lord lift vp his countenance vpon
thee, and giue thee peace.
m They shal pray in my Name for them.
27 So they shal put my [m] Name vpon the
children of Israél, and I wil blesse them.

CHAP. VII.

2 The heades or princes of Israél offre at the setting vp of the Tabernacle. 10 And at the dedicacion of the altar. 89 God speaketh to Mosés frō the Merciseat.

1 NOw when Mosés had finished the
setting vp of the Tabernacle, and
Exod.40,18.
*anointed it and sanctified it, and all the
instruments thereof, and the altar with all
*Or, vessels.
the *instrumēts thereof, and had anointed
them and sanctified them,
*Or, captainer.
2 Then the *princes of Israél, heades ouer
the houses of their fathers (they were the
princes of the tribes, who were ouer them
that were nombred) offred,
3 And broght their offring before ŷ Lord,
a Like horslitters to kepe the things, ŷ were caryed in them, from wether.
six [a] couered charets, and twelue oxen: o-
ne charet for two princes, and for euerie
one an oxe, and they offred them before
the Tabernacle.
4 And the Lord spake vnto Mosés, saying,
5 Take *these* of them, that they may be to
b That is, to carie things & stuffe in.
do the [b] seruice of the Tabernacle of the
Congregacion, and thou shalt giue them
vnto the Leuites, to euerie man according
vnto his office.
6 So Mosés toke the charets and the oxen,
and gaue them vnto the Leuites:
7 Two charets and foure oxen he gaue to
the sonnes of Gershón, according vnto
c For their vse to cary with.
their [c] office.
8 And foure charets and eyght oxen he gaue to ŷ sonnes of Merarí according vnto
their office, vnder the hād of Ithamár the
d The holie things of the Sāctuarie must be caryed vpō their shulders, and not drawen with oxē, Chap 4,15.
sonne of Aarón the Priest.
9 But to the sonnes of Koháth he gaue none, [d] because the charge of the Sanctuarie
belonged to them, *which* they did beare
vpon *their* shulders.
e That is, whē the first sacrifice was offred thereupon by Aarón, Leuit. 9,1.
10 ¶ The princes also offred in the [e] dedi-
cacion for the altar in the day that it was
anointed: then the princes offred their
offring before the altar.

11 And ŷ Lord said vnto Mosés, One prince one day, and another prince another
day shal offer their offring, for the dedicacion of the altar.
12 ¶ So then on the first day did ‖ Nahshón
‖ The offring of Nahshón.
the sonne of Amminadáb of the tribe of
Iudáh offer his offring.
13 And his offring *was* a siluer charger of
an hundreth and thirty *shekels* weight, a
siluer boule of seuenty shekels after the
shekel of the Sanctuarie, bothe ful of fine
floure, mingled with oyle, for a * meat of-
Leuit. 2,1.
fring,
14 An *incens* cup of golde of ten *shekels*, ful
of incens,
15 A yong bullocke, a ram, a lambe of a
yere olde for a burnt offring,
16 An he goat for a sin offring,
17 And for peace offrings, two bullockes,
fiue rams, fiue he goates, & fiue lambes of
a yere olde: this was the offring of Nahshón the sonne of Amminadáb.
18 ¶ The second day ‖ Nethaneél, the sonne
‖ The offring of Nethaneél.
of Zuár, prince of *the tribe* of Issachár did
offer:
19 Who offred for his offring a siluer charger of an hūdreth & thirty *shekels* weight,
a siluer boule of seuenty shekels after the
shekel of the Sanctuarie, bothe ful of fine
floure, mingled ŵ oyle, for a meat offring,
20 An *incens* cup of golde of ten *shekels*,
ful of incens,
21 A yong bullocke, a ram, a lambe of a yere olde for a burnt offring,
22 An he goat for a sin offring,
23 And for peace offrings, two bullockes, fiue rams, fiue he goates, fiue lābes of a yere
olde: this was the offring of Nethaneél
the sonne of Zuár.
24 ¶ The third day ‖ Eliáb the sonne of He-
‖ The offring of Eliáb.
lón prince of ŷ childrē of Zebulún *offred*.
25 His offring *was* a siluer charger of an
hundreth and thirty *shekels* weight, a siluer
boule of seuenty shekels, after the shekel
of the Sanctuarie, bothe ful of fine floure,
mingled with oyle, for a meat offring,
26 A golden *incens* cup of ten *shekels*, ful of
incens,
27 A yong bullocke, a ram, a lambe of a yere olde for a burnt offring,
28 An he goat for a sin offring,
29 And for peace offrings, two bullockes,
fiue rams, fiue he goates, fiue lambes of a
yere olde: this was the offring of Eliáb the
sonne of Helón.
30 ¶ The fourth day ‖ Elizúr ŷ sonne of She-
‖ The offring of Elizúr.
deúr prince of ŷ childrē of Reubén *offred*.
31 His offring *was* a siluer charger of an hū
dreth and thirty *shekels* weight, a siluer
boule of seuenty shekels, after the shekel
of the Sanctuarie, bothe ful of fine floure,
mingled with oyle, for a meat offring,
32 A goldē *incēs* cup of tē *shekels*, ful of incēs,

33 A yong bullocke, a ram, a lambe of a
yere olde for a burnt offring,
34 An he goat for a sin offring,
35 And for a peace offring, two bullockes,
fiue rams, fiue he goates, and fiue lambes
of an yere olde: this was the offring of E-
lizúr the sonne of Shedeúr.
36 ¶The fift day ‖Shelumiél the sonne of
Zurishaddái, prince of the children of Simeón *offred*.
37 His offring *was* a siluer charger of an hūdreth and thirty shekels weight, a siluer
boule of seuenty shekels, after the shekel
of the Sā̃ctuarie, bothe ful of fine floure,
mingled with oyle for a meat offring,
38 A golden *incens* cup of ten *shekels* ful of
incens,
39 A yong bullocke, a ram, a lambe of a yere olde for a burnt offring,
40 An he goat for a sin offring,
41 And for a peace offring, two bullockes,
fiue rams, fiue he goates, fiue lā̃bes of a yere olde: this was the offring of Shelumiél
the sonne of Zurishaddái.
42 ¶The sixt day ‖Eliasáph the sonne of
Deuél prince of the children of Gad *offred*.
43 His offring *was* a siluer charger of an
hundreth and thirty *shekels* weight, a siluer
boule of seuentie shekels, after the shekel
of the Sanctuarie, bothe ful of fine floure,
mingled with oyle for a meat offring,
44 A golden *incens* cup of ten *shekels* ful of
incens,
45 A yong bullocke, a ram, a lambe of a
yere olde, for a burnt offring,
46 An he goat for a sin offring,
47 And for a peace offring, two bullocks,
fiue rams, fiue he goates, fiue lambes of a
yere olde: this was the offring of Eliasáph
the sonne of Deuél.
48 ¶The seuenth day ‖Elishamá the sonne
of Ammiúd prince of the children of E-
phráim *offred*.
49 His offring *was* a siluer charger of an
hū̃dreth, & thirtie *shekels* weight, a siluer
boule of seuentie shekels, after the shekel
of the Sanctuarie, bothe ful of fine floure,
mingled with oyle, for a meat offring,
50 A golden *incens* cup of ten *shekels*, ful of
incens,
51 A yong bullocke, a ram, a lambe of a
yere olde for a burnt offring,
52 An he goat for a sin offring,
53 And for a peace offring, two bullocks, fiue rams, fiue he goates, fiue lambes of a
yere olde: this was the offring of Elishamá, the sonne of Ammiúd.
54 ¶The eyght day *offred* ‖ Gamliél the
sonne of Pedazúr, prince of the children
of Manasséh.
55 His offring *was* a siluer charger of an
hundreth & thirtie *shekels* weight, a siluer
boule of seuentie *shekels*, after the shekel
of the Sā̃ctuarie, bothe ful of fine floure,
mingled with oyle for a meat offring,
56 A golden *incens* cup of ten *shekels*, ful of
incens,
57 A yong bullocke, a ram, a lambe of a
yere olde for a burnt offring,
58 An he goat for a sin offring,
59 And for a peace offring, two bullockes,
fiue rams, fiue he goates, fiue lambes of a
yere olde: this was the offring of Gamliél
the sonne of Pedazúr.
60 ¶The ninth day ‖ Abidán the sonne of
Gideoní prince of the children of Beniamín *offred*.
61 His offring *was* a siluer charger of an
hundreth and thirty *shekels* weight, a siluer
boule of seuenty shekels, after the shekel
of the Sanctuarie, bothe ful of fine floure,
mingled with oyle for a meat offring,
62 A golden *incens* cup of ten *shekels*, ful
of incens,
63 A yong bullocke, a ram, a lambe of a
yere olde for a burnt offring,
64 An he goat for a sin offring,
65 And for a peace offring two bullocks,
fiue rams, fiue he goates, fiue lambes of a
yere olde: this was the offring of Abidán
the sonne of Gideoní.
66 ¶The tenth day ‖Ahiézer the sonne of
Ammishaddái, prince of the children of
Dan *offred*.
67 His offring *was* a siluer charger of an
hundreth and thirty *shekels* weight, a siluer
boule of seuenty shekels, after the shekel
of the Sactuarie, bothe ful of fine floure,
mingled with oyle for a meat offring,
68 A golden *incens* cup of ten *shekels* ful of
incens,
69 A yong bullocke, a ram, a lambe of a
yere olde for a burnt offring,
70 An he goat for a sin offring,
71 And for a peace offring, two bullocks,
fiue rams, fiue he goates, fiue lambes of a
yere olde: this was the offring of Ahiézer
the sonne of Ammishaddái.
72 ¶The eleuenth day ‖Pagiél the sonne
of Ocrán, prince of the childrē of Ashér
offred.
73 His offring *was* a siluer charger of an
hundreth and thirty *shekels* weight, a siluer boule of seuenty shekels, after the shekel of the Sā̃ctuarie, bothe ful of fine floure, mingled with oyle for a meat offring,
74 A golden *incens* cup of ten *shekels*, ful of
incens,
75 A yong bullocke, a ram, a lambe of a
yere olde for a burnt offring,
76 An he goat for a sin offring,
77 And for a peace offring, two bullocks,
fiue rams, fiue he goates, fiue lambes of a
yere olde: this was the offring of Pagiél
the sonne of Ocrán.

78 ¶The

‖ The offring of Shelumiél.

‖ The offring of Eliasáph.

‖ The offring of Elishamá.

‖ The offring of Gamliél.

‖ The offring of Abidán.

‖ The offring of Ahiézer.

‖ The offring of Pagiél, or Phegiel.

‖The offring of Ahirá.

78 ¶The twelueth day ‖Ahirá the sonne of
Enán, prince of the children of Naphtalí *offred*.
79 His offring *was* a siluer charger of an
hundreth & thirtie *shekels* weight, a siluer
boule of seuentie shekels, after the shekel
of the Sanctuarie, bothe ful of fine floure,
mingled with oyle, for a meat offring,
80 A golden *incens* cup of ten *shekels*, ful of
incens,
81 A yong bullocke, a ram, a lambe of a
yere olde, for a burnt offring.
82 An he goat for a sinne offring,
83 And for peace offrings two bullockes,
fiue rams, fiue he goats, fiue lambes of a
yere olde: this was the offring of Ahirá,
the sonne of Enán.
84 This was the [f] dedicacion of the Altar
by the princes of Isráel, when it was anointed: twelue chargers of siluer, twelue
siluer boules, twelue *incens* cups of golde,
85 Euerie charger, *conteining* an hundreth &
thirtie *shekels* of siluer, and euerie boule
seuentie: all the siluer vessel *conteined* two
thousand and foure hundreth *shekels*, after
the shekel of the Sanctuarie.
86 Twelue *incens* cups of golde ful of incẽs, *conteining* ten shekels euerie cup, after
the shekel of the Sanctuarie: all the golde
of the *incens* cups *was* an hundreth and
twentie *shekels*.
87 All the bullockes for the burnt offring
were twelue bullockes, the rams twelue,
the lambes of a yere olde twelue, with
their meat offrings, and twelue he goats
for a sinne offring.
88 And all the bullockes for the peace offrings *were* foure & twentie bullockes, the
rams sixtie, the he goats sixtie, the lambes
of a yere olde sixtie: this was the dedica-
ciõ of the Altar, after that it was [g] anointed.
89 And when Mosés wẽt into the [h] Tabernacle of the Cõgregacion, to speake with
God, he heard the voyce of one speaking
vnto him from the Merciseat, that was
vpon the Arke of the Testimonie [i] betwene the two Cherubíms, and he spake
to him.

f This was ẏ offring of the princes, when Aarón did dedicate the Altar.

g By Aarón.

h That is, the Sanctuarie.

i According as he had promised, Exod. 25,22.

CHAP. VIII.

2 The ordre of the lampes. 6 The purifying and offring of the Leuites. 24 The age of the Leuites, when thei are receiued to seruice, and when thei are dimissed.

1 AND the Lord spake vnto Mosés,
saying,
2 Speake vnto Aarón, and say vnto him,
When thou lightest the lampes, the seuen
lampes shal giue light towarde the [a] forefront of the Candelsticke.
3 And Aarón did so, lighting the lampes
thereof toward the forefront of the Cãdelsticke, as the Lord had commanded
Mosés.

a To that parte which is ouer against ẏ Candelsticke, Exod. 25,37.

4 And this was the worke of the Candelsticke, *euen* of golde beaten out with the
hammer, bothe the shaft, and the floures
thereof* was beatẽ out with the hammer:
[b] accordĩg to the paterne, which the Lord
had shewed Mosés, so made he the Candelsticke.
5 ¶And the Lord spake vnto Mosés, saying,
6 Take the Leuites from among the children of Isráel, and purifie them.
7 And thus shalt thou do vnto them, when
thou purifiest them, Sprinkle [c] water of
purificacion vpon them, & let them shaue
all their flesh, and wash their clothes: so
thei shalbe cleane.
8 Then thei shal take a yong bullocke with
his meat offring of fine floure, mingled
with oyle, and another yong bullocke
shalt thou take for a sinne offring.
9 Then thou shalt bring the Leuites before the Tabernacle of the Congregacion,
and assemble [d] all the Congregacion of
the children of Isráel.
10 Thou shalt bring the Leuites also before
the Lord, & the [e] children of Isráel shal
put their hands vpon the Leuites.
11 And Aarón shal offer the Leuites before
the Lord, as a shake offring of the childrẽ
of Isráel, that thei may execute the seruice of the Lord.
12 And the Leuites shal put their hands vpon the heades of the bullockes, and make
thou the one a sinne offring, & the other a
burnt offring vnto the Lord, that thou
maiest make an atonemẽt for the Leuites.
13 And thou shalt set the Leuites before
Aarón and before his sonnes, and offer
them as a shake offring to the Lord.
14 Thus thou shalt separate the Leuites
from among the children of Isráel, & the
Leuites shalbe * mine.
15 And afterward shal the Leuites go in, to
serue in the Tabernacle of the Congregacion, and thou shalt purifie them and
offer them, as a shake offring.
16 For thei are frely giuen* vnto me from
among the children of Isráel, for [f] suche
as open anie wombe: for all the firstborne
of the children of Isráel haue I taken thẽ
vnto me.
17 * For all the firstborne of the children
of Isráel are mine, bothe of man and of
beast: since the day that I smote euerie
firstborne in the land of Egypt, I sanctified them for my self.
18 And I haue taken the Leuites for all the
firstborne of the children of Isráel,
19 And haue giuen the Leuites as a gift vnto Aarón, and to his sonnes from among
the children of Isráel, to do the seruice of
the [g] children of Isráel in the Tabernacle of the Congregacion, and to make

Exod. 25,18.

b And not set together of diuers pieces.

c In Ebrewe, it is called the water of sinne, because it is made to purge sinne, as Chap. 19,9.

d That thou maiest do this in presence of them all.

e Meanĩg, certeine of them in the name of the whole.

Chap. 3,45.

Chap. 3,9.

f That is, thei that are ẏ first borne.

Exod. 13,2. luk. 2,20.

g Which seruice the Israelites shulde els do.

an atonement for the children of Iſraél,
that there be no plague among the children of Iſraél, when the children of Iſraél come nere vnto [h] the Sanctuarie.

h Becauſe the Leuites go into the Sāctuarie in their name.

20 ¶Thē Mosés and Aarón & all the Congregacion of the children of Iſraél did
with the Leuites, according vnto all that
the Lord had commanded Mosés concerning the Leuites: ſo did the children of
Iſraél vnto them.
21 So the Leuites were purified, and waſhed their clothes, & Aarón offred thē as a
ſhake offring before the Lord, & Aarón
made an atonemēt for thē, to purifie thē.
22 And after that, went the Leuites in to do
their ſeruice in the Tabernacle of ŷ Cōgregacion, [i] before Aarón & before his
ſonnes: as the Lord had commanded Mosés concerning the Leuites, ſo thei did
vnto them.

i In their preſence, to ſerue them.

23 ¶And ŷ Lord ſpake vnto Mosés, ſaying,
24 This alſo *belongeth* to the Leuites: from
fiue and twentie yere olde and vpwarde,
thei ſhal go in, to execute *their* office in
the ſeruice of the Tabernacle of the Cōgregacion.
25 And after the age of fiftie yere, thei ſhal
ceaſe from executing the [k] office, and
ſhal ſerue no more:
26 But thei ſhal miniſter [l] with their brethren in the Tabernacle of the Congregaciō, to kepe things committed to their
charge, but thei ſhal do no ſeruice: thus
ſhalt thou do vnto the Leuites touching
their charges.

k Suche office as was peineful, as to beare burthens and ſuche like.
l In ſinging pſalmes, inſtructing, counſeling and keping ŷ things in ordre.

CHAP. IX.

2 The Paſſeouer is commanded againe. 13 The puniſhment of him that kepeth not the Paſſeouer. 15 The cloude conducteth the Iſraelites through the wildernes.

1 AND the Lord ſpake vnto Mosés in
the wildernes of Sinái, in the firſt
moneth of the ſecōde yere, after thei were come out of the land of Egypt, ſaying,
2 The childrē of Iſraél ſhal alſo celebrate
the* Paſſeouer at the time appointed thereunto.
3 In the fourtēth day of this moneth at* e-
uē, ye ſhal kepe it in his due ſeaſon: according to [a] all the ordinances of it, and
according to all the ceremonies thereof
ſhal ye kepe it.

Exod.12,1. leui.23,5. nomb.28,16. deut.16,2.
Exod.12,6. deut.16,6.
a Euen in all pointes as the Lord hathe inſtitute it.

4 Then Mosés ſpake vnto the children of
Iſraél, to celebrate the Paſſeouer.
5 And thei kept the Paſſeouer in the fourtenth day of the firſt moneth at euen in ŷ
wildernes of Sinái: according to all that
the Lord had commanded Mosés, ſo did
the children of Iſraél.
6 ¶And certeine men were defiled [b] by a
dead man, that thei might not kepe the
Paſſeouer the ſame day: and thei came before Mosés and before Aarón the ſame
day.

b By touching a corps, or being at the buryal.

7 And thoſe men ſaid vnto him, We are
defiled by a dead man: wherefore are we
kept backe that we may not [c] offer an offring vnto the Lord in the time thereunto appointed among the children of Iſraél?

c Or celebrate the Paſſeouer the fourtenth day of the firſt moneth.

8 Then Mosés ſaid vnto them, Stand ſtil,
and I wil heare what the Lord wil cōmande concerning you.
9 ¶And the Lord ſpake vnto Mosés, ſaying,
10 Speake vnto the children of Iſraél, and
ſay, If anie among you, or of your poſteritie ſhalbe vncleane by the reaſon of a
corps, or be in a long iourney, [d] he ſhal
kepe the Paſſeouer vnto the Lord.
11 In the fourtēth day of the [e] ſeconde moneth at euen thei ſhal kepe it: with vnleauened bread and ſowre herbes ſhal thei
eat it.

d And can not come where ŷ Tabernacle is, when others kepe it.
e So that the vncleane, and thei that are not at home, haue a moneth longer grāted vnto them.

12 They ſhal leaue none of it vnto the
morning,* nor breake anie bone of it: according to all the ordinance of the Paſſeouer ſhal thei kepe it.

Exod.12,46. iohn.19,36.

13 But the man that is cleane and is not in
a [f] iourney, and is negligent to kepe the
Paſſeouer, the ſame perſone ſhalbe cut of
from his people: becauſe he broght not
the offring of the Lord in his due ſeaſon,
that man ſhal beare his" ſinne.

f When ŷ Paſſeouer is celebrate.
"Or, puniſhment of his ſinne.

14 And if a ſtranger dwel among you, and
wil kepe the Paſſeouer vnto the Lord, as
the ordinance of the Paſſeouer, & as the
maner thereof *is*, ſo ſhal he do:* ye ſhal haue one lawe bothe for the ſtranger, & for
him that was borne in the ſame land.

Exod.12,49.

15 ¶*And whē the Tabernacle was reared
vp, a cloude couered the Tabernacle, *namely* the Tabernacle of the Teſtimonie:
& at euen there was vpon the Tabernacle, as the [g] appearance of fire vntil morning.

Exod.40,34.
g Like a piller: read Exod.13,21.

16 So it was alwaie: the cloude couered it
by day, & the appearance of fire by night.
17 And when the cloude was taken vp from
the Tabernacle, then afterward the children of Iſraél iourneied: & in the place
where the cloude abode, there the children of Iſraél pitched their tentes.
18 At the" commandement of the [h] Lord
the children of Iſraél iourneied, and at
the commandement of the Lord thei pitched: as long as the cloude abode vpō the
Tabernacle,* they" laye ſtil.

"Ebr. mouthe.
h Who taught the whē to do by the cloude.
1.Cor.10,1.
"Ebr. camped.

19 And when the cloude taryed ſtil vpon
the Tabernacle a long time, the children
of Iſraél kept the [i] watch of the Lord, &
iourneyed not.
20 So when the cloude abode" a fewe daies
vpon the Tabernacle, thei abode in their
tents according to the commandement of
the Lord: for thei iourneyed at the commandement of the Lord.

i Thei waited whē the Lord wolde ſignifie ether their departure, or their abode by the cloude.
"Ebr. daies of nombre.

21 And

21 And thogh the cloude abode vpon the
Tabernacle from euen vnto the morning,
yet *if* the cloude was taken vp in the morning, thẽ they iourneyed: whether by day
or by night the cloude was taken vp, then
they iourneyed.
22 Or if the cloude taried two dayes or a
moneth, or a yere vpon the Tabernacle,
abiding thereon, the children of Israél *a-
bode stil, and iourneied not: but when it
was taken vp, they iourneyed.
23 At the commandemẽt of the Lord they
pitched, and at the commandement of the
Lord they iourneyed, keping the watch
of the Lord at the commandement of the
Lord by the [k] hand of Mosés.

Exod.40,36.

k Vnder the charge & gouernement of Mosés.

CHAP. X.

2 The vse of the siluer trumpettes. 11 The Israelites departe from Sinái. 14 The captaines of the hoste are nombred. 30 Hobáb refuseth to go with Mosés his sonne in lawe.

1 AND the Lord spake vnto Mosés,
saying,
2 Make thee two trumpets of siluer: of an
[a] whole piece shalt thou make them, that
thou maiest vse thẽ for the assembling of
the Congregacion, and for the departure
of the campe.
3 And whẽ they shal blowe with thẽ, all the
Congregacion shal assemble to thee before the dore of the Tabernacle of the Cõgregacion.
4 But if they blowe with one, then the
princes, *or* heads ouer the thousands of Israél shal come vnto thee.
5 But if ye blowe an alarme, then the cãpe
of thẽ that pitche on the [b] East parte, shal
go forwarde.
6 If ye blowe an alarme the seconde time,
thẽ the hoste of them ẏ lie on the [c] Southside shal marche: *for* they shal blowe an a-
larme when they remoue.
7 But in assembling the Congregacion, ye
shal blowe with out an alarme.
8 And the sonnes of Aarón the Priest shal
[d] blowe the trumpets, and ye shal haue thẽ
as a lawe for euer in your generacions.
9 And when ye go to warre in your land
against ẏ enemie that vexeth you, ye shal
blowe an alarme ẇ the trũpets, and ye shal
be remẽbred before the Lord your God,
and shal be saued from your enemies.
10 Also in the day of your [e] gladnes, and in
your feast daies, and in the beginning of
your monethes, ye shal also blowe the trũpets ″ ouer your burnt sacrifices, and ouer
your peace offrings, that they may be a
remembrance for you before your God: I
am the Lord your God.
11 ¶ And in the seconde yere, in the secõde
moneth, *and* in the twentieth *day* of the
moneth the cloude was taken vp from the
Tabernacle of the Testimonie.

a Or of worke beaten out ẇ the hammer.

b That is, the hoste of Iudáh and they that are vnder his ensigne.

c Meaning the hoste of Reubén.

d So that onely the Priests must blowe ẏ trumpets, so long as the Priesthode lasted.

e When ye reioyce that God hathe remoued anie plague.

″Or, when you offer burnt offrings.

12 And the children of Israél departed on
their ″ iourneis out of ẏ desert of Sinái, and
ẏ cloude rested in the wildernes of Parán.
13 So they [f] first toke their iourney at the cõ
mãdemẽt of the Lord, by ẏ hãd of Mosés.
14 ¶ * In the first place wẽt the standerd of
the hoste of the children of Iudáh, according to their armies: and * Nahshón the
sonne of Amminadáb *was* ouer his bãde.
15 And ouer the bande of the tribe of the
children of Issachár *was* Nethaneél the
sonne of Zuár.
16 And ouer the bande of the tribe of the
children of Zebulún *was* Eliáb the sonne
of Helón.
17 When ẏ Tabernacle was taken downe,
then the sonnes of Gershón, and the sonnes of Merarí wẽt forwarde bearing [g] the
Tabernacle.
18 ¶ After, departed the stãderd of the hoste
of Reubén accordĩg to their armies, & o-
uer his bãde *was* Elizúr ẏ sõne of Shedeúr.
19 And ouer the bande of the tribe of the
childrẽ of Simeón *was* Shelumiél the sonne of Surishaddái.
20 And ouer the bande of the tribe of the
children of Gád *was* Eliasáph the sonne
of Deuél.
21 The Kohathites also wẽt forwarde and
[h] bare the * Sanctuarie, & the [i] *former* did
set vp the Tabernacle against they came.
22 ¶ Then the standerd of the hoste of the
children of Ephráim went forwarde according to their armies, and ouer his bãde *was* Elishamá the sonne of Ammiúd.
23 And ouer the bande of the tribe of the
sonnes of Manasséh *was* Gamliél the sonne of Pedazúr.
24 And ouer the bande of the tribe of the
sonnes of Beniamín *was* Abidán the sonne of Gideoní.
25 ¶ Last, ẏ stãderd of the hoste of ẏ childrẽ
of Dan marched, [k] gatherĩg all the hostes
according to their armies: & ouer his bãde
was Ahiézer the sonne of Ammishaddái.
26 And ouer the bande of the tribe of the
children of Ashér *was* Pagiél the sonne
of Ocrán.
27 And ouer the bande of the tribe of the
children of Naphtalí *was* Ahirá the sonne of Enán.
28 [l] These were the remouings of the children of Israél according to their armies, when they marched.
29 ¶ After, Mosés said vnto [m] Hobáb the
sonne of Reuél ẏ Midianite, the father in
lawe of Mosés, We go into the place, of ẇ
ẏ Lord said, I wil giue it you: Come thou
with vs, and we wil do thee good: for the
Lord hathe promised good vnto Israél.
30 And he answered him, I wil not go: but
I wil departe to mine owne countrey, and
to my kinred.

″*Or, in keping this ordre in their iourneys.*

f Frõ Sinái to Parán, Chap. 33,1.

Chap.2,3.

Chap.1,7.

g With all the appertinances thereof.

h Vpon their shulders.

Chap.4,4.

i The Merarites and Gershonites.

k Leauing none behind nor anie of ẏ former that fainted in ẏ way.

l This was ẏ ordre of their hoste whẽ they remoued.

m Some thĩke that Reuél, Iethró, Hobáb, and Keni were all one: Kymhi saith ẏ Reuél was Iethros father: so Hobáb was Mosés father in law.

31 Thē he said, I praye thee, leaue vs not: for
thou knowest our cāping places in the wil
dernes: therefore ȳ maiest be "our guide.

"Ebr. eyes vnto vs.

32 And if thou go with vs, what goodnes ȳ
Lord shal shewe vnto vs, the same wil we
shewe vnto thee.

33 ¶ So they departed from the [n] mount of
the Lord, thre daies iourney: and the Arke of the couenant of the Lord wēt before them in the thre daies iourney, to searche out a resting place for them.

n Mount Sinái, or Horéb.

34 And the cloude of the Lord *was* vpon
them by day, when they went out of the
campe.

35 And when the Arke went forwarde, Mosés said, * [o] Rise vp, Lord, and let thine
enemies be scatered, and let them that hate thee, flee before thee.

Psal. 68, 2. o Declare thy might and power.

36 And when it rested, he said, Returne, ô
Lord, to the "manie thousands of Israél.

"Ebr to the ten thousand thousands.

CHAP. XI.

1 The people murmureth, and is punished with fire. 4 The people lusteth after flesh. 6 They lothe Manna. 11 The weake faith of Mosés. 16 The Lord deuideth the burthen of Mosés to seuenty of the Ancientes. 31 The Lord sendeth quailes. 33 Their lust is punished.

1 When the people became "murmurers, "it displeased the Lord: and
the Lord heard it, therefore his wrath was
kindled, and the fire of the Lord burnt
among them, and * consumed the vtmost
parte of the hoste.

"Ebr. as iniust complainers. "Ebr it was euil in the eares of the Lord. *Psal. 78, 21.*

2 Then the people cryed vnto Mosés: and
when Mosés prayed vnto the Lord, the fire was quenched.

3 And he called ȳ name of that place " Taberáh, because the fire of the Lord burnt
among them.

"Or, burning.

4 ¶ And a nomber of [a] people that was a-
mong them, fel a lusting, and [b] turned
away, and the children of Israél also wept
and said, Who shal giue vs flesh to eat?

a Which were of those strāgers that came out of Egypt with them, Exod. 12, 38. b From God.

5 We remember the fish which we did eat
in Egypt for [c] naught, the cucumbers, and
the pepons, and the lekes, and the onions,
and the garleke.

c For a smale price, or good cheape.

6 But now our soule is [d] dried away, we
can se nothing but this MAN.

d For the gready lust of flesh.

7 (The MAN also was as * coriāder sede, &
his coulour like the coulour of [e] bdeliū.

Exod. 16, 31. wisd. 16, 20. psal. 78, 24. ioh 6, 31. e Which is, a white perle or precious stone.

8 The people went about and gathered it,
and ground it in milles, or bet it in morters, and baked it in a cauldron, and made
cakes of it, and the taste of it was like vnto the taste of fresh oyle.

9 And when the dewe fel downe vpon the
hoste in the night, the MAN fel with it)

10 ¶ Then Mosés heard the people wepe
throughout their families, euerie man in
the dore of his tente, and the wrath of the
Lord was grieuously kindled: also Mosés
was grieued.

11 And Mosés said vnto ȳ Lord, Wherefore hast thou "vexed thy seruant? and why
haue I not founde [f] fauour in thy sight,
seing thou hast put the charge of all this
people vpon me?

"Or, euil intreated. f Or, wherein haue I displeased thee.

12 Haue I [g] conceiued all this people? or
haue I begotten them? that thou shuldest
say vnto me, Cary them in thy bosome (as
a nurse beareth ȳ sucking childe) vnto the
[h] land, for the which thou swarest vnto
their fathers?

g Am I their father, that none may haue ȳ charge of the but I? h Of Canáan promised by an othe to our fathers.

13 Where shulde I haue flesh to giue vnto
all this people? for they wepe vnto me,
saying, Giue vs flesh that we may eat.

14 I am not able to beare all this people a-
lone, for it is to heauie for me.

15 Therefore if thou deale thus with me, I
pray thee, if I haue founde fauour in thy
[i] sight, kil me, that I beholde not my miserie.

i I had rather dye, then to se my grief and miserie thus daily increase by their rebellion.

16 ¶ Then ȳ Lord said vnto Mosés, Gather
vnto me seuenty men of the Elders of Israél, whome thou knowest, that they are
the Elders of the people, & gouerners ouer
them, and bring them vnto the Tabernacle of the Congregacion, and let them
stand there with thee,

17 And I wil come downe, & talke with thee
there, [k] and take of the Spirit, which is
vpon thee, and put vpon them, and they
shal beare the burthē of the people with
thee: so thou shalt not beare it alone.

k I wil distribute my Spirit amōg them, as I haue done to thee.

18 Furthermore thou shalt say vnto the
people, [l] Be sanctified against tomorowe,
and ye shal eat flesh: for you haue wept
in the eares of the Lord, saying, Who shal
giue vs flesh to eat? for we were better in
Egypt: therefore the Lord wil giue you
flesh, and ye shal eat.

l Prepare your selues that ye be not vncleane.

19 Ye shal not eat one day nor two daies,
nor fiue daies, nether ten daies, nor twenty daies,

20 But a whole moneth, vntil it come out
at your nostrels, and be lothesome vnto
you, because ye haue [m] contemned the
Lord, which is [n] among you, and haue
wept before him, saying, Why came we
hither out of Egypt?

m Or, cast him of, because ye refused Manna which he appointed as moste mete for you. n Who leadeth and gouerneth you.

21 And Mosés said, Six hundreth thousand
fotemen *are there* of the people, [o] among
whome I am: & thou saiest, I wil giue thē
flesh, that they may eat a moneth long.

o Of whome I haue the charge.

22 Shal the shepe and the beues be slaine
for them, to finde them? ether shal all the
fish of the sea be gathered together for
them to suffise them?

23 And the Lord sayd vnto Mosés, Is * the
Lords hand shortened? thou shalt se now
whether my worde shal come to passe vnto thee, or no.

Isa. 50, 2. & 59. 1.

24 ¶ So Mosés went out, and tolde the people the wordes of the Lord, and gathered
seuenty men of the Elders of the people,
and set thē round about the Tabernacle.

25 Then

25 Thẽ the Lord came downe in a cloude,
and spake vnto him, and "toke of the Spirit, that was vpon him, and put it vpon the
seuenty Anciẽt men: and when the Spirit
rested vpon them, then they prophecied,
and did not p cease.

"Or, separated, as vers. 17.

p From that day the Spirit of prophecie did not faile them.

26 But there remained two of the men in
the hoste: the name of the one *was* Eldád,
and the name of the other Medád, and the
Spirit rested vpon them, (for they were
of them that were writẽ, and went not out
vnto the Tabernacle) & they prophecied
in the hoste.
27 Then there ran a yong man, and tolde
Mosés, and said, Eldád and Medád do prophecie in the hoste.
28 And Ioshúa the sonne of Nun the seruant of Mosés one of his q yong men,
answered and said, My lord Mosés, r forbid them.

q Or, a yong mã whome he had chosen from his youthe.

r Suche blinde zeale was in the Apostles, Mar. 9, 38. luk. 9, 49.

29 But Mosés said vnto him, Enuyest thou
for my sake? yea, wolde God that all the
Lords people *were* Prophetes, *&* that the
Lord wolde put his Spirit vpon them.
30 And Mosés returned into the hoste, he
and the Elders of Israél.
31 Then there went forthe a winde from
the Lord, and * broght quailes from the
Sea, and let them fall vpon the campe, a
daies iourney on this side, & a daies iourney on the other side, round about the hoste, and *they were* about two cubites aboue
the earth.

Exod. 16, 13. psal. 78, 26.

32 Then the people arose, all that day, and
all the night, and all the next day and gathered the quailes: he that gathered the
least, gathered ten f Homers ful, and they
spred them abroade for their vse round
about the hoste.

f Of Homer read Leui 27, 16. also it signifieth an heape, as Exod. 8, 14. iudg. 15, 15.

33 While the flesh was yet betwene their
tethe, before it was chewed, euẽ the wrath
of the Lord was kindled against the people, and the Lord * smote the people with
an exceading great plague.

Psal. 78, 31.

34 So the name of the place was called, "Kibróth-hattaauáh: for there they buryed
the people that fel a lusting.

"Or, graues of lust.

35 Frõ Kibróth-hattaauáh the people toke their iourney to Hazeróth, and abode
at Hazeróth.

CHAP. XII.

1 Aarón and Miriám grudge against Mosés. 10 Miriám is striken with leprosie, and healed at the prayer of Mosés.

1 AFterward Miriám and Aarón "spake
against Mosés, because of the womã
of Ethiopia whome he had maried (for he
had maried a a woman of Ethiopia)

"Or, murmured.

a Zipporáh was a Midianite, and because Midián bordered on Ethiopia, it is sometime in the Scripture cõprehended vnder this name.

2 And they said, What? hathe the Lord spoken but onely by Mosés? hathe he not spoken also by vs? and the Lord heard *this*.
3 (But Mosés *was* a very * b meke man, a-
boue all the men that were vpon the earth)

Eccle. 45, 4.

b And so bare w their grudgigs, althogh he knewe thẽ.

4 And by and by the Lord said vnto Mosés,
& vnto Aarón, & vnto Miriám, Come out
ye thre vnto the Tabernacle of the Congregacion: and they thre came forthe.
5 Then the Lord came downe in the piller
of the cloude, and stode in the dore of the
Tabernacle, & called Aarón and Miriám,
and they bothe came forthe.
6 And he said, Heare now my wordes, If
there be a Prophet of the Lord among
you, I wil be knowen to him by a c vision,
& wil speake vnto him by dreame.

c These were the two ordinarie meanes.

7 My seruãt Mosés *is* not so, who is faithful in d all mine house.

d In all Israél which was his Church.

8 Vnto him wil I speake * mouth to mouth,
and by vision, & not in darke wordes, but
he e shal se ỹ similitude of ỹ Lord. wherefore then were ye not afraied to speake a-
gainst my seruant, *euen* against Mosés?

Exod. 33, 11.

e So farre as anie man was able to comprehende, w he calleth his backe partes, Exod. 33, 23.

9 Thus the Lord was very angry with thẽ,
and departed.
10 Also the cloude departed from the f Tabernacle: & beholde, Miriám *was* leprous
like snowe: and Aarón loked vpõ Miriám,
and beholde, *she was* leprous.

f Frõ the dore of the Tabernacle.

11 Then Aarón said vnto Mosés, Alas, my
Lord, I beseche thee, lay not the sinne vpõ
vs, which we haue foolishly committed &
wherein we haue sinned.
12 Let her not, I pray thee, be as one g dead,
of whome the flesh is halfe consumed, whẽ
he commeth out of his mothers wombe.

g As a childe that commeth out of his mothers belly dead, hauing as it were but the skin.

13 Thẽ Mosés cryed vnto the Lord, saying,
O God, I beseche thee, heale her now.
14 ¶ And the Lord said vnto Mosés, If her
father had h spit in her face, shulde she not
haue bene ashamed seuen dayes? let her be
* shut out of the hoste seuen dayes, & after she shal be receiued.

h In his displeasure.

Leu. 13, 46.

15 So Miriám was shut out of the hoste seuen dayes, and the people remoued not, til
Miriám was broght in againe.

CHAP. XIII.

4 Certeine men are sent to searche the land of Canáan. 24 They bring of the frute of the land. 31 Caléb comforteth the people against the discouraging of the other Spies.

1 THen afterward the people remoued
from Hazeróth, & pitched in the wildernes of a Parán.

a That is, in Rithmá, w was in Parán, Chap. 33, 18.

2 ¶ And the Lord spake vnto Mosés, saying,
3 b Sẽd thou men out to search the land of
Canáan which I giue vnto the children
of Israél: of euerie tribe of their fathers
shal ye send a man, *suche as are* all rulers a-
mong them.

b After ỹ people had required it of Mosés, as it is Deu. 1, 22, then ỹ Lord spake to Mosés so to do.

4 Thẽ Mosés sent them out of the wildernes of Parán at the commandement of ỹ
Lord: all those men were "heades of the
children of Israél.

"Or, rulers.

5 Also their names are these: of the tribe
of Reubén, Shãmúa the sonne of Zaccúr;

6 Of the tribe of Simeón, Shaphát the sonne of Horí:
7 Of the tribe of Iudáh, Caléb the sonne
of Iephunnéh:
8 Of the tribe of Issachár, Igál the sonne
of Ioséph:
9 Of the tribe of Ephráim, ‖ Oshéa the
‖Or, Ioshúa.
sonne of Nun:
10 Of the tribe of Beniamín, Paltí the
sonne of Raphú:
11 Of the tribe of Zebulún, Gaddiél the
sonne of Sodí:
12 Of the tribe of Ioséph, *to wit*, of the tribe of Manasséh, Gaddí the sonne of Susí:
13 Of the tribe of Dan, Ammiél the sonne
of Gemallí:
14 Of the tribe of Ashér, Sethúr the sonne
of Michaél:
15 Of the tribe of Naphtalí, Nahbí the
sonne of Vophsí:
16 Of the tribe of Gad, Geuél the sonne
of Machí.
17 These are the names of the [c] mē, which
c Which in nomber were twelue, according to the twelue tribes.
Mosés sent to spie out the land: and Mosés
called the name of Oshéa the sonne of
Nun Iehoshúa.
18 So Mosés sent them to spie out the land
of Canáan, and said vnto thē, Go vp this
way toward the South, and go vp into ‖ the
‖Or, high countrey.
mountaines,
19 And consider the land what it is, and the
people that dwel therein, whether they be
strong or weake, ether few or many,
20 Also what the land *is* that they dwel in,
whether it be [d] good or bad: and what ci-
d Plentiful or baren.
ties *they be*, that they dwel in, whether they
dwel in tentes, or in walled townes:
21 And what the land *is*: whether it be fat
or leane, whether there be trees therein, or
not. And be of good courage, and bring
of the frute of the land (for then *was* the
time of the first ripe grapes)
22 ¶ So they went vp, & searched out the
land, from the wildernes of [e] Zin vnto
e Which was in the wildernes of Parán.
Rehób, to go to Hamáth,
23 And thei ascēded toward the South, and
came vnto Hebrón, where were Ahimán,
Sheshái and Talmái, the sonnes of [f] A-
f Which were a kinde of gyantes.
nák. And [g] Hebrón was buylt seuen yere
g Declaring ẏ antiquitie thereof: also Abrahám, Sará, Izhák & Iaakób were buryed there.
before Zoán in Egypt.
24 *Thē they came to the riuer of Eshcól,
Deu.1,24.
and cut downe thence a branche with one
clustre of grapes, and they bare it vpon
a barre betwene two, and *broght* of the pomegranates and of the figges.
25 That place was called the ‖ riuer Eshcól
‖*Or, the valley of Eshcol, that is, of grapes.*
because of the clustre of grapes, which
the children of Israél cut downe thence.
26 Then after fourty daies they turned a-
gaine from searching of the land.
27 And they went and came to Mosés and
to Aarón & vnto all the Cōgregacion of
the children of Israél, in the wildernes of
[h] Parán, to Kadésh, and broght to them,
h Called also Kadesh-berná
and to all the Congregacion tidings, and
shewed them the frute of the land.
28 And they tolde [i] him, and said, We came
i That is, Mosés.
vnto the land whether thou hast sente vs,
& surely it floweth with * milke & honie:
Exod.33,3.
and here is of the frute of it.
29 Neuertheles the people be strong that
dwel in the land, and the cities *are* walled
and exceading great: and moreouer, we
sawe the [k] sonnes of Anák there.
k Ahimán, Sheshái, and Talmái, whome Caléb slewe afterward.
30 The Amalekites dwel in ẏ Southecoū-
trey, and the Hittites, and the Iebusites,
and the Amorites dwel in the moūtaines,
and the Canaanites dwel by the Sea and
by the coste of Iordén.
31 Then Caléb stilled the people ‖ before
‖*Or, murmuring against Mosés.*
Mosés, & said, Let vs go vp atonce, and
possesse it: for vndoutedly we shal ouercome it.
32 But the men, that went vp with him,
said, We be not able to go vp against
the people: for they are stronger then we.
33 So they broght vp an euil reporte of the
lād which they had searched for the children of Israél, saying, The land which we
haue gone through to searche it out, is a
land that [l] eateth vp the inhabitants the-
l The gyants were so cruel that they spoiled & killed one another, and those that came to them.
reof: for all the people that we sawe in it,
are men of great stature.
34 For there we sawe gyātes, the sonnes of
Anák, *which come* of the gyantes, so that we
semed in our sight like greshoppers: and
so we were in their sight.

CHAP. XIIII.

1 The people murmure against Mosés. 10 They wolde haue stoned Caléb and Ioshúa. 13 Mosés pacifieth God by his praier. 45 The people that wolde entre into the land, contrarie to Gods wil, are slaine.

1 THen all the Congregacion lifted vp
their voice, and cryed: and [a] the peo-
a Such as were affraied at the reporte of the ten spies.
ple wept that night,
2 And all the children of Israél murmured against Mosés and Aarón: and the
whole assemblie said vnto them, Wolde
God we had dyed in the land of Egypt,
or in this wildernes: wolde God we were
dead.
3 Wherefore now hathe ẏ Lord broght vs
into this lād to fall vpon the sworde? our
wiues, and our children shal be [b] a praye:
b To our enemies the Canaanites.
were it not better for vs to returne into
Egypt?
4 And they said one to another, Let vs
make a captaine and returne into E-
gypt.
5 Then Mosés and Aarón [c] fel on their fa-
c Lamēting ẏ people & praying for them.
ces before all the assemblie of the Congregacion of the children of Israél.
6 *And Ioshúa the sonne of Nun, and Ca-
Eccle.46,9. 1.mac.2,56.
léb the sonne of Iephunnéh *two* of them
that searched the land, [d] rent their clo-
d For sorowe, hearing their blasphemie.
thes,

7 And

7 And ſpake vnto all the aſſemblie of the
children of Iſraél,ſaying, The land which
we walked through to ſearche it, is a very good land.
8 If the Lord loue vs,he wil bring vs into
this land, and giue it vs, which is a land
that floweth with milke and honie.
9 But rebel not ye againſt the Lord, nether feare ye the people of the land: for
they are *but* [e] bread for vs: their ſhielde is
departed from them,and the Lord is with
vs,feare them not.

e We ſhal eaſely ouercome them.

10 And all the multitude ſaid, [f] Stone thē
with ſtones: but the glorie of the Lord
appeared in the Tabernacle of the Congregacion,before all the children of Iſraél.

f This is the condition of thē that wolde perſuade in Gods cauſe,to be perſecuted of the multitude.

11 And the Lord ſaid vnto Moſés, How
long wil this people prouoke me,and how
long wil it be, yer they beleue me, for all
the ſignes which I haue ſhewed among
them?
12 I wil ſmite them with the peſtilence and
deſtroy them, and wil make thee a greater nacion and mightier then they.
13 But Moſés ſaid vnto the Lord,* When
the Egyptians ſhal heare it, (for thou
broghteſt this people by thy power from
among them)

Exod.32,12.

14 Then they ſhal ſay to the inhabitants of
this land,(*for* they haue heard that thou,
Lord,art amōg this people, & that thou,
Lord,art ſene " face to face, and that thy
cloude ſtandeth ouer them, and that thou
* goeſt before them by day time in a piller of a cloude, and in a piller of fire by
night)

" Ebr. eye to eye.
Exod.13,21.

15 That thou wilt kil this people as [g] one
man: ſo the heathen which haue heard
the fame of thee,ſhal thus ſay,

g So that none ſhal eſcape.

16 Becauſe the Lord was not *able to bring
this people into the land, which he ſware vnto them, therefore hathe he ſlaine
them in the wildernes.

Deut.9,28.

17 And now,I beſeche thee, let the power
of my Lord be great, according as thou
haſt ſpoken,ſaying,
18 The Lord is * ſlowe to angre, and of
great mercie, and * forgiuing iniquitie,
and ſinne,but not making *the wicked* innocent, & * viſiting the wickednes of the fathers vpon the children, in the third and
fourth *generacion*:

Exod.34,6. pſal.103,8. Pſal.142,2.
Exod.20,5. & 34,7.

19 Be merciful, I beſeche thee, vnto the
iniquitie of this people, according to
thy great mercy, and as thou haſt forgiuen this people from Egypt,euen vntil
nowe.
20 And the Lord ſaid, I haue forgiuen [h] it,
according to thy requeſt.
21 Notwithſtanding,as I liue,all the earth
ſhalbe filled with the glorie of the

h In that he deſtroied not them vtterly, but left their poſteritie and certeine to entre.

Lord.
22 For all thoſe men which haue ſene my
glorie, and my miracles which I did in E-
gypt,and in the wildernes, & haue tēpted
me this [i] ten times, and haue not obeied
my voyce,

i That is, ſondrie times and often.

23 Certeinely thei ſhal not ſe the land,whe-
reof I ſware vnto their fathers: nether
ſhal anie that prouoke me,ſe it.
24 But my ſeruant * Caléb, becauſe he
had another [k] ſpirit,& hathe folowed me
ſtil, euen him wil I bring into the land,
whether he went, and his ſede ſhal inherit it.

Ioſh.14,6.
k A meke and obedient ſpirit and not rebellious.

25 Now the Amalekites and the Canaanites [l] remaine in the valley: *wherefore* turne backe tomorowe, and get you into
the [m] wildernes, by the way of the red
Sea.

l And lie in wayte for you.
m For I wil not defend you.

26 ¶After,the Lord ſpake vnto Moſés and
to Aarón,ſaying,
27 *How long *ſhal I ſuffre* this wicked multitude to murmure againſt me? I haue heard the murmurings of the childrē of Iſraél,which they murmure againſt me.

Pſal.106,26.

28 Tel them, As* I liue (ſaieth the Lord)
I wil ſurely do vnto you,euen as ye haue
ſpoken in mine eares.

Chap. 26,65. & 32.10.

29 Your carkeiſes ſhal fall in this wildernes,& all you that were*counted through
all your nombers, from twentie yere olde
and aboue,which haue murmured againſt
me,

Deut.1,35.

30 Ye ſhal not douteles come into the lād,
for the which I * liſted vp mine hand, to
make you dwel therein, ſaue Caléb the
ſonne of Iephunnéh, and Ioſhúa the ſonne of Nun.

Gen.14,22.

31 But your children,(which ye ſaid ſhulde
be a praye) them wil I bring in, and they
ſhal know the land which ye haue refuſed:
32 But euen your carkeiſes ſhal fall in this
wildernes.
33 And your children ſhal [n] wander in the
wildernes,fourtie yeres,& ſhal beare your
[o] whoredomes,vntil your carkeiſes be waſted in the wildernes.

n The worde ſignifieth,to be ſhepherdes,or to wander like ſhepeherdes to and fro.
o Your infidelitie and diſobedience againſt God.

34 After the nomber of the dayes, in the
which ye ſearched out the land,*euen* fourtie dayes,* euerie day for a yere, ſhal ye
beare your iniquitie, for * fourtie yeres, and ye [p] ſhal fele my breache of pro-
miſe.

Ezek.4,6.
Pſal.95,10.
p Whether my promes be true or no.

35 I the Lord haue ſaid,Certeinely I wil do
ſo to all this wicked companie, that are
gathered together againſt me: *for* in this
wildernes they ſhalbe conſumed,and there they ſhal dye.
36 And the men which Moſés had ſent
to ſearche the land(which, when they came againe, made all the people to mur-

mure against him, and broght vp a slander
vpon the land)
37 Euē those men that did bring vp that vile slander vpon the lād, *shal dye by a plague before the Lord.

1.Cor.10,10. ebr.3,10. iude.5.

38 But Ioshúa the sonne of Nun, and Caléb
the sonne of Iephunnéh, of those mē that
went to searche the land, shal liue.
39 ¶ Then Mosés tolde these sayings vnto
all the children of Israél, and the people
sorowed greatly.
40 *And thei rose vp earely in the morning, and gat them vp into the top of the
mountaine, saying, Lo, we be ready, to
go vp to the place which the Lord hathe
promised: for we haue [q] sinned.

Deu.1,41.

q They cōfesse they sinned by rebelling against God, but consider not they offēded in goig vp without Gods commādemēt.

41 But Mosés said, Wherefore transgresse
ye thus the commandement of the Lord?
it wil not so come wel to passe.
42 Go not vp (for the Lord is not among
you) lest ye be ouerthrowen before your
enemies.
43 For the Amalekites and the Canaanites
are there before you, and ye shal fall by
ȳ sworde: for in as muche as ye are turned
awaie from the Lord, the Lord also wil
not be with you.
44 Yet they presumed [r] obstinatly to go vp
to the top of the mountaine: but the Arke
of the couenant of the Lord, and Mosés
departed not out of the campe.

r They colde not be staied by anie meanes.

45 Then the Amalekites and the Canaanites,
which dwelt in that mountaine, came
downe and smote them, * and consumed
them vnto Hormáh.

Deut.1,44.

CHAP. XV.

2 The offrings which the Israelites shulde offer whē they came into the land of Canáan. 32 The punishement of him that brake the Sabbath.

1 AND the Lord spake vnto Mosés, saying,
2 Speake vnto the children of Israél, and
say vnto them, *When ye be come into ȳ
[a] land of your habitacions, which I giue
vnto you,

Leu.23,10.

a Into the lād of Canáan.

3 And wil make an offring by fire vnto the
Lord, a burnt offrīg or a sacrifice * " to fulfil a vowe, or a fre offring, or in your feastes, to make a * swete sauour vnto ȳ Lord
of the heard, or of the flocke,

Leu.22,21.
"Or, separate.
Exod.29,18.

4 Then * let him that offereth his offring
vnto the Lord, bring a meat offring of a
tenth deale of fine floure, mingled with ȳ
fourth parte of an [b] Hin of oyle.

Leu.2,1.

b Read Exod. 29,40.

5 Also thou shalt prepare the fourthe parte
of an Hin of wine to be powred on a lambe, *appointed* for the burnt offring or *anie*
offring.
6 And for a ram, thou shalt for a meat offring, prepare two tēth deales of fine floure, mingled with the third parte of an Hin
of oyle.
7 And for a [c] drinke offring, thou shalt offer the third parte of an Hin of wine, for
a swete sauour vnto the Lord.

c The licour was so called, because it was powred on ȳ thing that was offred.

8 And whē thou preparest a bullocke for a
burnt offring, or for a sacrifice to fulfil a
vowe or a peace offring to the Lord,
9 Thē let him offer with ȳ bullocke a meat
offring of " thre tēth deales of fine floure,
mingled with halfe an Hin of oyle.

"Or, thre Omers.

10 And thou shalt bring for a drīke offring
halfe an Hin of wine, for an offring made
by fire of a swete sauour vnto the Lord.
11 Thus shal it be done for a bullocke, or for
a ram, or for a lambe, or for a kid.
12 According to the nomber [d] that ye prepare *to offer*, so shal ye do to euerie one according to their nomber.

d Euerie sacrifice of beastes must haue their meat offring & drinke offring, according to this proportion.

13 All that are borne of the coūtrey, shal do
these things thus, to offer an offring made
by fire of swete sauour vnto the Lord.
14 And if a stranger soiourne with you, or
whosoeuer be among you in your generacions, and wil make an offring by fire of a
swete sauour vnto the Lord, as ye do, so
he shal do.
15 *One ordinance *shalbe* bothe for you of
the Congregacion, and also for the stranger that dwelleth *with you, euen* an ordinance for euer in your generaciōs: as you are,
so shal the stranger be before the Lord.

Exod.12,49. chap.9,14.

16 One lawe and one maner shal serue bothe for you & for the strāger that soiourneth with you.
17 ¶ And the Lord spake vnto Mosés, sayīg,
18 Speake vnto the children of Israél, and
say vnto them, When ye be come into ȳ
land, to the which I bring you,
19 And when ye shal eat of the bread of the
lād, ye shal offer an heaue offring vnto the
Lord.
20 Ye shal offer vp a cake of the first of
your [e] dowe for an heaue offring: * as the
heaue offring of the barne, so ye shal lift
it vp.

e Which is made of the first corne ye gather.
Leu.23,14.

21 Of the first of your dowe ye shal giue
vnto ȳ Lord an heaue offring in your generacions.
22 ¶ And if ye [f] haue erred, & not obserued
all these cōmandementes, which the Lord
hathe spoken vnto Mosés,

f As by ouersight or ignorance, read Leu.4,2.

23 *Euen* all that the Lord hathe commāded
you by the hand of Mosés, from the first
day that the Lord commanded Mosés,
& henceforward among your generacions.
24 And if so be that oght be committed
ignorātly of the [g] Cōgregacion, then all
the Cōgregacion shal giue a bullocke for
a burnt offring, for a swete sauour vnto
the Lord, with the meat offring & drinke
offring thereto, according to the * maner,
and an he goat for a sin offring.

g Some read, from the eyes of the Cōgregaciō: that is, which is hid from the Cōgregacion.
Leu.4,8.

25 And the Priest shal make an atonement
for all the Congregacion of the children
of Israél, and it shalbe forgiuen them: for
it is ignorance: and thei shal bring their
offring for an offring made by fire vnto
the Lord, and their sinne offring before
the Lord for their ignorance.
26 Then it shalbe forgiuen all the Cōgregacion of the children of Israél, and the
stranger that dwelleth among them: for
all the people *were* in ignorance.
27 ¶*But if anie one persone sinne through
ignorance, then he shal bring a she goat
of a yere olde for a sinne offring.

Leui.4,27.

28 And the Priest shal make an atonement
for the ignorant persone, when he sinneth
by ignorãce before the Lord, to make reconciliacion for him: & it shalbe forgiuen
him.
29 He that is borne among the children of
Israél, and the stranger that dwelleth amōg them, shal haue bothe one lawe, who
so doeth sinne by ignorance.
30 ¶But the persone that doeth oght [a] presumptuously, whether he be borne in the
land, or a stranger, the same blasphemeth
the Lord: therefore that persone shal be
cut of from among his people,

a Ebr. with an hie hand: that is, in cōtempt of God.

31 Because he hathe dispised the worde of
the Lord, and hathe broken his commandemẽt: that persone shalbe vtterly cut of:
his [h] iniquitie shalbe vpon him.

h He shal susteine the punishmẽt of his sinne.

32 ¶And while the children of Israél were
in the wildernes, thei founde a man that
gathered stickes vpon the Sabbath day.
33 And thei that foũde him gathering stickes, broght him vnto Mosés & to Aarón,
and vnto all the Congregacion,
34 And thei put him in* warde: for it was
not declared what shulde be done vnto
him.

Leui.24,12.

35 Then the Lord said vnto Mosés, This
man shal dye the death: & let all the multitude stone him with stones without the
hoste.
36 And all the Congregacion broght him
without the hoste, and stoned him with
stones, and he dyed, as the Lord had commanded Mosés.
37 ¶And ẏ Lord spake vnto Mosés, saying
38 Speake vnto the children of Israél, and
byd them that thei * make them fringes
vpō ẏ borders of their garmẽts throughout their generacions, and put vpon the
fringes of the borders a rybãde of blewe
silke.

Deut.22,12. mat.23,5.

39 And he shal haue the fringes, that when
ye loke vpon thẽ, ye may remẽber all the
commandements of the Lord, & do thẽ:
& that ye seke not after your owne heart,
nor after your owne eies, after the which
ye go a [i] whoring:

i By leauing Gods commandements and followig your owne fātasies.

40 That ye may remember and do all my
commandements, and be holy vnto your
God.
41 I am the Lord your God, which broght
you out of the land of Egypt, to be your
God: I am the Lord your God.

CHAP. XVI.

1 The rebellion of Kórah, Dathan and Abirám. 31 Kórah and his companie perisheth. 41 The people the next day murmure. 49. 14700. are slaine for murmuring.

1 NOw *Kórah the sonne of Izhár, the
sonne of Koháth, the sonne of Leui "went a parte with Dathán, and Abirám the sonnes of Eliáb, & On the sonne
of Péleth, the sonnes of Reubén:

Chap.27,3. eccle.45,22. iude 11.

" Or, toke other with him.

2 And thei rose vp "against Mosés, with
certeine of the children of Israél, two
hundreth and fiftie captaines of the assemblie,* famous in the Congregacion &
men of renoume.

" Or, before Mosés.

Chap.26,9.

3 Who gathered them selues together against Mosés, and against Aarón, and said
vnto them, [a] *Ye take* to muche vpon you,
seing all the Congregacion is holy, [b] euerie one of them, and the Lord *is* among
them: wherefore then lift ye your selues
aboue the Congregacion of the Lord?

a Or, let it suffice you: meaning to haue abused them thus long.

b All are a like holy: therefore none oght to be preferred aboue other: thus the wicked reason against Gods ordinance.

4 But when Mosés heard it, he fel vpon
his face,
5 And spake to Kórah & vnto all his companie, saying, Tomorowe the Lord wil
shewe who is his, and who is holy, & who
oght to approche nere vnto him: & whome he hathe [c] chosen, he wil cause to come nere to him.

c To be the Priest & to offer.

6 This do *therefore*, Take you censers, *bothe*
Kórah, and all his companie,
7 And put fire therein, and put incens in
them before the Lord tomorowe: and the
man whome the Lord doeth chose, the same shalbe holy: [d] *ye take* to muche vpon
you, ye sonnes of Leuí.

d He laieth ẏ same to their charge iustely, wherewith thei wrõgfully charged hĩ.

8 Againe Mosés said vnto Kórah, Heare, I
pray you, ye sonnes of Leuí.
9 Semeth it a small thing vnto you that the
God of Israél hathe separated you from
the multitude of Israél, to take you nere
to him self, to do the seruice of the Tabernacle of the Lord, and to stand before
the Congregacion and to minister vnto
them?
10 He hathe also taken thee to [e] him, and
all thy brethren the sonnes of Leuí with
thee, and seke ye the office of the Priest
also?

e To serue in the Congregacion, as in the verse before.

11 For which cause, thou, and all thy companie are gathered together against the
Lord: and what is Aarón, that ye murmure against him?
12 ¶And Mosés sent to call Dathán, and
Abirám the sonnes of Eliáb: who answered, We wil not come vp.
13 Is it a small thing that thou hast broght

f Thus thei spake contẽpteously, preferring Egypt to Canáan.

vs out f of a land that floweth with milke
and hony, to kil vs in the wildernes, except thou make thy self Lord and ruler
ouer vs also?
14 Also thou hast not broght vs vnto a lãd
that floweth with milke and honie, nether
giuen vs inheritance of fieldes and vineyardes: wilt thou g put out ÿ eies of these
men? we wil not come vp.

g Wilt thou make thẽ, that searched ÿ lãd, beleue that thei sawe not ÿ, which thei sawe?

15 Thẽ Moses waxed verie angrie, & said
vnto the Lord, * Loke not vnto their offring, I haue not taken so muche as an asse frõ thẽ, nether haue I hurte anie of thẽ.

Gen.4,4.

16 And Moses said vnto Kórah, Be thou &
all thy companie h before the Lord: *bothe*
thou, thei, and Aarón tomorowe:

h At the dore of the Tabernacle.

17 And take euerie man his censor, and put
incens in them, and bring ye euerie man
his censor before the Lord, two hundreth
and fiftie censors: thou also and Aarón, e-
uerie one his censor.
18 So thei toke euerie man his censor, and
put fire in them, and laied incens thereon,
and stode in the dore of the Tabernacle
of the Cõgregacion with Moses & Aarón.
19 And Kórah gathered all the i multitude
against them vnto the dore of the Tabernacle of the Congregacion: then the glorie of the Lord appeared vnto all the Cõgregacion.

i All that were of there faction.

20 And the Lord spake vnto Moses and to
Aarón, saying,
21 Separate your selues frõ amõg this Cõgregacion, ÿ I may consume thẽ atonce.
22 And thei fel vpon their faces and said,
O God ÿ God of the spirits, "of all flesh,
hathe not one man *onely* sinned, and wilt
thou be wrath with all the Cõgregacion?

" *Or, of euerie creature.*

23 And the Lord spake vnto Moses, saying,
24 Speake vnto the Congregacion & say,
Get you away frõ about the Tabernacle
of Kórah, Dathán and Abirám.
25 Then Moses rose vp, & went vnto Dathán and Abirám, and the Elders of Israél
followed him.
26 And he spake vnto the Congregacion,
saying, Departe, I pray you, frõ the tentes
of these wicked men, and touche nothing
of theirs, lest ye perish k in all their sinnes.

k With them that haue committed so manie sinnes.

27 So thei gate them away frõ the Tabernacle of Kórah, Dathán and Abirám on
euerie side: and Dathán, & Abirám came
out and stode in the dore of their tentes
with their wiues, and their sonnes, & their
litle children.
28 And Moses said, Hereby ye shal knowe
that ÿ Lord hathe sent me to do all these
workes: for *I haue* not *done them* of mine
owne l minde.

l I haue not forged thẽ of mine owne braine.

29 If these mẽ dye the cõmune death of all
men, or if thei be visited after ÿ visitaciõ
of all men, the Lord hathe not sent me.
30 But if the Lord make m a newe thing, &

m Or, shewe a strange sight.

the earth open her mouth, & swalowe thẽ
vp ŵ all that thei haue, & thei go downe
quicke into "n ÿ pit, thẽ ye shal vnderstãd
that these men haue prouoked the Lord.

" *Or, hel.* n Or, depe & darcke places of the earth.

31 ¶ And as sone as he had made an end of
speaking all these wordes, euen the grou-
de claue a sunder that was vnder them,
32 And the earth * opened her mouthe, and
swalowed them vp, with their families, &
all the men that were with Kórah, and all
their goods.

Chap.27,3. deut.11,6. psal.106,17.

33 So thei & all that thei had, went downe
aliue into the pit, & the earth couered thẽ:
so thei perished from among the Cõgregacion.
34 And all Israél that were about thẽ, fled
at the crye of thẽ: for thei said, *Let vs flee*,
lest the earth swalowe vs vp.
35 But there came out a fire from the Lord,
and consumed the two hundreth and fiftie
men that offred the incens.
36 ¶ And ÿ Lord spake vnto Moses, saying,
37 Speake vnto Eleazár, the sonne of Aarón the Priest, that he take vp the censers
out of the burning, and skater the fire beyonde *the altar*: for thei are halowed,
38 The censers, *I say*, of these sinners, *that de-*
stroy. d o them selues: and let them make of
them broad plates for a couering of the
Altar: for they offred thẽ before the Lord,
therefore thei shalbe holy, and thei shalbe
p a signe vnto the children of Israél.

o Which were the occasiõ of their owne death.

p Of Gods iudgements against rebels.

39 Then Eleazár the Priest toke the brasen
cẽsers, which thei, that were burnt, had offred, and made broad plates of them for
a couering of the Altar.
40 *It is* a remembrance vnto the children
of Israél, that no stranger which is not of
the sede of Aarón, come nere to offer incens before the Lord, that he be not like
q Kórah and his companie, as the Lord
said to him by the hand of Moses.

q Who presumed aboue his vocacion.

41 ¶ But on the morowe all the multitude
of the children of Israél murmured a-
gainst Moses and against Aarón, saying,
Ye haue killed the people of the Lord.
42 And when the Cõgregacion was gathered against Moses & against Aarón, then
thei " turned their faces toward the Tabernacle of the Cõgregacion: & beholde,
the cloude couered it, & the glorie of the
Lord appeared.

" *Or, fled: towards Moses & Aarón.*

43 Then Moses and Aarón were come before the Tabernacle of the Cõgregaciõ.
44 ¶ And the Lord spake vnto Moses, sayĩg,
45 Get you vp from among this Congregacion: for I wil consume them quickely:
then thei fel vpon their faces.
46 And Moses said vnto Aarón, Take the
censer and put fire therein of the r Altar,
& put *therein* incens, & go quickely vnto
the Congregacion, & make an atonement
for them: for there is wrath gone out frõ

r For it was not lauful to take anie other fire, but of the Altar of burnt offring, Leui.10,1.

the Lord: the plague is begonne.
47 Then Aarón toke as Mosés commãded
him, and ran into the middes of the Congregacion, and beholde, the f plague was
begõne among the people, & he put in incens, & made an atonemẽt for the people.
48 And when he stode betwene the dead, &
thẽ that were aliue, ỹ g plague was stayed.
49 So they dyed of this plague fourtene
thousand and seuen hundreth, beside thẽ
that dyed in the conspiracie of Kórah.
50 And Aarón went againe vnto Mosés before the dore of the Tabernacle of the
Congregacion, & the plague was stayed.

f God had begõne to punishe ỹ people.

g God drewe backe his hãd & ceased to punishe them.

CHAP. XVII.

2 The twelue rods of the twelue princes of the tribes of Israél 9 Aarons rod buddeth, and beareth blossoms, 10 For a testimonie against the rebellious people.

1 AND the Lord spake vnto a Mosés, saying,
2 Speake vnto the childrẽ of Israél, & take
of euerie one of them a rod, after ỹ house
of their fathers, of all their princes according to the familie of their fathers, *euen*
twelue rods: *and* thou shalt write euerie
mans name vpon his rod.
3 And write Aarons name vpon the rod of
Leui: for euerie rod *shalbe* for the head of
the house of their fathers.
4 And thou shalt put thẽ in the Tabernacle of the Congregacion, before *the Arke*
of the Testimonie,* where I wil declare
my self to you.
5 And the mans rod, whome I b chose, shal
blossom: and I wil make cease from me
the grudgings of the children of Israél,
which grudge against you.
6 ¶ Then Mosés spake vnto the children of
Israél, & all their princes gaue him a rod,
one rod for euerie prince, according to ỹ
houses of their fathers, *euen* twelue rods,
& the rod c of Aarón *was* amõg their rods.
7 And Mosés laid the rods before the Lord
in the Tabernacle of the Testimonie.
8 And when Mosés on the morowe went
into the Tabernacle of the Testimonie,
beholde, the rod of Aarón d for the house of Leui was budded, and broght forthe
buddes, & broght forthe blossoms & bare ripe almondes.
9 Then Mosés broght out all the rods frõ
before the Lord vnto all the children of
Israél: and they loked vpon them, & toke
euerie man his rod.
10 ¶ After, ỹ Lord said vnto Mosés, *Bring
Aarons rod againe before the Testimonie to be kept for a tokẽ to the rebellious
children, & thou shalt cause their e murmurings to cease frõ me, ỹ they dye not.
11 So Mosés did as the Lord had commãded him: so did he.
12 ¶ And the children of Israél spake vnto
Mosés, saying, Beholde, f we are dead, we
perish, we are all lost.

a While he was in ỹ dore of the Tabernacle.

Exod.25,22.

b To be the chief Priest.

c Thogh Iosephs tribe was deuided into two in ỹ distributiõ of the land, yet here it is but one, and Leui maketh a tribe.

d To declare that God did chose ỹ house of Leui to serue him in ỹ Tabernacle.

Ebr.9,4.

e Grudging ỹ Aarón shulde be hie Priest

f The Chalde text describeth thus their murmuring: We dye by the sworde: the earth swaloweth vs vp, ỹ pestilẽce doeth consume vs.

13 Whosoeuer cõmeth nere, or approcheth
to the Tabernacle of the Lord, shal dye:
shal we be consumed and dye?

CHAP. XVIII.

1. 7 The office of Aarón & his sonnes, 2 With the Leuites. 8 The Priests parte of the offrings. 20 God is their portion. 26 The Leuites haue the tithes, and offer the tenthes thereof to the Lord.

1 AND ỹ Lord said vnto Aarón, Thou,
& thy sonnes and thy fathers house
with thee, shal beare a the iniquitie of the
Sanctuarie: bothe thou & thy sonnes with
thee shal beare ỹ iniquitie of your Priests
office.
2 And bring also with thee thy brethren of
the tribe of Leui of the familie of thy father, which shalbe ioyned with thee, and
minister vnto thee: but thou, and thy sonnes with thee *shal minister* before the Tabernacle of the Testimonie.
3 And they shal b kepe thy charge, euen the
charge of all ỹ Tabernacle: but they shal
not come nere the instruments of the Sãctuarie, nor to the altar, lest they dye, bothe they & you:
4 And they shal be ioyned with thee & kepe the charge of the Tabernacle of the
Congregacion for all ỹ seruice of the Tabernacle: & no c stranger shal come nere
vnto you.
5 Therefore shal ye kepe the charge of the
Sanctuarie, and the charge of the altar: so
there shal fall no more wrath vpon the
children of Israél.
6 For lo, I haue *taken your brethren ỹ Leuites frõ among ỹ children of Israél, *which*
as a gift of yours, are giuẽ vnto the Lord,
to do the seruice of the Tabernacle of the
Congregacion.
7 But thou, & thy sonnes with thee shal kepe your Priests office for all things of the
altar, and within the vaile: therefore shal
ye serue: *for* I haue made your Priests office "an office of seruice: therefore the strãger that commeth nere, shal be slaine.
8 ¶ Againe ỹ Lord spake vnto Aarón, Beholde, I haue giuen thee the keping of mine d offrings, of all the halowed things of
the childrẽ of Israél: vnto thee I haue giuen them for the anointings sake, and to
thy sonnes, for a perpetual ordinance.
9 This shalbe thine of ỹ moste holie thĩgs,
reserued from the e fire: all their offring of
all their meat offring, and of all their sin
offring, and of all their trespas offring, ŵ
they bring vnto me, that shalbe most holy vnto thee and to thy sonnes.
10 In the most f holy place shalt thou eat it:
euerie male shal eat of it: it is holy vnto
thee.
11 This also shalbe thine: the heaue offring
of their gift, with all the shake offrings
of the children of Israél: I haue giuen
them vnto thee & to thy sonnes & to thy

a If you trespas in anie thing concerning the ceremonies of the Sanctuarie, or your office, you shalbe punished.

b That is, the things, which are cõmitted to thee: or, ŵ thou doest enioyne them.

c Which was not of ỹ tribe of Leui.

Chap.3,45.

"Or, a gift.

d As the first frute, firstborne, & ỹ tẽthes.

e That ŵ was not burned, shulde be the Priests.

f That is, in ỹ Sanctuarie, betwene ỹ court & the Holiest of all.

g Read Leuit. 10,14.

g daughters ẘ thee, to be a duetie for euer:
all the cleane in thine house shal eat of it.

h That is, the chiefest, or the best.

12 All the h fat of the oyle, and all the fat
of the wine, and of the wheat, which they
shal offer vnto the Lord for their first frutes, I haue giuen them vnto thee.
13 And the first ripe of all that is in their
lād, which they shal bring vnto the Lord,
shalbe thine: all the cleane in thine house
shal eat of it.

Leuit. 27,28.

14 *Euerie thing separate from the cōmune vse in Israél, shal be thine.

Exod. 13,2. & 22,29. leu. 27,26. chap. 3,13.

15 All that *first* openeth the * matrice of a-
nie flesh, which they shal offer vnto the
Lord, of man or beast, shalbe thine: but
the first borne of man shalt thou redeme, and the first borne of the vncleane
beast shalt thou redeme.
16 And those that are to be redemed, shal tẙ
redeme from the age of a moneth, according to thy estimation, for the money of
fiue shekels, after the shekel of the Sanctuarie, * which is twentie gerahs.

Exod. 30,13. leu. 27,25. chap. 3,17. ezek. 45,12.

i Because thei are appointed for sacrifice.

17 But the first borne of a kowe, or the first
borne of a shepe, or the first borne of a
goat shalt thou not i redeme: *for* they are
holy: thou shalt sprinkle their blood at
the altar, and thou shalt burne theyr fat: *it
is* a sacrifice made by fire for a swete sauour vnto the Lord.

Exod. 29, 26. leui. 7,30.

18 And the flesh of them shalbe thine, * as
the shake breast, and as the right shulder
shalbe thine.
19 All the heaue offrings of the holy things
which the children of Israél shal offer vnto the Lord, haue I giuen thee, & thy sonnes, and thy daughters with thee, to be a
duetie for euer: *it is* a perpetual couenant
k of salt before the Lord, to thee and to
thy sede with thee.

k That is, sure, stable, & incorruptible.

l Of Canaan.

20 ¶ And the Lord said vnto Aarón, Thou
shalt haue none inheritance in their l land,
nether shalt thou haue anie parte among
them: * I am thy parte & thine inheritance
among the children of Israél.

Deu. 10,9. & 18 2. iosh. 13,14. ezek. 44,28.

21 For beholde, I haue giuē the childrē of
Leuí all the tenth in Israél for an inheritance, for their seruice which they serue in
the Tabernacle of the Congregacion.
22 Nether shal the children of Israél anie
more m come nere ẙ Tabernacle of the Cōgregacion, lest they susteine sinne, & dye.

m To serue therein: for ẙ Leuites are put in their place.

23 But the Leuites shal do the seruice in ẙ
Tabernacle of ẙ Cōgregaciō, & they shal
beare n their sinne: *it is* a lawe for euer in
your generacions, ẙ among the childrē of
Israél they possesse none enheritance.

n If they faile in their office, they shalbe punished.

24 For the tithes of the children of Israél,
which they shal offer as an offring vnto ẙ
Lord, I haue giuen the Leuites for an inheritance: therefore I haue said vnto thē,
Among the childrē of Israél ye shal possesse none inheritance.
25 ¶ And ẙ Lord spake vnto Mosés, sayĩg,
26 Speake also vnto the Leuites & say vnto
them, When ye shal take of the childrē of
Israél the tithes, ẘ I haue giuen you of thē
for your inheritance, then shal ye take an
heaue offring of that same for the Lord, *e-
uen* the tenth parte of the tithe.
27 And your heaue offrĩg shalbe rekened vn
to you, as the o corne of the barne, or as
the abundance of the wine presse.

o As acceptable as ẙ frute of your owne groūde, or vineyarde.

28 So ye shal also offer an heaue offring vn
to the Lord of all your tithes, which ye
shal receiue of the children of Israél, and
ye shal giue thereof the Lords heaue offring to Aarón the Priest.
29 Ye shal offer of all your p gifts all the
Lords heaue offrings: of all ẙ q fat of the
same *shal ye offer* the holy things thereof.

p Which ye haue receiued of the childrē of Israél.

q Read vers. 12.

30 Therefore thou shalt say vnto thē, Whē
ye haue offred the fat thereof, then it shalbe counted vnto the Leuites, as the encrease of the corne floore, or as ẙ encrease of
the wine presse.
31 And ye shal eat it in all r places, ye, and
your housholds: for it is your wages for
your seruice in the Tabernacle of the Cō
gregacion.

r As is in the 11. vers.

32 And ye shal s beare no sinne by the reason of it, when ye haue offred the fat of it:
nether shal ye pollute the holy t things of
the children of Israél, lest ye dye.

s Ye shal not be punished therefore.

t The offrings which the Israelites haue offred to God.

CHAP. XIX.

2 *The sacrifice of the red kowe.* 9 *The sprinkling water.*
11 *He that toucheth the dead.* 14 *The man that dyeth
in a tent.*

1 AND the Lord spake to Mosés, and to
Aarón, saying,
2 a This is the ordināce of the lawe, which
the Lord hathe cōmāded, saying, Speake
vnto the children of Israél that they bring
thee a red kowe without blemish, wherein
is no spot, vpon the which neuer came
yoke.

a According to this lawe & ceremonie, ye shal sacrifice ẙ red kowe.

3 And ye shal giue her vnto Eleazár the
Priest, that he may bring her * without the
hoste, and cause her to b be slaine before
his face.

Ebr. 13,11.

b By another Priest.

4 Then shal Eleazár the Priest take of her
blood with his * finger, & sprinkle it before the Tabernacle of the Congregacion
seuen times,

Ebr. 9,13.

5 And cause ẙ kowe to be burnt in his sight:
with her * skin, & her flesh, and her blood,
and her doung shal he burne *her*.

Exod. 29,14. leu. 4,11.

6 Then shal the Priest take ceder wood, &
hyssope and skarlet *lace*, and cast them in
the middes of the fire where the kowe
burneth.
7 Then shal the c Priest wash his clothes,
and he shal wash his flesh in water, and
then come into the hoste, and the Priest
shalbe vncleane vnto the euen.

c Meaning, Eleazár.

8 Also he that d burneth her, shal wash his
clo-

d The inferior Priest who killed her & burned her.

clothes in water, and wash his flesh in water, and be vncleane vntil euen.
9 And a man, *that is* cleane, shal take vp the
ashes of the kowe, & put them without the
hoste in a cleane place: and it shalbe kept
for the Congregacion of the children of
Israél for [e] a sprinkling water: it is a sinne
offring.

> e Or the water of seperation, because that they that were separate for their vnclennes, were sprinkled therewith & made cleane, Chap. 8,7. It is also called holy water, because it was ordeined to an holy vse, Chap. 5,17.

10 Therefore he that gathereth the ashes
of the kowe, shal wash his clothes, and remaine vncleane vntil euen: and it shalbe
vnto the children of Israél, and vnto the
stranger that dwelleth among them, a statute for euer.
11 He that toucheth the dead bodie of anie
man, shalbe vncleane euen seuen daies.
12 He shal purifie him selfe [f] therewith the
third day, and the seuenth day he shalbe
cleane: but if he purifie not him selfe the
third day, then the seuenth day he shal not
be cleane.

> f With the sprinkling water.

13 Whosoeuer toucheth the corps of anie
man that is dead, and purgeth not him
selfe, defileth ẏ Tabernacle of the Lord, &
that persone shalbe [g] cut of from Israél, be
cause the sprinkling water was not sprinkled vpon him: he shalbe vncleane, and his
vnclennes *shal remaine* stil vpon him.

> g So that he shulde not be estemed to be of the holy people, but as a polluted & excōmunicate persone.

14 This is the lawe, When a man dyeth in
a tent, all that come into the tent, and all
that is in the tent, shalbe vncleane seuen
dayes,
15 And all the vessels that be open, which
haue no [*] couering fastened vpō them, shal
be vncleane.

> * Ebr. a couering of cloth.

16 Also whosoeuer toucheth one that is
slaine with a sworde in ẏ fielde, or a dead
persone, or a bone of a dead man, or a graue, shalbe vncleane seuen dayes.
17 Therefore for an vncleane persone thei
shal take of the burnt ashes of the [h] sin offring, and [i] pure water shal be put thereto
in a vessel.
18 And a [k] cleane persone shal take hyssope
and dip it in the water, and sprinkle it vpon the tent, and vpon all the vessels, and
on the persones that were therein, and
vpon him that touched the bone, or ẏ slaine, or the dead, or the graue.

> h Of the red kowe burnt for sinne.
> i Water of ẏ fountaine or riuer.
> k One of the Priests which is cleane.

19 And the cleane persone shal sprinkle vpon the vncleane the third day, and the seuenth day, and he shal purifie him self the
seuenth day, & [l] wash his clothes, & wash
him selfe in water, & shalbe cleane at euē.

> l Because he had bene amōg them that were vncleane: or els had touched the water, as ver. 21.

20 But the man that is vncleane and purifieth not him selfe, that persone shalbe cut
of from amōg the Congregacion, because he hathe defiled the Sanctuarie of the
Lord: and the sprinkling water hathe not
bene sprinkled vpon him: *therefore* shal he
be vncleane.
21 And it shalbe a perpetual lawe vnto thē,
that he that sprinkleth the sprinkling water, shal wash his clothes: also he that toucheth the sprinkling water, shal be vncleane vntil euen.
22 And whatsoeuer the vncleane persone
toucheth, shal be vncleane: and the persone that toucheth [m] *him*, shalbe vncleane
vntil the euen.

> m That is vncleane.

CHAP. XX.

*1 Miriám dyeth. 2 The people murmure. 8 They ha-
ue water out of the rocke. 14 Edóm denyeth the Israelites passage. 25. 28 The death of Aarón, in whose
rowme Eleazár succedeth.*

1 THen the children of Israél came with
the whole Congregacion to the desert of Zin in the first [a] moneth, and the
people abode at Kadésh: where [b] Miriám
dyed, and was buryed there.
2 But there was no water for the Congregacion, and they [c] assembled them selues
against Mosés and against Aarón.
3 And the people chode with Mosés, and
spake, saying, Wolde God we had perished,
*when our brethren dyed before ẏ Lord.
4 *Why haue ye thus broght the Congregacion of the Lord vnto this wildernes,
ẏ both we, and our cattel shulde dye there?

> a This was fourtie yeres after their departure from Egypt.
> b Mosés and Aarons sister.
> c Another rebellion was in Raphidim, Exod. 17, and this was in Kadésh.
> Chap. 11,33.
> Exod. 17,2.

5 Wherefore now haue ye made vs to come vp frō Egypt, to bring vs into this miserable place, *which is* no place of sede, nor
figs, nor vines, nor pomgranates? nether is
there anie water to drinke.
6 Then Mosés and Aarón went from the
assemblie vnto the dore of the Tabernacle of the Congregacion, and fel vpon
their faces: and the glorie of the Lord appeared vnto them.
7 ¶ And ẏ Lord spake vnto Mosés, saying,
8 Take the [d] rod, and gather thou and thy
brother Aarón the Congregacion together, and speake ye vnto the rocke before
their eies, & it shal giue forthe his water,
and thou shalt bring them water out of
the rocke: so thou shalt giue the Congregacion, and their beastes drinke.

> d Wherewith thou didest miracles in Egypt, and didest deuide ẏ Sea.

9 Then Mosés toke the rod frō before the
Lord, as he had commanded him.
10 And Mosés and Aarón gathered ẏ Cōgregacion together before the rocke, and
Mosés sayd vnto them, Heare now, ye rebels: [e] shal we bring you water out of
this rocke?
11 Then Mosés lift vp his hand, and with
his rod he smote the rocke twise, and the
water came out abundantly: so the Congregacion, and their beasts dranke.

> e The punishment, which followed hereof, declared that Mosés & Aarón beleued not the Lords promes, as appeareth vers. 12.

12 ¶ Agayne the Lord spake vnto Mosés &
to Aarón, Because ye beleued me not, to
[f] sanctifie me in the presence of the children of Israél, therefore ye shal not bring
this Congregacion into the land which
I haue giuen them.
13 This is the water [g] of Meribáh, because
the children of Israél stroue with ẏ Lord,

> f That ẏ children of Israél shulde beleue and acknowledge my power, & so honour me.
> g Or, strife, & contencion.

h By shewing hi self almightie & maiteyning his glorie.
i Because Iaakób or Israél was Esaus brother, who was called Edóm.

and he h was sanctified in them.
14 ¶Then Mosés sent messengers from Kadésh vnto ŷ King of i Edóm, *saying*, Thus
saith thy brother Israél, Thou knowest
all the trauaile that we haue had,
15 How our fathers went downe into E-
gypt, and we dwelt in Egypt a long time,
where the Egyptians handled vs euil &
our fathers.
16 But when we cryed vnto the Lord, he heard our voyce, and sent an Angel, & hathe
broght vs out of Egypt, & beholde, we are
in ŷ citie Kadésh, in thine vtmost border.
17 I pray thee that we may passe through
thy countrey: we wil not go through the
fieldes nor the vineyardes, nether wil we
drinke of the water of the welles: we wil
go by the ″kings way, and nether turne
vnto the right hand nor to the left, vntil
we be past thy borders.

″Or, hie way.

18 And Edóm answered him, ″Thou shalt
not passe by me, lest I come out against
thee with the sworde.

″Or, come not.

19 Then the children of Israél said vnto
him, We wil go vp by the hie way: & if I
and my cattel drinke of thy water, I wil
then paye for it: I wil onely (without anie
harme) go through on my fete.
20 He answered againe, Thou shalt not
go through. Thẽ ″Edóm came out against
him with muche people, and with a mighty power.

″Or, the Edomites.

21 Thus Edóm denied to giue Israél passage through his coũtrie: wherefore Israél
k turned away from him.

k To passe by another way.

22 ¶And when the children of Israél with
all the Congregacion departed from *Kadésh, they came vnto the mount Hor.

Chap. 33, 37.

23 And the Lord spake vnto Mosés and to
Aarón in the mount Hor nere the coste
of the land of Edóm, saying,
24 Aarón shalbe l gathered vnto his people: for he shal not entre into the land, ŵ
I haue giuen vnto the children of Israél,
because ye ″disobeied my commandement
at the water ″of Meribáh.

l Read Gen. 25, 8.
″Or, rebelled.
″Or, strife.

25 Take *Aarón and Eleazár his sonne, &
bring them vp into the mount Hor,

Chap. 33, 38. deut. 32, 50.

26 And cause Aarón to put of his garmẽts
& put them vpon Eleazár his sonne: for
Aarón shal be gathered *to his fathers*, and
shal dye there.
27 And Mosés did as the Lord had cõmãded: & they went vp into the mount Hor,
in the sight of all the Congregacion.
28 And Mosés put of Aarons clothes, and
put them vpon Eleazár his sonne: *so Aarón dyed there in the top of the mõut: and
Mosés and Eleazár came downe from of
the mount.

Deu. 10, 6. & 32, 50.

29 When all the Congregacion sawe that
Aarón was dead, all the house of Israél
wept ″for Aarón thirtie dayes.

″Or, mourned.

CHAP. XXI.

3 *Israél vanquisheth King Arád. 6 The firy serpentes are sent for the rebellion of the people. 24. 33 Sihón and Og are ouercome in battel.*

1 WHen King *Arád the Canaanite,
which dwelt toward the South,
heard tel that Israél came by the a waie of
the spies, then foght he against Israél, and
toke of them prisoners.

Chap. 33, 40.
a By that way which their spies, that searched the dangers, found to be moste safe.

2 So Israél vowed a vowe vnto the Lord,
and said, If thou wilt deliuer *and* giue this
people into mine hand, then I wil vtterly
destroye their cities.
3 And the Lord heard the voyce of Israél,
and deliuered *them* the Canaanites: & they
vtterly destroyed them and their cities, &
called the name of the place ″Hormáh.

″Or, destruction.

4 ¶After, they departed from the mount
Hor by the way of the red Sea, to b compasse the land of Edóm: and the people
were sore grieued because of the way.

b For they were forbidden to destroy it, Deut. 2, 5.

5 And the people spake against God and
against Mosés, *saying*, Wherefore haue ye
broght vs out of Egypt, to dye in the wildernes? for *here is* nether bread nor water,
and our soule *lotheth this light c bread.
6 *Wherefore the Lord sent d firy serpentes among the people which stõg the people: so that manie of the people of Israél
dyed.

Chap. 11, 6.
c Meaning Mána, which they thoght did not nourish.
Wisd. 16, 1.
1. cor. 10, 9.
d For thei ŷ were stõg therwith, were so inflamed with the heat thereof, that they dyed.

7 Therefore the people came to Mosés and
said, We haue sinned: for we haue spoken against the Lord, and against thee:
praye to the Lord, that he take away the
serpents from vs: and Mosés prayed for
the people.
8 And the Lord said vnto Mosés, Make thee
a firy serpent, and set it vp ″for a signe,
that as manie as are bitten, may loke vpon
it, and liue.

″Or, vpon a pole.

9 *So Mosés made a serpent of brasse, and
set it vp for a signe: and when a serpent
had bitten a man, then he loked to the serpent of brasse, and ″liued.

2. Kin. 18, 4. ioh. 3, 14.
″Or, recouered.

10 *And the children of Israél departed
thence, and pitched in Obóth.

Chap. 33, 47.

11 ¶And they departed from Obóth, and
pitched ″in Iie-abarím, in the wildernes,
which is before Moáb on the Eastside.
12 ¶They remoued thence, and pitched
vpon the riuer of Záred.

″Or, in the heapes of Abarim, or, hilles.

13 ¶Thence they departed, and pitched on
the other side of Arnón, which is in the
wildernes, and commeth out of the costes
of the Amorites: (for Arnón *is* the border
of Moáb, betwene the Moabites and the
Amorites)
14 Wherefore it shalbe spoken in the boke
of e the battels of the Lord, ″what thing
he did in the red Sea, and in the riuers of
Arnón,
15 And *at* the streame of ŷ riuers that goeth
downe to ŷ dwelling of Ar, and lieth vpõ
the

e Which semeth to be the boke of the Iudges, or as some thinke, a boke which is lost.
″Or, (How God destroyed) Vaheb (the citie) with a whirlewinde, and the vallies of Arnon.

the border of Moáb.
16 ¶And from thence *they turned* to Beér:
the same is the well where the Lord said
vnto Mosés, Assemble the people, and I
wil giue them water.
17 ¶Then Israél sang this song, "Rise vp
well, [f] sing ye vnto it.
18 The princes digged this well, ye captaines of the people digged it, euen [g] the lawegiuer, with their staues. And from the
wildernes *they came* to Mattanáh,
19 ¶And from Mattanáh to Nahaliél, and
from Nahaliél to Bamóth,
20 ¶And frō Bamóth in the valley, that is
in the plaine of Moáb, to the top of Pisgáh that loketh toward Ieshimón.
21 ¶Then Israél sent messengers vnto Sihón, King of the Amorites, saying,
22 *Let me go through thy land: we wil not
turne aside into the fields, nor into the vineyardes, nether drinke of the waters of ye
welles: we wil go by the kings way, vntil
we be past thy countrei.
23 *But Sihón gaue Israél no licence to passe through his countrey, but Sihón assembled all his people, and went out against
Israél into the wildernes: and he came to
Iahóz, and foght against Israél.
24 *But Israél smote him with the edge of
the sworde, and conquered his land, from
Arnón vnto [h] Iabók, *euen* vnto the childrē of Ammón: for the border of the children of Ammón *was* [i] strong.
25 And Israél toke all these cities, & dwelt
in all the cities of the Amorites in Heshbón and in all the " villages thereof.
26 For [k] Heshbón was the citie of Sihón
the King of the Amorites, which had
foght before time against the King of the
Moabites, and had taken all his land out
of his hand, *euen* vnto Arnón.
27 Wherefore they that spake in prouerbes, say, Come to Heshbón, let the citie of
Sihón be buylt and repared:
28 For [l] a fire is gone out of Heshbón, *and*
a flame from the citie of Sihón, and hathe consumed Ar of the Moabites, *and*
the lords of Bamóth in Arnón.
29 Wo be to thee, Moáb: ô people of [m] Chemósh, thou art vndone: he hathe suffred his
sonnes to be pursued, and his daughters *to*
be in captiuitie to Sihón the King of the
Amorites.
30 Their " empire is lost from Heshbón
vnto Dibón, and we haue destroyed them
vnto Nóphah, which *reacheth* vnto Medebá.
31 ¶Thus Israél dwelt in the land of the
Amorites.
32 And Mosés sent to search out Iaazér,
and they toke the townes belōging thereto, and roted out the Amorites that were
there.

"Or, Spring.
f Ye that receiue the cōmoditie therof, giue praise for it.
g Mosés and Aarón heades of the people onely smote ye rocke with ye rod or staffe, which gaue water as a well, that were depe digged.
Deu. 2, 26. iudg. 11, 19.
Deu. 29, 7.
Iosh. 12, 2. psal. 134, 11. amos 2, 9.
h The riuer.
i For the people were talle and strong like gyāts. Deu. 2, 20.
" Ebr. daughters
k For if it had bene the Moabites, the Israelites might not haue possessed it, Deu. 2, 9.
l Meaning, warre.
m Chemósh was the Idole of the Moabites, 1 Kin. 11, 33: who was not able to defende his worshippers, wc toke ye idole for their father.
" Ebr. light.

33 ¶*And they turned and went vp toward
Bashán: & Og the King of Bashán came
out against them, he, and all his people, to
fight at Edréi.
34 Then the Lord said vnto Mosés, Feare
him not: for I haue deliuered him into
thine hand & all his people, and his land:
* and thou shalt do to him as thou didest
vnto Sihón the King of the Amorites,
which dwelt at Heshbón.
35 They smote him therefore, and his sonnes, and all his people, vntil there was none left him: so they conquered his land.

Deu. 3, 1. & 29, 7.
Psal. 135, 11.

CHAP. XXII.

1 King Balák sendeth for Balaám to curse the Israelites. 12 The Lord forbiddeth him to go. 22 The Angel of the Lord meteth him, & his asse speaketh. 38 Balaám protesteth that he wil speake nothing, but that which the Lord putteth in his mouthe.

1 After, the children of Israél departed
and pitched in the plaine of Moáb
on the [a] other side of Iordén from Ierichó.
2 ¶Now Balák the sonne of Zippór sawe
all that Israél had done to the Amorites.
3 And the Moabites were sore afraide of
the people, because they were manie, and
Moáb " freated against the children of
Israél.
4 Therefore Moáb said vnto the [b] Elders
of Midián, Now shal this multitude licke
vp all that are rounde about vs, as an oxe
licketh vp the grasse of the field: and Balák the sonne of Zippór *was* King of the
Moabites at that time.
5 *He sent menssengers therefore vnto Balaám the sonne of Beór to Pethór (which
is by the [c] riuer of the land of the childrē
of his folke) to call him, saying, Beholde, there is a people come out of Egypt,
which couer the face of the earth, and lie
ouer against me.
6 Come now therefore, I pray thee, *and*
curse me this people (for they are stronger then I) so it may be that I shal be able
to smite thē and to driue them out of the
lād: for I knowe that he, whome thou blessest, is blessed, and he whome thou cursest,
shalbe cursed.
7 And the Elders of Moáb, and the Elders
of Midián departed, hauing [d] *the rewarde*
of the soothsaying in their hand, and thei
came vnto Balaám, & tolde him the wordes of Balák.
8 Who answered them, Tary here this
night, and I wil giue you an answer, as the
Lord shal say vnto me. So [e] the princes
of Moáb abode with Balaám.
9 Then God came vnto Balaám, and said,
What men are these with thee?
10 And Balaám said vnto God, Balák the
sonne of Zippór, King of Moáb hathe
sent vnto me, *saying*,

a Being at Ierichó, it was beyonde Iordén: but where the Israelites were, it was on this side.
" Or, was vexed.
b Which were the heades & gouerners.
Iosh. 24, 9.
c To wit, Euphrátes, vpon ye which stode this citie Pethor.
d Thinking to bribe him wt giftes to curse the Israelites.
e Whome before he called Elders: meaning, the gouerners, & after calleth thē seruants: that is, subiectes to their King.

11 Beholde, *there is* a people come out of
Egypt and couereth the face of the earth:
come nowe, curse them for my sake: so it
may be that I shal be able to ouercome
them in battel, and to driue them out.
12 And God [f] said vnto Balaám, Go not
thou with them, nether curse the people,
for they are blessed.
13 And Balaám rose vp in the morning, and
said vnto the princes of Balák, Returne
vnto your land: for the Lord hathe refused to giue [g] me leaue to go with you.
14 So the princes of Moáb rose vp, and wẽt
vnto Balák, and said, Balaám hathe refused to come with vs.
15 ¶ Balák yet sent againe mo princes, and
more honorable then they.
16 Who came to Balaám, and said to him,
Thus saieth Balák the sonne of Zippór,
[h] Be not thou stayed, I pray thee, from cõ
ming vnto me.
17 For I wil promote thee vnto great honour, and wil do whatsoeuer thou sayest
vnto me: come therefore, I pray thee, curse me this people.
18 And Balaám answered, and sayd vnto
the seruantes of Balák, * If Balák wolde
giue me his house ful of siluer and golde,
I can not go beyonde the worde of the
Lord my God, to do lesse or more.
19 But nowe, I pray you, tary here this
night, that I may wit, what the Lord wil
say vnto me [i] more.
20 And God came vnto Balaám by night,
and said vnto him, If the mẽ come to call
thee, rise vp, *and* go with them: but onely
what thing I say vnto thee, that shalt
thou do.
21 So Balaám rose vp early, and sadled his
asse, and went with the princes of Moáb.
22 And the wrath of God was kindled, because he [k] went: & the Angel of the Lord
stode in the way to be against him, as he
rode vpon his asse, and his two seruantes
were with him.
23 And * when the asse sawe the Angel of ỹ
Lord stãd in the way, and his sworde drawen in his hand, the asse turned out of ỹ
waie and went into the field, but Balaám
smote the asse, to turne her into the way.
24 [l] Againe the Angel of the Lord stode
in a path of the vineyardes, *hauing* a wall
on the one side, and a wall on the other.
25 And when the asse sawe the Angel of
the Lord, she thrust her selfe vnto the
wall, and dasht Balaams fote against the
wall: wherefore he smote her againe.
26 Then the Angel of the Lord went further, and stode in a narowe place, where
was no way to turne, *ether* to the right
hand, or to the left.
27 And when the asse sawe the Angel of
the Lord, she "lay downe vnder Balaám:

f He warned him by a dreame ỹ he shulde not consent to the kings wicked request.

g Els he shewed him selfe willing, couetousnes had so blinded his heart.

h The wicked seke by all means to forther their naughty enterprises, thogh thei knowe that God is against them.

Chap 24,13.

i Because he tempted God to require hĩ cõtrary to his cõmandement, his petition was granted, but it turned to his owne cõdemnation.

k Moued rather with couetousnes, thẽ to obey God.

2.Pet.2,16. Iude 11.

l The seconde time.

"Or, fel.

therefore Balaám was very wrath, and
smote the asse with a staffe.
28 Then the Lord [m] opened the mouth of
the asse, and she said vnto Balaám, What
haue I done vnto thee, that thou hast
smitten me nowe thre times?
29 And Balaám said vnto the asse, Because thou hast mocked me: I wolde there were a sworde in mine hand, for now wolde
I kil thee.
30 And the asse said vnto Balaám, Am not
I thine asse, which thou hast ridden vpon
[n] since thy first time vnto this day? haue
I vsed at anie time to do thus vnto thee?
Who said, Nay.
31 And the Lord [o] opened the eies of Balaám, and he sawe the Angel of the Lord
stãding in the way with his sworde drawẽ
in his hand: then he bowed him selfe, and
fel flat on his face.
32 And the Angel of the Lord said vnto
him, Wherefore hast thou now smitten
thine asse thre times? beholde, I came out
to withstand thee, because *thy* [p] way is not
straight before me.
33 But the asse sawe me, and turned fro me
now thre times: for els, if she had not
turned fro me, surely I had euẽ now slaine thee, and saued her aliue.
34 Then Balaám said vnto the Angel of
the Lord, I haue sinned: for I wist not
that thou stodest in the way" against me:
now therefore if it displease thee, I wil
turne" home againe.
35 But the Angel said vnto Balaám, Go
with the men: but [q] what I say vnto thee,
that shalt thou speake. So Balaám went
with the princes of Balák.
36 And when Balák heard that Balaám came, he went out to mete him vnto a citie of Moáb, which is in the [r] border of
Arnón, euen in the vtmost coste.
37 Then Balák said vnto Balaám, Did I not
send for thee to call thee? wherefore camest thou not vnto me? am I not able in
dede to promote thee vnto honour.
38 And Balaám made answer vnto Balák,
Lo, I am come vnto thee, & can I now say
[s] anie thing at all? the worde that God
putteth in my mouth, that shal I speake.
39 So Balaám went with Balák, and thei
came vnto the citie of "Huzóth.
40 Then Balák offred bullockes, and shepe,
and sent *thereof* to Balaám, and to ỹ princes that were with him.
41 And on the morow Balák toke Balaám,
and broght him vp into the hie places of
[t] Baál, that thence he might se the vtmost
parte of the people.

m Gaue her power to speake.

n Since thou hast bene my master.

o For whose eyes the Lord doeth not opẽ, they can nether se his angre, nor his loue.

p Bothe thy heart is corrupt and thine ẽtreprise wicked.

"Or, before me, or, to mete me.

"Ebr. I wil returne to me.

q Because his heart was euil his charg was renued, that he shulde not pretend ignorãce.

r Nere the place, where the Israelites camped.

s Of my selfe I can speake nothing: onely what God reueleth, ỹ wil I vtter, seme it good or bad.

"Or, of stretes: or, a populous citie.

t Where the idole Baál was worshiped.

CHAP. XXIII.

1 Balaám causeth seuẽ Altars to be buylt. 5 God teacheth him what to answer. 8 In stede of cursing he blesseth Israél. 19 God is not like man.

And

1 AND Balaám said vnto Balák, Buylde me here seuen altars, and prepare
me here seuen bullockes, and seuen rams.
2 And Balák did as Balaám said, and [a] Balák and Balaám offred on *euerie* altar a bullocke and a ram.

a For among the Gentiles the Kings oft times vsed to sacrifice, as did ẏ Priests.

3 Then Balaám said vnto Balák, Stand by
the burnt offring, & I wil go, if so be that
the Lord wil come *and* mete me: & whatsoeuer he sheweth me, I wil tel thee: so he
"went forthe alone.

"Or, wẽt vp hier.

4 And God [b] met Balaám, and *Balaám* said
vnto him, I haue prepared seuen altars, &
haue offred vpon *euerie* altar a bullocke
and a ram.

b Appeared vnto him.

5 And the Lord [c] put an answer in Balaãs
mouth, and said, Go againe to Balák, and
say on this wise.

c Taught him what to say.

6 So when he returned vnto him, lo, he stode
by his burnt offring, he, & all the princes of Moáb.
7 Then he vttered his "parable, and said,
Balák the King of Moáb hathe broght me
from "Arám out of the mountaines of the
East, *saying*, Come, curse Iaakób for my
sake: come, and [d] detest Israél.

"Or, prophecie.

"Or, Syria.

d Cause that all men may hate & detest them.

8 How shal I curse, where God hathe not
cursed? or how shal I detest, *where* ẏ Lord
hathe not detested?
9 For frõ the top of the rocks I did se him,
and from the hils I did beholde him: lo,
the people shal dwel by them selues, and
shal not be rekened among the [e] nacions.
10 Who can tel the [f] dust of Iaakób, and
the nomber of the fourth parte of Israél?
Let me [g] dye the death of the righteous,
and let my last end be like his.

e But shal haue religion & lawes a parte.

f The infinite multitude, as the dust of the earth.

g The feare of Gods iudgements caused him to wish to be ioyned to the housholde of Abrahám thus ẏ wicked haue their consciences woũded when thei consider Gods iudgements.

11 Then Balák said vnto Balaám, What
hast thou done vnto me? I toke thee to curse mine enemies, and beholde, thou hast
blessed them altogether.
12 And he answered, and said, Must I not
take hede to speake that, which the Lord
hathe put in my mouth?
13 And Balák said vnto him, Come, I pray
thee, with me vnto an other place, whence
thou maiest se them, and thou shalt se but
the vtmost parte of them, and shalt not
se them all: therefore curse thẽ out of that
place for my sake.
14 ¶ And he broght him into "Sede-sophím
to the top of Pisgáh and buylt seuen altars, & offred a bullocke, & a ram on *euerie*
altar.

"Or, into the field of the that spied: to wit, lest the enemy shulde approche.

15 After, he said vnto Balák, Stand here by
thy burnt offring, and I wil mete *the Lord*
yonder.
16 And the Lord met Balaám, and * put an
answer in his mouth, and said, Go againe vnto Balák, and saie thus.

Chap. 22,35.

17 And when he came to him, beholde, he
stode by his burnt offring, and the princes
of Moáb with him: so Balák said vnto
him, What hathe the Lord said?
18 And he vttered his parable, & said, Rise vp, Balák, and heare: hearken vnto me,
thou sonne of Zippór.
19 [h] God *is* not *as* man, that he shulde lie,
nether *as* the sonne of man that he shulde repent: hathe he said, and shal he not
do it? and hathe he spoken, and shal he not
accomplish it?

h Gods enemies are cõpelled to confesse that his gouernement is iuste, constant, & without chãge or repentance.

20 Beholde, I haue receiued *commandement*
to blesse: for he hathe blessed, & I can not
alter it.
21 He seeth none iniquitie in Iaakób, nor
seeth no transgresion in Israél: the Lord
his God *is* with him, & the [i] ioyful shoute of a King *is* among them.
22 God broght them out of Egypt: their
strength *is* as an vnicorne.

i Thei triũphe as victorious Kings ouer their enemies.

23 For *there is* no sorcerie in Iaakób, nor
soothsaying in Israél: [k] according to this
time it shalbe said of Iaakób and of Israél, What hathe God wroght?
24 Beholde, the people shal rise vp as a liõ,
and lift vp him self as a yong lion: he shal
not lie downe, til he eat of the praie, and
til he drinke the blood of the slaine.

k Considering what God shal worke this time for the deliuerãce of his people, all the worlde shal wonder.

25 ¶ Then Balák said vnto Balaám, Nether
curse, nor blesse them at all.
26 But Balaám answered, and said vnto Balák, Tolde not I thee, saying, All that the
Lord speaketh, that must I do?
27 ¶ Againe Balák said vnto Balaám, Come,
I pray thee, I wil bring thee vnto another
[l] place, if so be it wil please God, that thou
maiest thence curse them for my sake.
28 So Balák broght Balaám vnto the top
of Peór, that loketh toward Ieshmón.

l Thus ẏ wicked imagine of God, that, that which he wil not grante in one place, he wil do it in another.

29 Then Balaám said vnto Balák, Make
me here seuen altars, and prepare me here
seuen bullockes, and seuen rams.
30 And Balák did as Balaám had said, and
offred a bullocke and a ram on *euerie* altar.

CHAP. XXIIII

5 Balaám prophecieth of the great prosperitie that shulde come vnto Israél: 17 Also of the cõming of Christ. 20 The destruction of the Amalekites, and of the Kenites.

1 WHen Balaám sawe that it pleased
the Lord, to blesse Israél, then he
went not, * as certeine times before, to fet
diuinacions, but set his face towarde the
[a] wildernes.

Chap. 23,3.

a Where the Israelites cãped.

2 And Balaám lift vp his eies, and loked
vpõ Israél, which dwelt accordĩg to their
tribes, and the Spirit of God came vpon
him.
3 * And he vttered his parable, and said,
Balaám the sonne of Beór hathe said, and
the man, whose eies [b] were shut vp, hathe
said,

Chap. 23,7.

b His eies were shut vp before in respect of ẏ cleare visions ẅ he sawe after: some read, were open.

4 He hathe said, which heard the wordes
of God, and sawe the vision of the Al-

mightie, and [c] falling *in a trance* had his
eies opened.
5 ¶How goodlie are thy tẽts, ô Iaakób, &
thine habitacions, ô Iſraél?
6 As the valleis, are thei ſtretched forthe, as
gardẽs by the riuers ſide, as the "aloe trees,
which the Lord hathe planted, as the ce-
dars, beſide the waters.
7 The [d] water droppeth out of his bucket,
and his ſede *ſhalbe* in many waters, & his
King ſhalbe hier then [e] Agág, & his kingdome ſhalbe exalted.
8 God broght him out of Egypt: his
ſtrength *ſhalbe* as an vnicorne: he ſhal eat
the nacions his enemies, and bruiſe their
bones, and ſhoote them through with his
arrowes.
9 *He coucheth *and* lieth downe as a yong
lyon, & as a lyon: who ſhal ſtirre him vp?
bleſſed is he that bleſſeth thee, and curſed
is he that curſeth thee.
10 Then Balák was verie angry ẇ Balaám,
and [f] ſmote his hands together: ſo Balák
ſaid vnto Balaám, I ſent for thee to curſe
mine enemies, and beholde, thou haſt bleſſed them now thre times.
11 Therefore now flee vnto thy place: I
thoght ſurely to promote thee vnto honour, but lo, the [g] Lord hathe kept thee
backe from honour.
12 Then Balaám anſwered Balák, Tolde I
not alſo thy meſſengers, which thou ſen-
teſt vnto me, ſaying,
13 If Balák wolde giue me his houſe ful of
ſiluer and golde, I can not paſſe the commandement of the Lord, to do *ether* good
or bad of mine owne minde? what the
Lord ſhal cõmãde, that ſame wil I ſpeake.
14 And now beholde, I go vnto my people: come, I wil " [h] aduertiſe thee what
this people ſhal do to thy folke in the later daies.
15 And he vttered his parable, and ſaid,
Balaám the ſonne of Beór hathe ſaid, and
the man whoſe eies were ſhut vp, hathe
ſaid.
16 He hathe ſaid that heard the wordes of
God, & hathe the knowledge of the moſte high, & ſawe the viſion of the Almightie, and falling *in a trance* had his eies opened:
17 I ſhal ſe him, but not now: I ſhal beholde him, but not nere: there ſhal come a
[i] ſtarre of Iaakób, and a ſcepter ſhal riſe
of Iſraél, and ſhal ſmite the [k] coaſtes of
Moáb, and deſtroye all the ſonnes of
[l] Shéth.
18 And Edóm ſhalbe poſſeſſed, and Seír
ſhalbe a poſſeſsion to their enemies: but
Iſraél ſhal do valiantly.
19 He alſo that ſhal haue dominiõ *ſhalbe* of
Iaakób, and ſhal deſtroye the remnant of
the [m] citie.

c Thogh he laye as in a ſlepe, yet the eies of his minde were open.
"Or, tentes.
d His proſperitie and poſteritie ſhalbe verie great.
e Which name was commẽ to the Kings of Amalék.
Gen. 49,9.
f In token of anger.
g Thus ẏ wicked burden God, whẽ thei cã not compas their wicked enterpriſes.
"Ebr, counſel.
h He gaue alſo wicked cõſel to cauſe ẏ Iſraelites to ſinne, that thereby God might forſake them, Chap. 31, 16.
i Meaning, Chriſt.
k That is, the princes.
l He ſhal ſubdue all that reſiſt: for of Shéth came Noáh, and of Noáh all the worlde.
m Of the Edomites.

20 ¶And when he loked on Amalék, he
vttered his parable, and ſaid, Amalék
was the [n] firſt of the nacions: but his later end *ſhal come* to deſtruction.
21 And he loked on the "Kenites, and vttered his parable, and ſaid, Strong is
thy dwelling place, and [o] put thy neſt in
the rocke.
22 Neuertheles, "the Kenite ſhalbe ſpoiled vntil Aſhúr cary thee away captiue.
23 Againe he vttered his parable, and
ſaid, Alas, [p] who ſhal liue when God
doeth this?
24 The ſhippes alſo ſhal *come* frõ the coaſtes of [q] Chittím and ſubdue Aſhúr, and
ſhal ſubdue Ebér, and [r] he alſo *ſhal come*
to deſtruction.
25 Then Balaám roſe vp, and went and
returned to his place: and Balák alſo went
his way.

CHAP. XXV.

2 The people committeth fornicacion with the daughters of Moab. 9 Phinehás killeth Zimri & Cozbi. 11 God maketh his couenant with Phinehás. 17 God commandeth to kil the Midianites.

1 NOw whiles Iſraél abode in Shittím,
the people began to cõmit whoredome with the [a] daughters of Moáb:
2 Which called ẏ people vnto the ſacrifice
of their gods, & the people ate, & bowed
downe to their gods.
3 And Iſraél [b] coupled him ſelf vnto Báal
Peór: wherefore the wrath of the Lord
was kindled againſt Iſraél:
4 And the Lord ſaid vnto Moſés, *Take
all the heades of the people, & hang them
vp "before the Lord [c] againſt the ſunne,
that the indignacion of the Lords wrath
may be turned from Iſraél.
5 Then Moſés ſaid vnto the Iudges of Iſraél, Euerie one ſlay his [d] men that were
ioyned vnto Báal Peór.
6 ¶And beholde, one of the children of Iſraél came and broght vnto his brethren a
Midianitiſh woman in the ſight of Moſés,
and in the ſight of all the Congregacion
of the children of Iſraél, [e] who wept before the dore of the Tabernacle of the
Congregacion.
7 *And when Phinehás the ſonne of Eleazár the ſonne of Aarón the Prieſt ſawe it,
he roſe vp from the middes of the Congregacion, and toke a "ſpeare in his hand,
8 And followed the man of Iſraél into the
tent, & thruſt them bothe through: *to wit,*
the man of Iſraél, and the womã, "through
her belly: ſo the plague ceaſed from the
children of Iſraél.
9 *And there dyed in that plague, foure &
twentie thouſand.
10 Then ẏ Lord ſpake vnto Moſés, ſaying,
11 *Phinehás ẏ ſonne of Eleazár, the ſonne
of Aarón the Prieſt, hathe turned mine
anger

n The Amalekites firſt made warre againſt Iſraél, as Chap. 14,45.
"Or, Midianites
o Make thy ſelf as ſtrong as thou canſt.
"Or, thou Kain ſhalt.
p Some read, Oh, who ſhal not periſh, when the enemie, *that is,* Antichriſt, ſhal ſet him ſelf vp as God?
q The Grecians, and Romains.
r Meaning, Eber, or the Iewes, for rebelling againſt God.
a With ẏ woman.
b Worſhipped the idole of ẏ Moabites, ẇ was in the hil Peór.
Deut. 4,3. ioſh. 22,17.
"Or, to the Lord.
c Openly in ẏ ſight of all.
d Let him ſe execuciõ done of them that are vnder his charge.
e Repenting ẏ thei had offended God.
Pſal. 106,30. 1. mac. 2,54.
"Or, iaueling.
"Or, in her tent, Chald. & Grek. in her ſecrets.
1. Cor. 10,8.
Pſal. 106,30.

f He was zealous to mainteine my glorie.

anger away from the children of Israél,
while he [f] was zelous for my sake among
them: therefore I haue not consumed the
children of Israél in my ielousie.

Eccle.45,24. 1.mac.2,54.

12 Wherefore saye *to him*, Beholde, * I giue
vnto him my couenant of peace,
13 And he shal haue it, and his sede after
him, *euen* the couenant of the Priests office
for euer, because he was zelous for his
God, and hathe made an [g] atonement for
the children of Israél.

g He hathe pacified Gods wrath.

14 And the name of the Israelite *thus* slayne,
which was killed with the Midianitish
woman, *was* Zimrí the sonne of Salú, prince
" of the familie of the Simeonites.

" Ebr. of the house of the father.

15 And the name of the Midianitish womã,
that was slaine, *was* Cozbí the daughter
of Zur, who *was* head ouer the people of
his fathers house in Midián.
16 ¶ Againe the Lord spake vnto Mosés,
saying,

Chap.31,2.

17 * Vexe the Midianites, and smite them:
18 For they trouble you with their [h] wiles,
wherewith thei haue beguiled you as concerning
Peór, & as concerning their sister
Cozbi the daughter of a prince of Midián,
which was slaine in the day of the
plague because of Peór.

h Causing you to cõmit both corporal and spiritual fornicacion by Balamscoũsel, Chap.31,16. reu.2,14.

CHAP. XXVI.

2 The Lord cõmandeth to nomber the children of Israél in the plaine of Moáb, from twẽty yere olde & aboue. 57 The Leuites and their families. 64 None of them, that were nombred in Sinai, go in to Canáan saue Caléb, and Ioshua.

a Which came for their whoredome & idolatrie.

1 And so after the [a] plague, the Lord
spake vnto Mosés, & to Eleazár the
sonne of Aarón the Priest, saying,

Chap.1,3.

2 Take the nomber of all the Congregacion
of the children of Israél * from twẽty
yere olde and aboue through out their
fathers houses, all that go forthe to warre
in Israél.
3 So Mosés & Eleazár the Priest spake vnto
them in the plaine of Moáb, by Iordén
[b] *towarde* Ierichó, saying,

b Where the riuer is nere to Ierichó.

Chap.1,1.

4 From twenty yere olde and aboue *ye shal
nomber the people*, as the * Lord had cõmanded
Mosés, and the children of Israél, whẽ
they came out of the land of Egypt.

Gen.46,9. exod 6,14. 1.chro.5,1. ‖Reubén.

5 ¶ * Reubén ỹ first borne of Israél: ỹ childrẽ
of ‖ Reubén *were*: Hanóch, *of whome came*
the familie of the Hanochites, *and* of
Pallú the familie of the Palluites:
6 Of Hesrón, the familie of the Hesronites:
of Carmí, the familie of ỹ Carmites.
7 These are ỹ families of the Reubenites:
and they were in nomber thre & fourtie
thousand, seuen hundreth and thirty.
8 And the sonnes of Pallú, Eliáb:
9 And the sonnes of Eliáb, Nemuél, & Dathán,
and Abirám: this Dathán and Abirám
were famous in the Congregacion,
and * stroue against Mosés and against Aarón
in [c] the assemblie of Kórah, whẽ they

Chap.16,2. c In that rebelliõ whereof Kórah was head.

stroue against the Lord.
10 And the earth opened her mouth, and
swalowed them vp with Kórah, when the
Congregacion dyed, what time the fire
consumed two hundreth and fifty men,
who were [d] for a signe:
11 Notwithstanding, *all* the sonnes of Kórah
dyed not.

d That is, for an example ỹ other shulde not murmure and rebelle against Gods ministers.

12 ¶ And the childrẽ of ‖ Simeón after their
families *were*: Nemuél, *of whome came* ỹ familie
of the Nemuelites: of Iamín, the familie
of the Iaminites: of Iachín, the familie
of the Iachinites:

‖Simeón.

13 Of Zérah, the familie of the Zarhites:
of Shaúl, the familie of the Shaulites.
14 These are the families of the Simeonites:
two and twenty thousand and two
hundreth.
15 ¶ The sonnes of ‖ Gad after their families
were: Zephón, *of whome came* ỹ familie
of the Zephonites: of Haggí, the familie
of the Haggites: of Shuní, the familie of
the Shunites:

‖Gad.

16 Of Ozní, the familie of the Oznites:
of Erí, the familie of the Erites:
17 Of Aród, the familie of the Arodites: of
Arelí, the familie of the Arelites.
18 These are the families of the sonnes of
Gad, according to their nombers, fourty
thousand and fiue hundreth.
19 ¶ The sõnes of ‖ Iudáh, Er & Onán: but Er
and Onán dyed in the land of [e] Canáan.

‖Iudáh. e Before Iaakób went into Egypt, Gen.38,3,& 7.

20 So were the sonnes of Iudáh after their
families: of Sheláh *came* the familie of the
Shelanites: of Phárez, ỹ familie of ỹ Pharzites,
of Zérah, the familie of ỹ Zarhites.
21 And the sonnes of * Pharéz *were*: of Hesrón,
the familie of ỹ Hesronites: of Hamúl,
the familie of the Hamulites.

Gen.46,12.

22 These are the families of Iudáh, after
their nombers, seuẽty ad six thousand and
fiue hundreth.
23 ¶ The sonnes of ‖ Issachár, after their families
were: Tolá, *of whome came* the familie
of the Tolaites: of Puá, the familie of
the Punites:

‖Issachár.

24 Of Iashúb ỹ familie of ỹ Iashubites: of
Shimrón the familie of the Shimronites.
25 These are the families of Issachár, after
their nombers, thre score and foure thousand
and thre hundreth.
26 ¶ The sonnes of ‖ Zebulún, after their families
were: of Séred, the familie of ỹ Sardites:
of Elón, the familie of the Elonites:
of Iahleél, the familie of the Iahleelites.

‖Zebulún.

27 These are the families of the Zebulunites,
after their nõbers, thre score thousand
and fiue hundreth.
28 ¶ The sonnes of Ioséph, after their families
were ‖ Manasséh and Ephráim.
29 The sonnes of Manasséh *were*: of * Machír,
ỹ familie of ỹ Machirites: & Machír
begate Gileád: of Gileád *came* ỹ familie

‖Manasséh. Iosh.17,1.

of the Giliadites.
30 These are the sonnes of Giliád: of Iezér,
the familie of the Iezerites: of Hélek, the
familie of the Helekites:
31 Of Asriél, the familie of the Asrielites:
of Shéchẽ, the familie of the Shichmites.
32 Of Shemidá, the familie of the Shemi-
daites: of Hépher, the familie of the He-
pherites.
Chap.27,1. 33 ¶ And *Zelophehád ỹ sonne of Hépher
had no sonnes, but daughters: and the names of the daughters of Zelophehád *were*
Mahláh, and Noáh, Hogláh, Milcáh and
Tirzáh.
34 These are the families of Manasséh, and
the nomber of them, two and fifty thousand and seuen hundreth.
‖Ephráim. 35 ¶ These are the sonnes of ‖ Ephráim after
their families: of Shutheláh *came* ỹ familie of the Shuthalhites: of Bechér, the familie of the Bachrites: of Táhan, the familie of the Tahanites.
36 And these are the sonnes of Shutheláh:
of Erán the familie of the Eranites.
37 These are ỹ families of the sonnes of E-
phráim after their nõbers, two and thirtie
thousand and fiue hundreth. these are the
sonnes of Ioséph after their families.
‖Beniamín. 38 ¶ *These are* the sonnes of ‖ Beniamín after
their families: of Belá *came* the familie
of the Baleites: of Ashbél, the familie of
the Ashbelites: of Ahirám, the familie of
the Ahiramites:
39 Of Shuphám, the familie of the Shupha-
mites: of Huphám, the familie of the Hu-
phamites.
40 And the sonnes of Belá were Ard and
Naamán: *of Ard came* the familie of the
Ardites, of Naamán, the familie of the
Naamites.
41 These are the sonnes of Beniamín after
their families, and their nombers, fiue and
fourty thousand and six hundreth.
‖Dan. 42 ¶ These are ỹ sonnes of ‖ Dan after their
families: of Shuhám *came* the familie of
the Shuhamites: these are the families of
Dan after their housholdes.
43 All the families of the Shuhamites *were*
after their nombers, thre score and foure
thousand, and foure hundreth.
‖Ashér. 44 ¶ The sonnes of ‖ Ashér after their families *were*: of Iimnáh, the familie of the
Iimnites: of Isuí, the familie of the Isu-
ites: of Beriáh, the familie of the Beriites.
45 The sonnes of Beriáh *were*, of Hebér the
familie of the Heberites: of Malchiél, the
familie of the Malchielites.
46 And the name of the daughter of Ashér
was Sárah.
47 These are the families of the sonnes of
Ashér after their nombers, thre and fifty
thousand and foure hundreth.
‖Naphtalí. 48 ¶ The sõnes of ‖ Naphtalí, after their families *were* of Iahzeél, the families of the
Iahzeelites: of Guni, the familie of the
Gunites.
49 Of Iézer, the familie of the Izrites: of
Shillém, the familie of the Shillemites.
50 These are the families of Naphtalí accordĩg to their housholdes, & their nõber,
fiue & fourty thousand & foure hũdreth.
51 These are the [f] nombers of the children
of Israél: six hundreth, and one thousand,
seuen hnndreth and thirty.
f This is the third time ỹ they are nombred.
52 ¶ And ỹ Lord spake vnto Mosés, saying,
53 Vnto these the lãd shal be deuided for an
inheritãce, according to ỹ nõber of ‖ names. ‖ Or, persones.
54 *To manie thou shalt giue the more inhe- Chap.33,54.
ritãce, and to fewe thou shalt giue lesse inheritance: to euerie one according to his
nomber shalbe giuen his inheritance.
55 Notwithstãding, the land shal be * deui- Iosh.11,23.
ded by lot: according to the names of the
tribes of their fathers thei shal inherit:
56 According to the lot shal the possession
thereof be deuided betwene manie & fewe.
57 ¶ *These also *are* the nõbers of the Le- Exod.6,17.
uites, after their families: of Gershón *came* the familie of the Gershonites: of Koháth the familie of the Kohathites: of
Merarí the familie of the Merarites.
58 These are the families of Leuí, the familie of the Libnites: the familie of ỹ Hebronites: the familie of the Mahlites: the
familie of the Mushites: the familie of the
Korhites: and Koháth begate Amrám.
59 And Amrás wife was called * Iochébed Exod.2,2.& 6,20.
the daughter of Leuí, ẇ was borne vnto
Leuí in Egypt: and she bare vnto Amrám
Aarón, & Mosés, and Miriám their sister.
60 And vnto Aarón were borne Nadáb, &
Abihú, Eleazár, and Ithamár.
61 *And Nadáb and Abihú dyed because Leu.10,2.
they offred strange fire before the Lord. chap.3,4
62 And their nombers were thre & twenty 1.chro.24,2.
thousand, all males from a moneth olde
and aboue: for they were not nombred a-
mong the childrẽ of Israél, because there
was none inheritance giuen them among
the children of Israél.
63 ¶ These are the nombers of Mosés and
Eleazár the Priest which nombred the
children of Israél in the plaine of Moáb,
nere Iordén, *toward* Ierichó.
64 And among these there was not a man
of them, [g] whome Mosés and Aarón the
Priest nõbred, whẽ they tolde the childrẽ
of Israél in the wildernes of Sinái.
g Wherein appeareth the great power of God, that so wonderfully increased his people.
65 For the Lord said of them, * They shal Chap.14,28.
dye in the wildernes: so there was not left 1.cor.10,6.
a man of them, saue Caléb the sonne of
Iephunnéh, & Ioshúa the sonne of Nun.

CHAP. XXVII.

1 The lawe of the heritage of the daughters of Zelophehád. 12 The land of promes is shewed vnto Mosés. 16 Mosés praieth for a gouerner to the people.

18 *Ioshúa is appointed in his stede.*

Chap.26.33. & 36.11. ios 17,3.

1 THen came the daughters of * Zelophehád, the sonne of Hépher, the sonne of Gileád, the sonne of Machír, the sõne of Manasséh, of the familie of Manasséh, the sonne of Ioséph, (and the names of
his daughters were these, Mahláh, Noáh,
and Hogláh, and Milcáh, and Tirzáh)
2 And stode before Mosés, and before E-
leazár the Priest, and before the princes,
and all the assembly, at the dore of ỳ Tabernacle of the Congregacion, saying,
3 Our father * dyed in the wildernes, and
he was not among the assemblie of them
that were assembled against ỳ Lord in the
cõpanie of Kórah, but dyed in his [a] sinne,
and had no sonnes.
4 Wherefore shulde the name of our father be taken away from among his familie, because he hathe no sonne? giue vs a
possession among the brethren of our
father.
5 Then Mosés broght their [b] cause before
the Lord.
6 And the Lord spake vnto Mosés, saying,
7 The daughters of Zelophehád speake
right: thou shalt giue them a possession to
inherit among their fathers brethrẽ, and
shalt turne the inheritance of their father vnto them.
8 Also thou shalt speake vnto the children
of Israél, saying, If a man dye & haue no
sonne, then ye shal turne his inheritance
vnto his daughter.
9 And if he haue no daughter, ye shal giue his inheritance vnto his brethren.
10 And if he haue no brethren, ye shal giue his inheritance vnto his fathers brethren.
11 And if his father haue no brethren, ye
shal giue his inheritãce vnto his next kinseman of his familie, and he shal possesse
it: and *this* shal be vnto the children of Israél a lawe of [c] iudgement, as the Lord
hathe commanded Mosés.
12 ¶ Againe ỳ Lord said vnto Mosés, * Go
vp into this mõut of Abarím, and beholde the land which I haue giuen vnto the
children of Israél.
13 And when thou hast sene it, thou shalt
be gathered vnto thy people also, * as Aarón thy brother was gathered.
14 For ye were * disobedient vnto my
worde in the desert of Zín, in the strife of
the assemblie, to sanctifie me in the waters
before their eyes. * That is the water of
" Meribáh in Kadésh in the wildernes of
Zín.
15 ¶ Then Mosés spake vnto the Lord,
saying,
16 Let the Lord God of [d] the spirits of all
flesh appoint a man ouer the Congregacion,

Chap.16.1. & 31.

a According as all mẽ dye, forasmuche as they are sinners.

b That is, their matter to be iudged, to knowe what he shulde determine, as he did all hard matters.

c Meaning an ordinance to iudge by.

Deu.32,49.

Chap.20,24.

Chap.20,12.

Exod 17,7.

" Or, strife.

d Who as he hathe created so he gouerneth the heartes of all mẽ.

17 Who may [e] go out and in before them,
& lead them out and in, that the Congregacion of the Lord be not as shepe, which
haue not a shepeherd.
18 And ỳ Lord said vnto Mosés, Take thee
Ioshúa the sonne of Nun, in whome is the
Spirit, and [f] put thine hands vpon him,
19 And set him before Eleazár the Priest,
and before all the Congregacion, and giue him a charge in their sight.
20 And [g] giue him of thy glorie, that all ỳ
Congregacion of the children of Israél
may obeie.
21 And he shal stand before Eleazár the
Priest, who shal aske counsel for him * by
the [h] iudgement of Vrím before the Lord:
at his worde they shal go out, and at his
worde they shal come in, *bothe* he, and all
the children of Israél with him & all the
Congregacion.
22 So Mosés did as the Lord had commãded him, & he toke Ioshúa, & set him before Eleazár the Priest, and before all the
Congregacion.
23 Then he put his hands vpon him, & gaue him a [i] charge, as the Lord had spoken
by the hand of Mosés.

e That is, gouerne them & do his duetie, as 2.chr.1,10.

f And so appoint him gouernour.

g Comend him to ỳ people as mete for ỳ office, & appointed by God.

Exod.28,30.

h According to his office: signifing that ỳ ciuile magistrat colde execute nothing but that ỳ he knewe to be ỳ wil of God.

i How he shulde gouerne hĩselfe in his office.

CHAP. XXVIII.

4 *The daiely sacrifice. 9 The sacrifice of the Sabbath, 11 Of the Moneth, 16 Of the Passeouer, 26 Of the first frutes.*

1 ANd the Lord spake vnto Mosés, saying,
2 Commande the children of Israél, and
say vnto them, Ye shal obserue to offer vnto me in their due season mine offring &
[a] my bread, for my sacrifices made by fire
for a swete sauour vnto me.
3 Also thou shalt say vnto them, * This is ỳ
offring made by fire which ye shal offer vn
to the Lord, two lambes of a yere olde
without spot, dayly, for a continual burnt
offring.
4 One lambe shalt thou prepare in ỳ morning, and the other lambe shalt thou prepare at euen.
5 * And the tẽth parte of an * Ephah of fine
floure for a * meatoffring mingled with ỳ
fourth parte of an * Hin of beaten oyle.
6 *This shalbe* a dailie burnt offring, as was
made in ỳ mõut Sinái for a swete sauour:
it is a sacrifice made by fire vnto the Lord.
7 And the drinkeoffring thereof the fourth
parte of an Hin for one lambe: in the holy
place cause to powre the drinke offring
vnto the Lord.
8 And the other lambe thou shalt prepare
at euẽ: as the meat offring of the morning
and as ỳ drinke offring thereof shalt thou
prepare *this* [b] *for* an offring made by fire of
swete sauour vnto the Lord.
9 ¶ But on the Sabbath day *ye shal offer* two
lambes of a yere olde, without spot, and

a By bread, he meaneth all maner of sacrifice.

Exod.29,38.

Exod.16,36.

Leui.2,1.

Exod.29,40.

b The meat offring & drinke offring of euening sacrifice.

c Of the measure Ephah.

two c tenth deales of fine floure for a meat
offring mingled with oyle, & the drinke
offring thereof.
10 *This is* the burnt offring of euerie Sabbath, beside the d continual burnt offring,
and drinke offring thereof.

d Which was offred euerie day at morning and at euening.

11 ¶And in the beginning of your monethes, ye shal offer a burnt offring vnto the
Lord, two yong bullockes, and a ram, and
seuē lambes of a yere olde, with out spot,
12 And thre tenth deales of fine floure for
a meat offring mingled with oyle for one
bullocke, and two tenth deales of fine
floure for a meat offring, mingled with
oyle for one ram,
13 And a tenth deale of fine floure mingled
with oyle for a meat offring vnto one lābe, for a burnt offring of swete sauour: *it is*
an offring made by fire vnto the Lord.

e That is, the wine that shal be powred vpon the sacrifice.

14 And their e drinke offrings shalbe halfe
an Hin of wine vnto one bullocke, & the
third parte of an Hin vnto a ram, and the
fourth parte of an Hin vnto a lābe: this is
ỷ burnt offring of euerie moneth, trough-
out the moneths of the yere.
15 And one he goat for a sin offring vnto
the Lord shalbe prepared, besides the continual burnt offring, & his drinke offring.

Exod.12,18. & 23,15. leu.23,5.

16 *Also the fourtenth day of the first moneth *is* the Passeouer of the Lord.
17 And in the fiftenth day of the same moneth is the feast: seuen daies shal vnleauened bread be eaten.

Leu.23,7.
f Or solemne assemblie.

18 In the * first day *shalbe* an holy f conuocacion, ye shal do no seruile worke *therein.*
19 But ye shal offer a sacrifice made by fire
for a burnt offring vnto the Lord, two
yong bullockes, one ram, and seuē lambes
of a yere olde: se that they be without blemish.
20 And their meat offring *shal be* of fine
floure mingled with oyle: thre tenth deales shal ye prepare for a bullocke, and two
tenth deales for a ram:
21 One tenth deale shalt thou prepare for
euerie lambe, *euen* for the seuen lambes.
22 And an he goat for a sin offring, to make an atonement for you.
23 Ye shal prepare these, beside the burnt
offring in the morning, which is a continual burnt sacrifice.

"Ebr. bread.

24 After this maner ye shal prepare through
out all the seuen dayes, for the " mainteining of the offring made by fire for a swete sauour vnto the Lord: it shal be done
beside the continual burnt offring and
drinke offring thereof.
25 And in the seuenth day ye shal haue an
holy conuocacion, *wherein* ye shal do no
seruile worke.

g In counting seuen wekes from the Passeouer to Witsontide, as Leuit.23,15.

26 ¶Also in ỷ day of your first frutes, when
ye bring a newe meat offrīg vnto ỷ Lord,
according to g your wekes ye shal haue
an holy cōuocacion, and ye shal do no seruile worke *in it*:
27 But ye shal offer a burnt offring for a
swete sauour vnto the Lord, two yōg bullockes, a ram, and seuen lambes of a yere
olde,
28 And their meat offring of fine floure
mingled with oyle, thre tenth deales vnto
a bullocke, two tenth deales to a ram,
29 And one tenth deale vnto euerie lambe
throughout the seuen lambes,
30 And an he goat to make an atonemēt for
you:
31 (Ye shal do this besides the cōtinual burnt
offring, and his meat offring:) "se they be
without blemish, with their drīke offrīgs.

"Ebr they shal be to you.

CHAP. XXIX.

1 Of the thre principal feasts of the seuenth moneth: to wit, the feast of trumpets. 7 The feast of reconciliacion. 12 And the feast of Tabernacles.

a Which conteineth part of September, & parte of October.
Leui.23,24.

1 MOreouer in the first *day* of the a seuenth moneth ye shal haue an holy
conuocacion: ye shal do no seruile worke
therein: *it shalbe a day of blowing the trū-
pets vnto you.
2 And ye shal make a burnt offring for a
swete sauour vnto the Lord: one yōg bullocke, one ram, & seuen lambes of a yere olde, without blemish.
3 And their meat offring *shalbe* of fine floure mingled with oyle, thre tēth deales vnto the bullocke, and two tenth deales vnto
the ram,
4 And one tenth deale vnto one lambe,
for the seuen lambes,
5 And an he goat for a sin offring to make
an atonement for you,

b Which must be offred in ỷ begining of euerie moneth.
c Which is for morning & euening.

6 Beside the burnt offring of the b moneth,
& his meat offring, and ỷ cōtinual c burnt
offring, and his meat offring & the drinke
offrings of the same, according to their
maner, for a swete sauour: *it is* a sacrifice
made by fire vnto the Lord.

Leui.16,30. & 23,27.
d Which is ỷ feast of reconciliacion.

7 ¶ * And ye shal haue in the tenth *day* of
ỷ seuenth moneth, an holy d cōuocacion:
and ye shal humble your soules, *and* shal
not do anie worke *therein*:
8 But ye shal offer a burnt offring vnto the
Lord for a swete sauour: one yong bullocke, a ram, and seuen lambes of a yere
olde: se they be without blemish.
9 And their meat offring shal be of fine
floure mingled with oyle, thre tenth deales to a bullocke, & two tenth deales to a
ram,
10 One tēth deale vnto euerie lābe, through
out the seuen lambes,

e That is, offred euerie morning & euening.
f Meaning the feast of ỷ Tabernacles.

11 An he goat for a sin offring, (beside ỷ sin
offring to make the atonement and the
continual e burnt offring and the meat offring thereof) & their drinke offrings.
12 ¶And in the fiftenth day of the seuēth
moneth ye shal haue an holy f cōuocaciō:
ye shal

ye shal do no seruile worke *therein*, but ye
shal kepe a feast vnto ÿ Lord seuen dayes.
13 And ye shal offer a burnt offring for a sacrifice made by fire of swete sauour vnto
the Lord, thirtene yong bullockes, two
rams, & fourtene lambes of a yere olde:
they shalbe without blemish.
14 And their meat offring shalbe of fine
floure mingled with oyle, thre tenth deales vnto euery bullocke of ÿ thirtene bullockes, two tenth deales to ether of ÿ two
rams,
15 And one tenth deale vnto eche of the
fourtene lambes,
16 And one he goat for a sin offring, beside
the continual burnt offring, his meat offring and his drinke offring.
17 ¶ And the ‖ seconde day *ye shal offer* twelue yong bullockes, two rams, fourtene
lambes of a yere olde without blemish,
18 With their meat offring & their drinke
offrings for the bullockes, for the rams, &
for the lambes according to their nomber, after the maner,
19 And an he goat for a sin offring (beside
the continual burnt offring and his meat
offring) and their drinke offrings.
20 ¶ Also the ‖ third day *ye shal offer* eleuen
bullockes, two rams, and fourtene lambes
of a yere olde without blemish,
21 With their meat offring & their drinke
offrings, for the bullockes, for the rams, &
for the lambes, after their nomber according to the [g] maner,
22 And an he goat for a sin offring, beside
the continual burnt offring, and his meat
offring and his drinke offring.
23 ¶ And the ‖ fourth day *ye shal offer* tē bullockes, two rams, & fourtene lambes of a
yere olde without blemish.
24 Their meat offrīg & their drinke offrīgs,
for the bullockes, for the rams, and for the
lambes according to their nomber after
the maner,
25 And an he goat for a sin offring, beside
the continual burnt offring, his meat offring and his drinke offring.
26 ¶ In the ‖ fifth day also *ye shal offer* nine
bullockes, two rams, *and* fourtene lambes
of a yere olde without blemish,
27 And their meat offring and their drinke
offrings for the bullockes, for the rams, &
for the lambes according to their nomber, after the maner,
28 And an he goat for a sin offring, beside
the continual burnt offring and his meat
offring and his drinke offring.
29 ¶ And in the ‖ sixt day *ye shal offer* eight
bullockes, two rams, & fourtene lambes
of a yere olde without blemish,
30 And their meat offring, & their drinke
offrings for the bullockes, for the rams, &
for the lambes according to their nōber,

‖ The seconde day of ÿ feast of Tabernacles.

‖ The third daie.

g According to the ceremonies appointed thereunto.

‖ The fourthe day.

‖ The fift day.

‖ The sixt day.

after the maner,
31 And an he goat for a sin offring, beside
the cōtinual burnt offrīg, his meat offring
and his drinke offrings.
32 ¶ In the ‖ seuenth day also *ye shal offer* seuen bullockes, two rams & fourtene lambes of a yere olde without blemish,
33 And their meat offring and their drinke
offrings for the bullockes, for the rams, &
for the lambes according to their nomber, after their maner,
34 And an he goat for a sin offring, beside
the continual burnt offring, his meat offring and his drinke offring.
35 ¶ In the ‖ eight day, ye shal haue * a solemne assemblie: ye shal do no seruile worke
therein,
36 But ye shal offer a burnt offring, a sacrifice made by fire for a swete sauour vnto
the Lord, one bullocke, one ram, & seuen
lambes of a yere olde without blemish,
37 Their meat offring and their drinke offrings for the bullocke, for the ram, & for
the lambes according to their nomber,
after the maner,
38 And an he goat for a sin offring, beside
the continual burnt offring, and his meat
offring, and his drinke offring.
39 These things ye shal do vnto ÿ Lord in
your feastes, beside your [h] vowes, & your
fre offrings, for your burnt offrings, & for
your meat offrings, & for your drinke offrings and for your peace offrings.

‖ The seuenth day.

‖ The eight day.

* *Leui. 23, 36.*

h Beside ÿ sacrifices ÿ you shal vowe or offer of your owne mindes.

CHAP. XXX.

3 Concerning vowes. 4 The Vowe of the maid, 7 Of the wife, 10 Of the widow, or deuorced.

1 THen Mosés spake vnto the childrē of
Israél according to all that the Lord
had commanded "him,
2 Mosés also spake vnto the heades of the
tribes [a] concerning the children of Israél,
saying, This is the thing which the Lord
hathe commanded,
3 Whosoeuer voweth a vow vnto ÿ Lord,
or sweareth an othe to bīde him "selfe by
a bonde, he shal not breake his "promes,
but shal do accordīg to all that proceadeth
out of his mouth.
4 If a woman also vowe a vowe vnto the
Lord, & bīde her selfe by a bōde, *being* in
her fathers house, in ÿ time of her youth,
5 And her father heare her vowe & bōde,
wherewith she hathe bounde her selfe, and
her father holde his [b] peace concerning
her, then all her vowes shal stand & euerie bonde, wherewith she hathe bounde
her selfe, shall stand.
6 But if her [c] father disalowe her the same
daye that he heareth all her vowes & bondes, wherewith she hathe bōude her selfe,
they shal not be of value, and the Lord wil
forgiue her, because her father disalowed
her.

" *Ebr. Mosés.*

a Because thei might declare them to the Israelites.

" *Ebr. his soule.*

" *Ebr. violate his worde.*

b For in so doing, he doeth approue her.

c By not approuing or cōsenting to her vowe.

7 And if she haue an housbād whē she voweth or [d] pronounceth *oght* with her lippes,
wherewith she bindeth her selfe,
8 If her housband heard it and holdeth his
peace cōcerning her, the same day he heareth it, then her vowe shal stand, and her
bondes wherewith she bindeth her selfe
shal stand in effect.
9 But if her housband disalowe her the same day that he heareth it, then shal he make her vowe which she hathe made, & that
that she hathe pronoūced with her lippes,
wherewith she bonde her [e] selfe, of none
effect: and the Lord wil forgiue her.
10 But euerie vowe of a widowe, and of her
that is deuorced (wherewith she hathe bōde her selfe) shal stand in [f] effect with her.
11 And if she vowed in her housbandes
[g] house, or bōde her selfe streictly with an
othe,
12 And her housband hathe heard it, & helde his peace concerning her, not disalow-
ing her, then all her vowes shal stand, &
euerie bonde, wherewith she boūd her selfe, shal stand in effect.
13 But if her housband disanulled them,
the same day that he heard them, nothing
that proceaded out of her lippes concerning her vowes or concerning "her bōdes,
shal stand in effect: *for* her housband hathe
disanulled them: and the Lord wil forgiue
her.
14 *So* euerie vowe, and euerie othe *or* bonde, *made* to [h] humble the soule, her housband may stablish it, or her housband
may breake it.
15 But if her housband holde his peace cō
cerning her frō [i] day to day, thē he stablisheth all her vowes and all her bondes
which she hathe made: he hathe cōfirmed
them because he held his peace concerning her the same day that he heard *them.*
16 But if he [k] breake them after that he hathe heard them, then shal he beare her
iniquitie.
17 These are the ordināces which the Lord
commanded Mosés, betwene a man & his
wife, & betwene the father and his daughter, *being* yong in her fathers house.

d Ether by othe, or solēne promise.

e For she is in subiectiō of her housbād, & can performe nothing without his consent.

f For thei are not vnder ẏ autoritie of ẏ man.

g Her housbād being aliue.

" Ebr. the bōdes of her soule.

h To mortifie her selfe by abstinence, or other bodely exercises.

i And warne her not the same day that he heareth it, as vers. 9.

k Not ẏ same day he heard them, but some day after, ẏ sinne shalbe imputed to him & not to her.

CHAP. XXXI.

8 Fiue Kings of Midián & Balaám are slaine. 18 Onely the maides are reserued aliue. 27 The praye is equally deuided. 49 A present giuen of Israél.

1 AND the Lord spake vnto Mosés, saying,
2 *Reuenge the children of Israél of the
Midianites, & afterward shalt thou be
*gathered vnto thy people.
3 And Mosés spake to the people, saying,
Harnes some of you vnto warre, and let
them go against Midián, to execute the
vengeance of the Lord [a] against Midián.
4 A thousād of euerie tribe through out all
the tribes of Israél, shal ye send to the
warre.
5 So there were taken out of the thousands
of Israél, twelue thousand prepared vnto
warre, of euerie tribe a thousand.
6 And Mosés sent them to the warre, *euen*
a thousand of euerie tribe, and *sent* [b] them
with Phinehás the sonne of Eleazár the
Priest to the warre & the holy instrumēts:
that is, the trumpets to blowe *were* in his
hand.
7 And they warred against Midián, as
the Lord had commanded Mosés, & slue
all the males.
8 They slue also ẏ Kings of Midián amōg
them that were slaine: *Eui and Rékem, &
Zur, & Hur & Réba fiue kīgs of Midián,
and thei slue [c] Balaám the sonne of Beór
with the sworde:
9 But the children of Israél toke the womē
of Midián prisoners, and their children, &
spoyled all their cattel, & all their flockes, and all their goods.
10 And they burnt all their cities, wherein
they dwelt, and all their " villages with
fire.
11 And they toke all the spoyle & all the
praye *bothe* of men & beastes.
12 And they broght the [d] captiues and that
which they had taken, and the spoyle vnto
Mosés and to Eleazár the Priest, and vnto
the Congregacion of the children of Israél, into the cāpe in the plaine of Moáb,
which was by Iordén *toward* Ierichó.
13 ¶ Then Mosés and Eleazár the Priest, &
all the princes of the Congregacion went
out of the campe to mete them.
14 And Mosés was angry with the captaines of the hoste, with the captaines ouer
thousands, & captaines ouer hundreds,
which came from the warre and battel.
15 And Mosés said vnto them, What? haue
ye saued all the [e] women?
16 Beholde, *these caused the children of
Israél through the *counsel of Balaám to
commit a trespas against the Lord, [f] as cō
cerning Peór, and there came a plague a-
mong the Congregacion of the Lord.
17 Now therefore, *slay all the males a-
mong the [g] children, & kil all the women
that haue knowen man by carnal copulation.
18 But all the women children that haue
not knowen carnal copulation, kepe aliue
for your selues.
19 And ye shal remaine without the hoste
seuē dayes, all that haue killed any persone, * and all that haue touched anie dead,
& purifie bothe your selues & your prisoners the third day and the seuenth.
20 Also ye shal purifie euerie garment and
all that is made of skins & all worke of
goates heere, & all things made of wood.

Chap. 25, 17.

Chap. 27, 13.

a As he had cōmāded, Chap. 25, 17: declaring also that ẏ iniurie done against his people is done against him.

b For his great zeale ẏ he bare to ẏ Lord, Chap. 25, 13.

Iosh. 13, 21.

c The false pphet who gaue counsel how to cause ẏ Israelites to offēd their God.

" Or, palaces & gorgious buyldings.

d As the women & litle children.

e As thogh he said, Ye oght to haue spared none.

Chap. 25, 2.
2. Pet. 2, 15.

f For worshipping of Peór.

Iudg. 21, 11.

g That is, all ẏ mē childrē.

Chap. 19, 11.

21 ¶ And Eleazár the Priest said vnto the
men of warre, which went to the battel,
This is the ordinance" of the lawe which
the Lord* commanded Mosés,
22 As for golde, and siluer, brasse, yron, tynne, and lead:
23 *Euen* all that may abyde the fire, ye shal
make it go through the fire, and it shalbe
cleane: yet, it shalbe h purified with * the
water of purificacion: and all that suffreth
not the fire, ye shal cause to passe by the
i water.
24 Ye shal wash also your clothes the seuenth day, and ye shalbe cleane: and afterward ye shal come into the Hoste.
25 ¶ And the Lord spake vnto Mosés, saying,
26 Take the summe of the praie that was
taken, *bothe* of persones and of cattel, thou
and Eleazár the Priest, & the chief fathers
of the Congregacion.
27 And deuide the praie ‖ betwene the soldiers that went to the warre, and all the
Congregacion.
28 And ȳ shalt take a tribute vnto the Lord
of the k men of warre, which went out
to battel: one persone of fiue hundreth,
bothe of the persones, and of the beues, &
of the asses, and of the shepe.
29 Ye shal take it of their halfe and giue it
vnto Eleazár ȳ Priest, *as* an heaue offring
of the Lord.
30 But of the halfe of the children of Israél thou shalt take l one, taken out of
fiftie, *bothe* of the persones, of the beues,
of the asses, and of the shepe, *euen* of all
the cattel: and thou shalt giue them vnto
the Leuites, which haue the charge of the
Tabernacle of the Lord.
31 And Mosés and Eleazár the Priest did
as the Lord had commanded Mosés.
32 And ȳ bootye, *to wit*, the rest of the praie
which the men of warre had spoiled, was
six hundreth seuentie and fiue thousand
shepe,
33 And seuentie and two thousand beues,
34 And thre score and one thousand asses,
35 And two and thirtie thousand persones,
in all of women that had" lyen by no man.
36 And the halfe, *to wit*, the parte of them
that went out to warre touching the nomber of shepe, was thre hundreth seuen and
thirtie thousand, and fiue hundreth.
37 And the m Lords tribute of the shepe
was six hundreth and seuentie and fiue.
38 And the beues *were* six and thirtie thousand, whereof the Lords tribute *was* seuētie and two.
39 And the asses *were* thirtie thousand and
fiue hundreth, whereof the Lords tribute
was thre score and one:
40 And n of persones sixtene thousand,
whereof ȳ Lords tribute *was* two & thirtie persones.
41 And Mosés gaue ȳ tribute of the Lords
offring vnto Eleazár the Priest, as ȳ Lord
had commanded Mosés.
42 And of the o halfe of the children of Israél, which Mosés deuided from the men
of warre,
43 (For the halfe that perteined vnto the
Congregacion) was thre hundreth thirtie
and seuen thousand shepe and fiue hundreth,
44 And six and thirtie thousand beues,
45 And thirtie thousand asses, and fiue hundreth,
46 And sixtene thousand persones.
47 Mosés, I say, toke of the halfe that perteined vnto the p children of Israél, one
taken out of fiftie, *bothe* of the persones &
of the cattel, and gaue them vnto the Leuites, which haue the charge of the Tabernacle of the Lord, as the Lord had
commanded Mosés.
48 ¶ Then the captaines which were ouer
thousands of the hoste, the captaines ouer
the thousands, and the captaines ouer the
hundreds came vnto Mosés:
49 And said to Mosés, Thy seruants haue
taken the summe of the men of warre
which are vnder " our autoritie, and there lacketh not one man of vs.
50 q We haue therefore broght a present
vnto the Lord, what euerie man founde of
iewels of golde, bracelets, and cheines,
rings, eare rings, and ornaments of the
legs, to make an atonement for our soules
before the Lord.
51 And Mosés and Eleazár the Priest toke
the golde of them, *and* all wroght iewels.
52 And all the golde of ȳ offring that thei
offred vp to the Lord, (*of the captaines*
ouer thousands and hundreds) *was* sixtene
thousand seuen hundreth & fiftie shekels,
53 (*For* the men of warre had spoiled, euerie man for him r self)
54 And Mosés and Eleazár the Priest toke the golde of the captaines ouer the
thousands, and ouer the hundreds, and
broght it into the Tabernacle of the Cōgregacion, for a s memorial of the children of Israél before the Lord.

" Or, conteined in the Lawe.
Chap. 19, 12.
h The third daie & before it be molten.
Chap. 19, 9.
i It shalbe washed.
‖ The praie is first deuided equally among all.
k Of the praie that falleth to the soldiers.
l The Israelites ẇ had not bene at warre, of euerie fiftieth paied one to the Lord: & ȳ soldiers, one of euerie fiue hundreth.
" Ebr. not knowē the bed of man.
m This is the porcion that ȳ soldiers gaue to the Lord.
n Meaning of the maides, or virgines which had not companied with man.
o Of that part which was giuē vnto them, in deuiding ȳ spoile.
p Which had not bene at warre.
" Ebr. vnder our hands.
q The captaines by this free offrig acknowledge ȳ great benefit of God in preseruing his people.
r And gaue no porciō to their captaines.
s That ȳ Lord might remember ȳ children of Israél.

CHAP. XXXII.

2 The request of the Reubenites and Gadites, 16 And their promes vnto Mosés. 20 Mosés granteth their request. 33 The Gadites, Reubenites, and halfe the tribe of Manasséh, conquer and buylde cities on this side Iordén.

1 NOw the children of a Reubén, and
the children of Gád had an exceading great multitude of cattel: and they
sawe the land of Iazér, and the land of
b Gileád, that it was an apt place for cattel.
2 Then the children of Gád, and the chil-

a Reubén came of Leáh, & Gad of Zilpáh her handmaide.
b Which mounteine was so named of the heape of stones ȳ Iaakób made as a signe of the couenant betwene him & Labán, Gen. 31, 47.

dren of Reubén came, & spake vnto Mosés and to Eleazár the Priest, and vnto the princes of the Congregacion, saying,
3 *The land of* Ataróth, and Dibón, and Iazér, and Nimráh, and Heshbón, and Eleeléh, and Shebám, and Nebó, and Beón,
4 Which countrey the Lord smote before the Congregacion of Israél, is a land *mete* for cattel, and thy seruants haue cattel:
5 Wherefore, said thei, If we haue founde grace in thy sight, let this land be giuen vnto thy seruãts for a possession, & bring vs not ouer Iordén.
6 And Mosés said vnto the childrẽ of Gad, and to the children of Reubén, Shal your brethren go to warre and ye tary here?
7 Wherefore now " discourage ye ẏ heart of the children of Israél, to go ouer into the land, which the Lord hathe giuen thẽ?
8 Thus did your fathers when I sent them from Kadésh-barnéa to se the land.
9 For * when they went vp euen vnto the " ryuer of Eshcól, and sawe the land: they discouraged the heart of the children of Israél, that thei wolde not go into the lãd, which the Lord had giuen them.
10 And the Lords wrath was kindled the same day, and he did sweare, saying,
11 " None of the men that came out of Egypt * from twentie yere olde and aboue, shal se the land for the which I sware vnto Abrahám, to Izhák, and to Iaakób, because thei haue not " wholie folowed me:
12 Except Caléb the sonne of Iephunnéh the Kenesite, & Ioshúa the sonne of Nun: for thei haue cõstantly folowed the Lord.
13 And the Lord was verie angry with Israél, and made them wander in the wildernes fortie yeres, vntil all the generacion that had done [c] euil in the sight of the Lord were consumed.
14 And beholde, ye are risen vp in your fathers steade *as* an encrease of sinneful mẽ, stil to augment the fearce wrath of the Lord, toward Israél.
15 For if ye turne away frõ following him, he wil yet againe leaue *the people* in ẏ wildernes, and [d] ye shal destroye all this folke.
16 And thei went nere to him and said, We wil buylde shepe foldes here for õ shepe, *and* for our cattel, and cities for our children.
17 But we our selues wil be ready armed *to go* before the children of Israél, vntil we haue broght them vnto their [e] place: but our children shal dwel in the defenced cities, because of the inhabitants of the land.
18 We wil not returne vnto our houses, vntil the children of Israél haue inherited, euerie man his inheritance.
19 Nether wil we inherit with thẽ beyõde Iordén and on that side, because our inheritance is fallen to vs on this side Iordén Eastward.
20 ¶ * And Mosés said vnto them, If ye wil do this thing, and go armed [f] before the Lord to warre:
21 And wil go euerie one of you in harnes ouer Iordén before the Lord, vntil he hathe cast out his [g] enemies from his sight:
22 And vntil the land be subdued before the Lord, then ye shal returne and be innocent toward the Lord, and toward Israél: and this land shalbe your possession [h] before the Lord.
23 But if ye wil not do so, beholde, ye haue sinned against the Lord, and be sure, that your sinne [i] wil finde you out.
24 Builde you *then* cities for your children and foldes for your shepe, and do that ye haue spoken.
25 Then the children of Gad & the children of Reubén spake vnto Mosés, sayĩg, Thy seruants wil do as my lord commandeth:
26 Our children, our wiues, our shepe, and all our cattel shal remaine there in the cities of Gileád,
27 But * thy seruants wil go euerie one armed to warre before the Lord for to fight, as my lord sayeth.
28 So concerning them, Mosés [k] commanded Eleazár the Priest, & Ioshúa the sonne of Nun, and the chief fathers of the tribes of the children of Israél:
29 And Mosés said vnto them, If the children of Gad, and the children of Reubén, wil go with you ouer Iordén, all armed to fight before the Lord, then when the land is subdued before you, ye shal giue them the land of Gileád for a possession:
30 But if thei wil not go ouer with you armed, then thei shal haue their possessions among you in the land of Canáan.
31 And the children of Gad, and the children of Reubén answered, saying, As the [l] Lord hathe said vnto thy seruants, so wil we do.
32 We wil go armed before the Lord into the land of Canáan: that the possession of our inheritance *may be* to vs on this side Iordén.
33 * So Mosés gaue vnto thẽ, *euen* to the childrẽ of Gad, & to the children of Reubén, & to half the tribe of Manasséh the sonne of Ioséph, ẏ kingdome of Sihón King of the [m] Amorites, and the kingdome of Og, King of Bashán, the land with the cities thereof and coastes, euen the cities of the countrey round about.
34 ¶ Then the children of Gad buylt Dibón, and Ataróth, and Aroér,
35 And Atróth, Shophán, and Iazér, and Iogbeháh.

Marginal notes:
" Ebr. breake.
Chap. 13, 24.
" Or, valley.
" Ebr. if anie of the men.
Chap. 14, 28.
" Or, perseuered & continued.
c Because thei murmured, nether wolde beleue their report, ẇ tolde ẏ trueth as concerning ẏ lãd.
d By your occasion.
e In the land of Canáan.
Iosh. 1, 13.
f Before the Arke of the Lord.
g That is, the inhabitants of the land.
h The Lord wil grante you this land ẇ ye require.
i Ye shal assuredly be punished for your sinne.
Iosh. 4, 12.
k Mosés gaue charge ẏ his promes made to the Reubenites & others shulde be performed after his death, so that thei brake not theirs.
l That is attributed to the Lord which his messenger speaketh.
Deut. 3, 12. iosh. 13, 8. & 22, 4.
m The Amorites dwelled on bothe sides of Iordén: but here he maketh mencion of them that dwelt on this side: & Iosh. 10, 12, he speaketh of them that inhabited beyonde Iordén.

This mappe properly apperteineth to the 33 Chap. of Nombres.

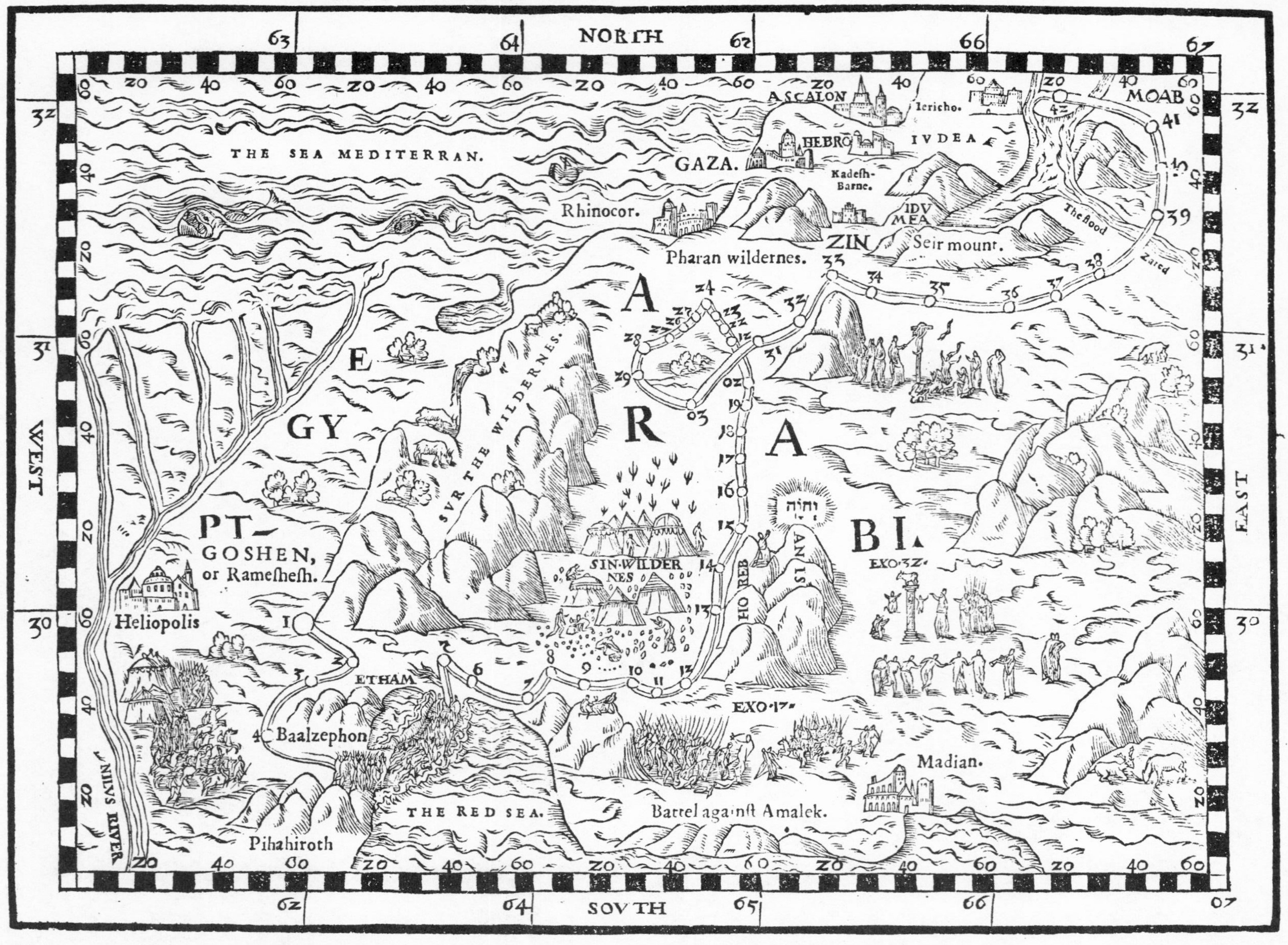

This mappe declareth the way, which the Israelites went for the space of fourtie yeres from Egypt through the wildernes of Arabia, vntil they entred into the land of Canaan, as it is mencioned in Exod. Nomb. & Deuter. It conteineth also the 42 places where they pitched their tentes, which are named Nomber. 33 with the obseruacion of the degrees, concerning the length and the breadth, and the places of their abode set out by nombers.

36 And Beth-nimráh, and Beth-harán, defenced cities: alſo ſhepe foldes.
37 And the childrē of Reubén built Heſhbón, and Elealéh, & Kiriatháim,
38 And Nébó, and Baal meón, and turned
their names, and Shibmáh: & gaue other
names vnto the cities which they built.

Gen 50,23.

39 And the children*of Machír the ſonne
of Manaſſéh went to Gileád, & toke it &
put out the Amorites that dwelt therein.
40 Then Moſés gaue Gileád vnto Machír
the ſonne of Manaſſéh, and he dwelt therein.

Deut.3,14.

41 *And Iaír the ſonne of Manaſſéh wēt &
toke the ſmal townes thereof, and called
them [n] Hauóth Iaír.

n That is, ẏ vil lages of Iair.

42 Alſo Nobáh went & toke Kenáth, with
the villages thereof and called it Nobáh,
after his owne name.

CHAP. XXXIII.

1 Two & fourtie iourneis of Iſrael are nōbred. 52 They are commanded to kil the Canannites.

a From whence they departed, and whether they came.

1 THeſe are the [a] iourneis of the childrē
of Iſraél, which went out of the land
of Egypt according to their bandes vnder the hand of Moſés and Aarón.
2 And Moſés wrote their going out by
their iourneyes according to the commādement of the Lord: ſo theſe are the iour
neies of their going out.

Exod.12,37.

3 Now they* departed frō Rameſés ẏ firſt
moneth, *euen* ẏ fifteth day of the firſt moneth, on the morowe after the Paſſeouer:
& the children of Iſraél went out with
an hie hand in the ſight of all the Egyptians.
4 (For the Egyptians buried all their firſt
borne, which the Lord had ſmitten amōg
them: vpon their [b] gods alſo the Lord did
execucion.)

b Ether meaning their idoles, or their men of autoritie.

5 And the children of Iſraél remoued from
Rameſés, and pitched in Succóth.

Exod. 13, 20.

6 And they departed from *Succóth, & pit
ched in Ethám, which is in the edge of the
wildernes.
7 And they remoued from Ethám, & turned againe vnto [c] Pi-hahiróth, which is
before Baal-zephón, and pitched before
Migdól.

c At ẏ commādement of the Lord Exo,14,2

8 And they departed from before Hahi-
róth, and* went through the middes of
the Sea into the wildernes, and went thre
dayes iourney in the wildernes of Ethám,
and pitched in Maráh.

Exod.15,22.

9 And they remoued from Maráh, and came vnto* Elím, and in Elím were twelue
fountains of water, and ſeuentie palme
trees, and they pitched there.

Exod.15,27.

10 And they remoued from Elím, and cam
ped by the red Sea.
11 And they remoued from the red Sea, &
laye in the * wildernes of Sin.

Exod. 16,1.

12 And they toke their iourney out of the
wildernes of Sín, and ſet vp their tentes in
Dophkáh.
13 And they departed from Dophkáh and
lay in Alúſh.
14 And they remoued from Alúſh, and lay
in* Rephidím, where was no water for ẏ *Exod 17,1.*
people to drinke.
15 And they departed from Rephidím, and
pitched in the*wildernes of Sinái. *Exod.19,1.*
16 And they remoued from the deſert of Si
nái, and pitched* in Kibróth Hattaauáh. *Chap.11, 34.*
17 And they departed frō Kibroth Hatta-
auáh, and lay at Hazeróth.
18 And they departed from Hazeróth, and
pitched in Rithmáh.
19 And they departed from Rithmáh, and
pitched at Rimmón Paréz.
20 *And they departed from Rimmón Pa- *Chap. 11,35.*
réz, and pitched in Libnáh. *& 13,1.*
21 And they remoued from Libnáh, & pitched in Riſſáh.
22 And they iourneied from Riſſáh, & pitched in Kehelatháh.
23 And they went from Kehelatháh, & pitched in mount Shápher.
24 And they remoued frō mount Shápher,
and lay in Haradáh.
25 And they remoued from Haradáh, and
pitched in Makhelóth.
26 And they remoued from Makhelóth, &
lay in Taháth.
27 And they departed from Taháth, & pitched in Taráh.
28 And they remoued from Taráh, & pitched in Mithkáh.
29 And they wēt from Mithkáh, & pitched
in Haſhmonáh.
30 And they departed from Haſhmonáh, &
lay in Moſeróth.
31 And they departed from Moſeróth, and
pitched in Bene-iaakán,
32 And they remoued from Bene-iaakán, &
lay in Hor-hagidgád.
33 And they went from Hor-hagidgád, &
pitched in Iotbáthah.
34 And they remoued from Iotbáthah, &
lay in Ebronáh.
35 And they departed from Ebronáh, and
lay in Ezion-gáber.
36 And they remoued from Ezion-gáber,
& pitched in the*wildernes of Zín, which *Chap.20,22.*
is Kadéſh.
37 And they remoued from Kadéſh, & pitched in mount Hor, in the edge of the lād
of Edóm.
38 *(And Aarón the Prieſt went vp into
mount Hor at the commandement of the *Chap.20,25.*
Lord, and died there, in the fourtieth ye- *deut.32,50.*
re after the children of Iſraél were come
out of the land of Egypt, in the firſt day
of the [d] fifth moneth.

d Which ẏ Ebrewes call Ab, and anſwereth to part of Iulie & part of Auguſt.

39 And Aarón was an hundreth, & thre and
twētie yere olde, whē he died ī moūt Hor.

Chap.21,1. 40 And *King Arád ẏ Canaanite, ẇ dwelt
in the South of the land of Canáan, heard of the cõming of ẏ childrẽ of Israél)
Chap.21,10. 41 And they departed from mounte* Hor,
and pitched in Zalmonáh.
42 And they departed from Zalmonáh, &
pitched in Punón.
43 And they departed from Punón, and
pitched in Obóth.
44 And they departed from Obóth, & pitched in Iie-abarím, in ẏ borders of Moáb.
Nom.21,4. 45 And they departed from *Iim, and pitched in Dibón-gad,
46 And thei remoued from Dibón-gad, &
lay in Almón-diblatháim.
47 And they remoued from Almon-dibla-
tháim, and pitched in the mounteines of
Abarím before Nebó.
48 And they departed from the mountei-
nes of Abarím, and pitched in the "playne of Moáb, by Iordén *toward* Ierichó.
"Or, field.
49 And they pitched by Iordén, from Beth-
Chap.25,1. ieshimóth vnto *Abel-shittím in the plaine of Moáb.
50 ¶ And the Lord spake vnto Mosés in the
plaine of Moáb, by Iordén *toward* Ierichó, saying,
51 Speake vnto the children of Israél, and
Deut.7,2. iosh.11,11. say vnto them, *When ye are come ouer
Iordén to entre in to the land of Canáan,
52 Ye shal then driue out all ẏ inhabitants
of the land before you, & destroy all their
[e] pictures, and breake a sunder all their i-
mages of metal, & plucke downe all their
hie places.

e Which were set vp in their hie places to worship.

53 And ye shal possesse the land and dwel
therein: for I haue giuen you the land to
possesse it.
54 And ye shal inherit the land by lot ac-
Chap.26,53. cording to your families: *to the more ye
shal giue more inheritance, & to the fewer
the lesse inheritance. where the lot shal
fall to anie mã, that shalbe his: according
to the tribes of your fathers shal ye inherit.
55 But if ye wil not driue out the inhabitants of the land before you, then those
ẇ ye let remaine of them, shal be * "prickes in your eies, and thornes in your sides,
and shal vexe you in the land wherein ye
dwel.

Iosh.23,13. iudg.2,3. "Or, kniues.

56 Moreouer, it shal come to passe, that I
shal do vnto you, as I thoght to do vnto
them.

CHAP. XXXIIII.

3 The coastes and borders of the land of Canáan. 17 Certeine men are assigned to deuide the land.

1 AND the Lord spake vnto Mosés, saying,
2 Commande the children of Israél, and
say vnto them, When ye come into the
land of Canáan, this is the [a] land that shal
fall vnto your inheritance: *that is*, the land
of Canáan with the coastes thereof.

a Meaning the description of the land.

3 *And your Southquarter shalbe from Iosh.15,1.
the wildernes of Zin to the borders of
Edóm: so that your Southquarter shalbe
from the salt Sea coast Eastward:
4 And the border shal compasse you from
the Southe "to Maaleh-akrabbím, and rea- "Or, ascending vp of scorpions.
che to Zin, & go out from the Southe to
Kadesh-barnéa: thence it shal stretch to
Hazar-addár, and go along to Azmón.
5 And the border shal compasse from Azmón vnto the [b] riuer of Egypt, and shal
go out to the sea.
6 And your Westquarter shal be the great
[c] sea: euen that border shalbe your West-
coast.

b Which was Nilus, or, as some thinke, Rhinocorura.

c Which is called Mediterraneum.

7 And this shal be your Northquarter: ye
shal marke out your border frõ the great
sea *vnto* mount [d] Hor.
8 From mount Hor ye shal point out til it
come vnto Hamáth, and the end of the
coast shalbe at Zedád.

d Which is a mounteine nere Tyre & Sidón & not ẏ Hor in the wildernes, where Aarón dyed.

9 And ẏ coast shal reache out to Ziphrón,
& go out at Hazar-enán. this shalbe your
Northquarter.
10 And ye shal marke out your Eastquarter
from Hazar-enán to Shephám.
11 And the coast shal go downe from Shephám to Ribláh, and from the Eastside of
Aín: and the same border shal descend &
go out at the side of the Sea of [e] Chinne-
réth Eastwarde.
12 Also that border shal go downe to Iordén, and leaue at the salt Sea. this shalbe
your land with the coastes thereof round
about.

e Which in ẏ Gospel is called ẏ lake of Gennazereth.

13 ¶ Then Mosés commanded the children of Israél, saying, This is the land
which ye shal inherit by lot, which ẏ Lord
commanded to giue vnto nine tribes and
halfe the tribe.
14 *For the tribe of the children of Reu- Chap.32,33. iosh.14,2.
bén, according to the housholdes of their
fathers, and the tribe of the children of
Gad, according to their fathers housholdes, and halfe the tribe of Manasséh, haue
receiued their inheritance.
15 Two tribes and an halfe tribe haue receiued their inheritãce on this side of Iordén *toward* Ierichó ful East.
16 ¶ Againe the Lord spake to Mosés, saying,
17 These are the names of the men which
shal deuide the lãd vnto you: Eleazár the
Priest, and Ioshúa the sonne of Nun.
18 And ye shal take also a [f] prince of euerie
tribe to deuide the land.
19 The names also of the men are these: Of
the tribe of Iudáh, Caléb the sonne of Iephunnéh.

f One of the heades or chiefe men of euerie tribe.

20 And of the tribe of the sonnes of Simeón, Shemuél the sonne of Ammihúd.
21 Of the tribe of Beniamín, Elidád the
sonne

sonne of Chislón.
22 Also of the tribe of the sonnes of Dan,
the prince Bukkí, the sonne of Ioglí.
23 Of the sonnes of Ioséph: of the tribe of
the sonnes of Manasséh, the prince Han-
niél the sonne of Ephód.
24 And of the tribe of ẙ sonnes of Ephráim, the prince Kemuél, ẙ sonne of Shiphtán.
25 Of the tribe also of ẙ sonnes of Zebulún, the prince Elizaphán, ẙ sonne of Par-
nách.
26 So of the tribe of ẙ sonnes of Issachár,
the prince Paltiél the sonne of Azzán.
27 Of the tribe also of ẙ sonnes of Ashér,
the prince Ahihúd the sonne of Shelo-
mí.
28 And of the tribe of the sonnes of Naphtalí, the prince Pedahél, the sonne of Ammihúd.
29 These are they, whome the Lord commanded to g deuide the inheritance vnto
the children of Israél, in the land of Canáan.

g And be iudges ouer euerie piece of grounde that shulde fall to anie by lot, to thintēt that all things might be done orderly & without contention.

CHAP. XXXV.

2 Vnto the Leuites are giuen cities and suburbes. 11 The cities of refuge. 16 The lawe of murther. 30 For one mans witnes shal no man be condemned.

1 AND the Lord spake vnto Mosés in ẙ
plaine of Moáb by Iordén, *toward*
Ierichó, saying,
2 *Commande the children of Israél, that
they giue vnto the a Leuites of the inheritãce of their possession, b cities to dwel
in: ye shal giue also vnto the Leuites the
suburbes of the cities round about them.
3 So they shal haue the cities to dwel in, &
their suburbes shalbe for their cattel, and
for their substance, & for all their beastes.
4 And the suburbes of the cities, which ye
shal giue vnto the Leuites, from the wall
of the citie outwarde, *shalbe* a thousand
cubites round about.
5 And ye shal measure without the citie of
the Eastside, c two thousand cubites: and
of the Southside, two thousand cubites: &
of the Westside, two thousand cubites: &
of the Northside, two thousand cubites: &
the citie *shalbe* in the middes. this shalbe
the measure of the suburbes of their cities.
6 And of the cities which ye shal giue vnto
the Leuites, **there shalbe* six cities for refuge, which ye shal appoint, that he which
killeth, may flee thither: & to them ye shal
adde two and fourty cities mo.
7 All the cities which ye shal giue to ẙ Leuites, *shalbe* eight and fourtie cities: them
shal ye giue with their suburbes.
8 And concerning the cities which ye shal
giue, of the possession of the children
of Israél: of many ye shal take mo, and
of fewe ye shal take lesse: euerie one shal
giue of his cities vnto the Leuites, accor-

Iosh.21,2.

a Because thei had no inheritance asigned them in ẙ lãd of Canáan.
b God wolde haue thē scatered through all ẙ land, because ẙ people might be preserued by the in ẙ obediēce of God & his lawe.

c So ẙ in all were thre thousand: and in the compasse of these two thousand they might plant & sowe.

Deut.4,41. iosh.21,3.

ding to his inheritance, which he inheri-
teth.
9 ¶ And the Lord spake vnto Mosés, saying,
10 Speake vnto the children of Israél, and
say vnto them, *When ye be come ouer
Iordén into the land of Canáan,
11 Ye shal appoint you cities, to be cities
of refuge for you, that the slayer, which
slayeth anie persone vnwares, may flee
thither.
12 And these cities shalbe for you a refuge
from the d auenger, that he which killeth,
dye not, vntil he stand before the Cõgregacion in iudgement.
13 And *of* the cities which ye shal giue, six
cities shal ye haue for refuge.
14 Ye shal appoint thre e on this side Iordén, and ye shal appoint thre cities in the
land of Canáan which shalbe cities of refuge.
15 These six cities shalbe a refuge for the
children of Israél, and for the stranger,
and for him that dwelleth among " you,
that euerie one which killeth anie persone vnwares, may flee thither.
16 *And if one f smite an other with an instrument of yron that he dye, he *is* a murtherer, & the murtherer shal dye ẙ death.
17 Also if he smite him by casting a g stone, wherewith he may be slaine, and he
dye, he is a murtherer, *and* the murtherer
shal dye the death.
18 Or if he smite him with an hãd weapon
of wood, wherewith he may be slaine, if he
dye, he is a murtherer, *and* the murtherer
shal dye the death.
19 The reuenger of the blood him selfe
shal slay the murtherer: when he meteth
him, he shal slay him.
20 But if he thrust him *of hate, or hurle at
him by laying of wait, that he dye,
21 Or smite him through enemitie with his
hand, that he dye, he that smote him shal
dye the death: *for* he is a murtherer: the reuenger of the blood shal slay the murtherer when he meteth him.
22 But if he pushed him "vnaduisedly, and
*not of hatred, or cast vpon him anie
" thing, without laying of wait,
23 Or anie stone (whereby he might be slaine) and sawe him not, or caused it to fall
vpon him, and he dye, & was not his enemie, nether soght him anie harme,
24 Then the Congregacion shal iudge betwene the slayer & the h auenger of blood
according to these lawes.
25 And the Congregacion shal deliuer the
slayer out of the hand of the auenger of
blood, and the Congregacion shal restore
him vnto the citie of his refuge, whither
he was fled: and he shal abide there vnto
the death of the i hie Priest, which is
anointed with the holy oyle.

Exod.21,13. deu.19,2. iosh.20,2.

d Meaning, frõ the next of ẙ kinred, who oght to pursue the cause.

e Among the Reubenites, Gadites, and halfe the tribe of Manasséh.

"*Ebr. among them.*

Exod.21,14.
f Wittingly, and willingly.

g That is, ẙ a big and dangerous stone: in Ebr. with a stone of his hand.

Deu.19,11.

"*Or, sodenly.*
Exod.21,13.
"*Ebr. instrument.*

h That is, his next kinsmã.

i Vnder this figure is declared, ẙ our sinnes colde not be remitted, but by the death of the hie Priest Iesus Christ.

26 But if the ſlayer come without the borders of the citie of his refuge, whither he
was fled,
27 And the reuenger of blood finde him
without the borders of the citie of his re
fuge, and the reuenger of blood ſlay the
[k] murtherer, he ſhal be giltles,
28 Becauſe he ſhulde haue remained in the
citie of his refuge, vntil the death of the
hye Prieſt: and after the death of the hie
Prieſt: the ſlayer ſhal returne vnto ẏ land
of his poſſeſsion.
29 So theſe things ſhalbe a [l] lawe of iudgement vnto you, throughout your generacions in all your dwellings.
30 Whoſoeuer killeth anie perſone, the *iud
ge* ſhal ſlay the murtherer, through * witneſſes: but * one witnes ſhal not teſtifie a-
gainſt a perſone to cauſe him to die.
31 Moreouer ye ſhal take no recompenſe
for the life of ẏ murtherer, which is [m] wor
thie to die: but he ſhal be put to death.
32 Alſo ye ſhal take no recōpēſe for him
that is fled to the citie of his refuge, that
he ſhuld come againe, and dwel in the
land, before the death of the hie Prieſt.
33 So ye ſhal not pollute the land wherein
ye ſhal dwel: ° for blood defileth the land:
and the land can not be [n] clenſed of the
blood that is ſhed therein, but by ẏ blood
of him that ſhed it.
34 Defile not therefore the land which ye
ſhal inhabite, for I dwel in the middes the
reof: for I the Lord dwel among the children of Iſraél.

k By the ſentence of the iudge.

l A lawe to iudge murthers done, ether of purpoſe or vnaduiſedly.

Deut.17,6. & 19,15. Mat.18,16. 2.cor.13.1.

m Which purpoſly hath cōmitted murther.

° *Or murther.*

n So God is mindful of the blood wrongfully ſhed ẏ he maketh his domme creatures to demande vengeance thereof.

CHAP. XXXVI.

6 *An ordre for the mariage of the daughters of Zelophehád. 7 The inheritance colde not be giuen from one
tribe to another.*

1 THen [a] the chief fathers of the familie
of the ſonnes of Gileád, the ſonne of
Machír the ſonne of Manaſſéh, of the families of the ſonnes of Ioſéph, came, and
ſpake before Moſés, and before the princes, the chief fathers of the children of
Iſraél,
2 And ſaid, * The Lord commanded [b] my
lord to giue the land to inherite by lot
to the children of Iſraél: and my lord was
commanded by the Lord, to giue the inhe
ritance of Zelophehád our brother vnto
his daughters.
3 If they be maried to anie of the ſonnes
of the *other* tribes of the childrē of Iſraél
then ſhal their inheritance be taken away
from the inheritāce of our fathers, & ſhal
be put vnto the inheritance of the tribe
whereof they ſhalbe: ſo ſhal it be taken a-
way from the lot of our inheritance.
4 Alſo when the [c] Iubile of the children
of Iſraél commeth, then ſhal their inheritance be put vnto the inheritance of the
tribe whereof they ſhalbe. ſo ſhal their inheritance be takē away from the inheritance of the tribe of our fathers.
5 Then Moſés commanded the children
of Iſraél, according to the worde of the
Lord, ſaying, The tribe of the ſonnes of
Ioſéph haue ſayd [d] wel.
6 This is the thing that the Lord hathe
commanded, concerning the daughters of
Zelophehád, ſaying, They ſhal be wiues,
to whome they thinke beſt, onely to the
familie of the tribe of their father ſhal
they mary:
7 So ſhal not the inheritance of the children of Iſraél remoue from tribe to tribe,
for euerie one of the children of Iſraél
ſhal ioyne him ſelfe to the inheritance of
the tribe of his fathers.
8 And euerie daughter that poſſeſſeth anie
[e] inheritance of the tribes of the children of Iſrael, ſhal be wife vnto one of
the familie of the tribe of her father:
that the children of Iſraél may enioye
euerie man the inheritance of their fathers.
9 Nether ſhal the inheritance go about
from tribe to tribe: but euerie one of the
tribes of the children of Iſraél ſhal ſticke
to his owne inheritance.
10 As the Lord commanded Moſés, ſo did
the daughters of Zelophehád.
11 For * Mahláh, Tirzáh, and Hogláh, and
Milcáh, and Noáh the daughters of Zelophehád were maried vnto their fathers
brothers ſonnes,
12 They were wyues *to certeine* of the families of the ſonnes of Manaſſéh the ſonne of Ioſéph: ſo their inheritance remained in the tribe of the familie of their
father.
13 Theſe are the [f] commandements and
lawes which the Lord commanded by the
hand of Moſés, vnto the children of Iſraél in the plaine of Moáb, by Iordén
toward Ierichó.

a It ſemeth ẏ ẏ tribes contended who might mary theſe daughters to haue their inheritāce: and therefore the ſonnes of Ioſéph propoſed the matter to Moſés.

Chap.27,1. ioſh.17,3.

b Meaning, Moſés.

c Signifying ẏ at no time it colde returne for in ẏ Iubile all things returned to their owne tribes.

d For the tribe colde not haue cōtinued if the inheritance which was the maintenance thereof ſhulde haue bene abalienated to others.

e When there is no male to inherite.

Chap.27,1.

f Touching the ceremonial and iudicial lawes.

THE

THE FIFTH BOKE OF Mosés, called* Deuteronomie.

* That is, a seconde lawe: so called, because the Lawe ŷ God gaue in mount Sinái, is here repeated, as thogh it were a newe Law, and this boke is a commentarie or exposition of the tē comaundemēts.

THE ARGUMENT.

The wonderful loue of God toward his Churche is liuely set forthe in this boke. For albeit through their ingratitude and sundry rebellions against God, for the space of forty yeres, Deu. 9,7, they had deserued to haue bene cut of from the nōber of his people, and for euer to haue bene depriued of the vse of his holy worde, & sacraments: yet he did euer preserue his Church euen for his owne mercies sake, and wolde stil haue his Name called vpon among them. Wherefore he bringeth them into the land of Canáan, destroyeth their enemies, giueth them their countrey, townes, and goodes, and exhorteth them by the example of their fathers (whose infidelitie, idolatrie, adulteries, murmurings and rebellion, he had moste sharpely punished) to feare and obey the Lord, to embrace and kepe his lawe without adding therunto or diminishing there from. For by his worde he wolde be knowē to be their God, and they his people: by his worde he wolde gouerne his Churche, and by the same they shulde learne to obey him: by his worde he wolde discerne the false Prophet from the true, light from darknes, error from knollage, and his owne people from all other nations and infideles: teaching them thereby to refuse and detest, destroy and abolish whatsoeuer is not agreable to his holy wil, seme it otherwise neuer so good or precious in the eyes of man. And for this cause God promised to raise vp Kings and gouernours for the setting forthe of this worde and preseruacion of his Churche: giuing vnto them an especial charge for the executing thereof: whome therefore he willeth to exercise them selues diligently in the continual studie and meditaciō of the same: that they might learne to feare the Lord, loue their subiects, abhorre couetousnes and vice, and whatsoeuer offendeth the maiestie of God. And as he had to fore instructed their fathers in all things apperteining, bothe to his spiritual seruice, and also for the maintenance of that societie which is betwene men: so he prescribeth here anewe, all suche lawes and ordinances, which ether concerne his Diuine seruice, or els are necessarie for a comon weale: appointing vnto euerie estate and degre their charge and duetie: aswel, how to rule and liue in the feare of God, as to nourish friendeship towarde their neighbours, and to preserue that ordre which God hathe established among men: threatening withall, moste horrible plagues to them that transgresse his commandements, and promising all blessings & felicitie to suche as obserue and obey them.

CHAP. I.

2 A brefe reharsal of things done before, frō Horéb vnto Kadesh-bernéa. 32 Moses reproueth the people for their incredulite. 44 The Israelites are ouer come by the Amorites because they fought against the commādement of the Lord.

These be ŷ wordes which
Mosés spake vnto all Israél, on a this side Iordén in
the wildernes, in the plaine,
b ouer against ŷ red Sea,
betwene Parán & Tóphel,
and Labán, and Hazeróth,
and Di-zaháb.
2 *There are* eleuē daies iourney from c Horéb vnto Kadésh-barnéa, by the way of
mount Seír.
3 And it came to passe in the first day of the
eleuenth moneth, in the forteth yere, that
Mosés spake vnto the children of Israél
according vnto al that the Lord had giuē
him in commandement vnto them,
4 After that he had slaine d *Sihón the King
of ŷ Amorites which dwelt in Heshbón,
and Og King of Bashán, which dwelt at
Ashtaróth in Edréi.
5 On this side Iordén in the land of Moáb
e begã Mosés to declare this Law, saying,
6 The Lord our God spake vnto vs in f Ho
réb, saying, Ye haue dwelt long ynough
in this mount,
7 Turne you and departe, and go vnto the
mountaine of the Amorites, and vnto all
places nere therunto: in the plaine, in the
mountaine, or in the valley: bothe South
ward, and to the sea side, to the land of ŷ
Canaanites, and vnto Lebanón: *euen* vnto
the great riuer, the riuer "Peráth.
8 Beholde, I haue set the land before you:
go in and *possesse that land which the
Lord sware vnto your fathers, Abrahám,
Izhák, and Iaakób, to giue vnto thē and
to their sede after them.
9 ¶ And I spake g vnto you the same time,
saying, I am not able to beare you my selfe alone:
10 The Lord your God hathe h multiplied
you: & beholde, ye are this day as the starres of heauen in nomber:
11 (The Lord God of your fathers make
you a thousand times so manie mo as ye
are, and blesse you, as he hathe promised
you)
12 How cã I alone i beare your cumbrance
and your charge, and your strife?
13 Bring you men of wisdome and of vnderstanding, and k knowen among your
tribes, and I wil make them rulers ouer
you:
14 Then ye answered me & said, The thing
is good that thou hast cōmanded *vs* to do.
15 So I toke the chief of your tribes l wise
and knowen mē, and made thē rulers ouer

a In the coūtrey of Moáb.

b So that the wildernes was betwene ŷ Sea and this plaine of Moab.

c In Horéb, or Sinái, forty yeres before this ŷ lawe was giuen: but because all ŷ were then of age and iudgemēt were now dead, Mosés repeateth the same to the youth which ether thē were not borne, or had not iudgement.

d By these examples of Gods fauour their mindes are prepared to receiue the Law.

Nom. 21, 24.

e The seconde time.

f In ŷ secōde yere, and secōde moneth, Nom. 10.11.

" Or, Euphrátes.

Gen. 15, 18. & 17, 7.

g By the consel of Iethro my father in lawe. Exod. 18, 19.

h Not so muche by ŷ cours of nature, as miraculously.

i Signifying how great a burden it is, to gouerne the people.

k Whose godlines and vprightnes is knowen.

l Declaring what sort of men oght to haue a publike charge, read Exod. 18, 21.

you, captaines ouer thouſands, and captaines ouer hundreds, & captaines ouer fifty, and captaines ouer ten, and officers a-
mong your tribes.
16 And I charged your iudges that ſame time, ſaying, Heare the *controuerſies* betwene
your brethren, and *iudge righteouſly betwene euerie man and his brother, and
the ſtranger that is with him.
17 Ye ſhal haue no reſpect of perſone in
iudgement, *but ſhal heare the ſmall aſwel as the great: ye ſhal not feare the face
of man: for the iudgemēt is m Gods: and
the cauſe that is to hard for you, bring vnto me, and I wil heare it.
18 Alſo I cōmanded you the ſame time all
the things which ye ſhulde do.
19 ¶ Then we departed from Horéb, and
went through all that great and terrible
wildernes, (as ye haue ſene) by the way of
ye mounteine of the Amorites, as the Lord
our God commanded vs: and we came to
Kadeſh barnéa.
20 And n I ſaid vnto you, ye are come vnto the mounteine of the Amorites, which
the Lord our God doeth giue vnto vs.
21 Beholde, the Lord thy God hathe layed
ye lād before thee: go vp & poſſeſſe it, as ye
Lord ye God of thy fathers hathe ſaid vnto thee: feare not, nether be diſcouraged.
22 ¶ o Then ye came vnto me euerie one, &
ſaid, We wil ſēd mē before vs, to ſearche
vs out the land and to bring vs worde a-
gaine, what way we muſt go vp by, and
vnto what cities we ſhal come.
23 So the ſaying pleaſed me wel, and I toke
twelue men of you, of euerie tribe one.
24 *Who departed, and went vp into the
mouteine, & came vnto the "riuer Eſhcól,
and ſearched out the *land*.
25 And toke of the frute of the lād in their
hands, and broght it vnto vs, and broght
vs worde againe, and p ſaid, It is a good
land, which the Lord our God doeth giue vs.
26 Notwithſtanding, ye wolde not go vp,
but were diſobedient vnto the commandement of the Lord your God,
27 And murmured in your tentes, and ſaid,
Becauſe the Lord q hated vs, therefore
hathe he broght vs out of the land of E-
gypt, to deliuer vs into the hand of the
Amorites, and to deſtroy vs.
28 Whether ſhal we go vp? our r brethrē
haue diſcouraged our hearts, ſaying, The
people *is* greater, and taller then we: the
cities *are* great and walled vp to heauen:
and moreouer we haue ſene the ſonnes of
the *Anakims there.
29 But I ſaid vnto you, Dread not, nor be
afraid of them.
30 The Lord your God, ſ who goeth before you, he ſhal fight for you, according
to all that he did vnto you in Egypt before your eyes,
31 And in the wildernes, where thou haſt ſene how the Lord thy God bare thee, as a
man doeth beare his ſonne, in all the way
which ye haue gone, vntil ye came vnto
this place.
32 Yet for all this ye did not beleue the
Lord your God,
33 *Who went in the way before you, to
ſearche you out a place to pitche your tētes in, in fire by night, ye ye might ſe what
way to go, and in a cloude by day.
34 Then the Lord heard the voyce of your
wordes, and was wroth, and ſware, ſaying,
35 *Surely there ſhal not one of theſe mē of
this froward generacion, ſe ye good land,
which I ſware to giue vnto your fathers,
36 Saue Caléb the ſonne of Iephūnéh: he
ſhal ſe it, *and to him wil I giue the land
that he hathe troden vpon, and to his children, becauſe he hathe cōſtantly followed
the Lord.
37 *Alſo the Lord was angry with me for
your ſakes, ſaying, *Thou alſo ſhalt not
go in thither,
38 But Ioſhúa the ſonne of Nun which
ſtādeth t before thee, he ſhal go in thither:
incourage him: for he ſhal cauſe Iſraél to
inherit it.
39 Moreouer, your u children, which ye
ſaid ſhulde be a pray, and your ſonnes,
which in that day had no knowledge betwene good and euil, they ſhal go in thither, and vnto them wil I giue it, and they
ſhal poſſeſſe it.
40 But as for you, turne backe, & take your
iourney into the wildernes by the way of
the red Sea.
41 Thē ye anſwered and ſaid vnto me, We
haue ſinned againſt the Lord, x we wil go
vp, and fight, according to all that ye Lord
our God hathe commanded vs: and ye armed you euerie man to the warre, & were
ready to go vp into the mounteine.
42 But the Lord ſaid vnto me, Say vnto thē,
Go not vp, nether fight, (for I am y not
amōg you) leſt ye fall before your enemies.
43 And whē I tolde you, ye wolde not heare, but rebelled againſt the commandemēt
of the Lord, and were preſumpteous, and
went vp into the mounteine.
44 Then the Amorites which dwelt in that
mounteine came out againſt you, & chaſed you (as bees vſe to do) and deſtroyed
you in Seír, *euen* vnto Hormáh.
45 And when ye came againe, ye wept before the Lord, but the Lord wolde not
z heare your voyce, nor incline his eares
vnto you.
46 So ye abode in Kadéſh a long time, according to the time that ye had remained
before.

Ioh.7,24. *Leu.19,15. chap.16,19. 1.ſam.17,7. prou.24,23. eccle.42.5. iam.2,2.*

m And you are his lieutenants.

n So that the faute was in them ſelues ye they dyd not ſoner poſſeſſe the inheritāce promiſed.

o Read Nōb. 13.1.

Nomb.13,24. "Or, valley of the cluſter of grapes.

p To wit, Caléb, & Ioſhúa: Moſés preferreth the better part to ye greater, that is, two to ten.

q Suche was the Iewes vnthankfulnes, that they coūted Gods eſpecial loue hatred.

r The other ten, not Caléb & Ioſhúa.

Nōb.13,29.

ſ Declaring ye to renoūce our owne force, & conſtantly to followe our vocation, and depend on the Lord, is ye true boldenes, and agreable to God.

Exod.13,21. *Nom.14,23.* *Ioſh.14,6.* *Nom.20,12. & 27,14. Chap.3,26. & 4,21, & 34,4.*

t Which miniſtreth vnto thee.

u Which were vnder twenty yere olde, as Nomb.14,31.

x This declareth mans nature, who wil do that which God forbiddeth, and wil not do that wc he cōmandeth.

y Signifying that man hath no ſtrength, but when God is at hand to helpe him.

z Becauſe ye rather ſhewed your hypocriſie, then true repentance: rather lamēting ye loſſe of your brethren, then repenting for your ſinnes.

CHAP.

CHAP. II.

1 Israél is forbidde to fight with the Edomites. 9 Moabites, 19 And Ammonites. 33 Sihón King of Heshbón is discomfited.

a They obeyed, after that God had chastised them.

b Eight and thirtie yere, as ver. 14.

1 THen [a] we turned, and toke our iourney into the wildernes, by the waie of
ye red Sea, as the Lord spake vnto me: and
we compassed mount Seír a [b] long time.
2 And the Lord spake vnto me, saying,
3 Ye haue compassed this mountaine long
ynough: turne you Northwarde.
4 And warne thou the people, saying, Ye
shal go through the [c] coast of your brethren the children of Esáu, which dwel in
Seír, and they shal be afraid of you: take
ye good hede therefore.

c This was ye seconde time: for before thei had caused the Israelites to returne, Nōb. 20, 21.

5 Ye shal not prouoke them: for I wil not
giue you of their land so muche as a fote
breadth, * because I haue giue mount Seír
vnto Esáu for a possession.

Gen. 36, 8.

6 Ye shal bye meat of them for money to
eat, and ye shal also procure water of the
for money to drinke.
7 For ye Lord thy God hathe [d] blessed thee
in all ye workes of thine hād: he knoweth
thy walking through this great wildernes,
& the Lord thy God hathe bene with thee
this fortie yere, *and* thou hast lacked nothing.

d And giuen thee meanes wherewith yu maiest make recompence: also God wil direct thee by his prouidēce, as he hathe done.

8 And when we were departed frō our brethren the children of Esáu which dwelt
in Seír, through the way of the ″plaine,
from Eláth, & from Ezion-gáber, we turned and went by the way of the wildernes
of Moáb.

″Or, wildernes.

9 Then the Lord said vnto me, Thou shalt
not ″ vexe Moáb, nether prouoke them to
battel: for I wil not giue thee of their lād
for a possession, because I haue giuen Ar
vnto the children [e] of Lot for a possessiō.

″Or, besiege.

e Which were the Moabites & Ammonites.

10 The [f] Emims dwelt therein in times
past, a people great, & many, and tall, as
the Anakíms.
11 They also were taken for gyantes as the
Anakíms: whome the Moabites call E-
míms.

f Signifying ye as these gyāts were driuē out for their finnes: so ye wicked whē their finnes are ripe can not auoide Gods plagues.

12 The Horíms also dwelt in Seír before
time, whome the children of Esáu chased
out and destroyed them before them, and
dwelt in their stede: as Israél shal do vnto
the land of his possession, which the Lord
hathe giuen them.
13 Now rise vp, *said I*, and get you ouer the
riuer * Zeréd: and we went ouer the riuer
Zeréd.

Nom. 21, 12.

14 The [g] space also wherein we came from
Kadesh-barnéa vntil we were come ouer
the riuer Zeréd, *was* eight and thirtie yeres, vntil all the generacion of the men of
warre were wasted out from among the
hoste, as the Lord sware vnto them.
15 For in dede the [h] hand of the Lord was
against them, to destroye them frō amōg
the hoste, til thei were consumed.

g He sheweth hereby, that as God is true in his promes: so his threatenīgs are not in vaine.

h His plague & punishment to destroye all ye were twentie yere olde and aboue.

16 ¶ So when all the men of warre were
consumed and dead from among the people:
17 Then the Lord spake vnto me, saying,
18 Thou shalt go through Ar the coast of
Moáb this day:
19 And thou shalt come nere ouer against
the children of Ammón: *but* shalt not lay
siege vnto them, nor moue warre against
them: for I wil not giue thee of the land
of the children of Ammón *anie* possession: for I haue giuen it vnto the children
of Lot for a possession.
20 That also was taken for a land [i] of gyants: *for* gyants dwelt therein a fore time,
whome the Ammonites called Zamzum-
míms:
21 A people *that was* great, & many, & tall,
as the Anakíms: but the Lord destroyed
them before them, & thei succeded them
in their inheritance, and dwelt in their
stede:

i Who called the selues Rephaims: that is, preseruers, or phisicians to heale & reforme vices: but were in dede Zamzūmíms, that is, wicked & abominable.

22 As he did to the children of Esáu which
dwel in Seír, when he destroyed the Horíms before them, & thei possessed them,
and dwelt in their stede vnto this day.
23 And the Auíms which dwelt in Haze-
rím *euen* vnto ″ Azzáh, the Caphtoríms
which came out of Caphtor destroyed
them, and dwelt in their stede.

″Or, Gaza.

24 ¶ Rise vp *therefore, said the Lord*: take
your iourney, and passe ouer the riuer Arnón: beholde, I haue giuen into thy hand
Sihón: the [k] Amorite, King of Heshbón, and his land: begin to possesse it and
prouoke him to battel.

k According to his promes made to Abrahám, Gen. 15, 21.

25 This day wil I [l] begin to send thy feare & thy dread, vpon all people vnder the
heauens, which shal heare thy fame & shal
tremble and quake before thee.

l This declareth that the hearts of men are in Gods hands ether to be made faint, or bolde.

26 Then I sent messengers out of the wildernes of Kedemóth vnto Sihón King of
Heshbón, with wordes of peace, saying,
27 ¶ * Let me passe through thy land: I wil
go by the hie way: I wil nether turne vnto
the right hand nor to the left.

Nom. 21, 21.

28 Thou shalt sel me meat for money, for
to eat, and shalt giue me water for money
for to drinke: onely I wil go through on
my fote,
29 (As the [m] children of Esáu which dwel
in Seír, and the Moabites which dwel in
Ar, did vnto me) vntil I be come ouer Iordén, into the land which ye Lord our God
giueth vs.

m Because nether intreaty nor exāples of others colde moue him, he colde not complaine of his iuste destructiō

30 But Sihón the King of Heshbón wolde
not let vs passe by him: for the Lord thy
God had [n] hardened his spirit, and made
his heart obstinat, because he wolde deliuer him into thine hand, as *appeareth* this
day.
31 And the Lord said vnto me, Beholde, I

n God, in his electiō & reprobacion doeth not onelie appoint ye ends, but the meanes tending to the same.

haue begonne to giue Sihón and his land
before thee: begin to possesse and inherit
his land.

Nomb.21,23.
32 *Then came out Sihón to mete vs, him
self with all his people to fight at Iaház.
33 But the Lord our God deliuered him
" into our power, and we smote him, and
his sonnes, and all his people.

" Ebr. before vs.

34 And we toke all his cities the same time, & destroyed euerie citie, mé, & ° women, & children: we let nothing remaine.
35 Onely the cattel we toke to our selues,
& the spoile of the cities which we toke.

° God had cursed Canáan & therefore he wolde not that anie of ẏ wicked race shulde be preserued.

36 From Aroér, which is by the banke of
the riuer of Arnón, & *from* ẏ citie that is
vpó the riuer, eué vnto Gileád: there was
not one citie that escaped vs: *for* the Lord
our God deliuered vp all " before vs.

" Or, into our hand.

37 Onely vnto the land of the children of
Ammón thou camest not, *nor* vnto anie
place of the " riuer Iabbók, nor vnto the
cities in the mountaines, nor vnto whatsoeuer the Lord our God forbade vs.

" Or, fourde.

CHAP. III.

3 Og King of Bashán is slaine. 11 The bignes of his bed. 18 The Reubenites and Gadites are commanded to go ouer Iordén armed before their brethren. 21 Ioshua is made captaine. 27 Moses is permitted to se the land, but not to enter, albeit he desired it.

1 THen we turned, and went vp by the
way of Bashán: * and Og King of
Bashán [a] came out against vs, he, and all
his people to fight at Edréi.

Nomb.21,33. chap.29,7.

a Therefore beside the cómandement of the Lord, thei had iuste occasió of his parte to fight agaist him.

2 And the Lord said vnto me, Feare him
not, for I wil deliuer him, and all his people, and his land into thine hand, & thou
shalt do vnto him, as thou didest vnto
*Sihón King of ẏ Amorites, which dwelt
at Heshbón.

Nomb.21,24.

3 So the Lord our God deliuered also vnto our hand, * Og the King of Bashán, &
all his people: and we smote him, vntil none was left him *aliue*,

Nomb.21,33.

4 And we toke all his cities the same time,
nether was there a citie which we toke not
from them, *euen* thre score cities, *and* all
the countrey of Argób, the kingdome of
Og in Bashán.
5 All these cities *were* fenced with hie
walles, gates and barres, beside [b] vnwalled townes a great many.

b As villages & smale towres.

6 And we ouerthrewe them, as we did vnto
Sihón King of Heshbón, destroying euerie citie, *with* men, [c] women, & children.
7 But all the cattel and the spoile of the cities we toke for our selues.

c Because this was Gods appointemét, therefore it may not be iudged cruel.

8 Thus we toke at that time out of the hád
of two Kings of the Amorites, the land
that was on this side Iordén from the riuer of Arnón vnto mount Hermón:
9 (Which Hermón the Sidoniás call Shirión, but the Amorites call it Shenír)
10 All the cities of the plaine and all Gileád, and all Bashán vnto Salcháh, and E-
dréi, cities of the kingdome of Og in
Bashán.
11 For onelie Og King of Bashán remained of the remnant of the gyants, [d] whose bed *was* a bed of yron: is it not at Rabbáth among the children of Ammón? the
length thereof *is* nine cubites, and foure
cubites the bredth of it, after the cubite
of a man.

d The more terrible ẏ this gyant was, the greater occasion had thei to glorifie God for ẏ victorie.

12 And this land *which* we possessed at that
time, from Aroér, which is by the riuer of
Arnón, and halfe mount Gileád, * and the
cities thereof, gaue I vnto the Reubenites
and Gadites.

Nomb.32,33.

13 And the rest of Gileád, and all Bashán,
the kingdome of Og, gaue I vnto the half
tribe of Manasséh: *euen* all the coútrey of
Argób with all Bashán, which is called,
The land of gyantes.
14 Iaír the sonne of Manasséh toke all the
countrey of Argób, vnto the coastes of
Geshurí, and called them after his owne
name, Bashán, Hauoth Iaír vnto [e] this
day.

e Meanig whé he wrote this historie.

15 And I gaue *parte* of Gileád vnto Machír.
16 And vnto the Reubenites and Gadites
I gaue *the rest* of Gileád, and vnto the riuer of Arnón, halfe the riuer and the borders, euen vnto the riuer [f] Iabbók, *which is*
the border of the children of Ammón:

f Which separateth ẏ Ammonites from the Amorites.

17 The plaine also and Iordén, & the borders from Chinnéreth euen vnto the Sea
of the plaine, *to wit*, the salt Sea " vnder the
springs of Pisgáh Eastwarde.

" Or, at Ashdoth-pisgáh.

18 ¶ And I commanded [g] you the same time, saying, The Lord your God hathe
giuen you this land to possesse it: ye shal
go ouer armed before your brethren the
children of Israél, all men of warre.

g That is, the Reubenites, Gadites, and half Manasséh, as Nomb.32,21.

19 Your wiues onelie, & your children, &
your cattel (for I knowe ẏ ye haue muche
cattel) shal abide in your cities, which I
haue giuen you,
20 Vntil the Lord haue giué rest vnto your
brethren as vnto you, and that thei also
possesse the land, which ẏ Lord your God
hathe giuen them beyond Iordén: thé shal
ye * returne euerie man vnto his possessió,
which I haue giuen you.

Iosh.22,4.

21 ¶ * And I charged Ioshúa the same time,
saying, Thine eies haue sene all that the
[h] Lord your God hathe done vnto these
two Kings: so shal the Lord do vnto all
the kingdomes whither thou goest.

Nomb.27,18.

h So that the victories came not by your owne wisdome strength or multitude.

22 Ye shal not feare thé: for the Lord your
God, he shal fight for you.
23 And I besoght the Lord the same time,
saying,
24 O Lord God, thou haste begonne to
shewe thy seruant thy greatnes and thy
mightie hand: for where is there a God in
heauen or in earth, that can [i] do like thy
workes,

i He speaketh according to ẏ common and corrupt speeche of them ẏ attribute that power vnto idoles ẏ onelie apperteineth vnto God.

"Or, wonders.

workes,and like thy "power?
25 I pray thee let me go ouer and se the
good land that is beyond Iordén, that
goodlie [k] mountaine,and Lebanón.
26 But ye Lord was angry with me for your
sakes,and wolde not heare me:and ye Lord
said vnto me, Let it suffice thee, speake no
more vnto me of this matter.
27 Get thee vp into the top of Pisgáh, and
[l] lift vp thine eyes Westward, and Northward,and
Southward, and Eastward, &
beholde it with thine eyes, for thou shalt
not go ouer this Iordén:
28 But charge Ioshúa,and incourage him,
and bolden him:for he shal go before this
people,and he shal deuide for inheritance
vnto them,the land which thou shalt se.
29 So we abode in the valley ouer against
Beth-Peór.

k He meaneth Zión, where ye temple shulde be buylt and God honored.

l As before he sawe by the spirit of prophecie ye good mountaine, w^c was Zión, so here his eyes were lifted vp aboue the ordre of nature to beholde all the plentiful lãd of Canáan.

CHAP. IIII.

1 An exhortacion to obserue the Lawe without adding thereto or diminishing. 6 Therein standeth our wisdome. 9 We must teache it to our children. 15 No image oght to be made to worship. 26 Threatenings against them that forsake the Law of God. 37 God chose the sede because he loued their fathers. 43 The thre cities of refuge.

1 NOw therefore hearken, ô Israél,vnto
the ordinances and to the lawes w^c I
teache you to [a] do,that ye may liue and
go in,& possesse the land, which the Lord
God of your fathers giueth you.
2 Ye shal [b] put nothing vnto the worde
which I commande you,nether shal ye take
[c] oght there from,that ye may kepe the
commandements of the Lord your God
which I commande you.
3 Your [d] eyes haue sene what the Lord did
because of Baal-Peór,for all the men that
followed Baal-Peór, the Lord thy God
hathe destroyed euerie one frõ amõg you.
4 But ye that did [e] cleaue vnto ye Lord your
God,are aliue euerie one of you this day.
5 Beholde, I haue taught you ordinances,
and lawes, as the Lord my God commanded
me, that ye shulde do euen so with in
the land whither ye go to possesse it.
6 Kepe them therefore , and do them: for
that is your [f] wisdome, and your vnderstanding
in the sight of the people, which
shal heare all these ordinances , and shal
say, "Onely this people *is* wise,and of vnderstanding
and a great nacion.
7 For what nacion *is so* great , vnto whome
the gods come so nere vnto them, as the
Lord our God *is* [g] *nere vnto vs*, in all that
we call vnto him for?
8 And what nacion *is so* great,that hathe ordinãces
and lawes so righteous, as all this
Lawe,which I set before you this day?
9 But take hede to thy selfe,and [h] kepe thy
soule diligently, that thou forget not the
things which thine eyes haue sene,& that
they departe not out of thine heart,all the

a For this doctrine standeth not in bare knowledge, but in practise of life.
b Thinke not to be more wise then I am.
c God wil not be serued by halues,but wil haue ful obedience.
d Gods iudgements executed vpõ other idolaters oght to serue for our instructiõ.
e And were not idolaters.

f Because all men naturally desire wisdome,he sheweth how to atteine vnto it.
"Or, surely.

g Helping vs, and deliuering vs out of all dangers.
h He addeth all these wordes to shewe that we can neuer be careful ynough to kepe the lawe of God and to teache it to our posteritie.

daies of thy life: but teache thẽ thy sonnes,and
thy sonnes sonnes:
10 *Forget not* the day that thou stodest before
the Lord thy God in Horéb , when ye
Lord said vnto me, Gather me the people
together, and I wil cause them heare my
wordes,that they may learne to feare me
all the dayes that they shal liue vpon the
earth , and that they may teache their
children:
11 Then came you nere &* stode vnder the
mountaine & the mountaine [i] burnt with
fire vnto the middes of heauen, *and there was*
darcknes,cloudes and mist.
12 And the Lord spake vnto you out of the
middes of the fire,*and* ye heard the voyce
of the wordes,but sawe no similitude, saue
a voyce.
13 Then he declared vnto you his couenant
which he commanded you to [k] do,*euen*
the ten commandements, and wrote them
vpon two tables of stone.
14 ¶ And the Lord commanded me that same
time, that I shulde teache you ordinãces
and lawes,which ye shulde obserue in
the land, whither ye go, to possesse it.
15 Take therefore good hede vnto your
"selues:for ye sawe no [l] image in the day
that the Lord spake vnto you in Horéb
out of the middes of the fire:
16 That ye corrupt not your selues, & make
you a grauen image *or* representacion
of anie figure : *whither it be* the likenes of
male or female,
17 The likenes of anie beast that is on earth
or the likenes of anie fethered foule that
flieth in the aire:
18 *Or* the likenes of anie thing that crepeth
on the earth, *or* the likenes of anie fish
that is in the waters beneth the earth,
19 And lest thou lift vp thine eyes vnto heauen,and
when thou seest the sunne and the
moone and the starres with all the hoste
of heauen, shuldest be driuen to worship
them and serue them, which the Lord thy
God hathe [m] distributed to all people vnder
the whole heauen.
20 But the Lord hathe takẽ you and broght
you out of the [n] yron fornace: out of Egypt
to be vnto him a people *and* inheritance,as
appeareth this day.
21 And the Lord was angry with me for
your wordes, and sware that I shulde not
go ouer Iordén,& that I shulde not go in
vnto that good land, which the Lord thy
God giueth thee for an inheritance.
22 For I must dye in this land,and shal not
go ouer Iordén:but [o] ye shal go ouer, and
possesse that good land.
23 Take hede vnto your selues, lest ye forget
the couenant of the Lord your God w^c
he made with you, & *lest* ye make you anie
grauen image , *or* likenes of anie thing, as

Exod.19,18.
i The law was giuen with fearefulmiracles, to declare bothe that God was the autor thereof,& also that no flesh was able to abide ye rigour of the same.

k God ioineth this condicion to his couenant.

"*Ebr. soules.*
l Signifying ye destruction is prepared for all them that make anie image to represent God.

m He hathe appointed thẽ for to serue mã

n He hathe deliuered you out of moste miserable slauerie, and frely chosen you for his children.

o Moses good affectiõ appeareth: in that that he, being depriued of suche an excellent treasure, doeth not enuie them that must enioye it.

the Lord thy God hathe charged thee.
24 For the Lord thy God is a [p] consuming
fire, *and* a ielous God.

p To those ẏ come not vnto him with loue and reuerence, but rebelle against him, Ebr 12,29.

25 ¶ When thou shalt beget children and
childrens children, and shalt haue remained long in the land, if ye [q] corrupt your
selues, and make anie grauen image, *or* likenes of anie thing, and worke euil in the
sight of the Lord thy God, to prouoke
him to angre,

q Meaning hereby all superstición and corruption of the true seruice of God.

26 I [r] call heauen and earth to recorde a-
gainst you this day, that ye shal shortely
perish from the land, whereúto ye go ouer
Iordén to possesse it: ye shal not prolong
your daies therein, but shal vtterly be destroyed.

r Thogh men wolde absolue you, yet the insensible creatures shalbe witnesses of your disobedience.

27 And the Lord shal [s] scatter you among
the people, & ye shalbe left fewe in nomber among the nacions, whether the Lord
shal bring you:

s So that his curse shal make his former blessings of none effect.

28 And there ye shal serue gods, *euen* the
worke of mans hand, wood, & stone, which
nether se, nor heare, nor eat, nor smel.
29 But if from thence thou shalt seke the
Lord thy God, thou shalt finde him, if
thou seke him with all thine [t] heart, and
with all thy soule.

t Not ẇ outward shew or ceremonie, but with a true cōfession, of thy fautes.

30 When thou art in tribulacion, and all
these things are come vpon thee, " at the
length, if thou returne to the Lord thy
God, and be obedient vnto his voyce,

" Ebr. in the later dais.

31 (For the Lord thy God is a merciful
God) he wil not forsake thee, nether destroye thee nor forget the couenant of thy
fathers, which he [u] sware vnto them.

u To certifie them the more of the assurance of their saluacion.

32 For inquire now of the daies ẏ are past,
which were before thee, since the day that
God created man vpon the earth, and
[x] *aske* from the one end of heauē vnto the
other, if there came to passe suche a great
thing as this, or whether anie suche like
thing hathe bene heard.

x Mans negligence is partely cause that he knoweth not God.

33 Did euer people heare ẏ voyce of God
speakīg out of the middes of a fire, as thou
hast heard, and liued?
34 Or hathe God assayed to go & take him
a nacion from among nacions, by [y] tentacions, by signes, and by wonders, and by
warre, and by a mighty hand, & by a stretched out arme, and by great feare, according vnto all that the Lord your God did
vnto you in Egypt before your eyes?

y By so manifest proffes ẏ none colde doute thereof.

35 Vnto thee it was shewed, that thou mightest [z] knowe, that the Lord he is God,
and that there is none but he alone.

z He sheweth the cause, why God wroght these miracles.

36 Out of heauē he made thee heare his voice to instruct thee, & vpō earth he shewed
thee his great fire, and thou heardest his
voyce out of the middes of the fire.
37 And because [a] he loued thy fathers,
therefore he chose their sede after them,
and hathe broght thee out of Egypt in his
sight, by his mighty power,

a Frely, & not of their desertes.

38 To thrust out nacions greater and mightier thē thou, before thee, to bring thee
in, *and* to giue thee their land for inheritance: as *appeareth* this day.
39 Vnderstand therefore this day, and consider in thine heart, that ẏ Lord, he is God
in heauen aboue, and vpon the earth beneth: there *is* none other.
40 Thou shalt kepe therefore his ordinances, and his commandements which I cōmande thee this day, that it may [b] go wel
with thee, and with thy childrē after thee,
and that thou maiest prolong thy dayes
vpon the earth, which the Lord thy God
giueth thee for euer.

b God promiseth rewarde not for our merites, but to incourage vs, and to assure vs that our labour shal not be lost.

41 ¶ Then Mosés separated thre cities on
this side of Iordén towarde the sonne rising:
42 That the slayer shulde flee thither,
which had killed his neighbour at vnwares, and hated him not in time past, might
flee, I say, vnto one of those cities, and
liue:
43 *That is,* * Bézer in the wildernes, in the
plaine countrey of the Reubenites: and
Ramóth in Gileád among the Gadites:
& Golán in Bashán among them of Manasséh.

Iosh. 20, 8.

44 ¶ So this is the lawe which Mosés set
before the children of Israél.
45 These are the [c] witnesses, and the ordinances, and the lawes which Mosés declared to the children of Israél after they came out of Egypt,

c The articles and pointes of the couenant.

46 On this side Iordén, in the valey ouer
against Beth-peór, in the land of Sihón
King of the Amorites, which dwelt at
Heshbón, whome Mosés and the children
of Israél * smote, after they were come out
of Egypt:

Nomb. 21, 24. chap. 1, 4.

47 And they possessed his land, and the lād
of * Og King of Bashán, two Kings of the
Amorites, which were on this side Iordén
toward the sonne rising:

Nomb. 21, 33. chap. 3, 3.

48 From Aroér, which is by the banke of
the riuer Arnón, euen vnto mount Sión,
which is Hermón,
49 And all the plaine by Iordén Estward,
euen vnto [d] the Sea, of the plaine, vnder
the * springs of pisgáh.

d That is, the salt Sea
Chap. 3, 17.

CHAP. V.

5 Mosés is the meane betwene God and the people. 6 The Lawe is repeted. 23 The people are afraide at Gods voyce. 29 The Lord wissheth that the people wolde feare him. 32 They must nether decline to the right hand nor left.

1 THen Mosés called all Israél, and said
vnto them, Heare ô Israél the ordināces and the lawes which I " propose to you
this day, that ye may learne them, and take hede to obserue them.

" Ebr. I speake in your eares.

2 * The Lord our God made a couenant
with vs in Horéb.

Exod. 19, 5.

3 The

a Some read, God made not this couenant, that is, in suche ample sort & with suche signes and wonders.
b So plainely that you nede not to doute thereof.

3 The Lord a made not this couenãt with
our fathers,*onely*,but with vs,*euen* with vs
all here aliue this day.
4 The Lord talked with you b face to face in the mount,out of the middes of the
fire.
5 (At that time I stode betwene the Lord
and you,to declare vnto you the worde of
the Lord: for ye were afraide at the sight
of the fire,& went not vp into the mount)
and he said,

Exod.20,2. leu.16,1. psal.96,7.
**Or,seruants.*
c God bindeth vs to serue him onely, without superstición and idolatrie.

6 ¶*I am the Lord thy God, which haue
broght thee out of the land of Egypt,frõ
the house of *bondage.
7 Thou shalt haue none c other gods before my face.
8 Thou shalt make thee no grauen image,
or anie likenes *of that* ẏ is in heauen aboue,
or which is in the earth beneth, or that is
in the waters vnder the earth.

Exod.34,7. ier.32,18.
d That is, of his honour,not permitting it to be giuen to other.

9 Thou shalt nether bowe thy self vnto
them,nor serue them: for* I the Lord thy
God am a d ielous God, visiting the iniquitie of the fathers vpon the children,
euen vnto the third and fourth *generacion*
of them that hate me:
10 And shewing mercie vnto thousands of
them that e loue me, and kepe my commandements.

e The first degre to kepe ẏ comandements is, to loue God.

11 Thou shalt not take the Name of the
Lord thy God in vaine: for the Lord wil
not holde him giltles, that taketh his Name in vaine.
12 Kepe the Sabbath day, to sanctifie it, as
the Lord thy God hathe cõmanded thee.
13 Six daies f thou shalt labour, and shalt
do all thy worke:

f Meaning, since God permitteth six daies to our labours, that we oght willingly to dedicat the seuẽth to serue him wholy.

14 But the seuẽth day *is* the Sabbath of the
Lord thy God : ẏ shalt not do anie worke *therein*,thou,nor thy sonne,nor thy daughter,nor thy man seruante, nor thy maide,nor thine oxe, nor thine asse, nether a-
nie of thy cattel, nor the stranger that is
within thy gates:that thy man seruãt and
thy maide may rest aswel as thou.
15 For,remember that thou wast a seruant
in the lãd of Egypt, and *that* the Lord the
God broght thee out thence by a mighty
hand and a stretched out arme : therefore
the Lord thy God commãded thee to obserue the Sabbath day.

g Not for a shewe, but ẇ true obediēce,and due reuerence.

16 ¶ g Honour thy father & thy mother,as
the Lord thy God hathe commãded thee
that thy daies may be prolonged,and that
it may go wel with thee vpoñ the land,
which the Lord thy God giueth thee.

Matth.5,21. Luk.18,20. Rom.13,9. Rom.7,7.
h He speaketh not onely of ẏ resolute wil, but that there be no motion or affection.

17 * Thou shalt not kil.
18 * Nether shalt thou commit adulterie.
19 * Nether shalt thou steale.
20 Nether shalt thou beare false witnes a-
gainst thy neighbour.
21 *Nether shalt h thou couet thy neighbours wife, nether shalt thou desire thy
neighbours house, his field, nor his man
seruant,nor his maid,his oxe,nor his asse,
nor oght that thy neighbour hathe.
22 ¶These wordes the Lord spake vnto all
your multitude in the mount out of the
middes of the fire, the cloude & the darkenes,with a great voyce,and i added nomore *thereto*: and wrote them vpon two
tables of stone, and deliuered them vnto
me.

i Teaching vs by his exãple to be contẽt ẇ his worde, & adde nothing thereto.

23 And when ye heard the voyce out of the
middes of the darkenes,(for ẏ mountaine
did burne with fire,) then ye came to me,
all the chief of your tribes, and your Elders:
24 And ye said,Beholde,the Lord our God
hath shewed vs his glorie & his greatnes,
& * we haue heard his voyce out of ẏ middes of the fire: we haue sene this day that
God doeth talke with man, and he* liueth.

Exod.19,19. Chap.4,33.

25 Now therefore, why shulde we dye: for
this great fire wil consume vs:if we heare
the voyce of the Lord our God anie more,we shal dye.
26 For what *flesh *was* there euer, that heard the voyce of the liuing God speaking
out of the middes of the fire as we *haue*,&
liued?

**Or,man.*

27 Go thou nere and heare all that ẏ Lord
our God saith : and declare thou vnto vs
all that the Lord our God sayeth vnto
thee*and we wil heare it,and do it.

Exod.20,19.

28 Then the Lord heard the voyce of your
wordes, when ye spake vnto me : and the
Lord said vnto me,I haue heard the voyce of the wordes of this people, which
they haue spoken vnto thee: they haue wel
said,all that they haue spoken.
29 *Oh k that there were such an heart in
them to feare me,and to kepe all my com
mandementes alway:that it might go wel
with them,and with their children for e-
uer.

k He requireth of vs nothing but obediẽce, shewing alsoẏ of our selues we are vnwilling thereunto.

30 Go, say vnto them, Returne you into
your tentes.
31 But stand thou here with me, & I wil tel
thee all the commandements, and the ordinances,and the lawes, which thou shalt
teache them:that they may do them in the
land which I giue them to possesse it.
32 Take hede therefore, that ye do as the
Lord your God hathe commanded you:
l turne not aside to the right hand nor to
the left,

l Ye shal nether adde nor diminishe.

33 *But* walke in all the wayes which the
Lord your God hath commanded you,
that ye may m liue,and that it may go wel
with you : & that ye may prolong your
dayes in the land which ye shal possesse.

m As by obedienc, God giueth vs all felicities so of disobeying God procede all our miseries.

CHAP. VI.

1 An exhortation to feare God, and kepe his commandemẽts, 5 Which is, to loue him with all thine heart. 7 The same must be taught to the posteritie. 16 Not to tempt God. 25 Righteousnes is coteined in the Lawe.

1 THese now are the cōmandements,or-
dinances, and "lawes, which the Lord
your God commanded *me* to teache *you*,
that ye might do them in the land whether ye go to possesse it:

"Or, iudgemēts.

2 That thou mightest [a] feare the Lord thy
God, and kepe all his ordinances, and his
commandements which I commāde thee,
thou, and thy sonne, and thy sonnes sonne all the dayes of thy life, euen that thy
dayes may be prolonged.

a A reuerent feare and loue of God, is the first beginning to kepe Gods cōmandemēts.

3 Heare therefore, ô Israél, and take hede
to do it, that it may go wel with thee, and
that ye may increase mightely [b] in the
land that floweth with milke and hony, as
the Lord God of thy fathers hathe promised thee.

b Which hathe the abundance of all things apperteining to mans life.

4 Heare, ô Israél, The Lord our God *is*
Lord onely,
5 And * thou shalt loue the Lord thy God
with all thine heart, and with all thy soule, and with all thy might.

Mat.22,37. mar.12,29. luk.10,27.

6 * And these wordes which I commande
thee this day, shalbe in thine heart.

Chap.11,18.

7 And thou shalt [c] rehearse them continually vnto thy children, and shalt talke
of them when thou tariest in thine house,
and as thou walkest by the way, and when
thou lyest downe, and when thou risest vp:

c Some read, ŷ shalt whet them vpon thy children: to wit, that they may printe thē more depely in memorie.

8 And thou shalt binde them for a signe
vpon thine hand, and they shalbe " as fron-
telets betwene thine eyes.

"Or, signes of remembrance.

9 Also thou shalt write them vpō the [d] postes of thyne house, and vpon thy gates.

d That when ŷ entrest in, thou maiest remember them.

10 And when the Lord thy God hathe
broght thee into the land, which he sware vnto thy fathers, Abrahám, Izhák, and
Iaakób, to giue to thee, with great and
goodly cities which thou buyldedst not,
11 And houses ful of all maner of goods
which thou filledst not, and wels digged
which thou diggedst not, vineyardes and
olive trees which thou plantedst not, and
when thou hast eaten and art ful,
12 [e] Beware lest thou forget the Lord, which
broght thee out of the land of Egypt, frō
the house of bondage.

e Let not welthe and ease cause thee for get Gods mercies, wherby thou wast deliuered out of miserie.

13 Thou shalt feare the Lord thy God, and
serue him, & shalt [f] sweare by his Name.

f We must feare God, serue him onely, and confesse his Name, which is done by swearing lawfully.

14 Ye shal not walke after other gods, *after anie* of the gods of the people which
are round about you,
15 (For the Lord thy God is a ielous God
among you:) lest the wrathe of the Lord
thy God be kindeled against thee, and destroy thee from the face of the earth.
16 ¶ Ye shal not [g] tempt the Lord your
God, as ye did tempt him in Massáh:

g By douting of his power refusing lauful meanes, & abusing his graces.

17 *But* ye shal kepe diligently the commā-
demēts of the Lord your God, and his testimonies, and his ordinances which he
hathe commanded thee,
18 And thou shalt do that which is right
and good in the [h] sight of the Lord: that
thou maiest prosper, and that thou maiest
go in, and possesse that good land which
the Lord sware vnto thy fathers,

h Here he cōdemneth all mans good intentions.

19 To cast out all thine enemies before
thee, as the Lord hathe said.
20 When [i] thy sonne shal aske thee in time
to come, saying, What meane these testimonies, and ordinances, and lawes, which
the Lord our God hathe commanded
you?

i God requireth not onely ŷ we serue him all our life, but also ŷ we take paine ŷ our posteritie may set forthe his glorie.

21 Then thou shalt say vnto thy sonne,
We were Pharaohs bondmen in Egypt:
but the Lord broght vs out of Egypt with
a mighty hand.
22 And the Lord shewed signes and wonders great & euil vpō Egypt, vpon Pharaóh, and vpon all his housholde, before our
eyes,
23 And [k] broght vs out from thence, to
bring vs in, and to giue vs the land which
he sware vnto our fathers.

k Nothing oght to moue vs more to true obedience thē ŷ great benefites ŵ we haue receiued of God.

24 Therefore the Lord hathe commanded
vs, to do all these ordinances, & to feare
ŷ Lord our God, that it may go euer wel
with vs, & that he may preserue vs a liue as at this present.
25 Moreouer, this shal be our [l] righteousnes before the Lord our God, if we take
hede to kepe all these commandements, as
he hathe commanded vs.

l But because none colde fully obey ŷ lawe, we must haue our recourse to Christ to be iustified by faith.

CHAP. VII.

1 The Israelites may make no couenant with the Gentiles. 5 They must destroy the idoles. 8 The electiō depē-deth on the fre loue of God. 19 The experience of the power of God oght to confirme vs. 25 To auoide all occasion of idolatrie.

1 WHen the Lord thy God shal bring
thee into the land whither thou
goest to possesse it, * & shal roote out manie nacions before thee: the Hittites, and
the Girgashites, & the Amorites, & the
Canaanites, & the Perizzites, & the Hiuites, and the Iebusites, seuen naciōs greater and mightier then thou,

Chap.31,3.

2 And the Lord thy God shal giue them
[a] before thee, then thou shalt smite them:
thou shalt vtterly destroy thē: thou shalt
make no * couenant with them, nor haue
compassion on them,

a Into thy power.

Exod.23,32. & 34,12.

3 Nether shalt thou make mariages with
them, nether giue thy daughter vnto
his sonne nor take his daughter vnto thy
sonne.
4 For " they wil cause thy sonne to turne a-
way from me, & to serue other gods: then
wil the wrath of the Lord waxe hote a-
gainst you and destroy thee sodenly.

"Or, anie of them.

5 But thus ye shal deale with them, [b] Ye
shal

b God wolde haue his seruice pure without all idolatrous ceremonies and superstitions.

shal ouerthrowe their altars, and breake
downe their pillers, and ye shal cut downe
their groues, & burne their grauen images with fire.

Chap.14,2. & 26,18. Exod.19,5. 1.pet.2,9.

6 *For thou art an holy people vnto the
Lord thy God, *the Lord thy God hathe
chosen thee, to be a precious people vnto him selfe, aboue all people that are vpon the earth.
7 The Lord did not set his loue vpon you,
nor chose you, because ye were mo in nōber then anie people: for ye were the few-
est of all people:

c Frely, findīg no cause in you more thē in others so to do.

8 But because ẏ Lord [c]loued you, & because he wolde kepe the othe which he had
sworne vnto your fathers, the Lord hathe
broght you out by a mighty hand and deliuered you out of the house of bondage from the hand of Pharaóh King of
Egypt,

d And so put difference betwene him & idoles.

9 That thou maiest knowe, [d] that the Lord
thy God, he is God, the faithful God ẇ
kepeth couenant and mercie vnto them
that loue him and kepe his commandements, *euen* to a thousand generacions,

e Meanīg, manifestly, or in this life.

10 And rewardeth [e] them to their face
that hate him, to bring them to destruction: he wil not deferre to rewarde him
that hateth him, to his face.
11 Kepe thou therefore the commandements, and the ordinances, and the lawes,
which I commande thee this day to do
them.
12 ¶For if ye hearken vnto these lawes, and
obserue and do them, then the Lord thy
God shal kepe with thee the couenant, &
the [f] mercy which he sware vnto thy fathers.

f This couenāt is grounded vpon his fre grace: therefore in recōpensing their obedience he hathe respect to his mercie & not to their merites.

13 And he wil loue thee, and blesse thee, &
multiplie thee: he wil also blesse the frute
of thy wombe, and the frute of thy land:
thy corne and thy wine, and thine oyle &
the increase of thy kine, and the flockes
of thy shepe in the land, which he sware
vnto thy fathers to giue thee.
14 Thou shalt be blessed aboue all people:
*there shalbe nether male nor female barē
among you, nor among your cattel.

Exod.23,26.

15 Moreouer, the Lord wil take away from
thee all infirmities, and wil put none of
the euil diseases of *Egypt (which ẏ knowest) vpon thee, but wil send them vpon
all that hate thee.

Exod.9,14.

16 Thou shalt therefore consume all people which the Lord thy God shal giue
thee: [g] thine eie shal not spare them, nether shalt thou serue their gods, for that
shalbe thy *destruction.

g We oght not to be merciful where God cōmandeth seueritie.

Exod.23,33.

17 If thou say in thine heart, These nacions
are mo then I, how can I cast them out?
18 Thou shalt not feare them, *but* remember what ẏ Lord thy God did vnto Pharaóh, and vnto all Egypt:
19 The great [*]tentacions which thine eyes
sawe, and the signes and wonders, and the
mightie hand & stretched out arme, whereby the Lord thy God broght thee out:
so shal the Lord thy God do vnto all the
people, whose face thou fearest.

*Or, plagues, or trials, as Chap. 29,3. exod.15,25. & 16,4.

20 *Moreouer, the Lord thy God wil send
[h] hornettes among them vntil they that
are left, and hide them selues from thee,
be destroied.

Exod.23,28. iosh.24,12.

h There is not so smale a creature, ẇ I wil not arme to fight on thy side against them.

21 Thou shalt not feare them: for the Lord
thy God *is* among you, a God mighty &
dreadful.
22 And the Lord thy God wil roote out
these nacions before thee by litle and litle:
thou maist not consume them at once, lest
the [i] beastes of the field increase vpō thee.

i So ẏ it is your cōmoditie ẏ God accomplish not his promes so sone as you wolde wish.

23 But the Lord thy God shal giue them
before thee, and shal destroy them with a
mighty destruction, vntil they be broght
to noght.
24 And he shal deliuer their Kīgs into thine hand, and thou shalt destroy their name from vnder heauen: there shal no man
be able to stand before thee, vntil thou
hast destroied them.
25 The grauen images of their gods shal
ye burne with fire, *and* *couet not the
siluer and golde, *that is* on them, nor take it vnto thee, lest thou [k] be snared therewith: for it is an abominacion *before* the
Lord thy God.

Iosh.7,1. 2.mac.12,40.

k And be intised to idolatrie.

26 Bring not therefore abominacion into thine house, lest thou be accursed like
it, *but* vtterly abhorre it, and counte it moste abominable: for it is *accursed.

Leui.27,21. nomb.21,3.

CHAP. VIII.

2 God humbleth the Israelites to trie what they haue in their hearts God chasticeth them as his childrē. 14 The heart oght not to be proude for Gods benefites. 19 The forgetfulnes of Gods benefites causeth destruction.

1 YE shal kepe all the commandements
ẇ I cōmande thee this day, for [a] to
do thē: that ye may liue, & be multiplied,
and go in, and possesse the land which the
Lord sware vnto your fathers.

a Shewing ẏ it is not ynough to heare ẏ worde, except we expresse it by exāple of life.

2 And thou shalt remember all the way
which ẏ Lord thy God led thee this fourty yere in the wildernes, for to humble
thee and to [b] proue thee, to knowe what
was in thine heart, whether thou woldest
kepe his commandements or no.

b Which is declared in afflictiōs, ether by paciēce, or by grudging against Gods visitation.

3 Therefore he humbled thee, and made
thee hungry, & fed thee with MAN, which
thou knewest not, nether did thy fathers
knowe it, that he might teache thee that
man liueth not by [c] bread onely, but by e-
uerie *worde* that proceadeth out of the
mouth of the Lord, doeth a man liue.

c Man liueth not by meat, but by ẏ power of God, ẇ giueth it strength to nourish vs.

4 Thy raymēt waxed not olde vpon thee,
nether did thy fote [d] swel those fourtie
yeres.

d As they ẏ go bare foted.

5 Knowe therefore in thine heart, that as a
man nourtereth his sonne, so the Lord thy
God [e] nourtereth thee.
6 Therefore shalt thou kepe the commandements of the Lord thy God, that thou
maiest walke in his wayes, and feare
him.
7 For the Lord thy God bringeth thee into
a good land, a lād in the which are riuers
of water and fountaines, & "depthes that
spring out of valeis and mountaines:
8 A land of wheat and barley, and of vineyardes, and figtrees, & pomgranates: a lād
of oyle oliue and honey:
9 A lād wherein thou shalt eat bread without scarcetie, nether shalt thou lacke anie
thing therein: a lād [f] whose stones *are* yrō,
& out of whose mountains thou shalt digge brasse.
10 And when thou hast eaten and filled
thy self, thou shalt [g] blesse the Lord thy
God for the good land, which he hath giuen thee.
11 Beware that thou forget not the Lord
thy God, not keping his commandemēts,
and his lawes, and his ordinances, which I
commande thee this day:
12 Lest *when* thou hast eaten and filled thy
selfe, & hast buylt goodly houses & dwelt
therein,
13 And thy beastes, and thy shepe are increased, and thy siluer and golde is multiplied, & all that thou hast is encreased,
14 Then thine heart [h] be lifted vp and thou
forget the Lord thy God, which broght
thee out of the land of Egypt, from the
house of bondage,
15 Who was thy guide in the great and ter
rible wildernes (*wherein were* firy serpēts,
and scorpions, and drought, where *was* no
water, *who broght forthe water for thee,
out of the rocke of flinte:
16 Who fed thee in ỹ wildernes with *MAN,
which thy fathers knewe not,) to humble
thee, and to proue thee, that he might do
thee good at thy latter end.
17 *Beware* lest thou say in thine heart, My
power, and the strength of mine owne hād
hathe prepared me this abundance.
18 But remember the Lord thy God: for it
is he which [i] giueth thee power to get
substance to establish his couenāt which
he sware vnto thy fathers, as *appeareth* this
day.
19 And if thou forget the Lord thy God,
and walke after other gods, & serue them,
and worship them, I [k] testifie vnto you
this day that ye shal surely perish.
20 As the naciōs which the Lord destroyeth before you, so ye shal perish, because
ye wolde not be obedient vnto the voyce
of the Lord your God.

e So ỹ his affli ctiōs are signes of his fatherly loue towarde vs.

"Or, meres.

f Where there are mines of metal.

g For to receiue Gods benefites, & not to be thankful, is to cōtēne God in them.

h By attributing Gods benefites to thine owne wisdome & labour, or to good fortune.

Nomb. 20, 11.

Exod. 16, 15.

i If things concerning this life procede onely of Gods mercie: muche more spiritual gifts & life euerlasting.

k Or, take to witnes ỹ heauen & ỹ earth, as Chap. 4, 26.

CHAP. IX.

4 God doeth them not good for their owne righteousnes, but for his owne sake. 7 Moses putteth them in remembrance of their sinnes. 17 The two tables are broken. 26 Moses prayeth for the people.

1 Heare ô Israél, Thou shalt passe o-
uer Iordén [a] this day, to go in &
to possesse nacions greater & mightier then thy selfe, & cities great & walled vp to heauen,
2 A people great and tall, *euen* the children
of the Anakims, whome thou knowest, and
of whome thou hast [b] heard say, Who can
stand before the children of Anák?
3 Vnderstand therefore that this day the
Lord thy God is he which [c] goeth ouer
before thee *as* a consuming fire: he shal destroy them, and he shal bring them downe
before thy face: so thou shalt cast thē out
and destroy them sodenly, as ỹ Lord hathe
said vnto thee.
4 Speake not thou in thine heart (after that
the Lord thy God hath cast them out before thee) saying, For my [d] righteousnes ỹ
Lord hathe broght me in, to possesse this
land: but for ỹ wickednes of these nacions
the Lord hathe cast them out before thee.
5 *For* thou entrest not to inherit their land
for thy righteousnes, or for thy vpright
heart, but for the wickednes of those natiōs, the Lord thy God doeth cast thē out
before thee, and that he might perfourme
the worde which the Lord thy God sware
vnto thy fathers, Abrahám, Izhák, and Iaakób.
6 Vnderstand therefore, that the Lord thy
God giueth thee not this good land to
possesse it for thy righteousnes: for thou
art a [e] stifnecked people.
7 ¶ Remember, & forget not, how ỹ prouo
kedst the Lord thy God to angre in the
wildernes: [f] since the day that thou didest
depart out of the land of Egypt, vntil ye
came vnto this place ye haue rebelled a-
gainst the Lord.
8 Also in Horéb ye prouoked the Lord to
angre so that ỹ Lord was wroth with you,
euen to destroy you.
9 When I was gone vp in to the mount, to
receiue the tables of stone, the tables, *I say,*
of ỹ couenāt, which the Lord made with
you: and *I abode in the moūt forty dayes
and fortie nightes, & I nether ate bread
nor yet dranke water:
10 *Then the Lord deliuered me two tables
of stone, written with the [g] finger of God,
and in them *was conteined* according to all
the wordes which the Lord had said vnto
you in the mounte out of the middes of
the fire, in the day of the assemblie.
11 And when the fortie dayes and fortie
nightes were ended, the Lord gaue me the
two tables of stone, the tables, *I say,* of the
coue-

a Meaning, shortely.

b By ỹ report of the spies, Nomb. 13, 29.

c To guide thee & gouerne thee.

d Man of him selfe can deserue nothing but Gods angre, & if God spare anie it cometh of his great mercie.

e Like stubberne oxen ẘ wil not endure their masters yoke.

f He proueth by ỹ lēgth of time, ỹ their rebelliō was moste great, & intolerable.

Exod. 24, 18. & 34. 28.

Exod. 31, 18.

g That is miraculously, & not by ỹ hand of men.

couenant.
12 And the Lord said vnto me, *Arise, get
thee downe quickely from hence: for thy
people which thou hast broght out of E-
gypt, haue [h] corrupt *their wayes*: thei are
sone turned out of the way, which I commanded them: thei haue made thẽ a molten image.

Exod 32,7.

[h] So sone as man declineth from the obedience of God, his waies are corrupt.

13 Furthermore, the Lord spake vnto me,
saying, I haue sene this people, and beholde, it is a stifnecked people.
14 [i] Let me alone, that I may destroye thẽ,
and put out their name from vnder heauẽ,
and I wil make of thee a mightie nacion,
and greater then thei be.

[i] Signifying ẏ the praiers of ẏ faithful are a barre to staie Gods angre, ẏ he cõsume not all.

15 So I returned, and came downe from the
Mount (& the Mount burnt with fire, and
the two Tables of the coucnãt *were* in my
two hands)
16 Then I loked, & beholde, ye had sinned
agaĩst the Lord your God: *for* ye had made you a moltẽ calf, *and* had turned quickely out of the [k] way which the Lord
had commanded you.

[k] That is, frõ the Lawe: wherein he declareth what is ẏ cause of our perdition.

17 Therefore I toke the two Tables, & cast
them out of my two hands, and brake thẽ
before your eies.
18 And I fel downe before the Lord, fortie
daies, and fortie nights, as before: I nether
ate bread nor dranke water, because of
all your sinnes, which ye had committed,
in doing wickedly in the sight of ẏ Lord,
in that ye prouoked him vnto wrath.
19 (For I was afraied of the wrath and indignacion, wherewith the Lord was moued against you, *euen* to destroye you) yet
the Lord heard me at that time also.
20 Likewise the Lord was verie angry with
Aarón, *euen* to [l] destroye him: but at that
time I praied also for Aarón.
21 And I toke your sinne, *I meane* the calfe
which ye had made, and burnt him with
fire, and stamped him and grounde him
smale, euen vnto verie dust: and I cast the
dust thereof into the riuer, that descended out of the [m] Mount.

[l] Whereby he sheweth what dãger thei are in, ẏ haue autoritie, & resist not wickednes

[m] Horéb, or Sinái.

22 Also *in Taberáh, and in *Massáh* and
in Kibrothhattaauáh ye prouoked ẏ Lord
to angre.

Nomb.11,1.
Exod.17,7.
Nomb.11,34.

23 Likewise when the Lord sent you from
Kadesh-barnéa, saying, Go vp, and possesse the land which I haue giuen you, thẽ
ye [n] rebelled against the commandemẽt
of the Lord your God, and beleued him
not, nor hearkened vnto his voyce.

[n] At the returne of ẏ spies.

24 Ye haue bene rebellious vnto the Lord,
since the daie that I knewe you.
25 Then I fel downe before the Lord [o] fortie daies and fortie nights, as I fel downe
before, because the Lord had said, that he
wolde destroye you.

[o] Whereby is signified that God requireth earnest continuãce in praiers.

26 And I praied vnto the Lord, and said,
O Lord God, destroye not thy people &
thine inheritance, which thou hast redemed through thy greatnes whome ẏ hast
broght out of Egypt by a mightie hand.
27 [p] Remember thy seruants Abrahám, Izhák, and Iaakób: loke not to the stuburnes
of this people, nor to their wickednes, nor
to their sinne,

[p] The godlie in their praiers grõude on Gods promes, & cõfesse their sinnes.

28 Lest the countrey, whence thou broghtest them, say, *Because the Lord was not
able to bring them into the land which he
promised them, or because he hated them,
he caried them out, to slaye them in the
wildernes.

Nom.14,16.

29 Yet thei are thy people, and thine inheritance, which thou broghtest out by thy
mightie power, and by thy stretched out
arme.

CHAP. X

5 The seconde tables put in the Arke. 8 The tribe of Leuí is dedicate to the seruice of the Tabernacle. 12 What the Lord requireth of his. 16 The circumcision of the heart. 17 God regardeth not the persone. 21 The Lord is the praise of Israél.

1 IN the same time the Lord said vnto
me, *Hewe thee two Tables of stone
lyke vnto the first, and come vp vnto me
into the Mount, and make thee an Arke of
wood,

Exod.34,1.

2 And I wil write vpon ẏ Tables the wordes that were vpon the first Tables, which
thou brakest, and thou shalt put them in
the Arke.
3 And I made an Arke of [a] shittím wood,
and hewed two Tables of stone like vnto
the first, and went vp into the Mountaine,
and the two Tables in mine hand.

[a] Which wood is of long continuance.

4 Then he wrote vpon the Tables according to the first writing (the ten commãdements, which the Lord spake vnto you
in the Mount out of the middes of the fire, in the daye of the [b] assemblie) and the
Lord gaue them vnto me.

[b] When you were assẽbled to receiue the Lawe.

5 And I departed, and came downe frõ the
Mount, & put the Tables in ẏ Arke which
I had made: and there thei be, as the Lord
commanded me.
6 ¶ And the children of Israél toke their
iourney from Beeróth of the children of
Iaakán to [c] Moserá, where Aarón dyed,
& was buryed, and Eleazár his sonne became Priest in his steade.

[c] This mountaine was also called Hor, Nomb.20,28.

7 ¶ From thence thei departed vnto Gudgodáh, and from Gudgodáh to Iotbáth a
land of running waters.
8 ¶ The same time the Lord separated the
tribe of Leuí to beare the Arke of the couenant of the Lord, *and* to stand before
the Lord, to [d] minister vnto him, and to
blesse in his Name vnto this day.
9 Wherefore Leuí hathe no parte nor inheritance with his brethren: *for* the Lord
is his [e] inheritance, as the Lord thy God
hathe promised him.

[d] That is, to offer sacrifices & to declare ẏ Lawe to the people.

[e] So God turned ẏ curse of Iaakób, Gen 49,7, vnto blessing.

10 And I taried in the Mount, as at the
first time, fortie daies and fortie nights,
and the Lord heard me at that time also,
and the Lord wolde not destroye thee.
11 But the Lord said vnto me, Arise, go
forthe in the iourney before the people,
that thei may go in and possesse the land,
which I sware vnto their fathers to giue
vnto them.
12 ¶ And now, Israél, what doeth the Lord
thy God [f] require of thee, but to feare
the Lord thy God, to walke in all his waies, and to loue him, and to serue the Lord
thy God with all thine heart, and with all
thy soule?

f For all our sinnes & transgressions God requireth nothing but to turne to him & obey him.

13 That thou kepe the commandements
of the Lord, and his ordinances, which
I commande thee this day, for thy
welth?
14 Beholde, heauen, and the heauen of heauens *is* the Lords thy God, and the earth,
with all that therein is.
15 [g] Notwithstanding, the Lord set his delite in thy fathers to loue them, and dyd
chose their sede after them, *euen* you aboue all people, as *appeareth* this day.

g Althogh he was Lord of heauē & earth, yet wolde he chuse none but you.

16 [h] Circumcise therefore the foreskin of
your heart, and harden your neks no
more.

h Cut of all your euil affectiōs, Iere. 4, 4.

17 For the Lord your God is God of gods,
and Lord of lords, a great God, mightie,
& terrible, which accepteth no * persones
nor taketh rewarde:

2. Chro. 19, 7. iob. 34, 19. rom. 2, 11.

18 Who doeth right vnto the fatherles and
widowe, and loueth the stranger, giuing
him fode and rayment.
19 Loue ye therefore the stranger: for ye
were strangers in the land of Egypt.
20 * Thou shalt feare the Lord thy God:
thou shalt serue him, and thou shalt cleaue vnto him, and [i] shalt sweare by his
Name.

Chap. 6, 13. mat. 4, 10.

i Read Chap. 6, 13.

21 He is thy praise, and he is thy God, that
hathe done for thee these great and terrible things, which thine eies haue sene.
22 Thy fathers went downe into Egypt
* with seuentie persones, & now the Lord
thy God hathe made thee, as the * starres
of the heauen in multitude.

Gen. 46, 27. exod. 1, 5. Gen. 15, 5.

CHAP. XI.

1 An exhortacion to loue God, and kepe his Lawe. 10 The praises of Canáan. 18 To meditate continually the worde of God. 19 To teache it vnto the children. 26 Blessing, and cursing.

1 Therefore thou shalt loue the Lord
thy God, and shalt kepe that, which
he commandeth to be kept: that is, his ordinances, and his Lawes, and his commãdements alwaie.
2 And [a] consider this day (*for I speake not*
to your children, which haue nether know-
ne nor sene) the chastisemēt of the Lord
your God, his greatnes, his mightie hand,
and his stretched out arme,

a Ye, which haue sene Gods graces wt your eies, oght rather to be moued, thē your children, wc haue onely heard of thē.

3 And his signes, and his actes, which he
did in the middes of Egypt vnto Pharaóh the King of Egypt and vnto all his
land:
4 And what he did vnto the hoste of the
Egyptians, vnto their horses and to their
charets, when he caused the waters of the
red Sea to ouerfloe them, as thei pursued
after you, and the Lord destroyed them
vnto this day:
5 And [b] what he did vnto you in the wildernes, vntil ye came vnto this place:

b Aswel cōcerning his benefites, as his corrections.

6 And what he did vnto Dathán and Abirám the sonnes of Eliáb the sonne of
Reubén, when the earth opened her
mouth, and swallowed them with their
housholdes and their tents, and all their
substance that " thei had in the middes of
all Israél.

" Ebr. was at their fete.

7 For your eies haue sene all the great actes of the Lord which he did.
8 Therefore shal ye kepe [c] all the commandements, which I commande you
this day, that ye may be strong, and go
in and possesse the land whether ye go to
possesse it:

c Because ye haue felt both his chastisements and his benefites.

9 Also that ye may prolong *your* daies in
the land, which the Lord sware vnto
your fathers, to giue vnto them and to
their sede, *euen* a land that floweth with
milke and honie.
10 ¶ For the land whether thou goest to
possesse it, is not as the land of Egypt, frō
whence ye came, where thou sowedst thy
sede, and wateredst it with " thy [d] fete as
a garden of herbes:

" Or, labour.

d As by making gutters for the water to come out of the riuer Nilus to water the land.

11 But the land whether ye go to possesse
it, *is* a land of mountaines and valleis,
& drinketh water of the raine of heauen.
12 This land doeth the Lord thy God care
for: the eies of the Lord thy God *are* alwaies vpon it, from the beginning of the
yere, euen vnto the end of the yere.
13 ¶ If ye shal hearken therefore vnto my
commandements, which I commande
you this day, that ye loue the Lord your
God & serue him with all your heart, and
with all your soule,
14 I also wil giue raine vnto your land in
due time, [e] the first raine and the latter,
that thou maiest gather in thy wheat, and
thy wine, and thine oyle.

e In the sede time, & toward haruest.

15 Also I wil sēd grasse in thy fields for thy
cattel, that thou maiest eat, and haue y-
nough.
16 But beware lest your heart [f] deceaue
you, and lest ye turne aside, and serue other
gods, and worship them,

f By diuising to your selues foolish deuocíōs according to your owne fantasies.

17 And so ỹ angre of the Lord be kindled
against you, and he shut vp the heauen,
that there be no raine, and that your land
yelde not her frute, & ye perish quickely
from

from the good land, which the Lord giueth you.
18 ¶ Therefore shal ye lay vp these my wor
des in your heart & in your soule, & *binde
them for a signe vpon your hand, ỹ they
maie be as a frontelet betwene your eyes,

Chap.6,6.

19 And ye shal *teache them your children,
speaking of thẽ, when thou sittest in thine
house, and when thou walkest by the waie,
and when thou liest downe, and when thou
risest vp.

Chap.4,10. & 6,6.

20 And thou shalt write them vpon the
postes of thine house, & vpon thy gates,
21 That your dayes maie be multiplied, &
the dayes of your children, in the land ẘ
the Lord sware vnto your fathers to giue
them, as long as [g] the heauens are aboue
the earth.

g As long as the heauens endure.

22 ¶ For if ye kepe diligently all these commandements, which I commande you to
do: *that is*, to loue the Lord your God to
walke in all his waies, & to cleaue vnto hĩ,
23 Then wil the Lord cast out all these nacions before you, and ye shal possesse great nacions and mightier then you.
24 *All the places whereõ the soles of [h] your
fete shal treade, shalbe yours: your coast
shalbe from the wildernes and from Lebanón, and from the Riuer, *euen* the riuer
Peráth, vnto the vttermost [i] Sea.

Iosh.1,3.
h This was accomplished in Dauids & Salomons time.
i Called mediterraneum.

25 No man shal stand against you: *for* the
Lord your God shal cast the feare and
dread of you vpon all the lãd that ye shal
tread vpon, as he hathe said vnto you.
26 ¶ Beholde, I set before you this day a
blessing and a curse:
27 *The blessing, if ye obey the commãdements of the Lord your God which I cõ
mande you this day:

Chap.28,2. & 30,1.

28 And ỹ curse, if ye wil not obey the cõmandements of the Lord your God, but
turne out of the way, which I commande
you this day, to go after other gods, ẘ ye
haue not [k] knowen.

k He reproueth ỹ malice of mẽ ẘ leaue that ẘ is certeine, to follow that ẘ is vncerteine.

29 ¶ Whẽ the Lord thy God therefore hathe broght thee into the land, whether
thou goest to possesse it, then thou shalt
put the *blessing vpon mount Gerizím,
and the curse vpon mount Ebál.

Chap.27,13. Iosh.8,33.

30 Are they not beyonde Iordén on ỹ parte,
[l] where the sunne goeth downe in the
land of the Canaanites, which dwel in the
plaine ouer against Gilgál, beside the
"groue of Moréh?

l Meáning in Samaria.
"Or, plaine.

31 For ye shal passe ouer Iordén, to go in
to possesse the land, which the Lord your
God giueth you, and ye shal possesse it, &
dwel therein.
32 Take hede therefore that ye *do all the
commandements and the lawes, which I
set before you this day.

Chap.5,32.

CHAP. XII.

*2 To destroy the idolatrous places. 5, 8 To serue God
where he commandeth and as he commandeth, and not
as men fantasie. 19 The Leuites must be nourished.
31 Idolaters burnt their children to their gods. 32 To
adde nothing to Gods worde.*

1 These are the ordinances & the lawes,
which ye shal obserue and do in the
land (which the Lord God [a] of thy fathers giueth thee to possesse it) as long as
ye liue vpon the earth.

a Whereby they are admonished to seke none other God.

2 *Ye shal vtterly destroy all the places
wherein the nacions which ye shal possesse, serued their gods vpon the hie mountains & vpon the hilles, and vnder euerie
grene tre.

Chap 7,5.

3 *Also ye shal ouerthrowe their altars, &
breake downe their pillers, & burne their
[b] groues with fire: & ye shal hewe downe
the grauen images of their gods, & abolish their names out of that place.

Iudg.2,2.
b Wherein they sacrificed to their idoles.

4 Ye shal [c] not so do vnto the Lord your
God,

c Ye shal not serue ỹ Lord ẘ superstitiõs.

5 But ye shal seke the place which the Lord
your God shal *chose out of all your tribes, to put his Name there, & there to
dwel, and thether thou shalt come,

1.Kin.8,29. 2.chro.6,5. & 7,12.

6 And ye shal brĩg thether your burnt offrings, and your sacrifices, & your tithes,
& the [d] offring of your hands, & your vowes, & your fre offrings & the first borne
of your kine & of your shepe.

d Meaning the first frutes.

7 And there ye shal eat [e] before the Lord
your God, and ye shal reioyce in all that
ye put your hãd vnto, *bothe* ye, & your hou
sholdes, because the Lord thy God hathe
blessed thee.

e Where his Arke shalbe.

8 Ye shal not do after all these things ỹ we
do [f] here this day: *that is*, euerie man whatsoeuer semeth him good in his owne eyes.
9 For ye are not yet come to rest, & to ỹ inheritãce ẘ the Lord thy God giueth thee.

f Not ỹ they sacrificed after their fantasies, but ỹ God wolde be serued more purely in ỹ lãd of Canáan.

10 But when ye go ouer Iordén, & dwel in
the land, which the Lord your God hathe
giuen you to inherit, & *when* he hathe giuen you [g] rest from all your enemies rounde about, & ye dwel in safetie,

g It had not bene ynough to cõquer, except God had maiteined thẽ in rest vnder his protectiõ.

11 When there shalbe a place which ỹ Lord
your God shal chose, to cause his Name
to dwel there, thether shal ye bring all
that I commãde you: your burnt offrings,
& your sacrifices, your tithes, and the offring of your hands, and all your "special
vowes which ye vow vnto the Lord:

"Or, that which ye chuse out for your vowes.

12 And ye shal reioyce before ỹ Lord your
God, ye, & your sonnes & your daughters,
& your seruants, and your maidens, and ỹ
Leuite that is within your gates: *for he
hathe no parte nor inheritance with you.

Chap.10,9.

13 Take hede that thou offer not thy burnt
offrings in euerie place that thou seest:
14 But in the place which the Lord shal
[h] chose in one of thy tribes, there thou
shalt offer thy burnt offrings, and there
thou shalt do all that I commande thee.

h As was declared euer by ỹ placing of ỹ Arke, as in Shilóh 243 yeres, or as some write, more the 300 yeres, & in other places til the temple was buylt.

15 Notwithstanding thou maist kil and eat
flesh in all thy gates, whatsoeuer thine
heart desireth, according to the [i] blessing
of the Lord thy God which he hathe giuen thee: *bothe* the vncleane and the cleane
may eat thereof, [k] as of the roe bucke, &
of the hart.

i As God hathe giuen thee power & abilitie.

k Euerie one might eat at home aswel ẏ beast appointed for sacrifice as ẏ other.

16 Onely ye shal not eat ẏ blood, *but* powre it vpon the earth as water.
17 ¶ Thou maiest not eat within thy gates
the [l] tithe of thy corne, nor of thy wine,
nor of thine oyle, nor ẏ first borne of thy
kine, nor of thy shepe, nether anie of thy
vowes which thou vowest, nor thy fre offrings, nor the offring of thine hands,

l Meaning, whatsoeuer was offred to ẏ Lord, might not be eaten, but where he had appointed.

18 But thou shalt eat it before the Lord thy
God, in the place which ẏ Lord thy God
shal chose, thou, and thy sonne, and thy
daughter, and thy seruant, and thy maid,
and the Leuite, that is within thy gates: and thou shalt reioyce before ẏ Lord
thy God, in all that thou puttest thine
hand to.

Eccles.7.32.

19 *Beware, that thou forsake not the Leuite, as long as thou liuest vpon the earth.
20 ¶ When the Lord thy God shal enlarge thy border, *as he hathe promised thee,
and thou shalt say, I wil eat flesh, (because
thine heart lõgeth to eat flesh) thou maist
eat flesh, whatsoeuer thine heart desireth.

Gen.28.14. chap.19.9.

21 If the place which the Lord thy God
hathe chosẽ to put his Name there, be far
from thee, thẽ thou shalt kil of thy bullockes, and of thy shepe which the Lord hathe giuen thee, as I haue commanded thee,
& thou shalt eat in thy gates, whatsoeuer
thine heart desireth.
22 Euen as the roe bucke and the hart is
eaten, so thou shalt eat them: *bothe* the vncleane & the cleane shal eat of thẽ alike.
23 Onely be "sure that thou eat not the blood: for the blood [m] is the life, and ẏ maist
not eat the life with the flesh.

"*Ebr. be strong or constant.*

m Because the life of beasts is in their blood.

24 *Therefore* thou shalt not eat it, *but* powre
it vpon the earth as water.
25 Thou shalt not eat it, that it may go
wel with thee, and with thy children after
thee, when thou shalt do that which is
right in the sight of the Lord:
26 But thine [n] holy things which thou hast,
and thy vowes thou shalt take vp, and come vnto ẏ place which ẏ Lord shal chose.

n That which thou wilt offer in sacrifice.

27 And thou shalt make thy burnt offrings
of the flesh, and of the blood vpon the altar of the Lord thy God, and the blood
of thine offrings shal be powred vpon the
altar of the Lord thy God, & thou shalt
eat the flesh.
28 Take hede, and heare all these wordes
which I command thee, ẏ it may go [o] wel
with thee, and with thy children after thee
for euer, when ẏ doest that which is good
& right in the sight of the Lord thy God.

o God by promes bindeth him selfe to do good to thẽ that obey his worde.

29 ¶ When the Lord thy God shal destroy
the nacions before thee, whether thou goest to possesse them, & thou shalt possesse
them and dwel in their land,
30 Beware, lest thou be taken in [p] a snare after thẽ, after that they be destroyed before thee, & lest thou aske after their gods,
saying, How did these nacions serue their
gods, that I may do so likewise?

p By followĩg their superstitions & idolatries, & thinkĩg to serue me thereby.

31 Thou shalt not do so vnto the Lord thy
God: for all abominacion, which the
Lord hateth, haue they done vnto their
gods: for they haue [q] burned bothe their
sonnes and their daughters with fire to
their gods.

q They thoght nothing to deare to offer to their idoles.

32 *Therefore* whatsoeuer I commande you,
take hede you do it: *thou shalt put nothing thereto, nor take oght therefrom.

Chap.4.2. iosh.1.7. prou.36.6. reu.22.18.

CHAP. XIII.

5 The inticers to idolatrie must be slaine, seme they neuer so holy, 6 So nere of kinred or frẽdship, 12 Or great in multitude or power.

1 IF there arise among you a prophet or a
dreamer of [a] dreames, (& giue thee a
signe or wondre,

a Which saith, that he hathe things receiled vnto him in dreames.

2 And the signe and the wondre, which he
hathe tolde thee, come to passe) sayĩg, [b] Let
vs go after other gods, which thou hast
not knowen, and let vs serue them,

b He sheweth whereunto ẏ false prophets tend.

3 Thou shalt not hearken vnto the wordes
of ẏ prophet, or vnto that dreamer of dreames: for ẏ Lord your God [c] proueth you,
to knowe whether ye loue the Lord your
god ẇ all your heart, and ẇ all your soule.

c God ordeineth all these things ẏ his may be knowen.

4 Ye shal walke after the Lord your God &
feare him, and shal kepe his commandements, and hearken vnto his voyce, and ye
shal serue him, & cleaue vnto him.
5 But that prophet, or ẏ dreamer of dreames he shal [d] be slaine, because he hathe
spoken to turne you away from the Lord
your God (ẇ broght you out of the land
of Egypt, and deliuered you out of the
house of bõdage) to thrust thee out of the
way, wherein the Lord thy God cõmãded thee to walke: so shalt thou take the
euil away forthe of the middes of thee.

d Being conuict by testimonies & cõdemned by the iudge.

6 ¶ If [e] thy brother, the sonne of thy mother, or thine owne sonne, or thy daughter, or the wife, *that lieth* in thy bosome, or
thy frende, which is as thine owne [f] soule,
entice thee secretly, saying, Let vs go and
serue other gods, (which thou hast not
knowen, thou, *I say*, nor thy fathers)

e All natural affections must giue place to Gods honour.

f Whome thou louest as thy life.

7 *Anie* of the gods of the people which are
rownde about you, nere vnto thee or far
of from thee, from the one end of ẏ earth
vnto the other:
8 Thou shalt not cõsent vnto him, nor heare him, nether shal thine eye pitie him,
nor shewe mercie, nor kepe him secret:
9 But ẏ shalt euẽ kil him: [g] thine hãd shalbe first vpõ him to put him to death, & thẽ

g As ẏ witnes is charged, Chap.17.7.

the

the hands of all the people.
10 And thou ſhalt ſtone him with ſtones, ẏ
he dye(becauſe he hathe gone about to
thruſt thee away frõ the Lord thy God,
which broght thee out of the land of E-
gypt,from the houſe of bondage)
11 That*all Iſraél may heare & feare,& do
no more anie ſuche wickednes as this a-
mong you.

Chap.17,13.

12 ¶If thou ſhalt heare ſay (concerning a-
nie of thy cities which the Lord thy God
hathe giuen thee to dwel in)
13 "Wicked men are gone out from amõg
you,& haue drawen away ẏ inhabitãts of
their citie,ſayĩg, Let vs go & ſerue other
gods,which ye haue not knowen,

" *Ebr. children of Belial.*

14 Then [h] thou ſhalt ſeke, & make ſearche
&enquire diligently:and if *it be* true , &
the thing certeine, that ſuche abominacion is wroght among you,

h Which art appointed to ſe fautes puniſhed.

15 Thou ſhalt euẽ ſlaye the inhabitãts of ẏ
citie with the edge of the ſworde:deſtroy
it vtterly, & all that is therein, & the cattel thereof with the edge of the ſworde.
16 And [i] thou ſhalt gather all the ſpoile of
it into the middes of the ſtrete thereof, &
burne with fire the citie & all the ſpoile
thereof euerie whit, vnto the Lord thy
God : and it ſhalbe an heape for euer : it
ſhal not be buylt againe.

i Signifying ẏ no idolatrie is ſo execrable, nor more grieuouſly to be puniſhed,then of them which once profeſſed God.

17 And there ſhal cleaue nothing of ẏ [k] dã-
ned thing to thine hãd, ẏ the Lord maie
turne from the fearcenes of his wrath , &
ſhewe thee mercie , and haue compaſsion
on thee and multiplie thee , as he hathe
ſworne vnto thy fathers:

k Of ẏ ſpoyle of ẏ idolatrous & curſed citie, Read Chap.7,26.

18 *When thou ſhalt obey the voyce of the
Lord thy God,and kepe all his commandements which I commãde thee this day,
that thou do that which is right in ẏ eies
of the Lord thy God.

CHAP. XIIII.

1 The maners of the Gentiles in marking thẽ ſelues for the dead,may not be folowed. 4 What meates are cleane to be eaten,and what not. 29 The tithes for the Leuite,ſtranger,fatherles,and widowe.

1 YE are the children of the Lord your
God. *Ye ſhal not cut your ſelues,
nor make you *anie* baldnes betwene your
eies for the dead.

Leuit.19,28.

2 *For thou art an holy people vnto ẏ Lord
thy God,& the Lord hathe choſen thee
to be a [a] precious people vnto him ſelfe,
aboue all the people that are vpon the
earth.

Chap 7,6. & 26,18.

a Therefore ẏ oghteſt not to followe ẏ ſuperſtitions of the Gentils.

3 ¶Thou ſhalt eat no maner of abominacion.
4 [b] Theſe are the beaſts , which ye ſhal eat,
the beſe,the ſhepe,and the goat,
5 The hart,& the roe bucke, and ẏ bugle,
and the wilde goat, & the vnicorne,& the
wilde oxe,and the chamois.
6 And euerie beaſt ẏ parteth the hooſe,and
cleaueth ẏ cliſt into two clawes,and *is* of ẏ
beaſts that cheweth ẏ cud,that ſhal ye eat.

b This ceremonial Lawe inſtructed ẏ Iewes to ſeke a ſpiritual purenes , euen in their meat & drinke.

7 But theſe ye ſhal not eat, of them that
chewe the cud,and of them that deuide &
cleaue ẏ hooſe *onely*:the camel,nor the hare,nor the cony: for they chewe the cud,
but deuide not the hooſe : *therefore* they
ſhalbe vncleane vnto you:
8 Alſo the ſwine, becauſe he deuideth the
hooſe, & cheweth not the cud, ſhalbe vncleane vnto you : ye ſhal not eat of their
fleſh,nor touche their dead carkeiſes.
9 ¶* Theſe ye ſhal eat, of all that are in
the waters: all that haue finnes and ſcales
ſhal ye eat.

Leuit.11,2.

10 And whatſoeuer hathe no finnes nor ſcales, ye ſhal not eat:it ſhalbe vncleane vnto you.
11 ¶Of all cleane birdes ye ſhal eat:
12 But theſe are thei , whereof ye ſhal not
eat: ẏ egle,nor ẏ goſhawke,nor ẏ oſprey,
13 Nor the glead nor the kite, nor the vul-
ture,after their kinde,
14 Nor all kinde of rauens,
15 Nor the oſtriche,nor ẏ nightcrowe,nor
ẏ "ſemeaw,nor the hawke after her kinde,
16 Nether the lytle owle, nor the great
owle,nor the redſhanke,

" *Or,cuckowe.*

17 Nor the pellicane,nor the ſwãne,nor ẏ
cormorant:
18 The ſtorcke alſo, and the heron in his
kinde,nor the lapwing,nor * the backe.
19 And euerie creping thing ẏ flieth , ſhalbe
vncleane vnto you:it ſhal not be eaten.

Leuit.11,20.

20 *But* of all cleane foules ye may eat.
21 Ye ſhal eat of nothing that [c] dyeth alone,but thou ſhalt giue it vnto the [d] ſtranger that is within thy gates, that he may
eat it:or thou maieſt ſel it vnto a ſtrãger:
for thou art an holy people vnto ẏ Lord
thy God. Thou ſhalt not * ſeeth a kid in
his mothers milke.

c Becauſe their blood was not ſhed,but remaineth in them.

d Which is not of thy religion.

Exod.23,19, and 34,26.

22 Thou ſhalt [e] giue the tithe of all the
increaſe of thy ſede, that commeth forthe of the field yere by yere.
23 And thou ſhalt eat before the Lord thy
God(in the place which he ſhal choſe to
cauſe his Name to dwel there)the tithe
of thy corne,of thy wine,and of thine oyle, and the firſt borne of thy kyne and of
thy ſhepe,that thou maieſt learne to feare the Lord thy God alway.

e The tithes were ordeined for the maintenance of the Leuites,which had none inheritance.

24 And if the way be to long for thee, ſo
that thou art not able to cary it, becauſe
the place is far from thee, where the Lord
thy God ſhal choſe to ſet his Name,[f] whẽ
the Lord thy God ſhal bleſſe thee.

f When he ſhal giue thee abilitie.

25 Then ſhalt thou make it in money, and
"take the money in thine hand,and go vnto the place which the Lord thy God ſhal
choſe.

" *Or,binde vp.*

26 And thou ſhalt beſtowe the money for
what ſoeuer thine heart deſireth : whe-

ther it be oxe, or shepe, or wine or strong
drinke, or whatsoeuer thine heart desireth:
g and shalt eat it there before ȳ Lord thy
God, and reioyce, *bothe* thou, & thine housholde.

g After the Priest hathe receiued ȳ Lords parte.

27 And the Leuite that is within thy gates,
shalt thou not forsake: for he hathe nether
parte nor inheritance with thee.

28 ¶ At the end of thre yere ȳ shalt h bring
forthe all the tithes of thine encrease of
ȳ same yere, & lay it vp within thy gates.

29 Then the Leuite shal come, because he
hathe no parte nor inheritance with thee,
& the stranger, and the fatherles, and the
widowe, which are within thy gates, and
shal eat, and be filled, that the Lord thy
God may blesse thee in all the worke of
thine hand which thou doest.

h Besides the yerely tithes that were giuē to ȳ Leuites, these were laide vp in store for ȳ poore.

CHAP. XV.

1 *The yere of releasing of debts. 5 God blesseth them that kepe his commandements. 7 To helpe the poore. 12 The fredome of seruants. 19 The first borne of the cattel must be offred to the Lord.*

1 AT the terme of seuen yeres thou
shalt make a fredome.

2 And this is the maner of ȳ fredome: euerie a creditour shal quite the lone of his
hād w̄ he hathe lent to his neighbour: he
shal not aske it againe of his neighbour,
nor of his brother: for *the yere* of ȳ Lords
fredome is proclamed.

a He shal onely release his dettors, w̄ are not able to pay for ȳ yere.

3 Of a stranger thou maist require it: but
ȳ which thou hast with thy brother, thine
hand shal remit:

4 b Saue when there shalbe no poore with
thee: for the Lord shal blesse thee in the
lād, which the Lord thy God giueth thee,
for an inheritance to possesse it:

b For if thy dettor be rich, he may be cōstrained to pay.

5 So that thou hearken vnto the voyce of
ȳ Lord thy God to obserue & do all these
commandements, which I commāde thee
this day.

6 For ȳ Lord thy God hathe blessed thee,
as he hathe promised thee: & * thou shalt
lend vnto manie nacions, but thou thy sel
fe shalt not borowe, & thou shalt reigne
ouer manie nacions, and they shal not reigne ouer thee.

Chap.28,12.

7 ¶ If one of thy brethrē with thee be poore "within anie of thy gates in thy land, w̄
the Lord thy God giueth thee, thou shalt
not harden thine heart, nor shut thine hād
from thy poore brother:

"*Or, anie of thy cities.*

8 *But thou shalt open thine hād vnto him,
and shalt lend him sufficient for his nede
which he hathe.

Matt.5,42. luke.6,34.

9 Beware ȳ there be not a wicked thoght
in thine heart, to say, The seuenth yere, ȳ
yere of fredome is at hand: therefore " it
grieueth thee to loke on thy poore brother, and thou giuest him noght, & he crie
vnto the Lord against thee, so that sinne
be in thee:

"*Ebr. thyne eie is euil.*

10 Thou shalt giue him, & let it not grieue
"thine heart to giue vnto him: for because
of this ȳ Lord thy God shal blesse thee in
all thy workes, & in all that thou puttest
thine hand to.

"*Ebr. let not thine heart be euil.*

11 c Because there shalbe euer *some* poore
in the land, therefore I commande thee,
saying, Thou shalt d open thine hand vnto thy brother, to thy nedie, and to thy
poore in thy land.

c To trie your charitie, Mat. 26,11.

d Thou shalt be liberal.

12 ¶ *If thy brother an Ebrewe sel him selfe
to thee, or an Ebrewesse, and serue thee six
yere, euē in the seuenth yere thou shalt let
him go fre from thee.

Exod.21,2. iere.34.14.

13 And when thou sendest him out fre frō
thee, ȳ shalt not let him go away emptie,

14 *But* shalt e giue him a liberal rewarde
of thy shepe, & of thy corne, & of thy wine: thou shalt giue him of that wherewith
the Lord thy God hathe blessed thee.

e In token ȳ thou doest acknowledg the benefite which God hathe giuen thee by his labours.

15 And remember that thou wast a seruant
in the land of Egypt, and the Lord thy
God deliuered thee: therefore I commāde thee this thing to day.

16 And if he say vnto thee, I wil not go a-
way from thee, because he loueth thee &
thine house, & because he is wel with thee,

17 *Then shalt thou take a naule, and perce
his eare through against the dore, and he
shal be thy seruāt f for euer: and vnto thy
mayd seruant thou shalt do likewise.

Exod.21,6.

f To the yere of Iubile, Leuit.25,40.

18 Let it not grieue thee, when thou lettest
him go out fre frō thee: for he hathe serued thee six yeres, *which is* the double worthe of g an hired seruant: & the Lord thy
God shal blesse thee in all ȳ thou doest.

g For the hired seruāt serued but thre yeres, and he six.

19 ¶ *All the first borne males that come of
thy cattel, & of thy shepe, thou shalt sanctifie vnto the Lord thy God. h Thou
shalt do no worke with thy first borne bullocke, nor sheare thy first borne shepe.

Exod.34,19.

h For they are the Lords.

20 Thou shalt eat it before the Lord thy
God yere by yere, in the place which the
Lord shal chose, *bothe* ȳ, & thine houshold.

21 *But if there be anie blemish therein, *as if
it be* lame, or blinde, or haue anie euil faut,
ȳ shalt not offer it vnto ȳ Lord thy God,

Leui.22,20. chap.17,1. eccl.35,14.

22 *But* shalt eat it within thy gates: the vncleane, and the cleane *shal eat it* alike, i as
the roe bucke, and as the heart.

i Thou shalt aswel eat thē, as ȳ roe bucke, and other wilde beasts.

23 Onely thou shalt not eat the blood thereof, *but* powre it vpon ȳ groūde as water.

CHAP. XVI.

1 *Of Easter, 10 Witsontide, 13 And the feast of tabernacles. 18 What officers oght to be ordeined. 21 Idolatrie forbidden.*

1 THou shalt kepe ȳ moneth of a Abib
& thou shalt celebrate the Passeouer
vnto the Lord thy God: for in the moneth of Abib the Lord thy God broght
thee out of Egypt by night.

a Read Exod. 13,4.

2 Thou shalt therefore b offer the Passeouer vnto the Lord thy God, of shepe and
bullockes * in the place where the Lord
shal

b Thou shalt eat the Easter Lambe.

Chap.12,5.

shal chose to cause his Name to dwel.

Exod.12,14.

3 Thou * shalt eat no leauened bread with
it: *but* seuen dayes shalt thou eat vnleauened bread therewith, *euen* the bread of
[c] tribulacion: for thou camest out of the
land of Egypt in haste, that thou maiest
remember the day when thou camest out
of ỹ land of Egypt, all ỹ dayes of thy life.

c Which signified that affliction, which ỹ haddest in Egypt.

4 And there shal be no leauen sene with
thee in all thy coastes seuen dayes long:
nether shal there remaine the night anie
of the flesh vntil the morning which thou
offredst the first day at euen.
5 Thou maiest [d] not offer the Passeouer
within anie of thy gates, which the Lord
thy God giueth thee:

d This was chiefly accōplished, when the tēple was buylt.

6 But in the place which ỹ Lord thy God
shal chose to place his Name, there thou
shalt offer the [e] Passeouer at euen, about
the going downe of the sunne, in the season that thou camest out of Egypt.
7 And thou shalt roste and eat it in ỹ place which the Lord thy God shal chose,
and shalt returne on the morow, and go
vnto thy tentes.

e Which was institute to put them in remēbrāce of their deliuerāce out of Egypt: & to continue them in the hope of Iesus Christ, of whome this lābe was a figure

8 Six dayes shalt thou eat vnleauened bread, and the seuenth day *shalbe* a solemne
assemblie to the Lord thy God: thou shalt
do no worke *therein*.
9 ¶ Seuen wekes shalt thou [f] nomber vnto
thee, and shalt begin to nomber the seuen
wekes, when thou beginst to put the sickel
to the corne:

f Beginning at the next morning after the Passeouer, Leuit.23,15. exo.13,4.

10 And thou shalt kepe the feast of wekes
vnto the Lord thy God, "*euen* a fre gift of
thine hād, which thou shalt giue vnto the
Lord thy God, as the Lord thy God hathe
blessed thee.

"*Or, as thou art able, willingly.*

11 And thou shalt reioyce before the Lord
thy God, thou and thy sonne, and thy
daughter, and thy seruant, and thy maid,
and the Leuite that is within thy gates, &
the stranger, and the fatherles, and the
widow, that are among you, in the place
which ỹ Lord thy God shal chose to place
his Name there,
12 And thou shalt remēber that thou wast
a seruant in Egypt: therefore thou shalt
obserue and do these ordinances.
13 ¶ Thou shalt [g] obserue the feast of the
Tabernacles seuen daies, when thou hast
gathered in thy corne, and thy wine.

g That is, the 15 day of the seuēth moneth, Leu.23,34.

14 And ỹ shalt reioyce in thy feast, thou,
and thy sonne, and thy daughter, and thy
seruant, and thy maid, and the Leuite, and
the stranger, and the fatherles, and the widow, that are within thy gates.
15 Seuen daies shalt ỹ kepe a feast vnto the
Lord thy God in the place which ỹ Lord
shal chose: whē ỹ Lord thy God shal blesse
thee in all thine increase, & in all ỹ workes
of thine hāds, ỹ shalt in anie case be glad.
16 ¶ * Thre times in the yere shal all ỹ males appeare before the Lord thy God in ỹ
place which he shal chose: in ỹ feast of the
vnleauened bread, & in ỹ feast of ỹ wekes,
& in the feast of the Tabernalces: & they
shal not appeare before the Lord empty.

Exod.23,15. & 34,20. ecclesi.16.6.

17 Euerie man *shal giue* according to the
gift of his [h] hand, and according to the
blessing of the Lord thy God, which he
hathe giuen thee.

h According to the abilitie that God hathe giuen him.

18 ¶ [i] Iudges and officers shalt thou make
thee in all thy cities, w̃ the Lord thy God
giueth thee, throughout thy tribes: & they
shal iudge ỹ people w̃ righteoꝰ iudgemēt.

i He gaue autoritie to that people for a time to chuse them selues magistrates.

19 Wrest not thou the Lawe, nor respect
anie persone, nether take rewarde: for the
rewarde blindeth the eyes of the wise, &
peruerteth the wordes of the iust.
20 That w̃ [k] is iust and right shalt thou followe, that thou maiest liue, & possesse the
lād which the Lord thy God giueth thee.

k The magistrat must constātly follow the tenor of the Lawe, and in nothing decline from iustice.

21 ¶ Thou shalt plāt thee no groue of anie
trees nere vnto the altar of the Lord thy
God, which thou shalt make thee.
22 Thou shalt set thee vp no " piller, which
thing the Lord thy God hateth.

"*Or, image.*

CHAP. XVII.

2 The punishment of the idolater. 9 Hard controuersies are broght to the Priest and the iudge. 12 The contemner must dye. 15 The election of the King. 16 & 17 What things he oght to auoide. 18 And what he oght to imbrace.

1 THou shalt offer vnto ỹ Lord thy God
no bullocke nor shepe wherein is [a] ble
mish *or* anie euil fauored thing: for that
is an abominaciō vnto ỹ Lord thy God.

a Thou shalt not serue God for facions sake, as hypocrites do.

2 ¶ If there be found amōg you in anie of
thy cities, which ỹ Lord thy God giueth
thee, man or [b] woman that hathe wroght
wickednes in the sight of the Lord thy
God, in transgressing his couenant,

b Shewing that the crime can not be excused by the frailtie of the persone.

3 And hathe gone & serued other gods, &
worshipped thē: as the sunne, or the moone, or anie of the hoste of heauen, which
I haue not [c] commanded,

c Whereby he condēneth all religion and seruing of God which he hathe not commanded.

4 And it be tolde vnto thee, and thou hast
heard it, then shalt thou inquire diligently: and if *it be* true, *and* the thing certeine,
ỹ suche abominacion is wroght in Israél,
5 Then shalt thou bring forthe that mā, or
that woman (which haue committed that
wicked thing) vnto thy gates, *whether it be*
man or woman, and shalt stone them with
stones, til they dye.
6 * At ỹ mouth of two or thre witnesses shal
he that is worthy of death, dye: *but* at the
mouth of one witnes, he shal not dye.

Nom.35,30. chap 19.15. mat.18,16. 2 cor.13,1.

7 The hands of the [d] witnesses shalbe first
vpō him, to kil him: and afterwarde the
hands of all the [e] people: so thou shalt
take the wicked away from among you.

d Whereby they declared that they testified ỹ trueth.

e To signifie a commune consent to mainteine Gods honour and true religion.

8 ¶ If there rise a matter to hard for thee in
iudgement betwene blood and blood, betwene plea and plea, betwene plague and
plague, in the matters of controuersie

within thy gates, then shalt thou arise,
and go vp vnto the place which the Lord
thy God shal chose,
9 And thou shalt come vnto the Priests of
the Leuites, & vnto the [f] iudge that shalbe in those dayes, and aske, and thei shal
shewe thee the sentence of iudgement,
10 And thou shalt do according to ẏ thing
which they of that place (which the Lord
hathe chosen) shewe thee, and thou shalt
obserue to do according to all that they
informe thee.
11 According to the Lawe, which they
shal teach thee, and according to the iudgemēt which thei shal tel thee, shalt [g] thou
do: thou shalt not decline from the thing
which they shal shewe thee, *nether* to the
right hand, nor to the left.
12 And that man that wil do presumpteously, not hearkening vnto the Priest (that
stādeth before the Lord thy God to [h] minister there) or vnto the iudge, that man
shal dye, and thou shalt take away euil frō
Israél.
13 So all the people shal heare and feare,
and do no more presumpteously.
14 ¶ When thou shalt come vnto the land
which the Lord thy God giueth thee, and
shalt possesse it, and dwel therein, if thou
say, I wil set a King ouer me, like as all
the nacions that are about me,
15 *Then* thou shalt make him King ouer
thee, whome the Lord thy God shal chose: from among thy brethren shalt thou
make a King ouer thee: thou shalt not set a
[i] stranger ouer thee, ẇ is not thy brother.
16 In anie wise he shal not prepare him manie horses, nor bring the people againe to
[k] Egypt for to increase the nōber of horses, seing the Lord hathe said vnto you,
Ye shal hensforthe go no more again that
way.
17 Nether shal he take him manie wiues,
lest his heart [l] turne away, nether shal he
gather him muche siluer and gold.
18 And when he shal sit vpon the throne of
his kingdome, then shal he write him this
[m] Lawe repeted in a boke, by the [n] Priests
of the Leuites.
19 And it shalbe with him, and he shal
read therein all dayes of his life, that he
may learne to feare the Lord his God, &
to kepe all the wordes of this Lawe, and
these ordinances, for to do them:
20 That his heart be not lifted vp aboue
his [o] brethren, and that he turne not from
the commandement, to the right hand or
to the left, *but* that he may prolong his
dayes in his kingdome, he, and his sonnes
in the middes of Israél.

f Who shal giue sentence as the Priests cōsel him by the Lawe of God.
g Thou shalt obey their sentence that the controuersie may haue an end.
h So long as he is the true minister of God, and pronoūceth according to his worde.
i Who is not of thy nacion, lest he change true religion into idolatrie, and bring thee to slauerie.
k To reuenge their iniuries, and to take thē of their best horses. 1. King 10,28.
l From the Lawe of God.
m Meaning, ẏ Deuteronomie.
n He shal cause it to be writ by them, or, he shal write it by their example.
o Whereby is mēt, that Kigs oght so to loue their subiects, as nature bindeth one brother to loue another.

CHAP. XVIII.

3 The portion of the Leuites. 6 Of the Leuite comming from another place. 9 To auoyde the abominacion of the Gentiles. 15 God wil not leaue thē without a true Prophet. 20 The false prophet shalbe slaine. 22 How he may be knowen.

1 THe Priests of the Leuites, *and* all the
tribe of Leuí * shal haue no parte nor Nomb.18,20.
inheritance with Israél, * *but* shal eat the Chap.10,9.
offrings of the Lord made by fire, and his 1.cor.9,13.
[a] inheritance.
2 Therefore shal they haue no inheritance
amōg their brethren: *for* the Lord is their
inheritance, as he hathe said vnto them.
3 ¶ And this shalbe ẏ Priests duetie of the
people, that they, which offer sacrifice,
whether *it be* bullocke or shepe, shal giue
vnto the Priest the [b] shulder, and the two
chekes, and the mawe.
4 The first frutes *also* of thy corne, of thy
wine, and of thine oyle, and the first of the
fleece of thy shepe shalt thou giue him.
5 For the Lord thy God hathe chosen him
out of all thy tribes, to stand and minister
in the Name of the Lord, him, & his sonnes for euer.
6 ¶ Also when a Leuite shal come out of
anie of thy cities of all Israél, where he
remained, and come with [c] all the desire
of his heart vnto the place, which the
Lord shal chose,
7 He shal then minister in the Name of ẏ
Lord his God, as all his brethren the Leuites, which remaine there before the
Lord.
8 They shal haue like porciōs to eat [d] beside that which commeth of his sale of his
patrimonie.
9 When thou shalt come into ẏ land which
the Lord thy God giueth thee, thou shalt
not learne to do after the abominacions
of those nacions.
10 Let none be founde among you that
maketh his sonne or his daughter to [e] go
through the fire, *or* that vseth witchcraft,
or a regarder of times, or a marker of the
flying of foules, or a sorcerer,
11 Or * a charmer, or that counselleth with Leu.20,27.
spirits, or a sothesayer, or that * asketh 1.Sam.28,7.
counsel at the dead.
12 For all that do suche things *are* abominaciō vnto the Lord, and because of these abominacions the Lord thy God doeth
cast them out before thee.
13 Thou shalt be [f] vpright therefore with
the Lord thy God.
14 For these nacions which thou shalt possesse, hearken vnto those that regarde the
times, & vnto sorcerers:" as for thee, the
Lord thy God hathe not suffered thee so.
15 ¶ * The Lord thy God wil raise vp vnto Act.7,37.
thee a [g] Prophet like vnto me, frō amōg
you, *euen* of thy brethrē: vnto him ye shal
hearken,
16 According to all that thou desiredst of
the Lord thy God in Horéb, in the day of
the

a That is, the Lords parte of his inheritance.
b The right shulder, Nom. 18,18.
c Meaning, to serue God vnfainedly, and not to seke ease.
d Not cōstreined to liue of him selfe.
e Signifying they were purged by this ceremonie of passing betwene two fires.
f Without hypocrisie, or mixture of false religion.
" Ebr. but thou not so.
g Meaning a continual successiō of Prophets, til Christ ẏ end of all Prophetes come.

Exod.20.19. the assemblie, when thou saidest, * Let me
heare the voyce of my Lord God no mo-
rè, nor se this great fire anie more, that I
dye not.
17 And the Lord said vnto me, Thei haue
wel spoken.
18 *I wil raise thē vp a Prophet from amōg
their brethren like vnto thee, and wil put
my wordes in his [h] mouth, and he shal
speake vnto them all that I shal commande him.
19 And whosoeuer wil not hearken vnto my
wordes, which he shal speake in my Name, I wil [i] require it of him.
20 But the prophet that shal presume to
speake a worde in my Name, which I haue
not cōmanded him to speake, or that speaketh in the name of other gods, euen the
same prophet shal dye.
21 And if thou thinke in thine heart, How
shal we knowe the worde which the Lord
hathe not spoken?
22 When a prophet speaketh in the Name of the Lord, if the thing [k] followe not
nor come to passe, that is the thing which
the Lord hathe not spokē, *but* the prophet
hathe spokē it presumpteously: thou shalt
not *therefore* be afrayed of him.

Iosh.1,45. act.3,21.

h Which promes is not onely made to Christ, but to all ŷ teache in his Name, Isa. 59,21.

i By executing punishmēt vpon him.

k Vnder this sure note he compriseth all ŷ other tokēs.

CHAP. XIX.

3 The frāchised townes. 14 Not to remoue thy neighbours bondes. 16 The punishment of him that beareth false witnes.

Chap.12,29.

1 WHē the Lord thy God *shal roote out the nacions, whose lād the
Lord thy God giueth thee, and thou shalt
possesse them, and dwel in their cities, and
in their houses,
2 *Thou shalt separate thre cities for thee
in the middes of thy land which the Lord
thy God giueth thee to possesse it.
3 Thou shalt [a] prepare thee the waie, & deuide the coastes of the land, which the
Lord thy God giueth thee to inherit, into
thre partes, that euerie [b] manslayer may
flee thether.
4 ¶ This also is ŷ cause wherefore the māslaier shal flee thether, and liue: whoso
killeth his neighbour ignorantly, & hated
him not in time passed:
5 As he that goeth vnto the wood with his
neighbour to hewe wood, and his hand
striketh with the axe to cut downe the
tre, if the head slip from the helue, and
hitte his neighbour that he dyeth, ŷ same
[c] shal flee vnto one of the cities, & liue,
6 Lest the * auenger of the blood followe
after the māslaier, while his heart is chafed, and ouertake him, because the way is
long, & slay him, althogh he be not * worthy of death, because he hated him not in
time passed.
7 Wherefore I cōmande thee, sayīg, Thou
shalt appoint out thre cities for thee.

Exod.21,13. nomb.35,9. iosh.20,2.

a Make an opē & readie way.

b Which killeth agaīst his wil, & bare no hatred in his heart.

c That murther be not cōmitted vpon murther.

Nomb.35,12.

Or, can not be iudged to death

8 And when the Lord thy God [d] enlargeth thy coastes (as he hathe sworne vnto
thy fathers) and giueth thee all the land
which he promised to giue vnto thy fathers,
9 (If thou kepe all these commandements
to do them, which I commandē thee this
day: *to wit*, that thou loue the Lord thy
God, and walke in his waies for euer) * thē
shalt thou adde thre cities mo for thee
besides those thre,
10 That innocent blood be not shed within thy land, which the Lord thy God giueth thee to inherit, [e] lest blood be vpon
thee.
11 ¶ But if a man hate his neighbour, and
laie waite for him, and rise against him, &
smite any man that he dye, and flee vnto any of these cities,
12 Then the [f] Elders of his citie shal send
and fet him thence, and deliuer him into
the hands of the auenger of the blood,
that he may dye.
13 Thine [g] eie shal not spare him, but thou
shalt put away *the crye* of innocent blood
from Israél, that it may go wel with thee.
14 ¶ Thou shalt not remoue thy neighbours marke, which thei of olde time haue
set in thine inheritance, that thou shalt inherit in the lād, which the Lord thy God
giueth thee to possesse it.
15 ¶ * One witnes shal not rise against a mā
for any trespas, or for any sinne, or for
any faute that he offendeth in, * *but* at the
mouth of two witnesses or at the mouth
of thre witnesses shal the matter be stablished.
16 ¶ If a false witnes rise vp against a man
to accuse him of trespasse,
17 Then bothe the men which striue together, shal stand before the [h] Lord, *euen*
before the Priests and the Iudges, which
shalbe in those daies,
18 And the Iudges shal make diligent inquisicion: and if the witnes be founde false, *and* hathe giuen false witnes against his
brother,
19 * Then shal ye do vnto him as he had
thoght to do vnto his brother: so thou
shalt take euil away forthe of the middes
of thee.
20 And the rest shal heare *this*, and feare,
and shal henceforthe cōmit no more any-
suche wickednes among you.
21 Therefore thine eie shal haue no compassion, *but* * life for life, eie for eie, tothe
for tothe, hand for hand, fote for fote.

d When thou goest ouer Iordén to possesse the whole lād of Canáan.

Iosh.20,7.

e Lest thou be punished for innocēt blood

f The Magistrates.

g Then whosoeuer pardoneth murther, offēdeth agaīst the worde of God.

Chap.17,6. mat.18,16. ioh.8,17. 2.Cor.13,1. ebr.10,28.

h Gods presēce is where his true ministers are assembled.

Prou.19,5. dan.13,62.

Exod.21,23. leui.24,20. mat.5,38.

CHAP. XX.

3 The exhortacion of the Priest when the Israelites go to battel. 5 The exhortacion of the officers shewing who shulde go to battel. 10 Peace must first be proclamed. 19 The trees that beare frute, must not be destroyed.

a Meaning, vpõ iuste occasion: for God permitteth not his people to fight whẽ it semeth good to them.

1 WHen [a] thou shalt go forthe to
warre against thine enemies, &
shalt se horses and charets, *and* people mo
then thou, be not afraied of them: for the
Lord thy God *is* with thee, which broght
thee out of the land of Egypt.
2 And whẽ ye are come nere vnto the battel, then the Priest shal come forthe to
speake vnto the people,
3 And shal say vnto them, Heare, ô Isráel:
ye are come this day vnto battel against
your enemies: * let not your hearts faint,
nether feare, nor be amased, nor adread of
them.

Chap 28,7.

b Is present to defend you wt his grace and power.

4 For the Lord your God [b] goeth with
you, to fight for you against your enemies,
and to saue you.
5 ¶ And let the officers speake vnto ye people, saying, What man *is there* that hathe
buylt a newe house, and hathe not [c] dedicate it? let him go and returne to his house lest he dye in the battel, and an other
man dedicate it.

c For when thei ẽtred first to dwel in an house, thei gaue thankes to God, acknowledging yt they had that benefite by his grace.

6 And what man *is there* that hathe plãted
a vineyard, and hathe [d] not eaten of the
frute? let him go and returne againe vnto
his house, lest he dye in the battel, & another eat the frute.

d The Ebrewe worde signifieth to make cõmune or prophane, Leui. 19,25.

7 And what man *is there* that hathe betrothed a wife, and hathe not taken her? let
him go and returne againe vnto his house,
lest he dye in battel, and another man take
her.
8 And let the officers speake further vnto
the people, & say, * Whosoeuer is afraied
and faint hearted, let him go and returne
vnto his house, lest his brethrens heart
faint like his heart.

Iudg.7,3.

9 And after ye the officers haue made an end
of speaking vnto the people, thei shal make captaines of the armie to gouerne the
people.
10 ¶ When thou comest nere vnto a citie to
fight against it, * thou shalt offer it peace.
11 And if it answer thee againe [e] peaceably, and open vnto thee, then let all the
people that is founde therein, be tributaries vnto thee, and serue thee.

Nomb.21,22. chap.2,26.
e If it accept peace.

12 But if it wil make no peace with thee,
but make warre against thee, then thou
shalt besiege it.
13 And the Lord thy God shal deliuer it
into thine hands, and thou shalt smite all
the males thereof with the edge of the
sworde.
14 Onely the women, and the children,
* and the cattel, and all that is in the citie,
euen all the spoile thereof shalt thou take
vnto thy self, and shalt eat the spoile of
thine enemies, which the Lord thy God
hathe giuen thee.

Iosh.8,2.

15 Thus shalt thou do vnto all the cities,
which are a great way of from thee, which
are not of the cities of these [f] nacions
here.

f For God had appointed that ye Canaanites shulde be destroyed, & made ye Israelites executers of his wil, Chap. 7,1.

16 But of ye cities of this people, which the
Lord thy God shal giue thee to inherit,
thou shalt saue no persone aliue,
17 But shalt vtterly destroye them: *to wit,*
the Hittites, and the Amorites, the Canaanites, & the Perizzites, the Hiuites,
and the Iebusites, as the Lord thy God
hathe commanded thee,
18 That they teache you not to do after all
their abominacions, which thei haue done
vnto their gods, and *so* ye shulde sinne a-
gainst the Lord your God.
19 ¶ When thou hast besieged a citie long
time, and made warre against it to take it,
destroye not the trees thereof, by smiting
an axe into them: for thou maiest eat of
them: therefore thou shalt not cut them
downe to further thee in the siege (for the
[g] tre of the field is mans *life*)
20 Onely those trees, which thou knowest
are not for meat, those shalt thou destroye
& cut downe, and make fortes against the
citie that maketh warre with thee, vntil
thou subdue it.

g Some read, For man *shalbe in steade* of the tre of ye field, to come out in ye siege against thee.

CHAP. XXI.

2 Inquisicion for murther. 11 Of the woman taken in warre. 15 The birthright can not be changed for affection 18 The disobedient childe. 23 The bodie may not hang all night.

1 IF one be founde [a] slayne in the land,
which the Lord thy God giueth thee
to possesse it, lying in the field, *and* it is not
knowen who hathe slayne him,
2 Then thine Elders and thy Iudges shal
come forthe, and measure vnto the cities
that are round about him that is slayne.

a This Lawe declareth how horrible a thĩg murther is, seing yt for one man a whole countrey shal be punished, except a remedy be founde.

3 And let the Elders of that citie, which is
next vnto the slayne man, take out of the
droue an heifer that hathe not bene put to
labour, nor hathe drawen in the yoke.
4 And let the Elders of that citie bring the
heifer vnto a ⁊ stonie [b] valley, which is
nether eared nor sowen, and strike of the
heifers necke there in the valley.

⁊ Or, rough.
b That the blood shed of the innocent beast in a sollitarie place, might make them abhorre the fact.

5 Also the Priests the sonnes of Leuí (whome the Lord thy God hathe chosen to
minister, and to blesse in the Name of the
Lord) shal come forthe, and by their worde shal all strife and plague be tryed.
6 And all the Elders of that citie that came nere to the slayne man, shal wash their
hands ouer the heifer that is beheaded in
the valley:
7 And shal testifie, and say, Our hands
haue not shed this blood, nether haue our
eies sene it.
8 [c] O Lord, be merciful vnto thy people
Isráel, whome thou hast redemed, and lay
no innocent blood to ye charge of thy people Isráel, & ye blood shalbe forgiuẽ them.
9 So shalt yu take away *the crye* of innocent
blood

c This was the prayer, which ye Priests made in the audiẽce of the people.

blood from thee, when thou ſhalt do that
which is right in the ſight of the Lord.
10 ¶When thou ſhalt go to warre againſt
thine enemies,and the Lord thy God ſhal
deliuer them into thine hands, and thou
ſhalt take them captiues,
11 And ſhalt ſe among the captiues a beautiful woman,and haſt a deſire vnto her, &
woldeſt take her to thy wife,
12 Then thou ſhalt bring her home to thine houſe, [d] and ſhe ſhal ſhaue her head,
and pare her nailes,
13 And ſhe ſhal put of the garment that ſhe
was taken in, and ſhe ſhal remaine in thine houſe, [e] and bewaile her father & her
mother a moneth lōg: and after that ſhalt
thou go in vnto her,and mary her,and ſhe
ſhal be thy [f] wife.
14 And if thou haue no fauour vnto her,
then ŷ maieſt let her go whether ſhe wil,
but thou ſhalt not ſel her for money, nor
make marchandiſe of her, becauſe thou
haſt humbled her.

d Signifying that her former life muſt be chāged before thei colde be ioyned to the people of God
e As hauing renounced parents and countrey.
f This onely was permitted in the warres: otherwiſe the Iſraelites colde not mary ſtrangers.

15 ¶If a man haue two wiues, one loued
and an other [g] hated, and they haue borne him children, bothe the loued and alſo the hated:if the firſt borne be the ſonne
of the hated,
16 Then when the time cōmeth, that he appointeth his ſonnes to be heyres of that
which he hathe,he may not make the ſonne of the beloued firſt borne ‖before the
ſonne of the hated, which is ŷ firſt borne:
17 But he ſhal acknowledge the ſonne of ŷ
hated for ŷ firſt borne, & giue him [h] double porcion of all that he hathe: for he is
the firſt of his ſtrength, and to [i] him belongeth the right of the firſt borne.

g This declareth that the pluralitie of wiues came of a corrupt affection.
‖Or, while the ſonne of the hated liueth.
h As muche as to two of the others.
i Except he be vnworthy, as was Reubén Iaakobs ſonne.

18 If anie man haue a ſonne that is ſtubburne and diſobedient, which wil not hearken
vnto the voyce of his father, nor the voyce of his [k] mother,and they haue chaſte-
ned him,and he wolde not obey them,
19 Then ſhal his father and his mother
take him, and bring him out vnto the Elders of his citie, and vnto the gate of the
place where he dwelleth,
20 And ſhal ſay vnto the Elders of his citie, This our ſonne is ſtubburne and diſobedient, *and* he wil not obey our admoni-
cion:he is a ryotour,and a dronkard.
21 Then all the men of his citie ſhal [l] ſtone him with ſtones vnto death: ſo thou
ſhalt take away euil from among you,that
all Iſraél may heare it and feare.
22 ¶If a man alſo haue cōmitted a treſpas
worthy of death, and is put to death, &
thou hangeſt him on a tre,
23 His body ſhal not remaine [m] all night
vpō ŷ tre,but thou ſhalt bury him ŷ ſame
day:for the * curſe of God *is* on him that
is hāged.Defile not therefore thy land,ŵ
ŷ Lord thy God giueth thee to inherit.

k For it is the mothers duetie alſo to inſtruct her children.
l Which death was alſo appointed for blaſphemers and idolaters: ſo that to diſobey the parents is moſte horrible.
m For Gods Lawe by his death is ſatiſfied, and nature abhorreth crueltie.
Gal.3,13.

CHAP. XXII.

1 He commandeth to haue care of our neighbours goods. 5 The woman may not weare mans apparel, nor man the womans. 6 Of the dam and her yong birdes. 8 Why thei ſhulde haue batelments. 9 Not to mixe diuers kinds together. 13 Of the wife not being founde a virgine. 22 The puniſhement of adulterie.

1 THou * ſhalt not ſe thy brothers oxe
nor his ſhepe go aſtray, and [a] withdrawe thy ſelfe from them, *but* ſhalt bring
them againe vnto thy brother.
2 And if thy brother be not [b] nere vnto
thee,or if thou knowe him not,then ŷ ſhalt
bring it into thine houſe, and it ſhal remaine with thee, vntil thy brother ſeke after it: then ſhalt thou deliuer it to him
againe.
3 In like maner ſhalt ŷ do with his [c] aſſe,
and ſo ſhalt thou do with his raiment,
and ſhalt ſo do with all loſte things of thy
brother,which he hathe loſte:if thou haſt
found them,thou ſhalt not withdrawe thy
ſelfe *from them.*

Exod.23,4.
a As thogh thou ſaweſt it not.
b Shewing, ŷ brotherly affectiō muſt be ſhewed,not onely to them that dwel nere vnto vs,but alſo to them which are farre of.
c Muche more art thou boūde to do for thy neighbours perſone.

4 ¶Thou ſhalt not ſe thy brothers aſſe nor
his oxe fall downe by the way, and withdraw thy ſelfe from them, *but* ſhalt lifte
them vp with him.
5 ¶The [d] woman ſhal not weare that
which perteineth vnto the man,nether ſhal
a man put on womans raiment:for all that
do ſo,*are* abominacion vnto the Lord thy
God.

d For that were to alter ŷ ordre of nature,& to deſpite God.

6 ¶If thou finde a birdes neſt in the way,
in anie tre, or on the ground, *whether they
be* yong or egges,and the dam ſitting vpō
the yong,or vpon the egges, [e] thou ſhalt
not take the dam with the yong,
7 *But* ſhalt in anie wiſe let the dam go and
take the yong to thee,ŷ thou maieſt proſper and prolong thy dayes.
8 ¶Whē thou buyldeſt a newe houſe,thou
ſhalt make a batelment on thy roof, that
thou lay not blood vpon thine houſe, if a-
nie man fall thence.

e If God deteſt crueltie done to litle birdes, how muche more to man, made according to his image?

9 ¶Thou ſhalt not [f] ſowe thy vineyard
with diuers kīdes of ſedes,leſt thou defile
the increaſe of the ſede which thou haſt
ſowen,and the frute of the vineyarde.
10 ¶Thou ſhalt not plowe with an oxe and
an aſſe together.
11 ¶Thou ſhalt not weare *a garment* of diuers ſortes,as of wollē and linē together.
12 ¶*Thou ſhalt make thee fringes vpon
the foure quarters of thy veſture, wherewith thou causereſt thy ſelfe.
13 ¶If a man take a wife,and when he hathe
lien with her,hate her,
14 And lay [g] ſlanderous things vnto her
charge, and bring vp an euil name vpon
her,and ſay, I toke this wife, and when I
came to her I found her not a maid,
15 Then ſhal the father of the maid and
her mother take & bring the ſignes of the

f The tenor of this Lawe is, to walke in ſimplicitie, & not to be curious of newe inuentions.
Nom.15,38.
g That is, be an occaſion ŷ ſhe is ſlādred.

maides virginitie vnto the Elders of the
citie to the gate.
16 And the maides father shal say vnto the
Elders, I gaue my daughter vnto this mã
to wife, and he hateth her:
17 And lo, he laieth slanderous things vnto
her charge, sayig, I foũd not thy daughter
a maid: lo, these *are the tokens* of my daughters
virginitie: and they shal spreade ẏ
[h] vesture before the Elders of the citie.
18 Thẽ the Elders of the citie shal take that
man and chastice him,
19 And shal condemne him in an hundreth
shekels of siluer, and giue them vnto the father
[i] of ẏ maid, because he hathe broght
vp an euil name vpõ a maid of Israél: &
she shalbe his wife, & he may not put her
away all his life.
20 ¶ But if this thing be true, that the maide
be not found a virgin,
21 Then they shal bring forthe the maide
to the dore of her fathers house, and the
men of her citie shal stone her with stones
to death: for she hathe wroght follie in Israél,
by playing the whore in her fathers
house: so thou shalt put euil away from
among you.
22 ¶ *If a man be found lying with a womã
maried to a man, then they shal dye euen
bothe twaine: *to wit*, the man that lay with
the wife, and the wife: so thou shalt put away
euil from Israél.
23 ¶ If a maide be betrothed vnto an housband,
and a man finde her in the towne
and lie with her,
24 Then shal ye bring them bothe out vnto
ẏ gates of the same citie, and shal stone
them with stones to death: the maide because
she cryed not, *being* in the citie, and
ẏ man, because he hathe "humbled his neighbours
wife: so thou shalt put away euil
from among you.
25 ¶ But if a man finde a betrothed maide
in the field, and force her, and lye with
her, then the man that lay with her, shal
dye alone:
26 And vnto the maide thou shalt do nothing,
because there is in the maide no
"cause of death: for as when a man riseth
against his neighbour and woundeth him
to death, so [k] is this matter.
27 For he found her in the fields: the betrothed
maide cryed, and there was no man
to succour her.
28 ¶ *If a man finde a maide that is not betrothed,
and take her, and lye with her, &
they be founde,
29 Then the man that lay with her, shal giue
vnto the maides father fifty *shekels* of
siluer: and she shal be his wife, because he
hathe humbled her: he can not put her away
all his life.
30 ¶ No man shal [l] take his fathers wife,
nor shal vncouer his fathers skirt.

h Meaning the shete, wherein the signes of her virginitie were.

i For the faute of the childe redoundeth to ẏ shame of the parents: therefore he was recompẽced when she was fautles.

Leuit.20,10.

"Or, defiled.

"Or, no faute worthy death.

k Meaning, ẏ the innocent can not be punished.

Exod.22,16.

l He shal not lye with his stepmother: meaning hereby all other degrees forbidden. Leu.18.

CHAP. XXIII.

1 What men might not be admitted to office. 9 What they oght to auoide when they go to warre. 15 Of the fugitiue seruant. 17 To flee all kinde of whoredome. 19 Of vsurie. 21 Of vowes. 24 Of the neighbours vine and corne.

1 None that is hurt by bursting, or that
hathe his priuie mẽbre cut of, [a] shal
entre into the Congregacion of the Lord.
2 [b] A bastard shal not entre into the Congregacion
of the Lord: euen to his tenth
generacion shal he not entre into the Cõgregacion
of the Lord.
3 * The Ammonites and the Moabites shal
not entre into the Congregacion of the
Lord: euen to their tenth generacion shal
they not entre into the Congregacion of
the Lord for euer,
4 Because they [c] met you not with bread
and water in the way, when ye came out
of Egypt, and because they hired against
thee Balaám the sonne of Beór, of Pethór
in Aram-naharáim, to curse thee.
5 Neuertheles, the Lord thy God wolde
not hearken vnto Balaám, but the Lord
thy God turned the curse to a blessing vnto
thee, because the Lord thy God loued
thee.
6 Thou [d] shalt not seke their peace nor
their prosperitie all thy daies for euer.
7 ¶ Thou shalt not abhorre an Edomite:
for he is thy brother, nether shalt thou
abhorre an Egyptian, because thou wast a
stranger in his land.
8 The children that are begotten [e] of thẽ
in their third generacion, shal entre into
the Congregacion of the Lord.
9 ¶ When thou goest out with the hoste against
thine enemies, kepe thee then from
all wickednes.
10 ¶ If there be among you anie that is vncleane
by that which commeth to him by
night, he shal go out of the hoste, and shal
not entre into the hoste,
11 But at euen he shal wash *him selfe* with
water, and when the sunne is downe, he
shal entre into the hoste.
12 ¶ Thou shalt haue a place also without
the hoste whether thou shalt [f] resorte,
13 And thou shalt haue a paddle among thy
weapõs, and when thou woldest sit downe
without, thou shalt dig therewith, and returning
thou shalt [g] couer thine excrements.
14 For the Lord thy God walketh in the
middes of thy campe to deliuer thee, and
to giue *thee* thine enemies before thee:
therefore thine hoste shalbe holy, that he
se no filthy thing in thee and turne away
from thee.
15 ¶ Thou shalt not [h] deliuer the seruant
vnto his master, which is escaped from his
master

a Ether to beare office, or to mary a wife.

b This was to cause them to liue chastely, that their posteritie might not be reiected.

Nom.22,5. nehem.13,1.

c Hereby he condẽneth all, that further not the childrẽ of God in their vocatiõ.

d Thou shalt haue nothing to do with them.

e If the fathers haue renounced their idolatrie, and receiued circumcision.

f For the necessitie of nature.

g Meaning hereby that his people shulde be pure bothe in soule and body.

h This is ment of the heathẽ, who fled for their masters crueltie and imbraced the true religion.

master vnto thee.
16 He shal dwel with thee, *euen* amóg you,
in what place he shal chose, in one of thy
"cities where it liketh him best: thou shalt
not vexe him.

"Ebr. gates.

17 ¶There shalbe no whore of the daughters of Israél, nether shal there be a who-
rekeper of the sonnes of Israél.
18 Thou shalt nether bring the [i] hire of a
whore, nor ẏ price of a dog into the house
of the Lord thy God for anie vowe: for
euen bothe these *are* abominacion vnto
the Lord thy God.

i Forbidding hereby that anie gaine gotten of euil things, shulde be applied to the seruice of God, Mic.1,7.

19 ¶*Thou shalt not giue to vsurie to thy
brother: *as* vsurie of money, vsurie of meat,
vsurie of anie thing that is put to vsurie.

Exod.22,25. Leu.25,36.

20 Vnto a [k] stranger thou maiest lend vpõ
vsurie, but thou shalt not lend vpon vsurie vnto thy brother, that the Lord thy
God may [l] blesse thee in all that thou settest thine hand to, in the lãd whether thou
goest to possesse it.

k This was permitted for a time for the hardenes of their heart.
l If thou shewe thy charitie to thy brother, God wil declare his loue toward thee.

21 ¶When thou shalt vowe a vow vnto ẏ
Lord thy God, thou shalt not be slacke to
pay it: for the Lord thy God wil surely
require it of thee, and *so* it shulde be sinne
vnto thee.
22 But when thou absteinest from vowing,
it shalbe no sinne vnto thee.
23 That which is gone out of thy lippes,
thou shalt [m] kepe and performe, as thou
hast vowed it willingly vnto the Lord thy
God: *for* thou hast spokẽ it with thy mouth.

m If the vowe be lauful and godly.

24 ¶When thou cõmest vnto [n] thy neighbours vineyard, then thou maiest eat grapes at thy pleasure, as muche as thou wilt:
but thou shalt put none in thy [o] vessel.

n Being hired for to labour.
o To bring home to thine house.

25 Whẽ thou cõmest into thy neighbours
corne * thou maiest plucke the eares with
thine hand, but thou shalt not moue a sickle to thy neighbours corne.

Mat.12,1.

CHAP. XXIIII.

1 Diuorcement is permitted. 5 He that is newly maried is exempted from warre. 6 Of the pledge. 14 Wages must not be reteined. 16 The good must not be punished for the bad. 17 The care of the stranger, fatherles and widowe.

1 WHen a mã taketh a wife, and marieth her, if so be she finde no fauour in his eyes, because he hathe espied
some filthines in her, [a] then let him write
her a bil of diuorcemẽt, and put it in her
hand, and send her out of his house.

a Hereby God approueth not that light diuorcemẽt, but permitteth it to auoide further inconuenience, Matth.19,7.

2 And whẽ she is departed out of his house, and gone her way, and mary with an o-
ther man,
3 And if the later housband hate her, and
write her a letter of diuorcement, and put
it in her hãd, and send her out of his house, or if the later man dye which toke her
to wife:
4 *Then* her first housband, which sent her
away, may not take her againe to be his
wife, after that she is [b] defiled: for that *is*
abominacion in the sight of the Lord, and
thou shalt not cause ẏ lãd to sinne, which ẏ
Lord thy God doeth giue thee to inherit.

b Seing that by dimitting her, he iudged her to be vncleane and defiled.

5 ¶When a man taketh a newe wife, he shal
not go a warfare, [c] nether shalbe charged
with anie busines, but shalbe fre at home
one yere, and reioyce with his wife which
he hathe taken.

c That they might learne to knowe one anothers conditions and so afterward liue in godly peace.

6 ¶No man shal take the nether nor ẏ vpper [d] milstone to pledge: for this gage is
his liuing.

d Nor anie thĩg, whereby a man getteth his liuing.

7 ¶If anie man be found stealing anie of
his brethren of the children of Israél, and
maketh marchãdise of him, or selleth him,
that these shal dye. so shalt thou put euil
away from among you.
8 ¶Take hede of the* plague of leprosie,
that thou obserue diligently, & do according to all that the Priests of the Leuites
shal teache you: take hede ye do as I commanded them.

Leui.13,2.

9 Remember what the Lord thy God did
vnto *Miriám by the way after that ye were come out of Egypt.

Nom.12,10.

10 ¶When ẏ shalt aske againe of thy neigh
bour anie thing lent, thou shalt not go [e] into his house to fet his pledge.
11 But thou shalt stand without, and the mã
that borowed it of thee, shal bring ẏ pledge out of the dores vnto thee.

e As thogh ẏ woldest appoint what to haue, but shalt receiue what he may spare.

12 Furthermore if it be a poore bodie, thou
shalt not slepe with his pledge,
13 *But* shalt restore him the pledge when ẏ
sunne goeth downe, ẏ he may slepe in his
rayment, & blesse thee: & it shalbe righteousnes vnto thee, [f] before ẏ Lord thy God.

f Thogh he wolde be vnthãkeful, yet God wil not forget it.

14 ¶Thou shalt not oppresse an hired seruant that is nedy and poore, *nether* of thy
brethren, nor of the stranger that is in thy
land within thy gates.
15 * Thou shalt giue him his hire for his
day, nether shal the sunne go downe vpon
it: for he is poore, & therewith susteineth
his life: lest he crye against thee vnto the
Lord, and it be sinne vnto thee.

Leui.19,13. tob.4,15.

16 ¶*The fathers shal not be put to death
for the children, nor the children put to
death for the fathers, but euerie man shalbe put to death for his owne sinne.

2.King.4,1. 2.chro.25,4. iere.31,29. ezech.18,20.

17 ¶Thou shalt not peruert the right of the
[g] stranger, *nor* of the fatherles, nor take a
widowes raiment to pledge.
18 But remember that thou wast a seruant
in Egypt, & how the Lord thy God deliuered thee thence. therefore I commande
thee to do this thing.

g Because the world did least esteme these sortes of people, therefore God hathe moste care ouer them.

19 ¶*When ẏ cuttest downe thine haruest
in thy field, & hast forgotten a sheafe in
the field, thou shalt not go againe to fet
it, *but* it shalbe for the stranger, for the fatherles, & for the widow: that the Lord
thy God may blesse thee in all the workes

Leui.19,9. & 23,22.

of thine hands.
20 Whē thou″ beatest thine oliue tre, thou
shalt not go ouer the boughes againe, *but*
it shalbe for the stranger, for ẏ fatherles,
and for the widow.

″Or, gatherest thine oliues.

21 When thou gatherest thy ″ vineyard,
thou shalt not gather the grapes cleane
after thee, *but* thei shalbe for the stranger,
for the fatherles and for the widow.

″Or, the grapes of thy vineyard.

22 And remember that thou wast [h] a seruāt
in the land of Egypt: therefore I cōmāde thee to do this thing.

h God iudged thē not mindeful of his benefite, except they were beneficial vnto others.

CHAP. XXV.

3 The beating of the offenders. 5 To raise vp sede to the kinseman. 11 In what case a womans hand must be cut of. 13 Of iust weights, and measures. 19 To destroy the Amalekites.

1 WHen there shal be strife betwene
men, & they shal come vnto iudgement, [a] and sentēce shalbe giuen vpon
them, and the righteous shalbe iustified,
and the wicked condemned,
2 Then if so be the wicked be worthy to
be beaten, the iudge shal cause him to lye
downe, [b] and to be beaten before his face,
according to his trespas, vnto a certeine
nomber.
3 [c] Forty *stripes* shal he cause him to haue
and not past, lest if he shulde excede and
beat him aboue that with manie stripes,
thy brother shulde appeare despised in thy
sight.

a Whether there be a plaintife or none, ẏ magistrates oght to trie out fautes and punishe according to the crime.
b When the crime deserueth not death.
c The iewes of superstition afterward toke one awaie, 2 Cor 11,24.

4 ¶ * Thou shalt not mosel the oxe that
treadeth out the corne.
5 ¶ *If brethren dwel together, and one of
thē dye & haue no childe, the wife of the
dead shal not mary without: *that is*, vnto a
stranger, but his [d] kinseman shal go in
vnto her, and take her to wife, and do the
kinsmans office to her.
6 And the first borne which she beareth,
shal succede in the name of his brother
which is dead, that his name be not put
out of Israél.
7 And if the man wil not take his kinse woman,
then let his kinswoman go vp to the
gate vnto the Elders, and say, My kinsmā
refuseth to raise vp vnto his brother a name in Israél: he wil not do the office of a
kinsman vnto me.
8 Thē the Elders of his citie shal call him,
and comen with him: if he stand and say,
I wil not take her,
9 Then shal his kinswomā come vnto him
in the presence of the Elders, and lose his
shooe from his fote, & spit in his face, and
answer, and say, So shal it be done vnto
that man, that wil not buyld vp his brothers house.
10 And his name shalbe called in Israél,
The house of him whose shooe is put of.
11 ¶ [e] When men striue together, one with
another, if the wife of the one come nere,

1.Cor.9,9. 1.tim.5,18.
Ruth 4,3. matt.22,24. mar.12,19. luk.20,27.

d Because the Ebrewe worde signifieth not ẏ natural brother, & the worde, that signifieth a brother, is takē also for a kinseman: it semeth that it is not ment that the natural brother shuld mary his brothers wife, but some other of ẏ kinred, ẏ was in that degre ẇ might mary.

e This lawe imported, ẏ godly shamefastnes be preserued: for it is an horrible thing to se a woman past shame.

for to rid her housband out of the hands
of him that smiteth him, and put forthe
her hand, and take him by his priuities,
12 Then thou shalt cut of her hand: thine
eie shal not spare her.
13 ¶ Thou shalt not haue in thy bagge two
maner of ″ weightes, a great & a small,
14 Nether shalt thou haue in thine house
diuerse ″ measures, a great and a small:
15 *But* thou shalt haue a right & iust weight:
a perfit & a iust measure shalt thou haue, that thy dayes may be lengthened in ẏ
lād, which the Lord thy God giueth thee.
16 For all that do suche things, *and* all that
do vnrighteously, *are* abominacion vnto
the Lord thy God.
17 ¶ *Remēber what Amalék did vnto thee *Exod.17,8.*
by ẏ way, whē ye were come out of Egypt:
18 How he met thee by the way, and smote
the hindmost of you, all that were feble
behind thee, when thou wast fainted and
weary, and he feared not God.
19 Therefore, when the Lord thy God hathe giuen thee rest from all thine enemies
round about in the land, which the Lord
thy God giueth thee for an inheritance to
possesse it, *then* thou shalt put out the [f] remembrance of Amalék from vnder hea-
uen: forget not.

″Ebr. stone and stone.
″Ebr. Ephah & ephah: read Exod.16,36.
f This was partely accomplished by Saúl, about 450 yeres afterward.

CHAP. XXVI.

3 The offring of the first frutes. 5 What they must protest when they offer them. 12 The tithe of the third yere. 13 Their protestation in offring it 19 To what honour God preferreth them which acknowledge him to be their Lord.

1 ALso when thou shalt come into the
lād which the Lord thy God giueth
thee for inheritance, & shalt possesse it &
dwel therein,
2 [a] Then shalt thou take of the first of all ẏ
frute of the earth, and bring it out of the
land that the Lord thy God giueth thee,
& put it in a basket, & go vnto the place,
which the Lord thy God shal chose to
[b] place his Name there.
3 And thou shalt come vnto the Priest, ẏ
shalbe in those daies, and say vnto him, I
acknowledge this day vnto the Lord thy
God, ẏ I am come vnto the coūtrey ẇ the
Lord sware vnto our fathers for to giue vs.
4 Then the Priest shal take the basket out
of thine hand, & set it downe before the
altar of the Lord thy God.
5 And thou shalt answer & say before the
Lord thy God, a [c] Syrian *was* my father,
who being ready to perish *for hungre*, went
downe into Egypt, and soiourned there
ẇ a smale companie, and grewe there vnto a naciō great, mighty, [d] & ful of people.
6 And the Egyptians vexed vs, and troubled vs, and laded vs with cruel bondage.
7 But when we [e] cryed vnto the Lord God
of our fathers, the Lord heard our voyce,
and

a By this ceremonie they acknowledged ẏ they receiued the lād of Canáan as a fre gift of God.
b To be called vpō, serued, & worshiped spiritually, Chap.12,5.
c Meaning Iaakób who serued 20 yeres in Syria.
d Onely by Gods mercie, & not by their fathers deseruings.
e Alledging ẏ promises made to our fathers, Abrahám, Izhák, & Iaakób.

and loked on our aduersitie, and on our
labour, and on our oppresion.
8 And the Lord broght vs out of Egypt in
a mightie hand, and a stretched out arme,
with great terriblenes, bothe in signes &
wonders.
9 And he hathe broght vs into this place,
and hathe giuen vs this land, *euen* a land
that floweth with milke and hony.
10 And now, lo, I [f] haue broght the first
frutes of the land which thou, ô Lord, hast
giuen me, and thou shalt set it before the
Lord thy God, and worship before ẏ Lord
thy God:

f In token of a thankful heart, & mindful of this benefite.

11 And thou shalt reioyce in all the good
things which ẏ Lord thy God hathe giuen vnto thee and to thine [g] housholde, ẏ
and the Leuite, and the stranger that is a-
mong you.

g Signifing ẏ God giueth vs not goods for our selues onely, but for their vses also, which are committed to our charge.

12 ¶ When thou hast made an end of tithing all the tithes of thine increase, the
third yere, *which is* the yere of tithing, and
hast giuen it vnto the Leuite, to the stranger, to the fatherles and to the widowe,
that they may eat within thy gates, and
be satisfied,
13 Then thou shalt [h] say before the Lord
thy God, I haue broght the halowed thing
out of mine house, & also haue giuē it vnto ẏ Leuites & to the strangers, to the fatherles, and to the widowe, according to
all thy *commandements which thou hast
commanded me: I haue [i] transgressed none of thy commandements, nor forgotten
them.

h Without hypocrisie.

Chap. 14, 27.

i Of malice & contempt.

14 I haue not eaten thereof in my [k] mourning, nor suffred oght to perish [l] through
vnclennes, nor giuen oght thereof for the
dead, *but* haue hearkened vnto ẏ voyce of
the Lord my God: I haue done [m] after all
that thou hast commanded me.

k Or, for anie necessitie.

l By putting them to anie prophane vse.

m As farre as my sinneful nature wolde suffer: for els, as Dauid & Paul say, there is not one iust, Psal. 14, 4, rom. 3, 10.

15 Loke downe from thine holy habitaciō,
euen from heauen, & blesse thy people Israél, and the land which thou hast giuen vs
(as thou swarest vnto our fathers) the lād
that floweth with milke and honie.
16 ¶ This day the Lord thy God doeth cōmande thee to do these ordinances, and
lawes: kepe them therefore, and do them
with [n] all thine heart, and with all thy soule.

n With a good & simple conscience.

17 *Thou hast set vp the Lord this day to
be thy God, and to walke in his wayes,
and to kepe his ordinances, and his commandements, and his lawes, and to hearken vnto his voice.

Chap. 7, 6. & 14, 2.

18 [o] And the Lord hathe set thee vp this
day, to be a precious people vnto him (as
he hathe promised thee) & that thou shuldest kepe all his commandements,

o Signifing ẏ there is a mutual bōde betwene God & his people.

19 And to make thee *high aboue all naciōs
(which he hathe made) in praise, & in name and in glorie, *& that thou shuldest be
an holie people vnto the Lord thy God,
as he hathe said.

Chap. 4, 7. Chap. 7, 6. ver. 13, 11.

CHAP. XXVII.

2 They are cōmanded to write the Law vpon stones for a remembrāce, 5 Also to buylde an altar. 13 The cursings are giuen on mount Ebál.

1 THen Mosés with the Elders of Israél
[a] commanded the people, saying, Kepe all the commandements, which I commande you this day.

a As Gods minister & charged ẇ the same.

2 And when ye shal passe ouer Iordén vnto
the land which the Lord thy God giueth
thee, thou shalt set thee vp great stones, &
plaister them with plaister,
3 [b] And shalt write vpon thē all the wordes of this Lawe, when thou shalt come
ouer, that thou maiest go into the land ẇ
the Lord thy God giueth thee: a lād that
floweth with mylke and hony, as the Lord
God of thy fathers hathe promised thee.

b God wolde ẏ his Law shulde be set vp in the borders of the lād of Canáan, that all ẏ loked thereō might knowe that ẏ land was dedicate to his seruice.

4 Therefore when ye shal passe ouer Iordén, ye shal set vp these stones, which I cō
mande you this day in moūt Ebál, & thou
shalt plaister them with plaister.
5 *And there shalt thou buyld vnto ẏ Lord
thy God an altar, *euen* an altar of stones: ẏ
shalt lift none [c] yron *instrument* vpon thē.

Exod. 20, 25. iosh. 8, 31.

6 Thou shalt make the altar of ẏ Lord thy
God of whole stones, and offer burnt offrings thereon vnto the Lord thy God.
7 And thou shalt offer peace offrings, and
shalt eat there and reioyce before ẏ Lord
thy God:

c The altar shulde not be curiously wroght, because it shulde cōtinewe but for a time: for God wolde haue but one altar in Iudáh.

8 And thou shalt write vpon the stones all
the wordes of this Lawe, [d] wel, and plainly.

d That euerie one may wel read it and vnderstand it.

9 ¶ And Mosés & the Priests of the Leuites spake vnto all Israél, saying, Take hede & heare, ô Israél: this day thou art become the people of the Lord thy God.
10 Thou [e] shalt hearken therefore vnto the
voyce of the Lord thy God, and do his cō
mandements and his ordinances, which I
commande thee this day.

e This condition God hathe boūde thee vnto, that if ẏ wilt be his people, thou must kepe his Lawes.

11 ¶ And Mosés charged the people the same day, saying,
12 These shal stand vpon moūt Gerizzím,
to blesse the people when ye shal passe o-
uer Iordén: Simeón, & Leuí, & Iudáh, &
Issachár, & [f] Ioséph, & Beniamín.

f Meaning Ephráim & Manasséh.

13 And these shal stand vpon mount Ebál
to [g] curse: Reubén, Gád, & Ashér, & Zebulún, Dan, & Naphtalí.

g Signifying, that if they wolde not obey God for loue, they shulde be made to obey for fear.

14 And the Leuites shal answer & say vnto
all the men of Israél with a loude voyce,
15 ¶ Cursed be ẏ mā ẏ shal make anie carued
or moltē [h] image, *which is* an abominacion
vnto ẏ Lord, the worke of ẏ hāds of ẏ craf
tesmā, & putteth it in a secret place: And
all the people shal answer, & say: So be it.

h Vnder this he conteineth all ẏ corruptiō of Gods seruice, & the trāsgresion of ẏ first table.

16 Cursed be he that [i] curseth his father
& his mother: And all the people shal say:
So be it.

i Or, contemneth: & this aperteineth to ẏ secōd table.

17 Cursed be he that remoueth his neighbours [k] marke: And all the people shal say:
So be it.
18 Cursed be he that maketh the [l] blinde
go out of the way: And all the people shal
say: So be it.
19 Cursed be he that hindreth the right of
the stranger, the fatherles, & the widowe:
And all the people shal say: So be it.
20 Cursed be he that lieth with his fathers
wife: for he hathe vncouered his fathers
[m] skirt: And all ẏ people shal say: So be it.
21 Cursed be he that lieth with anie beast:
And all the people shal say: So be it.
22 Cursed be he that lieth with his sister,
the daughter of his father, or the daughter of his mother: And all the people shal
say: So be it.
23 Cursed be he that lieth with his [n] mother in lawe: And all the people shal say:
So be it.
24 Cursed be he that smiteth his neighbour
[o] secretly: And all the people shal say: So
be it.
25 *Cursed be he that taketh a rewarde to
put to death innocent blood: And all the
people shal say: So be it.
26 *Cursed be he that confirmeth not all ẏ
wordes of this Lawe, to do them: And all
the people shal say: So be it.

k He condemneth all iniuries & extorsions.

l Meanig, that helpeth not & conseleth not his neighbour.

m In committing vilenie against him.

n Meaning his wiues mother.

o For God, ẏ seeth in secret, wil reuenge it.

Ezek. 22, 12.

Gala. 3, 10.

CHAP. XXVIII.

1 The promises to them that obey the commandements. 15 The threatenings to the contrarie.

1 IF *thou shalt obey diligently the voyce
of the Lord thy God, and obserue and
do all his commandemẽts, which I commande thee this day, then the Lord thy
God wil [a] set thee on high aboue all the
nacions of the earth.
2 And all these blessings shal come on thee,
and [b] ouertake thee, if thou shalt obey the
voyce of the Lord thy God.
3 Blessed shalt thou be in the [c] citie, & blessed also in the field.
4 Blessed shalbe the frute [d] of thy body, &
the frute of thy ground, and the frute of
thy cattel, the increase of thy kine, & the
flockes of thy shepe.
5 Blessed shalbe thy basket and thy dough.
6 Blessed shalt thou be, when [e] thou comest
in, and blessed also when thou goest out.
7 The Lord shal cause thine enemies that
rise agaĩst thee, to fall before thy face: they
shal come out against thee one way, & shal
flee before thee [f] seuen wayes.
8 The Lord shal commande the blessing
to be with thee in thy store houses, & in all
that thou settest thine [g] hand to, and wil
blesse thee in the land which the Lord thy
God giueth thee.
9 The Lord shal make thee an holy people
vnto him selfe, as he hathe sworne vnto
thee, if thou shalt kepe the commãdemẽts

Leu. 26, 3.

a He wil make thee the moste excellẽt of all people.

b When thou thinkest thy selfe forsa ẽ.

c Thou shalt liue welthely.

d Thy children & succession.

e All thine enterprises shal haue good successe.

f Meaning, manie waies.

g God wil blesse vs if we do our duetie, & not be ydle

of the Lord thy God, and walke in his
waies.
10 Thẽ all people of the earth shal se that ẏ
Name of the Lord is [h] called vpon ouer
thee, and they shalbe afraid of thee.
11 And the Lord shal make thee plenteous
in goods, in the frute of thy body, & in the
frute of thy cattel, and in the frute of thy
ground, in the land which the Lord sware
vnto thy fathers, to giue thee.
12 The Lord shal open vnto thee his good
treasure, *euen* the [i] heauẽ to giue rayne vnto thy land in due season, and to blesse all
the worke of thine hands: and thou shalt
lend vnto many nacions, but shalt not borowe thy self.
13 And the Lord shal make thee the head,
and not the ″tayle, and thou shalt be aboue onely, and shalt not be beneth, if thou
obey the commandements of the Lord
thy God, which I commãde thee this day,
to kepe and to do *them*.
14 But thou shalt not decline from anie of
the wordes, which I commande you this
day, *ether* to the right hand or to the left,
to go after other gods to serue them.
15 ¶*But if thou wilt not obey the voyce of
the Lord thy God, to kepe and to do all
his commandements & his ordinances, ẇ
I commande thee this day, thẽ all these
curses shal come vpon thee, and ouertake
thee.
16 Cursed shalt thou be in the towne, and
cursed also in the field.
17 Cursed shal thy basket be, & thy ″dough.
18 Cursed shalbe ẏ frute of thy body, and ẏ
frute of thy land, the increase of thy kine,
& the flockes of thy shepe.
19 Cursed shalt thou be when thou comest
in, and cursed also when thou goest out.
20 The Lord shal send vpon thee cursing,
trouble, and ″shame, in all that which thou
settest thine hand to do, vntil thou be destroyed, and perish quickely, because of ẏ
wickednes of thy workes whereby thou
hast forsaken me.
21 The Lord shal make the pestilence cleaue vnto thee, vntil he hathe cõsumed thee
from the land, whether thou goest to possesse it.
22 *The Lord shal smite thee with a consumption, and with ẏ feauer, and with a
burning ague, and with feruent heat,
″and with the sword, and with blasting,
and with the mildewe, and they shal pursue thee vntil thou perish.
23 And thine heauẽ that is ouer thine head,
shalbe [k] brasse, and the earth that is vnder
thee, yron.
24 The Lord shal giue thee for the raine
of thy land, dust and ashes: *euen* from ″hea-
uen shal it come downe vpon thee, vntil
thou be destroyed.

h In that he is thy God and thou art his people.

i For nothing in the earth is profitable, but whẽ God sendeth his blessings from heauen.

″Or, the lowest.

Leu. 26, 14. lament. 2, 17. mala. 2, 2. baru. 1, 20.

″Or, store.

″Or, rebuke.

Leui. 26, 16.

″Or, drought.

k It shal giue thee no more moysture, then if it were of brasse.

″Or, out of the ayre, as dust raised with winde.

25 *And* the Lord ſhal cauſe thee to fall before thine enemies: thou ſhalt come out
one way againſt them, and ſhalt flee ſeuen wayes before them, and ſhalt be [l] ſcatered through all the kingdomes of the
earth.

l Some read, yͧ ſhalt be a terrour & feare, when thei ſhal heare how God hathe plagued thee.

26 And thy [m] carkeis ſhal be meat vnto
all foules of the ayre, and vnto the beaſtes of the earth, and none ſhal fray them
away.

m Thou ſhalt be curſed bothe in thy life and in thy death: for yͤ buryal is a teſtimonie of the reſurrection, wͨ ſigne for thy wickednes yͧ ſhalt lacke.

27 The Lord wil ſmite thee with yͤ botche
of Egypt, and with the emeroides, & with
the ſkab, and with the itche, that thou
canſt not be healed.
28 And the Lord ſhal ſmite thee with madnes, and with blindnes, & with aſtonying
of heart.
29 Thou ſhalt alſo grope at noone daies, as
the [n] blinde gropeth in darckenes, & ſhalt
not proſper in thy waies: thou ſhalt neuer
but be oppreſſed with wrong, & be poul-
led euermore & no man ſhal ſuccour *thee*.

n In things moſte euident & cleare thou ſhalt lacke diſcretion & iudgement.

30 Thou ſhalt betrothe a wife, & another
man ſhal lie with her: thou ſhalt buylde an
houſe, and ſhalt not dwel therein: thou
ſhalt plant a vineyarde and ſhalt not "eat
the frute.

"Ebr. make it commune.

31 Thine oxe ſhal be ſlayne before thine
eies, and thou ſhalt not eat thereof: thine
aſſe ſhalbe violently takē away before thy
face, and ſhal not be reſtored to thee: thy
ſhepe ſhalbe giuen vnto thine enemies, &
no man ſhal reſcue *them* for thee.
32 Thy ſonnes and thy daughters ſhalbe
giuen vnto another people, and thine eies
[o] ſhal ſtil loke for them, euen til they fall
out, and there ſhal be no power in thine
hand.

o When they ſhal returne from their captiuitie.

33 The frute of thy land & all thy labours
ſhal a people, which thou knoweſt not, eat,
and thou ſhalt neuer but ſuffer wrong, and
violence alway:
34 So that thou ſhalt be mad for the ſight
which thine eies ſhal ſe.
35 The Lord ſhal ſmite thee in the knees, &
in the thighes, with a ſore botche, that
thou canſt not be healed: euen frō the ſole
of thy fote vnto the top of thine head.
36 The Lord ſhal bring thee & thy [p] King
(which thou ſhalt ſet ouer thee) vnto a nacion, which nether thou nor thy fathers
haue knowen, and there thou ſhalt ſerue
other gods: *euen* wood and ſtone,

p As he did Manaſſeh, Ioachim, Zedechias & others

37 And thou ſhalt *be a wonder, a prouerbe
& a cōmune talke among all people, whether the Lord ſhal cary thee.

Iere.24,9. & 25,9.

38 * Thou ſhalt cary out muche ſede into yͤ
field, and ſhalt gather but litle in: for the
greſhoppers ſhal deſtroye it.

Mich.6,15. ag.1,6.

39 Thou ſhalt plante a vineyarde and dreſ-
ſe it, but ſhalt nether drinke of the wine,
nor gather *the grapes*: for the wormes ſhal
eat it.
40 Thou ſhalt haue oliue trees in all thy
coaſtes, but ſhalt not anoint thy ſelf with
the oyle: for thine oliues ſhal "fall.

"*Or, be ſhaken, before thei be ripe.*

41 Thou ſhalt beget ſonnes, and daughters,
but ſhalt not haue them: for thei ſhal go
into captiuitie.
42 All thy trees and frute of thy lād [q] ſhal
the greſhopper conſume.

q Vnder one kinde he conteineth all the vermine, wͨ deſtroye the frutes of the land: and this is an euident token of Gods curſe.

43 The ſtranger that is among you, ſhal
clime aboue thee vp on hye, & thou ſhalt
come downe beneth alowe.
44 He ſhal lend thee, and thou ſhalt not
lend him: he ſhalbe the head, & thou ſhalt
be the taile.
45 Moreouer, all theſe curſes ſhal come vpon thee, and ſhal purſue thee and ouertake
thee, til thou be deſtroyed, becauſe thou
obeyedſt not the voyce of the Lord thy
God, to kepe his commandements, & his
ordinances, which he commanded thee:
46 And thei ſhalbe vpon [r] thee for ſignes
and wonders, and vpon thy ſede for euer,

r Gods plagues ſhalbe euident ſignes yͤ he is offended with thee.

47 Becauſe thou ſeruedſt not the Lord thy
God with ioyfulnes & with a good heart
for the abundance of all things.
48 Therefore thou ſhalt ſerue thine enemies
which the Lord ſhal ſend vpon thee, in
honger and in thurſt, and in nakednes, and
in nede of all things: & he ſhal put a yoke
of yron vpon thy necke vntil he haue deſtroyed thee.
49 The Lord ſhal bring a nacion vpō thee
from far, *euen* from the end of the worlde,
flying *ſwift* as an egle: a nacion whoſe
tongue thou ſhalt not vnderſtand:
50 A nacion of a "fierce countenāce, which
wil not regarde the perſone of the olde,
nor haue compaſsion of the yong.

"*Or, barbarous, cruel, or impudent.*

51 The ſame ſhal eat the frute of thy cattel, and the frute of thy land vntil thou be
deſtroied, and he ſhal leaue thee nether
wheat, wine, nor oyle, *nether* the "increaſe
of thy kyne, nor the flockes of thy ſhepe,
vntil he haue broght thee to noght.

"*Or, firſtborne of thy bullockes.*

52 And he ſhal beſiege thee in all thy cities, vntil thine hye and ſtrong walles fall
downe, wherein yͧ truſtedſt in all the land:
and he ſhal beſiege thee in all thy "cities
throughout all thy land, which the Lord
thy God hathe giuen thee.

"*Or, gates.*

53 *And thou ſhalt eat the frute of thy bodie: *euen* the fleſh of thy ſonnes and thy
daughters, which the Lord thy God
hathe giuen thee, during the ſiege and
ſtraitnes wherein thine enemie ſhal inclo-
ſe thee:

Leui.26,29. 2 king.6,29. lamen.4,10. baruk.2,3.

54 *So that* the man (that is tender and exceding deintie among you) *ſhalbe grieued
at his brother and at his wife, *that lyeth* in
his boſome, & at the remnant of his children, which he hathe yet left,

Chap.15,9.

55 For feare of giuing vnto anie of them
of the fleſh of his children, whome he ſhal

eat, because he hathe nothing left him in
that siege, and straitnes, wherewith thine
enemie shal besiege thee in all thy cities.

f As came to passe in ӯ daies of Iorám, King of Israél, 2.King 6,29, and when the Romains besieged Ierusalem.

56 The tender and deintie f woman a-
mong you, which neuer wolde venture to
set the sole of her fote vpon the grounde
(for her softnes and tédernes) shalbe grieued at her housband, *that lyeth* in her bosome, and at her sonne, & at her daughter,

t Hungre shal so bite her, ӯ she shal be ready to eat her childe before it be deliuered.

57 And at her t afterbyrth (that shal come out from betwene her fete) and at her
children, which she shal beare: for whẽ all
things lacke, she shal eat them secretly,
during the siege and straitnes, wherewith
thine enemie shal besiege thee ĩ thy cities.

u For he that offendeth in one, is giltie of all, Iam 2,10.

58 ¶If thou wilt not kepe and do u all the
wordes of this Lawe (that are written in
this boke) & feare this glorious & feareful
Name THE LORD THY GOD,
59 Then the Lord wil make thy plagues
wonderful, & the plagues of thy sede, *euen*
great plagues and of long continuance, &
sore diseases, and of long durance.
60 Moreouer, he wil bring vpõ thee all the
diseases of Egypt, whereof thou wast a-
fraied, and thei shal cleaue vnto thee.

x Declaring ӯ God hathe infinite meanes to plague the wicked, besides them that are ordinarie or written.

Chap.10,22.

61 And euerie sickenes, and euerie plague,
which is not x written in the boke of this
Lawe, wil the Lord heape vpon thee, vntil thou be destroyed.
62 And ye shalbe left fewe in nomber, where ye were as the *starres of heauẽ in multitude, because thou woldest not obey the
voyce of the Lord thy God.
63 And as the Lord hathe reioyced ouer
you, to do you good, & to multiplie you,
so he wil reioyce ouer you, to destroye
you, and bring you to noght, and ye shalbe rooted out of the land, whether thou
goest to possesse it.

y Signifying ӯ it is a singular gift of God to be in a place where as we may worship God purely & declare our faith & religion.

64 And the Lord shal y scatter thee amõg
all people, frõ the one end of the worlde
vnto the other, and there thou shalt serue
other gods, which thou hast not knowen
nor thy fathers, *euen* wood and stone.
65 Also amõg these nacions thou shalt finde no rest, nether shal the sole of thy fote
haue rest: for the Lord shal giue thee there a trembling heart, and *loking to returne*
til thine eies fall out, & a sorouful minde.

°Or, thou shalt be in doute of thy life.

66 And thy life shal ° hang before thee, and
thou shalt feare bothe night and day, and
shalt haue none assurance of thy life.
67 In the morning thou shalt say, Wolde
God it were euening, and at euening thou
shalt say, Wolde God it were morning,
for the feare of thine heart, which thou
shalt feare, and for the sight of thine eies,
which thou shalt se.

z Because thei were vnmindeful of that miracle, whẽ the Sea gaue place for thẽ to passe through.

68 And the Lord shal bring thee into Egypt
againe with z shippes by the way, whereof I said vnto thee, Thou shalt se it no
more againe: & there ye shal sel your selues vnto your enemies for bondemen and
bonde women, & there *shalbe* no byer.

CHAP. XXIX.

2 The people are exhorted to obserue the cõmandements. 10 The whole people from the hiest to the lowest are cõprehẽded vnder Gods couenãt 19 The punishmẽt of him that flatereth him selfe in his wickednes. 24 The cause of Gods wrath against his people.

1 THese are the a wordes of the couenant which the Lord cõmanded Moses to make with the children of Israél in
the lãd of Moáb beside the couenãt which
he had made with them in b Horéb.

a That is, the articles, or cõdicions.

b At the first giuing of the Lawe, which was fourtie yeres before.

2 ¶And Mosés called all Israél, & said vnto them, Ye haue sene all that the Lord
did before your eies in the land of Egypt
vnto Pharaóh and vnto all his seruants, &
vnto all his land,
3 The c great tentacions which thine
eies haue sene, those great miracles and
wonders:

c The profes of my power.

4 Yet the Lord hathe not d giuen you an
heart to perceiue, and eies to se, and eares
to heare, vnto this day.

d He sheweth that it is not in mãs power to vnderstand the mysteries of God, if it be not giuen him from aboue.

5 And I haue led you fourtie yere in the
wildernes: your clothes are not waxed olde vpon you, nether is thy shooe waxed
olde vpon thy fote.
6 Ye haue eaten no e bread, nether dronke wine, nor strong drinke, that ye might
knowe, how that I am ӯ Lord your God.

e Made by mans arte, but manna, which is called the bread of Angels.

7 After ye came vnto this place, and Sihón
King of Heshbón, and Og King of Bashán came out against vs vnto battel, and
we slewe them,
8 And toke their land, and gaue it for an
inheritance vnto the Reubenites, and to ӯ
Gadites, & to the half tribe of Manasséh.
9 *Kepe therefore the wordes of this couenãt & do them, that ye may prosper in all
that ye shal do.

Chap.4,6.

10 Ye stand this day euerie one of you before the Lord your f God: your heades
of your tribes, your Elders and your officers, *euen* all the men of Israél:

f Who knoweth your heartes, & therefore ye may not thinke to dissemble ẇ him.

11 Your children, your wiues, & thy stranger that is in thy campe frõ the hewer of
thy wood, vnto the drawer of thy water,
12 That thou shuldest g passe into the couenant of the Lord thy God, and into his
othe which the Lord thy God maketh
with thee this day,

g Alluding to them, ӯ when they made a sure couenant, deuided a beast in twaine, and past betwene the partes deuided, Gen.15, 10.

13 For to establish thee this day a people
vnto him self, & that he may be vnto thee
a God, as he hathe said vnto thee, and
as he hathe sworne vnto thy fathers, A-
brahám, Izhák, and Iaakób.
14 Nether make I this couenant, and this
othe with you onely,
15 But *aswel* with him that standeth here
with vs this day before ӯ Lord our God,
as with him h that is not here with vs
this day.

h Meaning, their posteritie.

16 For ye knowe, how we haue dwelt in the
land

land of Egypt, and how we passed through
the middes of the nacions, which ye passed by.
17 And ye haue sene their abóminacions &
their idoles (wood, and stone, siluer & golde) which were among them,
18 That there shulde not be amõg you mã
nor woman, nor familie, nor tribe, which
shulde turne his heart away this day from
the Lord our God, to go & serue the gods
of these naciõs, & that there shulde not be
amõg you [i] *anie* roote that bringeth fourth
gall and wormewood,
19 So that when he heareth the wordes of
this curse, he 'blesse him selfe in his heart,
saying, I shal haue peace, althogh I walke according to the stubbernes of mine
owne heart, thus adding [k] dronkennes to
thirst.
20 The Lord wil not be merciful vnto him,
but then the wrath of the Lord and his
ielousie shal smoke against that man, and
euerie curse that is written in this boke,
shal light vpon him, and the Lord shal put
out his name from vnder heauen,
21 And the Lord shal separate him vnto
euil out of all the tribes of Israél, according vnto all the curses of the couenant,
that is written in the boke of this Lawe.
22 So that the [l] generacion to come, *euen*
your children, that shal rise vp after you,
and the stranger that shal come from a far
land, shal say, when they shal se the plagues of this land, and the diseases thereof,
wherewith the Lord shal smite it:
23 (*For* all that lãd *shal* burne with brimstone and salt: it shal not be sowen, nor bring
fourth, nor anie grasse shal growe therein,
like as in the ouerthrowing of * Sodom,
& Gomoráh, Admáh, & Zeboím, which
the Lord ouerthrewe in his wrath and in
his angre)
24 Then shal all nacions say, *Wherefore
hathe the Lord done thus vnto this land?
how fearce *is* this great wrath?
25 And they shal answer, Because they haue
forsaken the couenant of the Lord God
of their fathers, which he had made with
them, when he broght them out of the lãd
of Egypt,
26 And went and serued other gods & worshipped them: *euen* gods which they knewe not, & 'which had giuen them nothing,
27 Therefore the wrath of the Lord waxed
hote against this land, to bring vpon it e-
uerie curse that is written in this boke.
28 And the Lord hathe rooted them out of
their land in angre, and in wrath, and in
great indignacion, and hathe cast them into another land, as *appeareth* this day.
29 The [m] secret things *belong* to the Lord
our God, but ỹ things reueiled *belong* vnto
vs, and to our children for euer, that we
may do all the wordes of this Lawe.

i Suche sinne, as the bitter frute thereof might choke & destroye you.

'Or, flatter.

k For as he ỹ is thirsty, desireth to drinke muche, so he ỹ followeth his appetites, seketh by all meanes, & yet can not be satisfied.

l Gods plagues vpon the stiffe rebell against him, shal be so strange, that all ages shalbe astonied.

Gene.19,25.

1.King.9,8. Ier.22,8.

'*Or, which had not giuen them a land to possesse.*

m Mosés herby reproueth their curiositie, which seke those things ỹ are only knowen to God: & their negligẽce, that regarde not that, ỹ God hath reueiled vnto them, as the Lawe.

CHAP. XXX.

1 Mercie shewed when thei repent. 6 The Lord doeth circumcise the heart 11 All excuse of ignorance is taken away. 19 Life and death is set before thẽ. 20 The Lord is their life which obey him.

1 NOw whẽ all these things shal come
vpon thee, *ether* the blessing or the
curse which I haue set before thee, and ỹ
shalt [a] turne into thine heart, among all ỹ
nacions whether the Lord thy God hathe
driuen thee,
2 And shalt returne vnto ỹ Lord thy God,
and obey his voyce in all that I commãde
thee this day: thou, & thy children with all
thine [b] heart and with all thy soule,
3 Then ỹ Lord thy God wil cause thy captiues to returne, and haue compassion vpon thee, & wil returne, to gather thee out
of all the people, where ỹ Lord thy God
had scatered thee.
4 Thogh thou werest cast vnto the vtmost
parte of [c] heauen, from thence wil ỹ Lord
thy God gather thee, & from thence wil
he [d] take thee,
5 And the Lord thy God wil bring thee
into the land which thy fathers possessed,
and thou shalt possesse it, and he wil shewe thee fauour, and wil multiplie thee a-
boue thy fathers.
6 And the Lord thy God wil [e] circumcise
thine heart, and the heart of thy sede, that
thou maist loue the Lord thy God with
all thine heart, and with all thy soule, that
thou maist liue.
7 And the Lord thy God wil lay all these
curses vpon thine enemies, and on them,
that hate thee, and that persecute thee.
8 [f] Returne thou therefore, & obey the voice of the Lord, & do all his commandements, which I commande thee this
day.
9 And ỹ Lord thy God wil make thee plẽ-
teous in euerie worke of thine hand, in ỹ
frute of thy body, and in the frute of thy
cattel, and in the frute of the land for thy
welth: for ỹ Lord wil turne againe & [g] reioyce ouer thee to do thee good, as he reioyced ouer thy fathers,
10 Because thou shalt obey the voyce of
the Lord thy God, in keping his commãdements, & his ordinãces, which are written in the boke of this Lawe, when thou
shalt returne vnto the Lord thy God with
all thine heart & with all thy soule.
11 ¶For this commandement which I commande thee this day, is [h] not hid frõ thee,
nether is it farre of.
12 It is not in heauẽ, that thou shuldest say,
*Who shal go vp for vs to heauen, and
bring it vs, and cause vs to heare it, that
we may do it?
13 Nether is it beyonde the [i] sea, that thou

a By calling to remẽbrãce, both his mercies & his plagues.

b In true repẽtance is none hypocrisie.

c Euen to the worldes end.

d And bring thee into thy countrey.

e God wil purge all thy wicked affections: ỹ thing is not in thine owne power to do.

f If we wil haue God to worke in vs with his holy Spirit, we must turne againe to him by repentance.

g He meaneth not that God is subiect to these pasiõs, to reioyce or to be sad: but he vseth this maner of speache to declare the loue ỹ he beareth vnto vs.

h The Law is so euidẽt that none can pretẽd ignorance.

Rom.10,6.

i By heauen & ỹ sea he meaneth places most farre distant.

shuldest say, Who shal go ouer the sea for
vs, & bring it vs, and cause vs to heare it,
that we may do it?

k Euen the Lawe & the Gospel.
l By faith in Christ.

14 But the [k] worde is verie nere vnto thee:
euen in thy mouth & in thine heart, for
to [l] do it.
15 Beholde, I haue set before thee this day
life & good, death and euil.

m So that to loue & obey God, is onely life & felicitie.
n He addeth these promises to signifie that it is for our profit ŷ we loue him, & not for his.

16 In that I commande thee this day, [m] to
loue the Lord thy God, to walke in his
wayes, & to kepe his commandements, &
his ordinances, & his lawes ŷ thou maiest
[n] liue & be multiplied, and that the Lord
thy God may blesse thee in the land, whether thou goest to possesse it.
17 But if thine heart turne away, so that ŷ
wilt not obey, but shalt be seduced & worship other gods, and serue them,
18 I pronounce vnto you this day that ye
shal surely perish, ye shal not prolõg your
dayes in the lãd whether thou passest ouer
Iordén to possesse it.

Chap. 4, 26.

19 *I call heauen & earth to recorde this
day against you, *that* I haue set before you
life and death, blessing and cursing. therfore [o] chose life, that *bothe* thou & thy sede
may liue,

o That is, loue & obey God: which thing is not in mãs power, but Gods spirit onely worketh it in his elect.

20 By louing the Lord thy God, by obeyĩg
his voyce, & by cleauing vnto him: for he
is thy life, and the length of thy dayes:
that thou maist dwel in the land which the
Lord sware vnto thy fathers, Abrahám,
Izhák and Iaakób, to giue them.

CHAP. XXXI.

1, 7 Mosés preparing him selfe to dye, appointeth Ioshúa to rule the people. 9 He giueth the Law to the Leuites, that they shulde read it to the people. 19 God giueth thẽ a song as a witnes betwene him & them. 23 God confirmeth Ioshúa. 29 Mosés sheweth them that they wil rebel after his death.

1 Then Mosés went & spake these wordes vnto all Israél,
2 And said vnto them, I am an hundreth &
twentie yere olde this day: I [a] can no more
go out & in: also ŷ Lord hathe said vnto
me, *Thou shalt not go ouer this Iordén.

a I can no longer execute mine office.
Nomb. 20, 12. chap. 3, 26.

3 The Lord thy God he wil go ouer before
thee: he wil destroy these nacions before
thee, & thou shalt possesse them. *Ioshúa,
he shal go before thee, as the Lord hathe
said.

Nom. 27, 18.

4 And the Lord shal do vnto thẽ, as he dyd
to *Sihón & to Og Kings of the Amorites, & vnto their lãd whome he destroyed.

Nom. 21, 24.

5 And the Lord shal giue thẽ [b] before you
that ye may do vnto them according vnto euerie *commandement, which I haue
commanded you.

b Into your handes.
Chap. 7, 2.

6 Plucke ″vp your hearts therefore, and be
strong: dread not, nor be afrayd of them:
for the Lord thy God him selfe doeth go
with thee: he wil not fayle thee, nor forsake thee.

″Or, be of good courage.

7 ¶ And Mosés called Ioshúa, and said vnto him in the sight of all Israél, Be [c] of a
good courage and strong: for thou shalt
go with this people vnto the land which
the Lord hathe sworne vnto their fathers,
to giue them, and thou shalt giue it them
to inherit.

c For he that must gouerne ŷ people, hathe nede to be valiant to represse vice, & constant to mainteine vertue.

8 And the Lord him selfe doeth [d] go before thee: he wilbe ŵ thee: he wil not fayle
thee, nether forsake thee: feare not *therefore*, nor be discomforted.

d Signifying that man can neuer be of good courage, except he be persuaded of Gods fauour & assistance.

9 ¶ And Mosés wrote this Lawe, and deliuered it vnto the Priestes ŷ sonnes of Leuí (which bare the Arke of the couenant
of the Lord) and vnto all the Elders of
Israél,
10 And Mosés commanded them, saying,
*Euerie seuenth yere *whẽ ŷ yere of fre-
dome *shalbe* in the feast of the Tabernacles:

Nehem. 8, 8. Chap. 15, 1.

11 When all Israél shal come to appeare
[e] before the Lord thy God, in the place
which he shal chose, thou shalt read this
Lawe before all Israél that they may heare it.

e Before ŷ Arke of the couenãt, which was the signe of Gods presence, & the figure of Christ.

12 Gather the people together: men, & women, and children, and thy stranger that is
within thy gates, that they may heare, and
that they may learne, and feare the Lord
your God, and kepe, and obserue all ŷ wordes of this Lawe,
13 And that their children which [f] haue not
knowen it, may heare it, and learne to feare the Lord your God, as long as ye liue
in the land, whether ye go ouer Iordén to
possesse it.

f Which were not borne whẽ the Lawe was giuen.

14 ¶ Then the Lord said vnto Mosés, Beholde, thy dayes are come, that thou must
dye: Call Ioshúa, & stãd ye in the Tabernacle of the Congregacion that I may giue him a ″charge. so Mosés & Ioshúa wẽt,
and stode in the Tabernacle of the Congregacion.

″*Or, commandement.*

15 And the Lord appeared in ŷ Tabernacle, in the piller of a [g] cloude: & the piller
of the cloude stode ouer the dore of the
Tabernacle.

g In a cloude that was facioned like a piller.

16 ¶ And ŷ Lord said vnto Mosés, Beholde,
thou shalt slepe with thy fathers, and this
people wil rise vp, and go a whoring after
the gods of a strange land (whether they
go) *to dwel* therein, & wil forsake me, and
breake my couenant which I haue made
with them.
17 Wherefore my wrath wil waxe hote a-
gainst them at ŷ day, & I wil forsake them,
& wil [h] hide my face frõ them: then they
shalbe consumed, and many aduersities &
tribulacions shal come vpon them: so then
they wil say, Are not these troubles come
vpon me, because God is not with me?

h That is, I wil take my fauour frõ thẽ: as to turne his face toward vs, is to shewe vs his fauour.

18 But I wil surely hide my face in ŷ day,
because of all the euil, which they shal cõmit, in ŷ they are turned vnto other gods.

19 Now

19 Now therefore write ye this [i] song for
you, and teache it the children of Isráél:
put it in their mouthes, that this song may
be my witnes against the children of Israél.

i To preserue you and your childrẽ frõ idolatrie, by remẽbring Gods benefites.

20 For I wil bring them into the lãd (which
I sware vnto their fathers) that floweth
with milke and honie, and they shal eat,
and fil them selues, and waxe fat: [k] then
shal they turne vnto other gods, and serue them, and contemne me, & breake my
couenant.

k For this is the nature of flesh, no lõger to obey God, then it is vnder the rod.

21 And then when manie aduersities and
tribulacions shal come vpon them, this
song shal [l] answer them to their face as a
witnes: for it shal not be forgotten out
of the mouthes of their posteritie: for I
knowe their imaginacion, which they go
about euen now, before I haue broght thẽ
into the land which I sware.

l That these euils are come vpon them, because they for soke me.

22 ¶ Mosés therefore wrote this song the same day and taught it the children of Israél.

23 And God gaue Ioshúa the sonne of Nun
a charge, and said, *Be strong, and of a good courage: for thou shalt bring the children of Isráél into the land, which I sware vnto them, and I wil be with thee.

Iosh.1,6.

24 ¶ And when Mosés had made an end of
writing the wordes of this Lawe in a boke vntil he had finished them,

25 Then Moses commanded the Leuites,
which bare the Arke of the couenant of ẏ
Lord, saying,

26 Take the boke of this Law, and put ye
it in the side of the Arke of the couenant
of the Lord your God, that it may be there for a [m] witnes against thee.

m Of thine infidelitie, whẽ ẏ shalt turne away frõ the doctrine conteined thereĩ.

27 For I knowe thy rebellion and thy stiffe
necke: beholde, I being yet aliue with you
this day, ye are rebellious against the
Lord: how muche more then after my
death?

28 Gather vnto me all the Elders of your
tribes, and your [n] officers, that I may
speake these wordes in their audience,
and call heauen and earth to recorde a-
gainst them.

n As gouerners, iudges, & magistrates.

29 For I am sure that after my death ye wil
vtterly be corrupt and turne from the
way, which I haue commanded you: therefore euil wil come vpon you at the
length, because ye wil commit euil in
the sight of ẏ Lord, by prouoking him to
angre through the [o] worke of your hãdes.

o By idolatrie, worshiping images, ẇ are the worke of your hãds.

30 Thus Mosés spake in the audiẽce of all
the Congregacion of Isráél the wordes
of this song, vntil he had ended them.

CHAP. XXXII.

7 The song of Mosés cõteining Gods benefites toward the people. 15 And their ingratitude toward him. 20 God menaceth them. 21 And speaketh of the vocation of the Gentiles. 46 Mosés commandeth to teache the Lawe to the childrẽ. 49 God forewarneth Mosés of his death.

1 HEarken, ye [a] heauẽs, and I wil speake:
and let the earth heare the wordes of
my mouth.

a As witnesses of this peoples ingratitude.

2 My [b] doctrine shal drop as the raine, *and*
my speache shal stil as doeth the dewe, as
the showre vpon the herbes, and as the
great raine vpon the grasse.

b He desireth that he may speake to Gods glorie, & that the people, as the grene grasse, may receiue the dewe of his doctrine.

3 For I wil publishe the Name of ẏ Lord:
giue ye glorie vnto our God.

4 Perfect is ẏ worke of the [c] mighty God:
for all his wayes *are* iudgement. God is
true, and without wickednes: iust, & righteous is he.

c The Ebrewe worde is rocke: noting ẏ God onelie is mightie, faithful, and constãt in his promes.

5 They haue corrupted them selues toward
him by their vice, not being his children,
but a frowarde and crooked generacion.

6 Do ye so rewarde ẏ Lord, ô foolish people and vnwise? is not he thy father, that
hathe boght thee? he hathe [d] made thee,
and proportioned thee.

d Not according to ẏ cõmune creaciõ, but by a new creature by his Spirit.

7 ¶ Remember the dayes of olde: consider
the yeres of so manie generaciõs: aske thy
father, and he wil shewe thee: thine Elders,
and they wil tel thee.

8 Whẽ the most hie *God* deuided to the nacions their inheritance, when he separated
ẏ sonnes of Adám, he appointed the borders of the [e] people according to the nomber of the children of Isráél.

9 For the Lords porcion *is* his people: Iaakób *is* the lot of his inheritance.

e When God by his prouidence deuided the worlde, he lẽt for a time that portiõ to the Canaanites, which shulde after be an inheritãce for all his people Isráél.

10 He founde him in the land of the wildernes, in a waste, and roaring wildernes:
he led him about, he taught him, *and* kept
him as the apple of his eye.

11 As an egle stereth vp her nest, [f] flotereth
ouer her birdes, stretcheth out her wings,
taketh them, *and* beareth them on her
wings,

f To teache them to flie.

12 *So* the Lord alone led him and there was
no * strange god with him.

*Or, god of strãge nacion.

13 He caried him vp to the hie places of the
[g] earth, that he might eat ẏ frutes of the
fields, and he caused him to sucke [h] hony
out of the stone and oyle out of the hard
rocke:

g Meaning of the lãd of Canáán, which was hie, in respect of Egypt.
h That is, abũdance of all things euen in the very rockes.

14 Butter of kine, and milke of shepe with
fat of the lambs, and rams fed in Bashán,
and goates, with the fat of the graines of
wheat, and the red * licour of the grape
hast thou dronke.

*Ebr. blood.

15 ¶ But *he that shulde haue bene* [i] vpright,
when he waxed fat, spurned with his hele:
thou art fat, thou art grosse, thou art laden with fatnes: therefore he forsoke God
that made him, and regarded not the strõg
God of his saluacion.

i He sheweth what is the principal end of our vocacion.

16 They prouoked him with [k] strange
gods: they prouoked him to angre with
abominacions.

k By chãging his seruice for their superstitions.

17 They offred vnto deuils, not to God,
but to gods whome they knewe not: [l] newe

l Scripture calleth newe, whatsoeuer mã inuẽteth, be the error neuer so olde.

gods that came newly vp, whome their fathers feared not.
18 Thou hast forgotten the mightie God,
that begate thee, & hast forgottē God that
formed thee.
19 The Lord then sawe it, and was angry,
for the prouocacion of his [m] sonnes and
of his daughters.

m He calleth the Gods children, not to honour them, but to shewe them from what dignitie they are fallen.

20 And he said, I wil hide my face frō thē:
I wil se what their end shalbe: for they a-
re a frowarde generacion, childrē in whome is no faith.
21 They haue moued me to ielousie with
that which is not God: they haue prouoked
me to angre with their vanities: * and I
wil moue them to ielousie with *those which*
are no [n] people: I wil prouoke them to angre with a foolish nacion.

Rom.10,19.

n Which I haue not fauoured, nor giuen my Lawes vnto them.

22 For fire is kindled in my wrath, & shal
burne vnto the bothome of hel, & shal cōsume the earth with her increase, & set on
fire the fundacions of the mountaines.
23 I wil spend plagues vpon them: I wil bestowe mine arrowes vpon them.
24 *They shalbe* burnt with hunger, and consumed with heat, and with bitter destruction: I wil also send the teeth of beastes
vpon them, with the venime of serpents *cre*
ping in the dust.
25 The sworde shal [o] kil them without, and
in the chambers feare bothe the yong mā
and the yong woman, the suckeling with
the man of graye heere.

o They shalbe slaine bothe in the field & at home.

26 I haue said, I wolde scatter thē abroade:
I wolde make their remembrance to cease
from among men,
27 Saue that I feared the furie of the enemie, lest their aduersaries shulde [p] waxe
proude, & lest they shulde say, Our hye
hand & not the Lord hathe done all this.

p Reioycing to se the godly afflicted, & attributing that to them selues ẇ is wroght by Gods hād.

28 For they are a nacion voyde of counsel,
nether is there *anie* vnderstanding in thē.
29 Oh that they were wise, *then* they wolde
vnderstād this: they wolde [q] cōsider their
later end.

q They wolde consider ẏ felicitie, that was prepared for them, if they had obeyed God.

30 Howe shulde one chase a thousand, and
two put tē thousād to flight, except their
strong God had solde them, & the Lord
had ″shut them vp?

″Or, deliuered them to their enemis.

31 For their god *is* not as our God, euen our
enemies being iudges.
32 For their vine *is* of the vine of Sodom, &
of the vines of Gomoráh: their grapes *are*
grapes of gall, their clusters *be* bitter.
33 Their [r] wine *is* the poyson of dragons,
and the cruel gall of aspes.

r The frutes of the wicked are as poyson, detestable to God and dangerous for man.

34 Is not this laid in store with me, & sealed vp among my treasures?
35 *Vengeance and recompense are mine:
their fote shal slide in due time: for the
daye of their destruction is at hand, and
the things that shal come vpon them, make haste.

Eccles.28,1. rom.12,19. ebr.10,30.

36 For the Lord shal iudge his people, and
″repent toward his seruants, when he seeth
that their power is gone, and none [s] shut
vp *in holde* nor left *abroad.*

″Or, change his minde.
s When nether strōg nor weake in a maner remaine.

37 When men shal say, Where are their
gods, their mightie God in whome they
trusted?
38 Which did eat the fat of their sacrifices,
and did drinke the wine of their drinke
offring? let them rise vp, and helpe you: let
him be your refuge.
39 Beholde now, for I, I am he, and there is
no gods with me: * I kil, and giue life: I
wounde, & I make whole: * nether is there *anie* that can deliuer out of mine hand.

1.King.2,6. tob.13,2. Wisd.16,13.

40 For I [t] lift vp mine hand to heauen, &
say, I liue for euer.

t That is, I sweare, read Gen.14,22.

41 If I whet my glittering sworde, and mine hand take holde on iudgement, I wil
execute vengeance on mine enemies, and
wil rewarde them that hate me.
42 I wil make mine arrowes dronke with
blood, (and my sworde shal eat flesh) for
the blood of the slaine, & of the captiues,
when I beginne to take vengeance of the
enemie.
43 *Ye nations, praise his people: for he wil
auenge the [u] blood of his seruants, and
wil execute vengeance vpon his aduersaries, and wil be merciful vnto his land,
and to his people.

Rom.15,10.
u Whether ẏ blood of Gods people be shed for their sinnes, or trial of their faith, he promiseth to reueng it.

44 ¶ Then Mosés came and spake all the
wordes of this song in the audience of
the people, he and ″Hoshéa the sunne of
Nun.

″Or, Ioshúa.

45 When Mosés had made an end of speaking all these wordes to all Israél,
46 Then he said vnto them, * Set your hearts vnto all the wordes which I testifie
against you this day, that ye may cōmande them vnto your childrē, that they may
obserue and do all the wordes of this
Lawe.

Chap.6,6. & 11,18.

47 For it is no [x] vaine worde concerning
you, but it is your life, and by this worde
ye shal prolong your dayes in the land,
whether ye go ouer Iordén to possesse it.

x For I wil performe my promes vnto you, Isa.55,10.

48 *And the Lord spake vnto Mosés the
selfe same day, saying,

Nom.27,12.

49 Go vp into this mountaine of Abarím,
vnto ẏ mount Nebó, which is in the land
of Moáb, that is ouer against Ierichó: and
beholde the land of Canáan, which I giue
vnto ẏ children of Israél for a possession,
50 And dye in the moūt which thou goest
vp vnto, and thou shalt be * gathered vnto thy people, * as Aarón thy brother
dyed in moūt Hor, and was gathered vnto his people,

Gen.25,8. Nom.20,25. & 33,38.

51 Because ye * trespassed against me amōg
the children of Israél, at the waters ″of
Meribáh, at Kadésh in the wildernes of
Zin: for ye [y] sanctified me not among the
children

Nom.20,12. & 27,14.
″Or, of strife.
y Ye were not earnest and cōstant to mainteine mine honour.

children of Iſraél.
52 Thou ſhalt therefore ſe the land before
thee, but ſhalt not go thither, *I meane*, into
ẏ land which I giue the childrẽ of Iſraél.

CHAP. XXXIII.

*1 Mosés before his death bleſſeth all the tribes of Iſraél.
26 There is no God like to the God of Iſraél. 29 Nor
anie people like vnto his.*

1 NOw this is the [a] bleſſing wherewith
Mosés the man of God bleſſed the
childrẽ of Iſraél before his death, & ſaid,
2 The Lord came from Sinái, and roſe vp
from Seír vnto them, *and* appeared clearely from mount Parán, and he came with
ten [b] thouſands of Saintes, *and* at his
right hand a firy Lawe for them.
3 Thogh he loue the people, *yet* [c] all
thy Saintes are in thine hands: & they are
humbled at [d] thy fete, to receiue thy
wordes.
4 Mosés cõmãded vs a Lawe for an [e] inheritãce of the Cõgregacion of Iaakób.
5 Thẽ "he was among the "righteous *people*,
as King, when the heades of the people,
and the tribes of Iſraél were aſſembled.
6 ¶ Let [f] Reubén liue, and not dye, thogh
his men be a ſmall nomber.
7 ¶ And thus *he bleſſed* Iudáh, & ſaid, Heare,
ô Lord, the voice of Iudáh, & bring him
vnto his people: his hands ſhalbe [g] ſufficient for him, if thou helpe him againſt
his enemies.
8 ¶ And of Leuí he ſaid, Let thy *Thũmím
& thine Vrím be w̄ thine holy one, whome
thou dideſt proue in Maſſáh, *and* dideſt
cauſe him to ſtriue at ẏ waters of Meribáh.
9 Who ſaid vnto his father and to his mother, [h] I haue not ſene him, nether knewe he his brethren, nor knewe his owne
children: for they obſerued thy worde, &
kept thy couenant.
10 Thei ſhal teache Iaakób thy iudgemẽts,
and Iſraél thy Lawe: they ſhal put incens
before thy face, & the burnt offring vpon
thine altar.
11 Bleſſe, ô Lord, his ſubſtance, and accept
the worke of his hands: [i] ſmite through
the loines of thẽ that riſe againſt him, and
of them that hate him, that they riſe not
againe.
12 ¶ Of Beniamín he ſaid, The beloued of
the Lord ſhal [k] dwel in ſafety by him: *the
Lord* ſhal couer him all the day long, and
dwel betwene his ſhulders.
13 ¶ And of Ioséph he ſaid, Bleſſed of the
Lord is *his* land for the ſwetenes of heauẽ,
for the dewe, and "for the depth lying beneth,
14 And for the ſwete increaſe of the ſunne,
and for the ſwete increaſe of the moone,
15 And for *the ſwetenes* of the top of the ancient mountaines, and for the ſwetenes of
the olde hilles,

[a] This bleſſing cõteineth not onely a ſimple prayer, but an aſſurance of the effect thereof.
[b] Meaning, infinit Angels.
[c] Ebr. his Saintes, that is the childrẽ of Iſraél.
[d] As thy diſciples.
[e] To vs and our ſucceſſors.
" *Or, Mosés.*
" *Or, Iſraél.*
[f] Reubẽ ſhalbe one of the tribes of Gods people, thogh for his ſinne his honour be diminiſhed & his familie but ſmale.
[g] Signifying that he ſhulde hardely obteine Iaakobs pmes, Gen. 49,8.
Exod. 28,30.
[h] He preferred Gods glorie to all natural affection, Exod 32,29.
[i] He declareth that the miniſters of God haue manie enemies, & therefore haue nede to be prayed for.
[k] Becauſe the temple ſhulde be buylt in Zion, w̄ was in the tribe of Beniamin, he ſheweth that God ſhulde dwel with him there.
" *Or, founteines.*

16 And for the ſwetenes of the earth, & abũdance thereof: & the good wil of him that
dwelt in the [l] buſhe, ſhal come vpon the
head of Ioséph, and vpon the top of the
head of him that was *ſeparated *from* his
brethren.
17 His beautie *ſhalbe like* his firſt borne bullocke, and "his hornes *as* the hornes of an
vnicorne: with them he ſhal ſmite the
people together, *euen* the ends of the
worlde: theſe are alſo the ten thouſands
of Ephráim, and theſe are the thouſands
of Manaſſéh.
18 ¶ And of Zebulún he ſaid, Reioyce, Zebulún, in thy [m] going out, and *thou*, Iſſha-
chár, in thy tentes.
19 They ſhal call the people vnto the "mountaine: there they ſhal offer the ſacrifices
of righteouſnes: for [n] they ſhal ſucke of
the abundance of the ſea, and of the treaſures hid in the ſand.
20 ¶ Alſo of Gad he ſaid, Bleſſed be he that
enlargeth Gad: he dwelleth as a lion, that
catcheth for his pray ẏ arme w̄ the head.
21 And he loked to him ſelfe at the beginning, becauſe there was a porcion of the
[o] Lawegiuer hid: yet he ſhal come with
the heads of the people, to execute the iuſtice of the Lord, & his iudgements with
Iſraél.
22 ¶ And of Dan he ſaid, Dan *is* a lions
whelpe: he ſhal leape from Baſhán.
23 ¶ Alſo of Naphtalí he ſaid, ô Naphtalí,
ſatiſfied with fauour, and filled with the
bleſſing of the Lord, poſſeſſe [p] the Weſt
and the South.
24 ¶ And of Aſhér he ſaid, Aſhér *ſhalbe* bleſſed with children: he ſhalbe acceptable
vnto his brethren, and ſhal dip his fote in
oyle.
25 Thy ſhooes *ſhalbe* [q] yron and braſſe,
and thy ſtrength *ſhal continue* as long as
thou liueſt.
26 ¶ There is none like God, ô righteous
people, which rideth vpon the heauens for
thine helpe, & on ẏ cloudes in his glorie.
27 The eternal God *is thy* refuge, and vnder
his armes thou arte for euer: he ſhal caſt
out the enemie before thee, and wil ſay,
Deſtroy *them*.
28 Thẽ Iſraél [r] the fouteine of Iaakób ſhal
dwel alone in ſafety in a land of wheat &
wine: alſo his heauẽs ſhal drop the dewe.
29 Bleſſed art thou, ô Iſraél: who is like vnto
thee, ô people ſaued by the Lord, ẏ ſhylde
of thine helpe, & which is ẏ ſworde of thy
glorie? therefore [ſ] thine enemies ſhalbe in
ſubiection to thee, & thou ſhalt tread vpõ
their hie places.

CHAP. XXXIIII.

*1 Mosés ſeeth all the land of Canáan. 5 He dyeth.
8 Iſraél wepeth. 9 Ioſhúa ſucedeth in Mosés rowme.
10 The praiſe of Mosés.*

[l] Which was, God appearing vnto Mosés, Exod. 3,2.
Gen. 49,26.
" *Or, ſtrength.*
[m] In thy proſperous viages vpon the ſea, Gen. 49,13.
" *Or, mõut Zión.*
[n] The tribe of Zebulún.
[o] So that the portion of the Gadites, and others on this ſide Iordén was Gods, thogh it was not ſo knowẽ.
[p] Meaning, nere the ſea.
[q] Thou ſhalt be ſtrong, or thy countrey ful of metal. It ſemeth that Simeón is left out becauſe he was vnder Iudáh, & his porciõ of his inheritãce, Ioſh. 19,9.
[r] Who was plentiful in iſſue as a founteine.
[ſ] Thine enemies for feare ſhal lie & faine to be in ſubiection.

1 THen Moſés went from the plaine of
Moáb vp into mount [a] Nebó vnto
the top of Piſgáh that is ouer againſt Ierichó: and the Lord ſhewed him * all the lãd
of Gileád, vnto Dan,
2 And all Naphtalí and the land of E-
phráim and Manaſséh, and all the land of
Iudáh, vnto the vtmoſt [b] ſea:
3 And the South, and the plaine of the valley of Ierichó, the citie of palmetrees, vnto Zoár.
4 And the Lord ſaid vnto him, * This is yͤ
land which I ſware vnto Abrahám, to Izhák & to Iaakób, ſaying, I wil giue it vnto
thy ſede: I haue cauſed thee to ſe it with
thine eyes, but yͧ ſhalt not go ouer thither.
5 So Moſés the ſeruant of the Lord dyed
there in the land of Moáb, according to yͤ
worde of the Lord.
6 And [c] he buryed hĩ in a valley in yͤ lãd of
Moáb ouer againſt Beth-peór, but no mã
knoweth of his ſepulchre vnto [d] this day.
7 Moſés was now an hũdreth & twẽty yere
olde whẽ he dyed: his eye was not dimme,
nor his natural force abated.
8 And the children of Iſraél wept for Moſés in the plaine of Moáb thirty dayes: ſo
the dayes of weping and mourning for
Moſés were ended.
9 And [e] Ioſhúa the ſonne of Nun was ful
of the ſpirit of wiſdome: for Moſés had
put his hands vpon him. And the children
of Iſraél were obedient vnto him, and did
as the Lord had commanded Moſés.
10 But there aroſe not a Prophet ſince in
Iſraél like vnto Moſés (whome the Lord
knewe [f] face to face)
11 In all the miracles and wonders which
the Lord ſent him to do in the land of E-
gypt before Pharaóh and before all his
ſeruants, and before all his land,
12 And in all that mighty [g] hand and all
that great feare, which Moſés wroght in
the ſight of all Iſraél.

a Which was a parte of mount Abarim, Nomb.27,12. *Chap.3,27. 2.mac.2,4.*

b Called, Mediterraneum.

Gen.12,7. & 13,15.

c To wit, the Angel of the Lord, Iude 9.

d That the iewes might not haue occaſion thereby to cõmit idolatrie.

e Hereby appeareth the fauour of God that leaueth not his Church deſtitute of a gouernour.

f Vnto whome the Lord did reueile him ſelfe ſo plainely.

g Meaning, the power of God working by Moſés in the wildernes.

THE BOKE OF IOSHVA.

THE ARGVMENT.

IN this boke the holy Goſt ſetteth moſte liuely before our eyes the accompliſhement of Gods promes, who as he promiſed by the mouthe of Moſes, that a Prophet ſhulde be raiſed vp vnto the people like vnto him, whome he willeth to obey, Deut.18,15: ſo he ſheweth him ſelfe here true in his promes, as at all other times, and after the deathe of Moſes his faithful ſeruant, he raiſeth vp Ioſhúa to be ruler and gouernour ouer his people, that nether they ſhulde be diſcouraged for lacke of a captaine, nor haue occaſion to diſtruſt Gods promiſes hereafter. And becauſe that Ioſhúa might be confirmed in his vocation, and the people alſo might haue none occaſion to grudge, as thogh he were not approued of God: he is adorned with moſte excellent giftes and graces of God, bothe to gouerne the people with counſel, and to defend them with ſtrength, that he lacked nothing which ether belonged to a valiant captaine or a faithful miniſter. So he ouercometh all difficulties and bringeth them in to the land of Canáan: the which according to Gods ordinance he deuideth among the people & appointeth their borders: he eſtabliſheth lawes and ordinances, and putteth them in remembrãce of Gods manifolde benefites, aſſuring them of his grace and fauour, if they obey God, and contrariewiſe of his plagues and vengeance, if they diſobey him. This hiſtorie doeth repreſent Ieſus Chriſt the true Ioſhúa, who leadeth vs into eternal felicitie, which is ſignified vnto vs by this land of Canáan. From the beginning of the Geneſis to the end of this boke are conteined 2597 yeres. For from Adám vnto the flood are 1656. from the flood vnto the departure of Abrahám out of Caldea, 363. and from thence to the death of Ioſeph 290. So that the Geneſis conteineth 2390. Exodus 140. the other thre bokes of Moſes 40. Ioſhúa 27. So the whole maketh 2597 yeres.

CHAP. I.

2 The Lord incourageth Ioſhúa to inuade the lãd. 4 The borders and limites of the lãd of the Iſraelites. 5 The Lord promiſeth to aſsiſt Ioſhúa, if he obey his worde. 11 Ioſhúa commandeth the people to prepare thẽ ſelues to paſſe ouer Iordén, 12 And exhorteth the Reubenites to execute their charge.

NOw after yͤ [a] death of Moſés the ſeruãt of the Lord,
yͤ Lord ſpake vnto Ioſhúa
the ſonne of Nun, Moſés
miniſter, ſaying,
2 Moſés my ſeruãt is de-
ad: now therefore ariſe,
go ouer this Iordén, thou, and all this people, vnto the land which I giue them, *that
is*, to the children of Iſraél.
3 * Euerie place that the ſole of your fote
ſhal tread vpon, haue I giuẽ you, as I ſaid
vnto Moſés.
4 * Frõ the [b] wildernes and this Lebanón
euen vnto yͤ great Riuer, the riuer * Peráth:
all the land of the [c] Hittites, euen vnto
the great [d] ſea toward the going downe
of the ſunne, ſhal be your coaſt.
5 There ſhal not a man be able to withſtãd
thee all the dayes of thy life: as I was with
Moſés, ſo wil I be with thee: * I wil not
leaue thee, nor forſake thee.

a The beginning of this boke dependeth on the laſt chap. of Deut, which was writen by Ioſhúa as a preparaciõ to his hiſtorie.

Chap.14,9.

Deut.11,24.

b Of Zin, called Kadéſh & Parán.

* Or, Euphrates.

c Meaning the whole land of Canáan.

d Called, Mediterraneum.

Ebr.13,5.

6 Be

6 Be ftrong and of a good courage: for vnto this people fhalt thou deuide the land
for an inheritance, which I fware vnto
their fathers to giue them.
7 Onely be thou ftrong, "and of a mofte
valiant courage, that thou maieft obferue
and do according to all the Lawe which
Mofés my feruant hathe commãded thee:
*thou fhalt not turne away from it to the
right hãd, nor to the left, that thou maieft
[e] profper whetherfoeuer thou goeft.

"Or, growe ftrõnger & ftronger.
Deut.5,32.
e He fheweth wherein confifteth true profperitie, euen to obey the worde of God.

8 Let not this boke of the Lawe departe
out of thy mouth, but meditate therein
day and [f] night, that thou maieft obferue & do according to all that is written
therein: for then fhalt thou make thy way
profperous, & then fhalt thou " haue good
fucceffe.

f Shewĩg that it was not poffible to gouerne wel without cõtinual ftudie of Gods worde.
"Or, gouerne wifely.

9 Haue not I commanded thee, faying, Be
ftrong and of a good courage, feare not
nor be difcouraged? for I the Lord thy
God *wilbe* with thee, whetherfoeuer thou
goeft.
10 ¶ Then Iofhúa commanded the officers
of the people, faying,
11 Paffe through the hofte, and commande
the people, faying, Prepare you vitailes:
for [g] after thre daies ye fhal paffe ouer
this Iordén, to go in to poffeffe the land,
which the Lord your God giueth you to
poffeffe it.

g Meaning, frõ the day ỳ this was proclaimed.

12 ¶ And vnto the Reubenites, and to the
Gadites, and to halfe the tribe of Manaf-
féh fpake Iofhúa, faying,
13 *Remember the worde, which Mofés the
feruant of the Lord commãded you, faying, The Lord your God hathe giuen you
reft, and hathe giuen you this [h] land.

Nomb 32,20.
h Which belonged to Sihón the King of the Amorites, & Og Kĩg of Bafhán.

14 ¶ Your wiues, your childrẽ, & your cattel fhal remaine in the land which Mofés
gaue you on " this fide Iordén: but ye fhal
go ouer before your brethren armed, all
that be men of warre, & fhal helpe them,
15 Vntil the Lord haue giuen your brethrẽ
reft, afwel as to you, & vntil thei alfo fhal
poffeffe the land, which ỳ Lord your God
giueth them: then fhal ye returne vnto the
land of your poffefsion and fhal poffeffe
it, which *land* Mofés the Lords feruant
[i] gaue you on this fide Iordén towarde
the funne rifing.

"Or, beyonde Iordén, frõ Ierichó.
i By your requeft, but yet by Gods fecret appointemẽt, Deut.33,21

16 Then thei anfwered Iofhúa, faying, All
that thou haft commanded vs, we wil do,
and whetherfoeuer thou fendeft vs, we
wil go.
17 As we obeyed Mofés in all things, [k] fo
wil we obey thee: onely the Lord thy God
be with thee as he was with Mofés.
18 Whofoeuer fhal rebelle againft thy cõmandement, and wil not obey thy wordes
in all that thou commandeft him, let him
be put to death: onely be ftrõg & of good
courage.

k Thei do not onely promife to obey him fo lõg as God is w̃ him: but to helpe to punifh all that rebelle againft him.

CHAP. II.

1 Iofhúa fendeth mẽ to fpie Ierichó, whome Rahab hideth. 11 She confeffeth the God of Ifraél. 12 She requireth a figne for her deliuerance. 21 The fpies returne to Iofhúa with comfortable tidings.

1 THen Iofhúa the fonne of Nun fent
out of [a] Shittím two men to fpie fe-
cretly, faying, Go, vewe the land, and *alfo*
Ierichó: and thei went, and * came into an
" harlots houfe, named Raháb, and lodged there.

a Which place was in the plaine of Moáb nere vnto Iordén.
Ebr.11,21.
iam.2,25.
"Or, tauerners houfe, or hofter.

2 Then reporte was made to the King of
Ierichó, faying, Beholde, there came men
hether to night, of the children of Ifraél,
to fpie out the countrey.
3 And the King of Ierichó fent vnto Raháb, faying, [b] Bring forthe the mẽ that are
come to thee, *and* w̃ are entred into thine houfe: for thei be come to fearche out
all the land.
4 (But the woman had taken the two men,
and hid them) Therefore faid fhe thus,
There came men vnto me, but I wift not
whence thei were.

b Thogh the wicked fe the hand of God vpon them, yet thei repẽt not, but feke how thei may by their power refift his meanes.

5 And whẽ thei fhut the gate in the darcke,
the men went out, whether the men went
I wote not: followe ye after thẽ quickely,
for ye fhal ouertake them.
6 (But fhe had broght thẽ vp to the [c] roofe
of the houfe, & hyd them with the ftalkes
of flaxe, which fhe had fpread abroade vpon the roofe)

c Meaning, vpon the houfe: for then their houfes were flat aboue, fo ỳ they might do their bufines thereupõ.

7 And certeine men purfued after them,
the way to Iordén, vnto the fourdes, and
affone as thei which purfued after them,
were gone out, thei fhut the gate.
8 ¶ And before thei were a flepe, fhe came
vp vnto them vpon the roofe,
9 And faid vnto thẽ men, I knowe that the
Lord hathe giuen you the land, and that
the [d] feare of you is fallen vpon vs, and
that all the inhabitants of the land faint
becaufe of you.

d For fo God p̃mifed, Deut. 28,7. chap.5,1.

10 For we haue heard, how the Lord* dryed
vp the water of the read Sea before you,
when you came out of Egypt, and what
you did vnto the two Kings of the Amorites, that were on the other fide Iordén,
vnto* Sihón and to Og, whome ye vtterly
deftroyed:

Exod.14,21.
Nomb.21,24.

11 And when we hearde it, our heartes "did
faint, and there remained no more " courage in anie becaufe of you: for [e] the
Lord your God, he is the God in heauen
aboue, and in earth beneth.

"Or, melted.
"Or, fpirit.
e Herein appeareth the great mercie of God, ỳ in this commune deftruction he wolde drawe a mofte miferable finner to repẽt & confeffe his Name.

12 Now therefore, I pray you, fweare vnto
me by the Lord, that as I haue fhewed you
mercie, ye wil alfo fhewe mercie vnto my
fathers houfe, and giue me a true token,
13 And that ye wil faue aliue my father and
my mother, and my brethren, and my fi-
fters, and all that thei haue: & that ye wil

"Or, liues.

deliuer our" soules from death.

f We warrant you on peine of our liues.

14 And the mē answered her, f Our life for
you to dye, if ye vtter not this our busines: and when the Lord hathe giuen vs the
land, we wil deale mercifully and truely
with thee.
15 Then she let them downe by a corde
through the windowe: for her house *was*
vpon the towne wall, and she dwelt vpon
the wall.
16 And she said vnto them, Go you into the
g mountaine, lest the pursuers mete with
you, & hyde your selues there thre daies,
vntil the pursuers be returned: thē afterward may ye go your way.

g Which was nere vnto the citie.

17 And the men said vnto her, h We wil
be blameles of this thine othe, which thou
hast made vs sweare.

h We shal be discharged of our othe, if ȳ doest performe this condicion that foloweth: for so shalt ȳ & thine be deliuered.

18 Beholde, when we come into the land,
thou shalt binde this corde of red threde
in the windowe, whereby thou lettest vs
downe, and thou shalt bring thy father &
thy mother, and thy brethren, and all thy
fathers housholde home to thee.
19 And whosoeuer then doeth go out at the
dores of thine house into the streat, i his
blood shal be vpon his head, and we wil
be gylteles: but whosoeuer shal be with
thee in the house, his blood shalbe on our
head, if anie hand touche him:

i He shal be giltie of his owne death.

20 And if thou vtter this our k matter, we
wil be quit of thine othe, which thou hast
made vs sweare.

k So ȳ others shulde thinke to escape by the same meanes.

21 And she answered, Accordīg vnto your
wordes so be it: then she sent them away,
and they departed, and she bounde the" red
corde in the windowe.

"Or, scarlet couleured.

22 ¶ And they departed, and came into the
mountaine, & there abode thre daies, vntil the pursuers were returned: & the pursuers soght them throughout all the way,
but founde them not.
23 So the two men returned, and descended from the mountaine, & passed l ouer,
and came to Ioshúa the sonne of Nun, &
tolde him all things that came vnto them.
24 Also they said vnto Ioshúa, Surely the
Lord hathe deliuered into our hands all
the land: for euē all the inhabitants of the
countrey faint because of vs.

l To wit, the riuer Iordén.

CHAP. III.

1 Ioshúa commandeth them to departe whē the Arke remoueth. 7 The Lord promiseth to exalt Ioshúa before the people. 9 Ioshuas exhortacion to the people. 16 The waters parte asunder whiles the people passe.

1 THen Ioshúa rose verie early, & they
remoued from Shittím, and came to
a Iordén, he, & all the children of Israél, &
lodged there, before they went ouer.
2 And after b thre daies the officers went
throughout the hoste,
3 And cōmāded the people, saying, Whē
ye se ȳ Arke of the couenant of the Lord
your God, and the Priests of the Leuites
bearing it, ye shal departe from your place, and go after it.

a Which according to the Ebrewes was in Marche, and about 40 daies after Moses death.

b Which time was giuen for to prepare thé vitailes, Chap. 1, 11.

4 Yet there shalbe a space betwene you &
it, about" two thousand cubites by measure: ye shal not come nere vnto it, that ye
may knowe the way, by the which ye shal
go: for ye haue not gone this way in times
past.

"Or, a myle.

5 (Now Ioshúa had said vnto the people,
* Sanctifie your selues: for tomorowe the
Lord wil do wonders among you)
6 Also Ioshúa spake vnto the Priests, saying, Take vp the Arke of the couenant,
and go ouer before the people: so thei toke
vp the Arke of the couenant, and went before the people.

Leui. 20, 7. nomb. 11, 18. 1. sam. 16, 5. chap 7, 13.

7 ¶ Then the Lord said vnto Ioshúa, This
day wil I begin to magnifie thee in the
sight of all Israél, which shal knowe,
that* as I was with Mosés, so wil I be with
thee.

Chap. 1, 5.

8 Thou shalt therefore cōmāde the Priests
that beare the Arke of the couenant, saying, When ye are come to the brinke of
the waters of Iordén, ye shal stand stil c in
Iordén.

c Euen in the chanel, where ȳ streame had runne, as vers. 17.

9 ¶ Then Ioshúa said vnto the children of
Israél, Come hether, and heare the wordes
of the Lord your God.
10 And Ioshúa said, d Hereby ye shal knowe
that the liuing God is among you, & that
he wil certeinly cast out before you the
Canaanites, and the Hittites, and the Hiuites, and the Perizzites, and the Gerga-
shites, and the Amorites, and the Iebusites.

d By this miracle in deuiding ȳ water.

11 Beholde, the Arke of the couenant of the
Lord of all the worlde passeth before you
into Iordén.
12 Now therefore take from among you
e twelue men out of the tribes of Israél,
out of euerie tribe a man.

e Which shulde set vp twelue stones in remembrance of the benefite.

13 And assone as the soles of the fete of the
Priests (that beare the Arke of the Lord
God the Lord of all the worlde) shal stay
in the waters of Iordén, the waters of Iordén shalbe cut of: for the waters that come from aboue, * shal stand stil vpon an
heape.

Psal. 114, 3.

14 ¶ Then when the people were departed
from their tentes to go ouer Iordén, the
Priests bearing the * Arke of the couenāt,
went before the people.

Act. 7, 45.

15 And as thei that bare the Arke came vnto Iordén, and the fete of the Priests that
bare the Arke were dipped in the brinke
of the water, (* for Iordén vseth to fil all
his f bankes all the time of haruest)

Eccl. 24, 36.

16 Then the waters that came downe from
aboue, stayed *and* rose vpon an heape and
departed far frō the citie of Adám, ȳ was
beside Zaretán: but the *waters* that came
downe

f Because the riuer was accustomed at this time to be ful, the miracle is so muche ȳ greater.

downe towarde the Sea of the wildernes,
euen the salt Sea, failed, *and* were cut of: so
ẏ people went right ouer against Ierichó.
17 But the Priests that bare the Arke of the
couenant of the Lord, stode drye within
Iordén, g ready prepared, and all the Israelites went ouer drye, vntil all the people
were gone cleane ouer through Iordén.

g Ether tarying til the people were past, or, as some read, sure, as though they had bene vpõ the drye land.

CHAP. IIII.

2 God cõmãded Ioshúa to set vp twelue stones in Iordén. 18 The waters returne to their olde course. 20 Other twelue stones are set vp in Gilgál. 21 This miracle must be declared to the posteritie.

1 AND when all the people were wholly
gone * ouer Iordén, (after the Lord
had spoken vnto Ioshúa, saying,

Deut.27,2.

2 Take you twelue men out of the people,
out of euerie tribe a man,
3 And commande you them, saying, Take
you hence out of the middes of Iordén,
out of the place where the Priests stode
in a a readines, twelue stones, which ye
shal take away with you, and leaue them
in the b lodging, where you shal lodge
this night)

a As Chap.3, 17.

b Meaning, ẏ place where they shulde campe.

4 Then Ioshúa called the twelue mẽ, whome
he had prepared of the children of
Israél, out of euerie tribe a man,
5 And Ioshúa said vnto them, Go ouer before
the Arke of the Lord your God, euẽ
through the middes of Iordén, & take vp
euerie man of you a stone vpõ his shulder
according vnto the nomber of the tribes
of the children of Israél,
6 That this may be a signe among you,
that when your c children shal aske their
fathers in time to come, saying, What
meane you by these stones?

c God cõmãdeth, that not onely we our selues profit by his wonderful workes, but that our posteritie may knowe ẏ cause thereof & glorifie his Name.

7 Then ye may answer them, That the
waters of Iordén were cut of before the
Arke of the couenant of the Lord: *for* whẽ
it passed through Iordén, the waters of
Iordén were cut of: therefore these stones
are a memorial vnto the children of
Israél for euer.
8 Then the children of Israél did euẽ so, as
Ioshúa had cõmanded, & toke vp twelue
stones out of the middes of Iordén, as the
Lord had said vnto Ioshúa, according to
the nõber of the tribes of the children of
Israél, & caried thẽ away with them vnto
the lodging, and layed them downe there.
9 And Ioshúa set vp d twelue stones in the
middes of Iordén, in the place where the
fete of the Priests, which bare the Arke of
the couenant, stode, and there haue they
continued vnto this day.

d Besides the twelue stones which were caried by the tribes and set vp in Gilgál.

10 ¶ So the Priests, ẇ bare the Arke, stode
in the middes of Iordén, vntil euerie thing
was finished that the Lord had cõmanded
Ioshúa to say vnto the people, according
to all that Mosés charged Ioshúa: then the
people hasted and went ouer.
11 When all the people were cleane passed
ouer, the Arke of the Lord went ouer also,
and the Priests e before the people.

e Meaning, in the presence or sight of the people.

12 * And the sonnes of Reubén, & the sonnes
of Gad, and halfe the tribe of Manasséh
went ouer before the children of Israél
armed, as Mosés had charged them.

Nomb.32,28.

13 Euen fourty thousand prepared for warre,
went before the f Lord vnto battel,
into the plaine of Ierichó.

f That is, the Arke.

14 That day the Lord magnified Ioshúa in
the sight of all Israél, & they "feared him,
as they feared Mosés all dayes of his life.

" Or, reuerenced him.

15 And the Lord spake vnto Ioshúa, saying,
16 Commande the Priests that beare the
g Arke of the Testimonie, to come vp out
of Iordén.

g Because the Arke testified Gods presence, and the tables of the Law coteined therein, signified Gods wil toward his people.

17 Ioshúa therefore cõmanded the Priests,
saying, Come ẏe vp out of Iordén.
18 And when the Priests that bare the Arke
of the couenant of the Lord were come
vp out of the middes of Iordén, and assone
as ẏ soles of the Priests fete were set on
the drye land, the waters of Iordén returned
vnto their place, and flowed ouer all
the bankes thereof, as they did before.
19 ¶ So the people came vp out of Iordén
the tenth *day* of the h first moneth, and
pitched in Gilgál, in the Eastside of Ierichó.

h Called Abib or Nisán, conteining parte of Marche, and parte of April.

20 Also the twelue stones, which they toke
out of Iordén, did Ioshúa pitche ĩ Gilgál.
21 And he spake vnto the children of Israél,
saying, When your children shal aske
their fathers in time to come, and say,
What *meane* these stones?
22 Thẽ ye shal shewe your childrẽ, and say,
Israél came ouer this Iordén on drye lãd:
23 For ẏ Lord your God dryed vp the waters
of Iordén before you, vntil ye were
gone ouer, as the Lord your God did the
red Sea, * which he dryed vp before vs, til
we were gone ouer,

Exod.14,21.

24 That all the people of the i world may
know that the hãd of the Lord is mightie,
that ye might feare the Lord your God
continually.

i Gods benefits serue for a forther condemnation to the wicked, & stirre vp his to reuerence him, and obey him.

CHAP. V.

1 The Canaanites are afraide of the Israelites. 2 Circumcision is commanded the seconde time. 10 The Passeouer is kept. 12 Manna ceaseth. 13 The Angel appeareth vnto Ioshúa.

1 NOw whẽ all ẏ Kings of the a Amorites,
which were beyonde Iordén
Westward, and all the Kings of the Canaanites,
which were by ẏ Sea, heard that
the Lord had dryed vp ẏ waters of Iordén
before the childrẽ of Israél vntil they were
gone ouer, their heart fainted: and there
was no courage in them anie more because
of the children of Israél.

a The Amorites were on bothe sides Iordén, whereof two Kings were slaine already on the side toward Moáb.

2 ¶ That same time ẏ Lord said vnto Ioshúa,
* Make thee sharpe kniues, b *and*

Exod.4,25.

b For now they had left it of, about 40 yeres.

returne, and circumciſe the ſonnes of Iſraél the ſecond time.
3 Then Ioſhúa made him ſharpe kniues &
circumciſed the ſonnes of Iſraél in [c] the
hil of the foreſkinnes.

c Gilgál was ſo called, becauſe they were there circumciſed.

4 And this is the cauſe why Ioſhúa circũciſed all the people, *euen* the males that
came out of Egypt,becauſe all the men of
warre were dead in the wildernes by the
way after they came out of Egypt.
5 For all the people that came out were
circumciſed:but all the people that were
borne in the wildernes by the way after
they came out of Egypt,were [d] not circũciſed.

d For they loked daily to remoue at the Lords cõmandement: which thing they ÿ were newe circũciſed, colde not do without great danger.

6 For the children of Iſraél walked fourty
yeres in the wildernes, til all the people
of the men of warre that came out of E-
gypt were conſumed,becauſe they obeyed
not the voyce of the Lord: vnto whome
the Lord ſware, that he wolde not ſhewe
thẽ the land, * which the Lord had ſworne vnto their fathers, that he wolde giue
vs, *euen* a land that floweth with milke
and honie.

Nom.14,23.

7 So their ſonnes whome he raiſed vp in
their ſteade,Ioſhúa circumciſed:for they
were vncircũciſed, becauſe they circumciſed them not by the way.
8 And when they had made an end of cir-
cũciſing all the people, they abode in the
places in the cãpe til they [e] were whole.

e For their ſore was ſo grieuous,that they were not able to remoue.

9 After, the Lord ſaid vnto Ioſhúa, This
day I haue taken away the [f] ſhame of E-
gypt from you : wherefore he called the
name of that place Gilgál,vnto this day.

f By bringing you into this promiſed land cõtrary to the wicked opiniõ of the Egyptians : or the foreſkin,whereby you were like to the Egyptians.

10 ¶ So the childrẽ of Iſraél abode in Gilgál,and kept the feaſt of the Paſſoeuer the
fourtenth day of the moneth at euen in the
plaine of Ierichó.
11 And they did eat of the corne of the lãd,
on the morow after the Paſſeouer, vnleauened bread,and parched corne in the ſame day.
12 And the MAN ceaſed on the morowe
after they had eaten of the corne of the
land , nether had the children of Iſraél
MAN anie more , but did eat of the frute
of the land of Canáan that yere.
13 ¶ And when Ioſhúa was by Ierichó , he
lift vp his eyes and loked: and beholde,
there ſtode a * man againſt him, hauing a
ſworde drawen in his hand : and Ioſhúa
went vnto him,& ſaid vnto him, Art thou
on our ſide,or on our aduerſaries?

Exod.23,23.

14 And he ſaid, Nay,but *as* a captaine of
the hoſte of the Lord am I now come: thẽ
Ioſhúa fel on his face to the earth , and
[g] did worſhip, and ſaid vnto him , What
ſaith my Lord vnto his ſeruant?

g In that that Ioſhúa worſhippeth him, he acknoledgeth him to be God: & in that that he calleth him ſelfe ÿ Lords captaine, he declareth him ſelfe to be Chriſt.

15 And the captaine of the Lords hoſte ſaid
vnto Ioſhúa, * Loſe thy ſhooe of thy fote: for the place whereon thou ſtandeſt,
is holy:and Ioſhúa did ſo.

Exod.3,5. ruth 4,7. act.7,33.

CHAP. VI.

3 The Lord inſtructeth Ioſhúa what he ſhulde do,as touching Ierichó. 6 Ioſhúa commandeth the Prieſts and warriers what to do. 20 The walles fall. 22 Raháb is ſaued. 24 All is burnt ſaue golde and metal. 26 The curſe of him that buyldeth the citie.

1 NOw Ierichó was [a] ſhut vp,& [b] cloſed,[c] becauſe of the children of Iſra-
él:none might go out nor entre in.

a That none colde go out.
b That none colde come in.
c For feare of the Iſraelites.

2 And ÿ Lord ſaid vnto Ioſhúa, Beholde,
I haue giuen into thine hand Ierichó and
the King thereof, *and* the ſtrong men of
warre.
3 All ye therefore *that be* men of warre,ſhal
compaſſe the citie, in going round about
ÿ citie [d] once: thus ſhal you do ſix dayes:

d Euerie day.

4 And ſeuen Prieſts ſhal beare ſeuen trompets of [e] rams hornes before the Arke:&
the ſeuenth day ye ſhal compaſſe the citie ſeuen times,and the Prieſts ſhal blowe
with the trompets.

e That the cõqueſt might not be aſſigned to mãs power, but to ÿ mercie of God, which ẘ moſt weake things can ouercome that , which ſemeth moſte ſtrong.

5 And when they make a lõg *blaſt* with the
rams horne,& ye heare the ſounde of the
trompet,all the people ſhal ſhoute with a
great ſhoute: then ſhal the wall of the citie fall downe flat,and the people ſhal aſ-
cend vp,euerie man ſtreight before him.
6 ¶ Then Ioſhúa the ſonne of Nun called
the Prieſts & ſaid vnto them, Take vp the
Arke of the couenant,& let ſeuen Prieſts
beare ſeuen trompets of rams hornes before the Arke of the Lord.
7 But he ſaid vnto the people, [f] Go and
compaſſe the citie: and let him that is armed,go forthe before ÿ Arke of the Lord.

f This is chiefely ment by the Reubenites,Gadites,& halfe the tribe of Manaſſéh.

8 ¶ And when Ioſhúa had ſpoken vnto the
people, the ſeuen Prieſts bare the ſeuen
trompets of rams hornes,and went forthe
before the Arke of the Lord, and blewe
with the trõpets, and the Arke of the couenant of the Lord followed them.
9 ¶ And the men of armes wẽt before the
Prieſts,that blewe the trompets:then the
[g] gathering *hoſte* came after the Arke, as
they went and blewe the trompets.

g Meaning the rerewarde, wherein was ẏ ſtãderd of the tribe of Dan, Nomb.10,15.

10 (Now Ioſhúa had commãded the people,ſaying,Ye ſhal not ſhoute, nether make anie noyſe with your voice,nether ſhal
a worde procede out of your mouth, vntil the day that I ſay vnto you, Shoute,
then ſhal ye ſhoute)
11 So the Arke of the Lord compaſſed the
citie,and went aboute it [h] once:then they
returned into the hoſte,and lodged in the
campe.

h For that day.

12 And Ioſhúa roſe early in the morning,
& the Prieſts bare the Arke of the Lord:
13 Alſo ſeuen Prieſts bare ſeuen trompets
of rams hornes, and went before the Arke
of the Lord, and going blewe with the
trompets:and the men of armes went before them,but the [i] gathering *hoſte* came
after

i The tribe of Dã was ſo called, becauſe it marched laſt, and gathered vp whatſoeuer was left of others.

after the Arke of the Lord, as they went
and blewe the trompets.
14 And the second day thei compassed the
citie once, and returned into the hoste:
thus they did six dayes.
15 And when the seuēth day came, they rose early, euē with the dawning of the day,
and compassed the citie after the same
maner [k] seuen times: onely that day they
compassed the citie seuen times.

k Besides euerie day once for the space of six dayes.

16 And when the Priests had blowen the
trompets the seuēth time, Ioshúa said vnto the people, Shoute: for the Lord hathe
giuen you the citie.
17 And ẏ citie shalbe [l] an execrable thing,
bothe it, and all that are therein, vnto the
Lord: onely Raháb the harlot shal liue,
she, and all that are with her in the house:
for she * hid the messengers that we sent.

l That is, appointed wholy to be destroyed.

Chap.2,4.

18 Notwithstāding be ye ware of the execrable thing, lest ye make your selues execrable, & in taking of the execrable thing,
make also the hoste of Israél * execrable,
and trouble it.

Leu.27,21. nom.21,2. deut 13,15.

19 But all siluer, and golde, and vessels of
brasse, and yron shalbe [m] consecrate vnto
the Lord, *and* shal come into the Lords
treasurie.

m And therefore cā not be put to anie priuate vse, but must be first molten, & then serue for the Tabernacle.

20 So the people shouted, when they had
blowen trompets: for whē the people had
heard the sounde of the trompet, they
shouted with a great shoute: and the * wall
fel downe flat: so the people went vp into
the citie, euerie man streight before him:
* and they toke the citie.

Ebr.11,30.

2.Mac.12,15.

21 And they vtterly destroyed all that was
in the citie, bothe man and woman, yong,
and olde, and oxe, and shepe, and asse, with
the edge of the sworde.
22 But Ioshúa had said vnto the two men
that had spied out the countrey, Go into
the harlots house, and bring out thence
the woman, and all that she hathe, * as ye
sware to her.

Chap.2,14. ebr.11,31.

23 So the yong men that were spies, * went
in, and broght out Rahāb, and her father
and her mother, and her brethren, and all
that she had: also they broght out all her
familie, and put them [n] without the hoste of Israél.

n For it was not lauful for strangers to dwel amōg ẏ Israelites, til they were purged.

24 After they burnt the citie with fire, and
all that was therein: onely the siluer and
the golde, and the vessels of brasse and
yron, they put vnto the treasure of the
[o] house of the Lord.

o Meaning, ẏ Tabernacle.

25 So Ioshúa saued Rahāb the harlot, and
her fathers housholde, & all that she had,
& she [p] dwelt in Israél euē vnto this day,
because she had hid the messengers, which
Ioshúa sent to spie out Ierichó.

p For she was maried to Salmón, prince of the tribe of Iudáh, Mat 1,5.

26 ¶ And Ioshúa sware at ẏ time, saying,
Cursed be the man before the Lord, that
riseth vp, and buyldeth this citie Ierichó:
[q] he shal lay the fundacion thereof in his
eldest sonne, & in his yōgest sonne shal he
set vp the gates of it.

q He shal buil de it to the destruction of all his stocke, ẇ thing was fulfilled in Hiél of Beth-él, 1.King.16,34.

27 So the Lord was with Ioshúa, and he
was famous through all the worlde.

CHAP. VII.

1 The Lord is angry with Achán. 4 They of Aí put the Israelites to flight. 6 Ioshúa prayeth to the Lord. 16 Ioshúa inquireth out him that sinned, and stoneth him & all his.

1 BVt the children of Israél committed
a trespasse in the [a] excommunicate
thing: for * Achán the sonne of Carmí, the
sonne of Zabdí, the sonne of Zérah of ẏ
tribe of Iudáh toke of the excōmunicate
thing: wherefore the wrath of the Lord
was kindled against the children of Israél.

a In taking ẏ ẇ was cōmanded to be destroied.

Chap.22,20. 1.chro.2,7.

2 And Ioshúa sent men from Ierichó to
[b] Aí, which is beside Bethauén, on the East
side of Beth-él, and spake vnto them, saying, Go vp, and vewe the countrey. And
the men went vp, and vewed Aí,
3 And returned to Ioshúa, and said vnto hī,
Let not all ẏ people go vp, *but* let as it were two or thre thousand mē go vp, & smite
Aí, and make not all the people to labour
thether, for they are fewe.

b This was a citie of the Amorites: for there was another so called among the Ammonites, Iere.49,3. The first Aí is called Aiath, Isa. 10,28.

4 So there went vp thether of the people
about thre thousand men, & they fled before the men of Aí.
5 And the [c] men of Aí smote of them vpon
a thirtie and six men: for they chased them
from before the gate vnto Shebarím, and
smote them in the going downe: wherefore the heartes of the people melted away
like water.

c God wolde by this ouerthrowe make thē more earnest to search out and punish the sinne committed.

6 ¶ Then Ioshúa rent his clothes, and fel
to the earth vpon his face before the Arke
of the Lord, vntil the euentide, he, and the
Elders of Israél, and put dust vpon their
heades.
7 And Ioshúa said, Alas, ô Lord God, wherefore hast thou broght this people ouer
Iordén, to deliuer vs into the hand of the
Amorites, and to destroy vs? wolde God
we had bene contēt to dwel on the [d] other
side Iordén.

d This infirmitie of his faith sheweth how we are inclined of nature to distrust.

8 Oh Lord, what shal I say, whē Israél turne their backes before their enemies?
9 For the Canaanites, and all the inhabitants of the land shal heare of it, and shal
compasse vs, and destroy our name out of
the earth: and what wilt thou do vnto
thy mightie [e] Name?

e When thine enemies shal blaspheme thee, & say, ẏ thou wast not able to defend vs from them.

10 ¶ And the Lord said vnto Ioshúa, Get
thee vp: wherefore liest thou thus vpon
thy face?
11 Israél hathe sinned, and they haue transgressed my couenant, which I commāded
them: for thei haue euē taken of the excōmunicate thing, and haue also stollen, and
dissembled also, & haue put it euen with

their owne ſtuffe.
12 Therefore the childrẽ of Iſraél can not
ſtande before their enemies, *but* haue turned their backes before their enemies, becauſe they be execrable: nether wil I be
with you anie more, except ye [f] deſtroy
the excommunicate from among you.
13 Vp *therefore*, ſanctifie the people, and ſay,
Sãctifie your ſelues againſt tomorowe: for
thus ſaith the Lord God of Iſraél, *There is*
an execrable thing among you, ô Iſraél,
therefore ye can not ſtand againſt your enemies, vntil ye haue put the [g] execrable
thing from among you.
14 In the morning therefore ye ſhal come
according to your tribes, and the tribe
which the Lord taketh, ſhal come according to the families: & the familie which
the Lord ſhal take, ſhal come by the hou-
ſholds: & the houſholde which the Lord
ſhal take, ſhal come man by man.
15 And he that is [h] taken with the excommunicate thing, ſhalbe burnt with fire, he,
& all that he hathe, becauſe he hathe tráſ-
greſſed the couenant of the Lord, and becauſe he hathe wroght foly in Iſrael.
16 ¶ So Ioſhúa roſe vp early in yͤ morning
& broght Iſraél by their tribes: & the tribe of Iudáh was taken.
17 And he broght the families of Iudáh, &
toke the familie of the Zarhites, and he
broght the familie of the Zarhites, man
by man, and Zabdí was taken.
18 And he broght his houſholde, man by
man, and Achán the ſonne of Carmí, the
ſonne of Zabdí, the ſonne of Zérah of the
tribe of Iudáh was taken.
19 Then Ioſhúa ſaid vnto Achán, My ſonne, I beſeche thee, giue glorie to the Lord
God of Iſraél, and [i] make confeſſion vnto him, and ſhewe me now what thou haſt
done: hide it not from me.
20 And Achán anſwered Ioſhúa, and ſaid,
In dede, I haue ſinned againſt the Lord
God of Iſraél, and thus, and thus haue I
done.
21 I ſawe among the ſpoyle a goodly [k] Ba-
bylonish garmẽt, & two hundreth ſhekels
of ſiluer, and a wedge of golde of fyftie
ſhekels weight, and I coueted them, and
toke them: and beholde, they lye hid in
the earth in the middes of my tent, & the
ſiluer vnder it.
22 ¶ Then Ioſhúa ſent meſſengers, which
ran vnto the tent, and beholde, it was hid
in his tent, and the ſiluer vnder it.
23 Therefore they toke them out of the tẽt,
and broght them vnto Ioſhúa, and vnto
all the children of Iſraél, and layed them
before the Lord.
24 Then Ioſhúa toke Achán the "ſonne of
Zérah, and the ſiluer, & the garment and
the [l] wedge of golde and his [m] ſonnes, &

f Then, to ſuffre wickednes vnpuniſhed is, to refuſe God willingly.

g Meaning the man that toke of the thing forbidden.

h That is, foũde gyltie, ether by lottes, or by the iudgement of Vrim, Nomb. 27,21.

i By declaring the trueth: for God is glorified when the trueth is confeſſed.

k Suche a riche garmẽt as the ſtates of Babylon did weare.

" Or, newewe.

l Some read, a plate: others, a rod, and ſome a tongue.

m This iudgement onely apperteineth to God, and to whome he wil reucile it: to man he hathe cõmanded not to puniſhe the childe for the fathers faute, Deut. 24,16.

his daughters, and his oxen, and his aſſes,
and his ſhepe, and his tent, and all that he
had: and all Iſraél with him broght them
vnto the valley of Achór.
25 And Ioſhúa ſaid, [n] In as muche as thou
haſt troubled vs, the Lord ſhal trouble
thee this day: and all Iſraél threwe ſtones
at him, and burned them with fire, & ſtoned them with ſtones.
26 And they caſt vpon him a great heape
of ſtones vnto this day: and *ſo* the Lord
turned from his fearce wrath: therefore
he called the name of that place, The valley of Achór, vnto this day.

CHAP. VIII.

3 The ſiege, 19 And winning of Aí. 29 The King thereof is hanged. 30 Ioſhúa ſetteth vp an altar. 32 He writeth the Lawe vpon ſtones, 35 And readeth it to all the people.

1 AFter, yͤ Lord ſaid vnto Ioſhúa, *Feare not, nether be thou faint hearted:
take all the men of warre with thee and a-
riſe, go vp to Aí: beholde, I haue giuen into thine hãd the King of Aí, and his people, and his citie, and his land.
2 And thou ſhalt do to Aí and to the King
thereof, as thou dideſt vnto * Ierichó and
to the King thereof: neuertheles yͤ ſpoyle
thereof and * the cattel thereof ſhal ye
take vnto you for a pray: thou ſhalt lie in
waite againſt the citie on the [a] backſide
thereof.
3 ¶ Then Ioſhúa aroſe, and all the men of
warre to go vp againſt Aí: and Ioſhúa
choſe out thirtie thouſand ſtrong men,
and valiant, and ſent them away by
night.
4 And he commanded them, ſaying, Beholde, ye [b] ſhal lye in wait againſt the citie on the backſide of the citie: go not very far frõ the citie, but be ye all in a readines.
5 And I and all the people that are with
me, wil approche vnto the citie: and when
they ſhal come out againſt vs, as they did
at the firſt time, then wil we flee before
them.
6 For they wil come out after vs, til we haue broght them out of the citie: for they
wil ſay, They flee before vs as at the firſt
time: ſo we wil flee before them.
7 Then you ſhal riſe vp from lying in wait
and "deſtroy the citie: for the Lord your
God wil deliuer it into your hand.
8 And when ye haue taken the citie, ye ſhal
ſet it on fire: according to the commãdement of the Lord ſhal ye do: beholde, I
haue charged you.
9 ¶ Ioſhúa then ſent them forthe, and they
went to lie in wait, and abode betwene
Beth-él and Aí, on the Weſtſide of Aí:
but Ioſhúa lodged that night [c] among the
people.

n He declareth yͭ this is Gods iudgemẽt, becauſe he had offended, and cauſed others to be ſlaine.

* Deut. 7,18. & 21,23.

* Chap. 6,21.

* Deut. 20,14.

a Meaning on the Weſtſide, as verſ. 9.

b God wolde not deſtroy Aí by miracle, as Ierichó, to the intent that other nations might feare yͤ power & police of his people.

" Or, driue out the inhabitãts of the citie.

c With yͤ reſt of the armie.

10 And Ioshúa rose vp early in ẏ morning,
and [d] nombred the people: and he and
the Elders of Isráel went vp before the
people *against* Aí.

d That is, vewed them & set them in a ray.

11 Also all the men of warre that were with
him wẽt vp & drue nere, and came against
the citie, & pitched on the Northside of
Aí: and there was a valley betwene them
and Aí.
12 And he toke about fiue thousand men,
[e] & set them to lie in wayt betwene Beth-
él & Aí, on the Westside of the citie.

e He sent these fewe, that the other ẃ lay in ambushe, might not be discouered.

13 And the people set all the hoste that was
on the Northside against the citie, & the
liers in wayte on the West, against the citie: & Ioshúa went the same night into ẏ
[f] middes of the valley.

f To the intent that they in ẏ citie might ẏ better discouer his armie.

14 ¶ And whẽ the King of Aí sawe it, then
the men of the citie hasted & rose vp early, and went out against Isráel to battel, he
& all his people at the time appointed, before the plaine: for he knewe not that *anie*
lay in waite against him on the backside
of the citie.
15 Then Ioshúa and all Isráel [g] *as* beaten
before thẽ, fled by the way of the wildernes.

g As they ẃ fayned to flee for feare.

16 And all the people of the citie were called together, to pursue after them: & they
pursued after Ioshúa, and were drawen a-
way out of the citie,
17 So that there was not a man left in Aí,
nor in Beth-él, that went not out after Israél: and they left the citie open, & pursued after Isráel.
18 Thẽ the Lord said vnto Ioshúa, [h] Stretche out the speare that is in thine hand
towarde Aí: for I wil giue it into thine
hand: and Ioshúa stretched out the speare
that he had in his hand, towarde the citie.

h Or, lift vp ẏ baner, to signifie when they shal inuade ẏ citie.

19 And thei that lay in waite, arose quickly
out of their place, & ran assone as he had
stretched out his hand, and they entred into the citie, and toke it, and hasted, and set
the citie on fire.
20 And the men of Aí loked behinde thẽ,
& sawe it: for lo, the smoke of the citie ascended vp *to heauen, and they had no
*power to flee this way or that way: for ẏ
people that fled to the wildernes, turned
backe vpon the pursuers.

*Or, towarde the heauen.
*Or, place.

21 When Ioshúa and all Isráel sawe that
they that lay in wait, had takẽ the citie, &
that the smoke of the citie mounted vp,
then they turned againe and slewe the mẽ
of Aí.
22 Also the [i] other issued out of the citie
against thẽ: so were they in the middes of
Isráel, these *being* on ẏ one side, & ẏ rest on
ẏ other side: & they slewe thẽ, so that they
let none of them *remaine nor escape.

i Which came out of the ambushe.

Deut.7,2.

23 And the King of Aí they toke aliue, &
broght him to Ioshúa.
24 And when Isráel had made an end of
slaying all the inhabitãts of Aí in ẏ field,
that is, in ẏ wildernes, where they chased
them, and when they were all fallen on the
edge of the sword, vntil they were consumed, all the Israelites returned vnto Aí, &
[k] smote it with the edge of the sworde.

k For the fire, ẃ they had before set in the citie, was not to consume it, but to signifie vnto Ioshúa ẏ they were entred.

25 And all that fel that day, bothe of men
and women, were twelue thousand, euen
all the men of Aí.
26 For Ioshúa drewe not his hand backe a-
gaine which he had stretched out with the
speare, vntil he had vtterly destroyed all ẏ
inhabitants of Aí.
27 *Onely the cattel & the spoyle of this
citie, Isráel toke for a pray vnto them selues, according vnto the worde of ẏ Lord,
which he commanded Ioshúa.

Nomb.30,22.

28 And Ioshúa burnt Aí, and made it an
heape for [l] euer, & a wildernes vnto this
day.

l That it colde neuer be buylt againe.

29 And ẏ King of Aí he hanged on a tre,
vnto the euening. And assone as ẏ sunne
was downe, Ioshúa cõmanded [m] that they
shulde take his carkeis downe frõ the tre,
and cast it at the entring of the gate of
the citie, and *lay thereon a great heape of
stones, *that remaineth* vnto this day.

m According as it was commanded, Deut.21,23.

Chap.7,25.

30 ¶ Then Ioshúa buylt an altar vnto the
Lord God of Isráel, in mount Ebál,
31 As Mosés the seruant of the Lord had
commanded the children of Isráel, as it is
written in ẏ * boke of the Lawe of Mosés,
an altar of whole stone, ouer which no mã
had lift an yron: and they offred thereon
burnt offrings vnto the Lord, & sacrificed
peace offrings.

Exod.20,25.
deu.27,5.

32 Also he wrote there vpon the stones,
a [n] rehearsal of the Lawe of Mosés, which
he wrote in the presence of the children of Isráel.

n Meaning the ten commandements, ẃ are the summe of ẏ whole Law.

33 And all Isráel (and their Elders, and officers & their iudges stode on this side of
the Arke, and on that side, before the Priests of the Leuites, which bare the Arke
of the couenant of the Lord) aswel the
stranger, as he that is borne in the countrey: halfe of them *were* ouer against
mount Gerizím, and halfe of them ouer
against moũt Ebál, * as Mosés the seruant
of the Lord had commanded before, that
they shulde blesse the people of Isráel.

Deut.11,29.
& 27,12.

34 Then afterward he red all the wordes
of the Lawe, the blessings and cursings, ac
cording to all that is written in the boke
of the Lawe.
35 There was not a worde of all that Mosés had commanded, which Ioshúa red
not before all the Congregacion of Israél, * aswel *before* the women and the children, as [o] the stranger that was conuersant among them.

Deut.31,12.

o So nether yong nor olde, man nor wom̃a were excepted from hearing ẏ worde of the Lord.

CHAP. IX.

1 Diuers Kings assemble them selues against Iosh́úa. 3 The craft of the Gibeonites. 15 Iosh́úa maketh a league with them. 23 For their craft they are condemned to perpetual sclauerie.

a In respect of the plaine of Moáb.

1 AND when all the Kings ẏ a were beyond Iordén, in the mountaines & in
the valleis, and by all the coastes of the
b great Sea ouer against Lebanón (*as* the
Hittites, & ẏ Amorites, the Canaanites,
the Perizzites, the Hiuites, & the Iebusites) heard thereof,

b The maigne Sea called Mediterraneum.

2 They gathered them selues together, to
fight against Iosh́úa, & against Isráél with
one "accord.

"Ebr. one mouthe.

3 ¶ *But the inhabitants of Gibeón heard
what Iosh́úa had done vnto Ierichó, and
to Aí.

*2. Sam. 21, 1.

4 And therefore they wroght craftely: for
they went, and fained them selues embassa
dours, and toke olde sackes vpon their asses, and olde bottels for wine, bothe rent
& c bounde vp,

c Because thei were all worne.

5 And olde shooes and clouted vpon their
fete: also the raiment vpon them *was* olde,
& all their prouision of bread was dried,
& mouled.

6 So they came vnto Iosh́úa into the hoste
to Gilgál, & said vnto him, and vnto the
men of Isráél, We be come from a farre
countrey: now therefore make a league
with vs.

7 Thẽ the men of Isráél said vnto the d Hiuites, It may be that thou dwellest among
vs, how then can I make a league with
thee?

d For ẏ Gibeonites and the Hiuites were all one people.

8 And they said vnto Iosh́úa, We are thy
seruãts. Then Iosh́úa said vnto thẽ, Who
are ye? & whence come ye?

9 And they answered him, From a very far
countrey thy seruants are come for e the
Name of the Lord thy God: for we haue
hearde his fame & all that he hathe done
in Egypt,

e Euen the idolaters for feare of death wil pretend to honor ẏ true God & receiue his religiõ.

10 And all that he hathe done to the two
Kings of the Amorites that were beyond
Iordén, to Sihón King of Heshbón, & to
Og King of Bashán, which were at Ash-
taróth.

11 Wherefore our Elders, and all the inhabitants of our cõtrey spake to vs, saying,
Take vitailes "with you for the iourney, &
go to mete them, & say vnto them, We are
your seruants: now therefore make ye a
league with vs.

"Ebr. in your hand.

12 This our f bread we toke it hot with vs
for vitailes out of our houses, the day we
departed to come vnto you: but now beholde, it is dried, and it is mouled.

f The wicked lacke no art nor spare no lies to set forth their policie, when they wil deceiue ẏ seruants of God.

13 Also these bottels of wine which we filled, *were* new, and lo, they be rent, and these
our garments and our shooes are olde, by
reason of the exceding great iourney.

14 ¶ And the g mẽ accepted *their tale* cõcerning their vitailes, & counseled not with
the mouth of the Lord.

g Some thinke that ẏ Israelites ate of their vitailes, & so made a league with them.

15 So Iosh́úa made peace with them, & made a league with thẽ, that he wolde suffer
them to liue: also the Princes of the Congregacion sware vnto them.

16 ¶ But at the end of thre daies, after they
had made a league with them, they heard
that they were their neighbours, and that
they dwelt among them.

17 And the children of Isráél toke their
h iourney, and came vnto their cities the
third day, and their cities *were* Gibeón, &
Chephiráh, & Beeróth & Kiriathiearím.

h Frõ Gilgál.

18 And the children of Isráél slewe them
not, because the Princes of the Congrega
cion had sworne vnto them by the Lord
God of Isráél: wherefore all the Congregacion i murmured against the Princes.

i Fearing lest for their faute the plague of God shuld haue light vpon them all.

19 Then all the princes said vnto all the
Congregacion, We haue sworne vnto thẽ
by the Lord God of Isráél: now therefore
we may not touche them.

20 *But* this we wil do to them, & let them
liue, lest the wrath be vpon vs because of
the k othe which we sware vnto them.

k This doeth not establish rash othes, but sheweth Gods mercie toward his, ẘ wolde not punish thẽ for this faute.

21 And the Princes said vnto them againe,
Let them liue, but they shal hewe wood, &
drawe water vnto all the Congregacion,
as the Princes appoint them.

22 Iosh́úa then called them, and talked ẘ
them, and said, Wherefore haue ye beguiled vs, saying, We are verie farre from
you, when ye dwel among vs?

23 Now therefore ye are cursed, and there
shal none of you be freed frõ being bondmen, and hewers of wood, and drawers of
water for l the house of my God.

l For the vses of the Tabernacle, & of the temple when it shalbe buylt.

24 And they answered Iosh́úa and said, Because it was tolde thy seruants, that the
Lord thy God had * commanded his seruant Mosés to giue you all the land, and
to destroy all the inhabitants of the land
out of your sight, therefore we were exceding sore afraid for our liues at the presence of you, & haue done this thing:

*Deut. 7, 1.

25 And beholde now we are in thine hand:
do as it semeth good & right in thine eies
to do vnto vs.

26 Euen so did he vnto them, and deliuered them out of the m hand of the children of Isráél, that they slewe them not.

m Who were minded to put them to death for feare of Gods wrath.

27 And Iosh́úa appointed them that same
daie *to be* hewers of wood, & drawers of
water for the Congregacion, & for the
n altar of the Lord vnto this day, in ẏ place which he shulde chuse.

n That is for ẏ sacrifices.

CHAP. X.

1 Fiue Kings make warre against Gibeón whome Iosh́úa discomfiteth. 11 The Lord rained hailestones and slewe manie. 12 The sunne standeth at Ioshuas prayer. 26 The fiue Kings are hanged. 29 Many mo cities & Kings are destroyed.

1 Now

1 NOw whē Adoni-zédek King of Ierusalém had heard how Ioshúa had
taken Ai and had destroyed it,(* *for* as he
had done to Ierichó and to the King thereof, so he had done to * Ai and to the
King thereof) and how the inhabitants of
Gibeón had made peace with Israél, and
were among them,

Chap.6,21.
Chap.8,3.

2 Then thei feared excedingly: for Gibeón was a great citie, as one of the roial
cities: for it was greater then Ai, and all
the men thereof *were* mightie.
3 Wherefore [a] Adoni-zédek King of Ierusalém sent vnto Hohám King of Hebrón, and vnto Pirám King of Iarmúth,
and vnto Iapía King of Lachísh, and vnto Debír King of Eglón, saying,
4 Come vp vnto me, and helpe me, that
we may smite Gibeón: for thei haue made
peace with Ioshúa and with the children
of Israél.

a That is, Lord of iustice: so tyrants take to thē selues glorious names, when in dede thei be verie enemies agaīst God and all iustice.

5 Therefore the fiue Kings of the Amorites, the King of Ierusalém, the King of
Hebrón, the King of Iarmúth, the King
of Lachísh, *and* the King of Eglón gathered them selues together, & went vp, thei
with all their hostes, & besieged Gibeón,
and made [b] warre against it.
6 And the mē of Gibeón sent vnto Ioshúa,
euē to the hoste to Gilgál, saying, Withdrawe not thine hand frō thy seruants: come vp to vs quickely, and saue vs, and helpe vs: for all the Kings of the Amorites
which dwel in the mountaines, are gathered together against vs.

b So enuious ẏ wicked are, when any departe frō their bande.

7 So Ioshúa ascended from Gilgál, he,
and all the people of warre with him, and
all the men of might.
8 ¶And the Lord said vnto Ioshúa, [c] Feare
them not: for I haue giuen them into thine hand: none of them shal stand against
thee.
9 Ioshúa therefore came vnto them sodenly: *for* he went vp from Gilgál all ẏ night.
10 And the Lord discomfited them before
Israél, & slewe them with a great slaughter at Gibeón, and chased them along the
way that goeth vp to Beth-horón, and
smote them to Azekáh and to Makkedáh.

c Lest Ioshúa shulde haue thoght ẏ God had sent this great power against him for his vnlauful league with ẏ Gibeonites, ẏ Lord here strengtheneth him.

11 And as thei fled frō before Israél, & were in the going downe to Beth-horón, ẏ
Lord cast downe great stones from heauē
vpō them, vntil Azekáh, & thei dyed: *thei*
were more that dyed with the [d] haylesto-
nes, then they whome the children of Israél slewe with the sworde.

d So we se ẏ all things serue to execute Gods vengeāce against the wicked.

12 ¶Then spake Ioshúa to the Lord, in the
day when the Lord gaue the Amorites
before the children of Israél, and he said
in the sight of Israél, * Sunne, staie thou
in Gibeón, and thou moone, in the valley
of Aialón.
13 And the sunne abode, & the moone stode

Isa.28,21. eccles.46,5.

stil, vntil the people auenged them selues
vpō their enemies: (Is not this written in
the boke of [e] Iashér) so the sunne abode
in the middes of the heauen, and hasted
not to go downe for a whole day.
14 And there was no day like that before it,
nor after it, that the Lord heard the voyce
of a man: for the Lord [f] fought for Israél.
15 ¶After, Ioshúa returned, and all Israél
with him vnto the campe to Gilgál:
16 But the fiue Kings fled and were hid in
a caue at Makkedáh.
17 And it was tolde Ioshúa, saying, The fiue Kings are foūde hyd in a caue at Makkedáh.

e Some read, in the boke of the righteous, meaning Mosés. The Chalde texte readeth in ẏ boke of the Lawe: but it is like ẏ it was a boke thus named ẇ is now lost.
f By taking away ẏ enemies heartes & destroying them with hailestones.

18 Then Ioshúa said, Roule great stones
vpon the mouthe of the caue, and set men
by it for to kepe them.
19 But stand ye not stil: followe after your
enemies, and " smite all the hindemost,
suffre them not to enter into their cities:
for the Lord your God hathe giuen them
into your hand.

" Ebr. cut of all their traine, or tayle.

20 And when Ioshúa and the children of
Israél had made an end of slaying them
with an exceding great slaughter til they
were consumed, and the rest that remained of them were entred into walled cities,
21 Then all the people returned to the cāpe, to Ioshúa at Makkedáh in [g] peace: no
man moued his tongue against the children of Israél.

g Or, in safetie: so that none gaue them as muche as an euil worde.

22 After, Ioshúa said, Open the mouthe of
the caue, & bring out these fiue Kings vnto me forthe of the caue.
23 And thei did so, and broght out those
fiue Kings vnto him forthe of the caue,
euen the King of Ierusalém, the King of
Hebrón, the King of Iarmúth, the King
of Lachísh, *and* the King of Eglón.
24 And when thei had broght out those
Kings vnto Ioshúa, Ioshúa called for all
the men of Israél, and said vnto the chief
of ẏ men of warre, which went with him,
Come nere, set your fete vpō the [h] neckes
of these Kings: & thei came nere and set
their fete vpon their neckes.
25 And Ioshúa said vnto them, Feare not,
nor be faint hearted, *but* be strong and of a
good courage: for thus wil the Lord do
to all your enemies, against whome ye
fight.

h Signifying what shulde become of the rest of Gods enemies, seing ẏ Kings them selues were not spared.

26 So then Ioshúa smote them, and slewe
them, and hanged them on fiue trees, and
thei hanged stil vpon the trees vntil the
euening.
27 And at the going downe of the sunne,
Ioshúa gaue commandement, that thei
shulde take * them downe of the trees, &
cast them into the caue (wherein thei had
bene hid) and thei layed great stones vpō
the caues mouthe, *which remaine* vntil this
day.

Deut.21,23. chap.8,29.

‖ Ioſhúa taketh Makkedáh.

28 ¶And that ſame day Ioſhúa toke ‖ Makkedáh and ſmote it with the edge of the
ſworde, & the King thereof deſtroyed he
with them, and " all the ſoules that were

" Or, euery perſone.

therein, he let none remayne: for he did to
the Kĩg of Makkedáh * as he had done vn-

* Chap. 6,21.

to the King of Ierichó.
29 Then Ioſhúa went from Makkedáh, and
all Iſraél with him vnto Libnáh, & fought
againſt Libnáh.

‖ Libnáh is taken.

30 And the Lord gaue ‖ it alſo & the King
thereof into the hãd of Iſraél: & he ſmote it with the edge of the ſworde, & all the
" ſoules ỳ were therein: he let none remaine

" Or, perſones.

in it: for he did vnto the King thereof, as
he had done vnto the King of Ierichó.
31 ¶And Ioſhúa departed from Libnáh, &
all Iſraél with him vnto Lachíſh, and beſieged it, and aſſalted it.

‖ Lachíſh is taken.

32 And the Lord gaue ‖ Lachíſh into ỳ hand
of Iſraél, which toke it the ſeconde day,
and ſmote it with the edge of the ſworde,
and all the ſoules that were therein, according to all as he had done to Libnáh.

‖ The King of Gézer is ſlayne.

33 ¶Then Horám King of ‖ Gézer came vp
to helpe Lachíſh: but Ioſhúa ſmote him
and his people, vntil none of his remained.
34 ¶And from Lachíſh Ioſhúa departed
vnto ‖ Eglón, and all Iſraél with him, and

‖ Eglón is taken.

thei beſieged it, and aſſalted it,
35 And they toke it the ſame day, & ſmote
it with the edge of the ſworde, and all the
ſoules ỳ were therein he vtterly deſtroyed
the ſame day, according to all that he had
done to Lachíſh.
36 Then Ioſhúa went vp from Eglón, and
all Iſraél with him vnto Hebrón, & they
fought againſt it.

‖ Hebrón is taken.

37 And when they had takẽ ‖ it, they ſmote
it with the edge of the ſworde, and the
King thereof, and all the cities thereof, &
all the ſoules that were therein: he left none remaining, according to all as he had
done to Eglón: for he deſtroyed it vtterly, and all the ſoules that were therein.
38 ¶So Ioſhúa returned, and all Iſraél with
him to Debír, and fought againſt it.

‖ Debír is taken.

39 And when he had taken ‖ it, & the King
thereof, and all the cities thereof, they
ſmote them with the edge of the ſworde,
& vtterly deſtroyed all the ſoules ỳ were
therein, he let none remaine: as he did to
Hebrón, ſo he did to Debír, & to the King
thereof, as he had alſo done to Libnáh, &
to the King thereof.
40 ¶So Ioſhúa ſmote all the hyl cõtreis,
and the Southcountreis, and the valleis, and the [i] hil ſides, & all their Kings,

[i] Some read, Aſhedóth, ỳ ſignifieth the deſcentes of ỳ hilles.

& let none remaine, but vtterly deſtroyed euery ſoule, as the Lord God of Iſraél had commanded.
41 And Ioſhúa ſmote them from Kadeſh-
barnéa euen vnto Azzáh, and all the countrey of Goſhén, euen vnto Gibeón.
42 And all theſe Kings, and their land did
Ioſhúa take at [k] one time, becauſe the

[k] In one battel.

Lord God of Iſraél fought for Iſraél.
43 Afterwarde, Ioſhúa and all Iſraél with
him returned vnto the campe in [l] Gilgál.

[l] Where ỳ Arke was, there to giue thãkes for their victories.

CHAP. XI.

1 Diuers Kings and cities, and countreis ouercome by Ioſhúa. 15 Ioſhúa did all that Moſes had commanded him. 20 God hardeneth the enemies heartes that they might be deſtroyed.

1 AND when Iabín King of Hazór
had heard this, then he [a] ſent to Iobáb King of Madón, and to the King of

[a] The more ỳ Gods power appeareth, the more ỳ wicked rage againſt it.

Shimrón, and to the King of Achſháph,
2 And vnto the Kings that were by the
North in the mountaines, and plaines
towarde the Southſide of [b] Cinneróth,

[b] Which the Euangeliſtes call the lake of Génezeréth, or Tiberias.

and in the valleis, and in the borders of
Dor Weſtwarde,
3 *And* vnto the Canaanites, *bothe* by Eaſt,
and by Weſt, and vnto the Amorites, and
Hittites, and Perizzites, and Iebuſites in
the mountaines, and vnto the Hiuites vnder [c] Hermón in the land of Mizpéh.

[c] Which was mount Sihón, as Deut. 4,48.

4 And they came out and all their hoſtes
with them, many people as the ſand that is
on the ſeaſhore for multitude, with horſes
and charets exceding many.
5 So all theſe Kings met together, & came
and pitched together at the waters of Meróm, for to fight againſt Iſraél.
6 ¶Thẽ the Lord ſaid vnto Ioſhúa, Be not
afraid for them: for to morowe about this
time wil I deliuer them all ſlayne befo.e
Iſraél: thou ſhalt [d] hough their horſes, &

[d] That nether thei ſhuld ſerue to the vſe of warre, nor the Iſraelites ſhulde put their truſt in them.

burne their charets with fire.
7 Then came Ioſhúa and all the men of
warre with him againſt them by the waters of Meróm ſodenly, and fel vpon
them.
8 And the Lord gaue them into the hand
of Iſraél: and they ſmote them, and chaſed them vnto great Zidón, and vnto
[e] Miſrephóthmáim, and vnto the val-

[e] Which ſignifieth, hot waters, or according to ſome, brine pittes.

ley of Mizpéh Eaſtwarde, & ſmote them
vntil thei had none remaining of them.
9 And Ioſhúa did vnto them as the Lord
bade him: he houghed their horſes, and
burnt their charets with fire.
10 ¶At that time alſo Ioſhúa turned backe,
and toke Hazór, and ſmote the King thereof with the ſworde: for Hazór beforetime was the head of all thoſe kingdomes.
11 Moreouer thei ſmote all the [f] perſones

[f] Bothe men & womẽ & children.

that were therein with the edge of the
ſworde, vtterly deſtroying *all*, leauing none aliue, and he burnt Hazór with fire.
12 So all the cities of thoſe Kings, and all
the Kings of them did Ioſhúa take, and
ſmote thẽ with the edge of the ſworde, &

vtterly

Nom.33,52. deu.7,2.
vtterly destroyed them,*as Mosés the seruant of the Lord had commanded.
13 But Israél burnt none of the cities that
g Which were strong by situation & not hurt by warre.
stode stil in their [g] strength, saue Hazór
onely,that Ioshúa burnt.
14 And all the spoyle of these cities and
the cattel the children of Israél toke for
h All mankide.
their praye, but they smote euerie [h] man
with the edge of ẙ sworde vntil they had
destroyed them,not leauing one a liue.
Exod.34,11. Deu.7,2.
15 ¶As the Lord* had commanded Mosés
his seruãt,so did Mosés*cõmande Ioshúa,
& so did Ioshúa:he left nothĩg vndone of
all that the Lord had commanded Mosés.
16 So Ioshúa toke all this land of the mountaines,and all the South,and all the lãd
of Goshén and the lowe countrey,and the
i That is, Samaria
plaine, & the [i] mountaine of Israél, and
the lowe countrey of the same,
k So called, because it was bare & without trees.
*Or, the valley of Gad.
17 From the mount [k] Halák, that goeth vp
to Seír,euen vnto * Baal-gád in ẙ valley of
Lebanón,vnder mount Hermón: and all
their Kings he toke,and smote them, and
slewe them.
18 Ioshúa made warre long time with all
those Kings,
19 Nether was there any citie that made
Chap.9,3.
peace with the children of Israél,*saue
those Hiuites that inhabited Gibeón:all
other they toke by battel.
l That is, to giue the ouer to the selues: and therefore thei colde not but rebelle against God & seke their owne destruction.
20 For it came of the Lord, to [l] harden
their heartes that they shulde come a-
gainst Israél in battel to the intent that
they shulde destroy them vtterly, *and* shewe them no mercy, but that they shulde
bring them to noght: as the Lord had cõmanded Mosés.
21 ¶And that same season came Ioshúa,
and destroyed the Anakíms out of the
mountaines: *as* out of Hebrón,out of Debír,out of Anáb,and out of all the mountaines of Iudáh,and out of all the mountaines of Israél: Ioshúa destroyed them
vtterly with their cities.
22 There was no Anakím left in the land
of the children of Israél: onely in Az-
m Out of the ẘ came Goliath,1.Sam.17,4.
záh, [m] in Gath,and in Ashdód were they
left.
23 So Ioshúa toke the whole land, according to all that the Lord had said vnto
Mosés: and Ioshúa gaue it for an inheri-
Nom.26,53.
tance vnto Israél*according to their porcions through their tribes: then the land
was at rest without warre.

CHAP. XII.

1. 7. What Kings Ioshúa and the children of Israél kil led on bothe sides of Iordén, 24 Which were in nomber thirtie and one.

1 AND these are the Kings of the land,
which the children of Israél smote
a From Gilgál where Ioshúa camped.
and possessed their land, on the [a] other
side Iordén toward ẙ rising of the sunne,
frõ the riuer Arnón, vnto mout Hermón,
and all the plaine Eastward.
2 *Sihón King of the Amorites,that dwelt Nom.21,24.
in Heshbón, hauing dominion from A- deu.3,6.
roér,which is beside the riuer of Arnón,
and from the middle of the riuer, & from
halfe Gileád vnto the riuer Iabbók,in the
border of the children of Ammón.
3 And frõ the plaine vnto the sea of Cinneróth Eastward,and vnto the Sea of the
*plaine,euẽ the salt Sea Eastward, the way *Or, wildernes.
to Bethieshimóth, & from the South vn-
der the *springs of*Pisgáh. *Or, hil sides.
4 ¶They *conquered* also the coast of Og Deu.3,17. & 4,49.
King of Bashán of the* remnant of the Deu 3,11.
gyãtes,ẘ dwelt at Ashtaróth, & at Edréi, chap.13,12.
5 And reigned in mount Hermón, and in
Salcáh,and in all Bashán, vnto the border of the Geshurites, and the Maachathites,& halfe Gileád, euen the border of
Sihón King of Heshbón.
6 Mosés the seruant of the Lord, and the
children of Israél smote them:* Mosés al- Nom.32,29.
so the seruãt of the Lord gaue *their land* for deu.3,12.
a possessiõ vnto ẙ Reubenites,& vnto the chap.13,8.
Gadites,and to halfe ẙ tribe of Manasséh.
7 ¶These also are the Kings of the countrey,ẘ Ioshúa and the children of Israél
smote on this side Iordén,Westward, frõ
Baal-gád in ẙ valley of Lebanón,euẽ vn-
to ẙ mount [b] Halák ẙ goeth vp to Seír, & b Read Chap. 11.vers.17.
Ioshúa gaue it vnto ẙ tribes of Israél for
a possession, according to their porciõs:
8 In the mountaines, and in the valleis,&
in the plaines,& in the *hil sides, & in the *Or, in Ashdóth.
wildernes, & in the Southe, *where were* the
Hittites, the Amorites, and the Canaanites,ẙ Perizzites, ẙ Hiuites,& ẙ Iebusites.
9 ¶*The King of Ierichó *was* one:* the Chap.6,2.
King of Ai which is beside Beth-él,one: Chap.8,29.
10 The*King of Ierusalém,one:the King Chap.10,23.
of Hebrón,one:
11 The King of Iarmúth,one:the King of
Lachísh,one:
12 The King of Eglón, one: the*King of Chap.10,33.
Gézer,one:
13 The*King of Debír, one: the King of Chap.10,38.
Géder,one:
14 The King of Hormáh,one:the King of
Arád,one:
15 The*King of Libnáh,one:the King of Chap.10,30.
Adullám,one:
16 The*King of Makkedáh,one:the King Chap.10,28.
of Beth-él,one: chap.8,17.
17 The King of Tappuáh,one:the King of
Hépher,one:
18 The King of Aphék, one: the King of
Lasharón,one:
19 The King of Madón,one:the*King of Chap.11,10.
Hazór,one:
20 The King of Shimron merón,one:the
King of Achsháph,one:
21 The King of Taanach,one:the King of
Megiddó,one:

22 The King of Kedéſh, one: the King of
Iokneám of "Carmél, one:
23 The King of Dor, in the countrey of
Dor, one: the * King of the nacions of Gilgál, one:
24 The King of Tirzáh, one. all the Kings
were thirty and one.

"Or, nere vnto Carmél.
Gen. 14, 1.

CHAP. XIII.

*3 The borders and coaſtes of the land of Canáan. 8 The
poſseßion of the Reubenites, Gadites, and of halfe the
tribe of Manaſséh. 14 The Lord is the inheritance of
Leui. 22 Balaám was ſlaine.*

1 NOw when Ioſhúa was olde, *&* [a] ſtri-
ken in yeres, the Lord ſaid vnto him,
Thou art olde & " growen in age, & there remaineth exceding much land to be
[b] poſſeſſed:
2 This is the land that remaineth, all the
"regions of the Philiſtíms, & all Geſhurí,
3 From "Nilus which is "in Egypt, euē vnto the borders of Ekrón Northward: this
is counted of the Canaanites, euen fiue
lordeſhippes of the Philiſtíms, the Azzi-
thites, and the Aſhdodites, the Eſhkeloni-
tes, the Gittites, and the Ekronites, and ỹ
Auites:
4 From the Southe, all the land of the Canaanites, and the " caue that is beſide the
Sidonians, vnto Aphék, *and* to the borders of the Amorites:
5 And the land of the Giblites, and all Lebanón, towarde the ſunne riſing from "Ba-
hal-gád vnder mount Hermón, vntil one
come to Hamáth.
6 All the inhabitants of the mountaines
frō Lebanón vnto [c] Miſrephothmáim, *&*
all the Sidonians, I wil caſt them out frō
before the children of Iſraél: onely deuide thou it by lot vnto the Iſraelites, to
inherit, as I haue commanded thee.
7 Now therefore deuide this land to inherit, vnto the nine tribes, and to the halfe
tribe of Manaſſéh.
8 *For* with *halfe* thereof the Reubenites and
the Gadites haue receiued their inheritāce, * which Moſés gaue them beyond Iordén Eaſtward, euen as Moſés the ſeruant
of the Lord had giuen them,
9 From Aroér that is on the brinke of the
riuer Arnón, and from the citie that is in
the middes of the "riuer, and all the plaine
of Medebá vnto Dibón,
10 And all the cities of Sihón King of the
Amorites, which reigned in Heſhbón, vnto the borders of the childrē of Ammón,
11 And Gileád, & the borders of the Geſhu
rites & of the Maachathites, & all mount
Hermón, with all Baſhán vnto Salcáh:
12 All the kingdome of Og in Baſhán, ẇ
reigned in Aſhtaróth and in Edréi: (who
remained of the * reſt of the gyantes) for
theſe did Moſés ſmite, and caſt them out.

a Beīg almoſte an hūdreth & ten yere olde.
"Ebr. commen into yeres.
b After that ỹ enemies are ouercome.
"Or, borders.
"Ebr. Shihór.
"Ebr vpon the face of Egypt.
"Ebr. Mearáh.
"Or, the plaine of Gad
c Read Chap. 11, 8.
Nom. 32, 33. deu. 3, 13. chap. 22, 4.
"Or, valley.
Deu. 3, 11. chap. 12, 4.

13 But the childrē of Iſraél [d] expelled not
ỹ Geſhurites nor the Maachathites: but ỹ
Geſhurites & ỹ Maachathites dwel amōg
the Iſraelites euen vnto this day.
14 Onely vnto the tribe of Leuí he gaue
none inheritance, *but* the ſacrifices of the
Lord God of Iſraél are [e] his inheritance,
as he ſaid vnto him.
15 ¶ Moſés then gaue vnto the tribe of the
children of Reubén *inheritance*, according
to their families.
16 And their coaſt was from Aroér, that is
on the brinke of the riuer Arnón, & frō
the citie that is in the middes of the riuer,
& all the plaine which is by Medebá:
17 Heſhbón with all the cities thereof, that
are in the plaine: Dibón and "Bamoth-bá-
al, and Beth-baal-meón:
18 And Iahazáh, & Kedemóth and Mepháath:
19 Kiriatháim alſo, & Sibmáh, & Zereth-
ſhahár in the mount of "Emek:
20 And Beth-peór, & * Aſhdoth piſgáh, &
Beth-ieſhimóth:
21 And all the cities of the plaine: and all
the kingdome of Sihón King of the A-
morites, which reigned in Heſhbón, whome Moſés ſmote * with the Princes of Midián, Euí, and Rekém, and Zur, and Hur,
and Réba, the dukes of Sihón, dwelling in
the countrey.
22 And [f] Balaám the ſonne of Beór ỹ ſouth-
ſayer did the children of Iſraél ſlaye with
the ſworde, among them that were ſlaine.
23 And the border of the children of Reubén was Iordén with the coaſtes. this was
the inheritance of the children of Reubén according to their families, with the
cities and their villages.
24 ¶ Alſo Moſés gaue *inheritance* vnto the
tribe of Gad, *euen* vnto the children of
Gád according to their families.
25 And their coaſtes were Iazér, and all the
cities of Gileád and halfe the land of the
children of Ammón vnto Aroér, which
is before Rabbáh:
26 And from Heſhbón vnto Ramóth,
Mizpéh, and Betoním: and from Mahanáim vnto the borders of Debír.
27 And in the valley Beth-arám, and Beth-
nimráh, and Succóth, and Zaphón, the
reſt of the kingdome of Sihón King of
Heſhbón, vnto Iordén and the borders e-
uen vnto the Sea coaſt of Cinéreth, [g] beyonde Iordén Eaſtward.
28 This is the inheritance of the children
of Gad, after their families, with the cities and their villages.
29 ¶ Alſo Moſés gaue *inheritance* vnto the
halfe tribe of Manaſſéh: and this belonged to the halfe tribe of the children of
Manaſſéh according to their families.

d Becauſe thei deſtroyed not all as God had cōmāded, they that remained, were ſnares & pricks to hurt thē, Nō. 33, 55. chap. 23, 13. iudg. 2, 3.
e Leuí ſhal liue by ỹ ſacrifices, Nō. 18, 21.
"Or, hie places of Baal.
"Or, the valley.
Deu. 3, 17.
Nom. 31, 8.
f So that bothe they, ẇ obeied wicked counſel & the wicked counſeller periſhed by ỹ iuſt iudgemēt of God.
g That is, in ỹ land of Moab.

30 And

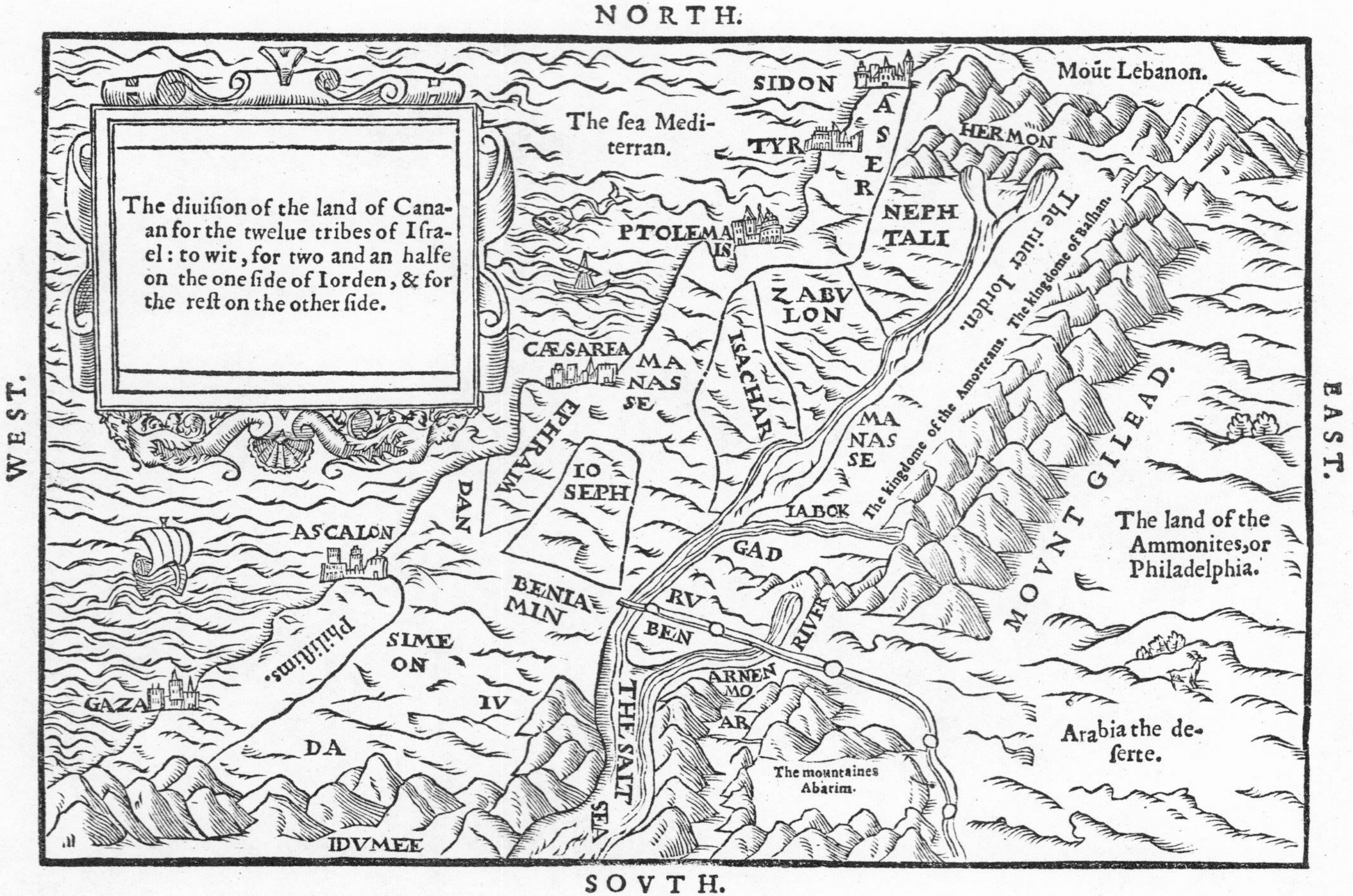

This mappe doeth apperteine to the Chap. 15 of Ioſhua.

30 And their border was from Mahanáim,
euen all Bashán, *to wit*, all the kingdome of
Og King of Bashán, and all the townes
of Iaír which are in Bashán, threscore cities,
31 And halfe Gileád, & Ashtaróth, & Edréi,
cities of the kingdome of Og in Bashán,
Nom.32,39. *were giuen* vnto the h children of Machír
h Meaning, his neuewes and posteritie.
the sonne of Manasséh, to halfe of the chil
dren of Machír after their families.
32 These are the heritages, which Mosés did distribute in the plaine of Moáb
beyonde Iordén, *towarde* Ierichó Estwarde.
Chap.18,7. 33 *But vnto the tribe of Leuí Mosés gaue
none inheritance: *for* the Lord God of Is-
Nom.18,20. raél is their inheritance, * as he said vnto
them.

CHAP. XIIII.

2 The land of Canáan was deuided among the nine tribes and the halfe. 6 Caléb requireth the heritage that was promised him. 13 Hebrón was giuen him.

1 THese also are the *places* which the
children of Israél inherited in the
Nom.34,17. lād of Canáan, *which Eleazár the Priest,
and Ioshúa the sonne of Nun and the
chief fathers of the tribes of the children
of Israél, distributed to them,
Nom.26,55. & 33,54. 2 *By the lot of their inheritance, as the
Lord had commanded by the hand of
Mosés, to giue to the nine tribes, and the
halfe tribe.
3 For Mosés had giuen inheritance vnto
a As Reubén & Gad & halfe the tribe of Manasséh.
a two tribes and an halfe tribe, beyonde
Iordén: but vnto the Leuites he gaue none inheritance among them.
b So thogh Leui lacked, yet were there stil twelue tribes by this meanes.
4 For the children of Ioséph were b two
tribes, Manasséh and Ephráim: therefore
they gaue no parte vnto the Leuites in the
lād, saue cities to dwel in, with the suburbes of the same for their beastes and their
substance.
Nom 35,2. 5 *As the Lord had commanded Mosés, so
the children of Israél did whē they deuided the land.
6 ¶ Then the children of Iudáh came vnto Ioshúa in Gilgál: and Caléb the sonne
of Iephūnéh the Kenezite said vnto him,
Thou knowest what the Lord said vnto
c Which was, that they two onely shulde enter into the lād, Nō.14,24.
Mosés the man of God, concerning c me
and thee in Kadesh-barnéa.
7 Fourty yere olde was I, when Mosés the
seruant of the Lord sent me from Kadesh-barnéa to espy the land, & I broght
him worde againe, as *I thoght* in mine
heart.
d Which were the ten other spies.
8 But my d brethren that went vp with me,
discouraged the heart of the people: yet I
followed stil the Lord my God.
9 Wherefore Mosés sware the same day,
saying, Certeinly the land whereon thy
fete haue troden, shal be thine inheritance, and thy childrens for euer, because
thou hast followed constantly the Lord
my God.
10 Therefore beholde now, the Lord hathe
kept me aliue, as he promised: this is the
fourty and fift yere since the Lord spake
this thing vnto Mosés, while the children
of Israél wandred in the wildernes: and
now lo, I am this day fourscore and fiue
yere olde:
11 And yet am as * strong at this time, as I Eccle.46,11.
was whē Mosés sent me: as strong as I was
then, so strong am I now, *ether* for warre,
or " for gouernement. " Ebr. to go out, and come in.
12 Now therefore giue me this mountaine
whereof the Lord spake in ŷ day (for thou
heardest in that daie, how the ° Anakíms ° Or, gyants.
were there, and the cities great and walled)
e if so be the Lord wil be with me, that I
may driue them out, as the Lord said. e This he spake of modestie & not of douting.
13 Then Ioshúa blessed him, and gaue vn-
to Caléb the sonne of Iephūnéh, Hebrón
for an inheritance.
14 * Hebrón therefore became ŷ inheritā- 1.Mac.2,56.
ce of Caléb the sonne of Iephunnéh the
Kenezite, vnto this day: because he followed cōstantly the Lord God of Israél.
15 And the name of * Hebrón *was* before- Chap.15,13.
time, Kiriath-arbá: which *Arbá* was a
f great man among the Anakíms: thus the f Ether for his power or persone.
land ceased from warre.

CHAP. XV.

1 The lotte of the children of Iudáh, and the names of the cities and villages of the same. 13 Calebs portion. 15 The request of Achsah.

1 THis then was the lot of the tribe of
the children of Iudáh by their fami-
lies: *euen* * to the border of Edóm and the Nomb.34,3.
wildernes of * Zin, Southward on the Nom.33,36.
Southcoast.
2 And their Southborder was the salt Sea
coast, from a the point that loketh South- a The Ebrewe worde signifieth tongue, whereby is ment ether the arme of the Sea that commeth into the land, or a rocke or cape that goeth into the Sea.
ward.
3 And it went out on the Southside toward
Maaleth-akrabbím, and went along to
Zin, and ascended vp on the Southside
vnto Kadesh-barnéa, and went along to
Hezrón, and went vp to Adár, and fet a
compasse to Karkáa.
4 From thence went it a long to Azmón, &
reached vnto the riuer of Egypt, and the
end of that coast was on the Westside:
this shalbe your Southcoast.
5 Also the Eastborder shalbe the salt Sea,
vnto the b end of Iordén: and the border b Meaning the mouth of the riuer where it runneth into ŷ salt Sea.
on the North quarter from the point of
the Sea, *and* from the end of Iordén.
6 And this border goeth vp to Beth-hoglá,
and goeth along by the Northside of
Beth-arabáh: so the border from thence
goeth vp to the c stone of Bohán the son- c Which was a marke to parte their countreyes.
ne of Reubén.
7 Againe this border goeth vp to Debír
frō the valley of Achór, & Northwarde,

turning toward Gilgál, that lyeth before
the going vp to Adummím, which is on ẏ
Southside of the riuer: also this border
goeth vp to the waters of "En-shémesh, &
endeth at *En-rogẽl.

"Or, the founteine of the sunne.
1.King.1,9.

8 Then this border goeth vp to the valley
of the sonne of Hinnóm, on the Southside
of the Iebusites: the same is Ierusalém. also this border goeth vp to the top of the
mountaine that lieth before the valley of
Hinnóm Westward, which is by the end
of the valley of the "gyãtes Northward.

"Ebr. Rephaim.

9 So this border compasseth from the top
of the mountaine vnto the founteine of ẏ
water of Nephtóah, and goeth out to the
cities of mount Ephrón: and this border
draweth to Baaláh, which is "Kiriath-iearím.

"Or, the citie of woods.

10 Then this border compasseth from Baaláh Westward vnto mount Seír, & goeth
along vnto the side of mount Iearím,
which is Chesalón on the Northside: so it
commeth downe to Beth-shémesh, and
goeth to Timnáh.
11 Also this border goeth out vnto the side
of Ekrón Northward: and this border
draweth to Shicrón, and goeth along to
mount Baaláh, & stretcheth vnto Iabneél:
& the endes of this coast are to the [d] Sea.

d Meanig toward Syria.

12 And the Westborder *is* to the great Sea:
so this border shalbe the bondes of the
childrẽ of Iudáh round about, according
to their families.
13 ¶ And vnto Caléb the sonne of Iephũnéh
did Iosʃhúa giue a parte amõg the childrẽ
of Iudáh, as the Lord commanded him,
euen *Kiriath-arbá of the father of Anák,
which is Hebrón.

Chap. 14,15.

14 And Caléb [e] droue thence thre sonnes
of Anák, Sheshái, and Ahimán, and Talmái, the sonnes of Anák.

e This was done after the death of Iosʃhúa, Iud. 1,10.

15 And he went vp thence to the inhabitãts
of Debír: and the name of Debír before
time *was* Kiriath-sépher.
16 Thẽ Caléb said, He ẏ smiteth Kiriath-
sépher, & taketh it, euẽ to him wil I giue
Achsáh my daughter to wife.
17 And Othniél, the sonne of Kenáz, the
"brother of Caléb toke it: and he gaue him
Achsáh his daughter to wife.

"Or, cousin.

18 And as she wẽt in *to him*, she moued him,
to aske of her father a field: [f] & she lighted
of her asse, & Caléb said vnto her, What
wilt thou.

f Because her housband taried to long.

19 Thẽ she answered, "Giue me a blessing:
for thou hast giuẽ [g] me the South coũtrei:
giue me also sprĩgs of water. And he gaue
her ẏ springs aboue & the sprĩgs benethe.

"Or, Grante me this petition.
g Because her countrey was baren, she desired of her father a field ẏ had springs.

20 This shalbe the inheritance of the tribe
of ẏ children of Iudáh according to their
families.
21 And the vtmost cities of the tribe of ẏ
children of Iudáh, toward the coastes
of Edóm Southward *were* Kabzeél, and
Eder, and Iagúr,
22 And Kináh, and Dimonáh, & Adadáh,
23 And Kédesh, and Hazór, and Ithnán,
24 Ziph, and Télem, and Bealóth,
25 And Hazór, Hadattáh, & Kerióth, Hes-
ron (which is Hazór)
26 Amám, and Shemá, and Moladáh,
27 And Hazár, Gaddáh, & Heshmón, and
Beth-pálet,
28 And Hasar-shuál, and Beershéba, and
Biziothiáh,
29 Baaláh, and Iím, and Azem,
30 And Eltolád, & Chesil, [h] and Hormáh,
31 And Ziklág, and Madmanná, and San-
sannáh,

h Which before was called Zepháth, Iud. 1,17.

32 And Lebaóth, and Shilhím, and Aín, &
Rimmón: all *these* cities *are* twenty & nine
with their villages.
33 ¶ In the lowe countrey *were* Eshtaól, and
Zoreáh, and Ashnáh,
34 And Zanoáh, & En-ganním, Tappúah,
and Enám,
35 Iarmúth, & Adullám, Socóh, & Azekáh,
36 And Sharáim, & Adithaim, & Gederáh,
and Gederotháim: fourtene cities with
their villages.
37 Zenám, & Hadasháh, and Migdal-gád,
38 And Dileám, and Mizpéh, and Iokthe̋él,
39 Lachísh, and Bozkáth, and Eglón,
40 And Cabbón, & Lahmám, & Kithlísh,
41 And Gederóth, Beth-dagón, and Naamáh, and Makkedáh: sixtene cities with
their villages.
42 Lebnáh, and Ethér, and Asʃhán,
43 And Iiphtáh, and Asʃhnáh, and Nezíb,
44 And Keiláh, and Aczib, and Mareshâh:
nine cities with their villages.
45 Ekrón with her "townes & her villages,

"Ebr. daughters.

46 From Ekrón, euen vnto the Sea, all that
lieth about Asʃhdód with their villages.
47 Asʃhdód with her townes and her villages: Azzáh with her townes and her villages, vnto the [i] riuer of Egypt, and the
great sea *was their* coast.

i Meaning, Nilus, as chap. 13,3.

48 ¶ And in the mountaines *were* Shamír,
and Iattír, and Socóh,
49 And Dannáh, and [k] Kiriath-sannáth,
(which is Debír)

k Which is also called Kiriath-sépher, vers. 15.

50 And Anáb, and Asʃhtemóh, and Aním,
51 And Góshen, and Holón, & Gilóh: eleuen cities with their villages.
52 Aráb, and Dumáh, and Esheán,
53 And Ianúm, and Beth-tappuáh, and A-
phekáh,
54 And Humtáh, and *Kiriath-arbá (which
is Hebrón) & Ziór: nine cities with their
villages.

Chap. 14,15.

55 Maón, Carmél, and Zíph, and Iuttáh,
56 And Izreél, and Iokdeám, and Zanóah,
57 Káin, Gibeáh, and Timnáh: ten cities
with their villages.
58 Halhúl, Beth-zúr, and Gedór,

59 And Maaráh, and Beth-anóth, and Elte-
kón: six cities with their villages.
60 Kiriath-báal, which is Kiriath-iearím,
& Rabbáh: two cities with their villages.
61 ¶ In the wildernes *were* Beth-arabáh,
Middín, and Secacáh,

l Of this citie the salt Sea hathe his name.

62 And Nibshán, and the l citie of salt, and
En-gedí: six cities with their villages.
63 Neuertheles, the Iebusites that were the
inhabitants of Ierusalém, colde not the
children of Iudáh cast m out, but the Iebusites dwel with the children of Iudáh
at Ierusalém vnto this day.

m That is, vtterly, thogh they slewe the moste parte, & burnt their citie. Iudg. 1, 8.

CHAP. XVI.

1 The lot or parte of Ephráim. 10 The Canaanite dwelled among them.

a That is, to Ephráim and his children: for Manassehs porcion followeth.

1 AND the lot fel to the a children of
Ioséph frő Iordén by Ierichó vnto
the water of Ierichó Eastwarde, & to the
wildernes that goeth vp from Ierichó by
the mount Beth-él:

Iudg. 1, 26.

2 And goeth out from Beth-él to * Luz, and
runneth alőg vnto the borders of Archia-
tároth,
3 And goeth downe Westward to the co-
aste of Iaphletí, vnto the coast of Beth-
horón the nether, and to Gézer: and the
ends b thereof are at the Sea.

b Of their inheritance.

4 So the children of Ioséph, Manasséh and
Ephráim c toke their inheritance.

c Seuerally, first Ephráim, and then Manasséh.

5 ¶ Also the borders of the children of
Ephráim according to their families, euen
the borders of their inheritãce on ẏ Eastside, were Atróth addár, vnto Beth-horón
the vpper.
6 And this border goeth out to the Sea vnto Michmetháh on the Northside, & this
border returneth Eastwarde vnto Taa-
náth shilóh, and passeth it on the Eastside
vnto Ianóhah,
7 And goeth downe from Ianóhah to A-
tároth, and Naaráth, and cometh to Ierichó, d and goeth out at Iordén.

d For so farre the coasts reache.

8 And this border goeth from Tappúah
Westward vnto the riuer Kanáh, and the
ends thereof are at the Sea: this is the inheritance of the tribe of the children of
Ephráim by their families.
9 And the e separate cities for the childrẽ
of Ephráim *were* among the inheritance
of the children of Manasséh: all the cities
with their villages.

e Because Ephraims tribe was farre greater then Manasséh, therefore he had mo cities.

10 And they cast not out the Canaanite
that dwelt in Gézer, but the Canaanite
dwelleth amőg the Ephraimites vnto this
day, and serue vnder tribute.

CHAP. XVII.

1 The porcion of the halfe tribe of Manasséh. 3 The daughters of Zelophehád. 13 The Canaanites are become tributaries. 14 Manasseh and Ephraim require a greater porcion of heritage.

1 THis was also the lot of the tribe of
Manasséh: for he was the * first borne
of Ioséph, *to wit*, of Machír ẏ first borne of

Genes. 46, 14.

Manasséh, *and* the father of Gileád: now
because he was a man of warre, he had Gileád and Bashán.
2 And also * of the a rest of the sonnes of
Manasséh by their families, *euen* of the
sonnes of Abiézer, and of the sonnes of
Hélek, and of the sonnes of Azriél, and of
the sonnes of Shéchem, and of the sonnes
of Hépher, and of the sonnes of Shemidá:
these *were* the males of Manasséh, the sonne of Ioséph according to their families.

Nom. 26, 29.

a For the other halfe tribe had their porcion beyonde Iordén

3 ¶ * But Zelophehád the sonne of Hépher,
the sonne of Gileád, the sonne of Machír,
the sonne of Manasséh, had no sonnes, but
daughters: and these are the names of his
daughters, Malháh, and Noáh, Hogláh,
Milcháh and Tirzáh:

Nom. 26, 33. & 27, 1. and 36, 2.

4 Which came before Eleazár the Priest,
and before Iosħúa the sonne of Nun, and
before the princes, saying, The Lord cő-
manded Mosés to giue vs an inheritance among our b brethren: therefore according to the cőmandement of the Lord
he gaue them an inheritance among the
brethren of their father.

b Among the of our tribe.

5 And there fel ten porcions to c Manasséh, beside the land of Gileád and Bashán,
which is on the otherside Iordén,
6 Because the daughters of Manasséh did
inherit among his sonnes: and Manassehs
other sonnes had the land of Gileád.

c In the land of Canáan: fiue to the males, and other fiue to the daughters of Zelophehád.

7 ¶ So the borders of Manasséh were from
Ashér to Michmetháh ẏ lieth before Shechém, & this border goeth on ẏ right hãd,
euen vnto the inhabitãts of En-tappúah.
8 The land of Tappúah belonged to Manasséh, but d Tappúah beside the border
of Manasséh *belongeth* to the sonnes of
Ephráim.

d Meaning, the citie it selfe.

9 Also this border goeth dowen vnto the
* riuer Kanáh Southward to the riuer: these cities of Ephráim *are* among the cities
of Manasséh: and the border of Manasséh
is on the Northside of the riuer, and the
ends of it are at the e Sea,

Or, the broke of reedes.

e That is, toward the maigne sea.

10 The South perteineth to Ephráim, and
the North to Manasséh, and the Sea is his
border: and they met together in f Ashér
Northward, and in Issachár Eastward.

f In the tribe of Ashér, and tribe of Issachár.

11 And Manasséh had in Issachár and in A-
shér, Beth-sheán, & her townes, & Ibleám,
& her townes, & the inhabitants of Dor
with the townes thereof, and the inhabitants of En-dór with the townes thereof,
& the inhabitants of Thaanách with her
townes, & the inhabitants of Megiddó ŵ
the townes of the same, *euen* thre cőutreis.
12 Yet the childrẽ of Manasséh g colde not
destroy those cities, but the Canaanites
dwelled stil in that land.
13 Neuertheles, when the children of Israél were strong, they put the Canaanites
vnder tribute, but cast thẽ not out wholly.

g For at the first they lacked courage, & after agreed with them on condicions contrary to Gods commandement.

14 Then the children of Ioséph spake vnto
Ioshúa, saying, Why hast thou giuen me
but one lot, and one porcion to inherit,
seing I am a great people, for as muche as
the Lord hathe [h] blessed me hetherto?

h According to my father Iaakobs prophecie, Genes. 48,19.

15 Ioshúa then answered them, If thou be
muche people, get thee vp to the wood, &
cut *trees* for thy selfe there in the land of
the Perizzites, and of the gyãts, [i] if moũt
Ephráim be tonarowe for thee.

i If this moũt be not large ynough, why doest not thou get more by destroying Gods enemies, as he hathe cõmanded?

16 Then the children of Iosépħ said, The
mountaine wil not be ynough for vs: and
all the Canaanites that dwel in the lowe
countrey haue charets of yron, aswel they
in Beth-sheán, and in the townes of the
same, as they in the valley of Izreél.
17 And Ioshúa spake vnto the house of Ioséph, to Ephráim, & to Manasséh, saying,
Thou art a great people, and hast great
power, *and* shalt not haue one lot.
18 Therefore the mountaine shalbe thine:
for it is a wood, and thou shalt cut it
downe: and the ends of it shalbe thine,[k] &
thou shalt cast out the Canaanites, thogh
they haue yron charets, *and* thogh they be
strong.

k So that thou shalt enlarge thy portion thereby.

CHAP. XVIII.

8 The Tabernacle set in Shilóh. 4 Certeine are sent to deuide the land to the other seuen tribes. 11 The lot of the children of Beniamin.

1 AND the whole Congregacion of the
children of Israél came together at
Shilóh: for they set vp the [a] Tabernacle of the Congregacion there, after the
land was subiect vnto them.

a For they had now remoued it from Gilgál and set it vp in Shilóh

2 Now there remained among the childrẽ
of Israél seuen tribes, to whome [b] they
had not deuided their inheritance.

b As Eleazár, Ioshúa & the heades of the tribes had done to Iudáh, Ephráim and halfe of Manasséh.

3 Therefore Ioshúa said vnto the children
of Israél, How long are ye so slacke to entre and possesse the land which the Lord
God of your fathers hathe giuen you?
4 Giue from among you for *euerie* tribe
thre men, that I may send them, and that
they may rise, and walke through the lãd,
and distribute it according to [c] their inheritance, and returne to me.

c That is, into seuen porsions, to euerie tribe one.

5 And that they may deuide it vnto them
into seuen partes, (Iudáh shal abide in his
coast at the South, and the house of Ioséph shal [d] stand in their coastes at the
North)

d For these had their inheritance already appointed.

6 Ye shal describe the land therefore into
seuen partes, & shal bring them hether to
me, & I wil cast lottes for you here before
the [e] Lord our God.

e Before the Arke of the Lord.

7 But the Leuites shal haue no part among
you: for the [f] Priesthode of the Lord is
their inheritance: also Gad and Reubén
& halfe the tribe of Manasséh haue receiued their inheritãce beyõde Iordén Eastward, which Moses the seruãt of the Lord
gaue them.

f That is, the sacrifices and offrings, Chap. 13,14.

8 ¶ Then the men arose, and went their
way: and Ioshúa charged them that went
to describe the land, saying, Departe, and
go through the land, and [g] describe it, and
returne to me, that I may here cast lots for
you before the Lord in Shilóh.

g By writing the names of euerie coũtrey and citie.

9 So the men departed, and passed through
the land, and described it by cities into seuen partes in a boke, and returned to Ioshúa into the campe at Shilóh.
10 ¶ Then Ioshúa [h] cast lots for them in
Shilóh before the Lord, and there Ioshúa
deuided the lãd vnto the children of Israél, according to their porcions:

h That euerie one shulde be contẽt w God's appointement.

11 ¶ And the lot of the tribe of the childrẽ
of Beniamín came forthe according to
their families, and the coast of their lot
lay [i] betwene the children of Iudáh, and
the children of Iosépħ.

i Their inheritance bordered vpon Iudáh and Iosépħ.

12 And their coast on the Northside was
from Iordén, and the border went vp to
the side of Ierichó on the Northparte, &
went vp through the mountaines Westward, and the endes thereof are in the wildernes of Beth-auén:
13 And this border goeth along from thẽce to Luz, *euen* to the Southside of Luz
(the same is [k] Beth-él) and this border
descendeth to Atroth-addár, nere the
moũt, that lieth on the Southside of Beth-
horón the nether.

k Which was in the tribe of Ephráim: another Beth-él was in the tribe of Beniamín.

14 So the border turneth, and compasseth
the corner of the Sea Southward, from the
moũt that lieth before Beth-horón Southward: and the ends thereof are at Kiriath-
báal (which is Kiriath-iearím) a citie of
the children of Iudáh: this is the Westquarter.
15 And the Southquarter *is* from the end
of Kiriath-iearím, and this border goeth
out "Westward, and cometh to the founteine of waters of Nephtóah.

"Or, to the Sea.

16 And this border descendeth at the end
of the mountaine, that lieth before the
valley of Bẽ-hinnóm, which is in the valley of the "gyantes Northward, & descẽ-
deth into the valley of Hinnóm by the side of "Iebusi Southward, and goeth downe to En-rogél,

"Or, Rephaim.

"Or, Ierusalém.

17 And compasseth from the North, and
goeth forthe to [l] En-shémesh, & stretcheth
to Gelilóth, which is toward the going vp
vnto Adummím, and goeth downe to the
* stone of Bóhan the sonne of Reubén.

l Which is in the tribe of Ephráim.

Chap. 15,6.

18 So it goeth alõg to the side ouer against
the plaine Northward, and goeth downe
into the plaine.
19 After, this border goeth along to the side of Beth-hogláh Northward: & the ends
thereof, *that is*, of the border, reache to the
point of the salt Sea Northward, *and* to
the [m] end of Iordén Southward: this is
the Southcoast.

m To the very streit, where the riuer runneth into ÿ salt Sea.

20 Also Iordén is the border of it on the
Eastside : this is the inheritance of the
children of Beniamín by the coastes thereof round about according to their families.
21 Now the cities of the tribe of the children of Beniamín according to their families, are Ierichó, and Beth-hogláh, and
the valley of Keziz,
22 And Beth-arabah, and Zemaráim, and
Beth-él,
23 And Auím, and Paráh, and Ophráh,
24 And Chephár, Ammonái, and Ophní, &
Gabá: twelue cities with their villages.
25 Gibeón, and Ramáh, and Beeróth,
26 And Mizpéh, and Chephiráh, and Mo-
záh,
27 And Rékem, and Irpeél, and Taraláh,
28 And Zelá, Eléph, and Iebusí, (which is
[n] Ierusalém) Gibeáth, *and* Kiriáth: fourtene cities with their villages: this is the
inheritance of the children of Beniamín
according to their families.

n Which was not wholly in the tribe of Beniamín, but part of it was also in ẏ tribe of Iudáh.

CHAP. XIX.

1 The porcion of Simeón, 10 Of Zebulún, 17 Of Issachár, 24 Of Ashér, 32 Of Naphtali, 40 Of Dan. 49 The possession of Ioshúa.

1 AND the seconde lot came out to Simeón, *euen* for the tribe of the children of Simeón according to their families: and their inheritãce was in the [a] middes of the inheritance of the children of
Iudáh.

a According to Iaakobs prophecie, that he shulde be scattered among ẏ other tribes, Gen. 49, 7.

2 Now thei had in their inheritance, Beer-
shéba, & Shéba, and Moladáh,
3 And Hazar-shuál, and Baláh, and Azem,
4 And Eltolád, and Bethúl, and Hormáh,
5 And Ziklág, and Beth-marcabóth, and
Hazar-susáh,
6 And Beth-lebaóth, and Sharuhén: thirtene cities with their villages.
7 Ain, Remmón, and Ether, & Ashán: foure
cities with their villages.
8 And all the villages that were round a-
bout these cities, vnto Baalathbeér, *and*
‖ Rámath Southwarde: this is the inheritance of the tribe of the children of Simeón according to their families.

‖ Or, Ramath-negeb.

9 Out of the porcion of the children of
Iudáh *came* the inheritance of the childrẽ
of Simeón: for the parte of the children
of Iudáh was to [b] muche for them: therefore the children of Simeón had their
inheritance within their inheritance.

b But this large porciõ was giuen them by Gods prouidẽce, to declare their increase in time to come.

10 ¶ Also the third lot arose for the children of Zebulún according to their families: and the coastes of their inheritãce
came to Saríd,
11 And their border goeth vp [c] Westwarde,
euen to Maraláh, and reacheth to Dabbá-
sheth, & meteth with the riuer that lyeth
before Iokneám,
12 And turneth from Saríd Eastwarde
towarde the sunne rising vnto the border
of Chislóth tabór, & goeth out to Daberáth, and ascendeth to Iaphía,

c Meaning, towarde the great Sea.

13 And from thence goeth along Eastwarde
towarde the sunne rising to Gittáh hépher to Ittáh kazín, and goeth forthe to
Rimmón, and turneth to Neáh.
14 And this border compasseth it on the
Northside to Hannathón, and the ends
thereof are in the valley of Iiphtah-él,
15 And Kattáth, and Nahallál, and Shimrón, and Idaláh, and [d] Beth-léhem: twelue
cities with their villages.

d There was another Beth-léhem in the tribe of Iudáh.

16 This is the inheritance of the children
of Zebulún according to their families:
that is, these cities and their villages.
17 ¶ The fourthe lot came out to Issachár,
euen for the children of Issachár according to their families.
18 And their coast was Izreélah, and Che-
sullóth, and Shuném,
19 And Hapharáim, and Shión, and Anaha-
ráth,
20 And Harabbíth, & Kishión, and Abez,
21 And Reméth, and [e] En-ganním, and
En-haddáh, and Beth-pazzéz.
22 And this coast reacheth to Tabór, and
Shahazimáth, and Beth-shémesh, and the
ends of their coast reache to Iordén: sixtene cities with their villages.
23 This is the inheritance of the tribe of
the childrẽ of Issachár according to their
families: *that is*, the cities, and their villages.

e There was another citie of this name in the tribe of Iudáh: for vnder diuers tribes certeine cities had all one name, and were distincted by the tribe onely.

24 ¶ Also the fifte lot came out for the tribe of the children of Ashér according to
their families.
25 And their coast was Helcáth, and Halí,
and Béten, and Achsháph,
26 And Alammélech, and Amád, & Mishe-
ál, and came to Carmél Westwarde, and
to Shihór libnáth,
27 And turneth towarde the sunne rising to
Beth-dagón, and commeth to [f] Zebulún, and to the valley of Iiphtah-él, towarde the Northside of Beth-emék, and
Neiél, and goeth out on the left side of
Cabúl,

f Ioineth to ẏ tribe of Zebulún, which lay more Eastwarde.

28 And to Ebrón, and Rehób, and Ham-
món, and Kanáh vnto great Zidón.
29 Then the coast turneth to Ramáh & to
the strong citie of [g] Zor, and this border turneth to Hosáh, and the endes thereof are at the Sea from Hebél to Ach-
zib,

g Which was Tyrus a strong citie in ẏ Sea.

30 Vmmáh also and Aphék, and Rehób:
two and twentie cities with their villages.
31 This is the inheritance of the tribe of
the children of Ashér according to their
families: *that is*, these cities and their villages.
32 ¶ The sixt lot came out to the childrẽ of

Naphtalí, *euen* to the children of Naphtalí according to their families.
33 And their coast was from [h] Héleph, *and*
from Allón in Zaananním, and Adami
nékeb, and Iabneél, euen to Lakúm, & the
ends thereof are at Iordén.

h These cities were in the countrey of Zaanannim.

34 So this coast turneth Westwarde to Az-
noth tabór, and goeth out from thence to
Hukkók, and reacheth to Zebulún on the
Southside, & goeth to Ashér on the Westside, and to Iudáh "by Iordén towarde the
sunne rising.

"Or, euen vnto Iordén.

35 And the strong cities *are* Ziddím, Zer, &
Hammáth, Rakkáth, and [i] Cinnéreth,
36 And Adamáh, & Ramáh, and Hazór,
37 And Kédesh, and Edréi, and En-hazór,
38 And Irón, and Migdal-él, Horém, and
Beth-anáh, and Beth-shémesh: ninetene
cities with their villages.

i Of the which ŷ lake of Genezaréth had his name.

39 This is the inheritance of the tribe of
ŷ childrẽ of Naphtalí according to their
families: *that is*, the cities & their villages.
40 ¶ The seuẽth lot came out for the tribe
of the children of Dan according to their
families.
41 And the coast of their inheritance was,
Zoráh, and Eshtaól, and Ir-shémesh,
42 And Shaalabbín, and Aiialón, & Ithláh,
43 And Elón, and Temnáthah, and Ekrón,
44 And Eltekéh, & Gibbethón, & Baaláh,
45 And Iehúd, and Bene-berák, and Gath-
rimmón,
46 And Me-iarkón, and Rakkón, with the
border that lyeth before [k] Iápho.

k Called Ioppe.

47 But the coastes of the children of Dan
fel out *to litle* for them: therefore the childrẽ of Dan went vp to [l] fight against Léshem, and toke it, and smote it with the
edge of the sworde, and possessed it, and
dwelt therein, and called Léshem, * Dan,
after the name of Dan their father.

l According as Iaakób had prophecied, Gen 49,17.

Iud. 18,29.

48 This is the inheritance of the tribe of
the children of Dan according to their
families: *that is*, these cities and their villages.
49 ¶ When thei had made an end of deuiding the land by the coastes thereof, then
the children of Israél gaue an inheritãce
vnto Ioshúa ŷ sonne of Nun among thẽ.
50 According to the worde of the Lord
thei gaue him the citie which he asked, *euẽ*
* Timnath-seráh in mount Ephráim: and
he buylt the citie and dwelt therein.

Chap. 24,30.

51 * These are the heritages which Eleazár
the Priest, and Ioshúa the sonne of Nun,
and the chief fathers of the tribes of the
children of Israél deuided by lot in Shilóh before the Lord at the dore of ŷ Tabernacle of the Cõgregaciõ: so thei made
an end of deuiding the countrey.

Nomb. 34,17

CHAP. XX.

1 The Lord commandeth Ioshúa to appoint cities of refuge. 3 The vse thereof. 7 And their names.

1 THe Lord also spake vnto Ioshúa,
saying,
2 Speake to the children of Israél, and say,
* Appoint you cities of refuge, whereof I
spake vnto you by the hand of Mosés,

Exod. 21,13. nomb. 35,9. deut. 19,2.

3 That the slayer ŷ killeth any persone [a] by
ignorance, *and* vnwittingly, may flee thether, & thei shal be your refuge from the
auenger of blood.

a At vnwares, & bearing him no grudge.

4 And he that doeth flee vnto one of those cities, shal stand at the entring of the
gate of the citie, and shal shewe his cause
"to the Elders of the citie: and thei shal
receiue him into the citie vnto them, and
giue him a place, ŷ he may dwel ŵ them.

"Ebr. in the eares of the Elders.

5 And if the [b] auenger of blood pursue
after him, thei shal not deliuer the slayer
into his hand because he smote his neighbour ignorantly, nether hated he him beforetime:

b That is, the nerest kinsmã of him that is slayne.

6 But he shal dwel in ŷ citie vntil he stand
before the Congregacion in [c] iudgement,
* or vntil the death of the hye Priest that
shalbe in those daies: then shal the slayer
returne, and come vnto his owne citie, and
vnto his owne house, *euen* vnto the citie
from whence he fled.

c Til his cause were proued.

Nomb. 35,25.

7 ¶ Then thei appointed Kédesh in "Galíl
in mount Naphtalí, & Shechém in mount
Ephráim, and Kiriath-arbá, (which is Hebrón) in the mountaine of Iudáh.

"Or, Galile.

8 And on the other side Iordén *towarde* Ierichó Eastwarde, thei appointed * Bézer
in the wildernes vpon the plaine, out of
ŷ tribe of Reubén, & Ramóth in Gileád,
out of the tribe of Gad, and Golán in Bashán, out of the [d] tribe of Manasséh.

Deut. 4,43. chap. 20,9.

d Out of the half tribe of Manasséh beyonde Iordén.

9 These were the cities appointed for all
the children of Israél, and for the stranger
that soiourned among them, that whosoeuer killed any persone ignorantly, might
flee thether, & not dye by the hand of the
auenger of blood, vntil he stode before
the [e] Congregacion.

e Before the Iudges.

CHAP. XXI.

41 The cities giuen to the Leuites, in nõber eight & fourtie. 44 The Lord according to his promes gaue the children of Israél rest.

1 THẽ came the "principal fathers of the
Leuites vnto Eleazár the Priest, and
vnto Ioshúa the sonne of Nun, and vnto
the chief fathers of the tribes of the children of Israél,

"Or, the chief of the fathers.

2 And spake vnto thẽ at Shilóh in the land
of Canaã, sayĩg, * The Lord cõmãded [a] by
the hãd of Mosés, to giue vs cities to dwel
in, ŵ the suburbes thereof for our cattel.

Nomb. 35,2.

a By Mosés, by whose ministerie God shewed his power.

3 So the children of Israél gaue vnto the
Leuites, out of their inheritãce at the cõmandement of the Lord these cities with
their suburbes.
4 And the lot came out for the families of
the [b] Kohathites: & the childrẽ of Aarón
the Priest, *which were* of the Leuites, had
by

b He meaneth thẽ that were Priests: for some were but Leuites.

by lot, out of the tribe of Iudáh, and out
of the tribe of Simeón, and out of the tribe of Beniamín [c] thirtene cities.

c Euerie tribe gaue mo or fewer cities according as their inheritāce was great or litle, Nom. 35,8.

5 And the rest of the children of Koháth
had by lot out of the families of the tribe
of Ephráim, and out of the tribe of Dan,
and out of the halfe tribe of Manasséh, ten
cities.
6 Also the children of Gershón *had* by lot
out of the families of the tribe of Issachár, and out of the tribe of Ashér, and out
of the tribe of Naphtalí, and out of the
halfe tribe of Manasséh in Bashán, thirtene cities.
7 The children of Merarí according to
their families *had* out of the tribe of Reubén, and out of the tribe of Gad, and out
of the tribe of Zebulún, twelue cities.
8 So the childrē of Israél gaue by lot vnto
the Leuites these cities with their suburbes, as the Lord had commanded by the
hand of Mosés.
9 ¶ And they gaue out of ye tribe of ye childrē
of Iudáh, & out of the tribe of the childrē
of Simeón, these cities wc are here named.
10 And they were the childrens of [d] Aarón
being of the families of the Kohathites, *&*
of the sonnes of Leuí, (for theirs was the
first lot)

d For Aarón came of Koháth, and therefore the Priests office remained in ye familie.

11 So they gaue thē Kiriath-arbá of the father of Anók (which is Hebrón) in the
mountaine of Iudáh, with the suburbes of
the same round about it.
12 (But the land of the citie, and the villages thereof, gaue they to * Caléb the sonne of Iephunnéh to be his possession)

Chap. 14,14. 1. chro. 6,56.

13 ¶ Thus they gaue to the [e] childrē of Aarón the Priest, a citie of refuge for the
slayer, *euen* Hebrón with her suburbes, &
Libnáh with her suburbes,

e That is, the Priest of the familie of the Kohathites, of whome Aarón was chief.

14 And Iattír with her suburbes, and E-
shtemóa and her suburbes,
15 And Holón with her suburbes, and Debír with her suburbes,
16 And Aín with her suburbes, and Iuttáh
wt her suburbes, Beth-shémesh wt her suburbes: nine cities out of those two tribes.
17 And out of the tribe of Beniamín *they*
gaue Gibeón with her [f] suburbes, Géba
with her suburbes,
18 Anathóth with her suburbes, and Almón
with her suburbes: foure cities.

f The suburbes were a thousand cubites from the wall of ye citie rounde about, Nom. 35,4.

19 All the cities of the children of Aarón
Priests, *were* thirtene cities with their suburbes.
20 ¶ But to the families of the children of
Koháth of the Leuites, [g] which were the
rest of the children of Koháth (for the cities of their lot were out of the tribe of
Ephráim)

g That were not Priests.

21 They gaue them the citie of refuge for
the slayer, [h] Shechém with her suburbes
in mounte Ephráim, and Gézer with her
suburbes,

h Hebrón and Shechém were the two cities of refuge vnder the Kohathites.

22 And Kibzáim with her suburbes, & Beth-
horón with her suburbes: foure cities.
23 And out of ye tribe of Dan, Eltekéh with
her suburbes, Gibethón wt her suburbes,
24 Aiialón with her suburbes, Gath-rimmón with her suburbes: foure cities.
25 And out of the [i] halfe tribe of Manasséh,
Tanách with her suburbes, & Gath-rimmón with her suburbes: two cities.

i Which dwelt in Canáan.

26 All the cities for the other families of the
children of Koháth *were* ten with their
suburbes.
27 ¶ Also vnto the children of Gershón of
the families of the Leuites, *they gaue* out
of ye halfe tribe of Manasséh, the citie of refuge for ye slayer, [k] Golán in Bashán with
her suburbes, & Beeshteráh with her suburbes: two cities.

k Golán and Kédesh were the cities of refuge vnder the Gershonites.

28 And out of the tribe of Issachár, Kishón
with her suburbes, Daberéh with her suburbes,
29 Iarmúth with her suburbes, En-ganním
with her suburbes: foure cities.
30 And out of the tribe of Ashér, Mishál wt
her suburbes, Abdón with her suburbes,
31 Helkáh with her suburbes, and Rehób
with her suburbes: foure cities.
32 And out of ye tribe of Naphtalí, the citie
of refuge for the slayer, Kédesh in ‖ Galíl
with her suburbes, & Hammoth-dór with
her suburbes, and Kartán with her suburbes: thre cities.

‖ Or, Galile.

33 All the cities of the Gershonites according to their families, *were* thirtene cities with their suburbes.
34 ¶ Also vnto the families of the children
of Merarí the [l] rest of the Leuites, *they*
gaue out of ye tribe of Zebulún, Iokneám
with her suburbes, *and* Kartáh with her
suburbes,
35 Dimnáh with her suburbes, Nahalál
with her suburbes: foure cities.

l They are here called the rest, because they are last nombred, and Merarí was ye yongest brother, Genes. 46,11.

36 And out of ye tribe of Reubén, [m] Bézer wt
her suburbes, and Iahazáh wt her suburbes,
37 Kedemóth with her suburbes, and Mepháath with her suburbes: foure cities.

m Bézer and Ramóth were the cities of refuge vnder the Merarites and beyonde Iordén, Chap. 20,8.

38 And out of the tribe of Gad *they gaue* for
a citie of refuge for the slayer, Ramóth in
Gileád with her suburbes, and Mahanáim
with her suburbes,
39 Heshbón with her suburbes, *and* Iazér
with her suburbes: foure cities in all.
40 So all the cities of the children of Merarí according to their families (which
were the rest of the families of the Leuites) were by their lot, twelue cities.
41 *And* all the cities of the Leuites [n] within the possession of the children of Israél
were eight and fourtie with their suburbes.
42 These cities lay euerie one *seuerally* with
their suburbes rounde about them: so

n Thus according to Iaakobs prophecie, they were scattered throughout ye coūtrei, which God vsed to this end, that his people might be instructed in the true religion.

were all these cities.
43 ¶So the Lord gaue vnto Israél all the
land, which he had sworne to giue vnto
their fathers: and they possessed it, and
dwelt therein.
44 Also the Lord gaue them rest round
about according to all that he had sworne
vnto their fathers: and there stode not a
man of all their enemies before them: *for*
the Lord deliuered all their enemies into
their hand.
45 *There failed nothing of all the good
things, which the Lord had said vnto the
house of Israél, *but* all came to passe.

Chap.23,15.

CHAP. XXII.

2 Reubén, Gad, and the halfe tribe of Manasséh are sent againe to their possessions. 10 They buyld an altar for a memorial. 15 The Israelites reproue thẽ. 21 Their answer for defense of the same.

1 THen [a] Ioshúa called the Reubenites,
and the Gadites, and the halfe tribe
of Manasséh,
2 And said vnto thẽ, Ye haue kept all that
Mosés the seruant of the Lord [b] commãded you, and haue obeyed my voyce in all
that I commanded you:
3 Ye haue not forsaken your brethren this
long season vnto this day, but haue diligently kept the commandement of the
Lord your God.
4 And now the Lord hathe giuen rest vnto
your brethren as he promised them: therefore now returne ye and go to your tẽtes,
to the land of your possession, which Mosés the seruant of the Lord *hathe giuen
you beyonde Iordén.
5 But take diligent hede, to do the commandement and Lawe, which Mosés the
seruant of the Lord commanded you: *that
is*, *that ye [c] loue the Lord your God, and
walke in all his wayes, and kepe his commandements, and cleaue vnto him, and
serue him with all your heart and with all
your soule.
6 So Ioshúa [d] blessed them and sent them
away, and they went vnto their tents.
7 ¶Now vnto *one* halfe of the tribe of Manasséh Mosés had giuen *a possession* in Bashán: and vnto the *other* halfe thereof gaue
Ioshúa among their brethren on this side
Iordén Westward: therefore whẽ Ioshúa
sent them away vnto their tẽtes, and blessed them,
8 Thus he spake vnto thẽ, saying, Returne
with muche riches vnto your tentes, and
with a great multitude of cattel, with siluer and with golde, with brasse and with
yron, and with great abundãce of raimẽt:
deuide the spoyle of your enemies with
your [e] brethren.
9 ¶So the children of Reubén, & the children of Gad, and halfe the tribe of Manasséh returned, and departed from the children of Israél from Shilóh (which is in
the land of Canáan) to go vnto the countrey of Gileád to the land of their possession, which they had obteined, according
to the worde of the Lord by the hand of
Mosés.
10 ¶And when they came vnto "the borders of Iordén (ẘ are in the land of Ca-
nãã) then the children of Reubén, and the
children of Gad, & the halfe tribe of Manasséh, buylt [f] there an altar by Iordén, a
great altar to se to.
11 ¶Whẽ the children of Israél heard saie,
Beholde, the children of Reubén, and the
children of Gad, and the halfe tribe of
Manasséh haue buylt an altar in the forefront of the land of Canáan vpõ the borders of Iordén at the passage of the children of Israél:
12 When the children of Israél heard it,
then the whole Congregacion of the
children of Israél gathered them together
at Shilóh to go vp [g] to warre against
them.
13 Then the children of Israél sent vnto
the children of Reubén, and to the children of Gad, and to the halfe tribe of Manasséh into the land of Gileád, Phinehás
the sonne of Eleazár the Priest,
14 And with him ten princes, of euerie chief
house a prince, according to all the tribes
of Israél: for euerie one *was* chief of their
fathers housholde among the "thousandes of Israél.
15 ¶So they wẽt vnto the children of Reubén, and to the children of Gad, and to the
halfe tribe of Manasséh, vnto the land of
Gileád, and spake with them, saying,
16 Thus saith [h] ẏ whole Congregacion of
the Lord, What transgression is this that
ye haue transgressed against the God of
Israél, to turne away this day from the
Lord, in that ye haue buylt you an altar
for to rebel this day against the Lord?
17 Haue we to litle for the wickednes * of
Peór, whereof we are not [i] clensed vnto
this day, thogh a plague came vpon the
Congregacion of the Lord?
18 Ye also are turned away this day from
the Lord: & seing ye rebel to day against
the Lord, euen tomorowe he wilbe wrath
with all the Congregacion of Israél.
19 Notwitstanding if the lãd of your possession be [k] vncleane, come ye ouer vnto
the land of the possessiõ of the Lord, wherein the Lords Tabernacle dwelleth, and
take possession among vs: but [l] rebel not
against the Lord, nor rebel not against vs
in buylding you an altar, beside the altar
of the Lord our God.
20 Did not Achán the sonne of Zérah trespasse grieuously in the execrable thing, &
wrath fel on * all the Congregacion of
Israél?

a After that ẏ Israelites enioyed the land of Canáan.

b Which was to go armed before their brethrẽ. Nom. 32,29.

Nom 32,33. chap.13,6.

Deut.10,12.

c He sheweth wherein consisteth the fulfilling of the Lawe.

d He commẽded thẽ to God & prayed for them.

e Which remained at home and went not to the warre, Nom 31,27. 1 sam.30,24.

"*Ebr Gelilóth, which countrey also was called Canáan because the Amorites dwelling there were called Canaanites.*

f That is, beyonde Iordén; for some time the whole countrey on bothe sides of Iordén is ment by Canáan.

g Suche now was their zeale, that they wolde rather lose their liues, then suffer the true religiõ to be chãged or corrupted.

"*Or, multitude.*

h Not only of ẏ princes, but also of the cõmune people.

Nom.25,4.

i Meaning, God is not fully pacified, for asmuche as no punishement cã be sufficiẽt for suche wickednes & idolatrie.

k In your iudgement.

l To vse anie other seruice then God hathe appointed, is to rebel against God, 1. Sam. 15,23.

Chap.7.1.

Israél? and this man alone m perished
not in his wickednes.
21 ¶Then the children of Reubén and the
children of Gad, & halfe the tribe of Manasséh answered, and said vnto the heades
ouer the thousandes of Israél,
22 The Lord God of gods, ŷ Lord God of
gods, he knoweth, and Israél him selfe shal
knowe: if by rebelliō, or by transgression
against the Lord we *haue done it*, saue thou
vs not this day.
23 If we haue buylt vs an altar to returne
away from the Lord, ether to offer thereō
burnt offring, or meat offring, or to offer
peace offrings thereon, let ŷ Lord n him
selfe require it:
24 And if we haue not *rather* done it for feare of *this* thing, saying, In time to come
your children might say vnto our childrē,
What haue ye to do with the Lord God
of Israél?
25 For ŷ Lord hathe made Iordén a border
betwene vs and you, ye children of Reubén, & of Gad: therefore ye haue no parte
in the Lord: so shal your children make
our children o cease from fearing the
Lord.
26 Therefore we said, We wil now go a-
bout to make vs an altar, not for burnt offring, nor for sacrifice,
27 But for a * witnes betwene vs and you,
and betwene our generacions after vs,
to execute the seruice of the Lord before
him in our burnt offrings, and in our sacrifices, and in our peace offrings, and
that your children shulde not say to our
children in time to come, Ye haue no parte in the Lord.
28 Therefore said we, If so be that they
shulde so say to vs or to our p generacions
in time to come, thē wil we answer, Beholde the facion of the altar of the Lord,
which our fathers made, not for burnt offring nor for sacrifice, but it is a witnes
betwene vs and you.
29 God forbid, that we shulde rebel against
the Lord, and turne this day away from
the Lord to buyld an altar for burnt offring, *or* for meat offring, or for sacrifice, saue the altar of the Lord our God,
that is before his Tabernacle.
30 ¶And when Phineás the Priest, and the
princes of the Congregacion and heades
ouer the thousandes of Israél which were
with him, heard the wordes, that the children of Reubén, and children of Gad, and
the children of Manasséh spake, " they
were wel content.
31 And Phinehás the sonne of Eleazár the
Priest said vnto the children of Reubén
and to ŷ children of Gad, & to the childrē
of Manasséh, This day we perceiue, that
ŷ Lord is q among vs, because ye haue not
done this trespas against the Lord: now
ye r haue deliuered the children of Israél
out of the hand of the Lord.
32 ¶Then Phinehás the sonne of Eleazár
the Priest with the princes returned from
the childrē of Reubén, and from the children of Gad, out of the land of Gileád,
vnto the land of Canáan, to the children
of Israél, and broght them answer.
33 And the saying pleased the children of
Israél: and the children of Israél "blessed
God, and "minded not to go against thē
in battel, for to destroy the land, wherein
the children of Reubén, and Gad dwelt.
34 Then the children of Reubén, and the
children of Gad called the altar "*Ed*: for it
shalbe a witnes betwene vs, that the Lord
is God.

m Signifying, that if manie offred for one mans faute, for the faute of manie all shulde suffre.

n Let him punishe vs.

o Or, to turne backe frō the true God.

Gen. 31,48. chap. 24,27.

p They signifie a wonderful care that they bare towarde their posteritie, that they might liue in the true seruice of God

" Ebr. it was good in their eyes.

q By preseruing vs & gouerning vs.

r Whome if ye had offended, he wolde haue punished with you.

" Or, praised.

" Ebr. said.

" Or, witnes.

CHAP. XXIII.

1 Ioshúa exhorteth the people, that they ioyne not thē selues to the Gentiles. 7 That they name not their idoles. 14 The promes, if they feare God. 15 And threatenings, if they forsake him.

1 AND along season after that ŷ Lord
had giuen rest vnto Israél from all
their enemies round about, & Ioshúa was
olde, and "striken in age,
2 Then Ioshúa called all Israél, & their Elders, and their heades, and their iudges,
and their officers, and said vnto them, I
am olde, & striken in age.
3 Also ye haue sene all that the Lord your
God hathe done vnto all these nacions
a before you, how the Lord your God him
selfe hathe fought for you.
4 Beholde, I haue "deuided vnto you by lot
these nacions that remaine, to be an inheritāce according to your tribes, from Iordén, with all the nacions that I haue destroyed, euē vnto ŷ great Sea "Westward.
5 And the Lord your God shal expel b thē
before you, & cast them out of your sight,
and ye shal possesse their land, as the Lord
your God hathe said vnto you.
6 Be ye therefore of a valiant courage, to
obserue and do all that is written in the
boke of the Lawe of Mosés, *that ye turne not therefrom to the right hand nor
to the left,
7 Nether company with these nacions: *that
is*, with them which are c left with you, nether make *mencion of the name of their
gods, d nor cause to sweare *by them*, nether
serue them nor bowe vnto them:
8 But sticke fast vnto the Lord your God,
as ye haue done vnto this day.
9 For the Lord hathe cast out before you
great nacions and mighty, and no man
hathe stand before your face hetherto.
10 *One man of you shal chase a thousand:
for the Lord your God, he fighteth for
you, as he hathe promised you.
11 Take good hede therefore vnto your

" Ebr. cōmen into yeres.

a Your eyes bearing witnes.

" Or, ouerthrowe these nacions.

" Ebr. at the sunne set.

b Which yet remaine & are not ouercome, as Chap 13,2.

Deut. 5,32. & 28,4.

c And not yet subdued.

Psal. 16,4.

d Let not the Iudges admit anothe, ŵ anie shal sweare by their idoles.

Leu. 26,8. deu. 32,30.

"selues, that ye loue the Lord your God.
12 Els, if ye go backe, and cleaue vnto the
rest of these nacions: *that is*, of them that
remaine with you, and shal "make mariages with them, and "go vnto them, & they
to you,
13 Knowe ye for certeine, that the Lord
your God wil cast out no more of these
nacions from before you: *but they shal
be a snare and destruction vnto you, and a
whip on your sides, and thornes in your
[e] eyes, vntil ye perish out of this good
land, which the Lord your God hathe giuen you.
14 And beholde, this day do I [f] entre into
the way of all the world, and ye knowe in
all your [g] heartes and in all your soules,
that *nothing hathe failed of all the good
things which the Lord your God promised you, *but* all are come to passe vnto you:
nothing hathe failed thereof.
15 Therefore as all "good things are come
vpon you, which the Lord your God promised you, so shal the Lord bring vpon
you euerie "euil thing, vntil he haue destroyed you out of this good land, which
the Lord your God hathe giuen you.
16 When ye shal [h] transgresse the couenant of the Lord your God, which he cōmanded you, and shal go, and serue other
gods, and bowe your selues to them, then
shal the wrath of ẏ Lord waxe hote against
you, and ye shal perish quickly out of the
good land which he hathe giuen you.

"Ebr. soules.
"Or, be of their affinitie.
"Or, haue conuersacion with thē.
Exod.23,33. nom 33,55. deut.7,15.
e Meaning, they shalbe a cōtinual grief vnto you, and so the cause of your destruction.
f I dye according to ẏ course of nature.
g Moste certeinly.
Chap.21,45.
"Or, promises.
"Or, threatnings.
h He sheweth that no euil cā come vnto man, except he offend God by disobedience.

CHAP. XXIIII.

2 Ioshúa rehearseth Gods benefites, 14 And exhorteth the people to feare God. 25 The league renued betwene God and the people. 29 Ioshúa dyeth. 32 The bones of Ioséph are buryed. 33 Eleazár dyeth.

1 AND Ioshúa assembled *againe* all the
[a] tribes of Israél to Shechém, & called the Elders of Israél, and their heades,
and their iudges, and their officers, & they
presented them selues before [b] God.
2 Then Ioshúa said vnto all the people,
Thus saith the Lord God of Israél, *Your
fathers dwelt beyonde the [c] flood in olde
time, *euen* Térah the father of Abrahám,
and the father of Nachór, and serued other gods.
3 And I toke your father Abrahám from
beyōde the flood, & broght him through
all the land of Canáan, and multiplied his
sede, and *gaue him Izhák.
4 And I gaue vnto Izhák, Iaakób & Esáu:
and I gaue vnto *Esáu mount Seír, to possesse it: but *Iaakób and his children wēt
downe into Egypt.
5 *I sent Mosés also and Aarón, and I plagued Egypt: & whē I had so done among
them, I broght you out.
6 So I *broght your fathers out of Egypt,
& ye came vnto the Sea, & the Egyptiās
pursued after your fathers with charrets
and horsemen vnto *the red Sea.
7 Then they cryed vnto the Lord, and he
put "a darcknes betwene you & the Egyptians, and broght the Sea vpon them, and
couered them: so your eyes haue sene what
I haue done in Egypt: also ye dwelt in
the wildernes [d] a long season.
8 After I broght you into the land of the
Amorites, which dwelt beyonde Iordén,
*and they fought with you: but I gaue thē
into your hand, and ye possessed their countrey, and I destroyed them out of your
sight.
9 *Also Balák the sonne of Zippór King
of Moáb arose and warred against Israél,
and sent to call Balaám the sonne of Beór for to curse you,
10 But I wolde not heare Balaám: therefore he blessed you, and I deliuered you out
of his hand.
11 And ye went ouer Iordén, and came vnto Ierichó, and the [e] mē of Ierichó fought
against you, the Amorites, & the Perizzites, & ẏ Canaanites, and the Hittites and
the Girgashites, the Hiuites and the Iebusites, and I deliuered them into your
hand.
12 And I sent *hornets before you, which
cast them out before you, *euen* the two
Kings of the Amorites, & not with thy
sworde, nor with thy bowe.
13 And I haue giuen you a land, wherein
ye did not labour, and cities which ye
buylt not, & ye dwel in them, & eat of the
vineyardes and oliue trees, which ye planted not.
14 Now therefore [f] feare the Lord, & serue him in vprightenes and in trueth, and
put away the gods, which your fathers serued beyonde the flood and in Egypt, and
serue ye the Lord.
15 And "if it seme euil vnto you to serue the
Lord, chuse you this day whome ye wil
serue, whether ẏ gods which your fathers
serued (that were beyonde the flood) or
the gods of the Amorites, in whose land
ye dwel: [g] but I and mine house wil serue
the Lord.
16 Then the people answered and said, God
forbid, that we shulde forsake the Lord, to
serue other gods.
17 For the Lord our God, he broght vs and
our fathers out of the land of Egypt,
from the house of bondage, and he did
those great miracles in our sight, and preserued vs in all the way that we went, and
among all the people through whome we
came.
18 And the Lord did cast out before vs all
the people, euē the Amorites which dwelt
in the land: *therefore* wil we also serue the
Lord, [h] for he is our God.

a That is, the nine tribes & the halfe.
b Before the Arke, which was broght to Shechém, whē they went to bury Iosephs bones.
Gen.11,32. iudi.5,6.
c Euphrátes in Mesopotamia, Gen.11,26.
Gen.21,2. & 25,25.
Gen.36,8.
Gen.46,6.
Exod.3,10.
Exod.12,37.
Exod.14,9.
"Or, a cloude.
d Euen fourtie yeres.
Nom.21,24.
Nom.22,5. deut.23,4.
e Because it was the chief citie, vnder it he conteineth all the countrey: els they of the citie fought not. Chap.3,14.
Exod.23,28. deut.7,20. chap.11,20.
f This is the true vse of Gods benefites, to learne thereby to feare & serue him with an vpright conscience.
"Ebr. if it be euil in your sight.
g This teacheth vs ẏ if all ẏ worlde wolde go frō God, yet euerie one of vs particularly is bonde to cleaue vnto him.
h How muche more are we bonde to serue God in Christ, by whom we haue receiued ẏ redemption of our soules?

19 And Ioſhúa ſaid vnto the people, Ye can
not ſerue ŷ Lord: for he is an holy God:
he is a ielous God: he wil not pardõ your
iniquitie nor your ſinnes.
20 If ye forſake the Lord and ſerue ſtrange
gods,*thẽ he wil returne & bring euil vpõ
you, and conſume you, after that he hathe
done you good.
21 And the people ſaid vnto Ioſhúa, Nay,
but we wil ſerue the Lord.
22 And Ioſhúa ſaid vnto the people, Ye a-
re witneſſes [i] againſt your ſelues, that ye
haue choſen you the Lord, to ſerue him: &
they ſaid, *We are* witneſſes.
23 Then put away now, *ſaid he*, the ſtrange
[k] gods which are among you, & bow your
hearts vnto the Lord God of Iſraél.
24 And the people ſaid vnto Ioſhúa, The
Lord our God wil we ſerue, and his voyce
wil we obey.
25 So Ioſhúa [l] made a couenant with the
people the ſame day, and gaue them an ordinance and lawe in Shechém.
26 And Ioſhúa wrote theſe wordes in the
boke of the Lawe of God, and toke a
great ſtone, and pitched it there vnder an
°oke that was in the Sanctuarie of the
Lord.
27 And Ioſhúa ſaid vnto all the people, Beholde, this ſtone ſhalbe a witnes vnto vs:
for it [m] hathe heard all the wordes of the
Lord which he ſpake with vs: it ſhalbe
therefore a witnes againſt you, leſt ye deny your God.
28 Thẽ Ioſhúa let the people departe, euerie man vnto his inheritance.
29 And after theſe things Ioſhúa the ſonne
of Nun, the ſeruant of the Lord dyed, being an hundreth and ten yeres olde.
30 And they buryed him in ŷ border of his
inheritance in *Timnath-ſeráh, which is
in mount Ephráim, on the Northſide of
mount Gáaſh.
31 And Iſraél [n] ſerued the Lord all the days
of Ioſhúa, and all the dayes of the Elders that ouerliued Ioſhúa, & which had
knowen all the workes of the Lord that
he had done for Iſraél.
32 And the *bones of Ioſéph, which the
children of Iſraél broght out of Egypt,
buryed they in Shechém in a parcel of
grounde which Iaakób boght of the *ſonnes of Hamór the father of Shechém, for
an hundreth pieces of ſiluer, and the children of Ioſéph had them in their inheritance.
33 Alſo Eleazár the ſonne of Aarón dyed,
whome they buryed in °the hil of Phinehás his ſonne, which was giuen him in mount Ephráim.

Chap. 23, 15.

i If you do ŷ cõtrarie, your owne mouthes ſhal condemne you.

k Out of your heartes and otherwiſe.

l By ioyning God and the people together: alſo he repeated the promiſes and threatenings out of ŷ Lawe.

° Or, elme.

m Rather thẽ mans diſsimulation ſhulde not be puniſhed, the dũme creatures ſhal crye for vengeance.

Chap. 19, 50.

n Suche are ŷ people cõmonly as their rulers are.

Gen. 50, 25. exod. 13, 19.

Gen. 33, 19.

° Ebr. Gibeath Phinchás.

THE BOKE OF IVDGES.

THE ARGVMENT.

Albeit there is nothing that more prouoketh Gods wrath, then mans ingratitude, yet is there nothing ſo diſpleaſant and heinous that can turne backe Gods loue from his Church. For now when the Iſraelites were entred into the land of Canáan, and ſawe the trueth of Gods promes performed, in ſtead of acknowledging his great benefites and giuing thankes for the ſame; they fell to moſte horrible obliuion of Gods graces, contrarie to their ſolemne promes made vnto Ioſhúa, and ſo prouoked his vengeance (as muche as in them ſtode) to their vtter deſtruction. Whereof as they had moſte euident ſignes by the mutabilitie of their ſtate: for he ſuffered them to be moſte cruelly vexed and tormented by tyrants: he pulled them from libertie, and caſt them into ſlauerie, to the intent they might fele their owne miſeries and ſo call vnto him and be deliuered. Yet to ſhewe that his mercies indure for euer, he raiſed vp from time to time ſuche as ſhulde deliuer them and aſſure them of his fauour and grace, if they wolde turne to him by true repentance. And theſe deliuerers the Scripture calleth Iudges, becauſe they were executers of Gods iudgements, not choſen of the people nor by ſucceſsion, but raiſed vp, as it ſemed beſt to God, for the gouernance of his people. They were twelue in nomber beſides Ioſhúa, and gouerned from Ioſhúa vnto Saúl the firſt King of Iſrael. Ioſhúa and theſe vnto the tyme of Saúl ruled 336 yeres. In this boke are manie notable points declared, but two eſpecially: firſt, the battel that the Church of God hathe for the maintenance of true religion againſt idolatrie and ſuperſtition: next, what great danger that commune wealth is in, when as God giueth not a magiſtrate to reteine his people in the purenes of religion and his true ſeruice.

CHAP. I.

1 After Iosh̃úa was dead, Iudáh was constitute captaine. 6 Adoni-bézek is take. 14 The request of Achsáh. 16 The children of Keni. 19 The Canaanites are made tributaries, but not destroyed.

1 After ÿ Iosh̃úa was dead,
ÿ childrẽ of Isráél [a] asked
the Lord, saying, [b] Who
shal go vp for vs against
the Canaanites, to fight
first against them?

[a] By the iudgement of Vrim: read Exo. 28,30 nom. 27, 21.1 sam. 28,6.
[b] Who shalbe our Captaine?

2 And the Lord said, Iudáh shal go vp: beholde, I haue giuen the land into his
hand.

3 And Iudáh said vnto Simeón his [c] brother, Come vp with me into my lot, that
we may fight against the Canaanites: and
I likewise wil go with thee into thy lot:
so Simeón went with him.

[c] For the tribe of Simeón had their inheritãce within ÿ tribe of Iudáh, Iosh. 19,1.

4 Then Iudáh went vp, and the Lord deliuered the Canaanites and the Perizzites
into their hands, and they slewe of them
in Bézek ten thousand men.

5 And they foũde [*] Adoni-bézek in Bézek:
and they fought against him, and slew the
Canaanites, and the Perizzites.

[*] *Or, the lord of Bézek.*

6 But Adoni-bézek fled, and they pursued
after him, and caught him, and [d] cut of the
thumbes of his hands and of his fete.

[d] This was Gods iust iudgement, as the tyrant him selfe confesseth, ÿ as he had done, so did he receiue, Leuit. 24,19.

7 And Adoni-bézek said, Seuentie Kings
hauing the thumbes of their hands and of
their fete cut of, gathered *bread* vnder my
table: as I haue done, so God hathe rewarded me. so they broght him to Ierusalém,
and there he dyed.

8 (Now the children of Iudáh had fought
against Ierusalém, and had takẽ it & smitten it with the edge of the sword, and had
set the [e] citie on fire)

[e] Which was afterward buylt againe, & possessed by ÿ Iebusites, 2. Sam. 5,6.

9 ¶ Afterwarde also the children of Iudáh
went downe to fight against the Canaanites, that dwelt in ÿ mountaine, and toward
the South, and in the lowe countrey.

10 And Iudáh wẽt against the Canaanites,
that dwelt in Hebrón, which Hebrón beforetime was called [*] Kiriath-arbá: and
they slewe [f] Sheshái, and Ahimán & Talmái.

[*] Iosh. 15,14.
[f] These thre were gyãts, & the children of Anák.

11 And from thence he went to the inhabitants of Debír, and the name of Debír
in olde time *was* Kiriath-sépher.

12 And Caléb said, He ÿ smiteth Kiriath-sépher, & taketh it, euen to him wil I giue
Achsáh my daughter to wife.

13 And Othniél the sonne of Kenáz Calebs yonger brother toke it, to whome he
gaue Achsáh his daughter to wife.

14 And whẽ she came *to him*, she moued him
to aske of her father a field, [g] and she lighted of her asse, and Caléb said vnto her,
What wilt thou?

[g] Read Iosh. 15,18.

15 And she answered him, Giue me a blessing: for thou hast giuen me a South countrey, giue me also springs of water: and
Caléb gaue her the springs aboue and
the springs beneth.

16 ¶ And the children of [h] Kení Mosés father in lawe went vp out of the citie of
the palmetrees with the children of Iudáh, into the wildernes of Iudáh, that lieth
in the South of Arád, and went and dwelt
among the people.

[h] This was one of the names of Mosés father in lawe, read Nom. 10, 29.

17 But Iudáh went with Simeón his brother, and they slewe the Canaanites that
inhabited Zepháth, and vtterly destroyed
it, and called the name of the citie [*] Hormáh.

[*] Nom. 21,3.

18 Also Iudáh toke [i] Azzáh with the coastes
thereof, & Askelón with the coastes thereof, and Ekrón with the coastes thereof.

[i] These cities & others were afterward possessed of the Philistims, 1. Sam. 6,17.

19 And the Lord was with Iudáh, and he
possessed the mountaines: for he colde not
driue out the inhabitants of the valleys,
because they had charets of yron.

20 And they gaue Hebrón vnto Caléb, as
[*] Mosés had said, and he expelled thence
the thre sonnes of Anák.

[*] Nom. 14,24. iosh. 14,13. & 15,14.

21 But the children of Beniamín did not
cast out the Iebusites, that [k] inhabited Ierusalém: therefore the Iebusites dwel with
the children of Beniamín in Ierusalém
vnto this day.

[k] For after ÿ the tribe of Iudáh had burnt it, they built it againe.

22 ¶ They also that were of the house of
Ioséph, went vp to Beth-él, and the Lord
was with them,

23 And the house of Ioséph caused to vewe Beth-él (and the name of the citie beforetime *was* [*] Luz)

[*] Gen. 28,19.

24 And the spies sawe a man come out of
the citie, & they said vnto him, Shewe vs,
we pray thee, the way into the citie, [*] and
we wil shewe thee mercie.

[*] Iosh. 2,14.

25 And when he had shewed them the way
into the citie, they smote the citie with ÿ
edge of the sword, but they let the man &
all his housholde departe.

26 Then the man went into the land of the
Hittites, and buylt a citie, and called the
name thereof Luz, which is the name thereof vnto this day.

27 ¶ [*] Nether did Manasséh destroy Beth-sheán with her townes, nor Taanách with
her townes, nor the inhabitants of Dor
with her townes, nor the inhabitants of Ibleám with her townes, nether the inhabitants of Megiddó with her townes:
[l] but the Canaanites dwelled stil in that
land.

[*] Iosh. 17,12.
[l] Wherefore God permitted the Canaanites to dwel stil in ÿ land, read Chap. 3,4.

28 Neuertheles when Israél was strõg, they
put the Canaanites to tribute, and expelled them not wholly.

29 ¶ [*] Likewise Ephráim expelled not the
Canaanites that dwelt in Gézer, but the
Canaanites dwelt in Gézer among them.

[*] Iosh. 16,10.

30 ¶ Nether did [m] Zebulún expel the inhabitants of Kitrón, nor the inhabitants
of

[m] That is the tribe of Zebulún, as is also to be vnderstãd of ÿ rest.

of Nahalól, but the Canaanites dwelt a-
mong them, and became tributaries.
31 ¶Nether did Ashér cast out the inhabitants of Acchó, nor the inhabitants of Zi-
dôn, nor of Ahláb, nor of Achzíb, nor of
Helbáh, nor of Aphík, nor of Rehób,
32 But the Asherites dwelt among the Canaanites the inhabitants of the land: for
thei did not driue them [n] out.
33 ¶Nether did Naphtalí driue out the inhabitants of Beth-shémesh, nor the inhabitants of Beth-anáth, but dwelt among
the Canaanites the inhabitãts of the lãd:
neuertheles the inhabitants of Beth-shémesh, and of Beth-anáth became tributaries vnto them.
34 And the Amorites "droue the children
of Dan into the mountaine: so that thei
suffred them not to come downe to the
valley.
35 And the Amorites " dwelt stil in mount
Héres in Aiialón, and in Shaalbím, and
when the [o] hand of Iosephs familie preuailed, thei became tributaries:
36 And the coast of the Amorites was from
Maaleh-akrabbím, *euen* from [p] Sélah and
vpwarde.

n But made them pay tribut as y others did.

"Or, afflicted them.

"Or, wolde dwel

o Meaning, when he was stronger then they.

p Which was a citie in Arabia, or, as some read, from the rocke.

CHAP. II.

1 The Angel rebuketh the people, because thei had made peace with the Canaanites. 11 The Israelites fel to idolatrie after Iosuas death. 14 Thei are deliuered into the enemies hands. 16 God deliuereth them by Iudges. 22 Why God suffred idolaters to remaine among them.

1 AND an [a] Angel of the Lord came
vp from Gilgál to Bochím, & said,
I made you to go vp out of Egypt, & haue
broght you vnto the land which I had
sworne vnto your fathers, and said, I wil
neuer breake my couenant with you.
2 *Ye also shal make no couenant with the
inhabitants of this land, * *but* shal breake
downe their altars: but ye haue not obeyed my voyce. Why haue ye done this?
3 Wherefore, I said also, I wil not cast thẽ
out before you, but thei shalbe* *as thornes*
vnto your sides, and their gods shalbe
"your destruction.
4 And when the Angel of the Lord spake
these wordes vnto all the children of Israél, the people lift vp their voyce, and
wept.
5 Therefore thei called the name of that
place, "Bochím, and offred sacrifices there
vnto the Lord.
6 ¶Now when Ioshúa had [b] sent the people away, the children of Israél went euerie mã into his inheritance to possesse the
land.
7 And the people had serued the Lord all
the daies of Ioshúa, and all the daies of
the Elders that outlyued Ioshúa, which
had sene all the great [c] workes of the
Lord that he did for Israél.

a That is, messenger, or Prophet, as some thinke, Phinehás.

Deut.7,2.

Deut.12,3.

Iosh.23,13.

"Or, snare.

"Or, weeping.

b After that he had deuided to euery man his porcion by lot, Iosh.24,28.

c Meaning, the wonders & miracles.

8 But Ioshúa the sonne of Nun the seruãt
of the Lord dyed, when he was an hũdreth
and ten yeres olde:
9 And thei buryed him in the coastes of his
inheritance, in [d] Timnath-héres in mount
Ephráim, on the Northside of mount
Gáash.
10 And so all that generacion was gathered
vnto their fathers, and an other generacion arose after them, which nether knewe
the Lord, nor yet the workes, which he
had done for Israél.
11 ¶Thẽ the children of Israél did wickedly in the sight of the Lord, and serued
[e] Baalím,
12 And forsoke the Lord God of their fathers, which broght them out of the land
of Egypt, & followed other gods, *euẽ* the
gods of the people that were round about
them, and bowed vnto them, & prouoked
the Lord to angre.
13 So thei forsoke the Lord, & serued Báal
and [f] Ashtaróth.
14 And the wrath of the Lord was hote a-
gainst Israél, and he deliuered them into
the hãds of spoilers, that spoiled them, &
he * solde them into the hands of their e-
nemies roũd about thẽ, so that thei colde
no longer stand before their enemies.
15 [g] Whersoeuer thei went out, the [h] hãd
of the Lord was sore against them, as the
Lord had said, & as the Lord had sworne
vnto them: so he punished them sore.
16 ¶Notwithstanding, the Lord raised vp
"Iudges, which" deliuered them out of the
hands of their oppressers.
17 But yet thei wolde not obey their Iudges: for thei went a whoring after other
gods, and worshipped them, *&* turned
quickely out of the [i] way, wherein their
fathers walked, obeying the commandements of the Lord: thei did not so.
18 And when the Lord had raised them vp
Iudges, the Lord was with the Iudge, and
deliuered them out of the hand of their
enemies all the daies of the Iudge (for the
Lord" had compassion of their gronings,
[k] because of them that oppressed them &
tormented them)
19 Yet* whẽ the Iudge was dead, thei returned, and " did worse then their fathers, in
following other gods to serue them and
worship them: thei ceased not from their
owne inuencions, nor from their rebellious way.
20 Wherefore the wrath of the Lord was
kindled against Israél, & he said, Because
this people hathe transgressed my couenant, which I commanded their fathers, &
hathe not obeyed my voyce,
21 Therefore wil I no more cast out before them any of the [l] nacions, which Ioshúa left when he dyed,

d Héres by turnĩg the letters backward is Seréh, as Iosh.24,30.

e That is, all maner of idoles.

f These were idoles, which had the forme of an ewe or shepe among the Sidonians.

Psal 44,13. isa.50,1.

g In all their enterprises.

h The vengeance.

"Or, Magistrates.

"Ebr. saued.

i Meaning, frõ the true religion.

"Ebr. repented.

k Seing their crueltie.

Chap.3,12.

"Ebr. corrupted them selues.

l As the Hiuites, Iebusites, Amorites, &c.

m So ŷ bothe outwarde enemies and false Prophets are but a tryal to proue ŏ faith, Deut.13,3.

22 That through them I may m proue Israél, whether they wil kepe the way of the Lord, to walke therein, as their fathers kept it, or not.
23 So the Lord left those nacions, & droue them not out immediatly, nether deliuered them into the hand of Ioshúa.

CHAP. III.

1 The Canaanites were left to trye Israél. 9 Othniél deliuereth Israél. 21 Ehúd killeth King Eglón. 31 Shamgár killeth the Philistims.

1 These now are the nacions which the Lord left, that he might proue Israél by them (*euen* as many *of Israél* as had not knowen all the a warres of Canáan,
2 Onely to make the generacions of the children of Israél to knowe, and to teache them warre, which douteles their predessessors knewe b not)
3 Fiue princes of the Philistims, and all the Canaanites, and the Sidonians, and the Hiuites that dwelt in mount Lebanón, from mount Báal hermón vnto one come to Hamáth.
4 And these remained to proue Israél by them, to wit, whether thei wolde obey the commandements of the Lord, which he commanded their fathers by the hand of Mosés.
5 And the children of Israél dwelt among the Canaanites, the Hittites, & the Amorites, and the Perizzites, and the Hiuites, and the Iebusites,
6 And thei toke c their daughters to be their wiues, and gaue their daughters to their sonnes, and serued their gods.
7 ¶ So ŷ children of Israél did wickedly in the sight of the Lord, & forgate the Lord their God, & serued Baalím, and d Asheróth.
8 Therefore the wrath of the Lord was kindled against Israél, and he solde them into the hād of Chushán rishatháim King of "Arám-naharáim, & the childrē of Israél serued Chushán rishatháim eight yeres.
9 ¶ And when the children of Israél cryed vnto the Lord, the Lord stirred vp a sauiour to the children of Israél, and he saued them, *euen* Othniél the sonne of Kenáz, Calebs yonger brother.
10 And the e Spirit of the Lord came vpō him, and he iudged Israél, and went out to warre: & the Lord deliuered Chushán rishatháim King of "Arám into his hand, and his hand preuailed against Chushán rishatháim.
11 So the land had rest f fourtie yeres, and Othniél the sonne of Kenáz dyed.
12 ¶ Thē the children of Israél againe cōmitted wickednes in ŷ sight of the Lord: & the Lord g strengthened Eglón King of Moáb against Israél, because thei had committed wickednes before the Lord.
13 And he gathered vnto him the children of Ammón, and Amalék, and went and smote Israél, and thei possessed the citie of palmetrees.
14 So the children of Israél serued Eglón King of Moáb eightene yeres.
15 But when the children of Israél cryed vnto the Lord, the Lord stirred them vp a sauiour, Ehúd the sonne of Gerá the sonne of "Iemini, a man "lame of his right hand: and the children of Israél sent a present by him vnto Eglón King of Moáb.
16 And Ehúd "made him a dagger with two edges of a cubite length, and he did girde it vnder his raymēt vpon his right thigh,
17 And he presented the gift vnto Eglón King of Moáb (and Eglón *was* a very fat man)
18 And whē he had now presented the present, he sent away the people that bare the present,
19 But he turned againe from the h quarris, that were by Gilgál, and said, I haue a secret errand vnto thee, ô King. Who said, Kepe i silence: and all that stode about him, went out from him.
20 Then Ehúd came vnto him, (& he sate alone in a somer parler, which he had) & Ehúd said, I haue a message vnto thee frō God. Then he arose out of his throne,
21 And Ehúd put forthe his left hand, and toke the dagger from his right thigh, and thrust it into his belly,
22 So that the hafte went in after the blade: and the fat closed about the blade, so that he colde not drawe the dagger out of his belly, but the dirt came out.
23 Then Ehúd gate him out "into the porche, and shut the dores of the parler vpon him, and locked them.
24 And when he was gone out, his seruants came: who seing that ŷ dores of the parler were locked, thei said, "Surely he doeth his easement in his somer chambre.
25 And thei taryed til thei were ashamed: and seing he opened not the dores of the parler, thei toke the keye, and opened thē, and beholde, their lord was fallen dead on the earth.
26 So Ehúd escaped (while thei taryed) and was passed the quarris, and escaped vnto Seiráth.
27 And when he came *home*, "he blewe a trumpet in mount Ephráim, and the children of Israél went downe with him from the mountaine, and he went before them.
28 Then said he vnto them, Followe me: for the Lord hathe deliuered your enemies, *euen* Moab into your hand. So they went downe after him, and toke the passages

a Which were acheued by ŷ hand of God, and not by the power of man.

b For thei trusted in God & he fought for them.

c Contrary to Gods commādement, Deut. 7,3.

d Trees or woods erected for idolatrie.

"Or, Mesopotamia.

e He was stirred vp by the Spirit of the Lord.

"Or, Syria.

f That is, 32. vnder Ioshúa, & 8. vnder Othniél.

g So ŷ the enemies of Gods people haue no power ouer them, but by Gods appointement.

"Or, Beniamite.
"Or, left hāded.

"Or, caused a dagger to be made.

h Or, as some read, from the places of idoles.

i Til all be departed.

"Or, haule.

"Ebr. he couereth his fete.

"Or, caused the trumpet to be blowen, Nomb. 10,2.

sages of Iordén toward Moáb, and suffred not a man to passe ouer.

"Or, strong, and big bodied.

29 And they slew of the Moabites the same
time about ten thousand mē, all "fed men,
and all *were* warriours, and there escaped
not a man.

"Ebr. humbled.
k Meaning, the Israelites.

30 So Moáb was "subdued that day, vnder
the hand of Isráél: and the k land had rest
foure score yeres.
31 ¶ And after him was Shamgár the sonne
of Anáth, which slewe of the Philistims
sixe hundreth men with an oxe l goade, &
he also deliuered Isráél.

l So that it is not the nōber, nor ẏ meanes ẏ God regardeth, when he wil get the victorie.

CHAP. IIII.

1 Isráél sinne and are giuē into the hands of Iabín. 4 Deboráh iudgeth Isráél and exhorteth Barák to deliuer the people. 15 Siserá fleeth, 17 And is killed by Iaél.

"Ebr. added, or continued to do euil.

1 AND the children of Isráél " began a-
gaine to do wickedly in the sight of
the Lord when Ehúd was dead.
2 And the Lord solde them into the hand
of a Iabín King of Canáan, that reigned
in Hazór, whose chief captaine *was called*
Siserá, which dwelt in b Harosheth of the
Gentiles.

a There was another Iabin, whome Ioshúa killed & burnt his citie Hazór, Iosh. 11, 13.
b That is, in a wood, or strōg place.

3 Then the children of Isráél cryed vnto
the Lord: (for he had nine hundreth charets of yron, and twentie yeres he had vexed the children of Isráél very sore)
4 ¶ And at that time Deboráh a Prophetesse the wife of Lapidóth c iudged Israél.

c By ẏ Spirit of prophecie, resoluing of controuersies, & declaring ẏ wil of God.

5 And this Deboráh dwelt vnder a palme
tre, betwene Ramáh and Beth-él in mōūt
Ephráim, & the children of Isráél came vp
to her for iudgement.
6 Then she sent and called Barák the sonne of Abinóam out of Kédesh of Naphtalí, and said vnto him, Hathe not ẏ Lord
God of Isráél d commanded, *saying*, Go,
and drawe toward mount Tabór, & take
with thee ten thousand men of the children of Naphtalí and of the children of
Zebulún?

d And reueiled vnto me by ẏ Spirit of prophecie.

* Psal. 83, 10.
"Or, valley.

7 And I wil drawe vnto thee to the * "riuer
Kishón Siserá, the captaine of Iabins armie with his charets, and his multitude, &
wil deliuer him into thine hand.
8 And Barák said vnto her, e If thou wilt
go with me, I wil go: but if thou wilt not
go with me, I wil not go.

e Fearing his owne weakenes & his enemies power, he desireth ẏ Prophetesse to go with him to assure him of Gods wil from time to time.

9 Then she answered, I wil surely go with
thee, but this iourney that thou takest, shal
not be for thine honour: for ẏ Lord shal
sel Siserá into ẏ hād of a womā. And Deboráh arose and went ẇ Barák to Kédesh.
10 ¶ And Barák called Zebulún and Naph
talí to Kédesh, & " he went vp on his fete
with ten thousand men, and Deboráh wēt
vp with him.

"Or, he led after him 10000. men.

"Or, posteritie.
* Nom. 10, 29.
"Ebr. frō Káin.

11 (Now Hébér the Kenite, which was of
the "children of * Hobáb the father in law
of Mosés, was departed from the " Kenites, and pitched his tent f vntil the plaine
of Zaanaim, which is by Kédesh)

f Meaning, ẏ he possessed a great parte of that countrey.

12 Thē they shewed Siserá, ẏ Barák ẏ sonne
of Abinóā was gone vp to mōūt Tabór.
13 And Siserá called for all is charets, *euen*
nine hundreth charets of yron, & all the
people that were with him frō Harosheth
of the Gentiles, vnto the riuer Kishón.
14 Then Deboráh said vnto Barák, g Vp:
for this is ẏ day that the Lord hathe deliuered Siserá into thine hand. Is not the
Lord gone out before thee? so Barák went
downe from mount Tabór, and ten thousand men after him.

g She stil encourageth hī to this entreprise by assuring him of Gods fauour & aide.

15 And the Lord destroyed Siserá and all
his charets, & all his hoste with the edge
of the sworde, before Barák, so that Siserá lighted downe of his charet, and fled
away on his fete.
16 But * Barák pursued after the charets,
& after the hoste vnto Harosheth of the
Gētiles: & all ẏ host of Siserá fel vpon ẏ
edge of ẏ sworde: there was not a mā left.

* Psal. 83, 10.

17 Howbeit, Siserá fled away on his fete to
the tent of Iaél the wife of h Hebér the
Kenite: (for peace *was* betwene Iabín the
King of Hazór, and betwene the house
of Hebér the Kenite)

h Whose ancesters were strāgers, but worshiped ẏ true God, & therefore were ioyned ẇ Isráél.

18 And Iaél wēt out to mete Siserá, & said
vnto him, Turne in, my Lord, turne into
me: feare not. And when he had turned in
vnto her into her tent, she couered him
with a "mantel.

"Or, blanket.

19 And he said vnto her, Giue me, I pray
thee, a litle water to drīke: for I am thirsty.
And she opened * a bottle of milke & gaue him drinke, and couered him.

* Chap. 5, 25.

20 Againe he said vnto her, Stande in the
dore of the tent, and when anie man doeth come and enquire of thee, saying, Is
i anie man here? thou shalt say, Nay.

i To wit, Siserá.
k That is, the pinne or stake, whereby it was fastened to the groūde.

21 Then Iaél Hebers wife toke a k nayle of
the tent, and toke an hammer in her hand,
and went softly vnto him, and smote the
naile into his temples, and fastened it into
the grounde, (for he was fast a slepe, and
wearie) and *so* he dyed.
22 And beholde, as Barák pursued after Siserá, Iaél came out to mete him, and said
vnto him, Come, and I wil shewe thee the
mā, whome thou seekest: and whē he came
into her *tent*, beholde, Siserá lay l dead, and
the naile in his temples.

l So he sawe ẏ a woman had the honour, as Deboráh prophecied.

23 So God broght downe Iabín the King
of Canáan that day before the children of
Isráél.
24 And the hand of the children of Isráél
"prospered, and preuailed against Iabín
the King of Canáan, vntil they had destroyed Iabín King of Canáan.

"Ebr. went and was strong.

CHAP. V.

1 The song and thankesgiuing of Deboráh and Barák after the victorie.

1 THen sang Deboráh, and Barák the
sonne of Abinóam the same day, saying,
2 Praise ye the Lord for the auenging of
Israél, & for the [a] people that offred thē
selues willingly.

a To wit, the two tribes of Zebulún and Naphtalí.

3 Heare, ye Kings, hearken ye princes: I, *e-
uen* I wil sing vnto ẏ Lord: I wil sing praise vnto the Lord God of Israél.
4 Lord, * when thou wentest out of Seír,
when thou departedst out of the field of
*Edóm, the earth trembled, & the heauēs
rained, the cloudes also dropped water.
5 *The mountaines melted before ẏ Lord,
**as did* that Sinái before the Lord God of
Israél.

Deu.4,11. *Deu.2,1.* *Psal.97,5.* *Exod.19,18.*

6 In the dayes of *Shamgár the sonne of
Anáth, in ẏ dayes of *Iaél the hye wayes
were [b] vnoccupied, and the trauelers walked through bywayes.

Chap.3,31. *Chap.4,18.*
b For feare of the enemies.

7 The townes were not inhabited: they decayed, *I say*, in Israél, vntil I Deboráh came vp, which rose vp a [c] mother in Israél.
8 They chose newe gods: then *was* warre in
the gates. Was there a [d] shilde or speare
sene among fourtie thousand of Israél?

c Miraculously stirred vp of God to pitie them & deliuer them.
d They had no heart to resist their enemies.

9 Mine heart *is set* on the gouerners of Israél, & on them that are willing among ẏ
people: praise ye the Lord.
10 Speake ye that ride on [e] white asses, ye ẏ
dwel [f] by Middín, and that walke by the
waye.

e Ye gouerners.
f As in dāger of your enemies.

11 For the noyse of the archers *appaised* a-
mōg the [g] drawers of water: there shal thei
rehearse ẏ righteousnes of the Lord, his
righteousnes of his townes in Israél: then
did the people of the Lord go downe to
the gates.

g For now you may drawe water without feare of your enemies.

12 Vp Deboráh, vp, arise, & sing a song: a-
rise Barák, & lead [h] thy captiuitie captiue,
thou sonne of Abinóam.

h To wit, thē ẏ kept thy people in captiuitie.

13 For they that remaine, haue dominiō o-
uer the mightie of the people: the Lord
hathe giuen me dominion ouer the strong.
14 Of Ephráim [i] their roote *arose* against A-
malék: & after thee, Ben-iamin *shal fight* a-
gainst thy people, *ô Amalek*: of Machír came rulers, and of Zebulún they that handle the penne of the [k] writer.

i Ioshúa first fought against Amalék, and Saul destroyed him.
k Euen ẏ learned did helpe to fight.

15 And the Princes of Issachár were with
Deboráh, & [l] Issachár, and also Barák: he
was set on his fete in the valley: for the diuisions of Reubén *were* great [m] thoghtes
of heart.

l Euē ẏ whole tribe.
m They merueiled, ẏ they came not ouer Iordén to helpe them.

16 Why abodest thou among the shepefoldes, to heare the bleatings of the flockes?
for the diuisions of Reubén *were* great
thoghtes of heart.
17 [n] Gileád abode beyonde Iordén: & why
doeth Dan remaine in shippes? Ashér sate on the seashore, and taried in his [o] decayed places.
18 *But* the people of Zebulún and Naphtalí haue ieoparde their liues vnto the death
in the hye places of the field.

n She reproueth all them that came not to helpe their brethren in their necessitie.
o Ether by beating of the sea, or by mining.

19 The Kings came & fought: thē fought
the Kings of Canáan in Taanách by the
waters of Megiddó: they receiued no gaine of [p] money.
20 They fought from heauen, *euen* the starres in their courses fought against Siserá.

p They wanne nothing, but lost all.

21 The riuer Kishón [q] swept them away,
that ancient riuer the riuer Kishón. ô my
soule, thou hast marched valiantly.

q As a besome doeth ẏ filth of ẏ house.

22 Then were the horsehoufes broken with
the oft beating together of their mighty
men.
23 Curse ye [r] Meróz: (said the Angel of the
Lord) curse the inhabitants thereof, because they came not to helpe the Lord, to
helpe the Lord against the mightie.

r It was a citie nere Tabor, where thei fought.

24 Iaél the wife of Hebér the Kenite shal
be blessed aboue *other* women: blessed
shal she be aboue women *dwelling* in tents.
25 He asked water, & she gaue him milke: she broght forthe [f] butter in a lordly
dish.

f Some read, churned milke in a great cup.

26 She put her hand to the naile, and her
right hand to the workemans hammer:
with the hammer smote she Siserá: she
smote of his head, after she had wounded,
& persed his temples.
27 He bowed him downe at her fete, he fel
downe, & lay stil: at her fete he bowed him
downe, and fel: and when he had sonke
downe, he lay there "dead.

"*Ebr. destroyed.*

28 The mother of Siserá loked out at a
windowe, and cryed through the lattesse,
Why is his charet so long a cōming? why
tary the "wheles of his charets?

"*Or, fete.*

29 Her wise ladyes answered her, Yea. [t] She
answered her selfe with her owne wordes,

t That is, she comforted her selfe.

30 Haue they not gotten, & they deuide
the spoyle? euerie man hathe a maide or
two. Siserá hathe a praye of diuers cou-
loured *garments*, a pray of sondry coulours
made of nedle worke: of diuers coulours
of nedle worke on bothe sides, [u] for the
chief of the spoyle.

u Because he was chief of ẏ armie.

31 So let all thine enemies perish, ô Lord:
but they that loue him, shal be as the [x] sunne when he riseth in his might. and the lād
had rest fortie yeres.

x Shal growe daily more & more in Gods fauour.

CHAP. VI.

1 Israél is oppressed of the Midianites for their wickednes. 14 Gideón is sent to be their deliuerer. 37 He asketh a signe.

1 AFterward the children of Israél com
mitted wickednes in the sight of the
Lord, and the Lord gaue thē into the handes of Midián seuen yeres.
2 And the hand of Midián preuailed a-
gainst Israél, [a] & because of the Midianites the children of Israél made them dē-
nes

a For feare of ẏ Midianites thei fled into ẏ dennes of the mountaines.

dennes in the mountaines, and caues, and
ſtrong holdes.
3 When Iſraél had ſowen, then came vp
the Midianites, the Amalekites, and they
of the "East, and came vpon them,
4 And camped by them, and deſtroyed the
frute of the earth, euen til thou come vnto
[b]Azzáh, & left no foode for Iſraél, nether
ſhepe, nor oxe, nor aſſe.
5 For they wẽt vp, and their cattel, and came with their tentes as greſhoppers in
multitude: ſo that they and their camels
were without nomber: and they came into the land to deſtroye it.
6 So was Iſraél excedingly impouerished
by the Midianites: therefore the [c]children
of Iſraél cryed vnto the Lord.
7 ¶And when the children of Iſraél cryed
vnto the Lord becauſe of the Midianites,
8 The Lord ſent vnto the children of Iſraél a Prophet, who ſaid vnto them, Thus
ſayeth the Lord God of Iſraél, I haue
broght you vp frõ Egypt & haue broght
you out of the houſe of bondage,
9 And I haue deliuered you out of the hãd
of the Egyptians, and out of the hand of
all that oppreſſed you, and haue caſt them
out before you, and giuen you their
land.
10 And I ſaid vnto you, I am the Lord your
God: * feare not the gods of the Amorites in whoſe land you dwel: but you haue
not obeyed my voyce.
11 ¶And the Angel of the Lord came, and
ſate vnder the oke which was in Ophráh,
that perteined vnto Ioáſh the father of
the Ezrites, and his ſonne Gideón threa-
ſhed wheat by the winepreſſe, "to hide it
from the Midianites.
12 Then the Angel of the Lord appeared
vnto him, and ſaid vnto him, The Lord *is*
with thee, thou valiant man.
13 To whome Gideón anſwered, [d]Ah my
Lord, if the Lord be with vs, why then
is all this come vpon vs? and where be
all his miracles which our fathers tolde
vs of, and ſaid, Did not the Lord bring
vs out of Egypt? but now the Lord
hathe forſaken vs, and deliuered vs into the hand of the Midianites.
14 And the [e]Lord loked vpon him, and
ſaid, Go in this thy [f]might, & thou ſhalt
ſaue Iſraél out of the hands of the Midianites: haue not I ſent thee?
15 And he anſwered him, Ah my Lord,
whereby ſhal I ſaue Iſraél? beholde, my
"father is poore in Manaſſéh, and I am the
leaſt in my fathers houſe.
16 Then the Lord ſaid vnto him, I wil therefore be with thee, and thou ſhalt ſmite
the Midianites, as one man.
17 And he anſwered him, I pray thee, if I
haue fouñde fauour in thy ſight, then ſhewe

" Or, of kedém.

b Euen almoſt ỹ whole cõtrey.

c This is the end of Gods puniſhemẽts, to call his to repentance ỹ they may ſeke for helpe of him.

* 2.King.17,38. iere.10,2.

" Or, to prepare his flight.

d This came not of diſtruſt, but of weakenes of faith, ŵ is in ỹ moſte perfect: for no man in this life can haue a perfect faith, but the children of God haue a true faith, whereby they be iuſtified.

e That is, Chriſt appearing in viſible forme.

f Which I haue giuen thee.

" Or, familie.

me [g]a ſigne, that thou talkeſt with me.
18 Departe not hence, I pray thee, vntil I
come vnto thee, and bring mine offring, &
lay it before thee. And he ſaid, I wil tary
vntil thou come againe.
19 ¶Then Gideón went in, & made ready
a kid, & vnleauened bread of an [h]Epháh
of floure, and put the fleſh in a baſket, and
put the broth in a pot, and broght it out
vnto him vnder the oke, and preſented it.
20 And the Angel of God ſaid vnto him,
Take the fleſh and the vnleauened bread,
and lay them vpon this ſtone, and powre
out the broth: and he did ſo.
21 ¶Thẽ the Angel of the Lord put forthe
the end of the ſtaffe that he held in his
hand, and touched the fleſh & the vnleauened bread: and there aroſe vp fire [i]out
of the ſtone, and conſumed the fleſh & the
vnleauened bread: ſo the Angel of the
Lord departed out of his ſight.
22 And when Gideón perceiued that it
was an Angel of the Lord, Gideón then
ſaid, Alas, my Lord God: * for becauſe I
haue ſene an Angel of the Lord face to
face, *I ſhal dye*.
23 And the Lord ſaid vnto him, Peace be
vnto thee: feare not, thou ſhalt not dye.
24 Then Gideón made an altar there vnto
the Lord, and called it, "Iehouáh ſhalóm:
vnto this day it is in Ophráh, of the father of the Ezrites.
25 ¶And the ſame night the Lord ſaid vnto him, Take thy fathers yong bullocke, &
another bullocke [k]of ſeuen yeres olde,
and deſtroy the altar of Báal that thy father hathe, and cut downe the groue that
is by it,
26 And buylde an altar vnto the Lord thy
God vpõ the top of this rocke, in a plaine
place: and take the ſeconde bullocke, and
offer a burnt offring with the wood of the
[l]groue, which thou ſhalt cut downe.
27 Then Gideón toke ten men of his ſeruants, and did as the Lord bade him: but
becauſe he feared to do it by day for his
fathers houſholde and the men of the citie, he did it by night.
28 ¶And when the men of the citie aroſe
early in the morning, beholde, the altar of
Báal was broken, and the groue cut downe
that was by it, and the [m]ſeconde bullocke
offred vpon the altar that was made.
29 Therefore they ſaid one to another,
Who hathe done this thing? & when they
inquired and aſked, they ſaid, Gideón the
ſonne of Ioáſh hathe done this thing.
30 Then the men of the citie ſaid vnto Ioáſh, Bring out thy ſonne, that he may dye:
for he hathe deſtroyed the altar of Báal,
& hathe alſo cut downe the groue that was
by it.
31 And Ioáſh ſaid vnto all that ſtode by

g So that we ſe how the fleſh is enemie vnto Gods vocatiõ, which can not be perſuaded without ſignes.

h Of Epháh read Exod. 16,36.

i By ỹ power of God onely, as in ỹ ſacrifice of Helias, 1.King.18,38.

* Exod.33,20. chap.13,22.

" Or, the Lord of peace.

k That is, as the Chalde text writeth, fed ſeuen yeres.

l Which growed about Baals altar.

m Meaning ỹ fat bul, which was kept to be offred vnto Báal.

him, Wil ye pleade Baals cause? or wil
ye saue him? [n] he that wil contend for hi,
let him dye or the morning. If he be God,
let him pleade for him selfe against him
that hathe cast downe his altar.
32 And in that day was Gideón called Ierubbáal, ӯ is, Let Báal plead for him selfe
because he hathe broken downe his altar.
33 Then all the Midianites & the Amalekites and they of the East, were gathered
together, and went & pitched in the valley of Izreél.
34 But the Spirit of the Lord "came vpon
Gideón,* & he blewe a trumpet, & [o] Abiézer was ioyned with him.
35 And he sent messengers through out all
Manasséh, which also was ioyned with hi,
and he sent messengers vnto Ashér, and to
Zebulún and to Naphtalí, and they came
vp to mete them.
36 Then Gideón said vnto God, [p] If thou
wilt saue Israél by mine hād, as thou hast
said,
37 Beholde, I wil put a fleece of wolle in ӯ
threshing place: if the dewe come on the
fleece onely, and it be drye vpon all the
earth, then shal I be sure, that ӯ wilt saue
Israél by mine hand, as thou hast said.
38 And so it was: for he rose vp early on ӯ
morowe, & thrust the fleece together, and
wringed the dewe out of the fleece, and
filled a bowle of water.
39 Againe Gideón said vnto God, Be not
angry with me, that* I may speake once
more: let me proue once againe, I pray
thee, with the fleece: let it now be drye o-
nely vpon the fleece, and let dewe be vpō
all the grounde.
40 And God did so that same night: for it
was [q] drye vpon the fleece onely and there
was dewe on all the grounde.

n Thus we oght to iustifie them, that are zelous of Gods cause, thogh all the multitude be against vs.

"Ebr. clad Gideón.

Nom. 10, 3. chap. 3, 27.

o The familie of Abiézer, whereof he was.

p This request proceded not of infidelitie, but ӯ he might be confirmed in his vocatiō.

Gen. 18, 32.

q Whereby he was assured ӯ it was a miracle of God.

CHAP. VII.

2 The Lord commandeth Gideón to send a way a great parte of his companie. 22 The Midianites are discomfited by a wonderous sort. 25 Oréb and Zeéb are slaine.

1 THen * Ierubbáal (who is Gideón)
rose vp early and all the people that
were with him, and pitched beside "the
well of Haród, so that the hoste of the Mi
dianites was on the Northside of them in
the valley by the hil of "Moréh.
2 And ӯ Lord said vnto Gideón, The peo
ple that are with thee, are to manie for me
to giue the Midianites into their handes,
lest Israél make their [a] vante against me,
and say, Mine hand hathe saued me.
3 Now therefore proclayme in the audience of the people, & say, * Whoso is time-
rous or feareful, let him returne, and departe early from mout Gileád. And there
returned of the people which were at mount Gileád, two and twentie thousand: so
ten thousand remained.

Chap. 8, 35.

"Ebr. En-haród.

"Ebr. Hammoréh.

a God wil not that anie creature depriue him of his glorie.

Deu. 20, 8. 1. mac. 3, 56.

4 And the Lord said vnto Gideón, The
people are yet to manie: bring thē downe
vnto the water, and I wil [b] trye them
for thee there: and of whome I say vnto
thee, This man shal go with thee, the same
shal go with thee: and of whomesoeuer I
say vnto thee, This man shal not go with
thee, the same shal not go.
5 So he broght downe the people vnto the
water. And ӯ Lord said vnto Gideón, As
manie as lappe the water with their tongues as a dog lappeth, them put by them
selues, & euerie one that shal bowe downe
his knees to [c] drinke, *put aparte.*
6 And the nomber of them that lapped *by*
putting their hands to their mouthes, *were*
thre hundreth men: but all the remnant of
the people kneled downe vpō their knees
to drinke water.
7 ¶ Then the Lord said vnto Gideón, By
these thre hundreth men that lapped, wil
I saue you, and deliuer the Midianites into thine hand: and let all the *other* [d] people
go euerie man vnto his place.
8 ¶ So the people toke vitailes "with thē,
and their trumpets: and he sent all the rest
of Israél, euerie man vnto his tent, " & reteined the thre hundreth men: and the hoste of Midián was beneth him in a valley.
9 ¶ And the same night the Lord said vnto
him, Arise, [e] get thee downe vnto the hoste: for I haue deliuered it into thine hād.
10 But if thou feare to go downe, *then* go
thou, & Phuráh thy seruant downe to the
hoste,
11 And thou shalt hearken, what they say,
and so shal thine hands be strong to go
downe vnto ӯ hoste. Thē went he downe
and Phuráh his seruāt vnto the outside of
the souldiars that were in the hoste.
12 ¶ And the Midianites, and the Amalekí-
tes and all* they of the East, lay in the valley like grashoppers in multitude, & their
camels *were* without nomber, as the sand
which is by the seaside for multitude.
13 And when Gideón was come, beholde,
a man tolde a dreame vnto his neighbour,
and said, Beholde, I dreamed a dreame, &
lo, a [f] cake of barley bread tombled from
aboue into the hoste of Midián, and came
vnto a tent, and smote it that it fel, and o-
uerturned it, that the tent fel downe.
14 And his fellowe answered, and said, This
is nothing els saue the sworde of Gideón
the sonne of Ioásh a man of Israél: *for* into
his hād hathe God deliuered Midián and
all the hoste.
15 ¶ When Gideón heard the dreame tolde, and the interpretacion of the same, he
[g] worshipped, and returned vnto the hoste of Iraél, & said, Vp: for the Lord hathe
deliuered into your hād ӯ hoste of Midiā.
16 And he deuided the thre hundreth men

b I wil giue thee a proofe to knowe thē, that shal go with thee.

c Let thē departe, as vnmete for this enterprise.

d That is, the one and thirtie thousand, and 700.

"Ebr. in their hands.

"Or, incouraged.

e Thus ӯ Lord by diuers meanes doth strēgthen him that he faint not in so great an enterprise.

Chap. 6, 33.

f Some read, a trembling noise of barley bread: meaning that one of no reputacion shulde make their great armie to treble.

g Or, gaue God thākes, as it is in the Chalde text.

into thre bandes, and gaue euerie man a
trumpet in his hãd with emptie pitchers,
and "lampes [h] within the pitchers.

"Or, fire brands.
h These weake meanes God vsed, to signifie that ẏ whole victorie came of him.

17 And he said vnto them, Loke on me, and
do likewise, whẽ I come to the side of the
hoste: euen as I do, so do you.
18 When I blowe with a trumpet and all
that are with me, blowe ye with trumpets
also on euerie side of the hoste, and say,
[i] For the Lord, and for Gideón.

i That is, the victorie shalbe the Lords and Gideons his seruant.

19 ¶ So Gideón and the hundreth men that
were with him, came vnto the outside of
the hoste in the beginning of the middle
watche, and they raised vp the watchemẽ,
and they blewe with their trumpets, and
brake the pitchers that were in their hãds.
20 And the thre companies blewe with
trumpets and brake the pitchers, and held
the lampes in their left hands, and the trũpets in their right hands to blowe withall:
and they cryed, The [k] sworde of the Lord
and of Gideón.

k Shal destroy the enemies.

21 And they stode, euerie man in his place
rounde about the hoste: and all the hoste
"ranne, and cryed, and fled.

"Or, broke their array.

22 And the thre hũdreth blewe with trumpets, & * the Lord set euerie mans sworde
vpon his [l] neighbour, and vpon all the
hoste: so the hoste fled to Beth-hashittáh
in Zereráh, *and* to the border of Abél
meholáh vnto Tabbáth.

*Isa. 9,4.
l The Lord caused the Midianites to kil one another.

23 Then the men of Israél being gathered
together out of Naphtalí, & out of Ashér,
and out of all Manasséh pursued after the
Midianites.
24 And Gideón sent messengers vnto all
mount Ephráim, saying, Come downe a-
gainst the Midianites, and take before thẽ
the [m] waters vnto Beth-baráh, and Iordén. Then all the men of Ephráim gathered together and toke the waters vnto
Beth-baráh, and Iordén.

m Meaning, ẏ passages or the foordes, that they shulde not escape.

25 And they toke two * princes of the Midianites, Oréb and Zeéb, and slewe Oréb
vpon the rocke Oréb, and slewe Zeéb at
[n] the winepresse of Zeéb, and pursued the
Midianites, and broght the heades of O-
réb & Zeéb to Gideón beyonde Iordén.

*Psal. 83,12. isa. 10,26.
n These places had their names of the actes that were done there.

CHAP. VIII.

1 *Ephráim murmureth against Gideón, 2 Who appeaseth them. 4 He passeth the Iordén. 16 He reuengeth him selfe on them of Succóth and Penuél. 27 He maketh an Ephód which was the cause of idolatrie. 30 Of Gideons sonnes and of his death.*

1 THen the men of Ephráim said vnto
him, [a] Why hast thou serued vs thus
that thou calledst vs not, when thou wentest to fight with the Midianites? and they
chode with him sharpely.
2 To whome he said, What haue I now
done in comparison of [b] you? is not [c] the
gleaning of grapes of Ephráim better, thẽ
the vintage of Abiézer?
3 God hathe deliuered into your hands the
princes of Midián, Oréb and Zeéb: and
what was I able to do in comparison of
you? and when he had thus spoken, then
their spirits abated toward him.

a They began to cauil, because he had the glorie of the victorie.
b Which haue slaine two princes, Oréb and Zeéb.
c This last acte of the whole tribe is more famous, then the whole enterprise of one man of one familie.

4 ¶ And Gideón came to Iordén to passe
ouer, he, and the thre hundreth men that
were with him, weary, yet pursuing *them*.
5 And he said vnto the men of Succóth,
Giue, I pray you, [d] morsels of bread vnto the people "that followe me (*for they be
weary*) that I may followe after Zébah, &
Zalmunná Kings of Midián.

d Or, some smale porciõ.
"Ebr. that are at my fete.

6 And the princes of Succóth said, Are the
[e] hands of Zébah and Zalmunná now in
thine hãds, that we shulde giue bread vnto thine armie?

e Because thou hast ouercome an handful, thinkest thou to haue ouercome ẏ whole.

7 Gideón then said, Therefore when the
Lord hathe deliuered Zébah & Zalmunná into mine hand, I wil "teare your flesh
with thornes of the wildernes and with
breers.

"Ebr. beat to pieces.

8 ¶ And he went vp thence to Penuél, and
spake vnto them likewise, and the men
of Penuél answered him, as the men of
Succóth answered.
9 And he said also vnto the men of Penuél, When I come againe [f] in peace, I
wil breake downe this towre.
10 ¶ Now Zébah and Zalmunná *were* [g] in
Karkór, and their hostes with them, about
fiftene thousand, all that were left of all ẏ
hostes of them of the East: for there was
slayne an hundreth and twentie thousand
men, that drewe swordes.

f Hauing gotten the victorie.
g A citie Eastward beyonde Iordén.

11 ¶ And Gideón went through them that
dwelt in [h] tabernacles on the Eastside of
Nóbah & Iogbeháh, and smote the hoste:
for the hoste was careles.

h He went by the wildernes where the Arabiãs dwelt in tentes.

12 And when Zébah and Zalmunná fled, he
followed after them, & toke the two Kings
of Midián, Zébah and Zalmunná, and discomfited all the hoste.
13 ¶ So Gideón ẏ sonne of Ioásh returned
from battel, [i] the sunne being *yet* hie,
14 And toke a seruant of the men of Succóth, and inquired of him: and he "wrote
to him the princes of Succóth & the Elders thereof, *euen* seuentie and seuen men.

i Some read, before ẏ sunne rose vp.
"Or, described.

15 And he came vnto the men of Succóth,
and said, Beholde Zébah and Zalmunná,
by whome ye vpbraided me, saying, Are ẏ
hands of Zébah & Zalmunná already in
thine hãds, that we shulde giue bread vnto thy weary men?
16 Then he toke the Elders of the citie, &
thornes of the wildernes & breers, & "did
teare the men of Succóth with them.
17 Also he brake downe the towre of * Penuél, and slewe the men of the citie.

"Ebr. brake in pieces, as one threshcth corne.
*1 King. 12,25.

18 ¶ Then said he vnto Zébah & Zalmunná, What maner of mẽ were they, whome
ye slew at Tabór? and they answered, "As
thou art, so were they: *euerie* one was like

"Or, they were like vnto thee.

the children of a King.
19 And he said, They were my brethren,
euen my [k] mothers children: as the Lord
liueth, if ye had saued their liues, I wolde
not slay you.
20 Then he said vnto Iéther his first borne sonne, Vp, and slay them: but the boy
drewe not his sworde: for he feared, because he was yet yong.
21 Then Zébah and Zalmunná said, Rise
thou, and fall vpon vs: for [l] as the man is,
so is his strength. And Gideón arose and
slewe Zébah and Zalmunná, & toke away
the [ʺ] ornaments, that were on their camels
neckes.
22 ¶ Then the men of Israél said vnto Gideón, Reigne thou ouer vs, bothe thou, &
thy sonne, & thy [m] sonnes sonne: for thou
hast deliuered vs out of ŷ hād of Midián.
23 And Gideón said vnto them, I wil not
reigne ouer you, nether shal my childe
reigne ouer you, *but* the Lord shal [n] reigne
ouer you.
24 Againe Gideón said vnto them, I wolde
desire a request of you, that you wolde giue
me euerie man the earings of his praye
(for they had golden earings because they
were Ismaelites)
25 And they answered, We wil giue them.
And they spred a garmēt, & did cast therein euerie man the earings of his praye.
26 And the weight of the golden earings
that he required, was a thousand and seuen
hundreth *shekels* of golde, beside collers,
[ʺ] and jewels, and purple raiment that was
on the Kings of Midián, and beside the
cheines, that were about their camels
neckes.
27 And Gideón made an [o] Ephód thereof,
and put it in Ophráh his citie: & all Israél wēt a whoring there after it, which was
the destruction of Gideón and his house.
28 Thus was Midián broght lowe before ŷ
childrē of Israél, so that they lift vp their
heads nomore: and the countrey was in
quietnes forty yeres in the dayes of Gideón.
29 ¶ Thē Ierubbáal the sonne of Ioásh wēt,
and dwelt in his owne house.
30 And Gideón had seuentie sonnes [ʺ] begottē of his body: for he had manie wiues.
31 And his concubine that was in Shechém,
bare him a sonne also, whose name he called Abimélech.
32 So Gideón the sonne of Ioásh dyed in a
good age, and was buryed in the sepulchre
of Ioásh his father in Ophráh, of the [p] father of the Ezrites.
33 But when Gideón was dead, the children
of Israél turned away and wēt a whoring
after Baalím, and made [q] Baal-beríth
their god.
34 And the children of Israél remembred

k We came all out of one belly: therefore I wil be reuenged.

l Meanīg, that they wolde be rid out of their paine at once, or els to haue a valiant man to put thē to death.

ʺOr, collers.

m That is, thy posteritie.

n His intent was to shewe him selfe thākeful for this victorie by restoring of religiō, which, because it was not according as God had cōmāded, turned to their destruction.

ʺOr, swete baldes.

o That is, suche things as perteined to ŷ vse of the tabernacle.

ʺEbr. which came out of his thigh.

p Which citie belonged to the familie of the Ezrites.

q That is Baal, to whome they had boūde them selues by couenant.

not the Lord their God, which had deliuered them out of the hands of all their
enemies on euerie side.
35 Nether [r] shewed they mercie on the
house of Ierubbáal, *or* Gideón, according
to all the goodnes which he had shewed
vnto Israél.

CHAP. IX.

1 Abimélech vsurpeth the kingdome, and putteth his brethren to death. 7 Iothám proposeth a parable. 23 Hatred betwene Abimélech & the Shechemites. 26 Gaál conspireth against him, and is ouercome. 53 Abimélech is wounded to death by a woman.

1 THen Abimélech the sonne of Ierubbáal went to Shechém vnto his [a] mothers brethren, and cōmuned with them,
and with all the familie, *and* house of his
mothers father, saying,
2 Say, I pray you, in the audience of all the
men of Shechém, whether is better for
you, that all ŷ sonnes of Ierubbáal, which
are seuentie persones, reigne ouer you,
ether that one reigne ouer you? Remember also, that I am your [b] bone, and your
flesh.
3 Then his mothers brethren spake of him
in the audiēce of all the men of Shechém,
all these wordes: and their heartes were
moued to followe Abimélech: for said
they, He is our brother.
4 And they gaue him seuentie pieces of siluer out of the house of Baal-beríth, wherewith Abimélech hired [ʺ] vaine and light
fellowes which followed him.
5 And he went vnto his fathers house at O-
phráh, and [c] slewe his brethren, the sonnes of Ierubbáal, *about* seuenty persones
vpon one stone: yet Iothám the yongest
sonne of Ierubbáal was left: for he hid
him selfe.
6 ¶ And all the men of Shechém gathered
together with all the house of [d] Milló, and
came and made Abimélech King in the
plaine, where the stone was erected in Shechém.
7 And when they tolde it to Iothám, he
went and stode in the top of mount Gerizím, and lift vp his voyce, and cryed, and
said vnto them, Hearken vnto me, you
men of Shechém, that God may hearken
vnto you.
8 [e] The trees wēt forthe to anointe a King
ouer them, and said vnto the oliue tre,
Reigne thou ouer vs.
9 But the oliue tre said vnto them, Shulde
I leaue my fatnes, wherewith by me they
honour God and man, and go to auance
me aboue the trees?
10 Then the trees said to the fig tre, Come
thou, *and* be King ouer vs.
11 But the fig tre answered them, Shulde I
forsake my swetenes, and my good frute,
and go to auance me aboue the trees?

r They were vnmindeful of God, and vnkynde toward him, by whome they had receyued so great a benefite.

a To practise with his kinsfolkes for the atteining of ŷ kingdome.

b Of your kinred by my mothers side.

ʺOr, idle felowes and vacabōds.

c Thus tyrāts to establishe their vsurped power spare not the innocent blood, 1. King 10, 7. 2. chro. 21, 4.

d Which was as the towne house or comōlial, which he calleth the towre of Shechém. vers. 49.

e By this parable he declareth, that those that are not ambitious, are moste worthy of honour, and that the ambitious abuse their honour bothe to their owne destruction and others.

12 Then

12 Then said the trees vnto the vine,Come
thou & be King ouer vs.
13 But the vine said vnto them, Shulde I
leaue my wine,whereby I cheare God and
man,and go to auance me aboue the trees?
‖Or,thistel,or breere.
14 Thē said all the trees vnto the bramble,
Come thou *and* reigne ouer vs.
15 And the bramble said vnto the trees, If
ye wil in dede anoint me King ouer you,
come,& put your trust vnder my shadow:
f Abimélech shal destroye the nobles of Shechém.
and if not,the [f] fire shal come out of the
bramble, and consume the cedres of Lebanón.
16 Now therefore,if ye do truely and vn-
corruptly to make Abimélech King, & if
ye haue dealt wel with Ierubbáal & with
his house, & haue done vnto him according to the deseruing of his hands,
''Ebr.he cast his life farre from him.
17 (For my father fought for you,and''ad-
uentured his life, & deliuered you out of
the hands of Midián.
18 And ye are risen vp against my fathers
house this day, and haue slayne his children, *about* seuentie persones vpon one
stone, & haue made Abimélech the sonne
of his maideseruant, King ouer the men
of Shechém,because he is your brother)
19 If ye then haue delt truely and purely
with Ierubbáal, and with his house this
g That he is your King,and you his subiectes.
day,then [g] reioyce ye with Abimélech,
and let him reioyce with you.
20 But if not, let a fire come out from A-
bimélech, and consume the men of Shechém and the house of Milló: also let a
fire come forthe frō the men of Shechém,
& from the house of Milló, and consume
Abimélech.
21 And Iothám ranne away,and fled,& wēt
to Beér and dwelt there for feare of Abimélech his brother.
22 So Abimélech reigned thre yere ouer
Israél.
h Because the people consented with the King in shedīg innocēt blood: therefore God destroyeth bothe the one & the other.
23 But God [h] sent an euil spirit betwene
Abimélech,and the men of Shechém:and
the mē of Shechém brake their promes to
Abimélech,
24 That the crueltie towarde the seuentie
sonnes of Ierubbáal & their blood might
come and be laide vpon Abimélech their
brother,which had slayne them,and vpon
ẏ men of Shechém, which had aided him
to kil his brethren.
25 So ẏ men of Shechém set men in waite
for him in the tops of the mountaines:
who robbed all that passed that way by
them:and it was tolde Abimélech.
26 Then Gáal the sonne of Ebéd came
with his brethren, and thei went to Shechém: and the men of Shechém put their
confidence in him.
i Before they were afrayed of Abimelechs power,& durst not go out of the citie.
27 Therefore thei [i] went out into the
field,& gathered in their grapes & troade
them, and made mery, and went into the
house of their gods,and did eat & drinke,
and cursed Abimélech.
28 Thē Gáal the sonne of Ebéd said,Who
is Abimélech? and who is Shechém, that
we shulde serue him? Is he not the sonne
of Ierubbáal? & Zebúl is his officer? Serue rather the men of Hamór the father of
Shechém: for why shulde we serue him?
29 Now wolde God this people were vnder mine hād:then wolde I put away Abi-
mélech. And he said to [k] Abimélech,In- k Braggingly as thogh he had bene present, or to his captaine Zebúl.
crease thine armie,and come out.
30 ¶And when Zebúl the ruler of the citie
heard the wordes of Gáal the sonne of E-
béd,his wrath was kindled.
31 Therefore he sent messengers vnto A-
bimélech ''priuely,saying,Beholde, Gáal ''Ebr.craftely.
the sonne of Ebéd and his brethren be co-
me to Shechém, and beholde,thei fortifie
the citie against thee.
32 Now therefore arise by night,thou and
ẏ people that is with thee, & lie in wayte
in the field.
33 And rise early in the morning as soone
as the sunne is vp, and assalt the citie: and
when he and the people that is with him,
shal come out agaīst thee,do to him''what ''Ebr.what thine hand can finde.
thou canst.
34 ¶So Abimélech rose vp,& all the people
that were with him by night:and thei laie
in waite agaīst Shechém in foure bandes.
35 Then Gáal the sonne of Ebéd went out
and stode in the entring of the gate of the
citie:and Abimélech rose vp, and the folke that were with him, frō liyng in waite.
36 And when Gáal sawe the people,he said
to Zebúl, Beholde, there come people
downe from the tops of the mountaines:
and Zebúl said vnto him,The [l] shadowe l Thou art afrayed of a shadowe.
of the mountaines seme men vnto thee.
37 And Gáal spake againe, & said,Se,there
come folke downe '' by the middle of the ''Ebr.by the nauel.
land, & an other band cometh by the way
of the plaine of ‖Meonením. ‖Or,charmers.
38 Then said Zebúl vnto him, Where is
now thy mouth,that said,Who is Abimélech,that we shulde serue him? Is not this
the people that thou hast despised?Go out
now,I pray thee, and fight with them.
39 And Gáal [m] went out before the men of m As their captaine.
Shechém, and fought with Abimélech.
40 But Abimélech pursued him, & he fled
before him, and many were ouerthrowen
and wounded, euen vnto the entring of
the gate.
41 And Abimélech dwelt at Arumáh: and
Zebúl thrust out Gáal and his brethren
that thei shulde not dwel in Shechém.
42 ¶And on the morowe, the people went
out into the field: which was tolde Abimélech.
43 And he toke the [n] people,and deuided n Which were of his companie.
them into thre bandes, and laid waite in

the fields,and loked,& beholde, the people were come out of the citie,& he rose
vp against them,and smote them.
44 And Abimélech, and the bandes that
were with him,russhed forwarde,& stode
in the entring of the gate of ye citie:and
ye two other bãdes ranne vpon all the people that were in the field and slewe them.
45 And whẽ Abimélech had fought against
the citie all that day,he toke the citie,and
slewe the people that was therein , & destroyed the citie and sowed o salt in it.

o That it shulde be vnfruteful and neuer serue to any vse.

46 ¶And when all the men of the towre of
Shechém heard it, thei entred into an
holde of the house of the god p Beríth.

p That is, of Baal-berith,as Chap.8,33.

47 And it was tolde Abimélech,that all the
men of the towre of Shechém were gathered together.
48 And Abimélech gate him vp to mount
Zalmón, he and all the people that were
with him: and Abimélech toke axes with
him and cut downe boughes of trees and
toke them, and bare them on his shulder,
and said vnto the folke that were with
him, What ye haue sene me do, make
haste,*and* do like me.
49 Thẽ all the people also cut downe euery
man his bough, and followed Abimélech,
& put them to the holde,and set the holde
on fire wt them:so all the men of the towre
of Shechém q dyed also, about a thousand
men and women.

q Meaning, yt all were destroyed, aswel thei in ye towre as the other.

50 ¶Then went Abimélech to Tebéz,and
besieged Tebéz,and toke it.
51 But there was a strong towre within the
citie, and thether fled all the men and
women,and all the chief of the citie, and
shut it to them, and went vp to the top of
the towre.
52 And Abimélech came vnto the towre &
fought against it,and went hard vnto the
dore of the towre to set it on fire.
53 But a certaine woman * cast a piece of a
milstone vpon Abimelechs head, & brake
his braine pan.

2.Sam.11,21.

54 Thẽ Abimélech called hastely his page
that bare his harnes, and said vnto him,
Drawe thy sworde & slay me,that mẽ say
not of me,A woman slewe him . And his
page r thrust him through,and he dyed.

r Thus God by suche miserable death taketh vengeãce on tyrãts euen in this life.

55 And when the men of Israél sawe that
Abimélech was dead,thei departed euery
man vnto his owne place.
56 Thus God rendred the wickednes of A-
bimélech,which he did vnto his father,in
slaying his seuenty brethren.
57 Also all the wickednes of the mẽ of Shechém did God bring vpon their heades.
So vpon thẽ came the f curse of Iothám
the sonne of Ierubbáal.

f For making a tyrant their king.

CHAP. X.

2 Tolá dyeth. 5 Iair also dyeth. 17 The Israelites are punished for their sinnes. 10 Thei crye vnto God, 16 And he hathe pitie on them.

1 AFter Abimélech there arose to defend Israél, Tolá, the sonne of Puáh, the sonne of " Dodó, a man of Issachár which dwelt in Shamír in mount
Ephráim.

"Or, his vncle.

2 And he " iudged Israél thre and twentie
yere and dyed , & was buryed in Shamír.

"Or, gouerned.

3 ¶And after him arose Iaír a Gileadite,&
iudged Israél two and twentie yere.
4 And he had thirtie sonnes that a rode on
thirty assecoltes, & thei had thirty cities,
which are called " Hauoth-Iaír vnto this
day,and are in the land of Gileád.

a Signifying, thei were men of autoritie.

"Or, the townes of Iair, as Deu. 3,14.

5 And Iaír dyed,& was buryed in Kamón.
6 ¶*And the childrẽ of Israél wroght wickednes againe in the sight of the Lord, &
serued Baalím and * Ashtaróth , and the
gods of " Arám , and the gods of Zidón,
and the gods of Moáb , and the gods of
the children of Ammón,and the gods of
the Philistíms, and forsoke the Lord and
serued not him.

Chap.2,11.& 3,7.& 4,1.& 6,1.& 13,1.
Chap.2,13.
"Or, Syria.

7 Therefore the wrath of the Lord was
kindled against Israél,and " he solde them
into the hands of the Philistíms,and into
the hands of the children of Ammón:

"Or, deliuered.

8 Who from that yere vexed and oppressed the children of Israél eightene yeres,
b *euen* all the children of Israél that were
beyonde Iordén,in the land of the Amorites, which is in Gileád.

b As the Reubenites, Gadites, & half the tribe of Manasséh.

9 Moreouer the children of Ammón went
ouer Iordén to fight against Iudáh, and a-
gainst Beniamín,and against the house of
Ephráim : so ye Israél was sore tormented.
10 Then the children of Israél c cryed vnto the Lord, saying , We haue sinned a-
gainst thee, euẽ because we haue forsaken
our owne God,and haue serued Baalím.

c Thei prayed to the Lord & confessed their sinnes.

11 And the Lord d said vnto the children
of Israél , *did not I deliuer you* from the E-
gyptiãs & frõ the Amorites, frõ the children of Ammón & from the Philistíms?

d By stirring them vp some Prophet, as Chap.6,8.

12 The Zidonians also, and the Amalekites,and the Maobites did oppresse you, &
ye cryed to me and I saued you out of
their hands.
13 Yet ye * haue forsaken me,and serued o-
ther gods : wherefore I wil deliuer you
nomore.

Deut.32,15. ierem.2,13.

14 Go, and crye vnto the gods which ye
haue chosen : let them saue you in the time of your tribulacion.
15 And the children of Israél said vnto the
Lord , We haue sinned : do thou vnto vs
whatsoeuer please thee:onely we pray thee
to deliuer vs e this day.

e That is, frõ this present danger.

16 Then they put away ye strange gods frõ
among thẽ & f serued ye Lord : & his soule was grieued for the miserie of Israél.

f This is true repentance to put away the euil,& to serue God aright.

17 Then the childrẽ of Ammón gathered
thẽ selues together,& pitched in Gileád:
and the children of Israél assembled them
selues,

selues,and pitched in Mizpéh.
18 And the people *and* princes of Gileád
said one to an other, Whosoeuer wil begin the battel against the childrē of Ammón,the same shal be * head ouer all the
inhabitants of Gileád.

Chap.11,6.

CHAP. XI.

1 Iphtáh being chased away by his brethren,was after made captaine ouer Israél. 30 He maketh a rashe vowe. 32 He vainquisheth the Ammonites. 39 And sacrificeth his daughter according to his vowe.

1 THen Gileád begate Iphtáh,& Iphtáh
the Gileadite was " a valiant man,
but the sonne of an" harlot.
2 And Gileads wife bare him sonnes, and
when ẏ womās childrē were come to age,
they thrust out Iphtáh,and said vnto him,
Thou shalt not inherit in our fathers hou-
se:for thou art ẏ sonne of a [a] strāge womā.
3 Then Iphtáh fled from his brethren, and
dwelt in the land of [b] Tob:and there gathered ydle fellowes to Iphtáh,and [c] went
out with him.
4 ¶And in processe of time the children of
Ammón made warre with Israél.
5 And whē the children of Ammón fought
with Israél, [d] the Elders of Gileád went
to fet Iphtáh out of the land of Tob.
6 And they said vnto Iphtáh, [e] Come and
be our captaine, that we may fight with
the children of Ammón.
7 Iphtáh then answered the Elders of Gileád,Did not ye hate me, and [f] expel me
out of my fathers house? how then come
you vnto me now in time of your tribulacion?
8 Then the Elders of Gileád said vnto
Iphtáh, Therefore we turne againe to thee
now,that thou maiest go with vs, & fight
against the children of Ammón,& be our
head ouer all the inhabitants of Gileád.
9 And Iphtáh said vnto the Elders of Gileád,If ye bring me home againe to fight
against ẏ children of Ammón,if the Lord
giue them before me,shal I be your head?
10 And ẏ Elders of Gileád said to Iphtáh,
The Lord " be witnes betwene vs, if we
do not according to thy wordes.
11 Then Iphtáh went with the Elders of
Gileád, and the people made him head
and captaine ouer them: and Iphtáh rehearsed all his wordes before the Lord in
Mizpéh.
12 ¶Then Iphtáh sent messengers vnto the
King of the children of Ammón, saying,
What hast thou to do with me, that thou
art come against me,to fight in my land?
13 And the King of the children of Ammón answered vnto the messengers of
Iphtáh,*Because Israél toke my lād, whē
they came vp frō Egypt,from Arnón vnto Iabbók, and vnto Iordén: now therefore restore those *lands* " quietly.

"Ebr.a man of mightie force.
"Or,vitailer.
a That is,of an harlot,as ver.1
b Where the gouernour of the countrey was called Tob.
c Ioyned with him, as some thinke, against his brethren.
d Or, ambassadours, sent for that purpose.
e Men oft times are constrained to desire helpe of them, whome before they haue refused.
f Oft tymes those thīgs,ẇ mē reiect, God choseth to do great enterprises by.
"Ebr.be the hearer.
Nomb.21,13.
"Ebr. in peace.

14 Yet Iphtáh sent messengers againe vnto the King of the children of Ammón,
15 And said vnto him, Thus saith Iphtáh,
*Israél toke not the land of Moáb, nor the
land of the children of Ammón.
16 But when Israél came vp from Egypt,
and walked through the wildernes vnto
the red Sea,then they came to Kadésh.
17 *And Israél sent messengers vnto the
King of Edóm, saying, Let me, I pray
thee,go through thy lād: but the King of
Edóm wold not consent: and also they
sent vnto the King of Moáb, but he wolde
not:therefore Israél abode in Kadésh.
18 Then thei went through the wildernes,
and compassed the land of Edóm,and the
land of Moáb,and came by the Eastside of
ẏ lād Moáb,and pitched on the other side
of Arnón,*and came not within ẏ coast of
Moáb: for Arnón *was* ẏ border of Moáb.
19 Also Israél*sent messengers vnto Sihón,
King of the Amorites,the King of Heshbón,& Israél said vnto him,Let vs passe,we pray thee,by thy lād vnto our"place.
20 But Sihón [g] cōsented not to Israél,that
he shulde go through his coast:but Sihón
gathered all his people together, and pyt-
ched in Iaház,and fought with Israél.
21 And the Lord God of Israél gaue Sihón
and all his folke into the hands of Israél,
and they smote thē: so Israél possessed all
the land of the Amorites, the inhabitants
of that countrey:
22 And they possessed* all the coast of the
Amorites,from Arnón vnto Iabbók, and
from the wildernes euen vnto Iordén.
23 Now therefore the Lord God of Israél hathe cast out the Amorites before his
people Israél,& shuldest thou possesse it?
24 Woldest not thou possesse that which
Chemósh thy god giueth thee to possesse?
So whomesoeuer the [h] Lord our God driueth out before vs, them wil we possesse.
25 *And art thou now farre better then Balák the sonne of Zippór King of Moáb?
did he not striue with Israél and fight a-
gainst them,
26 When Israél dwelt in Heshbón and in
her townes,and in Aroér & in her townes,
and in all the cities that are by the coasts
of Arnón,thre hundreth yeres?why did ye
not then recouer [i] them in that space?
27 Wherefore,I haue not offēded thee:but
thou doest me wrōg to warre against me.
The Lord the Iudge [k] be iudge this day
betwene the children of Israél, and the
children of Ammón.
28 Howebeit the King of the children of
Ammón hearkened not vnto the wordes
of Iphtáh,which he had sent him.
29 ¶Then the [l] Spirit of the Lord came
vpon Iphtáh,& he passed ouer to Gileád
and to Manasséh, and came to Mizpéh in

Deut.2,9.
Nom.20,14.
Nomb.21,13. & 22,24.
Deut.2,26.
"Or,countrey.
g He trusted the not to go through his countrey.
Deut.2,36.
h For we oght more to beleue and obey God, thē thou thine idoles.
Nom.22,2. deut.23,4. iosh.24,9.
i Meaning their townes.
k To punishe the offender.
l That is, the spirit of strength and zeale.

Gileád, and from Mizpéh in Gileád he
went vnto the children of Ammón.

m As the Apostle commendeth Iphtáh for his worthy entreprise in deliuering the people, Ebr. 11, 32: so by his rashe vowe & wicked performance of the same, his victorie was defaced: and here we se that the sinnes of the godly do not vtterly extinguish their faith.

30 And Iphtáh [m] vowed a vowe vnto the
Lord, and said, If thou shalt deliuer the
children of Ammón in to mine hands,
31 Thẽ that thing that commeth out of the
dores of mine house to mete me, when I
come home in peace from the children of
Ammón, shal be the Lords, and I wil offer it for a burnt offring.
32 And so Iphtáh went vnto the children
of Ammón to fight against them, and the
Lord deliuered them into his hands.
33 And he smote them from Aroér euẽ til ẏ
come to Minníth, twentie cities, and so
forthe to ᐟAbél of the vineyardes, with an
exceding great slaughter. Thus the childrẽ of Ammón were humbled before the
children of Israél.

ᐟOr, the plaine.

34 ¶ Now whẽ Iphtáh came to Mizpéh vnto his house, beholde, his daughter came
out to mete him with [n] timbrels and
dances, which was his onely childe: he had
none other sonne, nor daughter.

n According to the maner after the victorie.

35 And when he sawe her, he [o] rent his clothes, and said, Alas my daughter, thou hast
broght me low, & art of thẽ that trouble
me: for I haue opened my mouthe vnto
the Lord, and can not go backe.

o Being ouercome with blinde zeale, and not considering whether the vowe was lauful or no.

36 And she said vnto him, My father, if thou
haste opened thy mouthe vnto the Lord,
do with me as thou hast promised, seing
that the Lord hathe auenged thee of thine
enemies the children of Ammón.
37 Also she said vnto her father, Do thus
muche for me: suffre me two monethes,
that I may go to the mõutaines, and [p] bewaile my virginitie, I and my fellowes.

p For it was counted as a shame in Israél, to dye without children, and therefore they reioyced to be maryed.

38 And he said, Go: and he sent her away
two monethes: so she went with her companions, and lamented her virginitie vpõ
the mountaines.
39 And after the end of two monethes, she
turned againe vnto her father, who did
with her according to his vowe which he
had vowed, and she had knowen no man,
and it was a custome in Israél.
40 The daughters of Israél went yere by
yere to lament the daughter of Iphtáh the
Gileadite, foure dayes in a yere.

CHAP. XII.

6 Iphtáh killeth two & fortie thousand Ephraimites. 8 After Iphtáh succedeth Ibzán. 11 Elón. 13 And Abdón.

1 AND the men of Ephráim gathered
thẽ selues together, and went [a] Northward and said vnto Iphtáh, Wherefore
wentest thou to fight against the children
of Ammón, and didest not call [b] vs to go
with thee? we wil therefore burne thine
house vpon thee with fire.

a After they had passed Iordén.

b Thus ambicion enuieth Gods worke in others, as they did also agaist Gideón, Chap. 8, 1.

2 And Iphtáh said vnto thẽ, I and my people were at great strife with the children
of Ammón, and when I called you, ye deliuered me not out of their hands.
3 So when I sawe ẏ ye deliuered me not, [c] I
put my life in mine hãds, & went vpon the
children of Ammón: so ẏ Lord deliuered
them into mine hands. Wherefore thẽ are
ye come vpõ me now to fight against me?

c That is, I ventured my life, and when mãs helpe fayled, I put my trust onely in God.

4 Then Iphtáh gathered all the men of
Gileád, and fought with Ephráim: & the
men of Gileád smote Ephráim, because
they said, Ye Giliadites are runagates of
Ephráim [d] among the Ephraimites, *and*
among the Manassites.

d Ye ran frõ vs, and chose Gileád, & now in respect of vs, ye are nothing.

5 Also the Giliadites toke the passages of
Iordén before the Ephraimites, and when
the Ephraimites that were escaped, said,
Let me passe, then the men of Gileád said
vnto him, Art thou an Ephraimite? If he
said, Nay,
6 Thẽ said they vnto him, Say now [e] Shib-
bóleth: and he said, Sibbóleth: for he colde not so pronounce: then they toke him,
and slewe him at the passages of Iordén:
and there fel at that time of the Ephraimites two and forty thousand.

e Which signifieth, the fall of waters, or an eare of corne.

7 And Iphtáh iudged Israél six yere: then
dyed Iphtáh the Giliadite, and was buryed in *one* of the cities of Gileád.
8 ¶ After him [f] Ibzán of Beth-léhem iudged Israél,

f Some thinke that this was Boáz ẏ housband of Ruth.

9 Who had thirtie sonnes and thirtie daughters, *which* he sent out, and toke in thirtie daughters from abroad for his sonnes.
and he iudged Israél seuen yere.
10 Then Ibzán dyed, and was buryed at
Beth-léhem.
11 ¶ And after him iudged Israél Elón, a
Zebulonite, and he iudged Israél ten yere.
12 Then Elón the Zebulonite dyed, & was
buryed in Aiialón in the countrey of Zebulún.
13 ¶ And after him Abdón ẏ sonne of Hillél the Pirathonite iudged Israél.
14 And he had fortie sonnes & thirtie "ne-
uews that rode on seuentie ᐟ assecoltes: and
he iudged Israél eight yeres.

" Ebr. sonnes sonnes.

ᐟ Or, horsecoltes.

15 Then dyed Abdón the sonne of Hillél ẏ
Pirathonite, and was buryed in Pirathón,
in the land of Ephráim, in the mount of
the Amalekites.

CHAP. XIII.

1 Israél for their wickednes is oppressed of the Philistims. 3 The Angel appeareth to Manoahs wife. 16 The Angel commandeth him to sacrifice vnto the Lord. 24 The birth of Samsón.

1 BVt the children of Israél continued
to commit * wickednes in the sight
of the Lord, and the Lord deliuered them
into the hands of the Philistims fortie
yere.

Chap. 2, 11. & 3, 7. & 4, 1. & 6, 1. & 10, 6.

2 ¶ Then there was a man in Zoráh of the
familie of the Danites, named Manóah,
whose wife was [a] baren, and bare not.

a Signifying ẏ their deliuerãce came onely of God & not by mãs power.

3 And

3 And the Angel of the Lord appeared vnto the woman, and said vnto her, Beholde
now, thou art baren, and bearest not: but
thou shalt conceiue, and beare a sonne.
4 And nowe therefore beware * that thou
drinke no wine, nor strong drinke, nether
eat anie vncleane thing.

Nomb.6,2.

5 For lo, thou shalt conceiue and beare a
sonne, & no rasor shal * come on his head:
for the childe shalbe a [b] Nazarite vnto
God from his birth: and he shal begin to
saue Israél out of the hands of the Philistíms.

1.Sam.1,11.

b Meaning, he shulde be seperate from the worlde and dedicate to God.

6 ¶ Then the wife came, & tolde her housband, saying, A man of God came vnto
me, and the facion of him was like the facion of ẏ Angel of God exceding [c] fearful, but I asked him not whence he was,
nether tolde he me his name,
7 But he said vnto me, Beholde, thou shalt
conceiue, and beare a sonne, and now thou
shalt drinke no wine, nor strong drinke,
nether eat anie vncleane thing: for the
childe shal be a Nazarite to God from
his byrth to the day of his death.

c If flesh be not able to abide the sight of an Angel, how much lesse the presence of God?

8 Then Manóah [d] prayed to the Lord and
said, I pray thee, my Lord, let the man of
God, whome thou sentest, come againe
now vnto vs, and teache vs what we shal
do vnto the childe when he is borne.

d He sheweth him selfe ready to obey Gods wil, and therefore desireth to knowe farther.

9 And God heard the voyce of Manóah, &
the Angel of God came againe vnto the
wife, as she sate in the field, but Manóah
her housband was not with her.
10 ¶ And the wife made haste & ranne, and
shewed her housband and said vnto him,
Beholde, the man hathe appeared vnto me,
that came vnto me [e] to day.
11 And Manóah arose and went after his
wife, and came to the [f] man, and said vnto
him, Art thou the man that spakest vnto
the woman? and he said, Yea.
12 Then Manóah said, Now let thy saying
come to passe: *but* how shal we ordre the
childe, and do vnto him?
13 And ẏ Angel of the Lord said vnto Manóah, The woman must beware of all that
I said vnto her.

e It semeth ẏ the Angel appeared vnto her twise in one day

f He calleth him man, because he so semed, but he was Christ the eternal worde, which at his time appointed became man.

14 She may eat of nothing that cometh of
the vinetre: she shal not drinke wine nor
strong drinke, nor eat anie [g] vncleane
thing: let her obserue all that I haue commanded her.

g Anie thing forbidden by the Lawe.

15 Manóah then said vnto the Angel of
the Lord, I pray thee, let vs reteine thee,
vntil we haue made ready a kid for thee.
16 And the Angel of the Lord said vnto
Manóah, Thogh thou make me abide, I
wil not eat of thy bread, and if thou wilt
make a burnt offring, offer it vnto the
[h] Lord: for Manóah knewe not that it was
an Angel of the Lord.
17 Againe Manóah said vnto ẏ Angel of ẏ
Lord, What is thy name, ẏ whẽ thy saying is come to passe, we may honour thee?

h Shewing ẏ he soght not his owne honer, but Gods, whose messenger he was.

18 And ẏ Angel of the Lord said vnto him,
Why askest ẏ thus after my name, which
is *secret?

*Or, merueilouse?

19 Then Manóah toke a kid with a meat offring, and offred it vpon a stone vnto the
Lord: and *the Angel* did [i] wonderously,
whiles Manóah and his wife loked on.
20 For when the flame came vp towarde
heauen from the altar, the Angel of the
Lord ascended vp in the flame of the altar, and Manóah and his wife beheld it, &
fel on their faces vnto the ground.

i God sent fire from heauẽ to consume their sacrifice, to confirme their faith in his promes.

21 (So the Angel of the Lord did no more
appeare vnto Manóah and his wife) Thẽ
Manóah knewe that it was an Angel of ẏ
Lord.
22 And Manóah said vnto his wife, *We shal
surely dye, because we haue sene God.

Exod.33,20. chap.6,22.

23 But his wife said vnto him, If the Lord
wolde kil vs, he wolde not haue receiued
a [k] burnt offring, and a meat offring of our
hands, nether wolde he haue shewed vs all
these things, nor wolde now haue tolde vs
anie suche.
24 ¶ And the wife bare a sonne, and called
his name Samsón: and the childe grewe, &
the Lord blessed him.
25 And the Spirit of ẏ Lord began to *strég-
thẽ him in the hoste of Dan, betwene Zoráh, and Eshtaól.

k These graces ẏ we haue receiued of God, & his accepting of our obedience, are sure tokens of his loue toward vs, so ẏ nothing can hurt vs.

*Or, to come vpõ him at diuers times.

CHAP. XIIII.

1 Samsón desireth to haue a wife of the Philistíms. 6 He killeth a lyon. 12 He propoundeth a riddle. 19 He kylleth thirtie. 20 His wife forsaketh him and taketh another.

1 NOw Samsón went downe to Timnáth, and sawe a woman in Timnáth
of the daughters of the Philistíms,
2 And he came vp and tolde his father and
his mother, and said, I haue sene a woman
in Timnáth of the daughters of the Phili
stíms: now therefore *giue me her to wife.

*Ebr. take her for me to wife.

3 Thẽ his father and his mother said vnto
him, Is there [a] neuer a wife amõg ẏ daughters of thy brethren, and among all my
people, that thou must go to take a wife
of the vncircũcised Philistíms? And Samsón said vnto his father, Giue me her, for
she pleaseth me wel.

a Thogh his parẽts did iustely reproue him, yet it appeareth ẏ this was ẏ secret worke of the Lord, vers.4.

4 But his father and his mother knewe not
that it came of the Lord, that he shulde
seke an occasion against the [b] Philistíms:
for at that time the Philistíms reigned o-
uer Israél.

b To fight against thẽ for the deliuerãce of Israél.

5 ¶ Then went Samsón and his father and
his mother downe to Timnáth, and came
to ẏ vineyardes at Timnáth: & beholde,
a yong lyon roared vpon him.
6 And the Spirit of the Lord [c] came vpon
him, and he tare him, as one shulde haue
rent a kid, and had nothing in his hand, ne-

c Whereby he had strength & boldnes.

ther tolde he his father nor his mother
what he had done.
7 And he went downe,and talked with the
woman which was beautiful in the eyes of
Samsón.
8 ¶And within a *fewe* dayes, whẽ he returned" to receiue her, he went aside to se the
carkeis of the lyon:and beholde,there was
a swarme of bees,and hony in the body of
the lyon.

"*Or, to take her to his wife.*

9 And he toke thereof in his hands, and
went eating,and came to his father and to
his mother,and gaue vnto them, and they
did eat:but he tolde not them,that he had
taken the hony out of the bodie of ẏ lyon.
10 So his father went downe vnto the woman,and Samsón made there a [d] feast:
for so vsed the yong men to do.
11 And when [e] they sawe him,they broght
thirtie companions to be with him.
12 Then Samsón said vnto them,I wil now
put forthe a ridle vnto you: & if you can
declare it me within seuen dayes of the
feast,and finde it out,I wil giue you thirtie
shetes,and thirtie [f] change of garmẽts.
13 But if you cãnot declare it me, then shal
ye giue me thirtie shetes and thirtie change of garments. And they answered him,
Put forthe thy ridle,that we may heare it.
14 And he said vnto them, Out of the eater came meat,and out of the strong came
swetenes: & they colde not in thre dayes
expounde the ridle.

d Meaning, when he was maried.
e That is, her parents or friendes.
f To weare at feastes or solemne dayes.

15 And when the seuenth day was [g] come,
they said vnto Samsons wife, Entise thyne housband, that he may declare vs the
ridle, lest we burne thee and thy fathers house with fire. Haue ye called vs,
"to possesse vs? is it not *so*?
16 And Samsons wife wept before him,and
said,Surely thou hatest me and louest me
not: for thou hast put forthe a ridle vnto
the [h] children of my people,and hast not
tolde it me. And he said vnto her, Beholde, I haue not tolde it my father, nor my
mother,and shal I tel it thee?
17 Then Samsons wife wept before him
[i] seuen dayes, while their feast lasted:and
when the seuenth day came, he tolde her,
because she was importunate vpon him:
so she tolde the ridle to the children of
her people.
18 And the men of the citie said vnto him
the seuenth day before the sonne went
downe, What is sweter, then honie? and
what is stronger then a lyon? Then said he
vnto them, [k] If ye had not plowed wͭ my
heiffer,ye had not founde out my ridle.
19 And the Spirit of the Lord came vpon
him,and he went downe [l] to Ashkelón,and
slewe thirtie men of them & spoiled thẽ,
and gaue change of garments vnto them,
which expounded the ridle: & his wrath

g Or, drewe neretoir it was ẏ fourthe day.
"*Or, to imponerishe vs.*
h Vnto them which are of my nacion.
i Or, to the seuenth day, begynning at the fourthe.
k If ye had not vsed the helpe of my wife.
l Which was one of the fiue chief cities of the Philistims.

was kindled, and he went vp to his fathers house.
20 Thẽ Samsons wife was *giuen* to his companion,whome he had vsed as his friend.

CHAP. XV.

*4 Samsón tieth firebrãdes to the foxe tailes. 6 The Phili-
stims burnt his father in lawe & his wife. 15 With the
iawebone of an asse he killeth a thousand men. 19 Out
of a great tothe in the iawe God gaue him water.*

1 BVt within a while after, in the time of
wheat haruest, Sãsón visited his wife
with a kid,saying, I wil [a] go into my wife
into the chãber: but her father wolde not
suffre him to go in.
2 And her father said, I thoght that thou
haddest hated her: therefore gaue I her to
thy companion. Is not her yonger sister
fairer then she? take her, I pray thee, in
stead of the other.
3 Thẽ Samsón said vnto them, Now am I
more [b] blameles thẽ the Philistíms: therefore wil I do them displeasure.
4 ¶And Samsón went out,& toke thre hũdreth foxes,and toke firebrands,& turned
them taile to taile,and put a firebrand in
the middes betwene two tailes.
5 And when he had set the brandes on fier,
he sent them out into the standing corne
of the Philistíms, and burnt vp bothe the
[c] riekes & the standing corne with the vineyardes & oliues.
6 Then the Philistíms said, Who hathe
done this? And they answered,Samsón the
sonne in lawe of the [d] Timnite,because he
had taken his wife,& giuen her to his cõ-
paniõ. Then the Philistíms came vp and
[e] burnt her and her father with fire.
7 And Samsón said vnto them, Thogh ye
haue done this, yet wil I be auenged of
you,and then I wil cease.
8 So he smote them "hippe and thigh with
a mighty plague: then he went and dwelt
in the toppe of the rocke Etám.
9 ¶Then ẏ Philistíms came vp,& pitched
in Iudáh, & " were spred abroad in Léhi.
10 And the men of Iudáh said,Why are ye
come vp vnto vs? And they answered, To
[f] binde Samsón are we come vp, and to do
to him as he hathe done to vs.
11 Then thre thousand men of Iudáh wẽt
to the toppe of the rocke Etám,and said to
Sãsón,Knowest thou not that ẏ Philistíms
are rulers ouer vs? [g] Wherefore then hast ŷ
done thus vnto vs? And he answered thẽ, As
they did vnto me,so haue I done vnto thẽ.
12 Againe they said vnto hĩ, We are come
to binde thee,and to deliuer thee into the
hand of the Philistíms. And Samsón said
vnto them, Sweare vnto me, that ye wil
not fall vpon me your selues.
13 And they answered him, saying, No,
but we wil binde thee and [h] deliuer thee
vnto their hand, but we wil not kil thee.

a That is, I wil vse her as my wife.
b For through his father in laws occasion, he was moued againe to take vengeance of ẏ Philistims.
c Or, that ẏ was reaped & gathered.
d Or, ẏ citizẽ of Timnáth.
e So ẏ wicked punish not vice for loue of iustice, but for feare of dãger, ẘ els might come to them.
"*Or, horsemẽ & fotemen.*
"*Or, camped.*
f And so beig our prisoner, to punishe hi.
g Suche was their grosse ignorãce, that they iudged Gods great benefite to be a plague vnto them.
h Thus they had rather betray their brother, then vse ẏ meanes that God had giuẽ for their deliuerance.

And they bound him with two newe cordes,and broght him from the rocke.
14 When he came to Léhi, the Philistíms
shouted against him, and the Spirit of the
Lord came vpon him, and the cordes that
were vpon his armes,became as flaxe that
was burnt with fire: for the bandes losed
from his hands.
15 And he found a [i] newe iawebone of an
asse, and put forthe his hand, and caught
it,and slewe a thousand men therewith.

i That is,of an asse lately slaine.

16 Then Samsón said, With the iawe of
an asse *are* heapes vpon heapes: wͭ the iawe
of an asse haue I slayne a thousand men.
17 And when he had left speaking, he cast
away the iawebone out of his hand,& called that place,"Ramath-Léhi.
18 And he was sore a thirst, and [k] called on
the Lord,and said,Thou hast giuen this
great deliuerance into the hand of thy
seruant: and now shal I dye for thirst, and
fall into the hands of the vncircumcised?

"Or, the lifting vp of the iawe.
k Wherby appeareth, ỳ he did these thigs in faith,& so wͭ a true zeal to glorifie God & deliuer his coūtrey.

19 Then God brake the cheeke tothe, that
was in the iawe,and water came thereout:
and when he had dronke, his Spirit came
againe,and he was reuiued: wherefore the
name thereof is called, "En-hakkoré, wͨ
is in Léhi vnto this day.
20 And he iudged Israél in the dayes of ỳ
Philistíms twentie yeres.

"Or, the foūtaine of him that prayed.

CHAP. XVI.

3 *Samsón carieth away the gates of Azzáh. 18 He was deceiued by Deliláh. 30 He pulleth downe the house vpon the Philistíms, and dyeth with them.*

1 THen went Samsón to [a] Azzáh,& sawe
there "an harlot,& [b] went in vnto her.
2 And it was tolde to the Azzathites, Samsón is come hether. And they went about,
& layed wait for him all night in the gate
of the citie, and were quiet all the night,
saying, *Abide* "til the morning earely,and
we shal kil him.

a One of ỳ.5. chief cities of ỳ Philistíms.
"Or, vitailer.
b That is, he lodged wͭ her.
"Or, to the light of the morning.

3 And Samsón slept til midnight, & arose
at midnight,and toke the dores of the gates of the citie, and the two postes and lift
them away with the barres, and put them
vpon his shulders,and caried them vp to
the top of the mountaine that is before
Hebrón.
4 ¶ And after this he loued a woman by ỳ
"riuer of Sorék,whose name was Deliláh:
5 Vnto whome came the princes of ỳ Philistíms,and said vnto her,Entise him, and
se wherein his great strength *lieth*, and by
what meane we may ouercome him, that
we may binde him,and punishe him, and
euerie one of vs shal giue thee eleuen hundreth [c] *shekels* of siluer.

"Or, plaine.
c Of ỳ value of a shekel read Gen.23,15

6 ¶ And Deliláh said to Samsón, Tel me, I
pray thee,wherein thy great strength *lieth*,
and wherewith thou mightest be bounde,
to do thee hurt.
7 Samsón then answered vnto her, If they
binde me with seuen "greene cordes that
were neuer dryed, thē shal I be weake, and
be as an other man.

"Or, new withs.

8 And the princes of ỳ Philistíms broght
her seuē greene cordes that were not drye,
and she bound him therewith.
9 (And she had [d] men lying in wayte wͭ her
in ỳ chāber) Then she said vnto him, The
Philistíms *be* vpon thee, Samsón. And he
brake the cordes, as a thread of towe is
broken,when [e] it feleth fire: so his strēgth
was not knowen.

d Certeine Philistíms in a secret chamber.
e Whē fire cōmeth nere it.

10 ¶ After Deliláh said vnto Samsón, Se,ỳ
hast mocked me and tolde me lies. I pray
thee now, [f] tel me wherewith ỳ mightest
be bound.
11 Then he answered her, If they binde me
with newe ropes ỳ neuer were occupied,
then shal I be weake, and be as another
man.

f Thogh her falsehood tended to make him, lose his life,yet his affection so blinded him ỳ he colde not beware.

12 Deliláh therefore toke newe ropes, and
bound him therewith, and said vnto him,
The Philistíms be vpon thee, Samsón:(&
men lay in wait in the chāber)& he brake
them from his armes, as a threade.
13 ¶ Afterward Deliláh said to Samsón, Hetherto thou hast beguiled me, and tolde
me lies: tel me how thou mightest be bo-
und. [g] And he said vnto her, If thou plat-
tedst seuen lockes of mine head with the
threades of the woufe.
14 And she fastened it with a pinne, & said
vnto him, The Philistíms *be* vpon thee,
Samsón. And he awoke out of his slepe,
and went away with the "pinne of ỳ webbe
and the woufe.

g It is impossible,if we giue place to our wicked affections, but at lēgth we shal be destroied.
"Or, beame.

15 Againe she said vnto him, How canst
thou say, [h] I loue thee, when thine heart is
not with me? thou hast mocked me these
thre times,and hast not tolde me wherein
thy great strength *lieth*.

h For this Samsón vsed to saye, I loue thee.

16 And because she was importunate vpon
him with her wordes cōtinually,and vexed him,his soule was peined vnto ỳ death.
17 Therefore he tolde her all his [i] heart, &
said vnto her, There neuer came rasor
vpon mine head: for I am a Nazarite vnto
God frō my mothers wombe: therefore if
I be shauen,my strength wil go from me,
& I shal be weake,& be like all *other* men.
18 And whē Deliláh sawe that he had tolde
her all his heart,she sent, & called for the
Princes of ỳ Philistíms, saying, Come vp
once *againe*: for he hathe shewed me all his
heart. Then the princes of the Philistíms
came vp vnto her, and broght the money
in their hands.

i Thus his immoderate affectiōs towarde a wicked womā caused him to lose Gods excellent gifts,& become slaue vnto thē, whome he shulde haue ruled.

19 And she made him slepe vpō her knees,
& she called a man, & made him to shaue
of ỳ seuen lockes of his head,& she begā to
vexe hī, & his strength was [k] gone frō hī.
20 Then she said, The Philistíms *be* vpō
thee, Sāsón. And he awoke out of his slepe,

k Not for the losse of his heere, but for ỳ contempt of ỳ ordinance of God, wͨ was ỳ cause ỳ God departed from him.

and thoght, I wil go out now as at other
times, & shake my selfe, but he knewe not
that the Lord was departed from him.
21 Therefore the Philistims toke him, and
put out his eies, and broght him downe to
Azzáh, and bound him with fetters: and
he did grinde in the prison house.
22 And the heere of his head begã to [l] growe
againe after that it was shauen.

l Yet had he not his strẽgth againe, til he had called vpon God, and reconciled hi selfe.

23 Then the princes of the Philistims gathered them together for to offer a great
sacrifice vnto Dagón their god, and to reioyce: for they said, Our god hathe deliuered Samsón our enemie into our hãds.
24 Also when the people saw him, they praised their god: for they said, Our god hath
deliuered into our hands our enemie and
destroier of our countrey, ẘ hathe slaine
manie of vs.
25 And when their heartes were mery, they
said, Call Samsón, that he may make vs
pastime. So they called Samsón out of
the prison house, and he [m] was a laughing
stocke vnto them, and they set him betwene the pillers.

m Thus by Gods iust iudgements they are made slaues to infidels, which neglect their vocacion in defending the faithful.

26 Then Samsón said vnto the seruant that
led him by the hand, Lead me, that I may
touche the pillers that the house standeth
vpon, and that I may leane to them.
27 (Now the house was ful of men & women, and there *were* all the princes of the
Philistims: also vpon the roofe *were* about
thre thousand men & women that behelde
while Samsón "played)

"Or, was mocked

28 Then Samsón called vnto the Lord, and
said, ô Lord God, I pray thee, thinke vpon
me: ô God, I beseche thee, strengthen me
at this time onely, that I maye be "at once
[n] auenged of the Philistims for my two
eyes.

"Ebr. take one vengeance.

n According to my vocasion, which is to execute Gods iudgements vpon the wicked.

29 And Samsón layed holde on the two
middle pillers whereupõ the house stode,
and on which it was borne vp: on the one
with his right hand, and on the other with
his left.
30 Then said Samsón, [o] Let me lose my life
with the Philistims: and he bowed him ẘ
all his might, and the house fel vpon the
princes, and vpon all the people that were
therein. so the dead which he slue at his
death were mo then they which he had
slayne in his life.

o He speaketh not this of dispaire, but hũbling hi selfe for neglecting his office & ẙ offence thereby giuen.

31 Then his brethren, and all the house of
his father came downe and toke him, and
broght him vp & buryed him betwene Zoráh and Eshtaól, in the sepulchre of Manóah his father: now he had iudged Israél
twentie yeres.

CHAP. XVII.

3 Michahs mother according to her vowe made her sonne two idoles. 5 He made his sonne a Priest for his idoles. 10 And after he hired a Leuite.

1 THere [a] was a man of mount Ephráim,
whose name was Micháh,
2 And he said vnto his mother, The eleuen
hundreth *shekels* of siluer that were taken
from thee, for the which thou cursedst, &
spakedst it, euẽ in mine hearing, beholde,
the siluer *is* with me, I toke it. Then his
mother said, Blessed be my sonne of the
Lord.

a Some thike this historie was in ẙ time of Othniél, or as Iosephus writeth, immediatly after Ioshúa.

3 And when he had restored the eleuen hũdreth *shekels* of siluer to his mother, his mother said, I had dedicate ẙ siluer to ẙ Lord
of mine hand for my sonne, to make [b] a
grauen and molten image. Now therefore I wil giue it thee againe.
4 And whẽ he had restored the money vnto his mother, his mother toke two hundreth *shekels* of siluer, and gaue them to
the founder, which made thereof a grauẽ
and molten image, and it was in the house
of Micháh.

b Contrary to the commandement of God and true religion practised vnder Ioshúa, they forsoke ẙ Lord and fel to idolatrie.

5 And this man Micháh had an house of
gods, & made an * [c] Ephód, & * Teraphím,
and "consecrated one of his sonnes, who
was his Priest.
6 In those daies there was no [d] King in Israél, *but* euerie man did that, which was
good in his owne eies.

Chap 8,27.

c He wolde serue bothe God & idoles.

Gen. 31,19. ose. 3,4.

"*Ebr. filled the hand of one.*

d For where there is no magistrat fearing God, there can be no true religion, nor ordre.

7 ¶ There was also a yong mã out of Bethléhem Iudáh, [e] of the familie of Iudáh:
who was a Leuite, and soiourned there.
8 And the man departed out of the citie, *euẽ*
out of Beth-léhem Iudáh, to dwel where
he colde finde *a place*: and as he iourneied,
he came to mount Ephráim to the house
of Micháh.

e Which Bethléhem was in the tribe of Iudáh.

9 And Micháh said vnto him, Whence cõmest thou? And the Leuite answered him,
[f] I *come* from Beth-léhem Iudáh, and go to
dwel where I may finde *a place*.
10 Then Micháh said vnto him, Dwel ẘ
me, and be vnto me a father and a Priest,
and I wil giue thee ten *shekels* of siluer
by yere, and a sute of apparel, & thy meat
and drinke. So the Leuite went in.

f For in those daies ẙ seruice of God was corrupt in all estates and the Leuites were not loked vnto.

11 And the Leuite was [g] content to dwel ẘ
the man, and the yong man was vnto
him as one of his owne sonnes.
12 And Micháh consecrated the Leuite, &
the yong man was his Priest, and was in
the house of Micháh.
13 Then said Micháh, Now I knowe that ẙ
Lord wil be [h] good vnto me, seing I haue
a Leuite to my Priest.

g Not cõsidering that he forsoke ẙ true worshiping of God for to mainteine his owne belly.

h Thus ẙ idolaters persuade thẽ selues of Gods fanour, when in deede he doeth detest thẽ.

CHAP. XVIII.

2 The children of Dan send men to searche the land. 11 Then come the six hundreth & take the gods, and the Priest of Micháh awaie. 27 They destroy La'sh. 28 Thei buyld it againe, 30 And set vp idolatrie.

1 IN those dayes there was no [a] King in
Israél, and at the same time the tribe of
Dan soght them an inheritãce to dwel in:
for

a Meaning no ordinarie Magistrat, to punishe vice according to Gods worde.

for vnto that time *all* their inheritãce had
not fallen vnto them among the tribes of
Israél.
2 Therefore the children of Dan sent of
their familie, fiue men out of their coastes, *euen* men expert in warre, out of Zoráh & Eshtaól, to vewe the land and searche it out, and said vnto them, [b] Go, *and*
searche out the land. Then thei came to
mount Ephráim to the house of Micháh
and lodged there.

b For the porcion ẘ Ioshúa gaue them, was not sufficient for all their tribe.

3 When thei were in the house of Micháh,
thei knewe the [c] voyce of the yong man
the Leuite: and being turned inthether,
thei said vnto him, Who broght thee hether? or what makest thou in this place? &
what hast thou *to do* here?

c Thei knewe him by his speache that he was a strãger there.

4 And he answered them, Thus and thus
dealeth Micháh with me, and hathe hired
me, and I am his Priest.
5 Againe thei said vnto him, Aske counsel
now of god, that we may knowe whether
the way which we go, shal be prosperous.
6 And the Priest said vnto them, [d] Go in
peace: for ẏ Lord guideth your way which
ye go.
7 Then the fiue men departed and came
to Laish, and sawe the people that were
therein, which dwelt careles, after the maner of the Zidonians, quiet and sure, because no man " made any trouble in the
land, or vsurped any dominion: also they
were far from the Zidonians, and had no
busines with *other* men.

d Thus God granteth the idolaters sometime their requests to their destruction that delite in errors.

" *Ebr. made thẽ ashamed.*

8 ¶ So thei came againe vnto their brethrẽ
to Zoráh and Eshtaól: and their brethren
said vnto them, What haue ye *done*?
9 And thei answered, Arise, that we may
go vp against them: for we haue sene the
land, and surely it is very good, and [e] do
ye sit stil? be not slouthful to go and enter
to possesse the land.

e Lose ye this good occasion through your slouthfulnes?

10 (If ye wil go, ye shal come vnto a careles people, and the countrey *is* large) for
God hathe giuen it into your hand. *It is*
a place which doeth lacke nothing that is
in the worlde.
11 ¶ Then there departed thence of the familie of the Danites, from Zoráh and
from Eshtaól, six hũdreth men appointed
with instruments of warre.
12 And thei went vp, & pitched in Kiriáth
iearim in Iudáh: wherefore they called
that place, " Mahaneh-Dan vnto this day:
and it is behinde Kiriáth iearim.

" *Or the tentes of Dan.*

13 And thei went thence vnto mount E-
phráim, and came to the house of Micháh.
14 Then answered the fiue men, that wẽt to
spie out the countrey of Laish, and said
vnto their brethren, [f] Knowe ye not,
that there is in these houses an Ephód, &
Teraphím, and a grauen and a molten

f Because thei before had had good successe, thei wolde ẏ their brethrẽ shulde be encouraged by hearing ẏ same tidings.

image? Now therefore consider what ye
haue to do.
15 And thei turned thetherwarde and came
to the house of the yong man the Leuite,
euen vnto the house of Micháh, and saluted him peaceably.
16 And the six hundreth men appointed
with their weapons of warre, which were
of the children of Dan, stode by the entring of the gate.
17 Then the fiue men that went to spie out
the land, went inthether, *and* toke the
[g] grauen image and the Ephód, and the
Teraphím, and the molten image: and the
Priest stode in the entring of the gate
with the six hundreth men, that were appointed with weapons of warre,
18 And the other went into Michahs house
and fet the grauen image, the Ephód, and
the Teraphím, and the molten image.
Then said the Priest vnto them, What
do ye?

g So superstición blinded them, that thei thoght Gods power was in these idoles, & ẏ thei shulde haue good succes by them, thogh by violence & robbery they did take them awaye.

19 And thei answered him, Holde thy peace: laye thine hand vpon thy mouth, and
come with vs to be our father and Priest.
Whether is it better that thou shuldest be
a Priest vnto the house of one man, or
that thou shuldest be a Priest vnto a tribe
and to a familie in Israél?
20 And the Priests heart was glad, and he
toke the Ephód and the Teraphím, and
the grauen image, and went among the
[h] people.

h With the six hundreth men.

21 And they turned and departed, and put
the children and the cattel, and the substãce [i] before them.

i Suspecting them that did pursue them.

22 ¶ When thei were farre of frõ the house of Micháh, the men that were in the
houses nere to Michahs house, gathered
together, and pursued after the children
of Dan,
23 And cryed vnto the children of Dan:
who turned their faces, and said vnto Micháh, What ayleth thee, that thou makest
an outcrye?
24 And he said, Ye haue taken away my
[k] gods, which I made, and the Priest, and
go your waies: & what haue I more? how
then say ye vnto me, What aileth thee?

k This declareth what opinion the idolaters haue of their idoles.

25 And the children of Dan said vnto him,
Let not thy voyce be heard amõg vs, lest
" angry fellowes runne vpon thee, & thou
lose thy life with the liues of thine housholde.

" *Ebr. who haue their hearts bitter.*

26 So the children of Dan went their
waies: and when Micháh sawe that they
were to strong for him, he turned, & went
backe vnto his house.
27 And thei toke the [l] things which Micháh had made, and the Priest which he
had, and came vnto Laish, vnto a quiet
people and without mistrust, and smote
thẽ with the edge of the sworde & burnt

l Meaning, the idoles, as vers. 18.

the citie with fire:
°Or, deliuer thē. 28 And there was none to° helpe, because
m Which after was called Cesarea Philippi. m Laish was farre from Zidón, and they
had no busines with *other* men: also it was
in the valley that lyeth by Beth-rehób.
After, they buylt the citie, & dwelt therein,
Iosh. 19, 47. 29 *And called the name of the *citie Dan,
after the name of Dan their father which
was borne vnto Israél: howbeit the name
of the citie was Laish at the beginning.
30 Then the children of Dan set them vp
n Thus in steade of giuing glorie to God, thei attributed the victorie to their idoles, & honored them therefore. the n grauen image: and Ionathán the
sonne of Gershóm, the sonne of Manasséh and his sonnes were the Priests in the
tribe of the Danites vntil the day of the
o That is, til the Arke was taken, 1. Sam. 5, 1. o captiuitie of the land.
31 So they set them vp the grauen image,
which Micháh had made, all the while the
house of God was in Shilóh.

CHAP. XIX.

1 A Leuites wife being an harlot, forsoke her housband, and he toke her againe. 25 At Gibeáh she was moste vilenously abused to the death. 29 The Leuite cutteth her in pieces and sendeth her to the twelue tribes.

Chap. 17, 6. & 18, 1. 1 Also in those daies, * when there
was no King in Israél, a certaine
Leuite dwelt on the side of mount Ephráim, and toke to wife a * concubine out of
Gen. 25, 6. Beth-léhem Iudáh,
2 And his concubine played the whore
"Ebr. besides him: to wit, with others. " there, and went away from him vnto
her fathers house to Beth-léhem Iudáh,
and there cōtinued the space of foure moneths.
3 And her housband arose and went after
"Ebr. to her heart. her, to speake "friendly vnto her, and to
bring her againe: *he had* also his seruant
with him, and a couple of asses: and she
broght him vnto her fathers house, and
when the yong womans father sawe him,
°Or, at his meting. he reioyced° of his comming.
4 And his father in lawe, the yong womans
father reteined him: and he abode with
him thre daies: so they did eat & drinke,
and lodged there.
5 ¶ And when the fourth day came, thei a-
"Ebr. rose vp. rose early in the morning, & "he prepared
to departe: then the yong womans father
°Or, strengthen. said vnto his sonne in lawe, °Comforte
thine heart with a morsel of bread, and
then go your way.
6 So they sate downe, & did eat and drinke bothe of them together. And the a yōg
a That is, his concubines father. womans father said vnto the man, Be
content, I pray thee, and tary all night, &
let thine heart be mery.
7 And when the mā rose vp to departe, his
°Or, compelled him. father in lawe ° was earnest: therefore he
returned, and lodged there.
b Meanīg, that he shulde refresh him selfe with meate, as vers. 5. 8 And he arose vp early the fifte day to
departe, & the yong womans father said,
b Comforte thine heart, I pray thee: and
they taryed vntil after midday, and they
bothe did eat.
9 Afterwarde when the man arose to departe with his concubine and his seruant,
his father in lawe, the yong womans father said vnto him, Beholde now, the day
"Ebr. is weake. " draweth towarde euen: I pray you, tary
°Or, the day lodgeth. all night: beholde° the sunne goeth to rest:
lodge here, that thine heart may be mery, & tomorowe get you early vpon your
way, and go to thy c tent.
c To wit, to ŷ towne or citie where he dwelt. 10 But the man wolde not tary, but arose
and departed, & came ouer against Iebús,
(which is Ierusalém) and his two asses laden, and his concubine *were* with him.
11 When thei were nere to Iebús, the day
°Or, wet downe. ° was sore spent, and the seruant said vnto
his master, Come, I pray thee, & let vs turne into this citie of the Iebusites, & lodge
all night there.
12 And his master answered him, d We wil
d Thogh in these daies there were most horrible corruptiōs, yet very necessitie colde not cōpel thē to haue to do with them that professed not the true God. not turne into the citie of strangers that
are not of the children of Israél, but we
wil go forthe to Gibeáh.
13 And he said vnto his seruant, Come, and
let vs drawe nere to one of these places,
that we may lodge in Gibeáh or in Ramáh.
14 So they went forwarde vpon their way,
and the sunne went downe vpō them nere
to Gibeáh, which is in Beniamín.
15 ¶ Then thei turned thether to go in and
lodge in Gibeáh: and when he came, he
sate him downe in a strete of the citie: for
°Or, gathered them. there was no man that° toke them into his
house to lodging.
16 And beholde, there came an olde man
from his worke out of the field at euen,
and the man was of mount Ephráim, but
dwelt in Gibeáh: and the men of the place were the children of e Ieminí.
e That is, of ŷ tribe of Beniamin. 17 And when he had lift vp his eyes, he
°Or, a man walking. sawe a° wayfaring mā in the stretes of the
citie: then this olde man said, Whether
goest thou, and whence camest thou?
18 And he answered him, We came from
Beth-léhem Iudáh, vnto the side of mōut
Ephráim: from thence am I: and I went
to Beth-léhem Iudáh, and go *now* to the
f To Shilōh or Mizpéh, where the Arke was. f house of the Lord: and no man receiueth me to house,
19 Althogh we haue strawe and prouandre
for our asses, and also bread and wine for
me and thine handmayd, and for the boy
that is with thy seruant: we lacke nothing.
°Or, be of good comfort. 20 And the olde man said, ° Peace be with
thee: as for all that thou lackest, *shalt thou
finde* with me: onely abide not in the strete
all night.
21 ¶ So he broght him into his house, and
gaue foddre vnto the asses: & thei washed
their fete, & did eat and drinke.
22 And as they were making their hearts
mery,

mery,beholde,the men of the citie, ”wicked men beset the house round about, and
g smote at the dore,and spake to this olde
man the master of the house,saying,Bring
forthe the man that came into thine house
that we may knowe him.

”Ebr men of Belial:that is,giuen to all wickednes.
g To the intēt they might breake it.

23 And * this man the master of the house,
went out vnto them, and said vnto them,
Naye my brethren, do not so wickedly,I
pray you:seing that this man is come into mine house,do not this vilanie.

Gen.19,8.

24 Beholde, *here is* my daughter , a virgine,
and his concubine : them wil I bring out
now, h and humble them,and do with thē
what semeth you good : but to this man
do not this vilenie.

h That is,abuse them.

25 But the men wolde not hearken to him:
therefore the man toke his concubine,and
broght her out vnto them:and they knewe
her and abused her all the night vnto the
morning:& whē the day began to spring,
they let her go.
26 So ẏ woman came in the dawning of the
day,& i fel downe at the dore of the mās
house where her lord was,til the light day.
27 And her ° lord arose in the morning , &
opened the dores of the house, and went
out to go his way, and beholde , the woman his concubine *was* ° dead at the dore
of the house and her hands *lay* vpon the
thresholde.

i She fell downe dead, as vers.27.
°Or, housband.
°Or, fallen.

28 And he said vnto her, Vp and let vs go:
but she answered not . Then he toke her
vp vpon the asse,and the man rose vp,and
went vnto his k place.
29 And when he was come to his house, he
toke a knife, and laid hand on his concubine, and deuided her in pieces with her
bones into twelue partes , and sent her
through all quarters of Israél.

k Meaning, home vnto mount Ephráim.

30 And all that sawe it, said, There was no
l suche thing done or sene since the time
that the children of Israél came vp from
the land of Egypt vnto this day: consider
the matter,consult and giue sentence.

l For this was like the sin of Sodō, for the w God rained downe fire & brimstone from heauen.

CHAP. XX.

*1 The Israelites assemble in Mizpéh,to whome the Le-
uite declareth his wrong. 13 They sent for them that
did the vilenie. 25 The Israelites are twise ouercome,
46 And at length get the victorie.*

1 THen * all the childrē of Israél wēt out
and the Congregacion was gathered
together as a one man , from Dan to Beér
shéba, with the land of Gileád , vnto the
b Lord in Mizpéh.
2 And the ” chief of all the people *and* all
the tribes of Israél assembled in the Congregaciō of the people of God foure hūdreth thousand fotemen ẏ c drewe sword.
3 (Now the children of Beniamín heard
that the childrē of Israél were gone vp to
Mizpéh) Then the children of Israél
d said,How is this wickednes committed?

Osee 10,9.
a That is, all with one consent
b To aske counsel.
”Ebr. corners.
c Meaning mē able to handle their weapon.
d To the Leuite.

4 And the same Leuite, the womans housband that was slaine, answered and said, I
came vnto Gibeáh that is in Beniamín
with my concubine to lodge,
5 And the ° mē of Gibeáh arose against me,
and beset the house round about vpon me
by night,thinking to haue slaine me, and
haue forced my cōcubine that she is dead.
6 Then I toke my concubine, and cut her
in pieces, and sent e her through out all
the countrey of the inheritance of Israél:
for they haue committed abominacion
and vilenie in Israél.

°Or,chief,or lords.
e That is, her pieces, to euerie tribe a piece,Chap.19,9.

7 Beholde,ye are all children of Israél:gi-
ue your aduise,and counsel herein.
8 Thē all ẏ people arose as one mā,saying,
There shal not a man of vs go to his tent,
nether anie turne into his f house.
9 But now this is that thing which we wil
do to Gibeáh:*we wil go vp* by lot agaīst it,
10 And we wil take ten men of the hūdreth
throughout all the tribes of Israél, and
an hundreth of the thousand , and a thousand of ten thousand to bring g vitaile
for the people that they may do (when
they come to Gibeáh of Beniamín)accor-
ding to all the vilenie, that it hathe done
in Israél.

f Before we haue reuenged this wickednes.
g These onely shulde haue ẏ charge to prouide for vitaile for the rest.

11 ¶So all the men of Israél were gathered
against the citie,knit together,as one mā.
12 And the tribes of Israél sent mē through
all the h tribe of Beniamín,saying,What
wickednes is this ẏ is cōmitted amōg you?
13 Now therefore deliuer vs those wicked
men which are in Gibeáh, that we may
put them to death, and put away euil
from Israél:but the children of Beniamín
i wolde not obey the voyce of their brethren the children of Israél.
14 But the children of Beniamín gathered
them selues together out of the cities vnto
Gibeáh,to come out and fight against the
children of Israél.
15 ¶And the children of Beniamín were
nombred at that time out of the cities six
and twentie thousand men that drewe
sworde,beside the inhabitants of Gibeáh,
which were nombred seuen hundreth chosen men.

h That is,euerie familie of the tribe.
i Because they wolde not suffre the wicked to be punished, they declared them selues to maintaine thē in their euil,& therefore were all iustely punished.

16 Of all this people *were* seuen hundreth
chosen men , being * left handed : all these colde sling stones at an heere breadth,
and not faile.

Chap.3,15.

17 ¶Also ẏ men of Israél, beside Bēiamín,
were nōbred foure hundreth thousand mē
that drewe sworde,euen all men of warre.
18 And the children of Israél arose,& wēt
vp k to the house of God,& asked of God,
sayīg,Which of vs shal go vp first to fight
against the children of Beniamín?And the
Lord said,Iudáh *shalbe* first.
19 Then the childrē of Israél arose vp early and camped against Gibeáh.

k That is,to ẏ Arke, which was in Shilóh: some thinke, in Mizpéh , as vers.1.

20 And the men of Israél went out to battel against Beniamín, and the men of Israél put thẽ selues in array to fight against
them beside Gibeáh.
21 And the children of Beniamín came out
of Gibeáh, & slewe downe to the grounde
of the Israelites that day [l] two and twentie thousand men.
22 And the people, the men of Israél plucked vp their hearts, and set their battel a-
gaine in array in the place where they put
them in array the first day.
23 (For the children of Israél had gone vp
and wept before the Lord vnto ẏ euening,
and had asked of the Lord, saying, Shal I
go againe to battel against the children of
Beniamín my brethren? & the Lord said,
Go vp against them)
24 ¶ Then the children of Israél came nere
against the children of Beniamín the seconde day.
25 Also the seconde day Beniamín came
forthe to mete thẽ out of Gibeáh, & slewe
downe to the groũde of the childrẽ of Israél againe eightene thousand men: " all
they colde handle the sworde.
26 Then all the children of Israél went vp
& all the people came also vnto the house
of God, & wept and sate there before the
Lord & fasted that day vnto the euening,
and offred burnt offrings & peace offrings
before the Lord.
27 And the children of Israél asked the
Lord (for [m] there *was* the Arke of the couenant of God in those dayes,
28 And Phinehás the sonne of Eleazár, the
sonne of Aarón [n] stode before it at that
time) saying, Shal I yet go anie more to
battel against the childrẽ of Beniamín my
brethrẽ, or shal I cease? And the Lord
said, Go vp: for tomorowe I wil deliuer
them into your hand.
29 And Israél set men to lye in wait round
about Gibeáh.
30 And the children of Israél went vp a-
gainst the children of Beniamín the third
day, and put them selues in array against
Gibeáh, as at other times.
31 Then the children of Beniamín comming out against the people, were [o] drawẽ
from the citie: and they began to smite of
the people and kil as at other times, *euen*
by the wayes in the field (whereof one
goeth vp to the house of God, & the other
to Gibeáh) vpon a thirtie men of Israél.
32 (For the childrẽ of Beniamín said, They
are fallen before vs, as at the first. But the
children of Israél said, Let vs flee & plucke them away from the citie vnto the hie
[p] wayes)
33 And all the men of Israél rose vp out of
their place, & put them selues in array at
Baál tamár: and the men that lay in waite

l This God permitted, because the Israelites partely trusted to muche in their strength, and partely God wolde by this meanes punish their sinnes.

" Ebr. *all they drawing the sworde.*

m To wit, in Shilóh.

n Or, serued in the Priests office at those daies: for the Iewes write, that he liued thre hundreth yeres.

o By the policie of the children of Israél.

p Meaning, crosse wayes or paths to diuers places.

of the Israelites came forthe of their place, *euen* out of the medowes of Gibeáh,
34 And they came ouer against Gibeáh, ten
thousand chosẽn men of all Israél, & the
battel was sore: for they knewe not that
the [q] euil was nere them.
35 ¶ And ẏ Lord smote Beniamín before Israél, and the children of Israél destroyed
of the Beniamites the same day fiue and
twentie thousand and an hundreth men:
all they colde handle the sworde.
36 So the childrẽ of Beniamín sawe that they
were striken downe: for the men of Israél
[r] gaue place to the Beniamites, because
they trusted to the men that lay in wait,
which they had laid beside Gibeáh.
37 And they that lay in waite hasted, and
brake forthe towarde Gibeáh, and the
embushment " drewe them selues along,
and smote all the citie with the edge of
the sworde.
38 Also the men of Israél had appointed a
certaine time with the embushmẽts, that
they shulde make a great flame, *and* smoke
rise vp out of the citie.
39 And whẽ the men of Israél retired in the
battel, Beniamín began to [s] smite and kil
of the men of Israél about thirtie persones: for they said, Surely they are striken
downe before vs, as in the first battel.
40 But when the flame began to arise out
of the citie, *as* a piller of smoke, the Beniamites loked backe, and beholde, the flame of the citie began to ascende vp to
heauen.
41 Then ẏ men of Israél turned [t] againe,
and the men of Beniamín were astonied:
for they saw that euil was nere vnto thẽ.
42 Therefore they fled before the men of
Israél vnto the way of the wildernes,
but the battel ouertoke them: also they
which *came out* of the cities, slewe them
[u] among them.
43 *Thus* they compassed the Beniamites
about, *and* chased them " at ease, and ouer-
ran them, euen ouer against Gibeáh on
the Eastside.
44 And there were slaine of Beniamín eightene thousand mẽn, which were all men
of warre.
45 And they turned and fled to the wildernes vnto the rocke of Rimmón: and the
Israelites [x] glained of them by the way fiue thousand mẽ, & pursued after thẽ vnto
Gidóm, & slewe two thousand mẽ of thẽ,
46 So that all that were slaine that day of
Beniamín, were [y] fiue and twentie thousand men that drewe sworde, which were
all men of warre:
47 But six hundreth men turned & fled to
the wildernes, vnto the rocke of Rimmón
and abode in the rocke of Rimmón foure
moneths.

q They knewe not, that Gods iudgemẽt was at hand to destroy them.

r Retired, to drawe them after.

" Or, *made alõg sounde with a trumpet.*

s For they were waxen hardy by the two former victories.

t And withstode their enemies.

u For they were cõpassed in on euerie side.

" Or, *droue thẽm frõ their reste.*

x They slewe them by one & one, as they were scattered abroad.

y Besides eleuen hundreth that had bene slaine in the former battelles.

48 Then

48 Then the men of Israél returned vnto
the children of Beniamín, and smote thẽ
with the edge of the sworde frõ the mẽ of
the citie vnto the beasts, and all that came
to hand: also they set on fire all the [z] cities that they colde come by.

z If they belonged to the Beniamites.

CHAP. XXI.

1 The Israelites sweare that they wil not mary their daughters to the Beniamites. 10 They slay them of Iabésh Gileád, and giue their virgines to the Beniamites. 21 The Beniamites take the daughters of Shilóh.

1 MOreouer the men of Israél [a] sware in
Mizpéh, saying, None of vs shal giue his daughter vnto the Beniamites to
wife.

a This othe came of rashenes and not of iudgement: for after they brake it, in shewing secretly the meanes to mary with certaine of their daughters.

2 And the people came vnto the house of
God, & abode there til euen before God,
and lift vp their voices, and wept with
great lamentacion,
3 And said, ô Lord God of Israél, why is
this come to passe in Israél, that this day
one tribe of Israél shulde want?
4 ¶ And on the morowe the people rose vp
and made there an [b] altar, and offred
burnt offrings and peace offrings.

b According to their custome, when they wolde consult with the Lord.

5 Then the children of Israél said, Who
is he amõg all ẏ tribes of Israél, that came
not vp with the Congregacion vnto the
Lord? for they had made a great othe concerning him that came not vp to the
Lord to Mizpéh, saying, Let him dye the
death.
6 And the children of Israél [c] were sorie
for Beniamín their brother, & said, There is one tribe cut of from Israél this day.

c Or, repented that they had destroied their brethren, as appeareth vers. 15.

7 How shal we do for wiues to them that
remaine, seing we haue sworne by ẏ Lord,
that we wil not giue them of our daughters to wiues?
8 Also they said, Is there anie of the tribes
of Israél that [d] came not vp to Mizpéh
to the Lord? and beholde, there came none
of Iabésh Gileád vnto the hoste *and* to
the Congregacion.

d Cõdemning thẽ to be fauters of vice, which wolde not put their hand to punish it.

9 For when the people were vewed, beholde, none of the inhabitants of Iabésh Gileád were there.
10 Therefore the Congregacion sent thether twelue thousand men of the "moste
valiant, and commanded them, saying,
Go, and smite the inhabitants of Iabésh
Gileád with the edge of the sworde, bothe
women and children.

" Ebr. children of strength.

11 *And this is it that ye shal do: ye shal
vtterly destroy all the males and all the
women that haue lien by men.

Nomb. 31, 17.

12 And they founde among the inhabitants
of Iabésh Gileád foure hundreth maides,
virgins that had knowen no man by lying
with anie male: and they broght them vnto the hoste to Shilóh, which is in the land
of Canáan.
13 ¶ Thẽ the whole Congregacion [e] sent &
spake with the children of Beniamín that
were in the rocke of Rimmón, and called "peaceably vnto them:

e To wit, about foure monethes after ẏ discomfiture, Chap. 20, 47.
" Or, friendly.

14 And Beniamín came againe at ẏ time,
& they gaue them wiues which they had
saued aliue of the women of Iabésh Gileád: but they had not [f] so ynough for thẽ.

f For there lacked two hundreth.

15 And the people were sory for Beniamín,
because the Lord had made a breache in
the tribes of Israél.
16 Therefore the Elders of the Congregacion said, How shal we do for wiues to the
remnant? for the women of Beniamín
are destroyed.
17 And they said, *There must be* an [g] inheritance for them that be escaped of Beniamín, that a tribe be not destroyed out of
Israél.

g Beniamín must be reserued to haue ẏ twelft portiõ in ẏ inheritãce of Iaakób.

18 Howbeit we may not giue them wiues
of our daughters: for the children of
Israél had sworne, saying, Cursed be he,
that giueth a wife to Beniamín.
19 Therefore they said, Beholde, there is a
feast of the Lord euerie yere in Shilóh
in a place, which is on the [h] Northside of
Beth-él, and on the Eastside of the way
that goeth vp from Beth-él to Shechém,
and on the South of Lebonáh.

h He describeth the place where the maides vsed yerely to dance, as ẏ maner then was, & to syng Psalmes and songs of Gods workes emongs them.

20 Therefore thei commanded the childrẽ
of Beniamín, saying, Go, and lye in waite
in the vineyardes.
21 And when ye se that the daughters of
Shilóh come out to dance in dances, then
come ye out of the vineyardes, and catche
you euery man a wife of the daughters of
Shilóh, & go into the land of Beniamín.
22 And [i] when their fathers or their brethren come vnto vs to complaine, we wil
say vnto them, Haue pitie on thẽ for our
sakes, because we reserued not to eche mã
his wife in the warre, and because ye haue
not giuen vnto them hetherto, ye haue
sinned.

i Thogh they thoght hereby to persuade men that they kept their othe, yet before God it was broken.

23 And the children of Beniamín did so,
and toke wiues of them that dãced according to their [k] nomber: which they toke,
and went away, and returned to their inheritance, and repaired the cities & dwelt
in them.

k Meaning, two hũdreth.

24 So the childrẽ of Israél departed thẽce
at that time, euery man to his tribe, and to
his familie, and went out from thence e-
uerie man to his inheritance.
25 *In those dayes there was no King in Israél, *but* euerie man did that which was
good in his eyes.

Chap. 17, 6. & 18, 1. & 19, 1.

THE BOKE OF RUTH.

THE ARGUMENT.

This boke is intitled after the name of Ruth: which is the printipal persone spoken of in this treatise. Wherein also figuratiuely is set forthe the state of the Church which is subiect to manifolde afflictions, and yet at length God giueth good and ioyful yssue: teaching vs to abide with pacience til God deliuer vs out of troubles. Herein also is described howe Iesus Christ, who according to the flesh oght to come of Dauid, proceded of Ruth, of whome the Lord Iesus did vouchesaue to come, notwithstanding she was a Moabite of base condicion, and a stranger from the people of God: declaring vnto vs thereby that the Gentiles shulde be sanctified by him and ioyned with his people, and that there shulde be but one shepefolde, and one shepherde. And it semeth that this historie apperteineth to the time of the Iudges.

CHAP. I.

2 Elimélech goeth with his wife and childrẽ into the lãd of Moáb. 3 He and his sonnes dye. 19 Naomi and Ruth come to Beth-léhem.

IN the time that the iudges "ruled, there was a
dearth in the [a] land, and
a mã of Beth-léhem [b] Iudáh went for to soiourne in the coũtrei of Moáb, he, and his wife, and
his two sonnes.

" Ebr. iudged.

a In the land of Canáan.

b In ẏ tribe of Iudáh, which was also called Beth-léhẽ Ephráthah, because there was another citie so called in the tribe of Zebulún.

2 And the name of the mã *was* Elimélech,
and the name of his wife, Naomí: and the
names of his two sonnes, Mahlón, & Chilión, Ephrathites of Beth-léhem Iudáh:
and when they came into the land of Moáb, they continued there.
3 Then Elimélech the housbãd of Naomí
dyed, & she remained with her two sonnes,
4 Which toke them wiues of the [c] Moabites: the ones name *was* Orpáh, and the
name of the other Ruth: and they dwelled
there about ten yeres.
5 And Mahlón and Chilión dyed also
bothe twaine: so the woman was left *destitute* of her two sonnes, & of her housbãd.
6 ¶ Then she arose with her daughters in
lawe, and returned from the countrey of
Moáb: for she had heard say in the countrei of Moáb, that the Lord had [d] visited
his people, and giuen them bread.
7 Wherefore she departed out of the place
where she was, and her two daughters in
lawe with her, and they wẽt on their way
to returne vnto the land of Iudáh.
8 Thẽ Naomí said vnto her two daughters
in lawe, Go, returne eche of you vnto her
owne mothers house: ẏ Lord shewe fauour
vnto you, as ye haue done with the dead,
and with me.
9 The Lord grante you, that you may finde
[e] rest, ether of you in the house of her housband. And when she kissed them, they lift
vp their voyce and wept.
10 And they said vnto her, Surely we wil
returne with thee vnto thy people.
11 But Naomí said, Turne againe, my
daughters: for what cause wil you go with
me? are there anie mo sonnes in my wombe, that they may be your housbands?
12 Turne againe, my daughters: go your
way: for I am to olde to haue an housbãd.
if I shulde saie, I haue hope, & if I had an
housband this night: yea, if I had borne
sonnes,
13 Wolde ye tary for them, til they were of
age? wolde ye be differred for them from
taking of housbands? nay my daughters:
for it grieueth me "muche for your sakes ẏ
the hãd of ẏ Lord is gone out against me.
14 Then they lift vp their voyce, and wept
againe, and Orpáh [f] kissed her mother in
lawe, but Ruth abode stil with her.
15 And Naomí said, Beholde, thy sister in
lawe is gone backe vnto her people & vnto
her gods: [g] returne ẏ after thy sister in law.
16 And Ruth answered, Intreat me not to
leaue thee, nor to departe from thee: for
whither thou goest, I wil go: and where
thou dwellest, I wil dwel: thy people *shalbe*
my people, and thy God my God.
17 Where ẏ dyest, wil I dye, and there wil
I be buryed. the Lord do so to me & more
also, if *oght* but death departe thee & me.
18 ¶ When she sawe that she was stedfastly
minded to go with her, she left speaking
vnto her.
19 So they went bothe vntil they came to
Beth-léhẽ: & whẽ they were come to Beth-léhem, it was [h] noised of them through all
the citie, and thei said, Is not this Naomí?
20 And she answered thẽ, Call me not "Naomí, *but* call me "Mará: for the Almightie
hathe giuen me muche bitternes.
21 I wẽt out ful, & ẏ Lord hathe caused me
to returne empty: why call ye me Naomí,
seing the Lord hath hũbled me, & the Almighty hathe broght me vnto aduersitie.
22 So Naomí returned and Ruth ẏ Moabitesse her daughter in law with her, when
she came out of the countrei of Moáb: &
they came to Beth-léhem in the beginning of [i] barly haruest.

c By this wõderful prouidence of God Ruth became one of Gods housholde, of whome Christ came.

d By sending them plentie againe.

e Hereby it appeareth that Naomi by dwellĩg amõg idolaters was waxen colde in ẏ true zeale of God, ẇ rather hathe respect to the ease of ẏ body then to ẏ comfort of ẏ soule.

" Or, more then you.

f When she toke leaue & departed.

g No persuasions can preuaile to turne thẽ backe frõ God whome he hathe chosen to be his.

h Whereby appeareth ẏ she was of a great familie & of good reputation.

" Or, beautiful.

" Or, bitter.

i Which was in the moneth Nisan, that cõteineth part of March & parte of April.

CHAP. II.

1 Ruth gathereth corne in the fieldes of Bóaz. 15 The gẽtlenes of Bóaz toward her.

1 THen Naomis housband had a kinsman, one of great [a] power of the familie of Elimélech, & his name *was* Bóaz.
And

a Bothe for vertue, autoritie and riches.

2 And Ruth ẏ Moabitesse said vnto Naomí, I pray thee, let me go to ẏ field, & [b] gather eares of corne after hĩ, in whose sight
I find fauour. And she said vnto her, Go
my daughter.

b This her humilitie declareth her great affection toward her mother in lawe, for as muche as she spareth no painful diligence to get bothe their liuings.

3 ¶ And she went, & came & gleaned in ẏ
field after the reapers, & it came to passe,
that she met w̃ the portion of the field of
Bóaz, who was of ẏ familie of Elimélech.
4 And beholde, Bóaz came from Beth-léhem, and said vnto the reapers, The Lord
be with you: & thei answered him, The
Lord blesse thee.
5 Thẽ said Bóaz vnto his seruãt ẏ was appoĩted ouer ẏ reapers, Whose maid is this?
6 And the seruant that was appointed ouer
the reapers, answered, and said, It is the
Moabitish mayd, that came with Naomí
out of the countrey of Móab:
7 And she said vnto vs, I pray you, let me
gleane and gather after the reapers ″amõg
the sheaues: so she came, and hathe continued from that time in the morning vnto
now, saue ẏ she taried a litle in the house.

″Or, certaine handefuls.

8 ¶ Then said Bóaz vnto Ruth, Hearest
thou, my daughter? go to none other field
to gather, nether go from hence: but abide
here by my maidens.
9 [c] Let thine eyes be on the field that they
do reape, and go thou after the *maidẽs*. Haue I not charged the seruants, that they
touche thee not? Moreouer when thou art
a thirst, go vnto the vessels and brinke of
that which the seruants haue drawen.

c That is, Take hede in what field they do reape

10 Then she fel on her face, and bowed her
se lf to the ground, & said vnto im, How
haue I found fauour in thine eyes, that ẏ
shuldest knowe me, seing I am [d] a strãger?
11 And Bóaz answered, and said vnto her,
All is tolde and shewed me that ẏ hast
done vnto thy mother in law, since ẏ death
of thine housbãd, and how thou hast left
thy father and thy mother, and the land
where thou wast borne, and art come vnto
a people w̃ thou knewest not in time past.

d Euen of the Moabites, w̃ are enemies to Gods people.

12 The Lord recompence thy worke and a
ful reward be giuen thee of the Lord God
of Israél, vnder whose [e] wings thou art
come to trust.

e Signifiing ẏ she shal neuer want anie thĩg if she put her trust in God & liue vnder his protectiõ.

13 Then she said, Let me finde fauour in
thy sight, my lord: for ẏ hast cõforted me,
and spoken comfortably vnto thy maid,
thogh I be not like to one of thy maids.
14 And Bóaz said vnto her, At ẏ meale time
come thou hither, and eat of the bread, &
dip thy morsel in ẏ vinegre. And she sate
beside the reapers, and he reached her parched corne: and she did eat, and was suffised, and [f] left thereof.
15 ¶ And when she arose to gleane, Bóaz cõ
mãded his seruants, saying, Let her gather
among ẏ sheaues, and do not rebuke her.
16 Also let fall *some* of the sheaues for her,

f Which she broght home to her mother in lawe.

& let it lie, that she may gather it vp, and
rebuke her not.
17 So she gleaned in the field vntil euening,
and she threshed that she had gathered,
and it was about an *Ephàh of barly.

Exod.16,36.

18 ¶ And she toke it vp, & went into the citie, and her mother in lawe sawe what she
had gathered: also she [g] toke forthe, and
gaue to her that which she had reserued,
when she was suffised.

g To wit, of her bagg, as is in the Chalde texte.

19 Then her mother in lawe said vnto her,
Where hast thou gleaned to day? & where
wroghtest thou? blessed be he, that knewe
thee. And she shewed her mother in lawe,
with whome she had wroght, & said, The
mans name with whome I wroght to day,
is Bóaz.
20 And Naomí said vnto her daughter in
lawe, Blessed be he of the Lord: for he ceaseth not to do good to the liuing and to
the [h] dead. Againe Naomí said vnto her,
The mã is nere vnto vs, & of our affinitie.
21 And Ruth the Moabitesse said, He said
also certainly vnto me, Thou shalt be w̃
my seruãts, vntil they haue ended all mine haruest.

h To my housband & childrẽ, whẽ they were aliue, & now to vs.

22 And Naomí answered vnto Ruth her
daughter in lawe, It is best, my daughter,
that thou go out with his maids, that thei
″mete thee not in an other field.

″Or, fall vpon thee.

23 Thẽ she kept her by the maids of Bóaz,
to gather vnto the end of barly haruest, &
of wheat haruest, and ″ dwelt with her mother in lawe.

″Or, returned to her mother in lawe.

CHAP. III.

1 Naomí giueth Ruth counsel. 8 She slepeth at Bóaz fete.
12 He acknowledgeth him selfe to be her kinseman.

1 AFterward Naomi her mother in law
said vnto her, My daughter, shal not
I seke [a] rest for thee, that ẏ maiest prosper?
2 Now also is not Bóaz our kinsman, with
whose maids ẏ wast? beholde, he winow-
eth barly to night in the ″floore.

a Meaning, ẏ she wolde prouide her of an housband, w̃ whome she might liue quietly.

″Or, in the barne.

3 Wash thy selfe therefore, & anoint thee,
& put thy raiment vpõ thee, and get thee
downe to ẏ floore: let not ẏ [b] mã knowe of
thee, vntil he haue left eating & drinking.

b Bóaz, nor yet anie other

4 And when he shal slepe, marke the place
where he layeth him downe, & go, & vncouer the place of his fete, and lay thee
downe, & he shal tel thee what ẏ shalt do.
5 And she answered her, All that thou bid-
dest me, I wil do.
6 ¶ So she went downe vnto the floore, &
did according to all ẏ her mother in lawe
bade her.
7 And when Bóaz had eaten, and dronkẽ, &
[c] cheared his heart, he went to lie downe at
the end of the heape of corne, & she came
softely, & vncouered the place of his fete,
& lay downe.

c That is, had refreshed him selfe amõg his seruants.

8 And at midnight the man was afraied ″&
caught holde: & lo, a womã lay at his fete.

″Or, turned him selfe from one side to another.

9 Then he said, Who art thou? And she answered, I am Ruth thine hãdmaide: spread
therefore the wing of thy garment ouer
thine hãdmaid: for thou art the kinseman.
10 Then said he, Blessed be thou of the
Lord, my daughter: ẏ hast [d] shewed more
goodnes in the latter end, then at the beginning, in as muche as thou folowedst
not yong men, were they poore or riche.
11 And now, my daughter, feare not: I wil do
to thee all that thou requirest: for all the
citie of my people doeth knowe, that thou
art a vertuous woman.
12 And now, it is true that I am thy kinsman, howbeit there is a kinseman nearer
then I.
13 Tary to night, & when morning is come,
if he [e] wil do the duetie of a kinseman vnto thee, wel, let him do the kinsmans duetie: but if he wil not do the kinsemans
parte, then wil I do the duetie of a kinsmã,
as ẏ Lord liueth: slepe vntil the morning.
14 ¶ And she lay at his fete vntil the morning: & she arose before one colde knowe
another: for he said, Let no man knowe,
that a woman came in to the floore.
15 Also he said, bring the ″ shete that thou
hast vpon thee, and holde it. And when she
helde it, he measured six *measures* of
barly, and laied them on her, & went into the citie.
16 And whē she came to her mother in law,
she said, [f] Who art ẏ, my daughter? And
she tolde her all ẏ the mã had done to her,
17 And said, These six *measures* of barly gaue
he me: for he said to me, Thou shalt not
come empty vnto thy mother in lawe.
18 Then said she, My daughter, sit stil, vntil thou knowe how the thing wil fall: for
the man wil not be in rest, vntil he hathe
finished the matter this same day.

d Thou shewest thy selfe frõ time to time more vertuous.

e If he wil take thee to be his wife by ẏ title of affinitie, according to Gods law, Deu.25,5.

″ Or, mantel.

f Perceyuing by her coming home, that he had not taken her to his wife, she was astonied.

CHAP. IIII.

1 Bóaz speaketh to Ruths next kinseman touching her mariage. 7 The anciēt custome in Israél. 10 Bóaz maryeth Ruth, of whome he begetteth Obéd. 18 The generation of Phárez.

1 THen went Bóaz vp to the [a] gate, and
sate there, and beholde, the kinseman,
of whome Bóaz had spoken, came by: and
he said, [b] Ho, suche one, come, sit downe
here. And he turned, and sate downe.
2 Then he toke ten men of the Elders
of ẏ citie, & said, Sit ye downe here. And
they sate downe.
3 And he said vnto ẏ kinsman, Naomí, that
is come againe out of ẏ cōutrei of Moáb,
wil sel a parcel of lãd, which was our brother Elimélechs.
4 And I thoght to aduertise thee, saying,
Bye it before the ″ assistans, and before the
Elders of my people. If thou wilt redeme
it, redeme it: but if thou wilt not redeme
it, tel me: for I knowe that there is none [c] besides thee to redeme it, & I am after thee. Then he answered, I wil redeme it.
5 Then said Bóaz, What day thou byest ẏ
field of the hand of Naomí, thou must
also bye it of Ruth ẏ Moabitesse the wife
of the dead, to sterre vp the name of the
dead, vpon his [d] inheritance.
6 And the kinsman answered, I can not redeme it, lest I destroy mine owne inheritãce: redeme my right to thee, for I cã not
redeme it.
7 Now this was the maner beforetime in
Israél, concerning redeming and chãging,
for to stablish all things: a man did plucke
of his shooe, and gaue it his neighbour,
and this was a sure [e] witnes in Israél.
8 Therefore the kinsman said to Bóaz, Bye
it for thee: and he drue of his shooe.
9 And Bóaz said vnto the Elders and vnto
all the people, Ye are witnesses this day,
that I haue boght all ẏ was Elimélechs,
and all that was Chilións & Mahlóns, of
the hand of Naomí.
10 And moreouer, Ruth the Moabitesse the
wife of Mahlón, haue I boght to be my
wife, to sterre vp the name of ẏ dead vpō
his inheritance, and that the name of the
dead be not put out from among his brethren, and from the gate of his [f] place: ye
are witnesses this day.
11 And all the people that were in the gate,
& the Elders said, *We are* witnesses: the
Lord make the wife that cometh into thine house, like Rahél and like Leáh, which
twaine did buyld the house of Israél: and
that thou maiest do worthely in [g] E-
phráthah, and be famous in Beth-léhem,
12 And that thine house be like ẏ house of
Phárez (*whome Thamár bare vnto Iudáh) of the sede which the Lord shal giue
thee of this yong woman.
13 ¶ So Bóaz toke Ruth, and she was his
wife: and when he went in vnto her, the
Lord gaue, that she conceiued, and bare a
sonne.
14 And the women said vnto Naomí, Blessed *be* ẏ Lord, which hathe not left thee
this day without a kinsman, & [h] his name
shalbe continued in Israél.
15 And this shal bring thy life againe, and
cherish thine olde age: for thy daughter in
lawe which loueth thee, hathe borne vnto him, and she is better to thee then [i] seuen sonnes.
16 And Naomí toke the childe, and layed it in her lap, and became nource vnto it.
17 And *the women* her neighbours gaue
it a name, saying, There is a childe borne to Naomí, and called the name thereof
Obéd: the same was the father of Ishái,
the father of Dauid.

a Which was ẏ place of iudgement.

b The Ebrews here vse two wordes which haue no propre signification, but serue to note a certaine persone: as we say, ho, syrray, or ho, suche one.

″ Or, inhabitãts.

c For thou art the next of ẏ kinne.

d That his inheritance might beare his name that is dead.

e That he had resigned his right, Deut. 25,9.

f Or, of ẏ citie where he remained.

g Ephráthah & Beth-léhem are bothe one.

Gen. 38,29.

h He shal leaue a continual posteritie.

i Meaning, manie sonnes.

18 ¶ These

1.Chro.2,4. mat.1,3.
k This genealogie is broght in to proue that Dauid by succession came of the house of Iudáh.

18 ¶ These now are the generacions of
* k Phárez: Phárez begate Hezrón,
19 And Hezrón begate Ram, & Ram begate Amminadáb,
20 And Amminadáb begate Nahshón, and
Nahshón begate Salmáh,
21 And Salmón begate Bóaz, and Bóaz begate Obéd,
22 And Obéd begate Ishái, and Ishái begate Dauid.

THE FIRST BOKE OF Samuél.

THE ARGVMENT.

According as God had ordeined Deut. 17,14. that when the Israelites shulde be in the land of Canáan, he wolde appoint them a King: so here in this first boke of Samuel is declared the state of this people vnder their first King Saúl, who not content with that ordre, which God had for a time appointed for the gouernement of his Church, demanded a King, to the intent thei might be as other nacions & in a greater assurance as thei thoght: not because thei might the better thereby serue God, as being vnder the safegarde of him, which did represent Iesus Christ the true deliuerer: therefore he gaue them a tyrant and an hypocrite to rule ouer them, that they might learne, that the persone of a King is not sufficient to defend them, except God by his power preserue and kepe them. And therefore he punisheth the ingratitude of his people & sendeth the continual warres bothe at home and abroad. And because Saúl, whome of nothing God had preferred to the honour of a King, did not acknowledge Gods mercie towarde him, but rather disobeied the worde of God and was not zealous of his glorie, he was by the voyce of God put downe from his state, and Dauid the true figure of Messiáh placed in his steade, whose pacience, modestie, constancie, persecucion by open enemies, fained friends, and dissembling flatterers are left to the Church and to euery member of the same, as a paterne and example to beholde their state ad vocacion.

CHAP. I.

1 The genealogie of Elkanáh father of Samuél. 2 His two wiues. 5 Hannáh was baren and praied to the Lord. 15 Her answer to Elí. 20 Samuél is borne. 24 She doeth dedicate him to the Lord.

a There were two Ramaths, so that in this citie in mount Ephráim were Zophim: that is, the learned men and Prophets.

1 There was a man of one of the two a Ramathaím Zophím, of mout Ephráim, whose name was Elkanáh the sonne of Ierohám, the sonne of Elihú, the sonne of Tóhu, the sonne of Zuph, an Ephrathite:
2 And he had two wiues: the name of one was Hannáh, and the name of the other Peninnáh: and Peninnáh had childrẽ, but Hannáh had no children.

Deut.16,16.
b For the Arke was there at that time.

3 * And this man went vp out of his citie
euery yere, to worship & to sacrifice vnto
the Lord of hostes in b Shilóh, where
were the two sonnes of Elí, Hophní and
Phinehás Priests of the Lord.
4 And on a day, whẽ Elkanáh sacrifised, he
gaue to Peninnáh his wife and to all her
sonnes and daughters porcions,

c Some read, a porcion with an heauy chere.

5 But vnto Hãnáh he gaue a worthy c porcion: for he loued Hannáh, and the Lord had made her baren.
6 ¶ And her aduersarie vexed her sore, for asmucheas she vpbraided her, because the Lord had made her baren.
7 (And so did he yere by yere) & as oft as she wẽt vp to the house of ẏ Lord, thus she vexed her, that she wept and did not eat.
8 Then said Elkanáh her housbãd to her, Hannáh, why wepest thou? and why eatest thou not? & why is thine heart troubled? am not I better to thee then ten d sonnes?

d Let this suffice thee, that I loue thee no lesse, then if ẏ hadest many children.

9 So Hannáh rose vp after that they had eaten and dronke in Shilóh (and Elí the Priest sate vpõ a stole by one of ẏ postes of the e Temple of the Lord)

e That is, of ẏ house, where the Arke was.

10 And she was troubled in her minde, and praied vnto the Lord, and wept sore:
11 Also she vowed a vowe, & said, O Lord
of hostes, if thou wilt loke on the trouble
of thine handmayd, and remẽber me, and
not forget thine handmayd, but giue vnto
thine handmayd a manchilde, then I wil
giue him vnto the Lord all the daies of
his life, * and there shal no raser come
vpon his head.

Nomb 6,5. iudg.13,5.

12 And as she cõtinued praying before the Lord, Elí marked her mouth.
13 For Hãnáh spake in her heart: her lippes did moue onely, but her voyce was not heard: therefore Elí thoght she had bene dronken.
14 And Elí said vnto her, How long wilt thou be dronkẽ? Put away "thy dronkẽnes from thee.

"Ebr. thy wine.

15 Then Hannáh answered and said, Nay my lord, but I am a woman " troubled in spirit: I haue drõke nether wine nor strõg drinke, but haue * powred out my soule before the Lord.

"Ebr. of an hard spirit.
Psal.42,4.

16 Count not thine handmaid ″for a wicked woman: for of the abundance of my
complaint and my grief haue I ſpoken
hitherto.
17 Then Elí anſwered, and ſaid, Go in
peace, and the God of Iſraél grant thy
peticion that thou haſt aſked of him.
18 She ſaid againe, Let thine handmayd
finde [f] grace in thy ſight: ſo the woman
went her way, and did eat, and loked no
more ſad.
19 ¶ Then they roſe vp early, and worſhiped before the Lord, and returned, and
came to their houſe to Ramáh. Now Elkanáh knewe Hannáh his wife, and the
Lord [g] remembred her.
20 For in proceſſe of time Hannáh cõceiued, and bare a ſonne, and ſhe called his
name Samuél, Becauſe, *ſaid ſhe*, I haue aſked him of the Lord.
21 ¶ So the man [h] Elkanáh & all his houſe
went vp to offer vnto ẏ Lord the yerelie
ſacrifice, and his vowe:
22 But Hannáh went not vp: for ſhe ſaid
vnto her houſbãd, *I wil tary* vntil the childe be weined, then I wil bring him that
he may appeare before the Lord, & there
abide for euer.
23 And Elkanáh her houſband ſaid vnto
her, Do what ſemeth thee beſt: tary vntil
thou haſt weined him: onely the Lord accompliſh his [i] worde. So the woman a-
bode, and gaue her ſonne ſucke vntil ſhe
weined him.
24 ¶ And whẽ ſhe had weined him, ſhe toke
him with her with thre bullockes and an
*Epháh of floure and a bottle of wine, and
broght him vnto the houſe of the Lord in
Shilóh, and the childe was ″ yong.
25 And thei ſlewe a bullocke, and broght
the childe to Elí.
26 And ſhe ſaid, Oh my lord, as thy [k] ſoule
liueth, my lord, I am the womã that ſtode
with thee here praying vnto the Lord.
27 I praied for this childe, and the Lord
hathe giuen me my deſire which I aſked
of him.
28 Therefore alſo I haue ″ giuen him vnto
the Lord: as long as he liueth he ſhalbe
giuen vnto the Lord: and he [l] worſhiped the Lord there.

CHAP. II.

1 The ſong of Hannáh. 12 The ſonnes of Elí, wicked. 13 The newe cuſtome of the Prieſts. 18 Samuél miniſtreth before the Lord. 20 Elí bleſſeth Elkanáh and his wife. 23 Elí reproueth his ſonnes. 27 God ſendeth a Prophet to Elí. 31 Elí is menaced for not chaſtiſing his children.

AND Hannáh [a] praied, & ſaid, Mine
heart reioyceth in the Lord, mine
[b] horne is exalted in ẏ Lord: my mouth
is [c] enlarged ouer mine enemies, becauſe
I reioyce in thy ſaluacion.

″Ebr. for a daughter of Belial.

f That is, pray vnto the Lord for me.

g According to her peticiõ.

h This Elkanáh was a Leuite, 1. Chro. 6, 27. and as ſome write, once a yere thei accuſtomed to appeare before the Lord ẇ their families.

i Becauſe her praier toke effect, therefore it was called ẏ Lords promes.

Exod. 16, 36.

″Ebr. a childe.

k That is, moſt certeinly.

″Ebr. lent.

l Meaning, Elí gaue thãkes to God for her.

a After that ſhe had obteined a ſonne by prayer, ſhe gaue thankes.

b I haue recouered ſtrength & glorie by ẏ benefite of the Lord.

c I can anſwer them, that reproue my barennes.

2 There is none holy as the Lord: yea, there is none beſides thee, & there is no God
like our God.
3 Speake [d] no more preſumpteouſly: let
not arrogancie come out of your mouth:
for the Lord *is* a God of knowledge, and
by him enterpriſes are eſtabliſhed.
4 The bowe & the mightie men are broken, and the weake haue girde them ſelues with ſtrength.
5 Thei that were ful, are hired forthe for
[e] bread, & the hongrie are no more *hired*,
ſo that the baren hathe borne ″ ſeuen: and
ſhe that had many children, is feble.
6 *The Lord killeth and maketh aliue:
bringeth downe to the graue and raiſeth vp.
7 The Lord maketh poore and maketh
riche: bringeth lowe, and exalteth.
8 *He reiſeth vp the poore out of the duſt,
and lifteth vp the begger from the dong-
hil, to ſet *them* among [f] princes, and to
make them inherit the ſeat of glorie:
for the pillers of the earth are the
[g] Lords, and he hathe ſet the worlde vpon them.
9 He wil kepe the fete of his Sainctes, and
the wicked ſhal kepe ſilence in darckenes:
for in *his owne* might ſhal no man be
ſtrong.
10 The Lords aduerſaries ſhal be deſtroyed, and out of heauen ſhal he * thunder
vpon them: the Lord ſhal iudge the ends
of the worlde, and ſhal giue power vnto
his [h] King, and exalte the horne of his
Anointed.
11 And Elkanáh went to Ramáh to his
houſe, and the childe did miniſter vnto
the Lord [i] before Elí the Prieſt.
12 ¶ Now the ſonnes of Elí *were* wicked
men & [k] knewe not the Lord.
13 For the Prieſts cuſtome toward the people *was this*: when any mã offred ſacrifice,
the Prieſts ″ boy came, while the fleſh was
ſething and a fleſhoke with thre teth in
his hand,
14 And thruſt it into the kettle, or into the
caldren, or into the pan, or into ẏ pot: [l] all
that ẏ fleſhoke broght vp, the Prieſt toke
for him ſelf: thus thei did vnto all the Iſraelites, that came thether to Shilóh.
15 Yea, before they burnt the [m] fat, the
Prieſts boy came and ſaid to the man that
offred, Giue me fleſh to roſt for ẏ Prieſt:
for he wil not haue ſodden fleſh of thee,
but rawe.
16 And if any man ſaid vnto him, Let them
burne the fat according to the ″ cuſtome,
then take as muche as thine heart [n] deſireth: then he wolde anſwer, No, but thou
ſhalt giue it now: and if thou wilt not, I
wil take it by force.
17 Therefore the ſinne of the yong mẽ was
very

d In that ye condemne my barennes, ye ſhewe your pride againſt God.

e Thei ſel their labours for neceſſarie fode.

″Or, many.

Deut. 32, 39. wiſd. 16, 13. tob. 13, 2.

Pſal. 113, 7.

f He preferreth to honour and putteth downe according to his owne wil, though mans iudgement be contrary.

g Therefore he may diſpoſe all things according to his wil.

Chap. 7, 10.

h She grounded her prayer on Ieſus Chriſt ẏ was to come.

i In all ẏ Elí cõmãded him.

k That is, thei neglected his ordinance.

″Or, ſonne.

l Traſgreſsing the ordre appointed in the Lawe, Leui. 7, 31, for their bellies ſake.

m Which was cõmanded firſt to haue bene offred to God.

″Or, Lawe.

n Not paſsing for their owne profite ſo that God might be ſerued aright.

o Seing ȳ horrible abuse thereof.

very great before the Lord: for men o abhorred the offring of the Lord.
18 ¶ Now Samuél being a yong childe ministred before the Lord, girded with a linnen * Ephód.

Exod.28,4.

19 And his mother made him a litle coate, and broght it to him from yere to yere, when she came vp with her housband, to offer the yerely sacrifice.
20 And Elí blessed Elkanáh and his wife, & said, The Lord giue thee sede of this woman, for ″ the peticion that she asked of the Lord: and they departed vnto their place.

″Or, for the thing that she hathe lent to the Lord: to wit Samuel.

21 And the Lord visited Hannáh, so that she conceiued, and bare thre sonnes, and two daughters. And the childe Samuél grewe before the Lord.
22 ¶ So Elí was very olde, & heard all that his sonnes did vnto all Israél, & how they laye with the women that p assembled at the doore of the Tabernacle of the Congregacion.

p Which was (as the Ebrewes write) after their trauel, when they came to be purified, read Exod. 38,8. Leu. 12,6.

23 And he said vnto thẽ, Why do ye suche things? for of all this people I heare euil reportes of you.
24 *Do no more*, my sonnes: for it is no good reporte that I heare, *which is*, that ye make the Lords people to q trespasse.

q Because they cōtemne their duetie to God, vers. 17.

25 If one man sinne against an other, the iudge shal iudge it: but if a man sinne against the Lord, who wil pleade for him? Notwithstãding thei obeied not the voyce of their father, because ȳ Lord r wolde slaye them.

r So that to obey good admonitions is Gods mercie, & to disobey them, is his iust iudgement for sinne.

26 ¶ (Now the childe Samuél profited and grewe and was in fauour bothe with the Lord, and also with men)
27 And there came a mã of God vnto Elí and said vnto him, Thus saieth the Lord, Did not I plainely appeare vnto ȳ house of thy f father, when they were in Egypt in Pharohs house?

f To wit, Aarón.

28 And I chose him out of all the tribes of Israél to be my Priest, to offer vpon mine altar, and to burne incence, and to weare an Ephód before me, and * I gaue vnto the house of thy father all the offrings made by fire of the children of Israél.

Leu. 10,14.

29 Wherefore haue you t kiked against my sacrifice and mine offring, which I cōmanded in my Tabernacle, and honorest thy children aboue me, to make your selues fat of the first frutes of all the offrings of Israél my people?

t Why haue you cōtemned my sacrifices, and as it were trod them vnder fete.

30 Wherefore ȳ Lord God of Israél sayth, I said, ȳ thine house & the house of thy father shulde walke before me for euer: but nowe the Lord saith, u It shal not be so: for them that honour me, I wil honour, and they that despise me, shal be despised.

u Gods promises are onely effectual to suche as he giueth constancie vnto, to feare and obey him.

31 Beholde, the dayes come, that I wil cut of thine x arme, and the arme of thy fathers house, that there shal not be an olde man in thine house.

x Thy power and autoritie.

32 And thou y shalt se *thine* enemie in the habitation *of the Lord* in all things wherewith *God* shal blesse Israél, and there shal not be an olde man in thine house for euer.

y Thy posteritie shal se the glorie of the chief Priest translated to another, whome they shal ennie, 1. King. 2,27.

33 Neuertheles, I wil not destroy euery one of thine frõ mine altar, to make thine eyes to faile, & to make thine heart sorowful: and all the multitude of thine house shal ″ dye *when they be* men.

″Or, When they come to mans age.

34 And this shalbe a signe vnto thee, that shal come vpon thy two sonnes Hophní and Phinehás: in one day they shal dye bothe.
35 And I wil sterre me vp a z faithful Priest, that shal do according to mine heart and according to my minde: and I wil buylde him a sure house, and he shal walke before mine Anoynted for euer.

z Meaning, Zadók, who succeded Abiathár, and was the figure of Christ.

36 And all that are left in thine house, shal come and a bowe downe to him for a piece of siluer and a morsel of bread, and shal say, Appoint me, I pray thee, to one of the Priests offices, that I may eat a morsel of bread.

a That is, shal be inferior vnto him.

CHAP. III.

1 There was no manifest visiõ in the time of Elí. 4 The Lord calleth Samuél thre times, 11 And sheweth what shal come vpon Elí and his house. 18 The same declareth Samuél to Elí.

1 Now the childe Samuél ministred vnto the Lord a before Elí: and the worde of the Lord was b precious in those dayes: for there was no manifest vision.

a The Chalde text readeth, whiles Elí liued.
b Because there were very fewe Prophetes to declare it.

2 And at that time, as Elí laye in his c place, his eyes began to waxe dimme that he colde not se.

c In the court next to the Tabernacle.

3 And yer the d light of God went out, Samuél slept in the temple of the Lord, where the Arke of God was.

d That is, the lampes which burnt in the night.

4 Then the Lord e called Samuél: and he said, Here I am.

e Iosephus writeth that Samuél was twelue yere olde, when ȳ Lord appeared to him.

5 And he ran vnto Elí, and said, Here am I, for thou calledst me. But he said, I called thee not: go againe *and* slepe. And he went and slept.
6 And the Lord called once againe, Samuél. And Samuél arose, and went to Elí, & said, I am here: for thou didest call me. And he answered, I called the not, my sonne: go againe *and* slepe.
7 Thus *did* Samuél, before he knewe f the Lord, and before the worde of the Lord was reueiled vnto him.

f By vision.

8 And the Lord called Samuél againe the third time: and he arose, and went to Elí, and said, I am here: for thou hast called me. Then Elí g perceiued that the Lord had called the childe.

g Suche was the corruptiõ of those times that the chief Priest was become dul and negligent to vnderstãd the Lords appearing

9 Therefore Elí said vnto Samuél, Go *and* slepe: and if he call thee, then say, Speake

Lord, for thy seruant heareth. So Samuél
went, and slept in his place.
10 ¶ And the Lord came, & stode, and called as at other times, Samuél, Samuél. Thē
Samuél answered, Speake, for thy seruant
heareth.
11 ¶ Thē the Lord said to Samuél, Beholde,
I wil do a thing in Israél, whereof whosoeuer shal heare, his two eares shal [h] tingle.
12 In that day I wil raise vp against Elí all
things which I haue spoken concerning
his house: when I begin, I wil also make
an end.
13 And I haue tolde him that I wil iudge his
house for euer, for the iniquitie which he
knoweth, because his sonnes ran into a
slander, and he stayed them not.
14 Now therefore I haue sworne vnto the
house of Elí, that the wickednes of Elis
house, shal not be purged with sacrifice
nor offring [i] for euer.
15 Afterwarde Samuél slept vntil the morning, and opened the doores of the house
of the Lord, and Samuél feared to shewe
Elí the vision.
16 ¶ Then Elí called Samuél, and said, Samuél my sonne. And he answered, Here
I am.
17 Thē he said, What is it, that *the Lord* said
vnto thee? I pray thee, hide it not from
me. God [k] do so to thee, and more also,
if thou hide anie thing from me, of all that
he said vnto thee.
18 So Samuél tolde him euerie whit, & hid
nothing from him. Then he said, It is the
Lord: let him do what semeth him good.
19 ¶ And Samuél grewe, and the Lord was
with him, and let none of his wordes [l] fall
to the ground.
20 And all Israél from Dan to Beershéba
knewe" that faithful Samuél *was* the Lords
Prophet.
21 And the Lord appeared againe in Shilóh: for the Lord reueiled him selfe to Samuél in Shilóh by" his worde.

h God declareth what soden feare shal come vpon mē whē they shal heare that the Arke is taken and also se Elis house destroyed.

i Meaning, that his posteritie shulde neuer enioye ẏ chief Priests office.

k God punishe thee after this and that sort, except thou tel me trueth, Ruth 1,17.

l The Lord accomplished whatsoeuer he had said.

"Or, that Samuél was the faithful Prophet of the Lord.

"Ebr. by the worde of the Lord.

CHAP. IIII.

1 Israél is ouercome by the Philistims. 4 They do fet the Arke, wherefore the Philistims do feare. 10 The Arke of the Lord is taken 11 Elí and his childrē dye. 19 The death of the wife of Phinehás the sonne of Elí.

1 AND Samuél spake vnto all Israél: ‖ &
Israél went out against ẏ Philistíms
to battel and pitched beside" Ebén ézer:
and the Philistíms pitched in Aphék.
2 And ẏ Philistíms put them selues in array against Israél: and when they ioyned
the battel, Israél was smitten downe before the Philistíms: who slewe of the armie
in the field about foure thousand men.
3 So when the people were come into the
campe, the Elders of Israél said, [a] Wherefore hathe the Lord smitten vs this day
before the Philistíms? let vs bring ẏ Arke
of the couenant of the Lord out of Shilóh
vnto vs, that when it commeth among vs,
it may saue vs out of the hand of our enemies.
4 Thē the people sent to Shilóh, & broght
from thence the Arke of the couenant of
the Lord of hostes, who [b] dwelleth betwene the Cherubíms: and there were the
two sonnes of Elí, Hophní, & Phinehás,
with the Arke of the couenant of God.
5 And when the Arke of the couenāt of the
Lord came into the hoste, all Israél showted a mihgty showte, so that the earth rāg
againe.
6 And when the Philistíms heard the noise of the showte, they said, What meaneth
the sounde of this mighty showte in the
hoste of the Ebrewes? & they vnderstode,
that the Arke of the Lord was come into
the hoste.
7 And the Philistíms were afraid, and said,
God is come into the hoste: therefore said
thei, [c] Wo vnto vs: for it hathe not bene
so heretofore.
8 Wo vnto vs, who shal deliuer vs out of
the hand of these mighty Gods? these are
the Gods that smote the Egyptians with
all the plagues in the [d] wildernes.
9 Be strong and play the men, ô Philistíms,
that ye be not seruāts vnto the Ebrewes,
* as they haue serued you: be valiant therefore, and fight.
10 And the Philistíms fought, and Israél
was smitten downe, and fled euerie man
into his tent: and there was an exceding
great slaughter: for there fel of Israél
[e] thirtie thousand fotemen.
11 And the Arke of God was taken, and the
two sonnes of Elí, Hophní and Phinehás
dyed.
12 And there ran a man of Beniamín out of
the armie, and came to Shilóh the same
day with his clothes [f] rent, and earth
vpon his head.
13 And when he came, lo, Elí sate vpon a
seate by the way side, waiting: for his heart
[g] feared for the Arke of God: and when
the man came into the citie to tel it, all
the citie cryed out.
14 And when Elí heard the noise of the
crying, he said, What meaneth this noise
of the tumult? and the mā came in hastely,
and tolde Elí.
15 (Now Elí *was* fourescore and eightene
yere olde, and * his eyes were dimme that
he colde not se)
16 And the man said vnto Elí, I came from
the armie, and I fled this day out of the
hoste: and he said, What thing is done,
my sonne?
17 Then the messenger answered and said,
Israél is fled before the Philistíms, and
there hathe bene also a great slaughter
among

‖ From the departure of the Israelites out of Egypt, vnto the time of Samuél are about 390 yere.

"Or, stone of helpe, chap. 7, 12.

a For it may seme that this warre was vndertaken by Samuels commandement.

b For he vsed to appeare to the Israelites betwene the Cherubíms ouer the Arke of the couenant, Exod 25, vers. 17.

c Before we fought against men, and now God is come to fight against vs.

d For in the red Sea in ẏ wildernes the Egyptians were destroyed, which was ẏ last of all his plagues.

Iudg. 13, 1.

e Dauid alluding to this place Psal 77, 63 saieth they were cōsumed with fire: meaning they were sodenly destroyed.

f In token of sorrowe and mourning.

g Lest it shulde be taken of the enemies.

Chap. 3, 2.

among the people: and moreouer thy two
sonnes, Hophní and Phinehás [h] are dead,
and the Arke of God is taken.

h According, as God had afore said.

18 ¶ And whẽ he had made mencion of the
Arke of God, *Eli* fel from his seate backwarde by the side of the gate, & his necke
was broken, and he dyed: for he was an olde mã and heauye: and ″ he had iudged Israél fortie yeres.

″Or, gouerned.

19 And his daugter in lawe Phinehás wife
was with childe *nere* ″ her trauel: and when
she heard the report that the Arke of God
was taken, and that her father in lawe &
her housband were dead, she [i] bowed her
selfe, and traueled: for her paines came
vpon her.

″Or, to crye out.

i And setled her body toward her trauel

20 And about the time of her death, the women that stode about her, said vnto her,
Feare not: for thou hast borne a sonne: but
she answered not, nor regarded it.
21 And she named the childe ″ Ichabód,
saying, The glorie is departed from Israél, because the Arke of God was taken, &
because of her father in lawe and her
housband.

″Or, No glorie, or, where is the glorie.

22 She said againe, [k] The glorie is departed frõ Israél: for the Arke of God is takẽ.

k She vttered her great sorrowe by repeting her wordes.

CHAP. V.

2 The Philistíms bring the Arke into the house of Dagón, which idole fel downe before it. 6 The men of Ashdód are plagued. 8 The Arke is caryed into Gath and after to Ekrón.

1 THen the Philistíms toke the Arke of
God and caryed it from Ebén-ézer
vnto [a] Ashdód,
2 Euen the Philistíms toke the Arke of
God, and broght it into the house of [b] Dagón, and set it by Dagón.

a Which was one of the fiue principal cities of the Philistíms.
b Which was their chief idole, & as some write, from ỹ nauil downwarde was like a fishe, and vpwarde like a man.

3 And when they of Ashdód rose the next
day in the morning, beholde, Dagón was
fallen vpon his face on the grounde before the Arke of the Lord, and they toke vp
Dagón, and set him in his place againe.
4 Also they rose vp early in the morning
the next day, & beholde, Dagón was fallẽ
vpon his face on the grounde before the
Arke of the Lord, and the head of Dagón
and the two palmes of his hands *were* cut
of vpon the thresholde: onely the stumpe
of Dagón was left to him.
5 Therefore the Priests of Dagón, and all
that come into Dagons house [c] treade
not on the thresholde of Dagón in Ashdód, vnto this day.

c Thus in steade of acknowledging ỹ true God by this miracle, they fall to a farther superstición.

6 But the hand of the Lord was heauy vpõ
them of Ashdód, and destroyed them, and
smote them with *emerods, *bothe* Ashdód,
and the coastes thereof.

*Psal. 78, 66.

7 And whẽ the men of Ashdód sawe this,
they said, Let not the Arke of the God of
Israél abide with vs: for his hand is sore
vpon vs and vpon Dagón our god.
8 They sent therefore and gathered all the
princes of the Philistíms vnto them, and
said, [d] What shal we do with the Arke of
the God of Israél? And they answered, Let
the Arke of the God of Israél be caried
about vnto Gath: & thei caried the Arke
of the God of Israél about.

d Thogh thei had felt Gods power & were affraied thereof, yet they wolde farther trie hĩ, which thing God turned to their destruction & his glorie.

9 And when they had caried it about,
the hand of the Lord was against the citie with a very great destruction, and he
smote the men of the citie bothe small
and great, & they had emerods in their secret partes.
10 ¶ Therefore they sent the Arke of God
to Ekrón: and assone as the Arke of God
came to Ekrón, the Ekronites cryed out,
saying, They haue broght the Arke of ỹ
God of Israél to vs to slay vs and our
people.
11 Therefore they sent, and gathered together all the princes of the Philistíms and
said, Send [e] away the Arke of the God of
Israél, and let it returne to his owne place,
that it slay vs not and our people: for there
was a destruction & death through out all
the citie, & the hãd of God was very sore
there.

e The wicked, when they fele the hand of God, grudge & reiecte him, where ỹ godly humble them selues & crye for mercie.

12 And the men that dyed not, were smittẽ
with the emerods: and the crye of the citie went vp to heauen.

CHAP. VI.

1 The time that the Arke was with the Philistíms which they sent againe with a gift. 12 It commeth to Beth-shémesh. 17 The Philistíms offer golden emerods. 19 The men of Beth-shémesh are stricken for loking into the Arke.

1 SO the Arke of the Lord was in ỹ countrey of the Philistíms [a] seuen monethes.
2 And the Philistíms called the Priestes &
the sothsayers, saying, What shal we do
wͭ the Arke of the Lord? tel vs wherewith
we shal send it home againe?

a Thei thoght by continuãce of time ỹ plague wolde haue ceased and so wolde haue kept ỹ Arke stil.

3 And they said, If you send away the Arke
of ỹ God of Israél, send it not away emptie, but giue vnto it [b] a sinne offring: then
shal ye be healed, and it shalbe knowen to
you, why his hand departeth not from
you.

b The idolaters confesse there is a true God, who punisheth sinne iustely.

4 Then said they, What shalbe the sinne
offring, which we shal giue vnto it? And
they answered, Fiue golden emerods and
fiue golden mice, according to the nomber of ỹ Princes of the Philistíms: for one
plague *was* on you all, & on your princes.
5 Wherefore ye shal make the similitudes
of your emerods, and the similitudes of
your mice that destroye the lãd: so ye shal
giue glorie vnto the God of Israél, that
he may take his hãd from you, and from
your [c] gods, and from your land.

c This is Gods iudgement vpõ the idolaters, that knowing the true God thei worship him not aright.

6 Wherefore then shulde ye harden your
heartes, as the Egyptians and Pharaóh
hardened their heartes, when he wroght

Exod.12,31.

wonderfully among them, * did they not
let them go, and they departed?
7 Now therefore make a newe carte, and
take two melche kine, on whome there
hathe come no yoke: & tye the kine to the
carte, and bring the calues home from
them.
8 Then take the Arke of the Lord, and ſet
it vpon the carte, and put the [d] iewels of
golde which ye giue it for a ſinne offring
in a coffer by the ſide thereof, and ſend it
away, that it may go.

d Meaning ẏ goldē emerods and the golden mice.

9 And take hede, if it go vp by the way of
his owne coaſt to Beth-ſhémeſh, it is [e] he
that did vs this great euil: but if not, we
ſhal knowe then, that it is not his hād that
ſmote vs, *but* it was a [f] chance that happened vs.

e The God of Iſraél.

f The wicked attribute almoſt all thīgs to fortune and chance, whereas in dede there is nothing done without Gods prouidence & decree.

10 And the men did ſo: for they toke two
kine that gaue milke, and tyed them to the
carte and ſhut the calues at home.
11 So they ſet the Arke of the Lord vpon
the carte, and the coffer with the mice of
golde, and with the ſimilitudes of their
emerods.
12 And the kine went the ſtreight way to
Beth-ſhémeſh, & kept one path and lowed
as they went, & turned nether to the right
hand nor to the left: alſo the princes of the
Philiſtíms went after [g] thē, vnto the borders of Beth-ſhémeſh.

g For the trial of the matter.

13 Now they of Beth-ſhémeſh were reaping
their wheat harueſt in the valley, & they
lift vp their eyes, and ſpyed the Arke, and
reioyced when they ſawe it.
14 ¶ And the carte came into the fielde of
Ioſhúa a Bethſhemite, & ſtode ſtil there.
there was alſo a great ſtone, and [h] they
claue the wood of the carte and offred the
kine for a burnt offring vnto the Lord.

h To wit, the men of Beth-ſhémeſh, ẇ were Iſraelites.

15 And the Leuites toke downe the Arke of
the Lord, and the coffer that was with it,
wherein the iewels of golde were, & put
them on the great ſtone, and the men of
Beht-ſhémeſh offred burnt offring, and
ſacrificed ſacrifices that ſame day vnto
the Lord.
16 And when the fiue princes of the Philiſtíms had ſene it, they returned to Ekrón
the ſame day.
17 ¶ So theſe are the goldē emerods, which
the Philiſtíms gaue for a ſinne offring to
the Lord: for [i] Aſhdód one, for Gazá one,
for Aſkelón one, for Gath one, & for Ekrón one,
18 And goldē mice, according to the nomber of all the cities of the Piliſtíms, *belō-*
ging to the fiue princes, bothe of walled
townes and of townes vnwalled, vnto the
great *ſtone* of ‖ Abél, whereon they ſet the
Arke of the Lord: *which ſtone remaineth* vnto this day in the field of Ioſhúa the Bethſhemite.

i Theſe were the fiue principal cities of the Philiſtims which were not all cōquered vnto the time of Dauid.

‖ *Or, the plaine, or lamentation.*

19 And he ſmote of the men of Beth-ſhémeſh, becauſe they [k] had loked in the Arke of the Lord: he ſlewe euen among the
people fiftie thouſand men and thre ſcore and ten men. and the people lamented,
becauſe the Lord had ſlaine ẏ people with
ſo great a ſlaughter.

k For it was not lauful to anie other to touche or to ſe it, saue onely to Aarón & his ſonnes, Nom. 4,15 & 20.

20 Wherefore the men of Beth-ſhémeſh
ſaid, Who is able to ſtand before this holy Lord God? and to whome ſhal he go
from vs?
21 And they ſent meſſengers to the inhabitants of Kiriath-iearím, ſaying, The Philiſtíms haue broght againe the Arke of
the Lord: come ye downe & take it vp
to you.

CHAP. VII.

1 The Arke is broght to Kiriath-iearím. 3 Samuél exhorteth the people to forſake their ſinnes and turne to the Lord. 10 The Philiſtims fight againſt Iſraél & are ouercome. 16 Samuél iudgeth Iſraél.

1 THen the men of [a] Kiriath-iearím
came, and toke vp the Arke of the
Lord, and broght it into the houſe of Abi
nadáb in the hil: and they ſanctified Eleazár his ſonne, to kepe the Arke of the
Lord.

a A citie in ẏ tribe of Iudáh, called alſo Kiriath-bá-al, Ioſh. 15,60.

2 (For while the Arke abode in Kiriath-
iearím, the time was long, for it was twētie yeres) and all the houſe of Iſraél lamented [b] after the Lord.

b Lamented for their ſinnes & followed the Lord.

3 ¶ Thē Samuél ſpake vnto all the houſe of
Iſraél, ſaying, If ye be come againe vnto
the Lord with all your hearte, * put away
the ſtrange gods frō among you, & * Aſhtaróth, and direct your hearts vnto the
Lord, and ſerue him * onely, and he ſhal
deliuer you out of the hand of the Philiſtíms.

Ioſh. 24,15. *Iudg. 2,13.* *Deut. 6,4.* *mat. 4,10.*

4 Then the children of Iſraél did put away
* Baalím and Aſhtaróth, and ſerued the
Lord onely.

Iudg. 2,13.

5 And Samuél ſaid, Gather all Iſraél to
[c] Mizpéh, and I wil pray for you vnto ẏ
Lord.
6 And they gathered together to Mizpéh,
and [d] drewe water and powred it out before the Lord, and faſted the ſame day, &
ſaid there, We haue ſinned againſt the
Lord. And Samuél iudged the children of
Iſraél in Mizpéh.

c For Shilóh was now deſolate, becauſe the Philiſtíms had takē thence the Arke.

d The Chalde text hathe, ẏ thei drewe water out of their heart: that is, wept abūdātly for their ſinnes.

7 When the Philiſtíms heard that the children of Iſraél were gathered together to
Mizpéh, the princes of the Philiſtíms wēt
vp againſt Iſraél: and when the children
of Iſraél heard that, they were afraied of
the Philiſtíms.
8 And the children of Iſraél ſaid to Samuél, Ceaſe not to [e] crye vnto the Lord
our God for vs, that he may ſaue vs out of
the hand of the Philiſtíms.

e Signifying ẏ in the prayers of the godlie there oght to be a vehemēt zeale.

9 Then Samuél toke a ſucking lambe, and
offred it all together for a burnt offring

vnto the Lord, and Samuél cryed vnto
the Lord for Israél, and the Lord heard
him.
10 And as Samuél offred the burnt offring,
the Philistíms came to fight against Israél: but the Lord [f] thundred with a great
thundre that day vpon the Philistíms, &
scatred them: so they were slaine before Is
raél.

f Accordīg to the prophecie of Hannáh Samuels mother, Chap.2,10.

11 And the men of Israél went from Mizpéh and pursued the Philistíms, and smote
them vntil *they came* vnder Beth-car.
12 Then Samuél toke a stone and pitched it
betwene Mizpéh and [g] Shen, and called ŷ
name thereof, Ebén ézer, and he said, Hitherto hathe the Lord holpen vs.

g Which was a great rocke ouer against Mizpéh.

13 ¶So ŷ Philistíms were broght vnder, &
they came nomore againe into the coastes
of Israél: and the hand of the Lord was a-
gainst the Philistíms all the dayes of Samuél.
14 Also the cities which the Philistíms had
taken from Israél, were restored to Israél, from Ekrón euen to Gath: & Israél deliuered the coastes of the same out of the
hands of the Philistíms: & there was peace betwene Israél & the [h] Amorites.

h Meaning, ŷ Philistíms.

15 And Samuél iudged Israél all the dayes
of his life,
16 And went about yere by yere to Beth-
él, and Gilgál and Mizpéh, and iudged Israél in all those places.
17 Afterward he returned to Ramáh: for
there was his house, & there he iudged Israél: also he buylt an [i] altar there vnto the
Lord.

i Which was not cōtrarie to the Lawe: for as yet a certeine place was not appointed.

CHAP. VIII.

1 Samuél maketh his sones iudges ouer Israél, who followe not his steppes. 5 The Israelites aske a King. 11 Samuél declareth in what state they shulde be vnder the King. 19 Notwithstanding they aske one stil, & the Lord willeth Samuél to grant vnto them.

1 WHē Samuél was now become old,
he [a] made his sonnes iudges ouer
Israél.

a Because he was not able to beare the charge.

2 (And the name of his eldest sonne was
[b] Ioél, and the name of the seconde Abiáh)
euen iudges in Beer-shéba.

b Who was also called Vashni, 1 Chro.6,28.

3 And his sonnes walked not in his waies
but turned aside after lucre and * toke rewardes, and peruerted the iudgement.

Deut.16,19.

4 ¶Wherefore all the Elders of Israél gathered them together, & came to Samuél
vnto [c] Ramáh,

c For there his house was, Chap 7,17.

5 And said vnto him, Beholde, thou art old,
and thy sonnes walke not in thy waies:
* make vs now a King to iudge vs like all
nacions.

Ose.13,10. act.13,21.

6 But the thing [d] displeased Samuél, when
they said, Giue vs a King to iudge vs: and
Samuél prayed vnto the Lord.

d Because thei were not content wt the ordre ŷ God had appointed, but wolde be gouerned as were ŷ Gentiles.

7 And the Lord said vnto Samuél, Heare
the voice of the people in all that they shal
say vnto thee: for they haue not cast thee
away, but they haue cast me away, that I
shulde not reigne ouer them.
8 As thei haue euer done since I broght thē
out of Egypt euen vnto this day, (and haue forsaken me, and serued other gods) e-
uen so do they vnto thee.
9 Now therefore hearkē vnto their voyce:
howbeit yet [e] testifie vnto them & shewe
thē the maner of the King that shal reigne ouer them.

e To proue if they wil forsake their wicked purpose.

10 ¶So Samuél tolde all the wordes of the
Lord vnto the people that asked a King
of him.
11 And he said, This shalbe the [f] maner of
the King that shal reigne ouer you: he wil
take your sonnes, and appoint them to his
charets, and to be his horsmen, and *some*
shal runne before his charet.
12 Also he wil make them his captaines o-
uer thousandes and captaines ouer fifties,
and to eare his grounde, and to reape his
haruest, & to make instruments of warre,
and the things that serue for his charets.

f Not ŷ Kings haue this autoritie by their office, but that suche as reigne in Gods wrath shulde vsurpe this ouer their brethren cōtrary to the Law, Deu.17,20.

13 He wil also take your daughters and
make them apoticaries, and cookes and
bakers.
14 And he wil take your fieldes, and your
vineyardes, and your best oliue trees, and
giue them to his seruants.
15 And he wil take the tenth of your sede,
and of your vineyardes, and giue it to his
"Eunuches, and to his seruants.

"Or, chief officers.

16 And he wil take your men seruants and
your maid seruants, and the chief of your
yong men, and your asses, and put them
to his worke.
17 He wil take the tenth of your shepe, and
ye shalbe his seruants.
18 And ye shal crye out at that day, becausе
of your King, whome ye haue chosen
you, and the Lord wil not [g] heare you at
that day.

g Because ye repent not for your sinnes, but because ye smart for your afflictions, whereinto ye cast your selues willingly.

19 But ŷ people wolde not heare the voyce
of Samuél, but did say, Nay, but there
shalbe a King ouer vs.
20 And we also wil be like all *other* naciōs,
and our King shal iudge vs, & go out before vs, and fight our battels.
21 Therefore when Samuél heard all the
wordes of the people, he rehearsed them
in the eares of the Lord.
22 And the Lord said to Samuél, "Hearken vnto their voyce, and make them a
King. And Samuél said vnto the men of
Israél, Go euerie man vnto his citie.

"Or, grant their request.

CHAP. IX.

3 Saúl seking his fathers asses, by the counsel of his seruant goeth to Samuél. 9 The Prophets called Seers. 15 The Lord reueileth to Samuél Sauls comming, commanding him to annoint him King. 22 Samuél bringeth Saul to the feast.

a That is, bothe valiant & riche.
Chap.14,51. 1.chro.8,33.

1 THere was now a man of Beniamín
a mightie in power named *Kish the
sonne of Abiél, the sonne of Zerór, ỹ sonne of Bechoráth, the sonne of Aphíah, the
sonne of a man of Ieminí.

b So that it might seme ỹ God approued their request in appointing out suche a persone.

2 And he had a sõne called Saúl, a [b] goodly
yong man and a faire: so that among the
children of Israél there was none goodlier then he: from the shulders vpward he
was hier then anie of the people.
3 And the asses of Kish Saules father were
lost: therefore Kish said to Saúl his sonne,
Take now one of the seruants with thee,
and arise, go, and [c] seke the asses.

c All these circumstãces were means to serue vnto Gods prouidẽce, whereby Saúl (thogh not approued of God) was made King.

4 So he passed through mount Ephráim &
went through the land of Shalisháh, but
they found them not. Then they went
through the land of Shalím, and *there they*
were not: he went also through the land of
Ieminí, but they found them not.

d Where was Ramath-Zophim ỹ citie of Samuél.

5 When they came to the land of [d] Zuph,
Saúl said vnto his seruant that was with
him, Come and let vs returne, lest my father leaue *the care* of asses, and take thoght
for vs.
6 And he said vnto him, Beholde now, in
this citie is a man of God, and he is an honorable man: all that he saieth commeth
to passe: let vs now go thither, if so be that
he can shewe vs what way we may go.
7 Then said Saúl to his seruant, Wel then,
let vs go: but what shal we bring vnto the
man? For the bread is spent in our vessels,
and there is no present to bring to the mã
of God: what haue we?

Or, vitailes.

8 And the seruant answered Saúl againe, &
said, Beholde, I haue found about me the
fourth parte of a [e] shekle of siluer: that wil
I giue the man of God, to tel vs our way.

e Which is about fiue pence, read Gen. 23,15.

9 (Beforetime in Israél when a man went
to seke an answer of God, thus he spake,
Come, & let vs go to the [f] Seer: for *he that*
is called now a Prophet, was in ỹ olde time
called a Seer)

f So called, because he foresawe things to come.

10 Thẽ said Saúl to his seruant, Wel said,
come, let vs go: so they went into the citie where the man of God was.
11 ¶ And as thei were going vp the hie way
to the citie, they founde maydes that came out to drawe water, and said vnto thẽ,
Is there here a Seer?
12 And they answered them, and said, Yea:
lo, *he is* before you. make haste now, for he
came this day to the citie: for there is an
[g] offring of the people this day in the hie
place.

g That is, a feast after the offring, which shulde be kept in an hie place of ỹ citie appointed for ỹ vse.

13 When ye shal come into the citie, ye shal
finde him streight way yer he come vp to
the hie place to eat: for the people wil not
eat vntil he come, because he wil [h] blesse ỹ
sacrifice: and then eat they that be bidden
to the feast: now therefore go vp: for euẽ
now shal ye finde him.

h That is, giue thankes, & distribute the meat accordig to their custome.

14 Then they went vp into the citie, and
when they were come into the middes of
the citie, Samuél came out against them,
to go vp to the hie place.
15 ¶ *But the Lord had reueiled to Samuél
secretly (a day before Saúl came) saying,

Chap.15,1. act 13,21.
Ebr. in his eare.

16 Tomorowe about this time I wil send
thee a man out of the land of Beniamín:
him shalt thou anoint to be gouernour ouer my people Israél, ỹ he may [i] saue my
people out of the hands of the Philistíms:
for I haue loked vpon my people, & their
crye is come vnto me.

i Not withstãding their wickednes, yet God was euer mindful of his inheritance.

17 When Samuél therefore sawe Saúl, the
Lord answered him, Se, this is the man
whome I spake to thee of, he shal rule
my people.
18 Then went Saúl to Samuél in the middes of the gate, and said, Tel me, I pray
thee, where the Seers house is.
19 And Samuél answered Saúl, and said, I
am the Seer: go vp before me vnto the hie
place: for ye shal eat with me to day. and
tomorowe I wil let thee go, & wil tel thee
all that is in thine [k] heart.

k Meaning, all that ỹ desirest to knowe.

20 And as for thine asses ỹ were lost thre
dayes ago, care not for them: for they are
founde. and [l] on whome *is set* all the desire
of Israél? is it not vpon thee and on all
thy fathers house?

l Whome doeth Israél desire to be their Kĩg but thee.

21 ¶ But Saúl answered, and said, Am not I
the sonne of Ieminí of the smalest tribe of
Israél? & my familie *is* the least of all the
families of ỹ tribe of Beniamín. Wherefore then speakest thou so to me?
22 And Samuél toke Saúl and his seruant,
and broght them into the [m] chamber, and
made them sit in the chiefest place among
them that were bidden: which were about
thirtie persones.

m Where the feast was.

23 And Samuél said vnto the cooke, Bring
forthe the portion which I gaue thee, &
whereof I said vnto thee, Kepe it with
thee.
24 And the cooke toke vp the shoulder, &
that ẘ was [n] vpon it, & set it before Saúl.
And *Samuel* said, Beholde, that which is
left, set it before thee & eat: for hitherto
hathe it bene kept for thee, saying, Also I
[o] haue called the people. So Saúl did eat
with Samuél that day.

n That is, the shoulder ẘ ỹ breast, ẘ the Priest had for his familie in all peace offrings, Leu.10,14.
o That bothe by ỹ assẽbling of the people, & by ỹ meat prepared for thee, ỹ mighest vnderstãde ỹ I knewe of thy comming.

25 And whẽ they were come downe frõ the
hie place into ỹ citie, he communed with
Saúl vpon the top of the house:
26 And whẽ they arose early about ỹ spring
of ỹ day, Samuél called Saúl to the [p] top
of the house, saying, Vp, that I may send
thee away. And Saúl arose, and they went
out, bothe he, and Samuél.

p To speake ẘ him secretely: for ỹ houses were flat aboue.

27 And when they were come downe to the
end of the citie, Samuél said to Saúl, Bid
the seruant go before vs, (and he went)
but

but stand thou stil now, that I may shewe
thee q the worde of God.

q Gods commandement as concerning thee.

CHAP. X.

6 *Saúl is anointed King by Samuél. 9 God changeth Sauls heart and he prophecieth. 17 Samuél assembleth the people, and sheweth them their sinnes. 21 Saúl is chosen King by lot. 25 Samuél writeth the Kings office.*

a In the Lawe this anointing signified the gifts of ỹ holy Gost, whiche were necessarie for them ỹ shulde rule.

1 THen Samuél toke a viole of a oyle
and powred it vpon his head, & kissed him,and said, Hathe not the Lord anointed thee to be gouernour ouer his inheritance?
2 When thou shalt departe from me this
day,thou shalt finde two men by * Rahels
sepulchre in the border of Beniamin, euē
at Zelzáh, & thei wil say vnto thee, The
b asses which ỹ wentest to seke, are foūde:
& lo, thy father hathe left the care of the
asses,and soroweth for you,saying, What
shal I do for my sonne?

Gen 35,20.

b Samuél confirmeth him by these signes ỹ God hathe appoited him King.

3 Then shalt thou go forthe from thence
and shalt come to the "plaine of Tabór,
and there shal mete thee thre mē going vp
to God to Beth-el:one caryīg thre kiddes,
& another carying thre loaues of bread,
and another carying a bottle of wine:

"Or, oke.

4 And thei wil aske thee "if all be wel,and
wil giue thee the two *loaues of* bread,which
thou shalt receiue of their hands.

"Ebr. of peace.

5 After that shalt thou come to the c hil
of God, where is the garisons of the
Philistims: and when thou art come thether to the citie,thou shalt mete a companie of Prophets comming downe from
the hye place with a viole,and a tymbrel,
and a pipe,and an harpe before them, and
thei shal prophecie.

c Which was an hie place in the citie Kiriath-iearim, where the Arke was,Chap. 7,1.

6 Then the Spirit of the Lord wil come
vpon thee, and thou shalt prophecie with
thē, & shalt be turned into another man.
7 Therefore when these signes shal come
vnto thee, do as occasion shal serue: for
God *is* with thee.
8 And thou shalt go downe before me to
Gilgál: and I also wil come downe vnto
thee to offer burnt offrings, & to sacrifice
sacrifices of peace. * Tary for me seuen
daies, til I come to thee and shewe thee
what thou shalt do.

Chap. 13,8.

9 And whē he had turned his "backe to go
from Samuél, God gaue him another
d heart: & all those tokens came to passe
that same day.

"Ebr shoulder.

d He gaue him suche vertues as were mete for a King.

10 ¶ And whē thei came thether to the hil,
beholde, the companie of Prophets met
him, and the Spirit of God came vpon
him, and he "prophecied among them.

"Or, sang praises

11 Therefore all the people that knewe him
before,when thei sawe that he prophecied
among the Prophets, said eche to other?
What is come vnto the sonne of Kish?*is
Saúl also among the Prophets?

Chap. 19,24.

12 And one of the same place answered,and
said,But who is their e father? Therefore
it was a prouerbe, Is Saúl also among the
f Prophets?

e Meaning,that prophecie cōmeth not by succession,but is giuen, to whome it pleaseth God.

f Noting thereby him that from lowe degre commeth sodenly to honour.

13 And when he had made an end of prophecying, he came to the hie place.
14 And Sauls vncle said vnto him, and to
his seruāt, Whether went ye? And he said,
To seke the asses: and when we sawe that
thei were no where,we came to Samuél.
15 And Sauls vncle said, Tel me, I pray
thee,what Samuél said vnto you.
16 Then Saúl said to his vncle,He tolde vs
plainely that the asses were founde: but
concerning the kingdome whereof Samuél spake,tolde he him not.
17 ¶ And Samuél g assembled the people
vnto the Lord in Mizpéh,

g Bothe to declare vnto the their faute in asking a King, & also to shew Gods sentence therein.

18 And he said vnto the children of Israél,
Thus saith the Lord God of Israél, I haue broght Israél out of Egypt, and deliuered you out of the hand of the Egyptians, & out of the hands of all kingdomes
that troubled you.
19 But ye haue this day cast away your
God,who onely deliuereth you out of all
your aduersities and tribulacions: and ye
said vnto him, *No*, but appoint a Kīg ouer
vs. Now therefore stand ye before the
Lord according to your tribes and according to your thousands.
20 And when Samuél had gathered together all the tribes of Israél, the tribe of
Beniamín was h taken.

h That is, by casting of lots.

21 Afterwarde he assembled the tribe of
Beniamín according to their families, &
the familie of Matri was taken. So Saúl
the sonne of Kish was taken, and when
thei soght him, he colde not be founde.
22 Therefore thei asked the Lord againe,
if that man shulde yet come thether. And
the Lord answered, Beholde, he i hathe
hid him selfe among the stuffe.

i As thogh he were vnworthy and vnwilling.

23 And thei ranne, and broght him thence:
and when he stode among the people, he
was hier then any of the people from the
shoulders vpwarde.
24 And Samuél said to all the people,Se ye
not him, whome the Lord hathe chosen,
that there is none like him among all the
people? And all the people showted and
said," God saue the King.

"Ebr. let the King liue

25 Then Samuél tolde the people k the
duetie of the kingdome, and wrote it in
a boke, and layed it vp before the Lord,
& Samuél sent all the people away euery
man to his house.

k As it is writen in Deuteronomie Chap. 17,15.

26 Saúl also went home to Gibeáh,& there
followed him a band of men,whose heart
God had touched,
27 But the wicked men said, How shal he
saue vs? So thei despised him, and broght
him no presentes: but he l held his tōgue.

l Bothe to auoide seditiō, and also to winne them by paciēce.

CHAP. XI.

1 *Naháſh the Ammonite warreth againſt Iabéſh Gileád, who aſketh helpe of the Iſraelites. 6 Saúl promiseth helpe. 11 The Ammonites are ſlayne. 14 The kingdome is renued.*

a After that Saúl was choſen King: for feare of whome they aſked a King, as Chap 12,12.

1 THen Naháſh the Ammonite [a] came
vp, and beſieged Iabéſh Gileád: and
all the men of Iabéſh ſaid vnto Naháſh,
Make a couenant with vs, and we wil be
thy ſeruants.
2 And Naháſh the Ammonite anſwered
them, On this condicion wil I make a couenant with you, that I may thruſte out
all your [b] right eyes, & bring that ſhame
vpon all Iſraél.
3 To whome ỹ Elders of Iabéſh ſaid, Giue
vs ſeuen daies reſpet, that we may ſend
meſſengers vnto all the coaſtes of Iſraél:
& then if no man deliuer vs, we wil come
out to thee.
4 ¶ Then came the meſſengers to Gibeáh
of Saúl, & tolde theſe tidings in the eares
of the people: and all the people liſt vp
their voyces and wept.
5 And beholde, Saúl came following the
cattel out of the field, & Saúl ſaid, What
ayleth this people, ỹ thei wepe? And thei
tolde him the tidings of the mẽ of Iabéſh.
6 Then the Spirit of God [c] came vpon
Saúl, when he heard thoſe tidings, and he
was exceding angry,
7 And tooke a yoke of oxen, and hewed
them in pieces, and ſent them throughout
all the coaſtes of Iſraél by the hands of
meſſengers, ſaying, Whoſoeuer commeth
not forthe after Saúl, and after [d] Samuél,
ſo ſhal his oxẽ be ſerued. And the feare of
the Lord fel on the people, and thei came
out "with one conſent.
8 And when he nombred them in Bezék,
the children of Iſraél were thre hundreth
thouſand men: and the men of Iudáh
thirty thouſand.
9 Then [e] thei ſaid vnto the meſſengers
that came, So ſay vnto the men of Iabéſh
Gileád, Tomorowe by then the ſunne be
hote, ye ſhal haue helpe. And the meſſengers came and ſhewed it to the men of Iabéſh, which were glad.
10 Therefore the men of Iabéſh ſaid, Tomorowe we wil come out vnto [f] you, &
ye ſhal do with vs all that pleaſeth you.
11 ¶ And when the morowe was come, Saúl
put the people in thre bands, & thei came
in vpõ the hoste in the morning watch, &
ſlewe the Ammonites vntil the heate of
the day: and thei that remained, were ſcattered, ſo that two of them were not left
together.
12 Then the people ſaid vnto Samuél,
[g] Who is he that ſaid, Shal Saúl reigne
ouer vs? bring thoſe mẽ that we may ſlaye
them.

b This declareth, that the more nere that tyrants are to their deſtruction, the more cruel thei are.

c God gaue him the ſpirit of ſtrength & courage to go againſt this tyrant.

d He addeth Samuél, becauſe Saúl was not yet approued of all.

" Ebr. as one man.

e Meaning, Saúl & Samuél.

f That is, to ỹ Ammonites, diſſembling that thei had hope of aide.

g By this victorie the Lord wõne ỹ hearts of the people to Saúl.

13 But Saúl ſaid, There ſhal no man [h] dye
this day: for to day the Lord hathe ſaued
Iſraél.
14 ¶ Then ſaid Samuél vnto the people,
Come, that we may go to Gilgál, & renue
the kingdome there.
15 So all the people went to Gilgál, and
made Saúl King there before the Lord in
Gilgál: and there thei offred [i] peace offrings before the Lord: and there Saúl &
all the mẽ of Iſraél reioyced excedingly.

h By ſhewing mercie, he thoght to ouercome their malice.

i In ſigne of thankeſgiuing for ỹ victorie.

CHAP. XII.

1 *Samuél declaring to the people his integritie, reproueth their ingratitude. 19 God by miracle cauſeth the people to confeſſe their ſinne. 20 Samuél exhorteth the people to followe the Lord.*

1 SAmuél then ſaid vnto all Iſraél, Beholde, I haue [a] hearkened vnto your
voyce in all that ye ſaid vnto me, & haue
appointed a King ouer you.
2 Now therefore beholde, *your* King walketh [b] before you, and I am olde & graye
headed, and beholde, my ſonnes *are* with
you: and I haue walked before you from
my childehode vnto this day.
3 Beholde, here I am: *beare recorde of me
before the Lord and before his Anointed.
[c] Whoſe oxe haue I taken? or whoſe aſſe
haue I taken? or whome haue I done wrõg
to? or whome haue I hurte? or of whoſe
hand haue I receiued any bribe, to blinde
mine eies therwith, & I wil reſtore it you?
4 Then thei ſaid, Thou haſt done vs no
wrong, nor haſt hurt vs, nether haſt thou
taken oght of any mans hand.
5 And he ſaid vnto them, The Lord is witnes againſt you, and his [d] Anointed is
witnes this day, that ye haue foũde noght
in mine hands. And they anſwered, *He is*
witnes.
6 Then Samuél ſaid vnto the people, It is
the Lord that "made Moſés and Aarón, &
that broght your fathers out of the land
of Egypt.
7 Now therefore ſtand ſtil, that I may reaſon with you before the Lord according
to all ỹ "righteouſnes of the Lord, which
he ſhewed to you and to your fathers.
8 *After ỹ Iaakób was come into Egypt,
and your fathers cryed vnto the Lord,
then ỹ Lord *ſent Moſés and Aarón which
broght your fathers out of Egypt, and
made them dwel in this place.
9 *And when thei forgate the Lord their
God, he ſolde them into the hand of Si-
ſerá [e] captaine of the hoſte of Hazór and
into the hand of the Philiſtíms, and into
the hand of the King of Moáb, and they
foght againſt them.
10 And thei cryed vnto the Lord, and ſaid,
We haue ſinned, becauſe we haue forſakẽ
the Lord, and haue ſerued Baalím & Aſhtaróth. Now therefore deliuer vs out of
the

a I haue granted your peticion.

b To gouerne you in peace & warre.

Ecclеſ. 46,23.

c God wolde that this confeſsion ſhulde be a paterne for all them ỹ haue any charge or office.

d Your King, who is anointed by the cõmandement of the Lord.

" Or, exalted.

" Or, benefites.

Gen. 46,5.

Exod. 4,16.

Iudg. 4,2.

e Captaine of Iabins hoſte Kig of Hazór.

the hands of our enemies, and we wil ſerue thee.
11 Therefore the Lord ſent Ierubbáal [f] &
Bedán &*Iphtáh, & *Samuél, & deliuered
you out of the hands of your enemies on
euerie ſide, and ye dwelled ſafe.
12 Notwithſtanding when you ſawe, that
Naháſh the King of the children of Ammón came againſt you, ye ſaid vnto me,
[g] No, but a King ſhal reigne ouer vs: whẽ
yet the Lord your God was your King.
13 Now therefore beholde ẏ King whome
ye haue choſen *and* whome ye haue deſired: lo therefore, ẏ Lord hathe ſet a King
ouer you.
14 If ye wil feare the Lord and ſerue him,
and heare his voyce, and not diſobey the
worde of the Lord, bothe ye, & the King
that reigneth ouer you, ſhal [h] followe
the Lord your God.
15 But if ye wil not obey the voyce of the
Lord, but diſobey the Lords mouth, then
ſhal the hand of the Lord be vpon you, &
on your [i] fathers.
16 Now alſo ſtand and ſe this great thing
which the Lord wil do before your eyes.
17 Is it not nowe wheate harueſt? I wil call
vnto the Lord, and he ſhal ſend thundre
and raine, that ye may perceiue and ſe,
how that your wickednes is [k] great, which
ye haue done in the ſight of the Lord in
aſking you a King.
18 Then Samuél called vnto the Lord, and
the Lord ſent thundre and raine the ſame
day: and all the people feared the Lord &
Samuél excedingly.
19 And all the people ſaid vnto Samuél,
Pray for thy ſeruants vnto the Lord thy
God, that we dye not: for we haue ſinned
in aſking vs a King, beſide [l] all our *other*
ſinnes.
20 ¶ And Samuél ſaid vnto ẏ people, Feare
not. (ye haue in dede done all this wicked
nes, [m] yet departe not from following
the Lord, but ſerue ẏ Lord with all your
heart,
21 Nether turne ye backe: for *that ſhulde be*
after vaine things which can not profit
you, nor deliuer you, for they are but vanitie)
22 For the Lord wil not forſake his people
for his great Names ſake: becauſe it hathe
pleaſed ẏ Lord to make you [n] his people.
23 Moreouer God forbid, that I ſhulde
ſinne againſt the Lord, and ceaſe praying
for you, but I wil ſhewe you the good and
right way.
24 Therefore feare you the Lord, and ſerue him in the trueth with all your [o] hearts,
and conſider how great things he hathe
done for you.
25 But if ye do wickedly, ye ſhal periſh,
bothe ye, and your King.

f That is, Samſon, Iudg.13,25. *Iudg.7,32. Iudg.11,1. Chap.4,1.*

g Leauing God to ſeke helpe of man, Chap. 8,5.

h Ye ſhal be preſerued as they ẏ follow the Lords wil.

i Meaning, the gouernours.

k In that ye haue forſaken him, who hath all power in his hand, for a mortale man.

l Not onely at other times, but now chiefely.

m He ſheweth that there is no ſinne ſo great, but it ſhal be forgiuen, if the ſinner turne againe to God.

n Of his fre mercie, & not of your merites, and therefore he wil not forſake you.

o Vnfainedly and without hypocriſie.

CHAP. XIII.

3 The Philiſtíms are ſmittẽ of Saúl & Ionathán. 13 Saúl being diſobedient to Gods commandement is ſhewed of Samuél that he ſhal not reigne. 19 The great ſlauerie, wherein the Philiſtíms kept the Iſraelites.

1 Saúl now had bene King [a] one yere, &
he reigned [b] two yeres ouer Iſraél.
2 Then Saúl choſe him thre thouſand of
Iſraél: & two thouſand were with Saúl in
Michmáſh, and in mount Beth-él, and a
thouſand were with Ionathán in Gibeáh
of Beniamín: and the reſt of the people he
ſent euerie one to his tent.
3 And Ionathán ſmote the gariſon of the
Philiſtíms, that was in the [c] hil: and it came to the Philiſtíms eares: and Saúl blewe
the [d] trumpet throughout all the land,
ſaying, Heare, ô ye Ebrewes.
4 And all Iſraél heard ſay, Saúl hathe deſtroyed a gariſon of the Philiſtíms: wherefore Iſraél was had in abominaciõ with
the Philiſtíms: and the people gathered
together after Saúl to Gilgál.
5 ¶ The Philiſtíms alſo gathered them ſelues together to fight with Iſraél, thirtie
thouſand charets and ſix thouſand horſe-
mẽ: for the people *was* like the ſand which
is by the ſeas ſide in multitude, and came
vp, and pitched in Michmáſh Eastwarde
from [e] Beth-áuen.
6 And whẽ the men of Iſraél ſawe that they
were in a ſtraite (*for the people were in diſtreſ-
ſe*) the people hid thẽ ſelues in caues, & in
holdes, & in rockes, & towres, & in pittes.
7 And *ſome* of the Ebrewes went ouer Iordén vnto the land of [f] Gad & Gileád: and
Saúl was yet in Gilgál, and all the people
for feare followed him.
8 And he taried ſeuẽ dayes, according vnto the time that Samuél had appointed:
but Samuél came not to Gilgál, therefore
the people were [g] ſcatred from him.
9 And Saúl ſaid, Bring a burnt offring to
me and peace offrings: and he offred a
burnt offring.
10 And aſſone as he had made an end of
offring the burnt offring, beholde, Samuél
came: and Saúl went forthe to mete him,
to " ſalute him.
11 And Samuél ſaid, What haſt thou done?
Then Saúl ſaid, Becauſe I ſawe that the
people was [h] ſcatred from me, and that
thou cameſt not within the dayes appointed, and that the Philiſtíms gathered thẽ
ſelues together to Michmáſh,
12 Therefore ſaid I, The Philiſtíms wil
come downe now vpon me to Gilgál, and
I haue not made ſupplicacion vnto the
Lord. I was bolde therefore and offred a
burnt offring.
13 And Samuél ſaid to Saúl, Thou haſt done fooliſhly: thou haſt not kept the commandement of the Lord thy [i] God, which

a Whiles theſe things were done.

b Before he toke vpon him the ſtate of a King.

c Of Kiriath-iearim, where the Arke was, Chap.10,5.

d That euerie one ſhulde prepare them ſelues to warre.

e Which was alſo called Beth-él, in the tribe of Beniamin.

f Where the two tribes & the halfe remained.

g Thinking ẏ the abſence of ẏ Prophet was a ſigne, that they ſhulde loſe the victorie.

" *Ebr. bleſſe him.*

h Thogh theſe cauſes ſeme ſufficient in mans iugemẽt: yet becauſe they had not the worde of God, they turned to his deſtruction.

i Who willed thee to obey him and reſt vpon the wordes ſpoken by his Prophet.

he cōmãded thee: for the Lord had now
stablished thy kingdome vpon Israél for
euer.
14 But now thy kingdome shal not continue: the Lord hathe soght him a [k] man
after his owne heart, and ẏ Lord hathe cōmãded him to be gouernour ouer his people, because thou hast not kept that which
the Lord had commanded thee.

k That is, Dauid.

15 ¶ And Samuél arose, and gate him vp frō
Gilgál in [l] Gibeáh of Beniamín: & Saúl
nombred the people that were foūde with
him, about six hundreth men.

l And went to his citie Ramáh.

16 And Saúl and Ionathán his sonne, & the
people that were founde with them, had
their abiding in Gibeáh of Beniamín: but
the Philistíms pitched in Michmásh.
17 And there came out of the hoste of the
Philistíms ″thre bādes to destroy, one bāde turned vnto the way of Ophráh vnto
the land of Shuál,

″Or, the destroiers: to wit, the captaine came out with the bands.

18 And another bande turned toward the
way to Beth-horón, and the [m] thirde bāde turned toward the way of the coast that
loketh toward the valley of Zeboím, toward the wildernes.

m So that to mans iudgemēt these thre armies wold haue ouerrunne the whole countrey.

19 Thē there was no smith founde through
out all the land of Israél: for the Philistíms said, Lest the Ebrewes make them
swordes or speares.
20 Wherefore all the Israelites wēt downe
to the Philistíms, to sharpen euerie man
his share, his mattocke, & his axe and his
weding hooke.
21 Yet they had a file for the shares, and for
the mattockes, and for the pickeforkes, &
for the axes and for to sharpen the goades.
22 So when the day of battel was come, there was nether [n] sworde nor speare founde
in the hands of anie of the people that
were with Saúl & with Ionathán: but *onely*
with Saúl and Ionathán his sonne was
there founde.

n To declare that the victorie onely came of God & not by their force.

23 And the garison of the Philistíms came
out to the passage of Michmásh.

CHAP. XIIII.

14 Ionathán and his armour bearer put the Philistíms to flight. 24 Saúl bindeth the people by an othe, not to eat til euening. 32 The people eat with the blood. 38 Saúl wolde put Ionathán to death. 45 The people deliuer him.

1 THen on a day Ionathán the sonne of
Saúl said vnto the yong man that bare his armour, [a] Come and let vs go ouer
toward the Philistíms garison, that is
yonder on the otherside, but he tolde not
his father.

a By this exāple God wold declare to Israél that the victorie did not consist in multitude or armour, but onely came of his grace.

2 And Saúl taryed in the border of Gibeáh vnder a pomegranate tre, which was
in Migrón, and the people that were with
him, *were* about six hundreth men.
3 And Ahiáh the sonne of Ahitúb, *Icha-
bods brother, the sonne of Phinehás, the

*Chap. 4, 21.

sonne of Elí, was the Lords Priest in Shilóh, and ware an Ephód: and the people
knewe not that Ionathán was gone.
4 ¶ Now in the way whereby Ionathán
soght to go ouer to ẏ Philistíms garison,
there was a ″sharpe rocke on the one side,
and a sharpe rocke on the other side: the
name of the one *was* called Bozéz, & the
name of the other Séneh.

″Or, like a tothe.

5 The one rocke stretched frō the North
toward Michmásh, & the other *was* from
the South toward Gibeáh.
6 And Ionathán said to the yong man that
bare his armour, Come, and let vs go ouer
vnto the garison of these [b] vncircumcised: it may be that the Lord wil worke
with vs: for it is ″not hard to the Lord *to
saue with manie, or with fewe.

b To wit, the Philistíms.

″Or, none can let the Lord.

*2. Chro. 14, 11.

7 And he that bare his armour, said vnto
him, do all that is in thine heart: go where
it pleaseth thee: beholde, [c] I am with thee
as thine heart desireth.

c I wil follow thee whethersoeuer thou goest.

8 Then said Ionathán, Beholde, we go
ouer vnto those men, and wil shewe our
selues vnto them.
9 [d] If they say on this wise to vs, Tarie vntil we come to you, then we wil stand stil
in our place, and not go vp to them.
10 But if they say, Come vp vnto vs, then
we wil go vp: for * the Lord hathe deliuered them into our hand: and this shalbe a
signe vnto vs.

d This he spake by the Spirit of prophecie, forasmuche as hereby God gaue him assurance of the victorie.

*1. Mac. 4, 30.

11 So they bothe shewed them selues vnto
the garison of the Philistíms: and the Philistíms said, Se, the Ebrewes come out of ẏ
[e] holes wherein they had hid thē selues.

e Thus they spake cōtempteously, and by derision.

12 And the men of the garison answered
Ionathán, & his armour bearer, and said,
Come vp to vs: for we wil shewe you a
thing. Then Ionathán said vnto his armour bearer, Come vp after me: for the
Lord hathe deliuered them into the hand
of Israél.
13 So Ionathán went vp vpon [f] his hands
and vpon his fete, and his armour bearer
after him: and *some* fel before Ionathán, &
his armour bearer slewe *others* after him.

f That is, he crept vp, or went vp with all hast.

14 So the [g] first slaughter which Ionathán
and his armour bearer made, was about
twentie mē within that cōpasse, as it were
within halfe an acre of land which two
oxen plowe.

g The seconde was whē they slewe one another, and the third when ẏ Israelites chased them.

15 And there was a feare in the hoste, *and* in
the field, and amōg all the people: the garison also, and they that went out to spoile, were afrayed them selues: and the earth
[h] trembled: for it was *stricken* with feare by
God.

h In that the insensible creatures tremble for feare of Gods iudgement, it declareth how terrible his vengeance shalbe against his enemies.

16 ¶ Thē the watchmen of Saúl in Gibeáh
of Beniamín sawe: and beholde, the multitude was discomfited, and smitten as they
went.
17 Therefore said Saúl vnto the people
that

that were with him, Search now & se, who
is gone from vs. And whẽ they had nombred,
beholde, Ionathán and his armour
bearer were not there.
18 And Saúl said vnto Ahiáh, Bring hither
the Arke of God (for ẏ Arke of God was
at that time with the children of Israél)
19 ¶ And while Saúl talked vnto the Priest,
the noise, that was in the hoste of the Philistims,
spred farther abroade, & encreased:
therefore Saúl said vnto the Priest,
[i] Withdrawe thine hand.
20 And Saúl was assembled with all the
people that were with him, and they came
to the battel: & beholde, * euerie mans
sworde was against his fellowe, *and* there
was a very great discomfiture.
21 Moreouer ẏ Ebrewes that were with the
Philistíms before time, & were come with
them into all partes of the hoste, euẽ they
also turned to be with the [k] Israelites that
were with Saúl and Ionathán.
22 Also all the men of Israél which had
hid them selues in mount Ephráim when
they heard, that the Philistims were fled,
they followed after them in the battel.
23 And so the Lord saued Israél that day:
and the battel continued vnto Beth-áuen.
24 ¶ And at that time the men of Israél were
pressed *with hunger*: for Saúl charged
the people with an othe, saying, [l] Cursed
be the man ẏ eateth "foode til nyght, that
I may be auenged of mine enemies: so
none of the people tasted *anie* sustenance.
25 And all they of the lãd came to a wood,
where hony lay vpon the ground.
26 And the people came into the wood, &
beholde, the hony dropped, and no man
moued his hãd to his mouth: for the people
feared the [m] othe.
27 But Ionathán heard not when his father
charged the people with the othe: wherefore
he put forthe the end of the rod that
was in his hãd, and dipt it in an hony cõbe,
and put his hand to his mouth, and his
[n] eyes receyued sight.
28 Then answered one of the people, and
said, Thy father made ẏ people to sweare,
saying, Cursed be the man that eateth sustenance
this day: and the people were
"faint.
29 Then said Ionathán, My father hathe
[o] troubled the land: se now how mine eyes
are made cleare, because I haue tasted a
litle of this hony:
30 How muche more, if the people had eatẽ
to day of the spoile of their enemies which
they founde? for had there not bene now a
greater slaughter among the Philistims?
31 ¶ And they smote ẏ Philistíms that day,
from Michmásh to Aiialón: and the people
were exceding faint.
32 So the people turned to the spoyle, and
toke shepe, & oxen, and calues, & slewe thẽ
on the ground, and the people did eat thẽ
*with the blood.
33 Then men told Saúl, saying, Beholde, the
people sinne against the Lord, in that thei
eat with the blood. And he said, Ye haue
trespassed: [p] roule a great stone vnto me
this day.
34 Againe Saúl said, Go abroade among ẏ
people, & bid them bring me euerie man
his oxe, and euery mã his shepe, and slaye
them here, and eate and sinne not against
the Lord in eating with the blood. And
the people broght euery man his oxe in
his hand that night and slewe them there.
35 Then Saúl made an altar vnto the Lord,
& that "was the first altar that he made
vnto the Lord.
36 ¶ And Saúl said, Let vs go downe after
the Philistíms by night, and spoyle them
vntil the morning shine, and let vs not leaue
a mã of them. And they said, Do whatsoeuer
thou thinkest best. Then said the
Priest, Let vs [q] draw nere hither vnto God.
37 So Saúl asked of God, *saying*, Shal I go
downe after the Philistíms? wilt thou deliuer
them into the hands of Israél? But
he answered him not at that time.
38 ¶ And Saúl said, * All "ye chief of ẏ people,
come ye hither, and knowe, and se by
whome this sinne is done this day.
39 For as the Lord liueth, which saueth Israél,
thogh it be *done* by Ionathán my
sonne, he shal dye the death. But none of
all the people answered him.
40 Then he said vnto all Israél, Be ye on
one side, & I and Ionathán my sonne wil
be on the other side. And the people said
vnto Saúl, Do what thou thinkest best.
41 Then Saúl said vnto the Lord God of
Israél, Giue [r] a perfet *lot*. And Ionathán
& Saúl were taken, but the people escaped.
42 And Saúl said, Cast *lot* betwene me and
Ionathán my sonne. And Ionathán was
taken.
43 Then Saúl said to Ionathán, Tel me
what thou hast done. And Ionathán told
him, and said, I tasted a litle hony with ẏ
end of the rod, that was in mine hand, &
lo, I must dye.
44 Againe Saúl answered, God do so and
more also, vnles ẙ dye ẏ death, Ionathán.
45 And the people said vnto Saúl, [s] Shal
Ionathán dye, who hathe so mightely deliuered
Israél? God forbid. As ẏ Lord liueth
there shal not one heere of his head
fall to the ground: for he hathe wroght ẘ
God this day. So the people deliuered Ionathán
that he dyed not.
46 Thẽ Saúl came vp from the Philistíms:
& the Philistíms wẽt to their owne place.
47 ¶ So Saúl helde the kingdome ouer Israél,
and foght against all his ennemies on

[i] Let the Ephód alone: for I haue no leasure nowe to aske counsel of God, Nomb. 27,21.

Iudg. 7,21. 2. chro. 20,23.

[k] Thogh before for feare of the Philistims they declared them selues as ennemies to their brethren.

[l] Suche was his hypocrisie & arrogancie, ẏ he thoght to attribute to his policie ẏ, which God had giuen by the hand of Ionathán.

"Ebr. bread.

[m] That is, the punishement, if they brake their othe.

[n] Which were dimme before for wearines and hungre.

"Or, werie.

[o] By making this cruel lawe.

Leu. 7,26. & 19,26. deu. 12, 16.

[p] That the blood of the beasts ẏ shal be slaine, may be pressed out vpon it.

"Or, that Saúl began he to buylde an altar.

[q] To aske counsel of him.

Iudg. 20,2.

"Ebr. corners.

[r] Cause ẏ lot to fall on him ẏ hathe broke the othe: but he doeth not consider his presumptiõ in commanding the same othe.

[s] The people thoght it their duetie to rescue him, who of ignorance, had but broken a rashe lawe, and by whome they had receiued so great a benefite.

euerie side, against Moáb, and against the
children of Ammón, and against Edóm,
and against ẏ Kings of Zobáh, & against
the Philistíms: & whethersoeuer he went,
he "handled them as wicked men.
48 He gathered also an hoste & smote [t] A-
malék, & deliuered Israél out of the hāds
of them that spoiled them.
49 Now the sonnes of Saúl were Ionathán, [u] and Ishuí, and Malchishúa: and
the names of his two daughters, the elder
was called Meráb, and the yonger was named [x] Michál.
50 And ẏ name of Sauls wife was Ahinóam
the daughter of Ahimáaz: and the name
of his chief captaine was [y] Abnér the sonne of Ner, Sauls vncle.
51 And Kish *was* Sauls father: and Ner the
father of Abnér *was* the sonne of Abiél.
52 And there was sore warre against the
Philistíms all the dayes of Saúl: & [z] whomesoeuer Saul sawe to be a strong man, &
mete for the warre, he toke him vnto him.

"Or, ouercame them.
t As the Lord had commanded, Deu. 25,17.
u Called also Abinadáb, Chap. 31,2.
x Which was the wife of Dauid, Chap. 18,27.
y Whome Ioáb the captaine of Dauid slewe, 2. Sam. 3,27.
z As Samuél had forewarned Chap. 8,11.

CHAP. XV.

3 Saúl is commanded to slay Amalék. 9 He spareth Agág & the best things. 19 Samuél reproueth him. 28 Saúl is reiected of the Lord, and his kingdome giuen to another. 33 Samuél heweth Agág in pieces.

1 AFterwarde Samuél said vnto Saúl,
* The Lord sent me to anoint thee
King ouer his people ouer Israél: nowe
therefore [a] obey the voyce of the wordes
of the Lord.
2 Thus saith the Lord of hostes, I remember what Amalék did to Israél,* how they
layed *wait* for them in the way, as they came vp from Egypt.
3 Nowe *therefore* go, and smite Amalék, &
destroye ye all that perteineth vnto them,
and haue no cōpassion on them, but [b] slay
bothe man and woman, bothe infant and
suckeling, bothe oxe, and shepe, bothe camel, and asse.
4 ¶ And Saúl assembled the people, and
"nombred them in Telaím, two hundreth
thousand fotemen, and ten thousand men
of Iudáh.
5 And Saúl came to a citie of Amalék, "and
set watch at the riuer.
6 And Saúl said vnto the [c] Kenites, Go,
departe, *and* get you downe from among
the Amalekites, lest I destroy you with
them: for ye shewed [d] mercy to all the
children of Israél, when they came vp frō
Egypt: and the Kenites departed from a-
mong the Amalekites.
7 So Saúl smote the Amalekites from Hauiláh as thou commest to Shur, that is before Egypt,
8 And toke Agág the King of the Amalekites aliue, and destroyed all the people
with the edge of the sworde.
9 But Saúl and the people spared Agág, &
the better shepe, and the oxen, and the fat

Chap. 9,16.
a Because he hathe preferred thee to this honour, thou art boūd to obey him.
Exod. 17,14. nomb. 24,20.
b That this might be an exāple of Gods vengeance against thē that deale cruelly with his people.
"Or, knewe their nomber by the lambes, which they broght.
"Or, foght in the valley.
c Which were the posteritie of Iethró Mosés father in lawe.
d For Iethró came to visit them and gaue them good counsel, Exod. 18,19.

beastes, and the lambes, and all that was
good, & they wolde not destroye thē: but
euery thing that was vile & noght worthe,
that they destroyed.
10 ¶ Thē came the worde of the Lord vnto Samuél, saying,
11 It [e] repenteth me that I haue made Saúl
King: for he is turned frō me, & hathe not
performed my commandements. And Sa
muél was moued, & cryed vnto the Lord
all night.
12 And whē Samuél arose early to mete Saúl in the morning, one tolde Samuél, saying, Saúl is gone to Carmél: and beholde,
he hathe made him there a place, from
whence he returned, and departed, and is
gone downe to Gilgál.
13 ¶ Thē Samuél came to Saúl, & Saúl said
vnto him, Blessed be ẏ of the Lord, I haue
fulfilled the [f] cōmandement of the Lord.
14 But Samuél said, What meaneth then ẏ
bleating of the shepe in mine eares, & the
lowing of the oxen which I heare?
15 And Saúl āswered, Thei haue broght thē
from the Amalekites: for the people spared the best of the shepe, and of the oxen
to sacrifice them vnto the Lord thy God,
and the remnant haue we destroyed.
16 Againe Samuél said to Saúl, Let me tel
thee what the Lord hathe said to me this
night. And he said vnto him, Say on.
17 Then Samuél said, When thou wast [g] litle in thine owne sight, wast ẏ not made
the head of the tribes of Israél? for the
Lord anointed thee King ouer Israél.
18 And the Lord sent thee on a iourney, &
said, Go, and destroye those sinners the A-
malekites, and fight against them, vntil
thou destroye them.
19 Now wherefore hast thou not obeyed ẏ
voyce of the Lord, but hast turned to the
praye, and hast done wickedly in the sight
of the Lord?
20 And Saúl said vnto Samuél, Yea, I [h] haue
obeyd ẏ voyce of the Lord, & haue gone ẏ
way which the Lord sent me, and haue
broght Agág the King of Amalék, & haue
destroyed the Amalekites.
21 But ẏ people toke of the spoyle, shepe, &
oxen, & the chiefest of the things which
shulde haue bene destroyed, to offer vnto
the Lord thy God in Gilgál.
22 And Samuél said, Hathe ẏ Lord as great
pleasure in burnt offrings & sacrifices, as
whē the voyce of ẏ Lord is obeied? beholde, *to obey is better then sacrifice, and
to hearken *is better* then the fat of rammes.
23 For [i] rebellion *is as* the sinne of witchcraft, and transgresion is wickednes and
idolatrie. Because thou hast cast away the
worde of the Lord, therefore he hathe
cast away thee from being King.
24 Then Saúl said vnto Samuél, I haue sinned

e God in his eternal coūsel neuer chāgeth nor repenteth, as vers. 29. thogh he semeth to vs to repent, when anie thing goeth contrary to his temporal election.
f This is ẏ nature of hypocrites, to be impudēt against the trueth, to condemne others, & iustifie thē selues.
g Meaning of base conditiō, as Chap. 9,21.
h He standeth most impudētly in his owne defense bothe against God & his owne cōscience.
Eccles. 4,17. ose. 6,7. mat. 9,13. & 22,7.
i God hateth nothing more then the disobedience of his commādement, thogh ẏ intent seme neuer so good to man.

ned: for I haue transgressed the cómandement of the Lord, & thy wordes, because
I feared the people, & obeied their voyce.
25 Now therefore, I pray thee, take away my
[k] sinne, and turne againe with me, that I
may worship the Lord.

k This was not true repétance, but dissimulation, fearing ŷ losse of his kingdome.

26 But Samuél said vnto Saúl, I wil not returne with thee: for thou hast cast awaye
the worde of the Lord, & the Lord hathe
cast away thee, that thou shalt not be Kĩg
ouer Israél.
27 And as Samuél turned him selfe to go
away, he caught ŷ lap of his coat, & it rẽt.
28 Then Samuél said vnto him, The Lord
hathe rent the kingdome of Israél from
thee this day, & hathe giuen it to thy
[l] neighbour, that is better then thou.

l That is, to Dauid.

29 For in dede the [m] strength of Israél wil
not lie nor repent: for he is not a man that
he shulde repent.

m Meaning God, who mainteineth & preferreth his.

30 Then he said, I haue sinned: but honour
me, I pray thee, before the Elders of my
people, & before Israél, & turne againe ŵ
me, that I may worship the Lord thy God.
31 ¶ So Samuél turned againe, and followed
Saúl: and Saúl worshiped the Lord.
32 Thẽ said Samuél, Bring ye hither to me
Agág ŷ King of the Amalekites: & Agág
came vnto him "pleasantly, and Agág said,
Truely the [n] bitternes of death is passed.

" Or, in bonders.
n He suspected nothing lesse then death, or as some write, he passed not for death.

33 And Samuél said, * As thy sworde hathe
made women childeles, so shal thy mother
be childeles among other womẽ. And Samuél hewed Agág in pieces before the
Lord in Gilgál.

Exod. 17, 11. nomb. 14, 45.

34 ¶ So Samuél departed to [o] Ramáh, and
Saúl went vp to his house to Gibeáh of
Saúl.

o Where his house was.

35 And Samuél came nomore to [p] se Saúl
vntil ŷ day of his death: but Samuél mourned for Saúl, and the Lord [q] repented that
he made Saúl King ouer Israél.

p Thogh Saúl came where Samuel was, Chap. 19, 22.
q As ver. 11.

CHAP. XVI.

1 Samuél is reproued of God, & is sent to anoint Dauid. 7 God regardeth the heart. 13 The Spirit of the Lord commeth vpon Dauid. 14. The wicked spirit is sent vpon Saúl. 19 Saúl sendeth for Dauid.

1 THe Lord thẽ said vnto Samuél, How
long wilt ŷ mourne for Saúl, [a] seing
I haue cast him away from reigning ouer
Israél? fil thine horne with oyle and come,
I wil send thee to Ishái the Bethlehemite:
for I haue prouided me a King among
his sonnes.

a Signifying, ŷ we oght not to shewe our selues more pitiful then God, nor to lamẽt thẽ, whome he casteth of.

2 And Samuél said, How can I go? for if
Saúl shal heare it, he wil kil me. Then the
Lord answered, Take an heifer "ŵ thee, &
say, I am come [b] to do sacrifice to ŷ Lord.

" Ebr. in thine hand.
b That is, to make a peace offring, which might be done thogh ŷ Arke was not there.

3 And call Ishái to the sacrifice, and I wil
shewe thee what ŷ shalt do, & ŷ shalt anoit
vnto me him whome I name vnto thee.
4 So Samuél did ŷ the Lord bade him, &
came to Beth-léhem, and the Elders of the
towne were [c] astonied at his comming, &
said, Commest thou peaceably?

c Fearing, lest some grieuous crime had bene commited, because ŷ Prophet was not wonte to come thether.

5 And he answered, Yea: I am come to do
sacrifice vnto the Lord: sanctifie your selues, & come with me to the sacrifice. And
he sanctified Ishái and his sonnes, and called them to the sacrifice.
6 And when they were come, he loked on
Eliáb, and said, Surely the Lords [d] Anointed is before him.

d Thinking, ŷ Eliáb had bene appointed of God to be made King.

7 But the Lord said vnto Samuél, Loke not
on his coũtinance, nor on the height of his
stature, because I haue refused him: for
God seeth not as man seeth: for man loketh
on the outward appearance, but the Lord
beholdeth the * heart.

1. Chro 28, 29. ier. 11, 20. & 17, 10. & 20, 12. psal. 7, 10.

8 Then Ishái called Abinadáb, & made hĩ
come before Samuél. And he said, Nether
hathe the Lord chosen this.
9 Thẽ Ishái made Shámáh come. And he
said, Nether yet hathe ŷ Lord chosen hĩ.
10 Againe Ishái made his seuen sonnes to
come before Samuél: & Samuél said vnto
Ishái, The Lord hath chosẽ none of these.
11 Finally Samuél said vnto Ishái, "Are
there no more children *but these*? And he
said, There remaineth yet a litle one behinde, ŷ kepeth the shepe. Then Samuél
said vnto Ishái, * Send and fet him: for we
wil not sit downe, til he be come hither.

" *Ebr. are the children ended?*
2. Sam. 7, 8. psal. 78, 71. & 89, 21.

12 And he sent, and broght him in: and he
was ruddie, and of a good countinance, &
comelie visage. And ŷ Lord said, Arise, &
anoint him: for this is he.
13 Then Samuél toke the horne of oyle, &
anointed him in the middes of his brethren. And the * Spirit of the Lord "came
vpon Dauid, from that day forwarde: thẽ
Samuél rose vp, and went to Ramáh.

Act. 7, 46. & 13, 22.
" *Or, prospered.*

14 ¶ But the Spirit of the Lord departed
from Saúl, and an [e] euil spirit *sent* of the
Lord vexed him.

e The wicked spirits are at Gods commandement to execute his wil against ŷ wicked.

15 And Sauls seruãts said vnto hĩ, Beholde
now, ŷ euil spirit of God vexeth thee.
16 Let our lord therefore commande thy
seruants, *that are* before thee, to seke a man,
that is a conning player vpon the harpe:
that when the euil spirit of God commeth
vpon thee, he may playe with his hand, &
thou maiest be eased.
17 Saúl then said vnto his seruãts, Prouide
me a man, I pray you, that can play wel, &
bring him to me.
18 Then answered one of his seruants, and
said, Beholde, I haue sene a [f] sonne of Ishái,
a Bethlehemite, that can playe, & is strõg,
valiãt & a mã of warre & wise in matters,
& a comely persone, & ŷ Lord is with hĩ.

f Thogh Dauid was now anointed King by ŷ Prophet, yet God wolde exercise him in sondry sortes before he had the vse of his kingdome.

19 ¶ Wherefore Saúl sent messengers vnto
Ishái, & said, Send me Dauid thy sonne,
which is with the shepe.
20 And Ishái toke an asse *laden* with bread
& a flagon of wine & a kid, & sent thẽ by

the hand of Dauid his sonne vnto Saúl.
21 And Dauid came to Saúl, and "stode before him: and he loued him very wel, and
he was his armour bearer.

"Or, serued him.

22 And Saúl sent to Ishái, saying, Let Dauid now remaine with me: for he hathe
founde fauour in my sight.
23 And so when the *euil* spirit of God came vpon Saúl, Dauid toke an harpe and
plaied with his hand, & Saúl was g refreshed, & was eased: for the euil spirit departed from him.

g God wolde ŷ Saúl shulde receiue this benefite as at Dauids hād, ŷ his cōdemnation might be the more euident, for his cruel hate towarde him.

CHAP. XVII.

1 The Philistíms make warre against Israél. 10 Goliáth defieth Israél. 17 Dauid is sent to his brethren. 34 The strength and boldenes of Dauid. 47 The Lord saueth not by sworde nor speare. 50 Dauid killeth Goliáth and the Philistíms flee.

1 NOw the Philistíms gathered their
armies to battel, and came together
to Shochóh, which is in Iudáh, & pitched
betwene Shochóh and Azekáh, "in the coast of Dammím.

"Or, in Ephes dammim.

2 And Saúl, and the men of Israél assembled, and pitched in the valley "of Eláh, &
put them selues in battel array to mete the
Philistíms.

"Or, of the oke.

3 And the Philistíms stode on a mountaine
on the one side, and Israél stode on a mountaine on the other side: so a valley *was*
betwene them.
4 ¶ Then came a mā betwene them a bothe
out of the tentes of the Philistíms, named Goliáth of Gath: his height *was*
six cubits and an hand breadth,

a Betwene the two campes.

5 And had an helmet of brasse vpō his head, and a "brigandine vpon him: and the
weight of his brigandine *was* fiue thousand b shekels of brasse.

"Or, coate of plate.

6 And he had "bootes of brasse vpō his legges, & a shilde of brasse vpō his shoulders.
7 And the shafte of his speare *was* like a
weauers beame: and his speare head *weyed*
six hundreth shekels of yron: and one bearing a shilde went before him.

b That is, 156 lib. 4 onces, after halfe an once the shekel. & 600 shekels weight amounteth to 18 lib. 3 quarters.
"Or, greaues.

8 And he stode, and cryed against the hoste
of Israél, and said vnto them, Why are ye
come to set your battel in array? am not I
a Philistím, and you seruāts to Saúl? chose
you a mā for you, & let him come downe
to me.
9 If he be able to fight with me, and "kil
me, then wil we be your seruants: but if I
ouercome him, and kil him, then shal ye
be our seruants, and serue vs.

"Ebr. smite me.

10 Also the Philistím said, I defie the hoste
of Israél this day: giue me a man, that we
may fight "together.

"Or, hād to hād.

11 When Saúl and all Israél heard those
wordes of the Philistím, they were discouraged, and greatly afrayed.
12 ¶ Now this Dauid *was* the * sonne of an
Ephrathite of Beth-léhem Iudáh, named

Chap. 16, 1.

Ishái, which had eight sonnes: and "this mā
was taken for an olde man in the dayes
of Saúl.

"Or, he was counted among thē that bare office.

13 And the thre eldest sonnes of Ishái went
and followed Saúl to the battel: and the
names of his thre sonnes that wēt to battel, *were* Eliáb the eldest, & the next Abinadáb, and the third Shammáh.
14 So Dauid was the least: and the thre
eldest went after Saúl.
15 Dauid also c went, but he returned from
Saúl to fede his fathers shepe in Beth-léhem.

c To serue Saúl, as chap. 16, ver. 19.

16 And the Philistím drewe nere in ŷ morning, and euening, and continued fourtie
dayes.
17 And Ishái said vnto Dauid his sonne,
d Take now for thy brethren an Epháh of
this parched corne, and these ten cakes,
and runne to the hoste to thy brethren.
18 Also cary these ten fresh cheses vnto the
captaine, and loke how thy brethren fare,
and receiue their e pledge.

d Thogh Ishái mentone thīg, yet Gods prouidence directed Dauid to another end.

e If they haue laied anie thīg to gage for their necessitie, redeme it out.

19 (Then Saúl and they, and all the men of
Israél *were* in the valley of Eláh, fighting with the Philistíms)
20 ¶ So Dauid rose vp early in the mornīg,
and left the shepe with a keper, and toke
and went as Ishái had commanded him, &
came within the compasse of the hoste:
& the hoste went out in array, and showted in the battel.
21 For Israél and the Philistíms had put
them selues in array, armie against armie.
22 And Dauid left the things, which he
bare, vnder the hands of the keper of the
"cariage, and ran into the hoste, & came,
and asked his brethren "how they did.

"Ebr. vessels.
"Ebr. of peace.

23 And as he talked with them, beholde, the
man *that was* betwene the two *armies*, came vp, (whose name *was* Goliáth the Philistím of Gath) out of the "armie of the
Philistíms, and spake f suche wordes, &
Dauid heard them.

"Or, valleys.
f As are aboue rehearsed ver. 8, & 9.

24 And all the men of Israél, when they
sawe the man, ran away from him, & were
sore afrayed.
25 For euery man of Israél said, Sawe ye
not this man that cometh vp? euen to reuile Israél is he come vp: and to him that
killeth hī, wil the King giue great riches,
and wil giue him his * daughter, yea, and
make his fathers house g fre in Israél.

Iosh. 15, 16.
g From taxes, & paymentes.

26 ¶ Then Dauid spake to the men that
stode with him, and said, What shalbe done to the man that killeth this Philistím,
and taketh away the h shame from Israél?
for who is this vncircumcised Philistím,
that he shulde reuile the hoste of the liuing God?

h This dishonour ŷ he doeth to Israél.

27 And the people answered him after this
maner, saying, Thus shal it be done to
the

the man that killeth him.
28 And Eliáb his eldest brother heard whẽ
he spake vnto the men, & Eliáb was very
angry with Dauid, and said, Why camest
thou downe hether? and with whome hast
ẏ left those fewe shepe in the wildernes? I
knowe thy pride and the malice of thine
heart, that thou art come downe to se the
battel.
29 Then Dauid said, What haue I now
done? Is there not a [i] cause?
30 And he departed from him into the presence of another, and spake of the same
maner, and the people answered him according to the former wordes.
31 ¶And thei that heard the wordes which
Dauid spake, rehearsed them before Saúl,
which caused him to be broght.
32 So Dauid said to Saúl, Let no mãs heart
faile him, because of him: thy seruant wil
go, and fight with this Philistím.
33 And Saúl said to Dauid, Thou art not
[k] able to go against this Philistím to fight
with him: for thou art a boye, and he is a
man of warre from his youth.
34 And Dauid answered vnto Saúl, Thy
seruant kept his fathers shepe, and there
came a [l] lyon and likewise a beare, and
toke a shepe out of the flocke,
35 And I went out after him & smote him,
& toke it out of his mouth: and when he
arose against me, I caught him by the
bearde, and smote him, and slewe him.
36 So thy seruant slewe bothe the lyon, and
the beare: therefore this vncircumcised
Philistím shalbe as one of them, seing he
hath railed on ẏ hoste of the liuing God.
37 ¶Moreouer Dauid said, The Lord that
deliuered me out of the pawe of the lyon,
and out of the pawe of the beare, he wil
deliuer me out of the hand of this Philistím. Then Saúl said vnto Dauid, [m] Go,
and the Lord be with thee.
38 And Saúl put his rayment vpon Dauid,
and put an helmet of brasse vpõ his head,
and put a brigandine vpon him.
39 Thẽ girded Dauid his sworde vpon his
rayment, and "began to go: for he neuer
proued it: and Dauid said vnto Saúl, I can
not go with these: for I am not accustomed, wherefore Dauid put them of him.
40 Then toke he his [n] staffe in his hand,
and chose him fiue smothe stones out of a
brooke, and put them in his shepherdes
bag or skrippe, & his sling *was* in his hãd,
and he drewe nere to the Philistím.
41 ¶And the Philistím came & drewe nere
vnto Dauid, and the man that bare the
shield *went* before him.
42 Now when the Philistím loked about
and sawe Dauid, he disdeined him: for he
was but yong, ruddy & of a comely face.
43 And the Philistím said vnto Dauid, Am

i For his fathers sending was a iuste occasion, & also he felt him self inwardly moued by Gods Spirit.

k Here Satan proueth Dauids faith by the infidelitie of Saúl.

l Dauid by the experience ẏ he hathe had in time past of Gods helpe, nothing douteth to ouercome this dãger, seing he was zealous for Gods honour.

m For by these examples he sawe that the power of God was ẇ him.

" Or, assayed.

n To ẏ intent that by these weake meanes God might only be knowẽ to be ẏ autor of this victorie.

I a dog, that thou commest to me with
staues? And the Philistím [o] cursed Dauid
by his gods.
44 And ẏ Philistím said to Dauid, Come
to me, and I wil giue thy flesh vnto the
foules of the heauen, and to the beastes of
the field.
45 ¶Thẽ said Dauid to ẏ Philistím, Thou
commest to me with a sworde, and with a
speare, and with a shield, but I come to
thee in the Name of the Lord of hostes,
the God of the hoste of Israél, whome
thou hast railed vpon.
46 This [p] day shal the Lord close thee in
mine hand, and I shal smite thee, and take
thine head from thee, and I wil giue the
carkeises of the hoste of the Philistíms
this day vnto the foules of the heauen, &
to the beastes of the earth, ẏ all the worlde
may knowe that Israél hathe a God,
47 And that all this assemblie may knowe,
that the Lord saueth not with sworde nor
with speare (for the battel is the Lords) &
he wil giue you into our hands.
48 And when the Philistím arose to come
and drawe nere vnto Dauid, Dauid [q] hasted & ran to fight against the Philistím.
49 And Dauid put his hand in his bag, and
toke out a stone, & slang it and smote the
Philistím in his forehead, that the stone
sticked in his forehead, and he fel groue-
ling to the earth.
50 So Dauid * ouercame the Philistím
with a sling and with a stone, & smote the
Philistím, & slewe him, when Dauid had
no sworde in his hand.
51 Then Dauid ran, and stode vpon the
Philistím, and toke his sworde & drewe it
out of his sheath, and slewe him, & cut of
his head therewith. So whẽ the Philistíms
sawe, that their champion was dead, they
fled.
52 And the men of Israél and Iudáh arose,
and showted, and followed after the Philistíms, vntil thei came to the "valley, and
vnto the gates of Ekrón: and the Philistíms fel downe wounded by the way of
Shaaráim, euen to Gath and to Ekrón.
53 And the children of Israél returned frõ
pursuing the Philistíms, and spoiled their
tents.
54 And Dauid toke the head of the Philistím, and broght it to Ierusalém, and put
his armour in his "tent.
55 ¶When Saúl sawe Dauid go forthe a-
gainst the Philistím, he said vnto Abnér
the captaine of his hoste, Abnér, [r] whose
sonne is this yong man? and Abnér answered, As thy soule liueth, ô King, I can not
tel.
56 Thẽ the King said, Enquire thou whose
sonne this yong man is.
57 And when Dauid was returned from the

o He sware by his gods that he wolde destroye him.

p Dauid being assured bothe of his cause & of his calling, prophecieth of the destruction of the Philistims.

q Beĩg moued with a feruent zeale to be reuenged vpon this blasphemer of Gods Name.

Eccles. 47,4. 1. mac. 4,30.

" Or, Gai, the citie.

" Or, house at Beth-léhem.

r That is, of what familie & tribe is he? or els, he had forgotten Dauid, albeit he had receiued so great a benefit by him.

ſlaughter of ÿ Philiſtím, thē Abner toke
him, & broght him before Saúl with the
head of the Philiſtím in his hand.
58 And Saúl ſaid to him, Whoſe ſonne art
thou, thou yong man? And Dauid anſwered, I am the ſonne of thy ſeruant Iſhái
the Bethlehemite.

CHAP. XVIII.

1 The amitie of Ionathán and Dauid. 8 Saúl enuieth Dauid for the praiſe that the wome gaue him. 11 Saúl wolde haue ſlayne Dauid. 17 He promiſeth him Meráb to wiſe, but giueth him Michál. 27 Dauid deliuereth to Saúl two hundreth foreſkinnes of the Philiſtims. 29 Saúl feareth Dauid, ſeing that the Lord is with him.

1 AND when he had made an end of
ſpeaking vnto Saúl, the [a] ſoule of
Ionathán was knit with the ſoule of Dauid, and Ionathán loued him, as his owne
ſoule.
2 And Saúl toke him that day, and wolde
not let him returne to his fathers houſe.
3 Then Ionathán and Dauid made a couenant: for he loued him as his owne ſoule.
4 And Ionathán put of the robe that was
vpon him, and gaue it Dauid, and his garments, euen to his ſworde, & to his bowe,
and to his girdle.
5 And Dauid went out whetherſoeuer Saúl
ſent him, & behaued him ſelfe [b] wiſely:
ſo that Saúl ſet him ouer the mē of warre,
and he was accepted in the ſight of all the
people, and alſo in the ſight of Sauls ſeruants.
6 ¶ When thei came againe, and Dauid returned from the ſlaughter of the [c] Philiſtím, the women came out of all cities of
Iſraél, ſinging and danſing to mete King
Saúl, with timbrels, with *inſtrumēts of* ioye,
and with rebecks.
7 And the women [*] ſang by cours in their
playe, & ſaid, * Saúl hathe ſlayne his thouſand, and Dauid his ten thouſand.
8 Therefore Saúl was exceding wrath, and
the ſaying diſpleaſed him, & he ſaid, Thei
haue aſcribed vnto Dauid ten thouſand, &
to me thei haue aſcribed *but* a thouſand,
& *what can he haue* more ſaue the kīgdome?
9 Wherefore Saúl [d] had an eye on Dauid
from that day forwarde.
10 ¶ And on the morowe, the euil ſpirit of
God came vpon Saúl, & he [e] prophecied
in the middes of the houſe: and Dauid
plaied with his hand like as at other times,
and there *was* a ſpeare in Sauls hand.
11 And Saúl toke the ſpeare, and ſaid, I wil
ſmite Dauid *through* to ÿ wall. But Dauid
auoyded twiſe out of his preſence.
12 And Saúl was afraied of Dauid, becauſe
the Lord was with him, and was departed
from Saúl.
13 Therefore Saúl put him from him, and
made him a captaine ouer a thouſand, and
he went [f] out and in before the people.
14 And Dauid behaued him ſelfe wiſely in
all his waies: for the Lord *was* with him.
15 Wherefore when Saúl ſawe that he was
very wiſe, he was afraied of him.
16 For all Iſraél and Iudáh loued Dauid,
becauſe he went out and in before them.
17 ¶ Thē Saúl ſaid to Dauid, Beholde mine
eldeſt daughter Meráb, her I wil giue thee
to wife: onely be a valiant ſonne vnto me,
and [g] fight the Lords battels: for Saúl
thoght, Mine hand ſhal not be vpon him,
but the hand of the Philiſtíms ſhalbe vpon him.
18 And Dauid anſwered Saúl, What am I?
and what is my life, *or* the familie of my
father in Iſraél, that I ſhulde be ſonne in
lawe to the King?
19 Howbeit when Meráb Sauls daughter
ſhulde haue bene giuē to Dauid, [h] ſhe was
giuē vnto Adriél a Meholathite to wife.
20 ¶ Then Michál Sauls daughter loued
Dauid: and thei ſhewed Saúl, & the thing
pleaſed him.
21 Therefore Saúl ſaid, I wil giue him her,
that ſhe may be a [i] ſnare to him, and that
the hād of the Philiſtíms may be againſt
hī. Wherefore Saúl ſaid to Dauid, Thou
ſhalt this day be my ſonne in lawe in the
one of the twaine.
22 And Saúl cōmanded his ſeruants, Speake
with Dauid ſecretly, and ſay, Beholde, the
King hathe a fauour to thee, and all his
ſeruants loue thee: be now therefore the
Kings ſonne in lawe.
23 And Sauls ſeruants ſpake theſe wordes
in the eares of Dauid. And Dauid ſaid,
[k] Semeth it to you a light thing to be a
Kings ſonne in lawe, ſeing that I am a
poore man and of ſmall reputacion?
24 And then Sauls ſeruants broght him
worde againe, ſaying, Suche wordes ſpake
Dauid.
25 And Saúl ſaid, This wiſe ſhal ye ſay to
Dauid, The King deſireth no dowrie, but
an hūdreth foreſkinnes of the Philiſtíms,
to be auenged of the Kings enemies: for
Saúl thoght to make Dauid fall into the
hands of the Philiſtíms.
26 And when his ſeruāts tolde Dauid theſe
wordes, it pleaſed Dauid wel, to be the
[l] Kings ſonne in lawe: and the daies were
not expired.
27 Afterwarde Dauid aroſe with his men,
and went and ſlewe of the Philiſtíms two
hundreth men: and Dauid broght their
foreſkinnes, and [m] thei gaue them wholy
to the King that he might be the Kings
ſonne in lawe: therefore Saúl gaue him
Michál his daughter to wife.
28 Then Saúl ſawe, & vnderſtode that the
Lord *was* with Dauid, & that Michál the
daughter of Saúl loued him.
29 Thē Saúl was more & more [n] afraied of

a His affection was fully bent toward him.
b That is, he proſpered in all his doings.
c To wit, Goliáth.
* Ebr. anſwered, playing. Chap. 21,11. & 29,5. eccleſ. 47,7.
d Becauſe he bare him euie & hatred.
e That is, ſpake as a mā beſide him ſelfe: for ſo the people abuſed this worde, when thei colde not vnderſtand.
f Meaning, he was captaine ouer ÿ people.
g Fight againſt them ÿ warre againſt Gods people.
h By whome he had fiue ſonnes, which Dauid put to death at the requeſt of the Gibeonites, 2. Sam. 21,8.
i So his hypocriſie appeareth: for vnder pretence of fauour he ſoght his deſtructiō.
k Meaning, ÿ he was not able to endowe his wife with riches.
l Becauſe he thoght him ſelfe able to compaſſe the Kings requeſt.
m Meaning, Dauid and his ſoldiers.
n To be depriued of his kingdome.

Dauid, and Saúl became alway Dauids
enemy.
30 And when the princes of the Philistíms
went forthe, at their going forthe [o] Dauid behaued him selfe more wisely then
all the seruantes of Saúl, so that his name
was muche set by.

o That is Dauid had better successe agaist the Philistims then Sauls mē.

CHAP. XIX.

2 Ionathán declareth to Dauid the wicked purpose of Saúl. 11 Michál his wife saueth him. 18 Dauid commeth to Samuél. 23 The Spirit of prophecie commeth on Saúl.

1 THen Saúl spake to Ionathán his sonne, and to all his seruants, that they
shulde [a] kil Dauid: but Ionathán Sauls
sonne had a great fauour to Dauid.
2 And Ionathán tolde Dauid, saying, Saúl
my father goeth about to slaye thee: now
therefore, I pray thee, take hede vnto thy
selfe vnto the morning, and abide in a secret *place*, and hide thy selfe.
3 And I wil go out, and stand by my father
in the field where thou [b] art, and wil cōmune with my father of thee, and I wil se
what *he saith* and wil tel thee.
4 ¶ And Ionathán spake good of Dauid
vnto Saúl his father, and said vnto him,
Let not the King sinne against his seruāt,
against Dauid: for he hathe not sinned a-
gainst thee, but his workes haue bene to
thee very good.
5 For he "did * put his life in danger, and
slewe the Philistím, and the Lord wroght
a great saluation for all Israél: thou sawest
it, and thou reioysedst: wherefore then
wilt thou sinne against innocent blood, &
slaye Dauid without a cause?
6 Then Saúl hearkened vnto the voyce of
Ionathán, and Saúl [c] sware, As the Lord
liueth, he shal not dye.
7 So Ionathán called Dauid, and Ionathán shewed him all those wordes, & Ionathán broght Dauid to Saúl, and he was
in his presence as in times past.
8 ¶ Againe the warre began, and Dauid wēt
out and foght with the Philistíms, and
slewe them with a great slaughter, & they
fled from him.
9 ¶ And the euil Spirit of the Lord was
vpō Saúl, as he sate in his house hauing his
speare in his hand, and Dauid [d] played
with his hand.
10 And Saúl entended to smite Dauid to
the wall with the speare: but he turned a-
side out of Sauls presence, and he smote
the speare against the wall: but Dauid fled,
and escaped the same night.
11 Saúl also sent messengers vnto Dauids
house, to watche him, and to slaye him in
the morning: & Michál Dauids wife tolde
it him, saying, If thou saue not thy self
this night, tomorowe thou shalt be slaine.
12 So Michál [e] let Dauid downe through
a windowe: and he went, and fled, and
escaped.
13 Then Michál toke an image and layed
it in the bed, and put a pillowe stuffed with
goates *heere* vnder the head of it, and couered it with a cloth.
14 And when Saúl sent messengers to take
Dauid, she said, He is sicke.
15 And Saúl sent the messengers againe to
se Dauid, saying, Bring him to me in the
[f] bed, that I may slaye him.
16 And when the messengers were come in,
beholde, an image *was* in the bed, with
a pillowe of goates *heere* vnder the head
of it.
17 And Saúl said vnto Michál, Why hast
thou mocked me so, and sent away mine
enemy, that he is escaped? And Michál answered Saúl, He said vnto me, Let me go,
or els I wil kil thee.
18 ¶ So Dauid fled, and escaped, and came
to Samuél to Ramáh, and tolde him all
that Saúl had done to him: and he and Samuél went and dwelt in [g] Naióth.
19 But one tolde Saúl, saying, Beholde, Dauid *is* at Naióth in Ramáh.
20 And Saúl sent messengers to take Dauid: and when they sawe a companie of
Prophets prophecying, and Samuél standing [h] as appointed ouer them, the Spirit of God fel vpon the messengers of
Saúl, and they also [i] prophecied.
21 And whē it was tolde Saúl, he sent other
messengers, and they prophecied likewise:
againe Saúl sent the third messengers, and
they prophecied also.
22 Then went he him self to Ramáh, and
came to a great wel that is in Sechú, and
he asked, and said, Where are Samuél and
Dauid? and one said, Beholde, *they be* at
Naióth in Ramáh.
23 And he [k] went thither, *euen* to Naióth
in Ramáh, and the Spirit of God came
vpon him also, and he went prophecying
vntil he came to Naióth in Ramáh.
24 And he stript of his [l] clothes, and he
prophecied also before Samuél, and fel
[m] downe naked all that day and all that
night: therefore they say, * Is Saúl also a-
mong the Prophetes?

a Before Saúl soght Dauids life secretly, but now his hypocrisie bursteth forth to open crueltie.

b That I may giue thee warning what to do.

"Ebr. he put his soule in his hand.
Iudg.12,3.
1.sam 27,21.
psal.119,109.

c Whatsoeuer he pretended outwardly, yet his heart was ful of malice.

d He plaide on his harpe to mitigate ỹ rage of the euil Spirit, as Chap.16,23.

e Thus God moued bothe the sonne and daughter of this tyrant to fauour Dauid against their father.

f Beholde, how ỹ tyrāts to accomplish their rage, nether regarde othe nor frēdship, God nor man.

g Naióth was a schole where the worde of God was studyed, nere to Ramáh.

h Being their chief instructer.

i Chāged their mindes and praised God.

k With a minde to persecute them.

l His kingly apparel.

m He hūbled him selfe as other did.
Chap.10,11.

CHAP. XX.

1 Ionathán comforteth Dauid. 3 They renue their league. 33 Saúl wolde haue killed Ionathán. 38 Ionathán aduertiseth Dauid by thre arrowes of his fathers fury.

1 ANd Dauid [a] fled from Naióth in
Ramáh, and came and said before
Ionathán, What haue I done? what *is*
mine iniquitie? and what sinne haue I
committed before thy father, that he seketh my life?
2 And he said vnto him, God forbid, thou
shalt not dye: beholde, my father wil do

a For Saúl was stayed, & prophecied a day & a night by Gods prouidence, that Dauid might haue time to escape.

nothing great nor smale, but he wil "shew
it me: and why shulde my father hide this
thing from me? he wil not do it.

" Ebr. reueile it in mine eare.

3 And Dauid sware againe and said, Thy
father knoweth that I haue founde grace
in thine eyes: therefore he thinketh, Ionathán shal not knowe it, lest he be sory: but
in dede, as the Lord liueth, and as thy soule liueth, there is but a [b] steppe betwene
me and death.

b I am in great danger of death.

4 Then said Ionathán vnto Dauid, Whatsoeuer thy soule" requireth, that I wil do
vnto thee.

" Ebr. sayeth.

5 And Dauid said vnto Ionathán, Beholde,
tomorowe is the [c] first day of the moneth,
and I shulde sit with the King at meat:
but let me go, that I may hide my selfe in
the fields vnto the third *day* at euen.

c At what time there shulde be a solẽne sacrifice, Nõb. 28, 11: to the w they added peace offrings and feasts.

6 If thy father make mencion of me, then
say, Dauid asked leaue of me, ỹ he might
go to Beth-léhẽ to his owne citie: for there
is a [d] yerely sacrifice for all that familie.

d Read Chap. 1, 21.

7 And if he say thus, It is wel, thy seruant
shal haue peace: but if he be angry, be sure
that wickednes is concluded of him.
8 So shalt thou shewe mercy vnto thy seruant: * for thou hast ioyned thy seruant
into a couenant of the Lord with thee, &
if there be in me iniquitie, slaye thou me:
for why shuldest thou bring me to thy
father?

Chap. 18, 3. & 23, 18.

9 ¶ And Ionathán answered, God kepe ỹ
from thee: for if I knewe that wickednes
were [e] concluded of my father to come
vpon thee, wolde not I tel it thee?

e That he were fully determined.

10 Thẽ said Dauid to Ionathán, Who [f] shal
tel me? how *shal I knowe*, if thy father answere thee cruelly?

f If thy father do fauour me.

11 And Ionathán said to Dauid, Come
and let vs go out into the field: and they
twaine went out into the field.
12 Then Ionathán said to Dauid, O Lord
God of Israél, when I haue groped my fathers minde tomorowe at this time, *or*
with in this thre dayes, & if it be wel with
Dauid, and I then send not vnto thee, and
shewe it thee,
13 The Lord [g] do so & muche more vnto
Ionathán: but if my father haue minde to
do thee euil, I wil shewe thee also, & send
thee away, that thou mayest go in peace:
and the Lord be with thee as he hathe bene with my father.

g The Lord punishe me moste grieuously.

14 Likewise *I require* not whiles I liue: *for I
dout not* but thou wilt shewe me the mercy
of the Lord, [h] *that I dye not.*
15 But *I require* that thou cut not of thy mercie from mine house for euer: no, not whẽ
the Lord hathe destroyed the enemies of
Dauid, euerie one from the earth.
16 So Ionathán made a bonde with the
house of Dauid, *saying*, Let the Lord require it at the hands of Dauids enemies.

h I knowe ỹ if thou werest now preferred to ỹ kyngdome, thou woldest not destroy me, but shewe thy selfe friendly to my posteritie.

17 And againe Ionathán sware vnto Dauid,
because he loued him (for he loued him
as his owne soule)
18 Thẽ said Ionathán to him, Tomorowe
is ỹ first day of the moneth: and thou shalt
"be looked for, for thy place shalbe empty.

" Or, mencioned.

19 Therefore thou shalt hide thy selfe thre
dayes, *then* thou shalt go downe quickely
and come to the place where thou didest
hide thy selfe, when this matter was in
hand, & shalt remaine by the stone "Ezél.
20 And I wil shoote thre arrowes on the
side thereof, as thogh I shot at a marke.

" Ebr. of the way, because it serued as a signe to shewe the way to thẽ that passed by.

21 And after I wil send a boy, *saying*, Go, seke the arrowes. If I say vnto the boy, Se, ỹ
arrowes are on this side thee, bring them,
and come thou: for it is " wel with thee
and no hurt, *as* the Lord liueth.

" Ebr. peace.

22 But if I say thus vnto the boy, Beholde,
the arrowes are beyonde thee, go thy way:
for the [i] Lord hathe sent thee away.

i The Lord is the autour of thy departure.

23 As touching the thing which thou and
I haue spoken of, beholde, the Lord *be*
betwene thee and me for euer.
24 ¶ So Dauid hid him selfe in the field: &
when the first day of the moneth came,
the King sate to eat meat.
25 And the King sate, as at other times vpõ
his seat, euen vpon his seat by the wall: &
Ionathán arose, and Abnér sate by Sauls
side, but Dauids place was empty.
26 And Saúl said nothing that day: for he
thoght, Some thing hathe befallen him,
thogh he were [k] cleane, *or els* because he
was not purified.

k Yet he might haue some busines to let him.

27 But on the morowe which was the secõd
day of the moneth, Dauids place was emptie againe: and Saúl said vnto Ionathán
his sonne, Wherefore commeth not the
sonne of [l] Ishái to meat, nether yesterday
nor to day?

l Thus he speaketh contempteously of Dauid.

28 And Ionathán answered vnto Saúl, Dauid required of me, *that he might go* to Beth-
léhem.
29 For he said, Let me go, I pray thee: for
our familie *offreth* [m] a sacrifice in the citie, and my brother hathe sent for me:
therefore now if I haue found fauour in
thine eyes, let me go, I pray thee, & se my
[n] brethrẽ: this is the cause that he cõmeth
not vnto the Kings table.

m That is a peace offring.

n Meaning all his kinsfolke.

30 Then was Saúl angry with Ionathán, &
said vnto him, Thou [o] sonne of the wicked rebellious woman, do not I knowe,
that thou hast chosen the sonne of Ishái
to thy confusion and to the confusion *and*
shame of thy mother?

o Thou art euer contrary vnto me as thy mother is.

31 For as long as the sonne of Ishái liueth
vpon the earth, thou shalt not be stablished, nor thy kingdome: wherefore now
send and fet him vnto me, for he " shal
surely dye.

" Ebr. sonne of death.

32 And Ionathán answered vnto Saúl his
father,

p For it were to great tyrãnie to put one to death and not to shewe ŷ cause why.

father, and said vnto him, Wherefore shal
he p dye? what hathe he done?
33 And Saúl cast a speare at him to hit him,
whereby Ionathán knewe, that it was determined of his father to slaye Dauid.
34 ¶ So Ionathán arose from the table in a
great angre, and did eat no meat the secõd
day of the moneth: for he was sory for
Dauid, *and* because his father had reuiled him.

q For this was the third day, as it was agreed vpon, vers. 5.

35 On the next morning therefore Ionathán went out into the field, q at the time
appointed with Dauid, and a litle boy
with him.
36 And he said vnto his boy, Runne now,
seke the arrowes which I shoote, & as the
boy ran, he shot an arrowe beyonde him.
37 And when the boy was come to the place where the arrowe was that Ionathán
had shot, Ionathán cryed after the boy, &
said, Is not the arrowe beyond thee?

r By these wordes he admonished Dauid what he oght to do.

38 And Ionathán cryed after the boy, r Make spede, haste *and* stand not stil: and Ionathãs boy gathered vp the arrowes, and
came to his master,
39 But the boy knewe nothing: onely Ionathán and Dauid knewe the matter.

"Ebr. instruments.

40 Then Ionathán gaue his "bowe and arrowes vnto the boy that was with him,
& said vnto him, Go, carie them into the
citie.

f It semeth ŷ he had shot on the Northside of the stone, lest the boy shulde haue espied Dauid.

41 ¶ Assone as the boy was gone, Dauid
arose out of a place that was towarde the
f South, and fel on his face to the ground,
and bowed him selfe thre times: and they
kyssed one an other, and wept bothe twaine, til Dauid exceded.

t Which othe he calleth in the eight verse the couenãt of the Lord.

42 Therefore Ionathán said to Dauid, Go
in peace: that which we haue t sworne
bothe of vs in the Name of the Lord,
saying, The Lord be betwene me & thee,
and betwene my seede and betwene thy seede, *let it stand* for euer.
43 And he arose and departed, and Ionathán went into the citie.

CHAP. XXI.

1 Dauid fleeth to Nob to Ahimélech the Priest. 6 He getteth of him the shewbread to satisfie his hungre. 7 Doég Sauls seruant was present. 10 Dauid fleeth to King Achish, 13 And there faineth him selfe mad.

a Where the Arke thẽ was, to aske cõsel of the Lord.

1 THen came Dauid to a Nob, to Ahimélech the Priest, and Ahimélech was
astonyed at the meting of Dauid, and said
vnto him, Why art thou alone, and no mã
with thee?

b These infirmities that we se in the saints of God, teache vs that none hathe his iustice in him selfe, but receiueth it of Gods mercie.

2 And Dauid said to Ahimélech the Priest,
The b King hathe commanded me a certeine thing, and hathe said vnto me, Let
no man knowe whereabout I send thee, &
what I haue commanded thee, and I haue
appointed my seruants to suche *and* suche
places.
3 Now therefore if thou hast oght vnder
thine hand, giue me fiue *cakes of* bread, or
what commeth to hand.
4 And the Priest answered Dauid, & said,
There is no commune bread vnder mine
hand, but here is *halowed bread, if ŷ yong
men haue kept them selues, at least from
c women.

Exod 25,30. leu. 24,5. mat. 12,3.

c If they haue not companied wt their wiues.

5 Dauid then answered the Priest, and said
vnto him, Certeinly women haue bene separate frõ vs these two or thre dayes since I came out: and the d vessels of ŷ yong
men were holy, thogh the way were prophane, & how muche more then shal *euery
one* e be sanctified this day in the vessel?

d That is, their bodies.

e Shalbe more careful to kepe his vessel holy, when he shal haue eatẽ of this holy foode?

6 So the Priest gaue him halowed *bread*: for
there was no bread there, saue the shewbread that was takẽ from before the Lord,
to put hote bread there, the day that it was
taken away.
7 (And there was the same day one of the
seruãts of Saúl f abiding before the Lord,
named Doég the Edomite, the "chiefest of
Sauls herdemen)

f Tarying to worship before the Arke.

"Or, master of them that kept Sauls cattel.

8 And Dauid said vnto Ahimélech, Is there not here vnder thine hand a speare or a
sworde? for I haue nether broght my sworde nor mine harnes with me, because the
Kings busines required haste.
9 And ŷ Priest said, The sworde of Goliáth
the Philistím, whome thou slewest in the
*valley of Eláh, beholde, it is wrapt in a
clothe behinde the g Ephôd: if thou wilt
take that to thee, take it: for there is none
other saue that here, & Dauid said, There
is none to that, giue it me.

Chap. 17,2.

g Behide that place, where ŷ hie Priests garment lay.

10 And Dauid arose & fled the same day
from the h presence of Saúl, & went to A-
chísh the King of Gath.

h That is, out of Sauls dominion.

11 And the seruants of Achísh said vnto hĩ,
Is not this Dauid the *King of the land?
did they not sing vnto him in dances, saying, *Saúl hathe slaine his thousand, & Da
uid his ten thousand?

Chap. 17,9.

Chap. 18,7. & 29,5. eccles. 47,7.

12 And Dauid "considered these wordes,
& was sore afraid of Achísh the King of
Gath.

"Ebr. put these wordes in his heart.

13 And he chãged his behauiour before thẽ,
and fained him selfe mad in their hands,
& i scrabled on the dores of the gate, &
let his spetle fall downe vpon his bearde.

i By making markes and toyes.

14 Then said Achísh vnto his seruants, Lo,
ye se the mã is beside him selfe, wherefore
haue ye broght him to me?
15 Haue I nede of mad men, that ye haue
broght this fellowe to play the mad man
in my presence? k shal he come into mine
house?

k Is he mete to be in a Kings house?

CHAP. XXII.

1 Dauid hideth him selfe in a caue. 2 Many that were in trouble came vnto him. 9 Doég accuseth Ahimélech. 18 Saúl causeth the Priests to be slaine. 20 Abiathár escapeth.

1 DAuid therefore departed thence, and
saued him selfe in the caue [a] of A-
dullám: and when his brethren and all his
fathers house heard it, they went downe
thither to him.

a Which was in the tribe of Iudáh and nere to Beth-léhem.

2 And there gathered vnto him all mẽ that
were in trouble and all men that were in
det, & all those that were vexed in minde,
and he was their "prince, and there were
with him about foure hundreth men.

"Or, captaine.

3 ¶And Dauid went thence to Mizpéh in
[b] Moáb, and said vnto the King of Moáb,
I pray thee, let my father and my mother
come *and abide* with you, til I knowe what
God wil do for me.

b For there was another so called in Iudáh.

4 And he [c] broght them before the King
of Moáb, and they dwelt with him all the
while that Dauid kept him selfe in [d] the
holde.

c For he feared the rage of Saúl against his house.
d That is, in Mizpéh, which was a strong holde.

5 And the Prophet Gad said vnto Dauid,
Abide not in the holde, *but* departe & go
into the lãd of Iudáh. Thẽ Dauid departed and came into the forest of Háreth.

6 ¶And Saúl heard that Dauid was [e] discouered, and the men that were with him,
and Saúl remained in Gibeáh vnder a tre
in Ramáh, hauing his speare in his hand,
and all his men stode about him.

e That a great brute went on him.

7 And Saúl said vnto his seruãts that stode
about him, Heare now, ye sonnes [f] of Ieminí, wil the sonne of Ishái giue euerie
one of you fields and vineyardes? wil he
make you all captaines ouer thousands, &
captaines ouer hundreths?

f Ye that are of my tribe & linage.

8 That all ye haue cõspired against me, and
there is none that telleth me that my sonne hathe made a couenant with ÿ sonne of
Ishái? & there is none of you that is sory
for me, or sheweth me, that my [g] sonne
hathe stirred vp my seruant to lye in wait
against me, as *appeareth* this day.

g Hereby he wolde persuade the ÿ this cõspiracie was more horrible, where the sonne conspired against the father, and the seruant against his master.

9 ¶Thẽ answered Doég the Edomite (who
was appointed ouer the seruants of Saúl)
and said, I sawe the sonne of Ishái when
he came to Nob, to Ahimélech the sonne
of Ahitúb,

10 Who asked counsel of the Lord for him
& gaue him vitails, and he gaue him also
the sworde of Goliáth the Philistím.

11 Then the King sent to call Ahimélech
the Priest the sonne of Ahitúb, and all
his fathers house, *to wit*, [h] the Priests that
were in Nob: and they came all to the
King.

h Which were the remnant of the house of Elí, whose house God threatened to punishe.

12 And Saúl said, Heare now thou sonne
of Ahitúb. And he answered, Here I am,
my lord.

13 Then Saúl said vnto him, Why haue ye
conspired against me, thou and the sonne
of Ishái, in that thou hast giuen him vitaile, and a sworde, and hast asked counsel of
God for him, that he shulde rise against
me, & lye in waite as appeareth this day?

14 ¶And Ahimélech answered the King, &
said, Who is so faithful among all thy seruãts as Dauid, *being* also the Kings sonne
in lawe, & goeth at thy commandement,
and is honorable in thine house?

15 [i] Haue I this day first begon to aske counsel of God for him? be it far frõ me, let
not the King impute any thing vnto his
seruant, nor to all the house of my father:
for thy seruant knewe nothing of all this,
lesse nor more.

i Haue I not at other times also, whẽ he had great affaires, consulted w the Lord for him?

16 Then the King said, Thou shalt surely
dye, Ahimélech, thou, and all thy fathers
house.

17 And the King said vnto the "sergents
that stode about him, Turne, & slaye the
Priests of the Lord, because their hand also is with Dauid, and because they knewe
when he fled, and shewed it not to me. But
the seruãts of the King [k] wolde not moue
their hands to fall vpon the Priests of the
Lord.

"Or, footemen.

k For thei knewe ÿ thei oght not to obey ÿ wicked cõmandement of the King in slaying ÿ innocents.

18 Thẽ the King said to Doég, Turne thou
and fall vpon the Priests. And Doég the
Edomite turned, and ran vpon the Priests,
and slewe that same day foure score and
fiue persones that did weare a linen
Ephód.

19 Also Nob the citie of the Priests smote
he with the edge of the sworde, bothe
man and woman, bothe childe and suck-
ling, bothe oxe and asse, and shepe with
the edge of the sworde.

20 But one of the sonnes of Ahimélech the
sonne of Ahitúb (whose name *was* Abiathár) [l] escaped and fled after Dauid.

l This was Gods prouidence, who according to his promes preserued some of the house of Elí, Chap. 2, 33.

21 And Abiathár shewed Dauid, that Saúl
had slaine the Lords Priests.

22 And Dauid said vnto Abiathár, I knewe
it the same day, when Doég the Edomite
was there, that he wolde tel Saúl. I am the
cause *of the death* of all the persones of
thy fathers house.

23 Abide thou with me, *&* feare not: for
"he that seketh my life, shal seke thy life
also: for with me thou shalt be in sauegarde.

"Or, he that seketh thy life, shal take mine also.

CHAP. XXIII.

5 Dauid chaseth the Philistims from Keiláh. 13 Dauid departeth from Keiláh, and remaineth in the wildernes of Ziph. 16 Ionathán comforteth Dauid. 28 Sauls entreprise is broken in pursuing Dauid.

1 THen they tolde Dauid, saying, Beholde, the Philistíms fight against
[a] Keiláh, and spoyle the barnes.

a Which was a citie in the tribe of Iudáh, Iosh. 15, 44.

2 Therefore Dauid asked coũsel of ÿ Lord,
saying, Shal I go and smite these Philistíms? And the Lord answered Dauid, Go
and smite the Philistíms, and saue Keiláh.

3 And Dauids men said vnto him, Se, we be
afraied here in [b] Iudáh, how muche more
if we come to Keiláh against the hoste of
the

b That is, in ÿ middes of Iudáh, muche more whẽ we come to ÿ borders against our enemies.

the Philistíms?
4 Then Dauid asked counsel of the Lord
againe. And the Lord answered him, and
said, Arise, go downe to Keiláh: for I wil
deliuer the Philistíms into thine hand.
5 ¶ So Dauid and his men went to Keiláh,
and foght with the Philistíms, and broght
away theyr cattel, and smote them with a
great slaughter: thus Dauid saued the inhabitants of Keiláh.
6 (And whẽ Abiathár the sonne of Ahimé
lech * fled to Dauid to Keiláh, he broght
an [c] Ephód "with him)
7 ¶ And it was tolde Saúl that Dauid was
come to Keiláh, and Saúl said, God hathe
deliuered him into mine hand: for he is
shut in, seing he is come into a citie that
hathe gates and barres.
8 Thẽ Saúl called all the people together
to warre, for to go downe to Keiláh, and
to besiege Dauid and his men.
9 ¶ And Dauid hauing knowledge that Saúl imagined mischief against him, said to
Abiathár the Priest, [d] Bring the Ephód.
10 Then said Dauid, O Lord God of Israél, thy seruant hathe heard, that Saúl is
about to come to Keiláh to destroy the citie for my sake.
11 Wil the lords of Keiláh deliuer me
vp into his hãd? and wil Saúl come downe,
as thy seruant hathe heard? O Lord God
of Israél, I beseche thee, tel thy seruant.
And the Lord said, He wil come downe.
12 Thẽ said Dauid, Wil the "lords of Keiláh deliuer me vp and the men that are
with me, into the hand of Saúl? And the
Lord said, They wil deliuer thee vp.
13 ¶ Then Dauid and his men, which were
about six hundreth, arose, and departed out
of Keiláh, and went" whither they colde.
And it was tolde Saúl, that Dauid was fled
from Keiláh, and he left of his iourney.
14 And Dauid abode in the wildernes in
"holdes, and remained in a mountaine in
the wildernes of Ziph. And Saúl soght
him euerie day, but God [e] deliuered him
not into his hand.
15 And Dauid sawe that Saúl was come out
for to seke his life: & Dauid *was* in the wil
dernes of Ziph in the wood.
16 ¶ And Ionathán Sauls sonne arose and
went to Dauid into the wood, and comforted "him in God,
17 And said vnto him, Feare not: for the
hãd of Saúl my father shal not finde thee,
and thou shalt be [f] King ouer Israél, and I
shal be next vnto thee: and also Saúl my
father knoweth it.
18 So they twaine made a couenant before
the Lord: and Dauid did remaine in the
wood: but Ionathán went to his house.
19 ¶ Then came vp the Ziphíms to Saúl to
Gibeáh, sayĩg, Doeth not Dauid hide him

Chap.22,20.
c By Gods prouidence the Ephód was preserued & kept w Dauid the true King.
"Ebr. in his hãd
d To consult w the Lord by Vrim & Thummim.
"Or, gouernours.
"Or, to & fro, as hauing no certeine place to go to.
"Or, strõg places
e No power nor policie cã preuaile agaist Gods childrẽ, but when he appointeth ẏ time.
"Ebr. his hãde.
f Ionathán assureth Dauid, that God wil accõplish his pmes & ẏ his father striueth against his owne cõscience.

selfe by vs in holdes, in the wood in the
hil of Hachiláh, which is on the right side
"of Ieshimon?
20 Now therefore ô King, come downe according to all that thine heart can desire,
& our parte *shalbe* to deliuer him into the
Kings hands.
21 Then Saúl said, [g] Be ye blessed of the
Lord: for ye haue had compassion on
me.
22 Go, I pray you, and prepare yet better:
knowe and se his place where he "hanteth,
and who hathe sene him there: for it is
said to me, He is subtile, and crafty.
23 Se therefore, and knowe all the secret
places where he hideth him selfe, & come
ye againe to me with the certentie, and I
wil go with you: and if he be in the [h] land,
I wil searche him out throughout all the
thousands of Iudáh.
24 Thẽ they arose and went to Ziph before
Saúl, but Dauid and his men *were* in the
wildernes of Maón, in the plaine on the
right hand of Ieshimón.
25 Saúl also and his men went to seke him,
and they tolde Dauid: wherefore he came
downe vnto a rocke, and abode in the wildernes of [i] Maón. And when Saúl heard
that, he followed after Dauid in ẏ wildernes of Maón.
26 And Saúl and his men went on the one
side of the mountaine, and Dauid and his
men on the other side of the mountaine:
and Dauid made haste to get from the
presence of Saúl: for Saúl and his men cõ
passed Dauid & his men round about, to
take them.
27 But there came a [k] messenger to Saúl,
saying, Haste thee, and come: for the Philistíms haue inuaded the land.
28 Wherefore Saúl returned from pursuing Dauid, and went against the Philistíms. Therefore they called that place,
Sela-hammáhlekoth.

CHAP. XXIIII.

1 Dauid hid in a caue spareth Saúl. 10 He sheweth to Saúl his innocẽcie. 18 Saul acknowledgeth his faute. 22 He causeth Dauid to sweare vnto him to be fauorable to his.

1 AND Dauid went thence, and dwelt in
[a] holdes at En-gédi.
2 When Saúl was returned from the Philistíms, they tolde him, saying, Beholde,
Dauid *is* in the wildernes of [b] En-gédi.
3 Then Saúl toke thre thousand chosen
men out of all Israél, and went to seke Dauid and his men vpon the rockes *among* the
wilde goates.
4 And he came to the shepecoates by the
way where there was a caue and Saúl wẽt
in "to do his easement: and Dauid and
his men sate in the "inward partes of the
caue.

"Or, of the wildernes.
g The Lord recompence this friendship.
"Ebr. where his fote hathe bene.
h In your cõtrey of Ziph, w is in Iudah.
i Which was also in ẏ tribe of Iudáh, Iosh. 15,55.
k Thus ẏ Lord cã pul backe the bridel of the tyrants, & deliuer his out of the lions mouthe.
a That is, in strong places, w were defensed by nature.
b A citie of Iudáh, Iosh. 15,62.
"Ebr. to couer his fete.
"Ebr. in the sides.

c Here we se how ready we are to hasten Gods promes, if ye occasion serue neuer so litle.

5 And the men of Dauid said vnto him, Se,
the day is c come, whereof the Lord said
vnto thee, Beholde, I wil deliuer thine e-
nemie into thine hand, and thou shalt do
to him as it shal seme good to thee. Then
Dauid arose and cut of the lappe of Sauls
garment priuely.

d For seing it was his owne priuate cause, he repented yt he had touched his enemie.

6 And afterward Dauid d was touched in
his heart, because he had cut of the lappe
which was on Sauls *garment*.
7 And he said vnto his mē, The Lord kepe
me from doing that thing vnto my master
the Lords Anointed, to lay mine hand vpon him: for he is the Anointed of the
Lord.
8 So Dauid ouercame his seruants wt these
wordes, & suffred them not to arise against
Saúl: so Saúl rose vp out of the caue & wēt
away.
9 ¶ Dauid also arose afterward, & went out
of the caue, and cryed after Saúl, saying,
O my Lord ye King. And when Saúl loked
behinde him, Dauid inclined his face to
the earth, and bowed him selfe.

e Contrary to ye false report of them yt said, Dauid was Sauls enemie, he proueth hi selfe to be his friend.

10 And Dauid said to Saúl, e Wherefore giuest thou an eare to mēs wordes, that say,
Beholde, Dauid seketh euil against thee?
11 Beholde, this day thine eyes haue sene,
that the Lord had deliuered thee this day
into mine hand in the caue, and some bade
me kil thee, but I had compassiō on thee,
and said, I wil not lay mine hand on my
master: for he is the Lords Anointed.
12 Moreouer my father, beholde: beholde, I
say, the lappe of thy garmēt in mine hād:
for whē I cut of the lappe of thy garmēt,
I killed thee not. Vnderstand and se, that
there is nether euil nor wickednes in me,
nether haue I sinned against thee, yet thou
huntest after my soule to take it.
13 The Lord be iudge betwene thee & me,
and the Lord auenge me of thee, and let
not mine hand be vpon thee.

"Or, the prouerbe of an Ancient man.

14 According as the "olde prouerbe saith,
Wickednes procedeth from the wicked,
but mine hand be not vpon thee.
15 After whome is the King of Israél come
out? after whome doest thou pursue? after
a dead dog, & after a flye?
16 The Lord therefore be iudge, & iudge
betwene thee and me, and se, and plead
my cause, and " deliuer me out of thine
hand.

"Ebr. iudge.

17 When Dauid had made an end of speaking these wordes to Saúl, Saúl said, f Is
this thy voyce, my sonne Dauid? and Saúl
lift vp his voyce, and wept,

f Thogh he was a moste cruel enemie to Dauid, yet by his great gentlenes his conscience cōpelled him to yelde.

18 And said to Dauid, Thou art more righteous then I: for thou hast rendred me
good, and I haue rendred thee euil.
19 And thou hast shewed this day, that thou
hast dealt wel with me: forasmucheas whē
the Lord had closed me in thine hands,
thou killedst me not.
20 For who shal finde his enemy, and let
him departe "fre? wherefore the Lord rendre thee good for that thou hast done vnto
me this day.

"Ebr. a good way.

21 For now beholde, I g knowe that yu shalt
be King, and that the kingdome of Israél
shalbe stablished in thine hand.

g Thogh this tyrant saw and confessed the fauour of God toward Dauid, yet he ceaseth not to persecute him against his owne conscience.

22 Sweare now therefore vnto me by the
Lord, that yu wilt not destroy my seede after me, and that thou wilt not abolish my
name out of my fathers house.
23 So Dauid sware vnto Saúl, and Saúl wēt
home: but Dauid and his men went vp vnto the holde.

CHAP. XXV.

1 Samuél dyeth. 3 Nabál & Abigáil. 38 The Lord killeth Nabál. 43 Abigáil & Ahinóam Dauids wiues. 44 Michál is giuen to Phalti.

1 THen * Samuél dyed, and all Israél assembled, and mourned for him, & buryed him in his a owne house at Ramáh.
And Dauid arose and went downe to the
wildernes of Parán.

Chap. 28, 3. eccles. 46, 23.

a That is, amōg his owne kinred.

2 Now in b Maón *was* a man, who had his
possession in Carmél, and the man was
exceding mighty and had thre thousand
shepe, and a thousand goates: and he was
shering his shepe in Carmél.

b Maón and Carmél were cities in ye tribe of Iudáh. Carmél ye mouteine was in Galile.

3 The name also of the man *was* Nabál, &
the name of his wife Abigáil, and she was
a woman of singular wisdome, and beautiful, but the man *was* churlish, and euil cō-
ditioned, and was of the familie of Caléb.
4 And Dauid heard in the wildernes, that
Nabál did shere his shepe.
5 Therefore Dauid sent ten yong men, &
Dauid said vnto the yong men, Go vp to
Carmél, and go to Nabál, and aske him in
my name "how he doeth.

"Ebr. of peace.

6 And thus shal ye say c " for salutation,
Bothe yu, and thine house, and all that thou
hast, be in peace, welth, and prosperitie.

c Some read, so maiest thou liue in prosperitie the next yere, bothe thou, &c.

"Ebr. for life.

7 Beholde, I haue heard, that thou hast sherers: now thy shepherds were with vs, and
we did them no hurt, nether did they misse anie thing all the while they were in
Carmél.
8 Aske thy seruants & they wil shewe thee.
Wherefore let these yōg mē finde fauour
in thine eyes: (for we come in a good season) giue, I praye thee, whatsoeuer d commeth to thine hand vnto thy seruants, &
to thy sonne Dauid.

d Whatsoeuer yu hast ready for vs.

9 ¶ And when Dauids yong men came,
they tolde Nabál all those wordes in the
name of Dauid, and helde their peace.
10 Then Nabál answered Dauids seruāts,
and said, Who is Dauid? and who is the
e sonne of Ishái? there is manie seruants
now a dayes, that breake awaye euery mā
from his master.

e Thus ye couetous wretches, in stede of releuing ye necessitie of Gods children, vse to reuile their persones and condēne their cause.

11 Shal

11 Shal I then take my bread,& my water,
& my flesh that I haue killed for my sherers,and giue it vnto mẽ,whome I knowe
not whence thei be?
12 ¶ So Dauids seruants turned their way,
and went againe,and came,and tolde him
all those things.
13 And Dauid said vnto his men, Girde e-
uery man his sworde *about him*. And they
girded euery man his sworde:Dauid also
girded his sworde. And about foure hundreth men went vp after Dauid, and two
hundreth abode by the "cariage.
14 Now one of the seruants tolde Abigáil
Nabals wife,saying, Beholde, Dauid sent
messengers out of the wildernes to salute
our master,and he"rayled on them.
15 Notwithstanding the men were very
good [f] vnto vs,and we had no displeasure,
nether missed we any thing as long as we
were conuersant with them,when we were
in the fields.
16 Thei were as a wall vnto vs bothe by
night and by day, all the while we were
with them keping shepe.
17 Now therefore take hede, and se what
thou shalt do: for euil" wil surely come
vpon our master,and vpon all his familie:
for he is so wicked ŷ a man can not speake
to him.
18 ¶ Then Abigáil made haste, and toke
two hundreth" cakes, and two bottles of
wine,and fiue shepe ready dressed, & fiue
measures of parched corne, and an hundreth "frailes of raisins, and two hundreth of figges,and laded them on asses.
19 Then she said vnto her seruants, Go ye
before me:beholde, I wil come after you:
yet she tolde [g] not her housband Nabál.
20 And as she rode on her asse, she came
downe by a secret place of the mountaine,
and beholde, Dauid and his men came
downe against her,and she met them.
21 And Dauid said,In dede I haue kept all
in vaine that this fellowe had in the wildernes, so that nothing was missed of all
that perteined vnto him: for he hathe re-
quited me euil for good.
22 So and more also do God vnto the enemies of Dauid: *for* surely I wil not leaue of
all that he hathe, by the dawning of the
day,*any* that [h] pisseth against the wall.
23 And when Abigáil sawe Dauid, she hasted and lighted of her asse, & fel before
Dauid on her face, and bowed her selfe to
the grounde,
24 And fel at his fete,& said, Oh, my lord,
I *haue committed* the iniquitie, and I pray
thee,let thine handmaid speake"to thee,&
heare thou the wordes of thine hãdmayd.
25 Let not my lord, I pray thee, regarde
this wicked man Nabal: for as his name
is,so is he:" Nabál *is* his name, and foly *is*

" Ebr. vessel.
" Ebr. drone thẽ away.
f When we kept our shepe in the wildernes of Parán.
" Ebr is accomplished.
" Ebr. bread.
" Or, clusters.
g Because she knewe his crooked nature, ŷ he wolde rather haue perished, then consented to her enterprise.
h Meaning by this prouerbe, that he wolde destroye bothe smale & great.
" Ebr. in thine eares.
" Or, foole.

with him: but I thine handmayd sawe not
the yong men of my lord whome ŷ sentest.
26 Now therefore my lord, as the Lord liueth,and as thy soule liueth (the Lord, *I*
say,that hathe withholdẽ thee from comming to *shed* blood,and that [i] thine hand
shulde *not* saue thee)so now thine enemies
shalbe as Nabál, and thei that intende to
do my lord euil.
27 And now, this "blessing which thine
handmayd hathe broght vnto my lord,
let it be giuen vnto the yong mẽ,that"followe my lord.
28 I pray thee,forgiue the trespasse of thine handmayd: for the Lord wil make my
lord a [k] sure house,because my lord fighteth the battels of the lord and none euil
hathe bene founde in thee "in all thy life.
29 Yet [l] a man hathe risen vp to persecute
thee,and to seke thy soule, but the soule of
my lord shalbe bounde in the [m] bundel of
life with the Lord thy God:and the soule
of thine enemies shal *God* cast out, as out
of the midle of a sling.
30 And when the Lord shal haue done to
my lord all the good that he hathe promised thee, and shal haue made thee ruler
ouer Israél,
31 Then shal it be no grief vnto thee, nor
offence of minde vnto my lord, that he
hathe not shed blood causeles, nor that
my lord hathe [n] *not* preserued him selfe:&
whẽ the Lord shal haue dealt wel with my
lord,remember thine handmayd.
32 Then Dauid said to Abigáil, Blessed be
the Lord God of Israél, which sent thee
this day to mete me.
33 And blessed be thy counsel, and blessed
be thou, which haste kept me this day frõ
comming to *shed* blood, [o] and that mine
hand hathe *not* saued me.
34 For in dede, as the Lord God of Israél
liueth, [p] who hathe kept me backe from
hurting thee, except thou haddest hasted
and met me,surely there had not bene left
vnto Nabál by the dawning of the day,"
any that pisseth against the wall.
35 Then Dauid receiued of her hand that
which she had broght him, & said to her,
Go vp in peace to thine house:beholde, I
haue heard thy voyce,and haue "granted
thy peticion.
36 ¶ So Abigáil came to Nabál,& beholde,
he made a feast in his house,like the feast
of a King, and Nabals heart was mery
within him,for he was very drõken: wherefore she tolde him [q] nothing, nether
lesse nor more,vntil the morning arose.
37 Then in the morning when the wine
was gone out of Nabál, his wife tolde
him those wordes, & his heart dyed within him,and he was like [r] a stone.
38 And about ten daies after, the Lord

i That is, that thou shuldest not be reuẽged of thine enemie.
" Or, present.
" Ebr. walke at the fete.
k Cõfirme his kingdome to his posteritie.
" Ebr. from thy daies.
l To wit, Saúl.
m God shal preserue thee lõg in his seruice and destroye thine enemies.
n That he hathe not auẽged him selfe, which things wolde haue tormented his conscience.
o Read vers. 26
p He attributeth it to the Lords mercie, & not to him self ŷ he was staied.
" Ebr. receiued thy face.
q For he had no raison to consider, or giue thankes for this great benefite of deliuerance.
r For feare of ŷ great dãger.

smote Nabál, that he dyed.
39 ¶ Now when Dauid heard, that Nabál
was dead, he said, Blessed be the Lord that
hathe " iudged the cause of my rebuke of
the hand of Nabál, & hathe kept his seruant from euil: for the Lord hathe recompensed the wickednes of Nabál vpon his
owne head. Also Dauid sent to commune
with Abigáil to [f] take her to his wife.
40 And when the seruants of Dauid were
come to Abigáil to Carmél, they spake
vnto her, saying, Dauid sent vs to thee, to
take thee to his wife.
41 And she arose, and bowed her self on her
face to the earth, & said, Beholde, let thy
handmayd be a seruant to wash the fete of
the seruants of my lord.
42 And Abigáil hasted, and arose, and rode
vpon an asse, & her fiue maids " followed
her, and she went after the messengers of
Dauid, and was his wife.
43 * Dauid also toke Ahinóam of * Izreél, &
thei were bothe his wiues.
44 Now Saúl had giuē * Michál his daughter Dauids wife to Phaltí the sonne of
Láish, which was of [c] Gallím.

"Or, reuenged.

f For he had experience of her great godlines, wisdome & humilitie.

"Ebr. went at her fete.

Iosh. 15, 55.

2. Sam. 3, 15.

c Which was a place bordering on the countrey of ẏ Moabites.

CHAP. XXVI.

1 *Dauid was discouered vnto Saúl by the Ziphims.*
12 Dauid taketh awaye Sauls speare, and a pot of
water that stode at his head. 21 Saúl cōfesseth his sinne.

1 AGaine the Ziphims came vnto Saúl to Gibeáh, saying, * Doeth not
Dauid hide him selfe " in the hil of Hachiláh before " Ieshimón?
2 Then Saúl arose, and went downe to the
wildernes of Ziph, hauing thre thousand
[a] chosen men of Israél with him, for to
seke Dauid in the wildernes of Ziph.
3 And Saúl pitched in the hil of Hachiláh,
which is before Ieshimón by the waye
side. Now Dauid abode in the wildernes,
and he sawe that Saúl came after him into the wildernes.
4 (For Dauid had sent out spies, & vnderstode, that Saúl was come " in very dede)
5 Then Dauid arose, and came to the place
where Saúl had pitched, and *when* Dauid
beheld the place where Saúl lay, & * Abnér the sonne of Ner which was his chief
captaine, (for Saúl lay in the forte, and the
people pitched round about him.)
6 Then spake Dauid, & said to Ahimélech
the [b] Hittite, and to Abishái the sonne
of Zeruiáh, brother to [c] Ioáb, saying,
Who wil go downe with me to Saúl to
the hoste? Then Abishái said, I wil go
downe with thee.
7 So Dauid & Abishái came downe to the
people by night: and beholde, Saúl laye
sleping within the forte, & his speare did
sticke in the grounde at his " head: and
Abnér and the people lay round-about
him.

Chap. 23, 19.

"Or, in Gibeáh.

"Or, the wildernes.

a That is, of ẏ moste skilful and valiant soldiers.

"Or, to a certeine place.

Chap. 14, 50. & 17, 55.

b Who was a stranger & not an Israelite.

c Who afterwarde was Dauids chief captaine.

"Or, bolster.

8 ¶ Thē said Abishái to Dauid, God hathe
closed thine enemie into thine hand this
day: now therefore, I pray thee, let me
smite him once with a speare to ẏ earth,
and I wil not smite him [d] againe.
9 And Dauid said to Abishái, Destroye
him not: for who can lay his hande [e] on the
Lords anointed, and be giltles?
10 Moreouer Dauid said, As the Lord liueth, ether the Lord shal smite him, or his
day shal come to dye, or he shal descende
into battel, and perish.
11 The Lord kepe me from laying mine
hand vpō the Lords anointed: but, I pray
thee, take now the speare that is at his
head, and the pot of water, and let vs go
hence.
12 So Dauid toke the speare and the pot of
water from Sauls head, & thei gate them
away, and no man sawe it, nor marked it,
nether did any awake, but thei were all a-
slepe: for " the Lord had sent a dead slepe
vpon them.
13 Then Dauid went into the other side, &
stode on ẏ toppe of an hil a far of, a great
space being betwene them.
14 And Dauid cryed to the people, and to
Abnér the sonne of Ner, saying, " Hearest
thou not Abnér? Then Abnér answered,
and said, Who art thou that cryest to the
King?
15 ¶ And Dauid said to Abnér, Art not ẏ "
a [f] man? and who is like thee in Israél?
wherefore then hast thou not kept thy
lord the King? for there came one of the
folke in to destroye the King thy lord.
16 This is not wel done of thee: as the Lord
liueth, ye are " worthy to dye, because ye
haue not kept your master the Lords Anointed: and now se where the Kings speare is, and the pot of water that was at his
head.
17 And Saúl knewe Dauids voyce, & said,
Is this thy voyce, [g] my sonne Dauid? And
Dauid said, It is my voyce, my lord ô
King.
18 And he said, Wherefore doeth my lord
thus persecute his seruant? for what haue I
done? or what euil is in mine hand?
19 Now therefore, I beseche thee, let my
lord the King heare the wordes of his seruant. If the Lord haue stirred thee vp a-
gainst me, [h] let him smel the sauour of a
sacrifice: but if the children of men *haue*
done it, cursed be thei before the Lord: for
thei haue cast me out this day frō abiding
in the inheritāce of the Lord, saying, Go,
serue other [i] gods.
20 Now therefore let not my blood fall to
the earth before the face of the Lord: for
the King of Israél is come out to seke a
flye, as one wolde hunt a partriche in the
mountaines.

d Meaning, he wolde make him sure at one stroke.

e To wit, in his owne priuate cause: for Iehú slew two Kings at Gods appointment, 2. King. 9, 24.

"Ebr. the heauy slepe of the Lord was fallen vpō them.

"Ebr. answerest.

f Estemed moste valiant, and mete to saue the King?

"Ebr. sonnes of death.

g Hereby it appeareth, ẏ the hypocrite persecuted Dauid against his owne consciēce, and contrary to his promes.

h Let his angre towarde vs be pacified by a sacrifice.

i As muche as laye in them, they cōpelled him to idolatrie, because they forced hī to flee to the idolaters.

21 Then

21 Then said Saúl, I haue sinned : come a-
gaine, my sonne Dauid: for I wil do thee
nomore harme , because my soule was
[k] precious in thine eyes this day: beholde,
I haue done foolishly, and haue erred excedingly.
22 Then Dauid answered, & said, Beholde
the Kings speare, let one of the yong mẽ
come ouer and fet it.
23 And let the Lord rewarde euerie man
according to his [l] righteousnes & faithfulnes: for the Lord had deliuered thee into *mine* hãds this daie, but I wolde not lay
mine hand vpon the Lords anointed.
24 And beholde, like as thy life was muche
set by this day in mine eyes: so let my life
be set by in the eyes of the Lord, that he
may deliuer me out of all tribulacion.
25 Then Saúl said to Dauid, Blessed art
thou, my sonne Dauid : for thou shalt do
great things, and also preuaile. So Dauid
went his way, and Saúl returned to his
[m] place.

k Because thou saued st my life this day.

l Thus he protesteth his innocencie toward Saúl, not defending his iustice in the sight of God, in whose presence none is righteous, Psal 14,3. and 130,3.

m To Gibeáh of Beniamín.

CHAP. XXVII.

2 Dauid fleeth to Achísh King of Gath, who giueth him Ziklág. 8 Dauid destroyeth certeine of the Philistíms. 10 Achísh is deceyued by Dauid.

1 AND Dauid said in his heart, I shal
now [a] perish one day by the hand
of Saúl: is it not better for me that I saue
my selfe in the land of the Philistíms, and
that Saúl may haue no hope of me to seke
me anie more in all the coastes of Israél,
and *so* escape out of his hand?
2 Dauid therefore arose, and he, and the
six hundreth men that were with him, wẽt
vnto Achísh the sonne of Maóch King of
Gath.
3 And Dauid [b] dwelt with Achísh at Gath,
he, and his men, euerie man with his housholde, Dauid with his two wiues, Ahinóam the Izreelite, and Abigáil Nabals
wife the Carmelite.
4 And it was tolde Saúl that Dauid was
fled to Gath: so he soght nomore for him.
5 And Dauid said vnto Achísh, If I haue
now founde grace in thine eyes, [c] let them
giue me a place in some *other* citie of the
countrey, that I may dwel there: for why
shulde thy seruant dwel in the *head* citie
of the kingdome with thee?
6 Then Achísh gaue him Ziklág that same day: therefore Ziklág perteineth vnto
the Kings of Iudáh vnto this day.
7 ¶ And * the time that Dauid dwelt in the
countrey of the Philistíms, was foure moneths and certeine dayes.
8 Then Dauid and his men went vp, and
inuaded the [d] Geshurites, and the Girzi-
tes and the Amalekites : for they inhabited the land from the beginning, *from the*
way, as thou goest to Shur, euen vnto the
land of Egypt.

a Dauid distrusteth Gods protection, and therfore fleeth vnto the idolaters, who were enemies to Gods people.

b Thus God by his prouidence chãgeth the enemies hearts & maketh them to fauour hi, in their necessitie.

c Let thine officers appoint me a place.

*Ebr. the nõber of the dayes.

d These were the wicked Canaanites, whome God had appointed to be destroyed.

9 And Dauid smote the land, & left nether
man nor woman aliue, and toke shepe, &
oxen, and asses, and camels, and apparel,
and returned and came to Achísh.
10 And Achísh said, * Where haue ye bene
a rouing this day? And Dauid answered,
Against the Southe of Iudáh, and against
ÿ Southe of the [e] Ierameelites, & against
the Southe of the Kenites.
11 And Dauid saued nether man nor woman aliue, to bring them to Gath, saying,
Lest they shulde tel on vs, and say, So did
Dauid, and so *wil be* his maner all the while that he dwelleth in the countrey of the
Philistíms.
12 And Achísh beleued Dauid, saying, * He
hathe made his people of Israél vtterly to
abhorre him : therefore he shalbe my seruant for euer.

*Or, against whome.

e Which were a familie of ÿ tribe of Iudáh, 1.Chro 2,9.

*Or, he doeth surely abhorre his people.

CHAP. XXVIII.

2 Dauid hathe the chief charge promised about Achísh. 8 Saúl consulteth with a witche, and she causeth him to speake with Samuél, 18 Who declareth his ruine.

1 NOw at that time the Philistíms assembled their bandes and armie to
fight with Israél: therefore Achísh said to
Dauid, [a] Be sure, thou shalt go out with
me to the battel, thou, and thy men.
2 And Dauid said to Achísh, Surely thou
shalt knowe what thy seruant can do. And
Achísh said to Dauid, Surely I wil make
thee keper of mine head for euer.
3 * (Samuél was then dead, and all Israél
had lamented him, and buryed him in Ramáh his owne citie: and Saúl had [b] put
away the sorcerers, and the sothesayers
out of the land.)
4 Then the Philistíms assembled them
selues, and came, and pitched in Shuném:
and Saúl assembled all Israél, & they pitched in Gilbóa.
5 And when Saúl sawe the hoste of the Phi
listíms, he was afrayed, and his heart was
sore astonied.
6 Therfore Saúl asked counsel of ÿ Lord,
& the Lord answered him not, nether by
dreames, nor by [c] Vrim, nor yet by Prophetes.
7 ¶ Then said Saúl vnto his seruants, Seke
me a woman that hathe a familiar spirit,
that I may go to her, and aske of her. And
his seruants said to him, Beholde, there is
a woman at En-dor that hathe a familiar
spirit.
8 Then Saúl [d] changed him selfe, and put
on other raiment, and he went, and two mẽ
with him, and they came to the woman by
night: and he said, I pray thee, coniecture
vnto me by the familiar spirit, and bring
me him vp whome I shal name vnto thee.
9 And the woman said vnto him, Beholde,
thou knowest what Saúl hathe done, how
he hathe destroyed the sorcerers, and the

a Albeit it was a great grief to Dauid to fight against ÿ people of God, yet suche was his infirmitie, he durst not deny him.

Chap. 25,1.

b According to the cõmandemẽt of God, Exod. 22,18. & deut. 18,10.

c Meaning ÿ hie Priest, Exod. 28,30.

d He seketh not to God in his miserie, but is led by Satã to vnlawful meanes, which in his conscience he condemneth.

sothesayers out of the land: wherefore thē
sekest thou to take me in a snare to cause
me to dye?
10 And Saúl sware to her by the Lord,
saying, As the Lord liueth, no″harme shal
come to thee for this thing.

″Or, punishemēt.

11 Then said the womā, Whome shal I
bring vp vnto thee? And he answered,
Bring me vp [e] Samuél.
12 And when the woman sawe Samuél, she
cryed with a loude voyce, and the woman
spake to Saúl, saying, Why hast thou deceiued me? for thou art Saúl.
13 And the King said vnto her, Be not a-
frayed: for what sawest thou? And the woman said vnto Saúl, I sawe″gods ascēding
vp out of the earth.

e He speaketh according to his grosse ignorance, not considering ȳ state of the Saints after this life, and howe Satan hathe no power ouer thē.

″Or, an excellēt persone.

14 Then he said vnto her, What facion
is he of? And she answered, An olde man
cometh vp lapped in a mantel: and Saúl
knewe that it was [f] Samuél, and he enclined his face to the ground, & bowed him
selfe.

f To his imaginaciō, albeit it was Satan, who to blinde his eyes toke vpon him the forme of Samuél, as he cā do of an Angel of light.

15 ¶ And Samuél said to Saúl, Why hast ȳ
disquieted me, to bring me vp? Then Saúl
answered, I am in great distresse: for the
Philistíms make warre against me, & God
is departed frō me, and answereth me nomore, nether ″by Prophetes nether by
dreames: therefore I haue called thee, that
thou mayest tel me, what I shal do.

″Ebr. by the hād of Prophets.

16 Then said Samuél, Wherefore thē doest
thou aske of me, seing the Lord is gone
from thee, and is thine enemie?
17 Euen the Lord hathe done to [g] him, as
he spake *by mine″hand: for the Lord wil
rent the kingdome out of thine hand, and
giue it thy neighbour Dauid.

g That is, to Dauid.
Chap. 15,28.
″Or, ministerie.

18 Because thou obeiedst not the voyce of
the Lord, nor executedst his fearce wrath
vpon the Amalekites, therefore hathe the
Lord done this vnto thee this day.
19 Moreouer the Lord wil deliuer Israél
with thee into the hāds of the Philistíms:
[h] and tomorowe shalt thou and thy sonnes
be with me, & the Lord shal giue the hoste
of Israél into the hands of the Philistíms.

h Ye shal be dead, Chap. 31,6.

20 Then Saúl fel streyght way all along on
the earth, and was sore [i] afrayed because
of the wordes of Samuél, so that there was
no strength in him: for he had eaten no
bread all the day nor all the night.

i The wicked, whē they heare Gods iudgements, tremble and dispaire, but can not seke for mercie by repentance.

21 Then the woman came vnto Saúl, and
sawe that he was sore troubled, and said
vnto him, Se, thine handmayd hathe o-
beyed thy voyce, & I [k] haue put my soule
in mine hand, and haue obeyed thy wordes which thou saidest vnto me.

k I haue ventured my life.

22 Now therefore, I pray thee, hearken
thou also vnto the voyce of thine handmaid, and let me set a morsel of bread before thee, that thou mayest eat & get thee
strength, and go on thy iourney.
23 But he refused, and said, I wil not eat: but
his seruants and the woman together cōpelled him, & he obeied their voyce: so he
arose from the earth, and sate on the bed.
24 Now the woman had a fat calfe in the
house, and she hasted, and killed it, and
toke floure and kneaded it, and baked of it
[l] vnleauened *bread*.
25 Then she broght them before Saúl, and
before his seruants: and when they had
eaten, they stode vp, and went away the
same night.

l Because it required haste.

CHAP. XXIX.

4 *The princes of the Philistíms cause Dauid to be sent backe from the battel against Israél, because they distrusted him.*

1 SO the Philistíms were gathered together with all their armies in Aphék: &
the Israelites pitched″by the founteine,
which is in Izreél.

″Or, in Ain.

2 And the″princes of the Philistíms went
forthe by [a] hundreths and thousands, but
Dauid and his men came behinde with
Achísh.

″Or, captaines.

a According to their bandes, or ensignes.

3 Then said the princes of the Philistíms,
What *do* these Ebrewes *here*? And Achísh
said vnto the princes of the Philistíms, Is
not this Dauid ȳ seruant of Saúl the King
of Israél, who hathe bene with me these
dayes, [b] or these yeres, and I haue foūde
nothing in him, since he″dwelt with me
vnto this day?

b Meaning, a long tyme, ȳ is foure monethes and certeine dayes, Chap. 27,7.
″Ebr fell, as Gen. chap. 25,18.

4 But the princes of the Philistíms were
wrothe with him, & the princes of the Phi
listíms said vnto him, *Send this fellowe
backe, that he may go againe to his place
which thou hast appointed him, & let him
not go downe with vs to battel, lest that in
the battel he be an aduersarie to vs: for
wherewith shulde he obteine the fauour
of his master? shulde it not be with the
[c] heads of these men?

1. Chro. 12,19.

c Wolde not Saúl receiue him to fauour, if he colde betraye vs?

5 Is not this Dauid, of whome they sang in
dances, saying, *Saúl slewe his thousand,
and Dauid his ten thousand?

Chap. 18,7. & 21,11.

6 ¶ Thē Achísh called Dauid, & said vnto
him, As the Lord liueth, thou hast bene
vpright and good in my sight, when thou
[d] wentest out and in with me in the hoste,
nether haue I founde euil with thee, since
ȳ camest to me vnto this daye, but ″the
princes do not fauour thee.

d That is, was conuersant w me.
″Ebr thou art not good in the eyes of the princes.

7 Wherefore now returne, and go in peace, that thou displease not the princes of
the Philistíms.
8 ¶ And Dauid said vnto Achísh, But what
haue I done? and what hast thou founde
in thy seruant as long as I haue bene with
thee vnto this day, that I may [e] not go &
fight against the enemies of my lord the
King?
9 Achísh thē answered, and said to Dauid,
I knowe thou pleasest me, as an Angel of
God:

e This dissimulacion can not be excused: for it grieued him to go against ȳ people of God.

God: but the princes of the Philistíms haue said, Let him not go vp ẇ vs to battel.
10 Wherefore now rise vp early in ẏ morning with thy [f] masters seruants that are
come with thee: and when ye be vp early,
assone as ye haue light, departe.
11 So Dauid and his men rose vp early to
departe in the morning, and to returne into the land of the Philistíms: & the Philistíms went vp to Izreél.

f With them that fled vnto thee frō Saúl.

CHAP. XXX.

1 The Amalekites burne Ziklág. 5 Dauids two wiues are taken prisoners. 6 The people wolde stone him. 8 He asketh counsel of the Lord and pursuing his enemies, recouereth the praye. 24 He deuideth it equally, 26 And sendeth parte to his friends.

1 BVt when Dauid and his men were come to Ziklág [a] the third day, the A-
malekites had inuaded vpon the South,
euen vnto Ziklág, and had [b] smitten Ziklág, and burnt it with fire,
2 And had taken the women that were therein prisoners, bothe small and great, *and*
slewe not a man, but caryed them away,
and went their wayes.
3 ¶So Dauid and his men came to the citie, and beholde, it was burnt with fire, and
their [c] wiues, and their sonnes, and their
daughters were taken prisoners.
4 Then Dauid & the people that was with
him, lift vp their voyces and wept, vntil
they colde wepe nomore.
5 Dauids two wiues were taken prisoners
also, Ahinóam the Izreelite, and Abigáil
the wife of Nabál the Carmelite.
6 And Dauid was in great sorowe: for the
people [d] entended to stone him, because
the heartes of all the people were vexed
euerie mā for his sonnes and for his daughters: but Dauid comforted him selfe in
the Lord his God.
7 ¶And Dauid said to Abiathár the Priest
Ahimelechs sonne, I pray thee, bring me
the Ephód. And Abiathár broght the E-
phód to Dauid.
8 Then Dauid asked counsel at the Lord,
saying, Shal I followe after this companie? shal I ouertake them? And he answered him, Followe: for thou shalt surely
ouertake them, and [e] recouer all.
9 ¶So Dauid and the six hundreth mē that
were with him, wēt, and came to the riuer
Besór, where a parte of them abode:
10 But Dauid and foure hundreth men followed (for two hundreth abode behinde,
being to wearye to go ouer ẏ riuer Besór)
11 And they founde an Egyptiā in the field,
and broght him to Dauid, and gaue him
[f] bread and he did eat, and they gaue him
water to drinke.
12 Also they gaue him a fewe figs, and two
clusters of raisins: and when he had eaten,
his spirit came againe to him: for he had
eaten no bread, nor dronke anie water in

a After that he departed from Achish.

b That is, destroyed ẏ citie.

c For these onely remained in the citie, when the mē were gone to warre.

d Thus we se, ẏ in troubles & aduersitie we do not consider Gods prouidēce, but like raging beastes forget bothe our owne duetie and contēne Gods appointment ouer vs.

e Thogh God seme to leaue vs for a time, yet if we trust in him, we shal be sure to finde comforte.

f God by his prouidēce bothe prouided for the necessitie of this poore strāger, and made him a guide to Dauid to accōplishe his enterprise.

thre dayes, and thre nights.
13 ¶And Dauid said vnto him, To whome
belongest thou? and whence art thou? And
he said, I am a yong mā of Egypt, and seruant to an Amalekite: and my master left
me thre daies ago, because I fel sicke.
14 We roued vpon the South of Chéreth,
& vpon the *coast* belonging to Iudáh, and
vpon the South of Caléb, and we burnt
Ziklág with fire.
15 And Dauid said vnto him, Canst thou
bring me to this companie? And he said,
[g] Sweare vnto me by God, that thou wilt
nether kil me, nor deliuer me into the
hands of my master, and I wil bring thee
to this companie.
16 ¶And when he had broght him thither,
beholde, they lay scatered abroade vpon
all the earth, [h] eating and drinking, & dan-
sing, because of all ẏ great pray that thei
had taken out of the land of ẏ Philistíms,
and out of the land of Iudáh.
17 And Dauid smote them from the twilight, euen vnto the euening [i] of the next
morowe, so that there escaped not a man
of them, saue foure hundreth yong men,
which rode vpon camels, and fled.
18 And Dauid recouered all that ẏ Amalekites had takē: also Dauid rescued his two
wiues.
19 And thei lacked nothing, small or great,
sonne or daughter, or of the spoyle of all
that they had taken away: Dauid recouered them all.
20 Dauid also toke all the shepe, and the
oxē, *&* they draue them before his cattel,
and said, This is Dauids [k] praye.
21 ¶And Dauid came to the two hundreth
mē that were to wearie for to followe Dauid: whome they had made also to abide
at the riuer Besór: and they came to mete
Dauid, and to mete the people that were
with him: so when Dauid came nere to the
people, he saluted them.
22 Then answered all the euil and wicked
of the mē that went with Dauid, and said,
Because they went not with vs, therefore wil we giue them none of the praye,
that we haue recouered, saue to euery man
his [l] wife and his children: therefore let
them cary them away and departe.
23 Then said Dauid, Ye shal not do so, my
brethren, with that which the Lord hathe
giuen vs, who hathe preserued vs, and deliuered the companie that came against vs,
into our handes.
24 For who wil obey you in this matter? but
as his parte *is* that goeth downe to the battel, so *shal* his parte *be*, that tarieth by the
stuffe: they shal parte alike.
25 [m] So from that day forward hee made it
a statute and a lawe in Israél, vntil this
day.

g For othes were in all ages had in moste reuerence euen amōg the heathen.

h The wicked in their pōpe and pleasures consider not ẏ iudgement of God, which is thē at hand to smite them.

i Some reade, & vnto ẏ morowe of ẏ two *euenings*: that is, thre daies.

k Which the Amalekites had taken of others, & Dauid from thē besides the goods of Ziklág.

l Vnder these are comprehēded the cattel and goods, ẇ apperteined to euerie man.

m Some referre these wordes to Dauid, that he alleged an olde custome & law, as if it were writ, It is bothe now and hathe bene euer.

26 ¶When Dauid therefore came to Ziklág, he sent of the pray vnto the Elders
of Iudáh & to his friends, saying, Se, *there*
is a blessing for you of the spoyle of the
enemies of the Lord.
27 He sent to them of Beth-él, and to them
of South Ramóth, and to them of Iattír,
28 And to them of Aroér, and to them of
Siphmóth, and to them of Eshtemóa,
29 And to them of Rachál, and to them of
the cities of the Ierahmeelites, and to thē
of the cities of the Kenites,
30 And to them of Hormáh, & to them of
Chor-ashán, and to them of Athách,
31 And to them of Hebrón, and [n] to all the
places where Dauid and his men had
hanted.

n Shewing him selfe mindeful of their benefites towards him.

CHAP. XXXI.

4 Saúl killeth him selfe. 6 His children are slaine in the battel. 12 The men of Iabésh toke downe his body, which was hanged on the wall.

1 NOw *the Philistíms foght against
Israél, and the men of Israél fled a-
way from the Philistíms, & thei fel downe
″wounded in mount Gilbóa.

1.Chro.10,1.

″Or, slaine.

2 And the Philistíms preassed sore vpon
Saúl and his sonnes, and slewe Ionathán,
and Abinadáb, and Malchishúa Sauls
sonnes.
3 And when the battel went sore against
Saúl, the archers and bowemen″ hit him,
and he was sore″ wounded of the archers.

″Ebr. founde him.
″Or, afraied.

4 Then said Saúl vnto his armour bearer,
[a] Drawe out thy sworde, and thrust me
through therewith, lest the vncircumcised
come and thrust me through and mocke
me: but his armour bearer wolde not, for
he was sore afrayed. Therefore Saúl toke
a sworde and fel vpon it.

a So we se that his cruel life hathe a desperate end, as is comonly sene in them, that persecute the children of God.

5 And when his armour bearer sawe that
Saúl was dead, he fel likewise vpon his
sworde, and dyed with him.
6 So Saúl dyed, and his thre sonnes, and his
armour bearer, and all his men that same
day together.
7 ¶And when the mē of Israél that were on
the otherside of the [b] valley, and they of
the otherside [c] Iordén sawe that the men
of Israél were put to flight, and that Saúl
and his sonnes were dead, thē thei left the
cities, and ran away: & the Philistíms came and dwelt in them.

b Nere to Gilbóa.
c The tribes of Reubén and Gad, and halfe the tribe of Manasséh.

8 ¶And on the morowe when the Philistíms were come to spoyle them that were
slaine, they founde Saúl and his thre sonnes lying in mount Gilbóa,
9 And they cut of his head, and stripped
him out of his armour, and sent into the
land of the Philistíms on euerie side, that
they shulde [d] publish it in the temple of
their idoles, and among the people.

d In token of victorie, and triumphe.

10 And they layed vp his armour in ẏ house
of Ashtaróth, but they hāged vp his body
on the wall of Beth-shan.
11 ¶When the inhabitants of [e] Iabésh Gileád heard, what the Philistíms had done
to Saúl,

e Whome he had deliuered from their enemies, Chap. 11,11.

12 Thē they arose (as manie as were strong
men) & went all night and toke the body
of Saúl, & the bodies of his sonnes, from
the wall of Beth-shan, & came to Iabésh,
and *burnt them there,
13 And toke their bones & *buryed thē vnder a tre at Iabésh, & [f] fasted seuen dayes.

Ier.34,5.
2.Sam.2,4.
f Accordig to the custome of mourners.

THE SECONDE BOKE of Samuél.

THE ARGVMENT.

THis boke and the former beare the title of Samuel, because they conteine the conception, natiuitie and the whole course of his life, and also the liues and actes of two Kings, to wit, of Saúl and Dauid, whome he anointed and consecrated Kings by the ordinance of God. And as the first boke conteineth those things, which God broght to passe among this people vnder the gouernement of Samuel and Saúl: so this seconde boke declareth the noble actes of Dauid, after the death of Saúl, when he began to reigne, vnto the end of his kingdome: and how the same by him was wonderfully augmented: also his great troubles & dangers, which he susteined bothe within his house and without: what horrible & dangerous insurrections, vprores, & treasons were wroght against him, partely by false counselers, fained friends & flatterers, and partely by some of his owne children and people: and how by Gods assistance he ouercame all difficulties, and enioyed his kingdome in rest and peace. In the persone of Dauid the Scripture setteth forthe Christ Iesus the chief King, who came of Dauid according to the flesh, and was persecuted on euery side with outward and inward enemies, aswel in his owne persone, as in his members, but at length he ouercometh all his enemies and giueth his Church victorie against all power bothe spiritual & temporal: and so reigneth with them, King for euermore.

CHAP.

CHAP. I.

4 It was tolde Dauid of Sauls death. 15 He causeth him to be slaine that broght the tydings. 19 He lamenteth the death of Saúl and Ionathán.

1 AFter the death of Saúl,
when Dauid was returned from the *slaughter
of the Amalekites and
had bene two dayes in
Ziklág,

1.Sam.30,17.

2 Beholde, a man came the third day out of
the hoste from Saúl with his a clothes rēt,
and earth vpon his head: & when he came
to Dauid, he fel to the earth, and did obeisance.

a Seming to lament ẏ ouerthrowe of the people of Israel.

3 Then Dauid said vnto him, Whence cōmest thou? And he said vnto him, Out of
the hoste of Israél I am escaped.
4 And Dauid said vnto him, What is done?
I pray thee, tel me. Thē he said, ẏ the people is fled from the battel, and many of ẏ
people are ouerthrowen, and dead, and also Saúl and Ionathán his sonne are dead.
5 And Dauid said vnto the yong man, that
tolde it him, How knowest thou that Saúl
and Ionathán his sonne be dead?
6 Then the yong man that tolde him, answered, b As I came to mount Gilbóa, beholde, Saúl leaned vpon his speare. and lo,
the charets and "horsemen followed hard
after him.

b As I fled in the chase.

"Or, captaines.

7 And whē he loked backe, he sawe me, and
called me. And I answered, Here am I.
8 And he said vnto me, Who art thou? And
I answered him, I am an c Amalekite.
9 Then said he vnto me, I pray thee, come
vpon me, and slaye me: for anguish is
come vpon me, because my d life is yet
whole in me.
10 So "I came vpon him, and slewe him, &
because I was sure that he colde not liue,
after that he had fallen, I toke the crowne that was vpon his head, and the bracelet that was on his arme, and broght thē
hither vnto my lord.

c He was an Amalekite borne, but renoūced his cōtrey & ioyned with the Israelites.

d I am sory, because I am yet aliue.

"Ebr. I stode vpon him.

11 Then Dauid toke holde on his clothes,
*& rent them, and likewise all the men
that were with him.

Chap.3,31. & 13,31.

12 And they mourned and wept, and fasted
vntil euen, for Saúl and for Ionathán his
sonne, and for the people of the Lord, and
for the house of Israél, because they were
slaine with the sworde.
13 ¶ e Afterward Dauid said vnto the yong
man that tolde it him, Whence art thou?
And he answered, I am the sonne of a strāger an Amalekite.

e After the lamentation he examined him againe.

14 And Dauid said vnto him, * How wast
thou not afraied, to put forthe thine hand
to destroy the Anoynted of the Lord?

Psal.105,15.

15 Then Dauid called one of his yong mē,
& said, Go nere, and fall vpō him. And he
smote him that he dyed.
16 Thē said Dauid vnto him, f Thy blood
be vpon thine owne head: for thine owne
mouth hathe testified agaīst thee, saying,
I haue slaine the Lords Anointed.

f Thou art iustely punished for thy faute.

17 ¶ Then Dauid mourned with this lamētation ouer Saúl, and ouer Ionathán his
sonne,
18 (Also he bade them teache the children of
Iudáh to g shoote, as it is written in ẏ boke
of* " Iashér)

g That they might be able to match their enemies the Philistíms in that arte.

Iosh.10,13.

"Or, righteous.

19 O noble Israél, h he is slaine vpon thy
hie places: how are the mighty ouerthrowen?

h Meaning Saúl.

20 *Tel it not in Gath, nor publish it in
the stretes of Ashkelón, lest the daughters
of the Philistíms reioyce, lest the daughters of the vncircumcised triumphe.

Mich 1,10.

21 Ye mountaines of Gilbóa, vpon you *be*
nether dewe nor raine, nor i *be there* fields
of offrings: for there the shield of the
mightie is cast downe, the shield of Saúl,
as thogh he had not bene anoynted with
oyle.

i Let their fertile fieldes be baren, & bring forth no frute to offre to the Lord.

22 The bowe of Ionathán neuer turned
backe, nether did the sworde of Saúl returne empty from the blood of the slaine,
and from the fat of the mighty.
23 Saúl and Ionathán were louely and
pleasant in their liues, and in their
deathes they were not k deuided: they
were swifter the egles, they were strōge
then lions.

k They dyed bothe together in Gilbóa.

24 Ye daughters of Israél, wepe for Saúl,
which clothed you in skarlet, l with pleasures, and hanged ornaments of golde vpon your apparel.

l As riche garments, & costly iewels.

25 How were the mighty slaine in the middes of the battel? ô Ionathán, thou wast
slaine in thine hie places.
26 Wo is me for thee, my brother Ionathán: very kinde hast thou bene vnto me:
thy loue to me was wonderful, passing ẏ
loue of m women: how are the mighty ouerthrowen, and the weapons of warre destroyed?

m Ether towarde their housbandes, or their children.

CHAP. II.

4 Dauid is anoynted King in Hebrón. 9 Abnér maketh Ish-bósheth King ouer Israél. 15 The battel of the seruants of Dauid and Ish-bósheth. 32 The buryal of Asahél.

1 AFter this Dauid a asked counsel of
the Lord, saying, Shal I go vp into
anie of the cities of Iudáh? And the Lord
said vnto him, Go vp. And Dauid said,
Whither shal I go? He thē answered, Vnto
b Hebrón.

a By the meanes of the hie Priest, as 1.Sam.23,2. & 2.sam.5,19.

b Which citie was also called Kiriath árba, Iosh,14,15.

2 So Dauid went vp thither & his two wiues also, Ahinóam the Izreelite, and Abigáil Nabals wife the Carmelite.
3 And Dauid broght vp the men that were
with c him, euerie man with his housholde, and they dwelt in the cities of
Hebrón.

c In the time of his persecution.

4 ¶Then the men of Iudáh came, and there
they anoĩted Dauid King ouer the house
of Iudáh. And they tolde Dauid, saying,
*that the men of Iabésh Gileád buryed
Saúl.
5 And Dauid sent messengers vnto the mẽ
of Iabésh Gileád, & said vnto them, Blessed are ye of ỹ Lord, that ye haue shewed
suche kindenes vnto your lord Saúl, that
you haue buryed him.
6 Therefore now the Lord shewe mercie
and [d] trueth vnto you: and I wil recompence you this benefite, because ye haue
done this thing.
7 Therefore now let your hands be strõg,
and be you valiant: albeit your master Saúl be dead, yet neuerthelesse the house of
Iudáh hathe anointed me [e] King ouer
them.
8 ¶But Abnér the sonne of Ner that was
captaine of Sauls hoste, toke Ish-bósheth
the sonne of Saúl, and broght him to Mahanáim,
9 And made him King ouer Gileád, and o-
uer the Ashurites, and ouer Izreél, and
ouer Ephráim, and ouer Beniamín, and
ouer [f] all Israél.
10 Ish-bósheth Sauls sonne was fourty yere
olde when he began to reigne ouer Israél,
and reigned two yere: but the house of Iudáh followed Dauid.
11 (And the time which Dauid reigned in
Hebrón ouer the house of Iudáh, *was* seuẽ
yere and six [g] monethes)
12 ¶And Abnér the sonne of Ner, and the
seruants of Ish-bósheth the sonne of Saúl
went out of Mahanáim to Gibeón.
13 And Ioáb the sonne of Zeruiáh, and the
seruants of Dauid went out and met one
an other by the poole of Gibeón: and
they sate downe, the one on the one side
of the poole, and the other on the other
side of the poole.
14 Then Abnér said to Ioáb, Let the yong
men now arise, and [h] playe before vs. And
Ioáb said, Let them arise.
15 Then there arose and went ouer twelue
of Beniamín by nomber, which perteined
to Ish-bósheth the sonne of Saúl, and
twelue of the seruants of Dauid.
16 And euerie one caught [i] his fellowe
by the head, & *thrust* his sworde in his fellowes side, so they fel downe together:
wherefore the place was called ″Helkath-
hazzurím which is in Gibeón.
17 And the battel was exceding sore that
same day: for Abnér and the men of Israél
[k] fel before the seruants of Dauid.
18 And there were thre sonnes of Zeruiáh
there, Ioáb, and Abishái, and Asahél. And
Asahél was as light on foote as a wilde
roe.
19 And Asahél followed after Abnér, & in

*1 Sam. 31, 12.

d According to his promes, which is to recompẽce them that are merciful.

e So ỹ you shal not want a captaine & a defender.

f Ouer ỹ eleuen tribes.

g After this time was expired, he reigned ouer all ỹ countrey 33 yeres, Chap. 5, 5.

h Let vs se how they can handle their weapons.

i Meaning, his aduersarie.

″Or, the field of strong men.

k After that these foure & twentie were slaine.

going he turned nether to the right hand
nor to the left from Abnér.
20 Then Abnér loked behinde him, & said,
Art thou Asahél? And he answered, Yea.
21 Then Abnér said, Turne thee ether to ỹ
right hand or to the left, and take one of
the yong men, and take thee his ″weapons:
but Asahél wolde not departe from him.
22 And Abnér said to Asahél, Departe frõ
me: [l] wherefore shulde I smite thee to the
groũde? how thẽ shulde I be able to holde
vp my face to Ioáb thy brother?
23 And when he wolde not departe, Abnér
with the hindre end of the speare smote
him vnder the [m] fift *rib*, that the speare
came out behinde him: and he fel downe
there, and dyed in his place. And as manie
as came to the place where Asahél fel
downe and dyed, stode stil.
24 Ioáb also and Abishái pursued after Abnér: and the sunne went downe, when they
were come to ỹ hil Ammáh, that lieth before Gíah, by the way of the wildernes of
Gibeón.
25 And the children of Beniamín gathered
them selues together after Abnér, & were on an heape and stode on the top of an
hil.
26 Then Abnér called to Ioáb, and said,
Shal the [n] sworde deuoure for euer? knowest thou not, that it wil be bitternes in the
latter end? how long thẽ shal it be, or thou
bid the people returne frõ following their
brethren?
27 And Ioáb said, As God liueth, if thou
haddest not [o] spoken, surely euen in the
morning the people had departed euerie
one backe from his brother.
28 ¶ So Ioáb blewe a trumpet, and all the
people stode stil, and pursued after Israél
nomore, nether foght they anie more.
29 And Abnér and his men walked all that
night through the ″plaine, & wẽt ouer Iordén, & past through all Bithrón til they
came″ to Mahanaím.
30 Ioáb also returned backe from Abnér: &
whẽ he had gathered all the people together, there lacked of Dauids seruants ninetene men and Asahél.
31 But the seruãts of Dauid had smitten of
Beniamín, and of Abners men, *so that* thre
[p] hundreth and threscore men dyed.
32 And they toke vp Asahél, and buryed hĩ
in the sepulchre of his father, which was
in Beth-léhem: and Ioáb and his men wẽt
all night, and *when they came* to Hebrón,
the daie arose.

″Or, spoile.

l Why doest ỹ prouoke me to kil thee?

m Some read, in those partes, where as the liuely partes lye: as the heart, the lungs, ỹ liuer, the milt, and the gall.

n Shal we not make an end of murthering?

o If ỹ hadest not prouoked thẽ to battel, as vers. 14.

″Or, wildernes.

″Or, to the tẽts.

p Thus God wolde confirme Dauid in his kingdome by the destruction of his aduersaries.

CHAP. III.

1 Long warre betwene the houses of Saúl and Dauid. 2 The children of Dauid in Hebrón. 22 Abnér turneth to Dauid. 27 Ioáb killeth him.

1 THere was then [a] long warre betwene
the house of Saúl and the house of
Dauid:

a That is, without intermissiõ, induring two yeres, which was the whole reigne of Ish-bósheth.

Dauid: but Dauid waxed stronger, & the
house of Saúl waxed weaker.
2 ¶ And vnto Dauid were children borne
in Hebrón: and his eldest sonne was Amnón of Ahinóam the Izreelite,
3 And his secōde, *was* [b] Chileáb of Abigáil
the wife of Nabál the Carmelite: and the
third, Absalóm the sonne of Maacáh the
daughter of Talmái the King of Geshúr,
4 And the fourth, Adoniiáh the sonne of
Aggíth, and the fifth, Shephaciáh the sonne of Abitál,
5 And the sixt, Ithreám by Egláh Dauids
wife: these were borne to Dauid in [c] Hebrón.
6 ¶ Now while there was warre betwene
the house of Saúl and the house of Dauid, Abnér made all his power for ye house
of Saúl.
7 And Saúl had a concubine named Rizpáh, the daughter of Aiiáh. And *Ish-bósheth*
said to Abnér, Wherefore hast thou gone
in to my fathers concubine?
8 Thē was Abnér very wrothe for the wordes of Ish-bósheth, & said, Am I a [d] dogs
head, which against Iudáh do shew mercy this day vnto the house of Saúl thy father, to his brethren, & to his neighbours,
and haue not deliuered thee into the hand
of Dauid, that thou chargest me this day
with a faute concerning this woman?
9 [e] So do God to Abnér, and more also, except, as the Lord hathe sworne to Dauid,
euen so I do to him,
10 To remoue the kingdome frō the house of Saúl, that the throne of Dauid may
be stablished ouer Israél, and ouer Iudáh,
euen from Dan to Beer-shéba.
11 And he durst nomore answer to Abnér:
for he feared him.
12 ¶ Then Abnér sent messengers to Dauid " on his behalfe, saying, Whose is the
land? Who shulde *also* say, Make couenant
with me, & beholde, mine hand *shalbe* with
thee, to bring all Israél vnto thee.
13 Who said, Wel, I wil make a couenant
with thee: but one thing I require of thee,
that is, that you se not my face except thou
bring Michál Sauls daughter when thou
commest to se me.
14 ¶ Then Dauid sent messengers to Ish-
bósheth Sauls sonne, saying, Deliuer me
my wife Michál, which I maried for * an
hundreth foreskinnes of the Philistíms.
15 And Ish-bósheth sent, and toke her from
her housbād * Phaltiél the sonne of Laish.
16 And her housband went with her, and
came weping behinde her, vnto Bahurím:
then said Abnér vnto him, Go, & returne.
So he returned.
17 ¶ And Abnér had [f] communicaciō with
the Elders of Israél, saying, Ye soght for

b Who is called also Daniel, 1.Chro.3,1.
c Within seuē yeres and six moneths.
d Doest thou esteme me no more then a dog, for all my seruice done to thy fathers house?
e We se how the wicked cā not abide to be admonished of their fautes, but seke their displeasure, wc go about to bring them frō their wickednes.
" Or, secretly.
* 1.Sam.18,27.
* 1.Sam.25,44.
f Rather for malice that he bare towarde Ish-bósheth, then for loue he bare to Dauid.

Dauid in times past, that he might be
your King.
18 Now then do it: for the Lord hathe spoken of Dauid, saying, By the hand of my
seruant Dauid I wil saue my people Israél out of the hands of the Philistíms, and
out of the hands of all their enemies.
19 Also Abnér spake " to Beniamín, and afterwarde Abnér went to speake with Dauid in Hebrón, *concerning* all that Israél
was content with, and the whole [g] house of
Beniamín.
20 So Abnér came to Dauid to Hebrón,
hauing twenty men with him, and Dauid
made a feast vnto Abnér, and to the men
that were with him.
21 Then Abnér said vnto Dauid, I wil rise
vp, and go gather all Israél vnto my lord
ye King, that thei may make a couenāt with
thee, & that thou maiest reigne ouer all
that thine heart desireth. Then Dauid let
Abnér departe, who went " in peace.
22 ¶ And beholde, the seruants of Dauid
and Ioáb came [h] from the cāpe, & broght
a great pray with them (but Abnér was
not with Dauid in Hebrón: for he had sent
him away, and he departed in peace)
23 When Ioáb, and all the hoste that was
with him were come, men tolde Ioáb, saying, Abnér the sonne of Ner came to the
King, and he hathe sent him away, and he
is gone in peace.
24 Then Ioáb came to the King, and said,
[i] What hast thou done? beholde, Abnér
came vnto thee, why hast thou sent him
away, and he is departed?
25 Thou knowest Abnér the sōne of Ner:
for he came to disceiue thee, & to knowe
thy outgoing and ingoing, and to knowe
all that thou doest.
26 ¶ And when Ioáb was gone out frō Dauid, he sent messēgers after Abnér, which
broght him againe frō the well of Siriáh
vnknowing to Dauid.
27 And when Abnér was come againe to
Hebrón, * Ioáb toke him aside in the gate
to speake with him " peaceably, and smote
him vnder the fift *rib*, that he dyed, for the
blood of * Asahél his brother.
28 ¶ And when afterwarde it came to Dauids eare, he said, I and my kingdome are
[k] giltles before the Lord for euer, cōcerning the blood of Abnér the sonne of
Ner.
29 Let the blood fall on the head of Ioáb,
and on all his fathers house, that the house of Ioáb be neuer without some yt haue
running yssues, or lepre, or that leaneth on
a staffe, or that doeth fall on the sworde,
or that lacketh bread.
30 (So Ioáb and [l] Abishái his brother slewe
Abnér, because he had slayne their brother Asahél at Gibeón in battel)

" Ebr. in the eares of Beniamin.
g Who chalēged the kingdome, because of their father Saúl.
" Or, without harme.
h From warre against the Philistims.
i Here appeareth the malicious minde of Ioáb, who wolde haue had the King to slay Abnér for his priuate grudge.
* 1.King.2,5.
" Or, secretly.
* Chap 2,23.
k The Lord knoweth that I did not consent to his death.
l Abishái is said to slay him wt Ioáb, because he cōsented to ye murther.

31 And Dauid said to Ioáb, and to all the
people that were with him, Rēt your clothes, and put on sackecloth, and mourne
[m] before Abnér: and King Dauid him self
followed the beare.

m Meaning, before ẏ corps.

32 And when thei had buryed Abnér in Hebrón, the King lift vp his voyce, & wept
beside the sepulchre of Abnér, and all the
people wept.
33 And the King lamented ouer Abnér, and
said, Dyed Abnér as [n] a foole dyeth?
34 Thine hands were not bounde, nor thy
feete tyed in fetters of brasse: *but* as a mā
falleth before wicked men, *so* didest thou
fall. And all the people wept againe for
him.

n He declareth that Abnér dyed not as a wretch or vile persone, but as a valiant man might do, beīg traiterously deceiued by ẏ wicked.

35 Afterwarde all the people came to cause
Dauid eat [o] meat while it was yet day, but
Dauid sware, saying, So do God to me &
more also, if I taste bread, or oght els til
the sunne be downe.

o According to their custome, which was to banket at buryals.

36 And all the people knewe it, & it [p] pleased them: as whatsoeuer the King did,
pleased all the people.
37 For all the people and all Israél vnderstode that day, how that it was not the
Kings dede that Abnér the sonne of Ner
was slayne.

p It is expedient sometime not onely to conceiue inwarde sorrow, but also that it may appeare to others to the intent that they may be satisfied.

38 And the King said vnto his seruants,
Knowe ye not, that there is a prince and a
great man fallen this day in Israél?
39 And I am this day weake and *newely* anointed King: and these men the sonnes of
Zeruiáh be to ″hard for me: ẏ Lord reward
the doer of euil according to his wickednes.

″Or, cruel.

CHAP. IIII.

5 Baanáh and Recháb slaye Ish-bósheth the sonne of Saúl. 12 Dauid commandeth them to be slayne.

1 AND whē Sauls [a] sonne heard ẏ Abnér
was dead in Hebrón, then his hands
were [b] feble, and all Israél was afrayed,
2 And Sauls sonne had two men that were
captaines of bands: the one called Baanáh, and the other called Recháb, the sonnes of Rimmón a Beerothite of the children of Beniamín. (for [c] Beeróth was
reckened to Beniamín,
3 Because the Beerothites fled to [d] Gittáim, and soiourned there, vnto this day)
4 And Ionathán Sauls sonne had a sonne
that was lame on his feete: he was fiue
yere olde when the tidings came of Saúl
and Ionathán out of Israél: then his
nourse toke him, and fled away. And as
she made haste to flee, the childe fell, and
began to halt, and his name was Mephibósheth.

a That is, Ish-bósheth.

b Meaning, ẏ he was discouraged.

c The citie Beeróth was in the tribe of Beniamín, Iosh. 18, 25.

d After the death of Saúl, for feare of ẏ Philistims.

5 And the sonnes of Rimmón the Beerothite, Recháb and Baanáh went and came
in the heate of the day to the house of
Ish-bósheth (who slept on a bed at noone)
6 And beholde, Recháb and Baanáh his
brother came into the middes of the house, *as* they [e] wolde haue wheat, and they
[f] smote him vnder the fift *rib*, and fled.
7 For when they came into the house, he
slept on his bed in his bedchamber, and
they smote him, and slewe him, and beheaded him, and toke his head, and gate
them away through the ″ plaine all the
night.

e Thei disguised thē selues as marchants, which came to bye wheat.

f There is nothing so vile & dangerous, ẇ ẏ wicked wil not enterprise in hope of lucre & fauour.

″Or, wildernes.

8 And thei broght the head of Ish bósheth
vnto Dauid to Hebrón, and said to the
King, Beholde the head of Ish-bósheth
Sauls sonne thine enemie, who soght after
thy life: and the Lord hathe auenged my
lord the King this day of Saúl and of his
seed.
9 Then Dauid answered Recháb and Baanáh his brother, the sonnes of Rimmón
the Beerothite, and said vnto them, As
the Lord liueth, who hathe deliuered my
soule out of all aduersitie,
10 When one * tolde me, and said that
Saúl was dead, (thinking to haue broght
good tidings) I toke him and slewe him
in Ziklág, who thoght that I wolde haue
giuen him a rewarde for his tidings:

Chap. 1, 15.

11 How [g] muche more, when wicked men
haue slayne a righteous persone in his
owne house, & vpon his bed? shal I not
now therefore require his blood at your
hand, and take you from the earth?
12 Then Dauid commanded his yong men,
and they slewe them, and cut of their
hands and their feete, & hanged them vp
ouer the poole in Hebrón: but they toke
the head of Ish-bósheth, and buryed it in
the sepulchre of * Abnér in Hebrón.

g Forasmuche as nether the exāple of him that slew Saúl, nor duetie to their master, nor ẏ innocencie of the persone, nor reuerence of the place, nor time did moue thē. they deserued most grieuous punishment.

Chap. 3, 32.

CHAP. V.

3 Dauid is made King ouer all Israél. 7 He taketh the forte of Zión. 19 He asketh counsel of the Lord, 20 And ouercometh the Philistims twise.

1 THen * came all the tribes of Israél
to Dauid vnto Hebrón, & said thus,
Beholde, we are thy [a] bones and thy flesh.
2 And in time past when Saúl was our
King, thou leddest Israél in and out: and
the Lord hathe said to thee, * Thou shalt
feede my people Israél, and thou shalt be a
captaine ouer Israél.

1. Chro. 11, 1.

a We are of thy kinred, & most nere ioyned vnto thee.

Psal. 78, 71.

3 So all the Elders of Israél came to the
King to Hebrón: and King Dauid made
a couenant with them in Hebrón [b] before the Lord: and they anointed Dauid
King ouer Israél.

b That is, taking the Lord to witnes: for the Arke was as yet in Abinadabs house.

4 ¶ Dauid *was* thirty yere olde when he began to reigne: *and* he reigned fourty
yere.
5 In Hebrón he reigned ouer Iudáh * seuē
yere, and six moneths: and in Ierusalém
he reigned thirty and thre yeres ouer all
Israél and Iudáh.

Chap. 2, 11.

6 ¶ The King also and his men went to
Ierusalém vnto the Iebusites, ẏ inhabitāts
of

of the land: who spake vnto Dauid, saying,
Except thou take away the [c] blinde and
the lame, thou shalt not come in hither:
thinking ye Dauid colde not come thither.
7 But Dauid toke the forte of Zión: this is
the citie of Dauid.
8 Now Dauid had said ye same day, Whosoeuer smiteth the Iebusites, & getteth vp
to the gutters & *smiteth* the lame & blinde,
which Dauids soule hateth, *I wil preferre
him:* *therefore they said, The blinde and
the lame shal not [d] come into that house.
9 So Dauid dwelt in that forte, and called it
the citie of Dauid, and Dauid buylt roũd
about it, from [e] Milló, and inwarde.
10 And Dauid prospered and grewe: for
the Lord God of hostes *was* with him.
11 ¶ Hirám also King of "Tyrus sent messẽgers to Dauid, and cedar trees, and carpẽters, and masons for walles: and thei buylt
Dauid an house.
12 Then Dauid knewe, that the Lord had
stablished him King ouer Israél, and that
he had exalted his kingdome for his people Israels sake.
13 And Dauid toke him mo *concubines &
wiues out of Ierusalém, after he was come
from Hebrón, and mo sonnes and daughters were borne to Dauid.
14 *And these be the names of the sonnes
that were borne vnto him in Ierusalém:
Shammúa, and Shobáb, and Nathán, and
Salomón,
15 And Ibhár, and Elishúa, and Népheg,
and Iaphía,
16 And Elishamá, & Eliadá, and Eliphálet.
17 ¶ *But when the Philistims heard that
they had anointed Dauid King ouer Israél, all the Philistims came vp to seke Dauid: and when Dauid heard, he wẽt downe
to a forte.
18 But the Philistíms came, and spred them
selues in the valley of Repháim.
19 Then Dauid [f] asked coũsel of the Lord,
saying, Shal I go vp to the Philistíms?
wilt thou deliuer them into mine hands?
And the Lord answered Dauid, Go vp: for
I wil doutles deliuer the Philistims into
thine hands.
20 ¶ *Then Dauid came to Baal-perazím,
and smote them there, & said, The Lord
hathe deuided mine enemies asondre before me, as waters be deuided asondre: therefore he called the name of that place,
"Baal-perazím.
21 And there they left their images, & Dauid and his men *burnt them.
22 Againe the Philistims came vp, & spred
them selues in the valley of [g] Repháim.
23 And when Dauid asked counsel of the
Lord, He answered, Thou shalt not go vp,
but turne about behinde thẽ, & come vpon
them ouer against the mulbery trees.
24 And whẽ thou hearest the noyse of one
going in the toppes of the mulbery trees,
then remoue: for then shal the Lord go
out before thee, to smite the hoste of the
Philistims.
25 Then Dauid did so as the Lord had cõmanded him, and smote the Philistims frõ
Géba, vntil thou come to [h] Gázer.

CHAP. VI.

3 The Arke is broght forthe of the house of Abinadáb. 7 Vzzah is striken, & dyeth. 14 Dauid dãceth before it. 16 And is therefore despised of his wife Michál.

1 AGaine Dauid gathered together all
the "chosen men of Israél, *euen* thirtie
thousand,
2 *And Dauid arose & went wt all the people that were with him [a] frõ Baalé of Iudáh to bring vp from thence the Arke of
God, whose name is called by the Name
of the Lord of hostes, that dwelleth vpon
it betwene the Cherubims.
3 And they put the Arke of God vpon a
newe carte, and broght it out of the house
of Abinadáb that was in [b] Gibeáh. And
Vzzáh and Ahió the sonnes of Abinadáb
did driue the newe carte.
4 And when they broght the Arke of God
out of the house of *Abinadáb, that was at
Gibeáh, Ahió went before the Arke,
5 And Dauid and all the house of Israél
[c] played before the Lord on all *instruments*
made of firre, and on harpes, and on psalteries, and on timbrels, and on cornets, and
on cymbals.
6 ¶ *And whẽ they came to Nachons threshĩg floore, Vzzáh put his hãd to the Arke
of God, & helde it: for ye oxẽ did shake it.
7 And the Lord was very wrothe wt Vzzáh,
& God [d] smote him in ye same place for his
faute, & there he dyed by ye Arke of God.
8 And Dauid was displeased, because the
Lord had "smitten Vzzáh: and he called
the name of the place "Pérez Vzzáh vntil
this day.
9 Therefore Dauid that day feared the
Lord, and said, How shal the Arke of the
Lord come to me?
10 So Dauid wolde not bring the Arke of
the Lord vnto him into the citie of Dauid, but Dauid caryed it into the house of
Obed-edóm [e] a Gittite.
11 And the Arke of the Lord continued in
the house of Obed-edóm the Gittite, thre
moneths, and the Lord blessed Obededóm, and all his housholde.
12 ¶ And one tolde King Dauid, saying,
*The Lord hathe blessed the house of Obed-edóm, and all that he hathe, because
of the Arke of God: therefore Dauid went
and [f] broght the Arke of God from the
house of Obed-edóm, into the citie of Dauid with gladnes.
13 And when they that bare the Arke of the

---

c The childrẽ of God called idoles blinde and lame guides: therefore the Iebusites ment, that thei shulde proue that their gods were nether blinde nor lame.

1. Chro. 11,6.

d The idoles shulde entre no more into that place.

e He buylt from the towne house rounde about to his owne house, 1. Chro. 11,8.

"Ebr. Zor.

1. Chro. 3,9.

1. Chro. 3,5.

1. Chro. 14,8. & 11,16.

f By Abiathár the Priest.

Isa. 28,21.

"Or, the plaine of diuisions.

1. Chro. 14,12.

g Meaning, the valley of gyants, which Dauid called Baal perazim because of his victorie.

h Which was in the tribe of Beniamin, but the Philistims did possesse it.

"Or, chief.

1. Chro. 13,5.

a This was a citie in Iudáh called also Kiriath-iearim, Iosh. 15,9.

b Which was an hie place of the citie of Baalé.

1. Sam. 7,2.

c Praised God, and sang psalmes.

1. Chro. 13,10.

d Here we se what danger it is to followe good intẽtiõs, or to do anie thing in Gods seruice without his expresse worde.

"Ebr. made a breache.

"Or the diuision of Vzzáh.

e Who was a Leuite, & had dwelt in Gittáim, 1 Chro. 15,21.

1. Chro. 15,25.

f Meaning, he caused ye Leuites to beare it, according to the Lawe.

Lord had gone six spaces, he offred an oxe,
and a fat beast.
14 And Dauid dáced before the Lord with
all his might, and was girded with a linen g Ephód.
15 So Dauid and all the house of Israél,
broght the Arke of the Lord with showting,
and sounde of trumpet.
16 And as the Arke of the Lord came into
the citie of Dauid, Michál Sauls daughter
loked through a windowe, and sawe King
Dauid leape, and dance before the Lord,
and she h despised him in her heart.
17 And when they had broght in the Arke
of the Lord, they set it in his place, in the
middes of the tabernacle that Dauid had
pitched for it: thē Dauid offred burnt offrings, & peace offrings before the Lord.
18 And assone as Dauid had made an end
of offring burnt offrings & peace offrings,
he * blessed the people in the Name of the
Lord of hostes,
19 And gaue among all the people, *euen* a-
mong the whole multitude of Israél, aswel to the women as men, to euerie one a
cake of bread, and a piece of flesh, and a
bottel *of wine*: so all the people departed
euerie one to his house.
20 ¶ Then Dauid returned to i blesse his
house, and Michál the daughter of Saúl
came out to mete Dauid, and said, O how
glorious was the King of Israél this day,
which was vncouered to day in the eyes
of the maidens of his seruants, as a foole
vncouereth him selfe.
21 Then Dauid said vnto Michál, k *It was*
before the Lord, which chose me rather
then thy father, and all his house, and cōmanded me to be ruler ouer all the people
of the Lord, *euen* ouer Israél: and therefore wil I play before the Lord,
22 And wil yet be more vile then thus, and
wil be lowe in mine owne sight, and of the
very same maidseruants, which thou hast
spoken of, shal I be had in honour.
23 Therefore Michál the daughter of Saúl
had l no childe, vnto the day of her death.

g With a garment like to ẏ Priests garmēt.

h The worldlings are not able to cōprehend the mocions that moue the childrē of God.

1.Chro.16,2.

i That is, to pray for his house, as he had done for the people.

k It was for no worldely affection, but onely for that zeale that I bare to Gods glorie.

l Which was a punishment, because she mocked ẏ seruant of God.

CHAP. VII.

2 *Dauid wolde buylde God an house, but is forbidden by the Prophet Nathán. 8 God putteth Dauid in minde of his benefites. 12 He promiseth continuance of his kingdome and posteritie.*

1 AFterwarde * whē the King sate in his
house and the Lord had giuen him
rest round about from all his enemies,
2 The King said vnto Nathán the Prophet, Beholde, now I dwel in an house of
cedar trees, and the Arke of God remaineth within the a curtaines.
3 Then Nathán said vnto the King, Go,
and do all that is in thine heart: for the
Lord *is* with thee.
4 ¶ And the same night the worde of the

1.Chro.17,2.

a Within the Tabernacle couered ẘ skinnes, Exo.26,7.

Lord came vnto Nathán, saying,
5 Go, and tel my seruāt Dauid, Thus saieth
the Lord, b Shalt thou buyld me an house for my dwelling?
6 For I haue dwelt in no house since the time that I broght the children of Israél
out of Egypt vnto this day, but haue walked in a tent and tabernacle.
7 In all the *places* wherein I haue walked
with all the children of Israél, spake I one
worde with anie of the tribes of c Israél
when I commanded *the iudges* to fede my
people Israél? or said I, Why buyld ye not
me an house of cedar trees?
8 Now therefore so say vnto my seruant
Dauid, Thus sayeth the Lord of hostes, * I
toke thee from the shepecote following
the shepe, that thou mightest be ruler o-
uer my people, ouer Israél.
9 And I was with thee wheresoeuer thou
hast walked, and haue destroyed all thine
enemies out of thy sight, and haue made
thee a d great name, lyke vnto the name
of the great men that are in the earth.
10 (Also I wil appoint a place for my people Israél, and wil plant it, that they may
dwel in a place of their owne, and moue
e nomore, nether shal wicked people trouble them anie more as before time,
11 And since the time that I set iudges ouer
my people of Israél) and I wil giue thee
rest from all thine enemies: also the Lord
telleth thee, ẏ he wil make thee an house.
12 * And when thy dayes be fulfilled, thou
shalt slepe with thy fathers, & I wil set vp
thy seede after thee, which shal procede
out of thy body, and wil stablish his kingdome.
13 * He shal buyld an house for my Name,
and I wil stablish the throne of his kingdome for euer.
14 * I wilbe his father, & he shalbe my sonne: & * if he sinne, I wil chasten him with
the f rod of men, and with the plagues of
the children of men.
15 But my mercy shal not departe away frō
him, as I toke it from Saúl whome I haue
put away before thee.
16 And thine house shalbe stablished and
thy kingdome for euer before thee, *euen*
thy throne shalbe g stablished for euer.
17 According to all these wordes, and according to all this vision, Nathán spake
thus vnto Dauid.
18 Then King Dauid went in, and sate before the Lord, & said, Who am I, ô Lord
God, and what is mine house, that thou
hast broght me hitherto?
19 And this was yet a small thing in thy
sight, ô Lord God, therefore thou hast
spokē also of thy seruāts house for a great
while: but " doeth this apperteine to h mā,
ô Lord God?

b Meaning, he shulde not: yet Nathán speaking accordig to mās iudgement and not by the Spirit of prophecie, permitted him.

c As concerning the buylding of an house: meanig that without Gods expresse worde nothing oght to be attempted.

1.Sam.16,12. Psal.78,70.

d I haue made thee famous through all ẏ worlde.

e He promiseth the quietnes, if they wil walke in his feare and obedience.

1.King.8,20.

1 King.5,5. & 6,12. 1.chro.22,10.

Ebr.1,5. Psal.89,31.

f That is, gentely, as fathers vse to chastice their childrē.

g This was begon in Salomón as a figure, but accōplished in Christ.

" Ebr. is this the lawe of man?

h Cometh not this rather of thy fre mercie, then of anie worthines that can be in man?

20 And

20 And what can Dauid say more vnto thee?
for thou, Lord God, knowest thy seruant.
21 For thy wordes sake, and according to
thine owne heart hast thou done all these
great things, to make them knowen vnto
thy seruant.
22 Wherefore thou art great, ô Lord God:
for there is none like thee, nether is there
anie god besides thee, according to all
that we haue heard with our eares.
23 *And what one people in ẏ earth is like
thy people, like Israél: whose God went &
redemed thé to him selfe, that they might
be his people, and that he might make
him a name, & do for [i] you great things,
and terrible for thy [k] lãd, ô Lord, *euen* for
thy people, whome thou redemest to thee
out of Egypt, *from* the [l] nacions, and their
gods?
24 For thou hast [m] ordeined thy people
Israél to be thy people for euer: and thou
Lord art become their God.
25 Now therefore, ô Lord God, confirme
for euer the worde that thou hast spoken
concerning thy seruant and his house, and
do as thou hast said.
26 And let thy Name be magnified for e-
uer by them that shal say, The Lord of
hostes *is* the God ouer Israél: and let the
[n] house of thy seruant Dauid be stablished
before thee.
27 For thou, ô Lord of hostes, God of Israél, hast reueiled vnto thy seruant, saying, I
wil buyld thee an house: therefore hathe
thy seruant "bene bolde to pray this
prayer vnto thee.
28 Therefore now, ô Lord God, (*for* thou
art God, and thy wordes be true, and thou
hast tolde this goodnes vnto thy seruãt)
29 Therefore now let it please thee to blesse the house of thy seruant, that it may cõtinue for euer before thee: for thou, ô Lord
God, hast [o] spoken it: and let the house of
thy seruant be blessed for euer, with thy
blessing.

Deu.4,7.

i O Israél.

k And inheritance, which is Israél.

l From the Egyptians and their idoles.

m He sheweth that Gods fre election is the onely cause, why the Israelites were chosen to be his people.

n This praier is moste effectual, whẽ we chiefly seke Gods glorie, and the accõplishment of his promes.

"*Ebr. founde his heart disposed.*

o Therefore I firmely beleue it shal come to passe.

CHAP. VIII.

1 *Dauid ouercommeth the Philistims, and other strange nacions, and maketh them tributaries to Israél.*

1 AFter*this now, Dauid smote the Philistims, and subdued them, & Dauid
toke "the bridle of bondage out of [a] the
hand of the Philistims.
2 And he smote Moáb, and measured them
with a corde, and cast them downe to the
ground: he measured them with [b] two
cordes to put them to death, & with one
ful corde to kepe them aliue: so became
the Moabites Dauids seruants, and broght
gifts.
3 ¶Dauid smote also Hadadézer the sonne
of Rehób King of Zobáh as he went to
"recouer his border at ẏ riuer "Euphrátes.
4 And Dauid toke a thousand and seuen

1.Chro.18,1. psal.60,2.

"*Or, metheg-ammah.*

a So that they paied no more tribute.

b He slewe two partes, as it pleased him and reserued the third.

"*Or, enlarge.*

"*Ebr. Perath.*

hundreth horsemen, and twẽtie thousand
fotemen, and "destroyed all the charets, but
he reserued an hundreth charets of them.
5 ¶ Then came "the Aramites of "Dam-
mések to succour Hadadézer King of Zo
báh, but Dauid slewe of the Aramites two
and twentie thousand men.
6 And he put a garison in [c] Arám of Dãmé-
sek: and the Aramites became seruants to
Dauid, [d] and broght giftes. And the Lord
saued Dauid wheresoeuer he went.
7 And Dauid toke the shields of golde
that belonged to the seruants of Hadadézer, and broght them to [e] Ierusalém.
8 And out of Betah, and Berothái (cities
of Hadadézer) Dauid broght exceding
muche brasse.
9 ¶Then Tói King of "Hamáth heard how
Dauid had smitten all the hoste of Hadadézer,
10 Therefore Tói sent Iorám his sonne
vnto King Dauid, "to salute him, and to
"[f] reioyce with him because he had foght
against Hadadézer, and beaten him (for
Hadadézer had warre with Tói) who
"broght with him vessels of siluer, and
vessels of golde & vessels of brasse.
11 And King Dauid did dedicate them vnto the Lord with the siluer and golde that
he had dedicate of all the nacions, which
he had subdued:
12 Of "Arám, & of Moáb, and of the children of Ammón, & of the Philistims, and
of Amalék, and of the spoyle of Hadadézer the sonne of Rehób King of Zobáh.
13 So Dauid gate a name after that he returned, and had slaine of the Aramites in the
"valley of salt eightene thousand men.
14 And he put a garison in Edóm: throughout all Edóm put he soldiers, and all they
of Edóm became Dauids seruants: and ẏ
Lord kept Dauid "whethersoeuer he wẽt.
15 Thus Dauid reigned ouer all Israél, and
executed [g] iudgement and iustice vnto all
his people.
16 And Ioáb the sonne of Zeruiáh *was* ouer
the hoste, and Iosshaphát the sonne of Ahilúd was "recorder.
17 And Zadók the sonne of Ahitúb, and
Ahimélech the sonne of Abiathár *were* ẏ
Priests, and Seraiáh the scribe.
18 And Benaiahú the sonne of Iehoiadá "&
the [h] Cherethites & the Pelethites, & Da
uids sonnes were chief rulers.

"*Or, hoght the horses of the charets.*

"*Or, the Syriãs.*

"*Or, of Damascus: that is, which dwelt nere Damascus.*

c In that part of Syria, where Damascus was.

d They payed yerely tribute.

e For the vse of the tẽple.

"*Or, Antiochia.*

"*Ebr. to aske peace.*

"*Ebr. blesse him*

f For seing Dauid victorious, he was glad to intreat of peace.

"*Ebr. in his hãd*

"*Or, Syria, or Cœlosyria.*

"*Or, in Ge-melah.*

"*Or, in all his entreprises.*

g He gaue iudgement in controuersies, and was merciful towarde the people.

"*Or, writer of Chronicles.*

"*Or, was ouer the Cherethites.*

h The Cherethites & Pelethites were as the Kigs garde, and had charge of his persone.

CHAP. IX.

9 *Dauid restoreth all the landes of Saúl to Miphibósheth the sonne of Ionathán. 10 He appointeth Zibá to se to the profit of his landes.*

1 ANd Dauid said, Is there yet any man
left of the house of Saúl, that I may
shewe him mercy for [a] Ionathans sake?
2 And there was of the housholde of Saúl

a Because of mine othe and promes made to Ionathán, *1.Sam.20,15.*

a seruant whose name was Zibá, & when
they had called him vnto Dauid, ẏ King
said vnto him, Art thou Zibá? And he
said, I thy seruant *am he*.
3 Then the King said, Remaineth there
yet none of the house of Saúl, on whome
I may shewe the [b] mercy of God? Zibá
then answered the King, Ionathán hathe
yet a sonne* lame of his feete.
4 Then the King said vnto him, Where is
he? And Zibá said vnto ẏ King, Beholde,
he is in the house of Machír the sonne of
Ammiél of Lo-debár.
5 ¶ Then King Dauid sent, and toke him
out of the house of Machír the sonne of
[c] Ammiél of Lo-debár.
6 Now when Mephibósheth the sonne of
Ionathán, the sonne of Saúl was come
vnto Dauid, he fell on his face, and did
reuerence. And Dauid said, Mephibósheth? And he answered, Beholde thy seruant.
7 Then Dauid said vnto him, Feare not:
for I wil surely shewe thee kindenes for
Ionathán thy fathers sake, and wil restore
thee all the "fields of Saúl thy father, and
thou shalt eat bread at my table continually.
8 And he bowed him selfe, and said, What
is thy seruãt, that thou shuldest loke vpon
suche [d] a dead dog as I am?
9 Then the King called Zibá Sauls seruãt,
and said vnto him, I haue giuen vnto thy
masters "sonne all that perteined to Saúl
and to all his house.
10 Thou therefore and [e] thy sonnes, and
thy seruants shal till the land for him, and
bring in that thy masters sonne may haue
foode to eat. And Mephibósheth thy masters sonne shal eat bread alway at my table (now Zibá had fiftene sonnes, and
twentie seruants)
11 Then said Zibá vnto the King, According to all ẏ my lord the King hathe commanded his seruant, so shal thy seruãt do,
[f] that Mephibósheth may eat at my table,
as one of the Kings sonnes.
12 Mephibósheth also had a yõg sonne named Michá, & all that dwelled in ẏ house
of Zibá, *were* seruants vnto Mephibósheth.
13 And Mephibósheth dwelt in Ierusalém:
for he did eat cõtinually at the Kings table, and was lame on bothe his feete.

b Suche mercie, as shal be acceptable to God.

Chap. 4, 4.

c Who was also called Eliám, ẏ father of Bath-sheba Dauids wife.

" Or, landes.

d Meaning, a despised persone.

" Or, nephewe.

e Be ye provident ouerseers and gouerners of his lãds that they may be profitable.

f That Mephibósheth may haue all thigs at commandement as becõmeth a Kings sonne.

CHAP. X.

4 The messengers of Dauid are vilainously entreated of the King of Ammón. 7 Ioáb is sent against the Ammonites.

1 After this, the* King of the children
of Ammón dyed, & Hanún his sonne reigned in his stede.
2 Then said Dauid, I wil shewe kindenes
vnto Hanún the sonne of Nahásh, as his
father [a] shewed kĩdenes vnto me. And Da
uid sent his seruãts to cõforte him for his
father. So Dauids seruants came into the
land of the children of Ammón.
3 And the princes of the children of Ammón said vnto Hanún their lord, "Thinkest thou ẏ Dauid doeth honour thy father, that he hathe sent comforters to thee?
hathe not Dauid *rather* sent his seruants
vnto thee, [b] to searche the citie, and to spie
it out, and to ouerthrowe it?
4 Wherefore Hanún toke Dauids seruants,
and shaued of the halfe of their bearde, &
cut of their garments in the middle, euen
to their buttockes, and sent them away.
5 ¶ When it was tolde vnto Dauid, he sent
to mete them (for the men were excedig-
ly ashamed) and the King said, Tarie
at Ierichó, vntil your beardes be growen,
then returne.
6 ¶ And when the children of Ammón
sawe that they [c] stanke in the sight of Dauid, the children of Ammón sent and hired the "Aramites of the house of Rehób,
and the Aramites of Zobá, twentie thousand footemen, and of King Maacáh a
thousand men, & of Ish-tób twelue thousand men.
7 And when Dauid heard of it, he sent Ioáb, and all the hoste of the strong men.
8 And the children of Ammón came out,
& put their armie in array at the entring
in of the gate: & the Aramites of [d] Zobá,
and of Rehób, and of Ish-tób, and of Maacáh *were* by them selues in the field.
9 When Ioáb sawe that the fronte of the
battel was against him before and behinde, he chose of all the choise of Israél, and put them in array against the Aramites.
10 And the rest of the people he deliuered
into the hand of Abishái his brother, that
he might put them in array against the
children of Ammón.
11 And he said, If the Aramites be strõger
then I, thou shalt helpe me, & if the children of Ammón be to strong for thee, I
wil come and succour thee.
12 Be strong and let vs be valiant for [e] our
people, and for the cities of our God, and
let the Lord do that which is good in his
eyes.
13 Then Ioáb, & the people that was with
him, ioyned in battel with the Aramites,
who fled before him.
14 And when the children of Ammón sawe
that the Aramites fled, they fled also before Abishái, and entred into the citie. So
Ioáb returned from the children of Ammón, and came to Ierusalém.
15 ¶ And when the Aramites sawe that thei
were smitten before Israél, they gathered
them together.

1 Chro. 19, 2.

a The childrẽ of God are not vnmindeful of a benefit receiued.

" Ebr. In thine eyes doeth Dauid.

b Their arrogant malice wolde not suffer them to se the simplicitie of Dauids heart: therefore their counsel turned to the destruction of their coũtrey.

c That they had deserued Dauids displeasure, for ẏ iniurie done to his ambassadours.

" Or, Syrians.

d These were diuers parts of the coũtrey of Syria, whereby appeareth that the Syriãs serued, where thei might haue interteinement, as now the Sweitzers do.

e Here is declared wherefore warre oght to be vndertaken: for the defence of true religion and Gods people.

16 And

*Or, Hadadézer.
*Or, Euphrates.

16 And Hadarézer sent, and broght out the
Aramites that were beyonde the *Riuer: &
they came to Helám, and Shobách ŷ captaine
of the hoste of Hadarézer *went* before
them.
17 When it was shewed Dauid, then he gathered
f all Isráél together, and passed ouer
Iordén and came to Helám: and the Aramites
set thẽ selues in array against Dauid,
and foght with him:

f Meaning, the greatest parte.

18 And the Aramites fled before Israél: &
Dauid destroyed g seuen hundreth charets
of the Aramites, & fourtie thousand horsemen,
and smote Shobách the captaine of
his hoste, who dyed there.

g Which were ŷ chiefest & moste principal: for in all he destroyed 7000, as 1 Chro 19,18: or, the soldiers which were in 700 charets.

19 And when all the Kings, *that were* seruãts
to Hadarézer, sawe that they fell before
Israél, they made peace with Israél, and
serued them. and the Aramites feared to
helpe the children of Ammón anie more.

CHAP. XI.

1 The citie Rabbáh is besieged. 4 Dauid committeth adulterie. 17 Vriáh is slaine. 27 Dauid marieth Bathshéba.

1 AND when the yere was a expired in ŷ
time when Kings go forthe *to battel,*
Dauid sent *Ioáb, and his seruants with
him, & all Israél, who destroyed the children
of Ammón, and besieged Rabbáh:
but Dauid remained in Ierusalém.

a The yere following about the spring time.
1 Chro. 20,1.

2 ¶ And when it was euening tide, Dauid
arose out of his b bed, and walked vpon
the roofe of the Kings palace: and frõ
the roofe he sawe a woman washing her
selfe: and the womã was very beautiful to
loke vpon.

b Whereupon he vsed to rest at after none, as was red of Ish-bósheth, Chap. 4,7.

3 And Dauid sent and inquired what woman
it was: and *one* said, Is not this Bethshéba
ŷ daughter of Eliám, wife to Vriáh
the c Hittite?

c Who was not an Israelite borne, but conuerted to the true religion.

4 Then Dauid sent messengers, and toke
her away: and she came vnto him and he
lay with her: (now she was *purified from
her vnclennes) and she returned vnto her
house.

Leui. 15,19. & 18,19.

5 And ŷ womã cõceiued: therefore she sent
& d tolde Dauid, & said, I am with childe.

d Fearing lest she shulde be stoned according to the Law.

6 ¶ Then Dauid sent to Ioáb, *saying,* Send
me Vriáh the Hittite. And Ioáb sent Vriáh
to Dauid.
7 And when Vriáh came vnto him, Dauid
demanded him how Ioáb did, & how
the people fared, and how the warre prospered.
8 Afterwarde Dauid said to Vriáh, e Go
downe to thine house, and wash thy feete.
So Vriáh departed out of the Kings palace,
& the King sent a present after him.

e Dauid thoght that if Vriáh lay with his wife, his faute might be cloked.

9 But Vriáh slept at the dore of the Kings
palace with all the seruants of his lord,
and went not downe to his house.
10 Then they tolde Dauid, saying, Vriáh
went not downe to his house: and Dauid
said vnto Vriáh, Comest thou not from
thy iourney? why didest thou not go
downe to thine house?
11 Thẽ Vriáh answered Dauid, f The Arke
of Israél, and Iudáh dwel in tents: and
my lord Ioáb and the seruants of my lord
abide in the open fields: shal I then go into
mine house to eat and drinke, and lie
with my wife? *by* thy life, & *by* the life of
thy soule, I wil not do this thing.

f Hereby God wolde touche Dauids conscience, that seing the fidelitie & religiõ of his seruãt, he wolde declare him selfe so forgetful of God and iniurious to his seruant.

12 Then Dauid said vnto Vriáh, Tarie yet
this daye, and tomorowe I wil send thee
awaie. So Vriáh abode in Ierusalém that
day, and the morowe.
13 Then Dauid called him, & he did eat and
drinke before him, & he made him g drõke:
& at euen he went out to lie on his couche
with the seruants of his lord, but went not
downe to his house.

g He made hĩ drinke more liberally thẽ he was wonte to do, thinkĩg hereby he wolde haue lyen by his wife.

14 And on the morowe Dauid wrote a letter
to Ioáb, and sent it by the hand of Vriáh.
15 And he wrote *thus in the letter, h Put ye
Vriáh in the forefrõte of the strength of
the battel, & recule ye backe from him,
that he may be smitten, and dye.

*Ebr. saying.
h Except God cõtinually vpholde vs with his mightie Spirit, ŷ moste perfect fall headlong into all vice & abomination.

16 ¶ So whẽ Ioáb besieged ŷ citie, he assigned
Vriáh vnto a place, where he knewe
that strong men *were.*
17 And the men of the citie came out, and
foght with Ioáb: & there fell of the people
of the seruants of Dauid, & Vriáh the
Hittite also dyed.
18 Then Ioáb sent and tolde Dauid all the
things concerning the warre,
19 ¶ And he charged the messenger, saying,
When thou hast made an end of telling
the matters of the warre vnto the King,
20 *And if the Kings angre arise, so that he
say vnto thee, Wherefore approched ye vn
to ŷ citie to fight? knewe ye not that they
wolde hurle from the wall?

*Or, Thou shalt do this, if.

21 Who smote Abimélech sonne of i Ierubésheth?
did not a woman cast a piece of a
milstone vpon him from the wall, and he
dyed in Thebéz? why went you nye the
wall? Then say thou, Thy seruant Vriáh
the Hittite is also dead.

i Meaning, Gideón, Iudg. 9,52.

22 ¶ So the messenger went, and came and
shewed Dauid all that Ioáb had sent him
for.
23 And the messenger said vnto Dauid,
Certeinly the men preuailed against vs,
and came out vnto vs into the field, but
we *pursued them vnto the entring of the
gate.

*Ebr. were against them.

24 But ŷ shooters shot frõ the wall against
thy seruants, and *some* of the Kings seruants
be dead: and thy seruant Vriáh the
Hittite is also dead.
25 Then Dauid said vnto the messenger,
k Thus shalt thou say vnto Ioáb, Let not
this thing trouble thee: for the sworde de-

k He dissembleth with the messenger, to ŷ intent that nether his cruel commãdemẽt, nor Ioabs wicked obedience might be espied.

"Ebr. so and so.

uoureth "one aswel as another: make thy
battel more strong against the citie & destroy it, & encourage thou him.
26 ¶And when the wife of Vriáh heard
that her housband Vriáh was dead, she
mourned for her housband.
27 So when the mourning was past, Dauid
sent & toke her into his house, and she became his wife, and bare him a sonne: but
the thing that Dauid had done, "displeased the Lord.

"Ebr. was euil in the eyes of the Lord.

CHAP. XII.

1 Dauid reproued by Nathán confesseth his sinne. 18 The childe cōceiued in adulterie, dyeth. 24 Salomón is borne. 26 Rabbáh is taken. 31 The citizens are grieuously punished.

a Because Dauid lay nowe drowned in sinne, the louing mercie of God, which suffreth not his to perish, waketh his consciēce by this similitude, and bringeth him to repentance

1 THen the Lord [a] sent Nathán vnto Dauid, who came to him, and said vnto
him, There were two men in one citie, the
one riche, and the other poore.
2 The riche man had exceding many shepe
and oxen:
3 But the poore had none at all, saue one
litle shepe which he had boght, & nourished vp: and it grewe vp with him, and
with his children also, and did eat of his
owne morsels, & dranke of his owne cup,
and slept in his bosome, and was vnto him
as his daughter.
4 Now there came a "stranger vnto the
riche mā, who "refused to take of his owne
shepe, and of his owne oxen to dresse for
the stranger that was come vnto him, but
toke the poore mans shepe, and dressed it
for the man that was come to him.
5 Thē "Dauid was exceding wrothe with
the mā, and said to Nathán, As the Lord
liueth, the man that hathe done this thing,
"shal surely dye,
6 And he shal restore the lābe *foure folde,
because he did this thing, and had no pitie thereof.
7 Then Nathán said to Dauid, Thou art
the man. Thus sayth the Lord God of
Israél, *I anointed thee King ouer Israél,
and deliuered thee out of the hand of
Saúl,
8 And gaue thee thy lords [b] house, and thy
lords [c] wiues into thy bosome, and gaue
thee the house of Israél, and of Iudáh, &
wolde moreouer (*if that had bene* to litle)
haue giuen thee [d] suche and suche things.
9 Wherefore hast thou despised the commandement of the Lord, to do euil in his
sight? thou hast killed Vriáh the Hittite
with the sworde, and hast taken his wife *to
be* thy wife, and hast slaine him with the
sworde of the [e] children of Ammón.
10 Now therefore the sworde shal neuer
departe from thine house, because thou
hast despised me, and taken the wife of
Vriáh the Hittite to be thy wife.
11 Thus saith the Lord, Beholde, I wil raise

"Or, wayfaring man.
"Or, spared.
"Ebr. The angre of Dauid was kindeled.
"Ebr. is the childe of death.
Exod. 22,1.
2. Sam. 16,23.
b For Dauid succeded Saúl in his kingdome.
c The Iewes vnderstād this of Egláh and Michal, or of Rizpáh and Michál.
d That is, greater things thē these: for Gods loue and benefites increase toward his, if by their ingratitude they stay him not.
e Thou hast moste cruelly giuen him into the hands of Gods enemies.

vp euil against thee out of thine owne
house, and wil *take thy wiues before thine eyes, & giue them vnto thy neighbour,
and he shal lye with thy wiues in the sight
of this [f] sunne.
12 For thou didest it secretly: but I wil do
this thing before all Israél, and before the
sunne.
13 Then Dauid said vnto Nathán, *I haue
sinned against ȳ Lord. And Nathán said
vnto Dauid, The Lord also hathe [g] put
away thy sinne, thou shalt not dye.
14 Howbeit because by this dede thou hast
caused the enemies of the Lord to [h] blaspheme, the childe that is borne vnto thee
shal surely dye.
15 ¶So Nathán departed vnto his house:
and the Lord stroke the childe that V-
riahs wife bare vnto Dauid, and it was
sicke.
16 Dauid therefore besoght God for the
childe, and fasted and [i] went in, and laye
all night vpon the earth.
17 Then the Elders of his house arose *to
come* vnto him, and to cause him to rise
from the grounde: but he wolde not, nether did he eat [k] meat with them.
18 So on the seuenth day the childe dyed: &
the seruants of Dauid feared to tel him
that the childe was dead: for thei said, Beholde, while the childe was aliue, we spake
vnto him, and he wolde not hearken vnto
our voyce: how then shal we say vnto him,
The childe is dead, "to vexe *him* more?
19 But when Dauid sawe that his seruants
whispered, Dauid perceiued that ȳ childe
was dead: therefore Dauid said vnto his
seruāts, Is the childe dead? And they said,
He is dead.
20 Then Dauid [l] arose from the earth, &
washed and anointed him selfe, and changed his apparel, and came into the house
of the Lord, and worshiped, & afterward
came to his owne house, and bade that thei
shulde set bread before him, and he did
eat.
21 Then said [m] his seruāts vnto him, What
thing is this, that thou hast done? thou
didest fast and wepe for the childe, while
it was aliue, but whē the childe was dead,
thou didest rise vp, and eat meat.
22 And he said, While the childe was yet
aliue, I fasted, and wept: for I said, Who
can tel *whether* God wil haue mercie on
me, that the childe may liue?
23 But now being dead, wherefore shulde I
now fast? [n] Can I bring him againe anie
more? I shal go to him, but he shal not returne to me.
24 ¶And Dauid comforted Bath-shéba his
wife, and went in vnto her, and lay with
her, *and she bare a sonne, [o] & he called
his name Salomón: also ȳ Lord loued hī.

Deu. 28,30. chap. 16,22.
f Meaning, openly, as at none dayes.
Eccles. 47,13.
g For the Lord seketh but ȳ ȳ sinner wolde turne to him.
h In saying, that the Lord hathe appointed a wicked man to reigne ouer his people.
i To wit, to his priuie chāber.
k Thinking by his instāt praier that God wolde haue restored his childe, but God had otherwise determined.
"Ebr. & he wil do him selfe euil.
l Shewing that our lamentations oght not to be excessiue, but moderate: and ȳ we must praise God in all his doings.
m As they ȳ considered not that God granteth manie things to the sobbes & teares of ȳ faithful.
n By this consideration he appaised his sorrowe.
Mat. 1,6.
o To wit, the Lord, 1. Chro. 22,9.

25 *Therefore

25 For *the Lord* had sent by Nathán the
p Prophet: therefore q * he called his name Iedidiáh, because the Lord *loued him.*

p To call him Salomón. q Meaning, Dauid
1.Chro.22.9

26 ¶ Then Ioáb foght against Rabbáh of
the children of Ammón, and toke the ″ citie of the kingdome.

″ *Or, the chief citie.*

27 Therefore Ioáb sent messengers to Dauid, saying, I haue foght against Rabbáh,
and haue taken the citie of r waters.

r That is, the chief citie, & where all the cõduits are, is as good as taken

28 Now therefore gather the rest of the
people together, and besiege the citie, that
thou maiest take it, lest ″ the victorie be
attributed to me.

″ *Ebr. my name be called vpõ it.*

29 So Dauid gathered all the people together, and went against Rabbáh, and besieged it, and toke it.

30 *And he toke their Kings crowne from
his head, (which wayed a f talent of golde,
with precious stones) & it was *set* on Dauids head: and he broght away the spoile
of the citie in exceding great abundance.

1.Chro.20.2.
f That is, threscore pounde after ỹ weight of the cõmune talent.

31 And he caryed away the people that was
therein, and put them vnder t sawes, and
vnder yron harowes, and vnder axes of
yron, and cast them into the tyle kylne: e-
uen thus did he with all the cities of the
children of Ammón. Then Dauid and all
the people returned vnto Ierusalém.

t Signifying, ỹ as thei were malicious enemies of God, so he put them to cruel death.

CHAP. XIII.

14 Amnón Dauids sonne defileth his sister Tamár.
19 Tamár is comforted by her brother Absalóm.
29 Absalom therefore killeth Amnón.

1 NOw after this so it was, that Absalóm the sonne of Dauid hauing a
faire sister, whose name *was* a Tamár,
Amnón the sonne of Dauid loued her.

a Tamár was Absalōs sister both by father & mother, and Amnons onely by father.

2 And Amnón was so sore vexed, that he
fel sicke for his sister Tamár: for she was
a b virgin, & it semed harde to Amnón
to do any thing to her.

b And therefore kept in her fathers house, as virgins were accustomed.

3 But Amnón had a friend called Ionadáb, the sonne of Shimeáh Dauids brother: and Ionadáb was a very subtile man.
4 Who said vnto him, Why *art* thou the
Kings sonne so leane frõ day to day? wilt
thou not tel me? Then Amnón answered
him, I loue Tamár my brother Absalōs
sister.
5 And Ionadáb said vnto him, c Lye downe
on thy bed, and make thy selfe sicke: and
when thy father shal come to se thee, say
vnto him, I pray thee, let my sister Tamár come, and giue me meat, and let her
dresse meat in my sight, that I may se it,
and eat it of her hand.

c Here we se that there is no enterprise so wicked, ỹ can lacke coũsel to further it.

6 ¶ So Amnón laye downe, & made him
selfe sicke: and when the King came to se
him, Amnón said vnto the King, I pray
thee, let Tamár my sister come, & make
me a couple of d cakes in my sight, that I
may receiue meat at her hand.

d Meaning, some delicate & dentie meat.

7 Then Dauid sent home to Tamár, saying, Go now to thy brother Amnōs house, and dresse him meat.
8 ¶ So Tamár went to her brother Amnons house, and he laye downe: and she
toke ″ floure, and knead it, and made cakes
in his sight, and did bake the cakes.

″ *Or, paste.*

9 And she toke a panne, & e powred them
out before him, but he wolde not eat. Thẽ
Amnón said, Cause ye euery man to go
out from f me: so euery man went out frõ
him.

e That is, she serued them on a dishe.
f For ỹ wicked are ashamed to do that before mẽ, which thei are not afrayed to cõmit in ỹ sight of God.

10 Then Amnón said vnto Tamár, Bring
the meat into the chamber, that I may eat
of thine hand. And Tamár toke the cakes
which she had made, and broght them into the chamber to Amnón her brother.
11 And when she had set them before him
to eat, he toke her, and said vnto her, Come, lye with me, my sister.
12 But she answered him, Naye, my brother, do not force me: for no suche thing
* oght to be done in Israél: commit not
this folie.

Leui.18.9.

13 And I, ″ whether shal I cause my shame
to go: and thou shalt be as one g of the
fooles in Israél: now therefore, I pray
thee, speake to the King, for he wil not
denye me vnto thee.

″ *Or, How shal I put away my shame.*
g As a lewde & wicked persone.

14 Howbeit he wolde not hearkẽ vnto her
voyce, but being stronger then she, forced
her, and lay with her.
15 Then Amnón hated her excedingly, so
that the hatred wherewith he hated her,
was greater then the loue, wherewith he
had loued her: and Amnón said vnto her,
Vp, get thee hence
16 And she answered him, ″ There *is* no
cause: this euil (to put me away) is greater
then the other that thou didest vnto me:
but he wolde not heare her,

″ *Or, for this cause.*

17 But called his ″ seruant that serued him,
and said, Put this woman now out from
me, and locke the dore after her.

″ *Or, boye.*

18 (And she had a garment of h diuers
coulers vpon her: for with suche garmẽts
were the Kings daughters that were virgins, appareled) Then his seruant broght
her out, and locked the dore after her.

h For ỹ which was of diuers coulers or pieces in those dayes was had in greatest estimaciõ, Gen. 37.3 iudg.5.30.

19 And Tamár put ashes on her head &
rent the garment of diuers coulers which
was on her, and layed her hand on her
head, & went her way crying.
20 And Absalóm her brother said vnto
her, Hathe Amnón thy brother bene with
thee? Now yet be i styl, my sister: he is thy
brother: let not this thing grieue thine
heart. So Tamár remained desolate in
her brother Absaloms house.

i For thogh he conceiued soden vẽgeãce in his heart, yet he dissembled it til occasion serued, and comforted his sister.

21 ¶ But when King Dauid heard all these
things, he was very wrothe.
22 And Absalóm said vnto his brother
Amnón nether good nor bad: for Absalóm hated Amnón, because he had forced his sister Tamár.

23 ¶And after the time of two yeres, Absálóm had shepesherers in *Baal-hazór,
which is beside Ephráim, and [k] Absálóm
called all the Kings sonnes.

*Or, in the plaine of Hazór.
k To wit, to a banket, thinking thereby to fulfil his wicked purpose.

24 And Absálóm came to the King & said,
Beholde now, thy seruant hathe shepesherers: I pray thee, that the King with his
seruants wolde go with thy seruant.
25 But the King answered Absálóm, Naye
my sonne, I pray thee, let vs not go all, lest
we be chargeable vnto thee. Yet Absálóm
laye sore vpō him: howbeit he wolde not
go, but *thanked him.

*Ebr. blessed.

26 Thē said Absálóm, But, I pray thee, shal
not my brother [l] Amnón go with vs?
And the King answered him, Why shulde
he go with thee?

l Pretending to the King, ẏ Amnón was moste deare vnto him.

27 But Absálóm was instant vpon him, and
he sent Amnón with him, & all the Kings
children.
28 ¶Now had Absálóm commanded his
seruants, saying, Marke now whē Amnōs
heart is mery with wine, and when I say
vnto you, Smite Amnón, kil him, feare
not, for haue not [m] I commanded you?
be bolde therefore, and play the men.

m Suche is the pride of the wicked masters, that in all their wicked commandements they thinke to be obeyed.

29 And the seruants of Absálóm did vnto
Amnón, as Absálóm had commanded: &
all the Kings sonnes arose, and euery man
gate him vp vpon his mule, and fled.
30 ¶And while thei were in the way, tidīgs
came to Dauid, saying, Absálóm hathe
slayne all the Kings sonnes, and there is
not one of them left.
31 Then the King arose, and tare his garments, and lay on the [n] grounde, and all
his seruants stode by with their clothes
rent.

n Lamenting, as he that felt the wrath of God vpon his house, Chap. 12,10.

32 And Ionadáb the sonne of Shimeáh
Dauids brother answered and said, Let
not my lord suppose that thei haue slayne
all the yong men the Kings sonnes: for
Amnón onely is dead, *because Absálóm
had reported *so*, since he forced his sister
Tamár.

*Ebr. because it was put in Absaloms mouthe.

33 Now therefore let not my lord ẏ King
*take ẏ thing so grieuously, to thinke that
all the Kings sonnes are dead: *for Amnón onely is dead.

*Or, take it to heart.
*Or, but.

34 ¶Then Absálóm fled: & the yong man
that kept the watche, lift vp his eyes, and
loked, & beholde, there came muche people by the way of the hil side *behinde
him.

*Or, one after an other.

35 And Ionadáb said vnto the King, Beholde, the Kings sonnes come: as thy seruant said, [o] so it is.

o That onely Amnón is dead.

36 And assone as he had left speaking, beholde, the Kings sonnes came, and lift vp
their voyces, and wept: and the King also
and all his seruants wept excedingly sore.
37 But Absálóm fled away, and went to
[p] Talmái the sonne of Ammihúr King of
Geshúr: and *Dauid* mourned for his sonne
euery day.

p For Maachái his mother was the daughter of this Talmái, Chap 3,3.

38 So Absálóm fled, and went to Geshúr, &
was there thre yeres.
39 And King Dauid *desired to go forthe
vnto Absálóm, because he was pacified
concerning Amnón, seing he was dead.

*Or, ceased.

CHAP. XIIII.

2 Absálóm is reconciled to his father by the subteltie of Ioáb. 24 Absálóm may not se the Kings face 25 The beautie of Absálóm. 30 He causeth Ioabs corne to be burnt, and is broght to his fathers presence.

1 THen Ioáb the sonne of Zeruiáh perceiued, that the Kings [a] heart was
towarde Absálóm,

a That ẏ King fauoured him.

2 And Ioáb sent to Tekóah, and broght
thence a *subtile woman, & said vnto her,
I pray thee, faine thy selfe to mourne, and
now put on mourning apparel, & [b] anoint
not thy selfe with oyle: but be as a woman
that had now long time mourned for the
dead.

*Or, wise.
b In token of mourning: for thei vsed anointing to seme cheareful.

3 And come to the King, and speake of this
maner vnto him (for Ioáb *taught her
what she shulde say)

*Ebr. put words in her mouthe.

4 ¶Then the woman of Tekóah spake
vnto the King, and fel downe on her face
to the grounde, & did obeisance, and said,
*Helpe, ô King.

*Ebr. Saue.

5 Then the King said vnto her, What ayleth thee? And she answered, I am in dede
a *widowe, and mine housband is dead:
6 And thine hādmayd had two [c] sonnes, &
they two stroue together in the field: (and
there was none to parte them) so the one
smote the other, and slewe him.

*Ebr. a widowe woman.
c Vnder this parable she describeth the death of Amnón by Absálóm.

7 And beholde, the whole familie is risen
against thine handmayd, & thei said, Deliuer him that smote his brother, that we
may kil him for the [d] soule of his brother whome he slewe, that we may destroy
the heire also: so they shal quenche my
sparkle which is left, and shal not leaue to
mine housbād nether name nor posteritie
vpon the earth.

d Because he hathe slayne his brother, he oght to be slayne according to the Lawe, Gen 9, 6 exod 21,12.

8 And the King said vnto the woman, Go
to thine house, and I wil giue a charge for
thee.
9 Then the woman of Tekóah said vnto
the King, My lord, ô King, this [e] trespasse
be on me, and on my fathers house, & the
King and his throne *be* *giltles.

e As touching the breache of ẏ Lawe w punisheth blood, let me beare the blame.
*Or, innocent.

10 And ẏ King said, Bring him to me that
speaketh against thee, and he shal touche
thee nomore.
11 Then said she, I pray thee, let the King
[f] remember the Lord thy God, that thou
woldest not suffer many reuēgers of blood
to destroy, lest thei slaye my sōne. And he
answered, As the Lord liueth, there shal
not one heere of thy sonne fall to ẏ earth.

f Sweare that thei shal not reuenge the blood, which are many in nomber.

12 Then the woman said, I pray thee, let
thine hādmaid speake a worde to my lord
the

the King. And he ſaid, Say on.
13 Then the woman ſaid, Wherefore then
haſt thou [g] thoght ſuche a thing againſt
the people of God? or *why* doeth ẏ King,
as one which is fautie, ſpeake this thing,
that he wil not bring againe his baniſhed?

g Why doeſt thou giue contrary ſentence in thy ſonne Abſalóm?

14 For we muſt nedes dye, & *we are* as water
ſpilt on the grounde, which can not be
gathered vp againe: nether doeth God
*ſpare anie perſone, yet doeth he appoint
[h] meanes, not to caſt out from him him
that is expelled.

*Or, accept.

h God hathe pruided waies (as ſanctuaries) to ſaue thē oft times, whome man iudgeth worthy death.

15 Now therefore that I am come to ſpeake
of this thing vnto my lord the King,
the cauſe is that the people [i] haue made me
afraide: therefore thine handmaid ſaid,
Now wil I ſpeake vnto ẏ King: it may be
that the King wil performe the requeſt
of his handmaid.

i For I thoght they wolde kil this mine heir.

16 For the King wil heare, to deliuer his
handmaid out of the hand of the man that
wolde deſtroye me, and alſo my ſonne frō
the inheritance of God.
17 Therefore thine handmaid ſaid, The
worde of my lord the King ſhal nowe be
"comfortable: for my lord the King is
euen as an [k] Angel of God in hearing of
good & bad: therefore the Lord thy God
be with thee.

"Ebr. reſt.

k Is of great wiſdome to diſcerne right from wrong.

18 Then the King anſwered, and ſaid vnto
the woman, Hide not frō me, I pray thee,
the thing that I ſhal aſke thee. And ẏ woma
ſaid, Let my lord ẏ King now ſpeake.
19 And the King ſaid, Is not [l] the hand of
Ioáb with thee in all this? Then the woman
anſwered, & ſaid, As thy ſoul liueth,
my lord the King, I wil not turne to the
right hand nor to the left from oght that
my lord the King hathe ſpoken: for euen
thy ſeruāt Ioáb bade me, & he put all theſe
wordes in ẏ mouthe of thine handmaid.

l Haſt not thou done this by ẏ counsel of Ioáb?

20 For to the intent that I ſhulde [m] change
the forme of ſpeache, thy ſeruant Ioáb
hathe done this thīg: but *my lord is wiſe
according to the wiſdome of an Angel
of God to vnderſtand all things that are
in the earth.

m By ſpeaking rather in a parable thē plainely.

*Or, none can hide oght from the King.

21 ¶ And ẏ King ſaid vnto Ioáb, Beholde
now, I haue [n] done this thing: go then,
& bring the yong man Abſalóm againe.

n I haue grāted thy requeſt.

22 And Ioáb fel to the grounde on his face,
and bowed him ſelfe, and "thanked the
King. Then Ioáb ſaid, This day thy ſeruant
knoweth, that I haue founde grace
in thy ſight, my lord the King, in that
the King hathe fulfilled the requeſt of his
ſeruant.

"Ebr. bleſſed.

23 ¶ And Ioáb aroſe, and went to Geſhúr,
and broght Abſalóm to Ieruſalém.
24 And the King ſaid, Let him [o] turne to
his owne houſe, and not ſe my face. So
Abſalóm turned to his owne houſe, and
ſawe not the Kings face.

o Couering hereby his affection, and ſhewing ſome parte of iuſtice to pleaſe ẏ people.

25 Now in all Iſraél there was none to be
ſo muche praiſed for beautie as Abſalóm:
from the ſole of his foote euen to the top
of his head there was no blemiſh in him.
26 And whē he polled his head, (for at euerie
yeres end he polled it: becauſe it was
to heauy for him, therefore he polled it)
he weighed the heere of his head at two
hundreth [p] ſhekels by the Kings weight.

p Which weighed 6 l. 4. onces after halfe an once the ſhekel.

27 And Abſalóm had thre ſonnes, and one
daughter named Tamár, which was a faire
woman to loke vpon.
28 ¶ So Abſalóm dwelt ẏ ſpace of two yeres
in Ieruſalém, & ſawe not the Kings face.
29 Therefore Abſalóm ſent for Ioáb to
ſend him to the King, but he wolde not
come to him: and when he ſent againe, he
wolde not come.
30 Therefore he ſaid vnto his ſeruants, Beholde,
Ioáb hathe a *field by my place, &
hathe barly therein: go, & ſet it [q] on fire:
& Abſaloms ſeruants ſet the field on fire.

*Or, poſſeſsion.

q The wicked are impacient in their affections, & ſpare no vnlawful meanes to cōpaſſe them.

31 Then Ioáb aroſe, and came to Abſalóm
vnto his houſe, and ſaid vnto him, Wherefore
haue thy ſeruants burnt my field
with fire?
32 And Abſalóm anſwered Ioáb, Beholde,
I ſent for thee, ſaying, Come thou hither,
and I wil ſend thee to the King for to
ſay, Wherfore am I come from Geſhúr?
It had bene better for me to haue bene
there ſtil: now therefore let me ſe ẏ Kings
face: and [r] if there be anie treſpaſſe in me,
let him kil me.

r If I haue offended by reuenging my ſiſters diſhonour: thus the wicked iuſtifie them ſelues in their euil.

33 Then Ioáb came to the King, and tolde
him: and he called for Abſalóm, who came
to the King, and bowed him ſelfe to
the grounde on his face before the King,
and the King kiſſed Abſalóm.

CHAP. XV.

*3 The practiſes of Abſalóm to aſpire to the kingdome.
14 Dauid and his flee. 31 Dauids prayer. 34 Huſhái is ſent to Abſalóm to diſcouer his counſel.*

1 AFter this, Abſalóm "prepared him
charets and horſes, and fiftie men to
[a] runne before him.

"Ebr. made him.

a Which were as a garde to ſet forthe his eſtate.

2 And Abſalóm roſe vp early, and ſtode
hard by the entring in of the gate: & euerie
mā that had anie *matter, & came to ẏ
King for iudgement, him did Abſalóm
call vnto him, and ſaid, Of what citie art
thou? And he anſwered, Thy ſeruant *is* of
one of the [b] tribes of Iſraél.

*Or, controuerſie.

b That is, noting of what citie or place he was.

3 Thē Abſalóm ſaid vnto him, Se, thy matters
are good & righteous, but there is no
man *deputed* of the King to heare thee.
4 Abſalóm ſaid moreouer, [c] Oh ẏ I were
made iudge in the land, that euerie man ẇ
hathe anie matter or controuerſie, might
come to me, that I might do him iuſtice.
5 And when anie man came nere to him,
and did him obeiſance, he put forthe his
hand, and toke him, and kiſſed him.

c Thus by ſlander, flatterie, and faire promiſes the wicked ſeke preferrement.

6 And on this maner did Absalóm to all
Israél, that came to the King for iudgement: so Absalóm [d] stale the heartes of
the men of Israél.
7 ¶ And after [e] fortie yeres, Absalóm said
vnto the King, I pray thee, let me go to
Hebrón, and rendre my vowe which I haue vowed vnto the Lord.
8 For thy seruant vowed a vowe when I remained in Geshúr, in Arám, saying, If the
Lord shal bring me againe in dede to Ierusalém, I wil [f] serue the Lord.
9 And the King said vnto him, Go in peace. So he arose, and went to Hebrón.
10 ¶ Then Absalóm sent spies throughout
all the tribes of Israél, saying, When ye
heare the sounde of the trumpet, ye shal
say, Absalóm reigneth in Hebrón.
11 ¶ And with Absalóm went two hundreth
men out of Ierusalém, that were [g] called:
and they wēt in their simplicitie, knowing
nothing.
12 Also Absalóm sent for Ahithóphel the
Gilonite Dauids counseler, from his citie
Gilóh, while he offred sacrifices: and the
treason was great: for the people " encreased stil with Absalóm.
13 ¶ Then came a messenger to Dauid,
saying, The hearts of the men of Israél
are turned after Absalóm.
14 Then Dauid said vnto all his seruants
that were with him at Ierusalém, Vp, and
let vs flee: for we shal not escape frō [h] Absalóm: make spede to departe, lest he come sodenly and take vs, & bring euil vpō
vs, and smite the citie with the edge of
the sworde.
15 And the Kings seruants said vnto him,
Beholde, thy seruāts *are ready to do* according to all that my lord the King shal
"appoint.
16 So the King departed and all his housholde " after him, and the King left ten
concubines to kepe the house.
17 And the King went forthe and all the
people after him, and taryed in a " place
[i] farre of.
18 And all his seruāts went about him, and
all the [k] Cherethites and all the Pelethites and all ẏ Gittites, *euen* sixe hūdreth
men which were come after him frō Gath,
went before the King.
19 Then said the King to [l] Ittái the Gittite, Wherefore commest thou also with
vs? Returne and abide with the King, for
thou art a stranger: departe thou therefore to thy place.
20 Thou camest yesterday, and shulde I
cause thee to wander to day and go with
vs? I wil go whither I can: therefore returne thou, and cary againe thy [m] brethren:
mercie and [n] trueth *be* with thee.
21 And Ittái answered the King, and said,
As the Lord liueth, & as my lord the King
liueth, in what place my lord the King
shalbe, whether in death or life, euen there
surely wil thy seruant be.
22 Then Dauid said to Ittái, Come, & go
forwarde. And Ittái the Gittite went, and
all his men, and all the children that were
with him.
23 And all the countrey wept with a loude
voyce, and [o] all the people went forward,
but the King passed ouer the brooke Kidrón: and all the people wēt ouer towarde
the way of the wildernes.
24 ¶ And lo, Zadók also *was there*, and all the
Leuites with hym, [p] bearing the Arke of
the couenant of God: & they set downe ẏ
Arke of God, and Abiathár wēt [q] vp vntil
the people were all come out of the citie.
25 Then the King said vnto Zadók, Carie
the Arke of God againe into the citie: if I
shal finde fauour in the eyes of the Lord,
he wil bring me againe, & shewe me *bothe*
it, and the " Tabernacle thereof.
26 But if he thus say, I haue no delite in
thee, beholde, [r] here am I, let him do to
me as semeth good in his eyes.
27 The King said againe vnto Zadók the
Priest, Art not thou a * Seer? returne into
the citie in peace, & your two sonnes with
you: *to wit*, Ahimáaz thy sonne, and Ionathán the sonne of Abiathár.
28 Beholde, I wil tarie in the fieldes of the
wildernes, vntil there come some worde
from you to be tolde me.
29 Zadók therefore and Abiathár caryed
the Arke of God againe to Ierusalém, and
they taried there.
30 And Dauid went vp the mount of oliues
and wept as he went vp, and had his head
[s] couered, and wēt barefooted: and all the
people that was with him, had euerie man
his head couered, and as they went vp, they
wept.
31 Then one tolde Dauid, saying, Ahithóphel is one of them that haue conspired
with Absalóm: and Dauid said, ô Lord, I
pray thee, turne the [t] counsel of Ahithóphel into foolishnes.
32 ¶ Then Dauid came to the toppe of the
mount where he worshiped God: and beholde, Hushái the Archite came against
him with his coate torne, & hauing earth
vpon his head.
33 Vnto whome Dauid said, If thou go with
me, thou shalt be a burthen vnto me.
34 But if thou returne to the citie, and say
vnto Absalóm, I wil be thy [u] seruant, ô
King, (as I haue bene in time past thy fathers seruant, so wil I now be thy seruant)
then thou maiest bring me the counsel of
Ahithóphel to noght.
35 And hast thou not there with thee Zadók and Abiathár the Priests? therefore
whatsoeuer

d By intising them from his father to him selfe.
e Counting from the time that the Israelites had asked a King of Samuél.
f By offring a peace offring, ẇ was lawful to do in anie place.
g And byd to his feast in Hebrón.
" Ebr. went and increased.
h Whose heart he sawe that Satan had so possessed, that he wolde leaue no mischief vnattepted.
" Ebr. chose.
" Ebr. at his feete.
" Or, house.
i To wit, frō Ierusalém.
k These were as the Kings garde, or as some write, his counselers.
l Who, as some write, was the Kings sonne of Gath.
m Meaning, them of his familie.
n God requite thee thy friēdship and fidelitie.
o To wit, the six hundreth men.
p Which was the charge of the Kohathites, Nomb. 4,4.
q To stand by the Arke.
" Or, his tabernacle.
r The faithful in all their afflictions shewe them selues obedient to Gods wil.
* 1. Sam. 9,9.
s With asshes & dust in signe of sorrowe.
t The counsel of the crafty worldelings doeth more harme thē the open force of the enemie.
u Thogh Hushái dissembled here at the Kings requeste, yet may we not vse this exāple to excuse our dissimulacion.

whatsoeuer thou shalt heare out of the
Kings house, thou shalt shewe to Zadók
and Abiathár the Priests.
36 Beholde, there are with them their two
sonnes: Ahimáaz Zadoks *sonne*, and Ionathán Abiathars *sonne*: by them also shal ye
send me euerie thing that ye can heare.
37 So Husħái Dauids friend went into the
citie: and Absalóm came into Ierusalém.

CHAP. XVI.

1 The infidelitie of Zibá. 5 Shimeí curseth Dauid. 16 Husħái cometh to Absalóm. 21 The counsel of Ahithóphel for the concubines.

1 WHen Dauid was a litle past the
[a] toppe *of the hil*, beholde, Zibá the
seruant of Mephibóſheth met him with a
couple of asses sadled, and vpon them two
hundreth *cakes* of bread, and one hundreth
bunshes of raisins, & an hundreth of " dryed figges, and a bottel of wine.
2 And ẏ King said vnto Zibá, What meanest thou by these? And Zibá said, They
be [b] asses for the Kings housholde to ride on, and bread and dryed figges for the
yong men to eat, and wine, that the faint
may drincke in the wildernes.
3 And the King said, But where is thy masters sonne? Thẽ Zibá answered the King,
Beholde, he remaineth in Ierusalém: for
he said, This day shal the house of Israél
restore me the kingdome of my father.
4 Then said the King to Zibá, Beholde,
thine are all that *perteined* vnto Mephibósheth. And Zibá said, " I beseche thee, let
me finde grace in thy sight, my lord, ô
King.
5 ¶ And when King Dauid came to [c] Bahurím, beholde, thence came out a man of
the familie of the house of Saúl, named
Shimeí the sonne of Gerá: and he came
out, and cursed.
6 And he cast stones at Dauid, and at all
the seruants of King Dauid: and all the
people, and all the men of warre *were* on
his [d] right hand, and on his left.
7 And thus said Shimeí when he cursed,
Come forthe, come forthe thou " murtherer, and " wicked man.
8 The Lord hathe broght vpon thee all the
[e] blood of the house of Saúl, in whose stead
thou hast reigned: and the Lord hathe deliuered the kingdome into the hand of
Absalóm thy sonne: and beholde, thou
art *taken* in thy wickednes, because thou
art a murtherer.
9 Then said Abishái the sonne of Zeruiáh
vnto the King, Why doeth this * dead
dogge curse my lord the King? let me go,
I pray thee, and take away his head.
10 ¶ But the King said, What haue I to do
with you, ye sonnes of Zeruiáh: for he
curseth, euen because the Lord hathe
[f] bidden him curse Dauid: who darre then
say, Wherefore hast thou done so?
11 And Dauid said to Abishái, & to all his
seruants, Beholde, my sonne ẇ came out
of mine owne bowels, seketh my life: then
how muche more now may this sonne of
Iemini? Suffre him to curse: for the Lord
hathe bidden him.
12 It may be that the Lord wil loke on
" mine affliction, and [g] do me good for his
cursing this day.
13 And as Dauid and his men went by the
way, Shimeí went by the side of the mõutaine ouer against him, and cursed as he
went, and threwe stones against him, and
cast dust.
14 Then came ẏ King & all the people that
were with him weary, and refreshed them
selues [h] there.
15 ¶ And Absalóm, and all the people, the
men of Israél came to Ierusalém, & Ahithóphel with him.
16 And when Husħái the Archite Dauids
friend was come vnto Absalóm, Husħái
said vnto Absalóm, " God saue the King,
God saue the King.
17 Then Absalóm said to Husħái, Is this
thy kindenes to thy [i] friend? Why wentest
thou not with thy friend?
18 Husħái then answered vnto Absalóm,
Nay, but whome the Lord, & this people,
and all the men of Israél chuse, his wil I
be, and with him wil I dwell.
19 And " moreouer vnto whome shal I do
seruice? not to his sonne? as I serued before thy father, so wil I before thee.
20 ¶ Then spake Absalóm to Ahithóphel,
Giue counsel what we shal do.
21 And [k] Ahithóphel said vnto Absalóm,
Go in to thy fathers cõcubines, which he
hathe left to kepe the house: and when all
Israél shal heare, that thou art abhorred
of thy father, the hands of all that are
with thee, shalbe strong.
22 So they spred Absalóm a tent vpon the
top of the house, and Absalóm went in to
his fathers concubines in the sight of all
Israél.
23 And the counsel of Ahithóphel which he
counseled in those dayes, was like as one
had asked [l] counsel at the oracle of God:
so *was* all the coũsel of Ahithóphel bothe
with Dauid and with Absalóm.

CHAP. XVII.

7 Ahithophels counsel is ouerthrowen by Husħái. 14 The Lord had so ordeined. 19 The Priests sonnes are hid in the well. 22 Dauid goeth ouer Iordén. 23 Ahithóphel hangeth him selfe. 27 Thei bring vitails to Dauid

1 MOreouer Ahithóphel said to Absalóm, [a] Let me chuse out now twelue
thousand men, and I wil vp and follow after Dauid this night,
2 And I wil come vpõ him: for he is weary,

a Which was the hil of oliues, Chap 15, 30.

" Or, fig cakes.

b Cõmunely there are no viler traitours then they, ẇ vnder pretence of friendship accuse others.

" Ebr. I worship.

c Which was a citie in the tribe of Beniamin.

d That is, rounde about him.

" Ebr. man of blood.

" Ebr. man of Belial.

e Reproching him as thogh by his meanes Ish bósheth & Abnér were slaine.

1. Sam. 24, 15. & chap. 3, 8.

f Dauid felt ẏ this was the iudgement of God for his sinne, & therefore humbleth him selfe to his rod.

" Or, my teares.

g Meaning, ẏ the Lord wil send cõfort to his when they are oppressed.

h To wit, at Bahurím.

" Ebr. Let the King liue.

i Meaning, Dauid.

" Ebr the secõde time.

k Suspecting ẏ change of the kingdome, and so his owne ouerthrowe, he giueth suche counsel as might moste hindre his fathers reconciliation: and also declare to the people ẏ Absalóm was in hiest autoritie.

l It was so estemed for the successe thereof.

a The wicked are so gredy to execute their malice, that they leaue none occasion, that may further the same.

and weake handed: so I wil feare him, and
all the people that are with him, shal flee,
and I wil smite the King onely,
3 And I wil bring againe all the people vnto thee, *and* when all shal returne, (b the
man whome thou sekest *being slaine*) all the
people shalbe in peace.
4 And the saying " pleased Absalóm wel,
and all the Elders of Israél.
5 Thē said Absalóm, Call now Hushái the
Archite also, and let vs heare likewise
"what he sayeth.
6 So when Hushái came to Absalóm, Absalóm spake vnto him, saying, Ahithóphel hathe " spoken thus: shal we do after
his saying, or no? tel thou?
7 Hushái then answered vnto Absalóm,
The counsel that Ahithóphel hathe giuē,
is not c good at this time.
8 For, said Hushái, thou knowest thy father, and his men, that they be strong mē,
and are chafed in minde as a beare robbed
of her whelpes in the field: also thy father
is a valiant warriar, and wil not " lodge
with the people.
9 Beholde, he is hid now in some caue, or
in some place: and thogh some of them be
ouerthrowen at the first, yet the *people* shal
heare, and say, The people that followe
Absalóm, be " ouerthrowen.
10 Then he also that is valiant whose heart
is as the heart of a lion, shal " shrinke and
faint: for all Israél knoweth, that thy
father is valiant, and they which be with
him, stowte men.
11 Therefore my counsel is, that all Israél
be gathered vnto thee, from Dan euen to
Beer-shéba as the sand of the sea in nomber, and that thou go to battel in thine
owne persone.
12 So shal we come vpō him in some place,
where we shal finde him, and " we wil vpō
him as the dewe falleth on the ground: and
of all the men that are with him, we wil
not leaue him one.
13 Moreouer if he be gotten into a citie,
then shal all the men of Israél bring ropes
to that citie, and we wil drawe it into the
riuer, vntil there be not one smale stone
found there.
14 ¶ Then Absalóm and all the men of Israél said, The counsel of Hushái the Archite is better, then the counsel of Ahithóphel: for the Lord had " determined to
destroy the d good cousel of Ahithóphel,
that the Lord might e bring euil vpon
Absalóm.
15 Then said Hushái vnto Zadók and to
Abiathár the Priests, Of this and that maner did Ahithóphel and the Elders of Israél counsel Absalóm: and thus and thus
haue I counseled.
16 Now therefore send quickly, and shewe
Dauid, saying, Tary not this night in the
fieldes of the wildernes, but rather get
thee f ouer, least the King be deuoured &
all the people that are with him.
17 ¶ Now Ionathán and Ahimáaz abode
by " En-rogél: (for they might not be sene
to come into the citie) and a maid went,
and tolde g them, and they went and shewed King Dauid.
18 Neuertheles a yong man sawe them, and
tolde it to Absalóm. therefore they bothe
departed quyckly, & came to a mās house
in Bahurím, who had a well in his court,
into the which they went downe.
19 And h the wife toke and spred a couering ouer the welles mouthe, and spred
grounde corne thereon, that the thing
shulde not be knowen.
20 And when Absaloms seruants came to
the wife into the house, they said, Where
is Ahimáaz and Ionathán? And the woman answered them, They be gone ouer
the i broke of water. And when they had
soght them, and colde not finde them,
they returned to Ierusalém.
21 And assone as they were departed, the
other came out of the well and went and
tolde King Dauid, and said vnto him, Vp,
and get you quyckly ouer the water: for
k suche counsel hathe Ahithóphel giuen
against you.
22 Then Dauid arose, and all the people
that were with him, and they went ouer
Iordén l vntil the dawning of the day, so
that there lacked not one of them, that was
not come ouer Iordén.
23 ¶ Now whē Ahithóphel sawe that his counsel was not followed, he sadled his asse,
and arose, and he went home vnto his citie, and put his housholde in ordre, and
m hanged him selfe, and dyed, and was buryed in his fathers graue.
24 ¶ Then Dauid came to Mahanáim. And
Absalóm passed ouer Iordén, he, and all
the men of Israél with him.
25 And Absalóm made Amasá captaine
of the hoste in the stead of Ioáb: which
Amasá was a mans sonne named Ithrá an
Israelite, that wēt in to Abigál the daughter of n Naháſh, sister to Zeruiáh Ioabs
mother.
26 So Israél and Absalóm pitched in the
land of Gileád.
27 ¶ And when Dauid was come to Mahanáim, Shobí the sonne of Naháſh out of
Rabbáh of the children of Ammón, and
Machír the sonne of Ammiél out of Lo-
debár, and Barzelái the Gileadite out
of Rogél
28 o *Broght* beds, and basens, and earthen
vessels, and wheat, and barly, and floure,
and parched corne, & beanes, and lentils,
and parched corne,

b Meaning, Dauid.

" *Ebr. was right in the eyes of Absalóm.*

" *Ebr. what is in his mouthe.*

" *Or, giuen suche counsel.*

c Hushái sheweth him selfe faithful to Dauid, in that he reproueth this wicked counsel and purpose.

" *Or, tary all night.*

" *Ebr. haue a breache, or ruine.*

" *Ebr, melt.*

" *Or, we wil came against him.*

" *Or, commāded.*

d That counsel which semed good at the first to Absalóm, vers. 4.

e For by the cousel of Hushái he went to the battel where he was destroyed.

f That is, ouer Iordén.

" *Or, the well of Rogél.*

g Meaning, the message from their fathers.

h Thus God sendeth succour to his in their greatest dangers.

i The Chalde text readeth, now they haue passed the Iordén.

k To wit, to pursue thee with all haste.

l They traueled all night, & by morning had all their companie passed ouer.

m Gods iuste vengeance euē in this life is powred on them, which are enemies, traitours, or persecuters of his Church.

n Who was also called Ishái Dauids father.

o God sheweth hi selfe moste liberale to his, when they seme to be vtterly destitute.

29 And

29 And they broght hony, and butter, and
shepe, and chese of kine for Dauid and
for the people that were with him, to eat:
for they said, The people is hungry, &
weary, and thirsty in the wildernes.

CHAP. XVIII.

2 Dauid deuideth his armie into thre partes. 9 Absalóm is hanged slaine, and cast in a pit. 33 Dauid lamenteth the death of Absalóm.

a For certein of ẏ Reubenites, Gadites, & of the halfe tribe, colde not beare the insolencie of ẏ sonne against ẏ father, & therefore ioyned with Dauid.

1 THen Dauid [a] nōbred the people that
were with him, & set ouer them captaines of thousands and captaines of hundreths.
2 And Dauid sent forthe the third parte of
the people vnder the hand of Ioáb, and
the third parte vnder the hand of Abishái
Ioabs brother the sonne of Zeruiah: and
the *other* third parte vnder the hād of Ittái the Gittite. & the King said vnto the
people, I wil go with you my selfe also.
3 But the people answered, Thou shalt not
go forthe: for if we flee away, they wil not
regarde vs, nether wil they passe for vs,
thogh halfe of vs were slaine: but thou
[b] art now worthe tē thousand of vs: therefore now it is better that thou succour vs
out of the citie.

b Signifying, ẏ a good gouernour oght to be so deare vnto his people, that they wil rather lose their liues, thē ẏ oght shulde come vnto hī.

4 Then the King said vnto them, What
semeth you best, that I wil do. So ẏ King
stode by the gate side, and all the people
came out by hundreths and by thousands.
5 And the King commanded Ioáb and A-
bishái, and Ittai, saying, *Entreate* the yong
man Absalóm gently for my sake. and all
the people hearde when the King gaue all
the captaines charge concerning Absalóm.
6 So the people went out into the field to
meete Israél, & the battel was in ẏ [c] wood
of Ephraim:

c So called because ẏ Ephraimites (as some say) fed their cattel beyōde Iordén in this wood.

7 Where the people of Israél were slaine
before the seruants of Dauid: so there was
a great slaughter that day, *euen* of twentie
thousand.
8 ¶ For the battel was skatred ouer all the
countrey: and the wood deuoured muche
more people that day, then did the
sworde.
9 ¶ Now Absalóm met the seruants of Dauid, and Absalóm rode vpon a mule, and
the mule came vnder a great thicke oke:
and his head caught holde of the oke, and
he was taken vp ‖ betwene the heauen and
the earthe: & the mule that was vnder him
went away.

‖ This is a terrible example of Gods vengeance against them that are rebels or disobedient to their parents.

10 And one that sawe it, tolde Ioáb, saying,
Beholde, I sawe Absalóm hanged in an
oke.
11 Then Ioáb said vnto the man that tolde
him, And hast thou in dede sene? why then
didest not thou there smite him to the
ground, and I wolde haue giuen thee ten
*shekel, of siluer, and a girdle?

Gen.23,15.

12 Then the man said vnto Ioáb, Thogh I
shulde "receiue a thousand *shekels* of siluer in mine hād, yet wolde I not lay mine
hād vpon the Kings sonne: for in our hearing the King charged thee, and Abishái,
& Ittái, saying, Beware, lest anie *touche* the
yong man Absalóm.

" Ebr. weigh vpō mine hand.

13 If I had done it, *it had bene* the "danger
of my life: for nothing can be hid frō the
King: yea, ẏ thy selfe woldest haue bene
against me.

" Ebr. a lye against my soule.

14 Then said Ioáb, I wil not thus tary with
thee. And he toke thre dartes in his hand,
& thrust them" through Absalóm, while
he was yet aliue in the middes of the oke.

" Ebr. in the heart of Absalóm.

15 And ten seruāts that bare Ioabs armour,
compassed about and smote Absalóm, and
slewe him.
16 Then Ioáb [d] blewe the trumpet, and the
people returned from pursuing after Israél: for Ioáb helde backe the people.
17 And they toke Absalóm, and cast him
into a great [e] pit in the wood, and layed a
mighty great heape of stones vpon him:
and all Israél fled euerie one to his tent.

d For he had pitie of ẏ people, which was seduced by Absaloms flatterie.

e Thus God turned his vaine glorie to shame.

18 Now Absalóm in his life time had takē
and reared him vp a piller, which is in
the *Kings dale: for he said, I haue no
[f] sonne to kepe my name in remembrance.
& he called ẏ piller after his owne name,
and it is called vnto this day, Absaloms
place.

Gen.14,17.

f It semeth ẏ God had punished hī, in taking away his children, Chap.14,27.

19 ¶ Then said Ahimáaz the sonne of Zadók, I pray thee, let me runne, and beare
the King tidings that the Lord hathe "deliuered him out of the hand of his enemies.

" Ebr. iudged.

20 And Ioáb said vnto him, Thou [g] shalt
not be ẏ messenger to day, but thou shalt
beare tidings another time, but to day
thou shalt beare none: for the Kings sonne
is dead.

g For Ioáb bare a good affection to Ahimáaz, & douted how Dauid wold take the reporte of Absaloms death.

21 Thē said Ioáb to Cushí, Go, tel the Kīg,
what thou hast sene. And Cushí bowed
him selfe vnto Ioáb, and ran.
22 Thē said Ahimáaz the sonne of Zadók
againe to Ioáb, What, I pray thee, if I
also runne after Cushí? And Ioáb said,
Wherefore now wilt thou runne, my sonne, seing that thou hast no tidings to
bring?
23 Yet what if I runne? Then he said vnto
him, Rūne. So Ahimáaz ranne by the way
of the plaine, and ouerwent Cushí.
24 Now Dauid sate betwene ẏ two [h] gates.
And the watcheman went to the toppe of
the gate vpon the wall, & lift vp his eyes,
and sawe, and beholde, a man came rūning
alone.

h He sate in the gate of ẏ citie of Mahanáim.

25 And the watcheman cryed, & tolde the
King. And the King said, If he be alone,
"he bringeth tidings. And he came apase,
and drewe nere.

" Ebr. tidings are in his mouthe.

26 And the watcheman sawe an other man running, and the watcheman called vnto the porter, and said, Beholde, *another* man runneth alone. And the King said, He also bringeth tidings.

"Ebr. I se the running.

27 And the watcheman said, "Me thinketh the running of the formost *is* like the running of Ahimáaz the sonne of Zadók. Then the King said, He is a [i] good man, & commeth with good tidings.

i He had had experience of his fidelitie, Chap.17,21.

28 And Ahimáaz called, and said vnto the King, Peace *be with thee*: and he fel downe to the earth vpon his face before ẏ King, and said, Blessed be the Lord thy God, who hathe "shut vp the men that lift vp their hands against my lord the King.

"Or, deliuered vp.

29 And the King said, Is the yong man Absalóm safe? And Ahimáaz answered, Whē Ioáb sent the Kings [k] seruant, and *me* thy seruāt, I sawe a great tumulte, but I knewe not what.

k To wit, Chushi, who was an Ethiopian.

30 And the King said vnto him, Turne aside, & stand here. so he turned aside and stode stil.

31 And beholde, Cushí came, and Cushí said, "Tidings, my lord the King: for the Lord hathe deliuered thee this day out of the hand of all that rose against thee.

"Ebr. tidings is broght.

32 Then the King said vnto Cushí, Is the yong man Absalóm safe? And Cushí answered, The enemies of my lord ẏ King, & all that rise agaīst thee to do thee hurt, be as that yong man is.

33 And the King was [l] moued, and went vp to the chamber ouer the gate, and wept: & as he went, thus he said, O my sonne Absalóm, my sonne, my sonne Absalóm: wolde God I had dyed for thee, ô Absalóm, my sonne, my sonne.

l Because he considered bothe the iudgemēt of God against his sinne, & colde not otherwise hide his fatherly affectiō toward his sonne.

CHAP. XIX.

7 Ioáb encourageth the King. 8 Dauid is restored. 23 Shimeí is pardoned. 24 Mephibósheth meeteth the King. 39 Barzelái departeth. 41 Israél striueth with Iudah.

1 AND it was tolde Ioáb, Beholde, the King wepeth and mourneth for Absalóm.

2 Therefore the "victorie of that day was turned into mourning to all the people: for the people heard say that day, The King sorroweth for his sonne.

"Ebr. saluation, or, deliuerance.

3 And the people wēt that day into the citie "secretly, as people confounded hide them selues when they flee in battel.

"Or, by stealthe.

4 So the King [a] hid his face, and the King cryed with a lowde voyce, My sonne Absalóm, Absalóm my sonne, my sonne.

a As they do that mourne.

5 ¶ Then Ioáb came into [b] the house to the King & said, Thou hast shamed this day the faces of all thy seruāts, which this day haue saued thy life, and the liues of thy sonnes and of thy daughters, and the liues of thy wiues, and the liues of thy concubines,

b At Mahanáim.

6 In that thou louest thine enemies, & hatest thy friendes: for thou hast declared this day, that thou regardest nether thy "princes nor seruants: therefore this day I perceiue, that if Absalóm had liued, and we all had dyed this day, that thē it wolde haue "pleased thee wel.

"Or, captaines.

"Ebr. bene right in thine eyes.

7 Now therefore vp, come out, and speake "cōfortably vnto thy seruāts: for I sweare by the Lord, except thou come out, there wil not tary one man with thee this night: and that wil be worse vnto thee, then all ẏ euil that fel on thee from thy youthe hetherto.

"Ebr. to the heart of thy seruants.

8 Then the King arose, & sate in the [c] gate: and they tolde vnto all the people, saying, Beholde, the King doeth sit in the gate: & all the people came before the King: for Israél had fled euerie man to his tent.

c Where the moste resorte of the people haunted.

9 ¶ Then all the people were at [d] strife throughout all the tribes of Israél, saying, The King saued vs out of the hād of our enemies, & he deliuered vs out of the hand of the Philistims, and now he is fled out of the land for Absalóm.

d Euerie one blamed another & stroue who shulde first bring him home.

10 And Absalóm, whome we anoīted ouer vs, is dead in battel: therefore why are ye so slowe to bring the King againe?

11 But King Dauid sent to Zadók and to Abiathár the [e] Priests, saying, Speake vnto the Elders of Iudáh and say, Why are ye behind to bring ẏ King againe to his house, (for the saying of all Israél is come vnto the King, *euen* to his house)

e That they shulde reproue the negligence of ẏ Elders, seing the people were so forwarde.

12 Ye are my brethren: my bones and my flesh are ye: wherefore then are ye the last that bring the King againe?

13 Also say ye to Amasá, Art thou not my bone and my flesh? God do so to me and more also, if thou be not captaine of the hoste to me for euer in ẏ [f] roume of Ioáb.

f By this policie Dauid thoght ẏ by winning of the captaine, he shulde haue ẏ heartes of all the people.

14 So he bowed the heartes of all the men of Iudáh, as of one man: therefore they sent to the King, saying, Returne thou with all thy seruants.

15 ¶ So the King returned, & came to Iordén. And Iudáh came to Gilgál, for to go to meete the King, & to conduct him ouer Iordén.

16 ¶ And [g] Shimeí ẏ sonne of Gerá, the sonne of Iemíni, which was of Bahurím, hasted & came downe with the men of Iudáh to meete King Dauid,

g Who had before reuiled him, Chap. 16,13.

17 And a thousand men of Beniamín with him, and *Zibá the seruant of the house of Saúl, and his fiftene sonnes and twentie seruants with him: and they wēt ouer Iordén before ẏ King.

Chap.16,3.

18 And there wēt ouer a bote to carie ouer the Kings housholde, and to do him pleasure. Then Shimeí the sonne of Gerá fel before the King, when he was come ouer Iordén,

19 And said vnto ý King, Let not my lord
impute * wickednes vnto me, nor remember the thing that thy seruant did [h] wickedly when my lord the King departed
out of Ierusalém, that ý King shulde take
it to his heart.
20 For thy seruãt doeth knowe, that I haue
done amisse: therefore beholde, I am the
first this day of all the house of [i] Ioséph,
that am come to go downe to meete my
lord the King.
21 But Abishái the sonne of Zeruiáh answered, and said, Shal not Shimeí dye for
this, because he cursed the Lords anointed?
22 And Dauid said, What haue I to do with
you, ye sonnes of Zeruiáh, that this day ye
shulde be aduersaries vnto me? shal there
anie man dye this day in Israél? for do not
I knowe, that I am this day King ouer Israél?
23 Therefore the King said vnto Shimeí,
Thou shalt not dye, and the King sware
vnto him.
24 ¶ And Mephibósheth the sonne of Saúl
came downe to meete the King, and had
nether washed his feete, nor dressed his
bearde, nor washed his clothes from the
time the King departed, vntil he returned
in peace.
25 And when [k] he was come to Ierusalém,
& met the King, the King said vnto him,
Wherefore wentest not thou with me,
Mephibósheth?
26 And he answered, My lord the King, my
seruant disceiued me: for thy seruant said,
I wolde haue mine asse sadled to ride thereon for to go with the King, because thy
seruant *is* lame.
27 And he hathe * accused thy seruant vnto my lord the King: but my lord ý King
is as an [l] Angel of God: do therefore thy
pleasure.
28 For all my fathers house were [m] but
dead men before my lord the King, yet
didest thou set thy seruant among them
ý did eat at thine owne table: what right
therefore haue I yet to crye anie more
vnto the King?
29 And the King said vnto him, Why speakest thou anie more of thy matters? I haue
said, Thou, and Zibá deuide the [n] lands.
30 And Mephibósheth said vnto ý King,
Yea, let him take all, seing my lord the
King is come home in peace.
31 ¶ Then Barzillái the Gileadite came
downe from Rogelím, and went ouer Iordén with the King, to conduct him ouer
Iordén.
32 Now Barzillái was a very aged man, *euẽ*
fourescore yere olde, and he had prouided
the King of sustenance, while he lay at
Mahanáim: for he was a man of very great
substance.
33 And the Kĩg said vnto Barzillái, Come
ouer with me, & I wil feede thee with me
in Ierusalém.
34 And Barzillái said vnto ý King, " How
long haue I to lyue, that I shulde go vp
with the King to Ierusalém?
35 I am this day fourescore yere olde: and
cã I discerne betwene good or euil? Hathe
thy seruant anie taste in that I eat or in ý
I drinke? Can I heare anie more the voice
of singing men and women? wherefore
then shulde thy seruant be anie more a
[o] burthen vnto my lord the King?
36 Thy seruant wil go a litle way ouer Iordén with the King, and why wil the King
recompence it me with suche a rewarde?
37 I pray thee, let thy seruant turne backe
againe, that I may dye in mine owne citie, and *be buryed* in the graue of my father
and of my mother: but beholde thy seruãt
[p] Chimhám, let him go with my lord the
King, & do to him what shal please thee.
38 And the King answered, Chimhám shal
go with me, and I wil do to him that thou
shalt be content with: & whatsoeuer thou
shalt " require of me, that wil I do for
thee.
39 So all the people went ouer Iordén: and
the King passed ouer: and the King kissed
Barzillái, and " blessed him, and he returned vnto his owne place.
40 ¶ Then the King went to [q] Gilgál, and
Chimhám went with him, and all the people of Iudáh conducted the King, and
also halfe the people of [r] Israél.
41 And beholde, all the men of Israél came
to the King, & said vnto the King, Why
haue our brethren the men of Iudáh sto-
len thee away, and haue broght the King
and his housholde, and all Dauids men
with him ouer [s] Iordén?
42 And all the men of Iudáh answered the
men of Israél, Because the King is nere of
kin to vs: and wherefore now be ye angry
for this matter? haue we eatẽ of the Kings
cost, or haue we taken anie bribes?
43 And the men of Israél answered the mẽ
of Iudáh, and said, We haue ten partes in
the King, and haue also more *right* to Dauid then ye, Why then did ye despise vs,
" that our aduise shulde not be first had in
restoring our King? And the wordes of
the men of Iudáh were fearcer then the
wordes of the men of Israél.

CHAP. XX.

1 Shéba raiseth Israél against Dauid. 10 Ioáb killeth Amasá traiterously. 22 The head of Shéba is deliuered to Ioáb. 23 Dauids chief officers.

1 THen there was come [a] thither a wicked man (named Shéba the sonne of
Bichri, a man of Iemini) and he blewe the
trumpet, and said, We haue no parte in

*Chap. 16,15.

h For in his aduersitie he was his moste cruel enemie, & now in his prosperitie seketh by flatterie to crepe into fauour.

i By Ioséph he meaneth Ephráim, Manasséh, and Beniamin (whereof he was) because these thre were vnder one standerd, Nomb 2,18.

k When Mephibósheth being at Ierusalém had met the King.

*Chap. 16,3.

l Able for his wisdome to iudge in all matters.

m Worthy to dye for Sauls crueltie towarde thee.

n Dauid did euil in taking his lands from him before he knewe ý cause, but muche worse, that knowing the trueth, he did not restore them.

" *Ebr. how many daies are the yeres of my life?*

o He thoght it not meete to receiue benefites of him to whome he was not able to do seruice againe.

p My sonne.

" *Or, chuse.*

" *Or, bade him fare wel.*

q Where the tribe of Iudáh taryed to receiue him.

r Which had taken parte ẇ the King.

s Towarde Ierusalém.

" *Or, haue not we first spoken to bring home the King? vers. 11.*

a Where the ten tribes contended against Iudáh.

b As thei of Iudáh say.
c He thoght by speaking contepteously of the King, to stirre ỹ people rather to sedicion.
d Frō Gilgál, which was nere Iordén.
Chap. 16, 22.
e Who was his chief captaine in Ioabs roume, Chap. 19, 13.
f Ether them which had bene vnder Ioáb, or Dauids mē.
Chap. 8, 19.
g Which was his coat, that he vsed to weare in the warres.
"Ebr. peace.
"Ebr. doubled not his stroke.
h He stode by Amasá at Ioabs appointement.
i Vnto the citie Abél, which was nere to Bethmaacháh.

b Dauid, nether haue we inheritance in
ỹ sonne c of Ishái: euery man to his tents,
ô Israél.
2 So euery man of Israél went from Dauid
and followed Shéba the sonne of Bichrí:
but the men of Iudáh claue fast vnto their
King, from d Iordén euen to Ierusalém.
3 When Dauid then came to his house
to Ierusalém, the King toke the ten women
his * concubines, that he had left behinde
him to kepe the house, & put them
in warde, and fed them, but lay no more
with them: but they were enclosed vnto ỹ
day of their death, liuing in widowhode.
4 ¶ Thē said the King to e Amasá, Assemble
me the mē of Iudáh within thre daies,
and be thou here present.
5 So Amasá wēt to assemble Iudáh, but he
taried longer then the time which he had
appointed him.
6 Then Dauid said to Abishái, Now shal
Shéba the sonne of Bichrí do vs more
harme thē *did* Absalóm: take thou *therefore*
thy f lords seruants and followe after him,
lest he get him walled cities, & escape vs.
7 And there went out after him Ioabs mē,
and the * Cherethites and the Pelethites,
and all the mightie men: & thei departed
out of Ierusalém, to followe after Shéba
the sonne of Bichrí.
8 Whē thei were at the great stone, which
is in Gibeón, Amasá went before them, &
Ioabs g garment, that he had put on, was
girded vnto him, & vpon it was a sworde
girded, which hanged on his loines in the
sheath, & as he went, it vsed to falle out.
9 And Ioáb said to Amasá, Art thou in
" health, my brother? & Ioáb toke Amasá
by the beard with ỹ right hād to kisse him.
10 But Amasá toke no hede to the sworde
that was in Ioabs hand: for therewith he
smote him in the fift *rib*, and shed out his
bowels to the grounde, & " smote him not
the seconde time: so he dyed. then Ioáb &
Abishái his brother followed after Shéba
the sonne of Bichrí.
11 And one of Ioabs men h stode by him,
& said, He that fauoreth Ioáb, & he that
is of Dauids parte, *let him go* after Ioáb.
12 And Amasá wallowed in blood in the
middes of the way: & when the man sawe
that all the people stode stil, he remoued
Amasá out of the way into ỹ field, & cast
a cloth vpon him, because he sawe that
euery one that came by him, stode stil.
13 ¶ When he was remoued out of the way,
euery man went after Ioáb, to followe after
Shéba the sonne of Bichrí.
14 And he went through all the tribes of
Israél vnto Abél, and i Bethmaacháh and
all *places* of Berím: and thei gathered together,
and went also after him.
15 So thei came, and besieged him in Abél,
nere to Bethmaacháh: and thei cast vp a
mount against the citie, & the people thereof
stode on the ramper, and all the people
that was with Ioáb, k destroyed and
cast downe the wall.
16 Then cryed a wise woman out of the citie,
Heare, heare, I pray you, say vnto Ioáb,
Come thou hither, that I may speake
with thee.
17 And when he came nere vnto her, the
womā said, Art thou Ioáb? And he answered,
Yea. And she said to him, Heare the
wordes of thine handmayd. And he answered,
I do heare.
18 Then she spake thus, l Thei spake in the
olde time, saying, Thei shulde aske of Abél,
and so haue thei continued.
19 I am m *one* of them, that are peaceable
& faithful in Israél: and thou goest about
to destroye a citie, and a mother in Israél:
why wilt thou deuoure the inheritance
of the Lord?
20 And Ioáb answered, & said, God forbid,
God forbid it me, that I shulde deuoure,
or destroye it.
21 The n matter is not so, but a mā of mount
Ephráim (Shéba the sonne of Bichrí by
name) hathe lift vp his hand against the
King, *euen* against Dauid: deliuer vs him
onely, & I wil departe from the citie. And
the woman said vnto Ioáb, Beholde, his
head shalbe throwen to thee ouer the wall.
22 Then the woman went vnto all the people
with her wisdome, and thei cut of the
head of Shéba the sonne of Bichrí, & cast
it to Ioáb: then he blewe the trumpet, and
" thei retired from the citie, euery man to
his tent: and Ioáb returned to Ierusalém
vnto the King.
23 ¶ * Thē Ioáb *was* ouer all the hoste of Israél,
and Banaiáh the sonne of Iehoiadá
ouer the Cherethites & ouer ỹ Pelethites,
24 And Adorám ouer the tribute, and Ioshaphát
the sonne of Ahilúd the recorder,
25 And Sheiá *was* scribe, and Zadók and
Abiathár the Priests,
26 And also Irá the Iairite *was* o chief about
Dauid.

k That is, he went about to ouerthrowe it.
l She sheweth that the olde custome was, not to destroie a citie, before peace was offred, Deut. 20, 11.
m She speaketh in the name of ỹ citie.
n Hearing his faute tolde hī, he gaue place to reason and required onely him that was autor of the treason.
"Ebr. thei were scatered.
Chap. 8, 16.
o Ether in dignitie, or familiaritie.

CHAP. XXI.

1 Thre deare yeres. 9 The vengeance of the sinnes of Saúl lighteth on his seuē sonnes, which are hāged. 15 Foure great battels, which Dauid had against the Philistims

1 Then there was a famine in the daies
of Dauid, thre yeres " together: and
Dauid " asked counsel of the Lord, & the
Lord answered, *It is* for Saúl, and for *his*
bloodie house, because he slewe the a Gibeonites.
2 Then the King called the Gibeonites, &
said vnto thē (Now the Gibeonites were
not of the children of Israél, but * a remnant
of the Amorites, vnto whome the
children of Israél had sworne: but Saúl
soght

"Ebr. yere after yere.
"Ebr. soght the face of the Lord.
a Thinking to gratifie ỹ people, because these were not of the seede of Abrahám.
Iosh. 9, 3.

soght to slaye thẽ for his zeale toward the
children of Israél and Iudáh)
3 And Dauid said vnto the Gibeonites,
[b] What shal I do for you, and wherewith
shal I make the atonement, that ye may
blesse the inheritance of the Lord?
4 The Gibeonites then answered him,
We wil haue no siluer nor gold of Saúl
nor of his house, nether for vs shalt thou
kil [c] anie man in Israél. And he said, What
ye shal say, that wil I do for you.
5 Then they answered the King, The man
that consumed vs and that imagined euil
against vs, *so that* we are destroyed from
remaining in anie coste of Israél,
6 Let seuen men of his [d] sonnes be deliuered vnto vs, and we wil hang them vp
[e] vnto the Lord in Gibeáh of Saúl, the
Lords chosen. And the King said, I wil
giue them.
7 But the King had compassion on Mephibósheth the sone of Ionathán the sonne of
Saúl, because of the * Lords othe, that was
betwene them, *euen* betwene Dauid and
Ionathán the sonne of Saúl.
8 But the King toke the two sonnes of Rizpáh the daughter of Aiáh, whome she bare
vnto Saúl, *euen* Armoní & Mephibósheth
and the fiue sonnes of [f] Michál, the daughter of Saúl, whome she bare to Abriél the
sonne of Barzillái the Meholathite.
9 And he deliuered them vnto the hands of
the Gibeonites, which hãged them in the
mõutaine before the Lord: so they " dyed
all seuen together, and they were slaine in
the time of haruest: in the [g] first *dayes*, &
in the beginning of barly haruest.
10 Then Rizpáh the daughter of Aiáh toke [h] sackcloth & hãdged it vp for her vpõ
the rocke, from the beginning of haruest,
vntil [i] water dropped vpon them from
the heauen, and suffred nether the birdes
of the aire to " light on them by day, nor
beastes of the field by night.
11 ¶ And it was tolde Dauid, what Rizpáh
the daughter of Aiáh the concubine of
Saúl had done.
12 And Dauid went and toke the bones of
Saúl and the bones of Ionathán his sonne
from the citizens of Iabésh Gileád, which
had stollen them from the strete of Beth-
shán, where the Philistíms had * handged
them, when the Philistíms had slaine Saúl
in Gilbóa.
13 So he broght thence the bones of Saúl
and the bones of Ionathán his sonne, and
thei gathered the bones of them that were
hanged.
14 And the bones of Saúl and of Ionathán
his sonne buryed they in the countrei of
Beniamín in Zeláh, in the graue of Kish
his father: and when they had performed
all that the King had commanded, God

b Wherewith may your wrath be appeased, ẏ you may pray to God to remoue this plague from his people?

c Saue onely of Sauls stocke

d Of Sauls kinsemen.

e To pacifie ẏ Lord.

1.Sam.18,3.

f Here Michál is named for Meráb Adriels wife as appeareth 1.Sam 18, 19 for Michál was the wife of Paltiel, 1.Sam 25,44, & neuer had childe, 2.Sam.6,23.

"Ebr.fel.

g Which was in the moneth Abib or Nisan, which conteineth parte of Marche and parte of April.

h To make her a tẽt, wherein she prayed to God to turne away his wrath.

i Because drought was ẏ cause of this famine, God by sending of raine shewed ẏ he was pacified.

"Or, rest.

1.Sam.31,10.

was then [k] appeased with the land.
15 ¶ Againe the Philistíms had warre with
Israél: and Dauid went downe, and his
seruants with him, and they foght a-
gainst the Philistíms, and Dauid fainted.
16 Then Ishi-benób which was of the sonnes of [l] Haraph※áh (*the head* of whose
speare wayed thre hundreth [m] shekels of
brasse) cuẽ he being girded with a newe
sword, thoght to haue slaine Dauid.
17 But Abishái the sonne of Zeruiáh suc-
coured him, and smote the Philistím, and
killed him. Then Dauids men sware vnto him, saying, Thou shalt go no more
out with vs to battel, lest thou quenche the
[n] light of Israél.
18 ¶ And after this also there was a battel
with the Philistíms at [o] Gob, then Sib-
bechái the Hushathite slewe Saph, which
was one of the sonnes of Harapháh.
19 And there was yet *another* battel in Gob
with the Philistíms, where Elhanáh the
sonne of Iaare-oregím, a Bethlehemite
slewe [p] Goliáth the Gittite: the staffe
of whose speare *was* like a weauers beame.
20 Afterwarde there was also a battel in
Gath, where was a man of *a great* stature,
and had on euerie hand six fingers, and on
euerie foote six toes, foure and twentie in
nomber: who was also the sonne of Harapháh.
21 And when he reuiled Israél, Ionathán
the sonne of * Shimá the brother of Dauid slewe him.
22 These foure were borne to Harapháh
in Gath, and dyed by the hand of Dauid
and by the hands of his seruants.

CHAP. XXII.

2 Dauid after his victories praiseth God. 8 The angre of God toward the wicked. 44 He propheciesth of the reiection of the Iewes, and vocacion of the Gentiles.

1 AND Dauid spake the wordes of this
[a] song vnto the Lord, what time the
Lord had deliuered him out of the hands
of all his enemies, and out of the hand of
Saúl.
2 And he said, * The Lord is my [b] rocke
and my fortresse, and he that deliuereth
me.
3 God *is* my " strength, in him wil I trust: my
shield, and the horne of my saluacion, my
hie towre *and* my refuge: my sauiour,
thou hast saued me from violence.
4 I wil call on the Lord, who is worthy to
be praised: so shal I be safe from mine e-
nemies.
5 For the [c] pangs of death haue compassed me: the floods of vngodlines haue made me afraide.
6 The sorowes of the graue compassed me
about: the snares of death ouertoke me.

k For where ẏ magistrat suffreth fautes vnpunished, there the plague of God lyeth vpõ the land.

l That is, of ẏ race of Gyãts.

m Which amount to nine pounde thre quarters.

n For the glorie and welth of the contrey standeth in the preseruacion of the godly magistrate.

o Called Gézer, and Zaph is called Zippai, 1.Chro 20, 4.

p That is, Lahmí the brother of Goliáth, whome Dauid slewe, 1.Chro 20,5.

1.Sam.16,9.

a In token of the wonderful benefites, that he receiued of God.

Psal.18,2.

b By the diuersitie of these cõfortable names, he sheweth how his faith was strengthened in all tentacions.

"Or, rocke.

c As Dauid (who was the figure of Christ) was by Gods power deliuered frõ all dangers: so Christ and his Church shal ouercome moste greuous dãgers, tyrannie, and death.

7 *But* in my tribulation did I call vpon the
Lord, and crye to my God, & he did heare my voice out of his temple, & my crye
did enter into his eares.
8 Then the earth trembled and quaked: the
fundacions of the heauens moued, and
shoke, because he was angry.
9 [d] Smoke went out at his nostrels, and cōsuming [e] fire out of his mouth: coles were kindled thereat.
10 He [f] bowed the heauens also, and came
downe, and darkenes *was* vnder his feete.
11 And he rode vpon [g] Cherúb and did
flye, and he was sene vpon the wings of the
winde.
12 And he made darknes a tabernacle
rounde about him, *euen* the gatherings of
waters, *and* the cloudes of the aire.
13 At the brightnes of his presence [h] the
coles of fire were kindled.
14 The Lord thundred from heauen, & the
moste hye gaue his voyce.
15 He shot arrowes also, and scatred them:
to wit, lightning, and destroyed them.
16 The [i] chanels also of the sea appeared,
euen the fundacions of the worlde were
discouered by the rebuking of the Lord,
and at the blast of the breath of his nostrels.
17 He sent from aboue, *and* toke me: he
drewe me out of manie waters.
18 He deliuered me from my strong enemie, *and* from thē that hated me: for they
were to strong for me.
19 They [k] preuented me in the day of
my calamitie, but the Lord was my stay,
20 And broght me forthe into a large place: he deliuered me, because he fauored me.
21 The Lord rewarded me according to
my [l] righteousnes: according to the purenes of mine hands he recompenced me.
22 For I kept the wayes of the Lord, and
did not [m] wickedly against my God.
23 For all his lawes *were* before me, and his
statutes: I did not departe therefrom.
24 I was vpright also towarde him, and
haue kept me from my wickednes.
25 Therefore the Lord did rewarde me,
according to my righteousnes, according
to my purenes before his eyes.
26 With ŷ godlie thou wilt shewe thy selfe godlie: with the vpright man thou wilt
shewe thy selfe vpright.
27 With the pure thou wilt shewe thy selfe
pure, and with the [n] frowarde thou wilt
shewe thy selfe frowarde.
28 Thus thou wilt saue the poore people:
but thine eyes *are* vpon the hautie to hūble *them*.
29 Surely thou art my light, ô Lord: and
the Lord wil lighten my darkenes.
30 For by thee haue I broken through an
hoste, and by my God haue I leaped ouer
a wall.
31 The way of God is [o] vncorrupt: the
worde of the Lord is tryed *in the fire*: he is
a shield to all that trust in him.
32 For who is God besides the Lord? and
who is mighty, saue our God?
33 God is my strength in battel, and maketh my way vpright.
34 He maketh my feete like [p] hindes *feete*,
and hathe set me vpon mine hie places.
35 He teacheth mine hands to fight, so that
a bowe of [*] brasse is broken with mine
armes.
36 Thou hast also giuen me the shield of
thy saluacion, and thy louing kindenes
hathe caused me to increase.
37 Thou hast enlarged my steppes vnder
me, and mine heeles haue not slid.
38 I haue pursued mine enemies and destroyed them, and haue not turned againe
vntil I had consumed them.
39 Yea, I haue consumed them and thrust
them through, and they shal not arise, but
shal fall vnder my feete.
40 For thou hast [q] girded me with power
to battel, *and* them that arose against me,
hast thou subdued vnder me.
41 And thou hast giuen me the neckes of
mine enemies, that I might destroy them
that hate me.
42 They loked about, but there was none to
saue *them*, *euen* vnto the [r] Lord, but he answered them not.
43 Then did I beate thē as small as the dust
of the earth: I did tread them flat as the
clay of the streete, *and* did spread them
abroad.
44 Thou hast also deliuered me from the
contēcions of my [s] people: thou hast preserued me to be the head ouer nacions: the
people which I knewe not, do serue me.
45 Strangers [t] shalbe in subiection to me:
assone as they heare, they shal obey me.
46 Strangers shal shrinke away, and feare
in their priuie chambers.
47 Let the Lord liue, [u] and blessed *be*
my strength: and God, *euen* the force of
my saluacion be exalted.
48 *It is* God that giueth me *power* to reuēge me, and subdue the people vnder me,
49 And rescueth me from mine enemies: (ŷ
also hast lift me vp from them that rose
against me, thou hast deliuered me from
the cruel man.
50 Therefore I wil praise thee, ô Lord, among the [*] nacions, and wil sing vnto thy
Name)
51 *He is* the towre of saluaciō for his King,
and sheweth mercy to his Anointed, *euen*
to Dauid, and to his seede [*] for euer.

CHAP. XXIII.

1 The last wordes of Dauid. 6 The wicked shalbe pluckt

[d] That is, cloudes, and vapors.
[e] Lightening & thūdering.
[f] So it semeth when the aire is darcke.
[g] To flie in a moment through the worlde.
[h] By this description of a tempest he declareth the power of God against his enemies.
[i] He alludeth to the miracle of the red Sea.
[k] I was so beset, that all meanes semed to faile.
[l] Toward Saul and mine enemies.
[m] I attempted nothing without his commandement.
[n] Their wickednes is cause, that thou semest to forget thy wonted mercie.
[o] The maner ŷ God vseth to succour his, neuer faileth.
[p] He vseth extraordinarie meanes to make me winne moste strong holdes.
[*] Or, steele.
[q] He acknowledgeth that God was the autor of his victories, who gaue him strength.
[r] The wicked in their necessitie are compelled to flie to God, but it is to late.
[s] Meaning, of ŷ Iewes, who conspired against me.
[t] Not willingly obeyīg me, but dissemblingly.
[u] Let him shewe his power, that he is the gouernour of all the worlde.
Rom. 15, 9.
Chap. 7, 18.

pluckt vp as thornes. 8 The names and factes of his mighty men. 15 He desired water and wolde not drinke it.

a Which he spake after ẏ he had made the Psalmes.

1 THese also be the [a] last wordes of Dauid, Dauid the sonne of Ishái saith,
euen the man who was set vp on hie, the
Anointed of the God of Iaakób, and the
swete singer of Israél saith,
2 The Spirit of the Lord spake by me, and
his worde *was* in my [b] tongue.

b Meaning, he spake nothing but by the motion of Gods Spirit.

3 The God of Israél spake to me, ẏ stregth
of Israél said, *Thou shalt* beare rule ouer mẽ,
being iust, *and* ruling in the feare of God.
4 Euen as the morning light when ẏ sunne
riseth, the morning, I say, without clouds,
so shal mine house be, and not as the [c] grasse
of the earth *is* by the bright raine.

c Which groweth quickely and fadeth sone.

5 For so shal not mine house *be* with God:
for he hathe made with me an euerlasting
couenãt, persit in all points, and sure: therefore all mine health and whole desire *is*,
that he wil not make it [d] growe so.

d But that my kingdome may continue for euer accordig to his promes.

6 But the wicked *shal be* euerie one as thornes thrust away, because they can not be
taken with hands.
7 But the man that shal touche them, must
be defensed with yron, or with the shaft of
a speare: & they shal be burnt with fire in
the same place.
8 ¶ These *be* the names of the mighty men
whome Dauid had. He that sate in ẏ seate
of [e] wisdome being chief of the princes,
was Adinó of Ezní, he slewe eight hundreth at one time.

e As one of ẏ Kings counsel.

1.Chro.11,12.

9 And after him *was* * Eleazár the sonne of
Dodó, the sonne of Ahohí, one of the thre
worthies with Dauid, when thei ″ defied ẏ
Philistíms gathered there to battel, when
the men of Israél were [f] gone vp.

″Or, *assailed with dangers of their liues.*

f Meaning, fled from the battel.

10 He arose and smote the Philistíms vntil
his hand was weary, and his hand [g] claue
vnto the sworde: and the Lord gaue great
victorie the same day, and the people returned after him onely to spoile.

g By a crãpe which came of wearines and straining.

1.Chro.11,27.

11 After him *was* * Shammáh the sonne of
Agé the Hararite: for ẏ Philistíms assembled at a towne, where was a piece of a
field ful of lentils, and the people fled frõ
the Philistíms.
12 But he stode in the middes of the field,
and defended it, and slewe the Philistíms:
so the Lord gaue [h] great victorie.

h Who hathe nether respect to manie nor fewe, when he wil shewe his power.

13 ¶ Afterward thre of the thirty captaines
went downe, and came to Dauid in the
haruest time vnto the caue of Adullám, &
the hoste of the Philistíms pitched in the
valley ″ of Rephaim.

″Or, *Gyants.*

14 And Dauid *was* then in an holde, and the
garison of the Philistíms *was* then in
Beth-léhem.
15 And Dauid [i] longed, and said, Oh, that
one wolde giue me to drinke of the water
of the well of Beth-léhem, which is by the
gate.

i Being ouercome w wearines & thirst.

16 Thẽ the thre migty brake into the hoste
of the Philistíms, and drewe water out of
the well of Beth-léhem that was by the
gate, and toke & broght it to Dauid, who
wolde not drinke thereof, but [k] powred it
for an offring vnto the Lord,

k Bridelig his affection, and also desiring God not to be offended for ẏ rash enterprise.

17 And said, O Lord, be it far from me, that
I shulde do this. *Is* not this ẏ blood of the
men that wẽt in ieopardy of their liues?
therefore he wolde not drinke it. These
things did these thre mighty men.
18 ¶ * And Abishái the brother of Ioáb, the
sonne of Zeruiáh, was chief among ẏ thre,
and he lifted vp his speare against thre
hundreth, ″ and slewe them, and he had the
name among the thre.

1.Chro.11,20.

″*Ebr. slaine.*

19 For he was moste excellent of the thre,
and was their captaine. but he atteined
not vnto *the first* thre.
20 And Benaiáh the sonne of Iehoiadá the
sonne of ″ a valiant man, which had done
many actes, & *was* of Kabzeél, slewe two
strong men of Moáb: he went downe also,
and slewe a lion in the middes of a pit in
the time of snowe.

″*Or, Ish-hai.*

21 And he slewe an Egyptian a ″ mã of great
stature, and the Egyptian *had* a [l] speare in
his hand: but he went downe to him with
a staffe, and plucked the speare out of the
Egyptiãs hand, & slewe him with his owne
speare.

″*Or, a comely man.*

l Which was bigge as a weauers beame, 1.Chro.11,23.

22 These things did Benaiáh the sonne of
Iehoiadá, & had the name amõg the thre
worthies.
23 He was honorable among [m] thirty, but
he atteined not to the *first* thre: and Dauid
made him of his counsel.

m He was more valiant the ẏ 30 that follow, and not so valiant as the 6 before.

24 ¶ * Asahél the brother of Ioáb *was* one
of the thirty: Elhanán the sonne of Dodó of Beth-léhem:

Chap.2,18.

25 Shammáh the Harodite: Eliká the Harodite:
26 Hélez the * ″ Paltite: Irá the sonne of Ikkésh the Tekoite:

1 Chro.11,27.

″*Or, Pelonite.*

27 Abiézer the Anethothite: [n] Mebunnái ẏ
Husathite:

n Diuers of these had two names, as appeareth. 1.Chro.11. and also many more are there mencioned.

28 Zalmón an Ahohite: Maharái the Netophathite:
29 Héleb the sonne of Baanáh a Netophathite: Ittái the sonne of Ribái of Gibeáh of the children of Beniamín.
30 Benaiáh the Pirathonite: Hiddái of the
riuer of Gaásh:
31 Abi-álbon the Arbathite: Azmáueth the
Barhumite:
32 Elihabá the Shaalbonite: *of* the sonnes of
Iashén, Ionathán:
33 Shammáh the Hararite: Ahiám the sonne
of Sharár the Hararite:
34 Eliphélet the sonne of Ahasbái the sonne
of Maachathí: Eliám the sonne of Ahithó
phel the Gilonite:

35 Hezrái the Carmelite: Paarái the Ar-
bite:
36 Igál the sonne of Nathán of Zobáh:
Baní the Gadite:
37 Zélek the Ammonite: Naharái the Beerothite, the armour bearer of Ioáb the
sonne of Zeruiáh:
38 Irá the Ithrite Garéb the Ithrite:
39 Vriiáh the Hittite, [o] thirty and seuen
in all.

o These came to Dauid and helped to restore him to his kingdome.

CHAP. XXIIII.

1 Dauid causeth the people to be nombred. 10 He repenteth, and chuseth to fall into Gods hands. 15 Seuentie thousand perish with the pestilence.

1 AND the wrath of the Lord was [a] a-
gaine kindled against Israél, and
[b] he moued Dauid against them, in that he
said, Go, nomber Israél and Iudáh.
2 For the King said to Ioáb the captaine
of the hoste, which was with him, Go spedely now through all the tribes of Israél,
from Dan euen to Beer-shéba and nomber ye the people, that I may knowe the
[c] nomber of the people.
3 And Ioáb said vnto the King, The Lord
thy God increase the people an hundreth
folde mo then they be, and that the eyes
of my lord the King maye se it: but why
doeth my lord the King desire this thing?
4 Notwithstanding the Kings worde preuailed against Ioáb & against the captaines of the hoste: therefore Ioáb & the captaines of the hoste went out from the presence of the King, to nomber the people
of Israél.
5 ¶ And they passed ouer Iordén, and pitched in Aroér at the right side of the citie
that is in the middes of the ["] valley of Gad
and toward Iazér.
6 Then thei came to Gileád, and to ["] Tah-
tim hodshí, so they came to Dan Iaán, &
so about to Zidón,
7 And came to the fortresse of Tyrus and
to all the cities of the Hiuites and of the
Canaanites, and went toward the South
of Iudáh, euen to Beer-shéba.
8 So when they had gone about all the lãd,
they returned to Ierusalém at the end of
nine moneths and twentie dayes.
9 ¶ And Ioáb deliuered the nomber *and*
summe of the people vnto the King: and
there were in Israél [d] eight hũdreth thousand strong men that drewe swordes, and
the men of Iudáh were [e] fiue hundreth
thousand men.
10 Thẽ Dauids heart smote him, after that
he had nombred the people: and Dauid
said vnto the Lord, I haue sinned excedingly in that I haue done: therefore now,
Lord, I beseche thee, take away the trespasse of thy seruant: for I haue done very
foolishly.
11 ¶ And when Dauid was vp in the morning, the worde of the Lord came vnto
the Prophet Gad Dauids [f] Seer, saying,
12 Go, and say vnto Dauid, Thus sayth the
Lord, I offre thee thre things, chose thee
which of them I shal do vnto thee.
13 So Gad came to Dauid, and shewed hĩ,
and said vnto him, Wilt thou that [g] seuen
yeres famine come vpon thee in thy land,
or wilt thou flee thre moneths before
thine enemies, they following thee, or
that there be thre daies pestilence in thy
land? now aduise thee, and se, what answer
I shal giue to him that sent me.
14 ¶ And Dauid said vnto Gad, I am in a
wonderful straite: let vs fall now into
the hand of the Lord, (for his mercies
are great) and let me not fall into the hãd
of man.
15 So the Lord sent a pestilence in Israél,
from the morning euen to the time appointed: and there dyed of the people frõ
[h] Dan euen to Beer-shéba seuentie thousand men.
16 And when the Angel stretched out his
hand vpon Ierusalém to destroy it, the
Lord *repẽted of the euil, and said to the
Angel that destroyed the people, It is sufficient, [i] holde now thine hand. And the
Angel of the Lord was by the threshing
place of Araunáh the Iebusite.
17 And Dauid spake vnto the Lord (when
he sawe the Angel that smote the people)
& said, Beholde, I haue sinned, yea, I haue
done wickedly: but these shepe, what haue
they [k] done? let thine hand, I praye thee,
be against me & agaĩst my fathers house.
18 ¶ So Gad came the same day to Dauid,
and said vnto him, Go vp, reare an altar
vnto the Lord in the threshing floore of
Araunáh the Iebusite.
19 And Dauid (according to the saying of
Gad) went vp, as the Lord had commanded.
20 And Araunáh loked, and sawe the King
and his seruants comming towarde him,
and Araunáh went out, and bowed him
selfe before the King on his face to the
grounde,
21 And [l] Araunáh said, Wherefore is my
lord the King come to his seruant? Then
Dauid answered, To bye the threshing
floore of thee, for to buylde an altar vnto
the Lord, that the plague may cease from
the people.
22 Then Araunáh said vnto Dauid, Let my
lord the King take and offer what semeth
him good in his eyes: beholde the oxen for
the burnt offring, and charets, and the instruments of the oxen for wood.
23 All these things did Araunáh [m] *as* a Kĩg
giue vnto the King: & Araunáh said vnto the King, The Lord thy God be fauorable vnto thee.

a Before they were plagued with famine, Chap. 21,1.
b The Lord permitted Satan, as 1. Chro. 21,1.
c Because he did this to trie his power and so to trust therein, it offẽded God, els it was lawful to nõber ỹ people, Exod. 30 12, Nomb 1,2.
" Or, riuer.
" Or, to the nether lãd newly inhabited.
" Or, Iaan.
d According to Ioabs counte: for in all there were eleuen hũdreth thousand, 1 Chro. 21,5
e Concluding vnder thẽ the Beniamites: for els they had but foure hundreth & seuentie thousand, 1 Chro. 21,5.
f Whome God had appointed for Dauid and his time.
g For 3. yeres of famine were past for the Gibionites matter: this was ỹ 4 yere, to the which shulde haue bene added other. 3. yeres more, 1. Chro 21,12.
h Frõ the one side of the countrey to ỹ other.
* 1. Sam. 15, 11.
i The Lord spared this place, because he had chosen it to buylde his temple there.
k Dauid sawe not ỹ iust cause, why God plagued ỹ people, & therefore he offreth him selfe to Gods corrections, as the onely cause of this euil.
l Called also Ornán, 1. Chro. 21,22.
m That is, abũdantly, for as some write, he was King of Ierusalem before Dauid wãne ỹ towre.

24 Thē the King said vnto Araunáh, Not
so,but I wil by it of thee at a price, & wil
not offer burnt offring vnto the Lord my
God of that which doeth cost me nothīg.
So Dauid boght the threshing floore, and
the oxen for [n] fiftie shekels of siluer.
25 And Dauid buylt there an altar vnto the
Lord,and offred burnt offrings and peace
offrings, & the Lord was appeased toward
the land,& the plague ceased from Israél.

n Some write, that euery tribe gaue 50, wͨ make 600, or ỷ afterwarde he boght as muche as came to 550 shekels, 1. Chro. 21,25.

THE FIRST BOKE OF the Kings.

THE ARGUMENT.

Because the children of God shulde loke for no continual rest and quietnes in this worlde, the holy Gost setteth before our eyes in this boke the varietie and change of things, which came to the people of Israél from the death of Dauid, Salomón and the rest of the Kings, vnto the death of Aháb, declaring how that florishing kingdomes, except they be preserued by Gods protection, (who then fauoreth them when his worde is truely set forthe, vertue estemed, vice punished and concorde mainteined) fall to decay and come to naught: as appeareth by the diuiding of the kingdome vnder Robohám, and Ierobohám, which before were but all one people, and now by the iuste punishment of God were made two, whereof Iudáh and Beniamín claue to Robohám: and this was called the kingdome of Iudáh, and the other ten tribes helde with Ierobohám, and this was called the kingdome of Israél. The King of Iudáh had his throne in Ierusalém, and the King of Israél in Samaria, after it was buylte by Amri Ahabs father. And because our Sauiour Christ according to the flesh shulde come of the stocke of Dauid, the genealogie of the Kings of Iudáh is here described, from Salomón to Iorám the sonne of Iosaphát, who reigned ouer Iudáh in Ierusalém, as Aháb did ouer Israél in Samaria.

CHAP. I.

3 Abishág kepeth Dauid in his extreme age. 5 Adoniiáh vsurpeth the kingdome. 30 Salomón is anointed King. 50 Adoniiáh fleeth to the altar.

1 Now when King Dauid
was [a] olde,and striken in
yeres, they couered him
wͭ clothes,but no [b] heate
came vnto him.
2 Wherefore his seruāts
said vnto him, Let there
be soght for my lord the King a yong
virgin,and let her [*] stand before the King,
and cherish him: & let her lye in thy bosome,
that my lord the King may get
heate.
3 So they soght for a faire yong maid
throughout all the coastes of Israel, and
founde one Abishág [c] a Shunammite,and
broght her to the King.
4 And the maid was exceding faire,& cherished
the King,and ministred to him, but
the King knewe her not.
5 ¶ Then Adoniiáh the sonne of Haggíth
exalted him selfe,saying, I wil be King.
And he gate him charets and horsemen,&
[d] fifty men to runne before him.
6 And his father wolde not displease him
frō his [*] childehode,to say,Why hast thou
done so? And he was a very goodly mā, &
his mother bare him next after Absalóm.
7 And [*] he toke counsel of Ioáb the sonne
of Zeruiáh,and of Abiathár the Priest:&

a He was about 70 yere olde, 2 Sam. 5,4.
b For his natural heate was worne away with trauels.
* Or, serue him.
c Which citie was in the tribe of Issachár.
d Read, 2. Sam. 15,1.
* Ebr. daies.
* Ebr. his wordes were with Ioáb.

they [e] helped forward Adoniiáh.
8 But Zadók the Priest, and Benaiáh the
sonne of Iehoiadá, and Nathán the Prophet,&
Shimeí,& Reí,& ỷ men of might
wͨ were with Dauid,were not wͭ Adoniiáh.
9 Then Adoniiáh sacrificed shepe & oxen,
and fat cattel by the stone of Zohéleth,
which is by [*] En-rogél, and called all his
brethren the Kings sonnes, & all the men
of Iudáh the Kings seruants,
10 But Nathán the Prophet, & Benaiáh,
and the [f] mighty men, and Salomón his
brother he called not.
11 Wherefore Nathán spake vnto Bath-shéba
the mother of Salomón, saying, Hast
thou not heard, that Adoniiáh the sonne
*of Haggíth doeth reigne, and Dauid our
lord knoweth it not?
12 Now therefore come,& I wil now giue
thee counsel,how to saue thine owne [g] life,
and the life of thy sonne Salomón.
13 Go,and get thee in vnto King Dauid, &
say vnto him, didest not thou, my lord,
ô King,sweare vnto thine hādmaid,sayīg,
Assuredly Salomón thy sonne shal reigne
after me,and he shal sit vpon my throne?
why is then Adoniiáh King?
14 Beholde,while ỷ yet talkest there with
the King,I also wil come in after thee,&
[h] comfirme thy wordes.
15 ¶ So Bath-shéba went in vnto the King
into ỷ chāber,& the King was very olde,
and Abishág the Shunammite ministred
vnto the King.

e They toke his part & folowed him.
* Or, the fountaine.
f As the Cherethites & Pelethites.
* 2.Sam.3,4.
g For Adoniiah wil destroy thee and thy sonne, if he reigne.
h By declaring suche things, as may further the same.

16 And Bath-shéba bowed and made obeisance vnto the King. And the King said,
What is thy matter?
17 And she answered hĩ, My lord, thou swarest by the Lord thy God vnto thine hãdmaid, *saying*, Assuredly Salomón thy
sonne shal reigne after me, and he shal sit
vpon my throne.
18 And beholde, now *is* Adoniiáh King, &
now, my lord, ô King, thou knowest [i] it
not.

i The King being worne with age, cold not attend to ye affaires of the realme, & also Adoniiáh had many flatterers which kept it frõ the King.

19 And he hathe offred many oxen, and fat
cattel, and shepe, and hathe called all the
sonnes of the King, & Abiathár ye Priest,
& Ioáb the captaine of the hoste: but Salomón thy seruant hathe he not bidden.
20 And thou, my lord, ô King, *knowest* that
the eyes of all Israél *are* on thee, that thou
shuldest tel them, who shulde sit on the
throne of my lord the King after him.
21 For els whẽ my lord the King shal slepe
with his fathers, I and my sonne Salomón
shalbe [k] reputed "vile.

k And so put to death as wicked transgressers "Ebr sinners.

22 And lo, while she yet talked with the
King, Nathán also the Prophet came in.
23 And they tolde the King, saying, Beholde, Nathán the Prophet. And when he
was come in to ye King, he made obeisance before the King vpon his face [l] to the
grounde.

l Acknowledging him to be ye true & worthy King apoĩted of God as the figure of his Christ.

24 And Nathán said, My lord, ô King, hast
thou said, Adoniiáh shal reigne after me,
and he shal sit vpon my throne?
25 For he is gone downe this day, & hathe
slaine many oxen, and fat cattel, and shepe,
and hathe called all the Kings sonnes, &
the captaines of the hoste, & Abiathár the
Priest: and beholde, they eat & drinke before him, and say, "God saue King Adoniiáh.

"Ebr. let the King Adoniiáh liue.

26 But me thy seruãt, and Zadók the Priest
and Benaiáh the sonne of Iehoiadá, and
thy seruant Salomón hathe he not called.
27 Is this thing done by my lord the King,
& thou hast not shewed it vnto thy [m] seruant, who shulde sit on the throne of my
lord the King after him?

m Meaning, yt he oght in suche affaires enterprise nothing except he had consulted with the Lord.

28 ¶ Then King Dauid answered, & said,
Call me Bath-shéba. And she came into ye
Kings presence, and stoode before the
King.
29 And the King sware, saying, As ye Lord
liueth, who hathe redemed my soule out of
all aduersitie,
30 That as I [n] sware vnto thee by the Lord
God of Israél, saying, Assuredly Salomón thy sonne shal reigne after me, and
he shal sit vpon my throne in my place,
so wil I certeinly do this day.

n Moued by ye Spirit of God so to do, because he foresawe that Salomón shulde be ye figure of Christ.

31 Then Bath-shéba bowed her face to the
earth, & did reuerẽce vnto ye Kĩg, & said,
God saue my lord King Dauid for euer.
32 ¶ And King Dauid said, Call me Zadók the Priest, and Nathán the Prophet,
and Benaiáh the sonne of Iehoiadá. And
they came before the King.
33 Then the King said vnto them, Take
with you the [o] seruants of your lord, and
cause Salomón my sonne to ride vpon mine owne mule, & cary him downe to Gihón.

o Meaning, the Kings seruants & suche as were of his garde.

34 And let Zadók the Priest and Nathán
the Prophet anoint him there King ouer
Israél, and blowe ye the trumpet, and say,
God saue King Salomón.
35 Then come vp after him, that he may
come and sit vpon my throne: and he shal
be King in my steade: for I haue "appointed him to be prince ouer Israél and ouer
Iudáh.

"Ebr. cõmãded.

36 Then Benaiáh the sonne of Iehoiadá
answered the King, & said, So be it, & the
Lord God of my lord the King "ratifie it.

"Ebr. say so.

37 As the Lord hathe bene with my lord ye
King, so be he with Salomón, & exalt his
throne aboue the throne of my lord King
Dauid.
38 So Zadók the Priest, and Nathán the
Prophet, and Benaiáh the sonne of Iehoiadá, and the Cherethites & the Pelethites
wẽt downe, and caused Salomón to ride
vpon King Dauids mule, and broght him
to Gihón.
39 And Zadók the Priest toke an horne of
[p] oyle out of the Tabernacle, and anointed Salomón: and thei blewe the trumpet,
and all the people said, God saue King Sa
lomón.

p Wherewith they accustomed to anoint the Priestes & the holy instruments, Exod.30,23.

40 And all the people came vp after him,
and the people piped with pipes & reioyced with great ioye, so that the earth "rãg
with the sounde of them.

"Ebr. brake.

41 ¶ And Adoniiáh and all the gestes that
were with him, heard it: (and they had
made an end of eating) and when Ioáb
heard the sounde of the trumpet, he said,
What meaneth this noise & vprore in the
citie?
42 And as he yet spake, beholde, Ionathán
the sonne of Abiathár the Priest came: &
Adoniiáh said, Come in: for yu art "a worthy man, and bringest [q] good tidings.

"Ebr. a man of power.
q He praised Ionathán thinking to haue heard cõfortable newes, but God wroght things cõtrary to his expectation, and so did beat downe his pride.

43 And Ionathán answered, and said to A-
doniiáh, Verely our lord King Dauid hathe made Salomón King.
44 And the King hathe sent with him Zadók the Priest, and Nathán the Prophet,
and Benaiáh the sonne of Iehoiadá, and
the Cherethites, and the Pelethites, and
they haue caused him to ride vpon the
Kings mule.
45 And Zadók the Priest, and Nathán the
Prophet haue anointed him King in Gihón: and thei are gone vp frõ thence with
ioye, and the citie is moued: this is the
noise.

noise that ye haue heard.
46 And Salomón also sitteth on the throne
of the kingdome.
47 And moreouer the Kings seruants came
[r] to blesse our lord King Dauid, saying,
God make the name of Salomón more
famous then thy name, & exalt his throne aboue thy throne: therefore the King
worshiped vpon the [s] bed.

r To salute him & to pray & praise God for him.

s He gaue God thākes for the good successe.

48 And thus said the King also, Blessed be
the Lord God of Israél, who hathe made
one to sit on my throne this day, euen in
my sight.
49 Then all the gestes that were with A-
doniiáh, were afraied, and rose vp, & went
euery man his waye.
50 ¶ And Adoniiáh fearing the presence of
Salomón, arose and went, and toke holde
on the hornes of the [t] altar.

t Which Dauid his father had buylt in ẏ floore of Araunáh.

51 And one tolde Salomón, sayīg, Beholde,
Adoniiáh doeth feare King Salomón: for
lo, he hathe caught holde on the hornes of
ẏ altar, saying, Let King Salomón sweare
vnto me this day, that he wil not slaye his
seruant with the sworde.
52 Thē Salomón said, If he wil shewe him
selfe a worthy man, there shal not an heere
of him fall to the earth, but if wickednes
be found in him, he shal dye.
53 Thē King Salomón sent, & thei broght
him from the altar, and he came and did
obeisance vnto King Salomón. And Salomón said vnto him, Go to thine house.

CHAP. II.

1 Dauid exhorteth Salomón, and giueth charge as concerning Ioáb, Barzillái, and Shimei. 10 The death of Dauid. 17 Adoniiah asketh Abishag to wife. 25 He is slayne. 35 Zadók was placed in Abiathars roume.

1 THen the daies of Dauid drewe nere
that he shulde dye, and he charged
Salomón his sonne, saying,
2 I go the [a] waie of all the earth: be strong
therefore, and shewe thy selfe a man,
3 And take hede to ẏ [b] charge of the Lord
thy God, to walke in his waies, & kepe his
statutes, & his cōmandements, & his iudgemēts, & his testimonies, as it is written
in the Lawe of Moses, that thou maiest
*" prosper in all that thou doest, and in e-
uery thing whereunto thou turnest thee,

a I am ready to dye, as all men must.

b He sheweth how hard a thing it is to gouerne, and that none can do it wel, except he obey God.

Deut. 29,9. iosh. 1,7.

"Or, do wisely.

4 That the Lord may confirme his worde
which he spake vnto me, sayīg, If thy sonnes take hede to their way, that thei walke
before me in [c] trueth, with all their hearts,
and with all their soules, *" thou shalt not
(said he) want one of thy *posteritie* vpon
the throne of Israél.

c And without hypocrisie.

2 Sam. 7,12.

"Ebr. a man shal not be cut of to thee from of the throne.

5 Thou knowest also what Ioáb the sonne
of Zeruiáh did to me, and what he did to
the two captaines of the hostes of Israél,
vnto * Abnér the sonne of Ner, and vnto
* Amasá the sonne of Iethér: whome he
slewe, and [d] shed blood of battel in peace,
and [e] put the blood of warre vpon his
girdle that was about his loynes, & in his
shooes that were on his feete.

2 Sam. 3,27.

2 Sam. 20,10.

d He shed his blood in time of peace, as if there had bene warre.

e He put the bloody sworde into his sheathe.

6 Do therefore according to thy wisdome,
and let thou not his hoare head go downe
to the graue in peace.
7 But shewe kindenes vnto the sonnes of
* Barzillái the Gileadite, and let them be
among them that eat at thy table: [f] for so
thei came to me when I fled from Absalóm thy brother.

2. Sam. 19,31.

f That is, they delt mercifully with me.

8 ¶ And beholde, with thee * *is* Shimeí the
sonne of Gerá, the sonne of Ieminí, of Bahurím, which cursed me with an horrible
curse in ẏ day when I went to Mahanáim:
but he came downe to meete mē at Iorden, and I sware to him by the Lord, saying, * I wil not slaye thee with the sworde.

2. Sam. 16,5.

2. Sam. 19,23.

9 But thou shalt not count him innocent:
for thou art a wise man, and knowest what
thou oghtest to do vnto him: therefore
ẏ shalt cause his hoare head to go downe
to the graue with [g] blood.

g Let him be punished with death.

10 So * Dauid slept with his fathers, & was
buryed in the citie of Dauid.

Act. 2,29. & 13,36.

11 And the daies which Dauid * reigned
vpon Israél, *were* fourtie yeres: seuen yeres
reigned he in Hebrón, and thirty & thre
yeres reigned he in Ierusalém.

2 Sam. 5,4.

12 ¶ * Thē sate Salomón vpō the throne of
Dauid his father, and his kingdome was
stablished mightely.

2. Chro. 29,23

13 And Adoniiáh the sonne of Haggíth
came to Bath-shéba the mother of Salomón: and she said, [h] Commest thou peaceably? And he said, Yea.

h For she feared, lest he wolde worke treason against the King.

14 He said moreouer, I haue a sute vnto
thee. And she said, Say on.
15 Then he said, Thou knowest that the
kingdome was mine, and that all Israél set
[i] their faces on me, that I shulde reigne:
howbeit the kingdome is turned away, &
is my brothers: for it came to him by the
Lord.

i In signe of their fauour & consent.

16 Now therefore I aske thee one request,
" refuse me not. And she said vnto him,
Say on.

"Ebr. cause not my face to turne away.

17 And he said, Speake, I pray thee, vnto
Salomón the Kīg, (for he wil not say thee
naye) that he giue me Abishág the Shunammite to wife.
18 And Bath-shéba said, Wel, I wil speake
for thee vnto the King.
19 ¶ Bath-shéba therefore went vnto King
Salomón, to speake vnto him for Adoniiáh: and the King rose to meete her, and
[k] bowed him selfe vnto her, & sate downe
on his throne: and he caused a seat to be
set for the Kings mother, and she sate at
his right hand.

k In token of reuerence, and that others by his example might haue her in greater honour.

20 Then she said, I desire a smale request
of thee, say me not naye. Then the King
said vnto her, Aske on, my mother: for I

wil not say thee naye.
21 She said thē, Let Abishág the Shunāmite
be giuē to Adoniiáh thy brother to wife.
22 But King Salomón answered and said
vnto his mother, And why doest ẏ aske
Abishág ẏ Shunāmite for Adoniiáh? aske
for him the [l] kingdome also: for he is
mine elder brother, & hathe for him bothe
Abiathár the Priest, and Ioáb the sonne
of Zeruiáh.

l Meaning, that if he shulde haue granted Abishág, ẇ was so deare to his father, he wolde afterwarde haue aspired to the kingdome.

23 Thē King Salomón sware by the Lord,
saying, God do so to me and more also,
if Adoniiáh hathe not spoken this worde
against his owne life.
24 Now therefore as the Lord liueth, who
hathe established me, and set me on the
throne of Dauid my father, who also
hathe made me an house, as he *promised,
Adoniiáh shal surely dye this day.

2.Sam.7,12.

25 And King Salomón sent by the hand of
Benaiáh the sonne of Iehoiadá, and he
[*] smote him that he dyed.

*Or, fel vpō him

26 ¶ Then the King said vnto Abiathár
the Priest, Go to Anathóth vnto thine
owne [*] fields: for thou art [*] worthy of
death: but I wil not this day kil thee, because thou [m] barest the Arke of the Lord
God before Dauid my father, & because
thou hast suffred in all, wherein my father
hathe bene afflicted.

*Or, possessions. *Ebr. a man of death.

m When he fled before Absalóm, 2.Sam. 15,24.

27 So Salomón cast out Abiathár from being Priest vnto the Lord, that he might
*fulfil the wordes of the Lord, which he
spake against the house of Elí in Shilóh.

1.Sam.2,31.

28 ¶ Then tidings came to Ioáb: (for Ioáb
had [n] turned after Adoniiáh, but he turned not after Absalóm) and Ioáb fled vnto the Tabernacle of the Lord, & caught
holde on the hornes of the altar.

n He toke Adoniiahs parte whē he wolde haue vsurped the kingdome, Chap.1,7.

29 And it was tolde King Salomón, that
Ioáb was fled vnto the Tabernacle of the
Lord, & beholde, *he is* by the [o] altar. Thē
Salomón sent Benaiáh the sonne of Ieho-
iadá, saying, Go, fall vpon him.

o Thinking to be saued by ẏ holines of the place.

30 And Benaiáh came to the Tabernacle
of the Lord, & said vnto him, Thus saith
the King, Come out. And he said, Naye,
but I wil dye here. Then Benaiáh broght
the King worde againe, saying, Thus said
Ioáb, and thus he answered me.
31 And the King said vnto him, Do as he
hathe said, and [p] smite him, & burye him,
ẏ thou maiest take away the blood, which
Ioáb shed causeles, from me and from the
house of my father.

p For it was lawful to take ẏ wilful murtherer frō the altar, Exod. 21,14.

32 And the Lord shal bring his blood vpō
his owne head: for he smote two mē more
righteous & better then he, & slewe them
with the sworde, and my father Dauid
knewe not: *to wit*, * Abnér ẏ sonne of Ner,
captaine of the hoste of Israél, and * A-
masá the sonne of Iethér captaine of the
hoste of Iudáh.

2.Sam.3,27. 2.Sam.20,10.

33 Their blood shal therefore returne vpō
the [q] head of Ioáb, and on the head of his
sede for euer: but vpon Dauid, and vpon
his sede, and vpon his house, and vpon his
throne shal there be peace for euer frō the
Lord.

q Ioáb shalbe iustely punished for the blood that he hathe cruelly shed.

34 So Benaiáh the sonne of Iehoiadá went
vp, and smote him, and slewe him, and he
was buryed in his owne house in the wildernes.
35 And the King put Benaiáh the sonne of
Iehoiadá in his roume ouer ẏ hoste: & the
King set Zadók the [r] Priest in the roume
of Abiathár.

r And so toke the office of ẏ hie Priest frō the house of Eli, & restored it to ẏ house of Phinehas.

36 ¶ Afterwarde the King sent, and called
Shimeí, and said vnto him, Buylde thee
an house in Ierusalém, and dwel there, &
departe not thence anie whether.
37 For that day that thou goest out, & passest ouer the riuer of Kidrón, knowe assuredly, that thou shalt dye the death: thy
blood shalbe vpon thine owne head.
38 And Shimeí said vnto the King, The
thing is good: as my lord the King hathe
said, so wil thy seruāt do. So Shimeí dwelt
in Ierusalém many dayes.
39 And after thre yeres two of the [s] seruāts
of Shimeí fled away vnto Achísh sonne
of Maacháh King of Gath: & thei tolde
Shimeí, saying, Beholde, thy seruants *be* in
Gath.

s Thus God appointeth the waies & meanes to bring his iuste iudgements vpon the wicked.

40 And Shimeí arose, and sadled his asse,
and went to Gath to Achísh, to seke his
seruants: and [t] Shimeí went, and broght
his seruants from Gath.

t His couetous minde moued him rather to venture his life, thē to lose his worldely profit, which he had by his seruants.

41 And it was tolde Salomón, that Shimeí
had gone from Ierusalém to Gath, & was
come againe.
42 And the King sent and called Shimeí,
& said vnto him, Did I not make thee to
sweare by ẏ Lord, & protested vnto thee,
saying, That day that thou goest out, and
walkest anie whether, knowe assuredly ẏ
thou shalt dye the death? And thou saidest
vnto me, The thing is good, *that* I haue
heard.
43 Why then hast thou not kept the othe
of the Lord, & the cōmandement wherewith I charged thee?
44 The King said also to Shimeí, [u] Thou
knowest all the wickednes whereunto thine heart is priuie, that thou didest to Dauid my father: the Lord therefore shal
bring thy wickednes vpon thine owne
head.

u For thogh ẏ woldest denie, yet thine owne cōsciēce wold accuse thee, for reuiling & doing wrōg to my father, 2.Sam 16,5.

45 And let King Salomón be blessed, and
the throne of Dauid stablished before the
Lord for euer.
46 So the King commanded Benaiáh the
sonne of Iehoiadá: who went out & smote
him that he dyed. And the kingdome was
[x] stablished in the hand of Salomón.

x Because all his enemies were destroied

CHAP.

CHAP. III.

1 Salomón taketh Pharaohs daughter to wife. 5 The Lord appeareth to him, & giueth him wisdome. 17 The pleating of the two harlottes, and Salomons sentence therein.

2.Chro.1,1.
1 SAlomón * thē made affinitie with Pharaóh King of Egypt, and toke Paraohs
daughter, and broght her into the a citie of Dauid, vntil he had made an end of
buylding his owne house, and the house of
the Lord, and the wall of Ierusalém roūd
about.

a Which was Beth-léhem.

2 Onely the people sacrificed in b the hie
places, because there was no house buylt
vnto the Name of the Lord, vntil those
dayes.

b Where altars were appointed before the Temple was buylt to offer vnto the Lord.

3 And Salomón loued the Lord, walking in
the ordinācēs of Dauid his c father: onely
he sacrificed and offred incense in the hie
places.

c For his father had commāded him to obey the Lord & walke in his wayes, Chap. 2,3.

4 And the King wēt to d Gibeón to sacrifice there, for that was the chief hie place:
a thousand burnt offrings did Salomón
offer vpon that altar.

d For there ẏ Tabernacle was, 2 Chro. 1,3.

5 In Gibeón the Lord appeared to Salomón in a dreame by night: and God said,
Aske what I shal giue thee.

6 And Salomón said, Thou hast shewed
vnto thy seruant Dauid my father great
mercy, "when he walked before thee in
trueth, & in righteousnes, and in vprightnes of heart with thee: & thou hast e kept
for him this great mercy, and hast giuen
him a sonne, to sit on his throne, as *appeareth* this day.

"Or, as he walked.

e Thou hast performed thy promes.

7 And now, ô Lord, my God, thou hast made thy seruant King in stead of Dauid my
father: and I am but a yong childe, and
knowe not how to f go out and in.

f That is, to behaue my selfe in executing this charge of ruling.

8 And thy seruant *is* in the middes of thy
people, which ẏ hast chosen, euen a great
people which can not be tolde nor nombred for multitude.

2.Chro.1,10.
"Or, obedient.

9 * Giue therefore vnto thy seruant an "vnderstādīg heart, to iudge thy people, that
I may discerne betwene good & bad: for
who is able to iudge this thy g mighty
people?

g Which are so manie in nomber.

10 And this pleased the Lord wel, that Salomón had desired this thing.

11 And God said vnto him, Because thou
hast asked this thing, & hast not asked for
thy selfe long life, nether hast asked riches
for thy selfe, nor hast asked ẏ life of thine
h enemies, but hast asked for thy selfe vnderstanding to heare iudgement,

h That is, that thine enemies shulde dye.

12 Beholde, I haue done according to thy
wordes: lo, I haue giuen thee a wise and an
vnderstanding heart, so that there hathe
bene none like thee before thee, nether after thee shal arise the like vnto thee.

Matt.6,33.
wisdo.7,11.

13 And I haue also * giuen thee that, which
thou hast not asked, bothe riches and honour, so that among the Kings there "shalbe none like vnto thee all thy dayes.

"Or, hathe bene none.

14 And if thou wilt walke in my wayes, to
kepe mine ordinances and my commandements, * as thy father Dauid did walke,
I wil prolong thy dayes.

Chap.15,5.

15 And when Salomón awoke, beholde, it
was i a dreame, and he came to Ierusalém, and stode before the Arke of the couenant of the Lord, and offred burnt offrings and made peace offrings, and made
a feast to all his seruants.

i He knewe that God had appeared vnto him in a dreame.

16 ¶ Then came two "harlottes vnto the
King, and k stode before him.

"Or, vitailers.

k By this exāple it appeareth that God kept promes with Salomón in granting him wisdome.

17 And the one woman said, Oh my lord, I
& this woman dwel in one house, & I was
deliuered of a childe with her in ẏ house.

18 And the third day after that I was deliuered, this woman was deliuered also: and
we were in the house together: no stranger
was with vs in the house, saue we twaine.

19 And this womās sonne dyed in the night:
for she ouerlay him.

20 And she rose at midnight, and l toke my
sonne from my side, while thine hādmaid
slept, & layed him in her bosome, & layed
her dead sonne in my bosome.

l She stale the quicke childe away, because she might both auoide ẏ shame and punishement.

21 And when I rose in the morning to giue
my sonne sucke, beholde, he was dead: and
when I had wel cōsidered him in the morning, beholde, it was not my sonne, whome I had borne.

22 Then the other woman said, Nay, but
my sonne liueth, and thy sonne is dead:
againe she said, No, but thy sōne is dead, &
mine aliue: thus they spake before ẏ King.

23 Thē said the King, She sayth, this that
liueth is my sonne, & the dead is thy sonne: and ẏ other saith, Naye, but the dead
is thy sonne, and the liuing is my sonne.

24 Then ẏ King said, m Bring me a sworde:
& they broght out a sworde before ẏ King.

m Except God giue iudges vnderstādīg, the impudēcie of the trespacer shal ouerthrowe ẏ iust cause of the innocent.

25 And the King said, Deuide ye the liuing
childe in twaine, and giue the one halfe to
the one, and the other halfe to the other.

26 Then spake the woman, whose the liuing
childe was, vnto the King, for her compassion was kindled toward her sonne, &
she said, Oh my lord, giue her the liuing
childe, and n slay him not: but the other
said, Let it be nether mine nor thine, but
deuide it.

n Her motherly affectiō herein appeareth that she had rather endure the rigour of the lawe, then se her childe cruelly slaine.

27 Then the King answered, & said, Giue
her the liuing childe, and slay him not:
this is his mother.

28 And all Israél heard ẏ iudgement, which
the King had iudged, and they feared the
King: for they sawe that the wisdome of
God was in him to do iustice.

CHAP. IIII.

2 The princes and rulers vnder Salomón. 22 The pourueyance for his vitailes. 26 The nomber of his horses. 32 His bokes, and writings.

a That is, his chief officers.
b He was the ſonne of Achimais and Zadoks nephew.

1 AND King Salomón was King ouer
all Iſraél.
2 And theſe were [a] his princes, [b] Azariáh the ſonne of Zadók the Prieſt,
3 Elihóreph and Ahiáh the ſonnes of Shi-
ſhá ſcribes, Iehoſhaphát the ſonne of A-
hilúd, the recorder,
4 And Benaiáh the ſonne of Iehoiadá
was ouer the hoſte, and Sadók and [c] Abiathár Prieſts,
5 And Azariáh the ſonne of Nathán *was*
ouer the officers, and Zabúd the ſonne of
Nathán Prieſt *was* the Kings friend,
6 And Ahiſhár was ouer the houſholde: &
* Adonirám the ſonne of Abdá *was* ouer
the tribute.

c Not Abiathár, whome Salomón had put from his office, Chap. 2, 27, but another of that name.

Chap. 5, 14.

7 ¶ And Salomón had twelue officers ouer
all Iſraél, which prouided vitailes for the
King and his houſholde: eche man had a
moneth in the yere to prouide vitailes.
8 And theſe are their names: the ſonne of
Hur in mount Ephráim:
9 The ſonne of Dekár in Makáz, and in
Shaalbím and Beth-ſhémeſh, and "Elón
and Beth-hanán:

"Or, Elón in Beth-auán.

10 The ſonne of Héſed in Arubóth, to
whome perteined Sochóh, & all the land
of Hépher:
11 The ſonne of Abinadáb in all the regiõ
of Dor, which had Tapháth the daughter
of Salomón to wife.
12 Baaná the ſonne of Ahilúd in Taanách,
and Megiddó, & in all Beth-ſheán, which
is by Zartánah beneth Izreél, from Beth-
ſheán "to Abel-meholáh, euen til beyonde
ouer againſt Iokmeám:

"Or, to the plaine.

13 The ſonne of Géber in Ramóth Gileád,
& his were the townes of [d] Iaír, the ſonne of Manaſſéh, which are in Gileád, and
vnder him was the regiõ of Argób which
is in Baſhán: threſcore great cities with
walles and barres of braſſe.

d Which townes bare Iairs name, becauſe he toke them of the Canaanites, Nomb. 32, 41.

14 ¶ Ahinadáb the ſonne of Iddó *had* to
Mahanáim:
15 Ahimáaz in Naphtalí, and he toke Baſ-
máth the daughter of Salomón to wife:
16 Baanáh the ſonne of Huſhái in Aſhér
and in Alóth:
17 Iehoſhaphát the ſonne of Parúah in
[e] Iſſachár.
18 Shimeí the ſonne of Eláh in Beniamín:
19 Gebér the ſonne of Vri in the countrei
of Gileád, the land of Sihón King of the
Amorites, and of Og King of Baſhán, and
was officer alone in the land.

e Salomón obſerued not the diuiſion that Ioſhúa made, but deuided it as might beſt ſerue for his purpoſe.

20 Iudáh and Iſraél *were* manie, as the ſand
of the ſea in nomber, [f] eating, drinking,
and making meary.
21 *And Salomón reigned ouer all kingdomes, from the [g] Riuer *vnto* the land of the
Philiſtíms, and vnto the border of Egypt,
and they broght preſentes, and ſerued Salomón all the dayes of his life.

f They liued in all peace & ſecuritie.

Eccleſ. 47, 15.

g Which is Euphrátes.

22 And Salomons vitailes for one day were
thirtie "meaſures of fine floure, and threſcore meaſures of meale:
23 Ten fat oxen, and twentie oxen of the
paſtures, and an hundreth ſhepe, beſide
hartes, and buckes, and bugles, and fat
foule.

"Ebr. Corim.

24 For he ruled in all *the region* on the other
ſide of the Riuer, from Tiphſáh euen vnto "Azzáh, ouer all the [h] Kings on the o-
ther ſide the Riuer: & he had peace rou͂de
about him on euerie ſide.
25 And Iudáh and Iſraél dwelt without
feare, euerie man vnder his vine, and vnder his fig tre, from [i] Dan, euen to Beer-
ſhéba, all the dayes of Salomón.

"Or, Gaza.
h For they were all tributaries vnto him.
i Throughout all Iſraél.

26 ¶ And Salomón had *fortie thouſãd ſtal-
les of horſes for his charets, and twelue
thouſand horſemen.

2 Chro. 9, 25.

27 And theſe officers prouided vitaile for
King Salomón, and for all that came to
King Salomons table, euerie man his moneth, *and* they ſuffred to lacke nothing.
28 Barly alſo and ſtrawe for the horſes and
mules broght they vnto the place where
the officers were, euerie man according to
his charge.
29 ¶ * And God gaue Salomón wiſdome
and vnderſtanding exceding muche, and
a [k] large heart, euen as the ſand that is
on the ſea ſhore.
30 And Salomons wiſdome excelled the
wiſdome of all the children of the [l] Eaſt
and all the wiſdome of Egypt.
31 For he was wiſer then anie man: *yea*, then
were Ethán the Ezrahite, then Hemán,
then Chalcól, then Dardá the ſonnes of
Mahól: and he was famous throughout all
nacions rounde about.

Eccleſ. 47, 16.

k Meaning, great vnderſtanding and able to comprehend all things.

l To wit, the philoſophers & aſtronomers, ƿ were iudged moſte wiſe.

32 And Salomón ſpake thre thouſãd [m] prouerbes: and his ſongs were a thouſand and
fiue.
33 And he ſpake of trees, from the cedar tre
that is in Lebanón, euen vnto the [n] hyſſope that ſpringeth out of the wall: he
ſpake alſo of beaſtes, and of foules, and of
creping things, and of fiſhes.
34 And there came of all people to heare
the wiſdome of Salomón, frõ all Kings of
the earth, which had heard of his wiſdome.

m Which for the moſt parte are thoght to haue periſhed in the captiuitie of Babilón.

n From the hieſt to the loweſt.

CHAP. V.

*1 Hirám ſendeth to Salomón, and Salomón to him, pur-
poſing to buylde the houſe of God. 6 He prepareth ſtuffe for the buylding. 13 The nomber of the workemẽ.*

1 AND Hirám King of Tyrus ſent his
ſeruants vnto Salomón, (for he had
heard, that they had anoynted him King
in the roume of his father) becauſe Hirám
had euer loued Dauid.
2 *Alſo Salomón ſent to Hirám, ſaying,
3 Thou knoweſt that Dauid my father
colde not buylde an houſe vnto the Name of the Lord his God, for the warres

"Or, Zor.

2 Chro. 2, 3.

which were about him on euerie side, vntil
the Lord had put ″ them vnder the soles of
his fecte.

‖Or, his enemies

4 But now the Lord my God hathe giuen
me [a] rest on euerie side, *so that* there is nether aduersarie, nor euil to resiste.
5 And beholde, I purpose to buylde an house vnto the Name of the Lord my God,
*as the Lord spake vnto Dauid my father,
saying, Thy sonne, whome I wil set vpon
thy throne for thee, he shal buylde an
house vnto my Name.

a He declareth that he was bounde to set forthe Gods glorie, forasmuche as the Lord had sent him rest and peace.

2.Sam.7,13. 1.chro.22,10.

6 Now therefore cõmande, that they hewe
me cedar trees out of Lebanón, and my
seruants shal be with thy seruants, and vnto thee wil I giue the [b] hire for thy seruants, according to all that thou shalt ap
point: for thou knowest that there are none amõg vs, that can hewe timbre like vnto the Sidonians.

b This was his equitie, ȳ he wolde not receiue a benefite without some recompence.

7 ¶ And when [c] Hirám heard the wordes
of Salomón, he reioyced greatly, and said,
Blessed be the Lord this day, which hathe
giuen vnto Dauid a wise sonne ouer this
mightie people.

c In Hirám is prefigurate ȳ vocacion of ȳ Gentiles, who shulde helpe to buylde the Spiritual temple.

8 And Hirám sent to Salomón, saying, I
haue considered the things, for the which
thou sentest vnto me, and wil accomplish
all thy desire, concerning the cedar trees
and firre trees.
9 My seruãts shal bring them downe from
Lebanón to the sea: and I wil conueie thẽ
by sea ″ in rafts vnto the place that thou
shalt shewe me, and wil cause them to be
discharged there, and thou shalt receyue
them: now thou shalt do me a pleasure to
minister foode for [d] my familie.

‖Or, flotes.

d While my seruãts are occupied about thy busines.

10 So Hirám gaue Salomón cedar trees &
firre trees, *euen* his ful desire.
11 And Salomón gaue Hirám twẽtie thousand ″ measures of wheat for foode to his
housholde, and twentie measures of ″ beaten oyle. Thus muche gaue Salomón to
Hirám yere by yere.

″ Ebr. Corim.

‖Or, pure.

12 ¶ And ye Lord gaue Salomón wisdome
as he* promised him. And there was peace betwene Hirám and Salomón, and they
[e] two made a couenant.

Chap.3,12.

e As touching the furniture of wood, and vitailes.

13 ¶ And King Salomón raised a summe
out of all Israél, and the summe was thirty
thousand men:
14 Whome he sent to Lebanón, ten thousand a moneth by course: they were a moneth in Lebanón, & two moneths at home. And *Adonirám *was* ouer the summe.
15 And Salomón had seuentie thousand
that bare burdens, & fourescore thousand
masons in the mountaine,
16 Besides the ″ princes, whome Salomón

Chap.4,6.

‖Or, masters of the worke.

appointed ouer the worke, *euen* thre thousand and thre hundreth, which ruled the
people that wroght in the worke.
17 And the King commanded them, & they
broght great stones and costly stones to
make the fundacion of the house, *euen*
hewed stones.
18 And Salomons workemen, & the workemen of Hirám, and the [f] masons hewed &
prepared timbre and stones for the buyl
ding of the house.

f The Ebrewe worde is, Giblím, which some say, were excellent masons.

CHAP. VI.

1 The buylding of the Temple and the forme thereof. 12 The promes of the Lord to Salomón.

1 AND *in the foure hundreth and fourscore yere (after the children of Israél were come out of the land of Egypt)
and in the fourth yere of the reigne of Salomón ouer Israél, in the moneth [a] Zif,
(which is the seconde moneth) he buylt
the [b] house of the Lord.

2.Chro.3,1.

a Which moneth cõteineth parte of April & part of May.
b Whereby is ment the temple & the oracle.

2 And the house which Kĩg Salomón buylt
for the Lord, was thre score cubites long,
& twentie broade, and thirty cubites hie.
3 And the [c] porche before the Temple of the
house *was* twentie cubites long according
to the breadth of the house, and ten cubites broade before the house.

c Or the court where ȳ people prayed, ŵ was before the place where ȳ altar of burnt offrings stode.

4 And in the house he made windowes,
″ broade *without*, and narowe *within*.
5 And by the wall of the house he made
″ galleries rounde about, euen by the
walles of the house rounde about the Tẽple and [d] the oracle, and made chambres
rounde about.

‖Or, to open & to shut.

‖Or, lofts.

d Whẽce God spake betwene ȳ Cherubims, called also the moste holy place.

6 The nethermost gallerie *was* fiue cubites
broade, and the middlemost six cubites
broade, & the thirde seuẽ cubites broade:
for he made [e] restes rounde about without
the house, that *the beames* shulde not be fastened in the walles of the house.
7 And whẽ the house was buylt, it was bu
ylt of stone perfit, *before* it was broght, so
that there was nether hammer, nor axe,
nor any toole of yron heard in the house,
while it was in buylding.

e Which were certeine stones comming out of ȳ wall, as stayes for the beames to rest vpon.

8 The dore of the middle ″ chambre was
in the right side of the house, & men went
vp with winding steires into the middlemost, and out of the middlemost into the
third.

‖Or, gallerie.

9 So he buylt the [f] house and finished it, &
cieled the house being vawted with cieling of cedar trees.
10 And he buylt the galleries vpon all the
wall of the house of fiue cubites height, &
they were ioyned to the house with beames of cedar.
11 And the worde of the Lord came to Salomón, saying,

f In Exodus it is called the Tabernacle: & the temple is there called ȳ sanctuarie, and the oracle the moste holy place.

THE TEMPLE VNCOVERED.

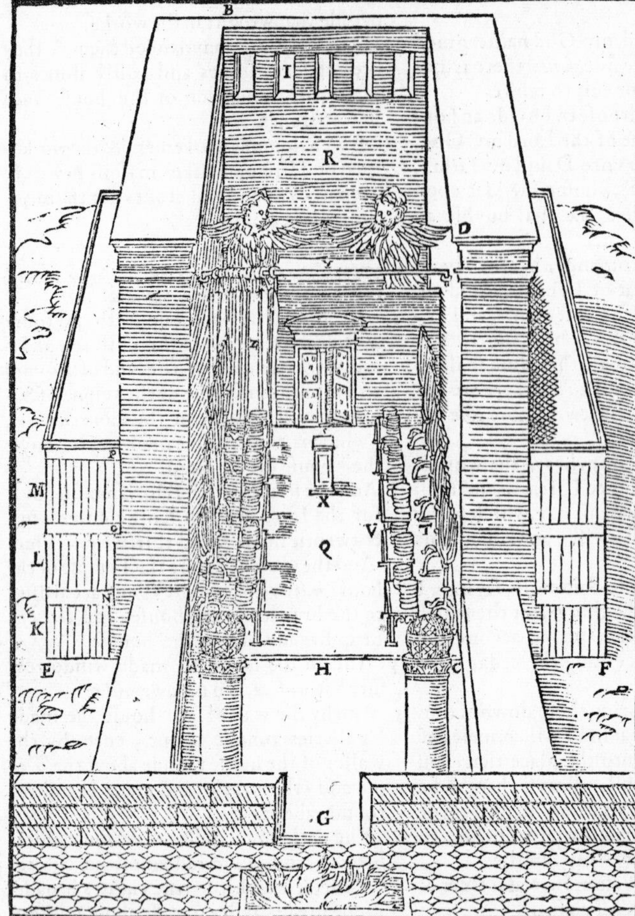

The cause why we vncouered and set open the Téple, without settig forthe the wall that is before it, is, that the ordre of those things that are within, might be sene more liuely.
A B. The length of the Temple of threscore cubites.
A C. The breadth of twétie cubites within, and not measuring the thickenes of the walles. This also was the length of ẏ porche without ẏ Téple.
C D. The height of thirtie cubites.
E F. The chambers of the Priests, which cōpassed about the Téple on thre sides, South, West and North, and were of thre heights.
G H. The breadth of the porche, ten cubites.
I The Windowes of the Temple.
K The first chamber was fiue cubites broad.
L. The seconde six.
M. The third seuen.
N O P. The rests or stayes of the walle, which bare vp the postes that did separate chamber from chamber.
Q. The holy place
R. The holiest of all, where the Arke of the couenant was Y
S. The gate to enter into the moste holy place.
T. The fiue Candelstickes on euerie side of the Téple.
V. The ten tables on bothe the sides for the shewe bread.
X. The incense altar.

12 Cōcerning this house which thou buyldest, if thou wilt walke in mine ordināces,
and execute my iudgements, and kepe all
my commandements, to walke in them,
then wil I performe vnto thee my pro-
mes,*which I promised to Dauid thy fa- (2 Sam.7,13.)
ther.
13 And I wil g dwel among the children of (g According as he promised vnto Moses, Exo.25,22.)
Israél, and wil not forsake my people Is-
raél.
14 So Salomón buylt the house and finished it,
15 And buylt the walles of the house within, with bordes of cedre tre from the pa-
uement of the house vnto h the walles of (h Meaning vnto the roofe, which was also cieled.)
the cieling, and within he couered them
with wood and couered the floore of the
house with plankes of firre.
16 And he buylt twentie cubites in the sides of the house with bordes of cedre, frō
the floore to the walles, and he prepared *a*
place within it for ẏ oracle, *euen* the moste
holy place.
17 But the i house, that is, the temple before (i For when he spake of the house in ẏ first verse, he ment bothe the oracle & the Téple.)
it was fourtie cubites *long*.
18 And the cedre of the house within was
kerued with "knoppes, and grauen with ("Or, wilde cucumers.)
flowres: all *was* cedre, *so that* no stone was
sene.
19 ¶ Also he prepared the place of the ora-
cle in the middes of the k house within, to (k That is, in ẏ moste inwarde place of the house.)
set the Arke of the couenant of the Lord
there.
20 And the place of the oracle within *was*
twentie cubites long, and twentie cubites
broad, and twentie cubites hie, and he couered it with pure golde, and couered the
altar with cedre.
21 So Salomón couered the house within
with pure golde: and he "shut the place of ("For he drewe through the chaines of golde before.)
the oracle with chaines of golde, and co-
uered it with golde.
22 And he ouerlaied the house with golde,
l vntil all the house was made perfit. also (l Meaning the altar of incense, Exod 30,3.)
he couered ẏ whole altar, that was before
the oracle, with golde.

23 And

THE TEMPLE COVERED.

This figure representeth the great court separated into thre partes, whose separatiō was made of thre orders of hewē stone & one of cedre bordes. In the first court towarde the West was the Tēple A. The seconde court B. was for the Priests, called the inner court In this stode the altar of burnt offring. D which was twētie cubites long and as muche broad, & ten of length. 2.Chr.4,1. There was also ten caldrons: fiue on the one side, and fiue on the other. E. and on the Southe side stode the Sea. F. 2.Chro.4,2. C the court of the people, which 2 Chro.4,9. is called the great porche, and Act.3,11 the porche of Salomon. This court is oft in the newe Testamēt taken for the Temple, Matt.21,23. act.3,2. In this court Christ preached, & chased thence thē that boght and solde. G. A skaffolde of brasse, whereon Salomon praied that the people might se him, & the better vnderstand him: it was fiue cubites long, fiue cubites broad, & thre of height. 2.Chro.6,13. H the gate on the Eastside, called the gate of Sur or Seir. 2.Kin.11,6. and the gate of the fundation 2.Chro.23,5. It is also called beautiful Act.3,2. because the Prince entred onely thereat into the court, and not the people, Ezek.44,3. for the people entred in by the Southe gate and North gate.

23 And within the oracle he made two Che
rubíms of ⁿolive tre, ten cubites hie.
24 The wing also of the one Cherúb *was*
fiue cubites, & the wing of the other Cherúb *was* fiue cubites: from the vttermost
parte of *one* of his wings vnto the vttermost parte of the *other* of his wings, *were*
ten cubites.
25 Also the other Cherúb was of ten cubites: bothe ỳ Cherubíms were of one measure and one syse.
26 *For* the height of the one Cherúb *was*
ten cubites, and so *was* the other Cherúb.
27 And he put the Cherubíms within the
inner house, *and the Cherubíms stretched
out their wings, so that the wing of ỳ one
touched the one wall, and the wing of
the other Cherúb touched the other wall:
and their *other* wings touched one another in the middes of the house.
28 And he ᵐ ouerlaied the Cherubíms with
golde.
29 And he carued all the walles of ỳ house
round about with grauen figures of Che
rubíms and of palme trees, and grauen
flowres within and without.
30 And the floore of the house he couered
with golde within and without.
31 An in the entring of the oracle he made
two dores of olive tre: *and* the vpper poste
& side postes *were* fiue square.
32 The two dores also *were* of olive tre, &
he graued them with grauing of Cherubíms and palme trees, and grauen flowres,
and couered thē with golde, & laied ⁿ thin
golde vpon the Cherubíms and vpon the
palme trees.
33 And so made he for the dore of the Temple postes of olive tre foure square.
34 But the two dores *were* of firre tre, the
two sides of the one dore *were* ⁿrounde,
& the two sides of ỳ other dore *were* roūd.

ⁿOr, pine tree.

*Exod.25,20.

m For the other ỳ Moses made of beatē golde, were takē away with the other iewels by their enemies, whome God permitted diuers times to ouercome thē for their great sinnes.

n So that the facion of the carued worke might stil appeare.

ⁿOr, folding.

35 And he graued Cherubíms, and palme
trees and carued flowres and couered the
carued worke with golde, finely wroght.
36 ¶And he buylt the [o] court within with
thre rowes of hewed stone, and one rowe
of beames of cedar.
37 In the fourth yere was the fundacion
of the house of the Lord laied in the moneth of Zif:
38 And in the eleuenth yere in the moneth
of [p] Bul, (which is the eight moneth) he
finished the house with all the furniture
thereof, and in euerie point: so was he seuẽ
yere in buylding it.

o Where the Priests were, & was thus called in respect of the great court, wͨ is called Act. 3,11. yͤ porche of Salomón, where yͤ people vsed to pray.

p Which conteineth part of October and parte of Nouember.

CHAP. VII.

1 The buylding of the houses of Salomón. 15 The excellent workemanship of Hirám in the pieces which he made for the Temple.

1 BVt Salomón was buylding his owne
house * thirtene yeres, and [a] finished
all his house.

*Chap. 9,10.

a After he had buylt the Temple.

THE FIRST FIGVRE OF THE KINGS HOVSE IN THE VVOOD OF LEBANON.

This figure is made without wall or porche, that the ordre of the pillers within might be sene. A. B. The length of an hundreth cubites. B. C. The breadth of fifty. A. D. The height of thirtie. E. F. G. H. The foure rowes of pillers. I. The postes which stayed on the pillers.

THE SECONDE FIGVRE OF THE SAME HOVSE.

This seconde figure sheweth the maner of the house without, and the porche thereof, which was fiftie cubites long, A. B. and thirtie broad. C. D.

b For ẏ beautie of the place and great abundance of cedre trees ẏ went to the buylding thereof, it was cōpared to moũt Lebanón in Syria: this house he vsed in sōmer for pleasure & recreacion.

c There were as many, & like proporcion on the one side as on ẏ other, & at euery end euen thre in a rowe one aboue another.

2 He buylt also an house b *called* the forest of Lebanón, an hundreth cubites lōg,
and fiftie cubites broade, and thirtie cubites hie, vpon foure rowes of cedre pillers,
and cedre beames *were laied* vpon the pillers.
3 And it was couered aboue with cedre vpō
the beames, that lay on the fourtie & fiue
pillers, fiftene in a rowe.
4 And the windowes *were* in thre rowes, &
windowe *was* c against windowe in thre
rankes.
5 And all the dores, and the side postes *with*
the windowes were foure square, & win
dowe was ouer against windowe in thre
rankes.
6 And he made a porche of pillers fiftie cubites long, and thirtie cubites broade, and
the porche was before d them, *euen* before
them *were* thirtie pillers.
7 ¶ Then he made a porche e for the throne, where he iudged, *euen* a porche of iudgement, & it was cieled with cedre from
pauement to pauement.
8 And in his house, where he dwelt, *was* an
other hall more inwarde then the porche
ẇ. was of the same worke. Also Salomón
made an house for Pharaohs daughter
(* whome he had taken to wife) like vnto
this porche.
9 All these were " of costely stones, hewed by measure, *and* sawed with sawes
within and without, from the fundacion
vnto f the *stones* of an " hand breadth, & on
the outside to the great courte.
10 And the fundaciō *was* of costely stones,
& great stones, *euen* of stones of ten cubites, and stones of eight cubites.
11 g Aboue also *were* costely stones, squared
by rule, and *boardes* of cedre.
12 ¶ And the great courte round about *was*
with thre rowes of hewed stones, and a
rowe of cedre beames: h so *was it* to the
inner courte of the house of the Lord, &
to the porche of the house.
13 ¶ Then King Salomón sent, and fet *one*
Hirám out of " Tyrus.
14 He was a widowes sonne of the tribe of
Naphtalí, his father being a mā of Tyrus,
and wroght in brasse: i he was ful of wisdome, and vnderstāding, & knowledge to
worke all maner of worke in brasse: who
came to King Salomón, and wroght all
his worke.
15 ¶ For he cast two pillers of brasse: the
height of a piller was eightene cubites, &
a threade of twelue cubites did compasse
" ether of the pillers.
16 And he made two " chapiters of molten
brasse to set on the toppes of the pillers:
the height of one of the chapiters *was* fiue
cubites, and the height of the other chapiter *was* fiue cubites.

d Before the pillers of the house.

e For his house, which was at Ierusalém.

Chap. 3, 1.

" *Or, precious.*

f Which were rests & staies for the beames to lie vpon.

" *Or, spanne.*

g Frō the fundaciō vpward.

h As the Lords house was buylt, so was this: onely the great courte of Salomons house was vncouered.

" *Or, Zór.*

i Thus when God wil haue his glorie set forthe, he raiseth vp men & giueth them excellent gifts for the accomplishement of ẏ same, Exod. 31, 2.

" *Ebr. the seconde.*

" *Or, pummels.*

THE FORME OF THE PILLER.

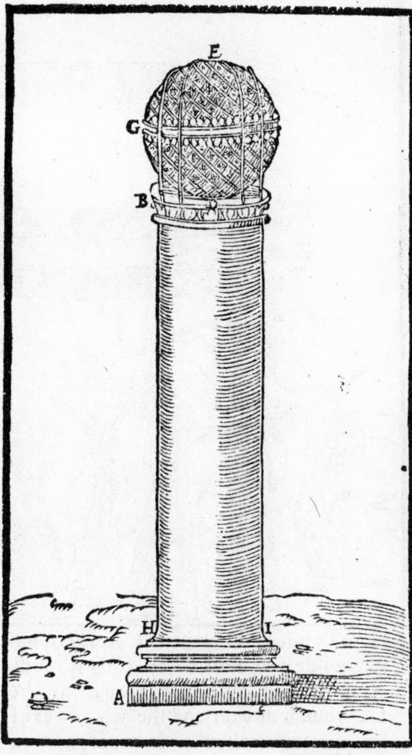

A B The height of a piller eighten cubites: the compasse of a piller was twelue cubites.
D E The height of the chapiter or rounde balle vpō the piller of fiue cubites height.
G In ẏ middes were two rowes of pomegranates: ẏ rest is the networke & flowre delices or roses.

17 He made grates like networke, & " writhē
worke like chaines for the chapiters that
were on the toppe of the pillers, *euen* seuen
for the one chapiter, & seuen for the other
chapiter.
18 So he made the pillers and two rowes of
pomegranates rounde about in the one
grate to couer the chapiters that were
vpon the toppe. And thus did he for the
other chapiter.
19 And the chapiters that were on ẏ toppe
of the pillers *were* after k lilye worke in
the porche, foure cubites.
20 And the chapiters vpon the two pillers
had also aboue, " ouer against the bellie
" within ẏ networke *pomegranates*: for two
hundreth pomegranates were in the *two*
rankes about vpō " ether of the chapiters.
21 And he set vp the pillers in the l porche
of ẏ Temple. And when he had set vp the
right piller, he called the name thereof
m Iachín: and when he had set vp the left
piller, he called the name thereof n Bóaz.
22 And vpon the top of the pillers *was*
worke of lilyes: so was the workemanship
of the pillers finished.
23 ¶ And he made a molten o sea ten cubites
wide from brim to brim, round in compasse, and fiue cubites hie, and a line of
thirtie cubites did compasse it about.

" *Or, cordes like chaines.*

k As was sene communely wroght in costelie porches.

" *Or, rounde about the middes.*

" *Or, beyonde.*

" *Ebr. the seconde.*

l Which was in the inner court betwene the Temple & the oracle.

m That is, he wil stablish, to wit, his promes towarde this house.

n That is, in strength: meaning, ẏ power thereof shal continue.

o So called for the hugenes of the vessel.

THE SEA OR GREAT CALDRON.

A B Ten cubites frõ one side to the other.
C D The height of fiue cubites.
F The two rowes, which cõpassed ẏ vessel about, and were garnished w bulles heades, wherein were pipes, to auoyde the water.

24 And vnder the brim of it *were* knoppes
like wilde cucumers compassing it roũde
about, ten in one cubite, compassing the
sea* rounde about: and the two rowes of
knoppes were cast, when it was molten.
25 It stode on twelue bulles, thre loking
towarde the North, and thre towarde the
West, and thre towarde the South, & thre
towarde the East: and the sea *stode* aboue
vpon them, & all their hinder partes were
inwarde.
26 It was ° an hand breadth thicke, and the
brim thereof was like the worke of the
brim of a cup with flowres of lilies: it cõteined two thousand p Baths.
27 ¶And he made ten bases of brasse, one
base *was* foure cubites long, and foure cubites broade, and thre cubites hie.
28 ¶And ẏ worke of the bases was on this
maner, Thei had borders, and the borders
were betwene the ledges:
29 And on the borders that were betwene
the ledges, were lyons, bulles and Cherubíms: and vpon the ledges there was a base
aboue: and beneth the lyons, and bulles
were addicions made of thinne worke.
30 And euery base had foure brasen wheles,
and plates of brasse: and the foure corners
had " vndersetters: vnder the caldrõ were
vndersetters molten at the side of euery
addicion.
31 And q the mouth of it *was* within the
chapiter and aboue *to measure* by the cubite: for the mouth thereof *was* rounde
made like a base, & it was a cubite & halfe
a cubite: & also vpon the mouth thereof
were grauen workes, whose borders *were*
foure square, & not rounde.
32 And vnder the borders *were* foure wheles, and the axeltrees of the wheles *ioyned*
to the base: and the height of a whele *was*
a cubite and halfe a cubite.
33 And the facion of the wheles was like
the facion of a charet whele, their axeltrees, and their naues and their " felloes, &
their spokes *were* all molten.
34 And foure vndersetters *were* vpon the
foure corners of one base: & the vndersetters thereof were of the base *it selfe*.
35 And in the toppe of the base was a roũde r compasse of halfe a cubite hie roũde
about: and vpon the toppe of the base the
ledges thereof and the borders thereof
were of the same.
36 And vpon the tables of the ledges thereof, and on the borders thereof he did
graue Cherubíms, lyons and palmetrees,
on the side of euery one, and addicions
rounde about.
37 Thus made he the ten bases, *Thei* had all
one casting, one measure, *and* one syse.
38 ¶Thẽ made he f ten caldrons of brasse,
one caldron conteined fourtie Baths: and
euery caldron *was* foure cubites, one caldron *was* vpon one base throughout the
ten bases.
39 And he set the bases, fiue on the right side
of the house, & fiue on the left side of the
house. And he set the sea on the right sid
of the t house Eastwarde towarde ẏ South

2.Chro.4,3.

° Or, a spanne.

p Bath and Epháh seme to be bothe one measure, Ezek.45,11. euery Bath cõteined about ten pottels.

" Ebr. shulders.

q The mouth of the great base or frame entred into ẏ chapiter, or piller ẏ bare vp ẏ caldron.

" Or, rings.

r Which was called the piller, chapiter, or smale base, wherein the caldron stode.

f To kepe waters for ẏ vse of the sacrifices.

t To wit, of ẏ Tẽple or Sãctuarie.

40 ¶ And Hirám made caldrons, and beſo-
mes and baſens, & Hirám finiſhed all the
worke that he made to King Salomón for
the houſe of the Lord:
41 To wit, two pillers and *two* bowles of
the chapiters that were on the toppe of the
two pillers, and two grates to couer the
two bowles of the chapiters which were
vpon the toppe of the pillers,
42 And foure hundreth pomegranates for
the two grates, euē two rowes of pomegranates for euerie grate to couer the two
bowles of the chapiters, that were vpon
the pillers.
43 And the ten baſes, & ten caldrons vpon
the baſes,

THE FORME OF THE CALDRONS.

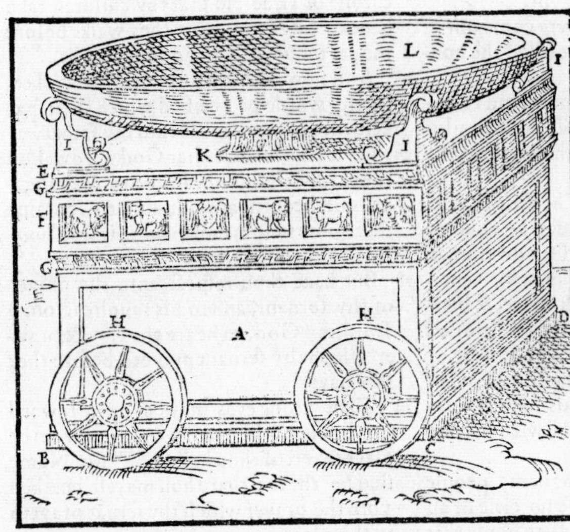

A B C The baſe whereupon ſtode the caldrons which were thre cubites long.
C B. Foure cubites broade,
B E Thre cubites high.
F. The imboſement and figures of lions, bulles, Cherubims.
G. The border of workemanſhip folding to and fro.
H The foure wheles, which had a cubite and an halfe of height.
I. The foure ſtayes or vpholds, which were vpon the baſe whereupon the caldron ſtode
K The rounde bothom of a cubite and halfe long, which did vpholde the caldron in the middes.
L. The caldron.

44 And the ſea, & twelue bulles vnder that
ſea,
45 And pottes, and beſoms and baſens: &
all theſe veſſels, which [u] Hirám made
to King Salomón for the houſe of the
Lord, were of ſhining braſſe.
46 In the plaine of Iordén did ẏ King caſt
thē in [″] clay betwene Succóh & Zarthán.
47 And Salomón left *to weigh* all the veſſels becauſe of the exceding abundance,
nether colde the weight of the braſſe be
counted.
48 So Salomón made all the veſſels that
perteined vnto the houſe of the Lord, the
[x] golden altar, and the golden table, whereon the ſhewbread was,
49 And the candelſtickes, fiue at the right
ſide, and fiue at the left, before the oracle
of pure golde, and the flowres, and the lāpes, and the ſnoffers of golde,
50 And the bowles, [y] and the hookes, and
the baſens, & the ſpoones, & the aſhpan-
nes of pure golde, and the hinges of golde
for the dores of the houſe within, *euen* for
the moſt holy place, *and* for the dores of
the houſe, *to wit*, of the Temple.
51 So was finiſhed all the worke that King
Salomón made for ẏ houſe of the Lord,
and Salomón broght in the things which
*Dauid his father had dedicated: ẏ ſiluer,
and the golde and the veſſels, *and* layed
them among the treaſures of the houſe of
the Lord.

u By this name alſo Hirám the King of Tyrus was called.

″Or, thicke earth.

x This was done accordīg to the forme ẏ the Lord preſcribed vnto Moſes in Exodus.

y Some take this for ſome inſtrument of muſike.

2. Chro. 5, 1.

CHAP. VIII.

4 The Arke is borne into the Tēple. 10 A cloude filleth the Temple. 15 The King bleſſeth the people.

1 THen* King Salomón aſſembled the
Elders of Iſraél, euen all the heads of
the tribes, the chief fathers of the childrē
of Iſraél vnto [″] him in Ieruſalém, for to
[a] bring vp the Arke of the couenant of the
Lord from the citie of Dauid, which is
Zión.
2 And all the mē of Iſraél aſſembled vnto
King Salomón at the feaſt in the moneth
of [b] Ethaním, which is the ſeuēth moneth.
3 And all the Elders of Iſraél came & the
Prieſts toke the Arke.
4 They bare the Arke of the Lord, and thei
bare ẏ Tabernacle of the Congregacion,
& all the holy veſſels that were in the Tabernacle: thoſe did the Prieſts & Leuites
bring vp.
5 And King Salomón and all the Congregacion of Iſraél, that were aſſembled vnto
him, *were* with him before the Arke, offrīg
ſhepe & beeues, which colde not be tolde,
nor nombred for multitude.
6 So the [c] Prieſts broght the Arke of the
couenant of the Lord vnto his place, into
the oracle of the houſe, into ẏ moſte holy
place, euē vnder ẏ wings of ẏ Cherubíms.
7 For the Cherubíms ſtretched out their
wings ouer the place of the Arke, and the
Cherubíms couered the Arke, & the barres thereof aboue.

2 Chro. 5, 2.

″Ebr. Salomōn.

a For Dauid broght it frō Obed-edóm & placed it in ẏ Tabernacle ẇ he had made for it, 2. Sam. 6, 17.

b Conteining part of Septēber and parte of October, in the which moneth they held thre ſolemne feaſts, Nom. 29, 1.

c That is, the Kohathites, Nom 4, 5

d They drewe thē onely out ſo farre as they might be ſene: for they might not pul them altogether out, Exo. 25,15.
e For it is like that the enemies, when they had the Arke in their hands, toke away the rod of Aarón and the pot with Man.
Exod.40,34.

8 And they [d] drew out the barres, that the
ends of the barres might appeare out of
the Sanctuarie before the oracle, but they
were not ſene without: and there they are
vnto this day.
9 Nothing *was* in the Arke [e] ſaue the two
tables of ſtone which Mosés had put there
at Horéb, where the Lord made a couenãt
with the children of Iſraél, whẽ he broght
them out of the land of Egypt.
10 And when the Prieſts were come out of
the Sanctuarie, the * cloude filled the houſe
of the Lord,
11 So that the Prieſts colde not ſtand to miniſter,
becauſe of the cloude: for the glorie
of the Lord had filled the houſe of the
Lord.

2.Chro.6,1.

12 Then ſpake Salomón, The Lord * ſaid,
that he wolde dwel in the darcke cloude.
13 I haue buylt thee an houſe to dwel in, an
habitacion for thee to abide in for [f] euer.

f He ſpake according to the tenor of Gods promes, which was cōdicionally, ỹ they ſhulde ſerue him aright.

14 ¶ And the King turned his face, & bleſſed
all the Congregacion of Iſraél: for all
the Congregacion of Iſraél ſtode *there*.
15 And he ſaid, Bleſſed be the Lord God of
Iſraél, who ſpake with his mouth vnto
Dauid my father, and hathe with his hãd
fulfilled it, ſaying,
16 Since the day that I broght my people
Iſraél out of Egypt, I choſe no citie of all
ỹ tribes of Iſraél, to buylde an houſe that
my Name might be there: but I haue choſen
* Dauid to be ouer my people Iſraél.

2.Sam.7,11.

17 And it was in the heart of Dauid my father
to buyld an houſe to the Name of
the Lord God of Iſraél.
18 And the Lord ſaid vnto Dauid my father,
Where as it was in thine heart to
buylde an houſe vnto my Name, thou dideſt
wel, that thou waſt ſo minded:
19 Neuertheles thou ſhalt not buylde the
houſe, but thy ſonne, that ſhal come out of
thy loynes, he ſhal buylde the houſe vnto
my Name.

"Ebr. confirmed.

20 And the Lord hathe made "good his
worde that he ſpake: and I am riſen vp in
the roume of Dauid my father, and ſit on
ỹ throne of Iſraél, as the Lord promiſed,
and haue buylt the houſe for the Name of
the Lord God of Iſraél.
21 And I haue prepared therein a place for
the Arke, wherein is the [g] couenant of
the Lord which he made with our fathers,
whẽ he broght thẽ out of ỹ lãd of Egypt.

g The two tables wherein the articles of the couenant were writen.
2.Chro.6,13.

22 ¶ Then Salomón ſtode before * the altar
of the Lord in the ſight of all the
Congregaciõ of Iſraél, and ſtretched out
his hands towarde heauen,

2.Mac.2,8.

23 And ſaid, *O Lord God of Iſraél, there
is no god like thee in heauen aboue, or in
the earth beneth, thou that kepeſt couenãt
& mercy with thy ſeruants that walke before
thee with [h] all their heart,

h Vnfaynedly and without all hypocriſie.

24 Thou that haſt kept with thy ſeruant
Dauid my father, that thou haſt promiſed
him: for thou ſpakeſt with thy mouth &
haſt fulfilled it with thine hand, as appeareth
this day.
25 Therefore now, Lord God of Iſraél, kepe
with thy ſeruãt Dauid my father that thou
haſt promiſed him, ſaying, * Thou ſhalt
not want a man in my ſight to ſit vpon ỹ
throne of Iſraél: ſo that thy children take
hede to their way, that they walke before
me, as thou haſt walked in my ſight.

Chap.2,4.

26 And now, ô God of Iſraél, I pray thee,
let thy worde be verified, which thou ſpakeſt
vnto thy ſeruant Dauid my father.
27 [i] Is it true in dede that God wil dwel on
the earth? beholde, the heauens, & the heauens
of heauens are not able to containe
thee: how muche more *vnable* is this houſe
that I haue buylt?

i He is rauiſhed with the admiracion of Gods mercies, who being incomprehẽſible and Lord ouer all, wil become familiar with men.

28 But haue thou reſpect vnto the prayer
of thy ſeruant, and to his ſupplicacion, ô
Lord, my God, to heare the crye & prayer
which thy ſeruant prayeth before thee
this day:
29 That thine eyes may be open toward
this houſe, night and day, *euen* towarde the
place whereof thou haſt ſaid, * My Name
ſhal be there: that thou mayeſt hearken
vnto the prayer which thy ſeruãt prayeth
in this place.

Deut.12,11.

30 Heare thou therefore the ſupplicacion
of thy ſeruant, and of thy people Iſraél,
which pray in this place, and heare thou "in
the place of thine habitacion, *euen* in heauen,
and when thou heareſt, haue mercy.

"Or, from.

31 ¶ When a man ſhal treſpaſſe againſt his
neighbour, and [k] he lay vpon him an othe
to cauſe him to sweare, and "the ſwearer
ſhal come before thine altar in this houſe,

k To wit, the iudge, or neighbour.
"Ebr. the othe.

32 Then heare thou in heauen, and [l] do &
iudge thy ſeruants, that thou cõdemne the
wicked to bring his way vpon his head, &
iuſtifie the righteous, to giue him according
to his righteouſnes.

l That is, make it knowen.

33 ¶ When thy people Iſraél ſhalbe ouerthowen
before the enemie, becauſe they
haue ſinned againſt thee, and turne againe
to thee, and [m] confeſſe thy Name, and
pray and make ſupplicacion vnto thee in
this houſe,

m Acknowledge thy iuſt iudgement, & praiſe thee.

34 Then heare thou in heauen, and be merciful
vnto the ſinne of thy people Iſraél,
and bring thẽ againe vnto the land, which
thou gaueſt vnto their fathers.
35 ¶ When heauẽ ſhalbe [n] ſhut vp, & there
ſhalbe no raine becauſe they haue ſinned
againſt thee, and ſhal pray in this place,
and confeſſe thy Name, and turne from
their ſinne, when thou doeſt afflict them,

n So that there be a drought to deſtroy the frutes of the land.

36 Then heare thou in heauen, & pardone
the ſinne of thy ſeruants and of thy people
Iſraél (when thou haſt taught them the
good

good way wherein they may walke) and
giue raine vpon the land that thou hast
giuen to thy people to inherit.
37 ¶When there shalbe famine in the lād,
when there shalbe pestilence, when there
shalbe blasting mildewe, greshopper *or*
caterpiller, when their enemie shal besiege them in the "cities of their land, *or*
anie plague *or* anie sickenes,
38 *Then* what prayers, *and* supplicacion soeuer shalbe made of anie man *or* of all thy
people Israél, when euerie one shal knowe
the plague in his owne [o] heart, & stretch
forthe his hands in this house,
39 Heare thou then in heauen, in thy dwelling place, and be merciful, and do, and
giue euerie mā according to all his wayes,
as thou knowest his heart (for thou onely
knowest the hearts of all the children of
men)
40 That they may feare thee as lōg as they
liue in the land, which thou gauest vnto
our fathers.
41 Moreouer as touching the [p] stranger
that is not of thy people Israél, who shal
come out of a farre countrei for thy Names sake,
42 (Whē they shal heare of thy great Name, and of thy mighty hand, and of thy
stretched out arme) and shal come & pray
in this house,
43 Heare thou in heauen thy dwelling place, and do according to all that the stranger calleth for vnto thee: that all ẏ people of the earth may knowe thy Name, &
feare thee, as do thy people Israél: and
that they may knowe, that thy [q] Name is
called vpon in this house which I haue
buylt.
44 ¶When thy people shal go out to battel against their enemie by the way that
thou shalt send them, and shal pray vnto
the Lord **towarde* the way of ẏ citie which
thou hast chosen, & *towarde* the house that
I haue buylt for thy Name,
45 Heare thou then in heauen their prayer
and their supplicacion, and "iudge their
cause.
46 If they sinne against thee (* for there is
no man that sinneth not) & thou be angry
with them, & deliuer them vnto the enemies, so that they carie them away prisoners vnto the land of the enemies, ether
farre or nere,
47 Yet "if they turne againe vnto their
heart in the land (to the which they be caryed away captiues) and returne and pray
vnto thee [r] in the land of them that caryed them away captiues, saying, We
haue sinned, we haue transgressed, and done wickedly,
48 If they turne againe vnto thee with all
their heart, and with all their soule in the
land of their enemies, which led thē away
captiues, and pray vnto thee *towarde* [s] the
way of their land, which thou gauest vnto
their fathers, *& towarde* ẏ citie which thou
hast chosen, and the house, which I haue
buylt for thy Name,
49 Then heare thou their prayer and their
supplicacion in heauē thy dwelling place,
and "iudge their cause,
50 And be merciful vnto thy people that
haue sinned against thee, & vnto all their
iniquities (wherein they haue transgressed
against thee) and cause that thei, which led
them away captiues, may [t] haue pitie and
compassion on them:
51 For they be thy people, and thine inheritance, which thou broghtest out of Egypt
from the middes of the yron fornace.
52 Let thine eies be open vnto the prayer
of thy seruant, and vnto the praier of thy
people Israél, to hearken vnto them, in all
that they call for vnto thee.
53 For thou didest separate them to thee
from among all people of the earth for
an inheritāce, as thou saidest by the hand
of Mosés thy seruant, whē thou broghtest
our fathers * out of Egypt, ô Lord God.
54 And when Salomón had made an end
of praying all this [u] prayer and supplicacion vnto the Lord, he arose from before
the altar of the Lord, from kneling on his
knees, and stretching of his hands to heauen,
55 And stode and blessed all the Congregacion of Israél with a loude voice,
saying,
56 Blessed be the Lord that hathe giuen
rest vnto his people Israél, according to
all ẏ he promised: there hathe not failed
one worde of all his good promes which
he promised by the hand of Mosés his seruant.
57 The Lord our God be with vs, as he was
with our fathers, that he forsake vs not,
nether leaue vs,
58 That he may [x] bowe our hearts vnto hī,
that we may walke in all his waies, & kepe
his commandements, and his statutes, and
his lawes, which he commanded our fathers.
59 And these my wordes, ẇ I haue praied
before ẏ Lord, be nere vnto the Lord our
God day and night, that he defende the
cause of his seruant, and the cause of his
people Israél " alway as the matter requireth,
60 That all the people of the earth may
knowe, that the Lord is God, *&* none o-
ther.
61 Let your heart therefore be perfit with
the Lord our God to walke in his statutes,

"*Ebr. in the lād of their gates.*

o For suche are most mete to receiue Gods mercies

p He meaneth suche as shulde be turned frō their idolatrie to serue the true God.

q That this is the true religion wherewith ẏ wilt be worshiped.

Dan. 6, 1.

"*Or, mainteine their right.*

2. Chro 6, 36. ecclesi. 7, 21. 1 ioh. 1, 7.

"*Or, if they repent.*

r Thogh the Temple was ẏ chief place of prayer, yet he secludeth not them, that being let with necessitie call vpon him in other places.

s As Daniel did, Dan. 6, 10.

"*Or, auenge their wrong.*

t He vnderstode by faithe ẏ God of enemies wolde make friends vnto them ẏ did conuert vnto him.

Exod. 19, 6.

u Salomón is a figure of Christ, who cōtinually is the Mediator betwene God and his Church.

x He concludeth that man of him selfe is enemie vnto God, and ẏ all obedience to his lawe procedeth of his mere mercie.

"*Ebr the thing of a day in his day.*

& to kepe his commandemēts, as this day.
62 ¶ Thē the King & all Israél with him
offred sacrifice before the Lord.
2.Chro.7,3. 63 *And Salomón offred a sacrifice of peace
offrings which he offred vnto the Lord, *to
wit*, two & twentie thousand beeues, and
an hundreth & twentie thousand shepe:
so the King and all the children of Israél
y Before the oracle, where the Arke was. dedicated the y house of the Lord.
64 The same day did the King halowe the
midle of the courte, that was before the
house of ŷ Lord: for there he offred burnt
offrings, and the meat offrings, and the
2.Chro.7,7. fat of the peace offrings, because the*brasen altar that was before the Lord, was to
litle to receiue the burnt offrings, and the
meat offrings, and the fat of the peace
offrings.
65 And Salomón made at that time a feast
and all Israél with him, a very great Cō-
z That is, frō North to South: meanig all the countrey. gregaciō, euen frō the entring in of z Hamáth vnto the riuer of Egypt, before the
Lord our God, a seuen dayes and seuen
dayes, *euen* fourtene dayes.
a Seuen dayes for the dedicacion, and seuen for the feast. 66 And the eight day he sent the people a-
way: and they "thanked the King and
"Ebr. blessed. went vnto their tentes ioyous and with
glad heart, because of all the goodnes that
the Lord had done for Dauid his seruant,
and for Israél his people.

CHAP. IX.

2 The Lord appeareth the seconde time to Salomón.
11 Salomón giueth cities to Hirám. 20 The Canaa-
nites become tributaries. 28 He sendeth forthe a na-
uie for golde.

2.Chro.7,11. 1 WHen * Salomón had finished the
buylding of the house of ŷ Lord,
and the Kings palace, and all that Salomón desired and minded to do,
2 Then the Lord appeared vnto Salomón
Chap.3,5. ŷ seconde time, as he *appeared vnto him
at Gibeón.
3 And ŷ Lord said vnto him, I haue heard
thy prayer and thy supplicacion, that thou
hast made before me: I haue halowed this
Chap.8,29. deut.12,11. house (which thou hast buylt) to * put my
Name there for euer, and mine eyes, and
mine heart shal be there perpetually.
a If ŷ walke in my feare, & withdrawe thy selfe from the commune maner of men which follow their sensualitie. 4 And a if thou wilt walke before me (as
Dauid thy father walked in purenes of
heart, & in righteousnes) to do according
to all that I haue commāded thee, *and* kepe my statutes, and my iudgements,
5 Then wil I stablish the throne of thy
kingdome vpō Israél for euer, as I promi-
2.Sam.7,12. 1.chro.22,10. sed to Dauid thy father, saying, * Thou
shalt not want a man vpon the throne of
Israél.
b God declareth that disobedience against him is ŷ cause of his displeasure, & so of all miserie. 6 *But* if ye and your children turne away
from me, and wil b not kepe my commā-
demēts, *and* my statutes, (which I haue set
before you) but go and serue other gods,
and worship them,
7 Then wil I cut of Israél from the land,
which I haue giuen them, and the house
which I haue halowed *for my Name, wil Ier.7,14.
I cast out of my sight, and Israél shalbe a
c prouerbe, and a cōmune talke among all
people.
c The worlde shal make of you a mockig stocke for the vile contempt and abusing of Gods most liberal benefites.
8 Euen this hie house shalbe *so*: euerie one
that passeth by it, shal be astonied, and shal
hisse, and they shal say, * Why hathe the
Lord done thus vnto this land and to this
house? Deut.29,24. ier.22,8.
9 And they shal answer, Because they forsoke the Lord their God, which broght
their fathers out of the land of Egypt,
and haue taken holde vpon other gods,
and haue worshiped them, and serued
them, therefore hathe the Lord broght
vpon them all this euil.
10 *And at the end of twentie yeres, when 2.Chro.8,1.
Salomón had buylded the two houses, the
house of the Lord, and the Kings palace,
11 (*For the which* Hirám the King of "Tyrus "Or, Zor.
had broght to Salomón timber of cedre,
and firre trees, and golde, and whatsoeuer
he desired) then King Salomón gaue to
Hirám twētie cities in the lād of "Galil. "Or, Galile.
12 And *Hirám came out from Tyrus to se
the cities which Salomón had giuen him,
and they pleased him not.
13 Therefore he said, What cities are these
which thou hast giuen me, my brother?
And he called them the land of "Cabúl "Or, dirtie, or, baren.
vnto this day.
14 And Hirám had sent the Kīg d six score
e talents of golde.
d For his tribute towarde the buylding
e The commō talent was about threscore poūde weight.
15 ¶ And this is the cause of ŷ tribute why
Kīg Salomón raised tribute, *to wit*, to buylde ŷ house of the Lord, & his owne house,
and f Milló, and the wall of Ierusalém, &
Hazór, and Megiddó, and Gézer.
f Milló was as ŷ towne house or place of assemblie which was open aboue.
16 Pharaóh King of Egypt had come vp,
and taken Gézer, and burnt it with fire,
& slewe the Canaanites, that dwelt in the
citie, and gaue it for a present vnto his
daughter Salomons wife.
17 (Therefore Salomón buylt Gézer and
Beth-horón the nether,
18 And Baaláth and Tamór in the wildernes of the land,
19 And all the cities g of store, that Salo- g Cities for his munitions of warre.
món had, euen cities for charets, and ci-
ties for horsemen, and *all* that Salomón
desired & wolde buyld in Ierusalém, and
in Lebanón and in all the land of his dominion)
20 All the people that were h left of the
Amorites, Hittites, Perizzites, Hiuites, &
Iebusites, which were not of the childrē
of Israél:
h These were as bondmen & payed, what was required, ether labour or money.
21 *To wit*, their children that were left after
them

them in the land, whome the children of
Israél were not able to destroye, those did
Salomón make tributaries vnto this day.
22 But of the children of Israél did Salomón *make no bondmen: but they were
men of warre and his seruants, and his
princes, and his captaines, and rulers of his
charets and his horsemen.
23 These were the princes of the officers,
that were ouer Salomons worke: *euen* [i] fiue
hundreth and fiftie, and they ruled yͤ people that wroght in the worke.
24 ¶ And Pharaohs daughter came vp frō
the citie of Dauid vnto the house which
Salomón had buylt for her: thē did he buylde Milló.
25 And thrise a yere did Salomón offer
burnt offrings and peace offrings vpon
the altar which he buylt vnto the Lord: &
he burnt incense vpon *the altar*, that was
before the Lord, when he had finished the
house.
26 ¶ Also King Salomón made a nauie of
shippes in Ezeon-géber, which is beside
Elóth, and the brincke of the red Sea, in
the land of Edóm.
27 And Hirám sent with the nauie his seruants, yͭ were mariners, & had knowledge
of the sea, with the seruants of Salomón.
28 And they came to Ophír and fet from
thence [k] foure hundreth and twenty talēts
of golde, & broght it to King Salomón.

Leui.25,39.

i The ouersee-ers of Salomons workes were deuided into 3. partes. the first cōteined. 3300. yͤ seconde 300. and yͤ 3. 250, which were Israelites: so here are conteined the two last parts, which make 550.

k In yͤ 2 Chro. 8, 18. is made mencion of thirtie mo, wͨ seme to haue bene employed for their charges.

CHAP. X.

1 The quene of Sabá commeth to heare the wisdome of Salomón. 18 His royal throne 23 His power and magnificence.

1 AND the *quene of [a] Shebá hearing
the fame of Salomón (concerning
the Name of the Lord) came to proue
him with hard questions,
2 And she came to Ierusalém with a very
great traine, *&* camels that bare swete o-
dors, and golde exceding muche, & precious stones: and she came to Salomón,
and communed with him of all that was
in her heart.
3 And Salomón declared vnto her all her
questions: nothing was hid frō the King,
which he expounded not vnto her.
4 Then the quene of Shebá sawe all Salomons wisdome, and the house that he had
buylt.
5 And the [b] meat of his table, and the sitting of his seruants, and the ordre of his
ministers, & their apparel, & his drinking
vessels, and his burnt offrings, that he offred in the house of the Lord, and "she
was greatly astonied.
6 And she said vnto the King, It was a true
worde that I heard in mine owne land of

1.Chro.9,1. mat.12,42. luk.11,31.

a Iosephus saith that she was quene of Ethiopia, and yͤ Shebá was the name of yͤ chief citie of Meroé, which is an yland of Nilus.

b That is, the whole ordre, and trade of his house.

"*Ebr. there was no more spirit in her.*

thy sayings, and of thy wisdome.
7 Howbeit I beleued not this reporte, til I
came, and had sene it with mine eyes: but
lo, the one halfe was not tolde me: *for* thou
hast more wisdome and prosperitie, thē
I haue heard by reporte.
8 Happy are thy men, happy are these thy
seruants, which stand euer before thee, and
heare thy [c] wisdome.
9 Blessed be the Lord thy God, which [d] loued thee, to set thee on the throne of Israél, because the Lord loued Israél for e-
uer and made thee King, to do [e] equitie
and righteousnes.
10 And she gaue the King six score talents
of golde, and of swete odors exceding
muche, and precious stones. There came
no more suche abūdance of swete odors,
as the quene of Shebá gaue to King Salomón.
11 The nauie also of Hirám (that caried
golde from Ophír) broght likewise great
plenty of * Almuggím trees from Ophír
and precious stones.
12 And the King made of the Almuggím
trees pillers for the house of the Lord, &
for the Kings palace, and made harpes &
psalteries for singers. There came no more suche Almuggím trees, nor were anie
more sene vnto this day.
13 And King Salomón gaue vnto the quene
of Shebá, whatsoeuer she wolde aske, besides that, which Salomón gaue her" of
his kinglie liberalitie: so she returned &
went to her owne countrey, *bothe* she, and
her seruants.
14 ¶ Also the weight of golde, that came to
Salomón in one yere, was six hundreth
thre score and six * talents of golde,
15 Besides that *he had* of marchant men and
of the marchandises of them that solde
spices, and of all the Kings of Arabia, &
of the princes of the [f] countrey.
16 And King Salomón made two hundreth targats of beaten golde, six hun
dreth *shekels* of golde went to a targat:
17 And thre hundreth shields of beaten
golde, thre pounde of golde went to one
shield: and the King put them in yͤ * house
of the wood of Lebanón.
18 ¶ Then the King made a great throne
of yuerie, and couered it with the best
golde.
19 And the throne had six steps, and the top
of the throne *was* round behinde, & there
were [g] stayes on ether side on the place of
the throne, and two lions standing by the
stayes.
20 And there stode twelue lions on the six
steps on ether side: there was not the like
made in any kingdome.

c But muche more happie are they, wͨ heare the wisdome of God reueiled in his worde.

d It is a chief signe of Gods fauour, when godlie & wise rulers sit in yͤ throne of iustice.

e This is the cause, why Kings are appointed.

2.Chro. 9,10.

"*Ebr. by the hād of the King.*

Exod.25,39.

f To wit, of Arabia, which for the great abundance of all things was called, happy.

Chap.7,2.

g As the chaire bowes, or places to leane vpon.

THE ROYAL THRONE OF SALOMON.

21 And all King Salomons drinking vesſels *were* of golde, and all the veſſels of
the houſe of the wood of Lebanón *were*
of pure golde . none *were* of ſiluer : *for* it
was nothing eſtemed in the daies of Salomón.
22 For the King had on the ſea the nauie of
Tharſhíſh with the nauie of Hirám: once
in thre yere came ẏ nauie of [h] Tharſhíſh,
& broght golde and ſiluer, yuerie, & apes
and peacockes.

h By Tharſhíſh is ment Cilicia, ẇ was abundant in varietie of precious things.

23 So King Salomón exceded all ẏ Kings
of the earth bothe in riches and in wiſdome.
24 And all the worlde ſoght to ſe Salomón,
to heare his wiſdome, which God had put
in his heart,
25 And thei broght euery man his preſent,
veſſels of ſiluer, and veſſels of golde , and
raiment , and armour, and ſwete odors,
horſes and mules, from yere to yere.
26 Then Salomón gathered together *charets and horſemen: and he had a thouſand
and foure hundreth charets , and twelue
thouſand horſemen, whome he placed in
the charet, cities, and with the King at Ieruſalém.

2.Chro.1,14.

27 And the King ″ gaue ſiluer in Ieruſalém
as ſtones, and gaue cedres as the wilde figtrees that growe abundantly in the plaine.

″Or, he made ſiluer as plenteous as ſtones.

28 Alſo Salomón had horſes broght out of
Egypt, and fine linen : ″ the Kings marchants receiued the linen for a price.

″Or, for the companie of the Kings marchãts did receiue a nomber at a price.

29 There came vp and went out of Egypt
some charet, *worthe* ſix hundreth *ſhekels* of
ſiluer: that is, one horſe, an hundreth and
fiftie. and thus they broght *horſes* to all the
Kings of the Hittites and to the Kings of
Arám by their ″ meanes.

″Ebr. handes.

CHAP. XI.

1 Salomón hathe a thouſand wiues and concubines, which bring him to idolatrie. 14 His God raiſeth vp aduerſaries againſt him. 43 He dyeth.

1 BVt Kĩg Salomón loued *many [a] outlandiſh women: bothe the daughter
of Pharaóh, & the women of Moáb, Ammón, Edóm, Zidón and Heth,

Deu.17,17. eccleſ.47,2.

a Which were idolaters.

2 Of the nacions, whereof the Lord had
ſaid vnto the children of Iſraél, *Go not
ye in to them, nor let thẽ come in to you:
for ſurely they wil turne your hearts after
their gods . to them, *I ſay*, did Salomón
ioyne in loue.

Exod.34,16.

3 And he had ſeuen hundreth wiues, *that
were* ″ princeſſes and thre hundreth [b] concubines, and his wiues turned away his
heart.

″Or, quenes.

b To whome perteined no dowry.

4 For when Salomón was olde, his wiues
turned his heart after other gods, ſo ẏ his
heart was not [c] perfit with the Lord his
God, as *was* the heart of Dauid his father.

c He serued not God with a pure heart,

5 For Salomón followed* Aſhtaróth the
god of ẏ Zidonians, & [d] Milcóm the abominacion of the Ammonites.

Iudg.2,13.

d Who was alſo called Molech ver.7. read. 2. King.23,10.

6 So Salomón wroght wickednes in the
ſight of the Lord, but continued not to
follow the Lord, as *did* Dauid his father.
7 Then did Salomón buylde an hie place

for

e Thus the Scripture termeth, whatsoeuer man doeth reuerence and serue as God.

for Chemósh the [e] abominació of Moáb,
in the mountaine that is ouer against Ierusalém, and vnto Mólech the abomination of the children of Ammón.
8 And so did he for all his outlandish wiues,
which burnt incense and offred vnto their gods.
9 Therefore the Lord was angry with Salomón, because he had turned his heart from the Lord God of Israél, *which had appeared vnto him twise,

Chap.3,5.& 9,3.
Chap.6,12.

10 And had giuen him a *charge concerning this thing, that he shulde not followe other gods: but he kept not that, which the Lord had commanded him.
11 Wherefore the Lord said vnto Salomón, Forasmucheas [f] this is done of thee, and thou hast not kept my couenant, and my statutes (which I commanded thee) *I wil surely rent the kingdome fró thee, and wil giue it to thy seruant.

f That thou hast forsaken me & worshiped idoles.

Chap.12,15.

12 Notwithstanding in thy daies I wil not do it, because of Dauid thy father, but I wil rent it out of the hand of thy sonne:
13 Howbeit I wil not rent all ẏ kingdome, *but* wil giue one [g] tribe to thy sonne, because of Dauid my seruant, and because of Ierusalém, which I haue chosen.

g Because the tribes of Iudáh & Beniamin had their possessiós mixed, thei are here taken as one tribe.

14 ¶ Then the Lord stirred vp an aduersarie vnto Salomón, *euen* Hadád the Edomite, of the Kings [h] seede, which was in Edóm.

h Of the King of Edoms stocke.

2.Sam.8,14.

15 *For when Dauid was in Edóm, & Ioáb the captaine of the hoste had smitten all the males in Edóm, and was gone vp to bury the [i] slayne,

i Of the Edomites.

16 (For six moneths did Ioáb remaine there, and all Israél, til he had destroyed all the males in Edóm)
17 Then this Hadád [k] fled and certeine other Edomites of his fathers seruants with him, to go into Egypt, Hadád being yet a litle childe.

k Thus God reserued this idolater to be a scourge to punishe his peoples sinnes.

18 And they arose out of Midián, & came to Parán, and toke men with them out of Parán, and came to Egypt vnto Pharaóh King of Egypt, which gaue him an house, and appointed him vitailes, and gaue him land.
19 So Hadád [l] founde great fauour in the sight of Pharaóh, & he gaue him to wife the sister of his owne wife, *euen* the sister of Tahpenés the quene.

l God broght him to honour that his power might be more able to cópasse his enterprises against Salomós house.

20 And the sister of Tahpenés bare him Genubáth his sonne, whome Tahpenés wayned in Pharaohs house: & Genubáth was in Pharaohs house among the sonnes of Pharaóh.
21 And when Hadád heard in Egypt, that Dauid slept with his fathers, & that Ioáb the captaine of the hoste was dead, Hadád said to Pharaóh, Let me departe, that I may go to mine owne countrey.
22 But Pharaóh said vnto him, What hast thou lacked with me, that thou woldest thus go to thine owne countrey? And he answered, Nothing, but in any wise let me go.
23 ¶ *And God stirred him vp *another* aduersarie, Rezón the sonne of Eliadáh, which [m] fled from his lord Hadadézer King of Zobáh.

2.Sam.8,3.

m Whé Dauid had discófited Hadadézer & his armie.

24 And he gathered men vnto him, & had bene captaine ouer the companie, when Dauid slewe them. And thei went to Damascus, and dwelt there, [n] and thei made him King in Damascus.

n To wit, the mé, whome he had gathered vnto him.

25 Therefore was he an aduersarie to Israél all the daies of Salomón: besides the euil that Hadád *did*, he also abhorred Israél, and reigned ouer Arám.
26 ¶ *And Ieroboám ẏ sonne of Nebát an Ephrathite of Zeréda Salomons seruant (whose mother was called Zeruáh a widowe) lift vp his hand against the King.

2.Chro.13,6.

27 And this was the cause that he lift vp *his* hand against the King, *When* Salomón buylt Milló, he repared the broken places of the citie of Dauid his father.
28 And this man Ieroboám was a man of strength and courage, and Salomón seing that the yong mã was mete for the worke, he made him [o] ouerseer of all the laboure of the house of Ioséph.

o He was ouerseer of Salomós workes for the tribe of Ephráim and Manasséh.

29 And at that time, when Ieroboám went out of Ierusalém, the Prophet Ahiiáh the Shilonite founde him in the way, hauing a newe garment on him, and thei two were alone in the field.
30 Then Ahiiáh caught the newe garment that was on him, and [p] rent it in twelue pieces,

p By these visible signes ẏ Prophetes wolde more depely printe their message into their hearts, to whome thei were sent.

31 And said to Ieroboám, Take vnto thee ten pieces: for thus sayth the Lord God of Israél, Beholde, I wil rẽt the kingdome out of the hands of Salomón, & wil giue ten tribes to thee.
32 But he shal haue one tribe for my seruãt Dauids sake, and for Ierusalém the citie, which I haue chosen out of all the tribes of Israél,
33 Because thei haue forsaken me, and haue worshiped Ashtaróth the god of the Zidonians, & Chemósh the god of the Moabites, and Milcóm the god of the Ammonites, & haue not walked in my wayes (to *do right in mine eyes, and my statutes, & my lawes) as *did* Dauid his father.

*Or, to do that, that pleaseth me.

34 But I wil not take the whole kingdome out of his hãd: for I wil make him prince all his life long for Dauid my seruants sake, whome I haue chosen, & who kept my commandements and my statutes.
35 *But I wil take the kingdome out of his sonnes hand, and wil giue it vnto thee, *euẽ* the ten tribes.

Chap.12,17.

36 And vnto his sonne wil I giue one tribe,
that Dauid my seruant maye haue a [a]light
alwaie before me in Ierusalém the citie,
which I haue chosen me, to put my Name there.
37 And I wil take thee, & thou shalt reigne, "euen as thine heart desireth, & shalt
be King ouer Israél.

[a] He hathe respect vnto the Messiáh, w̄ shulde be the bright starre ẏ shulde shine through all ẏ worlde.
" Ebr. in all that thy soule.

38 And if thou harkē vnto all that I commande thee, and wilt walke in my waies,
and do right in my sight, to kepe my statutes and my commandements, as Dauid
my seruant did, then wil I be with thee, &
buylde thee a sure house, as I buylt vnto
Dauid, and wil giue Israél vnto thee.
39 And I wil for [r] this afflict the seede of
Dauid, [s] but not for euer.
40 ¶ Salomón soght therefore to kil Ieroboám, and Ieroboám arose, and fled into Egypt vnto Shishák King of Egypt,
and was in Egypt vntil the death of Salomón.

[r] For this idolatrie that Salomón hathe committed.
[s] For ẏ whole spiritual kīgdome was restored in Messiáh.

41 And the rest of the wordes of Salomón, & all that he did, and his wisdome,
are thei not writen in the [t] boke of the
actes of Salomón?
42 The time that Salomón reigned in
Ierusalém ouer all Israél, was fourtie
yere.
43 And Salomón slept with his fathers and
was buryed in the citie of Dauid his father: and Rehoboám his sonne reigned in
his steade.

[t] Which boke, as is thoght, was lost in their captiuitiē.

CHAP. XII.

1 Rehoboám succedeth Salomón. 8 He refuseth the counsel of the Ancient. 20 Ieroboám reigneth ouer Israél. 21 God commandeth Rehoboám not to fight. 28 Ieroboám maketh golden calues.

1 AND * Rehoboám went to Shechém:
for all Israél were come to Shechém, to make him King.

* 2.Chro.10,1.

2 And when Ieroboám the sonne of Nebát heard of it (who was yet in Egypt)
* whether Ieroboám had fled from King
Salomón, and "dwelt in Egypt,

* Chap.11,40.
" Or, returned from Egypt.

3 Then thei sent and called him: and Ieroboám and all the Congregacion of Israél came, and spake vnto Rehoboám,
saying,
4 Thy father made our * yoke grieuous:
now therefore make thou the grieuous
seruitude of thy father, and his sore yoke
which he put vpon vs, [a] lighter, & we wil
serue thee.

* Chap.4,7.
[a] Oppresse vs not w̄ so great charges, which we are not able to susteine.

5 And he said vnto them, Departe yet for
thre dayes, then come againe to me. And
the people departed.
6 And King Rehoboám toke counsel with
the olde men that "had stande before Salomón his father, while he yet liued, and
said, What counsel giue ye, that I may
make an answer to this people?
7 And thei spake vnto him, saying, If thou
be a [b] seruant vnto this people this day,
and serue them, and answer them, and
speake kinde wordes to them, thei wil be
thy seruants for euer.

" Or, had bene of his ancient counsellers.
[b] Thei shewed him that there was no way to winne ẏ peoples hearts, but to grante thē their iuste peticion.

8 But he forsoke the counsel that the olde
men had giuen him, and asked counsel of
the yong men, that had bene broght vp
with him, and waited on him.
9 And he said vnto them, [c] What counsel
giue ye, that we may answer this people,
which haue spoken to me, saying, Make
the yoke, which thy father did put vpon
vs, lighter?

[c] There is nothing harder for them, that are in autoritie, thē to bridel their affections, and followe good counsel.

10 Then the yong men that were broght
vp with him, spake vnto him, sayīg, Thus
shalt thou say vnto this people, that haue
spoken vnto thee, and said, Thy father
hathe made our yoke heauie, but make
thou it lighter vnto vs: euē thus shalt thou
say vnto thē, My "least parte shalbe [d] bigger then my fathers loynes.

" Or, litle singer.
[d] I am muche more able to kepe you in subiection thē my father was.

11 Now where as my father did burdē you
with a grieuous yoke, I wil yet make your
yoke heauier: my father hathe chastised
you with rods, but I wil correct you with
"scourges.

" Or, scorpions.

12 ¶ Then Ieroboám and all the people
came to Rehoboám the third day, as the
King had [e] appointed, sayīg, Come to me
againe the third day.

[e] The people declare their obedience in this, that they wolde attempt nothing before ẏ King had giuen thē iuste occasion.

13 And the King answered the people sharpely, and left the olde mens counsel that
thei gaue him,
14 And spake to them after the counsel of
the yong men, saying, My father made
your yoke grieuous, and I wil make your
yoke more grieuous: my father hathe
chastised you with rods, but I wil correct
you with scourges.
15 And the King hearkened not vnto the
people: for "it was the ordinance of the
Lord, that he might performe his saying,
which the Lord had spoken by * Ahiiáh
the Shilonite vnto Ieroboám the sonne
of Nebát.

" Or, the Lord was the cause.
* Chap.11,11.

16 So when all Israél sawe that the King
regarded them not, the people answered
the King thus, saying, What porciō haue
we in [f] Dauid? we haue none inheritance
in the sonne of Ishái. To your tents, ô
Israél: now se to thine owne house, Dauid.
So Israél departed vnto their tents.

[f] Thogh their cause were good, yet it is moste hard for the people to bridel their affectiōs, as these vile wordes declare.

17 Howbeit ouer the children of Israél,
which dwelt in the cities of Iudáh, did
Rehoboám reigne stil.
18 ¶ Now the King Rehoboám sent Adorám the receiuer of the tribute, and all Israél stoned him to death: then King Rehoboám "made spede to get him vp to his
charet, to flee to Ierusalém.

" Ebr strengthened him selfe.

19 And Israél rebelled against the house
[g] of Dauid vnto this day.
20 ¶ And when all Israél had heard that Ieroboám

[g] By the iuste iudgement of God for Salomons sinnes.

roboám was come againe, they sent and
called him vnto the assemblie, and made
him King ouer all Israél: none followed
the house of Dauid, but the tribe of Iudáh *onely.

Chap.11,13.

21 And whē Rehoboám was come to Ierusalém, he [h] gathered all the house of Iudáh with the tribe of Beniamín an hundreth and four score thousand of chosen men (which were good warriours) to fight against the house of Israél & to bring the kingdome againe to Rehoboám the sonne of Salomón.

h For as yet he perceiued not that the Lord had so appointed it.

22 *But the worde of God came vnto Shemaiáh the [i] man of God, saying,

2.Chro.11,2.

i That is, the Prophet.

23 Speake vnto Rehoboám the sonne of Salamón King of Iudáh, and vnto all the house of Iudáh and Beniamín, and the remnant of the people, saying,

24 Thus sayth the [k] Lord, Ye shal not go vp, nor fight against your brethren the children of Israél: returne euerie man to his house: for this thing is done by me. They obeied therefore the worde of the Lord and returned, and departed, according to the worde of the Lord.

k Who of his iust iudgemēt wil punishe ẏ trespasser, and of his mercie spare the innocent people.

25 ¶ Then Ieroboám buylt Shechém in mount Ephraím, and dwelt therein, & wēt from thence, and buylt Penuél.

26 And Ieroboám thoght in his heart, Now shal the kingdome returne to the house of Dauid.

27 If this people go vp and do sacrifice in the house of the Lord [l] at Ierusalém, thē shal the heart of this people turne againe vnto their lord, *euen* to Rehoboám King of Iudáh: so shal they kil me and go againe to Rehoboám King of Iudáh.

l He feared lest his people shulde haue by this meanes bene entised to rebelle against him.

28 Whereupon the King toke counsel, and made two calues of golde, and said vnto them, [m] It is to muche for you to go vp to Ierusalém: beholde, ô Israél, thy gods, which broght thee vp out of the land of Egypt.

m So craftie are the carnal persuasions of princes, when they wil make a religion to serue to their appetite.

29 And he set the one in Beth-él, and the other set he in Dan.

30 And this thing turned to sinne: for the people wēt (because of ẏ one) euē to Dan.

31 Also he made an [n] house of hye places, and made Priests of the lowest of the people, which were not of the sonnes of Leuí.

n That is, a temple, where altars were buylt for idolâtrie.

32 And Ieroboám made a feast the [o] fiftēth day of the eight moneth, lyke vnto ẏ feast that is in Iudáh, and offred on the altar. So did he in Beth-él and offred vnto the calues that he had made: and he placed in Beth-él the Priests of the hie places, which he had made.

o Because he wolde the more binde the peoples deuociō to his idolatrie, he made a newe holy day, besides those that the Lord had appointed in ẏ Lawe.

33 And he offred vpon the altar, which he had made in Beth-él, the fiftēth day of the eight moneth (*euen* in the moneth which he had forged of his owne heart) & made a solēne feast vnto the childrē of Israél: & he went vp to the altar, to burne incense.

CHAP. XIII.

1 Ieroboám is reprehended of the Prophet. 4 His hand dryeth vp. 15 The Prophet is seduced. 24 And is killed of a lyon. 33 The obstinacie of Ieroboám.

1 AND beholde, there came [a] a man of God out of Iudáh (by the commandement of the Lord) vnto [b] Beth-él, and Ieroboám stode by the altar to offer incense.

a That is, a Prophet.

b Not that ẏ was called Luz in Beniamín, but another of that name.

2 And he cryed against the altar by the cōmandemēt of the Lord, and said, O altar, altar, thus sayth ẏ Lord, Beholde, a childe shal be borne vnto the house of Dauid, *Iosiáh by name, and vpon thee shal he sacrifice the Priests of the hie places that burne incense vpon thee, and they shal burne mens bones vpon thee.

2.King.23,17

3 And he gaue a signe ẏ same time, saying, This is the [c] signe, that the Lord hathe spoken, Beholde, the altar shal rent, and the asshes that are vpon it, shal "fall out.

c By this signe ye shal knowe that ẏ Lord hathe sent me.

"Or, be powred out.

4 And whē the King had heard the saying of the man of God, which he had cryed against ẏ altar in Beth-él, Ieroboám stretched out his hand from the altar, saying, [d] Lay holde on him: but his hād which he put forthe against him, dryed vp, & he colde not pull it in againe to him.

d The wicked rage against ẏ Prophetes of God, whē they declare them Gods iudgements.

5 The altar also claue asundre, & the asshes fel out from the altar, according to the signe, which the man of God had giuen by the "commandement of the Lord.

"Ebr. mouthe.

6 Then the King answered, and said vnto the man of God, [e] I beseche thee, pray vnto the Lord thy God, and make intercession for me, that mine hand may be restored vnto me. And the man of God besoght the Lord, and the Kings hand was restored, and became as it was afore.

e Thogh the wicked humble thē selues for a time, whē they fele Gods iudgemēts, yet after they returne to their olde malice & declare that they are but vile hypocrites.

7 Thē the King said vnto the mā of God, Come home with me, that thou maist "dine, and I wil giue thee a rewarde.

"Or, take sustenance.

8 But the man of God said vnto the King, If thou woldest giue me halfe thine house, I wolde not go in with thee, nether wolde I eat bread nor drinke water in this place.

9 For so "was it charged me by the worde of the Lord, saying, [f] Eat no bread nor drinke water, nor turne againe by the same way that thou camest.

"Or, he charged me: to wit, an Angel.

f Seing he had the expresse worde of God, he oght not to haue declined there from, nether for the persuasion of man nor Angel.

10 So he went another way & returned not by the way that he came to Beth-él.

11 ¶ And an olde Prophet dwelt in Beth-él & his sonnes came, & tolde him all ẏ workes, ẏ the mā of God had done that day in Beth-él, & the wordes which he had spokē vnto the King, tolde they their father.

12 And their father said vnto them, What way went he? and his sonnes "shewed him what way the man of God went, which came from Iudáh.

"Ebr. loked.

13 And he said vnto his sonnes, Sadle me
the asse. Who sadled him the asse, and he
rode thereon,
14 And went after the man of God, and
founde him sitting vnder an oke: and he
said vnto him, Art thou the man of God
that camest frō Iudáh? And he said, "Yea.
15 Then he said vnto him, g Come home
with me, and eat bread.
16 But he answered, I may not returne with
thee, nor go in with thee, nether wil I eat
bread nor drinke water with thee in this
place.
17 For it was charged me by the worde of
the Lord, *saying*, Thou shalt eat no bread,
nor drinke water there, nor turne againe
to go by the way that thou wentest.
18 And he said vnto him, I am a Prophet
also as thou art, and an h Angel spake vnto me by the worde of the Lord, saying,
Bring him againe with thee into thine
house, that he may eat bread and drinke
water: *but* he lied vnto him.
19 So he went againe with him, and did eat
bread in his house, and dranke water.
20 And as they sate at the table, the worde
of the Lord came vnto the Prophet, that
broght him againe.
21 And he cryed vnto the man of God that
came from Iudáh, saying, Thus saith the
Lord, i Because thou hast disobeyed the
mouth of the Lord, and hast not kept the
commandemēt which the Lord thy God
commanded thee,
22 But camest backe againe, and hast eaten
bread & dronke water in the place (whereof he did say vnto thee, Thou shalt eat no
bread nor drinke anie water) thy carkeis
shal not come vnto the sepulchre of thy
fathers.
23 ¶And when he had eaten bread and
drōke, he sadled him the asse, to wit, to the
Prophet whome he had broght againe.
24 And when he was gone, k a lyon met
him by the way, and slewe him, and his
bodie was cast in the way, and the asse
stode thereby: the lyon stode by the corps
also.
25 And beholde, men that passed by, sawe
the carkeis cast in the way, and the lyon
standing by the corps: and they came and
tolde it in the towne where the olde Prophet dwelt.
26 And when the Prophet, that broght him
backe againe from the way, heard thereof,
he said, It is the man of God, who hathe
bene disobedient vnto the commandemēt
of the Lord: therefore the Lord hathe deliuered him vnto the lyon, which hathe
rent him and slaine him, according to the
worde of the Lord, which he spake vnto
him.
27 ¶And he spake to his sonnes, saying,
Sadle me the asse. And they sadled him.
28 And he went and founde his body cast in
the way, and the asse and the lyon stode by
the corps: and the lyon had l not eaten
the body, nor torne the asse.
29 And ẏ Prophet toke vp the body of the
man of God, and layed it vpon the asse,
and broght it againe, and the olde Prophet came to the citie, to lament and
bury him.
30 And he layed his body in his m owne
graue, & they lamented ouer him, *saying*,
Alas, my brother.
31 And when he had buryed him, he spake
to his sonnes, saying, When I am dead,
bury ye me also in the sepulchre, wherein
the man of God is buryed: laye my bones
beside his bones.
32 For that thing which he cryed by the
worde of the Lord against the altar that
is in Beth-él, and against all the houses of
the hie places, which are in the cities of
Samaria, shal surely come to passe.
33 *Howbeit* after this, Ieroboám n conuerted not from his wicked way, but turned againe, and made of the lowest of the
people Priests of the hie places. Who
wolde, might "cōsecrate him selfe, and be
of the Priests of the hie places.
34 And this thing turned to sinne vnto the
house of Ieroboám, euen to roote it out,
and destroy it from the face of the earth.

CHAP. XIIII.

1 Ieroboám sendeth his wife disguised to Ahiiáh the Prophet, who declareth vnto him the destruction of his house. 22 Iudáh is punished by Shishak.

1 At that time Abiiáh the sonne of Ieroboám fel sicke.
2 And Ieroboám said vnto his wife, Vp, I
pray thee, a & disguise thy selfe, that they
knowe not that thou art the wife of Ieroboám, and go to Shilóh: for there is A-
hiiáh the Prophet, which tolde me * that
I shulde be King ouer this people,
3 And take "with b thee ten loaues and
craknels, and a bottel of hony, and go to
him: he shal tel thee what shal become of
the yong man.
4 And Ieroboams wife did so, and arose, &
went to Shilóh, and came to the house of
Ahiiáh: but Ahiiáh colde not se, for his
" sight was decayed for his age.
5 Thē the Lord said vnto Ahiiáh, Beholde,
the wife of Ieroboám commeth to aske a
thing of thee for her sonne, for he is sicke:
thus and thus shalt thou say vnto her: *for*
when she cōmeth in, she shal feine her selfe
to be c another.
6 Therefore when Ahiiáh heard the sound
of her fete as she came in at the dore, he
said, Come in, thou d wife of Ieroboám:
why feinest ẏ thus thy selfe to be another?
I am sent to thee *with* heauy tidings.

"*Ebr. I am.*

g This he did of a simple minde, thinkīg it his duetie to declare friēdship to a Prophet.

h His faute is here double: first in ẏ ẏ he suffreth not the Prophete to obey Gods expresse cōmandement: and next, that he faineth to haue a reuelaciōn to the cōtrary.

i God wolde reproue his foly by him, who was the occasion to bring him into error.

k By this fearful exāple, God setteth forthe, how dangerous a thing it is for men to behaue them selues coldely, or deceitfully in their charge whereūto God hathe called them.

l To declare that this was onely the iudgemēt of God: for if the lyon had done it for hūgre, he wolde also haue deuoured the body.

m Which he had prepared for him selfe.

n So the wicked profit not by Gods threatnings, but go backewarde & become worse and worse, 2. Tim. 3, 13.

" *Ebr. fil his hand.*

a His owne cōscience bare him witnes, ẏ the Prophet of God wolde not satisfie his aff&tiōs which was a wicked man.

Chap. 11, 31.

"*Ebr. in thine hand.*

b According to the custome whē they wēt to aske cōnsel of Prophetes, 1. Sam. 9, 7.

"*Ebr. eyes stode.*

c Then the wife of Ieroboám.

d For God ofttimes discloseth vnto his the craft and subteltie of ẏ wicked.

7 Go,

7 Go, tel Ieroboám, Thus saith the Lord
God of Israél, Forasmuche as I haue exalted
[e] thee from among the people, and
haue made thee prince ouer my people
Israél,

e Which wast but a seruant.

8 And haue rent the kingdome away from
the house of Dauid, and haue giuẽ it thee,
and thou hast not bene as my seruant Dauid,
which kept my commandements, and
followed me with all his heart, and did
onely that which was right in mine eyes,
9 But hast done euil aboue all that were
before thee (for thou hast gone and made
thee other gods, and [f] molten images, to
prouoke me, and hast cast me behinde thy
backe)

f To wit, two calues.

10 Therefore beholde, I wil bring euil vpõ
the house of Ieroboám, and wil cut of frõ
Ieroboám him that * [g] pisseth against
the wall, aswel him that [h] is shut vp, as
him that is left in Israél, & wil swepe away
the remnant of the house of Ieroboám,
as a man swepeth away doung, til it be
all gone.

Chap. 21, 21. & 2. king. 9, 8.
g Euery male euen to the dogs, 1. Sam 25, 22.
h Aswel him that is in the strong holde, as him that is abroad.

11 The dogs shal eat him of Ieroboams
stocke that dyeth in the citie, and the foules
of the aire shal eat him that dyeth in the
field: [i] for the Lord hathe said it.

i They shal lacke the honour of buryal in token of Gods malediction.

12 Vp therefore & get thee to thine house:
for whẽ thy feete entre into the citie, the
childe shal dye.
13 And all Israél shal mourne for him, and
bury him: for he onely of Ieroboám shal
come to the graue, because in him there is
founde [k] some goodnes towarde ỹ Lord
God of Israél in the house of Ieroboám.

k In the middes of ỹ wicked God hath some, on whome he doeth bestowe his mercies.

14 Moreouer, the Lord shal stir him vp a
King ouer Israél, which shal destroy the
house of Ieroboám in that day: [l] what?
yea, euen now.

l The Lord wil beginne to destroy it out of hand.

15 For the Lord shal smite Israél, as when a
rede is shaken in the water, and he shal
wede Israél out of this good land, which
he gaue to their fathers, and shal scatre
them beyonde the [m] Riuer, because they
haue made them groues, prouoking the
Lord to angre.

m Meaning, Euphrates.

16 And he shal giue Israél vp, because of
the sinnes of Ieroboám, who did sinne, and
[n] made Israél to sinne.

n The people shal not be excused, when they do euil at ỹ comandemẽt of their gouernours.

17 ¶ And Ieroboams wife arose, and departed,
and came to Tirzáh, and when she came
to the thresholde of the house, the yõg
man dyed,
18 And they buryed him, and all Israél lamented
him, according to the worde of
the Lord, which he spake by the hand of
his seruant Ahiiáh the Prophet.
19 And the rest of Ieroboams actes, how he
warred, & how he reigned, beholde, they
are writen in the boke of the Chronicles
of the Kings of Israél.
20 And the dayes which Ieroboám reigned,
were two and twentie yere: and he [o] slept
with his fathers, & Nadáb his sonne reigned
in his steade.

o The Lord smote him ỹ he dyed, 2. Chro. 13, 20.

21 ¶ Also Rehoboám the sonne of Salomón
reigned in Iudáh. Rehoboám was one and
fourtie yere olde, when he begã to reigne,
and reigned seuentene [p] yere in Ierusalém
the citie, which the Lord did chuse
out of all the tribes of Israél, to put his
Name there: and his mothers name was
Naamáh an Ammonite.

p And dyed before Ieroboám about 4. yeres.

22 And Iudáh wroght wickednes in the
sight of the Lord: & they prouoked him
more ŵ their sinnes, which thei had committed,
″then all that which their fathers
had done.

″*Or, besides all that their fathers had done by their sinnes.*

23 For they also made them hie places, and
images, and groues on euery hye hil, and
vnder euerie grene tre.
24 There were also Sodomites [q] in ỹ land,
they did according to all the abominacions
of the nacions, which the Lord had
cast out before the children of Israél.

q Where idolatrie reigneth, all horrible vices are committed, til at length Gods iust iudgemẽt destroy them vtterly.

25 ¶ And in the fift yere of King Rehoboám,
Shishák King of Egypt came vp against
Ierusalém,
26 And toke the treasures of the house of ỹ
Lord, & the treasures of the Kings house,
and toke away all: also he caried away all
the shields of golde *which Salomón had
made.

Chap. 10, 16.

27 And King Rehoboám made for them
brasen shields, and committed them vnto
the hands of the chief of the garde,
which waited at the dore of the Kings
house.
28 And when the King went into the house
of the Lord, the garde bare them, and
broght them againe into the garde chamber.
29 And the rest of ỹ actes of Rehoboám, &
all that he did, are they not writen in [r] the
boke of the Chronicles of the Kings of
Iudáh?
30 And there was warre betwene Rehoboám
and Ieroboám [s] continually.
31 And Rehoboám slept with his fathers, &
was buryed with his fathers in the citie of
Dauid: his mothers name *was* Naamáh an
[t] Ammonite. And Abiiám his sonne reigned
in his steade.

r Which bokes were caled the bokes of Shemaiáh and Iddó the Prophetes, 2. Chro 12, 15.
s That is, all ỹ dayes of Rehoboams life.
t Whose idolatrie Rehoboám her sonne followed.

CHAP. XV.

1 Abiiám reigneth ouer Iudáh. 9 Asá succedeth in his roume 16 The battel betwene Asá and Baashá. 24 Iehoshaphát succedeth Asá. 25 Nadáb succedeth Ieroboám. 28 Baashá killeth Nadab.

1 AND in the eightene yere of King *Ieroboám
the sonne of Nebát, reigned
Abiiám ouer Iudáh.

2. Chro. 11, 22.

2 Thre yere reigned he in Ierusalém, and
his mothers name *was* Maacháh ỹ daughter
of [a] Abishalóm.

a Some thinke that this was Absalóm Salomons sonne.

3 And he walked in all the sinnes of his fa-

ther, which he had done before him: and
his heart was not perfit with the Lord his
God as the heart of Dauid his father.
4 But for Dauids sake did ẏ Lord his God
giue him a [b] light in Ierusalém, and set vp
his sonne after him, and established Ierusalém,
5 Because Dauid did that which was right
in the sight of the Lord, and turned from
nothing that he commanded him, all the
dayes of his life, *saue onely in the matter of Vriáh the Hittite.
6 And there was warre betwene Rehoboám
and Ieroboám as long as he liued.
7 The rest also of the actes of Abiiám, and
all that he did, are they not writen in the
*boke of the Chronicles of the Kings of
Iudáh? there was also warre betwene Abiiám, and Ieroboám.
8 And Abiiám slept with his fathers, & they
buryed him in the citie of Dauid: & Asá
his sonne reigned in his steade.
9 ¶*And in the twentie yere of Ieroboám
King of Israél reigned Asá ouer Iudáh.
10 He reigned in Ierusalém one & fourtie
yere, and his [c] mothers name *was* Maacháh,
the daughter of Abishalóm.
11 And Asá did right in ẏ eyes of the Lord,
as *did* Dauid his father.
12 And he toke away the Sodomites out of
the land, and put away all the idoles that
his fathers had made.
13 And he [d] put downe Maacháh his mother
also from her estate, because she had made
an idole in a groue: & Asá destroyed her
idoles, & burnt thẽ by the broke Kidrón.
14 But they put not downe the hie places.
Neuertheles Asas heart was [e] vpright
with the Lord all his dayes.
15 Also he broght in the holy vessels of his
father, & the things that he had dedicate
vnto the house of the Lord, siluer, & golde
and vessels.
16 ¶And there was warre betwene Asá and
Baashá King of Israél all their dayes.
17 Then Baashá King of Israél went vp
against Iudáh, and buylt [f] Ramáh, so that
he wolde let none go out or in to Asá
King of Iudáh.
18 Then Asá toke all the siluer & the gold
ẏ was left in the treasures of the house of
the Lord, and the treasures of the Kings
house, and deliuered them into the hands
of his seruants, and King Asá sent them to
*Ben-hadád the sonne of Tabrimón, the
sonne of Hezión King of *Arám that
dwelt at Damascus, saying,
19 *There is* a couenant betwene me and
thee, *and* betwene my father and thy father: beholde, I haue sent vnto thee a present of siluer, and golde: come, breake thy
couenant with Baashá King of Israél, that
he may [g] departe from me.

b Meaning, a sonne to reigne ouer Iudáh.
2.Sam.11,4. & 12,9.
2.Chro.13,3.
2.Chro.14,1.
c That is, his grand mother, as Dauid is oft times called father of the, whose grand father he was.
d Nether kinred nor autoritie oght to be regarded, when they blaspheme God & become idolaters, but must be punished.
e For in that that he suffred them to worship God in other places, then he had appointed, it came of ignorance and not of malice.
f Of the same purpose that Ieroboám did because the people shulde not go vp to Ierusalém lest they shulde followe Asá.
2.Chro.16,2.
*Or, Syria.
g And vexe me no longer.

20 So Ben-hadád hearkened vnto King Asá, and sent the captaines of the hostes,
which he had against the cities of Israél,
and smote Iión, and Dan, and Abélbethmaacháh, and all Cinneróth, with all the
land of Naphtalí.
21 And when Baashá heard thereof, he left
buylding of Ramáh, and dwelt in Tirzáh.
22 Then King Asá "assembled all Iudáh,
" none excepted. & they toke the stones of
Ramáh, & the timber thereof, wherewith
Baashá had buylt, & King Asá buylt with
them Géba of Beniamín and Mizpáh.
23 And the rest of all the actes of Asá, and
all his might and all that he did, and the
cities which he buylt, are they not writẽ
in the boke of the Chronicles of ẏ Kings
of Iudáh? but in his olde age he was diseased in his [h] feete.
24 And Asá slept with his fathers, and was
buryed with his fathers in the citie of Dauid his [i] father. And Iehoshaphát his sonne
reigned in his steade.
25 And Nadáb the sonne of Ieroboám began to reigne ouer Israél the secõde yere
of Asá King of Iudáh, and reigned ouer
Israél two yere.
26 And he did euil in the sight of the Lord,
walking in the way of his father, & in his
sinne wherewith he made Israél to sinne.
27 And Baashá the sonne of Ahiiáh of the
house of Issachár conspired against him,
& Baashá slewe him at Gibbethón, which
belonged to the Philistíms: for Nadáb &
all Israél laied siege to Gibbethón.
28 Euen in the third yere of Asá King of
Iudáh did Baashá slay him, and reigned
in his steade.
29 And when he was King, he [k] smote all
the house of Ieroboám, he left non aliue
to Ieroboám, vntil he had destroyed him,
according to the *worde of ẏ Lord which
he spake by his seruant Ahiiáh the Shilonite,
30 Because of ẏ sinnes of Ieroboám which
he committed, and wherewith he made Israél to sinne, by his [l] prouocation, wherewith he prouoked the Lord God of Israél.
31 And the residue of the actes of Nadáb
and all that he did, are they not writen in
the boke of the Chronicles of the Kings
of Israél?
32 And there was warre betwene Asá & Baashá King of Israél, all their dayes.
33 In the third yere of Asá King of Iudáh,
began Baashá the sonne of Ahiiáh to reigne ouer all Israél in [m] Tirzáh, *and reigned*
foure and twentie yeres.
34 And he did euil in the sight of the Lord,
walking in the way of Ieroboám, & in his
sinne, wherewith he made Israél to sinne.

"Or, made a proclamation.
"Ebr. none innocent.
h He had the goute & put his trust rather in phisitians then in the Lord, 2.Chro.16,12.
i His great grãde father.
k So God stirred vp one tyrant to punish the wickednes of another.
Chap.14,10.
l By causing ẏ people to commit idolatrie with his calues, & so prouoking God to angre.
m Which was ẏ place where the Kings of Israel remained.

CHAP.

CHAP. XVI.

1 Of Baashá, 6 Eláh, 9 Zimrí, 16 Omrí. 31 Achab marieth Iezebél. 34 Ierichó is buylt againe.

1 THen the worde of the Lord came to
Iehú the sonne of Hanáni against
Baashá, saying,
2 [a] Forasmucheas I exalted thee out of the
dust, & made thee captaine ouer my people Isráel, and thou hast walked in the way
of Ieroboám, and hast made my people
Isráel to sinne, to prouoke me with their
sinnes,
3 Beholde, I wil take away the posteritie of
Baashá, and the posteritie of his house,
and wil make [b] thine house like the * house
of Ieroboám the sonne of Nebát.
4 *He that dyeth of Baashas *stocke* in the citie, him shal the dogs eat: and that man
of him which dyeth in the fields, shal the
foules of the ayre eat.
5 And the rest of the actes of Baashá and
what he did, and his "power, are they not
writen in the boke of the * Chronicles of
the Kings of Isráel?
6 So Baashá slept with his fathers, & was
buryed in Tirzáh, & Eláh his sonne reigned in his steade.
7 And [c] also by the hand of Iehú the sonne of Hanáni the Prophet came the worde of the Lord to Baashá, & to his house,
that he shulde be like the house of Ieroboám, euen for all the wickednes that he
did in the sight of the Lord, in prouoking
him with the worke of his hands, and because he killed [d] him.
8 ¶In the six and twentie yere of Asá Kíg
of Iudáh began Eláh the sonne of Baashá
to reigne ouer Isráel in Tirzáh, *& reigned*
two yere.
9 And his seruant Zimrí, captaine of halfe
his charets conspired against him, as he
was in Tirzáh drinking, til he was dronken in the house of [e] Arzá stuarde of his
house in Tirzáh.
10 And Zimrí came & smote him & killed
him in the seuen and twenty yere of Asá
King of Iudáh, & reigned in his steade.
11 ¶And when he was King, and sate on his
throne, he slewe all ẏ house of Baashá, not
leauing thereof one to pisse against a
wall, nether of his kinsfolkes nor of his
friends.
12 So did Zimrí destroy all the house of
Baashá, according to the worde of ẏ Lord
which he spake against Baashá by the hād
of Iehú the [f] Prophet,
13 For all the sinnes of Baashá, and sinnes
of Eláh his sonne, which they sinned and
made Isráel to sinne, and prouoked the
Lord God of Isráel with their vanities.
14 And the rest of the actes of Eláh, and
all that he did, are they not writen in the
boke of the Chronicles of the Kings of
Isráel?
15 ¶In the seuen and twentie yere of Asá
King of Iudáh did Zimrí reigne seuen
dayes in Tirzáh, and the people was then
in the hoste [g] besieging Gibbethón, which
belonged to the Philistims.
16 And the people of the hoste heard say,
Zimrí hathe conspired, & hathe also slaine
the Kíg. Wherefore all Isráel made Omrí the captaine of the hoste King ouer Isráel that same day, *euen* in the hoste.
17 Then Omrí went vp from Gibbethón,
and all Isráel with him, and they besieged
[h] Tirzáh.
18 And whē Zimrí sawe, that the citie was
taken, he went into the palace of the
Kings house, and "burnt him selfe and the
Kings house with fire, & so dyed,
19 For his sinnes which he sinned, in doing that which is euil in the sight of the
Lord, in walking in the way of Ieroboám,
and in his sinnes which he did, causing
Isráel to sinne.
20 And the rest of the actes of Zimrí, and
his treason that he wroght, are they not
writen in the boke of the Chronicles of
the Kings of Isráel?
21 Thē were ẏ people of Isráel deuided into two partes: *for* [i] halfe ẏ people followed
Tibní the sonne of Ginàth to make him
King, & the other halfe followed Omrí.
22 But the people that followed Omrí, preuailed against the people that followed
Tibní the sonne of Ginath: so Tibní dyed, and Omrí reigned.
23 In the one and thirtie yere of Asá King
of Iudáh began Omrí to reigne ouer Israél, *& reigned* twelue yere. Six yere reigned he in Tirzáh.
24 And he boght the moūtaine "Samaria of
one Shémer for two talents of siluer, and
buylt in the mountaine, and called the name of the citie, which he buylt, after the
name of Shémer, lord of the mountaine
Samaria.
25 But Omrí did euil in the eyes of the
Lord, and did [k] worse then all that were
before him.
26 For he walked in all the way of Ieroboám the sonne of Nebát, and in his sinnes
wherewith he made Isráel to sinne in prouoking the Lord God of Isráel with their
vanities.
27 And the rest of the actes of Omrí, that
he did, and his strēgth that he shewed, are
they not writen in the boke of the Chronicles of the Kings of Isráel?
28 And Omrí slept with his fathers, & was
buryed in [l] Samaria: and Aháb his sonne
reigned in his steade.
29 Now Aháb the sonne of Omrí began to reigne ouer Isráel, in the eight
and thirtie yere of Asá King of Iudáh:

a Thus spake Iehú to Baashá in the Name of the Lord.

b Meanig, the house of Baashá.

Chap. 15, 29.
Chap 14, 11.

"Or, valiātnes.
2.Chro 16, 1.

c That is, the Prophet did his message.

d Meaning, Nadáb Ieroboams sonne.

e The Chalde text hathe thus, Drinking til he was drōken in the temple of Arzá ẏ idole by his house in Tirzáh.

f Bothe Hanáni his father and he were Prophetes.

g Which siege had continued from the time of Nadáb Ieroboās sonne.

h Where Zimrí kept hi selfe in holde.

"*Ebr. burnt the Kigs house vpon him.*

i That is, the people which were not at ẏ siege of Gibbethón. for there they had chosen Omrí.

"*Or, Shemeron.*

k For suche is the nature of idolatrie, ẏ the superstitiō thereof doeth daily increase, & the elder it is, the more abominable it is before God and his Church.

l He was the first King that was buryed in Samaria, after that the Kigs house was burnt in Tirzáh.

and Aháb ẏ sonne of Omrí reigned ouer
Israél in Samaria two and twentie yere.
30 And Aháb the sonne of Omrí did worse in the sight of the Lord then all that
were before him.
31 For was it a light thing for him to walke
in the sinnes of Ieroboám the sonne of
Nebát, except he toke Iezebél also the
daughter of Eth-báal King of the Zidonians to [m] wife, and went and serued Báal,
and worshiped him?
32 Also he reared vp an altar to Báal in the
house of Báal, which he had buylt in Samaria.
33 And Aháb made a groue, and Aháb proceded, and did prouoke the Lord God of
Israél more then all the Kings of Israél
that were before him.
34 In his dayes did Hiél the Bethelite buylde [n] Ierichó: he laied the fundació thereof in Abirám his eldest sonne, and set
vp the gates thereof in his yongest sonne
Segúb, according to ẏ worde of the Lord
which he spake "by Ioshúa the sonne of
Nun.

m By whose meanes he fel to all wicked, & strange idolatrie, & cruel persecution.

n Read Iosh. 6,26.

" Ebr. by the hád of Ioshua.

CHAP. XVII.

1 Eliáh forewarneth of the famine to come. 4 He is fed of rauens. 9 He is sent to Zarephath, where he restoreth his hostesse sonne to life.

1 AND Eliáh the Tishbite one of the
inhabitants of Gileád said vnto A-
háb, *As the Lord God of Israél liueth,
before whome I [a] stád, there shalbe nether
dewe nor rayne these yeres, but [b] accordīg
to my worde.
2 ¶ And the worde of the Lord came vnto
him, saying,
3 Go hence, and turne thee Eastwarde, and
hide thy selfe in the "riuer Cheríth, that is
ouer against Iordén,
4 And thou shalt drinke of the riuer: and
I haue commanded the [c] rauens to feede
thee there.
5 So he went and did according vnto the
worde of the Lord: for he went, and remained by the riuer Cheríth that is ouer
against Iordén.
6 And the rauens broght him bread & flesh
in the morning, and bread and flesh in the
euening, and he dranke of the riuer.
7 And after a while, the riuer dryed vp, because there fel no raine vpon the earth.
8 ¶ And the [d] worde of the Lord came vnto him, saying,
9 *Vp, *and* get thee to Zarepháth, which is
in Zidón, and remaine there: beholde, I
haue commanded a widowe there to su-
staine thee.
10 So he arose, and went to Zarepháth: and
when he came to the gate of the citie, beholde, the widowe was there [e] gathering
stickes: & he called her, & said, Bring me,
I pray thee, a litle water in a vessel, that
I may drinke.
11 And as she was going to fet it, he called
to her, and said, Bring me, I pray thee, a
morsel of bread in thine hand.
12 And she said, As the Lord thy God liueth, I haue not a cake, but euen an hande-
ful of meale in a barel, and a litle oyle in a
cruse: and beholde, I am gathering "a fewe
stickes for to go in, and dresse it for me &
my sonne, that we may eat it, and [f] dye.
13 And Eliáh said vnto her, Feare not, come,
do as thou hast said, but make me thereof
a litle cake first of all, and bring it vnto
me, and afterwarde make for thee, and thy
sonne.
14 For thus saith the Lord God of Israél,
[g] The meale in ẏ barel shal not be wasted,
nether shal the oyle in the cruse be diminished, vnto the time that the Lord send
raine vpon the earth.
15 So she went, and did as Eliáh said, and
she did eat: so did he and her house [h] for a
certeine time.
16 The barel of the meale wasted not, nor
the oyle was spent out of the cruse, according to the worde of the Lord, which he
spake by the hand of Eliáh.
17 ¶ And after these things, the sonne of the
wife of the house fel sicke, and his sicknes
was so sore, "that there was no [i] breath left
in him.
18 And she said vnto Eliáh, What haue I to
do with thee, ô thou man of God? art thou
come vnto me to call my sinne to remembrance, and to slaye my sonne?
19 And he said vnto her, Giue me thy sonne. and he toke him out of her bosome, &
caried him vp into a chamber, where he
abode, and laied him vpon his owne
bed.
20 Thé he called vnto the Lord, & said, O
Lord my God, hast thou [k] punished also
this widowe, with whome I soiourne, by
killing her sonne?
21 And he stretched him selfe vpon the
childe thre times, and called vnto ẏ Lord,
and said, O Lord my God, I pray thee,
let this childes soule come into him a-
gaine.
22 Thé the Lord heard the voyce of Eliáh,
and the soule of the childe came into him
againe, and he reuiued.
23 And Eliáh toke the childe, and broght
him downe out of the chamber into the
house, and deliuered him vnto his mother, and Eliáh said, Beholde, thy sonne liueth.
24 And the woman said vnto Eliáh, Now
[l] I knowe that thou art a man of God, and
that the worde of the Lord in thy mouth
is true.

Eccles 48,3. Iam. 5,16.

a That is, whome I serue.

b But as I shal declare it by Gods reuelation.

" Or, broke.

c To strengthen his faith against persecution, God promiseth to fede him miraculously.

d As the troubles of the Saints of God are many, so his mercie is euer at hand to deliuer thé.

Luk. 4,25.

e All this was to strengthen the faith of Eliáh to the intent that he shulde loke vpon nothing worldely, but onely trust on Gods prouidence.

" Ebr. two.

f For there is no hope of any more sustenance.

g God receiueth no benefite for the vse of his, but he promiseth a moste ample recópense for the same.

h That is, til he had raine & foode on the earth.

" Or, that he dyed.

i God wolde trye whether she had learned by his merciful prouidéce to make him her onely staye and comforte.

k He was afraide, lest Gods Name shuld haue be ne blasphemed and his ministers contemned, except he shulde haue continued his mercies, as he had begonne thé, specially while he there remained.

l So hard a thing it is to depéd on God, except we be confirmed by miracles.

CHAP. XVIII.

1 Eliáh is sent to Aháb. 13 Obadiáh hideth an hundreth

Pro-

Prophetes. 40 Eliiáh killeth all Baals prophetes. 45 He obteineth raine.

1 AFter many daies, the worde of the
Lord came to Eliiáh, in the [a] third
yere, saying, Go, shewe thy selfe vnto A-
háb, and I wil send raine vpon the earth.

a After that he departed from the riuer Cherith.

2 And Eliiáh went to shewe him selfe vnto
Aháb, and *there was* a great famine in Samaria.
3 And Aháb called Obadiáh the gouernour of his house: (and Obadiáh [b] feared
God greatly)

b God had begone to worke his feare in his heart, but had not yet broght him to that knowledge, wc is also requisit of the godly: yt is, to professe his Name openly.

4 For when Iezébel destroyed the Prophetes of the Lord, Obadiáh toke an hũdreth
Prophetes, & hid them, by fiftie in a caue,
and he fed them with bread and water.
5 And Aháb said vnto Obadiáh, Go into
the land, vnto all the fountaines of water,
and vnto all the riuers, if so be that we
may finde grasse to saue the horses & the
mules aliue, lest we depriue *the land* of the
beastes.
6 And so thei deuided the land betwene
them to walke through it. Aháb went one
way by him selfe, and Obadiáh went another way by him selfe.
7 ¶And as Obadiáh was in the way, beholde, Eliiáh [c] met him: & he knewe him,
and fel on his face, and said, Art not thou
my lord Eliiáh?

c God pitieth oft times the wicked for ye godly sake, & causeth Eliiáh to mete with Obadiáh, that the benefite might be knowen to be granted for Gods children sake.

8 And he answered him, Yea, go tel thy
lord, Beholde, Eliiáh *is here.*
9 And he said, What haue I sinned, that
thou woldest deliuer thy seruant into the
hand of Aháb, to slaye me?
10 As the Lord thy God liueth, there is no
naciõ or kĩgdome, whether my lord hathe
not sent to seke thee: and when thei said,
He is not here, he toke an othe of ye kingdome and nacion, if thei had not founde
thee.
11 And now thou saist, Go, tel thy lord, Beholde, Eliiáh *is here.*
12 And when I am gone frõ thee, the Spirit of the Lord shal cary thee into some
place that I do not knowe: so when I come
and tel Aháb, if he can not finde thee, then
wil he kil me: but I thy seruant [d] feare the
Lord from my youth.

d I am none of the wicked persecuters, yt thou shuldest procure vnto me suche displeasure, but serue God and fauour his children.

13 Was it not tolde my lord, what I did
when Iezébel slewe the Prophetes of the
Lord, how I hidde an hundreth men of
the Lords Prophetes by fifties in a caue, &
fed them with bread and water?
14 And now thou saiest, Go, tel thy lord,
Beholde, Eliiáh *is here,* that he may slaye
me.
15 And Eliiáh said, As the Lord of hostes
liueth, before whome I stand, I wil surely
shewe [e] my selfe vnto him this day.

e By my presence I wil declare yt thou hast tolde him the trueth.

16 ¶So Obadiáh went to mete Aháb, and
tolde him: and Aháb wẽt to mete Eliiáh.
17 And when Aháb sawe Eliiáh, Aháb said
vnto him, Art thou he that troubleth Israél?
18 And he answered, I haue not troubled Israél, but [f] thou, and thy fathers house, in
that ye haue forsaken the cõmandements
of the Lord, and thou hast followed Baalím.

f The true ministers of God oght not onely not to suffer ye trueth to be vniustely sklãdered, but to reproue boldly ye wicked sklãderers without respect of persone.

19 Now therefore send, and gather to me
all Israél vnto mount Carmél, and the
prophetes of Báal foure hũdreth & fiftie,
& the prophetes of the groues foure hundreth, which eat at Iezebels table.
20 ¶So Ahab sent vnto all the children of
Israél, & gathered the prophetes together
vnto mount Carmél.
21 And Eliiáh came vnto all the people, &
said, How long [g] halt ye betwene two opinions? If the Lord be God, followe him:
but if Báal be he, then go after him. And
the people answered him not a worde.

g Be constant in religion, & make it not as a thing indiferẽt whether ye followe God or Báal, or whether ye serue God wholly or in parte.

22 Then said Eliiáh vnto ye people, I onely
remaine a Prophet of the Lord: but Baals
prophetes are foure hundreth & fiftie mẽ.
23 Let them therefore giue vs two bullocks,
and let them chuse the one, and cut him
in pieces, and laye him on the wood, but
put no fyre *vnder,* and I wil prepare the o-
ther bullocke, and laye him on the wood,
and wil put no fyre *vnder.*
24 Then call ye on the name of your god,
and I wil call on the Name of the Lord:
and thẽ the God that answereth [h] by fyre,
let him be God. And all the people answered, and said, It is wel spoken.

h By sending downe fire frõ heauẽ to burne ye sacrifice.

25 And Eliiáh said vnto the prophetes of
Báal, Chuse you a bullocke, and prepare
him first, (for ye are many) & call on the
name of your gods, but put no fyre *vnder.*
26 So thei toke the one bullocke, yt was giuen them, & thei prepared it, & called on
ye name of Báal, from morning to noone,
saying, O Báal, heare vs: but there was no
voyce, nor anie to answer: and thei [i] leapt
vpon the altar that was made.

i As men rauished wt some strange spirit.

27 And at noone Eliiáh mocked them, and
said, Crye loud: for he is a [k] god: ether he
talketh or pursueth *his enemies,* or is in his
iourney, or it may be that he slepeth, and
must be [l] awaked.

k You esteme him as a god.

l He mocketh their beastly madnes, which thinke that by anie instance or sute ye dead & vile idoles cã helpe their worshipers in their necessities.

28 And they cryed loude, and cut them selues as their maner was, with kniues and
lancets, til the blood gusshed out vpon
them.
29 And when mydday was passed, and thei
had prophecied vntil the offring of the
euening sacrifice, there was nether voyce,
nor one to answer, nor anie that regarded.
30 And Eliiáh said vnto all the people, Come to me. And all ye people came to him.
And he repared the altar of the Lord that
was broken downe.
31 And Eliiáh toke twelue stones, accordĩg
to the nomber of the tribes of the sonnes

of Iaakób, (vnto whome the worde of the
Lord came, saying, * Israél shalbe thy name)

Gen. 32,28. 2. king. 17,34.

32 And with the stones he buylt an altar in
the Name of the Lord: & he made a ditche rounde about the altar, as great as
wolde conteine two " measures of sede.

" Ebr. Sats, which some thinke conteine about thre pottels & a third parte a piece.

33 And he put the wood in order, & hewed
the bullocke in pieces, and layed him on
the wood,
34 And said, Fil foure barels with water, &
powre it on the burnt offring and on the
wood. Againe he said, Do so againe. And
thei did so the seconde time. And he said,
Do it the third time. And thei did it the
third time.
35 And the water ran rounde about the altar: & m he filled the ditche w water also.
36 And when thei shulde offer the *euening*
sacrifice, Eliiáh the Prophet came, & said,
Lord God of Abrahám, Izhák and of Israél, let it be knowen this day, that thou
art the God of Israél, and that I am thy
seruant, and that I haue done all these
things at thy commandement.

m Hereby he declared the excellẽt power of God, who contrary to nature colde make ẏ fyre burne euen in the water, to the intent thei shulde haue none occasion to doute, that he is ẏ onelie God.

37 Heare me, ô Lord, heare me, and let this
people knowe that thou art ẏ Lord God,
and that thou hast turned their heart a-
gaine n at the last.

n Thogh God suffer his to runne in blindenes & error for a time, yet at the length he calleth thẽ home to him by some notorious signe & worke.

38 Then the fyre of the Lord fel, and consumed the burnt offring, and the wood, &
the stones, and the dust, and licked vp the
water that was in the ditche.
39 And when all the people sawe it, thei fel
on their faces, and said, The Lord is God,
the Lord is God.
40 And Eliiáh said vnto them, Take the
prophetes of Báal, let o not a man of them
escape. And they toke them, and Eliiáh
broght them to the broke Kishón, & slewe
them there.

o He commanded them that as they were truely persuaded to confesse ẏ onely God: so thei wolde serue him w all their power & destroye the idolaters his enemies.

41 ¶ And Eliiáh said vnto Aháb, Get thee
vp, eat and drinke, for *there is* a sounde of
muche raine.
42 So Aháb went vp to eat and to drinke,
and Eliiáh went vp to the top of Carmél:
and he crouched vnto the earth, and put
his face betwene his knees,
43 And said to his seruant, Go vp now and
loke towarde the way of the Sea. And he
went vp, and loked, and said, There is nothing. Againe he said, Go againe p seuen
times.

p As Gods Spirit moued him to pray, so was he strengthened by the same, that he did not faint, but continued stil til he had obteined.

44 And at ẏ seuenth time he said, Beholde,
there ariseth a litle cloude out of the sea
like a mans hand. Then he said, Vp, and
say vnto Aháb, Make readie *thy charet*, and
get thee downe, that the raine stay thee
not.
45 And " in the meane while the heauen was
blacke with cloudes & winde, & there was
a great raine. Then Aháb went vp & came
to Izreél.

" Or, here and there.

46 And the hãd of the Lord was on Eliiáh,
and he girded vp his loynes, and ran q before Aháb til he came to Izreél.

q He was so strengthened w Gods Spirit, that he ran faster then the charet was able to runne.

CHAP. XIX.

5 Eliiáh fleing from Iezébel, is nourished by the Angel of God. 15 He is commanded to anoint Hazaél, Iehu, and Elishá.

1 NOw Aháb tolde Iezébel all that E-
liiáh had done, & how he had slayne all the a prophetes with the sworde.

a To wit, of Báal.

2 Then Iezébel sent a messenger vnto E-
liiáh, saying, b The gods do so to me and
more also, if I make not thy life like one
of their liues by to morowe this time.

b Thogh the wicked rage against Gods children, yet he holdeth them backe ẏ they can not execute their malice.

3 ¶ When he sawe that, he arose, and went
" for his life, & came to Beer-shéba, which
is in Iudáh, and left his seruant there.

" Or, whether his minde led him.

4 But he went a daies iourney into the wildernes, and came and sate downe vnder a
iuniper tre, & desired that he might dye,
and said, It is now ynough: ô Lord, c take
my soule, for I am no better, then my fathers.

c So hard a thing it is to bridel our impaciẽcie in affliction that ẏ saincts colde not ouercome the same.

5 And as he laie and slept vnder the iuniper tre, beholde now, an Angel touched
him, and said vnto him, Vp, *&* eat.
6 And when he loked about, beholde, there
was a cake baken on the coles, and a pot
of water at his head: so he did eat and
drinke, and returned and slept.
7 And the Angel of the Lord came againe
the seconde time, and touched him, and
said, Vp, *&* eat: for d thou hast a great
iourney.

d He declareth ẏ except God had nourished him miraculously, it had not bene possible for him to haue gone this iourney.

8 ¶ Then he arose, and did eat and drinke,
and walked in the strength of that meat
fourtie daies & fourtie nights, vnto Horéb the mount of God.
9 And there he entred into a caue, & lodged there: and beholde, the Lord spake to
him, and said vnto him, What doest thou
here, Eliiáh?
10 And he answered, I haue e bene very ielous for the Lord God of hostes: for the
children of Israél haue forsaken thy couenant, broken downe thine altars, and
slayne thy Prophetes with the sworde, * &
I onely am left, and thei seke my life to
take it away.

e He complaineth, that the more zealous ẏ he shewed him self to maintei ne Gods glorie, the more cruelly was he persecuted.

Rom. 11,12.

11 And he said, Come out, and stand vpon
the mount before the Lord. And beholde,
the Lord went by, and a mightie strong
winde rent the mountaines, and brake the
rockes before the Lord: *but* the Lord was
f not in the winde: and after the winde *came* an earthquake: *but* the Lord was not
in the earthquake:
12 And after the earthquake *came* fyre: *but*
the Lord was not in the fyre: & after the
fyre *came* a stil and soft voyce.
13 And whẽ Eliiáh heard it, he couered his
face with his mantel, & went out, & stod
in the entring in of the caue: & beholde,
there

f For the nature of man is not able to come nere vnto God, if he shulde appeare i his strẽgth & ful maiestie, & therefore of his mercie he submitteth him selfe to our capacitie.

there came a voyce vnto him, and said,
What doest thou here, Eliiáh?
14 And he answered, I haue bene very ielous for ẏ Lord God of hostes, g because
the children of Israél haue forsakē thy couenant, cast downe thine altars and slaine
thy Prophetes with the sworde, & I onely
am left, and they seke my life to take it
away.

g We oght not to depend on the multitude in mainteining Gods glorie, but because our duetie so requireth, we oght to do it.

15 And the Lord said vnto him, Go, returne by the wildernes vnto Damascus, and
when thou commest *there*, anoynt Hazaél
King ouer "Arám.

"Or, Syria.

16 And Iehú the sonne of Nimshí shalt
thou anoint King ouer Israél: & Elishá the
sonne of Shaphat of Abél Meholáh shalt
thou anoynt to be Prophet in thy roume.
17 And * him that escapeth frō the sworde
of Hazaél, shal Iehú slaye: and him that
escapeth from the sworde of Iehú, shal E-
lisha slay.

2. King. 9, 1. eccles. 48, 8.

18 Yet wil * I leaue seuē thousand in Israél,
euen h all the knees that haue not bowed
vnto Báal, and euerie mouthe that hathe
not kissed him.

Rom. 11, 4.

h He declareth that wicked dissemblers and idolaters are not his.

19 ¶ So he departed thence, and founde E-
lishá ẏ sōne of Shaphát who was plowing
with twelue yoke of oxen before him, and
was with the twelft: & Eliiáh went towards him, and cast his mantel vpon him.
20 And he left the oxen, & ran after Eliiáh,
and said, i Let me, I pray thee, kisse my
father and my mother, and then I wil followe thee. Who answered him, Go, returne: for what haue I done to thee?
21 And when he wēt backe againe frō him,
he toke a couple of oxen, and slewe them,
and sod their flesh with the k instruments
of the oxen, and gaue vnto the people, &
they did eat: then he arose and went after
Eliiáh, and ministred vnto him.

i Thogh this natural affection is not to be cōtemned, yet it oght not to moue vs whē God calleth vs to serue him.

k He wolde not stay til wood was broght, so great was his desire to followe his vocation.

CHAP. XX.

1 *Samaria is besieged. 13 The Lord promiseth the victorie to Aháb by a Prophet. 31 The King of Israél made peace with Ben-hadád, and is reproued therefore by the Prophet.*

1 THen Bē-hadád the King of "Arám assembled all his armie, and two and
thirtie a Kings with him, with horses, &
charets, and went vp, and besieged "Samaria, and foght against it.

"Or, Syria.

a That is, gouernours, and rulers of prouinces.

"Or, Shomerón.

2 And he sent messengers to Aháb King
of Israél, into the citie,
3 And said vnto him, Thus sayeth Ben-hadád, Thy siluer and thy golde his mine:
also thy women, and thy faire children
are mine.
4 And the King of Israél answered, and
said, My lord King, according to thy saying, b I am thine, and all that I haue.
5 And when the messengers came againe,
they said, Thus comandeth Ben-hadád, &
sayth, When I shal send vnto thee, and
cōmande, thou shalt deliuer me thy siluer
& thy golde, & thy women, & thy childrē,
6 c Or els I wil send my seruants vnto thee
by to morow this time: and they shal searche thine house, and the houses of thy seruants: and whatsoeuer is pleasant in thine
eyes, they shal take it in their hands, and
bring it away.

b I am content to obey and pay tribute.

c He wolde not accept his answer, except he did out of hand deliuer whatsoeuer he shulde aske: for he soght an occasion, how to make warre against him.

7 Then the King of Israél sent for all the
Elders of the land, and said, Take hede, I
pray you, and se how he seketh mischief:
for he sent vnto me for my wiues, and for
my children, and for my siluer, and for my
golde, and I denyed him not.
8 And all the Elders, & all the people said
to him, Hearkē d not vnto him, nor cōsēt.
9 Wherefore he said vnto the messengers
of Ben-hadád, Tel my lord the King, All
that thou didest send for to thy seruant
at the first time, that I wil do, but this thīg
I may not do. And the messengers departed, and broght him an answer.

d They thoght it their dueties rather to venter their liues, then to grant to that thing which was not lawful, onely to satisfie the lust of a tyrāt.

10 And Ben-hadád sent vnto him, & said,
The gods do so to me & more also, if the
e dust of Samaria be ynough to all ẏ peo
ple ẏ followe me, for euerie mā an hādful.
11 And the King of Israél answered, and
said, Tel *him*, Let not him that girdeth *his*
harnes, boast hī selfe, as he ẏ f putteth it of.
12 And when he heard ẏ tidings, as he was
with the Kings drinking in the pauilions,
he said vnto his seruāts, Bring forthe "*your*
engines, and thei set them against the citie.

e Muche lesse shal there be founde anie pray, that is worthe anie thing, when they shalbe so manie.

f Boast not before the victorie be gotten.

"Or, Put your selues in ordre.

13 ¶ And beholde, there came a Prophet
vnto Aháb King of Israél, saying, Thus
saith ẏ Lord, Hast thou sene all this great
multitude? beholde, I wil deliuer it into
thine hand this day, that ẏ maiest knowe,
g that I am the Lord.
14 And Aháb said, By whome? And he said,
Thus saith the Lord, By the seruants of
the princes of the prouinces. He said a-
gaine, Who shal ordre the battel? And he
answered, Thou.

g Before God went about by signes and miracles to pul Aháb frō his impietie, and now againe by wonderful victories.

15 ¶ Then he nombred the seruants of the
princes of the prouinces, and they were
two hundreth, two and thirtie: & after thē
he nombred the whole people of all the
children of Israél, *euen* seuen thousande.
16 And they wēt out at noone: but Ben-hadád did drinke til he was dronken in the
tents, *bothe* he & the Kings: *for* two & thirtie Kings helped him.
17 So the h seruants of the princes of the
prouinces went out first: & Ben-hadád sent
out, and they shewed him, saying, There
are men come out of Samaria.

h That is, yong men trained in the seruice of princes.

18 And he said, Whether they be come out
for peace, take them aliue: or whether they
be come out to fight, take them yet aliue.
19 So they came out of the citie, *to wit*, the ser
uants of the princes of the prouinces, and
the hoste which followed them.

20 And they slewe euerie one his "enemie:
and the "Aramites fled, and Israél pursued
them: but Ben-hadád the King of Arám
escaped on an horse with *his* [i] horsemen.
21 And the King of Israél went out, and
smote the horses and charets, and with a
great slaughter slewe he the Aramites.
22 (For there had come a Prophet to the
King of Israél, & had said vnto him, Go,
be of good courage, and consider, and take
hede what thou doest: for when the yere is
gone about, the King of Arám wil come
vp against thee)
23 ¶ Thẽ the seruants of the King of Arám
said vnto him, Their [k] gods are gods of
the mountaines, and therefore they ouercame vs: but let vs fight against them in
the plaine, and douteles we shal ouercome
me them.
24 And this do, Take the Kings away, euerie one out of his place, and place captaines for them.
25 And nomber thy selfe an armie, like the
armie that thou hast lost, with suche horses, and suche charets, and we wil fight a-
gainst them in the plaine, and douteles we
shal ouercome thẽ: and he hearkened vnto
their voyce, and did so.
26 And after the yere was gone about, Ben-
hadád nombred the Aramites, and went
vp to Aphék to fight against Israél.
27 And the children of Israél were nombred, and were all [l] assembled and went
against them, and the children of Israél
pitched before them, like two litle flockes
of kiddes: but the Aramites filled the countrey.
28 And there came a man of God, and spake
vnto the King of Israél, saying, Thus
sayth the Lord, Because the Aramites
haue said, The Lord is the God of the
mountaines, and not God of the valleis,
therefore wil I deliuer all this great multitude into thine hand, and ye shal knowe
that [m] I am the Lord.
29 And they pitched one ouer against the
other seuen dayes, & in the seuẽth day the
battel was ioyned: and the children of Israél slewe of the Aramites an hundreth
thousand fotemen in one day.
30 But the rest fled to Aphék into the citie:
and there fel a wall vpon seuen & twentie
thousand men that were left: and Ben-hadád fled into the citie, and came into "a
secret chamber.
31 ¶ And his seruantes said vnto him, Beholde now, we haue heard say that the
Kings of the house of Israél are merciful
Kings: we pray thee, let vs put sackecloth
about our [n] loynes, and ropes about our
heades, and go out to the King of Israél:
it may be that he wil saue thy life.
32 Thẽ they girded sackecloth about their
loynes, and *put* ropes about their heades,
and came to the King of Israél, and said,
Thy seruant Ben-hadád saith, I pray thee,
let me liue: and he said, Is he yet aliue? he
is my brother.
33 Now the men toke diligent hede, "if they
colde catche *anie thing* of him, and made
haste, & said, Thy brother [o] Ben-hadád.
And he said, Go, bring him. So Bẽ-hadád
came out vnto him, and he caused him to
come vp vnto the charet.
34 And *Ben-hadád* said vnto him, The cities, which my father toke frõ thy father,
I wil restore, and thou shalt make stretes
for thee in [p] Damascus, as my father did
in Samaria. Then *said Aháb*, I wil let thee
go with this couenant. So he made a couenant with him, and let him go.
35 ¶ Then a certeine man of the "children
of the Prophetes said vnto his neighbour
by the cõmandemẽt of the Lord, [q] Smite
me, I pray thee. But the man refused to
smite him.
36 Then said he vnto him, Because thou
hast not obeyed the voyce of the Lord,
beholde, assone as thou art departed from
me, a lyon shal [r] slay thee. So when he
was departed from him, a lyon found
him and slewe him.
37 Then he found another man, and said,
Smite me, I pray thee. And the man smote
him, and in smiting wounded *him*.
38 So the Prophet departed, and waited for
the King by the way, and disguysed him
selfe with asshes vpon his face.
39 And when the King came by, he cryed
vnto the King, and said, [s] Thy seruant
went into the middes of the battel: and
beholde, there went away a man, whome
another man broght vnto me, & said, Kepe
this man: if he be lost, and want, thy life
shal go for his, or els thou shalt paye a talent of siluer.
40 And as thy seruant had here and there
to do, he was gone: and the King of Israél
said vnto him, So shal thy iudgement be:
thou hast giuen sentence.
41 And he hasted, and toke the asshes away
from his face: & the King of Israél knew
him that he was of the Prophetes:
42 And he said vnto him, Thus saith the
Lord, *Because thou hast let go out of *thine*
hands a man whome I appointed to dye,
thy life shal go for his life, and thy people
for his people.
43 And the King of Israél went to his house heauy and in displeasure, and came to
"Samaria.

"Ebr. man.

"Or, Syrians.

i With them ẏ were appointed for the preseruaciõ of his persone.

k Thus ẏ wicked blaspheme God in their furie, whome notwithstãding he suffreth not vnpunished.

l All they, ẇ were in ẏ battel of the former yere, ver. 15.

m Who am of like power in the valley, as I am on the hills, and can aswel destroy a multitude ẇ fewe as with manie.

"Ebr from chãber to chamber.

n In signe of submission, and that we haue deserued death, if he wil punishe vs ẇ rigour.

"Or, and caught it of him.

o He is aliue

p Thou shalt appoint in my chief citie what thou wilt, and I wil obey thee.

"Or, of the disciples.

q By this external signe he wolde more liuely touche ẏ Kings heart.

r Because thou hast transgressed the commandement of the Lord.

s By this parable he maketh Aháb cõdemne him selfe, who made a couenant with Gods enemie, and let him escape, whome God had appointed to be slaine.

Chap. 22, 38.

"Or, Shomerón.

CHAP. XXI.

8 Iezébel commandeth to kil Nabóth for the Vineyard, that he refused to sel to Aháb. 19 Eliiáh reproueth Aháb, and he repenteth.

1 After

"Or, at this time.

1 A "Fter these things Nabóth the Izreelite had a vineyarde in Izreél, hard
by the palace of Aháb King of Samaria.
2 And Aháb spake vnto Nabóth, saying,
[a] Giue me thy vineyarde, that I may make
me a garden of herbes thereof, because it
is nere by mine house: and I wil giue thee
for it a better vineyarde then it is: *or* if it
please thee, I wil giue thee the worthe of
it in money.
3 And Nabóth said to Aháb, The Lord
kepe me from giuing the inheritãce of my
fathers vnto thee.
4 Then Aháb came into his house heauy &
in displeasure, because of the worde which
Nabóth the Izreelite had spokẽ vnto him.
for he had said, I wil not giue thee the inheritance of my fathers, and he lay [b] vpon
his bed and turned his face and wolde
eat no bread.
5 Then Iezébel his wife came to him and
said vnto him, Why is thy spirit so sad ẏ
thou eatest no bread?
6 And he said vnto her, Because I spake
vnto Nabóth the Izreelite, and said vnto
him, Giue me thy vineyarde for money,
or if it please thee, I wil giue thee *another*
vineyarde for it: but he answered, I wil
not giue thee my vineyarde.
7 Then Iezébel his wife said vnto him,
[c] Doest thou now gouerne the kingdome
of Israél? vp, eat bread, and "be of good
chere, I wil giue thee the vineyard of Nabóth the Izreelite.
8 ¶ So she wrote letters in Ahabs name, &
sealed them with his seale, and sent the
letters vnto the Elders, and to the nobles
that were in his citie dwelling wᵗ Nabóth.
9 And she wrote in the letters, saying, Proclaime a [d] fast, and set Nabóth amõg the
chief of the people,
10 And set two wicked men before him, and
let thẽ witnes against him, saying, Thou
didest blaspheme God and the King: thẽ
cary him out, and stone him that he may
dye.
11 And the [e] men of his citie, *euen* the Elders and gouernours, which dwelt in his
citie, did as Iezébel had sent vnto them: as
it was writẽ in the letters, which she had
sent vnto them.
12 They proclaimed a fast, and set Nabóth
among the chief of the people,
13 And there came two wicked men, & sate
before him: and the wicked men witnessed
against Nabóth in the presence of the
people, saying, Nabóth did "blaspheme
God and the King. Thẽ they caryed him
away out of the citie, and stoned him with
stones, that he dyed.
14 Then they sent to Iezébel, saying, Nabóth is stoned and is dead.
15 ¶ And when Iezébel heard that Nabóth
was stoned and was dead, Iezébel said to
Aháb, [f] Vp, & take possession of the vineyard of Nabóth the Izreelite, which
he refused to giue thee for money: for
Nabóth is not aliue, but is dead.
16 And when Aháb heard that Nabóth was
dead, he rose to go downe to the vineyard
of Nabóth the Izreelite, to take possession of it.
17 ¶ And the worde of the Lord came vnto Eliiáh the Tishbite, saying,
18 Arise, go downe to mete Aháb King of
Israél, which is in Samaria. lo, *he is* in the
vineyarde of Nabóth, whether he is gone downe to take possession of it.
19 Therefore shalt thou say vnto him, Thus
saith the Lord, [g] Hast thou killed, and also gotten possession? And thou shalt speake vnto him, saying, Thus sayth the Lord,
[h] In the place where dogs licked the blood
of Nabóth, shal dogs licke euẽ thy blood
also.
20 And Aháb said to Eliiáh, Hast thou
founde me, ô mine enemie? And he answered, I haue founde *thee*: for thou hast solde
thy selfe to worke wickednes in the sight
of the Lord.
21 * Beholde, I wil bring euil vpon thee, &
wil take away thy posteritie, and wil cut
of from Aháb him that *pisseth against ẏ
wall, aswel him that is * shut vp, as him
that is left in Israél,
22 And I wil make thine house like ẏ house
of *Ieroboám the sonne of Nebát, & like
the house of *Baashá the sonne of Ahiiáh,
for the prouocacion wherewith thou hast
prouoked, and made Israél to sinne.
23 And also of Iezébel spake the Lord, saying, *The dogs shal eat Iezébel, "by the
wall of Izreél.
24 The dogs shal eat him of Ahabs *stocke*,
that dyeth in the citie: and him that dyeth
in the fields, shal the foules of the ayre
eat.
25 But there was none like Aháb, who did
[i] sell him selfe, to worke wickednes in the
sight of the Lord: whome Iezébel his
wife prouoked.
26 For he did excedĩg abominably in following idoles, accordĩg to all that the Am
morites did, whome the Lord cast out before the children of Israél.
27 Now when Aháb heard those wordes,
he rent his clothes, and put sackecloth vpõ
"him and fasted, and lay in sackecloth and
went [k] softely.
28 And the worde of the Lord came to E-
liiáh the Tishbite, saying,
29 Seest thou how Aháb is humbled before
me? because he submitteth him selfe before me, I wil not bring that euil in his dayes,
but in his [l] sonnes dayes wil I bring e-
uil vpon his house.

a Thogh Ahabs tyrannie be condemned by the holy Spirit, yet he was not so rigorous that he wolde take from another man his right without ful recompence.

b Thus ẏ wicked consider not what is iust & lawful, but fret inwardely, when they can not haue their inordinate appetites satisfied.

c As thogh she said, Thou knowest not what it is to reigne. Commaunde, and intreat not.

"Ebr. let thine heart be mery.

d For thẽ they vsed to inquire of mẽs fautes: for none cold fast truely that were notorious sinners.

e Thus the worldelings contrary to Gods cõmãdemẽt, who willeth not to cõsent to the shedding of innocẽt blood, obey rather ẏ wicked commandemẽts of princes then the iust Lawes of God.

"Ebr. blesse.

f This example of monstreous crueltie the holy Gost leaueth to vs to the intent ẏ we shulde abhorre all tyrannie, and specially in them, whome nature & kinde shulde moue to be pitiful and inclined to mercie.

g Doest thou thinke to haue anie aduantage by murthering of an innocent?

h This was fulfilled in Iorám his sonne, as. 2. Kin. 9, 25.

Chap. 14, 10. 2. king. 9, 8.
1. Sam. 25, 22.
Chap. 14, 10.
Chap. 15, 29.
Chap. 16, 3.
2. Kin. 9, 33.
"Or, fortresse, or, possession.

i By the wicked counsel of his wife, he became a vile idolater and cruel murtherer, as one that gaue him selfe wholly to serue sinne.

"Ebr. his flesh.
k In token of mourning, or, as some read, bare foted.

l Meaning, in Iorams time, 2. Kin. 9, 26.

CHAP. XXII.

2 Iehoshaphát & Aháb fight against the King of Syria. 15 Micháiah sheweth the King what shalbe the successe of their enterprise. 24 Zedkiiáh the false prophet smiteth him. 34 Aháb is slaine. 40 Ahazia his sonne succedeth. 41 The reigne of Iehoshaphát, 51 and Iorám his sonne.

1 AND * they continued [a] thre yere
without warre betwene Arám and
Israél.
2 And in the third yere did Iehoshaphát the
King of Iudáh [b] come downe to the King
of Israél.
3 (Then the King of Israél said vnto his
seruãts, Knowe ye not that [c] Ramóth Gileád was ours? and we staye, and take it not
out of the hand of the King of Arám?)
4 And he said vnto Iehoshaphát, Wilt
thou go with me to battel against Ramóth
Gileád? And Iehoshaphát said vnto the
King of Israél, [d] I am as thou art, my
people as thy people, and mine horses as
thine horses.
5 Then Iehoshaphát said vnto the King of
Israél, [e] Aske counsel, I pray thee, of the
Lord to day.
6 Then the King of Israél gathered the
[f] Prophetes vpon a foure hundreth men,
and said vnto them, Shal I go against Ramóth Gileád to battel, or shal I let it alone? And they said, Go vp: for the Lord shal
deliuer it into the hands of the King.
7 And Iehoshaphát said, Is there here neuer a Prophet of the [g] Lord more, that
we might inquire of him?
8 And the King of Israél said vnto Iehoshaphát, There is yet one man (Micháiah the
sonne of Imláh) by whome we may aske
counsel of the Lord, but [h] I hate him: for
he doeth not prophecie good vnto me, but
euil. And Iehoshaphát said, Let not the
King say so.
9 Then the King of Israél called an [i] Eunuche, & said, Call quickely Micháiah the
sonne of Imláh.
10 And the King of Israél & Iehoshaphát
the King of Iudáh sate ether *of them* on his
throne in their [k] apparel in the voyde
place at the entring in of the gate of Samaria, and all the Prophetes prophecied
before them.
11 And Zidkiiáh the sonne of Chenaanáh
made him [l] hornes of yron, & said, Thus
sayth the Lord, With these shalt thou
push the Aramites, vntil thou hast consumed them.
12 And all the Prophetes prophecied so,
saying, Go vp to Ramóth Gileád, & prosper: for the Lord shal deliuer it into the
Kings hand.
13 ¶ And the messenger that was gone to
call Micháiah spake vnto him, saying, Beholde now, the wordes of the Prophetes

2.Chro.18,1.
a Ben-hadád the King of Syria and Aháb made a peace, which indured thre yeres.
b To se and visite him.
c The Kings of Syria kept Ramóth before this league was made by Ben-hadád: therefore he thoght not him selfe boũde thereby to restore it.
d I am ready to ioyne & go with thee, and all mine is at thy commandement.
e He semed ye he wolde not go to the warre, except God approued it, yet when Micháh cõunseled the contrarie, he wolde not obey.
f Meaning, the false prophetes, which were flatterers & serued for lucre, whome Iezébel had assembled and kept after the death of those whome Elias slewe.
g Iehoshaphát did not acknowledge ye false Prophetes to be Gods ministers, but did contemne them.
h Whereby we se that the wicked cã not abide to heare the trueth, but hate the Prophetes of God & molest thẽ.
i Read Genes. 37,36.
k In their kinglie apparel.
l The true Prophetes of God were accustomed to vse signes for the confirmacion of their doctrine, Isa. 20, 2. iere 7,2. Wherein the false Prophetes did imitate them, thinking thereby to make their doctrine more commendable.

declare good vnto the King with " [m] one
accorde: let thy worde therefore, I pray
thee, be like the worde of one of them, &
speake thou good.
14 And Micháiah said, As the Lord liueth,
whatsoeuer the Lord sayth vnto me, that
wil I speake.
15 ¶ So he came to the King, and the King
said vnto him, Micháiah, shal we go agaĩst Ramóth Gileád to battel, or shal we
leaue of? And he answered him, [n] Go vp, &
prosper: and the Lord shal deliuer it into
the hand of the King.
16 And the King said vnto hĩ, How oft shal
I charge thee, that thou tel me nothĩg but
that which is true in the Name of ye Lord.
17 Then he said, I sawe all Israél scatred
vpon the moũtaines, as shepe that had no
shepherd. And the Lord said, [o] These haue no master, let euery man returne vnto
his house in peace.
18 (And the King of Israél said vnto Iehoshaphát, Did I not tel thee, that he wolde
prophecie no good vnto me, but euil?)
19 Againe he said, Heare thou therefore ye
worde of the Lord. I sawe the Lord sit
on his throne, & all the [p] hoste of heauen
stode about him on his right hand and on
his left hand.
20 And the Lord said, Who shal " entise Aháb that he may go and fall at Ramóth
Gileád? And one said on this maner, and
another said on that maner.
21 Then there came forthe a spirit, & [q] stode before the Lord, and said, I wil entise
him. And the Lord said vnto him, Wherewith?
22 And he said, I wil go out, and be a [r] false
spirit in the mouthe of all his prophetes.
Thẽ he said, Thou shalt entise *him*, & shalt
also preuaile: go forthe, and do so.
23 Now therefore beholde, the Lord hathe
put a lying spirit in the mouthe of all these thy prophetes, and the Lord hathe appointed euil against thee.
24 Then Zidkiiáh ye sonne of Chenaanáh
came nere & smote Micháiah on ye cheke,
and said, * [s] When went the Spirit of the
Lord from me, to speake vnto thee?
25 And Micháiah said, Beholde, yu shalt se
in that day, when thou shalt go from chãber to chamber to hide thee.
26 And the King of Israél said, Take Micháiah, & cary hĩ vnto Amón ye gouernour
of ye citie, and vnto Ioásh the Kings sonne,
27 And say, thus sayth the King, Put this
man in the prison house, & fede him with
[t] bread of affliction, & with water of affliction, vntil I returne in peace.
28 And Micháiah said, If yu returne in peace, the Lord hathe not spoken by me. And
he said, [u] Hearken all ye people.
29 So the King of Israél & Iehoshaphát the
King

" *Ebr. mouthe.*
m This is the commune argument of ye wicked, who thinke that none shulde speake against a thing, if the greater parte approue it, be they neuer so vngodlie.
n He speaketh this in derisiõ, because ye Kĩg attributed so muche to the false prophetes, meaning yt by experience he shulde trye that thei were but flatterers.
o It is better thei returne home, thẽ to be punished and scatred, because thei take warre in hand without Gods counsel & approbacion.
p Meaning, his Angels.
" *Or, persuade & deceiue.*
q Here we se yt though ye deuil be euer readie to bring vs to destructiõ, yet he hathe no further power then God giueth him.
r I wil cause all his prophetes to tel lies.
2.Chro.18,23.
s Thus ye wicked wolde seme that none were in ye fauour of God, but they, and yt God hathe giuen his graces to none so muche as to thẽ.
t Let him be pyned away wt hungre & be fed wt a smale portion of bread & water.
u That when ye shal se these things come to passe, ye may giue God the glorie & knowe that I am his true Prophet.

Kĩg of Iudáh wẽt vp to Ramóth Gileád.
30 And the King of Iſraél ſaid to Iehoſhaphát, I wil change mine apparel, and wil
entre into the battel, but put thou on thine apparel. And the King of Iſraél changed him ſelfe, and went into the battel.
31 And the King of Arám commanded his
two & thirtie captaines ouer his charrets,
ſaying, Fight nether with ſmal, nor great,
ſaue onely againſt the King of Iſraél.
32 And when the captaines of the charets
ſawe Iehoſhaphát, they ſaid, Surely it is ỹ
King of Iſraél, & they turned to fight a-
gainſt him: and Iehoſhaphat [x] cryed.
33 And when the captaines of the charets
ſawe that he was not the King of Iſraél,
they turned backe from him.
34 Then a *certeine* man drue a bowe "mightely and ſmote the King of Iſraél betwene the ioyntes "of his brigádine. Wherefore he ſaid vnto his charet man, Turne
thine hãd & cary me out of the hoſte: for I
am "hurt.
35 And the battel encreaſed that day, and
the [y] King ſtode ſtil in his charet againſt
the Aramites, and dyed at euen: and the
blood ran out of the woũde into the middes of the charet.
36 And there went a proclamatiõ through
out ỹ [z] hoſte about the going downe of the
ſunne, ſaying, Euery man to his citie, and
euery man to his owne countrei.
37 So the King dyed, and was broght to Samaria, & they buryed ỹ King in Samaria.
38 And one waſhed the charet in the poole
of Samaria & the doggs licked vp his blood (& "they waſhed his armoure) accordĩg
*vnto the worde of the Lord w̃ he ſpake.
39 Cõcerning the reſt of the actes of Aháb
& all that he did, & ỹ yuorie houſe, which
he buylt, & all the cities that he buylt, are
they not writen in the boke of the Chronicles of the Kings of Iſraél?
40 So Aháb ſlept with his fathers, & Ahaziáh his ſonne reigned in his ſteade.
41 ¶*And Iehoſhaphát the ſonne of Aſá began to reigne vpon Iudáh in the fourth
yere of Aháb King of Iſraél.
42 Iehoſhaphát was fiue and thirtie yere olde, when he began to reigne, and reigned
fiue and twentie yere in Ieruſalém. And
his mothers name was Azubáh the daughter of Shilhí.
43 And he walked in all the wayes of Aſá
his father, and declined not therefrom, but
did that which was right in the eyes of
the Lord. Neuertheles [a] the hie places were not taken away: *for* the people offred ſtil
and burnt incenſe in the hie places.
44 And Iehoſhaphát made peace with the
King of Iſraél.
45 Concerning the reſt of the actes of Iehoſhaphát, and his worthie dedes that he
did, and his battels which he foght, are
they not writen in the boke of the Chronicles of the Kings of Iudáh?
46 And the Sodomites, which remained in
the dayes of his father Aſá, he put cleane
out of the land.
47 There was then no King in Edóm: the
[b] deputie was King.
48 Iehoſhaphát made ſhippes of [c] Tharſhíſh
to ſaile to [d] Ophir for golde, but they wẽt
not, for the ſhippes were broken at Ezión
Gáber.
49 Then ſaid Ahaziáh the ſonne of Aháb
vnto Iehoſhaphát, Let my ſeruãts go with
thy ſeruãts in ỹ ſhippes. But Iehoſhaphát
wolde not.
50 And Iehoſhaphát did ſlepe with his fathers, & was buryed with his fathers in the
citie of Dauid his father and Iehorám his
ſonne reigned in his ſteade.
51 ¶Ahaziáh the ſonne of Aháb began to
reigne ouer Iſraél in Samaria, the ſeuen-
tenth yere of Iehoſhaphát King of Iudáh,
& reigned two yeres ouer Iſraél.
52 But he did euil in the ſight of the Lord,
and walked in the way of his father, & in
the way of his mother, and in the way of
Ieroboám the ſonne of Nebát, which made Iſraél to ſinne.
53 For he ſerued Báal and worſhipped him,
& prouoked the Lord God of Iſraél vnto
wrath, "according vnto all that his father
had done.

x That is, to ỹ Lord for helpe.

"Or, in his ſimplicitie & ignorantly.

"Ebr. & betwene the brigandine.

"Ebr. ſicke.

y To wit, Aháb King of Iſraél.

z Of the Iſraelites.

"Or, the harlots waſhed it.

Chap. 21, 19.

2. Chro. 20, 31.

a Meaning, ỹ he was led w̃ an error, thinking that they might ſtil ſacrifice to the Lord in thoſe places, aſwel as thei did before the Temple was buylt.

b In the time of this King Idumea was ſubiect to Iudáh & was gouerned, by whome thei of Iudáh appoited.

c By Tharſhíſh the Scripture meaneth Cilicia & all ỹ Sea called Mediterraneum

d Ioſephus writeth that Ophir is in India, where the Egyptians & Arabians traffike for golde.

"Or, in all pointes as his father did.

THE SECONDE BOKE of the Kings.

THE ARGUMENT.

This ſeconde boke conteineth the actes of the Kings of Iudáh and Iſraél: to wit, of Iſraél, from the death of Aháb vnto the laſt King Hoſhéa, who was impriſonned by the King of Aſſyria, & his citie Samaria taken, & the tẽ tribes by the iuſte plague of God for their idolatrie & diſobedience to God led into captiuitie. And alſo of Iudáh, frõ the reigne of Iehorám ſonne of Iehoſhaphát vnto Zedechiá who for contemning the Lords cõmandement by his Prophetes, & neglecting his ſundry admonitions, by famine & other meanes was taken by his enemies, ſawe his ſonnes moſte cruelly ſlaine before his face, & his owne eyes put out, as the Lord had declared to him before by his Prophet Ieremie: and alſo by the iuſte vengeance of God for contempt of his worde Ieruſalém was deſtroyed, the Temple burnt, and he and all his people were led away captiues into Babylon. In this boke are notable examples of Gods fauour towardes those rulers and people which obey his Prophetes and imbrace his worde: and contrary wise of his plagues towardes those commune weales which neglect his ministers and do not obey his commandements.

CHAP. I.

2 Ahaziáh by a fall falleth sicke & cōsulteth with Baál-zebúb. 3 He is reproued by Eliáh. 10 The captaines ouer fiftie were sent to Eliiáh, whereof two were burnt with fire frō heauen by his prayer. 17 Ahaziáh dyeth, and Iehorám his brother succedeth him.

1 WHen Moáb rebelled a-
gaist Israél after the death of Aháb:
2 And [a] Ahaziáh fel
through the lattesse win
dowe in his vpper chā-
ber which was in Sama-
ria: so he was sicke: thē he sent messengers,
to whome he said, Go, & enquire of [b] Baal-zebúb the god of Ekrón, if I shal recouer of this my disease.
3 Then the Angel of the Lord said to
Eliiáh the Tishbite, Arise, & go vp to
mete the messengers of the King of Samaria, and saye vnto them, [c] Is it not because there is no God in Israél, that ye go
to inquire of Baal-zebúb the god of Ekrón?
4 Wherefore thus sayth the Lord, Thou
shalt not come downe from the bed on
which thou art gone vp, but shalt dye the
death. So Eliiáh departed.
5 And the messengers returned vnto him,
to whome he said, Why are ye now returned?
6 And they answered him, There came a
man and met vs, and said vnto vs, Go, *and*
returne vnto the King which sent you, and
say vnto him, Thus sayth the Lord, [d] Is it
not because there is no God in Israél, that
thou sendest to enquire of Baal-zebúb
the god of Ekrón? Therefore thou
shalt not come downe from the bed, on
which thou art gone vp, but shalt dye the
death.
7 And he said vnto them, What maner of
man was he which came and met you, and
tolde you these wordes?
8 And they said vnto hī, He was an [e] heerie
man, and girded with a girdle of lether a-
bout his loynes. Then said he, It is Eliiáh
the Tishbite.
9 Therefore *the King* sent vnto him a captaine ouer fiftie with his fifty *men*, who
went vp vnto him: *for* beholde, he sate on
the toppe [f] of a mountaine, & he said vnto
him, O man of God, the King hathe commanded *that* thou come downe.
10 But Eliiáh answered, & said to the captaine ouer the fiftie, If that I be a man of
God, let fyre come downe frō the heauē,
and deuoure thee and thy fyftie. [g] So fyre
came downe from the heauen and deuoured him and his fiftie.

a So that he was punished for his idolatrie after two sortes: for the Moabites, wͤ were wonte to pay him tribute, rebelled, & he fel downe at a grate wͤ was vpon his house to giue light bento the.
b The Philistims, wͤ dwelt at Ekrón, worshipped this idole, wͤ signifieth, ẏ god of flies, thinking that he colde preserue them from the bitig of flies: or els he was so called, because flies were ingēdred in great abundance of the blood of ẏ sacrifices that were offred to that idole.
c He sheweth that idolaters haue not the true God, for els they wolde seke to none but to him alone.
d Ignorance is the mother of error and idolatrie.
e Some thinke ẏ this is ment of his garmēts wͤ were rough & made of heere.
f To wit, Carmel.
g He declareth what power Gods worde hathe in the mouthe of his seruants, when they threaten Gods iudgements against the wicked.

11 Againe also he sent vnto him another
captaine ouer fiftie, with his fifty. Who
spake, and said vnto him, [h] O man of God,
thus the King commandeth, Come downe
quickly.
12 But Eliiáh answered & said vnto them,
[i] If I be a man of God, let fyre come downe from the heauen, and deuoure thee and
thy fiftie. So fyre came downe from the
heauen, and deuoured him and his fiftie.
13 ¶ Yet againe he sent the third captaine
ouer fifty wͭ his fifty. And the third captaine ouer fifty went vp & came, & fel on his
knees before Eliiáh, & besoght him, & said
vnto him, O man of God, I pray thee, let
my [k] life and the life of these thy fifty
seruantes be [l] precious in thy sight.
14 Beholde, there came fyre downe from
the heauen and deuoured the two former
captaines ouer fifty with their fifties: therefore let my life now be precious in thy
sight.
15 And the Angel of the Lord said vnto
Eliiáh, Go downe wͭ him, be [m] not afrayd
of his presence. So he arose, and wēt downe with him vnto the King.
16 And he said vnto him, Thus saith the
Lord, Because thou hast sent messengers
to inquire of Baal-zebúb the God of Ekrón, (was it not because there was no
God in Israél to inquire of his worde)
therefore thou shalt not come downe of
the bed, on which thou art gone vp, but
shalt dye the death.
17 So he dyed according to the worde of ẏ
Lord which Eliiáh had spoken. And [n] Iehorám begā to reigne in his steade, in the
seconde yere of Iehorám the sonne of Iehoshaphát King of Iudáh, because he had
no sonne.
18 Concerning the rest of the actes of Ahaziáh, that he did, are thei not writen in the
boke of the Chronicles of the Kings of
Israél?

CHAP. II.

8 Eliiáh deuideth the waters with his cloke. 11 He is taken vp into heauen. 13 Elishá taketh his cloke & deuideth Iordén. 20 The bitter and venemous waters are healed. 23 The children that mocke Elishá, are rent in pieces with beares.

1 AND when the Lord wolde take vp E-
liiáh into heauē by a whirle wind, E-
liiáh went with Elishá from [a] Gilgál.
2 Then Eliiáh said to Elishá, Tary here, I
pray thee: for the Lord hathe sent me
to Beth-él. But Elishá said, As the Lord
liueth, & as thy soule liueth, I wil not leaue thee. So they came downe to Beth-él.

h He spake this in mockery, & therefore prouoked Gods wrath so muche the more.
i Meanīg, that God wolde shewe by effect, whether he was a true Prophet or not.
k Which humble my selfe before God & his seruant.
l That is, spare my life & let me not dye as the other two.
m Thus ẏ Lord giueth boldenes to his that they feare not the threatnigs of tyrants, wͤ otherwise of them selues are afraide to do Gods message.
n Iehoshaphát going to battel against the Syrians, made his sonne Iehorám King in the 17 yere of his reigne: and in the 18 yere, wͤ was the seconde yere of his sonne, Iehorám ẏ sonne of Aháb reigned in Israél: and in the fifthe yere of this Iehorám Iehoshaphát dyed and the kingdome of Iudáh was cōfirmed to his sonne.
a Which was ẏ place where the childrē of Israél were circumcised after they came ouer Iordén & had bene fourtie yeres in ẏ wildernes, as Iosh. 5,9.

3 And

b So called because they are begotten as it were anewe by the heauenlie doctrine.
c That is, frõ being any more thine head: for to be as ỹ head, is to be the master, as to be at the fete, is to be a scholar.
d For ỹ Lord had reueiled it vnto him.

3 And the [b] children of the Prophetes that
were at Beth-él, came out to Elishá, and
said vnto him, Knowest thou that ỹ Lord
wil take thy master from [c] thine head this
day? And he said, Yea, I [d] knowe it: holde
ye your peace.
4 Againe Eliiáh said vnto him, Elishá,
tary here, I pray thee: for the Lord hathe
sent me to Ierichó. But he said, As ỹ Lord
liueth, and as thy soule liueth, I wil not
leaue thee. So thei came to Ierichó.
5 And the children of the Prophetes that
were at [e] Ierichó, came to Elishá, & said
vnto him, Knowest thou, that the Lord
wil take thy master from thine head this
day? And he said, Yea, I knowe it: holde ye
your peace.
6 Moreouer Eliiáh said vnto him, Tary, I
pray thee, here: for the Lord hathe sent me
to Iordén. But he said, As the Lord liueth,
& as thy soule liueth, I wil not leaue thee.
So they went bothe *together*.
7 And fiftie men of the sonnes of the Prophetes went and stode on the other side a-
farre of, and thei two stode by Iordén.
8 ¶ Then Eliiáh toke his cloke, and wrapt
it together, and smote the [f] waters, and
they were deuided hether and thether, &
thei twaine went ouer on the drye land.
9 Now when thei were passed ouer, Eliiáh
said vnto Elishá, Aske what I shal do for
thee before I be taken from thee. And E-
lishá said, I pray thee, Let thy Spirit [g] be
double vpon me.
10 And he said, Thou hast asked an hard
thing: *yet* if thou se me when I am taken
from thee, thou shalt haue it so: & if not,
it shal not be.
11 And as thei went walking and talking,
beholde, there *appeared* a charet of fyre,
and horses of fyre, and did separate them
twaine. * So Eliiáh went vp by a whyrle-
winde into [h] heauen.
12 And Elishá sawe it, and he cryed, My
father, my father, the charet of Israél, and
the horsemen thereof: & he sawe him no
more: and he toke his *owne* clothes, & rent
them in two pieces.
13 ¶ He toke vp also the cloke of Eliiáh
that fel from him, and returned, and stode
by the banke of Iordén.
14 After, he toke the cloke of Eliiáh, that
fel from him, and smote the waters, and
said, Where is the Lord God of Eliiáh,
and he him selfe? Againe also he smote
the waters, and thei were separated this
waye and that waye: and Elishá went
ouer.
15 And when the children of the Prophetes, which were at Ierichó, sawe him on
the other side, they said, [i] The Spirit of
Eliiáh doeth rest on Elishá: and they came
to mete him, & fel to the grounde before
him,

e Not onely at Beth-él, but at Iericho and other places were there Prophetes, ẇ had scholars, whome they instructed and brogħt vp in ỹ true feare of God.

f To wit, of Iordén.

g Let thy Spirit haue double force in me, because of these dãgerous times: or let me haue twise so muche as ỹ rest of the Prophetes: or thy spirit beĩg deuided into thre partes, let me haue two.

Eccles. 48, 13. 1 mac. 2, 58.
h Thus God hathe left a testimonie in all ages bothe before the Lawe, in the Lawe, & in the time of the Gospel of ỹ resurrectiõ.

i The Spirit of prophecie is giuen to him, as it was to Eliiáh.

16 And said vnto him, Beholde now, there
be with thy seruants fiftie strong men: let
them go, we pray thee, and seke thy [k] master, if so be the Spirit of the Lord hathe
taken him vp, and cast him vpon some
mountaine, or into some valley. But he
said, [l] Ye shal not send.
17 Yet they were instant vpon him, til he
was ashamed: wherefore he said, Send. So
thei sent fiftie mẽ, which soght thre daies,
but founde him not.
18 Therefore thei returned to him, (for he
taried at Ierichó) and he said vnto them,
Did not I say vnto you, Go not?
19 ¶ And the men of the citie said vnto E-
lishá, Beholde, we pray thee: the situacion
of this citie is pleasant, as thou, my lord,
seest, but the water *is* noght, & the groũde
*baren.
20 Then he said, Bring me a newe cruse, &
put salt therein. And they broght it to
him.
21 And he went vnto the spring of the waters, and cast there [m] the salt, and said,
Thus saith the Lord, I haue healed this
water: death shal no more come thereof,
nether barennes *to the grounde*.
22 So the waters were healed vntil this
day, according to ỹ worde of Elishá which
he had spoken.
23 ¶ And he wẽt vp from thẽce vnto Beth-
él. And as he was going vp the waye, litle
children came out of the citie, and mocked him, and said vnto him, Come vp, thou
balde head, come vp, thou balde head.
24 And he turned backe, & loked on them,
and [n] cursed them in the Name of the
Lord. And two beares came out of the
forest, and tare in pieces two and fourtie
children of them.
25 So he went from thence to mount Carmél, and from thence he returned to Samaria.

k Meaning, Eliiáh: for they thoght his bodie had bene cast in some mountaine.

l Because the fact was extraordinarie, thei douted where he was become, but Elishá was assured ỹ he was taken vp to God.

*Or, killeth the inhabitants.

m Thus God gaue him power, euẽ cõtrary to nature, to make that water profitable for mãs vse, ẇ before was hurtful.

n Perceiuing their malicious heart against the Lord and his worde, he desireth God to take vengeance of that iniurie done vnto him.

CHAP. III.

1 The reigne of Iehorám. 6 He and Iehoshaphát go to warre against Moab, which rebelled. 13 Elishá reproueth him, 17 And giueth their beste water 24 The Moabites are ouercome. 27 Their King sacrificeth his sonne.

1 NOw Iehorám the sonne of Aháb
began to reigne ouer Israél in Samaria, the [a] eightenth yere of Iehoshaphát
King of Iudah, & reigned twelue yeres.
2 And he wroght euil in the sight of the
Lord, but not like his father nor like his
mother: for he toke away the image of
Báal that his father had made.
3 Neuertheles, he cleaued vnto [b] the sinnes
of Ieroboám, the sonne of Nebát, ẇ made
Israél to sinne, & departed not therefrõ.
4 ¶ Then [c] Meshá King of Moáb had store of shepe, and rendred vnto the King
of Israél an hundreth thousand lambes,

a Read the annotaciõ in the 1 Chap. & 17. verse.

b He sacrificed to ỹ goldẽ calues, that Ieroboám had made.

c This was done after ỹ Dauid had made the Moabites tributaries to his successers.

& an hundreth thousand rams with the woll.
5 But when Aháb was deade, the King of
Moáb rebelled against the King of Israél.
6 Therefore King Iehorám went out of
Samaria the same season, and nombred all
Israél,
7 And went, and sent to Iehoshaphát King
of Iudáh, saying, The Kig of Moáb hathe
rebelled against me: wilt thou go with me
to battel against Moáb? And he answered,
I wil go vp: *for* [d] I am, as thou art, my people, as thy people, *and* mine horses as thine
horses.
8 Then said he, What way shal we go vp?
And he answered, The way of the wildernes of Edóm.
9 ¶ So went the King of Israél & the King
of Iudáh, and the [e] King of Edóm, and
when they had compassed the way seuen
daies, thei had no water for the hoste, nor
for the cattel that "followed them.
10 Therefore the King of Israél said, Alas,
that the Lord hathe called these thre Kigs,
to giue them into the hand of Moáb.
11 But Iehoshaphát said, Is there not here a
Prophet of the Lord, that we may inquire of the Lord by him? And one of the
King of Israels seruants answered, & said,
Here is Elishá the sonne of Shaphát, which
[f] powred water on the hands of Eliiáh.
12 Then Iehoshaphát said, [g] The worde of
the Lord is with him. Therefore the King
of Israél, and Iehoshaphát, and the King
of Edóm went downe to him.
13 And Elishá said vnto the King of Israél, [h] What haue I to do with thee? Get
thee to the Prophetes of thy father and to
the Prophetes of thy mother. And the
King of Israél said vnto him, [i] Naye: for
the Lord hathe called these thre Kings, to
giue them into the hand of Moáb.
14 Then Elishá said, As the Lord of hostes
liueth, in whose sight I stand, if it were
not, that I regarde the presence of Iehoshaphát the King of Iudáh, I wolde [k] not
haue loked towarde thee, nor sene thee.
15 But now bring me a minstrel. And when
the minstrel [l] played, the hand of the
Lord came vpon him.
16 And he said, Thus saith the Lord, Make
this valley ful of dyches.
17 For thus saith the Lord, Ye shal nether
se winde nor se raine, yet the valley shal
be filled with water, that ye may drinke,
bothe ye and your cattel, and your beastes.
18 But this is a [m] small thing in the sight of
the Lord: for he wil giue Moáb into your
hand.
19 And ye shal smite euerie strong towne
and euerie chief citie, and shal fel euerie
fayre tre, and shal stop all the fountaines
of water, and [n] marre euerie good field
with stones.
20 And in the morning when the meat offring was offred, beholde, there came water by the way of Edóm: and the countrey
was filled with water.
21 And when all the Moabites heard that
the Kings were come vp to fight against
them, thei gathered all that was able " to
put on harnes, and vpwarde, and stode in
their border.
22 And thei rose early in the morning, whē
the sunne arose vpō the water, & the Moabites sawe the water ouer against them, as
red as blood.
23 And thei said, [o] This is blood: the Kings
are surely slayne, and one hathe smiten
another: now therefore, Moáb, to the spoile.
24 And when thei came to the hoste of Israél, the Israelites arose vp, and smote the
Moabites, so that thei fled before them,
but they [p] inuaded them, and smote
Moáb.
25 And they destroyed the cities: and on
all the good field euerie mā cast his stone,
& filled them, & thei stopte all the fountaines of water, and felled all the good
trees: onely in [q] Kir-haráseth left they
the stones thereof: howbeit thei wēt about
it with slings, and smote it.
26 And when the King of Moáb sawe that
the battel was to sore for him, he toke with
him seuen hundreth men that drewe the
sworde to breake through vnto the King
of Edóm: but thei colde not.
27 Thē he toke his eldest sonne, that shulde
haue reigned in his steade, & [r] offred him
for a burnt offring vpon the wall: so that
Israél was sore grieued, and thei departed
from him, and returned to their countrey.

d Read 1. King. 22,4.

e Meaning, the Viceroy or Lieutenant of the King of Iudáh, read 1. King. 22,48.

" Ebr. that were at their fete.

f That is, who was his seruāt.

g He is able to instruct vs what is Gods wil in this point.

h He knewe that this wicked King wolde haue but vsed his counsel to serue his turne, & therefore he disdained to answer him.

i The wicked esteme not the seruants of God, but when they are driuē by very necessitie & feare of the present danger.

k God suffreth his worde to be declared to the wicked, because of the goldlie that are among thē.

l He sāg songs to Gods glorie, and so stirred vp the Prophetes heart to prophecie.

m He wil not onely miraculously giue you waters, but your enemies also into your hand.

n Thogh God bestowe his benefites for a time vpon his enemies, yet he hathe his seasons, when he wil take them away, to the intent thei might se his vengeance, which is prepared against them.

" Ebr. to girde him selfe with a girdle.

o The sodeine ioye of the wicked is but a preparacion to their destructiō, which is at hand.

p Meaning, they followed them into the townes.

q Which was one of the principal cities of the Moabites, wherein they left nothing, but the walles.

r Some referre it to the King of Edōs sonne, whome they say he had taken in the skirmish, but rather it semed to be his owne sonne, whome he offred to his gods to pacifie them, which barbarous crueltie moued the Israelites hearts of pitie to departe.

CHAP. IIII.

4 God increaseth the oyle to the poore widowe by Elishá. 12 He obteineth for the Shunammite a sonne at Gods hand. 28 Who dying, 32 He raiseth him vp agayne. 40 He maketh swete the pottage. 42 And multiplieth the loaues.

1 AND one of the wiues [a] of the sonnes of the Prophetes cryed vnto E-
lishá, saying, Thy seruāt mine housband
is dead, and thou knowest, that thy seruant
did [b] feare the Lord: and the creditour
is come to take my two sonnes to be his
[c] bondemen.
2 Then Elishá said vnto her, What shal I
do for thee? tel me, what hast thou at home. And she said, Thine handmayd hathe
nothing at home, saue a [d] pytcher of oyle.
3 And he said, Go, and borowe thee vessels
abroade of all thy neighbours, emptye
vessels, *&* spare not.
4 And when thou art come in, thou shalt
shut the dore vpon thee & vpon thy sonnes, and powre out into [e] all those vessels
and set aside those that are ful.

a Read Chap. 2,3.

b And therefore fel not into det by vnthriftines or prodigalitie, but by the hand of the Lord.

c Because I am poore and not able to pay.

d Thus God suffreth his many times to be broght to extreme necessitie, before he succor them, that afterwarde they may the more praise his mercie.

e The Prophet declareth hereby vnto her, that God neuer faileth to prouide for his seruants, their wiues & children, if they trust in him.

5 So she departed from him, and shut the
dore vpon her, and vpon her sonnes. And
they broght to her, and she powred out.
6 And when the vessels were ful, she said
vnto her sonne, Bring me yet a vessel. And
he said vnto her, There is no mo vessels.
And the oyle [f] ceased.
7 Then she came and tolde the man of
God. And he said, Go, *and* sel the oyle, &
pay them that thou art in det vnto, and liue thou and thy children of the [g] rest.
8 ¶ And on a time Elishá came to Shuné, &
there a woman of great *estimation* cõstrained him to eat bread: and as he passed by,
he turned in thether to eat bread.
9 And she said vnto her housbãd, Beholde,
I knowe now, that this is an holie man
of God that passeth by vs continually.
10 Let vs make [h] him a litle chamber, I
pray thee, with walles, and let vs set him
there a bed and a table & a stole, and a cã-
dlesticke, that he may turne in thether whẽ
he commeth to vs.
11 ¶ And on a day, he came thether and turned into the chamber, and laye therein,
12 And said to Gehazí his seruãt, Call this
Shunammite: and when he called her, she
stode before him.
13 Then he said vnto him, Say vnto her
now, Beholde, thou hast had all this great
care for vs, [i] what shal we do for thee?
Is there anie thing to be spoké for thee to
the King or to the captaine of the hoste?
And she answered, I [k] dwel among mine
owne people.
14 Againe he said, What is then to be done
for her? Then Gehazí answered, In dede
she hathe [l] no sonne, and her housband is
olde.
15 Thẽ said he, Call her. And he called her,
and she stode in the dore.
16 And he said, *At this time appointed, according to the time of life, thou shalt embrace a sonne. And she said, Oh my lord,
thou man of God, do not lye vnto thine
handmaid.
17 So the womã conceiued, and bare a sonne at that same season, according to the time of life, that Elishá had said vnto her.
18 ¶ And when the childe was growen, it fel
on a day, that he went out to his father, *&*
to the reapers.
19 And he said to his father, [m] Mine head,
mine head. Who said to *his* seruant, Beare him to his mother.
20 And he toke him and broght him to his
mother, & he sate on her knees til noone,
and dyed.
21 Then she went vp, and layed him on the
bed of the man of God, and shut *the dore*
vpon him, and went out.
22 ¶ Then she called to her housband, and
said, Send with me, I pray thee, one of the

f To augment and increase in the vessels.

g God here did not onely prouide for his seruãt, that his dets shulde be payed, & so kept his doctrine and professiõ without slãder, but also for his wife and children

h Which shulde be separate from the rest of the house, that he might more cõmodiously giue him selfe to study and prayers.

i Thus the seruants of God are not vnthankful for ẏ benefites they receyue

k I am contẽt with that that God hathe sẽt me, and can want nothing that one cã do for another.

l Which then was a reproche & therefore he wolde ẏ his master shulde pray to God for her that she might be fruteful.

Gen.18,10.

m His head aked sore, and therefore he cryed thus.

yong mẽ & one of the asses: for I wil haste
to the man of God, and come againe.
23 And he said, Wherefore wilt thou go to
him to day? *it is* nether [n] newe moone
nor Sabbath day. And she answered, "All
shalbe wel.
24 Then she sadled an asse, and said to her
seruant, Dryue, and go forwarde: stay not
for me to get vp, except I bid thee.
25 ¶ So she went, & came vnto the man of
God to mount Carmél. And whẽ the man
of God saw her "ouer against him, he said
to Gehazí his seruant, Beholde, the Shunammite.
26 Runne now, I say, to mete her, and say
vnto her, Art thou in helthe? is thine housband in helthe? *&* is the childe in helthe?
And she answered, We are in helthe.
27 And when she came to the man of God
vnto the mountaine, she [o] caught him by
his fete: and Gehazí went to her, to thrust
her away: but the man of God said, Let her
alone: for her soule is "vexed within her,
and the Lord hathe hid it from me, and
hathe not tolde it me.
28 Then she said, Did I desire a sonne of
my lord? did I not say? Disceiue me not.
29 Thẽ he said to Gehazí, Girde thy loynes, and take my staffe in thine hand, and
go thy way: [p] if thou mete anie, salute him
not: and if anie salute thee, answer him
not: and lay my staffe vpon the face of the
childe.
30 And the mother of the childe said, As the
Lord liueth, and as thy soule liueth, I wil
not leaue thee. Therefore he arose, and
followed her.
31 But Gehazí was gone before thẽ, & had
layed the staffe vpõ the face of the childe,
but he nether spake nor heard: wherefore
he returned to mete him and tolde him,
saying, The childe is not waken.
32 ¶ Then came Elishá into the house, and
beholde, the childe was dead, and layed
vpon his bed.
33 He went in therefore, and shut the dore
vpon them twaine, and prayed vnto the
Lord.
34 After he went vp, and [q] lay vpon the
childe, and put his mouth on his mouth,
and his eyes vpon his eyes, and his hands
vpon his hands, and stretched him selfe
vpon him, & the flesh of the childe waxed
warme.
35 And he wẽt *from him*, and walked vp and
downe in the house, & went vp and spred
him selfe vpon him: then the childe nee-
sed [r] seuen times, and opened his eyes.
36 Then he called Gehazí, and said, Call
this Shunammite. So he called her, which
came in vnto him. And he said vnto her,
Take thy sonne.
37 And she came, and fel at his fete, and

n For at suche times the people were wõte to resorte to ẏ Prophetes for doctrine and consolacion.

"Ebr. peace.

"Or, farre of.

o In token of humilitie and ioy that she had met with him

"Ebr. her soule is in bitternes.

p Make suche spede that nothing may let thee in ẏ way, Luk.10,4.

q The like did Eliiah to the widowes sõne at Sarephta. 1. King.17,21. and S Paul Act.20, to signifying ẏ care that oght to be in them, that beare the worde of God and are distributers of the spiritual life.

r Meaning, oftentimes.

bowed her selfe to the grounde, and toke
vp her sonne, and went out.
38 Afterwarde Elishá returned to Gilgál,
and a famine *was* in the [f] land, and the
childrẽ of the Prophetes dwelt with him.
And he said vnto his seruant, Set on the
great pot, and seethe pottage for the children of the Prophetes.
39 And one went out into the field, to gather herbes, and founde, *as it were*, a wilde
vine, and gathered thereof [t] wilde gour-
des his garment ful, and came and shred
them into the pot of pottage: for they
knewe it not.
40 So they powred out for the men to eat:
and when they did eat of the pottage, they
cryed out, and said, O thou man of God,
[u] death *is* in the pot: and they colde not eat
thereof.
41 Thẽ he said, Bring meale. And he cast it
into the pot, and said, Powre out for the
people, that they may eat: & there was none euil in the pot.
42 ¶Then came a man from Baal-shalísha,
and broght the man of God bread of the
first frutes, *euen* twentie loaues of barly, &
ful eares of corne in ỹ huske. And he said,
Giue vnto the people, that they may eat.
43 And his seruant answered, How shulde
I set this before an hundreth men? He
said againe, Giue it vnto the people that
they may eat: for thus sayth the Lord,
They shal eat, and there [x] shal remaine.
44 So he set it before them, and thei did eat,
and left ouer, according to the worde of
the Lord.

f That is, in the land of Israél.

t Which the Apoticaries call colloquintida, and is moste vehement and dangerous in purging.

u They feared ỹ they were poysoned, because of the bitternes.

x It is not the quantitie of bread that satisfieth, but ỹ blessing that God giueth.

CHAP. V.

1 *Naamán the Syrian is healed of his leprosie. 16 Elishá refuseth his gifts. 27 Gehazí is striken with leprosie, because he toke money, & raimẽt of Naamán.*

1 NOw was there one Naamán captaine
of the hoste of the King of Arám, a
great man, and honorable in the sight of
his lord, because that by him ỹ Lord had
[a] deliuered the Aramites. He also was a
mightie man *and* valiant, *but* a lepre.
2 And the Aramites had gone out by bandes, & had taken a litle maid of the land
of Israél, and she "serued Naamans wife.
3 And she said vnto her mastres, Wolde
God my lord *were* with the [b] Prophet
that is in Samaria. he wolde soone deliuer
him of his leprosie.
4 And [c] he went in, and tolde his lord,
saying, Thus and thus saith the maid that
is of the land of Israél.
5 And the King of Arám said, Go thy way
thether, and I wil send a letter vnto the
King of Israél. And he departed, and
[d] toke "with him ten talents of siluer, and
six thousand *pieces* of golde, and ten chãge of raiments,
6 And broght the letter to the King of Israél to this effect, Now when this letter is
come vnto thee, vnderstãd, that I haue sent
thee Naamán my seruãt, that thou mayest
heale him of his leprosie.
7 And when the King of Israél had red the
letter, he rent his clothes, and said, Am I
God, to kil and to giue life, that he doeth
send to me, that I shulde heale a man from
his leprosie? wherefore considre, I pray
you, and se how he seketh a quarel against
me.
8 But when Elishá the man of God had
heard that the King of Israél had rent his
clothes, he sent vnto the King, saying,
[e] Wherefore hast thou rẽt thy clothes? Let
him come now to me, and he shal knowe,
that there is a Prophet in Israél.
9 ¶Then Naamán came with his horses, &
with his charets, and stode at the dore of
the house of Elishá.
10 And Elishá sent a messenger vnto him,
saying, Go and wash thee in Iordén seuen
times, and thy flesh shal come againe to
thee, and thou shalt be cleansed.
11 But Naamán was [f] wroth & went away,
and said, Beholde, I thoght with my selfe, He wil surely come out, and stand, and
call on the Name of the Lord his God &
put his hand on the place, and heale the
leprosie.
12 Are not Abanáh and Pharpár, riuers of
Damascus, better then all the waters of Israél? may I not wash me in them, and be
cleansed? So he turned, and departed in
displeasure.
13 But his seruants came, and spake vnto
him, and said, [g] Father, *if* the Prophet had
cõmãded thee a great thing, woldest thou
not haue done it? how muche rather then,
whẽ he saith to thee, Wash, and be cleane?
14 Then went he downe, and *washed him
selfe seuen times in Iordén, according to
the saying of the mã of God: and his flesh
came againe, like vnto the flesh of a litle
childe, and he was cleane.
15 ¶And he turned againe to the man of
God, he, and all his companie, and came &
stode before him and said, Beholde, now I
know that *there is* no God in all ỹ worlde,
but in Israél: now therefore, I pray thee,
take "a rewarde of thy seruant.
16 But he said, As the Lord liueth (before
whome I stãd) I wil not receiue it. And he
wolde haue constrained him to receiue it,
[h] but he refused.
17 Moreouer Naamán said, Shal there not
be giuẽ to thy seruant two mules loade of
this earth? for thy seruant wil hencefor the
offer nether burnt sacrifice, nor offring
vnto anie other god, saue vnto the Lord.
18 Herein the Lord be [i] merciful vnto thy
seruant, that when my master goeth into
the house of Rimmón, to worship there,
and

a Here appeareth that amõg the infideles God hath his, and also that the infideles haue them in estimation, ỹ do good to their coũtrey.

" Ebr. she was before.

b Meaning, Elishá.

c That is, Naamán tolde it to the King of Syria.

d To giue this as a present to the Prophet.

" Ebr. in his hand.

e The Prophet rebuketh the King because he did not cõsider that God was true in his promes & therefore wolde not leaue his Church destitute of a Prophet, whose prayers he wolde heare, and to whome other shulde haue recourse for comforte.

f Mans reason murmureth, when it considereth onely the signes and outwarde things & hathe not regarde to the worde of God, which is there conteined.

g This declareth that seruants oght to reuerence and loue their masters as childrẽ their fathers, and likewise masters toward their seruants muste be affectioned as towarde their children.

*Luk. 4, 27.

" Ebr. blessing.

h So the Lord commandeth that they that receiue freely shulde giue also freely.

i He feleth his conscience woũded in being present at idoles seruice, and therefore desireth God to forgiue hĩ, lest others by his example might fall to idolatrie: for as for his owne parte he cõfesseth that he wil neuer serue anie, but the true God.

and leaneth on mine hand, and I bowe
my selfe in the house of Rimmón: when
I do bowe downe, *I say*, in the house of
Rimmón, the Lord be merciful vnto thy
seruant in this point.
19 Vnto whome he said, k Go in peace.
So he departed frõ him about halfe a daies
iourney of grounde.

k The Prophet did not approue his act, but after ye commune maner of speche, he biddeth him fare wel.

20 And Gehazí the seruant of Elishá the
mã of God said, Beholde, my master hathe
spared this Aramite Naamán, receiuing
not those things at his hãd that he broght:
as the Lord liueth, I wil run after him, and
take somewhat of him.
21 So Gehazí followed spedely after Naamán. And when Naamán sawe him running after him, l he light downe from the
charet to mete him, and said, Is all wel?

l Declaring thereby what honour and affectiõ he bare to the Prophet his master.

22 And he answered, All is wel: my master
hathe sent me, saying, Beholde, there be
come to me, euen now from mounte E-
phráim two yong men of the children of
the Prophetes: giue them, I pray thee, a
talent of siluer, and two chãge of garmẽts.
23 And Naamán said, Yea, take two talẽts:
and he compelled him, and bounde two talents of siluer in two bags, with two change of garments, and gaue them vnto two
of his seruãts, that they might beare them
before him.
24 And when he came to *the towre, he toke
them out of their hãds, and layed them in
the house, and sent away the men: m and
they departed.

* Or, fortresse, or, secret place.

m Naamans seruants.

25 ¶ Then he went in, and stode before his
master. And Elishá said vnto him, Whẽce
commest thou, Gehazí? And he said, Thy seruant went no whether.
26 But he said vnto him, n Went not mine
heart *with thee* when the man turned againe from his charet to mete thee? Is this a
time to take money, and to receiue garments, o and oliues, and vineyardes, and
shepe, and oxen, and men seruants, and
maid seruants?
27 The leprosie therefore of Naamán shal
cleaue vnto thee, & p to thy sede for euer.
And he wẽt out from his presence a lepre
white as snowe.

n Was not I present with thee in spirit?

o That is, money to by possessions with: meaning, yt it is detestable in the seruants of God to haue couetous mindes.

p To be an example to all suche, as by whose couetousnes Gods worde might be slandered.

CHAP. VI.

6 Elishá maketh yrõ to swimme aboue the water. 8 He discloseth the King of Syrias counsel to the King of Israél. 13 Who sending certeine to take him, were kept fast in Samaria. 24 Samaria is besieged and endureth extreme famine.

1 AND the childrẽ of the Prophetes said
vnto Elishá, Beholde, we pray thee,
the place where we dwel with thee, is to
litle for vs.
2 Let vs now go to Iordén, that we may take thence euerie man a a beame, and make
vs a place to dwel in. And he answered,
Go.

a Or a piece of wood fit to buylde with.

3 And one said, vouchsafe, I pray thee, to
go with thy seruants. And he answered, I
wil go.
4 So he went with them, and when they came to Iordén, they cut downe wood.
5 And as one was felling of a tre, the *yron
fel into the water: thẽ he cryed, & said, A-
las master, it was but borowed.

* Or, the axe head.

6 And the man of God said, Where fel it?
And he shewed him the place. Then he cut
downe *a piece* of wood, and cast in thether,
and he caused the yron to b swimme.
7 Then he said, Take it vp to thee. And he
stretched out his hand, and toke it.
8 Then the King of Arám warred against
Israél and toke counsel with his seruants,
and said, In c suche and suche a place *shal
be* my campe.

b God wroght this miraculously to confirme the autoritie of Elishá, to whome he had giuen suche abundãce of his Spirit.

c Meaning, yt he wolde lie in ambushe & take the Israelites at vnwares.

9 Therefore the man of God sent vnto the
King of Israél, saying, Beware thou go
not ouer to suche a place: for there the A-
ramites are come downe.
10 So the King of Israél sent to the place
which the man of God tolde him, & warned him of, and d saued him selfe from
thence, not once, nor twise.
11 And the heart of the King of Arám was
troubled for this thing: therefore he called his seruants and said vnto them, Wil
ye not shew me, which of vs *bewraieth our
counsel* to the King of Israél?

d The wicked conspire nothing so craftely, but God can reueile it to his seruãts & cause their counsel to be disclosed.

12 Then one of his seruants said, None, my
lord, ô King, but Elishá the Prophet that
is in Israél, telleth the King of Israél, *euen*
the wordes that thou speakest in thy e priuie chamber.
13 And he said, Go, and espie where he is,
that I may send and fetch him. And one
tolde him, sayĩg, Beholde, *he is* in Dothán.

e There is nothing so secret that thou canst go about, but he knoweth it, & discouereth it vnto his King.

14 ¶ So he sent thether horses, and charets,
and a f mightie hoste: and they came by
night, and compassed the citie.
15 And when the seruant of the mã of God
arose early to go out, beholde, an hoste
compassed the citie with horses and charets. Then his seruant said vnto him, Alas
master, how shal we do?
16 And he answered, g Feare not: for they
that be with vs, are mo then they that be
with them.
17 Then Elishá prayed, & said, Lord, I beseche thee, opẽ his eyes, h that he maie see.
And the Lord opened the eyes of the seruãt, & he loked, & beholde, the mountaine
was ful of horses & charets of fyre round
about Elishá.
18 So i they came downe to him, but Elishá
prayed vnto the Lord, & said, Smite this
people, I pray thee, with blĩdenes. And he
smote them with blindenes, according to
the worde of Elishá.
19 And Elishá said vnto them, This is not
the way, nether is this the citie: followe

f Thogh it had bene nothing in mans iudgment to haue taken Elishá, yet ye wicked euer doute & thĩke thei are neuer able to prepare power ynoug, thogh it be but against one, or a fewe.

g For he was assured of Gods helpe, & that millions of Angels camped about the godlie to deliuer them.

h That he may beholde how thou hast prepared an armie to rescue vs.

i Meaning, the Syrians his enemies, which came downe, thinking them selues sure of him.

me,and I wil lead you to the man whome
ye seke. But he [k] led them to Samaria.

k Thus he did being led by the Spirit of God & not because he soght his owne reuengance, but onely to set forthe ӯ glorie of God.

20 And when they were come to Samaria,
Elishá said, Lord,opē their eyes that they
may se. And the Lord opened their eyes,
and they sawe, and beholde, *they were* in
the middes of Samaria.
21 And the King of Israél said vnto Elishá
when he sawe them, [l] My father, shal I
smite them,shal I smite them?

l The wicked vse reuerent & graue wordes towardes the seruāts of God, when they thinke to haue anie commoditie by them, thogh in their heart they cā not abyde thē.

22 And he answered, Thou shalt not smite
them: doest thou not smite them that thou
hast taken with thy sworde, & with thy
bowe? *but* set bread and water before thē,
that they may eat and drinke and go to
their master.
23 And he made great preparacion for thē:
& when they had eaten & dronken,he sent
them away:and they went to their master.
So the bands of Arám came [m] nomore
into the land of Israél.

m For this gētle intreatie & the miracle wroght by the Prophet, did more preuaile for commune quietnes, then if they had bene ouercome in battel: for they returned no more at that time to fight against Israél, or in that Kings dayes.

24 But afterwarde Ben-hadád King of A-
rám gathered all his hoste,and went vp,&
besieged Samaria.
25 So there was a great famine in Samaria:
for lo,they besieged it vntil an asses head
was at foure score *pieces* of siluer, and the
fourth parte of a kab of dooues [n] doung
at fiue *pieces* of siluer.

n The Ebrewes write, ӯ they burned it in ӯ siege for lacke of wood.

26 And as the King of Israél was going
vpon the wall,there cryed a woman vnto
him,saying,Helpe,my lord, ô King.
27 And he said, *Seing* the Lord doeth not
succour thee,how shulde I helpe thee with
the [o] barne,or with the wine presse?

o Meaning, anie kinde of vitaile, as corne and wine, &c.

28 Also ӯ King said vnto her, What aileth
thee? And she answered, This woman said
vnto me, Giue thy sonne, that we may eat
him to day, and we wil eat my sonne tomorowe.
29 *So we sod my sonne, and did eat him:
and I said to her the day after, Giue thy
sonne,that we may eat him, but she hathe
hid her sonne.

*Deut.28,57.

30 And when the King had heard ӯ wordes
of the woman, he rent his clothes, (and as
he went vpon the wall, the people loked,
and beholde, he had sackecloth ‖within
[p] vpon his flesh)

‖Or, vnder his clothes.

p Thus hypocrites, when they fele Gods iudgements, thinke to please hī with outward ceremonies, whome in prosperitie they wil not knowe.

31 And he said, God do so to me and more
also,if the head of Elishá the sōne of Shaphát shal stand on him this day.
32 (Now Elishá sate in his house, and the
Elders sate with him) And *the King* sent a
man before him: *but* before the messenger
came to him,he said to the Elders, Se ye
not how this [q] murtherers sonne hathe
sent to take away mine head? take hede
when the messenger commeth,& shut the
dore,and hādle him roughly at the dore:
is not the sound of his masters fete behind
him?

q Meaning, Iehorám Achabs sonne who killed the Prophetes & caused Naboth to be stoned.

33 While he yet talked with thē, beholde,
the messenger came downe vnto him, &
said, Beholde,this euil cōmeth of ӯ Lord:
[r] shulde I attend on the Lord any longer?

r So the wicked fall into a rage & desperation, if they finde not sodeine remedy against their afflictions.

CHAP. VII.

1 Elishá prophesieth plentie of vitaile and other things to Samaria. 6 The Syrians runne away, and haue no man following them. 17 The prince that wolde not beleue the worde of Elishá is troden to death.

1 THen Elishá said, Heare ye the worde
of the Lord: thus saith the Lord,
[a] Tomorowe this time a measure of fine
floure *shalbe* solde for a shekel, and two
measures of barly for a shekel in the gate
of Samaria.

a The godlie are euer assured of Gods helpe in their necessities, but the times and houres are onely reueled by Gods Spirit.

2 Then a prince, on whose hand the King
[b] leaned, answered the man of God, and
said, Thogh the Lord wolde make [c] windowes in the heauē, colde this thing come
to passe? And he said, Beholde, thou shalt
se it with thine eyes, but ӯ shalt not [d] eat
thereof.

b To whome the King gaue the charge & ouersight of things, as vers.17.

c He mocketh at ӯ Prophetes wordes, saying that if God rained downe corne frō heauen ӯ this colde not come to passe.

d Thy infidelitie shalbe punished herein, whē thou shalt se this miracle & yet not be partaker thereof.

3 Now there were foure leprouse men at
ӯ [e] entring in of ӯ gate: and they said one
to another, Why sit we here vntil we dye?

e For it was commanded in the Lawe that they shulde dwel aparte & not amōg their brethren, Leui.13,46.

4 If we say, We wil entre into the citie, the
famine is in the citie, & we shal dye there:
and if we sit here, we dye also. Now therefore come, and let vs fall into the campe
of the Aramites: if thei saue our liues, we
shal liue: & if they kil vs, we are but dead.
5 So they rose vp in the twilight, to go to
the campe of the Aramites: and when thei
were come to the vtmoste parte of the
campe of the Aramites, lo, there was no
man there.
6 For the Lord had caused the campe of ӯ
Aramites to heare a [f] noise of charets & a
noise of horses, & a noise of a great armie, so ӯ they said one to another, Beholde, the King of Israél hathe hired against
vs the Kings of the Hittites, & the Kings
of the Egyptians to come vpon vs.

f Thus God nedeth no great preparacion to destroy the wicked, thogh they be neuer so many for he can scater them with a smale noise or shaking of a leafe.

7 Wherefore they arose, and fled in the
twilight, & left their tentes & their horses, & their asses, *euen* the campe as it was,
and [g] fled for their liues.

g The wicked nede no greater enemie thē their owne cōscience to pursue them.

8 And when these lepers came to ӯ vtmost
part of the campe, they entred into one
tent, and did eat and drinke, and caried
thence siluer and golde, and raiment, and
went and hid it: after they returned, and
entred into another tent, & caried thence
also, and went, and hid it.
9 Then said one to another, We do not
wel: this day is a day of good tidings, and
we holde our peace. if we tary til day
light, some ‖mischief wil come vpon vs.
Now therefore come, let vs go, and tel
the Kings housholde.

‖Or, we shalbe punished for our faute.

10 So they came, & called vnto the porters
of the citie, & tolde thē, saying, We came
to the campe of the Aramites, & lo, there
was no man there, nether voyce of mā, but
horses

horses tyed and asses tyed : and the tentes
are as they were.
11 And the porters cryed and declared to
the Kings house within.
12 Then the King arose in the night, and
said vnto his seruants, [h] I wil shewe you
now, what the Aramites haue done vnto
vs. They knowe that we are affamished,
therefore they are gone out of the campe
to hide them selues in the field, saying,
When thei come out of the citie, we shal
catche them aliue, and get into the citie.
13 And one of his seruants answered, and
said, Let men take now fiue of the horses
that remaine, & are left in the *citie*, (beholde, they are euen as all the [i] multitude of
Israél that are left therein : beholde, *I say*,
they are as the multitude of the Israelites that are cõsumed) & we wil send to se.
14 So they toke *two charets of horses, and
the King sent after the hoste of the Aramites, saying, Go and se.
15 And they went after them vnto Iordén,
and lo, all the way was ful of clothes and
vessels which the Aramites had cast from
them in their haste : & the messengers returned, and tolde the King.
16 Then the people went out and spoiled
the campe of the Aramites: so a measure
of fine floure was at a shekel, and two measures of barly at a shekel [k] according to ŷ
worde of the Lord.
17 And the King gaue the prince (on whose
hand he leaned) the charge of the gate, &
the people [l] trode vpon him in the gate,
and he dyed, as the man of God had said,
which spake it, when the King came downe to him.
18 And it came to passe, as the man of God
had spoken to the King, sayĩg, Two measures of barly at a shekel and a measure of
fine floure shalbe at a shekel, tomorowe a-
bout this time in the gate of Samaria.
19 But the prince had answered the man
of God, and said, Thogh the Lord wolde
make windowes in the heauen, colde it
come so to passe? And he said, Beholde,
ŷ shalt se it with thine eies, but thou shalt
not eat thereof.
20 And so it came vnto him : for the people trode vpon him in the gate, and he
dyed.

h He mistrusted ŷ Prophetes wordes, & therefore colde beleue nothing, as thei which are more politike then godlie euer cast more perils then nedeth.

i There are no more left, but thei, or the rest are consumed with the famine as the rest of the people.

*Or, *two horses of the charet, which were accustomed to drawe in the charet.*

k Which he spake by the mouthe of Elishá. vers. 1.

l As the people preaced out of ŷ gate to runne to ŷ Syrians tentes where they had heard was meat, & great spoile left.

CHAP. VIII.

1 Elishá prophecieth vnto the Shunammite the dearth of seuen yere. 12 He prophecieth to Hazaél that he shalbe King of Syria. 15 He reigneth after Benhadád. 16 Iehorám reigneth ouer Iudah. 20 Edóm falleth from Iudáh. Ohoziáh succedeth Iehorám.

1 THen spake Elishá vnto the woman,
*whose sonne he had restored to life,
saying, Vp, and go, thou, and thine house,
and soiourne where thou [a] canst soiourne:
for the Lord hathe called for a famine, &
it cõmeth also vpon the land seuen yeres.
2 And the woman arose, and did after the
saying of the man of God, and went bothe
she & her housholde and soiourned in the
land of the Philistíms seuen yeres.
3 ¶ And at the seuen yeres end, the woman
returned out of the land of the Philistíms
and went out [b] to call vpon the King for
her house and for her land.
4 And the King talked with Gehazí the
seruãt of the man of God, saying, Tel me,
I praye thee, all the great actes, that Elishá
hathe done.
5 And as he tolde [c] the King, how he had
restored one dead to life, beholde, the woman, whose sonne he had raised to life,
called vpon the King for her house & for
her land. Then Gehazí said, My lord, ô
King, this is the woman, and this is her
sonne, whome Elishá restored to life.
6 And when the King asked the womã, she
tolde him: so the King appointed her an
Eunuche, saying, Restore thou all that are
hers, and all the [d] frutes of *her* landes since
ŷ day she left the land, euẽ vntil this time.
7 ¶ Then Elishá came to Damascus, & Ben-
hadád the King of Arám was sicke. & one
tolde him, saying, The man of God is
come hether.
8 And the King said vnto Hazaél, Take
a present in thine hand, and go mete the
man of God, that thou maiest inquire of
the Lord by him, saying, Shal I recouer
of this disease?
9 ¶ So Hazaél went to mete him, and toke
the present in his hand, and of euerie [e] good thing of Damascus, *euen* the burden
of fourty camels, and came and stode before him, and said, Thy sonne Ben-hadád
King of Arám hathe sent me to thee, saying, Shal I recouer of this disease?
10 And Elishá said to him, Go, *&* say vnto
him, Thou shalt [f] recouer: howbeit ŷ Lord
hathe shewed me, that he shal surely dye.
11 And he loked vpon him stedfastely til
Hazaél was ashamed, and the man of God
wept.
12 And Hazaél said, Why wepeth my lord?
And he answered, Because I knowe the e-
uil that thou shalt do vnto the children of
Israél: *for* their strong cities shalt thou set
on fyre, and their yõg men shalt thou slay
with the sworde, and shalt dashe their infants *against the stones*, & rent in pieces their
women with childe.
13 Then Hazaél said, What? is thy seruant a
[g] dog, that I shulde do this great thing?
And Elishá answered, The Lord hathe
shewed me, ŷ thou shalt be Kĩg of Arám.
14 ¶ So he departed from Elishá, and came
to his master, who said to him, What said
Elishá to thee? And he answered, He tolde
me that thou shuldest recouer.

Chap. 4,35.
a Where thou canst finde a commodious place to dwel, where as is plentie.

b That is to complaine on the which had taken her possessiõs whiles she was absẽt.

c Gods wõderful prouidence appeareth in this that he caused ŷ King to be desirous to heare of hĩ, whome before he contemned, & also hereby prepared an entrance to the poore widowes sute.

d The King caused that to be iustely restored which was wrongfully holden frõ her.

e Of all the chiefest & precious things of ŷ coũtrey.

f Meanĩg that he shulde recouer, of this disease: but he knewe ŷ this messenger Hazaél shulde slaie him to obteine the kingdome.

g That I shulde be without all humanitie and pitie.

15 And on the morow he toke a thicke cloth
and dipt it in water, and [h] spread it
on his face, and he dyed: & Hazaél reigned in his steade.
16 ¶ * Now in the fifte yere of Iorám the
sonne of Aháb King of Israél, and of Iehoshaphát King of Iudáh, [i] Iehorám the
sonne of Iehoshaphát King of Iudáh began [k] to reigne.
17 He was two and thirtie yere olde, when
he began to reigne: and he reigned eight
yere in Ierusalém.
18 And he walked in the wayes of the Kīgs
of Israél, as did the house of Aháb: for ye
[l] daughter of Aháb was his wife, and
he did euil in the sight of the Lord.
19 Yet the Lord wolde not destroy Iudáh,
for Dauid his seruants sake, * as he had
promised him to giue him a light & to
his children for euer.
20 ¶ In those dayes Edóm [m] rebelled from
vnder the hand of Iudáh, & made a King
ouer them selues.
21 Therefore Iorám went to Zaír, and all
his charets with him, & he arose by night,
and smote the Edomites which were a-
bout him with the captaines of the charets, and the people fled into their tentes.
22 So Edóm rebelled from vnder the hand
of Iudáh vnto this day. then [n] Libnáh rebelled at that same time.
23 Concerning the rest of the actes of Iorám and all that he did, are they not writen in the boke of the Chronicles of the
Kings of Iudáh?
24 And Iorám slept with his fathers, & was
buryed with his fathers in the citie of
Dauid. And * Ahaziáh his sonne reigned
in his steade.
25 ¶ In the twelft yere of Iorám the sonne
of Aháb King of Israél did Ahaziáh the
sonne of Iehorám King of Iudáh begin
to reigne.
26 [o] Two and twentie yere olde was Ahaziáh when he began to reigne, & he reigned one yere in Ierusalém, & his mothers
name *was* Athaliáh ye daughter of Omrí
King of Israél.
27 And he walked in the way of the house
of Aháb, and did euil in the sight of the
Lord, like the house of Aháb: for he was
the sonne in lawe of the house of Aháb.
28 And he went with Iorám the sonne of
Aháb to warre agaīst Hazaél King of A-
rám in [p] Ramóth Gileád, and the Aramites smote Iorám.
29 And King Iorám returned to be healed
in [q] Izreél of the wounds which the Aramites had giuen him at Ramah, when he
foght against Hazaél King of Arám.
And Ahaziáh the sonne of Iehorám King
of Iudáh went downe to se Iorám the
sonne of Aháb in Izreél, because he was
sicke.

h Vnder pretence to refresh or ease him, he styfled him with this cloth.
2.Chro 21, 4.
i Read Chap. 1,17.
k He was cōfirmed in his kingdome after his fathers death.
l The holy Gost sheweth hereby what danger it is to ioyne with infideles.
2.Sam.7,13.
m Which had bene subiect from Dauids time vntil this time of Iehoram.
n This was a citie in Iudáh giuen to the Leuites, Iosh. 21,13, and after turned from King Iehorám because of his idolatrie.
2.Chro. 22,1.
o Which is to be vnderstand, that he was made King, when his father reigned, but after his fathers death he was confirmed King, whē he was fourtie two yere olde, as 2.Chr.22,2.
p Which was a citie in ye tribe of Gad beyonde Iordén.
q This is a citie belonging to the tribe of Isschár.

CHAP. IX.

6 Iehú is made King of Israél, 24 And killeth Iehorám the King thereof, 27 And Ahaziáh, otherwise called Ochozias, the King of Iudáh, 33 And causeth Iezébel to be cast downe out of a window, and the dogs did eat her.

1 THen Elishá the Prophet called one of
the children of the Prophetes, and
said vnto him, * [a] Girde thy loynes and
take this boxe of oyle in thine hand, and
get thee to Ramóth Gileád.
2 And when thou commest thether, loke
where *is* Iehú the sonne of Iehoshaphát,
the sonne of Nimshí, and go, and make
him arise vp from among his brethren, &
lead him" to a secret chamber.
3 Then take the boxe of oyle, and powre it
on his head, & say, Thus sayeth the Lord,
I haue anointed thee for King ouer Israél.
then open the dore, and flee without anie
tarying.
4 So the seruant of the Prophet gate him
to Ramóth Gileád.
5 And whē he came in, beholde, the captaines of the armie were sitting. And he said,
I haue a message to thee, ô captaine. And
Iehú said, Vnto which of all vs? And he
answered, To thee, ô captaine.
6 And he arose, and went into the house,
and he powred the oyle on his head, and
said vnto him, Thus saith the Lord God
of Israél, I haue [b] anointed thee *for* King
ouer the people of the Lord, *euen* ouer Israél.
7 And thou shalt smite the house of Aháb
thy master, that I may auenge the blood
of my seruants the Prophetes, & the blood of all the seruants of the Lord * of the
hand of Iezebel.
8 For the whole house of Aháb shalbe destroyed: and * I wil cut of from Aháb, him
that maketh water against the wall, aswel
him that is shut vp, as him that is left in
Israél.
9 And I wil make the house of Aháb like
the house * of Ieroboám the sonne of Nebát, & like the house * of Baashá the sonne
of Ahiiáh.
10 And the dogs shal eat Iezébel in the
field of Izreél, and there shalbe none to
burye her. And he opened the dore, and
fled.
11 ¶ Then Iehú came out to the [c] seruants
of his lord. And *one* said vnto him, Is all
wel? wherefore came this [d] mad fellowe
to thee? And he said vnto them, Ye knowe
the man, and what his talke was.
12 And thei said, It is false, tel vs it now.
Then he said, Thus and thus spake he to
me, saying, Thus saith the Lord, I haue
anointed thee for King ouer Israél.

1.Kin.19, 19.
a Prepare thy selfe to go diligently about thy busines: for in those countreis they vsed long garments, which they tucked vp, when they wēt about earnest busines.
" Ebr. from chāber to chamber.
b This annointing was for Kings, Priests & Prophetes, which were all figures of Messiáh, in whome these thre offices were accomplished.
1.Kin.21, 21.
1.Kin.14, 10. & 21,21.
1.Kin.14, 10. & 21,30.
1.King.16, 3.
c That is, the rest of the armie, whome he called before, his brethren. vers.2.
d In this estimation the worlde hathe the ministers of God. notwithstādig for asmuche as ye worlde hathe euer slandered the children of God, (yea they called ye sonne of God a deceiuer & said he had ye deuil) therefore they oght not to be discouraged.

13 Then they made haste, and toke euerie
man his garment, and put it vnder him
on the top of the staires, and blewe the
trumpet, saying, Iehú is King.
14 So Iehú the sonne of Iehoshapát the
sonne of Nimshí cõspired against Iorám
(Now Iorám kept Ramóth Gileád, he &
all Israél because of Hazaél Kĩg of Arám.
15 And *King Iorám returned to be healed in Izreél of the woundes, which the
Aramites had giuen him, when he foght
with Hazaél King of Arám) and Iehú
said, If it be your mindes, let no man departe and escape out of the citie, to go &
tel in Izreél.
16 So Iehú gate vp into a charet, and went
to Izreél: for Iorám laye there, and [e] Ahaziáh King of Iudáh was come downe to
se Iorám.
17 And the watcheman that stode in the
towre in Izreél, spyed the companie of Iehú as he came, and said, I se a companie.
And Iehorám said, Take a horseman and
send to mete them, that he may say, Is it
peace?
18 So there went one on horsebacke to mete
him, and said, Thus saith the King, Is it
peace? And Iehú said, What hast thou to
do with peace? *turne behinde me. And
the watchemã tolde, saying, The messenger came to them, but he commeth not
againe.
19 Then he sent out another on horsebacke, which came to them, and said, Thus
saith the King, Is it peace? And Iehú answered, What hast thou to do with peace?
turne behinde me.
20 And the watchman tolde, saying, He came to them *also*, but commeth not againe,
and the marching *is* like the marching of
Iehú the sonne of Nimshí: for he mar-
cheth [f] furiously.
21 ¶ Then Iehorám said, Make readie: and
his charet was made readie. And Iehorám King of Israél and Ahaziáh King of
Iudáh went out ether of them in his charet against Iehú, and met him in the field
of Nabóth the Izreelite.
22 And when Iehorám sawe Iehú, he said,
Is it peace, Iehú? And he answered, What
[g] peace? the whoredomes of thy mother
Iezébel, and her witchcraftes *are* yet in
great nomber.
23 Then Iehorám turned his hand, & fled,
and said to Ahaziáh, O Ahaziáh, *there is*
treason.
24 But Iehú toke a bowe in his hand, and
smote Iehorám betwene the shulders, that
the arowe went through his heart: and he
fel downe in his charet.
25 Thẽ said *Iehú* to Bidkár a captaine, Take, *&* cast him in some place of the field of
Nabóth the Izreelite: for I remember

Chap. 8, 29.

e God had thus ordeined, as is red 2. Chro. 22, 7. ÿ this wicked & idolatrous King, who was more ready to gratifie wicked Iorám, thẽ to obey ÿ wil of God, shulde perish wt him, by whose meanes he thoght to haue bene stronger.

Or, followe me.

f As one that went earnestly about his enterprise.

g Meanĩg that forasmuche as God is their enemie because of their sinnes, that he wil euer stirre vp some to reuenge his cause.

that when I and thou rode together after
Aháb his father, the Lord *layed this burden vpon him.
26 *Surely I haue sene yesterday the blood
of Nabóth, and the blood of his [h] sonnes,
said the Lord, and I wil render it thee in
this field, saith the Lord: now therefore
take *and* cast him in the field, according to
the worde of the Lord.
27 But when Ahaziáh the King of Iudáh
sawe this, he fled by the way of the gardẽ
house: and Iehú pursued after him, & said,
Smite him also in the charet: *& thei smote
him* in the going vp to Gur, which is by
Ibleám. And he fled to [i] Megiddó, and
there dyed.
28 And his seruants caryed him in a charet
to Ierusalém, & buryed him in his sepulchre with his fathers in ÿ citie of Dauid.
29 ¶ And in the [k] eleuenth yere of Iorám
the sonne of Aháb, begã Ahaziáh to reigne ouer Iudáh.
30 And when Iehú was come to Izreél, Iezébel heard of it, and peinted her face, and
tired her head,[l] & loked out at a wyndow.
31 And as Iehú entred at the gate, she said,
Had [m] Zimri peace, wc slewe his master?
32 And he lift vp his eyes to the windowe,
and said, Who is on my side, who? Then
two *or* thre of her *Eunuches loked vnto
him.
33 And he said, Cast her downe: and they
cast her downe, [n] and he sprinkled of her
blood vpon the wall, and vpon the horses,
and he trode her vnder fote.
34 And whẽ he was come in, he did eat and
drinke, and said, Visite now yonder cursed
woman, and bury her: for she is a [o] Kings
daughter.
35 And thei went to bury her, but thei foũde no more of her then the skul & the fete,
and the palmes of her hands.
36 Wherefore they came againe and tolde
him. And he said, This is the worde of the
Lord, which he spake *by his seruãt Eliiáh
the Tishbite, saying, *In the field of Izreél shal the dogs eat the flesh of Iezébel.
37 And the carkeis of Iezébel shalbe as
doung vpõ the grounde in the field of Izreél, so ÿ none shal say, [p] This is Iezébel.

CHAP. X.

6 Iehú causeth the seuentie sonnes of Aháb to be slayne, 13 And after that fourty and two of Ahaziahs brethren 25 He killeth also all the priests of Baal. 35 After his death his sonne reigneth in his steade.

1 AHáb had now seuentie [a] sonnes in
Samaria. And Iehú wrote letters, &
sent to Samaria vnto the rulers of Izreel,
& to the Elders, and to the bringers vp of
Ahabs children, to this effect,
2 Now when this letter commeth to you,
(for ye haue with you your masters sonnes, ye haue with you bothe charets and

Or, spake this prophecie against him.

1. King. 21, 29

h By this place it is euidẽt, that Iezébel caused bothe Nabóth & his sonnes to be put to death ÿ Aháb might enioye his vineyarde more quietly: for els his children might haue claimed possession.

i After that he was wounded in Samaria he fled to Megiddó, which was a citie of Iudáh.

k That is, eleuen whole yeres: for Chap. 8, 25 before, when he said that he began to reigne the twelfte yere of Iorám, he taketh parte of ÿ yere for the whole.

l Being of an hautie & cruel nature, she wolde stil reteine her princelie state and dignitie.

m As thogh she wolde say, Can any traitor, or any ÿ riseth against his superior, haue good successe: read 1. King 16, 10.

Or, chief seruants.

n This he did by the mocion of the Spirit of God, ÿ her blood shulde be shed, that had shed the blood of innocents, to be a spectacle and example of Gods iudgements to all tyrants.

o To wit, of ÿ Kĩg of Zidon, 1. King. 16, 31.

Ebr. by the hand of

1. King. 21, 23

p Thus Gods iudgements appeare euen in this worlde against thẽ that suppresse his worde & persecute his seruants.

a The Scripture vseth to call thẽ sonnes wc are ether children, or nephewes.

horses, and a defensed citie, and armour)
3 Cōsider therefore which of your masters
sonnes is best and moste mete, & [b] set him
on his fathers throne, and fight for your
masters house.

b He wrote this to proue them whether thei wolde take his parte or no.

4 But thei were excedingly afraied, & said,
Beholde, two Kings colde not stand before him, how shal we then stand?
5 And he that was gouernour of *Ahabs*
house, and he that ruled the citie, and the
Elders, and the bringers vp of the childrē
sent to Iehú, saying, We are thy seruants,
and wil do all that thou shalt byd vs: we
wil make no King: do what semeth good
to thee.
6 ¶ Then he wrote another letter to them,
sayĩg, If ye be mine, & wil obey my voice,
[c] take the heades of the men *that are* your
masters sonnes, and come to me to Izreél
by tomorowe this time. (Now the Kings
sonnes, *euen* seuenty persones *were* with
the great men of the citie, which broght
them vp)

c God as a iuste iudge punisheth the wicked children of wicked parents vnto the thirde & fourt generacion.

7 And when the letter came to them, they
toke the Kings sonnes, and slewe the seuenty persones, and laied their heades in
baskets, and sent them vnto him to Izreél.
8 ¶ Then there came a messenger & tolde
him, saying, Thei haue broght the heades
of the Kings sonnes. And he said, Let thē
lay them on two heapes at the entring in
of the gate vntil the morning.
9 And whē it was day, he went out, & stode
& said to all the people, Ye be [d] righteous:
beholde, I conspired against my master, &
slewe him: but who slewe all these?
10 Knowe now that there shal fall vnto the
earth nothing of the worde of the Lord,
which the Lord spake concerning ỳ house
of Aháb: for the Lord hathe broght to
passe the things that he spake " by his seruant * Eliiáh.

d Ye can not iustely cōdēne me for the Kings death, seing ye haue done the like to his posteritie: for ỳ Lord commanded me, and moued you to execute this his iudgement.
" Ebr. by the hand of.
* 1. King. 21, 29

11 So Iehú slewe all that remayned of the
house of Aháb in Izreél, and all that were
great with him, and his familiars and
his [e] priests, so that he let none of his remaine.

e Meaning, ỳ were the idolatro' priests.

12 ¶ And he arose, and departed and came
to Samaria. *And* as Iehú was in the waye
by an house where the shepherdes did
shere,
13 He met with the brethren of Ahaziáh
King of Iudáh and said, Who are ye? And
thei answered, We are the brethren of A-
haziáh, & go downe to salute the children
of the King and the children of the quene.
14 And he said, Take them aliue. And thei
toke them aliue, & slewe them at the weil
beside the house where ỳ shepe are shorne,
euen two and fourtie men, and he [f] left not
one of them.

f Thus Gods vengeance is vpon thē that haue any parte or familiaritie with the wicked.

15 ¶ And when he was departed thence, he
met with Iehonadáb the sonne of Recháb
comming to mete him, and he [g] " blessed
him, and said to him, Is thine heart vpright, as mine heart is toward thine? And
Iehonadáb answered, Yea, douteles. *Then*
giue me thine hand. And when he had giuen him his hand, he toke him vp to him
into the charet.

g For he feared God and lamented the wickednes of those times: therefore Iehú was glad to ioyne with him: of Recháb read Iere. 35, 2.
" Or, praised God for him.

16 And he said, Come with me, and se the
zeale that I haue for the Lord: so they
made him ryde in his charet.
17 And when he came to Samaria, he slewe
all that remained vnto Aháb in Samaria,
til he had destroyed him, according to the
worde of the Lord, which he spake to E-
liiáh.
18 Then Iehú assembled all the people, and
said vnto them, Aháb serued [h] Báal a
litle, *but* Iehú shal serue him muche
more.
19 Now therefore call vnto me all the prophetes of Báal, all his seruants, and all his
priests, and let not a man be lacking: for I
haue a great sacrifice for Báal: whosoeuer
is lacking, he shal not liue. But Iehú did
it by a subtiltie to destroye the seruants
of Báal.

h Here Báal is taken for Ashteróth the idole of the Zidonians, ỳ Iezébel caused to be worshiped, as it is also so vsed. 1. King. 16, 32. & 22, 54.

20 And Iehú said, " Proclaime a solemne
assēblie for Báal. And thei proclaimed it.

" Ebr. sanctifie.

21 So Iehú sent vnto all Israél, and all the
seruants of Báal came, and there was not a
mā left that came not. And thei came into
the house of Báal, & the house of Báal was
ful from end to end.
22 Then he said vnto him that had ỳ charge of the vestrie, Bring forthe vestements
for all the seruāts of Báal. And he broght
them out vestements.
23 And when Iehú went, & Iehonadáb the
sonne of Recháb into the house of Báal,
he said vnto the seruants of Báal, Searche
diligently, and loke, lest there be here with
you *any* of the [i] seruants of the Lord, but
the seruants of Báal onely.
24 And when thei went in to make sacrifice
& burnt offrĩg, Iehú appointed fourescore
men without, and said, If anie of the men
whome I haue broght into your hands,
escape, " his soule *shalbe* for his soule.

i Thus God wolde haue his seruants preserued, and idolaters destroyed: as in his Lawe he giueth expresse commādement, Deut. 13.
" Or, he shal dye for him.

25 And when he had made an end of the
burnt offring, Iehú said to the garde, and
to the captaines, Go in, slaye them, let not
a man come out. And they smote thē with
the edge of the sworde. And the garde, and
the captaines cast them out, & went vnto
the [k] citie, *where was* the temple of Báal.

k Which citie was nere to Samaria.

26 And they broght out the images of the
temple of Báal, and burnt them.
27 And they destroyed the image of Báal,
and threwe downe the house of Báal, and
made a iakes of it vnto this day.
28 So Iehú destroyed Báal out of Israél.
29 But frō the sinnes of Ieroboám ỳ sonne
of

of Nebát which made Israél to sinne, Iehú departed not frõ them, *nether from* the
golden calues that were in Beth-él and
that were in Dan.
30 ¶ And the Lord said vnto Iehú, Because
thou hast diligently executed that which
was right in mine eyes, *and* hast done vnto
the house of Aháb according to all thĩgs
that were in mine heart, *therefore* shal thy
[l] sonnes vnto the fourte *generacion* sit on
the throne of Israél.
31 But Iehú regarded not to walke in ỹ lawe
of ỹ Lord God of Israél with all his heart:
for he departed not from the sinnes of Ie-
robeám which made Israél to sinne.
32 In those dayes the Lord began to "lothe
Israél, and Hazaél smote them in all the
coastes of Israél,
33 From Iordén Eastwarde, *euen* all the land
of Gileád, the Gadites, and the Reubenites, and them that were of Manasséh, from
Aroér (which is by the riuer Arnón) and
Gileád and Bashán.
34 Concerning the rest of the actes of Iehú, and all that he did, and all his valiant
dedes, are they not writen in the boke of
the Chronicles of the Kings of Israél?
35 And Iehú slept with his fathers, and they
buryed him in Samaria, and Iehoaház his
sonne reigned in his steade.
36 And the time that Iehú reigned ouer Israél in Samaria is eight and twẽtie yeres.

l Thus God approueth & rewardeth his zeale, in executing Gods iudgement, albeit his wickednes was afterward punished.

"Or, to cut them of.

CHAP. XI.

1 Athaliáh putteth to death all the Kings sonnes, except Ioásh the sonne of Ohoziáh. 4 Ioash is appointed King 15 Iehoiada causeth Athaliah to be slaine 17 He maketh a couenant betwene God and the people. 18 Baal and his priests are destroyed.

1 THen* Athaliáh ỹ mother of Ahaziáh
whẽ she saw that her sonne was dead,
she arose, & destroyed all the [a] Kings sede.
2 But Iehoshéba ỹ daughter of King Iorám,
and sister to Ahaziáh [b] toke Ioásh the sonne of Ahaziáh, & stale him from among
the Kings sonnes that shulde be slaine,
bothe him and his nource, *keping them* in the
bed [c] chãber, and they hid him from A-
thaliáh, so that he was not slaine.
3 And he was with her hid in the house of
the Lord six yere: and Athaliáh did reigne
ouer the land.
4 ¶* And the seuẽth yere [d] Iehoiadá sent &
toke the captaines ouer hundreths, with
other captaines and them of the garde, and
caused them to come vnto him into the
house of the Lord, & made a couenãt with
thẽ, & toke an oth of them in the house of
the Lord, & shewed thẽ the Kings sonne.
5 And he cõmanded thẽ, saying, This is it
that ye must do, The third parte of [e] you,
that cometh on the Sabbath, shal [f] warde
towarde the Kings house.
6 And *another* third parte in ỹ gate of [g] Sur:
and *another* third parte in the gate behinde

2.Chro.22,10.

a Meaning all ỹ posteritie of Iehoshaphát, to whome the kingdome apperteined. thus God vsed the crueltie of this woman to destroye the whole familie of Aháb.

b The Lord promised to mainteine the familie of Dauid and not to quenche the light thereof: therefore he moued the heart of Iehoshéba to preserue him

c Where the Priests did lye.

2.Chro.23,3.

d The chief Priest Iehoshebas housbãd.

e Of the Leuites, which had charge of the keping of the Tẽple and kept watche by course.

f That none shulde come vpon thẽ, while they were crowning the King

g Called the East gate of the Temple.

them of the garde: & ye shal kepe watche
"in the house of Massáh.
7 And two partes of you, *that is*, all that [h] go
out on the Sabbath day, shal kepe ỹ watche
of the house of the Lord about the King.
8 And ye shal compasse the King round a-
bout, euerie man with his weapon in his
hand, and whosoeuer commeth within the
ranges, let him be slaine: be you with the
King, as he goeth out and in.
9 ¶ And the captaines of the hundreths did
according to all that Iehoiadá the Priest
cõmanded, & they toke euerie man his mẽ
that entred in *to their charge* on the [i] Sabbath with them that went out *of it* on the
Sabbath, and came to Iehoiadá the Priest.
10 [k] And the Priest gaue to the captaines of
hundreths the speares and the shields that
were King Dauids, and were in the house
of the Lord.
11 And the garde stode, euerie mã with his
weapon in his hand, from the right side of
the house to the left side, about the altar &
about the house, round about the King.
12 Then he broght out [l] the Kings sonne,
and put the crowne vpõ him and *gaue him*
[m] the Testimonie, & they made him King:
also they annointed him, and clapt their
hands, and said, God saue the King.
13 ¶ And when Athaliáh heard the noyse of
the running of the people, she came in to
the people in the house of the Lord.
14 And when she loked, beholde, the King
stode by a [n] piller, as the maner was, and
the princes and the trũpeters by the King,
and all the people of the land reioyced, &
blue with trumpets. Then Athaliáh rent
her clothes, and cryed, Treason, treason.
15 But Iehoiadá the Priest commanded the
captaines of the hũdreths that had the rule of the hoste, and said vnto them, Haue
her forthe " of the ranges, & he that [o] followeth her, let him dye by the sworde: for
the Priest had said, let her not be slayne
in the house of the Lord.
16 Then they layed hãds on her, & she went
by the way, by the which the horses go to the
house of ỹ King, and there was she slaine.
17 And Iehoiadá made a couenant betwene
the Lord and [p] the King, and the people,
that they shulde be the Lords people: likewise betwene the [q] King and ỹ people.
18 Then all the people of the land wẽt into
the house of Báal, and destroyed it with
his altars, & his images brake they downe
courageously, and slewe Mattán the priest
of Báal before the [r] altars: & the [s] Priest
set a garde ouer the house of the Lord.
19 Then he toke the captaines of hũdreths,
and the *other* captaines, and the garde, and
all the people of the land: and they broght
the King from the house of the Lord, and
came by ỹ way of the gate of ỹ garde to ỹ

"Or, that none breake his ordre.

h Whose charge is ended.

i Read vers. 5, and 7.

k To wit, Iehoiadá.

l That is, Ioásh, which had bene kept secret six yeres.

m Meaning, ỹ Lawe of God, which is his chiefcharge & whereby onely his throne is established.

n Where the Kings place was in the Temple.

"Or, out of the Temple.

o To take her parte.

p That bothe the King and ỹ people shulde mainteine the true worship of God and destroy all idolatrie.

q That he shulde gouerne, and they obey in the feare of God.

r Euen in the place where he had blasphemed God and thoght to haue bene holpẽ by his idole, there God powred his vengeance vpõ him

s To wit, Iehoiadá.

Kings house: & he sate him downe on the
throne of the Kings.
20 And all the people of the land reioyced,
and the citie was in quiet. e for they had
slaine Athaliáh with the sworde beside
the Kings house.
21 Seuen yere olde was Iehoásh when he
began to reigne.

e Which by her crueltie & persecuciõ had vexed ỹ whole land before.

CHAP. XII.

6 Iehoásh maketh prouision for the repairing of the Tẽple. 16 He stayeth the King of Syria by a present frõ comming against Ierusalém. 20 He is killed by two of his seruants.

2.Chro.14,1.

1 IN *the seuẽth yere of Iehú Iehoásh began to reigne, and reigned fourty yeres
in Ierusalém, and his mothers name was
Zibiáh of Beer-shéba.
2 And Iehoásh did that which was good in
the sight of the Lord all his time that a Iehoiadá the Priest taught him.
3 But b the hie places were not taken away:
for the people offred yet and burnt incense in the hie places.
4 ¶ And Iehoásh said to the Priests, All the
siluer of dedicate things that be broght to
the house of the Lord, *that is*, the money of
them that are vnder the c counte, the money that euerie man is set at, *and* all the
money that one offreth willingly, and
bringeth into the house of the Lord,
5 Let the Priests take it to them, euerie mã
of his acquaintance: and they shal repaire
the broken d places of the house, wheresoeuer anie decaye is found.
6 ¶ Yet in the thre and twentieth yere of
King Iehoásh the Priests had not mẽded
that which was decayed in the Temple.
7 Then King Iehoásh called for Iehoiadá
the Priest, and the *other* Priests, and said
vnto them, Why repaire ye not the ruines
of the Temple? now therefore e receiue
nomore money of your acquaintance, excepte ye deliuer it to *repaire* the ruines of
the Temple.
8 So the Priests consented to receiue nomore money of the people, nether to repaire the decayed places of the Temple.
9 Then Iehoiadá the Priest toke a chest &
bored an hole in the lid of it, and set it
beside the altar, on the f right side, as euerie man commeth into the Temple of the
Lord. And the Priests that kept the "dore,
put therein all the money that was broght
into the house of the Lord.
10 And when they sawe there was muche
money in the chest, the Kings secretary
came vp & the hie Priest, and put it vp
after that they had tolde the money that
was founde in the house of the Lord,
11 And they gaue the money made ready
into the hands of them, g that vndertoke
the worke, *and* that had the ouersight of
the house of the Lord: and they payed it
out to the carpenters and buylders that
wroght vpon the house of the Lord,
12 And to the masons and hewers of stone,
and to bye tymber and hewed stone, to
repaire that was decayed in the house of
the Lord, and for all that which was layed
out for the reparacion of the Temple.
13 Howbeit there was h not made for the
house of the Lord bowles of siluer, instrumẽts of musike, basons, trumpets, nor anie
vessels of golde, or vessels of siluer of the
money that was broght into the house of
the Lord.
14 But they gaue it to the workemẽ, which
repaired therewith the house of the Lord.
15 Moreouer, they rekened not with the
men, into whose hands they deliuered that
money to be bestowed on workmen: for
they dealt faithfully.
16 The money of the trespasse offring and
the money of the sinne offrings was not
broght into ỹ house of the Lord: *for* it was
the Priests.
17 ¶ Then came vp Hazaél King of Arám,
and foght against Gath and toke it, and
Hazaél set his face to go vp to Ierusalém.
18 And Iehoásh King of Iudáh toke all the
i hallowed things that Iehoshaphát, & Iehorám, and Ahaziáh his fathers Kings of
Iudáh had dedicate, and that he him selfe
had dedicated, and all the golde that was
foũde in the treasures of the house of the
Lord and in the Kings house, and sent it
to Hazaél King of Arám, and he departed
from Ierusalém.
19 Concerning the rest of the actes of Ioásh and all that he did, are they not writen in the boke of the Chronicles of the
Kings of Iudáh?
20 ¶ And his seruants arose and wroght
treason, and k slewe Ioásh in the house of
l Milló, when he came downe to Sillá:
21 Euen "Iozachár the sonne of Shimeath,
and Iehozabád the sonne of Shomér his
seruants smote him, and he dyed: and they
buryed him with his fathers in the citie
of Dauid. And Amaziáh his sonne reigned
in his steade.

a So long as rulers giue eare to the true ministers of God, they prosper.
b So hard a thing it is for them, that are in autoritie to be broght to the perfit obedience of God.
c That is, the money of redéption, Exod. 30,12: also the money which the Priest valued ỹ vowes at. Leu. 27,2, & their fre liberalitie.
d For the Tẽple which was buylt an hundreth fiftie & fiue yeres before, had many things decaied in it, bothe by the negligence of the Kings his predecessors, and also by ỹ wickednes of the idolaters.
e He taketh from them the ordering of ỹ money because of their negligence.
f That is, on the Southside.
"Or, vessel.
g For the King had appointed other which were mete for that purpose, Chap. 22,5.
h For these men had onely the charge of the reparacion of the Tẽple, and the rest of ỹ money was broght to the King, who caused these afterwarde to be made, 2 Chro. 24,14.
i After the death of Iehoiadá Ioásh fel to idolatrie therefore God reiecteth him, and stirreth vp his enemie against him, whome he pacified with ỹ treasures of the Temple: for God wolde not be serued with those gifts, seing the Kings heart was wicked.
k Because he had put Zacharie the sonne of Iehoiadá to death, 2. Chro. 24,25.
l Read 2 Sam. 5,9
"Or, Iozabád.

CHAP. XIII.

3 Iehoaház the sonne of Iehú is deliuered into the hãds of the Syrians. 5 He prayeth vnto God and is deliuered. 9 Ioásh his sonne reigneth in his steade. 24 Hazaél dyeth. 26 Elishá dyeth.

1 IN the thre and twentieth yere of Ioásh
the sonne of Ahaziáh King of Iudáh,
Iehoaház the sonne of Iehú begã to reigne ouer Israél in Samaria, *and he reigned*
seuentene yere.
2 And he did euil in the sight of the Lord,
and followed the sinnes of Ieroboám the
sonne of Nebát, ỹ made Israél to a sinne,
and departed not therefrom.
3 And the Lord was angry with Israél, and
deli-

a By worshiping the calues, which Ieroboám did erect in Israél.

deliuered them into the hand of Hazaél
King of Arám, and into the hand of Ben-
hadád the sonne of Hazaél, all [b] *his* dayes.
4 And Iehoaház besoght the Lord, and the
Lord heard him: for he sawe the trouble
of Israél, wherewith the King of Arám
troubled them.
5 (And the Lord gaue Israél a [c] deliuerer,
so that they came out from vnder the subiection of the Aramites. And the children
of Israél [d] dwelt in their tentes as " before time.
6 Neuertheles they departed not from the
sinnes of the house of Ieroboám which
made Israél sinne, *but* walked in them. euen
the [e] groue also remained stil in Samaria)
7 For he had left of the people to Iehoaház but fiftie horsemen, and ten charets, &
ten thousand fotemen, because the King
[f] of Arám had destroyed them, and made
them like dust beaten to poudre.
8 Concerning the rest of the actes of Iehoaház and all that he did, and his valiãt
dedes, are they not writen in the boke of
the Chronicles of the Kings of Israél?
9 And Iehoaház slept with his fathers, and
they buryed him in Samaria, and Ioásh
his sonne reigned in his steade.
10 ¶ In the seuẽ and thirtieth yere of Ioásh
King [g] of Iudáh began Iehoásh the sonne of Iehoaház to reigne ouer Israél in
Samaria, *and reigned* sixtene yere,
11 And did euil in the sight of the Lord:
for he departed not from all the sinnes of
Ieroboam the sonne of Nebát that made
Israél to sinne, but he walked therein.
12 Concerning the rest of the actes of Ioásh
and all that he did, and his valiant dedes,
and how he foght against Amaziáh King
of Iudáh, are they not writen in the boke
of the Chronicles of the King of Israél?
13 And Ioásh slept with his fathers, & Ieroboam sate vpon his seat: & Ioásh was buryed in Samaria amõg ẏ Kings of Israél.
14 ¶ When Elishá fel sicke of his sicknes,
whereof he dyed, Ioash the King of Israél
came downe vnto him, and wept vpon his
face, & said, [h] O my father, my father, the
charet of Israél, & the horsmẽ of ẏ same.
15 Thẽ Elishá said vnto him, Take a bowe
and arowes. And he toke vnto him bowe
and arowes.
16 And he said to the King of Israél, Put
thine hand vpon the bow. And he put his
hand vpon it. And Elishá put his hands
vpon the Kings hands,
17 And said, Open the windowe [i] Eastward. And when he had opened it, Elishá
said, Shote. And he shot. And he said, *Beholde* the arowe of the Lords deliuerance
& the arowe of deliuerãce against Arám:
for thou shalt smite ẏ Aramites in Aphék,
til thou hast consumed them.

b While Iehoaház liued.

c To wit, Ioásh the sonne of Iehoaház.

d Safely and without danger.

" Ebr. as yesterday and before yesterday.

e Wherein thei did cõmit their idolatrie, & which the Lord had commãded to be destroyed, Deu. 16, 20.

f That is, Hazaél and Benhadád his sonne, as vers 3; read of Hazaél Chap. 8, 12.

g His chief purpose is to describe the kingdome of Iudáh & how God performed his promes made to the house of Dauid but by the way he sheweth how Israél was afflicted and punished for their great idolatrie, who though they had now degenerat, yet God bothe by sending thẽ sundry Prophetes and diuers punishments did call them vnto him againe.

h Thus thei vsed to call ẏ Prophetes and seruãts of God by whome God blessed his people, as chap. 2, 12. meaning that by their prayers thei did more prosper their countrey, thẽ by force of armes.

i That is, toward Syria, so that he did not onely prophecie with wordes, but also cõfirmed him by these signe that he shulde haue ẏ victorie.

18 Againe he said, Take the arowes. And he
toke them. And he said vnto the King of
Israél, Smite the ground. And he smote
thrise, and ceased.
19 Then the man of God was [k] angry with
him, and said, Thou shuldest haue smiten
fiue or six times, so thou shuldest haue smiten Arám, til thou hadest consumed it,
where now thou shalt smite Arám but
thrise.
20 ¶ So Elishá dyed, & they buryed him.
And *certeine* bands of the Moabites came
into the land that yere.
21 And as they were burying a man, beholde, they sawe the souldiers: therefore they
cast the man into the sepulchre of Elishá. And when the man was downe, & touched the bones of Elishá, *he [l] reuiued &
stode vpon his fete.
22 ¶ But Hazaél King of Arám vexed Israél
all the daies of Iehoaház.
23 Therefore the Lord had mercie on thẽ,
and pitied them, and had respect vnto thẽ
because of his couenant with Abrahám,
Izhák, and Iaakób, and wolde not destroy
them, nether cast he them from him as
[m] yet.
24 So Hazaél the King of Arám dyed:
and Ben-hadád his sonne reigned in his
steade.
25 Therefore Iehoásh ẏ sonne of Iehoaház
returned, and toke out of the hãd of Ben-
hadád the sonne of Hazaél ẏ cities which
he had taken away by warre out of the
hand of Iehoaház his father: *for* thre times
did Ioásh beat him, and restored the cities
vnto Israél.

k Because he semed content to haue victorie against the enemies of God for twise or thrise, and had not a zeale to ouercome them continually and to destroy them vtterly.

Eccles. 48, 14.

l By this miracle God cõfirmed the autoritie of Elishá whose doctrine in his life they contemned, ẏ at this sight they might returne & imbrace the same doctrine.

m That is, vntil their sinnes were come to a ful measure, & there was no more hope of amẽdment.

CHAP. XIIII.

1 Amaziáh the King of Iudáh putteth to death them that slewe his father. 7 And after smiteth Edóm. 15 Ioásh dyeth, and Ieroboam his sonne succedeth him. And after him reigneth Zachariah.

1 THe secõde yere of Ioásh sonne of Iehoaház King of Israél reigned *Amaziáh the sonne of Ioásh King of Iudáh.
2 He was fiue and twentie yere olde when
he began to reigne, and reigned nine and
twentie yere in Ierusalém, & his mothers
name *was* Iehoadán of Ierusalém.
3 And he did [a] vprightly in the sight of
the Lord, yet not like Dauid his father, *but*
did according to all that Ioásh his father
had done.
4 Notwithstanding the hie places were
not taken away: *for* as yet the people did
sacrifice & burnt incense in the hie places.
5 ¶ And when the kingdome was confirmed in his hãd, *he slewe his seruãts which
had killed the King his father.
6 But the children of those that did slay
him, he [b] slewe not, according vnto that that
is writen in the boke of the Lawe of Moses, wherein the Lord commanded, saying,

2. Chro. 25, 1.

a In the beginnĩg of his reigne he semed to haue an outward shewe of godlines, but afterwarde he became an idolater, & worshiped the idoles of ẏ Idumeãs.

Chap. 12, 20.

b Because thei nether consented nor were partakers with their fathers in that act.

Deut. 24,16. ezek.18,20.

*The fathers shal not be put to death for
the children,nor the children put to death
for the fathers : but euerie mã shal be put
to death for his owne sinne.
7 He slewe also of c Edóm in the valley of
salt ten thousand,and toke "*the citie* of Séla
by warre, & called the name thereof Iok-
théel vnto this day.
8 ¶ Then Amaziáh sent messengers to Iehoásh the sonne of Iehoaház, sõne of Iehú
King of Israél, saying, Come, d let vs se
one another in the face.
9 Then Iehoásh the King of Israél sent to
Amaziáh King of Iudáh, saying, The thistle that is in Lebanón, sent to the e cedre
that is in Lebanón, saying, Giue thy daughter to my sonne to wife : and the wilde
beast that was in Lebanón, went and trode
downe the thistle.
10 *Because* thou hast smiten Edóm, thine
heart hathe made thee proude: f brag of
glorie, & tarye at home . why doest thou
prouoke to *thine* hurt, that thou shuldest
fall,and Iudáh with thee?
11 But Amaziáh wolde not heare:therefore
Iehoásh King of Israél went vp: and he &
Amaziáh King of Iudáh sawe one another in the face at Beth-shémesh which is
in Iudáh.
12 And Iudáh was put to the worse before
Israél, and they fled euerie man to their
tentes.
13 But Iehoásh King of Israél toke Amaziáh King of Iudáh,the sonne of Iehoásh
the sonne of Ahaziáh, at Beth-shémesh,&
"came to Ierusalém, and brake downe the
wall of Ierusalém frõ the gate of Ephráim
to the corner gate,foure hundreth cubites.
14 And he toke all the golde and siluer,and
all the vessels that were foũde in the house of the Lord, and in the treasures of the
Kings house,and the children that were in
g hostage, and returned to Samaria.
15 Concerning the rest of the actes of Iehoásh which he did and his valiant dedes,
and how he foght with Amaziáh King of
Iudáh, are they not writen in the boke of
the Chronicles of the Kings of Israél?
16 And Iehoásh slept with his fathers, and
was buryed at Samaria among the Kings
of Israél:and Ieroboám his sonne reigned
in his steade.
17 ¶ And Amaziáh the sonne of Ioásh King
of Iudáh,liued after the death of Iehoásh
sonne of Iehoaház King of Israél fiftene
yere.
18 Concerning the rest of the actes of Amaziáh,are they not writen in the boke of the
Chronicles of the Kings of Iudáh?
19 But they wroght treason against him in
Ierusalém, and he fled to h Lachish,but
they sent after him to Lachish, and slewe
him there.

c For the Idumeans,whome Dauid had broght to subiection, did rebelle in the time of Iehorã sonne of Iehoshaphát.

"*Or, the towre, or,rocke.*

d Let vs fight hãd to hand & trye it by battel,and not destroye one anothers cities.

e By this parable Iehoásh cõpareth him selfe to a cedre tre because of his great kigdome ouer ten tribes, and Amaziáh to a thistle, because he ruled but ouer two tribes, and the wilde beasts are Iehoashs souldiers that spoiled the cities of Iudáh.

f Brag of thy victorie, so ỳ thou tarie at home and anoye me not.

"*Or, broght him.*

g That is, ỳ the Israelites had giuen to them of Iudáh for an assurance of peace.

h Which citie Roboám buylt in Iudáh for a forteresse, 2.Chro 11,9.

20 And they broght him on horses, and he
was buryed at Ierusalém with his fathers
in the citie of Dauid.
21 Then all the people of Iudáh toke i A-
zariáh,which was sixtene yere olde, and
made him King for his father Amaziáh.
22 He buylt k Eláth, and restored it to Iudáh,after ỳ the Kĩg slept with his fathers.
23 ¶ In the fiftenth yere of Amaziáh the
sonne of Ioásh King of Iudáh, was Ieroboám the sonne of Ioásh made Kĩg ouer
Israél in Samaria, & *reigned* one and fourtie yere.
24 And he did euil in the sight of the Lord:
for he departed not from all the l sinnes of
Ieroboám the sonne of Nebát, which
made Israél to sinne.
25 He restored the coast of Israél,from the
entring of Hamáth, vnto ỳ Sea of the wildernes, accordĩg to ỳ worde of the Lord
God of Israél,which he spake"by his seruant Ionáh the sonne of Amittái the Prophet,which was of Gath Hépher.
26 For the Lord sawe the exceding bitter
affliction of Israél,so that there was none
m shut vp,nor any left, nether yet any that
colde helpe Israél.
27 Yet the Lord " had not decreed to put
out the name of Israél from vnder the
heauen:therefore he preserued them by ỳ
hand of Ieroboám the sonne of Ioásh.
28 Concerning the rest of the actes of Ieroboám,and all that he did, and his valiãt
dedes, & how he foght, and how he restored Damascus,and n Hamáth to Iudáh
in Israél,are they not writen in the boke
of the Chronicles of the Kings of Israél?
29 So Ieroboám slept with his fathers, *euen*
with the Kings of Israél , and Zachariáh
his sonne reigned in his steade.

CHAP. XV.

1 Azariáh the King of Iudáh becommeth a leper. 3 Of Iothám.10 Shallúm,14 Menahém,23 Pekahiah,30 Vzziáh,31 Iothám, 38 And Aház.

1 IN the "seuen & twẽtieth yere of Ieroboám King of Israél,begã Azariáh,son-
ne of Amaziáh King of Iudáh to reigne.
2 Sixtene yere olde was he, when he was
made King,and he reigned two and fiftie
yere in Ierusalém:and his mothers name
was Iecholiáh of Ierusalém.
3 And he did a vprightly in the sight of the
Lord,according to all that his father Ama
ziáh did.
4 But the hie places were not put away : *for*
the people yet offred, and burned incense
in the hie places.
5 And the Lord b smote the King : and he
was a leper vnto the day of his death,and
dwelt in an house aparte, and Iothám the
Kings sonne gouerned the house, & c iudged the people of the land.
6 Concerning the rest of the actes of Azariáh,

i Who is also called Vzziáh, 2 Chro.26,1.

k Which is also called Elanón or Eloth.

l Because this idolatrie was so vile and almoste incredible , that mẽ shulde forsake ỳ liuing God to worship calues, ỳ worke of mãs hãds,therefore the Scripture doeth oft times repeat it in the reproche of all idolaters.

"*Ebr by the hand of.*

m Read.1.Kig. 14,10.

"*Ebr.had not spoken.*

"*Ebr in the twẽtieth yere & seuenth yere.*

a So long as he gaue eare to Zachariáh the Prophet

b His father & grand father were slaine by their subiects and seruãts, & he,because he wolde vsurpe the Priests office contrarie to Gods ordinance, was smitẽ immediatly by the hand of God with the leprosie, 2,Chro 26, 21.

c As viceroy or deputie to his father.

riáh, and all that he did, are they not writen in the boke of the Chronicles of the
Kings of Iudáh?
7 So Azariáh slept with his fathers & they
buryed him with his fathers in the citie of
Dauid, and Iothám his sonne reigned in
his steade.
8 ¶ In the eight and thirtieth yere of Azariáh King of Iudáh did Zachariáh the
sonne of Ieroboám reigne ouer Israél in
Samaria six [d] monethes,
9 And did euil in the sight of the Lord, as
did his fathers: *for* he departed not from
the sinnes of Ieroboám the sonne of Nebát, which made Israél to sinne.
10 And Shallúm the sonne of Iabésh conspi
red against him, & smote him in the sight
of the people, and killed [e] him, & reigned
in his steade.
11 Concerning the rest of the actes of Zachariáh, beholde, thei are writē in ẏ boke
of the Chronicles of the Kings of Israél.
12 This was the *worde of the Lord, which
he spake vnto Iehú, sayīg, Thy sonnes shal
sit on the throne of Israél vnto ẏ fourte *generacion* after thee. And it came so to passe.

d He was the fourtē in descent from Iehú, who reigned according to Gods promes, but in him God began to execute his wrath against ẏ house of Iehú.
e Zachariáh was the last in Israél, ẏ had the kingdome by succession, saue onely Pekahiáh ẏ sonne of Menahém who reigned but two yeres.
Chap. 10,30.

13 ¶ Shallúm the sonne of Iabésh began
to reigne in the nine and thirtieth yere of
Vzziáh King of Iudáh: and he reigned
the space of a moneth in Samaria.
14 For Menahém the sonne of Gadí went
vp from Tirzáh, and came to Samaria, &
smote Shallúm the sonne of Iabésh in Samaria, & slew him, & reigned in his stead.
15 Concerning the rest of the actes of Shal
lúm, and the treason which he wroght, beholde, they are writen in the boke of the
Chronicles of the Kings of Israél.
16 ¶ Then Menahém destroyed [f] Tiphsáh,
and all that were therein, and the coastes
thereof from Tirzáh, because they opened not to him, and he smote it, and ript
vp all their women with childe.

f Which was a citie of Israél that wolde not receiue him to be Kīg.

17 The nine and thirtieth yere of Azariáh
King of Iudáh, began Menahém the sonne
of Gadí to reigne ouer Israél, *& reigned*
ten yeres in Samaria.
18 And he did euil in the sight of the Lord,
and departed not all his dayes from the
sinne of Ieroboám the sonne of Nebát,
which made Israél to sinne.
19 ¶ Thē Phul the King of Asshúr came
against the [g] land: & Menahém gaue Phul
a thousand [h] talents of siluer, that his hād
might be with him, & establish the kingdome in his hand.
20 And Menahém exacted the money in Israél, that all men of substance shulde giue
the King of Asshúr fifty shekels of siluer
a piece: so the King of Asshúr returned &
taried not there in the land.
21 Concerning the rest of the actes of Menahém, and all that he did, are they not

g That is, of Israél
h In steade of seking helpe of God, he wēt about by money to purchase the fauour of this King beīg an infidele, & therefore God forsoke him, & Phul sone afterwarde brake promes, destroyed his coūtrey & led his people away captiue.

writen in the boke of the Chronicles of
the Kings of Israél?
22 And Menahém slept with his fathers, &
Pekahiáh his sonne did reigne in his stead.
23 ¶ In the fiftieth yere of Azariáh King of
Iudáh, begā Pekahiáh the sonne of Menahém to reigne ouer Israél in Samaria, *&*
reigned two yere.
24 And he did euil in the sight of ẏ Lord:
for he departed not frō the sinnes of Ieroboám the sonne of Nebát, which made
Israél to sinne.
25 And Pékah the sonne of Remaliáh, his
captaine cōspired against him, and smote
him in Samaria in the place of the Kings
palace with [i] Argób and Ariéh, and with
him fifty men of the Gileadites: so he killed him, and reigned in his steade.

i Which were of the same conspiracie.

26 Concerning the rest of the actes of Pekahiáh, and all that he did, beholde, they
are writen in the boke of the Chronicles
of the Kings of Israél.
27 In the two and fiftieth yere of Azariáh
King of Iudáh began Pékah the sonne of
Remaliáh to reigne ouer Israél in Samaria, *and reigned* twentie yere.
28 And he did euil in the sight of the Lord:
for he departed not from the sinnes of Ieroboám the sonne of Nebát, that made
Israél to sinne.
29 In the dayes of Pékah King of Israél,
[k] came Tigláth Pilesér King of Asshúr,
and toke Iión, & Abél, Beth-maacháh, &
Iánoah, and Kedésh, and Hazór, and Gileád, and Galiláh, *&* all the land of Naphtalí, and caried them away to Asshúr.

k For God stirred vp Phul & Tigláth Pilesér against Israél for their sinnes, 1. Chro. 5,26.

30 And Hoshéa the sonne of Eláh wroght
treason against Pékah the sonne of Rema
liáh, and smote him, and slewe him, & reigned in his steade in the twentieth yere of
Iothám the sonne of Vzziáh.
31 Concerning the rest of the actes of Pékah, and all that he did, beholde, they are
writen in the boke of the Chronicles of
the Kings of Israél.
32 ¶ *In the second yere of Pékah the sonne
of Remaliáh Kīg of Israél, began Iothám
sonne of 'Vzziáh Kīg of Iudáh to reigne.
33 Fiue and twentie yere olde was he, whē he
began to reigne, and he reigned sixtene
yere in Ierusalém: and his mothers name
was Ierushá the daughter of Zadók.

2. Chro. 27, 1.
'Or, *Azariáh.*

34 And he did vprightly in the sight of the
Lord: he did according [l] to all that his fa
ther Vzziáh had done.
35 But the hie places were not put away: *for*
the people yet offred & burnt incense in ẏ
hie places: he buylt the hiest gate of the
house of the Lord.
36 Cōcerning the rest of ẏ actes of Iothám,
& all ẏ he dyd, are thei not writē in ẏ boke of the Chronicles of ẏ Kīgs of Iudáh?
37 In [m] those dayes the Lord began to

l He shewetii ẏ his vprightnes was not suche, but ẏ he had many and great fautes.
m After the death of Iothám.

send against Iudáh Rezín the King of A-
rám, and [n] Pekáh the sonne of Remaliáh.
38 And Iothám slept with his fathers, and
was buryed with his fathers in the citie of
Dauid his father, & Aház his sonne reigned in his steade.

n Which slewe of Iudáh in one day six score thousand fighting men, 2.Chro. 28,6, because they had forsaken the true God.

CHAP. XVI.

3 Aház King of Iudáh consecrateth his sonne in fyre. 5 Ierusalém is besieged. 9 Damascus is taken and Rezín slaine. 11 Idolatrie 19 The death of Aház. 20 Hezechiáh succedeth him.

1 THe seuententh yere of Pekáh the sonne of Remaliáh, [a] Aház the sonne of
Iothám King of Iudáh began to reigne.
2 Twentie yere olde was Aház, when he
began to reigne, and he reigned sixtene
yere in Ierusalém, and did not vprightely
in the sight of the Lord his God, like Dauid his father:
3 But walked in the way of the Kings of
Israél, yea, & made his sonne to [b] go thorow the fyre, after the abominations of the
heathē, whome the Lord had cast out before the children of Israél.
4 Also he offred and burnt incense in the
hie places and on the hilles, & vnder euerie grene tre.
5 *Then Rezín King of Arám and Pekáh
sonne of Remaliáh Kīg of Israél came vp
to Ierusalém to fight: & they besieged A-
ház, but colde not ouercome [c] him.
6 At the same time Rezín King of Arám
restored [d] Eláth to Arám, and droue the
Iewes frō Eláth: so the Aramites came to
Eláth, and dwelt there vnto this day.
7 Then Aház sent [e] messengers to Tigláth
Pilesár King of Asshúr, saying, I am thy
seruant and thy sonne: come vp, and deliuer me out of the hand of the King of
Arám, and out of the hand of the King of
Israél which rise vp against me.
8 And Aház toke the siluer and the golde
that was foūde in the [f] house of the Lord,
and in the treasures of the Kings house,
and sent a present vnto the King of Asshúr.
9 And the King of Asshúr consented vnto him: and the King of Asshúr went vp
against Damascus. and when he had takē
it, he caried the people away to Kir, and
slewe Rezín.
10 And King Aház went vnto Damascus
to mete Tigláth Pilesár King of Asshúr:
and when King Aház sawe the altar that
was at Damascus, he sent to Vriiáh the
Priest the patern of the altar, and the facion of it, and all the workemanship
thereof.
11 And Vriiáh the Priest made an altar [g] in
all pointes like to that which King Aház
had sent from Damascus, so did Vriiáh
the Priest against King Aház came from
Damascus.

a This was a wicked sonne of a godlie father, as of him againe came godlie Ezekiáh, and of him wicked Manasséh, saue that God in ye end shewed him mercie. thus we se how vncerteine it is to depend on the dignitie of our fathers.

b That is, offred hī to Moléch, or made him to passe betwene two fyres, as ye maner of the Gētiles was, Leu. 21,18, Deu. 18, 10.

Isa.7,1.

c For ye Lord preserued the citie and his people for his promes sake made to Dauid.

d Which citie Azariáh had taken from the Aramites and fortified it, Chap.14,22.

e Contrary to the admonitiō of ye Prophet, Isai. Isa.7,4.

f Thus he spared not to spoile the Temple of God to haue succour of men, and wolde not once lift his heart toward God to desire his helpe, nor yet heare his Prophetes coūsel.

g We se that there is no price so wicked, but he shal finde flatterers & false ministers to serue his turne.

12 So when the King was come from Damascus, the Kīg sawe the altar: & the King
drewe nere to the altar and offred [h] thereon.
13 And he burnt his burntoffring, and his
meat offring, & powred his drinkoffring,
and sprinkled the blood of his peace offrings besides the altar,
14 And *set it* by the brasen altar which was
before the Lord, and broght it in farther
before the house betwene the altar and the
house of the Lord, & set it on the [i] Northside of the altar.
15 And King Aház commāded Vriiáh the
Priest and said, Vpon the great altar set
on fyre in the morning the burntoffring,
and in the euen the meat offring, and the
Kings burnt offring and his meat offring,
with the burntoffring of all the people of
the land, and their meat offring, and their
drinkoffrings: and powre thereby all the
blood of the burnt offring, and all the
blood of the sacrifice, and the [k] brasen
altar shalbe for me to inquire *of God*.
16 And Vriiáh the Priest did according to
all that King Aház had commanded.
17 And King Aház brake the borders of
the bases, and toke the caldrons from of
them, and toke downe the sea from the
brasen oxen that were vnder it, and put it
vpon a pauement of stones.
18 And the [l] vaile for the Sabbáth (that
they had made in the house) & the Kings
entrie without turned he to the house of
the Lord, [m] because of ye King of Asshúr.
19 Concerning the rest of the actes of A-
ház, which he did, are they not writen in
the boke of the Chronicles of the Kings
of Iudáh?
20 And Aház slept with his fathers, & was
buryed with his fathers in the citie of Dauid, & Hezekiáh his sonne reigned in his
steade.

h Ether offrings for peace or prosperitie, or of thankes giuing, as Leui 3,1, or els meaning the morning and eueníg offríg, Exod 29,38, Nom 28,3: and thus he contēned the meanes and the altar which God had commanded by Salomón, to serue God after his owne fantasie.

i That is, at ye right hand as men went into the Temple.

k Here he establisheth by cōmandemēt his owne wicked procedings, & doeth abolish the commandement & ordinance of God.

l Or tent, wherein they lay on ye Sabbath which had serued their weeke in the Temple and so departed home.

m Ether to flatter the King of Asyria, when he shulde thus se him change the ordināce of God, or els that the Temple might be a refuge for him if ye King shulde sodēly assaile his house.

CHAP. XVII.

3 Hoshéa King of Israél is taken, 4 And he and all his realme broght to the Assyrians, 18 For their idolatrie. 24 Lions destroie the Assyriās that dwelt in Samaria. 29 Euerie one worshipeth the God of his nation, 35 Contrary to the commandement of God.

1 IN the twelfte yere of Aház King of
Iudáh began Hoshéa the sonne of E-
láh to reigne in Samaria ouer Israél, *and
reigned* nine yeres,
2 And he did euil in the sight of the Lord,
[a] but not as the Kings of Israél, that were
before him.
3 And Shalmanéser King of Asshúr came
vp against him, and Hoshéa became his
seruant, and gaue him presents.
4 And the King of Asshúr founde treason
in Hoshéa: for he had sent messengers to
So King of Egypt, and broght no present
vnto the King of Asshúr, [b] as *he had done*
yerely:

a Thogh he inuented no newe idolatrie or impietie as others did, yet he soght for helpe at the Egyptians wc God had forbidden.

b For he had payed tribute for the space of eight yeres.

yerely: therefore the King of Aſſhúr ſhut
him vp, and put him in priſon.
5 Then the King of Aſſhúr came vp
throughout all the land, and went againſt
Samaria, and beſieged it thre yere.
6 ¶ *In the ninth yere of Hoſhéa, the King
of Aſſhúr toke Samaria, and caryed Iſraél away vnto Aſſhúr, and put them in Ha-
láh, and in Habór by the riuer of Gozán,
and in the cities of the [c] Medes.
7 For when the children of Iſraél [d] ſinned
againſt the Lord their God, which had
broght them out of the land of Egypt,
from vnder the hand of Pharaóh King of
Egypt, and feared other gods,
8 And walked according to the facions of
the heathen, whome the Lord had caſt out
before the children of Iſraél, and *after the
maners* of the Kings of Iſraél, which they
vſed,
9 And the children of Iſraél had done ſecretly things that were not vpright before the Lord their God, and throughout all
their cities had buylt hie places, *bothe* from
the towre [e] of the watche, to the defen-
ſed citie,
10 And had made them images and groues
vpon euerie hie hil, and vnder euerie
grene tre,
11 And there burnt incenſe in all the hie
places, as did the heathē, whome the Lord
had taken away before them, and wroght
wicked things to angre the Lord,
12 And ſerued idoles: whereof the Lord
had ſaid vnto them, *Ye ſhal do no ſuche
thing,
13 Notwithſtanding the Lord teſtified to
Iſraél, and to Iudáh " by all the Prophetes, and by all the Seers, ſaying, *Turne
from your euil waies, & kepe my cōmandements & my ſtatutes, according to all
the Lawe, which I commanded your fathers, and which I ſent to you by my ſeruants the Prophetes.
14 Neuertheles they wolde not obey,
*but hardened their neckes, like to the nec-
kes of their [f] fathers, that did not beleue
in the Lord their God.
15 And thei refuſed his ſtatutes and his couenant, that he made with their fathers,
and his teſtimonies (wherewith he witneſſed vnto them) and they followed vanitie,
and became vaine, & followed the heathē
that were rounde about them: concerning
whome, the Lord had charged them, that
they ſhulde not do like them.
16 Finally they left the commandements
of the Lord their God, and made them
molten images, **euen* two calues, & made
a groue, and worſhiped all the [g] hoſte of
heauen, and ſerued Báal.
17 And thei made their ſonnes and their
daughters [h] paſſe through the fyre, and v-

Chap.18,10.

c For at this time ỳ Medes and Perſians were ſubiect to ỳ Aſsyriās.

d He ſetteth forth at legth the cauſe of this great plague & perpetual captiuitie, to admoniſh all people and nacions to cleaue to the Lord God, and onely worſhip him for feare of like iudgement.

e Meaning, throughout all their borders.

Deut.4,19.

" Ebr by the hand of.

Iere.18,11 & 25,5.& 35,15

Deut.31,27.

f So that to alledge the autoritie of our fathers or great antiquitie, except we can proue ỳ they were godlie, is but to declare that we are ỳ childrē of the wicked.

Exod.32,8. 1.King.12,28

g That is, the ſunne, ỳ moone & ſtarres, Deut 4,19

h Read Chap. 16,3.

ſed witchcraft and enchantements, yea,
[i] ſolde them ſelues, to do euil in the ſight
of the Lord, to angre him.
18 Therefore ỳ Lord was exceding wroth
with Iſraél, and put them out of his ſight,
and none was left but the tribe of Iudáh
[k] onely.
19 Yet Iudáh kept not the commandemēts
of the Lord their God, but walked according to the facion of Iſraél, which they
vſed.
20 Therefore the Lord caſt of all the ſede
of Iſraél, and affli&ed them, & deliuered
them into the hands of ſpoylers, vntil he
had caſt them out of his [l] ſight.
21 [m] For he cut of Iſraél from the houſe of
Dauid, and they made Ieroboám the ſonne of Nebát King: & Ieroboám drewe Iſraél away from following the Lord and
made them ſinne a great ſinne.
22 For the children of Iſraél walked in all
the ſinnes of Ieroboám, which he did, *and*
departed not therefrom,
23 Vntil the Lord put Iſraél away out of
his ſight, as he had ſaid " by all his ſeruāts
the * Prophetes, & caryed Iſraél away out
of their land to Aſſhúr vnto this day.
24 And the King of Aſſhúr broght folke
from Babél, and from [n] Cutháh, and
from Auá, and from Hamáth, and from
Sepharuáim, and placed them in the cities
of Samaria in ſteade of the children of Iſraél: ſo they poſſeſſed Samaria, and dwelt
in the cities thereof.
25 ¶ And at the beginning of their dwellīg
there, thei [o] feared not the Lord: therefore
the Lord ſent lyons among them, which
ſlewe them.
26 Wherefore they ſpake to the King of
Aſſhúr, ſaying, The nacions which thou
haſt remoued, and placed in the cities of
Samaria, knowe not the maner of ỳ God
of the land: therefore he hathe ſent lyons
among them, and beholde, they ſlay them,
becauſe they knowe not the maner of the
God of the land.
27 Then the King of Aſſhúr commanded,
ſaying, Cary thether one of the prieſts,
whome ye broght thence, and let him go
and dwel there, & teache them the maner
of the God [p] of the countrey.
28 So one of the prieſts, which they had
caryed from Samaria, came and dwelt in
Beth-él, and taught them how thei ſhulde
feare the Lord.
29 Howbeit euerie naciō made their gods,
and put them in the houſes of the hie places, which the Samaritās had made, euerie
nacion in their cities, wherein thei dwelt.
30 For the men of Babél made [q] Succóth-
Benóth: and the men of Cuth made Ner-
gál, and the men of Hamáth made Aſhi-
má.

i Read of this phraſe, 1. Kig. 21,20, & 25.

k No whole tribe was left but Iudáh, & thei of Beniamín & Leui, ỳ remained, were coūted with Iudáh.

l Out of the land where he ſhewed ỳ greateſt tokens of his preſence & fauour

m That is, God cut of the ten tribes, 1. King. 12,16.

" Ebr. by the hand of.

Iere.25,9.

n Of theſe peoples came the Samaritās, whereof mencion is ſo muche made in ỳ Goſpel, & with whome ỳ Iewes wolde haue nothing to do, Ioh 4,9.

o That is, thei ſerued him not: therefore, leſt they ſhuld blaſpheme hī, as thogh there were no God, becauſe he chaſtiſed ỳ Iſraelites, he ſheweth his mightie power among the by this ſtrāge puniſhment.

p That is, how to worſhip hī: thus ỳ wicked rather thē to loſe their cōmodities, wil change to all religions.

q Meaning, ỳ euery coūtrey ſerued that idole, which was moſte eſtemed in that place whence they came.

31 And the Auims made Nibház, and Tar-
ták: and the Sepharuims burnt their children in the fyre to Adrammélech, and A-
nammélech the gods of Sepharuáim.
32 Thus they feared the Lord, and appointed out priests out of them selues for the
hie places, who prepared for them *sacrifices*
in the houses of the hie places.
33 They [r] feared the Lord, but serued their
gods after the maner of the nacions whome they caryed thence.
34 Vnto this day they do after the olde maner: they nether feare God, nether do after
[f] their ordinances nor after their customes, nor after the Lawe, nor after the cōmandement, which the Lord commanded
the children of Iaakób, * whome he named Isráel,
35 And w̃ whome the Lord had made couenāt, & charged them, saying, * Feare none
other gods, nor bowe your selues to them,
nor serue them, nor sacrifice to them:
36 But feare the Lord which broght you
out of the lād of Egypt with great power,
and a stretched out arme: him feare ye, and
worship him, and sacrifice to him.
37 Also kepe ye diligently the statutes and
the ordinances, and the Lawe, and the cōmandement, which he wrote for you, that
ye do them continually, & feare not other
gods.
38 And forget not the couenant that I haue
made w̃ you, nether feare ye other gods,
39 But feare the Lord your God, and he wil
deliuer you out of the hands of all your
enemies.
40 Howbeit they obeyed not, but did after
their olde custome.
41 So these [t] nacions feared the Lord, and
serued their images *also*: so *did* their children, and their childrens children: as did
their fathers, *so* do they vnto this day.

r That is, thei had a certein knowledge of God & feared him, because of the punishment, but thei continued stil idolaters, as do ẏ Papists, which worship bothe God & idoles: but this is not to feare God as appeareth vers. 34.

f He meaneth this by the Israelites, to whome he had giuē his commandements.

Gen. 32,28. *1 king. 18,31.* *Iudg. 6,10.* *iere 10,2.*

t That is, these strangers, w̃ were sent into Samaria by ẏ Assyrians.

CHAP. XVIII.

4 Ezekiáh King of Iudáh putteth downe the brasen serpent, & destroyeth the idoles. 7 And prospereth. 11 Israél is caryed away captiue. 30 The blasphemie of Saneherib.

2. Chro. 28,27 & 29,1.

1 NOw in * the third yere of Hoshéa,
sonne of Eláh King of Israél, Hezekiáh the sonne of Aház King of Iudáh
began to reigne.
2 He was fiue and twentie yere olde when
he began to reigne, and reigned nine and
twētie yere in Ierusalém. His mothers name also was Abí ẏ daughter of Zachariáh,
3 And he did [a] vprightly in the sight of the
Lord, according to all that Dauid his father had done.
4 He toke away the hie places, and brake
the images, and cut downe the groues,
& brake in pieces the * brasen serpent that
Mosés had made: for vnto those dayes the
children of Israél did burne incense to

a Althogh thei of Iudáh were giuen to idolatrie and impietie, as thei of Israél were, yet God for his ꝓmes sake was merciful vnto the throne of Dauid: & yet by his iudgement towarde the other, prouoked them to repentance.

Nomb. 21,8.

it, and he called it [b] Nehushtán.
5 He trusted in the Lord God of Israél: so
that after him was none like him among
all the Kings of Iudáh, nether were there
anie suche before him.
6 For he claue to the Lord & departed not
from him, but kept his commandements,
which the Lord had commanded Mosés.
7 So the Lord was with him, *and* he prospered in all things, which he toke in hand:
also he rebelled against the King of Asshúr, and serued him not.
8 He smote the Philistims vnto Azzáh, &
the coastes thereof, [c] from the watche
towre vnto the defensed citie.
9 ¶ * And in the fourte yere of King Hezekiáh, (which was the seuēth yere of Hoshéa sonne of Eláh King of Israél) Shalmanéser King of Asshúr came vp against
Samaria, and besieged it.
10 And after thre yeres they toke it, *euen* in
the sixt yere of Hezekiáh: that is, * ẏ ninth
yere of Hoshéa King of Israél was Samaria taken.
11 Thē the King of Asshúr did cary away
Israél vnto Asshúr, and put them in Ha-
láh and in Habór, *by* the riuer of Gozán,
and in the cities of the Medes,
12 Because they wolde not obey the voyce
of the Lord their God, but transgressed
his couenant: *that is*, all that Mosés the seruant of the Lord had commanded, and
wolde nether obey nor do them.
13 ¶ * Moreouer, in the fourtenth yere of
King Hezekiáh Sancheríb Kīg of Asshúr
came vp against all the strōg cities of Iudáh, and toke them.
14 Then Hezekiáh King of Iudáh sent
vnto the King of Asshúr to Lachísh, saying, [d] I haue offended: departe from me,
& what thou layest vpon me, I wil beare
it. And the King of Asshúr appointed vnto Hezekiáh King of Iudáh thre hundreth talents of siluer, and thirty talents
of golde.
15 Therefore Hezekiáh gaue all the siluer
that was founde in the house of the Lord,
and in the treasures of the Kings house.
16 At the same season did Hezekiáh pul of
the plates of the dores of the Temple of
the Lord, and the pillers (which the said
Hezekiáh King of Iudáh had couered o-
uer) and gaue them to the King of Asshúr.
17 ¶ And the King of Asshúr sent [e] Tartán, and Rab-sarís, and Rabshakéh from
Lachísh to King Hezekiáh with a great
hoste against Ierusalém. And they went
vp, and came to Ierusalém, and when they
were come vp, they stode by the condite
of the vpper poole, which is by the path of
the fullers field,
18 And called to the King. Then came out

b That is, a piece of brasse: thus he calleth ẏ serpent by contempt, w̃ notwithstāding was set vp by ẏ worde of God, & miracles were wroght by it: yet whē it was abused to idolatrie, this good King destroyed it, not thinking it worthie to be called a serpent, but a piece of brasse.

c Read Chap. 17,9.

Chap. 17,3.

Chap. 17,6.

2. Chro. 32,1. isa. 36,1. eccles. 48,19.

d As his zeale was before praised, so his weakenes is here set forth ẏ none shulde glorie in him selfe.

e After certeine yeres when Hezekiáh ceased to send ẏ tribute appointed by ẏ King of ẏ Assyrians, he sēt his captaines & armie against him.

to

to them Eliakím the sonne of Hilkiáh,
which was stewarde of the house,& Shebnáh the chanceller, and Ioáh the sonne
of Asáph the "recorder.
19 And Rabshakéh said vnto them, Tel ye
Hezekiáh, I pray you, Thus sayth the
great King, eue the great King of Asshúr,
What confidéce is this wherein ŷ trustest?
20 Thou thinkest, Surely I haue "eloquence, [f] but counsel and strength are for the
warre. On whome then doest thou trust,
that thou rebellest against me?
21 Lo, thou trustest now in this broken staffe
of rede, to wit, on [g] Egypt, on which if a
man leane, it wil go into his hād, & pearce it: so is Pharaóh King of Egypt vnto all
that trust on him.
22 But if ye say vnto me, We trust in ŷ Lord
our God, is not that he whose hie places,
and whose altars Hezekiáh hathe [h] taken
away, and hathe said to Iudáh and Ierusalém, Ye shal worship before this altar in
Ierusalém?
23 Now therefore giue [i] hostages to my
lord the King of Asshúr, and I wil giue
thee two thousand horses, if thou be able
to set riders vpon them.
24 For how canst thou despise anie captaine of the least of my masters seruāts, & put
thy trust on Egypt for charets and horsemen?
25 Am I now come vp without the [k] lord
to this place, to destroye it? the lord said
to me, Go vp against this lād, & destroy it.
26 Then Eliakím the sonne of Hilkiáh and
Shebnáh, and Ioáh said vnto Rabshakéh,
Speake, I pray thee, to thy seruants in the
"Aramites language, for we vnderstand it,
and talke not with vs in the Iewes tongue, in the audience of the people that are
on the wall.
27 But Rabshakéh said vnto thē, Hathe my
master sent me to thy master and to thee
to speake these wordes, and not to the men
which sit on the wall, that they may eat
their owne doung, & drinke" their owne
pisse with you?
28 So Rabshakéh stode and cryed with a
loude voyce in the Iewes language, & spake, saying, Heare the wordes of the great
King, of the King of Asshúr.
29 Thus sayth the King, Let not Hezekiáh disceiue you: for he shal not be able
to deliuer you "out of mine hand.
30 Nether let Hezekiáh make you to trust
in the Lord, saying, The Lord wil surely
deliuer vs, and this citie shal not be giuen
ouer into the hand of the King of Asshúr.
31 Hearken not vnto Hezekiáh: for thus
saith the King of Asshúr, Make" appointement with me, and come out to me, that
euerie man may eat of his owne vine, and
euerie man of his owne figtre, and drinke
euerie man of the water of his owne well,
32 Til [l] I come, and bring you to a land
like your owne land, euen a land of wheat
and wine, a land of bread and vineyardes,
a land of oliues oyle, & hony that ye may
liue and not dye: and obey not Hezekiáh,
for he disceiueth you, saying, The Lord
wil deliuer vs.
33 Hathe anie of the gods of the naciōs deliuered his land out of the hand of the
King of Asshur?
34 Where is the god of Hamáh, and of Arpád? where is the god of Sepharuáim, Hená and Iuáh? how haue they deliuered Samaria out of mine hand?
35 Who are they among all the gods of the
naciōs, that haue deliuered their land out
of mine hand, that the [m] Lord shulde deliuer Ierusalém out of mine hand?
36 But the people held their peace, and
answered not him a worde: for the Kings
commandement was, saying, Answer ye
him not.
37 Then Eliakím, the sonne of Hilkiáh ŵ
was stewarde of the house & Shebnáh the
chanceller, and Ioáh the sonne of Asáph
the recorder came to Hezekiáh with their
clothes rent, and tolde him the wordes of
Rabshakéh.

"Or, writer of Chronicles, or, secretarie.

"Ebr. talke of the lippes.

f Thou thinkest ŷ wordes wil serue to persuade thy people, or to moue my master

g Egypt shal not onely be able not to succour thee, but shalbe an hurt vnto thee.

h Thus the idolaters thinke that Gods religion is destroyed, when superstition & idolatrie are reformed.

i Meaning ŷ it was best for hi to yelde to the King of Assyria, because his power was so small that he had not mē to fournish two thousand horses.

k The wicked alwayes in their prosperitie flatter thē selues, ŷ God doeth fauour thē. Thus he speaketh to feare Ezekiáh that by resisting him, he shulde resist God.

"Or, Syrians.

"Ebr. the water of their fete.

"Or, by his hand

"Ebr. blessing: meaning the cōditions of peace.

l He maketh him selfe so sure, that he wil not grant them truce, except they rendre them selues to him to be led away captiues.

m This is an execrable blasphemie against the true God, to make him equal with ŷ idoles of other nacions: therefore God did moste sharpely punish it.

CHAP. XIX.

6 God promiseth by Isaiáh victorie to Hezekiáh. 35 The Angel of the Lord killeth an hundreth and foure score and fiue thousand men of the Assyrians. 37 Saneherib is killed of his owne sonnes.

1 AND *when King Hezekiáh heard it,
he rent his clothes and put on sackeclothe, & came into the house of ŷ Lord,
2 And sent Eliakim which was ŷ stewarde
of the house, and Shebnáh the chanceller,
and the Elders of the Priests clothed in
sackeclothe [a] to Isaiáh the Prophet the
sonne of Amóz.
3 And they said vnto him, Thus sayth Hezekiáh, This day is a day of tribulacion
and of rebuke, & blasphemie: for the children are come to [b] the birth, and there is
no strength to bring forthe.
4 If so be the Lord thy God hathe heard
all the wordes of Rabshakéh, whome the
the King of Asshúr his master hathe sent
to raile on the liuing God, and to reproche him with wordes which the Lord thy
God hathe heard, thē lift thou vp t' y prayer for the [c] remnant that are left.
5 ¶ So the seruants of King Hezekiáh came
to Isaiáh.
6 And Isaiáh said vnto them, So shal ye say
to your master, Thus sayth the Lord, Be
not afrayed of the wordes which thou hast
heard wherewith the seruāts of the King
of Asshúr haue blasphemed me.
7 Beholde, I wil send a blast [d] vpon him,
& he shal heare a noyse, & returne to his

*Isa. 37.1.

a To heare some newe prophecie and to haue comforte of him.

b The dangers are so great ŷ we can nether auenge this blasphemie, nor helpe our selues, no more thē a womā in her trauel.

c Meaning Ierusalém ŵ onely remained of all the cities of Iudáh.

d The Lord can with one blast blowe away all the strength of mā and" turne it into dust.

owne land: & I wil cause him to fall vpon
the sworde in his owne land.
8 ¶So Rabshakéh returned, and founde
the King of Asshúr fighting against Libnáh: for he had heard that he was departed from Lachísh.
9 [e] He heard also men say of Tirhákah
King of *Ethiopia, [f] Beholde, he his come
out to fight against thee: he therefore departed and sent *other* messengers vnto
Hezekiáh, saying,
10 Thus shal ye speake to Hezekiáh Kĩg of
Iudáh, & say, Let not thy [g] God disceiue
thee in whome thou trustest, saying, Ierusalém shal not be deliuered into the hand
of the King of Asshúr.
11 Beholde, thou hast heard what the Kings
of Asshúr haue done to all lands, how they
haue destroyed them: and shalt thou be
deliuered?
12 Haue the gods of the heathẽ deliuered
them which my fathers haue destroyed? *as*
Gozán, and Harán, and Rézeph, and the
childrẽ of Eden, which were in Thelasár?
13 Where is the King of Hamáth, and the
King of Arpád, and the King of the citie
of Sepharuaim, Hená and Iuá?
14 ¶So Hezekiáh receiued the letter of the
hand of the messengers, and red it: & Hezekiáh wẽt vp into the house of the Lord,
and Hezekiáh spred it before the [h] Lord.
15 And Hezekiáh [i] prayed before ŷ Lord,
and said, O Lord God of Israél, which
dwellest betwene the Cherubíms, thou art
very God alone ouer all the kingdomes
of the earth: thou hast made the heauen &
the earth.
16 Lord, [k] bowe downe thine eare, and
heare: Lord open thine eyes and beholde,
and heare the wordes of Sancheríb, who
hathe sent to blaspheme the [l] liuing God.
17 Trueth it is, Lord, that the Kings of Asshúr haue destroyed the nacions and their
lands,
18 And haue set fyre on their gods: for they
were no gods, but the worke of mans hãds,
euen wood and stone: therefore they destroyed them.
19 Now therefore, O Lord our God, I
beseche thee, saue thou vs out of his hand,
that all the [m] kingdomes of ŷ earth may
knowe, that thou, ô Lord, art onely God.
20 ¶Then Isaiáh the sonne of Amóz sent
to Hezekiáh, saying, Thus sayth ŷ Lord
God of Israél, I haue heard that which
thou hast prayed me, concerning Saneheríb King of Asshúr.
21 This is the worde that the Lord hathe
spoken against him, O [n] virgine, daughter of Zión, he hathe despised thee, *and*
laughed thee to scorne: ô daughter of Ierusalém, he hathe shaken his head at thee.
22 Whome hast thou railed on? and whome

e That is, Saneherib.
*Or, blacke Mores.
f For ŷ Kings of Ethiopia & Egypt ioyned together against ŷ King of Assyria because of his oppression of other countreys.
g The more nere that the wicked are to their destruction, the more they blaspheme.
h Before the Arke of the couenant.
i He sheweth what is the true refuge & succour in all dangers, to wit, to flee to the Lord by ernest prayer.
k Shew by effect that thou wilt not suffer thy Name to be blasphemed.
l By this title he discerneth God from all idoles and false gods.
m He sheweth for what end the faithful desire of God to be deliuered: to wit, ŷ he may be glorified by their deliuerance.
n Because as yet Ierusalém had not bene taken by the enemie, therefore he calleth her virgine.

hast thou blasphemed? and against whome
hast thou exalted thy voyce, and lifted vp
thine eyes on hye? *euen* [o] against the Holy one of Israél.
23 By thy messengers thou hast railed on
the Lord, and said, By the multitude of
my charets I am come vp to the top of
the mountaines, by the sides of Lebanón,
and wil cut downe the hie cedres thereof,
and the faire fyrre trees thereof, and I wil
go into the [p] lodging of his borders, and
into the forest of *his Cármel.
24 I haue digged, and dronke the waters of
others, and with the plant of my feete haue I dryed all the *floods closed in.
25 Hast thou not heard, how I haue of olde
time made it, and haue formed it long a-
go? [q] and shulde I nowe bring it, that it
shulde be destroyed, *and layed* on ruinous
heapes, *as* cities defensed?
26 Whose [r] inhabitãts haue small power,
and are afraied, and confounded: they are
like the grasse of the field, and grene herbe, *or* grasse on the house toppes, or as
corne blasted before it be growen.
27 I knowe thy dwelling, yea, thy goying
out, and thy comming in, and thy fury a-
gainst me.
28 And because thou ragest against me, and
thy tumult is come vp to mine eares, I
wil put mine [s] hoke in thy nostrels, and my
bridel in thy lippes, & wil bring thee backe againe the same way thou camest.
29 And this shalbe a [t] signe vnto thee, *ô*
Hezekiáh, Thou shalt eat this yere suche
things as growe of thẽ selues, and the next
yere suche as growe without sawing, and
the third yere sowe ye and reape, & plant
vineyardes, and eat the frutes thereof.
30 And the remnant that is escaped of the
house of Iudáh, shal againe take [u] roote
downewarde, and beare frute vpwarde.
31 For out of Ierusalém shal go a remnant,
and some that shal escape out of mount
Zión: the [x] zeale of the Lord of hostes
shal do this.
32 Wherefore thus saith the Lord, concerning the King of Asshúr, He shal not entre into this citie, nor shote an arow there,
nor come before it with shield, nor cast a
mount against it:
33 *But* he shal returne the way he came, and
shal not come into this citie, sayth the
Lord.
34 For I wil defend this citie to saue it for
mine owne sake, & for Dauid my seruants
sake.
35 ¶*And the same night the Angel of the
Lord went out and smote in the campe of
Asshúr an hundreth foure score and fyue
thousand: so when they rose early in the
morning, beholde, they were all dead
corpses.

o God counteth that iniurie done to him, and wil reuenge it ŷ is done to anie of his Saintes.
p Meaning Ierusalém, ŵ Isaiáh calleth the hight of his borders, to wit, of Iudáh, Isa. 37,24.
*Or, pleasant countrey.
*Or, the waters of cities besieged.
q He declareth that forasmuche as he is ŷ autor and beginning of his Church, he wil neuer suffer it vtterly to be destroyed, as other cities and kingdomes.
r Thus he describeth the wicked, which for a time florish, and afterwarde fade and decay like flowres.
s I wil bridel thy rage and turne thee to & fro as pleaseth me.
t God did not onely promes him the victorie, but giueth him a signe to confirme his faith.
u The Lord wil multiplie in great nomber that small remnant of Iudáh that is escaped.
x The loue, ŷ God beareth toward his Church, shal ouercome the counsels and enterprises of men.

Isa. 37.36. tobi. 1,21. eccl. 48,24. 1. mac. 7,41. 2. mac. 8,19.

36 So

36 So Saneheríb King of Asshúr departed,
and went his way, and returned, and dwelt
in Niniuéh.
37 And as he was in the temple worshiping Nisróch his god, Adramélech and
Sharézer his sonnes [y] slewe him with the
sworde: and they escaped into the land of
Ararát, ad Esarhaddón his sonne reigned in his steade.

y This was ẏ iuste iudgemēt of God for his blasphemie, that he shulde be slaine before that idole, whome he preferred to the liuing God, & by them, by whome he oght by nature to haue bene defended.

CHAP. XX.

1 Hezekiáh is sicke, and receyueth the signe of his health. 12 He receyueth rewardes of Berodách, 13 Sheweth his treasures, and is reprehēded of Isaiáh. 22 He dyeth and Manasséh his sonne reigneth in his steade.

1 ABout that time *was Hezekiáh sicke
vnto death: and ẏ Prophet Isaiáh the
sonne of Amóz came to him, and said vnto him, Thus sayth the Lord, Put thine
house in an ordre: for thou shalt dye, and
not liue.
2 Then he turned his face to the [a] wall, &
prayed to the Lord, saying,
3 I beseche thee, ô Lord, remember now,
how I haue walked before thee in trueth
& with a [b] perfit heart, and haue done that
which is good in thy sight: and Hezekiáh
[c] wept sore.
4 ¶And afore Isaiáh was gone out into
the middle of the court, the worde of the
Lord came to him, saying,
5 Turne againe, and tel Hezekiáh the captaine of my people, Thus sayth the Lord
God of Dauid thy father, I haue heard
thy [d] prayer, *and* sene thy teares: beholde,
I haue healed thee, *and* the third day
thou shalt go vp to the [e] house of the
Lord,
6 And I wil adde vnto thy dayes fiftene yere, & wil deliuer thee and this citie out of
the hand of the King of Asshúr, and wil
defend this citie for mine owne sake, and
for Dauid my seruants sake.
7 Then Isaiáh said, Take a [f] lompe of drye
figs. And they toke it, and layed it on the
boyle, and he recouered.
8 ¶For Hezekiáh had said vnto Isaiáh,
What *shalbe* the signe that the Lord wil
heale me, and that I shal go vp into the
house of the Lord the third day?
9 And Isaiáh answered, This signe shalt
thou haue of the Lord, that the Lord wil
do that he hathe spoken, *Wilt thou* that the
shadowe go forwarde ten degrees, or go
backe ten degrees?
10 And Hezekiáh answered, It is a light
thing for the shadowe to passe forwarde
ten degrees: not so *then*, but let the shadowe [g] go backe ten degrees.
11 And Isaiáh the Prophet called vnto the
Lord, and he broght againe the shadowe
tē degrees backe by the degrees whereby
it had gone downe in the [h] dial of Aház.
12 ¶*The same season Berodách Baladán

2 Chro.32,24 isa.38,1. eccles.48,46.

a That his minde might not be troubled.

b Meaning, without all hypocrisie.

c Not so muche for his owne death, as for feare that idolatrie shulde be restored, which he had destroyed, and so Gods Name be dishonored.

d Because of his vnfained repentance & prayer God turned away his wrath.

e To giue thākes for thy deliuerance.

f He declareth ẏ albeit God cā heale without other medecines, yet he sheweth that he wil not haue these inferior meanes contemned.

g Let the sunne go so manie degrees backe that ẏ houres may be so manie the fewer in the Kings dial

h Which dial was set in the top of the stayres that Aház had made.

Isa.39,1.

the sonne of Baladán King of Babél, sent
letters and a [i] present to Hezekiáh: for he
had heard how that Hezekiáh was sicke.
13 And Hezekiáh heard them, and shewed
them all his treasure house, *to wit*, the siluer,
& the golde, & the spices, and the precious
ointment, & all the house of his armour,
and all that was founde in his treasures:
there was nothing in his house, and in all
his [k] realme, that Hezekiáh shewed them
not.
14 Then Isaiáh the Prophet came vnto
King Hezekiáh, and said vnto him, What
said these men? and from whence came
they to thee? And Hezekiáh said, They be
come from a farre countrey, *euen* from Babél.
15 Then said he, What haue they sene in
thine house? And Hezekiáh answered, All
that is in mine house haue they sene: there is nothing among my treasures, that
I haue not shewed them.
16 And Isaiáh said vnto Hezekiáh, Heare
the worde of the Lord.
17 Beholde, the dayes come, that all that is
in thine house, and whatsoeuer thy fathers
haue laied vp in store vnto this day, * shal
be caried into Babél: Nothing shalbe left,
saith the Lord.
18 And of thy sonnes, that shal procede out
of thee, & which thou shalt beget, shal
they take away, and they shalbe eunuches
in the palace of the King of Babél.
19 Then Hezekiáh said vnto Isaiáh, The
worde of the Lord which thou hast [l] spoken, is good: for said he, Shal it not *be good*,
if [m] peace and trueth be in my dayes?
20 Concerning the rest of the actes of He
zekiáh, and all his valiant dedes, and how
he made a poole & a cōdite, & broght water into the citie, are they not writen in
the boke of the Chronicles of the Kings
of Iudáh?
21 And Hezekiáh slept with his fathers: &
Manasséh his sonne reigned in his steade.

i Moued with the fauour ẏ God shewed to Hezekiáh, & also because he had declared him selfe enemie to Saneheríb his enemie which was now destroied.

k Beīg moued with ambition and vaine glorie, & also because he semed to reioyce in ẏ friendship of him ẏ was Gods enemie & an infidele.

2.Kin.24,13. & 25,13. iere.27,19.

l He acknowledgeth Isaiáh to be the true Prophet of God, and therefore humbleth him selfe to his worde.

m Seīg ẏ God hathe shewed me this fauour to grant me quietnes durīg my life: for he was afraied lest ẏ enemies shulde haue had occasion to reioyce, if the Church had decaied in his time, because he had restored religion.

CHAP. XXI.

3 King Manasséh restoreth idolatrie, 16 And vseth great crueltie. 18 He dyeth, and Amón his sonne succedeth, 23 Who is killed of his owne seruants. 26 After him reigneth Iosiáh.

1 MAnasséh *was twelue yere olde whē
he began to reigne, and reigned fiftie and fiue yere in Ierusalém: his mothers
name also was Hephzi-báh.
2 And he did euil in the sight of the Lord
after the abominacion of the heathen,
whome the *Lord had cast out before the
children of Israél.
3 For he went backe and buylt the hie places, *which Hezekiáh his father had destroied: and he erected vp altars for Báal,
and made a groue, as did Aháb King of

2.Chro.33,1.

Deu.18,9.

Chap.18,4.

Iſraél,and worſhiped all the hoſte of heauen and ſerued them.
4 Alſo he* buylt altars in the houſe of the
Lord,of the which the Lord ſaid,*In Ieruſalém wil I put my Name.
5 And he buylt altars for all the hoſte of the
heauen in the two courtes of the houſe of
the Lord.
6 And he cauſed his ſonnes [a] to paſſe
through the fyre, and gaue him ſelfe to
witchcraft and ſorcerie,and he vſed them
that had familiar ſpirits and were ſothe-
ſayers, and did muche euil in the ſight of
the Lord to angre him.
7 And he ſet the image of the groue, that
he had made,in the houſe,whereof ẏ Lord
had ſaid to Dauid and to Salomón his
ſonne,* In this houſe, and in Ieruſalém,
which I haue choſen out of all the tribes
of Iſraél,wil I put my Name for euer.
8 Nether wil I make ẏ feete of Iſraél moue anie more out of the land,which I gaue
their fathers: ſo that they wil [b] obſerue
and do all that I haue commanded them,
& according to all the Lawe that my ſeruant Moſés commanded them.
9 Yet they obeyed not, but Manaſſéh led
them out of the way,to do more wickedly
then did the heathen people, whome the
Lord deſtroyed before the children of
Iſraél.
10 Therefore the Lord ſpake by his ſeruãts
the Prophetes,ſaying,
11 *Becauſe that Manaſſéh King of Iudáh
hathe done ſuche abominaciõs, and hathe
wroght more wickedly then all that the
Amorites(which were before him) did, &
hathe made Iudáh ſinne alſo ẇ his idoles,
12 Therefore thus ſaith the Lord God of
Iſraél, Beholde,I wil bring an euil vpon
Ieruſalém and Iudáh,that whoſo heareth
of it,bothe his eares ſhal [c] tingle.
13 And I wil ſtretch ouer Ieruſalém the line [d] of Samaria, and the plommet of the
houſe of Aháb: and I wil wipe Ieruſalém,
as a man wipeth a diſh, which he wipeth,
and turneth it vpſide downe.
14 And I wil forſake the [e] remnant of mine inheritance, and deliuer them into the
hãd of their enemies,and they ſhalbe robbed & ſpoiled of all their aduerſaries,
15 Becauſe they haue done euil in my ſight,
and haue prouoked me to angre, ſince the
time their fathers came out of Egypt vntil
this day.
16 Moreouer Manaſſéh ſhed [f] innocent
blood exceding muche, til he repleniſhed
Ieruſalém from corner to corner, beſide
his ſinne wherewith he made Iudáh to ſinne,and to do euil in the ſight of the Lord.
17 Concerning the reſt of the actes of Manaſſéh, and all that he did, and his ſinne
ẏ he ſinned, are they not writen in ẏ boke

Iere.32,34. 2.Sam.7,10.

a Read Chap. 16,3.

1.King.8,29. & 9,3. 2.king.7,10.

b Therefore ſeing they obeyed not the cõmãdemẽt of God,they were iuſtly caſt forthe of that lãd which thei had but on cõdicion.

Iere.15,4.

c Meaning, ẏ whoſoeuer ſhal heare of this great plague,ſhalbe aſtoniſhed.

d As I haue deſtroyed Samaria and the houſe of Aháb,ſo wil I deſtroye Iudáh.

e Meaning Iudáh and Beniamín, which were onely left of the reſt of the tribes.

f The Ebrewes write that he ſlewe Iſaiáh ẏ Prophet, who was his father in Lawe.

of the Chronicles of the Kings of Iudáh?
18 And Manaſſéh ſlept with his fathers,and
was buryed in ẏ gardẽ of his owne houſe,
euen in the garden of Vzzá:and Amón his
ſonne reigned in his ſteade.
19 ¶ *Amón was two and twentie yere olde,when he began to reigne,and he reigned two yere in Ieruſalém: his mothers
name alſo was Meſhullémeth the daughter of Harúz of Iotbáh.
20 And he did euil in the ſight of the Lord,
as his father Manaſſéh did.
21 For he walked in all the waie,that his father walked in, and ſerued the idoles that
his father ſerued,and worſhiped them.
22 And he forſoke the Lord God of his fa
thers, and walked not in the [g] way of the
Lord.
23 And the ſeruants of Amón conſpired
againſt him, and ſlewe the King in his
owne houſe.
24 And the people of the land ſlewe all
them that had conſpired againſt King
Amón, and the people made Ioſiáh his
ſonne King in his ſteade.
25 Concerning the reſt of the actes of A-
món,which he did, are they not writen
in the boke of ẏ Chronicles of the Kings
of Iudáh?
26 And "they buryed him in his ſepulchre
in the garden of Vzzá:and Ioſiáh his ſonne reigned in his ſteade.

2.Chro.33,20.

g That is, according to his cõmandemẽts.

"Or, he buryed him, to wit, Ioſiáh his ſonne.

CHAP. XXII.

4 Ioſiáh repareth the Temple. 8 Helkiáh findeth the boke of the Lawe, and cauſeth it to be preſented to Ioſiáh. 12 Who ſendeth to Huldáh the propheteſſe to inquire the Lords wil.

1 IOſiáh was*eight yere olde when he began to reigne, and he reigned one and
thirtie yere in Ieruſalém. His mothers
name alſo was Iedidáh the daughter of A-
daiáh of Bozcáth.
2 And he did vprightly in the ſight of the
Lord,& [a] walked in all the wayes of Dauid his father, and bowed nether to the
right hand,nor to the left.
3 ¶ And in the eightenth yere of King Ioſiáh, the King ſent Shaphán the ſonne of
Azaliáh the ſonne of Meſhullám the chã
celler to the houſe of the Lord,ſaying,
4 Go vp to Hilkiáh the hie Prieſt, that he
may "ſumme the ſiluer which is broght into the houſe of the Lord, which the kepers of the" [b] dore haue gathered of the
people.
5 And let them [c] deliuer it into the hand
of them that do the worke, *and* haue the
ouerſight of the houſe of the Lord: let
them giue it to them that worke in the
houſe of the Lord, to repaire the decaied
places of the houſe:
6 *To wit,* vnto the artificers and carpenters
& maſons,and to bie tymber, and hewed
ſtone

2.Chro.34,1.

a His zeale was propheciedof, & his name mencioned by Iaddó the Prophet, more then thre hundreth yeres before, 1.King.13,2: and being but eight yere olde,he ſoght ẏ God of his father Dauid, 2.Chro.34,3.

"Or, coyne, as vers.9.

"Or,veſſel.

b Certeine of the Prieſts were appointed to this office, as Chap.12,9.

c From the time of Ioáſh for the ſpace of 224 yeres the Temple remained without reparatiõ through the negligence of ẏ Prieſts. this declareth that they that haue a charge and execute it not, oght to haue it taken from them.

ſtone to repaire the houſe.
7 Howbeit let no rekening be made with
them of the money, that is deliuered into
their hand: for they deale [d] faithfully.
8 And Hilkiáh the hie Prieſt said vnto
Shaphán the chanceller, I haue founde
the [e] boke of the Lawe in the houſe of the
Lord: and Hilkiáh gaue the boke to Shaphán,
and he red it.
9 So Shaphán the chanceller came to the
King, and broght him worde againe, &
said, Thy seruãts haue "gathered the money,
that was founde in the houſe, and
haue deliuered it vnto the hands of them
that do the worke, *and* haue the ouerſight
of the houſe of the Lord.
10 Alſo Shaphán the chanceller ſhewed
the King, sayĩg, Hilkiáh the Prieſt hathe
deliuered me a boke. And Shaphán red
it before the King.
11 And when the King had heard the wordes
of the boke of the Lawe, he rent his
clothes.
12 Therefore the King commanded Hilkiáh
the Prieſt, and Ahikám the ſonne of
Shaphán, and Achbór the ſonne of Michaiáh,
and Shaphán the chanceller, and
Aſahiáh the Kings ſeruant, saying,
13 Go ye *and* [f] inquire of the Lord for me,
and for the people, and for all Iudáh, concerning
the wordes of this boke that is
founde: for great is the wrath of the Lord
that is kindled againſt vs, becauſe our fathers
haue not obeyed the wordes of this
boke, to do according vnto all that which
is writen therein for vs.
14 ¶ So Hilkiáh the Prieſt and Ahikám,
and Achbór and Shaphán, and Aſahiáh
went vnto Huldáh the Propheteſſe the
wife of Shallúm, the ſonne of Tikuáh,
the ſonne of Harhás keper of the wardrobe:
(and ſhe dwelt in Ieruſalém in the
[g] colledge) and they communed with her.
15 And ſhe anſwered them, Thus ſayth
the Lord God of Iſraél, Tel the man that
ſent you to me,
16 Thus ſayth the Lord, Beholde, I wil
bring euil vpon this place, and on the inhabitants
thereof, *euen* all the wordes of
ỹ boke which ỹ King of Iudáh hathe red,
17 Becauſe they haue forſaken me, and haue
burnt incenſe vnto other gods, to
anger me with all the [h] workes of their
hands: my wrath alſo ſhalbe kindled againſt
this place, and ſhal not be quenched.
18 But to the King of Iudáh, who ſent you
to inquire of the Lord, ſo ſhal ye ſay vnto
him, Thus ſayth the Lord God of Iſraél,
The wordes that thou haſt heard, *ſhal
come to paſſe.*
19 *But* becauſe thine heart did [i] melt, and
thou haſt humbled thy ſelfe before the

d So God prouided him of faithful ſeruãts, ſeing he went about ſo zealouſly to ſet forthe the worke of God.
e This was the copie that Moſés left them, as appeareth 2 Chro 34,14. which ether by the negligence of the Prieſts had bene loſt, or els by the wickednes of idolatrous Kings had bene aboliſhed.
"Ebr. melted.
f Meaning to ſome Prophet whome God reueleth the knowledge of things vnto, as Ier. 21,1. thogh at other times they inquired the Lord by Vrim & Thũmim.
g Or, the houſe of doctrine ẇ was nere to the Temple, & where the learned aſſembled to intreat the Scriptures, & the doctrine of the Prophetes.
h The workes of mans hand here ſignifie all that mã inuenteth beſide the worde of God, ẇ are abominable in Gods ſeruice.
i Meaning that he did repent, as they, that do not repent, are ſaid to harden their heart, Pſal. 95,8.

Lord, when thou heardeſt what I ſpake againſt
this place, and againſt the inhabitãts
of the ſame, *to wit*, that it ſhulde be deſtroyed
and accurſed, and haſt rent thy
clothes, and wept before me, I haue alſo
heard it, ſayth the Lord.
20 Beholde therefore, I wil gather thee to
thy fathers, and thou ſhalt be put in thy
graue in [k] peace, and thine eyes ſhal not
ſe all the euil, which I wil bring vpon this
place. Thus they broght the King worde
againe.

CHAP. XXIII.

2 Ioſiáh readeth the Lawe before the people. 3 He maketh a couenant with the Lord. 4 He putteth downe the idoles, after he had killed their prieſts. 22 He kepeth Paſſeouer. 24 He deſtroyeth the coniurers. 29 He was killed in Megiddó. 30 And his ſonne Iehoaház reigneth in his ſteade. 33 After he was taken, his ſonne Iehoiakím was made King.

1 Then *the King [a] ſent, and there gathered
vnto him all the Elders of Iudáh
and of Ieruſalém.
2 And the King went vp into the houſe of
the Lord, with all the men of Iudáh and
all the inhabitãts of Ieruſalém with him,
and the Prieſts and Prophetes, and all the
people bothe ſmall & great: and he red in
their eares all the wordes of the boke of
the couenant, which was found in the houſe
of the Lord.
3 And the King ſtode by [b] the piller, and
made a [c] couenant before the Lord, that
they ſhulde walke after the Lord, and kepe
his commandements, and his teſtimonies,
and his ſtatutes with all *their* heart, &
with all *their* ſoul, that they might accompliſh
the wordes of this couenant writen
in this boke. And all ỹ people ſtode to the
couenant.
4 Then the King commanded Hilkiáh the
hie Prieſt and the [d] Prieſts of the ſecond
ordre, and the kepers of the dore, to bring
out of the Temple of the Lord all the
veſſels that were made for Báal, and
for the groue, and for all the hoſte of heauen,
and he burnt them without Ieruſalém
in the fields of Kedrón, and caryed
[e] the powdre of them into Beth-él.
5 And he put downe ỹ [f] Chemerím, whome
the Kings of Iudáh had fouded to burne
incẽſe in the hie places, & in the cities of
Iudáh, and about Ieruſalém, & alſo them
that burnt incenſe vnto Báal, to the ſunne
and to the moone, and to the planets, &
to all the hoſte of heauen.
6 And he broght out the [g] groue from the
Tẽple of the Lord without Ieruſalém vnto
the valley Kedrón, and burnt it in the
valley Kedrón, and ſtampt it to powdre,
and caſt the duſt thereof vpon the [h] graues
of the children of the people.
7 And he brake downe ỹ houſes of ỹ ſodomites,
that were in the houſe of the Lord,

k Whereupon we may gather that the angre of God is ready agaĩſt the wicked, when God taketh his ſeruants out of this worlde.
2.Chro.34,30
a Becauſe he ſawe the great plagues of God that were threatned, he knewe no more ſpedie waye to auoide them, then to turne to God by repentance, ẇ can not come but of faith, and faith by hearĩg of ỹ worde of God.
b Where the King had his place, Chap. 11,14.
c As Ioſhúa did, Ioſ. 24.22
d Meaning the ẇ were next in dignitie to ỹ hie Prieſt.
e In contempt of that altar, which Ierobo-ám had there buylt to ſacrifice to his calues.
f Meaning the prieſts of Báal, which were called Chemirims, ether becauſe thei ware blacke garments, or els were ſmoked with burning incenſe to idoles.
g He remoued that groue ẇ idolaters for deuotion had planted nere vnto the Temple, contrarie to the commãdement of the Lord, Deu 16, 20. or as ſome read, the ſimilitude of a groue which was hanged in the Temple.
h Bothe in cõtempt of the idoles, & reproche of them ẇ had worſhiped them in their liues.

where the women woue hangings for the
groue.
8 Also he broght all the priestes out of the
cities of Iudáh, and defiled the hie places
where the priests had burnt incense, *euen*
from Géba to Beer-shéba, and destroied
the hie places of the gates, that were in ȳ
entring in of the gate of Ioshúa the gouernour of the citie which was at the left
hand of the gate of the citie.
9 Neuertheles the priests of the hie places [i] came not vp to the altar of the Lord
in Ierusalém, saue onely thei did eat of the
vnleauened bread among their brethren.
10 He defiled also [k] Tópheth, which was
in the valley of the children of Hinnóm,
that no man shulde make his sonne or his
daughter passe through ȳ fyre to Mólech.
11 He put downe also the [l] horses that the
Kings of Iudáh had giuen to the sunne at
the entring in of the house of the Lord,
by the chamber of Nethan-mélech the
eunuche, which was *ruler* of the suburbes,
and burnt the charets of the sunne with
fyre.
12 And the altars that were on the top of
the chamber of Aház, which the Kings
of Iudáh had made, and the altars which
Manasséh had made in the two courtes of
the house of the Lord, did the Kĩg breake
downe, and hasted thence, and cast the dust
of them in the *brooke Kedrón.
13 Moreouer the King defiled the hie places that were before Ierusalém and on the
right hand of the [m] mount of corruption
(which *Salomón the King of Israél had
buylt for Ashtóreth the idole of the Zido
nians, and for Chemósh the idole of the
Moabites, and for Milchóm the abomination of the children of Ammón)
14 And he brake the images in pieces, and
cut downe the groues and filled their places with the bones of men.
15 Furthermore [n] the altar that was at Beth-
él, & the hie place made by Ieroboám the
sonne of Nebát, which made Israél to sinne, bothe this altar and also the hie place
brake he downe, & burnt the hie place, &
stampt it to powder and burnt the groue.
16 And as Iosiáh turned him selfe, he spied
the graues, that were in the mount, and
sent and toke the bones out of the graues,
and burnt them vpon the altar, and polluted it, according to the worde of the Lord
that the [o] man of God proclaimed which
cryed the same wordes.
17 Thẽ he said, What title is that which I
se? And the mẽ of the citie said vnto him,
It is the sepulchre of the man of God,
which came from Iudáh, and tolde these
things that thou hast done to the altar of
Beth-él.
18 Thẽ said he, Let him alone: let none remoue his bones. So his bones were saued
with the bones of the [p] Prophet that came
from Samaria.
19 Iosiáh also toke away all the houses of
the hie places, which were in the cities of
Samaria, which the Kings of Israél had
made to angre *the Lord*, and did to them
according to all the factes that he had
done in Beth-él.
20 And he sacrificed all the priests of the
hie places, that were there vpõ the altars,
and burnt mens bones vpon them, and returned to Ierusalém.
21 ¶ Then the King commanded all the
people, saying, *Kepe the Passeouer vnto
the Lord your God, *as it is writen in the
boke of this couenant.
22 And there was no Passeouer holden [q] like that from the daies of the Iudges that
iudged Israél, nor in all the dayes of the
Kings of Israél, and of the Kings of Iudáh.
23 And in the eightenth yere of King Iosiáh was this Passeouer celebrated to the
Lord in Ierusalém.
24 Iosiáh also toke away them that had
familiar spirits, & the sothesayers, and the
images, and the idoles, & all the abominacions that were espied in the land of Iudáh & in Ierusalém, to performe the wordes of the * Lawe, which were writen in
the boke that Hilkiáh the Priest founde in
the house of the Lord.
25 Like vnto him was there no King before him, that turned to the Lord with all
his heart, and with all his soule, & with all
his might according to all the Lawe of
Mosés, nether after him arose there anie
like him.
26 Notwithstanding the Lord turned not
from the [r] fearcenes of his great wrath
wherewith he was angrie agaĩst Iudáh, because of all the prouocacions wherewith
Manasséh had prouoked him.
27 Therefore the Lord said, I wil put Iudáh also out of my sight, as I haue put a-
way Israél, and wil cast of this citie Ierusalém, which I haue chosen, and the house
whereof I said, * My Name shalbe there.
28 Concenring the rest of the actes of Iosiáh, and all that he did, are they not writen in the boke of the Chronicles of the
Kings of Iudáh?
29 ¶ *In his dayes Pharaóh Nechóh King
of Egypt went vp against the King of Asshúr to the riuer Peráth. And Kĩg Iosiáh
[s] went against him, whome when *Pharaóh*
sawe, he slewe him at Megiddó.
30 Then his seruants caried him dead from
Megiddó, and broght him to Ierusalém,
& buryed him in his owne sepulchre. And
the people of the land toke Iehoaház the
sonne of Iosiáh, and annointed him, and
made

i Because that those that had forsaken the Lord to serue idoles, were not mete to minister in the seruice of the Lord for the instruction of others.

k Which was a valley nere to Ierusalém, & signifieth a tabret, because they smote on the tabret while their children were burning, that their crye shulde not be heard, where after Iosiáh commanded carions to be cast.

l The idolatrous Kĩgs had dedicate horses & charets to the sunne either to carie ȳ image thereof about as the heathen did, orels to sacrifice thẽ, as a sacrifice moste agreable.

*Or, valley

m That was ȳ mõt of oliues, so called because it was ful of idoles.

1.King.11,7.

n Which Ieroboám had buylt in Israél, 1.King.12,28.

o According to the prophecie of Iaddó, 1.King.13,2.

p Meaning ȳ Prophet ẇ came after him, and caused him to eat contrary to ȳ commandemẽt of the Lord, ẇ were bothe two buryed in one graue, 1.King.13,31.

2.Chro.35,1. 3.esdr.1,1. Exod.12,3. deut.16,2.

q For the multitude & zeale of the people with the great preparation.

Leui.20,27. deut.18,11.

r Because of ȳ wicked heart of the people, ẇ wolde not turne vnto him by repentance.

1.King.8,29. & 9,3. 2.king.7,10.

2.Chro.35,20.

s Because he passed through his countrey, he feared lest he wolde haue done him harme, and therefore wolde haue staied hĩ, yet he consulted not with ȳ Lord, & therefore was slain.

made him King in his fathers steade.
31 *Iehoaház *was* thre and twentie yere olde
when he began to reigne, & reigned thre
moneths in Ierusalém. His mothers name
also was Hamutál the daughter of Ieremiáh of Libnáh.
32 And he did euil in the sight of the Lord,
accordĩg to all that his [t] fathers had done.
33 And Pharaóh Nechóh put him in bonds
[u] at Ribláh in the land of Hamath, [*] while
he reigned in Ierusalém, and put the land
to a tribute of an hundreth talents of siluer, and a talent of golde.
34 ¶ And Pharaóh Nechóh made Eliakím
the sonne of Iosiáh King in steade of Iosiáh his father, and turned his name to Iehoiakím, and toke Iehoaház away, which
when he came to Egypt, dyed there.
35 And Iehoiakím gaue the siluer and the
golde to Pharaóh, and taxed the land to
giue the money, according to the cõmandement of Pharaóh: he leuyed of euerie
man of the people of the land, according
to his vallue, siluer and golde to giue vnto Pharaóh Nechóh.
36 Iehoiakím was fiue and twentie yere olde, whẽn he began to reigne, & he reigned
eleuen yeres in Ierusalém. His mothers
name also was Zebudáh the daughter of
Pedaiáh of Rumáh.
37 And he did euil in the sight of the Lord,
according to all that his fathers had done.

*2.Chro.36,1.
t Meaning, the wicked Kings before
u Which was Antiochia in Syria, called also Hamáth.
*Or, that he shulde not reigne.

CHAP. XXIIII.

1 Iehoiakím made subiect to Nebuchad-nezzár rebelleth. 3 The cause of his ruine and all Iudahs. 6 Iehoiachín reigneth. 15 He and his people are caryed vnto Babylon. 17 Zedekiah is made King.

1 IN his [a] dayes came Nebuchad-nezzár
King of Babél vp, and Iehoiakím became his seruant thre yere: afterwarde he
turned, and rebelled against him.
2 And the Lord sent against him bandes of
the Caldees, & bandes of the Aramites,
and bandes of the Moabites, and bandes
of the Ammonites, & he sent them agaĩst
Iudáh, to destroye it, * according to the
worde of the Lord, which he spake by his
seruants the Prophetes.
3 Surely by the [b] cõmandement of ỷ Lord
came this vpon Iudáh, that he might put
them out of his sight for the sinnes of Manasséh, according to all that he did,
4 And for the innocent blood that he shed,
(for he filled Ierusalém w̃ innocent blood)
therefore the Lord wolde not pardone it.
5 Concerning the rest of the actes of Iehoiakím, & all that he did, are thei not writẽ
in the boke of the Chronicles of ỷ Kings
of Iudáh?
6 So Iehoiakím [c] slept with his fathers, and
Iehoiachín his sõne reigned in his steade.
7 ¶ And the King of Egypt came no more
out of his land: for the King of Babél had
taken from the riuer of Egypt, vnto the
riuer [*] Peráth, all that perteined to the
King of Egypt.
8 ¶ Iehoiachin *was* eightene yere olde, whẽ
he began to reigne, and reigned in Ierusalém thre moneths. His mothers name also
was Nehushtá, the daughter of Elnathán
of Ierusalém.
9 And he did euil in the sight of the Lord,
according to all that his father had done.
10 * In that time came the seruants of Nebuchad-nezzár King of Babél vp against
Ierusalém: so the citie was besieged.
11 And Nebuchad-nezzár King of Babél
came against the citie, & his seruants did
besiege it.
12 Thẽ Iehoiachín the King of Iudáh [d] came out against the King of Babél, he, and
his mother, and his seruants, and his princes, and his eunuches: and the King of
Babél toke him in the eight yere [e] of his
reigne.
13 *And he caryed out thence all the treasures of the house of the Lord, and the treasures of the Kings house, and brake all the
vessels of golde, which Salomón King of
Israél had made in the Tẽple of the Lord,
as the Lord had said.
14 And he caryed away all Ierusalém, and
all the princes, and all the strong men of
warre, *euen* ten thousand into captiuitie, &
all the workemen, & conning mẽ: so none
remained sauing the poore people of the
land.
15 * And he caryed away Iehoiachín into
Babél, and the Kings mother, & the Kings
wiues, and his eunuches, and the mightie
of the land caryed he away into captiuitie from Ierusalém to Babél,
16 And all the men of warre, *euen* seuen
thousand, and carpenters, & lockesmithes
a thousand: all that were strong and apt
for warre, did the King of Babél bring to
Babél captiues.
17 ¶*And the King of Babél made Mattaniáh his vncle King in his steade, & changed his name to Zedekiáh.
18 Zedekiáh was one & twentie yere olde,
when he began to reigne, and he reigned
eleuẽ yeres in Ierusalém. His mothers name also was Hamutál the daughter of Ieremiáh of Libnáh.
19 And he did euil in the sight of the Lord,
according to all that Iehoiakím had
done.
20 Therefore certeinly the wrath of the
Lord was against Ierusalém & Iudáh vntil
he cast them out of his [f] sight. And Zedekiáh rebelled against the King of Babél.

a In the end of ỷ third yere of his reigne, and in the beginning of the fourte, Dan.1,1.
Chap. 20,17. & 23,27.
b Thogh God vsed these wicked tyrãts to execute his iuste iudgemẽts, yet they are not to be excused, because thei proceded of ambicion & malice.
c Not that he was buryed w̃ his fathers, but he dyed in the way, as they led him prisoner towarde Babylon: read Iere 22,19.
*Or, Euphrates.
*Dan.1,1.
d That is, yelded him selfe vnto him by ỷ counsel of Ieremie.
e In the reigne of the King of Babylon.
Chap.20,17. Isa.39,6.
2.Chro.36,10. Esther 2,6.
Iere.37,1. & 52,1.
f Out of Ierusalém and Iudáh into Babylón.

CHAP. XXV.

1 Ierusalém is besieged of Nebuchad-nezzár, & taken. 7 The sonnes of Zedekiáh are slayne before his eyes, &

after are his owne eyes put out. 21 Iudáh is broght to Babylón. 25 Gedoliáh is slayne. 27 Iehoiachín is exalted.

Iere.39,1.& 52,4.
a That is, of Zedekiáh.
b Which the Ebrewes call Tebét, and it côteineth part of December & parte of Ianuarie.
*Or, a mount.

1 AND *in the [a] ninthe yere of his reigne, the [b] tenth *moneth & tenth* day of
the moneth Nebuchad-nezzár King of
Babél came, he, & all his hoste against Ierusalém, and pitched against it, and they
buylt * fortes against it rounde about it.
2 So the citie was besieged vnto the eleuēth
yere of King Zedekiáh.
3 And the ninthe *day* of the moneth the famine was [c] sore in the citie, so that there
was no bread for the people of the land.
4 Then the citie was broken vp, and all
the men of warre *fled* by night, by the
waye of the [d] gate, *which is* betwene two
walles that was by the Kings garden: now
the Caldees *were* by the citie rounde a-
bout: *and the King* went by the way of the
wildernes.
5 But the armie of the Caldees pursued after the King, and toke him in the deserts
of Ierichó, and all his hoste was scatred
from him.
6 Then they toke the King, and caryed
him vp to the King of Babél to Ribláh,
where they [e] gaue iudgement vpon him.
7 And they slewe the sonnes of Zedekiáh
before his eyes, and put out the eyes of
Zedekiáh, and bounde him in chaines, &
caryed him to Babél.
8 ¶ And in the fift moneth, & [f] seuenth *day*
of the moneth, which was the nintenth
yere of King Nebuchad-nezzár King of
Babél, came Nebuzar-adán * chief steward
and seruant of the King of Babél, to Ierusalém,
9 And burnt the house of the Lord, and the
Kings house, and all the houses of Ierusalém, & all the great houses burnt he with
fyre.
10 And all the armie of the Caldees that
were with the chief stewarde, brake downe
the walles of Ierusalém rounde about.
11 And the rest of the people that were left
in the citie, and those that were fled and
[g] fallen to the King of Babél, with the
remnant of the multitude, did Nebuzar-
adán chief stewarde carye away captiue.
12 But the chief stewarde left of the poore
of the land to dresse the vines, and to til
the land.
13 * Also the pillers of brasse that were in
the house of the Lord, and the bases, and
the brasen Sea that was in the house of the
Lord, did the Caldees breake, and caryed
the brasse of them to Babél.
14 The pottes [h] also and the besomes, and
the instruments of musike, and the incense
asshes, & all the vessels of brasse that they
ministred in, toke they away.
15 And the asshe pannes, and the basens, *and*
all that was of golde, & that was of siluer,
toke the chief stewarde away,
16 With the two pillers, one Sea & the bases, which Salomón had made for the house of the Lord: the brasse of all these vessels was without weight.
17 *The height of the one piller was eightene cubites, and the chapiter thereon *was*
brasse, and the height of the chapiter *was*
with networke thre cubites, and pomegranates vpon the chapiter rounde about, all
of brasse: and likewise *was* the seconde piller with the networke.
18 And the chief stewarde toke Seraiáh the
chief Priest, and Zephaniáh the [i] seconde
Priest, and the thre kepers of the dore.
19 And out of the citie he toke an eunuche
that had the ouersight of the mē of warre,
and [k] fiue men of them that were in the
Kings presence, which were founde in the
citie, and Sophér captaine of the hoste,
who mustred the people of the land, and
threscore men of the people of the land,
that were founde in the citie.
20 And Nebuzar-adán the chief stewarde
toke them, and broght them to the King
of Babél to Ribláh.
21 And the King of Babél smote them, and
slewe them at Ribláh in the land of Hamáth. So Iudáh was caryed away captiue
out of his owne land.
22 *Howbeit there remained people in the
land of Iudáh, whome Nebuchad-nezzár
King of Babél left, & made Gedaliáh the
sonne of Ahikám the sonne of Shaphán
ruler ouer them.
23 Thē when all the captaines of the hoste
& *their* men heard, that the King of Babél
had made Gedaliáh gouernour, thei came
to Gedaliáh to Mizpáh, to wit, Ishmaél
the sonne of Nethaniáh, and Iohanán the
sonne of Káreah, and Seraiáh the sonne of
Tanhúmeth ẏ Netophathite, & Iaazaniáh ẏ sonne of Maachathí, thei & their mē.
24 And Gedaliáh [l] sware to thē, & to their
men, and said vnto them, Feare not to be
the seruants of the Caldees: dwel in the
land, and serue the King of Babél, and ye
shal be wel.
25 *But in the seuenth moneth Ishmaél the
sonne of Nethaniáh the sonne of Elishamá of the Kings sede, came, and ten men
with him, & smote Gedaliáh, & he dyed,
and so did he the Iewes, and the Caldees
that were with him at Mizpáh.
26 Then all the people bothe small & great
and the captaines of the armie arose, and
came to [m] Egypt: for they were afrayed of
the Caldees.
27 Notwithstanding in the seuen and thirtieth yere after, [n] Iehoiachín King of Iudáh was caryed away in the twelft moneth
& the seuen and twentith *day* of the moneth, Euil-merodách King of Babél in the
yere

c In so muche ẏ the mothers did eat their children, Lament.4,10.
d Which was a posterne dore or some secret gate to issue out at.
e Or condēned hī for his periurie & treasō, 2.Chro.36,13.
f Ieremie writeth Chap.52,12 the tenth day, because ẏ fyre continued frō the seuenth day to ẏ tēth.
*Or, captaine of the garde.
g While the siege indured.
Chap.20,17. iere.27,22.
h Of these read Exod. 27,3.
1.King 7,15. iere.52,21. 2.chro.3,15.
i That is, one appointed to succede in the hie Priests rowme, if he were sicke or els otherwise letted.
k Ieremie maketh mencion of seuen, but here he speaketh of them that were the chiefest.
Iere.40,5.& 9.
l That is, he did exhorte them in the Name of the Lord, according to Ieremies coūsel, to submit them selues to Nebuchad-nezzár, seing it was the reueled wil of the Lord.
Iere.41,1.
m Contrary to Ieremies coūsel, Iere.40,41 & 42,43.
n Thus lōg was he, his wife, & his childrē in Babylón, whome Nebuchad nezzars sonne, after his fathers death, preferred to honour: thus by Gods prouidence the sede of Dauid was reserued euen vnto Christ.

yere that he began to reigne, did lift vp
the head of Iehoiachín King of Iudáh out
of the prison,
28 And spake kindely to him, & set his throne aboue the throne of the Kings that were with him in Babél,
29 And changed his prisongarments: and
he did continually eat bread before him,
all the dayes of his life.
30 And his [o] porciō was a cōtinual porcion
giuen him by the King, euerie day a certein, all the dayes of his life.

o Meaning, ẏ he had an ordinarie in the court.

THE FIRST BOKE OF the "Chronicles," or Paralipoménon.

"Ebr. Wordes of dayes.
"Or, of things omitted, to wit, in the bokes of the Kings.

THE ARGUMENT.

The Iewes comprehend bothe these bokes in one, which the Grecians because of the length deuide into two: and they are called Chronicles, because they note briefly the histories from Adám to the returne from their captiuitie in Babylón. But these are not those bokes of Chronicles, which are so oft mencioned in the bokes of Kings of Iudáh and Israél, which did at large set forthe the storie of bothe the kingdomes, and afterward perished in the captiuitie: but an abridgement of the same, and were gathered by Esra, as the Iewes write, after their returne frō Babylón. This fyrst boke conteineth a brief rehearsal of the children of Adám vnto Abrahám, Izhák, Iaakób, and the twelue Patriarches, chiefly of Iudáh and of the reigne of Dauid, because Christ came of him according to the flesh. And therefore it setteth forthe the more amply his actes, bothe cōcerning ciuil gouernement, and also the administracion, and care of things concerning religion, for the good successe whereof he reioyceth, and giueth thankes to the Lord.

CHAP. I.

1 The genealogie of Adám and Nóah vntil Abrahám. 27 And from Abrahám to Esau. 35 His children. 43 Kings and dukes came of him.

1 ADám,[a] Sheth, Enósh,
2 Kenán, Mahalaleél, Ié-
red,
3 Henóch, Methushélah,
Lámech,
4 Nóah, [b] Shem, Ham, &
Iápheth.
5 ¶*The sonnes of Iápheth were Gómer,
and Magóg, and Madái, and Iauán, and
Tubál, and Méshech, and Tirás.
6 And the sonnes of Gómer, Ashchenáz, &
"Iphath and Togarmáh.
7 Also the sonnes of Iauán, Elisháh and
Tarshisháh, Kittím, and "Dodaním.
8 ¶The sonnes of Ham were Cush and
Mizráim, Put and Canáan.
9 And the sonnes of Cush, Sibá and Hauiláh, and Sabtá, and Raamáh, and Sabte-
chá. Also the sonnes of Raamáh were Shebá and Dedán.
10 And Cush begate [c] Nimród, who begā
to be mighty in the earth.
11 And Mizráim begate Ludím and Ana-
mím, Lehabím and Naphtuhím:
12 Pathrusim also, & Casluhím, of whome
came the Philistíms, and Caphtorím.
13 Also Canáan begate Zídon his first
borne, and Heth,
14 And the Iebusite, and the Amorite, and
the Girgashite,
15 And the Hiuuite, and the Arkite and
the Simite,
16 And the Aruadite, & the Zemarite, and
the Hamathite.
17 ¶*The sonnes of Shem were Elám and

a Meaning that Sheth was Adams sonne & Enósh Sheths sonne.
b It had bene sufficient to haue named Shem, of whome came Abrahám and Dauid, but because the worlde was restored by these thre, mencion is also made of Ham and Iápheth.
Gen. 10,2.
"Or, Riphath.
"Or, Rodanim.
c Who first did lift vp him self aboue others, Genes. 10,8.
Gen. 10,22. & 11,10.

Asshúr, and Arpachshád, and Lud, and
[d] Arám, and Vz, and Hul and Géther, and
Méshech.
18 Also Arpachshád begate Shélah, & Shé-
láh begate [e] Eber.
19 Vnto Eber also were borne two sonnes:
the name of the one was Péleg: for in his
dayes was the earth deuided: and his brothers name was Ioktán.
20 Then Ioktán begate Almodád and Shéleph, and Hazermáueth and Iérah,
21 And Hadorám and Vzál and Dikláh,
22 And Ebál, and Abimaél, and Shebá,
23 And Ophír, and Hauiláh and Iobáb: all
these were the sonnes of Ioktán.
24 [f]Shem, [g] Arpachshád, Shélah,
25 Eber, Péleg, Rehú,
26 Serúg, Nahór, Teráh,
27 *Abrám, which is Abrahám.
28 ¶The sonnes of Abrahám were Izhák,
and Ishmaél.
29 These are their generacio̅s. *The eldest
sonne of Ishmaél was Nebaióth, and Kedár, and Adbeél, and Mibsám,
30 Mishmá, and Dumáh, Massá, "Hadád, and
Temá,
31 Ietúr, Naphísh and Kédemah: these are
the sonnes of Ishmaél.
32 ¶And Keturáh Abrahams [h] cōcubine
bare sonnes, Zimrán, and Iokshán, & Medán, and Midián, and Ishbák, & Shúah: and
the sonnes of Iokshán, Shebá, and Dedán.
33 And the sonnes of Midián were Epháh,
& Ephár, & Henóch, & Abidá, & Eldaáh:
*all these are the sonnes of Keturáh.
34 *And Abrahám begate Izhák: the sonnes
of Izhák, Esáu, and Israél.
35 ¶The sonnes of Esáu were [i] *Elipház,
Reuél, and Ieúsh, and Iaalám, and Kórah.

d Of whome came the Syrians, and therefore thei are called Aramites through out all ẏ Scripture.
e Of him came ẏ Ebrewes which were afterwarde called Israelites of Israél, which was Iaakób: and Iewes of Iudáh, because of the excellencie of that tribe.
f He repeateth Shem againe, because he wolde come to the stocke of Abrahám.
g Who came of Shem, and of him Shélah.
Gen. 16,11. & 17,5. & 21,2.
Gen. 25,13.
"Or, Hadar.
h Read Gene. 25,2.
Gen. 25,4.
Gen. 21,2.
i These were borne of thre diuers mothers, read Gen 36,4.
Gen. 36,9.

36 The sonnes of Elipház, Temán, and O-
már, *Zephí, and Gatám, Kenáz, and
k Timná, and Amalek.

*Or, Zephô.
k Which was Elepház concubine: read Gen.36,12.

37 The sonnes of Reuél, Náhath, Zérah,
Shammáh and Mizzáh.
38 And the sonnes of l Seír, Lotán, and Shobál, and Zibeón, and Anáh, and Dishón,
and Ezér and Dishán.

l He is also called Seír the Horite, which inhabited mount Seír, Gen.36,20.

39 And the sonnes of Lotán, Horí, and Ho-
mám, and Timná Lotans sister.
40 The sonnes of Shobál *were* Alián, and
Manáhath, and Ebál, Shephí, and Onám.
And the sonnes of Zibeón, Aiáh & Anáh.
41 The sonne of Anáh *was* Dishón. And
the sonnes of Dishón, Amrán, & Eshbán,
and Ithrán, and Cherán.
42 The sonnes of Ezér *were* Bilhán, and
Zaauán, *and* Iaakán. The sonnes of Dishón *were* Vz, and Arán.
43 ¶ And these were the m Kings that reigned in the land of Edóm, before a King
reigned ouer the children of Israél, *to wit*,
Béla the sonne of Beór, and the name of
his citie *was* Dinhábah.

m He maketh mẽciõ of the Kings that came of Esáu, according to Gods promes made to Abrahám cõcerning him, that Kings shulde come of him. These eight Kings reigned one after another in Idumea vnto the time of Dauid, who conquered their countrey.

44 Thẽ Béla dyed, and Iobáb the sonne of
Zérah of n Bozráh reigned in his steade.

n Which was the principal citie of the Edomites.

45 And whẽ Iobáb was dead, Husshám of ÿ
lãd of the Temanites reigned in his stead.
46 And when Husshám was dead, Hadád
the sonne of Bedád which smote Midián
in the field of Moáb, reigned in his stead,
and the name of his citie *was* Auíth.
47 So Hadád dyed, and Samláh of Mashre-
cáh reigned in his steade.
48 And Samláh dyed, and Shaúl of Rehobóth by the riuer reigned in his steade.
49 And when Shaúl was dead, Báal-hanán
the sonne of Achbór reigned in his steade.
50 And Báal-hanán dyed, and Hadád reigned in his steade, & the name of his citie
was *Paí, & his wiues name Mehetabél the
daughter of Matréd the daughter of Mezaháb.

*Or, Paú.

51 Hadád dyed also, and there were dukes in Edóm, duke Timná, duke *Aliáh,
duke Iethéth,

*Or, Aluáh.

52 Duke Aholibamáh, duke Eláh, duke
Pinón,
53 Duke Kenáz, duke Temán, duke Mibzár,
54 Duke Magdiél, duke Irám: these were
the dukes of Edóm.

CHAP. II.

1 *The genealogie of Iudáh vnto Ishái the father of Dauid.*

Gen.29,32. & 30,5. & 35,18.
Gen.38,3. & 46,12. chap.4,1.

1 THese are the sõnes of Israél, *Reubén,
Simeón, Leuí and Iudáh, Isshachár, &
Zebulún,
2 Dan, Ioséph, and Beniamín, Naphtalí,
Gad, and Ashér.
3 *The sonnes of a Iudáh, Er, and Onán, &
Sheláh. These thre were borne to him of
the daughter of Shúa ÿ Cananite: but Er
the eldest sonne of Iudáh was euil in the
sight of the Lord, and he slewe him.

a Thogh Iudáh was not Iaakobs eldest sonne, yet he first beginneth at him, because he wolde come to the genealogie of Dauid, of whome came Christ.

4 *And Thamár his daughter in lawe bare
him Phárez, and Zérah: so all the sonnes of
Iudáh were fyue.

Gen.38,29. mat.1,3.

5 *The sõnes of Phárez, Hezrón & Hamúl.

Ruth.4,18.

6 The sonnes also of Zeráh *were* *Zimrí,
and b Ethán, and Hemán, and Calcól, and
Dára, which were fiue in all.

*Or, Zabdi.
b Of these read 1 Kings 4,31.

7 And ÿ sonne of Carmí, *Achár that troubled Israél, transgresing in the thing excommunicate.

*Or, Achán. Iosh.7,1.

8 The sonne also of Ethán, Azariáh.
9 And the sonnes of Hezrón that were borne vnto him, Ierahmeél, and c Ram and
Chelubái.

c Whome S. Matth. calleth Arám, Mat.1,3

10 And Ram begate Aminadáb, and Aminadáb begate Nashón d prince of the
children of Iudáh,

d That is, chief of the familie.

11 And Nahshón begate Salmá, and Salmá
begate Bóaz,
12 And Bóaz begate Obéd, and Obéd begate *Ishái,

*Or, Iesse.

13 *And Ishái begate his eldest sonne Eliáb,
and Abinadáb the seconde, and *Shimma
the third,

1.Sam.16,19. & 17,12.
*Or, Shammáh.

14 Nathaneél the fourt, Raddái the fift,
15 Ozém the sixt, *and* Dauid the seuent.
16 Whose sisters *were* Zeruiáh & Abigáil.
And the sonnes of Zeruiáh, Abishái, and
Ioáb, and Asahél.
17 And Abigáil bare Amasá: and the father
of Amasá *was* Iethér an Ishmeelite.
18 ¶ And e Caléb the sonne of Hezrón begate Ierióth of Azubáh *his* wife, and her
sonnes are these, Iesher, and Shobáb, and
Ardón.

e Who was called the sonne of Hezrón, vers.9.

19 And when Azubáh was dead, Caléb toke
vnto him Ephráth, which bare him Hur.
20 *And Hur begate Vrí, and Vrí begate
Bezaleél.

Exod.31,2.

21 And afterwarde came Hezrón to the
daughter of Machír the father of f Gileád,
and toke her when he was threscore yere
olde, and she bare him Segúb.

f Who was prince of mounte Gileád, read Nom. 32,40.

22 And Segúb begate Iaír, which had thre
and twentie cities in the land of Gileád.
23 And Gesshúr with Arám toke the townes of Iaír g from them, *and* Kenáth and
the townes thereof, *euen* threscore cities.
All these were the sonnes of Machír, the
father of Gileád.

g That is, the Geshurites & Syrians toke the townes from Iairs children.

24 And after that Hezrón was dead at
h Caléb Ephrátah, then Abiáh Hezrons
wife bare him also Ashúr the i father of
Tekóa.

h Which was a towne named of the housbãd and wife, called also Beth-léhem Ephrátah.
i Meaning the chief & prince.

25 And the sonnes of Ierameél the eldest
sonne of Hezrón were Ram the eldest,
then Bunáh, & Orén & Ozén *and* Ahiiáh.
26 Also Ierahmeél had another wife named Ataráh, which was the mother of
Onám.
27 And the sonnes of Ram the eldest sonne of Ierahmeél were Máaz, and Iamín
and

and Ekar.
28 And the sonnes of Onám were Shammái
and Iadá. And the sonnes of Shãmái, Nadáb and Abishúr.
29 And the name of the wife of Abishúr
was called Abiháil, and she bare him Ah-
bán and Molíd.
30 The sonnes also of Nadáb *were* Séled
and Appáim : but Séled dyed without
children.
31 And the sonne of Appáim *was* Ishí, and
the sonne of Ishí, Sheshán, and the sonne
of Sheshán, [k] Ahlái,
32 And the sonnes of Iadá the brother of
Shammái *were* Iéther and Ionathán: but
Iéther dyed without children.
33 And the sonnes of Ionathán *were* Péleth
and Zazá. These were the sonnes of Ierahmeél.
34 And Sheshán had no sonnes, but daughters. And Sheshán had a seruant that was
an Egyptian named Iarhá.
35 And Sheshán gaue his daughter to Iarhá his seruant to wife, and she bare him
Attái.
36 And Attái begate Nathán, and Nathán
begate Zabád,
37 And Zabád begate Ephlál, & Ephlál begate Obéd,
38 And Obéd begate Iehú, and Iehú begate Azariáh,
39 And Azariáh begate Hélez, and Hélez
begate Eleasáh,
40 And Eleasáh begate Sisamái, & Sisamái
begate Shallúm,
41 And Shallúm begate Iekamiáh, & Iekamiáh begate Elishamá.
42 Also the sonnes of Caléb, the brother of
Ierahmeél, *were* Meshá his eldest sonne,
which was the [l] father of Ziph: & the sonnes of Maresháh the father of Hebrón.
43 And the sonnes of Hebrón *were* Kórah
and Tappúah, and Rékem and Shéma.
44 And Shéma begate Ráham the father
of Iorkoám: and Rékem begate Shammái.
45 The sonne also of Shammái *was* Maón:
and Maón *was* the father of Beth-zúr.
46 And Epháh a [m] concubine of Caléb
bare Harán and Mozá, and Gazéz: Harán
also begate Gazéz.
47 The sonnes of Iahdái *were* Régem, and
Iothám, and Geshán, & Pélet, and Epháh,
and Sháaph.
48 Calebs concubine Maacháh bare Shé-
ber and Tirhanáh.
49 She bare also Sháaph, the father of Mad-
mannáh, *and* Sheuá the father of Mach-
benah, and the father of Gibeá. *And
Achsáh was Calebs daughter.
50 ¶ These were the sonnes of Caléb the
sonne of Hur ẏ eldest sonne of Ephráthah,
Shobál the father of Kiriáth-iearím.
51 Salmá the father of Beth-léhem, *and* Ha-
réph the father of Beth-gadér.
52 And Shobál the father of Kiriath-iearím had sonnes, and he" was the ouerseer
of halfe Hammenóth.
53 And the families of Kiriath-iearím *were*
the Ithrites, and the Puthites, and the Shu
mathites, & the Mishraites. of them came
the Zarreathites, and the Eshtaulites.
54 The sonnes of Salmá of Beth-léhem,
and the Netophathite, the [n] crownes of
the house of Ioáb, and" halfe the Manahthites *and* the Zorites.
55 And the families of the [o] Scribes dwelling at Iabéz, the Tirathites, the Shim-
meathites, the Shuchathites, which are
the [p] Kenites, that came of Hammáth the
father of the house of Rechab.

k Who dyed whiles his father was alyue and therefore it is said, vers. 34 that Sheshán had no sonnes.

l That is, the chief gouernor or prince of ẏ Ziphims, because the prince oght to haue a fatherlie care and affection toward his people.

m This difference was betwene the wife and the cõcubine, that the wife was takẽ with certeine solemnities of mariage, and her children did inherit: the concubine had no solemnities in mariage, nether did her children inherit, but had a porcion of goods or money giuen thẽ.

*Iosh. 15,17.

"Or, he that sawe the halfe, because the prince oght to ouerse his subiectes.

n Meaning, the chief & principal.

"Or, the Zorites, the halfe of the Manahthites.

o Which were men learned and expert in the Lawe.

p Read Nóm. 10,29, & iudg. 1,16.

CHAP. III.

1 *The genealogie of Dauid, and of his posteritie vnto the sonnes of Iosiáh.*

1 THese also were the sonnes of [a] Dauid, which were borne vnto him in
Hebrón: the eldest Amnón of Ahinóam,
the Izraelitesse: the second [b] Daniél of A-
bigáil the Carmelitesse.
2 The third Absalóm the sonne of Maacháh daughter of Talmái King of Geshúr: the fourt Adoniiáh the sonne of
Haggíth:
3 The fift Shephatiáh of Abitál: the sixt
Ithreám by Egláh his wife.
4 *These* six were borne vnto hĩ in Hebrón:
and there he reigned seuen yere and six
moneths: and in Ierusalém he reigned
thre and thirtie yere.
5 And these foure were borne vnto him in
Ierusalém, Shimeá, and Shobáb, and Nathán, and [c] Salomón of [d] Bathshúa the
daughter of Ammiél:
6 Ibhár also, and [e] Elishamá, and Eliphálet,
7 And Nógah, and Népheg, and Iaphía,
8 And Elishamá, and Eliadá, and Eliphélet,
nine *in nomber.*
9 *These are* all the sonnes of Dauid, besides
the sonnes of the concubines, & Thamár
their sister.
10 ¶ And Salomons sonne *was* Rehoboám,
whose sonne *was* Abiáh, *and* Asá his sonne, *and* Iehoshaphát his sonne,
11 *And* Iorám his sonne, *and* Ahaziáh his
sonne, *and* Ioásh his sonne,
12 *And* Amaziáh his sonne, & Azariáh his
sonne, & Iothám his sonne,
13 *And* Aház his sonne, & Hezekiáh his
sonne, & Manasséh his sonne,
14 *And* Amón his sonne, & Iosiáh his
sonne.
15 ¶ And of the sonnes of Iosiáh, the [f] eldest *was*" Iohanán, the seconde Iehoiakím, the thirde Zedekiáh, *and* the fourt
Shallúm.
16 And the sonnes of Iehoiakím *were* Ie-

a He returneth to the genealogie of Dauid, to shewe that Christ came of his stocke.

b Which 2. Sam. 3,3. is called Cheleáb, borne of her, that was Nabals wife the Carmelite.

c Onely Salomón was Dauids natural sonne, ẏ other thre were Vriahs, whome Dauid made his by adoption. he that was begotten in adulterie & dyed ẏ eight day, is not rekened among Dauids sonnes.

d Called also Bathshéba the daughter of Eliám: so thei gaue them diuerse names.

e Elishamá, or Elishúa. 2. Sam 5,15: & Eliphélet dyed, & Dauid named those sonnes, which were next borne, by the same names: in the boke of Kigs his children are mencioned which were aliue, and here bothe they ẏ were aliue & dead.

f So called because he was preferred to ẏ dignitie royal before his brother Iehoiakim, ẇ was the elder.

"Or, Iehoaház, 2. King. 23,30.

coniáh his sonne, *and* Zedekiáh his sonne.
17 And the sonnes of Ieconiáh, Assir *and*
Shealtiél his sonne:
18 Malchirám also and Pedaiáh, & Shenazár, Iecamiáh, Hoshamá, and Nedabiáh.
19 And the sonnes of Pedaiáh *were* [g] Zerubbabél, and Shimmeí: and the sonnes of
Zerubbabél *were* Meshullám, and Hananiáh, and Shelomíth their sister,
20 And Hashubáh, & Ohél, and Berechiáh,
& Hazadiáh, & Iushabhésed, fiue *in nõber*.
21 And the sonnes of Hananiáh *were* Pelatiáh, and Iesaiáh: the sonnes of Rephaiáh, the sonnes of Arnán, the sonnes of
Obadiáh, the sonnes of Shechaniáh.
22 And the sonne of Shechaniáh *was* Shemaiáh: and the sonnes of Shemaiáh *were*
Hattúsh and Igeál, and Baríah, and Neariáh and Shaphát, [h] six.
23 And the sonnes of Neariáh *were* Elioenái, and Hezekiiáh, and Azrikám, thre.
24 And the sonnes of Elioenái *were* Hodaiáh, and Eliashíb, and Pelaiáh, and Akkúb,
and Iohanán, and Delaiáh and Anáni,
seuen.

g S. Mat. saith that Zorobabél was sonne of Zalathiél, meaning that he was his neuewe according to the Ebrewe speache: for he was Pedaiahs sonne.

h So that Shemaiáh was Shechaniahs natural sonne, & the other fiue his neuewes, & in all were six.

CHAP. IIII.

1 The genealogie of the sonnes of Iudáh. 5 Of Ashúr. 9 Of Iabéz and his prayer. 11 Of Chelúb. 24 And Simeón: their habitacions. 38 And conquests.

1 The [a] sonnes of Iudáh *were* * Phárez,
Hezrón, and Carmí, and Hur, and
Shobál.
2 And Reaiáh the sonne of Shobál begate
Iáhath, and Iáhath begate Ahumái, and
Láhad: these are the families of the Zoreathites.
3 And these were of the father of Etám,
Izreél, and Ishmá and Idbásh: and the name of their sister *was* Hazlelepóni.
4 And Penuél *was* the father of Gedór,
and Ezér the father of Husháh: these are
the sonnes of Hur the [b] eldest sonne of Ephrátah, the father of Beth-léhem.
5 But Ashúr the father of Tekóa had two
wiues, Heleáh, and Naaráh.
6 And Naaráh bare him Ahuzám, & Hépher, and Temení and Haashtarí: these
were the sonnes of Naaráh.
7 And the sonnes of Heleáh *were* Zéreth,
Iezóhar and Ethnán.
8 Also Coz begate Anúb, and Zobebáh, &
the families of Aharhél ỹ sõne of Harúm.
9 But Iabéz was more honorable then
his brethren: and his mother called his
name [c] Iabéz, saying, Because I bare him
in sorowe.
10 And Iabéz called on the God of Israél,
saying, If thou wilt blesse me in dede, and
enlarge my coastes, and [d] *if* thine hand be
with me, and thou wilt cause me *to be deliuered* from euil, that I be not hurt. And
God granted the thing that he asked.
11 ¶ And Chelúb the brother of Shuáh begate Mehír, ẇ was the father of Eshtón.
12 And Eshtón begate Beth-raphá, & Paseáh, & Tehinnáh the father of the citie
of Naháshi: these are the men of Recháh.
13 ¶ And ỹ sonnes of Kenáz *were* Othniél &
Zeraiáh, & ỹ sonne of Othniél, Hatháth.
14 And Meonothái begate Ophráh. And
Seraiáh begate Ioáb the [e] father of the valley of craftesmen: for they were craftesmen.
15 ¶ And the sonnes of Caléb the sonne of
[f] Iephunnéh *were* Irú, Eláh, and Náam.
And the sonne of Eláh *was* Kenáz.
16 And the sonnes of Iehaleél *were* Ziph,
and Zipháh, Tiriá, and Asareél.
17 And the sonnes of Ezráh *were* Iéther &
Méred, and Ephér, and Ialón, and he begate Miriám, and Shammái, and Ishbáh the
father of Eshtemóa.
18 Also his [o] wife Iehudiiáh bare Iéred the
father of Gedór, and Héber the father of
Sochó, and Iekuthiél the father of Zanóah: and these are the sonnes of Bithiáh
the daughter of Pharaóh [o] which Méred
toke.
19 And the sonnes of the wife of Hodiáh,
the sister of Nahám the father of Keiláh
were the Garmites, & Eshtemóa the Maachathite.
20 And the sonnes of Shimón *were* Amnón
and Rinnáh, Ben-hanám and Tilón. And
the sonnes of Ishí *were* Zohéth, and Benzohéth.
21 ¶ * The sonnes of Sheláh, the sonne of
Iudáh *were* Er the father of Lecáh, & Laadáh the father of Maresháh, and the families of the housholdes of thẽ that wroght
fine linen in the house of Ashbéa.
22 And Iokím and the men of Chozebá &
Ioásh, and Saraph, which had the dominiõ
in Moáb, and [o] Iashúbi Léhem. *These* also
are ancient things.
23 These were potters, and dwelt among
plants & hedges: [g] there thei dwelt with
the King for his worke.
24 * The sonnes of Simeón *were* Nemuél,
and Iamín, Iaríb, Zérah, & [h] Shaúl.
25 Whose sonne *was* Shallúm, & his sonne,
Mibsám, & his sonne Mishmá.
26 And the sonnes of Mishmá, Hamuél *was*
his sonne, Zacchúr his sonne, & Shimeí
his sonne.
27 And Shimeí had sixtene sonnes, and six
daughters, but his brethren had not many
children, nether was all their familie like
to the children of Iudáh in multitude.
28 And they dwelt at [i] Beer-shéba, & at Moladáh, and at Hazár Shuál,
29 And at Bilháh, and at Ezém, and at Toládh,
30 And at Bethuél, and at Hormáh, and at
Ziklág,
31 And at Beth-marcabóth, and at Hazár
Susím,

a Meaning, they came of Iudáh, as neuewes & kinsmen: for onely Phárez was his natural sonne.

Gen. 38,29. & 46,12. chap. 2,4.

b The first borne of his mother, & not the eldest sonne of his father.

c Otherwise called Othniel, Iudg. 1,13.

d It is to be vnderstãd, that then he wolde accõplish his vowe which he made.

e The Lord of ỹ valley where the artificers did worke.

f Called also Esrón.

o Or, she bare, meaning the seconde wife of Ezráh.

o Or, of whome he had Méred.

Gen. 38,1.

o Or, of the inhabitants of Léhem.

g They were King Dauids gardiners and serued him in his workes.

Gen. 46,10. exod. 6,15.

h His sonne O had is here omitted.

i These cities belonged to ỹ tribe of Iudáh Iosh. 19,1. and were giuen to the tribe of Simeón.

Susím, at Beth-bireí, & at Shaaráim. these
were their cities vnto the reigne of [k] Dauid.
32 And their townes *were* Etám, and Aín,
Rimmón, and Tóchẽ, & Ashán, fiue cities.
33 And all their townes that were round a-
bout these cities vnto Báal, These are their
habitations and the declaration of their
genealogie,
34 And Meshobáb and Iamléch, & Ioshāh
the sonne of Amashiáh,
35 And Ioél and Iehú the sonne of Ioshi-
biáh, ẏ sonne of Seraiáh, ẏ sonne of Asiél,
36 And Elionái, and Iaakóbah, & Ieshoha-
iáh, and Asaiáh, and Adiél and Iesimiél &
Benaiáh,
37 And Zizá the sonne of Shiphéi, the sonne of Allón, the sonne of Iedaiáh, the sonne of Shimrí, the sonne of Shemaiáh.
38 These were famous princes in their families, and increased greatly their fathers
houses.
39 And they [l] went to the entring in of Gedór, euen vnto the East side of the valley,
to seke pasture for their shepe.
40 And thei found fat pasture & good, & a
wide land, bothe quiet and fruteful: for
they of Ham had dwelt there before.
41 And these described by name, came in ẏ
dayes of Hezekiáh Kĩg of Iudáh, & smote
their tents, and the inhabitants that were
founde there, and destroyed them vtterly
vnto this day, and dwelt in their rowme,
because there was pasture there for their
shepe.
42 And besides these, fiue hundreth men of
the sonnes of Simeón went to mõut Seír,
and Pelatiáh, & Neariáh, and Rophaiáh,
and Vzziél the sonnes of Ishí *were* their
captaines,
43 And the rest of Amalék that had [m] escaped, and they dwelt there vnto this day.

k Then Dauid restored them to the tribe of Iudáh.

l For the tribe of Simeón was so great in nõber ẏ in the time of Ezekiáh thei soght newe dwellĩgs vnto Gedór, which is in the tribe of Dán.

m And were not slaine by Saúl & Dauid.

CHAP. V.

1 The birthright taken from Reubén and giuen to the sonnes of Ioséph. 3 The genealogie of Reubén, 11 And Gad, 23 And of the halfe tribe of Manasséh.

1 THe sonnes also of Reubén the eldest
sonne of Israél (for he was the eldest,
*but had defiled his fathers bed, *therefore*
his birthright was giuen vnto the [a] sonnes
of Ioséph the sonne of Israél, so that the
genealogie is not rekened after *his* birthright.
2 For Iudáh preuailed aboue his brethren,
& of him *came* [b] the prince, but the birthright *was* Iosephs)
3 *The sonnes of Reubén the eldest sonne
of Israél *were* Hanóch & Pallú, Hezrón
and Carmí.
4 The sonnes of Ioél, Shemaiáh his sonne,
Gog his sonne, *and* Shimeí his sonne,
5 Micháh his sonne, Reaiáh his sonne, *and*
Báal his sonne,

Gen. 35,22. & 49,4.

a Because thei were made two tribes, thei had a double portion.

b That is, he was ẏ chiefest of all ẏ tribes according to Iaakobs prophecie, Gen. 49,8, & because Christ shulde come of him.

Gen. 46,9. exod. 6,14. nomb. 26,5.

6 Beeráh his sonne: whome Tilgáth Pilne-
éser King of Asshúr [c] caryed away: he was
a prince of the Reubenites.
7 And when his brethren in their families rekened the genealogie of their generacions, Ieiél and Zechariáh *were* the
chief,
8 And Béla the sonne of Azáz, the sonne
of Shéma, the sonne of Ioél, which dwelt
in [d] Aroér, euẽ vnto Nebó & Báal-meón.
9 Also Eastwarde he inhabited vnto the
entring in of the wildernes from the riuer "Peráth: for they had muche cattel in
the land of Gileád.
10 And in the dayes of Saúl they warred
with the [e] Hagarims, which fell by their
hands: and they dwelt in their tents in
all the East partes of Gileád.
11 ¶ And the children of Gad dwelt ouer
against them in the land of Bashán, vnto
Salcháh.
12 Ioél *was* the chiefest, and Shaphám the
seconde, but Iaanái & Shaphát *were* in Bashán.
13 And their brethrẽ of the house of their
fathers *were* Michaél, & Meshullám, & She
bá, & Sorái, and Iacán & Ziá, & Ebér, seuẽ.
14 These are the children of Abiháil, the
sonne of Hurí, the sonne of Iaroáh, the
sonne of Gileád, the sonne of Michaél, the
sonne of Ieshishái, the sonne of Iahdó,
the sonne of Buz.
15 Ahí the sonne of Abdiél, the sonne of
Guní *was* chief of the housholde of their
fathers.
16 And they dwelt in Gileád in [f] Bashán, &
in the townes thereof, and in all the suburbes of Sharón, by their borders.
17 All these were rekened by genealogies
in the dayes of Iothám King of Iudáh, &
in the dayes of Ieroboám King of Israél.
18 ¶ The sonnes of Reubén and of Gad, &
of halfe the tribe of Manasséh of those ẏ
were valiant men, able to beare shield, &
sworde, and to drawe a bowe, exercised in warre, were foure & fourtie thousand, seuen hundreth and threscore, that
went out to the warre.
19 And they made warre with ẏ Hagarims,
with [g] Ietúr, & Naphísh and Nodáb.
20 And they were [h] holpen against them, &
the Hagarims were deliuered into their
hand, and all that were with them: for thei
cryed to God in the battel, and he heard
them, because they trusted in him.
21 And they led away their cattel, *euẽ* their
camels fiftie thousand, and two hundreth,
& fiftie thousand shepe, and two thousand
asses, and of "persones an hundreth thousand.
22 For many fel downe wounded, because
the warre *was* of God. And they dwelt in
their steades vntil the [i] captiuitie.

c To wit, in ẏ time of Vzziiáh King of Israél, 2. Kings 15,29.

d These places were beyonde Iordén toward the East in the land, giuẽ to the Reubenites.

"Or, Euphrates.

e The Ishmaelites that came of Hagár Abrahams concubine.

f Bothe the hole countrey & one peculiar citie were called by this name Bashán.

g These twaine were ẏ sonnes of Ishmaél, Gene. 25,13.

h To wit, by the Lord, that gaue them the victorie.

"Ebr. soules of men.

i Meaning the captiuitie of ẏ tẽ tribes vnder Tilgáth-Pilneéser.

23 And the children of the halfe tribe of
Manasséh dwelt in the land, from Bashán
vnto [k] Báal Hermón, and Senír, and vnto
mount Hermón: *for* they increased.

k Otherwise called, Báalgad.

24 And these were the heades of the housholdes of their fathers, euen Epher and
Ishí, and Eliél and Azriél, and Ieremiáh,
and Hodauiáh, and Iahdiél, strong men,
valiant & famous, heades of the housholdes
des of their fathers.
25 But they transgressed against the God
of their fathers, and went a whoring after
the gods of the people of the land, whome God had destroied before them.
26 And God of Isráel [l] stirred vp the spirit
of Pul King of Asshúr, and the spirit of
Tilgáth Pilneesér King of Asshúr, and
he caried them awaye: *euen* the Reubenites, and the Gadites, and the halfe tribe
of Manasséh, and broght them vnto * Ha-
láh and Habór, and Hará, and to the riuer Gozán, vnto this day.

l Thus God stirred vp the wicked and vsed them, as instruments to execute his iuste iudgemēt agaist sinners, althogh they were led w̄ malice & ambitiō.

2.King.18,11.

CHAP. VI.

10 The genealogie of the sonnes of Leuí. 31 Their ordre in the ministerie of the Tabernacle. 49 Aarón & his sonnes Priests. 54, 57. Their habitations.

1 The sonnes of Leuí *were* Gershón,
Koháth, and Merarí.
2 * And the sonnes of Koháth, Amrám, Izhár, and Hebrón and Vzziél.

Gen.46,11. exod.6,17. chap.23,6.

3 And the children of Amrám, Aarón, and
Mosés and Miriám. And the sonnes of
Aarón, * Nadáb, and Abihú, & * Eleazár,
and Ithamár.

Leuit.10,1. Nomb.20,25.

4 Eleazár begate Phinehás. Phinehás begate Abishúa,
5 And Abishúa begate Bukkí, & Bukkí begate Vzzí,
6 And Vzzí begate Zerahiáh, and Zarahi-
áh begate Miraióth.
7 Meraióth begate Amariáh, and Amariáh
begate Ahitúb,
8 And Ahitúb begate [a] Zadók, and Zadók
begate Ahimáaz,
9 And Ahimáaz begate Azariáh, and Azariáh begate Iohanán,
10 And Iohanán begate Azariáh (it was he
that was [b] Priest in the house that Salomón buylt in Ierusalém)
11 And Azariáh begate Amariáh, and Ama
riáh begate Ahitúb,
12 And Ahitúb begate Zadók, and Zadók
begate Shallúm,
13 And Shallúm begate Hilkiáh, and Hilkiáh begate Azariáh,
14 And Azariáh begate Seraiáh, and Seraiáh begate Iehozadák,

a Which was the Priest after that Abiathár was deposed, according to the prophecie of Eli the Priest, 1 Sam.2,31.
b And did valiatly resist Kīg Vzziáh, who wolde haue vsurped the Priests office, 2.Chro.26,17.

15 And [c] Iehozadák departed whē the Lord
caried away into captiuitie Iudáh and Ierusalém by the hand of Nebuchad-nezzár.

c That is, he was led into captiuitie with his father Seraiáh the hie Priest, 2.Kig. 25,18.

16 ¶ The sonnes of Leuí *were* Gershóm,
Koháth and Merarí.
17 And these be the names of the sonnes of
Gershóm, Libní, and Shimeí.
18 And the sonnes of Koháth *were* Amrám, and Izhár, and Hebrón and Vzziél.
19 The sonnes of Merarí, Mahlí and Mushí: and these are the families of Leuí cōcerning their fathers.
20 Of Gershóm, Libní his sonne, Iaháth
his sonne, Zimmáh his sonne,
21 Ioáh his sonne, Iddó his sonne, Zérah his
sonne, Ieaterái his sonne.
22 The sonnes of Koháth, [d] Aminadáb his
sonne, * Kórah his sonne, Assír his
sonne,

d Who semeth to be called Izhár, Exod. 6,21.

Nomb.16,1.

23 Elkanáh his sonne, and Ebiasáph his sonne, and Assír his sonne,
24 Taháth his sonne, Vriél his sonne, Vzziáh his sonne, and Shaúl his sonne,
25 And the sonnes of Elkanáh, Amasái, and
Ahimóth.
26 Elkanáh. the sonnes of Elkanáh, Zophái
his sonne, and Náhath his sonne,
27 Eliáb his sonne, Ierohám his sonne, Elkanáh his sonne,
28 And the sonnes of Samuél, ỹ eldest [e] Vash-
ní, then Abiáh.

e Who is also called Ioél, 1. Sam.8,2. & the 33 verse of this chapter.

29 ¶ The sonnes of Merarí *were* Mahlí,
Libní his sonne, Shimeí his sonne, Vzzáh
his sonne,
30 Shimeá his sonne, Haggiáh his sonne,
Asaiáh his sonne.
31 And these be they whome Dauid set for
to sing in the house of the Lord, after that
the Arke had [f] rest.
32 And thei ministred before the Tabernacle, euen the Tabernacle of the Congregation with [g] singing, vntil Salomón had
buylt the house of the Lord in Ierusalém: then they continued in their office,
according to their custome.

f After it was broght to that place where ỹ Tēple shulde be built & was nomore caryed to & fro.
g Read Exod. 27,21.

33 And these ministred with their children:
of the sonnes of Koháth, Hemán a singer, the sonne of Ioél, the sonne of Shemuél,
34 The sonne of Elkanáh, the sonne of Ierohám, the sonne of Eliél, the sonne of
Tóah,
35 The sonne of Zuph, the sonne of Elkanáh, the sonne of Máhath, the sonne of
Amasái,
36 The sonne of Elkanáh, the sonne of Ioél, the sonne of Azariáh, the sonne of Zephaniáh,
37 The sonne of Táhath, the * sonne of Assír, the sonne of Ebiasáph, the sonne of
Kórah,

* Or, nephew.

38 The sonne of Izhár, the sonne of Koháth, the sonne of Leuí, the sonne of Israél.
39 And his * brother [h] Asáph stode on his
right hand: & Asáph was the sonne of Berechiáh, the sonne of Shimeá,

* Or, cousin.
h Meaning the cousin of Hemán, vers.33.

40 The

40 The ſonne of Michaél, the ſonne of Ba-
aſeiáh, the ſonne of Malchiáh,
41 The ſonne of Ethní, the ſonne of Zérah,
the ſonne of Adaiáh,
42 The ſonne of Ethán, the ſonne of Zimmáh, the ſonne of Shimeí,
43 The ſonne of Iáhath, the ſonne of Gerſhóm, the ſonne of Leuí.
44 And their brethren the ſonnes of Merarí *were* on the left hand, *euen* Ethán the
ſonne of Kiſhí, the ſonne of Abdí, the ſonne of Mallúch,
45 The ſonne of Haſhabiáh, the ſonne of
Amaziáh, the ſonne of Hilkiáh,
46 The ſonne of Amzí, the ſonne of Baní,
the ſonne of Shámer,
47 The ſonne of Mahlí, the ſonne of Mu-
ſhí, the ſonne of Merarí, ẏͤ ſonne of Leuí.
48 ¶ And their [i] brethren the Leuites were
[k] appointed vnto all the ſeruice of the
Tabernacle of the houſe of God,
49 But Aarón and his ſonnes burnt incenſe
vpon the altar of burnt offring, and on the
altar of incenſe, for all that was to do in
the moſte holy place, and to make an atonement for Iſraél, according to all that
Moſés the ſeruant of God had commanded.
50 Theſe are alſo the ſonnes of Aarón, E-
leazár his ſonne, Phinehás his ſonne, Abiſhúa his ſonne,
51 Bukkí his ſonne, Vzzí his ſonne, Zeráhi-
áh his ſonne,
52 Meraióth his ſonne, Amariáh his ſonne,
Ahitúb his ſonne,
53 Zadók his ſonne, & Ahimáaz his ſonne.
54 ¶ And theſe are the [l] dwelling places of
them throughout their townes & coaſtes,
euen of the ſonnes of Aarón for the familie of the Kohathites, for the [m] lot was
theirs.
55 So thei gaue them [n] Hebrón in the land
of Iudáh and the ſuburbes thereof rounde
about it.
56 But the field of the citie, and the villages thereof thei gaue to Calèb the ſonne
of Iephunnéh.
57 And to the ſonnes of Aarón they gaue
the cities *of Iudáh* for [o] refuge, *euen* Hebrón and Libná with their ſuburbes, and
Iattír, and Eſhtemóa with their ſuburbes,
58 And [p] Hilén with her ſuburbes, & Debir with her ſuburbes,
59 And Aſhán and her ſuburbes, and Beth-
ſhémeſh and her ſuburbes:
60 ¶ And of the tribe of Beniamín, Gebá
and her ſuburbes, and [q] Alémeth with her
ſuburbes, & Anathóth with her ſuburbes:
all their cities *were* thirtene cities by their
families.
61 And vnto the ſonnes of [r] Kohāth the
remnant of the familie of the tribe, *euen*

i The Leuites are called the ſingers brethren, becauſe they came of ẏͤ ſame ſtocke.
k Read Nomb 4,4.

l Or, cities ẇͤ were giuen to the Leuites.
m Thei were firſt appoited, and prepared for.
n Which was alſo called, Kiriath-arbá, Gen 23,2 ioſh. 21,11.

o That he ẏͤ had killed a man might flee thereunto for ſuccour til his cauſe were tryed, Deu 19, 2.
p Which Ioſhúa calleth Holón, Ioſh. 24,15.
q Or, Almón, Ioſh. 21,18
r That is, thei gaue a portion to ẏͤ Kohathites, ẇͤ were the remnant of the tribe of Leuí, out of ẏͤ halfe tribe of Manaſſéh and out of Ephráim, verſ. 66.

of the halfe tribe of the halfe of Manaſſéh, by lot ten cities.
62 And to the ſonnes of Gerſhóm accordíg
to their families out of the tribe of Iſſachár, and out of the tribe of Aſhér, & out
of the tribe of Naphtalí, and out of the
tribe of Manaſſéh in Baſhán, thirtene cities.
63 Vnto the ſonnes of Merarí accordíg
to their families out of the tribe of Reubén, and out of the tribe of Gad, and out
of the tribe of Zebulún, by lot twelue
cities.
64 Thus the children of Iſraél gaue to the
Leuites cities with their ſuburbes.
65 And they gaue by lot out of the tribe of
ẏͤ children of Iudáh, & out of the tribe of
the children of Simeón, & out of the tribe of the children of Beniamín, theſe cities, which thei called by *their* names.
66 And they of the families of the ſonnes
of Koháth, had cities *and* their coaſtes out
of the tribe of Ephráim.
67 *And they gaue vnto them cities of refuge, Shechém in mount Ephráim, & her
ſuburbes, and Gézer and her ſuburbes,
68 Iokmeám alſo and her ſuburbes, & Beth-
horón with her ſuburbes,
69 And Aialón and her ſuburbes, and Gath
Rimmón and her ſuburbes,
70 And out of the halfe tribe of Manaſſéh,
″Aner and her ſuburbes, and ″ Bileám and
her ſuburbes, for the families of the remnant of the ſonnes of Koháth.
71 Vnto the ſonnes of [ſ] Gerſhóm out of the
familie of the halfe tribe of Manaſſéh,
Golán in Baſhán, & her ſuburbes, & ″Aſh-
taróth with her ſuburbes,
72 And out of the tribe of Iſſachár, ″ Ké-
deſh and her ſuburbes, Daberáth and her
ſuburbes,
73 ″Ramóth alſo and her ſuburbes, and ″ A-
ném with her ſuburbes,
74 And out of the tribe of Aſhér, Maſhál
and her ſuburbes, and Abdón and her ſuburbes,
75 And Hukók and her ſuburbes, and Rehób and her ſuburbes,
76 And out of the tribe of Naphtalí, Ké-
deſh in Galilea & her ſuburbes, & ″ Ham-
món and her ſuburbes, and ″ Kiriatháim
and her ſuburbes.
77 Vnto the reſt of the children of Merarí
were giuen out of the tribe of Zebulún,
″Rimmón and her ſuburbes, ″ Tabór and
her ſuburbes,
78 And on the other ſide Iordén *by* Ierichó,
euen on the Eaſtſide of Iordén, out of the
tribe of Reubén, Bézer in the wildernes
with her ſuburbes, and Iahzáh with her
ſuburbes,
79 And Kedemóth with her ſuburbes, and
Mepháath with her ſuburbes,

Ioſh. 21,21.

″Or, Taanách, Ioſh. 21,25.
″Or, Gath-rimmón.
ſ Who in the firſt verſe is called alſo Gerſhón.
″Or, Beeſhterāh, Ioſh. 21,27.
″Or, Kiſhón, Ioſh. 21,28.
″Or, Iarmúth, Ioſh 21,29.
″Or, Engannim, Ioſh. 21,29.
″Or, Helkáh, Ioſh. 21,31.
″Or, Ammoth-dor, Ioſh. 21,32.
″Or, Kartán, Ioſh. 21,32.
″Or, Iokneám.
″Or, Kartáh, Ioſh. 21,34.

80 And out of the tribe of Gad Ramóth in
Gileád with her suburbes, and Mahanáim
with her suburbes,
81 And Heshbón with her suburbes, & Iaazér with her suburbes.

CHAP. VII.

8 The genealogie of Issachár, Beniamín, 13 Naphtalí, 14 Manasséh, 20 Ephráim, 30 And Ashér.

1 AND the sónes of Issachár *were* Tolá
& "Puáh, [a] Iashúb, & Shimrón, foure.
2 And the sonnes of Tolá, Vzzí, and Rephaiáh, and Ieriél, and Iahmái, & Iibsám,
and Shemuél, heades in the housholdes of
their fathers. Of Tolá *were* valiant men of
warre in their generacions, [b] whose nomber *was* in the daies of Dauid two & twentie thousand, and six hundreth.
3 And the sonne of Vzzí *was* Izrahaiáh, & ỹ
sonnes of Izrahaiáh, Michaél, & Obadiáh,
and Ioél, & Isshiáh, [c] fiue men all princes.
4 And with them in their generacions after the housholde of their fathers *were*
bands of mẽ of warre for battel, six & thirtie thousand: for thei had many wiues and
children.
5 And their "brethren among all the families of Issachár *were* valiãt men of warre,
rekened in all by their genealogies foure
score and seuen thousand.
6 ¶ The *sonnes* of Beniamín *were* Béla, &
Bécher, and [d] Iediaél, [e] thre.
7 And the sonnes of Béla, Ezbón, & Vzzí,
and Vzziél, and Ierimóth, & Irí, fiue heads
of the housholdes of their fathers, valiant
men of warre, and were rekened by their
genealogies, two and twentie thousand &
thirtie and foure.
8 And the sonnes of Bécher, Zemiráh, and
Ioásh, and Eliézer, and Elioenái, & Omrí,
& Ierimóth, & Abiáh, & Anathóth, & A-
láмеth: all these were the sónes of Bécher.
9 And thei were nombred by their genealogies according to their generacions, and
the chief of the houses of their fathers,
valiant men of warre, twentie thousand &
two hundreth.
10 And the sonne of Iediaél *was* Bilhán,
and the sonnes of Bilhán, Ieúsh, and Beniamín, and Ehúd, and Chenaanáh, and Zethán, and Tharshísh, and Ahisháhar.
11 All these were ỹ sonnes of Iediaél, chief
of the fathers, valiant men of warre, seuẽ-
tene thousand & two hundreth, marching
in battel aray to the warre.
12 And Shuppím, & Huppím *were* the sonnes of "Ir, *but* Hushim *was* the sonne [f] of
"another.
13 ¶ The sonnes of Naphtalí, Iahziél, and
Guní, and Iézer, and "Shallúm [g] of the sonnes of Bilháh.
14 The sóne of Manasséh *was* Ashriél whome she bare vnto him, *but* his concubine of
Arám bare Machír the * father of Gileád.

"Or, Phuuah.
a Who also is called Iob, Gen. 46,13.
b That is, their nomber was founde th' great whẽ Dauid nõbred the people, 2. Sam. 24,1.
c Meaning, the foure sonnes, & the father.
"Or, kinsmen.
d Called also Ashbél, Gen. 46,21. Nomb. 26,38.
e Which were the chief: for els there were seuen in all, as appeareth, Gen. 46,21.
"Or, Irí.
f Meaning, ỹ he was not the sonne of Beniamín, but of Dan, Gen. 46,23
"Or, of Ahér.
"Or, Shillém, Gen. 46,34.
g These came of Dan and Naphtalí, w͑ were the sonnes of Bilháh. Gen. 46,23
Nomb. 26,31. Iosh. 17,1.

15 And Machír toke to wife *the sister* of Huppím & Shuppím, and the name of their sister was Maacháh. And the name of the
secóde *sonne* was Zelophchád, and Zelophchád had daughters.
16 And Maacháh the wife of Machír bare
a sonne, and called his name "Péresh, and
the name of his brother was Shéresh: and
his sonnes *were* Vlám and Rakém.
17 And ỹ sonne of Vlám *was* Bedán. These were the sonnes of Gileád the sonne of
Machír, the sonne of Manasséh.
18 And [h] his sister Molécheth bare Ishód, &
Abiézer, and Mahaláh.
19 And the sonnes of Shemidá *were* Ahián,
and Shéchem, and Likhí, and Aniám.
20 ¶ The sonnes also of Ephráim *were*
Shuthélah, & Béred his sonne, & Táhath
his sonne, and his sonne Eladáh, & Táhath
his sonne,
21 And Zabád his sonne, and Shuthélah his
sonne, and Ezér, and Eleád: and the men of
[i] Gath that were borne in the land, slewe
them, because thei came downe to take a-
way their cattel.
22 Therefore Ephráim their father mourned many dayes, and his "brethren came to
comforte him.
23 And when he went in to his wife, she
conceiued, and bare him a sonne, & he called his name Beriáh, because afflictiõ was
in his house.
24 And his "daughter *was* Sheráh, which
buylt Beth-horón the nether, and the vpper, and Vzzén Sheeráh.
25 And Réphah *was* his [k] sonne, & Résheph,
and Télah his sonne, & Táhan his sonne,
26 Laadán his sonne, Ammihúd his sonne,
Elishamá his sonne,
27 Non his sonne, Iehoshúa his sonne,
28 And their possesiõs & their habitacions
were Beth-él, and the villages thereof, and
Eastwarde Naarán, and Westwarde Gézer with the villages thereof, Shechém also and the villages thereof, vnto "Azzáh &
the villages thereof,
29 And by the places of the children of
Manasséh, Beth-sheán & her villages, Taanách and her villages, Megiddó and her
villages, Dor and her villages. In those
dwelt the children of Ioséph the sonne of
Israél.
30 ¶ * The sonnes of Ashér *were* Imnáh, &
Isuáh, and Ishuái, & Beriáh, & Sérah their
sister.
31 And the sonnes of Beriáh, Héber, and
Malchiél, w͑ is the father of Birzáuith.
32 And Héber begate Iaphlét, and Shomér,
and Hothám, and Shuáh their sister.
33 And the sonnes of Iaphlét *were* Pasách,
and "Bimhál, and Ashuáth: these were
the children of Iaphlét.
34 And the sonnes of Shámer, Ahí, & Roh-
gáh,

"Or, Iezér, Nomb. 26,30.
h Meaning, the sister of Gileád.
i Which was one of the fiue pricipal cities of the Philistims, slewe ỹ Ephraimites.
"Or, kinsfolkes.
"Or, neece.
k To wit, of Ephráim.
"Or, Adaiáh.
Gen. 46,17.
"Or, Kimhál.

gáh, Iehubbáh, and Arám.
35 And ẏ sonnes of his brother Hélem were
Zopháh, and Iimná, and Shélesh & Amál.
36 The sonnes of Zopháh, Suáh, and Har-
népher, and Shuál, and Berí, and Imráh,
37 Bézer and Hod, and Shammá, and Shil-
sháh, and Ithrán, and Beerá.
38 And the sonnes of Iéther, Iephunnéh, &
Pispá and Ará.
39 And the sonnes of Vllá, Haráh, and Ha-
niél, and Riziá.
40 All these were the children of Ashér, the
heads of their fathers houses, noble men,
valiant mē of warre *and* chief princes, and
thei were rekened by their genealogies for
warre and for battel to the nomber of six
and twentie thousand men.

CHAP. VIII.

1 The sonnes of Beniamin, 33 and race of Saúl.

1 Beniamin also [a] begate Béla his eldest
sonne, Ashbél the seconde, and Aha-
ráh the thirde,
2 Noháh the fourte, and Raphá the fifte.
3 And the sonnes of Béla were Addár, and
Gerá, and Abihúd,
4 And Abishúa, and Naamán and Ahóah,
5 And Gerá, and Shephuphán, and Hurám.
6 ¶ And these are the sonnes of Ehúd: these
were the chief fathers of those that inhabited Géba: and [b] they were caryed away
captiues to Monáhath,
7 And Naamán, and Ahiáh, and Gerá, he
caryed them away captiues: and [c] he begate Vzzá and Ahihúd.
8 And Shaharáim begate *certeine* in the
coūtrey of Moáb, after he had sent [d] away
Hushím and Baará his wiues.
9 He begate, I say, of Hodésh his wife, Iobáb and Zibiá, and Meshá, and Malchám,
10 And Ieúz & Shachiá and Mirmá: these
were his sonnes *and* chief fathers.
11 And of Hushí he begate Ahitúb & Elpáal.
12 And the sonnes of Elpáal *were* Eber, and
Mishám and Shámed (which buylt Onò,
and Lod, and the villages thereof)
13 And Beriáh and Shéma (which were the
chief fathers among the inhabitants of
Aialón: they draue away the inhabitants
of Gath)
14 And Ahió, Shasák and Ierimóth,
15 And Sebadiáh, and Aŕád, and Ader,
16 And Michaél, & Ispáh, & Iohá, the sonnes of Beriáh,
17 And Zebadiáh, & Meshullám, & Hizkí,
and Héber,
18 And Ishmerái and Izliáh, and Iobáb, the
sonnes of Elpáal,
19 Iakím also, and Zichrí, and Sabdí,
20 And Elienái, and Zillethái, and Eliél,
21 And [*] Adaiáh, and Beraiáh, and Shimráth the sonnes of Shimeí,
22 And Ishpán, and Eber, and Eliél,
23 And Abdón, and Zichrí, and Hanán,
24 And Hananiáh, & Elám, & Antothiiáh,
25 Iphedeiáh & Penuél ẏ sonnes of Shasják,
26 And Shásherái, & Shehariáh & Athaliáh,
27 And Iaareshiáh, and Eliáh, and Zichrí,
the sonnes of Ierohám.
28 These were the chief [e] fathers according to their generations, *euen* princes,
which dwelt in Ierusalém.
29 And at [*] Gibeón dwelt the father of Gibeón, & ẏ name of his wife *was* Maacháh.
30 And his eldest sonne *was* Abdón, then
Zur, and Kish, and Báal, and Nadáb,
31 And Gidór, and Ahió, and Zácher.
32 And Miklóth begate Shimeáh: these also dwelt with their brethren in Ierusalém,
euen by their brethren.
33 And [f] Ner begate Kish, and Kish begate
Saúl, and Saúl begate Ionathán, and
Malchishúa, & Abinadáb, and [g] Eshbáal.
34 And the sonne of Ionathán *was* [h] Merib-báal, and Merib-báal begate Micáh.
35 And the sonnes of Micáh *were* Pithón, &
Mélech, and Taréa and Aház.
36 And Aház begate Iehoadáh, and Iehoadáh begate Alémeth, and Azmáueth, and
Zimrí, and Zimri begate Mozá,
37 And Mozá begate Bineáh, whose sonne
was Ráphah, *and* his sonne Eleasáh, *and* his
sonne Azél.
38 And Azél had six sonnes, whose names
are these, Azrikám, Bocherú and Ishmaél,
and Sheariáh, and Obádiáh, and Hanán:
all these were the sonnes of Azél:
39 And the sonnes of Eshek his brother *were*
Vlám his eldest sonne, Iehush the secōde,
and Eliphélet the third.
40 And the sonnes of Vlám *were* valiant
men of warre which shot with the bowe,
and had manie sonnes and nephewes, an
hundreth and fiftie: all these were of the
sonnes of Beniamin.

CHAP. IX.

1 All Israél and Iudáh nombred. 10 Of the Priests, and Leuites, 11, 18 And of their offices.

1 Thus all Israél were nōbred by their
genealogies: & beholde, thei are writen in the boke of the Kings of Israél and
of Iudáh, *and* they were [a] caryed away to
Babél for their transgression.
2 ¶ And the chief inhabitants that dwelt in
their owne possessions, *and* in their owne
cities, *euen* Israél the Priests, the Leuites,
and the [b] Nethinims.
3 And in Ierusalém dwelt of the children
of Iudáh, & of the children of Beniamín, &
of the children of Ephráim, & Manasséh.
4 Vthái ẏ sonne of Amihúd ẏ sōne of Omrí the sonne of Imrí, the sonne of Baní: of
the childrē of Phárez, the sonne of Iudáh.
5 And of Shiloní, Asaiáh the eldest, and his
sonnes.
6 And of the sonnes of Zérah, Ieuél, and
their brethren six hundreth and ninetie.

a He continueth in ẏ description of ẏ tribe of Beniamin, because his purpose is to set forth the ẏ genealogie of Saúl.

b Meaning the inhabitants of the citie Géba.

c To wit, Ehúd.

d After he had put away his two wiues.

* Or, Araiáh.

e The chief of the tribe of Beniamin that dwelt in Ierusalém.

* Chap. 9,35.

f Who in the 1.Sam 9,1. is called Abiél.

g He is also named Ishbósheth, 2 Samu. 2,9.

h He is likewise called Mephibósheth 2.Sam. 9,6.

a Hitherto he hathe described their genealogies before they wēt into captiuitie, and now he describeth their historie after their returne.

b Meaning the Gabionites, ẘ serued in the Temple, read Iosh. 9,23.

7 And of the sonnes of Beniamín, Sallú,
the sonne of Meshullám, the sonne of Hodauiáh, the sonne of Hasenuáh,
8 And Ibneiáh the sonne of Ierohám, and
Eláh the sonne of Vzzí, the sonne of Michrí, & Meshullám the sonne of Shephatiáh, the sonne of Reuél, the sonne of
Ibniiáh.
9 And their brethren according to their
generacions nine hundreth, fiftie and six:
all these men were ″ chief fathers in the
housholdes of their fathers.
10 ¶ And of the Priests, Iedaiáh, and Iehoiaríb, and Iachín,
11 And Azariáh the sonne of Hilkiáh, the
sonne of Meshullám, the sonne of Zadók,
the sonne of Meraióth, the sonne of Ahitúb the [c] chief of the house of God,
12 And Adaiáh the sonne of Ierohám, the
sone of Pashhúr, the sonne of Malchiiáh,
and Maasái the sonne of Adiél, ẏ sonne of
Iahzérah, the sonne of Meshullám, ẏ sonne of Meshillemíth, the sonne of Immér.
13 And their brethrẽ the chief of the housholdes of their fathers a thousand, seuen
hundreth and thre score valiãt men, for ẏ
[d] worke of the seruice of the house of God.
14 ¶ And of the Leuites, Shemaiáh the sonne of Hasshúb, the sonne of Azrikám, the
sone of Hashabiáh of the sones of Merarí,
15 And Bakbakkár, Héresh and Galál, and
Mattaniah the sonne of Michá, the sonne
of Zichrí, the sonne of Asáph,
16 And Obadiáh the sonne of Shemaiáh,
the sonne of Galál, ẏ sonne of Ieduthún,
and Berechiáh, the sonne of Asá, the sonne
of Elkanáh, that dwelt in the villages of
the Netophathites.
17 ¶ And the porters *were* Shallúm, and Akkúb, and Talmón, and Ahimán, and their
brethren: Shallúm *was* the chief.
18 For they were porters to this time by
companies of the children of Leuí vnto
the [e] Kings gate Eastwarde.
19 And Shallúm the sonne of Kóre the sonne of Ebiasáph the sonne of Kórah, & his
brethren the Korathites (of the house of
their father) *were* ouer the worke, *and* office to kepe the gates of the [f] Tabernacle:
so their families *were* ouer the hoste of the
Lord, keping the entrie.
20 And Phinehás the sonne of Eleazár was
their guide, and the Lord *was* with him.
21 Zechariáh the sonne of Meshelemiáh
was the porter of the dore of the Tabernacle of the Congregacion.
22 All these were chosen for porters of the
gates, two hundreth and twelue, which
were nombred according to their genealogies by their townes. Dauid established
these and Samuél the Seer ″ in their perpetual office.
23 So they and their children had the ouersight of the gates of ẏ house of ẏ Lord, euẽ
of the house of the Tabernacle by wardes.
24 The porters were in foure quarters
Eastward, Westward, Northward and
Southward.
25 And their brethren, *which were* in their
townes, came at [g] seuen dayes from time
to time with them.
26 For these foure chief porters were in
perpetual office, and were of the Leuites
and had charge of the ″ chambers, & of the
treasures in the house of God.
27 And they laye round about the house of
God, because the charge *was* theirs, & they
caused it to be opened euerie morning.
28 And certeine of them had the rule of the
ministring vessels: for they broght them
in by tale, and broght them out by tale.
29 Some of them also were appointed
ouer the instruments, and ouer all the vessels of the Sanctuarie, and of the [h] floure,
and the wine, and the oyle, and the incense, and the swete odours.
30 And certeine of the sonnes of the Priests
made ointments of swete odours.
31 And Mattithiáh one of the Leuites which
was the eldest sonne of Shallúm the Korhite, had the charge of the thĩgs that were
made in the fryingpan.
32 And other of their brethren the sonnes
of Koháth had ẏ ouersight of the * shewbread to prepare it euerie Sabbath.
33 And these are the singers, the chief fathers of the Leuites, *which dwelt* in the chãbers, [i] and had none other charge: for
they had to do in that busines day and
night.
34 These were the chief fathers of the Leuites according to their generacions, and
the principal which dwelt at Ierusalém.
35 * And in Gibeón dwelt ″ the father of
Gibeón, Ieiél, and the name of his wife *was*
Maacháh.
36 And his eldest sonne *was* Abdón, then
Zur, & Kish, & Báal, and Ner, & Nadáb,
37 And Gedór, and Ahió, and Zechariáh,
and Miklóth.
38 And Miklóth begate Shimeám: they also dwelt with their brethren at Ierusalém,
euen by their brethren.
39 And * Ner begate Kish, & Kish begate
Saúl, and Saúl begate Ionathán and Malchishúa, and Abinadáb and Eshbáal.
40 And the sonne of Ionathán *was* Meribbáal: and Merib-báal begate Micáh.
41 And the sonnes of Micáh *were* Píthon, &
Mélech and Tahréa.
42 And Aház begate [k] Iaráh, and Iaráh
begate Alémeth, and Azmáueth & Zimrí, and Zimrí begate Mozá.
43 And Mozá begate Bineá, whose sonne
was Rephaiáh, and his sonne *was* Eleasáh,
and his sonne Azél.

″ *Or, chief of the families.*

c That is, he was the hie Priest.

d To serue in the Temple, euerie one according to his office.

e So called because the King came into the Tẽple thereby, & not the commune people.

f Their charge was, that none shulde entre into those places, ẇ were onely appointed for ẏ Priests to minister in.

″ *Or, for their fidelitie.*

g They serued wekely, as Ezek. 4, 10.

″ *Or, opening of the dores.*

h Whereof ẏ meat offring was made, Leuit. 2, 1.

Exod. 25, 30.

i But were cõtinually occupied in singing praises to God

Chap. 8, 29.
″ *Or, Abigibeón.*

1. Sam. 14, 51. chap. 8, 33.

k Who was also called Iehoadáh chap. 8, 36.

44 And Azél had six sonnes, whose names
are these, Azrikám, Bocherú, & Ismaél, &
Sheariáh, and Obadiáh, and Hanán: these
are the sonnes of Azél.

CHAP. X.

1 The battel of Saúl against the Philistims. 4 In which he dyeth, 5 And his sonnes also. 13 The cause of Sauls death.

1.Sam.31,1.

1 THen * the Philistims foght against
Israél: and the men of Israél fled before the Philistims, and fel downe slaine
in mount Gilbóa.
2 And the Philistims pursued after Saúl &
after his sonnes, and the Philistims smote
Ionathán, and Abinadáb, & Malchishúa
the sonnes of Saúl.
3 And the battel was sore against Saúl, and
the archers hit him, and he was "wounded
of the archers.
4 Then said Saúl to his armour bearer,
Drawe out thy sworde, and thrust me
through therewith, lest these vncircũcised
come & mocke at me: but his armour bearer wolde not, for he was sore afraid: therefore Saúl toke the sworde & fel vpõ it.
5 And when his armour bearer sawe that
Saúl was dead, he fel likewise vpon the
sworde, and dyed.
6 So Saúl dyed and his thre sonnes, and
all his house, they dyed together.
7 And when all the men of Israél that were
in the valley, sawe how they fled, and that
Saúl and his sonnes were dead, they forsoke their cities, & fled away, and the Phi
listims came, and dwelt in them.
8 And on the morowe when the Philistims
came to spoile them that were slaine, they
found Saúl & his sonnes "lying in mount
Gilbóa.
9 And when they had stript him, they toke
his head and his armour, and sent them
into the land of the Philistims round a-
bout, to publish it vnto their idoles, and
to the people.
10 And they laied vp his armour in ÿ house
of their god, and set vp his head in the
house of [a] Dagón.
11 ¶ Whẽ all thei of Iabésh Gileád heard
all that the Philistims had done to Saúl,
12 Then they arose (all the valiant men)
and toke the body of Saúl, and the bodies of his sonnes, and broght them to
Iabésh, and buryed the bones of them vnder an oke in Iabésh, and fasted seuen
dayes.
13 So Saúl dyed for his transgression, that
he committed against the Lord, * euen a-
gainst the worde of the Lord, which he
kept not, and in that he soght and asked
counsel of a "* familiar spirit,
14 And asked not of the Lord: therefore he
slewe him, and turned the kingdome vnto
Dauid the sonne of Ishái.

"Ebr. founde.

"Ebr. fallen.

a Which was the idole of ÿ Philistims, & from the belly downeward had the forme of a fish & vpwarde of a man.

1.Sam.15,23.

"Or, witche and sorceresse.
1.Sam.28,8.

CHAP. XI.

3 After the death of Saúl is Dauid anointed in Hebrón. 5 The Iebusites rebell against Dauid, from whome he taketh the towre of Zión. 6 Ioáb is made captaine. 10 His valiant men.

1 THen * all Israél [a] gathered them selues to Dauid vnto Hebrón, saying,
Beholde, we are thy bones and thy flesh.
2 And in time past, euen when Saúl was
King, thou leddest Israél out and in: and
the Lord thy God said vnto thee, Thou
shalt fede my people Israél, and thou shalt
be captaine ouer my people Israél.
3 So came all the Elders of Israél to ÿ King
to Hebrón, & Dauid made a couenãt with
thẽ in Hebrón before the Lord. And they
anointed Dauid King ouer Israél, * according to the worde of the Lord by the
hand of Samuél.
4 ¶ And Dauid & all Israél went to Ierusalém, which is Iebús, where *were* the Iebusites, the inhabitants of the land.
5 And the inhabitants of Iebús said to Dauid, Thou shalt not come in hither. Neuer
theles Dauid toke the towre of Zión,
which is the citie of Dauid.
6 And Dauid said, * Whosoeuer smiteth ÿ
Iebusites first, shal be the chief & captaine. So Ioáb the sonne of Zeruiáh wẽt first
vp, and was captaine.
7 And Dauid dwelt in the towre: therefore
thei called it the citie of Dauid.
8 * And he buylt the citie on euerie side, frõ
Milló euen round about: & Ioáb repaired
the rest of the citie.
9 And Dauid prospered, & grewe: for the
Lord of hostes *was* with him.
10 ¶ * These also are the chief of the valiant
men that were with Dauid & ioyned their
force with him in his kingdome ŵ all Israél, to make him King ouer Israél, according to the worde of the Lord.
11 And this is the nomber of the valiant mẽ
whome Dauid had, Iashobeám the sonne
of Hachmoní, the [b] chief among thirty:
he lift vp his speare against thre hundreth,
whome he slewe at one time.
12 And after him *was* Eleazár the sonne of
"Dódo the Ahohite, which was one of the
thre valiant men.
13 He was with Dauid at Pas-dammím, &
there the Philistims were gathered together to battel: and there was a parcel of
ground ful of barly, and the people fled
before the Philistims.
14 And thei stode in ÿ middes of the field,
[c] and saued it, and slewe the Philistims: so
the Lord gaue a great victorie.
15 ¶ And thre of the [d] thirtie captaines wẽt
to a rocke to Dauid, into the caue of A-
dullám. And the armie of the Philistims
camped in the valley of Rephaím.
16 And when Dauid *was* in the holde, the
Philistims garison *was* at Beth-léhem.

2.Sam.5,1.
a This was after the death of Ishbósheth Sauls sonne, whẽ Dauid had reigned ouer Iudáh seuen yeres and six moneths in Hebrón, 2. Sam. 5,5.

1.Sam.16,13.

2.Sam.5,8.

2.Sam.5,9.

2.Sam.23,8.

b Meaning the moste excellẽt & best estemed for his valiãtnes: some read, the chief of the princes.
"Or, his vncle.

c This act is referred to Shamáh, 2.Sam.23,11. ŵ semeth was the chiefest of these.
d That is Eleazár & his two companions.

2.Sam 23,15. 17 And Dauid longed, and said, * Oh, that
one wolde giue me to drinke of the water
of the well of Beth-léhem that is at the
gate.
18 Then these thre brake thorowe the hoste
of the Philistims, and drewe water out of
the well of Beth-léhem that was by the
gate, and toke it and broght it to Dauid:
but Dauid wolde not drinke of it, but
powred it *for an oblacion* to the Lord,
19 And said, Let not my God suffer me to
do this: shulde I drinke the [e] blood of these
mẽs liues: for they haue broght it with the
ieopardye of their liues: therefore he wolde not drinke it: these things did these thre
mightie men.
20 ¶ And Abshái the brother of Ioáb, he
was chief of the thre, and he lift vp his
speare against thre hũdreth, *and* slewe thẽ,
and had the name among the thre.
21 Among the thre he was more honorable then the two, & he was their captaine:
* but he attained not vnto the *first* thre.
22 Benaiáh the sonne of Iehoiadá (the sonne of a valiant man) which had done manie actes, *and was* of Kabzeél, he slewe two
" strong men of Moáb: he went downe also
and slewe a lion in the middes of a pit in
time of snow.
23 And he slewe an Egyptian, a mã of great
stature, *euen* fiue cubites long, and in the
Egyptiãs hand *was* a speare like a weauers
beame: and he went downe to him with a
staffe, and plucked the speare out of the
Egyptians hand, and slewe him with his
owne speare.
24 These things did Benaiáh the sonne of
Iehoiadá, & had the name among the thre
worthies.
25 Beholde, he was honorable among thirtie, but he attained not vnto the [f] *first* thre.
* And Dauid made him of his counsel.
26 ¶ These also *were* valiant men of warre,
Asahél the brother of Ioáb, Elhanán the
sonne of Dodó of Beth-léhem,
27 [g] Shammóth the Harodite, Hélez the
Pelonite,
28 Irá the sonne of Ikkésh the Tekoite,
Abiézer the Antothite,
29 [h] Sibbecái the Husathite: Ilái ỹ Ahohite,
30 Maharái the Netophathite, Héled the
sonne of Baanáh the Netophathite,
31 Ithái the sonne of Ribái of Gibeáh of
the children of Beniamín, Benaiáh the Pirathonite,
32 Hurái of the riuers of Gáash, Abiél the
Arbathite,
33 Azmáueth the Baharumite, Elihabá the
Shaalbonite,
34 The sonnes of Hashém the Gizonite,
Ionathán the sonne of Shagéh the Harite,
35 Ahiám the sonne of Sacár the Hararite,
Eliphál the sonne of Vr,

e That is, this water, for the which they vẽtured their blood.

2.Sam.23,19.

" Or, lions.

f Meaning, those thre ỹ broght the water to Dauid.

2.Sam.23,23.

g Called also Shemmóah, 2.Sam 23,25.

h He is also called Mebunnái, 2.Sam.23,27.

36 Hépher the Mecherathite, Ahiiáh the Pe
lonite,
37 Hezró the Carmelite, Naarái the sonne
of Ezbái,
38 Ioél the brother of Nathán, Mibhár the
sonne of Haggerí,
39 Zélek the Ammonite, Nahrái the Bero-
thite, the armour bearer of Ioáb, the sonne of Zeruiáh,
40 Ira the Ithrite, Garíb the Ithrite,
41 Vriáh the Hittite, Zabád the sonne of
Ahlái,
42 Adiná the sonne of Shizá the Reubenite,
a captaine of the Reubenites, and thirtie
with him,
43 Hanán the sonne of Maacháh, and Ioshaphát the Mithnite,
44 Vziá the Ashterathite, Shamá and Ieiél
the sonnes of Othám the Aroerite,
45 Iediaél the sonne of Shimrí, and Iohá
his brother the Tizite,
46 Eliél the Mahauite, and Ieribái and Io-
shauiáh the sonnes of Elnáam, & Ithmáh
the Moabite,
47 Eliél and Obéd, and Iaasiél the Meso-
baite.

CHAP. XII.

1 Who they were that went with Dauid when he fled from Saúl. 14 Their valiantnes. 23 Thei that came vnto him vnto Hebrón out of euerie tribe to make him King.

1 THese also are they that came to Dauid to [a] Ziklág, while he was yet kept
close, because of Saúl the sonne of Kish:
and they were among the valiant and helpers of the battel.
2 Thei were weaponed with bowes, & colde vse ỹ right and the left hãd with stones
and with arrowes *&* with bowes, *and were*
of Sauls [b] brethren, *euen* of Beniamín.
3 The chief *were* Ahiézer, and Ioásh the
sonnes of Shemaáh a Gibeathite, and Ie-
ziél, and Pélet the sonnes of Asmáueth,
Beracháh and Iehú the Antothite,
4 And Ishmaiáh the Gibeonite, a valiant
man among thirtie, & aboue the thirtie,
and Ieremiáh, and Iehaziél, and Iohanán,
and Ioshabád the Gederathite,
5 Eluzái, and Ierimóth, and Bealiáh, and
Shemariáh, and Shephatiáh, the Haru-
phite,
6 Elkanáh, and Ishiáh, and Azariél, and Ioé-
zer, Iashobeám of Hakorehím,
7 And Ioeláh, and Zebadiáh, the sonnes of
Ierohám of " Gedór.
8 And of the Gadites there separated them
selues some vnto Dauid into the holde of
the wildernes, valiant men of warre, *and*
mẽ of armes, *&* *apt* for battel, which colde
handle " speare and shield, and their faces
were like the faces of [c] lyons, and *were* like
the roes in the mountaines in swiftenes,
9 Ezér the chief, Obadiáh the seconde,
Eliáb

a To take his parte against Saúl, who persecuted him.

b That is, of the tribe of Beniamin, where of Saúl was, & wherein were excellẽt throwers ỹ slings, Iudg.20,16.

" Or, Gedóah.

" Or, buckler.

c Meanig fearce, & terrible.

Eliáb the third,

10 "Mishmanáh the fourte, Ieremiáh the
fifte,
11 Attái the sixt, Eliél the seuente,
12 Ionan in the eight, Elzabád the ninte,
13 Ieremiáh the tente, Macbannái the eleuente.
14 These were the sonnes of Gad, captaines of the hoste: one of the least *colde resist* an hundreth, and the greatest a thousand.
15 These are they that went ouer Iordén in
the [d] first moneth whẽ he had filled ouer
all his bankes, and put to flight all them
of the valley, towarde the East and the
West.
16 And there came of the children of Beniamín, and Iudáh to the holde vnto Dauid,
17 And Dauid went out to mete them, and
answered and said vnto them, If ye be come peaceably vnto me to helpe me, mine
heart shalbe knit vnto you, but if you *come*
to betray me to mine aduersaries, *seing*
there is no wickednes in mine hãdes, the
God of our fathers beholde it, and rebuke it.
18 And the [e] spirit came vpon Amasái,
which was the chief of thirtie, *and he said,*
Thine *are we*, Dauid, & with thee, ô sonne
of Ishái. Peace, peace be vnto thee, and
peace be vnto thine helpers: for thy God
helpeth thee. Thẽ Dauid receiued them, &
made them captaines of the garison.
19 ¶ And of Manasséh *some* fel to Dauid,
when he came with the Philistims against
Saúl to battel, but they [f] helped them
not: for the princes of the Philistims * by
aduisement sent him away, saying, He
wil fall to his master Saúl "for our heades.
20 As he went to Ziklág, there fel to him
of Manasséh, Adnáh, and Iozabád, and Lediaél, and Michaél, and Iozabád, and Elihú, & Ziltái, heades of the thousands that
were of Manasséh.
21 And thei helped Dauid against [g] that bãde: for thei were all valiant men and were
captaines in the hoste.
22 For at that time day by day there came
to Dauid to helpe him, vntil it was a great
hoste, like the hoste of [h] God.
23 And these are the nombers of the captaines that were armed to battel, & came to
Dauid to Hebrón to turne the kingdome
of Saúl to him, according to the worde of
the Lord.
24 The children of Iudáh that bare shield
& "speare, *were* six thousand & eight hundreth armed to the warre.
25 Of the children of Simeón valiant men
of warre, seuen thousand and an hundreth.

"Or, Mashmanáh.

d Which ỹ Ebrewes called Nisán or Abib, coteining halfe Marche and halfe April, when Iordén was wõte to ouerflowe his bãkes, read Iosh.3,15.

e The spirit of boldenes and courage moued him to speake thus.

f They came onely to helpe Dauid & not to succour the Philistims, ỽ were enemies to their countrey

1 Sam.29,4.

"Or, on the ieopardie of our heades.

g To wit, of ỹ Amalekites ỽ had burned ỹ citie Ziklág. 1.Sam.30,9.

h Meaning, mightie or strong: for the Ebrewes say a thing is of God, when it is excellent.

"Or, buckler.

26 Of the children of Leuí foure thousand and six hundreth.
27 And Iehoiadá *was* the chief of them of
[i] Aarón: and with him thre thousand and
seuen hundreth.
28 And Zadók a yong man very valiant,
and of his fathers housholde *came* two and
twentie captaines.
29 And of the children of Beniamín the
brethrẽ of Saúl thre thousand: for a great
parte of them vnto that time [k] kept the
warde of the house of Saúl.
30 And of the children of Ephraím twẽtie
thousand, & eight hundreth valiant men
& famous men in the housholde of their
fathers.
31 And of the halfe tribe of Manasséh
eightene thousand, which were appointed by name to come and make Dauid
King.
32 And of the children of Issachár which
were men that had vnderstanding of the
[l] times, to knowe what Israél oght to do:
the heades of them *were* two hundreth, &
all their brethren were at their commandement.
33 Of Zebulún that went out to battel, expert in warre, & in all instruments of
warre, fiftie thousand "which colde set the
battel in aray: they were not of "a double
heart.
34 And of Naphtalí a thousand captaines,
and with them with shield and speare seuẽ
& thirtie thousand.
35 And of Dan expert in battel, eight and
twentie thousand, and six hundreth.
36 And of Ashér that went out to the battel and were trained in the warres, fourtie
thousand.
37 And of the otherside of Iordén of the
Reubenites and of the Gaddites, and of
the halfe tribe of Manasséh with all instruments of warre to fight with, an hundreth and twentie thousand.
38 [m] All these men of warre "that colde lead
an armie, came with "vpright heart to Hebrón to make Dauid King ouer all Israél:
& all the rest of Israél *was* of one accorde
to make Dauid King:
39 And there they were with Dauid thre
dayes, eating and drinking: for their [n] brethren had prepared for them.
40 Moreouer they that were nere them vntil Issachár, and Zebulún, and Naphtalí broght bread vpon asses, and on camels,
and on mules, and on oxen, *euen* meat,
floure, figges, & reisins, and wine & oyle,
& beues and shepe abundantly: for there
was ioye in Israél.

i Of the Leuites which came by descent of Aarón.

k That is, the greatest nomber toke Sauls parte.

l Men of good experience, ỽ knewe at all times what was to be done.

"Or, set them selues in aray.

"Ebr. heart and heart.

m So that his whole hoste were thre hundreth twẽtie & two thousand, two hundreth twenty & two.

"Or, fight in their aray.

"Or, with a good courage.

n The rest of the Israelites.

CHAP. XIII.

7 *The Arke is broght againe from Kiriathiearim to Ierusalém. 9 Vzzá dyeth because he touched it.*

1 AND Dauid counseled with the captaines of thousands & of hundreths,
& with all the gouernours.
2 And Dauid said to all the Cōgregacion
of Israél, If it seme good to you, and that
it procedeth of the Lord our God, we wil
send to and fro vnto our brethren, that a-
re left in all the land of Israél (for with
them are the Priests and the Leuites in
ȳ cities *and* their suburbes) that thei may
assemble them selues vnto vs.
3 And we wil bring againe the [a] Arke of our
God to vs: for we soght not vnto it in the
dayes of Saúl.
4 And all the Congregacion answered, Let
vs do so: for the thing semed good in the
eyes of all the people.
5 ¶ *So Dauid gathered all Israél together
frō "Shihór in Egypt, euē vnto the entring
of Hamáth, to bring the Arke of God
from [b] Kiriath-iearím.
6 And Dauid went vp & all Israél to "Baaláth, in Kiriath-iearím, ȳ was in Iudáh,
to bring vp from thence the Arke of God
the Lord that dwelleth betwene the Cherubims, where his name is called on.
7 And they caried the Arke of God in a
newe cart out of the house of Abinadáb:
and Vzzá and Ahió [c] guided the cart.
8 And Dauid and all Israél plaied before
[d] God with all *their* might, bothe w̄ songs
& with harpes, and with violes, and with
timbrels and with cimbales and with trū-
pets.
9 ¶ And when they came vnto the thresshing floore of [e] Chidón, Vzzá put forthe
his hand to holde the Arke, for the oxen
did shake it.
10 But the wrath of the Lord was kindled
against Vzzá, and he smote him, because
he laied his hand vpon ȳ Arke: so he dyed
there [f] before God.
11 And Dauid was angrie, because the Lord
had made a breache in Vzzá, and he called
the name of that place Pérez-vzzá vnto
this day.
12 And Dauid feared God that day, sayīg,
How shal I bring in to me the Arke of
God?
13 Therefore Dauid broght not the Arke
to him into the citie of Dauid, but caused it to turne into the house of [g] Obéd
Edóm the Gittite.
14 So the Arke of God remained in the
house of Obéd Edóm, *euen* in his house
thre moneths: and the Lord blessed the
house of Obéd Edóm, and all that he
had.

a His first care was to restore religiō, which had in Sauls dayes bene corrupted & neglected.

2.Sam.6,2.

"Or, Nilus.

b That is, frō Gibeá, where the inhabitāts of Kiriath iearím had placed it in the house of Abinadáb, 2 Sam. 6,3.

"Or, Baale, read 2.Sam. 6,2.

c The sonnes of Abinadáb.

d That is, before the Arke where God shewed hī selfe: so that the signe is taken for the thing signified, w̄ is cōmune to all sacramēts bothe in the olde & newe testament.

e Called also Nachón, 2.Sa. 6,6.

f Before ȳ Arke for vsurpīg that w̄ did not apperteine to his vocation: for this charge was giuē to the Priests, Nom. 4,15, so ȳ here all good intentions are cōdemned, except thei be cōmanded by the worde of God.

g Who was a Leuite, & called Gittite, because he had dwelt at Gath.

CHAP. XIIII.

1 Hirám sendeth wood and workemen to Dauid. 4 The names of his children. 8. 14. By the counsel of God he goeth against the Philistims & ouercommeth thē. 15 God fighteth for him.

1 THen *sent Hirám the King of "Tyrus messengers to Dauid, & cedre
trees, with masons & carpēters to buylde
him an house.
2 Therefore Dauid knewe that the Lord
had confirmed him King ouer Israél, &
that his kingdome was lift vp on hie, because of his [a] people Israél.
3 ¶ Also Dauid toke mo wiues at Ierusalém, & Dauid begate mo sonnes & daughters.
4 And these are the names of the children
which he had at Ierusalém, Shammúa, and
Shobáb, Nathán, & Salomón,
5 And Ibhár, and Elishúa, and [b] Elpálet,
6 And Nógah, and Népheg and Iaphía,
7 And Elishamá, and "Beeliadá, and Eliphálet.
8 But when the Philistims heard that Dauid was anointed King ouer Israél, all ȳ
Philistims came vp to seke Dauid. And
when Dauid heard, he went out against
them.
9 And the Philistims came, and spred them
selues in the valley of Rephaím.
10 Then Dauid asked counsel at God, saying, Shal I go vp against ȳ Philistims, &
wilt thou deliuer them into mine hand?
And the Lord said vnto him, Go vp: for I
wil deliuer them into thine hand.
11 So they came vp to Báal-perazím & Dauid smote them there: and Dauid said, God
hathe deuided mine enemies with mine
hād, as waters are deuided: therefore thei
called the name of that place, [c] Báal-perazím.
12 And there they had left their gods: and
Dauid said, Let them euen be burnt with
fyre.
13 Againe the Philistims came and spred
them selues in the valley.
14 And whē Dauid asked againe cousel at
God, God said to him, Thou shalt not go
vp after them, *but* turne away from them,
that thou maiest come vpon them ouer a-
gainst the mulbery trees.
15 And when thou hearest the noise of one
going in the toppes of the mulbery trees,
then go out to battel: for God is gone
forthe before thee, to smite the hoste of
the Philistims.
16 So Dauid did as God had commanded
him: and they smote the hoste of the
Philistims from Gibeón euen to Gézer.
17 And the fame of Dauid went out into all lands and the Lord broght the feare
of him vpon all nacions.

2.Sam.5,11.

"Ebr. Zor.

a Because of Gods promes made to the people of Israél.

b Elpálet and Nógah are not mencioned, 2. Sam 5, 14 so there are but eleuen & here thirtene.

"Or, Eliadá.

c That is, the valley of diuisions, because the enemies were dispersed there like waters.

CHAP. XV.

1 Dauid prepareth an hoste for the Arke. 4 The nomber and ordre of the Leuites. 16 The singers are chosen

sen out among them. 25 Thei bring againe the Arke with ioye. 29 Dauid dancing before it, is despised of his wife Michál.

a That was in the place of ý citie called Zión, 2.Sam. 5,8.

Nomb.4,2 & 20.

1 AND Dauid made him houses in the
a citie of Dauid, and prepared a
place for the Arke of God, and pitched
for it a tent.
2 Then Dauid said, * None oght to cary
the Arke of God, but the Leuites: for the
Lord hathe chosen them to beare the Arke of the Lord, and to ministre vnto him
for euer.
3 ¶ And Dauid gathered all Israél together
to Ierusalém to bring vp the b Arke of the
Lord vnto his place, which he had ordeined for it.

b From ý house of Obéd Edóm, 2 Sam. 6,10.

4 And Dauid assembled the sonnes of Aarón, and the Leuites.
5 Of the sonnes of Koháth Vriél the chief,
and his [*] brethren six score.

* Or, kinsmen.

6 Of the sõnes of Merarí, Asaiáh the chief,
and his brethren two hundreth & twentie.
7 Of the sonnes of Gershóm, Ioél the
chief, and his brethren an hundreth and
thirtie.
8 Of the sonnes of c Elizaphán, Shemaiáh the chief, and his brethren two hundreth.
9 Of the sonnes of d Hebrón, Eliél the
chief, and his brethren foure score.
10 Of the sonnes of Vzziél, Amminadáb
the chief, and his brethren an hundreth &
twelue.

c Who was ý sonne of Vzziél, ý fourte sonne of Koháth, Exod. 6, 21 & Nomb. 3,30.
d The third sonne of Koháth, Exod. 6,19.

11 ¶ And Dauid called Zadók & Abiathár
the Priests, and of the Leuites, Vriél, A-
saiáh and Ioél, Shemaiáh, and Eliél, and
Amminadáb:
12 And he said vnto thẽ, Ye are the chief fathers of the Leuites: e sanctifie your selues,
and your brethren, and bring vp the Arke
of the Lord God of Israél vnto the *place*
that I haue prepared for it.
13 For * because ye were not there at ý first,
the Lord our God made a breache among
vs: for we soght him not after *due* f ordre.

e Prepare your selues, & be pure, abstei ne from all things whereby ye might be polluted, & so not able to come to ý Tabernacle.
Cha.13,10.
f According as he hathe appointed in the Lawe.

14 So the Priests and the Leuites sanctified
them selues to bring vp the Arke of the
Lord God of Israél.
15 ¶ And the sonnes of the Leuites bare the
Arke of God vpon their shulders with
the barres, as Mosés had commanded, *according to the worde of the Lord.

Exod.25,15.

16 And Dauid spake to the chief of the Leuites, that they shulde appoint *certeine* of
their brethren to sing with g instruments
of musike, with violes and harpes, & cymbales, that thei might make a sounde, and
lift vp their voyce with ioye.
17 So the Leuites appointed Hemán the
sonne of Ioél, and of his brethren Asáph
the sonne of Berechiáh, and of the sonnes
of Merarí their brethren, Ethán the sonne
of Kushaiáh,

g These instruments & other ceremonies, ẘ thei obserued, were instructions of their infãcie, which cõtinued to ý comming of Christ.

18 And with them their brethren in the
h seconde degre, Zechariáh, Ben, and Iaa-
ziél, and Shemiramóth, and Iehiél, and
Vnní, Eliáb, and Benaiáh, and Maasiáh, &
Mattithiáh, and Elipheléh, and Mikneáh,
and Obéd Edóm, and Ieiél the porters.

h Which were inferior in dignitie.

19 So Hemán, Asáph & Ethán *were* singers
to make a sounde with cymbales of brasse,
20 And Zechariáh, and Aziél, and Shemiramóth, and Iehiél, and Vnní, and Eliáb,
and Maashiáh, and Benaiáh with violes
on i Alamóth,
21 And Mattithiáh, & Elipheléh, and Mikneáh, and Obéd Edóm, and Ieiél, and A-
zaziáh, with harpes k vpon Sheminíth le-
nazzéah.
22 But Chenaniáh the chief of the Leuites
had l the charge, bearing the burden in the
charge, for he was able to instruct.
23 And Berechiáh & Elkanáh were porters
for the Arke.
24 And Shecaniáh and Iehoshaphát and
Nethaneél and Amashái, and Zachariáh,
and Benaiáh, and Eliézer the Priests did
blowe with trumpets before the Arke of
God, and Obéd Edóm and Iehiáh *were*
porters m for the Arke.

i This was an instrument of musike, or a certeine tune, whereũto thei accustomed to sing Psalmes.
k Which was ý eight tune, ouer the which he ý was most excellent had charge.
l To wit, to appoint psalmes, & songs to thẽ that sung.
m With Berechiáh & Elkanáh, vers. 23.

25 *So Dauid and the Elders of Israél and
the captaines of thousands went to bring
vp the Arke of the couenant of the Lord
from the house of Obéd Edóm with
ioye.

2.Sam.6,12.

26 And because that God n helped the Leuites that bare the Arke of the couenant
of the Lord, thei offred o seuen bullockes
and seuen rams.
27 And Dauid had on him a linen garmẽt, as all the Leuites that bare the Arke,
and the singers and Chenaniáh that had
the chief charge of the singers: and vpon
Dauid *was* a linen p Ephód.

n That is, gaue them strength to execute their office.
o Besides the bullocke and the fat beast, which Dauid offred at euery sixt pase. 2. Sam. 6,13.
p Read 2.Sam. 6,14.

28 Thus all Israél broght vp ý Arke of the
Lords couenant with shouting and sõude
of trumpets & with cornet, & with cymbales, making a sounde with violes & with
harpes.
29 And when the Arke of the q couenant
of the Lord came into the citie of Dauid,
Michál the daughter of Saúl loked out at
a windowe, & sawe King Dauid dancing
and playing, and * she despised him in her
heart.

q It was so called because it put the Israelites in remembrance of the Lords couenant made with them.
2 Sam.6,16.

CHAP. XVI.

1 The Arke being placed, thei offer sacrifices. 4 Dauid ordeineth Asáph and his brethren to minister before the Lord. 8 He appointeth a notable Psalme to be sung in praise of the Lord.

1 SO *thei broght in the Arke of God, &
set it in the middes of the Tabernacle
that Dauid had pitched for it, and thei offred burnt offrings and peace offrings before God.

2.Sam.6,17.

2 And when Dauid had made an end of offring ŷ burnt offring & the peace offrings,
he [a] blessed the people in the Name of the
Lord.
3 And he dealt to euerie one of Israél bothe
man and woman, to euerie one a cake of
bread, and a piece of flesh, and a bottel of
wine.
4 And he appoĩted certeine of the Leuites
to minister before the Arke of the Lord,
and to [b] rehearse and to thanke and praise
the Lord God of Israél,
5 Asáph the chief, and next to him Zechariáh, Ieiél, and Shemiramóth, and Iehiél,
and Mattithiáh, and Eliáb, and Benaiáh, &
Obéd Edóm, euen Ieiél with instruments,
violes and harpes, and Asáph to make a
sounde with cymbales,
6 *And* Benaiáh and Iahaziél Priests, with
trumpets continually before the Arke of
the couenant of God.
7 Then at that time Dauid did [c] appoint
at the beginning to giue thankes to the
Lord by the hãd of Asáph & his brethrẽ.
8 *Praise the Lord *&* call vpon his Name:
declare his [d] workes among the people.
9 Sing vnto him, sing praise vnto him, *and*
talke of all his [e] wonderful workes.
10 Reioyce in his holy Name: let the hearts
of them that seke the Lord reioyce.
11 Seke the Lord and his strength: seke his
face continually.
12 Remember his maruelous workes that
he hathe done, his wonders, and the [f] iudgements of his mouth,
13 O sede of Israél his seruant, ô the children of Iaakób his [g] chosen.
14 He is the Lord our God: his iudgemẽts
are throughout all the earth.
15 Remember his couenant for euer, *&* the
worde, which he commanded to a thousand generacions:
16 *Which he made with Abrahám, and his
othe to Izhák:
17 And hathe confirmed it to Iaakób for a
Lawe, *&* to Israél for an euerlasting couenant,
18 Saying, To thee wil I giue the land of
Canáan, the "lot of your inheritance.
19 When ye were [h] fewe in nomber, yea, a
very fewe, and strangers therein,
20 And walked about from nacion to nacion, and from *one* kingdome to another
people,
21 He suffred no mã to do them wrong, but
rebuked [i] Kings for their sakes, saying,
22 Touche not mine [k] anointed, and do
my [l] Prophetes no harme.
23 *Sing vnto the Lord all the earth: declare his saluacion from day to day.
24 Declare his glorie among the nacions,
and his wonderful workes among all people.

a He called vpon the Name of God desiring him to prosper ŷ people, and giue good successe to their beginnings.

b To wit, Gods benefites towarde his people.

c Dauid gaue thẽ this Psalme to praise ŷ Lord, signifying that in all our ẽterprises the Name of God oght to be praised and called vpon.

Psal.105,1. isa.12,4.

d Whereof this is ŷ chiefest that he hathe chosen him selfe a Church to call vpõ his Name.

e Who of his wonderful prouidence hathe chosen a fewe of the stocke of Abrahám to be his children.

f In ouercomming Pharaóh, which iudgements were declared by Gods mouthe to Mosés.

g Meaning hereby that the promes of adoption onely apperteineth to ŷ Church.

Gen 22,16. luk.1,73.ebr.6,17.

" *Ebr. coarde, whereby parcels of lands were measured.*

h Meaning, frõ the time that Abrahám entred, vnto the time, ŷ Iaakób went into Egypt for famine.

i As Pharaóh & Abimélech.

k Mine elect people & them whome I haue sanctified.

l To whome God declared his worde, & thei declared it to their posteritie.

Psal.96,1.

25 For the Lord *is* great and muche to be
praised, and he is to be feared aboue all
gods.
26 For all the gods of the people *are* [m] i-
doles, but the Lord made the heauens.
27 Praise and glorie *are* before him: power
and beautie *are* in his place.
28 Giue vnto the Lord, ye families of the
people: giue vnto the Lord glorie and
power.
29 Giue vnto the Lord the glorie of his
Name: bring an offring and come before
him, *&* worship the Lord in the glorious
Sanctuarie.
30 [n] Tremble ye before him, all the earth:
surely the worlde shal be stable *and* not
moue.
31 Let the [o] heauens reioyce, and let the
earth be glad, and let them say among the
nacions, The Lord reigneth.
32 Let the sea roare, and all that therein is:
let the field be ioyful and all that is in it.
33 Let the trees of the wood thẽ reioyce at
the presence of the Lord: for he commeth
to [p] iudge the earth.
34 Praise the Lord, for he is good, for his
mercie *endureth* for euer.
35 And say ye, Saue vs, ô God, our saluaciõ,
and gather vs, & deliuer vs from the heathẽ, that we may praise thine holy Name,
and [q] glorie in thy praise.
36 Blessed *be* the Lord God of Israél for
euer and euer: and let all people say, [r] So
be it, and praise the Lord.
37 ¶ Then he left there before the Arke of
the Lords couenant Asáph and his brethren to minister continually before the
Arke, that which was to be done euerie
day:
38 And Obéd Edóm and his brethren,
thre score and eight: and Obéd Edóm
the sonne of Ieduthún, and Hosáh *were*
porters.
39 And Zadók the Priest and his brethren
the Priests *were* before the Tabernacle of
the Lord, in the hie place that was at Gibeón,
40 To offer burnt offrings vnto the Lord,
vpon the burnt offring altar continually, in the morning and in the euening, e-
uen according vnto all that is writen in
the Lawe of the Lord, which he commanded Israél.
41 And with them [s] were Hemán, and Ieduthún, and the rest that were chosen,
(which were appointed by names) to praise the Lord, because his mercie *endureth*
for euer.
42 Euen with them *were* Hemán and Ieduthún to make a sounde with the cornets &
with the cymbales, with excellent instruments of musike: and the sonnes of Ieduthún were at the gate.

m His strong faith appeareth herein ŷ thogh all the worlde wolde follow idoles, yet he wolde cleaue to the liuing God.

n Hũble your selues vnder ŷ mightie hãd of God.

o He exhorteth the dumme creatures to reioyce wt him in cõsidering ŷ greatnes of the grace of God.

p To restore all things to their estate.

q He esteemeth this to be the chiefest felicitie of man.

r He willeth all the people bothe in heart and mouthe to cõsent to these praises.

s With Zadók and the rest of the Priests.

43 And

t Declaring ẏ after our duetie to God we are chiefly bounde to our owne houſe, for the which as for all other thigs, we oght to pray vnto God, and inſtruct our families to praiſe his Name.

43 And all the people departed, euerie man
to his houſe: & Dauid returned to t bleſſe his houſe.

CHAP. XVII.

3 Dauid is forbidden to buylde an houſe vnto the Lord. 12 Chriſt is promiſed vnder the figure of Salmón. 18 Dauid giueth thankes. 23 And prayeth vnto God.

2.Sam.7,2.

a Wel buylt & faire.

1 NOw *afterwarde whē Dauid dwelt in
his houſe, he ſaid to Nathán ẏ Prophet, Beholde, I dwel in an houſe of a cedre trees, but the Arke of the Lords couenant remaineth vnder b curtaines.

b That is, in tents couered with ſkinnes

c As yet God had not reueled to the Prophet what he purpoſed concerning Dauid: therefore ſeig God fauored Dauid, he ſpake what he thoght

d After that Nathán had ſpoken to Dauid.

e That is, in a tent which remoued to and fro.

f Meaning, whereſoeuer his Arke went, which was a ſigne of his preſence.

2 Then Nathán ſaid to Dauid, Do c all
that is in thine heart: for God is with thee.
3 And the ſame d night euen the worde of
God came to Nathán, ſaying,
4 Go, and tel Dauid my ſeruāt, Thus ſaith
the Lord, Thou ſhalt not buylde me an
houſe to dwel in:
5 For I haue dwelt in no houſe, ſince the
day ẏ I broght out the children of Iſraél
vnto this day, but I haue bene from e tent
to tent, and from habitacion *to habitacion.*
6 Whereſoeuer I haue f walked with all
Iſraél, ſpake I one worde to anie of the
iudges of Iſraél (whome I commanded to
fede my people) ſaying, Why haue ye not
buylt me an houſe of cedre trees?
7 Now therefore thus ſhalt thou ſay vnto
my ſeruant Dauid, Thus ſaith the Lord of
hoſtes, I toke thee frō the ſhepecoate g &
from following the ſhepe, that thou ſhuldeſt be a prince ouer my people Iſraél.
8 And I haue bene ẇ thee whetherſoeuer
thou haſt walked, and haue deſtroyed all
thine enemies out of thy ſight, and haue
*made thee a name, like the name of the
great men that are in the earth.
9 (Alſo I wil appoint a place for my people Iſraél, & h wil plant it, that they may
dwel in their place, and moue nomore:
nether ſhal the "wicked people *vexe thē
anie more, as at the beginning,
10 And ſince the time that I commanded
iudges ouer my people Iſraél) And I wil
ſubdue all thine enemies: therefore I ſay
vnto thee, that the Lord wil i buylde
thee an houſe.
11 And when thy dayes ſhalbe fulfilled to
go with thy fathers, then wil I raiſe vp
thy ſede after thee, which ſhal be of thy
ſonnes, and wil ſtabliſh his kingdome.
12 He ſhal buylde me an houſe, and I wil
ſtabliſh his throne for k euer.
13 I wil be his father and he ſhalbe my ſonne, and I wil not take my mercie away frō
him, as I toke it from him that was before
l thee.
14 But I wil eſtabliſh him in mine houſe, &
in my kingdome for euer, and his throne
ſhalbe ſtabliſhed for euer,
15 According to all theſe wordes, and ac-

g Of a ſhepherd of ſhepe I made thee a ſhepherd of mē, ſo ẏ thou cameſt not to this dignitie through thine owne merites, but by my pure grace.

*Or, gotten thee fame.

h Make them ſure that they ſhal not remoue.

"Ebr. ſonnes of iniquitie.

*Or, conſume.

i Wil giue thee great poſteritie.

k That is, vnto the coming of Chriſt: for the theſe ſignes ſhulde ceaſe.

l Which was Saul.

cording to all this viſion. So Nathán ſpake to King Dauid.
16 ¶ And Dauid the King m went in and
*ſate before the Lord and ſaid, Who am
I, ô Lord God, and what is mine houſe,
that thou haſt broght me n hetherto.
17 Yet thou eſteming this a ſmale thing, ô
God, haſt alſo ſpoken concerning the
houſe of thy ſeruant for a great while, and
haſt regarded me according to the eſtate
of a man of o hye degre, ô Lord God.
18 What can Dauid *deſire* more of thee for
the honour of thy ſeruāt? for thou knoweſt
thy ſeruant.
19 O Lord, for thy ſeruants ſake, euen according to thine p heart haſt thou done
all this great thing to declare all magnificence.
20 Lord, there *is* none like thee, nether *is*
there anie god beſides thee, according to
all that we haue heard with our eares.
21 Moreouer what one nacion in the earth
is like thy people Iſraél, whoſe God went
to redeme thē *to be* his people, & to make
thy ſelfe a Name, *and to do* great and terrible things by caſting out naciōs from before thy people, whome thou haſt deliuered out of Egypt?
22 For thou haſt ordeined thy people Iſraél
to be thine owne people for euer, and thou
Lord art become their God.
23 Therefore now Lord, let the thing that
thou haſt ſpoken concerning thy ſeruant
& concerning his houſe, be cōfirmed for
euer, and do as thou haſt ſaid,
24 And let thy Name be ſtable & magnified for euer, that it may be ſaid, The Lord
of hoſtes, God of Iſraél, *is* the God of
q Iſraél, & let the houſe of Dauid thy ſeruant be ſtabliſhed before thee.
25 For thou, ô my God, haſt r reueled vnto the eare of thy ſeruant, that thou wilt
buylde him an houſe: therefore thy ſeruant hathe "bene bolde to pray before
thee.
26 Therefore now Lord (*for* thou art ſ God,
and haſt ſpoken this goodnes vnto thy
ſeruant)
27 Now therefore, it hathe pleaſed thee to
bleſſe the houſe of thy ſeruant, that it may
be before thee for euer: for thou, ô Lord,
haſt bleſſed it, & it ſhalbe bleſſed for euer.

m He wēt into ẏ tent where ẏ Arke was, ſhewing what we oght to do whē we receiue anie benefites of the Lord.

*Or, remained.

n Meaning, to this kinglie eſtate.

o Thou haſt promiſed a kingdome that ſhal continue to me and my poſteritie, and that Chriſt ſhal prosede of me.

p Frely, and according to the purpoſe of thy wil, without anie deſeruing.

q That is, he ſheweth him ſelfe in dede to be their God, by deliuering them from dangers, & preſeruing them.

r Thou haſt declared vnto me by Nathán the Prophet.

"Ebr hathe founde.

ſ And canſt not breake promes.

CHAP. XVIII.

1 The battel of Dauid againſt the Philiſtims, 2 And againſt Moab, 3 Zobah, 5 Arám, 12 And Edóm.

1 AND after this Dauid ſmote the Philiſtims, and ſubdued them, and toke
a Gath, and the villages thereof out of the
hand of the Philiſtims.
2 And he ſmote Moáb, and the Moabites
became Dauids ſeruants, and *broght
giftes.
3 ¶ And Dauid ſmote *Hadarézer King of

a Which 2.Sam.8,1 is called the bridle of bondage, because it was a ſtrong towne, and kept the countrey round about in ſubiection.

*Or, payed tribute

*Or, Hadadézer.

Zobáh vnto Hamáth, as he wēt to stablish
his border by the riuer* Peráth.

*Or, Euphrates.

4 And Dauid toke from him a thousand
charets, and seuen thousand horsemen, &
twētie thousand fotemen, and *destroyed
all the charets, but he reserued of them an
hundreth charets.

2.Sam.8,4.

5 ¶ Then came the Aramites of Damascus
to succour Hadarézer King of Zobáh, but
Dauid slewe of the Aramites two and
twentie thousand.

6 And Dauid put *a garison* in Arám of
*Damascus, and the Aramites became
Dauids seruants, and broght giftes: and
the Lord [b] preserued Dauid wheresoeuer
he went.

*Or, Darmések.

b That is, in all things that he enterprised.

7 And Dauid toke the shields of golde that
were of the seruants of Hadarézer, and
broght them to Ierusalém.

8 And from [c] Tibháth, and from Chun
(cities of Hadarézer) broght Dauid exceding muche brasse, wherewith Salomón made the brasen* Sea, and the pillers and the vessels of brasse.

c Which 2 Samuél 8, 8 are called Betáh & Berothái.

1.King.7,23. iere.52,20.

9 ¶ Thē Tóu King of Hamáth heard how
Dauid had smiten all the hoste of Hadarézer King of Zobáh:

10 Therefore he sent [d] Hadóram his sonne to King Dauid, to salute him, and to
reioyce with him, because he had foght
against Hadarézer, & beatē him (for Tóu
had warre with Hadarézer) *who broght* all
vessels of golde, and siluer and brasse.

d Called also Iorám, 2.Sam. 8,10.

11 And King Dauid did dedicate them vnto the Lord, with the siluer and golde that
he broght from all the nacions, from [e] E-
dóm, and from Moáb, and from the children of Ammón, and from the Philistims,
and from Amalék.

e Because the Edomites and the Syrians ioyned their power together, it is said 2.Sam.8, 12, ẏ the Aramites were spoiled.

12 ¶ And Abishái the sonne of Zeruiáh
smote of Edóm in the salte valley [f] eightene thousand,

f Which is vnderstād that Ioáb slewe twelue thousand, as is in the title of the threscore psal. and Abisái the rest.

13 And he put a garison in Edóm, and all
the Edomites became Dauids seruants: &
the Lord preserued Dauid wheresoeuer
he went.

14 So Dauid reigned ouer all Israél, and
executed iudgemēt and iustice to all his
people.

15 And Ioáb the sonne of Zeruiáh was ouer
the hoste, and Iehoshaphát the sonne of A-
hilúd recorder,

16 And Zadók the sonne of Ahitúb, and
Abimélech the sonne of Abiathár *were*
the Priests, and* Shaushá the scribe,

*Or, Seraiáh.

17 *And Benaiáh the sonne of Iehoiadá was
ouer the [g] Cherethites and the Pelethites: and the sonnes of Dauid *were* chief
about the King.

2.Sam.8,17.

g Read 2. Sam.8,18.

CHAP. XIX.

4 Hanún King of the childrē of Ammón doeth great iniuries to the seruants of Dauid. 6 He prepareth an armie against Dauid, 15 And is ouercome.

1 AFter this also *Nahásh the King of
the children of Ammón dyed, & his
sonne reigned in his steade.

2.Sam.10,1.

2 And Dauid said, I wil shewe kindnes vnto Hanún the sonne of Nahásh, because
his [a] father shewed kindenes vnto me. And
Dauid sent messengers to comforte him
for his father. So the seruants of Dauid
came into the land of the childrē of Ammón to Hanún to comforte him.

a Because Nahásh receiued Dauid & his cōpanie, when Saul persecuted him, he wolde now shewe pleasure to his sonne for the same.

3 And the princes of the children of Ammón said to Hanún, Thinkest thou that
Dauid doeth honour thy father, that he
hathe sent comforters vnto thee? Are not
his seruants come to thee to [b] searche, to
seke and to spie out the land?

b Thus ẏ malicious euer interpret the purpose of the godlie in the worst sense.

4 Wherefore Hanún toke Dauids seruāts,
and [c] shaued them, and cut of [d] their garments by the halfe vnto the buttocks, and
sent them away.

c They shaued of the halfe of their beardes, 2. Samu 10,4.

d To put thē to shame and vilanie, where as the ambassadoursoght to haue bene honored: and because the Iewes vsed to weare side garments and beards, they thus diffigured thē to make them odious to others.

5 And there went *certeine* and tolde Dauid
concerning the men: and he sent to mete
them (for the men were excedingly ashamed) & the King said, Tary at Ierichó,
vntil your beardes be growen: thē returne.

6 ¶ When the children of Ammón sawe
that they *stanke in the sight of Dauid, thē
sent Hanún and the children of Ammón
a thousand talents of siluer to hyre them
charets & horsemen out* of Arám Naharáim and out of Arám, Maacháh, and out
of [e] Zobáh.

*Or, had made them selues to be abhorred of Dauid.

2.Sam.10,8.

e Which were fiue in all.

7 And they hyred them two and thirtie
thousand charets, & the King of Maacháh
and his people, which came and pitched
before [f] Medebá: and the children of
Ammón gathered them selues together
from their cities, and came to the battel.

f Which was a citie of the tribe of Reubén beyonde Iordén.

8 ¶ And when Dauid heard, he sent Ioáb &
all the hoste of the valiant men.

9 And the children of Ammón came out,
and set their battel in araye at the gate of
the citie. And the Kings that were come,
were by them selues in the field.

10 When Ioáb sawe that the fronte of the
battel was against him before & behinde,
then he chose out of all the choise of Israél, and set him selfe in araye to mete the
Aramites.

11 And the rest of the people he deliuered
vnto the hand of Abishái his brother, and
they put them selues in araye against the
children of Ammón.

12 And he said, If Arám be to strōg for me,
then thou shalt succour me: & if the children of Ammón preuaile against thee, thē
I wil succour thee.

13 Be strong, and let vs shewe our selues valiant for our [g] people, and for the cities
of our God, & let the Lord do that which
is good in his owne sight.

g He declareth, that where the cause is euil, the courage can not be valiant, and that in good causes men oght to be courageous & cōmit the successe to God.

14 So Ioáb and the people that was with
him, came nere before the Aramites vnto
the

the battel, and they fled before him.
15 And when the children of Ammón sawe
that the Aramites fled, they fled also before Abisháí his brother, and entred into
the citie: so Ioáb came to Ierusalém.
16 ¶ And when the Aramites sawe that they
were discomfited before Israél, they sent
messengers and caused the Aramites to
come forthe that were beyonde the [h] riuer: & Shophách the captaine of the hoste
of Hadarézer *went* before them.
17 And when it was shewed Dauid, he gathered all Israél, and went ouer Iordén, &
came vnto thē, and put him selfe in araye
against them: and whē Dauid had put him
selfe in battel araye to mete the Aramites,
they foght with him.
18 But the Aramites fled before Israél, and
Dauid destroyed of the Aramites [i] seuen
thousand charets, and fortie thousand
fotemen, and killed Shophách the captaine of the hoste.
19 And when the seruāts of Hadarézer sawe
that they fel before Israél, they made peace with Dauid, and serued him. And the
Aramites wolde nomore succour the children of Ammón.

h That is, Euphrates.

i For this place read 2.Sam. 10,18.

CHAP. XX.

1 Rabbáh destroyed. 3 The Ammonites tormented. 4 The Philistims are thrise ouercome with their gyants.

1 AND *whē the yere was expired, in the
time that Kings go out *a warrefare*,
Ioáb caried out the strength of the armie,
and destroyed the countrey of the children of Ammón, and came and besieged
[a] Rabbáh (but Dauid taryed at Ierusalém)
and Ioáb smote Rabbáh and destroyed it.
2 *Thē Dauid toke ẏ crowne of their Kīg
from of his head, and founde it the weight
of a [b] talēt of golde, with precious stones
in it: and it was *set* on Dauids head, and he
broght away the spoile of the citie exceding muche.
3 And he caryed away the people that were
in it, and cut them with sawes, and with
harowes of yron, and with axes: euen thus
did Dauid with all the cities of the children of Ammón. Then Dauid and all the
people came againe to Ierusalém.
4 ¶ *And after this also there arose warre
at "Gézer with the Philistims: then Sib-
becháí the Hushathite slewe "Sippái, of
the children of "Haraphāh, and they were
subdued.
5 And there was yet *another* battel with the
Philistims: and Elhanán the sonne of Iaír
slewe [c] Lahmí, the brother of Goliáth ẏ
Gittite, whose speare staffe *was* like a weauers beame.
6 And yet againe there was a battel at
Gath, where was a man of a *great* stature,
and his fingers *were* by [d] sixes, *euen* foure
and twenty, and was also the sonne of Haraphāh.
7 And when he reuiled Israél, Iehonathán
the sonne of Shimeá Dauids brother did
slea him.
8 These were borne vnto Haraphāh at
Gath, and fel by the hand of Dauid: and
by the hands of his seruants.

2.Sam. 11,1.

a Which was the chief citie of the Ammonites.

2.Sam. 12,29.

b Which mounteth about the vallue of seuē thousād & seuentie crownes, which is about threscore pounde weight.

2.Sam. 21,18.

"Or, Gob. 2.Sam. 21,18.

"Or, Saph.

"Or, Raphāim, or, the gyants.

c Read 2 Sam. 21,19.

d Meaning, ẏ he had six a piece on hāds and fete.

CHAP. XXI.

1 Dauid causeth the people to be nombred. 14 And there dye seuentie thousand men of the pestilence.

1 AND [a] Satan stode vp against Israél,
and prouoked Dauid to nomber Israél.
2 Therefore Dauid said to Ioáb, and to the
rulers of the people, Go & nomber Israél
from [b] Beer-shéba euen to Dan, and bring
it to me, that I may know the nomber of
them.
3 And Ioáb answered, The Lord increase
his people an hundreth times so many as
they be, ô my lord the King: are they not
all my lords seruants? wherefore doeth
my lord require this thing? why shulde he
be a cause of [c] trespasse to Israél.
4 Neuertheles the Kings worde preuailed
against Ioáb. And Ioáb departed and wēt
through all Israél, and returned to Ierusalém.
5 And Ioáb gaue the nomber & summe of
the people vnto Dauid: & all Israél were
[d] eleuen hundreth thousand men ẏ drewe
sworde: and Iudáh was [e] foure hundreth
and seuentie thousand men that drewe
sworde.
6 But the Leuites and Beniamín counted
he not among them: for the Kings worde
was abominable to Ioáb.
7 ¶ And God was displeased with this thīg:
therefore he smote Israél.
8 Then Dauid said vnto God, I haue sinned greatly, because I haue done this
thing: but now, I beseche thee, remoue the
iniquitie of thy seruant: for I haue done
very foolishly.
9 And the Lord spake vnto Gad Dauids
"Seer, saying,
10 Go and tel Dauid, saying, Thus sayth
the Lord, I offre thee thre things: chose
thee one of them, that I may do it vnto
thee.
11 So Gad came to Dauid, and said vnto
him, Thus sayth the Lord, Take to
thee
12 Ether thre yeres famine, or thre moneths to be destroyed before thine aduersaries, and the sworde of thine enemies
"to take *thee*, or els the sworde of ẏ Lord
and pestilence in the land thre dayes, that
ẏ Angel of the Lord may destroy througH-
out all the coastes of Israél: now therefore aduise thee, what worde I shal
bring againe to him that sent me.

a He tempted Dauid in setting before his eyes his excellencie & glorie, his power & victories, read 2.Sam. 24,1.

b That is, frō Southe to North.

c It was a thing indifferent & vsual to nomber the people, but because he did it of an ambitious minde, as thogh his strength stode in his people, God punished him.

d Ioáb partely for grief and partly through negligence gathered not the whole sūme as it is here declared.

e In Samuél is mentiō of thirtie thousand more: ẇ was ether by ioyning to them some of the Beniamites, ẇ were mixed ẇ Iudáh, or as ẏ Ebrewes write, here ẏ chief & princes are left out.

"Or, Prophet.

"Or, smite thee.

13 And Dauid ſaid vnto Gad, I am in a wõderful ſtrait. let me now fall into the hand
of the Lord: for his mercies *are* exceding
great, & let me not fall into ẏ hand of mã.
14 So the Lord ſent a peſtilence in Iſraél,
and there fell of Iſraél ſeuentie thouſand
men.
15 ¶ And God ſent the Angel into Ieruſalém to deſtroye it. And [f] as he was deſtroying, the Lord behelde, and [g] repented of the euil and ſaid to the Angel that
deſtroyed, It is now ynough, let thine hãd
ceaſe. Then the Angel of the Lord ſtode
by the threſſhing floore of ‖ Ornán the
Iebuſite.

f Read 2. Sam. 24,16

g When God draweth backe his plagues, he ſemeth to repent, read Gen. 6,6.

‖ Or, *Araunáh.*

16 And Dauid lift vp his eyes, and ſawe the
Angel of the Lord ſtãd betwene the earth
and the heauen with his ſworde drawen
in his hand, *and* ſtretched out towarde Ieruſalém. Then Dauid and the Elders of
Iſraél, which were clothed in ſacke, fell
vpon their faces.
17 And Dauid ſaid vnto God, Is it not I
that commanded to nomber the people?
It is euen I that haue ſinned and haue
committed euil, but theſe ſhepe what haue they done? ô Lord my God, I beſeche
thee, let thine hand be on me and on my
fathers houſe, and not on [h] thy people for
their deſtruction.

h Thus he bothe ſheweth a true repentãce and a fatherlie care toward his people, ẇ deſireth God to ſpare them and to puniſh him and his.

18 ¶ Thẽ the Angel of the Lord cõmanded
Gad to ſay to Dauid, that Dauid ſhulde
go vp, and ſet vp an altar vnto the Lord
in the threſſhing floore of Ornán the Iebuſite.
19 So Dauid went vp according to ẏ ſaying
of Gad, which he had ſpokẽ in the Name
of the Lord.
20 And Ornán turned about, and ſawe the
Angel, and his foure ſonnes *that were* with
him, [i] hid them ſelues, and Ornán threſ-
ſhed wheat.

i If man hide him ſelfe at ẏ ſight of an Angel which is a creature, how muche leſſe is a ſinner able to appeare before the face of God?

21 And as Dauid came to Ornán, Ornán
loked and ſawe Dauid and went out of the
threſſhing floore, and bowed him ſelfe to
Dauid with his face to the ground.
22 And Dauid ſaid to Ornán, Giue me the
place of *thy* threſſhing floore, that I may
buylde an [k] altar therein vnto the Lord:
giue it me for ſufficient money, that the
plague may be ſtayed from the people.

k Thus he did by the cõmãdemẽt of God, as verſ 18. for els it had bene abominable except he had other Gods worde, or reuelacion.

23 Then Ornán ſaid vnto Dauid, Take it
to thee, and let my lord the King do that
which ſemeth him good: lo, I giue thee
bullockes for burnt offrings, & threſſhing
inſtruments for wood, & wheat for meat
offring, I giue it all.
24 And King Dauid ſaid to Ornán, Not
ſo: but I wil bye it for ſufficient [l] money:
for I wil not take that which is thine for ẏ
Lord, nor offer burnt offrĩgs without coſt.

l That is, as muche as it is worthe: for hauing ynough of his owne & yet to haue takẽ of another mans goods to offer vnto the Lord, it had bene theft and not acceptable to God.

25 So Dauid gaue to Ornán for that place
[m] ſix hũdreth ſhekels of golde by weight.

m Read 2. Samu. 24,24.

26 And Dauid buylt there an altar vnto the
Lord, and offred burnt offrings, and peace
offrings, and called vpon the Lord, and he
[n] anſwered him by fyre from heauẽ vpon
the altar of burnt offring.

n God declared ẏ he heard his requeſt in that he ſent downe fire frõ heauen: for els thei might vſe no fire in ſacrifice, but of ẏ which was reſerued ſtil vpõ ẏ altar, Leui. 6, 13 & came downe from heauen, Leui. 9,24. as appeared by the puniſhement of Nadáb and Abihú, Leu. 10,1.

27 And when the Lord had ſpoken to the
Angel, he put vp his ſworde againe into
his ſhethe.
28 At that time when Dauid ſawe that the
Lord had heard him in the threſſhĩg floore of Ornán the Iebuſite, then he ſacrificed there.
29 (But the Tabernacle of the Lord which
Moſés had made in the wildernes, and the
altar of burnt offring *were* at that ſeaſon
in the hie place at Gibeón.
30 And Dauid colde not go before it to aſke counſel at God: for he was afraied of
the ſworde of the Angel of the Lord)

CHAP. XXII.

2 Dauid prepareth things neceſſarie for the buylding of the Tẽple 6 He cõmandeth his ſonne Salomón to buylde the Tẽple of the Lord, which thing he him ſelfe was forbidden to do. 9 Vnder the figure of Salomón Chriſt is promiſed.

1 AND Dauid ſaid, This is the [a] houſe
of the Lord God, & this is the altar
for the burnt offring of Iſraél.

a That is, the place wherein he wil be worſhiped.

2 And Dauid commanded to gather together the [b] ſtrangers that were in the land
of Iſraél, and he ſet maſons to hewe and
poliſh ſtones to buylde the houſe of God.

b Meaning, cũning men of other nations ẇ dwelt among the Iewes.

3 Dauid alſo prepared [c] muche yron for the
nailes of the dores & of the gates, and
for the ioynings, and abundance of braſſe
paſsing weight,

c To wit, ẇ weighed fiftie ſhekels of golde. 2. Chr. 3,9.

4 And cedre trees without nomber: for
the Zidonians and they of Tyrus broght
muche cedre wood to Dauid.
5 And Dauid ſaid, Salomón my ſonne is
yong and tender, and we muſt buylde an
houſe for the Lord, magnifical, excellent
and of great fame and dignitie throughout all countreis. I wil *therefore* now prepare for him. So Dauid prepared very much
before his death.
6 Then he called Salomón his ſonne, and
charged him to buylde an houſe for the
Lord God of Iſraél.
7 And Dauid ſaid to Salomón, *My ſonne,
I purpoſed with my ſelfe to buyld an houſe to the Name of the Lord my God,

2. Sam. 7, 2.

8 But the worde of the Lord came to me,
ſaying, * [d] Thou haſt ſhed muche blood, &
haſt made great battels: thou ſhalt not
buylde an houſe vnto my Name: for thou
haſt ſhed muche blood vpon the earth in
my ſight.

Chap. 28,3.

d This declareth how greatly God deteſteth the ſheding of blood, ſeĩg Dauid for this cauſe is ſtaied to buylde the Temple of the Lord, albeit he enterpriſed no warre, but by Gods cõmãdemẽt & againſt his enemies.

9 Beholde, a ſonne is borne to thee, which
ſhalbe a mã of reſt, for I wil giue him reſt
from all his enemies round about: therefore his name is Salomón: and I wil ſend
peace and quietnes vpon Iſraél in his
dayes.

10 *He

2.Sam.7,13. 1.king.5,5.

10 *He shal buylde an house for my Name,
and he shal be my sonne, and I wil be his
father, and I wil establish the throne of
his kingdome vpon Israél for euer.
11 Now *therefore* my sonne, the Lord shalbe
with thee, and thou shalt [e] prosper, and
thou shalt buylde an house to the Lord
thy God, as he hathe spoken of thee.
12 Onely the Lord giue thee [f] wisdome &
vnderstanding, and giue thee charge ouer
Israél, euen to kepe the Law of the Lord
thy God.
13 Then thou shalt prosper, if thou take hede
to obserue the statutes and the iudgements
which the Lord commanded Mosés
for Israél: be strong and of good courage:
feare not, nether be afraied.
14 For beholde, according to my [g] pouertie
haue I prepared for the house of the
Lord an hundreth thousand talents of
golde, and a thousand thousand talents of
siluer, and of brasse and of yron passing
weight: for there was abundance: I haue
also prepared timbre and stone, and thou
maiest prouide more thereto.
15 Moreouer thou hast workmen with thee
ynough, "hewers of stone, and workemen
for timbre, and all men expert in euerie
worke,
16 Of golde, of siluer, *and* of brasse, and of
yron there is no nomber. [h] Vp *therefore*,
& be doing, & the Lord wil be with thee.
17 Dauid also commanded all the princes
of Israél to helpe Salomón his sonne,
saying,
18 Is not the Lord your God with you,
& hathe giuen you rest on euerie side? for
he hathe giuen the [i] inhabitants of the
land into mine hand, & the land is subdued
before ẏ Lord & before his people.
19 Now set [k] your hearts and your soules
to seke the Lord your God, and arise, and
buylde the Sanctuarie of the Lord God
to bring the Arke of the couenant of the
Lord, and the holy vessels of God into
the house buylt for ẏ Name of the Lord.

e He sheweth that there can be no prosperitie, but when the Lord is wt vs.

f These are onely the meanes whereby Kings gouerne their subiectes aright, & wherby the realmes doprosper and florish.

g For Dauid was poore in respect of Salomón.

"Or, masons, & carpenters.

h That is, go about it quickely.

i The nations round about.

k For els he knewe that God wolde plague them, & not psper their labours except they soght wt all their hearts to set forthe his glorie.

CHAP. XXIII.

1 Dauid being olde, ordeineth Salomón King. 3 He causeth the Leuites to be nombred, 4 And assigneth them to their offices 13 Aaron and his sonnes are for the hie Priest. 14 The sonnes of Mosés.

1.King 1,30.

1 SO when Dauid was olde and ful of
daies, * he made Salomón his sonne
King ouer Israél.
2 And he gathered together all the princes
of Israél with the Priests and the Leuites.
3 And the Leuites were nombred from the
age of thirtie yere and aboue, and their
nomber according to their summe was
eight and thirtie thousand men.
4 Of these foure and twentie thousand
were set to "aduāce the worke of the house
of the Lord, and six thousand were ouerseers
and iudges.
5 And foure thousand *were* porters, & foure
thousand praised ẏ Lord with instrumēts
which "he made to praise *the Lord*.
6 *So Dauid deuided offices vnto them, *to
wit*, to the sonnes of Leuí, to * Gershón,
Koháth, and Merarí.
7 Of the Gershonites *were* "Laadán and
Shimeí.
8 The sonnes of Laadán, the chief *was* Iehiél,
and Zethám and Ioél, thre.
9 The sonnes of Shimeí, Shelomíth, and
Haziél and Harám, thre: these were the
chief fathers of Laadán.
10 Also the sonnes of Shimeí *were* Iáhath,
Ziná, Ieúsh, and Beriáh: these foure were
the sonnes of Shimeí.
11 And Iáhath was the chief, & "Zizáh the
seconde, but Ieúsh & Beriáh had not many
sonnes: therefore they were in the families
of *their* father, counted but as one.
12 ¶ The sonnes of Koháth *were* Amrám,
Izhár, Hebrón and Vzziél, foure.
13 *The sonnes of Amrám, Aarón and Mosés:
and Aarón was separated to [a] sanctifie
the moste holy place, he & his sonnes for
euer to burne incense before the Lord, to
minister to him, and to blesse in his Name
for euer.
14 ¶ Mosés also the man of God, & his
children were named with the [b] tribe of
Leuí.
15 The sonnes of Mosés *were* Gershóm,
and Eliézer,
16 Of the sōnes of * Gershóm *was* Shebuél
the chief.
17 And the sonne of Eliézer *was* Rehabiáh
the [c] chief: for Eliézer had none other
sonnes: but the sonnes of Rehabiáh were
very many.
18 The sonne of Izhár *was* Shelomíth the
chief.
19 The sonnes of Hebrón *were* Ieriáh the
first, Amariáh the seconde, Iahaziél the
third, and Iekamiám the fourt.
20 The sonnes of Vzziél *were* Micháh the
first, and Isshiáh the seconde.
21 ¶ The sonnes of Merarí *were* Mahlí
and Mushí. The sonnes of Mahlí, Eleazár
and Kish.
22 And Eleazár dyed, and had no sonnes,
but daughters, and their [d] brethren the
sonnes of Kish toke them.
23 The sonnes of Mushí *were* Mahlí, and
Edér, and Ierimóth, thre.
24 These were the sonnes of Leuí according
to the house of their fathers, *euen*
the chief fathers according to their offices,
according to the nomber of names &
their summe that did the worke for the
seruice of the house of the Lord from the
age of [e] twenty yeres and aboue.

"Or, to haue care ouer.

"Ebr. I made, meaning Dauid.

Chap 6,1. Exod.6,17.

"Or, Libni. Chap.6,17.

"Or, Ziza.

Exod.2,2. & 6,20. ebr.5,5.

a That is, to serue in the moste holy place & to cōsecrate ẏ holy things.

b Thei were but of the ordre of the Leuites & not of the Priests as Aarōs sonnes.

Exod.2,22. & 18,3.

c The Scripture vseth to call chief or ẏ first borne, although he be alone & there be none borne after, Matt.1,25.

d Meaning their cousins.

e Dauid did chose the Leuits twise, first at the age of thirtie, as ver. 3, & againe afterwarde at twentie, as the necessitie of ẏ office did require: at ẏ beginning they had no charge in the Temple, before thei were fiue and twentie yere olde, and had none after fiftie, Nōb.10,24.

25 For Dauid said, The Lord God of Israél hathe giuen rest vnto his people, that
they may dwel in Ierusalém for euer.
26 And also the Leuites shal nomore beare
the Tabernacle and all the vessels for the
seruice thereof.
27 Therefore according to the last wordes
of Dauid, the Leuites were nõbred from
twentie yere and aboue,
28 And their office *was* vnder the hand of
the sonnes of Aarón, for the seruice of
the house of the Lord in the courtes, and
chambers, and in the [f] purifying of all holy things, and in the worke of the seruice
of the house of God,
29 Bothe for the shewebread, and for the
fine floure, for the meat offring, and for
the vnleauened cakes, and for the fryed
things, and for that which was rosted, and
for all measures and cise,
30 And for to stand euerie morning, to giue thankes and to praise the Lord, & likewise at euen,
31 And to offer all burnt offrings vnto the
Lord, in the Sabbaths, in the moneths,
and at the appointed times, according to
the nomber & according to their custome
continually before the Lord,
32 And that they shulde kepe the charge of
the Tabernacle of the Congregacion, and
the charge of the holie place, and the
charge of the sonnes of Aarón their brethren in the seruice of the house of the
Lord.

f In wasshing and cleansing all the holy vessels.

CHAP. XXIIII.

Dauid assigneth offices vnto the sonnes of Aarón.

1 THese are also the *diuisions of the
sonnes of Aarón, The sonnes of
Aarón *were* Nadáb, and Abihú, Eleazár,
and Ithamár.
2 But Nadáb and Abihú dyed [a] before
their father, and had no childrẽ: therefore
Eleazár and Ithamár executed ẏ Priests
office.
3 And Dauid distributed them, euen Zadók of the "sonnes of Eleazár, and Ahimélech of the sonnes of Ithamár according to their offices in their ministration.
4 And there were found mo of the sonnes
of Eleazár by the "nomber of men, then of
the sonnes of Ithamár: and they deuided
them, *to wit*, among the sonnes of Eleazár,
sixtene heades, according to the housholde of their fathers, and among the sonnes
of Ithamár, according to the housholde
of their fathers, eight.
5 Thus they distributed them by lot the
one from the other, and so the rulers of the
Sanctuarie and the rulers *of the house* of
God *were* of the sonnes of Eleazár and
of the sonnes of Ithamár.
6 And Shemaiáh the sonne of Nethaneél

Leui.10,4. nom.3,4. & 26,6.

a Whiles their father yet liued.

"Or, cousins.

"Ebr. heades.

the scribe of the Leuites, wrote them before the King and the princes, and Zadók
the Priest, and Ahimélech the sonne of
Abiathár, and *before* the chief fathers of
the Priests and of the Leuites, one familie being reserued for Eleazár, & another
reserued for Ithamár.
7 And the first [b] lot fel to Iehoiaríb, and
the second to Iedaiáh,
8 The third to Harím, the fourt to Seo-
rím,
9 The fift to Malchiiáh, the sixt to Miia-
mín,
10 The seuent to Hakkóz, the eight to A-
[c] biiáh,
11 The ninte to Iesshúa, the tent to Shecaniáh,
12 The eleuent to Eliáship, the twelft to
Iakím,
13 The thirtente to Huppáh, the fourtente
to Ieshebeáb,
14 The fiftente to Bilgáh, the sixtente to
Immér,
15 The seuentente to Hezír, the eightente
to Happizzér,
16 The ninetente to Pethahiáh, the twentieth to Iehezekél,
17 The one and twentie to Iachín, the two
and twentie to Gamúl,
18 The thre and twẽtie to Deliáh, the foure and twentie to Maaziáh.
19 These were their ordres according to
their offices, when they entred into the
house of the Lord according to their custome vnder [d] the hand of Aarón their father, as the Lord God of Israél had commanded him.
20 ¶ And of the sonnes of Leuí that remai
ned of the sonnes of Amrám, *was* Shubaél,
of the sonnes of Shubaél, Iedeiáh,
21 Of Rehabiáh, *euen* of the sonnes of Rehabiáh, the first Isshiiáh,
22 Of Izharí, Shelomóth, of the sonnes of
Shelomóth, Iáhath,
23 And *his* sonnes Ieriáh *the first*, Amariáh
the seconde, Iahaziél the thirde, *and* Ie-
kameám the fourt,
24 The sonne of Vzziél *was* Micháh, the
sonne of Micháh *was* Shamír,
25 The brother of Micháh *was* Isshiiáh, the
sonne of Isshiiáh, Zechariáh,
26 The sonnes of Merarí *were* Mahlí and
Mushí, the sonne of Iaaziiáh *was* Benó,
27 The sonnes of Merarí of Iahaziáh *were*
Benó, and Shóham, and Zaccúr and I-
brí.
28 Of Mahlí *came* Eleazár, which had no
sonnes.
29 Of Kish, the sonne of Kish *was* Ierahmeél,
30 And the sonnes of [e] Mushí *were* Mahlí,
and Edér, and Ierimóth: these were sonnes
of the Leuites after the housholde of their
fathers.

b This lot was ordeined to take away all occasiõ of enuie or grudgig of one against another.

c Zacharie the father of Iohn Baptist was of this course or lot of Abiá, Luk.1,5.

d By the dignitie that God gaue to Aarón.

e Which was the seconde sonne of Merari.

31 And

f That is, euerie one had ẏ dignitie, ẇ fel vnto him by lot.

31 And these also cast f lottes ẇ their brethren the sonnes of Aarón before King
Dauid, and Zadók and Ahimélech and the
chief fathers of the Priests, and of the Leuites, *euen* the chief of the families agaĩst
their yonger brethren.

CHAP. XXV.

The singers are appointed, with their places & lottes.

a The singers were deuided into foure and twentie courses, so that euery course or ordre conteined twelue, & in all there were 288, as vers. 7.

1 SO Dauid & the captaines of ẏ armie
a separated for the ministerie the sonnes of Asáph, and Hemán, and Ieduthún,
who shulde *sing* prophecies with harpes,
with violes, and with cymbales, and their
nomber was *euen* of the men for the office
of their ministerie, *to wit*,
2 Of the sonnes of Asáph, Zaccúr, and Ioséph, & Nethaniáh, & Asharélah the sonnes of Asaph *were* vnder the hand of A-
sáph, *which sang* prophecies by the " commission of the King.

"Ebr. hands.

3 Of Ieduthún, the sonnes of Ieduthún,
Gedaliáh, & Zerí, and Ieshaiáh, Ashabiáh
and Mattithiáh, b six, vnder the hands of
their father: Ieduthún *sang* c prophecies
with an harpe, for to giue thankes and to
praise the Lord.

b Whereof one is not here nombred.
c Meaning, Psalmes and songs to praise God.

4 Of Hemán, the sonnes of Hemán, Bukkiáh, Mattaniáh, Vzziél, Shebuél, and Ierimóth, Hananiáh, Hanáni, Eliáthah,
Giddálti, & Romámti-ézer, Ioshbekáshah,
Mallóthi, Hothir & Mahazióth.
5 All these were the sonnes of Hemán the
Kings " Seer in the wordes of God to lift
vp the " horne: and God gaue to Hemán
fourtene sonnes and thre daughters.

"Or, Prophet.
"Or, power, meaning of the King.
"Or, gouernemẽt.

6 All these were vnder the " hand of their
father, singing in the house of ẏ Lord with
cymbales, violes & harpes, for the seruice
of the house of God, & Asáph, and Ieduthún, and Hemán *were* at the Kings " cõmandement.

"Ebr. hand.

7 So was their nomber with their brethren
that were instruct in the songs of ẏ Lord,
euen of all that were conning, two hundreth foure score and eight.
8 And thei cast lottes, d charge against *charge*, aswel e small as great, the cunning man
as the scholer.
9 And the first lot fell to f Ioséph, *which was*
of Asáph, the seconde, to Gedaliáh, who
with his brethren and his sonnes were
twelue.
10 The third, to Zaccúr, *he*, his sonnes and
his brethren *were* twelue.
11 The fourte, to " Izrí, *he*, his sonnes & his
brethren twelue.
12 The fift, to Nethaniáh, *he*, his sonnes &
his brethren twelue.
13 The sixt, to Bukkiáh, *he*, his sonnes & his
brethren twelue.
14 The seuent, to Iesharélah, *he*, his sonnes
and his brethren twelue.
15 The eight, to Ieshaiáh, *he*, his sonnes and
his brethren twelue.

d Who shulde be in euery companie and course.
e Without respect to age or cunning.
f So that he serued in the first turne, and the rest euery one as his turne followed, orderly.
"Or, the Leuites.

16 The nint, to Mattaniáh, *he*, his sonnes &
his brethren twelue.
17 The tent, to Shimeí, *he*, his sonnes and
his brethren twelue.
18 The eleuent, to Azaréel, *he*, his sonnes
and his brethren twelue.
19 The twelft, to Ashabiáh, *he*, his sonnes
and his brethren twelue.
20 The thirtent, to Shubaél, *he*, his sonnes
and his brethren twelue.
21 The fourtent, to Mattithiáh, *he*, his sonnes and his brethren twelue.
22 The fiftent, to Ierimóth, *he*, his sonnes
and his brethren twelue.
23 The sixtente, to Hananiáh, *he*, his sonnes
and his brethren twelue.
24 The seuentente, to Ioshbekáshah, *he*, his
sonnes and his brethren twelue.
25 The eightente, to Hananí, *he*, his sonnes
and his brethren twelue.
26 The ninetente, to Mallóthi, *he*, his sonnes and his brethren twelue.
27 The twẽtieth, to Eliáthah, *he*, his sonnes
and his brethren twelue.
28 The one and twentieth, to Hothír, *he*,
his sonnes and his brethren twelue.
29 The two and twentieth, to Giddálti, *he*,
his sonnes and his brethren twelue.
30 The thre and twentieth, to Mahazióth,
he, his sonnes and his brethren twelue.
31 The foure and twentieth, to Romámti-
ézer, *he*, his sonnes & his brethren twelue.

CHAP. XXVI.

1 The porters of the Temple are ordeined, euerie man to the gate, which he shulde kepe. 20 And ouer the treasure.

1 COncerning the " diuisions of the porters, of the Korhites, Meshelemiáh
the sonne of Koré of the sonnes of a A-
sáph.
2 And the sonnes of Meshelemiáh, Zechariáh the eldest, Iediaél the seconde, Zebadiáh the third, Iathniél the fourt,
3 Elám the fift, Iehohanán the sixt, & Eli-
ehoenái the seuent.
4 And of the sonnes of Obéd Edóm, Shemaiáh the eldest, Iehozabád the seconde,
Ioáh the third, and Sacár the fourt, and
Nethaneél the fift,
5 Ammiél the sixt, Issachár the seuent,
Peulthái the eight: for God had b blessed
him.
6 And to Shemaiáh his sonne, were sonnes
borne, that c ruled in the house of their
father, for thei were men of might.
7 The sonnes of Shemaiáh *were* Othní, and
Rephaél, and Obéd, Elzabád & his brethren strong men: Elihú also, & Semachiáh.
8 All these were of the " sonnes of Obéd E-
dóm, thei and their sonnes and their brethren mightie and d strong to serue, *euen*

"Or, courses, and turnes.
a This Asáph was not the notable musitian, but another of ẏ name called also Ebiasaph, Chap 9,37. & 9,19. & also Iasaph.
b In giuing him many children.
c Or like their fathers house, meaning worthie men and valiant.
"Or, nephewes.
d And mete to serue in the office of the portership.

thre score and two of Obéd Edóm.
9 And of Meshelemiáh sonnes and brethrē
eightene mightie men.
10 And of Hosáh of the sonnes of Merarí
the sonnes *were* Shúri the chief,& (thogh
he was not the eldest, yet his father made
him the chief)
11 Helkiáh the seconde, Tebaliáh the third,
& Zechariáh the fourt: all the "sonnes &
the brethren of Hosáh *were* thirtene.
12 Of these *were* the "diuisions of the porters of the chief men, *hauing* the charge
e against their brethrē, to serue in the house of the Lord.
13 And thei cast lottes bothe smale & great
for the house of their fathers, for euerie
gate.
14 And the lot on the Eastside fel to "Shelemiáh: thē thei cast lottes for Zechariáh his
sonne f a wise counseler, and his lot came
out Northwarde:
15 To Obéd Edóm Southwarde, and to his
sonnes the house of g Asuppím:
16 To Shuppím and to Hosáh Westwarde
with ý gate h of Shallécheth by the paued
strete that goeth vpwarde, warde ouer a-
gainst warde.
17 Eastwarde *were* six Leuites, & Northwarde foure a day, *and* Southwarde foure a
daye, and towarde Asuppím i two & two.
18 In k Parbár towarde ý West *were* foure
by the paued strete, and two in Parbár.
19 These are the diuisions of the porters of
the sonnes of Koré, and of the sonnes of
Merarí.
20 ¶ And of the Leuites, Ahiiáh *was* ouer
the treasures of the house of God, and o-
uer the treasures of the dedicate things.
21 Of the sonnes of Laadán the sonnes of
the Gershúnites *descending* of Laadán, the
chief fathers of Laadán *were* Gershúnni
& Iehielí.
22 The sonnes of Iehielí *were* Zethán and
Ioél his brother, *appointed* ouer the treasures of the house of the Lord.
23 Of the l Amramites, of the Izharites,
of the Hebronites *and* of the Ozielites.
24 And Shebuél the sonne of Gershóm, the
sonne of Mosés, a ruler ouer the treasures.
25 And of his "brethren, *which came* of Eliézer, was Rehabiáh his sonne, and Ieshaiáh
his sonne, and Iorám his sonne, and Zichrí
his sonne, and Shelomíth his sonne.
26 Which Shelomíth & his brethren *were*
ouer all the treasures of ý dedicate things,
which Dauid the King, and the chief fathers, the captaines ouer thousands, and
hundreths, and the captaines of the armie
had m dedicate.
27 (*For* of the battels and of the spoiles
they did dedicate to mainteine the house
of the Lord)
28 And all that Samuél the Seer had dedi-

*Or, cousins.

*Or, courses.

e According to their turnes, aswel the one as the other.

*Or, Meshelemiáh.

f One experte and mete to kepe ý gate.

g This was an house, where they vsed to resort to consulte of things cōcerning the Temple, as a Conuocacion house.

h Whereat they vsed to cast out ý filth of the citie, Isa.6,13.

i Meanīg, two one daye and two another.

k Which was an house wherein they kept the instrumēts of the Tēple.

l These also had charge ouer the treasures.

*Or, cousins.

m According as the Lord commanded, Nomb.31,28.

cate, and Saúl the sonne of Kish and Abnér the sonne of Ner, and Ioáb the sonne
of Zeruiáh, *and* whosoeuer had dedicate
anie thing, it was vnder the hand of Shelo-
mith, and his brethren.
29 Of the Izharites *was* Chenaniáh & his
sonnes, for the busines n without ouer Israél, for officers and for iudges.
30 Of the Hebronites, Ashabiáh and his
brethren, men of actiuitie, a thousand, and
seuen hundreth were officers for Israél beyonde Iordén Westwarde, in all the busines of the Lord, and for the seruice o of
the King.
31 Among the Hebronites *was* Iediáh the
chiefest, euen the Hebronites by his generacions according to the families. And in
the fourtieth yere of the reigne of Dauid
thei were soght for: and there were founde among them men of actiuitie at Iazér
in Gileád.
32 And his p brethren men of actiuitie, two
thousand & seuen hundreth chief fathers,
whome King Dauid made rulers ouer the
Reubenites, & the Gadites, and the halfe
tribe of Manasséh, for euerie matter *perteining* to q God, and for the Kings busines.

n Meaning of things ý were out of ý citie.

o That is, for the Kings house.

p To wit, the cousins of Iediáh.

q Bothe in spiritual and tēporal thigs.

CHAP. XXVII.

Of the princes and rulers that ministred vnto the King.

1 THe childrē of Israél also after their
nomber, *euen* the chief fathers and
captaines of thousands and of hundreths,
and their officers that serued the King by
diuers "courses, a which came in & went
out, moneth by moneth throughout all the
moneths of the yere: in euerie course *were*
foure and twentie thousand.
2 Ouer the first course for the first moneth
was Iashobeám the sonne of Zabdiél: and
in his course *were* foure and twentie thousand.
3 Of the sonnes of Pérez *was* the chief o-
uer all the princes of the armies for the
first moneth.
4 And ouer the course of the seconde moneth was Dodái, an Ahohite, & *this was* his
course, & Mikióth *was* b a captaine, and in
his course *were* foure & twétie thousand.
5 The captaine of the third hoste for the
third moneth *was* Benaiáh the sonne of
Iehoiadá the chief Priest: & in his course
were foure and twentie thousand.
6 This Benaiáh was mightie amōg * thirtie and aboue the thirtie, and in his course
was Amizabád his sonne.
7 The fourt for the fourt moneth *was* A-
sahél the brother of Ioáb, and Zebadiáh
his sonne after him: and in his course *were*
foure and twentie thousand.
8 The fift for the fift moneth *was* prince
Shamhúth the Izrahite: and in his course
foure and twentie thousand.

*Ebr. diuisions, or bandes.

a Which executed their charge and office, which is ment by comming in and going out.

b That is, Dodais lieutenāt.

* 2.Sam.23,20. & 22,23.

9 The

9 The sixt for the sixt moneth *was* Irá the
sonne of Ikkésh the Tekoite: and in his
course foure and twentie thousand.
10 The seuent for the seuent moneth *was*
Hélez the Pelonite, of the sonnes of E-
phráim: and in his course foure and twentie thousand.
11 The eight for the eight moneth *was* Sibbecái the Hushathite of the Zarhites: and
in his course foure and twentie thousand.
12 The nint for the nint moneth *was* A-
biézer the Anethothite of the sonnes of
″Ieminí: and in his course foure and twentie thousand.

″Or, Beniamin.

13 The tent for the tent moneth *was* Maharái, the Netophathite of the Zarhites:
and in his course foure and twentie thousand.
14 The eleuent for the eleuent moneth
was Benaiáh the Pirathonite of the sonnes
of Ephráim: and in his course foure and
twentie thousand.
15 The twelft for the twelft moneth *was*
Heldái the Netophathite, of Othniél: &
in his course foure & twentie thousand.
16 ¶ Moreouer [c] *the rulers* ouer the tribes
of Israél ouer, the Reubenites *was* ruler,
Eliézer the sonne of Zichri: ouer the Shi-
meonites, Shephatiáh the sonne of Maacháh:

c Meaning, besides these twelue captaines.

17 Ouer ẏ Leuites, Hashabiáh the sonne of
Remuél: ouer *them* of Aharón, & Zadók:
18 Ouer Iudáh, Elihú of the brethré of Dauid: ouer Issachár, Omrí the sonne of Michaél:
19 Ouer Zebulún, Ishmaiáh the sonne of
Obadiáh: ouer Naphtali, Ierimóth the
sonne of Azriél:
20 Ouer the sonnes of Ephráim, Hoshéa
the sonne of Azazziáh: ouer the halfe tribe of Manasséh, Ioél ẏ sonne of Pedaiáh:
21 Ouer the [d] *other* halfe of Manasséh in
Gileád, Iddó the sōne of Zechariáh: ouer
Beniamín, Iaasiél the sonne of Abnér:
22 Ouer Dan, Azariél ẏ sonne of Ierohám.
these are the prīces of the tribes of Israél.

d Which is beyonde Iordén in respect of Iudáh: also one captaine was ouer the Reuoenites & the Gadites.

23 ¶ But Dauid toke not the nōber of them
from twentie yere olde and vnder, because the Lord had said that he wolde increase Israél like vnto ẏ starres of the heauēs.
24 And *Ioáb the sonne of Zeruiáh began
to nomber: but he finished it not, [e] because there came wrath for it against Israél, nether was the nomber put into the
[f] Chronicles of King Dauid.

Chap.21,7.

e And the cōmandement of the King was abominable to Ioáb, Chap. 21,6.

f The Ebrewes make bothe these bokes of Chronicles but one, & at this verse make the middes of the boke, as touching the nōber of verses.

25 And ouer the Kings treasures *was* Azma-
uéth the sonne of Adiél: and ouer the treasures in the fields, in the cities and in the
villages & in the towres *was* Iehonathán
the sonne of Vzziáh:
26 And ouer the workemen in the field
that tilled the grounde, *was* Ezrí the sonne
of Chelúb:
27 And ouer them that dressed the vines,
was Shimeí the Ramathite: and ouer
that which apperteined to the vines, and
ouer the store of the wine *was* Sabdí the
Shiphmite:
28 And ouer ẏ oliuetrees and mulberie trees
that were in the valleies, *was* Báal Hanán
the Gederite: & ouer the store of the oyle
was Ioásh:
29 And ouer the oxen that fed in Sharón,
was Shetrái the Sharonite: & ouer the oxē
in ẏ valleies *was* Shaphat ẏ sōne of Adlái:
30 And ouer the camels *was* Obíl the Ish-
maelite: and ouer the asses *was* Iehdeiáh
the Meronothite:
31 And ouer the shepe *was* Iazíz the Hage-
rite: all these were the rulers of the substāce that was King Dauids.
32 And Iehonathán Dauids vncle a man of
counsel and of vnderstanding (for he was
a [g] scribe) & Iehiél the sonne of Hachmoní *were* with the Kings [h] sonnes.
33 And Ahitóphel *was* the Kings cōuseler,
and Hushái the Archite the Kings friend.
34 And [i] after Ahitóphel *was* Iehoiadá the
sonne of Benaiáh and Abiathár: and captaine of the Kings armie *was* Ioáb.

g That is, a man learned in the worde of God.

h To be their scholemasters and teachers.

i After that Ahitóphel had hāged him selfe, 2 Samu. 17,23 Iehoiada was made counseler.

CHAP. XXVIII.

3 Because Dauid was forbidden to buylde the Tēple, he willeth Salomón and the people to performe it, 8 Exhorting him to feare the Lord.

1 NOw Dauid assembled all the princes
of Israél: the princes of the tribes, &
the captaines of the bandes that serued the
King, and the captaines of thousands &
the captaines of hundreths, and the rulers
of all the substance, and possession of the
King, & of his sonnes, with the ″eunuches,
and the mightie, and all the mē of power,
vnto Ierusalém.

″Or, chief seruants, Gen 37, 36.

2 And King Dauid stode vp vpon his fete,
and said, Heare ye me, my brethren & my
people: I purposed to haue buylt an house
of [a] rest for the Arke of the couenant of
the Lord, & for a *footestole of our God,
and haue made ready for the buylding,
3 But God said vnto me, *Thou shalt not
buylde an house for my Name, because
thou hast bene a mā of warre, & hast shed
blood.

a Where the Arke shulde remaine and remoue nomore to and fro.

Psal 99,5.

2 Sam. 7,13.

chap.22,8.

4 Yet as the Lord God of Israél chose me
before all the house of my father, to be
King ouer Israél for euer (for in Iudáh
wolde he chuse a prince, & of the house of
[b] Iudáh is the house of my father, & amōg
the sonnes of my father he delited in me
to make me King ouer all Israél)

b According to the prophecie of Iaakób, Gen. 49,8.

5 *So of all my sonnes (for the Lord hathe
giuen me manie sonnes) he hathe euē chosen Salomón my sonne to sit vpō the throne of the kingdome of ẏ Lord ouer Israél.

Wisd.9,7.

6 And he said vnto me, Salomón thy sōne,
he shal buylde mine house & my courtes:

for I haue chosen him to be my sonne, and
I wil be his father.
7 I wil stablish therefore his kingdome
for euer: if he indeuoure him selfe to do
my commandements, and my iudgemẽts,
as [c] this day.
8 Now therefore in the sight of all Israél
the Congregacion of the Lord, and in the
audience of our God, kepe and seke for all
the cõmandements of the Lord your God,
that ye may possesse this [d] good land, and
leaue it for an inheritance for your children after you [e] for euer.
9 And thou, Salomón my sõne, knowe thou
the God of thy father, and serue him with
a perfit hearte, and with a willing minde:
* for the Lord searcheth all hearts, and vnderstandeth all the imaginacions of thoghtes: if thou seke him, he wil be founde of
thee, but if thou forsake him, he wil cast
thee of for euer.
10 Take hede now, for the Lord hathe
chosen thee to buylde [f] the house of the
Sanctuarie: be strong *therefore*, and [g] do it.
11 ¶ Then Dauid gaue to Salomón his sonne the paterne of the porche and of the
houses thereof, and of the closets thereof, and of the galeries thereof, and of the
chambers thereof that are within, and of
the house of the merciseate,
12 And the paterne of all that "he had in
his minde for the courtes of the house
of the Lord, and for all the chambers
rounde about, for the treasures of the house of God, and for the treasures of the dedicate things,
13 And for the courses of the Priests, and of
the Leuites, and for all the worke for the
seruice of the house of the Lord, and for
all the vessels of the ministerie of the house of the Lord.
14 *He gaue* of golde by weight, for *the vessels*
of golde, for all the vessels of all maner
of seruice, *and* all the vessels of siluer by
weight, for all maner vessels of all maner
of seruice.
15 The weight also of golde for the [h] candlestickes, and golde for their lãpes, with
the weight for euerie candlesticke, & for
the lampes thereof, & for the cãdlestickes
of siluer by the weight of the candlesticke,
and the lampes thereof, according to the
vse of euerie candlesticke,
16 And the weight of the golde for the tables of shewbread, for euerie table, & siluer
for the tables of siluer,
17 And pure golde for the fleshokes, & the
bowles, and "plates, & for basens, golde in
weight for euerie basen, and for siluer basens by weight for euerie basen,
18 And for the altar of incense, pure golde
by weight, and golde for the paterne of
[i] the charet of the Cherubs that spred thẽ

c If he continue to kepe my Lawe and departe not therefrom, as he doeth hitherto.

d To wit, of Canáan.

e He declareth that nothing can separat them frõ the commoditie of this lãd bothe for thẽ selues & their posteritie, but their sinnes & iniquitie.

1.Sam.16,7. psal.7,10. iere.11,20. & 17,10. & 20,12.

f Meaning, for his Arke.

g Put it in execucion.

"*Ebr. that were in his spirit with him.*

h That is, the tẽ cãdlesticks, 1.King.7,49.

"*Or, couerings.*

i Meaning, of the merciseat which couered the Arke, which was called the charet because the Lord declared him selfe there

selues, and couered the Arke of the coue-
nante of the Lord:
19 All, *said he*, by writing *sent* to me [k] by
the hand of the Lord, *which* made me vnderstand all the workemanship of the
paterne.
20 And Dauid said to Salomón his sonne,
Be strong, and of a valiant courage and do
it: feare not, nor be afraied: for the Lord
God, *euen* my God *is* with thee: he wil not
leaue thee nor forsake thee til thou hast
finished all the worke for the seruice of
the house of the Lord.
21 Beholde also, the cõpanies of the Priests
and the Leuites for all the seruice of the
house of God, euen *they shalbe* with thee
for the whole worke, [l] with euerie fre heart that is skilful in anie maner of seruice. The princes also and all the people *wil
be* "wholly at thy commandement.

CHAP. XXIX.

2 The offring of Dauid and of the princes for the buylding of the Temple. 10 Dauid giueth thankes to the Lord. 20 He exhorteth the people to do the same. 22 Salomón is created King. 28 Dauid dyeth, and Salomón his sonne reigneth in his steade.

1 MOreouer Dauid the King said vnto
all the Cõgregaciõ, God hathe chosen Salomón mine onelie sonne yong and
tendre, & the worke *is* great: for this house
is not for man, but for the [a] Lord God.
2 Now I haue prepared with all my power
for the house of my God, golde for *vessels*
of golde, and siluer for *them* of siluer, and
brasse for *things* of brasse, yron for *things* of
yron, and wood for *things* of wood & onix
stones, and stones to be set, and carbuncle
stones and of diuers colour, and all precious stones, & marble stones in abũdãce.
3 Moreouer because I haue [b] delite in the
house of my God, I haue of mine owne
golde and siluer, which I haue giuẽ to the
house of my God, beside all that I haue
prepared for the house of the Sanctuarie,
4 Euen [c] thre thousand talents of golde
of the golde of Ophír, and seuen thousand
talents of fined siluer to ouerlay the walles of the houses.
5 The golde for the *things* of golde, and
the siluer for *things* of siluer, and for all
the worke by the hands of artificers: and
who is [d] willing " to fil his hand to day
vnto the Lord?
6 So the Princes of the families, and the
princes of the tribes of Israél, & the captaines of thousands & of hundreths, with the
rulers of ẏ Kings worke, offred willingly,
7 And they gaue for the seruice of the house of God fiue thousand talents of golde,
and ten thousand pieces, and ten thousand
talents of siluer, and eightene thousand talents of brasse, and one hundreth thousand
talents of yron.

k For all this was left in wrting in the boke of ẏ Lawe, Exod 5,40. ẇ boke the King was bounde to put in execucion, Deut. 17,19.

l That is, euerie one wil be ready to helpe thee with those gifts that God hathe giuen him.

"*Ebr at all thy wordes.*

a And therefore it oght to be excellent in all pointes.

b His great zeale toward the furtherãce of the Tẽple made him to spare no expenses, but to bestowe his owne peculiar treasure.

c He sheweth what he had of his owne store for ẏ Lords house.

d He was not onely liberal him selfe, but prouoked others to set forthe ẏ worke of God.

"*Or, to offer.*

8 And

8 And they with whome *precious* stones were
[e] founde, gaue them to the treasure of the
house of the Lord, by the hand of Iehiél
the Gershunnite.
9 And the people reioyced when they offred
willingly: for they offred willingly
vnto the Lord, with a [f] perfite heart. And
Dauid the King also reioyced with great
ioye.
10 Therefore Dauid blessed the Lord before
all the Congregacion, & Dauid said,
Blessed *be* thou, ô Lord God, of [g] Israél
our father, for euer and euer.
11 Thine, ô Lord, *is* greatnes and power,
and glorie, and victorie and praise: for all
that is in heauen & in earth *is thine*: thine
is the kingdome, ô Lord, and thou excel-
lest as head ouer all.
12 Bothe riches and honour *come* of thee,
& thou reignest ouer all, and in thine hād
is power and strength, and in thine hand it
is to make great, and to giue strength vnto all.
13 Now therefore our God, we thanke thee,
and praise thy glorious Name.
14 But who am I, and what is my people,
that we shulde be able to offer willingly
after this sorte? for all things [h] come of
thee: and of thine owne hand we haue giuen thee.
15 For we are [i] strangers before thee, and
soiourners, like all our fathers: our dayes
are like the shadowe vpon the earth, and
there is none "abiding.
16 O Lord our God, all this abundance
that we haue prepared to buylde thee an
house for thine holy Name, is of thine
hand and all *is* thine.
17 I knowe also, my God, that thou *tryest
the heart, and hast pleasure in righteousnes: I haue offred willingly in ȳ vprigh-
nes of mine heart all these things: now
also haue I sene thy people which are
founde here, to offer vnto thee willingly
with ioye.
18 O Lord God of Abrahám, Izhák and
Israél our fathers, kepe this for euer in the
[k] purpose, *and* the thoghts of the heart of
thy people, and prepare their hearts vnto
thee.
19 And giue vnto Salomón my sonne a perfit heart to kepe thy commandements, thy
testimonies, and thy statutes, and to do
all things, and to buylde the house which
I haue prepared.
20 ¶ And Dauid said to all the Congregaciō, Now blesse the Lord your God. And
all the Congregacion blessed the Lord
God of their fathers, and bowed downe
their heades, & worshipped the Lord and
the [l] King.
21 And they offred sacrifices vnto the Lord,
and on the morowe after that day, they
offred burnt offrings vnto the Lord, *euen*
a thousand yong bullockes, a thousand
rammes, & a thousand sheepe, with their
[m] drinke offrings, and sacrifices in abundāce for all Israél.
22 And they did eat and drinke before the
Lord the same day with greate ioye, and
they made Salomón the sonne of Dauid
King the seconde time, and anointed him
prince before the Lord, and Zadók for
the hie Priest.
23 So Salomón sate on the [n] throne of the
Lord, as King in steade of Dauid his father, and prospered: and all Israél o-
beyed him.
24 And all the princes and men of power,
and all the sonnes of King Dauid "submitted them selues vnder King Salomón.
25 And the Lord magnified Salomón in
dignitie, in the sight of all Israél, and gaue him so glorious a kingdome, as no
King had before him in Israél.
26 ¶ *Thus Dauid the sonne of Ishái reigned ouer all Israél.
27 And the space that he reigned ouer Israél, *was* fourtie yere: seuen yere reigned
he in Hebrón, and thre & thirtie yere reigned he in Ierusalém:
28 And he dyed in a good age, ful of dayes,
riches and honour, and Salomón his sonne
reigned in his steade.
29 Concerning the actes of Dauid the
King first and last, beholde, they are writen in the boke of Samuél the Seer, and in
the boke of [o] Nathán the Prophete, and
in the boke of Gad the Seer,
30 With all his reigne and his power,
and [p] times that went ouer him, and ouer
Israél and ouer all the kingdomes of the
earth.

e Meaning, thē that had anie.
f That is, with a good courage & without hypocrisie.
g Which did reueile thy selfe to our father Iaakób.
h We gaue thee nothing of our owne, but that which we haue receiued of thee: for whether ȳ gifts be corporal or spiritual, we receiue them all of God, and therefore must giue him the glorie.
i And therefore haue this land but lent to vs for a time.
"Ebr. *waiting for them to returne.*
1.Sam.16,7. chap.28,9.
k Cōtinue thē in this good minde, that they may serue thee willingly.
l That is, did reuerence to the King.
m Meaning, all kide of licour which they mingled, with their sacrifices, as wine, oyle, &c.
n This declareth that the Kings of Iudáh were figures of Christ, who was the true anointed, & to whome God gaue the chief gouernment of all things.
"*Ebr. gaue the hand.*
1.King.2,11.
o The bokes of Nathán & Gad are thoght to haue bene lost in the captiuitie.
p Meaning, the troubles and griefs.

THE SECONDE BOKE of the Chronicles.

THE ARGUMENT.

THis seconde boke conteineth briefely in effect that, which is comprehended in the two bokes of the Kings: that is, from the reigne of Salomón to the destruction of Ierusalém, and the carying away of the people captiue into Babylon. In this storie are certeine things declared and set forthe more copiously then in the bokes of the Kings, and therefore serue greatly to the vnderstanding of the Prophetes. But thre things are here chiefly to be considered. First that the godlie Kings, when they sawe the plagues of God prepared against their countrey for sinne, had recourse to the Lord, and by earnest prayer were heard, and the plagues remoued. The seconde how it is a thing that greatly offendeth God, that suche as feare him and professe his religion, shulde ioyne in amitie with the wicked. And thirdely how the good rulers euer loued the Prophetes of God, and were very zealous to set forthe his religion throughout all their dominions, and contrarie wise the wicked hated his ministers, deposed them, and for the true religion and worde of God, set vp idolatrie, and serued God according to the fantasie of men. Thus haue we hitherto the chief actes from the beginning of the worlde to the buylding againe of Ierusalém, which was the two and thirtieth yere of Darius, and conteine in the whole, thre thousand, foure hundreth foure score and eight yeres, and six moneths.

CHAP. I.

6 The offring of Salomón at Gibeón. 9 He prayeth vnto God to giue him wisdome. 11 Which he giueth him and more. 14 The nomber of his charets and horses, 15 And of his riches.

1 THé Salomón the sõne of
Dauid was [a]cõfirmed in
his kingdome: & ỹ * Lord
his God *was* with him, &
magnified him highlie.

[a] Or, established, and strong.
1. King. 3,1.

2 And Salomón [a] spake
vnto all Israél, to the captaines of thousands, and of hũdreths and
to the iudges, and to all the gouernours in
all Israél, *euen* the chief fathers.

a That is, he proclaimed a solemne sacrifice, and commãded that all shulde be at the same.

3 So Salomón and all the Congregacion
with him went to the hye place that was
at [b] Gibeón: for there was the Tabernacle
[c] of the Cõgregacion of God which Mosés the seruant of the Lord had made in
the wildernes.

b Read 1. King. 3,4
c So called, because that God thereby shewed certeine signes to the congregacion of his presence.

4 But the Arke of God had Dauid broght
vp from Kiriath-iearím, when Dauid had
made preparacion for it: for he had pitched a tent for it in Ierusalém.
5 Moreouer the [d] brasen altar * that Bezaleél the sonne of Vrí, the sonne of Hur had
made, did he set before the Tabernacle of
the Lord: and Salomón and the Cõgregacion soght it.

d Which was for the burnt offrings, Exod. 27,1
Exod. 38,1.

6 And Salomón offred there before ỹ Lord
vpon the brasen altar that was in the Tabernacle of the Congregacion: * euen a
thousand burnt offrings offred he vpon it.

1. King. 3,4.

7 ¶ The same night did God appeare vnto
Salomón, and said vnto him, Aske what I
shal giue thee.
8 And Salomón said vnto God, Thou hast
shewed great mercie vnto Dauid my father
and hast made me to reigne in his steade.
9 Now *therefore*, ô Lord God, let thy promes
vnto Dauid my father be [e] true: for thou
hast made me King ouer a great people,
like to the dust of the earth.
10 Giue me now wisdome and knowledge,
ỹ I may [f] go out & go in before this people: for who cã iudge this thy great people?
11 And God said to Salomón, Because this
was in thine heart, & thou hast not asked
riches, treasures nor honour, nor the [g] liues of thine enemies, nether yet hast asked
long life, but hast asked for thee wisdome
& knowledge that thou mightest iudge
my people, ouer whome I haue made thee
King,

e Performe thy pmes made to my father concerning me.
f That I may gouerne this people, read 1. Chro. 27,1.
g That is, to be reuéged on thine enemies.

12 Wisdome & knowledge is granted vnto
thee, and I wil giue thee riches and treasures and honour, so that there hathe not bene the like amõg the Kings ẘ were before
thee, nether after thee shal there be ỹ like.
13 Then Salomón came from the hie place,
that was at Gibeón, to Ierusalém from before the Tabernacle of the Congregaciõ,
and reigned ouer Israél.
14 * And Salomón gathered the charets &
horsmen: and he had a thousand and foure
hũdreth charets, & twelue thousand horsmen, whome he placed in the [h] charet cities, and with the King at Ierusalém.

2. King. 10,26
h Which were cities appointed to kepe & mainteine the charets

15 And the King gaue siluer and golde at
Ierusalém as [i] stones, & gaue cedre trees
as the wilde fig trees, that are abundantly
in the plaine.

i He caused so great plentie that it was no more estemed then stones.

16 Also Salomón had horses broght out of
Egypt and * fine linen: [k] the Kings marchãts receiued the fine linen for a price.

Isai. 19,9.
ezek. 27,7.
k Read 1. Kig. 10,28.

17 They came vp also and broght out of
Egypt *some* charet, *worthe* six hundreth *shekels* of siluer, that is an horse for an hundreth and fiftie: & thus they broght *horses*
to all the Kings of the Hittites, and to the
Kings of Arãm by their [a] meanes.

[a] Ebr. hands.

CHAP. II.

2 The nomber of Salomons workemen to buylde the Temple. 3 Salomón sendeth to Hirám the King of Tyrus for wood and workemen.

1 THé Salamón determined to buyld an
house for the Name of the Lord, &
an [a] house for his kingdome.

[a] Or, palace.

2 And Salomón tolde out seuentie thousand that bare burdens, and foure score
thousand men to hewe *stones* in the mountaine, and thre thousand and [a] six hũdreth
to oursee them.

a Which is to be vnderstand of all sorte of officers & ouerseers: for els the chief officers were but 3300, as 1. King. 5,16.

3 And Salomón sent to [b] Hurám the King of
Tyrus, sayĩg, As thou hast done to Dauid
my father, & * didest send him cedre trees
to buyld hĩ an house to dwel in, *so do to me*.
4 Beholde, I buyld an house vnto the Name of ỹ Lord my God, to sanctifie it vnto
him,

[b] Or, Hirám.
2. Sam. 5, 11.

him, & to burne swete incése before him,
and for the continual shewbread, & for ÿ
burnt offrings of the morning & euening,
on the Sabbath daies,& in the newe moneths, and in the solemne feastes of the
Lord our God: this is a perpetual thing
for Israél.
5 And the house which I buyld, *is* great: for
great *is* our God aboue all gods.
6 Who is he thẽ that can be able to buyld
him an house, when the heauen, and the
heauen of heauens can not conteine him?
who am I then ÿ I shulde buyld hĩ an house? but *I do it* to burne [b] incense before him.
7 Send me now therefore a cunning man
that can worke in golde, in siluer, and in
brasse, and in yron, and in purple, and *crimosin and blewe silke, and that can graue
in grauen worke with the cunning men ÿ
are with me in Iudáh and in Ierusalém,
whome Dauid my father hathe prepared.
8 Send me also cedre trees, firre trees and
[c] *Algummím trees from Lebanón: for I
knowe that thy seruants can skill to hewe
timbre in Lebanón: and beholde, my seruants *shalbe* with thine,
9 That they may prepare me timbre in a-
bundãce: for the house which I do buyld,
is great and wonderful.
10 And beholde, I wil giue to thy seruants
the cutters and the hewers of timbre twẽ
tie thousand* measures of beaten wheat,
and twentie thousand measures of barly,
and twentie thousand baths of wine, and
twentie [d] thousand baths of oyle.
11 Then Hurám King of Tyrus answered
in writing which he sent to Salomón, Because the Lord hathe loued his people, he
hathe made thee King ouer them.
12 Hurám said moreouer, Blessed *be* the
Lord God of Israél which made the heauen and the earth, and that hathe giuen vn
to Dauid the King a [e] wise sonne, that hathe discretion, prudence and vnderstanding to buylde an house for the Lord, and
a palace for his kingdome.
13 Now therefore I haue sent a wise man,
& of vnderstãding of my father Hurams,
14 *The sonne of a woman of the [f] daughters of Dan: and his father was a man of
Tyrus, & he can skill to worke in golde,
in siluer, in brasse, in yron, in stone, and in
timbre, in purple, in blewe silke, and in fine
linen and in crimosin, and can graue in all
grauen workes, and broder in all broydred worke that shalbe giuẽ him, with thy
cunning men, and with the cunning men
of my lord Dauid thy father.
15 Now therefore the wheat and the barly,
the oyle & the wine, which my lord hathe
spoken of, let him send vnto his seruants.
16 And we wil cut wood in Lebanón as
muche as thou shalt nede, and wil bring it
to thee in *raftes by the sea to *Iaphó, so
thou maiest cary them to Ierusalém.
17 ¶ And Salomón nõbred all the strangers that were in the land of Israél, after
the nombring that his father Dauid had
nombred them: and they were founde an
hundreth and thre and fiftie thousand, and
six hundreth.
18 And he set seuentie thousand of them to
the burden, and fourescore thousand to
hewe *stones* in the mountaine, & thre thousand and six hundreth ouerseers to cause
the people to worke.

CHAP. III.

The Temple of the Lord, and the porche are buylded, with other things thereto belonging.

1 SO *Salomón began to buyld the house
of the Lord in Ierusalém, in mount
[a] Moriáh which had bene declared vnto
Dauid his father, in the place that Dauid
prepared in the thresshing floore of *Ornán the Iebusite.
2 And he began to buyld in the seconde
moneth & the seconde day, in the fourt
yere of his reigne.
3 And these are the *measures, whereon* Salomón groũded to buyld the house of God:
the length of cubites after the first [b] measure *was* threscore cubites, & the breadth
twenty cubites:
4 And the porche, ÿ was before the length
in the fronte [c] of the breadth *was* twentie
cubites, and the height *was* an [d] hundreth
and twẽtie, & he ouerlaied it within with
pure golde.
5 And the greater house he syled with firre
tree which he ouerlaied with good golde,
& graued thereon palmetrees & chaines.
6 And he ouerlaied ÿ house with precious
stone for beautie: and the golde *was* golde of [e] Paruáim.
7 The house, I say, the beames, postes, and
walles thereof and the doores thereof o-
uerlaied he with golde, and graued Cherubims vpon the walles.
8 ¶ He made also ÿ house of the moste holy
place: the length thereof *was* in the fronte
of the breadth of the house, twentie cubites, and the breadth thereof twentie cubites: and he ouerlaied it with the best
golde, of six hundreth talents.
9 And the weight of the nailes *was* fiftie
shekels of golde, and he ouerlaied the chãbers with golde.
10 ¶ And in the house of the moste holy
place he made two Cherubims wroght
like children, and ouerlaied them with
golde.
11 * And the wings of the Cherubims *were*
twentie cubites long: the one wing *was* fiue cubites, reaching to the wall of the
house, and the other wing fiue cubites,
reaching to ÿ wing of the other Cherúb.

b That is, to do that seruice which he hathe commãded, signifying that none is able to honour & serue God in that perfectiõ as his maiestie deserueth.
*Or, skarlet.
c Some take it for brasil, or the wood called Ebenum, others for corall.
*Or, Almuggim
*Ebr. corim.
d Of Bath read 1. King. 7,26. it is called also Ephá. but Ephá is to measure drye things, as bath is a measure for licours.
e The very heathen confessed that it was a singular gift of God, when he gaue to any nation a King that was wise & of vnderstãding. albeit it appeareth that this Hirám had ÿ true knowledge of God.
f It is also writen, that she was of the tribe of Naphtali, 1. Kig, 7 14. which may be vnderstand that by reason of the cõfusion of tribes, ẇ then began to be, thei maried in diuers tribes, so that by her father she might be of Dan, and by her mother of Naphtali.
*Or, shippes.
*Or, Ioppe.
1. King. 7,23.
a Which is ÿ moũtain where Abrahám thoght to haue sacrificed his sonne, Gen. 22,2.
2. Sam. 24,16.
b According to the whole length of the Temple, comprehending ÿ most holy place ẇ the rest.
c It conteined as muche as did ÿ breadth of ÿ Temple, 1 King 6,3.
d Frõ the fundacion to the top: for in the boke of Kings mentiõ is made, from the fundatiõ to ÿ first stage.
e Some thinke it is ÿ place which is called Perú.
1. King. 6,19.

12 Likewise the wing of the other Cherúb
was fiue cubites, reaching to the wall of
the house, and the other wing fiue cubites
ioyning to the wing of the other Cherúb.
13 The wings of these Cherubims were
spred abroad twentie cubites: they stode
on their fete and their faces *were* toward
the house.
14 ¶He made also [f] the vaile of blewe silke
and purple, and crimosin, and fine linen,
& wroght Cherubims thereon.
15 ¶And he made before the house two pil
lers [g] of fiue and thirtie cubites hie: and
the chapiter that was vpon the top of *eche*
of them, *was* fiue cubites.
16 He made also chaines for the oracle, and
put them on the heades of the pillers, and
made an [h] hundreth pomegranates, and
put them among the chaines.
17 And he set vp the pillers before the Tẽple, one on the right hand & the other on
the left, and called that on the right hand
Iachín, and that on the left hand Bóaz.

f Which separated the Temple from the moste holy place.

g Euerie one was eightẽ cubites long, but the halfe cubite colde not be sene: for it was hid in the roundenes of the chapiter, & therefore he giueth to euerie one but 17, and an halfe.

h For euerie piller an hundreth, read. 1.King. 7,20.

CHAP. IIII.

1 The altar of brasse. 2 The molten Sea. 6 The caldrons. 7 The candlestickes, &c.

1 AND [*] he made an altar of brasse twẽtie cubites long, and twentie cubites
broade, and ten cubites hie.
2 And he made a molten [a] Sea of ten cubites from brim to brim, rounde in cõpasse,
and fiue cubites hie: and a line of thirtie
cubites did compasse it about.
3 And vnder [b] it was the facion of oxen
which did compasse it round about, [c] ten
in a cubite compassing the Sea about: two
rowes of oxen were cast when it was molten.
4 It stode vpon twelue oxen: thre loked
toward the North, and thre loked toward
the West, & thre loked toward the South,
and thre loked toward the East, and the
Sea *stode* about vpon them, and all their
hinder partes were inwarde.
5 And the thickenes thereof *was* an hand
breadth, and the brim thereof *was* like the
worke of the brim of a cup, with floures
of [*] lilies: it conteined [d] thre thousand
baths.
6 ¶He made also ten caldrons, and put fiue on the right hand, and fiue on the left,
to wash in them & to clense in them that
which apperteined to the burnt offrings:
but the Sea *was* for ẏ Priestes to wash in.
7 ¶And he made ten candlestickes of golde (according to [e] their forme) and put
them in the Tẽple, fiue on the right hãd,
and fiue on the left.
8 ¶And he made ten tables, & put them in
the Temple, fiue on the right hand, & fiue
on the left: and he made an hundreth basens of golde.

Leu.6,9.

a A great vessel of brasse, so called because of the great quantitie of water, ẇ it conteined, 1. King 7,23.

b Meaning, vnder the brim of the vessel, as.1, Kĩg, 7,24.

c In the length of euery cubite were tẽ heades or knoppes which in all are 300.

Or, floure delyces.

d In ẏ first boke of Kings, chap. 7, 26 mẽcion is onely made of two thousand: but the lesse nõber was takẽ there, & here according as the measures proued afterward is declared.

e Euen as thei shulde be made.

9 And he made the court of the Priestes, &
the great [f] court and dores for the court,
and ouerlayed the dores thereof with
brasse.
10 And he set ẏ Sea on the right side Eastward toward the South.
11 And Hurám made [*] pottes and besomes
and basens, and Hurám finished the worke that he shulde make for Kĩg Salomón
for the house of God,
12 *To wit,* two pillers, & the bowles & ẏ chapiters on the toppe of the two pillers, and
two grates to couer the two bowles of the
chapiters which were vpon the toppe of
the pillers:
13 And foure hundreth pomegranates for
the two grates, two rowes of pomegranates for euerie grate to couer the two bowles of the chapiters, that were vpon the
pillers.
14 He made also bases, and made caldrons
vpon the bases:
15 *And* a Sea, and twelue bulles vnder it:
16 Pottes also and besomes, and fleshokes,
and all these vessels made Hurám [g] his father, to King Salomón for the house of
the Lord of shining brasse.
17 In the plaine of Iordén did the King
cast them in claye betwene Succóth and
Zeredáthah.
18 And Salomón made all these vessels in
great abundance: for the weight of brasse
colde not be rekened.
19 And Salomón made all the vessels that
were for the house of God: the golden altar also & the tables, whereon the [h] shewbread stode.
20 Moreouer the candlestickes, with their
lampes to burne them after the maner, before the oracle, of pure golde.
21 And the floures and the lampes, and the
snoffers of golde, which was fine golde.
22 And the [*] hookes, and the basens, and the
spones, and the ashpans of pure golde:
the entrie also of ẏ house & dores thereof
within, *euen* of the moste holy place: and
the dores of the house, *to wit,* of the Temple *were* [i] of golde.

f Called also the porche of Salomón. Act. 3,11. It is also taken for the Temple where Christ preached, Mat.21, 23.

Or, caldrons.

g Whome Salomón reuerenced for ẏ giftes that God had giuẽ hĩ, as a father: he had ẏ same name also that Hurám the Kĩg of Tyrus had, his mother was a Iewesh & his father a Tyriã. Some read, for his father, the autor of this worke.

h In Ebrewe, the bread of ẏ faces, because they were set before ẏ Arke, where ẏ Lord shewed his presence.

Or, instrumẽts of Musike.

i That is, couered ẇ plates of golde.

CHAP. V.

1 The things dedicated by David, are put in the Temple. 2 The Arke is broght into the Temple. 10 What was within it. 12 They sing praise to the Lord.

1 SO [*] was all the worke finished that Salomón made for the house of ẏ Lord,
and Salomón broght in the things that
Dauid his father had dedicated, with the
siluer and the golde, and all the vessels, &
put them among the treasures of the house of God.
2 Then Salomón assembled the Elders of
Israél, and all the heades of the tribes, the
chief fathers of the children of Israél vnto Ierusalém to bring vp the Arke of the

1.King.7,51. & 8,1.

coue-

a Read 2 Sam. 6,12.

couenant of the Lord from the [a] citie of
Dauid, which is Zión.
3 And all the mē of Israél assembled vnto
the King at the [b] feast: it was in the seuent [c] moneth.
4 And all the Elders of Israél came, & the
Leuites toke vp the Arke.
5 And thei caryed vp the Arke and the Tabernacle of the Congregacion: and all the
holy vessels that were in the Tabernacle,
those did the Priests & Leuites bring vp.
6 And King Salomón and all the Congregacion of Israél that were assembled vnto
him, *were* before the Arke, offring shepe &
bullockes, which colde not be tolde nor
nombred for multitude.
7 So the Priests broght the Arke of the
couenant of the Lord vnto his place, into
the Oracle of the house, into the moste
Holy place, *euen* vnder the wings of the
Cherubims.
8 For the Cherubims stretched out *their*
wings ouer the place of the Arke, and the
Cherubims couered the Arke and the barres thereof aboue.
9 And they drewe out the barres, that the
ends of the barres might be sene out of
the Arke before the Oracle, but they were
not sene″without: and there they are vnto
this day.
10 Nothing *was* in the Arke, saue [d] the two
Tables, which Mosés gaue at Horéb,
where the Lord made a couenant with the
children of Israél, when they came out of
Egypt.
11 And when the Priests were come out of
the Sāctuarie (for all the Priests that were
present, were [e] sanctified *and* did not waite
by course.
12 And the Leuites the singers of all sortes,
as of Asáph, of Hemán, of Ieduthún & of
their sonnes and of their brethren, being
cladde in fine linen, stode with cymbales,
& with violes and harpes at the East end
of the altar, and with them an hundreth &
twentie Priests blowing with trumpets:
13 And thei were [f] as one, blowing trumpets,
and singing, and made one sounde to be
heard in praising and thanking the Lord,
and when they lift vp *their* voyce with
trumpets and with cymbales, and with instruments of musike, and when they praised the Lord, *singing*, [g] For he is good, because his mercie *lasteth* for euer) then the
house, *euen* the house of the Lord was filled with a cloude,
14 So that the Priests colde not stand to
ministre, because of the cloude: for the
glorie of the Lord had filled the house of
God.

b When the things were dedicate and broght into the Temple.

c Called in Ebrew Ethanī, cōteining part of September and parte of October, 1.King. 8,2. wͨ moneth the Iewes called ȳ first moneth, because, they say, that the worlde was created in ȳ moneth, & after they came frō Egypt thei began at Marche: but because this opiniō is vncerteine, we make Marche euer the first, as best writers do.

″Or, without the Oracle.

d For Aarons rod and Māna were taken thence before it was broght to this place.

e Were prepared to serue the Lord.

f They agreed all in one tune

g This was ȳ effect of their songs.

CHAP. VI.

3 Salomón blesseth the people. 4 He praiseth the Lord. 14 He praieth vnto God for those that shal pray in the Temple.

1 THé*Salomón [a] said, The Lord hathe
said that he wolde dwel in the darke
cloude:
2 And I haue buylt thee an house to dwel
in, an habitacion for thee to dwel in for
euer.
3 And the King turned his face, & blessed
all the Congregacion of Israél (for all the
Congregacion of Israél stode *there*)
4 And he said, Blessed *be* the Lord God of
Israél, who spake with his mouthe vnto
Dauid my father, & hathe with his″hand
fulfilled it, saying,
5 Since the day that I broght my people
out of the land of Egypt, I chose no citie
of all the tribes of Israél to buylde an
″house, that my Name might be there, nether chose I anie man to be a ruler ouer
my people Israél:
6 But I haue chosen Ierusalém, that my
Name might be there, and haue chosen
Dauid to be ouer my people Israél.
7 *And it was in the heart of Dauid my father to buylde an house vnto the Name of
the Lord God of Israél,
8 But the Lord said to Dauid my father,
Where as it was in thine heart to buylde
an house vnto my Name, thou didest wel,
that″thou wast so minded.
9 Notwithstanding thou shalt not buylde
the house, but thy sonne which shal come
out of thy loynes, he shal buylde an house
vnto my Name.
10 And the Lord hathe performed his
worde that he spake: and I am risen vp in
the roume of Dauid my father, and am set
on the throne of Israél as the Lord promised, and haue buylt an house to the Name of the Lord God of Israél.
11 And I haue set the Arke there, wherein is
the [b] couenant of the Lord, that he made
with the children of Israél.
12 ¶ And ȳ King [c] stode before the altar of
the Lord, in the presence of all the Congregacion of Israél, and stretched out his
hands,
13 (For Salomón had made a brasen skaffolde & set it in the middes of the courte
of fiue cubites long, & fiue cubites broade,
and thre cubites of height, and vpon it he
stode, and kneled downe vpon his knees
before all the Congregacion of Israél, &
[d] stretched out his hands towarde heauen)
14 And said, O Lord God of Israél,* there
is no God like thee in heauen nor in earth,
which kepest couenant, and mercie vnto
thy seruants, that walke before thee with
all their heart.
15 Thou that hast kept with thy seruant
Dauid my father, that thou hast promised
him: for thou spakest with thy mouthe, &
hast fulfilled it with thine″hād, as *appeareth*
this day.

1.King.8,12.

a After ȳ he had sene the glorie of the Lord in the cloude.

″*Or, power.*

″*Or, Temple.*

2.Sam.7,5.

″*Ebr. that it was in thine heart.*

b Meaning, ȳ two Tables, wherein is cōteined the effect of the couenant, that God made wͭ our fathers.

c On a skaffolde that was made for that purpose, that he praying for the whole people might be heard of all.

d Bothe to giue thākes for the great benefites of God bestowed vpō him, and also to pray for ȳ perseuerance & prosperitie of his people.

2.Mac.2,8.

″*Or, in effect, or by thy power.*

16 Therefore now Lord God of Israél, kepe with thy seruant Dauid my father, that
thou hast promised him, saying, Thou
"shalt not wāt a man in my sight, that shal
sit vpon the throne of Israél: so that thy
sonnes take hede to their waies, to walke
in my Lawe, as ẏ hast walked before me.
17 And now, ô Lord God of Israél, let thy
worde be verified, which thou spakest vnto thy seruant Dauid.
18 (Is it true in dede that God wil dwel
with man on earth? beholde, the * heauens,
and the heauens of heauens are not able
to conteine thee: how muche more *vnable*
is this house, which I haue buylt?)
19 But haue thou respect to the prayer of
thy seruant, & to his supplicacion, ô Lord
my God, to heare the crye & prayer which
thy seruant prayeth before thee,
20 That thine [e] eyes may be open toward
this house day and night, *euen* toward the
place, whereof thou hast said, That thou
woldest put thy Name there, that thou
maiest hearken vnto the prayer, which thy
seruant prayeth in this place.
21 Heare thou therefore the supplicacion
of thy seruant, and of thy people Israél,
which they praye in this place: and heare
thou in the place of thine habitacion, *euen*
in heauen, and when thou hearest, be merciful.
22 ¶ * When a man shal sinne against his
[f] neighbour, and he lay vpon him an othe
to cause him to sweare, and the " swearer
shal come before thine altar in this house,
23 Then heare thou in heauen, and do, and
iudge thy seruants, in recompensing the
wicked to bring his way [g] vpon his head,
and in iustifying the righteous, to giue
him according to his righteousnes.
24 ¶ And when thy people Israél shalbe o-
uerthrowen before the enemie, because
they haue sinned against thee, and turne
againe, and "confesse thy Name, and pray,
and make supplicacion before thee in this
house,
25 Then heare thou in heauen, and be merciful vnto the sinne of thy people Israél,
and bring thē againe vnto the land which
thou gauest to them and to their fathers.
26 When heauen shalbe shut vp, and there
shalbe no raine, because they haue sinned
against thee, and shal pray in this place, &
confesse thy Name, and " turne from their
sinne, when thou doest afflict them,
27 Then heare thou in heauen, and pardone
the sinne of thy seruants, and of thy people Israél (whē thou hast taught them the
good way wherein thei may walke) & giue
raine vpon thy land, which thou hast giuē
vnto thy people for an inheritance.
28 ¶ * When there shalbe famine in the lād,
when there shalbe pestilence, blasting, or
mildewe, when there shalbe greshopper, or
caterpiller, when their enemie shal besiege them" in the cities of their land, *or* any
plague or any sicknes,
29 *Then* what prayers *and* supplicacion
soeuer shal be made of any man, or of all
thy people Israél, when euerie one shal
knowe his owne plague, and his owne disease, and shal stretche forthe his hands
toward this house,
30 Heare thou then in heauen, thy dwelling
place, and be merciful, and giue euerie mā
according vnto all his wayes, as thou doest knowe his [h] heart (for ẏ onely knowest
the hearts of the children of men)
31 That they may feare thee, and walke in
thy wayes as long as they liue in the land
which thou gauest vnto our fathers.
32 ¶ Moreouer as touching the stranger
which is not of thy people Israél, who shal
come out of a farre coūtrey for thy great
Names sake, & thy mightie hand, and thy
stretched out arme: when they shal come
and [i] pray in this house,
33 Heare thou in heauē thy dwelling place,
and do according to all that the stranger
calleth for vnto thee, that all the people of
the earth may knowe thy Name, and feare
thee like thy people Israél, and that they
may knowe, that thy Name is called vpon
in this house which I haue buylt.
34 ¶ When thy people shal go out to battel
against their enemies, by the way that
[k] thou shalt send them, and they praye to
thee, "in the way toward this citie, which
thou hast chosen, euen toward the house
which I haue buylt to thy Name,
35 Then heare thou in heauen their prayer
and their supplicacion, and iudge their
cause.
36 If thei sinne against thee (* for there is
no man that sinneth not) and thou be angrie with them and deliuer them vnto the
enemies, and thei take them & cary them
away captiue vnto a land farre or nere,
37 If they "turne againe to their heart in
the land whether they be caryed in captiues, and turne & pray vnto thee in the lād
of their captiuitie, sayīg, We haue sinned,
we haue transgressed and haue done wickedly,
38 If they turne againe to thee with all
their heart, and with all their soule in the
land of their captiuitie, whether they haue
caryed them captiues, & pray toward their
lād, which thou gauest vnto their fathers,
and *toward* the citie which thou hast chosen, and toward the house which I haue
buylt for thy Name,
39 Then heare ẏ in heauen, in the place of
thine habitacion their prayer & their supplicacion, & "iudge their cause, & be merciful vnto thy people, which haue sinned
against thee.

"*Ebr. a man shal not be cut of.*

1.*King.8,27.*

e That thou maiest declare in effect, that thou hast a continual care ouer this place.

1.*King.8,31.*

f By reteining any thing frō him, or els by denyīg that ẘ he hathe left him to kepe, or do him any wrong.

"*Ebr. othe.*

g Meaning, to giue him that which he hath deserued.

"*Or, praise.*

"*Or, toward this place.*

Chap.20,8.

"*Ebr. in the land of their gates.*

h He declareth that the prayers of hypocrites can not be heard, nor of any but of thē, which pray vnto God with an vnfained faith and in true repentance.

i He sheweth ẏ before God there is no acceptiō of persone, but all people ẏ feareth him and worketh righteousnes, is accepted, Act. 10,35.

k Meanīg that none oght to enterprise any warre, but at ẏ Lords cōmandemēt, that is, ẘ is lawful by his worde.

"*Or, according to the maner of this citie.*

1.*King.8,46.*
eccles.7,21.
1.*Iohn.1,8.*

"*Or, repent.*

"*Or, mainteine their right.*

40 Now my God, I beseche thee, let thine
eyes be open, and thine eares attent vnto
the prayer *that is made* in this place.
41 *Now therefore arise, ô Lord God, *to come*
into thy [l] rest, thou, and the Arke of thy
strength: ô Lord God, let thy Priests be
clothed with [m] saluacion, and let thy
Sainctes reioyce in goodnes.
42 O Lord God, refuse not the face of
[n] thine anointed: remember the mercies
promised to Dauid thy seruant.

*Psal.132,8.

l That is, into thy Temple.

m Let them be preserued by thy power and made vertuous and holy.

n Heare my prayer, which am thine anointed King.

CHAP. VII.

1 The fyre consumeth the sacrifice. 2 The glorie of the Lord filleth the Temple. 12 He heareth his prayer, 17 And promiseth to exalt him and his throne.

1 AND* whẽ Salomón had made an end
of praying, [a] fyre came downe from
heauen, and consumed the burnt offring &
the sacrifices: and the glorie of the Lord
filled the house,
2 So that the Priests colde not enter into
the house of the Lord, because the glorie
of the Lord had filled the Lords house.
3 And when all the children of Israél saw
the fyre, and the glorie of the Lord come
downe vpon the house, they bowed them
selues with *their* faces to the earth vpon
the pauement, and worshiped and praised
the Lord, *saying*, For he is good, because
his mercie *lasteth* for euer.
4 *Then the King and all the people offred
sacrifices before the Lord.
5 And King Salomón offred a sacrifice of
two and twentie thousand bullockes, and
an hundreth and twentie thousand shepe.
so the King and all the people dedicated
the house of God.
6 And the Priests waited on their offices, &
the Leuites with the instruments of musike
of the Lord, which King Dauid had
made to praise ẏ Lord, Because his mercy
lasteth for euer: when Dauid praised *God*
"by them, the Priests also blewe trumpets
ouer against them: and all they of Israél
stode by.
7 Moreouer Salomón halowed the middle
of the court that was before the house of
the Lord: for there he had prepared burnt
offrings, and the fat of the peace offrings,
because the brasen altar which Salomón
had made, was not able to receiue ẏ burnt
offring, and the meat offring, and the fat.
8 And Salomón made [b] a feast at that time
of seuen dayes, & all Israél with him,
a very great Congregacion, from the entring
in of Hamáth, vnto the riuer of
Egypt.
9 And in the eight day they [c] made a solẽne
assemblie: for they had made the dedicacion
of the altar seuen dayes, and the
feast seuen dayes.
10 And the [d] thre and twentieth day of the
seuent moneth, he sent the people away
into their tents, ioyous & with glad heart,
because of the goodnes that the Lord had
done for Dauid and for Salomón, and for
Israél his people.
11 *So Salomón finished the house of the
Lord, and the Kings house, and all that came
into Salomons heart to make in the
house of the Lord: and he prospered in his
house.
12 ¶ And the Lord * appeared to Salomón
by night and said to him, I haue heard thy
prayer, and haue chosen this place for my
selfe to be an house of sacrifice.
13 If I shut the heauen that there be no raine,
or if I commande the grashopper to
deuore the land, or if I send pestilence among
my people,
14 If my people, among whome my Name
is called vpon, do humble them selues, &
praye, and seke my presence, and turne frõ
their wicked wayes, then wil I heare in
heauen, and be merciful to their sinne, and
wil [e] heale their land.
15 Then mine eyes shalbe open and mine
eares attent vnto the prayer *made* in this
place.
16 For I haue now chosen and sanctified
this house, that my Name may be there
for euer: and mine eyes and mine heart
shalbe there perpetually.
17 And if thou wilt walke before me, as Dauid
thy father walked, to do according
vnto all that I haue commanded thee, and
shalt obserue my statuts & my iudgemẽts,
18 Then wil I stablish the throne of thy
kingdome, according as I made the couenãt
with Dauid thy father, saying, *Thou
shalt not want a man to be ruler in Israél.
19 But if ye turne away, and forsake my statutes
and my commandemẽts which I haue
set before you, and shal go and serue
other gods, and worship them,
20 Then wil I plucke them vp out of my
land, which I haue giuen them, and this
house which I haue [f] sanctified for my
Name, wil I cast out of my sight, and wil
make it to be a prouerbe and a commune
talke among all people.
21 And this house which is moste hie, shalbe
an astonishment to euerie one ẏ passeth by
it, so that he shal say, Why hathe the Lord
done thus to this land, and to this house?
22 And they shal answer, Because they forsoke
the Lord God of their fathers, which
broght them out of the land of Egypt,
and haue taken holde on other gods, and
haue worshiped them, and serued them,
therefore hathe he broght all this euil vpon
them.

*2.Mac 2,10.

a Hereby God declared that he was pleased with Salomons prayer.

*1.King.8,65.

" Ebr. by their hande.

b The feast of the Tabernacles which was kept in the seuent moneth.

c They assembled to heare the worde of God after that they had remained seuen dayes in the bouthes or Tabernacles.

d They had leaue to departe ẏ two & twẽtieth day, 1.King. 8, 66, but they went not away til the next day.

*1.King.9,1.

*Nom.12,6.

e I wil cause ẏ pestilence to cease & destroy the beasts that hurt the frutes of the earth, and send raine in due season.

*Chap.6,16.

f Which thig declareth that God had more respect to their saluatiõ, then to the aduancement of his owne glorie: & where as men abuse those things, which God hathe appointed to set forthe his praise, he doeth withdrawe his graces thence.

CHAP. VIII.

2 The cities that Salomón buylt. 7 People that were made tributarie vnto him. 12 His sacrifices. 17 He sendeth to Ophir.

1.King.9,10.
a Signifying ỷ he was twetie yere in buylding them.

1 AND* after [a] twentie yere when Salomón had buylt the house of the
Lord, and his owne house,
2 Then Salomón buylt the cities that Hurám [b] gaue to Salomón, and caused the
children of Israél to dwel there.

b That is, ỷ Hirám gaue againe to Salomón because they pleased him not: and therefore called them Cabúl, ỷ is, dirt or filth, 1 King 9,13.

3 And Salomón went to Hamáth Zobáh,
and ouercame it.
4 And he buylt Tadmór in the wildernes,
& repaired all [c] the cities of store which
he buylt in Hamáth.

c Meaning, of municions and treasures for the warre.

5 And he buylt [d] Beth-horón the vpper, &
Beth-horón ỷ nether, cities defensed with
walles, gates and barres:

d That is, he repaired and fortified them for they were buylt long before by Seeráh a noble womã of the tribe of Ephráim, 1. Chro.6,24.

6 Also Baaláth, and all the cities of store
that Salomón had, and all the charet cities, and the cities of the horsemen, and
euerie pleasant place that Salomón had a
minde to buylde in Ierusalém, & in [e] Lebanón, and throughout all the land of his
dominion,

e Read 1. King.7,2.

7 *And* all the people that were left of the
Hittites, and the Amorites, and Perizites,
and the Hiuuites, and the Iebusites, which
were not of Israél,
8 *But* of their children which were left after
them in the land, whome the children of
Israél had not consumed, euen thẽ did Salomón make "tributaries vntil this day.

"Ebr. to come vp to tribute.

9 But of the childrẽ of Israél did Salomón
make no seruants for his worke: for they
were mẽ of warre, and his chief princes, &
the captaines of his charets & of his horsemen.
10 So these were the chief of the officers
which Salomón had, *euen* [f] two hundreth
and fiftie that bare rule ouer the people.

f For in all there were 3300, but here he meaneth of them that had the principal charge, read. 1 King.9,23.

11 ¶ Thẽ Salomón broght vp the daughter
of Pharaóh out of the citie of Dauid, into
the house that he had buylt for her: for he
said, My wife shal not dwel in the house of
Dauid King of Israél: for it is holy, because that the Arke of the Lord came vnto it.
12 ¶ Then Salomón offred burnt offrings
vnto the Lord, on the * altar of the Lord,
which he had buylt before the porche,

Chap.4,1.

13 To * offer according to the commandement of Mosés "euerie day, in the Sabbaths, and in the newe moones, and in the
solemne feastes, [g] thre times in the yere,
that is, in the feast of ỷ vnleauened bread,
and in the feast of the wekes, and in the
feast of the Tabernacles.

Exod.29,39.
"Or, after the maner of euerie day.
g Read Leuit. 23.

14 And he set the courses of the Priests to
their offices, according to ỷ ordre of Dauid his father, & the Leuites in their watches, for to praise and minister before the
Priests euerie day, & the porters by * their
courses, at euerie gate: for so *was* the commandement of Dauid the man of God.

1.Chro.24,1.

15 And they declined not from the commandement of the King, concerning the
Priests & the Leuites, touching all things,
and touching the treasures.
16 ¶ Now Salomón had made prouisiõ for
all the [h] worke, from the day of the fundacion of the house of the Lord, vntil it
was finished: *so* the house of the Lord was
perfite.

h Bothe for the matter & also ỷ workemaship.

17 Then went Salomón to Ezion-géber, &
to Elóth by ỷ [i] seaside in ỷ land of Edóm.

i Meaning, the red sea.

18 And Hurám sent him by the hands of his
seruants, shippes, and seruants that had
knowledge of the sea: and they went with
ỷ seruãts of Salomón to Ophír, & broght
thence [k] four hundreth and fiftie talents
of golde, and broght them to King Salomón.

k Which summe is thoght to mount to thre millions & six hundreth thousand crownes: for here is menciõ made of thirtie mo, then are spoken of 1. King 9,28.

CHAP. IX.

1.9 The Quene of Shebá cometh to se Salomón & bringeth giftes. 13 His yerely reuenues. 30 The time of his reigne 31 His death.

1.King.10,1. mat.12,14. luk.11,31.
a To knowe whether his wisdome were so great as the reporte was.

1 AND* when the Quene of Shebá heard
of the fame of Salomón, she came to
[a] proue Salomón with harde questions at
Ierusalém, with a verie great traine, and
camels that bare swete odours and muche
golde, and precious stones: and when she
came to Salomón, she cõmuned with him
of all that was in her heart.
2 And Salomón declared her all her questions, and there was [b] nothing hid from
Salomón, which he declared not vnto her.

b There was no question so hard that he did not solue.

3 Then the Quene of Shebá sawe the wisdome of Salomón, and the house that he
had buylt,
4 And the meat of his table, and the sitting
of his seruants, and the ordre of his way-
ters, and their apparel, and his butlers,
and their apparel, and his "burnt offrings,
which he offred in the house of the Lord,
and she was "greatly astonied.

"Or, galleries whereby he went vp.
"Ebr. there was no more spirit in her.

5 And she said to the King, *It was* a true
worde which I heard in mine owne land
of thy "sayings, and of thy wisdome:

"Or, actes.

6 Howbeit I beleued not their reporte, vntil I came, and mine eyes had sene it: and
beholde, the one halfe of thy great wisdome was not tolde me: *for* thou excedest
the fame that I heard.
7 Happie are thy men, and happie are these thy seruants, which stande before thee
all way, and heare thy wisdome.
8 Blessed be ỷ Lord thy God, which loued
thee, to set thee on his [c] throne as King,
in the stead of the Lord thy God: because
thy God loueth Israél, to establish it for
euer, therefore hathe he made thee King
ouer them, to execute iudgemẽt & iustice.

c Meaning, that the Israelites were Gods peculiar people, & that Kings are the lieutenants of God, which oght to grante vnto him the superioritie, and minister iustice to all.

9 Then she gaue the King six score talents
of golde, and of swete odours exceding
muche and precious stones: nether was
there suche swete odours *since,* as the Quene of Shebá gaue vnto King Salomón.
10 And the seruants also of Hurám, and the
seruants of Salomón which broght golde
from

d Read Chap. 2,8.

from Ophír,broght [d] Algumím wood &
precious stones.
11 And the King made of the Algumím
wood [e] staires in the house of the Lord,&
in the Kings house,and harpes and violes
for singers: and there was no suche sene
before in the land of Iudáh.
12 And King Salomón gaue to the Quene
of Shebá euerie pleasant thing that she
asked, [f] besides for that which she had
broght vnto the King: so she returned and
went to her owne countrey, *bothe* she, and
her seruants.
13 ¶ Also the weight of golde that came to
Salomón in one yere, was six hũdreth thre
score and six talents of golde,
14 Besides that which chapmen and marchants broght: and all the Kings of Arabia,& the princes of the countrey broght
golde and siluer to Salomón.
15 And King Salomón made two hundreth
targats of beaten golde,& [g] six hundreth
shekels of beaten golde went to one targat,
16 And thre hundreth shields of beaten
golde, thre hũdreth [h] *shekels* of golde went
to one shield, and the King put them in
the house of the wood of Lebanón.
17 And the King made a great throne of
yuorie and ouerlaied it with pure golde.
18 And the throne had six steppes, with a
footestole of golde [i] fastened to the throne, and stayes on ether side on the place of
the seate, and two lions standing by the
[k] stayes.
19 And twelue lions stode there on the six
steppes on ether side: there was not the like made in anie kingdome.
20 And all King Salomõs drinking vessels
were of golde, and all the vessels of the
house of the wood of Lebanón *were* of
pure golde: *for* siluer was nothing estemed
in the dayes of Salomón.
21 For the Kings shippes went to Tarshísh
with the seruants of Hurám, euerie thre
yere once came the shippes of [l] Tarshísh,
and broght golde, and siluer, yuorie, and
apes, and pecockes.
22 So King Salomón excelled all ỹ Kings
of the earth in riches and wisdome.
23 And all the Kings of the earth soght the
presence of Salomón, to heare his wisdome that God had put in his heart.
24 And they broght euerie man his present,
vessels of siluer, and vessels of golde, and
raiment, armour, & swete odours, horses,
and mules, from yere to yere.
25 And Salomón had [m] foure thousand
stalles of horses, and charets, and twelue
thousand horsemen, whome he bestowed
in the charet cities, and with the King at
Ierusalém.
26 And he reigned ouer all the Kings from
the [″] Riuer euen vnto the land of the Philistims, and to the border of Egypt.
27 And the King gaue siluer in Ierusalém,
[n] as stones, & gaue cedre trees as the wilde fig trees, that are abundant in the
plaine.
28 And they broght vnto Salomón horses
out of Egypt, and out of all lands.
29 Cõcerning the rest of the actes of Salomón first & last, are they not writen in the
boke of Nathán the Prophet, and in the
prophecie of Ahiiáh the Shilonite, and in
the visions of [″] Ieedó the Seer [o] against
Ieroboám the sonne of Nebát?
30 And Salomón reigned in Ierusalém ouer
all Israél fourty yeres.
31 And Salomón * slept with his fathers, &
they buryed him in the citie of Dauid his
father: and Rehoboám his sonne reigned
in his steade.

e Or, pillers: meaning, the garnishing & trimming of ỹ stayres or pillers.

f That is, ẘ the King gaue her for recompense of that treasure which she broght.

g Which summe mounteth to 2400 crownes of the sunne, Budeus de asse.

h Or, pounds, called mine, whereof euerie one semed to make an hundreth shekels.

i That is, the steppes & the fotestole were fastened to the throne.

k Vpon the pommels or knoppes.

l Which coũtrey of ỹ best writers is thoght to be Cilicia, read 1. King. 10,22.

m That is, ten horses in euerie stable, which in all mount to fourtie thousand, as 1. King. 4,26

″ Or, Euphrates.

n The abũdãce of these tẽporal treasures in Salomõs kingdome is a figure of the spiritual treasures, which ỹ elect shal enioye in ỹ heauens vnder the true Salomón Christ.

″ Or, Iddó.

o That is, ẘ prophecied against him.

1. King. 11,41

CHAP. X.

4.14 The rigour of Rehoboám. 13 He followeth lewde counsel. 16 The people rebelle.

1 THen * Rehoboám [a] wẽt to Shechém:
for to Shechém came all Israél to make him King.
2 And when Ieroboám the sonne of Nebát
heard it, (which was in Egypt, whether he
had fled frõ the presence of Salomón the
King) he returned out of Egypt.
3 And they sent and called him: so came Ieroboám and all Israél, and cõmuned with
Rehoboám, saying,
4 Thy father [b] made our yoke grieuous:
now therefore make ỹ the grieuous seruitude of thy father, and his sore yoke,
that he put vpon vs, lighter, and we wil
serue thee.
5 And he said to thẽ, *Departe* yet thre dayes,
thẽ come againe vnto me. And the people
departed.
6 And King Rehoboám toke counsel with
the olde men that had stand before Salomón his father, while he yet liued, saying,
What counsel giue ye that I may answer
this people?
7 And they spake vnto him, saying, If thou
be kinde to this people, and please them,
and speake louing wordes to them, they
wil be thy seruants for euer.
8 But he left the coũsel of the ancient men
that they had giuen him, and toke counsel
of the yong mẽ that were broght vp with
him, and [c] waited on him.
9 And he said vnto them, What counsel giue ye, that we may answer this people, ẘ
haue spoken to me, saying, Make the yoke
which thy father did put vpon vs, lighter?
10 And the yong men that were broght vp
with him, spake vnto him, saying, Thus
shalt thou answer the people that spake
to thee, saying, Thy father made our yoke
heauy, but make thou it lighter for vs.

1. King. 12,1.

a After the death of Salomón.

b That is, hãdeled vs rudely. It semeth that God hardened their heartes, so that they thus murmured without cause: which declareth also the incõstãcie of the people.

c Or, that stode by him, that is, which were of his counsel and secretes.

d Or, litle finger: meaning ÿ he was of farre greater powe r thē was his father.

thus shalt thou say vnto them, My [d] least
parte shal be bigger then my fathers
loynes.
11 Now where as my father did burdē you
ŵ a grieuous yoke, I wil yet increase your
yoke: my father hathe chastised you with
roddes, but I *wil correct you* with "scourges.
12 ¶ Then Ieroboám and all the people came to Rehoboám the third day, as the
King had appointed, saying, Come againe to me the third day.
13 And the King answered them sharpely:
and King Rehoboám left the counsel of
the ancient men,
14 And spake to them after the counsel of
the yong men, saying, My father made
your yoke grieuous, but I wil increase it:
my father chastised you with roddes, but
I *wil correct you* with scourges.
15 So the King hearkened not vnto the
people: for it was the [e] ordinance of God
that the Lord might performe his saying,
which he had spoken " by Ahiiáh the Shilonite to Ieroboám the sonne of Nebát.
16 So when all Israél sawe that the King
wolde not heare them, the people answered the King, saying, *What portion haue
we in Dauid? for we haue none inheritance in the sonne of Ishái. O Israél, euerie man to your tents: now se to thine ōwe
ne house, Dauid. So all Israél departed to
their tents.
17 Howbeit Rehoboám reigned ouer the
children of Israél, that dwelt in the cities
of Iudáh.
18 Then King Rehoboám sent Hadorám
that was "ouer the tribute, & the children
of Israél stoned him with stones, that he
dyed: then King Rehoboám "made spede
to get him vp to his charet, to flee to Ierusalém.
19 And Israél rebelled against the house of
Dauid vnto this day.

"Or, scorpions.

e Gods wil imposeth suche a necessitie to ÿ second causes, that nothing cā be done but according to the same, and yet mans wil worketh as of it selfe, so that it can not be excused in doing euil, by alledging that it is Gods ordinance.

"Ebr. by the hād

1. Kin. 12, 16.

"Or, receyuer.

"Ebr. strēgthened him selfe.

CHAP. XI.

4 Rehoboám is forbidden to fight against Ieroboám. 5 Cities which he buylt 21 He hath eightene wiues, & threscore concubines, and by them eight and twentie sonnes, and threscore daughters.

1 AND *whē Rehoboám was come to Ie
rusalém, he gathered of the house of
Iudáh and [a] Beniamín nine score thousand chosen men of warre to fight against
[b] Israél, & to bring the kingdome againe
to Rehoboám.
2 But the worde of the Lord came to Shemaiáh the man of God, saying,
3 Speake vnto Rehoboám, the sonne of Salomón King of Iudáh, and to all Israél
that are in Iudáh, and Beniamín, saying,
4 Thus sayth the Lord, Ye shal not go vp,
nor fight against your brethren: returne
euerie man to his house: for this thing is
done of me. They obeied therefore the

1. Kin. 12, 20.

a That is, the halfe tribe of Beniamin: for the other halfe was gone after Ieroboám.

b Meaning the ten tribes ŵ rebelled.

worde of the Lord, and returned from
going against Ieroboám.
5 And Rehoboám dwelt in Ierusalém, and
[c] buylt strong cities in Iudáh.
6 He buylt also Beth-léhem, and Etám, and
Tekóa,
7 And Beth-zúr, and Shocó, & Adullám,
8 And Gath, and Mareshá, and Ziph,
9 And Adoráim, and Lachísh, and Azekáh,
10 And Zoráh, & Aialón & Hebrón, which
were in Iudáh & Beniamín, strōg cities.
11 And he" repaired the strong holdes and
put captaines in them, and store of vitaile, and oyle and wine.
12 And in all cities he put shields & speares, & made them exceding strong: so Iudáh and Beniamín were his.
13 ¶ And the Priests and the Leuites that
were in all Israél, "resorted vnto him out
of all their coastes.
14 For the Leuites left their suburbes and
their possession, and came to Iudáh and
to Ierusalém: *for Ieroboám and his sonnes had cast them out from ministring in
the Priests office vnto the Lord.
15 *And he ordeined him Priests for the
hie places, and for the [d] deuils and for the
calues which he had made.
16 And after ÿ Leuites there came to Ierusalém of all ÿ tribes of Israél, suche as set
their [e] hearts to seke ÿ Lord God of Israél,
to offer vnto ÿ Lord God of their fathers.
17 So they strengthened the kingdome of
Iudáh, and made Rehoboám the sonne of
Salomón mightie, thre yere long: for thre
yere they [f] walked in the way of Dauid &
Salomón.
18 ¶ And Rehoboám toke him Mahaláth
the daughter of Ierimóth the sonne of
Dauid to wife, & Abiháil the daughter of
Eliáb the sonne of Ishái,
19 Which bare him sonnes Ieúsh, and Shemariáh, and Záham.
20 And after her he toke Maakáh ÿ daughter of Absalóm which bare him Abiiáh,
and Atthái, and Zizá, and Shelomíth.
21 And Rehoboám loued Maakáh ÿ daughter of Absalóm aboue all his wiues & his
concubines: for he toke eightene wiues, &
thre score concubines, and begate eight
and twētie sonnes, & threscore daughters.
22 And Rehoboám made [g] Abiiáh the sōne
of Maakáh the chief ruler among his brethren: for he thoght to make him King.
23 And he taught him: and dispersed all
his sonnes throughout all the countreis of
Iudáh and Beniamín vnto euerie strong
citie: and he gaue them abundance of vitaile, and [h] desired many wiues.

c Or, repaired them & made them strong, to be more able to resist Ieroboám.

"Or, strēgthened

"Ebr. stode.

Chap. 13, 9.

1. Kin. 12, 31.

d Meaning, idoles, read Isa. 34, 15.

e Which were zealous of true religion, & feared God.

f So long as they feared God, and set forth his worde, they prospered.

g Called also Abiiam, who reigned thre yere, 1. Ki. 15, 2.

h He gaue him selfe to haue many wiues.

CHAP. XII.

1 Rehoboám forsaketh the Lord and is punished by Shishák. 5 Shemaiáh reproueth him. 6 He hūbleth him selfe.

se.7 God sendeth him succour. 9 Shishák taketh his treasures.13 His reigne and death.16 Abiiáh his sonne succedeth him.

1 AND when "Rehoboám had established the kingdome & made it strōg,
he forsoke the Lawe of the Lord,and [a] all
Israél with him.
2 Therefore in the fift yere of King Rehoboám,Shishák the King of Egypt came
vp against Ierusalém(because they had
transgressed against the Lord)
3 With twelue hundreth charets, and thre
score thousand horsmē,& the people were
without nomber,that came with him from
Egypt,*euen* the Lubims,[b] Sukkiims,& the
"Ethiopians.
4 And he toke the strōg cities which were
of Iudáh,and came vnto Ierusalém.
5 ¶ Then came Shemaiáh the Prophet to
Rehoboám, and to the princes of Iudáh,
that were gathered together in Ierusalém,
because of Shishák, and said vnto them,
Thus sayth the Lord , Ye haue forsaken
me,[c] therefore haue I also left you in the
hands of Shishák.
6 Then the princes of Israél, and the Kīg
humbled them selues,and said, The Lord
is [d] iuste.
7 And when the Lord sawe that they humbled them selues , the worde of the Lord
came to Shemaiáh,saying, They haue hūbled them selues , *therefore* I wil not destroye them, but I wil send them deliuerāce shortely,& my wrath shal not "be powred out vpon Ierusalém by the hand of
Shishák.
8 Neuertheles they shalbe his seruants : so
shal thei know my [e] seruice, & the seruice
of the kingdomes of the earth.
9 ¶ Then Shishák King of Egypt came
vp against Ierusalém,and toke the treasures of the house of the Lord,and the treasures of the Kings house:he toke *euen* all,
and he caryed away the shields of golde,
*which Salomón had made.
10 In stead whereof King Rehoboám made shields of brasse,and committed them
to the hāds of the chief of the garde, that
waited at the dore of the Kings house.
11 And when the King entred into the house of the Lord , the garde came and bare
them and broght them againe vnto the
garde chamber.
12 And because he [f] humbled him selfe,the
wrath of the Lord turned from him, that
he wolde not destroye all together . And
also in Iudáh the things prospered.
13 *So King Rehoboám was strong in Ieru
salém and reigned: for Rehoboám was one
& fourtie yere olde, whē he begā to reigne,
& reigned [g] seuentene yeres in Ierusalém,
the citie which the Lord had chosen out
of all the tribes of Israél to put his Name

"Or, when the Lord had established Rehoboáms kīgdome.

a For suche is the inconstancie of the people that for ẏ moste part thei follow the vices of their gouernours.

b Which were a people of Africa called ẏ Troglodites, because they dwelled in holes.

"Or, blacke Mores.

c Signifying ẏ no calamitie can come vnto vs except we forsake God, & ẏ he neuer leaueth vs til we haue cast him of.

d And therefore doeth iustely punish you for your sinnes.

"Ebr. drop downe.

e He sheweth that Gods punishments are not to destroy his vtterly,but to chastise thē, to bring them to ẏ knowledge of them selues & to knowe how much better it is to serue God thē tyrants.

Chap.9,16.

f Which declareth that God seketh not the death of a sinner, but his cōuersiō, Ezek. 18,32.& 33,11.

1.Kin.14,21.

g That is, twelue yeres after that he had bene ouercome by Shishák, ver.2.

there . And his mothers name was Naamáh an Ammonitesse.
14 And he did euil:for he prepared not his
heart to seke the Lord.
15 The actes also of Rehoboám , first and
last,are they not writen in the "boke of
Shemaiáh the Prophet,and Iddó ẏ Seer,
in rehearsing the genealogie ? & there *was*
warre alway betwene Rehoboám & Ieroboám.
16 And Rehoboám slept with his fathers,
and was buryed in the citie of Dauid, and
Abiiáh his "sonne reigned in his stead.

"Ebr. sayings.

"Or, Abiam.

CHAP. XIII.

1 Abiiáh maketh warre against Ieroboám. 4 He sheweth the occasion.12 He trusteth in the Lord and ouercometh Ieroboám.21 Of his wiues and children.

1 IN the eightente yere of King Ieroboám began Abiiáh to reigne ouer [a] Iudáh.
2 He reigned thre yere in Ierusalém:(his
mothers name also was [b] Michaiáh the
daughter of [c] Vriél of Gibeá) and there
was warre betwene Abiiáh and Ieroboám.
3 And Abiiáh set the battel in aray with
the armie of valiant men of warre, *euen*
foure hundreth thousand chosen men. Ieroboám also set the battel in aray against
him with eight hundreth thousand chosen men which were strong *and* valiant.
4 And Abiiáh stode vp vpon mount [d] Ze-
meráim,which is in mount Ephráim, and
said,O Ieroboám,& all Israél , heare you
me,
5 Oght you not to knowe that the Lord
God of Israél hathe giuen the kingdome ouer Israél to [e] Dauid for euer, *euen* to
him and to his sonnes by a couenant [f] of
salt?
6 And Ieroboám the sonne of Nebát the
seruant of Salomón the sonne of Dauid
is risen vp,and hathe *rebelled against his
lord.
7 And there are gathered to him [g] vaine
men *&* "wicked, and made them selues
strong against Rehoboám the sonne of
Salomón : for Rehoboám was [h] *but* a
childe and " * tender hearted, & colde not
resist them.
8 Now therefore ye thinke that ye be able
to resist against the kingdome of the
Lord , *which is* in the hands of the sonnes
of Dauid,and ye be a great multitude , &
the golden calues *are* with you which Ieroboám made you for gods.
9 * Haue ye not driuen away the Priests of
the Lord the sonnes of Aarón and the Le
uites , and haue made you Priests like the
people of *other* countreis? whosoeuer commeth to " consecrate with a [i] yong bullocke and seuen rams , the same may be a
Priest of them that are no gods.

a He meaneth Iudáh and Beniamin.

b Or, Maachá, 1. King.15,2.

c Called also Abshalóm, or, Abshalóm was her grandefather. 1 Ki.15,2.

d Which was one of the toppes of mount Ephráim.

e And therefore whosoeuer doeth vsurpe it or take it frō ẏ stocke, trāsgresseth the ordinance of ẏ Lord.thus like an hypocrite he alledged ẏ worde of God for his aduantage.

f That is, perpetual, because that thing, which is salted, is preserued from corruptiō: he meaneth also that it was made solemnely & cōfirmed by offring of sacrifices, where as thei vsed salt according as was ordeined, Nom.18,19.

1.Kin.11, 26.

g This worde in ẏ Chalde tongue is Racha, which our Sauiour vseth, Matt.5,22.

"*Ebr. childrē of Belial.*

h Meaning, in heart and courage.

"*Or, fainte hearted.*

Leui.26,36.

1.King 12,31. chap.11,14.

"*Ebr fil his hād*

i He sheweth the nature of idolaters ẇ take no trial of the vocation, life & doctrine of their ministers, but thinke the moste vilest & greatest beastes sufficient, to serue their turne.

10 But we belong vnto the Lord our God,
& haue not forsaken him,& the Priests the
sonnes of Aarón minister vnto the Lord,
and the Leuites in *their* office.
11 And they burne vnto the Lord euerie
[k] morning and euerie euening burnt offrings and swete incense, and the bread is
set in order vpon the pure table,& thecá-
dlesticke of golde with the lápes thereof,
to burne euerie euening: for we kepe the
watche of the Lord our God: but ye haue
forsaken him,

k As it was appointed in the Lawe, Exod. 29,39.

12 And beholde, this God [l] *is* with vs, as a
captaine, & his Priests with the sounding
trumpets, to crye an alarme against you.
O ye children of Israél, fight not against
the Lord God of your fathers: for ye
shal not prosper.

l Because their cause was good & approued by the Lord, thei douted not of the successe and victorie.

13 ¶ But Ieroboám caused an ambushment
[m] to compasse, & come behinde them,
when thei were before Iudáh, and the ambushment behinde them,

m Contemnīg ẏ good coūsel ẇ came of the Spirit of God, he thoght to haue ouercome by deceite.

14 Then Iudáh loked, and beholde, the bat
tel *was* before and behinde them, and they
cryed vnto the Lord, and the Priests blewe
with the trumpets,
15 And the men of Iudáh gaue a shoute: &
euen as the men of Iudáh shouted, God
"smote Ieroboám and also Israél before
Abiiáh and Iudáh.

"Or, gaue him the ouerthrowe.

16 And the children of Israél fled before
Iudáh, and God deliuered them into their
hand.
17 And Abiiáh and his people slewe a great
slaughter of them, so that there fel downe wounded of Israél fiue hundreth thousand chosen men.
18 So the children of Israél were broght
vnder at that time: and the childrē of Iudáh preuailed, [n] because they staied vpon
the Lord God of their fathers.
19 And Abiiáh pursued after Ieroboám, &
toke cities from him, *euen* Bethél, and the
"villages thereof, and Ieshanáh with her
villages, and Ephrón with her villages.

n He sheweth that the stay of all kingdomes & assurance of victories depende vpon our trust & cōfidence in the Lord.

"Ebr. daughters.

20 And Ieroboám recouered no strength
againe in the dayes of Abiiáh, but ẏ Lord
plaged him, and he dyed.
21 So Abiiáh waxed mightie, and maried
fourtene wiues, and begate two and twentie sonnes, and sixtene daughters.
22 The rest of the actes of Abiiáh and his
maners and his sayings are writen in the
storie of the Prophet Iddó.

CHAP. XIIII.

3 Asá destroieth idolatrie & commandeth his people to serue the true God. 11 He praieth vnto God when he shulde go to fight. 12 He obteineth the victorie.

1.King.15,8.

1 SO* Abiiáh slept with his fathers, & thei
buryed him in the citie of Dauid, & Asá
his sonne reigned in his steade: in whose
dayes the land was quiet ten yere.
2 And Asá did that was good and right in
the
the eyes of the Lord his God.
3 For he toke away the altars of the strange
gods & the hie places, & brake downe the
images, and cut downe the [a] groues,
4 And cōmanded Iudáh to seke the Lord
God of their fathers, & to do *according* to
the Lawe and the commandement.

a Which were planted contrary to the Lawe, Deut. 16,20.

5 And he toke away out of all the cities of
Iudáh the hie places, & the images: therefore the kingdome was [b] quiet before
him.
6 He buylt also strong cities in Iudáh, because the land was in rest, and he had no
warre in those yeres: for the Lord had giuen him rest.

b He sheweth that the rest & quietnes of kigdomes stādeth in abolishig idolatrie, and aduancing true religion.

7 Therefore he said to Iudáh, Let vs buyld
these cities and make walles about, and
towres, gates, and barres, whiles the lád is
[c] before vs: because we haue soght ẏ Lord
our God, we haue soght him, and he hathe
giuen vs rest on euerie side: so they buylt
and prospered.

c Whiles we haue the ful gouernement thereof.

8 And Asá had an armie of Iudáh that bare shields and speares, thre hundreth thousand, and of Beniamín that bare shields &
drewe bowes, two hundreth & foure score
thousand: all these were valiant men.
9 ¶ And there came out against then Zérah
[d] of Ethiopia with an hoste of ten hūdreth
thousand, and thre hundreth charets, and
came vnto [e] Mareshāh.

d The King of Ethiopia or Egypt.

e Which was a citie in Iudáh, Iosh.15, 44: where Michaiáh ẏ Prophet was borne.

10 Then Asá went out before him, and thei
set the battel in aray in the valley of Ze-
pháthah beside Mareshāh.
11 And Asá* cryed vnto the Lord his God,
& said, Lord, it is nothīg with thee to helpe "with many, *or* with no power: helpe vs,
ô Lord our God: for we rest on thee, and
in thy Name are we come against this mul
titude: ô Lord, thou art our God, [f] let not
man preuaile against thee.

1.King.14,8.

"Or, against many, without power.

f Thus ẏ childrē of God nether trust in their owne power or policie, nether feare the strength & subtiltie of their enemies, but consider ẏ cause and se whether their entreprises tēd to Gods glorie, & thereupō assure thē selues of ẏ victorie by him, ẇ is onely almightie, & can turne all flesh into dust ẇ the breath of his mouthe.

12 ¶ So ẏ Lord smote the Ethiopians before Asá and before Iudáh, and the Ethiopians fled.
13 And Asá and the people that was with
him, pursued them vnto Gerár. And the E-
thiopians hoste was ouerthrowen, *so that*
there was no life in them: for they were
destroyed before the Lord and before his
hoste: & they caryed away a mighty great
spoile.
14 And they smote all the cities round a-
bout Gerár: for the [g] feare of the Lord
came vpon them, and they spoiled all the
cities, for there was exceding muche spoile in them.

g The Lord had strike thē with feare.

15 Yea, and they smote the tents of cattel, &
caryed away plentie of shepe and camels,
and returned to Ierusalém.

CHAP. XV.

1 The exhortatiō of Azariáh. 8 Asá purgeth his coūtrey of idolatrie. 11 He sacrificeth with the people. 14 Thei sweare together to serue the Lord. 16. He deposeth his

mo-

ther for her idolatrie.

1 THen the Spirit of God came vpon
[a] Azariáh the ſonne of Odéd.
2 And he went out to mete Aſá, and ſaid
vnto him, O Aſá, and all Iudáh, and Beniamín, heare ye me. The Lord *is* with you,
while ye be with him: and if ye ſeke him,
he wil be founde of you, but if ye forſake
him, he wil forſake you.
3 Now for a long ſeaſon Iſraél *hathe bene*
without the [b] true God, & without Prieſt
to teache and without Lawe.
4 But *whoſoeuer* returned in his affliction to
the Lord God of Iſraél, and ſoght him,
he [c] was founde of them.
5 And in that time there *was* no peace to
him, that did go out and go in: but great
troubles *were* to all the inhabitants of the
earth.
6 For nacion was deſtroyed of nacion, and
citie of citie: for God troubled them with
all aduerſitie.
7 Be ye ſtrong therefore, and let not your
hādes be weake: for your [d] worke ſhal haue
a rewarde.
8 ¶ And when Aſá heard theſe wordes, and
the prophecie of Odéd the Prophet, he
was encouraged, and toke away the abominacions out of all the land of Iudáh, &
Beniamín, and out of the cities which he
had taken of mount Ephráim, and he renued the altar of the Lord, that was before the porche of the Lord.
9 And he gathered all Iudáh & Beniamín,
& the ſtrangers with thē out of Ephráim,
and Manaſſéh & out of Simeón: for there
fell many to him out of Iſraél, when they
ſawe that the Lord his God *was* with him.
10 So they aſſembled to Ieruſalém in the
[e] third moneth, in the fiftente yere of the
reigne of Aſá.
11 And they offred vnto the Lord the ſame
time of the [f] ſpoyle, *which* thei had broght,
euen ſeuen hundreth bullockes, and ſeuen
thouſand ſhepe.
12 And they made a couenant to ſeke the
Lord God of their fathers, with all their
heart, and with all their ſoule.
13 And [g] whoſoeuer wil not ſeke the Lord
God of Iſraél, ſhal be ſlaine, whether he
were ſmall or great, man or woman.
14 And they ſware vnto the Lord with a
loude voyce, and with ſhouting and with
trumpets, and with cornets.
15 And all Iudáh reioyced at the othe: for
they had ſworne vnto the Lord with all
their heart, and ſoght him with a whole
deſire, and he was [h] founde of them. And
the Lord gaue them reſt rounde about.
16 ¶ And King Aſá depoſed Maacháh *his*
[i] mother from her regēcie, becauſe ſhe had
made an idole in a groue: and Aſá brake
downe her idole, & ſtamped it, and burnt

a Who was called Odéd, as his father was, verſ. 8.

b For the ſpace of twelue yeres vnder Rehoboám, and thre yeres vnder Abiiáh, religiō was neglected and idolatrie planted.

c He ſheweth, that notwithſtanding the wickednes of tyrāts & their rage, yet God hath his, whome he heareth in their tribulacion, as he deliuered his from Zeráh King of the Ethiopians, & out of all other dangers, when thei called vpon the Lord

d Your confidence & truſt in God ſhal not be fruſtrat

e Called Shiuán, conteinīg parte of May and parte of Iune

f Which they had taken of the Ethiopiās.

g Theſe were the wordes of their couenāt, which cōmanded all idolaters to be put to death according to the Lawe of God, Deut 13.

h So long as thei ſerued hī aright, ſo long did he preſerue & proſper them.

i Or grādmother: & herein he ſhewed ỹ he lacked zeale: for ſhe oght to haue dyed bothe by the couenant, and by the Lawe of God: but he gaue place to fooliſh pitie, & wolde alſo ſeme after a ſorte to ſatiſfie the Lawe.

it at the broke Kidrón.
17 But the hie places were not [k] taken away
out of [l] Iſraél: yet the heart of Aſá was
[m] perfite all his dayes.
18 Alſo he broght into the houſe of God
the things that his father had dedicate, &
that he had dedicate, ſiluer, and golde, &
veſſels.
19 And there was no warre vnto the fiue &
thirtieth yere of the reigne of Aſá.

CHAP. XVI.

2 *Aſá for feare of Baaſhá King of Iſraél, maketh a couenant with Benhadád King of Arám. 7 He is reproued by the Prophet, 10 Whome he putteth in priſon. 12 He putteth his truſt in the Phiſitians. 13 His death.*

1 IN the ſix & thirtieth yere of the reigne of Aſá came [a] Baaſhá King of Iſraél vp againſt Iudáh, and buylt [b] Ramáh
to let none paſſe out or go in to Aſá King
of Iudáh.
2 Then Aſá broght out ſiluer and golde
out of the treaſures of the houſe of the
Lord, and of the Kings houſe, and ſent to
Benhadád King of Arám that dwelt at
*Damaſcus, ſaying,
3 There *is* a couenant betwene me & thee,
and betwene my father and thy father: beholde, I haue ſent thee ſiluer and golde:
come, [c] breake thy league with Baaſhá
King of Iſraél that he may departe from
me.
4 And Benhadád hearkened vnto King
Aſá, and ſent the captaines of the armies
which he had, againſt the cities of Iſraél.
And they ſmote Iión, and Dan, and Abel-
máim, and the ſtore cities of Naphtalí.
5 And when Baaſhá heard it, he left buylding of Ramáh, and let his worke ceaſe.
6 Then Aſá the King toke all Iudáh, and
caryed away the ſtones of Ramáh and the
tymbre thereof, wherewith Baaſhá did
buyld, and he buylt therewith Géba and
Mizpáh.
7 ¶ And at that ſame time Hanáni the *Seer
came to Aſá King of Iudáh, and ſaid vnto him, Becauſe thou haſt reſted vpon the
King of Arám, and not reſted in the Lord
thy God, therefore is the hoſte of the Kīg
of Arám eſcaped out of thine hand.
8 *The Ethiopians and the Lubims, were
they not a great hoſte with charets and
horſemen, exceding many? yet becauſe
thou dideſt reſt vpon the Lord, he deliuered them into thine hand.
9 *For the eies of the Lord beholde all the
earth to ſhewe him ſelfe ſtrong with them
that are of perfite heart toward him: thou
haſt thē done fooliſhly in this: therefore
from henſforthe thou ſhalt haue warres.
10 Thē Aſá was wroth with the Seer, & put
him into a "priſon: for he was [d] diſpleaſed with him, becauſe of this thing. And
Aſá oppreſſed *certeine* of the people at the

k Which partely came through lacke of zeale in hī, partly through the negligence of his officers, & partely by the ſuperſtitiō of the people, that all were not taken away.

l Becauſe that God was called the God of Iſraél by reaſon of his promes to Iaakób: therefore Iſraél is ſome time taken for Iudáh, becauſe Iudáh was his chief people.

m In reſpect of his predeceſſors.

a Who reigned after Nadáb the ſonne of Ieroboám.

b He fortified it with walles and ditches: it was a citie in Beniamín nere to Gibeón.

*Or, Darmeſek.

c He thoght to repulſe his aduerſarie by an vnlawful meanes, ỹ is, by ſeking helpe of infideles, as they ỹ ſeke ỹ Turkes amitie, thinkīg thereby to make thē ſelues more ſtrong.

*Or, Prophet.

Chap. 14, 9.

2. Mac. 9, 5. & 12, 22.

"Ebr. priſon houſe.

d Thus in ſtead of turning to God by repentance, he diſdained the admonicion of ỹ Prophet, and puniſhed him, as the wicked do when they be tolde of their fautes.

same time.
11 And beholde, the actes of Asá first and
last, lo, they are writen in the boke of the
Kings of Iudáh and Israél.
12 ¶And Asá in the nine and thirtieth yere
of his reigne was″ diseased in his fete, *and*
his disease was″ e extreme: yet he soght not
the Lord in his disease, but to the f Phisicians.
13 So Asá slept with his fathers, and dyed in
the one and fourtieth yere of his reigne.
14 And they buryed him in *one* of his sepulchres,
which he had made for him selfe
in the citie of Dauid, & laied him in the
bed, which they had filled with swete odours
and diuerse kindes *of spices*, made by
the arte of the apoticarie: and they burnt
him with an exceding great fyre.

″Or, goutie, or swollen.
″Or, to the top of his head.
e God plagued his rebellion, & hereby declareth that it is nothing to begine wel, except we so cōtinue to the ēd, that is, zealous of Gods glorie, and put our whole trust in him.
f He sheweth that it is in vaine to seke to ẏ Phisitiās, except first we seke to God to purge our sinnes, which are the chief cause of all our diseases, & after vse the helpe of ẏ phisitiā, as a meane by whome God worketh.

CHAP. XVII.

1 Iehoshaphát trusting in the Lord, prospereth in riches and honour. 6 He abolisheth idolatrie. 7 And causeth the people to be taught. 11 He receiueth tribute of strangers. 13 His munitions and men of warre.

1 AND Iehoshaphát his sonne reigned
in his stead, and preuailed against
Israél.
2 And he put garisons in all the strong cities
of Iudáh, and set bands in the land of
Iudáh and in the cities of Ephráim, which
Asá his father had taken.
3 And the Lord was with Iehoshaphát, because
he walked in the a first wayes of his
father Dauid, and soght not b Baalím,
4 But soght the Lord God of his father,
and walked in his commandements, and
not after the ″ trade of Israél.
5 Therefore the Lord stablished the kingdome
in his hand, and all Iudáh broght
presents to Iehoshaphát, so that he had of
riches and honour in abundance.
6 And he c lift vp his heart vnto the wayes
of the Lord, and he toke awaie moreouer
the hie places & the groues out of Iudáh.
7 ¶And in the third yere of his reigne he
sent his princes, Ben-háil, and Obadiáh, &
Zechariáh, and Nethaneél, and Michaiáh,
that they shulde d teache in the cities of
Iudáh,
8 And with them Leuites, Shemaiáh, and
Nethaniáh, and Zebadiáh, and Asahél, &
Shemiramóth, and Iehonathán, and Adoniiáh,
and Tobiiáh, and Tob-adoniiáh,
Leuites, and with them Elishamá and Iehorám
Priests.
9 And they taught in Iudáh, and had the
boke of the Lawe of the Lord with them,
& went about throughout all the cities of
Iudáh, and taught the people.
10 And the feare of the Lord fell vpon all
the kingdomes of the lands ẏ were rounde
about Iudáh, and they e foght not against
Iehoshaphát.
11 Also *some* of the Philistims broght Iehoshaphát
gifts and tribute siluer, and the
Arabiás broght him flockes, seuē thousād,
and seuen hundreth rams, and seuen thousand,
and seuen hundreth he gotes.
12 So Iehoshaphát prospered and grewe vp
on hie: and he buylt in Iudáh palaces and
cities of store.
13 And he had great workes in the cities of
Iudáh, and men of warre, & valiant men
in Ierusalém.
14 And these are the nombers of them after
the house of their fathers, In Iudáh
were captaines of thousands, Adnáh the
captaine, and ″ with him of valiant men
thre hundreth thousand.
15 And ″ at his hand Iehohanán a captaine,
and with him two hundreth & foure score
thousand.
16 And at his hand Amasiáh the sonne of
Zichrí, which f willingly offred him selfe
vnto the Lord, and with him two hūdreth
thousand valiant men.
17 And of Beniamin, Eliadá a valiant mā,
and with him armed men with bowe and
shield two hundreth thousand.
18 And at his hand Iehozabád, & with him
an hundreth and foure score thousand armed
to the warre.
19 These g waited on the King, besides
those which the King put in the strong
cities throughout all Iudáh.

a That is, his vertues: meaning, before he had cōmitted ẇ Bath-shéba and against Vriáh.
b Soght not helpe at strāge gods
″Ebr. worke.
c He gaue him selfe wholy to serue ẏ Lord.
d He knewe it was in vaine to professe religion, except suche were apointed which colde instruct the people in the same, and had autoritie to put away all idolatrie.
e Thus God prospereth all suche that ẇ a pure heart seke his glorie, and kepeth their enemies in feare ẏ thei cā not be able to execute their rage against them.
″Ebr. in his hand.
″Or, next to him.
f Meaning, he was a Nazarian.
g That is, they were as his ordinarie garde.

CHAP. XVIII.

1 Iehoshaphát maketh affinitie with Aháb. 10 Foure hūdreth Prophetes cōusel Aháb to go to warre. 16 Michaiáh is against them 23 Zidkiah smiteth him. 25 The King putteth him in prison. 29 The effect of his prophecie.

1 AND * Iehoshaphát had riches & honour
in abundance, but he was ioyned
in a affinitie with Aháb.
2 And after certeine b yeres he went downe
to Aháb to Samaria: & Aháb slewe shepe
and oxen for him in great nomber, & for
the people that he had with him, and entised
him to go vp vnto c Ramóth Gileád.
3 And Aháb King of Israél said vnto Iehoshaphát
Kīg of Iudáh, Wilt thou go with
me to Ramóth Gileád? And he answered
him, I am as thou art, & my people as thy
people, & we wil ioyne ẇ thee in the warre.
4 And Iehoshaphát said vnto the King of
Israél, Aske counsel, I pray thee, at the
d worde of the Lord this day.
5 Therefore the King of Israél gathered
of e Prophetes foure hundreth men, and
said vnto them, Shal we go to Ramóth
Gileád to battel, or shal I cease? And they
said, Go vp: for God shal deliuer it into
the Kings hand.
6 But Iehoshaphát said, Is there here neuer
a Prophet more of the Lord ẏ we might
inquire of him?
7 And ẏ King of Israél said vnto Iehoshaphát,

*1.King.22,3.
a For Iorám Iehoshaphats sonne maried Ahabs daughter.
b That is, the third yere, 1.King.22,2.
c To recouer it out of the hands of the Syrians.
d Heare the aduise of some Prophet, to knowe whether it be Gods wil.
e Which were the Prophetes of Báal, signifying that the wicked esteme not but flatterers and suche as wil beare with their inordinate affections.

phát, There is yet one man, by whome we
may aske counsel of the Lord, but I [f] hate
him: for he doeth not prophecie good
vnto me, but allway euil: it is Michaiáh
the sonne of Imlá. Thē Iehoshaphát said,
Let not the King say [g] so.
8 And the King of Israél called an eunuche, and said, Call quickly Michaiáh the
sonne of Imlá.
9 ¶ And the King of Israél, and Iehoshaphát
phát King of Iudáh sate ether of them on
his throne clothed in *their* [h] apparel: they
sate euen in the threshing floore at the entring in of the gate of Samaria: & all the
Prophetes prophecied before them.
10 And Zidkiáh the sonne of Chenaanáh
made him [i] hornes of yron, & said, Thus
saith ẏ Lord, With these shalt thou push ẏ
Aramites vntil thou hast consumed them.
11 And all the Prophetes prophecied so,
saying, Go vp to Ramóth Gileád, & prosper: for the Lord shal deliuer it into the
hand of the King.
12 ¶ And the messenger that wēt to call Michaiáh, spake to him, saying, Beholde, the
wordes of the Prophetes *declare* good to
ẏ King with one [k] accorde: let thy worde
therfore, I pray thee, be lyke one of theirs,
and speake thou good.
13 And Michaiáh said, As the Lord liueth,
whatsoeuer my God saith, ẏ wil I speake.
14 ¶ So he came to the King, and the King
said vnto him, Michaiáh, shal we go to Ra
móth Gileád to battel, or shal I leaue of?
And he said, [l] Go ye vp, and prosper, and
they shal be deliuered into your hand.
15 And the King said to him, How oft shal I
charge thee, that thou tel me nothing but
the trueth in the Name of the Lord?
16 Then he said, I sawe all Israél scatered
in the mountaines, as shepe that haue no
shepheard: and the Lord said, [m] These
haue no master: let thē returne euerie man
to his house in peace.
17 And the King of Israél said to Iehoshaphát, Did I not tel thee, that he wolde not
prophecie good vnto me, but euil?
18 Againe he said, Therefore heare ye the
worde of the Lord: I sawe the Lord sit
vpon his throne, and all the [n] hoste of
heauen standing at his right hand, and at
his left.
19 And the Lord said, Who shal" persuade
Aháb King of Israél, that he may go vp
and fall at Ramóth Gileád? And one spake and said thus, and another said that.
20 Thē there came forthe a spirit and stode before the Lord, and said, I wil persuade him. And the Lord said vnto him,
Wherein?
21 And he said, I wil go out, and be a false
spirit in the mouthe of all his Prophetes.
And [o] he said, Thou shalt persuade, and

f Yet the true ministers of God oght not to cease to do their duetie, thogh the wicked magistrates can not abide them to speake the trueth.

g Meaning, ẏ he oght not to refuse to heare anie that was of God.

h That is, in their maiestie and royal apparel.

i Read 1. King. 22,11.

k Thinking, ẏ where as foure hundreth Prophetes had agreed in one thing, that he being but one man, and in least estimatiō durst not gaine say it.

l He spake this by derisiō of the false Prophetes, as the King wel perceiued.

m He prophecieth how the people shulde be dispersed & Aháb sleane.

n Meaning, his Angels.

" Or, deceiue.

o That is, the Lord.

shalt also preuaile: go forthe and do so.
22 Now therefore beholde, the Lord hathe
put a [p] false spirit in the mouthe of these
thy Prophetes, & the Lord hathe determined euil against thee.
23 Then Zidkiáh the sonne of Chenaanáh
came nere, and smote Michaiáh vpon the
[q] cheke, and said, By what way wēt the spirit of ẏ Lord frō me, to speake with thee?
24 And Michaiáh said, Beholde, thou shalt
se that day whē thou shalt go from chamber to chamber to hide thee.
25 And the King of Israél said, Take ye
Michaiáh, and carie him to Amón the gouernour of the citie, & to Ioásh the Kings
sonne,
26 And say, Thus saith the King, Put this
man in the prison house, & fede him with
bread of [r] affliction and with water of affliction vntil I returne in peace.
27 And Michaiáh said, If thou returne in
peace, the Lord hathe not spoken by me.
And " he said, Heare, all ye people.
28 So the King of Israél and Iehoshaphát
the King of Iudáh wēt vp to Ramóth Gileád.
29 And the King of Israél said vnto Iehoshaphát, I wil [s] change my selfe, and entre into the battel: but put thou on thine
apparel. So the King of Israél chāged him
selfe, and they went into the battel.
30 And the King of Arám had commanded
the captaines of the charets that were with
him, saying, Fight you not with small nor
great, but against ẏ King of Israél onely.
31 And when the captaines of the charets
sawe Iehoshaphát, they said, It is the King
of Israél: and they compassed about him
to fight. But Iehoshaphát [t] cryed, & ẏ Lord
helped him & moued them *to departe* from
him.
32 For when the captaines of the charets
sawe that he was not the King of Israél,
they turned backe from him.
33 Then *a certeine* man drewe a bowe" my-
ghtely, & smote the King of Israél betwene the ioyntes" of his brigādine: therefore he said to his charetman, Turne thine
hand, and carie me out of the hoste: for I
am hurt.
34 And the battel increased that day: and
the King of Israél [u] stode stil in his charet against the Aramites vntil euen, and
dyed at the time of ẏ sunne going downe.

CHAP. XIX.

4 After Iehoshaphát was rebuked by the Prophet, he called againe the people to the honoring of the Lord. 5 He appointeth iudges and ministers, 9 And exhorteth them to feare God.

1 AND Iehoshaphát the King of Iudáh returned" safe to his house in Ierusalém.
2 And Iehú ẏ sonne of Hanáni the Seer wēt

p So they that wil not beleue ẏ trueth, God sendeth strong delusion, that they shulde beleue lyes, 2. Thess. 2,10.

q By this crueltie his ambicion and hypocrisie was discouered: the hypocrites boast of ẏ Spirit which they haue not, and declare their malice against thē, in whome the true Spirit is.

r Kepe him streictly in prison, and let him fele hungre and thirst.

" Or, Michaiáh.

s Thus ẏ wicked thinke by their owne subtiltie to escape Gods iudgements, ẇ he threateneth by his worde.

t He cryed to the Lord by acknowledging his faute in going with this wicked King to warre against the worde of the Lord by his Prophet, and also by desiring mercie for the same.

" Ebr. in his simplicitie, or ignorantly.

" Or, betwene the habergine.

u He dissembled his hurt, that his souldiers might fight more corragiously.

" Ebr. in peace.

out to mete him, and ſaid to King Iehoſ-
ſhaphát, [a] Woldeſt thou helpe the wicked, and loue them that hate the Lord?
therefore for this thing yͤ wrath " of the
Lord is vpon thee.
3 Neuertheles good things are founde in
thee, becauſe thou haſt takẽ away the groues out of the land, and haſt prepared thine heart to ſeke God.
4 ¶ So Iehoſhaphát dwelt at Ieruſalém, &
returned and went [b] through the people
from Beer-ſhebá to mount Ephráim, and
broght them againe vnto the Lord God
of their fathers.
5 And he ſet iudges in the land throughout
all the ſtrong cities of Iudáh, citie by
citie,
6 And ſaid to the iudges, Take hede what
ye do: for ye execute not the iudgements
of man, but of the Lord, & *he wilbe* [c] with
you in the cauſe *and* iudgement.
7 Wherefore now let the feare of yͤ Lord
be vpon you: take hede, & do it: for there
is no [d] iniquitie with the Lord our God,
nether * reſpect of perſones, nor receiuing
of rewarde.
8 Moreouer in Ieruſalém did Iehoſhaphát
ſet of the Leuites, and of the Prieſts and
of the chief of the families of Iſraél, for
the iudgement and cauſe of the Lord: and
they [e] returned to Ieruſalém.
9 And he charged them, ſaying, Thus ſhal
ye do in the feare of the Lord faithfully
and with a perfite heart.
10 And in euerie cauſe that ſhal come to
you of your brethren that dwel in their
cities, betwene [f] blood and blood, betwene
lawe and precept, ſtatutes and iudgemẽts,
ye ſhal iudge them, and admoniſh them that
they treſpaſſe not againſt the Lord, that
[g] wrath come not vpon you and vpõ your
brethrẽ. Thus ſhal ye do & treſpaſſe not.
11 And beholde, Amariáh the Prieſt *ſhalbe* yͤ
chief ouer you in all matters of the Lord,
& Zebadiáh the ſonne of Iſhmaél, a ruler
of the houſe of Iudáh, *ſhalbe* for all the
[h] Kings affaires, & the Leuites *ſhalbe* officers [i] before you. Be of courage, and do
it, and the Lord ſhalbe with the [k] good.

a He declareth that the wrath and iudgment of God is ouer all ſuche, that supporte the wicked, and rather ſhewe not in dede yͤ they are enemies to all ſuche as hate yͤ Lord.
" Ebr. wrath frõ the Lord.
b He viſited all his cõutrei and broght his people from idolatrie to yͤ knowledge of the true God.
c Bothe to preſerue you, if you do iuſtely, or to puniſh you, if you do the contrarie.
d He wil declare by the ſharpenes of yͤ puniſhement, that he hateth all iniquitie.
Deu. 10,17. iob. 34,19. act. 10,34. rom. 2,11. gal. 2,6. ephe. 6,9. col. 3,26. 1. pet. 1,17.
e The Prieſts and Leuites wͨ ſhulde iudge matters according to the worde of the Lord.
f That is, to trye whither yͤ murther was done at vnwares or els on ſet purpoſe, Nomb. 35,11. deut. 4,41.
g Meaning, yͤ God wolde puniſh them moſte ſharpely, if thei wold not execute iuſtice aright.
h Shalbe chief ouerſeer of yͤ publike affaires of the realme.
i Thei ſhal haue the handeling of inferiour cauſes.
k God wil aſſiſt them that do iuſtice.

CHAP. XX.

3 Iehoſhaphát and the people pray vnto the Lord. 22 The maruelous victorie that the Lord gaue him againſt his enemies. 30 His reigne and actes.

1 AFter this alſo came the children of
Moáb and the children of Ammón,
and with them of the [a] Ammonites a-
gainſt Iehoſhaphát to battel.
2 Thẽ there came that tolde Iehoſhaphát,
ſaying, There cometh a great multitude
againſt thee from beyonde the [b] Sea, out
of Arám: and beholde, they be in Hazzón
Tamár, which is En-gédi.
3 And Iehoſhaphát feared, and ſet him ſelfe
[c] to ſeke the Lord, and proclaimed a faſt
throughout all Iudáh.
4 And Iudáh gathered them ſelues together to aſke counſel of the Lord: they came euẽ out of all the cities of Iudáh to inquire of the Lord.
5 And Iehoſhaphát ſtode in the Congregacion of Iudáh and Ieruſalém in the houſe
of the Lord before the new court,
6 And ſaid, O Lord God of our fathers, art
not thou God in heauen? and reigneſt not
thou on all the kingdomes of the heathẽ?
and in thine hand is power and might, &
none is able to withſtand thee.
7 Dideſt not thou our God caſt out the
inhabitants of this land before thy people
Iſraél, and [d] gaueſt it to the ſede of Abrahám thy friend for euer?
8 And they dwelt therein, and haue buylt
thee a Sanctuarie therein for thy Name,
ſaying,
9 *If euil come vpon vs, *as* the [e] ſworde of
iudgement, or peſtilence, or famine, we wil
ſtand before this houſe and in thy preſence (for thy Name [f] is in this houſe) &
wil crye vnto thee in our tribulacion, and
thou wilt heare and helpe.
10 And now beholde, the children of *Ammón and Moáb, and mõut Seír, by whome
thou woldeſt not let Iſraél go, when they
came out of the land of Egypt: but they
turned aſide from them, and deſtroyed
them not:
11 Beholde, I ſay, thei rewarde vs, in cõming
to caſt vs out of thine inheritance, which
thou haſt cauſed vs to inherit.
12 O our God, wilt thou not iudge them?
for there is no ſtrẽgth in vs *to ſtand* before
this great multitude that cõmeth againſt
vs, nether do we know what to do: but our
eyes [g] are towarde thee.
13 And all Iudáh ſtode [h] before the Lord
with their yong ones, their wiues, and
their children.
14 And Iahaziél the ſonne of Zechariáh the
ſonne of Benaiáh, the ſonne of Ieiél, the
ſõne of Mattaniáh, a Leuite of the ſonnes
of Aſáph *was there*, vpon whome came [i] the
Spirit of the Lord, in the middes of the
Congregacion.
15 And he ſaid, Hearken ye, all Iudáh, & ye
inhabitants of Ieruſalém, and thou, King
Iehoſhaphát: thus ſaith the Lord vnto
you, Feare you not, nether be afraied for
this great multitude: for the [k] battel *is* not
yours, but Gods.
16 Tomorowe go ye downe againſt them:
beholde, they come vp by the cleft of Ziz,
and ye ſhal finde them at the end of the
broke before the wildernes of Ieruél.
17 Ye ſhal not nede to fight in this *battel*:
*ſtand ſtil, moue not, and beholde the " ſal-
uacion of the Lord towarde you: ô Iudáh,
and

a That is, yͤ côterfaited yͤ Ammonites in langage & apparel. The Hebrews thinke that they were yͤ Amalekites, but as may appeare by the 20 verſe, they were the Idumeans of moũt Seir.
b Called the dead ſea where God deſtroyed the fiue cities for ſinne.
c This declareth what the feare of the godlie is, wͨ is as a pricke to ſtirre them to prayer, and to depend on yͤ Lord, where as it moueth the wicked ether to ſeke after worldly meanes & policies, or els to fall into deſpaire.
d He grounded his prayer vpõ Gods power, whereby he is able to helpe, and alſo on his mercie, which he wil cõtinue toward his, for as muche as he hathe once choſen them and begonne to ſhewe his graces towarde them.
1. King. 8,37. chap. 6,28.
e Meanĩg, warre which cometh by Gods iuſte iudgements for our ſinnes.
f That is, it is here called vpon, and thou declareſt thy preſence and fauour.
Deu. 2,9. nehem. 13,1.
g We onely put our truſt in thee and waite for our deliuerance frõ heauen.
h That is, before the Arke of yͤ couenant.
i Which was moued by the Spirit of God to prophecie.
k They fight againſt God & not againſt you: therefore he wil fight for you.
Exod. 14,13.
" Or, deliuerãce.

and Ierusalém, feare ye not, nether be a-
fraied: tomorowe go out against them,
and the Lord *wilbe* with you.

l Declaring his faith and obedience to the worde of the Lord, and giuing thankes for the deliuerance promised.

18 ¶Then Iehoshaphát [l] bowed downe
with his face to the earth, and all Iudáh &
the inhabitants of Ierusalém fell downe
before the Lord, worshiping the Lord.
19 And the Leuites of the children of the
Kohathites and of the children of the
Corhites stode vp to praise the Lord God
of Israél with a loude voice on hie.
20 And when they arose early in the morning, they went forthe to the wildernes of
Tekóa: & as they departed, Iehoshaphát
stode and said, Heare ye me, ô Iudáh, and
ye inhabitãts of Ierusalém: put your trust
in the Lord your God, and ye shalbe assured: beleue his [m] Prophetes, and ye shal
prosper.

m Giue credit to their wordes and doctrine.

21 And whẽ he had consulted with the people, and appointed singers vnto the Lord,
& them that shulde praise *him that is* in the
beautiful Sanctuarie, in going forthe before the men of armes, & saying, [n] Praise
ye the Lord, for his mercie *lasteth* for euer,
22 And when they began to shoute, and to
praise, the Lord laied ambushmẽts against
the childrẽ of Ammón, Moáb, and [o] moũt
Seír, which were come against Iudáh, and
they slewe one another.

n This was a psalme of thãkes giuing, ӯ they vsed cõmunely to sing whẽ they praised the Lord for his benefites, and was made by Dauid, Psal, 136.

o Meaning, the Idumeans, ӯ dwelt in moũt Seír.

23 For the children of Ammón and Moáb
rose against the inhabitãts of mount Seír,
to slea & to destroye *them*: and when they
had made an end of the inhabitãts of Seír,
euerie one helped to [p] destroy another.

p Thus the Lord according to Iehoshaphats praier declared his power, when he deliuered his by causing their enemies to kil one another.

24 And when Iudáh came toward Mizpáh
in the wildernes, they loked vnto the multitude: and beholde, the carkeises were fallen to the earth, and none escaped.
25 And when Iehoshaphát and his people
came to take away the spoyle of them, thei
found amõg them in abundance bothe of
substance & also of bodies *ladẽ* with precious iewels, which thei toke for thẽ selues, til they colde cary nomore: they were
thre dayes in gathering of the spoile: for
it was muche.
26 And in the fourte day thei [q] assembled
them selues in the valley of Berachâh: for
there thei blessed the Lord: therefore thei
called the name of that place, The vallei
of Berachâh vnto this day.

q To giue thãkes to the Lord for the victorie: and therefore the valley was called Berachâh, that is, blessing or thãkes giuing, which was also called the valley of Iehoshaphát, Ioel 3, 2. & 12, because the Lord iudged ӯ enemies according to Iehoshaphats praier.

27 Thẽ euerie man of Iudáh & Ierusalém
returned with Iehoshaphát their head, to
go againe to Ierusalém with ioye: for the
Lord had made thẽ to reioyce ouer their
enemies.
28 And they came to Ierusalém with violes, and with harpes, and with trumpets,
euen vnto the house of the Lord.
29 And the [r] feare of God was vpon all the
kingdomes of the earth, when they had
heard that the Lord had foght against the
enemies of Israél.

r He declareth hereby, that ӯ workes of God bring euer cõforte or deliuerance to his, & feare or destructiõ to his enemies.

30 So ӯ kingdome of Iehoshaphát was quiet, & his God gaue him rest on euery side.
31 ¶And *Iehoshaphát reigned ouer Iu- 1.Kin.22,42.
dáh, and *was* fiue & thirtie yere olde, whẽ
he began to reigne: and reigned fiue and
twẽtie yere in Ierusalém, and his mothers
name was Azubáh the daughter of Shilhí.
32 And he walked in the [s] waye of Asá his
father, and departed not therefrom, doing
that which was right in the sight of the
Lord.

s Meaning, in his vertues & those waies, wherein he folowed God.

33 Howbeit the hie places were [t] not taken
away: for the people had not yet prepared
their hearts vnto the God of their fathers.

t If the great care and diligence of this good Kīg was not able vtterly to abolish all superstition & idolatrie out of this people, but that they wolde stil reteine their filth and idolatrie, how muche lesse are they able to reforme euil, ӯ ether haue litle zeale, or not suche as he had: thogh herein he was not to be excused?

34 Concerning ӯ rest of the actes of Iehoshaphát first and last, beholde, thei are wri
ten in the boke of Iehú the sonne of Hanáni, which *is mencioned in the boke of
the Kings of Israél.
35 ¶Yet after this did Iehoshaphát King
of Iudáh ioyne him selfe with Ahaziáh
King of Israél, who was giuen to do euil.
36 And he ioyned with him, to * make shippes to go to Tarshish: and thei made the
shippes in Ezión Gabér.
37 Then Eliézer the sonne of Dodauáh of 1.King.16,1
Mareшáh prophecied agaĩst Iehoshaphát, 1.Kin.22,49.
saying, Because thou hast [u] ioyned thy self
with Ahaziáh, the Lord hathe broken thy
workes. and the shippes were broken, that
thei were not able to go to Tarshísh.

u Thus God wolde not haue his to ioyne in societie with idolaters & wicked mẽ.

CHAP. XXI.

1 Iehoshaphát dyeth. 3 Iehorám succedeth him, 4 Which killeth his brethrẽ. 6 He was broght to idolatrie. 11 And seduceth the people. 16 He is oppressed of the Philistims. 18 His miserable end.

1 IEhoshaphát thẽ slept with his fathers,
and was buryed with his fathers in the
citie of Dauid: and Iehorám his sonne
reigned in his stead.
2 And he had brethren the sonnes of Iehoshaphát, Azariáh, and Iehiél, & Zechariáh,
and Azariáh, and Michaél, & Shephatiáh.
All these were the sonnes of Iehoshaphát
King of [a] Israél.

a Read chap. 15, 17 how by Israél is ment Iudáh.

3 And their father gaue them great giftes
of siluer and of golde, and of precious
things, with strong cities in Iudáh, but the
kingdome gaue he to Iehorám: for he was
the eldest.
4 *And Iehorám rose vp vpõ the kĩgdome 2.King.8,16.
of his father, and made him selfe strõg, &
[b] slewe all his brethren with the sworde,
and also of the princes of [c] Israél.

b Because the wicked liue euer in feare & also are ambitious, they become cruel, & spare not to murther them, whome by nature they oght moste to cherish & defend.

c Meaning, of Iudáh & Beniamin.

5 Iehorám was two and thirtie yere olde,
when he began to reigne, and he reigned
eight yere in Ierusalém.
6 And he walked in the waye of the Kings
of Israél, as the house of Aháb had done:
for he had the daughter of Aháb to [d] wife,
and he wroght euil in the eies of ӯ Lord.

d So that we se how it cã not be ӯ we shulde ioyne with ӯ wicked & serue God.

7 Howbeit the Lord wolde not destroy
the house of Dauid,because of the * couenant that he had made with Dauid , and
because he had promised to giue a light
to him,and to his sonnes for euer.

2.Sam.7,12. 1.king 2,4. & 9,5. 2 king.8,19. chap.6,16.

8 ¶In his dayes Edóm rebelled frõ vnder
the hand of Iudáh,and made a King ouer
them.
9 And Iehorám wẽt forthe with his princes,
and all his charets with him : & he rose vp
by night,and smote Edóm,which had cõpassed him in, and the captaines of the
charets.
10 But Edóm rebelled from vnder the hãd
of Iudáh vnto this day. thẽ did e Libnah
rebell at the same time from vnder his
hand, because he had forsaken the Lord
God of his fathers.

e Read 2 King. 8,22.

11 ¶Moreouer he made hie places in the
mountaines of Iudáh, and caused the inhabitants of Ierusalém to commit f fornicacion,and compelled Iudáh *thereto*.
12 And there came a writing to him from
g Eliáh the Prophet , saying , Thus saith
the Lord God of Dauid thy father, Because thou hast not walked in the waies of Iehoshaphát thy father, nor in the wayes of
Asá King of Iudáh,
13 But hast walked in the way of the Kings
of Israél, and hast made Iudáh and the inhabitants of Ierusalém to go a whoring,
as the house of Aháb went a whoring, and
hast also sleane thy brethrẽ of thy fathers
house,which were better then thou,

f Meaning,idolatrie, because that the idolater breaketh promes with God, as doeth the adulteresse to her housband.
g Some thinke that this was Elishá, so called,because he had the Spirit in abundance, as had Eliáh.

14 Beholde,with a great plague wil ẏ Lord
smite thy people, and thy children, & thy
wiues,and all thy substance,
15 And thou shalt be in great diseases in the
disease of thy bowels, vntil h thy bowels
fall out for the disease,day by day.
16 ¶So the Lord stirred vp against Iehoram
the spirit of the Philistims, and the
Arabians that were beside the i Ethiopiãs.
17 And they came vp into Iudáh, and brake into it, and caried away all the substãce that was founde in the Kings house, &
his sonnes also,and his wiues,so that there
was not a sonne left him,saue k Iehoaház,
the yongest of his sonnes.
18 And after all this , the Lord smote him
in his bowels with an incurable disease.
19 And in processe of time , euen after the
ẽd of two yeres,his guttes fell out with his
disease: so he dyed of sore diseases : & his
people made no burning for him like the
burning of his fathers.
20 When he began to reigne, he was two
and thirtie yere olde,and reigned in Ierusalém eight yere, l and liued without being desired: yet they buryed him in the
citie of Dauid, but not among the sepulchres of the Kings.

h We se this example daily practised vpõ them that fall away frõ God, and become idolaters and murtherers of their brethrẽ.
i There were other Arabiãs in Africa Southward toward Egypt.
k Called also Ahaziáh, as Chap 22,1, or Azariáh,ver.6
l That is,as some write, he was not regarded, but deposed for his wickednes & idolatrie: so that his sonne reigned 22 yeres, (his father yet lyuĩg) without honour & after his fathers death he was cõfirmed to reigne stil, as Chap.22,2.

CHAP. XXII.

1 Ahaziáh reigneth after Iehorám. 8 Iehú King of Israél killeth Ahaziah. 10 Athaliah putteth to death all the Kings linage. 11 Ioash escapeth.

1 AND * the inhabitants of Ierusalém
made Ahaziáh his yõgest sonne Kĩg
in his stead: for the armie ẏ came a with
the Arabians to the campe, had sleane all
the eldest: therefore Ahaziáh the sonne of
Iehorám King of Iudáh reigned.
2 Two and b fourty yere olde *was* Ahaziáh
whẽ he began to reigne,& he reigned c one
yere in Ierusalém. and his mothers name
was Athaliáh the daughter d of Omrí.
3 He walked also in the waies of the house
of Aháb: for his mother counseled him to
do wickedly.
4 Wherefore he did euil in the sight of
the Lord , like the house of Aháb : for
they were his e counselers after the death
of his father,to his destruction.
5 And he walked after their counsel, and
went with Iehorám the sonne of Aháb
King of Israél to fight against Hazaél
King of Arám at Ramóth Gileád: and the
Aramites smote Iorám.
6 ¶And he returned to be healed in Izreél , because of the woũdes wherewith thei
had wounded him at Ramáh, when he
foght with Hazaél King of Arám . Now
Azariáh the sonne of Iehorám King of
Iudáh went downe to se Iehorám the sonne of Aháb at Izreél , because he was diseased.

2.King.8,24.
a Meaning,the Philistims.
b Read Chap. 21,20.
c That is, after the death of his father.
d She was Ahabs daughter, who was the sonne of Omri.
e He sheweth, that it must nedes followe that the rulers are suche as their counselers be, & that there can not be a good Kĩg, that suffreth wicked counselers.

7 And the destruction of Ahaziáh f came
of God in that he wẽt to Iorám: for when
he was come,he went forthe with Iehorám
against Iehú the sonne of Nimshí, * whome the Lord had anointed to destroye
the house of Aháb.
8 Therefore when Iehú * executed iudgement vpon the house of Aháb, and foũde
the princes of Iudáh and the sonnes of
the brethren of Ahaziáh that waited on
Ahaziáh,he slewe them also.
9 And he soght Ahaziáh, and they caught
hĩ where he was hid in Samaria, & broght
him to Iehú , and slewe him , and buryed
him,because, said thei, he is the sonne of
g Iehoshaphát,which soght the Lord with
all his heart. So the house of Ahaziáh was
not able to reteine the kingdome.
10 ¶* Therefore when Athaliáh the mother
of Ahaziáh sawe that her sonne was dead,
she arose and h destroyed all the Kings sede of the house of Iudáh.
11 But Iehoshabeáth the daughter of the
King, toke Ioásh the sonne of Ahaziáh,
and stale him from among the Kings sonnes,that shulde be sleane,and put him and
his nurce in the bed chamber : so Iehoshabeáth the daughter of Kĩg Iehorám
the wife of Iehoiadá the Priest (for she
was

f Hereby we se how nothĩg can come to any , but by Gods prouidẽce & as he hathe appointed, & therefore he causeth all meanes to serue to his wil.
2.King.9,7.
* Or, toke vengeance.
g This was ẏ iuste plague of God, because he ioyned him selfe ẇ Gods enemies : yet God to declare the worthines of Iehoshaphát his grandfather, moued thẽ to giue him ẏ honour of buryal.
2 King 11,1.
h To the intẽt ẏ there shulde be none to make title to the crowne, & so she might vsurpe the gouernement.

was the sister of Ahaziáh) hid him from A-
thaliáh: so she slewe him not.
12 And he was with them hid in the [i] house
of God six yeres, whiles Athaliáh reigned
ouer the [k] land.

i Meaning, in the chamber, where the Priests and Leuites slept, & kept their courses weekly in ẏ Teple.
k To wit, of Iudáh.

CHAP. XXIII.

1 Ioásh the sonne of Ahaziáh is made King. 3 Athaliáh is put to death 17 The Temple of Baal is destroied. 19 Iehoiada appointeth ministers in the Temple.

2.King.11,4.
a Or the reigne of Athaliáh, or after ẏ death of Ahaziáh.

1 AND * [a] in the seuente yere Iehoiadá
waxed bolde, and toke the captai-
nes of hundreths, *to wit*, Azariáh the sonne
of Ierohám, and Ishmaél the sonne of Iehohanán, and Azariáh the sonne of Obéd,
and Maasiáh the sonne of Adaiáh, and E-
lishaphát the sonne of Zichri in couenant
with him.
2 And they went about in Iudáh, & gathered the Leuites out of all the cities of Iudáh, and the chief fathers [b] of Israél: and
they came to Ierusalém.
3 And all the Congregacion made a couenant with the King in the house of God:
& he said vnto them, Beholde, the Kings
sonne muste reigne, * as ẏ Lord hathe said
of the sonnes of Dauid.
4 This is it that ye shal do, The third parte
of you that come on the Sabbath of the
Priests, and the Leuites, *shalbe* porters of
the dores.
5 And *another* third parte towarde the
Kings house, and *another* third parte
at the * gate of the [c] fundacion, and all
the people *shalbe* in ẏ courtes of the house of the Lord.
6 But let none come into the house of the
Lord, saue the Priests, and the Leuites that
minister: they shal go in, for they are holy:
but all the people shal kepe the watch of
the Lord.
7 And the Leuites shal compasse the Kĩg
round about, and euerie mã with his weapon in his hand, and he that entreth [d] into the house, shalbe sleane, and be you
with the King, when he commeth in, and
when he goeth out.
8 ¶ So the Leuites and all Iudáh did according to all things that Iehoiadá the Priest had commanded, and toke euery man
his men that came on the Sabbath, with
them that [e] went out on the Sabbath: for
Iehoiadá the Priest did not discharge
the courses.
9 And Iehoiadá the Priest deliuered to
the captaines of hundreths speares, and
shields, and bucklers which had bene
King Dauids, and were in the house of
God.
10 And he caused all the people to stãd (euerie man with his weapon in his hand) from
the right side of the house, to the left side
of the house by the altar and by the [f] house
rounde about the King.

b Meaning of Iudah & Beniamin: read why they are called Israél, Chap.15,17
2.Sam.7,12. 1.king.2,4. chap.21,7.
2.King.11,6.
c Which was the chief gate of the Temple toward ẏ East
d Meaning, to make any tumulte or to hinder their enterprise.
e Which had finished their course on the Sabbath, & so the other part entred to kepe their turne.
f Meaning, the moste holy place where ẏ Arke stode.

11 Then they broght out the Kings sonne,
ne, and put vpon him the crowne and *gaue him* the [g] testimonie, and made him
King. And Iehoiadá and his sonnes
anointed him, and said, God saue the
King.
12 ¶ But when Athaliáh heard the noise
of the people running and praising the
King, she came to the people into the
house of the Lord.
13 And whẽ [*] she loked, beholde, the King
stode by his piller at the entring in, & the
princes & the trumpers by the King, &
all the people of the land reioyced, and
blewe the trumpets, and the singers *were*
with instruments of musike, and they that
colde sing praise: then Athaliáh rent her
clothes, and said, [h] Treason, treason.
14 Then Iehoiadá the Priest broght out
the captaines of hundreths that were gouerners of the hoste, and said vnto them,
Haue her forthe of the ranges, & he that
[i] followeth her, let him dye by ẏ sworde:
for the Priest had said, Slea her not in the
house of the Lord.
15 So they layed hands on her: and when
she was come to the entring of the horsegate by the Kings house, thei slewe her
there.
16 ¶ And Iehoiadá made a [k] couenant betwene him, and all the people, and the
King, that they wolde be the Lords people.
17 And all the people went to the house of
Báal, and [l] destroyed it, and brake his altars and his images, and slewe [m] Mattán the Priest of Báal before the altars.
18 And Iehoiadá appointed officers for
the house of the Lord, vnder the [*] hands
of the Priests and Leuites, whome Dauid had distributed for the house of
the Lord, to offer burnt offrings vnto
the Lord, * as it is writen in the Lawe
of Mosés, with reioycing and singing
by the appointement of Dauid.
19 And he set porters by the gates of the
house of the Lord, that none that was
vncleane in any thing, shulde entre in.
20 And he toke the captaines of hundreths,
and the noble men, and the gouerners
of the people, and all the people of the
land, and he caused the King to come
downe out of the house of the Lord, and
they went through [n] the hie gate of the
Kings house, and set the King vpon the
throne of the kingdome.
21 Then all the people of the land reioyced, & the citie was quiet, [o] after that thei
had sleane Athaliáh with the sworde.

g That is, the boke of the Law, or as some read, they put vpon him his royal apparel.
* Or, sawe the King standing.
h Declaring her vile impudēcie, which hauing vniustly, & by murther vsurped the crowne, wolde stil haue defeated the true possessor, and therefore called true obediēce, treason.
i To ioyne with her partie, & to mainteine her autoritie.
k That they wolde onely serue him and renounce all idolatrie.
l According to their couenant made to the Lord.
m As the Lord commanded in his Lawe bothe for the persone and also the citie, Deu. 13,9 & 15.
* Or, charge.
Nomb.28,3.
n Which was the principal gate, that the King might be sene of all the people.
o For where a tyrant & an idolater reigneth, there can be no quietnes: for ẏ plagues of God are euer amõg such people.

CHAP. XXIIII.

4 Ioásh repaireth the house of the Lord. 17 After the death of Iehoiada he falleth to idolatrie 21 He stoneth to death Zechariah the Prophet. 25 Ioásh is killed of his owne seruāts 27 After him reigneth Amaziáh.

2.King.12,1. 1 IOásh* *was* seuen yere olde when he began to reigne, and he reigned fourtie
yere in Ierusalém: and his mothers name
was Zibiáh of Beer-shéba.
2 And Ioásh did vprightly in the sight of
the Lord, all the dayes of [a] Iehoiadá the
Priest.
3 And Iehoiadá [″] toke him two wiues, and
he begate sonnes and daughters.
4 ¶ And afterward it came into Ioásh minde, to renue the house of the Lord.
5 And he assembled the Priestes and the
Leuites, & said to them, Go out vnto the
cities of Iudáh, and gather of all [b] Israél
money to repaire the house of your God,
from yere to yere, and haste the thing: but
the Leuites hasted not.
6 Therefore the King called Iehoiadá,
the [c] chief, and said vnto him, Why hast
thou not required of the Leuites to bring
in out of Iudáh and Ierusalém * the taxe
of Mosés the seruant of the Lord, and of
the Congregacion of Israél, for the Tabernacle of the testimonie?
7 For [d] wicked Athaliáh, & her children
brake vp the house of God: and all the
things that were dedicate for the house of
the Lord, did thei bestowe vpon Baalím.
2.King.12,9. 8 Therefore the King commanded, * and
they made a chest, and set it at the gate of
the house of the Lord.
9 And they made proclamacion through
Iudáh and Ierusalém, to bring vnto the
Lord * the taxe of Mosés the seruant of
God, *laied* vpon Israél in the wildernes.
10 And all the princes and all the people
reioyced, and broght in, and cast into the
chest, vntil they had finished.
11 And when it was time, [e] thei broght the
chest vnto the Kings officer by the hand
of the Leuites: and when they sawe that
there was muche siluer, then ẏ Kings Scribe (& one appointed by ẏ hie Priest) came
and emptied the chest, and toke it, and caried it to his place againe: thus they did
day by day, and gathered siluer in abundance.
12 And the King and [f] Iehoiadá gaue it to
suche as did the labour & worke in the
house of the Lord, and hyred masons
and carpenters to repaire the house of
the Lord: *they gaue it* also to workers of
yron and brasse, to repaire the house of
the Lord.
13 So the workemen wroght, and the worke
[″] amended through their hands: and they
restored the house of God to his state, &
strengthened it.
14 And when they had finished it, they
broght the rest of the siluer before the
King and Iehoiadá, and he made thereof
[g] vessels for the house of the Lord, *euen*
vessels to minister, bothe morters & *incen-*
se cuppes, and vessels of golde, and of siluer: and they offred burntoffrings in the
house of the Lord continually all the
dayes of Iehoiadá.
15 ¶ But Iehoiadá waxed olde, and was ful
of daies and dyed. An hundreth and thirtie yere olde *was he* when he dyed.
16 And thei buryed him in the citie of Dauid with the [h] Kings, because he had done
good in Israél, and toward God and his
house.
17 ¶ And after the death of Iehoiadá, came the [i] princes of Iudáh, and did reuerēce to the King, & the King hearkened vnto them.
18 And they left the house of the Lord
God of their fathers, and serued groues
and idoles: and wrath came vpon Iudáh
and Ierusalém, because of this their trespas.
19 And *God* sent Prophetes among them, to
bring them againe vnto the Lord: and
thei [k] made protestation among them, but
they wolde not heare.
20 And the Spirit of God came vpon Zechariáh the sonne of Iehoiadá the Priest,
which stode [l] aboue the people, and said
vnto them, Thus saith God, Why transgresse ye the commandements of ẏ Lord:
surely it shal not prosper: because ye haue forsaken the Lord, he also hathe forsaken you.
21 Then they conspired against him and
stoned him with stones at the [m] commandement of the King, in the court of the
house of the Lord.
22 Thus Ioásh the King remembred not ẏ
kindenes which Iehoiadá his father had
done to him, but slewe his sonne. And whē
he dyed, he said, The Lord [n] loke vpō it, &
require it.
23 ¶ And when the yere was out, the hoste
of Arám came vp against him, and thei
came against Iudáh and Ierusalém, & destroyed all the princes of the people frō
among the people, and sent all the spoile
of them vnto the King of Damascus.
24 Thogh the armie of Arám came with a
small company of mē, yet the Lord deliuered a very great armie into their hand,
because they had forsaken the Lord God
of their fathers: and they [o] gaue sentence
against Ioásh.
25 And when thei were departed from him,
(for thei left him in great diseases) his
owne seruants conspired against him for
the blood of the [p] children of Iehoiadá
the Priest, and slewe him on his bed, and
he dyed, and they buryed him in the citie of Dauid: but they buryed him not in
the

a Who was a faithful counseler, and gouerned him by the worde of God.

″ Or, gaue him two wiues.

b He meaneth not the ten tribes, but onely the two tribes of Iudáh and Beniamin.

c For he was the hie Priest.

Exod.30,13.

d The Scripture doeth terme her thus, because she was a cruel murtherer, and a blasphemous idolatresse.

Exod.30,13.

e Such as were faithful mē, whome the King had appointed for that matter.

f Signifying, ẏ this thing was done by aduise and counsel, and not by any one mās affection.

″ Ebr. a medicine was vpon the worke, meanīg, it was repaired.

g For the wicked Kings his predecessours and Athaliáh had destroied the vessels of the Temple, or turned thē to ẏ vse of their idoles.

h Signifying, that thei colde not honour hī to muche, who had so excellently serued in ẏ worke of ẏ Lord, and in the affaires of ẏ cōmune wealth.

i Which were flatterers, and knewe now ẏ the King was destitute of hī who did watche ouer him as a father, & therefore broght him to moste vile idolatrie.

k They toke heauē & earth and all creatures to witnes, that except they returned to the Lord, he wolde moste grieuously punish their infidelitie & rebellion.

l In a place aboue the people to the intēt ẏ he might be heard.

m There is no rage so cruel & beastely as of them whose heartes God hathe hardened, and ẘ delite more in superstition & idolatrie, then in the true seruice of God & pure simplicitie of his worde.

n Reuenge my death & require my blood at your hands: or, he speaketh this by prophecie, because he knewe that God wolde do it. This Zacharie is also called the sonne of Barachie Mat. 23, 35, because his progenitours were Iddó, Barachiáh, Iehoiadá, &c.

o That is, reproued & checked him, and handeled him rigorously.

p Meanīg Zacharie, ẘ was one of Iehoiadas sonnes & a Prophet of the Lord.

the ſepulchres of the Kings.
26 And theſe are they that conſpired agaĩſt
him, Zabád the ſõne of Shimráth an Am-
moniteſſe, and Iehozabád the ſonne of
Shimrĩth a Moabiteſſe.
27 But [q] his ſonnes, and the ſumme of the
taxe *gathered* by him, and the [r] fundacion
of the houſe of God, beholde, they are
writen in the ſtorie of the boke of the
Kings. And Amaziáh his ſonne reigned
in his ſtead.

q That is, concernĩg his ſonnes, &c.
r That is, the reparacion.

CHAP. XXV.

3 Amaziáh putteth them to death which ſlewe his father. 10 He ſendeth backe them of Iſraél. 11 He ouercõmeth the Edomites. 14 He falleth to idolatrie. 17 And Ioáſh King of Iſraél ouercommeth Amaziáh. 27 He is ſlayne by a conſpiracie.

1 AMaziáh was fiue and twentie yere
olde, when he began to reigne, & he
reigned nine and twentie yere in * Ieruſalém: & his mothers name *was* Iehoad-
dán, of Ieruſalém.
2 And he did [a] vprightly in the eyes of the
Lord, but not with a perfite heart.
3 And when the kingdome was eſtabliſhed
vnto him, he ſlewe his ſeruants, that had
ſlayne the King his father.
4 But he ſlewe not their children, but *did*,
as it is writen in the Law, *&* in the boke
of Moſés, where the Lord commanded,
ſaying, * The fathers ſhal not dye for the
[b] children, nether ſhal the children dye
for the fathers, but euerie man ſhal dye
for his owne ſinne.
5 ¶ And Amaziáh aſſembled Iudáh, and
made them captaines ouer thouſands, &
captaines ouer hundreths according to
the houſes of their fathers, throughout all
Iudáh and Beniamín: & he nombred them
from [c] twentie yere olde and aboue, and
founde among them thre hundreth thouſand choſen mẽ, to go forthe to the warre,
and to handle ſpeare and ſhield.
6 He hyred alſo an hundreth thouſand valiant men [d] out of Iſraél for an hundreth
talents of ſiluer.
7 But a man of God came to him, ſaying,
O King, let not the armie of Iſraél go
with thee: for the Lord is not [e] with Iſraél, *nether* with all the houſe of Ephráim.
8 If [f] not, go thou on, do it, make thy ſelfe
ſtrõg to the battel, *but* God ſhal make thee
fall before ỹ enemie: for God hathe power
to helpe, and to caſt downe.
9 And Amaziáh ſaid to the man of God,
What ſhal we do then for the hundreth
talents, ẘ I haue giuen to the hoſte of Iſraél? Then ỹ man of God anſwered, The
Lord is able to [g] giue thee more then this.
10 So Amaziáh ſeparated thẽ, *to wit*, the armie that was come to him out of Ephráim, to returne to their place: wherefore
their wrath was kindled greatly againſt

2.King 14,2.
a Meaning, in reſpect of his predeceſſers, albeit he had his imperfections.
Deut.24,16. 2.king.14,6. iere.31,30. ezek.18,20.
b That is, for ỹ faute wherefore ỹ childe is puniſhed, except he be culpable of the ſame.
c So many as were able men to beare weapons & go to the warre.
d That is, out of the ten tribes, which had ſeparated them ſelues before, bothe from God and their true King.
e And therefore to thinke to haue helpe of thẽ, whome the Lord fauoreth not, is to caſt of the helpe of the Lord.
f If thou wilt not giue credit to my wordes.
g He ſheweth that if we depẽd onely vpõ God, we ſhal not nede to be troubled with theſe worldlie reſpects: for he wil giue at all times that ẘ ſhalbe neceſſarie, if we obey his worde

Iudáh, and they returned to their places
with great angre.
11 Then Amaziáh was encouraged, and led
forthe his people, & went to the ſalt valley, and ſmote of the children of [h] Seír,
ten thouſand.
12 And *other* ten thouſand did the children
of Iudáh take aliue, and caryed them to
the toppe of a [i] rocke, and caſt thẽ downe
from the toppe of the rocke, and they all
burſt to pieces.
13 But the men of the [k] armie, which A-
maziáh ſent away, that they ſhulde not go
with his people to battel, fell vpon the cities of Iudáh from Samaria vnto Beth-
horón, and ſmote thre thouſand of them,
and toke muche ſpoyle.
14 Now after that Amaziáh was come frõ
the ſlaughter of the Edomites, he broght
the gods of the children of Seír, and ſet
them vp to be his gods, and [l] worſhiped
them, and burned incenſe vnto them.
15 Wherefore the Lord was wroth with A-
maziáh, and ſent vnto him a Prophet,
which ſaid vnto him, Why haſt ỹ ſoght
the gods of the people, which were not a-
ble to [m] deliuer their owne people out of
thine hand?
16 And as he talked with him, [n] he ſaid
vnto him, Haue thei made thee ỹ Kings
counſeler? ceaſe thou: why ſhulde they
[o] ſmite thee? And the Prophet ceaſed, but
ſaid, I knowe that God hathe determined
to deſtroye thee, becauſe thou haſt done
this, and haſt not obeyed my counſel.
17 ¶ Then Amaziáh King of Iudáh toke
counſel, and ſent to Ioáſh the ſonne of
Iehoaház, the ſonne of Iehú King of Iſraél, ſaying, Come, [p] let vs ſe one another
in the face.
18 But Ioáſh King of Iſraél ſent to Amaziáh King of Iudáh, ſaying, The thiſtle
that is in Lebanón, ſent to the cedre that
is in Lebanón, ſaying, * Giue thy daughter to my ſonne to wife: & the wilde beaſt
that was in Lebanón went & trode downe
the thiſtle.
19 Thou thinkeſt: lo, thou haſt ſmiten E-
dóm, and thine heart lifteth thee vp to
bragge: abide now at home: why doeſt
thou prouoke to *thine* hurt, that thou ſhuldeſt fall, and Iudáh with thee?
20 But Amaziáh wolde not heare: for [q] it
was of God, that he might deliuer them
into *his* hand, becauſe they had ſoght the
gods of Edóm.
21 So Ioáſh the King of Iſraél went vp: &
he, and Amaziáh King of Iudáh ſawe one
another in the face at Bethſhémeſh, which
is in Iudáh.
22 And Iudáh was put to the worſe before
Iſraél, and they fled euerie man to his
tents.

h For the Idumeans whome Dauid had broght to ſubiectiõ, rebelled vnder Iehorám Iehoſhaphats ſonne.
i In the 2.Kĩg. 14,7 this rocke is called ỹ citie Selá.
k That is, the hũdreth thouſand of Iſraél.
l Thus where he ſhulde haue giuen the praiſe to God for his benefites and great victorie, he fel from God, and did moſt vilely diſhonour hĩ.
m He proueth that whatſoeuer can not ſaue hĩ ſelfe, nor his worſhipers, is no God but an idole.
n Meaning, the King.
o So hard it is for the carnal man to be admoniſhed for his faute, that he contẽneth, mocketh & threateneth him that warneth him: yea, impriſoneth him & putteth him to death, 2.Chro 16,10. & 18,26 & 24,21
p That is, let vs trye ỹ matter hand to hand: for he was offended, that the armie of the Iſraelites, whome he had in wages, & dimiſſed by the counſel of the Prophet, had deſtroyed certeine of the cities of Iudáh.
2.King.14,9.
q Thus God oft times plagueth by thoſe meanes, wherein mẽ moſte truſt, to teache them to haue their recourſe onely to him: and to ſhewe his iudgemẽts, moueth their hearts to folowe ỹ which ſhalbe their deſtruction.

23 But Ioásh the King of Israél toke Amaziáh King of Iudáh, the sonne of Ioásh,
the sonne of Iehoaház in Bethshémesh, &
broght him to Ierusalém, & brake downe
the wall of Ierusalém, from the gate of E-
phráim vnto the corner gate, foure hundreth cubites.
24 And *he toke* all the golde and the siluer,
and all the vessels that were founde in the
house of God with [r] Obéd Edóm, and in
the treasures of the Kings house, and the
children that were in hostage, & returned
to Samaria.
25 ¶ And Amaziáh the sonne of Ioásh Kīg
of Iudáh liued after the death of Ioásh
sonne of Iehoaház King of Israél, fiftene
yere.
26 Cōcerning the rest of the actes of Amaziáh first & last, are they not writen in the
boke of the Kings of Iudáh and Israél?
27 Now after the time that Amaziáh did
turne away from the Lord, * they wroght
treason against him in Ierusalém: & when
he was fled to Lachísh, thei sēt to Lachísh
after him, and slewe him there.
28 And thei broght him vpon horses, & buryed him with his fathers in the citie of
Iudáh.

r Meaning, the successers of Obéd Edóm: for the house bare the name of the chief father.

2.King.14,19

CHAP. XXVI.

1.5 Vzziáh obeying the Lord, prospereth in his enterprises. 16 He waxeth proude & vsurpeth the Priests office. 19 The Lord plagueth him. 20 The Priests driue him out of the Temple, & exclude him out of the Lords house. 23 His buryal, and his successour.

1 THen* all ẏ people of Iudáh toke [a] Vzziáh, which was sixtene yere olde, &
made him King in the stead of his father
Amaziáh.
2 He buylt [b] Elóth, & restored it to Iudáh
after that the King slept with his fathers.
3 * Sixtene yere olde *was* Vzziáh, when he
began to reigne, and he reigned two and
fiftie yere in Ierusalém, and his mothers
name *was* Iecoliáh of Ierusalém.
4 And he did vprightly in the sight of the
Lord, according to all that his father A-
maziáh did.
5 And he soght God in the dayes of [c] Zechariáh (which vnderstode the visions of
God) and when as [d] he soght the Lord,
God made him to prosper.
6 For he went forthe and foght against the
Philistims and brake downe the wall of
Gath, and the wall of Iabnéh, and the wall
of Ashdód, and buylt cities in Ashdód,
and among the Philistims.
7 And God helped him against the Philistims, and against the Arabians that dwelt
in Gur-báal and Hammeuním.
8 And the Ammonites gaue [e] giftes to Vzziáh, and his name spred to the entring in
of Egypt: for he did moste valiantly.
9 Moreouer Vzziáh buylt towres in Ieru-

2.King.14,21
a Called also Azariáh.

b He fortified it and made it strong: this citie was also called Eláth & Elanón, nere to ẏ red Sea.

2.King.15,2.

c This was not that Zechariáh that was the sonne of Iehoiadá, but some other Prophet of that name.

d For God neuer forsaketh any ẏ seketh vnto him, and therefore man is the cause of his owne destruction.

e That is, thei payed tribute in signe of subiection.

salém at the corner gate, and at the valley
gate, & at the * [f] turning, and made them
strong.
10 And he buylt towres in the wildernes,
and digged many [*] cisternes: for he had
muche cattel bothe in the valleis and
plaines, plowmen, and dressers of vines in
the mountaines, and in [g] Carmél: for he
loued housbandrie.
11 Vzziáh had also an hoste of fighting mē
that wēt out to warre by bādes, according
to the counte of their nomber vnder the
hand of Ieiél the scribe, and Maaseiáh the
ruler, & vnder the hand of Hananiáh, one
of the Kings captaines.
12 The whole [h] nomber of the chief of the
families of the valiāt men *were* two thousand and six hundreth.
13 And vnder their hand *was* the armie for
warre, thre hundreth and seuen thousand,
and fiue hundreth that foght valiantly to
helpe the King against the enemie.
14 And Vzziáh prepared them throughout
all the hoste, shields, and speares, and helmets, and brigandines, and bowes, and stones to sling.
15 He made also verie [*] artificial engins in
Ierusalém, to be vpon the towres and vpō
the corners, to shote arowes and great stones: and his name spred farre abroade, because *God* did helpe him meruelously, til
he was mightie.
16 ¶ But when he was strong, his heart [i] was
lift vp to *his* destruction: for he transgressed against the Lord his God, & went into
the Temple of the Lord to burne incense
vpon the altar of incense.
17 And Azariáh ẏ Priest went in after him,
and with him foure score Priests of the
Lord, valiant men.
18 And they withstode Vzziáh the King, &
said vnto him, * It perteineth not to thee,
Vzziáh, to burne incense vnto the Lord,
but to ẏ Priests the sonnes of Aarón, that
are consecrated for to offer incense: [k] go
forthe of the Sanctuarie: for thou hast trā-
gressed, and thou shalt haue none honour
of the Lord God.
19 Then Vzziáh was wroth, and had incense in his hand to burne it: & while he was
wroth with the Priests, the leprosie rose vp
in his forehead before the Priests in the
house of the Lord beside the incēse altar.
20 And whē Azariáh the chief Priest with
all the Priests loked vpon him, beholde,
he was leprous in his forehead, and they
caused him hastely to departe thence: and
he was euen compelled to go out, because
the Lord had smiten him.
21 * And Vzziáh the King was a lepre vnto
the day of his death, and dwelt as a lepre
in an [l] house aparte, because he was cut of
frō the house of the Lord: & Iothám his
sonne

Nehem.3,19. & 24.
f Where as ẏ walle or towre turneth.
* Or, pittes.

g That is, in mount Carmél, or, as the worde signifieth, in the fruteful field. it is also taken for a grene eare of corne, when it is ful, as Leui.2,14.

h Of ẏ chief officers of the Kings house, or of the captaines and sergeants for warre.

* Ebr. engins by the inuention of an inuentiue man.

i Thus prosperitie causeth men to trust in them selues, & by forgetting him, which is the autor thereof, procure their owne perdicion.

Nomb.18,7.

k Thogh his zeale semed to be good & also his intencion, yet because they were not gouerned by the worde of God, he did wickedly, and was therefore bothe iustely resisted & also punished.

2.King.15,5.
l According to the commandement of the Lord Leui. 13,46.

sonne *ruled* ouer the Kings house, and iudged the people of the land.
21 Concerning the rest of the actes of Vzziáh, first and last, did Isaiáh the Prophet
the sonne of Amóz write.
23 So Vzziáh slept with his fathers, and
they buryed him with his fathers in the
field of the buryal, which perteined to the
Kings: for they said, He [m] is a lepre. And
Iothám his sonne reigned in his stead.

m And therefore was buryed aparte in the same field, but not in the same sepulchres with his predecessers.

CHAP. XXVII.

1 Iothám reigneth, and ouercometh the Ammonites. 8 His reigne & death. 9 Aház his sonne reigneth in his stead.

1 IOthám * *was* fyue & twentie yere olde
when he began to reigne, and reigned
sixtene yere in Ierusalém, and his mothers
name *was* Ierusháh the daughter of Zadók.
2 And he did vprightly in the sight of the
Lord according to all that his father Vzziáh did, saue that he entred not into the
[a] Temple of the Lord, and the people did
yet [b] corrupt *their waies*.
3 He buylt the hye [c] gate of the house of
the Lord, and he buylt very muche on the
wall of the castel.
4 Moreouer he buylt cities in the mountaines of Iudáh, and in the forests he buylt
palaces and towres.
5 And he foght with the King of the children of Ammón, and preuailed against
them. And the children of Ammón gaue
him the same yere an hundreth talents of
siluer, and ten thousand " measures of
wheat, and ten thousand of barly: this did
the children of Ammón giue him" bothe
in the second yere and the third.
6 So Iothám became mightie [d] because he
directed his way before the Lord his God.
7 Concerning the rest of the actes of Iothám, and all his warres and his wayes, lo,
they are writen in the boke of the Kings
of Israél, and Iudáh.
8 He was fyue and twentie yere olde when
he began to reigne, and reigned sixtene
yere in Ierusalém.
9 And Iothám slept with his fathers, and
they buryed him in the citie of Dauid: &
Aház his sonne reigned in his stead.

* 2.King.15,33

a To wit, to offer incense against þ worde of God, which thing is spokē to the comendacion of Iothám.

b They were not cleane purged from idolatrie.

c Which was six score cubites hie, & was for the height called Ophel: it was at þ East gate, and mencion is made of it, chap.3,4.

" Ebr. Corim.

" Or, yerely.

d He sheweth that all prosperitie cometh of God, who neuer faileth, when we put our trust in him.

CHAP. XXVIII.

1 Aház an idolater is giuen into the hands of the Syriās, and the King of Israél. 9 The Prophet reproueth the Israelites crueltie. 18 Iudah is molested with enemies. 23 Aház increaseth his idolatrie. 26 His death and successour.

1 AHáz * *was* twentie yere olde when
he began to reigne, and reigned sixtene yere in Ierusalém, and did not vprightly in the sight of the Lord, like Dauid
his "father.
2 But [a] he walked in the wayes of þ Kings
of Israél and made euen molten images
for [b] Baalím.

* 2.King.16,2.

" Or, predecessour.

a He was an idolatre, like them.

b As the idolaters haue certeine chief idoles, who are as patrons: (as were these Baalím) so haue they others which are inferior & do represent þ great idoles.

3 Moreouer he burnt incense in the valley
of Ben-hinnóm, & " burnt his sonnes with
fyre, after the abominacions of the heathē
whome the Lord had cast out before the
children of Israél.
4 He sacrificed also and burnt incense in
the hie places, and on hilles, and vnder
euerie grene tre.
5 Wherefore the Lord his God deliuered
him into the hand of the King of the A-
ramites, and they smote him, and toke of
his, " manie prisoners, and broght them
to Damascus: and he was also deliuered
into the hand of the King of Israél, which
smote him with a great slaughter.
6 For [c] Pekáh the sonne of Remaliáh, slewe
in Iudáh six score thousand in one day, all
" valiant men, because they had forsaken
the Lord God of their fathers.
7 And Zichrí a " mightie man of Ephráim
slewe Maaseiáh the Kings sonne, and Azrikám the gouernour of the house, and Elkanáh the seconde after the King.
8 And the children of Israél toke prisoners
of their brethren, [d] two hundreth thousand of women, sonnes and daughters, and
caryed away muche spoile of them, and
broght the spoile to Samaria.
9 ¶ But there was a Prophet of the Lords,
(whose name *was* Odéd) and he went out
before the hoste that came to Samaria, &
said vnto them, Beholde, [e] because the
Lord God of your fathers is wroth with
Iudáh, he hathe deliuered them into your
hand, and ye haue slaine them in a rage,
that reacheth vp to heauen.
10 And now ye purpose to kepe vnder the
children of Iudáh and Ierusalém, as seruants and handmaides vnto you: but are
not you *suche, that* [f] sinnes *are* with you before the Lord your God?
11 Now therefore heare me, and deliuer the
captaines againe, which ye haue takē prisoners of your brethren: for þ fearce wrath
of the Lord *is* toward you.
12 Wherefore certeine of the chief of the
children of [g] Ephráim, Azariáh the sonne of Iehohanán, Berechiáh the sonne of
Meshillemóth, and Iehizkiáh the sonne of
Shallúm, and Amasá the sonne of Hadlái,
stode vp against them that came from the
warre,
13 And said vnto thē, Bring not in the captiues hether: for *this shalbe* [h] a sinne vpon
vs *against* the Lord: ye entēd to adde more to our sinnes and to our trespasse, thogh
our trespasse be great, & the fearce wrath
of God is against Israél.
14 So the armie left the captiues and the
spoile before the princes and all the Congregacion.
15 And the mē that were [i] named by name,
rose vp and toke the prisoners, and with

" Or, made them passe through the fyre, as Cha. 33,6 leu.18,21.

" Ebr. a great captiuitie.

c Who was Kīg of Israél.

" Ebr. sonnes of strength.

" Or, tyrant.

d Thus by the iuste iudgemēt of God Israél destroyed Iudáh.

e For they thoght they had ouercome them by their owne valiantnes, & did not consider that God had deliuered them into their hāds, because Iudáh had offended him.

f May not God aswel punish you for your sinnes, as he hathe done these men for theirs, seing yours are greater?

g Which tribe was now greatest, and had moste autoritie.

h God wil not suffre this sinne, which we comit against him, to be vnpunished.

i Whose names were rehearsed before, vers.12.

the ſpoile clothed all that were naked a-
mong them, and arayed them, and ſhod
them, and gaue them meat and gaue them
drinke, and [k] anointed them, and caryed
all that were feble of them vpon aſſes, &
broght them to Ierichó the citie of Palmetrees to their [l] brethren: ſo they returned to Samaria.

k Ether for their woundes or wearines.

l To them of the tribe of Iudáh.

16 ¶ At that time did King Aház ſend vnto
the [m] Kings of Aſſhúr, to helpe him.
17 (For the Edomites came moreouer, and
ſlewe of Iudáh, & caryed away captiues.
18 The Philiſtims alſo inuaded the cities in
the lowe countrey, and towarde the South
of Iudáh, and toke Bethſhémeſh and Aialón, and Gederóth and Shochó, with the
villages thereof, & Timnáh, with her villages, and Gimzo, with her villages, and
they dwelt there.

m To Tilgath Pilneéſer, and thoſe Kings ỹ were vnder his dominion, 2. King.16,7.

19 For the Lord had humbled Iudáh, becauſe of Aház King of [n] Iſraél: for he
had broght vengeance vpon Iudáh and
had grieuouſly tranſgreſſed againſt the
Lord)
20 And Tigláth Pilneéſer King of Aſſhúr
came vnto him who troubled him and did
not ſtrengthen him.
21 For Aház "toke a porcion * out of the
houſe of the Lord and out of the Kings
houſe and of the princes, and gaue vnto ỹ
King of Aſſhúr: yet it helped him not.
22 And in the time of his tribulacion did
he yet treſpaſſe more againſt the Lord,
(this is King Aház)
23 For he ſacrificed vnto the gods of Damaſcus, which [o] plagued him, & he ſaid,
Becauſe the gods of the Kings of Arám
helped them, I wil ſacrifice vnto them, &
they wil [p] helpe me: yet they were his
ruine, and of all "Iſraél.
24 And Aház gathered the veſſels of the
houſe of God, and brake the veſſels of the
houſe of God, and ſhut vp the dores of the
houſe of the Lord, and made him altars in
euerie corner of Ieruſalém.
25 And in euerie citie of Iudáh he made hie
places, to burne incenſe vnto other gods,
and prouoked to angre the Lord God of
his fathers.
26 Concerning the reſt of his actes, and all
his wayes firſt and laſt, beholde, they are
writen in the boke of the Kings of Iudáh,
and Iſraél.
27 And Aház ſlept with his fathers, & they
buryed him in the citie "of Ieruſalém, but
broght him not vnto the [q] ſepulchres of
the Kings of Iſraél: and Hezekiáh his ſonne reigned in his ſteade.

n He meaneth Iudáh, becauſe Aház forſoke the Lord and ſoght helpe of the infideles. read of Iſraél taken for Iudáh chap.15, 17.

" Ebr. diuided. 2.King.16,8.

o As he falſely ſuppoſed.

p Thus the wicked meaſure Gods fauour by proſperitie & aduerſitie: for if idolaters proſper, they make their idoles gods, not conſidering ỹ God puniſheth them oft times whome he loueth, & giueth his enemies good ſucceſſe for a time, whome afterwarde he wil deſtroye.

" Or, Iudáh and Beniamin.

" Or, in Ieruſalém.

q They buryed him not in the citie of Dauid where were ỹ ſepulchres of the Kings.

CHAP. XXIX.

3. 5 Hezekiáh repareth the Temple and aduertiſeth the Leuites of the corruption of religion. 12 The Leuites prepare the Temple. 20 The King and his princes ſacrifice in the Temple. 25 The Leuites ſing praiſes. 31 The oblacion of the people.

1 HEzekiáh * began to reigne, when he
was fyue and twentie yere olde, and
reigned nine and twentie yere in Ieruſalém: and his mothers name *was* "Abiiáh the
daughter of Zechariáh.
2 And he did vprightly in the ſight of the
Lord, according to all that Dauid his father had done.
3 He opened the [a] dores of the houſe of
the Lord in the firſt yere and in the [b] firſt
moneth of his reigne, and repared them.
4 And he broght in the Prieſts and the Leuites, and gathered them into the Eaſt
ſtrete,
5 And ſaid vnto them, Heare me, ye Leuites: ſanctifie now your ſelues, and ſanctifie
the houſe of ỹ Lord God of your fathers,
and carye forthe [c] the filthines out of the
Sanctuarie.
6 For our fathers haue treſpaſſed, and done
euil in the eyes of the Lord our God, and
haue forſaken him, and turned away their
faces from the Tabernacle of the Lord, &
turned their backes.
7 They haue alſo ſhut the dores of the
porche, and quenched the lampes, and haue nether burnt incenſe, nor offred burnt
offrings in the Sanctuarie vnto the God of
Iſraél.
8 [d] Wherefore the wrath of the Lord hathe
bene on Iudáh and Ieruſalém: & he hathe
made them a "ſcatering, a deſolacion, and
an hiſsing, as ye ſe with your eyes.
9 For lo, our fathers are fallẽ by ỹ ſworde,
and our ſonnes, & our daughters, and our
wiues *are* in captiuitie for the ſame cauſe.
10 Now "I purpoſe to make a couenant
with the Lord God of Iſraél, that he may
[e] turne away his fearce wrath from vs.
11 Now my ſonnes, be not deceiued: for
the Lord hathe * choſen you to ſtand before him, to ſerue him, and to be his miniſters, and to burne incenſe.
12 ¶ Then the Leuites aroſe, Maháth the
ſonne of Amaſhái, and Ioél the ſonne of
Azariáh of the ſonnes of the Kohathites
and of the ſonnes of Merari, Kiſh the ſonne of Abdí, and Azariáh the ſonne of Ie-
halelél: and of the Gerſhonites, Ioáh the
ſonne of Zimmáh, and Edén the ſonne of
Ioáh:
13 And of the ſonnes of Elizaphán, Shimrí,
and Iehiél: & of the ſonnes of Aſáph, Zechariáh, and Mattaniáh:
14 And of the ſonnes of Hemán, Iehiél, and
Shimeí: and of the ſonnes of Ieduthún,
Shemaiáh and Vzziél.
15 And they gathered their brethren, and
ſanctified them ſelues & came according
to the commandement of the King, *and* "by
the wordes of the Lord, for to clenſe the
houſe of the Lord.

2.King.18,1.

" Or, Abi.

a Which Aház had ſhut vp, Chap.28, 24.

b This is a notable example for all princes, firſt to eſtabliſh the pure religion of God, and to procure that ỹ Lord may be honored and ſerued aright.

c Meaning all the idoles, altars, groues & whatſoeuer was occupied in their ſeruice, and where with the Temple was polluted.

d He ſheweth that the contempt of religion is the cauſe of all Gods plagues.

" Or, a nodding of the head and mockerie.

" Ebr. it is in mine heart.

e He proueth by the iudgements of God vpon thoſe ỹ haue contemned his worde, that there is no way to auoyde his plagues, but by cõforming the ſelues to his wil.

Nom.18,6.

" Or, concerning the things of the Lord.

16 And the Prieſts went into the inner partes of the houſe of the Lord,to [f] clenſe it,
& broght out all the vnclennes that they
founde in the Temple of the Lord , into
the courte of the houſe of the Lord : and
the Leuites toke it,to carie it out vnto the
broke Kidrón.

f Frõ the pollucions and filth that Aház had broght in.

17 They began the firſt *day* of the [g] firſt
moneth to ſanctifie it,and the eight day of
the moneth came they to the porche of ŷ
Lord:ſo they ſanctified the houſe of the
Lord in eight dayes,and in the ſixtẽte day
of the firſt moneth they made an end.

g Which conteined parte of Marche and parte of April.

18 ¶Then they went in to Hezekiáh the
King , and ſaid, We haue clenſed all the
houſe of the Lord and the altar of burnt
offring,with all the veſſels thereof, & the
[*] ſhewbread table , with all the veſſels
thereof:

Or,table where the bread was ſet in ordre.

19 And all the veſſels which King Aház
had caſt aſide when he reigned, *and* tranſgreſſed,haue we prepared and ſanctified:
and beholde, they are before the altar of
the Lord.
20 ¶And Hezekiáh the King [h] roſe early,
and gathered the princes of the citie, and
went vp to the houſe of the Lord.
21 And they broght ſeuen bullockes, and
ſeuen rams , and ſeuen lambes , and ſeuen
hegoates, for a * ſin offring for the kingdome, and for the ſanctuarie, and for Iudáh . And he commanded the Prieſts the
ſonnes of Aarón,to offer *them* on the altar
of the Lord.

h By this maner of ſpeache the Ebrewes meane a certeine dilıgẽce & ſpede to do a thing,& whẽ there is no delay.

Leui.4,14.

22 So they ſlewe the bullockes,and ŷ Prieſts
receiued the blood,& [i] ſprinkled it vpon
the altar:they ſlewe alſo the rams & ſprinkled the blood vpon the altar, and they
ſlewe the lambes , and they ſprinkled the
blood vpon the altar.

i For without ſprinkling of blood nothing colde be ſanctified, Ebr.9,21.exod.24,8.

23 Then they broght the hegoates for the
ſinne offring before the King & the Cõgregacion , [k] and they laied their hands
vpon them.
24 And the Prieſts ſlewe them , & with the
blood of them they clẽſed the altar to reconcile all Iſraél : for the King had commanded for all Iſraél the burnt offring &
the ſinne offring.

k That is,the King and the Elders,as Leu.4,15 for they that offred a ſinne offring , muſt lay their hands vpon it, to ſignifie that they had deſerued that death,and alſo that they did conſecrat it to God to be thereby ſanctified, Exod. 29,10.

25 He appointed alſo the Leuites in the
houſe of the Lord with cymbales, with
violes,and with harpes,*according to the
commandement of Dauid , and Gad the
Kings Seer,and Nathán the Prophet: for
the [l] commandement *was* by the hand of
the Lord,*and* by the hãd of his Prophetes.

1.Chro.16,4.

l This thing was not appoĩted of mã, but it was the commandemẽt of God.

26 And the Leuites ſtode with the inſtruments of Dauid, and the Prieſts with the
trumpets.
27 And Hezekiáh commanded to offer the
burnt offring vpon the altar : & when the
burnt offring begã,the ſong of the [m] Lord
began with the trumpets, and the inſtruments [n] of Dauid King of Iſraél.

m The Pſalme which Dauid had appointed to be ſung for thãkes giuing.

n Which Dauid had appointed to praiſe ŷ Lord with.

28 And all the Congregacion worſhiped,
ſinging a ſong,and thei blewe the trum-
pets:all this *continued* vntil the burnt offring was finiſhed.
29 And when they had made an end of offring,the King and all that were preſent
with him,bowed them ſelues,and worſhiped.
30 ¶Thẽ Hezekiáh the King & the princes
commanded the Leuites to praiſe the
Lord with the [o] wordes of Dauid , and
of Aſáph the Seer . ſo thei praiſed with
ioye , and thei bowed them ſelues , and
worſhiped.

o With that pſalme whereof mencion is made 1.Chro. 16,8.

31 And Hezekiáh ſpake,and ſaid , Now ye
haue ''conſecrate your ſelues to the Lord:
come nere and bring the ſacrifices and *of-*
frings of praiſe into the houſe of the Lord.
And the Congregacion broght ſacrifices,
and *offrings* of praiſes,and euerie man that
was willing in heart,*offred* burnt offrings.

''Ebr filled your hands.

32 And the nomber of the burnt offrings,
which the Congregacion broght,was ſe-
uẽtie bullockes,an hundreth rammes, *and*
two hundreth lambes : all theſe were for
a burnt offring to the Lord:
33 And for [p] ſanctification ſix hundreth bul
lockes, and thre thouſand ſhepe.

p That is, for the holy offrings.

34 But the Prieſts were to fewe, & were not
able to flay all the burnt offrings:therefo-
re their brethren the Leuites did helpe
them,til they had ended the worke, & vntil *other* Prieſts were ſanctified:for the Leuites were [q] more vpright in heart to ſanctifie them ſelues,then the Prieſts.

q Meanĩg, were more zealous to ſet forward the religion.

35 And alſo the burnt offrings were many
with the *fat of the peace offrings and the
drinke offrings for the burnt offring. ſo
the ſeruice of the houſe of the Lord was
ſet in order.

Leu.3,2.

36 Then Hezekiáh reioyced & all the people,that God had made the people ſo [r] rea
dy:for the thing was done ſodenly.

r He ſheweth that religion can not procede,except God touche the heart of the people.

CHAP. XXX.

1.13 The keping of the Paſſeouer by the Kings cõmã-
dement. 6 He exhorteth Iſraél to turne to the Lord.
18 He praieth for the people.24 His oblation and the
princes.27 The Leuites bleſſe the people.

1 AND Hezekiáh ſent to all Iſraél , and
Iudáh,and alſo wrote letters to [a] E-
phráim and Manaſſéh,that thei ſhulde come to the houſe of the Lord at Ieruſalém,
to kepe the Paſſeouer vnto the Lord God
of Iſraél.

a Meaning all Iſraél whome Tilgáth Pilneéſar had not taken away into the captiuitie, 2 King.15,29.

2 And the King and his princes and all the
Congregacion had taken counſel in Ieruſalém to kepe the Paſſeouer in the [b] ſecõde moneth.
3 For thei colde not kepe it at this time,
becauſe there were not Prieſts ynow ſanctified,nether was the people gathered to
Ieruſalém.

b Thogh thei oght to haue done it in the firſt moneth, as Exod.12,18. nom.9,3 ,yet if any were not cleane , or els had a long iornei,thei might differ it vnto the ſecõde moneth, as Nom. 9,10.

4 And the thing pleaſed the King, and
all the Congregacion.
5 And they decreed to make proclamacion
throughout all Iſraél from c Beerſhéba
euen to Dan, that they ſhulde come to kepe the Paſſeouer vnto the Lord God of
Iſraél at Ieruſalém: for they had not done
it of a great *time*, d as it was writen.
6 ¶ So the poſtes went with letters by the
commiſsion of the King, and his princes,
throughout all Iſraél and Iudáh, and with
the commandement of the King, ſaying,
Ye childrē of Iſraél, turne againe vnto the
Lord God of Abrahám, Izhák, and Iſraél,
and e he wil returne to the remnant that
are eſcaped of you, out of the hands of the
Kings of Aſſhúr.
7 And be not ye like your fathers, and like
your brethren, which treſpaſſed againſt
the Lord God of their fathers: *and* therefore he made them deſolate, as ye ſe.
8 Be not ye now ſtifnecked like your fathers, *but* f giue the hād to the Lord & come into his Sāctuarie, which he hathe ſanctified for euer, and ſerue the Lord your
God, and the fearcenes of his wrath ſhal
turne away from you.
9 For if ye returne vnto ẏ Lord, your brethren and your children *ſhal finde* mercie
before them that led them captiues, and
they ſhal g returne vnto this land: for the
Lord your God is gracious and merciful,
and wil not turne away his face from you,
if ye conuert vnto him.
10 ¶ So the poſtes went from citie to citie
through the land of Ephráim and Manaſſéh, euen vnto Zebulún: but they h laughed them to ſcorne, and mocked them.
11 Neuertheles diuers of Aſhér, and Manaſſéh, and of Zebulún ſubmitted them
ſelues, and came to Ieruſalém.
12 And the hand of God was in Iudáh, ſo
that he gaue them one i heart to do the cōmandemēt of the King, and of the rulers,
according to the worde of the Lord.
13 And there aſſembled to Ieruſalém muche
people, to kepe the feaſt of ẏ vnleauened
bread in the ſeconde moneth, a very great
aſſemblie.
14 ¶ And they aroſe, & toke away the k altars that were in Ieruſalém: and all thoſe
for incenſe toke they away, and caſt them
into the broke Kidrón.
15 Afterward they ſlewe the Paſſeouer the
fourtente *day* of the ſeconde moneth: and
the Prieſts and Leuites were l aſhamed,
and ſanctified them ſelues, and broght the
burnt offrings into the houſe of the Lord.
16 And they ſtode in their place after their
maner, according to the Law of Moſés
the man of God: *and* the Prieſts ſprinkled
the m blood, *receiued* of the hands of the
Leuites.
17 Becauſe there were manie in the Cōgregacion that were not ſanctified, therefore
the Leuites had the charge of the killing
of ẏ Paſſeouer for all that were not cleane, to ſanctifie it to the Lord.
18 For a multitude of the people, *euen* a mul
titude of Ephráim, & Manaſſéh, Iſſachár
& Zebulún had not clenſed them ſelues,
yet did eat the Paſſeouer, *but* not as it was
writen: wherefore Hezekiáh prayed for
them, ſaying, The n good Lord be merciful toward *him*,
19 That prepareth his whole heart to ſeke ẏ
Lord God, the God of his fathers, thogh
he be not *clenſed*, according to the purificacion of the Sanctuarie.
20 And the Lord heard Hezekiáh, & o healed the people.
21 And the children of Iſraél that were pre
ſent at Ieruſalém, kept the feaſt of the vnleauened bread ſeuen dayes wͭ great ioye,
and the Leuites, and the Prieſts praiſed
the Lord, day by day, ſinging with lowde
inſtruments vnto the Lord.
22 And Hezekiáh "ſpake comfortably vnto
all ẏ Leuites that had good knowledge *to*
ſing vnto the Lord: & they did eat in that
feaſt ſeuen dayes, & offred peace offrings,
& praiſed the Lord God of their fathers.
23 And the whole aſſemblie toke counſel to
kepe it other ſeuen dayes. So thei kept it
ſeuen dayes with ioye.
24 For Hezekiáh King of Iudáh had giuen
to the Congregacion a p thouſand bullockes, and ſeuen thouſand ſhepe. And
the princes had giuen to the Congregacion a thouſand bullockes, and ten thouſand ſhepe: and many Prieſts were ſanctified.
25 And all the Congregaciō of Iudáh reioyced with the Prieſts and the Leuites, &
all the Congregacion that came out of
Iſraél, and the ſtrangers that came out of
the land of Iſraél, & that dwelt in Iudáh.
26 So there was great ioye in Ieruſalém: for
ſince the time of Salomón the ſonne of
Dauid King of Iſraél there *was* not the
like thing in Ieruſalém.
27 Then the Prieſts and the Leuites aroſe, and q bleſſed the people, and their voyce was heard, and their prayer came vp vn
to heauen, to his holy habitacion.

CHAP. XXXI.

1 The people deſtroye idolatrie. 2 Hezekiáh appointeth Prieſts & Leuites. 4 And prouideth for their liuing. 13 He ordeineth ouerſeers to diſtribute to euerie one his portion.

1 And whē all theſe thīgs were finiſhed,
all Iſraél that were founde in ẏ cities
of Iudáh, went out & a brake the images, &
cut downe the groues, & brake downe the
hie places, and the altars through out all
Iudáh & Beniamín, in Ephráim alſo, and
Manaſſéh,

c Frō one end of the land to ẏ other, North and South.

d In ſuche ſort and perfectiō, as God had appointed.

e He wil haue compaſſion on them, and preſerue them.

f Submit your ſelues to the Lord, and rebelle no more.

g God wil not onely preſerue you, but through your repentance reſtore your brethren, which for their ſinnes he gaue into the handes of the enemies.

h Thogh the wicked mocke at the ſeruants of God, by whome he calleth thē to repētāce, as Gen. 19,14, yet the worde ceaſeth not to fructifie in the heartes of Gods elect.

i He ſheweth the cauſe why ſome obey & ſome mocke at Gods calling, to wit, becauſe his Spirit is with the one ſort & moueth their heart, & the other are left to them ſelues.

k Which declareth that we muſt put away thoſe things wherewith God is offended, before we can ſerue him aright.

l Seing their owne negligēce (who ſhulde haue bene more prompt) & the readines of the people, Chap. 29,36.

m To wit, of the lambe of the Paſſeouer.

n He knewe, ẏ faith and ſinceritie of heart was more agreable to God, then the obſeruatiō of theſe ceremonies, & therefore he praied vnto God to pardon this faute vnto the people, which did not offend of malice but of ignorance.

o That is, did accept thē as purified.

" Ebr. ſpake to the heart.

p This great liberalitie declareth how Kings, princes & all they, to whome God hathe giuen wherewith, oght to be moſte ready to beſtowe it in ſetting forthe of Gods glorie.

q According to that which is writen Nō. 6,23, whē thei ſhulde dimiſſe the people.

a According to the comandemēt of the Lord, Deut. 7,25. ioſh. 7,1. 2.mac. 12,40.

Manasséh, vntil they had made an end: afterward all the [b] childrē of Israél returned
euerie mā to his possession, into their owne cities.

b That is, all they which came to the Passeouer.

2 And Hezekiáh appointed the courses of
the Priests and Leuites by their turnes, e-
uerie man according to his office, *bothe*
Priests & Leuites, for the burnt offring &
peace offrings, to minister & to giue thankes, and to praise in the gates of the [c] tents
of the Lord.

c That is, in ỳ Temple where thei assembled as in a tent.

3 (And the Kings porcion *was* of his owne substance for the burnt offrings, *euen*
for the burnt offrīgs of the morning & of
the euening, and the burnt offrings for the
Sabbaths, and for the new moones, & for
the solemne feastes, * as it is writen in the
Law of the Lord)

Nom.28,3. & 9.

4 He commāded also the people that dwelt
in Ierusalém, to giue a [d] parte to the Priests, and Leuites, that they might be [e] encouraged in the Law of the Lord.

d The tithes & first frutes for the maintenāce of ỳ Priests and Leuites.

e That their mindes might not be intangled with prouision of wordely thīgs, but ỳ they might wholy & cherefully serue the Lord.

5 ¶ And whē the commādement was "spred,
the children of Israél broght abundance
of first frutes, of corne, wine, & oyle, & honie, & of all the increase of the field, and
the tithes of all things broght they abundantly.

" Or, published.

6 And the children of Israél & Iudáh that
dwelt in ỳ cities of Iudáh, thei also broght
the tithes of bullockes and shepe, and the
holy tithes [f] ẇ were cōsecrate vnto ỳ Lord
their God, & laid them on [g] many heapes.

f Which they had dedicate to the Lord by a vowe.

g For the relief of the Priests, Leuites, widowes, pupilles, fatherlesse, strangers & suche as were in necessitie.

7 In the third moneth they began to laye
the fundacion of the heapes, and finished
them in the seuent moneth.

8 ¶ And when Hezekiáh & the princes came, and sawe the heapes, thei [h] blessed the
Lord and his people Israél.

h Thei praised the Lord, and praied for all prosperitie to his people.

9 And Hezekiáh questioned ẇ the Priests
and the Leuites concerning the heapes.

10 And Azariáh ỳ chief Priest of the house of Zadók answered him, & said, Since
the people begā to bring the offrings into
the house of the Lord, we haue [i] eaten &
haue bene satisficed, & there is left in abūdāce: for the Lord hathe blessed his people, and this abundance that is left.

i He sheweth that this plēteous liberalitie is expediēt for ỳ maintenance of the ministers, and that God therefore prospereth his people, & increaseth by his blessing that which is giuē.

11 ¶ And Hezekiáh cōmanded to prepare
chambers in the house of the Lord: and
they prepared them,

12 And caryed in the first frutes, and the
tithes, & the dedicate things faithfully: &
ouer thē *was* Conaniáh the Leuite, ỳ chief,
and Shimeí his brother the seconde.

13 And Iehiél, and Azaziáh, & Náhath, &
Asahél, & Ierimóth, and Iozabád, and E-
liél, and Ismachiáh, and Máhath, and Benaiáh *were* ouerseers " by the appointement of Conaniáh, and Shimeí his brother, & by the cōmandement of Hezekiáh
the King, and of Azariáh the chief of the
house of God.

" Ebr. by the hand.

14 And Koré the sōne of Imnáh the Leuite porter toward the East, *was* ouer the
things ỳ were willingly offred vnto God,
to distribute the oblations of the Lord, &
the holy things that were consecrate.

15 And at his hand *were* Edén, & Miniamín,
& Ieshúa, & Shemaiáh, Amariáh, and Shechaniáh, in the cities of the Priests, to distribute with fidelitie to their brethrē by
courses, bothe to the great and small,

16 Their daily porcion: beside their generacion being males [k] from thre yere olde
and aboue, *euen* to all that entred into the
house of the Lord to their office in their
charge, according to their courses:

k Who had also a portion & alowance in this distribution.

17 Bothe to the generaciō of the Priests after the house of their fathers, & to the Le
uites from twentie yere olde & aboue, according to their charge in their courses:

18 And to the generacion of all their children, their wiues, & their sonnes and their
daughters throughout all the Congregacion: for by their [l] fidelitie are thei partakers of the holy things.

l Meanīg, that ether by the faithful distributions of the officers, euerie one had their parte in the thīgs that were offred, or els that their wiues & childrē were relieued, because the Leuites were faithful in their office, and so depended on them.

19 Also to the sonnes of Aarón, the Priests,
which were in ỳ fields & suburbes of their
cities, in euerie citie the men that were ap
pointed by names, shulde giue porcions
to all the males of the Priests, and to all
the generacion of the Leuites.

20 And thus did Hezekiáh throughout all
Iudáh, and did wel, and vprightly, & truely before the Lord his God.

21 And in all the workes that he began for
the seruice of the house of God, bothe in
the Law and in the commandements, to
seke his God, he did it with all his heart, &
prospered.

CHAP. XXXII.

1 Sanneherib inuadeth Iudáh. 3 Hezekiáh prepareth for the warre. 7 He exhorteth the people to put their trust in the Lord. 9 Sanneherib blasphemeth God. 20 Hezekiáh prayeth. 21 The Angel destroieth the Assyrians, and the King is slaine. 25 Hezekiáh is not thankful toward the Lord. 33 His death.

1 AFter these things faithfully *described*,
* Sanneheríb King of Asshúr came
and entred into Iudáh, and besieged the
strōg cities, & thoght to " winne them for
him selfe.

2. Kin. 18, 13. isai. 30, 1. eccles. 48, 20.

" Ebr. breake them vp.

2 When Hezekiáh sawe that Sanneheríb
was come, & that his " purpose *was* to fight
against Ierusalém,

" Ebr. face.

3 Then he toke counsel with his princes
and his nobles, to stoppe the water of the
fountaines without the citie: and they did
helpe him.

4 So many of the people assembled them
selues, and stopt all the fountaines, and
the riuer that ran through the middes
of the countrey, saying, Why shulde the
Kings of Asshúr come, and finde muche
water?

"Ebr. he was strengthened.

a He made a double wall.
b Read 2.Sam. 5,9.
c Some read, swordes or daggers.

"He spake to their heart.

5 "And he toke courage, and buylt all the
broken wall, and made vp the towres, &
another wall without, & repared a Milló
in the b citie of Dauid, and made many
c dartes and shields.
6 And he set captaines of warre ouer the
people and assembled them to him in the
broad place of the gate of the citie, and
"spake comfortably vnto them, saying,
7 Be strong and couragious: feare not, nether be afraied for the King of Asshúr, nether for all the multitude that is with
him: for there *be* mo with vs, then *is* with
him.

d That is, the power of man.
e This declareth that Ezekiáh did euer put his trust in God, and yet made him selfe strong and vsed lawful meanes, lest he shulde seme to tempt God.
2.Kin.18,17.
f While he besieged Lachish.

8 With him *is* an d arme of flesh, but with
vs *is* the e Lord our God for to helpe vs,
and to fight our battels. Then the people
were confirmed by the wordes of Hezekiáh King of Iudáh.
9 *After this, did Sanneheríb King of Asshúr send his seruants to Ierusalém (while
he was f against Lachísh, and all his domi
nion with him) vnto Hezekiáh King of Iu
dáh and vnto all Iudáh that were at Ierusalém, saying,
10 Thus saith Sanneheríb the King of
Asshúr, Wherein do ye trust, that ye wil
remaine in Ierusalém, *during* the siege?
11 Doeth not Hezekiáh entice you to giue
ouer your selues vnto death by famine &
by thirst, saying, The Lord our God shal
deliuer vs out of the hand of the King of
Asshúr?

g Thus ẏ wicked put no difference betwene true religion & false, God & idoles: for Hezekiáh onely destroied idolatrie & placed true religion thus ẏ Papists slander the seruãts of God: for when they destroie idolatrie, they say that they abolish religion.
h This is his blasphemie, ẏ he wil compare the liuig God to vile idoles
i When man hathe prosperitie, he swelleth in pride and thinketh him selfe able to resist and ouercome euẽ God him self.
k Herein we se that when ẏ wicked speake euil of the seruants of God, they care not to blaspheme God him self: for if they feared God, they wolde loue his seruants.

12 Hathe not ẏ same Hezekiáh takẽ awaie
his hie places and his g altars and cõmã
ded Iudáh and Ierusalém, saying, Ye shal
worship before one altar, and burne incẽse vpon it?
13 Knowe ye not what I and my fathers haue done vnto all the people of *other* countreies? Were the gods of the nations of
other lands able to deliuer their land out
of mine hand?
14 Who is he of all the h gods of those nacions (that my fathers haue destroied)
that colde deliuer his people out of mine
hand? that your God shulde be able to deliuer you out of mine hand?
15 Now therefore let not Hezekiáh deceiue you, nor seduce you after this sorte, ne
ther beleue ye him: for none of all ẏ gods
of any nacion or kingdome was able to
deliuer his people out of i mine hand and
out of ẏ hand of my fathers: how muche
lesse shal your gods deliuer you out of mine hand?
16 And his seruants spake yet more against
the Lord God, & against his k seruant Hezekiáh.
17 He wrote also letters, blaspheming the
Lord God of Israél and speaking against
him, saying, As the gods of the nacions of
other countreis colde not deliuer their people out of mine hand, so shal not the God
of Hezekiáh deliuer his people out of mine hand.
18 Then they l cryed with a loude voyce in
the Iewes speache vnto the people of Ierusalém that were on the wall, to feare thẽ
and to astonish them, that they might take the citie.
19 Thus they spake against the God of Ierusalém, as against the gods of the people
of the earth, *euen* the m workes of mans
hands.
20 But Hezekiáh the King, and the Prophet
Isaiáh the sonne of Amóz n praied agaĩst
this and cryed to heauen.
21 And the Lord sent an Angel which destroied all the valiant men, and the prĩces
and o captaines of the hoste of the King
of Asshúr: so he returned "with shame to
his owne land. And when he was come into the house of his god, they that came
forthe of his p owne bowels, slewe him there with the sworde.
22 So the Lord saued Hezekiáh and the inhabitants of Ierusalém from the hand
of Sanneheríb King of Asshúr, and from
the hand of all *other*, and "mainteined thẽ
on euerie side.
23 And many broght offrings vnto ẏ Lord
to Ierusalém, and presents to Hezekiáh
King of Iudáh, so that he was q magnified
in the sight of all nacions from thence
forthe.
24 *In those dayes Hezekiáh was sicke vnto the death, and praied vnto the Lord,
who spake vnto him, and gaue him r a
signe.
25 But Hezekiáh did not rendre accordĩg
to the rewarde *bestowed* vpon him: for his
heart f was lift vp, and wrath came vpon
him, and vpon Iudáh and Ierusalém.
26 Notwithstanding Hezekiáh humbled
him selfe (after that his heart was lifted
vp) he and the inhabitants of Ierusalém,
and the wrath of the Lord came not vpon them in the daies of Hezekiáh.
27 Hezekiáh also had excedĩg muche riches
& honour, & he gate him treasures of siluer, & of golde, and of precious stones, &
of swete odours, and of shields, and of
all pleasant vessels:
28 And of store houses for the increase of
wheat, and wine and oyle, and stalles for
all beastes, and "rowes for the "stables.
29 And he made him cities, and *had* possession of shepe and oxen in abundance: for
God had giuen him substance exceding
muche.
30 This same Hezekiáh also stopped the
vpper water springs of t Gihón, and led
thẽ streight vnderneth toward ẏ citie of
Dauid Westward. so Hezekiáh prospered
in all his workes.

31 But

l Their wordes are writẽ 2.King 18,19.
m Which were inuẽted, made and autorized by man.
n This sheweth what is ẏ best refuge in all troubles & dangers.
o To the nomber of an hundreth fourescore and fiue thousand, as 2.King. 19,35.
"Ebr. with shame of face.
p Meanĩg, Adramélech, and Sharézer his sonnes.
"Or, gouerned.
q Thus after trouble, God sendeth cõfort to all them ẏ patiẽtly waite on him, and cõstãtly put their trust in his mercies.
2.King.20,1. isa.38,1.
r To confirme his faith in Gods promes, who declared to him by his Prophet that his life shulde be prolonged fiftene yere.
f He was lifted vp with ẏ pride of his victorie & treasures, & shewed them for an ostentation to the ambassadours of Babylon.
"Or, ranges, and partitions.
"Or, rackes.
t Which also was called Siloe, whereof mencion is made Isa.8,6. ioh.9,7.

31 But becauſe of the ambaſſadours of the
princes of Babél, which ſent vnto him to
enquire of the wondre that was done in
the land, God left him to [u] trye him, & to
knowe all that was in his heart.
32 Concerning the reſt of the actes of Hezekiáh, and his goodnes, beholde, thei are
writen in the viſion of Iſhaiáh the Prophet, the ſonne of Amóz, in the boke of
the Kings of Iudáh and Iſraél.
33 So Hezekiáh ſlept with his fathers, and
they buryed him in the higheſt ſepulchre
of the ſonnes of Dauid: and all Iudáh and
the inhabitants of Ieruſalém did him honour at his death: and Manaſséh his ſonne
reigned in his ſtead.

u Here we ſe the cauſe, why the faithful are tempted, ẘ is to trye whether they haue faith or no, and that they may fele the preſence of God, who ſuffreth them not to be ouercome by tentacions, but in their weakenes miniſtreth ſtrength.

CHAP. XXXIII.

2 Manaſséh an idolater. 9 He cauſeth Iudáh to erre. 11 He is led away priſoner into Babylón. 12 He praieth to the Lord, and is deliuered. 14 He aboliſheth idolatrie. 16 And ſetteth vp true religion. 20 He dyeth and Amón his ſonne ſucedeth, 24 Whome his owne ſeruants ſlay.

1 MAnaſséh *was* twelue yere olde, * whé
he began to reigne, and he reigned
fiue and fiftie yere in Ieruſalém:
2 And he did euil in the ſight of the Lord,
like the abominacions of the heathen,
* whome the Lord had caſt out before the
children of Iſraél.
3 For he went backe and buylt the hie places, * which Hezekiáh his father had broken downe: * and he ſet vp altars for Baa-
lim, and made groues, and worſhiped all
the hoſte of the heauen, and ſerued them.
4 Alſo he buylt altars in the houſe of the
Lord, whereof the Lord had ſaid, * In Ieruſalém ſhal my Name be for euer.
5 And he buylt altars for all the hoſte of
the heaué in the two courtes of the houſe
of the Lord.
6 [a] And he cauſed his ſonnes to paſſe
through ẏ fyre in the valley of Ben-hinnóm: he gaue him ſelfe to witchcraft and
to charming, and to ſorcerie, and he vſed
them that had familiar ſpirits, and ſothe-
ſayers: he did verie muche euil in ẏ ſight
of the Lord to angre him.
7 He put alſo the karued image, which he
had made, in the houſe of God: whereof
God had ſaid to Dauid and to Salomón
his ſonne, * In this houſe & in Ieruſalém,
which I haue choſen before all the tribes
of Iſraél, wil I put my Name for euer,
8 Nether wil * I make the foote of Iſraél to
remoue any more out of the land which I
haue appointed for your fathers, ſo that
they take hede, & do all that I haue commanded them, according to the Law and
ſtatutes and iudgements by the [b] hand of
Moſés.
9 So Manaſséh made Iudáh and the inha-
bitáts of Ieruſalém to erre, & to do worſe
then the heathen, whome the Lord had
deſtroyed before the children of Iſraél.
10 ¶ And the Lord ſpake [c] to Manaſséh &
to his people, but they wolde not regarde.
11 Wherefore the Lord broght vpon them
the captaines of the hoſte of the King of
Aſſhúr, which toke Manaſséh & *put him* in
fetters, and bounde him in chaines, and caryed him to Babél.
12 And when he was in tribulació, he prayed to the Lord his God, and humbled him
ſelfe greatly before ẏ God of his fathers,
13 And prayed vnto him: and *God* was [d] entreated of him, and heard his prayer, and
broght him againe to Ieruſalém into his
kingdome: thé Manaſséh knewe that the
Lord was God.
14 Now after this he buylt a wall without
the citie of Dauid, on the Weſtſide of
[e] Gihón in the valley, eué at the entrie of
the fiſh gate, & compaſſed about [f] Ophél,
and raiſed it very hie, and put captaines of
warre in all the ſtrong cities of Iudáh.
15 And he toke away the ſtrange gods and
the image out of the houſe of the Lord,
and all the altars that he had buylt in the
mount of the houſe of the Lord, and in
Ieruſalém, and caſt them out of the citie.
16 Alſo he prepared the [g] altar of ẏ Lord,
and ſacrificed thereon peace offrings, and
of thankes, and commanded Iudáh to ſerue the Lord God of Iſraél.
17 Neuertheles the people did ſacrifice ſtil
in the hie places, but vnto ẏ [h] Lord their
God.
18 ¶ Concerning the reſt of the actes of
Manaſséh, and his [i] prayer vnto his God,
and the wordes of the Seers, that ſpake to
him in the Name of the Lord God of Iſraél, beholde, thei are *writen* in the boke of
the Kings of Iſraél.
19 And his prayer and how *God* was intreated of him, and all his ſinne, and his treſpaſſe, and the places wherein he buylt hie
places, and ſet groues and images (before
he was humbled) beholde, they are writen
in the boke of ″ the Seers.
20 So Manaſséh ſlept with his fathers, and
they buryed him in his owne [k] houſe: and
Amón his ſonne reigned in his ſtead.
21 ¶ Amón *was* two and twentie yere olde,
when he began to reigne, and reigned two
yere in Ieruſalém.
22 But he did euil in the ſight of the Lord,
as did Manaſséh his father: for Amón ſacrificed to all the images, which Manaſséh
his father had made, and ſerued them,
23 And he humbled not him ſelf before the
Lord, as Manaſséh his father had humbled
him ſelfe: but this Amón treſpaſſed more
and more.
24 And his ſeruants * conſpired againſt
him, and ſlewe him in his owne houſe.

2.King.21,1. — *Deut.18,9.* — *2 King.18,4.* — *Iere.32,34.* — *2.King.21,5.* — *1 King.8,29. & 9,3. 2.king 7,10. & 21,7.* — *2.Sam.7,10.* — *2.King.21,23*

a Read 2 King. 16,3.

b By the charge giué to Moſés.

c Meaning, by his Prophetes, but their hearts were not touched to beleue & repent without the ẘ the preaching of the worde taketh no place.

d Thus afflictió giueth vnderſtáding: for he that hated God in his proſperitie, now in his miſerie he ſeketh vnto him.

e Read Chap. 32,30.

f Read Chap. 27,3.

g Which Salomón had cauſed to be made.

h Thus by ignorance they were deceiued thinking it nothing to kepe the altars, ſo that thei worſhiped God: but it is idolatrie to worſhip God anie otherwiſe then he hathe appointed.

i Which albeit that it is not conteined in the Ebrew, yet becauſe it is here mécioned & is writé in the Greke, we haue placed it in ẏ end of this boke.

″ Or, Hozai.

k Becauſe he had ſo horribly offended againſt ẏ Lord, they did not burye him in ẏ ſepulchres of the Kings, but in the garden of the Kings houſe.

25 But the people of the land slewe all thē
that had conspired against King Amón:
and the people of the land made Iosiáh
his sonne King in his stead.

CHAP. XXXIIII.

3 Iosiáh destroyeth the idoles. 8 And restoreth the Temple. 14 The boke of the Lawe is founde. 21 He sendeth to Huldáh the prophetesse for counsel. 27 God heareth his prayer. 31 He maketh a couenant with God.

1 IOsiáh* *was* eight yere olde whē he began to reigne, and he reigned in Ierusalém one and thirtie yere.
2 And he did vprightly in the sight of the
Lord, and walked in the wayes of [a] Dauid
his father, and bowed nether to the right
hand nor to the left.
3 And in the eight yere of his reigne (when
he was yet a [b] childe) he began to seke after the God of Dauid his father: and in
the twelft yere he began to purge Iudáh,
and Ierusalém from the hie places, and the
groues, and the kerued images, and moltē
images:
4 And they brake downe [c] in his sight the
altars of Baalím, and he caused to cut
downe the images that were on hie vpon
them: he brake also the groues, & the kerued images, and the molten images, and
stampt them to poudre, and strowed it vpon the graues of them that had sacrificed
vnto them.
5 Also he burnt the [d] bones of the Priests
vpon their altars, and purged Iudáh and
Ierusalém.
6 And in ỹ cities of Manasséh, & Ephráim,
and Simeón, euen vnto Naphtalí, with
their maules *they brake all* rounde about.
7 And when he had [e] destroyed the altars
and the groues, and had broken and stamped to poudre the images, and had cut
downe all the idoles throughout all the
land of Israél, he returned to Ierusalém.
8 ¶ * Then in the eightente yere of his
reigne when he had purged the land and
the Temple, he sent Shaphán the sonne of
Azaliáh, and Maaseáh the gouernour of
the citie, and Ioáh the sonne of Ioaház the
recorder, to repare the house of the Lord
his God.
9 And when they came to Hilkiáh the hie
Priest, they deliuered the money that was
broght into the house of God, which the
Leuites that kept the dore, had gathered
at the hand of Manasséh, and Ephráim, &
of all the residue of Israél, and of all Iudáh and Beniamín, and ' of the inhabitāts
of Ierusalém.
10 And they put it in the hands of them
that shulde do the worke & had the ouersight in the house of the Lord: and they
gaue it to the workemen that wroght in
the house of the Lord, to repare & amende the house.

2.King.22,1.

a He followed Dauid in all pointes that he followed ỹ Lord.

b When he was but sixtene yere olde, he shewed him selfe zealous of Gods glorie, & at twētie yere olde he abolished idolatrie and restored ỹ true religion.

c Which sheweth that he wolde se the reformacion wͭ his owne eies.

d Read 2.Kīg. 23,16.

e This great zeale of this godlie King ỹ holie Gost setteth forthe as an example & paterne to other Kings & rulers, to teache thē what God requireth of them.

2.King.22,3.

' *Or, thei returned to Ierusalém*, meaning, Shaphán, &c.

11 Euen to the workemen & to the buylders
gaue they it, to bye hewed stone and timber for couples & for beames of the [f] houses, which the Kings of Iudáh had destroyed.
12 And the men did the worke [g] faithfully,
and the ouerseers of them *were* Iaháth
and Obadiáh the Leuites, of the children
of Merarí, and Zechariáh, and Meshullám, of the children of the Kohathites to
set it forwarde: and of the Leuites all that
colde skil of instruments of musike.
13 And *they were* ouer the bearers of burdēs,
and them that set forwarde all the workemen in euerie worke: and of the Leuites
were scribes, & officers and porters.
14 ¶ And when they broght out the money
that was broght into the house of the
Lord, Hilkiáh the Priest foūde the [h] boke
of the Law of the Lord *giuen* by the hād
of Mosés.
15 Therefore Hilkiáh answered and said to
Shaphán the chanceler, I haue founde the
boke of the Lawe in the house of the
Lord: and Hilkiáh gaue the boke to
Shaphán.
16 And Shaphán caryed the boke to [i] the
King, and broght the King worde againe,
saying, All that is committed to the hand
of thy seruants, that do they.
17 For they haue gathered the money that
was founde in the house of the Lord, and
haue deliuered it into the hands of the
ouerseers, and to the hands of the workemen.
18 Also Shaphán the chanceler declared to
the King, saying, Hilkiáh the Priest hathe
giuen me a boke, & Shaphán red it before
the King.
19 And when the King had heard the wordes of the Lawe, he [k] tare his clothes.
20 And the King commanded Hilkiáh, and
Ahikám the sonne of Shaphán, & Abdón
the sonne of Micáh, & Shaphán the chanceler, and Asaiáh the Kings seruant, saying,
21 Go *and* enquire of the Lord for me, and
for the rest in Israél and Iudáh, concerning the wordes of this boke that is founde: for great *is* the wrath of the Lord ỹ is
fallen vpon vs, because our [l] fathers haue
not kept the worde of the Lord, to do after all that is writen in this boke.
22 Then Hilkiáh and they that the King
had appointed, went to Huldáh the prophetesse the wife of Shallúm, the sonne of
' Tokháth, the sonne of " Hasráh keper of
the [m] wardrobe (and she dwelt in Ierusalém within the [n] colledge) and they
communed hereof with her.
23 And she answered them, Thus saith
the Lord God of Israél, Tel ye [o] the man
that sent you to me,

f For there were many porcions and pieces annexed to the Temple.

g Meaning, ỹ they were in suche credite for their fidelitie, that they made none acōptes of that which thei receiued, 2.Kīg. 22,9.

h Read 2 Kīg. 22,8.

i For ỹ King was commanded to haue continually a copie of this boke, & to read therein day & night, Deut. 17,18.

k For sorow that ỹ worde of God had bene so long suppressed, and ỹ people kept in ignorance, cōsidering also the curses cōteined therein against ỹ trāsgressours.

l Thus ỹ godlie do not only lament their owne sinnes, but also that their fathers and predecessours haue offended God.

' *Or, Tikuáh.*

" *Or, Harhas.*

m Meaning, ether of the Priests apparel, or of the Kings.

n Read hereof 2.King.22,15.

o That is, to the King.

24 Thus saith the Lord, Beholde, I wil brĩg
euil vpon this place, and vpon the inhabitants thereof, *euen* all the curses, that are
writen in the boke which they haue red
before the King of Iudáh:
25 Because they haue forsakẽ me, and burnt
incẽse vnto other gods, to angre me with
all the workes of their [p] hands, therefore
shal my wrath fall vpon this place, & shal
not be quenched.
26 But to the King of Iudáh, who sent you
to enquire of the Lord, so shal ye say vnto
him, Thus saith the Lord God of Israél,
The wordes which thou hast heard, *shal
come to passe.*
27 *But* because thine heart did [q] melt, and
thou didest humble thy self before God,
whẽ thou heardest his wordes against this
place and against the inhabitants thereof,
and humbledst thy selfe before me and
tarest thy clothes, and weptest before me,
I haue also heard it, saith the Lord.
28 Beholde, I wil gather thee to thy fathers,
and thou shalt be put in thy graue in peace, and thine eyes shal not se all the euil,
which I wil bring vpon this [r] place, and
vpon the inhabitants of the same. Thus
they broght the King worde againe.
29 ¶ Then the King sent and gathered all
the Elders of Iudáh and Ierusalém.
30 And the King went vp into the house
of the Lord, and all the men of Iudáh, and
the inhabitants of Ierusalém, and the
Priests and the Leuites, and all the people
frõ the greatest to the [s] smallest, and he
red in their eares all the wordes of the boke of the couenant that was founde in the
house of the Lord.
31 And the King stode by his piller, and
made a couenant before the Lord, to walke after the Lord, and to kepe his cõmã-
dements, and his testimonies, and his statutes, with all his heart, and with all his
soule, & ẏ he wolde accõplish the wordes
of the couenant writen in the same boke.
32 And he caused all that were founde in
Ierusalém, and Beniamín to stand to it: &
the inhabitants of Ierusalém did according to the couenant of God, *euen* the
God of their fathers.
33 So Iosiáh toke away all the abominacions out of all the countreis that perteined to the children of Israél, and compelled all [t] that were found in Israél, to serue
the Lord their God: *so* all his daies they
turned not backe from the Lord God of
their fathers.

p This she speaketh in cõtempt of the idolaters, who contrarie to reason and nature make that a god, which they haue made, and framed with their owne hands.

q This declareth what is ẏ end of Gods threatnings, to call his to repentance, & to assure the vnrepentant of their destruction.

r It may appeare that very fewe were touched wᵗ true repentance, seing that God spared thẽ for a time onely for the Kings sake.

s Forasmuch as nether yõg nor olde colde be exẽpted frõ the curses cõteined therein, if they did transgresse, he knewe it apperteined to all & was his duetie to se it red to all sortes, that euerie one might learne to auoyde those punishements by seruing God arights.

t Because he had charge ouer all & must answer for euerie one that perished, he thoght it his duetie to se ẏ all shulde make professiõ to receiue the worde of God

CHAP. XXXV.

1 *Iosiáh kepeth the Passeouer. 2 He setteth forth the Gods
seruice. 20 He fighteth against the King of Egypt, &
dyeth. 24 The people bewayle him.*

1 MOreouer *Iosiáh kept a Passeouer
vnto the Lord in Ierusalém, & they
slewe the [a] Passeouer in the fourtente
day of the first moneth.
2 And he appointed the Priests to their
charges, and incouraged them to the seruice of the house of the Lord,
3 And he said vnto ẏ Leuites, that [b] taught
all Israél and were sanctified vnto ẏ Lord,
Put the holy Arke in the house which Salomón the sonne of Dauid King of Israél did buyld: it *shal be* no more a [c] burden vpon your shulders: serue now the
Lord your God and his people Israél,
4 And prepare your selues by the houses of
your fathers according to your courses, as
*Dauid the King of Israél hathe writen,
& according to the writing of Salomón
his sonne,
5 And stand in the Sanctuarie according
to the diuisiõ of the families of your brethren ''the children of the people, and *after*
the diuision of the familie of the Leuites:
6 So kil the Passeouer, and sanctifie your
selues, and [d] prepare your brethren that
they may do according to the worde of
the Lord by the hand of Mosés.
7 Iosiáh also gaue to the ''people shepe, lãbes and kiddes, all for the Passeouer, *euen*
to all that were present, to the nomber of
thirty thousand, & thre thousand bullockes: these were of the Kings substance.
8 And his princes offred willingly vnto the
people, to the Priests & to the Leuites: Hilkiáh, and Zechariáh, and Iehiél, rulers of
the house of God, gaue vnto ẏ Priests for
the Passeouer, *euen* two thousand and six
hundreth *shepe*, & thre hũdreth bullockes.
9 [e] Conaniáh also and Shemaiáh and Nethaneél his brethren, and Hashabiáh and
Ieiél, & Iozabád, chief of the Leuites gaue vnto the Leuites for the Passeouer, fyue
thousand *shepe*, & fyue hũdreth bullockes.
10 Thus the seruice was prepared, and
the Priests stode in their places, also the
Leuites in their ordres according to the
Kings commandement:
11 And thei slewe the Passeouer, & ẏ Priests
[f] sprinkled *the blood* with their hands, & the
Leuites flayed *them*.
12 And they toke away *from* the [g] burnt offring to giue it according to the diuisions
of the families of the children of the people, to offer vnto the Lord, as it is writen
in the boke of Mosés, & so of ẏ bullockes.
13 And *they rosted the Passeouer with fyre, according to the custome, but the sanctified things they sod in pottes, pannes,
and caulderns, & distributed them quickely to all the people.
14 Afterwarde also they prepared for thẽ
selues & for the Priests: for the Priests the
sonnes of Aarón *were occupied* in offring of
burnt offrĩgs, & the fat vntil night: therefore the Leuites prepared for thẽ selues, &

2.King.23,21

a The Scripture vseth in sondrie places to call the lambe the Passeouer, which was but the signe of ẏ Passeouer, because in all sacraments the signes haue the names of the things which are signified.

b So that the Leuites charge was not onely to minister in ẏ Tẽple, but also to instruct the people in the worde of God.

c As it was before the Tẽple was buylt: therefore your office onely is now to teache the people, & to praise God.

1 Chro.23,2. & 25,26.

'' Or, the people.

d Exhorte euerie one to examine them selues, that they be not vnmete to eat of the Passeouer.

'' Ebr. sonnes of the people.

e So ẏ euerie one, and of all sortes gaue of that they had a liberal porciõ to the seruice of God.

f Meaning of ẏ lãbe, which was called the Passeouer: for onely ẏ Priests might sprikle, and in necessitie the Leuites might kil the sacrifice.

g They reserued for the people that wᶜ was not expedient to be offred, that euerie man might offer peace offrings, and so haue his portion.

Exod.12,8.

for the Priests the sonnes of Aarón.
15 And the singers the sonnes of Asáph
stode in their standing * according to the
commandement of Dauid, and Asáph, and
Hemán, and Ieduthún the Kings [h] Seer:
and the porters at euerie gate, who might
not departe from their seruice: therefore
their brethren the Leuites prepared for
them.
16 So all the seruice of the Lord was prepared the same day, to kepe the Passeouer,
and to offer burnt offrings vpon the altar
of the Lord, according to the commandement of King Iosiáh.
17 And the childrẽ of Israél that were present, kept the Passeouer the same time, and
the feast of the vnleauened bread seuen
dayes.
18 And there was no Passeouer kept like
that, in Israél, from the dayes of Samuél
the Prophet: nether did all ẏ Kings of Israél kepe suche a Passeouer as Iosiáh kept,
and the Priests and the Leuites, & all Iudáh, and Israél that were "present, and the
inhabitants of Ierusalém.
19 This Passeouer was kept in [i] the eightente yere of the reigne of Iosiáh.
20 ¶ * After all this, when Iosiáh had prepared the Tẽple, Nechó King of Egypt
came vp to fight against [k] Carchemish
by " Peráth, and Iosiáh went out against
him.
21 But he sent messengers to him, saying,
What haue I to do with thee, thou King
of Iudáh? *I come* not against thee this day,
but against the house " of mine enemie,
and God commanded me to make haste:
leaue of *to come* against God, which is with
me, lest he destroye thee.
22 But Iosiáh wolde not turne his face frõ
him, but [l] chãged his apparel to fight with
him, and hearkened not vnto the wordes
of Nechó, which were of the mouth of
God, but came to fight in the valley of
Megiddó.
23 And the shoters shot at King Iosiáh: thẽ
the King said to his seruants, Cary me
away, for I am very sicke.
24 So his seruants toke him out of that charet, & put him in the seconde charet which
he had, and when they had broght him
to Ierusalém, he dyed, and was buryed in
the sepulchres of his fathers: and all Iudáh and Ierusalém [m] mourned for Iosiáh.
25 And Ieremiáh lamented Iosiáh, and all
singing men and singing women mourned for Iosiáh in their lamẽtacions to this
day, and made the same for an ordinance
vnto Israél: and beholde, they be writen
in the [n] lamentacions.
26 Concerning the rest of the actes of Iosiáh and his goodnes, *doing* as it was writẽ
in the Law of the Lord,

1.Chro.25,1.

h Meaning herby his Prophet, because he appointed the Psalmes & prophecies ẏ were to be sung.

" *Ebr.founde.*

i Which was in the six and twentieth yere of his age.

2.King.23,29

k Which was a citie of the Assyrians, and Iosiáh fearing lest he passing through Iudáh, wolde haue taken his kingdome, made warre against him and consulted not the Lord.

" *Or, Euphrates.*

" *Ebr of my battel.*

l That is, armed him selfe, or disguised him selfe because he might not be knowẽ.

m The people so muche lamented ẏ losse of this good King, that after whẽ there was anie great lamentation, this was spokẽ of as a prouerbe, read Zach. 12,11.

n Which some thinke Ieremie made, wherein he lamẽteth the state of the Church after this Kĩgs death.

27 And his dedes, first and last, beholde, thei
are writen in the boke of the Kings of Israél and Iudáh.

CHAP. XXXVI.

1 After Iosiáh, reigneth Iehoaház. 4 After Iehoaház, Iehoiakím. 8 After him Iehoiachin. 11 After him, Zedekiáh. 14. 17 In whose time all the people were caryed away to Babél, for contemning the admonicions of the Prophetes. 22 And were restored againe the seuentieth yere after by King Cyrus.

1 THen * the people of the land toke Iehoaház the sonne of Iosiáh, and made
him Kĩg in his fathers stead in Ierusalém.
2 Iehoaház *was* thre and twentie yere olde
when he began to reigne, and he reigned
thre [a] moneths in Ierusalém.
3 And the King of Egypt toke him away at
Ierusalém, and condemned the land in an
[b] hundreth talents of siluer, & a talent of
golde.
4 ¶ And the King of Egypt made Eliakím
his brother King ouer Iudáh and Ierusalém, and turned his name to Iehoiakím:
and Nechó toke Iehoaház his brother, and
caryed him to Egypt.
5 Iehoiakím *was* fyue and twentie yere olde
when he began to reigne, and he reigned
eleuen yere in Ierusalém, and did [c] euil in
the sight of the Lord his God.
6 Against him came vp Nebuchadnezzár
King of Babél, & bounde him with chaines to carye him to Babél.
7 Nebuchadnezzár also * caryed of ẏ vessels of the house of the Lord to Babél, and
put them in his Temple at Babél.
8 Concerning the rest of the actes of Iehoiakím, and his abominaciõs which he did,
& [d] that which was founde vpõ him, beholde, they are writen in the boke of the
Kings of Israél and Iudáh, & Iehoiachín
his sonne reigned in his steade.
9 ¶ Iehoiachín *was* [e] eight yere olde when
he began to reigne, and he reigned thre
moneths and ten dayes in Ierusalém, and
did euil in the sight of the Lord.
10 And when the yere was out, King Nebuchadnezzár sent and broght him to Babél with the precious vessels of the house
of the Lord, and he made Zedekiáh his
"brother King ouer Iudáh and Ierusalém.
11 Zedekiáh *was* one and twẽtie yere olde,
whẽ he began to reigne, and reigned eleuẽ
yere in Ierusalém.
12 * And he did euil in the sight of ẏ Lord
his God, and humbled not him self before
Ieremiáh the Prophet at the commandement of the Lord,
13 But he rebelled moreouer against Nebuchadnezzár, which had caused him to
sweare by God: and he hardened his necke
& made his heart obstinate that he might
not returne to the Lord God of Israél.
14 All the chief of the Priests also and of
the people trespassed wonderfully, according

2.King.28,30

a For thre moneths after ẏ death of Iosiáh came Nechó to Ierusalém & so the plagues began, which Huldáh & the Prophets forewarned shulde come vpon Ierusalém.

b To pay this as a yerely tribute.

c Because he, and the people turned not to God by his first plague, he broght a newe vpon him, and at length rooted them out.

2.King.24.13

d He meaneth superstitious markes which were founde vpon his bodie, when he was dead: ẇ thing declared how depely idolatrie was rooted in his heart, seing he bare the markes in his flesh.

e That is, he begã his reigne at eight yere olde, and reigned ten yeres when his father was aliue, and after his fathers death, which was the eightente yere of his age he reigned alone thre moneths and ten dayes.

" *Or, vncle.*

2.King.24,17

iere.52,2.

ding to all the abominacions of the heathen, and polluted the houſe of the Lord which he had ſanctified in Ieruſalém.
15 Therefore the Lord God of their fathers ſent to thē "by his meſſengers, [f] riſing early and ſending: for he had compaſſion on his people, and on his habitacion.
16 But they mocked the meſſengers of God and deſpiſed his wordes, and miſuſed his Prophetes, vntil the wrath of the Lord aroſe againſt his people, and til there was no [g] remedie.
17 For he broght vpon them the King of the Caldeans, who ſlewe their yong men with the ſworde [h] in the houſe of their Sāctuarie, and ſpared nether yong man, nor virgine, ancient, nor aged. *God* [i] gaue all into his hand,
18 And all ẏ veſſels of ẏ houſe of God great & ſmall, and the treaſures of the houſe of ẏ Lord, and the treaſures of the King, and of his princes: all theſe caryed he to Babél.
19 And they burnt the houſe of God, and brake downe the wall of Ieruſalém, and burnt all the palaces thereof with fyre, & all the precious veſſels thereof: to deſtroye *all*.
20 And thei that were left by the ſworde, caryed he away to Babél, and they were ſeruants to him and to his ſonnes, vntil the kingdome of the [k] Perſians had rule,
21 To fulfil the worde of the Lord by the [l] mouth of Ieremiáh, vntil the lād had her fil of her Sabbaths: *for* all the dayes that ſhe lay deſolate, ſhe kept Sabbath, to fulfil ſeuentie yeres.
22 ¶ *But in ẏ [m] firſt yere of Cyrus King of Perſiá (when the worde of the Lord *ſpoken* by the mouth of Ieremiáh, was finiſhed) the Lord ſtirred vp the ſpirit of Cyrus King of Perſia, and he made a proclamacion through all his kingdome, and alſo by writing, ſaying,
23 Thus ſayth Cyrus King of Perſia, All ẏ kingdomes of the earth hathe the Lord God of heauen giuen me, and he hathe [n] commanded me to buyld him an houſe in Ieruſalém, that is in Iudáh. Who is among you of all his people, with whome the Lord his God *is* let him go vp.

" *Ebr. by the hād of his.*
f By this phraſe the ſcripture meaneth often times and diligently, as Iere.11,7. 25,3, & 4.265,.& 32, 33.
g Til God colde no longer ſuffer their ſinnes, but muſte nedes puniſh them.
h Whether thei fled, thinking to haue bene ſaued for the holines thereof.
i Which is not becauſe God approueth him which yet is the miniſter of his iuſtice, but becauſe God wolde by his iuſte iudgemēt puniſh this people: for this King was led with ambicion and vaine glorie, whereunto were ioyned furie and crueltie: therefore his worke was condēnable, notwithſtanding it was iuſte and holy on Gods parte, who vſed this wicked inſtrument to declare his iuſtice.
k Whē Cyrus King of Perſia, had made the Babylonians ſubiect.
l Who threatned the vengeāce of God, and 70 yeres captiuitie, ẇ he calleth the Sabbaths or reſt of the lād, Iere.25,11.
Iere.25,13. & 29,10. 3.Eſdr.1,1.
m In the firſt yere that he reigned ouer the Caldeans.
n God had ſo prophecied aboue an hundreth yeres, before Cyrus was borne, Iſa. 44,28, that Ieruſalém & the Temple ſhulde be buylt againe by Cyrus his anointed: ſo called, becauſe God vſed his ſeruice for a time to deliuer his Church.

THE PRAYER OF MANASSÉH King of the Iewes.

O Lord almightie, God of our fathers, Abram, Iſaac and Iacob, and of their righteous ſede, which haſt made heauen and earth with all their ornament, which haſt bound the ſea by the worde of thy commandement, which haſt ſhut vp the depe and ſealed it by thy terrible and glorious Name, whome all do feare & tremble before thy power: for the maieſtie of thy glorie can not be borne, & thine angrie threatning toward ſinners is importable, but thy merciful promes is vnmeaſurable & vnſearcheable. For thou art the moſte high Lord, of great compaſſiō, long ſuffring & moſte merciful, & repēteſt for mās miſeries. Thou, ô Lord, accordīg to thy great goodnes haſt promiſed [a] repentance & forgiuenes to them that ſinne againſt thee, & for thine infinite mercies haſt appointed repentance vnto ſinners that thei may be ſaued. Thou therefore, ô Lord, that art the God of the iuſte, haſt not appointed repentance to the iuſte, *as* to Abram, and Iſaac and Iacob, which haue not [b] ſinned againſt thee, but thou haſt appointed repentance vnto me that am a ſinner: for I haue ſinned aboue the nōber of the ſand of the ſea. My tranſgreſsions, ô Lord, are multiplied: my tranſgreſsions are exceding many: and I am not worthy to beholde & ſe the height of the heauēs for the multitude of mine vnrighteouſnes. I am bowed downe with many yrō bādes, that I cā not lift vp mine head, nether haue any releaſe. For I haue prouoked thy wrath and done euil before thee. I did not thy wil, nether kept I thy commandements. I haue ſet vp abominations & haue multiplied offenſes. Now therefore I bowe the kne of mine heart, beſechīg thee of grace. I haue ſinned, ô Lord, I haue ſinned, & I acknowledge my trāſgreſsiōs: but I humbly beſeche thee, forgiue me: ô Lord, forgiue me, & deſtroye me not with my tranſgreſsions. Be not angry with me for euer by reſeruing euil for me, nether condemne me into the lower partes of the earth. For thou art the God, *euen* the God of them that repent: and in me thou wilt ſhewe all thy goodnes: for thou wilt ſaue me that am vnworthy, according to thy great mercie: therefore I wil praiſe thee for euer all the dayes of my life. for all the power of the heauens praiſe thee, & thine is the glorie for euer & euer, Amen.

This prayer is not in the Ebrewe, but is tranſlated out of the Greke.
a Thou haſt promiſed that repētance ſhal be the way for thē to returne to thee.
b He ſpeaketh this in cōpariſon of him ſelfe & thoſe holy fathers which haue their commēdacion in the Scriptures, ſo that in reſpect of him ſelf he calleth their ſinnes nothing, but attributeth vnto them righteouſnes.

EZRA.

THE ARGVMENT.

As the Lord is euer merciful vnto his Church, and doeth not punish them, but to the intent they shulde se their owne miseries, and be exercised vnder the crosse, that they might contemne the worlde and aspire vnto the heauens: so after that he had visited the Iewes and kept thē now in bondage seuentie yeres in a strange countrey among insideles and idolaters, he remembred his tendre mercies and their infirmities, and therefore for his owne sake raised them vp a deliuerer, and moued bothe the heart of the chief ruler to pitie them, and also by him punished suche, which had kept them in seruitude. Notwithstanding lest they shulde growe into a contempt of Gods great benefite, he kepeth them stil in exercise, and raiseth domestical enemies, which endeuour as muche as they can to hindre their moste worthie enterprises: yet by the exhortacion of the Prophetes they went forward by litle and litle til their worke was finished. The autor of this boke was Ezra, who was Priest, and scribe of the Law, as chap. 7, 6. he returned to Ierusalém the sixt yere of Darius, who succeded Cyrus, that is, more then fourtie yeres after the returne of the first vnder Zerubbabél, when the Temple was buylt. He broght with him a great companie, and muche treasures, with letters to the Kings officers for all suche things as shulde be necessarie for the Temple: and at his cōming he redressed that which was amisse, and set the things in good ordre.

CHAP. I.

1 Cyrus sendeth againe the people that was in captiuitie. 8 And restoreth them their holy vessels.

1 Now *in ẏ first yere of
Cyrus King of Persia (ẏ
the worde of the Lord,
spoken by the [b] mouth of
Ieremiáh, might be accō
plished) the Lord stirred
vp the [c] spirit of Cyrus
King of Persia, and he made a proclamacion through all his kingdome, and also
by writing, saying,
2 Thus saith Cyrus King of Persia, The
Lord God of heauen hathe giuen me [d] all
the kingdomes of the earth, and he hathe
commanded me to buyld him an house in
Ierusalém, which is in Iudáh.
3 Who is he among you of all his people
with whome his God is? let him go vp to
Ierusalém which is in Iudáh, and buyld
the house of the Lord God of Israél: he is
the God, which is in Ierusalém.
4 And euerie one that remaineth in anie
place (where he soiourneth) [e] let the
men of his place relieue him with siluer
& with golde, and with substance, & with
cattel, [f] *and* with a willing offring, for the
house of God that is in Ierusalém.
5 Then the chief fathers of Iudáh & Benia
mín, & the Priests & Leuites rose vp, with
all thē whose spirit God had raised to go
vp, to buyld the house of the Lord which
is in Ierusalém.
6 And all [g] they that were about thē, strēgthened their hands with vessels of siluer,
with golde, with substance & with cattel,
& with precious thīgs, besides all that was
willingly offred.
7 Also the King Cyrus broght forthe the
vessels of the house of the Lord, * which
Nebuchadnezzár had takē out of Ierusalém, & had put thē in ẏ house of his god.

2.Chro.36,2. 3.ez.2,1.iere. 33,12 & 29,10
a After that he and Darius had wonne Babylón.
b Who promised thē deliuerance after that seuentie yeres were past, Ier. 25,11.
That is, moued him, and gaue him heart.
d For he was chief Monarche, and had manie nacions vnder his dominion, which this heathen King cōfesseth to haue receiued of the liuing God.
e If any through pouertie were not able to returne, the Kings cōmissiō was that he shulde be furnished wᵗ necessaries.
f Which they them selues shulde send toward the reparation of ẏ Temple.
g The Babylonians & Chaldeans gaue them these presents: thus rather then the children of God shulde want for their necessities, he wolde stirre vp the heart of the very infideles to helpe them.
2.Kin.25,13, 2.chro.36,7. ier.27,19. dan.1,2.

8 Euen thē did Cyrus King of Persia brīg
forthe by the hād of Mithredáth the treasurer, and counted thē vnto [h] Sheshbazzár
the prince of Iudáh.
9 And this is the nomber of them, thirtie
basins of golde, a thousand basins of siluer,
nine and twentie [i] kniues,
10 Thirtie bowles of golde, & of siluer
bowles of the secōd sorte, foure hundreth
and ten, & of other vessels, a thousand.
11 All the vessels of golde & siluer *were* fiue thousand & foure hūdreth. Sheshbazzár broght vp all [k] with thē of the captiuitie that came vp frō Babél to Ierusalém.

CHAP. II.

The nomber of them that returned from the captiuitie.

1 These * also are the sonnes [a] of the prouince, that went vp out of ẏ captiuitie (whome Nebuchadnezzár Kīg of Babél had caried away vnto Babél) & retur
ned to Ierusalém, & to Iudáh, euerie one
vnto his citie,
2 Which came with [b] Zerubbabél, *to wit*, Ieshúa, Nehemiáh, Seraiáh, Reelaiáh, [c] Mor
decái, Bilshán, Mispár, Biguái, Rehúm,
Baanáh. The nomber of the men [d] of the
people of Israél *was*,
3 The sonnes of Paróshe, two thousand, an
hundreth, seuentie and two:
4 The sonnes of Shephatiáh, thre hundreth
seuentie and two:
5 The sonnes of Aráh, seuen hundreth, and
seuentie and fiue:
6 The sonnes of *Paháth Moáb, of the sonnes of Ieshúa & Ioáb, two thousand, eight
hundreth and twelue:
7 The sonnes of Elám, a thousand, two hūdreth, and foure and fiftie:
8 The sonnes of Zattú, nine hundreth, and
fiue and fourtie:
9 The sonnes of Zaccái, seuen hundreth,
and threscore:
10 The sonnes of Baní, six hundreth, and
two and fourtie:

h So the Chaldeās called Zerubbabél, who was the chief gouernour, so that ẏ preeminence stil remained in the house of Dauid.
i Which serued to kill the beastes that were offred in sacrifice.
k With ẏ Iewes ẏ had bene kept captiues in Babylón.
Nehe.7,6. 3.esdr.5,7.
a Meaning Iudea, wᶜ was a prouince, ẏ is, a countrey which was in subiection.
b Zerubbabél was chief captaine, Ieshúa the hie Priest, & Nehemiáh a man of great autoritie went not now but came after. 54 yeres.
c This was not that Mordecái wᶜ was Esters kinsman.
d Meaning of the commune people.
Or, of the duke of Moáb.

11 The

11 The sonnes of Bebái, six hundreth, and
thre and twenty:
12 The sonnes of Azgád a thousand, two hú
dreth, and two and twentie:
13 The sonnes of Adonikám, six hundreth,
thre score and six:
14 The sonnes of Biguái, two thousand, &
six and fiftie:
15 The sonnes of Adín, foure hundreth &
foure and fiftie:
16 The sonnes of Atér of [e]Hizkiáh, ninetie
and eight:
17 The sonnes of Bezái, thre hundreth, &
thre and twentie:
18 The sonnes of Ioráh, an hundreth, and
twelue:
19 The sonnes of Hasshúm, two hundreth
and thre and twentie:
20 The sonnes of Gibbár, ninetie and fiue:
21 [f] The sonnes of Beth-léhem, an húdreth
and thre and twenty:
22 The men of Netopháh, six & fiftie:
23 The men of Anothóth, an hundreth &
eight & twentie:
24 The sõnes of Azmáueth, two & fourtie:
25 The sonnes of Kiriáth arím, of Chephiráh, & Beeróth, seuen hundreth & thre
and fourtie:
26 The sonnes of Haramáh and Gába, six
hundreth, and one and twentie:
27 The men of Michmás, an hundreth, and
two and twentie:
28 The sonnes of Beth-él & Ai, two hundreth, and thre and twentie:
29 The sonnes of Nebó, two and fiftie:
30 The sonnes of Magbísh, an hundreth
and six and fiftie:
31 The sonnes of the other Elám, a thousand, and two hundreth, & foure & fiftie:
32 The sonnes of Harím, thre hundreth &
twentie:
33 The sonnes of Lod-hadíd, & Onó, seuẽ
hundreth, and fiue and twentie:
34 The sonnes of Ierichó, thre hundreth
and fiue and fourtie:
35 The sonnes of Senáah, thre thousand, six
hundreth and thirtie.
36 ¶ The [g]Priests: of the sonnes of Iedaiáh
of the house of Ieshúa, nine hundreth seuentie and thre:
37 The sonnes of Immér, a thousand and
two and fiftie:
38 The sonnes of Pashúr, a thousand, two
hundreth and seuen and fourtie:
39 The sonnes of Harím, a thousand and
seuentene.
40 ¶ ‖ The Leuites: the sonnes of Ieshúa, &
Kadmiél of the sonnes of Hodauiáh, seuentie and foure.
41 ¶ ‖ The singers: the sonnes of Asáph, an
hundreth and eight and twentie.
42 ¶ ‖ The sonnes of the porters: the sonnes
of Shallúm, the sonnes of Atér, the sonnes
of Talmón, the sonnes of Akkúb, ye sonnes
of Hatitá, the sonnes of Shobái: all *were*
an hundreth and nine ad thirtie.
43 ¶ The [h]Nethinims: the sonnes of Zihá, ye
sonnes of Hasuphá, ye sonnes of Tabbaóth,
44 The sonnes of Kerós, ye sonnes of Sia-
há, the sonnes of Padón,
45 The sonnes of Lebanáh, the sonnes of
Hagabáh, the sonnes of Akkúb,
46 The sonnes of Hagab, the sonnes of Shã
lái, the sonnes of Hanán,
47 The sonnes of Giddél, the sonnes of
Gáhar, the sonnes of Reaiáh,
48 The sonnes of Rezín, the sonnes of Nekodá, the sonnes of Gazzám,
49 The sonnes of Vzzá, the sonnes of Paséah, the sonnes of Besái,
50 The sonnes of Asnáh, the sonnes of Meuním, the sonnes of Nephusím,
51 The sonnes of Bakbúk, the sonnes of Ha
kupá, the sonnes of Harhúr,
52 The sonnes of Bazlúth, the sonnes of
Mehidá, the sonnes of Harshá,
53 The sonnes of Barcós, the sonnes of Si-
sará, the sonnes of Thámah,
54 The sonnes of Nezíah, the sonnes of
Hatiphá,
55 The sonnes of Salomons [i]seruants, the
sonnes of Sotái, the sonnes of Sophéreth,
the sonnes of Perudá,
56 The sonnes of Iaaláh, the sonnes of Dar
kón, the sonnes of Giddél,
57 The sonnes of Shephatiáh, the sonnes
of Hattíl, the sonnes of Pochéreth Haz-
zebaím, the sonnes of Amí.
58 All the Nethinims, and the sonnes of Sa
lomons seruants *were* thre hundreth ninetie and two.
59 ¶ And these went vp from Telmeláh, &
from Telharshá, Cherúb, Addán, & Immér, but they colde not discerne their fathers house and their sede, whether they
were of Israél.
60 The sonnes of Delaiáh, the sonnes of
Tobiáh, the sonnes of Nekodá, six hundreth and two and fiftie.
61 And of the sonnes of ye Priests, ye sonnes
of Habaiáh, the sonnes of Coz, the sonnes of [k]Barzillái: which toke of ye daughters of Barzillái the Giliadite to wife, and
was called after their name.
62 These soght their writing of the genealogies, but they were not found: therefore were they put from the Priesthode.
63 And [l]Tirsháthá said vnto them, that
thei shulde not eat of the moste holy thĩg,
til there rose vp a Priest with [m]Vrím &
Thummím.
64 The whole Congregacion together *was*
two and fourtie thousand, thre hundreth
and thre score,
65 Beside their seruants and their maides: of whome *were* seuen thousand,

e Which were of the posteritie of Hezekiáh.

f That is, inhabitants: for so this word (Sonne) signifieth, whẽ it is ioyned with the names of places.

g Before he hathe declared the two tribes of Iudáh and Beniamín, & now commeth to ye tribe of Leui & beginneth at ye Priests.

‖ The Leuites.

‖ The Singers.

‖ The Porters.

h So called because thei were giuen to the Temple, to cut wood & beare water for the vse of the sacrifices, & came of the Gibionites wc were appointed to this vse by Ioshúa, Iosh. 9,23.

i Which came of them that Salomón had appointed for the worke of the Temple.

k Of him is made mẽciõ 2 Sam. 17,27. & 19,31: & because ye Priests office was had in contempt, these wolde haue changed their estate by their name, & so by Gods iuste iudgemẽt lost bothe the estimation of the worlde & the dignitie of their office.

l This is a Chalde name & signifieth hĩ yt hathe autoritie ouer others.

m Read Exo. 28,30.

thre hundreth and seuen and thirtie: and
among them *were* two hundreth singing
men and singing women.
66 Their horses *were* seuen hundreth, & six
and thirty: their mules, two hundreth and
fiue and fourtie:
67 Their camels foure hũdreth and fiue &
thirtie: their asses, six thousand, seuen hũdreth and twentie.
68 And *certeine* of the chief fathers, when
they came to the house of the Lord, which
was in Ierusalém, thei offred willingly for
the house of God, to set it vp vpon his fundacion.
69 Thei gaue after their habilitie vnto ẏ
treasure of the worke, *euen* one and threscore thousand [n] drammes of golde, and
fiue thousand [o] pieces of siluer and an hundreth Priests garments.
70 So the Priests & the Leuites, and a *certeine* of the people, and the singers, & the
porters, and the Nethiníms dwelt in their
cities, and all Israél in their cities.

n Which mount to of our money 24826. li. 13, shil. 4. d. esteming the french crowne at 6. shil 4 d. for the dramme is ẏ eight part of an ounce, & the ounce the eight part of a marke.

o Which are called mine, & conteine a piece two markes so 5000 mines make 550000. frankes, which mount to of our many 69666, li. 13. shil 4 d. so that ẏ whole some was 94493 li. 26. shil. 8 d.

CHAP. III.

1 Thei buyld the altar of God 6 Thei offer to the Lord. 7 Thei prepare for the Tẽple, 11 And sing vnto the Lord.

1 AND * when the [a] seuent moneth was
come, and the children of Israél *were* in their cities, the people assembled
them selues as one man vnto Ierusalém.
2 Then stode vp Ieshúa the sonne of Iozadák, and his brethren the Priests, and Zerubbabél the [b] sonne of Shealtiél, and his
brethren, & buylded the altar of the God
of Israél, to offer burnt offrings thereon,
as it is writen in the Law of Mosés the
man of God,
3 And they set the altar vpõ this bases (for
feare *was* among them, because of the people of those countreies) therefore they offred burnt offrings thereõ vnto the Lord,
euen burnt offrings in the morning and at
euen.
4 They kept also the feast of the Tabernacles, as it is writen, and the burnt offring * daily, by nomber according to the
custome day by day,
5 And afterward [d] the continual burnt offring, bothe in the new moneths and
in all the feast dayes that were consecrate
vnto the Lord, and in all the oblations
willingly offred vnto the Lord.
6 From the first day of the seuent moneth
began they to offer burnt offrings vnto
the Lord: but the fundacion of the Temple of the Lord was not laied.
7 They gaue money also vnto the masons,
and to the workemen, and meat and drinke, and oyle vnto them of Zidón and of
Tyrus, to bring thẽ cedre wood from Lé-
banón to the sea vnto * Iaphó, according
to the grant that they had of Cyrus King
of Persia.

3. Esdr. 5, 47.

a Called Tishri, ẇ answereth to part of September & parte of October.

b Meanĩg, nephewe: for he was the sonne of Pedaiáh. read 1. Chro. 3, 19.

* In the place where Salomón had placed it.

Exod. 23, 16.

d That is, after the feast of Tabernacles.

* Or, Ioppe.

8 ¶ And in the seconde yere of their comming vnto the house of God in Ierusalém in the [e] second moneth began Zerubbabél the sonne of Shealtiél, and Ieshúa
the sonne of Iozadák, and the remnant of
their brethren the Priests and the Leuites,
& all they that were come out of the captiuitie vnto Ierusalém, and appointed the
Leuites from twenty yere olde & aboue,
to set forward the worke of the house of
the Lord.
9 And Ieshúa [f] stode with his sonnes, and
his brethren, & Kadmiél with his sonnes,
& the sonnes of Iudáh together to set for
ward the workemen in the house of God,
and the sonnes of Henadád with their
sonnes, and their brethren the Leuites.
10 And when the buylders laied the fundacion of the Temple of the Lord, thei appointed the Priests in their apparel with
trumpets, and the Leuites the sonnes of
Asáph with cymbales, to praise the Lord,
* after the ordinance of Dauid King of
Israél.
11 Thus they sang when they gaue praise,
and when they gaue thankes vnto the
Lord, For he is good, for his mercie *endureth* for euer toward Israél. And all ẏ people shouted with a great shoute, whẽ thei
praised the Lord, because the fundacion
of the house of the Lord was layed.
12 Many also of the Priests and the Leuites and the chief of the fathers, ancient
men, which had sene the first house, (when
the fundacion of this house was layed before their eies) [g] wept with a loude voyce: and many shouted a loude for ioye,
13 So that the people colde not discerne the
sounde of the shoute for ioye, from the
noyce of the weping of the people: for the
people shouted with a loude crye, and the
noyce was heard farre of.

e Which moneth conteined parte of April and parte of May. for in the meane season they had prouided for thĩgs necessarie for the worke.

f They gaue them exhortations & encouraged euerie man forward in the worke.

2. Chro. 16, 8.

g Because thei sawe that it was nothĩg so glorious as that Temple, which Salomón had buylt, notwithstanding Aggeus cõforteth them & prophecieth that it shalbe more beautiful thẽ the first: meaning the spiritual Temple, ẇ are the members of Christes bodie.

CHAP. IIII.

2 The buylding of the Temple is hindred & how. 11 Letters to Artaxerxes, and the answer.

1 BUt [a] the aduersaries of Iudáh and Béiamín heard, that the children of the
captiuitie buylded the Temple vnto the
Lord God of Israél.
2 And thei came to Zerubbabél, & to ẏ chief
fathers, and said vnto them, We wil buylde with you: for we seke the Lord your
God as ye *do*: & we haue sacrificed vnto
him since the time of Esár Haddón King
of Asshúr which broght vs vp hither.
3 Then Zerubbabél, and Ieshúa, and the
rest of the chief fathers of Israél, said vnto them, It is not for you, but for vs to
buyld the house vnto our God: [b] for we
our selues together wil buyld it vnto the
Lord God of Israél, as King Cyrus the
King of Persia hathe commanded vs.

a Meaning, the inhabitants of Samaria, whome ẏ King of Assyria had placed in the steade of ẏ ten tribes 2. King. 17, 24. & 19, 37. These professed God, but worshiped idoles also, and therefore were the greatest enemies to the true seruants of God.

b For thei perceiued what their pretence was, to wit, to erect idolatrie in steade of true religion.

4 Whe-

''Ebr. made their hands weake.

4 Wherefore the people of ỳ land'' discouraged the people of Iudáh, and troubled
them in buylding,

c They bribed the gouerners vnder the King, to hĩder their worke. thus they that halte, can not abide, ỳ God shulde be purely serued.

5 And they [c] hyred counselers against thẽ,
to hinder their deuice, all the daies of
Cyrus King of Persia, euẽ vntil the reigne of Darius King of Persia.

d He was also called Artaxerxes, which is a Persian name. some thĩke it was Cambises Cyrus sonne, or Darius, as vers. 5.

6 And in the reigne of [d] Ahashuérósh (in the
beginning of his reigne) wrote thei an ac
cusation against the inhabitants of Iudáh
and Ierusalém.

e Called Artaxerxes, w^c^ signifieth in ỳ Persiã tõgue, an excellent warriour.

7 And in the dayes of [e] Artahshásh̃te, Mithredáth, Tabeél, & the rest of their companiõs wrote when it was peace vnto Ar-
tahshásh̃te King of Persia, & the writing
of the letter was the Aramites writing, &
the thing declared *was* in the language of
the Aramites.

'Or, counseler.

8 Rehúm the ' chancelour, and Shimshái
the scribe wrote a lettre against Ierusalém to Artahshásh̃te ỳ King, in this sorte.
9 Then *wrote* Rehúm the chancelour, and
Shimshái the scribe, & their companions

f These were certeine peple, which the Assyrians placed in Samaria in stead of the ten tribes.

[f] Dinaié, and Apharsathcaié, Tarpelaié,
Apharsaié, Archeuaié, Bablaié, Shushan-
chaié, Dehaué, Elmaié,

g Some thinke it was Sanneherib, but rather Salmanasár.

10 And the rest of the people whome the
great & noble [g] Asnappár broght ouer, &
set in the cities of Samaria, and other that
are beyonde the [h] Riuer and [i] Cheéneth.

h To wit, Euphrates, & he meaneth in respect of Babél ỳ they dwelt beyonde it.

i Which were a certeine people ỳ enuyed the Iewes.

11 ¶ This is the copie of the letter that
they sent vnto King Artahshásh̃te, THY
SERVANTS the men beyonde the Riuer and Cheéneth, *salute thee*.
12 Be it knowen vnto the King that the
Iewes, which came vp from thee to vs, are
come vnto Ierusalém (a citie rebellious &
wicked) & buylde, & laye the fundacions
of the walles, and haue ioyned the fundacions.
13 Be it knowen now vnto the King, that if
this citie be buylt, & the fundaciõs of the
walles layed, thei wil not giue tolle, tribute, nor [k] custome: so shalt thou hinder the
Kings tribute.

k Meaning, the gifts that are wonte to be giuen to Kings whẽ they passe by any cõtrey.

''Ebr. In the Chalde, we haue eaten the salt of the palace.

14 Now therefore because'' we haue bene
broght vp in the *Kings* palace, it was not
mete for vs to se the Kings dishonour: for
this cause haue we sent and certified the
King,
15 That one may searche in the boke of the
Chronicles of thy fathers, and thou shalt
finde in the boke of the Chronicles, and
perceiue that this citie is rebellious and
noysome vnto Kings and prouinces, and
that thei haue moued sedicion of olde time, for the which cause this citie was destroyed.
16 We certifie the King *therefore*, that if
this citie be buylded, and the fundacion of
the walles layed, by this meanes the porcion beyonde the Riuer shal not be thine.
17 ¶ The King sent an answer vnto Rehúm
the chancelour, and Shimshái the scribe,
and to the rest of their companions that
dwelt in Samaria, and vnto the other beyonde the Riuer, [l] Shelám & [m] Cheéth.

l Some read for Shelám, salutacion or greting.

m Called also Cheeneth, as vers. 11.

18 ¶ The letter which ye sent vnto vs, hathe
bene openly red before me,
19 And I haue commanded and they haue
searched, and founde, that this citie of
olde time hathe made insurrectiõ against
Kings, and hathe rebelled, and rebellion
hathe bene committed therein.
20 There haue bene mightie Kings also o-
uer Ierusalém, which haue ruled ouer all
beyonde the Riuer, and tolle, tribute, and
custome was giuen vnto them.
21 Make ye now a decree, that those men
may cease, and that the citie be not buylt,
til I haue giuen *another* commandement.
22 Take hede now that ye faile not to do
this: why shulde domage growe to hurt
the King?
23 When the copie of King Artahshásh̃tes
lettre was red before Rehúm & Shimshái
the scribe, & their companions, they went
vp in all the haste to Ierusalém vnto the
Iewes, and caused them to cease by force
and power.
24 Then [n] ceased the worke of the house
of God, which was in Ierusalém, and did
stay vnto the secõde yere of Darius King
of Persia.

n Not all together: for the Prophetes exhorted thẽ to continue, but they vsed lesse diligence because of the troubles.

CHAP. V.

1 Haggái & Zechariáh do prophecie. 3 The worke of the Temple goeth forwarde contrary to the minde of Tatnái. 6 His lettres to Darius.

'Or, Haggeus. Hag. 1, 1. 3. esdr 6, 6.

1 THẼ ' * Haggái a Prophet & Zechariáh
the sonne of Iddó a Prophet prophecied vnto the Iewes that were in Iudáh, &
Ierusalém, in the Name of the God of Israél, *euen* vnto them.
2 Then Zerubbabél the sonne of Shealtiél, & Ieshúa the sonne of Iozadák arose,
and began to buylde the house of God at
Ierusalém, and with them *were* the Prophetes of God, which [a] helped them.

a Which incouraged thẽ to go forward & accused thẽ that they were more careful to buyld their owne houses, then zealous to buylde the Tẽple of God.

3 ¶ At the same time came to them Tatnái,
which was captaine beyonde the Riuer, &
Shether-boznái and their companions, &
said thus vnto them, Who hathe giuen
you commandemẽt to buylde this house,
and to lay the fundacions of these walles?
4 [b] Then said we vnto them after this maner, What are the names of the men that
buylde this buylding?

b That is, the enemies asked this, as ver. 10.

5 But the [c] eye of their God was vpon the
Elders of the Iewes, that they colde not
cause them to cease, til the matter came
to Darius: and then they answered by letters thereunto.

c His fauour & the spirit of strength.

6 The copie of the lettre, that Tatnái captaine beyond the Riuer, and Shether-boznái and his companions Apharsechaié,
(which were beyonde the Riuer) sent vnto
King Darius.

7 They sent a lettre vnto him, wherein it
was writen thus, VNTO DARIVS the
King, all peace.
8 Be it knowen vnto the King, that we wẽt
into the prouince of Iudea, to the house
of the great God, which is buylded with
"great stones, and beames are layed in the
walles, and this worke is wroght spedely,
and prospereth in their hands.
9 Then asked we those Elders, and said vnto
them thus, Who hathe giuen you commandement
to buyld this house, and to
laye the fundacion of these walles?
10 We asked their names also, ỳ we might
certifie thee, & that we might write the
names of the men that were their rulers.
11 But thei answered vs thus, & said, We are
the seruants of ỳ God of heauen & earth,
& buyld the house that was buylt of olde
& many yeres ago, which a [d] great King
of Israél *buylded, & founded it.
12 But after that our fathers had prouoked
the God of heauen vnto wrath, * he gaue
them ouer into the hand of Nebuchadnezzár
King of Babél the Caldean, and
he destroyed this house, and caryed the
people away captiue vnto Babél.
13 But in the [e] first yere of Cyrus King of
Babél, Kĩg Cyrus made a decree to buyld
this house of God.
14 And the vessels of golde & siluer of the
house of God, which Nebuchadnezzár
toke out of the Tẽple, that was in Ierusalém,
and broght them into the Temple of
Babél, those did Cyrus the King take out
of the Tẽple of Babél, & they gaue them
vnto *one* [f] Sheshbazzár by his name, whome
he had made captaine.
15 And he said vnto him, Take these vessels
and go thy way, & put them in the Temple
that is in Ierusalém, and let the house
of God be buylt in his place.
16 Then came the same Sheshbazzár and
layed the fundacion of the house of God,
which is in Ierusalém, and since that time
euen vntil now, hathe it bene in buylding,
yet is it not finished.
17 Now therefore if it please the King, let
there be searche made in the house of the
Kings [g] treasures, which is there in Babél,
whether a decree hathe bene made by
King Cyrus, to buylde this house of God
in Ierusalém, and let the King send *his*
minde concerning this.

"Or, marble.
d To wit, Salomón.
1. King 6,2. 2 chro. 3,2.
2. King. 24,2. & 25,9.
e Read Chap. 1,1.
f Read Chap. 1, 8.
g Meaning, in the librarie, or places where laye the registers, or recordes of times.

CHAP. VI.

At the commandement of Darius King of Persia, after the Temple was buylded and dedicate, the children of Israél kepe the feast of vnleauened bread.

1 THen *King Darius gaue commandement,
and they made searche in the
"librarie of the treasures, which were
there layed vp in Babél.
2 And there was founde in a [a] coffre (in the
palace that was in the prouince of the Medes)
a volume, & therein was it thus writẽ,
as a memorial,
3 IN THE FIRST yere of King Cyrus,
King Cyrus made a decree for the house
of God in Ierusalém, Let the house be
buylt, *euen* the place where they offred sacrifices,
& let the walles thereof be ioyned
together: let the height thereof *be* thre
score cubites, & the breadth thereof thre
score cubites,
4 Thre" orders of " great stones, and one
order of tymbre, and let the expences be
giuen of the Kings house.
5 And also let them render ỳ vessels of the
house of God (of golde & siluer, ẘ Nebuchadnezzár
toke out of the Tẽple, which
was in Ierusalém, and broght vnto Babél)
and let [b] him go vnto the Temple that is
in Ierusalém to his place and put them in
the house of God.
6 Therefore Tatnái captaine beyonde the
Riuer, and Shethár Boznái, (& their companions
Apharsecaié, which are beyonde
the Riuer) be ye farre [c] from thence.
7 Suffre ye the worke of this house of God,
that the captaine of the Iewes & the Elders
of the Iewes may buylde this house
of God in his place.
8 For I haue giuen a commandement what
ye shal do to the Elders of these Iewes for
the buylding of this house of God, that of
the reuenues of the King, which is of the
tribute beyonde the Riuer, there be incontinently
expenses giuen vnto these mẽ
that they [d] cease not.
9 And that which thei shal haue nede of, let
it be giuen vnto them day by day, whether
it be yong bullockes, or rams, or lambs for
the burnt offrings of the God of heauen,
wheat, salt, wine, & oyle, according to the
appointemẽt of the Priests that are in Ierusalém,
that there be no faute,
10 That they may haue to offer swete odours
vnto the God of heauen, and pray
for the Kings life, and for his sonnes.
11 And I haue made a decree, ỳ whosoeuer
shal alter this sentence, the wood shal be
pulled downe from his house, and shalbe
set vp, & he shal be hanged thereon, & his
house shal be made a dung hil for this.
12 And the God that hathe caused his Name
[e] to dwel there, destroye all Kings and
people that put to their hand to alter, *and*
to destroye this house of God, which is in
Ierusalém. I Darius haue made a decree,
let it be done with spede.
13 ¶ *Then Tatnái the captaine beyonde
the Riuer, & Shethár Boznái and their cõpanions,
according to that which Darius
had sent, so thei did spedely.
14 So the Elders of the Iewes buylded, and
they prospered by the prophecying of
[f] Haggái

1. Esdr. 6,21.
"Ebr. house of bokes.
a Wherein were the actes of the Kings of Medes and Persians.
"Or, rewes, or courses.
"Or, marble.
b Meanig, Zerubbabél, to whome he giueth charge.
c Medle not with them, nether hinder them.
d For lacke of money.
e Who hathe appointed that place to haue his name called vpõ there.
1. Esdr. 7,1.

f Whome God ſtired vp to aſſure them that he wolde giue their worke good ſucceſſe.

[f] Haggái the Prophet, and Zechariáh the
ſonne of Iddó, and they buylded and finiſhed it, by the appointemẽt of the God
of Iſraél, and by the commandement of
Cyrus and Darius, & Artahſháſhte King
of Perſia.

g This is the twelft moneth, and conteineth parte of Februarie and parte of Marche.
h And the two and fortieth after their firſt returne.

15 And this houſe was finiſhed the third
day of the moneth [g] Adar, which was
[h] the ſixt yere of ẏ reigne of King Darius.
16 ¶ And the children of Iſraél, the Prieſts,
& the Leuites, and the reſidue of the children of the captiuitie kept the dedicacion
of this houſe of God with ioye,
17 And offred at the dedicació of this houſe of God an hundreth bullockes, two
hundreth rams, foure hundreth lambes &
twelue goates, for the ſinne of all Iſraél,
according to the nomber of the tribes of
Iſraél.
18 And they ſet the Prieſts in their ordre,
and the Leuites in their courſes ouer the
ſeruice of God in Ieruſalém, as it is writen in the * boke of Moſés.

Nomb.3.6. & 8.9.

19 And the children of the captiuitie kept
the Paſſeouer on the fourtente *day* of the
firſt moneth.
20 (For the Prieſts & the Leuites were purified all together) & they killed the Paſſeouer for all the children of the captiuitie, & for their brethren the Prieſts, & for
them ſelues.
21 So the children of Iſraél which were come againe out of captiuitie, and all ſuche
as had [i] ſeparated them ſelues vnto them,
from the filthines of the heathen of the
lád, to ſeke ẏ Lord God of Iſraél, did eat,
22 And they kept the feaſt of vnleauened
bread ſeuen dayes with ioye: for the Lord
had made them glad, and turned the heart
of the King of [k] Aſſhúr vnto them, to
"incourage them in the worke of the houſe of God, *euen* the God of Iſraél.

i Which were of the heathé and forſaked their idolatrie to worſhip the true God.
k Meaning, Darius who was King of ẏ Medes, Perſiás and Aſſyrians.
" Ebr. to ſtrengthen their handes.

CHAP. VII.

1 By the commãdement of the King, Ezrá and his companiõs come to Ieruſalém. 27 He giueth thãkes to God.

1 NOw after theſe things, in the reigne
of [a] Artahſháſhte King of Perſia,
was Ezrá the ſonne of Seraiáh, the ſonne
of Azariáh, the ſonne of Hilkiáh,
2 The ſonne of Shallúm, the ſonne of Zadók, the ſonne of Ahitúb,
3 The ſonne of Amariáh, the ſonne of Azariáh, the ſonne of Meraióth,
4 The ſonne of Zeraiáh, the ſonne of Vzzí, the ſonne of Bukkí,
5 The ſonne of Abiſhúa, the ſonne of Phinehás, the ſonne of Eleazár, the ſonne of
[b] Aarón, the chief Prieſt.
6 This Ezrá came vp from Babél, and was
a [c] ſcribe prompt in the Law of Moſés,
which the Lord God of Iſraél had giuen,
and the King gaue him all his requeſt
according to the hand of the Lord his
God *which was* vpon him.

a The Ebrewes write, that diuers of the Kings of Perſia were called by this name, as Pharaóh was a cõmune name to the Kĩgs of Egypt, and Ceſar to ẏ Emperours Romain.
b Ezrá deduceth his kinred, til he cõmeth to Aarón, to proue that he came of him.
c He ſheweth here what a ſcribe is, who had charge to write the Law & to expoũde it, whome Marke calleth a ſcribe, Mar. 12, 28. Mat. and Luke call him a lawier, or doctor of the Law, Mat. 22, 35. Luk. 10, 25.

7 And there went vp *certeine* of the children of Iſraél, and of the Prieſts, and the
Leuites, and the ſingers, and the porters,
and the Nethinims vnto Ieruſalém, in the
ſeuent yere of King Artahſháſhte.
8 And he came to Ieruſalém in the [d] fift
moneth, which was in the ſeuent yere [e] of
the King.

d That conteined parte of Iulie and parte of Auguſt.
e Of King Darius.

9 For vpon the firſt *day* of the firſt moneth
began he to go vp from Babél, and on the
firſt *day* of the fift moneth came he to Ieruſalém, according to the good hand of
his God *that was* vpon him.
10 For Ezrá had prepared his heart to ſeke
the Law of the Lord, and to do it, & to teache the precepts & iudgements in Iſraél.
11 ¶ And this is the copie of the letter that
King Artahſháſhte gaue vnto Ezrá the
Prieſt *&* ſcribe, *euẽ* a writer of the wordes
of the cõmandements of the Lord, and of
his ſtatutes ouer Iſraél.
12 ARTAHSHASHTE King of Kings to
Ezrá ẏ Prieſt & perfite ſcribe of the Law
of the God of heauen, and to [f] Cheéneth.
13 I haue giuen cõmandement, that euerie
one, that is willing in my kingdome of
the people of Iſraél, and of the Prieſts, and
Leuites [g] to go to Ieruſalém with thee,
ſhal go.
14 Therefore art thou ſent of the King and
his ſeuen counſelers, to [h] enquire in Iudáh
and Ieruſalém, according to the Law of
thy God, which is in [i] thine hand,
15 And to carie the ſiluer and the golde, ẇ
the King and his coũſelers willingly offer
vnto the God of Iſraél (whoſe habitacion
is in Ieruſalém)

f Some take this for the name of a people, ſome for time or continuance meaning ẏ the King wiſhed him long life.
g Which remained as yet in Babylon, & had not returned with Zerubbabél.
h To examine who liued according to the Law.
i Whereof thou art expert.

16 And all the ſiluer and golde that thou
canſt finde in all the prouince of Babél,
with the fre offring of the people, and that
which the Prieſts offre willingly to ẏ houſe of their God which is in Ieruſalém,
17 That thou maieſt bye ſpedely with this
ſiluer, bullockes, rams, lambes, with their
meat offrings and their drinke offrings: &
thou ſhalt offer thẽ vpon the altar of the
houſe of your God, which is in Ieruſalém.
18 And whatſoeuer it pleaſeth thee & thy
brethrẽ to do with the reſt of the ſiluer,
and golde, do ye it according to the wil of
your [k] God.
19 And the veſſels that are giuen thee for
the ſeruice of the houſe of thy God, thoſe
deliuer thou before God in Ieruſalém.
20 And the reſidue that ſhalbe nedeful for
the houſe of thy God, which ſhalbe mete
for thee to beſtowe, thou ſhalt beſtowe it
out of the Kings treaſure houſe,
21 And I King Artahſháſhte haue giuen commandement to all the treaſurers
which are beyonde [l] the Riuer, that
whatſoeuer Ezrá the Prieſt and ſcribe

k As ye know beſt may ſerue to Gods glorie.
l Which was the Riuer Euphrates, and they were beyonde it in reſpect of Babylon.

of the Law of ẏ God of heauē shal require of you, that it be done incontinently,
22 Vnto an hundreth talents of siluer, vnto
an hundreth " measures of wheat, and vnto
an hundreth baths of wine, and vnto an
hundreth m baths of oyle, and salt without writing.

"Ebr. Corim.

m Read 1. King 7,26, and 2. Chro.2,10.

23 Whatsoeuer *is* by the commandement
of the God of heauen, let it be done spedely for the house of the God of heauen: for
why shulde he be wrath n against the realme of the King, and his children?
24 And we certifie you, that vpon anie of
ẏ Priests, Leuites, singers, porters, Nethinims, or ministers in this house of God,
there shal no gouernour lay vpon them
tolle, tribute nor custome.

n This declareth that the feare of Gods iudgemēts caused him to vse this liberalitie, and not the loue that he bare to Gods glorie or affection to his people.

25 And thou Ezrá (after the wisdome of thy
God, ẏ is in thine hand) o set iudges & arbiters, which may iudge all ẏ people that
is beyond the Riuer, *euen* all that knowe
the Law of thy God, & teache ye *them* that
knowe it not.

o He gaue Ezrá ful autoritie to restore all things according to the worde of God, and to punish thē that resisted and wolde not obeie.

26 And whosoeuer wil not do the Law of
thy God, and the Kings law, let him haue
iudgement without delay, whether it be
vnto death, or to banishment, or to confiscation of goods, or to imprisonement.
27 p Blessed *be* the Lord God of our fathers,
which so hathe put in the Kings heart, to
beautifie the house of the Lord that is in
Ierusalém,

p Thus Ezrá gaue God thākes for that he gaue him so good successe in his affaires by reason of the King.

28 And hathe enclined mercie towarde me,
before the King and his counselers, and
before all the Kings mightie princes: and
I was comforted by the hand of the Lord
my God *which was* vpon me, and I gathered the chief of Israél to go vp with me.

CHAP. VIII.

8 The nomber of them that returned to Ierusalém with Ezrá. 21 He causeth thē to fast. 24 He admonisheth the Priests of their duetie. 31 What they did when they came to Ierusalém.

1. Esdr. 8,31.

1 THese * are now the chief fathers of
thē, and the genealogie of them that
came vp with me from Babél, in the reigne of King a Artahshashte.

a Read Chap. 7,1.

2 Of the sonnes of Phinehás, Gershóm: of
the sonnes of Ithamár, Daniél: of the sonnes of Dauíd, Hattúsh:
3 Of the sonnes of Shechaniáh, of the sonnes of Pharósh, Zechariáh, and with him
the counte of the males, an hundreth and
fiftie.
4 Of the sonnes of " Pahath Moáb, Eliho-
enái, the sonne of Zerahiáh, and with him
two hundreth males.

"*Or, captaine of Moáb.*

5 Of the sonnes of Shechaniáh, the sonne
of Iahaziél, and with him thre hundreth
males.
6 And of the sonnes of Adin, Ebed the sonne of Ionathán, and with him fiftie males.
7 And of the sonnes of Elám, Ieshaiáh the
sonne of Athaliáh, and with him seuentie
males.
8 And of the sonnes of Shephatiáh, Zebadiáh the sonne of Michaél, and with him
foure score males.
9 Of the sonnes of Ioáb, Obadiáh the sonne of Iehiél, and with him two hundreth
and eightene males.
10 And of the sonnes of Shelomíth the sonne of Iosiphiáh, and with him an hūdreth
and thre score males.
11 And of the sonnes of Bebái, Zechariáh,
the sonne of Bebái, & with him eight and
twentie males.
12 And of the sonnes of Azgád, Iohanán
the sonne of Hakkatán, and with him an
hundreth and ten males.
13 And of the sonnes of Adonikám, *that were* the b last, whose names are these: Eliphélet, Iehiél and Shemaiáh, and with thē
thre score males.

b That came to go with Ezrá.

14 And of the sonnes of Biguái, Vthái, and
Zabbúd, and with them seuentie males.
15 And I gathered them to the c Riuer that
goeth toward Ahauá, and there abode we
thre dayes: then I vewed the people, and
the Priests, and founde there none of the
sonnes of Leuí.

c To that place of Euphrates, where Ahauá the riuer entreth into it.

16 Therefore sent I to Eliézer, to Ariél, to
Shemeiáh, & to Elnathán, & to Iaríb, and
to Elnathán, and to Nathán, and to Zechariáh, and to Meshullám the chief, and
to Ioiaríb and to Elnathán, men of vnderstanding,
17 And I gaue them commandement, to
Iddó the d chiefest at the place of Case-
phiá, and I " tolde them the wordes that
they shulde speake to Iddó, *and* to his brethren the Nethinims at the place of Ca-
siphiá, that they shulde cause the ministers
of the house of our God to come vnto vs.

d He was the chiefest that taght there ẏ Law of God vnto the Leuites.

"*Ebr. put worde in their mouth.*

18 So by the good hand of our God *which
was* vpon vs, they broght vs a man of vnderstanding of the sonnes of Mahalí the
sonne of Leuí, the sonne of Israél, and She
rebiáh with his sonnes and his brethren,
euen eightene.
19 Also Hashabiáh, and with him Ieshaiáh
of the sonnes of Merarí, with his brethren,
and their sonnes twentie.
20 And of the e Nethinims, whome Dauid had set, and the princes for the seruice of the Leuites, two hundreth and twētie of the Nethinims, which all were named by name.

e Read Chap. 2,42.

21 And there at the Riuer, by Ahauá, I proclaimed a fast, that we might humble f our
selues before our God, and seke of him a
right waye for vs, and for our children, &
for all our substance.

f He sheweth that the end of fasting is to hūble the body to the spirit, which muste procede of the heart lyuely touched, or els it is but hypocrisie.

22 For I was g ashamed to require of the
King an armie and horsemen, to helpe vs
against the enemie in the way, because we
had

g He thoght it better to cōmit him selfe to the protection of God, then by seking these ordinarie meanes, to giue an occasion to others to thinke that he did doute of Gods power.

had spoken to the King, saying, The hand
of our God *is* vpon all them that seke him,
in goodnes, but his power and his wrath *is*
against all them that forsake him.
23 So we fasted, and besoght our God for
this: and he was intreated of vs.
24 Then I separated twelue of the chief of
the Priests, Sherebiáh, *and* Hashabiáh, and
ten of their brethren with them,
25 And weighed thē the siluer & the golde,
& the vessels, *euen* the offring of the house
of our God, *which* the King and his coū-
selers, and his princes, and all Israél that
were present had offred.
26 And I weighed vnto their hand six hundreth and fifty [h] talents of siluer, and in
siluer vessel, an hundreth talents, *and* in
golde, an hundreth talents:
27 And twentie basins of golde, of a thousand [i] drammes, and two vessels of shining brasse very good, and precious as
golde.
28 ¶ And I said vnto thē, Ye are consecrate
vnto the Lord, and the vessels *are* consecrate, and the golde and the siluer *are* frely offred vnto the Lord God of your fathers.
29 Watche ye, & kepe *them* vntil ye weigh
them before the chief Priests and the Leuites, and the chief fathers of Israél in Ierusalém in the chambers of the house of
the Lord.
30 So the Priests and the Leuites receiued
the weight of the siluer and of the golde,
and of the vessels to bring *them* to Ierusalém, vnto the house of our God.
31 ¶ Then we departed from the Riuer of
Ahauá on the twelft *day* of the first moneth, to go vnto Ierusalém, and the hand
of our God was vpon vs, and deliuered vs
from the hand of the enemie, and of suche
as layed [k] waite by the way.
32 And we came to Ierusalém, and abode
there thre dayes.
33 And on the fourte day was the siluer
weighed, and the golde and the vessel
in the house of our God by the hand of
Meremóth the sonne of Vriáh the Priest,
and with him *was* Eleazár the sonne of
Phinehás, and with them *was* Iozabád the
sonne of Ieshúa, and Noadiáh the sonne
of Binnúi the [l] Leuites,
34 By nomber and by weight of euerie one,
and all the weight was writen at the same
time.
35 Also the childrē of the captiuitie, which
were come out of captiuitie, offred burnt
offrīgs vnto the God of Israél, twelue bullockes for all Israél, ninetie and six rams,
seuentie and seuen lambes, *and* twelue he
goates for sinne: all *was* a burnt offring of
the Lord.
36 And they deliuered the Kings commis-

h Read 1.Kin. 9,14.

i Read Chap. 2,69.

k This declared that their iourney was ful of danger, and yet God deliuered thē according to their prayer.

l This was a takē of a good conscience & of his integritie, that he wolde haue witnesses of his fidelitie.

sion vnto the Kīgs officers, & to the captaines beyonde the Riuer: and they promoted the people, and the house of God.

CHAP. IX.

1 Ezrá complaineth on the people that had turned them selues from God, and maryed with the Gentiles. 5 He praieth vnto God.

1 WHen *as these things were done, ȳ
rulers came to me, saying, The
people of Israél, and the Priests and the
Leuites are not [a] separated from the people of the lands (as touching their abominacions) *to wit*, of the Canaanites, the
Hittites, the Perizzites, the Iebusites, the
Ammonites, the Moabites, the Egyptians,
and the Amorites.
2 For they haue taken their daughters to
them selues, and to their sonnes, and they
haue mixed the holy sede with the people
of the lands, and the hād of the [b] princes
& rulers hathe bene chief in this trespasse.
3 But when I heard this saying, I rent my
clothes and my garment, and pluckt of the
heere of mine head, and of my beard, &
sate downe [c] astonied.
4 And there assembled vnto me all that
feared the wordes of the God of Israél,
because of the transgresion of them of
the captiuitie. And I sate downe astonied
vntil the *euening sacrifice.
5 And at the euenīg sacrifice I arose vp frō
mine heuines, & when I had rent my clothes and my garment, I fel vpon my knees,
and spred out mine hands vnto the Lord
my God,
6 And said, O my God, I am cōfounded &
ashamed, to lift vp mine eyes vnto thee
my God: for our iniquities are increased
ouer [d] our head, & our trespasse is growen
vp vnto [e] the heauen.
7 From the dayes of our fathers haue we
bene in a great trespasse vnto this day, &
for our iniquities haue we, our Kings, *and*
our Priests bene deliuered into the hand
of ȳ Kings of the lands, vnto the sworde,
into captiuitie, into a spoyle, and into cōfusion of face, as *appeareth* this day.
8 And now for a litle space grace hathe bene shewed from the Lord our God, in
causing a remnant to escape, & in giuing
vs a [f] nayle in his holy place, that our God
may light our eyes, & giue vs a litle reui-
uing in our seruitude.
9 For *thogh* we were bondemen, yet our God
hathe not forsaken vs in our bondage, but
hathe enclined mercie vnto vs in the sight
of the Kings of Persia, to giue vs life, *and*
to erect the house of our God, and to redresse the desolate places thereof, and to
giue vs a wall in Iudáh and in Ierusalém.
10 And now, our God, what shal we say after this? for we haue forsaken thy commādements.

3.Esdr.9,69.

a From the time they came home vnder Zerubbabél vntil ȳ commīg of Ezrá, they had degenerate contrary to the Lawe of God, and maried where it was not lawful, Deu.7,3.

b That is, the gouerners are the chief beginners hereof.

c As one douting whether God wolde cōtinue his benefites toward vs or els destroy this which he had begone.

Exod.29,39. nomb.28,3.

d That is, we are drowned in sinne.

e They so excede that thei can not growe greater.

f In giuing vs a restīg place. it is a similitude takē of thē that remaine stil in a place, which smite nailes to hang things vpon, Isa.22,23.

Exod.23,32. & 34,12,15. deu.7,23.

11 Which thou hast commanded by thy
seruants the Prophetes, saying, * The lãd
whereunto ye go to possesse it, is an vncleane land, because of the filthines of the
people of the lands, which by their abominaciõs, *and* by their vnclennes haue filled it from corner to corner.

12 Now therefore shal ye not giue your
daughters vnto their sonnes, nether shal
ye take their daughters vnto your sonnes,

Deut.23,5.

nor seke their * peace nor wealth for euer,
that ye may be strõg and eat the goodnes
of the land, and leaue it for an inheritance
to your sonnes for euer.

13 And after all that is come vpon vs for
our euil dedes, and for our great trespasses
(seing that thou our God hast staied *vs*
from being benethe [g] for our iniquities, &
hast giuen vs suche deliuerance)

g Hast not vtterly cast vs downe and destroied vs for our sinnes, Deu.28,13.

14 Shulde we returne to breake thy cõmandements, and ioyne in affinitie with the
people of suche abominaciõs? woldest not
thou be angrie toward vs til thou haddest
cõsumed *vs*, so that there *shulde be* no remnant nor anie eskaping?

15 O Lord God of Isráel, thou art iuste, for
we haue bene [h] reserued to escape, as *ap-*
peareth this day: beholde, we are before
thee in our trespasse: therefore we can not
stand before thee because of it.

h He sheweth that God is iuste in punishing his people, & yet merciful in reseruing a residue to whome he sheweth fauour.

CHAP. X.

1 The people repent and turne, and put away their strange wiues.

3.Esdr.8,92.

1 WHiles * Ezrá prayed thus, & [a] confessed him selfe weping, and falling downe before ẏ house of God, there
assembled vnto him of Isráel a very great
Congregacion of men and women & children: for the people wept with a great lamentacion.

a He confessed his sinnes and the sinnes of the people.

2 Then Shechaniáh the sonne of Iehiél one
of the sonnes of Elám, answered, and said
to Ezrá, We haue trespassed against our
God, and haue taken strange wiues of the
people of the land, yet now there is [b] hope
in Isráel concerning this.

b Meaning, that God wolde receiue thẽ to mercie.

3 Now therefore let vs make a couenant
with our God, to put away [c] all the wiues
(and suche as are borne of them) according to the counsel of the Lord, and of
those that feare the commandements of
our God, and let it be done according to
the Law.

c Which are strangers and maried contrarie to the Law of God.

4 Arise: for the matter [d] belongeth vnto
thee: we also wil be with thee: be of comforte and do it.

d Because God hathe giuen thee autoritie, & learning to persuade ẏ people herein and to cõmande them.

5 ¶ Then arose Ezrá, and caused the chief
Priests, the Leuites, & all Isráel, to sweare
that they wolde do according to this
worde. So they sware.

3.Esdr.9,1.

6 * And Ezrá rose vp from before the house
of God, and went into the chambre of Iohanán the sonne of Eliashib: he went euen
thither, *but* he did eat nether bread, nor
dronke water: for he mourned, because of
the trãsgression of thẽ of the captiuitie.

7 And they caused a proclamacion to go
throughout Iudáh and Ierusalém, vnto
" all them of the captiuitie, that they shulde assemble them selues vnto Ierusalém.

" Ebr. sonnes of the captiuitie.

8 And whosoeuer wolde not come within thre dayes according to the counsel of
the princes and Elders, all his substance
shulde be " forfait, & he shulde be separate
from the Congregacion of them of the
captiuitie.

" Or, cõdemned.

9 ¶ Then all the men of Iudáh & Beniamín assembled them selues vnto Ierusalém within thre dayes, which was the twẽtieth *day* of the [e] ninte moneth, and all
the people sate in the strete of the house
of God, trembling for this matter, and
for the [f] raine.

e Which conteined part of Nouember & part of December.

f For the season was giuen to raine, & so ẏ wether was more sharpe & colde, and also their conscience touched them.

10 And Ezrá the Priest stode vp, and said
vnto them, Ye haue transgressed, and haue taken strange wiues, to [g] increase the
trespasse of Isráel.

g Ye haue layed one sinne vpon another.

11 Now therefore [h] giue praise vnto the
Lord God of your fathers, and do his wil
and separate your selues from the people
of the land, & from the strange wiues.

h Read Iosh. 7,19.

12 And all the Congregacion answered, &
said with a loude voyce, So wil we do according to thy wordes vnto vs.

13 But the people are many, and it is a ray-
nie wether, and we are not able to stand
without, neither *is it* the worke of one day
or two: for we are many that haue offended in this thing.

14 Let our rulers stand therefore [i] before
all the Congregacion, and let all them
which haue taken strange wiues in our cities, come at the time appointed, and with
them the Elders of euerie citie and the
iudges thereof, til the fierce wrath of our
God for this matter turne away from vs.

i Let them be appointed to examine this matter.

15 Then were appointed Ionathán the sonne of Asah-él, and Iahaziáh the sonne of
Tikuáh ouer this matter, and Meshullám
and Shabbethái the Leuites helped them.

16 And thei of the captiuitie did so and [k] departed, *euen* Ezrá the Priest, *&* the mẽ *that*
were chief fathers to the familie of their
fathers by name, and sate downe in the
first daye of the tente moneth to examine
the matter.

k Thei went to the chief cities to sit on this matter ẇ was thre moneths in finishing.

17 And vntil the first day of ẏ first moneth
they were finishing the busines with all
the men that had taken strange wiues,

18 And of the sonnes of the Priests there
were men founde, that had taken strange
wiues, *to wit*, of the sonnes of Ieshúa, the
sonne of Iozadák, & of his brethren, Maaseiáh, A Eliézer, and Iaríb and Gedaliáh.

19 And thei gaue [l] their hãds, that thei wolde

l As a token that thei wolde kepe promes & do it.

de put away their wiues,and they that had
trespassed,*gaue* a rāme for their trespasse.
20 And of the sonnes of Immér, Honaní,
and Zebadiáh.
21 And of the sonnes of Harím, Maaseiáh,
and Eliiáh, and Shemaiáh,and Iehiél,and
Vzziáh.
22 And of the sonnes of Pashúr, Elioenái,
Maaseiáh, Ishmaél, Nethaneél, Iozabád,
and Elasáh.
23 And of the Leuites,Iozabád and Shimeí
& Kelaiáh,(which is Kelitáh) Pethahiáh,
Iudáh and Eliézer.
24 And of the singers,Eliashíb. And of the
porters,Shallúm,and Telém,and Vrí.
25 And of [m] Israél: of the sonnes of Parósh,Ramiáh,and Iesiáh, and Malchiáh,
and Miámin,and Eleazár,and Malchiiáh,
and Benaiáh.
26 And of the sonnes of Elám, Mattaniáh,
Zechariáh,and Iehiél,and Abdí,and Iere-
móth,and Eliáh.
27 And of the sonnes of Zattú, Elioenái,
Eliashíb,Mattaniáh,and Ierimóth,& Zabád,and Azizá.
28 And of the sonnes of Bebái,Iehohanán,
Hananiáh,Zabbái,Athlái.

m Meaning, of ẏ comune people: for before he spake of the Priests & Leuites.

29 And of the sonnes of Baní,Meshullám,
Mallúch, and Adaiáh, Iashúb,and Sheál,
Ieramóth.
30 And of the sonnes of ‖ Paháth Moáb,
Adná, & Chelál, Benaiáh,Maaseiáh,Mat
taniáh,Bezaleél,& Binnúi,and Manasséh.
31 And of the sonnes of Harím, Eliézer,
Ishiiáh,Malchiáh,Shemaiáh,Shimeón,
32 Beniamín,Mallúch,Shamariáh.
33 Of the sonnes of Hashúm, Mattenái,
Mattattáh,Zabád,Eliphélet,Ieremái,Me-
nasséh,Shimeí.
34 Of the sonnes of Baní, Maadái, Amrám,and Vél,
35 Banaiáh,Bediáh,Chellúh,
36 Vaniáh, Meremóth,Eliashíb,
37 Mattaniáh, Mattenái,and Iaasau,
38 And Banní & Bennúi,Shimeí,
39 And Shelemiáh,& Nathán, & Adaiáh,
40 Machnadebái, Shashái,Sharái,
41 Azareél, and Shelemiáh, Shemariáh,
42 Shallúm,Amariáh,Ioséph.
43 Of the sonnes of Nebó, Ieiél, Mattithiáh, Zabád,Zebiná,Iadaú,& Ioél, Benaiáh.
44 All these had taken strange wiues: and
among thē were womē that had [n] childrē.

‖ Or, the captaine of Moab.

n Which also were made illegitimate because the mariage was vnlawful.

NEHEMIAH.

THE ARGUMENT.

God doeth in all ages and at all times set vp worthy persones for the commoditie and profite of his Church, as now within the compasse of seuentie yeres he raised vp diuers excellent men for the preseruation of his people, after their returne from Babylon, as Zerubbabél, Ezrá, and Nehemiáh. Whereof the first was their captaine to bring them home, and prouided that the Temple was buylded: the seconde reformed their maners and planted religion: & the third buylded vp the walles, deliuered the people from oppression, and prouided that the Law of God was put in execution among them. He was a godlie man and in great autoritie with the King, so that the King fauoured him greatly, and gaue him moste ample letters for the accomplishement of all things which he colde desire. This boke is also called of the latins the seconde of Ezrá, because he was the writer thereof.

CHAP. I.

1 Nehemiáh bewaileth the calamitie of Ierusalém. 5 He confesseth the sinnes of the people,& prayeth God for them

1 THe wordes of Nehe-
miáh the sonne of Ha-
chaliáh, in the moneth
[a] Chisleu, in the twen-
tieth yere, as I was
in the palace of Shu-
shán,
2 Came Hanáni,one of my [b] brethren, he &
the men of Iudáh, and I asked them concerning the Iewes that were deliuered,
which were of the residue of ẏ captiuitie,
and concerning Ierusalém.
3 And they said vnto me, The residue that
are left of the captiuitie there in the [c] prouince,*are* in great affliction and in reproche,and the wall of Ierusalém *is* broken
downe,& the gates thereof are burnt with
fyre.
4 And when I heard these wordes,I sate
downe and wept, and mourned *certeine*
dayes,and I fasted and prayed before the
God of heauen,
5 And said, *O Lord God of heauen, the
great and terrible God, that kepeth couenant and mercie for them that loue
him, and obserue his commandements,
6 I pray thee,let thine eares be attent,and
thine eyes open, to heare the prayer of
thy seruant,which I pray before thee dayly, day & night for the children of Israél
thy seruants, & confesse the sinnes of the
children of Israél,which we haue sinned

a Which conteineth part of Nouember & part of December, and was their ninth moneth.

b A Iewe as I was.

c Meaning, in Iudea.

* Dan. 9,4.

againſt thee, bothe I & my fathers houſe
haue ſinned:
7 We haue "grieuouſly ſinned againſt thee,
and haue not kept the commandements,
nor the ſtatutes, nor the iudgements,
ẘ thou commandedſt thy ſeruant Moſés.
8 I beſeche thee, remember the worde that
thou commandedſt thy ſeruant Moſés,
ſaying, Ye wil tranſgreſſe, and I wil ſcatre
you abroade among the people.
9 But if ye turne vnto me, and kepe my cōmandements, and do them, thogh your
ſcatering were to the vttermoſt parte of
the heauē, *yet* wil I gather you from thēce
and wil bring you vnto the place that I
haue choſen, to place my Name there.
10 Now theſe are thy ſeruants & thy people, whome thou haſt redemed by thy
great power, and by thy mighty hand.
11 O Lord, I beſeche thee, let thine eare
now hearken to the prayer of thy ſeruant,
and to the prayer of thy ſeruāts, who deſire to [d] feare thy Name, and, I pray thee,
cauſe thy ſeruant to proſper this day, and
giue him fauour in the preſence of [e] this
man: for I was the Kings butler.

"Ebr. corrupted.

Deut. 30, 4.

d That is, to worſhip thee.

e To wit, the King Artahſhaſhte.

CHAP. II.

1 After Nehemiáh had obteined letters of Artaxerxes, 11 He came to Ieruſalém, 17 And buylded the walles.

1 NOw in the moneth [a] Niſan in the
twētieth yere of King [b] Artahſhaſhte, the wine *ſtode* before him, and I toke
vp the wine, and gaue it vnto the King,
now I was not *before time* ſad in his preſence.
2 And the King ſaid vnto me, Why is thy
countenance ſad, ſeing thou art not ſicke? this is nothing, but ſorowe of heart.
Then was I ſore afraied,
3 And I ſaid to the King, God ſaue the
King for euer: why ſhulde not my countenance be ſad, when the citie & houſe of
ẏ ſepulchres of my fathers lieth waſte &
the gates thereof are deuoured with fyre?
4 And the King ſaid vnto me, For what
thing doeſt thou require? Then I praied
[c] to the God of heauen,
5 And ſaid vnto the King, If it pleaſe the
King, and if thy ſeruant haue founde fauour in thy ſight, *I deſire* that thou woldeſt
ſend me to Iudáh vnto the citie of the ſepulchres of my fathers, that I may buylde it.
6 And the King ſaid vnto me, (the quene
alſo ſitting by him) How long ſhal thy
iourney be? and when wilt thou come a-
gaine? So it pleaſed the King, and he ſent
me, and I ſet him a time.
7 After I ſaid vnto the King, If it pleaſe ẏ
King, let them giue me letters to the captaines beyonde the "Riuer, that they may
conuaye me ouer, til I come into Iudáh,

a Which was ẏ firſt moneth of the yere & cōteineth part of Marche & part of April.

b Who is alſo called Darius: read Ezr. 7, 1.

c I deſired God in mine heart to proſper mine enterpriſe.

"Or, Euphrates.

8 And letters vnto Aſáph the keper of the
Kings "parke, that he may giue me timber
to buylde the gates of the palace (which
apperteined to the houſe) & for the walles
of the citie, and for the houſe that I ſhal
entre into. And the King gaue me according to [d] the good hand of my God vpon me.
9 ¶ Then came I to the captaines beyond
the Riuer, & gaue them the Kings letters.
And the King had ſent captaines of the
armie and horſmen with me.
10 But [e] Sanballát the Horonite, and Tobiáh a ſeruant an Ammonite heard it, and
it grieued thē ſore, that there was come a
man which ſoght the wealth of the children of Iſraél.
11 So I came to Ieruſalém, and was there
thre dayes.
12 And I roſe in the night, I, and a few mē
ẘ me: for I tolde no man, what God had
put in mine heart to do at Ieruſalém, and
there was not a beaſt with me, ſaue the
beaſt whereon I rode.
13 And I went out by night by the gate of
the valley, and *came* before the draggon
well, and to the dung porte, and vewed the
walles of Ieruſalém, how they were broken downe, and the portes thereof deuoured with the fyre.
14 Then I went forthe vnto the gate of ẏ
"fountaine, and to the Kings fiſh poole, &
there was no roume for the beaſt that was
vnder me to paſſe.
15 Then went I vp in the night by the
broke, & vewed the wall, and turned backe, and comming backe, I entred by the
gate of the valley and returned.
16 And the rulers knewe not whether I was
gone, nor what I did, nether did I as yet
tel it vnto the Iewes, nor to the Prieſts,
nor to the noble men, nor to the rulers, nor
to the reſt that laboured in the worke.
17 Afterward I ſaid vnto them, Ye ſe the
miſerie that we are in, how Ieruſalém lieth
waſte, and the gates thereof are burnt
with fyre: come and let vs buylde the wall
of Ieruſalém, that we be no more [f] a reproche.
18 Then I tolde them of the hand of my
God, (which was good ouer me) and
alſo of the Kings wordes that he had ſpoken vnto me. And they ſaid, Let vs riſe, &
buylde. So they [g] ſtrengthened their hand
to good.
19 But whē Sanballát the Hōronite, & Tobiáh the ſeruant an Ammonite, and [h] Ge-
ſhém the Arabian heard it, they mocked
vs and deſpiſed vs, and ſaid, What a thīg
is this that ye do? Wil ye [i] rebell againſt
the King?
20 Then anſwered I them, and ſaid to thē,
The God of heauen, he wil proſper vs, &
we

"Or, paradiſe.

d As God moued me to aſke, & as he gaue me good ſucceſſe therein.

e Theſe were great enemies to the Iewes & labored alwaies bothe by force & ſubtiltie to ouercome them, & Tobiáh becauſe his wife was a Ieweſſe, had aduertiſement euer of their affaires and ſo wroght them great trouble.

"Or, conduit.

f That is, contemned of other natiōs, as thogh God had forſaken vs.

g They were incouraged & gaue them ſelues to do wel, & to trauel in this worthy enterpriſe.

h Theſe were thre chief gouerners vnder ẏ King of Perſia beyōde Euphrates.

i Thus ẏ wicked when thei wil burthen ẏ children of God, euer lay treaſon vnto their charge, bothe becauſe it maketh thē moſte odious to the worlde, & alſo ſtirreth ẏ hatred of princes moſte againſt them.

k Nether ye are of the nõber of the children of God (to whome he hathe appointed this citie onely) nether did anie of your predecessours euer feare God.

we his seruants wil rise vp and buylde: but
as for you, ye haue no porcion nor right,
nor [k] memorial in Ierusalém.

CHAP. III.

The nomber of them that buylded the walles.

1 THen arose Eliashib the hie Priest
with his brethren the Priests, & they
buylt the shepegate: thei [a] repared it, & set
vp the dores thereof: euen vnto the towre
of Meáh repared they it, & vnto the towre of Hananeél.

a In Ebrewe, thei sanctified it, that is, they finished it, and so dedicated it to the Lord by prayer, in desiring him to maiteine it.

2 And next vnto him buylded the men of
Ierichó, and beside him Zaccúr the sonne
of Imrí.
3 But the fish porte did the sonnes of Senaáh buylde, which also layed the beames
thereof, and set on the dores thereof, the
lockes thereof, and the barres thereof.
4 And next vnto thẽ fortified Merimóth,
the sonne of Vriiáh, the sonne of Hakkóz:
and next vnto them fortified Meshullám,
the sonne of Berechiáh, the sonne of Meshezabeél: and next vnto them fortified
Zadók, the sonne of Baaná:
5 And next vnto them fortified the Tekoites: but the great men of them [b] put not
their neckes to the worke of their lords.

b The riche & mightie wolde not obey thẽ, which were appointed officers in this worke, nether wolde thei helpe thereũto

6 And the gate of the * olde *fishpoole* fortified Iehoiadá the sonne of Paséah, & Meshullám the sõne of Besodaiáh: thei layed
the beames thereof, and set on the dores
thereof, and the lockes thereof, and the
barres thereof.

Isa.22,11.

7 Next vnto them also fortified Melatiáh
the Gibeonite, & Iadón ẏ Meronothite,
men of Gibeón, and of Mizpáh, vnto the
[c] throne of the Duke, *which was* beyonde
the Riuer.

c Vnto ẏ place where the Duke was wonte to sit in iudgement, who gouerned the countrey in their absence.

8 Next vnto him fortified Vzziél the sonne of Harhohiáh * of the golde smithes:
next vnto him also fortified Hananiáh,
the sonne * of Harakkahím, and they repared Ierusalém vnto the broad wall.

* *Or, of Zorephim.*
* *Or, of the apoticaries.*

9 Also next vnto them fortified Rephaiáh,
the sonne of Hur, the ruler of the halfe
parte of Ierusalém.
10 And next vnto him fortified Iedaiáh the
sonne of Harumáph, euen ouer against
his house: and next vnto him fortified
Hattúsh, the sonne of Hashabniáh.
11 Malchiiáh the sonne of Harím, and Hashúb the sonne of Paháth Moáb fortified
the seconde * portion, & the towre of the
fornaces.

* *Or, measure.*

12 Next vnto him also fortified Shallúm,
the sonne of Halloésh, the ruler of the
halfe parte of Ierusalém, he, & his daughters.
13 The valley gate fortified Hanún, & the
inhabitants of Zanuáh: thei buylt it, and
set on the dores thereof, ẏ lockes thereof,
& the barres thereof, euen a thousand cubites on the wall vnto the dung porte.
14 But the dung porte fortified Malchiáh,
the sonne of Recháb, the ruler of ẏ fourte
parte of Beth-haccárem: he buylt it, & set
on the dores thereof, the lockes thereof, &
the barres thereof.
15 But the gate of the fountaine fortified
Shallún, the sonne of Col-hozéh, the ruler of ẏ fourte parte of Mizpáh: he buylded it, and couered it, and set on the dores
thereof, the lockes thereof, and the barres
thereof, and the wall vnto the fishpoole
of * Sheláh by the Kings garden, and vnto
the steppes that go downe from the citie
of Dauid.

* *Or, Siloh.*

16 After him fortified Nehemiáh the sonne of Azbúk, the ruler of the halfe parte
of Beth-zúr, vntil the otherside ouer against the sepulchres of Dauid, and to the
fishpoole that was repared, and vnto the
house of the mightie.
17 After him fortified the Leuites, Rehúm
the sonne of Baní, and next vnto him fortified Hashabiáh the ruler of the halfe
parte of Keiláh in his quarter.
18 After him fortified their brethren: Bauái, the sonne of Henadád the ruler of the
halfe parte of Keiláh:
19 And next vnto him fortified Ezer, the
sonne of Ieshúa the ruler of Mizpáh, the
other portion ouer against the going vp
to the [d] corner of the armoure.

d Where the weapons and armour of the citie laye.

20 After him was earnest Barúch the sonne
of Zacchái, & fortified another portion
from the corner vnto the dore of the house of Eliashib the hie Priest.
21 After him fortified Merimóth, the sonne of Vriiáh, the sonne of Hakkóz, another portion from the dore of the house
of Eliashib, euen as long as the house of
Eliashib extended.
22 After him also fortified the Priests, the
men of [e] the plaine.

e Which dwelt in ẏ plaine countrey by Iorden & Ierichó.

23 After them fortified Beniamín, & Hashúb ouer against their house: after him
fortified Azariáh, the sonne of Maaseiáh,
the sonne of Ananiáh, by his house.
24 After him fortified Binnúi, the sonne of
Henadád another portiõ, from the house
of Azariáh vnto the turning and vnto the
corner.
25 Palál, the sonne of Vzái, from ouer against the corner, and the high towre, that
lyeth out from the Kings house, which is
beside the courte of the prison. After him,
Pedaiáh, the sonne of Parósh.
26 And the [f] Nethinims they dwelt in the
fortresse vnto the *place* ouer against the
water gate, Eastward, & to the towre that
lyeth out.

f Read Ezra. Chap.2,43.

27 After him fortified ẏ Tekoites another
portion ouer against the great towre, that
lyeth out, euen vnto the wall of the fortresse.

28 Frõ aboue the horſegate forthe fortified
ẏ Prieſts,euerie one ouer agaĩſt his houſe.
29 After them fortified Zadók the ſonne of
Immér ouer againſt his houſe: and after
him fortified Shemaiáh,the ſonne of Shechaniáh the keper of the Eaſtgate.
30 After him fortified Hananiáh,the ſonne
of Shelemiáh,& Hanún,the ſonne of Za-
láph,the g ſixt,another portion: after him
fortified Meſhullám, the ſonne of Berechiáh,ouer againſt his chamber.
31 After him fortified Malchiáh the gold-
ſmithes ſonne, vntil the houſe of the Nethinims,& of the marchants ouer againſt
the gate h Miphkád, and to the chamber
in the corner.
32 And betwene the chamber of the corner
vnto the ſhepegate fortified the goldſmi-
thes and the marchants.

g Meaning,the ſixt of his ſonnes.

h Which was the place of iudgement, or execution.

CHAP. IIII.

7 The buylding of Ieruſalém is hindred, 15 But God breaketh their enterpriſe. 17 The Iewes buylde with one hand,and holde their weapons in the other.

1 BVt when Sanballát heard that we
buylded the wall,then was he wroth
and ſore grieued,and mocked the Iewes,
2 And ſaid before his a brethren and the
armie of Samaria, thus he ſaid, What do
theſe b weake Iewes? wil they fortifie thẽ
ſelues? wil thei ſacrifice? wil thei finiſh it
in a day? wil they make the ſtones whole
againe out of ẏ heapes of duſt,ſeing they
are burnt?
3 And Tobiáh the Ammonite *was* beſide
him,and ſaid, Althogh they buylde, *yet* if
a foxe go vp, he ſhal euen breake downe
their ſtony wall.
4 c Heare,ô our God (for we are deſpiſed)
and turne their ſhame vpon their owne
head, and giue them vnto a pray d in the
land of their captiuitie,
5 And couer not their e iniquitie,nether let
their ſinne be put out in thy preſence: for
thei haue prouoked *vs* before the buylders.
6 So we buylt the wall,and all the wall was
ioyned vnto the * halfe thereof, and the
heart of the people was to worke.
7 ¶ But when Sanballát,and Tobiáh,& the
Arabians,and the Ammonites,& the Aſh-
dodims heard that the walles of Ieruſalém
were repared,(for the breaches begã to be
ſtopped)then thei were verie wroth,
8 And conſpired altogether to come and to
fight againſt Ieruſalém,& to ** hinder thẽ.
9 Then we prayed vnto our God, and ſet
watchemen by them, day & night,becauſe
of them.
10 And Iudáh ſaid,The ſtrength of ẏ bearers is weakened,and there *is* muche earth,
ſo that we are not able to buylde the wall.
11 Alſo our aduerſaries had ſaid, Thei ſhal
not knowe, nether ſe, til we come into the
middes of them and ſlaye them,and cauſe

a Of his companions that dwelt in Samaria.
b Thus the wicked, that conſider not ẏ Gods power is euer in a readines for the defẽce of his, mocke thẽ as thogh thei were weake and feble.
c This is the remedie that the childrẽ of God haue againſt the deriſiõ & threatnings of their enemies, to flee to God by prayer.
d Let them be ſpoiled & led away captiue.
e Let thy plagues declare to the worlde ẏ thei ſet them ſelues againſt thee, & agaĩſt thy Church: thus he prayeth,onely hauing reſpect to Gods glorie,& not for any priuate affection, or grudge.
* Or, halfe height.
** Ebr. make to ſtay, meaning the people.

the worke to ceaſe.
12 But when the Iewes(which dwelt beſide
them)came,they tolde vs f ten times,g Frõ
all places whence ye ſhal returne, *they wil
be* vpon vs.
13 Therefore ſet I in the lower places behinde the wall vpon ẏ toppes of the ſtones,
& placed ẏ people by their families, with
their ſwordes,their ſpeares & their bowes,
14 Then I beheld, and roſe vp,& ſaid vnto
the princes,& to the rulers,& to the reſt of
the people, Be not afraied of them: h remẽber the great Lord, & feareful, & fight
for your brethren, your ſonnes, and your
daughters,your wiues,and your houſes.
15 And when our enemies heard that it was
knowen vnto vs, then God broght their
counſel to noght, & we turned all againe
to the wall,euerie one vnto his worke.
16 And frõ that day,halfe of the yong men
did the labour, and the other halfe parte
of them helde the ſpeares, and ſhields, &
bowes,and habergins: and the rulers *ſtode*
i behinde all the houſe of Iudáh.
17 They that buylded on the wall,and they
that bare burdens, *&* they that laded, did
the worke with one hand,& with the other
helde the ſworde.
18 For euerie one of the buylders *had* his
ſworde girde on his loynes,& *ſo* buylded:
& he that blewe the trũpet, *was* beſide me.
19 Then ſaid I vnto the princes, and to the
rulers, and to the reſt of the people, The
worke is great and large, and we are ſeparated vpon the wall, one farre from another.
20 In what place *therefore* ye heare the ſoũd
of the trumpet, k reſorte ye thither vnto
vs: our God ſhal fight for vs.
21 So we laboured in the worke, and halfe
of them helde the ſpeares,from the appearing of the morning, til the ſtarres came
forthe.
22 And at the ſame time ſaid I vnto the
people, Let euerie one with his ſeruant
lodge within Ieruſalém,that they may be
a watche for vs in the night,and labour in
the day.
23 So nether I,nor my brethren,nor my ſeruants,nor the mẽ of the warde,(which followed me) none of vs did put of our clothes,ſaue euerie one put them of l for waſ-
ſhing.

f That is, oftentimes.
g Thei,which broght the tidĩgs,ſaid thus, Whẽ you leaue your worke, & go ether to eat, or to reſt, your enemies wil aſſaile you.
h Who is euer at hand to deliuer his out of danger,and therefore ſeīg thei ſhulde fight for the maintenãce of Gods glorie & for the preſeruation of their owne liues & of theirs, he incourageth them to play the valiãt mẽ
i To ouerſee them & to incourage them to their worke.
k Meaning, to reſiſt their enemies,if nede required.
l That is, whẽ they purified them ſelues,or els when they waſhed their clothes.

CHAP. V.

1 The people are oppreſſed and in neceſsitie. 6 Nehemiáh remedieth it. 14 He toke not the portion of others that had ruled before,leſt he ſhulde grieue the people.

1 NOw there was a great crye of the
people, and of their wiues a againſt
their brethren the Iewes.
2 For there were that ſaid, We,our ſõnes &
our daughters are many,therefore we take
vp b corne,that we may eat and liue.
3 And there were that ſaid, We muſt gage

a Againſt the riche, which oppreſſed thẽ.
b This is the cõplaint of ẏ people,ſhewig to what extremitie thei were broght vnto

our lands,& our vineyardes,& our houses
and take vp corne for the famine.
4 There were also that said, We haue borowed money for the Kings [c] tribute *vpon*
our lands and our vineyardes.
5 And now our flesh *is* as [d] the flesh of
our brethrẽ,& our sonnes as their sonnes:
and lo,we bring into subiection our sonnes,and our daughters,as seruãts,and there be of our daughters *now* in subiection,
and there *is* no power [e] in our hands: for
other mẽ *haue* our lãds & our vineyardes.
6 Then was I very angrie when I heard
their crye and these wordes.
7 And I thoght in my minde, and I rebuked the princes, and the rulers, and said
vnto them, You laie [f] burdens euerie one
vpon his brethren:and I set a great [g] assemblie against them,
8 And I said vnto them, We(according to
our abilitie) haue redemed our brethren
the Iewes,which were solde vnto the hea-
then:and wil you sell your brethren againe,or shal they be [h] solde vnto vs? Then
helde they their peace, and colde not
answere.
9 [i] I said also, That which ye do,is not
good. Oght ye not to walke in the feare of our God, for the [k] reproche of the
heathen our enemies?
10 For euen I, my brethren, and my seruãts
do lend them money & corne:I pray you,
let vs leaue of this "burden.
11 Restore,I pray you, vnto them this day
their lands,their vineyardes, their oliues,
and their houses, and *remit* the hundreth
parte of the siluer and of the corne, of the
wine,& of the oyle [l] that ye exact of thẽ.
12 Then said they, We wil restore it, and
wil not require it of them: we wil do as
thou hast said. Then I called the Priests,&
caused them to sweare,that they shulde do
according to this promes.
13 So I shooke my lappe,& said,So let God
shake out euerie man that wil not performe this promes from his house,and from
his labour:euen thus let him be shakẽ out,
and emptied. And all the Congregacion
said,Amen,and praised the Lord: and the
people did according to this promes.
14 And frõ the time that *the King* gaue me
charge to be gouernour in the land of Iudáh from the twentieth yere,euẽ vnto the
two and thirtieth yere of King Artahshá-
shte,*that is*, twelue yere,I, and my brethrẽ
haue not eatẽ the [m] bread of ỹ gouernour.
15 For the former gouernours that were
before me, had bene chargeable vnto the
people, and had taken of them bread and
wine, besides fourtie shekels of siluer:yea,
and their seruants bare rule ouer the people: but so did not I, because of the feare
of God.

c To pay our tribute to the King of the Persiãs,which was exacted yerely of vs.
d By nature ỹ riche is no better thẽ the poore.
e We are not able to redeme thẽ,but for pouertie are cõstrayned to hier thẽ to others.
f You presse thẽ with vsurie and seke how to bring all things into your hands.
g Bothe because they shulde be moued with pitie, seing how manie were by them opprest, and also heare the iudgement of others, ŵ shulde be as it were witnesses of their dealing toward their brethrẽ.
h Seing God hathe once deliuered thẽ frõ the bõdage of the heathen, shal we make them our slaues?
i Meaning, Nehemiáh.
k Who by this occasion wil blaspheme the Name of God seing that our actes are no better then theirs.
" Or, vsurie.
l Which ye take of them for the lone.
m I receiued not that porcion,and diet, which the gouernours, that were before me, exacted: wherein he declareth that he rather soght ỹ wealth of the people, then his owne commoditie.

16 But rather I fortified *a porcion* in the worke of this wall, and we boght no land, and
all my seruants came thether together vnto the worke.
17 Moreouer there *were* at my table an hundreth and fiftie of the Iewes, and rulers,
which came vnto vs from among the heathen that are about vs.
18 And there was prepared daiely an oxe,&
six chosen shepe, & birdes were prepared
for me,and "within ten dayes wine for all
[n] in abundance. Yet for all this I required
not the bread of the gouernour: for the
bondage was grieuous vnto this people.
19 Remember me, ô my God,in goodnes,
according to all that I haue done for this
people.

" Or, once in ten dayes.
n Where as at other times they had by measure, at this time they had most liberally.

CHAP. VI.

8 Nehemiáh answereth with great wisdome,and zeale to his aduersarie. 11 He is not discouraged by the false Prophetes.

1 AND when Sanballát, and Tobiáh, &
Géshem the Arabian, and the rest of
our enemies heard that I had buylt ỹ wall,
& that there were no mo [a] breaches the-
rein(thogh at that time I had not set vp
the dores vpon the gates)
2 Thẽ sent Sanballát and Géshẽ vnto me,
saying, Come thou that we may mete together in the villages in the plaine of O-
nó:and they thoght to do me euil.
3 Therefore I sent messengers vnto them,
saying, I haue a great worke to do,& I can
not come downe: [b] why shulde the worke cease,whiles I leaue it,and come downe
to you?
4 Yet they sent vnto me foure times after
this sorte. And I answered them after the
same maner.
5 Then sent Sanballát his seruant after this
sorte vnto me the fift time, with an open
letter in his hand,
6 Wherein was writẽ, It is reported amõg
the heathen,and "Gashmú hathe said it,
that thou and the Iewes thinke to rebell,
for the which cause thou buyldest the wall
and thou wilt be their King according to
these [c] wordes.
7 Thou hast also ordeined [d] the Prophetes to preache of thee at Ierusalém,sayĩg,
There is a King in Iudáh: and now according to these wordes it shal come to the
Kings eares:come now therefore, and let
vs take counsel together.
8 Thẽ I sent vnto him,saying,It is not done
according to these wordes ỹ thou sayest:
for thou fainest them of thine owne heart.
9 For all thei afraied vs,saying, Their hãds
shal be weakened frõ ỹ worke,& it shal not
be done:now therefore "incourage ỹ me.
10 ¶ And I came to the house of Shemaiáh ỹ
sõne of Delaiáh the sonne of Mehetabeél,
& he was [e] shut vp,& he said,Let vs come

a That is,that they were ioined together, as Chap.4,6.
b Meaning,ỹ if he shulde obei their request,the worke,which God had appoĩted, shulde cease: shewing hereby that we shulde not cõmit our selues to the hãds of the wicked.
" Or, Géshem.
c As the fame goeth.
d Thou hast bribed,and set vp false Prophetes, to make thy selfe King,and so to defraude the King of Persia of that subiection, which you ogh vnto him.
" Ebr. strẽgthen then mine hãd.
e As thogh he wolde be secret to the intent that he might pray vnto God with greater libertie,and receiue some reuelation,which in him was but hypocrisie.

together into ŷ houſe of God in the middes of the Tẽple, and ſhut the dores of the
Temple: for they wil come to ſlay thee:
yea, in ŷ night wil they come to kil thee.
11 Then I ſaid, [f] Shulde ſuche a man as I,
flee? Who is he, being as I am, that wolde
go into the Temple to liue? I wil not
go in.
12 And lo, I perceiued, that God had not
ſent him, but that he pronoũced this prophecie againſt me: for Tobiáh and Sanballát had hyred him.
13 Therefore was he hyred, that I might be
afrayed, and do thus, and ſinne, and that
they might haue an euil reporte that they
might reproche me.
14 My God, remember thou Tobiáh, and
Sanballát according vnto theſe their workes, and Noadiáh the [g] Propheteſſe alſo,
and the reſt of the Prophetes that wolde
haue put me in feare.
15 ¶ Notwithſtanding the wall was finiſhed on the fiue & twentieth *day* of [h] Elúl,
in two and [i] fiftie dayes.
16 And whẽ all our enemies heard thereof,
euen all the heathen ŷ were about vs, thei
were afrayed, & their courage failed thẽ:
for they knewe, ŷ this worke was wroght
by our God.
17 And in theſe dayes *were* there manie of
the princes of Iudáh, whoſe [k] letters wẽt
vnto Tobiáh, and thoſe of Tobiáh came
vnto them.
18 For there *were* manie in Iudáh, that were
ſworne vnto him: for he was the ſonne in
law of Shechaniáh, the ſonne of Aráh: &
his ſonne Iehonathán had the daughter
of Meſhullám, the ſonne of Berechiáh.
19 Yea, they ſpake in his praiſe before me, &
tolde him my wordes, & Tobiáh ſent letters to put me in feare.

f He douted not but God was able to preſerue him, & knewe that, if he had obeyed this counſel, he ſhuld haue diſcouraged all the people: thus God giueth power to his, to reſiſt falſe prophecies thogh they ſeme to haue neuer ſo great probabilitie.

g Very grief cauſed him to pray againſt ſuche, which vnder the pretence of being the miniſters of God, were aduerſaries to his glorie, and went about to ouerthrow his Church, declaring alſo hereby that where there is one true miniſter of God, ŷ deuil hathe a great ſorte of hierlings.

h Which was the ſixt moneth and conteined parte of Auguſt, and parte of Sept.

i After that I had ſent Sanballát his anſwere.

k Thus the Church of God hathe euermore enemies within it ſelfe, which are more dangerous then the outwarde and profeſſed enemie.

CHAP. VII.

1 *After the wall once buylded, is the watche appointed.*
6 *They that returned from the captiuitie are nõbred.*

1 NOw [*] when the wall was buylded, & I
had ſet vp the dores, and the porters,
and the ſingers and the Leuites were appointed,
2 Then I commanded my brother Hanáni
and Hananiáh the prince of the palace in
Ieruſalém (for he was doutles a faithful
man, and feared God aboue manie)
3 And I ſaid vnto them, Let not the gates
of Ieruſalém be opened, vntil the heat of
the ſunne: and while [a] they ſtand by, let
them ſhut the dores, and [**] make them faſt:
and I appointed wardes of the inhabitans
of Ieruſalém, euerie one in his warde, and
euerie one ouer againſt his houſe.
4 Now the citie *was* large and great, but
the people *were* fewe therein, and the houſes were not buylded.
5 And my God put into mine heart, and I

* Eccleſ. 49, 15.

a To wit, thei that are mencioned, ver. 2.

** *Ebr. holde thẽ, meaning til the barres were put in.*

gathered the princes, and the rulers, & the
people, to counte their genealogies: and I
founde a boke of the genealogie of them,
[*] which came vp at the firſt, and founde
writen therein,
6 Theſe are the [b] ſonnes of ŷ prouince that
came vp from the captiuitie that was caryed away (whome Nebuchadnezzár
King of Babél had caried away) and they
returned to Ieruſalém & to Iudáh, euerie
one vnto his citie.
7 They which came with Zerubbabél, Ieſhúa, Nehemiáh, [c] Azariáh, Raamiáh,
Nahamáni, Mordecái, Bilſhán, Miſpé-
reth, Biguái, Nehúm, Baanáh. *This is* the
nõber of the men of the people of Iſraél.
8 The ſonnes of Paróſh, two thouſand an
hundreth ſeuentie and two.
9 The ſonnes of Shephatiáh, thre hundreth ſeuentie and two.
10 The ſonnes of Aráh, ſix hundreth fiftie
and two.
11 The ſonnes of [*] Paháth Moáb of the ſonnes of Ieſhúa, & Ioáb, two thouſand, eight
hundreth and eightene.
12 The ſonnes of Elám, a thouſand, two
hundreth fiftie and foure.
13 The ſonnes of Zattú, eight hundreth &
fyue and fourtie.
14 The ſonnes of Zacchái, ſeuen hundreth
and thre ſcore.
15 The ſonnes of Binnúi, ſix hundreth and
eight and fourtie.
16 The ſonnes of Bebái, ſix hundreth and
eight and twentie.
17 The ſonnes of Azgád, two thouſand, thre
hundreth and two and twentie.
18 The ſonnes of Adonikám, ſix hundreth
thre ſcore and ſeuen.
19 The ſonnes of Biguái, two thouſand thre
ſcore and ſeuen.
20 The ſonnes of Adín, ſix hundreth, and
fyue and fiftie.
21 The ſonnes of Atér of Hizkiáh, ninetie
and eight.
22 The ſonnes of Haſhúm, thre hundreth
and eight and twentie.
23 The ſonnes of Bezái, thre hundreth and
foure and twentie.
24 The ſonnes of Haríph, an hundreth and
twelue.
25 The [d] ſonnes of Gibeón, ninetie and
fyue.
26 The men of Beth-léhem & Netopháh,
an hundreth foure ſcore and eight.
27 The men of Anathóth, an hundreth and
eight and twentie.
28 The men of Beth-azmáueth, two and
fourtie.
29 The men of Kiriath-iearím, Chephiráh
and Beeróth, ſeuen hundreth, and thre and
fourtie.
30 The men of Ramáh and Gába, ſix hundreth

* Ezr. 2, 2.

b That is, the inhabitants of Iudáh.

c Azariáh in Ezrá is called Seraiáh, and Raamiáh, Reeliáh, chap. 2, 2.

* *Or, the captaine of Moáb.*

d That is, the inhabitants of Gibeón.

dreth and one and twentie.
31 The men of Michmás, an hundreth and
two an twentie.
32 The men of Beth-él and Ai, an hundreth
and thre and twentie.
33 The men [e] of the other Nebó, two and
fiftie.

e For there were two cities of this name.

34 The sonnes of the other Elám, a thousand, two hundreth and foure and fiftie.
35 The sonnes of Harím, thre hundreth &
twentie.
36 The sonnes of Ierichó, thre hundreth
and fyue and fourtie.
37 The sonnes of Lod-hadíd and Onó, seuen hundreth, and one and twentie.
38 The sonnes of Senaáh, thre thousand,
nine hundreth and thirtie.
39 The Priests: the sonnes of Iedaiáh of the
house of Ieshúa, nine hundreth seuentie &
thre.
40 The sonnes of Immér, a thousand and
two and fiftie.
41 The sonnes of Pashúr, a thousand, two
hundreth and seuen and fourtie.
42 The sonnes of Harím, a thousand and
seuentene.
43 ¶ The Leuites: the sonnes of Ieshúa of
Kadmiél, and of the sonnes of ″Hodiuáh,
seuentie and foure.

″Or, Hodaiáh.

44 ¶ The singers: the children of Asáph,
an hundreth, and eight and fourtie.
45 The porters: the sonnes of Shallúm, the
sonnes of Atér, the sonnes of Talmón,
ẏ sonnes of Akkúb, the sonnes of Hatitá,
the sonnes of Shobái, an hundreth and
eight and thirtie.
46 ¶ The [f] Nethinims: the sonnes of Zihá, the sonnes of Hashuphá, the sonnes of
Tabaóth,

f Read Ezrá 2,58.

47 The sonnes of Kerós, the sonnes of Siá,
the sonnes of Padón,
48 The sonnes of Lebaná, the sonnes of Hagabá, the sonnes of Shalmái,
49 The sonnes of Hanán, the sonnes of
Giddél, the sonnes of Gáhar,
50 The sonnes of Reaiáh, the sonnes of Rezín, the sonnes of Nekodá,
51 The sonnes of Gazzám, the sonnes of
Vzzá, the sonnes of Paséah,
52 The sonnes of Besái, the sonnes of Meuním, the sonnes of Nephishesim,
53 The sonnes of Bakbúk, the sonnes of Hakuphá, the sonnes of Harhúr,
54 The sonnes of Bazlíth, the sonnes of
Mehidá, the sonnes of Harshá,
55 The sonnes of Barkós, the sonnes of Sisserá, the sonnes of Támah,
56 The sonnes of Nezíah, the sonnes of
Hatiphá,
57 The sonnes of Salomons seruants, the
sonnes of Sotái, the sonnes of Sophéreth,
the sonnes of Peridá,
58 The sonnes of Iaalá, the sonnes of Darkón, the sonnes of Giddél,
59 The sonnes of Shephatiáh, the sonnes
of Hattíl, the sonnes of Pochéreth of Zebaím, the sonnes of Amón.
60 All the Nethinims, and the sonnes of
Salomons seruants *were* thre hũdreth, ninetie and two.
61 ¶ And these came vp from Tel-meláh,
Tel-hareshá, Cherúb, Addón, and Immér: but thei colde not shew their fathers
house, nor their sede, *or* if they were of Israél.
62 The sonnes of Delaiáh: the sonnes of
Tobiáh, the sonnes of Nekodá, six hundreth and two and fourtie.
63 And of the Priests: the sonnes of Habaiáh, the sonnes of Hakkóz, the sonnes of
Barzillái, which toke one of the daughters
of Barzillái the Giliadite to wife, & was
named after their name.
64 These soght their writing of the genealogies, but it was not founde: therefore they were put from the Priesthode.
65 And [g] the Tirsháthа said vnto thẽ, that
they shulde not eat of the most holy, til
there rose vp a Priest with * Vrím and
Thummím.

g Meaning, Nehemiáh: for Tirshatha in ẏ Chalde tõgue signifieth a butler.

Exod. 28,30.

66 All the Congregacion together *was* two
and fourtie thousand, thre hundreth and
threscore,
67 Besides their seruants and their maids,
which were seuen thousand, thre hũdreth
and seuen and thirtie: and they had two
hundreth and fiue and fourtie singing
men and singing women.
68 Their horses *were* seuen hundreth & six
and thirtie, & their mules two hundreth
and fiue and fourtie.
69 The camels foure hundreth and fiue &
thirtie, & six thousand, seuen hundreth &
twentie asses.
70 And certeine of the chief fathers gaue
vnto the worke. The Tirsháthа gaue to
the treasure, a thousand [h] drammes of golde, fiftie basins, fiue hundreth and thirtie
Priests garments.

h Read Ezrá 2,69.

71 And *some* of the chief fathers gaue vnto
the treasure of the worke, twentie thousand drammes of golde and two thousand and two hundreth ″ pieces of siluer.

″Or, mines.

72 And the rest of the people gaue twentie
thousand drammes of golde, & two thousand pieces of siluer, & thre score and seuen Priests garments.
73 And the Priests and Leuites, & the porters and the singers and the rest of the
people and the Nethinims, and all Israél
dwelt in their cities: and when the [i] seuent
moneth came, the children of Israél were
in their cities.

i Which conteined parte of September & parte of October.

CHAP. VIII.

1 *Ezrá gathereth together the people, and readeth to the*

the Law. 12 They reioyce in Israél for the knowledge of the worde of God. 15 They kepe the feast of Tabernacles or boothes.

1 AND all the people assembled them
selues "together, in ỹ streat that was
before the watergate, and they spake vnto
Ezrá the [a] scribe, that he wolde bring the
boke of the Law of Mosés, which the Lord
had commanded to Israél.

" Ebr. as one man.

a Read Ezrá 7,5.

2 And Ezrá the Priest broght the Law before the Congregacion bothe of men and
women, and of all that [b] colde heare and
vnderstand it, in the first day of the seuent moneth,

b Which had age and discretion to vnderstand.

3 And he red therein in the streat that was
before the watergate (from the morning
vntil [c] the midday) before men and women, and of them that vnderstode it, and
the eares of all the people *hearkened* vnto
the boke of the Law.

c This declareth the great zeale, that the people had to heare ỹ worde of God.

4 And Ezrá the scribe stode vpon a pulpit of wood, which he had made for the
preaching, & beside him stode Mattithiáh,
and Shéma, and Ananiáh, and Vriiáh, &
Hilkiáh, and Maaseiáh on his right hãd,
and on his left hand Pedaiáh, & Mishaél,
and Malchiáh, and Hashúm, and Hashba-
dána, Zechariáh, *and* Meshullám.

5 And Ezrá opened the boke before all the
people: for he was [d] aboue all the people:
and when he opened it, all the people stode vp.

d To the intent that his voyce might be the better heard.

6 And Ezrá praised ỹ Lord the great God,
and all the people answered, Amen, Amẽ,
with lifting vp their hãds: & they bowed
them selues, and worshiped the Lord
with their faces toward the grounde.

7 Also Ieshúa, and Baní, and Sherebiáh, Iamín, Akkúb, Shabbethái, Hodiiáh, Maaseiáh, Kelitá, Azariáh, Iozabád, Hanán, Pelaiáh, & the Leuites caused the people to
vnderstand the Law, and the people *stode*
in their place.

8 And they red in the boke of the Law of
God distinctly and gaue the sense, & caused them to vnderstand the reading.

9 Then Nehemiáh (which is Tirsháthа)
and Ezrá the Priest & scribe, and the Leuites that instructed the people, said vnto
all the people, This daye is holy vnto the
Lord your God: mourne not, nether wepe:
for all the people [e] wept, whẽ they heard
the wordes of the Law.

10 He said also vnto them, Go, *and* eat of
the fat, & drinke the swete, and send parte
vnto them, for whome none *is* [f] prepared:
for this day is holy vnto our Lord: be ye
not sory therefore: for the [g] ioye of the
Lord is your strength.

11 And the Leuites made silence throughout all the people, saying, Holde your peace: for ỹ day is holy, be not sad therefore.

12 Then all the people went to eat and to

e In considering their offenses against the Law. Therefore the Leuites do not reproue them for mourning, but assure thẽ of Gods mercies for asmuche as they are repentant.

f That is, remember the poore.

g Reioyce in the Lord, and he wil giue you strength.

drinke, and to send away parte, & to make
great ioye, because they had vnderstand
the wordes that they had taught them.

13 And on the secõde day the chief fathers
of all the people, the Priests and the Leuites were gathered vnto Ezrá the scribe,
that he also might instruct them in the
wordes of the Law.

14 And thei founde writẽ in the Law, (that
the Lord had commanded by Mosés) that
the childrẽ of Israél shulde dwell in *boothes in the feast of the seuent moneth,

* Leui.23,34.

15 And that thei shulde cause it to be declared and proclaimed in all their cities, and
in Ierusalém, saying, Go forthe vnto the
mount, and bring oliuebranches, and pi-
nebranches, and branches of "myrtus, and
palmebranches, and branches of thicke
trees, to make boothes, as it is writen.

" Or, goodly brãches, as Leu.23, 40.

16 So the people went forthe and broght *thẽ*
& made them boothes, euerie one vpon
the [h] rofe of his house, and in their courts,
and in the courts of the house of God, &
in the strete by the watergate, and in the
strete of the gate of Ephráim.

h For their houses were made flat aboue, read Deu.22,8.

17 And all the Cõgregacion of them ỹ were come againe out of the captiuitie, made
boothes, & sate vnder the boothes: for since the [i] time of Ieshúa the sonne of Nun
vnto this day, had not the children of Israél done so, & there was very great ioye.

i Which was almost a thousand yeres.

18 And he red in the boke of the Law of
God euerie day, from the first daye vnto
the last daye. And thei kept the feast seuen
dayes, & on the eight daye a solẽne assemblie, according vnto the maner.

CHAP. IX.

1 The people repent, & forsake their strange wiues. 5 The Leuites exhorte them to praise God, 6 Declaring his wonders, 26 And their ingratitude, 30 And Gods great mercies toward them.

1 IN the foure & twentieth day of this
[a] moneth the children of Israél were assembled with * fasting, & with sackecloth,
and earth vpon them.

a Meaning, the seuent.

* 3. Esdr. 9,4.

2 (And they that were of the sede of Israél were separated from all the "strãgers)
& thei stode and confessed their sinnes and
the iniquities of their fathers.

" Ebr. strange children.

3 And they stode vp in their place and red
in the boke of the Law of the Lord their
God foure times on the day, and thei [b] cõfessed and worshiped ỹ Lord their God
foure times.

b Thei made cõfessiõ of their sinnes & vsed praiers.

4 Then stode vp vpon the staires of the
Leuites Ieshúa, and Baní, Kadmiél, Sheba
niáh, Bunní, Sherebiáh, Baní & Chenáni,
& cryed with a loude voice vnto the Lord
their God.

5 And ỹ Leuites said, *euẽ* Ieshúa & Kadmiél, Baní, Hashabniáh, Sherebiáh, Hodiiáh,
Shebaniáh & Pethahiáh, Stãd vp, & praise ỹ Lord your God for euer, & euer, & let
them

them praise thy glorious Name, ô God, which
excelleth aboue all thãksgiuing & praise.
6 Thou art Lord alone: thou hast made hea
uen, and the heauen of all heauens, with
all their hoste, the earth, and all thĩgs that
are therein, the seas, & all that are in thẽ,
and thou preseruest them all, and the hoste
of the heauen worshipeth thee.
7 Thou art, ô Lord, the God, that hast cho-
Gene.11,31. sen Abrám, & broghtest him out of * Vr in
Gen.17,5. Caldea * and madest his name Abrahám,
8 And foundest his heart faithful before
Gen.15,18. thee, * and madest a couenant with him, to
giue vnto his sede the land of the Canaanites, Hittites, Amorites, & Perizzites, &
Iebusites, and Girgashites, and hast performed thy wordes, because thou art iust.
Exod.3,7. 9 * Thou hast also considered the affliction of our fathers in Egypt, and heard
their crye by the red Sea,
10 And shewed tokens and wonders vpon
Pharaóh, and on all his seruants, & on all
the people of his land: for thou knewest
that thei dealt proudely agaĩst thẽ: therefore thou madest thee a Name, as *appeareth* this day.
Exod.14,21. 11 * For thou didest breake vp the Sea before them, and they went through the mid-
des of the Sea on drye lãd: and those that
pursued them, hast thou cast into the bottoms as a stone, in the mightie waters:
Exod.13,21. 12 And * leddest thẽ in the daye with a piller of a cloude, & in the night with a piller of fyre to giue them light in the way
that thei went.
Exod.20,1. 13 * Thou camest downe also vpon mount
Sinái, and spakest vnto them from heauen,
& gauest them right iudgements, & true
lawes, ordinãces & good commandemẽts,
14 And declaredst vnto thẽ thine holy Sabbath, and commandedst them precepts, &
ordinances, and laws, by the hand of Mosés thy seruant:
Exod.16,15. 15 * And gauest them bread from heauen
Exod.17,6. for their hungre, * & broghtest forthe water for them out of the rocke for their
Deu.1,8. thirst: & * promisedst them that thei shulde
go in, & take possession of the land: for the
which thou haddest lift vp thine hand for
to giue them.
16 But thei and our fathers behaued them
selues proudely and hardened their necke,
so that they hearkened not vnto thy commandements,
17 But refused to obey, and wolde not remember thy maruelous workes that thou
hadest done for them, but hardened their
neckes and had in their heades to returne to their bondage by their rebellion:
but thou, ô God of mercies, gracious and
ful of compassion, of long suffring and
of great mercie, yet forsokest them not.
18 Moreouer when they made them a moltẽ calfe (and said, This is thy god ý broght
thee vp out of the land of Egypt) & committed great blasphemies,
19 Yet thou for thy great mercies forsokest
them not in the wildernes: * the piller of Exod.13,21.
the cloude departed not from them by nom.14,14.
day to lead them the way, nether the pil- 1.cor.10,1.
ler of fyre by night, to shewe them light, &
the way whereby they shulde go.
20 Thou gauest also thy good Spirit to instruct them, & withheldest not thy MAN
from their mouth, and gauest them water
for their thirst.
21 Thou didest also fede thẽ fourtie yeres
in ý wildernes: thei lacked nothĩg: * their Deut.8,4.
clothes waxed not olde, and their fete
c swelled not.
22 And thou gauest them kingdomes and
people, and d scatteredst them into corners: so they possessed * the land of Sihón
and the land of the King of Heshbón, &
the land of Og King of Bashán.
23 And thou didest multiplie their childrẽ,
like the starres of the heauen, & broghtest them into the lãd, whereof thou hadest spoken vnto their fathers, that they
shulde go, and possesse it.
24 So the children went in, and possessed
the land, and thou subduedst before them
the inhabitants of the land, *euen* the Canaanites, and gauest them into their hãds,
with their Kings and the people of the
land, that they might do with them what
they wolde.
25 And they toke their strõg cities and the
fat land, and possessed houses, full of all
goods, cisternes digged out, vineyardes,
& oliues, and trees for fode in abundance,
and they did eat, and were filled, and became fat, & liued in pleasure through thy
great goodnes.
26 Yet they were disobedient, and rebelled
against thee, & cast thy Law behinde their
backes & slewe thy Prophetes (which e pro
tested among them to turne them vnto
thee) and committed great blasphemies.
27 Therefore thou deliueredst them into
the hand of their enemies that vexed thẽ:
yet in the time of their affliction, when
they cryed vnto thee, thou heardest them
from the heauen, and through thy great
mercies thou gauest them sauiours, who
saued them out of the hand of their aduersaries.
28 But when they had f rest, they returned
to do euil before thee: therefore leftest
thou them in the hand of their enemies,
so that thei had the dominion ouer them,
yet when they conuerted and cryed vnto
thee, thou heardest them from heauen, and
deliueredst them according to thy great
mercies many times,
29 And protestedst among them that thou

c Thogh the way was tedious & long.

d Meaning the heathen whome he droue out.

Nom.21,26.

e Taking heauen and earth to witnes that God wolde destroye thẽ, except thei returned, as 2. Chro.24,19.

f He declareth how Gods mercies euer contended with the wickednes of the people, who euer in their prosperitie forgate God.

mightest bring thẽ againe vnto thy Law:
but they behaued them selues proudely,
and hearkened not vnto thy commandements, but sinned against thy iudgements (* which a man shulde do and liue in them) and g pulled away the shuldre, and were stifnecked, and wolde not
h heare.
30 Yet thou " didest forbeare them many
yeres, and protestedst among them by thy
Spirit, *euen* by the hand of thy Prophetes,
but they wolde not heare: therefore gauest
thou them into the hand of the people of
the lands.
31 Yet for thy great mercies, thou hast not
consumed them, nether forsaken them:
for thou art a gracious and merciful
God.
32 Now therefore our God, * thou great
God, mightie and terrible, that kepest couenant and * mercie, let not all the affliction that hathe come vnto vs, seme a litle before thee, *that is*, to our Kings, to our
princes, & to our Priests, and to our Prophetes and to our fathers, & to all thy peo
ple since the time of the Kings of i Asshúr
vnto this day.
33 Surely thou art iust in all that is come
vpon vs: for thou k hast delt truely, but we
haue done wickedly.
34 And our Kings and our princes, our
Priests and our fathers haue not done thy
Law, nor regarded thy commandements
nor thy protestatiõs, wherewith thou hast
l protested among them.
35 And they haue not serued thee in their
kingdome, and in thy great goodnes that
thou shewedst vnto them, and in the large and fat land which thou settest before
them, and haue not conuerted from their
euil workes.
36 Beholde, we are seruants this day, &
the lãd that thou gauest vnto our fathers,
to eate the m frute thereof, and the goodnes thereof, beholde, we are seruants therein.
37 And it yeldeth muche frute vnto ẏ Kĩgs
whome thou hast set ouer vs, because of
our sinnes: and they haue dominion ouer
our bodies and ouer our cattel at their
pleasure, and we are in great affliction.
38 Now because of all this we make n a sure
couenãt, and write it, and our princes, our
Leuites *and* our Priests seale vnto it.

Leui. 18, 5. ezek. 20, 11. roma. 10, 5. gal. 3, 12.

g Which is a similitude taken of oxen, ẏ shrinke at the yoke or burdẽ, as Zach. 7, 11.

h When thou didest admonish them by thy Prophets.

" Ebr. thou didst prolong vpon thẽ many yeres.

Exod. 34, 6.

Psal. 143, 2.

i By whome we were led away into captiuitie, & haue bene appoĩted to be slaine, as Ester 3, 13.

k He confesseth that all these things came to them iustely for their sinnes, but he appealeth frõ Gods iustice to his mercies.

l That thou woldest destroy them, except thei wolde returne to thee.

m That is, to be the lords thereof.

n Thus by affliction they promes to kepe Gods commandements, whereunto they colde not be broght by Gods great benefites.

CHAP. X.

1 The names of them that sealed the couenant betwene God and the people.

1 NOw thei that sealed *were* Nehemiáh
the " Tirsháthe the sonne of Hacha-
liáh, and Zidkiiáh,
2 Seraiáh, Azariáh, Ieremiáh,
3 Pashúr, Amariáh, Malchiáh,
4 Hattúsh, Shebaniáh, Mallúch,

" Or, butler.

5 Harím, Merimóth, Obadiáh,
6 Daniél, Ginnethón, Barúch,
7 Meshullám, Abiiáh, Miamín,
8 Maaziáh, Bilgái, Shemaiáh: these are a the
Priests.
9 ¶ And the Leuites: Ieshúa the sonne of
Azaniáh, Binnúi, of the sonnes of Henadád Kadmiél.
10 And their brethrẽ, Shebaniáh, Hodiiáh,
Kelitá, Pelaiáh, Hanán,
11 Michá, Rehób, Hashabiáh,
12 Zaccúr, Sherebiáh, Shebaniáh,
13 Hodiáh, Baní, Beninu.
14 ¶ The chief of the people *were* Parósh,
" Paháth Moáb, Elám, Zattú, Baní,
15 Bunní, Azgád, Bebái,
16 Adoniáh, Biguái, Adín,
17 Atér, Hizkiiáh, Azzúr,
18 Hodiáh, Hashúm, Bezái,
19 Haríph, Anathóth, Nebái,
20 Magpiásh, Meshullám, Hezír,
21 Meshezabeél, Zadók, Iaddúa,
22 Pelatiáh, Hanán, Anaiáh,
23 Hoshéa, Hananiáh, Hashúb,
24 Hallohésh, Pilehá, Shobék,
25 Rehúm, Hashabnáh, Maaseiáh,
26 And Ahiiáh, Hanán, Anán,
27 Mallúch, Harím, Baanáh.
28 And the rest of the people, the Priests,
the Leuites, the porters, the singers,
the b Nethinims, and all that were c separated from the people of the lands
vnto the Law of God, their wiues, their
sonnes, and their daughters, all that colde
vnderstand.
29 The chief of them d receiued it for
their brethren, & they came to e the curse
and to the othe to walke in Gods Law,
which was giuen by Mosés the seruant of
God, to obserue and do all the commãdements of the Lord our God and his iudgements and his statutes:
30 And that we wolde not giue our daughters to the people of the land, nether take
their daughters for our sonnes.
31 And *if* the people of the land broght ware on the Sabbath or anie vitailes to sel,
f that we wolde not take it of them on
the Sabbath and on the holy dayes: * and
that we wolde let the seuent yere be fre,
and the debtes of euerie " persone.
32 And we made statutes for our selues to
giue by the yere the third parte of a shekel for the seruice of the house of our
God,
33 For the g shewebread, and for the daiely
offring, and for the daiely burnt offring,
the Sabbaths, the newe moones, for the
solemne feastes, and for the things that
were sanctified, and for the sinne offrings
to make an atonement for Israél, and for
all the worke of the house of our God.
34 We cast also lottes for the offrĩg of the

a Which subscribed to kepe ẏ promes.

" Or, captaine of Moáb.

b Read Ezrá 2, 43.

c Which beĩg idolaters forsoke their wickednes & gaue thẽ selues to serue God.

d They made the othe in ẏ name of the whole multitude.

e Whereunto they gaue thẽ selues, if thei brake ẏ Law, as Deut. 28, 15.

f Which notwithstanding thei brake sone after, as Nehem. 13, 23.

Leu. 25, 4. deut. 15, 1.

" Ebr. hand.

g This declareth wherefore thei gaue this third part of the shekel, which was besides the halfe shekel, that thei were boũde to pay, Exod. 30, 13.

wood.

wood, *euen* ẏ Prieſts, the Leuites & ẏ people to bring it into ẏ houſe of our God, "by
the houſe of our fathers, yerely at ẏ times
appointed, to burne it vpõ the altar of the
Lord our God, as it is writen in the Law,
35 And to bring the firſt frutes of our land,
and the firſt of all the frutes of all trees,
yere by yere, into the houſe of the Lord,
36 And the firſtborne of our ſonnes, and of
our cattel, as it is [h] writen in the Law, and
the firſtborne of our bullockes and of our
ſhepe, to bring it into the houſe of our
God, vnto the Prieſts that miniſter in the
houſe of our God,
37 And that we ſhulde bring the firſt frute
of our dough, and our offrings, & the frute
of euerie tre, of wine and of oyle, vnto the
Prieſts, to the chãbers of the houſe of our
God: and the tithes of our land vnto the
Leuites, that the Leuites might haue the
tithes in all the cities of our [i] trauail.
38 And the Prieſt, the ſonne of Aarón ſhal
be with the Leuites, when the Leuites take
tithes, and the Leuites ſhal* bring vp the
tenth parte of the tithes vnto the houſe
of our God, vnto the chambers of the
treaſure houſe.
39 For the children of Iſraél, and the children of Leuí ſhal bring vp the offrings of
the corne, of the wine, & of the oyle, vnto
the chambers: and there *ſhalbe* the veſſels
of the Sanctuarie, and the Prieſts that miniſter, and the porters, and the ſingers, and
[k] we wil not forſake the houſe of our God.

"Or, into the houſe of.

h By this rehearſal is mẽt that there was no parte nor ceremonie in the Law, wherẽto thei did not binde thẽ ſelues by couenant.

i Whereſoeuer we laboured, or traueled, there the tithes were due vnto the Lord bothe by the Law and according to ẏ othe & couenant that we made.

Nomb. 18, 26

k We wil not leaue it deſtitute of that, ẏ ſhalbe neceſſarie for it.

CHAP. XI.

1 Who dwelled in Ieruſalém after it was buylded, 21 And who in the cities of Iudáh.

1 And the rulers of the people dwelt
in Ieruſalém: the other people alſo
caſt lottes, [a] to bring one out of ten to
dwel in Ieruſalém the holy citie, and nine
partes *to be* in the cities.
2 And the people thanked all the men that
were willing to dwel in Ieruſalém.
3 Theſe now are the chief of the prouince,
that dwelt in Ieruſalém, but in ẏ cities of
Iudáh, euerie one dwelt in his owne poſ-
ſeſſion in their cities of Iſraél, the Prieſts
and the Leuites, and the Nethinims, & the
ſonnes of Salomons ſeruants.
4 And in Ieruſalém dwelt *certeine* of the
childrẽ of Iudáh, & of the childrẽ of Beniamín. Of the ſonnes of Iudáh, Athaiáh,
the ſonne of Vziiáh, the ſonne of Zechariáh, the ſonne of Amariáh, the ſonne of
Shephatiáh, the ſonne of Mahaleél, of the
ſonnes of [b] Pérez,
5 And Maaſeiáh the ſonne of Barúch, the
ſonne of Col Hozéh, the ſõne of Hazaiáh,
the ſonne of Adaiáh, the ſonne of Ioiaríb,
ẏ ſonne of Zechariáh, the ſõne of "Shiloní.
6 All the ſonnes of Pérez that dwelt at Ieruſalém, *were* foure hundreth, thre ſcore
and eight valiant men.
7 Theſe alſo are the ſonnes of Beniamín,
Sallú, the ſõne of Meſhullám, the ſonne of
Ioéd, the ſonne of Pedaiáh, the ſonne of
Kolaiáh, the ſonne of Maaſeiáh, the ſonne
of Ithiél, the ſonne of Ieſhaiáh.
8 And after him Gabái, Sallái, nine hundreth and twentie and eight.
9 And Ioél the ſonne of Zichrí *was* gouernour ouer them: and Iudáh, the ſonne of
Senuáh *was* the ſeconde ouer the citie:
10 Of the Prieſts, Iedaiáh, the ſonne of Ioiaríb, Iachín.
11 Seraiáh, the ſonne of Hilkiáh, the ſonne
of Meſhullám, the ſonne of Zadók, the
ſonne of Meraióth, the ſonne of Ahitúb
[c] *was* chief of the houſe of God.
12 And their brethren [d] that did the worke
in the Temple, *were* eight hundreth, twentie and two: and Adaiáh, the ſonne of Ierohám, the ſonne of Pelaliáh, the ſonne of
Amzí, the ſonne of Zechariáh, the ſonne
of Paſhúr, the ſonne of Malchiáh:
13 And his brethren, chief of the fathers,
two hundreth and two and fourtie: and
Amaſhſai the ſonne of Azareél, the ſonne
of Ahazái, the ſonne of Meſhilemóth, the
ſonne of Immér:
14 And their brethren valiant men, an hundreth & eight & twentie: and their ouerſeer *was* Zabdiél the ſõne" of Hagedolím.
15 And of the Leuites Shemaiáh, the ſonne
of Haſhúb, the ſonne of Azrikám, the ſonne of Haſhabiáh, the ſonne of Bunní.
16 And Shabbethái, and Iozabád of the
chief of the Leuites *were* ouer the workes
of the houſe of God without.
17 And Mattaniáh, the ſonne of Michá, the
ſonne of Zabdí, the ſonne of Aſáph *was*
the chief to [e] begin the thankeſgiuing *&*
prayer: and Bakbukiáh the ſeconde of his
brethren, and Abdá, the ſonne of Shammúa, the ſonne of Galál, the ſonne of Ieduthún.
18 All the Leuites in the holy citie *were* two
hundreth foure ſcore & foure.
19 And ẏ porters Akkúb, Talmón & their
brethrẽ that kept the [f] gates *were* an hundreth twentie & two.
20 And the [g] reſidue of Iſraél, of ẏ Prieſts,
& of the Leuites *dwelt* in all the cities of
Iudáh, euerie one in his inheritance.
21 And the Nethinims dwelt in the" fortres,
& Zihá, & Giſpá *was* ouer the Nethinims.
22 And the ouerſeer of the Leuites in Ieruſalém *was* Vzzí the ſonne of Baní, the ſonne of Aſhabiáh, the ſonne of Mattaniáh,
the ſonne of Michá: of the ſonnes of A-
ſáph ſingers *were* ouer the worke of the
houſe of God.
23 For it *was* the Kings commandement
concerning thẽ, that faithful *prouiſion ſhulde
be* for the ſingers euerie day.

a Becauſe their enemies dwelt rounde about them, thei prouided that it might be repleniſhed with men, and vſed this policie, becauſe there were fewe ẏ offred them ſelues willingly.

b Which came of Pérez the ſonne of Iudáh.

"Or, of a Shilonite.

c That is, was the hie Prieſt.

d That ſerued and miniſtred in the Tẽple.

"Or, of one of the great men.

e That is, he begã the pſalme, & was the chanter.

f Meaning, of the Temple.

g Of them, ẏ dwelt not in Ieruſalém.

"Or, Ophel.

24 And Pethahiáh ẏ sonne of Meshezabeél,
of the sonnes of Zérah, the sonne of Iudáh [h] *was* at the Kings hand in all matters
concerning the people.

h Was chief about the Kig for all his affaires.

25 And in the villages in their lands, *some* of
the children of Iudáh dwelt in Kiriáth-
arbá, and in the villages thereof, and in
Dibón, and in the villages thereof, and in
Iekabzeél, and in the villages thereof,
26 And in Ieshúa, and in Moladáh, and in
Beth-pálet,
27 And in Hazér-shuál, and in Beer-shéba,
and in the villages thereof,
28 And in Ziklág, and in Mechonáh, and in
the villages thereof,
29 And in En-rimmón, & in Zareáh, and in
Iarmúth,
30 Zanóah, Adullám, and in their villages,
in Lachísh, and in the fields thereof, at A-
zekáh, & in the villages thereof: and they
dwelt from Beer-shéba vnto the valley of
Hinnóm.
31 And the sonnes of Béiamín from Géba,
in Michmásh, & Aiiá, & Beth-él, & in the
villages thereof,
32 Anathóth, Nob, Ananiáh,
33 Hazór, Ramáh, Gittáim,
34 Hadíd, Zeboím, Nebalát,
35 Lod & Onó, in the carpenters valley.
36 And of the Leuites *were* diuisions in Iudáh and in Beniamín.

CHAP. XII.

1 The Priests and Leuites, which came with Zerubbabél vnto Ierusalém, are nõbred. 27 And the wall is dedicated.

1 THese also are the Priests & the Leuites that [a] went vp with Zerubbabél,
the sonne of Shealtiél, and Ieshúa: *to wit,*
Seraiáh, Ieremiáh, Ezrá,

a From Babylon to Ierusalém.

2 Amariáh, Mallúch, Hattúsh,
3 Shecaniáh, Rehúm, Merimóth,
4 Iddó, Ginnethó, Abiiáh,
5 Miamín, Maadiáh, Bilgáh,
6 Shemaiáh, & Ioiaríb, Iedaiáh,
7 Sallú, Amók, Hilkiiáh, Iedaiáh: these were the [b] chief of the Priests, & of their brethren in the daies of Ieshúa.

b Next in dignitie to ẏ hie Priests, and ẇ were of the stocke of Aarón.

8 And the Leuites, Ieshúa, Binnúi, Kadmiél, Sherebiáh, Iudáh, Mattaniáh [c] *were* ouer
the thankesgiuings, he, & his brethren.

c Had charge of them that sang the Psalmes.

9 And Bakbukiáh and Vnní, *&* their brethren *were* about them in the [d] watches.

d They kept their wardes and watches according to their turnes, as 1.Chro.23,6.

10 And Ieshúa begate Ioiakím: Ioiakím also
begate Eliashíb, & Eliashíb begate Ioiadá,
11 And Ioiadá begate Ionathán, & Ionathán begate Iaddúa.
12 And in the daies of Ioiakím were *these,*
the chief fathers of the Priests: vnder [e] Seraiáh *was* Meraiáh, vnder Ieremiáh, Hananiáh,

e That is, next to Seraiáh, or rather of that ordre, which was called after the name of Seraiáh.

13 Vnder Ezrá, Meshullám, vnder Amariáh,
Iehohanán,
14 Vnder Melicú, Ionathán, vnder Shebaniáh, Ioséph,
15 Vnder Harím, Adná, vnder Meraióth,
Helkái,
16 Vnder Iddó, Zechariáh, vnder Ginni-
thón, Meshullám,
17 Vnder [f] Abiiáh, Zichrí, vnder Miniamín, *&* vnder Moadiáh, Piltái,

f Whereof was Zacharie John Baptists father.

18 Vnder Bilgáh, Shāmúa, vnder Shemaiáh,
Iehonathán,
19 Vnder Ioiaríb, Mattenái, vnder Iedaiáh,
Vzzí,
20 Vnder Sallái, Kallái, vnder Amók, Eber,
21 Vnder Hilkiáh, Hashabiáh, vnder Iedaiáh, Nethaneél.
22 In ẏ daies of Eliashíb, Ioiadá, & Iohanán
and Iaddúa *were* the chief fathers of the
Leuites writen, and the Priests in the reigne of Darius the Persian.
23 The sõnes of Leuí, the chief fathers *were*
writen in the boke of the Chronicles euen
vnto the daies of Iohanán the sonne of E-
liashíb.
24 And the chief of the Leuites *were* Hashabiáh, Sherebiáh, and Ieshúa the sonne
of Kadmiél, & their brethren about them
to giue praise and thankes, according to
the ordinance of Dauid the man of God,
warde ouer [g] against warde.

g That is, one after another, and euerie one in his course.

25 Mattaniáh and Bakbukiáh, Obadiáh, Meshullám, Talmón *and* Akkúb *were* porters
keping the warde at the thresholdes of the
gates.
26 These were in the daies of Ioiakím the
sonne of Ieshúa, the sonne of Iozadák, &
in the daies of Nehemiáh the captaine, &
of Ezrá the Priest and scribe.
27 And in the dedicacion of the wall at Ierusalém they soght the Leuites out of all
their places to bring them to Ierusalém to
kepe the dedicacion and gladnes, bothe
with thankesgiuings and with songs, cymbales, violes and with harpes.
28 Then the " singers gathered them selues
together bothe from the plaine countrey
about Ierusalém, and from the villages of
[h] Netophathí,

" *Ebr. sonnes of the singers.*

29 And from the house of Gilgál, and out
of the countreis of Géba, and Azmáueth:
for the singers had buylt thẽ villages rounde about Ierusalém.

h Whiche were a certeine familie & had their possessions in ẏ fields. 1.Chro.2,54.

30 And the Priests & Leuites were purified,
and clensed the people, and the gates, and
the wall.
31 And [i] I broght vp the princes of Iudáh
vpon the wall, & appointed two great cõpanies to giue thankes, and the *one* went
on the right hand of the wall towarde the
dung gate.

i Meaning, Nehemiáh.

32 And after them went Hoshaiáh, & halfe
of the princes of Iudáh,
33 And Azariáh, Ezrá and Meshullám,
34 Iudáh, Beniamín, and Shemaiáh, and Ieremiáh,
35 And of the Priests sonnes with trumpets,
Zechariáh

Zechariáh the sonne of Ionathán, the sonne of Shemaiáh, the sonne of Mattaniáh,
the sonne of Michaiáh, the sonne of Zaccúr, the sonne of Asaph.
36 And [k] his brethren, Shemaiáh, and Azareél, Milalái, Gilalái, Maái, Nethaneél, &
Iudáh, Hanáni, with ẏ musical instruments
of Dauid the man of God: and Ezrá the
scribe *went* before them.
37 And to the gate of the fountaine, euen
ouer against them went they vp by [l] the
staires of the citie of Dauid, at the going
vp of the wall beyonde the house of Dauid, euen vnto the water gate Eastwarde.
38 And the seconde companie of them that
gaue thankes, went on the other side, and I
after them, and the halfe of the people *was*
vpon the wall, *and* vpon the towre of the
furnaces euen vnto the broade wall.
39 And vpon the gate of Ephraím, and vpō
the olde gate, and vpon the fishgate, and
the towre of Hananeél, and the towre of
Meáh, euen vnto the shepegate: and they
stode in the gate of the warde.
40 So stode the two companies (of them
that gaue thankes) in the house of God, &
I and the halfe of the rulers with me.
41 The Priests also, Eliakím, Maaseiáh, Miniamín, Michaiáh, Elioenái, Zechariáh,
Hananiáh, with trumpets,
42 And Maaseiáh, and Shemaiáh, & Eleazár, and Vzzí, and Iehohanán, and Malchiiáh, and Elám, & Ezer: and the singers
" sang loude, hauing Izrahiáh which *was*
the ouerseer.
43 And the same day they offred great sacrifices and reioyced: for God had giuen
them great ioye, so that bothe the women,
and the children were ioyful: and the ioye
of Ierusalém was heard farre of.
44 Also at the same time were men appointed [m] ouer the chambers of the store for
the offrings (for the first frutes, and for the
tithes) to gather in to thē out of the fields
of the cities, the porcions of the Law for
the Priests and the Leuites: for Iudáh reioyced for the Priests & for the Leuites,
that serued.
45 And bothe the singers and the Leuites
kept the warde of their God, & the warde
of the purification according to the commandement of Dauid, *and* Salomón his
sonne.
46 * For in the dayes of Dauid and Asaph,
of olde *were* chief singers, and songs of
praise and thankesgiuing vnto God.
47 And in the dayes of Zerubbabél, and in
the dayes of Nehemiáh did all Israél giue porcions vnto the singers and porters,
euerie day his porcion, and they gaue the
holy things vnto the Leuites, and the Leuites [n] gaue the holy things vnto the sonnes of Aarón.

k That is, the brethren of Zaccúr.

l Which was the going vp to the mount Zión, which is called the citie of Dauid.

" Ebr. caused to heare.

m Which were chambers appointed by Hezekiáh to put in the tithes, and suche thinges, 2. Chro.31,11, and now were repared againe for the same vse.

* 1.Chro.15,16.

n That is, the tenth parte of the tithes.

CHAP. XIII.

1 The Law is red. 3 They separate from them all strāgers. 15 Nehemiáh reproueth them that breake the Sabbath. 30 An ordinance to serue God.

1 AND on that day did they read in the
boke of Moses, in the audiēce of the
people, & it was founde writē therein, that
the Ammonite, and the Moabite * shulde
not enter into the Congregacion of God,
2 Because they met not the children of Israél ẇ bread & with water, * but hired Balaám agaīst thē, that he shulde curse thē: &
our God turned the curse into a blessing.
3 Now when they had heard the Law, they
separated from Israél [a] all those that
were mixed.
4 ¶ And before [b] this had the Priest Eliashib the ouersight of the chamber of the
house of our God, being [c] kinsman to
Tobiáh:
5 And he had made him a great chamber &
there had thei aforetime laid the offrings,
the incense, and the vessels, and the tithes
of corne, of wine, and of oyle (appointed
for the Leuites, and the singers, & the porters) and the offrings of the Priests.
6 But in all this *time* was not I in Ierusalém:
for in the two and thirtieth yere of [d] Artahshashte King of Babél, came I vnto the
King, and " after certeine dayes I obteined
of the King.
7 And when I was come to Ierusalém, I
vnderstode [e] ẏ euil that Eliashib had done
for Tobiáh, in that he had made him a
chāber in the court of the house of God,
8 And it grieued me sore: therefore I cast
forth all ẏ vessels of the house of Tobiáh
out of the chamber.
9 And I commanded them to cleanse the
chambers: and thether broght I againe
the vessels of the house of God with the
meat offring and the incense.
10 And I perceiued that the porcions of
the Leuites had not bene giuen, and that
euerie one was fled to his lād, *euen* the Leuites & singers that executed the worke.
11 Thē reproued I the rulers & said, Why
is the house of God forsakē? And I assembled them, and set them in their place.
12 Then broght all Iudáh the tithes of corne & of wine, & of oyle vnto ẏ treasures.
13 And I made treasurers ouer ẏ treasures,
Shelemiáh the Priest, & Zadók the scribe,
& of the Leuites, Pedaiáh, & vnder their
hand Hanán the sonne of Zaccúr the sonne of Mattaniáh: for they were counted
faithful, and their office was to distribute
vnto their brethren.
14 Remember me, ô my God, herein, and
wipe not out my [f] kindenes that I haue
shewed on the house of my God, and on
the offices thereof.
15 In those daies saw I in Iudáh thē, ẏ trode

* Deu.23,3.

* Nomb.22,5.

a That is, all suche, which had ioyned in vnlawful mariage, and also those, with whome God had forbiddē them to haue societie.

b That the separation was made.

c He was ioined in affinitie with Tobiáh the Ammonite, and enemie of the Iewes.

d Called also Darius, Ezrá 7,1.

" Or, at the yeres end.

e Thus we se to what inconueniences the people fall into, when they are destitute of one that hathe the fear of God, seing that their chief gouernour was but awhile absent, and yet they fel into suche great absurdities: as appeareth also, Exo. 32,1.

f He protesteth that he did his ductie with a good consciēce, yet he dothe not iustifie him selfe herein, but desireth God to fauour him, and to be merciful vnto him for his owne godnes sake, as verse 22.

wine presses on ye Sabbath, & that broght
in sheaues, and which laded asses also with
wine, grapes, and figges and all burdens,
and broght them into Ierusalém vpon the
Sabbath day: and [g] I protested to them in
the day that they solde vitailes.
16 There dwelt men of Tyrus also therein,
which broght fish and all wares, and solde
on the Sabbath vnto the children of Iudáh
euen in Ierusalém.
17 Then reproued I the rulers of Iudáh, &
said vnto them, What euil thing is this
that ye do, and breake the Sabbath daye?
18 Did not your fathers [h] thus, and our God
broght all this plague vpon vs, and vpon
this citie? yet ye increase the wrath vpon
Israél, in breaking the Sabbath?
19 And when the gates of Ierusalém began
to be [i] darke before the Sabbath, I commanded
to shut the gates, and charged,
that they shulde not be opened til after the
Sabbath, and *some* of my seruants set I at
the gates, that there shulde no burden be
broght in on the Sabbath daye.
20 So the chapmen and marchants of all
marchandise remained once or twise all
night without Ierusalém.
21 And I protested among them, and said
vnto them, Why tary ye all night about
the wall? If ye do it once againe, I wil lay
hands vpon you. Frō that time came they
nomore on the Sabbath.
22 ¶ And I said vnto the Leuites that they
shulde clense them selues, and that they
shulde come and [k] kepe the gates, to sanctifie
the Sabbath day. Remember me, ô
my God, cōcerning this, and pardone me
according to thy great mercie.

g I declared vnto thē, that God wolde not suffer suche transgressours of his Law to be vnpunished.

h Was not this a great cause, why God plagued vs in times past? meaning, that if they trāsgressed now in the same againe, their plague shulde be greater.

i About the time that the sunne went downe: for the Sabbath lasted from the sunne goingdowne of the one day, to ye sunne setting of the other.

k Meaning, of the Tēple that none, that was vncleane, shulde entre.

23 In those dayes also I sawe Iewes that maried
wiues of [l] Ashdód, of Ammón, and of
Moáb.
24 And their children spake halfe in the
speache of Ashdód, & colde not speake in
the Iewes language, and according to the
language of the *one* people, & of the *other*
people.
25 Then I reproued them, and [m] cursed
them, and smote certeine of them, and pulled
of their heere, & toke an othe of them
by God, Ye shal not giue your daughters
vnto their sonnes, nether shal ye take of
their daughters vnto your sonnes, nor for
your selues.
26 *Did not Salomón the King of Israél
sinne by these things? yet among manie
nacions was there no King like him: for
he was beloued of his God, and God had
made him King ouer Israél: yet strange
women caused him to sinne.
27 *Shal we then obey vnto you, to do all
this great euil, and to transgresse against
our God, *euen* to mary strange wiues?
28 And *one* of the sonnes of Ioiadá the sonne
of Eliashíb the hye Priest was the sonne
in law of Sanballát the Horonite: but I
chased him from me.
29 Remember them, ô my God, that [n] defile
the Priesthode, and the couenant of the
Priesthode, and of the Leuites.
30 Then clensed I them from all strangers,
and appointed the wardes of the Priests &
of the Leuites, euerie one in his office,
31 And for the offring of the wood at times
appointed, & for the first frutes. Remember
me, ô my God, [o] in goodnes.

l Which was a citie of the Philistims, & they had maried wiues thereof, and so had corrupted their speache, and religion.

m That is, I did excommunicate them, & driue thē out of the Cōgregacion.

1.King.3,7.

1.King.11,1.

n Punish thē according to their faute, & euil example, which they haue giuen to the rest of thy people, cōtrarie to their vocation.

o That is, to shewe mercie vnto me.

ESTER.

THE ARGVMENT.

Because of the diuersitie of names, whereby they vsed to name their Kings, and the supputation of yeres, wherein the Ebrewes, and the Grecians do varie, diuers autors write diuersly as touching this Ahashuerósh, but it semeth Daniel 6,1, and 9,1. that he was Darius King of the Medes, and sonne of Astyages, called also Ahashuerósh, which was a name of honour, and signified great and chief, as chief head. Herein is declared the great mercies of God toward his Church: who neuer faileth them in their greatest dangers, but when all hope of worldely helpe faileth, he euer stirreth vp some, by whome he sendeth comfort, and deliuerance. Herein also is described the ambition, pride and crueltie of the wicked, when they come to honour, and their sodeyn fall when they are at highest: and how God preserueth, and preferreth them which are zealous of his glorie, and haue a care and loue towarde their brethren.

CHAP.

CHAP. I.

3 *King Ahaſhuerósh maketh a royal feaſt, 10 Wherũto the Quene Vaſhti wil not come. 19 For which cauſe ſhe is diuorced. 20 The Kings decree touching the preeminence of man.*

a Called alſo Darius, who was now the ſouereing Monarch, & had ẏͤ gouernemẽt of the Medes, Perſians and Chaldeans. ſome thinke he was Darius Hyſtaſpis ſonne, called alſo Artaxerxes.
b Daniél chap. 6, 1. maketh mẽcion but of ſix ſcore, leauing out the nomber that is vnperfit, as the Scripture in diuers places vſeth.
c That is, had reſt, and quietnes.
Nehem. 1, 1.

1 IN the dayes of [a] Ahaſhuerósh (this is Ahaſhuerósh that reigned,
from India euen vnto
Ethiopia, ouer an [b] hũdreth, and ſeuen and
twentie prouinces)
2 In thoſe dayes when the King Ahaſhuerósh [c] ſate on his throne, which was in
the palace of* Shuſhán,
3 In the thirde yere of his reigne, he made
a feaſt vnto all his princes and his ſeruãts,
euen the power of Perſia and Media, and
to the captaines and gouernours of the
prouinces *which were* before him,
4 That he might ſhewe the riches & glorie of his kingdome, and the honour of his
great maieſtie manie dayes, *eũ* an hũdreth
and foure ſcore dayes.
5 And when theſe dayes were expired, the
King made a feaſt to all the people that
were found in the palace of Shuſhán, bothe vnto great and ſmall, ſeuen dayes, in
the courte of the garden of the Kings
palace,
6 *Vnder* an hanging of white, grene, and
blewe *clothes*, faſtened with cordes of fine
linen and purple, in ſiluer rings, and pillers
of marble: the [d] beddes *were* of golde,
and of ſiluer vpon a pauement of porphyre, and marble and alabaſter, and blewe
coulour.
7 And they gaue them drinke in veſſels of
golde, and changed veſſel after veſſel, and
royal wine in abundance according to the
[e] power of the King.
8 And the drinking *was* by an ordre, none
might [f] compel: for ſo the King had appointed vnto all the officers of his houſe,
that they ſhulde do according to euerie
mans pleaſure.
9 ¶ The Quene Vaſhtí made a feaſt alſo
for the womẽ in the royal houſe of King
Ahaſhuerósh.
10 Vpon the [g] ſeuent day when the King
was mery with wine, he commanded Mehumán, Bizthá, Harboná, Bigthá, and Abagthá, Zethár, and Carcás, the ſeuen eunuches (that ſerued in the preſence of Kĩg
Ahaſhuerósh)
11 To bring Quene Vaſhtí before the King
with ẏͤ crowne royal, that he might ſhewe
the people and the princes her beautie:
for ſhe was faire to loke vpon.
12 But the Quene Vaſhtí refuſed to come
at the Kings worde, * which he had giuen
in charge to the eunuches: therefore the
King was very angrie, and his wrath kindled in him.

d Which they vſed in thoſe countreis in ſtead of tables
e As was beſeming for ſo magnifical a King.
f None might be cõpelled to drinke more then it pleaſed him.
g Which was the laſt day of the feaſt that the King made for ẏͤ people, as verſe 5.
*Ebr. which was in the hãd of the eunuches.

13 Then the King ſaid to the wiſe men,
[h] that knewe the times (for ſo was the Kĩgs
maner towardes all that knewe the lawe
and the iudgement:
14 And the next vnto him *was* Carſhená,
Shethár, Admátha, Tarſhiſh, Méres, Marſená & Memucán the ſeuen princes of Perſia and Media, which ſawe the [i] Kings face, and ſate the firſt in the kingdome)
15 What ſhal we do vnto ẏͤ Quene Vaſhtí
according to the lawe, becauſe ſhe did not
according to the worde of the King Ahaſhuerósh by the commiſsion of the eunuches?
16 Then Memucán anſwered before the
King and the princes, The Quene Vaſhtí
hathe not onely done [k] euil againſt the
King, but againſt all the princes, & agaĩſt
all the people that are in all the prouinces
of King Ahaſhuerósh.
17 For the [l] acte of the Quene ſhal come abrode vnto all women, ſo that they ſhal
deſpiſe their houſbãds in their owne eies,
and ſhal ſay, The King Ahaſhuerósh cõmanded Vaſhtí the Quene to be broght
in before him, but ſhe came not.
18 So ſhal the [m] princeſſes of Perſia & Media this day ſay vnto all the Kings Princes, whẽ thei heare of the acte of the Quene: thus *ſhal there be* muche deſpitefulnes
and wrath.
19 If it pleaſe the King, let a royal decree
procede from him, and let it be writen among the ſtatutes of Perſia, and Media
(and let it not be tranſgreſſed) that Vaſhtí come [n] nomore before King Ahaſhuerósh: and let the King giue her royal eſtate vnto her companion that is better
then ſhe.
20 And when the decree of the King which
ſhalbe made, ſhalbe publiſhed throughout
all his kingdome (thogh it be [o] great) all
the women ſhal giue their houſbands honour, bothe great and ſmall.
21 And this ſaying pleaſed the King & the
princes, & the King did according to the
worde of Memucán.
22 For he ſent letters into all the prouinces
of the King, into euerie prouince accordĩg to the writĩg thereof, & to euerie people after their language, that euerie man
ſhulde [p] beare rule in his owne houſe, and
that he ſhulde publiſh it in the language
of that ſame people.

h That had experience of things, as thei had learned by diligent marking in cõtinuance of time.
i Which were his chief counſelers, that might haue alwaies acceſſe to him.
k By her diſobedience ſhe hathe giuen an example to all women to do the like to their houſbands.
l That is, her diſobedience.
m Meaning, ẏͤ thei wolde take firſt occaſiõ hereof to do ẏͤ like, & that ẏͤ reſt of womẽ wolde by continuance do ẏͤ ſame.
n Let her be diuorced & another made Quene.
o For he had vnder him an hundreth twẽtie and ſeuen countreis.
p That is, that ẏͤ wiſe ſhulde be ſubiect to the houſband and at his cõmandement.

CHAP. II.

2 *After the Quene is put away, certeine yong maides are broght to the King 14 Eſtér pleaſeth the King, & is made Quene. 22 Mordecái diſcloſeth vnto the King thoſe that wolde betray him.*

1 AFter theſe things, when the wrath of
King Ahaſhuerósh was appeaſed, he
[a] remembred Vaſhtí, & what ſhe had do-

a That is, he called ẏͤ matter againe into cõmunicatiõ.

b By the ſeuẽ wiſe men of his counſel.

ne, and what was decreed [b] againſt her.
2 And the Kings ſeruants that miniſtred
vnto him, ſaid, Let them ſeke for the King
beautiful yong virgins,
3 And let ẏ King appoint officers through
all the prouinces of his kingdome, and let
thẽ gather all the beautiful yong virgins
vnto the palace of Shuſhán, into the houſe of the women, vnder the hand of Hegé the Kings eunuche, [c] keper of the women, to giue them their things [d] for purification.
4 And the maid that ſhal pleaſe the King,
let her reigne in the ſtead of Vaſhtí. And
this pleaſed the King, and he did ſo.
5 ¶ In the citie of Shuſhán, there was a certeine Iewe, whoſe name *was* Mordecái
the ſonne of Iaír, the ſonne of Shimeí, the
ſonne of Kiſh a man of Iemini,
6 Which had bene caryed away from Ieruſalém *with the captiuitie that was caryed away with Iekoniáh King of Iudáh
(whome Nebuchadnezzár King of Babél
had caryed away)
7 And he nouriſhed Hadaſſáh, that is Eſtér,
his vncles daughter: for ſhe had nether father nor mother, and the maid was faire,
and beautiful to loke on: & after the death
of her father, and her mother, Mordecái
toke her for his owne daughter.
8 And when the Kings commandement, &
his decree was publiſhed, and manie maides were broght togeher to the palace of
Shuſhán, vnder the hãd of Hegé, Eſtér was
broght alſo vnto the Kings houſe vnder ẏ
hand of Hegé the keper of the women.
9 And the maid pleaſed him, and ſhe founde fauour in his ſight: therefore he cauſed
her things for purificatiõ to be giuen her
ſpedely, and her ‖ ſtate, and ſeuen comely
maides to be giuen her out of the Kings
houſe, and he gaue change to her and to
her maides of the beſt in the houſe of the
women.
10 *But* Eſtér ſhewed not her people and her
kinred: for Mordecái had charged her,
that ſhe ſhulde not tel it.
11 And Mordecái walked [e] euerie day before the courte of the womens houſe, to
knowe if Eſtér did wel, and what ſhulde be
done with her.
12 And when the courſe of euerie maid came, to go in to King Ahaſhueróſh, after
that ſhe had bene twelue moneths according to the maner of the women (for ſo
were the dayes of their purifications accompliſhed, ſix moneths with oyle of
myrrhe, & ſix moneths with ſwete odours
and in the purifying of the women:
13 And thus went the maids vnto the King)
whatſoeuer ſhe required, was [f] giuen her,
to go with her out of the womens houſe
vnto the Kings houſe.

c The abuſe of theſe cõtreis was ſo great, that they inuented manie meanes to ſerue the luſtes of princes, and therefore, as they ordeined wicked lawes that the King might haue whoſe daughters he wolde, ſo they had diuers houſes appointed, as one for them, whiles they were virgines, another whẽ they were concubines, & for the Quenes another.

d Read what this purification was, verſ. 13.

2. *Kin. 24, 15.*

‖ *Ebr. portions.*

e For thogh ſhe was taken away by a cruel law, yet he ceaſed not to haue a fatherlie care ouer her, and therefore did reſort oft times to heare of her.

f What apparel ſhe aſked of the eunuch, that was he bounde to giue her.

14 In the euening ſhe went, and on the morow ſhe returned into the ſeconde houſe
of the women vnder the hand of Shaaſh-
gáz the Kings eunuche, which kept the
cõcubines: ſhe came into the King nomore, except ſhe pleaſed the King, & that ſhe
were called by name.
15 Now when the courſe of Eſtér ẏ daughter of Abihaíl the vncle of Mordecái
(which had taken her as his owne daughter) came, ẏ ſhe ſhulde go in to the King,
ſhe deſired nothing, but what ‖ Hegé the
Kings eunuche the keper of the women
[g] ſaid: and Eſtér founde fauour in the ſight
of all them that loked vpon her.
16 ¶ So Eſtér was takẽ vnto King Ahaſhueróſh into his houſe royal in the tenth moneth, which is the [h] moneth Tebéth, in the
ſeuent yere of his reigne.
17 And the King loued Eſtér aboue all the
women, and ſhe founde grace and fauour
in his ſight more then all the virgins: ſo
that he ſet the crowne of the kingdome
vpõ her head, & made her Quene in ſteade of Vaſhtí.
18 Then the King made a great feaſt vnto
all his princes and his ſeruants *which was*
[i] the feaſt of Eſtér and gaue reſt [k] vnto the
prouinces, and gaue giftes, according to
[l] the power of a King.
19 And when the virgins were gathered the
[m] ſeconde time, then Mordecái ſate in the
Kings gate.
20 Eſtér had not yet ſhewed her kinred nor
her people, as Mordecái had charged her:
for Eſtér did after the worde of Mordecái, as when ſhe was nouriſhed with
him.
21 ¶ In thoſe daies when Mordecái ſate in
the Kings gate, two of the Kings eunuches, Bigthán and Téreſh, which kept
the dore, were wroth, & ſoght to lay [n] hand
on the King Ahaſhueróſh.
22 And the thing was knowẽ to Mordecái,
and he tolde it vnto Quene Eſtér, and E-
ſtér certified the King thereof in Mordecais name: and when inquiſitiõ was made,
it was founde ſo: therefore thei were bothe
hanged on a tre: and it was writen in
the boke of the [o] Chronicles before the
King.

‖ *Or, Hegai.*

g Wherein her modeſtie appeared becauſe ſhe ſoght not apparel to cõmend her beautie, but ſtode to ẏ eunuches appoĩtment.

h Which conteined part of December & part of Ianuarie.

i That is, made for her ſake.

k He releaſed their tribute.

l That is, great & magnifical.

m That is, at the mariage of Eſtér, which was ẏ ſeconde mariage of ẏ King.

n Meaning, to kil him.

o In the Chronicles of the Medes & Perſiãs, as Chap. 10, 2.

CHAP. III.

1 Hamán, after he was exalted, obteined of the King, that all the Iewes ſhulde be put to death, becauſe Mordecái had not done him worſhip as other had.

1 AFter theſe things did King Ahaſhueróſh promote Hamán the ſonne of
Hammedátha the Agagite, & exalted hĩ,
and ſet his ſeat aboue all the princes that
were with him.
2 And all the Kings ſeruants that were at
the Kings gate, bowed their knees, & re-
uerẽced Hamán: for the Kĩg had ſo cõmã

ded

ded cōcerning him: but Mordecái [a] bowed
not the knee, nether did reuerence.
3 Then the Kings seruants which were at
the Kings gate said vnto Mordecái, Why
transgressest thou the Kings commandement?
4 And albeit they spake daiely vnto hī, yet
he wolde not heare them: therefore they
[b] tolde Hamán, that they might se how
Mordecais matters wolde stād: for he had
tolde them, that he was a Iewe.
5 And when Hamán sawe that Mordecái
bowed not the knee vnto him, nor did reuerence vnto him, then Haman was ful of
wrath.
6 Now he "thoght it to litle to lay hands
onely on Mordecái: & because they had
shewed him the people of Mordecái, Hamán soght to destroye all the Iewes, that
were throughout the whole kingdome of
Ahashuerósh, *euen* ẏ people of Mordecái.
7 In the first moneth (that is the moneth
[c] Nisán) in the twelft yere of King A-
hashuerósh, they cast Pur (that is a lot)
[d] before Hamán, from day to day, and frō
moneth to moneth, *vnto* the twelft moneth, that is the moneth [e] Adár.
8 Then Hamán said vnto King Ahashuerósh, There is a people scatred, and dispersed among the people in all the prouin
ces of thy kingdome, and their lawes *are*
diuers from all people, and they do not
obserue the [f] Kings lawes: therefore it is
not the Kings profite to suffre them.
9 If it please the King, let it be writen
that they may be destroyed, & I wil "paye
ten thousand talents of siluer by the hāds
of them that haue the charge of this busines to bring it into the Kings treasurie.
10 Then the King toke his ring from his
hand and gaue it vnto Hamán the sonne
of Hammedátha the Agagite the Iewes
aduersarie.
11 And the King said vnto Hamán, Let ẏ
siluer be thine, and the people to do with
them as it pleaseth thee.
12 Then were the Kings "scribes called on
the thirtent day of the first moneth, and
there was writen (according to all that
Hamán commanded) vnto the Kings officers, and to the captaines that were ouer
euerie prouince, and to the rulers of euerie people & to euerie prouince, accordīg
to the writing thereof, & to euerie people
according to their language: in the name
of King Ahashuerósh was it writen, and
sealed with the Kings ring.
13 And the lettres were sent "by postes into
all the Kings prouinces, to rote out, to kill
and to destroye all the Iewes, bothe yong
and olde, children and women, in one day
vpon the thirtent day of the twelft moneth, (which is the moneth Adar) and to

a The Persiās maner was to knele downe and reuerence their Kings, & suche as he apposited in chief autoritie, ẇ Mordecái wolde not do to this ambitious & proude mā.

b Thus we se that there is none so wicked, but thei haue their flaterers to accuse the godlie.

"Ebr. despised in his eyes.

c Which answereth to parte of Marche and parte of April.

d To knowe what moneth and day shulde be good to enterprise this thing, that it might haue good successe: but God disapointed their lettes & expectation.

e Conteining part of Februarie, & parte of Marche.

f These be the two argumēts which commonly ẏ worldelings & the wicked vse toward prīces agaīst ẏ godly, that is, ẏ contempt of their laws, & diminishig of their profit: without respect how God is ether pleased or displeased.

"Ebr. weigh.

"Or, secretaries.

"Ebr the hands of postes.

spoile them as a pray.
14 The contents of the writing *was*, that
there shulde be giuen a cōmandemēt in
all prouinces, & published vnto all people, that thei shulde be ready against the
same day.
15 And the postes compelled by the Kings
cōmandement went forthe, and the commandement was giuē in the palace at Shu
shán: and the King and Hamán sate drinking, but the [g] citie of Shushán was in
perplexitie.

g To wit, the Iewes, ẏ were in Shushán.

CHAP. IIII.

1 Mordecái giueth the Quene knowledge of the cruel decree of the King against the Iewes. 16 She willeth that they pray for her.

1 NOw when Mordecái perceiued all
that was done, Mordecái rent his
clothes, and put on sackecloth, & ashes, and
went out into the middes of the citie, &
cryed with a great crye, and a bitter.
2 And he came euē before the Kings [a] gate,
but he might not entre within the Kings
gate, being clothed with sackecloth.
3 And in euerie prouince, & place, whether
the Kings charge and his commission came, there *was* great sorowe among the Iewes, and fasting, & weping and mournīg,
and "many laye in sackecloth & in ashes.
4 ¶ Then Esters maides and her eunuches
came and tolde it her: therefore the Quene was very heauy, and she sent raiment
to clothe Mordecái, and to take away his
sackecloth frō him, but he receiued ẏt not.
5 Then called Estér Hatách *one* of ẏ Kīgs
eunuches, whome he "had appointed to
serue her, and gaue him a commandement vnto Mordecái, to knowe what it
was, and why it was.
6 So Hatách wēt forthe to Mordecái vnto
the streat of the citie, which was before
the Kings gate.
7 And Mordecái tolde hī of all that which
had come vnto him, and of the "summe
of the siluer that Hamán had promised to
paye vnto the Kings treasures, because of
the Iewes, for to destroye them.
8 Also he gaue him the "copie of the writīg
& commission that was giuen at Shushán,
to destroye thē that he might shewe it vnto Estér and declare it vnto her, and to
charge her, that she shulde go in to the
King, & make peticion and supplication
before him for her people.
9 ¶ So when Hatách came, he tolde Estér
the wordes of Mordecái.
10 Then Estér said vnto Hatách, and com
manded him, *to say* vnto Mordecái,
11 All the Kings seruants and the people
of the Kings prouinces do knowe, that
whosoeuer, man or woman, that commeth
to the King into the inner court, which
is not called, there *is* a lawe of his,

a Because he wolde aduertise Estér of this cruel proclamation.

"Ebr. sackcloth & ashes were spred for many.

"Ebr. had caused to stand before her.

"Ebr. declaration.

"Or, contents.

that he shal dye, except him to whome the King holdeth out the golden rod,
that he may liue. Now I haue not bene called to come vnto the King these thirtie dayes.
12 And they certified Mordecái of Esters wordes.
13 And Mordecái said, that thei shulde answer Estér *thus*, Thinke not with thy self that thou shalt escape in the Kings house, more then all the Iewes.
14 For if thou holdest thy peace at this time, "comfort and deliuerãce [b] shal appeare to the Iewes out of another place, but thou and thy fathers house shal perish: and who knoweth whether thou art come to ỳ kingdome for [c] such a time?
15 Then Estér commãdẽd to answer Mordecái,
16 Go, & assemble all the Iewes that are found in Shushán, & fast ye for me, & eat not, nor drĩke in thre dayes, day nor night. I also and my maides wil fast likewise, and so wil I go in to the King, which is not according to the Law: and if I perish, [d] I perish.
17 So Mordecái went his way, and did according to all that Estér had commanded him.

"Ebr breathĩg.
b Thus Mordecái spake in ỳ confidence of that faith, ẇ all Gods children oght to haue: which is that God wil deliuer them, thogh all worldely meanes faile.
c For to deliuer Gods Churche out of these present dãgers.
d I wil put my life in danger & referre the successe to God, seig it is for his glorie & the deliuerance of his Church.

CHAP. V.

1 Estér entreth in to the King, and biddeth him and Hamán to a feast. 11 Hamán prepareth a galous for Mordecái.

1 AND on the third [a] day Estér put on her royal apparel, and stode in the court of the Kings palace within, ouer against the Kings house: and the King sate vpon his royal throne in the Kings palace ouer against the gate of the house.
2 And when the King sawe Estér the Quene standing in the court, she found fauour in his sight: & the Kĩg [b] helde out the goldẽ sceptre ỳ was in his hãd: so Estér drewe nere, and touched the toppe of the sceptre.
3 Then said the King vnto her, What wilt thou, Quene Estér? & what is thy request? it shalbe euen giuen [c] thee to the halfe of the kingdome.
4 Then said Estér, If it please the King, let the King and Hamán come this day vnto the bãket, ỳ I haue prepared for him.
5 And the Kĩg said, Cause Hamán to make hast that he maie do as Estér hathe said. So the King and Hamán came to the bãket that Estér had prepared.
6 And the King said vnto Estér at the banket of [d] wine, What is thy peticion, that it may be giuen thee? and what is thy request? it shal euen be performed vnto the halfe of the kingdome.
7 Then answered Estér, and said, My peticion and my request *is*,
8 If I haue founde fauour in the sight of the King, and if it please the King to giue me my peticion, and to performe my request, let the King and Hamán come to the banket that I shal prepare for them, & I wil do tomorowe according to the Kĩgs [e] saying.
9 ¶ Then went Hamán forth the same day ioyful & with a glad heart. But when Hamán sawe Mordecái in the Kĩgs gate, that he stode not vp, nor moued for him, then was Hamán ful of indignacion at Mordecái.
10 Neuertheles Hamán refrained him self: and when he came home, he sent, and called for his friends, and Zéresh his wife.
11 And Hamán tolde them of the glorie of his riches, and the multitude of his children, and all the things wherein the King had [f] promoted him, and how that he had set him aboue the princes and seruants of the King.
12 Hamán said moreouer, Yea, Estér the Quene did let no man come in with the King to the banket that she had prepared, saue me: and tomorowe am I bidden vnto her also with the King.
13 But all this doeth nothing auaile me, as long as I se Mordecái the Iewe sitting at the Kings gate.
14 Then said Zéresh his wife and all his friends vnto him, Let them make a tre of fiftie [g] cubites hie, and tomorowe speake thou vnto the King, that Mordecái may be hanged thereon: thẽ shalt thou go ioyfully with the King vnto the banket. And the thing pleased Hamán, and he caused to make the tre.

a To wit, after that the Iewes had begõne to fast.
b Which was a signe ỳ her comming was agreable vnto him, as Chap. 4,11.
c Meaning hereby, ỳ what soeuer she asked, shuld be granted, as Mar. 6,23.
d Because thei vsed to drinke excessiuely in their bankets, they called the bãket by the name of that, which was moste in vse or estemed
e I wil declare what thing I demande.
f Thus ỳ wicked when thei are promoted, in stead of acknowledging their charge & humbling thẽ selues, waxe ambitious disdainful and cruel.
g Meaning, ỳ hieghest that colde be founde.

CHAP. VI.

1 The King turneth ouer the chronicles, and findeth the fidelitie of Mordecái, 10 And commandeth Hamán, to cause Mordecái to be had in honour.

1 THE same night "the King slept not, & he commanded to bring the boke of the records & the chronicles: and thei were red before the King.
2 Then it was founde writen that Mordecái *had tolde of Bigtána, & Téresh two of the Kings eunuches, kepers of the dore, who soght to lay hands on the King Ahashuerósh.
3 Thẽ the King said, What honour & dignitie hathe bene giuen to Mordecái [a] for this? And the Kings seruants that ministred vnto him, said, There is nothing done for him.
4 And the King said, Who is in the court? (Now Hamán was come into the inner court of the Kings house, that he might speake vnto the King to [b] hang Mordecái on the tre that he had prepared for him.)
5 And the Kings seruants said vnto him, Beholde, Hamán standeth in the court. And the King said, Let him come in.

"Ebr. the Kings slepe departed.
Chap. 2, 22.
a For he thoght it vnworthie his estate to receiue a benefite, & not reward it.
b Thus while the wicked imagine the destruction of others, thei thẽ selues fall into the same pit.

6 And

6 And when Hamán came in, the King said
vnto him, What shalbe done vnto the mã,
whome the King wil honour? Thẽ Hamán
thoght in his heart, To whome wolde the
King do honour more then to me?
7 And Hamán answered the King, The
man whome the King wolde honour,
8 Let thẽ bring *for him* royal apparel, which
the King *vseth* to weare, and the [c] horse
that the King rydeth vpon, and that the
crowne royal may be set vpon his head.

c Meanĩg hereby, that the King shulde make him next vnto him self, as Ioseph hereby was knowen to be next to Pharaóh, Gen 41, 42.

9 And let the rayment and the horse be deliuered by the hand of one of the Kings
moste noble princes, and let them apparel
the man (whome the King wil honour) &
cause him to ride vpon the horse through
the strete of the citie, & proclaime before
him, Thus shal it be done vnto the man,
whome the King wil honour.
10 Then the King said to Hamán, Make
haste, take the raymẽt & the horse as thou
hast said, & do so vnto Mordecái ẏ Iewe,
that sitteth at the Kings gate: let nothing
faile of all that thou hast spoken.
11 So Hamán toke the raymẽt & the horse,
and arayed Mordecái, and broght him on
horse backe through the strete of the citie, and proclaimed before him, Thus shal
it be done to the man whome the King
wil honour.
12 And Mordecái came againe to ẏ Kings
gate, but Hamán hasted home mourning
and his head couered.
13 And Hamán tolde Zéresh his wife, & all
his friends all that had befallen him. Thẽ
said his wise men, and Zéresh his wife vnto him, If Mordecái *be* of the sede of the
Iewes, before whome thou hast begõne to
fall, thou shalt not preuaile against him,
[d] but shalt surely fall before him.

d Thus God sometime putteth in the mouthe of the very wicked, to speake that thĩg, which he hathe decreed shal come to passe.

14 And while they were yet talking with
him, came the Kings eunuches and hasted
to bring Hamán vnto the bãket that Estér
had prepared.

CHAP. VII.

3 The quene biddeth the King & Hamán againe & praieth for her selfe and her people. 6 She accuseth Hamán and he is hanged on the gallows, which he had prepared for Mordecái.

1 SO the King and Hamán came to banket with the Quene Estér.
2 And the King said againe vnto Estér on
the seconde day at the banket of [a] wine,
What is thy peticion, Quene Estér, that it
may be giuẽ thee? and what is thy request?
It shalbe euen performed vnto the halfe
of the kingdome.

a Read Chap. 5,6.

3 And Estér the Quene answered, and said,
If I haue founde fauour in thy sight, ô
King, and if it please the King, let my life
be giuen me at my peticion, & my people
at my request.
4 For we are solde, I, and my people, to be
destroyed, to be slayne and to perish: but
if we were solde for seruants, & for handmaides, I wolde haue helde my tongue:
althogh the aduersarie colde not [b] recõpense the Kings losse.
5 Thẽ King Ahashuerósh answered, & said
vnto ẏ Quene Estér, Who is he? & where
is he that "presumeth to do thus?

b Hamán colde not so muche profite ẏ King by this his malice, as he shulde hinder him by ẏ losse of the Iewes, & the tribute which he hath of them.

" *Ebr. filleth his heart.*

6 And Estér said, The aduersarie and enemie is this wicked Hamán. Then Hamán
was afraied before the King & the Quene.
7 And the King arose from the banket of
wine in his wrath, *& went* into the palace
garden: but Hamán stode vp, to make request for his life to ẏ Quene Estér: for he
sawe that there was a [c] mischief prepared
for him of the King.
8 And when the King came againe out of
the palace garden, into the house where
they dranke wine, Hamán was [d] fallen
vpon the bed whereon Estér *sate*: therefore
the King said, Wil he force ẏ Quene also
before me in the house? As the worde wẽt
out of the Kings mouthe, they [e] couered
Hamans face.
9 And Harbonáh one of the eunuches, said
in the presence of the King, Beholde, there standeth yet the tre in Hamans house
fiftie cubites hie, which Hamán had prepared for Mordecái, that spake [f] good for
the King. Then the King said, Hang him
thereon.
10 So they hanged Hamán on the tre, that
he had prepared for Mordecái: then was
the Kings wrath pacified.

c His consciẽce did accuse him that as he had conspired the death of innocents, so the vengeance of God might fall vpon him for the same.

d He fel downe at the beddes fete or couche, whereupon she sate, and made request for his life

e This was the maner of the Persians, when one was out of the Kings fauour.

f Which discouered the conspiracie agaĩst ẏ King, Chap. 2,2.

CHAP. VIII.

1 After the death of Hamán was Mordecái exalted. 14 Comfortable lettres are sent vnto the Iewes.

1 THe same day did King Ahashuerósh
giue the house of Hamán the aduersarie of the Iewes vnto the Quene Estér.
And Mordecái [a] came before the King: for
Estér tolde what he was [b] vnto her.
2 And the King toke of his ring, which he
had taken from Hamán, and gaue it vnto
Mordecái: and Estér set Mordecái ouer
the house of Hamán.

a That is, was receiued into the Kings fauour and presence.

b That he was her vncle and had broght her vp.

3 And Estér spake yet more before ẏ King,
and fell downe at his fete weping, and besoght him that he wolde put away the
[c] wickednes of Hamán the Agagite, and
his deuise that he had imagined against
the Iewes.
4 And the King helde out the goldẽ [d] sceptre toward Estér. Then arose Estér, and
stode before the King,
5 And said, If it please the King, and if I
haue founde fauour in his sight, and the
thing be acceptable before the King, and
I please him, let it be writen, that the lettres of the deuise of Hamán the sonne of
Ammedátha the Agagite may be called a-
gaine, which he wrote to destroye ẏ Iewes,

c Meaning, ẏ he shulde abolish ẏ wicked decrees, which he had made for the destruction of the Iewes.

d Read Chap. 5,2.

that are in all the Kings prouinces.
6 For how can I suffer and se the euil, that
shal come vnto my people? Or how can I
suffer and se the destruction of my kinred?
7 And the King Ahashuerósh said vnto
ӯ Quene Estér, & to Mordecái the Iewe,
Beholde, I haue giuen Estér the house of
Hamán, whome they haue hanged vpon
the tre, because he ″ layed hand vpon the
Iewes.

″Or, went about to slay the Iewes.

8 Write ye also for the Iewes, as it liketh
you in the Kings name, and seale it with
the Kings ring, (for the writings writen
in the Kings name, and sealed with the
Kings ring, may no [e] man reuoke)
9 Thē were the Kings scribes called at the
same time, euē in the third moneth, that is
the moneth [f] Siuán, on the thre & twētieth
day thereof: and it was writen, according
to all as Mordecái commanded vnto the
Iewes and to the prouinces, & captaines,
and rulers of the princes, which were from
India euen vnto Ethiopia, an hundreth &
seuen and twentie prouinces, vnto euerie
prouince, according to the [g] writing thereof, and to euerie people after their speache, and to the Iewes, according to their
writing, and according to their language.

e This was ӯ lawe of the Medes & Persians, as Dan. 6,15: notwithstanding the King reuoked the former decree grãted to Hamán, for Esters sake.
f Which conteineth parte of May and parte of Iune.
g That is, in suche letters & lãguage, as was vsual in euerie prouince.

10 And he wrote in the King Ahashuerósh
name, and sealed it with the Kings ring: &
he sent lettres by postes on horsebacke &
that rode on *beastes* of price, *as* dromedaries & ″ coltes of mares.

″Or, mules.

11 Wherein the King granted the Iewes (in
what cities soeuer they were) to gather
them selues together, & to stand for [h] their
life, & to roote out, to slay & to destroye
all the power of the people & of the prouince that vexed them, *bothe* children and
women, and to spoyle their goods:

h That is, to defend them selues against all that wolde assaile them.

12 Vpon one day in all the prouinces of
King Ahashuerósh, *euen* in the thirtent
day of the twelft moneth, which is the
moneth [i] Adár.
13 The copie of the writing *was*, how there
shulde be a commandement giuen in all
and euerie prouince, published among all
the people, and that the Iewes shulde be
readie against that day to [k] auenge them
selues on their enemies.

i Which hath parte of Februarie & part of Marche.
k The King gaue them libertie to kill all ӯ did oppresse them.

14 *So* the postes rode vpon *beastes* of price,
& dromedaries, & wēt forthe with spede,
to execute the Kings commandement, &
the decree was giuen at Shushán ӯ palace.
15 And Mordecái went out from the King
in royal apparel of blewe, and white, and
with a great crowne of golde, and with a
garment of fine linen and purple, and the
citie of Shushán reioyced and was glad.
16 *And* vnto the Iewes was come light and
[l] ioye and gladnes, and honour.
17 Also in all and euerie prouince, and in
all and euerie citie and place, *where* the
Kings cōmādement & his decree came,
there was ioye and gladnes to the Iewes, a
feast and good day, and many of the people of the lād [m] became Iewes: for the feare of the Iewes fell vpon them.

l He sheweth by these wordes that follow what this light was.
m Cōformed them selues to the Iewes religion.

CHAP. IX.

1 At the commandement of the King the Iewes put their aduersaries to death. 14 The ten sonnes of Hamán are hanged. 17 The Iewes kepe a feast in remēbrance of their deliuerance.

1 SO in the twelft moneth, which is
the moneth Adár, vpon the thirtent
day of the same, when the Kings commādement and his decree drewe nere to be
put in execution, in the day that the enemies of the Iewes hoped to haue power
ouer them (but it [a] turned contrary: for
the Iewes had rule ouer them that hated
them)
2 The Iewes gathered thē selues together
into their cities throughout all the prouinces of the King Ahashuerósh, to laye
hand on suche as soght their hurt, and no
man colde withstande them: for the feare
of them fell vpon all people.

a This was by Gods great prouidence, who turneth ӯ ioye of the wicked into sorow, & the teares of the godlie into gladnes.

3 And all the rulers of the prouinces, & the
princes and the captaines, and the officers
of the King [b] exalted the Iewes: for the
feare of Mordecái fell vpon them.

b Did thē honour, & shewed thē friendship.

4 For Mordecái was great in the Kīgs house, and the reporte of him went through
all the prouinces: for this man Mordecái
waxed greater and greater.
5 Thus the Iewes smote all their [c] enemies
with strokes of the sworde and slaughter,
and destruction, and did what they wolde
vnto those that hated them.

c Which had cōspired their death by the permission of the wicked Hamán.

6 And at Shushán the palace slewe ӯ Iewes
and destroyed [d] fiue hundreth men,
7 And Parshandátha, and Dalphón, and
Aspátha,
8 And Porátha, and Adaliá, and Aridá-
tha,
9 And Parmáshta, and Arisái, and Aridái,
and Vaiezátha,
10 The ten sonnes of Hamán, the sonne of
Ammedátha, the aduersarie of the Iewes
slewe they: but they layed not their hāds
[e] on the spoyle.

d Besides those thre hundreth, ӯ they slewe the seconde day, as vers. 15.

11 On the same day came the nomber of
those that were slayne, vnto the palace of
Shushán before the King.
12 And the King said vnto the Quene Estér,
The Iewes haue slayne in Shushán the
palace and destroyed fiue hundreth men,
and the ten sonnes of Hamán: what haue
they done in the rest of the Kings prouinces? and what is thy peticion, that it
may be giuen thee? or what is thy request
moreouer, that it may be performed?
13 Then said Estér, If it please the King,
let it be granted also tomorowe to the
Iewes that are in Shushán, to do according

e Whereby they declared, that this was Gods iust iudgement vpon ӯ enemies of his Church, forasmucheas they soght not their owne gaine, but to execute his vengeance.

[f] vnto

f vnto this dayes decree, that they may
hang vpon the tre Hamans ten sonnes.
14 And the King charged to do so, and the
decree was giuen at Shushán, and they hãged Hamans ten sonnes.
15 ¶ So the Iewes that were in Shushán, assembled them selues vpon the fourtent
day of the moneth Adár, and slewe thre
hũdreth men in Shushán, but on the spoile
they layed not their hand.
16 And the rest of the Iewes that were in
the Kings prouinces assembled thẽ selues,
and stode for g their liues, and had rest
from their enemies, & slewe of them that
hated them, h seuentie and fyue thousand:
but they layed not their hãd on the spoile.
17 *This they did* on the i thirtente day of
the moneth Adár, and rested the fourtẽte
day thereof, and kept it a daye of feasting and ioye.
18 But the Iewes that were in Shushán, assembled them selues on the thirtẽte *day*,
& on the fourtente thereof, & thei rested
on the fiftente of the same, & kept it a day
of feasting and ioye.
19 Therefore the Iewes of the villages that
dwelt in the vnwalled townes, k kept
the fourtente day of the moneth Adár
with ioye and feasting, *euen* a ioyful day,
and euerie one sent presents vnto his neighbour.
20 ¶ And Mordecái wrote l these wordes,
and sent letters vnto all the Iewes that
were through all the prouinces of the
King Ahashuerósh, *bothe* nere and farre,
21 Inioining them that they shulde kepe
the fourtente day of the moneth Adár,
and the fiftente day of the same, euerie
yere.
22 According to the dayes wherein the Iewes rested from their enemies, and the
moneth which was turned vnto them frõ
sorow to ioye, and from mourning into a
ioyful day, to kepe them the dayes of feasting, and ioye, and m to send presents
euerie man to his neighbour, and giftes to
the poore.
23 And the Iewes promised to do as they
had begonne, and as Mordecái had writen
vnto them,
24 Because Hamán the sonne of Hammedátha the Agagite all the Iewes aduersarie, had imagined against the Iewes, to destroye them, & had n cast Pur (that is a lot)
to consume and destroye them.
25 And whẽ o she came before the King, he

f This she requireth not for desire of vengeance, but ẏ zeale to se Gods iudgemẽts executed against his enemies.

g Read Chap. 8,11.

h Meaning, ẏ they laide hãdes on none, ẏ were not the enemies of God.

i Meaning, in all places sauing in Shushán.

k As ẏ Iewes do, euẽ to this day, calling it in the Persians language Purim, that is the day of lots.

l The Iewes gather hereof that Mordecái wrote this storie, but it semeth that he wrote but onely these letters, and decrees that followe.

m He setteth before our eies the vse of this feast, which was for the remembrance of Gods deliuerãce, the maintenance of mutual frẽdship, and relief of the poore.

n Read Chap. 3,7.

o That is, Estér.

cõmanded by letters, Let his wicked p deuise (which he imagined against ẏ Iewes)
turne vpon his owne head, and let them
hang him and his sonnes on the tre.
26 Therefore they called these dayes Purím, by the name of Pur, *and* because of all
the wordes of this lettre, and of that which
they had sene besides this, & of that which
had come vnto them.
27 The Iewes *also* ordeined, and promised
for them and for their sede, and for all that
ioined vnto them, that they wolde not
"faile to obserue those q two dayes euerie
yere, according to their writing, and according to their season,
28 And that these dayes shulde be remembred, and kept throughout euerie generation and euerie familie, and euerie prouince, and euerie citie: euen these dayes of
Purím shulde not faile among the Iewes,
and the memorial of them shulde not perish from their sede.
29 And ẏ Quene Estér the daughter of A-
biháil & Mordecái the Iewe wrote with
all "autoritie (to cõfirme this letter of Purím the seconde time)
30 And he sent letters vnto all the Iewes
to the hundreth and seuen and twentie
prouinces of the kingdome of Ahashuerósh, with r wordes of peace and trueth,
31 To confirme these dayes of Purím according to their seasons, as Mordecái the
Iewe and Estér the Quene had appointed
them, and as they had promised for them
"selues and for their sede with s fasting
and prayer.
32 And the decree of Estér confirmed these wordes of Purím, & was writen in the
boke.

CHAP. X.

The estimation and autoritie of Mordecái.

1 AND the King Ahashuerósh layed a
tribute vpon the land, and vpon the
yles of the sea.
2 And all the actes of his power, and of his
might, and the declaration of the dignitie
of Mordecái, wherewith the King magnified him, are they not writen in the boke
of the Chronicles of the Kings of Media
and Persia?
3 For Mordecái the Iewe was the seconde
vnto King Ahashuerósh, and great amõg
the Iewes, and a accepted amõg the multitude of his brethren, who procured the
welth of his people, & spake peaceably to
all his sede.

p These are ẏ wordes of the Kings commãdemẽt to disanull Hamans wicked enterprise.

" Or, *transgresse*.

q Meaning the fourtente, and the fiftẽte day of the moneth Adár.

" Or *strength, or efficacie*.

r Which were letters declaring vnto the quietnes, and assurance, and putting them out of doute, and feare.

" Ebr. *soules*.

s That they wolde obserue this feast with fasting, & earnest prayer, which in Ebrewe is signified by this worde (their crye.)

a These thre pointes are here set forth as commendable, and necessarie for him, that is in autoritie: to haue the fauour of the people: to procure their welth, & to be gentle, and louing toward them.

IOB.

THE ARGVMENT.

IN this historie is set before our eyes the example of a singular pacience. For this holy man Iob was not onely extremely afflicted in outwarde things and in his body, but also in his minde, and conscience by the sharpe tentations of his wife, and chief friends: which by their vehement wordes, and subtil disputations broght him almoste to dispaire: for they set forthe God as a seuere iudge, and mortal enemie vnto him, which had caste him of, therefore in vaine he shulde seke vnto him for succour. These friends came vnto him vnder pretence of consolation, and yet they tormented him more then did all his affliction. Notwithstanding he did constantly resist them, and at length had good successe. In this storie we haue to marke that Iob mainteineth a good cause, but handeleth it euil: againe his aduersaries haue an euil matter, but they defend it craftely. For Iob helde that God did not alway punish men according to their sinnes, but that he had secret iudgements, whereof man knewe not the cause, and therefore man colde not reason against God therein, but he shulde be conuicted. Moreouer he was assured that God had not reiected him, yet through his great torments, & affliction he brasteth forthe into manie inconueniencies bothe of wordes and sentences, and sheweth him selfe as a desperate man in manie things, and as one that wolde resist God: and this is his good cause which he doeth not handel wel. Agayne the aduersaries mainteine with manie goodlie argumēts, that God punisheth continually according to the trespas, grounding vpon Gods prouidence, his iustice, and mans sinnes, yet their intention is euil: for they labour to bring Iob into dispaire, and so they mainteine an euil cause. Ezekiél commendeth Iob as a iuste man, Ezek. 14,14, and Iames setteth out his pacience for an example, Iam. 5,11.

CHAP. I.

1 The holines, riches, and care of Iob for his children. 10 Satán hathe permission to tempt him. 13 He tēpteth him by taking away his substance, and his children. 20 His faith and pacience.

1 THere was a mā in the lād
of [a] Vz called Iob, and
this mā [b] was an vpright
and iuste man, [c] one that
feared God, & eschewed
euil.
2 And he had seuē sonnes,
and thre daughters.
3 His [d] substance also was seuen thousand
shepe, and thre thousand camels, and fyue
hundreth yoke of oxen, and fyue hundreth
she asses, and his familie was verie great,
so that this man was the greatest of all the
"men of [e] the East.
4 And his sonnes went and banketted in
their houses, euerie one his day, and sent, &
called their thre sisters to eat & to drinke
with them.
5 And when the dayes of their banketting
were gone about, Iob sent, and [f] sanctified thē, and rose vp early in the morning,
and [g] offred burnt offrings *according* to the
nomber of thē all. For Iob thoght, It may
be that my sonnes haue sinned, and [h] blasphemed God in their hearts: thus did Iob
[i] euerie day.
6 ¶ Now on a day when the [k] children of
God came and stode [l] before the Lord,
Satán [m] came also among them.
7 Then the Lord said vnto Satán, Whēce
[n] commest thou? And Satán answered the
Lord, saying, [o] From cōpassing the earth
to and fro, and from walking in it.
8 And the Lord said vnto Satán, Hast thou
not cōsidered my seruant Iob, how none *is*
like him in the earth? an vpright and iust
man, one that feareth God, and escheweth
euil?
9 Thē Satán answered the Lord, and said,
Doeth Iob feare God for [p] noght?
10 Hast thou not made [q] an hedge about him
and about his house, and about all that he
hathe on euerie side? thou hast blessed the
worke of his hands, and his substance is
encreased in the land.
11 But stretche out now thine hand and
[r] touche all that he hathe, *to se* if he wil not
blaspheme thee to [s] thy face.
12 Then the Lord said vnto Satán, Lo, all
that he hathe *is* in [t] thine hand: onely vpō
him selfe shalt thou not stretch out thine
hād. So Satán departed from the [u] presence of the Lord.
13 ¶ And on a day, when his sonnes and his
daughters were eating and drinking wine
in their eldest brothers house,
14 There came a messenger vnto Iob, and
said, The oxen were plowing, and the asses feding in their places,
15 And the [x] Shabeans came violently, &
toke them: yea, they haue slaine the seruants with the edge of the sworde: but I
onely am escaped alone to tel thee.
16 And

a That is, of ye countrey of Idumea, as Lamen. 4,21, or bordering thereupon: for ye land was called by the name of Vz the sonne of Dishán the sonne of Seír, Genes. 36,28.
b Forasmuche as he was a Gētile and not a Iewe, & yet is pronounced vpright, and without hypocrisie, it declareth that amōg the heathen God hath his.
c Hereby is declared, what is ment by an vpright, and iuste man.
d His childrē and riches are declared, to commend his vertue in his prosperitie, & his paciēce, & constācie whē God had takē them frō him.
" Ebr. children.
e Meaning, the Arabiās, Chaldeans, Idumeans, &c.
f That is, cōmāded them to be sanctified: meaning, that they shulde consider the fautes, that they had committed, & recōcile them selues for the same.
g That is, he offred for euerie one of his children an offring of reconciliaciō, which declared his religiō toward God, & the care that he had toward his children.
h In Ebrewe it is, and blessed God, which is some time taken for blaspheming and cursing, as here, and 1. King. 21,10 and 13, &c.
i While the feast lasted.
k Meaning, the Angels which are called the sonnes of God, because they are willing to execute his wil.
l Because our infirmitie cā not comprehend God in his maiestie, he is set forthe vnto vs as a King, that our capacitie may be able to vnderstand that, ŵ is spokē of him.
m This declareth that although Satán be aduersarie to God, yet he is compelled to obey him, and do him all homage, without whose permission, & apointement he cā do nothing.
n This questiō is asked for our infirmitie: for God knewe whence he came.
o Herein is described the nature of Satán, which is euer ranging for his pray, 1. Pet. 5,8.
p He feareth thee not for thine owne sake, but for the cōmoditie that he receiueth by thee.
q Meaning, ye grace of God, which serued Iob as a ramparte against all tentations.
r This signifieth that Satán is not able to touche vs, but it is God that must do it.
s Satán noteth the vice, whereunto mē are cōmonly subiect: that is, to hide their rebellion, and to be contēt with God in the time of prosperitie, which vice is disclosed in the time of their aduersitie.
t God giueth not Satán power ouer man to gratifie him, but to declare that he hathe no power ouer man, but that which God giueth him.
u That is, went to execute that which God had permitted him to do: for els he can neuer go out of Gods presence.
x That is, the Arabians.

[y] Which thĩg was also done by ỹ craft of Satán to tempt Iob the more grieuously, for asmuche as he might se, that not onely men were his enemies, but that God made war re against him.
[z] This last plague declareth, that whẽ one plague is past which semeth hard to be borne, God can send vs another farre more grieuous, to trye his, & teache them obedience.
[a] Which came not of impaciẽcie, but declareth that the children of God are not insensible like blockes, but ỹ in their paciẽce they fele affliction, and grief of minde: yet they kepe a meane herein, and rebell not against God, as the wicked do.

16 And whiles he was yet speaking, another came, and said, The [y] fyre of God
is fallen from the heauen, and hathe burnt
vp the shepe and the seruants, and deuoured them: but I onely am escaped alone,
to tel thee.
17 And whiles he was yet speaking, another
came, and said, The Caldeans set out thre
bandes, and fel vpon the camels, and haue
taken them, and haue slaine the seruants
with the edge of the sworde: but I onely
am escaped alone to tel thee.
18 And whiles he was yet speaking, came an
other, & said, Thy [z] sonnes, & thy daughters were eating, & drinking wine in their
eldest brothers house,
19 And beholde, there came a great winde
from beyond the wildernes, and smote the
foure corners of the house, which fel vpon
the childrẽ, and they are dead, and I onely am escaped alone to tel thee.
20 Then Iob arose, and [a] rent his garmẽt,
and shaued his head, and fel downe vpon
the grounde, and worshiped,
21 And said, *Naked came I out of my mothers wombe, & naked shal I returne [b] thether: the Lord hathe giuen, and the Lord
hathe taken it: [c] blessed be the Name of
the Lord.
22 In all this did not Iob sinne, nor charge God [d] foolishly.

Eccle. 5, 14. 1. tim. 6, 7.

b That is, into the belly of ỹ earth, which is the mother of all.
c Hereby he confesseth that God is iuste, and good, all thogh his hãd be sore vpon him. d But declared that God did althing according to iustice and equitie.

CHAP. II.

6 Satán hathe permission to afflict Iob. 9 His wife tẽpteth him to forsake God. 11 His thre friends visite him.

a That is, the Angels, as Chap. 1, 6.
b Read Chap. 1, 13.

1 AND on a day the [a] children of God
came and stode before the Lord, and
[b] Satán came also among them, and stode
before the Lord.
2 Then the Lord said vnto Satán, Whence
commest thou? And Satán answered the
Lord, and said, From cõpassing the earth
to and fro, and from walking in it.
3 And the Lord said vnto Satán, Hast thou
not considered my seruant Iob, how none
is like him in the earth? * an vpright and
iuste man, one that feareth God, and es-
chueth euil? for yet he continueth in his
vprightnes, [c] althogh thou mouedst me
against him, to destroye [d] him without
cause.
4 And Satán answered the Lord, and said,
[e] Skin for skin, & all that euer a mã hathe,
wil he giue for his life.
5 But stretche now out thine hand, and touche his [f] bones and his flesh, *to se* if he
wil not blaspheme thee to thy face.
6 Then the Lord said vnto Satán, Lo, he
is in thine hand, but saue [g] his life.
7 ¶ So Satán departed from the presence of the Lord, and smote Iob with sore
[h] boyles, from the sole of his fote vnto his
crowne.
8 And he toke a [i] potsharde to scrape him,
and he sate downe among the ashes.
9 Thẽ said his [k] wife vnto him, Doest thou
[l] continue yet in thine vprightnes? [m] Blaspheme God, and dye.
10 But he said vnto her, Thou speakest like
a foolish woman: what? shal we receiue
good at the hand of God, and not [n] receiue euil? In all this did not Iob sinne with
his [o] lippes.
11 Now when Iobs thre [p] friends heard of
all this euil that was come vpon him, thei
came euerie one from his owne place, *to
wit*, Elipház the Temanite, and Bildád the
Shuhite, and Zophár the Naamathite: for
thei were agreed together to come to lament with him, and to comfort him.
12 So whẽ they lift vp their eyes a farre of,
they knewe him not: therefore thei lift vp
their voyces and wept, and euerie one of
them rent his garment, & sprinkled [q] dust
vpon their heades toward the heauen.
13 So thei sate by him vpon the grounde seuen dayes, and seuen nights, & none spake
a worde vnto him: for they sawe, that the
grief *was* very [r] great.

Ezek. 14, 14.
c He proueth Iobs integritie by this that he ceased not to feare God whẽ his plagues were grieuously vpon him.
d That is, whẽ ỹ hadst noght against him, or whẽ thou wast not able to bring thy purpose to passe.
e Hereby he mẽt that a mãs owne skinne is dearer vnto him then another mans.
f Meaning his owne persone.
g Thus Satán can go no further in punishing thẽ God hathe limited vnto him.

h This sore was moste vehemẽt, wherewith also God plagued the Egyptians, Exo. 9, 9. and threateneth to punish the rebellious people, Deut. 28, 27. so that this tentation was moste grieuous: for if Iob had measured Gods fauour by the vehemencie of his disease, he might haue thoght ỹ God had cast him of.
i As destitute of all other helpe and meanes, and wonderfully afflicted with the sorowe of his disease.
k Satán vseth the same instrumẽt agaĩst Iob, as he did against Adám.
l Meaning, What gainest thou to serue God, seing he thus plagueth thee as thogh he were thine enemie? This is ỹ moste grieuous tentation of the faithful, when their faith is assailed, and when Satán goeth about to persuade them, that thei trust in God in vayne.
m For death was appointed to the blasphemer, & so she ment that he shulde be sone ridde out of his peine. n That is, to be pacient in aduersitie, as we reioice, when he sendeth prosperitie, & so to acknowledge him to be bothe merciful and iuste. o He so brideled his affections, that his tõgue through impaciencie did not murmure against God. p Which were men of autoritie, wise and learned, and as the Septuagint write, Kings, and came to comfort him, but when they saw how he was visited, they conceiued an euil opinion of him, as thogh he had bene but an hypocrite, and so iustely plagued of God for his sinnes. q This was also a ceremonie, which they vsed in those contreis, as the renting of their clothes in signe of sorowe &c.
r And therefore thoght that he wolde not haue hearkened to their counsel.

CHAP. III.

1 Iob complaineth and curseth the day of his birth. 11 He desireth to dye, as thogh death were the end of all mãs miserie.

1 AFterward [a] Iob opened his mouthe,
and [b] cursed his day.
2 And Iob cryed out, and said,
3 Let the daye [c] perish, wherein I was borne, and the night when it was said, There
is a manchilde conceiued.
4 Let ỹ day be darkenes, let not God [d] regarde it from aboue, nether let the light
shine vpon it,
5 *But* let darkenes, & the [e] shadowe of death
staine it: let the cloude remaine vpon it, &
let them make it feareful as a bitter day.
6 Let darkenes possesse that night, let it
not be ioined vnto the dayes of the yere,
nor let it come into the count of the moneths.
7 Yea, desolate be that night, & let no ioye
be in it.
8 Let them that curse the day, (beĩg [f] ready to renue their mourning) curse it.

a The seuen dayes ended, Chap. 2, 13.
b Here Iob beginneth to fele his great imperfection in this battel betwene the Spirit and ỹ flesh, Rom. 7, 18, and after a maner yeldeth, yet in the end he getteth victorie, thogh he was in the meane time greatly wounded.
c Mẽ oght not to be weary of their life, & cursse it, because of the infirmities that it is subiect vnto, but because they are giuẽ to sinne and rebellion against God.
d Let it be put out of the nõber of dayes, and let it not haue the light of the sunne to separate it from the night.
e That is, moste obscure darknes, which maketh them afraied of death, that are in it. f Which cursse the day of their birth, let them lay that cursse vpon this night.

9 Let the starres of that twilight be dim,
through darkenes of it: let it loke for
light, but haue none: nether let it g se
"the dawning of the daye,
10 Because it shut not vp the dores of my
mothers wombe: nor hid sorowe from mine
eyes.
11 hWhy dyed I not in ӯ birth? or why dyed
I not, when I came out of the wombe?
12 Why did the knees preuent me? and why
did I sucke the breastes?
13 For *so* shulde I now haue i lyen and bene
quiet, I shulde haue slept then, *and* bene
at rest,
14 With the Kings and counsellers of the
earth, which haue buylded them selues
k desolate places:
15 Or with the princes that had golde, *&*
haue filled their houses with siluer.
16 Or *why* was I not hid, as an vntimely
birth, *ether* as infants, *which* haue not sene
the light?
17 The wicked l haue there ceased from
their tyrānie, and there they that laboured
valiantly, are at rest.
18 The m prisoners rest together, *and* heare
not the voyce of the oppressour.
19 There are small & great, and the seruāt
is fre from his master.
20 Wherefore is the light giuen to him
that is in miserie? and n life vnto them that
haue heauy hearts?
21 Which long for death, & if it come not,
they wolde euen search it more thē treasures:
22 Which ioye for gladnes *and* reioyce,
when they can finde the graue.
23 *Why is the light giuen* to the mā whose way
is o hid, & whome God hathe hedged in?
24 For my sighing cometh before I eat, and
my rorings are powred out like the water.
25 For the thing I p feared, is come vpon
me, and the thing that I was afrayed of, is
come vnto me.
26 I had no peace, nether had I quietnes,
nether had I rest, q yet trouble is come.

g Let it be alwais night, and neuer se day. "Ebr. the eye liddes of the morning. h This & that which followeth declareth that when mā giueth place to his passiōs, he is not able to stay nor kepe measure, but rūneth headling into all euil, except God call him backe. i The vehemēcie of his afflictions made him to vtter these wordes, as though death were the end of all miseries and as if there were no life after this, wc he speaketh not as thogh it were so, but ӯ infirmities of his flesh caused him to brast out into this error of the wicked. k He noteth the ambition of thē, which for their pleasure, as it were, change the order of nature, and buylde in moste barē places, because they wolde hereby make their names immortal. l That is, by death ӯ crueltie of the tyrants hathe ceased. m All they ӯt susteine anie kinde of calamitie and miserie in this worlde: which he speaketh after the iudgement of the flesh. n He sheweth that the benefites of God are not cōfortable, except the heart be ioiful, and the conscience quieted. o That seeth not how to come out of his miseries, because he depēdeth not on Gods prouidence. p In my prosperitie I loked euer for a fall, as is come now to passe. q The feare of troubles that shulde insue, caused my prosperitie to seme to me as nothing, and yet I am not exempted from trouble.

But now it is come vpon thee, & thou art
grieued: it toucheth thee, & thou art troubled.
6 Is not this thy c feare, thy confidence,
thy pacience, and the vprightnes of thy
wayes?
7 Remember, I pray thee: who *euer* perished
being an d innocēt? or where were the vpright destroied?
8 As I haue sene, they that e plowe iniquitie, and sowe wickednes, reape the same.
9 With the f blast of God they perish, and
with the breath of his nostrilles are they
consumed.
10 The roring of the g lion, and the voice
of the lionesse, and the teeth of the lions
whelpes are broken.
11 The lion perisheth for lacke of praye,
and the lions whelpes are scatred a-
brode.
12 But a thing was broght to me h secretly,
and mine eare hathe receiued a litle thereof.
13 In the thoghts of the visions of the
night, when slepe falleth on men,
14 Feare came vpon me, and dread which
made all my bones i to tremble.
15 And the winde passed before me, & made the heeres of my flesh to stand vp.
16 *Then* stode *one*, and I knewe not his face:
an image *was* before mine eyes, *&* in k silence heard I a voyce, *saying*,
17 Shal man be more l iust then God? or
shal a man be more pure then his maker?
18 Beholde, he founde no stedfastnes in
his Seruants, & laied folie vpon his m Angels.
19 How muche more in them that dwel in
houses of n clay, whose fundacion is in the
dust, which shalbe destroyed before the
moth?
20 They be destroyed from o the morning
vnto the euening: they perish for euer,
p without regarde.
21 Doeth not their dignitie go away with
them? do they not dye, and that without
q wisdome.

c This he concludeth that Iob was but an hypocrite & had no true feare nor trust in God. d He concludeth that Iob was reproued, seing that God handeled him so extremely, which is the argument that the carnal men make against the children of God. e They that do euil, can not but receiue euil. f He sheweth that God nedeth no great preparation to destroye his enemies: for he can do it with the blast of his mouthe. g Though men according to their office do not punish tyrants (whome for their crueltie he compareth to lions, and their children to their whelpes) yet God bothe is able, and his iustice wil punish them. h A thing that I knewe not before, was declared vnto me by vision: that is, that whosoeuer thinketh him selfe iuste, shal be founde a sinner, whē he commeth before God. i In these visions which God sheweth to his creatures, there is euer a certeine feare ioyned, that the autoritie thereof might be had in greater reuerence. k When all things were quiet, or when the feare was somewhat aswaged, as God appeared to Eliáh. 1. King. 19,12. l He proueth that if God did punish the innocent, the creature shulde be more iuste then the Creator, which were a blasphemie. m If God finde imperfection in his Angels, when they are not mainteined by his power, how muche more shal he lay foly to mans charge, when he wolde iustifie him selfe against God? n That is, in this mortal body, subiect to corruption, 2. Cor. 5,1. o They se death continually before their eies, and daily approching toward them. p No man for all this doeth consider it. q That is, before that any of them were so wise as to thinke on death.

CHAP. IIII.

5 Iob is reprehended of impaciencie. 7 And vniustice. 17 And of the presumption of his owne righteousnes.

1 THē Elipház the Temanite answered,
and said,
2 If we assay to commune with thee, wilt
thou be grieued? but a who can withholde
him self from speaking?
3 Beholde, thou hast taught manie, & b hast
strengthened the wearie hands.
4 Thy wordes haue confirmed him that
was falling, & thou hast strengthened the
weake knees.

a Seing this thine impaciencie. b Thou haste comforted oshers in their afflictions, and canst not now comfort thy selfe.

CHAP. V.

1.2 Elipház sheweth the difference betwene the children of God & the wicked. 3 The fall of the wicked. 9 Gods power who destroieth the wicked and deliuereth his.

1 CAll now, if anie wil a answer thee, &
to which of the Saintes wilt thou
turne?
2 Douteles b angre killeth the foolish, and
enuie slayeth the idiote.

a He willeth Iob to cōsider ӯ example of all thē that haue liued or do liue godly, whether any of thē be like vnto hī in raging against God as he doeth. b Murmuring against God in afflictions increaseth the peine, and vttereth mans folie.

3 I haue ſene the [c] fooliſh wel rooted, & ſodenly I [d] curſed his habitacion, *ſaying*,
4 His [e] children ſhalbe farre from ſaluatiõ,
and they ſhalbe deſtroied in the [f] gate, and
none ſhal deliuer them.
5 The hungrie ſhal eat vp his harueſt: yea,
thei ſhal take it from among the [g] thornes,
and the thirſtie ſhal drinke vp their ſubſtance.
6 For miſerie commeth not forthe of the
duſt, [h] nether doeth affliction ſpring out
of the earth.
7 But man is borne vnto [i] trauail, as the
ſparkes flye vpward.
8 But I wolde inquire [k] at God, and turne my talke vnto God:
9 Which [l] doeth great things and vnſearcheable, *and* marueılous things without
nomber.
10 He [m] giueth raine vpon the earth, and
powreth water vpon the ſtretes,
11 And ſetteth vp on hie them that be lowe,
that the ſorowful may be exalted to ſaluation.
12 He ſcatereth the deuiſes of the craftie:
ſo that their hands can not accõpliſh that
which they do enterpriſe.
13 *He taketh the wiſe in their craftines, &
the counſel of the wicked is made fooliſh.
14 They mete with [n] darkenes in the day
time, and [o] grope at noone day, as in the
night.
15 But he saueth the [p] poore frõ the ſworde,
from their [q] mouth, and from the hand of
the violent man,
16 So that the poore hathe *his* hope, but iniquitie ſhal [r] ſtop her mouth.
17 Beholde, bleſſed *is* the man whome God
correcteth: therefore refuſe not thou the
chaſtiſing of the Almightie.
18 For he maketh the wounde, and bindeth
it vp: he ſmiteth, and his hãds make whole.
19 He ſhal deliuer thee [ſ] in ſix troubles, and
in the ſeuent the euil ſhal not touche thee.
20 In famine he ſhal deliuer thee frõ death:
and in battel from the power of the
ſworde.
21 Thou ſhalt be hid from the ſcourge of ỹ
tongue, and thou ſhalt not be affraied of
deſtruction when it cometh.
22 *But* thou ſhalt [t] laugh at deſtruction and
dearth, & ſhalt not be afrayd of the beaſt
of the earth.
23 For the ſtones of the field [u] ſhalbe in league with thee, and the beaſtes of the field
ſhal be at peace with thee.
24 And thou ſhalt knowe, that peace *ſhalbe*
in thy tabernacle, & thou ſhalt viſite thine habitacion, and ſhalt not [x] ſinne.

c That is, the ſinner that hathe not the feare of God.
d I was not moued wͭ his pſperitie, but knewe that God had curſed him & his.
e Thogh God ſometime ſuffer the fathers to paſſe in this worlde, yet his iudgemẽts wil light vpõ their wicked children.
f By publicke iudgemẽt thei ſhalbe condẽned, and none ſhal pitie thẽ.
g Thogh there be but two or thre eares left in the hedges, yet theſe ſhalbe taken from him.
h That is, the earth is not ỹ cauſe of barennes and mans miſerie, but his owne ſinne.
i Which declareth that ſinne is euer in our corrupt nature: for before ſinne it was not ſubiect to peine & afflictiõ.
k If I ſuffred as thou doeſt, I wolde ſeke vnto God.
l He counſeleth Iob to hũble him ſelfe vnto God, to whome all creatures are ſubiect, and whoſe workes declare that man is inexcuſable, except he glorifie God in all his workes.
m He ſheweth by particular exãples, what the workes of God are.
*1 Cor. 3.19.
n In things plaine and euident thei ſhewe them ſelues fooles in ſtead of wiſe men
o This declareth that God puniſheth the worldely wiſe, as he threatened, Deu. 28, 29.
p That is, he that humbleth him ſelfe before God.
q He cõpareth the ſklãder of the wicked to ſharpe ſwordes.
r If the wicked be compelled at Gods workes to ſtoppe their mouthes, muche more thei ỹ profeſſe God.
ſ He wil ſend trouble after trouble, that his children may not for one time, but continually truſt in him: but they ſhal haue a comfortable iſſue, euen in the greateſt and the laſt, which is here called the ſeuent.
t Where as the wicked lament in their troubles, thou ſhalt haue occaſion to reioice.
u When we are in Gods fauour, all creatures ſhal ſerue vs.
x God ſhal ſo bleſſe thee that thou ſhalt haue occaſion to reioice in all things, and not to be offended.

25 Thou ſhalt perceiue alſo, that thy ſede
ſhalbe great, & thy poſteritie as the graſſe
of the earth.
26 Thou ſhalt go to thy graue in [y] a ful age,
as a ricke *of corne* cometh in due ſeaſon *into*
the barne.
27 Lo, [z] thus haue we inquired of it, *and* ſo
it is: heare this and knowe it for thy ſelf.

y Thogh the children of God haue not alwaies this promes performed, yet God doeth recompence it otherwiſe to their aduantage.
z We haue learned theſe pointes by experience, that God puniſheth not the innocent, that man can not compare in iuſtice with him, that ỹ hypocrites ſhal not long proſper, and that the affliction which man ſuſteineth, commeth for his owne ſinne.

CHAP. VI.

1 Iob anſwereth, that his peine is more grieuous then his faute. 8 He wiſheth death. 14 He cõplaineth of his frẽds.

1 BVt Iob anſwered, and ſaid,
2 Oh that my grief were wel weighed,
and my miſeries were laied together in
the [a] balance.
3 For it wolde be now heauyer thẽ the ſand
of ỹ ſea: therefore my wordes are [b] ſwal-
lowed vp.
4 For the arowes of the Almightie *are* in
me, ỹ venime whereof doeth drinke vp my
ſpirit, & the terrours of God [c] fight agaĩſt
me.
5 Doeth the [d] wilde aſſe braye when he hathe graſſe? or loweth the oxe when he hathe foddre?
6 That which is [e] vnſauery, ſhal it be eaten
without ſalt? or is there any taſte in the
white of an egge?
7 Suche things as my ſoule refuſed to touche, as *were* ſorowes, are my meate.
8 Oh that I might haue my [f] deſire, & that
God wolde graunt me the thing that I
long for!
9 That is, that God wolde deſtroye me:
that he wolde let his hãd go, & cut me of.
10 Then ſhulde I yet haue comfort, (thogh
I burne with ſorowe, let him not ſpare)
[g] becauſe I haue not denyed the wordes
of the Holie one.
11 What power haue I that I ſhulde endure? or what is mine [h] end, if I ſhulde prolong my life?
12 Is my ſtrẽgth the ſtrength of ſtones? *or* is
my fleſh of braſſe?
13 Is it not ſo, that there is in me no [i] helpe?
and that [*] ſtrength is taken from me?
14 He that is in miſerie, oght to be comforted of his neighbour: but mẽ haue forſaken the feare of the Almightie.
15 My brethren haue deceiued me as a [k] brooke, & as the riſing of the riuers they paſſe away.
16 Which are blackiſh with yce, & wherein the ſnowe is hid.
17 But in time thei are dryed vp with heat
& are conſumed: and when it is hote they
faile out of their places,

Kk.iiii.

a To knowe whether I cõplaine without iuſt cauſe.
b My grief is ſo great, that I lacke wordes to expreſſe it.
c Which declareth that he was not onely afflicted in body, but wounded in conſciẽce, which is ỹ greateſt battel that the faithful can haue.
d Thinke you that I crye without cauſe, ſeing ỹ brute beaſtes do not cõplaine when thei haue what thei wolde?
e Can a mans taſte delite in that ỹ hath no ſauour? meaning that none take pleaſure in affliction, ſeing thei can not away with things that are vnſauery to ỹ mouth.
f Herein he ſinneth double, bothe in wiſhing through impacience to dye, and alſo in deſiring of God a thing which was not agreable to his wil.
g That is, let me dye at once, before I come to diſtruſt in Gods pmes through mine impaciẽcie.
h He feareth leſt he ſhulde be broght to inconueniencies, if his ſorowes ſhulde continue.
i Haue I not ſoght to helpe my ſelfe as muche as was poſſible?
*Or, wiſdome, or Law.
k He compareth thoſe friends which comfort vs not in miſerie, to a broke, which in ſommer, when we nede waters, is drye: in winter is hard froſen, & in ỹ time of raine, when we haue no nede, ouerfloweth with water.

18 Or thei departe from their way & course,
yea, they vanish and perish.
19 Thei that go to Temá, [l] considered thē,
& thei that go to Shebá, waited for them.
20 *But* they were confounded: when thei ho
ped, thei came thether and were ashamed.
21 Surely now are ye *like* [m] vnto it: ye haue
sene *my* feareful plague, and are afrayed.
22 Was it because I said, Bring vnto me? or
giue a rewarde to me of your [n] substance?
23 And deliuer me from the enemies hand,
or ransom me out of the hand of tyrants?
24 Teach me, & I wil [o] holde my tongue: &
cause me to vnderstand, wherein I haue
erred.
25 How [p] stedfast are the wordes of righteousnes? and what can any of you iustely
reproue?
26 Do ye imagine to reproue [q] wordes, that
the talke of the afflicted shulde be as the
winde?
27 Ye make your wrath to fall vpon the fatherles, and digge a pit for your friend.
28 Now therefore be content to [r] loke vpon me: for I wil not lye before your face.
29 Turne, I pray you, let there be none iniquitie: returne, I say, & *ye shal se* yet my
righteousnes in that behalfe. Is there iniquitie in my tōgue? doeth not my mouthe
fele sorowes?

l Thei that passe thereby to go into ẏ hote countreies of Arabia, thinke to finde water there, to quēch their thirst, but they are deceiued.
m That is, like to this broke, which deceiueth them, that thinke to haue water there in their nede, as I loked for cōsolation at your hands.
n He toucheth ẏ worldelings, which for no necessitie wil giue parte of their goods, and muche more these men, which wolde not giue him comfortable wordes.
o Shewe me wherein I haue erred, and I wil confesse my faute.
p He ẏ hathe a good cōsciēce, doeth not shrinke at the sharpe wordes or reasonings of others, excepte thei be able to persuade him by reason.
q Do you cauill at my wordes, because I shulde be thoght to speake foolishly, which am now in miserie?
r Consider whether I speake as one that is driuen to this impaciencie through very sorowe, or as an hypocrite, as you condemne me.

CHAP. VII.

1 Iob sheweth the shortenes and miserie of mans life.

1 IS there not an appointed time to man
vpon earth? and *are not* his dayes as the
dayes of an [a] hyreling.
2 As a seruant longeth for the shadowe, &
as an hyreling loketh for *the end* of his
worke,
3 So haue I had as an inheritance the [b] moneths of vanitie, and peineful nights haue bene appointed vnto me.
4 If I laied me downe, I said, When shal
I arise? and measurīg the euening I am e-
uen ful with tosing to and fro vnto the
dawning of the day.
5 My flesh is [c] clothed with wormes & filthines of the dust: my skin is rent, & become horrible,
6 My dayes are swifter thē [d] a weauers shit-
tle, and they are spent without hope.
7 Remember that my life is but a winde, &
that mine eye shal not returne to se pleasure.
8 The eye that hathe sene me, shal se me no
more: thine eyes *are* vpon me, and I shalbe
no longer.
9 [e] *As* the cloude vanisheth & goeth away,
so he that goeth downe to the graue, shal
[f] come vp nomore.
10 He shal returne nomore to his house,
nether shal his place knowe him anymore.
11 Therefore I wil not [g] spare my mouthe,
but wil speake in the trouble of my spirit,
& muse in the bitternes of my minde.
12 Am I a sea [h] or a whalefish, that thou kepest me in warde?
13 When I say, My couche shal relieue me,
& my bed shal bring *comfort* in my meditation,
14 Then fearest thou me [i] with dreames,
and astonishest me with visions.
15 Therefore my soule [k] choseth rather to
be strangled & to dye, then *to be in* my bones.
16 I abhorre it, I shal not liue alway: [l] spare me then, for my daies *are* but vanitie.
17 What is man, that thou [m] doest magnifie him, and that thou settest thine heart
vpon him?
18 And doest visit him euerie morning, and
tryest him euerie moment?
19 How long wil it be *yer* thou departe frō
me? thou wilt not let me alone whiles I
may swallowe my spetle.
20 I haue [n] sinned, what shal I do vnto thee?
ô thou preseruer of men, why hast thou
set me *as a marke* against thee, so that I
am a burden vnto my self?
21 And why doest thou not pardone my tres
pas? and take away mine iniquitie? for now
shal I slepe in the dust, and if thou sekest
me in the morning, I shal [o] not be *founde*.

a Hathe not an hyred seruant some rest and ease? then in this my continual tormēt I am worse then an hyreling.
b My sorowe hathe continued from moneth to moneth, and I haue loked for hope in vaine.
c This signifieth that his disease was rare and moste horrible.
d Thus he speaketh in respect of the breuitie of mās life, which passeth without hope of returnīg: incōsideratiō whereof he desireth God to haue compassion on hī.
e If thou beholde me in thine angre, I shal not be able to stand in thy presence.
f Shal nomore enioye this mortal life.
g Seing I can by nonother meanes cōfort my selfe, I wil declare my grief by wordes. and thus he speaketh as one ouercome with grief of minde.
h Am not I a poore wretch? what nedest thou then to lay so muche peine on me?
i So that I cā haue no rest, night nor day.
k He speaketh as one ouercome wᵗ sorowe, and not of iudgement, or of the examination of his faith.
l Seing my terme of life is so shorte, let me haue some rest and ease.
m Seing that mā of him selfe is so vile, why doest thou giue him that honour to contende against him?
n After all tentations faith brasteth forthe & leadeth Iob to repentance: yet it was not in suche perfection, that he colde bridel him selfe frō reasoning with God, because that he stil tryed his faith.
o That is, I shalbe dead.

CHAP. VIII.

1 Bildád sheweth that Iob is a sinner, because God punisheth the wicked, and preserueth the good.

1 THen answered Bildád the Shuhite,
and said,
2 How long wilt thou talke of these thīgs?
& howlōg shal the wordes of thy mouthe
[a] *be as* a mightie winde?
3 Doeth God peruert iudgement? or doeth
the almighty subuert iustice?
4 If thy sonnes haue sinned against him, &
he hathe sent them into the place of their
[b] iniquitie,
5 *Yet* if thou [c] wilt early seke vnto God, &
pray to the Almighty,
6 If thou be pure and vpright, then surely
he wil awake vp vnto thee, & he wil make
the habitation of thy righteousnes prospe
rous.
7 And thogh thy beginning [d] be smale,
yet thy later end shal greatly increase.
8 [e] Inquire therefore, I pray thee, of the
former age, and prepare thy selfe to searche of their fathers.
9 (For we are but [f] of yesterday, and are
igno-

a He declareth that their wordes which wolde diminesh any thīg frō the iustice of God, is but as a puft of winde that vanisheth away.
b That is, hathe rewarded thē according to their iniquitie: meaning, that Iob oght to be warned by the exāple of his children, that he offend not God.
c That is, if ẏ turne betime whiles God calleth thee to repentance.
d Thogh the beginnings be not so pleasant, as thou woldest desire, yet in the end thou shalt haue sufficient occasion to cōtent thy self.
e He willeth Iob to examine all antiquitie, and he shal finde it true which he here saith.
f Meaning, that it is not ynough to haue the experience of our selues, but to be confirmed by the examples of them that went before vs.

ignorant: for our dayes vpon earth *are* but
a ſhadow)
10 Shal not thei teache thee & tel thee, and
vtter the wordes of their heart?
11 Can a [g] ruſh growe without myre? or,
can the graſſe growe without water?
12 Thogh it were in grene & not cut downe, yet ſhal it wither before anie other
herbe.
13 So *are* the paths of all that forget God,
and the hypocrites hope ſhal periſh.
14 His confidence alſo ſhal be cut of, & his
truſt *ſhalbe, as* the houſe of a [h] ſpyder.
15 He ſhal leane vpon his houſe, but it ſhal
not ſtand: he ſhal holde him faſt by it, yet
ſhal it not endure.
16 The [i] *tre* is grene before the ſunne, and
the branches ſpread ouer the garden thereof.
17 The rotes thereof are wrapped about
the fountaine, & are folden *about* the houſe
of ſtones.
18 If *anie* plucke it from his place, and it
[k] denie, *ſaying,* I haue not ſene thee,
19 Beholde, it wil reioyce [l] by this meanes,
that it may growe in another molde.
20 Beholde, God wil not caſt away an vpright man, nether wil he take the wicked
by the hand,
21 Til he haue filled thy mouthe w^t [m] laughter, and thy lippes with ioye.
22 They that hate thee, ſhalbe clothed
with ſhame, & the dwelling of the wicked
ſhal not *remaine*.

g As a ruſh can not growe without moiſtnes, ſo can not the hypocrite, becauſe he hathe not faith, which is moiſtened with Gods Spirit.
h Which is to day, and to morowe ſwept away
i He cōpareth the iuſte to a tre, which althogh it be remoued out of one place vnto another, yet floriſheth: ſo the affliction of the godlie turneth to their profite.
k That is, ſo ŷ there remaine nothing there to proue whether ŷ tre had growen there, or no.
l To be planted in another place, where it may growe at pleaſure.
m If thou be godlie, he wil giue thee occaſion to reioyce, & if not, thine afflictiō ſhal increaſe.

CHAP. IX.

1 Iob declareth the mightie power of God, and that mās righteouſnes is nothing.

1 THen Iob anſwered, and ſaid,
2 I knowe verely that it is ſo: for how
ſhulde man *compared* vnto God, be [a] iuſtified?
3 If he wolde diſpute with him, he colde
not anſwer him one thing of a [b] thouſand.
4 He is wiſe in heart, & mightie in ſtrength:
who hathe bene fearce agaiſt him & hathe
proſpered?
5 He remoueth the moūtaines & they fele
not when he ouerthroweth them in his
wrath.
6 He [c] remoueth the earth out of her place, that the pillers thereof do ſhake.
7 He commandeth the ſunne, and it riſeth
not: he cloſeth vp the ſtarres, as vnder a
ſignet.
8 He him ſelf alone ſpreadeth out the heauens, and walketh vpon the height of the
ſea.
9 He maketh *the ſtarres* [d] Arcturus, Orion,
and Pleiades, and the climats of ŷ South.
10 He doeth great things, and vnſearcheable: yea, meruelous things without nomber.

a Iob here anſwereth to ŷ point of Eliphaz and Bildads oracion, touching the iuſtice of God & his innocēcie, confeſsing God to be infinit in iuſtice, and man to be nothing in reſpect.
b Of a thouſand things, ŷ God colde lay to his charge, mā can not anſwer him one.
c He declareth what is the infirmitie of mā by ŷ mightie and incompreheſible power that is in God, ſhewing what he colde do, if he wolde ſet forthe his power.
d These are ŷ names of certeine ſtarres, whereby he meaneth that all ſtarres bothe knowen & vnknowen are at his appointement.

11 Lo, when he goeth [e] by me, I ſe him not:
& when he paſſeth by, I perceiue him not.
12 Beholde, when he taketh a pray, [f] who
can make him to reſtore it? who ſhal ſay
vnto him, What doeſt thou?
13 God [g] wil not withdrawe his angre &
the moſte mightie helpes [h] do ſtoupe vnder him.
14 How muche leſſe ſhal I anſwer him? or
how ſhulde I finde out [i] my wordes with
him?
15 For thogh I were iuſte, yet colde I [k] not
anſwer, *but* I wolde make ſupplicacion to
my Iudge.
16 If I [l] crye, and he anſwer me, *yet* wolde
I not beleue, that he heard my voyce.
17 For he deſtroyeth me with a tempeſt, &
woundeth me [m] without cauſe.
18 He wil not ſuffer me to take my breath,
but filleth me with bitternes.
19 If *we ſpeake* of ſtrength, beholde, he is
[n] ſtrong: if *we ſpeake* of iudgement, who
ſhal bring me in to plaide?
20 If I wolde iuſtifie my ſelf, mine owne
mouth ſhal condemne me: [o] if I wolde be
perfite, he ſhal iudge me wicked.
21 *Thogh* I were perfite, *yet* I knowe not my
ſoule: *therefore* abhorre I my lyfe.
22 This is one point: therefore I ſaid, He
deſtroyeth the [p] perfite and the wicked.
23 If the ſcourge ſhulde ſodenly [q] ſlaie,
ſhulde *God* [r] laugh at the puniſhment of
the innocent?
24 The earth is giuen into the hand of the
wicked: he [ſ] couereth the faces of the iudges thereof: if not, where [t] is he? or who
is he?
25 My daies haue bene more ſwift then a
poſte: they haue fled, & haue ſene no good
thing.
26 They are paſſed *as* with the moſte ſwift
ſhippes, and as the egle that flieth to the
praye.
27 If [u] I ſay, I wil forget my complaint, I
wil ceaſe from my wrath, & comfort me,
28 *Then* I am afrayed of all my ſorowes,
knowing that thou wilt not iudge me innocent.
29 *If* I be wicked, why [x] labour I thus in
vaine?
30 If I [y] waſh my ſelf with ſnowe water,
and purge mine hands moſte cleane,
31 Yet ſhalt thou plonge me in the pit, and
mine owne [z] clothes ſhal make me filthy.
32 For he is not a man as I am, that I ſhulde

e I am not able to cōprehend his workes, which are commune and daily before mine eyes, muche leſſe in thoſe things, which are hid and ſecret.
f He ſheweth that whē God doeth execute his power, he doeth it iuſtely, for aſmuch as none can controle him.
g God wil not be appeaſed for oght that man can laie for him ſelf for his iuſtification.
h That is, all ŷ reaſons that men can laie to approue their cauſe.
i How ſhulde I be able to anſwer him by eloquence: whereby he noteth his friends, that albeit thei were eloquent in talke, yet thei felt not in heart, that which thei ſpake.
k Meaning, in his owne opinion, ſignifyīg that man wil ſometime flatter him ſelf to be righteo*, which before God is abominacion
l Whiles I am in my pangs, I can not but braſt forthe into many inconueniences, althogh I know ſtil that God is iuſt.
m I am not able to fele my ſinnes ſo great, as I fele the weight of his plagues: & this he ſpeaketh to condemne his dulnes, and to iuſtifie God.
n After he hathe accuſed his owne weakenes, he contineweth to iuſtifie God and his power.
o If I wolde ſtande in mine owne defence, yet God hathe iuſte cauſe to condemne me, if he examine mine heart, & conſcience.
p If God puniſh according to his iuſtice, he wil deſtroye aſwel them that are coūted perfite, as them that are wicked. q To wit, the wicked. r This is ſpoken according to our apprehenſion, as thogh he wolde ſay, If God deſtroye but the wicked, as chap 5,3, why ſhulde he ſuffer the innocēts to be ſo long tormented by them? ſ That they can not ſe to do iuſtice. t That can ſhewe the contrary? u I thinke not to fall into theſe affections, but my ſorowes bring me to theſe manifolde infirmities, & my conſcience condemneth me. x Why doeth not God deſtroye me at once? thus he ſpeaketh according to the infirmitie of the fleſh. y Thogh I ſeme neuer ſo pure in mine owne eyes, yet all is but corruption before God z Whatſoeuer I wolde vſe to couer my filthines with, ſhal diſcloſe me ſo muche more.

answer him, *if* we come together to iudgement.
33 Nether is there any vmpire [a] that might
laie his hand vpon vs bothe.
34 Let him take his rod away frō me, & let
not his feare astonish me:
35 *Then* wil I speake, & feare him not: [b] *but*
because I am not so, I holde me stil.

a Which might make an accorde betwene God and me, speaking of impaciencie, & yet confessing God to be iust in punishing him.
b Signifying ŷ Gods iudgements kepe him in awe.

CHAP. X.

1 Iob is weary of his life, and setteth out his fragilitie before God. 20 He desireth him to stay his hand. 22 A description of death.

1 MY soule is cut of [a] thogh I liue: I
wil leaue my [b] complaint vpon my
self, & wil speake in the bitternes of my
soule.
2 I wil say vnto God, [c] Condēne me not:
shewe me, wherefore thou contendest with
me.
3 Thinkest thou it [d] good to oppresse me,
& to cast of the [e] labour of thine hands,
and to fauour the [f] counsel of the wicked?
4 Hast thou [g] carnal eyes? or doest thou se
as man seeth?
5 Are thy dayes as mans [h] dayes? or thy yeres, as the time of man?
6 That thou inquirest of mine iniquitie, &
searchest out my sinne.
7 Thou knowest that I can not do [i] wickedly: for none can deliuer me out of thine
hand.
8 Thine [k] hands haue made me, and facioned me wholy rounde about, & wilt thou
destroye me?
9 Remember, I pray thee, that thou hast
made me as [l] the clay, and wilt thou bring
me into dust againe?
10 Hast thou not powred me out as mylke?
and turned me to cruds like chese?
11 Thou hast clothed me with skinne and
flesh, and ioyned me together with bones
and sinewes.
12 Thou hast giuen me life, and [m] grace: &
thy [n] visitacion hathe preserued my spirit.
13 Thogh thou hast hid these things in thine heart, *yet* I knowe [o] ŷ it is so with thee.
14 If I haue sinned, then thou wilt streight-
ly loke vnto me, and wilt not holde me
giltles of mine iniquitie.
15 If I haue done wickedly, wo vnto me: if
I haue done righteously, I wil not [p] lift
vp mine head, being ful of confusion, because I se mine affliction.
16 But let it increase: hunt thou me as a lyon: returne & shewe thy self [q] maruelous
vpon me.

a I am more like to a dead man then to one ŷ liueth.
b I wil make an ample declaratiō of my tormēts, accusing my self & not God.
c He wolde not that God shulde procede against him by his secret iustice, but by the ordinarie meanes that he punisheth others.
d Is it agreable to thy iustice to do me wrong?
e Wilt thou be without compassion?
f Wilt thou gratifie ŷ wicked & condēne me?
g Doest thou this of ignorance?
h Art thou inconstant and changeable, as the times, to daie a friend, to morowe an enemie?
i By affliction thou kepest me as in a prison, & restraynest me from doing euil, nether can any set me at libertie.
k In these eight verses following he describeth the mercie of God in the wōderful creation of man: & therefrō groūdeth that God shulde not shew him self rigorous against him.
l As brittel as a pot of clay.
m That is, reason and vnderstanding, and many other giftes whereby man excelleth all earthlie creatures.
n That is, thy fatherlie care & prouidence, whereby thou preseruest me, and without the which I shulde perish streight way.
o Thogh I be not fully able to comprehend these things, yet I must nedes confesse that it is so.
p I wil alway walke in feare and humilitie, knowing that none is iuste before thee.
q Iob being sore assalted in this battel betwene the flesh and the Spirit, brasteth out into these affections, wishing rather short dayes then long peine.

17 Thou renuest thy plagues against me,
and thou increasest thy wrath against me:
[r] changes and armies *of sorowes* are against
me.
18 Wherefore thē hast thou broght me out
of the wombe? Oh that I had perished,
and that none eye had sene me!
19 *And* that I were as I had not bene, *but*
broght from the wombe to the graue.
20 Are not my dayes fewe? let him [s] cease,
and leaue of frō me, that I may take a litle
comfort,
21 Before I go and shal not [t] returne, *euen*
to the land of darkenes and shadowe of
death:
22 Into a lād, *I say*, darke as darkenes it self,
& into the shadow of death, where is none
[u] order, but the light *is there* as darkenes.

r That is, diuersitie of diseases and in great abundāce, shewīg that God hathe infinite meanes to punish mā.
s He wisheth ŷ God wolde leaue of his affliction, considerīg his great miserie & the breuitie of his life.
t He speaketh thus in ŷ persone of a sinner, that is ouercome with passions & ŷ the feling of Gods iudgements, & therefore can not apprehēd in ŷ state the mercies of God & cōfort of the resurrection.
u No distinctiō betwene light and darkenes, but where all is verie darkenes it self.

CHAP. XI.

1 Iob is vniustly reprehended of Zophár. 7 God is incōprehensible. 14 He is merciful to the repentant. 18 Their assurance that liue godlie.

1 THen answered Zophár the Naamathite, and said,
2 Shulde not the multitude of wordes be
answered? or shulde a great [a] talker be iustified?
3 Shulde men holde their peace at thy lyes?
and when thou mockest *others*, shal none
make thee ashamed?
4 For thou hast said, [b] My doctrine is pure,
and I am cleane in thine eyes.
5 But oh, that God wolde speake and open
his lippes against thee!
6 That he might shewe thee the [c] secrets of
wisdome, how ŷ hast *deserued* double, accordīg to right: knowe therefore that God
hathe forgoten thee for thine iniquitie.
7 Canst thou by searching finde out God?
canst thou finde out the Almightie to *his*
perfection?
8 The heauens are hie, what canst thou do?
[d] it is deper then the hel, how canst thou
knowe it?
9 The measure thereof is longer then the
earth, and it is broder then the sea.
10 If he cut of and [e] shut vp, or gather together, who can turne him backe?
11 For he knoweth vaine men, and seeth iniquitie, & him that vnderstandeth nothing.
12 Yet vaine man wolde be wise, thogh man
newe borne is like a wilde asse [f] colte.
13 If thou [g] prepare thine heart, & stretche
out thine hands towarde him:
14 If iniquitie be in thine [h] hand, put it
farre away, & let no wickednes dwel in thy
tabernacle.
15 Then truely shalt thou lift vp thy [i] face
without

a Shulde he persuade by his great talke, that he is iuste?
b He chargeth Iob with this, that he shulde say, that the thing, which he spake, was true, and that he was without sinne in ŷ sight of God.
c Which is, not to stand in iustifying of thy self: he signifieth that man wil neuer be ouercome, whiles he reasoneth with another, and therefore God must breake of the controuersie, and stop mans mouth.
d That is, this perfection of God, & if man be not able to comprehend the height of the heauē, the depth of hel, the length of the earth, the breadth of the sea, which are but creatures: how can he atteine to the perfection of the Creator?
e If God shulde turne the state of thigs, and establish a newe ordre in nature, who colde cōtrole him?
f That is, without vnderstanding: so that whatsoeuer gifts he hathe afterwarde, come of God and not of nature.
g If thou repent, pray vnto him.
h Renounce thine owne euil workes, and se that they offend not God, our whome thou hast charge.
i He declareth what quietnes of conscience and successe in all things suche shal haue, which turne to God by true repentāce.

without ſpot, and ſhalt be ſtable, & ſhalt
not feare.
16 But thou ſhalt forget *thy* miſerie, and remember it as waters that are paſt.
17 Thine age alſo ſhal appeare more *cleare*
then the noone day: thou ſhalt ſhine *and*
be as the morning.
18 And thou ſhalt be bolde, becauſe there is
hope: and thou ſhalt dig pittes, *and* ſhalt
lye downe ſafely.
19 *For when thou takeſt thy reſt, none ſhal
make thee afraied: yea, manie ſhal make
ſute vnto thee.
20 But the eyes [k] of the wicked ſhal faile,
and their refuge ſhal periſh, and their hope *ſhalbe* ſorowe of minde.

Leuit.26,5.

k He ſheweth that contrarie things ſhal come vnto them that do not repent.

CHAP. XII.

1 Iob accuſeth his friends of ignorance. 7 He declareth the might, and power of God. 17 And how he changeth the courſe of things.

1 THen Iob anſwered, and ſaid,
2 In dede becauſe that ye are the people *onely*, [a] wiſdome muſt dye with you.
3 But I haue vnderſtanding aſwel as you, &
am not inferior vnto you: yea, who knoweth not ſuche things?
4 *I am [b] as one mocked of his neighbour,
who calleth vpon God, and he [c] heareth him: the iuſte *and* the vpright is laughed to ſcorne.
5 [d] He that is ready to fall, *is as* a lampe
deſpiſed in the opinion of the riche.
6 The tabernacles of robbers do proſper,
and they are in ſauetie, that prouoke God,
" whome God hathe enriched with his
hand.
7 Aſke now the beaſtes, [e] and they ſhal
teache thee, and the foules of the heauen,
and they ſhal tel thee:
8 Or ſpeake to the earth, and it ſhal ſhewe
thee: or the fiſhes of the ſea, and they ſhal
declare vnto thee.
9 Who is ignorant of all theſe, but that the
hand of the Lord hathe made theſe?
10 In whoſe hand is the ſoule of euerie
liuing thing, and the breath of all " mankinde.
11 Doeth not the eares [f] diſcerne the wordes? and the mouth taſte meat for it
ſelf?
12 Among the [g] ancient *is* wiſdome, and in
the length of dayes *is* vnderſtanding.
13 With him *is* wiſdome and ſtrength: he
hathe counſel and vnderſtanding.
14 Beholde, he wil breake downe, and it can
not be buylt: he ſhutteth a man vp, and he
can not be loſed.
15 Beholde, he withholdeth the waters, and
thei drye vp: but when he ſendeth thē out,
they deſtroye the earth.
16 With him *is* ſtrength and wiſdome: he
that is deceiued, and that [h] deceiueth, a-
re his.
17 He cauſeth the counſelers to go *as* ſpoiled, and maketh the iudges fooles.
18 [i] He loſeth [k] the colar of Kings, and girdeth their loines with a girdle.
19 He leadeth away the princes *as* a pray, &
ouerthroweth the mightie.
20 He taketh away the ſpeache from the
[l] faithful *counſelers*, & taketh away the iudgement of the ancient.
21 He powreth cōtempt vpon princes and
maketh the ſtrēgth of the mightie weake.
22 He diſcouereth the depe places from
their darkenes, & bringeth forthe the ſhadowe of death to light.
23 He [m] increaſeth the people, and deſtroyeth them: he inlargeth the nacions, &
bringeth them in againe.
24 He taketh away the hearts of them that
are the chief ouer the people of the earth,
and maketh them to wāder in the wildernes out of the way.
25 They grope in the darke without light:
& he maketh them to ſtagger like a dronken man.

a Becauſe you fele not that, wͨ you ſpeake, you thinke yͤ whole ſtādeth in wordes, and ſo flatter your ſelues as thogh none knewe anie thing, or colde knowe but you.

Prou.14,2.

b He reproueth theſe his friends of two fautes: the one yͭ thei thoght thei had better knowledge thē in dede they had, & yͤ other that in ſtead of true cōſolatiō they did deride, and deſpiſe their friend in his aduerſitie.

c The which neighbour being a mocker, and a wicked man, thinketh that no man is in Gods fauour but he, becauſe he hathe all thīgs that he deſireth.

d As the riche eſteme not a light, or torche that goeth out, ſo is he deſpiſed that falleth from proſperitie to aduerſitie.

" *Ebr. to whome God hathe broght in with his hand.*

e He declareth to them that did diſpute agaīſt him, that their wiſdome is cōmune to all, & ſuche as yͤ very brute beaſts do dailie teache.

" *Or, fleſh.*

f He exhorteth them to be wiſe in iudging, and aſwel to know the right vſe why God hathe giuen them eares, as he hathe done a mouth. g Thogh men by age, and continuance of time atteine to wiſdome, yet it is not comparable to Gods wiſdome, nor able to comprehend his iudgements, wherein he anſwereth to that, which was alledged, Chap 8,8.

h He ſheweth that there is nothing done in this worlde without Gods wil, and ordinance: for els he ſhulde not be almightie.

i He taketh wiſdome frō them.

k He abateth the honour of princes, and bringeth them into the ſubiectiō of others.

l He cauſeth that their wordes haue no credit, which is when he wil puniſh ſinne

m In this diſcourſe of Gods wonderful workes Iob ſheweth that whatſoeuer is done in this worlde, bothe in yͤ ordre and chāge of thīgs is by Gods wil and appointement: wherein he declareth that he thinketh wel of God, and is as able to ſet forthe his power in wordes as they that reaſoned againſt, were.

CHAP. XIII.

1 Iob compareth his knowledge with the experiēce of his friends. 16 The penitent ſhalbe ſaued, and the hypocrite condemned. 20 He prayeth vnto God that he wolde not handle him rigorouſly.

1 LO, mine eye hathe ſene all *this*: mine
eare hathe heard, and vnderſtand it.
2 I knowe alſo aſmuche as you knowe: I
am not inferior vnto you.
3 But I wil ſpeake to the Almightie, and I
deſire [a] to diſpute with God.
4 For in dede ye forge lyes, and all you are
[b] phiſicions of no value.
5 Oh, that you wolde holde your tongue,
that it might be imputed to you for wiſdome!
6 Now heare my diſputation, and giue eare to the arguments of my lippes.
7 Wil ye ſpeake [c] wickedly for Gods *defence*, and talke deceitfully for his cauſe?
8 Wil ye accept his perſone? or wil ye contend for God?
9 Is it wel yͭ he ſhulde ſeke of you? wil you
make a lye for him, as one lyeth for a mā?
10 He wil ſurely reproue you, if ye do ſecretly accept anie perſone.
11 Shal not his excellēcie make you afraid?
and his feare fall vpon you?
12 Your [d] memories may be cōpared vnto
aſhes, *and* your bodies to bodies of claye.
13 Holde your tōgues in my preſence, that
I may ſpeake, and let come vpon what wil.
14 Wherefore do I [e] take my fleſh in my
tethe, and put my ſoule in mine hand?
15 Lo, thogh he ſlay me, *yet* wil I truſt in him,
and I wil reproue my wayes in his ſight.

Chap XIII.

a For althogh he knewe that God had a iuſtice, wͨ was manifeſt in his ordinarie working, and another in his ſecret counſel, yet he wolde vtter his affectiō to God, becauſe he was not able to vnderſtand the cauſe why he did thus puniſh him

b You do not wel applye your medicine to the diſeaſe.

c He cōdēneth their zeale wͨ had not knowledge, nether regarded they to cōfort him, but alwaie grated on Gods iuſtice, as thogh it was not euidently ſene in Iob, except they had vndertakē the probation thereof.

d Your fame ſhal come to nothing.

e Is not this a manifeſt ſigne of mine affliction, and that I do not complaine without cauſe, ſeing yͭ I am thus tormēted as thogh I ſhulde teare mine owne fleſh, & put my life in dāger

16 He shal be my saluation also: for the
[f] hypocrite shal not come before him.
17 Heare diligently my wordes, and marke
my talke.
18 Beholde now: *if* I prepare me to iudgement, I knowe that I shal be [g] iustified.
19 Who is he, that wil pleade [h] with me? for
if I now holde my tongue, I [i] dye.
20 But do not these two things vnto me: thẽ
wil I not hide my self from thee.
21 [k] Withdrawe thine hand from me, and
let not thy feare make me afraied.
22 Then call thou, and I wil answer: or let
me speake, and answer thou me.
23 How manie are [l] mine iniquities and
sinnes? shewe me my rebellion, and my
sinne.
24 Wherefore hidest thou thy face, and takest me for thine enemie?
25 Wilt thou breake a leafe driuen to and
fro? and wilt thou pursue the drye stubble?
26 For thou writest bitter things against me,
and makest me to possesse [m] the iniquities
of my youth.
27 Thou puttest my fete also in the [n] stockes, and lokest narowly vnto all my paths,
and makest the printe *thereof* in the [*] heeles of my fete.
28 Suche one consumeth like a roten thing,
and as a garment that is motheaten.

f Whereby he declareth that he is not an hypocrite as thei charged him.
g Thas is, cleared, and not cast of for my sinnes, as you reason.
h To proue yͭ God doeth thus punish me for my sinnes.
i If I defend not my cause, euerie mã wil condemne me.
k He sheweth what these two thĩgs are.
l His pãgs thus moue him to reason wͭ God, not denying but that he had sinned: but he desired to vnderstand what were his great sinnes yͭ had deserued suche rigour, wherein he offended, that he wolde knowe a cause of God why he did punish him.
m Thou punishest me now for the fautes that I cõmitted in my youth.
n Thou makest me thy prisoner, and doest so presse me that I can not stirre hãd nor fote.
*Ebr. rotes.

CHAP. XIIII.

1 *Iob describeth the shortenes and miserie of the life of man. 14 Hope susteineth the godlie. 22 The condition of mans life.*

1 MAn [a] yͭ is borne of woman, is of short
continuance, and ful of trouble.
2 He shooteth forthe as a flowre, and is
cut downe: he vanisheth also as *a shadow,
& continueth not.
3 *And* yet thou openest thine eyes vpõ suche [b] one, and causest me to entre into
iudgement with thee.
4 *Who can bring a cleane thing out of
filthines? there is not one.
5 Are not his dayes determined? the nõber
of his moneths *are* with thee: thou hast
appointed his boundes, which he can not
passe.
6 Turne from him that he may cease vntil
his desired day, [c] as an hyreling.
7 For there is hope of a tre, if it be cut
downe, that it wil yet sproute, and the
branches thereof wil not cease.
8 Thogh yͤ rote of it waxe olde in the earth
& the stocke thereof be dead in yͤ groũde,
9 *Yet* by the sent of water it wil bud, and
bring forthe bowes like a plant.
10 [d] But man is sicke, and dyeth, & man perisheth, and where is he?
11 *As* the waters passe from the sea, and as
the flood decayeth and dryeth vp,
12 So man slepeth and riseth not: *for* he shal
not wake againe, nor be raised from his
slepe til the heauen be nomore.
13 Oh that thou woldest hide me in the graue, and kepe me secret, vntil thy [e] wrath
were past, *and* woldest giue me terme, and
[f] remember me.
14 If a man dye, shal he liue againe? All the
dayes of mine appointed tima wil I waite, til [g] my changing shal come.
15 Thou shalt call *me*, and I shal [h] answer
thee: thou louest the worke of thine owne
hands.
16 But now thou *nombrest my steps, *and*
doest not delay my sinnes.
17 Mine iniquitie is sealed vp, *as* in a [i] bagge, and thou addest vnto my wickednes.
18 And surely *as* the moũtaine that falleth,
cometh to noght, and the [k] rocke that is
remoued from his place:
19 *As* the water breaketh the stones, *when*
thou ouerflowest the things which growe
in the dust of the earth: so thou destroyest
the hope of man.
20 Thou preuailest alway against him, so
that he passeth away: he changeth his face when thou castest him away.
21 And he knoweth not if his sonnes shalbe
honorable, nether shal he vnderstand concerning thẽ, whether they shalbe of lowe
degre,
22 But *while* his [l] flesh *is* vpon him, he shalbe sorowful, and *while* his soule *is* in him,
it shal mourne.

a Taking occasion of his aduersaries wordes, he describeth yͤ state of mãs life from his birth to his death.
Chap. 8, 9.
Psal. 144, 4.
b His meaning is, that seing that man is so fraile a creature, God shulde not handle him so extremely: wherein Iob sheweth yͤ wickednes of the flesh, whẽ it is not subiect to the Spirit.
Psal. 51, 7.
c Vntil yͤ time that thou hast appointed for him to dye, wͨ he desireth, as the hyreling waiteth for yͤ end of his labour to receyue his wages.
d He speaketh not here as thogh he had not hope of yͤ immortalitie, but as a mã in extreme peine, when reason is ouercom by affections & torments.
e Hereby he declareth that the feare of Gods iudgement was the cause why he desired to dye.
f That is, release my peines and take me to mercie.
g Meaning, vnto the day of the resurrectiõ whẽ he shulde be changed, & renued.
h Thogh I be afflicted in this life, yet in the resurrection I shal fele thy mercies, and answer when thou callest me.
Prou. 5, 21.
i Thou layest thẽ all together & suffrest none of my sinnes vnpunished.
k He murmureth through yͤ impaciẽcie of yͤ flesh against God, as thogh he vsed as great seueritie against him as against yͤ hard rockes, or waters yͭ ouerflowe so that hereby all the occasion of his hope is taken away.
l Yet whiles he liueth, he shalbe in peine & miserie.

CHAP. XV.

1 *Eliphàz reprehendeth Iob, because he ascribeth wisdome, and purenes to him self. 16 He describeth the curse that falleth on the wicked, rekoning Iob to be one of the nomber.*

1 THen answered Eliphàz the Temanite, and said,
2 Shal a wise man speake wordes of the
[a] winde, and fil his belly [b] with the East
winde?
3 Shal he dispute with wordes not comely?
or with talke that is not profitable?
4 Surely thou hast cast of [c] feare, and
restrainest prayer before God.
5 For thy mouth declareth thine iniquitie, seing thou hast chosen [d] the tongue
of the crafty.
6 Thine one mouth condemneth thee, and
not I, and thy lippes testifie against
thee.
7 Art thou the [e] first man, that was borne?
and wast thou made before the hils?
8 Hast thou heard the secret counsel of
God, and doest thou restraine wisdome
[f] to thee?
9 What knowest thou that we knowe not?
and vnderstandest that is not in vs?
10 With vs are bothe ancient and very
aged men, farre older then thy father.
11 *Seme* the consolations of God [g] smale
vnto thee? is this thing strange vnto thee?

a That is, vaine wordes, & without consolation?
b Meaning, wͭ matters that are of none importãce which are forgotten assone as they are vttered, as the East winde drieth vp the moisture assone as it falleth.
c He chargeth Iob as thogh his talke caused mẽ to cast of the feare of God & prayer.
d Thou speakest as do the mockers, and contemners of God.
e That is, the moste ancient, and so by reason the moste wise?
f Art thou onely wise?
g He accuseth Iobs pride, and ingratitude, yͭ wil not be cõforted by God, nor by their counsel.

12 Why

12 Why doeth thine heart [h] take thee away,
and what do thine eyes meane,
13 That thou answerest to God [**] at thy
pleasure, and bringest *suche* wordes out of
thy mouth?
14 What is man, that he shulde be cleane?
and he that is borne of woman, that he
shulde [i] be iust?
15 Beholde, he founde no stedfastnes in his
Saintes: yea, the heauens are not cleane in
his sight.
16 How muche more *is* man abominable, &
filthie, which [k] drinketh iniquitie like
water?
17 I wil tel thee: heare me, and I wil declare that which I haue sene:
18 Which wise men haue tolde, *as they haue*
heard of their fathers, and haue not kept it
secret:
19 To whome alone the land was [l] giuen &
no stranger passed through them.
20 The wicked man is continually as one
that trauelleth of childe, and the nomber
[m] of yeres is hid from the tyrant.
21 A soũd of feare *is* in his eares, *&* in his pro
speritie ẏ destroyer shal come vpon him.
22 He beleueth not to returne out of [n] darkenes: for he seeth the sworde before him.
23 He wãdreth [o] to and fro for bread where *he may*: he knoweth that the day of darkenes is prepared at hand.
24 Affliction and [p] anguish shal make him
afraid: they shal preuaile against him as a
King ready to the battel.
25 For he hathe stretched out his hãd agaĩst
God, and made him self strong against
the Almightie.
26 *Therefore God* shal runne vpon him, *euen*
vpõ his necke, & against the moste thicke
part of his shield.
27 Because he hathe couered his face with
[q] his fatnes, & hathe collopes in *his* flãcke.
28 Thogh he dwel [r] in desolate cities, *and*
in houses which no man inhabiteth, but
are become heapes,
29 He shal not be riche, nether shal his substance continue, nether shal he prolong
the [s] perfection thereof in the earth.
30 He shal neuer departe out of darkenes: ẏ
flame shal drye vp his branches, & he shal
go away with the breath of his mouth.
31 He [t] beleueth not that he erreth in vanitie: therefore vanitie shalbe his change.
32 His branche shal not be grene, but shalbe cut of before his day.
33 *God* shal destroy him as the vine her sower
[u] grape, and shal cast him of, as the oliue
doeth her flowre.
34 For the congregacion of the hypocrite
shalbe desolate, & fyre shal deuoure the
houses of [x] bribes.
35 *For thei* [y] conceiue mischief and bring
forthe vanitie, & their bellie hathe prepared deceite.

h Why doest thou stand in thine owne conceite?
** *Ebr. in thy spirit.*
i His purpose is to proue, ẏ Iob as an vniust man & an hypocrite is punished for his sinnes, like as he did before, Chap 4,18.
k Which hathe a desire to sinne as he ẏ is thirstie to drinke.
l Who by their wisdome so gouerned, ẏ no stranger inuaded them, & so the land semed to be giuẽ to them alone.
m The cruel man is euer in danger of death, and is neuer quiet in conscience.
n Out of that miserie where into he once falleth.
o God doeth not onely impouerish the wicked oft times: but euen in their prospe ritie he punisheth thẽ with a gredines euer more to gather: which is as a beggerie.
p He sheweth what weapons God vseth against ẏ wicked which lift vp thẽ selues against him, to wit, terror of conscience, & outward afflictions.
q That is, he was so puft vp with great prosperitie, & abundance of all things, that he forgate God: noting, ẏ Iob in his felicitie had not the true feare of God.
r Thogh he buylde, & repare ruinous places to get him fame, yet God shal bring all to naught, and turne his great prosperitie into extreme miserie.
s Meaning, ẏ his sumpteous buyldings shulde neuer come to perfection.
t He standeth so in his owne conceite, that he wil giue no place to good counsel, therefore his owne pride shal bring him to destruction.
u As one that gathereth grapes before they be ripe.
x Which were buylt or mainteined by powling, and briberie.
y And therefore all their vaine deuises shal turne to their owne destructio.

CHAP. XVI.

1 Iob moued by the importunacie of his friends. 7 Counteth in what extremitie he is. 19 And taketh God witnes of his innocencie.

1 BVt Iob answered, and said,
2 I haue oft times heard suche things:
miserable comforters are ye all.
3 Shal there be none ẽd of wordes of [a] winde? or what maketh thee bolde so to [b] answer?
4 I colde also speake as ye do: (but wolde
God your [c] soule were in my soules stead)
I colde kepe you companie in speaking,
and colde [d] shake mine head at you,
5 But I wolde strengthen you [e] with my
mouth, and the comfort of my lips shulde
aswage *your sorowe*.
6 Thogh I speake, my sorowe [f] can not be
aswaged: thogh I cease, what release haue I?
7 But now [g] he maketh me weary: *o God*, thou
hast made all my [h] congregacion desolate,
8 And hast made me ful of [i] wrĩkles which
is a witnes thereof, and my leannes riseth
vp in me, testifying *the same* in my face.
9 [k] His wrath hathe torne *me*, and he hateth me, *&* gnasheth vpon me with his teeth: mine enemie hathe sharpened his eies
against me.
10 They haue opened their mouthes vpon
me, & smitten me on the [l] cheke in reproche: thei gather thẽ selues together agaĩst
me.
11 God hathe deliuered me to the vniust,
and hathe made me to turne out of the
way by the [m] hands of the wicked.
12 I was in welth, but he hathe broght me
to noght: he hathe taken me by the necke,
and beaten me, and set in me as a marke
for him self.
13 His [n] archers compasse me round about:
he cutteth my reines, & doeth not spare,
and powreth my gall [o] vpon the grounde.
14 He hathe broken me with one breaking
vpon another, and runneth vpon me like a
gyant.
15 I haue sowed a sackecloth vpõ my skin,
and haue abased mine [p] horne vnto the
dust.
16 My face is withered with weping, & the
shadow of death *is* vpon mine eies,
17 Thogh *there be* no wickednes in [q] mine
hands, and my prayer [r] *be* pure.
18 O earth, couer not thou my [s] blood, and
let my crying finde no place.
19 For lo, now my [t] witnes *is* in the heauen,
and my record *is* on hie.

a Which serue for vaine ostentation and for no truecõfort.
b For Elipház did replie against Iobs answer.
c I wolde you felt ẏ which I do.
d That is, mocke at your miserie, as you do at mine.
e If this were in my power, yet wolde I comfort you, and not do as ye do to me.
f If thei wolde say, Why doest thou not then comfort thy selfe? he answereth, ẏ the iudgemẽts of God are more heauy, then he is able to aswage ether by wordes or silence.
g Meaning, God.
h That is, destroyed most of my familie.
i In token of sorowe and grief.
k That is, God by his wrath: and in this diuersitie of wordes & his stile he expresseth how grieuous ẏ hãd of God was vpon him.
l That is, hathe handeled me moste contẽpteously: for so smiting on the cheke signified, 1. King. 22,24. Mar. 14, 65.
m Thei haue led me whither thei wolde.
n His manifold afflictions.
o I am wounded to ẏ heart.
p Meaning, his glorie was broght lowe.
q Signifying, ẏ he is not able to cõprehend the cause of this his grieuous punishment.
r That is, vnfained, and without hypocrisie.
s Let my sinne be knowen, if I be suche a sinner as mine aduersaries accuse me, and let me finde no fauour.
t Thogh man condemne me, yet God is witnes of my cause.

20 My friends [u] speake eloquently a-
gainst me: *but* mine eye powreth out *teares*
vnto God.
21 Oh that a man might [x] pleade with
God, as man with his neighbour!
22 For the yeres accounted come, and I shal
go the way, whence I shal not returne.

CHAP. XVII.

1 Iob sayth that he consumeth away, and yet doeth paciently abide it. 10 He exhorteth his friends to repentance, 13 Shewing that he loketh but for death.

1 MY breath is corrupt: my daies are cut
of, and the graue *is ready* for me.
2 There are none but [a] mockers with me,
and mine eye continueth in [b] their bitternes.
3 [c] Laye downe now *and* put me in suretie
for thee: who is he, that [d] wil touche mine
hand?
4 For thou hast hid their heart from [e] vnderstanding: therefore shalt thou not set
them vpon hie.
5 [f] For the eyes of his children shal faile,
that speaketh flaterie to *his* friends.
6 He hathe also made me a [g] byworde of
the people, and I am as a tabret [h] before
them.
7 Mine eye therefore is dim for grief, and
all my strength *is* like a shadowe.
8 The righteous shal be astonied at [i] this,
and the innocent shalbe moued against
the hypocrite.
9 But the righteous wil holde his [k] waye,
and he whose hands are pure, shal increase *his* strength.
10 All [l] you therefore turne you, and come now, and I shal not finde one wise a-
mong you.
11 My dayes are past, mine enterprises are
broken, *and* the thoghts of mine heart
12 Haue changed the [m] night for the day,
and the light that approched, for darkenes.
13 Thogh I hope, [n] *yet* the graue shalbe mine house, *and* I shal make my bed in the
darke.
14 I shal say to corruption, Thou art my
[o] father, *and* to the worme, Thou art my
mother and my sister.
15 Where is then now mine hope? or who
shal consider the thing, that I hoped for?
16 [p] They shal go downe into the bottome
of the pit: surely, it shal lye together in
the dust.

u Vse painted wordes in stead of true consolation.
x Thus by his great torments he is caryed away, and brasteth out into passions, and speaketh vnaduisedly, as thogh God shulde intreat man more gently, seing he hathe but a short time here to liue.

Chap. XVII.
a In stead of cōforte, being now at deaths dore, he had but them that mocked at hī, and discouraged him.
b I se stil that they seke but to vexe me.
c He reasoneth with God as a mā beside him selfe to the intēt ỹ his cause might be broght to light.
d And answer for thee?
e That these mine afflictiōs are thy iuste iudgements, thogh man know not the cause.
f He that flattereth a man, and onely iudgeth him happy in his prosperitie, shal not him self onely, but in his posteritie be punished.
g God hathe made all the worlde to speake of me, because of mine afflictions.
h That is, as a continual sounde in their eares.
i To wit, whē they se ỹ godlie punished: but in the end they shal come to vnderstanding, and knowe what shal be the reward of the hypocrite.
k That is, wil not be discouraged, considering that the godlie are punished aswel as the wicked.
l Iob speaketh to the thre, ỹ came to cōfort him.
m That is, haue broght me sorow in stead of cōfort.
n Thogh I shulde hope to come from aduersitie to prosperitie, as your discours pretedeth.
o I haue nomore hope in father, mother, sister, or anie worldely thing: for the dust and wormes shalbe to me in stead of them.
p All worldely hope, and prosperitie faile, which you say, are onely signes of Gods fauour: but seing that these things perish, I se mine hope in God, and in the life euerlasting.

CHAP. XVIII.

1 Bildád rehearseth the peines of the vnfaithful and wicked.

1 THen answered Bildád the Shuhite, &
said,
2 When wil [a] ye make an end of *your* wordes? [b] cause vs to vnderstand, & thē we wil
speake.
3 Wherefore are we counted as beastes, &
are vile in your sight?
4 *Thou art* [c] *as one* that teareth his soule in his
anger. Shal the [d] earth be forsaken for thy
sake? or ỹ rocke remoued out of his place?
5 Yea, the light of the wicked shalbe [e] quēched & ỹ sparke of his fyre shal not shine.
6 The light shalbe darke in his dwelling,
and his candel shalbe put out with him.
7 The steppes of his stregth shalbe restrai
ned, and his owne counsel shal cast him
downe.
8 For he is taken in the net by his fete, &
he [f] walketh vpon the snares.
9 The grenne shal take him by the heele, &
the thefe shal come vpon him.
10 A snare is laid for him in the grounde, &
a trappe for him in the way.
11 Fearfulnes shal make him afraid on euery side, and shal driue him to his fete.
12 His strength shalbe [g] famine: & destruction shalbe readie at his side.
13 It shal deuoure the partes of his skinne,
& the [h] first borne of death shal deuoure
his strength.
14 His hope shalbe roted out of his dwelling, & shal cause him to go to the [i] King
of feare.
15 *Feare* shal dwel in his house (because it
is not [k] his) [l] *and* brimstone shalbe scatred vpon his habitacion.
16 His rotes shalbe dryed vp beneth, and
aboue shal his branche be cut downe.
17 His remembrance shal perish from the
earth, and he shal haue no name in the
strete.
18 They shal driue him out of the [m] light
vnto darkenes, and chase him out of the
worlde.
19 He shal nether haue sonne nor nephewe
among his people, nor any posteritie in
his dwellings.
20 The posteritie shalbe astonied at his
[n] day, & feare shal come vpon the anciēt.
21 Surely suche are the habitacions of the
wicked, and this is the place of him that
knoweth not God.

a Which counte your selues iuste? as Chap. 12, 4.
b Whome you take to be but beastes, as Chap 12, 7.
c That is, like a mad man.
d Shal God chāge the ordre of nature for thy sake, by dealing wͭ thee otherwise then he doeth with all men?
e When ỹ wicked is in his pͬsperitie, thē God changeth his state: & this is his ordinarie workīg for their sinnes.
f Meaning that the wicked are in continual danger.
g That which shulde nourish him, shalbe consumed by famine.
h That is, some strong and violēt death that consume his strength: or as ỹ Ebrew worde signifieth, his membres or parts.
i That is, with most great feare.
k Meaning, not truely come by.
l Thogh all ỹ worlde wolde fauour hī, yet God wolde destroie him & his.
m He shal fall from prosperitie to aduersitie.
n When thei shal se what came vnto hī.

CHAP. XIX.

1 Iob reproueth his friends, 15 And reciteth his miseries & grieuous peines. 25 He assureth him selfe of the generall resurrection.

1 BVt Iob answered, and said,
2 How long wil ye vexe my soule, and
torment me with wordes?
3 Ye haue now [a] ten times reproched me,
& are not ashamed: ye are impudēt toward me.
4 And thogh I had in dede erred, mine errour [b] remaineth with me.
5 But in dede if ye wil aduāce your selues
against

a That is, many times, as Nehem. 4, 12.
b That is, I my self shalbe punished for it, or you haue not yet confuted it.

c He braſteth out againe into his paſsiōs and declareth ſtil that his afflictiō cometh of God, thogh he be not able to fele ÿ cauſe in him ſelf.
d Meaning, out of his afflictiōs
e Meaning, his children and whatſoeuer was dere vnto him in this worlde
f Which is pluckt vp, and hathe no more hope to grow.
g His manifolde afflictions.
h Mine houſhold ſeruāts: by all theſe loſſes Iob ſheweth that touching the fleſh he had great occaſion to be moued.
i Which were hers & mine.
k Beſides theſe great loſſes & moſte cruel vnkindenes, he was touched in his owne perſon as followeth.
l All my fleſh was cōſumed.
m Seing I haue theſe iuſt cauſes to complaine, condemne me not as an hypocrite, ſpecially ye ŵ ſhulde comfort me.
n Is it not ynough ÿ God doeth puniſh me except you by reproches increaſe my ſorowe?
o To ſe my body puniſhed, except ye trouble my minde?
p He proteſteth that notwithſtanding his ſore paſsions, his religion is perfite, & that he is not a blaſphemer, as thei iudged hī.
q I do not ſo iuſtifie my ſelfe before the worlde, but I knowe that I ſhal come before the great iudge, who ſhalbe my deliuerer & Sauiour.
r Herein Iob declareth plainely that he had a ful hope, that bothe the ſoule and body ſhulde enioye the preſence of God in the laſt reſurrection.

against me, & rebuke me for my reproche,
6 Knowe now, ÿ God hathe [c] ouerthrowen
me, & hathe compaſſed me with his net.
7 Beholde, I crye out of violēce, but I haue
none anſwer: I crye but there *is* no iudgement.
8 He hathe hedged vp my waye that I can
not [d] paſſe, and he hathe ſet darkenes in
my paths.
9 He hathe ſpoiled me of mine honour, &
taken the [e] crowne away from mine head.
10 He hathe deſtroied me on euerie ſide & I
am gone: & he hathe remoued mine hope
like [f] a tre.
11 And he hathe kīdled his wrath agaīſt me,
and counteth me as one of his enemies.
12 His [g] armies came together, and made
their way vpon me, & camped about my
tabernacle.
13 He hathe remoued my brethren farre frō
me, and alſo mine acquaintance were ſtrāgers vnto me.
14 My neighbours haue forſaken me, and
my familiars haue forgotten me.
15 [h] They that dwel in mine houſe, and my
maides toke me for a ſtranger: for I was a
ſtranger in their ſight.
16 I called my ſeruāt, but he wolde not anſwer, *thogh* I praied him with my mouth.
17 My breath was ſtrange vnto my wife,
thogh I praied her for the childrens ſake
of mine [i] owne body.
18 The wicked alſo deſpiſed me, *&* when I
roſe, they ſpake againſt me.
19 All my ſecret friēds abhorred me, & thei
whome I loued, are turned againſt me.
20 My bone [k] cleaueth to my ſkin & to my
fleſh, and I haue eſcaped with the [l] ſkinne
of my tethe.
21 Haue pitie vpon me: haue [m] pitie vpon
me, (ô ye my friends) for the hād of God
hathe touched me.
22 Why do ye perſecute me, as [n] God? and
are not ſatiſfied with my [o] fleſh?
23 Oh that my wordes were now writen! oh
that thei were writen euen in a boke!
24 *And* grauen with [p] an yron pēne in lead,
or in ſtone for euer.
25 For I am ſure, that my [q] Redemer liueth,
and he ſhal ſtand the laſt on the earth.
26 And thogh after my ſkin *wormes* deſtroy
this *bodie*, yet ſhal I ſe God [r] in my fleſh.
27 Whome I my ſelf ſhal ſe, and mine eies
ſhal beholde, and non other *for me, thogh* my
reines are conſumed within me.
28 But ye ſaid, Why is he perſecuted? And
there was [ſ] a depe matter in me.
29 Be ye afraid of the ſworde: for ÿ ſworde
wil be [t] auenged of wickednes, that ye may
know that there is a iudgement.

CHAP. XX.

1 Zophár ſheweth, that the wicked and the couetous ſhal haue a ſhorte end, 22 Thogh for a time they floriſh.

1 Thē anſwered Zophár the Naamathite
and ſaid,
2 Douteles my thoghts cauſe me to anſwer, and therefore I make haſte.
3 I haue heard [a] the correction of my reproche: therefore ÿ ſpirit of mine vnderſtanding cauſeth me to anſwer.
4 Knoweſt thou not this of olde? *&* ſince
God placed man vpon the earth?
5 That the reioycing of the wicked *is* ſhorte, & that the ioye of hypocrites is but a
moment?
6 Thogh [b] his excellencie mounte vp to
the heauen, and his head reache vntō the
cloudes,
7 *Yet* ſhal he periſh for euer, like his dung,
and they which haue ſene him, ſhal ſay,
Where is he?
8 He ſhal flee away as a dreame, & thei ſhal
not finde him, and ſhal paſſe away as a viſion of the night.
9 So that the eye which had ſene him, ſhal
do ſo no more, and his place ſhal ſe him
no more.
10 His children ſhal [c] flatter the poore, and
his hands ſhal [d] reſtore his ſubſtance.
11 His bones are ful *of the ſinne* of his youth,
& [e] it ſhal lye downe with him in the duſt.
12 Whē wickednes [f] was ſwete in his mouthe, *&* he hid it vnder his tongue,
13 *And* fauoured it, and wolde not forſake
it, but kept it cloſe in his mouth,
14 *Then* his meat in his bowels was turned:
the gall of aſpes *was* in the middes of hī.
15 He hathe deuoured ſubſtāce, and he ſhal
vomit it: *for* God ſhal drawe it out of his
belly.
16 He ſhal ſucke the [g] gall of aſpes, *and* the
vipers tongue ſhal ſlaye him.
17 He ſhal not ſe the [h] riuers, *nor* the floods
& ſtreames of hony and butter.
18 He ſhal reſtore ÿ labour, & ſhal deuoure nomore: *euen* according to the ſubſtance *ſhalbe* his exchange, [i] and he ſhal enioye
it nomore.
19 For he hathe vndone *manie*: he hathe forſaken the poore, *&* hathe ſpoiled houſes
which he buylded not.
20 Surely he ſhal fele no quietnes in his
body, *nether* ſhal he reſerue of that which
he deſired.
21 There ſhal none of his [k] meat be left:
therefore none ſhal hope for his goods.
22 Whē he ſhalbe filled with his abundāce,
he ſhalbe in paine, *&* the hand [l] of all the
wicked ſhal aſſaile him.
23 He ſhalbe about to fil his belly, *but God*
ſhal ſend vpō hī his fearce wrath, [m] & ſhal
cauſe to raine vpō him, *euen* vpō his meat.
24 He ſhal flee from the yron weapons, *and*
the bowe of ſtele ſhal ſtrike him through.

a He declareth that two thīgs moued him to ſpeake: to wit, becauſe Iob ſemed to touche him, & becauſe he thoght he had knowledge ſufficient to confute him.
b His purpoſe is to proue Iob to be a wicked man, & an hypocrite, becauſe God puniſhed him, and changed his proſperitie into aduerſitie,
c Where as ÿ father through ambition & tyrannie oppreſſed the poore, the children through pouertie & miſerie ſhal ſeke fauour at ÿ pore.
d So that the thing, which he hathe taken away by violēce, ſhalbe reſtored againe by force.
e Meanig, that he ſhal cary nothing away with him, but his ſinne
f As poyſon ŷ is ſwete in the mouthe bringeth deſtruction, when it cometh into ÿ body: ſo all vice at ÿ firſt is pleaſant, but afterward God turneth it to deſtruction.
g He compareth euil gotten goods to ÿ venim of aſpes, which ſerpent is moſte dangerous: noting that Iobs great riches were not truely come by, & therefore God did plague him iuſtely for the ſame.
h Thogh God giue to all other abundance of his bleſſings, yet he ſhal haue no parte thereof.
i That is, theſe rauenors & ſpoilers of ÿ poore ſhal enioye their theft but for a time: for after God wil take it from them and cauſe thē to make reſtitutiō, ſo ÿ it is but an exchāge
k He ſhal leaue nothing to his poſteritie.
l The wicked ſhal neuer be in reſt: for one wicked man ſhal ſeke to deſtroy another.

ſ Thogh his friends thoght ÿ he was but perſecuted of God for his ſinnes, yet he declareth that there was a deper conſideration: to wit, the tryal of his faith & pacience, and ſo to be an example for others
t God wilbe reuenged of this haſtie iudgement, whereby you condemne me.

m Some read, vpon his fleſh, alluding to Iob, whoſe fleſh was ſmiten with a ſcabbe.

25 *The arowe* is drawen out, and cometh
forthe of the [n] body, and shineth of his
gall, *so* feare cometh vpon him.
26 [o] All darkenes shalbe hid in his secret
places: the fyre that is not [p] blowen, shal
deuoure him, *and* that which remaineth
in his tabernacle, shalbe destroied.
27 The heauen shal declare his wickednes,
and the earth shal rise vp against him.
28 The [q] increase of his house shal go away:
it shal flowe away in the day of his wrath.
29 This is the porcion of the wicked man
from [r] God, & the heritage *that he shal haue*
of God for his [s] wordes.

n Some read, of ẏ quiuer.
o All feare & sorow shal light vpō him, when he thinketh to escape.
p That is, fyre frō heauen, or ẏ fyre of Gods wrath.
q Meaning, ẏ children of ẏ wicked shal flowe away like riuers and be dispersed in diuers places.
r Thus God wil plague the wicked.
s Agaīst God, thinking to excuse him selfe and to escape Gods hand.

CHAP. XXI.

7 Iob declareth how the prosperitie of the wicked maketh them proude, 15 In so muche that they blaspheme God. 16 Their destruction is at hand. 23 None oght to be iudged wicked for affliction, nether good for prosperitie.

1 BVt Iob answered, and said,
2 Heare diligently my wordes, and this
[a] shalbe in stead of your consolations.
3 Suffre me, that I may speake, and when I
haue spoken, mocke on.
4 Do I *direct* my talke to man? If it [b] were
so, how shulde not my spirit be troubled?
5 Marke me, and be abashed, and lay your
hand vpon *your* [c] mouth.
6 Euen when I remember, I am afraied, &
feare taketh holde on my flesh.
7 Wherefore do the wicked [d] liue, *and*
waxe olde, and growe in welth?
8 Their sede is established in their sight
with them, and their generacion before
their eies.
9 Their houses are peaceable without feare,
and the rod of God is not vpon them.
10 Their bullocke gendreth, & faileth not:
their cowe calueth, and casteth not her
calfe.
11 They send forthe their children [e] like
shepe, and their sonnes dance.
12 They take the tabret and harpe, and reioyce
in the sounde of the organs.
13 They spend their daies in welth, and sodenly
[f] they go downe to the graue.
14 Thei say also vnto God, Depart frō vs:
for we desire not the [g] knowledge of thy
waies.
15 Who is the Almightie, that we shulde
serue him? and what profite shulde we haue,
if we shulde pray vnto him?
16 Lo, their welth is not in their hand: [h] *therefore*
let the counsel of the wicked [i] be farre
from me.
17 How oft shal the candel of the wicked
be put out? and their destructiō come vpon
them? he wil deuide *their* liues in his
wrath.
18 They shal be as stubble before the winde,
and as chaffe that the storme caryeth
away.

a Your diligēt marking of my wordes shalbe to me a great consolation.
b As thogh he wolde say, I do not talke with man, but with God, who wil not answer me, & therefore my minde mustnedes be troubled.
c He chargeth them as thogh they were not able to cōprehēd this his feling of Gods iudgement, & exhorteth thē therefore to silence.
d Iob proueth against his aduersaries that God punisheth not straight waies the wicked, but oft times giueth thē long life, and prosperitie: so that we must not iudge God iuste or vniust by the things that appeare to our eye.
e Thei haue store of children, lustie & helthful, & in these pointes he answereth to that which Zophár alledged before.
f Not beīg tormented with long sickenes.
g Thei desire nothing more thē to be exēpt from all subiection that thei shulde beare to God: this Iob sheweth his aduersaries, ẏ if they reason onely by ẏ which is sene by commune experience, ẏ wicked that hate God, are better delt ẇ all, then they that loue him.
h It is not their owne, but God onely lendeth it vnto them.
i God kepe me from their prosperitie.

19 God wil lay vp the sorow *of the father*
for his children: when he rewardeth him,
he shal knowe it.
20 [k] His eies shal se his destruction, and he
shal drinke of the wrath of ẏ Almightie.
21 For what pleasure hathe he in his house
after him, when the nomber of his moneths
is cut of?
22 Shal any teache [l] God knowledge, who
iudgeth the hiest things?
23 One [m] dyeth in his ful strength, being in
all ease and prosperitie.
24 His breasts are full of milke, and his bones
runne ful of marowe.
25 And another [n] dyeth in the bitternes of
his soule, and neuer eateth with pleasure.
26 They shal slepe bothe in [o] the dust, and
the wormes shal couer them.
27 Beholde, I know your thoghts, and the
enterprises, *where with* ye do me wrong.
28 For ye say, Where is the princes [p] house?
and where is the tabernacle of the wickeds
dwelling?
29 May ye not [q] aske thē that go by ẏ way?
and ye can not denie their signes.
30 But the wicked is kept vnto the day of
[r] destructiō, *&* they shal be broght forthe
to the day of wrath.
31 Who shal declare his waie [s] to his face?
and who shal rewarde him for that he
hathe done?
32 Yet shal he be broght to the graue, and
remaine in the heape.
33 The [t] slimie valley shalbe swete vnto hī,
and euerie man shal drawe after him, as
before him there were innumerable.
34 How thē comfort [u] ye me in vaine, seīg
in your answers there remaine but lyes?

k When God recompenseth his wickednes he shal knowe ẏ his prosperitie was but vanitie
l Who sendeth to the wicked prosperitie, & punisheth the godlie.
m Meanīg, the wicked.
n To wit, the godlie.
o As concerning their bodies: and this he speaketh according to ẏ commune iudgement.
p Thus thei called Jobs house in derision, concluding ẏ it was destroied because he was wicked.
q Which through long trauailing haue experience & tokens hereof, to wit, that the wicked do prosper & the godlie liue in affliction.
r Thogh the wicked florish here, yet God wil punish hī in the last day.
s Thogh men do flatter him, and none dare reproue him in this worlde, yet death is a tokē that God wil bring him to an account.
t He shal be glad to lie in a slimie pit, ẇ before colde not be content with a royal palace.
u Saying, that the iust in this worlde haue prosperitie & ẏ wicked aduersitie.

CHAP. XXII.

5 Elipház affirmeth that Iob is punished for his sinnes. 6 He accuseth him of vnmercifulnes, 13 And that he denied Gods prouidence. 21 He exhorteth him to repentance.

1 THen Elipház the Temanite answered,
and said,
2 May a man be [a] profitable vnto God, as
he that is wise, may be profitable to him
self?
3 * Is it any thing vnto the Almightie,
that thou art righteous? or is it profitable
to him, that thou makest thy wayes vpright?
4 Is it for feare [b] of thee that he wil accuse
thee? or go with thee in to iudgement?
5 Is not thy wickednes great, & thine iniquities
innumerable?
6 For thou hast taken the [c] pledge from thy
brother for noght, and spoiled the clothes
of the naked.
7 To suche as were weary, thou hast not giuen
water to drinke, and hast withdrawen
bread from the hungrie.

a Thogh ẏ men were iuste, yet God colde haue no profite of this his iustice: and therefore when he punisheth him, he hathe no regard to his iustice, but to his sinne.
Chap. 35, 7.
b Lest ẏ shuldest reproue or hurt him?
c Thou hast bene cruel, and without charitie, & woldest do nothing for the poore, but for thine owne aduantage.

8 But

8 But the mightie man [d] had the earth, and
he that was in autoritie, dwelt in it.
9 Thou hast cast out widowes emptie, and
the armes of [e] the fatherles were broken.
10 Therefore snares *are* rounde about thee,
and feare shal sodenly trouble thee:
11 Or darkenes that thou shuldest not se,
and [f] abũdance of waters shal couer thee.
12 Is not God on [g] hie in the heauen? & beholde the height of the [h] starres how hie
they are.
13 But thou saiest, How shulde God [i] know?
can he iudge through the darke cloude?
14 The cloudes hide him that he can not
se, and he walketh in the circle of heauen.
15 Hast thou marked the way of ye worlde,
[k] wherein wicked men haue walked?
16 Which were [l] cut downe before the time, whose fundacion *was as* a riuer that
ouerflowed:
17 Which said vnto God, Departe from
vs, and *asked* what the Almightie colde do
for them.
18 Yet he [m] filled their houses with good
things: but let the counsel of the wicked
be farre from me.
19 The righteous shal se *them*, and shal reioyce, [n] and the innocent shal laugh them
to scorne.
20 Surely [o] our substance is hid: but the fyre hathe deuoured the remnant of [p] them.
21 Therefore acquaint thy self, I pray thee,
[q] with him, and make peace: thereby thou
shalt haue prosperitie.
22 Receiue, I pray thee, the law of his
mouth, and laie vp his wordes in thine
heart.
23 If thou returne to the Almightie, thou
shalt [r] be buylt vp, *&* thou shalt put iniquitie farre from thy tabernacle.
24 Thou shalt lay vp golde for [s] dust, and
the golde of Ophir, as the flints of the
riuers.
25 Yea, the Almightie shalbe thy defence,
and thou shalt haue plentie of siluer.
26 And thou shalt thẽ delite in the Almightie, and lift vp thy face vnto God.
27 Thou shalt make thy prayer vnto him,
and he shal heare thee, and thou shalt rendre thy vowes.
28 Thou shalt also decree a thing, & he shal
establish it vnto thee, and the [t] light shal
shine vpon thy waies.
29 [u] When *others* are cast downe, then shalt
thou say, I am lifted vp: and *God* shal saue
the humble persone.
30 The innocent shal deliuer the [x] yland,
and it shalbe preserued by the purenes of
thine hands.

d When thou wast in power and autoritie, thou didst not iustice, but wrong

e Thou hast not onely not shewed pitie, but oppressed them

f That is, manifolde afflictions.

g He accuseth Iob of impietie & cõtempt of God, as thogh he wolde say, If thou passe not for men, yet consider the height of Gods maiestie

h That so muche the more by that excellent worke yu maist feare God and reuerence him

i He reproueth Iob as thogh he denied Gods prouidẽce, and that he colde not se ye thĩgs that were done in this worlde.

k How God hath punished them from the beginning?

l He proueth Gods prouidence by the punishement of the wicked, whome he taketh away before they can brĩg their wicked purposes to passe.

m He answereth to that, which Iob had said Chap. 21, 7 that the wicked haue prosperitie in this worlde: desiring that he might not be partaker of ye like.

n The iust reioyce at the destruction of the wicked for two causes: first, because God sheweth him self iudge of the worlde, & by this meanes continueth his honour and glorie: secõdly, because God sheweth that he hathe care ouer his in that he punisheth their enemies.

o That is, the state and preseruation of ye godlie is hid vnder Gods wings.

p Meaning, of the wicked. q He exhorteth Iob to repentance and to returne to God. r God wil restore vnto thee all thy substance.
s Which shalbe in abundance like dust. t That is, the fauour of God.
u God wil deliuer his when the wicked are destroyed rounde about them, as in the flood and in Sodom. x God wil deliuer a whole countrey from peril, euen for the iuste mans sake.

CHAP. XXIII.

2 Iob affirmeth that he bothe knoweth and feareth the power and sentence of the Iudge. 10 And that he is not punished onely for his sinnes.

1 BVt Iob answered and said,
2 Thogh my talke be this day in
[a] bitternes, *and* my plague greater thẽ my
groning,
3 Wolde God *yet* I knewe how to finde
him, I wolde entre vnto his place.
4 I wolde pleade the cause before him, and
fil my mouth with arguments.
5 I wolde knowe the wordes, *that* he wolde
answer me, and wolde vnderstand what he
wolde say vnto me.
6 Wolde he [b] plead against me with *his*
great power? No, but he wolde [c] put
strength in me.
7 [d] There the righteous might reason with
him, so I shulde be deliuered for euer frõ
my Iudge.
8 [e] Beholde, *if* I go to the East, he is not
there: if to the West, yet I can not perceiue him:
9 *If* to the North where he worketh, yet I
can not se him: he wil hide him self in the
South, and I can not beholde him.
10 But he knoweth my [f] way, *and* tryeth me,
and I shal come forthe like the golde.
11 My fote hathe followed his steppes: his
way haue I kept, and haue not declined.
12 Nether haue I departed from the commandement of his lippes, *&* I haue [g] estemed the wordes of his mouth more then
mine appointed fode.
13 Yet he is in one *minde*, and who can [h] turne him? yea, he doeth what his minde desireth.
14 For he wil performe that, which is decreed of me, and [i] many suche things *are*
with him.
15 Therefore I am troubled at his presence,
& in considering it, I am afrayed of him.
16 For God [k] hathe softened mine heart, &
the Almightie hathe troubled me.
17 For I am not cut of in [l] darkenes, but
he hathe hid the darkenes from my face.

a He sheweth the iuste cause of his cõplaining, & as touching that Elpház had exhorted him to returne to God, chap. 22, 21, he declareth that he desireth nothing more: but it semed that God wolde not be foũde of him.

b Vsing his absolute power & saying, Because I am God, I may do what I wil.

c Of his mercie he wolde giue me power to answer hĩ.

d When he of his mercie hathe giuen strength to maĩteine their cause.

e Meaning, yt if he consider Gods iustice, he is not able to cõprehende his iudgemẽts on what side or parte soeuer he turneth him self.

f God hathe this preeminẽce aboue me that he knoweth my waye: to wit, that I am innocent, and I am not able to iudge of his workes: he sheweth also his confidẽce, that God doeth visite him for his profite.

g His worde is more precious vnto me, then the meat wherewith the bodie is susteined.

h Iob confesseth that at this present he felt not Gods fauour, and yet was assured, that he had appointed him to a good end. i In many pointes man is not able to atteine to Gods iudgements. k That I shulde not be without feare. l He sheweth the cause of his feare, which is, that he being in trouble, seeth none end, nether yet knoweth the cause.

CHAP. XXIIII.

2 Iob describeth the wickednes of men, and sheweth what curse belongeth to the wicked, 12 How all things are gouerned by Gods prouidence, 17 And the destruction of the wicked.

1 HOw shulde not the times [a] be hid frõ
the Almightie, seing that thei which
knowe him, se not his [b] daies?
2 *Some* remoue the land markes, that robbe
the flockes and fede *thereof.*
3 They lead away the asse of the fatherles:
and take the widowes oxe to pledge.

a Thus Iob speaketh in his passions and after the iudgement of the flesh: that is, ye he seeth not the things that are done at times, nether yet hathe a peculiar care ouer all, because he punisheth not the wicked, nor reuengeth the godlie.

b When he punisheth the wicked and rewardeth the good.

4 They make the poore to turne out of the
way, ſo that the poore of the earth hide
them ſelues [c] together.
5 Beholde, *others as* wilde aſſes in the wildernes, go forthe to their buſines, and [d] riſe earely for a pray: the wildernes [e] *giueth* him
& his children fode.
6 They reape [f] his prouiſiõ in the field, but
thei gather the late [g] vĩtage of the wicked.
7 Thei cauſe the naked to lodge without
garmẽt, & without couering in the colde.
8 They are wet with the ſhowres of the
mountaines, [h] and thei imbrace the rocke
for want of a couering.
9 They plucke the fatherles [i] frõ the breaſt,
and take the pledge [k] of the poore.
10 They cauſe him to go naked without
clothing, and take the gleining from the
hungrie.
11 Thei ẏ make oyle [l] betwene their walles,
and treade their winepreſſes, ſuffer thirſt.
12 Mẽ [m] crye out of the citie, & the ſoules of
the ſlayne [n] crye out: yet God doeth [o] not
charge them with follie.
13 Theſe are thei, that abhorre the [p] light:
thei knowe not the waies thereof, nor continue in the paths thereof.
14 The murtherer riſeth earely *&* killeth
the poore and the nedie: and in the night
he is as a thefe.
15 The eye alſo of the [q] adulterer waiteth
for the twylight, and ſaith, None eye ſhal
ſe me, and diſguiſeth his face.
16 Thei digge through houſes in the darke,
which they marked for them ſelues in the
day: they knowe not the light.
17 But the morning *is* euen to them as the
ſhadow of death: if one knowe thẽ, *they are*
in the terrours of the ſhadowe of death.
18 He is ſwift vpon the [r] waters: their [ſ] porcion ſhalbe curſed in the earth: he wil not
beholde the way of the vineyardes.
19 *As* the drye grounde & heat cõſume the
ſnowe waters, *ſo ſhal* the graue [t] the ſinners.
20 [u] The pitiful man ſhal forget him: the
worme *ſhal fele* his ſwetenes: he ſhalbe no
more remẽbred, & the wicked ſhalbe broken like a tre.
21 He [x] doeth euil intreat the baren, that
doeth not beare, nether doeth he good to
the widowe.
22 He draweth alſo ẏ [y] mightie by his powre, *&* whẽ he riſeth vp, none is ſure of life.
23 Thogh men giue him aſſurance to be in
ſauetie, yet his eyes *are* vpon their wayes.
24 Thei are exalted for a litle, but thei are
gone, and are broght lowe as all *others*: thei
are deſtroyed, and cut of as the top of an
eare of corne.

c And for crueltie & oppreſſion dare not ſhewe their faces.
d That is, ſpare no diligẽce.
e He and his, liue by robbing and murdering.
f Meaning the poore mans.
g Signifying, that one wicked man wil not ſpoile an other, but for neceſsitie.
h The poore are driuen by the wicked into rockes and holes, where thei cã not lie drye for the rayne.
i That is, they ſo powle and pille ẏ poore widowe, ẏ ſhe can not haue to ſuſteine her ſelf, that ſhe may be able to giue her childe ſucke.
k That is, his garment, wherewith he ſhulde be couered or clad.
l In ſuche places, ẇ are appointed for ẏ purpoſe: meaning, ẏ thoſe that labour for ẏ wicked, are pined for hungre.
m For ẏ great oppreſsion & extortion.
n Crye out & call for vengeance.
o God doeth not condemne ẏ wicked, but ſemeth to paſſe ouer it by his lõg ſilẽce.
p That is, Gods worde, becauſe they are reproued thereby.
q By theſe particular vices, & the licẽce thereũto, he wolde proue ẏ God puniſheth not ẏ wicked & rewardeth the iuſte.
r He fleeth to the waters for his ſuccour.
ſ They thinke that all the worlde is bent againſt them, & dare not go by the hie way.
t As the drye grounde is neuer ful with waters, ſo wil thei neuer ceaſe ſinning, til thei come to the graue.
u Thogh God ſuffer the wicked for a time, yet their end ſhal be moſte vile deſtruction, & in this point Iob cometh to him ſelf and ſheweth his confidence.
x He ſheweth why the wicked ſhal not be lamented, becauſe he did not pitie others.
y He declareth that after that the wicked haue deſtroyed the weakeſt, thei wil do like to the ſtronger, and therefore are iuſtely preuented by Gods iudgements.

25 But if it be not [z] ſo, where is he? *or* who
wil proue me a lyer, & make my wordes of
no value?

z That is, that contrary to your reaſoning no man can giue a perfite reaſon of Gods iudgements, let me be reproued.

CHAP. XXV.

Bildád proueth that no man is cleane nor without ſinne before God.

1 THen anſwered Bildád the Shuhite, &
ſaid,
2 [a] Power & feare *is* with him, that maketh
peace in his hie places.
3 Is there any nomber in his armies? & vpõ
whome [b] ſhal not his light ariſe?
4 And how may a man [c] be iuſtified with
God? or how can he be cleane, that is borne of woman?
5 Beholde, he wil giue no light to the moone, [d] and the ſtarres are vncleane in his
ſight.
6 How muche more man, a worme, euẽ the
ſonne of man, *which is but* a worme?

Chap. XXV.
a His purpoſe is to proue, ẏ albeit God trye and afflict the iuſte, yet ſone after he ſendeth proſperitie, & becauſe he did not ſo to Iob, he concludeth that he is wicked.
b Who cã hide him frõ his preſence?
c That is, be iuſte in reſpect of God?
d If God ſhew his power, the moone & ſtarres cã not haue that light, ẇ is giuen thẽ, muche leſſe cã man haue any excellẽcie, but of God.

CHAP. XXVI.

Iob ſheweth that man can not helpe God, & proueth it by his miracles.

1 BVt Iob anſwered, and ſaid,
2 [a] Whome helpeſt thou? him that
hathe no power? ſaueſt thou the arme that
hathe no ſtrength?
3 Whome counſeleſt thou? him that hathe
no wiſdome? thou [b] ſheweſt right wel as
the thing is.
4 To whome doeſt ẏ declare *theſe* wordes?
or whoſe ſpirit [c] cometh out of thee?
5 The [d] dead things are formed vnder the
waters, and nere vnto them.
6 The graue is [e] naked before him, & there
is no couering for [f] deſtruction.
7 He ſtretcheth out the [g] North ouer the
emptie place, and hangeth the earth vpon
nothing.
8 He bindeth the waters in his cloudes, and
the cloude is not broken vnder them.
9 He holdeth backe the face of his throne:
[h] and ſpreadeth his cloude vpon it.
10 He hathe ſet bondes about the waters,
vntil the [i] day and night come to an end.
11 The [k] pillers of heauen tremble and
quake at his reproſe.
12 The ſea is calme by his power, & by his
vnderſtanding he ſmiteth ẏ pride *thereof.*
13 His Spirit hathe garniſhed the heauẽs, *&*
his hand hathe formed ẏ crooked [l] ſerpẽt.
14 Lo, theſe are parte of his wayes: but
[m] how litle a portion heare we of him? and
who can vnderſtand his feareful power?

Chap. XXVI.
a Thou cõcludeſt nothing: for nether ẏ helpeſt me, ẇ am deſtitute of all helpe, nether yet ſpeakeſt ſufficiẽtly on Gods behalfe, who hathe no nede of thy defence.
b But ẏ doeſt not applie it to ẏ purpoſe.
c That is, moueth thee to ſpeake this?
d Iob beginneth to declare the force of Gods power & prouidence in the mines and metals in the depe places of the earth.
e There is nothing hid in ẏ bottom of the earth, but he ſeeth it.
f Meaning, the graue wherein thĩgs putrifie.
g He cauſeth ẏ whole heauen to turne about ẏ North pole.
h That is, he hideth ẏ heauens, which are called his throne.
i So lõg as this worlde endureth.
k Not that heauẽ hathe pillers to vpholde it, but he ſpeaketh by a ſimilitude, as thogh he wolde ſay, The heauen it ſelf is not able to abide his reproche.
l Which is a figure of ſtarres facioned like a ſerpent, becauſe of the crookednes.
m If theſe fewe things, which we ſe daily with our eyes, declare his great power and prouidence, how muche more wolde they appeare, if we were able to comprehend all his workes?

CHAP XXVII.

3 The conſtancie and perfitnes of Iob. 13 The rewarde of the wicked and of the tyrants.

1 MOreouer Iob proceeded and continued his parable, ſaying,

2 The

2 The liuing God hathe taken away my
a iudgement: for the Almightie hathe put
my soule in bitternes.
3 Yet so lōg as my breath is in me, and the
Spirit of God in my nostrels,
4 My lips surely shal speake no wickednes,
b and my tongue shal vtter no deceit.
5 God forbid, that I shulde c iustifie you:
vntil I dye, I wil neuer take away mine
d innocencie from my self.
6 I wil kepe my righteousnes, and wil not
forsake it: mine heart shal not reproue me
of my e dayes.
7 Mine enemie shalbe as the wicked, & he
that riseth against me, as the vnrighteous.
8 For what f hope hathe the hypocrite whē
he hathe heaped vp riches, if God take a-
way his soule?
9 Wil God heare his crye, when trouble
cometh vpon him?
10 Wil he set his delite on the Almightie?
wil he call vpon God at all times?
11 I wil teach you *what is* in ẏ hād of g God,
& I wil not conceil that which is with the
Almightie.
12 Beholde, all ye your selues h haue sene it:
why then do you thus vanish i in vanitie?
13 This is the k porcion of a wicked man
with God, & the heritage of tyrāts, *which*
they shal receiue of the Almightie.
14 If his children be in great nomber, the
sworde *shal destroy* them, and his posteritie
shal not be satisfied with bread.
15 His remnant shal be buryed in death, &
his widowes l shal not wepe.
16 Thogh he shulde heape vp siluer as the
dust, and prepare raiment as the clay,
17 He may prepare it, but the iuste shal put
it on, and the innocēt shal deuide ẏ siluer.
18 He buyldeth his house as the m mothe,
and as a lodge that the watchman maketh.
19 When the riche man slepeth, n he shal
not be gathered *to his fathers*: they opened
their eyes, and he was gone.
20 Terrours shal take him as waters, *and* a
tempest shal carie him away by night.
21 The East wind shal take him away, & he
shal departe: and it shal hurlle him out of
his place.
22 And *God* shal cast vpon him & not spare,
thogh he wolde faine flee out of his hand.
23 *Euerie man* shal clap their hands at him,
and hisse at him out of their place.

a He hathe so sore afflicted me, that mē cā not iudge of mine vprightnes: for thei iudge onely by outward signes.
b Howsoeuer men iudge of me, yet wil I not speake cōtrarie to that, which I haue said, and so do wickedly in betraying the trueth.
c Which condemne me as a wicked mā, because ẏ hād of God is vpō me
d I wil not cōfesse that God doeth thus punish me for my sinnes.
e Of my life past.
f What aduātage hathe the dissembler to gaine neuer so much, seing he shal lose his owne soule?
g That is, what God reserueth to him self, & whereof he giueth not the knowledge to all.
h That is, these secret iudgements of God, and yet do not vnderstand them
i Why mainteine you thē this erroar?
k Thus wil God ordre the wicked, & punish him, euen vnto his posteritie.
l None shal lament him.
m Which bredeth in another mans possession or garmēt, but is sone shaken out.
n He meaneth that the wicked tyrants shal not haue a quiet death, nor be buried honorably.

CHAP. XXVIII.

Iob sheweth that the wisdome of God is vnsercheable.

1 THe siluer surely hathe his vaine, a &
the golde his place, *where* thei take it.
2 Yron is taken out of the dust, and brasse
is molten out of the stone.
3 *God* putteth an end to darknes, b & he tryeth the perfectiō of all things: he setteth a
bōde of darkenes, & of ẏ shadow of death.
4 The flood breaketh out against the c in-

a His purpose is to declare that man may atteine in this worlde to diuers secrets of nature, but mā is neuer able to comprehēd the wisdome of God.
b There is nothing but it is cōpassed within certeine limites, & hathe an end, but Gods wisdom.
c Meanig him that dwelleth thereby.

habitant, *and the waters* d forgotten of the
fote, being higher thē mā, are gone away.
5 Out of the same earth cometh e bread, &
vnder it, as it were fyre is turned vp.
6 The stones thereof *are* a place f of saphirs, and the dust of it *is* golde.
7 There is a path which no foule hathe
knowen, nether hathe the kites eye sene it.
8 The lions whelps haue not walked it, nor
the lion passed thereby.
9 He putteth his hand vpon the g rockes, &
ouerthroweth the moūtaines by ẏ rootes.
10 He breaketh riuers in the rockes, and his
eye seeth euerie precious thing.
11 He bindeth the floods, that they do not
ouerflowe, & the thing that is hid, bringeth he to light.
12 But where is wisdome foūde? h & where
is the place of vnderstanding?
13 Man knoweth not i the price thereof: for
it is not found in the land of the liuing.
14 The depth saith, It is not in me: the sea
also saith, It is not with me.
15 k Golde shal not be giuen for it, nether
shal siluer be weighed for ẏ price thereof.
16 It shal not be valued with the wedge of
golde of Ophir, *nor* with the precious o-
nix, nor the saphir.
17 The golde nor the christal shal be equal
vnto it, nor the exchange *shalbe* for plate
of fine golde.
18 No mencion shalbe made of coral, nor
of the l gabish: for wisdome is more precious then perles.
19 The Topaz of Ethiopia shal not be e-
qual vnto it, nether shal it be valued with
the wedge of pure golde.
20 Whence thē cometh wisdome? and where is the place of vnderstanding,
21 Seing it is hid from the eyes of all the liuing, & is hid frō the m foules of ẏ heauē?
22 Destruction and death say, We haue heard the fame thereof with our eares.
23 But God vnderstādeth the n way thereof,
and he knoweth the place thereof.
24 For he beholdeth the ends of ẏ worlde,
& seeth all that is vnder heauen,
25 To make the weight of the windes, & to
weigh the waters by measure.
26 When he made a decree for the raine, &
a way for the lightening of the thunders,
27 Then did he se it, and counted it: he prepared it and also considered it.
28 And vnto man he said, Beholde, * the
o feare of the Lord is wisdome, and to departe from euil *is* vnderstanding.

d Which a mā can not wade through.
e That is, corne, and vnder nethe is brimstone or cole, which easely conceiueth fyre.
f He alludeth to the mines and secrets of nature, which are vnder the earth, whereinto nether foules nor beastes cā entre.
g After that he hathe declared the wisdome of God in the secretes of nature, he describeth his power.
h Thogh Gods power, & wisdome may be vnderstand in earthly thīgs, yet his heauēlie wisdome can not be atteined vnto.
i It is to hie a thing for man to atteine vnto in this worlde.
k It cā nether be boght for golde, nor precious stones, but is onely ẏ gift of God.
l Which is thoght to be a kinde of precious stone.
m Meaning, ẏ there is no natural meanes, whereby man might atteine to the heauenlie wisdome: which he meaneth by the foules, that flie hie.
n He maketh God onely ẏ autor of this wisdome, and the giuer thereof.
* Prouerb. 1,7.
o He declareth that mā hathe so muche of this heauenlie wisdome, as he sheweth by fearing God, and departing from euil.

CHAP. XXIX.

1 Iob complaineth of the prosperitie of the time past. 7. 21. His autoritie. 12 Iustice and equitie.

1 SO Iob proceded and continued his parable, saying,
2 Oh that I were as " in times past, when
God preserued me!

" Ebr. monethes before.

3 When his [a] light shined vpō mine head:
& when by his light I walked through the
[b] darkenes,
4 As I was in the dayes of my youth: when
[c] Gods prouidēce *was* vpō my tabernacle:
5 When the Almightie was yet with me, *&*
my children rounde about me:
6 When I washed my paths [d] with butter, and when the rocke powred me out riuers of oyle:
7 When I went out to the gate, *euen* to the
iudgemēt seat, *and when* I caused them to
prepare my seat in the strete.
8 The yong men sawe me, and [e] hid them
selues, and the aged arose, *and* stode vp.
9 The princes stayed talke, and laied their
hand on their [f] mouth.
10 The voyce of princes was hid; and their
tongue cleaued to ẏ roofe of their mouth.
11 And when the [g] eare heard me, it blessed
me: and when the eye sawe *me*, it gaue witnes to [h] me.
12 For I deliuered the [i] poore that cryed,
and the fatherles, and him that had none
to helpe him.
13 [k] The blessing of him that was ready to
perish, came vpon me, and I caused the
widowes heart to reioyce.
14 I put [l] on iustice, and it couered me: my
iudgement *was* as a robe, and a crowne.
15 I was the eyes to the blinde, and I was
the fete to the lame.
16 I was a father vnto the poore, and *when*
I knewe not the cause, I soght it out diligently.
17 I brake also the chawes of the vnrighteous man, and pluckt the praye out of his
tethe.
18 Then I said, I shal dye in my [m] nest, and
I shal multiplie *my* dayes as the sande.
19 *For* my roote is [n] spred out by the water,
and the dewe shal lye vpon my branche.
20 My glorie shal renue toward me, and
my bowe shal be restored in mine hand.
21 Vnto me men gaue eare, and waited, and
helde their tongue at my counsel.
22 After my wordes thei replied not, & my
talke [o] dropped vpon them.
23 And they waited for me, as for the raine, and they opened their mouth [p] as for
the latter raine.
24 *If* I [q] laughed on them, they beleued it
not: nether did they cause the light of my
countenance [r] to fall.
25 I appointed out [s] their way, and did sit
as chief, and dwelt as a King in the armie,
and like him that comforteth ẏ mourners.

a When I felt his fauour.
b I was fre from afflictiō.
c That is, semed by euidēt tokens to be more present with me.
d By these similitudes he declareth the great prosperitie, that he was in, so that he had none occasion to be suche a sinner as they accused him.
e Being ashamed of their lightnes, and afraied of my grauitie.
f Acknowledging my wisdome.
g All that heard me, praised me.
h Testifying ẏ I did good iustice.
i Because his aduersaries did so much charge him with wickednes, he is cōpelled to rendre a coūte of his life.
k That is, I did succour him ẏ was in destresse, and so he had cause to praise me.
l I delited to do iustice as others did, to weare costely apparel.
m That is, at home in my bed without all trouble, and vnquietnes.
n My felicitie doeth increase.
o That is, was pleasant vnto them.
p As the drye grounde thirsteth for the raine.
q That is, thei thoght it not to be a iest, or thei thoght not ẏ I wold cōdescēd vnto thē.
r They were afraied to offend me, and cause me to be angrie.
s I had them at commandement.

CHAP. XXX.

Iob complaineth that he is contemned of the moste contemptible, 11. 21. Because of his aduersitie and affliction. 23 Death is the house of all flesh.

1 BVt now they that are yonger then I,
[a] mocke me: *yea*, thei whose fathers I
haue refused to set with the [b] dogges of
my flockes.
2 For where to shulde the strength of their
hands haue serued me, *seing* age [c] perished
in them?
3 For pouertie and famine *they were* solitarie, fleing into the wildernes, *which is* darke, desolate and waste.
4 They cut vp *nettels by the bushes, and
the iuniper rootes *was* their meat.
5 Thei were [d] chased forthe from among
men: they showted at them, as at a thefe.
6 Therefore they dwelt in the clefts of riuers, in the holes of the earth and rockes.
7 They roared among the bushes, and vnder the thistels they gathered them selues.
8 *They were* the children of fooles and the
children of villaines, which were more vile then the earth.
9 And now am I their [e] song, & I am their
talke.
10 They abhorre me, *and* flee farre from
me, and spare not to spit in my face.
11 Because that *God* hathe losed my [f] corde
and humbled me, [g] they haue losed the
bridel before me.
12 The youth rise vp at my right hād: they
haue pusht my fete, and haue trode on me
as on the [h] paths of their destruction.
13 They haue destroyed my paths: they
toke pleasure at my calamitie, they had
none [i] helpe.
14 They came as a great breache *of waters*,
and [k] vnder this calamitie they come on
heapes.
15 Feare is turned vpō me: *and* thei pursue
my soule as the winde, and mine health
passeth away as a cloude.
16 Therefore my soule is now [l] powred
out vpon me, and the dayes of affliction
haue taken holde on me.
17 [m] It perceth my bones in the night, and
my sinewes take no rest.
18 For the great vehemencie is my garmēt
chāged, *which* compasseth me about as the
colar of my coate.
19 [n] He hathe cast me into the myre, and I
am become like ashes and dust.
20 When I crye vnto thee, ẏ doest not heare me, nether regardest me, *whē* I stād vp.
21 Thou turnest thy self [o] cruelly against
me, and art enemie vnto me with the
strength of thine hand.
22 Thou takest me vp *and* causest me to ride vpon the [p] winde, and makest my
*strength to faile.
23 Surely I know that thou wilt bring me
to death, and to the house appointed for
all the liuing.
24 Doutles none can stretche his hand
[q] vnto the graue, thogh they crye in his
destruction.
25 Did not I wepe with him ẏ was in trouble?

a That is, mine estate is chāged, & where as before the ancient men were glad to do me reuerence, the yong men now contemne me.
b Meaning, to be my shepherdes, or to kepe my dogges.
c That is, their fathers dyed for famine before they came to age.
*Or, malowe.
d Iob sheweth that these that mocked him in his afflictiō, were like to their fathers, wicked, and lewde fellowes, suche as he here describeth.
e They make songs of me, & mocke at my miserie.
f God hathe takē frō me ẏ force, credit & autoritie, wherewith I kept them in subiection.
g He said that the yong men whē they saw him, hid them selues, as chap. 29,8, and now in his miserie they were impudent and licencious.
h That is, thei soght by all meanes how thei might destroye me.
i They nede none to helpe them.
k By my calamitie they toke an occasiō against me.
l My life faileth me, and I am as halfe dead.
m Meaning, sorowe.
n That is, God hathe broght me into contempt.
o He speaketh not thus to accuse God, but to declare the vehemencie of his affliction, whereby he was caryed beside hi self.
p He compareth his afflictions to a tēpest, or whirle winde.
*Or, wisdome, or Law.
q None can deliuer me thence thogh they lament at my death.

ble? was not my soule in heauines for the
poore?
26 Yet when I loked for good, [r] euil came
vnto me: and when I waited for light,
there came darkenes.
27 My bowels did boyle without rest: *for* the
dayes of affliction are come vpon me.
28 I wẽt mourning [s] without sunne: I stode
vp in the congregacion [t] *and* cryed.
29 I am a brother to the [u] dragons, and a
companion to the ostriches.
30 My skinne is blacke vpõ me, and my bones are burnt with [x] heat.
31 Therefore mine harp is turned to mourning, and mine organs into the voyce of
them that wepe.

r In stead of cõforting they mocked at me.
s Not deliting in anie worldely thing, no not so muche, as in the vse of the sunne.
t Lamenting the that were in affliction, & mouing others to pitie them.
u I am like ÿ wilde beastes that desire moste solitarie places.
x With the heat of affliction.

CHAP. XXXI.

Iob reciteth the innocencie of his liuing, and nomber of his vertues, which declareth what oght to be the life of the faithful.

1 I Made a couenant with mine [a] eyes:
why thẽ shulde I thinke on [b] a maid?
2 For what porcion *shulde I haue* of God
from aboue? and *what* inheritance of the
Almightie from on hie?
3 Is not destruction to the wicked & strãge
punishement to [c] the workers of iniquitie?
4 Doeth not he beholde my wayes and tell
all my steppes?
5 If I haue walked in vanitie, or if my fote
hath made haste to deceit,
6 Let God weigh me in the iuste balance,
and he shal knowe mine [d] vprightnes.
7 If my step hathe turned out of the way,
or mine heart hathe [e] walked after mine
eye, or if anie blot hathe cleaued to mine
hands,
8 Let me sowe, & let another [f] eat: yea, let
my plants be rooted out.
9 If mine heart hathe bene deceiued by a
woman, or if I haue layed wayte at the dore of my neigbour,
10 Let my wife [g] grinde vnto another mã,
and let other men bowe downe vpon her.
11 For this is a wickednes, and iniquitie to
be condemned.
12 Yea, this is a fyre that shal deuoure [h] to
destruction, and which shal roote out all
mine increase,
13 If I did contemne the iudgement of my
seruant, and of my maid, when they [i] did
contend with me.
14 What then shal I do when [k] God stãdeth vp? and when he shal visite *me*, what
shal I answer?
15 He that hathe made me in the wombe,
hathe he not made [l] him? hathe not he a-
lone facioned vs in the wombe?
16 If I restrained the poore of *their* desire,
or haue caused the eyes of the widowe
[m] to faile,
17 Or haue eaten my morsels alone, & the
fatherles hathe not eaten thereof,

a I kept mine eyes from all wanton lokes.
b Wolde not God then haue punished me?
c Iob declareth that the feare of God was a bridel to stay him from all wickednes.
d He sheweth wherein his vprightnes stãdeth: that is, in as muche as he was blameles before men, & sinned not against the second table.
e That is, hathe accomplished the lust of mine eye.
f According to the curse of the Law, Deu. 28,33.
g Let her be made a slaue.
h He sheweth that albeit mã neglect the punishement of adulterie, yet the wrath of God wil neuer cease til suche be destroyed.
i When they thoght them selues euil intreated by me.
k If I had oppressed others, how shulde I haue escaped Gods iudgement?
l He was moued to shewe pitie vnto seruants, because they were Gods creatures as he was.
m By long waiting for her request.

18 (For from my youth he hathe growẽ vp
with me [n] as *with* a father, & from my mothers wombe I haue bene a guide vnto
her)
19 If I haue sene anie perish for want of clo
thing, or any poore without couering,
20 If his loines haue not blessed me, because
he was warmed w͛ the fleece of my shepe,
21 If I haue lift [o] vp mine hand against the
fatherles, when I sawe that I might helpe
him in the gate,
22 Let mine [p] arme fall frõ my shulder, &
mine arme be broken from the bone.
23 For Gods punishment was [q] fearful vnto me, and I colde not *be deliuered* from his
highnes.
24 If I made golde mine hope, or haue said
to the wedge of golde, *Thou* art my confidence,
25 If I reioyced because my substance was
great, or because mine hand had gotten
muche,
26 If I did beholde the [r] sunne, when it shined, or the moone, walking in *her* brightenes,
27 If mine heart did flatter me in secret, or
if my mouth did kisse mine [s] hand,
28 (This also had bene an iniquitie to be
condemned: for I had denyed the God
[t] aboue)
29 If I reioyced at his destruction that hated me, or was moued *to ioye* when euil came vpon him,
30 Nether haue I suffred my mouth to
sinne, by wishing a cursse vnto his soule.
31 Did not the men of my [u] tabernacle say,
Who shal giue vs of his flesh? we can not
be satisfied.
32 The strãger did not lodge in the strete,
but I opened my dores vnto him, that wẽt
by the way.
33 If I haue hid [x] my sinne, as Adam, concei
ling mine iniquitie in my bosom,
34 Thogh I colde haue made afraied a
great multitude, yet the most contemptible of the families did [y] feare me: so I kept
[z] silence, and went not out of the dore.
35 Oh that I had some to heare me! beholde
my [a] signe that the Almightie wil witnes
for me: thogh mine aduersarie shulde
write a boke *against me*,
36 Wolde not I take it vpon my shulder,
& binde it as [b] a crowne vnto me?
37 I wil tel him the nomber of my goings,
and go vnto him as to a [c] prince.
38 If my land [d] crye against me, or the forrowes thereof complaine together,
39 If I haue eaten the frutes thereof without siluer: or if I haue grieued [e] the soules
of the masters thereof,
40 Let thistles growe in stead of wheat, &
cokle in the stead of barly.

THE [f] VVORDES OF IOB ARE ENDED.

n He nourished ÿ fatherles & mainteined the widowes cause.
o To oppresse him & do him iniurie.
p Let me rott in pieces.
q I refrained not from sinning for feare of men, but because I feared God.
r If I was proude of my worldelie prosperitie & felicitie, which is ment by the shining of the sunne & brightenes of the moone.
s If mine owne doings delited me.
t By putting confidence in any thing, but in him alone.
u My seruants moued me to be reuẽged of mine enemie, yet did I neuer wish him hurt.
x And not confessed it frely: whereby it is euident that he iustified hĩselfe before men and not before God.
y That is, I reuerenced the moste weake & contemned & was afraied to offend them.
z I suffred the to speake euil of me and wẽt not out of my house to reuẽge it.
a This is a sufficient token of my righteousnes, that God is my witnes and wil iustifie my cause.
b Shulde not this boke of his accusatiõs be a praise & condemnation to me?
c I wil make him a coũte of all my life, without feare.
d As thogh I had withholden their wages that labored in it.
e Meaning, that he was no briber nor extorcioner.
f That is, the talke which he had with his thre frieds.

CHAP. XXXII.

1 *Elihú reproueth them of foly. 8 Age maketh not a man wise, but the Spirit of God.*

1 SO these thre men ceased to answer
Iob, because he [*] estemed him selfe
iust.
2 Thẽ the wrath of Elihú the sonne of Barachél the [a] Buzite, of ẏ familie of [b] Ram,
was kindled: his wrath, *I say*, was kindled
against Iob, because he iustified him self
[c] more then God.
3 Also his anger was kindled against his
thre friends, because they colde not finde
an answer, *and* yet condemned Iob.
4 (Now Elihú had waited til Iob had spoken: for [d] they were more ancient in yeres
then he).
5 So when Elihú sawe, that there was none
answer in the mouth of the thre men, his
wrath was kindled.
6 Therefore Elihú the sonne of Barachél,
the Buzite answered, and said, I am yong
in yeres, and ye are ancient: therefore I
douted, and was afrayed to shewe you mine opinion.
7 *For* I said, The dayes [e] shal speake, and
the multitude of yeres shal teache wisdome.
8 Surely there is a spirit in man, [f] but the
inspiracion of the Almightie giueth vnderstanding.
9 Great men are not *alway* wise, nether do
the aged *all way* vnderstand iudgement.
10 Therefore I say, Heare me, *and* I wil
shewe also mine opinion.
11 Beholde, I did waite vpon your wordes
& hearkened vnto your knowledge, whiles you soght out [g] reasons.
12 Yea, when I had considered you, lo, there
was none of you that reproued Iob, nor
answered his wordes:
13 Lest ye shulde say, We haue [h] founde
wisdome: *for* God hathe cast him downe,
& no man.
14 Yet hathe [i] he not directed *his* wordes
to me, nether wil I answer [k] him by your
wordes.
15 *Then* they fearing, answered nomore, *but*
left of their talke.
16 When I had waited (for they spake not,
but stode stil *and* answered nomore)
17 *Then* answered I in my turne, & I shewed mine opinion.
18 For I am ful of [l] matter, & the spirit
within me compelleth me.
19 Beholde, my bellie *is* as the wine, which
hathe no vent, & like the newe bottels
that brast.
20 *Therefore* wil I speake, that I may take
breath: I wil open my lippes, and wil answer.
21 I wil not now accept the persone of mã,
[m] nether wil I giue titles to man.
22 For I may not giue [n] titles, *lest* my Maker
shulde take me away sodenly.

[*] *Ebr. was iust in his owne eyes*

[a] Which came of Buz ẏ sonne of Nahór Abrahams brother.
[b] Or, as the Chalde paraphrast readeth, Abrám.
[c] By making him self innocent, and by charging God of rigour.
[d] That is, the thre mẽcioned before.
[e] Meaning, the ancient, which haue experiẽce
[f] It is a special gift of God that man hathe vnderstanding, and cometh nether of nature nor by age.
[g] To proue ẏ Iobs afflictiõ came for his sinnes.
[h] And flatter your selues, as thogh you had ouercome him.
[i] To wit, Iob.
[k] He vseth almost the like arguments, but without tanting, and reproches.
[l] I haue conceiued in my minde great store of reasons.
[m] I wil nether haue regarde to riches, credit nor autoritie, but wil speake the verie trueth.
[n] The Ebrew worde signifieth to change the name, as to call a foole a wise man: meaning that he wolde not cloke the trueth to flatter men.

CHAP. XXXIII.

1 *Elihú accuseth Iob of ignorance. 14 He sheweth that God hathe diuers meanes to instruct man and to drawe him from sinne. 19. 29 He afflicteth man and sodenly deliuereth him. 26 Man being deliuered, giueth thankes to God.*

1 WHerefore, Iob, I pray thee, heare
my talke and hearken vnto all my
wordes.
2 Beholde now, I haue opened my mouth:
my tongue hathe spoken in my mouth.
3 My wordes *are* in the vprightenes of mine heart, and my lippes shal speake pure
knowledge.
4 The [a] Spirit of God hathe made me, &
the breath of the Almightie hathe giuen
me life.
5 If thou canst giue me answer, prepare
thy selfe & stand before me.
6 Beholde, I am according to thy wish in
[b] Gods stead: I am also formed of the clay.
7 Beholde, my terrour shal not feare thee,
nether shal mine hãd [c] be heauy vpõ thee.
8 Douteles thou hast spoken in mine eares,
and I haue heard the voyce of *thy* wordes.
9 I am [d] cleane, without sinne: I am innocent, and there is none iniquitie in me.
10 Lo, he hathe founde occasions against
me, and counted me for his enemie.
11 He hathe put my fete in the stockes, and
loketh narowly vnto all my paths.
12 Beholde, in this hast thou not done right:
I wil answer thee, ẏ God is greater thẽ mã.
13 Why doest thou striue against him? for
he doeth not [e] giue account of all his
matters.
14 For God speaketh [f] once or twise, & one
seeth it not.
15 In dreames & [g] visions of the night, whẽ
slepe falleth vpon men, and they slepe vpon *their* beddes,
16 Then he openeth the eares of mẽ, euen
by their corrections, *which* he [h] had sealed,
17 That he might cause man to turne away
from *his* enterprise, and that he might hide
the [i] pride of man,
18 And kepe backe his soule frõ the pit, &
ẏ his life shulde not passe by the sworde.
19 He is also striken with sorow vpon his
bed, and the grief of his bones *is* sore,
20 So that his [k] life causeth him to abhorre
bread, and his soule daintie meat.
21 His flesh faileth that it can not be sene,
& his bones *which* were not sene, clatter.
22 So his soule draweth to the graue, & his
life [l] to the buriers.
23 If there be a [m] messenger with him, *or* an
interpreter, one of a thousand [n] to declare
vnto man his righteousnes,
24 Then wil he haue [o] mercie vpon him,

Chap. XXXIII.
[a] I confesse ẏ power of God, & am one of his therefore thou oghtest to heare me.
[b] Because Iob had wished to dispute his cause with God, Chap 16,21, so that he might do it without feare, Elihú sayth, he wil reason in Gods stead, whome he nedeth not to feare, because he is a man made of the same matter that he is.
[c] I wil not handle thee so roughly as these others haue done.
[d] He repeateth Iobs wordes, whereby he protested his innocencie in diuers places, but specially in the 13, 16 & 30 Chap.
[e] The cause of his iudgemẽts is not alwayes declared to man
[f] Thogh God by sondrie examples of his iudgements speake vnto man, yet the reason thereof is not knowen: yea & thogh God shulde speake, yet he is not vnderstand.
[g] God, saith he, speaketh cõmunely, ether by visions to teache vs the cause of his iudgements, or els by afflictiõs, or by his messenger.
[h] That is, determined to send vpon thẽ.
[i] He sheweth for what end God sendeth afflictions: to beat downe mãs pride, & to turne frõ euil.
[k] That is, his painful & miserable life.
[l] To them that shal burie hĩ.
[m] A man sent of God to declare his wil.
[n] A singular man, & as one chosen out of a thousand, ẇ is able to declare the great mercies of God vnto sinners: & wherein mans righteousnes standeth, which is through the iustice of Iesus Christ & faith therein.
[o] He sheweth that it is a sure toke of Gods mercie towards sinners, whẽ he causeth his worde to be preached vnto thẽ.

and wil ſaie,[p]Deliuer him, that he go not
downe into the pit: for I haue receiued
a reconciliation.
25 Thē ſhal his fleſh be [q] as freſh as a childs,
& ſhal returne as in yͤ daies of his youth.
26 He ſhal pray vnto God, and he wil be
fauourable vnto him,and he ſhal ſe his face with ioy: for he wil rendre vnto man
his [r] righteouſnes.
27 He loketh vpon mē,and if one ſay, I haue ſinned,and [ſ] peruerted righteouſnes,
and it did not profit [t] me,
28 [u]He wil deliuer his ſoule from going into the pit,and his life ſhal ſe the light.
29 Lo,all theſe thīgs wil God worke [x] twiſe
or thriſe with a man,
30 That he may turne backe his ſoule frō
the pit,to be illuminate in the light of the
liuing.
31 Marke wel, ô Iob, & heare me: kepe ſilence,and I wil ſpeake.
32 If there be [y]matter, anſwer me, & ſpeake:
for I deſire to [z] iuſtifie thee.
33 If thou haſt not,heare me: holde thy tongue,and I wil teache thee wiſdome.

p That is, the miniſter ſhal by the preaching of the worde pronouce vnto him yͤ forgiuenes of his ſinnes.
q He ſhal fele Gods fauour and reioyce: declarīg hereby, wherein ſtandeth the true ioy of the faithful: and yͭ God wil reſtore hī to health of body, which is a token of his bleſsing.
r God wil forgiue his ſinnes and accept hī as iuſte.
ſ That is, done wickedly.
t But my ſinne hathe bene the cauſe of Gods wrath toward me.
u God wil forgiue the penitent ſinner.
x Meaning, oft times, euen as oft as a ſinner doeth repent.
y If thou doute of any thing, or ſe occaſion to ſpeake againſt it.
z That is, to ſhewe thee, wherein mans iuſtification conſiſteth.

CHAP. XXXIIII.

5 Elihú chargeth Iob, that he called him ſelfe righteous. 12 He ſheweth that God is iuſt in his iudgemēts. 24 God deſtroyeth the mightie. 30 By him the hypocrite reigneth.

1 MOreouer Elihú anſwered,and ſaid,
2 Heare my wordes,ye [a] wiſe men, and
hearkē vnto me, ye that haue knowledge.
3 For the eare tryeth the wordes,as yͤ mouth
taſteth meat.
4 Let vs ſeke [b] iudgement among vs,& let
vs knowe among our ſelues what is good.
5 For Iob hathe ſaid, I am righteous, and
God hathe taken [c] away my iudgement.
6 Shulde I lye in my [d] right? my *wounde* of
the arowe is [e] grieuous without *my* ſinne.
7 What mā is like Iob, that drinketh [f] ſcor-
nefulnes like water?
8 Which goeth in the [g] companie of them
that worke iniquitie, & walketh with wicked men?
9 For he hathe ſaid, [h] It profiteth a mā nothing that he ſhulde [i]walke with God.
10 Therefore hearken vnto me, ye men of
wiſdome, God forbid yͭ wickednes *ſhulde*
be in God, and iniquitie in the Almightie.
11 For he wil rendre vnto man *according* to
his worke, & cauſe euerie one to finde according to his way.
12 And certeinly God wil not do wickedly,
nether wil the Almightie peruert iudgement.
13 Whome[x] hathe he appointed ouer yͤ earth
beſide him ſelf? or who hathe placed the
whole worlde?
14 If [k] he ſet his heart vpon *man*, and gather
vnto him ſelf his ſpirit [l] and his breath,

a Which are eſtemed wiſe of the worlde.
b Let vs examine the matter vprightly.
c That is, hathe afflicted me without meaſure.
d Shulde I ſay, I am wicked, being an innocent?
e I am ſorer puniſhed, then my ſinne deſerueth.
f Which is compelled to receiue the reproche & ſcornes of many for his fooliſh wordes.
g Meanīg, that Iob was like to the wicked, becauſe he ſemed not to glorifie God, & ſubmit him ſelfe to his iudgements.
h He wraſteth Iobs wordes, who ſaid tha Gods childrē are oft times puniſhed i this worlde, & the wicked go fre.
i That is, liue godly, as Gen. 5,22
Chap 36.23.
k To deſtroye him.
l The breath of life, which he gaue man.

15 All fleſh ſhal periſh together, and man
ſhal returne vnto duſt.
16 And if yͧ haſt vnderſtanding, heare this
& hearken to the voyce of my wordes.
17 Shal he that hateth iudgement, [m] gouerne? & wilt thou iudge him wicked that
is moſte iuſt?
18 Wilt thou ſay vnto a Kīg, *Thou art* [n] wic
ked? or to princes, *Ye are* vngodlie?
19 *How muche leſſe* to him that accepteth
not the perſones of princes, & regardeth
not the riche, more then the poore? for thei
be all the worke of his hands.
20 They ſhal dye ſodenly,[o] and the people
ſhalbe troubled at midnight,[p] & they ſhal
paſſe forthe and take away the mightie
without hand.
21 For his eyes *are* vpon the wayes of man,
and he ſeeth all his goings.
22 There is no darkenes nor ſhadowe of death, that the workers of iniquitie might be
hid therein.
23 For he wil not lay on man ſo muche,
that he ſhulde [q] entre into iupgemēt with
God.
24 He ſhal breake the mightie without [r] ſeking, and ſhal ſet vp other in their ſteade.
25 Therefore ſhal he declare their [ſ] workes:
he ſhal turne the [t] night, and they ſhalbe
deſtroyed.
26 He ſtriketh them as wicked men in the
places of the [u] ſeers,
27 Becauſe they haue turned backe from
him, and wolde not conſider all his waies:
28 So that they haue cauſed the voyce of
the poore to [x]come vnto him, and he hathe
heard the crye of the afflicted.
29 And when he giueth quietnes, who can
make trouble? and when he hideth his face, who can beholde him, whether *it be*
vpon nacions, or vpon a man onely?
30 Becauſe the [y] hypocrite doeth reigne,
& becauſe the people are ſnared.
31 Surely *it apperteineth* vnto God [z] to ſay, I
haue pardoned, I wil not deſtroye.
32 [a] But if I ſe not, teache thou me: if I haue done wickedly, I wil do no more.
33 Wil he performe the thing through
[b] thee? for thou haſte reproued [c] it, becauſe that thou haſt choſen, and not I. now
ſpeake what thou knoweſt.
34 Let men of vnderſtanding tel me, and
let a wiſe man hearken vnto me.
35 Iob hathe not ſpoken of knowledge, nether were his wordes according to wiſdome.
36 I deſire that Iob may be [d] tryed, vnto the end touching the anſwers for wicked men.
37 For he [e] addeth rebellion vnto his ſinne: he clappeth his hāds among vs, & multiplieth his wordes againſt God.

m If God were not iuſt, how colde he gouerne the worlde?
n If man of nature feare to ſpeake euil of ſuch as haue power, thē muche more oght thei to be afraid to ſpeake euil of God.
o When they loke not for it
p The meſſengers or viſitation that God ſhal ſend.
q God doeth not afflict man aboue meaſure, ſo that he ſhulde haue occaſion to cōtend with hī.
r For all his creatures are at hand to ſerue him, ſo that he nedeth not to ſeke for anie other armie.
ſ Make them manifeſt that they are wicked.
t Declare the thīgs that were hid.
u Meanīg, opēly in the ſight of all men
x By their crueltie & extortion
y When tyrāts ſit in the throne of iuſtice yͤ vnder pretēce of executing iuſtice are but hypocrites & oppreſſe the people, it is a ſigne that God hathe drawen backe is coūtenance and fauour from that place.
z Onely it belōgeth to God to moderat his corrections, & not vnto man.
a Thus Elihú ſpeaketh in yͤ perſone of God, as it were mockīg Iob becauſe he wolde be wiſer then God.
b Wil God vſe thy counſel in doing his workes?
c Thus he ſpeaketh in yͤ perſone of God, as thogh Iob ſhulde chuſe & refuſe afflictiō at his pleaſure.
d That he may ſpeake as muche as he can, that we may anſwer him & all the wicked that ſhal vſe ſuche arguments.
e He ſtandeth ſtubbernly in the maītenāce of his cauſe.

CHAP. XXXV.

6 Nether doeth godlines profite, or vngodlines hurt God, but man. 13 The wicked crye vnto God and are not heard.

1 ELihú ſpake moreouer, and ſaid,
2 Thikeſt thou this right, that thou haſt
ſaid, I am [a] more righteous then God?
3 For thou haſt ſaid, What profiteth it thee
and what auaileth it me, *to purge me* from
my ſinne?
4 *Therefore* wil I anſwer thee, and thy [b] com
panions with thee.
5 Loke vnto the heauen, and ſe and beholde the [c] cloudes *which* are hier then thou.
6 If thou ſinneſt, what doeſt thou [d] againſt
him, yea, when thy ſinnes be many, what
doeſt thou vnto him?
7 If thou be righteous, what giueſt thou
vnto him? or what receiueth he at thine
hand?
8 Thy wickednes *may hurt* a man as thou
art: thy rigteouſnes *may profite* the ſonne of
man.
9 They cauſe many that are oppreſſed, [e] to
crye, *which* crye out for the violence of the
mightie.
10 But none ſaith, Where is God that made me, which giueth ſongs in the night?
11 Which teacheth vs more thẽ the beaſtes
of the earth, and giueth vs more wiſdome
then the foules of the heauen.
12 Then they crye becauſe of the violence
of the wicked, but [f] he anſwereth not.
13 Surely God wil not heare vanitie, nether
wil the Almightie regarde it.
14 Althogh thou ſayeſt *to God*, Thou wilt not
regarde it, [g] yet iudgement *is* before him:
truſt thou in him.
15 But now becauſe his angre hathe not viſited, nor called to cõut *the euil* with great
extremitie,
16 Therefore Iob [h] openeth his mouth in
vaine, and multiplieth wordes without
knowledge.

CHAP. XXXVI.

2 Elihú ſheweth the power of God. 6 And his iuſtice, 9 And wherefore he puniſheth. 13 The propertie of the wicked.

1 ELihú alſo proceded and ſaid,
2 Suffre me a litle, & I wil inſtruct thee:
for *I haue* yet to ſpeake on Gods behalfe.
3 I wil fetche [a] my knowledge a farre of, &
wil attribute righteouſnes vnto my Maker.
4 For truely my wordes ſhal not be falſe,
& he that is [b] perfite in knowledge, *ſpeaketh* with thee.
5 Beholde, the mightie God caſteth away
none that is [c] mightie & valiant of courage.
6 [d] He mainteineth not the wicked, but he
giueth iudgement to the afflicted.
7 He withdraweth not his eies from the
righteous, but *thei are* with [e] Kings in the
throne, where he placeth them for euer:
thus they are exalted.
8 And if thei be bound in fetters & tyed
with the cordes of affliction,
9 Then wil he ſhewe them their [f] worke
and their ſinnes, becauſe they haue bene
proude.
10 He openeth alſo their eare to diſcipline,
and commandeth them that they returne
from iniquitie.
11 * If they obey and ſerue him, they
ſhal end their dayes in proſperitie, & their
yeres in pleaſures.
12 But if they wil not obey, they ſhal paſſe
by the ſworde, & periſh [g] without knowledge.
13 But the hypocrites [h] of heart increaſe the
wrath: *for* thei [i] call not when he bindeth
them.
14 Their ſoule dyeth in [k] youth, & their
life among the whoremongers.
15 He deliuereth the poore in his afflictiõ,
and openeth their eare in trouble.
16 Euen ſo wolde he haue taken thee out of
the ſtreight place *into* a broad place & not
ſhut vp beneth? and [l] that which reſteth vpon thy table, had bene ful of fat.
17 But thou art ful of the [m] iudgement of
the wicked, *thogh* iudgement and equitie
mainteine *all things*.
18 [n] For *Gods* wrath is, leſt he ſhulde take thee
away in *thine* abundance: for no multitude
of giftes can deliuer thee.
19 Wil he regarde thy riches? *he regardeth*
not golde, nor all them that excell in
ſtrength.
20 [o] Be not careful in the night, how he deſtroieth the people out of their place.
21 Take thou hede: loke not to [p] iniquitie:
for thou haſt choſen it rather then affliction.
22 Beholde, God exalteth by his power:
what teacher is like him?
23 Who hathe appointed to him his way?
or who can ſay, Thou haſt done wickedly?
24 Remember that thou magnifie his worke, which men beholde.
25 All men ſe it, and men beholde it [q] a
farre of.
26 Beholde, God *is* excellent, [r] & we knowe
him not, nether can the nomber of his yeres be ſearched out.
27 When he reſtraineth the droppes of water, the raine [ſ] powreth downe by the vapour thereof,
28 Which *raine* the cloudes do droppe &
let fall abundantly vpon man.
29 Who cã knowe the diuiſiõs of the cloudes & the thunders of his [t] tabernacle?
30 Beholde he ſpreadeth his light vpon
[u] it, and couereth the [x] bottome of the
ſea.

31 For

a Iob neuer ſpake theſe wordes: but becauſe he mainteined his innocencie, it ſemed as thogh he wolde ſay, that God tormented him without iuſt cauſe.
b Suche as are in the like errour.
c If thou canſt not controle the cloudes, wilt thou preſume to inſtruct God?
d Nether doeth thy ſinne hurt God, nor thy iuſtice profite hĩ: for he wil be glorified without thee.
e The wicked may hurt man and cauſe him to crie, who if he ſoght to God, which ſendeth comfort, ſhulde be deliuered.
f Becauſe thei pray not in faith as feling Gods mercies.
g God is iuſt, howſoeuer ỹ iudgeſt of hĩ.
h For if he did puniſh thee, as thou deſerueſt, thou ſhuldeſt not be able to open thy mouth.
Chap XXXVI.
a He ſheweth that when we ſpeake of God we muſt lift our ſpirits more hie, then our natural ſenſe is able to reache.
b Thou ſhalt perceiue that I am a faithful inſtructour, & that I ſpeake to thee in ỹ name of God.
c Strong and conſtant, & of vnderſtãding: for theſe are ỹ gifts of God, & he loueth them in man: but for aſmuche as God puniſhed now Iob, it is a ſigne that theſe are not in hĩ.
d Therefore he wil not preſerue the wicked: but to the humble & afflicted heart he wil ſhewe grace.
e He preferreth the godlie to honour.
f He wil moue their heartes to fele their ſinnes ỹ thei may come to him by repentance as he did Manaſſeh.
Iſa 1,19.
g That is, in their follie or obſtination, & ſo ſhalbe cauſe of their owne deſtruction.
h Which are maliciouſly bẽt agaĩſt God and flatter thẽ ſelues in their vices.
i When they are in afflictiõ they ſeke not to God for ſuccour, as Aſa. 2.Chro.16,12. reuel.16,11.
k Thei dye of ſome vile death and that before they come to age.
l If thou hadeſt bene obedient to God, he wolde haue broght thee to libertie & welth.
m Thou art altogether after the maner of the wicked: for thou doeſt murmure againſt ỹ iuſtice of God.
n God doeth puniſh thee, leſt thou ſhuldeſt forget God in thy welth and ſo periſh
o Be not thou curious in ſeking the cauſe of Gods iudgements, when he deſtroyeth any.
p And ſo murmur againſt God through impaciencie.
q The workes of God are ſo manifeſt, that a man may ſe thẽ a farre of and knowe God by the ſame.
r Our infirmitie hindereth vs ſo, that we can not atteine to the perfite knowledge of God.
ſ That is, the raine cometh of thoſe droppes of water, which he kepeth in ỹ cloudes.
t Meaning, of the cloudes, ỹ he calleth ỹ Tabernacle of God.
u Vpon the cloude.
x That men cã not come to ỹ knowledge of ỹ ſprings thereof.

31 For thereby he iudgeth [y] the people, and
giueth meat abundantly.
32 He couereth the light with the cloudes,
and commandeth them to go [z] against it.
33 [a] His companion sheweth him thereof,
and there is angre in rising vp.

CHAP. XXXVII.

2 Elihú proueth that the vnsearcheable wisdome of God is manifest by his workes, 4 As by the thunders, 6 The snowe, 9 The whirle winde, 11 And the rayne.

1 AT this also mine heart is [a] astonied,
& is moued out of his place.
2 Heare the [b] sounde of his voyce, and the
noyse that goeth out of his mouth.
3 He directeth it vnder the whole heauen,
and his light vnto the ends of the worlde.
4 After it a noyse soundeth: he thundreth
with the voyce of his maiestie, and he wil
not stay [c] them when his voyce is heard.
5 God thundreth marueloussly w^t^ his voyce:
he worketh great things, which we knowe
not.
6 For he saith to the snowe, Be thou vpon ỹ
earth: [d] likewise to the smale raine and to
the great raine of his power.
7 With the force *thereof* he [e] shutteth vp
euerie man, that all men may knowe his
worke.
8 Then the beasts go into the denne, and
remaine in their places.
9 The whirle wi[n]de cometh out of ỹ South,
and the colde from the [f] North winde.
10 At the breath of God the frost is giuen,
& the breadth of the waters [g] *is* made narrowe.
11 He maketh also the cloudes to [h] labour,
to water *the earth*, & scatereth the cloude
of [i] his light.
12 And it is turned about by his gouernemēt, that thei may do whatsoeuer he commandeth them vpon the whole worlde:
13 Whether it be for [k] punishmēt, or for his
land, or of mercie, he causeth it to come.
14 Hearken vnto this, ô Iob: stand and consider the wonderous workes of God.
15 Didest thou knowe when God disposed
them? and caused the [l] light of his cloude
to shine?
16 Hast thou knowen the [m] varietie of the
cloude, & the wonderous workes of him,
that is perfite in knowledge?
17 *Or* how thy clothes are [n] warme, when he
maketh the earth quiet through the South
winde?
18 Hast thou stretched out ỹ heauens, which
are strong, & as a molten [o] glasse?
19 Tel vs what we shal say vnto him: *for* we
can not dispose *our matter* because of [p] darkenes.
20 Shal it be [q] tolde him when I speake? or
shal mā speake when he shalbe [r] destroied?
21 And now men se not the light, [s] which
shineth in the cloudes, but the winde passeth and clenseth them.
22 The [t] brightnes cometh out of ỹ North:
the praise *thereof is* to God, which is terrible.
23 *It is* the Almightie: we cā not finde him
out: *he is* excellent in power & iudgement,
& abundant in iustice: he [u] afflicteth not.
24 Let men therefore feare him: *for* he wil
not regarde any that are wise in their owne
conceit.

CHAP. XXXVIII.

God speaketh to Iob, and declareth the weakenes of man in the consideration of his creatures by whose excellencie the power, iustice and prouidence of the Creator is knowen.

1 THen answered the Lord vnto Iob
out of the [a] whirle winde, & said,
2 Who is this that [b] darkeneth the counsel
by wordes without knowledge?
3 Gird vp now thy loynes like a man: I [c] wil
demande of thee and declare thou vnto
me.
4 Where wast thou when I layed the [d] fundacions of the earth? declare, if thou hast
vnderstanding,
5 Who hathe layed the measures thereof, if
thou knowest, or who hathe stretched the
line ouer it:
6 Where vpon are the fundacions thereof
set: or who layed the corner stone thereof:
7 When the starres of the morning [e] praised *me* together, and all the [f] children of
God reioyced:
8 Or *who* hathe shut vp the sea with dores,
when it yssued and came forthe *as* out of
the wombe:
9 When I made the cloudes *as* a couering
thereof, and darkenes *as* the [g] swadeling
bandes thereof:
10 When I stablished my commandement
vpon it, and set barres and dores,
11 And said, Hetherto shalt thou come, but
no farther, and here [h] shal it staye thy
proude waues.
12 Hast thou commanded the [i] morning
since thy dayes? hast thou caused the morning to knowe his place?
13 That it might take holde of the corners
of the earth, and that the wicked might be
[k] shaken out of it?
14 It is turned as clay to facion, [l] & all stand
vp as a garment.
15 And from the wicked their light shalbe
taken away, and the hie arme shalbe broken.

y He sheweth that the raine hathe double vse: the one ỹ it declareth Gods iudgements, when it doeth ouerflowe any places, & ỹ other that it maketh ỹ lād fruteful.
z That is, one cloude to dash agaīst another.
a The colde vapour sheweth him: that is, the cloude of the hote exhalaciō, which being taken in ỹ colde cloude mouñteth vp towarde the place where ỹ fyre is, and so angre is ingendred: ỹ is, noise and thunder claps.

Chap. XXXVII.
a At the maruelling of the thunder, and lightenings: whereby he declareth that the faithful are liuely touched with the maiestie of God, whē they beholde his workes.
b That is, the thunder, whereby he speaketh to men to waken their dulnes and to bring them to the consideracion of his workes.
c Meaning, the raines and thunders.
d So ỹ nether smale raine nor great, snowe nor anie thing els cometh without Gods appointement.
e By raines & thunders God causeth men to kepe them selues within their houses.
f In Ebrewe it is called ỹ scatering winde, because it driueth away the cloudes & purgeth the ayre.
g That is, is frosen vp and dryed.
h Gather the vapours, and moue to & fro to water the earth.
i That is, the cloude ỹ hath lightenīg in it.
k Raine, colde, heat, tempestes and suche like are sent of God, ether to punish mā, or to profite ỹ earth, or to declare his fauour toward man, as Chap. 36, 31.
l That is, the lightning to breake forthe in the cloudes?
m Which is some time changed into raine, or snowe, or haile or suche like.
n Why thy clothes shulde kepe thee warme, when the South winde bloweth, rather then when anie other winde bloweth?
o For their clearenes.
p That is, our ignorance: signifying that Iob was so presumpteous that he wolde controle the workes of God.

q Hathe God nede that anie shulde tel him when mā murmureth agaīst him?
r If God wolde destroye a man, shulde he repine?
s The cloude stoppeth the shining of ỹ sunne, that mā cā not se it til the winde haue chased away ỹ cloude: and if man be not able to atteine to the knowledge of these things, how muche lesse of Gods iudgements?
t In Ebrewe, golde: meanīg faire wether and cleare as golde.
u Meaning, without cause.

Chap. XXXVIII.
a That his wordes might haue greater maiestie, and ỹ Iob might knowe with whome he had to do.
b Which by seking out the secret coūsel of God by mans reason, maketh it more obscure & sheweth his owne folie
c Because he had wished to dispute with God, Chap. 13, 3, God reasoneth with him to declare his rashnes.
d Seig he colde not iudge of those thīgs, ỹ were done so long before he was borne, he was not able to cōprehend all Gods workes: muche lesse the secret causes of his iudgements.
e The starres and dumme creatures are said to praise God, because his power, wisdome and goodnes is manifest & knowē therein.
f Meaning, the Angels.
g As thogh ỹ great sea were but as a litle babe in the hands of God to turne to & fro.
h That is, Gods decree and commandement, as verse 10.
i To wit, to rise, since thou wast borne?
k Who hauing in the night bene giuen to wickednes, can not abide the light but hide them selues.
l The earth which semed in the night to haue no forme, by the rising of the sunne is as it were created a newe, and all things therein clad with newe beautie.

16 Hast thou entred into the bottomes of
the sea? or hast thou walked to seke out the
[m] depth?
17 Haue the gates of death bene opened vnto thee? or hast thou sene the gates of the
shadow of death?
18 Hast thou perceiued the breadth of the
earth? tel if thou knowest all this.
19 Where is the way *where* light dwelleth?
and where is the place of darkenes,
20 That thou [n] shuldest receiue it in the
boundes thereof, and that thou shuldest
knowe the paths to the house thereof?
21 Knewest thou it, because thou wast then
borne, & *because* the nomber of thy daies *is*
great?
22 Hast thou entred into the treasures of
the snowe? or hast thou sene the treasures
of the hayle,
23 Which I haue [o] hid against the time of
trouble, against the day of warre & battel?
24 By what way is the light parted, *which*
scattereth the East winde vpon the earth?
25 Who hathe deuided the spowtes for the
raine? or the way for the lightening of the
thunders,
26 To cause it to raine on the earth where
no man is, & in the wildernes where there
is no man?
27 To fulfil the wilde & waste place, & to
cause the bud of the herbe to sprĩg forthe?
28 Who is the father of the raine? or who
hathe begotten the droppes of the dewe?
29 Out of whose wombe came the yce?
who hathe ingẽdred the frost of ỹ heauen?
30 The waters are hid [p] as *with* a stone: and
the face of the depth is frosen.
31 Cãst thou restraine the swete *influences* of
[q] ỹ Pleiades? or loose the bãds of [r] Orión?
32 Canst thou bring forthe [s] Mazzaróth in
their time? canst thou also guide [t] Arctú-
rus with his sonnes?
33 Knowest thou the course of heauen, or
cãst thou set [u] the rule thereof in ỹ earth?
34 Canst thou lift vp thy voyce to ỹ cloudes that the abundance of water may couer thee?
35 Cãst ỹ sende the lightenĩgs that thei may
walke, & say vnto thee, Lo, here we are?
36 Who hathe put wisdome in the [x] reines?
or who hathe giuen ỹ heart vnderstanding?
37 Who can nomber cloudes by wisdome?
or who can cause to cease the [y] bottels of
heauen,
38 When the earth groweth into hardenes,
[z] and the clottes are fast together?

m If thou art not able to seke out ỹ depth of the sea, how muche lesse art thou able to cõprehend ỹ counsel of God?

n That ỹ mighteest appoint it his way and limites.

o To punish mine enemies with them, as Exod. 9,18. iosh. 10,11.

p The yce couereth it, as thogh it were paued with stone.

q Which starres arise when the sunne is in Taurus, which is the spring time, & bring floures.

r Which starre bringeth in winter.

s Certeine starres so called: some thinke they were the twelue signes.

t The North starre ẘ those that are about him?

u Canst thou cause ỹ heauẽlie bodies to haue anie power ouer the earthlie bodies?

x In the secret partes of mã.

y That is, the clouds, wherein the water is conteined as in bottels.

z For when God doeth not open these bottels, the earth cometh to this inconuenience.

CHAP. XXXIX.

The bountie and prouidence of God, which extendeth euen to the yong rauens, giueth manful occasion to put his cõfidence in God. 37 Iob confesseth & hũbleth him self.

1 W[a]Ilt thou hunt the praye for the
lyon? or fil the appetite of ỹ lyons
whelpes,
2 When they couche in their places, & remaine in the couert to lye in waite?
3 Who prepareth for the rauen his meat,
when his byrdes [b] crye vnto God, wande-
ring for lacke of meat?
4 Knowest thou the time when the wilde
goates bring forthe yong? or doest thou
marke when the [c] hindes do calue?
5 Canst thou nomber the moneths that
they [d] fulfil? or knowest thou the time whẽ
they bring forthe?
6 They bowe them selues: they [e] bruise their
yong and cast out their sorowes.
7 *Yet* their yong waxe fat, and growe vp
with corne: they go forthe and returne not
vnto them.
8 Who hathe set the wilde asse at libertie?
or who hathe loosed the bondes of the
wilde asse?
9 *It is I* which haue made the wildernes
his house, and the [f] salt places his dwellings.
10 He derideth the multitude of the citie:
he heareth not the crye of the driuer.
11 He seketh out the mountaine for his pasture, & searcheth after euerie grene thĩg.
12 Wil the vnicorne [g] serue thee? or wil he
tary by thy crybbe?
13 Canst thou binde the vnicorne with his
band *to labour* in ỹ forrowe? or wil he plowe
the valleis after thee?
14 Wilt ỹ trust in him, because his strength
is great, and cast of thy labour vnto
him?
15 Wilt thou beleue him, that he wil bring
home thy sede, and gather it vnto thy
barne?
16 *Hast thou giuen* the pleasant wings vnto
the pecockes? or wings & fethers vnto the
ostriche?
17 Which leaueth his egges in the earth &
maketh [h] them hote in the dust,
18 And forgetteth that the fote might scater them, or that the wilde beast might
breake them.
19 He sheweth him self cruel vnto his yong
ones, *as* they were not his, *and* is without
feare, as if he trauailed [i] in vaine.
20 For God hathe depriued him of [k] wisdome, & hathe giuen him no parte of vnderstanding.
21 When [l] time *is*, he mounteth on hye: he
mocketh the horse and his rider.
22 Hast thou giuen the horse strength? *or*
couered his necke with [m] neying?
23 Hast thou made him afraied as the grashoper? his strong neying is feareful.
24 He [n] diggeth in the valley, & reioyceth
in *his* strength: he goeth forthe to mete the
harnest *man*.
25 He mocketh at feare, & is not afraied, &
turneth not backe from the sworde,
26 *Thogh* the quiuer rattle against him, the
glittering

a After he had declared Gods workes in the heauens, he sheweth his maruelous prouidence in earth, euẽ toward the brute beasts.

b Read Psal. 147,9.

c He chiefly maketh mencion of wilde goates & hindes, because they brĩg forthe their yong with moste difficultie

d That is, how lõg they go ẘ yong?

e Thei bring forthe with great difficultie.

f That is, the baren grounde where no good frutes growe.

g Is it possible to make the vnicorne tame? signifiing that if man can not rule a creature, that it is muche more impossible ỹ he shulde appoint the wisdome of God, whereby he gouerneth all the worlde.

h Thei write ỹ the ostrich couereth her egges in ỹ sand, and because ỹ cõutrey is hote and the sunne stil kepeth them warme, they are hatched.

i If he shulde take care for them.

k That is, to haue a care, & natural affection toward his yong.

l When the yong ostrich is growen vp, he out runneth the horse.

m That is, giuẽ hĩ courage? which is ment by neying and shaking his mane: for ẘ his breath he couereth his necke.

n He beateth ẘ his hoofe.

glittering speare and the shield.
27 He [o] swalloweth the grounde for fearcenes and rage, and he beleueth not that it
is the noyse of the trumpet.
28 He saith among the trumpets, Ha, ha:
he smelleth the battel a farre of, and the
noyse of the captaines, and the shouting.
29 Shal the hauke flie by thy wisdome, *stretching out* his wyngs toward the [p] South?
30 Doeth the egle mount vp at thy cōmandement, or make his nest on hye?
31 She abideth and remaineth in the rocke,
euen vpon the top of the rocke, and the
tower.
32 From thence she spieth for meat, *and* her
eyes beholde a farre of.
33 His yong ones also sucke vp blood: and
where the slaine *are*, there is she.
34 Moreouer the Lord spake vnto Iob, and
said,
35 Is this to [q] learne to striue with the
Almightie? he that reproueth God, let him
answer to it.
36 ¶ Then Iob answered the Lord, saying,
37 Beholde, I am [r] vile: what shal I answer
thee? I wil lay mine hand vpō my mouth.
38 Once haue I spoken, but I wil answer no
more, yea twise, but I wil procede no farther.

o He so riddeth ȳ groūde that it semeth nothing vnder him.

p That is, whē colde cometh, to flie into the warme countreis.

q Is this the way for a man that wil learne to striue w̄ God? which thing he reproueth in Iob.

r Whereby he sheweth that he repented, & desired pardon for his fautes.

CHAP. XL.

2 How weake mans power is, being compared to the workes of God: 10 Whose power appeareth in the creation, and gouerning of the great beastes.

1 AGaine the Lord answered Iob out of
* the whirlewinde, and said,
2 Gird vp now thy loynes like a man: I wil
demāde of thee, & declare thou vnto me.
3 Wilt thou disanul [a] my iudgement? or wilt
thou condemne me, that thou mayest be
iustified?
4 Or hast thou an arme like God? or doest
thou thunder with a voyce like him?
5 Decke thy self now with [b] maiestie and
excellencie, & araye thy self with beautie
and glorie.
6 Cast abroad the indignacion of thy
wrath, and beholde euerie one that is
proude, and abase him.
7 Loke on euerie one that is arrogant, *and*
bring him low: and destroy the wicked in
their place.
8 Hide them in the dust together, & binde
[c] their faces in a secret place.
9 Then wil I confesse vnto thee also, that
thy right hand can [d] saue thee.
10 ¶ Beholde now [e] Behemóth, (whome I
made [f] with thee) which eateth [g] grasse
as an oxe.
11 Beholde now, his strength *is* in his loines,
and his force *is* in the nauil of his belly.
12 *When* he taketh pleasure, his taile is like
a cedre: ȳ sinewes of his stones are wrapt
together.
13 His bones are *like* staues of brasse, *and*
his small bones like staues of yron.
14 [h] He is the chief of the wayes of God:
[i] he that made him, wil make his sworde to
approche vnto him.
15 Surely the mountaines bring him forthe
grasse, where all the beasts of the field
playe.
16 Lyeth he vnder the trees in the couert of
the rede and fennes?
17 Can the trees couer him with their shadowe? or can the willowes of the riuer cōpasse him about?
18 Beholde, he spoileth the riuer, [k] and hasteth not: he trusteth that he can drawe vp
Iordén into his mouth.
19 He taketh it with his eyes, and thrusteth
his nose through whatsoeuer meteth him.
20 ¶ Canst thou draw out [l] Liuiathán with
an hooke, and with a line which thou shalt
cast downe vnto his tongue?
21 Canst thou cast an hooke into his nose?
canst thou perce his iawes with an angle?
22 Wil he make manie [m] prayers vnto thee,
or speake thee faire?
23 Wil he make a couenant with thee? *and*
wilt thou take [n] him as a seruant for euer?
24 Wilt thou play with him as with a bird?
or wilt thou binde him for thy maides?
25 Shal the companions banket with him?
shal they deuide him among the marchants?
26 Canst thou fill the basket with his skinne? or the fishpanyer with his head?
27 Laye thine hand vpon him: remember
[o] the battel, *and* do nomore so.
28 Beholde, [p] his hope is in vaine: *for* shal
not one perish euen at the sight of him?

Chap. 38, 1.

a Signifying that they that iustifie them selues, condēne God as iniust.

b Meaning, ȳ these were ꝓpre vnto God, and belonged to no man.

c Cause them to dye if thou canst.

d Prouing hereby ȳ whosoeuer attributeth to him self power, & abilitie to saue him self, maketh him self God.

e This beast is thoght to be the eliphāt, or some other, w̄ is vnknowen.

f Whome I made aswel as thee.

g This cōmēderir the prouidēce of God toward mā: for if he were giuen to deuoure as a liō, nothing were able to resist him or contēt him.

h He is one of the chiefest workes of God amōg ȳ beasts.

i Thogh man dare not come nere him, yet God can kil him.

k He drinketh at leasure, and feareth no body.

l Meaning, the whale.

m Bacause he feareth lest thou shuldest take him.

n To do thy busines, & be at thy cōmandement?

o If thou once consider the danger, thou wilt not medle with him.

p To wit, that trusteth to take him.

CHAP. XLI.

1 By the greatnes of this monstre Liuiathán God sheweth his greatnes, and his power, which nothing can resist.

1 NOne *is* so fearce that dare stirre him
vp. Who is he then that can stand
[a] before me?
2 Who hathe preuented me that I shulde
[b] make an end? All vnder heauen is mine.
3 I wil not kepe silence *concerning* [c] his
partes, nor *his* power, nor his comely proportion.
4 Who can discouer the face [d] of his garment? or who shal come to him with a double [e] bridel?
5 Who shal [f] open the dores of his face?
his teeth are feareful round about.
6 The maiestie *of his scales is like* strong
shields, *and* are sure sealed.
7 One is set to another, that no winde can
come betwene them.
8 One is ioyned to another: they sticke together, that they can not be sondred.
9 His niesings [g] make the light to shine, &
his eyes *are* like ȳ eye lids of the morning.
10 Out of his mouth go lampes, *and* spar-

a If none dare stand against a whale, which is but a creature, who is able to cōpare with God the Creator?

b Who hathe taught me to accōplish my worke?

c The partes, and members of the whale.

d That is, who dare pul of his skinne?

e Who dare put a bridel in his mouth?

f Who dare loke in his mouth?

g That is, casteth out flames of fyre.

kes of fyre leape out.
11 Out of his nostrelles cometh out smoke,
as out of a boyling pot or caldron.
12 His breath maketh the coles burne: for a
flame goeth out of his mouth.
13 In his necke remaineth strength, & [h] labour is reiected before his face.
14 The members of his bodie are ioyned:
they are strong in them selues, *and* can not
be moued.
15 His heart is as strong as a stone, and as
hard as the nether milstone.
16 The mightie are afraied of his maiestie,
and for feare they faint in them selues.
17 When the sworde doeth touche him, he
wil not rise vp, *nor for* the speare, dart nor
habergeon.
18 He estemeth yron as strawe, and brasse as
rotten wood.
19 The archer can not make him flee: the
stones of the sling are turned into stubble
vnto him.
20 The dartes are counted as straw: and
he laugheth at the shaking of the speare.
21 Sharpe stones [i] are vnder him, and he
spreadeth sharpe things vpon the myre.
22 He maketh the depth to [k] boyle like a
pot, and maketh the sea like *a pot* of oyntment.
23 He maketh a path to [l] shine after him:
one wolde thinke the depth as an hore
head.
24 In the earth there is none like him: he is
made without feare.
25 He beholdeth [m] all hie things: he is a
King ouer all the children of pride.

CHAP. XLII.

6 The repentance of Iob. 9 He prayeth for his friends. 12 His goods are restored double vnto him. 13 His children, age and death.

1 Then Iob answered the Lord, and
said,
2 I knowe that thou canst do all things,
and that there is no [a] thoght hid from
thee.
3 Who is he that hideth counsel without
[b] knowledge? therefore haue I spokẽ that I
vnderstode not, *euen* things to wonderful
for me, [c] and *which* I knewe not.
4 Heare, I beseche thee, and I wil speake: I
wil demande of thee, [d] and declare thou
vnto me.
5 I haue [e] heard of thee by the hearing of
the eare, but now mine eye seeth thee.
6 Therefore I abhorre *my self*, and repent in
dust and ashes.
7 ¶ Now after that the Lord had spoken
these wordes vnto Iob, the Lord also said
vnto Eliphàz the Temanite, My wrath is
kindled against thee, and against thy two
friẽds: for ye haue not spokẽ of me ẏ thing
that is [f] right, like my seruant [g] Iob.
8 Therefore take vnto you now seuen bullockes, and seuen rams, and go to my seruant Iob, & offer vp for your selues a burnt
offring, and my seruant Iob shal [h] pray
for you: for I wil accept him, lest I shulde
put you to shame, because ye haue not spokẽ of me the thing, which is right, like my
seruant Iob.
9 So Eliphàz the Temanite, and Bildád
the Shuhite, *and* Zophár the Naamathite
went, and did according as the Lord had
said vnto them, and the Lord accepted
Iob.
10 ¶ Then the Lord turned the [i] captiuitie of Iob, when he prayed for his friẽds:
also the Lord gaue Iob twise so muche as
he had before.
11 Then came vnto him all his [k] brethrẽ,
and all his sisters, and all they that had bene of his acquaintance before, and did eat
bread with him in his house, and had com
passion of him, and comforted him for all
the euil, that the Lord had broght vpon
him, and euerie man gaue him a [*] piece of
money, & euerie one an earing of golde.
12 So the Lord blessed the last dayes of Iob
more then the first: for he had [l] fourtene thousand shepe, and six thousand camels, and a thousand yoke of oxen, and a
thousand she asses.
13 He had also seuen sonnes, and thre daughters.
14 And he called the name of one [m] Iemi-
máh, and the name of the second [n] Ke-
ziáh, and the name of the thirde [o] Keren-
happúch.
15 In all the land were no women founde so
faire as the daughters of Iob, and their father gaue them inheritance among their
brethren.
16 And after this liued Iob an hundreth
and fourtie yeres, and sawe his sonnes, and
his sonnes sonnes, *euen* foure generacions.
17 So Iob dyed, being olde, & ful of dayes.

h Nothing is peinful or hard vnto him

i His skinne is so hard that he lieth with as great ease on the stones as in the myre.

k Ether he maketh ẏ sea to seme as it boiled by his wallowing, or els he spowteth water in suche abundance, as it wolde seme that the sea boyled.

l That is, a white froth, & shinĩg streame before him.

m He despiseth all other beasts, & monsters, & is the proudest of all others.

Chap. XLII.

a No thoght so secret, but thou doest se it, nor anie thing that ẏ thinkest, but thou canst brĩg it to passe.

b Is there anie but I? for this God laid to his charge, Chap. 38,2.

c I cõfesse herein mine ignorance, and that I spake I wist not what.

d He sheweth that he wil be Gods scholer to learne of him.

e I knewe thee onely before by hearesay: but now thou hast caused me to fele what ẏ art to me, that I may resigne my self ouer vnto thee.

f You toke in hand an euil cause, in ẏ you condẽned him by his outward afflictiõs and not comforted him ẇ my mercies.

g Who had a good cause, but handeled it euil.

h When you haue reconciled your selues to him for the fautes that you haue committed against him, he shal pray for you, & I wil heare him.

i He deliuered him out of the affliction wherein he was.

k That is, all his kinred, read Chap. 19,13.

Or, lambe, or money so marked.

l God made him twise so riche in cattel as he was afore, & gaue him as manie children, as he had taken from him.

m That is, of long life, or beautiful as ẏ day.

n As pleasant as cassia, or swete spice.

o That is, the horne of beautie.

THE

THE *PSALMES of Dauid.

* Or, Praises according to the Ebrewes: and were chiefly institute to praise, and giue thankes to God for his benefites. Thei are called the Psalmes, or Sōgs of Dauid because the moste parte were made by him.

THE ARGVMENT.

This boke of Psalmes is set forthe vnto vs by the holie Gost to be estemed as a moste precious treasure, wherein all things are conteined that apperteine to true felicitie: aswel in this life present as in the life to come. For the riches of true knowledge, and heauenlie wisdome are here set open for vs, to take thereof moste abundantly. If we wolde knowe the great, and hie maiestie of God, here we may se the brightnes thereof shine moste clearely. If we wolde seke his incomprehensible wisdome, here is the schole of the same profession. If we wolde comprehend his inestimable boūtie, and approche nere thereunto, and fil your hands with that treasure, here we may haue a moste liuely, and comfortable taste thereof. If we wolde knowe wherein standeth our saluation, and how to atteine to life euerlasting, here is Christ our onely redemer, and mediator moste euidently described. The riche man may learne the true vse of his riches. The poore man may fynde ful contentation. He that wil reioyce, shal knowe the true ioe, and how to kepe measure therein. They that are afflicted and oppressed, shal se wherein standeth their comforte, and how they oght to praise God when he sendeth them deliuerance. The wicked and the persecuters of the children of God shal se how the hand of God is euer against them: and thogh he suffer them to prosper for a while, yet he brideleth them, in somuche as they can not touche an heere of ones head, except he permit them, and how in the end their destruction is moste miserable. Briefly, here we haue moste present remedies against all tentations, and troubles of minde and conscience, so that being wel practised herein, we may be assured against all dangers in this life, liue in the true feare, and loue of God, and at length atteine to that incorruptible crowne of glorie, which is laid vp for all them that loue the comming of our Lord Iesus Christ.

PSALME I.

Whether it was Esdras, or anie other that gathered the Psalmes into a boke, it semeth he did set this Psalme first in maner of a preface, to exhorte all godlie men to studie, and meditate the heauenlie wisdome. For the effect hereof is, 1 That they be blessed, which giue them selues wholy all their life to the holy Scriptures. 4 And that the wicked contemners of God, thogh they seme for a while happie, yet at length shal come to miserable destruction.

1 Blessed *is* the man that
doeth not walke in the
[a] counsel of the wicked,
nor stand in the way of
sinners, nor sit in the seat
of the scorneful:
2 But his delite *is* in the
*Law of the Lord, & in his [b] Law doeth he
meditate day and night.
3 For he shal be like a* tre planted by the
riuers of waters, that wil bring forthe her
frute in due season: whose leafe shal not
fade: so [c] whatsoeuer he shal do, shal prosper.
4 [d] The wicked *are* not so, but as the chaffe,
which the winde driueth away.
5 Therefore the wicked shal not stand in
the [e] Iudgem[e]nt, nor sinners in the assemblie of the righteous.
6 For the Lord [f] knoweth the way of the
righteous, and the way of the wicked shal
perish.

a When a man hathe giuē once place to euil counsel, or to his owne cōcupiscence, he beginneth to forget him self in his sin, & so falleth into contēpt of God, which cōtempt is called the seat of the scorners.
Deut.6,6. iosh.1,8. pro.6,20.
b In the holie Scriptures.
Iere.17,8.
c Gods children are so moystened euer with his grace, ỹ whatsoeuer cometh vnto them, tendeth to their saluation.
d Thogh the wicked seme to beare the swinge in this worlde, yet the Lord driueth them downe that thei shal not rise nor stand in the companie of the righteous.
e But tremble, when they fele Gods wrath.
f Doeth approue and prosper, like as not to knowe, is to reproue and reiect.

PSAL. II.

1 The Prophet Dauid reioyceth that notwithstanding his enemies rage, yet God wil cōtinue his kingdome for euer & aduāce it euen to the end of the worlde, 10 And therefore exhorteth Kings and rulers, that they wolde humbly submit them selues vnder Gods yoke, because it is in vaine to resiste God. Herein is figured Christs kingdome.

1 Why do the [a] heathen * rage, & the
people murmur in vaine?
2 The Kings of the earth band them selues,
and the princes are assembled together against the Lord, and against his *Christ.
3 [b] Let vs breake their bands, and cast their
cords from vs.
4 * *But* he that dwelleth in the heauen shal
laugh: the Lord shal haue thē in derisiō.
5 [c] Then shal he speake vnto them in his
wrath, & vexe them in his sore displeasure,
saying,
6 *Euen* I haue set my King vpon Zión mine holie mountaine.
7 I wil declare the [d] decree: *that is,* the Lord
hathe said vnto me,* Thou art my Sonne:
this [e] day haue I begotten thee.
8 Aske of me, & I shal giue thee the heathé
for thine inheritance, and the [f] endes of
the earth for thy possession.
9 *Thou shalt krush them with a sceptre of
yron, & breake them in pieces like a potters vessel.
10 [g] Be wise now therefore, ye Kings: be
learned ye Iudges of the earth.
11 Serue the Lord in feare, and reioyce in
trembling.
12 [h] Kisse the Sonne, lest he be angrie, and
ye [i] perish in the waie, when his wrath shal

a The conspiracie of ỹ Gentiles, ỹ murmuring of the Iewes, & power of Kings can not preuaile against Christ.
Act.4,25.
* Or, anointed.
b Thus the wicked say, ỹ they wil cast of the yoke of God & of his Christ.
Prou.1,26.
c Gods plagues wil declare that in resisting his Christ, they foght against him.
d To shewe that my vocation to the kingdome is of God.
Act.13,23. ebr.1,5.
e That is to say, as touching mans knowledge, be cause it was ỹ first time that Dauid appeared to be elected of God. So is it applied to Christ in his first comming & manifestatiō to the worlde.
f Not onely ỹ Iewes but the Gentiles also.
Reue.2,27.
g He exhorteth all rulers to repent in time.
h In signe of hommage.
i When the wicked shal say, Peace & reste, seming yet to be but in the midway of their purposes, then shal destructiō sodenly come, 2. Thessa.5,3.

suddenly burne.blessed *are* all that trust in
him.

PSAL. III.

1 Dauid driuẽ forthe of his kingdome, was greatly tormẽted in minde for his sinnes against God: 4 And therefore calleth vpon God, & waxeth bolde through his promeses against the great railings and terrors of his enemies yea, against death it self, which he sawe present before his eyes. 7 Finally he reioyceth for the good successe, that God gaue him, and all the Church.

A Psalme of Dauid, when he fled from his sonne Absalóm.

1 LOrd, how are mine aduersaries [a] increased? how manie rise against me?
2 Manie saye to my soule, *There is* no helpe
for him in God. [b] Sélah.
3 But thou Lord art a buckler for me: my
glorie, and the lifter vp of mine head.
4 I did call vnto the Lord with my voyce,
and he heard me out of his holie moũtaine. Sélah.
5 I laied me downe & slept, *and* rose vp a-
gaine: for the Lord susteined me.
6 I wil not be afrayed for [c] ten thousand
of the people, that shulde beset me round
about.
7 O Lord, arise: helpe me, my God: for
thou hast smitten all mine enemies vpon
the cheke bone: thou hast broken the teeth
of the wicked.
8 [d] Saluaciõ *belongeth* vnto the Lord, & thy
blessing *is* vpon thy people. Sélah.

a This was a token of his stable faith, that for all his troubles he had his recours to God.
b Sélah here signifieth a lifting vp of the voyce, to cause vs to consider the sentence, as a thing of great importance.
c When he cõsidered the trueth of Gods promes, and tried the same, his faith increased marueloussly.
d Be the dangers neuer so great or manie, yet God hathe euer meanes to deliuer his.

PSAL. IIII.

1 When Saúl persecuted him, he called vpõ God, trusting moste assuredly in his promes, and therefore boldely reproueth his enemies, who wilfully resisted his dominion, 7 And finally preferreth the fauour of God before all worldelie treasures.

[a] To him that excelleth on Neginóth. A Psal-me of Dauid.

1 HEare me when I call, [b] ô God of
my righteousnes: thou hast set me at
libertie, *when I was* [c] in distres: haue mercie vpon me and hearken vnto my prayer.
2 O ye [d] sonnes of men, how long *wil ye*
turne my glorie into shame, [e] louing vanitie *and* seking lyes? Sélah.
3 For be ye sure that the Lord hathe chosen
to him self [f] a godlie man: the Lord wil
heare when I cal vnto him.
4 [g] Tremble, and sinne not: examine your
owne heart vpon your bed, and be [h] stil.
Sélah.
5 [i] Offer the sacrifices of righteousnes, and
trust in the Lord.
6 Manie saye, Who wil shew vs *anie* [k] good?
but Lord, lift vp the light of thy countenãce vpon vs.
7 Thou hast giuen me more ioye of heart,
then *they haue had*, when their wheat and
their wine did abunde.
8 I wil laye me downe, & also slepe in peace: for thou, Lord, [l] onely makest me dwel
in sauetie.

a Among thẽ that were appointed to sing the Psalmes, and to play on the instruments, one was appoited chief to set ẏ tune, & to begine: who had the charge, because he was moste excellent, and he begã this Psal. on the instrument called Neginóth, or in a tune so called.
b Thou ẏ art ẏ defender of my iust cause.
c Bothe of mĩde and body.
d Ye that thinke your selues noble in this worlde.
e Thogh your enterprises please you neuer so muche, yet God wil bring them to noght.
f A King that walketh in his vocation.
g For feare of Gods Iudgemẽt.
h Cease your rage.
i Serue God purely and not with outward ceremonies.
k The multitude seke worldlie welth, but Dauid setteth his felicitie in Gods fauour.
l This worde in Ebrew may be referred to God, as it is here translated, or to Dauid, signifying that he shulde dwel as ioyfully alone, as if he had manie about him, because the Lord is with him.

PSAL. V.

1 Dauid oppressed with the crueltie of his enemies, and fearing greater dangers, calleth to God for succour, shewing how requisite it is that God shulde punish the malice of his aduersaries. 7 After being assured of prosperous succes, he conceiueth comfort, 12 Concluding that when God shal deliuer him, others also shal be partakers of the same mercies.

To him that excelleth vpon ° Nehilóth. A Psalme of Dauid.

° Or, a musical instrument or tune.

1 HEare my wordes, ô Lord: vnderstand
my [a] meditation.
2 Hearken vnto the voice of my crye, my
King & my God: for vnto thee do I praie.
3 Heare my voice in the morning, ô Lord:
for in the morning will I direct *me* vnto
thee, and I wil [b] wait.
4 For thou art not a God that loueth [c] wic
kednes: nether shal euil dwel with thee.
5 [d] The foolish shal not stand in thy sight:
for thou hatest all them that worke iniquitie.
6 Thou shalt destroy them that speake lyes:
the Lord wil abhorre the bloodie man and
deceitful.
7 But I [e] wil come into thine house in the
multitude of thy mercie: & in thy feare
wil I worship towarde thine holie Tẽple.
8 Lead me, ô Lord, in thy righteousnes,
[f] because of *mine* enemies: make thy waie
plaine before my face.
9 For no cõstancie *is* in their mouth: within, thei are very corruption: their * throte
is an open sepulchre, & they flatter with
their tongue.
10 Destroye them, ô God: ° let them [g] fall
from their counsels: cast them out for the
multitude of their iniquities, because thei
haue rebelled against thee.
11 And [h] let all them that trust in thee, reioyce & triumphe for euer, & couer thou
them: and let them, that loue thy Name,
reioyce in thee.
12 For thou Lord wilt ° blesse the righteous,
& with fauour [i] wilt compas him, as with
a shield.

a That is, my vehemẽt praier and secret complaint & sighings.
b With pacience & trust til I be heard.
c Seing that God of nature hateth wickednes, he must nedes punish the wicked & saue the godlie.
d Which rũne moste ragigly after their carnal affections.
e In ẏ deepest of his tentations he putteth his ful cõfidẽce in God.
f Because ẏ art iust, therefore lead me out of the dãgers of mine enemies.
* Rom.3,13.
° Or, cause them to erre.
g Let their deuises come to noght.
h Thy fauour towarde me shal confirme the faith of all others.
° Or, giue good successe.
i So that he shal be safe frõ all dãgers.

PSAL. VI.

1 When Dauid by his sinnes had prouoked Gods wrath, and now felt not onely his hand against him, but also conceiued the horrors of death euerlasting, he desireth forgiuenes, 6 Bewailing that if God toke him awaie in his indignation, he shulde lacke occasion to praise him as he was wont to do, whiles he was among men. 9 Then suddenly feling Gods mercie, he sharpely rebuketh his enemies which reioyced in his affliction.

To him that excelleth on Neginóth vpon the eight tune. A Psalme of Dauid.

1 O Lord, * [a] rebuke me not in thine
angre, nether chastise me in thy
wrath.

* Ier.10,24.
a Thogh I deserue destructi on, yet let thy mercie pitie my fraltie.

2 Haue

b For my whole stregth is abated.
c His conscie͂ce is also touched with the feare of Gods iudgement.

2 Haue mercie vpon me, ô Lord, for I
am weake: ô Lord heale me, for my [b] bones are vexed.
3 [c] My soule is also sore troubled: but
Lord how long wilt thou delay?
4 Returne, ô Lord: deliuer my soule: saue
me for thy mercies sake.

d He lamenteth that occasion shulde be taken fro͂ him to praise God in the Congregation.

5 For in [d] death *there is* no remembrance
of thee: in the graue who shal praise
thee?
6 I fainted in my mournĩg: I cause my bed
euery night to swimme, & watter my couche with my teares.

*Or, mine eye is eaten as it were with wormes.
e God sendeth comfort and boldnes in affliction, that we may triumphe ouer our enemies.

7 "Mine eye is dimmed for despite, & sunke
in because of all mine enemies.
8 [e] Awaie from me all ye workers of iniquitie: for the Lord hathe heard the voyce
of my weping.
9 The Lord hathe heard my peticion: the
Lord wil receiue my praier.
10 All mine enemies shal be confunded &
sore vexed: thei shal be turned backe, *and*
put to shame [f] suddenly.

f When the wicked thinke that the godlie shal perish, God deliuereth them suddenly and destroyeth their enemies.

PSAL. VII.

1 Being falsely accused by Chush one of Sauls kinsemen, he calleth to God to be his defender, 2 To whome he commendeth his innocencie, 9 First shewing that his conscience did not accuse him of anie euil towards Saul: 10 Next that it touched Gods glorie to awarde sentence against the wicked. 12 And so entring into the consideration of Gods mercies and promes, he waxeth bolde and derideth the vaine enterprises of his enemies, 16 Threatening that it shal fall on their owne necke that which they haue purposed for others.

"Or, kinde of tune.
"Or, accusatio͂.
2.Sam.16,7.

*"Shigaion of Dauid, which he sang vnto the Lord, concerning the " wordes of * Chush the sonne of Iemini.*

1 O Lord my God, in thee I put me trust:
saue me from all that persecute me,
and deliuer me.

a He desireth God to deliuer him fro͂ the rage of cruel Saul.
b Wherewith Chush chargeth me.

2 Lest [a] he deuoure my soule like a lion,
and teare it in pieces, while there is none
to helpe.
3 O Lord my God, if I haue done [b] this
thing: if there be *anie* wickednes in mine hands,

c If I reuerenced not Saul for affinities sake & preserued his life, 1.Sam.26,8.

4 [c] If I haue rewarded euil vnto him that
had peace with me, (yea I haue deliuered him that vexed me without cause)
5 *Then* let the enemie persecute my soule
& take it: yea, let him treade my life downe vpon the earth, and lay mine [d] honour
in the dust. Sélah.

d Let me not onely dye, but be dishonored for euer.

6 Arise, ô Lord, in thy wrath, and lift vp
thy selfe against the rage of mine enemies, and awake for me *according* to
the [e] iudgement *that* thou hast appointed.

e In promising me ÿ kĩgdome
f Not onely for mine, but for thy Church sake declare thy power.
g As touching my behauiour toward Saul & mine enemies.

7 So shal the Congregacion of the people
compasse thee about: for their sakes therefore [f] returne on hie.
8 The Lord shal iudge the people: iudge
thou me, ô Lord, according to my [g] righteousnes, and according to mine innocencie, *that is* in me.
9 Oh let the malice of the wicked come
to an end: but guide thou the iust: for the
righteous God tryeth the [h] hearts and
reines.

h Thogh they pretend a iuste cause against me, yet God shal iudge their hypocrisie.

10 My defence *is* in God, who preserueth
the vpright in heart.
11 God iudgeth the righteous, & him that
contemneth God, [i] euerie day.

i He doeth co͂tinually call ÿ wicked to repenta͂ce by some signes of his iudgementes.
k Except Saul turne his minde, I dye: for he hath bothe men and weapo͂s to destroy me, Thus co͂siderĩg his great dãger, he magnifieth Gods grace.
Isa.59,4. iob.15,35.

12 Except [k] he turne, he hathe whet his
sworde: he hathe bent his bowe and made
it readie.
13 He hathe also prepared him deadly weapons: he wil ordeine his arrowes for them
that persecute *me*.
14 * Beholde, he shal trauail with wickednes: for he hathe conceiued mischief, but
he shal bring forthe a lye.
15 He hathe made a pit and digged it, and
is fallen into the pit *that* he made.
16 His mischief shal returne vpon his owne head, and his crueltie shal fall vpon his
owne pate.
17 I wil praise the Lord according to his
[l] righteousnes, and wil sing praise to the
Name of the Lord moste high.

l In keping faithfully his promes ŵ me.

PSAL. VIII.

1 The Prophet considering the excellent liberalitie and fatherlie prouidence of God towards man, whome he made, as it were a god ouer all his workes, doeth not onely giue great thankes, but is astonished with the admiration of the same, as one nothing able to compasse suche great mercies.

To him that excelleth on " Gittith. A Psalme of Dauid.

"Or, kinde of the instrume͂t, or tune.
"Or, noble or maruelous.

1 O Lord our Lord, how "excellent is
thy Name in all the worlde! which
hast set thy glorie aboue the heauens.
2 Out of the [a] mouth of babes and sucke-
lings hast thou "ordeined strength, because of thine enemies, that thou mightest
" stil the enemie and the auenger.

a Thogh the wicked wolde hide Gods praises, yet ÿ very babes are suffície͂t witnesses of the same.
"Or, established.
"Or, confunde.

3 When I beholde thine heauens, *euen* the
workes of thy fingers, the moone and the
starres which thou hast ordeined,
4 What is [b] man, *say I*, that thou art mindful of him? and the sonne of mã, that thou
visitest him?
5 For thou hast made him a litle lower thẽ
[c] God, and crowned him with glorie and
worship.

b It had bene sufficient for him to haue set forthe his glorie by the heaue͂s, thogh he had not come so low as to man, which is but dust.
c Touchĩg his first creation.

6 Thou hast made him to haue dominion
in the workes of thine hands: thou hast
put all things vnder his fete:
7 All [d] shepe and oxen: yea, and the beastes
of the field:
8 The foules of the aire, and the fish of
the sea, & that which passeth through the
paths of the seas.
9 O Lord our Lord, how excellent is thy
Name in all the worlde!

d By the temporal gifts of mans creation he is led to co͂sider the benefites which he hathe by his regeneration through Christ

PSAL. IX.

1 After he had giuen thankes to God for the sundrie

victories that he had sent him against his enemies, and also proued by manifolde experience how readie God was at hãd in all his troubles. 14 He being now likewise in danger of newe enemies, desireth God to helpe him according to his wonte, 17 And to destroy the malicious arrogancie of his aduersaries.

To him that excelleth vpon ″ *Muth Labbén. A Psalme of Dauid.*

1 I Wil praise the Lord with my a whole
heart: I wil speake of all thy maruerlous workes.
2 I wil be glad, and reioyce in thee: I wil
sing praise to thy Name, ô moste high,
3 For that mine enemies are turned backe:
they shal fall, and perish at thy presence.
4 For b thou hast mainteined my right
& my cause: thou art set in the throne, *and*
iudgest right.
5 Thou hast rebuked the heathen: thou hast
destroied the wicked: ŷ hast put out their
name for euer and euer.
6 c O enemie, destructions are come to a
perpetual end, and thou hast destroied the
cities: their memorial is perished with
them.
7 But the Lord ″shal sit for euer: he hathe
prepared his throne for iudgement.
8 For he shal iudge the worlde in righteousnes, *&* shal iudge the people with equitie.
9 The Lord also wil be a refuge for the
d poore, a refuge in *due* time, *euen* in affliction.
10 And thei that knowe thy Name, wil trust
in thee: for thou, Lord, hast not failed thẽ
that seke thee.
11 Sing praises to the Lord, which dwelleth
in Zión: shewe the people his workes.
12 For e when he maketh inquisition for
blood, he remembreth it, *&* forgetteth not
the complaint of the poore.
13 Haue mercie vpon me, ô Lord: consider
my trouble, *which I suffre* of them that hate
me, thou that liftest me vp from the gates
of death.
14 That I maie shewe all thy praises within
the f gates of the daughter of Zión, *&* reioyce in thy saluacion.
15 The heathen are g sunken downe in the
pit, *that* thei made: in the net that they hid,
is their fote taken.
16 h The Lord is knowẽ by executing iudgement: the wicked is snared in the worke
of his owne hands. ″ Higgaión. Sélah.
17 The wicked shal turne into hel, *&* all
nations that forget God.
18 For the poore shal not be alwaie forgotten: the hope i of the afflicted shal not perish for euer.
19 Vp Lord: let not man preuaile: let the
heathen be iudged in thy sight.
20 Put them in feare, ô Lord, that the heathen maie know that they are but k men.
Sélah.

″ *Or, kinde of instrument, or tune: or for the death of Labbén or Goliath.*
a God is not praised, except the whole glorie be giuen to him alone.
b Howsoeuer ŷ enemie seme for a time to preuaile, yet God preserueth the iust.
c A derision of ŷ enemie, that mindeth nothing but destructiõ: but the Lord wil deliuer his, & bring him into iudgement.
″ *Or, reigne as Iudge.*
d Our miseries are meanes to cause vs to fele Gods present care ouer vs.
e Thogh God reuengeth not sodenly the wrõg done to his, yet he suffreth not the wicked vnpunished.
f In the open assemblie of the Church.
g For God ouerthroweth the wicked in their entreprises.
h The mercie of God toward his Saints must be declared, & the fall of the wicked must alwaies be cõsidered.
″ *Or, this is worthy to be noted.*
i God promiseth not to helpe vs before we haue felt the crosse.
k Which thei can not learne without ŷ feare of thy Iudgement.

PSAL. X.

1 He complaineth of the fraude, rapine, tyrannie, and all kindes of wrong, which worldelie men vse, assigning the cause thereof, that wicked men, being as it were drunken with worldelie prosperitie, and therefore setting aparte all feare and reuerence towardes God, thinke they may do all things without controwling. 15 Therefore he calleth vpon God to send some remedie against these desperat euils, 16 And at length comforteth him selfe with hope of deliuerance.

1 WHy standest thou farre of, ô Lord,
& hidest thee in a *due* time, *eue͂* in
affliction?
2 The wicked with pride doeth persecute
the poore: let them be taken in the crafts
that they haue imagined.
3 For the wicked hathe b made boast of his
owne hearts desire, and the couetous blesseth *him selfe*: he contemneth the Lord.
4 The wicked is so proude that he seketh
not *for God*: he thinketh alwaies, There is
no God.
5 His waies alwaie prosper: thy Iudgemẽts
are hie aboue his sight: therefore ″ defieth
he all his enemies.
6 He saieth in his heart, I shal ″ neuer be moued, c nor be in danger.
7 His mouth is ful of cursing and disceite
and fraude: vnder his tongue is mischief &
iniquitie.
8 d He lieth in waite in the villages: in the
secret places doeth he murther the innocent: his eies are bent against the poore.
9 He lieth in wait secretly, *euen* as a lyon in
his denne: he lieth in waite to spoile the
poore: he doeth spoile the poore, when he
draweth him into his net.
10 He crowcheth *&* boweth: therefore heapes of the e poore do fall by his might.
11 He hathe said in his heart, God hathe
forgotten, he hideth awaie his face, *&* wil
neuer se.
12 f Arise, ô Lord God: lift vp thine hand:
forget not the poore.
13 Wherefore doeth the wicked contemne
God? he saieth in his heart, Thou wilt not
g regarde.
14 *Yet* thou hast sene it: for thou beholdest
mischief and wrong, that thou maiest h take it into thine hãds: the poore cõmitteth
him selfe vnto thee: *for* thou art the helper
of the fatherles.
15 Breake thou the arme of the wicked and
malicious: searche his wickednes, *&* thou
shalt finde i none.
16 The Lord *is* King for euer and euer: the
k heathen are destroyed forthe of his
land.
17 Lord, thou hast heard the desire of the
poore: thou preparest their heart: thou bẽdest thine eare *to them*,
18 l To iudge the fatherles and poore, that
earthlie man ″ cause to feare no more.

a So sone as we enter into affliction, we thinke God shulde helpe vs, but that is not alwaies his due time.
b The wicked man reioyceth in his owne lust: he boasteth when he hathe that he wolde: he braggeth of his wit & welth, & blesseth him selfe, and thus blasphemeth the Lord.
″ *Or, puffeth at.*
″ *Or, not be moued because he was neuer in euil.*
c The euil shal not touche me, Isa. 28,15. or els he speaketh thus because he neuer felt euil.
d He sheweth that ŷ wicked haue many meanes to hide their crueltie, and therefore oght more to be feared.
e By the hypocrisie of thẽ that haue autoritie the poore are deuoured.
f He calleth to God for helpe, because wickednes is so farre ouergrowen ŷ God must now helpe or neuer.
g Therefore ŷ must nedes punish this their blasphemie.
h To iudge betwene the right and the wrong.
i For ŷ hast vtterly destroied him.
k The hypocrites, or suche as liue not after Gods law, shalbe destroyed.
l God helpeth when mãs helpe ceaseth.
″ *Or, destroy no more man vpon the earth.*

PSAL. XI.

1 This psalme conteineth two partes. In the first Dauid sheweth how harde assaltes of tentacions he susteined, & in how great anguish of minde he was, when Saúl did persecute him. 4 Then next he reioyceth that God sét him succour in his necessitie, declaring his iustice aswel in gouerning the good, and the wicked men, as the whole worlde.

¶ *To him that excelleth.* A Psal. *of Dauid.*

1 IN the Lord put I my trust: how say ye
then to my soule, [a] Flee to your mountaine *as* a birde?
2 For lo, the wicked bend their bowe, *and*
make readie their arrowes vpō the string,
that thei may secretly shoote at thē, which
are vpright in heart.
3 For the [b] fundaciōs are cast downe: what
hathe the [c] righteous done?
4 The Lord *is* in his holie palace: ŷ Lords
throne *is* in the heauen: his eyes [d] wil consider: his eye lids wil trye the children of
men.
5 The Lord wil trye the righteous: but the
wicked & him that loueth iniquitie, doeth
his soule hate.
6 Vpon the wicked he shal raine snares,
[e] fyer, and brimstone, & stormie tempest:
this is the [f] porcion of their cup.
7 For the righteous Lord loueth righteousnes: his countenance doeth beholde ŷ iust.

a This is the wicked counsel of his enemies to him & his cōpanions, to driue him from the hope of Gods pmes

b All hope of succour is taken awaie.

c Yet am I innocent and my cause good.

d Though all things in earth be out of order, yet God wil execute iudgement from heauen.

e As in the destruction of Sodóm and Gomorrha.

f Which they shal drinke euen to the dregs, Ezek. 23,34.

PSAL. XII.

1 The Prophet lamenting the miserable estate of the people, and the decay of all good order, desireth God spedely to send succour to his children. 7 The comforting him self and others with the assurance of Gods helpe he cōmendeth the constant veritie that God obserueth in keping his promises.

¶ *To him that excelleth vpon the eight tune. A Psalme of Dauid.*

1 HElpe Lord, for there is not [a] a godlie
man left: for the faithful are failed
from among the children of men.
2 They speake deceitfully euerie one with
his neighbour, [b] flattering with their lippes, *and* speake with a double heart.
3 The Lord cut of all flattering lippes, &
the tongue that speaketh proude things:
4 Which haue said, [c] With our tongue
wil we preuaile: our lippes are our owne:
who is lord ouer vs?
5 [d] Now for the oppresion of the nedie,
& for the sighes of the poore, I wil vp saieth the Lord, *and* wil [e] set at libertie him,
whome the wicked hathe snared.
6 The wordes of the Lord *are* pure wordes, *as* ŷ siluer, tryed in a fornace of earth,
fined seuen folde.
7 Thou wilt kepe [f] them, ô Lord: thou wilt
preserue him from this generaciō for euer.
8 The wicked walke on euerie side: when
they are exalted, [g] *it is* a shame for the
sonnes of men.

a Which dare defende the trueth, & shew mercie to the oppressed.

b He meaneth ŷ flaterers of the courte, ŵ hurt him more with their tongues then with their weapons.

c They thinke thē selues able to persuade whatsoeuer they take in hand

d The Lord is moued with the complaits of his, & deliuereth in the end from all dangers.

e Because the Lordes worde and promes is true & vnchāgeable, he wil performe it & preserue the poore from this wicked generation.

f That is, thine, thogh he were but one man.

g For thei suppres ŷ godlie and mainteine the wicked.

PSAL. XIII.

1 Dauid as it were ouercome with sundrie and newe afflictions, fleeth to God as his onelie refuge 3 And so at the length being encouraged through Gods promises, he conceiueth moste sure confidence against the extreme horrors of death.

¶ *To him that excelleth. A Psalme of Dauid.*

1 HOw long wilt ŷ forget me, ô Lord,
[a] for euer? how long wilt thou hyde
thy face from me?
2 How long shal I take [b] cōusel within my
self, *hauing* wearines daiely in mine heart?
how long shal mine enemie be exalted a-
boue me?
3 Beholde, & heare me, ô Lord my God:
lighten mine eyes, that I slepe not in
death:
4 Lest mine enemie saie, I haue [c] preuailed against him: & they that afflict me, reioyce when I slide.
5 But I trust in thy [d] mercie: mine heart shal
reioyce in thy saluacion: I wil sing to the
Lord, because he hathe [e] delt louingly
with me.

a He declareth ŷ his afflictiōs lasted a long time, & ŷ his faith fainted not.

b Chāging my purpose as the sickemā doeth his place.

c Which might turne to Gods dishonour, if he did not defend his.

d The mercie of God is the cause of our saluacion.

e Bothe by the benefites past and by others to come.

PSAL. XIIII.

1 He describeth the peruerse nature of men, which were so growen to licēciousnes, that God was broght to vtter contempt. 7 For the which thing althogh he was greatly grieued, yet being persuaded that God wolde send some present remedie, he comforteth him self & others.

¶ *To him that excelleth.* A Psalme *of Dauid.*

1 THe foole hathe said in his heart, [a] *There is* no God: thei haue [b] corrupted,
and done an abominable worke: *there is*
none that doeth good.
2 The Lord loked downe from heauen
vpon the children of men, to se if there
were anie that wolde vnderstand, and seke
God.
3 [c] All are gone out of the way: they are all
corrupt: there is none that doeth good, no
not one.
4 Do not all ŷ workers of iniquitie knowe
that they eat vp my people, *as* they eat
bread? they call not vpon the Lord.
5 [d] There they shal be taken with feare,
because God *is* in the generacion of the
iust.
6 You haue made [e] a mocke at the counsel of the poore, because the Lord *is* his
trust.
7 Oh giue saluacion vnto [f] Israél out of
Zión: when the Lord turneth the captiuitie of his people, *then* Iaakób shal reioyce, and Israél shal be glad.

Psal. 53.

a He sheweth that the cause of all wickednes is to forget God.

b There is nothing but disorder & wickednes among them.

c Dauid here maketh comparison betwene the faithful and the reprobat: but S. Paul speaketh the same of all mē naturally, Rom. 3,10

d Where they thinke them selues moste sure.

e You mocke them that put their trust in God.

f He prayeth for the whole Church, whome he is assured God wil deliuer: for none but he onely can do it.

PSAL. XV.

1 This Psalme teacheth on what conditiō God did chuse the Iewes for his peculiar people, and wherefore he placed his Temple among them, which was to the intent that they by liuing vprightely and godly, might witnes that they were his special and holie people.

¶ *A Psalme of Dauid.*

1 LOrd, who shal dwel in thy Tabernacle? who shal rest in thine holie Mou-
tayne?

a First God requireth vprightenes of life, next doĩg wel to others, and thirdely trueth and simplicitie in our wordes.

2 He that [a] walketh vprightly and worketh righteousnes, and speaketh the trueth in his heart.
3 He that sclandreth not with his tongue, nor doeth euil to his neighbour, nor receiueth a false reporte against his neighbour.

b He that flattereth not the vngodlie in their wickednes.

4 [b] In whose eyes a vile persone is cõtemned, but he *honoreth* them that feare the Lord: he that sweareth to his *owne* hinderance and changeth not.

c To the hinderance of his neighbour.
d That is, shal not be cast forthe of the Church as hypocrites.

5 He that [c] giueth not his money vnto vsurie, nor taketh rewarde against the innocent: he that doeth these things, [d] shal neuer be moued.

PSAL. XVI.

1 *Dauid prayeth to God for succour, not for his workes, but for his faiths sake. 4 Protesting that he hateth all idolatrie, taking God onelie for his comfort and felicitie. 8 Who suffreth his to lacke nothing.*

*Or, a certeine tune.

¶ [*] *Michtám of Dauid.*

a He sheweth that we can not call vpon God, except we trust in hĩ.
b Thogh we cã not enriche God, yet we must bestowe Gods gifts to the vse of his children.

1 PReserue me, ô God: for in thee do I [a] trust.
2 *O my soule*, thou hast said vnto the Lord, Thou art my Lord: my [b] weldoing *extendeth* not to thee,
3 *But* to the Saints that are in the earth, and to the excellent: all my delite is in them.

c As grief of conscience & miserable destruction.
d He wolde nether by outwarde professiõ nor in heart nor in mouth cõsent to their idolatries.

4 The [c] sorowes of them, that offer to another *god*, shal be multiplied: [d] their offrings of blood wil I not offer, nether make mẽcion of their names with my lippes.
5 The Lord *is* the porcion of mine inheritance and of my cup: thou shalt mainteine my lot.

e Wherewith my porcion is measured.

6 The [e] lines are fallen vnto me in pleasant places: yea, I haue a faire heritage.

f God teacheth me continually by secret inspiraciõ
g The faithful are sure to perseuere to the end.

7 I wil praise the Lord, who hathe giuen me counsel: my [f] reines also teache me in the nights.
8 I haue set the Lord alwayes before me: for he is at my right hand: *therefore* I [g] shal not slide.

h That is, I reioyce bothe in bodie & in soule.
i This is chiefly ment of Christ, by whose resurrection all his mẽbers haue immortalitie.
k Where God fauoreth, there is perfite felicitie.

9 Wherefore [h] mine heart is glad and my tongue reioyceth: my flesh also doeth rest in hope.
10 For thou [i] wilt not leaue my soule in the graue: nether wilt thou suffer thine holie one to se corruption.
11 Thou wilt shewe me the path of life: in thy [k] presence *is* the fulnes of ioye: *and* at thy right hãd there *are* pleasures for euermore.

PSAL. XVII.

1 *Here he complaineth to God of the cruel pride and arrogancie of Saul, and the rest of his enemies, who thus raged without anie cause giuen on his parte. 6 Therefore he desireth God to reuenge his innocencie, and deliuer him.*

¶ *The prayer of Dauid.*

a My righteo[us] cause.

1 HEare [a] the right, ô Lord, cõsider my crye: hearken vnto my prayer of lips vnfained.

b The vengeãce that ÿ shalt shewe against mine enemies.

2 Let my [b] sentence come forthe from thy presence, & let thine eyes beholde equitie.

c When thy Spirit examined my conscience.
d I was innocent towarde mine enemie bothe in dede and thoght.

3 Thou hast [c] proued & visited mine heart in the night: thou hast tryed me, & foundest nothing: *for* I was purposed that my [d] mouth shulde not offend.

e Thogh the wicked prouoked me to do euil for euil, yet thy worde kept me backe.

4 Concerning the workes of men, by the [e] wordes of thy lippes I kept me from the paths of the cruel man.
5 Stay my steps in thy paths, that my fete do not slide.

f He was assured that God wolde not refuse his request.

6 I haue called vpon thee: [f] surely thou wilt heare me, ô God: incline thine eare to me, & hearken vnto my wordes.

g For all rebell against thee, ÿ trouble thy Churche.

7 Shewe thy maruelous mercies, *thou* that art the Sauiour of them that trust *in thee*, from suche as [g] resist thy right hand.
8 Kepe mẽ as the apple of the eye: hide me vnder the shadow of thy wings,
9 From the wicked that oppresse me, *from mine* enemies, which compasse me rounde about for [h] *my* soule.

h For their crueltie can not be satisfied but with my death.
i Thei are puft vp with pride, as the stomake that is choked with fat.

10 They are inclosed in their owne [i] fatt, *and* they haue spoken proudly with their mouth.
11 They haue compassed vs now in our steps: they haue set their eyes to bring downe to the grounde:

k Stop his rage
*Or, which is thy sworde.
l By thine heauenlie power.
*Or, whose tyrãnie hathe to lõg endured.

12 Like as a lyon that is gredie of praye, & as it were a lyons whelpe lurking in secret places.
13 Vp Lord, [k] disapoint him: cast him downe: deliuer my soule from the wicked *with thy sworde,

m And fele not the smart that Gods children oft times do.
n This is ÿ ful felicitie, comforting against all assaltes, to haue the face of God & fauorable countenãce opened vnto vs.
o And am deliuered out of my great troubles.

14 Frõ men by thine [l] hand, ô Lord, from men* of the worlde, who haue their [m] porcion in this life, whose belies thou fillest with thine hid treasure: their childrẽ haue ynough, and leaue the rest of their substãce for their children.
15 *But* I wil beholde [n] thy face in righteousnes, & when I [o] awake, I shalbe satisfied with thine image.

PSAL. XVIII.

1 *This Psalme is the first beginning of his gratulacion, and thankesgiuing in the entring into his kingdome, wherein he extolleth & praiseth moste highly the maruelous mercies and grace of God, who hathe thus preserued and defended him. 32 Also he setteth forthe the image of Christs kingdome, that the faithful may be assured that Christ shal alwayes conquer & ouercome by the vnspeakeable power of his Father, thogh all the whole worlde shulde striue there against.*

¶ *To him that excelleth. A Psalme of Dauid the seruant of the Lord, which spake vnto the Lord the wordes of this song (in the day that the Lord deliuered him from the hand of all his enemies, & from the hand of Saul) and said,*

2.Sam.22,1.
a He vseth this deuersitie of names, to shewe ÿ as the wicked haue many meanes to hurt, so God hathe manie waies to helpe

1 I *Wil loue thee derely, ô Lord my strength.
2 [a] The Lord *is* my rocke, and my fortresse, and

and he that deliuereth me, my God & my
strength: in him wil I trust, my shield, the
horne also of my saluaciō, & my refuge.
3 I wil call vpon the Lord, which is worthie to be [b] praised: so shal I be safe from
mine enemies.
4 The [c] sorowes of death compassed me,
and the floods of wickednes made me a-
fraied.
5 The * sorowes of the graue haue cōpassed
me about: the snares of death ouertoke me.
6 *But* in my trouble did I call vpon the
Lord, and cryed vnto my God: he heard
my voyce out of his Temple, and my
crye did come before him, *euen* into his e-
ares.
7 [d] Then the earth trembled, and quaked:
the fundacions also of the mōutaines moued and shoke, because he was angrie.
8 Smoke went out at his nostrels, and a [e] cōsuming fyre out of his mouth: coles were
kindled thereat.
9 He bowed the heauens also and came
downe, and [f] darkenes *was* vnder his fete.
10 And he rode vpon [g] Cherúb and did
flie, and he came flying vpon the wings of
the winde.
11 He made darkenes his [h] secret place, &
his pauilion rounde about him, *euen* darkenes of waters, *and* cloudes of the aire.
12 At the brighnes of his presence his
cloudes passed, hailestones & coles of fyre.
13 The Lord also thundred in the heauen,
and the Highest gaue [i] his voyce, hailestones and coles of fyre.
14 Then he sent out [k] his arrowes & scatered them, and he increased lightnings
and destroyed them.
15 And the chanels of waters were sene, and
the [l] fundaciōs of the worlde were discouered at thy rebuking, ô Lord, at the blasting of the breath of thy nostrels.
16 He hathe sent downe from aboue *and* taken me: he hathe drawen me out of manie
[m] waters.
17 He hathe deliuered me from my [n] strōg
enemie, and from them which hate me: for
they were [o] to strong for me.
18 They preuented me in the daye of my
calamitie: but the Lord was my stay.
19 He broght me forthe also into a large
place: [p] he deliuered me because he fauored me.
20 The Lord rewarded me according to
my [q] righteousnes: according to the purenes of mine hands he recompensed me:
21 Because I kept the wayes of the Lord, &
did not wickedly against my God.
22 For all his Lawes *were* before me, and I
did not cast away his [r] commandements
from me.
23 I was vpright also with him, & haue kept
me from my [s] wickednes.

b For none cā obteine their requests of God, ÿ ioyne not his glorie with their petition.
c He speaketh of the dāgers and malice of his enemies, frō the which God had deliuered him.
* Or, cordes, or cables.
d A descriptiō of the wrath of God against his enemies after he had heard his praiers.
e He sheweth how horrible Gods iudgements shalbe to the wicked.
f Darknes signifieth the wrath of God, as the cleare light signifieth Gods fauour.
g This is described at large Psal. 104.
h As a King angrie with ÿ people, wil not shew him self vnto them.
i Thundred, lightened, and hailed.
k His lightenings.
l That is, the depe bottoms were sene, whē the red Sea was deuided.
m Out of sundrie, and great dangers.
n To wit, Saúl.
o Therefore God sent me succour.
p The cause of Gods deliuerance is his onelie fauour & loue to vs.
q Dauid was sure of his righteous cause and good behauiour toward Saul & his enemies, & therefore was assured of Gods fauour & deliuerance.
r For all his dangers he exercised him self in the Law of God.
s I nether gaue place to their wicked tentations, nor to mine owne affections.

24 Therefore ÿ Lord rewarded me according to my righteousnes, & according to
the purenes of mine hands in his sight.
25 With the [t] godlie thou wilt shewe thy
self godlie: with the vpright mā thou wilt
shewe thy self vpright.
26 With the pure thou wilt shewe thy self
pure, & with the frowarde thou wilt shewe
thy self froward.
27 Thus thou wilt saue the poore people,
& wilt [u] cast downe the proude lokes.
28 Surely thou wilt light my candel: the
Lord my God wil lighten my darkenes.
29 For by thee I haue [x] broken through
an hoste, and by my God I haue leaped
ouer a wall.
30 The waye of God is vncorrupt: the
[y] worde of the Lord is tryed *in the fyre*: he
is a shield to all that trust in him.
31 For who is God besides the Lord? and
who is mightie saue our God?
32 God girdeth me with strength, and maketh my [z] waye vpright.
33 He maketh my fete like hindes *fete*, and
setteth me vpon mine [a] high places.
34 He teacheth mine hands to fight: so that
a bowe of * brasse is broken with mine
armes.
35 Thou hast also giuē me ÿ [b] shield of thy
saluacion, and thy right hand hathe stayed
me, and thy [c] louing kindenes hathe caused me to increase.
36 Thou hast enlarged my steppes vnder
me, and mine heles haue not slid.
37 [d] I haue pursued mine enemies, and takē
them, and haue not turned againe til I had
consumed them.
38 I haue wounded thē, that they were not
able to rise: they are fallen vnder my fete.
39 For thou hast girded me with strength
to battel: them, that rose against me, thou
hast subdued vnder me.
40 And thou hast [e] giuen me the neckes of
mine enemies, that I might destroye them
that hate me.
41 They [f] cryed, but there was none to saue
them, euen vnto the Lord, but he answered
them not.
42 Then I did beate them smale as the dust
before the winde: I did tread them flat as
the claye in the stretes.
43 Thou hast deliuered me from the contentions of the people: thou hast made
me the head of the [g] heathen: a people, *whome* I haue not [h] knowen, shal serue me.
44 As sone as thei heare, thei shal obey me:
the strangers shal [i] be in subiection to me.
45 Strangers shal [k] shrinke away, & feare
in their priuie chambers.
46 Let the Lord liue, and blessed be my
strength, and the God of my saluacion be
exalted.

t Here he speaketh of God accordīg to our capacitie, who sheweth mercie to his & punisheth the wicked, as is said also, Leuit. 26, 21.
u When their sinne is come to the ful measure.
x He attributeth it to God that he bothe gate the victorie in ÿ field, & also destroyed the cities of his enemies.
y Be the dangers neuer so manie or great, yet Gods promes must take effect.
z He giueth good successe to all mine enterprises
a As towres and fortes, which he toke out of the hands of Gods enemies.
* Or, stele.
b To defend me frō dāgers.
c He attributeth the beginning, continuāce & increase in weldoing onely to Gods fauour.
d Dauid declareth that he did nothing besides his vocation, but was stirred vp by Gods Spirit to execute his iudgements.
e Thou hast giuē thē into mine hands to be slaine.
f Thei that reiect ÿ crye of the afflicted, God wil also reiect them, whē thei crye for helpe: for ether peine or feare cause those hypocrites to crye.
g Which dwelt roūd about me
h The kingdome of Christ is in Dauids kīgdome prefigured: who by ÿ preaching of his worde bringeth all to his subiection.
i Or, lye: signifying a subiection constrained & not voluntarie.
k Feare shal cause them to be afraied & come forthe of their secret holes & holdes to seke pardō.

47 *It is* God that giueth me *power* to auẽge me,and subdueth the people vnder me.

48 O my deliuerer from mine enemies, euen thou hast set me vp from them, that rose against me: thou hast deliuered me from the [l] cruel man.

49 Therefore [m] I wil praise thee,ô Lord, among the nations, and wil sing vnto thy Name.

50 Great deliuerances giueth he vnto his King,& sheweth mercie to his anointed, *euen* to Dauid,and to his [n] sede for euer.

l That is, Saul, who of malice persecuted hĩ.
m This prophecie apperteineth to the kingdome of Christ,and vocation of the Gentiles, as Rom.15,9.
n This did not properly apperteine to Salomón, but to Iesus Christ.

PSAL. XIX.

1 To the intent he might moue the faithful to a deeper consideration of Gods glorie,he setteth before their eyes the moste exquisite workemanship of the heauens with their proportion,and ornaments: 8 And afterward calleth thẽ to the Law,wherein God hathe reueiled him self more familiarly to his chosen people. The which peculiar grace by commending the Law he setteth forthe more at large.

¶ *To him that excelleth. A Psalme of Dauid.*

1 THe [a] heauens declare the glorie of God, and the firmament sheweth the worke of his hands.

2 [b] Daie vnto daie vttereth the same, and night vnto night teacheth knowledge.

3 *There is* no speache nor [c] language, *where* their voyce is not heard.

4 Their [d] line is gone forthe through all the earth, and their wordes into the ends of the worlde: in them hathe he set a tabernacle for the sunne.

5 Which commeth forthe as a bridegrome out of his [e] chambre, *and* reioyceth like a mightie man to runne *his* race.

6 His going out *is* from the end of the heauen, and his compas *is* vnto the ends of the same, & none is hid from the heate thereof.

7 The [f] Law of the Lord is perfite, conuerting the soule: the testimonie of the Lord is sure, and giueth wisdome vnto the simple.

8 The statutes of the Lord *are* right and reioyce the heart: the commandement of the Lord *is* pure, and giueth light vnto the eyes.

9 The feare of the Lord *is* cleane, and indureth for euer: the iudgements of the Lord *are* [g] trueth: they are righteous [h] all together,

10 And more to be [i] desired then golde, yea,then muche fine golde: swetter also thẽ honie and the honie combe.

11 Moreouer,by them *is* thy seruant made circumspect, *&* in keping of them there *is* great [k] rewarde.

12 Who can vnderstand *his* [l] fautes? clense me from secret *fautes*.

13 Kepe thy seruant also from [m] presumpteous sinnes: let them not reigne ouer me: [n] so shal I be vpright, and made cleane from muche wickednes.

14 Let the wordes of my mouth, and the [o] meditation of mine heart be acceptable in thy sight, ô Lord, my strength, and my redeemer.

a He reprocheth vnto mã his ingratitude, seing ŷ heauens, which are dumme creatures, set forthe Gods glorie.
b The continual successe of the daye & the night is sufficiẽt to declare Gods power and goodnes.
c The heauens are a scholemaster to all natiõs, be they neuer so barbarous.
d The heauens are as a line of great capital letters to shewe vnto vs Gods glorie.
e Or, vaile. The maner was that the bride and bridegrome shuld stand vnder a vaile together, & after come forthe ŵ great solemnitie and reioycing of ŷ assemblie.
f Though the creatures can not serue, yet this oght to be sufficient to lead vs vnto him.
g So that all mãs inuentiõs and intenciõns are lies.
h Euerie one without exception.
i Except Gods worde be estemed aboue all worldlie things, it is contemned.
k For God accepteth our indeuour, though it be farre vnperfite.
l Then there is no rewarde of duetie, but of Grace: for where sinne is, there death is the rewarde.
m Which are done purposly and of malice.
n If thou suppresse my wicked affections by thine holie Spirit.
o That I may obey thee in thoght, worde and dede.

PSAL. XX.

1 A prayer of the people vnto God,that it wolde please him to heare their King & receiue his sacrifice, which he offred before he went to battel against the Ammonites.

¶ *To him that excelleth. A Psalme of Dauid.*

1 THe [a] Lord heare thee in the daye of trouble: the [b] Name of the God of Iaakób defende thee:

2 Send thee helpe from the Sanctuarie, and strengthen thee out of Zión.

3 Let him remember all thine offrings, and [c] turne thy burnt offrings into asshes. Sélah:

4 *And* grante thee according to thine heart, and fulfil all thy purpose:

5 *That* we may reioyce in thy [d] saluacion, and set vp the banner in the Name of our God, *when* the Lord shal performe all thy petitions.

6 Now [e] know I that the Lord wil helpe his anointed, *and* wil heare him from his [f] Sanctuarie, by the mightie helpe of his right hand.

7 Some *trust* in chariots, and some in horses: but we wil remember the Name of the Lord our God.

8 [g] They are broght downe and fallen, but we are risen, and stande vpright.

9 Saue Lord: [h] let the King heare vs in the day that we call.

a Hereby Kings are also admonished to call to God in their affaires.
b The vertue, power & grace of God.
c In token ŷ thei are acceptable vnto him.
d Granted to the King, in whose wealth our felicitie standeth.
e The Church feeleth that God hathe heard their petition.
f As by the visible Sãctuarie Gods familiaritie appeared toward his people, so by the heauenlie is ment his power & maiestie.
g The worldelings that put not their onely trust in God.
h Let the King be able to deliuer vs by thy strength, when we seke vnto him for succour.

PSAL. XXI.

1 Dauid in the persone of the people praiseth God for the victorie, attributing it to God, and not to the strength of man. Wherein the holie Gost directeth the faithful to Christ, who is the perfection of this kingdome.

¶ *To him that excelleth. A Psalme of Dauid.*

1 THe King shal [a] reioyce in thy strẽgth, ô Lord: yea, how greatly shal he reioyce in thy saluation!

2 Thou hast giuen him his hearts desire, & hast not denied *him* the request of his lippes. Sélah.

3 For thou [b] didest preuent him with liberal blessings, *&* didest set a crowne of pure golde vpon his head.

4 [c] He asked life of thee, *and* thou gauest him a long life for euer and euer.

5 His glorie *is* great in thy saluaciõ: dignitie and honour hast thou layed vpon him.

6 For thou hast set him *as* [d] blessings for euer: thou hast made him glad with the ioye of thy countenance.

7 Because the King trusteth in the Lord, and in the mercie of the most High, he shal not slide.

8 [e] Thine hand shal finde out all thine ene-

a Whẽ he shal ouercome his enemies, and so be assured of his vocatiõ.
b Thou declaredst thy liberal fauour toward him before he praied.
c Dauid did not onely obteine life, but also assurance that his posteritie shulde reigne for euer.
d Thou hast made him thy blessings to others, & a perpetual exãple of thy fauour for euer.
e Here he describeth the power of Christs kingdome against the enemies thereof.

mies, *and* thy right hand shal finde out thẽ that hate thee.

9 Thou shalt make them like a fyrie ouen in time of thine angre: the Lord shal destroy them in his [f] wrath, and the fyer shal deuoure them.

10 Their frute shalt thou destroy from the earth, and their sede from the children of men.

11 For they [g] intended euil against thee, *and* imagined mischief, *but* they shal not preuaile.

12 Therefore shalt thou put them [h] aparte, & the strings of thy bowe shalt thou make ready against their faces.

13 [i] Be thou exalted, ô Lord, in thy strẽgth: so wil we sing and praise thy power.

f This teacheth vs paciently to endure the crosse til God destroye the aduersarie.

g Thei laied as it were their nets to make Gods power to giue place to their wicked enterprises.

h As a marke to shote at.

i Mainteine thy Church against thine aduersaries, ý we may haue ample occasiõ to praise thy Name.

PSAL. XXII.

1 Dauid cõplained because he was broght into suche extremities, that he was past all hope, but after he had rehearsed the sorowes & griefs, wherewith he was vexed, 10 He recouereth him self frõ the bottomles pit of tentations and groweth in hope. And here vnder his owne persone he setteth forthe the figure of Christ, whome he did forese by the spirit of prophecie, that he shulde maruelously & strangely be dejected & abased, before his Father shulde raise & exalte him againe.

¶ To him that excelleth vpon [*] Aiieleth Hasshahar. A Psalme of Dauid.

1 MY [a] God, my God, why hast thou forsaken me, & art so farre from mine health, *and* from the wordes of my [b] roaring?

2 O my God, I crye by daie, but thou hearest not, & by night, but [*] haue no audiẽce.

3 But thou art holie, and doest inhabite the [c] praises of Israél.

4 Our fathers trusted in thee: they trusted, and thou didest deliuer them.

5 They called vpon thee, and were deliuered: they trusted in thee, and were not cõfounded.

6 But I am a [d] worme, & not a man: a shame of men, and the contẽpt of the people.

7 All they that se me, haue me in derision: they make a mowe & nod the head, *saying*,

8 [*] He trusted in the Lord, let him deliuer him: let him saue him, seig he loueth him.

9 But ý didest drawe me out of the [e] wombe: thou gauest me hope, *euen* at my mothers breasts.

10 I was cast vpon thee, *euen* from [f] the wombe: thou art my God from my mothers belly.

11 Be not farre from me, because trouble is nere: for *there is* none to helpe *me*.

12 Manie yong bulles haue compassed me: mightie [g] bulles of Bashán haue closed me about.

13 They gape vpon me with their mouthes, *as* a ramping and roaring lion.

14 I am like [h] water powred out, and all my bones are out of ioynt: mine heart is like waxe: it is molten in the middes of my bowels.

* *Or, the hinde of the morning, & this was the name of some commune song.*

a Here appeareth tha horrible conflict, which he susteined betwene faith & desperation.

b Being tormented with extreme anguith.

* *Or, I cease not.*

c He meaneth the place of praising, euen the Tabernacle: or els it is so called, because he gaue ý people cõtinually occasiõ to praise him.

d And seming moste miserable of all creatures, ẘ was mẽt of Christ. And herein appeareth the vnspeakable loue of God toward man, that he wolde thus abase his Sonne for our sakes.

* *Ebr. rolled vpõ God.*

Matt. 27,43.

e Euen frõ my birth thou hast giuen me occasion to trust in thee.

f For except Gods prouidẽce preserue ý infants, they shulde perish a thousand times in the mothers wombe.

g He meaneth, that his enemies were so fat, proude and cruel, that they were rather beastes then men. h Before, he spake of the crueltie of his enemies, and now he declareth the inwarde griefs of ý minde, so that Christ was tormented, bothe in soule and bodie.

15 My strẽgth is dryed vp like a potsheard, and my tongue cleueth to my iawes, and ý [i] hast broght me into the dust of death.

16 For dogges haue compassed me, & the assemblie of the wicked haue inclosed me: they [k] perced mine hands and my fete.

17 I maie tel all my bones: *yet* thei beholde, *and* loke vpon me.

18 They parte my garments among them, and cast lottes vpon my vesture.

19 But be not thou farre of, ô Lord, my strength: hasten to helpe me.

20 Deliuer my soule from the sworde: my [l] desolate *soule* from the power of the dog.

21 [m] Saue me from the lions mouth, and answer me *in sauing me* from the hornes of the vnicornes.

22 [*] I wil declare thy Name vnto my brethren: in the middes of the Congregaciõ wil I praise thee, *saying*,

23 [n] Praise the Lord, ye that feare him: magnifie ye him, all the sede of Iaakób, & feare ye him, all the sede of Israél.

24 For he hathe not despised nor abhorred ý affliction of the [o] poore: nether hathe he hid his face from him, but when he called vnto him, he heard.

25 My praise *shalbe* of thee in the great Cõgregation: my [p] vowes wil I performe before them that feare him.

26 [q] The poore shal eat and be satisfied: thei that seke after the Lord, shal praise him: your heart shal liue for euer.

27 All the ends of the worlde shal remembre *them selues*, and turne to the Lord: and all the kinreds of the nations shal worship before thee.

28 For the kingdome *is* the Lords, and he ruleth among the nations.

29 All thei that be fat [r] in the earth, shal eat and worship: all they that go downe into the dust, shal bowe before him, [s] euen he that can not quicken his owne soule.

30 [t] *Their* sede shal serue him: it shalbe coũted vnto the Lord for a generation.

31 Thei shal come, & shal declare his righteousnes vnto a people that shal be borne, because he hathe [u] done it.

PSAL. XXIII.

1 Because the Prophet had proued the great mercies of God at diuerse times, and in sundrie maners, he gathereth a certeine assurance, fully persuading him self that God wil continue the verie same goodnes towards him for euer.

¶ A Psalme of Dauid.

1 THe Lord *is* my [*] shepherd, [a] I shal not want.

2 He maketh me to rest in grene pasture, & leadeth me by the stil waters.

3 He [b] restoreth my soule, & leadeth me in

i Thou hast suffred me to be without all hope of life.

k Thus Dauid cõplaineth as though he were nailed by his enemies bothe hands & fete but this was accomplished in Christ.

l My life ý is solitarie, left alone & forsakẽ of all, Psal. 35,17, & 25,16.

m Christ is deliuered ẘ a more mightie deliuerance by ouercomming death, then if he had not tasted death at all.

Ebr. 2,12.

n He promiseth to exhorte the Church ý thei by his example might praise ý Lord.

o The poore afflicted are cõforted by this example of Dauid, or Christ.

p Which were sacrifices of thankesgiuing, which they offred by Gods commandemẽt when thei were deliuered out of any great danger.

q He doeth allude stil to the sacrifice.

r Thogh ý poore be first named, as ver. 26, yet ý welthie are not separated frõ the grace of Christs kingdome.

s In whome there is no hope that he shal recouer life: so nether poore nor riche, quicke nor dead shalbe reiected from his kingdome.

t Meaning the posteritie, ẘ the Lord kepeth as a sede to the Church to continue his praise among men.

u That is, God hathe fulfilled his promes.

Isa. 40,11. ier. 23,5. ezek. 34,23. ioh. 10,11. 1 pet 2,25.

a He hathe care ouer me & ministreth vnto me all things.

b He comforteth or refresheth me.

the c paths of righteousnes for his Names sake.
4 Yea, thogh I shulde walke through the
valley of the d shadow of death, I wil feare
no euil: for thou art with me: thy rod and
thy staffe, they comfort me.
5 Thou doest prepare a e table before me
in the sight of mine aduersaries: thou doest f anoint mine head with oyle, *and* my
cup runneth ouer.
6 Douteles kindenes, & mercie shal follow
me all the dayes of my life, and I shal remaine a long season in the g house of the
Lord.

c Plaine, or streight waies.
d Thogh he were in dãger of death, as ỹ shepe that wãdreth in the darke valley without his shepherd.
e Albeit his enemies soght to destroy him, yet God deliuereth him, & dealeth moste liberally with him in despite of them.
f As was the maner of great feastes.
g He setteth not his felicitie in the pleasures of this worlde, but in ỹ feare & seruice of God.

PSAL. XXIIII.

1 *Albeit the Lord God hathe made, and gouerneth all the worlde, yet towards his chosen people his gracious goodnes doeth moste abundantly appeare, in that among thẽ he wil haue his dwelling place. Which thogh it was appointed among the children of Abrahám, yet onely thei do entre aright into this Sanctuarie, which are the true worshipers of God, purged from the sinful filth of this worlde. 7 Finally he magnifieth Gods grace for the buylding of the Temple, to the end he might stirre vp all the faithful to the true seruice of God.*

¶ *A Psalme of Dauid.*

1 The earth* *is* the Lords, and all that
therein is: the worlde and they that
dwel therein.
2 For he hathe founded it vpon the a seas:
and established it vpon the floods.
3 Who shal ascende into the mountaine of
the Lord? and who shal stand in his holie
place?
4 *Euen he that hathe* innocẽt hãds, & a pure
heart: which hathe not lift vp his minde
vnto vanitie, nor sworne deceitfully.
5 He shal receiue a blessing frõ the Lord, &
righteousnes frõ the God of his saluaciõ.
6 This is the b generation of them that
seke him, of them that seke thy face, *this is*
Iaakób. Sélah.
7 c Lift vp your heades ye gates, and be ye
lift vp ye euerlasting dores, and the King
of glorie shal come in.
8 Who is this King of glorie? the Lord,
strong and mightie, *euẽ* the Lord mightie
in battel.
9 Lift vp your heades, ye gates, and lift vp
your selues, ye euerlasting dores, & the King
of glorie shal come in.
10 Who is this King of glorie? the Lord of
hostes, he is the King of glorie. Sélah.

Deu.10,14. iob.28,25. 1.cor.10,27.
a He noteth two thĩgs: the one that the earth to mans iudgement semeth aboue the waters: & next, that God miraculously preserueth the earth, that it is not drowned with the waters, which naturally are aboue it.
b Thogh circũcision separate the carnal sede of Iaakób from the Gẽtils, yet he ỹ seketh God, is ỹ true Iaakób & the verie Israelite.
c Dauid desireth the buylding vp of the Tẽple, wherein the glorie of God shulde appeare, and vnder the figure of this Tẽple he also prayeth for ỹ spiritual Tẽple, which is eternal, because of the promes which was made to ỹ Tẽple, as is writẽ, Psal.132,14.

PSAL. XXV.

1 *The Prophet touched with the consideration of his sinnes, and also grieued with the cruel malice of his enemies, 6 Prayeth to God moste feruently to haue his sinnes forgiuen, 7 Especially suche as he had commited in his youth. He begynneth euerie verse according to the Ebrewe letters two or thre except.*

¶ A Psalme *of Dauid.*

1 Vnto thee, a ô Lord, lift I vp my
soule.
2 My God, I b trust in thee: let me not be
confounded: let not mine enemies reioyce
ouer me.
3 * So all that hope in thee, shal not be asha
med: *but* let them be confounded, that trãsgresse without cause.
4 c Shew me thy waies, ô Lord, & teache
me thy paths.
5 Lead me forthe in thy trueth, and teache
me: for thou art the God of my saluacion:
in thee do I trust d all the daie.
6 Remember, ô Lord, thy tendre mercies,
and thy louing kindenes: for thei haue bene for euer.
7 Remember not the e sinnes of my youth,
nor my rebellions, *but* according to thy
kindenes remember thou me, *euen* for thy
goodnes sake, ô Lord.
8 Gracious and righteous *is* the Lord: therefore wil he f teache sinners in the waie.
9 Them that be meke, wil he g guide in iudgement, and teache the humble his waie.
10 All the paths of the Lord *are* mercie &
trueth vnto such as kepe his couenant and
his testimonies.
11 For thy h Names sake, ô Lord, be merciful vnto mine iniquitie, for it is great.
12 What i man is he that feareth the Lord?
him wil he teache the waie *that* he shal
k chuse.
13 His soule shal dwel at l ease, and his sede
shal inherite the land.
14 The m secret of the Lord *is reueiled* to
them, that feare him: and his couenant to
giue them vnderstanding.
15 Mine eies *are* euer toward the Lord: for
he wil bring my fete out of the net.
16 Turne thy face vnto me, and haue mercie vpon me: for I am desolate and poore.
17 The sorowes of mine heart n are enlarged: drawe me out of my troubles.
18 Loke vpon mine affliction & my trauel,
and forgiue all my sinnes.
19 Beholde mine o enemies, for thei are ma
ny, and they hate me with cruel hatred.
20 Kepe my soule, & deliuer me: let me not
be confounded, for I trust in thee.
21 Let p mine vprightenes and equitie preserue me: for mine hope is in thee.
22 Deliuer Israél, ô God, out of all his troubles.

a I put not my trust in anie worldlie thing.
b That thou wilt take awaie mine enemies, which are thy rods.
Isa.28,16. rom.10,11.
c Reteine me in ỹ faith of thy promes, that I swerue not on any side.
d Constantly, and against all tentations.
e He confesseth ỹ his manifolde sinnes were the cause that his enemies did thus persecute hĩ, desiring that the cause of the euil may be taken awaie, to the intent, that ỹ effect may cease.
f That is, call them to repentance.
g He wil gouerne & cõfort them that are truely hũbled for their sinnes.
h And for none other respect.
i Meaning, the nomber is very small.
k He wil direct such ẘ his Spirit to followe the right waie.
l He shal prosper bothe in spiritual and corporal thĩgs
m His counsel conteined in his worde, whereby he declareth that he is ỹ protector of the faithful.
n My grief is increased because of mine enemies cruel tie
o The greater that his afflictions were, & the more that his enemies increased, the more nere felt he Gods helpe
p For as muche as I haue behaued my selfe vprightly toward mine enemies, let them knowe that thou art the defender of my iust cause.

PSAL. XXVI.

1 *Dauid oppressed with many iniuries, finding no helpe in the worlde, calleth for aide from God: & assured of his integritie toward Saúl, desireth God to be his iudge, & to defend his innocencie. 6 Finally he maketh menciõ of his sacrifice, which he wil offre for his deliuerance, & desireth to be in the cõpanie of the faithful in the Cõgregaciõ of God, wheñe he was banished by Saúl, promising integritie of life, & open praises & thãkesgiuing.*

¶ A Psalme *of Dauid.*

1 Iudge me, a ô Lord, for I haue walked in
mine innocencie: my trust hathe bene
also in the Lord: *therefore* shal I not slide.
2 Proue me, ô Lord, and trye me: examine
my

a He fleeth to God to be the Iudge of his iust cause, seĩg there is no equitie among men.

my [b] reines, and mine heart.
3 For thy [c] louing kindenes *is* before mine eyes: therefore haue I walked in thy trueth.
4 I haue not [d] hanted with vaine persones, nether kept cōpanie with the dissemblers.
5 I haue hated the assemblie of the euil, & haue not companied with the wicked.
6 I wil [e] wash mine hands in innocencie, ô Lord, and compasse thine altar,
7 That I maie declare with the voice of thankesgiuing, and set forthe all thy wonderous workes.
8 O Lord, I haue loued the habitation of thine house, and the place where thine honour dwelleth.
9 [f] Gather not my soule with the sinners, nor my life with the bloodie men:
10 In whose hands *is* [g] wickednes, and their right hand is ful of bribes.
11 But I wil walke in mine innocēcie: redeme me *therfore*, and be merciful vnto me.
12 My fote standeth in [h] vprightnes: I wil praise thee, ô Lord, in the Congregations.

b My very affections & inward motions of the heart.
c He sheweth what stayed him, ẏ he did not recōpence euil for euil.
d He declareth that thei can not walke in simplicitie before God, that delite in the companie of ẏ vngodlie.
e I wil serue thee wͭ a pure affection, and with the godlie that sacrifice vnto thee.
f Destroye me not in ẏ ouerthrowe of the wicked.
g Whose cruel hands do execute the malicious deuises of their hearts.
h I am preserued from mine enemies by ẏ power of God, and therefore wil praise him openly.

PSAL. XXVII.

1 Dauid maketh this psalme being deliuered from great perils, as appeareth by the praises and thankesgiuing annexed: 6 Wherein we may se the constant faith of Dauid against the assaltes of all his enemies. 7 And also the end wherefore he desireth to liue and to be deliuered, onely to worship God in his Congregation.

¶ A Psalme *of Dauid.*

1 THe Lord *is* my [a] light and my saluation, whome shal I feare? the Lord *is* the strength of my life, of whome shal I be afraid?
2 When the wicked, *euen* mine enemies and my foes came vpon me to eat vp my flesh they stumbled and fel.
3 Thogh an hoste pitched against me, mine heart shulde not be afraid: thogh warre be raised against me, I wil trust in [b] this.
4 [c] One thing haue I desired of the Lord, that I wil require, *euen* that I may dwel in the house of the Lord all the dayes of my life, to beholde the beautie of the Lord, & to visite his Temple.
5 For in the time of trouble he shal hide me in his Tabernacle: in the secret *place* of his pauilion shal he hide me, & set me vp vpon a rocke.
6 [d] And now shal he lift vp mine head aboue mine enemies roūd about me: therfore wil I offer in his Tabernacle sacrifices of ioye: I wil sing and praise the Lord.
7 Hearken vnto my voice, ô Lord, *when* I crye: haue mercie also vpon me and heare me.
8 *When thou saidest,* [e] Seke ye my face, mine heart answered vnto thee, O Lord, I wil seke thy face.
9 Hide not *therefore* thy face from me, nor cast thy seruant awaie in displeasure: thou hast bene my succour: leaue me not, nether forsake me, ô God of my saluation.
10 [f] Thogh my father and my mother shulde forsake me, yet the Lord wil gather me vp.
11 Teache me thy waie, ô Lord, and leade me in a right path, because of mine enemies.
12 Giue me not vnto the [g] lust of mine aduersaries: for there are false witnesses rise vp against me, & suche as speake cruelly.
13 *I shulde haue fainted,* except I had beleued to see the goodnes of the [h] Lord in the land of the liuing.
14 [i] Hope in the Lord: be strong, & he shal comfort thine heart, & trust in the Lord.

a Because he was assured of good successe in all his dangers, and that his saluation was surely laid vp ī God, he feared not the tyrānie of his enemies.
b That God wil deliuer me, & giue my faith ẏ victorie.
c The losse of countrie, wife & all worldely commodities greue me not in respect of this one thīg, that I may not praise thy Name in the middes of the Cōgregacion.
d Dauid assured him selfe by the Spirit of prophecie that he shulde ouercome his enemies and serue God in his Tabernacle.
e He groundeth vpō Gods promes & sheweth that he is most willing to obey his cōmandement.
f He magnifieth Gods loue towarde his, which farre passeth the most tender loue of parēts towards their children.
g But ether pacifie their wrath, or bridel their rage.
h In this present life before I dye, as Isa. 38, 11.
i He exhorteth him self to depēde on ẏ Lord, seing he neuer failed in his promises.

PSAL. XXVIII.

1 Being in great feare & heauines of heart to se God dishonored by the wicked he desireth to be rid of them. 4 And cryeth for vengeance against them: & at length assureth him selfe, that God hathe heard his praier. 9 Vnto whose tuition he commendeth all the faithful.

¶ A Psalme *of Dauid.*

1 VNto thee, ô Lord, do I crye: ô my strength, be not deafe toward me, lest, if thou answer me not, I be [a] like them that go downe into the pit.
2 Heare the voice of my petitions, when I crye vnto thee, when I holde vp mine hāds toward thine [b] holy Oracle.
3 [c] Drawe me not awaie with the wicked, and with the workers of iniquitie: which speake friendly to their neighbours, when malice *is* in their hearts.
4 [d] Reward them according to their dedes, and according to the wickednes of their inuentions: recompense them after the worke of their hands: rēder them their rewarde.
5 For thei regard not the workes of ẏ Lord, nor the operation of his hands: *therefore* [e] breake them downe, & buylde thē not vp.
6 [f] Praised *be* the Lord, for he hathe heard the voice of my petitions.
7 The Lord *is* my strength and my shield: mine heart trusted in him, and I was helped: therefore mine heart shal reioyce, & with my song wil I praise him.
8 The Lord *is* [g] their strength, and he is the strength of the deliuerances of his anointed.
9 Saue thy people, and blesse thine inheritāce: fede them also, & exalt thē for euer.

a He counteth him selfe as a dead man, til God shew his fauour toward him, and grāte him his petition.
b He vsed this outward meanes to helpe ẏ weaknes of his faith: for in ẏ place was the Arke, and there God promised to shewe the tokens of his fauour.
c Destroy not the good with the bad.
d He thus praieth in respect of Gods glorie, & not for his owne cause, being assured, that God wolde punish the persecuters of his Church.
e Let them be vtterly destroyed, as Malach. 1, 4.
f Because he felt the assurāce of Gods help in his heart, his mouth was opened to sing his praises.
g Meaning, his soldiers, who were as meanes, by whome God declared his power.

PSAL. XXIX.

1 The Prophet exhorteth the princes and rulers of the worlde, (which for the moste parte thinke there is no God) 3 At the least to feare him for the thunders & tempestes, for feare whereof all creatures tremble. 11 And thogh thereby God threateneth sinners, yet is he alwaies merciful to his, & moueth thē thereby to praise his Name.

¶ A Psalme *of Dauid.*

1 GIue vnto the Lord, ye [a] sonnes of the mightie: giue vnto the Lord glorie and strength.

a He exhorteth ẏ proude tyrants to hūble thē selues vnder Gods hand, and not to be inferiour to brute beasts & dūme creatures.

2 Giue vnto the Lord glorie *due* vnto his
Name: worship the Lord in the glorious
Sanctuarie.
3 The [b] voice of the Lord *is* vpon the waters: the God of glorie maketh it to thũder: the Lord *is* vpon the great waters.
4 The voice of the Lord *is* mightie: the
voice of the Lord *is* glorious.
5 The [c] voice of the Lord breaketh the cedres: yea, the Lord breaketh the cedres of
Lebanón.
6 He maketh thẽ also to leape like a calfe:
Lebanón *also* and [d] Shirión like a yong
vnicorne.
7 The voice of the Lord deuideth the [e] flames of fyre.
8 The voice of the Lord maketh the wildernes to tremble: the Lord maketh the
wildernes of [f] Kadésh to tremble.
9 The voice of the Lord maketh the hindes
to [g] calue, & [h] discouereth the forests: *therefore* in his [i] Temple doeth euerie man
speake of *his* glorie.
10 The Lord sitteth vpon the [k] flood, and
the Lord doeth remaine King for euer.
11 The Lord shal giue strẽgth vnto his people: ye Lord shal blesse his people wt peace.

b The thunder clappes, that are heard out of ye cloudes, oght to make the wicked to treble for feare of Gods angre.
c That is, the thunderbolte breaketh the moste strong trees, and shal men thinke their power to be able to resist God?
d Called also Hermón.
e It causeth ye lightenings to shote & glyde.
f In places most desolate, where as semeth there is no presence of God.
g For feare maketh them to cast their calues.
h Maketh the trees bare, or perceth ye most secret places.
i Thogh ye wicked are nothĩg moued wt these sights, yet ye faithful praise God.
k To moderat ye rage of the tempest & waters, that they destroy not all.

PSAL. XXX.

1 *When David was deliuered from great danger, he rendred thankes to God, exhorting others to do the like, and to learne by his example, that God is rather merciful then seuere and rigorous towards his children. 8 And also that the fall from prosperitie to aduersitie is sudden. 9 This done, he returneth to praier, promising to praise God for euer.*

¶ * *A Psalme* or *song of the dedication of the* [a] *house of David.*

1 I Wil magnifie thee, ô Lord: [b] for thou
hast exalted me, and hast not made my
foes to reioyce ouer me.
2 O Lord my God, I cryed vnto thee, and
thou hast [c] restored me.
3 O Lord, thou hast broght vp my [d] soule
out of the graue: thou hast reuiued me frõ
them that go downe into the pit.
4 Sing praises vnto the Lord, ye [e] his Saints,
and giue thankes [f] before the remembrãce of his Holines.
5 *For *he endureth but* a while in his angre: *but*
in his fauour *is* life: weping maie abide at
euening, but ioye *cometh* in the morning.
6 And in my [g] prosperitie I said, I shal
neuer be moued.
7 *For* thou Lord of thy goodnes hadest
made my [h] mountaine to stand strong: *but*
you didest hide thy face, *and* I [i] was troubled.
8 *Then* cryed I vnto thee, ô Lord, and prayed to my Lord.
9 What profit *is there* in my blood, whẽ I go
downe to ye pit? shal the dust [k] giue thãkes
vnto thee? or shal it declare thy trueth?

2.Sam.7,2.
a After that Absalóm had polluted it wt moste filthie fornication.
b He condemneth them of great ingratitude, which do not praise God for his benefites.
c Restored frõ ye rebellion of Absalóm.
d Meaning yt he escaped death moste narowly.
e The worde signifieth thē, yt haue receiued mercie & shew mercie liberally vnto others.
f Before his Tabernacle.
Psal.145,8. isai.54,7. 2.cor.4,17.
g I put to muche confidẽce in my quiet state, as Ier.31, 18. 2 chr.32,24.
h I thoght yu hadest established me in Zíon moste surely.

i After that yu hadest withdrawen thine helpe, I felt my miserie. k David meaneth that the dead are not profitable to the Congregacion of the Lord here in earth: therefore he wolde liue to praise his Name, which is the end of mans creation.

10 Heare, ô Lord, and haue mercie vpon
me: Lord, be thou mine helper.
11 Thou hast turned my mourning into
ioye: thou hast loosed my sacke & girded
me with gladnes.
12 Therefore shal *my* [l] tongue praise thee
and not cease: ô Lord my God, I wil giue thankes vnto thee for euer.

l Because thou hast preserued me, ye my tongue shulde praise thee. I wil not be vnmindeful of my duetie.

PSAL. XXXI.

1 *David deliuered from some great dãger, first rehearseth what meditation he had by the power of faith, when death was before his eies, his enemie being ready to take him. 15 Then he affirmeth that the fauour of God is alwaies readie to those that feare him. 20 Finally he exhorteth all the faithful to trust in God and to loue him, because he preserueth and strẽgtheneth them, as they may se by his example.*

¶ *To him that excelleth. A Psalme of David.*

1 IN * thee, ô Lord, haue I put my trust: 2.Sam.23,24
let me neuer be confounded: deliuer
me in thy [a] righteousnes.
2 Bowe downe thine eare to me: make haste
to deliuer me: be vnto me a strong rocke,
& an house of defence to saue me.
3 For thou art my rocke and my fortres:
therefore for thy Names sake direct me &
guide me.
4 Drawe me out of the [b] net, that they haue laied priuely for me: for thou art my
strength.
5 Into thine [c] hand I commende my spirit:
for thou hast redemed me, ô Lord God of
trueth.
6 I haue hated them that giue them selues
to deceitful vanities: for I [d] trust in the
Lord.
7 I wilbe glad and reioyce in thy mercie:
for thou hast sene my trouble: thou hast
knowen my soule in aduersities,
8 And thou hast not shut me vp in the hãd
of ye enemie, *but* hast set my fete at [e] large.
9 Haue mercie vpon me, ô Lord: for I am
in trouble: mine [f] eye, my soule & my bel
lie are consumed with grief.
10 For my life is wasted with heauines, and
my yeres with mourning: my strength
faileth for my peine, & my bones are consumed.
11 I was a [g] reproche among all mine enemies, but specially among my neighbours: and a feare to mine acquaintance,
[h] who seing me in the strete, fled from
me.
12 I am forgotten, as a dead man out of
minde: I am like a broken vessel.
13 For I haue heard the railing of [i] great
men: feare *was* on euerie side, while they
conspired together against me, *&* consulted to take my life.
14 But I trusted in thee, ô Lord: I said,
[k] Thou art my God.
15 My [l] times are in thine hand: deliuer me
from the hand of mine enemies, and from
them that persecute me.

a For thẽ God declareth him self iuste, whẽ he preserueth his according as he hathe promised.
b Preserue me from the craftie counsels & subtil practises of mine enemies.
c He desireth God not onely to take care for him in this life, but that his soule may be saued after this life.
d This affectiõ oght to be in all Gods children, to hate whatsoeuer thing is not grounded vpõ a sure trust in God, as deceitful and vaine.
e Largenes signifieth cõfort, as straitnes sorow and peril.
f Meanĩg, that his sorow and torment had continued a great while.
g Mine enemies had drawen all mẽ to their parte against me, euẽ my chief friends.
h Thei were afraied to shew mẽ anie token of frendship.
i Thei yt were in autoritie, condemned me as a wicked doer.
k I had this testimonie of conscience, yt thou woldest defend mine innocencie.
l Whatsoeuer changes come, thou gouernest them by thy prouidence.

16 Make thy face to ſhine vpon thy ſeruāt,
& ſaue me through thy mercie.
17 Let me not be confounded, ô Lord: for
I haue called vpon thee: let the wicked be
put to confuſion, & m to ſilence in ẏ graue.
18 Let the lying lippes be made dumme,
which cruelly, proudely & ſpitefully ſpeake againſt the righteous.
19 How great is thy goodnes, which thou
n haſt laied vp for them, that feare thee! &
done to them, that truſt in thee, *euen* before the ſonnes of men!
20 Thou doeſt hide them" o priuely in thy
preſence from the pride of men: thou kepeſt them ſecretly in thy Tabernacle frō
the ſtrife of tongues.
21 Bleſſed *be* the Lord: for he hathe ſhewed
his maruelous kindenes towarde me in a
p ſtrong citie.
22 Thogh I ſaid in mine q haſte, I am caſt
out of thy ſight, yet ẏ heardeſt the voyce
of my praier, when I cryed vnto thee.
23 Loue ye the Lord all his " Saints: *for* the
Lord preſerueth the faithful, and rewardeth abundantly the proude doer.
24 All ye that truſt in the Lord, be r ſtrong,
and he ſhal eſtabliſh your heart.

m Let death deſtroy them to the intent ẏ thei may hurt no more.
n The treaſures of Gods mercie are alwaies laied vp in ſtore for his childrē, albeit at all times thei do not enioye them.
" Ebr. *in the ſecret of thy face.*
o That is, in a place where thei ſhal haue thy cōfort, & be hid ſafely from the enemies pride.
p Meaning, there was no citie ſo ſtrong to preſerue hī, as ẏ defence of Gods fauour.
q And ſo by my raſhnes & infidelitie deſerued to haue bene forſaken.
" Or, *ye that fele his mercies.*
r Be conſtant in your vocation, and God wil confirme you with heauenlie ſtregth.

PSAL. XXXII.

1 Dauid puniſhed with grieuous ſicknes for his ſinnes, counteth them bleſſed, to whome God doeth not impute their tranſgreſsions. 5 And after that he had confeſſed his ſinnes and obteined pardon, 6 He exhorteth the wicked men to liue godly, 11 And the good to reioyce.

¶ A Pſalme *of Dauid to giue* a *inſtruction.*

1 BLeſſed *is he* whoſe wickednes is b forgiuen, & whoſe ſinne is couered.
2 Bleſſed *is* the man, vnto whome the Lord
imputeth not iniquitie, & in whoſe ſpirit
there is no guile.
3 When I helde my c tongue, my bones
conſumed, *or* when I d roared all the day,
4 (For thine hād is heauie vpon me, daie &
night: & my moiſture is turned into the
drought of ſummer. Sélah)
5 *Then* I e acknowledged my ſinne vnto thee,
nether hid I mine iniquitie: *for* I thoght, I
wil confeſſe againſt my ſelf my wickednes
vnto the Lord, and thou forgaueſt the puniſhment of my ſinne. Sélah.
6 Therefore ſhal euerie one, that is godlie,
make his praier vnto thee in a f time, when
thou maieſt be founde: ſurely in the flood
of great waters g they ſhal not come nere
him.
7 Thou art my ſecret place: thou preſer-
ueſt me from trouble: thou compaſſeſt me
about with ioyful deliuerance. Sélah.
8 I wil h inſtruct thee, & teache thee in the
way, that thou ſhalt go, & I wil guide thee
with mine eye.
9 Be ye not like an horſe, *or* like a mule,
which vnderſtand not: whoſe i mouthes
thou doeſt binde with bit and bridel, leſt
they come nere thee.
10 Many ſorowes *ſhal come* to the wicked:
but he, that truſteth in the Lord, mercie
ſhal compaſſe him.
11 Be glad ye righteous, & k reioyce in the
Lord, and be ioyful all ye, that are vpright
in heart.

Pſal. XXXII.
a Concerning the fre remiſſion of ſinnes, which is the chiefeſt point of our faith.
b To be iuſtified by faith, is to haue our ſinnes frely remitted, and to be reputed iuſt, Rom. 4, 6.
c Betwene hope and deſpaire.
d Nether by ſilence nor crying foūd I eaſe: ſignifyīg, that before the ſinner be reconciled to God, he feeleth a perpetual torment.
e He ſheweth that as Gods mercie is the onelie cauſe of forgiuenes of ſinnes, ſo the meanes therof are repentance and confeſſion, which procede of faith.
f When neceſſitie cauſeth him to ſeke to thee for helpe, Iſa 55, 6.
g To wit, the waters and great dangers.
h Dauid promiſeth to make the reſt of Gods childrē partakers of ẏ benifites, which he felt, & that he wil diligētly loke and take care to direct them in the waie of ſaluation.
i If men cau rule brute beaſtes, thinke thei, that God wil not bridle and tame their rage?
k He ſheweth that peace & ioy of cōſciēce in the holie Goſt is ẏ frute of faith.

PSAL. XXXIII.

1 He exhorteth good men to praiſe God for that he hathe not onely created all things, and by his prouidence gouerneth the ſame, but alſo is faithful in his promiſes. 10 He vnderſtandeth mans heart, and ſcatereth the counſel of the wicked, 16 So that no man can be preſerued by anie creature or mans ſtrength: but they, that put their confidence in his mercie, ſhalbe preſerued frō all aduerſities.

1 REioyce in the Lord, ô ye righteous:
for it a becometh vpright men to be
thankeful.
2 Praiſe ẏ Lord with harpe: ſing vnto him
with viole & b inſtrument of ten ſtrings.
3 Sing vnto him a new ſong: ſing cherefully with a loude voyce.
4 For the c worde of the Lord *is* righteous,
and all his d workes *are* faithful.
5 He e loueth righteouſnes & iudgement:
the earth is ful of the goodnes of ẏ Lord.
6 By the worde of the Lord were the heauens made, and all the hoſte of them by the
breath of his mouth.
7 He f gathereth the waters of the ſea together as vpon an heape, and laieth vp the
depths in *his* treaſures.
8 Let all the earth feare the Lord: let all thē
that dwel in the worlde, feare him.
9 For he ſpake, & it was done: he commanded, and it " ſtode.
10 The Lord breaketh the g counſel of the
heathen, & bringeth to noght the deuiſes
of the people.
11 The counſel of the Lord ſhal ſtand for
euer, & the thoghts of his heart through
out all ages.
12 Bleſſed *is* that nacion, whoſe h God is
the Lord: *euen* the people, *that* he hathe
choſen for his inheritance.
13 The Lord i loketh downe from heauen,
& beholdeth all the children of men.
14 From the habitacion of his dwelling he
beholdeth all them, that dwel in the earth.
15 He k facioneth their hearts euerie one,
& vnderſtandeth all their workes.
16 The l King is not ſaued by the multitude of an hoſte, *nether* is the mightie mā
deliuered by great ſtrength.
17 A horſe is a vaine helpe, and ſhal not deliuer *anie* by his great ſtrength.
18 Beholde, m the eye of the Lord *is* vpon
them that feare him, & vpon them, that
truſt in his mercie,

a It is the duetie of the godlie to ſet forthe ẏ praiſes of God for his mercie & power ſhewed towarde thē.
b To ſing on inſtrumēts was a parte of the ceremonial ſeruice of the Tēple, which doeth no more apperteine vnto vs, then the ſacrifices, cenſings & lights.
c That is, coūſel or cōmandement in gouerning the worlde.
d That is, the effect & execution.
e Howſoeuer ẏ worlde iudgeth of Gods workes, yet he doeth all thigs accordig to iuſtice & mercie.
f By the creation of ẏ heauens & beautiful ornamēt, with the gathering alſo of the waters he ſetteth forthe the power of God, that all creatures might feare him.
" Or, *was created.*
g No counſel can preuail againſt God, but he defeateth it & it ſhal haue euil ſucces.
h He ſheweth that all our felicitie ſtādeth in this, that ẏ Lorde is our God.
i He proueth that all things are gouerned by Gods prouidence & not by fortune.
k Therfore he knoweth their wicked enterpriſes.
l If Kings and the mightie of the worlde can not be ſaued by worldlie meanes, but onely by Gods prouidence, what haue others to truſt in, that haue not like meanes?
m God ſheweth that towarde his of his mercie, which man by no meanes is able to compaſſe.

19 To deliuer their soules from death, and
to preserue them in famine.
20 [n] Our soule waiteth for the Lord: *for* he
is our helpe and our shield.
21 Surely our heart shal reioyce in him, because we trusted in his holie Name.
22 Let thy mercie, ô Lord, be vpon vs, as
we trust in thee.

n Thus he speaketh in ỳ name of the whole Church, which onely depend on Gods prouidence.

PSAL. XXXIIII.

After Dauid had escaped Achish, according as it is writen in the 1. Sam. 21, 11, whome in this title he calleth Abimélech (which was a general name to all the Kings of the Philistims) he praiseth God for his deliuerance, 3 Prouoking all others by his example to trust in God, to feare & serue him: 14 Who defendeth the godlie with his Angels, 15 And vtterly destroyeth the wicked in their sinnes.

¶ A Psalme *of Dauid, when he changed his behauiour before Abimélech, who droue him awaie, & he departed.*

1 I Wil [a] alwaie giue thankes vnto the
Lord: his praise *shalbe* in my mouth
continually.
2 My soule shal glorie in the Lord: the [b] hũble shal heare it, and be glad.
3 Praise ye the Lord with me, and let vs
magnifie his Name together.
4 I soght the Lord, and he heard me: yea, he
deliuered me out of all my [c] feare.
5 They [d] shal loke vnto him, and runne *to*
him: and their faces shal not be ashamed,
saying,
6 This poore man cryed, & the Lord heard
him, and saued him out of all his troubles.
7 The [e] Angel of the Lord pitcheth roũde
about them, that feare him, and deliuereth
them.
8 Taste ye & se, how gracious the Lord is:
blessed *is* the man that trusteth in him.
9 Feare the Lord, ye his Saints: for nothing
wanteth to them that feare him.
10 The [f] lyons do lacke and suffer hungre,
but they, which seke the Lord, shal [g] want
nothing that is good.
11 Come children, hearken vnto me: I wil
teache you the [h] feare of the Lord.
12 * What man is he, that desireth life, and
loueth *long* daies for to [i] se good?
13 Kepe thy tongue from euil, and thy lippes, that they speake no guile.
14 Eschew euil and do good: seke peace &
followe after it.
15 The eyes of the Lord *are* vpon the righteous, & his eares *are open* vnto their crye.
16 *But* the [k] face of the Lord *is* against them
that do euil, to cut of their remembrance
from the earth.
17 *The righteous* crye, and the Lord heareth
them, and deliuereth them out of all their
troubles.
18 The Lord is nere vnto them that are of
a [l] contrite heart, and wil saue suche as be
afflicted in spirit.
19 Great *are* the troubles of the righteous:
but ỳ Lord deliuereth him out of thẽ all.
20 [m] He kepeth all his bones: not one of
them is broken.
21 *But* malice shal slay the [n] wicked: & thei
that hate the righteous, shal perish.
22 The Lord [o] redemeth the soules of his
seruants: & none, ỳ trust in him, shal perish.

a He promiseth neuer to become vnmindeful of Gods great benefite for his deliuerance.
b Thei ỳ are beaten downe with the experience of their owne euils.
c Which I cõceiued for the dangers wherein I was.
d Thei shalbe bolde to flee to thee for succour, whẽ thei shal se thy mercies towarde me.
e Thogh Gods power be sufficient to gouerne vs, yet for mans infirmitie he appointeth his Angels to watche ouer vs.
f The godlie by their paciẽt obediẽce pfit more then thei, which rauine & spoile.
g If thei abide the last tryal.
h That is, the true religiõ & worship of God.
1. Pet. 3, 10.
i Seing all mẽ naturally desire felicitie, he wondereth why thei cast them selues willingly into miserie.
k The angre of God doeth not onely destroie the wicked, but also abolisheth their name for euer.
l When thei seme to be swallowed vp w afflictions, the God is at hãd to deliuer them.
m And as Christ saith, all the heeres of his head.
n Their wicked entreprises shal turne to their owne destruction.
o For when thei seme to be ouercome with great dãgers & death it self, then God sheweth him self their redemer.

PSAL. XXXV.

So long as Saul was enemie to Dauid, all that had anie autoritie vnder him to flatter their King (as is the course of the worlde) did also moste cruelly persecute Dauid: against whome he praieth God to pleade & to auenge his cause, 8 That they may be taken in their nets & snares, which thei laied for him, that his innocẽcie may be declared, 27 And that the innocent, which taketh parte with him, maie reioyce & praise the Name of the Lord, that thus deliuereth his seruãt. 28 And so he promiseth to speake forthe the iustice of the Lord, & to magnifie his Name all the dayes of his life.

A Psalme *of Dauid.*

1 PLeade thou my [a] cause, ô Lord, with
them that striue with me: fight thou
against them, that fight against me.
2 [b] Laie hand vpon the shield and buckler,
and stand vp for mine helpe.
3 Bring out also the speare and stoppe *the*
waie against them, that persecute me: saie
vnto my [c] soule, I am thy saluacion.
4 Let thẽ be confounded & put to shame,
that seke after my soule: let them be turned backe, and broght to confusion, that
imagine mine hurt.
5 Let them be as chaffe before the winde,
and let the Angel of the Lord [d] scater
them.
6 Let their waie be darke & slipperie: & let
the Angel of the Lord persecute them.
7 For [e] without cause thei haue hid the pit
and their net for me: without cause haue
they digged *a pit* for my soule.
8 Let destruction come vpon [f] him at vnwares, & let his net, that he hathe laied priuely, take him: let him fall into [g] the same
destruction.
9 Thẽ my soule shalbe ioyful in the Lord:
it shal reioyce in his saluacion.
10 All my [h] bones shal saie, Lord, who is like vnto thee, which deliuerest the poore
from him, that is to strong for him! yea,
the poore and him that is in miserie, from
him that spoileth him!
11 [i] Cruel witnesses did rise vp: thei asked
of me things that I knewe not.
12 They rewarded me euil for good, to
[k] haue spoiled my soule.
13 Yet I, when thei were sicke, I was clothed
with a sacke: I humbled my soule with fasting: and [l] my praier was turned vpon my
bosome.
14 I behaued my selfe as to *my* friend, *or* as
to my brother: I humbled my selfe, mourning as one that bewaileth his mother.
15 But in mine [m] aduersitie thei reioyced,
& gathered them selues together: the abiects

Psal. XXXV.
a He desireth God to vndertake his cause against them that did persecute him and sclander him.
b Albeit God can with his breath destroy all his enemies, yet ỳ holie Gost attributeth vnto him these outward weapons to assure vs of his pſent power.
c Assure me against these tentatiõs, that thou art ỳ autor of my saluation.
d Smite them with the spirit of giddines that their entreprises may be foolish, & thei receiue iuste rewarde.
e Shewing ỳ we may not call God to be a reuenger, but onely for his glorie, & whẽ our cause is iuste.
f When he promiseth to him selfe peace.
g Which he prepared against the children of God.
h He attributeth his deliuerance onely to God, praising him therfore bothe in soule & body.
i That wolde not suffre me to purge my self.
k To haue taken from me all comfort & broght me into dispaire.
l I prayed for them with inward affectiõ, as I wolde haue done for my selfe: or, I declared mine affection with bowing downe mine head.
m When thei saw me ready to slip and as one that halted for infirmitie.

iects assembled them selues against me, &
I knewe not: thei tare [n] me & ceased not,
16 With the false skoffers at [o] bankets,
gnashing their teeth against me.
17 Lord, how long wilt thou beholde *this?*
deliuer my soule from their tumulte, *euen*
my desolate *soule* from the lions.
18 *So* wil I giue thee thankes in a great Cōgregacion: I wil praise thee among muche people.
19 Let not them that are mine enemies, vniustly reioyce ouer me, nether let them
[p] winke with the eye, that hate me without
a cause.
20 For they speake not as friends: but they
imagine deceitful wordes against the
"quiet of the land.
21 And they gaped on me with their mouthes, saying, Aha, aha, [q] our eye hathe sene.
22 Thou hast sene it, ô Lord: kepe not silēce: be not farre from me, ô Lord.
23 Arise and wake to my iudgement, *euen*
to my cause, my God, and my Lord.
24 Iudge me, ô Lord my God, according
to thy [r] righteousnes, and let them not
reioyce ouer me.
25 Let them not saye in their hearts, [s] O
our soule reioyce: nether let them saye,
We haue deuoured him.
26 Let them be confounded, and put to
shame [t] together, that reioyce at mine
hurt: let them be clothed [u] with cōfusion
and shame, that lift vp them selues against
me.
27 *But* let thē be ioyful & glad, [x] that loue
my righteousnes: yea, let them saye alwaie,
Let the Lord be magnified, which loueth
the [y] prosperitie of his seruant.
28 And my tōgue shal vtter thy righteousnes, & thy praise euerie day.

n With their railing wordes
o The worde signifieth cakes: meaning that the proud courtears at their deinty feasts skoff, raile, and conspire his death
p In token of contempt and mocking
"Or, clefter of the earth: meaning him self & others in their miserie.
q Thei reioyced as thogh they had now sene Dauid ouerthrowen.
r It is the iustice of God to giue to the oppressers affliction & tormēt, & to ẏ oppressed, aide and relief, 2. Thes. 1, 6.
s Because we haue that, ẇ we soght for, seing he is destroyed.
t That is, at once, were thei neuer so manie or mightie.
u This praier shal alwaies be verified against them, ẏ persecute the faithful.
x That at least fauour my right, thogh they be not able to helpe me.
y He exhorteth ẏ Church to praise God for the deliuerance of his seruants, & for the destructiō of his aduersaries.

PSAL. XXXVI.

1 The Prophet grieuously Vexed by the wicked, doeth cō-plaine of their malicious wickednes. 6 Then he turneth to cōsider the vnspeakable goodnes of God towards all creatures: 9 But specially towards his children, that by the faith thereof he maie be comforted & assured of his deliuerance by this ordinarie course of Gods worke, 13 Who in the end destroyeth the wicked & saueth the iuste.

¶ *To him that excelleth.* A Psal. *of David, the seruant of the Lord.*

1 WIckednes saieth to ẏ wicked mā,
[a] euen in mine heart, *that there is* no
feare of God before his eyes.
2 For he [b] flattereth him self in his owne
eyes, while his iniquitie is found *worthie*
to be hated.
3 The wordes of his mouthe *are* iniquitie
and [c] deceite: he hathe left of to vnderstand & to do good.
4 He [d] imagineth mischief vpon his bed:
he setteth him selfe vpon a waie, *that is* not
good & doeth not abhorre euil.

a I se euidētly by his dedes, that sinne pusheth forward ẏ reprobat frō wickednes to wickednes, albeit he go about to couer his impietie.
b Thogh all other detest his vile sinne, yet he himself seeth it not.
c The reprobat mocke at holsome doctrine and put not difference betwene good and euil.
d By describing at large the nature of the reprobat, he admonisheth the godlie to beware of these vices.

5 Thy [e] mercie, ô Lord, *reacheth* vnto the
heauens, *and* thy faithfulnes vnto the
cloudes.
6 Thy righteousnes *is* like the " mightie
mountaines: thy iudgemēts *are like* a great
[f] deepe: thou, Lord, doest saue man and
beast.
7 How excellent is thy mercie, ô God!
therefore the children of men trust vnder
the shadowe of thy wings.
8 They shal be [g] satisfied with the fatnes of
thine house, & thou shalt giue them drinke out of the riuer of thy pleasures.
9 For with thee *is* the well of life, & in thy
light shal we se light.
10 Extend thy louing kindenes vnto them
that [h] knowe thee, and thy righteousnes
vnto them that are vpright in heart.
11 Let not the [i] fote of pride come against
me, and let not the hand of the wicked mē
moue me.
12 [k] There they are fallen that worke iniquitie: they are cast downe, and shal not
be able to rise.

e Thogh wickednes semeth to ouerflowe all the worlde, yet by thine heauenlie prouidence thou gouernest heauen & earth.
"Ebr. the mountains of God: for whatsoeuer is excellent, is thus called.
f The depth of thy prouidence gouerneth all things, and disposeth thē, albeit the wicked seme to ouerwhelme the worlde.
g Onely Gods children haue ynough of all things both cōcerning this life & the life to come.
h He sheweth who are Gods childrē, to wit, they ẏ know him, and lead their liues vprightly.
i Let not the proude aduance him self against me, nether ẏ power of the wicked driue me away
k That is, in their pride wherein they flatter them selues.

PSAL. XXXVII.

1 This Psalme conteineth exhortation & consolation for the weake, that are grieued at the prosperitie of the wicked, & the affliction of the godlie. 7 For how prosperously soeuer the wicked do liue for the time, he doeth affirme their felicitie to be vaine and transitorie, because they are not in the fauour of God, but in the end they are destroyed as his enemies, 11 And how miserably that the righteous semeth to liue in the worlde, yet his end is peace, & he is in the fauour of God, he is deliuered from the wicked & preserued.

¶ A Psalme *of David.*

1 FReate not [a] thy self because of the
wicked men, nether be enuious for the
euil doers.
2 For they shal soone be [b] cut downe like
grasse, and shal wither as the grene herbe.
3 [c] Trust thou in the Lord & do good: dwel
in the land, & thou shalt be fed assuredly.
4 And delite thy self in the Lord, and he
shal giue thee thine hearts desire.
5 [d] Commit thy waye vnto the Lord, and
trust in him, and he shal bring it to passe.
6 And he shal bring forthe thy righteousnes as the light, & thy [e] iudgement as the
noone daye.
7 Waite paciently vpon the Lord & hope
in him: freat not thy self for him [f] which
prospereth in his waye: *nor* for the mā that
bringeth *his* entreprises to passe.
8 Cease from angre, & leaue of wrath: freat
not thy selfe [g] also to do euil.
9 For euil doers shalbe cut of, and they
that waite vpon the Lord, they shal inherite the land.
10 [h] Therefore yet a litle while, and the

a He admonisheth vs nether to vexe our selues for the prosperous estate of ẏ wicked, nether to desire to be like thē to make our state the better.
b For Gods iudgemēt cutteth downe their state in a moment.
c To trust in God, and do according to his wil, are sure tokens, that his prouidence wil neuer faile vs.
d Be not led by thine owne wisdome, but obey God, and he wil finish his worke in thee.
e As the hope of ẏ dailight causeth vs not to be offended with the darkenes of the night: so oght we paciently to trust that God wil cleare our cause and restore vs to our right.
f When God suffreth the wicked to prosper, it semeth to the flesh that he fauoreth their doings.
g Meaning, except he moderate his affectiōs, he shalbe led to do as they do.
h He correcteth the impaciencie of our nature, which can not abide til the fulnes of Gods time be come.

wicked shal not *appeare*, and thou shalt loke after his place, and he shal not *be founde*.
11 But *meeke men shal possesse the earth,
and shal haue their delite in the multitude of peace.
12 [i] The wicked practiseth against the iust,
and gnasheth his teeth against him.
13 *But* the Lord shal laugh him to scorne: for
he seeth, that his daye is coming.
14 The wicked haue drawne *their* sworde,
and haue bent their bowe, to cast downe
the poore and nedie, *and* to slay suche as be
of vpright conuersation.
15 *But* their sworde shal entre into their
owne heart, & their bowes shal be broken.
16 [k] A small thing vnto the iust man is better, then great riches to the wicked *and*
mightie.
17 For the armes of the wicked shalbe broken: but the Lord vpholdeth the iust men.
18 The Lord [l] knoweth ȳ dayes of vpright
men, and their inheritance shalbe perpetual.
19 They shal not be cōfounded in the perilous time, and in the dayes of famine they
shal haue [m] ynough.
20 But the wicked shal perish, and the enemies of the Lord shalbe consumed as the
[n] fat of lambes: *euen* with the smoke shal
they consume awaye.
21 The wicked boroweth and payeth not
againe: but the righteous is merciful, and
[o] giueth.
22 For suche as be blessed *of God*, shal inherit the land, & they that be cursed of him,
shalbe cut of.
23 [p] The paths of man are directed by the
Lord: for he loueth his waye.
24 Thogh he [q] fall, he shal not be cast of:
for the Lord putteth vnder his hand.
25 I haue bene yong and am olde: yet I saw
neuer the righteous forsaken, nor his [r] sede begging bread.
26 *But* he is euer merciful and lendeth, and
his sede *enioyeth* the blessing.
27 Flee from euil and do good, and dwel
for euer.
28 For the Lord loueth iudgement, & forsaketh not his Saints: they shalbe preserued for euermore: but the sede of the wicked shalbe cut of.
29 The righteous mē shal inherit the land,
and dwel therein [s] for euer.
30 The [t] mouth of the righteous wil speake of wisdome, and his tongue wil talke of
iudgement.
31 *For* the Law of his God *is* in his heart, &
his stepp:s shal not slide.
32 The wicked watcheth the righteous, and
seketh to slay him.
33 *But* ȳ Lord wil not leaue him in his hād,
nor condemne him, when he is [u] iudged.
34 Waite thou on the Lord, and kepe his
waye, & he shal exalt thee, that thou shalt
inherit the lād: when the wicked men shal
perish, thou shalt se.
35 I haue sene the wicked strong, & spreading him self like a grene baye tre.
36 Yet he [x] passed away, and lo, he was
gone, and I soght him, but he colde not be
founde.
37 [y] Marke the vpright man, and beholde
the iust: for the end of *that* man *is* peace.
38 But the transgressours shalbe destroyed
together, *and* the end of the wicked shalbe cut of.
39 But the [z] saluation of the righteous mē
shalbe of the Lord: he *shalbe* their strength
in the time of trouble.
40 For the Lord shal helpe them, and deliuer them: he shal deliuer them from the
wicked, and shal saue them, because they
trust in him.

PSAL. XXXVIII.

1 Dauid lying sicke of some grieuous disease, acknowledgeth him self to be chastised of the Lord for his sinnes, & therefore praieth God to turne away his wrath. 5 He vttereth the greatnes of his grief by manie wordes & circumstances, as wounded with the arrowes of Gods ire, forsaken of his friends, euil intreated of his enemies. 22 But in the end with firme confidence he commendeth his cause to God, & hopeth for spedie helpe at his hand.

¶ *A Psalme of Dauid for* [a] *remembrance.*

1 O Lord, rebuke me not in thine [b] angre, nether chastise me in thy wrath.
2 For thine [c] arrowes haue light vpon me,
and thine hand lyeth vpon me.
3 There *is* nothing sounde in my flesh, because of thine angre: nether *is* there rest in
my bones because of my [d] sinne.
4 For [e] mine iniquities are gone ouer mine head, & as a weightie burden they are
to heauie for me.
5 My woundes are putrified, and corrupt
because of [f] my foolishnes.
6 I am bowed, *and* croked very sore: I go
"mourning all the daye.
7 For my reines are ful of burning, & there *is* nothing sounde in my flesh.
8 I am weakened and sore broken: I [g] roare for the verie grief of mine heart.
9 Lord, *I powre* my whole desire before thee,
and my sighing is not hid from thee.
10 Mine heart "panteth: my strength faileth
me, and the light of mine eyes, euen [h] thei
are not mine owne.
11 My louers and my friends stand aside
from my plague, and my [i] kinsmen stand
a farre of.
12 They also, that seke after my life, laye
snares, and they that go about to do me
euil, talke wicked things and imagine deceite continually.

Matt. 5,5.

i The godlie are assured ȳ the power and craft of the wicked shal not preuail against them, but fall on their owne neckes, & therfore oght paciently to abide Gods time, & in the meane while bewaile their sinnes, & offer vp their teares as a sacrifice of their obedience.

k For thei are daily fed as w̄ Manna frō heauen, & haue sufficient, when ȳ wicked haue neuer ynough, but euer hūgre.

l God knoweth what dangers hang ouer his, & by what meanes to deliuer them.

m For God wil giue them cōtented mindes, & that w̄ shalbe necessarie.

n They shal vanish awaye suddenly: for they are fed for the daie of slaughter.

o God so furnisheth him with his blessing, that he is able to helpe others.

p God prospereth the faithful, because they walke in his waies with an vpright cōscience.

q When God doeth exercise his faith w̄ diuers tentations.

r Thogh the iust man dye, yet Gods blessings are extended to his posteritie, and thogh God suffer some iuste man to lacke temporal benefites, yet he recōpenseth him with spiritual treasures.

s They shal continually be preserued vnder Gods wings, and haue at least inwarde rest.

t These thre pointes are required of the faithful, that their talke be godlie, ȳ Gods Law be in their heart, & that their life be vpright.

u For thogh it be sometime so expedient both for Gods glorie & their saluation, yet he wil approue their cause, & reuenge their wrong.

x So that the prosperitie of the wicked is but as a cloude, which vanisheth away in a moment.

y He exhorteth the faithful to marke diligently the exāples bothe of Gods mercies, & also of his iudgemēts.

z He sheweth that ȳ pacient hope of the godlie is neuer in vaine, but in the end hathe good succes, thogh for a time God proue them by sundrie tentations.

a To put him self & others in minde of Gods chastisement for sinne.

b He desireth not to be exēpted frō Gods rod, but that he wolde so moderate his hand, that he might be able to beare it.

c Thy sickenes, wherewith thou hast visited me.

d Dauid acknowledgeth God to be iuste in his punishments because his sins had deserued muche more.

e He cōfesseth his sins, Gods iustice, & maketh prayer his refuge.

f That rather gaue place to mine owne lustes, then to the wil of God

"*Or, blacke, as one that is disfigured & consumed with sicknes.*

g This exāple warneth vs neuer to despaire, be the torment neuer so great: but alwaies to crye vnto God with sure trust for deliuerance.

"*Ebr. Runneth about, or, is tossed to & fro: meaning that he was destitute of all helpe & counsel.*

h My sight faileth me for verie sorowe.

i Partely for feare, and partely for pride they denied all duetie and friendship.

13 But I as [k] a deafe man heard not, and
am as a dumme man, *which* openeth not
his mouth.
14 Thus am I as a man, that heareth not, &
in whose mouth *are* no reprofes.
15 For on thee, ô Lord, do I waite: thou wilt
heare *me*, my Lord, my God.
16 For I said, *Heare me*, lest they reioyce o-
uer me: *for* [l] when my fote slippeth, they
extoll them selues against me.
17 Surely I am ready to [m] halte, and my sorow *is* euer before me.
18 When I declare my peine, & am sorie
for my sinne,
19 Then mine [n] enemies are aliue & are
mightie, and they that hate me wrongfully are manie.
20 They also, that rewarde euil for good,
are mine aduersaries, because I followe
[o] goodnes.
21 Forsake me not, ô Lord: be not thou farre from me, my God.
22 Haste thee to helpe me, ô my Lord, my
[p] saluation.

k For I can haue no audiēce before mē, and therefore paciently waite for the helpe of God.

l That is, if they se ỹ thou succour me not in time, they wil mocke & triumph, as thogh thou hadest forsaken me.

m I am without hope to recouer my strength.

n In my greatest miserie they most reioyce.

o He had rather haue the hatred of all ỹ worlde, thē to faile in anie parte of his duetie to God-ward.

p Which art the autor of my saluation: & this declareth that he prayed w̃ sure hope of deliuerance.

PSAL. XXXIX.

1 *David vttereth with what great grief & bitternes of minde he was driuen to these outragious complaints of his infirmities. 2 For he confesseth that when he had determined silence, that he brast forthe yet into wordes that he wolde not, through the greatnes of his grief. 4 Then he rehearseth certeine requestes which taste of the infirmitie of mã, 8 And mixeth with thē manie prayers: but all do shewe a minde wonderfully troubled, that it maye plainely appeare how he did striue mightely against death and desperation.*

¶ *To the excellent* musician [a] *Ieduthún. A Psalme of David.*

1 I Thoght, [b] I wil take hede to my
waies, that I sinne not with my tõgue:
I wil kepe my mouth brideled, while the
wicked is in my sight.
2 I was dumme and spake nothing: I kept
silence *euen* from good, [c] and my sorow
was more stirred.
3 Mine heart was hote within me, *and* while
I was musing, the fyre kindled, & [d] I spake with my tongue, *saying*,
4 Lord, let me know mine end, & the measure of my dayes, what it is: let me know
how long I haue to liue.
5 Beholde, thou hast made my dayes as an
hand breadth, and mine age as nothing in
respect of thee: surely euerie man *in his best*
state is altogether [e] vanitie. Sélah.
6 Douteles man walketh in a shadowe, and
disquieteth him self in vaine: he heapeth
vp *riches*, & cã not tel who shal gather thē.
7 And now Lord, what waite I for? mine
hope is euen in thee.
8 Deliuer me from all my transgresions,
and make me not a rebuke vnto the
[f] foolish.
9 I shulde haue bene dumme, and not haue

a This was one of ỹ chief singers, 1.Chr. 16,41.

b Albeit he had appointed with him self paciently to haue taryed Gods leasure, yet the vehemencie of his peine caused him to breake his purpose.

c Thogh whē the wicked ruled, he thoght to haue kept silence, yet his zeale caused him to change his minde.

d He confesseth, that he grudged agaist God, considering the greatnes of his sorowes, & the shortnes of his life.

e Yet David offended in ỹ that he reasoned w̃ God, as thogh that he were to seuere towarde his weake creature.

f Make me not a mockĩg stocke to the wicked, or wrap me not vp w̃ the wicked, when they are put to shame.

opened my mouth, because [g] thou didest it.
10 Take thy plague away from me: for I
am consumed by the stroke of thine hãd.
11 When thou with rebukes doest chastise
man for iniquitie, thou as a moth [h] makest
his [i] beautie to consume: surely euerie mã
is vanitie. Sélah.
12 Heare my praier, ô Lord, & hearken vn
to my crye: kepe not silence at my teares,
for I am a stranger with thee, & a soiourner as all my fathers.
13 Stay *thine angre* from me, that I maie recouer my strength, [k] before I go hence &
be not.

g Seing my troubles came of thy prouidēce, I oght to haue endured thē paciently.

h Thogh thine open plagues light not euermore vpõ them, yet thy secret cursse cõtinually freteth them.

i The worde signifieth all ỹ he desireth, as health, force, strength, beautie, and in whatsoeuer he hathe delite, so that the rod of God taketh away all that is desired in this worlde.

k For his sorow caused him to thinke that God wolde destroy him vtterly: whereby we se how hard it is for the verie Saintes to kepe a measure in their wordes, when death & despaire assaile them.

PSAL. XL.

1 *David deliuered from great danger, doeth magnifie and praise the grace of God for his deliuerance, & cõmendeth his prouidence towards all mankinde. 5 Then doeth he promise to giue him self wholly to Gods seruice, & so declareth how God is truely worshiped. 14 Afterward he giueth thankes & praiseth God, & hauing complained of his enemies, with good courage he calleth for aide and succour.*

¶ *To him that excelleth. A Psalme of David.*

1 I Waited [a] paciently for the Lord, & he
inclined vnto me, and heard my crye.
2 He broght me also out of the [b] horrible
pit, out of the myrie claie, and set my fete
vpon the rocke, and ordered my goings.
3 And he hathe put in my mouth [c] a new
song of praise vnto our God: manie shal
se it and feare, and shal trust in the Lord.
4 Blessed *is* the man, that maketh the Lord
his trust, and regardeth [d] not the proude,
nor suche as turne aside to lies.
5 [e] O Lord my God, thou hast made thy
wonderful workes *so* manie, that none can
counte in ordre to thee thy thoghts toward vs: I wolde declare, & speake *of them*,
but thei are mo then I am able to expresse.
6 Sacrifice and offring thou didest not desire: (*for* [f] mine eares hast thou prepared)
burnt offring and sin offring hast thou not
required.
7 [g] Then said I, Lo, I come: *for* in the rolle of the boke it *is* writen of me,
8 I desired to do thy good wil, ô my God:
yea, thy Law is within mine heart.
9 I haue declared *thy* righteousnes in the
[h] great Congregation: lo, I wil not refrei-
ne my lippes: ô Lord, thou knowest.
10 I haue not hid thy righteousnes within
mine heart, *but* I haue declared thy [i] trueth
and thy saluation: I haue not conceiled
thy mercie and thy trueth from the great
Congregation.

a Thogh God differred his helpe, yet he paciently abode, til he was heard.

b He hathe deliuered me frõ moste great dãgers.

c That is, a special occasiõ to praise him: for Gods benefites are so manie occasiõs for vs to praise his Name.

d To follow their example, which he must nedes do, that trusteth not onely in the Lord.

e David goeth from one kĩde of Gods fauour to the contemplation of his prouidēce ouer all, & confesseth that his counsels towards vs are farre aboue our capacities: we cã not so much as tel them in ordre.

f Thou hast opened mine eares to vnderstand the spiritual meaning of the sacrifices: and here David esteemeth the ceremonies of the Law nothing in respect of the spiritual seruice.

g When thou hadest opened mine eares & heart, I was readie to obei thee, being assured that I was writen in the boke of thine elect for this end.

h In the Church, assembled in ỹ Sanctuarie.

i David here nõbreth 3 degrees of our saluaciõ: Gods mercie, whereby he pitieth vs: his righteousnes, which signifieth his continual protection, and his trueth, whereby appeareth his constant fauour, so that hereof procedeth our saluation.

11 Withdrawe not thou thy tendre mercie
from me, ô Lord: let thy mercie and thy
trueth alway preserue me.
12 For innumerable troubles haue compassed me: my sinnes haue taken suche holde
vpon me, that I am not able to loke vp:
yea, they are mo in nomber then the heeres of mine head: therefore mine heart
hathe [k] failed me.
13 Let it please thee, ô Lord, to deliuer me:
make haste, ô Lord, to helpe me.
14 Let them be [l] confounded & put to shame together, ỷ seke my soule to destroye
it: let them be driuẽ backeward and put to
rebuke, that desire mine hurt.
15 Let them be [m] destroyed for a rewarde
of their shame, ẇ saye vnto me, Aha, aha.
16 Let all thẽ, that seke thee, reioyce and be
glad in thee: & let thẽ, that loue thy saluation,
saye alway, [n] The Lord be praised.
17 Thogh I be poore and nedie, the Lord
thinketh on me: thou art mine helper & my
deliuerer: my God, make no tarying.

k As touching the iudgement of the flesh, I was vtterly destitute of all counsel: yet faith inwardly moued mine heart to praye.
l He desireth that Gods mercie maye contend for him against the rage of his enemies.
m Let the same shame, and cõfusion light vpon them, ẇ they intended to haue broght vpon me.
n As the faithful alwayes praise God for his benefites: so the wicked mocke Gods children in their afflictiõs

PSAL. XLI.

1 *David being grieuously afflicted, blesseth them, that pitie his case, 9 And complaineth of the treason of his
owne friends & familiares, as came to passe in Iudas,
Iohn 13,18. After he feling the great mercies of God
gently chastising him, & not suffering his enemies to
triumph against him, 13 Giueth moste heartie thankes vnto God.*

¶ *To him that excelleth. A Psalme of David.*

1 Blessed *is* he that [a] iudgeth wisely of
the poore: the Lord shal deliuer him
in the time of trouble.
2 The Lord wil kepe him, & preserue him
aliue: he shalbe blessed vpon the earth, &
thou wilt not deliuer him vnto the wil of
his enemies.
3 The Lord wil strengthen him vpon the
[b] bed of sorowe: thou hast turned all his
[c] bed in his sickenes.
4 *Therefore* I said, Lord haue mercie vpon
me: heale my soule, for I haue sinned a-
gainst thee.
5 Mine enemies [d] speake euil of me, *saying*,
When shal he dye, and his name perish?
6 And if he come to se me, he speaketh
[e] lies, *but* his heart heapeth iniquitie within hĩ, *&* whẽ he cometh forthe, he telleth it.
7 All they that hate me, whisper together
against me: *euen* against me do they imagine mine hurt.
8 [f] A mischief is light vpon him, & he that
lieth, shal no more rise.
9 Yea, my " familiar friend, whome I trusted, which did eat of my bread, [g] hathe
lifted vp the hele against me.
10 Therefore, ô Lord, haue mercie vpõ me,
& raise me vp: so I shal rewarde them.
11 By this I know that thou fauorest me,
because mine enemie doeth not triumph
against me.
12 And as for me, thou vpholdest me [h] in

a Not cõdemning him as accursed, whome God doeth visite, knowing that there are diuers causes, why God layeth his hãd vpõ vs: yea, & afterwarde he restoreth vs.
b When for sorow & grief of minde he casteth him self vpon his bed.
c Thou hast restored him in his sicke bed & set him comfort.
d That is, curse me, and can not haue their cruel hate quẽched, but with my shameful death.
e For pretending to cõfort me, he conspireth my death in his heart, & braggeth thereof.
f The enemies thoght by his sharpe punishments ỷ God was become his mortal enemie.
" Ebr. *The man of my peace.*
g As Dauid felt this falshod, and as it was chiefly accomplished in Christ, Iohn 13,18, so shal his mẽbers cõtinually proue the same.
h Meaning, ether in prosperitie of life, or in ỷ true feare of God against all tentations.

mine integritie, and doest set me before
thy [i] face for euer.
13 Blessed *be* ỷ Lord God of Israél worlde
without end. [k] So be it, euen so be it.

PSAL. XLII.

1 *The Prophet grieuously complaineth, that being letted
by his persecutors he colde not be present in the Cõgrega
ciõ of Gods people, protesting that althogh he was sepa
rated in bodie frõ them, yet his heart was thitherwarde
affectioned 7 And last of all he sheweth, that he was not
so farre ouercome with these sorowes & thoghts, 8 But
that he continually put his confidence in the Lord.*

¶ *To him that excelleth.* A Psalme *to giue instruction*, [a] cõmitted *to the sonnes of Kórah.*

1 As the hart braieth for the riuers of
water, so [b] pãteth my soule after thee,
ô God.
2 My soule thirsteth for God, *euen* for the
liuing God: when shal I come and appeare *before* the presence of God?
3 [c] My teares haue bene my meat daie and
night, while they daiely say vnto me,
Where is thy God?
4 When I remẽbred [d] these things, I powred out my verie heart, because I had gone
with the multitude, *&* led them into the
House of God with the voice of singing,
& praise, as a multitude ỷ kepeth a feast.
5 Why art thou cast downe, my soule, and
vnquiet within me? [e] waite on God: for I
wil yet giue him thankes for the helpe of
his presence.
6 My God, my soule is cast downe within
me, [f] because I remember thee, from the
land of Iordén, and Hermoním, *and* from
the mount Mizár.
7 *One* [g] depe calleth *another* depe by ỷ noise of thy water spoutes: all thy waues and
thy floods are gone ouer me.
8 The Lord [h] wil grante his louing kinde
nes in the daie, and in the night shal I sing
of hĩ, *euẽ* a praier vnto ỷ God of my life.
9 I wil saie vnto God, *which is* my rocke,
Why hast thou forgotten me? why go I
mournig, when the enemie oppresseth *me*?
10 My [i] bones are cut a sunder, while mine
enemies reproche me, saying daiely vnto
me, Where is thy God?
11 [k] Why art thou cast downe, my soule? &
why art thou disquieted within me? waite
on God: for I wil yet giue him thankes: *he
is* my present helpe, and my God.

PSAL. XLIII.

1 *He praieth to be deliuered from them which conspire
against him, that he might ioyfully praise God in his
holie Congregacion.*

1 Iudge [a] me, ô God, & defend my cause
against the vnmerciful [b] people: deliuer
me from the deceitful and wicked man.
2 For thou art the God of my strẽgth: why
hast thou put me awaie? why go I so mourning, when the enemie oppresseth *me*.
3 Send thy [c] light and thy trueth: let them
lead me: let thẽ bring me vnto thine holy
Mountaine and to thy Tabernacles.

i Shewing me euident signes of thy Fatherlie prouidence.
k By this repetition he stirreth vp ỷ faithful to praise God.
Psal. XLII.
a As a treasure to be kept of thẽ, which were of the nõber of the Leuites.
b By these similitudes of thirst & pantĩg he sheweth his feruent desire to serue God in his Tẽple.
c As others take pleasure in eating & drinking, so he was altogether giuen to weping.
d That is, how I led ỷ people to serue thee in thy Tabernacle, & now seing my contrarie estate, I dye for sorow
e Thogh he susteined grieuous assaltes of the flesh to cast hĩ into despaire, yet his faith grounded on Gods accustomed mercies, getteth the victorie.
f That is, whẽ I remember thee in this lãd of my bãnishment among ỷ mountaines.
g Afflictions came so thicke vpon me, that I felt my self as ouerwhelmed: whereby he sheweth there is no end of our miserie, til God be pacified, & send remedie.
h He assureth him selfe of Gods helpe in time to come.
i That is, I am moste grieuously tormented.
k This repetition doeth declare ỷ David did not ouercome at once: to teache vs to be constant for asmuche as God wil certeinly deliuer his.
Psal. XLIII.
a He desireth God to vndertake his cause against the enemies, but chiefly that he wolde restore him to the Tabernacle.
b That is, the cruel companie of mine enemies.
c To wit, thy fauour, which appeareth by the performance of thy promises.

4 Then [d] wil I go vnto the altar of God,
euen vnto the God of my ioy *&* gladnes:
and vpon the harpe wil I giue thankes vn
to thee, ô God, my God.
5 Why art thou cast downe, my soule? and
why art thou disquieted within me? [e] waite
on God: for I wil yet giue him thankes,
be is my present helpe, and my God.

PSAL. XLIIII.

1 The faithful remember the great mercie of God toward his people. 9 After, thei complaine, because thei fele it no more. 17 Also thei alledge the couenant made with Abraham, for the keping whereof thei shewe what grieuous things thei suffred. 23 Finally they praie vnto God not to contemne their affliction, seing the same redoundeth to the contempt of his honour.

¶ *To him that excelleth.* A Psalme *to giue instructiõ, committed to the sonnes of Kórah.*

1 WE haue heard with our [a] eares, ô
God: our fathers haue tolde vs the
workes, *that* thou hast done in their daies,
in the olde time:
2 *How* thou hast driuen out the [b] heathen
with thine hand, and planted [c] them: *how*
thou hast destroyed the [d] people, and caused [e] them to growe.
3 For thei inherited not the land by their
owne sworde, nether did their owne arme
saue them: but thy right hand, & thine arme and the light of thy countenance, because thou didest [f] fauour them.
4 Thou art my King, ô God: send helpe
vnto [g] Iaakób.
5 [h] Through thee haue we thrust backe our
aduersaries: by thy Name haue we troadẽ
downe them that rose vp against vs.
6 For I do not trust in my bowe, nether can
my sworde saue me.
7 But thou hast saued vs from our aduersaries, & hast put thẽ to confusion ŷ hate vs.
8 *Therefore* wil we praise God continually,
& wil confesse thy Name for euer. Sélah.
9 But *now* thou art farre of, and puttest vs
to [i] confusion, & goest not forthe with our
armies.
10 Thou makest vs to turne backe from the
aduersarie, and thei, which hate vs, spoile
*for them selues.
11 *Thou giuest vs [k] as shepe to be eaten, &
doest scater vs among the nations.
12 Thou sellest thy people [l] without gaine,
and doest not increase their price.
13 Thou makest vs a reproche to our neighbours, a ieste and a laughing stocke to thẽ
that are round about vs.
14 Thou makest vs a prouerbe among the
nations, & a nodding of the head among
the people.
15 My [m] confusion *is* daiely before me, and
the shame of my face hathe couered me,
16 For the voice of the sclanderer and rebu
ker, for the enemie and [n] auenger.
17 All this is come vpon vs, yet do we not
[o] forget thee, nether deale we falsely concerning thy couenant.
18 Our heart is not turned backe: nether
our steppes gone out of thy paths,
19 Albeit thou hast smiten vs downe into
the place of *dragons, and couered vs with
the shadowe of death.
20 If we haue forgottẽ ŷ Name of our God,
& holden vp our hãds to a [p] strange god,
21 Shal not God [q] searche this out? for he
knoweth the secrets of the heart.
22 Surely for thy sake [r] are we slaine cõtinually, & are coũted as shepe for ŷ slaughter.
23 Vp, why slepest thou, ô Lord? awake, be
not farre of for euer.
24 Wherefore hidest thou thy face? *&* for-
gettest our miserie and our affliction?
25 For our soule is [f] beaten downe vnto the
dust: our belly cleueth vnto the grounde.
26 Rise vp for our succour, and redeme vs
for thy [t] mercies sake.

PSAL. XLV.

1 The maiestie of Salomón, his honour, strength, beautie, riches & power are praised, & also his mariage with the Egyptian being an heathen woman is blessed, 10 If that she can renoũce her people & the loue of her countrey and giue her selfe wholly to her housband. Vnder the which figure the wonderful maiestie & increase of the kingdome of Christ and the Church his spouse now taken of the Gentiles is described.

¶ *To him that excelleth on* [a] *Shoshannim a song of* [b] *loue to giue instruction*, committed *to the sonnes of Kórah.*

1 MIne heart wil vtter forthe a good
matter: I wil intreat *in* my workes of
the King: my tongue *is as* the penne of a
swift writer.
2 Thou art [c] fairer thẽ the childrẽ of men:
grace is powred in thy lippes, because God
hathe blessed thee for euer.
3 Girde thy sworde vpon *thy* thigh, ô moste
mightie, *to wit*, thy worship & thy glorie,
4 And prosper with thy glorie: [d] ride vpon
the worde of trueth and of mekenes *&* of
righteousnes: so thy right hand shal teache thee terrible things.
5 Thine arrowes *are* sharpe *to perce* the heart
of the Kings enemies: *therefore* the people
shal fall vnder thee.
6 Thy [e] throne, ô God, *is* for euer and euer:
the scepter of thy kingdome *is* a scepter
of righteousnes.
7 Thou louest righteousnes, and hatest wic
kednes, because God, *euen* thy God hathe
[f] anointed thee with the oile of gladnes
aboue thy felowes.
8 All thy garments *smell* of myrrhe and a-
loes, *and* cassia, *when thou comest* out of the
yuorie palaces, [g] where thei haue made
thee glad.
9 Kings daughters *were* amõg thine hono-

d He pmiseth to offre a solẽne sacrifice of thankesgiuing in token of his great deliuerance.

e Whereby he admonisheth ŷ faithful not to relent, but constantly to waite on the Lord, thogh their troubles be lõg & great.

a This psalme semeth to haue bene made by some excellẽt Prophet for ŷ vse of the people, when the Church was in extreme miserie, ether at their returne from Babylon, or vnder Antiochus, or in suche like affliction.
b That is, the Canaanites.
c To wit, our fathers.
d Of Canáan.
e That is, our fathers.
f Gods fre mercie & loue is ŷ onelie foũtaine & beginning of the Church, Deut. 4,37.
g Because ŷ art our King, therefore deliuer thy people from their miserie.
h Because thei & their forefathers made bothe one Church thei applie ŷ to thẽ selues, which before thei did attribute to their fathers
i As thei confessed before, ŷ their strength came of God, so now thei acknowledge ŷ this affliction came by his iust iudgemẽt.
*Or, at their pleasure.
Rom. 8,36.
k Knowing God to be autor of this calamitie, they murmure not, but seke remedie at his hands, who wounded thẽ.
l As sclaues ŵ are solde for a low price, nether lokest ŷ for him that offreth moste, but takest the first chapman.
m I dare not lift vp mine head for shame.
n Meaning, the proude and cruel tyrant.

o Thei boaste not of their vertues, but declare that thei rest vpon God in the middes of their afflictions: who punished not now their sinnes, but by hard afflictions called them to the consideration of the heauenlie ioyes.
*Or, whales: meaning the bottomles seas of tentations. here we se the power of faith, which can be ouercome by no perils.
p Thei shewe that thei honored God aright because thei trusted in him alone.
q Thei take God to witnes ŷ thei were vpright to himward.
r The faithful make this their cõfort, that ŷ wicked punish them not for their sinnes, but for Gods cause, Matt. 5, 10. 1 Pet. 4,14.
f There is no hope of recouerie, except thou put to thine hande & raise vs vp.
t Which is ŷ onelie & sufficient ransom to deliuer bothe the bodie and soule from all kide of sclauerie & miserie.

Psal. XLV.
a This was a certeine tune or an instrumẽt.
b Of that perfite loue that oght to be betwene ŷ housband & the wife.
c Salomõs beautie and eloquence to winne fauour with his people, and his power to ouercome his enemies, is here described.
d He alludeth to them ŷ ride in chariots in their triũphes, shewing ŷ the quiet state of a kingdome stãdeth ĩ trueth, mekenes & iustice, not in worldelie põpe and vanitie.
e Vnder this figure of this kingdome of iustice is set forthe ŷ euerlasting kingdome of Christ
f Hathe established thy kingdome as the figure of Christ, which is the peace & ioye of the Church.
g In the which palace the people made thee ioyful to se them giue thankes & reioyce for thee.

rable-*wiues*:vpon thy right hand did stand
the [h] Quene in a vesture of golde of O-
phír.
10 [i]Hearken,ô daughter, and consider, and
incline thine eare: forget also thine owne
people and thy fathers house.
11 So shal the Kĩg haue pleasure in thy beautie : for he is thy Lord, and reuerence
thou him.
12 And the [k] daughter of "Tyrus *with* the riche of the people shal do homage before
thy face with presents.
13 The Kings daughter is all glorious
[l] within: her clothing is of broydered
golde.
14 She shal be broght vnto the King in raiment of nedle worke: the virgins *that follow*
after her, & her companiõs shal be broght
vnto thee.
15 With ioye and gladnes shal thei be
broght, *and* shal enter into the Kings palace.
16 In steade of thy fathers shal thy [m] children be: ŷ shalt make thẽ princes [n] through
all the earth.
17 I wil make thy [o] Name to be remembred
through all generations : therefore shal ŷ
people giue thãkes vnto thee worlde without end.

PSAL. XLVI.

1 A song of triumph or thankesgiuing for the deliuerãce of Ierusalém, after Sennaherib with his armie was driuẽ awaie, or some other like sudden and maruelous deliuerance by the mightie hãd of God. 8 Whereby the Prophet commending this great benefite, doeth exhorte the faithful to giue them selues wholly into the hand of God, douting nothing but that vnder his protection thei shal be safe against all the assautes of their enemies, because this is his delite to asswage the rage of the wicked, when thei are moste busie against the iust.

¶ *To him that excelleth vpon* [a] *Alamóth a song committed to the sonnes of Kórah.*

1 GOd *is* our "hope and strength, & helpe in [b] troubles, readie to be founde.
2 Therefore wil not we [c] feare, thogh the
earth be moued, and thogh the mountaines fall into the middes of the sea.
3 *Thogh* the waters thereof [d] rage & be troubled & the mountaines shake at the surges of the same. Sélah,
4 *Yet there is* a [e] Riuer, whose streames shal
make glad ŷ Citie of God: *euen* ŷ Sanctua
rie of the Tabernacles of the moste High.
5 God *is* in the middes of it: *therefore* shal it
not be moued : God shal helpe it [f] verie
early.
6 *When* the nations raged, & the kingdomes were moued, *God* "thundred, & the
earth melted.
7 The Lord of hostes *is* [g] with vs: the God
of Iaakób *is* our refuge. Sélah.
8 Come, & beholde the workes of ŷ Lord,
[h] what desolations he hathe made in the
earth.
9 He maketh warres to cease vnto the ends
of the worlde: he breaketh the bowe and
cutteth the speare, & burneth the chariots
with fyre.
10 Be [i] stil and knowe that I am God: I wil
be exalted among the heathen, & I wil be
exalted in the earth.
11 The Lord of hostes *is* with vs : the God
of Iaakób *is* our refuge. Sélah.

PSAL. XLVII.

1 The Prophet exhorteth all people to the worship of the true and euerliuing God, cõmending the mercie of God toward the posteritie of Iaakób: 9 And after prophecieth of the kingdome of Christ in this time of the Gospel.

¶ *To him that excelleth. A Psalme* committed *to the sonnes of Kórah.*

1 ALl people [a] clap your hands: sing
loude vnto God with a ioyful voice.
2 For the Lord *is* high, & terrible : a great
King ouer all the earth.
3 He hathe [b] subdued the people vnder vs,
and the nations vnder our fete.
4 He hathe chosen [c] our inheritance for vs:
euen the glorie of Iaakób whome he loued. Sélah.
5 God is gone vp with triumph, *euen* the
Lord, with the [d] sounde of the trumpet.
6 Sing praises to God, sing praises: sing
praises vnto our King, sing praises.
7 For God *is* the King of all the earth: sing
praises *euerie one* that hathe [e] vnderstanding.
8 God reigneth ouer the heathen: God sitteth vpon his holie throne.
9 The princes of the people are gathered
vnto the people of the God of Abrahám:
for the shields of the worlde *belong* to
God: he [f] is greatly to be exalted.

PSAL. XLVIII.

1 A notable deliuerance of Ierusalém from the hand of manie Kings is mentioned, for the which thankes are giuen to God, and the state of that citie is praised, that hathe God so presently at all times readie to defend thẽ. The Psalme semeth to be made in the time of Ahaz, Ioshaphát, Asá or Ezechiáh: for in their times chiefly was the citie by foren princes assalted.

¶ [a] *A song or Psalme* commited *to the sonnes of Kórah.*

1 GReat *is* the Lord, and greatly to be
praised, in the [b] Citie of our God, *e-
uen* vpon his holie Mountaine.
2 Mount Zión, *lying* Northward, *is* faire in
situation: *it is* the [c] ioye of the whole earth,
and the citie of the great King.
3 In the palaces thereof God is knowen for
a [d] re-

h Thogh he had many Kĩgs daughters among his wiues, yet he loued Pharaohs daughter best.
i Vnder the figure of Pharaohs daughter he sheweth ŷ ŷ Church must cast of all carnal affections to obey Christ onely.
k He signifieth that diuers of them, that be riche, shalbe benefactours to the Church, albeit thei giue not perfite obedience to ŷ Gospel.
"Or, Zor.
l There is nothing fained, nor hypocritical, but she is glorious bothe within & without: and howbeit ŷ Church hath not at all times this outwarde glorie, the faute is to be imputed onely to their owne ingratitude.
m Thei shal haue greater graces then their fathers.
n He signifieth the great cõpasse of Christs kingdome, ŵ shalbe sufficiẽt to enriche all his membres.
o This must onely be referred to Christ and not to Salomón.

a Which was ether a musical instrument or a solemne tune, vnto the ŵ this psalme was sung.
"Or, protection.
b In all maner of troubles God sheweth his spedie mercie and power in defending his.
c That is, we wil not be ouercome with feare.
d Thogh the afflictions rage neuer so muche, yet the riuers of Gods mercies bring sufficient comfort to his.
e The riuer of Shiloáh, ŵ passed through Ierusalém: meaning thogh ŷ defence seme neuer so smale, yet if God haue appointed it, it is sufficient.
f Alwaies when nede requireth. "Ebr. gaue his voice. g Thei are assured that God can and wil defend his Church from all dangers and enemies.

h To wit, how oft he hathe destroied his enemies & deliuered his people.
i He warneth thẽ that persecute ŷ Church to cease their crueltie : for els thei shal fele that God is to strong for them, against whome thei fight.

a Here is figured Christ, vnto whome all his shulde giue willing obedience, & who wolde shew hĩ self terrible to the wicked.
b He hathe made ŷ Iewes, who were the kepers of the Law and Prophets, scholemasters to the Gentiles, that thei shulde with gladnes obey them.
c God hathe chosen vs aboue all other nations to enioye a moste glorious inheritance.
d He doeth allude vnto the trumpets, that were blowne at solemne feastes : but he doeth further signifie the triumph of Christ and his glorious ascension into the heauens. e He requireth that vnderstanding be ioyned with singing, lest the Name of God be profaned with vaine crying. f He praiseth Gods highnes, for that he ioyneth the great princes of the worlde, whome he calleth shields to the felowship of his Church.

a Some put this difference betwene a song and Psalme, saying that it is called a song, whẽ there is no instrument, but the voice: and the psalme, the cõtrary. The song of the Psalme is whẽ the instrumẽts beginne, & the voice followeth. The Psalme of the song, the contrary. b Albeit God shew his wonders through all the worlde, yet he wil be chiefly praised in his Church. c Because the words of saluation came thence to all them that shulde beleue.

a [d] refuge.
4 For lo, the Kings were [e] gathered, & wẽt
together.
5 When thei sawe [f] it, thei marueiled: thei
were astonied, & suddenly driuen backe.
6 Feare came there vpon them, & sorowe,
as vpon a woman in trauaile.
7 *As* with an East winde thou breakest the
shippes [g] of Tarshish, *so were they destroyed.*
8 As we haue [h] heard, so haue we sene in
the Citie of the Lord of hostes, in the Citie of our God: God wil stablish it for e-
uer. Sélah.
9 We waite for thy louĩg kindenes, ô God,
in the middes of thy Temple.
10 O God, according vnto thy Name, so is
thy praise vnto the [i] worldes end: thy right
hand is ful of righteousnes.
11 Let [k] mount Zion reioyce, & the daughters of Iudah be glad, because of thy iudgements.
12 [l] Compasse about Zión, and go rounde
about it, & tel the towres thereof.
13 Marke wel the wall thereof: beholde her
towres, that ye maie tel your posteritie.
14 For this God *is* our God for euer & euer:
he shal be our guide vnto the death.

d Except God were ȳ defence thereof, nether situacion nor municion colde preuaile. e Thei conspired & went against Gods people. f The enemies were afraid at the sight of ȳ Citie. g That is, of Cilicia, or of ȳ sea called Mediterraneum. h To wit, of our fathers, so haue we proue:or, God hathe performed his promes. i In all places where thy Name shalbe heard of, mẽ shal praise thee, whẽ thei heare of thy maruelo[us] workes. k Let Ierusalém & ȳ cities of Iudea reioyce for thy iust iudgemẽts against thine enemies. l For in this outward defẽce & strength Gods blesiſgs did also appeare: but ȳ chief is to be referred to Gods fauour and secret defence, who neuer leaueth his.

PSAL. XLIX.

1 The holie Gost calleth all men to the consideration of mans life, 7 shewing them not to be moste blessed, that are moste wealthie, & therefore not to be feared: but contrary wise he lifteth vp our mindes to consider how all things are ruled by Gods prouidence: 14 Who as he iugeth these worldlie misers to euerlasting torments, 15 So doeth he preserue his & wil rewarde thẽ in the day of the resurrection, 2 Thess. 1,6.

¶ *To him that excelleth. A psalme* committed *to the sonnes of Kórah.*

1 Heare [a] this, all *ye* people: giue eare,
all ye that dwel in the worlde,
2 Aswel lowe as hie, bothe riche & poore.
3 My mouth shal speake of wisdome, and
the meditacion of mine heart *is* of knowledge.
4 I wil incline mine eare to a parable, *and*
vtter my graue matter vpon the harpe.
5 Wherefore shulde I [b] feare in the euil
daies, *when* iniquitie shal compasse me a-
bout, *as at* mine heles?
6 They trust in their [c] goods, & boast them
selues in the multitude of their riches.
7 Yet a man can by no meanes redeme *his*
brother: he can not giue his ransome to
God,
8 (So [d] precious is the redemption of their
soules, [e] and the continuance for euer)
9 That he may liue stil for euer, & not se
the graue.
10 For he seeth that wisemen [f] dye, & also
that the ignorant and foolish perish, and
leaue their riches for [g] others.
11 *Yet* they thinke, their houses, & their habitacions *shal continue* for euer, *euen* from
generacion to generacion, and [*] call *their*
lands by their names.
12 But man shal not continue in honour: he
is like the [h] beasts *that* dye.
13 This their waie *vttereth* their foolishnes:
yet their posteritie [i] delite in their talke.
Sélah.
14 [k] Like shepe thei lie in graue: [l] death
deuoureth thẽ, & the righteous shal haue
dominacion ouer them in the [m] morning:
for their beautie shal consume, *when they*
shal go from their house to graue.
15 But God shal deliuer my soule from the
power of the graue: [*] for he wil receiue
me. Sélah.
16 Be not thou afraied when one is made
riche, & when the glorie of his house is
increased.
17 *For he shal take nothing awaie when he
dyeth, nether shal his pompe descend after him.
18 For while he liued, [*] he reioyced him
self: and [m] men wil praise thee, when thou
makest muche of thy self.
19 [*] [n] He shal enter into the generacion of
his fathers, [o] & they shal not liue for euer.
20 Man *is* in honour, and [p] vnderstandeth
not: he is like to beasts *that* perish.

a He wil intreat how God gouerneth the worlde by his prouidence w[hich] cã not be perceiued by the iudgement of the flesh. b Thogh wickednes reigne & enemies rage, seing God wil execute his iudgemẽts against ȳ wicked in time cõuenient. c To trust in riches is more madnes, seing they cã nether restore life nor prolong it. d That is, so rare, or not to be founde, as prophecie was pretious in the daies of Eli, 1.Sam.3,1. e Meaning, it is impossible to liue for euer: also that life and death are onely in Gods hands. f In that that death maketh no difference betwene the persones. g That is, not to their children, but to strangers. Yet the wicked profit not by these examples, but stil dreame an immortalitie in earth.

Or, labour that their name may be famous in earth. h As touching ȳ death of the bodie. i They speake & do the same thing ȳ their fathers did. k As shepe are gathered into ȳ folde, so shal thei be broght to the graue. l Because they haue no parte of life euerlasting. m Christs cõming is as the morning, when the elect shal reigne with Christ their head ouer the wicked. *Or, because he hathe receiued me.* *Iob 27,19. 1.tim.6,7.* *Ebr. he blessed his soule.* m The flatterers praise thẽ ȳ liue in delites & pleasures. *Or, his soule.* n And not passe the terme appointed for life. o Bothe thei & their fathers shal liue here but a while & at length dye for euer. p He condemneth mans ingratitude, who hauĩg receiued excellẽt giftes of God, abuseth them like a beast to his owne condemnacion.

PSAL. L.

1 Because the Church is alwaie ful of hypocrites, 8 Which do imagine that God wilbe worshiped with outward ceremonies onely, without the heart: and especially the Iewes were of this opinion, because of their figures and ceremonies of the Law, thinking that their sacrifices were sufficient, 21 Therefore the Prophet doeth reproue this grosse errour, & pronounceth the Name of God to be blasphemed, where holines is set in ceremonies. 23 For he declareth the worship of God to be spiritual, whereof are two principal partes, inuocation, & thankesgiuing.

¶ *A Psalme of* [a] *Asaph.*

1 The God of gods, *euen* ȳ Lord hathe
spoken and called the [b] earth frõ the
rising vp of ȳ sunne vnto the going downe
thereof.
2 Out of Zión, *which is* the [c] perfection of
beautie, hathe God shined.
3 Our God shal come and shal not kepe silence: [d] a fyre shal deuoure before him, &
a mightie tempest shal be moued rounde
about him.
4 He shal call the heauen aboue, and [e] the
earth to iudge his people.
5 Gather my [f] Saints together vnto me,
those that make a couenant with me with
[g] sacrifice.
6 And the heauens shal declare his righteousnes: for God is Iudge him self. Sélah.
7 Heare, ô my people, & I wil speake: *heare,*
ô Israél, and I wil testifie vnto thee: *for I*
am God, *euen* thy God.

PSAL. L. a Who was ether the autor, or a chief singer, to whome it was cõmitted. b To plead against his dissembling people before heauen and earth. c Because God had chosen it to haue his Name there called vpon, and also his image shined there in ȳ doctrine of ȳ Law. d As when God gaue his Law in mount Sinai, he appeared terrible with thunder and tempest, so wil he appeare terrible to take a count for the keping thereof. e As witnesses aginst the hypocrites. f God in respect of his elect, calleth the whole bodie holie, Saints & his people. g Which shulde knowe that sacrifices are seales of the couenant betwene God and his people, and not set religion therein.

h For I passe not for sacrifices, except ẏ true vse be there, which is to confirme your faith in my promises.
i Thogh he did delite in sacrifice, yet had he no nede of mans helpe thereunto.
k Thogh mans life for the infirmitie thereof hathe nede of fode, yet God, whose life quickneth all the worlde, hathe no nede of suche meanes.
l Shew thy self mindeful of Gods benefites by thankesgiuing.
m Why doest thou fained to be of my people and talkest of my couenant, seing thou art but an hypocrite?
n And to liue according to my worde.
o He sheweth what are the frutes of them that contemne Gods word.
p He noteth the crueltie of hypocrites, ẇ spare not in their talke or iudgemẽt their owne mothers sonne.
q I wil write all thy wicked dedes in a role and make thee to read & acknoledge thẽ whether thou wilt or no.
r Vnder the ẇ is conteined faith and inuocation.
s As God hathe appointed.
t That is, declare my self to be his Sauiour.

8 I wil not h reproue thee for thy sacrifices,
or thy burnt offrings, *that haue not bene cō-*
tinually before me.
9 I wil take no bullocke out of thine house,
nor goates out of thy foldes.
10 i For all the beasts of the forest are mine,
and the beasts on a thousand mountaines.
11 I knowe all the foules on the mountaines:
& the wilde beasts of the field are mine.
12 If I be hungrie, I wil not tel thee: for the
worlde is mine, and all that therein is.
13 k Wil I eat the flesh of bulles? or drinke
the blood of goates?
14 Offre vnto God praise, & l paie thy vowes vnto the moste High,
15 And call vpon me in the daie of trouble:
so wil I deliuer thee, & thou shalt glorifie
me.
16 But vnto the wicked said God, m What
hast thou to do to declare mine ordinances, that thou shuldest take my couenant
in thy mouth,
17 Seing thou hatest n to be reformed, and
hast cast my wordes behinde thee?
18 For whẽ thou seest a thefe, o thou runnest
with him, and thou art partaker with the
adulterers.
19 Thou giuest thy mouth to euil, & with
thy tongue thou forgest deceite.
20 Thou p sittest, *and* speakest against thy
brother, *and* sclanderest thy mothers sonne.
21 These things hast thou done, & I helde
my tongue: *therefore* thou thoghtest that I
was like thee: *but* I wil reproue thee, and
q set *them* in order before thee.
22 Oh consider this, ye that forget God,
lest I teare you in pieces, & there be none
that can deliuer *you*.
23 He that offreth r praise, shal glorifie me:
and to him, that s disposeth his waie aright,
wil I t shewe the saluacion of God.

PSAL. LI.

1 When Dauid was rebuked by the Prophet Nathán, for his great offences, he did not onely acknowledge the same to God with protestation of his natural corruptiō and iniquitie, but also left a memorial thereof to his posteritie. 7 Therefore first he desireth God to forgiue his sinnes, 10 And to renue in him his holie Spirit, 13 With promes that he wil not be vnmindeful of those great graces. 18 Finally fearing lest God wolde punish the whole Church for his faute he requireth that he wolde rather increase his graces towards the same.

a To reproue him because he had cōmited so horrible sinnes, and lien in the same without repentãce more thẽ a whole yere.
b As his sinnes were manifolde & great, so he requireth that God wolde giue him the feling of his excellent and abundant mercies.
c My sinnes sticke so fast in me, that I haue nede of some singular kinde of washing.

¶ *To him that excelleth. A psalme of Dauid, when the Prophet Nathán a came vnto him, after he had gone in to Bath shéba.*

1 Haue mercie vpon me, ô God, b according to thy louing kindenes: according to the multitude of thy compassions put awaie mine iniquities.
2 Wash me c throughly from mine iniquitie, and clense me from my sinne.
3 For I d knowe mine iniquities, & my sinne *is* euer before me.
4 Against thee, against thee onely haue I
sinned, & done euil in thy sight, that thou
maiest be iuste when thou e speakest, *and*
pure when thou iudgest.
5 Beholde, I was borne in iniquitie, and in
sinne hathe my mother conceiued me.
6 Beholde, thou f louest trueth in ẏ inwarde
affections: therefore hast thou taught me
wisdome in the secret *of mine heart*.
7 Purge me with * hyssope, and I shal be
cleane: wash me, & I shalbe whiter then
snowe.
8 Make me to heare g ioye and gladnes, *that*
the h bones, *which* thou hast broken, maie
reioyce.
9 Hide thy face from my sinnes, and put
awaie all mine iniquities.
10 i Create in me a cleane heart, ô God, &
renue a right spirit within me.
11 Cast me not awaie from thy presence,
and take not thine holie Spirit from me.
12 Restore to me the ioye of thy saluacion,
and stablish me with *thy* k fre Spirit.
13 *Then* shal I teache thy l waies vnto the
wicked, and sinners shal be conuerted vnto
thee.
14 Deliuer me from m blood, ô God, *which*
art the God of my saluacion, *and* my tongue shal sing ioyfully of thy righteousnes.
15 n Open thou my lippes, ô Lord, and my
mouth shal shewe forthe thy praise.
16 For thou desirest no sacrifice, thogh I
wolde giue it: thou delitest not in burnt
offring.
17 The sacrifices of God *are* a o contrite
spirit: a contrite & a broken heart, ô God,
thou wilt not despise.
18 Be fauourable vnto p Zión for thy good
pleasure: buylde the walles of Ierusalém.
19 Then shalt thou accept the sacrifices of
q righteousnes, *euen* the burnt offring and
oblation: then shal they offer calues vpon
thine altar.

d My cōscience accuseth me, so that I can haue no rest, til I be reconciled.
e When thou giuest sentence agaĩst sinners, thei must nedes confesse thee to be iust and them selues sinners.
f He cōfesseth that God, who loueth purenes of heart, maie iustely destroy man, who of nature is a sinner, much more him, whome he had instructed in his heauẽlie wisdome.
Leuit. 14, 6.
g He meaneth Gods comfortable mercies towards repentant sinners.
h By ẏ bones he vnderstandeth all strength of soule and bodie, which by cares and mourning are consumed.
i He cōfesseth ẏ when Gods Spirit is colde in vs, to haue it againe reuiued is as a new creation.
k Which maie assure me that I am drawen out of ẏ sclauerie of sinne.
l He promiseth to endeuour that others by his example may turne to God.
m From the murder of Vriiáh, and the others that were slaine ẇ him, 2. Sam. 11, 17.
n By giuing me occasion to praise thee, when thou shalt forgiue my sinnes.
o Which is a wounding of ẏ heart, proceding of faith, which seketh vnto God for mercie.
p He praieth for the whole Church, because through his sinne it was in danger of Gods iudgement.
q That is, iust & lawful, applied to their right end, ẇ is the exercise of faith & repentance.

PSAL. LII.

1 Dauid describeth the arrogant tyrannie of his aduersarie Doeg: who by false surmises caused Ahimélch with the rest of the Priests to be slayne 5 Dauid prophecieth his destruction, 6 And incourageth the faithful to put their confidence in God, whose iudgements are moste sharpe against his aduersaries. 9 And finally he rendreth thankes to God for his deliuerance. In this Psalme is liuely set forthe the kingdome of Antichrist.

¶ *To him that excelleth. A Psalme of Dauid to giue instruction. When Doeg the Edomite came & shewed Saúl, & said to him, Dauid is come to the house of Ahimélech.*

1 Why boastest thou thy self in *thy*
wickednes, ô a man of power?
the louing kindnes of God *indureth* daily.

a O Doeg, ẇ hast credit ẇ the tyrãt Saúl, & hast power to murther the Saints of God

2 Thy tongue imagineth b mischief, *and is*
like a sharpe rasor, ŷ cutteth deceitfully.
3 Thou doest loue euil more thē good, *and*
lies, more thē to speake ŷ "trueth. Sélah.
4 Thou louest all wordes that maye destroye, ô deceitful tongue!
5 So shal God c destroye thee for euer: he
shal take thee and plucke thee out of *thy*
tabernacle, & d rote thee out of the land
of the liuing. Sélah.
6 The e righteous also shal se it, f and
feare, and shal laugh at him, *saying*,
7 Beholde the man that toke not God for
his strength, but trusted vnto the multitude of his riches, & put his strength " in
his malice.
8 But I shalbe like a g grene oliue tre in
the house of God: *for* I trusted in the mercie of God for euer and euer.
9 I wil alway praise thee, for that thou hast
done h *this*, & I wil "hope in thy Name, because it is good before thy Saints.

PSAL. LIII.

1 He describeth the crooked nature, 4 The crueltie,
5 And punishment of the wicked, when they loke not
for it, 6 And desireth the deliuerance of the godlie,
that they maie reioyce together.

¶ *To him that excelleth on* a *Mahaláth*. A
Psalme *of Dauid to giue instruction.*

1 The foole hathe said in his heart, *There*
is b no God. they haue corrupted and
done abominable wickednes: *there is* none
that doeth good.
2 God loked downe from heauen vpon the
children of men, to se if there were anie
that wolde vnderstand, and c seke God.
3 *Euerie one is gone backe: they are altogether corrupt: there is none that doeth
good, no not one.
4 Do not the d workers of iniquitie knowe
ŷ they eat vp my people *as* they eat bread?
they call not vpon God.
5 There they were afraied for feare, *where*
no e feare was: for God hathe scatered
the f bones of him that besieged thee:
thou hast put them to confusion, because
God hathe cast them of.
6 Oh giue saluacion vnto Israél out of
Zión: when God turneth the captiuitie of
his people, *then* Iaakób shal reioyce, & Israél shal be glad.

PSAL. LIIII.

1 Dauid broght into great danger by the reason of the
Ziphims, 5 Calleth vpon the Name of God to destroye
his enemies, 6 Promising sacrifice and fre offrings for
so great deliuerance.

¶ *To him that excelleth on Neginóth.* A Psalme *of Dauid, to giue instruction. When the Zi-*
phims came & said vnto Saúl, Is not Dauid
hid among vs?

1 Saue me, ô God, a by thy Name, and by
thy power iudge me.
2 O God, heare my prayer: hearken vnto
the wordes of my mouth.
3 For b strangers are risen vp against me,
& c tyrants seke my soule: they haue not
set God before them. Sélah.
4 Beholde, God *is* mine helper: the Lord *is*
with d them that vpholde my soule.
5 He shal reward euil vnto mine enemies:
oh cut them of in thy e trueth!
6 *Then* I wil sacrifice f frely vnto thee: I wil
praise thy Name, ô Lord, because it is good
7 For he hathe deliuered me out of all trou
ble, and mine eye hathe g sene *my desire*
vpon mine enemies.

PSAL. LV.

1 Dauid being in great heauines & distresse cōplaineth
of the crueltie of Saúl. 13 And of the falsehode of his
familiar acquaintance, 17 Vttering moste ardent af-
fections to moue the Lord to pitie him. 22 After being
assured of deliuerāce, he setteth forthe the grace of God
as thogh he had already obteined his request.

¶ *To him that excelleth on Neginóth.* A Psalme *of Dauid to giue instruction.*

1 Heare a my prayer, ô God, & hide not
thy self from my supplication.
2 Hearkē vnto me, & answer me: I mourne
in my prayer, and make a noise,
3 For the b voyce of the enemie, & for the
vexation of the wicked, because c they
haue broght iniquitie vpon me, & furiously hate me.
4 Mine heart trembleth within me, and the
terrors of death are fallen vpon me.
5 Feare and trembling are come vpon me,
& an horrible feare hathe d couered me.
6 And I said, Oh that I had wings like a
dooue: then wold I e flie away and rest.
7 Beholde, I wolde take my flight farre of,
& lodge in the wildernes. Sélah.
8 He wolde make haste for my deliuerance
f from the stormie winde and tempest.
9 Destroye, ô Lord, *and* g deuide their tongues: for I haue sene crueltie and strife in
the citie.
10 Daye and night they go about it vpon
the walles thereof: bothe h iniquitie and
mischief *are* in the middes of it.
11 Wickednes *is* in ŷ middes thereof: deceit
& guile departe not from her stretes.
12 Surely mine i enemie did not diffame
me: for I colde haue borne it: nether did
mine aduersarie exalt him self against me:
for I wolde haue hid me from him.
13 But *it was* thou, ô man, euen my k companion, my guide and my familiar:
14 Which delited in consulting together,
and went into the House of God as companions.
15 Let death sease vpon them: let them l go
downe quicke into the graue: for wickednes *is* in their dwellings, *euen* in the middes
of them.
16 *But* I wil call vnto God, & the Lord wil
saue me.
17 Euening and morning, & at noone wil

b Thy malice moueth thee by craftie flateries & lies to accuse and destroye the innocents.
"*Or, righteousnes.*
c Thogh God forbeare for a time, yet at length he wil recompēse thy falsehode.
d Albeit thou seme to be neuer so sure setled.
e For the eies of ŷ reprobate are shut vp at Gods iudgements.
f With ioyful reuerēce, seig ŷ he taketh their parte against the wicked.
"*Or, in his substance.*
g He reioyceth to haue a place among the seruants of God, ŷ he maie growe in the knowledge of godlines.
h Executed this vengeāce.
"*Or, waite vpon thy grace and promes.*
Psal. LIII.
a Which was an instrumēt or kinde of note.
b Where as no regarde is had of honestie or dishonestie, of vertue nor of vice, there the Prophet pronounceth that the people haue no God
c Whereby he cōdemneth all knowledge & vnderstāding, ŷ tendeth not to seke God.
Rom. 3,10.
d Dauid pronoūceth Gods vengeance against cruel gouerners, who hauing charge to defende and preserue Gods people, do moste cruelly deuoure them.
e When they thoght there was none occasiō to feare, the sudden vēgeance of God lighted vpō thē
f Be the enemies power neuer so great, nor ŷ dāger so fearesul, yet God deliureth his in due time
Psal LIIII.
1. Sam. 23,11.
a He declareth that when all meanes do faile, God wil deliuer, euen as it were by miracle thē that call vnto him with an vpright conscience.

b To wit, the Ziphims.
c Saul and his armie, which were like cruel beastes & colde not be satisfied but by his death.
d Be they neuer so fewe, as he was with Ionathán.
e According to thy faithful promes for my defence.
f For hypocrites serue God for feare, or vpon conditions.
g We may lawfully reioyce for Gods iudgemēts against the wicked, if our affections be pure.
a The earnestnes of his praier declareth the vehemēcie of his grief, in so muche as he is compelled to burst out into cryes.
b For ŷ threatenings of Saúl & his adherēts.
c They haue diffamed me as a wicked persone: or, they haue imagined my destructiō.
d There was no parte of hī that was not astonied with extreme feare.
e Feare had driuē hī to so great distres, that he wished to be hid in some wildernes, & to be banished from that kingdome, ŵ God had promised that he shulde enioye.
f From ŷ cruel rage & tyrānie of Saúl.
g As in the cōfusiō of Babylon, when the wicked cōspired against God.
h All laws & good ordres are broken, & onelie vice & dissolutiō reigneth vnder Saúl.
i If mine open enemie had soght mine hurt, I colde ŷ better haue auoyded him.
k Which was not onely ioyned to me in friēdship & coūsel in worldlie matters, but also in religion.
l As Kórah, Dathán & Abirám.

I praye, m & make anoise, & he wil heare
my voyce.
18 He hathe deliuered my soule in peace frō
the battel, *that was* against me: for n manie
were with me.
19 God shal heare and afflict them, euen he
that reigneth of olde, Sélah. because they
o haue no changes, therefore they feare not
God.
20 He p layed his hand vpon suche, as be
at peace with him, *and* he brake his couenant.
21 *The wordes* of his mouth were softer thē
butter, yet warre *was* in his heart: his wordes were more gentle then oyle, yet they
were swordes.
22 Cast thy " burden vpon the Lord, and
he shal nourish thee: he wil not suffer the
righteous to fall for q euer.
23 And thou, ô God, shalt bring thē downe
into the pit of corruptiō: the blooddie, &
deceitful men shal not liue r halfe their
dayes: but I wil trust in thee.

m Which signifieth a feruent minde & sure truste to obteine his petitiō, which thing made him earnest at all times in praier.
n Euē the Angels of God foght on my side agaīst mine enemies, 2. King. 6,16.
o But their pꝛosperous estate stil cōtinueth.
p I did not pꝛouoke him, but was at peace with him, yet he made warre against me.
" Or, gift: to wit, which thou woldest that God shulde giue thee
q Thogh for their bettering & trial he suffer thē to slip for a time.
r Thogh they sometime liue lōger, yet their life is cursed of God, vnquiet & worse then anie death.

PSAL. LVI.

1 Dauid being broght to Achish the King of Gath, 2. Samu. 21,12, complaineth of his enemies, demandeth succour. 3 Putteth his trust in God & in his promises, 12 And promiseth to performe his vowes, which he had takē vpō him, whereof this was the effect to praise God in his Church.

¶ *To him that excelleth.* A Psalme *of Dauid on Michtám, concerning the* a *dumme dooue in a farre countrei, when the Philistims toke him in Gath.*

1 BE merciful vnto me, ô God, for b mā
wolde swallow me vp: he fighteth cōtinually *and* vexeth me.
2 Mine enemies wolde daiely swallow me
vp: for manie fight against me, ô thou
moste High.
3 When I was afraid, I trusted in thee.
4 I wil reioyce in God, *because* of his c worde, I trust in God, *&* wil not feare what
flesh can do vnto me.
5 Mine owne d wordes grieue *me* daily: all
their thoghts *are* agaīst me to do me hurt.
6 e They gather together, and kepe them
selues close: thei marke my steppes, because they waite for my soule.
7 f They *thinke* they shal escape by iniquitie: ô God, cast *these* people downe in *thine*
angre.
8 Thou hast counted my wandrings: put
my g teares into thy bottel: are they not
in thy registre?
9 When I crye, then mine enemies shal
turne backe: this I know, for God *is* with
me.
10 I wil reioyce in God *because of his* worde:
in the Lord wil I reioyce *because of his*
worde.
11 In God do I trust: I wil not be afraid
what man can do vnto me.

a Being chased by the furie of his enemies into a strāge countrie, he was as a dūme dooue, not seking reuengeance.
b He sheweth that it is ether now time, or neuer, ẏ God helpe him: for all ẏ worlde is against him & readie to deuoure him.
c He staieth his conscience vpō Gods promes, thogh he se not present helpe.
d All my cōsels haue euil successe & turne to mine owne sorowe.
e As all the worlde agaīst one man, & can not be saciat, except they haue my life.
f They thinke not onely to escape punishmēt, but ẏ more wicked thei are, the more impudent they waxe.
g If God kepe the teares of his Saints in store, muche more wil he remēber their blood to auēge it: & thogh tyrants burne the bones, yet can thei not blot the teares & blood out of Gods registre.

12 h Thy vowes *are* vpon me, ô God: I wil
rendre praises vnto thee.
13 For thou hast deliuered my soule from
death, and also my fete from falling, that I
maye i walke before God in the k light
of the liuing.

h Hauīg receiued ẏ which I required, I am boūde to paye my vowes of thākesgiuing, as I promised.
i As mindeful of his great mercies, & giuing him thākes for ẏ same
k That is, in this life and light of the sunne.

PSAL. LVII.

1 Dauid being in the desert of Ziph, where the inhabitāts did betraye him, & at length in the same caue with Saúl, 2 Calleth moste earnestly vnto God with ful cōfidence, that he wil performe his promes & take his cause in hād: 5 Also that he wil shew his glorie in the heauens and the earth against his cruel enemies. 9 Therefore doeth he rendre laude & praise.

¶ *To him that excelleth.* a *Destroye not.* A Psalme *of Dauid on Michtám.* * *When he fled
from Saúl in the caue.*

1 HAue mercie vpon me, ô God, haue
mercie vpō me: for my soule trusteth
in thee, and in the shadow of thy wings
wil I " trust, til *these* b afflictions ouerpasse.
2 I wil call vnto the moste high God, *euen*
to the God, that c performeth *his promes*
toward me.
3 He wil send from d heauen, and saue me
from the reprofe of him that wolde swallow me. Sélah. God wil send his mercie,
and his trueth.
4 My soule *is* among lions: I lie *among* the
childrē of men, that are set on fyre: whose
teeth *are* e speares and arrowes, and their
tongue a sharpe sworde.
5 f Exalte thy self, ô God, aboue the heauē,
& let thy glorie *be* vpon all the earth.
6 They haue layed a net for my steppes:
g my soule is pressed downe: they haue
digged a pit before me, *&* are fallen into
the middes of it. Sélah.
7 Mine heart is h prepared, ô God, mine
heart is prepared: I wil sing & giue praise.
8 Awake my i tongue, awake viole & harpe: I wil awake early.
9 I wil praise thee, ô Lord, among the people, *and* I wil sing vnto thee among the
nations.
10 For thy mercie is great vnto the heauēs,
and thy trueth vnto the k cloudes.
11 Exalt thy self, ô God, aboue the heauens,
and let thy glorie be vpon all the earth.

a This was ether the beginning of a certeine song, or the wordes, ẇ Dauid vttered, whē he stayed his affection.
1. Sam. 24,4.
" Or, dwel moste safly
b He cōpareth the afflictions, ẇ God layeth vpon his children, to a storme, that commeth & goeth.
c Who leaueth not his workes begō vnperfit.
d He wolde rather deliuer me by a miracle, then that I shulde be ouercome.
e He meaneth their calūnies & false reportes.
f Suffer me not to be destroyed to the contempt of thy Name.
g For verie feare, seing the great dangers on all sides.
h That is, wholly bēt to giue thee praise for my deliuerance.
i He sheweth ẏ bothe his heart shal praise God and his tōgue shal cōfesse him, and also ẏ he wil vse other meanes to prouoke him self forwarde to the same.
k Thy mercies do not onely apperteine to the Iewes, but also to the Gentiles.

PSAL. LVIII.

1 He describeth the malice of his enemies, the flatterers of Saúl, who bothe secretly & openly soght his destruction, frō whome he appealeth to Gods iudgement, 10 Shewing that the iuste shal reioyce, when they se the punishement of the wicked to the glorie of God.

¶ *To him that excelleth. Destroye not.* A Psal.
of Dauid on Michtám.

1 IS it true? ô a Congregacion, speake ye
iustly? ô sonnes of men, iudge ye
vprightly?
2 Yea, rather ye imagine mischief in *your*
heart: b your hands execute crueltie vpō
the earth.

a Ye cōselers of Saúl, who vnder pretēce of consulting for ẏ commune welth conspire my death being an innocent.
b Ye are not ashamed to execute ẏ crueltie publikely, ẇ ye haue imagined in your heartes.

3 The

3 The wicked [c] are ſtrangers from the wōbe: *euen* from the belly haue they erred, &
ſpeake lies.
4 Their poiſon is euen like the poiſon of a
ſerpent: like the deafe [d] adder *that* ſtoppeth his eare.
5 Which heareth not the voyce of the inchanter, thogh he be moſte expert in charming.
6 Breake their [e] teeth, ô God, in their mouthes: breake the iawes of the yong lions,
ô Lord.
7 Let them [f] melt like the waters, let thē
paſſe away: when he ſhooteth his arrowes,
let them be as broken.
8 Let him conſume like a ſnaile that melteth, *& like* ỳ vntimelie frute of a woman,
that hathe not ſene the ſunne.
9 [g] As rawe fleſh before your pottes fele *the*
fyre of thornes: *ſo* let him carie them away
as with a whirle winde in *his* wrath.
10 The righteous ſhal [h] reioyce when he
ſeeth the vengeance: he ſhal waſh his fete
in the [i] blood of the wicked.
11 And men ſhal ſay, [k] Verely there is
frute for the righteous: doutles there is a
God that iudgeth in the earth.

c That is, enemies to the people of God euen frō their birth.
d They paſſe in malice, and ſubtiltie the craftie ſerpēt, ẘ colde preſerue him ſelfe by ſtoppīg his eare from the inchanter.
e Take away all occaſiōs & meanes, wherby they hurt.
f Conſidering Gods diuine power he ſheweth that God in a moment can deſtroye their force, whereof they bragge.
g As fleſh is takē rawe out of ỳ pot before the water ſeeth: ſo he deſireth God to deſtroye their entrepriſes before thei brīg them to paſſe.
h With a pure affection.
i Their puniſhment & ſlaughter ſhalbe ſo great.
k Seing God gouerneth all by his prouidēce, he muſte nedes put difference betwene the godlie, and the wicked.

PSAL. LIX.

1 *Dauid being in great danger of Saúl, who ſent to ſlay him in his bed, prayeth vnto God: 3 Declareth his innocencie, & their furie. 5 Deſiring God to deſtroye all thoſe that ſinne of malicious wickednes. 11 Whome thogh he kepe aliue for a time to exerciſe his peeple, yet in the end he wil cōſume thē in his wrath. 13 That he maye be knowen to be the God of Iaakób to the end of the worlde. 16 For this he ſingeth praiſes to God, aſſured of his mercies.*

¶ *To him that excelleth. Deſtroye not.* A Pſalme *of Dauid on* [a] *Michtam.* * *When Saúl ſent & they did watche the houſe to kil him.*

1 O My God, [b] deliuer me from mine
enemies: defend me from them that
riſe vp againſt me.
2 Deliuer me from the wicked doers, and
ſaue me from the bloodḋie men.
3 For lo, they haue layed waite for my ſoule: the mightie men are gathered againſt
me, not for mine [c] offenſe, nor for my ſinne, ô Lord.
4 They runne and prepare them ſelues
without a faute *on my parte*: ariſe *there-*
fore to aſsiſt me, and beholde.
5 Euen thou, ô Lord God of hoſtes, ô God
of Iſraél awake to viſite all the heathen, &
be not [d] merciful vnto all that tranſgreſſe
maliciouſly. Sélah.
6 They go to and fro in the euening: they
barcke like [e] dogs, and go about the citie.
7 Beholde, they [f] brag in their talke, *and*
ſwordes *are* in their lippes: for Who, *ſay*
they, doeth heare?
8 But thou, ô Lord, ſhalt haue them
in deriſion, *and* thou ſhalt laugh at all the
heathen.

a Read pſal. 16
1. Sam. 19, 11.
b Thogh his enemies were euen at hand to deſtroye hī, yet he aſſured him ſelf that God had wayes ynough in his hād to deliuer him.
c For I am innocent to thē wardes, & haue not offended them.
d Seing it aperteineth to Gods iudgements to puniſh ỳ wicked, he deſireth God to execute his vengeāce on ỳ reprobat, who maliciouſly perſecute his Church.
e He cōpareth their crueltie to hūgrie dogs ſhewing that they are neuer wearie in doīg euil.
f They boaſt opēly of their wicked deuiſes, and euerie worde is as a ſworde: for thei nether feare God, nor are aſhamed of men.

9 [g] He is ſtrong: *but* I wil waite vpon thee:
for God *is* my defence.
10 My merciful God wil [h] preuent me: God
wil let me ſe *my deſire* vpon mine enemies.
11 Slay thē [i] not, leſt my people forget it: *but*
ſcater them abroad by thy power, & put
them downe, ô Lord our ſhield,
12 *For* the ſinne of their mouth, & the wordes of their lippes: and let them be taken
in their pride, euen for their periurie and
lies, *that* thei ſpeake.
13 [l] Conſume *them* in *thy* wrath: conſume
them that thei be no more: and let them
know that God ruleth in Iaakób, *euen* vnto the ends of the worlde. Sélah.
14 And in the euening they [m] ſhal go to and
fro, & barcke like dogs, & go about the citie.
15 Thei ſhal runne here and there for meat:
& ſurely they ſhal not be ſatiſfied, thogh
thei tarie all night.
16 But I wil ſing of thy [n] powr, & wil praiſe thy mercie in the mornīg: for thou haſt
bene my defence and refuge in the day of
my trouble.
17 Vnto thee, ô my [o] Strength, wil I ſing:
for God is my defence, *and* my merciful
God.

g Thogh Saúl haue neuer ſo great power, yet I knowe ỳ thou doeſt bridel him: therefore wil I paciently hope on thee.
h He wil not faile to ſuccour me, when nede requireth.
i Altogether, but by litle & litle, that the people ſeing oftē times thy iudgmēts may be mindeful of thee.
k That in their miſerie & ſhame thei may be as glaſſes and examples of Gods vēgeāce.
l When thy time ſhal come, and when thei haue ſufficiētly ſerued for an example of thy vengeance vnto other.
m He mocketh at their vaine entrepriſes, being aſſured ỳ thei ſhal not bring their purpoſe to paſſe.
n Which dideſt vſe the policie of a weake woman to confounde the enemies ſtrength, as 1 Sam. 19, 12.
o Confeſsing him ſelfe to be voide of all vertue and ſtrength, he attributeth the whole to God.

PSAL. LX.

1 *Dauid being now King ouer Iudáh and hauing had manie victories, ſheweth by euident ſignes, that God elected him King, aſſuring the people that God wil proſper thē, if they approue the ſame. 11 After he praieth vnto God to finiſh that that he hathe begonne*

¶ *To him that excelleth vpon* [a] *Shuſhan Eduth,* or *Michtám.* A Pſal. *of Dauid to teache.* * *When he foght againſt Aram Naharaím, and againſt* ° *Arám* [b] *Zobáh, whē Ioab returned and ſlew twelue thouſand Edomites in the ſalt vallei.*

1 O God, thou haſt caſt vs out, thou haſt
[c] ſcatered vs, thou haſt bene angrie,
turne againe vnto vs.
2 Thou haſt made the land to tremble, and
haſt made it to [d] gape: heale the breaches
thereof, for it is ſhaken.
3 Thou haſt [e] ſhewed thy people heauie
things: thou haſt made vs to drinke the wine of giddines.
4 *But now* thou haſt giuen [f] a banner to thē
that feare thee, that it maie be diſplaied
becauſe of *thy* trueth. Sélah.
5 That thy beloued may be deliuered, help
with thy right hand and heare me.
6 God hathe ſpoken in his [g] holines: *therefo-*
re I wil reioyce: I ſhal deuide Shechém, &
meaſure the valley of Succóth.
7 Gileád *ſhalbe* mine, and Manaſſéh *ſhalbe*
mine: Ephráim alſo *ſhalbe* the [h] ſtrength

a Theſe were certeine ſongs after the note whereof this pſalme was ſung.
2 Sam. 8, 1. & 10, 1. 1. chro. 18, 1.
° *Or, Syria, called Meſopotamia.*
b Called alſo Sophene ẘ ſtādeth by Euphrates.
c For when Saúl was not able to reſiſt ỳ enemie, ỳ people fled hether & thether: for thei colde not be ſafe in their owne houſes.
d As cleft ẘ an earth quake
e Thou haſt handled thy people ſharply in taking from them ſenſe and iudgement, in that thei aided Saúl the wicked King, and purſued him, to whome God had giuen the iuſt title of the realme.
f In making me King, thou haſt performed thy promes, which ſemed to haue loſt the force.
g It is ſo certeine, as if it were ſpoken by an oracle, that I ſhal poſſeſſe theſe places, which Saúl had left to his children.
h For it was ſtrong and wel peopled.

of mine head: [i] Iudáh *is* my lawgiuer.
8 Moáb *shalbe* my [k] wash pot: ouer Edóm
wil I cast out my shoe: [l] Palestina shew
thy self ioyful for me.
9 Who wil lead me into the [m] strong citie?
who wil bring me vnto Edóm?
10 Wilt not thou, ô God, *which* hadest cast
vs of, & didest not go forthe, ô God, with
our armies?
11 Giue vs helpe against trouble: for vaine
is the helpe of man.
12 Through God we shal do valiantly: for
he shal treade downe our enemies.

i Dauid meaneth, that in this tribe his kigdome shalbe established, Gen. 49,10.
k In most vile subiection.
l For ȳ wilt dissemble, and faine as thogh ȳ werest glad.
m He was assured that God wolde giue hĩ ȳ strong cities of his enemies wherein they thoght thẽ selues sure.

PSAL. LXI.

1 Whether that he were in danger of the Ammonites, or being pursued of Absalóm, here he cryeth to be heard & deliuered, 7 And confirmed in his kingdome. 8 He promiseth perpetual praises.

¶ *To him that excelleth on Neginóth.* A Psalme *of Dauid.*

1 Heare my crye, ô God: giue eare vnto
my praier.
2 From [a] the ends of the earth wil I crye
vnto thee: whẽ mine heart is opprest, bring
me vpõ the rocke that is [b] higher then I.
3 For thou hast bene mine hope, *&* a strõg
tower against the enemie.
4 I wil dwel in thy Tabernacle for euer, *&*
my trust shal be vnder the couering of
thy wings. Sélah.
5 For thou, ô God, [c] hast heard my desires:
thou hast giuẽ an heritage vnto those that
feare thy Name.
6 Thou shalt giue the King a [d] long life:
his yeres *shalbe* as manie ages.
7 He shal dwell before God for euer: prepare
[e] mercie & faithfulnes *that* they may
preserue him.
8 So wil I alway sing praise vnto thy Name
in performing daiely my vowes.

a From ȳ place, where I was banished, being driuen out of the Citie & Temple by my sonne Absalóm.
b Vnto the ẘ without thy helpe I cã not atteine.
c There is nothing ȳ doeth more strẽgthẽ our faith, then the remembrãce of Gods succour in times past.
d This chiefly is referred to Christ, who liueth eternally not onely in him self, but also in his members.
e For the stabilitie of my kingdome stãdeth in thy mercie & trueth.

PSAL. LXII

This Psalme partely conteineth meditatiõs, whereby Dauid incourageth him self to trust in God against the assalts of tentations And because our mindes are easely drawẽ from God by the alluremẽts of the worlde he sharply reproueth this vanitie, to the intent he might cleaue fast to the Lord.

¶ *To the excellent* musician * *Ieduthún*. *A Psalme of Dauid.*

1 Yet [a] my soule kepeth silence vnto
God: of him *cometh* my saluacion.
2 [b] Yet he is my strength and my saluaciõ,
& my defence: *therefore* I shal not muche be
moued.
3 How lõg wil ye imagine mischief against
a [c] man? ye shalbe all slaine: *ye shalbe* as a
bowed wall, *or* as a [d] wall shaken.
4 Yet they consulte to cast him downe frõ
his dignitie: their delite is in lies, thei blesse
with their mouthes, but curse with their
hearts. Sélah.
5 [e] Yet my soule kepe thou silẽce vnto God:
for mine hope *is* in him.
6 Yet is he my strength, & my saluacion, *&*
my defence: *therefore* I shal not be moued.
7 In God *is* my saluacion and my [f] glorie, ȳ
rocke of my strength: in God *is* my trust.
8 Trust in him alwaie, ye people: [g] powre
out your hearts before him, *for* God *is* our
hope. Sélah.
9 Yet the children of men *are* vanitie, the
chief mẽ *are* lies: to lay thẽ vpon a balance
thei are altogether lighter thẽ vanitie.
10 Trust not in oppresion nor in roberie:
[h] be not vaine: if riches increase, set not
your heart thereon.
11 God spake [i] once or twise, I haue heard
it, that power *belongeth* vnto God,
12 And to thee, ô Lord, mercie: for thou [k] rewardest
euerie one accordĩg to his worke.

1.Chro.16,41.
a Thogh Satã tempted him to murmure against God, yet he bridled his affections, & resisting vpõ Gods promes, beareth his crosse paciently.
b It appeareth by the oft repetition of this worde, that ȳ Prophet abode manifolde tentations, but by resting on God & by patience he ouercame them all.
c He meaneth him self, being the mã whome God had appointed to ȳ kingdome.
d Thogh ye seme to be in honour, yet God wil suddely destroye you.
e Dauid was greatly moued with these troubles: therefore he stirreth vp him self to trust in God.
f These vehement & often repetitiõs were necessarie to strengthen his faith against ȳ horrible assaltes of Satán.
g He admonisheth vs of our wicked nature, which rather hide our sorow, & bite on the bridle, then vtter our grief to God to obteine remedie.
h Giue your selues wholy to God by putting awaie all things ȳ are cõtrarie to his Lawe.
i He hathe plainely borne witnes of his power, so ȳ none nedeth to doute therof.
k So that the wicked shal fele thy power, and the godlie thy mercie.

PSAL. LXIII.

1 Dauid, after he had bene in great danger by Saúl in the desert of Ziph, made this psalme. 3 Wherein he giueth thankes to God for his wonderful deliuerance, in whose mercies he trusted, euen in the middes of his miseries, 9 Prophecying the destruction of Gods enemies: 11 And contrariwise happines to all them that trust in the Lord.

¶ *A Psalme of Dauid. When he was in the* [a] *wildernes of Iudáh.*

1 O God, thou art my God, early wil I seke
thee: my soule [b] thirsteth for thee:
my flesh longeth greatly after thee in a
baren and drye land without water.
2 Thus [c] I beholde thee *as* in the Sanctuarie,
when I beholde thy power & thy glorie.
3 For thy louing kindenes *is* better then life:
therefore my lippes shal praise thee.
4 Thus wil I magnifie thee *all* my life, *and*
lift vp mine hands in thy Name.
5 My soule shal be satisfied, as with [d] marow
and fatnes, and my mouth shal praise *thee*
with ioyful lippes,
6 When I remember thee on my bed, *&*
when I thinke vpon thee in the *night* watches.
7 Because thou hast bene mine helper, therefore
vnder the shadow of thy wings wil
I reioyce.
8 My soule cleaueth vnto thee: *for* thy right
hand vpholdeth me.
9 Therefore they that seke my soule to destroy
it, they shal go into the lowest partes
of the earth.
10 [f] They shal cast him downe with the edge
of the sworde, *&* thei shal be a portiõ
for foxes.
11 But the King shal reioyce in God, *and*
all that [g] sweare by him shal reioyce *in him*:
for the mouth of them that speake lies,
shal be stopped.

a To wit, of Ziph, 1. Sam. 23,14.
b Thogh he was bothe hũgrie & in great distres, yet he made God his sufficiencie & aboue all meate & drinke.
c In this miserie I exercise my self in the contemplatiõ of thy power & glorie, as if I were in thy Sanctuarie.
d The remembrance of thy fauour is more swete vnto me then all the pleasures and denties of the worlde.
e He assureth him selfe by the Spirit of God to haue ȳ gift of constãcie.
f He pphecieth of the destructiõ of Saúl, & the that take his parte, whose bodies shal not be buried, but be deuoured with wilde beastes.
g All ȳ sweare by God aright, or professe him, shal reioyce in this worthie King.

PSAL. LXIIII.

1 Dauid praieth against the furie and false reportes of his enemies. 7 He declareth their punishement & destruction, 10 To the comfort of the iust and the glorie of God.

¶ To him that excelleth. A Psalme of Dauid.

1 HEare my [a] voice, ô God, in my praier:
preserue my life from feare of the e-
nemie.
2 Hide me from the [b] conspiracie of the
wicked, *and* from the [c] rage of the workers
of iniquitie.
3 Which haue whet their tongue like a
sworde, and shot *for* their arrowes [d] bitter
wordes:
4 To shote at the vpright in secret: thei
shote at him suddenly, and [e] feare not.
5 Thei [f] encourage them selues *in* a wicked
purpose: thei cōmune together to laie sna
res priuely, *and* saie, Who shal se them?
6 Thei haue soght out iniquities, *and* haue
accomplished that which thei soght out,
euen euerie one [g] *his secret thoghts*, and the
depth of *his* heart.
7 But God wil shote an arrow at them suddenly: their strokes shal be *at once*.
8 Thei shal cause their owne tongue to fall
vpon them: *and* whosoeuer shal se them,
shal [h] flee awaie.
9 And all men shal se it, and declare the
worke of God, and thei shal vnderstand,
what he hathe wroght.
10 *But* the righteous [i] shal be glad in the
Lord, & trust in him: and all that are vpright of heart, shal reioyce.

a In that he calleth to God with his voice, it is a signe that his praier was vehement, & that his life was in danger.
b That is, frō their secret malice.
c To wit, their outward violēce.
d False reportes & sclāders
e To be without feare of God & reuerēce of man, is a signe of reprobation.
f The more that the wicked se Gods childrē in miserie, the more bolde, & impudent are thei in oppressing them.
g There is no waie so secret & subtil to do hurt, which thei inuented not for his destructiō.
h To se Gods heauie iudgements against them, and how he hathe caught them in their owne snares.
i When thei shal consider that he wilbe fauourable to thē, as he was to his seruant Dauid.

PSAL. LXV.

1 *A praise and thankesgiuing vnto God by the faithful.
who are signified by Zion, 4 For the chusing, preseruation and gouernance of them, 9 And for the plentiful
blessings powred forthe vpon all the earth, but specially
toward his Church.*

*¶ To him that excelleth. A Psalme or song of
Dauid.*

1 OGod, [a] praise waiteth for thee in Zión, & vnto thee shal the vowe be performed.
2 *Because thou* hearest the praier, vnto thee
shal all [b] flesh come.
3 Wicked dedes [c] haue preuailed against
me: *but* thou wilt be merciful vnto our trās
gresions.
4 Blessed *is he, whome* thou chusest and causest to come *to thee*: he shal dwell in thy
courts, *and* we shal be satisfied with the
pleasures of thine House, *euen* of thine ho
lie Temple.
5 O God of our saluacion, thou wilt [d] answer vs with feareful *signes* in *thy* righteous
nes, ô *thou* the hope of all the ends of the
earth, and of them that are farre of in the
[e] sea.
6 He stablisheth the moūtaines by his power:
and is girded about with strength.
7 He appeaseth the [f] noise of the seas *and*
the noise of the waues thereof, and the
tumultes of the people.
8 Thei also, that dwell in the vttermost par
tes *of the earth*, shalbe afraid of thy signes:
thou shalt make [*] the East and the West
to reioyce.
9 Thou [g] visitest the earth, and waterest it:
thou makest it very riche: the [h] Riuer of
God is ful of water: thou preparest them
corne: for so thou appointest [i] it.
10 Thou [k] waterest abūdantly the forrowes
thereof: thou causest *the raine* to descend
into the valleis thereof: thou makest it soft
with showres, & blessest the bud thereof.
11 Thou crownest the yere with thy goodnes, and thy steps drop fatnes.
12 They drop *vpon* the pastures of the wilder
nes: & the hils shal be cōpassed with gladnes.
13 The pastures are clad with shepe: the valleis also shal be couered with corne: *therefore* they showte for ioye, [l] and sing.

a Thou giuest daiely new occasion to thy Church to praise thee.
b Not onely the Iewes, but also the Gentiles in the kigdome of Christe.
c He imputeth it to his sins & to the sins of the people, that God, who was accustomed to assiste them, withdraweth his succour from them.
d Thou wilt declare thy self to be the preseruer of thy Church in destroying thine enemies, as thou didest in the red Sea.
e As of all barbarous nations and farre of.
f He sheweth that there is no parte nor creature in the worlde, which is not gouerned by Gods power & prouidence.

*Ebr. The going forthe of the morning & of the euening.
g To wit, with raine.
h That is, Shiloah, or, the raine.
i Thou hast appoited the earth to brig forthe fode to mans vse.
k By this description he sheweth that all the ordre of nature is a testimonie of Gods loue towarde vs, who causeth all creatures to serue our necessitie.
l That is, the dumme creatures shal not onely reioyce for a time for Gods benefites, but shal continually sing.

PSAL. LXVI.

1 *He prouoketh all men to praise the Lord and to consider his workes. 6 He setteth forthe the power of
God to affray the rebels, 10 And sheweth how God
hathe deliuered Israél from great bondage and affi-
ctions. 13 He promiseth to giue sacrifice. 16 And
prouoketh all men to heare what God hathe done for
him and to praise his Name.*

¶ To him that excelleth. A song, or Psalme.

1 REioyce in God, [a] all ye *inhabitants* of
the earth.
2 Sing forthe the glorie of his Name: make
his praise glorious.
3 Saie vnto God, How terrible art thou *in*
thy workes! through the greatnes of thy
power shal thine enemies be [b] in subiection vnto thee.
4 All the worlde shal worship thee, & sing
vnto thee, *euen* sing of thy Name. Sélah.
5 [c] Come and beholde the workes of God:
he is terrible in *his* doing toward [d] the sonnes of men.
6 He hathe turned the Sea into drye land:
thei passe through the riuer on fote: there
did we reioyce in him.
7 He ruleth the worlde with his power: his
eies beholde the natiōs: the rebellious shal
not [e] exalt them selues. Sélah.
8 Praise our God, ye people, and make the
voice of his praise to be heard.
9 Which [f] holdeth our soules in life, and
suffereth not our fete to slippe.
10 For thou, ô God, hast proued vs, thou
hast tryed vs as siluer is tryed.
11 Thou hast broght vs into the [g] snare, &
laied a strait *chaine* vpon our loins.
12 Thou hast caused men to ride ouer our
heades: we wēt into fyre & into water, but
thou broghtest vs out into a wealthie *place*.
13 I wil go into thine [h] House with burnt
offrings, & wil paie thee my vowes,
14 Which my lippes haue promised, &
my mouth hathe spoken in mine afflictiō.
15 I wil offer vnto thee the burnt offrings of

a He prophecieth that all natiōs shal come to the knowledge of God, who then was onely knowen in Iudea.
b As the faithful shal obey God willigly: so the infideles for feare shal dissemble thē selues to be subiect.
c He toucheth the slothful dulnes of mā, who is colde in the consideratiō of Gods workes.
d His prouidēce is wonderful in mainteining their estate.
e He proueth that God wil extend his grace also to the Gētiles, because he punisheth among them such as wil not obey his callig.
f He signifieth some special benefite, that God had shewed to his Church of the Iewes in deliuering thē frō some great dāger: whereof or of the like he promiseth that the Gentiles shal be partakers.
g The condition of the Church is here descrībed, which is to be led by Gods prouidēce into troubles, to be subiect vnder tyrants, & to enter into manifolde dangers. h The duetie of the faithful is here described, which are not vnmindeful to rendre God praise for his benefites.

fat rams with incẽse: I wil prepare bullockes and goates. Sélah.

16 [i] Come & hearken, all ye that feare God,
& I wil tel you what he hathe done to my
soule.

17 I called vnto him with my mouth, and
he was exalted with my tongue.

18 [k] If I regarde wickednes in mine heart,
the Lord wil not heare me.

19 But God hathe heard *me*, & considered
the voice of my praier.

20 Praised *be* God, which hathe not put
backe my praier, nor his mercie from me.

i It is not ynough to haue receiued Gods benefites & to be mindeful thereof, but also we are boũde to make others to profit thereby & praise God.
k If I delite in wickednes, God wil not heare me: but if I confesse it, he wil receiue me.

PSAL. LXVII.

1 *A praier of the Church to obteine the fauour of God & to be lightened with his countenance. 2 To the end that his waie & iudgements maie be knowen throughout the earth 7 And finally is declared the kingdome of God, which shulde be vniuersally erected at the comming of Christ.*

¶ *To him that excelleth on Neginóth. A Psal. or song.*

1 God be merciful vnto vs, and blesse
vs, & [a] cause his face to shine among
vs. Sélah.

2 That [b] they maie knowe thy waie vpon
earth, & thy sauing health among all nations.

3 Let the people praise thee, ô God: let all
the people praise thee.

4 [c] Let the people be glad and reioyce: for
thou shalt iudge ỹ people righteously, &
gouerne the nations vpon the earth. Sélah.

5 Let the people praise thee, ô God: let all
the people praise thee.

6 *Thẽ* shal [d] ỹ earth bring forthe her increase,
& God, *euen* our God shal blesse vs.

7 God shal blesse vs, and all the ends of the
earth [e] shal feare him.

a That is, moue our heartes w̃ his holy Spirit, ỹ we maie fele his fauour towards vs.
b That bothe Iewes & Gẽtiles maie know Gods couenãt made w̃ them.
c By these oft repetitions he sheweth, ỹ the people can neuer reioyce sufficiẽtly, & giue thãkes for the great benefites that thei shal receiue vnder the kingdome of Christ.
d He sheweth, ỹ where God fauoreth, there shalbe abundãce of all other things.
e Whẽ thei fele his great benefites bothe spiritual & corporal towards them.

PSAL. LXVIII.

1 *In this psalme Dauid setteth forthe as in a glasse the wonderful mercies of God towarde his people: 5 Who by all meanes & moste strange sortes declared him self to them. 15 And therefore Gods Church by reason of his promises, graces and victories doeth excel without comparison all worldlie things. 34 He exhorteth therefore all men to praise God for euer.*

¶ *To him that excelleth. A psalme or song of Dauid.*

1 God [a] wil arise, & his enemies shalbe
scattered: thei also that hate him, shal
flee before him.

2 As the smoke vanisheth, *so* shalt ỹ driue
them awaie: & as waxe melteth before the
fyre, *so* shal ỹ wicked perish at the presence
of God.

3 [b] But the righteous shalbe glad, & reioyce
before God: yea, thei shal leape for
ioye.

4 Sing vnto God, & sing praises vnto his
Name: exalt him, that rideth vpon the
heauens, in his Name [c] Iah, & reioyce before
him.

5 *He is* a Father of the fatherles, and a Iudge
of the widowes, *euen* God in his holie
habitation.

a The Prophet sheweth that albeit God suffreth ỹ wicked tyrãts to oppresse his Church for a time, yet at lẽgth he wil be reuenged of them.
b He sheweth that whẽ God declareth his power against ỹ wicked, that it is for the cõmoditie & saluation of his Church, w̃ praise him therefore.
c Iah & Iehouáh are the names of God, w̃ do signifie his essence & maiestie incõprehẽsible, so that herby is declared, ỹ all idols are but vanitie, & that ỹ God of Israél, is ỹ onely true God.

6 God [d] maketh the solitarie to dwell in families,
& deliuereth them that were prisoners
in stockes: but the rebellious shal
dwell in a [e] drye land.

7 [f] O God, when thow wentest forthe before
thy people: when thou wẽtest through
the wildernes, (Sélah)

8 The earth shoke, and the heauẽs dropped
at the presence of this God: *euen* Sinái *was
moued* at the presence of God, *euen* the
God of Israél.

9 Thou, ô God, sendest a gracious raine *vpon*
thine inheritance, & thou didest refresh
it when it was wearie.

10 Thy Congregation dwelled therein: *for*
thou, ô God, hast of thy [g] goodnes prepared
it for the poore.

11 The Lord gaue matter to the [h] women
to tel of the great armie.

12 Kings of the armies did flee: thei did flee
& [i] she that remained in the house, deuided
the spoile.

13 Thogh ye haue lien among [k] pots, *yet shal
ye be as* the wings of a dooue that is couered
with siluer, and whose fethers *are like*
yelowe golde.

14 When the Almightie scatered Kings
[l] in it, it was white as the snow in Zalmón.

15 [m] The mountaine of God *is like* the mountaine
of Bashán: *it is* an high Mountaine,
as mount Bashán.

16 [n] Why leape ye, ye high mountaines? as
for this Mountaine, God deliteth to dwell
in it: yea, the Lord wil dwell in it for euer.

17 The charets of God *are* twentie thousand
thousand Angels, *and* the Lord is among
them, *as* in the Sanctuarie of Sinái.

18 Thou art gone vp on high: thou hast [o] led
captiuitie captiue, *and* receiued giftes for
men: yea, euen the rebellious *hast thou led*,
that the Lord God might dwell *there*.

19 Praised *be* the Lord, *euen* the God of our
saluacion, *which* ladeth vs daiely *with benefites*.
Sélah.

20 This *is* our God, *euen* the God that saueth
vs: and to the Lord God *belong* the
[p] issues of death.

21 Surely God wil wound the head of his
enemies, & the heerie pate of him that
walketh in his sinnes.

22 The Lord hathe said, I wil bring *my people*
againe from [q] Bashán: I wil bring them
againe from the depths of the Sea:

23 That thy foote maie be dipped in blood,
& the tongue of thy dogges *in the blood* of
the enemies, *euen* in [r] it.

24 Thei haue sene, ô God, thy [s] goings, the
goings of my God, & my King, *which art*

d He giueth childrẽ to thẽ, ỹ be childeles, and increaseth their families.
e Which is baren of Gods blessĩgs, w̃ before thei had abused.
f He teacheth ỹ Gods fauour peculiarly belongeth to his Church, as appeareth by their wonderful deliuerãce out of Egypt.
g God blessed the land of Canáan because he had chosen that place for his Church.
h The facion then was that women sang songs after the victorie, as Miriám, Deboráh Iudith and others.
i The pray was so great ỹ not onely the soldiers, but womẽ also had parte thereof.
k Thogh God suffer his Church for a time to lie in blacke darkenes, yet he wil restore it and make it moste shinĩg & white.
l In ỹ land of Canáan, where his Church was.
m Zíon the Church of God doeth excell all worldlie things, not in põpe & outwarde shewe, but by the inwarde grace of God, w̃ there remaineth because of his dwellĩg there.
n Why boast ye of your strẽgth & beautie against this Mountaine of God?
o As God ouercame the enemies of his Church, toke the prisoners, and made the tributaries: so Christ, w̃ is God manifested in flesh, subdued Satã & sinne vnder vs, & gaue vnto his Church moste liberal giftes of his Spirit, Ephe. 4, 8.
p In moste extreme dangers God hathe infinite waies to deliuer his.
q As he deliuered his Church once frõ Og of Bashán, & other tyrãts, & frõ the dãgers of ỹ red Sea, so wil he stil do as oft as necessitie requireth.
r That is, in ỹ blood of that great slaughter, where dogges shal lap blood.
s That is, how ỹ, which art chief King, goest out with thy people to warre, and giuest them the victorie.

in the Sanctuarie.
25 The t singers went before, the plaiers of
instruments after: in the middes *were* the
maides playing with timbrels.
26 Praise ye God in the assemblies, & the
Lord, *ye that are* of the foūtaine u of Israél.
27 There *was* x litle Beniamín *with* their
y ruler, & the princes of Iudáh *with* their
assemblie, the princes of Zebulún, & the
princes of Naphtalí.
28 Thy God hathe appointed thy strēgth:
stablish, ô God, that, *which* ẏ hast wroght
in vs,
29 z Out of thy Temple vpon Ierusalém: &
Kings shal bring presents vnto thee.
30 Destroye the cōpanie of the spearemen,
& multitude of the mightie bulles with
the calues of the people, that a tread vnder
fete pieces of siluer: scater the people that
delite in warre.
31 *Then* shal ẏ princes come out b of Egypt:
Ethiopia shal haste to stretch her hāds vnto God.
32 Sing vnto God, ô ye kingdomes of the
earth: sing praise vnto the Lord, (Sélah)
33 To him that rideth vpon the moste high
heauens, *which were from* the beginning:
beholde he wil send out by his c voyce a
mightie sounde.
34 Ascribe the power to God: *for* his maiestie *is* vpon Israél, & his strength *is* in the
cloudes.
35 O God, thou art d terrible out of thine
holie e places: the God of Israél is he that
giueth strength and power vnto the people: praised *be* God.

t He describeth the ordre of the people, whē thei went to the Temple to giue thākes for the victorie.
u Which come of ẏ Patriarke Iaakób.
x Beniamín is called litle, because he was ẏ yongest sonne of Iaakób.
y Who was some chief ruler of the tribe.
z Declare out of thine holie palace thy power for the defence of thy Church Ierusalém.
a He desireth that the pride of the mightie may be destroied, ẇ accustomed to garnish their shoes ẇ siluer: & therfore for their glitering pompe thoght thē selues aboue all men.
b He pphecieth ẏ the Gentiles shal come to ẏ true knowledge & worship of God.
c By his terrible thunders he wil make him self to be knowen ẏ God of all ẏ worlde.
d In shewing fearful iudgemēts against thine enemies for the saluatiō of thy people.
e He alludeth to ẏ Tabernacle ẇ was deuided into thre partes.

PSAL. LXIX.

1 The cōplaints, prayers, feruent zeale & great anguish of Dauid is set forthe as a figure of Christ & all his mēbers: 21 The malicious crueltie of the enemies, 22 And their punishment also, 26 Where Iudas & suche traitors are accursed. 30 He gathereth courage in his affliction & offreth praises vnto God, 32 Which are more acceptable then all sacrifices: whereof all the afflicted maie take cōfort. 35 Finally he doeth prouoke all creatures to praises, prophecying of the kingdome of Christ, & the preseruacion of the Church, where all the faithful, 37 And their sede shal dwel for euer.

¶ *To him that excelleth vpon* a *Shoshannim*. A
Psalme of *Dauid*.

1 SAue me, ô God: for the b waters are
entred euen to *my* soule.
2 I sticke fast in the depe myre, where no
c staie *is*: I am come into depe waters, and
the streames runne ouer me.
3 I am wearie of crying: my throte is drye:
mine d eyes faile, whiles I waite for my
God.
4 They that hate me without a cause, are
mo then the heeres of mine head: thei that
wolde destroye me, *and* are mine enemies
e falsely, are mightie, so that I restored that
which I f toke not.

a Of Shoshaním read Psal. 45.
b Dauid signifieth by the waters, in what great dangers he was, out of ẏ which God did deliuer hī.
c No firmitie or stablenes to settle my fete.
d Thogh his senses failed him, yet his faith was constant & incouraged him stil to praie.
e Comdemning me giltles.
f Thei iudged me pore innocent as a thief and gaue my goods to others as thogh I had stollen them.

5 O God, thou knowest my g foolishnes, &
my fautes are not hid from thee.
6 Let not them that trust in thee, ô Lord
God of hostes, be ashamed for h me: let
not those that seke thee, be confounded
through me, ô God of Israél.
7 For thy sake haue I suffred reprofe: shame
hathe coucred my face.
8 I am become a stranger vnto my brethrē,
euen an aliant vnto my mothers sonnes.
9 i For the zeale of thine house hathe eaten
me, and the rebukes of them that rebuked
thee, are fallen vpon me.
10 I k wept and my soule fasted, but that
was to my reprofe.
11 I put on a sacke also: and I became a prouerbe vnto them.
12 They that l sate in the gate, spake of me,
and the drunkards sang *of me*.
13 But Lord, *I make* my praier vnto thee in
an m acceptable time, *euen* in the multitude of thy mercie: ô God, heare me in the
trueth of thy saluacion.
14 Deliuer me out of the myre, that I sinke
not: let me be deliuered from thē that hate
me, and out of the n depe waters.
15 Let not ẏ waterflood drowne me, nether
let the depe swallowe me vp: and let not
the pit shut her mouth vpon me.
16 Heare me, ô Lord, for thy louing kindenes is good: turne vnto me according to
the multitude of thy tendre mercies.
17 And o hide not thy face from thy seruāt,
for I am in trouble: make hast & heare me.
18 Drawe nere vnto my soule & redeme it:
deliuer me because of mine enemies.
19 Thou hast knowen my reprofe and my
shame, & my dishonour: all mine p aduersaries *are* before thee.
20 Rebuke hathe broken mine heart, and I
am ful of heauines, and q I loked *for some* to
haue pitie *on me*, but there was none: and
for comforters, but I founde none.
21 For thei gaue me gall in my meat, and
in my thirst thei gaue me vinegre to
drinke.
22 Let their r table be a snare before them,
and their prosperitie *their* ruine.
23 Let their eyes be blinded that thei se not:
and make their s loynes alwaie to tremble.
24 Powre out thine angre vpon them, & let
thy wrathful displeasure take them. *
25 *Let their t habitacion be voide, & let
none dwell in their tentes.
26 For thei persecute him, whome thou hast
smiten: and they adde vnto the sorowe of
them, whome thou hast wounded.
27 Lay u iniquitie vpon their iniquitie, &
let them not come into thy righteousnes.
28 Let them be put out of the x boke of life,

g Thogh I be giltie to thee warde, yet am I innocēt towarde them.
h Let not mine euil intreatie of the enemies be an occasiō, ẏ the faithful fall frō thee.
i When I sawe thine enemies pretend thy Name onely in mouth, and in their life denie the same, thine holie Spirit thrust me forwarde, to reproue thē & defend thy glorie.
k My zeale moued me to lamēt & praie for my saluation.
l The more he foght to wine them to God, the more thei were against him both poore and riche.
m Knowing that albeit I suffer now trouble, yet ẏ hast a time, wherein ẏ hast appointed my deliuerance.
n He sheweth a liuelie faith, in that ẏ he assureth hī self, ẏ God is fauorable to hī, whē he semeth to be angrie: & at hand, when he semeth to be farre of.
o Not that he feared ẏ God wold not heare him, but ẏ care made him to thinke that God differred long.
p Thou seest ẏ I am beset as a shepe among manie wolues.
q He sheweth ẏ it is in vaine to put ō trust in men in our great necessities, but ẏ our comfort onely dependeth of God: for man rather increaseth ō sorowes, then dimisheth them, John 19,29.
r He desireth God to execute his iudgements against the reprobate, ẇ can not by anie meanes be turned, Rom. 11,9.
s Take bothe iudgement and power frō thē.
Act. 1,20.
t Punish not onely them, but their posteritie, which shalbe like vnto them.
u By their continuance and increasing in their sinnes let it be knowen that they be of the reprobate.
x They which semed by their profession to haue bene writen in thy boke, yet by their frutes proue the contrarie, let them be knowen as reprobate.

nether let them be writen with the righteous.
29 When I am poore & in heauines, thine
helpe, ô God, shal exalt me.
30 I wil praise the Name of God with a
song, & magnifie him with thankesgiuig.
31 *This* also shal please the Lord better thẽ
a y yong bullocke, that hathe hornes and
hoofes.
32 The humble shal se *this*, *&* thei that seke
God, shalbe glad, & your heart shal liue.
33 For the Lord heareth the poore, and despiseth not his z prisoners.
34 Let heauen & earth praise him: the seas
and all that moueth in them.
35 For God wil saue Ziôn, and buylde the
cities of Iudáh, that men maie dwell there
and haue it in possession.
36 The a sede also of his seruants shal inherit it: and thei that loue his Name, shal
dwell therein.

PSAL. LXX.

1 He praieth to be right spedely deliuered. 2 He desireth the shame of his enemies, 4 And the ioyful comfort of all those that seke the Lord.

¶ *To him that excelleth*. A Psalme *of Dauid to put in* a *remembrance*.

1 O* God, b *haste thee* to deliuer me: make
haste to helpe me, ô Lord.
2 Let them be c confounded & put to shame, that seke my soule: let them be turned
backewarde and put to rebuke, that desire
mine hurt.
3 Let thẽ be turned backe for a rewarde of
their d shame, which said, Aha, aha.
4 *But* let all those that seke thee, be ioyful &
glad in thee, and let all that loue thy saluacion, saie alwaies, God be praised.
5 Now I am e poore and nedie: ô God, make haste to me: thou art mine helper, and
my deliuerer: ô Lord, make no tarying.

PSAL. LXXI.

1 He praieth in faith, established by the worde of the promes. 5 And confirmed by the worke of God from his youth. 10 He complaineth of the crueltie of his enemies, 17 And desireth God to continue his graces towarde him, 22 Promising to be mindeful and thankeful for the same.

1 IN * a thee, ô Lord, I trust: let me neuer
be ashamed.
2 Rescue me and deliuer me in thy b righteousnes: incline thine eare vnto me and
saue me.
3 Be thou my strong rocke, whereunto I
maie alwaie resorte: thou c hast giuẽ commandement to saue me: for thou art my
rocke, and my fortresse.
4 Deliuer me, ô my God, out of the hand
d of the wicked: out of the hand of the euil
and cruel man.
5 For thou art mine hope, ô Lord God, *euen*
my e trust from my youth.
6 Vpon thee haue I bene staied from the
wombe: thou art he that toke me out of
my mothers bowels: my praise shal be alwaies of thee.
7 I am become as it were a f monstre vnto
manie: but thou art my sure trust.
8 Let my mouth be filled with thy praise, *&*
with thy glorie euerie daie.
9 Cast me not of in the time of g age: forsake me not when my strength faileth.
10 For mine enemies speake of me, & they
that laie waite for my soule, take their counsel together,
11 Saying, h God hathe forsaken him: pursue and take him, for their is none to deliuer *him*.
12 Go not farre frõ me, ô God: i my God,
haste thee to helpe me.
13 Let them be confounded *and* consumed
that are against my soule: let them be couered with reprofe & confusion, that seke
mine hurt.
14 But I wil waite continually, & wil praise thee more and more.
15 My mouth shal daily rehearse thy righteousnes, *and* thy saluacion: k for I knowe
not the nomber.
16 I wil l go forwarde in the strength of
the Lord God, *and* wil make mention of
thy righteousnes, *euen* of thine onely.
17 O God, thou hast taught me from my
youth euen vntil now: *therefore* wil I tel of
thy wonderous workes,
18 m Yea, euen vnto *mine* olde age and graie
head, ô God: forsake me not, vntil I haue
declared thine arme vnto *this* generation,
& thy power to all them, that shal come.
19 And thy n righteousnes, ô God, *I wil exalt* on high: for ȳ hast done great things:
o ô God, who is like vnto thee!
20 Which hast shewed me great troubles
and p aduersities, *but* thou wilt returne
and reuiue me, and wilt come againe, *and*
take me vp from the depth of the earth.
21 Thou wilt increase mine honour, & returne *and* comfort me.
22 Therfore wil I praise thee *for* thy q faithfulnes, ô God, vpon instrument *and* viole:
vnto thee wil I sing vpon the harpe, ô Holie one of Israél.
23 My lippes wil reioyce when I sing vnto
thee, and my r soule, which thou hast deliuered.
24 My tongue also shal talke of thy righteousnes daily: for they are confounded &
broght vnto shame, that seke mine hurt.

PSAL. LXXII.

1 He praieth for the prosperous estate of the kingdome of Salomón, who was the figure of Christ. 4 Vnder whome shal be righteousnes peace and felicitie, 10 Vnto whome all Kings and all nations shal do homage, 17 Whose name and power shal indure for euer, & in whome all nations shalbe blessed.

y There is no sacrifice, ȳ God more esteemeth, then thankesgiuing for his benefites.
z For as he deliuered his seruant Dauid, so wil he do all ȳ are in destres, and call vpon him.
a Vnder the tẽporal promes of the land of Canáan he cõprehẽdeth the promes of life euerlasting to the faithful & their posteritie.

Psal. LXX.
a Which might put him in remembrance of his deliuerãce.
Psal. 40,14.
b He teacheth vs to be earnest in praier, thogh God seme to stay: for at his time he wil heare vs.
c He was assured that the more thei raged, the nerer thei were to destruction & he the nerer to his deliuerãce.
d Hereby we are taught not to mocke at others in their miserie, lest ȳ same fall on ô owne necks.
e Because he had felt Gods helpe before, he groundeth on experience and boldely seketh vnto him for succour.

Psal. LXXI.
Psal. 31.
a He praieth to God ŵ ful assurance of faith, ȳ he wil deliuer him from his aduersaries
b By declaring thy self true of promes.
c Thou hast infinite meanes, & all creatures are at thy commandement: therefore shew some signe, whereby I shalbe deliuered.
d That is, frõ Absolóm, Ahithóphel & that conspiracie.
e He strengtheneth his faith by the experience of Gods benefites, who did not onely preserue him in his mothers belly, but toke him thence, & euer since hathe preserued him.

f All ȳ worlde wondereth at me because of my miseries, aswel thei in autoritie, as the cõmon people, yet being assured of thy fauour I remained stedfast.
g Thou that didst helpe me in my youth, when I had more strẽgth, helpe me now so muche the more in mine olde age & weakenes.
h Thus the wicked bothe blaspheme God & triũph against his Saints, as thogh he had forsakẽ them, if he suffer thẽ to fall into their hands.
i In callĩg him his God, he putteth backe ȳ false reportes of the aduersaries, that said, God had forsaken him.
k Because thy benefites toward me are innumerable, I can not but cõtinually meditate & reheharse them.
l I wil remaine stedfast, being vpholden with ȳ power of God.
m He desireth ȳ as he hathe begonne, he wolde so continue his benefites, ȳ his liberalitie maie haue perfite praise.
n Thy iust performãce of thy promes.
o His faith breaketh through all tentacions, & by this exclamatiõ he praiseth ȳ power of God.
p As he confesseth that God is the onelie autor of his deliuerance: so he acknowledgeth that these euils were sent vnto him by Gods prouidence.
q He cõfesseth ȳ his long tariance was wel recompensed, when God performed his promes.
r For there is no true praising of God, except it come frõ the heart: and therefore he promiseth to delite in nothing, but wherein God maie be glorified.

A Psalme

¶A Psalme [a] *of Salomón.*

1 Giue thy [b] iudgements to the King,
ô God, and thy righteousnes to the
Kings [c] sonne.
2 *Then* shal he iudge thy people in righteousnes, and thy poore with equitie.
3 The [d] mõutaines and the hils shal bring
peace to the people by iustice.
4 He shal [e] iudge the poore of the people:
he shal saue the children of the nedie, and
shal subdue the oppressor.
5 They shal [f] feare thee as long as the sunne and moone endureth, from generation
to generation.
6 He shal come [g] downe like the raine
vpon the mowen grasse, & as the showres
that water the earth.
7 In his daies shal the righteous florish, &
abundance of peace *shalbe* so long as the
moone endureth.
8 His dominion shalbe also from [h] sea to
sea, and from the Riuer vnto the ends of
the land.
9 They that dwell in the wildernes, shal
knele before him, and his enemies shal licke the dust.
10 The Kings of [i] Tarshish & of the yles
shal bring presentes: the Kings [k] of Shebá
and Sebá shal bring giftes.
11 Yea, all Kings shal worship him: all nations shal serue him.
12 For he shal deliuer the poore when he
cryeth: the nedie also, and him that hathe
no helper.
13 He shalbe merciful to the poore and
nedie, and shal preserue the soules of the
poore.
14 He shal redeme their soules from deceit
and violence, and [l] deare shal their blood
be in his sight.
15 Yea, he shal liue, and vnto him shal
they giue of the [m] golde of Shebá: they
shal also praye for him continually, *and*
daily blesse him.
16 An handful of corne shalbe *sowen* in the
earth, *euen* in the top of the mountaines,
and the [n] frute thereof shal shake like *the*
trees of Lebanón: and the *children* shal florish out of the citie like the grasse of the
earth.
17 His name shalbe for euer: his name shal
indure as long as the sunne: all natiõs shal
blesse [o] him, and be blessed in him.
18 Blessed *be* the Lord God, *euen* the God
of Israél, which onely doeth [p] wonderous
things.
19 And blessed *be* his glorious Name for
euer: and let all the earth be filled with his
glorie. So be it, euen so be it.

HERE END THE [q] praiers of Dauid,
the sonne of Ishái.

a Cõposed by Dauid as touching ỹ reigne of his sonne Salomón.
b Endue the King with the Spirit of wisdome & iustice that he reigne not as do the worldelie tyrants.
c To wit, to his posteritie.
d Whẽ iustice reigneth, euen ỹ places moste barren shal be enriched with thy blessings.
e He sheweth wherefore the sworde is committed to Kings: to wit, to defend the innocent and suppresse the wicked.
f The people shal imbrace thy true religion, whẽ thou giuest a King, that ruleth according to thy worde.
g As this is true in all godlie Kings: so is it chiefly verified in Christ, who wͭ his heauenlie dewe maketh his Church euer to florish.
h That is, frõ the red Sea to the sea called Syriacum, and frõ Euphrates forwarde: meaning, ỹ Christs kingdome shulde be large & vniuersal.
i Of Cilicia & of all other countreis beyõd the sea, which he meaneth by the yles
k That is, of Arabia ỹ riche coũtrei, wherof Shebá was a parte bordering vpon Ethiopia.
l Thogh tyrants passe not to shed blood, yet this godlie King shal preserue his subiects from all kinde of wrong
m God wil bothe prosper his life, & also make the people moste willing to obeie him.
n Vnder suche a King shalbe moste great plentie, bothe of frute & also of the increase of mankinde.
o They shal praie to God for his continuãce, & know that God doeth prosper them for his sake.
p He confesseth that excepte God miraculously preserue his people, that nether the King nor the kingdome can continue.
q Concerning his sonne Salomón.

PSAL. LXXIII.

The Prophet teacheth by his example that nether the worldelie prosperitie of the vngodlie, 14 Nor yet the affliction of the good oght to discourage Gods children: but rather oght to moue vs to consider our Fathers prouidence, and to cause vs to reuerence Gods iudgements, 19 For asmuche as the wicked vanish away, 24 And the godlie enter into life euerlasting. 28 In hope whereof he resigneth him self into Gods hands.

¶A *Psalme* committed *to Asaph.*

1 Yet [a] God is good to Israél: *euen*, to
the pure in heart.
2 As for me, my fete were almost gone: my
steps had welnere slipt.
3 For I freated at the foolish, *when* I sawe
the prosperitie of the wicked.
4 For there are [b] no bands in their death,
but they are lustie & strong.
5 They are not in trouble *as other* men, nether are they plagued with *other* men.
6 [c] Therefore pride *is* as a chaine vnto thẽ,
& crueltie coucreth them *as* a garment.
7 Their eyes stand out for fatnes: " they
haue more then heart can wish.
8 They are licencious, and speake wickedly of *their* oppresion: thei talke presumpteously.
9 They [d] set their mouth against heauen, &
their tongue walketh through the earth.
10 Therefore his [e] people turne hither: for
waters of a ful *cup* are wrung out to them.
11 And they [f] say, How doeth God know
it? or is there knowledge in ỹ moste High?
12 Lo, these are the wicked, yet prosper thei
alway, & increase in riches.
13 Certeinly I haue clensed mine heart in
vaine, and washed mine hands in innocencie.
14 For daily haue I bene punished, and chastened *euerie* morning.
15 If I say, [g] I wil iudge thus, beholde
the generaciõ of thy children: I haue trespaced.
16 Thẽ thoght I to knowe this, *but* it was to
peinful for me,
17 Vntil I went into the [h] Sanctuarie of
God: *then* vnderstode I their end.
18 Surely thou hast set them in slipperie
places, *and* castest them downe into desolation.
19 How suddenly are they destroyed, perished & [i] horribly consumed,
20 As a dreame when one awaketh! ô Lord,
when [k] thou raisest vs vp, thou shalt make their image despised.
21 Certeinly mine heart was vexed, & I was
pricked in my reines:
22 So foolish was I and ignorant: I was a
[l] beast before thee.
23 Yet I was alway [m] with thee: thou hast

a As it were betwene hope & despaire he brasteth forthe into this affectiõ, being assured ỹ God wolde cõtinue his fauour toward suche as were godlie in dede, and not hypocrites.
b The wicked in this life liue at pleasure, & are not drawen to death like prisoners: that is by sickenes, wͨ is deathes messẽger.
c They glorie in their pride as some do in their chaines: & in crueltie, as some do in apparel.
" *Ebr. They passe the desires of the heart.*
d They blaspheme God & feare not his power, & raile vpon men, because they esteme thẽ selues aboue all others.
e Not onely ỹ reprobate, but also ỹ people of God often times fall backe, seing ỹ prosperous estate of the wicked, and are ouerwhelmed with sorowes, thinking ỹ God cõsidereth not aright the state of the godlie.
f Thus ỹ flesh moueth euẽ ỹ godlie to dispute with God touchĩg their poore estate & the prosperitie of the wicked.
g If I giue place to this wicked thoght, I offẽd against thy prouidence, seing ỹ disposest all things moste wisely, and preseruest thy children in their greatest dangers.
h Vntil I entred into thy schole & learned by thy worde & holie Spirit, ỹ thou orderest all things moste wisely & iustly.
i By thy feareful iudgement.
k When thou openest our eies to consider thy heauenlie felicitie, we contemne all their vaine pompe.
l For the more that mã goeth about by his owne reason to seke out Gods iudgements, ỹ more doeth he declare him self a beast.
m By faith I was assured that thy prouidence did watche alwayes ouer me to preserue me.

holden *me* by my right hand.
24 Thou wilt guide me by thy counsel, &
afterwarde receiue me to glorie.
25 Whome haue I in [n] heauen *but thee*? and
I haue desired none in ẏ earth with thee.
26 My flesh faileth and mine heart *also*: *but*
God *is* the stregth of mine heart, and my
[o] porcion for euer.
27 For lo, they that withdrawe them selues
from thee, shal perish: thou destroyest all
them that [p] go a whoring from thee.
28 As for me, it is good for me [q] to drawe
nere to God: *therefore* I haue put my trust
in the Lord God, that I may declare all
thy workes.

n He soght nether helpe nor cōfort of anie saue of God onely.
o He teacheth vs to denie our selues, to haue God our whole sufficiencie, & onely cōtentement.
p That is, forsake thee to seke others.
q Thogh all ẏ worlde shrinke from God, yet he promiseth to trust in him and to magnifie his workes.

PSAL. LXXIIII.

1 *The faithful complaine of the destruction of the Church & true religion,* 2 *Under the name of Zión, and the Temple destroyed:* 11 *And trusting in the might & fre mercies of God,* 20 *By his couenant,* 21 *They require helpe & succour for the glorie of Gods holie Name; for the saluacion of his poore afflicted seruants,* 23 *And the confusion of his proude enemies.*

¶ A Psalme *to giue instruction*, committed
to Asáph.

1 O God, [a] why hast thou put vs away
for euer? *why* is thy wrath kindled a-
gainst the shepe of thy pasture?
2 Thinke vpon thy Congregacion, *which*
thou hast possessed of olde, & on the [b] rod
of thine inheritance, *which* thou hast redemed, & on this mount Zión, wherein
thou hast dwelt.
3 Lift vp thy ″ strokes, that thou maiest for
euer destroye euerie enemie that doeth
euil to the Sanctuarie.
4 Thine aduersaries roare in the middes
of thy Congregacion, & [c] set vp their
banners for signes.
5 *He that* [d] *lifted* the axes vpon the thicke
trees, was renoumed, as one, that broght a
thing to perfection:
6 But now they breake downe the carued
worke thereof with axes and hammers.
7 They haue cast thy Sanctuarie into the
fyre, & *rased it* to the ground, *and* haue defiled the dwelling place of thy Name.
8 They said in their [e] hearts, Let vs destroye them altogether: they haue burnt
all the Synagogues of God in the land.
9 We se not our signes: there is not one
Prophet more, nor anie with vs that knoweth [f] how long.
10 O God, how long shal the aduersarie reproche *thee*? shal the enemie blaspheme
thy Name for euer?
11 Why withdrawest thou thine hand, euen
thy right hād? *drawe it* out of thy bosome,
& [g] consume them.
12 Euen God *is* my King of olde, working
saluacion [h] in the middes of the earth.
13 Thou didest diuide ẏ Sea by thy power:
thou brakest the heades of the [i] dragons
in the waters.
14 Thou brakest the head of [k] Liuiathán
in pieces, *and* gauest him to be [l] meat for
the people in wildernes.
15 Thou brakest vp the fountaine and riuer:
thou dryedst vp mightie riuers.
16 The [m] daye is thine, and the night is
thine: thou hast prepared the light and
the sunne.
17 Thou hast set all the borders of ẏ earth:
thou hast made somer and winter.
18 Remember this, *that* the enemie hathe
reproched the Lord, and the foolish people hathe blasphemed thy Name.
19 Giue not the soule of thy [n] turtle dooue
vnto the beast, & forget not the Congregacion of thy poore for euer.
20 Consider *thy* couenant: for [o] the darke
places of the earth are ful of the habitacions of the cruel.
21 Oh let not the oppressed returne ashamed, *but* let the poore & nedie praise thy
Name.
22 Arise, ô God: mainteine thine [p] owne
cause: remember thy dailie reproche by
the foolish man.
23 Forget not the voyce of thine enemies:
for the tumulte of them, that rise against
thee, ″ ascendeth continually.

a The Church of God being oppressed by the tyrannie ether of ẏ Babylonians, or of Antiochus, praieth to God by whose hād this yoke was laied vpon them for their sinnes.
b Which inheritance ẏ hast measured out for thy self as with a line or rod.
″ Or, fete.
c They haue destroyed thy true religion & spread their banners in signe of defiance.
d He cōmendeth the Temple for ẏ costlie matter, the excellent workemanship & beautie therof ẇ notwihstāding the enemies did destroye.
e They incouraged one another to crueltie, ẏ not onely Gods people might be destroyed, but also his religion vtterly in all places suppressed.
f They lamēt ẏ they haue no Prophet amōg them to shewe them how lōg their miseries shulde endure.
g They ioyne their deliuerāce with Gods glorie & power, knowing that the punishment of the enemie shulde be their deliuerance.
h Meaning, in the sight of all the worlde.
i To wit, Pharaohs armie.
k Which was a great mōstre of the sea, or whale, meanīg Pharaóh.
l His destrucion did reioyce thē as meat refresheth the bodie.
m Seing that God by his prouidence gouerneth & disposeth all thīgs, he gathereth ẏ he wil take care chiefly for his children.
n He meaneth ẏ Church of God, ẇ is exposed as a pray to the wicked.
o That is, all places where thy worde shineth not, there reigneth tyrānie & ambitiō.
p He sheweth that God can not suffer his Church to be oppressed, except he lose his owne right.
″ Or, increaseth more and more.

PSAL. LXXV.

1 *The faithful do praise the Name of the Lord,* 2 *Which shal come to iudge at the time appointed,* 8 *When the wicked shalbe put to confusion, and drinke of the cup of his wrath.* 10 *Their pride shalbe abated, & the righteous shalbe exalted to honour.*

¶ *To him that excelleth.* [a] *Destroye not. A*
Psalme or song committed *to Asáph.*

1 WE wil praise thee, ô God, we wil
praise *thee*, for thy Name *is* nere:
therefore [b] they wil declare thy wonderous workes.
2 [c] When I shal take a conuenient time, I
wil iudge righteously.
3 The earth and all the inhabitans thereof
are dissolued: *but* I wil establish the pillers
[d] of it. Sélah.
4 I said vnto the foolish, Be not so foolish,
and to the wicked, Lift not vp the horne.
5 Lift not vp your [e] horne on high, nether
speake with a stiffe necke.
6 For to come to preferment *is* nether from
the East, nor from the West, nor from the
South,
7 But God *is* the iudge: he maketh low and
he maketh hie.
8 For in the hand of the Lord *is* a [f] cup, and
the wine is red: it is ful mixt, and he powreth out of the same: surely all the wicked
of the earth shal wring out & drinke the
dregs thereof.

9 But

a Read Psal. 57,1
b He declareth how ẏ faithful shal euer haue iust occasiō to praise God, for asmuche as in their nede thei shal fele his power at hand to helpe them.
c When I se my time (saith God) to helpe your miseries, I wil come & set all things in good ordre.
d Thogh all things be broght to ruine, yet I can restore & preserue them.
e The Prophet warneth ẏ wicked that they wolde not set them selues against Gods people, seing ẏ God at his time destroyeth them that rule wickedly.
f Gods wrath is compared to a cup of strōg & delicate wine, wherewith the wicked are made so dronke, that by drinking til they come to the verie dregs, they are vtterly destroyed.

9 But I wil declare for euer, and sing praises vnto the God of Iaakób.

10 All the hornes of the wicked also wil I breake: *but* the hornes of the [g] righteous shalbe exalted.

g The godlie shal better prosper by their innocent simplicitie, then the wicked shal by all their craft, & subteltie.

PSAL. LXXVI.

1 This Psalme setteth forthe the power of God & care for the defence of his people in Ierusalém, in the destruction of the armie of Saneherib: 11 And exhorteth the faithful to be thankeful for the same.

¶ *To him that excelleth on Neginóth. A Psalme or song committed to Asáph.*

1 GOd is [a] knowen in Iudáh: his Name *is* great in Israél.

2 For in [b] Shalém is his Tabernacle, and his dwelling in Zión.

3 There brake he the arrowes of the bowe, the shield and the sworde and the battel. Sélah.

4 Thou art more bright and puissant, then [c] the mountaines of pray.

5 The stoute harted are spoiled: they haue slept their slepe, & all the men of strength haue not [d] founde their hands.

6 At thy rebuke, ô God of Iaakób, bothe the chariot and horse are cast a slepe.

7 Thou, *euen* thou art to be feared: and who shal stand in thy [e] sight, when thou art angrie!

8 Thou didest cause *thy* iudgement to be heard from heauen: *therefore* the earth feared and was stil,

9 When thou, ô God, arose to iudgement, to [f] helpe all the meke of the earth. Sélah.

10 Surely the [g] rage of man shal turne to thy praise: the remnant of the rage shalt thou restraine.

11 Vowe & performe vnto the Lord your God, all *ye* that be [h] rounde about him: let thẽ bring presents vnto him that oght to be feared.

12 He shal [i] cut of the spirit of princes: he is terrible to the Kings of the earth.

a He declareth ỷ Gods power is euidẽtly sene in preseruĩg his people and destroying his enemies.
b Which after ward was called Ierusalém.
c He cõpareth the kingdomes ful of extortiõ & rapine to ỷ mountaines ỷ are ful of rauening beasts.
d God hathe takẽ their spirits & strength from them, as thogh their hãds were cut of.
e God w̃ a looke is able to destroye all ỷ power & actiuitie of ỷ enemies, were thei neuer so manie or mightie.
f To reuenge ỷ wrõgs done to thy Church.
g For the end shal shewe ỷ ỷ enemie was able to bring nothing to passe, also ỷ shalt bridle their rage, ỷ they shal not compasse their purpose.
h To wit, the Leuites ỷ dwel about the Tabernacle, or ỷ people, among whome he doeth dwell.
i The Ebrewe worde signifieth, to vintage, or gather grapes: meaning that he shal make the counsels and entreprises of wicked tyrants foolish and vaine.

PSAL. LXXVII.

1 The Prophet in the name of the Church rehearseth the greatnes of his affliction, and his grieuous tentations, 6 Whereby he was driuen to this end to consider his former conuersation, 11 And the continual course of Gods workes in the preseruation of his seruants, & so he confirmeth his faith against these tentations.

¶ *For the excellent* musician **Ieduthún. A Psalme* committed *to Asáph.*

1 MY [a] voyce *came* to God, when I cryed: my voyce *came* to God, and he heard me.

2 In the day of my trouble I soght ỷ Lord: "my sore ranne & ceased not in the night: my soule refused comfort.

3 I did thinke vpon God, and was [b] troubled: I prayed, and my spirit was ful of anguish. Sélah.

* 1.Chro.16,41. psal.39,& 62
a The Prophet teacheth vs by his exãple to flee vnto God for helpe in our necessities
" *Or, mine hand was stretched out*
b He sheweth ỷ we must paciently abide, althogh God deliuer vs not out of our troubles at ỷ first cry.

4 Thou kepest mine eies [c] waking: I was astonied and colde not speake.

5 *Then* I considered the daies of olde, *and* the yeres of ancient time.

6 I called to remembrance my [d] song in the night: I cõmuned with mine owne heart, and my spirit searched [e] diligently.

7 Wil the Lord absent him self for euer? & wil he shewe no more fauour?

8 Is his [f] mercie cleane gone for euer? doeth his promes faile for euer more?

9 Hathe God forgotten to be merciful? hathe he shut vp his tẽder mercies in displeasure? Sélah.

10 And I said, This is my [g] death: *yet I remẽbred* the yeres of the right hãd of the most High.

11 I remembred the workes of the Lord: certeinly I remembred thy wonders of olde.

12 I did also meditate all thy workes, & did deuise of thine Actes, *saying,*

13 Thy waie, ô God, *is* [h] in the Sanctuarie: who is so great a [i] God as *our* God!

14 Thou art the God that doest wonders: thou hast declared thy power among the people.

15 Thou hast redemed thy people w̃ *thine* arme, *euen* the sonnes of Iaakób and Ioséph. Sélah.

16 The [k] waters sawe thee, ô God: the waters sawe thee, *and* were afraied: yea, the depths trembled.

17 The cloudes powred out water: the heauens gaue a [l] sounde: yea, thine arrowes went abroad.

18 The voice of thy thundre was round about: the lightenĩgs lightened the worlde: the earth trembled and shoke.

19 Thy waie *is* in the Sea, and thy paths in the great waters, and thy fotesteps are not [m] knowen.

20 Thou didest leade thy people like shepe by the hand of Mosés and Aarón.

c Meanĩg that his sorowes were as watchmen ỷ kept his eies frõ slepĩg.
d Of thankesgiuĩg, w̃ I was accustomed to sing in my prosperitie.
e Bothe ỷ causes why I was chastened, and when my sorowes shulde haue an end.
f As if he shulde saie, It is impossible: wherby he exhorteth him selfe to pacience.
g Thogh I first douted of my life, yet considering that God had his yeres, ỷ is, chãge of times, & was accustomed also to lift vp them, whome he hathe beaten, I toke heart againe.
h That is, in heauen, wherunto we must ascẽd by faith, if we wil kno we ỷ waies of God.
i He condemneth all ỷ worship anie thĩg saue ỷ onely true God, whose glorie appeareth through the worlde.
k He declareth, wherin ỷ power of God was declared, when he deliuered ỷ Israelites through the red Sea.
l That is, thũdered & lightened.
m For when ỷ hadest broght ouer thy people, the water returned to her course & ỷ enemies that thoght to haue followed thẽ, colde not passe through. Exod.14,19.

PSAL. LXXVIII.

1 He sheweth how God of his mercie chose his Church of the posteritie of Abrahám, 8 Reproching the stubburne rebellion of their fathers, that the children might not onely vnderstand, 11 That God of his fre mercie made his couenant with their ancetours, 17 But also seing them so malicious and peruerse, might be ashamed and so turne wholly to God. In this Psalme the holie Gost hathe comprehẽded, as it were, the summe of all Gods benefites, to the intent the ignorant and grosse people might se in fewe wordes the effect of the whole histories of the Bible.

¶ A Psalme *to giue* [a] *instruction* committed *to Asáph.*

1 HEare my [b] doctrine, ô my people: incline your eares vnto the wordes of my mouth.

2 I wil open my mouth in a parable: I wil declare high sentences of olde.

a Read psalme 32.
b The Prophet vnder the name of a teacher calleth ỷ people his, & the doctrine his, as Paul calleth ỷ Gospel his, whereof he was but ỷ preacher, as Rom. 2,16. & 16,25.

3 Which we haue heard and knowen, and
our [c] fathers haue tolde vs.
4 We wil not hide them from their children, *but* to the generacion to come we wil
shewe the praises of the Lord, his power
also, and his wonderful workes that he
hathe done:
5 How he established a [d] testimonie in
Iaakób, and ordeined a Law in Israél,
which he commanded our fathers, that
they shulde teache their children:
6 That the [e] posteritie might knowe it, *and*
the children, which shulde be borne,
shulde stand vp, & declare it to their children:
7 That they might [f] set their hope on
God, and not forget the workes of God
but kepe his commandements:
8 And not to be as their [g] fathers, a disobedient and rebellious generation: a generation that set not their heart aright, and
whose spirit was not faithful vnto God.
9 The children of [h] Ephráim being armed
& shooting with the bowe, turned backe
in the day of battel.
10 They kept not the couenant of God, but
refused to walke in his Law,
11 And forgate his Actes, and his wonderful workes that he had shewed them.
12 He did maruelous things in the sight of
their [i] fathers in the land of Egypt: *euen*
in the field of Zóan.
13 *He deuided the Sea, and led them
through: he made also the waters to stand
as an heape.
14 *In the daietime also he led them with
a cloude, and all the night with a light of
fyer.
15 *He claue the rockes in the wildernes,
and gaue them drinke as of the great
depths.
16 *He broght floods also out of the stonie
rocke, so that he made the waters to descend like the riuers.
17 Yet they [k] sinned stil against him, and
prouoked the Highest in the wildernes,
18 And tempted God in their heartes in
[l] requiring meat for their lust.
19 *They spake against God also, saying,
Can God [m] prepare a table in the wildernes?
20 *Beholde, he smote the rocke, that the
water gushed out, and the streames ouerflowed: can he giue bread also? or prepare
flesh for his people?
21 Therefore the Lord heard and was angrie, and the *fyer was kindled in Iaakób,
and also wrath came vpon Israél,
22 Because they beleued not in God, and
[n] trusted not in his helpe.

c Which were the people of God.
d By the testimonie & Law he meaneth ẏ Law writen, which they were commãded to teache their childrẽ, Deu. 6,7.
e He sheweth wherin ẏ children shulde be like their fathers, that is, in mainteining Gods pure religion.
f He sheweth wherein ẏ vse of this doctrine standeth: in faith, in ẏ meditation of Gods benefites & in obedience.
g Thogh these fathers were the sede of Abrahám & the chosen people, yet he sheweth by their rebellion, prouocation, falsehode & hypocrisie, that the childrẽ oght not to followe their exãples.
h By Ephráim he meaneth also the rest of the tribes, because thei were moste in nomber: whose punishmẽt declareth that they were vnfaithful to God, and by their multitude and autoritie had corrupt all others.
i He proueth that not onely the posteritie, but also their forefathers were wicked and rebellious to God.
Exod. 14,21.
Exod. 14,24.
Exod. 17,6. num. 20,11. psal. 105,41. 1. Cor. 10,4. wisd. 11,4.
k Their wicked malice colde be ouercome by no benefites, which were great & manie.
l Then to require more thẽ is necessarie, & to separate Gods power from his wil, is to tempt God. *Nomb 11,1.
m Thus when we giue place to sinne, we are moued to doute of Gods power, except he wil alwayes be ready to serue our lust. *Exod. 17,6 nomb. 20,11. psal. 105,41. 1 cor. 10, 4. *Nomb 11,1.
n That is, in his Fatherlie prouidence, whereby he careth for his and prouideth sufficiently.

23 Yet he had commanded the [o] cloudes a-
boue, and had opened the dores of heauen,
24 And had rained downe MAN vpon thẽ
for to eat, and had giuen them of the
wheat of heauen.
25 *Man did eat the bread of Angels: he sent
them meat ynough.
26 He caused the [p] Eastwinde to passe in the
heauen, and through his power he broght
in the Southwinde.
27 He rained flesh also vpon them as
dust, and feathered foule as the sand of
the sea.
28 And he made it fall in ẏ middes of their
campe, *euen* round about their habitations.
29 So thei did eat and were wel filled: for he
gaue them their desire.
30 They were not turned from their
[q] lust, *but* the meat *was* yet in their mouthes,
31 When the wrath of God came euen vpon them, and slew [r] the strongest of them,
and smote downe the chosen men in Israél.
32 For all this, thei [f] sinned stil, and beleued
not his wonderous workes.
33 Therefore their daies did he cõsume in
vanitie, and their yeres hastely.
34 And when he [t] slewe them, thei soght hĩ
& they returned, & soght God early.
35 And thei remembred that God *was* their
strength, & the moste high God their redemer.
36 But thei flattered him with their mouth
and dissembled with him with their tongue.
37 For their [u] heart was not vpright with
him: nether were they faithful in his couenant.
38 Yet he being merciful [x] forgaue *their* iniquitie, and destroied *them* not, but oft times called backe his angre, and did not
stirre vp all his wrath.
39 For he remembred that thei were flesh:
yea, a winde that passeth and commeth not
againe.
40 How oft did they prouoke him in the
wildernes? *&* grieue him in the desert?
41 Yea, they [y] returned, and tempted God,
and [z] limited the Holie one of Israél.
42 Thei [a] remembred not his hand, *nor* the
daie when he deliuered them from the e-
nemie,
43 *Nor* him that set his signes in Egypt, &
his wonders in the field of Zóan,
44 And turned their riuers into blood, and
their floods, that thei colde not drinke.
45 He sent [b] a swarme of flies among them,
which deuoured them, & frogs, which destroyed them.

o So that thei had ẏ, which was necessarie & sufficiẽt: but their lust made them to couet that which thei knewe God had denied them.
Ioh. 6,31. 1. cor. 10,3.
p God vsed ẏ meanes of the winde to teach them, that all elements were at his cõmandement, & that no distance of place colde let his working.
q Suche is the nature of concupiscence, ẏ the more it hathe, ẏ more it lusteth.
r Thogh other were not spared, yet chiefly thei suffred, ẏ trusted in their strength agaist God.
f Thus sinne by continuãce maketh men insensible, so ẏ by no plagues thei can be amended.
t Suche was their hypocrisie, that thei soght vnto God for feare of punishmẽt thogh in their heart thei loued him not.
u Whatsoeuer commeth not from the pure fountaine of ẏ heart, is hypocrisie.
x Because he wolde euer haue some remnant of a Church to praise his Name in earth, he suffred not their sinnes to ouercome his mercie.
y That is, thei tempted him oft times.
z As thei all do ẏ measure the power of God by their capacitie.
a The forgetfulnes of Gods benefits is the rote of rebellion & all vice.
b This worde signifieth a confused mixture of flies and venemous wormes. Some take it for all sortes of serpents: some for all wilde beastes.

46 He [c] gaue alſo their frutes vnto the caterpiller, and their labour vnto the grashopper.
47 He deſtroied their vines with haile, &
their wilde figgetrees with the haile-
ſtone.
48 He gaue their cattel alſo to the haile,
and their flockes to the thunderboltes.
49 He caſt vpon them the fiercenes of his
angre, indignation and wrath, and vexation by the ſending out of [d] euil Angels.
50 He made awaie to his angre: he ſpared
not their ſoule from death, *but* gaue their
life to the peſtilence,
51 And ſmote all the firſtborne in Egypt,
euen the [e] beginning of *their* ſtrength in
the tabernacles of [f] Ham.
52 But he made his people to go out like
ſhepe, and led them in the wildernes like a
flocke.
53 Yea, he caried them out ſafely, and they
[g] feared not, and the Sea couered their e-
nemies.
54 And he broght them vnto the borders
of his [h] Sanctuarie: *euen* to this Mountaine, *which* his right hand purchaſed.
55 *He caſt out the heathen alſo before thẽ
and cauſed them to fall to the lot of *his* inheritance, and made the tribes of Iſraél
to dwell in their tabernacles.
56 Yet they tempted, and prouoked the
moſt high God, and kept not his teſtimonies,
57 But turned backe and delt [i] falſely like
their fathers: thei turned like a deceitful
bowe.
58 And thei [k] prouoked him to angre with
their high places, & moued him to wrath
with their grauen images.
59 God heard *this* and was wroth, & greatly abhorred Iſraél,
60 So that he [l] forſoke the habitation of
Shiló, *euẽ* the Tabernacle where he dwelt
among men,
61 And deliuered his [m] power in to captiuitie, and his beautie into the enemies hand.
62 And he gaue vp his people to the ſworde, and was angrie with his inheritance.
63 The fyer [n] deuoured their choſen men,
and their maides were not [o] praiſed.
64 Their Prieſts fell by the ſworde, & their
[p] widowes lamented not.
65 But the Lord awaked as one out of ſlepe,
and as a ſtrong man that after *his* [q] wine
cryeth out,
66 And ſmote his enemies in the hinder *par*
tes, and put them to a perpetual ſhame.
67 Yet he refuſed the tabernacle of [r] Ioſeph,
and choſe not the tribe of Ephráim:
68 But choſe the tribe of Iudáh, *&* mount

c He repeteth not here all ẏ miracles that God did in Egypt, but certeine w̃ might be ſufficient to conuince the people of malice & ingratitude
d So called, ether of the effect: that is, of puniſhing the wicked, or els becauſe thei were wicked ſpirits, whome God permitted to vexe men
e The firſtborne are ſo called, as Gen. 49,3.
f That is, Egypt: for it was called Mizráim or Egypt of Mizráim, that was the ſonne of Ham
g That is, thei had none occaſion to feare, for aſmucheas God deſtroied their enemies and deliuered them ſafely.
h Meanig Canáan, w̃ God had conſecrate to him ſelfe, & appointed to his people.
Ioſh.11,1. & 13,7.
i Nothing more diſpleaſeth God in ẏ children, thẽ when thei cõtinue in ẏ wickednes, which their fathers had bigõne.
k By ſeruing God otherwiſe then he had appointed.
l For their ingratitude he ſuffred ẏ Philiſtims to take the Arke, w̃ was the ſigne of his preſẽce, frõ amõg thẽ.
m The Arke is called his power & beautie, becauſe thereby he deféded his people, & beautifully appeared vnto them
n Thei were ſuddenly deſtroyed, 1.Sam. 4,10.
o Thei had no mariage ſongs: ẏ is, thei were not maried.
p Ether thei were ſlaine before, or taken priſoners of their enemies, & ſo were forbidden.
q Becauſe thei were drunken in their ſinnes, thei iudged Gods pacience to be a ſlombring, as thogh he were drunken: therefore he anſwering their beaſtlie iudgement, ſaith, he wil awake and take ſudden vengeance.
r Shewing that he ſpared not altogether the Iſraelites, thogh he puniſhed their enemies.

Zión which he loued.
69 And he [ſ] buylt his Sanctuarie as an high
palace, like the earth, which he ſtabliſhed
for euer.
70 He choſe Dauid alſo his ſeruant, & toke
him from the ſhepefoldes.
71 Euen from behinde the ewes with yong
broght he him to fede his people in Iaakób, and his inheritance in Iſraél.
72 So [t] he fed them according to the ſimplicitie of his heart, and guided them by the
diſcretion of his hands.

ſ By buylding the Temple & eſtabliſhing ẏ kingdome, he declareth that the ſignes of his fauour were among thẽ.
t He ſheweth wherein a Kĩgs charge ſtãdeth: to wit, to prouide faithfully for his people, to guide them by counſel, & defend them by power.

PSAL. LXXIX.

1 The Iſraelites complaine to God for the great calamitie and oppreſsion that thei ſuffred by Gods enemies. 8 And confeſsing their ſinnes, flee to Gods mercies with ful hope of deliuerance, 10 Becauſe their calamities were ioyned with the contẽpt of his Name, 13 For the which thei promes to be thankeful.

¶ *A Pſalme* committed *to Aſaph.*

1 O God, [a] the heathen are come into
thine inheritance: thine holie Temple haue they defiled, *&* made Ieruſalém
heapes *of ſtones.*
2 The [b] dead bodies of thy ſeruants haue
thei giuen to be meat vnto foules of the
heauen: *and* the fleſh of thy Saincts vnto the beaſtes of the earth.
3 Their blood haue thei ſhed like waters ro-
und about Ieruſalém, and there was none
to [c] burye them.
4 We are a reproche to our [d] neighbours,
euen a ſcorne and deriſion vnto them that
are round about vs.
5 Lord, how long wilt thou be angrie for
euer? ſhal thy gelouſie [e] burne like fyer?
6 *Powre out thy wrath vpon the heathen
that haue not knowen thee, and vpon the
kingdomes that haue not called vpon thy
Name.
7 For thei haue deuoured Iaakób and made
his dwelling place deſolate.
8 Remember not againſt vs the [f] former
iniquities, *but* [g] make haſte *&* let thy tendre mercies preuent vs: for we are in great
miſerie.
9 Helpe vs, ô God of our [h] ſaluacion, for
the glorie of thy Name, and deliuer vs,
and be merciful vnto our ſinnes for thy
names ſake.
10 Wherefore ſhulde the heathen ſaie,
Where is their God? let him be knowen
among the heathen in our ſight by the
vengeance of the blood of thy ſeruants
that is ſhed.
11 Let the ſighĩg of the [i] priſoners come be
fore thee: according to thy mightie arme
preſerue [k] the children of death,
12 And render to our neighbours ſeuen
folde into their boſome their reproche,
wherewith they haue reproched thee, ô
Lord.
13 So we thy people, and ſhepe of thy

a The people crye vnto God againſt ẏ barbarous tyrãnie of ẏ Babylonians, who ſpoiled Gods inheritance, polluted his Tẽple, deſtroied his religion & murthered his people.
b The Prophet ſheweth to what extremities God ſuffreth ſometime his Church to fall, to exerciſe their faith before he ſet to his hand to deliuer them.
c Their frends & kinſfolkes durſt not burie them for feare of ẏ enemies.
d Whereof ſome came of Abrahám, but were degenerate: & others were open enemies to thy religion, but thei bothe laughed at our miſeries.
e Wilt ẏ vtterly conſume vs for our ſinnes, before ẏ takeſt vs to mercie?
Iere.10,25.
f Which we & our fathers haue committed.
g And ſtaie not til we haue recõpenced for our ſinnes.
h Seig we haue none other Sauiour, nether can we helpe our ſelues, and alſo by our ſaluacion thy Name ſhalbe praiſed, therefore, o Lord, helpe vs.
i Who thogh in reſpect of God thei were iuſtly puniſhed for their ſinnes, yet in cõſideration of their cauſe, were vniuſtly murthered.
k Which were captiues amõg their enemies, & colde loke for nothĩg but death.

pasture shal praise thee for euer: and from
generation to generation [l] we wil set forthe thy praise.

l We oght to desire no benefite of God, but on this condition to praise his Name, Isa. 43,21.

PSAL. LXXX.

1 A lamentable praier to God to helpe the miseries of his Church, 8 Desiring him to consider their first estate, when his fauour shined towards them, to the intent that he might finish that worke which he had begonne.

¶ *To him that excelleth on Shoshannim Eduth.* *A Psalme* committed *to Asaph.*

1 HEare, [a] ô thou Shepherd of Israél,
thou that leadest Ioséph like shepe:
shew *thy* brightnes, thou that sittest betwene the [b] Cherubims.
2 Before Ephráim and Beniamín and Manasséh stirre vp thy strength, and come to
helpe vs.
3 [c] Turne vs againe, ô God, and cause thy
face to shine that we maie be saued.
4 O Lord God of hostes, how long wilt
thou be [d] angrie against the praier of thy
people?
5 Thou hast fed thẽ with the bread of teares, and giuen them teares to drinke with
greate measure.
6 Thou hast made vs a [e] strife vnto our
neighbours, and our enemies laugh *at vs* a-
mong them selues.
7 [f] Turne vs againe, ô God of hostes: cause thy face to shine, and we shalbe saued.
8 Thou hast broght a [g] vine out of Egypt:
thou hast cast out the heathen, and planted it.
9 Thou madest roume for it, and didest
cause it to take roote, and it filled the
land.
10 The mountaines were couered with the
shadow of it, and the boughs thereof *were*
like the "goodlie cedres.
11 She stretched out her branches vnto the
Sea, and her boughes vnto the [h] Riuer.
12 Why hast thou *then* broken downe her
hedges, so that all thei, which passe by the
waie, haue plucked her?
13 The wilde [i] bore out of the wood hathe
destroied it, and the wilde beastes of the
field haue eaten it vp.
14 Returne we beseche thee, ô God of hostes: loke downe [k] from heauen and beholde and visit this vine,
15 And the vineyarde, that thy right hand
hathe planted, and the yong vine, *which*
thou madest [l] strong for thy self.
16 It is burnt with fyer *and* cut downe: *and*
they perish at the [m] rebuke of thy countenance.
17 Let thine hand be vpon ẏ [n] man of thy
right hand, *and* vpon the sonne of man,
whome thou madest strong for thine owne
self.

a This psalme was made as a praier for to desire God to be merciful to the tentribes.
b Moue their hearts ẏ thei may returne to worship God aright: ẏ is in ẏ place where thou hast appointed.
c Ioyne thy whole people & all thy tribes together againe.
d The faithful feare Gods angre, when thei perceiue that their praiers are not forthwith heard.
e Our neighbours haue cõtinual strife & warre agaĩst vs.
f Because that repentãce onely commeth of God, thei moste instantly & oft times call to God for it as a meane, whereby thei shalbe saued.
g Seing that of thy mercie thou hast made vs a moste deare possessiõ to thee, & we through our sinnes are made open for wilde beastes to deuour vs, declare againe thy loue & finish ẏ worke that thou hast begonne.
" Ebr. Cedres of God.
h To wit, Euphrates.
i That is, aswel thei ẏ hate our religion as thei ẏ hate our persones.
k Thei gaue not place to tentatiõ, knowing that albeit there were no helpe in earth, yet God was able to succour them frõ heauen.
l So ẏ no power can preuaile against it, & ẘ as a yong bud thou raisest vp againe as out of the burnt ashes.
m Onely when thou art angrie, and not with the sworde of the enemie.
n That is, vpon this vine, or people, whome thou hast planted with thy right hand, that thei shulde be as one man or onetbodie.

18 So wil not we go backe from thee: [o] reuiue thou vs, and we shal call vpon thy
Name.
19 Turne vs againe, ô Lord God of hostes:
cause thy face to shine and we shalbe saued.

o For none cã call vpõ God, but suche as are raised vp, as it were, from death to life & regenerate by ẏ holie Spirit.

PSAL. LXXXI.

1 An exhortatiõ to praise God bothe in heart & voice for his benefites, 8 And to worship him onely. 11 God condẽneth their ingratitude, 12 And sheweth what great benefites thei haue lost through their owne malice.

¶ *To him that excelleth vpon* [a] *Gittith.* A psalme committed *to Asaph.*

1 SIng [b] ioyfully vnto God our strength:
sing loude vnto the God of Iaakób.
2 Take the song and bring forthe the timbrel, the pleasant harpe with the viole.
3 Blowe the trumpet in the [c] newmoone,
euen in the time appointed, at our feast-
daie.
4 For this is a statute for Israél, *&* a Law
of the God of Iaakób.
5 He set this in [d] Ioséph for a testimonie,
when he came out of the land of Egypt,
where I heard a language, that [e] I vnderstode not.
6 I haue withdrawen his shulder from the
burden, *&* his hands haue left the [f] pottes.
7 Thou calledst in affliction and I deliuered thee, *and* [g] answered thee in the secret
of the thunder: I proued thee at the waters of "Meribáh. Séláh.
8 [h] Heare, ô my people, and I wil protest vn
to thee: ô Israél, if thou wilt hearken vnto me,
9 Let there be no strange god in thee, nether worship thou anie strange god.
10 For I am the Lord thy God, ẘ broght
thee out of the land of Egypt: [i] open thy
mouth wide and I wil fil it.
11 But my people wolde not heare my voice, and Israél wolde none of me.
12 So I gaue them vp vnto the hardenes of
their heart, *&* thei haue walked in their
owne counsels.
13 [k] Oh that my people had hearkened vnto me, *&* Israél had walked in my waies.
14 I wolde sone haue humbled their enemies, and turned mine hand [l] against their
aduersaries.
15 The haters of the Lord shulde haue bene
subiect vnto him, and their time [m] shulde
haue endured for euer.
16 And *God* wolde haue fed them with the
[n] fat of wheat, and with honie out of the
rocke wold I haue sufficed thee.

a An instrumẽt of musicke broght from Geth.
b It semeth ẏ this psal. was appointed for solẽne feastes & assemblies of the people, to whome for a time these ceremonies were ordeined, but now vnder the Gospel are abolished.
c Vnder this feast he cõprehendeth all other solemne daies.
d That is, in Israél: for Iosephs familie was counted the chief before that Iudáh was preferred.
e God speaketh in ẏ persone of the people, because he was their leader.
f If thei were neuer able to giue sufficient thãkes to God for this deliuerance frõ corporal bõdage, how muche more are we indetted to hĩ for our spiritual deliuerãce from the tyrannie of Satã & sinne?
g By a strange & wonderful facion.
" Or, contention, Exod. 17,16.
h He condemneth all assemblies, where ẏ people are not attentiue to heare Gods voice, & to giue obedience to the same.
i God accuseth their incredulitie, because thei opened not their mouthes to receiue Gods benefites in suche abundance as he powreth them out.
k God by his worde calleth all, but his secret election appointeth, who shal heare with frute.
l If their sinnes had not letted.
m If the Israelites had not broken couenant with God, he wolde haue giuen them victorie against their enemies.
n That is, with moste fine wheat and abundance of honie.

PSAL. LXXXII.

*1 The Prophet declaring God to be present among the Iudges and Magistrates, 2 Reproueth their parcia-
litie,*

litie, 3 And exhorteth them to do iustice. 5 But seing none amendement, 8 He desireth God to undertake the matter & execute iustice him self.

¶ *A Psalme* committed *to Asaph.*

1 GOd standeth in the assemblie of
[a] gods: he iudgeth among gods.
2 How long wil ye iudge vniustly, and accept the persones of the [b] wicked? Sélah.
3 Do right to the poore and fatherles: do
iustice to the poore and nedie.
4 Deliuer the poore and [c] nedie: saue *them*
from the hand of the wicked.
5 They knowe not & vnderstand nothing:
they walke in darknes, *albeit* all the [d] fundacions of the earth be moued.
6 I haue said, Ye are gods, and ye all are
children of the most High.
7 [e] But ye shal dye as a man, & ye princes,
shal fall like others.
8 O God, arise, *therefore* iudge thou the
earth: for thou shalt inherite [f] all nations.

PSAL. LXXXIII.

1 The people of Israél praie vnto the Lord to deliuer thē from their enemies bothe at home and farre of, which imagined nothing but their destruction. 9 And thei desire that all suche wicked people maie, according as God was accustomed, be stricken with the stormie tempest of Gods wrath, 18 That thei maie knowe that the Lord is moste high vpon the earth.

¶ *A song, or Psalme* committed *to Asaph.*

1 KEpe [a] not thou silence, ô God: be not
stil and cease not, ô God.
2 For lo, thine [b] enemies make a tumulte: &
they yᵗ hate thee, haue lifted vp the head.
3 Thei haue taken craftie counsel against
thy people, and haue consulted against
thy [c] secret ones.
4 Thei haue said, Come and let vs [d] cut
them of from being a nation: and let the
name of Israél be no more in remēbrance.
5 For thei haue consulted together [e] in
heart, & haue made a league [f] agaīst thee:
6 The tabernacles of Edóm, & the Ishmaelites, Moáb and the Agarims:
7 Gebál and Ammón, and Amaléch, the
Philistims with the inhabitants of ″Ty-
rus:
8 Asshúr also is ioyned with thē: thei haue
bene an arme to the children [g] of Lot.
Sélah.
9 Do thou to them as vnto the [h] Midianites: as to Siserá & as to Iabín at the riuer
of Kishón.
10 Thei perished at En-dór, & were [i] dongue for the earth.
11 Make thē, *euen* their princes like * Oréb
and like Zeéb: yea, all their princes like
Zébah and like Zalmuná.
12 Which haue said, Let vs take for our possession the [k] habitacions of God.

a The Prophet sheweth that if princes and judges do not their duetie, God, whose autoritie is aboue them, wil take vengeāce on them.
b For theues and murderers finde fauour in iudgemēt, whē the cause of yᵉ godlie can not be heard.
c Not onely whē they crye for helpe, but whē their cause requireth aide & support.
d That is, all things are out of ordre, ether by their tyrānie or carcles negligence.
e No title of honour shal excuse you, but you shalbe subiect to Gods iudgement, and rēder a compt as wel as other men.
f Therefore no tyrant shal plucke thy right & autoritie frō thee.

Psal. LXXXIII
a This Psalme semeth to haue bene cōposed, as a forme of praier against the dangers that the Church was in in the daies of Iehoshaphát.
b He calleth them Gods enemies, wᶜ are enemies to his Church
c The elect of God are his secret ones: for he hideth thē in the secret of his tabernacle, & preserueth them frō all dangers.
d Thei were not content to take yᵉ Church as prisoner, but soght vtterly to destroy it.
e By all secret meanes.
f Thei thoght to haue subuerted thy coūsel, wherein yᵉ perpetuitie of the Church was established.
″Or, Zor.
g The wicked nes of the Ammonites & Moabites is descri bed, in yᵗ they prouoked these other natiōs to fight against the Israelites their brethren.
h By these examples, thei were cōfirmed that God wolde not suffer his people to be vtterly destroied, Iudg. 7, 21 and 4, 15.
i Troden vnder fete as myre. *Iud. 7, 25. 8, 21.
k That is, Iudea: for where his Church is, there dwelleth he among them.

13 O my God, make thē like vnto a [l] whele,
& as the stubble before the winde.
14 As the fyer burneth the forest, and as the
flame setteth the mountaines on fyre:
15 So persecute them with thy tempest, and
make them afraied with thy storme.
16 Fil their faces with shame, that thei maie
[m] seke thy Name, ô Lord.
17 Let them be confounded and troubled
for euer: yea, let them be put to shame and
perish,
18 That they maie [n] knowe that thou, which
art called Iehouáh, art alone, *euen* the moste High ouer all the earth.

PSAL. LXXXIIII.

1 Dauid driuen forthe of his countrey, 2 Desireth moste ardently to come againe to the Tabernacle of the Lord & the assemblie of the Saints to praise God, 4 Pronouncing them blessed that maie so do. 6 Then he praiseth the courage of the people, that passe through the wildernes to assemble them selues in Zión. 10 Finally with praise of this matter & confidence of Gods goodnes he endeth the Psalme.

¶ *To him that excelleth vpon Gittith. A Psalme* committed *to the sonnes of Kórah.*

1 O [a] Lord of hostes, how amiable *are*
thy Tabernacles!
2 My soule longeth, yea, & fainteth for the
[b] courtes of the Lord: *for* mine heart and
my flesh reioyce in the liuing God.
3 Yea, the sparowe hathe foūde *her* an house, and the swallowe a nest for her, where
she maie lay her yong: *euen* by thine [c] altars, ô Lord of hostes, my King *and* my
God.
4 Blessed *are* thei that dwell in thine house: they wil euer praise thee. Sélah.
5 Blessed *is* the man, whose [d] strength *is* in
thee, & in whose heart *are thy* waies.
6 They going through the vale of [e] Bacá,
make welles therein: the raine also couereth the pooles.
7 They go from [f] strength to strength, *til*
euerie one appeare before God in Zión.
8 O Lord God of hostes, heare my praier:
hearken, ô God of Iaakób. Sélah.
9 Beholde, ô God, our shield, & loke vpon
the face of thine [g] Anointed.
10 For [h] a daie in thy courtes is better thē
a thousand *other where*: I had rather be a
dore keper in the House of my God, then
to dwell in the tabernacles of wickednes.
11 For the Lord God is the sunne & shield
vnto vs: the Lord wil giue grace & glorie,
& no [i] good thing wil he withholde from
them that walke vprightly.
12 O Lord of hostes, blessed *is* the mā that
trusteth in thee.

PSAL. LXXXV.

1 Because God withdrewe not his rods from his Church after their returne from Babylon, first they put him in minde of their deliuerance, to the intent that he shulde not leaue the worke of his grace vnperfite. 5 Next thei

l Because the reprobat colde by no meanes be amēded, he praieth yᵗ thei maie vtterly be destroied, be vnstable & led with all windes.
m That is, be compelled by thy plagues to confesse thy power.
n Thogh they beleue not, yet thei maie proue by experiēce, that it is in vaine to resist against thy counsel in establishing thy Church.

a Dauid complaineth yᵗ he can not haue accesse to the Church of God to make profession of his faith & to profit in religion.
b For none but the priests colde enter in to the Sāctuarie, & the rest of the people into the courtes.
c So that the poore birdes haue more libertie then I.
d Who trusteth nothing in him self, but in thee onely, & learneth of thee to rule his life.
e That is, of mulberie trees which was a baren place: so that they which passed through, must dig pits for water: signifying yᵗ no lets can hinder thē that are fully bent to come to Christs Church, nether yet that God wil euer faile them.
f Thei are neuer wearie, but increase in strēgth & courage til thei come to Gods House.
g That is, for Christs sake, whose figure I represent.
h He wolde wish to liue but one daie rather in Gods Church, then a thousand among yᵉ worldelings.
i But wil from time to time increase his blessings towards his more and more.

complaine of their long affliction: 8 And thirdly they reioyce in hope of felicitie promised. 9 For their deliuerãce was a figure of Christs kingdome, vnder the which shulde be perfite felicitie.

¶ *To him that excelleth. A Psalme cõmitted to the sonnes of Kórah.*

1 LOrd, thou hast bene [a] fauourable vnto
thy land: thou hast broght againe the
captiuitie of Iaakób.
2 Thou hast forgiuen the iniquitie of thy
people, *and* [b] couered all their sinnes. Sélah.
3 Thou hast withdrawen all thine angre, &
hast turned backe from the [c] fiercenes of
thy wrath.
4 Turne vs, ô God of our saluacion, & release thine angre towards vs.
5 Wilt thou be angrie with vs [d] for euer? &
wilt thou prolong thy wrath from one generacion to another?
6 Wilt thou not turne againe *and* quicken
vs, that thy people maie reioyce in thee?
7 Shewe vs thy mercie, ô Lord, and grante
vs thy [e] saluacion.
8 I wil hearkẽ what the Lord God wil saie:
for he wil speake [f] peace vnto his people,
& to his Saints, that they turne not againe
to folie.
9 Surely his saluacion is nere to them that
feare him, that glorie maie dwell in our
land.
10 Mercie and trueth shal mete: righteousnes and peace shal kisse *one another.*
11 [g] Trueth shal bud out of the earth, and
righteousnes shal loke downe frõ heauen.
12 Yea, the Lord shal giue good things, and
our land shal giue her increase.
13 [h] Righteousnes shal go before him, and
shal set her steps in the waie.

a Thei confesse that Gods fre mercie was the cause of their deliuerance, because he loued the land, which he had chosen.
b Thou hast buryed them that thei shal not come into iudgement.
c Not onely in withdrawing thy rod, but in forgiuig our sinnes, & in touching ye hearts to confesse them.
d As in times past thei had felt Godsmercies: so now being oppressed by the lõg continuance of euils, thei pray vnto God, that according to his nature he wolde be merciful vnto thẽ.
e He confesseth that our saluation commeth onely of Gods mercie.
f He wil send all prosperitie to his Church, when he hathe sufficiently corrected thẽ: also by his punishments the faithful shal learne to beware that thei returne not to like offences.
g Thogh for a time God thus exercise them with his rods, yet vnder the kingdome of Christ thei shulde haue peace & ioye.
h Iustice shal then florish & haue fre course & passage in euerie place.

PSAL. LXXXVI.

1 Dauid sore afflicted & forsaken of all prayeth feruently for deliuerance: sometimes rehearsing his miseries, 5 Sometimes the mercies receiued. 11 Desiring also to be instructed of the Lord, that he maie feare him and glorifie his Name. 14 He complaineth also of his aduersaries, & requireth to be deliuered from them.

¶ *A prayer of Dauid.*

1 INcline [a] thine eare, ô Lord, *and* heare
me: for I am poore and nedie.
2 Preserue thou my soule, for I am [b] merciful: my God, saue thou thy seruant, that
trusteth in thee.
3 Be merciful vnto me, ô Lord: for I [c] crye
vpon thee continually.
4 Reioyce the soule of thy seruant: for vnto thee, ô Lord, do I lift vp my soule.
5 For thou, Lord, art good and [d] merciful,
& of great kindenes vnto all them, that call
vpon thee.
6 Giue eare, Lord, vnto my prayer, & [e] hearken to the voyce of my supplicacion.
7 In the daye of my trouble I wil call vpõ
thee: for thou hearest me.
8 Among the gods there is none like thee,
ô Lord, and there [f] is none *that can do* like
thy workes.
9 All nations, whome thou hast made, shal
come and [g] worship before thee, ô Lord,
and shal glorifie thy Name.
10 For thou art great and doest wonderous
things: thou art God alone.
11 [h] Teache me thy waie, ô Lord, *and* I wil
walke in thy trueth: knit mine heart vnto
thee, that I maie feare thy Name.
12 I wil praise thee, ô Lord my God, with
all mine heart: yea, I wil glorifie thy Name for euer.
13 For great is thy mercie towarde me, and
thou hast deliuered my soule from [i] the
lowest graue.
14 O God, the proude are risen against me,
and the assemblies of violent men haue
[k] soght my soule, and haue not set thee before them.
15 But thou, ô Lord, art a pitiful God and
merciful, slowe to angre and great in kindenes and trueth.
16 Turne vnto me, and haue mercie vpon
me: giue thy strength vnto thy seruant, &
saue the [l] sonne of thine handmaid.
17 Shewe a token of *thy* goodnes towarde
me, that they which hate me, maie se it, &
be ashamed, because thou, ô Lord, hast
holpen me and comforted me.

a Dauid persecuted of Saûl, thus praied, leauing the same to the Church as a monumẽt, how to seke redresse agaīst their miseries.
b I am not enemie to thẽ, but pitie thẽ, thogh thei be cruel toward me.
c Which was a sure token ye he beleued ye God wolde deliuer him.
d He doeth confesse that God is good to all, but onely merciful to poore sinners.
e By crying and calling continually, he sheweth how we maie not be wearie, thogh God grante not forthewith our request, but that we must earnestly, and often call vpon him.
f He cõdẽneth all idoles, forasmuche as thei can do no workes to declare that thei are gods.
g This proueth ye Dauid praied in the name of Christ ye Messias, of whose kingdome he doeth here prophecie.
h He cõfesseth him self ignorant til God hathe taught him, and his heart variable & seperat frõ God, til God ioyne it to hĩ & cõfirme it in his obediẽce.
i That is, from moste great danger of death: out of the which none, but onely the mightie hand of God, colde deliuer him.
k He sheweth that there can be no moderation nor equitie, where proude tyrants reigne & that the lacke of Gods feare is as a priuiledge to all vice and crueltie.
l He boasteth not of his owne vertues, but cõfesseth that God of his fre goodnes hathe euer bene merciful vnto him & giuen him power against his enemies, as to one of his owne housholde.

PSAL. LXXXVII.

1 The holie Gost promiseth that the condition of the Church, which was in miserie after the captiuitie of Babylon, shulde be restored to great excellencie, 4 So that there shulde be nothing more comfortable then to be nombred among the members thereof.

¶ *A Psalme or song committed to the sonnes of Kórah.*

1 GOd laied his [a] fundacions among the
holie mountaines.
2 The Lord loueth ye gates of Zíon aboue
all the habitacions of Iaakób.
3 [b] Glorious things are spoken of thee, ô
Citie of God. Sélah.
4 I wil make mention of [c] Raháb and Babél among them that knowe me: beholde
Palestina & Tyrus with Ethiopia, [d] There is he borne.
5 And of Zíon it shalbe said, [e] Manie are
borne in her: and he, *euen* the most High
shal stablish her.
6 The Lord shal count, when he [f] writeth
the people, He was borne there. Sélah.
7 Aswel the singers as the plaiers on instruments *shal praise thee*: all my [g] springs *are*
in thee.

Psal. LXXXVII.
a God did chose that place among the hils to establish Ierusalém & his Temple.
b Thogh thy glorious estate do not yet appeare, yet waite wt pacience & God wil accomplish his promes.
c That is, Egypt & these other contreis shal come to ye knowledge of God.
d It shalbe said of him, ye is regenerat & come to the Church, ye he is as one that was borne in the Church.
e Out of all quarters they shal come into the Church and be counted as citizens. f When he calleth by his worde them into the Church, whome he had elected and writen in his boke. g The Prophet setteth his whole affections and comfort in the Church.

PSAL. LXXXVIII.

1 A grieuous complaint of the faithful, sore afflicted

by

by sicknes, persecutions & aduersitie: 7 Being as it were left of God without anie consolation. 13 Yet he calleth on God by faith & strieueth against desperation, 18 Complaining him self to be forsaken of all earthlie helpe.

¶ *A song or Psalme of* * *Hemán the Ezrahite to giue instruction,* committed *to the sonnes of Kórah for him that excelleth vpon Maláth* [a] *Leannoth.*

1 O Lord God of my saluació, I crye day
and night [b] before thee.
2 Let my prayer enter into thy presence:
incline thine eare vnto my crye.
3 For my soule is filled with euils, and my
life draweth nere to the graue.
4 I am counted among them that go downe
vnto the pit, *and* am as a man without
strength:
5 [c] Fre amóg the dead, like the slaine lying
in the graue, whome thou remembrest no
more, and they are cut of from thine
[d] hand.
6 Thou hast laied me in the lowest pit, in
darkenes, & in the depe.
7 Thine indignation lieth vpon me, and
thou hast vexed me with all thy [e] waues.
Sélah.
8 Thou hast put away mine [f] acquaintance
farre fró me, & made me to be abhorred
of them: [g] I am shut vp, and can not
get forthe.
9 [h] Mine eye is sorowful through mine affliction:
Lord, I call daiely vpon thee: I
stretche out mine hands vnto thee.
10 Wilt thou shewe [i] a miracle to ý dead?
or shal the dead rise & praise thee? Sélah.
11 Shal thy louing kindenes be declared
in the graue? *or* thy faithfulnes in destruction?
12 Shal thy wonderous workes be knowen
in the darke? and thy righteousnes in the
land [k] of obliuion?
13 But vnto thee haue I cryed, ô Lord, and
early shal my praier come before thee.
14 Lord, why doest thou reiect my soule, &
hidest thy face from me?
15 I am afflicted and at the point of death:
[l] from *my* youth I suffer thy terrours, douting
of my life.
16 Thine indignations go ouer me, & thy
feare hathe cut me of.
17 They came round about me daiely like
water, & compassed me together.
18 My louers and friends hast thou put away
from me, *and* mine acquaintance [*] hid
them selues.

* 1.King 4,31. psal.53.
a That is, to humble. It was ý beginning of a song, by the tune whereof this Psalme was sung
b Thogh many crye in their sorowes, yet they crye not earnestly to God for remedie as he did: whome he cófessed to be ý autor of his saluacion.
c For he that is dead, is fre from all cares & busines of this life: & thus he saieth because he was vnprofitable for all matters concernĩg mãs life, and as it were cut of fró this worlde.
d That is, fró thy prouidence & care, wis ment accordĩg to ý iudgemẽt of the flesh.
e The stormes of thy wrath haue ouerwhelmed me.
f He attributeth ý losse & displeasure of his friends to Gods prouidẽce, whereby he partely punisheth and partely trieth his.
g I se none end of my sorowes
h Mine eies & face declare my sorowes.
i He sheweth ý the time is more cõueniẽt for God to helpe, whẽ mẽ call vnto him in their dãgers thẽ to tary til thei be dead & then raise thẽ vp againe.
k That is, in ý graue, where onely the bodie lieth without all sense and remembrance.
l I am euer in great dangers & sorowes, as thogh my life shulde vtterly be cut of euerie moment.
* Ebr. were in darknes.

PSAL. LXXXIX.

1 *With manie wordes doeth the Prophet praise the goodnes of God, 23 For his testament & couenant, that he had made betwene him and his elect by Iesus Christ the sonne of Dauid: 38 Then doeth he complaine of the great ruine, and desolation of the kingdome of Dauid, so that to the outwarde appearance the promes was brokẽ. 46 Finally he praieth to be deliuered fró his afflictions, making mention of the shortnes of mans life, & confirming him self by Gods promises.*

¶ A Psalme *to giue instruction, of Ethán the Ezrahite.*

1 I Wil [a] sing the mercies of the Lord for
euer: with my mouth wil I declare thy
trueth from generacion to generacion.
2 For I [b] said, Mercie shalbe set vp for euer:
thy trueth shalt thou [c] stablish in the
verie heauens.
3 [d] I haue made a couenãt with my chosen:
I haue sworne to Dauid my seruant,
4 Thy sede wil I stablish for euer, and set
vp thy throne from generacion to generacion.
Sélah.
5 O Lord, euen the [e] heauens shal praise
thy wonderous worke: yea, thy trueth in
the [f] Congregacion of the Saints.
6 For who is equal to the Lord in the heauen!
& *who* is like the Lord among the
[g] sonnes of the gods!
7 God is verie terrible in the assemblie of
the [h] Saints, and to be reuerenced aboue
all, *that are* about him.
8 O Lord God of hostes, who is like vnto
thee, *which art* a mightie Lord, and thy
trueth *is* about thee!
9 [i] Thou rulest the raging of the sea: when
the waues thereof arise, thou stillest them.
10 Thou hast beaten downe Rahab as a mã
slaine: thou hast scatered thine enemies
with thy mightie arme.
11 The heauens are thine, the earth also is
thine: thou hast laied the fundacion of the
worlde, and all that therein is.
12 Thou hast created the North and the
South: [k] Tabór and Hermón shal reioice
in thy Name.
13 Thou hast a mightie arme: strong is
thine hand, & high is thy right hand.
14 [l] Righteousnes & equitie *are* the stablishment
of thy throne: mercie ad trueth go
before thy face.
15 Blessed *is* the people, that can [m] reioyce
in thee: they shal walke in the light of thy
[n] countenance, ô Lord.
16 They shal reioyce cõtinually in thy Name,
and in thy righteousnes shal they exalt
them selues.
17 For thou art the [o] glorie of their strẽgth,
and by thy fauour our hornes shalbe exalted.
18 For our [p] shield *apperteineth* to the Lord,
and our King to the Holie one of Israél.
19 Thou spakest thẽ in a vision vnto [q] thine
Holie one, and saidest, I haue laied helpe
vpon one that is [r] mightie: I haue exalted
one chosen out of the people.

a Thogh ý horrible confusió of thĩgs might cause them to despaire of Gods fauours yet the manifolde exãples of his mercies cause them to trust in God, thogh to mans iudgemẽt thei sawe none occasion.
b As he that surely beleued in heart.
c As thine inuisible heauen is not subiect to anie alteracion & chãge: so shal ý trueth of thy promes be vnchãgeable.
d The Prophet sheweth what was ý promes of God, wheró he grounded his faith.
e The Angels shal praise thy power & faithfulnes in deliuering thy Church.
f That is, in ý heauens.
g Meaning, ý Angels.
h If the Angels treble before Gods maiestie & infinite iustice, what earthlie creature by oppressing the Church, dare set him selfe against God?
i For as he deliuered the Church by ý red Sea, & by destroying Rahab, that is, ý Egyptians: so wil he eftsone deliuer it, whẽ the dangers be great.
k Tabór is a moũtaine Westwarde fró Ierusalẽ, & Hermón Eastwarde: so the Prophet signifieth ý all partes & places of the worlde shal obey Gods power for the deliuerance of his Church.
l For hereby he iudgeth the world & sheweth him self a merciful Father & faithful protector vnto his.
m Feling in their conscience that God is their Father. n They shalbe preserued by thy Fatherlie prouidence. o In that they are preserued and continue, they oght to giue the praise and glorie onely to thee. p In that that our King hathe power to defend vs, it is the gift of God. q To Samuél and to others, to assure that Dauid was thy chosen one r Whome I haue bothe chosen and giuen him strength to execute his office, as vers. 21.

20 I haue founde Dauid my seruant: with
mine holie oyle haue I anointed him.
21 Therefore mine hand shalbe established
with him, and mine arme shal strengthen
him.
22 The enemie shal not oppresse him, nether shal the wicked hurt him.
23 But I wil [f] destroye his foes before his
face, and plague them that hate him.
24 My trueth also and my [t] mercie *shalbe*
with him, and in my Name shal his [u] horne be exalted.
25 I wil set his hand also in the sea, and his
right hand in the [x] floods.
26 He shal crye vnto me, Thou art my
[y] Father, my God and the rocke of my
saluacion.
27 Also I wil make him my first borne, higher then the Kings of the earth.
28 My mercie wil I kepe for him for euermore, and my couenāt shal stand fast with
him.
29 His sede also wil I make to endure [z] for
euer, and his throne as the dayes of heauē.
30 But if his children forsake my Lawe, and
walke not in my iudgements:
31 *If they breake my statutes, and kepe not
my commandements:
32 Then wil I visit their transgresion with
the rod, and their iniquitie with strokes.
33 [a] Yet my louing kindenes wil I not take
from him, nether wil I falsifie my trueth.
34 My couenant wil I not breake, nor [b] alter the thing that is gone out of my
lippes.
35 I haue sworne once by mine holines,
"that I wil not faile Dauid, *saying*,
36 His sede shal endure for euer, and his
throne *shalbe* as the sunne before me.
37 He shalbe established for euermore as
the moone, & *as* a faithful [c] witnes in the
heauen. Sélah.
38 But thou hast reiected and abhorred, thou
hast bene angrie with thine Anointed.
39 Thou hast [d] broken the couenant of thy
seruant, *&* profaned his [e] crowne, *casting
it* on the grounde.
40 Thou hast broken downe all his walles:
thou hast layed his fortresses in ruine.
41 All that go by the way, spoile him: he is
a rebuke vnto his neighbours.
42 Thou hast set vp the right hand of his
enemies, *and* made all his aduersaries to
reioyce.
43 Thou hast also turned the edge of his
sworde, and hast not made him to stand in
the battel.
44 Thou hast caused his dignitie to decay,
and cast his throne to the grounde.
45 The dayes of his [f] youth hast thou
shortened, *and* couered him with shame.
Sélah.

f Thogh there shalbe euermore enemies against Gods kingdome, yet he promiseth to ouercome them.
t I wil mercifully performe my promises to hī, notwithstanding his infirmities & offences.
u His power, glorie & estate.
x He shal enioye the land round about.
y His excellēt dignitie shal appeare herein that he shal be named the sonne of God, & ẏ first borne, wherein he is a figure of Christ.
z Thogh for ẏ sinnes of the people ẏ state of this kigdome decayed: yet God reserued stil a rote, til he had acōplished this promes in Christ.
*2.Sam.7,14.
a Thogh the faithful āswer not in all poīts to their profession, yet God wil not breake his couenant with them.
b For God in promising hathe respect to his mercie and not to mans power in performing.
"Ebr. if I lie vnto Dauid: which is a maner of othe.
c As long as ẏ sunne & moone endure, they shalbe witnesses to me of this promes.
d Because of ẏ horrible cōfusion of things, the Prophet cōplaineth to God as thogh he sawe not ẏ performance of his promes. And thus dischargīg his cares on God, he resisteth doute & impaciēcie.
e By this he meaneth ẏ horrible dissipation and renting of ẏ kingdome, which was vnder Ieroboám: or els by ẏ Spirit of prophecie Ethán speaketh of those great miseries, ẇ came sone afterwarde to passe at the captiuitie of Babylon. f He sheweth that ẏ kingdome failed before it came to perfection or was ripe.

46 [g] Lord, how long wilt thou hide thy self,
for euer? shal thy wrath burne like fyre?
47 Remember [h] of what time I am: wherefore shuldest thou creat in vaine all the
children of men?
48 What man liueth, & shal not se death?
shal he deliuer his soule from the hand of
the graue? Sélah.
49 Lord, where are thy former mercies, *which*
thou swarest vnto Dauid in thy trueth?
50 Remember, ô Lord, the rebuke of thy seruants, which I beare in my [i] bosome of all
the mightie people.
51 For [k] thine enemies haue reproched *thee*,
ô Lord, because they haue reproched the
[l] fotesteppes of thine Anointed.
52 Praised *be* the Lord for euermore. So
be it, euen so be it.

PSAL. XC.

1 Mosés in his praier setteth before vs the eternal fauour of God toward his. 3 Who are nether admonished by the breuitie of their life, 7 Nor by his plagues to be thankeful. 12 Therefore Mosés praieth God to turne their hearts & continue his mercies toward them, & their posteritie for euer.

¶ *A praier of Mosés, the* [a] *man of God.*

1 LOrd, thou hast bene our [b] habitacion
from generacion to generacion.
2 Before the [c] mountaines were made, and
before thou hadest formed the earth, & the
worlde, euen from euerlasting to euerlasting thou art *our* God.
3 Thou [d] turnest man to destructiō: againe
thou saiest, Returne, ye sonnes of Adám.
4 [e] For a thousand yeres in thy sight *are* as
yesterdaie when it is past, and *as* a watche
in the night.
5 Thou hast [f] ouerflowed them: they are
as a slepe: in the morning he groweth like
the grasse:
6 In the morning it florisheth and groweth, *but* in the euening it is cut downe and
withereth.
7 For we [g] are consumed by thine angre,
and by thy wrath are we troubled.
8 Thou hast set our iniquities before thee,
and our secret sinnes in the light of thy
countenance.
9 For all our dayes are past in thine angre:
we haue [h] spent our yeres as a thoght.
10 The time of our life *is* threscore yeres &
ten, and if they be of strength, [i] foure
score yeres: yet their strength *is* but labour
and sorowe: for it is cut of quickely, and
we flee away.
11 [k] Who knoweth the power of thy wrath?
for according to thy feare *is* thine angre.
12 Teache vs so to nomber our dayes, that
we maie applie *our* hearts vnto [l] wisdome.
13 Returne (ô Lord, [m] how long?) and be
"pacified toward thy seruants.

g The Prophet in ioynig praier ẇ his complaint, sheweth ẏ his faith neuer failed.
h Seing mans life is short, & ẏ hast created mā to bestowe thy benefites vpon him, except thou haste to helpe, death wil preuent thee.
i He meaneth ẏ Gods enemies did not onely sclander him behinde his backe: but also mocked him to his face, & as it were cast their iniuries in his bosome.
k So he calleth the that persecute ẏ Church.
l They laugh at vs, ẇ paciētly waite for ẏ comming of thy Christ.
a Thus the Scripture vseth to call the Prophetes.
b Thou hast bene as an house and defence vnto vs in all our troubles & trauailes now this foure hūdreth yeres.
c Thou hast chosen vs to be thy people before ẏ fundacions of the worlde were laied.
d Mosés by lamenting the fraültie & shortnes of mās life moueth God to pitie.
e Thogh man thinke his life long, ẇ is in dede moste short, yea, thogh it were a thousand yeres: yet ī Gods sight it is as nothing, and as the watche ẏ lasteth but thre houres.
f Thou takest thē away suddenly as with a flood.
g Thou callest vs by thy rods to consider the shortnes of our life, & for our sinnes thou abbridgest our daies
h Our daies are not onely short, but miserable, forasmuch as our sinnes daily prouoke thy wrath.

i Meaning, according to the commune state of life. k If mans life for the breuitie be miserable, muche more, if thy wrath lie vpō it, as they, which feare thee, onely knowe. l Which is, by considering the shortnes of our life & by meditating the heauenlie ioyes. m Meaning, wilt ẏ be angrie? "Or, take comfort in thy seruants.

14 Fil

14 Fil vs with thy mercie in the morning:
ſo ſhal we reioyce and be glad all our
dayes.
15 Comfort vs according to the dayes that
thou haſt afflicted vs, & *according* to the
yeres that we haue ſene euil.
16 [n] Let thy worke be ſene toward thy ſeruants, & thy glorie vpon their [o] childrē.
17 And let the [p] beautie of ÿ Lord our God
be vpon vs, and [q] direct thou the worke
of our hands vpon vs, euen direct the worke of our hands.

n Euen thy mercie, ŵ is thy chiefeſt worke.
o As Gods p̄miſes apperteined aſwel to their poſteritie, as to thē, ſo Moſes praieth for the poſteritie
p Meaning ÿ it was obſcured, whē he ceaſed to do good to his Church.
q For except ÿ guide vs ŵ thine holie Spirit, our entrepriſes cā haue no good ſucces.

PSAL. XCI.

1 Here is deſcribed in what aſſurance he liueth that putteth his whole truſt in God, & committeth him ſelf wholly to his protection in all tentations. 14 A promes of God to thoſe that loue him, know him and truſt in him, to deliuer them, & giue them immortal glorie.

1 WHoſo dwelleth in the [a] ſecret of
the moſte High, ſhal abide in the
ſhadowe of the Almightie.
2 [b] I wil ſay vnto the Lord, O mine hope,
and my fortres: *he is* my God, in him wil I
truſt.
3 Surely he wil deliuer thee frō the [c] ſnare of the hunter, *and* from the noiſome peſtilence.
4 He wil couer thee vnder his wings, and
thou ſhalt be ſure vnder his feathers: his
[d] trueth ſhalbe thy ſhield and buckler.
5 [e] Thou ſhalt not be afraid of the feare of
the night, *nor* of the arrowe that flieth by
daye:
6 *Nor* of the peſtilence that walketh in the
darknes: *nor* of the plague that deſtroyeth
at noone daye.
7 A thouſand ſhal fall at thy ſide, and ten
thouſand at thy right hand, *but* it ſhal not
come nere thee.
8 Douteles with thine [f] eyes ſhalt thou beholde and ſe the rewarde of the wicked.
9 For thou *haſt ſaid*, The Lord *is* mine hope:
thou haſt ſet the moſte high for thy refuge.
10 There ſhal none euil come vnto thee,
nether ſhal anie plague come nere thy
tabernacle.
11 [g] For he ſhal giue his Angels charge ouer
thee to kepe thee in all thy waies.
12 They ſhal beare thee in their hands, that
thou hurt not thy fote againſt a ſtone.
13 Thou ſhalt walke vpon the liō and aſpe:
the [h] yong lion and the dragon ſhalt thou
tread vnder fete.
14 [i] Becauſe he hathe loued me, therefore
wil I deliuer him: I wil exalt him becauſe he hathe knowen my Name.
15 He ſhal call vpō me, & I wil heare him:
I wil be with him in trouble: I wil deliuer
him, and glorifie him.

a He ÿ maketh God his defence & truſt, ſhal perceiue his protection to be a moſte ſure ſafegarde.
b Beīg aſſured of this protection he praieth vnto the Lord.
c That is, Gods helpe is moſte readie for vs, whether Satān aſſaile vs ſecretly, ŵ he calleth a ſnare; or openly, which is here ment by the peſtilence.
d That is, his faithful kepīg of promes to helpe thee in thy neceſſitie
e The care ÿ God hathe ouer his, is moſte ſufficiēt to defende them from all dangers.
f The godlie ſhal haue ſome experience of Gods iudgements againſt ÿ wicked euen in this life, but fully thei ſhal ſe it at ÿ day, whē all things ſhalbe reueiled.
g God hathe not appointed euerie mā one Angel, but manie to be miniſters of his p̄uidēce to kepe his & defend them in their vocation, ŵ is the waye to walke in without tempting God.
h Thou ſhalt not onely be preſerued frō all euil, but ouercome it whether it be ſecret or open
i To aſſure the faithful of Gods protection, he bringeth in God to confirme the ſame.

16 With [k] long life wil I ſatiſfie him, and
ſhewe him my ſaluacion.

k For he is contēted with that life, that God giueth: for by death, ÿ ſhortnes of this life is recompenſed ŵ immortalitie.

PSAL. XCII.

1 This pſalme was made to be ſung on the Sabbath, to ſtirre vp the people to acknowledge God and to praiſe him in his workes: the Prophet reioyceth therein. 6 But the wicked is not able to conſider that the vngodlie, whē he is moſte floriſhing, ſhal moſte ſpedely periſh. 12 In the end is deſcribed the felicitie of the iuſt, planted in the houſe of God to praiſe the Lord.

¶ *A Pſalme or ſong for the* [a] *Sabbath daie.*

1 IT is a good thing to praiſe the Lord,
and to ſing vnto thy Name, ô moſte
High,
2 To declare thy louing kindenes in the
[b] morning, and thy trueth in the night,
3 Vpon an [c] inſtrument of ten ſtrings, and
vpō the viole with the ſong vpon the harpe.
4 For thou, Lord, haſt made me glad by thy
[d] workes, & I wil reioyce in the workes of
thine hands.
5 O Lord, how glorious are thy workes! &
thy thoghts are verie depe.
6 An [e] vnwiſe man knoweth it not, and a
foole doeth not vnderſtand this,
7 (When the wicked growe as the graſſe,
and all the workers of wickednes do floriſh) that thei ſhal be deſtroied for euer.
8 But thou, ô Lord, art [f] moſte high for euer
more.
9 For lo, thine enemies, ô Lord: for lo, thine
enemies ſhal periſh: all the workers of iniquitie ſhalbe deſtroied.
10 [g] But thou ſhalt exalt mine horne, like
the vnicornes, & I ſhalbe anointed with
freſh oile.
11 Mine eie alſo ſhal ſe *my deſire* againſt mine enemies: and mine eares ſhal heare *my
wiſh* againſt the wicked, that riſe vp a-
gainſt me.
12 The righteous ſhal [h] floriſh like a palme tre, & ſhal growe like a cedre in Lebanón.
13 Suche as be planted in the Houſe of the
Lord, ſhal floriſh in ÿ courts of our God.
14 Thei ſhal ſtil bring forthe frute in *their*
[i] age: thei ſhalbe fat and floriſhing,
15 To declare that the Lord my rocke is
righteous, and that none iniquitie *is* in
him.

Pſal. XCII.
a Which teacheth that the vſe of ÿ Sabbath ſtandeth ī praiſing God, and not onely in ceaſing frō worke.
b For Gods mercie & fidelitie in his p̄miſes toward his, binde thē to praiſe him continually bothe daie & night.
c Theſe inſtrumēts were thē permitted, but at Chriſts comming aboliſhed.
d He ſheweth what is ÿ vſe of the Sabbath daie: to wit, to meditate Gods workes.
e That is, the wicked conſider not Gods workes, nor his iudgemēts againſt them, & therfore moſte iuſtly periſh.
f Thy iudgements are moſte conſtant againſt the wicked and paſſe our reache
g Thou wilt ſtrengthen thē ŵ all power, & bleſſe them ŵ all felicitie.
h Thogh the faithful ſeme to wither and be cut downe by the wicked: yet thei ſhal growe againe and floriſh in the Church of God, as the cedres do in mount Lebanon.
i The childrē of God ſhal haue a power aboue nature, & their age ſhal brīg forthe moſte freſh frutes.

PSAL. XCIII.

1 He praiſeth the power of God in the creation of the worlde, & beateth downe all people which lift them vp againſt his maieſtie, 5 And prouoketh to conſider his promiſes.

1 THe Lord [a] reigneth, & is clothed with
maieſtie: the Lord is clothed, & girded with power: the worlde alſo ſhalbe eſtabliſhed, that it can not be moued.
2 Thy [b] throne is eſtabliſhed of olde: thou
art from euerlaſting.
3 [c] The floods haue lifted vp, ô Lord: the
floods haue lifted vp their voice: the

Pſal. XCIII.
a As God by his power and wiſdome hath made and gouerneth the worlde: ſo muſte the ſame be our defence againſt all enemies & dāgers.
b Whereſ thou ſitteſt & gouerneſt ÿ worlde.
c Gods power appeareth in ruling the furious waters.

floods lift vp their waues.
4 The waues of the sea *are* maruelous
through the noise of manie waters, *yet* the
Lord on high is more mightie.
5 Thy [d] testimonies are verie sure: holines becommeth thine House, ô Lord, for
euer.

PSAL. XCIIII.

1 He praieth vnto God against the violence and arrogancie of tyrants. 10 Warning them of Gods iudgements. 12 Then doeth he comfort the afflicted by the good issue of their afflictions, as he felt in him self, & did se in others, & by the ruine of the wicked, 23 Whome the Lord wil destroye.

1 O Lord God [a] the auenger, ô God
the auenger, shewe thy self [b] clearely.
2 Exalt thy self, ô Iudge of the worlde, &
render a rewarde to the proude.
3 Lord, how lōg shal the wicked, how lōg
shal the wicked [c] triumph?
4 They prate & speake fiercely: all the
workers of iniquitie vante them selues.
5 They [d] smite downe thy people, ô Lord,
and trouble thine heritage.
6 They slaie the widow and the stranger,
and murther the fatherles.
7 [e] Yet they saie, The Lord shal not se: nether wil the God of Iaakób regarde it.
8 Vnderstand ye vnwise amōg the people:
and ye fooles, when wil ye be wise?
9 He that [f] planted the eare, shal he not
heare? or he that formed the eye, shal he
not se?
10 Or he that chasticeth the [g] nations, shal
he not correct? he that teacheth mā knowledge, *shal he not knowe?*
11 The Lord knoweth the thoghts of man,
that they are vanitie.
12 Blessed *is* the man, whome thou [h] chasti-
cest, ô Lord, and teachest him in thy Law,
13 That thou maiest giue him rest from the
dayes of euil, whiles the pit is digged for
the wicked.
14 Surely ẏ Lord wil not faile his people,
nether wil he forsake his inheritance.
15 For [i] iudgement shal returne to iustice,
and all the vpright in heart *shal followe* after it.
16 Who wil rise vp with me against the
wicked? *or* who wil take my parte against
the workers of iniquitie?
17 If the Lord had not [k] holpen me, my
soule had almoste dwelt in silence.
18 When I said, [l] My fote slideth, thy mercie, ô Lord, staied me.
19 In the multitude of my [m] thoghts in
mine heart, thy comfortes haue reioyced
my soule.
20 Hathe the throne of iniquitie [n] feloship
with thee, which forgeth wrong for a law?

d Besides Gods power & wisdome in creating, and gouerning, his great mercie also appeareth in ẏ he hathe giuen his people his worde and couenant.

a Whose office it is to take vēgeance on the wicked.
b Shewe by effect ẏ thou art Iudge of the worlde to punish ẏ wicked.
c That is, brag of their crueltie & oppressiō: or, esteme them selues aboue all other.
d Seing the Church was thē so sore oppressed, it oght not to seme strange to vs, if we se it so now, & therefore we muste call to God to take our cause in hand.
e He sheweth that they are desperat in malice, forasmuchas they feared not God, but gaue thē selues wholly to do wickedly
f He sheweth that it is impossible, but God shulde heare, se & vnderstand their wickednes.
g If God punish whole nations for their sins, it is mere folie for anie one man, or els a fewe to thinke that God wil spare thē.
h God hathe care ouer his and chasticeth them for their welth, ẏ they shulde not perish for euer with the wicked.
i God wil restore the state & gouernemēt of things to their right vse, & then the godlie shal followe him cherefully.
k He complaineth of them, which wolde not helpe him to resiste the enemies: yet was assured that Gods helpe wolde not faile. l Whē I thoght there was no way but death. m In my trouble & destresse I euer founde thy present helpe. n Though the wicked iudges pretend iustice in oppressing the Church, yet they haue not that autoritie of God.

21 Thei gather them together against the
soule of the righteous, and condemne the
innocent blood.
22 But the Lord is my refuge, and my God
is the rocke of mine hope.
23 And he wil recompense thē their wickednes, and [o] destroie them in their owne malice: *yea,* ẏ Lord our God shal destroie thē.

PSAL. XCV.

1 An earnest exhortation to praise God 4 For the gouernement of the worlde, and the election of his Church. 8 An admonition not to followe the rebellion of the olde fathers, that tempted God in the wildernes: 11 For the which thei might not enter into the land of promes.

1 Come, let vs reioice vnto the Lord: let
vs sing [a] aloude vnto the rocke of our
saluacion.
2 Let vs come before his face with praise:
let vs sing loude vnto him with psalmes.
3 For the Lord *is* a great God, and a great
King aboue all [b] gods.
4 In whose hād *are* ẏ depe places of ẏ earth,
& the [c] heights of the mountaines *are* his:
5 To whome the sea *belongeth*: for he made it, and his hands formed the drye
land.
6 Come, let vs [d] worship and fall downe, &
knele before the Lord our maker.
7 For he is our God, and we are the people
of his pasture, & the shepe of his [e] hand:
to daie, if ye wil heare his voice,
8 [f] Harden not your heart, as *in Meribáh,
& as in the daie of *Massáh in thē wildernes.
9 Where your fathers tempted me, proued
me, thogh thei had sene my worke.
10 Fortie yeres haue I contended with *this*
generacion & said, Thei are a people that
[g] erre in heart, for thei haue not knowen
my waies.
11 Wherefore I sware in my wrath, *saying,*
Surely they shal not enter into my [h] rest.

PSAL. XCVI.

1 An exhortation bothe to the Iewes and Gentiles to praise God for his mercie. And this specially oght to be referred to the kingdome of Christ.

1 Sing [a] vnto the Lord a newe song: sing
vnto the Lord, all the earth.
2 Sing vnto the Lord, & praise his Name:
declare his saluacion from daie to daie.
3 Declare his glorie among all nations, *and*
his wonders among all people.
4 For the Lord *is* [b] great and muche to be
praised: he is to be feared aboue all gods.
5 For all the gods of the people *are* *idoles:
but the Lord [c] made the heauens.
6 [d] Strēgth & glorie *are* before him: power and beautie *are* in his Sanctuarie.
7 Giue vnto ẏ Lord, ye families of ẏ people: giue vnto the Lord glorie & [e] power.
8 Giue vnto the Lord the glorie of his
Name: bring [f] an offring, and entre into

o It is a great token of Gods iudgemēt, whē the purpose of the wicked is broken, but moste, when thei are destroied ī their owne malice.

Psal. XCV.
a He sheweth ẏ Gods seruice standeth not in dead ceremonies, but chiefly in the sacrifice of praise & thankesgiuing.
b Euen ẏ Angels (who in respect of men are thoght as gods) are nothing in his sight: much lesse the idols, ẏ mans braine inuenteth.
c All things are gouerned by his prouidence.
d By these thre wordes he signifieth one thing: meaning ẏ thei muste wholly giue them selues to serue God.
e That is, the flocke whome he gouerneth with his owne hād. He sheweth wherī thei are Gods flocke: that is, if thei heare his voice.
f By the contēning of Gods worde
*Or, strife: for whe re of the place was so called, Nom. 14,22.
*Or, tentation, read Exod. 17,7
g Thei were without iudgement & reason.
h That is, into the land of Canáan, where he promised them rest.

Psal XCVI.
a The Prophet sheweth that the time shal come, that all natiōs shal haue occasion to praise ẏ Lord for ẏ reueiling of his Gospel.
b Seīg he wil reueile hī selfe to all natiōs cōtrary to their owne expectation, they oght all to worship him contrary to their owne imaginatiōs, & onely as he hathe appointed.
*Or, vanities.
c Then the idoles, or whatsoeuer made not the heauens, are not God. d God can not be knowen, but by his strength and glorie: the signes whereof appeare in his Sanctuarie. e As by experience ye se that it is onely due vnto him.
f By offring vp your selues wholly vnto God, declare that you worship him onely.

his courtes.
9 Worship the Lord in the glorious San-
ctuarie:tremble before him all the earth.
10 Saie amõg the [g] nations, The Lord reigneth: surely the worlde shalbe stable, *and*
not moue, & he shal iudge the people [h] in
righteousnes.
11 Let the heauens reioyce,& let the earth
be glad: let the sea roare, and all that therein is.
12 Let the field be ioyful, and all that is in
it:let all the [i] trees of the wood then reioyce
13 Before the Lord: for he commeth, for he
commeth to iudge the earth: he wil iudge
the worlde with righteousnes, & the people in his trueth.

g He prophecieth that the Gentils shalbe partakers w the Iewes of Gods promes.
h He shal regenerate them anewe with his Spirit, and restore them to the image of God
i If the insensible creatures shal haue cause to reioyce, when God appeareth, much more we, from whome he hathe taken malediction & sinne.

PSAL. XCVII.

1 The Prophet exhorteth all to reioyce for the comming of the kingdome of Christ, 7 Dreadful to the rebels & idolaters, 8 And ioyful to the iust, whome he exhorteth to innocencie, 12 To reioycing and thankesgiuing.

1 THe [a] Lord reigneth: let the earth re-
ioyce:let the [b] multitude of the yles
be glad.
2 [c] Cloudes and darkenes *are* round about
him:righteousnes and iudgement *are* the
fundation of his throne.
3 There shal go a fyer before him, and burne vp his enemies round about.
4 His lightnigs gaue light vnto ỹ worlde:
the earth sawe it and was [d] afraid.
5 The mountaines melted like waxe at the
presence of the Lord, at the presence of
the Lord of the whole earth.
6 The heauens declare his righteousnes,
and all the people se his glorie.
7 [e] Confounded be all they that serue grauen images, & that glorie in idoles: worship him [f] all ye gods.
8 Zión heard of it, and was glad: and the
[g] daughters of Iudáh reioyced, because of
thy iudgements, ô Lord.
9 For thou, Lord, art moste high aboue all
the earth: thou art muche exalted aboue
all gods.
10 Ye that [h] loue the Lord, hate euil: he pre
serueth the soules of his Saints: he wil deliuer them from the hand of the wicked.
11 [i] Light is sowen for the righteous, and
ioye for the vpright in heart.
12 Reioyce ye righteous in the Lord, and
giue thankes for his holie [k] remembrance.

a He sheweth ỹ where God reigneth, there is all felicitie and spiritual ioye.
b For the Gospel shal notbe only preached in Iudea, but through all yles & cõtreis.
c He is thus described to kepe his enemies in feare, which cõmonly contemne Gods power.
d This feare bringeth not the wicked to true obediẽce, but maketh them to runne awaie from God.
e He signifieth ỹ Gods iudgements are in a readines to destroy the idolaters.
f Let all that which is estemed in ỹ worlde, fall downe before hĩ.
g The Iewes shal haue occasiõ to reioyce ỹ the Gentiles are made partakers w them of Gods fauour.
h He requireth two thigs of his childrẽ: the one ỹ thei detest vice, the other ỹ thei put their trust in God for their deliuerance.
i Thogh Gods deliuerance appeare not suddenly, yet it is sowen and laied vp in store for them.
k Be mindeful of his benefites and onely trust in his defence.

PSAL. XCVIII.

1 An earnest exhortation to all creatures to praise the Lord for his power, mercie and fidelitie in his promes by Christ, 10 By whome he hathe communicated his saluation to all nations.

¶ *A Psalme.*

1 SIng [a] vnto the Lord a new song: for he
hathe done maruelous things: *his
right hand, and his holie [b] arme haue gotten him the victorie.
2 The Lord declared his [c] saluation: his
righteousnes hathe he reueiled in ỹ sight
of the nations.
3 He hathe [d] remembred his mercie and his
trueth toward the house of Israél: all the
ends of the earth haue sene the saluation
of our God.
4 All the earth, sing ye loude vnto ỹ Lord:
crye out and reioyce, and sing praises.
5 Sing praise to the Lord vpon the harpe,
euen vpon the harpe with a singing voice.
6 With [e] shalmes and sounde of trumpets
sing loude before the Lord the King.
7 Let the sea roare, and all that therein is,
the worlde, and thei that dwell therein.
8 Let the floods clap their hands, & let the
mountaines reioyce togethr
9 Before the Lord: for he is come to iudge
the earth: with righteousnes shal he iudge
the worlde, and the people with equitie.

a That is, some song newly made in token of their wonderful deliuerãce by Christ.
Isai.59,16.
b He p̃serueth his Church miraculously.
c For the deliuerance of his Church.
d God was moued by none other meanes to gather his Church of the Iewes and Gentiles, but because he wolde performe his p̃mes.
e By this repetition & earnest exhortation to giue praises with instruments, & also of the dũme creatures, he signifieth ỹ the worlde is neuer able to praise God sufficiently for their deliuerance.

PSAL. XCIX.

1 He commendeth the power, equitie and excellencie of the kingdome of God by Christ ouer the Iewes and Gẽtiles, 5 And prouoketh them to magnifie the same & to serue the Lord, 6 Following the example of the ancient Fathers, Mosés, Aarón, Samuél, who calling vpon God, were heard in their praiers.

1 THe Lord reigneth, let the [a] people trẽ
ble:he sitteth *betwene* ỹ *Cherubims,
let the earth be moued.
2 The Lord *is* great in Zión, & he is high
aboue all the people.
3 Thei shal [b] praise thy great and fearefuI
Name (*for* it is holie)
4 And the Kigs power, that loueth iudgement:*for* thou hast prepared equitie: thou
hast executed iudgement & iustice in Iaakób.
5 Exalt the Lord our God, and fall downe
before his [c] fotestole:*for* he is holie.
6 Mosés & Aarón *were* among his Priests,
[d] and Samuél among suche as call vpon his
Name:these called vpon the Lord, & he
heard them.
7 He spake vnto thẽ in the cloudie piller:
thei kept his testimonies, & the Lawe *that*
he gaue them.
8 Thou heardest them, ô Lord our God:
thou wast a fauourable God vnto them,
thogh ỹ didest take vengeance for [e] their
inuentions.
9 Exalt the Lord our God, and fall downe
before his holie Mountaine: for the Lord
our God is holie.

a When God deliuereth his Church, all ỹ enemies shal haue cause to tremble.
Exod.25,22.
b Thogh the wicked rage against God, yet the godlie shal praise his Name, & mightie power.
c That is, before his Temple or Arke, where he promised to heare, when they worshipped him, as now he promiseth his spiritual presẽce, wheresouer his Church is assembled.
d Vnder these thre he comprehendeth ỹ whole people of Israél, with whome God made his promes.
e For the more liberally ỹ God dealeth with his people, the more doeth he punish them that abuse his benefites.

PSAL. C.

1 He exhorteth all to serue the Lord, 3 Who hathe chosen vs & preserued vs, 4 And to entre into his assemblies to praise his Name.

A psalme of praise.

1 SIng [a] ye loude vnto the Lord, all the
2 earth.
Serue the Lord with gladnes:come before him with ioyfulnes.
3 Knowe ye that euen the Lord is God:he
hathe [b] made vs, & not we our selues: *we*
are his people, and the shepe of his pasture.
4 [c] Enter into his gates with praise, & into
his courtes with reioycing: praise him
and blesse his Name.
5 For the Lord is good:his mercie *is* [d] euerlasting, and his trueth *is* from generacion
to generacion.

a He prophecieth ý Gods benefite in calling the Gentiles, shalbe so great that thei shal haue wonderful occasiõ to praise his mercie & reioyce.
b He chiefly meaneth, touching the spiritual regeneration, whereby we are his shepe and people.
c He sheweth that God wil not be worshiped, but by that meanes, which he hathe appointed.
d He declareth that we oght neuer to be wearie in praising him, seing his mercies toward vs last for euer.

PSAL. CI.

1 Dauid describeth what gouernement he wil obserue in his house and kingdome. 5 He wil punish and correct, by rooting forthe the wicked. 6 And cherishing the godlie persones.

A Psalme of Dauid.

1 I Wil [a] sing mercie and iudgement: vnto
thee, ô Lord, wil I sing.
2 I wil do wisely in the perfite waie [b] til
ý comest to me: I wil walke in ý vprightnes of mine heart in the middes of mine house.
3 I wil set no wicked thing before mine
eies: I hate [c] the worke of them that fall
awaie: it shal not cleaue vnto me.
4 A froward heart shal depart from me: I
wil knowe none euil.
5 Him, that priuely [d] sclandereth his neigh
bour, wil I destroie: hĩ that hathe a proude
loke and high heart, I can not *suffer*.
6 Mine eies *shalbe* vnto the [e] faithful of the
land, that they maie dwell with me: he
that walketh in a perfite waie, he shal serue me.
7 There shal no deceitful persone dwell
within mine house: he that telleth lies, shal
not remaine in my sight.
8 [f] Betimes wil I destroy all the wicked of
the land, that I maie cut of all the workers of iniquitie from the Citie of the
Lord.

a Dauid considereth what maner of King he wolde be, whẽ God shulde place him in the throne, promising openly, that he wolde be merciful and iust.
b Thogh as yet ý differrest to place me in the kĩglie dignitie, yet wil I giue my self to wisdome & vprightnes being a priuate man.
c He sheweth that magistrates do not their dueties, except thei be enemies to all vice.
d In promising to punish these vices, which are moste pernicious in thẽ that are about Kings, he declareth that he wil punish all.
e He sheweth what is ý true vse of the sworde: to punish the wicked and to mainteine the good.
f Magistrates must immediatly punish vice, lest it growe to farther inconuenience. and if heathen Magistrates are bounde to do this, how muche more thei that haue the charge of the Church of God?

PSAL. CII.

1 It semeth that this praier was appointed to the faithful to praie in the captiuitie of Babylon. 16 A consolation for the building of the Church: 18 Whereof followeth the praise of God to be published vnto all posteritie. 22 The conuersion of the Gentiles, 28 And the stabilitie of the Church.

¶ *A praier [a] of the afflicted, when he shalbe in distres, and powre forthe his meditation before the Lord.*

a Whereby is signified, that albeit we be in neuer so great miseries, yet there is euer place left for praier.

1 O Lord, heare my praier, and let my
[b] crye come vnto thee.
2 Hide not thy face from me in the time of
my trouble: incline thine eares vnto me:
when I call, make haste to heare me.
3 For my daies are [c] consumed like smoke,
and my bones are burnt like an herth.
4 Mine heart is smitten and withereth like
grasse, because I forgate [d] to eat my bread.
5 For the voice of my groning my bones
do cleaue to my skin.
6 I am like a [e] pelicane of the wildernes: I
am like an owle of the deserts.
7 I watche and am as a sparowe alone vpõ
the house toppe.
8 Mine enemies reuile me daiely, & they
ý rage agaĩst me, haue [f] sworne agaĩst me.
9 Surely I haue [g] eaten ashes as bread, and
mingled my drinke with weping,
10 Because of thine [h] indignation and thy
wrath: for thou hast heaued me vp, and cast
me downe.
11 My daies *are* like a shadowe that fadeth,
and I am withered like grasse.
12 But thou, ô Lord, doest [i] remaine for e-
uer, and thy remembrance from generaciõ
to generacion.
13 Thou wilt arise & haue mercie vpon Zión: for the time to haue mercie thereon,
for the [k] appointed time is come.
14 For thy seruãts delite in the [l] stones thereof, and haue pitie on the dust thereof.
15 Then the heathen shal feare the Name
of the Lord, & all the Kings of the earth
thy glorie,
16 Whẽ the Lord shal buylde vp Zión, &
shal appeare [m] in his glorie,
17 *And* shal turne vnto the praier of the
desolate, and not despise their praier.
18 This shalbe writen for the generacion
to come: & the people, which shalbe [n] created, shal praise the Lord.
19 For he hathe loked downe frõ the height
of his Sanctuarie: out of the heauen did
the Lord beholde the earth,
20 That he might heare the mourning of
the prisoner, and deliuer the [o] children of
death:
21 That thei maie declare the Name of the
Lord in Zión, and his praise in Ierusalém,
22 When the people shalbe gathered [p] together, and the kingdomes to serue the
Lord.
23 He [q] abated my strength in the waie, &
shortened my daies.
24 *And* I said, O my God, take me not
away

b He declareth that in our praier we must liuely fele that, which we desire and stedfastly beleue to obteine.
c These excessiue kindes of speache shew how muche ý affliction of ý Church oght to wounde the heartes of the godlie.
d My sorowes were so great, that I passed not for mine ordinarie fode.
e Euer mourning, and solitarie, casting out fearful cryes.
f Haue conspired my death.
g I haue not risen out of my mourning to take my refection.
h He sheweth that the afflictions did not onely thus moue him, but chiefly the feling of Gods displeasure.
i How soeuer we be frailes, yet thy promes is sure & the remembrãce thereof shal confirme vs for euer.
k That is, the seuẽtie yeres, which by the prophet Ieremie ý didest appoint, Ier. 29,12.
l The more ý the Church is in miserie and desolation, the more oght the faithful to loue and pitie it.
m That is, when he shal haue drawen his Church out of the darkenes of death.
n The deliuerance of the Church is a moste excellẽt benefite & therefore he cõpareth it to a newe creation: for in their banishment the bodie of the Church semed to haue bene dead, which by deliuerance was as it were created anewe.
o Who now in their banishement colde loke for nothing but death.
p He sheweth that Gods Name is neuer more praised, then when religion florisheth, and the Church increaseth: which thing is chiefly accomplished vnder the kingdome of Christ.
q The Church lamẽt that thei se not the time of Christ, which was promised, but haue but fewe yeres and short daies.

away in the middes of my daies: thy yeres
endure from generacion to generacion.
25 Thou hast aforetime laied the fundation of the earth, and the heauens *are* ye worke of thine hands.
26 [r] Thei shal perish, but thou shalt endure:
euen thei all shal waxe olde as doeth a garment: as a vesture shalt thou change them,
and thei shalbe changed.
27 But thou art the same, and thy yeres shal
not faile.
28 The children of thy seruants shal continue, and their sede shal stand [s] fast in thy
sight.

r If heauen & earth perish, muche more man shal perish: but the Church by reason of Gods promes endureth for euer.
s Seing yu hast chosen thy Church out of the worlde, & ioyned it to thee, it can not but continue for euer: for yu art euerlastig.

PSAL. CIII.

1 He prouoketh all to praise the Lord, which hathe pardoned his sinnes, deliuered him from destruction, and giuen him sufficient of all good things. 10 Then he addeth the tender mercies of God, which he sheweth like a moste tender Father towards his childrē, 14 The frailtie of mans life. 20 An exhortation to man and Angels to praise the Lord.

¶ A Psalme *of David*.

1 MY soule, [a] praise yu the Lord, & all that
is within me, *praise* his holie Name.
2 My soule, praise thou the Lord, and forget not all his benefites.
3 Which [b] forgiueth all thine iniquitie, &
healeth all thine infirmities.
4 Which redemeth thy life from ye [c] graue,
and crowneth thee with mercie and compassions.
5 Which satisfieth thy mouth with good
things: and thy [d] youth is renued like the
egles.
6 The Lord executeth righteousnes and
iudgement to all that are oppressed.
7 He made his waies knowen vnto [e] Mosés,
& his workes vnto the children of Israél.
8 The Lord is ful of compassion and mercie, slowe to angre and of great kindenes.
9 He wil not alwaie [f] chide, nether kepe *his*
angre for euer.
10 He hathe not [g] dealt with vs after our
sinnes, nor rewarded vs according to our
iniquities.
11 For as high as the heauen is aboue the
earth, so great is his mercie toward them
that feare him.
12 As farre as [h] the East is from the West:
so farre hathe he remoued our sinnes from
vs.
13 As a father hathe compassiō on his children, so hathe the Lord compassion on
them that feare him.
14 For he knoweth whereof we be made: he
remembreth that we are but dust.
15 The daies of [i] mā are as grasse: as a flower of the field, so florisheth he.
16 For the winde goeth ouer it, and it is gone, and the place thereof shal knowe it no
more.
17 But the louing kindenes of the Lord *en-*
dureth for euer & euer vpon them that feare him, and his [k] righteousnes vpon childrens children,
18 Vnto them that kepe his [l] couenant, and
thinke vpon his commandements to do
them.
19 The Lord hathe prepared his throne in
heauen, and his kingdome ruleth ouer
all.
20 Praise the Lord, ye [m] his Angels, that excel in strength, that do his commandement in obeying the voice of his worde.
21 Praise the Lord, all ye his hostes, ye his
seruants that do his pleasure.
22 Praise the Lord, all ye his workes, in all
places of his dominion: my soule, praise
thou the Lord.

a He wakeneth his dulnes to praise God, shewing yt both vnderstanding & affectiōs, minde & heart are to litle to set forthe his praise.
b This is the beginning and chiefest of all benefites: remission of sinne.
c For before yt we haue remission of our sinnes, we are as dead mē in the graue.
d As the egle, whether beake ouergroweth, sucketh blood, and so is renued in strength, euen so God miraculously giueth strēgth to his Church aboue all mās expectation.
e As to his chief minister & next to his people.
f He sheweth first his seuere iudgement, but so sone as the sinner is humbled, he receiueth him to mercie.
g We haue prouē by cōtinual experience, yt his mercie hathe euer preuailed against our offences.
h As great as the worlde is, so ful is it of signes of Gods mercies toward his faithful, when he hathe remoued their sinnes.
i He declareth that mā hathe nothīg in him selfe to moue God to mercie, but onely the confession of his infirmitie & miserie.
k His iuste & faithful kepīg of his promes.
l To whome he giueth grace to feare hī, & to obey his worde.
m In that that we, which naturally are slowe to praise God, exhort the Angels, wc willigly do it, we stirre vp our selues to consider our duetie, & awake out of our sluggishnes.

PSAL. CIIII.

1 An excellent Psalme to praise God for the creation of the worlde & the gouernance of the same by his maruelous prouidence. 35 Wherein the Prophet praieth against the wicked, who are occasions that God diminished his blessings.

1 MY soule, praise thou ye Lord: ô Lord
my God, thou art exceding great, yu
art [a] clothed with glorie & honour.
2 Which couereth him self with light as
with a garment, & spreadeth the heauens
like a curtaine.
3 Which laieth the beames of his chābers
in the waters, and maketh the cloudes his
chariot, and walketh vpon the wings of
the winde.
4 Which [b] maketh the spirits his messengers, & a flaming fyre his ministers.
5 He set the earth vpon her fundacions, so yt
it shal neuer moue.
6 Thou coueredst it with ye [c] deepe as with
a garment: the [d] waters wolde stand aboue
the mountaines.
7 *But* at thy rebuke thei flee: at the voice of
thy thunder thei haste awaie.
8 *And* the moūtaines ascend, & the valleis
descend to the place which thou hast established for them.
9 *But* thou hast set them a bonde, which thei
shal not passe: thei shal not returne to couer the earth.
10 He sendeth the springs into the valleis,
which runne betwene the mountaines.
11 Thei shal giue drinke to all the [e] beastes
of the field, and the wilde asses shal quenche their thirst.
12 By these [f] springs shal the foules of the
heauen dwell, and sing among the brāches.
13 He watereth the mountaines from his
[g] chambers, & the earth is filled with the
frute of thy workes.
14 He causeth grasse to growe for the cattel, and herbe for the vse of [h] man, that he
maie bring forthe bread out of the earth,
15 And wine *that* maketh glad the heart of
man, & oyle to make the face to shine,

a The Prophet sheweth that we nede not to enter into the heauēs to seke God, for asmuch as all the ordre of nature, with ye proprietie and placing of the elements, are moste liuely mirrours to se his maiestie in.
b As the Prophet here sheweth yt all visible powers are readie to serue God: so the Apostle to ye Ebr. 1, 7 beholdeth in this glasse, how ye verie Angels also are obedient to his cōmandement.
c Thou makest the sea to be an ornament vnto ye earth.
d If by thy power yu didest not bridle the rage of ye waters, it were not possible, but the whole worlde shulde be destroied.
e If God prouide for ye verie beastes, much more wil he extend his prouident care to man.
f There is no part of the worlde so baren, where moste euident signes of Gods blessings appeare not.
g From the cloudes.
h He describeth Gods prouident care ouer man, who doeth not only prouide necessarie thigs for him, as herbes & other meat: but also thigs to reioyce and comforte him, as wine & oyle or ointmēts.

& bread *that* strengtheneth mans heart.
16 The high trees are satisfied, *euen* the cedres of Lebanón, which he hathe planted,
17 That the birdes maie make their nestes
there: the storke dwelleth in the firre trees.
18 The high mountaines *are* for the *goates:
the rockes *are* a refuge for the conies.
19 He appointed the[i] moone for certeine
seasons: [k] the sunne knoweth his going
downe.
20 Thou makest darkenes, and it is night,
wherein all the beastes of the forest crepe
forthe.
21 The lions roare after their praie, and seke their meate[l] at God.
22 *When* the sunne riseth, they retire, and
couche in their dennes.
23 [m] *Then* goeth man forthe to his worke,
and to his labour vntil the euening.
24 O Lord, how[n] manifolde are thy workes! in wisdome hast thou made them all:
the earth is ful of thy riches.
25 *So is* this sea great & wide: *for* therein *are*
things creping innumerable, bothe smale
beastes and great.
26 There go ỹ shippes, *yea*, that *Liuiathán,
whome thou hast made to plaie therein.
27 [o] All these waite vpon thee, that thou
maiest giue them fode in due season.
28 Thou giuest it to them, & thei gather it:
thou openest thine hand, & thei are filled
with good things.
29 *But if* thou[p] hide thy face, thei are troubled: *if* thou take awaie their breath, they
dye and returne to their dust.
30 *Againe if* thou[q] send forthe thy spirit,
thei are created, and thou renuest the face
of the earth.
31 Glorie be to the Lord for euer: let the
Lord reioyce in his workes.
32 He loketh on the earth and it trembleth:
he toucheth ỹ mountaines, & thei[r] smoke.
33 I wil sing vnto the Lord *all* my life: I wil
praise my God, while I liue.
34 Let my wordes be acceptable vnto him:
I wil reioyce in the Lord.
35 Let the sinners be[ſ] consumed out of the
earth, & the wicked til there be no more: ô
my soule, praise thou the Lord. Praise ye
the Lord.

PSAL. CV.

He praiseth the singular grace of God, who hathe of all the people of the worlde chosen a peculiar people to him self, and hauing chosen them, neuer ceaseth to do them good, euen for his promes sake.

1 PRaise ỹ Lord, & call vpon his Name:
[a] declare his workes amōg the people.
2 Sing vnto him, sing praise vnto him, &
talke of all his wonderous workes.
3 Reioyce in his holie Name: let the heart
of them that seke the Lord, reioyce.
4 Seke the Lord & his[b] strength: seke his
face continually.
5 Remembre his[c] maruelous workes, that
he hathe done, his wonders and the[d] iudgements of his mouth,
6 Ye sede of Abrahám his seruant, ye children of Iaakób, which are his elect.
7 He is the Lord our God: his iudgements
are through all the earth.
8 He hathe alwaie remembred his couenant
& promes, that he made to a thousand generacions,
9 *Euen* that which he[e] made with Abrahám
and his othe vnto Izhák:
10 And *since* hathe confirmed it to Iaakób
for a law, & to Israél for an euerlasting
couenant,
11 Saying, [f] Vnto thee wil I giue the land
of Canáan, the lot of your inheritance.
12 Albeit thei were fewe in nomber, *yea*, verie fewe & strangers in the land,
13 And walked about from nacion to nació,
from *one* kingdome to another people,
14 *Yet* suffred he no man to do them wrong,
but reproued[g] Kīgs for their sakes, *saying*,
15 Touche not mine[h] anointed, and do my
[i] Prophetes no harme.
16 Moreouer he called a famine vpon the
land, & vtterly brake the[k] staf of bread.
17 *But* he sent a man before them: Ioséph
was solde for a slaue.
18 Thei helde his fete in the stockes, & he
was laied in yrons,
19 Vntil[l] his appointed time came, & the
counsel of the Lord had tryed him.
20 The King sent and losed him: *euen* the
Ruler of the people deliuered him.
21 He made him Lord of his house, and ruler of all his substance,
22 That he shulde binde his[m] princes vnto his wil, & teache his Ancients wisdome.
23 Then Israél came to Egypt, and Iaakób
was a stranger in the land of Ham.
24 And he increased his people excedingly,
and made them stronger then their oppressers.
25 [n] He turned their heart to hate his people, and to deale craftely with his seruāts.
26 *Then* sent he Mosés his seruant, & Aarón whome he had chosen.
27 Thei shewed among them the message
of his signes, and wonders in the land of
Ham.
28 He sent darkenes, and made it darke: and
thei were not[o] disobedient vnto his commission.
29 *He turned their waters into blood, and
slewe their fish.
30 *Their land broght forthe frogs, *euen* in
their Kings chambers.
31 He[p] spake, & there came swarmes of flies
& lice in all their quarters.
32 He gaue them[q] haile for raine, & flames of fyre in their land.
33 He smote their vines also and their fig-

*Or, does, roes, & suche like.
i As to separat the night from the daie, & to note daies, moneths & yeres.
k That is, by his course, ether farre or nere, it noteth sommer, winter and other seasons.
l That is, they onely finde meat accordīg to Gods prouidence, who careth euē for the brute beastes.
m To wit, whē the daie springeth: for the light is as it were a shield to defend man against the tyrānie and fiercenes of beastes.
n He confesseth that no tongue is able to expresse Gods workes, nor minde to comprehende them.
*Or, Whale.
o God is a moste nourishing Father, who prouideth for all creatures their daielie fode.
p As by thy presence all things haue life: so, if thou withdrawe thy blessings, thei all perish.
q As ỹ death of creatures sheweth ỹ we are nothing of our selues: so their generacion declareth ỹ we receiue all things of our Creator.
r Gods merciful face giueth strength to ỹ earth, but his seuere countenance burneth ỹ mountaines.
ſ Who infect ỹ worlde, & so cause God ỹ he can not reioyce in his workes.
Psal. CV.
a Forasmuch as the Israelites were excepted frō the commune condemnation of the worlde, and were elected to be Gods people, ỹ Prophet willeth them to shewe them selues mindeful by thākesgiuing.
b By ỹ strength & face, he meaneth ỹ Arke where God declared his power and his presence.

c Which he hathe wroght in the deliuerance of his people.
d Because his power was therby as liuely declared, as if he shulde haue declared it by mouth.
e The promes which God made to Abrahám to be his God, and the God of his sede after him, he renued and repeted it againe to his sede after him.
f He sheweth ỹ thei shulde not enioye the lād of Canáan by anie other meanes, but by reason of his couenāt made with their fathers.
g That is, the King of Egypt and the King of Gerár, Gen. 12,17, & 20,3.
h Those whome I haue sanctified to be my people.
i Meaning the olde fathers, to whome God sheweth him self plainely, and who were setters forthe of his worde.
k Ether by sending scarsetie, or by taking awaie ỹ stregth & nourishment thereof.
l So long he suffred aduersitie, as God had appoīted, and til he had tryed sufficiētly his paciēce.
m That ỹ verie princes of the countrey shulde be at Iosephs cōmandemēt & learne wisdome at him.
n So it is in God, ether to moue ỹ hearts of the wicked to loue or to hate Gods children.
o Meanīg, Mosés and Aarón.
Exod. 7, 20.
Exod. 8, 6.
p So that this vermine came not by fortune, but as God had appoīted, & his Prophet Mosés spake.
q It was strāge to se raine in Egypt, muche more it was fearful to se haile.

trees, and brake downe the trees in their
coaſtes.
34 [r] He ſpake, and the graſhoppers came, &
caterpillers innumerable,
35 And did eat vp all the graſſe in their lãd,
and deuoured the frute of their grounde.
36 *He ſmote alſo all the firſt borne in their
land, *euen* the beginning of all their
ſtrength.
37 He broght them forthe alſo with ſiluer
and golde, and there was [ſ] none feble a-
mong their tribes.
38 Egypt was [t] glad at their departing: for
the feare of them had fallen vpon them.
39 He ſpred a cloude to be a couering, and
fyre to giue light in the night.
40 They [u] asked, and he broght quailes,
& he filled them with the bread of heauẽ.
41 He opened the rocke, and the waters
flowed out, *and* ran in the drye places *like*
a riuer.
42 For he remembred his holie [x] promes
to Abrahám his ſeruant,
43 And he broght forthe his people with
[y] ioye, & his choſen with gladnes,
44 And gaue them the lands of the heathẽ,
and they toke the labours of the people in
poſſeſsion,
45 That they might [z] kepe his ſtatutes, and
obſerue his Lawes. Praiſe ye the Lord.

r He ſheweth ẏ all creatures are armed againſt mã, whẽ God is his enemie: as at his cõmandement the graſhoppers deſtroyed the land.
Exod 12,29.
ſ When their enemies felt Gods plagues, his childrẽ by his prouidẽce were exẽpted.
t For Gods plagues cauſed them rather to departe ẇ the Iſraelites then ẇ their liues.
u Not for neceſsitie, but for ſatiſfying of their luſt.
x Which he confirmeth to the poſteritie, in whome after a ſorte the dead liue and enioye the promiſes.
y When the Egyptians lamẽted & were deſtroyed.
z This is the end, why God preſerueth his Church, becauſe they ſhulde worſhip, and call vpon him in this worlde.

PSAL. CVI.

1 *The people diſperſed vnder Antiochus do magnifie the goodnes of God among the iuſte and repentãt:* 4 *Deſiring to be broght againe into the land by Gods merciful viſitation.* 8 *And after the manifolde maruels of God wroght in their deliuerance forthe of Egypt, and the great ingratitude of the people rehearsed,* 47 *Thei do pray & deſire to be gathered from amõg the heathẽ to the intent thei may praiſe the Name of the God of Iſraél.*

¶ *Praiſe ye the Lord.*

1 Praiſe [a] ye ẏ Lord becauſe he is good,
for his mercie *endureth* for euer.
2 Who can expreſſe the noble actes of the
Lord, *or* ſhewe forthe all his praiſe?
3 Bleſſed *are* they that [b] kepe iudgement,
and do righteouſnes at all times.
4 Remember me, ô Lord, with the [c] fauour
of thy people: viſit me with thy ſaluacion,
5 That I may ſe the felicitie of thy choſen,
and reioyce in the ioye of thy people, and
glorie with thine inheritance.
6 We haue [d] ſinned with our fathers: we
haue committed iniquitie, *and* done wickedly.
7 Our fathers vnderſtode not thy wõders
in Egypt, nether remembred they ẏ multitude of thy mercies, but rebelled at the
Sea, *euen* at the red Sea.
8 Neuertheles he [e] ſaued them for his Names ſake, that he might make his power to
be knowen.

a The Prophet exhorteth the people to praiſe God for his benefites paſt, ẏ thereby their mindes maie be ſtrẽgthened agaĩſt all preſent troubles & deſpaire.
b He ſheweth that it is not ynough to praiſe God with mouth, except ẏ whole hearte agre therunto, and all our life be thereunto framed.
c Let ẏ good wil that thou beareſt to thy people, extend vnto me, that thereby I maie be receiued in to the number of thine.
d By earneſt confeſsion aſwel of their owne, as of their fathers ſinnes, they ſhew that they had hope that God according to his promes wolde pitie them.
e The ineſtimable goodnes of God appeareth in this, that he wolde change the ordre of nature, rather then his people ſhulde not be deliuered, althogh they were wicked.

9 And he rebuked the red Sea, and it was
dryed vp, and he led them in the depe, as in
the wildernes.
10 And he ſaued them frõ the aduerſaries
hand, and deliuered them from the hand
of the enemie.
11 *And the waters couered their oppreſ-
ſors: not one of them was left.
12 Then [f] beleued they his wordes, & ſang
praiſe vnto him.
13 But incontinently they forgate his workes: they waited not for his [g] counſel,
14 But luſted with concupiſcẽce in the wildernes, & tempted God in the deſert.
15 Then he gaue them their deſire: but he
ſent [h] leannes into their ſoule.
16 They enuied Moſés alſo in the tentes, &
Aarón the holie one of the Lord.
17 *Therefore* the earth opened and [i] ſwalow-
ed vp Dathán, and couered the companie
of Abirám.
18 And the fyre was kindled in their aſſemblie: the flame burnt vp the wicked.
19 They made a calfe in Horéb, & worſhiped the molten image.
20 Thus they turned their [k] glorie into
the ſimilitude of a bullocke, that eateth
graſſe.
21 They forgate God their Sauiour, which
had done great things in Egypt,
22 Wonderous workes in the land of Ham,
and fearful things by the red Sea.
23 Therefore he minded to deſtroye them,
had [l] not Moſés his choſen ſtand in the
breache before hĩ to turne away his wrath,
left he ſhulde deſtroye *them*.
24 Alſo they contemned that [m] pleaſant
land, & beleued not is worde,
25 But murmured in their tentes, & hearkened not vnto the voyce of the Lord.
26 Therefore [n] he lifted vp his hãd againſt
them, to deſtroye them in the wildernes,
27 And to deſtroye their ſede among the
nacions, and to ſcater them throughout
the countreis.
28 They ioyned them ſelues alſo vnto
[o] Baal-peór, & did eat the offrings of the
[p] dead.
29 Thus they [q] prouoked *him* vnto angre
with their owne inuentions, and the plague brake in vpon them.
30 But [r] Phinehás ſtode vp, and executed
iudgement, and the plague was ſtaied.
31 *And it was [ſ] imputed vnto him for righteouſnes from generacion to generaciõ
for euer.
32 They angred him alſo at the waters of
*Meribáh, ſo that [t] Moſés was puniſhed
for their ſakes,
33 Becauſe they vexed his ſpirit, ſo that he
ſpake vnaduiſedly with his lippes.
34 Nether deſtroyed they the people, as ẏ
Lord had commanded them,

Exod.14,27.
f The wõderful workes of God cauſed thẽ to beleue for a time and to praiſe him.
g They wolde preuẽt his wiſdome and prouidence.
h The abũdance that God gaue thẽ, profited not, but made thẽ pine away, becauſe God curſed it.
i By ẏ greatnes of the puniſhment the hainous offence maie be cõſidered: for they that riſe againſt Gods miniſters, rebel agaĩſt him.
k He ſheweth ẏ all idolaters renounce God to be their glorie, when in ſtead of him they worſhip anie creature, muche more wood, ſtone, metal or calues.
l If Moſés by his intercesſiõ had not obteined Gods fauour againſt their rebelliõs
m That is, Canáan, ẇ was as it were an earneſt penie of ẏ heauenlie inheritance.
n That is, he ſware. Sõtime alſo it meaneth to puniſh.
o Which was ẏ idole of the Moabites.
p Sacrifices offred to ẏ dead idoles.
q Signifying, ẏ whatſoeuer man inuenteth of him ſelf to ſerue God by, is deteſtable & prouoketh his angre.
r When all other neglected Gods glorie, he in his zeale killed ẏ adulterers & preuented Gods wrath.
Nom.25,13.
ſ This acte declared his liuelie faith, & for his faiths ſake was accepted.
Nom.20,2.
pſal.95,8.
t If ſo notable a Prophet of God eſcape not puniſhmẽt thogh others prouoked him to ſinne, how muche more ſhal they be ſubiect to Gods iudgement, which cauſe Gods children to ſin?

35 But were mingled among the heathen, &
learned their workes,
36 And serued their idoles, which were their
ruine.
37 Yea, they offred their [u] sonnes, and their
daughters vnto diuels,
38 And shed innocent blood, *euen* the blood
of their sonnes, and of their daughters,
whome they offred vnto the idols of Canáan, and the land was defiled with blood.
39 Thus were they steined with their owne
workes, and went [x] a whoring with their
owne inuentions.
40 Therefore was the wrath of the Lord
kindled against his people, & he abhorred
his owne inheritance.
41 And he gaue them into the hand of the
heathen: and they that hated them, were
lords ouer them.
42 Their enemies also oppressed them, and
they were humbled vnder their hand.
43 Manie [y] a time did he deliuer them, but
they prouoked him by their counsels: therefore they were broght downe by their
iniquitie.
44 Yet he sawe when they were in afflictiō,
and he heard their crye.
45 And he remembred his couenāt toward
them, and [z] repēted according to the mul
titude of his mercies,
46 And gaue them fauour in the sight of all
them, that led them captiues.
47 Saue vs, ô Lord our God, and [a] gather
vs from among the heathen, that we maie
praise thine holie Name, and glorie in
thy praise.
48 Blessed *be* the Lord God of Israél for
euer & euer, and let all the people say, So
be it. Praise ye the Lord.

u He sheweth how mōstruo' a thīg idolatrie is, w̃ can winne vs to things abhorring to nature, where as Gods worde can not obteine moste smale things.

x Then true chastitie is to cleaue wholly & onely vnto God.

y The Prophet sheweth ỹ nether by menaces, nor pmisses we can come to God, except we be all together newly reformed, & ỹ his mercie ouercouer and hide our malice.

z Not ỹ God is changeable in him self, but that then he semeth to vs to repent, whē he altereth his punishment, & forgiueth vs.

a Gather thy Church, w̃ is dispersed, and giue vs constācie vnder the crosse, that w̃ one cōsent we may all praise thee.

PSAL. CVII.

1 The Prophet exhorteth all those that are redemed by the Lord, & gathered vnto him to giue thankes. 9 For this merciful prouidence of God, gouerning all things at his good pleasure. 20 Sending good & euil, prosperitie and aduersitie to bring men vnto him 42 Therefore as the righteous thereat reioyce, so shal the wicked haue their mouthes stopped.

1 PRaise [a] the Lord, because he is good:
for his mercie *endureth* for euer.
2 Let them, [b] which haue bene redemed
of the Lord, shewe how he hathe deliuered
them from the hand of the oppresser,
3 And gathered them out of the lāds, from
the East and from the West, from the
North and from the *South.
4 *When* they wandered in the desert & wildernes out of the way, *and* founde no citie
to dwell in,
5 [c] Bothe hungrie & thirstie, their soule
fainted in them.
6 Then they cryed vnto the Lord in their
trouble, *and* he deliuered them from their
distres,
7 And led thē forthe by the right way, that
they might go to a citie of habitacion.
8 Let them *therefore* cōfesse before the Lord
his louing kindenes, & his wonderful workes before the sonnes of men.
9 For he satisfied the thirstie soule, and filled the hungrie soule with goodnes.
10 They, that dwell in darkenes and in the
shadowe of death, being bounde in miserie and yron,
11 Because they [d] rebelled against the wordes of the Lord, and despised the counsel
of the moste High,
12 When he humbled their heart with heauines, *then* they fell downe and there was
no helper.
13 Then they [e] cryed vnto the Lord in
their trouble, *and* he deliuered them from
their distres.
14 He broght them out of darkenes, and
out of the shadowe of death, and brake their
bands a sunder.
15 Let them *therefore* confesse before the
Lord his louing kindenes, & his wonderful workes before the sonnes of men.
16 For he hathe broken ỹ [f] gates of brasse,
and brast the barres of yron a sundre.
17 [g] Fooles by reason of their transgression
& because of their iniquities are afflicted.
18 Their soule abhorreth all meat, & they
are broght to deaths dore.
19 Then they crye vnto the Lord in their
trouble, & he deliuereth them from their
distres.
20 [h] He sendeth his worde and healeth
them, and deliuereth them from their
[i] graues.
21 Let them *therefore* confesse before the
Lord his louing kindenes, & his wonderful workes before the sonnes of men,
22 And let them offer sacrifices of [k] praise,
and declare his workes with reioycing.
23 They that go downe to the [l] sea in shippes, & occupie by the great waters,
24 They se the workes of the Lord, & his
wonders in the depe.
25 For he commandeth and raiseth the
stormie winde, and it lifteth vp the waues
thereof.
26 They mounte vp to the heauē, & descēd
to the depe, so that their soule [m] melteth
for trouble.
27 They are tossed to and fro, and stagger
like a drunken man, and all their [n] cunning is gone.
28 Then they crye vnto the Lord in their
trouble, *and* he bringeth them out of their
distres.
29 He turneth the storme to calme, so that
the waues thereof are stil.
30 When they are [o] quieted, they are glad, &
he

a This notable sentence was in the beginning vsed, as the fote or tenour of the song, w̃ was oftentimes repeted.

b As this was true in ỹ Iewes, so is there none of Gods elect, ỹ fele not his helpe in their necessitie.

*Or, *from the Sea: meaning the red Sea, which is on the South parte of the land.*

c He sheweth that there is none affliction so grieuous, out of the which God wil not deliuer his, and also exhorteth them, that are deliuered, to be mindeful of so great a benefite.

d Then ỹ true way to obeie God, is to followe his expresse cōmandement: also hereby all are exhorted to descēde into thē selues, forasmuch as none are punished, but for their sinnes.

e He sheweth that the cause why God doeth punish vs extremely, is because we cā be broght vnto him by none other meanes.

f When there semeth to mās iudgement no recouerie, but all things are broght to despaire, thē God chiefly sheweth his mightie power.

g Thei ỹ haue no feare of God, by his sharp rods are broght to call vpon him and so finde mercie.

h By healing thē he declareth his good wil toward them.

i Meanīg their diseases, w̃ had almost broght thē to the graue & corruption.

k Praise and confession of Gods benefits are the true sacrifices of the godlie.

l He sheweth by ỹ sea what care God hathe ouer man, for in that ỹ he deliuereth thē from the great dangers of the sea, he deliuereth them, as it were, from a thousand deaths.

m Their feare & danger is so great.

n When their arte & meanes faile thē, they are compelled to cōfesse that onely Gods puidēce doeth preserue them.

o Thogh before euerie drop semed to fight one against an other, yet at his cōmandement they are astil, as thogh they were frosen.

he bringeth them vnto the hauen, where
they wolde be.
31 Let thē *therefore* confesse before the Lord
his louing kindenes, and his wonderful
workes before the sonnes of men.
32 And let them exalt him in the [p] Congregacion of the people, and praise him
in the assemblie of the Elders.
33 He turneth the floods into a wildernes,
and the springs of waters into drienes,
34 *And* a fruteful land into [*] barrennes for
the wickednes of them that dwell therein.
35 *Againe* he [q] turneth the wildernes into
pooles of water, & the drye land into water springs.
36 And there he placeth the hungrie, and
they buyld a citie to dwell in,
37 And sowe the fields, & plant vineyardes, which bring forthe fruteful [r] increase.
38 For he blesseth them, and they multiplie
excedingly, and he diminisheth not their
cattel.
39 [s] Againe *men* are diminished, and broght
lowe by oppression, euil and sorowe.
40 He powreth [t] contempt vpon princes,
and causeth them to erre in desert places
out of the way.
41 Yet he raiseth vp the poore out of miserie, and maketh him families like a flocke
of shepe.
42 The [u] righteous shal se it, and reioyce,
and all iniquitie shal stop her mouth.
43 Who is wise that he maie obserue these
things? for they shal vnderstād the louing
kindenes of the Lord.

p This great benefite oght not onely to be considered particularly, but magnified in all places & assemblies.
*Or, salteness.
q For the loue ȳ he beareth to his Church he changeth ȳ ordre of nature for their commoditie.
r Cōtinual increase & yearlie.
s As God by his prouidēce doeth exalte men, so doeth he also hūble them by afflictiōs to knowe them selues.
t For their wickednes and tyrānie he causeth ȳ people & subiects to contēne them.
u They, whose faith is lightened by Gods Spirit, shal reioyce to se Gods iudgements against the wicked & vngodlie.

PSAL. CVIII.

This Psalme is composed of two other Psalmes before, the seuen and fiftieth & the sixtieth. The matter here conteined is, 1 That David giueth him self with heart and voyce to praise the Lord, 7 And assureth him self of the promes of God concerning his kingdome ouer Israél, and his power against other nacions: 11 Who thogh he seme to forsake vs for a time, yet he alone wil in the end cast downe our enemies.

¶ *A song or Psalme of David.*

1 O God, mine heart *is* [a] prepared, so *is*
[*] my tongue: I wil sing & giue praise.
2 Awake viole & harpe: I wil awake early.
3 I wil praise thee, ô Lord, amōg the [b] people, and I wil sing vnto thee among the
nacions.
4 For thy mercie is great aboue the heauēs,
and thy trueth vnto the cloudes.
5 [c] Exalt thy self, ô God, aboue the heauēs,
and *let* thy glorie *be* vpon all the earth,
6 That thy beloued maie be deliuered:
[d] helpe with thy right hand and heare me.
7 God hathe spoken in his [e] holines: *therefore* I wil reioyce, I shal diuide Shechém
and measure the valley of Succóth.

a This earnest affection declareth that he is fre frō hypocrisie, and ȳ sluggishnes staieth hī not.
*Or, my glorie, because it chiefly setteth forthe the glorie of God.
b He prophecieth of ȳ calling of ȳ Gentiles: for except thei were called, they colde not heare the goodnes of God
c Let all the worlde se thy iudgements, in that thou art God ouer all, & so cōfesse that thou art glorious.
d Whē God by his benefites maketh vs partakers of his mercies, he admonisheth vs to be earnest in praier to desire him to continue and finish his graces.
e As he hathe spoken to Samuél concerning me, so wil he shewe him self constant, and holie in his promes, so that these nacions following shalbe subiect vnto me.

8 Gileád *shalbe* mine, *and* Manasséh *shalbe*
mine: Ephráim also *shalbe* the strength of
mine head: Iuda *is* my Lawegiuer.
9 *Móab *shalbe* my washpot: ouer Edóm wil
I cast out my shoe: vpon Palestina wil I
triumph.
10 Who wil leade me into the strong citie?
who wil bring me vnto Edóm?
11 [f] Wilt not thou, ô God, *which* haddest
forsaken vs, & didest not go forthe, ô God,
with our armies?
12 Giue vs helpe against trouble: for vaine
is the helpe of man.
13 Through God we shal do valiantly: for
he shal tread downe our enemies.

*Psal. 60,8.
f From ȳ sixte verse of this psalme vnto ȳ last read ȳ exposicion in the threscore psalme, and fifte verse.

PSAL. CIX.

1 David being falsely accused by flatterers vnto Saúl, praieth God to helpe him and to destroy his enemies. 8 And vnder thē he speaketh of Iudas the traitour vnto Iesus Christ, and of all the like enemies of the children of God: 27 And desireth so to be deliuered, that his enemies maie knowe the works to be of God. 30 Then doeth he promise to giue praises vnto God.

¶ *To him that excelleth. A Psalme of David.*

1 HOlde not thy tongue, ô God of my
[a] praise.
2 For the mouth of the wicked, and the
mouth *ful* of deceit are opened vpon me:
thei haue spoken to me with a lying tongue.
3 Thei compassed me about also with wordes of hatred, and foght against me without a cause.
4 For my friendship thei were mine aduersaries,[b] but I gaue my self to praier.
5 And they haue rewarded me euil for
good, and hatred for my friendship.
6 [c] Set thou the wicked ouer him, and let ȳ
aduersarie stand at his right hand.
7 When he shalbe iudged, let him be con
demned, and let his [d] praier be turned into
sinne.
8 Let his daies be fewe, and let another
take his [e] charge.
9 Let his children be fatherles, & his wife
a widowe.
10 Let his children be vagabunds & begge
and seke *bread, comming out* of their places
destroied.
11 Let [f] the extorcioner catche all ȳ the hathe, and let the strangers spoile his labour.
12 Let there be none to extend mercie vn
to him: nether let there be anie to shewe
mercie vpon his fatherles children.
13 Let his posteritie be destroied, & in the
generacion following let their name be
put out.
14 [g] Let the iniquitie of his fathers be had
in remembrance with the Lord: and let
not the sinne of his mother be done awaie.

a Thogh all ȳ worlde condēne me, yet thou wilt approue mine innocencie, & that is a sufficiēt praise to me.
b To declare ȳ I had none other refuge, but thee, in whome my cōscience was at rest.
c Whether it were Doeg or Saúl, or some familiar friēd ȳ had betraied hī, he praieth not of priuate affection, but moued by Gods Spirit, ȳ God wolde take vengeāce vpon him.
d As to the elect all things turne to their profite: so to ȳ reprobat euen those things, ȳ are good, turne to their damnation.
e This was chiefly accōplished in Iudas, Act. 1. 20.
f He declareth that ȳ curse of God lieth vpō the extorcioners: who thīking to enriche their children by their vnlawful gotten goods, are by Gods iust iudgement depriued of all.
g Thus punisheth the Lord to the third, and fourth generacion the wickednes of the parents in their wicked children.

15 *But* let them alway be before the Lord,
that he maie cut of their memorial from
the earth.
16 Because [h] he remembred not to shewe
mercie, but persecuted the afflicted and
poore man, and the sorowful hearted to
slaye him.
17 As he loued cursing, [i] so shal it come
vnto him, & as he loued not blessing, so
shal it be farre from him.
18 As he clothed him self with cursing like a raiment, so shal it come into his
bowels like water, and like oyle into his
bones.
19 Let it be vnto him as a garment to couer
him, and for a girdle, wherewith he shalbe
alwaie girded.
20 Let this be the rewarde of mine aduersarie [k] from the Lord, and of them, that
speake euil against my soule.
21 But thou, ô Lord my God, deale with me
according vnto thy [l] Name: deliuer me,
(for thy mercie is good)
22 Because I am poore and nedie, and mine
heart is wounded within me.
23 I departe like ÿ shadowe that declineth,
and am shaken of as the [m] grashopper.
24 My knees are weake through fasting, &
my flesh [n] hathe lost *all* fatnes.
25 I became also a rebuke vnto them: they
that loked vpon me, shaked their heads.
26 Helpe me, ô Lord my God: [o] saue me
according to thy mercie.
27 And they shal knowe, that this is thine
hand, & *that* thou, Lord, hast done it.
28 *Thogh* they [p] curse, yet thou wilt blesse:
they shal arise and be confounded, but
thy seruant shal reioyce.
29 Let mine aduersaries be clothed with
shame, and let them couer thẽ selues with
their confusion, as with a cloke.
30 I wil giue thãkes vnto the Lord greatly
with my [q] mouthe, and praise him amõg
the multitude.
31 For he wil stand at the right hand of the
poore, to saue him from them that wolde
[r] condemne his soule.

h He sheweth ÿ God accustometh to plague them after a strange sort, ÿ shewe them selues cruel toward other.
i Thus giueth the Lord to euerie mã the thing, wherin he deliteh, ÿ the reprobate can not accuse God of wrõg, when thei are giuen vp to their lusts and reprobat mindes.
k For being destitute of mans helpe, he fully trusted in the Lord, that he wolde deliuer him.
l As ÿ art named merciful, gracious and long suffring, so shewe thy self in effect.
m Meaning, ÿ he hathe no staie nor assurance in this worlde.
n For hungre, that came of sorow, he was leane, and his natural moysture failed hĩ.
o The more grieuous ÿ Satan assailed him, the more earnest & instant was he in praier.
p They shal gaine nothing by cursing me.
q Not onely in cõfessing it secretly in my self, but also in declaring it before all the Cõgregacion.
r Hereby he sheweth ÿ he had not to do ŵ them, that were of litle power, but ŵ the iudges and princes of the worlde.

PSAL. CX.

1 *Dauid prophecieth of the power and euerlasting kingdome giuẽ to Christ,* 4 *And of his Priesthode, which shulde put an end to the Priesthode of Leui.*

¶ *A Psalme of Dauid.*

1 The [a] Lord said vnto my Lord, Sit
thou at my right hand, vntil I make
thine enemies thy fotestole.
2 The Lord shal send the rod of thy power
out of [b] Zión: be thou ruler in the middes of thine enemies.
3 Thy people *shal come* willingly at the time *of assembling*: [c] thine armie in holie
beautie: the youth of thy wombe *shalbe* as
the morning dewe.
4 The Lord sware and wil not repent,
Thou art a Priest for euer after the ordre
of [d] Melchi-zédek.
5 The Lord, *that is* at thy right hand, shal
wounde Kings in the daie of his wrath.
6 He shalbe Iudge among the heathen: he
shal fil *all* with dead bodies, *and* smite the
[e] head ouer great countreis.
7 He shal [f] drinke of the brooke in ÿ waie:
therefore shal he lift vp *his* head.

a Iesus Christ in the two & twentie of Matt. giueth the interpretacion hereof, & sheweth ÿ this cã not properly be applied vnto Dauid, but to him self.
b And thence it shal stretch through all the worlde: & this power chiefly standeth in the preaching of his worde.
c By thy worde thy people shalbe assembled into thy Church, whose increase shalbe so abundant & wonderful, as the drops of the dewe.
d As Melchizédek ÿ figure of Christ was bothe King & Priest: so the effect can not be accomplished in anie King, saue onely in Christ, 2 Chro. 26, 21.
e No power shalbe able to resist him.
f Vnder this similitude of a captaine, that is so gredie to destroie his enemies, that he wil not scarse drinke by the waie, he sheweth how God wil destroy his enemies.

PSAL. CXI.

1 *He giueth thankes to the Lord for his merciful workes toward his Church,* 10 *And declareth wherein true wisdome and right knowledge consisteth.*

¶ *Praise ye the Lord.*

1 I Wil [a] praise the Lord with my whole
heart in the assemblie and Congregacion of the iust.
2 The workes of the Lord *are* [b] great, and
oght to be soght out of all them that loue
them.
3 His worke *is* beautiful and glorious, and
his righteousnes endureth for euer.
4 He hathe made his wonderful workes to
be had in remembrance: the Lord *is* merci
ful and ful of compassion.
5 He hathe giuen [c] a *portion vnto thẽ that
feare him: he wil euer be mindeful of his
couenant.
6 He hathe shewed to his people the power of his workes in giuing vnto them the
heritage of the heathen.
7 The [d] workes of his hands *are* trueth and
iudgement: all his statutes are true.
8 Thei are stablished for euer & euer, and
are done in trueth and equitie.
9 He sent redemption vnto his people: he
hathe commanded his couenant for euer:
holie and feareful *is* his Name.
10 [e] The beginning of wisdome *is* the feare
of the Lord: all they that obserue [f] them,
haue good vnderstanding: his praise endu
reth for euer.

a The Prophet declareth that he wil praise God bothe priuatly & opẽly, & that from ÿ heart, as he ÿ consecrateth hi selfe wholly & onely vnto God.
b He sheweth ÿ Gods workes are a sufficient cause, wherefore we shulde praise him, but chiefly his benefites toward his Church.
c God hathe giuen to his people all that was necessarie for thẽ, & wil do stil euẽ for his couenants sake. and in this sense the Ebrewe worde is takẽ, Prou. 30, 8. & 31, 15.
*Or, praie, & fode.
d As God promised to take the care of his Church: so in effect doeth he declare him selfe iust and true in ÿ gouernement of the same.
e Thei onely are wise, that feare God, and none haue vnderstanding, but thei that obey his worde.
f To wit, his commandements, as vers. 7.

PSAL. CXII.

1 *He praiseth the felicitie of thẽ, that feare God,* 10 *And condemneth the cursed state of the contemners of God.*

¶ *Praise ye the Lord.*

1 Blessed *is* the man, that [a] feareth the
Lord, & deliteth greatly in his commandements.
2 His sede shalbe mightie vpon earth: the
generaciõ of the righteous shalbe blessed.
3 [b] Riches and treasures *shalbe* in his house,
and his righteousnes endureth for euer.
4 Vnto the [c] righteous ariseth light in darkenes: *he is* merciful and ful of compassiõ
and righteous.

a He meaneth that reuerent feare, which is in ÿ children of God, which causeth them to delite onely in ÿ worde of God.
b The godlie shal haue abũdance & contentement, because their heart is satisfied in God onely.
c The faithful in all their aduersities knowe that all shal go wel with them: for God wilbe merciful and iuste.

5 A good

5 A good man *is* merciful and [d] lendeth, *and* wil measure his affaires by iudgement.

6 Surely he shal neuer be moued: *but* the righteous shalbe had in euerlasting remembrance.

7 He wil not be afraid of euil tidings: *for* his heart is fixed, & beleueth in the Lord.

8 His heart is stablished: *therefore* he wil not feare, vntil he se *his desire* vpon his enemies.

9 He hathe [e] distributed *and* giuen to the poore: his righteousnes remaineth for euer: his [f] horne shalbe exalted with glorie.

10 The wicked shal se it and be angrie: he shal gnash with his teeth, and [g] consume awaie: the desire of the wicked shal perish.

PSAL. CXIII.

1 An exhortacion to praise the Lord for his prouidence. 7 In that that contrarie to the course of nature he worketh in his Church.

¶ *Praise ye the Lord.*

1 Praise, ô ye seruãts of the Lord, [a] praise the Name of the Lord.

2 Blessed be the Name of the Lord from hence forthe and for euer.

3 The Lords Name is praised from the rising of the sunne vnto the going downe of the same.

4 The Lord is high aboue all [b] nacions, & his glorie aboue the heauens.

5 Who is like vnto the Lord our God, that hathe his dwelling on high!

6 Who abaseth him self to beholde *things* in the heauen and in the earth.

7 He raiseth the nedie out of the dust, & lifteth vp the [c] poore out of the dung,

8 That he maie set him with the princes, *euen* with the princes of his people.

9 He maketh the baren woman to dwell with a familie, & a ioyful mother of children. Praise ye the Lord.

PSAL. CXIIII.

1 How the Israelites were deliuered forthe of Egypt, & of the wonderful miracles, that God wroght at that time. Which put vs in remembrance of Gods great mercie toward his Church, who, when the course of nature faileth, preserueth his miraculously.

Exod. 14,21.

1 When [*] Israél went out of Egypt, & the house of Iaakób from the [a] barbarous people,

2 Iudáh was [b] his sanctificacion, & Israél his dominion.

3 The Sea sawe it and fled: Iordén was turned backe.

4 The [c] moũtaines leaped like rams, & the hilles as lambs.

5 What ailed thee, ô Sea, that thou fleddest? ô Iordén, *why* wast thou turned backe?

d He sheweth what is ỹ frute of mercie: to lend frely & not for gaine, & so to measure his doings, that he maie be able to helpe where nede requireth, and not to bestowe all on hĩ self.

e The godlie pinche not nigardely, but distribute liberally, as the necessitie of ỹ poore requireth, & as his power is able.

f His power & prosperous estate.

g The blessigs of God vpon his children shal cause the wicked to dye for enuie.

a By this oftẽ repeticion he stirreth vp our colde dulnes to praise God, seing his workes are so wõderful, & that we are created for the same cause.

b If Gods glorie shine through all ỹ world, & therfore of all oght to be praised, what great condemnation were it to his people, among whome chiefly it shineth, if they shulde not earnestly extoll his Name?

c By preferrĩg the poore to high honour, and giuing the barrẽ childrẽ, he sheweth ỹ God worketh not onely in his Church by ordinarie meanes, but also by miracles.

a That is, frõ thẽ that were of a strãge langage.

b The whole people were witnesses of his holie maiestie, in adopting them, and of his mightie power in deliuering them.

c Seing that these deade creatures felt Gods power, & after a sorte sawe it, muche more his people oght to consider it & glorifie him for the same.

6 Ye mountaines, *why* leaped ye like rams, *and ye* hilles as lambs?

7 The [d] earth trembled at the presence of the Lord, at the presence of the God of Iaakób.

8 Which [e] turneth the rocke into waterpooles, & the flint into a fountaine of water.

PSAL. CXV.

1 A praier of the faithful oppressed by idolatrous tyrãts against whome they desire that God wolde succour thẽ. 9 Trusting moste constantly that God wil preserue thẽ in this their nede seing that he hathe adopted and receiued them to his fauour. 18 Promising finally that thei wil not be vnmindful of so great a benefite, if it wolde please God to heare their praier, & deliuer them by his omnipotent power.

1 Not [a] vnto vs, ô Lord, not vnto vs, but vnto thy Name giue the glorie, for thy louing mercie *and* for thy trueths sake.

2 Wherefore shal the heathen saie, [b] Where is now their God?

3 But our God *is* in heauen: he doeth what soeuer he [c] wil.

4 Their idoles *are* [d] siluer and golde, *euen* the worke of mens hands.

5 Thei haue a mouth and speake not: thei haue eyes and se not.

6 Thei haue eares and heare not: thei haue noses and smell not.

7 Thei haue [e] hands and touche not: thei haue fete and walke not: nether make thei a sounde with their throte.

8 Thei that make them are [f] like vnto thẽ: *so are* all that trust in them.

9 O Israél, trust thou in the Lord: *for* he is their helpe and their shield.

10 [g] O house of Aarón, trust ye in ỹ Lord: *for* he is their helpe and their shield.

11 Ye that feare the Lord, trust in the Lord: *for* he is their helper and their shield.

12 The Lord hathe bene mindeful of vs: he wil blesse, he [h] wil blesse the house of Israél, he wil blesse the house of Aarón.

13 He wil blesse them that feare the Lord, bothe smal and great.

14 The Lord wil encrease *his graces* toward you, euẽ toward you and toward your children.

15 Ye are blessed of the Lord, which [i] made the heauen and the earth.

16 The [k] heauens, *euen* the heauens *are* the Lords: but he hathe giuen the earth to the sonnes of men.

17 The dead praise not the Lord, nether anie that [l] go downe into the *place of* silence.

18 But we wil praise the Lord from hence forthe and for euer. Praise ye the Lord.

d Oght then his people to be insensible, when thei se his power & maiestie?

e That is, caused miraculously water to come out of the rocke in moste abũdance, Exod. 17,6.

a Because God promised to deliuer them, not for their sakes, but for his Name, Isa. 48,11, therfore they grounde their praier vpon this promes.

b Whẽ ỹ wicked se ỹ God accomplisheth not his p̃mes, as thei imagine, thei thinke there is no God.

c No impediments can let his worke, but he vseth euen ỹ impedimẽts to serue his wil.

d Seing that nether ỹ matter, nor ỹ forme can commẽd ỹ idoles, it followeth ỹ there is nothig, why thei shulde be estemed.

e He sheweth what great vanitie it is to aske helpe of thẽ, which not onely haue no helpe in them, but lacke sense and reason.

f As muche without sense, as blockes & stones.

g For thei were appointed by God as instructers & teachers of faith and religion for others to followe.

h That is, he wil continue his graces toward his people.

i And therfore doeth stil gouerne & cõtinue all thĩgs therein.

k And thei declare ynough his sufficiẽcie, so ỹ the worlde serueth hĩ nothing, but to shewe his fatherlie care toward men.

l Thogh the dead set forthe Gods glorie, yet he meaneth here, that thei praise hĩ not in his Church and Congregacion.

PSAL. CXVI.

1 Dauid being in great danger of Saúl in the desert of Maón, perceiuing the great and inestimable loue of God toward him, magnifieth suche great mercies. 13 And protesteth that he wil be thãkeful for the same.

1 I [a] Loue ẏ Lord, because he hathe heard
my voice *and* my praiers.
2 For he hathe inclined his eare vnto me,
when I did call *vpon him* [b] in my daies.
3 *When* the snares of death compassed me,
and the griefs of the graue caught me: whẽ
I founde trouble and sorowe,
4 Then I called vpon the Name of the
Lord, *saying*, I beseche thee, ô Lord, deliuer my soule.
5 The Lord *is* [c] merciful & righteous, and
our God *is* ful of compassion.
6 The Lord preserueth the simple: I was in
miserie and he saued me.
7 Returne vnto thy rest, ô [d] my soule: for ẏ
Lord hathe bene beneficial vnto thee,
8 Because thou hast deliuered my soule
from death, mine eies from teares, & my
fete from falling.
9 I shal [e] walke before the Lord in the land
of the liuing.
10 [f] I beleued, therefore did I speake: *for* I
was sore troubled.
11 I said in my [g] feare, All men are lyers.
12 What shal I rendre vnto the Lord for
all his benefites toward me?
13 I wil [h] take the cup of saluacion, and
call vpon the Name of the Lord.
14 I wil paie my vowes vnto ẏ Lord, *euen*
now in the presence of all his people.
15 Precious in the sight of the Lord *is* the
[i] death of his Saints.
16 Beholde, Lord: for I am thy seruant, I
am thy seruant, & the sonne of thine hand
maied: thou hast broken my bonds.
17 I wil offer to thee a sacrifice of praise, &
wil call vpon the Name of the Lord.
18 I wil paie my [k] vowes vnto the Lord,
euen now in the presence of all his people,
19 In the courtes of the Lords house, *euen*
in the middes of thee, ô Ierusalém. Praise
ye the Lord.

a He granteth ẏ no pleasure is so great, as to fele Gods helpe in our necessitie, nether that anie thĩg more stirreth vp our loue toward him.
b That is, in cõueniẽt time to seke helpe, ẇ was whẽ he was in distres.
c He sheweth forthe ẏ frute of his loue in calling vpon him, cõfessing him, to be iust & merciful, & to helpe them ẏ are destitute of aide & cõusel.
d Which was vnquieted before, now rest vpõ the Lord: for he hathe bene beneficial towards thee.
e The Lord wil preserue me, & saue my life.
f I felt all these things, and therefore was moued by faith to cõfesse thẽ, 2. Cor. 4, 13.
g In my great distresse I thoght God wolde not regarde man, ẇ is but lies and vanitie, yet I ouercame this tentacion, and felt ẏ cõtrarie.
h In the Law thei vsed to make a bãket, whẽ thei gaue solẽne thãkes to God, and to take the cup & drinke in signe of thankesgiuing.
i I perceiue ẏ God hathe a care ouer his, so that he bothe disposeth their death and taketh an account.
k I wil thanke him for his benefites: for that is a iuste paiement, to confesse that we owe all to God.

PSAL. CXVII.

1 He exhorteth the Gentiles to praise God, because he hathe accomplished aswel to them as to the Iewes, the promes of life euerlasting by Iesus Christ.

Rom. 15, 11.

1 ALL * nacions, praise ye the Lord: all
ye people, praise him.
2 For his louing kindenes is great toward
vs, and the [a] trueth of the Lord *endureth*
for euer. Praise ye the Lord.

a That is, the moste certeine & cõtinual testimonies of his fatherlie grace.

PSAL. CXVIII.

1 Dauid reiected of Saúl and of the people, at the time appointed obteined the kingdome. 4 For the which he biddeth all them, that feare the Lord, to be thankeful. And vnder his persone in all this was Christ liuely set forthe, who shulde be of his people reiected.

1 PRaise [a] ye ẏ Lord, because he is good:
for his mercie *endureth* for euer.
2 Let Israél now saie, That his mercie *en-*
dureth for euer.
3 Let the house of Aarón now saie, That
his mercie *endureth* for euer.
4 Let them, that feare the Lord, now saie,
That his mercie *endureth* for euer.
5 I called vpon the Lord in [b] trouble, *and*
the Lord heard me, *and set me* at large.
6 The Lord *is* with me: *therefore* I wil not
feare what [c] man can do vnto me.
7 The Lord *is* with me among them that
helpe me: therefore shal I se *my desire* vpon
mine enemies.
8 It is better to trust in the Lord, then to
haue confidence [d] in man.
9 It is better to trust in the Lord, then to
haue confidence in princes.
10 All nacions haue compassed me: but in
the Name of the Lord shal I destroie
them.
11 Thei haue compassed me, yea, they haue
compassed me: but in the Name of the
Lord I shal destroie them.
12 Thei came about me like bees, *but* they
were quenched as a fyre of thornes: for in
the Name of the Lord I shal destroie
them.
13 [e] Thou hast thrust sore at me, that I
might fall: but the Lord hathe holpen
me.
14 The Lord *is* my strength and [f] song: for
he hathe bene my deliuerance.
15 The [g] voice of ioye and deliuerance
shalbe in the tabernacles of the righteous,
saying, The right hand of the Lord hathe
done valiantly.
16 The right hand of the Lord is exalted:
[h] the right hand of the Lord hathe done
valiantly.
17 I shal not dye, but liue, and declare the
workes of the Lord.
18 The Lord hathe chastened me sore, but
he hathe not deliuered me to death.
19 Open ye vnto me the [i] gates of righteousnes, *that* I maie go in to thẽ, & praise the Lord.
20 This is the gate of the Lord: the righteous shal entre into it.
21 I wil praise thee: for thou hast heard me,
and hast bene my deliuerance.
22 *The stone, *which* the buylders [k] refused,
is the head of the corner.
23 This was the Lords doing, & it is maruelous in our eyes.
24 This is the [l] daie, *which* the Lord hathe
made: let vs reioyce and be glad in it.
25 [m] O Lord, I praie thee, saue now: ô Lord,
I praie thee now giue prosperitie.

a Because God by creating Dauid King, shewed his mercie toward his afflicted Church, ẏ Prophet doeth not onely hĩ self thanke God, but exhorteth all ẏ people to do the same.
b We are here taught, that ẏ more ẏ troubles oppresse vs, the more oght we to be instãt ĩ praier.
c Beĩg exalted to this estate, he assured him selfe to haue mã euer to be his enemie. Yet he douted not, but God wolde maĩteine him because he had placed him.
d He sheweth ẏ he had trusted in vaine, if he had put his confidence in man, to haue bene preferred to ẏ kĩgdome, & therefore he put his trust in God & obteined.
e He noteth Saúl his chief enemie.
f In ẏ he was deliuered, it came not of him selfe, nor of ẏ power of man, but onely of Gods fauour: therefore he wil praise hĩ.
g He pmiseth bothe to rẽdre graces him self, & to cause others to do ẏ same, because ẏ in his persone the Church was restored.
h So that all, ẏ are bothe farre & nere, maie se his mightie power.
i He willeth the dores of ẏ Tabernacle to be opened, ẏ he maie declare his thankeful minde.

Isa. 28, 16. mat. 21, 42. act. 4, 11. rom. 9, 33. 1. pet. 2, 6.

k Thogh Saúl and the chief powers refused me to be King, yet God hathe preferred me aboue them all.
l Wherein God hathe shewed chiefly his mercie by appointing me King, and deliuering his Church.
m The people praie for the prosperitie of Dauids kingdome, who was the figure of Christ.

26 Blessed *be he*, that cometh in the Name
of the Lord: [n] we haue blessed you out of
the house of the Lord.
27 The Lord *is* mightie, and hathe giuen
vs [o] light: binde the sacrifice with cordes
vnto the hornes of the altar.
28 Thou art my God, and I wil praise thee,
euen my God: therefore I wil exalt thee.
29 Praise ye the Lord, because he is good:
for his mercie *endureth* for euer.

n Which are the priests and haue the charge thereof, as Nomb. 6,23.
o Because he hathe restored vs from darkenes to light, we wil offer sacrifices and praises vnto him.

PSAL. CXIX.

1 *The Prophet exhorteth the children of God to frame their liues according to his holie worde. 123 Also he sheweth wherein the true seruice of God standeth: that is, whē we serue him according to his worde, & not after our one fantasies.*

ALEPH.

1 Blessed *are* [a] those that are vpright in
their waie, & walke in the Lawe of ẏ
Lord.
2 Blessed *are* thei that kepe his testimonies, & seke him with their whole heart.
3 Surely they worke [b] none iniquitie, *that*
walke in his waies.
4 Thou hast commanded to kepe thy precepts diligently.
5 [c] Oh that my waies were directed to kepe thy statutes.
6 Then shulde I not be confounded, when
I haue respect vnto all thy commandements.
7 I wil praise thee with an vpright [d] heart,
when I shal learne the [e] iudgements of thy
righteousnes.
8 I wil kepe thy statutes: forsake me not
[f] ouerlong.

BETH.

9 Wherewith shal a [a] yong mā redresse his
waie? in taking hede *thereto* according to
thy worde.
10 With my whole heart haue I soght thee:
let me not wander from thy commandements.
11 I haue [b] hid thy promes in mine heart,
that I might not sinne against thee.
12 Blessed art thou, ô Lord: teache me thy
statutes.
13 With my lippes haue I declared all the
iudgements of thy mouth.
14 I haue had as great [c] delite in the waie of
thy testimonies, as in all riches.
15 I wil meditate in thy precepts, and consider thy waies.
16 I wil delite in thy statutes, & I wil not
forget thy worde.

GIMEL.

17 Be benificial vnto thy seruāt, *that* I maie
[a] liue and kepe thy worde.
18 Open mine eies, that I maie se the wonders of thy Law.
19 I am a [b] stranger vpon earth: hide not
thy commandements from me.
20 Mine heart breaketh for ẏ desire to thy
iudgements alwaie.
21 Thou [c] hast destroied the proude: cursed
are they that do erre from thy commandements.
22 Remoue from me shame and contempt:
for I haue kept thy testimonies.
23 [d] Princes also did sit, & speake against
me: *but* thy seruant did meditate in thy statutes.
24 Also thy testimonies *are* my delite, &
my counselers.

DALETH.

25 My soule cleaueth to the [a] dust: quicken
me according to thy worde.
26 I haue [b] declared my waies, and thou
heardest me: teache me thy statutes.
27 Make me to vnderstand the waie of thy
precepts, and I wil meditate in thy wōde-
rous workes.
28 My soule melteth for heauines: raise me
vp according vnto thy [c] worde.
29 Take from me the [d] waie of lying, and
grant me graciously thy Law.
30 I haue chosen the waie of trueth, & thy
iudgements haue I laied *before me*.
31 I haue cleaued to thy testimonies, ô
Lord: confounde me not.
32 I wil runne the waie of thy commandements, when ẏ [e] shalt enlarge mine heart.

HE.

33 Teache [a] me, ô Lord, the waie of thy statutes, and I wil kepe it vnto the end.
34 Giue me vnderstanding, and I wil kepe
thy Law: yea, I wil kepe it with *my* whole
[b] heart.
35 Direct me in the path of thy commādements: for therein is my delite.
36 Incline mine heart vnto thy testimonies,
and not to [c] couetousnes.
37 Turne awaie mine [d] eyes from regarding
vanitie, & quicken me in thy waie.
38 Stablish thy promes to thy seruant, because he feareth thee.
39 Take awaie [e] my rebuke that I feare: for
thy iudgements *are* good.
40 Beholde, I desire thy commandements:
[f] quicken me in thy righteousnes,

VAV.

41 And let thy [a] louing kindenes come vnto me, ô Lord, & thy saluacion according
to thy promes.
42 So shal I [b] make answer vnto my blasphe
mers: for I trust in thy worde.
43 And take not the worde of trueth vtterly
out of my mouth: for I wait for thy iudgements.
44 So shal I alwaie kepe thy Lawe for euer
and euer.
45 And I wil [c] walke at libertie: for I seke

Psal. CXIX.
a Here thei are not called blessed, which thinke themselues wise in their owne iudgement, nor which imagine to themselues a certeine holines, but thei whose cōuersation is without hypocrisie.
b For thei are ruled by Gods Spirit and imbrace no doctrine but his.
c Dauid acknowledgeth his imperfection, desiring God to reforme it that his life maie be conformable to Gods worde.
d For true religion stādeth in seruing God without hypocrisie.
e That is, thy precepts, ẇ cōteine perfite righteousnes.
f He refuseth not to be tryed by tentations, but he feareth to faint, if God succor not his infirmitie in time.
a Because youth is most giuen to licenciousnes, he chiefly warneth them to frame their liues betime to Gods worde.
b If Gods worde be grauen in ẏ heartes, we shalbe more able to resist the assaltes of Satān: and therefore the Prophet desireth God to instruct him daiely more & more therein.
c The Prophet doeth not boast of his vertues, but setteth forthe an exāple for others to followe Gods worde & leaue worldelie vanities. a He sheweth that we oght not to desire to liue but to serue God, and that we can not serue him aright, except he open our eyes and mindes. b Seing mans life in this worlde is but a passage, what shulde become of him, if thy worde were not his guide?

c In all ages ẏ hast plagued all suche, ẇ maliciously & contempteously depart from thy trueth.
d When the powers of the worlde gaue false sentence against me, thy worde was a guide & counseler to teache me what to do, & to comfort me.
a That is, it is almost broght to the graue, & without thy worde I can not liue.
b I haue confessed mine offences, and now depend wholly on thee.
c If God did not mainteine vs by his worde, ô life wolde drop awaie like water.
d Instruct me in thy worde, whereby my minde maie be purged frō vanitie & taught to obey thy wil.
e By this he sheweth ẏ we can nether chose good, cleaue to Gods word, nor runne forwarde in his waie, except he make ô hearts large to receiue his grace, & willīg to obey.
a He sheweth that he cā not followe on to ẏ end, except God teache him oft times and lead him forwarde.
b Not onely in outward cōuersation, but also ẇ inward affection.
c Hereby meaning all other vices, because ẏ couetousnes is the rote of all euil.
d Meaning, all his senses.
e Let me not fall to thy dishonour, but let mine heart stil delite in thy gracious worde.
f Giue me strength to cōtinue in thy worde euen to the end.
a He sheweth ẏ Gods mercie and loue is the first cause of our saluacion.
b By trusting in Gods worde he assureth him self to be able to confute the sclanders of his aduersaries. c Thei, that simply walke after Gods worde, haue no lets to intangle them, where as thei that do contrary, are euer in nets and snares.

thy precepts.
46 I wil speake also of thy testimonies before [d] Kings, and wil not be ashamed.
47 And my delite shalbe in thy commandements, which I haue loued.
48 Mine hands also wil I lift vp vnto thy
commandements, which I haue loued, and
I wil meditate in thy statutes.

ZAIN.

49 Remẽbre [a] the promes *made* to thy seruãt, wherein thou hast caused me to trust.
50 It is my comfort in my trouble: for thy
promes hathe quickened me.
51 The [b] proude haue had me excedingly
in derision: *yet* haue I not declined from
thy Law.
52 I remembred thy [c] iudgements of olde,
ô Lord, and haue bene comforted.
53 [d] Feare is come vpon me for the wicked,
that forsake thy Law.
54 Thy statutes haue bene my songs in the
house of my [e] pilgrimage.
55 I haue remembred thy Name, ô Lord,
in the [f] night, and haue kept thy Law.
56 [g] This I had because I kept thy precepts.

CHETH.

57 O Lord, *that art* my [a] porcion, I haue determined to kepe thy wordes.
58 I made my supplication in thy presence
with *my* whole heart: be merciful vnto me
according to thy promes.
59 I haue considered my [b] waies, & turned
my fete into thy testimonies.
60 I made haste and delayed not to kepe
thy commandements.
61 The bands of the wicked haue [c] robbed
me: *but* I haue not forgotten thy Law.
62 At midnight wil I rise to giue thankes
vnto thee, because of thy righteous iudgements.
63 I am [d] companion of all them that feare
thee, and kepe thy precepts.
64 The earth, ô Lord, is ful of thy mercie:
[e] teache me thy statutes.

TETH.

65 O Lord, thou hast delt [a] graciously with
thy seruant according vnto thy worde.
66 Teache me good iudgement and knowledge: for I haue beleued thy commandements.
67 Before I was [b] afflicted, I went astraie:
but now I kepe thy worde.
68 Thou art good and gracious: teache me
thy statutes.
69 The proude haue imagined a lie against
me: *but* I wil kepe thy precepts with *my*
whole heart.
70 [c] Their heart is fat as grease: *but* my delite is in thy Law.
71 It is [d] good for me that I haue bene afflicted, that I maie learne thy statutes.

d He sheweth ỹ the children of God oght not to suffer their Fathers glorie to be obscured by the vaine pompe of princes.

a Thogh he fele Gods hãd stil to lie vpon him, yet he resteth on his promes & comforteth him self therein.
b Meaning the wicked, ỽ cõtemne Gods worde, & tread his religiõ vnder fote.
c That is, the exãples, whereby thou declarest thy self to be iudge of the worlde.
d That is, a vehement zeale to thy glorie, & indignacion against ỹ wicked.
e In the course of this life and sorowful exile
f Eueñ when other slepe.
g That is, all these benefits.
a I am persuaded ỹ to kepe thy Law is an heritage and great gaine for me
b He sheweth ỹ none can imbrace ỹ worde of God, except he consider his owne imperfections and waies.
c They haue gone about to drawe me into their cõpanie.
d Not onely in mutual cõsent, but also with aide & succour.
e For ỹ knowledge of Gods worde is a singular token of his fauour.
a Hauing proued by experience that God was true in his promes, he desireth that he wolde increase in hĩ knowledge and iudgement.
b So Ieremie saith, ỹ before the Lord touched him, he was like a calfe vntamed: so that the vse of Gods rods is to call vs home to God.
c Their heart is indurate & hardened, puffed vp with prosperitie & vaine estimacion of them selues.
d He confesseth that before that he was chastened, he was rebellious, as mã by nature is.

72 The Law of thy mouth is better vnto
me, then thousands of golde and siluer.

IOD.

73 Thine hands haue [a] made me and facioned me: giue me vnderstanding *therefore*,
that I maie learne thy commandements.
74 So thei ỹ [b] feare thee, seing me shal reioyce, because I haue trusted in thy worde.
75 I knowe, ô Lord, that thy iudgements
are right, and that thou hast afflicted me
" iustly.
76 I praie thee that thy mercie maie comfort me according to thy promes vnto thy
seruant.
77 Let thy tender mercies come vnto me,
that I maie [c] liue: for thy Law *is* my delite.
78 Let the proude be ashamed: for thei haue dealt wickedly *and* falsely with me: *but*
I meditate in thy precepts.
79 Let suche as feare thee [d] turne vnto me,
and thei that [e] knowe thy testimonies.
80 Let mine heart be vpright in thy statutes, that I be not ashamed.

CAPH.

81 My soule [a] fainteth for thy saluacion: *yet*
I waite for thy worde.
82 Mine eyes faile for thy promes, saying,
When wilt thou comfort me?
83 For I am like a [b] bottel in the smoke: *yet*
do I not forget thy statutes.
84 How manie are the [c] daies of thy seruãt?
when wilt thou execute iudgement on thẽ
that persecute me?
85 The proude haue [d] digged pittes for me,
which is not after thy Law.
86 All thy commandements *are* true: they
persecute me falsely: [e] helpe me.
87 They had almost consumed [f] me vpon
the earth: but I forsoke not thy precepts.
88 Quicken me according to thy louing
kindenes: so shal I kepe the testimonie of
thy mouth.

LAMED.

89 O Lord, thy worde endureth for euer
in [a] heauen.
90 Thy trueth *is* from generacion to generacion: thou hast laied the fundacion of
the earth, and it abideth.
91 Thei [b] continue *euen* to this daie by thine ordinances: for all *are* thy seruants.
92 Except thy Law had bene my delite, I
shulde now haue perished in mine affliction.
93 I wil neuer forget thy precepts: for by
them thou hast quickened me.
94 I am [c] thine, saue me: for I haue soght
thy precepts.
95 The wicked haue waited for me to destroye me: *but* I wil consider thy testimonies.
96 I [d] haue sene an end of all perfection:
but thy commandement *is* exceding large.

a Because God leaueth not his worke, that he hathe begon, he desireth a newe grace: ỹ is, ỹ he wolde continue his mercies.
b When God sheweth his grace towarde anie, he testifieth to others that he faileth not them that trust in him.
" *Ebr. in trueth.*
c He declareth, ỹ when he felt not Gods mercies, he was as dead.
d That is, be comforted by mine exãple
e He sheweth that there can be no true feare of God without the knowledge of his worde.
a Thogh my strength faile me, yet my soule groneth and sigheth, resting stil in thy worde.
b Like a skynbottel or bladder that is parched in the smoke.
c How long wilt ỹ afflict thy seruant?
d They haue not onely oppressed me violẽtly, but also craftely cõspired agaĩst me.
e He assureth him self, that God wil deliuer his & destroy suche as vniustly persecute them.
f Finding no helpe in earth, he lifteth vp his eyes to heauen.
a Because none shulde esteme Gods worde according to the changes of things in this worlde, he sheweth that it abideth in heauen & therefore is immutable.
b Seing the earth and all creatures remaine in that estate, wherein ỹ hast created them, muche more thy trueth remaineth cõstant & vnchangeable.
c He proueth by effect, ỹ he is Gods childe, because he seketh to vnderstand his worde.
d There is nothing so perfite in earth, but it hathe an end: onely Gods worde lasteth for euer.

MEM.

97 Oh how loue I thy Law! [a] it is my meditacion continually.
98 By thy commandements thou hast made me wiser then mine enemies: for they
are euer with me.
99 I haue had more [b] vnderstanding then
all my teachers: for thy testimonies *are* my
meditacion.
100 I vnderstode more then the ancient,
because I kept thy precepts.
101 I haue refrained my fete from euerie
euil way, that I might kepe thy worde.
102 I haue not declined frō thy iudgemēts:
for [c] thou didest teache me.
103 How swete are thy promises vnto my
mouth! *yea*, more then honie vnto my
mouth.
104 By thy precepts I haue gotten vnderstanding: therefore I hate all the wayes of
falsehode.

NVN.

105 Thy worde *is* a [a] lanterne vnto my fete, and a light vnto my path.
106 I haue [b] sworne and wil performe it, ẏ
I wil kepe thy righteous iudgements.
107 I am verie sore afflicted: ô Lord, quicken me according to thy worde.
108 O Lord, I beseche thee accept the [c] fre
offrings of my mouth, and teache me thy
iudgements.
109 My [d] soule is continually in mine hād:
yet do I not forget thy Law.
110 The wicked haue layed a snare for me:
but I swarued not from thy precepts.
111 Thy testimonies haue I takē *as* an [e] heritage for euer: for they are the ioye of mine heart.
112 I haue applied mine heart to fulfil thy
statutes alwaie, *euen* vnto the end.

SAMECH.

113 I hate [a] vaine inuentions: but thy Law
do I loue.
114 Thou art my refuge and shield, *and* I
trust in thy worde.
115 [b] Awaie from me, ye wicked: for I wil
kepe the commandements of my God.
116 Stablish me according to thy promes,
that I maye liue, and disapoint me not of
mine hope.
117 [c] Staie thou me, and I shalbe safe, and I
wil delite continually in thy statutes.
118 Thou hast troden downe all them that
departe from thy statutes: for their [d] deceit
is vaine.
119 Thou hast taken away all the wicked of
the earth *like* [e] drosse: therefore I loue thy
testimonies.
120 My flesh [f] trembleth for feare of thee,
and I am afraied of thy iudgements.

AIN.

121 I haue executed iudgement and iustice:
leaue me not to mine oppressours.
122 [a] Answer for thy seruant in that, which
is good, *and* let not the proude oppresse
me.
123 Mine eyes haue failed *in waiting* for thy
saluacion, and for thy iuste promes.
124 Deale with thy [b] seruant according to
thy mercie, & teache me thy statutes.
125 I am thy seruant: grante me *therefore*
vnderstanding, that I maie knowe thy testimonies.
126 It is [c] time for the Lord to worke: *for*
they haue destroyed thy Law.
127 Therefore loue I thy commandements aboue golde, yea, aboue moste fine golde.
128 Therefore I esteme all thy precepts mo
ste iuste, and hate all false [d] waies.

PE.

129 Thy testimonies *are* [a] wonderful: therefore doeth my soule kepe them.
130 The entrance into thy [b] wordes sheweth light, *and* giueth vnderstanding to the
simple.
131 I opened my mouth & [c] panted, because
I loued thy commandements.
132 Loke vpō me and be merciful vnto me,
as thou vsest to do vnto those that loue
thy Name.
133 Direct my steppes in thy worde, and
let none iniquitie haue dominion ouer
me.
134 Deliuer me from the oppression of mē,
and I wil kepe thy precepts.
135 Shewe the light of thy countenance
vpon thy seruant, and teache me thy statutes.
136 Mine eyes gush [d] out with riuers of
water, because they kepe not thy Law.

TSADDI.

137 Righteous art thou, ô Lord, and iuste
are thy iudgements.
138 Thou hast commanded [a] iustice by thy
testimonies and trueth especially.
139 * My zeale hathe euen consumed me,
because mine enemies haue forgoten thy
wordes.
140 Thy worde is proued [b] moste pure,
and thy seruant loueth it.
141 I am [c] smale and despised: *yet* do I not
forget thy precepts.
142 Thy righteousnes *is* an euerlasting righteousnes, and thy Law *is* trueth.
143 Trouble and anguishe are come vpon me: *yet are* thy commandements my
delite.
144 The righteousnes of thy testimonies *is*
euerlasting: grante me vnderstanding, &
I shal [d] liue.

KOPH.

145 I haue [a] cryed with *my* whole heart: heare me, ô Lord, & I wil kepe thy statutes.
146 I called vpon thee: saue me, and I wil

a He sheweth ẏ we can not loue Gods worde, except we exercise our selues therein and practise it.
b Whosoeuer doeth submit him self onely to Gods worde, shal not onely be safe against ẏ practises of his enemies, but also learne more wisdome, thē they ẏ professe it, & are mē of experience.
c So then of our selues we cā do nothing, but whē God doeth inwardely instruct vs ẇ his Spirit, we fele his graces sweter then honie.
a Of our selues we are but darkenes, and can not se, except we be lightened with Gods worde.
b So all the faithful oght to binde them selues to God by a solemne othe and promes, to stir vp their zeale to imbrace Gods worde.
c That is, my praiers & thākesgiuing, ẇ sacrifice Hosea calleth ẏ calues of the lippes, Chap. 14 vers. 3.
d That is, I am in continual danger of my life.
e I estemed no wordlie thīgs, but made thy worde mine inheritance.
a Whosoeuer wil imbrace Gods worde aright, must abhorre all fātasies & imaginacions bothe of him self & of others.
b And hinder me not to kepe the Law of ẏ Lord.
c He desireth Gods cōtinual assistance lest he shulde faint in this race, ẇ he had begon.
d The craftie practises of thē that contemne thy Law, shal be broght to noght.
e Which infected thy people, as drosse doeth ẏ metal.
f Thy iudgements do not onely teache me obedience, but cause me to feare, cōsidering mine owne weakenes, which feare causeth repentance.

a Put thy self betwene mine enemies & me, as if thou were my pledge.
b He boasteth not that he is Gods seruant, but herby putteth God in minde, that as he made him his by his grace, so he wolde cōtinue his fauour toward him.
c The Prophet sheweth ẏ whē the wicked haue broght all things to confusion, and Gods worde to vtter contempt, then is it Gods time to helpe & sēd remedie.
d That is, whatsoeuer dissenteth frō the puritie of thy worde.
a Conteining high & secret mysteries, so ẏ I am moued ẇ admiracion & reuerence.
b The simple idiotes, ẏ submit thē selues to God, haue their eyes opened, and their mindes illuminated so sone as they begin to read Gods worde.
c My zeale toward thy worde was so great.
d He sheweth what oght to be the zeale of Gods childrē, when they se his worde contemned.
a We can not confesse God to be righteo⁹, except we liue vprightly and truely, as he hathe commāded.
* Psal. 69, 10. 2. pet. 2, 1.
b Golde hathe nede to be fined, but thy worde is perfection it self.
c This is the true trial, to praise God in aduersitie.
d So that the life of man without the knowledge of God is death.
a He sheweth that all his affectiōs & wholē heart were bent to God ward for to haue helpe in his dangers.

kepe thy testimonies.
147 I preuẽted the morning light,& cryed:
for I waited on thy worde.
148 Mine eyes b preuent the *night* watches
to meditate in thy worde.
149 Heare my voice according to thy louing kindenes: ô Lord, quicken me according to thy " iudgement.
150 They drawe nere, that followe after
c malice,*and* are farre from thy Law.
151 Thou art nere, ô Lord: for all thy commandements *are* true.
152 I haue knowen long since d by thy testimonies, that thou hast established them
for euer.

RESH.

153 Beholde mine afflictiõ, and deliuer me:
for I haue not forgotten thy Law.
154 Pleade my cause, and deliuer me: quicken me according vnto thy a worde.
155 Saluacion *is* farre from the wicked, because they seke not thy statutes.
156 Great are thy tender mercies, ô Lord:
quicken me according to thy b iudgements.
157 My persecutours and mine oppressours
are manie: *yet* do I not swarue from thy
testimonies.
158 I sawe the transgressours & was c grieued, because they kept not thy worde.
159 Consider, ô Lord, how I d loue thy precepts: quicken me according to thy louing
kindenes.
160 The e begining of thy worde is trueth,
and all the iudgements of thy righteousnes *endure* for euer.

SCHIN.

161 Princes haue a persecuted me without
cause, but mine heart stode in awe of thy
wordes.
162 I reioyce at thy worde, as one that findeth a great spoile.
163 I hate falsehode and abhorre it, *but* thy
Lawe do I loue.
164 b Seuen times a daie do I praise thee,
because of thy righteous iudgements.
165 They, c that loue thy Law, shal haue
great prosperitie, and they shal haue none
hurt.
166 Lord, I haue d trusted in thy saluacion,
and haue done thy commandements.
167 My soule hathe kept thy testimonies:
for I loue them excedingly.
168 I haue kept thy precepts and thy testimonies: e for all my waies *are* before
thee.

TAV.

169 Let my complaint come before thee, ô
Lord, *and* giue me vnderstãding, a according vnto thy worde.
170 Let my supplicatiõ come before thee,
and deliuer me according to thy promes.
171 My lippes shal b speake praise, when
thou hast c taught me thy statutes.
172 My tongue shal intreate of thy worde:
for all thy commandements *are* righteous.
173 Let thine hãd helpe me: for I haue chosen thy precepts.
174 I haue longed for thy saluaciõ, ô Lord,
and thy Law *is* my delite.
175 Let my soule liue, & it shal praise thee,
and thy d iudgements shal helpe me.
176 I haue e gone astraye like a lost shepe:
seke thy seruant, for I do not forget thy
commandements.

b He was more earnest in ŷ studie of Gods worde, then they, that kept the watche, were in their charge.
" Or, custome.
c He sheweth the nature of the wicked to be to persecute agaĩst their conscience.
d His faith is grounded vpõ Gods worde, that he wolde euer be at hãd when his children be oppressed.
a For without Gods promes there is no hope of deliuerance.
b According to thy promes made in the Law, ŵ because the wicked lacke, they cã haue no hope of saluacion.
c My zeale cõsumed me, whẽ I sawe their malice & contempt of thy glorie.
d It is a sure signe of our adoption, whẽ we loue the Law of God.
e Since ŷ first promised, euen to the end all thy sayings are true.
a The threatenings & persecutiõs of princes colde not cause me to shrinke to cõfesse thee, who met more feare then men.
b That is, oftẽ & sondrie times.
c For their cõsciẽce assureth them, that thei please thee, whereas they, that loue not thee, haue the contrarie.
d He sheweth ŷ we must first haue faith, before we can worke & please God.
e I had no respect of mẽ, but set thee alwaies before mine eies, as ŷ iudge of my doings.
a As thou hast promised to be the scholemaster vnto all them, ŷ depẽd vpon thee.
b The worde signifieth to powre forthe continually.
c All his praier, & desire is, to profit in ŷ worde of God.
d That is, thy provident care ouer me, and wherewith ŷ wilt iudge mine enemies.
e Beig chased to and fro by mine enemies, and hauing no place to rest in.

PSAL. CXX.

1 The prayer of Dauid being vexed by the false reportes of Sauls flatterers. 5 And therefore he lamenteth his long abode among those infideles, 7 Who were giuen to all kinde of wickednes and contention.

¶ *A song of* a *degrees.*

1 I Called vnto the Lord in my b trouble,
and he heard me.
2 Deliuer my soule, ô Lord, frõ lying lippes, *and* from a deceitful tongue.
3 What doeth *thy* c deceitful tongue bring
vnto thee? or what doeth it auaile thee?
4 *It is as* the d sharpe arrowes of a mightie
man, and *as* the coles of iuniper.
5 Wo is to me that I remaine in e Méshech, & dwell in the tentes of f Kedár.
6 My soule hathe to long dwelt with him
that hateth peace.
7 I *seke* g peace, and when I speake *thereof*,
they are *bent* to warre.

a That is, of lifting vp the tune & rising in singing.
b Albeit the children of God oght to reioyce, when they suffer for righteousnes sake, yet it is a great grief to the flesh to heare euil for wel doing.
c He assured him self that God wolde turne their craft to their owne destruction.
d He sheweth that there is nothing so sharpe to perce, nor so hote to set on fyre as a sclãderous tongue.
e These were people of Arabia, which came of Iaphét, Gen. 10, 2.
f That is, of the Ishmaelites.
g He declareth what he meaneth by Mésheeh, and Kedár: to wit, the Israelites which had degenerate from their godlie fathers and hated and contended against the faithful.

PSAL. CXXI.

1 This Psalme teacheth that the faithful oght onely to loke for helpe at God, 7 Who onely doeth mainteine, preserue and prosper his Church.

¶ *A song of degrees.*

1 I Wil lift mine eyes " vnto the mountaines, from whence mine helpe shal
come.
2 Mine helpe *commeth* from the Lord,
which hathe made the a heauen and the
earth.
3 He wil not suffer thy fote to slippe: *for* he
that kepeth thee, wil not b slumber.
4 Beholde, he that kepeth Israél, wil nether
slumber nor slepe.
5 The Lord *is* thy keper: the Lord *is* thy
shadowe at thy right hand.
6 The sunne shal not c smite thee by daie,
nor the moone by night.
7 The Lord shal preserue thee from all
euil: he shal kepe thy soule.
8 The Lord shal preserue thy d going out,
and thy comming in from hence forthe
and for euer.

" *Or, aboue the moũtaines: meaning, that there is nothĩg so high in this worlde, wherein he can trust, but onely in God.*
a He accuseth mans ingratitude, ŵ cã not depẽd on Gods power.
b He sheweth that Gods prouidence not onely watcheth ouer his Church in general, but also ouer euerie mẽber therof.
c Nether heate nor colde, nor anie incommoditie shalbe able to destroie Gods Church: albeit for a time they maie molest it.
d Whatsoeuer thou doest enterprise, shal haue good successe.

PSAL. CXXII.

1 Dauid reioyceth in the name of the faithful, that God hathe

hathe accomplished his promes, and placed his Arke in
Zión. 5 For the which he giueth thankes. 8 And
praieth for the prosperitie of the Church.

¶ *A song of degrees*, or Psalme *of Dauid*.

1 I [a] Reioyced, when they said to me, We
wil go into the house of the Lord.
2 Our [b] fete shal stand in thy gates, ô Ierusalém.
3 Ierusalém *is* buylded as a citie, that is
[c] compact together in it self:
4 Whereunto [d] the tribes, *euen* the tribes
of the Lord go vp *according* to the testimonie to Israél, to praise the Name of the
Lord.
5 For there are thrones set for iudgement,
euen the thrones of the house of [e] Dauid.
6 Praie for the peace of Ierusalém: let thẽ
prosper that loue thee.
7 Peace be within thy [f] walles, & prosperitie within thy palaces.
8 For my [g] brethren and neighbours sakes I wil wish thee now prosperitie.
9 Because of the House of the Lord our
God, I wil procure thy welth.

a He reioyceth ẏ God had appointed a place, where ẏ Arke shulde stil remaine.
b Which were wonte to wander to and fro, as the Arke remoued.
c By ẏ artificial ioyning & beautie of the houses, he meaneth ẏ cõcord, & loue ẏ was betwene the citizens.
d All the tribes according to Gods couenant shal come and praye there.
e In whose house God placed ẏ throne of iustice, and made it a figure of Christs kingdome.
f The fauour of God prosper thee bothe within and without.
g Not onely for mine owne sake, but for all ẏ faithful.

PSAL. CXXIII.

1 *A praier of the faithful, which were afflicted ether in*
Babylon or vnder Antiochus by the wicked worlde-
lings and contemners of God.

¶ *A song of degrees*.

1 I Lift vp mine eyes to thee, that dwellest in the heauens.
2 Beholde, as the eyes of [a] seruants *loke* vnto the hand of their masters, *and* as the
eyes of a maiden vnto the hãd of her mastres: so our eyes *waite* vpon the Lord our
God vntil he haue mercie vpon vs.
3 Haue mercie vpon vs, ô Lord, haue mercie vpon vs: for we haue [b] suffred to muche contempt.
4 Our soule is filled to ful of the mocking
of the welthie, & of the despitefulnes of
the proude.

a He compareth ẏ condition of ẏ godlie to seruants that are destitute of all helpe, assurĩg that whẽ all other helpes faile, God is euer at hand and like him self.
b He declareth that whẽ ẏ faithful are so ful, ẏ they can no more endure the oppressions, and scornings of ẏ wicked, there is alwaie helpe aboue, if ẘ hungrie desires they call for it.

PSAL. CXXIIII.

1 *The people of God, escaping a great peril, do acknow*
ledge them selues to be deliuered, not by their owne for-
ce, but by the power of God. 4 They declare the great-
nes of the peril. 6 And praise the Name of God.

¶ *A song of degrees* or Psalme *of Dauid*.

1 IF the Lord had not [a] bene on our side,
(maie Israél now say)
2 If the Lord had not bene on our side, whẽ
men rose vp against vs,
3 They had then swallowed vs vp [b] quicke, whẽ their wrath was kindled against vs.
4 Then the [c] waters had drowned vs, *and*
the streame had gone ouer our soule:
5 Then had the swelling waters gone ouer
our soule.
6 Praised *be* the Lord, which hathe not giuen vs *as* a praye vnto their teeth.
7 Our soule is escaped, euen as a birde out
of the [d] snare of the foulers: the snare
is broken and we are deliuered.
8 Our helpe *is* in the Name of the Lord,
which hathe made heauen and earth.

a He sheweth that God was readie to helpe at nede, & that there was none other waie to be saued, but by his onelie meanes.
b So vnable were we to resist.
c He vseth moste propre similitudes to expresse the great danger ẏ ẏ Church was in, & out of ẏ ẘ God miraculously deliuered them.
d For the wicked did not oney furiously rage agaist the faithful, but craftely imagined to destroye them.

PSAL. CXXV.

1 *He describeth the assurance of the faithful in their af-*
flictions, 4 And desireth their welth, 5 And the destru-
ction of the wicked.

¶ *A song of degrees.*

1 THei that trust in the Lord, *shalbe as*
mount Zión, *which* can not be [a] remoued, *but* remaineth for euer.
2 *As* the mountaines *are* about Ierusalém:
so *is* the Lord about his people from hence
forthe and for euer.
3 For the [b] rod of the wicked shal not rest
on the lot of the righteous, lest the righ
teous put forthe their hand vnto wicked
nes.
4 Do wel, ô Lord, vnto those that be good
and true in their hearts.
5 [c] But these that turne aside by their croked *waies*, them shal the Lord leade with
the workers of iniquitie: *but* peace *shalbe*
vpon Israél.

a Thogh the worlde be subiect to mutacions, yet the people of God shal stand sure & be defended by Gods prouidence.
b Though God suffer his to be vnder ẏ crosse, lest thei shulde imbrace wickednes, yet this crosse shal not so rest vpon thẽ, that it shulde driue thẽ frõ hope.
c He desireth God to purge his Church from hypocrites & suche as haue no zeale of the trueth.

PSAL. CXXVI.

1 *This psalme was made after the returne of the peple*
from Babylon, and sheweth that the meane of their
deliuerance was wonderful after the seuentie yeres of
captiuitie forespoken by Ieremie chap. 25,12. & 29,10.

¶ *A song of degrees* or Psalme *of Dauid*.

1 WHen the Lord broght againe the
captiuitie of Zión, we were like
them that [a] dreame.
2 Then was our mouth [b] filled with laughter, and our tongue with ioye: then said
thei among the [c] heathẽ, The Lord hathe
done great things for them.
3 The Lord hathe done great things for
vs, *whereof* we reioyce.
4 O Lord, bring againe our captiuitie, as
the [d] riuers in the South.
5 Thei that sowe in teares, shal reape in
ioye.
6 Thei went weping and caried [e] precious
sede: *but* thei shal returne with ioye and
bring their sheaues.

a Their deliuerance was as a thing incredible, and therefore toke awaie all excuse of ingratitude.
b He sheweth how ẏ godlie oght to reioyce, when God gathereth his Church or deliuereth it.
c If the infideles confesse Gods wonderful worke, the faithful cã neuer shewe thẽ selues sufficiẽtly thankeful.
d It is no more impossible to God to deliuer his people, then to cause the riuers to runne in the wildernes and barren places.
e That is, sede which was scarse & dere: meaning, that thei which trusted in Gods promes to returne, had their desire.

PSAL. CXXVII.

1 *He sheweth that the whole estate of the worlde, bothe*
domestical and political standeth by Gods mere proui-
dence and blessig. 3 And that to haue children wel
nurtred is an especial grace and gift of God.

¶ *A song of degrees* or Psalme *of Salomón*.

1 EXcept the Lord [a] buylde the house,
thei labour in vaine that buylde it:
except the Lord kepe the [b] citie, the keper watcheth in vaine.
2 It is in vaine for [c] you to rise early, & to
lye downe late, & eat ẏ bread [d] of sorow:
but he wil surely giue [e] rest to his beloued.
3 Beholde, children are the inheritance of
the Lord, *and* the frute of the wombe *his*

a That is, gouerne & dispose all things perteining to ẏ familie.
b The publike estate of ẏ cõmune welth.
c Which watches, & wardes, & are also magistrates, & rulers of ẏ citie.
d Ether that, ẘ is gotten by hard labour, or eaten with grief of minde.
e Not excempting them from labour, but making their labours comfortable, and as it were a rest.

rewarde.
4 As *are* the arrowes in the hand of the
strong man : so *are* the [f] children of
youth.
5 Blessed *is* the man, that hathe his quiuer
ful of them: *for* they [g] shal not be ashamed,
when they speake with *their* enemies in
the gate.

f That is, indued w^t^ stregth & vertues frō God: for these are signes of Gods blessigs, & not ye nōber. g Suche children shalbe able to stop their aduersaries mouthes, whē their godlie life is maliciously accused before iudges.

PSAL. CXXVIII.

1 *He sheweth that blessednes apperteineth not to all vniuersally, but to them onely that feare the Lord, and walke in his wayes.*

¶ *A song of degrees.*

1 Blessed *is* euerie one that feareth the
Lord and walketh in his [a] wayes.
2 When thou eatest the labours of thine
[b] hands, thou shalt be blessed, and it shalbe
wel with thee.
3 Thy wife *shalbe* as the fruteful vine on
the sides of thine house, *and* thy [c] children like the oliue plants round about thy
table.
4 Lo, surely thus shal the man be blessed,
that feareth the Lord.
5 The Lord out of Ziōn shal [d] blesse thee
and thou shalt se the welth of [e] Ierusalém
all the dayes of thy life.
6 Yea, thou shalt se thy children's children,
and peace vpon Israél.

a God approueth not our life, except it be reformed, according to his worde. b The worlde esteemeth them happie, w^c^ liue in welth, and ydlenes: but ye holie Gost approueth them best, y^t^ liue of the meane ꝓfit of their labours. c Because Gods fauour appeareth in none outward thig more thē in increase of children, he promiseth to enriche the faithful with this gift. d Because of the spiritual blessing, which God hathe made to his Church, these temporal things shalbe granted e For except God blessed his Church publikely, this priuat blessing were nothing.

PSAL. CXXIX.

1 *He admonisheth the Church to reioyce thogh it be afflicted.* 4 *For by the righteous Lord it shalbe deliuered,* 6 *And the enemies for all their glorious shewe, shal suddenly be destroyed.*

¶ *A song of degrees.*

1 They haue often times afflicted me
frō my youth (may [a] Israél now say)
2 They haue often times afflicted me from
my youth: but they colde not preuaile a-
gainst me.
3 The plowers plowed vpon my backe, *and*
made long forrowes.
4 *But* the [b] righteous Lord hathe cut the
cordes of the wicked.
5 They that hate Ziōn, shalbe all ashamed
and turned backwarde.
6 [c] They *shalbe* as ye grasse on the house toppes, w^c^ withereth afore it cōmeth forthe.
7 Whereof the mower filleth not his hand,
nether the glainer his lap:
8 [d] Nether they, which go by, say, The bles
sing of the Lord *be* vpon you, *or*, We blesse
you in the Name of the Lord.

a The Church now afflicted oght to remēber, how her conditiō hathe euer bene such from the beginning: to be molested most grieuously by ye wicked: yet in time it hath euer bene deliuered b Because God is righteous, he can not but plague his aduersaries, and deliuer his, as oxen out of ye plowe. c The enemies y^t^ lift thē selues most high, and as it were, approche nere to ye sunne, are cōsumed with the heate of Gods wrath, because they are not grounded in godlie humilitie. d That is, ye wicked shal perish and none shal passe for thē.

PSAL. CXXX.

1 *The people of God from their bottomles miseries do crye vnto God and are heard* 3 *They confesse their sinnes and flee vnto Gods mercie.*

¶ *A song of degrees.*

1 Ovt of the [a] depe places haue I called
vnto thee, ô Lord.
2 Lord, heare my voyce: let thine eares attend to the voice of my praiers.
3 If thou, ô Lord, straitly markest iniquities, ô Lord, [b] who shal stand?
4 But mercie *is* with thee, that thou [c] maiest
be feared.
5 I haue waited on the Lord : my soule hathe waited, and I haue trusted in his worde.
6 My soule *waiteth* on the Lord more then
the mornīg watche watcheth for the morning.
7 Let Israél waite on the Lord: for with the
Lord *is* [d] mercie, and with him *is* great redemption.
8 And he shal redeme Israél from all his
iniquities.

a Beig in great distresse and sorowe. b He declareth y^t^ we can not be iust before God, but by forgiuenes of sinnes. c Because of nature y^u^ art merciful: therfore the faithful reuerence thee. d He sheweth to whome the mercie of God doeth apperteine: to Israél, that is to the Church, & not to the reprobate.

PSAL. CXXXI.

1 *Dauid charged with ambition and gredie desire to reigne, protesteth his humilitie & modestie before God, and teacheth all men, what thei shulde do.*

¶ *A song of degrees or Psalme of Dauid.*

1 Lord, [a] mine heart is not hawtie, nether
are mine eies loftie, nether haue I
walked in great [b] matters and hid from
me.
2 Surely I haue behaued my self, like one
wained frō his mother, and kept silence: I
am in my self as one that is [c] wained.
3 Let Israél waite on the Lord from hence
forthe and for euer.

a He setteth forthe his great humilitie, as an example to all rulers and gouerners. b Which passe the measure & limites of his vocation. c He was voide of ambitiō & wicked desires.

PSAL. CXXXII.

1 *The faithful, grounding on Gods promes made vnto Dauid, desire that he wolde establish the same, bothe as touching his posteritie and the buylding of the Temple, to praie there as was forespoken, Deut. 12,5.*

¶ *A song of degrees.*

1 Lord, remēber Dauid with all his [a] affliction.
2 Who sware vnto the Lord, *&* vowed vn
to the mightie *God* of Iaakób, *saying,*
3 I [b] wil not enter into the tabernacle of
mine house, nor come vpon my palet *or*
bed,
4 Nor suffer mine eyes to slepe, nor mine
eye lids to slumber,
5 Vntil I finde out a place for the [c] Lord, an
habitacion for the mightie *God* of Iaakób.
6 Lo, we heard of it in [d] Ephráthah, *&* foūde it in the fields of the forest.
7 We wil entre into his Tabernacles, *and*
worship before his fotestole.
8 Arise, ô Lord, *to come* into thy [e] rest, thou,
and the Arke of thy strength.
9 Let thy Priests be clothed with [f] righteousnes, and let thy Saintes reioyce.
10 For thy [g] seruant Dauids sake refuse not
the face of thine Anointed.
11 The Lord hathe sworne in trueth vnto
Dauid, and he wil not shrinke from it,

a That is, with how great difficultie he came to the kigdome, & w^t^ how great zeale & care he went about to build thy Temple. b Because the chief charge of the King was to set forthe Gods glorie, he sheweth, y^t^ he colde take no rest, nether wolde go about anie worldelie thing, were it neuer so necessarie, before he had executed his office. c That is, the Arke, w^c^ was a signe of Gods presence. d The cōmune brute was that ye Arke shulde remaine in Ephráthah: y^t^ is, in Beth-léhem a plentiful place: but after we perceiued y^t^ y^u^ woldest place it in Ierusalém, which was barren as a forest & cōpassed about onely with hilles. e That is, Ierusalém, because, that afterward his Arke shulde remoue to none other place. f Let the effect of thy grace bothe appeare in the Priests & in the people. g As thou first madest promes to Dauid, so continue it to his posteritie, that whatsoeuer thei shal aske for their people, it maie be granted.

saiyng, Of the frute of thy bodie wil I set
vpon thy throne.
12 If thy sonnes kepe my couenant,and my
testimonies, that I shal teache them , their
sonnes also shal sit vpon thy throne for
[h] euer.
13 For the Lord hathe chosẽ Zión,& loued
to dwell in it,*saying*,
14 This is my rest for euer: here wil I
dwell,for I haue a [i] delite therein.
15 I wil surely blesse her vitailes, & wil satisfie her poore with bread,
16 And wil clothe her Priests with [k] saluacion , and her Saintes shal showte for
ioye.
17 There wil I make the [l] horne of Dauid
to bud: *for* I haue ordeined a light for mine Anointed.
18 His enemies wil I clothe with shame,
but on him his crowne shal florish.

h Because this can not be acco̅plished but in Christ,it followeth that ye p[ro]mes was spiritual.
i Meaning,for his owne sake, & not for the plentifulnes of the place: for he promiseth to blesse it,declaring before, y^t^ it was barre.
k That is,with my protection, whereby thei shalbe safe.
l Thogh his force for a time semed to be broken, yet he promiseth to restore it.

PSAL. CXXXIII.

1 This psalme conteineth the commendacion of brotherlie amitie among the seruants of God.

¶ A song of degrees or Psalme *of Dauid.*

1 BEholde,how good and how comelie a
thĩg it is, brethren to dwell euen [a] together.
2 *It is* like to the precious [b] ointment vpon
the head , that runneth downe vpon the
beard,*euen* vnto Aarons beard, which wẽt
downe on the border of his garments:
3 *And* as the dewe of [c] Hermón,which fal
leth vpon the moũtaines of Zión: for [d] there the Lord appointed the blessing & life
for euer.

a Because the greatest parte were against Dauid , though some fauoured him, yet when he was established King, at le̅gth thei ioyned all together like brethren: & therefore he sheweth by these similitudes the commoditie of brotherlie loue
b The ointment was a figure of the graces,which come fro̅ Christ the head vnto his Church.
c By Hermón & Zión he meaneth the plentiful countrei about Ierusalém.
d Where there is suche concorde.

PSAL. CXXXIIII.

1 He exhorteth the Leuites,watching in the Temple, to praise the Lord.

¶ A song of degrees.

1 BEholde,praise ye the Lord,all ye [a] ser
uants of the Lord, ye that by night
stand in the House of the Lord.
2 Lift vp your [b] hands to the Sanctuarie,&
praise the Lord.
3 The Lord,that hathe [c] made heauen and
earth,blesse thee out of Zión.

a Ye y^t^ are Leuites & chiefly appointed to this office.
b For their charge wasnot onely to kepe ye Temple, but to praie there & to giue God thankes.
c And therefore hathe all power,blesse thee with his Fatherlie loue declared in Zión. Thus the Leuites vsed to praise the Lord,and blesse the people.

PSAL. CXXXV.

1 He exhorteth all the faithful , of what estate so euer thei be,to praise God for his maruelous workes,12 And specially for his graces toward his people , wherein he hathe declared his maiestie. 15 To the confusion of all idolaters and their idoles.

¶ Praise ye the Lord.

1 PRaise the Name of the Lord : ye seruants of the Lord,praise *him*.
2 Ye y^t^ stand in the [a] House of the Lord,&
in the [b] courtes of the House of our God,
3 Praise ye ye Lord : for the Lord is good:
sing praises vnto his Name: for it is a comelie thing.
4 For the Lord hathe [c] chosen Iaakób to
him selfe, *and* Isráel for his chief treasure.
5 For I knowe that the Lord *is* great , and
that our Lord *is* aboue all gods.
6 Whatsoeuer pleased the Lord, that [d] did
he in heauen and in earth,in the sea, & in
all the depths.
7 He bringeth vp the cloudes from the
ends of the earth,and maketh the* lightnings with the raine : he draweth forthe
the winde out of his treasures.
8 *He smote the first borne of Egypt bothe of man and beast.
9 He hathe sent tokens and wonders into
the middes of thee, ô Egypt,vpon Pharaóh,and vpon all his seruants.
10 *He smote manie nacions,& slewe migh
tie Kings:
11 *As* Sihón King of the Amorites,and Og
King of Bashán , and all the kingdomes
of Canáan:
12 And [e] gaue their land for an inheritance,*euen* an inheritance vnto Isráel his peo
ple.
13 Thy Name,ô Lord , *endureth* for euer: ô
Lord,thy remembrance *is* from generation to generation.
14 For the Lord wil [f] iudge his people, and
be pacified towards his seruants.
15 The [g] idoles of the heathen *are* siluer &
golde, *euen* the worke of mens hands.
16 Thei haue a mouth,& speake not : thei
haue eyes and se not.
17 Thei haue eares and heare not,nether is
there anie breath in their mouth.
18 Thei that make them,are like vnto them:
so are all that trust in them.
19 Praise the Lord,ye house of Isráel:prai-
se the Lord,ye house of Aarón.
20 Praise the Lord , ye house of Leuí : ye
that feare the Lord,praise the Lord.
21 Praised *be* the Lord out of Zión , which
dwelleth in Ierusalém . Praise ye the
Lord.

a Ye Leuites y^t^ are in his Sanctuarie.
b Meaning the people: for the people and Leuites had their courtes, which were places of the Temple separate.
c That is,hath frely loued the posteritie of Abrahám.
d He ioyneth Gods power w^t^ his wil, to the intent that we shulde not separat them: & hereby he willeth Gods people to depend on his power, w^c^ he co̅firmeth by examples.
Ier.10.12.
exod.12,19.
Nom.21.5. & 24.33.
e He sheweth what frute the godlie co̅ceiue of Gods power, whereby thei se how he destroyeth his enemies,& deliuereth his people.
f That is, gouerne & defende his people.
g By shewing what punishment God appointeth for ye heathen idolaters , he warneth his people to beware the like offence,seing ye idoles haue nether power nor life, & y^t^ their deliuerance came not by idoles, but by ye mightie power of God. read psal 115. vers.4.

PSAL. CXXXVI.

1 A moste earnest exhortation to giue thankes vnto God for the creation and gouernance of all things which sta̅deth in confessing that he giueth vs all of his mere liberalitie.

1 PRaise ye ye Lord , because he is good:
for his [a] mercie *endureth* for euer.
2 Praise ye the God of gods: for his mercie
endureth for euer.
3 Praise ye the Lord of lords: for his mercie *endureth* for euer.
4 Which onelie doeth great wonders : for
his mercie *endureth* for euer:
5 Which by *his* wisdome made the heauẽs:
for his mercie *endureth* for euer:
6 Which hathe stretched out the earth

a By this repetition he sheweth that ye least of Gods benefites bideth vs to thankesgiuĩg: but chiefly his mercie, w^c^ is principally declared towards his Church.

vpon the waters: for his [b] mercie *endureth*
for euer:
7 Which made great lights: for his mercie
endureth for euer:
8 *As* the sunne to rule the daie: for his mer
cie *endureth* for euer:
9 The moone and the starres to gouerne
the night: for his mercie *endureth* for euer:
10 Which smote Egypt with their first bor
ne (for his mercie *endureth* for euer)
11 And [c] broght out Israél from among
them (for his mercie *endureth* for euer)
12 With a mightie hand and [d] stretched
out arme: for his mercie *endureth* for e-
uer:
13 Which diuided the red Sea in two partes: for his mercie *endureth* for euer:
14 And made Israél to passe through the
middes of it: for his mercie *endureth* for
euer:
15 And ouerthrewe Pharaóh and his hoste
in the red Sea: for his mercie *endureth* for
euer:
16 Which led his people through the [e] wildernes: for his mercie *endureth* for euer:
17 Which smote great Kings: for his mercie *endureth* for euer:
18 And slewe [f] mightie Kings: for his mercie
endureth for euer:
19 *As* Sihón King of the Amorites: for his
mercie *endureth* for euer:
20 And Og the King of Bashán: for his mer
cie *endureth* for euer:
21 And gaue their land for an heritage: for
his mercie *endureth* for euer:
22 *Euen* an heritage vnto Israél his seruant:
for his mercie *endureth* for euer:
23 Which remembred vs in our [g] base estate: for his mercie *endureth* for euer:
24 And hathe rescued vs from our oppressours: for his mercie *endureth* for euer:
25 Which giueth foode to all [h] flesh: for
his mercie *endureth* for euer.
26 [i] Praise ye the God of heauen: for his
mercie *endureth* for euer.

b This was a cõmune kinde of thãkesgiuĩg, wͨ the whole people vsed, when thei had receiued anie benefite of God, as 2. Chr. 7,6. & 20,21: meaning yͭ God was not onely merciful to their fathers, but also continued yͤ same to their posteritie.
c Gods merciful prouidence toward mã appeareth in all his creatures, but chiefly in that that he deliuered his Church from yͤ thraldome of their enemies.
d In doĩg such a worke as was neuer done before, nor that anie other colde do.
e Where for yͤ space of fortie yeres he shewed infinite and moste strange wonders.
f Declaring therby that no power nor autoritie was so dere vnto him, as the loue of his Church.
g In our greatest afflictiõ & sclauerie, whẽ we loked for nothing lesse then to haue had anie succour.
h Seing yͭ God prouideth, euẽ for the beastes: muche more hathe he care ouer his.
i Seing that all ages haue had most plaine testimonies of Gods benefites.

PSAL. CXXXVII.

1 The people of God in their banishment seing Gods true religion decaie, liued in great anguish and sorowe of heart: the which grief the Chaldeans did so litle pitie, 3 That thei rather increased the same daiely with tauntes, reproches and blasphemies against God. 7 Wherefore the Israelites desire God, first to punish the Edomites, who prouoked the Babylonians against them. 8 And moued by the Spirit of God, prophecie the destruction of Babylon, where thei were handled so tyrannously.

1 BY the riuers of Babél we [a] sate, and
there we wept, when we remembred
Zión.
2 We hanged our harpes vpõ the willowes
in the middes [b] thereof.
3 Then thei that led vs captiues, [c] required
of vs songs and mirth, when we had hanged vp *our harpes, saying,* Sing vs *one* of the
songs of Zión.
4 How shal we sing, *said we*, a song of the
Lord in a strange land?
5 [d] If I forget thee, ô Ierusalém, let my
right hand forget *to play*.
6 If I do not remembre thee, let my tongue cleaue to the rofe of my mouth: *yea*,
if I preferre not Ierusalém to my [e] chief
ioye.
7 Remember the children of [f] Edóm, ô
Lord, in the [g] daie of Ierusalém, which
said, Rase it, rase it to the fundacion
thereof.
8 O daughter of Babél, worthie to be destroied, blessed *shal he be* yͭ rewardeth thee,
as thou hast serued vs.
9 [h] Blessed *shal he be* that taketh & dasheth
thy children against the stones.

a That is, we abode a long time: & albeit yͭ the countrei was pleasant, yet colde it not staie our teares, nor turne vs frõ the true seruice of our God.
b To wit, of that countrey.
c The Babylonians spake thus in mocking vs, as thogh by our silence we shulde signifie that we hoped no more in God.
d Albeit the faithful are touched with their particular griefs, yet the cõmune sorowe of the Church is moste grieuous vnto them, & are suche as thei can not but remember and lament.
e The decaie of Gods religion ĩ their coũtrei was so grieuous, that no ioye colde make them glad, except it were restored.
f According as Ezekiel 25,13, & Ieremie 49, 7 vers. prophecied: & Abdias vers. 10 sheweth that the Edomites, wͨ came of Esau, cõspired with yͤ Babyloniãs against their brethren & kinsfolke.
g Whẽ thou didest visit Ierusalém.
h He alludeth to Isaies prophecie chap. 13, & 16. vers. promising good succes to Cyrus and Darius, whome ambition moued to fight against Babylón: but God vsed them as his rods to punish his enemies.

PSAL. CXXXVIII.

1 Dauid with great courage praiseth the goodnes of God toward him, the which is so great, 4 That it is knowen to forren princes, who shal praise the Lord together with him. 6 And he is assured to haue like comfort of God in the time following, as he hathe had heretofore.

¶ A Psalme *of Dauid*.

1 I Wil praise thee with my whole heart:
euen before the [a] gods wil I praise
thee.
2 I wil worship toward thine holie [b] Temple and praise thy Name, because of thy
louing kindenes and for thy trueth: for
thou hast magnified thy Name aboue all
things by thy worde.
3 When I called, then thou heardest me, &
hast [c] increased strength in my soule.
4 All the [d] Kings of the earth shal praise
thee, ô Lord: for they haue heard the wordes of thy mouth.
5 And thei shal sing of the waies of the
Lord, because the glorie of the Lord *is*
great.
6 For the Lord is high: yet he beholdeth
the lowely, but the proude he knoweth [e] a
farre of.
7 Thogh I walke in the middes of trouble,
yet wilt thou reuiue me: thou wilt stretch
forthe thine hand vpon the wrath of mine
enemies, and thy right hand shal saue me.
8 The Lord wil [f] performe *his worke*
toward me: ô Lord, thy mercie *endureth* for
euer: forsake not the workes of thine
hands.

a Euen in the presence of Angels & of thẽ, yͭ haue autoritie among mẽ.
b Bothe yͤ Tẽple & ceremonial seruice at Christs cõming were abolished: so that now God wil be worshiped onely in spirit and trueth.
c Thou hast strengthened me against mine outward & inward enemies.
d All yͤ worlde shal confesse yͭ thou hast wonderfully pserued me, & performed thy promes.
e Distance of place can not hinder God to shewe mercie to his, and to iudge the wicked, thogh thei thinke yͭ he is farre of.
f Thogh mine enemies rage neuer so much, yet the Lord, wͨ hathe begon his worke in me, wil cõtinue his grace to yͤ end.

PSAL. CXXXIX.

1 Dauid to cleanse his heart from all hypocrisie sheweth that there is nothing so hid, which God seeth not, 13 Which he confirmeth by the creation of man. 14 After declaring his zeale and feare of God, he protesteth to be enemie to all them that contemne God.

¶ *To him that excelleth. A Psalme of Dauid.*

1 O Lord, thou hast tryed me and knowē
me.
2 Thou knowest my [a] sitting & my rising:
thou vnderstandest my thoght a farre of.
3 Thou [b] compassest my paths, and my lying downe, and art accustomed to all my
waies.
4 For there is not a worde in my [c] tongue,
but lo, thou knowest it wholly, ô Lord.
5 Thou holdest me strait behinde and before, and laiest thine [d] hand vpon me.
6 *Thy* knowledge is to wonderful for me:
it is so high that I can not *atteine* vnto it.
7 Whether shal I go from thy [e] Spirit? or
whether shal I flee from thy presence?
8 If I ascend into heauen, thou art there: if
I lie downe in hel, thou art there.
9 Let me take the wings of the morning, &
dwell in the vttermost partes of the sea:
10 Yet thether shal thine [f] hand lead me, &
thy right hand holde me.
11 If I saie, Yet the darkenes shal hide me,
euen the night *shalbe* [g] light about me.
12 Yea, the darkenes hideth not from thee:
but the night shineth as the daie: ŷ darknes
and light are bothe alike.
13 For thou hast [h] possessed my reines: ŷ
hast couered me in my mothers wombe.
14 I wil praise thee, for I am [i] fearfully &
wonderously made: marueulous *are* thy
workes, and my soule knoweth it wel.
15 My bones are not hid from thee, thogh
I was made in a secret *place*, & facioned
[k] beneth in the earth.
16 Thine eyes did se me, when I was without forme: [l] for in thy boke were all things
writen, *which* in continuance were facioned, when there was none of them *before*.
17 How [m] dere therefore are thy thoghts vnto me, ô God! how great is ŷ summe of thē!
18 If I shulde counte them, thei are mo then
the sand: whē I wake, [n] I am stil with thee.
19 Oh that thou woldest slay, ô God, ŷ wicked and bloodie men, *to whome I saie*, Departe ye from me:
20 Which speake wickedly of thee, & beīg
thine enemies are lifted vp in vaine.
21 Do not I [o] hate them, ô Lord, that hate
thee? and do not I earnestly contend with
those that rise vp against thee?
22 I hate them with an vnfained hatred, as
they were mine *vtter* enemies.
23 Trye me, ô God, and knowe mine heart:
proue me and knowe my thoghts,
24 And consider if there be anie [p] waie of
wickednes in me, and lead me in the [q] waie
for euer.

a He cōfesseth ŷ nether our actiōs, thoghtes or anie parte of our life can be hid to God, thogh he seme to be farre of.
b So that thei are euidently knowē to thee.
c Thou knowest my meanig before I speake.
d Thou so guidest me with thine hand, ŷ I can turne no waie, but where thou appointest me.
e From thy power and knowledge?
f Thy power doeth so fast holde me, that I can escape by no meanes from thee.
g Thogh darkenes be an hinderance to mans sight, yet it serueth thine eyes as wel as the light.
h Thou hast made me in all partes & therfore must nedes knowe me.
i Considering thy wonderful worke in forming me, I can not but praise thee & feare thy mightie power.
k That is, in my mothers wōbe: ŵ he cōpareth to the inward partes of the earth.
l Seing that ŷ didest knowe me before I was composed of ether flesh or bone, much more now must ŷ knowe me when ŷ hast facioned me.
m How oght we to esteme ŷ excellēt declaration of thy wisdome in ŷ creaciō of mā?
n I cōtinually se newe occasiōs to meditate in thy wisdome and to praise thee.
o He teacheth vs boldely to contemne all the hatred of the wicked & friendship of ŷ worlde, whē thei wolde let vs to serue God syncerely.
p Or anie henous waie or rebellious: meaning, that thogh he were subiect to sinne: yet was he not giuen to wickednes and to prouoke God by rebellion.
q That is, continue thy fauour towards me to the end.

PSAL. CXL.

1 Dauid complaineth of the crueltie, falsehode & iniuries of his enemies. 8 Against the which he praieth vnto the Lord and assureth him self of his helpe and succour. 12 Wherefore he prouoketh the iust to praise the Lord, & to assure them selues of his tuition.

¶ *To him that excelleth. A psalme of Dauid.*

1 Deliuer me, ô Lord, from the euil man:
preserue me from the [a] cruel man:
2 Which imagine euil things in *their* [b] heart, & make warre continually.
3 Thei haue sharpened their tongues like a
serpent: [c] adders poyson *is* vnder their lippes. Sélah.
4 Kepe [d] me, ô Lord, from the hands of the
wicked: preserue me from the cruel man,
which purposeth to cause my steppes to
slide.
5 The proude haue laid a snare for me &
spred a net with cordes in my pathwaie, &
set grennes for me. Sélah.
6 *Therefore* I said vnto the Lord, Thou art
my God: heare, ô Lord, the voice of my
praiers.
7 O Lord God the strength of my saluacion, thou [e] hast couered mine head in the
daie of battel.
8 Let not ŷ wicked haue his desire, ô Lord:
[f] performe not his wicked thoght, *lest* thei
be proude. Sélah.
9 *As for* [g] the chief of them, that compasse
me about, let the mischief of their owne
lippes come vpon them.
10 Let coles fall vpon them: let [h] him cast
them into the fyre, & into the depe pittes,
that thei rise not.
11 *For* ŷ backebiters shal not be established
vpon the earth: euil shal [i] hunt the cruel
man to destruction.
12 I knowe that the Lord wil auenge the
afflicted, & iudge the poore.
13 Surely the righteous shal praise thy Name, & the iust shal [k] dwell in thy presence.

PSAL. CXLI.

1 Dauid being grieuously persecuted vnder Saúl, onely fleeth vnto God to haue succour, 3 Desiring him to bridle his affections, that he maie paciently abide til God take vengeance of his enemies.

¶ *A Psalme of Dauid.*

1 O Lord, I [a] call vpō thee: haste thee vnto me: heare my voyce, when I crye
vnto thee.
2 Let my praier be directed in thy sight *as*
incense, & the [b] lifting vp of mine hands
as an euening sacrifice.
3 Set a watche, ô Lord, before my mouth,
& kepe the [c] dore of my lippes.
4 Incline not mine heart to euil, that I
shulde commit wicked workes with men
that worke iniquitie: and let me not eat of
their [d] delicates.
5 Let the righteous smite me: *for that is* a benefite: & let [e] him reproue me, & *it shalbe* a
precious oyle, that shal not breake mine
head: for within a while I shal euen [f] praie
in their miseries.
6 When their iudges shalbe cast downe in

a Which persecuteth me of malice & without cause.
b That is, by their false cauillacions and lies thei kīdle ŷ hatred of the wicked agaīst me.
c He sheweth what weapons ŷ wicked vse, when power & force faile thē.
d He declareth what is ŷ remedie of the godlie, when thei are oppressed by the worldelings.
e He calleth to God with liuelie faith, being assured of his mercies, because he had before time prouen, that God helped him euer in his dangers.
f For it is in Gods hand to ouerthrowe ŷ counsels & enterprises of ŷ wicked.
g It semeth ŷ he alludeth to Saúl.
h To wit, God: for Dauid saw ŷ thei were reprobat & that there was no hope of repentance in thēm.
i Gods plagues shal light vpō him in suche sort, ŷ he shal not escape.
k That is, shalbe defended & preserued by thy Fatherlie prouidence & care.

Psal. CXLI.

a He sheweth ŷ there is none other refuge in ō necessities, but onely to flee vnto God for comfort of soule.
b He meaneth his earnest zeale & iesture, ŵ he vsed in praier: alluding to the sacrifices, which were by Gods commādement offred in ŷ olde Law.
c He desireth God to kepe his thoghts & waies ether from thinking or executing vengeance.
d Let not their prosperitie allure me to be wicked as thei are.
e He colde abide all corrections, that came of a louing heart.
f By pacience I shal se the wicked so sharpely handled, that I shal for pitie praie for them.

stonie places, thei shal [g] heare my wordes,
for thei are swete.
7 Our bones lie scattered at the [h] graues
mouth, as he that heweth *wood*, or diggeth
in the earth.
8 But mine eyes *loke* vnto thee, ô Lord God:
in thee is my trust: leaue not my soule destitute.
9 Kepe me from the snare, *which* thei haue
laied for me, and from the grennes of the
workers of iniquitie.
10 Let the wicked fall into [i] his nettes [k] together, whiles I escape.

g The people, which followed their wicked rulers in persecuting ẏ Prophet, shal repent & turne to God, when they se their wicked rulers punished.
h Here appeareth ẏ Dauid was miraculously deliuered out of manie deaths, as 2.Cor.1,9.
i Into Gods nettes, wherby he catcheth ẏ wicked I their owne malice.
k So that none of thē escape.

PSAL. CXLII.

1 The Prophet nether astonied with feare, nor caried awaie with angre, nor forced by desperation, wolde kil Saúl, but with a quiet minde directed his earnest praier to God, who did preserue him.

¶ A Psalme *of Dauid, to giue instruction*, & *a prayer, when he was in the caue.*

1 I Cryed vnto the Lord with my voyce:
with my voyce I [a] praied vnto ẏ Lord.
2 I powred out my meditacion before him,
& declared mine afflictiō in his presence.
3 Thogh my spirit "was in perplexitie in
me, yet thou knewest my path: in ẏ waie,
wherein I walked, haue thei priuely laied
a snare for me.
4 I loked vpon my right hand, & behelde,
but there was none that wolde knowe me:
all refuge failed me, & none "cared for my
soule.
5 *Then* cryed I vnto thee, ô Lord, & said,
Thou art mine [b] hope, & my porcion in ẏ
land of the liuing.
6 Hearken vnto my crye, for I am broght
verie lowe: deliuer me from my persecuters, for thei are to strong for me.
7 Bring my soule out of [c] prisō, that I maie
praise thy Name: *then* shal the righteous
[d] come about me, when thou art beneficial vnto me.

a Dauids pacience & instāt praier to God cōdēneth their wicked rage, which in their troubles ether despaire and murmur agaīst God, or els seke to others, thē to God, to haue redres in their miseries.
"*Ebr. Was foldē or wrapped in me: meaning, as a thing that colde haue none yssue.*
"*Or, soght for my soule.*
b Thogh all meanes failed him, yet he knewe ẏ God wolde neuer forsake him.
c For he was on all sides beset ẇ his enemies, as thogh he had bene in a most strait prison.
d Ether to reioyce at my wonderful deliuerance, or to set a crowne vpon mine head.

PSAL. CXLIII.

1 An earnest praier for remission of sinnes, acknowledging that the enemies did thus cruelly persecute him by Gods iust iudgement. 8 He desireth to be restored to grace, 10 To be gouerned by his holie Spirit, that he maie spende the remnant of his life in the true feare & seruice of God.

¶ *A Psalme of Dauid.*

1 Heare my praier, ô Lord, & hearken
vnto my supplicacion: answer me in
thy [a] trueth & in thy [b] righteousnes.
2 (And entre not into iudgement with thy
seruant: for in thy [c] sight shal none that liueth, be iustified)
3 For the enemie hathe persecuted my soule: he hathe smiten my life downe to the
earth: he hathe laied me in the darkenes,
as thei that haue bene dead [d] long ago:
4 And my spirit was in perplexitie in me,
& mine [e] heart within me was amased.

a That is, as ẏ hast promised to be faithful in thy promes to all that trust in thee.
b That is, according to thy fre goodnes, whereby thou defēdest thine.
c He knewe ẏ his afflictions were Gods messingers to call him to repentance for his sinnes, thogh toward his enemies he was innocent, & ẏ in Gods sight all men are sinners.
d He acknowledgeth that God is the onelie & true phisicion to heale him: & that he is able to raise him to life, thogh he were dead long ago, & turned to asshes.
e So that onely by faith, & by the grace of Gods Spirit he was vpholden.

5 *Yet* do I remember the time [f] past: I meditate in all thy workes, *yea*, I do meditate in
the workes of thine hands.
6 I stretche forthe mine hands vnto thee:
my soule desireth after thee, as the thirstie
land. Selah.
7 Heare me spedely, ô Lord, *for* my spirit
faileth: hide not thy face from me, els I
shalbe like vnto them that go downe into
the pit.
8 Let me heare thy louing kindenes in the
[g] morning, for in thee is my trust: [h] shewe
me the waie, that I shulde walke in, for
I lift vp my soule vnto thee.
9 Deliuer me, ô Lord, from mine enemies:
for [i] I hid me with thee.
10 Teache me to [k] do thy wil, for thou art
my God: let thy good Spirit lead me vnto
the land of [l] righteousnes.
11 Quicken me, ô Lord, for thy Names
sake, & for thy righteousnes bring my
soule out of trouble.
12 And for thy mercie [m] slay mine enemies,
and destroie all them that oppresse my
soule: for I am thy [n] seruant.

f To wit, thy great benefites of olde, & the manifolde examples of thy fauour toward thine.
g That is, spedely & in due season.
h Let thine holie Spirit counsel me how to come forthe of these great cares & troubles
i I hid my self vnder the shadow of thy wīgs, ẏ I might be defēded by thy power
k He cōfesseth that bothe the knowledge & obedience of Gods wil commeth by ẏ Spirit of God, who teacheth vs by his worde, giueth vnderstāding by his Spirit, & frameth our hearts by his grace to obey him.
l That is, iustly & aright. for so sone as we decline from Gods wil, we fall into errour
m Which shal be a signe of thy Fatherlie kindenes toward me.
n Resigning my selfe wholly vnto thee, and trusting in thy protection.

PSAL. CXLIIII.

1 He praiseth the Lord with great affection and humilitie for his kingdome restored, and for his victories obteined, 5 Demanding helpe and the destruction of the wicked. 9 Promising to acknowledge the same with songs of praises, 15 And declareth wherein the felicitie of anie people consisteth.

¶ A Psalme *of Dauid.*

1 Blessed *be* the Lord my strength, ẇ
[a] teacheth mine hands to fight, & my
fingers to battel.
2 *He is* my goodnes & my fortres, my tower
& "my deliuerer, my shield, and in him I
trust, which subdueth my [b] people vnder
me.
3 Lord, what is man that thou [c] regardest
him! *or* the sonne of man that thou thinkest vpon him!
4 Man is like to vanitie: his daies *are* like a
shadowe, that vanisheth.
5 [d] Bowe thine heauens, ô Lord, and come
downe: touche the mountaines & thei shal
smoke.
6 [e] Cast forthe the lightening and scatter
them: shote out thine arrowes, and consume them.
7 Send thine hand from aboue: deliuer me,
and take me out of the great [f] waters, *and*
from the hand of strangers,
8 Whose mouth talketh vanitie, and their
right hand *is* a right hand [g] of falsehode.
9 I wil sing a [h] newe song vnto thee, ô God,
& sing vnto thee vpon a viole, & an instrument of ten strings.
10 *It is he* that giueth deliuerance vnto

Psal. CXLIIII
a Who of a poore shepherd hathe made me a valiant warriour and mightie conquerour.
"*Ebr. my deliuerer vnto me: for the Prophet can not satisfie him self with any wordes.*
b He cōfesseth that nether by his owne autoritie, power nor policie his kīgdome was quiet, but by the secret grace of God.
c To giue vnto God iust praise is to confesse our selues to be vnworthie of so excellent benefites, & ẏ he bestoweth them vpon vs of his fre mercie.
d He desireth God to continue his graces & to send helpe for the presēt necessitie.
e By these maner of speaches he sheweth that all the lettes in the worlde can not hinder Gods power, which he apprehended by faith.
f That is, deliuer me from ẏ tumultes of them that shulde be my people, but are corrupt in their iudgemēt & enterprises, as thogh thei were strangers.
g For thogh thei shake hands, yet thei kepe not promes.
h That is, a rare & excellent song, as thy great benefites deserue.

Kings,& rescueth Dauid his [i] seruãt frõ
the hurtful sworde.
11 Rescue me, and deliuer me from the hãd
of strangers, whose mouth talketh vanitie,
and their right hand *is* a right hand of falsehode:
12 That our [k] sonnes *maye be* as the plantes growing vp in their youth, & our daughters as the corner *stones*, grauen after the
similitude of a palace:
13 That our [l] corners *may be* ful, *and* abunding with diuers sortes, *and* that our shepe
may bring forthe thousands and tẽ thousand in our stretes:
14 That our [m] oxen may be strong to labour: that their be none inuasiõ, nor going
out, nor no crying in our stretes.
15 Blessed *are* the people, that be [n] so, *yea*,
blessed *are* the people, whose God is the
Lord.

i Thogh wicked Kings be called Gods seruãts, as Cyrus, Isa. 45,1, forasmuche as he vseth thẽ to execute his iudgements: yet Dauid because of Gods prmes, and they, that rule godly, are pperly so called, because they serue not their owne affections, but set forthe Gods glorie.
k He desireth God to continue his benefites toward his people, counting the procreaciõ of children and their good educatiõ among ye chiefest of Gods benefites.
l That the verie corners of our houses may be ful of store for the great abundance of thy blessings. m He attributeth not onely the great commodities, but euen the least also to Gods fauour. n And if God giue not to all his children all these blessings, yet he recompenseth them with better things.

PSAL. CXLV.

This Psalme was composed, when the kingdome of Dauid florished. 1 Wherein he describeth the wonderful prouidence of God, aswel in gouerning man, as in preseruing all the rest of his creatures. 17 He praiseth God for his iustice & mercie, 18 But specially for his louing kindenes toward those that call vpon him, that feare him, and loue him: 21 For the which he promiseth to praise him for euer.

¶ A Psalme of Dauid, of praise.

1 O My God *and* King, [a] I wil extoll
thee, and wil blesse thy Name for e-
uer and euer.
2 I wil blesse thee daily, and praise thy Name for euer and euer.
3 [b] Great *is* the Lord, & moste worthie to
be praised, and his greatnes *is* incomprehensible.
4 Generacion shal praise thy workes vnto
[c] generacion, and declare thy power.
5 I wil meditate of the beautie of thy glorious maiestie, & thy wonderful workes,
6 And they shal speake of the power of thy
[d] feareful Actes, and I wil declare thy
greatnes.
7 They shal breake out into the mencion
of thy great goodnes, & shal sing aloude
of thy righteousnes.
8 *The Lord is gracious and [e] merciful,
slowe to angre, and of great mercie.
9 The Lord is good to all, & his mercies
are ouer all his workes.
10 All thy workes praise thee, ô Lord, and
thy Saints blesse thee.
11 [f] They shewe the glorie of thy kingdome and speake of thy power,
12 To cause his [g] power to be knowen to
the sonnes of men, & the glorious renome
of his kingdome.
13 Thy * kingdome *is* an euerlasting kingdome, & thy dominion *endureth* throughout all ages.
14 The Lord vpholdeth all [h] that fall, and
lifteth vp all that are readie to fall.
15 The eyes of [i] all waite vpon thee, and
thou giuest them their meat in due season.
16 Thou openest thine hand, and fillest all
things liuing of *thy* good pleasure.
17 The Lord *is* [k] righteous in all his waies,
and holie in all his workes.
18 The Lord *is* nere vnto all that call vpon
him: *yea*, to all that call vpon him in
[l] trueth.
19 He wil fulfil the [m] desire of them that
feare him: he also wil heare their crye, &
wil saue them.
20 The Lord preserueth all them that loue
him: but he wil destroye all the wicked.
21 My mouth shal speake the praise of the
Lord, and all [n] flesh shal blesse his holie
Name for euer and euer.

a He sheweth what sacrifices are pleasant & acceptable vnto God: euen praise & thãkesgiuing, and seing that God stil cõtinueth his benefites towards vs, we oght neuer to be wearie in praising him for the same.
b Herby he declareth ye all power is subiect vnto God, & ye no worldlie promotion oght to obscure Gods glorie.
c Forasmuche as the end of mans creation, & of his preseruatiõ ĩ this life is to praise God, therefore he requireth, ye not onely we our selues do this, but cause all other to do the same.
d Of thy terrible iudgemẽts against the wicked.
Exod. 34,6.
e He describeth after what sorte God sheweth him self to all his creatures, thogh our sinnes haue prouoked his vengeance against all: to wit, merciful, not onely in pardoning the sinnes of his elect, but in doing good euen to the reprobate, albeit they cã not fele the swete comfort of the same. f The praise of thy glorie appeareth in all thy creatures: & thogh ye wicked wolde obscure ye same by their silẽce, yet ye faithful are euer mindeful of the same.
g He sheweth ye all thĩgs are out of ordre, but onely where God reigneth.
Luk. 1,33. dan. 7,14.
h Who being in miserie and afflictiõ wolde fainte and fall away, if God did not vpholde them, and therefore they oght to reuerence him, that reigneth in heauen, and suffer them selues to be gouerned by him.
i To wit, aswel of man, as of beast.
k He praiseth God, not onely for that he is beneficial to all his creatures, but also in that that he iustly punisheth ye wicked, & mercifully examineth his by the crosse, giuing them strength & deliuering them. l Which onely apperteineth to the faithful: and this vertue is contrarie to infidelitie, douting, impaciencie and murmuring.
m For they wil aske or wish for nothing, but according to his wil, 1. Ioh 5, 14. n That is, all men shalbe bounde to praise him.

PSAL. CXLVI.

1 Dauid declareth his great zeale that he hathe to praise God, 3 And teacheth, not to trust in man, but onely in God almightie. 7 Which deliuereth the afflicted, 9 Defendeth the strangers, comforteth the fatherles, and the widowes, 10 And reigneth for euer.

¶ Praise ye the Lord.

1 PRaise thou the Lord, ô my [a] soule.
2 I wil praise the Lord during my life: as long as I haue anie being, I wil sing
vnto my God.
3 Put not your trust in [b] princes, *nor* in the
sonne of mã, for there is none helpe in hĩ.
4 His breath departeth, & he returneth to
his earth: then his [c] thoghts perish.
5 Blessed *is* he, that hathe the God of Iaakób for his helpe, whose hope *is* in ye Lord
his God.
6 Which made [d] heauen & earth, the sea,
and all that therein is: which kepeth *his* fidelitie for euer:
7 Which executeth iustice [e] for the oppressed: which giueth bread to the hũgrie:
the Lord looseth the prisoners.
8 The Lord giueth sight to the blinde: the
Lord raiseth vp the croked: the Lord
[f] loueth the righteous.
9 The Lord kepeth the [g] strangers: he re-
lieueth the fatherles and widowe: but he
ouerthroweth the way of the wicked.

a He stirreth vp him self, & all his affectiõs to praise God.
b That God may haue the whole praise. wherin he forbiddeth all vaine cõfidẽce, shewing ye of nature we are more enclined to put our trust in creatures, then in God ye Creator.
c As their vaine opinions, whereby they flattered them selues, and so imagined wicked entreprises.
d He encourageth ye godlie to trust onely in the Lord, bothe for that his power is able to deliuer them from all danger, & for his promes sake his wil is moste readie to do it.
e Whose faith & paciẽce for a while he tryeth, but at length he punisheth ye aduersaries, that he may be knowen to be iudge of the worlde. f Thogh he visit them by affliction, hungre, imprisonment and suche like, yet his Fatherlie loue and pitie neuer faileth them, yea, rather to his these are signes of his loue.
g Meaning all them, that are destitute of worldelie meanes and succour.

10 The Lord shal [h] reigne for euer: ô
Zión, thy God *endureth* from generacion
to generacion. Praise ye the Lord.

h He assureth the Church ÿ God reigneth for euer for ÿ preseruatiō of the same.

PSAL. CXLVII.

1 The Prophet praiseth the bountie, wisdome, power, iustice & prouidence of God vpō all his creatures. 2 But specially vpon his Church, which he gathereth together after their dispersion. 19 Declaring his worde and iudgements so vnto them, as he hathe done to none other people.

1 PRaise ye the Lord, for it is good to sing
vnto our God: for it is [a] a pleasant
thing, & praise is comelie.
2 The Lord doeth buyld vp [b] Ierusalém,
& gather together the dispersed of Israél.
3 He healeth those that are [c] broken in heart, and bindeth vp their sores.
4 He [d] counteth the nomber of the starres,
& calleth them all by their names.
5 Great *is* our Lord, and great *is his* power:
his wisdome is infinite.
6 The Lord releueth the meke, & abaseth
the wicked to the [e] grounde.
7 Sing vnto the Lord with praise: sing vpō
the harpe vnto our God,
8 Which [f] couereth the heauē with cloudes and prepareth raine for the earth, and
maketh the grasse to growe vpon the mountaines:
9 Which giueth to beastes their fode, *and*
to the yong rauens that [g] crye.
10 He hathe not pleasure in the [h] strength
of an horse, nether deliteth he in the legges of man.
11 *But* the Lord deliteth in them that feare
him, and attend vpon his mercie.
12 Praise the Lord, ô Ierusalém: praise thy
God, ô Zión.
13 For he hathe made the barres of thy gates [i] strong, *and* hathe blessed thy childrē
within thee.
14 He setteth peace in thy borders, & satisfieth thee with the " floure of wheat.
15 He sendeth forthe his [k] commandemēt
vpon earth, *and* his worde runneth verie
[l] swiftly.
16 He giueth snow like wool, & scattereth
the hoare frost like asshes.
17 He casteth forthe his yce like morsels:
who can abide the colde thereof?
18 He sendeth his worde and melteth thē:
he causeth his winde to blowe, & the waters flowe.
19 He sheweth his [m] worde vnto Iaakób,
his statutes and his iudgements vnto
Israél.
20 He hathe not dealt so with euerie nacion,
nether haue they [n] knowen *his* iudgemēts.

a He sheweth wherI we oght to exercise our selues continually, & to take our pastime: to wit, in praising God. b Because the Lord is ÿ foūder of ÿ Church, it can not be destroyed, thogh ÿ members thereof be dispersed, and seme, as it were, for a time to be cut of. c With affliction or sorow for sinne. d Thogh it seme to man incredible, that God shulde assemble his Church, being so dispersed, yet nothing cā be to hard to him, that can nōber & name all the starres. e For the more high that the wicked clime, the greater is their fall in the end. f He sheweth by the exāples of Gods mightie power, goodnes & wisdome, that we cā neuer wāt moste iust occasiō to praise God. g For their crying is as it were a confession of their nede, which cā not be relieued but by God onely: then if God shew himself mindeful of ÿ moste cōtēptible foules, can he suffer them to dye ŵ famine, whome he hathe assured of life euerlasting? h Thogh to vse lawful meanes is bothe ꝓfitable & pleaseth God, yet to put our trust in them, is to defraude God of his honour. i He doeth not onely furnish his Church ŵ all things necessarie, but preserueth also the same, & maketh it strong against all outward force. " *Ebr. fat.* k His secret working in all creatures is as a cōmandemēt to kepe thē in ordre, & to giue thē mouing & force. l For immediatly & without resisting all things obei him. m As before he called Gods secret working in all his creatures his word: so he meaneth here, by his worde, ÿ doctrine of life euerlasting, ŵ he hathe left to his Church, as a moste precious treasure. n The cause of this difference is Gods fre mercie, which hathe elected his in his Sonne Christ Iesus to saluacion: & his iuste iudgemēt, whereby he hathe appointed the reprobate to eternal damnation.

Praise ye the Lord.

PSAL. CXLVIII.

1 He prouoketh all creatures to praise the Lord in heauē and earth and all places. 14 Specially his Church for the power that he hathe giuen to the same after that he had chosen them and ioyned them vnto him.

¶ *Praise ye the Lord.*

1 PRaise ye the Lord from the heauen:
praise ye him in the high places.
2 Praise ye him, all ye [a] his Angels: praise
him, all his armie.
3 Praise ye him, [b] sunne and moone: praise
ye him all bright starres.
4 Praise ye him, [c] heauens of heauens, &
[d] waters, that be aboue the heauens.
5 Let them praise the Name of the Lord:
for he cōmāded, and they were created.
6 And he hathe established them for euer
and euer: he hathe made an ordinance,
which shal not passe.
7 Praise ye the Lord frō the earth, *ye* [e] dragons and all depths:
8 [f] Fyre and haile, snowe and vapors, stormie winde, which execute his worde:
9 Mountaines and all hilles, fruteful trees
and all cedres:
10 Beastes and all cattel, creaping things &
feathered foules:
11 [g] Kings of the earth and all people, princes and all iudges of the worlde:
12 Yong men and maidens, also olde men
and children:
13 Let them praise the Name of the Lord:
for his Name onely is to be exalted, *and*
his praise aboue the earth and the heauēs.
14 For he hathe exalted the [h] horne of his
people, *which is* a praise for all his Sainctes,
euen for the [i] children of Israél, a people
that is nere vnto him. Praise ye the Lord.

a Because thei are mēbers of ÿ same bodie, he setteth thē before our eyes, ŵ are moste willīg herunto, and by their prompt obedience teache vs to do our duetie. b In that Gods glorie shineth in these insensible creatures, this their beautie is as a cōtinual praising of God. c Not ÿ there are diuers heauens, but because of the spheres and of the situacion of the fixed starres & planets, he cōprehendeth by this worde ÿ whole heauē. d That is, the raine, which is in the midle regiōn of the aire, which he here comprendeth vnder the name of the heauens. e Meaning, ÿ great and mōstruous fishes, as whales and suche like. f Which come not by chance or fortune, but by Gods appointed ordinance. g For the greater giftes that anie hathe receiued, and the more high that one his preferred, the more bound is he to praise God for the same, but nether high nor lowe condition or degre can be exempted from this duetie. h That is, thē dignitie, power and glorie of his Church. i By reason of his couenant made with Abrahám.

PSAL. CXLIX.

1 An exhortation to the Church to praise the Lord for his victorie and conquest that he giueth his Saints against all mans power.

¶ *Praise ye the Lord.*

1 SIng ye vnto the Lord [a] a new song: let
his praise *be heard* in the Congregacion
of Saints.
2 Let Israél reioyce in him that [b] made
him, and let the children of Zión reioyce
in their [c] King.
3 Let them praise his Name with the flute:
let them sing praises vnto him with the
timbrel and harpe.
4 For the Lord hathe pleasure in his people: he wil make the meke glorious by deliuerance.
5 Let the Saints be ioyful with glorie: let
them sing loude vpon their [d] beddes.

a For his rare and manifolde benefites bestowed on his Church. b In that that they were preferred before all other nacions, it was as a newe creaciō, & therefore Psal 95,6. thei were called the worke of Gods hāds. c For God as he is the Creator of ÿ soule & bodie so wil he ÿ both two serue him, & ÿ his people be continually subiect vnto him as to their moste lawful King. d He alludeth to that continual rest, and quietnes, which they shulde haue, if they wolde suffre God to rule them.

6 Let the high Actes of God be in their
mouth, and a two edged sworde in their
hands,
7 [e] To execute vengeance vpon the heathen,& corrections among the people:
8 To binde [f] their Kings in chaines, and
their nobles with fetters of yron,
9 That they maye execute vpon them the
iudgement that is [g] writen: this honour
shalbe to all his Saints. Praise ye the Lord.

e This is chiefly accomplished in the kingdome of Christ, when Gods people for iuste causes execute Gods iudgements against his enemies: & it giueth no libertie to anie to reuenge their priuate iniuries. f Not onely the people, but the Kings, that were their enemies, shulde be destroyed g Hereby God bindeth the hands and mindes of all his to enterprise no farther then he appointeth.

PSAL. CL.

1 *An exhortacion to praise the Lord without cease by all maner of wayes for all his mightie, and wonderful workes.*

¶ *Praise ye the Lord*

1 PRaise ye God in his [a] Sanctuarie:
praise ye him in the [b] firmament of
his power.
2 Praise ye him in his mightie Actes: praise ye hĩ accordĩg to his excellẽt greatnes.
3 Praise ye him in the sounde of the [c] trũpet: praise ye him vpon the viole and the
harpe.
4 Praise ye him with timbrel & flute: praise ye him with virginales and organs.
5 Praise ye him with sounding cymbals:
praise ye him with high sõuding cymbals.
6 Let euerie thing that hathe [d] breath praise the Lord. Praise ye the Lord.

a That is, in ye heauen. b For his wõderful power appeareth in ye firmament, wc in Ebr. is called a stretchĩg out or spreading abroad, wherein the mightie worke of God shineth. c Exhorting ye people onely to reioyce in praising God, he maketh mẽcion of those instruments, wc by Gods cõmãdemẽt were appointed in the olde Law, but vnder Christ the vse thereof is abolished in the Church. d He sheweth that all the ordre of nature is bound to this duetie, and muche more Gods childrẽ, who oght neuer to cease to praise him, til they be gathered into that kingdome, which he hathe prepared for his, where they shal sing euerlasting praise.

THE *PROVERBES of Salomón.

*This worde Prouerbe, or Parable signifieth a graue & notable sentẽce, worthie to be kept in memorie: and is some time taken in the euil parte for a mocke, or scoffe.

THE ARGVMENT.

THe wonderful loue of God toward his Church is declared in this boke: forasmuche as the summe and effect of the whole Scriptures is here set forthe in these brief sentences, which partly conteine doctrine, and partely maners, and also exhortacions to bothe. Whereof the nine first chapters are as a preface ful of graue sentences, and depe mysteries, to allure the haerts of men to the diligent reading of the parables that follow: which are left as a moste precious iewel to the Churche, of those thre thousand parables mencioned 1. King. 4,32, and were gathered and commit to writing by Salomons seruants and indited by him.

CHAP. I.

1 *The power and vse of the worde of God 7 Of the feare of God and knowledge of his worde 10 We may not consent to the intisings of sinners 20 Wisdome complaineth that she is contemned. 24 The punishment of them that contemne her.*

1 THe Parables of Salomón
the sonne of Dauid King
of Israél,
2 To knowe wisdome, [a] &
instruction, to vnderstand
the wordes [b] of knowledge,
3 To receiue [c] instruction to do wisely, *by*
[d] iustice and iudgement and equitie,
4 To giue vnto the [e] simple sharpenes of
wit, & to the childe knowledge and discretion.
5 A wise man shal heare and increase in
learning, and a man of [f] vnderstanding,
shal atteine vnto wise counsels,
6 To vnderstand a parable, and the interpretation, the wordes of the wise, & their
darke sayings.
7 ¶ *The feare of ye Lord *is* ye beginnĩg of
knowledge: *but* fooles despise wisdome &
instruction.
8 My sonne, heare thy [g] fathers instruction,
and forsake not thy [h] mothers teaching.
9 For thei shalbe "a comelie ornament vnto
thine head, and *as* chaines for thy necke.
10 ¶ My sonne, [i] if sinners do intise thee,
consent thou not.
11 If they say, Come with vs, we wil lay
wait for [k] blood, & lie priuelie for the innocent without a cause:
12 We wil swallowe thẽ vp aliue like a [l] gra
ue euen whole, as those that go downe
into the pit:
13 We shal finde all precious riches, & fil
our houses with spoile:
14 Cast in thy lot among vs: we wil all haue
one [m] purse:
15 My sonne, walke not thou in the way
with them: refraine thy fote from their
[n] path.
16 For their fete runne to euil, & make hast
to shed blood.
17 Certeinly *as* without cause the net is
spred before ye eyes of all that hathe wing:
18 So they laye wait for blood & lie priuelie for [o] their liues.

a That is, what we oght to knowe & followe, & what we oght to refuse. b Meaning the worde of God wherein is the onelie true knowledge. c To learne to submit our selues to the correction of those that are wise. d By liuing iustely and rendring to euery man that wc apperteineth vnto him. e To suche as haue not discrecion to rule them selues f As he sheweth ye these parables conteining the effect of religion as touching maners & doctrine do apperteine to the simple peple, so doeth he declare that the same is also necessarie for them that are wise and learned. *Psal. 111,10. eccl. 1,16.

g He speaketh this in ye Name of God, wc is the vniuersal Father of all creatures, or in the Name of the pastor of ye Churche, who is as a father h That is, of ye Church, wherein the faithful are begotten by the incorruptible sede of Gods worde. "Ebr. increase of grace. i To wit, the wicked, which haue not the feare of God. k He speaketh not onely of ye sheding of blood with hand, but of all craftie practises which tẽde to the detriment of our neighbour. l As the graue is neuer satiat so the auarice of the wicked and their crueltie hathe none end. m He sheweth whereby the wicked are allured to ioyne together, because they haue euerie one parte of the spoile of the innocent n That is, haue nothing at all to do with them o He sheweth that there is no cause to moue these wicked to spoile the innocent, but their auarice and crueltie.

19 Suche *are* the wayes of euerie one that
is gredie of gaine: he wolde take away the
p life of the owners thereof.
20 ¶ q Wisdome cryeth without: she vttereth her voyce in the r stretes.
21 She calleth in the hye *strete among* the
prease in the entrings of the gates, & vttereth her wordes in the citie, *saying*,
22 O ye s foolish, how long wil ye loue foolishnes? & the skorneful take their pleasure in skorning, & the fooles hate knowledge?
23 (Turne you at my correction: lo, I wil
powre out my minde vnto you, & make
you vnderstand my wordes)
24 Because I haue called, and ye refused: I
haue stretched out mine hand, and none
wolde regarde.
25 But ye haue despised all my counsel, &
wolde none of my correction.
26 I wil also t laugh at your destruction,
and mocke, when your feare cometh.
27 When u your feare cometh like *sudden*
desolation, and your destruction shal come, like a whirle winde: when affliction &
anguish shal come vpon you,
28 Then shal they call vpon me, but I wil
not answer: they shal seke me early, but
they shal not x finde me,
29 Because they hated knowledge, and did
not chuse the feare of the Lord.
30 Thei wolde none of my cousel, *but* y despised all my correction.
31 Therefore shal they eat of the z frute of
their owne way, and be filled with their
owne deuises.
32 For a ease slayeth the foolish, and the
prosperitie of fooles destroyeth them.
33 But he that obeieth me, shal dwell safely,
& be quiet from feare of euil.

p Whereby he concludeth ẏ the couetous man is a murtherer.
q This wisdome is the eternal worde of God.
r So that none can pretend ignorance.
s Wisdome reproueth thre kindes of mē: the foolish or simple, which erre of ignorāce, and ẏ mockers, that can not suffer to be taught, & ẏ fooles which are drowned in worldelie lustes, & hate the knowledge of godlines.
t This is spoken according to our capacitie, signifying that the wicked, ẇ mocke & iest at Gods worde, shal haue the iuste rewarde of their mocking.
u That is, your destruction, ẇ thing you feared.
x Because thei soght not with an affection to God, but for ease of their owne grief.
y Shewing ẏ without faith and obedience we cā not call vpon God aright.
z They shal feele what cōmoditie their wicked life shal giue thē.
a That is, the prosperitie, & sensualitie, wherein they delite.

CHAP. II.

1 Wisdome exhorteth to obey her. 5 She teacheth the feare of God. 6 She is giuen of God. 10 She preserueth from wickednes.

1 MY sonne, if thou wilt receiue my wordes, and a hide my commandements
within thee,
2 And cause thine eares to hearken vnto
wisdome, & encline b thine heart to vnderstanding,
3 (For if thou callest after knowledge, c &
cryest for vnderstanding:
4 If thou sekest her as siluer, and searchest
for her as for d treasures,
5 Then shalt thou vnderstand the feare of
the Lord, and finde the e knowledge of
God.
6 For the Lord giueth wisdome, out of his
mouth *commeth* knowledge and vnderstanding.
7 He * preserueth the state of ẏ righteous:
he is a shield to them that walke vprightly,
8 That they may kepe the wayes of iudgement: and he preserueth the way of his
Saincts)
9 Then shalt thou vnderstand righteousnes, and iudgement, and equitie, & euerie
good path.
10 ¶ Whē wisdome entreth into thine heart,
and knowledge deliteth thy soule,
11 *Then* shal f counsel preserue thee, & vnderstanding shal kepe thee,
12 And deliuer thee from the euil way, *and*
from the man that speaketh froward
things,
13 *And from* them that leaue the g waies of
righteousnes to walke in the waies of darkenes:
14 Which reioyce in doing euil, & delite
h in the frowardnes of the wicked,
15 Whose waies are croked and they are
lewde in their paths.
16 And it shal deliuer thee from the strange i woman, *euen* from the stranger, which
flattereth with her wordes.
17 Which forsaketh the k guide of her
youth, and forgetteth the l couenant of
her God.
18 Surely her m house tendeth to death, &
her paths vnto n the dead.
19 All thei that go vnto her, returne not a-
gaine, nether take they holde of the waies
of life.
20 Therefore walke thou in the waie of
good men, & kepe the waies of the righteous.
21 For the iust shal dwell in the o land, and
the vpright men shal remaine in it.
22 But the wicked shalbe cut of from the
earth and the transgressers shalbe rooted
out of it.

a That is, kepe them in thine heart.
b If thou giue thy self to the true knowledge of God without hypocrisie.
c Meaning, ẏ we must seke the knowledge of God with care and diligence.
d Shewing ẏ no labour muste be spared.
e This (sayth he) is the true wisdome to knowe, & feare God.
* Or, hideth the saluation.
f The worde of God shal teache thee & counsel thee how to gouerne thy self.
g That is, the worde of God, ẇ is the onelie light, to followe their owne fantasies ẇ are darkenes.
h Whē thei se anie giuen to euil as thei are.
i Meanīg, that wisdome, ẇ is the worde of God, shal preserue vs from all vices: naming this vice of whoredome whereū to mā is moste prone.
k That is, her housband, ẇ is her head & guide to gouerne her, frō whome she oght not to depart, but remaine in his subiection.
l Which is, the promes made in mariage.
m Her acquaītance ẇ her familiars & thē that haunte her.
n To thē that are dead in bodie and soule.
o They shal ēioye the tēporal & spiritual promises of God, as ẏ wicked shalbe voyde of them.

CHAP. III.

1 The worde of God giueth life. 5 Trust in God. 7 Feare him. 9 Honour him. 11 Suffre his correction. 22 To them that followe the worde of God, all things shal succede wel.

1 MY sonne, forget not thou my Law,
but let thine heart kepe my commādements.
2 For thei shal increase the length of thy
a daies and the yers of life, and *thy* prosperitie.
3 Let not b mercie and trueth forsake thee:
binde them on thy c necke, & write them
vpon the table of thine d heart.
4 So shalt thou finde fauour and good vnderstanding in the sight of God and
man.
5 ¶ Trust in the Lord with all thine heart,
and leane not vnto thine owne wisdome.
6 In all thy waies acknowledge him, and
he shal direct thy waies.
7 ¶ Be not wise in thine owne eyes: *but* feare
the Lord, and departe from euil.
8 *So* health shalbe vnto thy e nauel, and
marow

Deut. 8,1. & 30,16.
a Lōg life is ẏ blessig of God ẇ he giueth to his, so farre forthe as it is expedient for them.
b By mercie & trueth, he meaneth the commandements of the first & secōd table: or els the mercie & faithfulnes ẏ we oght to vse towarde our neighbours.
c Kepe thē as a moste precious iewel.
d Haue them euer in remembrance.
e By this parte he comprehēdeth the whole bodie, as by health he meaneth all the benefites promised in the Law both corporal and spiritual.

marow vnto thy bones.
9 [f] Honour the Lord with thy riches, and
with the first *frutes* of all thine increase.
10 So shal thy barnes be filled with abundance, and thy presses shal [g] burst with
newe wine.
11 ¶ My sonne, refuse not the chastening
of ẏ Lord, nether be grieued with his correction.
12 *For ẏ Lord correcteth him, whome he
loueth, euē as the father *doeth* the childe in
whome he deliteth.
13 Blessed *is* the man that findeth wisdome,
and the man that getteth vnderstanding.
14 For the marchandise thereof is better
then the marchandise of siluer, and the
gaine thereof *is better* then golde.
15 It is more precious then pearls: and all
things that thou canst desire, are not to be
compared vnto her.
16 Length of daies *is* in her right hand, [h] &
in her left hand riches and glorie.
17 Her waies *are* waies of pleasure, and all
her paths prosperitie.
18 She is a tre [i] of life to them that laie holde on her, and blessed *is* he that reteineth
her.
19 The Lord by wisdome hathe laied the
[k] fundacion of the earth, and hathe stablished the heauens through vnderstanding.
20 By his knowledge the deapths are broken vp, and the cloudes droppe downe the
dewe.
21 My sonne, let not *these things* departe frō
thine eies, *but* obserue wisdome, and counsel.
22 So thei shalbe life to thy soule, and grace vnto thy *necke.
23 Thē shalt thou walke safely by thy waie:
and thy fote shal not stumble.
24 If ẏ sleapest, thou shalt not be afraied,
and when thou slepest, thy slepe shalbe
swete.
25 Thou shalt not feare for *anie* suddē feare, nether for the [l] destruction of the wicked, when it cometh.
26 For the Lord shal be for thine assurance,
& shal preserue thy fote from taking.
27 ¶ Withholde not the good from [m] the
owners thereof, thogh there be power
in thine hand to do it.
28 Saie not vnto thy neighbour, Go & come
againe, and to morowe wil I giue *thee*, if
thou *now* haue it.
29 ¶ Intēde none hurt agaīst thy neighbour,
seing he doeth dwell [n] without feare by
thee.
30 ¶ Striue not with a man causeles, when
he hathe done thee no harme.
31 ¶ Be not [o] enuious for the wicked man,
nether chuse anie of his waies.

[f] As was commanded in the lawe, Exod. 23, 19. deut. 26, 2. & by this thei acknowledged that God was the giuer of all things, and that thei were ready to bestowe all at his cōmandement.
[g] For to the faithful distributer God giueth in greater abundance.
Ebr. 12, 5.
Reuel. 3, 17.
[h] Meaning, ẏ he that seketh wisdome: that is, suffreth him self to be gouerned by the worde of God, shal haue all ꝓsperitie both corporal and spiritual.
[i] Which bringeth forthe suche frute ẏ thei that eat thereof, haue life: and he alludeth to the tre of life in Paradise.
[k] Hereby he sheweth ẏ this wisdome, whereof he speaketh, is euerlasting, because it was before all creatures, & ẏ all thīgs, euen the whole worlde were made by it.
*Or, throte, read chap. 1, 9.
[l] For whē God destroieth the wicked, he wil saue his, as he did Lot in Sodom
[m] Not onely from them to whome ẏ possession belongeth, but also thou shalt not kepe it from them, ẇ haue nede of the vse thereof.
[n] That is, putteth his trust in thee.
[o] Desire not to be like vnto him.

32 For the froward *is* abominacion vnto
the Lord: but his [p] secret *is* with the righteous.
33 The curse of the Lord *is* in the house
of the wicked: but he blesseth the habitation of the righteous.
34 With the skorneful [q] he skorneth, but
he giueth grace vnto the humble.
35 The wise shal inherite glorie: but fooles
dishonour, *thogh* they be exalted.

CHAP. IIII.

1 *Wisdome and her frutes oght to be searched.* 14 *The way of the wicked must be refused.* 20 *By the worde of God the heart, eyes and course of life must be guided.*

1 Heare, ô ye children, the instruction
of a [a] father, and giue eare to learne
vnderstanding.
2 For I do giue you a good doctrine: *therefore* forsake ye not my law.
3 For I was my fathers sonne, tender and
[b] dere in the sight of my mother,
4 When he [c] taught me, and said vnto me,
Let thine heart holde fast my wordes: kepe my commandements, and thou shalt
liue.
5 Get wisdome: get vnderstanding: forget
not, nether decline from the wordes of my
mouth.
6 Forsake her not, and she shal kepe thee:
loue her and she shal preserue thee.
7 [d] Wisdome *is* the beginning: get wisdome
therefore: and aboue all thy possession get
vnderstanding.
8 Exalt her, and she shal exalt thee: she
shal bring thee to honour, if thou embrace
her.
9 She shal giue a comelie ornament vnto
thine head, *yea*, she shal giue thee a crowne
of glorie.
10 ¶ Heare my sonne, and receiue my wordes, and the yeres of thy life shalbe manie.
11 I haue [e] taught thee in the waie of wisdome, *and* led thee in the paths of righteousnes.
12 When thou goest, thy gate shal not be
[f] strait, and when thou runnest, thou shalt
not fall.
13 Take holde of instruction, & leaue not:
kepe her, for she is thy life.
14 ¶ Entre not into the way of the wicked, &
walke not in the waie of euil men.
15 Auoide it & go not by it: turne from it,
& passe by.
16 For thei can not [g] slepe, except thei haue
done euil, and their slepe departeth, except
thei cause *some* to fall.
17 For they eat the bread of [h] wickednes,
and drinke the wine of violence.
18 But the way of ẏ righteous shineth as the
light, that [i] shineth more and more vn-

[p] That is, his couenant & fatherlie affectiō ẇ is hid & secret from the worlde.
[q] He wil shewe by his plagues that their skornes shal turne to their owne destruction, as Chap. 1, 26.
[a] He speaketh this in the persone of a preacher & minister, ẇ is as a father vnto ẏ people, read Chap 1, 8.
[b] In Ebrewe it is Onely: for thogh she had thre others by Vriiáh, yet Salomón was onely her sonne by Dauid.
[c] Meaning Dauid his father.
[d] He sheweth that we must first begin at Gods worde, if so be we wil ẏ other things prosper with vs. cōtrarie to the iudgement of the worlde, which make it their last study or els, care not for it at all.
[e] Salomón declareth what care his father had to bring him vp in the true feare of God: for this was Dauids protestation
[f] Thou shalt walke at libertie without offence.
[g] Meaning, that to do euil is more propre & natural to the wicked, then to slepe, eat or drinke.
[h] Gotten by wicked meanes and cruel oppression.
[i] Signifying ẏ the godlie increase dayly in knowledge & perfection, til thei come to ful perfection, ẇ is whē thei shalbe ioyned to their head in the heauens.

to the perfite daie.
19 The waie of the wicked *is* as the darkenes: they knowe not wherein thei shal
fall.
20 ¶ My sonne, harkē vnto my wordes, encline thine eare vnto my sayings.
21 Let them not departe from thine eyes,
but kepe them in the middes of thine
heart.
22 For thei are life vnto those that finde
them, and helthe vnto all their [k] flesh.
23 Kepe thine heart with all diligence: for
thereout cometh [l] life.
24 Put awaie from thee a frowarde mouth,
and put wicked lippes farre from thee.
25 Let thine eyes beholde the right, and
let thine eyeliddes direct thy way before
thee.
26 [m] Pondre the path of thy fete, & let all
thy waies be ordred aright.
27 Turne not to the right hand, nor to the
left, *but* remoue thy fote from euil.

k That is, thei shal haue health of body. vnder the which all other blessings promised in ye lawe are conteined.
l For as the heart is ether pure or corrupt, so is the whole course of mans life.
m Kepe a mesure in all thy doings.

CHAP. V.

3 Whoredome forbiddē, 9 And prodigalitie. 15 He willeth a mā to liue on his labours & to helpe others, 18 To loue his wife. 22 The wicked taken in their owne wickednes.

1 MY sonne, hearken vnto my wisdome,
and encline thine eare vnto my
"knowledge,
2 That thou maiest regarde counsel, and
thy lippes obserue knowledge.
3 For the lippes [a] of a strange woman drop
as an honie combe, and her mouth is more
soft then [b] oyle.
4 But the end of her is bitter as worme
wood, & sharpe as a two edged sworde.
5 Her [c] fete go downe to death, and her step
pes take holde on hel.
6 She weigheth not the way of life: her
paths are [d] moueable: thou cāst not knowe
them.
7 Heare ye me now therefore, ô children, &
departe not from the wordes of my mouthe.
8 Kepe thy waie farre from her, and come
not nere the dore of her house,
9 Lest thou giue thine [e] honour vnto others,
and thy yeres to the cruel:
10 Lest the stranger shulde be filled with
thy strength, and thy [f] labours be in the
house of a stranger,
11 And thou mourne at thine end, (when
thou hast consumed thy flesh and thy
bodie)
12 And saie, How haue I hated instruction,
and mine heart despised correction!
13 And haue not obeied the voice of them
that taught me, nor inclined mine eare to
them that instructed me!
14 I was almost [g] broght into all euil in the
middes of the Congregacion & assemblie.

"Or, vnderstādig
a That is, an harlot which giueth her self to another then to her housband.
b By oyle and honie he meaneth flatterig and craftie inisements.
c All her doīgs lead to destruction.
d She hathe euer newe meanes to allure to wickednes.
e That is, thy strength and goods to her yt wil haue no pitie vpon thee: as is red of Samson, & the prodigal sonne
f The goods gotten by thy trauail.
g Althogh I was faithfully instructed in ye trueth, yet had I almoste fallē to vtter shame and destructiō, notwithstādig my good briging vp in the assemblie of the godlie.

15 ¶ Drinke the water of [h] thy cisterne,
and of the riuers out of the middes of thine owne well.
16 Let thy fountaines flowe forthe, and the
riuers of waters in the stretes.
17 But let them be thine, *euen* [i] thine onely, and not the strangers with thee.
18 Let thy [k] fountaine be blessed, and reioyce with the wife of thy [l] youth.
19 *Let her be as* the louing hinde and pleasant roe: let her breasts satisfie thee at all
times, & delite in her loue continually.
20 For why shuldest thou "delite, my sonne,
in a strange woman, or embrace the bosome of a stranger?
21 For the waies of mā *are* before the [m] eyes
of the Lord, and he pondereth all his pathes.
22 His owne iniquities shal take the wicked
him self, and he shalbe holden with the
cordes of his owne sinne.
23 He shal [n] dye for faute of instruction, &
shal go astray through his great folie.

h He teacheth vs sobrietie, exhorting vs to liue of our owne labours & to be beneficial to ye godlie that want.
i Distribute them not to the wicked & infideiles, but reserue them for thy self, thy familie & them that are of the housholde of faith.
k Thy childrē wc shal come of thee in great abundāce, shewing yt God blesseth mariage and curseth whoredome.
l Which thou didest marie in thy youth.
"Or, go astray with a stranger?
m He declareth that except man do ioyne to his wife bothe in heart and in outward conuersation, that he shal not escape the iudgements of God.
n Because he wil not giue eare to Gods worde and be admonished.

CHAP. VI.

1 Instruction for suerties. 6 The slouthful and sluggish is stirred to worke. 12 He describeth the nature of the wicked. 16 The things that God hateth. 20 To obserue the worde of God. 24 To flee adulterie.

1 MY sonne, if thou be suertie for thy
neighbour, & hast striken hāds with
the stranger,
2 Thou art [a] snared with the wordes of thy
mouth: thou art *euen* taken with the wordes of thine owne mouth.
3 Do this now, my sonne, and deliuer thy
self: seing thou art come into the hand of
thy neighbour, go, and humble thy self, &
solicit thy friends.
4 Giue no slepe to thine eyes, nor slumber
to thine eyeliddes.
5 Deliuer thy self as a doe from the hand
of the hunter, and as a birde from the hand
of the fouler.
6 ¶ Go to [b] the pismire, ô sluggard: beholde her waies, and be wise.
7 For she hauing no guide, gouernour, nor
ruler,
8 Prepareth her meat in the sommer, & gathereth her fode in haruest.
9 *How long wilt thou slepe, ô sluggard?
when wilt thou arise out of thy slepe?
10 *Yet* a litle slepe, a litle slumber, [c] a litle
folding of the hands to slepe.
11 Therefore thy pouertie cometh as one
that [d] trauaileth by the waie, & thy necessitie like [e] an armed man.
12 The vnthriftie man [f] & the wicked man
walketh with a frowarde mouth.
13 He maketh a signe with his eyes: he "signi
fieth

a He forbiddeth vs not to become suretie one for another, accordig to the rule of charitie, but yt we cōsider for whome and after what sort, so that the creditour may not be defrauded.
b If the word of God cā not instruct thee, yet learne at the littel pismire to labour for thy self and not to burden others.
Chap. 24, 32.
c He expresseth liuely ye nature of the sluggards, wc though they slepe neuer so lōg yet haue neuer ynough, but euer seke occasiōs thereunto.
d That is suddēly, & when yu lokest not for it.
e It shal come in such sort as thou art not able to resist it.
f He sheweth to what inconuenience the idle persones & sluggardes come, by calling them vnthriftie or the men of Belial & sclāderous.
"Ebr. speaketh.

fieth with his fete: he [g] instructeth with
his fingers.
14 Lewde things *are* in his heart: he imagineth euil at all times, *and* raiseth vp contentions.
15 Therefore shal his destructiō come spedely: he shalbe destroyed suddenly without recouerie.
16 ¶ These six things doeth the Lord hate:
yea, his soule abhorreth seuen:
17 The hautie eyes, a lying tongue, and the
hands that shede innocent blood,
18 An heart that imagineth wicked enterprises, [h] fete that be swift in running to
mischief,
19 A false witnes that speaketh lyes, & him
that raiseth vp cōtentions amōg *brethrē.
20 ¶ My sonne, kepe thy fathers commandement, and forsake not thy mothers instruction.
21 Binde them alway vpon thine [i] heart, *and*
tye them about thy necke.
22 It shal leade thee, when thou walkest: it
shal watch for thee, when thou slepest, *and*
when thou wakest, it shal talke with thee.
23 For the [k] commandement *is* a lanterne,
and instruction a light: and [l] corrections
for instruction *are* the waie of life,
24 To kepe thee from the wicked woman,
& from the flatterie of the tongue of a
strange woman.
25 Desire not her beautie in thine heart, nether let her take thee with her [m] eyeliddes.
26 For because of the whoorish womā *a man
is broght* to a morsel of bread, & a woman
wil hunte for the precious life of a man.
27 [n] Can a man take fyre in his bosome, &
his clothes not be burnt?
28 Or can a man go vpon coles, and his fete
not be burnt?
29 So he that goeth in to his neighbours
wife, shal not be innocent, whosoeuer toucheth her.
30 Men do not [o] despise a thief, when he
stealeth, to satisfie his [p] soule, because he
is hungrie.
31 But if he be founde, he shal restore seuen
folde, *or* he shal giue all the substance of
his house.
32 But he that committeth adulterie with a
woman, he "is destitute of vnderstanding:
he ỹ doeth it, destroyeth his owne soule.
33 He shal finde [q] a wounde and dishonour,
& his reproche shal neuer be put away.
34 For ielousie *is* ỹ rage of a man: therefore
he wil not [r] spare in the day of vēgeance.
35 He can not beare the sight of anie raunsome: nether wil he consent, thogh thou
augment the giftes.

g Thus all his gesture tedeth to wickednes.

h Meaning, the raging affections, which carie a man away in suche sort that he cā not tel what he doeth.

*Or, neighbours.

i Read Chap. 3.3.

k By the commandement he meaneth the worde of God: & by the instruction, the preaching and declaration of the same, w̃ is cōmitted to ỹ Church.

l And reprehē sions whē the worde is preached bring vs to life.

m With her wanton lokes and gesture.

n Meaning, ỹ she wil neuer cease, til she haue broght thee to beggerie, & thē seke thy destructiō.

o He approueth not theft, but sheweth that it is not so abominable as whoredome, forasmuche as theft might be redemed: but adulterie was a perpetual infamie, and death by the Law of God.

p Meanīg, for very necessitie

"Ebr. faileth in heart.

q That is, death appointed by ỹ Law.

r He sheweth that man by nature seketh his death, that hathe abused his wife, and so concludeth that nether Gods Law nor the law of nature admitteth any raunsome for the adulterie.

CHAP. VII.

1 *An exhortacion to wisdome and to the worde of God,*
5 *Which wil preserue vs from the harlot,* 6 *Whose
maners are described.*

1 MY sonne, kepe my wordes, and hide
my commandements with thee.
2 Kepe my commandements, & thou shalt
liue, and mine instruction as the [a] apple of
thine eyes.
3 Binde them vpon thy fingers, *and* write
them vpon the table of thine heart.
4 Saie vnto wisdome, Thou art my sister:
and call vnderstanding *thy* kinswoman,
5 That they maie kepe thee from the strange woman, *euen* from the stranger that is
smothe in her wordes.
6 ¶ [b] As *I was* in the windowe of mine
house, I loked through my windowe,
7 And I sawe among the fooles, *and* considered among the children a yong man destitute of vnderstanding,
8 Who passed through the strete by her
corner, and went toward her house,
9 In the twilight in the euening, when the
night began to be [c] blacke and darke.
10 And beholde, there met him a woman
with an harlots *behauiour, and *subtil in
heart.
11 (She [d] is babling and lowde: whose fete
can not abide in her house.
12 Now *she is* without, now in the stretes, &
lieth in waite at euerie corner)
13 So she caught him & kissed him & "with
an impudent face said vnto him,
14 I haue [e] peace offrings: this [f] day haue
I paied my vowes.
15 Therefore came I forthe to mete thee, ỹ
I might seke thy face: & I haue foūde thee.
16 I haue deckt my bed with ornaments,
*carpets and laces of Egypt.
17 I haue perfumed my bed with myrrhe,
aloes, and cynamom.
18 Come, let vs take our fil of loue vntil the
mornīg: let vs take our pleasure in daliāce.
19 For *mine* housband is not at home: he is
gone a iourney farre of.
20 He hathe taken "with him a bagge of
siluer, *and* wil come home at the day appointed.
21 Thus with her great craft she caused
him to yelde, & with her flattering lippes
she entised him.
22 And he followed her straightwaies, as an
[g] oxe that goeth to the slaughter, & [h] as a
foole to the stockes for correction,
23 Til a darte strike through his liuer, as a
birde hasteth to the snare, not knowing
that "he is in danger.
24 ¶ Heare me now therefore, ô children,
and hearken to the wordes of my mouth.
25 Let not thine heart decline to her waies:
wander thou not in her paths.
26 For she hathe caused manie to fall downe
wounded, *and* the [i] strong men *are* all slayne by her.
27 Her house is the waie * vnto the graue,
which goeth downe to the chambers of
death.

a By this diuersitie of wordes he meaneth ỹ nothing oght to be so dere vnto vs, as the worde of God, nor ỹ we loke on any thing more, nor mīde any thing so muche.

b Salomon vseth this parable to declare their folie, ỹ suffer thē selues to be abused by harlottes.

c He sheweth that there was almost none so impudent, but they were afraid to be sene, and also their owne cōsciences did accuse them, which caused them to seke the night to couer their filthines.

*Or, garment.

*Or, hid.

d He describeth certeine condicions, w̃ are peculiar to harlottes.

"Ebr. she strēgthened her face

e Because that in peaceoffrīgs a portion returned to them, ỹ offred, she sheweth him that she hath meat at home to make good chere with: or els she wolde vse some cloke of holines, til she had goten him in her snares.

f Which declareth that harlottes outwardly wil seme holie & religious: bothe because they may the better deceiue others, and also thinking by obseruing of ceremonies & offrings to make satisfactiō for their sinnes.

*Or, karued worke.

"Ebr. in his hād

g Which thinking he goeth to the pasture, goeth willigly to his owne destructiō.

h Which goeth cherefully, not knowing that he shalbe chastised.

"Ebr. it is for his life.

i Nether wit nor strength cā deliuer thē that fall into the hands of the harlot.

Chap. 2, 18.

CHAP. VIII.

*1 Wisdome declareth her excellēcie. 11 Riches. 15 Power
22 Eternitie. 32 She exhorteth all to loue and followe
her.*

1 DOeth * not [a] wisdome crye? and vnderstanding vtter her voyce?
2 She standeth in the top of the high places by the way in the place of the paths.
3 She cryeth besides [b] the gates before the
citie at the entrie of the dores,
4 O men, I call vnto you, and *vtter* my voice to the children of men.
5 O *ye* foolish men, vnderstand wisdome,
and *ye*, ô fooles, be wise in heart.
6 Giue eare, for I wil speake of excellent
things, and the opening of my lippes *shal
teache* things that be right.
7 For my mouth shal speake the trueth, and
my lippes abhorre wickednes.
8 All the wordes of my mouth *are* righteous: there is no lewdenes, nor frowardē-
nes in them.
9 Thei are all [c] plaine to him that wil vnderstand, and straight to them that wolde
finde knowledge.
10 Receiue mine instruction, and not siluer,
and knowledge rather then fine golde.
11 For wisdome is better then precious stones: and all pleasures are not to be compared vnto her.
12 I wisdome dwell with [d] prudence, and I
finde forthe knowledge *and* counsels.
13 The feare of the Lord *is* to hate [e] euil
as pride, and arrogancie, and the euil waie:
and a mouth *that speaketh* lewde things, I
do hate.
14 I haue counsel and wisdome: I am vnderstanding, & I haue strength.
15 By me, Kings [f] reigne, and princes decree iustice.
16 By me princes rule and the nobles, *and*
all the iudges of the earth.
17 I loue them that loue me: & thei that seke
me [g] early, shal finde me.
18 Riches and honour *are* with me: [h] *euen*
durable riches and righteousnes.
19 My frute is better then golde, *euen* thē fine golde, and my reuenues *better* then fine
siluer.
20 I cause to walke in the waie of righteousnes, & in the middes of the paths of
[i] iudgement,
21 That I maie cause them that loue me, to
inherite substance, and I wil fil their treasures.
22 The Lord hathe possessed me in the beginning of his waie: *I was* [k] before his workes of olde.
23 I was set vp from euerlasting, from the
beginning & before the earth.
24 When there were no depths, was I begotten, when there were no fountaines
abunding with water.

Chap. 1, 20.

a Salomón declareth that man is cause of his owne perdition, and that he can pretend no ignorãce, for asmuche as God calleth to all men by his worde, and by his workes to followe vertue and to flee frō vice.

b Where the people did moste resort, and which was ỷ place of iustice.

c Meanĩg, that the worde of God is easie vn to all, that haue a desire vnto it, & ẇ are not blinded by the prince of this worlde.

d That is, except a man haue wisdome, ẇ is ỷ true know ledge of God, he can nether be prudent nor good counseller

e So that he ỷ doeth not hate euil, feareth not God.

f Whereby he declareth that honors, dignitie or riches come not of mans wisdome or industrie, but by the pro uidēce of God

g That is, studie the worde of God diligently, and ẇ a desire to profite.

h Signifying ỷ he chiefly meaneth the spiritual treasures and heauenlie riches.

i For there can be no true iustice or iudgement, which is not directed by this wisdome.

k He declareth hereby the diuinitie & eternitie of this wisdome, ẇ he magnifieth and praiseth through this boke: meaning thereby ỷ eternal Sonne of God Iesus Christ our Sauiour, whome S. Iohn calleth the worde ỷ was in ỷ begining, Iohn 1, 1.

25 Before the mountaines were setled: &
before the hilles, was I begotten.
26 He had not yet made the earth, nor the
open places, nor the height of the dust in
the worlde.
27 When he prepared the heauens, I was
[l] there, when he set the compas vpon the
depe.
28 When he established the cloudes aboue,
when he confirmed the fountaines of the
depe,
29 When he gaue his decree to the sea, that
the waters shulde not passe his commandement: when he appointed the fundacions of the earth,
30 Then [m] was I with him *as* a nourisher,
and I was daily *his* delite reioycing alwaie
before him,
31 And toke my [n] solace in the compasse of
[o] his earth: & my delite *is* with the childrē
of men.
32 Therefore now hearken, ô children, vnto
me: for blessed *are thei that* kepe my waies.
33 Heare instruction, and be ye wise, & refuse it not: blessed *is* the man that heareth
me, watching daily at my gates, & giuing
attendance at the postes of my dores.
34 For he that findeth me, findeth life, and
shal obteine fauour of the Lord.
35 But he that sinneth against me, hurteth
his owne soule: & all that hate me, loue
death.

l He declareth the eternitie of the Sonne of God, which is ment by this worde Wisdome, who was before all time and euer present ẇ the Father.

m Some read a chief worker: signifying that this Wisdome, euen Christ Iesus, was equal ẇ God his Father, and created, preserued and stil worketh ẇ him, as Ioh. 5, 17.

n Whereby is declared that the worke of ỷ creation was no peine, but a solace vnto the wisdome of God.

o By earth, he meaneth man, which is the worke of God in whome wisdome toke pleasure: in somuche as for mans sake ỷ Diuine Wisdome toke mans nature, and dwelt among vs, & filled vs with vnspeakeable treasures: and this is that solace & passetime whereof is here spoken.

CHAP. IX.

*2 Wisdome calleth all to her feast. 7 The scorner wil not
be corrected. 10 The feare of God. 13 The conditions
of the harlot.*

1 WIsdome hathe buylt her [a] house,
& hewen out her [b] seuen pillers.
2 She hathe killed her vitailes, drawen her
wine, and [c] prepared her table.
3 She hathe sent forthe her [d] maidens *and*
cryeth vpon the highest places of the citie, *saying*,
4 Whoso is [e] simple, let him come hether, &
to him ỷ is destitute of wisdome, she saith,
5 Come, & eat of my [f] meat, and drinke of
the wine *that* I haue drawen.
6 Forsake *your way*, ye foolish, and ye shal
liue: & walke in ỷ waie of vnderstanding.
7 He that reproueth a scorner, purchasseth
to him self shame: and he that rebuketh the
wicked, *getteth* him self [g] a blot.
8 Rebuke not a [h] scorner, lest he hate thee:
but rebuke a wise man, & he wil loue thee.
9 Giue *admonicion* to the wise, and he wil be
the wiser: teache a righteous man, & he wil
increase in learning.
10 The beginning of wisdome *is* ỷ feare of
the Lord, & the knowledge of holy thĩgs,
is [i] vnder-

a Christ hathe prepared him a Church.

b That is, many chief staies and principal partes of his Church, as were the Patriarkes, Prophetes, Apostles, Pastors & Doctors.

c He compareth wisdome with great princes ỷ kepe opē house for all ỷ come.

d Meanĩg true preachers, ẇ are not infected with mās wisdome

e He that knoweth his owne ignorance and is voide of malice.

f By the meat and drinke, is ment the worde of God and the ministratiō of the sacramēts, whereby God nourisheth his seruants in his house, ẇ is ỷ Church.

g For the wicked wil contemne him & labour to diffame him.

h Meaning, them that are incorrigible, which Christ calleth dogs & swine; or he speaketh this in comparison, not that ỷ wicked shuld not be rebuked, but he sheweth their malice, and the smale hope of profite.

is [i] vnderstanding.
11 For thy dayes shalbe multiplied by me,
and the yeres of thy life shalbe augmẽted.
12 If thou be wise, thou shalt be wise for
[k] thy self, *and if* thou be a scorner, thou a-
lone shalt suffre.
13 ¶ A [l] foolish woman *is* troublesome: she
is ignorant, and knoweth nothing.
14 But she sitteth at the dore of her house
on a seat in the hye places of the citie,
15 To call them that passe by the way, that
go right on their way, *saying*,
16 Who so is simple, let him come hether,
and to him that is destitute of wisdome,
she saith also,
17 Stollen waters are swete, and hid bread
is pleasant.
18 But he knoweth not, that the dead *are*
there, *and that* her ghestes *are* in the depth
of hel.

i He sheweth what true vnderstanding is, to know ẏ wil of God in his worde, ẇ is ment by holie things.
k Thou shalt haue the chief profite, and comoditie thereof.
l By ẏ foolish woman, some vnderstand, the wicked preachers, who cõterfait ẏ worde of God, as appeareth vers. 16, ẇ were the wordes of the true pͣchers, as vers. 4: but their doctrine is but as stollẽ waters: meanĩg that they are but mens traditions, which are more pleasant to ẏ flesh then ẏ worde of God: and therefore they them selues boast thereof.

CHAP. X.

In this chapter and all that followe vnto the thirtieth, the wise man exhorteth by diuers sentences, which he calleth parables, to followe vertue, and flee vice: and sheweth also what profite cometh of wisdome, & what hinderance proceadeth of foolishnes.

THE PARABLES OF SALOMON.

Chap 15,20.

1 A Wise * sonne maketh a glad father:
but a foolish sonne *is* an heauines to
his mother.
2 The treasures of wickednes [a] profite
nothing: but righteousnes deliuereth frõ
death.
3 The Lord wil [b] not famish the soule of
the righteous: but he casteth away the substance of the wicked.
4 A "slouthful hand maketh poore: but the
hand of the diligent maketh riche.
5 He that gathereth in sommer, *is* the sonne
of wisdome: *but* he that slepeth in haruest,
is the sonne of confusion.
6 Blessings *are* vpon the head of the righteous: but iniquitie shal couer the mouth
of [c] the wicked.
7 The memorial of the iuste *shalbe* blessed:
but the name of the wicked shal [d] rotte.
8 The wise in heart wil receiue commãdemẽts: but the foolish in "talke shalbe beatẽ.
9 He that walketh vprightly, walketh "boldely: but he that peruerteth his waies, shal
be knowen.
10 He that [e] winketh with the eye, worketh sorowe, and he that is [f] foolish in talke, shalbe beaten.
11 The mouth of a righteous man is a well
spring of life: but iniquitie couereth the
mouth of the wicked.
12 Hatred stirreth vp contentions: *but loue couereth all trespasses.
13 In the lippes of him that hathe vnderstãding wisdome is foũde, and [g] a rod shalbe
for the backe of him that is destitute of

a That is, wickedly gotten.
b Thogh he suffer ẏ iuste to want for a time, yet he wil send him comforte in due season.
"Or, deceiful.
c When their wickednes shalbe discouered, thei shal be as dumme, & not knowe what to say.
d Shal be vile and abhorred bothe of God and man, contrarie to their owne expectation, ẇ thinke to make their name immortal.
"Ebr. lippes.
"Or, surely.
e He that beareth a faire countenance, & imagineth misch ief in his heart, as Chap 6,13.
f For the corruption of his heart is knowẽ by his talke.
1. Cor. 13,4.
1. pet. 4,8.
g That is, God wil finde him out to punish him.

wisdome.
14 Wise men laye vp knowledge: but the
mouth of the foole *is* a present destruction.
15 The riche mans goods are his [h] strong
citie: *but* the feare of the nedie *is* their pouertie.
16 The labour of the righteous *tendeth* to
life: *but* the reuenues of the wicked to
sinne.
17 He that regardeth instruction, *is in* the
way of life: but he that refuseth correctiõ,
goeth out of the way.
18 He that dissembleth hatred with lying
lippes, and he that inuenteth sclandre, is a
foole.
19 In manie wordes there can not wãt iniquitie: but he that refraineth his lippes,
is wise.
20 The tongue of the iuste man *is as* fined
siluer: *but* the heart of the wicked *is* litle
worthe.
21 The lippes of the righteous do [i] fede manie: but fooles shal dye for want of wisdome.
22 The blessing of the Lord, it maketh riche, and he doeth adde [k] no sorowes
with it.
23 *It is* as a passe time to a foole to do wickedly: but wisdome *is* vnderstanding to a
man.
24 That which the wicked feareth, shal come vpon him: but *God* wil grante the desire
of the righteous.
25 As the whirle winde passeth, so *is* the wic
ked no more: but the righteous *is as* an
euerlasting fundacion.
26 As vinegre *is* to ẏ teeth, and as smoke to
the eyes, so *is* the slouthful to them that
[l] send him.
27 The feare of the Lord increaseth the
dayes: but the yeres of the wicked [m] shalbe diminished.
28 The pacient abiding of the righteous
shalbe gladnes: but the hope of the wicked
shal perish.
29 The way of the Lord *is* strength to the
vpright mã: but feare shalbe for the workers of iniquitie.
30 The righteous shal [n] neuer be remoued:
but the wicked shal not dwell in the land.
31 The mouth of the iuste shalbe fruteful
in wisdome: but the tongue of the frowarde shal be cut out.
32 The lippes of the righteous knowe what
is acceptable: but the mouth of the wicked *speaketh* frowarde things.

CHAP. XI.

1 FAlse [a] balances *are* an abominacion
vnto the Lord: but a perfite "weight
pleaseth him.
2 When pride cometh, then cometh [b] shame: but with the lowlie *is* wisdome.

h And so maketh him bolde to do euil, where as pouertie brideleth the poore from manie euil things.
i For they speake trueth and edifie manie by exhortations, admonition and counsel.
k Meaning ẏ all worldlie things bring care, & sorow, where as they that feele the blessings of God, haue none.
l He is but a trouble, and grief to him ẏ setteth him about anie busines.
m The time of their prosperitie shalbe short, because of their great fall, thogh thei seme to liue long.
n They enioye in this life by faith, and hope their euerlasting life.
a Vnder this worde he condẽneth all false weights, measures and deceit.
"Ebr. stone.
b When man forgetteth him self, and thinketh to be exalted aboue his vocation, then God bringeth him to confusiõ

3 The vprightenes of the iuste shal guide
them:but the frowardnes of the transgressers shal destroye them.
4 *Riches auaile not in the day of wrath:
but righteousnes deliuereth from death.
5 The righteousnes of the vpright shal direct his way: but the wicked shal fall in
his owne wickednes.
6 The righteousnes of the iuste shal deliuer them:but the transgressers shalbe takẽ
in *their* owne wickednes.
7 *When a wicked man dyeth,*his* hope perisheth, and the hope of the vniust shal
perish.
8 The righteous escapeth out of trouble,&
the wicked shal come in his c stead.
9 An d hypocrite with *his* mouth hurteth
his neighbour:but the righteous shalbe deliuered by knowledge.
10 In the prosperitie of the righteous the
citie e reioyceth, and when the wicked
perish,*there is* ioye.
11 By the *blesing of ẏ righteous, the citie
is exalted:but it is subuerted by the mouth
of the wicked.
12 He that despiseth his neighbour,is destitute of wisdome: but a man of vnderstanding wil f kepe silence.
13 He that goeth about *as* a sclãderer,disco-
uereth a secret:but he that is of a faithful
heart,conceileth a matter.
14 Where no counsel is,the people fall:but
where manie g counselers are, *there is* health.
15 He shal be sore vexed,that is suretie for
a h stranger, and he i that hateth suretie-
ship, is sure.
16 A *gracious woman atteineth honour,&
the strong men atteine riches.
17 He that is merciful, k rewardeth his
owne soule:but he that troubleth his owne
*flesh,*is* cruel.
18 The wicked worketh a disceitful worke:
but he that soweth righteousnes,*shal receiue* a sure rewarde.
19 As righteousnes *leadeth* to life:so he that
followeth euil,*seketh* his owne death.
20 They that are of a froward heart,*are* abomination to the Lord:but they that are
vpright in *their* way,*are* his delite.
21 l *Thogh* hand *ioyne* in hãd,the wicked shal
not be vnpunished: but the sede of the righteous shal escape.
22 *As* a iewel of golde in a swines snoute:*so
is* a faire woman,which *lacketh discretiõ.
23 The desire of the righteous *is* onely
good: *but* the hope of the wicked m *is* indignacion.
24 There is that scatereth,n and is more increased: but he that spareth more o then
is right,surely *cometh* to pouertie.
25 The *liberal persone shal haue plentie:
and he that watereth,shal also haue raine.

Ezek.7,19. ecclus.5,10.
Wisd.5,15.
c That is,shal enter into trouble.
d A dissembler that pretẽdeth friendship,but is a priuie enemie.
e The coũtrey is blessed, where there is godlie men, & they oght to reioyce, when the wicked are takẽ away.
Or,prosperitie.
f Wil not make light report of others.
g Where God giueth store of men of wisdome, and counsel.
h Whose conuersation he knoweth not.
i He ẏ doeth not without iudgement,and consideratiõ of the circumstãces put him self in danger, as Chap.6,1.
Or,modest.
k Is bothe good to him self, and to others.
Or,neighbour.
l Thogh they make neuer so manie friends, nor thinke thẽ selues neuer so sure, yet they shal not escape.
Or,is of vncomely behauiour.
m They cã loke for nothing but Gods vengeance.
n Meaning thẽ, that giue liberally, whome God blesseth.
o That is,the niggard.
Ebr. the soule of blessing shalbe made fat.

26 He that withdraweth the corne,the people wil curse him:but blesing *shal be* vpon
the head of him that p selleth corne.
27 He that seketh good things, getteth fauour: but he that seketh euil,it shal come
to him.
28 He that trusteth in his riches, shal fall:
but the righteous shal florish as a leafe.
29 He that troubleth his owne q house,shal
inherite ẏ winde,and the foole *shalbe* r seruant to the wise in heart.
30 The frute of the righteous *is as* a tre of
life, and he that s winneth soules, *is* wise.
31 Beholde, the righteous shalbe t recompensed in the earth:how muche more the
wicked and the sinner?

CHAP. XII.

1 HE that loueth instructiõ,loueth know-
ledge:but he that hateth correction,*is*
a foole.
2 A good man getteth fauoure of the Lord:
but the man of wicked imaginacions wil
he condemne.
3 A man can not be established by wickednes: but the a roote of the righteous shal
not be moued.
4 A *verteous woman *is* the crowne of her
housband: but she that maketh *him* ashamed,*is* as corruption in his bones.
5 The thoghts of the iuste *are* right:but the
counsels of the wicked are disceitful.
6 The talking of the wicked *is* to lie in wait
for blood:but the mouth of the righteous
wil b deliuer them.
7 *God* ouerthroweth the wicked, and they
are not:but the house of ẏ righteous shal
stand.
8 A man shalbe commended for his wis-
dome:but the froward of heart shalbe despised.
9 He that is despised, c and *is* his owne seruant, is better thẽ he that boasteth him self
and lacketh bread.
10 A righteous man d regardeth the life
of his beast:but the mercies of the wicked
are cruel.
11 *He that tilleth his land, shal be satisfied
with bread:but he that followeth the idle,
is destitute of *vnderstanding.
12 The wicked desireth the e net of euils:
but the f roote of the righteous giueth
frute.
13 The euil man is snared by the wickednes of *his* lippes,but the iust shal come out
of aduersitie.
14 A man shal be satiate with good things
by the frute of *his* mouth, and the recompense of a mans hands shal *God* giue vnto
him.
15 The way of a foole *is* g right in his owne eyes: but he that heareth counsel, *is*
wise.
16 A foole in a day shal be knowen by his
angre:

p That prouideth for ẏ vse of them that are in necessitie.
q The couetous men ẏ spare their riches to the hinderance of their families,shalbe depriued thereof miserably.
r For thogh ẏ wicked be riche, yet are thei but sclaues to ẏ godlie, ẘ are the true possessers of ẏ giftes of God.
s That is,bringeth them to the knowledge of God.
t Shal be punished as he deserueth, as 1.Pet.4,18.
a They are so grounded in ẏ fauour of God, that their rote shal prosper continually.
Ebr. strong,or painful.
b As their cõscience is vpright, so shal they be able to speake for them selues against their accusers.
c The poore man that is cõtemned, & yet liueth of his owne trauail.
d Is merciful, euen to the very beast that doeth him seruice.
Chap.28,19. ecclus.20,30.
Or,defence.
e Continually imagineth meanes how to do harme to others.
f Meanĩg,their heart within, which is vpright, and doeth good to all.
g He standeth in his owne cõceit, and condemneth all others in respect of him self.

h Which brideleth his affections.

angre: but he [h] that couereth shame, *is*
wise.
17 He that speaketh trueth, wil shewe righteousnes: but a false witnes *vseth* disceit.

Chap. 14, 5.
i Which seke nothing more then to prouoke others to angre.

18 * There is that speaketh *wordes* like the
prickings of [i] a sworde: but the tongue
of wise men *is* health.
19 The lippe of trueth shalbe stable for euer:
but a lying tongue *varieth* incontinently.
20 Disceit *is* in the heart of them that imagine euil: but to the counsellers of peace
shalbe ioye.
21 There shal none iniquitie come to the
iuste: but the wicked are ful of euil.
22 The lying lippes *are* an abomination to
the Lord: but they that deale truely *are*
his delite.
23 A wise man conceileth knowledge: but ẏ
heart of the fooles publisheth foolishnes.

Chap. 10, 4.

24 * The hand of the diligent shal beare
rule: but the idle *shalbe* vnder tribute.
25 Heauines in the heart of mā doeth bring
it downe: but a [k] good worde reioyceth it.
26 The righteous [l] *is* more excellent then
his neighbour: but the way of the wicked
wil disceiue them.
27 The disceitful man rosteth not, that he
[m] toke in hunting: but the riches of the diligent man *are* precious.
28 Life *is* in the way of righteousnes, and *in*
that pathway *there is* no death.

k That is, wordes of cōfort, or a chereful minde, which is declared by his wordes, reioyceth a mā, as a couetous minde killeth him.
l That is, more liberal in giuing.
m Althogh he get muche by vnlawful meanes, yet wil he not spend it vpon him self.

CHAP. XIII.

1 A Wise sonne *wil obey* the instruction
of his father: but a skorner wil heare
no rebuke.
2 A man shal eat good things by the frute
[a] of *his* mouth: but the soule of the tres-
passers *shal suffer* violence.
3 He that kepeth his mouthe, kepeth his
life: *but* he that openeth his lippes, destruction *shalbe* to him.
4 The sluggarde [b] lusteth, but his soule
hathe noght: but the soule of the diligent
shal haue plentie.
5 A righteous man hateth lying wordes: but
the wicked causeth sclander and shame.
6 Righteousnes preserueth the vpright of
"life: but wickednes ouerthroweth the
sinner.
7 There is that maketh him self riche, and
hathe nothing, & that maketh him self
poore, hauing great riches.
8 A mā *wil giue* his riches for the rausome
of *his* life: but the poore [c] cā not heare the
reproche.
9 The light of the righteous reioyceth:
but the candle of the wicked shalbe put
out.
10 Onely by pride [d] doeth *man* make contention: but with the wel aduised *is* wisdome.
11 The [e] riches of vanitie shal diminish: but
he that gathereth with [f] the hand, shal in-

a If he vse his tōgue to Gods glorie, and the profite of his neighbour, God shal blesse him.
b He euer desireth, but taketh no peines to get anie thing.
"Ebr. waye.
c For his pouertie, he is not able to escape the threatings, which ẏ cruel oppressers vse against him.
d Whē as euerie man cōtendeth to haue ẏ preeminēce, & wil not giue place to another.
e That is, goods euil gotten.
f That is, ẇ his owne labour.

crease *them*.
12 The hope that is differred, *is* the fainting
of the heart: but when the desire commeth, *it is as* a tre of life.
13 He that despiseth [g] the worde, he shalbe
destroied: but he that feareth the cōmādement, he shal be rewarded.
14 The instruction of a wise man *is as* the
well spring of life, to turne away from the
snares of death.
15 Good vnderstāding maketh acceptable:
but the way of the disobedient *is* hated.
16 Euerie wise man wil worke by knowledge: but a foole wil spread abroad follie.
17 *A wicked messenger falleth [h] into euil:
but a faithful ambassadour *is* preseruation.
18 Pouertie and shame *is* to him that refuseth instructiō: but he that regardeth correction, shal be honored.
19 A desire accōplished deliteth the soule:
but *it is* an abominatiō to fooles to departe from euil.
20 He that walketh with the wise, shalbe
wise: but a companion of fooles shalbe
[i] afflicted.
21 Afflictiō followeth sinners: but vnto the
righteous *God* wil recompense good.
22 The good mā shal giue inheritance vnto *his* childrens children: and the [k] riches
of the sinner is laied vp for the iuste.
23 Muche foode *is* in the field of the [l] poore:
but *the field* is destroyed without discretiō.
24 * He ẏ spareth his rod, hateth his sonne:
but he that loueth him, chasteneth him betime.
25 The righteous eateth to the contenta-
tiō of his minde: but the bellie of the wicked shal want.

g Meaning, ẏ worde of God, whereby he is admonished of his duetie.
Chap. 25, 13.
h Bringeth manie inconueniēces bothe to him selfe and to others.
i As he is partaker of their wickednes & beareth with their vices, so shal he be punished alike as thei are.
k Read Iob, 27, 16.
l God blesseth the labour of the poore & cōsumeth their goods, which are negligent, because thei thinke thei haue ynough.
Chap. 23, 13. eccle. 30, 1.

CHAP. XIIII.

1 A Wise woman [a] buyldeth her house:
but the foolish destroieth it with her
owne hands.
2 * He that walketh in his [b] righteousnes,
feareth the Lord: but he that is lewde in
his waies, despiseth him.
3 In the mouth of the foolish *is* the [c] rodde
of pride: but the lippes of the wise preserue them.
4 Where none [d] oxen *are*, there the crib *is*
emptie: but muche increase *cometh* by the
strength of the oxe.
5 A faithful witnes wil not lye: but a false
recorde wil speake lyes.
6 A scorner [e] seketh wisdome, and *findeth*
it not: but knowledge *is* easie to him that
wil vnderstand.
7 Departe from the foolish man, when thou
perceiuest not *in him* the lippes of knowledge.
8 The wisdome of the prudent *is* to vnderstand his way: but the foolisnes of the
fooles *is* disceit.

a That is, taketh peine to profite her familie and to do that which concerneth her duetie in her house.
Iob. 12, 4.
b That is in vprightnes of heart and without hypocrisie.
c His proude tongue shal cause him to be punished.
d By the oxe is ment labour, and by ẏ cribbe the barne: meaning, without labour there is no profite.
e For ẏ maintenance of his owne ambitiō and not for Gods glorie, as Simon magus.

f Doeth not knowe ẏ grie-nousnes therof nor Gods iudgemẽts against the same.

g As a mans conscience is witnes of his owne grief: so another cã not feele the ioye and comforte, which a man feeleth in him self.

Chap.16,25.

9 The foole maketh a mocke [f] of sinne:but
among the righteous *there is* fauour.
10 The heart knoweth the [g] bitternes of
his soule, and the stranger shal not medle
with his ioye.
11 The house of ẏ wicked shalbe destroyed:
but the tabernacle of the righteous shal
florish.
12 * There is a way which semeth right to
a man:but the yssues thereof *are* the wayes
of death.
13 Euen in laughing the heart is sorowful,
[h] and the end of that mirth *is* heauines.
14 The heart that declineth, [i] shalbe saciate with his owne wayes: but a good man
shal departe from him.
15 The foolish wil beleue euerie thing:but
the prudent wil consider his steppes.
16 A wise man feareth, and departeth from
euil:but a foole rageth,and is careles.
17 He that is hastie to angre, committeth
folie,and a "busie bodie is hated.
18 The foolish do inherite folie: but the
prudent are crowned with knowledge.
19 The euil shal bowe before the good,and
the wicked [k] at the gates of the righteous.
20 The poore is hated euen of his owne
neighbour:but the friends of the riche *are*
manie.
21 The sinner despiseth his neighbour:
but he that hathe mercie on the poore,*is*
blessed.
22 Do not they erre that imagine euil? but
to them that thinke on good things,*shalbe*
mercie,and trueth.
23 In all labour there is abundance:but the
talke of the lippes *bringeth* onely want.
24 The crowne of the wise *is* their riches,&
the folie of fooles *is* foolishnes.
25 A faithful witnes deliuereth soules: but
a disceiuer speaketh lies.
26 In ẏ feare of ẏ Lord *is* an assured strẽgth,
and his children shal haue hope.
27 The feare of the Lord *is as* a well spring
of life,to auoide the snares of death.
28 In the multitude of the [l] people is the
honour of a King,and for the want of people *cometh* the destruction of the prince.
29 He that is slowe to wrath,*is* of great wisdome : but he that is of an hastie minde,
exalteth folie.
30 A sound heart *is* the life of the "flesh:but
enuie *is* the rotting of the bones.
31 *He that oppresseth the poore, reproueth
him that made him:but he honoreth him
that hathe mercie on the poore.
32 The wicked shalbe cast away for his
malice: but the righteous hathe hope [k] in
his death.
33 Wisdome resteth in the heart of him
that hathe vnderstanding , and is knowen
[m] in the middes of fooles.

h He sheweth that the alluremẽt vnto sinne semeth swete,but the end thereof is destruction.

i He that forsaketh God, shal be punished,and made wearie of his sinnes wherein he delited.

"Ebr. the mã of imaginations.

k If this come not daiely to passe,we muste consider that it is because of our sinnes, ẇ let Gods working.

l That is,the strength of a King standeth in manie people.

"Or,bodie.

Chap.17,5.

m For as muche as thei are conuict thereby, and put to silence.

34 Iustice exalteth a nation, "but sinne is a
shame to the people.
35 The pleasure of a King *is* in a wise ser-
uãt:but his wrath shalbe toward him that
is lewde.

"Or,& the mercie of the people is a sacrifice for sinne.

CHAP. XV.

1 A* Soft answer putteth away wrath:
but grieuous wordes stirre vp angre.
2 The tongue of the wise vseth knowledge aright : but the mouth of fooles *bableth out foolishnes.
3 The eyes of the Lord *in* euerie place
beholde the euil and the good.
4 A wholsome tongue *is as* a tre of life: but
the frowardnes thereof *is* the breaking of
the minde.
5 A foole despiseth his fathers instructiõ:
but he that regardeth correctiõ,is prudẽt.
6 The house of the righteous *hathe* muche
treasure : but in the reuenues of the wicked is [a] trouble.
7 The lippes of the wise do spread abroad
knowledge : but the heart of the foolish
doeth not so.
8 The [b] sacrifice of the wicked *is* abomination to the Lord:but the praier of ẏ righteous is acceptable vnto him.
9 The way of the wicked is an abominacion vnto the Lord : but he loueth him ẏ
followeth righteousnes.
10 Instructiõ is euil to him that [c] forsaketh
the way,& he ẏ hateth correctiõ,shal dye.
11 [d]Hel & destruction *are* before the Lord:
how much more the hearts of the sonnes
of men?
12 A scorner loueth not him that rebuketh
him,nether wil he go vnto the wise.
13 * A ioyful heart maketh a chereful coun-
tenance:but by the sorow of the heart the
minde is heauie.
14 The heart of him that hathe vnderstanding,seketh knowledge : but the mouth of
the foole is fed with foolishnes.
15 All ẏ daies of the afflicted *are* euil: but a
good "conscience *is* a continual feast.
16 *Better *is* a litle with ẏ feare of the Lord,
thẽ great treasure and trouble therewith.
17 Better *is* a dinner of grene herbes where
loue *is*, then a stalled oxe and hatred therewith.
18 *An angrie man stirreth vp strife:but he
that is slowe to wrath, appeaseth strife.
19 The way of a slouthful man *is* as an hedge of [e] thornes:but the way of ẏ righteous
is plaine.
20 *A wise sonne reioyceth the father: but a
foolish man despiseth his mother.
21 Foolishnes *is* ioye to him that is destitute of vnderstanding : but a man of vnderstanding walketh vprightly.
22 Without counsel thoghtes come to
nought:but [f] in the multitude of counsellers there is stedfastnes.

Chap.25,15.

Vers.28.

a For thogh thei haue muche,yet it is ful of trouble & care.

b That thing is abominable before God, ẇ the wicked thinke to be moste excellẽt, and whereby thei thinke moste to be accepted

c He that swarueth from the worde of God, can not abide to be admonished.

d There is nothing so depe, or secret that can be hid frõ the eyes of God,much lesse mẽs thoghts

Chap. 17, 22.

"Ebr heart.

Psal.37,16.

Chap. 29, 22.

e That is,he euer findeth some let or stay, and dare not go forward.

Chap.10,1.

f Read Chap. 11,14.

23 A ioye *cometh* to a man by the answer of
his mouth: and how good *is* a worde [g] in
due season?
24 The waie of life *is* on high to the prudēt,
to auoide from hel beneth.
25 The Lord wil destroy the house of the
proude men: but he wil stablish the borders of the widowe.
26 The thoghts of the wicked are abominatiō to the Lord: but the pure *haue* [h] pleasant wordes.
27 He ẏ is gredie of gaine, troubleth his owne house: but he ẏ hateth giftes, shal liue.
28 The heart of the righteous studieth to
answer: but ẏ wicked mans mouth bableth
euil things.
29 The Lord is farre of from the wicked:
but he heareth the praier of ẏ righteous.
30 The light of ẏ eies reioyceth the heart,
& a good name maketh the bones fat.
31 The eare that hearkeneth to the [i] correction of life, shal lodge among the wise.
32 He that refuseth instruction, despiseth
his owne soule: but he that obeieth correction, getteth vnderstanding.
33 The feare of the Lord *is* the instructiō
of wisdome: & before honour *goeth* [k] humilitie.

CHAP. XVI.

1 THe [a] preparations of the heart *are* in
man: but the answer of the tongue *is*
of the Lord.
2 All the waies of a mā *are* [b] cleane in his o-
wne eies: but the Lord pōdereth ẏ spirits.
3 "Cōmit thy workes vnto the Lord, & thy
thoghts shal be directed.
4 The Lord hathe made all things for his
owne sake: yea, euē the wicked for the day
of [c] euil.
5 All that are proude in heart, *are* an abomination to the Lord: *thogh* * hand *ioyne* in
hand, he shal not be vnpunished.
6 By [d] mercie and trueth iniquitie shalbe
forgiuē, and by the feare of the Lord they
departe from euil.
7 When the waies of a man please ẏ Lord,
he wil make also his enemies at peace
with him.
8 *Better is a litle with righteousnes, then
great reuenues without equitie.
9 The heart of mā [e] purposeth his way: but
the Lord doeth direct his steppes.
10 A diuine sentence *shalbe* in the lippes of
the King: his mouth shal not transgresse in
iudgement.
11 *A true weight and balance are of the
Lord: all the weights of the bagge *are*
his [f] worke.
12 It is an abomination to Kings to commit wickednes: for the throne is stablished
[g] by iustice.
13 Righteous lippes are the delite of Kīgs,
and the King loueth him that speaketh
right things.

g If we wil ẏ our talke be cōfortable, we muste waite for time and season.

h That is, holsome and profitable to the hearers.

i That suffreth him self to be admonished by Gods worde, ẇ bringeth life: and so amendeth.

k Meanīg, that God exalteth none, but them that are truely humbled.

Chap. XVI.

a He derideth ẏ presumptiō of man, who dare attribute to him self anie thing, as to prepare his heart or suche like, seing that he is not able to speake a worde, except God giue it hī.

b He sheweth hereby, that man flattereth him self in his doings: callīg that vertue ẇ God termeth vice.

"Ebr. role.

c So that the iustice of God shal appeare to his glorie, euē in the destruction of the wicked.

Chap. 11, 21.

d Their vpright and repenting life shal be a tokē that their sinnes are forgiuen.

Chap. 15, 16. Psal. 37, 16.

e He sheweth the folie of mā ẇ thinketh ẏ his waies are in his owne hand: & yet is not able to remoue one fote except God giue force.

Chap. 11, 1.

f If they be true and iuste, thei are Gods worke & he deliteth therein, but other wise if thei be false, thei are the worke of the deuil, and to their condēnation that vse them.

g They are appointed by God to rule according to equitie and iustice.

14 The wrath of a King *is as* [h] messengers
of death: but a wise man wil pacifie it.
15 In the light of the Kings countenance *is*
life: and his fauour *is* [i] as a cloude of the
latter raine.
16 *How muche better is it to get wisdome
then golde? and to get vnderstanding, is
more to be desired then siluer.
17 The path of the righteous is to decline
from euil, & he kepeth his soule, that kepeth his way.
18 Pride *goeth* before destruction, and an
high minde before the fall.
19 Better it is to be of humble mind with
the lowlie, then to deuide the spoiles with
the proude.
20 He that is wise in *his* busines, shal finde
good: and * he that trusteth in the Lord, he
is blessed.
21 The wise in heart shalbe called prudēt:
& [k] the swetenes of the lippes shal increase doctrine.
22 Vnderstanding *is* a well sprīg of life vnto
them that haue it: and the [l] instruction of
fooles *is* folie.
23 The heart of the wise guideth his mouth
wisely, and addeth doctrine to his lippes.
24 Faire wordes *are as* an honie combe,
swetenes to the soule, & health to the bones.
25 *There is a way that semeth right vnto
man: but the yssue thereof *are* the waies of
death.
26 The persone that trauaileth, trauaileth
for him self: for his mouth " craueth it of
him.
27 A wicked man diggeth vp euil, and in
his lippes *is* like [m] burning fyre.
28 A froward persone soweth strife: and a
tale teller maketh diuision among princes.
29 A wicked man disceiueth his neighbour,
and leadeth him into the way that is not
good.
30 [n] He shutteth his eyes to deuise wickednes: he moueth his lippes, & bringeth euil
to passe.
31 Age is a crowne of glorie, *when* it is
founde in the way of [o] righteousnes.
32 He that is slowe vnto angre, is better thē
the mightie man: and he that ruleth his
owne minde, *is better* then he that winneth
a citie.
33 The lot is cast into the lappe: but the
whole disposition thereof *is* [p] of the Lord.

CHAP. XVII.

1 BEtter is a drye morsel, if peace *be* with
it, then an house ful of [a] sacrifices *with*
strife.
2 *A discrete seruant shal haue rule ouer a
lewde sonne, and he shal deuide the [b] heritage among the brethren.

h That is, he findeth out manie meanes to execute his wrath.

i Which is moste cōfortable to the drye grounde, Deu. 11, 14.

Chap. 8, 11.

Psal. 125, 1.

k The swete wordes of cōsolation, ẇ come forthe of a godlie heart.

l Ether that ẇ the wicked teache others, or els it is folie to teache them that are malicious.

Chap. 14, 12.

"Ebr. boweth vpon him.

m For he cōsumeth him self and others.

n With his whole indeuour he laboreth to bring his wickednes to passe.

o That is, whē it is ioyned ẇ vertue: or els the elder that ẏ wicked are, the more thei are to be abhorred.

p So that there is nothing ẏ oght to be attribute to fortune: for all things are determined in ẏ counsel of God which shal come to passe.

Chap. XVII.

a For where as were manie sacrifices, there were manie portions giuen to the people, wherewith thei feasted.

Eccle. 10, 30.

b That is, shal be made gouernour ouer the children.

3 *As is* ỹ fining pot for ſiluer, & the fornace for golde, ſo the Lord tryeth ỹ hearts.
4 The wicked giueth hede to falſe lippes,
& a lyer hearkeneth to the naughtie tongue.

Chap.14,31.

5 *He that mocketh the poore, reprocheth
him, that made him: and he that reioyceth
at deſtruction, ſhal not be vnpuniſhed.
6 Childrens children are the crowne of ỹ
elders: and the glorie of the children *are*
their fathers.

''*Ebr. the lippe of excellencie.*

7 ''Hie talke becōmeth not a foole, muche
leſſe a lying talke a prince.
8 A rewarde *is as* a ſtone pleaſant in the
eyes of thē that haue it: it proſpereth, whether ſoeuer it [c] turneth.

c The reward hathe great force to gaine ỹ heartes of men.

9 He that couereth a tranſgreſsion, ſeketh
loue: but he that repeateth a matter, ſepa-
rateth the [d] prince.

d He that admoniſheth the prince of his faute, maketh him his enemie.

10 A reprofe entreth more into him that
hathe vnderſtanding, then an hundreth
ſtripes into a foole.
11 A ſedicious perſone ſeketh onely euil, &
a cruel [e] meſſenger ſhal be ſent againſt
him.

e By the meſſenger is mēt ſuche meanes, as God vſeth to puniſh the rebelles.

12 *It is better* for a mā to mete a beare robbed of her whelpes, then [f] a foole in his
folie.

f Whereby he meaneth the wicked in his rage, who hathe no feare of God.

13 *He that rewardeth euil for good, euil
ſhal not departe from his houſe.

Rom.12,17. 1.theſſ.5,15. 1.pet.3,9.

14 The beginning of ſtrife *is as* one that
openeth the waters: therefore or the contention be medled with, leaue of.
15 *He that iuſtifieth the wicked, and he ỹ
condemneth the iuſt, euen thei bothe are
abominacion to the Lord.

Iſa.5,23. Chap.24,24.

16 Wherefore is there a [g] price in the hand
of the foole to get wiſdome, and *he hathe*
none heart?

g What auaileth it the wicked to be riche, ſeing he ſetteth not his minde to wiſdome?

17 A friend loueth at all times: and [h] a brother is borne for aduerſitie.

h So that he is more then a friend, euen a brother ỹ helpeth in time of aduerſitie.

18 A man deſtitute of vnderſtanding [i] toucheth the hand, and becometh ſuretie for
his neighbour.

i Read Chap. 6,1

19 He loueth trāſgreſsiō, that loueth ſtrife:
and he that exalteth his [k] gate, ſeketh deſtruction.

k Lifteth vp hī ſelf aboue his degre.

20 The frōwarde heart findeth no good:
and he that hathe a naughtie tongue, ſhal
fall into euil.
21 He that begetteth a foole, *getteth* him ſelf
ſorowe, and the father of a foole can haue
no ioye.

Chap.15,13.

22 *A ioyful heart cauſeth good health: but
a ſorowful minde dryeth the bones.

l That is, ſecretly & out of the boſome of the riche.

23 A wicked man taketh a gift out of the
[l] boſome to wreſt the waies of iudgement.

Eccl.2,14, & 8,1.

24 * Wiſdome *is* in the face of him that
hathe vnderſtanding: but the eyes of a
foole *are* in the [m] corners of the worlde.

m That is, wander to & fro & ſeke not after wiſdome.

25 A fooliſh ſonne is a grief vnto his father,
and a * heauines to her that bare him.

Chap.10,1.

26 Surely it is not good to condemne the
iuſte, nor that the princes ſhulde ſmite *ſuche* [n] for equitie.

n For their wel doing.

27 He that hathe knowledge, ſpareth his
wordes, and a man of vnderſtanding *is*
of an excellent ſpirit.
28 Euen a foole (when he holdeth his peace) is counted wiſe, and he that ſtoppeth
his lippes, prudent.

CHAP. XVIII.

1 FOr the deſire *thereof* he wil [a] ſeparate
him ſelf to ſeke it, & occupie him ſelf
in all wiſdome.

a He ỹ loueth wiſdome, wil ſeparate him ſelf from all impediments, and giue him ſelf wholly to ſeke it.

2 A foole hathe no delite in vnderſtanding: but that his heart may be [b] diſcouered.

b That is, that he may talke licenciouſly of whatſoeuer cometh to minde.

3 When the wicked commeth, then commeth [c] contempt, and with the vile man
reproche.

c Meaning, ſuche one as cōtemneth all others.

4 The wordes of a mans mouth *are like* depe [d] waters, & the well ſpring of wiſdome
is like a flowing riuer.

d Which can neuer be drawne emptie, but bring euer profite.

5 It is not good to [e] accept the perſone of
the wicked, to cauſe the righteous to fall
in iudgement.

e That is, to fauour him & ſupport him.

6 A fooles lippes come with ſtrife, and his
mouth calleth for ſtripes.

f Thei are ſone beleued & enter moſt depely.

7 A fooles mouth *is* his owne deſtruction,
and his lippes *are* a ſnare for his ſoule.
8 The wordes of a tale bearer *are* as flatterings, and thei go downe into [f] the bowels
of the bellie.

g He ſheweth what is the refuge of ỹ godlie againſt all troubles.

Chap.10,15. Chap.16,18. Eccle.11,8.

9 He alſo that is ſlouthful in his worke, is
euen the brother of him that is a great
waſter.
10 The Name of the Lord *is* a ſtrong towre:
the righteous runneth [g] vnto it, and is exalted.

h The minde can wel beare the infirmitie of the bodie, but when the ſpirit is wounded, it is a thig moſte hard to ſuſteine.

11 *The riche mans riches *are* his ſtrong citie: and as an hie wall in his imagination.
12 * Before deſtruction the heart of a man
is hautie, and before glorie *goeth* lowlines.

i Getteth him libertie to ſpeake, & fauour of them that are moſte in eſtimation.

13 *He that anſwereth a matter before he
heare it, it is folie and ſhame vnto him.

k He that ſpeaketh firſt, is beſt heard of ỹ wicked iudge, but when his aduerſarie inquireth out ỹ matter, it turneth to his ſhame.

14 The ſpirit of a man wil ſuſteine his infirmitie: but [h] a wounded ſpirit, who can
beare it?
15 A wiſe heart getteth knowledge, and the
eare of the wiſe ſeketh learning.

l If a controuerſie can not otherwiſe be decided, it is beſt to caſt lottes to knowe whoſe ỹ thing ſhalbe.

16 A mans gift [i] enlargeth him, and leadeth him before great men.
17 [k] *He that is* firſt in his owne cauſe, *is* iuſt:
then cometh his neighbour, and maketh
inquirie of him.

m Appeaſeth their controuerſie, ẇ are ſo ſtoute that can not otherwiſe be pacified.

18 The lot [l] cauſeth contentions to ceaſe,
& [m] maketh a particion among the mightie.

n Which for ỹ ſtrength thereof wil not bowe nor yelde.

19 A brother offended *is harder to winne*
then a ſtrong citie, & *their* contentions *are*
like the [n] barre of a palace.
20 With the frute of a mans mouthe ſhal
his

his bely be satisfied & with the increase of
his lippes shal he be filled.
21 Death and life *are* in the power of the
tongue,and they that [o] loue it,shal eat the
frute thereof.
22 He that findeth a [p] wife,findeth a good
thing, and receiueth fauour of the Lord.
23 The poore speaketh *with* prayers:but the
riche answereth roughly.
24 A man *that hathe* frieds,*oght* to shewe him
self friendly : for a friend is nerer [q] then a
brother.

[o] By the vsing of the tongue wel or euil, cometh the frute thereof ether good or bad.
[p] He that is ioyned with a vertuous woman in mariage, is blessed of ye Lord, as Chap 19,14.
[q] That is, oftetimes suche are foūd yt are more readie to do pleasure thē he yt is more bounde by duetie.

CHAP. XIX.

1 BEtter * is ye poore that walketh in his
vprightnes, then he that abuseth his
lippes,and is a foole.
2 For without knowledge the minde is not
good, and he that hasteth with his fete,sinneth.
3 The foolishnes of a man peruerteth his
way,& his heart freateth against ye Lord.
4 Riches gather manie friends:but the poore
is separated from his neighbour.
5 * A false witnes shal not be vnpunished :
& he that speaketh lies,shal not escape.
6 Manie reuerence the face of the prince,&
euerie man *is* friend to him that giueth
giftes.
7 All ye brethren of the poore do hate him:
how muche more wil his friends departe
farre from him?thogh he be instant [a] with
wordes,*yet* they wil not.
8 He yt possesseth vnderstanding, [b] loueth
his owne soule,& kepeth wisdome to finde
goodnes.
9 A false witnes shal not be vnpunished: &
he that speaketh lyes,shal perish.
10 [c] Pleasure is not comelie for a foole,
muche lesse for a seruāt to haue rule ouer
princes.
11 The discretion of a man differreth his
angre:and his glorie *is* [d] to passe by an offence.
12 *The Kings wrath *is* like the roaring of
a lyon:but his fauour *is* like the dewe vpon
the grasse.
13 * A foolish sonne *is* the calamitie of his
father,* and the contentions of a wife *are*
like a continual [e] dropping.
14 House and riches *are* the inheritance of
the fathers: but * a prudent wife *cometh* of
the Lord.
15 Slouthfulnes causeth to fall a slepe,and a
disceitful persone shal be affamished.
16 He that kepeth the commandement, kepeth
his owne soule : *but* he that despiseth
his waies,shal dye.
17 He that hathe mercie vpon the poore,
lendeth vnto the Lord : and the Lord wil
recōpense him that which he hathe giuē.
18 Chasten thy sonne while there is hope,
and let not thy soule spare for his murmuring.

Chap.28,6.
Deu.19 19. dan.13,60.
[a] To haue cōfort of them.
[b] He that is vpright in iudgemēt, findeth fauour of God
[c] The fre vse of things, are not to be permitted to him that can not vse them aright.
[d] That is, to couer it by charitie and to do therin as maie moste serue to Gods glorie.
Chap.20,2.
Chap.17,21.
Chap.21,9.
[e] As raine yt droppeth and rotteth the house.
Chap.18,22.

19 *A man* of muche angre shal suffer punishment
: & thogh thou [f] deliuer *him*, yet
wil *his angre* come againe.
20 Heare counsel, and receiue instruction,
that thou maiest be wise in thy latter end.
21 Manie deuices *are* in a [g] mans heart : but
the counsel of the Lord shal stand.
22 That that is to be desired of a man, *is* his
[h] goodnes, and a poore man is better then
a lyer.
23 The feare of the Lord *leadeth* to life:and
he that is filled *therewith*, shal continue, &
shal not be visited with euil.
24 * The slouthful hideth his hand in *his*
bosome,and wil not put it to his mouth againe.
25 * Smite a scorner, and [i] the foolish wil
beware : and reproue the prudent,and he
wil vnderstand knowledge.
26 He that destroyeth *his* father,*or* chaseth
away *his* mother, *is* a lewde and shameful
childe.
27 My sonne, heare no more the instructiō,
that causeth to erre from the wordes of
knowledge.
28 A wicked witnes mocketh at iudgemēt,
and the mouth of the wicked [k] swalloeth
vp iniquitie.
29 *But* iudgemēts are prepared for the scorners,
& stripes for the backe of the fooles.

[f] Thogh for a time he giue place to counsel, yet sone after wil he giue place to his raging affections.
[g] Mans deuice shal not haue succes, except God gouerne it, whose purpose is vnchangeable.
[h] That is, that he be honest: for the poore man that is honest, is to be estemed aboue ye riche which is not verteous
Chap.26,15.
Chap.21,11.
[i] That is, the simple and ignorant men learne, when thei se the wicked punished.
[k] Taketh a pleasure and delite therein, as gluttons & drunkardes in delicate meats and drinkes.

CHAP. XX.

1 WIne [a] *is* a mocker & strong drinke
is raging: & whosoeuer is deceiued
thereby, is not wise.
2 * The feare of the King *is* like the roarīg
of a lyon: he that prouoketh him vnto
angre, [b] sinneth against his owne soule.
3 *It is* a mans honour to cease from strife:
but euerie foole wil be medling.
4 The slouthful wil not plowe, because of
winter: *therefore* shal he begge in sommer,
but haue nothing.
5 The counsel in the heart of [c] man *is like*
depe waters : but a man that hathe vnderstanding,
wil drawe it out.
6 Manie men wil boast, euerie one of his
owne goodnes: but who can finde a faithful
man?
7 He that walketh in his integritie, *is* iuste:
& blessed *shal* his children *be* after him.
8 A King that sitteth in the throne of iudgement,
[d] chaseth away all euil wt his eyes.
9 * Who can say, I haue made mine heart
cleane, I am cleane from sinne?
10 Diuers " weightes, and diuers measures,
bothe [e] these are euen abominacion vnto
the Lord.
11 A childe also is knowen by his doings,
whether his worke be pure and right.
12 The Lord hathe made bothe these, euen
the eare to heare, and the eye to se.
13 Loue not slepe, lest thou come vnto pouertie
: open thine eyes, *and* thou shalt be

[a] By wine here is ment him that is giuen to wine, and so by strōg drinke.
Chap.19,12.
[b] Putteth his life in danger.
[c] It is hard to finde out: for it is as depe waters, whose bottome can not be found: yet the wise mā wil knowe a man ether by his wordes or maners.
[d] Where righteous iudgement is executed, there sinne ceaseth and vice dare not appeare.
1 King.8,46. 2 chro.6,36. eccles.7,21. 1.iohn.1,8.
" *Ebr. stone and stone, ephah & ephah*
[e] Read Chap. 16,11.

ſatiſfied with bread.
14 It is naught, it is naught, ſaith the byer:
but when he is gone a parte, he boaſteth.
15 There is golde, and a multitude of precious ſtones: but the lippes of knowledge
are a precious iewel.
16 *Take his [f] garment, that is ſuretie for
a ſtranger, and a pledge of him for the
ſtranger.
17 The bread of deceit *is* ſwete to a man:
but afterwarde his mouth ſhalbe filled
with grauel.
18 Eſtabliſh the thoghts by counſel: and by
counſel make warre.
19 He that goeth about *as* a ſclanderer, diſcouereth* ſecrets: therefore medle not wͭ
him that flattereth with his lippes.
20 *He that curſeth his father or his mother, his light ſhalbe put out in obſcure
darkenes.
21 An heritage *is* haſtely gotten at the beginning, but the end thereof ſhal not be
bleſſed.
22 Say not thou,* I wil recompenſe euil: *but*
waite vpon the Lord, and he ſhal ſaue
thee.
23 *Diuers weightes *are* an abominacion
vnto the Lord, and diſceitful balances *are*
not good.
24 *The ſteppes of man *are ruled* by the
Lord: how can a man then vnderſtand his
owne way?
25 It is a deſtruction for a man to [g] deuoure that which is ſanctified, and after the
vowes to inquire.
26 A wiſe King ſcattereth the wicked, and
causeth the [h] whele to turne ouer them.
27 The [i] light of the Lord *is* the breth of
man, and ſercheth all the bowels of the
bellie.
28 *Mercie and trueth preſerue the King:
for his throne ſhalbe eſtabliſhed wͭ mercie.
29 The beautie of yong mẽ *is* their ſtrẽgth,
and the glorie of the aged *is* the graye
head.
30 [k]The blewenes of the wounde ſerueth to
purge the euil, and the ſtripes within the
bowels of the bellie.

CHAP. XXI.

1 THe [a] Kings heart *is* in the hand of the
Lord, *as* the riuers of waters: he turneth it whetherſoeuer it pleaſeth him.
2 Euerie* way of a man *is* right in his owne
eyes: but the Lord pondereth the hearts.
3 *To do iuſtice and iudgement is more
acceptable to the Lord then ſacrifice.
4 A hautie loke, and a proude heart, *which is*
the *[b] light of the wicked, *is* ſinne.
5 The thoghts of the diligent *do* ſurely
bring abundance: but [c] whoſoeuer is haſtie,
cometh ſurely to pouertie.
6 *The gathering of treaſures by a diſceitful tongue *is* vanitie toſſed to and fro of
them that ſeke death.
7 The [d] robberie of the wicked ſhal deſtroye them: for thei haue refuſed to execute iudgement.
8 The way of ſome *is* peruerted and ſtrange: but of the pure man, his worke *is* right.
9 *It is better to dwell in a corner of ẏ houſe toppe, then with a contentious woman
in a * wide houſe.
10 The ſoule of the wicked wiſheth euil:
and his neighbour hathe no fauour in his
eyes.
11 [e] When the ſcorner is puniſhed, the fooliſh is wiſe: and when one inſtructeth the
wiſe, he wil receiue knowledge.
12 The righteous [f] teacheth the houſe of
the wicked: *but God* ouerthroweth the wicked for *their* euil.
13 He that ſtoppeth his eare at the crying
of the poore, he ſhal alſo crye and not be
heard.
14 A [g] gift in ſecret pacifieth angre, and a
gift in the boſome great wrath.
15 It is ioye to the iuſt to do iudgement:
but deſtruction *ſhalbe* to the workers of iniquitie.
16 A man that wandereth out of the way of
wiſdome, ſhal remaine in the congregaciõ
of the dead.
17 He that loueth paſtime, *ſhalbe* a poore
man: *&* he that loueth wine & oyle, ſhal
not be riche.
18 The [h] wicked *ſhalbe* a ranſome for the
iuſt, and the trãſgreſſour for the righteous.
19 *It is better to dwell in the wildernes,
then with a contentious & angrie womã.
20 In ẏ houſe of the wiſe is a pleaſant treaſure and [i] oyle: but a fooliſh man deuoureth it.
21 He that followeth after righteouſnes &
mercie, ſhal finde life, righteouſnes, and
glorie.
22 A [k] wiſe man goeth vp into the citie of
the mightie, and caſteth downe ẏ ſtrength
of the confidence thereof.
23 He that kepeth his mouth and his tõgue,
kepeth his ſoule from afflictions.
24 Proude, hautie *&* ſcorneful *is* his name
that worketh in *his* arrogancie wrath.
25 The deſire of the ſlouthful [l] ſlaieth him:
for his hands refuſe to worke.
26 He coueteth gredely, but the righteous
giueth, and ſpareth not.
27 The* ſacrifice of the wicked *is* an abominaciõ: how muche more when he bringeth it with a wicked minde?
28 *A falſe witnes ſhal periſh: but he that
heareth, [m] ſpeaketh continually.
29 A wicked man hardeneth his face: but
the iuſte, he wil direct his way.
30 There is no wiſdome, nether vnderſtanding, nor counſel againſt the Lord.
31 The horſe is prepared againſt the daie

Chap.27,13.
f Teache him wit, that he caſt not him ſelf raſhly into danger.
Chap.11,13.
Exod.21,17.
leuit.20,9.
mat.15,4.
Deut.32,35.
chap.17,13.
& 24,29.
rom.12,17.
1.theſſ.5,15.
1.pet.3,9.
Chap.11,1.
& verſ.10.
Ierem.10,23.
g That is, to applie it, or take it to his owne vſe, which was appointed to Gods, and thẽ inquire how thei maie be exempted frõ the faute.
h Which was a kinde of puniſhment then vſed.
i The worde of God giueth life vnto man, and cauſeth vs to ſe & trye the ſecrets of our darke hearts, Ebr. 4,12.
Chap 29,14.
k Sharpe puniſhement, ẏ perceth euen the inward partes, is profitable for the wicked, to bring them to amendement.
Chap. XXI.
a Thogh Kings ſeme to haue all things at commandement, yet are thei not able to bring their owne purpoſes to paſſe anie otherwiſe thẽ God hathe appointed: much leſſe are the inferiours able.
Chap.16,2.
Mich.6,8.
*Or, plowing.
b That is, the thing whereby he is guided, or which he bringeth forthe as the frute of his worke.
c He that goeth raſhely about his buſines and without counſel.
Chap.13,11.

d He meaneth this chiefly of iudges and princes which leaue that vocation whereunto God hath called them, & powle their ſubiects to mainteine their luſtes.
Chap.19,13.
& 25,24.
*Or, in a great familie.
e Read Chap. 19,25.
f Thogh the godlie admoniſh thẽ bothe by wordes & example of life, yet the wicked wil not amend, til God deſtroie them.
g To do a pleaſure to the angrie man pacifieth him.
h God ſhal cauſe that to fall on their owne heads, wͨ they intẽded agaiſt the iuſt, by deliuering the iuſte and putting the wicked in their places.
Eccle 25,23.
i Meaning, abundance of all things.
k Wiſdome ouercometh ſtrẽgth & confidẽce in worldelie things.
l He thinketh to liue by wiſhing and deſirĩg all things, but wil take no peine to get oght.
Chap.15,8.
iſa.1,13.
eccleſ.34,21.
Chap.19,5.
m He maie boldely teſtifie the trueth that he hathe heard.

of battel: but saluacion *is* of the Lord.

CHAP. XXII.

1 A *good name is to be chosen aboue
great riches, and [a] louing fauour is
aboue siluer and aboue golde.
2 *The riche and poore [b] mete together:
the Lord *is* the maker of them all.
3 *A prudent man seeth the [c] plague, and
hideth him self: but the foolish go on stil,
and are punished.
4 The rewarde of humilitie, & the feare of
God *is* riches, and glorie, and life.
5 Thornes *and* snares *are* in the way of the
frowarde: *but* he that regardeth his soule,
wil departe farre from them.
6 Teache a childe [d] in the trade of his
way, and when he is olde, he shal not departe from it.
7 The riche ruleth ỹ poore, and ỹ borower
is seruant to the man that lendeth.
8 He that soweth iniquitie, shal reape affliction, & the [e] rodde of his angre shal faile.
9 *He that hathe a good [f] eye, he shalbe blessed: for he giueth of his bread vnto ỹ pore.
10 Cast out the scorner, and strife shal go
out: so contention and reproche shal cease.
11 He that loueth purenes of heart *for* the
grace of his lips, the [g] King *shalbe* his fried.
12 The eyes of the Lord [h] preserue knowledge: but he ouerthroweth the wordes of
the transgressour.
13 The slouthful man saith, [i] A lyon *is* without, I shal be slaine in the strete.
14 The mouth of strange wome *is as* a depe
pit: he with whome ỹ Lord is angrie, [k] shal
fall therein.
15 Foolishnes is bounde [l] in the heart of a
childe: but the rodde of correction shal
driue it away from him.
16 He that oppresseth the poore to increase him self, & giueth vnto the riche, *shal* surely come to pouertie.
17 ¶ Incline thine eare, & heare ỹ wordes of
the wise, and applie thine heart vnto my
knowledge.
18 For *it shalbe* pleasant, if thou kepe them in
thy bellie, & *if* they be directed together
in thy lippes.
19 That thy confidéce may be in [m] ỹ Lord,
I haue shewed thee this day: thou therefore *take hede*.
20 Haue not I writé vnto thee [n] thre times
in counsels and knowledge,
21 That I might shewe thee the assurãce of
the wordes of trueth to answer the wordes
of trueth to them that send to thee?
22 Robbe not ỹ poore, because he is poore,
nether oppresse ỹ afflicted "in iudgemét.
23 For the Lord *wil defende their cause, &
spoile the soule of those that spoile them.
24 Make [o] no friẽdship with an angrie mã,
nether go with the furious man,
25 Lest thou learne his wayes, and receiue

Eccles.7,2.
a Which cometh by wel doing.
Chap.29,13.
b Liue together, and haue nede the one of the other.
Chap 27,12.
c That is, the punishment, ẘ is prepared for the wicked, & fleeth to God for succour.
d Bring him vp vertuously, and he shal so continue.
e His autoritie, whereby he did oppresse others, shal be taken from him.
Eccles 31,28.
f He that is merciful, and liberal.
g He sheweth that princes shuld vse their familiaritie, whose conscience is good, and their talke wise and godlie.
h Fauour the ỹ loue knowledge.
i He derideth thé that inuét vaine excuses, because they wolde not do their duetie.
k So God punisheth one sinne by another, when he suffreth the wicked to fall into the acquaintance of an harlot.
l He is naturally giuen vnto it.
m He sheweth what the end of wisdome is: to wit, to direct vs to the Lord.
n That is, sundrie times.
"Ebr. in the gate
Chap.23,11.
o Haue not to do with him ỹ is not able to rule his affections: for he wolde hurt thee by his euil conuersation.

destruction to thy soule.
26 Be not thou of them that [p] touche ỹ hãd,
nor among thé that are suretie for debts.
27 If thou hast nothing to paye, why *causest
thou* ỹ he shuld take thy bed frõ vnder thee?
28 Thou shalt not *remoue the anciét boú-
des which thy fathers haue made.
29 Thou seest that a diligent mã in his busines standeth before Kings, *and* standeth
not before the base sorte.

CHAP. XXIII.

1 When thou sittest to eat with a ruler, [a] consider diligently what is
before thee,
2 [b] And put the knife to thy throte, if thou
be a man giuen to the appetite.
3 Be not desirous of his deintie meats: [c] for
it is a disceiuable meat.
4 Trauail not to muche to be riche: *but* cease from thy [d] wisdome.
5 Wilt thou cast thine eyes vpon it, which
is nothing? for *riches* taketh her to her win-
ges, as an egle, and flieth into the heauen.
6 Eat ỹ not the bread of him that hathe an
[e] euil eye, nether desire his deintie meats.
7 For as thogh he thoght it in his heart, so
wil he say vnto thee, Eat and drinke: but
his heart is not with thee.
8 Thou shalt vomit thy [f] morsels that thou
hast eaten, and thou shalt lose thy swete
wordes.
9 Speake not in the eares of a foole: for he
wil despise the wisdome of thy wordes.
10 *Remoue not the ancient boundes, and
entre not into the fields of the fatherles.
11 For he that redemeth thé, is mightie: he
wil *defende their cause against thee.
12 Applie thine heart to instruction, & thine eares to the wordes of knowledge.
13 *Withholde not correctiõ frõ the childe: if thou smite him with the rod, he shal
not dye.
14 Thou shalt smite him with the rodde,
and shalt deliuer his soule from [g] hel.
15 My sonne, if thine heart be wise, mine
heart shal reioyce and I also.
16 And my reines shal reioyce, when thy
lippes speake righteous things.
17 *Let not thine heart be enuious against
sinners: but *let it be* in the feare of the Lord
continually.
18 For surely there is an end, [h] and thy hope shal not be cut of.
19 O thou my sonne, heare, and be wise, &
guide thine heart in the [i] way.
20 Kepe not companie with" dronkards,
nor with "gluttons.
21 For ỹ drõkard & ỹ glutton shalbe poore,
& the sleper shalbe clothed with ragges.
22 Obey thy father that hathe begoté thee,
& despise not thy mother whé she is olde.
23 Bye [k] the trueth, but sel it not: *likewise* wis
dome, and instruction, and vnderstãding.

p Which rashely put thé selues in danger for others, as Chap.6,1.
Deut.27,17.
chap.23,10.
a Eat with sobrietie.
b Bridel thine appetite, as it were by force and violence.
c For oft times the riche, whé they bid their inferiours to their tables, it is not for the loue they beare them, but for their owne secret purposes.
d Bestowe not the giftes that God hathe giuen thee, to get wordelie riches.
e That is, couetous, as contrarie a good eye is také for liberal, as Chap.22,9.
f He wil not cease, til he hathe done thee some harme, & his flattering wordes shal come to no vse.
Deut.27,17.
chap.22,28.
Chap.22,23.
Chap 13,24. & 19,18.
eccl.30,1.
g That is from destruction.
Psal 37,1.
chap.24,1.
h The prosperitie of ỹ wicked shal not continue.
i In the obseruation of Gods cómandeméts.
"Ebr. wine bibbers.
"Ebr deuourers of flesh.
k Spare no cost for trueths sake, nether departe from it for anie gaine.

24 The father of the righteous shal greatly
reioyce, & he that begetteth a wise childe,
shal haue ioye of him.
25 Thy father and thy mother shalbe glad,
and she that bare thee, shal reioyce.
26 My sonne, giue me [l] thine heart, and let
thine eyes delite in my wayes.

[l] Giue thy self wholly to wisdome.

27 *For a whore *is as* a depe ditche, & a strãge woman *is as* a narow pit.

Chap.22,14.

28 *Also she lieth in waite as for a pray,
[m] and she increaseth the transgressers a-
mong men.

Chap.7,8.

[m] She seduceth manie, & causeth them to offend God.

29 To whome is wo? to whome is sorowe?
to whome is strife? to whome is murmuring? to whome are woundes without cause? & to whome is the rednes of the eyes?
30 *Euen* to them that tarie long at the wine,
to them that go, [n] and seke mixt wine.

[n] Which by art make wine stronger, and more pleasant.

31 Loke not thou vpon the wine, when it is
red, & when it sheweth his colour in the
cuppe, *or* goeth downe pleasantly.
32 In the end thereof it wil bite like a serpent, and hurt like a cockatrise.
33 Thine [o] eyes shal loke vpõ strãge womẽ,
and thine heart shal speake lewde things.

[o] That is, drõkennes shal bring thee to whoredome.

34 And thou shalt be as one that slepeth in
the middes of the [p] sea, and as he that slepeth in the top of the mast.

[p] In suche great danger shalt thou be.

35 They haue striken me, *shalt thou say*, *but* I
was not sicke: they haue beaten me, *but* I
knewe not, when I awoke: *therefore* wil I
[q] seke it yet stil.

[q] Thogh drõkennes make them more insensible then beasts, yet cã they not refraine.

CHAP. XXIIII.

1 BE* not thou enuious against euil men,
nether desire to be with them.

Psal.37,1. chap.23,17.

2 For their heart imagineth destructiõ, and
their lippes speake mischief.
3 Through wisdome is an house buylded,
and with vnderstanding it is established.
4 And by knowledge shal the chambers be
filled with all precious, & pleasant riches.
5 A wise man *is* strong: for a man of vnderstanding encreaseth *his* strength.
6 *For with counsel thou shalt enterprise
thy warre, and in the multitude of them
that can giue counsel, *is* health.

Chap.20,18.

7 Wisdome is hie to a foole: *therefore* he cã
not open his mouth in the [a] gate.

[a] In the place where wisdome shulde be shewed.

8 He that imagineth to do euil, men shal
call him an autor of wickednes.
9 The wicked thoght of a foole *is* sinne, and
the scorner *is* an abominacion vnto men.
10 *If* thou be [b] faint in the day of aduersitie, thy strength *is* smal.

[b] Man hathe no tryal of his strength til he be in troubles.

11 Deliuer them that are drawen [c] to death:
and wilt thou not preserue them that are
led to be slaine?

[c] None can be excused, if he helpe not the innocent whẽ he is in dãger.

12 If thou say, Beholde, we knewe not of it:
he that põdereth the hearts, doeth not he
vnderstand it? and he that kepeth thy soule, knoweth he it not? wil not he also recompense euerie man according to his
workes?

13 My sonne, eat [d] honie, for it is good, and
the honie combe, *for it is* swete vnto thy
mouth.

[d] As honie is swete & pleasant to ỹ tast, so wisdome is to the soule.

14 So shal the knowledge of wisdome be
vnto thy soule, if thou finde it, and there
shalbe an [*] end, and thine hope shal not be
cut of.

[*] Or, rewarde.

15 Lay no waite, ô wicked man, against the
house of the righteous, and spoyle not his
resting place.
16 For a iuste man [e] falleth seuen times, &
riseth againe: but the wicked fall into
mischief.

[e] He is subiect to manie perils: but God deliuereth him.

17 Be thou not glad when thine enemie fal
leth, and let not thine heart reioyce when
he stumbleth,
18 Lest the Lord se it, and it displease him,
and he turne his wrath [f] from him.

[f] To be auenged on thee.

19 *Freat not thy self because of the malicious, nether be enuious at the wicked.

Psal.37,1. chap.23,17.

20 For there shal be none end *of plagues* to
the euil man: *the light of the wicked shalbe put out.

Chap 13,9.

21 My sonne, feare the Lord, and the King,
& meddle not with thẽ that are sedicious.
22 For their destruction shal rise suddenly,
& who knoweth the ruine of thẽ [g] bothe?

[g] Meaning, ether of ỹ wicked, and sedicious, as vers. 19, and 21, or of them that feare not God nor obey their King.

23 ALSO THESE THINGS PER-
TEINE TO THE WISE, It is not good
" to haue respect of anie persone in iudgement.

" Ebr. to knowe the face.

24 He that saith to the wicked, *Thou art
righteous, him shal the people curse, and
the multitude shal abhorre him.

Chap.17,15. isa.5,23.

25 But to them that rebuke *him*, shalbe pleasure, and vpon them shal come the blessing
of goodnes.
26 They shal kisse the lippes of him that
answereth vpright wordes.
27 Prepare thy worke without, and make
ready thy things in the field, [h] and after,
buylde thine house.

[h] Be sure of ỹ meanes how to compasse it before ỹ take anie enterprise in hand.

28 Be not a witnes against thy neighbour
without cause: for wilt thou deceiue with
thy lippes?
29 *Say not, I wil do to him, as he hathe done to me, I [i] wil recompense euerie man
according to his worke.

Chap 20,22.

[i] He sheweth what is the nature of ỹ wicked, to reuenge wrong for wrong.

30 I passed by the field of the slouthful, &
by the vineyarde of the man destitute of
vnderstanding.
31 And lo, it was all growen ouer with thornes, & nettles had couered the face thereof, and the stone wall thereof was broken
downe.
32 Then I beholde, *and* I considered it wel:
I loked vpon it, *and* [k] receiued instructiõ.

[k] That I might learne by another mans faute.

33 *Yet* a litle slepe, [l] a litle slumber, a litle
folding of the hands to slepe.

[l] Read Chap. 6,10.

34 So thy pouertie cometh *as* one that trauaileth by the way, and thy necessitie like an armed man.

CHAP.

CHAP. XXV.

1 THESE ARE ALSO PA-
rables of Salomón, which the a men of
Hezekiáh King of Iudáh b copied out.

2 THe glorie of God *is* to c conceile a
thing secret: but the d Kings honour
is to searche out a thing.
3 The heauens in height, and the earth in
depenes, and the e Kings heart can no man
searche out.
4 Take the f drosse from the siluer, and
there shal procede a vessel for the finer.
5 Take g away the wicked from the King,
and his throne shalbe stablished in righteousnes.
6 Boast not thy self before the King, and
stand not in the place of great men.
7 *For it is better, that it be said vnto thee,
Come vp hither, thẽ thou to be put lower
in the presence of the prince whome thine
eyes haue sene.
8 Go not forthe hastely to strife, lest thou
knowe not what to do in the end thereof,
when thy neighbour hathe put thee to
shame.
9 Debate thy matter with thy neighbour, &
discouer not the secret to another,
10 Lest he that heareth it, put thee to shame,
and thine infamie do not h cease.
11 A worde spokẽ in his place, *is like* appels
of golde with pictures of siluer.
12 He that reproueth the wise, & the obedient eare, *is as* a golden earing and an ornament of fine golde.
13 As the i colde of the snow in the time of
haruest, *so is* a faithful messenger to them
that send him: for he refresheth the soule
of his masters.
14 A man that boasteth of false liberalitie,
is like k cloudes and winde without raine.
15 A prince is pacified by staying l of angre, and a softe tõgue breaketh ỹ m bones.
16 *If* thou haue founde honie, eat that is
n sufficient for thee, lest thou be ouerful,
and vomit it.
17 Withdrawe thy fote from thy neighbours house, lest he be weary of thee, and
hate thee.
18 A man that beareth false witnes against
his neighbour, *is like* an hammer & a sword-
de, and a sharpe arrowe.
19 Cõfidence in an vnfaithful man in time
of trouble *is like* a broken tothe and a sli-
ding fote.
20 He ỹ taketh away the garmẽt in ỹ colde
season, *is like* vineger *powred* vpõ o nitre, or
like him ỹ singeth songs to an heauie heart.
21 *If he that hateth thee be hungrie, giue
him bread to eat, and if he be thirstie, giue
him water to drinke.
22 For thou shalt lay p coles vpon his head,
and the Lord shal recompense thee.

a Whome Hezekiáh appointed for this purpose.
b That is, gathered out of diuers bokes of Salomón.
c God doeth not reueile ỹ cause of his iudgements to man.
d Because the King ruleth by the reueiled worde of God, ỹ cause of his doings must appeare, & therefore he must vse diligence in trying out of causes.
e He sheweth ỹ it is to hard for man to atteine to ỹ reason of all the secret doings of ỹ King: euẽ when he is vpright, & doeth his dutie.
f When vice is remoued frõ a King, he is a mete vessel for the Lords vse.
g It is not ynough that he be pure him self, but ỹ he put away others that be corrupted.
Luk. 14, 10.
h Lest where as thou thinkest by this meanes to haue an end of ỹ matter, it put thee to farther trouble.
i In the time of great heat when men desire colde.
k Which haue an outward appearance, and are nothing within.
l By not ministring occasion to prouoke him farther.
m That is, the heart ỹ is bent to angre, as Chap. 15, 1.
n Vse moderatly the pleasures of this worlde.
o Which melteth it, and cõsumeth it. "Or, alume.
Rom. 12, 19.
p Thou shalt as it were by force ouercome him, in so muche that his owne cõsciẽce shal moue hi to acknowledge thy benefites, and his heart shalbe inflamed.

23 *As* the Northwind driueth away the raine, *so* doeth an angrie coũtenance ỹ sclan-
dering tongue.
24 *It is better to dwell in a corner of the
house toppe, then with a contentious woman in a wide house.
25 *As are* the colde waters to a wearie soule,
so is good newes from a farre countrey.
26 A righteous man falling downe before
the wicked, *is like* a troubled well, and a
corrupt spring.
27 It is not good to eat muche honie: *so to
search their owne glorie *is not* glorie.
28 A man that refraineth not his appetite,
is like a citie which is q broken downe, &
without walles.

CHAP. XXVI.

1 AS the snow in the sommer, and as the
raine in the haruest *are not mete*, *so* is
honour vnsemely for a foole.
2 As the sparow by fleing, and the swalowe
by flying *escape*, so the curse *that is* causeles,
shal not come.
3 Vnto the horse *belongeth* a whip, to the asse
a bridle, and a rodde to the fooles backe.
4 Answer not a foole a according to his foo
lishnes, lest thou also be like him.
5 Answer a foole b according to his foolishnes, lest he be wise in his owne " conceite.
6 He that sendeth a message by the hand of
a foole, *is as* he that cutteth of c the fete,
d and drinketh iniquitie.
7 *As* they that lift vp the legges of the
lame, *so is* a parable in a fooles mouth.
8 As the closing vp of a *precious* stone in an
heape of stones, *so is* he that giueth glorie
to a foole.
9 *As* a thorne standing e vp in the hand of
a drunkard, *so is* a parable in the mouth
of fooles.
10 f The excellent that formed all things,
bothe rewardeth the foole and rewardeth
the transgressers.
11 *As a dogge turneth againe to his owne
vomite, *so* a foole turneth to his foolishnes.
12 Seest thou a man wise in his owne conceite? g more hope *is* of a foole then of
him.
13 The slouthful man saith, h A lyon *is* in
the waye: a lyon *is* in the stretes.
14 *As* the dore turneth vpon his henges, *so
doeth* the slouthful man vpon his bed.
15 *The slouthful hideth his hand in *his*
bosome, *and* it grieueth him to put it a-
gaine to his mouth.
16 The sluggard is wiser in his owne conceit, then seuen *men* that can rendre a reason.
17 He that passeth by and medleth with
the strife *that belongeth* not vnto him, *is as*
on that taketh a dogge by the eares.

Chap. 21, 19.
Eccle. 3, 22.
q And so is in extreme danger.
a Consent not vnto him in his doings.
b Reproue hĩ as the matter requireth.
"Ebr. eyes.
c To wit, of the messenger, whome he sendeth.
d That is, receiueth domage thereby.
e Whereby he bothe hurteth him selfe and others.
f Meanĩg, God
2. Pet. 2, 22.
g For ỹ foole wil rather be counseled thẽ he: also ỹ foole sinneth of ignorance and the other of malice.
h Read Chap. 22, 13.
Chap. 19, 24.

18 As he that faineth him self mad, casteth
fyre brandes, arrowes and mortal things,

i Which dissembleth him self to be that he is not.

19 So *dealeth* the deceitful man [i] with his
friend and saith, Am not I in sporte?
20 Without wood the fyre is quenched, &
without a tale bearer strife ceaseth.

Eccl.38,12.

21 *As the cole *maketh* burning coles, and
wood a fyre, so the contentious man *is apt*
to kindle strife.

Chap.18,8.

22 *The wordes of a tale bearer *are* as flatterings, and they go downe into the bowels of the bellie.
23 *As* siluer drosse ouerlayed vpon a pot-
shard, *so are* burning lippes, and [k] an euil
heart.

k They wil sone breake out and vtter the selues.

24 He that hateth, wil counterfait with his
lippes, but in his heart he layeth vp deceit.
25 Thogh he speake fauorably, beleue him
not: for *there are* [l] seuen abominacions in
his heart.

l Meaning manie: he vseth y nõber certeine for the vncerteine.

26 Hatred may be couered by deceit: *but*
the malice thereof shalbe discouered in
the [m] Congregacion.

m In the assemblie of the godlie.
Ecclesi.10,8.
Eccl.27,30.

27 *He that diggeth a pit, shal fall therein,
and he that rolleth a stone, it shal returne vnto him.
28 A false tongue hateth the afflicted, and a
flattering mouth causeth ruine.

CHAP. XXVII.

a Delaye not the time, but take occasion when it is offred.

1 BOast not thy self of to [a] morowe: for
thou knowest not what a day may
bring forthe.
2 Let another man praise thee, and not thine owne mouth: a stranger, and not thine
owne lips.

Ecclesi.22,18.

3 *A stone *is* heauie, and the sand weightie:
but a fooles wrath *is* heauier then them
bothe.
4 Angre *is* cruel, and wrath *is* raging: but
who can stand before [b] enuie?

b For the enuious are obstinate and cã not be reconciled.
c They are flattering, and seme friẽdful.
Iob.6,6.

5 Open rebuke *is* better then secret loue.
6 The woundes of a louer *are* faithful, and
the kisses of an enemie *are* [c] pleasant.
7 *The persone that is ful, despiseth an honie combe: but vnto the hungrie soule e-
uerie bitter thing is swete.
8 As a birde that wandereth from her nest,
so *is* a man that wandereth from his owne
place.
9 *As* ointement and perfume reioyce the
heart, so *doeth* the swetenes of a mans friẽd
by heartie counsel.
10 Thine owne friend and thy fathers friẽd
forsake thou not: nether entre into thy brothers [d] house in the day of thy calamitie:

d Trust not to anie worldelie helpe in the day of thy trouble.

for better is a neighbour *that is* nere, then a
brother farre of.
11 My sonne, be wise, & reioyce mine heart,
that I may answer him that reprocheth
me.

e Read Chap. 22,3.

12 [e] A prudent man seeth the plague, and
hideth him self: *but* the foolish go on stil,
and are punished.
13 *Take his garment that is suretie for a Chap.20,16.
stranger, & a pledge of him for the strã-
ger.
14 He that "praiseth his friend with a lowe- "Ebr.blesseth.
de voyce, rising [f] early in the morning, it

f Hastely and without cause.

shalbe counted to him as a curse.
15 *A cõtinual dropping in the day of rai- Chap.19,20. & 21,9.
ne, and a contentious woman are a like.
16 He that hideth her, hideth the winde, &
she is as the oyle in his right hand, that vttereth it self.
17 Yron sharpeneth yron, so doeth [g] man

g One hastie man prouoketh another to angre.

sharpen the face of his friend.
18 He that kepeth the figge tre, shal eat the
frute thereof: so he that waiteth vpon his
master, shal come to honour.
19 As in water face *answereth* to face, [h] so the
heart of man to man.

h There is no difference betwene man & mã by nature, but onely the grace of God maketh the difference.

20 The graue and destruction can neuer be
ful, so *the eyes of man can neuer be satisfied.
21 *As *is* the fining pot for siluer & the for- Eccl.14,9.
nace for golde, so *is* euerie man according Chap.17,3.
to his [i] dignitie.

i That is, he is ether knowen to be ãbitious and glorious, or humble and modest.

22 Thogh thou shuldest braye a foole in a
morter among wheat brayed with a pe-
stel, *yet* wil not his foolishnes departe
from him.
23 Be diligẽt to knowe the state of thy flocke, and take hede to the heards.
24 For riches *remaine* not alwaye, nor
the crowne from generation to generation.
25 The heye discouereth it self, and the
grasse appeareth, and the herbes of the
mountaines are gathered.
26 The [k] lambes *are* for thy clothing, and
the goats *are* the price of the field.

k This declareth the great goodnes of God towardes man, & the diligence that he requireth of him for y preseruation of his giftes.

27 And let the milke of the goats *be* sufficient for thy foode, for the foode of thy
familie, and for the sustinance of thy maides.

CHAP. XXVIII.

1 THe wicked [a] flee when none pursueth: but the righteous are bolde as a
lyon.

a Becausetheir owne consciẽce accuseth them.

2 For the transgresion of the land [b] *there*
are manie princes thereof: but by a man
of vnderstanding and knowledge *a real-*
me likewise endureth long.

b The state of the commune weale is oftetimes chãged.

3 A poore man, if he oppresse the poore,
is like a raging raine, that *leaueth* no foode.
4 They that forsake the Law, praise the
wicked: but thei that kepe the Law, set thẽ
selues against them.
5 Wicked men vnderstand not iudgement:
but they that seke the Lord, vnderstand all
things.
6 *Better is the poore that walketh in his Chap.19,1.
vprightnes, then he that peruerteth *his*
waies, thogh he be riche.

7 He

7 He that kepeth the law, *is* a childe of vnderstanding: but he that fedeth the gluttons, shameth his father.
8 He that increaseth his riches by vsurie
and interest, gathereth [c] them for him that
wilbe merciful vnto the poore.

c For God wil take awai the wicked vsurer, & giue his goods to him that shal bestowe them wel.

9 He that turneth away his eare from hearing the Law, euen his praier shalbe [d] abominable.

d Because it is not of faith, w^c^ is grounded of Gods word, or Law, w^c^ the wicked contemne.

10 He that causeth the righteous to go a-
stray by an euil way, shal fall into his owne pit, and the vpright shal inherit good
things.
11 The riche man is wise in his owne conceit: but the poore that hathe vnderstanding, can trye [e] him.

e And iudge y^t^ he is not wise.

Chap. 29, 2.

12 * When righteous men reioyce, *there is*
great glorie: but when the wicked come
vp, the man [f] is tryed.

f He is knowẽ by his doings to be wicked.

13 He that hideth his sinnes, shal not prosper: but he that confesseth, and forsaketh
them, shal haue mercie.
14 Blessed *is* the man that [g] feareth alwaye:
but he that hardeneth his heart, shal fall
into euil.

g Which standeth in awe of God and is afraid to offẽd him.

15 *As* a roaring lyon, and an hũgrie beare,
so is [h] a wicked ruler ouer the poore people.

h For he can neuer be satisfied, but euer oppresseth and spoileth.

16 A prince destitute of vnderstanding, is
also a great oppressour: but he that hateth
couetousnes, shal prolong *his* daies.
17 A man that doeth violence against the
blood of a persone, shal flee vnto the graue, *and* thei shal not [i] stay him.

i None shalbe able to deliuer him.

18 He that walketh vprightly, shalbe saued: but he that is froward in *his* waies,
shal once fall.

Chap. 12, 11. eccl. 20, 30.

19 *He that tilleth his land, shal be satisfied
with bread: but he y^t^ followeth the ydle,
shal be filled with pouertie.

Chap. 13, 11. & 20, 21.

20 A faithful man shal abounde in blessings, & *he that maketh haste to be riche,
shal not be innocent.
21 To haue respect of persones is not good:
for *that* man wil transgresse for a piece of
[k] bread.

k He wil be abused for nothing.

22 A man with a wicked [l] eye hasteth to riches, and knoweth not, that pouertie shal
come vpon him.

l Meaning him that is couetous.

23 He that rebuketh a man, shal finde more fauour at the length, then he that flattereth with *his* tongue.
24 He that robbeth his father and mother,
& saith, it is no transgresion, is the companion of a man that destroieth.
25 He that is of a proude heart, stirreth vp
strife: but he that trusteth in the Lord, shal
be [m] fat.

m Shal haue all things in abundance.

26 He that trusteth in his owne heart, is a
foole: but he that walketh in wisdome,
shalbe deliuered.
27 He that giueth vnto the poore, shal not
lacke: but he that hideth his eyes, *shal haue*
many curses.

Chap. 29, 2.

28 *When the wicked rise vp, men hide thẽ
selues: but when thei perish, the righteous
increase.

CHAP. XXIX.

1 A Man that hardeneth his necke, when
he is rebuked, shal suddenly be des-
stroied and can not be cured.

Chap. 28, 12. & 28.

2 * When the righteous [*] are in autoritie,
the people reioyce: but when the wicked
beareth rule, the people sigh.

*Or, are increased.

Luk. 15, 13.

3 A mã that loueth wisdome, reioyceth his
father: * but he that fedeth harlots, wa-
steth *his* substance.
4 A King by iudgement mainteineth the
countrey: but a man *receiuing* giftes, destroieth it.
5 A man y^t^ flattereth his neighbour, [a] spreadeth a net for his steppes.

a He y^t^ giueth eare to ye flatterer, is in dãger as ye bird is before ye fouler.

6 In the transgresion of an euil man *is* his
[b] snare: but the righteous doeth sing and
reioyce.

b He is euer ready to fall into ye snare y^t^ he layeth for others.

7 The righteous knoweth the cause of the
poore: *but* the wicked regardeth not know
ledge.
8 Scornful men bring a citie into a snare:
but wise men turne away wrath.
9 *If* a wise man contend with [c] a foolish
man, whether he be angrie or laugh, there *is* no rest.

c He can beare no admonitiõ, in what sorte soeuer it is spoken.

10 Bloodie men hate him that is vpright:
but the iuste haue care of his soule.
11 A foole powreth out all his minde: but a
wise man kepeth it in til afterwarde.
12 Of a prince that hearkeneth to lyes, all
his seruants *are* wicked.

Chap. 22, 2.

13 * The poore and the vsurer mete together, *and* the Lord lighteneth bothe their
eyes.

Chap. 20, 28.

14 *A King that iudgeth the poore in trueth, his throne shalbe established for e-
uer.
15 The rodde and correction giue wisdome: but a childe set at libertie, maketh his
mother ashamed.
16 When the wicked are increased, transgresion increaseth: but the righteous shal
se their fall.
17 Correct thy sonne and he wil giue thee
rest, and wil giue pleasures to thy soule.
18 [d] Where there *is* no vision, the people
decay: but he that kepeth the Law, *is* blessed.

d Where there are not faithful ministers of the worde of God.

19 A [e] seruant wil not be chastised with
wordes: thogh he vnderstand, yet he wil
not [*] answere.

e He y^t^ is of a seruile & rebellious nature.

*Or, regarde.

20 Seest thou a man hastie in his matters? *there is* more hope of a foole, then
of him.
21 He that delicately bringeth vp his seruãt

from youth, at length he wil be euen *as*
his sonne.
Chap 15,18.
22 *An angrie man stirreth vp strife, and a
furious man abundeth in transgression.
Iob.22,29.
23 *The pride of a man shal bring him
lowe: but the humble in spirit shal enioye
glorie.
24 He that is partener with a thief, hateth
his owne soule: he heareth cursing, and declareth it not.
25 The feare of man bringeth a [f] snare: but
he that trusteth in ẏ Lord, shalbe exalted.
26 Manie do seke the face of the ruler: but
euerie mās [g] iudgement *commeth* from the
Lord.
27 A wicked man *is* abominaciō to the iust,
and he that is vpright in *his* way, *is* abominacion to the wicked.

f He ẏ feareth man more thē God falleth into a snare & is destroyed.
g He nedeth not to flatter ẏ ruler: for what God hathe appointed, that shal come to him.

CHAP. XXX.

2 To humble our selues in consideration of Gods workes. 5 The worde of God is perfite. 11 Of the wicked & hypocrites. 15 Of things that are neuer saciate. 18 Of others that are wonderful.

THE WORDES OF [a] AGVR THE SONNE OF IAKEH.

1 THe prophecie *which* the mā spake vnto Ithiél, *euen* to [b] Ithiél, and Vcál.
2 Surely I am more [c] foolish then anie man,
and haue not the vnderstanding of a man
in me.
3 For I haue not learned wisdome, nor atteined to the knowledge of holie things.
4 Who hathe ascended vp to [d] heauen,
and descended? Who hathe gathered
the winde in his fist? Who hathe bounde
the waters in a garmēt? Who hathe establi
shed all ẏ ends of the worlde? What is his
name, & what is his sonnes name, if thou
canst tel?
Psal.19,8.
5 *Euerie worde of God is pure: he is a
shield to those, that trust in him.
Deut.4,2. & 12,32.
6 *Put nothing vnto his wordes, lest he
reproue thee, and thou be founde a
lyer.
7 Two [e] things haue I required of thee: deny me them not before I dye.
8 Remoue farre frō me vanitie and lies: giue me not pouertie, nor riches: fede me
with foode conuenient for me,
9 Lest I be ful, and denie *thee*, and say,
[f] Who is the Lord? or lest I be poore and
steale, and take the Name of my God *in
vaine*.
10 Accuse not a seruant vnto his master,
lest he curse thee, [g] when thou hast offended.
11 *There is* a generacion that curseth their
father, and doeth not blesse their mother.
12 *There is* a generacion that are pure in
there owne conceit, and *yet* are not washed
from their filthines.

a Who was an excellent man in vertue and knowledge in the time of Salomón.
b Which were Agurs scholers or friēds.
c Herein he declareth his great humilitie who wolde not attribute anie wisdome to hī self, but all vnto God.
d Meaning, to knowe the secretes of God, as thogh he wolde saye, None.
e He maketh this request to God.
f Meaning, ẏ they that put their trust in their riches, forget God, & that by to muche wealth mē haue an occasion to ẏ same.
g In accusing him without cause.

13 *There is* a generacion, whose eyes are hautie, and their eye liddes are lifted vp.
14 *There is* a generacion, whose teeth *are as*
swordes, and their chawes *as* kniues to eat
vp the afflicted out of the earth, and the
poore from among men.
15 The horse leache hathe two [h] daughters
which crie, Giue, giue. There be thre thīgs
that wil not be satisfied: *yea*, foure that say
not, It is ynough.
16 The graue, & the baren wombe, the earth
that can not be satisfied with water, and
the fyre that saith not, It is ynough.
17 The eye that mocketh *his* father and des
piseth the instructiō of *his* mother, let the
rauens [i] of the valley picke it out, and the
yong egles eat it.
18 There be thre things hid from me: yea,
foure that I knowe not.
19 The way of an egle in the aire, the waie
of a serpent vpon a stone, the waie of a
shippe in the middes of the sea, and the
way of a man with a maide.
20 Suche is the way also of an aduouterous
woman: she eateth & [k] wipeth her mouth,
and saith, I haue not committed iniquitie.
21 For thre things the earth is moued: yea,
for foure it can not susteine it self:
22 For [l] a seruant when he reigneth, and a
foole when he is filled with meat,
23 For the hateful woman, when she is maried, and for a handmaid that is [m] heire to
her mastres.
24 These be foure smal things in the earth,
yet thei are [n] wise and ful of wisdome:
25 The pismires a people not strong, yet
prepare they their meat in sommer:
26 The conies a people not mightie, yet
make they their houses in the rocke:
27 The greshopper hathe no King, yet go
thei forthe all by bandes:
28 The spider taketh holde [o] with *her* hāds,
and is in Kings palaces.
29 There be thre things that order wel
their going: yea, foure are comelie in
going,
30 A lyon which is strong among beastes,
and turneth not at the sight of anie:
31 A lustie grayhound, and a goat, and a
King against whome there is no rising
vp.
32 If thou hast bene foolish in lifting thy
self vp, and if thou hast thoght wickedly, *lay* thine hand [p] vpon *thy* mouth.
33 When one churneth milke, he bringeth
forthe butter: and he that wringeth his
nose, causeth blood to come out: so he that
forceth wrath, bringeth forthe strife.

h The leach hathe two forkes in her tongue, which here he calleth her two daughters, whereby she sucketh ẏ blood: and is neuer satiate: euen so are the couetous extorsioners insatiable.
i Which haunte in the valley for carions.
k She hath her desires, & after counterfaiteth as thogh she were an honest woman.
l These comunely abuse the state whereunto thei are called.
m Which is maried to her master after the death of her mastres.
n Thei conteine great doctrine & wisdome.
o If man be not able to cōpasse these cōmune thigs by his wisdome, we can not attribute wisdome to man but folie.
p Make a stay & cōtinue not in doing euil.

CHAP. XXXI.

2 He exhorteth to chastitie and iustice. 10 And sheweth the conditions of a wise and worthy woman.

The

1 THE WORDES OF KING
[a] Lemuél: The [b] prophecie which his
mother taught him.
2 WHat my sonne! and what the sonne of [c] my wombe! and what, ô
sonne of my desires!
3 Giue not thy strength vnto womẽ, [d] nor
thy waies, *which is* to destroy Kings.
4 It is not for Kings, ô Lemuél, it is not for
Kings to drinke wine, nor for princes
[e] strong drinke,
5 Lest he drinke, and forget the decree, and
change the iudgement of all the children
of affliction.
6 Giue ye strong drinke vnto him, that is
readie to perish, and wine vnto them that
haue grief of heart.
7 Let him drinke, that he may forget [f] his
pouertie, and remember his miserie no
more.
8 Open thy mouth for the [g] domme in the
cause of all the children of destruction.
9 Open thy mouth: iudge righteously, and
iudge the afflicted, and the poore.
10 ¶ Who shal finde a vertuous woman? for
her price *is* farre aboue the pearles.
11 The heart of her housband trusteth in
her, and he shal haue no nede of [h] spoile.
12 She wil do him good, and not euil all
the daies of her life.
13 She seketh wooll and flaxe, and laboreth
cherefully with her hands.
14 She is like the shippes of marchants: she
bringeth her fode from a farre.
15 And she riseth, whiles it is yet night: and
giueth * the porcion to her housholde, and
the [i] ordinarie to her maids.
16 She considereth a field, and [k] getteth it:
& with the frute of her hands she plãteth
a vineyarde.
17 She girdeth her loynes with strength, &
strengtheneth her armes.
18 She feleth that her marchandise is good:
her candle is not put out by night.
19 She putteth her hands to the wherue, &
her hands handle the spindle.
20 She stretcheth out her hand to the poore,
and putteth forthe her hands to the nedie.
21 She feareth not the snowe for her familie: for all her familie is clothed with * skarlet.
22 She maketh her self carpets: fine linen &
purple *is* her garment.
23 Her housband is knowen in the [l] gates,
when he sitteth with the Elders of ỳ land.
24 She maketh * shetes, and selleth them, &
giueth girdels vnto the marchant.
25 [m] Strength and honour *is* her clothing,
and in the latter day she shal reioyce.
26 She openeth her mouth with wisdome,
and the [n] law of grace *is* in her tongue.
27 She ouerseeth ỳ waies of her housholde,
and eateth not the bread of ydlenes.
28 Her children rise vp, and [o] call her blessed: her housband also shal praise her, *saying*,
29 Manie daughters haue done vertuously:
but thou surmountest them all.
30 Fauour *is* disceitful, and beautie *is* vanitie: *but* a woman that feareth the Lord, she
shal be praised.
31 Giue [p] her of the frute of her hands, and
let her owne workes praise her in ỳ [q] gates.

a That is, of Salomón, who was called Lemuél, that is, of God because God hád ordeined him to be King ouer Israél.
b The doctrine, which his mother Bathshéba taught him.
c By this often repitition of one thing she declareth her motherlie affection.
d Meaning, ỳ women are the destruction of Kings, if thei haunte them.
e That is, the King must not giue him self to wantõnes & neglect his office, which is to execute iudgement.
f For wine doeth comfort the heart, as Psal 104,15.
g Defend their cause that are not able to helpe them selues.
h He shal not nede to vse anie vnlawful meanes to gaine his liuing.
* Or, meat, as Psal. 111,5.
i She prepareth their meat betime.
k She purchaseth it with ỳ gaines of her trauail.
* Or, with double.
l In the assemblies and places of iudgement.
* Or, linen cloth.
m After that he had spokẽ of the apparel of the bodie, he now declareth the apparel of the spirit.
n Her tongue is as a boke whereby one might learne manie good things: for she deliteth to talke of the worde of God.
o That is, do her reuerence.
p Confesse her diligent labours and cõmende her therefore.
q For as much as the moste honorable are clad in the apparel that she made.

ECCLESIASTES, OR the Preacher.

THE ARGVMENT.

Salomón, as a preacher and one that desired to instruct all in the way of saluacion, describeth the deceiuable vanities of this worlde, that man shulde not be addicted to anie thing vnder the sunne, but rather inflamed with the desire of the heauenlie life: therefore he confuteth their opinions, which set their felicitie, ether in knowledge, or in pleasures, or in dignitie and riches, shewing that mans true felicitie consisteth in that that he is vnited with God and shal inioye his presence: so that all other things must be reiected, saue in as muche as thei farther vs to atteine to this heauenlie treasure, which is sure and permanent, and can not be founde in anie other saue in God alone.

CHAP. I.

2 *All things in this worlde are ful of vanitie, and of none
indurance. 13 All mans wisdome is but folie and
grief.*

1 THe wordes of the [a] Preacher, the sonne of Dauid
King in Ierusalém.
2 [b] Vanitie of vanities,
saith ỳ Preacher: vanitie
of vanities, all *is* vanitie.
3 What remaineth vnto mã in all his [c] trauail, which he suffreth vnder the sunne?
4 *One* generacion passeth, and *another* generacion succedeth: but the earth remaineth
for [d] euer.
5 The sunne riseth, & the sunne goeth downe, & draweth to his place, where he riseth.
6 The [e] winde goeth toward ỳ South, & cõpasseth toward ỳ North: the winde goeth
round about, & returneth by his circuites.
7 *All the riuers go into the sea, yet the sea
is not ful: *for* the riuers go vnto the place,

a Salomón is here called a Preacher, or one that assẽbleth the people, because he teacheth the true knowledge of God, & how men oght to passe their life in this trãsitorie world.
b He condemneth the opinions of all mẽ that set felicitie in anie thing, but in God alone, seing that in this worlde all things are as vanitie and nothing.
c Salomón doeth not condemne mans labour or diligence, but sheweth that there is no ful contentation in anie thing vnder ỳ heauen, nor in anie creature, for asmuche as all things are trãsitorie.
d One man dieth after another, and the earth remaineth longest, euen to the last daie, which yet is subiect to corruption.
e By the sunne, winde and riuers he sheweth that the greatest labour and longest hathe an end, and therefore there can be no felicitie in this worlde.
* Eccles. 40,11.

&.i.

[f] whence thei returne, and go.
8 All things are ful of labour: man can not
vtter it: the eye is not satisfied with seing,
nor the eare filled with hearing.
9 [g] What is it that hathe bene? that that
shalbe: & what is it that hathe bene done?
that which shalbe done: and there *is* no
new thing vnder the sunne.
10 Is there anie thing, whereof one may
say, Beholde this, it is newe? it hathe bene
alreadie in the olde time ỹ was before vs.
11 There is no memorie of ỹ former, nether
shal there be a remẽbrance of the later that
shalbe, with them that shal come after.
12 ¶ [h] I the Preacher haue bene King ouer
Israél in Ierusalém:
13 And I haue giuen mine heart to search
& finde out wisdome by all things that are
done vnder the heauen: (this sore trauail
hathe God giuen to the sonnes of men,
[i] to humble them thereby)
14 I haue considered all the workes that are
done vnder the sunne, and beholde, all *is*
vanitie, and vexacion of the spirit.
15 That which is [k] croked, can none make
straight: & that ẘ faileth, cã not be nõbred.
16 I thoght in mine heart, & said, Beholde,
I am become great, and excel in wisdome
all them that haue bene before me in Ierusalém: and mine heart hathe sene muche
wisdome and knowledge.
17 And I gaue mine heart to knowe wisdome & knowledge, [l] madnes & foolishnes: I
knewe also ỹ this is a vexaciõ of the spirit.
18 For in ỹ multitude of wisdome *is* muche
[m] grief: & he that encreaseth knowledge,
encreaseth sorowe.

f The sea ẘ compasseth all the earth, filleth the veines thereof, the ẘ powre out springs and riuers into the sea againe.
g He speaketh of times & seasons & things done in them, which as thei haue bene in times past, so come thei to passe againe.
h He proueth that if anie colde haue atteined to felicitie in this worlde by labour and studie, he chiefly shulde haue obteined it, because he had giftes and aydes of God thereunto aboue all other
i Man of nature hathe a desire to knowe, and yet is not able to come to the perfection of knowledge, ẘ is the punishmẽt of sinne, to humble man, and to teache him to depende onely vpon God.
k Man is not able by all his diligence to cause things to go other wise then thei do: nether can he nombre the fautes that are committed, muche lesse remedie them.
l That is, vaine things, which serued vnto pleasure, wherin was no commoditie, but grief & trouble of conscience.
m Wisdome & knowledge can not be come by without great peine of bodie and minde: for when a man hathe atteined to the hiest, yet is his minde neuer fully content: therefore in this worlde is no true felicitie.

CHAP. II.

Pleasures, sumptuous buyldings, riches and possessiõs are but vanitie. 14 The wise and the foole haue bothe one end, touching the bodelie death.

1 I Said in mine heart, Go to now, I wil
proue [a] thee with ioye: therefore take
thou pleasure in pleasant things: & beholde, this also is vanitie.
2 I said of laughter, Thou art mad: and of
ioye, What is this that thou doest?
3 I soght in mine heart "to giue my self to
wine, & to lead mine heart in [b] wisdome,
and to take holde of folie, til I might se
where is that goodnes of the children of
men, which they "enioye vnder the sunne:
the *whole* nomber of the daies of their life.
4 I haue made my great workes: I haue buylt me houses: I haue plãted me vineyards.
5 I haue made me gardens and "orchardes,
and planted in them trees of all frute.
6 I haue made me cisternes of water, to
watter therewith the woods that growe
with trees.

a Salomón maketh this discours with hĩself, as thogh he wolde trye whether there were contentation in ease and pleasures.
" Ebr. drawe my flesh to wine.
b Albeit I gaue my self to pleasures, yet I thoght to kepe wisdome & the feare of God in mine heart, and gouerne mine affaires by the same.
" Ebr. do.
" Ebr. paradises

7 I haue gotten seruants & maids, and had
children *borne* in the [c] house: also I had
great possession of beues and shepe aboue
all that were before me in Ierusalém.
8 I haue gathered vnto me also siluer and
golde, and the chief treasures of Kings &
prouinces: I haue prouided me mẽ singers
and women singers, and the [d] delites of the
sonnes of men, *as* a woman [e] taken captiue,
and women taken captiues.
9 And I was great, and encreased aboue all
that were before me in Ierusalém: also my
wisdome [f] remained with me.
10 And what soeuer mine eyes desired, I
withhelde it not from thẽ: I withdrew not
mine heart from anie ioye: for mine heart
reioyced in all my labour: and this was
my [g] portion of all my trauail.
11 Thẽ I loked on all my workes that mine
hands had wroght, and on the trauail that
I had labored to do: and beholde, all *is* vanitie and vexacion of the spirit: and there
is no profite vnder the sunne.
12 ¶ And I turned to beholde [h] wisdome, &
madnes and folie: (for who is the man that
"wil come after the King in things, which
men now haue done?)
13 Then I sawe that there is profite in wisdome, more then in folie: as the light is
more excellent then darkenes.
14 *For the wise mans [i] eyes *are* in his head,
but the foole walketh in darkenes: yet I
knowe also that the same [k] condition falleth to them all.
15 Then I thoght in mine heart, It befalleth vnto me, as it befalleth to the foole.
Why therefore do I thẽ labour to be more wise? And I said in mine heart, that this
also is vanitie.
16 For there shalbe no remembrance of the
wise, nor of the foole [l] for euer: for that
that now is, in the daies to come shal all be
forgotten. And [m] how dyeth the wise man,
as doeth the foole?
17 Therefore I hated life: for the worke ỹ is
wroght vnder ỹ sũne is grieuous vnto me:
for all *is* vanitie, & vexacion of the spirit.
18 I hated also all my labour, wherein I had
trauailed vnder ỹ sũnne, which I shal leaue to the man that shalbe after me.
19 And who knoweth whether he shalbe
wise or foolish? yet shal he haue rule ouer
all my labour, wherein I haue trauailed, &
wherein I haue shewed my self wise vnder
the sunne. This is also vanitie.
20 Therefore I went about to make mine
heart [n] abhorre all the labour, wherein I
had trauailed vnder the sunne.
21 For there is a man whose trauail is in
wisdome, & in knowledge and in equitie:
yet to a mã that hathe not trauailed herein, shal he [o] giue his portion: this also is
vanitie and a great grief.

c Meaning, of the seruants or sclaues, ẘ he had boght: so the childrẽ borne in their seruitude, were the masters.
d That is, what soeuer men take pleasure in.
e Which were the most beautiful of them that were taken in warre, as Judges. 5, 30. Some vnderstand by these wordes, noe women but instruments of musike.
f For all this God did not take his gift of wisdome from me.
g This was ỹ frute of all my labour, a certeine pleasure mixt with care, which he calleth vanitie in the next verse.
h I bethoght with my self whether it were better to followe wisdome, or mine owne affectiõs and pleasures, which he calleth madnes.
" Or, compare with the King.
* Prou. 17, 24.
i He foreseeth things, ẘ the foole can not for lacke of wisdome.
k For bothe dye & are forgotten, as verse 16, or they bothe alike haue prosperitie or aduersitie.
l Meaning, in this worlde.
m He wondereth that men forget a wise man, being dead, assone as thei do a foole.
n That I might seke the true felicitie which is in God.
o Among other griefs this was not ỹ least to leaue that which he had gotten by great trauail, to one ỹ had taken no peine therefore, and whome he knewnot whether he were a wise man or a foole.

22 For

22 For what hathe man of all his trauail
and grief of his heart, wherein he hathe
trauailed vnder the sunne?
23 For all his dayes are sorowes, and his trauail grief. his heart also taketh not rest in
the night, which also is vanitie.
24 There *is* no profite to mã: but that he eat,
and drinke, and [p] delite his soule with the
profite of his labour: I sawe also this, that
it was of the hand of God.
25 For who colde eat, and who colde haste
to [q] outward things more then I?
26 Surely to a mã that is good in his sight,
God giueth wisdome, and knowledge, and
ioye: but to the sinner he giueth peine, to
gather, and to heape to giue to him that is
good before God: this is also vanitie, &
vexacion of the spirit.

p When man hathe all laboured, he can get no more then fode, and refreshing, yet he confesseth also that this cometh of Gods blessing, as Chap. 3, 13.
q Meaning, to pleasures.

CHAP. III.

1 All things haue their time. 14 The workes of God are perfite, and cause vs to feare him. 17 God shal iudge bothe the iuste, and iniuste.

1 TO all things *there is* an [a] appointed time, and a time to euerie purpose vnder the heauen.
2 A time to be borne, & a time to dye: a time to plant, and a time to plucke vp that,
which is planted.
3 A time to slay, and a time to heale: a time
to breake downe, and a time to buylde.
4 A time to wepe, and a time to laugh: a time to mourne, and a time to dance.
5 A time to cast away stones, and a time to
gather stones: a time to embrace, and a time to be farre from embracing.
6 A time to seke, and a time to lose: a time
to kepe, and a time to cast away.
7 A time to rẽt, & a time to sowe: a time to
kepe silence, and a time to speake.
8 A time to loue, and a time to hate: a time
of warre, and a time of peace.
9 What profite *hathe* he that worketh, of ẏ
thing wherein he trauaileth?
10 I haue sene the trauail that God hathe
giuen to the sonnes of men [b] to humble
them thereby.
11 He hathe made euerie thing beautiful in
his time: also he hathe set the [c] worlde in
their heart, yet can not man finde out the
worke that God hathe wroght from the
beginning euen to the end.
12 I knowe that there is nothing good in thẽ,
but to reioyce, & to do good in his life.
13 And also that euerie mã eateth and drinketh, and seeth the commoditie of all his
labour. this is the [d] gift of God.
14 I knowe that what soeuer God shal do, it
shalbe for euer: to it can no man adde, and
frõ it can none diminish: for God hathe
done it, ẏ they shulde feare before him.
15 What is that that hathe bene? that is
now: & that that shalbe, hathe now bene:
for God [f] requireth that which is past.

a He speaketh of this diuersitie of time for two causes, first to declare ẏ there is nothing in this worlde perpetual: next to teache vs not to be grieued, if we haue not all things at once according to our desires, nether enioye them so long as we wolde wish.
b Read Chap. 3, 13.
c God hathe giuen man a desire, and affection to seke out the things of this worlde and to labour therein.
d Read Chap. 2, 24 and these places declare that we shulde do all things with sobrietie, & in ẏ feare of God, forasmuche as he giueth not his giftes to ẏ intẽt that they shulde be abused.
e That is, man shal neuer be able to let Gods worke, but as he hathe determined, so it shal come to passe.
f God onelie causeth that, ẇ is past, to returne.

16 And moreouer I haue sene vnder the
sunne the place of iudgement, where *was*
wickednes, and the place of iustice where
was iniquitie.
17 I thoght in mine heart, God wil iudge
the iuste & the wicked: for time is [g] there
for euerie purpose and for euerie worke.
18 I considered in mine heart the state of
the children of men that God had [h] purged them: yet to se to, they are in thẽ selues *as* beasts.
19 For the condition of the children of mẽ,
and the conditiõ of beastes *are* euẽ *as* one
[i] cõdition vnto them. As the one dyeth, so
dyeth the other: for they haue all one breath, and there is no excellencie of man a-
boue the beast: for all *is* vanitie.
20 All go to one place, and all was of the
dust, and all shal returne to the dust.
21 Who [k] knoweth whether the spirit of
man ascende vpward, and the spirit of the
beast descend downeward to the earth?
22 Therefore I se that there is nothing
better then ẏ a man shulde [l] reioyce in his
affaires, because ẏ is his portion: For who
shal brĩg him to se what shalbe after him?

CHAP. IIII.

1 The innocents are oppressed. 4 Mans labours are ful of abuse and vanitie. 9 Mans societie is necessarie. 13 A yong man poore, and wise is to be preferred to an olde King that is a foole.

1 SO [a] I turned, and cõsidered all the oppressions that are wroght vnder the
sunne, & beholde, the teares of the oppressed, and none comforteth them: and *lo*, the
strength *is* of the hand of them that oppresse them, and none comforteth them.
2 Wherefore I praised the [b] dead which
now are dead, aboue the liuing, which a-
re yet aliue.
3 And *I counte* him [c] better then them bothe, which hathe not yet bene: for he hathe
not sene the euil workes which are wroght
vnder the sunne.
4 Also I behelde all trauail, and all [d] perfection of workes that this is the enuie of a
man against his neighbour: this also *is* vanitie and vexacion of spirit.
5 The foole foldeth his hands, and [e] eateth
vp his owne flesh.
6 Better is an handful with quietnes, then
two handfuls with labour and vexacion of
spirit.
7 Againe I returned, and sawe vanitie vnder the sunne.
8 There is one *alone*, and there *is* not a secõde, which hathe nether sonne nor brother,
yet *is* there none end of all his trauail, nether cã his eye be satisfied with riches: nether *doeth he thinke*, For whome do I trauail
and defraude my soule of pleasure? this also is vanitie, and this is an euil trauail.
9 [f] Two *are* better then one: for they haue

g Meaning, ẏ God, how soeuer man neglect his duetie.
h And made them pure in their first creation.
i Man is not able by his reason, & iudgement to put difference betwene man & beast, as touching those things whereunto both are subiect: for the eye cã not iudge anie other wise of a man being dead, thẽ of a beast, ẇ is dead: yet by ẏ worde of God and faith we easely knowe the diuersitie, as vers. 21.
k Meanĩg, that reason cã not comprehend ẏ which faith beleueth herein
l By the often repetition of this sentẽce, as Chap. 2, 24 & chap 3, 12, and 22. chap. 5, 17 & chap 8, 15 he declareth that mã by reason cã cõprehend nothing better in this life thẽ to vse the giftes of God soberly & cõfortably: for to knowe farther is a special gifte of God reueiled by his Spirit.

Chap IIII.
a He maketh here another discours with him self cõcerning the tyrãnie of them ẏ oppressed the poore.
b Because thei are no more subiect to these oppresions
c He speaketh according to ẏ iudgemẽt of ẏ flesh, ẇ cã not abide to fele, or se troubles.
d The more profit ẏ the worke is, the more is it enuied of ẏ wicked.
e For ydlenes he is cõpelled to destroye him self.
f Forasmuche as when mã is alone, he can nether helpe him self nor others, he sheweth ẏ mẽ oght to liue in mutual societie, to ẏ intent thei may be profitable one to another, & ẏ their things may encrease.

better wages for their labour.
10 For if they fall, the one wil lift vp his fellowe: but wo vnto him *that is* alone: for he
falleth, and there *is* not a seconde to lift
him vp.
11 Also if two slepe *together*, then shal they
haue heat: but to one how shulde there be
heat?
12 And if one ouercome him, two shal stande against him: and a threfolde [g] coard is
not easely broken.
13 Better is a poore and wise childe, then an
olde and foolish King, which wil no more
be admonished.
14 For out of the [h] prison he cometh forthe
to reigne: when as he that is [i] borne in his
kingdome, is made poore.
15 I behelde all the liuing, which walke vnder the sunne, [k] with the seconde childe,
which shal stande vp in his place.
16 There is none [l] end of all the people, *nor*
of all that were before them, and they that
come after, shal not reioyce in him: surely
this is also vanitie and vexation of spirit.
17 Take hede to thy [m] foote when thou entrest into he House of God, and be more
nere to heare then to giue the sacrifice of
[n] fooles: for they knowe not that they do
euil.

g By this prouerbe he declareth how necessarie it is, ẏ men shulde liue in societie.
h That is, frõ a poore, & base estate, or out of trouble, & prison, as Ioseph did, Gen 41,14
i Meaning, ẏ is borne a King.
k Which follow, & flatter ẏ Kings sonne, or him ẏ shal succede: to enter into credit with them in hope of gaine.
l They neuer cease by all meanes to crepe into fauour: but when they obteine not their greadie desires, they thinke thẽ selues abused, as other haue bene i time past, and so care no more for him.
m That is, ẇ what affection thou comest to heare ẏ worde of God.
n Meaning, of the wicked, ẇ thinke to please God ẇ ceremonies, and haue nether faith nor repẽtance.

CHAP. V.

1 Not to speake lightely, chiefely in Gods matters. 9 The couetous can neuer haue ynough. 11 The laborers slepe is swete. 14 Man when he dyeth, taketh nothing with him. 18 To liue ioyfully, and with a contẽted minde is the gift of God.

1 BE not [a] rash with thy mouth, nor let
thine heart be hastie to vtter a thing
before God: for God *is* in the heauens, and
thou art on ẏ earth: therefore let thy wordes be [b] fewe.
2 For *as* a dreame cometh by the multitude
of busines: so the voyce of a foole *is* in the
multitude of wordes.
3 *When thou hast vowed a vowe to God,
deferre not to pay it: for he deliteth not in
fooles: paye *therefore* ẏ thou hast [c] vowed.
4 It is better that thou shuldest not vowe,
then that thou shuldest vowe and not
paye it.
5 Suffer not thy mouth to make thy [d] flesh
to sinne: nether say before the [e] Angel, that
this is ignorance: wherefore shal God be
angrie by thy voyce, & destroye the worke of thine hands?
6 For in the multitude of dreames, & vanities *are* also manie wordes: but feare thou
God.
7 If in a countrey thou seest the oppressiõ
of the poore, and the defrauding of iudgement and iustice, be not astonied at the
matter: for he that is [f] higher then the
highest, regardeth, and *there be* higher then
they.

a Ether i vowing or in praying: meaning ẏ we shulde vse all reuerẽce to God warde.
b He heareth thee not for thy manie wordes sake, or often repetitions, but considereth thy faith, and feruent minde.
Deut.23,21.
c He speaketh of vowes, ẇ are approued by Gods worde, and serue to his glorie.
d Cause not thy self to sinne by vowing rashely: as thei do ẇ make a vowe to liue vnmaried, and suche like.
e That is, before Gods messenger whẽ he shal examine thy doing: as thogh thy ignorãce shulde be a iust excuse.
f Meaning, ẏ God wil redresse these things, & therfore we must depẽd vpõ hĩ.

8 And the [g] abundance of the earth is ouer
all: the King [h] *also consisteth* by the field that
is tilled.
9 He that loueth siluer, shal not be satisfied
with siluer, & he that loueth riches, *shalbe*
without the frute *therof*: this also is vanitie.
10 Whẽ goods encrease, they are encreased
that eat them: and what good cometh to
the owners thereof, but the beholding *thereof* with their eyes?
11 The slepe of him that trauaileth, *is* swete,
whether he eat litle or muche: but the [i] sa-
cietie of the riche wil not suffer him to
slepe.
12 There is an euil sickenes *that* I haue sene
vnder the sunne: *to wit*, riches [k] reserued to
the owners thereof for their euil.
13 And these riches perish by euil trauail, &
he begetteth a sonne, and in his [l] hand *is*
nothing.
14 *As he came forthe of his mothers belly, he shal returne naked to go as he came,
& shal beare away nothing of his labour,
which he hathe caused to passe by his hãd.
15 And this also is an euil sickenes *that* in all
pointes as he came, so shal he go, and what
profite hathe he that he hathe trauailed for
the [m] winde?
16 Also all his dayes he eateth in [n] darkenes with muche grief, and *in* his sorow &
angre.
17 Beholde then, what I haue sene good,
that it is comelie to [o] eat, and to drinke, &
to take pleasure in all his labour, wherein
he trauaileth vnder the sunne, ẏ *whole* nõber of the dayes of his life, which God giueth him: for this is his portion.
18 Also to euerie man to whome God hathe
giuen riches and treasures, and giueth him
power to eat thereof, and to take his parte,
and to enioye his labour: this is the gift of
God.
19 Surely he wil not muche remember the
dayes of his [p] life, because God answereth
to the ioye of his heart.

g The reuenues of ẏ earth are to be preferred aboue all things, ẇ appertaine to this life.
h Kings and princes cã not mainteine their estate without tillage, ẇ thig cõmẽdeth ẏ excellencie of tillage.
i That is, his great abũdãce of riches, or ẏ surfeting, ẇ cometh by his great feding.
k When couetous men heape vp riches, which turne to their destruction.
l He doeth not enioye his fathers riches.
Iob.1,21.
Wisd.7,6.
1.tim.6,7.
m Meaning, in vaine, & without profit.
n In affliction, and grief of minde.
o Read Chap. 3,22.
p He wil take no great thoght for the peines that he hathe endured in time past.

CHAP. VI.

The miserable estate of him to whome God hathe giuen riches, and not the grace to vse them.

1 THere is an euil, which I sawe vnder
the sunne, and it is muche among mẽ:
2 A man to whome God hathe giuen riches
and treasures and honour, and he wanteth
nothing for his soule of all that it desireth:
but [a] God giueth him not power to eat
thereof, but a strange man shal eat it vp:
this is vanitie, and this is an euil sickenes.
3 If a man beget an hundreth *children* and
liue manie yeres, and the dayes of his yeres
be multiplied, and his soule be not [b] satisfied with good things, and he be not
[c] buryed, I say that an vntimelie frute is
better then he.
4 For [d] he cometh into vanitie and goeth
into

a He sheweth that it is the plague of God when ẏ riche man hathe not a liberal hearte to vse his riches.
b If he cã neuer haue ynough.
c As we se oftentimes, that ẏ couetous mã ether falleth into crimes ẏ deserue death, or is murthered or drowned or hangeth himself or such like, & so lacketh the honour of buryal which is the last office of humanitie.
d Meaning, ẏ vntimelie frute whose life did nether profite or hurt anie.

into darkenes: & his name shalbe couered
with darkenes.
5 Also he hathe not sene ŷ sunne, nor knowē
it: *therefore* this hathe more rest then the
other.
6 And if he had liued a thousād yeres twise tolde, and had sene no good, shal not all
go to one place?
7 All the labour of mā *is* for his mouth: yet
the [e] soule is not filled.
8 For what hathe the wise man more then
the foole? what hathe ŷ poore that [f] knoweth how to walke before the liuing?
9 The [g] sight of the eye is better then to
walke in the lustes: this also is vanitie and
vexacion of spirit.
10 What is that that hathe bene? the name
thereof is now named: and it is knowen
that it is man: and he can not striue with
him that is [h] stronger then he.

e His desire & affection.
f That knoweth to vse his goods wel in the iudgement of men.
g To be content with that which God hathe giuen, is better then to followe the desires that neuer can be satisfied.
h Meaning, God who wil make him to fele that he is mortal.

CHAP. VII.

Diuers precepts to followe that which is good, and to auoide the contrarie.

1 SVrely there be manie things that increase vanitie: & what auaileth it mā?
2 For who knoweth what is [a] good for man
in the life & in the nomber of the dayes
of the life of his vanitie, seing he maketh
thē as a * shadow? For who can shewe vnto
man what shalbe after him vnder ŷ sunne?
3 * A good name *is better* then a good oyntment, and the day of [b] death, then the day
that one is borne.
4 It is better to go to the house of [c] mourning, then to go to the house of feasting,
because this is the end of all men: and the
liuing shal lay it to his heart.
5 Angre is better then laughter: for by a
sad loke the heart is made better.
6 The heart of the wise *is* in the house of
mourning: but the heart of fooles *is* in the
house of mirth.
7 Better it is to heare the rebuke of a wise
man, then that a mā shulde heare the song
of fooles.
8 For like the noise of the [d] thornes vnder
the pot, so *is* the laughter of the foole: this
also is vanitie.
9 Surely oppresiō maketh a wise mā [e] mad:
and the rewarde destroyeth the heart.
10 The [f] end of a thing is better then the
beginning thereof, & the pacient in spirit
is better then the proude in spirit.
11 Be not ŷ of an hastie spirit to be angrie:
for angre resteth in the bosome of fooles.
12 Say not thou, Why is it that the former
daies were better thē these? for thou doest
not enquire [g] wisely of this thing.
13 Wisdome is good with an [h] inheritāce,
and excellent to them that se the sunne.
14 For *man shal rest* in the shadowe of wisdome, & in ŷ shadowe of siluer: but the excellencie of the knowledge of wisdome
giueth life to the possessers thereof.
15 Beholde the worke of God: for who can
make * straight that which he hathe made
croked?
16 In the day of wealth be of good comfort,
& in the day of affliction [i] consider: God
also hathe made this contrary to that, to
the intent that mā shulde finde [k] nothing
after him.
17 I haue sene all things in the daies of my
vanitie: there is a iuste man that perisheth
in his [l] iustice, and there is a wicked man
that continueth long in his malice.
18 Be not thou iuste [m] ouermuche, nether
make thy self ouer wise: wherefore shuldest thou be desolate?
19 Be not thou wicked [n] ouermuche, nether
be thou foolish: wherefore shuldest thou
perish not in thy time?
20 It is good that thou laie holde on [o] this:
but yet withdrawe not thine hand from
[p] that: for he that feareth God, shal come
forthe of them all.
21 Wisdome shal strengthen the wise man
more then ten mightie princes that are in
the citie.
22 * Surely there is no man iust in the earth,
that doeth good and sinneth not.
23 Giue not thine [q] heart also to all ŷ wordes that men speake, lest thou do heare thy
seruant cursing thee.
24 For often times also thine heart knoweth that thou likewise hast ″ cursed others.
25 All this haue I proued by wisdome: I
thoght I wil be wise, but it went farre from
me.
26 It is farre of, what maie [r] it be? and it is a
profound depenes, who can finde it?
27 I haue compassed about, *bothe* I and mine
heart to knowe and to enquire and to searche wisdome and reason, and to knowe the
wickednes of folie, and the foolishnes of
madnes,
28 And I finde more bitter then death the
woman whose heart is *as* nettes & snares,
and her hands, *as* bands: he that is good before God, shalbe deliuered from her, but ŷ
sinner shalbe taken by her.
29 Beholde, saith the Preacher, this haue I
founde, *seking* one by one to [s] finde ŷ cōute:
30 And yet my soule seketh, but I finde it
not: I haue founde one man of a thousand:
but a woman among them all haue I not
founde.
31 Onely lo, this haue I founde, that God
hathe made man righteous: but they haue
soght manie [t] inuentions.

Chap VII
a There is no state, wherein man can liue to haue perfite quietnes in this life.
Iob 14,2.
psal.145,4.
Prou.22,1.
b He speaketh thus after the iudgement of ŷ flesh, which thinketh death to be the end of all euils: or els, because ŷ this corporal death is the entring into life euerlastig.
c Where we maie se ŷ hād of God & learne to examine our liues.
d Which crackel for a while and profite nothing.
e A man that is estemed wise, when he falleth to oppresion, becōmeth like a beast.
f He noteth their lightne: ŵ entreprise a thing, & suddenly leaue it of againe.
g Murmure not agaīst God when he sendeth aduersities for mans sinnes.
h He answereth to them ŷ esteme not wisdome, except riches be ioyned therewith, shewing that bothe are the giftes of God, but that wisdome is farre more excellent & maie be without riches.

Chap.1,15.
i Consider wherfore God doethe send it and what maie comfort thee.
k That man shulde be able to controlle nothing in his workes.
l Meaning, that cruel tyrants put the godlie to death and let the wicked go fre.
m Boast not to muche of thine owne iustice and wisdome.
n Tarie not long when ŷ art admonished to come out of the waie of wickednes.
o To wit, on these admonitions that go before.
p Consider what desolation & destructiō shal come, if thou do not obeie them.
1.King.8,46.
2.chro.6,48.
prou.20,9.
1.iohn.1,8.
q Credit them not, nether care for them.
″ *Or, spoken euil of others.*
r Meaning, wisdome.
s That is, to come to a conclusion.
t And so are cause of their owne destruction

CHAP. VIII.

2 To obey Princes and Magistrates. 17 The workes of God passe mans knowledge.

1 WHo is as the wise man? and who
knoweth the interpretacion of a
thing? the wisdome of a man doeth make

his [a] face to shine: and the [b] strength of
his face shalbe changed.
2 I *aduertise thee* to take hede to the [c] mouth
of the King, and to the worde of the othe
of God.
3 [d] Haste not to go forthe of his sight: stand
not in an euil thing: for he wil do whatsoeuer pleaseth him.
4 Where the worde of the King is, *there is*
power, and who shal say vnto him, What
doest thou?
5 He that kepeth the commandement, shal
knowe none euil thing, and the heart of
the wise shal knowe the [e] time and iudgement.
6 For to euerie purpose there is a time and
iudgement because the [f] miserie of man
is great, vpon him.
7 For he knoweth not that which shalbe: for
who can tel him when it shalbe?
8 Man is not lord [g] ouer the spirit to reteine the spirit: nether hathe he power in
the day of death, nor deliuerance in the
battel, nether shal wickednes deliuer the
possessers thereof.
9 All this haue I sene, and haue giuen mine
heart to euerie worke, which is wroght vnder the sunne, *and I sawe* a time that man
ruleth ouer man to his owne [h] hurt.
10 And likewise I sawe the wicked buryed,
and [i] they returned, and they that came
from the holie [k] place, were yet forgotten
in the citie where they had done right: this
also is vanitie.
11 Because sentence against an euil worke
is not [l] executed spedely, therefore the heart of the children of men is fully set in thē
to do euil.
12 Thogh a sinner do euil an hūdreth times,
and *God* prolongeth *his dayes*, yet I knowe
that it shalbe wel with them that feare the
Lord, and do reuerence before him.
13 But it shal not be wel to the wicked,
nether shal he prolong *his* dayes: *he shalbe*
like a shadowe, because he feareth not before God.
14 There is a vanitie, which is done vpō the
earth, that there be righteous men to whome it cometh according to the [m] worke
of the wicked: and there be wicked men to
whome it cometh according to the worke
of the iuste: I thoght also that this is
vanitie.
15 And I praised ioye: for there is no goodnes to man vnder the sunne, saue [n] to eat,
and to drinke and to reioyce: for this is
adioyned to his labour, the dayes of his life that God hathe giuen him vnder the
sunne.
16 When I applied mine heart to knowe
wisdome, and to beholde the busines that
is done on earth, that nether day nor night
the eyes of man take slepe,
17 Then I behelde ẏ whole worke of God,
that mā can not finde out the worke that
is wroght vnder the sunne: for the which
man laboreth to seke it, and can not finde it: yea, and thogh the wise man thinke
to knowe it, he can not finde it.

CHAP. IX.

*1 By no outward thing can man knowe whome God lo-
ueth or hateth. 12 No man knoweth his end. 16 Wisdome excelleth strength.*

1 I haue surely giuen mine heart to all this,
and to declare all this, that the iuste, &
the wise, and their workes *are* in the hand
of God: & no man knoweth ether loue or
[a] hatred of all *that is* before them.
2 All things *come* alike to all: and the same
condition *is* to the iuste and to the wicked,
to the good and to the pure, & to the polluted, & to him that sacrificeth, & to him
that sacrificeth not: as *is* the good, so *is* the
sinner, he that sweareth, as he that feareth
an othe.
3 This is euil among all that is done vnder the sunne, that there is one [b] condition to all, and also the heart of the sonnes
of men is ful of euil, and madnes *is* in their
hearts whiles they liue, and after that, *they*
go to the dead.
4 Surely whosoeuer is ioyned to all the liuing, there is hope: for it is better to a [c] liuing dog, then to a dead lyon.
5 For the liuing knowe that they shal dye,
but the dead knowe nothing at all: nether
haue they anie more a rewarde: for their
remembrance is forgotten.
6 Also their loue, and their hatred, & their
enuie is now perished, and they haue no
more portion foreuer, in all that is done
vnder the sunne.
7 Go, eat thy bread with ioye, & drinke thy
wine with a chereful heart: for God now
[d] accepteth thy workes.
8 At all times let thy garments be [e] white,
and let not oyle be lacking vpon thine
head.
9 " * Reioyce with the wife whome ẏ hast
loued all the dayes of the life of thy vanitie, ẇ *God* hathe giuen thee vnder thē
sunne all the dayes of thy vanitie: for this
is thy portion in the life, & in thy trauail
wherein thou laborest vnder the sunne.
10 All that thine hand shal finde to do, do
it with *all* thy power: for there is nether
worke nor inuention, nor knowledge, nor
wisdome in the graue whether thou goest.
11 I returned, & I sawe vnder the sunne that
the race is not to the swift, nor the battel
to the strōg, nor yet bread to the wise, nor
also riches to men of vnderstādīng, nether
yet fauour to men of knowledge: but time
and [f] chance cometh to them all.
12 For nether doeth man knowe his [g] time,
but as the fishes, which are taken in an euil
net,

a That is, doeth get him fauour & prosperitie.
b Whereas before he was proude and arrogant, he shal become humble and meke.
c That is, that thou obey the King, & kepe the othe that thou hast made for the same cause.
d Withdrawe not thy selfe lightly from the obedience of thy prince.
e That is, whē time is to obey, and how farre he shulde obey.
f Man of him self is miserable, and therefore oght to do nothing to increase the same, but to worke all things by wisdome, & counsel.
g Man hathe no power to saue his owne life, & therefore must not rashely cast him self into danger.
h As cometh oft times to tyrāts, and wicked rulers.
i That is, others as wicked as they.
k They that feared God, & worshiped hī according as he had appointed.
l Where iustice is delayed, there sinne reigneth.
m Which are punished as thogh they were wicked, as Chap. 7,16.
n Read Chap. 5,22.

a Meaning, what things he oght to chuse or refuse: or mā knoweth not by these outward things, ẏ is by prosperitie or aduersitie, whome God doeth fauour or hate: for he sendeth them aswel to the wicked as to the godlie.
b In outward things as riches, and pouertie, sicknes, & helth there is no differēce betwene the godlie, & the wicked: but ẏ difference is that ẏ godlie are assured by faith of Gods fauour & assistance.
c He noteth ẏ Epicures, and carnal men, ẇ made their bely their god, & had no pleasure but in this life, wishing rather to be an abiect, & vile persone in this life, then a man of autoritie, and so to dye, which is ment by the dog and lyon.
d They flatter them selues to be in Gods fauour, because they haue all things in abūdance.
e Reioyce, be mery, and spare for no cost. thus speake ẏ wicked belligods.
" Ebr. regarde the life.
* Chap. 5, 18.
f Thus ẏ worldelings say to proue that all things are lawful for thē and attribute that to chance and fortune, ẇ is done by the prouidence of God.
g That is, he doeth not forese what shal come.

net, & as the birdes that are caught in the
snare: so are the children of men snared in
the euil time when it falleth vpon them
suddenly.
13 I haue also sene this wisdome vnder the
sunne, and it is great vnto me.
14 A litle citie and fewe men in it, and a
great King came against it, and compassed it about, and buylded fortes against it.
15 And there was founde therein a poore
and wise man, and he deliuered the citie
by his wisdome: but none remembred this
poore man.
16 Then said I, Better is wisdome then
strength: yet the wisdome of the poore is
despised, and his wordes are not heard.
17 The wordes of the wise are more heard
in quietnes, then the crye of him that ruleth among fooles.
18 Better is wisdome then weapons of warre: but one sinner destroyeth muche good.

CHAP. X.

*1 The difference of foolishnes and wisdome. 11 A sclan-
derer is like a serpent that can not be charmed. 16 Of
foolish Kings, and dronken princes. 17 And of good
Kings and princes.*

1 Dead flies cause to stinke, and putrifie
the ointment of the apoticarie: *so doeth*
a litle folie him that is in estimation for
wisdome, *and* for glorie.
2 The heart of a [a] wise mã *is* at his right hãd:
but the heart of a foole *is* at his left hand.
3 And also whẽ the foole goeth by the way,
his heart faileth, and he [b] telleth vnto all
that he is a foole.
4 If the [c] spirit of him that ruleth, rise vp
against thee, leaue not thy place: for gentlenes pacifieth great sinnes.
5 There is an euil *that* I haue sene vnder the
sunne, as an [d] error that procedeth frõ the
face of him that ruleth.
6 Folie is set in great excellencie, and the
[e] riche set in the lowe place.
7 I haue sene seruants on horses and princes walking as seruants on the grounde.
8 *He that diggeth a pit, shal fall into it, &
he that breaketh the hedge, a serpent shal
bite him.
9 He ỳ remoueth stones, shal hurt him self
thereby, & he that cutteth wood, shalbe in
danger thereby.
10 If the yron be blunt, and one hathe not
whet the edge, he must then put to more
[f] strength: but the excellencie to direct a
thing *is* wisdome.
11 If the serpent bite, when he is not charmed: no better is a babler.
12 The wordes of the mouth of a wise man
haue grace: but the lippes of a foole deuoure him self.
13 The beginning of ỳ wordes of his mouthe *is* foolishnes, and the latter end of his
mouth *is* wicked madnes.

a So that he doeth all thĩgs wel, & iustly, where as the foole doeth ỳ contrary
b By his doĩgs he bewraieth him self.
c If thy superiour be angry with thee, be thou discrete, & not moued
d Meaning, ỳ it is an euil thing whẽ thei that are in autoritie, faile, & do not their duetie
e They that are riche in wisdome and vertue.
*Psal.7,16. prou.26,27. eccles.27,30.
f Without wisdome what soeuer a man taketh in hãd, turneth to his owne hurte.

14 For the foole multiplieth wordes, *saying*,
Man knoweth not what shalbe: and who
can tel him what shalbe after him?
15 The labour of the foolish doeth weary
him: for he knoweth not to go into the
[g] citie.
16 Wo to thee, ô land, when thy King *is*
a [h] childe, and thy princes [i] eat in the morning.
17 Blessed art thou, ô land, when thy King
is the sonne [k] of nobles, and thy princes
eat in time, for strength and not for dronkennes.
18 By slouthfulnes ỳ roofe of the house goeth to decay, and by the ydlenes of the
hands the house droppeth through.
19 Thei prepare bread for laughter, and
wine comforteth the liuing, but siluer answereth to all.
20 Curse not the Kĩg, no not in thy thoght,
nether curse the riche in thy bed chamber: for the [l] foule of the heauen shal cary
the voice, & that which hathe wings, shal
declare the matter.

g The ignorance & beastlines of ỳ wicked is such, ỳ thei knowe not cõmune thĩgs, & yet wil thei discusse hie matters.
h That is, without wisdome and coũsel.
i Are giuen to their lustes & pleasures.
k Meanĩg, whẽ he is noble for vertue & wisdome & with the giftes of God.
l Thou canst not worke euil so secretly, but it shal be knowen.

CHAP. XI.

*1 To be liberal to the poore. 4 Not to doute of Gods pro-
uidẽce 8 All worldelie prosperitie is but vanitie. 9 God
wil iudge all.*

1 Cast thy bread vpon the [a] waters: for
after manie daies thou shalt finde it.
2 Giue a portion to seuen, & also to eight:
for thou knowest not what euil shalbe vpon the earth.
3 If the [b] cloudes be ful, they wil powre
forthe raine vpon the earth: and if the
[c] tre do fall towarde the South, or toward
the North, in the place that the tre falleth,
there it shalbe.
4 He that obserueth the [d] winde, shal not
sowe, and he that regardeth the cloudes,
shal not reape.
5 As thou knowest not which is the way of
the spirit, *nor* how the bones *do growe* in
the wombe of her that is with childe: so
thou knowest not the worke of God that
worketh all.
6 In the morning sowe thy sede, and in the
euening let not thine hand [e] rest: for thou
knowest not whether shal prosper, this or
[f] that, or whether bothe shalbe alike good.
7 Surely the light is a pleasant thing: and
it is a good thing to the eyes to se ỳ sunne.
8 Thogh a man liue manie yeres, *and* in
them all he reioyce, yet he shal remember
the daies of [g] darkenes, because thei are
manie, all that cometh *is* vanitie.
9 [h] Reioyce, ô yong man, in thy youth, &
let thine heart chere thee in the daies of
thy youth: and walke in the waies of thine
heart, and in the sight of thine eyes: but
knowe that for all these things, God wil
bring thee to iudgement.

a That is, be liberal to the poore, & thogh it seme to be as a thing ventred on ỳ sea, yet it shal brĩg thee profite.
b As the cloudes that are ful, powre out raine, so theriche that haue abũdance, must distribute it liberally.
c He exhorteth to be liberal, while we liue: for after there is no power
d He that feareth inconueniences, when necessitie requireth, shal neuer do his duetie.
e Be not weary of weldoing.
f That is, ỳ of thy workes are moste agreable to God.
g That is, of affliction & trouble.
h He derideth them that set their delite in worldelie pleasures, as thogh God wolde not call them to an accounte.

&.iiii.

i To wit, angre, and enuie.
k Meaning, carnal lustes whereunto youth is giuen.
Chap. XII.
a Before thou come to a continual miserie: for when the cloudes remaine after ẏ raine, mans grief is increased.
b The hands, which kepe ẏ bodie.
c The legs.
d The tethe.
e The eyes.
f The lippes, or mouth.
g When the chawes shal scarse open & not be able to chewe nomore
h He shal not be able to slepe
i That is, the winde pipes, or the eares shalbe deafe & not able to heare singing.
k To climbe hie because of their weakenes, or thei stoupe downe, as thogh they were afraid lest anie thing shulde hit them.
l Thei shal trẽble as thei go, as thogh they were afraied.
m Their head shalbe as white as the blossomes of an almonde tre.
n Thei shalbe able to beare nothing.

10 Therefore take away [i] grief out of thine heart, and cause euil [k] to departe from
thy flesh: for childeholde & youth *are* vanitie.

CHAP. XII.

1 To thinke on God in youth and not to differre til age. 7 The soule returneth to God 11 Wisdome is the gift of God and consisteth in fearing him and keping his commandements.

1 Remember now thy Creator in the
daies of thy youth, whiles the euil
daies come not, nor the yeres approche,
wherein thou shalt say, I haue no pleasure
in them:
2 Whiles the sunne is not darke, nor the
light, nor the moone, nor the starres, nor
the [a] cloudes returne after the raine:
3 When the [b] kepers of the house shal trem
ble, and the [c] strong men shal bowe them
selues, and the [d] grinders shal cease, because thei are fewe, and they waxe darke that
[e] loke out by the windowes:
4 And the [f] dores shal be shut without by
the base sounde of the [g] grinding, and he
shal rise vp at the voice of the [h] birde:
& all the [i] daughters of singing shalbe a-
based.
5 Also thei shalbe afraied of the [k] hie
thing, and feare *shalbe* in [l] the way, and
the almonde tre shal [m] florish and the
[n] grashopper shalbe a burden, and concupiscence shalbe driuen away: for man goeth to the house of his age, and the mourners go about in the strete.
6 Whiles the [o] siluer corde is not lengthened, nor the golden [p] ewer broken, nor the
[q] pitcher brokẽ at the [r] well, nor the [s] whele broken at the [t] cisterne:
7 And dust returne to the earth as it was,
and the [u] spirit returne to God that gaue it.
8 Vanitie of vanities, saith the Preacher,
all *is* vanitie.
9 And the more wise the Preacher was, the
more he taught the people knowledge, &
caused them to heare, & searched forthe,
and prepared manie parables.
10 The Preacher soght to finde out pleasant wordes, & an vpright writing, euẽ the
wordes of trueth.
11 The wordes of the wise are like goades,
and like nailes [x] fastened by the masters of
the assemblies, *which* are giuẽ by one [y] pastour.
12 And of other thĩgs besides these, my sonne, take thou hede: for there is none end in
making manie [z] bokes: and muche reading
is a wearines of the flesh.
13 Let vs heare the end of all: feare God &
kepe his commandements: for this is the
whole *duetie* of man.
14 For God wil bring euerie worke vnto
iudgement, with euerie secret thing, whether it be good or euil.

o Meaning the marowe of the backe bone & the sinewes.
p The litle skine that couereth the braine, ẇ is in colour like gold.
q That is, the vaines.
r Meaning, the liuer.
s Which is the head.
t That is, the heart, out of ẏ which ẏ head draweth the powers of life.
u The soule incontinently ether goeth to ioy or tormẽt, & slepeth not as the wicked imagine.
x Which are well applied by ẏ ministers, whome he calleth masters.
y That is, by God.
z These things can not be cõprehended in bokes, or learned by studie, but God must instruct the heart that ẏ maiest onely knowe ẏ wisdome is the true felicitie, & the way thereunto is to feare God.

AN "EXCELLENT SONG which was Salomons.

" Ebr. a song of songs: so called because it is the chiefest of those 1005, which Salomón made as is mencioned, 1 King. 4,32.

THE ARGVMENT.

IN this Song, Salomón by moste swete and comfortable allegories and parables describeth the perfite loue of Iesus Christ, the true Salomón and King of peace, and the faithful soule or his Church, which he hathe sanctified and appointed to be his spouse, holy, chast and without reprehension. So that here is declared the singular loue of the bridegrome toward the bride, and his great and excellent benefites wherewith he doeth enriche her of his pure bountie and grace without anie of her deseruings. Also the earnest affection of the Church which is inflamed with the loue of Christ desiring to be more and more ioyned to him in loue, and not to be forsaken for anie spot or blemish that is in her.

a This is spoken in the persone of the Church, or of the faithful soule, inflamed with ẏ desire of Christ, whome she loueth.
b The felingof thy great benefites.
c Thei that are pure in heart & conuersation.
d The faithful confesse that thei can not come to Christ except thei be drawen.

CHAP. I.

1 The familiar talke and mystical communication of the spiritual loue betwene Iesus Christ and his Church. 6 The domestical enemies that persecute the Church.

1 Let [a] hi kisse me with the
kisses of his mouth: for
thy loue is better then
wine.
2 Because of the [b] sauour
of thy good ointments
thy name *is as* an oint-
ment powred out: therefore the [c] virgines
loue thee.
3 [d] Drawe me: we wil runne after thee: the
King hathe broght me into his [e] chambers: we wil reioyce and be glad in thee:
we wil remember thy loue more then wine: the righteous do loue thee.
4 I am [f] blacke, ô daughters of Ierusalém,
but comelie, as the frutes of [g] Kedár, *&*
as the [h] curtines of Salomón.
5 Regarde ye me not because I am [i] blacke:
for the [k] sunne hathe loked vpon me. The
[l] sonnes of my mother were angrie against
me: thei made me the keper of the vines:
but I [m] kept not mine owne vine.
6 Shewe me, [n] *o thou*, whome my soule loueth,

e Meaning, the secret ioye ẏ is not knowen to the worlde.
f The Church confesseth her spots & sinne, but hathe confidence in ẏ fauour of Christ.
g Kedár was Ishmaels sõne, of whome came the Arabians ẏ dwelt in tentes.
h Which within were all set with precious stones & iewels.
i Consider not the Church by ẏ outward appearance.
k The corruption of nature through sinne, and afflictions.
l Mine owne brethren, ẇ shulde haue moste fauoured me.
m She confesseth her owne negligence.
n The spouse feling her faute, fleeth to her housband onely for succour.

ueth, where thou fedest, where thou liest at
noone: for why shulde I be as she that turneth aside to ÿ flockes of o thy cópanions?
7 p If thou knowe not, ô thou the fairest a-
mong women, get thee forthe by the steppes of the flocke, and fede thy kiddes by
the tents of the shepherdes.
8 I haue compared thee, ô my loue, to the
troupe of horses in ÿ q charets of Pharaóh.
9 Thy chekes are comelie ŵ rowes of stones, and thy necke with chaines.
10 We wil make thee borders of golde with
studdes of siluer.
11 r Whiles the King was at his repast, my
spikenarde gaue the smel thereof.
12 My welbeloued *is as* a bundle of myrrhe
vnto me: he shal lye betwene my s breastes.
13 My welbeloued *is as* a clustre of camphi-
re vnto me in the vines of Engédi.
14 My loue, beholde, ÿ art t faire: beholde,
ÿ art faire: thine eyes *are like* the dooues.
15 My welbeloued, beholde, thou art faire
and pleasant: also our u bed is grene: the
beames of our house *are* cedres.

o Whome thou hast called to the dignitie of pastures, and thei set forthe their owne dreames in stead of thy doctrine.
p Christ speaketh to his Church, bidding thē that are ignorāt, to go to the pastors to learne.
q For thy spiritual beautie and excellēcie there was no worldelie treasure to be compared vnto thee.
r The Church reioyceth that she is admitted to the companie of Christ.
s He shal be moste deare vnto me.
t Christ accepteth his Churche and commendeth her beautie.
u That is, the heart of the faithful where in Christ dwelleth by his Spirit.

CHAP. II.

3 The Church desireth to rest vnder the shadowe of Christ. 8 She heareth his voyce. 14 She is compared to the dooue, 15 And the enemies to the foxes.

1 I Am the rose of the field, & the lilie of
the valleis.
2 Like a lilie among the thornes, so *is* my
a loue among the daughters.
3 b Like the apple tre amóg the trees of the
forest: so *is* my welbeloued among the sonnes *of men*: vnder his shadowe had I delite,
& sate downe: and his frute *was* swete vnto
my mouth.
4 He broght me into the wine celler, and
loue *was* his banner ouer me.
5 Stay me with flagons, and comfort me
with apples: for I am sicke of loue.
6 His left hand *is* vnder mine head, & his
right hand doeth imbrace me.
7 c I charge you, ô daughters of Ierusalém,
by the roes & by the hindes of the field,
that ye stirre not vp, nor waké *my* loue, vntil she please.
8 d *It is* the voice of my welbeloued: beholde, he cometh leaping by the mountaines,
and skipping by the hilles.
9 My welbeloued is like a roe, or a yong
heart: lo, he e standeth behinde our wall, loking forthe of the windowes, shewing him
selfe through the f grates.
10 My welbeloued spake & said vnto me, A-
rise, my loue, my faire one, & come thy way.
11 For beholde, g winter is past: the raine is
changed, and is gone away.
12 The flowers appeare in ÿ earth: the time
of the singing of birdes is come, & the voice of the turtle is heard in our land.
13 The figtre hathe broght forthe her yong
figges: & the vines with *their* small grapes
haue cast a sauour: arise my loue, my faire
one, and come away.
14 My dooue, that art in the h holes of the
rocke, in ÿ secret places of ÿ staires, shewe
me thy sight, let me heare thy voice: for
thy voyce is swete, and thy sight comelie.
15 Take vs ÿ foxes, ÿ i litle foxes, ŵ destroy
the vines: for our vines *haue* smale grapes.
16 My welbeloued *is* mine, and I am his:
he fedeth among the lilies,
17 Vntil ÿ day breake, & the shadowes flee
away: returne, my welbeloued, & be like a
k roe, or a yong hart vpon the mountaines of Béther.

a Thus Christ preferreth his Church aboue all other thigs
b The spouse testifieth her great desire toward her housband, but her strēgth faileth her, and therefore she desireth to be comforted, & felt it.
c Christ chargeth them ŵ haue to do in the Church, as it were by a solemne othe, that thei trouble not the quietnes thereof.
d This is spoken of Christ, who toke vpō him our nature to come to helpe his Church.
e For asmuche as his diuinitie was hid vnder the cloke of our flesh.
f So that we can not haue ful knowledge of him in this life.
g That is, sinne and error is driuen backe by the comming of Christ which is here described by ÿ spring time, when all things florish.
h Thou that art ashamed of thy sinnes, come & shewe thy self vnto me.
i Suppresse ÿ heretikes whiles thei are yong, that is, when thei beginne to shewe their malice & destroy ÿ vine of the Lord.
k The Church desireth Christ to be moste ready to helpe her in all dangers.

CHAP. III.

1 The Church desireth to be ioyned inseparably to Christ her housband. 6 Her deliuerance out of the wildernes.

1 IN my bed by a night I soght him that
my soule loued: I soght him, but I foú-
de him not.
2 I wil rise *therefore* now, and go about in
the citie, by the stretes & by the open places, & wil b seke him that my soule loueth:
I soght him, but I founde him not.
3 The c watchemen that went about the citie, founde me: *to whome I said,* Haue you
sene him whome my soule loueth?
4 When I had past a litle from them, then I
founde hī whome my soule loued: I toke
holde on him and left him not, til I had
broght him vnto my mothers house into
the chamber of her that conceiued me.
5 d I charge you, ô daughters of Ierusalém,
by the roes and by the hindes of the field,
that ye stirre not vp, nor waké *my* loue vntil she please.
6 Who is she that commeth vp out of the
e wildernes like pillers of smoke perfumed
with myrrhe and incense, & with all the
"spices of the marchant?
7 Beholde his f bed, which is Salomons:
threscore strong men *are* round about it,
of the valiant men of Israél.
8 Thei all handle the sworde, & *are* expert
in warre, euerie one *hathe* his sworde vpon
his thigh for the feare g by night.
9 King Salomón made him selfe a *palace
of the trees of Lebanón.
10 He made the pillers thereof of siluer, &
ÿ pauemēt thereof of golde, the hangings
therof of purple, whose middes *was* paued
ŵ the loue of ÿ daughters of Ierusalém.
11 Come forthe, ye h daughters of Zión, &
beholde the King Salomón ŵ the i crowne, wherewith his mother crowned him in
the day of his mariage, and in the day of
the gladnes of his heart.

a The Church by night, ÿ is in troubles seketh to Christ, but is not incōtinetly heard.
b Shewing ÿ althogh we be not heard at ÿ first, yet we must stil cōtinue in prayer til we fele cōfort.
c Which declareth, that we must seke vnto all, of whome we hope to haue anie succour.
d Read Chap. 2,7.
e This is referred to the Church of Israél, ŵ was led by the wildernes fortie yeres.
" Ebr. powdre.
f By the bed is ment the Tēple, which Salomón made.
g He alludeth to the watche, which kept ÿ Temple.
* Or, charet.
h All ye, that are of the nōber of ÿ faithful.
i Christ become man was crowned by ÿ loue of God ŵ the glorious crowne of his diuinitie.

CHAP. IIII.

1 The praises of the Church. 7 She is without blemish in his sight. 9 The loue of Christ towardes her.

1 BEholde, thou art a faire, my loue: behol
de, thou art faire: thine eies *are like* the
dooues: among thy lockes * thine heere is

a Because Christ deliteth in his Church, he comendeth all that is in her.
* Chap. 6,4.

like the [b] flocke of goates, ẇ loke downe
from the mountaine of Gileád.
2 Thy tethe *are* like a flocke of *shepe* in good
ordre, which go vp frō ẏ washing : which
euerie one bring out twinnes, and none is
baren among them.
3 Thy lippes are like a threde of skarlet &
thy talke is comelie: thy temples *are* within thy lockes as a piece of a pomegranate.
4 Thy necke is as the towre of Dauid buylt
for defense: a thousand shields hang therein, *and* all the targates of the strong
men.
5 Thy two [c] breastes *are* as two yong roes
that are twinnes, feding among the lilies.
6 Vntil the day breake, and the shadowes
flee away, I wil go into the mountaine of
myrrhe and to the mountaine of incense.
7 Thou art all faire, my loue, and there is
no spot in thee.
8 [d]Come with me from Lebanón, *my* spouse, *euen* with me from Lebanón, *and* loke
from the top of Amanáh, from the top of
Shenír and Hermón, from the dennes of
the lyons *and* from the mountaines of the
leopardes.
9 My [e] sister, *my* spouse, thou hast wounded mine heart: thou hast wounded mine
heart with one of thine [f] eyes, & with a
chaine of thy necke.
10 My sister, *my* spouse, how faire is thy
loue? how muche better is thy loue then
wine? & the sauour of thine ointmēts thē
all spices?
11 Thy [g] lippes, *my* spouse, droppe *as* honie
combes: honie and milke are vnder thy
tōgue, & the sauour of thy garments *is* as
the sauour of Lebanón.
12 My sister my spouse *is as* a garden inclosed, as a spring shut vp, *and* a fountaine
sealed vp.
13 Thy plantes *are as* an orcharde of pomegranates with swete frutes, *as* camphi-
re, spikenarde,
14 *Euen* spikenarde, and safran, calamus,
& synamom with all the trees of incense, myrrhe and aloes, with all the chief
spices.
15 [h] O fountaine of the gardens, ô well of
liuing waters, and the springs of Lebanón.
16 Arise, ô [i] North, and come ô South,
and blowe on my garden that the spices
thereof may flowe out: let my welbeloued come to his garden, and eat his pleasant frute.

CHAP. V.

1 Christ calleth his Church to the participation of all his treasures. 2 She heareth his Voyce. 6 She confesseth her nakednes. 10 She praiseth Christ her housband.

1 I am come into my [a] gardē, my sister, my
spouse: I gathered my myrrhe with my

[b] He hathe respect to the multitude of the faithful, ẇ are manie in nomber.

[c] Wherein are knowledge, & zeale, two precious iewels.

[d] Christ promiseth his Church to call his faithful from all the corners of the worlde.

[e] Christ calleth his Churche sister in respect that he had taken the flesh of man.

[f] In that he made his Church beautiful, & riche, he loued his giftes in her.

[g] Because of thy confession and thankesgiuing.

[h] The Church confesseth that all her glorie, & beautie cometh of Christ who is ẏ true fountaine of all grace.

[i] She desireth Christ to comforte her, and so powre the graces of his Spirit vpō her, which Spirit is ment by the North and South winde.

Chap. V.

[a] The garden signifieth the kingdome of Christ where he prepareth the banket for his elect.

spice: I ate mine honie cōbe with mine honie, I dranke my wine with my milke: eat,
ô friends, drinke, and make you mery, ô
welbeloued.
2 [b] I slepe, but mine heart waketh, *it is* the
voyce of my welbeloued that knocketh,
saying, Open vnto me, my sister, my loue,
my dooue, my vndefiled: for mine head is
ful of dewe, and my lockes with the drop
pes of the [c] night.
3 I haue put of my [d] coate, how shal I put
it on? I haue washed my fete, how shal I
defile them?
4 My welbeloued put in his hand by the
hole *of the dore*, & "mine heart was affectioned toward him.
5 I rose vp to opē to my welbeloued, & mine hāds did droppe downe myrrhe, & my
[e] fingers pure myrrhe vpon the handels of
the barre.
6 I opened to my welbeloued: but my welbeloued was gone, & past: mine heart was
gone when he did speake: I soght him, but
I colde not finde him: I called him, but he
answered me not.
7 The [f] watchemen that went about the
citie, founde me: they smote me & wounded me: the watchemen of the walles toke
away my vaile from me.
8 I charge you, [g] ô daughters of Ierusalém,
if you finde my welbeloued, that you tel
him that I am sicke of loue.
9 [h] O the fairest among women, what is
thy welbeloued more then *other* welbeloued? what is thy welbeloued more then
another louer, that thou doest so charge vs?
10 My welbeloued is white and ruddy, the
chiefest of ten thousand.
11 His [i] head *is as* fine golde, his lockes cur-
led, & blacke as a rauen.
12 His eyes *are* like dooues vpō the riuers of
waters, which are washt with milke, & remaine by the ful *vessels*.
13 His chekes *are* as a bed of spices, *and as*
swete flowres, & his lippes *like* lilies dropping downe pure myrrhe.
14 His hands *as* rings of golde set with the
"chrysolite his bellie like white yuorie couered with saphirs.
15 His leggs *are as* pillers of marble, set
vpon sockets of fine golde: his countenāce as Lebanón, excellent as the cedres.
16 His mouth *is as* swete things, and he is
wholy delectable: this is my welbeloued, &
this is my louer, ô daughters of Ierusalém.
17 [k] O the fairest among womē, whether is
thy welbeloued gone? whether is thy welbeloued turned aside, that we may seke
him with thee?

CHAP. VI.

2 The Church assureth her selfe of the loue of Christ. 3 The praises of the Church. 8 She is but one and vndefiled.

[b] The spouse saith that she is troubled ẇ the cares of worldly thīgs, which is ment by sleping

[c] Declaring ẏ long pacience of the Lord toward sinners

[d] The spouse confesseth her nakednes, and that of her self she hathe nothing: or seing that she is once made cleane, she promiseth not to defile her self againe.

" *Ebr. My bowels were moued towards him.*

[e] The spouse ẇ shulde be anointed of Christ, shal not finde him if she thinke to anoint him ẇ her good workes.

[f] These are ẏ false teachers, ẇ wounde ẏ conscience ẇ their traditiōs

[g] She asketh of them which are godlie (for asmuche as ẏ law & saluatiō shulde come out of Zion & Ierusalē) that thei wolde direct her to Christ.

[h] Thus say they of Ierusalém.

[i] She describeth Christ to be of perfite beautie, & comelines.

" *Ebr. Tarshish.*

[k] Hearing of ẏ excellencie of Christ, ẏ faithful desire to knowe how to finde him.

1 MY welbeloued is gone downe into
his [a] garden to the beds of ſpices,to
fede in the gardens,and to gather lilies.
2 I am my welbelоueds , and my welbeloued is mine,who fedeth among the lilies.
3 Thou art beautiful,my loue,as [b] Tirzáh,
comelie as Ierusalém,terrible as an armie
with banners.
4 [c] Turne away thine eyes frõ me: for they
ouercome me: * thine heere is like a flocke
of goats , which loke downe from Gileád.
5 Thy tethe *are* like a flocke of ſhepe,which
go vp from the waſhing,which euerieone
brĩg out twins , & none is barẽ amõg thẽ.
6 Thy temples *are* within thy lockes as a
piece of a pomegranate.
7 There are [d] threſcore Quenes & foreſcore
concubines , & of the dameſels without
nomber.
8 *But* my dooue is alone, & my vndefiled,
ſhe is the onelie *daughter* of her mother,
and ſhe is deare to her that bare her : the
daughters haue ſene her and counted her
bleſſed:*euen* the Quenes and the concubines, and thei haue praiſed her.
9 [e] Who is ſhe that loketh forthe as the
morning,faire as the moone , pure as the
ſunne,terrible as an armie with banners!
10 I went downe to the [f] garden of nuttes,
to ſe the frutes of the valley , to ſe if the
vine budded , *and if* the pomegranates
floriſhed.
11 [g] I knewe nothing, my ſoule ſet me [h] as
the charets of my noble people.
12 Returne,returne, ô [i] Shulamite,returne:
returne that we may beholde thee. What
ſhal you ſe in the Shulamite, *but* as the cõpanie of an armie?

CHAP. VII.

1 The beautie of the Church in all her members. 10 She is aſſured of Chriſts loue towardes her.

1 HOw beautiful are thy [a] goings with
ſhoes,ô princes daughter:the iointes
of thy thighs *are* like iewels : the worke
of the hand of a cunning workeman.
2 Thy nauel *is as* a rounde cuppe that wan
teth not lickour:thy belly *is as* an heape of
wheat compaſſed about with lilies.
3 [b] Thy two breaſtes *are* as two yong roes
that are twinnes.
4 Thy necke *is* like a towre of yuorie:thi-
ne eyes *are like* ỹ fiſh pooles in Heſhbón
by the gate of Bath-rabbim:thy noſe *is* as
the towre of Lebanón,that loketh toward
Damaſcus.
5 Thine head vpon thee *is* as ſkarlet , and
the buſhe of thine head like purple : the
King *is* tyed [c] in the * rafters.
6 How faire art thou, and how pleaſant art
thou,ô *my* loue,in pleaſures!
7 This thy ſtature is like a palme tree , and
thy breaſtes like cluſters.
8 I ſaid , I wil go vp into the palme tre , I

[a] That is , is conuerſant here in earth amõg men.

[b] Which was a faire & ſtrõg citie, 1. King. 14,17.

[c] This declareth the exceding loue of Chriſt toward his Church.

Chap.4,1.

[d] Meaning , ỹ the giftes are infinite which Chriſt giueth to his Church: or that his faithful are manie in nomber.

[e] He ſheweth that the beginning of the Church was ſmale, but ỹ it grewe vp to a great multitude.

[f] He wẽt downe into ỹ Synagogue to ſe what frutes came of ỹ Lawe, & ỹ Prophets.

[g] I founde nothing but rebellion.

[h] I ran as ſwift as the nobles of my people in their charets.

[i] O ye people of Ieruſalém: for Ieruſalém was called Shalém, which ſignifieth peace.

Chap.VII.

[a] He deſcribeth the comelie beautie of the Church in euerie part, ỹ is to be vnderſtand ſpiritually.

[b] Read Chap. 4,5.

[c] He deliteth to come nere thee and to be in thy companie.

* Or, galeries.

wil take holde of her boughes : thy breaſtes ſhal now be like the cluſters of the vi-
ne:and the ſauour of thy noſe like apples,
9 And the rouſe of thy mouth like good
wine,which goeth ſtraight to my welbelo
ued,& cauſeth the lippes of the ancient to
ſpeake.
10 [d] I am my welbeloueds,and his deſire is
toward me.
11 Come,my welbeloued,let vs go forthe
into the field:let vs remaine in ỹ villages.
12 Let vs get vp early to the vines,let vs ſe
if the [e] vine floriſh,*whether* it hathe budded the ſmale grape,*or whether* the pomegranates floriſh:there wil I giue thee my
loue.
13 The mãdrakes haue giuẽ a ſmel,& in our
gates are all ſwete things, newe & olde:
my welbeloued , I haue kept *them* for thee.

CHAP. VIII.

2 The Church wil be taught by Chriſt. 3 She is vpholden by him. 6 The vehement loue wherewith Chriſt loueth her. 11 She is the vine that bringeth forth frute to the ſpiritual Salomón, which is Ieſus Chriſt.

1 OH [a] that thou wereſt as my brother ỹ
ſucked the breaſtes of my mother :I
wolde finde thee without , I wolde kiſſe
thee,then thei ſhulde not deſpiſe * thee.
2 I wil lead thee & bring thee into my mothers houſe:*there* thou ſhalt teache me: &
I wil cauſe thee to drinke ſpiced wine , &
newe wine of the pomegranate.
3 [b] His left hand *ſhalbe* vnder mine head, &
his right hand ſhal embrace me.
4 [c] I charge you,ô daughters of Ieruſalém,
that you ſtirre not vp,nor waken *my* loue,
vntil ſhe pleaſe.
5 (Who is this that commeth vp out of the
wildernes,leaning vpon her welbeloued?)I
raiſed thee vp vnder an apple tre:there thy
mother conceiued thee: there ſhe conceiued that bare thee.
6 [d] Set me as a ſeale on thine heart , & as a
ſignet vpon thine arme: for loue *is* ſtrong
as death:ielouſie is cruel as the graue : the
coles thereof *are* fyrie coles, & a vehemẽt
flame.
7 Muche water cã not quenche loue,nether
can the floods drowne it : if a man ſhulde
giue all the ſubſtãce of his houſe for loue,
they wolde greatly contemne it.
8 [e] We haue a litle ſiſter,and ſhe hathe no
breaſtes:what ſhal we do for our ſiſter whẽ
ſhe ſhalbe ſpoken for?
9 [f] If ſhe be a walle,we wil buylde vpõ her
a ſiluer palace:and if ſhe be a dore, we wil
kepe her in with bordes of cedre.
10 [g] I am a walle & my breaſtes *are* as tow-
res:then was I in his eyes as one that findeth peace.
11 [h] Salomón had a vine in Baal-hamón: he
gaue the vineyard vnto kepers: euerie one
bringeth for the frute thereof a thouſand
pieces of ſiluer. &.vi.

[d] This ỹ ſpouſe ſpeaketh.

[e] If the people that are called to Chriſt, brĩg forthe anie frute.

[a] The Church called of the Gentiles,ſpeaketh thus to ỹ Church of Ieruſalém.

* Or, me.

[b] Read Chap. 2,6.

[c] Read Chap. 3,5.

[d] The ſpouſe deſireth Chriſt to be ioyned in perpetual loue with him.

[e] The Iewiſh Church ſpeaketh this of ỹ Church of the Gentiles.

[f] If ſhe be ſure & faſt, ſhe is mete for the houſband to dwel in.

[g] The Church promiſeth fidelitie & conſtancie.

[h] This is the vineyarde of ỹ Lord hired out, Mat.21,33.

12 *But* my vineyarde which is mine, *is* before me:to thee, ô Salomón, *apperteineth* a
thousand *pieces of siluer*,& two thousan to
them that kepe the frute thereof.
13 O thou that dwellest in the [i] gardens, the
companions hearken vnto thy voyce: cause me to heare it.
14 O my welbeloued,[k] flee away, and be like vnto the roe, or to the yong heart vpon
the mountaines of spices.

i Christ dwelleth in his Church whose voyce ÿ faithful heare.

k The Church desireth Christ that if he depart from the, yet that he wolde haste to helpe them in their troubles

ISAIAH.

THE ARGVMENT.

God, according to his promes Deut.18,15. that he wolde neuer leaue his Church destitute of a Prophet, hathe from time to time accomplished the same: whose office was not onely to declare vnto the people the things to come, whereof thei had a special reuelation, but also to interpret & declare the Law, and to applie particularly the doctrine, conteined brifely therein, to the vtilitie & profite of those, to whome thei thoght it chiefly to apperteine, and as the time and state of things required. And principally in the declaration of the Lawe they had respect to thre things, which were the grounde of their doctrine: First to the doctrine conteined briefly in the two tables: secondely to the promises & threatenings of the Law: & thirdely, to the couenant of grace & reconciliation, grouded vpon our Sauiour Iesus Christ, who is the end of the Law. Whereunto thei nether added nor diminished, but faithfully expounded the sense and meaning thereof. And according as God gaue them vnderstanding of things, thei applied the promises particularly for the comfort of the Church and the members thereof, and also denounced the menaces against the enemies of the same: not for anie care or regarde to the enemies, but to assure the Church of their sauegarde by the destruction of their enemies. And as touching the doctrine of reconciliation they haue more cleare-ly intreated it then Moses, and set forthe more liuely Iesus Christ, in whome this couenant of reconciliation was made. In all these things Isaiáh did excell all the Prophetes, and was moste diligent to set out the same, with moste vehement admonitions, reprehensions, and consolations: euer applying the doctrine, as he sawe that the disease of the people required. He declareth also manie notable prophecies which he had receiued of God, as touching the promes of the Messiáh, his office, and his kingdome. Also of the fauour of God toward his Church, the vocation of the Gentiles, and their vnion with the Iewes. Which are as moste principal pointes conteined in this boke, and a gathering of his sermons that he preached. Which after certeine daies that thei had stand vpon the Tenple dore (for the maner of the Prophetes was to set vp the summe of their doctrine for certeine dayes that the people might the better marke it, as Isa.8,1. & Habak.2,2.) the Priests toke it downe and reserued it among their registers: and so by Gods prouidence these bokes were preserued as a monument to the Church for euer. As touching his persone and time, he was of the Kings stocke: for Amoz his father was brother to Azariáh King of Iudáh, as the best writers agre, and prophecied more then 64 yeres from the time of Vzziáh vnto the reigne of Manasséh, whose father in lawe he was (as the Ebrewes write) and of whome he was put to death. And in reading of the Prophetes this one thing among other is to be obserued, that thei speake of things to come as thogh thei were now past, because of the certeintie thereof, and that thei colde not but come to passe, because God had ordeined them in his secret counsel, and so reueiled them to his Prophetes.

CHAP. I.

2 Isaiáh reproueth the Iewes of their ingratitude and stubbernes, that nether for benefites nor punishmēt wolde amend. 11 He sheweth why their sacrifices are reiected, and wherein Gods true seruice standeth. 24 He prophecieth of the destruction of Ierusalém, 25 And of the restitution thereof.

1 
A [a] vision of Isaiáh, the
sonne of Amóz, which
he sawe [b] concerning
Iudáh and Ierusalém:
in the daies of [c] Vzziáh,
Iothám, Aház & Heze-
kiáh Kings of Iudáh.
2 Heare, ô [d] heauens, and hearken, ô earth:
for the Lord hathe said, I haue nourished
and broght vp [e] children, but they haue rebelled against me.
3 The [f] oxe knoweth his owner, and the asse his masters cryb, *but* Israél hathe not
knowen: my people hathe not vnderstand.
4 Ah, sinful nacion, a people laden with iniquitie: a [g] sede of the wicked, corrupt childrē: thei haue forsaken the Lord: thei haue
prouoked the [h] holy one of Israél to anger:
they are gone backwarde.
5 Wherefore shulde ye be [i] smitten anie
more? for ye fall away more and more: the
whole [k] head is sicke, and the whole heart
is heauie.
6 From the [l] sole of the foote vnto the
head, there *is* nothing whole therein, *but*
woundes, & swelling, and sores ful of corruption: thei haue not bene wrapped, [m] nor
bounde vp, nor mollified with oyle.
7 Your land is waste: your cities *are* burnt
with fyre: strangers deuoure your land in
your presence, and *it is* desolate like the o-
uerthrowe [n] of strangers.
8 And the daughter of [o] Zión shal remaine like a cotage in a vineyarde, like a lodge in a garden of cucumbers, & like a besieged citie.
9 Except the Lord of hostes [p] had reserued
vnto vs, euen a smale remnant: we shulde
haue bene [q] as Sodóm, & shulde haue bene like vnto Gomoráh.
10 Heare the worde of the Lord, ô [r] princes of Sodóm: hearken vnto the Law of
our God, ô people of Gomoráh.
11 What haue I to do with the multitude of
your sacrifices, saith the Lord? I am ful of
the burnt offrings of rams, & of the fat of
fed beastes: and I [s] desire not the blood of
bullockes, nor of lambes, nor of goates.
12 Whē ye come to appeare before me, who
required this of your hāds to tread in my
courtes?
13 Bring no mo oblacions, [t] in vaine: incēse is an abominacion vnto me: I can not
suffer *your* newe moones, nor sabbaths, *nor*
solemne daies (*it is* iniquitie) nor solemne
assemblies.
14 My soule hateth your [u] newe moones &
your appointed feasts: they are a burden
vnto me: I am weary to beare *them*.
15 And whē you shal stretch out your hāds,
I wil hide mine eyes from you: and thogh
ye make manie prayers, I wil not heare: *for*
your hands are ful [x] of blood.
16 [y] Wash you, make you cleane: take away
the euil of your workes from before mine
eyes: cease to do euil.
17 Learne to [z] do wel: seke iudgement, relieue the oppressed: iudge the fatherles &
defend the widowe.
18 Come now, [a] & let vs reasō together, saith
the Lord: thogh your sinnes were as crim-
sin, they shalbe made [b] white as snowe:
thogh they were red like skarlet, they shal
be as woll.
19 If ye [c] consent and obey, ye shal eat the
good *things* of the land.
20 But if ye refuse and be rebellious, ye
shalbe deuoured with the sworde: for the
mouth of the Lord hathe spoken it.
21 How is the [d] faithful citie become an
harlot? it was ful of iudgement, & iustice
lodged therein, but now [e] *thei are* murtherers.
22 Thy [f] siluer is become drosse: thy wine
is mixt with water.
23 Thy princes *are* rebellious and companions of [g] theues: euerie one loueth gifts,
& followeth after rewards: they iudge not
the fatherles, nether doeth the widowes
cause come before them.
24 Therefore saith the Lord God of hostes, the [h] mightie one of Israél, Ah, I wil
[i] ease me of mine aduersaries, and auenge
me of mine enemies.
25 Then I wil turne mine hand vpon thee,
and burne out thy drosse, til it [k] be pure, &
take away all thy tynne.
26 [l] And I wil restore thy iudges as at the
first, and thy coūsellers as at the beginnig:

a That is, a reuelatiō or prophecie, which was one of the two meanes, whereby God declared him selfe to his seruants in olde time, as Nomb. 12,6: & therefore the Prophetes were called Seers, 1 Sam 9,9.
b Isaiáh was chiefly sent to Iudáh and Ierusalém, but not onely: for in this boke are prophecies concerning other nations also.
c Called also Azariáh 2. King. 15,1. of these Kings read 2. King. from Chap 14 vnto Chap. 21, and 2. Chro. from Chap. 25. vnto Chap. 33
d Because mē were obstinate and insensible, he calleth to ẏ dumme creatures, which were more prompte to obey Gods worde, as Deu 32,1
e He declareth his great mercie towarde ẏ Iewes, for asmuche as he chose them aboue all other nations to be his people & childrē, as Deu 10,15.
f The moste brute and dul beasts do more acknowledg their duetie toward their masters, then my people do toward me, of whome thei haue receiued benefits without cōparison.
g Thei were not onely wicked, as were their fathers, but vtterly corrupt, and by their euil example infected others.
h That is, him ẏ sanctifieth Israél.

t Without faith & repentance.
u Your sacrifices offred in the new moones & feastes: he condēneth hereby hypocrites, which thinke to please God with ceremonies, & they them selues are voide of faith and mercie.
x He sheweth that where mē be giuen to auarice, deceit, crueltie & extorsion, which is ment by blood, there God wil shew his angre, and not accept them, thogh they seme neuer so holy, as Chap 59,3.
y By this outward washig, he meaneth ẏ spiritual: exhorting the Iewes to repent & amend their liues.
z This kinde of reasoning, by the seconde table, the Scriptures vse in manie places against the hypocrites, who pretend moste holines & religion in worde, but when their charitie & loue toward their brethren shuld appeare, thei declare ẏ thei haue nether faith nor religion.
a To knowe if I do accuse you without cause.
b Lest sinners shulde pretend anie rigour on Gods parte, he onely willeth thē to be pure in heart, & he wil forgiue all their sinnes, were thei neuer so manie or great.
c He sheweth that whatsoeuer aduersitie man indureth, it oght to be attributed to his owne incredulitie and disobedience.

i What auaileth it to seke to amend you by punishment, seing the more I correct you, the more ye rebell? k By naming the chief partes of the bodie, he signifieth, that there was no parte of the whole bodie of the Iewes fre from his roddes. l Euerie parte of the bodie, aswel the least as the chiefest was plagued. m Their plagues were so grieuous that they were incurable, and yet they wolde not repent. n Meaning, of them, that dwell farre of, which, because they loke for no aduantage of that, which remaineth, destroye all before them. o That is, Ierusalém. p Because that he wil euer haue a Church to call vpon his Name q That is, all destroyed. r Ye that for your vices deserued all to be destroyed as they of Sodóm, saue that God of his mercie reserued a litle nomber, Lam. 3,22 s Althogh God commanded these sacrifices for a time, as aides and exercises of their faith: yet because the people had not faith nor repentance, God detesteth them, Psal. 50,14. ier. 6,20. amos 5,21. mich. 6,7.

d That is, Ierusalém, which had promised fidelitie vnto me, as a wife to her housband. e Giuen to couetousnes and extorcion, which he signified before by blood, vers. 15
f Whatsoeuer was pure in thee before, is now corrupt, thogh thou haue an outward shewe g That is, they mainteine the wicked & the extorcioners, & not onely do not punish them, but are them selues suche. h When God wil shewe him self merciful to his Church, he calleth him self, The holie one of Israél: but when he hathe to do with his enemies, he is called Mightie, as against whome no power is able to resist. i I wil take vengeance of mine aduersaries the Iewes, and so satisfie my desire by punishing them. Which thing yet he doeth with a grief because of his couenant.
k Lest the faithful among them shulde be ouercome with this threatning, he addeth this consolacion. l It is onely the worke of God to purifie the heart of man, which thing he doeth because of his promes, made concerning the saluacion of his Church.

afterwarde shalt thou be called a citie of
righteousnes,& a faithful citie.
27 Zión shalbe redemed in iudgement, and
they that returne in her, in [m] iustice.
28 And the [n] destruction of the trangressours and of the sinners shalbe together:
and thei that forsake the Lord, shalbe consumed.
29 For thei shal be cōfounded for the [o] okes,
which ye haue desired, and ye shalbe ashamed of the gardens, that ye haue chosen.
30 For ye shalbe as an oke, whose leafe fadeth: & as a garden that hathe no water.
31 And the strong shalbe as [p] towe, and the
maker thereof, as a sparke: and they shal
bothe burne together, & none shal quenche *them*.

m By iustice is meant Gods faithful promes, wͨ is the cause of ẏ deliuerance of his Church.
n The wicked shalnot bepartakers of Gods promes, Psal. 92,9.
o That is, the trees & pleasant places, where ye commit idolatrie, which was forbidden, Deut. 16,22.
p The false god, wherein ye put your cōfidence, shal be consumed as easely, as a piece of towe.

CHAP. II.

2 The Church shalbe restored by Christ, and the Gentiles called. 6 The punishment of the rebellious & obstinate.

1 THe worde that Isaiáh the sonne of Amóz sawe vpon Iudáh and Ierusalém.
2 *It [a] shalbe in the last daies, that the moūtaine of the house of the Lord shalbe prepared in the top of the moūtaines, & [b] shal
be exalted aboue the hilles, & all nacions
shal [c] flowe vnto it.
3 And manie people shal go, & say, Come,
and let vs go vp to [d] the mountaine of the
Lord, to the house of the God of Iaakób, &
he wil teache vs his waies, and we wil walke in his paths: for the [e] Law shal go forthe
of Zión, and the worde of the Lord from
[f] Ierusalém,
4 And [g] he shal iudge among the natiōs, &
[h] rebuke manie people: thei shal [i] breake
their swordes also into mattockes, & their
speares into sithes: nacion shal not lift vp
a sworde against nacion, nether shal they
learne [k] to fight anie more.
5 O house of Iaakób, come ye, and let vs
[l] walke in the light of the Lord.
6 Surely thou [m] hast forsaken thy people,
the house of Iaakób, because thei are [n] ful
of the East *maners*, and *are* sorcerers as the
Philistims, [o] and abunde with strange
children.
7 Their land also was ful of [p] siluer and
golde, and there *was* none end of their
treasures: and their land was ful of horses,
and their charets *were* infinite.
8 Their land also was ful of idoles: they
worshipped the worke of their owne hāds,
which their owne fingers haue made.

*Mich. 4,1.
a The decre and ordinance of God, touching the restauracion of the Church, wͨ is chiefly ment of the time of Christ.
b In an euidēt place to be sene and discerned.
c When the kingdome of Christ shalbe enlarged by ẏ preaching of the doctrine. Here also is declared the zeale of the children of God, when they are called.
d Alluding to mount Zion, where the visible Church then was.
e Meaning, the whole doctrine of saluaciō.
f This was accomplished, whē the Gospel was first preached in Ierusalém, and from thence went through all ẏ worlde.
g The Lord, wͨ is Christ, shal haue all power giuen him.
h That they may acknowledge their sinnes, & turne to him.
i He sheweth the frute of the peace, which the Gospel shulde bring: to wit, that men shulde do good one to another, where as before they were enemies.
k He speaketh not against the vse of weapons and lawful warre, but sheweth how the hearts of the godlie shalbe affected one toward another: which peace and loue doeth beginne and growe in this life, but shal be perfited, when we are ioyned with our head Christ Iesus.
l Seing the Gentiles wil be so readie, make you haste and shewe them the way to worship God.
m The Prophet seing the smale hope, that the Iewes wolde conuert, complaineth to God, as thogh he had vtterly forsaken them for their sinnes.
n Ful of the corruptions that reigned chiefly in the East partes.
o They altogether giue them selues to the facions of other nacions.
p The Prophet first condemned their superstition and idolatrie: next their couetousnes, and thirdly, their vaine trust in worldelie meanes.

9 And a man bowed him self, and a man
[q] hūbled him self: therefore [r] spare thē not.
10 Enter into the rocke, & hide thee in the
dust from before the feare of the Lord,
and from the glorie of his maiestie.
11 The hie loke of man shalbe humbled,
and the loftines of men shalbe abased, &
ẏ Lord onely shalbe exalted in [s] that day.
12 For the day of the Lord of hostes *is* vpon all the proude and hautie, and vpon all
that is exalted: and it shalbe made lowe.
13 Euen vpon all the cedres of Lebanón,
that are hie and exalted, and vpon all the
okes of Bashán,
14 And vpon all the high [t] mountaines, &
vpon all the hilles that are lifted vp,
15 And vpon euerie hie towre, and vpon euerie strong wall,
16 And vpon [u] all the shippes of Tarshísh,
and vpon all pleasant pictures.
17 And the hautines of men shalbe broght
lowe, and the loftines of men shalbe abased, and the Lord shal onely be exalted in
that day.
18 And the idoles wil he vtterly destroye.
19 Then they shal go * into the holes of the
rockes, and into the caues of the earth,
from before the feare of the Lord, & from
the glorie of his maiestie, when he shal arise to destroye the earth.
20 At that day shal man cast away his siluer
idoles, and his golden idoles (which they
had made them selues to worship them)
[x] to the mowles and to the backes,
21 To go into the holes of the rockes, and
into the toppes of the ragged rockes from
before the feare of the Lord, and from the
glorie of his maiestie, when he shal rise to
destroy the earth.
22 Cease you from the man whose [y] breath
is in his nostrelles: for wherein is he to be
estemed?

q He noteth the nature of the idolaters, which are neuer satisfied in their superstitions.
r Thus ẏ Prophet spake, beīg inflamed with the zeale of Gods glorie, & that he might feare them wͭ Gods iudgement.
s Meaning, assone as God shal begin to execute his iudgements.
t By high trees & mountaines are ment them ẏ are proude, and loftie, and thinke them selues moste strong in this worlde.
u He cōdēneth their vaine cōfidence, which they had in strong holdes, & in their riche marchandise, wͨ broght in vaine pleasures, wherewith mēs mindes became effeminate.
*Hoséah. 10, 8. luk. 23,30. reuel. 6,16. & 9,6.
x They shal cast them into moste vile and filthie places, when thei perceiue ẏ they are not able to helpe them.
y Cast of your vaine confidēce of man, whose life is so fraile, that if his nose be stopped, he is dead, & consider that you haue to do with God.

CHAP. III.

1 For the sinne of the people God wil take away the wise men, and giue them foolish princes. 14 The couetousnes of the gouernours. 16 The pride of the women.

1 FOr lo, the Lord God of hostes wil
take away from Ierusalém and from
Iudáh the stay [a] and the strength: *euen* all
the stay of bread, and all the stay of water,
2 The strong man, and the man of warre,
[b] the iudge and the Prophet, the prudent
and the aged,
3 The captaine of fiftie, and the honorable,
and the counseler, and the cunning artificer, and [c] the eloquent man.
4 And I wil appoint [d] children *to be* their
princes, and babes shal rule ouer them.
5 The people shalbe [e] oppressed one of another, & euerie one by his neighbour: the
childrē shal presume against the anciēt, &
the vile against the honorable.

Chap. III.
a Because thei trusted ī their abundance & prosperitie, he sheweth that thei shulde be taken frō thē.
b The tēporal gouernour & the minister.
c By these he meaneth that God wolde take away euerie thing that was in any estimacion, and wherein they had anie occasion to vāte them selues.
d Not onely in age, but in wit, maners knowledge & strength.
e For lacke of good regimēt and ordre.

6 When

6 When euerie one shal [f] take holde of his
brother of the house of his father, & say,
Thou hast clothing: thou shalt be our prīce, and let this fall be vnder thine hand.
7 In that day he shal [g] sweare, saying, I can
not be an helper: for there is no bread in
mine house, nor clothing: *therefore* make
me no prince of the people.
8 Douteles Ierusalém is fallen, and Iudáh
is fallen downe, because their tongue and
workes *are* against the Lord, to prouoke
the eyes of his glorie.
9 The [h] tryal of their coūtenance testifieth
against them, yea, thei declare their sinnes,
as Sodóm, they hide them not. Wo be
vnto their soules: for they haue rewarded
euil vnto them selues.
10 [i] Say ye, Surely it shalbe wel with ẏ iuste:
for they shal eat the frute of their workes.
11 Wo be to the wicked, it shalbe euil *with
him*: for the rewarde of his hādes shalbe giuen him.
12 [k] Children *are* extorcioners of my people, and women haue rule ouer them: ô my
people, they that lead thee, cause thee to
erre, and destroye the way of thy paths.
13 The Lord standeth vp to pleade, yea, he
standeth to iudge the people.
14 The Lord shal entre into iudgemēt with
the [l] Anciēts of his people and the princes
thereof: for ye haue eaten vp the vineyarde: the spoyle of the poore *is* in your
houses.
15 What haue ye to do, that ye beat my peo
ple to pieces, [m] and grinde the faces of the
poore, saith the Lord, *euen* the Lord of
hostes?
16 The Lord also saith, [n] Because the daughters of Zión are hautie, and walke with
[o] stretched out neckes, and with [p] wandring eyes, walking and [q] minsing as they
go, and making a [r] tinkeling with their
fete,
17 Therefore shal the Lord make the heads
of the daughters of Zión balde, and the
Lord shal discouer their secret partes.
18 In that day shal the Lord take away the
ornament of the slippers, & the calles, &
the rounde tyres,
19 The swete balles, and the brasselets, and
the bonnets,
20 The tyres of the head, and the sloppes, &
the head bands, & the tablets, & ẏ earings,
21 The rings and the mufflers,
22 The costelie apparel and the vailes, and
the wimpels, and the crisping pinnes,
23 And the glasses and the fyne linen, and
the hoodes, and the [s] launes.
24 And in stead of swete sauour, there shalbe stinke, and in stead of a girdle, a rent,
& in stead of dresing of ẏ heere, baldnes,
and in stead of a stomacher, a girding of
sacke cloth, & burning in stead of beautie.

f He sheweth that this plague shalbe so horrible, that cōtrarie to the cōmune maner of men, ŵ by nature are ambitious, none shalbe founde able or willīg to be their gouernour.
g Feare shal rather cause hī to forsweare him self, thē to take suche a dāgerous charge vpon him.
h When God shal examine their dedes, whereupō thei now set an impudent face, he shal finde the marke of their impietie in their forehead
i Be ye that are godlie assured ẏ God wil defēd you in ẏ middes of these troubles
k Because the wicked people were more addicte to their princes, thē to ẏ cōmādemēts of God, he sheweth ẏ he wolde giue thē suche princes, by whome thei shulde haue no helpe, but that shulde be manifest tokēs of his wrath, because they shuld be foles & effeminate.
l Meaning, that the rulers and gouerners had destroyed his Church, & not preserued it, according to their duetie.
m That is, ye shewe all crueltie against them.
n He menaceth ẏ people, because of ẏ arrogancie and pride of their women, which gaue them selues to all wantōnes & dissolution.
o Which declared their pride
p As a signe, ẏ they were not chaste.
q Which shewed their wnatōnes.
r Thei delited thē in slippers ẏ did creake, or had litle plates sowed vpon them, ŵ tynckled as they went.
s In rehearsing all these thigs particularly, he sheweth the lightnes & vanitie of suche as can not be content ŵ comelie apparel according to their degre.

25 Thy men [t] shal fall by the sworde, & thy
strength in the battel.
26 Then shal her gates mourne and lamēt,
and she, being desolate, shal sit vpon the
grounde.

CHAP. IIII.

1 *The smale remnant of men after the destruction of Ierusalém. 2 The graces of God vpō them that remaine.*

1 AND in that day shal [a] seuen women take holde of one man, saying,
We wil eat our owne bread, and we wil
weare our owne garments: onely [b] let vs
be called by thy name, & take away our
[c] reproche.
2 In that day shal the [d] budde of the Lord
be beautiful and glorious, and the frute of
the earth shalbe excellent and pleasant for
them that are escaped of Israél.
3 Then he that shalbe left in Zión, and he
ẏ shal remaine in Ierusalem, shal be called
holie, *and* euerie one shalbe [e] written a-
mong the liuing in Ierusalém,
4 When the Lord shal wash the filthines
of the daughters of Zión, & purge the
[f] blood of Ierusalém out of ẏ middes thereof by the spirit of [g] iudgement, and by
the spirit of burning.
5 And the Lord shal creat vpon euerie place of mount Zión, and vpō the assemblies
thereof, [h] a cloude and smoke by day, and
the shining of a flaming fyre by night:
for vpon all the [i] glorie *shalbe* a defense.
6 And a couering shalbe for a shadowe in
the day for the heat, and a place of refuge
and a couert for ẏ storme [k] & for the raine.

t Meaning, ẏ God wil not onely punish ẏ women, but their housbādes, ŵ haue suffred this dissolutenes, and also ẏ cōmune weale, ŵ hath not remedied it.

Chap. IIII.
a When God shal execute this vengeance, there shal not be one man foūde to be ẏ head to manie women, & thei contrarie to womanly shamefastnes, shal seke vnto men, and offer them selues to anie condition.
b Be thou our housband, and let vs be called thy wiues.
c For so they thoght it to be without an head & housband.
d He comforteth ẏ Church in this desolatiō, which shal spring vp like a bud, signifying that Gods graces shulde be as plentiful towarde the faithful, as thogh they sprang out of the earth, as Chap 45,8. Some by the bud of ẏ Lord meane Christ.
e He alludeth to the boke of life, whereof read Exod. 32, 32: meaning Gods secret counsel, wherein his elect are predestinate to life euerlasting.
f That is, the crueltie, extorsion, auarice, and all wickednes.
g When things shalbe redressed, that were amisse
h He alludeth to the piller of the cloude, Exod. 13, 21: meaning that Gods fauour & protection shulde appeare in euerie place.
i The faithful are called the glorie of God, because his image, and tokens of his grace shine in them
k God promiseth to be the defense of his Church against all troubles and dangers.

CHAP. V.

1 *Under the similitude of the vine he describeth the state of the people, 8 Of their auarice. 11 Their drūkennes. 13 Of their captiuitie.*

1 NOw wil [a] I sing to my [b] beloued a sōg of
my beloued to his vineyard, * My beloued had a [c] vineyard in a verie fruteful hil,
2 And he hedged it, and gathered out the
stones of it, and he planted it with the best
plants, [d] and he buylt a towre in ẏ middes thereof, & made a wine presse therein:
thē he loked ẏ it shulde bring forthe grapes: but it broght [e] forthe wilde grapes.
3 Now therefore, ô inhabitants of Ierusalém & mē of Iudah, iudge, I pray you, [f] betwene me, and my vineyarde.
4 What colde I haue done anie more to my
vineyarde ẏ I haue not done vnto it? why
haue I loked that it shulde bring forthe
grapes, & it bringeth forthe wilde grapes?
5 And now I wil tel you what I wil do to
my vineyard: I [g] wil take away ẏ hedge.

a The Prophet by this song doeth set before ẏ peoples eyes their ingratitude, and Gods mercie.
b That is, to God.
Iere. 2, 21.
mat. 21, 33.
c Meaning, ẏ he had plāted his Church in a place moste plentiful and abundant.
d He spared no diligence nor cost.
e In ẏ seuenth verse he declareth what thei were.
f He maketh thē iudges in their owne cause, for asmuche as it was euidēt ẏ they were the cause of their owne ruine.
g I wil take no more care for it: meaning ẏ he wolde take frō thē his worde & ministers, & all other cōfortes, & send them contrarie plagues.

thereof, & it ſhal be eaten vp: I wil breake
the wall thereof, & it ſhal be trodē downe:
6 And I wil lay it waſte: it ſhal not be cut, nor
digged, but briers, & thornes ſhal growe
vp: I wil alſo commande the cloudes that
they raine no raine vpon it.
7 ¶ Surely the vineyarde of the Lord of
hoſtes *is* the houſe of Iſraél, and the men
of Iudáh *are* his pleaſant plant, and he loked for [h] iudgemēt: but beholde oppreſsiō:
for righteouſnes, but beholde [i] a crying.
8 Wo vnto thē that ioyne houſe to houſe,
and lay field to field, til there be no [k] place,
that ye may be placed by your ſelues in
the middes of the earth.
9 *This is* in mine [l] eares, *ſaith* the Lord of
hoſtes. Surely manie houſes ſhalbe deſolate, *euē* great, & fayre without inhabitāt.
10 For ten acres of vines ſhal yelde one
[m] bath, & the ſede of an [n] hómer ſhal yelde
an [o] epháh.
11 ¶ Wo vnto them, that [p] riſe vp early to
followe drunkennes, and to them that cōtinue vntil [q] night, *til* the wine do infla-
me them.
12 And the harpe and viole, timbrel, and pipe, and wine *are* in their feaſtes: but they
regarde not the [r] worke of ỷ Lord, nether
conſider the worke of his hands.
13 Therefore my people [ſ] is gone into captiuitie, becauſe they had [t] no knowledge,
and the glorie thereof *are* men famiſhed,
& the multitude thereof is dryed vp with
thirſt.
14 Therefore [u] hel hathe inlarged it ſelf,
and hathe opened his mouth, without
meaſure, and their glorie, and their multitude, and their pompe, and he that reioyceth among them, ſhal deſcende *into it*.
15 And man ſhalbe broght downe, and man
ſhalbe humbled, euē the eyes of the proude ſhalbe humbled.
16 And the Lord of hoſtes ſhalbe exalted
in iudgement, and the holie God ſhalbe
ſanctified in iuſtice.
17 Then ſhal [x] the lambes fede after their
maner, and the ſtrangers ſhal eat the deſolate places of the fat.
18 ¶ Wo vnto them, that drawe iniquitie wͭ
[y] cordes of vanitie, and ſinne, as with cart
ropes:
19 Which ſay, [z] Let him make ſpede: let him
haſten his worke, that we may ſe it: & let
the coūſel of the holie one of Iſraél drawe
nere and come, that we may knowe it.
20 Wo vnto them that ſpeake good of
euil, [a] and euil of good, which put darkenes for light, and light for darkenes, that
put bitter for ſwete, and ſwete for ſowre.

h Iudgement and righteouſnes are true frutes of the feare of God, and therefore in the cruel oppreſſers there is no religion.
i Of them that are oppreſſed.
k To wit, for the poore to dwell in.
l I haue heard the cōplaint, and crye of ỷ poore.
m Which cōteineth about tē pottels: ſo ỷ euerie acre ſhulde but yelde one pottel.
n Which conteineth an hūdreth pottels.
o An Epháh conteineth ten pottels, & is in drye things as muche as bath is in licours.
p That ſpare no peine nor diligence to followe their luſtes.
q Which are neuer weary of their riotīg and exceſsiue pleaſures: but vſe all meanes to prouoke to the ſame.
r They regarde not the prouident care of God ouer them, nor for what end he hathe created them.
ſ That is, ſhal certeinly go: for ſo the Prophetes vſe to ſpeake, as thogh the thīg which ſhal come to paſſe, were done already.
t Becauſe thei wolde not obey the worde of God.
u Meaning, ỷ graue ſhal ſwallowe vp them that ſhal dye for hungre and thirſt, and yet for all this great deſtruction it ſhal neuer be ſaciate.
x God comforteth ỷ poore lambes of his Church, wͨ had bene ſtrangers in other coūtreis, promiſing that they ſhulde dwel in thoſe places againe, whereof thei had bene depriued by the fat, and cruel tyrants.
y Which vſe all allurements, occaſions, and excuſes to harden their conſcience in ſinne.
z He ſheweth what are the wordes of the wicked, when they are menaced with Gods iudgements, 2. Pet. 3, 4.
a Which are not aſhamed of ſinne, nor care for honeſtie, but are growen to a deſperate impietie.

21 Wo vnto them that are [b] wiſe in their
owne eyes, and prudent in their owne
ſight.
22 Wo vnto them that are [c] mightie to
drinke wine, and to them that are ſtrong
to powre in ſtrong drinke:
23 Which iuſtifie the wicked for a rewarde,
and take away the righteouſnes of the righteous from him.
24 Therefore as ỷ flame of fyre deuoureth
the ſtubble, and *as* the chaffe is conſumed
of the flame: *ſo* their [d] roote ſhalbe as rottennes, and their budde ſhal riſe vp like
duſt, becauſe they haue caſt of the Law of
the Lord of hoſtes, and contemned the
worde of the holie one of Iſraél.
25 Therefore is the wrath of the Lord kindled againſt his people, & he hathe ſtretched out his [e] hand vpon them, and hathe
ſmitten them that ỷ mountaines did trē-
ble: and their karcaſes were torne in the
middes of the ſtretes, *&* for all this his
wrath was not turned away, but his hand
was ſtretched out ſtil.
26 And he wil lift vp a ſigne [f] vnto the nations a farre, and wil hiſſe vnto them from
the end of the earth: & beholde, they ſhal
come haſtely with ſpede.
27 None ſhal [g] faint nor fall among them:
none ſhal ſlumber nor ſlepe, nether ſhal
the girdle of his loynes be loſed, nor [h] the
latchet of his ſhoes be broken:
28 Whoſe arrowes ſhalbe ſharpe, & all his
bowes bent: his horſe hoofes ſhalbe thoght
like flint, & his wheles like a whirle wide.
29 His roaring *ſhalbe* like a lyon, and he ſhal
roare like lyons whelpes: they ſhal [i] roare,
and lay holde of the pray: thei ſhal take it
away, and none ſhal deliuer it.
30 And in that day they ſhal roare vpon
them, as the roaring of the ſea: & if [k] they
loke vnto the earth, beholde darkenes, *and*
ſorow, and the light ſhalbe darkened in
their [l] ſkie.

b Which are contemners of all doctrine & admonition.
c Which are neuer weary, but ſhew their ſtrength, and bragge in glottonie and drūkennes.
d Bothe they and their poſteritie, ſo that nothing ſhalbe left.
e He ſheweth that God had ſo ſore puniſhed this people, that the dumme creatures, if they had bene ſo plagued, wolde haue bene more ſenſible, and therefore his plagues muſt continue, til they begin to fele them
f He wil make ỷ Babyloniās to come agaīſt thē at his becke, and to fight vnder his ſtāderd.
g They ſhalbe prompt, and luſtie to execute Gods vengeāce.
h The enemie ſhal haue none impediment.
i Whereby is declared the crueltie of the enemie.
k The Iewes ſhal finde no ſuccour.
l In the land of Iudáh.

CHAP. VI.

1 Iſaiáh ſheweth his vocation by the Viſion of the diuine maieſtie. 9 He ſheweh the obſtinacie of the people. 11 The deſtruction of the land. 13 The remnant reſerued.

1 IN the yere of the death of King Vzziáh, [a] I ſawe alſo the Lord ſitting vpō
an [b] high throne, and lifted vp, and the
lower [c] partes thereof filled the temple.
2 The Seraphims [d] ſtode vpon it: euerie
one had ſix wings: with twaine he couered
his [e] face, and with twaine he couered his
[f] fete, and with twaine he did [g] flie.
3 And one cryed to another, and ſaid, [h] Ho-

a God ſheweth not him ſelf to mā in his maieſtie, but according as mās capacitie is able to cōprehend him: that is by viſible ſignes, as Iohn Baptiſt ſawe the holie Goſt in the forme of a dooue.

b As a iudge ready to giue ſentence. c Of his garment, or of his throne. d They were Angels ſo called, becauſe they were of a fyrie colour, to ſignifie ỷ they burnt in the loue of God, or were light as fyre to execute his wil. e Signifying, that they were not able to endure the brightnes of Gods glorie. f Whereby was declared that man was not able to ſe the brightnes of God in them. g Which thing declareth the prompt obedience of the Angels to execute Gods cōmandement. h This oft repetition ſignifieth, that the holy Angels can not ſatiſfie them ſelues in praiſing God, to teache vs that in all our liues we ſhulde giue our ſelues to the continual praiſe of God.

ly, holy, holy *is* ẏ Lord of hostes: the whole
i worlde is ful of his glorie.
4 And the lintels of the dore chekes k moued at the voyce of him that cryed, and
the house was filled with smoke.
5 Then I said, l Wo is me: for I am vndone, because I am a man of polluted lippes, and I dwell in the middes of a people
of polluted lippes: for mine eyes haue sene
the King *and* Lord of hostes.
6 Then flewe one of the Seraphims vnto
me with an hote cole in his hand, *which* he
had takẽ from the m altar with the tongs:
7 And he touched my mouth, & said, Lo,
this hathe touched thy lippes, and thine
iniquitie shalbe taken away, and thy n sinne shalbe purged.
8 Also I heard the voyce of the Lord, saying, Whome shal I send? and who shal go
for vs? Then I sayd, Here am I, send me.
9 And he said, Go, and say vnto this people, o Ye shal heare in dede, but ye shal
not vnderstand: ye shal plainly se, & not
perceiue.
10 Make the heart of this people fat, make
their eares heauie, and shut their eyes, lest
they se with their eyes, & heare with their
eares, and vnderstand with their hearts,
and conuert, and he heale them.
11 Then said I, Lord, p how long? And he
answered, Vntil the cities be wasted without inhabitant, and the houses without
man, and the land be vtterly desolate,
12 And the Lord haue remoued men farre
away, and *there be* a great desolation in the
middes of the land.
13 But yet in it *shalbe* q a tenth, and shal returne, and shalbe eaten vp as an elme r or
as an oke, which haue a substance in them,
when they cast *their leaues: so* the holie sede
shalbe the substance thereof.

i His glorie doeth not onely appeare in ẏ heauens, but through all ẏ worlde, and therefore all creatures are bouñde to praise him.
k Which thĩgs were to confirme the Prophet, that it was not the voyce of man: and by the smoke was signified the blindenes ẏ shulde come vpon the Iewes.
l He speaketh this for two causes: ẏ one, because he ẏ was a mortal creature, and therefore had more nede to glorifie God then the Angels, did it not: and the other, because ẏ more nere ẏ man approcheth to God, the more doeth he knowe his owne sinne, & corruption.
m Of ẏ burnt offrings where the fyre neuer went out.
n This declareth that man can not rendre true obedience to God, til he haue purged vs.
o Whereby is declared that for the malice of man God wil not immediatly take away his worde, but he wil cause it to be preached to their condemnation, when as they wil not learne thereby to obey his wil, and be saued: hereby he exhorteth the ministers to do their duetie, and answereth to the wicked murmurers, that through their owne malice their heart is hardned, Mat. 13, 14. act 28, 26. rom. 11, 8.
p As he was moued with the zeale of Gods glorie, so was he touched with a charitable affection toward the people.
q Meaning, the tenth parte: or as some write, it was reueiled to Isaiáh for the confirmation of his prophecie, that ten Kings shulde come before their captiuitie, as were from Vzziáh to Zedekiáh.
r For the fewenes they shal seme to be eaten vp: yet they shal after florish as a tre, which in winter loseth his leaues, and semeth to be dead, yet in sommer is fresh, and grene.

CHAP. VII.

1 Ierusalém besieged. 4 Isaiáh comforteth the King. 14 Christ is promised.

1 AND in the dayes of * Aház, the sonne
of Iothám, the sonne of Vzziáh King
of Iudáh, Rezín the King of ″Arám a came vp, and Pekáh the sonne of Remaliáh
King of Israél, to Ierusalém to fight a-
gainst it, but he colde not ouercome it.
2 And it was tolde the house of b Dauid,
saying, Arám is ioyned with c Ephráim:
therefore his heart was d moued, and the
heart of his people, as the trees of the
forest are moued by the winde.
3 ¶ Then said the Lord vnto Isaiáh, Go
forthe now to mete Aház (thou and e She-
ar-iashúb thy sonne) at the end of the
conduit of the vpper poole, in the path of
the fullers field,
4 And say vnto him, Take hede, & be stil:
feare not, nether be faint hearted for the
two tailes of these smoking f fyrebrandes,
for the furious wrath of Rezín and of A-
rám, and of Remaliahs sonne:
5 Because Arám hathe taken wicked counsel against thee, & Ephráim, & Remaliahs
sonne, saying,
6 Let vs go vp against Iudáh, & let vs wa-
kẽ them vp, and make a breche therein for
vs, and set a King in the middes thereof,
euen the sonne of g Tabeál.
7 Thus saith the Lord God, It shal not
stand, nether shal it be.
8 For the head of Arám *is* Damascus, and
the head of Damascus *is* Rezín: and within fiue & h threscore yere, Ephráim shalbe
destroied from being a people.
9 And the head of Ephráim *is* Samaria, and
the head of Samaria *is* Remaliahs sonne. If
ye beleue not, surely ye shal not be established.
10 ¶ And the Lord spake againe vnto Aház,
saying,
11 Aske i a signe for thee of the Lord thy
God: aske it, *ether* in the depth or in the
height aboue.
12 But Aház said, I wil not aske, nether
wil I k tempt the Lord.
13 Thẽ he said, Heare you now, ô house of
Dauid, Is it a smale thing for you to grieue l men, that ye wil also grieue my God?
14 Therefore the Lord m him self wil giue
you a signe. Beholde, the virgine shal conceiue and beare a sonne, and she shal call
his name ″Immánu-él.
15 n Butter and honie shal he eat, til he haue knowledge to refuse the euil, & to chuse the good.
16 For afore ẏ o childe shal haue knowledge to eschewe the euil, and to chuse the
good, the land, that thou abhorrest, shalbe
forsaken of bothe her Kings.
17 The Lord shal bring vpon thee, and vpon thy people, and vpon thy fathers house
(the daies that haue not come frõ the daie
that p Ephráim departed from Iudáh) *e-
uen* the King of q Asshúr.
18 And in that day shal the Lord hisse for
the r flie that is at the vttermoste parte of
the floods of Egypt, & for the bee which
is in the land of Asshúr,
19 And thei shal come and shal light all in
the desolate valleis, and in the holes of the
rockes, and vpon all thornie places, and

* 2.King. 16, 5.
″Or, Syria.
a To wit, the seconde time: for in the first battel Aház was ouercome.
b Meaning, ẏ Kings house.
c That is, Israél, because ẏ tribe was the greatest, Gene. 48, 19.
d For feare.
e That is to say, The rest shal returne: ẇ name Isaiáh gaue his sonne, to signifie, that ẏ rest of the people shulde returne out of their captiuitie.
f Which haue but a litle smoke and shal quickely be quenched.
g Which was an Israelite & as semeth, enemie to the house of Dauid.
h Counting from ẏ fiue & twentieth yere of ẏ reigne of Vzziáh, at what time Amos prophecied this thĩg, and now Isaiáh confirmeth that the Israelites shulde be led into perpetual captiuitie, ẇ thing came to passe within twentie yere after that Isaiáh did this message.
i For the confirmation of this thing, that thine enemies shalbe destroyed & thou preserued.
k Not to beleue Gods worde without a signe is to tẽpt God: but to refuse a signe whẽ God offreth it for ẏ aide & helpe of our infirmitie, is to rebel against him.
l You thinke you haue to do ẇ men, whẽ ye contemne Gods messengers: but it is God, against whome you bend your selues.
m Forasmuche as thou art vnworthy, ẏ Lord for his owne promes sake wil giue a signe ẇ shalbe that Christ the Sauiour of his Church & the effect of all signes & miracles shalbe reueiled.
″*Or, God with vs, which name can agre to none, but to him, that is bothe God and man.*
n Meanĩg, that Christ is not onely God, but man also, because he shal be nourished as other men, vntil ẏ age of discretiõ.
o Not meanĩg Christ, but anie childe: for before a childe can come to the yeres of discretiõ, the Kĩgs of Samaria and Syria shal be destroied.
p Since the time that the twelue tribes rebelled vnder Roboám.
q In whome thou hast put thy trust.
r Meaning, the Egyptians: for by reason the countrei is hote and moiste, it is ful of flies, as Assyria is ful of bees.

vpon all busshie [f] places.
20 In that day shal the Lord shaue with a
raser that is hired, *euen* by them beyonde
the Riuer, by the King of Asshúr, the head
and the heere of the [t] fete, and it shal cōsume the beard.
21 And in the same day shal a mā [u] nourish
a yong kowe, and two shepe.
22 And for the [x] abundance of milke, that
they shal giue, he shal eat butter: for butter and honie shal euerie one eat, which is
left within the land.
23 And at the same day euerie place, wherein
shalbe a thousand vines, shalbe at a thousand *pieces* of siluer: *so* it shalbe for the briers and for the thornes.
24 With arrowes and with ŷ [y] bowe shal one
come thether: because all the land shal be
briers and thornes.
25 But on [z] all the mountaines, which shalbe digged with ŷ mattocke, there shal not
come thether the feare of briers & thornes: but they shalbe for the sending out of
bullockes and for the treading of shepe.

f Signifying, ŷ no place shalbe fre frō thē.
t That is, that which is from ŷ belly downeward: meaning, that he wolde destroy bothe great & smale.
u He that before had a great nomber of cattel, shalbe content ŵ one kowe & two shepe.
x The nomber of men shal be so smale, that a fewe beastes shalbe able to nourish all abundantly.
y As thei that go to seke wilde beastes among the busshes.
z The moūtaines contrarie to their wonte, shalbe tilled by suche as shal flee to them for succour.

CHAP. VIII.

8 The captiuitie of Israél & Iudáh by the Assyrians. 6 The infidelitie of the Iewes. 9 The destruction of the Assyrians. 14 Christ the stone of stombling to the wicked. 19 The worde of God must be inquired at.

1 MOreouer, ŷ Lord said vnto me, Take thee a [a] great role, and write in
it [b] with a mans penne, Make spede to the
spoyle: haste to the pray.
2 Then I toke vnto me [c] faithful witnesses
to recorde, Vriáh the Priest, and Zechariáh the sonne of Ieberechiáh.
3 After, I came vnto the [d] Prophetesse, ŵ
conceiued, and bare a sonne. Then said
the Lord to me, Call his name, [*] Mahér-
shalál hash-baz.
4 For before the [e] childe shal haue knowledge to crye, My father, and my mother,
[f] he shal take away the riches of Damascus
and the spoile of Samaria, before the Kīg
of Asshúr.
5 ¶ And ŷ Lord spake yet againe vnto me,
saying,
6 Because this people hathe refused the
waters of [g] Shiloáh that runne softely, and
reioyce with Rezín, and the sonne of Remaliáh,
7 Now therefore beholde, the Lord bringeth vp vpon thē the waters of [h] the Riuer
mightie and great, *euen* the King of Asshúr with all his glorie, and he shal come
vp vpon all their riuers, and go ouer all
their bankes,
8 And shal breake into Iudáh, *&* shal ouerflowe and passe through, *&* shal come vp
to the [i] necke, & the stretching out of his
wings shal fil the breadth of thy land,

a That ŷ maiest write in great letters to the intent it may be more easely red.
b Meaning, after the cōmune faciō: because all men might read it.
c Because the thing was of great importance, he toke these to witnesses, which were of credit ŵ ŷ people, whē he set this vp vpon the dore of the temple, albeit Vriáh was a flatterig hypocrite, 2. King. 16, 11.
d Meaning, to his wife, & this was done in a vision.
Or, Make spede to the spoile: haste to the pray.
e Before anie childe be able to speake.
f That is, the armie of Assyria.
g Which was a fountaine at the fote of moūt Zión, out of ŷ which rā a smale riuer through ŷ citie: meaning ŷ they of Iudáh, distrusting their owne power, which was smale, desired such power and riches as they sawe in Syria and Israél. h That is, the Assyrians, which dwel beyonde Euphrates. i It shalbe ready to drowne them.

ô [k] Immánu-él.
9 Gather together on heapes, ô ye [l] people,
and ye shalbe broken in pieces, and hearkē
all ye of farre countreis: girde your selues, and you shalbe broken in pieces: girde
your selues, & you shalbe broken in pieces.
10 Take counsel together, yet it shalbe
broght to naught: pronounce a decre, yet
shal it not stand: for God is with vs.
11 For ŷ Lord spake thus to me in takīg [m] of.
mine hād, & taught me, ŷ I shulde not walke in the way of this people, saying,
12 Say ye not, A [n] confederacie to all them,
to whome this people saith a confederacie, nether feare you [o] their feare, nor be a-
fraied of them.
13 [p] Sanctifie the Lord of hostes, and let him
be your feare, and let him be your dread,
14 And he shalbe as a [q] Sanctuarie: *but* as a
stōbling stone & as a rocke to fall vpon, to
bothe the houses of Israél, *&* as a snare &
as a net to the inhabitants of Ierusalém.
15 And manie among them shal stomble,
and shal fall and shal be broken and shalbe
snared & shalbe taken.
16 [r] Binde vp the testimonie: seale vp the
Law among my disciples.
17 Therefore I wil wait vpō the Lord that
hathe hid his face from the house of Iaakób, and I wil loke for him.
18 Beholde I, and the [s] children whome the
Lord hathe giuē me, *are* as signes & as wōders in Israél, [t] by ŷ Lord of hostes, which
dwelleth in mount Zión.
19 And whē thei shal say vnto you, Enquire at them that haue a spirit of diuination,
and at the south saiers, which whisper and
murmur, [u] Shulde not a people enquire at
their God? from the [x] liuing to the dead?
20 To the [y] Lawe, and to the testimonie, if
they speake not according to this worde: *it*
is because there *is* no [z] light in them.
21 Thē he that is afflicted & famished, shal
go to and fro in [a] it: & when he shalbe hungrie, he shal euen freat him self, [b] and curse his King and his gods, & shal loke vpwarde.
22 And whē he shal loke to the earth, beholde trouble, & [c] darkenes, vexacion *&* anguish, and he *is* driuen to darkenes.

k He speaketh this to Messiáh, or Christ, in whome the faithful were comforted, and who wolde not suffer his Churche to be destroied vtterly.
l To wit, ye ŷ are enemies to the Church, as the Assyrians, Egyptians, Syrians &c.
m To encourage me that I shulde not shrīke for the infidelitie of this people, and so neglect mine office.
n Consent not ye that are godlie, to the league & frīdship that this people seke ŵ strangers & idolaters.
o Meaning, ŷ thei shulde not feare ŷ thing that thei feared, ŵ haue no hope in God.
p In putting your trust onely in him, in calling vpon him in aduersitie, patiently loking for his helpe, and fearīg to do anie thing contrarie to his wil.
q He wil defēd you which are his elect, & reiect all the rest, which is ment of Christ against whome ŷ Iewes shuld stomble and fall, Luk. 2, 34. rom. 9, 33. 1 pet. 2, 7.
r Thogh all forsake me, yet ye that are mine, kepe my worde sure sealed in your hearts.
s Meaning, thē that were willing to heare and obeie the worde of God, whome ŷ worlde hated as thogh thei were monsters and not worthie to liue.

t This was a consolation in their troubles, knowing that nothing colde come vnto them, but by the wil of the Lord. u Answer the wicked thus, Shulde not Gods people seke succour onely at him? x That is, wil thei refuse to be taught of the Prophet, who is the mouth of God, and seke helpe at the dead, which is the illusion of Satan. y Seke remedie in the worde of God where his wil is declared? z Thei haue no knowledge, but are blinde leaders of ŷ blinde. a That is, in Iudáh, where thei shulde haue had rest, if thei had not thus grieuously offended God. b In whome afore thei put their trust. c Thei shal thinke ŷ heauen and earth & all creatures are bent against thē to trouble thē.

CHAP. IX.

1 The vocation of the Gentiles. 6 A prophecie of Christ. 14 The destruction of the ten tribes for their pride and contempt of God.

1 YEt [a] the darkenes shal not *be* according to the affliction, [b] that it had
when at the first he touched lightly the

a He comforteth the Churche againe after these great threatnings, promising to restore them to great glorie in Messiáh.
b Wherewith Israél was punished, first by Tigláth-pilesar, which was a light scourge in respect of that which thei suffred afterward by Shalma-neser, who caried the Israelites awaie captiues.

land of Zebulún and the land of Naphtalí,nor afterward *when* he was more grie
uous by ỳ way of the sea beyonde Iordén
in Galile of [c] the Gentiles.
2 The people that [d] walked in darkenes,ha-
ue sene a great [e] light: thei that dwelled
in the land of the shadow of death, vpon
them hathe the [f] light shined.
3 Thou hast [g] multiplied the natiō, & not
increased *their* ioye: thei haue reioyced
before thee according to the ioye in haruest, & as men reioyce whē they diuide a
spoile.
4 For [h] the yoke of their burdē, & the staffe
of their shulder & the rodde of their oppressour hast thou broken as in the day of
Midian.
5 Surely euerie battel of the warriour *is*
with noise,& with tumbling of garmēts
in blood: but *this* shalbe [i] with burning
and deuouring of fyre.
6 For vnto vs a Childe is borne, & vnto vs
a sonne is giuē:& the gouernement is vpō
his shuldēr,& he shal call his name Wonderful, Coūseller, The mightie God, The
euerlastīg [k] Father, The prince of peace,
7 The increase of *his* gouernement and
peace shal haue none end:he shal sit vpō
the throne of Dauid, & vpon his kingdome, to order it, and to stablish it with
iudgement and with iustice, from hence
forthe,*euē* for euer: [l] the zeale of the Lord
of hostes wil performe this.
8 ¶ The Lord hathe sent a worde into Iaakób,and it hathe lighted vpon [m] Israél.
9 And all the people shal knowe,*euē* Ephráim,and the inhabitant of Samaria, that
saie in ỳ pride & presumptiō of ỳ heart,
10 The [n] brickes are fallē,but we wil buylde it with hewen stones: the wilde figtrees
are cut downe, but we wil change thē into cedres.
11 Neuertheles the Lord wil raise vp the
aduersaries of [o] Rezín against him,& ioine his enemies together.
12 Arám before & the Philistims behind,
and thei shal deuoure Israél with open
mouth: *yet* for all this his wrath is not turned awaie, but his hand *is* stretched out
stil.
13 For the people turneth not vnto him that
smiteth thē, nether do thei seke the Lord
of hostes.
14 Therefore wil the Lord cut of from
Israél head and taile, branch and rush in
one daie.
15 The ancient and the honorable man,he
is the head: & the prophet that teacheth
lies,he is the taile.

c Where as ỳ Iewes & Gentiles dwelt together by reason of those twentie cities, which Salomón gaue to Hyram.
d Which were captiue in Babylón:& ỳ Prophet speaketh of that thing, which shulde come to passe threscore yeres after, as thogh it were nowe done.
e Meaning,the cōfort of their deliuerance.
f This captiuitie & deliuerāce were figures of our captiuitie by sinne, and of our deliuerance by Christ through the preaching of the Gospel, Mat 4,15
g Their nomber was greater when thei went into captiuitie then when thei returned, but their ioye was greater at their returne, Hag.2,10.
h Thou gauest them perfite ioye, by deliuering them & by destroying ỳ tyrants that had kept them in cruel bondage, as thou didest deliuer them by Gidion from the Midianites, Iudg.7,22.
i He speaketh of the deliuerance of his Church, ẘ he hathe deliuered miraculously from his enemies,but specially by the comming of Christ,of whome he ꝓpheciеth in the next verse.
k The autor of eternitie, and by whome the Church and euerie member thereof shalbe preserued for euer,and haue immortal life.
l His singular loue and care for his elect.
m This is another prophecie against thē of Samaria, ẘ were mockers and contēners of Gods promises and menaces.
n We were but weake,when the enemie ouercame vs, but we wil make our selues so strong,that we wil nether care for our enemies,nor feare Gods threatenings
o Rezin King of Syriáh,who was in league with Israél,was slaine by the Assyrians,after whose death Arám,that is,the Syrians were against Israél,which on the other side were assailed by the Philistims.

16 For the leaders of the people cause thē
to erre:and thei that are led by them, are
deuoured.
17 Therefore shal the Lord haue no pleasure in their yong men, nether wil he
haue compassion of their fatherles and of
their widowes: for euerie one is an hypocrite and wicked, and euerie mouth speaketh folie: *yet* for all this his wrath is not
turned awaie,but his hand *is* stretched out
stil.
18 For wickednes [p] burneth as a fyre: it deuoureth ỳ briers & the thornes & wil kindle in the thicke places of the forest: and
thei shal mounte vp *like* the lifting vp of
smoke.
19 By the wrath of the Lord of hostes shal
the land be darkened,and the people shalbe as ỳ meat of the fyre:no mā shal [q] spare
his brother.
20 And he shal snatche at the right hand,&
be hungrie:& he shal eat on the left hand,
and shal not be satisfied: euerie one shal
eat the [r] flesh of his owne arme.
21 Manasséh,Ephráim: & Ephráim Manasséh,*and* thei bothe shalbe against Iudáh:
yet for all this his wrath is not turned a-
waie, but his hand *is* stretched out stil.

p Wickednes as a bellowse kindleth the fyre of Gods wrath, which consumeth all his obstinate enemies.
q Thogh there were no foren enemie, yet thei shal destroy one another.
r Their gredines shal be insatiable, so that one brother shal eat vp another,as thogh he shul deeat his owne flesh.

CHAP. X.

1 Of wicked lawe makers. 5 God wil punish his people by the Assyrians and after destroie them. 21 The remnant of Israél shalbe saued.

1 WO vnto them that decre wicked decrees, & [a] write grieuous
things,
2 To kepe backe the poore from iudgemēt,
and to take awaie the iudgement of the
poore of my people,that widowes maie be
their praie, and that thei maie spoile the
fatherles.
3 What wil ye do now in the daie of visitation,& of destruction, which shal come
frō [b] farre?to whome wil ye flee for helpe?
and where wil ye leaue your [c] glorie?
4 [d] Without me *euerie one* shal fall among
them ỳ are boūde,& thei shal fall downe
among the slaine: *yet* for all this his wrath
is not turned awaie, but his hand *is* stretched out stil.
5 ¶ O [e] Asshúr,the rodde of my wrath:and
ỳ staffe in their hands is mine indignatiō.
6 I wil send [f] him to a dissembling nation,
and I wil giue him a charge against the
people of my wrath to take the spoile &
to take the praie, and to treade them vnder fete like the myre in the strete.
7 But he thinketh not so, nether doeth
his heart esteme it so: but he imagineth to
destroye and to cut of not a fewe nacions.

a Which write and pronoūce a wicked sentēce to oppresse the poore:meaning that the wicked magistrates, which were the chief cause of mischief, shulde be first punished.
b To wit,from Assyria.
c Your riches & autoritie, ỳ thei maie be safe, and that ye maie receiue them againe
d Because thei haue forsaken me, some shal go into captiuitie, and the rest shalbe slaine.
e God calleth for the Assyrians to be ỳ executioners of his vengeance
f That is, the Assyrians against the Iewes, which are but hypocrites:& in this sixt and seuenth verse is declared ỳ difference of ỳ worke of God & of ỳ wicked in one verie thing and act:for Gods intention is to chastice them for their amendement, and the Assyrians purpose is to destroie them to enriche them selues:thus in respect of Gods iustice,it is Gods worke,but in respect of their owne malice, it is the worke of the deuil.

8 For he ſaith, Are not my princes all together Kings?
9 Is not Calnó as [g] Carchemíſh? Is not Ha
máth like Arpád? Is not Samaria as Damaſcus?
10 Like as mine hãd hathe founde the kingdomes of the idoles, ſeing their idoles *were*
aboue Ieruſalém, and aboue Samaria:
11 Shal not I, as I haue done to Samaria, &
to the idoles thereof, ſo do to Ieruſalém
and to the idoles thereof?
12 ¶ But when the Lord hathe accõpliſhed
[h] all his worke vpon mount Zión and Ieruſalém, I wil viſit the frute of the proude heart [i] of the King of Aſſhúr, and his
glorious and proude lokes,
13 Becauſe he ſaid, By the power of mine
owne hand haue I done it, and by my wiſdome, becauſe I am wiſe: therefore I haue
remoued the borders of the people, and
haue ſpoiled their treaſures, and haue pulled downe the inhabitants like a valiant
man.
14 And mine hand hathe founde as a neſt
the riches of the people, and as one gathereth egges that are left, *ſo* haue I gathered all the earth: and there was none to
moue the wing or to open the mouth, or to
whiſper.
15 Shal the [k] axe boaſt it ſelf againſt him
ỹ heweth therewith? or ſhal the ſawe exalt it ſelf againſt him that moueth it? as
if the rod ſhulde lift vp it ſelf againſt him
that taketh it vp, *or* the ſtaffe ſhulde exalt
it ſelf, *as it were* no wood.
16 Therefore ſhal the Lord God of hoſtes
ſend among his fat men, leanenes, and vnder his glorie he ſhal kindle a burning, like the burning of fyre.
17 And the light of Iſraél ſhalbe as a [l] fyre,
and the Holy one thereof as a flame, and
it ſhal burne, and deuoure [m] his thornes
and his briers in one day:
18 And ſhal conſume the glorie of his foreſt, & of his fruteful fields bothe ſoule
[n] and fleſh: and he ſhalbe as the [o] fainting
of a ſtanderd bearer.
19 And the reſt of the trees of his foreſt
ſhalbe fewe, that a childe may tel them.
20 ¶ And at that day ſhal the remnant of
Iſraél, and ſuch as are eſcaped of the houſe
of Iaakób, ſtaye no more vpon him that
ſmote them, but ſhal [p] ſtay vpon the Lord,
the holy one of Iſraél in trueth.
21 The remnant ſhal returne, *euen* the remnant of Iaakób vnto the mightie God.
22 For thogh thy people, ô Iſraél, be as the
ſand of the ſea, *yet* ſhal the remnant of thẽ
returne. The conſumption [q] decreed ſhal
ouerflowe with righteouſnes.
23 For the Lord God of hoſtes ſhal make
the conſumption, euen [r] determined, in
the middes of all the land.

g Seing that I haue ouercome, aſwel one citie as another, ſo that none colde reſiſt, ſhal Ieruſalém be able to eſcape mine hands?

h Whẽ he hathe ſufficiently chaſtiſed his people (for he beginneth at his owne houſe) thẽ wil he burne the roddes.

i Meaning, of Saneherib.

k Here we ſe that no creature is able to do anie thing, but as God appointeth him, & that they are all but his inſtruments to do his worke, thogh the intentions be diuerſe, as ver. 6.

l Meaning, that God is a light to comfort his people, & a fyre to burne his enemies

m That is, the Aſſyrians.

n To wit, bodie and ſoule vtterly.

o When ỹ battel is loſt and the ſtanderd taken.

p This is the end of Gods plagues towards his, to bring them to him and to forſake all truſt in others.

q This ſmale nomber, w̃ ſemed to be conſumed, and yet according to Gods decre is ſaued, ſhalbe ſufficient to fil all the worlde with righteouſnes.

r God wil deſtroye this lãd as he hathe determined, and after ſaue a ſmale portiõ.

24 Therefore thus ſaith the Lord God of
hoſtes, O my people, that dwelleſt in Zión, be not afraied of Aſſhúr: he ſhal ſmite
thee with a rod, and ſhal lift vp his ſtaffe
againſt thee after the maner of [ſ] Egypt:
25 But yet a very litle time, and the wrath
ſhalbe conſumed, and mine angre in their
deſtruction.
26 And the Lord of hoſtes ſhal raiſe vp a
ſcourge for him, according to the plague
of [t] Midian in the rocke Oréb: and *as* his
ſtaffe *was* vpon the [u] Sea, ſo he wil lift it
vp after the maner of Egypt.
27 And at that day ſhal his burdẽ be taken
away from of thy ſhulder, & his yoke frõ
of thy necke: & the yoke ſhalbe deſtroyed
becauſe of [x] the anointing.
28 He is come [y] to Aiáth: he is paſſed into Migrón: at Michmáſh ſhal he lay vp
his armour.
29 They haue gone ouer the foorde: they
lodged in the lodging at Gebá: Ramáh
is afraied: Gibeáh of Saúl is fled away.
30 Lift vp thy voice, ô daughter Gallím,
cauſe Laiſh to heare, ô poore Anathóth.
31 Madmenáh is remoued: the inhabitãts of
Gebím haue gathered them ſelues together.
32 Yet there is a time ỹ he wil ſtay at Nob:
he ſhal lift vp his hand toward the mount
of the daughter Zión, the hil of Ieruſalém.
33 Beholde, the Lord God of hoſtes ſhal
cut of the [z] bough with feare, and thei of
highſtature ſhalbe cut of, and the hie ſhalbe humbled.
34 And he ſhal cut away the thicke places of
the foreſt with yron, & Lebanón ſhal haue a mightie fall.

ſ As ỹ Egyptians did puniſh thee.

t Read Chap. 9, 4.

u When the Iſraelites paſſed through by ỹ lifting vp of Moſes rod, & the enemies weredrowned, Exod. 14, 28.

x Becauſe of ỹ promes made to that kingdome, whereby Chriſts kingdome was prefigured.

y He deſcribeth by what way the Aſsyriãs ſhulde come againſt Ieruſalém to cõfirme ỹ faithful, whẽn it ſhulde come to paſſe, that as their plague was come, ſo ſhuldẽ thei be deliuered.

z Feare & deſtruction ſhal come vpon Iudáh: for the princes and ỹ people ſhal all be led awaie captiues.

CHAP. XI.

1 Chriſt borne of the roote of Iſhái. 2 His Vertues and kingdome. 6 The frutes of the Goſpel. 10 The calling of the Gentiles.

1 BVt there ſhal come a [a] rod forthe of ỹ
ſtocke of Iſhái, & a graſe ſhal growe
out of his rootes.
2 And the Spirit of the Lord ſhal reſt vpon
him: the Spirit of wiſdome and vnderſtan
ding, the Spirit of counſel & ſtrength, the
Spirit of knowledge, and of the feare of
the Lord,
3 And ſhal make him prudent in the feare
of the Lord: for he ſhal not iudge after
the ſight of his eyes, nether reproue by
the hearing of his eares.
4 But with righteouſnes ſhal he iudge the
poore, and with equitie ſhal he reproue for
the meke of the earth: and he ſhal [b] ſmite
the earth with the rodde of his mouth, &
with the breath of his lippes ſhal he ſlaye
the wicked.
5 And iuſtice ſhalbe the girdle of his loynes, & faithfulnes the girdle of his raines.

a Becauſe the captiuitie of Babylon was a figure of ỹ ſpiritual captiuitie vnder ſinne, he ſheweth that our true deliuerance muſt come by Chriſt for as Dauid came out of Iſhái a mã without dignitie: ſo Chriſt ſhulde come of a poore carpenters houſe as out of a dead ſtocke, Chap. 53. 2

b All theſe properties can agre to none but onely vnto Chriſt: for it is he that toucheth the heartes of the faithful and mortifieth their concupiſcences: & to the wicked he is ỹ ſauour of death & to them that ſhal periſh: ſo ỹ all ỹ worlde ſhal be ſmitten w̃ this rodde, w̃ is his worde.

6 The [c] wolfe also shal dwell with the lãbe,
and the leoparde shal lye with the kid, and
the calfe, and the lyon, and the fat beast
together, and a litle childe shal lead them.
7 And the kowe and the beare shal fede:
their yong ones shal lie together: and the
lyon shal eat strawe like the bullocke.
8 And the sucking childe shal play vpon ỹ
hole of the aspe, & the wained childe shal
put his hand vpon the cockatrice hole.
9 Then shal none hurt nor destroy in all the
mountaine of mine holines: for the earth
shalbe ful of the knowledge of the Lord,
as [d] the waters that couer the sea.
10 And in that day ỹ roote of Ishái, which
shal stand vp for a signe vnto the [e] people,
the naciõs shal seke vnto it, & his [f] rest shal
be glorious.
11 And in the same day shal the Lord *stretch
out* his hand [g] againe the second time, to
possesse the remnant of his people, (which
shalbe left) of Asshúr, and of Egypt, and
of Pathros, and of Ethiopia, and of Elám,
& of Shineár, and of Hamáth, and of the
yles of the sea.
12 And he shal set vp a signe to the nacions,
and assemble the dispersed of Israél, and
gather the scattered of Iudáh from the
foure corners of the worlde.
13 The hatred also of Ephráim shal departe, and the aduersaries of Iudah shalbe cut
of: Ephráim shal not enuie [h] Iudáh, nether
shal Iudáh vexe Ephráim:
14 But they shal flee vpon the shoulders of
the Philistims toward the West: they shal
spoyle them of the East together: Edóm
& Moáb shalbe the stretching out of their
hands, & the children of Ammón *in* their
obedience.
15 The Lord also shal vtterly destroye the
[i] tongue of the Egyptians sea, & with his
mightie winde shal lift vp his hand [k] ouer
the riuer, and shal smite him in *his* seuen
streames, and cause men to walke *therein*
with shoes.
16 And there shalbe a path to the remnant
of his people, which are left of Asshúr, like as it was vnto Israél in the day that he
came vp out of the land of Egypt.

CHAP. XII.

A thankesgiuing of the faithful for the mercies of God.

1 AND thou [a] shalt say in that day, O
Lord, I wil praise thee: thogh thou
wast angrie with me, thy wrath is turned
away, and thou comfortest me.
2 Beholde, God *is* my [b] saluaciõ: I wil trust,
and wil not feare: for the Lord God *is* *my
strength and song: he also is become my
saluacion.
3 Therefore with ioy shal ye [c] drawe waters
out of the welles of saluacion.
4 And ye shal say in that day, * Praise the
Lord: call vpon his Name: declare his
workes among the people: make mention
of them, for his Name is exalted.
5 Sing vnto the Lord, for he hathe done
excellent things: this is knowen in all the
worlde.
6 Crye out, and shoute, [d] ô inhabitant of
Zión: for great *is* the holy one of Israél in
the middes of thee.

CHAP. XIII.

The Medes and Persians shal destroye Babylon.

1 THE [a] burden of Babél, which Isaiáh
the sonne of Amóz did se.
2 Lift vp a stãdard vpon the hie mountaine: lift vp the voyce vnto them: wagge
the [b] hãd, that thei may go into the gates
of the nobles.
3 I haue cõmanded them, that I haue [c] sanctified: and I haue called the mightie to
my wrath, *&* thẽ that reioyce in my [d] glorie.
4 The noyse of a multitude *is* in the mountaines, like a great people: a tumultuous
voyce of the kingdomes of the naciõs gathered together: the Lord of hostes nom-
breth the hoste of the battel.
5 They come from a farre countrey, from
the end of the heauen: *euen* the Lord with
the [e] weapons of his wrath to destroy the
whole land.
6 Howle [f] you, for the day of the Lord is
at hand: it shal come as a destroyer from
the Almightie.
7 Therefore shal all hands be weakened, &
all mens hearts shal melt,
8 And thei shalbe afrayed: anguish & sorow
shal take *them*, and they shal haue peine, as
a woman that trauaileth: euerie one shalbe
amased at his neighbour, and their faces
shalbe like [g] flames of fyre.
9 Beholde, the daye of the Lord cometh,
cruel, with wrath and fierce angre to lay
the land waste: and he shal destroy the sinners out of it.
10 For the [h] starres of heauen and the planets thereof shal not giue their light: the
sũne shalbe darkened in his going forthe,
and the moone shal not cause her light to
shine.
11 And I wil visite the wickednes vpon the
[i] worlde, and their iniquitie vpon the wicked, and I wil cause the arrogancie of the
[k] proude to cease, and wil cast downe the
pride of tyrants.
12 I wil make a [l] man more precious then
fine golde, euen a man aboue the wedge of
golde of Ophír.
13 Therefore I wil shake the heauen, and the
earth shal remoue out of her place in the
wrath of the Lord of hostes, and in the day

c Mẽ because of their wicked affections are named by the names of beasts, wherein the like affections reigne: but Christ by his Spirit shal reforme them, & worke in them suche mutual charitie, that they shal be like lambes, fauoring & louing one another, and cast of all their cruel affectiõs, Chap. 65,25.

d It shalbe in as great abundance as the waters in the sea.

e He prophecieth of the calling of the Gentiles.

f That is, his Church, ŵ he also calleth his rest, Psal. 132,14.

g For God first deliuered his people out of Egypt, and now ꝓmiseth to deliuer thẽ out of their enemies hãds, as from ỹ Parthians, Persians, Chaldeans, & them of Antiochia, among whome thei were dispersed: & this is chiefly mẽt of Christ, who calleth his people, being dispersed through all ỹ worlde.

h Here he describeth the consent that shalbe in his Church, and their victorie against their enemies.

i Meaning, a corner of the sea, ỹ entreth into the land, and hathe the forme of a tõgue.

k To wit, Nilus, the great riuer of Egypt, which entreth into ỹ sea with seuẽ streames.

Chap XII.

a He sheweth how ỹ Church shal praise God, whẽ thei are deliuered from their captiuitie.

b Our saluaciõ standeth onely in God, who giueth vs an assured confidence, constãcie & occasion to praise him for the same.

*Exod 15,2. psal.118,14.

c The graces of God shalbe so abundant, that ye may receiue them in as great plentie, as waters out of a fountaine that is ful.

*1 Chron.16,8.

d Ye that are of the Church.

a That is, the great calamitie, which was prophecied to come on Babél, as a moste grieuous burdẽ, ŵ thei were not able to beare In these 12 Chapters following, he speaketh of ỹ plagues, wherewith God wolde smite these strange nacions, (whome thei knew) to declare that God chastised ỹ Israelites as his children, & these other as his enemies: & also that if God spare not these that are ignorant, ỹ they must not thinke strange, if he punished them, ŵ haue knowledge of his Law and kepe it not.

b To wit, to ỹ Medes & the Persians.

c That is, prepared & appointed to execute my iudgements.

d Which willingly go about ỹ worke, whereunto I appoint thẽ, but how the wicked do this, read Chap 10, 6.

e The armie of the Medes & the Persiãs against Babylon.

f Ye Babylonians.

g The Babylonians angre, & grief shalbe so muche, that their faces shal burne as fyre

h They that are ouercome, shal thinke ỹ all the powers of heauen and earth are against them, Ezek.32,7. ioel. 3,15. mat.24,29

i He compareth Babylon to the whole worlde, because they so estemed them selues by reason of their great empire

k He noteth the principal vice, whereunto they were moste giuen, as are all that abunde in welth.

l He noteth the great slaughter ỹ shalbe, seing the enemie shal nether for golde, or siluer spare a mans life, as vers. 17.

of his fierce angre.
14 And [m] it shalbe as a chased doe, and as a
shepe that no man taketh vp. euerie man
shal turne to his owne people, and flee e-
che one to his owne land.
15 Euerie one that is found, shalbe striken
through: and whosoeuer ioyneth him self,
shal fall by the sworde.
16 *Their [n] children also shalbe broken in
pieces before their eies: their houses shalbe spoiled, and their wiues rauished.
17 Beholde, I wil stirre vp the Medes agaīst
them, which shal not regard siluer, nor be
desirous of golde.
18 With bowes also shal they destroie the
children, & shal haue no compassion vpō
the frute of the wombe, and their eies shal
not spare the children.
19 And Babél the glorie of kingdomes, the
beautie and pride of the Chaldeans, shalbe
as the destruction of God * in Sodóm &
Gomoráh.
20 It shal not be inhabited for euer, nether
shal it be dwelled in from generacion to
generacion: nether shal the [o] Arabian pitche his tēts there, nether shal the shepherdes make their foldes there.
21 But [p] Ziim shal lodge there, and their
houses shalbe ful of Ohim: Ostriches shal
dwell there, & the Satyrs shal dance there.
22 And Iim shal crye in their palaces, and
dragons in their pleasant palaces: and the
time thereof is readie to come, & the dayes thereof shal not be prolonged.

m Meanīg, the power of Babylon with their hired souldiers.

*Psal.137,9.

n This was not accomplished when Cyrus toke Babylon, but after the death of Alexandre ẏ Great.

*Genes.19,25. ier.50,40.

o Who vseth to go from countrey to coūtrey to finde pasture for their beasts, but there shal thei finde none

p Which were ether wilde beasts, or foules, or wicked spirits, whereby Satan deluded man, as by the fairies, gobblins and suche like fantasies

CHAP. XIIII.

1 The returne of the people from captiuitie. 4 The derision of the King of Babylon. 11 The death of the King. 29 The destruction of the Philistims.

1 For [a] the Lord wil haue compassion
of Iaakób, and wil yet chuse Israél,
and cause them to rest in their owne land:
and the stranger [b] shal ioyne him self vnto them, and they shal cleaue to the house
of Iaakób.
2 And the people shal receiue thē & bring
them to their owne place, & the house of
Israél shal possesse them in the land of the
Lord, for [c] seruants & handmaids: & they
shal take thē prisoners, whose captiues thei
were, & haue rule ouer their oppressors.
3 ¶ And in that day whē the Lord shal giue thee rest from thy sorow, and from thy
feare, and from the sore bondage, wherein
thou didest serue,
4 Then shalt thou take vp this prouerbe
against the King of Babél, and say, How
hathe the oppressor ceased? and the golde
thirstie Babél rested?
5 The Lord hathe broken the rodde of the
wicked, *and* the sceptre of the rulers:
6 Which smote the people in angre with a
continual plague, & ruled the nations in
wrath: if anie were persecuted, he did [d] not
let.

a He sheweth why God wil hast to destroy his enemies: to wit, because he wil deliure his Church.

b Meaning, ẏ the Gentiles shalbe ioyned with the Churche and worship God.

c Signifying ẏ ẏ Iewes shuld be superiours to the Gētiles, & ẏ thei shulde be broght vnder the seruice of Christ by the preaching of the Apostles, whereby all are broght to the subiectiō of Christ, 2 Co 10,5.

d That is, he suffred all violence and iniuries to be done.

7 The whole worlde is at [e] rest & is quiet:
they sing for ioye.
8 Also the fyrre trees reioyced of thee, &
the cedres of Lebanón, *saying*, Since thou
art laide downe, no hewer came vp against vs.
9 Hell beneth is moued for thee to [f] mete
thee at thy comming, raising vp the dead
for thee, *euen* all the princes of the earth,
and hathe raised from their thrones all
the Kings of the nations.
10 All thei shal crye, and say vnto thee, Art
thou become weake also as we? art thou
become like vnto vs?
11 Thy pompe is broght downe to the graue, & the sounde of thy violes: the worme
[g] is spread vnder thee, and the wormes
couer thee.
12 How art thou fallen from heauē, ô [h] Lucifer, sonne of the morning? & cut downe to the grounde, which didest cast lottes
vpon the nations?
13 Yet thou saidest in thine heart, I wil ascend into heauen, and exalt my throne
aboue beside the starres of God: I wil sit
also vpon the mount of the Congregacion in the sides of the [i] North.
14 I wil ascēd aboue ẏ height of the cloudes, & I wil be like the moste high.
15 But thou shalt be broght downe to the
graue, to the sides of the pit.
16 Thei that se thee, shal [k] loke vpon thee &
consider thee, *saying*, Is this the man that
made the earth to tremble, & that did
shake the kingdomes?
17 He made the worlde as a wildernes, and
destroied the cities thereof, & opened not
[l] the house of his prisoners.
18 All the Kings of the nacions, *euen* they
all slepe in glorie, euerie one in his owne
house.
19 But thou art [m] cast out of thy graue like
an abominable branche: *like* the raimēt of
those ẏ are slaine, & thrust thorowe with
a sworde, which go downe to the stones of
the pit, as a carkeise troden vnder fete.
20 Thou shalt not be ioyned wᵗ them in the
graue, because ẏ hast destroied thine owne
land, & slaine thy people: the sede of the
wicked shal not be renoumed for euer.
21 [n] Prepare a slaughter for his children,
for the iniquitie of their fathers: let them
not rise vp nor possesse the land, nor fil the
face of the worlde with enemies.
22 ¶ For I wil rise vp against thē (saith the
Lord of hostes) and wil cut of from Babél the name and the remnant and the
sonne, and the nephewe, saith the Lord:
23 And I wil make it a possession to ẏ *hedgehog, and pooles of water, and I wil swepe it with the besome of destruction, saith
the Lord of hostes.
24 The Lord of hostes hathe sworne, sayīg,
Sure-

e Meanīg, that when tyrants reigne, there can be no rest nor quietnes, and also how detestable a thīg tyrānie is, seing the insensible creatures haue occasion to reioyce at their destructiō

f As thogh thei feared lest thou shuldest trouble the dead, as ẏ didest the lyuing: and here he derideth ẏ proude tyrannie of the wicked, which knowe not ẏ all creatures wish their destruction that thei maie reioyce.

g In stead of thy costly carpets and coue rings.

h Thou that thoghtest thy self most glorious, and as it were, placed in ẏ heauē: for ẏ morning starre, that goeth before the sunne, is called lucifer to whome Nebuchad-nezzar is compared.

i Meaning, Ierusalém, whereof the Temple was on the North side, as psal.48 2. whereby he meaneth that tyrāts fight against God, when thei persecute his Church, and wolde set thē selues in his place.

k In marueling at thee.

l To set them at libertie: noting his crueltie.

m Thou wast not buryed in the sepulchre of thy fathers thy tyrannie was so abhorred.

n He calleth to the Medes and Persians and all those that shulde execute Gods vengeance.

*Or tortes.

Surely like as I haue purposed, so shal it
come to passe, and as I haue consulted, it
shal stand:
25 [o] That I wil breake to pieces Asshúr in
my land, and vpon my mountaines wil I
treade him vnder fote: so ẏ his yoke shal
departe from [p] them, and his burden shal
be taken from of their shuldre.
26 This is the counsel that is cōsulted vpō
the whole worlde, and this is the hād stretched out ouer all the nacions,
27 Because the Lord of hostes hathe determined it, and who shal disanul it? and his
hand is stretched out, and who shal turne
it away?
28 ¶ In the yere that King Aház dyed, was
this [q] burden.
29 Reioyce not, (thou whole [r] Palestina)
because the rod of him that did beat thee,
is brokē: for out of the serpents roote shal
come forthe a cockatrise, and the frute
thereof *shalbe* a fyrie flying serpent.
30 For the [s] first borne of the poore shalbe
fed, & the nedie shal lye downe in safety:
and I wil kil thy roote with famine, & [t] it
shal slay thy remnant.
31 Howle, ô gate, crye ô citie: thou whole
land of Palestina art dissolued, for there
shal come from the [u] North a smoke,
and none *shalbe* alone, [x] at his time appointed.
32 What shal then one answer [y] ẏ messengers of the Gentiles? That the Lord hathe
stablished [z] Zión, & the poore of his people shal trust in it.

o As I haue be gōne to destroy the Assyrians in Saneherib, so wil I continue, & destroye them wholy, when I shal deliuer you from Babylón.
p Frō ẏ Iewes.
q Read Chap. 13,1.
r He willeth ẏ Philistims not to reioyce because ẏ Iewes are diminished in their power: for their strēgth shalbe greater then euer it was.
s The Israelites, ẇ were broght to moste extreme miserie.
t To wit, my people.
u That is, frō the Iewes, or Assyrians: for they were bothe North from Palestina.
x But they shalbe all ready, and ioine together.
y Which shal come to enquire of the state of the Church.
z Thei shal answer, ẏ ẏ Lord doeth defend his Church, & thē that ioyne them selues thereunto.

CHAP. XV.

A prophecie against Moáb.

1 THe [a] burden of Moáb. Surely [b] Ar of
Moáb was destroyed & broght to silence in a night: surely Kir of Moáb was
destroyed, & broght to silence in a night.
2 [c] He shal go vp to the temple, and to Dibón to the hie places to wepe: for [d] Nebó
and for Medebá shal Moáb howle: vpon
all [e] their heads *shalbe* baldenes, and euerie
beard shauen.
3 In their stretes shal they be girded with
sackecloth: on the toppes of their houses,
and in their stretes euerie one shal howle,
and come downe with weping.
4 And Heshbón shal crye, & Elealéh: their
voyce shalbe heard vnto Iáhaz: therefore
ẏ warriers of Moáb shal showte: the soule
of euerie one shal lament in him self.
5 Mine [f] heart shal crye for Moáb: his fugitiues *shal flee* vnto Zóar, [g] an heiffer of
thre yere olde: for they shal go vp ẇ weping by the mounting vp of Luhith: and
by the way of Horonáim they [h] shal raise
vp a crye of destruction.

a Read Chap. 13,1.
b The chief citie, whereby the whole countrey was ment.
c The Moabites shal flee to their idoles for succour, but it shalbe to late.
d Which were cities of Moáb
e For as in the West partes ẏ people vsed to let their heere growe long, when they mourned, so in the East partes they cut it of.
f The Prophet speaketh this in the persone of the Moabites, or as one that felt the great iudgement of God that shulde come vpon them.
g Meaning, that it was a citie that euer liued in pleasure, and neuer felt sorowe.
h He describeth the miserable dissipation, and flight of the Moabites.

6 For the waters of Nimrim shal be dryed
vp: therefore the grasse is withered, the
herbes consumed, & there was no grene
herbe.
7 Therefore what *euerie man* hathe left, &
their substance shal they beare to ẏ [i] broke of the willowes.
8 For the crye went rounde aboute ẏ borders of Moáb: & the howling thereof
vnto Eglaím, & the skriking thereof vnto
Beer Elím,
9 Because the waters of Dimón shalbe ful
[k] of blood: for I wil bring more vpon Dimón, euen lyons [l] vpon him that escа-
peth of Moáb, and to the remnant of the
land.

i To hide thē selues, & their goods there.
k Of thē that are slaine.
l So that by no meanes they shulde escape the hand of God: thus wil God punish ẏ enemies of his Church.

CHAP. XVI.

The causes wherefore the Moabites are destroyed.

1 SEnd [a] ye a lambe to the ruler of the
worlde from the rocke of the wildernes, vnto the mountaine of the daughter
Zión.
2 For it shalbe as a birde that [b] flyeth, and a
nest forsaken: the daughters of Moáb shal
be at the foordes of Arnón.
3 Gather a counsel, execute iudgement:
[c] make thy shadowe as the night in the
midday: hide them that are chased out:
bewraye not him that is fled.
4 Let my banished dwel with thee: Moáb be
thou their couert from the face of the destroyer: for the extorcioner [d] shal end:
the destroyer shalbe consumed, & the oppressour shal cease out of the land.
5 And in mercie shal the throne be prepared, [e] and he shal sit vpon it in stedfastnes, in the tabernacle of Dauid, iudging, and seking iudgement, and hasting
iustice.
6 We haue heard of the pride of Moáb (he
is verie proud) *euen* his pride, and his arrogancie, and his indignacion, *but* his [f] lies
shal not *be* so.
7 Therefore shal Moáb howle vnto Moáb:
euerie one shal howle: for the fundacions
of Kir-haréseth shal ye mourne, yet thei
shal be [g] striken.
8 For the vineyardes of Heshbón are cut
downe, & the vine of Sibmáh: [h] the lords
of the heathen haue broken the principal
vines thereof: they are come vnto [i] Iaazér:
they wandred in the wildernes: her goodlie branches stretched out them selues, &
went ouer the sea.
9 Therefore wil [k] I wepe with the weping
of Iaazér, & of ẏ vine of Sibmáh, ô Heshbón: and Elealéh, I wil make thee drunke
with my teares, because vpon thy sommer
frutes, and vpon thy haruest [l] a showting
is falln.

a That is, offer a sacrifice: whereby he derideth their long delay, which wolde not repent whē the Lord called thē, shewing them that it is now to late, seing the vengeance of God is vpō thē.
b There is no remedie, but you must flie.
c He sheweth what Moáb shulde haue done, when Isráel their neighbour was in affliction, to whome because they wolde giue no shadowe nor cōfort, they are now left cōfortles.
d The Assyrians shal oppresse the Israelites, but for a while.
e Meaning, Christ.
f Their vaine confidence, & proude bragges shal deceiue them, as Ier 48,2
g For all your mourning, yet the citie shalbe destroyed, euen vnto the fundations.
h That is, the Assyrians, and other enemies.
i Meaning, ẏ the countrey of Moáb was now destroyed and all the precious thīgs thereof were caried into the borders, yea, into other countreys, and ouer the sea.
k He sheweth that their plague was so great, that it wolde haue moued anie man to lament with them, as Psal. 141,5.
l The enemies are come vpon thee, and showte for ioye, when they carie thy commodities from thee, as Ier 48,33.

10 And gladnes is taken away, & ioye out
of the plentiful field: and in the vineyardes shalbe no singing nor shouting for
ioye : the treader shal not tread wine in
the wine presses: I haue caused the reioycing to cease.
11 Wherefore, my [m] bowels shal sounde like an harpe for Moáb, and mine inwarde
partes for Ker-háresh.
12 And when it shal appeare that Moáb
shalbe wearie of his hie places, then shal
he come to his [n] temple to pray, but he
shal not preuaile.
13 This is the worde that the Lord hathe
spoken against Moáb since that time.
14 And now the Lord hathe spoken, saying,
[o] In thre yeres, as the yeres of a [p] hyreling,
and the glorie of Moáb shalbe contẽned
in all the great multitude, & the remnãt
shalbe very smale *&* feble.

m For verie sorow and cõpassion.
n They shal vse all meanes to seke helpe of their idoles & all in vaine: for Chemóz their great god shal not be able to helpe them.
o He appointed a certeine time to punish the enemies in.
p Who wil obserue iustely ye time, for the which he is hyred, & serue no longer, but wil euer long for it.

CHAP. XVII.

A prophecie of the destruction of Damascus and Ephráim. 7 Calamitie moueth to repentance.

1 The [a] burden of [b] Damascus. Beholde, Damascus is taken away from
being a citie, for it shalbe a ruinous heape.
2 The cities of [c] Aroér *shalbe* forsaken: they
shalbe for ye flockes: for thei shal lye *there*,
and none shal make them afraide.
3 The munition also shal cease from [d] E-
phráim, & the kingdome from Damascus,
and the remnant of Arám shalbe as the
[e] glorie of the children of Israél, saith the
Lord of hostes.
4 And in that day the glorie of [f] Iaakób
shalbe impouerished, and the fatnes of his
flesh shal be made leane.
5 And it shalbe as when the haruest man
gathereth [g] the corne, and reapeth the eares with his arme, and he shalbe as he that
gathereth the eares in the valley of [h] Repháim.
6 Yet a gathering of grapes shal [i] be left
in it, as the shaking of an oliue tre, two *or*
thre beries *are* in the top of the vpmoste
boughs, *&* foure *or* fiue in the hye branches of the frute thereof, saith the Lord
God of Israél.
7 At that day shal a man loke to his [k] maker, and his eyes shal loke to the holie one
of Israél.
8 And he shal not loke to the altars, the
workes of his owne hands, nether shal he
loke to those things, which his owne fingers haue made, as groues and images.
9 In that day shal the cities of their stregth
be as the forsaking of boughs & brãches,
which [l] they did forsake, because of the

a Read Chap. 13,1.
b The chief citie of Syria.
c It was a coũtrey of Syria by the riuer Arnón.
d It semeth ye the Prophet wolde cõfort ye Church in declaring the destructiõ of these two Kings, of Syria & Israél, when as they had conspired ye ouerthrowe of Iudáh.
e The ten tribes gloried in their multitude, and alliãce with other nacions: therefore he saith yt they shal be broght downe and the Syriãs also.
f Meaning of ye ten tribes, wc boasted them selues of their nobilitie, psperitie, strẽgth & multitude.
g As the abũdance of corne doeth not feare the haruest men yt shulde cut it downe: no more shal ye multitude of Israél make ye enemies to shrĩke, whome God shal appoint to destroye them.
h Which valley was plentiful & fertile.
i Because God wolde haue his couenãt stable, he promiseth to reserue some of this people, and to bring them to repentance. k He sheweth that Gods corrections euer bring forthe some frute, and cause his to turne from their sinnes, and to humble them selues to him. l As the Canaanites left their cities, whẽ God did place the Israelites there, so the cities of Israél shal no more be able to defend their inhabitants, then busshes, when God shal send the enemie to plague them.

childrẽ of Israél, & there shalbe desolatiõ.
10 Because thou hast forgotten the God
of thy saluacion, and hast not remembred
the God of thy strength, therefore shalt
thou set pleasant plants, and shalt graffe
strange [m] vine branches:
11 In the day shalt thou make thy plant to
growe, and in the morning shalt thou make thy sede to florish : *but* the haruest shal
be gone in the day [n] of possession, and
there shalbe desperate sorow.
12 [o] Ah, the multitude of manie people, they
shal make a sounde like the noyse of the
sea: for the noyse of the people shal make a
sounde like the noyse of mightie waters.
13 The people shal make a sounde like the
noyse of manie waters: *but God* shal [p] rebuke them, and they shal flee farre of, and
shalbe chased as the chaffe of the mountaines before the winde, and as a rolling
thing before the whirle winde.
14 And lo, in the euening there *is* [q] trouble:
but afore the morning it is gone. This is
the porcion of them that spoile vs, and the
lot of them that robbe vs.

m Which are excellent, and broght out of other countreys.
n As the Lord threatneth the wicked in his Law, Leuit. 26,16.
o The Prophet lamenteth, considering the horrible plague yt was prepared against Israél by ye Assyriãs, which were infinite in nõber, and gathered of many nacions.
p He addeth this for ye cõsolation of the faithful, which were in Israél.
q He compareth ye enemies ye Assyrians to a tẽpest, which riseth ouer night, and in the morning is gone.

CHAP. XVIII.

1 Of the enemies of the Church. 7 And of the vocation of the Gentiles.

1 Oh, the [a] land shadowing with wings,
which is beyonde the riuers of E-
thiopia,
2 Sending ambassadours by the sea, euẽ in
vessels of [b] redes vpon the waters, *saying*,
[c] Go, ye swift messengers, to a nacion that
is scatred abroad, and spoiled, vnto a terrible [d] people from their beginning euẽ
hitherto : a nacion by litle and litle, euen
troden vnder fote, whose land the [e] floods
haue spoiled.
3 All ye the inhabitants of the worlde and
dwellers in the earth, shal se when [f] he setteth vp a signe in the mountaines, and whẽ
he bloweth the trumpe, ye shal heare.
4 For so the Lord said vnto me, I wil [g] rest
& beholde in my tabernacle, as [h] the heat
drying vp the raine, *&* as a cloude of dewe
in the heat of haruest.
5 For afore the haruest when the floure is
finished, & the frute is riping in the floure, then he shal cut downe the branches
with hookes, and shal take away, *&* cut of
the boughs:
6 They shal be left together vnto the foules of the mountaines, and to the [i] beastes
of the earth: for the foule shal sommer vpõ
it, and euerie beast of the earth shal winter
vpon it.
7 At that time shal a [k] present be broght

a He meaneth that parte of Ethiopia, which eth toward ye sea, wc was so ful of shippes that the seales (which he cõpareth to wings) semed to shadow the sea.
b Which in those coũtreis were great: inso muche as they made shippes of thẽ for swiftenes.
c This may be taken yt they sent other to comforte the Iewes, and to promise them helpe against their enemies, and so ye Lord did threaten to take away their strength that ye Iewes shulde not trust therein: or that they did solicite ye Egyptians, & promised thẽ aide to go against Iudah.
d To wit, the Iews, who because of Gods plagues made all other nacions afraid of the like, as God threatened, Deu. 28,37. e Meaning the Assyrians, as Chap. 8,7. f When yt Lord prepareth to fight against ye Ethiopians g I wil stay a while from punishing ye wicked. h Which two seasons are moste profitable for the riping of frutes: whereby he meaneth, yt he wil seme to fauour them, & giue them abundance for a time, but he wil suddenly cut them of. i Not onely mẽ shal contẽne them, but the brute beasts. k Meaning, that God wil pitie his Church, and receiue that litle remnant as an offring vnto him self.

vnto the Lord of hostes,(a people that is
scatred abroad, and spoiled, and of a terrible people from their beginning hitherto, a nacion, by litle and litle euen troden
vnder fote, whose lãd the riuers haue spoiled) to the place of the Name of the Lord
of hostes, *euen* the mount Zión.

CHAP. XIX.

1 The destruction of the Egyptians by the Assyrians. 18 Of their conuersion to the Lord.

1 THe [a] burden of Egypt. Beholde, the
Lord [b] rideth vpon a swift cloude, &
shal come into Egypt, & ỹ idoles of Egypt
shal be moued at his presence, & the heart
of Egypt shal melt in the middes of her.
2 And I wil set the Egyptians against the
Egyptiãs: so euerie one shal [c] fight against
his brother, and euerie one against his
neighbour, citie against citie, & kingdome against kingdome.
3 And the [d] spirit of Egypt shal faile in the
middes of her, and I wil destroye their counsel, and they shal seke at the idoles, & at
the sorcerers, & at them that haue spirits
of diuination, and at the southsayers.
4 And I wil deliuer the Egyptians into the
hand of cruel lords, and a mightie King
shal rule ouer them, saith the Lord God of
hostes.
5 Then the waters of the sea shal [e] faile, &
the riuer shal be dryed vp, and wasted.
6 And the riuers [f] shal go farre away: the
riuers of defense shalbe emptyed & dryed
vp: the redes & flagges shalbe cut downe.
7 The grasse in the riuer, *and* at the [g] head
of the riuers, and all that groweth by the
riuer, shal wither, & be driuen away, and
be no more.
8 The fishers also shal [h] mourne, and all
they that cast angle into the riuer, shal lament, and they that spread their net vpon
the waters, shalbe weakened.
9 Moreouer, they that worke in flax of diuers sortes, shalbe confounded, and they
that weaue nettes.
10 For their nettes shalbe broken, and all
they, ỹ make ponds, *shalbe* heauie in heart.
11 Surely ỹ princes of [i] Zoán *are* fooles: the
counsel of the wise counselers of Pharaóh
is become foolish: how say ye vnto Pharaóh, I [k] am the sonne of the wise? I am the
sonne of the ancient Kings?
12 Where are now thy wise men, that they
may tel thee, or may know what the Lord
of hostes hathe determined agaĩst Egypt?
13 The princes of Zoán are become fooles:
the princes of [l] Noph are deceiued, they
haue deceiued Egypt, *euen* the [m] corners
of the tribes thereof.
14 The Lord hathe mingled among them
the spirit [n] of errours: and thei haue caused
Egypt to erre in euerie worke thereof, as a
dronken man erreth in his vomite.
15 Nether shal there be anie worke ĩ Egypt,
which the head maie [o] do, nor the taile, the
branche nor the rush.
16 In that daie shal Egypt be like vnto women: for it shalbe afraide & feare because
of the mouing of the hand of the Lord of
hostes, which he shaketh ouer it.
17 And the land of Iudáh shalbe a feare
[p] vnto Egypt: euerie one ỹ maketh mencion of it, shalbe afraid thereat, because of
the counsel of the Lord of hostes, which
he hathe determined vpon it.
18 In that daie shal fiue cities in the land of
Egypt [q] speake the language of Canáan,
and shal [r] sweare by the Lord of hostes:
one shalbe called the citie of [s] destruction.
19 In that daie shal the altar of the Lord be
in the middes of the land of Egypt, and [t] a
piller by the border thereof vnto ỹ Lord.
20 And it shalbe for a signe and for a witnes vnto the Lord of hostes in the land of
Egypt: for thei shal crye vnto the Lord, because of the oppressers, and he shal send
them [u] a Sauiour and a great man, and shal
deliuer them.
21 And the Lord shalbe knowen of the E-
gyptiãs, and the Egyptians shal knowe the
Lord in that daie, and do [x] sacrifice & ob
lacion, & shal vowe vowes vnto the Lord,
and performe *them*.
22 So the Lord shal smite Egypt, he shal
smite and heale it: for he shal returne vnto the Lord, and he shalbe intreated of thẽ,
and shal heale them.
23 In that daie shal there be a path frõ ỹ E-
gypt to Asshúr, & Asshúr shal come into
Egypt, & Egypt into Asshúr: so the Egyptians shal worship with Asshúr.
24 In that daie shal Isráel be the third with
Egypt and Asshúr, *euen* a blessing in the
middes of the land.
25 For the Lord of hostes shal blesse it, saying, Blessed *be* my people Egypt and Asshúr, the worke of mine hands, and Isráel
mine inheritance.

CHAP. XX.

2 The thre yeres captiuitie of Egypt and Ethiopia descri- bed by the thre yeres going naked of Isaiáh.

1 IN the yere that [a] Tartán came to [b] Ashdód, (whẽ [c] Sargón King of Asshúr sẽt
him) and had foght against Ashdód, and
taken it,
2 At the same time spake the Lord by the
hand of Isaiáh the sonne of Amóz, saying,
Go, and lose the [d] sackeclothe from thy
loynes, and put of thy shoe from thy fote.

a Read Chap. 13,1.
b Because the Egyptians trusted in the defense of their countrey, in ỹ multitude of their idoles, & in the valiantnes of their men, the Lord sheweth that he wil come ouer all their munitions in a swift cloude, and that their idoles shal trẽble at his comming, and that mens hearts shal faint.
c As he caused the Ammonites, Moabites, and Idumeans to kil one another, whẽ thei came to destroye the Church of God, 2. Chron. 20,22 chap. 49 26.
d Meaning, their policie, and wisdome.
e He sheweth ỹ the sea & Nilus their great riuer, whereby thei thoght thẽ selues most sure, shulde not be able to defend them frõ his angre, but that he wolde send the Assyrians amõg thẽ that shulde kepe them vnder as sclaues.
f For Nilus rã into the sea by seuẽ streames, as thogh they were so manie riuers.
g The Ebrewe worde is mouth, whereby they meane the spring, out of the ŵ the water gusheth as out of a mouth.
h The Scriptures vse to describe the destruction of a countrey by taking away of the commodities thereof, as by vines, flesh, fish, and suche other things, whereby countreis are enriched.
i Called also Tanes, a famous citie vpon Nilus.
k He noteth the flatterers of Pharaóh: who persuaded the King that he was wise, and noble, and that his house was moste ancient, and so he flattered him self, saying, I am wise.
l Or Memphis, others Alexandria, and now called the great Caira.
m The principal vpholders thereof are the chiefest cause of their destructiõ.

n For the spirit of wisdome he hathe made thẽ drõken & giddie with ỹ spirit of errour.
o Nether the great nor the smale, ỹ strong nor ỹ weake.
p Considering that through their occasion the Iewes made not God their defence, but put their trust in them, & were therefore now punished, they shal feare lest the like light vpon them
q Shal make one confessiõ of faith with the people of God: by the speache of Canáan meaning, the language, wherein God was then serued.
r Shal renoũce their superstitiõs & protest to serue God a right.
s Meaning, of six cities fiue shulde serue God, and the sixt remaine in their wickednes: & so of the sixt parte there shulde be but one lost.
t There shalbe euident signes & tokens, that Gods religiõ is there: which maner of speach is taken of the Patriarkes and anciẽt times, when God had not as yet appointed the place, and ful maner how he wolde be worshiped.
u This declareth that this ꝓphecie shulde be accomplished in the time of Christ.
x By these ceremonies he comprehendeth the spiritual seruice vnder Christ.
y By these two nacions, which were then chief enemies of the Church, he sheweth that the Gẽtiles, & the Iewes shulde be ioyned together in one faith and religion, and shulde be all one folde vnder Christ their shepherd.

a Who was a captaine of Saneherib, 2 Kĩg 18.
b A citie of ỹ Philistims.
c The Ebrewes write that Saneherib was so called.
d Which signifieth that ỹ Prophet did lament the miserie that he sawe prepared, before the thre yeres, that he went naked and bare foted.

And he did so, walking naked and barefote.
3 And the Lord said, Like as my seruant
Isaiáh hathe walked naked,& barefote thre
yeres, *as* a signe & wondre vpon Egypt,&
Ethiopia,
4 So shal the King of Asshúr take away the
captiuitie *of* Egypt, and the captiuitie of
Ethiopia, *bothe* yong men and olde men,
naked and barefote, with their buttockes
vncouered,to the shame of Egypt.
5 And they shal feare, and be ashamed of
[e] Ethiopia their expectation,and of Egypt
[f] their glorie.
6 Thẽ shal ỹ inhabitãt of this [g] yle saye in
that day, Beholde, suche is our expectation,whether we fled for helpe to be deliuered from the King of Asshúr, and how
shal we be deliuered?

e In whose aide thei trusted.
f Of whome they boasted, and glorted.
g Meaning Iudea,which was cõpassed about with their enemies,as an yle with waters.

CHAP. XXI.

1 Of the destruction of Babylon by the Persiãs and Medes. 11 The ruine of Idumea, 13 And of Arábia.

1 THe burden of [a] the desert sea. As the
whirlwindes in the South vse to passe from the wildernes, *so* shal it [b] come
from the horrible land.
2 A grieuous vision was shewed vnto me,
The [c] transgressour *against* a trãsgressour,
and the destroyer *against* a destroyer. Go
vp [d] Elám, besige Media: I haue caused all
the mourning [e] thereof to cease.
3 Therefore are my loynes filled w̃ sorow:
sorowes haue taken me as the sorowes of
a woman that trauaileth: I was bowed
downe when I hearde it, & I was amased
when I sawe it.
4 Mine heart failed: fearfulnes troubled
me: the night [g] of my pleasures hathe he
turned into feare vnto me.
5 Prepare thou the table: watche in ỹ watche towre: eat, drinke: [h] arise, ye princes,
anoynt the shield.
6 For thus hathe the [i] Lord said vnto me,
Go, set a watchman, to tel what he seeth.
7 And he sawe a charet with two horsemen: [k] a charet of an asse, & a charet of a
camel: and he hearkened & toke diligent
hede.
8 And he cryed, A [l] lyon: my lord, I stand
continually vpon the watch towre in the
day time, and I am set in my watch euerie
night:
9 And beholde, this mans charet cometh
with two horsemen. And [m] he answered
and said, * Babél is fallen: it is fallen, and
all the images of her gods hathe he broken vnto the grounde.
10 O [n] my threshing, and the " corne of my
floore. That which I haue heard of the
Lord of hostes, the God of Israél, haue I
shewed vnto you.
11 ¶ The burden of [o] Dumáh. He calleth vn
to me out of [p] Seír, Watchman, what was
in the night? Watchman, what was in the
night?
12 The watchman said, The [q] morning cometh, & also the night. If ye wil aske, enquire: returne & come.
13 ¶ The burdẽ against Arabia. In [r] the forest of Arabia shal ye tary all night, *euen*
in the waies of Dedanim.
14 O inhabitants of the land of Temá, brĩg
forthe [s] water to mete the thirstie, *and*
preuent him that fleeth with his bread.
15 For they flee from the drawen swordes,
euen from the drawen sworde, and from
the bent bowe, and from the grieuousnes
of warre.
16 For thus hathe ỹ Lord said vnto me, Yet
a yere [t] according to the yeres of an [u] hyreling, & all the glorie of Kedár shal fayle.
17 And the residue of the number of the
strong archers of the sonnes of [x] Kedár
shalbe fewe: for the Lord God of Israél
hathe spoken it.

a On the sea side betwene Iudea,& Chaldea was a wildernes,whereby he meaneth Chaldea.
b That is, the ruine of Babylon by the Medes, and Persians.
c The Assyriãs and Chaldeãs, which had destroyed other nations, shal be ouercome of the Medes & Persians, and this he prophecied an hundreth yere before it came to passe.
d By Elám, he meaneth the Persians.
e Because thei shal finde no succour, they shal mourne no more, or, I haue caused them to cease mournĩg, whome Babylon had afflicted.
f This the Prophet speaketh in ỹ persone of the Babylonians.
g He prophecieth ỹ death of Belshazar, as Dan 5,30. who in the middes of his pleasures was destroyed.
h Whiles they are eating, and drinking they shalbe commãded to runne to their weapons.
i To wit, in a vision by the spirit of prophecie. k Meaning charets of men of warre, and others that caryed the baggage. l Meaning, Darius which ouercame Babylon. m The watcheman, whome Isaiáh set vp, tolde him, who came toward Babylón, and the Angel declared that it shulde be destroyed: all this was done in a vision. * Iere.51,8. reuel,14,8.
n Meaning, Babylon. " Ebr. sonne.
o Which was a citie of the Ishmaelites & was so named of Dumáh, Gen. 25,14.
p A mountaine of the Idumeans.
q He describeth the vnquietnes of ỹ people of Dumáh, who were night and day in feare of their enemies, and euer ran to and fro to enquire newes.
r For feare, the Arabians shal flee into the woods, and he appointeth what way thei shal take.
s Signifying ỹ for feare they shal not tary to eat or drike.
t He appoiteth them respit for one yere only and then they shulde be destroied.
u Read Chap. 16,14. x Which was the name of a people of Arabia: and by the horrible destruction of all these nations, he teacheth ỹ Iewes that there is no place for refuge or to escape Gods wrath, but onely to remaine in his Church, and to liue in his feare.

CHAP. XXII.

1 He prophecieth of the destruction of Ierusalém by Nebuchadnezzár. 15 A threatening against Shebna. 20 To whose office Eliakím is preferred.

1 THe burden of the [a] valley of vision.
What [b] aileth thee now that thou art
wholy gone vp vnto the house toppes?
2 Thou that art ful of [c] noise, a citie ful of
brute, a ioyous citie: thy slaine men shal
not *be* slaine [d] with sworde, nor dye in battel.
3 All thy princes shal flee together from
ỹ bowe: thei shal be [e] bound: all that shalbe
founde in thee, shalbe bounde together,
which haue fled from [f] farre.
4 [g] Therefore said I, Turne away from me:
I wil wepe bitterly: labour not to comfort me for the destruction of the daughter of my people.
5 For *it is* a day of trouble, and of ruine, &
of perplexitie by the Lord God of hostes
in the valley of vision, breaking downe
the citie: and a [h] crying vnto the mountaines.
6 ¶ And Elám [i] bare the quiuer in a mans
charet with horsemen, and Kir vncouered
the shield.
7 And thy chief valleis were ful of charets,
& the horsemen set them selues in aray

a Meaning, Iudea, w̃ was cõpassed about with mountaines, and was called the valley of visions, because of the Prophetes, w̃ were alwaies there, whome thei named Seers.
b He speaketh to Ierusalém, whose inhabitants were fled vp to ỹ house toppes for feare of their enemies.
c Which wast wonte to be ful of people and ioye.
d But for hungre.
e And led into captiuitie.
f Which haue fled from other places to Ierusalém for succour.
g He sheweth what is the duetie of the godlie, when Gods plagues hang ouer the Church, and specially of the ministers, Ier. 9,1. h That is, the showte of the enemies whome God had appointed to destroy the citie. i He putteth thẽ in minde how God deliuered them once from Saneherib, who broght the Persiãs & Cyreniãs with him, that thei might by returning to God auoyd that great plague which they shulde els suffer by Nebuchad-nezzár.

against the gate.
8 And he discouered the [k] couering of Iudáh:& thou didest loke in that day to the
armour of the house of the forest.
9 And ye haue sene [l] the breaches of the citie of Dauid: for thei were manie, and ye
gathered the waters of the lower poole.
10 And ye nombred the houses [m] of Ierusalém,and the houses haue ye broken downe to fortifie the wall,
11 And haue also made a ditch betwene the
two walles, for the [n] waters of the olde
poole,and haue not loked vnto the maker
[o] thereof,nether had respect vnto him that
formed it of olde.
12 And in that day did yͤ Lord God of hostes call vnto weping & mourning, & to
baldnes and girding with sackecloth.
13 And beholde,ioye and gladnes, slaying
oxen and killing shepe, eating flesh, and
drinking wine,[p] eating and drinking: for
to morowe we shal dye.
14 And it was declared in the eares of the
Lord of hostes. Surely this iniquitie shal
not be purged from you,til ye dye, saith
the Lord God of hostes.
15 Thus saith the Lord God of hostes, Go,
get thee to that [q] treasurer,to Shebná, the
steward of the house, *& say*,
16 What hast thou to do here? and whome
hast thou [r] here? that thou shuldest here
hewe thee out a sepulchre, as he yͭ heweth
out his sepulchre in an hie place, or that
graueth an habitacion [s] for him self in a
rocke?
17 Beholde,the Lord wil carye thee awaye
with a great captiuitie,and wil surely couer thee.
18 He wil surely rolle & turne thee like a
ball in a large countrey: there shalt thou
dye, and there the charets of thy glorie
shalbe the [t] shame of thy lords house.
19 And I wil dryue thee from thy statiō,&
out of thy dwelling wil he destroy thee.
20 And in that day wil I [u] call my seruant
Eliakím the sonne of Hilkiáh,
21 And with thy garments wil I clothe
him, and with thy girdle wil I strengthen
him: thy power also wil I commit into his
hād,and he shalbe a father of the inhabitants of Ierusalém, and of the house of
Iudáh.
22 And the [x] keye of the house of Dauid wil
I laie vpon his shoulder: so he shal open&
no man shal shut: and he shal shut,and no
man shal open.
23 And I wil fasten him as a [y] naile in a sure
place, and he shalbe for the throne of
glorie to his fathers house.
24 And thei shal hang vpon him all the
glorie of his fathers house, *euen* of the
nephewes and posteritie [z] all smale vessels,from the vessels of the cuppes,euen to
all the instruments of musike.
25 In that daie, saith the Lord of hostes,
shal the [a] naile,that is fastened in the sure
place, departe & shal be broken, and fall:
and the burden,that was vpon it, shalbe
cut of: for the Lord hathe spoken it.

k The secret place where yͤ armour was:to wit,in the house of yͤ forest, 1 King.2.
l Ye fortified the ruinous places,which were neglected in time of peace: meaning, the whole citie & the citie of Dauid which was within the compasse of yͤ other.
m Ether to pul downe suche as might hurt, or els to knowe what men thei were able to make.
n To prouide if nede shulde be of water.
o To God that made Ierusalém: that is, thei trusted more in these worldely meanes then in God
p In stead of repentance ye were ioyful & made great chere,contemnīg the admonitions of the Prophetes,saying,Let vs eat and drinke:for our Prophetes say, that we shal dye to morowe.
q Because the Ebrew worde doeth also signifie one that doeth nourish & cherish,there are of the learned that thinke, yͭ this wicked man did nourish secret frendship with the Assyriās and Egyptians, to betray yͤ Church and to prouide for him self against all dangers:in yͤ meane season he packt craftely & gate of the best offices into his hand vnder Hezekiáh, euer aspiring to the hiest.
r Meaning, yͭ he was a stranger and came vp of nothīg.
s Where as he thoght to make his name immortal by his famous sepulchre, he dyed moste miserably among the Assyrians.
t Signifying yͭ whatsoeuer dignitie the wicked atteine vnto, at length it wil turne to the shame of those Princes,by whome thei are preferred.
u To be steward againe, out of the which office he had bene put by the craft of Shebná.
x I wil commit vnto him the ful charge & gouernement of the Kings house.
y I wil establish him & confirme him in his office: of this phrase read Ezra 9,9.
z Meanīg that bothe smale & great that shal come of Eliakím, shal haue praise & glorie by this faithful officer.
a He meaneth Shebna, who in mans iudgement shulde neuer haue fallen.

CHAP. XXIII.

1 A prophecie against Tyrus. 17 A promise that it shal be restored.

1 THe [a] burden of Tyrus. Howle, ye
shippes of [b] Tarshísh: for [c] it is destroi
ed,so yͭ there is none house: none shal come
from the land of [d] Chittím: it is [e] reueiled
vnto them.
2 Be stil,ye that dwell in the yles: the marchants of Zidón,& such as passe ouer the
sea,haue [f] replenished thee.
3 The [g] sede of Nilus *growing* by the abundance of waters,& the haruest of the riuer *was* her reuenues, and she was a marte
of the nations.
4 Be ashamed, thou Zidón: for the [h] sea
hathe spoken, *euen* the strength of the sea,
saying, I haue not [i] trauailed,nor broght
forthe childrē, nether nourished yong mē
nor broght vp virgins.
5 When the fame commeth to the Egyptians, they shalbe [k] sorie,concerning the
rumor of Tyrus.
6 Go you ouer to [l] Tarshísh: howle,ye that
dwell in the yles.
7 Is not this that your glorious *citie*? her
antiquitie *is* of ancient daies: her owne
fete shal lead her a farre of to be a soiourner.
8 Who hathe decreed this against Tyrus
(that [m] crowneth *men*) whose marchāts *are*
princes? whose chapmen *are* the nobles of
the worlde?
9 The Lord of hostes hathe decreed this,
to staine the pride of all glorie, and to
bring to contempt all them that be glorious in the earth.
10 Passe through thy land like a flood *to* yͤ
[n] daughter of Tarshísh: there is no more
strength.
11 He stretched out his hand vpon the sea:
he shoke the kingdomes: the Lord hathe
giuen a commandement concerning the
place of marchādise, to destroye the power thereof.
12 And he said, Thou shalt no more reioyce
when yͭ art oppressed: [o] ô virgin [p] daughter of Zidón: rise vp,go ouer vnto Chittím: yet there thou shalt haue no rest.
13 Beholde the land of the Chaldeans: this
was no people: [q] Asshúr founded it by the
inhabitants of the wildernes: thei set vp
the towres thereof,they raised the palaces

a Read Chap. 13,1.
b Ye of Cilicia yͭ come thether for marchandise.
c Tyrus is destroied by Nebuchadnezzár
d By Chittim thei ment all the yles and countreis Westward from Palestina.
e All mē knowe of this destruction.
f Haue haunted thee & enriched thee.
g Meaning,the corne of Egypt which was fed by yͤ ouerflowing of Nilus.
h That is,Tyrus,which was the chief port of the Sea.
i I haue no people left in me,and am as a baren womā that neuer had childe.
k Because these two countreis were ioined in league together.
l Tyrus willeth other marchants to go to Cilicia and to come no more there.
m Who maketh her marchāts like princes.
n Thy strength wil no more serue thee: therefore flee to other countreis for succour.
o For Tyrus was neuer touched nor afflicted before.
p Because Tyrus was buylt by them of Zidón.
q The Chaldeans which dwelt in tentes in the wildernes, were gathered by yͤ Assyrians into cities.

thereof & her[r] broght it to ruine.
14 Howle ye shippes of Tarshish, for your
[s] strength is destroyed.
15 And in that daie shal Tyrus be forgottē
seuentie yeres, (according to the yeres of
one King) at the end of[t] seuētie yeres shal
Tyrus[u] sing as an harlot.
16 Take an harpe, & go about the citie:
(thou harlot that hast bene forgotten)
[x] make swete melodie, sing mo songs that
thou maiest be remembred.
17 And at the end of seuentie yeres shal
the Lord visite Tyrus, & she shal returne
to her[y] wages, and shal commit fornication with all the kingdomes of the earth,
that are in the worlde.
18 Yet her occupying and her wages shal
be[z] holie vnto ẏ Lord: it shal not be laied
vp nor kept in store, but her marchandise
shal be for thē that dwell before the Lord,
to eat sufficiently, and to haue durable
clothing.

r The people of ẏ Chaldeans destroyed the Assyrians: whereby the Prophet meaneth, that seig the Chaldeās were able to ouercome the Assyrians, ẇ were so great a nation, much more shal these two nations of Chaldea & Assyria be able to ouerthrowe Tyrus.
s That is, Tyrus, by whome ye are enriched.
t Tyrus shal lie destroied 70. yeres, which he calleth the reigne of one King, or a mās age.
u Shal vse all craft and subtiltie to entise men againe to her.
x She shal labour by all meanes to recouer her first credit, as an harlot when she is long forgotten, seketh by all meanes to enterteine her louers.
y Thogh she haue bene chastised of the Lord, yet she shal returne to her olde wicked practises, & for gaine shal giue her self to all mens lusts like an harlot
z He sheweth that God yet by the preaching of the Gospel wil call Tyrus to repentance, & turne her heart from auarice and filthie gaine vnto the true worshiping of God and liberalitie toward his Saints.

CHAP. XXIIII.

A prophecie of the curse of God for the sinnes of the people. 13 A remnant reserued, shal praise the Lord.

1 Beholde, the Lord maketh the[a] earth
emptie, & he maketh it waste: he turneth it vpside downe, & scattereth abroad
the inhabitants thereof.
2 And there shalbe like people, like[b] Priest,
and like seruant, like master, like maide, li-
ke mastresse, like byer, like seller, like lender, like borrower, like giuer, like taker to
vsurie.
3 The earth shalbe cleane emptied, and vtterly spoyled: for the Lord hathe spoken
this worde.
4 The earth lamenteth and fadeth away:
the worlde is febled & decayed: the proude people of the earth are weakened.
5 The earth[c] also deceiueth, because of the
inhabitāts thereof: for thei trāsgressed the
lawes: they changed the ordinances, *and*
brake the euerlasting couenant.
6 Therefore hathe the[d] curse deuoured the
earth, and the inhabitants thereof are desolate. Wherefore the inhabitants of the
land are[e] burned vp, and fewe mē are left.
7 The wine faileth, ẏ vine hathe no might:
all that were of mery heart, do mourne.
8 The mirth of tabrets ceaseth: the noise of
them that reioyce, endeth: the ioye of the
harpe ceaseth.
9 They shal not drinke wine with mirth:
strong drinke shalbe bitter to them that
drinke it.
10 The citie of[f] vanitie is broken downe:
euerie house is shut vp, that no man may
come in.
11 There is a crying for wine in the stretes:
all ioye is darkened: the[g] mirth of the
worlde is gone away.
12 In the citie is left desolacion, & the gate
is smitten with destruction.
13 ¶ Surely thus shal it be in the middes of
the earth, among the people,[h] as the shaking of an oliue tre, *and* as the grapes
when the vintage is ended.
14 They shal lift vp their voyce: thei shal
shoute for the magnificence of the Lord:
they shal reioyce from[i] the sea.
15 Wherefore praise ye ẏ Lord in the valleis, *euē* the Name of the Lord God of Israél, in the yles of the sea.
16 From the vttermost parte of the earth
we haue heard praises, *euen* glorie to the
[k] Iuste, & I said,[l] My leanenes, my leanenes, wo is me: the transgressors haue offended: yea, the transgressors haue grieuously
offended.
17 Feare, and the pit, and the snare *are* vpon
thee, ô inhabitant of the earth.
18 And he that fleeth from the noise of the
feare, shal fall into the pit: & he that commeth vp out of the pit, shalbe taken in the
snare: for the[m] windowes from on high are
open, and the fundacions of the earth do
shake.
19 The earth is vtterly broken downe: the
earth is cleane dissolued: the earth is moued excedingly.
20 The earth shal rele to & fro like a dronken man, and shalbe remoued like a tent,
and the iniquitie thereof shalbe heauie vpon it: so that it shal fall, and rise no more.
21 ¶ And in that day shal the Lord[n] visite ẏ
hoste aboue that is on hie, euen the Kings
of the worlde that are vpon the earth.
22 And thei shalbe gathered together, as the
prisoners in the pit: and thei shalbe shut vp
in the prison, & after manie daies shal thei
be[o] visited.
23 [p] Then the moone shalbe abasshed, & the
sunne ashamed, when the Lord of hostes
shal reigne in mount Zión and in Ierusalém: and glorie shalbe before his ancient
men.

a This prophecie is as a cōclusiō of that, which hathe bene threatened to the Iewes & other nacions from the 13 Chap: & therefore by ẏ earth he meaneth those lands, which were before named.
b Because this was a name of dignitie, it was also applied to thē, which were not of Aarōs familie, & so signifieth also a man of dignitie, as 2. Sam. 8,18. and 20,25 1 chron. 18,17. and by these wordes the Prophet signifieth an horrible confusion, where there shalbe nether religiō, order nor policie, Hosea. 4,9.
c That is, rendreth not her frute for the sinne of ẏ peole, whome ẏ earth deceiued of their nouriture, because they deceiued God of his honour.
d Writen in the Law, as Leui. 26,14. deut. 28,16. thus the Prophetes vsed to applie particularly the menaces, and promises which are general in the Law.
e With heat and drought, or els, that they were consumed with the fyre of Gods wrath.
f Which as it was without ordre, so now shulde it be broght to desolacion and confusion: and this was not onely ment of Ierusalém, but of all ẏ other wicked cities.
g Because thei did not vse Gods benefits aright, their pleasures shulde faile, and they fall to mourning
h He comforteth the faithful, declaring that in this great desolacion the Lord wil assemble his Church, ẇ shal praise his name, as Chap 10,22.
i From ẏ vtmost coastes of the worlde, where ẏ Gospel shal be preached, as vers. 16.
k Meaning, to God, who wil publish his Gospel through all ẏ worlde.
l I am consumed with care, considering the afflictiō of the Church, bothe by forē enemies & domestical. Some read, my secret, my secret: that is, it was reueiled to ẏ Prophet, that the good shulde be p̄serued & the wicked destroyed.
m Meaning, ẏ Gods wrath, and vengeance shulde be ouer & vnder them: so that thei shuld not escape no more then thei did at Noahs flood.
n There is no power so high or mightie, but God wil visite him ẇ his roddes.
o Not with his roddes, as vers. 21, but shalbe cōforted.
p When God shal restore his Church, the glorie thereof shal so shine and his ministers (which are called his ancient men) that the sunne and the moone shal be darke in comparison thereof.

CHAP. XXV.

A thankesgiuing to God in that that he sheweth him self iudge of the worlde, by punishing the wicked & mainteining the godlie.

1 O Lord, thou[a] art my God: I wil exalte thee, I wil praise thy Name: for
thou hast done wonderful things, *according*
to

a Thus the Prophet giueth thankes to God, because he wil bring vnder subiectiō these nacions by his corrections, & make them of his Church, ẇ before were his enemies.

to the counsels of olde, with a stable trueth.
2 For thou hast made of a [b] citie an heap, of
a strong citie, a ruine: *euen* the palace [c] of
strangers of a citie, it shal neuer be buylt.
3 Therefore shal the [d] mightie people giue
glorie vnto thee: the citie of the strong
nacions shal feare thee.
4 For thou hast bene a strength vnto the
poore, *euen* a strength to the nedie in his
trouble, a refuge against the tempest, a
shadowe against the heate: for the blast
[e] of the mightie is like a storme *against* the
wall.
5 Thou shalt bring downe the noise of the
strangers, [f] as the heat in a drye place: he
wil bring downe the song of the mightie,
as [g] the heat in the shadowe of a cloude.
6 And in this [h] mountaine shal the Lord of
hostes make vnto all people a feast of fat
things, *euen* a feast of fined *wines*, & of fat
things ful of marowe, of *wines* fined & purified.
7 And he wil destroye in this mountaine
[i] the couering that couereth all people, &
the vaile that is spred vpon all nacions.
8 He wil destroye death for euer: and the
Lord God wil [k] wipe away the teares frō
all faces, and the rebuke of his people wil
he take away out of all the earth: for the
Lord hathe spoken it.
9 And in that day shal men say, Lo, this is
our God: we haue waited for him, and he
wil saue vs. This is the Lord, we haue waited for him: we wil reioyce and be ioyful
in his saluacion.
10 For in this mountaine shal the hand of
the Lord rest, and [l] Moáb shalbe threshed
vnder him, euen as strawe is threshed in
[m] Madmenáh.
11 And he shal stretch out his hand in the
middes of thē (as he that swimmeth, stretcheth *them* out to swimme) and with the
strength of his hands shal he bring downe
their pride.
12 The defense also of the height of thy
walles shal he bring downe and lay lowe,
& cast them to the grounde, *euen* vnto the
dust.

b Not onely of Ierusalém, but also of these other cities, wc haue bene thine enemies.
c That is, a place where as all vagabōdes may liue without danger, and as it were, at ease, as in a palace.
d The arrogāt and proude, wc before wolde not knowe thee, shal by thy correctiōs feare & glorifie thee.
e The rage of the wicked is furious, til God breake yt force thereof.
f Meaning, yt as the heat is abated by the raine, so shal God bring downe the rage of the wicked.
g As a cloude shadoweth frō ye heat of the sunne, so shal God aswage ye reioycing of ye wicked agaist the godlie.
h To wit, in Zión, whereby he meaneth his Church, wc shulde vnder Christ be assembled of the Iewes and the Gentiles, and is here described vnder the figure of a costely banket, as Mat 22,2.
i Meanīg that ignorance and blidenes, whereby we are kept backe frō Christ.
k He wil take away all occasions of sorow & fil his with perfite ioye, Reuel. 7,17. & 21,4.
l By Moáb are ment all the enemies of his Church.
m There were two cities of this name: one in Iudáh, 1. Chron. 2,49, and another in the land of Moáb, Iere 48,2. which semeth to haue bene a plentiful place of corne. Chap. 10,31.

CHAP. XXVI.

A song of the faithful, wherein is declared, in what consisteth the saluacion of the Church, and wherein they oght to trust.

1 IN that day shal [a] this song be sung in
the land of Iudáh, We haue a strong
citie: [b] saluacion shal *God* set for walles &
bulwarkes.
2 [c] Opē ye the gates that the righteous naciō, which kepeth the trueth, may entre in.
3 By an assured [d] purpose wilt thou preserue
perfite peace, because thei trusted in thee.
4 Trust in the Lord for euer: for in ye Lord
God *is* strength for euer more.
5 For he wil bring downe them that dwell
on hie: [e] the hie citie he wil abase: *euen* vnto the grounde wil he cast it downe and
bring it vnto dust.
6 The fote shal treade it downe, *euen* the
fete of the [f] poore, *and* the steps of the
nedie.
7 The way of the iuste *is* righteousnes:
thou wilt make equal the righteous path
of the iust.
8 Also we, ô Lord, haue waited for thee in
the way of thy [g] iudgements: the desire of
our soule *is* to thy Name, & to the remembrance of thee.
9 With my soule haue I desired thee in the
night, and with my spirit within me wil I
seke thee in the mornīg: for seing thy iudgements *are* in the earth, the inhabitants
of the worlde shal learne [h] righteousnes.
10 Let mercie [i] be shewed to the wicked,
yet he wil not learne righteousnes: in ye lād
of vprightnes wil he do wickedly, and wil
not beholde the maiestie of the Lord.
11 O Lord, they wil not beholde thine hie
hand: *but* thei shal se it, and be confounded
with [k] the zeale of the people, & the fyre
of thine [l] enemies shal deuoure them.
12 Lord, vnto vs thou wilt ordeine peace:
for thou also hast wroght all our workes
for vs.
13 O Lord our God, *other* [m] lords beside thee
haue ruled vs, *but* we wil remember thee
onely, & thy Name.
14 The [n] dead shal not liue, *nether* shal the
dead arise, because thou hast visited and
scattered them, & destroyed all their memorie.
15 Thou hast encreased [o] ye nacion, ô Lord:
thou hast encreased the nacion: thou art
made glorious: thou hast enlarged all the
coastes of the earth.
16 Lord, in trouble haue thei [p] visited thee:
they powred out a prayer when thy chastening *was* vpon them.
17 Like as a woman with childe, that draweth nere to the trauail, is in sorow, & cryeth in her peines, so haue we bene in thy
[q] sight, ô Lord.
18 We haue conceiued, we haue borne in
peine, as thogh we shulde haue broght forthe [r] winde: there was no helpe in ye earth,
nether did the inhabitants of [s] the worlde
fall.
19 ¶ [t] Thy dead men shal liue: *euen* with my
bodie shal thei rise. Awake, & sing, ye that
dwell in dust: for thy [u] dewe *is as* the dewe

a This song was made to comfort the faithful, when their captiuitie shulde come, assuring them also of their deliuerance, for the which they shulde sing this song.
b Gods protection and defence shalbe sufficient for vs.
c He assureth the godlie to returne after the captiuitie to Ierusalém.

d Thou hast decreed so, & thy purpose cā not be chāged.
e There is no power so hie, that can let God, when he wil deliuer his.
f God wil set the poore afflicted ouer ye power of the wicked.
g We haue cōstantly abid in ye aduersities wherewith yu hast afflicted vs.
h Meaning, yt by afflictions mē shal learne to feare God.
i The wicked thogh God shewe them euident signes of his grace, shalbe neuer the better.
k Through enuie & indignacion againſt thy people.
l The fyre & vēgeāce, wherewith thou doest destroye thine enemies.
m The Babylonians, which haue not gouerned according to thy worde.
n Meaning, yt the reprobat, euen in this life shal haue the beginning of euerlasting death.
o To wit, the companie of ye faithful by the calling of the Gentiles.
p That is, the faithful by thy roddes were moued to pray vnto thee for deliuerance.
q To wit, in extreme sorowe.
r Our sorowes had none end, nether did we enioye the cōfort, that we loked for.
s The wicked and men without religion were not destroyed.
t He comforteth the faithful in their afflictiōs, shewing them that euen in death they shal haue life: and that they shulde moste certeinly rise to glorie: the contrarie shulde come to the wicked, as vers. 14.

u As herbes, dead in winter, florish againe by the raine in the spring time: so thei ye lie in the dust, shal rise vp to ioye when thei fele ye dewe of Gods grace.

of herbes,& the earth shal cast out ỳ dead.
20 Come,my people : [x] entre thou into thy
chambers,and shutte thy dores after thee:
hide thy self for a very litle while, vntil
the indignacion passe ouer.
21 For lo , the Lord cometh out of his place, to visite the iniquitie of the inhabitãts
of the earth vpon them: and the earth shal
disclose her [y] blood,and shal no more hide
her slayne.

x He exhorteth the faithful to be pacient in their afflictions,and to waite vpon Gods worke.
y The earth shal vomit & cast out the innocent blood, which it hath drunke,that it may crye for vengeance against the wicked.

CHAP. XXVII.

A prophecie against the kingdome of Satán, 2 And of the ioye of the Church for their deliuerance.

1 IN that [a] day the Lord with his sore &
great and mightie [b] sworde shal visite
Liuiathán,that percing serpent , euen Liuiathán,that croked serpent,& he shal slay
the dragon that is in the sea.
2 In that day sing of the vineyarde [c] of red
wine.
3 I the Lord do kepe it : I wil watter it e-
uery moment: lest anie assaile it,I wil kepe
it night and day.
4 Angre [d] is not in me: who wolde set the
briers and the thornes *against* me in battel?
I wolde go through them , I wolde burne
them together.
5 Or wil he [e] fele my strength, that he may
make peace with me,& be at one with me?
6 [f] Here after, Iaakób shal take rote: Israél
shal florish and growe,and the worlde shal
be filled with frute.
7 Hathe he smitten [g] him as he smote those
that smote him ? or is he slayne according
to the slaughter of them that were slayne
by him?
8 In [h] measure in the branches thereof wilt
thou cõtend wͭ it, *when* he bloweth with his
rough winde in the day of the East winde.
9 By this therefore shal ỳ iniquitie of Iaakób be purged , and this is all the [i] frute,
the taking away of his sinne : when he shal
make all the stones of the altars, as chalke
stones,broken in pieces,*that* the groues and
images may not stand vp.
10 Yet the [k] defensed citie *shalbe* desolate,
& the habitacion *shalbe* forsaken, and left
like a wildernes. There shal the calfe fede,
and there shal he lie,& consume the branches thereof.
11 When the boughs of it are drye, they
shalbe broken:the [l] women come, and set
them on fyre:for it is a people of none vn-
derstanding:therefore he that made them,
shal not haue compassion of them,and he
that formed them, shal haue no mercie on
them.
12 And in that day shal the Lord thresh frõ

Chap.XXVII.
a At the time appointed.
b That is , by his mightie power and by his worde. He prophecieth here of the destruction of Satán and his kingdome vnder the name of Liuiathán, Asshúr and Egypt.
c Meaning, of the best wine, which this vineyarde , that is ỳ Church, shulde bring forthe as moste agreable to the Lord.
d Therefore he wil destroy ỳ kingdome of Satán,because he loueth his Church for his owne mercies sake,& cã not be angrie wͭ it,but wisheth that he may powre his angre vpon ỳ wicked infideles,whome he meaneth by briers & thornes.
e He marueleth,that Israél wil not come by gentlenes , except God make thẽ to fele his rods,& so brĩg thẽ vnto him.
f Thogh I afflict & diminish my people for a time, yet shal the rote spring againe & bring forthe in great abundance.
g He sheweth that God punisheth his in mercie, & his enemies in iustice.
h That is,thou wilt not destroie the rote of thy Church thogh ỳ branches thereof seme to perish by the sharpe winde of affliction.

i He sheweth that there is no true repentance, nor ful reconciliacion to God,til the heart be purged from all idolatrie , and the monuments thereof destroyed. k Notwithstanding his fauour that he wil shewe them after , yet Ierusalém shalbe destroyed,and grasse for cattel shal growe in it l God shal not haue nede of mightie enemies : for the verie women shal do it,to their great shame.

the chanel of the [m] Riuer vnto the riuer
of Egypt , and ye shalbe gathered, one by
one , ô children of Israél.
13 In that day also shal the great trumpe be
[n] blowen,and they shal come, which perished in the land of Asshúr : and they that
were chased into the land of Egypt, and
they shal worship the Lord in the holy
mount at Ierusalém.

m He shal destroy all from Euphrates to Nilus : for some fled toward Egypt,thiking to haue escaped.
n In the time of Cyrus, by whome they shulde be deliuered : but this was chiefly accõplished vnder Christ.

CHAP. XXVIII.

Against the pride & dronkennes of Israél. 9 The vntowardnes of them that shulde learne the worde of God. 24 God doeth all things in time and place.

1 WO to the [a] crowne of pride, the
dronkards of Ephráim : for his
glorious beautie *shalbe* a fading floure , wͨ
is vpon the head of the [b] valley of them
that be fat,& are ouercome with wine.
2 Beholde, the Lord hathe a mightie and
[c] strong *hoste*, like a tempest of haile , & a
whirlwinde that ouerthroweth,like a tempest of mightie waters ỳ ouerflowe,which
throwe to the grounde mightely.
3 They shalbe troden vnder fote, *euen* the
crowne *and* the pride of the dronkards of
Ephráim.
4 For his glorious beautie shalbe a fading
floure , which is vpon the head of the vallei of them that be fat,*and* as [d] ỳ hastie frute afore sommer,which whẽ he that loketh
vpon it,seeth it, while it is in his hand, he
eateth it.
5 In that day shal the Lord of hostes be for
a crowne of glorie, and for a diademe of
beautie vnto the [e] residue of his people:
6 And for a spirit of iudgemẽt to him that
sitteth in iudgement, & for [f] strength vnto
thẽ that turne away the battel to the gate.
7 But [g] thei haue erred because of wine, &
are out of the way by strong drinke : the
Priest & the Prophet haue erred by strong
drinke : they are swallowed vp with wine:
they haue gone astray through strong
drinke:thei faile in vision:thei stomble in
iudgement.
8 For all *their* tables are ful of filthy vomi-
ting:no place *is cleane*.
9 [h] Whome shal he teache knowledge? and
whome shal he make to vnderstand the
things that he heareth ? them that are weined from the milke *and* drawen from the
breasts.
10 For [i] precept *must be* vpon precept, precept vpon precept, line vnto line,line vnto
line,there a litle & there a litle.
11 For with a stammering [k] tongue & with
a strange lãguage shal he speake vnto this
people.
12 Vnto whome [l] he said, [m] This is the rest:
[n] giue rest to him that is wearie:and this is
the refreshing,but thei wolde not heare.

Chap XXVIII
a Meaning,the proude kingdome of the Israelites, wͨ were dronken with worldly prosperitie.
b Because the Israelites for the most parte dwelt in plentiful valleis, he meaneth here by ỳ valley of them,ỳ had abundãce of worldelie prosperitie, & were,as it were , crowned therewith , as with garlãds.
c He semeth to meane the Assyrians, by whome ỳ ten tribes were caryed away.
d Which is not of long cõtinuance , but is sone ripe, & first eaten.
e Signifying, ỳ the faithful,wͨ put not their trust in anie worldely prosperitie,but made God their glorie, shalbe preserued.
f He wil giue counsel to the gouernour, & strength to the captaine , to driue the enemies in at their owne gates.
g Meaning,the hypocrites, wͨ were among them,& were all together corrupt in life & doctrine, wͨ is here ment by dronkẽnes & vomiting.
h For there was none that was able to vnderstãd anie good doctrine: but were foolish, & as vnmete as yong babes.
i They must haue one thig oft times told.
k Let one teache what he can, yet they shal no more vnderstãd him, thẽ if he spake in a strange language l That is,the Prophet,whome God shulde send. m This is the doctrine,whereupon ye oght to stay & rest. n Shewe to them that are wearie and haue nede of rest, what is the true rest.

13 Therefore

13 Therefore shal the worde of the [o] Lord
be vnto them precept vpon precept, precept vpon precept, line vnto line, line vnto line, there a litle & there a litle, that
they may go, and fall backewarde, and be
broken and be snared and be taken.
14 Wherefore, heare the worde of the Lord,
ye scorneful men ÿ rule this people, which
is at Ierusalém.
15 Because ye haue said, We haue made a
[p] couenant with death, & ŵ hell are we at
agrement: thogh a scourge runne ouer, &
passe through, it shal not come at vs: for
we haue made [q] falshode our refuge, and
vnder vanitie are we hid,
16 Therefore thus saith the Lord God,
Beholde, I wil lay in Zión a stone, a [r] tryed
stone, a precious corner stone, a sure fundacion. He that beleueth, [s] shal not make
haste.
17 Iudgement also wil I laye to the rule, &
[t] righteousnes to the balãce, and the [u] haile shal swepe away the vaine confidence,
and the waters shal ouerflowe [x] the secret
place.
18 And your couenant with death shalbe
disanulled, & your agrement with hel shal
not stand: when a scourge shal runne ouer
and passe through, then shal ye be trodde
downe by it.
19 When it passeth ouer, it shal take you a-
way: for it shal passe through euerie morning in the day, and in the night, and there
shalbe onely [y] feare to make *you* to vnderstand the hearing.
20 For the bed is [z] streict that it can not suffise, and the couering narowe that one cã
not wrap him self.
21 For the Lord shal stand as in mount [a] Pe
razím: he shalbe wrath as in the valley [b] of
Gibeón, ÿ he may do his worke, his strange worke, and bring to passe his acte, his
strange acte.
22 Now therefore be no mockers, lest your
bonds increase: for I haue heard of the
Lord of hostes a consumption, euen determined vpon the whole earth.
23 Hearken ye, and heare my voyce: hearkẽ
ye, and heare my speache.
24 Doeth the plow man plow all the day,
to sowe? doeth he opẽ, and breake the clottes of his grounde?
25 When he hathe made it [c] plaine, wil he
not then sowe the fitches, and sowe cummin, and cast in wheat by measure, & the
appointed barly and rye in their place?
26 For his God doeth instruct him to haue
discrecion, *and* doeth teache him.
27 For fitches shal not be thresshed with a
thresshing instrument, nether shal a cart

o Because thei wil not receiue the worde of God, when it is offred, it commeth of their owne malice, if after their hearts be so hardened, that they care not for it, as before Chap 6,9.
p They thoght they had shiftes to auoid Gods iudgemẽts, and that they colde escape thogh all other perished
q Thogh the Prophetes cõdemned their idoles, & vaine trust, of falsehode, & vanitie, yet the wicked thoght in them selues that thei wolde trust in these things.
r That is, Christ, by whome all ÿ buylding must be tryed, and vpholden, Psal. 118,22 mat 21, 42. act 4, 11. rom. 9,31. 1. pet. 2,6.
s He shal be quiet, and seke none other remedies, but be content with Christ.
t In the restitution of his Church, iudgement, and iustice shal reigne.
u Gods corrections and affliction.
x Afflictiõ shal discouer their vaine confidẽce, which they kept secret to them selues.
y Terrour and destructiõ shal make you to learne that, ŵ exhortations and gentlenes colde not brĩg you vnto.
z Your affliction shalbe so sore, that you are not able to endure it.
a When Dauid ouercame the Philistims, 2. Samuel 5.20. 1. chro 14,11
b Whete Ioshuá discomfited fiue Kings of the Amorites, Iosh. 10,12.
c As ÿ plowe man hathe his appointed time, and diuers instruments for his labour, so hathe the Lord for his vengeance: for he punisheth some at one time, and some at another, some after one sorte and some after another, so that his chosen sede is beaten, and tryed, but not broken, as are the wicked.

whele be turned about vpon the cummin:
but the fitches are beaten out with a staffe,
and cummin with a rod.
28 Bread *corne* when it is thresshed, he doeth
not alway thresh it, nether doeth the whele of his cart *stil* make a noyse, nether wil he
breake it with the tethe thereof.
29 This also cometh from the Lord of hostes, which is wonderful in counsel, & excellent in workes.

CHAP. XXIX.

1 A prophecie against Ierusalém. 13 The vengeance of God on them that followe the traditions of men.

1 AH [a] altar, altar of the citie that Dauid dwelt in: adde yere vnto yere:
[b] let them kil lambes.
2 But I wil bring the altar into distres, and
there shalbe heauines & sorow, and it shalbe vnto me like [c] an altar.
3 And I wil besege thee as a circle, & fight
against thee on a mount, & wil cast vp ramparts against thee.
4 So shalt thou be humbled, & shalt speake out of the [d] grounde, and thy speache
shal be *as* out of the dust: thy voyce also
shalbe out of the grounde like him that
hathe a spirit of diuination, and thy talking shal whisper out of the dust.
5 Moreouer, the multitude of thy [e] strangers shal be like smale dust, and the multitude of strong men shalbe as chaffe that
passeth away, and it shalbe in a moment,
euen suddenly.
6 Thou shalt be visited of ÿ Lord of hostes
with thundre, and shaking, and a great
noyse, a whirlwinde, and a tempest, and a
flame of a deuouring fyre.
7 And the [f] multitude of all the nacions ÿ
fight against the altar, shalbe as a dreame
or vision by night: euen all they that make
the warre against it, and strong holds a-
gainst it, and laye sege vnto it.
8 And it shalbe like as an hũgrie man dreameth, and beholde, [g] he eateth: and when
he awaketh, his soule is emptie: or like as
a thirstie man dreameth, and lo, he is drinking, and when he awaketh, beholde, he is
fainte, and his soule longeth: so shal the
multitude of all nacions be that fight a-
gainst mount Zión.
9 [h] Stay your selues, and wonder: they are
blinde, & make *you* blinde: they are dronken, but not with wine: they stagger, but
not by strong drinke.
10 For the Lord hathe couered you with a
spirit of slomber, and hathe shut vp your
eyes: the Prophetes, and your chief Seers
hathe he couered.
11 And the vision of them all is become vnto you, as the wordes of a boke that is sealed vp, which they deliuer to one that can
read, saying, Read this, I pray thee. Then
shal he say, I can [i] not: for it is sealed.

a The Ebrewe worde Ariel signifieth the lyon of God, & signifieth ÿ altar, because the altar semed to deuoure the sacrifice ÿ was offred to God, as Ezek. 43,16.
b Your vaine confidence in your sacrifices shal not last long.
c Your citie shalbe ful of blood, as an altar whereon they sacrifice.
d Thy speache shalbe no more so loftie, but abased, & low as the very charmers, ŵ are in lowe places, and whisper, so ÿ their voyce cã scarse be heard.
e Thine hired souldiers, in whome ŷ trustest, shalbe destroyed as dust or chaffe in a whirlewinde.
f The enemies ÿ I wil bring to destroye thee, and that, which thou makest thy vaine trust, shal come at vnwares, euen as a dreame in the night. Some read, as if this were a comfort to the Church for ÿ destruction of their enemies.
g That is, he thinketh that he eateth.
h Muse hereon as long as ye list, yet shal ye finde nothing, but occasion to be astonied: for your Prophetes are blinde, and therefore can not direct you.
i Meaning, ÿ it is all alike, ether to read, or not to read, except God open ÿ heart to vnderstãd,

12 And the boke is giuen vnto him that can
not read, saying, Read this, I pray thee.
And he shal say, I can not read.
13 Therefore the Lord said, Because this
people [k] come nere vnto me with their
mouth, and honour me with their lippes,
but haue remoued their heart far frō me,
and their [l] feare toward me was taught
by the precept of men,
14 Therefore beholde, I wil againe do a
maruelous worke in this people, *euen* a
maruelous worke, and a wonder: for the
wisdome of their wisemen shal [m] perish,
and the vnderstanding of their prudent
men shalbe hid.
15 Wo vnto them that [n] seke depe to hide
their counsel from the Lord: for their workes are in darknes, and they say, Who seeth
vs? and who knoweth vs?
16 Your turning *of deuises* shal it not be estemed [o] as the potters claye? for shal ỹ worke say of him that made it, He made me
not? or the thing formed, say of him that
facioned it, He had none vnderstanding?
17 Is it not yet but a litle while, and Lebanón shalbe [p] turned into Carmél? & Carmél shalbe counted as a forest?
18 And in that day shal the deafe heare the
wordes of the boke, & the eyes of the blind
shal se out of obscuritie, and out of darkenes.
19 The meke in the Lord shal receiue ioye
againe, and the poore men shal reioyce in
the holie one of Israél.
20 For the cruel man shal cease, and the
scorneful shalbe consumed: and all that
hasted to iniquitie, shalbe cut of:
21 Which made a man to sinne in ỹ [q] worde, & toke him in a snare: which reproued
them in the gate, and made the iuste to fall
without cause.
22 Therefore thus saith the Lord vnto the
house of Iaakób, *euen* he that redemed A-
brahám, Iaakób shal not now be confounded, nether now shal his face be pale.
23 But when he seeth his children, the worke of mine hāds, in the middes of him, they
shal sanctifie my Name, and sanctifie the
holie one of Iaakób, & shal feare the God
of Israél.
24 Then they that erred in spirit, [r] shal haue vnderstanding, and they that murmured, shal learne doctrine.

k Because thei are hypocrites & not syncere in heart, as Mat. 15,8.
l That is, their religion was learned by mās doctrine, & not by my worde.
m Meaning, ỹ where as God is not worshiped according to his worde, bothe magistrates, and ministers are but fooles, & without vnderstanding.
n This is spoken of thē, ẇ in heart despised Gods worde, & mocked at the admonitions, but outwardly bare a good face.
o For all your craft, saith the Lord, you can not be able to escape mine hands no more thē the claye, that is in the potters hands, hathe power to deliuer it self.
p Shal there not be a chāge of all things? and Carmél, that is a plentiful place in respect of that it shalbe then, may be taken, as a forest, as Chap. 32,15. & thus he speaketh to comfort the faithful.
q They that went about to finde faute ẇ the Prophetes wordes, and wolde not abide admonitions, but wolde intāgle thē and bring thē into danger.
r Signifying, ỹ except God giue vnderstāding, & knowledge, man can not but stil erre, and murmure against him.

CHAP. XXX.

1 He reproueth the Iewes which in their aduersitie Used their owne counsels, and soght helpe of the Egyptians 10 Despising the Prophetes. 16 Therefore he sheweth what destruction shal come vpon them. 18 But offreth mercie to the repentant.

1 WO to the [a] rebellious children,
saith the Lord, that take counsel,
but not of me, and [b] couer with a couering, but not by my spirit, that they may
lay sinne vpon sinne:
2 Which walke forthe to go downe into
Egypt (& haue not asked at my mouth) to
strengthen them selues with the strength
of Pharaóh, and trust in the shadowe of
Egypt.
3 But the strength of Pharaóh shalbe your
shame, & the trust in ỹ shadowe of Egypt
your confusion.
4 For his [c] princes were at Zóan, and his
ambassodours came vnto Hanés.
5 They shalbe all ashamed of the people ỹ
can not profite them, nor helpe nor do thē
good, but *shalbe* a shame and also a reproche.
6 ¶ The [d] burden of the beastes of the
South, in a land of trouble and anguish,
from whence shal come the yong and olde
lyon, the viper and fyrie flying serpent *a-
gainst them* that shal beare their riches vpō
the shoulders of the coltes, and their treasures vpon the bounches of the camels, to
a people that can not profite.
7 For the Egyptians are vanitie, and they
shal helpe in vaine. Therefore haue I
cryed vnto [e] her, Their strength [f] *is* to sit
stil.
8 Now go, & write [g] it before them in a ta
ble, & note it in a boke that it may be for
the [h] last day for euer and euer:
9 That it is a rebellious people, lying children, & children that wolde not [i] heare
the Law of the Lord.
10 Which say vnto the Seers, Se not: and
to the Prophetes, Prophecie not vnto vs
right things: *but* speake flattering things
vnto vs: prophecie [k] errours.
11 Departe out of the way: go aside out of
the path: cause the holie one of Israél to
cease from vs.
12 Therefore thus saith the holie one of Israél, Because you haue cast of this worde, and trust in [l] violence, and wickednes,
and stay thereupon,
13 Therefore this iniquitie shalbe vnto you
as a breache that falleth, *or* a swelling in
an hie wall, whose breaking cometh suddenly in a moment.
14 And the breaking thereof is like ỹ breaking of a potters pot, which is brokē without pitie, and in the breaking thereof is
not founde [m] a sheard to take fyre out of
the herth, or to take water out of the pit.
15 For thus said the [n] Lord God, the holie
one of Israél, In rest and quietnes shal ye
be saued: in quietnes and in confidence
shalbe your strength, but ye wolde not.
16 For ye haue said, No, but we wil flee away
vpon [o] horses. Therefore shal ye flee. We
wil ride vpon the swiftest. Therefore shal
your persecuters be swifter.
17 A thousand *as* one *shal flee* at the rebuke
of one:

a Who cōtrarie to their ꝓmes, take not me for their protectour, & contrarie to my commandement, seke helpe at strangers.
b They seke shiftes to cloke their doings, and not godlie meanes.
c The chief of Israél went into Egypt in ambaisie to seke helpe, and abode at these cities.
d That is, a heauy sentence or prophecie against the beasts that caried their treasures into Egypt, by the wildernes, ẇ was South frō Iudáh: signifying that if ỹ beastes shulde not be spared, the men shulde be punished muche more grieuously.
e To wit, to Ierusalém.
f And not to come to & fro to seke helpe.
g That is, this prophecie.
h That it may be a witnes, against them for all posteritie.
i He sheweth what was the cause of their destruction, & bringeth also all miserie to mā: to wit, because they wolde not heare the worde of God, but delited to be flattered, and led in errour.
k Threaten vs not by ỹ worde of God, nether be so rigorous, nor talke vnto vs in the name of the Lord, as Ier. 11,21.
l Meaning, in their stubbernes against God, and the admonitiōs of his Prophetes.
m Signifying, that the destruction of the wicked shalbe without recouerie.
n Oft times by his Prophetes he put you in remembrance of this, ỹ you shulde onely depēd on him.
o We wil trust to escape by our horses.

of one : at the rebuke of fiue shal ye flee,
til ye be left as a shippe mast vpon the
[p] top of a mountaine, and as a beaken vpō
an hill.
18 Yet therefore wil ẏ Lord waite, that he
may haue [q] mercy vpon you, and therefore wil he be exalted, that he may haue cōpassion vpon you: for the Lord *is* the God
of [r] iudgement. Blessed *are* all they that
waite for him.
19 Surely a people shal dwell in Ziōn, & in
Ierusalém: thou shalt wepe no more: he wil
certeinly haue mercie vpō thee at ẏ voyce of thy crye: whē he heareth thee, he wil
answer thee.
20 And when the Lord hathe giuē you the
bread of aduersitie, and the water of afflictiō, thy raine shalbe no more kept backe,
but thine eyes shal se thy ″ raine.
21 And thine eares shal heare a worde behinde thee, saying, This is the way, [s] walke ye in it, when thou turnest to the right
hand, and when thou turnest to the left.
22 And ye shal [t] pollute the couering of the
images of siluer, and the riche ornament
of thine images of golde, & cast thē away
as a menstruous cloth, and thou shalt say
vnto it, [u] Get thee hence.
23 Then shal he giue raine vnto thy sede,
when thou shalt sowe the groūde, & bread
of the increase of the earth, and it shalbe
fat and as oyle: in that day shal thy cattel
be fed in large pastures.
24 The oxen also and the yong asses, that
til the grounde, shal eat cleane prouendre,
which is winowed with the shouel and
with the fanne.
25 And vpon euerie hie [x] mountaine, and
vpon euerie hie hil shal there be riuers &
streames of waters, in the day of the great
slaughter, when the towers shal fall.
26 Moreouer, the light of the moone shalbe
as the light of the [y] sunne, and the light
of the sunne shal be seuen folde, and like
the light of seuen dayes in the day that
the Lord shal binde vp the breache of his
people, & heale the stroke of their woūde.
27 Beholde, [z] the Name of the Lord commeth from farre, his face is burning, and
the burden thereof *is* heauie: his lippes are
ful of indignacion, and his tongue *is* as a
deuouring fyre.
28 And his Spirit *is* as a riuer ẏ ouerfloweth
vp to ẏ necke: it diuideth asondre, to fanne the nations with the fanne of [a] vanitie,
and there *shalbe* a bridle to cause them to
erre in the chawes of the people.
29 *But* there shalbe a song vnto you as in
the [b] night, whē a solemne feast is kept: &
gladnes of heart, as he that cometh with a
pipe to go vnto the mount of the Lord, to
the mightie one of Israél.
30 And the Lord shal cause his glorious

p Whereas all the trees are cut downe saue two or thre to make mastes.
q He commēdeth the great mercies of God who with paciēce waiteth to call sinners to repentance.
r Not onely in punishing, but in vsing moderation in the same, as Ier.10, 24, and 30,11.
″Or, instructour.
s God shal direct all thy wayes, and appoīt thee how to go ether hether or thether.
t Ye shal cast away your idoles, which you haue made of golde, & siluer with all that belongeth vnto them, as a moste filthy thing and polluted
u Shewing that there can be no true repentāce except both in heart and dede we shewe our selues enemies to idolatrie.
x By these diuerse maners of speache he sheweth ẏ the felicitie of the Church shalbe so great, ẏ none is able sufficiently to expresse it.
y When the Church shalbe restored, ẏ glorie thereof shal passe seuē times ẏ brightnes of ẏ sunne: for by the sunne and moone, which are two excellent creatures, he sheweth what shalbe the glorie of the children of God in the kingdome of Christ.
z This threatning is against the Assyrians, the chief enemies of the people of God
a To driue thee to nothing: and thus God consumeth the wicked by ẏ meanes, whereby he clenseth his.
b Ye shal reioice at the destruction of your enemies, as they that sing for ioye of the solemne feast, which began in the euening.

voyce to be heard, & shal declare the lighting downe of his arme with the angre of
his countenance, and flame of a deuouring
fyre, with scattering & tempest, and haile stones.
31 For with the voyce of the Lord shal Asshúr be destroyed, which smote with the
[c] rodde.
32 And in euerie place that the staffe shal
passe, it shal [d] cleaue fast, which the Lord
shal lay vpon him with [e] tabrets and harpes: and with battels, & lifting vp *of hands*
shal he fight [f] against it.
33 For [g] Tōphet is prepared of olde: it is e-
uē prepared for the [h] King: he hathe made it [i] depe and large: the burning thereof *is* fyre & muche wood: the breth of
the Lord, like a riuer of brimstone, doeth
kindle it.

c Gods plague
d It shal destroy.
e With ioye & assurance of ẏ victorie.
f Against Babél: meaning ẏ Assyrians and Babylonians.
g Here it is taken for hel, where the wicked are tormented. read 2. King.23,10.
h So that their estate or degre can not exept the wicked.
i By these figuratiue speaches he declareth ẏ condition of ẏ wicked after this life.

CHAP. XXXI.

1 He curseth them that forsake God, and seke for the helpe of men.

1 WO vnto them that [a] go downe into Egypt for helpe, and stay vpon
horses, and trust in charettes, because they
are manie, and in horsemen, because they
be very strong: but thei loke not vnto the
holie one of Israél, nor [b] seke vnto the
Lord.
2 But he yet is [c] wisest: therefore he wil
bring euil, and not turne backe his worde,
but he wil arise against the house of the
wicked, and against the helpe of them that
worke vanitie.
3 Now the Egyptians *are* men, & not God,
and their horses flesh and not spirit : and
when the Lord shal stretche out his hand,
the [d] helper shal fall, and he that is holpē
shal fall, and thei shal altogether faile.
4 For thus hathe the Lord spoken vnto me,
As the lion or lions whelpe roareth vpon
his praie, against whome *if* a multitude of
shepherds be called, he wil not be afraide at their voice, nether wil humble him
self at their noise: so shal the Lord of hostes come [e] downe to fight for mount Ziōn, and for the hill thereof.
5 As birdes that flie, so shal the Lord of
hostes defend Ierusalém by defending and
deliuering, by passing through & preseruing it.
6 O ye children of Israél, turne againe, in
asmuche as ye are [f] sunken depe in rebellion.
7 For in that day euerie man shal [g] cast out
his idoles of siluer, and his idoles of golde, which your hands haue made you, *euē* a
sinne.
8 Thē shal Asshúr fall by [h] the sworde, not
of man, nether shal the sworde of man

a There were two special causes, why ẏ Israelites shulde not ioyne amitie with ẏ Egyptiās: first, because the Lord had commanded them neuer to returne thether, Deu 17,16. & 28,68, lest they shulde forget the benefite of their redemption: & secōdly, lest they shulde be corrupted with the superstitiō & idolatrie of the Egyptians, and so forsake God, Ier.2,18.
b Meanīg, that thei forsake the Lord, that put their trust in worldlie things: for thei can not trust in bothe.
c And knoweth their craftie enterprises & wil bring all to naught.
d Meaning, bothe the Egyptians and the Israelites.
e He sheweth the Iewes, that if thei wolde put their trust in him, he is so able, that none can resist his power : and so careful ouer thē, as a bird ouer her yōg, which euer flieth about them for their defence: which similitude the Scripture vseth in diuerse places, as Deut.32,11. matt.23,37.
f He toucheth their conscience that thei might earnestly fele their grieuous sinnes and so truely repent, forasmuche as now thei are almost drowned and past recouerie.
g By these frutes your repentance shalbe knowen, as Chap.2,18.
h When your repentāce appeareth.

deuoure him, and he shal fle frō the sworde,and his yong men shal faint.
9 And he shal go for feare to his [i] towre,&
his princes shal be afraide of the standart,
saith the Lord, whose [k] fyre is in Zión,
and his fornace in Ierusalém.

i This was accomplished sone after whē Saneherib armie was discomfited, and he fled to his castel in Niniuéh for succour.
k To destroye his enemies.

CHAP. XXXII.

The conditions of good rulers and officers described by the gouernement of Hezekiah, who was the figure of Christ.

1 BEholde, [a] a King shal reigne in iustice,& the princes shal rule [b] in iudgement.
2 And *that* man shalbe as an hiding place
from the winde,and as a refuge for the tē-
pest:as riuers of water in a drye place, *and*
as the shadowe of a great rocke in [c] a wearie land.
3 The eyes of [d] the seing shal not be shut,
and the eares of them that heare, shal
hearken.
4 And the heart of the foolish shal vnderstand knowledge,and the tongue of the
stutters shalbe ready to speake distinctly.
5 A [e] nigarde shal no more be called liberal,nor the churle riche.
6 But the nigarde wil speake of nigardnes,
and his heart wil worke iniquitie, and do
wickedly, and speake falsely against the
Lord,to make emptie the hungrie soule,
and to cause the drinke of the thirstie to
faile.
7 For the weapons of the churle *are* wic-
ked:he diuiseth wicked counsels,to vndo
the poore with lying wordes:and to speake *against* the poore in iudgement.
8 But the liberal man wil diuise of liberal
things,and he wil continue *his* liberalitie.
9 ¶ Rise vp, ye womē that are at ease:heare
my voyce, ye [f] careles daughters: hearkē
to my wordes.
10 Ye womē,that are careles, shalbe in feare [g] aboue a yere in dayes: [h] for the vintage shal faile, & the gathering shal come
no more.
11 Ye women,that are at ease,be astonied:
feare, ô ye careles womē:put of the clothes:
make bare,and girde *sacke clothe* vpon the
loynes.
12 Men shal lament for the [i] teates, *euen*
for the pleasant fields, & for the fruteful
vine.
13 Vpon the land of my people shal growe
thornes & briers: yea, vpon all the houses of ioye in the citie of reioycing,
14 Because the palace shalbe forsaken, *and*
the ″noyse of ẏ citie shalbe left:the towre
& fortressē shal be dennes for euer, & the
delite of wilde asses, *and* a pasture for
flockes,
15 Vntil the [k] Spirit be powred vpon vs

a This prophecie is of Hezekiáh who was a figure of Christ, & therefore it oght chiefly to be referred to hi.
b By iudgemēt and iustice is mēt an vpright gouernement, bothe in policie & religiō.
c Where men are wearie w̄ traueling, for lacke of water.
d He promiseth to giue the true light, which is the pure doctrine of Gods worde,& vnderstāding,and zeale of the same, contrarie to ẏ threatnings against ẏ wicked,Chap.6,9, & 29,10.
e Vice shal no more be called vertue,nor vertue estemed by power, and riches.
f He prophecieth of suche calamitie to come,that thei wil not spare the women & children, and therefore willeth them to take hede and prouide.
g Meaning, ẏ the affliction shulde continue long, and when one yere were past, yet they shulde loke for newe plagues.
h God wil take from you ẏ meanes and occasions,which made you to contemne him: to wit,abundāce of worldly goods.
i By the teates he meaneth ẏ plētiful fieldes, whereby men are nourished,as children with the teate: or the mothers for sorow, & leanenes shal lacke milke.
″Or,multitude.
k That is,when the Church shal be restored:thus the Prophetes after they haue denou̅ced Gods iudgements against the wicked,vse to comfort the godlie,lest they shulde faint.

from aboue,and the wildernes become a
fruteful field, & the [l] plenteous field be
counted as a forest.
16 And iudgemēt shal dwell in the desert,&
iustice shal remaine in the fruteful field.
17 And the worke of iustice shalbe peace,
euen the worke of iustice & quietnes, and
assurance for euer.
18 And my people shal dwell in the tabernacle of peace and in sure dwellings,& in
safe resting places.
19 Whē it haileth,it shal fall on the forest,
and the [m] citie shalbe set in the lowe place.
20 Blessed are ye [n] that sowe vpon all waters,and [o] driue *thether* the fete of the oxe
and the asse.

l The field which is now fruteful,shalbe but as a baren forest in comparison of ẏ it shalbe then, as Chap.29,17. which shalbe fulfilled in Christs time: for then they that were before as the baren wildernes, being regenerat,shalbe frutful,and they that had some beginning of godlines, shal bring forthe frutes in such abundance, ẏ their former life shal seme but as a wildernes, where no frutes were.
m They shal not nede to buylde it in hie places for feare of the enemie:for God wil defend it and turne away the stormes from hurting of their commodities.
n That is,vpon fat ground & wel watered,which bringeth forth in abundance:or in places which before were couered with waters,and now made dry for your vses.
o The fields shal be so rancke,that they shal send out their cattel to eat vp the first croppe, which abundance shalbe signes of Gods fauour and loue towards them.

CHAP. XXXIII.

The destruction of them, by whome God hathe punished his Church.

1 WO to thee that [a] spoilest,and wast
not spoiled: and doest wickedly,
and thei did not wickedly against thee:
whē thou shalt [b] cease to spoile,thou shalt
be spoyled: when thou shalt make an end
of doing wickedly, [c] they shal do wickedly against thee.
2 [d] O Lord, haue mercie vpon vs, we haue
waited for thee:be thou, *which wast* [e] their
arme in the morning,our helpe also in time of trouble.
3 At the noise of the tumult, the [f] people
fled:at thine [g] exalting the nations were
scatered.
4 And your spoile shal be gathered *like* the
gathering of [h] caterpillers: and [i] he shal
go against him like the leaping of grashoppers.
5 The Lord is exalted: for he dwelleth on
hie:he hathe filled Zión with iudgement
and iustice.
6 And there shalbe stabilitie of [k] thy times,
strength,saluacion, wisdome & knowledge: *for* ẏ feare of the Lord shalbe his treasure.
7 Beholde, [l] their messengers shal crye
without,and the [m] ambassadours of peace
shal wepe bitterly.
8 The [n] paths are waste: the waifaring
man ceaseth: he hathe broken the coue-
nant:he hathe contemned the cities:he regarded no man.
9 The earth mourneth and fainteth:Leba-
nón is a shamed,and hewen downe: [o] Sha-

a Meaning the enemies of the Church, as were ẏ Chaldeās, and Asyrians: but chiefly of Saneherib, but not onely.
b Whē thine appointed time shal come that God shal take away thy power: & that which thou hast wrongfully gotten,shalbe giuen to others,as Amoz 5.11.
c The Chaldeans shal do like to the Asyrians, as the Asyrians did to Israél: and the Medes, & Persians shal do the same to the Chaldeās.
d He declareth hereby what is the chief refuge of the faithful when troubles come to pray & seke helpe of God.
e Which helpedst our fathers so sone as they called vpon thee.
f That is, the Asyrians fled before the armie of ẏ Chaldeās,or ẏ Chaldeans for feare of the Medes and Persians.
g When thou, ô Lord, didest lift vp thine arme to punish thine enemies.
h Ye that as caterpillers destroied with your nomber ẏ whole worlde, shal haue no strength to resist your enemies the Chaldeans,but shal be gathered on an heape and destroied.
i Meaning the Medes & Persians against the Chaldeans.
k That is,in the daies of Hezekiáh.
l Sent from Saneherib.
m Whome thei of Ierusalém sent to intreat of peace.
n These are the wordes of the ambassadours,when thei returne from Saneherib.
o Which was a plentiful countrei,meaning,that Saneherib wolde destroy all.

rón is like a wildernes,and Baſhán is ſhaken and Carmél.
10 Now wil I p ariſe, ſaith the Lord : now
wil I be exalted,now wil I lift vp my ſelf.
11 q Ye ſhal conceiue chaffe,& bring forthe
ſtubble:the fyre of your breth ſhal deuoure you.
12 And the people ſhalbe *as* the burning of
lime:& *as* the thornes cut vp,ſhal they be
burnt in the fyre.
13 Heare,ye that are r farre of, what I haue
done,& ye that are nere,knowe my power.
14 The ſ ſinners in Zión are afraied:a feare
is come vpon the hypocrites : who among
vs ſhal dwell with the deuourĩg fyre?who
among vs ſhal dwell with the euerlaſting
burnings?
15 He that walketh in iuſtice, and ſpeaketh
righteous thĩgs,refuſing gaine of oppreſſion,ſhaking his hands from taking of giftes, ſtopping his eares from hearing of
blood, and ſhutting his eyes from ſeing
euil.
16 He ſhal dwell on t hye: his defence *ſhalbe*
the munitions of rockes:bread ſhalbe giuen him,& his waters ſhal be ſure.
17 Thine eyes ſhal u ſe the King in his glorie : they ſhal beholde the land x farre of.
18 Thine heart y ſhal meditate feare, Where
is the ſcribe?where is the receauer?where is
he that counted the towres?
19 Thou ſhalt not ſe a fierce people, a people of a darke ſpeache,that thou canſt not
perceiue,& of a ſtammering tongue that
thou canſt not vnderſtand.
20 Loke vpon Zión the citie of our ſolemne feaſtes:thine eyes ſhal ſe Ieruſalém a
quiet habitacion,a Tabernacle that can
not be remoued : & the ſtakes thereof can
neuer be taken away, nether ſhal any of
the cordes thereof be broken.
21 For ſurely there the mightie Lord *wilbe*
vnto vs,*as* a place z of floods & brode riuers, whereby ſhal paſſe no ſhippe with o-
res,nether ſhal great ſhip paſſe thereby.
22 For the Lord *is* our iudge, the Lord *is*
our law giuer:the Lord *is* our King,he wil
ſaue vs.
23 Thy a cordes are looſed: they colde not
wel ſtrengthen their maſt, nether colde
thei ſpread the ſaile:thẽ ſhal the b pray be
deuided for a great ſpoyle : *yea*, the lame
ſhal take awaie the pray.
24 And none inhabitant ſhal ſay, I am ſic-
ke:the people that dwell therein,ſhal haue
their iniquitie forgiuen.

p To helpe & deliuer my Church.
q This is ſpoken againſt the enemies, who thoght all was their owne:but he ſheweth ẏ their enterpriſe ſhal be in vaine,& that ẏ fyre, ẇ they had kĩdled for others,ſhulde cõſume them.
r His vẽgeance ſhalbe ſo great that all ẏ worlde ſhal talke thereof.
ſ Which do not beleue the wordes of the Prophet & the aſſurance of their deliuerance.
t Meaning that God wilbe a ſure defence to all them that liue according to his worde.
u Thei ſhal ſe Hezekiáh deliuered frõ his enemies & reſtored to honour & glorie.
x Thei ſhalbe no more ſhut in as thei were by Sanheríb, but go where it pleaſeth thẽ.
y Before ẏ this libertie cometh, ẏ ſhalt thinke ẏ thou art in great dãger: for ẏ enemie ſhal ſo ſharpely aſſaile you, ẏ one ſhal cry, Where is the clarke that writeth ẏ names of thẽ ẏ are taxed? another, Where is the receiuer? another ſhal crye for him ẏ valueth ẏ riche houſes, but God wil deliuer you from this feare.
z Let vs be cõtẽt ẇ this ſmale riuer of Shiloáh, & not deſire the great ſtreames & riuers, whereby ẏ enemies may bring in ſhippes & deſtroy vs.
a He derideth ẏ Aſsyrians & enemies of the Church, declaring their deſtructiõ as thei that periſh by ſhipwracke.
b He conforteth ẏ Church, & ſheweth ẏ thei ſhalbe enriſhed ẇ all benefites both of bodie & ſoule.

CHAP. XXXIIII.

1 He ſheweth that God puniſheth the wicked for the loue that he beareth toward his Church.

1 COme nere, ye a nations and heare, and
hearken, ye people: let the earth heare and all that is therein, the worlde and
all that procedeth thereof.

Chap. XXXIIII.
a He prophecieth of ẏ deſtruction of ẏ Edomites, and other natiõs which were enemies to the Church.

2 For the indignation of the Lord *is* vpon
all nations,and *his* wrath vpon all their
armies:he hathe b deſtroied thẽ & deliuered them to the ſlaughter.
3 And their ſlaine ſhalbe caſt out , and
their ſtincke ſhal come vp out of their bodies,and the mountaines ſhalbe melted
with their blood.
4 And all the hoſte of heauen c ſhal be diſſolued, and the heauens ſhal be folden like a boke : and all their hoſtes ſhal fall as
the leafe falleth from the vine, and as it
falleth from the figtre.
5 For my ſworde ſhalbe d dronken in the
heauen:beholde,it ſhal come downe vpon
Edóm,euen vpon the people of e my curſe to iudgement.
6 The ſworde of the Lord is filled with
blood:it is made fat with the fat & with
the blood of the f lambes and the goats,
with the fat of the kidneis of the rams:
for the Lord hathe a ſacrifice in g Bozráh,
and a great ſlaughter in the land of E-
dóm.
7 And the h vnicornes ſhal come downe
with them and the heiffers with the bulles,
and their land ſhal be drenkẽ with blood,
and their duſt made fat with fatnes.
8 For *it is* the day of the Lords vengeance,
and the yere of recompẽce for the iudgement of Zión.
9 And the riuers thereof ſhalbe turned in
to pitch,& the duſt thereof into i brimſtone,and the land thereof ſhalbe burning
pitch.
10 It ſhal not be quenched night nor day:
the ſmoke thereof ſhal go vp euermore: it
ſhal be deſolate from generation to gene-
ration:none ſhal paſſe through it for euer.
11 But the pelicane k & the hedgehog ſhal
poſſeſſe it, and the great owle, & the rauẽ
ſhal dwell in it,& he ſhal ſtretch out vpon
it the line l of vanitie, and the ſtones of
emptines.
12 m The nobles thereof ſhal call to the
kingdome,and there ſhalbe none,and all
the princes thereof ſhalbe *as* nothing.
13 And it ſhal bring forthe thornes in ẏ palaces thereof,nettles & thiſtles in ẏ ſtrong
holdes thereof,and it ſhalbe an habitacion
for dragons and a court for oſtriches.
14 There ſhal n mete alſo Ziím and Iim,and
the Satyre ſhal crye to his fellowe,and the
ſhriche owle ſhal reſt there, & ſhal finde
for her ſelf a quiet dwelling.
15 There o ſhal the owle make her neſt,and
lay,and hatche,and gather thẽ vnder her
ſhadowe: there ſhal ẏ vultures alſo be gathered,euerie one with her make.
16 Seke in the p boke of the Lord & read:
none of q theſe ſhal faile, none ſhal want
her make: for r his mouth hathe cõmanded,
& his verie Spirit hathe gathered them.

b God hathe determined in his counſel & hathe giuẽ ſentence for their deſtruction.
c He ſpeaketh this in reſpect of mans iudgement, who in great feare & horrible troubles thinketh that heauen & earth periſheth.
d I haue determined in my ſecret counſel & in the heauẽs to deſtroy thẽ til my ſworde be weary with ſhedĩg blood.
e Thei had an opiniõ of holines becauſe thei came of the Patriarke Izhák, but in effect were accurſed of God & enemies vnto his Church, as ẏ Papiſts are.
f That is, bothe of yong & olde, poore & riche of his enemies.
g That famous citie ſhalbe cõſumed as a ſacrifice burnt to aſſhes.
h The mightie & riche ſhal be as wel deſtroyed as the inferiours.
i He alludeth to ẏ deſtructiõ of Sodóm and Gomoráh, Gen.19,24.
k Read Chap. 13,21. and Zephan. 2,14.
l In vaine ſhal anie man go about to buylde it againe.
m Meaning, there ſhalbe nether order nor policie, nor ſtate of cõmune weale.
n Read Chap. 13, 21.
o Signifying, ẏ Idumea ſhulde be an horrible deſolation and barẽ wildernes
p That is, in ẏ Lawe where ſuche curſes are threatned againſt ẏ wicked.
q To wit, beaſtes and foules
r That is, the mouthe of ẏ Lord.

17 And he hathe cast the [f] lot for them, and
his hãd hathe diuided it vnto them by line: thei shal possesse it for euer: from gene
racion to generacion shal thei dwell in it.

CHAP. XXXV.

1 The great ioye of them that beleue in Christ. 3 Their office which preache the Gospel. 8 The frutes that followe thereof.

1 THe [a] desert and the wildernes shal reioyce: and the waste grounde shalbe
glad and florish as the rose.
2 It shal florish abundantly & shal greatly reioyce also and ioy: the glorie of Lebanón shalbe giuen vnto it: the beautie
of [b] Carmél, and of Sharón, they shal
[c] se the glorie of the Lord, & the excellēcie of our God.
3 [d] Strengthen the weake hands, & comfort
the feble knees.
4 Say vnto them that are feareful, Be you
strōg, feare not: beholde, your God commeth with [e] vengeance: *euen* God with a
recompence, he wil come and saue you.
5 Thē shal the eyes of the [f] blinde be lightened, and the eares of the deafe be opened.
6 Then shal the lame man leape as an hart,
& the dōme mans tongue shal sing: for in
the [g] wildernes shal waters breake out, &
riuers in the desert.
7 And the drye grounde shal be as a poole,
and the thirstie (as springs of water in the
habitation of dragōs: where thei lay) *shal
be* a place for redes and rushes.
8 And there shalbe a path and a way, and
the way shalbe called [h] holy: the polluted
shal not passe by it: for [i] he shalbe with
them, and walke in the way, and the fooles
shal not erre.
9 There shalbe [k] no lyon, nor noisome beastes shal ascend by it, nether shal they be
founde there, that the redemed may
walke.
10 Therefore the [l] redemed of the Lord
shal returne and come to Zión with praise: and euerlasting ioy shal be vpon their
heads: thei shal obtaine ioy and gladnes, &
sorowe and mourning shal flee away.

f He hathe giuen the beastes and foules Idumea for an inheritance.

a He propheciety of the ful restauratiō of the Church bothe of the Iewes and Gentiles vnder Christ, which shalbe fully accomplished at ẏ last day: albeit as yet it is cōpared to a desert and wildernes.
b The Church wͨ was before compared ro a baren wildernes, shal by Christ be made moste plenteous and beautiful.
c He sheweth ẏ the presence of God is the cause that the Church doeth bring forthe frute and florish.
d He willeth all to encourage one an other, and specially the ministers to exhort & strēgthen the weake, ẏ thei may paciently abide the comīg of God, wͨ is at hand.
e To destroy your enemies.
f When the knowledge of Christ is reueiled.
g They ẏ were baren & destitute of ẏ graces of God, shal haue them giuen by Christ.
h It shalbe for ẏ Saīts of God & not for the wicked.
i God shal lead and guide them, alluding to the bringing forthe of Egypt.
k As he threatened to the wicked to be destroied hereby, Chap. 30, 6.
l Whome the Lord shal deliuer from the captiuitie of Babylon.

CHAP. XXXVI.

1 Saneheríb sendeth Rabshakéh to besege Ierusalém. 15 His blasphemies against God.

1 NOw [a] in the [b] fourtenth yere of King
Hezekiáh, Saneheríb Kīg of Asshúr
came vp against all the strong cities of
Iudáh, and toke them.
2 And the King of Asshúr sent Rabshakéh
frō Lachísh toward Ierusalém vnto Kīg
Hezekiáh, with a great hoste, and he stode
by the conduite of the vpper poole in the
path of the fullers field.

a This historie is rehearsed, because it is as a seale & confirmation of the doctrine afore, bothe for the threatnings & pmises: to wit, that God wolde suffer his Church to be afflicted, but at length wolde send deliuerance.
b When he had abolished supersticion, & idolatrie, & restored religion, yet God wolde exercise his Church to trye their faith and pacience.

3 Then came forthe vnto him Eliakím the
sonne of Hilkiáh the [c] steward of the house, and Shebná [d] the chanceller, and Ioah
the sonne of Asáph the recorder.
4 And [e] Rabshakéh said vnto them, Tel
you Hezekiáh, I pray you, Thus saith the
great King, the King of Asshúr, What
confidence is this, wherein thou trustest?
5 I saie, [f] Surely *I haue* eloquence, *but* counsel and strength *are* for the warre: on whome then doest thou trust, that thou rebellest against me?
6 Lo, thou trustest in this broken staffe of
rede on Egypt, whereupon if a man leane,
it wil go into his hand, and perce it: so *is*
[g] Pharaóh King of Egypt, vnto all that
trust in him.
7 But if thou say to me, We trust in the
Lord our God. Is not that he, whose hie
places and whose altars Hezekiáh toke
downe, and said to Iudáh and to Ierusalém, Ye shal worship before this altar?
8 Now therefore giue hostages to my lord
the King of Asshúr, & I wil giue thee two
thousand horses, if thou be able on thy
parte to set riders vpon them.
9 For how canst thou "despise anie captaine of the [h] least of my lords seruants? and
put thy trust on Egypt for charets and for
horsemen?
10 And am I now come vp without ẏ Lord
to this land to destroy it? The Lord said
vnto me, [i] Go vp against this land & destroy it.
11 ¶ Then said Eliakím, and Shebná and Io
áh vnto Rabshakéh, [k] Speake, I pray thee,
to thy seruants in the Aramites language,
(for we vnderstand it) and talke not with
vs in the Iewes tongue, in the audience of
the people that are on the wall.
12 Then said Rabshakéh, Hathe my master
sent me to thy master, & to thee to speake
these wordes, and not to the men that sit
on the wall? that they may eat their owne
doung, and drinke their owne " pisse with
you?
13 So Rabshakéh stode, & cryed with a loude voyce in the Iewes language, and said,
Heare the wordes of the great King, of ẏ
King of Asshúr.
14 Thus saith the King, Let not Hezekiáh
deceiue you: for he shal not be able to deliuer you.
15 Nether let Hezekiáh make you to
trust in the Lord, saying, The Lord wil
surely deliuer vs: this citie shal not be giuen ouer into the hand of the King of
Asshúr.
16 Hearken not to Hezekiáh: for thus saith
the King of Asshúr, Make [l] appointment
with me, and come out to me, that euerie
man may eat of his owne vine, and euerie
man of his owne figtre, and drinke euerie

c For he was now restored to his office, as Isaiáh had prophecied, Chap. 22, 20.
d This declareth that there were fewe godlie to be founde in the Kīgs house, whē he was driuen to send this wicked man in suche a weightie matter.
e Saneheribs chief captaine.
f He speaketh this in the persone of Hezekiáh, falsely charging him, that he put his trust in his wit and eloquence, where as his onelie confidēce was in the Lord.
g Satan labored to pul the godlie King from one vaine confidence to another: to wit, from trust in ẏ Egyptiās, whose power was weake & wold deceiue them: to yelde him self to ẏ Asyrians and so not to hope for any helpe of God.
" Or, turne backe
h He reprocheth to Hezekiáh his smale power, which is not able to resist one of Saneheribs least captaines
i Thus the wicked to deceiue vs, wil pretend the Name of ẏ Lord: but we must trye the spirits, whether thei be of God or no.
k Thei were afraid, lest by his wordes he shulde haue stirred the people against the King, and also pretended to growe to some appointement with him.
" Ebr. the water of their fete.
l The Ebrewe word signifieth blessing: whereby this wicked captaine wolde haue psuaded ẏ people, that their condition shulde be better vnder Saneheríb then vnder Hezekiáh.

man the water of his owne well,
17 Til I come and bring you to a land like
your owne land, *euen* a land of wheat and
wine, a land of bread and vineyardes,
18 Lest Hezekiáh disceiue you, saying, The
Lord wil deliuer vs. Hathe anie of ỳ gods
of the naciōs deliuered his land out of the
hand of the King of Asshúr?
19 Where is the god of [m] Hamáth, and of
Arpád? Where is the god of Sepharuáim?
or how haue they deliuered Samaria out
of mine hand?
20 Who is he among all the gods of these
lands, that hathe deliuered their countrey
out of mine hand, that the Lord shulde
deliuer Ierusalém out of mine hand?
21 Then they [n] kept silence, and answered
him not a worde: for the Kings commandement was, saying, Answer him not.
22 Then came Eliakím the sonne of Hilkiáh the steward of the house, and Shebná
the chanceller, and Ioáh the sonne of A-
saph the recorder, vnto Hezekiáh with rēt
clothes, and tolde him the wordes of Rabshakéh.

CHAP. XXXVII.

2 *Hezekiáh asketh counsel of Isaiáh, who promiseth him the Victorie. 10 The blasphemie of Saneherib. 16 Hezekiahs prayer. 36 The armie of Saneherib is slayne of the Angel. 38 And he him self of his owne sonnes.*

1 And * whē the King Hezekiáh heard
it, he [a] rent his clothes, and put on
sackecloth & came into the House of the
Lord.
2 And he sent Eliakím the steward of the
house, and Shebná the chanceller, with the
Elders of the Priests, clothed in sackeclothe vnto [b] Isaiáh the Prophet, the sonne of
Amóz.
3 And they said vnto him, Thus saith Hezekiáh, This day is a day of tribulacion &
of rebuke and blasphemie: for the children
are come to the [c] birth, and there is no
strength to bring forthe.
4 If so be the Lord thy God hathe [d] heard
the wordes of Rabshakéh, whome the
King of Asshúr his master hathe sent to
raile on ỳ liuing God, & to reproche him
with wordes which ỳ Lord thy God hathe
heard, then [e] lift thou vp *thy* praier for the
remnant that are left.
5 So the seruants of the King Hezekiah came to Isaiáh.
6 And Isaiáh said vnto them, Thus say vnto your master, Thus saith the Lord, Be
not afraied of the wordes that thou hast
heard, wherewith the seruants of the King
of Asshúr haue blasphemed me.
7 Beholde, I wil send a blast vpon him, &
he shal heare a [f] noise, and returne to his
owne land, and I wil cause him to fall by

m That is, of Antiochia in Syria, of the which these two other cities also were: whereby we se how euery towne had his peculiar idole and how the wicked make God an idole, because they do not vnderstād that God maketh them his scourge & punissheth cities for sinne.

n Not that thei did not shewe by euident signes ỳ thei did detest his blasphemie: for thei had now rent their clothes, but they knewe it was in vaine to vse lōg reasoning with this infidele, whose rage thei shulde haue so much more prouoked.

Chap. XXXVII.

* 2. King 19, 1.

a In signe of grief and repentance.

b To haue cōfort of him by the worde of God, that his faith might be confirmed and so his prayer be more earnest: teaching hereby that in all dāgers these two are the onelie remedies, to seke vnto God and his ministers.

c We are in as great sorowe as a woman ỳ trauaileth of childe, and can not be deliuered.

d That is, wil declare by effect that he hathe heard it: for when God differreth to punish, it semeth to the flesh, that he knoweth not ỳ sinne, or heareth not the cause.

e Declaring, ỳ the ministers office doeth not onely stād in cōforting by the worde, but also in praying for the people.

f Of the Egyptians and Ethiopians, that shal come and fight against him.

the sworde in his owne land.
8 ¶ So Rabshakéh returned, and founde the
King of Asshúr fighting against [g] Libnáh:
for he had heard that he was departed frō
Lachish.
9 He heard also men say of Tirhakáh, Kīg
of Ethiopia, *Beholde*, he is come out to
fight against thee: and when he heard it, he
sent *other* messengers to Hezekiáh, saying,
10 Thus shal ye speake to Hezekiáh King
of Iudáh, saying, Let not thy God [h] deceiue thee, in whome thou trustest, saying,
Ierusalém shal not be giuen into the hand
of the King of Asshúr.
11 Beholde, thou hast heard what ỳ Kings
of Asshúr haue done to all lands in destroying them, & shalt thou be deliuered?
12 Haue the gods of the nacions deliuered
them, which my fathers haue destroyed?
as [i] Gozán, and [k] Harán, and Rézeph, and
the children of Eden, which were at Te-
lassár?
13 Where is the King of Hamáth, and the
King of Arpád, and the King of the citie
of Sepharuáim, Hena and Iuáh?
14 ¶ So Hezekiáh receiued the letter of the
hand of the messengers and red it, and he
went vp into the House of the Lord, and
Hezekiáh spred it before the Lord.
15 And Hezekiáh praied vnto the Lord,
saying,
16 O Lord of hostes, God of Israél, which
[l] dwellest betwene the Cherubims, thou
art very God alone ouer all the kīgdomes
of the earth: thou hast made the heauen &
the earth.
17 Encline thine eare, ô Lord, and heare: o-
pen thine eyes, ô Lord, and se, and heare
all the wordes of Saneherib, who hathe
sent to blaspheme the liuing God.
18 Trueth it is, ô Lord, that the Kings of
Asshúr haue destroyed all lands, & [m] their
countrey,
19 And haue cast their gods in the fyre: for
they were no gods, but the worke of mans
hands, *euen* wood or stone: therefore they
destroyed them.
20 Now therefore, ô Lord our God, saue
thou vs out of his hand, that [n] all the kingdomes of the earth may knowe, that thou
onely art the Lord.
21 ¶ Then Isaiáh the sonne of Amóz sent
vnto Hezekiáh, saying, Thus saith ỳ Lord
God of Israél, Because thou hast prayed
vnto me, concerning Saneherib King of
Asshúr,
22 This is the worde that the Lord hathe
spoken against him, O [o] virgine, daughter
of Zión, he hathe despised thee, *&* laughed thee to scorne: ô daughter of Ierusalém, he hathe shaken his head at thee.
23 Whome hast thou railed on & blasphemed? and against whome hast thou exalted

g Which was a citie toward Egypt, thinkīg thereby to haue stayed ỳ force of his enemies.

h Thus God wolde haue him to vtter a moste horrible blasphemie before his destruction: as to call the autor of all trueth, a deceiuer: some gather hereby ỳ Shebnáh had disclosed vnto Saneherib ỳ answer ỳ Isaiáh sent to the King.

i Which was a citie of the Medes.

k Called also Charre a citie in Mesopotamia, whence Abrahám came after his fathers death.

l He groūdeth his praier on Gods promes, who promised to heare them from betwene the Cherubīs.

m Meaning, of the ten tribes.

n He declareth for what cause he praied, ỳ they might be deliuered: to wit, ỳ God might be glorified thereby through all ỳ worlde.

o Whome God had chosen to him self, as a chaste virgine, and ouer whome he had care to preserue her from ỳ lusts of ỳ tyrāt, as a father wolde haue ouer his daughter.

thy voyce,& lifted vp thine eyes on hie?*e-*
uen against the [p] holy one of Israél.
24 By thy seruants hast thou railed on the
Lord, and said, By the multitude of my
charets I am come vp to the top of the
mountaines to the sides of Lebanón, and
wil cut downe the hie cedres thereof, *and*
the faire fyrre trees thereof, and I wil go
vp to the heights of his toppe & to the forest of his fruteful places.
25 I haue digged [q] & dronke the waters, &
with the plant of my fete haue I dryed all
the riuers closed in.
26 Hast thou not heard how I haue of olde
time made it, [r] and haue formed it long
ago? & shulde I now bring it, that it shulde be destroyed, *and layed* on ruinous heapes, *as* cities defensed?
27 Whose inhabitants" haue smale power,
& are afraied & confounded: thei are like
the grasse of the field and grene herbe, *or*
grasse on the house toppes, or corne blasted [s] afore it be growen.
28 But I knowe thy dwelling, & thy [t] going
out, and thy comming in, and thy furie a-
gainst me.
29 Because thou ragest against me, and thy
tumult is come vp vnto mine eares, therefore wil I put mine [u] hoke in thy nostrels,
and my bridle in thy lippes, and wil bring
thee backe againe the same way yᵗ [x] camest.
30 And this shalbe a [y] signe vnto thee, *o*
Hezekiáh, Thou shalt eat this yere suche
as groweth of it self: and the [z] second
yere, suche things as grow without sowĩg:
and in the third yere, sow ye and reape, &
plant vineyardes, & eat the frute thereof.
31 And [a] the remnant that is escaped of the
house of Iudáh, shal againe take roote
downeward and beare frute vpward.
32 For out of Ierusalém shal go a remnant,
& thei that escape out of mount Zión: the
zeale of the Lord of hostes shal do this.
33 Therefore thus saith the Lord, concerning yᵉ King of Asshúr, He shal not enter
into this citie, nor shoote an arrowe there, nor come before it with shield, nor cast
a mount against it.
34 By the same way that he came, he shal
returne, and not come into this citie, saith
the Lord.
35 For I wil defend this citie to saue it, for
mine owne sake, & for my seruãt [b] Dauids
sake.
36 ¶ * Then the Angel of the Lord went
out, and smote in the campe of Asshúr an
hundreth, foure score, and fiue thousand:
so when they arose early in the morning,
beholde, thei were all dead corpses.
37 So Sanchérib King of Asshúr departed,
and went away and returned and dwelt at
[c] Nineuéh.
38 And as he was in the temple worshiping
of Nisróch his god, Adramélech & Sharézer his sonnes slewe him wᵗ the sworde,
and they escaped into the land of ° Ararát:
and [d] Esarháddon his sonne reigned in his
stead.

CHAP. XXXVIII.

1 Hezekiáh is sicke. 5 He is restored to health by the Lord, and liueth fiftene yeres after. 10 He giueth thankes for his benefit.

1 ABout * that [a] time was Hezekiáh sicke
vnto the death, and the Prophet I-
saiáh sonne of Amóz came vnto him, and
said vnto him, Thus saith the Lord, Put
thine house in an ordre, for thou shalt dye,
and not liue.
2 Then Hezekiáh [b] turned his face to the
wall, and praied to the Lord,
3 And said, I beseche thee, Lord, remember
now how I haue walked before thee in trueth, & with a perfite heart, and haue done
that which is good in thy sight: & Hezekiáh wept sore.
4 ¶ Then came the worde of the Lord to
Isaiáh, saying,
5 Go, & say vnto Hezekiáh, Thus saith the
Lord God of Dauid thy father, I haue
heard thy praier, & sene thy teares: beholde, I wil adde vnto thy daies fiftene yeres.
6 And I wil deliuer thee [c] out of the hand
of the King of Asshúr, and this citie: for
I wil defend this citie.
7 And [d] this signe shalt thou haue of the
Lord, that yᵉ Lord wil do this thing, that
he hathe spoken,
8 Beholde, I wil bring againe yᵉ shadowe of
the degrees (whereby it is gone downe in
yᵉ dial of Aház by the [e] sunne) ten degrees
backeward: so the sũne returned by tẽ degrees, by thē degrees it was gone downe.
9 [f] The writing of Hezekiáh King of Iudáh, when he had bene sicke, and was recouered of his sickenes.
10 I said in yᵉ [g] cutting of of my daies, I shal
go to yᵉ gates of the graue: I am depriued
of the residue of my yeres.
11 I said, [h] I shal not se the Lord, *euen* the
Lord in the land of the liuing: I shal se
man no more amõg the inhabitants of the
worlde.
12 Mine habitacion is departed, and is remoued from me, like a shepherds tent: I
[i] haue cut of like a weauer my life: he wil
cut me of from the height: from day [k] to
night, thou wilt make an end of me.
13 I rekened [l] to the morning: but he brake

p Declaring hereby that they that are enemies to Gods Church, fight against him; whose quarel his Church onely mainteineth.
q He boasteth of his policie, in that that he can finde meanes to nourish his armie: and of his power, in that that his armie is so great, that it is able to drye vp whole riuers, and to destroy the waters, wᶜ the Iewes had closed in.
r Signifying, yᵗ God made not his Church to destroy it, but to preserue it, & therefore he saieth that he formed it of olde, euẽ in his eternal counsel, which cã not be chãged.
"Ebr. are short in hand.
s He sheweth that the state and power of moste florishĩg cities ẽdureth but a momẽt in respect of the Church, wᶜ shal remaine for euer, because God is yᵉ mainteiner therof.
t Meaning, his counsels & enterprises.
u Because Saneherib shewed him self, as a deuouring fish & furious beast, he vseth these similitudes, to teache how he wil take him and guide him.
x Thou shalt loose thy labour.
y God giueth signes after two sortes: some go before the thing, as yᵉ signes yᵗ Moses wroght in Egypt, which were for the confirmacion of their faith: and some go after yᵉ thing, as yᵉ sacrifice, wᶜ they were commãded to make thre daies after their departure: & these later are to kepe the benefits of God in our remembrance, of the which sorte this here is. z He promiseth that for two yeres the grounde of it self shulde fede them. a They whome God had deliuered out of the hands of the Assyrians, shal prosper: and this properly belongeth to the Church. b For my promes sake made to Dauid.

2.King.19,35. 2.chro.23,21. tob.1,21. eccles.48,24. 1.mac.7,41. 2.mac.8,19.

c Which was the chiefest citie of the Assyrians
°Or Armenia.
d Who was also called Sardanapalus in whose daies ten yeres after Saneheribs death, the Chaldeans ouercame yᵉ Assyrians by Merodách their King.
Chap. XXXVIII.
2.King.20,1. 2.chro.32,24.
a Sone after that the Assyrians were slayne; so that God wil haue the exercise of his childrẽ continual, that thei may learne only to depend vpõ God & aspire to yᵉ heauens.
b For his heart was touched wᵗ feare of Gods iudgement, seing he had appointed him to dye, so quickely after his deliuerance frõ so great calamitie, as one vnworthie to remaine in yᵗ estate, & also foreseing the great change, yᵗ shulde come in the Church, forasmuche as he left no sonne to reigne after him: for as yet Manasséh was not borne: & when he reigned, we se what a tyrant he was.
c He doeth not onely promise to prolong his life, but to giue him rest & quietnes from the Assyrians, who might haue renued their armie to reuenge their former discomfiture.
d For Hezekiáh had asked for yᵉ confirmaciõ of his faith a signe, as vers.22 and 2.King 20,8: whereunto he was moued by yᵉ singular mocion of Gods Spirit.
e Read 2.Kĩg 20,10.

f He left this song of his lamentacion & thankesgiuing to all posteritie, as a monument of his owne infirmitie & thãkeful heart for Gods benefites, as Dauid did, Psal 51. g At what time it was tolde me, that I shulde dye. h I shal no more praise the Lord here in his Temple among the faithful: thus God suffreth his dearest children to want his consolacion for a time, yᵗ his grace afterward may the more appeare whẽ thei fele their owne weakenes. i By my sinne I haue prouoked God to take my life from me. k That is, in one day, or shortly. l Ouer night I thoght yᵗ I shulde liue til morning, but my pangs in the night persuaded me the contrarie: he sheweth the horrour, that the faithful haue when they apprehend Gods iudgement against their sinne.

all my bones, like a lion: from daie to
night wilt thou make an end of me.
14 Like a crane *or* a swalow, so did I [m] chatter:
I did mourne as a doue: mine eies were lift
vp on hie: ô Lord, [n] it hathe oppressed me,
comfort me.
15 What shal I saie? [o] for he hathe said it
to me, and he hathe done it: I shal walke
[p] weakely all my yeres in the bitternes of
my soule.
16 O Lord, [q] *to them* that ouerliue them, &
to all *that are* in them, the life of my spirit
shalbe knowen, that thou causedst me to
[r] slepe and hast giuen life to me.
17 Beholde, for [s] felicitie I had bitter grief,
but it was thy pleasure *to deliuer* my soule
from the pit of corruption: for thou hast
cast all my [t] sinnes behinde thy backe.
18 For [u] the graue cã not cõfesse thee: death
can not praise thee: thei that go downe
into the pit, can not hope for thy trueth.
19 *But* the liuing, the liuing, he shal confesse thee, as I *do* this day: the father to the
[x] children shal declare thy trueth.
20 The Lord *was ready* to saue me: therefore
we wil sing my song, all the dayes of ỹ our
life in the House of the Lord.
21 Thẽ said Isaiáh, Take a lumpe of drye
figges and [z] laie it vpon the boile, and he
shal recouer.
22 Also Hezekiáh [a] had said, What is the
signe, that I shal go vp into the House of
the Lord?

m I was so opprest with sorowe, that I was not able to vtter my wordes, but onely to grone & sigh.
n To wit, sorow, and grief bothe of bodie and minde.
o God hathe declared by his Prophet ỹ I shal dye, and therefore I wil yelde vnto him.
p I shal haue no release, but continual sorowes whiles I liue.
q They that shal ouerliue the men that are now aliue, and all they ỹ are in these yeres shal acknowledge this benefite.
r That after that thou hadest condemned me to death, thou restoredst me to life.
s Where as I thoght to haue liued in rest and ease, being deliuered from mine enemie, I had grief vpon grief.
t He estemeth more the remission of his sinnes, & Gods fauour then a thousand liues.
u For asmuche as God hathe placed man in this worlde to glorifie him, the godlie take it as a signe of his wrath when their dayes were shortened, ether because that they semed vnworthie for their sinnes to liue longer in his seruice, or for their zeale to Gods glorie, seing that there is so fewe in earth, that do regarde it, as Psal. 6,5 and 115,17
x All posteritie shal acknowledge, and according to their duetie toward their children shal instruct them in thy graces, & mercies toward me
y He sheweth what is the vse of the Congregacion and Church: to wit, to giue the Lord thankes for his benefites.
z Read 2. King 20,7.
a As vers. 7.

CHAP. XXXIX.

Hezekiáh is reproued, because he shewed his treasures vnto the ambassadours of Babylon.

1 AT *the same time, [a] Merodách Baladán, the sonne of Baladán, King
of Babél, sent [b] letters, & a present to Hezekiáh: for he had heard that he had bene
sicke, and was recouered.
2 And Hezekiáh was [c] glad of them, and
shewed them the house of the treasures,
the siluer, and the golde, and the spices, &
the precious ointement, and all the house
of his armour, and all that was found in his
treasures: there was nothing in his house,
nor in all his kingdome that Hezekiáh
shewed them not.
3 Thẽ came Isaiáh the Prophet vnto King
Hezekiáh, and said vnto him, What said
these men? and from whence came they to
thee? And Hezekiáh said, They are come
from a farre countrey vnto me, from
Babél.
4 Thẽ said he, What haue [d] they sene in
thine house? And Hezekiáh answered, All
that is in mine house haue they sene: there
is nothing among my treasures, that I haue not shewed them.
5 And Isaiáh said to Hezekiáh, Heare the
worde of the Lord of hostes,
6 Beholde, the dayes come that all that is in
thine house, and which thy fathers haue
laid vp in store vntil this day, shalbe [e] caryed to Babél: nothing shalbe left, saith the
Lord.
7 And of thy sonnes, that shal procede out
of thee, & which thou shalt beget, shal
they take away, and they shalbe [f] eunuches
in the palace of the King of Babél.
8 [g] Then said Hezekiáh to Isaiáh, The worde of the Lord is good, which thou hast
spoken: and he said, Yet let there be peace,
and trueth in my dayes.

*2. King. 20,12.
a This was ỹ first King of Babylõ, which ouercame the Assyrians in ỹ tenth yere of his reigne.
b Partely moued with ỹ greatnes of ỹ miracle, partely because he shewed him self enemie to his enemies, but chiefly, because he wolde ioine with thẽ whome God fauoured, and haue their helpe, if occasion serued.
c Read 2. King. 20,13, & 2. chr. 32,25.
d He asketh him of the particulers to make him vnderstand the craft of the wicked, which he before being ouercome with their flatterie, and blinded with ambition colde not se.
e By the grieuousnes of the punishment is declared how greatly God detesteth ambition & vaine glorie.
f That is, officers and seruants.
g Read 2. King. 20,19.

CHAP. XL.

2 Remission of sinnes by Christ 3 The comming of Iohn Baptist. 18 The Prophet reproueth the idolaters and them that trust not in the Lord.

1 COmfort [a] ye, comfort ye my people,
wil your God say.
2 Speake comfortably to Ierusalém, & crye
vnto her, that her [b] warrefare is accomplished, that her iniquitie is pardoned:
for she hathe receiued of the Lords hand
[c] double for all her sinnes.
3 A [d] voyce cryeth in the [e] wildernes, [f] Pre
pare ye the way of the Lord: make streight
in the desert a path for our God.
4 Euerie valleie shalbe exalted, and euerie
[g] mountaine and hill shalbe made lowe: &
the croked shalbe streight, and the rough
places plaine.
5 And ỹ glorie of the Lord shalbe reueiled,
and all [h] flesh shal se it together: for the
mouth of the Lord hathe spoken it.
6 A [i] voyce said, Crye. And he said, What
shal I crye? All flesh *is* grasse, and all the
[k] grace thereof *is* as ỹ floure of the field.
7 The grasse withereth, the floure fadeth,
because the [l] Spirit of the Lord bloweth
vpon it: surely the people *is* grasse.
8 The grasse withereth, ỹ floure fadeth: but
the [m] worde of our God shal stãd for euer.
9 ¶ O Zión, that bringest good tidigs, get
thee vp into the hie [n] mountaine: ô Ierusalém, that bringest good tidings, lift vp
thy voyce with strength: lift it vp, be not
afraide: say vnto the cities of Iudáh, Beholde [o] your God.
10 Beholde, the Lord God wil come with

a This is a cõsolacion for the Church, assuring them that thei shalbe neuer destitute of Prophetes, whereby he exhorteth the true ministers of God that thẽ were, & those also that shulde come after him, to comfort the poore afflicted, and to assure them of their deliuerãce bothe of body and soule.
b The time of her affliction.
c Meaning, sufficiẽt, as chap. 61,7 & ful correction, or double grace, where as she deserued double punishment.
d To wit, of ỹ Prophetes.
e That is, in Babylon, and other places where they were kept in captiuitie, and miserie.
f Meaning, Cyrus and Darius which shulde deliuer Gods people out of captiuitie, and make them a ready way to Ierusalém: & this was fully accõplished, whẽ Iohn ỹ Baptist broght tidings of Iesus Christs cõming, who was the true deliuerer of his Church frõ sinne and Satán, Mat 3,3.
g Whatsoeuer may let or hinder this deliuerance, shalbe remoued.
h This miracle shalbe so great, that it shalbe knowen through all the worlde.
i The voyce of God, which spake to the Prophete Isaiáh.
k Meaning, all mans wisdome and natural powers, Iohn. 1,10. 1. pet. 1,24.
l The Spirit of God shal discouer the vanitie in all that seme to haue anie excellencie of them selues.
m Thogh cõsidering ỹ frailtie of mans nature manie of ỹ Iewes shulde perish & so not be partakers of this deliuerance, yet Gods promise shulde be fulfilled, & they that remained, shulde fele ỹ frute thereof.
n To publish this benefite through all the worlde.
o He sheweth at one worde the perfection of all mans felicitie, which is to haue Gods presence.

power, and [p] his arme shal rule for him:
beholde,his wages *is* with him,& his worke before him.
11 He shal fede his flocke like a shepherd:
he shal gather the lambes with his arme,&
carie them in his bosome, *and* shal guide
them with [q] yong.
12 Who hathe measured the waters in his
[r] fist?and counted heauen with the spanne,
and comprehended the dust of the earth
in a measure?and weighed the mountaines
in a weight,and the hilles in a balance?
13 Who hathe instructed the Spirit of the
Lord?or *was* [s] his cousélour *or* taught him?
14 Of whome toke he counsel, and *who* instructed him and taught him in the way of
iudgement? or taught him knowledge, &
shewed vnto him ỹ way of vnderstãding?
15 Beholde,the nations *are* as a droppe of a
bucket, and are counted as the dust of the
balãce:beholde,he taketh away the yles as
a litle dust.
16 And Lebanón *is* not sufficient for fyre,
nor the beastes thereof sufficient for a
burnt offring.
17 All nations before him *are* as [t] nothing,
and they are counted to him,lesse then nothing,and vanitie.
18 To whome then [u] wil ye liken God? or
what similitude wil ye set vp vnto him?
19 The workeman melteth an image,or the
goldesmith beateth it out in golde, or ỹ
goldesmith *maketh* siluer plates.
20 Doeth not [x] the poore chuse out a tre
that wil not rote,for an oblation? he seketh
also vnto him a cunning workeman, to
prepare an image, that shal not be moued.
21 Knowe ye nothĩg? haue ye not heard [y] it?
hathe it not bene tolde you from the beginning? haue ye not vnderstãd it by the
[z] fundacion of the earth?
22 He sitteth vpon the circle of the earth,&
the inhabitãts thereof *are* as grashoppers,
he stretcheth out the heauẽs,as a curtaine,
& spreadeth thẽ out,as a tent to dwell in.
23 He bringeth the princes to nothing, *and*
maketh the iudges of the earth,as vanitie,
24 As thogh they were not plãted, as thogh
they were not sowen,as thogh their stocke
toke no roote in the earth: for he did euẽ
[a] blow vpon them, and they withered, and
the whirle winde wil take them away as
stubble.
25 To whome now wil ye liken me, that I
shulde be like *him*, saith the holie one?
26 Lift vp your eyes on hie, and beholde,
who hathe created these things,and bringeth [b] out their armies by nomber, and
calleth them all by names? by the greatnes
of *his* power and mightie strength nothing
faileth.
27 Why saiest thou, ô Iaakób, and speakest
ô Israél, [c] My waye is hid from the Lord,

p His power shalbe sufficient without helpe of anie other,and shal haue all meanes in him self to bring his wil to passe.

q He shal shewe his care & fauour ouer them that are weake, and tender.

r Declaring ỹ as God onely hathe all powerso doeth he vse ỹ same for ỹ defence, and maintenãce of his Church.

s He sheweth Gods infinite wisdome for ỹ same end and purpose.

t He speaketh all this to the intent ỹ they shulde nether feare man nor put their trust in anie, saue onely in God.

u Hereby he armeth them against ỹ idolatrie, wherewith they shulde be tempted in Babylon.

x He sheweth the rage of the idolaters seing that the poore that haue not to suffise their owne necessities, wil defraude them selues to serue their idoles.

y Haue ye not the worde of God,ẘ plainely condẽneth idolatrie?

z Cã you not learne by ỹ visible creatures whome God hathe made to serue your vse, that you shuld not serue them nor worship them?

a So that his power appeareth in euerie place whereso euer we turne our eyes.

b Who hathe set in order ỹ infinit nomber of the starres.

c He rebuketh the Iewes,because thei did not rest on the prouidence of God,but thoght ỹ he had forsaken them in their troubles.

and my iudgement is passed ouer of my
God.
28 Knowest thou not? or hast thou not heard,
that the euerlasting God,the Lord hathe
created the [d] ends of the earth? he nether
fainteth,nor is weary: there *is* no searching
of his [e] vnderstanding.
29 *But* he giueth strẽgth vnto him that fainteth, & vnto him that hathe no strength,
he encreaseth power.
30 [f] Euen the yong men shal faint, and be
wearie,and the yong men shal stumble and
fall.
31 But they that waite vpon the Lord, shal
renue *their* strength: they shal lift vp the
wings as the egles: they shal runne, & not
be wearie,& they shal walke and not faint.

d And therefore all power is in his hãd to deliuer when his time cometh

e Shewing ỹ man muste paciently abide, & not curiously seke out the cause of Gods delay in our afflictions.

f They ỹ trust in their owne vertue, and do not acknowledge that all cometh of God.

CHAP. XLI.

2 Gods mercie in chusing his people. 6 Their idolatrie. 27 Deliuerance promised to Zión.

1 KEpe [a] silence before me, ô ylands, &
let the people [b] renue *their* strength:
let them come nere, and let them speake:
let vs come together into iudgement.
2 Who raised vp [c] iustice from the East,
& called him to his fote? *and* gaue the nacions before him,and subdued the Kings?
he gaue them as dust to his sworde, & as
scatred stubble vnto his bowe.
3 He pursued them,and passed safely by the
way that he had not gone with his fete.
4 Who hathe wroght and done it? he that
calleth the [d] generations from the beginning. I the Lord *am* the [e] first,and with the
last I am the same.
5 The yles sawe it,& did [f] feare & the ends
of the earth were abashed, drewe nere,and
[g] came.
6 Euerie man helped his neighbour and
said to his brother, [h] Be strong.
7 So the workeman comforted the founder
& he that smote ẘ the hammer,him that
smote by course, sayĩg,It is ready for the
sodering,& he fastened it with nailes that
it shulde not be moued.
8 ¶ But thou, Israél, art my [i] seruant, & thou
Iaakób, whome I haue chosen, the sede of
Abrahám my friend.
9 For I haue taken thee from the ends of
the earth,and called thee before the chief
thereof, and said vnto thee, Thou art my
seruant: I haue chosen thee, and not cast
thee away.
10 Feare thou not, for I am with thee: be
not afraid,for I am thy God: I wil strengthen thee, and helpe thee, and wil susteine
thee with the [k] right hand of my iustice.
11 Beholde,all they ỹ prouoke thee, shalbe
ashamed,and confounded: they shalbe as
nothing,& they that striue with thee,shal
perish.
12 Thou shalt seke thẽ and shalt not [l] finde
them:

a God,as thogh he pleaded his cause ẘ all nacĩos,requireth silence that he may be heard in his right.

b That is,gather all their power & supportes.

c Who called Abrahám(who was the paterne of Gods iustice in deliuering his Churche) from the idolatrie of ỹ Chaldeans to go to and fro at his cõmandement,& placed him in the land of Canáan?

d Who hathe created man & mainteined his succesion.

e Thogh the worlde set vp neuer so manie gods, yet they diminish nothing of my glorie: for I am all one, vnchãgeable, ẘ haue euer bene, and shalbe for euer.

f Considering mine excellent workes among my people.

g They assembled them selues,and conspired against me to mainteine their idolatrie.

h He noteth ỹ obstinacie of ỹ idolaters to maiteine their superstitions.

i And therefore oghtest not to pollute thy self with the superstitiõ of the Gẽtiles.

k That is, by the force of my promes in ỹ performãce whereof I wil shewe my self faithful and iuste.

l Because they shalbe destroyed.

them: *to wit*, the men of thy strife, *for* they
shalbe as nothing, and the men that warre
against thee, as a thing of naught.
13 For I the Lord thy God wil holde thy
right hand, saying vnto thee, Feare not, I
wil helpe thee.
14 Feare not, thou [m] worme, Iaakób, & ye
men of Israél: I wil helpe thee, saith the
Lord & thy redemer ȳ holie one of Israél.
15 Beholde, I wil make thee a roller, and a
newe threshing instrument hauing tethe:
thou shalt thresh the [n] mountaines, and
bring them to poudre, and shalt make the
hilles as chaffe.
16 Thou shalt fanne them, & the winde shal
carye them away, & the whirlwinde shal
scater them: and thou shalt reioyce in the
Lord, & shalt glorie in the holy one of
Israél.
17 *When* [o] the poore and the nedie seke water, and there *is* non (their tongue faileth
for thirst: I the Lord wil heare them: I the
God of Israél wil not forsake them)
18 I wil open riuers in the toppes of the
hilles, and fountaines in the middes of the
valleis: I wil make the wildernes as a
poole of water, & the waste [p] lād as springs
of water.
19 I wil set in the wildernes the cedre, the
shittah tre, & the myrre tre & the pine tre,
& I wil set in the wildernes the fyrre tre,
the elme and the boxe tree together.
20 Therefore let them se and knowe, and
let them consider and vnderstand together that the hand of the Lord hathe done
this, and the holie one of Israél [q] hathe created it.
21 [r] Stand to your cause, saith the Lord:
bring forthe your strong reasons, saith the
King of Iaakób.
22 Let thē bring thē forthe, & let thē tel vs
what shal come: let them shewe the former
things what thei be, that we maie consider
them, and knowe the later end of them: e-
ther declare vs things for to come.
23 Shewe the things that are to come hereafter, that we may know that you are gods:
yea, do good or do euil, that we may declare it, and beholde it together.
24 Beholde, ye are of no value, & your making is of naught: *man* hathe [s] chosen an a-
bomination by them.
25 ¶ I haue raised vp [t] from the North, and
he shal come: from the East sunne shal [u] he
call vpon my Name, and shal come vpon
[x] princes as vpon claye, and as the potter
treadeth myre vnder the fote.
26 Who hathe declared frō the beginning,
that we may knowe? or before time, that
we may say, He is righteous? Surely there
is none that sheweth: surely there is none
ȳ declareth: surely there is none that heareth [y] your wordes.
27 *I am* the first, *that saith* to Zión, Beholde,
beholde [z] them: and I wil giue to Ierusalém [a] one that shal bring good tidings.
28 But when [b] I beheld, there was none, &
when I enquired of them, there *was* no co
unselour, & whē I demanded of them, thei
answered not a worde.
29 Beholde, they are all vanitie: their worke is of nothing, their images are winde &
confusion.

m Thus he calleth thē because they were contēned of all the worlde, & that they considering their owne poore estate, shulde seke vnto him for helpe
n I wil make thee able to destroye all thine enemies, be thei neuer so mightie: and this chiefly is referred to ȳ kingdome of Christ
o That is, thei that shalbe afflicted in the captiuitie of Babylon.
p God wil rather change ȳ order of nature, then they shulde want anie thing that cry to him by true faith in their miseries: declaring to them hereby ȳ they shal lacke nothing by the way, whē they returne from Babylon.
q That is, hathe appointed, & determined ȳ it shal come so to passe.
r He biddeth the idolaters to proue their religion, and to bring forthe their idoles, ȳ they may be tryed whether thei knowe all things, and cā do all thīgs: ẘ if they can not do, he concludeth that they are no gods, but vile idoles
s So that a mā can not make an idole, but he must do that, which God detesteth, and abhorreth: for he chuseth his owne deuises, and forsaketh the Lords.
t Meaning, the Chaldeans.
u That is, Cyrus, who shal do all thing in my Name, & by my direction: whereby he meaneth that both their captiuitie, and deliuerance shal be ordered by Gods prouidēce and appointement.
x Bothe of the Chaldeans and others.
y Meaning, ȳ none of the gētiles gods can worke anie of these things.
z That is, ȳ Israelites, which returne from ȳ captiuitie.
a To wit, a continual succession of Prophetes & ministers
b Whē I loked whether ȳ idoles colde do these things, I fōde that they had nether wisdome nor power to do anie thing: therefore he concludeth that all are wicked, that trust in suche vanitie.

CHAP. XLII.

1 The obedience and humilitie of Christ. 6 Why he was sent into the worlde. 11 The vocation of the Gentiles.

1 Beholde, [a] my seruant: [b] I wil stay vpon
him: mine elect, *in whome* my soule [c] deliteth: I haue put my Spirit vpon him: he
shal bring forthe [d] iudgement to the Gentiles.
2 He shal not [e] crye, nor lift vp, nor cause
his voyce to be heard in the strete.
3 A [f] bruised rede shal he not breake, and
the smoking [g] flax shal he not quenche: he
shal bring forthe iudgement in [h] trueth.
4 He shal not faile nor be discouraged til
he haue [i] set iudgement in the earth: and
the [k] yles shal wait for his law.
5 Thus saith God the Lord (he that crea
ted the heauens and spred them abrode:
he that stretched forthe the earth, and the
buddes thereof: he that giueth breth vn
to the people vpon it, and spirit to them
that walke therein)
6 I the Lord haue called thee in [l] righteous
nes, and wil holde [m] thine hand, and I wil
kepe thee, and giue thee for a [n] couenant
of the people, & for a light of the Gentiles,
7 That thou maiest open the eies of the
blinde, & brīg out the prisoners from the
prison: and them that sit in darkenes, out
of the prison house.
8 I am the Lord, this is my Name, and my
[o] glorie wil I not giue to another, nether
my praise to grauen images.
9 Beholde, the former things are [p] come to
passe, and newe things do I declare: before
they come forthe, I tel you of them.
10 Sing vnto the Lord a newe song, & his
praise from the end of the earth: ye that
go downe to the sea, and all that is therein:
the yles and the inhabitants thereof.
11 Let the wildernes and the cities thereof
lift vp *their voice*, the townes that [q] Kedár

a That is, Christ, who in respect of his mahode is called here seruant The Prophetes vse to make mencion of Christ after that thei haue declared anie great promes, because he is the fundacion whereupon all the promises are made & ratified
b For I haue committed all my power to him, as to a moste faithful steward Some read, I wil establish him: to wit, in his office, by giuing him the fulnes of my Spirit.
c He onely is acceptable vnto me & they that come vnto me by him. for there is no nother meanes of reconciliatiō, Mat. 12, 18. eph. 1, 4.
d He shal declare him self gouernour ouer the Gentils, & call them by his worde and rule them by his Spirit
e His cōming shal not be ẘ pompe and noise, as earthlie princes.
f He wil not hurt the weake and feble, but support & comfort them
g Meaning the weke of a lampe, or candel which is almost out, but he wil cherish it and snoffe it, that it may shine brighter.
h Althogh he fauour the weake yet wil he not spare the wicked, but wil iudge them according to trueth and equitie.
i Til he haue set all things in good order
k The Gentiles shalbe desirous to receiue his doctrine.
l Meaning, vnto a lawful and iust vocation.
m To assist and guide thee.
n As him, by whome the promise, made to all nations in Abrahám, shal be fulfilled
o I wil not suffer my glorie to be diminished: which I shuld do, if I were not faithful in performing the same, and the idolaters thereby wolde extol their idoles aboue me.
p As in time past I haue bene true in my promises, so wil I be in time to come.
q Meaning the Arabians, vnder whome he comprehendeth all the people of the East.

doeth inhabite: let the inhabitants of the
rockes sing: let them shoute from the top
of the mountaines.
12 Let them giue glorie vnto the Lord, &
declare his praise in the ylandes.
13 The Lord shal go forthe as a [r] gyant: he
shal stirre vp *his* courage like a mã of warre: he shal shoute and crye, & shal preuaile against his enemies.
14 I haue a long time holden my peace: I
haue bene stil & refrained my self: *now*
wil I crye like a [s] trauailing woman: I wil
destroye and deuoure at once.
15 I wil make waste mountaines, and hilles,
and drye vp all their herbes, and I wil make the floods ylandes, and I wil drye vp
the pooles.
16 ¶And I wil bring the [t] blinde by a way,
that they knew not, & leade them by paths
that they haue not knowen: I wil make
darknes light before them, and croked
things streight. These things wil I do vnto them, and not forsake them.
17 They shalbe turned backe: they shalbe
greatly ashamed, that trust in grauẽ images, and say to the molten images, Ye are
our gods.
18 ¶Heare, ye deafe: and ye blinde, regarde,
that ye may se.
19 Who is blinde but my [u] seruant? or deafe as my [x] messenger, that I sent? who is
blinde as the [y] perfite, and blinde as the
Lords seruant?
20 Seig manie things, but thou kepest them
not? opening the eares, but he heareth not?
21 The Lord is willing for his righteousnes sake *that* he may magnifie the Law, &
exalt it.
22 But this people is [z] robbed and spoiled,
and shalbe all snared in dongeons, & they
shalbe hid in prison houses: thei shalbe for
a pray, and none shal deliuer: a spoile, and
none shal say, [a] Restore.
23 Who amõg you shal hearken to [a] this, &
take hede, and heare for [b] afterwardes?
24 Who gaue Iaakób for a spoile, and Israél to the robbers? Did not the Lord, because we haue sinned against him? for they
wolde not walke in his wayes, nether be
obedient vnto his Law.
25 Therefore he hathe powred vpon him
his fierce wrath, and the strength of battel:
and it set him on fyre round about, and he
knewe not, and it burned him vp, yet he cõsidered not.

r He sheweth the zeale of ŷ Lord, and his power in the conseruatiõ of his Church.
s I wil haste to execute my vengeance, ŵ I haue so long differred, as a woman that desireth to be deliuered whẽ she is in trauail.
t That is, my poore people, which are in perplexitie & care.
u To wit, Israél, ŵ shulde haue moste light because of my Law.
x The Priest to whome my worde is cõmitted, which shulde not onely heare it him self, but cause others to heare it.
y As ŷ Priests & Prophetes that shulde be lights to others.
z Because thei wil not acknowledge this benefite of the Lord, who is ready to deliuer them, he suffreth them to be spoiled of their enemies through their owne faute and incredulitie.
a There shalbe none to succour them, or to wil the enemie to restore that, ŵ he hathe spoiled.
b Meaning, Gods wrath.

CHAP. XLIII.

3 The Lord comforteth his people. He promiseth deliuerance to the Iewes. 11 There is no God but one alone.

1 BVt now thus saith the Lord, [a] that
created thee, ô Iaakób: and he that
formed thee, ô Israél, [b] Feare not: for I haue redemed thee: I haue called thee by thy
name, thou art mine.
2 When thou passest through the [c] waters,
I wil be with thee, & through the floods,
that thei do not ouerflowe thee. When
thou walkest through the verie fyre, thou
shalt not be burnt, nether shal the flame
kindle vpon thee.
3 For I am the Lord thy God, the holy
one of Israél, thy Sauiour: I gaue [d] E-
gypt for thy ransome, Ethiopia, and Sebá
for thee.
4 Because thou wast precious in my sight,
& thou wast honorable, and I loued thee,
therefore wil I giue [e] man for thee, & people for thy sake.
5 Feare not, for I am with thee: I wil bring
thy sede from the [f] East, and gather thee
from the West.
6 I wil saie to the North, Giue: and to the
South, Kepe not backe: bring my sonnes
from farre, and my daughters from the endes of the earth.
7 Euerie one shalbe called by my [g] Name:
for I created him for my glorie, formed
him and made him.
8 I wil bring forthe the blinde people, and
thei shal haue eyes, and the deafe, & they
shal haue eares.
9 Let all the nacions be gathered [h] together, and let the people be assembled:
who among them can declare this and
shewe vs former things? let them bring
forthe their [i] witnesses, ŷ thei maie be iustified: but let them [k] heare, and saie, It *is*
trueth.
10 You [l] are my witnesses, saith the Lord,
and my [m] seruant, whome I haue chosen:
therefore ye shal knowe and beleue me &
ye shal vnderstand that I am: before me
there was no God formed, nether shal
there be after me.
11 I, *euen* I, am the Lord, & beside me there
is no Sauiour.
12 I haue declared, and I haue saued, and
I haue shewed, when there was no
strange *god* among you: therefore you are
my witnesses, saith the Lord, that I am
God.
13 Yea, before the day *was*, I am, and there
is none that can deliuer out of mine hãd:
I wil do it, and who shal let it?
14 Thus saith the Lord your redemer, the
holy one of Israél, For your sake I haue
sent to Babél, and [n] broght it downe: they
are all fugitiues and the Chaldeans crye
in [o] the shippes.
15 I am the Lord your holy one, the creator
of Israél, your King.

a After these threatnings he promiseth deliuerance to his Church, because he hathe regenerate them, adopted them & called them.
b When thou seest dangers and conspiracies on all sides, remember this benefite and the loue of thy God, and it shal encourage thee.
c By water & fyre, he meaneth all kinds of troubles and perils.
d I turned Saneheribs power against these countreies and made thẽ to suffer that afflictiõ which thou shuldest haue done, and so were as the payment of thy ransome, Cha. 37,9.
e I wil not spare anie man rather then thou shuldest perish: for God more estemeth one of his faithful, then all the wicked in the worlde.
f He propheciet of their deliuerance from the captiuitie of Babylon, and so of the calling of the vniuersal Church, alluding to that which is writen Deut 30,3.
g Meaning, that he colde not be vnmindful of them, except he wolde neglect his owne Name & glorie.
h Signifying, that no power can resist him in doing this miraculous worke, nor all their idoles are able to do the like, as Chap. 41,22.
i To proue that the things, which are spoken of them, are true.
k Shewing, that the malice of the wicked hindereth them, in the knowledge of the trueth because thei wil not heare when God speaketh by his worde.
l The Prophetes and people to whome I haue giuen my Law.
m Meaning, specially Christ and by him, all ŷ faithful.
n By Darius and Cyrus.
o Thei shal crye when thei wolde escape by water, seing ŷ the course of Euphrates is turned another way by ŷ enemie.

16 Thus saith the Lord which maketh a
way in p the Sea, and a path in the mightie q waters.
17 When he r bringeth out the ſ charet, &
horse, the armie & the power lie together,
& shal not rise: thei are extinct, and quenched as towe.
18 Remember ye not the former things, nether regarde the things of olde.
19 Beholde, I do a newe thing: nowe shal it
come forthe: shal you not knowe it? I wil
euē make awaie in the t desert & floods in
the wildernes.
20 The wilde u beasts shal honour me, the
dragons and the ostriches, because I gaue
water in the desert & floods in the wilder
nes to giue drinke to my people, euen to
mine elect.
21 This people haue I formed for my self:
thei shal shewe forthe my praise.
22 And thou hast not x called vpō me, ô Iaakób, but thou hast y wearied me, ô Israél.
23 Thou z hast not broght me the shepe of
thy burntoffrings, nether hast thou honored me with thy sacrifices. I haue not caused thee to serue with an offring, nor wearied thee with incense.
24 Thou boghtest me no swete a sauour wt
monie, nether hast thou made me drunke
with the fatte of thy sacrifices, but thou
hast made me b to serue with thy sinnes, &
wearied me with thine iniquities.
25 I, *euen* I, am he that putteth awaie thine
iniquities for mine owne sake, & wil not
remember thy sinnes.
26 Put me in c remembrance: let vs be iudged together: count thou that thou maiest
be iustified.
27 Thy d first father hathe sinned, and thy
e teachers haue transgressed against me.
28 Therefore I haue f prophaned the rulers
of the Sanctuarie, and haue made Iaakób
a curse, and Israél a reproche.

p When he deliuered Israél from Pharaóh, Exod.14,22. q When the Israelites passed through Iordén, Iosh.3,17. r Whē he deliuered his people out of Egypt. ſ Pharaóh & his mightie armie. t Meanīg, that their deliuerāce out of Babylón shulde be more famous then that from Egypt was, Ier.23,7. hag.2,10. 2.cor.5,17. reuel 21,5. u Thei shal haue suche abundance of all things as they returne home, euen in ye drye and baren places, that the verie beasts shal fele my benefites, & shal acknowledge thē: muche more mē oght to be thankeful for the same. x Thou hast not worshipped me as yu oghtest to haue done. y Because thou hast not willingly receiued that which I did commande thee, thou didest grieue me. Whereby he sheweth that his mercies were the onelie cause of their deliurāce, forasmuch as thei had deserued the cōtrary. z Meaning, in true faith & obedience. a Ether for ye composition of the swete ointement, Exod,30,34, or for the swete incense, Exod,30,7. b Thou hast made me to beare an heauie burden by thy sinnes. c If I forget anie thing that may make for thy iustification, put me in remembrance & speake for thy self. d Thine ancestres. e Thy Priests and thy Prophets. f That is, reiected, abhorred and destroied them in the wildernes, and at other times.

CHAP. XLIIII.

5 The Lord promiseth comfort and that he wil assemble his Church of diuers nations. 9 The Vanitie of idoles. 17 The beastlines of idolaters,

1 YEt now heare, ô Iaakób my seruant,
and Israél, whome I haue chosen.
2 Thus saith the Lord, that made thee, and
formed a thee from the wōbe: he wil helpe
thee. Feare not, ô Iaakób, my seruant, and
thou righteous, b whome I haue chosen.
3 For I wil powre water vpon c the thirstie,
& floods vpon the drie ground: I wil powre my Spirit vpon thy sede, and my blessing vpon thy buddes,
4 And thei d shal growe as among the grasse, & as the willowes by the riuer of waters.
5 One shal say, I am ye Lords: another e shal
be called by the name of Iaakób: & another shal subscribe with his hand vnto the
Lord, and name him self by the name of
Israél.
6 Thus saith the Lord the King of Israél
& his redemer, the Lord of hostes, f I am ye
first, and I am the last, and without me *is*
there no God.
7 And who is like me, that shal g call, and
shal declare it, and set h it in order before
me, since I appointed the i ancient people?
and what is at hand, and what things are to
come? let k them shewe vnto them.
8 Feare ye not, nether be afraied: haue not
I tolde thee of olde, and haue declared it?
l you are euen my witnesses, whether
there be a God beside me, and that there
is no God that I knowe not.
9 All thei that make an image, are vanitie, and m their delectable things shal nothing profite: & thei are their owne witnesses, n that thei se not nor knowe: therefore thei shalbe confounded.
10 Who hathe made o a god, or molten an
image, that is p profitable for nothing?
11 Beholde, all that are of the q felowship
thereof, shalbe cōfounded: for theworke-
men them selues are men: let them all
be gathered together, and r stand vp, *yet*
thei shal feare, and be confounded together.
12 The smith *taketh* an instrument, & worketh in the coles, and facioneth it with
hammers, & worketh it with the strength
of his armes: yea, he is an ſ hungred, & his
strength faileth: he drinketh no water, &
is faint.
13 The carpenter stretcheth out a line: he
facioneth it with a red thread, he planeth
it, and he purtreieth it with the compasse,
and maketh it after the figure of a man,
& according to the beautie of a man that
it maie remaine in t an house.
14 He wil hewe him downe cedres, and take the pine tre and the oke, and taketh
courage among the trees of the forest: he
planteth a fyrre tre, and the raine doeth
nourish it.
15 And man burneth thereof: for he wil

a He created & chose thee from the begīning of his owne mercie, & before yu coldest merite anie thing. b Whome God accepteth as righteous: or which hadest occasion thereunto because of the Law, and of thine holy vocation. c Because man of him self is as the drye and baren land, he promiseth to moisten him with the waters of his holy Spirit, Ioel.2,28. ioh.7,38. act.2,17.

d That is, thy children and posteritie shal increase wonderfully after their deliuerance from Babylon. e By this diuersitie of speche he meaneth one thing that is, that the people shalbe holy & receiue the true religion of God, as Psal.87,5. f I am alwaies like my self, that is, merciful toward my Church, and moste able to maīteine it, as chap. 41,4, & 48,12 reuel.1,17 & 22,13. g And appoint them that shal deliuer the Church. h That is, declare vnto me how I oght to procede herein. i God calleth the Israelites ancient, because he preferred them to all other in his eternal election. k Meaning, their idoles. l Read Chap.43,10. m Whatsoeuer thei bestowe vpon their idoles to make thē to seme glorious. n That is, the idolaters seing their idoles blīde, must nedes be witnesses of their owne blindenes, and feling that thei are not able to helpe them, must confesse that thei haue no power. o Meaning, that whatsoeuer is made by the hand of man, if it be estemed as God, is moste detestable. p Whereby appeareth their blasphemie, which call images the bokes of the laitie, seing that thei are not onely here called vnprofitable, but Chap.41,24 abominable: and Iere. calleth them the worke of errors, ier.10,15. Habak. a lying teacher.2,18. q That is, which by any way consent either to the making or worshipping, r Signifying, that the multitude shal not then saue the idolaters, when God wil take vengeance, although thei excuse them selues thereby among men. ſ He describeth the raging affection of the idolaters, which forget their owne necessities to set forthe their deuocion toward their idoles. t To place it in some Temple.

takē thereof and [u] warme hĩ ſelf: he alſo
kindleth it and baketh bread, yet he maketh a god, and worſhipeth it: he maketh it
an idole and boweth vnto it.
16 He burneth the halfe thereof euen in
the fyre, *&* vpon the halfe thereof he [x] eateth fleſh: he roſteth the roſte and is ſatiſfied: alſo he warmeth him ſelf and ſaith,
Aha, I am warme, I haue bene at the fyre.
17 And ỹ reſidue thereof he maketh a god,
euen his idole: he boweth vnto it and worſhipeth and praieth vnto it, and ſaith, De
liuer me: for thou art my god.
18 Thei haue not knowen, nor vnderſtand:
[y] for *God* hathe ſhut their eyes that thei can
not ſe, *and* their hearts, that thei can not vn
derſtand.
19 And none " conſidereth in his heart, nether *is* there knowledge nor vnderſtãdĩg
to ſaie, I haue burnt halfe of it, euẽ in the
fyre, & haue baked bread alſo vpon ỹ coles
thereof: I haue roſted fleſh, and eaten it, &
ſhal I make the reſidue thereof an abominacion? ſhal I bowe to the ſtocke of a
tre.
20 He fedeth [z] of aſhes: a ſeduced heart
hathe deceiued him, that he can not deliuer his ſoule, nor ſay, Is their not a lye in
my right hand?
21 [a] Remembre theſe (ô Iaakób and Iſraél)
for ỹ art my ſeruant: I haue formed thee:
thou art my ſeruãt: ô Iſraél forget me not.
22 I haue put awaie thy trãſgreſsions like a
cloude, and thy ſinnes, as a miſt: turne vnto me, for I haue redemed thee.
23 [b] Reioyce, ye heauens: for the Lord hathe
done it: ſhoute, ye lower partes of ỹ earth:
braſt forthe into praiſes, ye mountaines,
ô foreſt and euerie tre therein: for ỹ Lord
hathe redemed Iaakób and wilbe glorified in Iſraél.
24 Thus ſaith the Lord thy redemer & he
that formed thee from the wombe, I am
the Lord, that made all things, that ſpred
out the heauens alone, and ſtretched out
the earth by my ſelf.
25 I deſtroye the [c] tokens of the ſoothſaiers
and make them that coniecture, fooles, &
turne the wiſe men backward, and make
their knowledge fooliſhnes.
26 ¶ He confirmeth the worde of his [d] ſeruant and performeth the counſel of his
meſſengers, ſaying to Ieruſalém, Thou
ſhalt be inhabited: and to the cities of Iudáh, ye ſhalbe buylt vp, and I wil repaire
the decaied places thereof.
27 He ſaith to the [e] depe, Be drye and I wil
drye vp thy floods.
28 He ſaith to [f] Cyrus, *Thou art* my ſhepherd:
& he ſhal reforme all my deſire, ſayĩg alſo
to Ieruſalém, Thou ſhalt be buylt: and to
the Temple, Thy fundacion ſhalbe ſurely
laied.

u He ſetteth forth the obſtinacie and malice of the idolaters, ỽ thogh thei ſe by dailie experience ỹ their idoles are no better thẽ the reſt of ỹ matter whereof thei are made, yet thei refuſe the one parte & make a god of ỹ other, as the papiſts make their cake, god and the reſt of their idoles.

x That is, he ether maketh a table or trenchers.

y The Prophet giueth here an anſwer to all them that wonder how it is poſsible that anie ſhulde be ſo blinde to commit ſuch abomination, ſaying, ỹ God hathe blinded their eyes, and hardened their hearts.

" Ebr. turneth.

z He is abuſed as one ỹ wold eat aſhes, thinking to ſatiſfie his hungre.

a Shewing ỹ mans heart is moſt enclined to idolatrie, & therefore he warneth his people by theſe exãples, that thei ſhulde not cleaue to anie but to the liuing God whẽ thei ſhulde be among the idolaters

b He ſheweth that the worke of ỹ Lord toward his people ſhalbe ſo great that ỹ inſenſible creatures ſhalbe moued therewith.

c He armeth them againſt ỹ ſothe ſayers of Babylon, ỽ wolde haue borne them in hand, that thei knew by ỹ ſtarres that God wolde not deliuer them, and that Babylon ſhulde ſtand.

d Of Iſaiáh & the reſt of his Prophetes, ỽ did aſſure the Church of Gods fauour & deliuerance.

e He ſheweth that Gods worke ſhulde be no leſſe notable in this their deliuerance, then when he broght them out of Egypt through the Sea.

f To aſſure them of their deliuerance, he nameth the perſone, by whome it ſhulde be more then an hundreth yere before he was borne.

CHAP. XLV.

1 The deliuerance of the people by Cyrus. 9 God is iuſt in all his workes. 20 The calling of the Gentiles.

1 THus ſaith the Lord vnto [a] Cyrus his
[b] anointed, whoſe right hand I haue
holden [c] to ſubdue nations before him:
therefore wil I weakẽ the loynes of Kĩgs
and open the dores before him, & the gates ſhal not be ſhut.
2 I wil go before thee & make ỹ [d] croked
ſtreight: I wil breake the braſen dores, &
burſt the yron barres.
3 And I wil giue thee ỹ treaſures of darkenes, and the things hid in ſecret places,
that thou maiſt [e] knowe that I am the
Lord which call thee by thy name, euen
the God of Iſraél.
4 For Iaakób my ſeruants [f] ſake, and Iſraél
mine elect, I wil euẽ call *thee* by thy name
& name thee, thogh thou haſt not knowen
me.
5 I am the Lord and there is none other:
there is no God beſides me: I [g] girded thee
thogh thou haſt not knowen me,
6 That thei maie knowe from the riſing of
the ſunne & from the Weſt, that there is
none beſides me. I am the Lord, and there
is none other.
7 I forme the [h] light and creat darkenes: I
make peace & creat euil: I the Lord do all
theſe things.
8 Ye heauens, ſend the dewe from aboue, &
let ỹ cloudes drop downe [i] righteouſnes:
let the earth open, and let ſaluacion and
iuſtice growe forthe: let it bring them
forthe together: I the Lord haue [k] created
him.
9 [l] Wo be vnto him that ſtriueth with his
maker, the potſherd ỽ the potſherds of the
earth: ſhal the claie ſaie to him that facioneth it, What makeſt ỹ? or thy worke, [m] it
hathe none hands?
10 Wo vnto him that ſaith to *his* father,
What haſt thou begotten? or to *his* mother, What haſt thou broght forthe?
11 Thus ſaith the Lord, the holy one of Iſraél, and his maker, Aſke me [n] of things
to come concerning my ſonnes, and concerning the workes of mine hands: commande you me.
12 I haue made the earth, and created man
vpon it: I, whoſe hands haue ſpred out

a To aſſure ỹ Iewes of their deliuerãce againſt ỹ great tentations that thei ſhulde abide, he nameth ỹ perſone and ỹ meanes.

b Becauſe Cyrus ſhulde execute ỹ office of a deliuerer, God called hĩ his anointed for a time, but after another ſort thẽ he called Dauid.

c To guide hĩ in ỹ deliuerance of my people

d I wil take away all impediments and lettes.

e Not that Cyrus did knowe God to worſhip hĩaright, but he had a certeine particular knowledge, as profane men may haue, of his power, & ſo was compelled to deliuer Gods people.

f Not for anie thing, that is in thee, or for thy worthines.

g I haue giuen thee ſtrength, power & autoritie.

h I ſend peace and warre, pſperitie & aduerſitie, as Amos 3,6.

i He comforteth the Iewes as if he wolde ſay, thogh whẽ ye loke to the heauens and earth for ſuccour, ye ſe nothing now but ſignes of Gods wrath, yet I wil cauſe thẽ to bring forth moſte certeine tokens of your deliuerance, & of the performance of my promes, which is mẽt by righteouſnes.

k I haue appointed Cyrus to this vſe & purpoſe.

l Hereby he brideleth their impaciencie, which in aduerſitie & trouble murmure againſt God and wil not tarie his pleaſure: willing that man ſhulde matche with his like and not contend againſt God m That is, it is not perfitely made. n In ſtead of murmuring, humble your ſelues and aſke what ye wil for the conſolation of my children, and you ſhalbe ſure of it, as ye are of theſe things which are at your commandement. Some read it with an interrogation, and make it the application of the ſimilitude.

the heauens, I haue euen commanded all
their [o] armie.
13 I haue raised [p] him vp in righteouſnes, &
I wil direct all his waies: he ſhal buylde
my citie, and he ſhal let go my captiues,
not [q] for price nor reward, ſaith the Lord
of hoſtes.
14 Thus ſaith the Lord, The labour [r] of E-
gypt, and the marchandiſe of Ethiopia, &
of the Sabeans, men of ſtature ſhal come
vnto thee, and thei ſhalbe [ſ] thine: thei ſhal
followe thee, *and* ſhal go in chaines: they
ſhal fall downe before thee, and make ſupplicacion vnto thee, *ſaying*, Surely God is
in thee, and there *is* none other God beſides.
15 Verely thou, ô God, [t] hideſt thy ſelf, ô
God, the Sauiour of Iſraél.
16 All they ſhalbe aſhamed and alſo confounded: they ſhal go to confuſion together, that are the makers of images.
17 *But* Iſraél ſhalbe ſaued in the Lord, with
an euerlaſting ſaluacion: ye ſhal not be a-
ſhamed nor confounded worlde without
end.
18 For thus ſaith the Lord (that created
heauen, God him ſelf, that formed ẏ earth,
and made it: he that prepared it, he created
it not in vaine: he formed it to be [u] inhabited) I am the Lord, and there *is* none o-
ther.
19 I haue not ſpoken in ſecret, *nether* [x] in a
place of darkenes in the earth: I ſaid not
in vaine vnto ẏ ſede of Iaakób, Seke you
me: I the Lord do ſpeake righteouſnes, &
declare righteous things.
20 Aſſemble your ſelues, and come: drawe
nere together, [y] ye abiect of the Gentiles:
they haue no knowledge, that ſet vp the
wood of their idole, and pray vnto a god,
that can not ſaue them.
21 Tel ye and bring them, & let them take
counſel together, who hathe declared this
from the beginning? *or* hathe tolde it of
olde? Haue not I the Lord? & there *is* none
other God beſide me, a iuſt God, & a Sauiour: there *is* none beſide me.
22 Loke vnto me, and ye ſhal be ſaued: all
[z] the ends of the earth ſhal be ſaued: for I
am God, and there *is* none other.
23 I haue ſworne by my ſelf: the worde is
gone out of my mouth in [a] righteouſnes,
and ſhal not returne, That euerie [b] knee
ſhal bowe vnto me, *and* euerie tongue ſhal
ſweare *by me*.
24 Surely [c] he ſhal ſay, In the Lord haue I
righteouſnes and ſtrength: he ſhal come
vnto him, and all that [d] prouoke him, ſhal
be aſhamed.
25 The whole ſede of Iſraél ſhalbe iuſtified, and glorie in the Lord.

o That is, the ſtarres. p To wit, Cyrus, that I may ſhewe by him ẏ faithfulnes of my promes in deliuering my people. q Meaning, frely & without ranſome, or any grieuous condicion. r Theſe people were tributaries to ẏ Perſians, & ſo Kīg Artahſhaſtte gaue this money towarde the buylding of the Tēple, Ezra.7,21. ſ Where as to fore thei were thine enemies, thei ſhal now honour thee, and thou ſhalt rule them: ẇ was accompliſhed in the time of Chriſt. t Hereby he exhorteth the Iewes to paciencie, thogh their deliuerāce be differred for a time: ſhewing that they ſhulde not repēt their long pacience, but ẏ wicked and idolaters ſhalbe deſtroied. u To wit, of mā, but chiefly of his Church. x As do the falſe gods, ẇ giue vncerteine anſwers. y All ye idolaters, which thogh you ſeme to haue neuer ſo muche worldelie dignitie, yet in Gods ſight you are vile & abiect. z He calleth the idolaters to repentance, willing them to loke vnto him with the eye of faith. a That is, that ẏ thing, which I haue promiſed, ſhalbe faithfully performed. b The knowledge of God and the true worſhiping ſhalbe through all the world, Rom 14,11. phil.2,10. whereby he ſignifieth that we muſt not onely ſerue God in heart, but declare the ſame alſo by outward profeſſiō. c Meaning, the faithful ſhal fele & confeſſe this. d All the cōtemners of God.

CHAP. XLVI.

1 The deſtruction of Babylon and of their idoles. 3 He calleth the Iewes to the conſideracion of his workes.

1 BEl is bowed downe: [a] Nebó is fallen:
their idoles were vpon the [b] beaſtes,
and vpon the cattel: they which did beare
you, *were* laden with a wearie burden.
2 [c] They are bowed downe, & fallen together: for thei colde not rid thē of the burden, & their [d] ſoule is gone into captiuitie.
3 Heare ye me, ô houſe of Iaakób, & all that
remaine of the houſe of Iſraél, which are
[e] borne of me *from* the wombe, and broght
vp of me *from* the birth.
4 Therefore vnto olde age, I the ſame, euē
I wil beare you vntil the hore heeres: I haue made *you*: I wil alſo beare *you*, and I wil
carye you [f] and I wil deliuer *you*.
5 ¶ To whome wil ye make me like, or make me equal, or [g] compare me, that I ſhulde be like him?
6 They drawe golde out of the bagge and
weigh ſiluer in the balance, *and* hyre a
goldſmith to make a god of it, & they
bowe downe, and worſhip it.
7 They beare it vpon the ſhoulders: they
cary him and ſet him in his place: ſo doeth
he ſtand, & can not remoue from his place. Thogh one crye vnto him, yet can he
not anſwer, nor deliuer him out of his tribulacion.
8 Remember this, and be aſhamed: bring it
againe [h] to minde, ô you tranſgreſſers.
9 Remember the former things of olde: for
I am God, and there *is* none other God,
and there *is* nothing like me,
10 Which declare the laſt thing from the
beginning: and from of olde, the things
that were not done, ſaying, My coūſel ſhal
ſtand, & I wil do whatſoeuer I wil.
11 I call a [i] birde from the Eaſt, & the man
of my [k] counſel from far: as I haue ſpoken,
ſo wil I bring it to paſſe: I haue purpoſed
it, and I wil do it.
12 Heare me, ye ſtubburne hearted, that are
farre from [l] iuſtice.
13 I bring [m] nere my iuſtice: it ſhal not be
farre of, and my ſaluacion ſhal not tary:
for I wil giue ſaluacion in Zión, *and* my
glorie vnto Iſraél.

a Theſe were the chief idoles of Babylō. b Becauſe thei were of golde and ſiluer, the Medes & Perſians caryed them away. c The beaſts that caryed ẏ idoles, fel downe vnder their burden. d He derideth the idoles, ẇ had nether ſoule nor ſenſe. e He ſheweth the difference betwene the idoles and the true God: for thei muſt be caryed of others, but God him ſelf caryeth his, as Deut.32,11. f Seing I haue begotten you, I wil nouriſh and preſerue you for euer. g The people of God, ſeing their owne calamitie & the floriſhing eſtate of the Babyloniās, ſhulde be tempted to thinke that their God was not ſo mightie as the idoles of their enemies: therefore he deſcribeth the original of all the idoles, to make them to be abhorred of all men: ſhewing that the moſte that can be ſpoken in their cōmendaciō is but to ꝑue them vile, Bar.6,25. h Become wiſe, meaning ẏ all idolaters are without wit or ſenſe, like mad mē. i That is, Cyrus, which ſhal come, as ſwift as a birde and fight againſt Babylon. k Him by whome I haue appointed to execute that, which I haue determined. l Which by your incredulitie wolde let the performance of my promes. m He ſheweth that mans incredulitie can not aboliſh the promes of God, Rom.3,3.

CHAP. XLVII.

The deſtruction of Babylon and the cauſes wherefore.

1 COme downe and ſit in the duſt: ô
[a] virgine, daughter Babél, ſit on the
grounde: there is no [b] throne, ô daughter
of the Chaldeans: for thou ſhalt no more
be called, Tendre and delicate.
2 Take the mille ſtones, & [c] grinde meale:

a Which haſt liued in wealth, & wantōnes, and haſt not yet bene ouercome by any enemie. b Thy gouernement ſhalbe taken from thee. c Thou ſhalt be broght to moſte vile ſeruitude: for to turne the mille was the office of ſlaues.

loose thy lockes: [d] make bare the fete: vncouer ẏ legge, & passe through the floods.
3 Thy filthines shalbe discouered, and thy
shame shalbe sene: I wil take vengeance,
and I wil not mete *thee as* a [e] man.
4 [f] Our redemer, the Lord of hostes *is* his
Name, the holy one of Israél.
5 [g] Sit stil, and get thee into darkenes, ô
daughter of the Chaldeans: for thou shalt
no more be called, The ladie of kingdomes.
6 I was wrath with my people: I haue polluted mine inheritance, and giuen them
into thine hand: thou didest shewe them
no [h] mercie, but thou didest lay thy very
heauie yoke vpon the ancient.
7 And thou saidest, I shalbe a ladie for e-
uer, so that thou didest not set thy minde
to these things, nether didest thou remember the latter end thereof.
8 Therefore now heare, thou that art giuen
to pleasures, & dwellest careles, She saith
in her heart, I am and none els: I shal not
sit *as* a widdow, nether shal knowe ẏ losse
of children.
9 But these two things shal come to thee
suddenly on one day, the losse of children
and widdowehead: they shal come vpon
thee in their [i] perfection, for the multitude
of thy diuinacions, & for the great abundance of thine inchanters.
10 For thou hast trusted in thy wickednes:
thou hast said, None seeth me. Thy [k] wisdome & thy knowledge, thei haue caused
thee to rebell, and thou hast said in thine
heart, I am, and none els.
11 Therefore shal euil come vpon thee, and
thou shalt not know the morning thereof:
destruction shal fall vpō thee, which thou
shalt not be able to put away: destruction
shal come vpon thee suddenly, or thou beware.
12 Stand now among thine inchanters, and
in the multitude of thy sothesayers (with
whome thou hast [l] wearied thy self from
thy youth) if so be thou maiest haue profite, *or* if so be thou maiest haue strength.
13 Thou art wearied in the multitude of
thy counsels: let now the astrologers, the
starre gasers, & pronosticatours stand vp,
and saue thee from these things, that shal
come vpon thee.
14 Beholde, they shalbe as stubble: the fyre
shal burne them: thei shal not deliuer their
owne liues from the power of the flame:
there *shal be* no coles [m] to warme at, *nor*
light to sit by.
15 Thus shal they serue thee, with whome
thou hast wearied thee, *euē* thy marchants
from thy youth: euery one shal wander to
his owne [n] quarter: none shal saue thee.

d The things wherin she setteth her greatest pride shal be made vile, euen from the head to the fote.
e I wil vse no humanitie nor pitie toward thee.
f The Israelites shal confesse, that the Lord doeth this for his Church sake.
g For very shame, & hide thy self.
h Thei abused Gods iudgements thinkīg that he punished ẏ Israelites, because he wolde vtterly cast them of, and therefore in stead of pitying their miserie, thou didist increase it.
i So that thy punishment shalbe so great, as is possible to be imagined.
k Thou didest thinke ẏ thine owne wisdome & policie wolde haue saued thee.
l He derideth their vaine cōfidence, ẏ put their trust in any thing, but in God, condēnig also suche vaine sciēces, which serue to no vse, but to delude the people and to bring them frō depending onely in God
m They shal vtterly perish and no parte of thē remaine.
n They shal flee euery one to that place, wh he thoght by his speculacions to be moste sure: but that shal deceiue them.

CHAP. XLVIII.

1 The hypocrisie of the Iewes is reproued. 11 The Lord alone wil be worshipped. 20 Of their deliuerance out of Babylon.

1 Heare ye this, ô house of Iaakób,
which are [a] called by the name of
Israél, and are come out of [b] the waters of
Iudáh: which sweare by the Name of the
Lord, and make mencion of the God of
Israél, *but* not in trueth, nor in righteousnes.
2 For they are called of the holy citie, and
staie them selues [c] vpon the God of Israél, whose Name *is* the Lord of hostes.
3 I haue declared the former things of olde, and they went out of my mouth, and I
shewed [d] them: I did them suddenly, and
they came to passe.
4 Because I knewe, that [e] thou art obstinate, and thy necke *is* an yron sinew, and thy
browe brasse,
5 Therefore I haue declared it to thee of
olde: before it came to passe, I shewed [f] it
thee, lest thou shuldest say, Mine idole
hathe done them, and my carued image,
and my molten image hathe commanded
them.
6 Thou hast heard, beholde all this, & wil
not ye [g] declare it? I haue shewed thee new
things, euen now, and hid things, which
thou knewest not.
7 They are created now, and not of olde,
and euen before this thou heardest them
not, lest ẏ shuldest say, Beholde, I [h] knewe
them.
8 Yet thou heardest thē not, nether didest
knowe them, nether yet was thine eare o-
pened of olde: for I knewe that thou woldest grieuously transgress: therefore haue I called thee a transgressour from the
[i] wombe.
9 For my Names sake wil I differ my
wrath, and for my praise wil I refraine it
from thee, [k] that I cut thee not of.
10 Beholde, I haue fined thee, but [l] not as
siluer: I haue [m] chosen thee in the fornace
of affliction.
11 For mine owne sake, for mine owne sake
wil I do it: for how shulde *my Name* [n] be
polluted? [o] surely I wil not giue my glorie
vnto another.
12 Heare me, ô Iaakób & Israél, my called,
[p] I am, I am the first, and I am the last.
13 Surely mine hād hathe layed the fundacion of the earth, & my right hand hathe
spanned the heauens: when I call them,
[q] they stand vp together.
14 All you, assemble your selues, & heare:
which among them hathe declared these
things? The Lord hathe loued [r] him: he wil

a He detecteth their hypocrisie, which vaunted them selues to be Israelites & were not so in dede.
b Meaning, the fountaine and stocke
c They make a shew, as thogh they wolde haue none other God
d He sheweth that thei colde not accuse him in anie thing, for asmuche as he hadperformed whatsoeuer he had promised.
e I haue done for thee more then I promised, that thy stubbernes and impudencie might haue bene ouercome.
f How ẏ shuldest be deliuered out of Babylon.
g Wil he not acknowledge this my benefite & declare it vnto others?
h Shewing ẏ mans arrogancie is the cause why God doeth not declare all thigs at once, lest thei shuld attribute this knowledge to their owne wisdome.
i From ẏ time that I broght thee out of Egypt: for that deliuerance was as ẏ birth of the Church.
k As it was my fre mercie ẏ I did chuse thee: so is it my fre mercie that must saue thee.
l For I had respect to thy weakenes and infirmitie: for in siluer there is some purenes, but in vs there is nothing, but drosse.
m I toke thee out of the fornace where thou shuldest haue bene consumed
n God ioyneth the saluacion of his with his owne honour: so that they can not perish, but his glorie shulde be diminished, as Deut.32,27.
o Read Chap.42,8
p Read 41,4
q To obey me, & to do whatsoeuer I commande them.
r Meaning, Cyrus, whome he had chosen to destroy Babylon.

do

do his wil in Babél, and his arme *shalbe* a-
gainst the Chaldeans.
15 I, *euen* I haue spoken it, and I haue called
him: I haue broght him, and his waie shal
prosper.
16 Come nere vnto me: heare ye this: I haue
not spoken it in secret frō the [s] beginning:
from the time that the thing was, I was
there, and now the Lord God and his spirit hathe [t] sent me.
17 Thus saith the Lord thy redemer, the
Holie one of Israél, I am the Lord thy
God, which teache thee [u] to profite, & lead
thee by the waie, that thou shuldest go.
18 Oh that thou hadest hearkened to my
commandements, then had thy prosperitie
bene as the flood, and thy righteousnes as
the waues of the sea.
19 Thy sede also had bene as the sande, and
ỹ frute of thy bodie like the grauel thereof: his [x] name shulde not haue bene cut of
nor destroied before me.
20 [y] Go ye out of Babél: flee ye from the
Chaldeans, with a voice of ioye: tel and de
clare this: shewe it forthe to the end of the
earth: saye ye, The Lord hathe redemed
his seruant Iaakób.
21 And thei [z] were not thirstie: he led them
through the wildernes: he caused ỹ waters
to flowe out of the rocke for them: for he
claue the rocke, and the water gushed out.
22 There is no [a] peace, saith the Lord, vnto
the wicked.

s Since the time that I declared my self to your fathers.
t Thus ỹ Prophet speaketh for him self, & to assure them of these thīgs.
u What things shal do thee good.
x That is, the prosperous estate of Israél.
y After that he had forewarned them of their captiuitie, and of the cause thereof, he sheweth them the great ioye, ỹ shal come of their deliuerance.
z He sheweth that it shalbe as easy to deliuer them, as he did their fathers out of Egypt
a Thus he speaketh that the wicked hypocrites shulde not abuse Gods promes in whome was nether faith, nor repentāce, as Chap. 57, 21.

CHAP. XLIX.

The Lord exhorteth all nacions to beleue his promises. 6 Christ is the saluacion of all that beleue, and wil deliuer them from the tyrannie of their enemies.

1 Heare ye me, ô yles, & hearkē, ye people frō farre. The Lord hathe called
[a] me from [b] the wombe, and made mencion
of my name from my mothers bellie.
2 And he hathe made my mouth like a
sharpe [c] sworde: vnder the shadowe of his
hād hathe he [d] hid me, and made me a chosen shafte & hid me in his quiuer,
3 And said vnto me, Thou art my seruant,
[e] Israél, for I wil be glorious in thee.
4 And I said, I haue [f] labored in vaine: I haue spent my strength in vaine and for nothing: but my iudgement *is* with the Lord,
and my worke with my God.
5 And now saith the Lord, that formed
me frō the wombe to be his seruant, that I
maie bring Iaakób againe to him (thogh
Israél be not gathered, [g] yet shal I be glori
ous in the eyes of the Lord: and my God
shalbe my strength)
6 And he said, It is a smale thing that thou
shuldest be my seruant, to raise vp the tribes of Iaakób, and to restore the desolations of Israél: I wil also giue [h] thee for a
light of the Gentiles, that thou maiest be
my saluacion vnto the end of the worlde.
7 Thus saith the Lord the redemer of Israél, & his Holie one, to him that is despised in soule, to a nation that is abhorred,
to a [i] seruant of rulers, Kings shal se, and
[k] arise, and princes shal worship, because
of the Lord, that is faithful: and the Holie
one of Israél, which hathe chosen thee.
8 Thus saith the Lord, [l] In an acceptable
time haue I heard thee, and in a day of saluacion haue I helped thee: and I wil preserue thee, and wil giue [m] thee for a couenant of the people, that thou maiest raise
vp the [n] earth, and obteine the inheritance
of the desolate heritages:
9 That thou maiest say to ỹ [o] prisoners, Go
forthe: and to them that are in darkenes,
Shewe your selues: they shal fede in the
wayes, & their [p] pastures shalbe in all the
toppes of the hilles.
10 They shal not be hūgrie, nether shal thei
be thirstie, nether shal the heat smite thē
nor the sunne: for he that hathe compassion [q] on them, shal lead them: euen to the
springs of waters shal he driue them.
11 And I wil make all my mountaines, as a
way, & my paths shalbe exalted.
12 Beholde, these shal come frō farre: & lo,
these from the North and from the West,
and these from the land of [r] Sinim.
13 Reioyce, ô [s] heauens: and be ioyful, ô
earth: brast forthe in to praise, ô mountaines: for God hathe comforted his people,
& wil haue mercie vpon his afflicted.
14 But Zión said, The Lord hathe [t] forsa
ken me, and my Lord hathe forgottē me.
15 Can a woman forget her childe, and not
haue compassion on the sonne of her wōbe? thogh they shulde forget, yet wil I not
forget thee.
16 Beholde, I haue grauē thee vpon the palme of *mine* [u] hands: thy [x] walles *are* euer in
my sight.
17 Thy buylders make [y] haste: thy destroyers and they that made thee waste, are departed from thee.
18 Lift vp thine eyes rounde about & beholde: all these gather thē selues together
& come to thee: as I liue, saith the Lord,
thou shalt surely [z] put thē all vpō thee as a
garmēt, & gird thy self wt thē like a bride.
19 For thy desolations, & thy waste places,
& thy land destroyed, shal surely be now
narrow for them ỹ shal dwell in it, & thei
that did deuoure thee, shalbe farre away.
20 The children of thy barennes shal say
againe in thine eares, The place is straict
for me: giue place to me that I may dwell.
21 Thē shalt ỹ say in thine heart, Who hathe
begotten me these, seing I am baren and

a This is spoken in the persone of Christ to assure the faithful, that these promises shulde come to passe: for they were all made in him, and in him shulde be performed.
b This is mēt of the time, ỹ Christ shulde be manifested to the worlde, as Psal 2, 7.
c By the sworde, and shafte, he signifieth ỹ vertue and efficacie of Christs doctrine
d God hathe takē me to his protection and defence: this chiefly is mēt of Christ, and may also be applied to ỹ ministers of his worde.
e By Israél is mēt Christ, & all the body of ỹ faithful as the members and their head.
f Thus Christ in his members complaineth, that his labour, and preaching take none effect, yet he is contented, ỹ his doings are approued of God.
g Thogh the Iewes refuse my doctrine, yet God wil approue my ministerie.

h To declare my Gospel to the Gentiles, Cha. 42, 6. act. 13, 47. luk. 2, 31.
i Meaning, the Iewes whome tyrants kept in bondage.
k The benefit of their deliuerance shalbe so great, that great, & smale shal acknowledge it, & reuerēce God for it
l Thus he speaketh of his Church, when he wolde shew his mercie toward it, 2. Cor. 6, 2.
m Meaning, Christ alone.
n Signifying, ỹ before Christ renue ỹ earth by his worde, there is nothing, but cōfusiō & disorder.
o To thē that are in the prison of sinne, & death.
p Being in Christs protection, they shal be safe against all dangers, & fre from the feare of the enemies.
q Meaning, ỹ there shulde be nothīg in their way from Babylon, ỹ shulde hinder or hurt them: but this is accomplished spiritually.
r Meaning, ỹ South coūtrey, so that Christ shal deliuer his from all the partes of the worlde.
s Read Chap. 44, 23.
t He obiecteth what ỹ faithful might say in their long affliction, and answereth thereunto to comfort them, with a moste proper similitude, and ful of consolatiō.
u Because I wolde not forget thee.
x Meaning, ỹ good order of policie & discipline.
y I haue a cōtinual care to buylde thee vp againe, & to destroye thine enemies.
z He sheweth what are the ornamēts of ỹ Church: to haue manie childrē, which are assembled by the worde of God & gouerned by his Spirit.

desolate, a captiue and a wanderer to and
fro? & who hathe nourished thẽ? beholde,
I was left alone: whence are these?
22 Thus saith the Lord God, Beholde, I wil
lift vp mine hand to the [a] Gentiles and set
vp my standart to the people, and they
shal bring thy sonnes in *their* armes: and
thy daughters shalbe caryed vpon *their*
shoulders.
23 And Kīgs [b] shalbe thy nourcing fathers,
and Quenes shalbe thy nources: thei shal
worship thee with *their* faces toward the
earth, and licke vp the [c] dust of thy fete: &
thou shalt knowe that I am the Lord: for
they shal not be ashamed ẏ waite for me.
24 Shal the praie be [d] taken from the mightie? or the iust captiuitie deliuered?
25 But thus saith the Lord, [e] Euen the captiuitie of the mightie shalbe taken awaie: &
the praie of the tyrant shalbe deliuered:
for I wil contend with him that conten-
deth with thee, & I wil saue thy children,
26 And wil fede them that spoile thee, with
[f] their owne flesh, and they shalbe drunken with their owne blood, as with swete
wine: & all flesh shal knowe that I ẏ Lord
am thy Sauiour & thy redemer, the mightie one of Iaakób.

a He sheweth, ẏ Christ wil not onely gather this great nõber of the Iewes, but also of the Gentiles
b Meaning, ẏ Kings shalbe cõuerted to ẏ Gospel and bestow their power, & autoritie for the preseruation of the Church.
c Being ioyned with the Church, they shal hũble thẽ selues to Christ their head, and giue him all honour.
d He maketh this as an obiectiõ, as thogh the Chaldeãs were strong, & had them in iuste possessiõ.
e This is, the answer to their obiectiõ, ẏ none is strõger then the Lord, nether hathe a more iuste title vnto them.
f I wil cause them to destroye one another, as Iud. 7, 22. 2 chro. 20, 22. chap. 19, 2.

CHAP. L.

1 The Iewes forsaken for a time. 2 Yet the power of God is not diminished. 5 Christs obediẽce & victorie.

1 THus saith the Lord, Where is that
[a] bil of your mothers diuorcement,
[b] whome I haue cast of? or who is the creditour [c] to whome I solde you? Beholde, for
your iniquities are ye solde, and because
of your transgressions is your mother forsaken.
2 Wherefore [d] came I, & there was no mã?
I called, and none answered: is mine hand
so [e] shortened, that it can not helpe? or haue
I no power to deliuer? beholde, at my rebuke I drye vp the Sea: I make the floods
desert: their fish rotteth for want of water, and dyeth for thirst.
3 I clothe the heauẽs with darknes, & make
a [f] sacke their couering.
4 The Lord God hathe giuen [g] me a tõgue
of the learned, that I shulde knowe *to minister* a worde in time to him ẏ is [h] weary:
he wil raise me vp in the morning: in the
morning he wil waken mine eare to heare,
[i] as the learned.
5 The Lord God hathe opened mine eare
and I was not rebellious, nether turned
I backe.

a Meaning, ẏ he had not forsaken her, but through her owne occasiõ, as Hosea. 2, 2.
b Which shulde declare, ẏ I haue cut her of: meaning, ẏ they colde shewe none.
c Signifying ẏ he solde them not for anie det or pouertie, but ẏ they solde thẽ selues to sinnes to bie their owne lustes, & pleasures.
d He came by his Prophetes and ministers, but thei wolde not beleue their doctrine and conuert.
e Am I not as able to helpe you, as I haue holpen your fathers of olde, when I dryed vp ẏ red Sea, and killed the fish in the riuers, & also afterwarde in Iorden?
f As I did in Egypt in tokẽ of my displeasure, Exod. 10, 21
g The Prophet doeth represente here the persone and charge of them that are iustely called to the ministerie of Gods worde.
h To him that is oppressed by affliction and miserie.
i As they that are taught, and made mete by him.

6 I gaue my backe vnto the [k] smiters, and
my chekes to the nippers: I hid not my
face from shame and spitting.
7 For the Lord God wil helpe me, therefore shal I not be confounded: therefore
haue I set my face like a flint, and I knowe
that I shal not be ashamed.
8 He is nere that iustifieth me: who wil cõtend with me? Let vs stand together: who
is mine aduersarie? let him come nere
to me.
9 Beholde, the Lord God wil helpe me:
who is he that can condemne me? lo, thei
shal waxe olde as a garment: the mothe
shal eat them vp.
10 [l] Who is amõg you that feareth ẏ Lord?
let him heare the voyce of his seruant: he
that walketh in darkenes, & hathe no light,
let him trust in the Name of the Lord, &
stay vpon his God.
11 Beholde, all you kindle [m] a fyre, and are
compassed about with sparkes: walke in ẏ
light of your fyre, and in the sparkes that
ye haue kindled. This shal ye haue of mine hand: ye shal lie downe in sorowe.

k I did not shrinke from God for anie persecution or calamitie. Whereby he sheweth, that the true ministers of God can loke for none other recompence of ẏ wicked but after this sorte and also what is their comfort.
l Shewing ẏ it is a rare thing that anie shulde obey aright Gods true ministers, thogh they labour to bring thẽ frõ hel to heauen.
m You haue soght consolation by your owne deuises, & haue refused the light, and consolation, ẇ God hathe offred: therefore ye shal remaine in sorowe, and not be cõforted.

CHAP. LI.

1 To trust in God alone by Abrahams example. 7 Not to feare men. 17 The great affliction of Ierusalém, & her deliuerance.

1 HEare me, ye [a] that follow after righteousnes, & ye that seke the Lord:
loke vnto the [b] rocke, *whence* ye are hewen,
and to the hole of the pit, *whence* ye are
digged.
2 Consider Abrahám your father, and Saráh that bare you: for I called him alone,
& blessed him, and increased him.
3 Surely the Lord shal comfort Zión: he
shal comfort all her desolations, and he
shal make her desert [c] like Eden, and her
wildernes like the garden of the Lord:
ioye and gladnes shalbe founde therein:
praise, and the voyce of singing.
4 Hearken ye vnto me, my people, and giue eare vnto me, ô my people: for a [d] Law
shal procede from me, and I wil bring forthe my iudgement for the light of the
people.
5 My [e] righteousnes is nere: my saluacion
goeth forthe, and mine [f] armes shal iudge
the people: the yles shal waite for me, and
shal trust vnto mine arme.
6 Lift vp your eyes to the heauens, and loke vpon the earth beneth: for the [g] heauens shal vanish away like smoke, and the
earth shal waxe olde like a garment, and
thei that dwell therein, shal perish in like
maner: but my saluacion shalbe for euer,
& my righteousnes shal not be abolished.
7 Hearken vnto me, ye that knowe righteousnes, the people in whose heart *is* my
Law. Feare ye not the reproche of men,
nether be ye afraied of their rebukes.

a He comforteth ẏ Church, that thei shulde not be discouraged for their smale nomber.
b That is, to Abrahám, of whome ye were begotten, & to Saráh, of whome ye were borne.
c As plẽtiful as Paradise, Genes. 2, 3.
d I wil rule, & gouerne my Church by my worde, and doctrine.
e The time, ẏ I wil accomplish my promes.
f My power, and strength.
g He forewarneth them of the horrible changes & mutations of all things, & how he wil preserue his Church in the middes of all these dangers.

8 For

8 For the mothe ſhal eat thē vp like a garment , and the worme ſhal eat them like
woll: but my righteouſnes ſhal be for euer,
and my ſaluacion from generacion to generacion.
9 Riſe vp, riſe vp, and put on ſtrength, ô arme of the Lord: riſe vp, as [h] in the olde time in the generacions of the worlde. Art
not thou the ſame, that haſt cut [i] Rahâb,
and wounded the [k] dragon?
10 Art not thou the ſame, which hath dryed
the Sea, *euen* the waters of the great depe,
making the depth of the Sea a way for the
redemed to paſſe ouer?
11 Therefore the redemed of the Lord ſhal
[l] returne, and come with ioye vnto Zión,
and euerlaſting ioye ſhalbe vpon their
head: they ſhal obteine ioye, & gladnes: &
ſorowe and mourning ſhal flee away.
12 I, *euen* I, am he, that comfort you. Who
art thou, that thou ſhuldeſt feare a mortal
man, and the ſonne of man, which ſhalbe
made as graſſe?
13 And forgeteſt the Lord thy maker, that
hathe ſpred out the heauens, and laide the
fundacions of the earth? and haſt feared
continually all the day, becauſe of the rage of the oppreſſour, which is ready to deſtroye? Where is now the rage of the oppreſſour?
14 The captiue [m] haſteneth to be looſed,
and that he ſhulde not dye in the pit, nor
that his bread ſhulde faile.
15 And I am the Lord thy God that diuided the Sea, when his waues roared: the
Lord of hoſtes *is* his Name.
16 And I haue put my wordes in thy [n] mouthe, and haue defended thee in the ſhadow
of mine hand, that I may plant ȳ [o] heauēs,
and laye the fundacion of the earth, & ſay
vnto Zión, Thou art my people.
17 Awake, awake, and ſtand vp, ô Ieruſalém,
which haſt drūke at the hand of the Lord
the [p] cup of his wrath: thou haſt drunken
the dregges of the cup of trembling, and
wrung them out.
18 There is none to guide her among all
ȳ ſonnes, whome ſhe hathe broght forthe:
there *is* none that taketh her by the hand of
all the ſonnes that ſhe hathe broght vp.
19 Theſe two [q] things are come vnto thee:
who wil lament thee? deſolation and deſtruction, and famine, and the ſworde: by
whome ſhal I comforte thee?
20 Thy ſonnes haue fainted, and lie at the
head of all the ſtretes as a wilde bulle in a
net, and are full of the wrath of the Lord,
& rebuke of thy God.
21 Therefore heare now this, thou miſerable and drunken, but [r] not with wine.
22 Thus ſaith thy Lord God, euen God
that pleadeth the cauſe of his people, Beholde, I haue taken out of thine hand the

h He putteth them in remēbrance of his great benefite for their deliuerance out of Egypt ȳ thereby they might learne to truſt in him conſtantly.
i Meaning Egypt. Pſal. 87,4.
k To wit, Pharaóh, Eze 29,3.
l From Babylon.
m He comforteth them by ȳ ſhort time of their baniſhement: for in ſeuentie yeres they were reſtored, and the greateſt empire of the worlde deſtroyed.
n Meaning, of Iſaiáh, and of all true miniſters, who are defended by his protection.
o That all things may be reſtored in heauen, and earth, Epheſ. 1,10.
p Thou haſt bene iuſtely puniſhed and ſufficiently, as Chap 40,2. and this puniſhement in the elect is by meaſure, & accordīg as God giueth grace to beare it: but in the reprobate it is ȳ iuſt vēgeance of God to driue them to an inſenſiblenes & madnes, as Ierem. 25,15.
q Whereof the one is outward, as of ȳ things ȳ come to ȳ body: as warre & famine: & ȳ other is inward, & aperteineth to, the mīde: that is, to be without comfort: therefore he ſaith, how ſhalt thou be comforted?
r But ŵ trouble & feare.

cuppe of trembling, *euen* the dregges of the
cuppe of my wrath: thou ſhalt drinke it no
more.
23 But I wil put it into their hād that ſpoile thee: which haue ſaid to thy ſoule, Bowe
downe, that we may go ouer, and thou haſt
laid thy bodie as the ground, and as the
ſtrete to them that went ouer.

CHAP. LII.

1 A conſolation to the people of God. 7 Of the meſſengers thereof.

1 ARiſe, ariſe: put on thy ſtrength, ô
Zión: put on the garments of thy
beautie, ô Ieruſalém, the holy citie:
for hence forthe there ſhal no [a] more come
into thee the vncircumciſed and the vncleane.
2 Shake thy ſelf from the [b] duſt: ariſe, and
ſit downe, ô Ieruſalém: looſe the bandes
of thy necke, ô thou captiue daughter,
Zión.
3 For thus ſaith the Lord, Ye were ſolde
for [c] naught: therefore ſhal ye be redemed
without money.
4 For thus ſaith the Lord God, My people
went [d] downe afore time into Egypt to ſo-
iourne there, and Aſſhúr [e] oppreſſed them
without cauſe.
5 Now therefore what haue I here, ſaith
the Lord, that my people is takē away for
naught, and thei that rule ouer them, make
them to howle, ſaith the Lord? & my Name all the day continually is [f] blaſphemed?
6 Therefore my people ſhal knowe my
Name: therefore *thei ſhal knowe* in that
day, that I am he that do ſpeake: beholde,
it is I.
7 How [g] beautiful vpon the mountaines are
the fete of him, that declareth & publiſheth peace? that declareth good tidings,
& publiſheth ſaluacion, ſaying vnto Zión, Thy God reigneth?
8 [h] The voice of thy watchmen *ſhalbe
heard*: thei ſhal lift vp their voyce, and
ſhout together: for thei ſhal ſe eye to eye,
when the Lord ſhal bring againe Zión.
9 O ye deſolate places of Ieruſalém, be
glad and reioyce together: for the Lord
hathe comforted his people: he hathe redemed Ieruſalém.
10 The Lord hathe made [i] bare his holy arme in the ſight of all the Gentiles, and all
the ends of the earth ſhal ſe the ſaluacion
of our God.
11 [k] Departe, departe ye: go out from thēce
and touche no vncleane thing: go out of
the middes of her: be ye cleane, that [l] beare
the veſſels of the Lord.

a No wicked tyrant, ŵ ſhal ſubuert Gods true religiō, & oppreſſe the conſciences.
b Put of ȳ garments of ſorowe & heauines, & put on the apparel of ioy & gladnes.
c The Babylonians paied nothīg to me for you: therefore I wil take you againe without ranſome.
d Whē Iaakób went thether in time of famine.
e The Egyptians might pretend ſome cauſe to oppreſſe my people becauſe thei wēt thether and remained among them, but the Aſſyrians haue no title to excuſe their tyrannie by: and therefore wil I puniſh them more thē I did the Egyptiās.
f To wit, by ȳ wicked, which thinke that I haue no power to deliuer thē.
g Signifying ȳ the ioye and good tidīgs of their deliuerance ſhulde make their affliction in the meane time more eaſy: but this is chiefly mēt of the ſpiritual ioy, as Nah. 1,15. rom. 10,35.
h The Prophets ŵ are thy watchmē, ſhal publiſh this thy deliuerance: this was begō vnder Zerubbabél, Ezrá & Nehemiáh, but was accōpliſhed vnder Chriſt.
i As ready to ſmite his enemies & to deliuer his people.
k He warneth the faithful not to pollute them ſelues with the ſuperſtitions of the Babylonians, as Chap. 48,20. 2. cor. 6,17.
l For the time is at hand, that the Prieſts and Leuites chiefly (and ſo by the all the people which ſhalbe as Leuites in this office) ſhal cary home the veſſels of the Temple, which Nebuchadnezzár had taken away.

12 For ye ſhal not go out [m] with haſte, nor
departe by fleing away: but the Lord wil
go before you, and the God of Iſraél wil
gather you together.
13 Beholde, my [n] ſeruant ſhal proſper: he
ſhalbe exalted and extolled, & be veryhie.
14 As manie were aſtonied at thee (his viſage was ſo [o] deformed of men, and his
forme of the ſonnes of men) ſo [p] ſhal he
ſprincle manie nations: the Kings ſhal
ſhut their [q] mouths at him: for that which
had not bene tolde them, ſhal they ſe,
and that which they had not heard, ſhal
they [r] vnderſtand.

m As your fathers did out of Egypt.
n Meaning, Chriſt by whome our ſpiritual deliuerãce ſhulde be wroght, whereof this was a figure.
o In the corrupt iudgement of man Chriſt in his perſone was not eſtemed.
p He ſhal ſpread his word through manie natiõs.
q In ſigne of reuerence, and as being aſtoniſhed at his excellencie.
r By the preaching of the Goſpel.

CHAP. LIII.

1 Of Chriſt and his kingdome, whoſe worde fewe wil beleue. 6 All men are ſinners. 11 Chriſt is our righteouſnes, 12 And is dead for our ſinnes.

1 WHo [a] wil beleue our report? and
to whome is the [b] arme of the
Lord reueiled?
2 But he ſhal growe vp before him as a
branche, & as a [c] roote out of a drye [d] grounde: he hathe nether forme nor beautie:
whẽ we ſhal ſe him, there ſhalbe no forme
that we ſhulde deſire him.
3 He is deſpiſed and reiected of mẽ: he is a
man ful of ſorows and hathe experience
of [e] infirmities: we hid as it were our faces
from him: he was diſpiſed and we eſtemed
him not.
4 Surely he hathe borne our infirmities, &
caried [f] our ſorowes: yet we did iudge hĩ,
as [g] plagued, and ſmitten of God, & humbled.
5 But he was wounded for our tranſgreſ-
ſions, he was broken for our iniquities: the
[h] chaſtiſemẽt of our peace *was* vpon him,
and with his ſtripes we are healed.
6 All we like ſhepe haue gone aſtraie: we haue turned euerie one to his owne way, and
the Lord hathe layed vpon him the [i] iniquitie of vs all.
7 He was oppreſſed & he was afflicted, yet
did he not [k] opẽ his mouth: he is broght as
a ſhepe to the ſlaughter, and as a ſhepe before her ſhearer is dumme, ſo he openeth
not his mouth.
8 He was taken out from [l] priſon, and frõ
iudgement: [m] & who ſhal declare his age?
for he was cut out of the lãd of the liuĩg:
for the tranſgreſsion of my people was he
plagued.
9 [n] And he made his graue with ẏ wicked,
and with the riche in his death, thogh he
had done no wickednes, nether *was* anie
deceite in his mouth.
10 Yet the Lord wolde breake him, & make him ſubiect to infirmities: whẽ [o] he ſhal
make his ſoule an offring for ſinne, he ſhal
ſe *his* ſede & ſhal prolong *his* daies, and the
wil of the Lord ſhal proſper in his hand.
11 He ſhal ſe of the [p] trauaile of his ſoule,
& ſhalbe ſatiſfied: by his knowledge ſhal
my [q] righteous ſeruant iuſtifie manie: for
he ſhal beare their iniquities.
12 Therefore wil I giue him a portion with
the great, and he ſhal deuide the ſpoyle
with the ſtrong, because he [r] hathe powred out his ſoule vnto death: and he was
counted with the tranſgreſſers, and he bare the ſinne [ſ] of many, and praied for the
treſpaſſers.

a The Prophet ſheweth, ẏ verie fewe ſhal receiue this their preaching of Chriſt, and of their deliuerãce by him, Ioh. 12,38 rom 10. 16.
b Meaning, ẏ none can beléue, but whoſe hearts God toucheth with the vertue of his holie Spirit.
c The beginning of Chriſts kingdome ſhalbe ſmale, and contemptible in ẏ ſight of man, but it ſhal growe wonderfully, and floriſh before God.
d Read Chap. 11,1.
e Which was by Gods ſingular prouidence for the comforte of ſinners, Ebr 4,15.
f That is, the puniſhement due to our ſinnes: for the ẇ he hathe both ſuffred, & made ſatiſfactiõ, Mat 8, 17, 1. pet.2,24.
g We iudged euil, thinking that he was puniſhed for his owne ſinnes, & not for ours.
h He was chaſtiſed for our reconciliation, 1.Cor. 15,3.
i Meaning, the puniſhement of our iniquitie, & not the faute it ſelf.
k But willingly, & paciently obeyed his fathets appointement, Mat 26,63. act 8,32.
l From the croſſe, and graue after that he was condemned.
m Thogh he dyed for ſinne, yet after his reſurrection he ſhal liue for euer, and this his death is to reſtore life to his members, Rom. 6,9.
n God the Father deliuered him into the hands of the wicked, and to the powers of the worlde to do with him what they wolde.
o Chriſt by offring vp him ſelf ſhal giue life to his Church, & ſo cauſe them to liue ẇ him for euer.
p That is, the frute & effect of his labour, ẇ is ẏ ſaluaciõ of his Church.
q Chriſt ſhal iuſtifie by faith through his worde, whe-re as Moſes cõlde not iuſtifie by the Lawe.
r Becauſe he hũbled him ſelf, therefore he ſhalbe exalted to glorie, Phil. 2,7.
ſ That is, in all that beleue in him.

CHAP. LIIII.

1 Mo of the Gentiles ſhal beleue the Goſpel then of the Iewes. 7 God leaueth his for a time, to whome afterward he ſheweth mercie.

1 REioyce, ô [a] baren that didest not beare: breake forthe into ioye & reioyce,
thou that dideſt not trauaile with childe:
for the [b] deſolate hathe mo children then
the maried wife, ſaith the Lord.
2 [c] Enlarge the place of thy tentes, and let
them ſpread out the curtaines of thine habitacions: ſpare not, ſtretch out thy cordes, and make faſte thy ſtakes.
3 For thou ſhalt increaſe on the right hand
and on the left, and thy ſede ſhal poſſeſſe
ẏ Gentiles & dwell in the deſolate cities.
4 Feare not: for ẏ ſhalt not be aſhamed, nether ſhalt ẏ be confounded: for ẏ ſhalt not
be put to ſhame: yea, ẏ ſhalt forget ẏ ſhame
of thy [d] youth, & ſhalt not remẽber the reproche of thy [e] widdowhead anie more.
5 For he that [f] made thee, *is* thine houſbãd
(whoſe Name *is* the Lord of hoſtes) and
thy redemer the holie one of Iſraél, ſhalbe
called the God of the whole [g] worlde.
6 For the Lord hathe called thee, being as
a woman forſaken, and afflicted in ſpirit,
and *as* a [h] yong wife when thou waſt refuſed, ſaith thy God.
7 For a litle while haue I forſaken thee,
but with great compaſsion wil I gather
thee.
8 For a moment, in *mine* angre, I hid my
face from thee for a litle ſeaſon, but with
euerlaſting mercie haue I had compaſsiõ
on thee, ſaith the Lord thy redemer.
9 For this is vnto me *as* the [i] waters of Noáh: for as I haue ſworne that the waters of
Noáh ſhulde no more go ouer the earth,
ſo haue I ſworne that I wolde not be angrie with thee, nor rebuke thee.
10 For the mountaines ſhal remoue and the
hilles ſhal fall downe: but my mercie ſhal

Chap. LIIII.
a After ẏ he hathe declared the death of Chriſt, he ſpeaketh to the Church, becauſe it ſhulde fele ẏ frute of ẏ ſame, & calleth her baren, becauſe ẏ in the captiuitie ſhe was as a widdowe without hope to haue anie children.
b The Church in this her affictiõ, & captiuitie ſhal brĩg forth mo children then whẽ ſhe was at libertie: or this may be ſpoken by admiratiõ, conſidering ẏ great nomber ẏ ſhulde come of her. Her deliuerãce vnder Cyrus was as her childe hode, & therefore this was accompliſhed, when ſhe came to her age, ẇ was vnder ẏ Goſpel.
c Signifying, ẏ for ẏ great nõber of childrẽ, ẏ God ſhulde giue her, ſhe ſhulde ſeme to lacke roume to lodge them.
d The afflictions which thou ſuffred at the beginning.
e When as ẏ waſt refuſed for thy ſinnes, Chap. 50,1.
f That did regenerate thee by his holy Spirit.
g His glorie ſhal ſhine through the whole worlde, which ſemed before to be ſhut vp in Iudea.
h As a wife which waſt forſaken in thy youth.
i As ſure as the promes that I made to Noáh, that the waters ſhulde no more ouerflowe the earth.

not

not depart from thee, nether shal the couenant of my peace fall away, saith the
Lord, that hathe compassion on thee.
11 O thou afflicted and tossed with tempest, that hast no comfort, beholde, I wil
lay thy stones with [k] the carbuncle, and lay
thy fundacion with saphirs,
12 And I wil make thy windowes of * e-
meraudes, and thy gates shining stones,
and all thy borders of pleasant stones.
13 And all thy children *shal be* [l] taught of
the Lord, and muche peace shalbe to thy
children.
14 In [m] righteousnes shalt thou be established, & be farre from oppressiō: for thou
shalt not feare it: and frō feare, for it shal
not come nere thee.
15 Beholde, *the enemie* shal gather him self,
but without me: whosoeuer shal gather
him self in thee, [o] against thee, shal fall.
16 Beholde, I haue created the [p] smith that
bloweth the coles in the fyre, and him
that bringeth forthe an instrument for his
worke, and I haue created the destroyer
to destroye.
17 But all the weapons that are made a-
gainst thee, shal not prosper: and euerie
tongue that shal rise against thee in iudgement, thou shalt condemne. This is the
heritage of the Lords seruants, and their
righteousnes *is* of me, saith the Lord.

k Hereby he declareth ye excellent estate of ye Church vnder Christ.
* Or, iaspar, or, pearle.
l By ye hearing of his worde & inward mouing of his Spirit.
m In stabilitie and surenes so y^t it shal stand for euer.
n And therefore shal not preuaile.
o Meaning, ye domestical enemies of the Church as are the hypocrites
p Signifyi̅g hereby ye man ca̅ do nothing but so farre as God giueth power: for seig that all are his creatures, he must nedes gouerne and guide them.

CHAP. LV.

1 An exhortation to come to Christ. 8 Gods counsels are not as mans 12 The ioy of the faithful.

1 HO, euerie one y^t [a] thirsteth, come ye
to the waters, and ye that haue [b] no
siluer, come, bie and eat: come, I saie, bie
[c] wine and milke without siluer and without monei.
2 Wherefore do ye laie out siluer & not for
bread? [d] & your labour without beig satisfied? hearke̅ diligently vnto me, & eat that
which is good, and let your soule delite in
[e] fatnes.
3 Encline your eares, and come vnto me:
heare, and your soule shal liue, and I wil
make an euerlasting couenant with you,
euen the [f] sure mercies of Dauid.
4 Beholde, I gaue [g] him for a witnes to the
people, for a prince and a master vnto the
people.
5 Beholde, thou shalt call a nation that thou
knowest not, [h] and a nation that knewe not
thee, shal ru̅ne vnto thee, because of ye Lord
thy God, and the holie one of Israél: for
he hathe glorified thee.
6 Seke ye the Lord while he maie [i] be founde: call ye vpon him while he is nere.
7 Let the wicked [k] forsake his waies, and the
vnrighteous his owne imaginations, and
returne vnto the Lord, and he wil haue
mercie vpon him: and to our God, for he
is verie readie to forgiue.
8 For my [l] thoghts *are* not your thoghts,
nether *are* your waies my waies, saith the
Lord.
9 For as the heauens are hier the̅ the earth,
so are my waies hier then your waies, and
my thoghts aboue your thoghts.
10 Surely as the raine cometh downe and
the snowe from heauen, and returneth not
thether, but watereth the earth and maketh
it to bring forthe and budde, that it maie
giue sede to the sower, and bread vnto
him that eateth,
11 So shal my [m] worde be, that goeth out
of my mouth: it shal not returne vnto me
voyde, but it shal accomplish that which I
wil, and it shal prosper in the thing whereto I sent it.
12 Therefore ye shal go out with ioye, and
be led forthe with peace: the [n] mountaines
and the hils shal breake forthe before you
into ioye, and all the trees of the field shal
clappe *their* hands.
13 For thornes there shal growe fyrre trees:
for nettles shal growe the myrrhe tree,
and it shalbe to the Lord [o] for a name, *and*
for an euerlasting [p] signe that shal not be
taken awaie.

Chap. LV.
a Christ by proposing his graces & gifts to his Church exempteth ye hypocrites w^c are ful with their imagined workes, & the Epicures, w^c are ful with their worldelie lusts & so thirst not after these waters.
b Signifying, y^t Gods benefits can not be boght for money.
c By waters, wine, milke & bread, he meaneth all thigs necessarie to ye spiritual life, as these are necessarie to this corporal life
d He reproueth their ingratitude, which refuse those things y^t God offreth willigly, and in the meane time spare nether cost nor labour to obteine those, which are nothing profitable.
e You shalbe fed abundantly.
f The same couenant, w^c through my mercie, I ratified & confirmed to Dauid that it shulde be eternal, 2. Sam 7, 13. act. 13, 34.
g Meaning, Christ, of whome Dauid was a figure.
h To wit, the Gentiles, w^c before thou didest not receiue to be thy people.
i When he offreth him self by the preaching of his worde.
k Hereby he sheweth that repentance must be ioyned with faith, & how we can not call vpon God aright, except ye frutes of our faith appeare.
l Althogh you are not sone reconciled one to another & iudge me by your selues, yet I am most easie to be reconciled, yea I offer my mercies to you.
m If these smale things haue their effect, as daiely experie̅ce sheweth, muche more shal my promes w^c I haue made & co̅firmed, brig to passe the thing which I haue spoke̅ for your deliuerance.
n Read Chap. 44, 23. 49, 13.
o To set forth his glorie.
p Of Gods deliuerance, & y^t he wil neuer forsake his Church.

CHAP. LVI.

1 An exhortacion to iudgement and iustice. 10 Against Shepherds that deuoure their flocke.

1 THus saith ye Lord, [a] Kepe iudgeme̅t &
do iustice: for my saluacio̅ is at ha̅d to
come & my [b] righteousnes to be reueiled.
2 Blessed *is* the man that doeth this, and
the sonne of man which laieth holde on
it: he that kepeth the [c] Sabbath and polluteth it not, and kepeth his hand from doing anie euil.
3 And let not the sonne of the stranger,
which [d] is ioyned to the Lord, speake and
say, The Lord hathe surely separat me fro̅
his people: nether let the Eunuch say, Beholde, I am a drye tre.
4 For thus saith the Lord vnto the Eunuches, that kepe my Sabbaths, and chuse the
thing that pleaseth me, and take holde of
my couenant,
5 Euen vnto the̅ wil I giue in mine [e] House
& within my walles, a place and a [f] name
better then of the sonnes & of the daughters: I wil giue them an euerlasting name,
that shal not be put out.
6 Also the strangers that cleaue vnto the
Lord, to serue him, & to loue the Name of
the Lord, & to be his seruants: euerie one
that kepeth the Sabbath, & polluteth it not
& imbraceth my couenant,
7 The̅ wil I bring also to mine holy moun
taine, & make them ioyful in mine House
of praier: their burnt [g] offrings and their
sacrifices *shalbe* accepted vpon mine altar:
for mine House shalbe called an house of
praier for [h] all people.

Chap. LVI.
a God sheweth what he requireth of the after y^t he hathe deliuered the̅: to wit, ye workes of charitie whereby true faith is declared.
b Which I wil declare toward you & powre into your hearts by my Spirit.
c Vnder ye Sabbath he co̅prehendeth the whole seruice of God & true religion.
d Let none thinke him self vnmete to receiue ye graces of ye Lord: for ye Lord wil take awaie all impediments, and wil forsake none w^c wil kepe his true religion & beleue in him.
e Meaning, in his Church.
f Thei shalbe called after my people & be of ye same religion: yea vnder Christ ye dignitie of ye faithful shalbe greater the̅ ye Iewes were at y^t time
g Hereby he meaneth ye spiritual seruice of God, to whome ye faithful offer continual thankesgiuing, yea the̅ selues & all y^t they haue as a liuely & acceptable sacrifice.
h Not onely for ye Iewes but for all others, Matt. 21, 13.

8 The Lord God ſaith, which gathereth
the ſcatered of Iſraél, Yet wil I gather to
them thoſe that are to be gathered to thẽ.
9 All ye [i] beaſtes of the field, come to deuoure, *euen* all ye beaſts of the foreſt.
10 Their [k] watchemen are all blinde: they
haue no knowledge: thei are all domme
doggs: thei can not barke: thei lie & ſlepe
and delite in ſleping.
11 And theſe gredie doggs can neuer haue
ynough: and theſe ſhepherds can not vnderſtand: *for* they all loke to their owne
way, euerie one for his aduantage, & for
his owne purpoſe.
12 Come, I wil bring wine, and we wil fil
our ſelues with ſtrong drinke, and to [l] morowe ſhalbe as this daie, *and* muche more
abundant.

i Meaning, the enemies of the Church, as the Babylonians, Aſsyrians, &c. thus he ſpeaketh to feare yͤ hypocrites & to aſſure the faithful, that when this cometh, thei may knowe it was tolde them before.

k He ſheweth that his affliction ſhal come through yͤ faute of yͤ gouernours, Prophetes & paſtors, whoſe ignorance, negligence, auarice & obſtinacie prouoked Gods wrath againſt them.

l We are wel yet, and tomorowe ſhal be better: therefore let vs not feare the plagues before they come: thus the wicked contemned the admonitions and exhortations which were made them in the Name of God.

CHAP. LVII.

2 God taketh awaie the good, that he ſhulde not ſe the horrible plagues to come 3 Of the wicked idolaters, 9 And their vaine confidence.

1 THe righteous periſheth, and no man
conſidereth it in heart: and merciful
men are taken awaie, and no man vnderſtandeth that the righteous is taken awaie
[a] from the euil *to come.*
2 [b] Peace ſhal come: thei ſhal reſt in their
beddes, *euerie one* that walketh before him.
3 But you [c] witches children, come hither,
the ſede of the adulterer and of yͤ whore.
4 On whome haue ye ieſted? vpon whome
haue ye gaped and thruſt out your tongue? are not ye rebellious children, *and* a
falſe ſede?
5 Inflamed with idoles vnder euerie grene
tree? and ſacrificing the [d] children in the
valleis vnder the toppes of the rockes?
6 Thy porcion *is* in the ſmooth ſtones [e] of
the riuer: thei, thei are thy lotte: euen to
them haſt thou powred a drinke offring:
thou haſt offred a ſacrifice. Shulde I delite in [f] theſe?
7 Thou haſt made thy [g] bed vpon a verie
hie mountaine: thou wenteſt vp thether,
euen thether wenteſt thou to offre ſacrifice.
8 Behinde the [h] dores alſo and poſtes haſt
thou ſet vp thy remembrance: for thou
haſt diſcouered thy ſelf *to another* then me,
and wenteſt vp *and* dideſt [i] enlarge thy
bed, & make a couenant betwene thee and
them, and louedſt their bed in *euerie* place

a From yͤ plague that is at hand, & alſo becauſe God wil puniſh the wicked.

b The ſoule of the righteous ſhal be in ioye & their bodie ſhal reſt in yͤ graue vnto the time of yͤ reſurrection, becauſe thei walked before the Lord.

c He threateneth the wicked hypocrites, who vnder the pretence of yͤ name of Gods people derided Gods worde & his promiſes: boaſting openly that thei were yͤ childrẽ of Abrahám, but becauſe they were not faithful & obedient as Abrahám was, he calleth thẽ baſtards, & the childrẽ of ſorcerers, wͨ forſoke God and fled to wicked meanes for ſuccour.

d Read Leui 18,21. 2 King, 23,10.

e Meaning, euerie place was polluted with their idolatrie: or euerie faire ſtone that they founde, thei made an idole of it.

f In the ſacrifices which you, offring before theſe idoles, thoght you did ſerue God.

g To wit, thine altars, in an open place like an impudent harlot that careth not for the ſight of her houſband

h In ſtead of ſetting vp the worde of God in the open places on the poſtes & dores to haue it in remembrance, Deut. 6, 9. & 27, 1. thou haſt ſet vp ſignes and markes of thine idolatrie in euerie place.

i That is, dideſt increaſe thine idolatrie more and more.

where thou ſaweſt it.
9 Thou wenteſt [k] to the Kigs with oyle, &
dideſt increaſe thine oyntmentes & ſend
thy meſſengers farre of, and dideſt humble
thy ſelfe vnto hel.
10 Thou wearied ſt thy ſelf in thy manifold
iourneis, *yet* ſaideſt thou not, [l] There is no
hope: thou [m] haſt founde life by thine hãd,
therefore thou waſt not grieued.
11 And whome dideſt thou reuerence or
feare, ſeing thou haſt [n] lied vnto me, and
haſt not remẽbred me, nether ſet thy minde
thereon? is it not *becauſe* I holde my peace, and that of long [o] time? therefore thou
feareſt not me.
12 I wil declare thy [p] righteouſnes & thy
workes, and thei ſhal not profite thee.
13 When thou cryeſt, let them that thou
haſt gathered together deliuer thee: but yͤ
winde ſhal [q] take thẽ all away: vanitie ſhal
pul them awaie: but he that truſteth in me,
ſhal inherit the land, and ſhal poſſeſſe mine holie Mountaine.
14 [r] And he ſhal ſaie, Caſt vp, caſt vp: prepare the waie: take vp the ſtõbling blockes
out of the waie of my people.
15 For thus ſaith he, that is hie and excellẽt,
he that inhabiteth yͤ eternitie, whoſe Name is the Holie one, I dwell in the hie &
holie place: with him alſo that is of a contrite and humble ſpirit to reuiue the ſpirit of the humble, and to giue life to them
that are of a contrite heart.
16 For I wil not contende for euer, nether
wil I be alwaies wrath, [ſ] for yͤ ſpirit ſhulde
faile before me: and I haue made the
breathe.
17 For his wicked [t] couetouſnes I am angrie with him, & haue ſmitẽ him: I hid me
& was angrie, yet he went awaie, & turned
after the waie of his owne heart.
18 I haue ſene his waies, and wil [u] heale
him: I wil leade him alſo, & reſtore cõfort
vnto him, and to thoſe that lament him.
19 I creat the [x] frute of yͤ lippes *to be* peace:
peace vnto them that are [y] farre of, and to
them that are nere, ſaith the Lord: for I
wil heale him.
20 But the wicked *are* like the raging ſea,
that cã [z] not reſt, whoſe waters caſt vp myre and dirt.
21 There is no peace, ſaith my God, to the
wicked.

CHAP. LVIII.

1 The office of Gods miniſters. 2 The workes of the hypocrites. 6 The faſt of the faithful. 13 Of the true Sabbath.

1 CRye a [a] loud, ſpare not: lift vp thy
voyce like a trumpet, and ſhewe my
people their tranſgreſsion, & to the houſe of Iaakób, their ſinnes.
2 Yet thei [b] ſeke me daily, & wil knowe my
waies, euen as a nacion that did righte-

k Thou dideſt ſeke the fauour of yͤ Aſsyrians by giftes and preſents, to helpe thee againſt yͤ Egyptians: & when thei failed, yͧ ſoughteſt to yͤ Babylonians & more and more dideſt torment thy ſelf.

l Althogh yͧ saweſt all thy labours to be in vaine, yet woldeſt yͧ neuer acknowledge thy faute & leaue of.

m He derideth their vnprofitable diligẽce wͨ thoght to haue made all ſure, & yet were deceiued.

n Broken promes with me.

o Meaning, yͤ yͤ wicked abuſe Gods lenitie & growe to farther wickednes.

p That is, thy naughtines, idolatries & impieties: which yͤ wicked call Gods ſeruice: thus he derideth their obſtinacie.

q Meaning, yͤ Aſsyrians & other, whoſe helpe thei loked for.

r God ſhal ſay to Darius and Cyrus.

ſ I wil not vſe my power againſt fraile mã whoſe life is but a blaſt.

t That is, for yͤ vices & fautes of yͤ people, wͨ is ment here by couetouſnes.

u Thogh thei were obſtinat, yet I did not withdraw my mercie from them.

x That is, I frame yͤ ſpeache & wordes of my meſſengers wͨ ſhal bring peace.

y As wel to hĩ yͭ is in captiuitie as to him yͭ remaineth at home.

z Their euil conſcience doeth euer torment them, & therefore they cã neuer haue reſt, read Cha. 48, 22.

Chap. LVIII. a The Lord thus ſpeaketh to yͤ Prophet, willing him to vſe all diligence & ſeueritie to rebuke the hypocrites.

b They wil ſeme to worſhip me and haue outward holines.

ously, and had not forsaken the statutes of
their God: thei aske of me the ordinances
of iustice: they wil drawe nere vnto God,
saying,
3 [c] Wherefore haue we fasted, & thou seest
it not? we haue punished our selues, & thou
regardest it not. Beholde, in ẏ day of your
fast you wil seke [d] *your* wil, and require all
your dettes.
4 Beholde, ye fast to strife and debate, and
to smite with the fist of wickednes: ye
shal not fast as *ye do* to day, to make your
voyce be [e] heard aboue.
5 Is it suche a fast, that I haue chosen that
a man shulde afflict his soule for a day, &
to bowe downe his head, as a bulle rush,
and to lie downe in sackecloth and asshes?
wilt thou call this a fasting, or an acceptable day to the Lord?
6 Is not this ẏ fasting, that I haue chosen,
to loose the bands of wickednes, to take of
the heauy burdens, & to let the oppressed
go fre, and that ye breake euery [f] yoke?
7 Is it not to deale thy bread to the hungry, & that thou bring the poore that wander, vnto thine house? when thou seest the
naked, that thou couer him, and hide not
thy self from [g] thine owne flesh?
8 Then shal thy [h] light breake forthe as
the morning, and thine health shal growe
spedely: thy [i] righteousnes shal go before
thee, *and* the glorie of the Lord shal embrace thee.
9 Then shalt thou call, and the Lord shal
answer: thou shalt crye and he shal say,
Here I am: if thou take away from the
middes of thee the yoke, the putting forthe of the [k] finger, and wicked speaking:
10 If thou [l] powre out thy soule to the
hungry, & refresh the troubled soule: then
shal thy light spring out in the [m] darkenes,
and thy darkenes *shalbe* as the none day.
11 And the Lord shal guide thee cōtinually, and satisfie thy soule in drought, and
make fat thy bones: and thou shalt be like a
watred garden, and like a spring of water,
whose waters faile not.
12 And they shalbe of thee, that shal buylde
the olde [n] waste places: thou shalt raise vp
the fundacions for manie generacions, &
ẏ shalt be called the repairer of ẏ breache
& the restorer of the paths to dwell in.
13 If thou [o] turne away thy fote from the
Sabbath, from doing thy wil on mine holy
day, & call the Sabbath a delite, to consecrat it, *as* glorious to the Lord, and shalt
honour him, not doing thine owne waies,
nor seking thine owne wil, nor speaking a
vaine worde,
14 Then shalt thou delite in the Lord, and
I wil cause thee to mounte vpon the hie
places of the earth, and fede thee with the
heritage of Iaakób thy father: for ẏ mouth
of the Lord hathe spoken it.

c He setteth forthe the malice and disdaine of ẏ hypocrites, ẇ grudge against God, if their workes be not accepted.

d Thus he conuinceth the hypocrites by the secōde table & by their duetie toward their neighbour that thei haue nether faith nor religion.

e So long as you vse contētion & oppression, your fasting & praier shal not be heard.

f That you leaue of all your extorsions.

g For in him thou seest thy self as in a glasse.

h That is, the prosperous estate, wherewith God wil blesse thee.

i The testimonie of thy goodnes shal appeare before God & mā.

k Whereby is mēt all maner of iniurie.

l That is, haue compassiō on their miseries.

m Thine aduersitie shalbe turned into prosperitie.

n Signifying ẏ of the Iewes shulde come suche, as shuld buylde againe ẏ ruines of Ierusalém & Iudea: but chiefly this is ment of the spiritual Ierusalém: whose buylders were the Apostles.

o If thou refraine thy self from thy wicked workes.

CHAP. LIX.

1 The wicked perish through their owne iniquities. 12 The confession of sinnes. 16 God alone wil preserue his Church, thogh all men faile.

1 Beholde, * the Lords hand is not shortened, that it can not saue: nether is
his eare heauy, that it can not heare.
2 But * your iniquities haue separated betwene you and your God, and your sinnes
haue hid *his* face from you, that he wil not
heare.
3 For your hands are defiled with [a] blood,
and your fingers with iniquitie: your lippes haue spoken lies & your tongue hathe
murmured iniquitie.
4 No man calleth for iustice: no man [b] con-
tendeth for trueth: they trust in vanitie, &
speake vaine things: thei cōceiue mischief,
and [c] bring forthe iniquitie.
5 They hatche cockatrice [d] egges, & weaue
the spiders [e] webbe: he that eateth of their
egges, dyeth, and that which is trod vpon,
breaketh out into a serpent.
6 Their webbes shalbe no garment, nether
shal they couer them selues with their labours: *for* their workes *are* workes of iniquitie, and the worke of crueltie *is* in their
hands.
7 Their fete runne to euil, and they make
haste to shed innocēt blood: their thoghts
are wicked thoghts: desolacion & destruction *is* in their paths.
8 The way of peace they knowe not, and
there *is* none equitie in their goings: thei
haue made them croked paths: whosoeuer
goeth therein, shal not knowe peace.
9 Therefore is [f] iudgement farre from vs,
nether doeth [g] iustice come nere vnto vs:
we waite for light, but lo, it *is* darkenes, for
brightnes: *but* we walke in darkenes.
10 We grope for the wall like the [h] blinde,
and we grope as one without eyes: we stōble at the none day as in the twilight: *we*
are in solitarie places, as dead men.
11 We roare all like [i] beares, and mourne
like doues: we loke for equitie, but there *is*
none: for health, *but* it is farre from vs.
12 For our trespaces are manie before thee,
and our [k] sinnes testifie against vs: for our
trespaces *are* with vs, and we knowe our
iniquities
13 In trespacing & lying against the Lord,
and we haue departed away frō our God,
& haue spoken of crueltie and rebellion,
concerning and vttering out of the heart
false [l] matters.
14 Therefore [m] iudgement is turned backeward, and iustice standeth farre of: for
trueth is fallen in the strete, and equitie
can not enter.
15 Yea, trueth faileth, and he that refreineth
from euil, maketh him self [n] a pray: and

Nomb. 11, 23. chap. 50, 2.

Iere. 5, 25.

a Read Chap. 1, 15.

b All mē winke at the iniuries & oppressions, & none go about to remedie them.

c According to their wicked deuises, they hurt their neighbours.

d Whatsoeuer cometh from thē, is poyson and bringeth death.

e Thei are profitable to no purpose.

f That is, Gods vengeāce to punish our enemies.

g Gods protection to defēd vs.

h We are altogether destitute of counsel and can finde no end of our miseries.

i We expresse our sorowes by outwarde signes, some more some lesse.

k This confession is general to the Church to obteine remissiō of sinnes, & the Prophetes did not exempt them selues frō the same.

l To wit, against our neighbours.

m There is nether iustice nor vprightnes among men.

n The wicked wil destroye him.

when the Lord sawe it, it displeased him,
that there *was* no iudgement.
16 And when he saw that there *was* no mã,
he wondred that none wolde offer him
self. ° Therefore his arme did ᵖ saue it, &
his righteousnes it self did susteine it.
17 For he put on righteousnes, as an habergeon, and an q helmet of saluacion vpon
his head, and he put on the garments of
vengeance for clothing, & was clad with
zeale as a cloke.
18 As *to make* recompence, as to requite the
furie of the aduersaries *with* a recompence to his enemies: he wil fully repaire the
r ylands.
19 So shal they feare the Name of the Lord
from the West, and his glorie from the rising of the sunne: for the enemie shal ſ come like a flood: *but* the Spirit of the Lord
shal chase him away.
20 And the Redemer shal come vnto Zión,
and vnto t them that turne from iniquitie
in Iaakób, saith the Lord.
21 And I wil *make* this my couenant with
them, saith the Lord, My Spirit that is vpon thee, & my wordes, which I haue put in
thy mouth, u shal not departe out of thy
mouth, nor out of the mouth of thy sede,
nor out of the mouth of the sede of thy sede, saith the Lord, from hence forthe euen
for euer

CHAP. LX.

3 The Gentiles shal come to the knowledge of the Gospel. 5 Thei shal come to the Church in abundance. 16 They shal haue abundance, thogh they suffer for a time.

1 ARise, *ó Ierusalém*: be bright, for thy
a light is come, & the glorie of the
Lord is risen vpon thee.
2 For beholde, darkenes shal couer ye b earth,
and grosse darkenes the people: but the
Lord shal arise vpon thee, and his glorie
shalbe sene vpon thee.
3 And the Gentiles shal walke in c thy light,
& Kings at ye brightnes of thy rising vp.
4 Lift vp thine eyes rounde about, & beholde: all d these are gathered, & come to
thee: thy sonnes shal come from farre, and
thy daughters shalbe nourished at *thy* side.
5 Then thou shalt se and shine: thine heart
shalbe astonied e & enlarged, because the
multitude of the sea shalbe conuerted vnto thee, and the riches of the Gentiles shal
come vnto thee.
6 The f multitude of camels shal couer
thee: and the dromedaries of Midián & of
Epháh: all they of Shebá shal come: they
shal bring golde & incense, and shewe forthe the praises of the Lord.
7 All the shepe g of Kedár shalbe gathered
vnto thee: ye rams of Nebaióth shal serue
thee: thei shal come vp to be accepted vpon mine h altar: and I wil beautifie the

o Meaning, to do iustice & to remedie the things ye were so farre out of order.
p That is, his Church: or his arme did helpe it self, and did not seke aide of any other.
q Signifying ye God hathe all meanes at hãd to deliuer his Church, and to punish their enemies.
r To wit, your enemies, w dwel in diuers places, and beyonde the sea.
ſ He sheweth ye there shalbe great afflictiõ in ye Church, but God wil euer deliuer his.
t Whereby he declareth that the true deliuerance from sinne & Satán belongeth to none, but to ye children of God, whome he iustifieth.
u Because the doctrine is made profitable by the vertue of the Spirit, he ioyneth the one with ye other, and promiseth to giue them bothe to his Church for euer.
Chap. LX.
a The time of thy prosperitie and felicitie: where as speaking of Babylon he cõmãded her to go downe, Chap. 47, 1.
b Signifying, ye all men are in darkenes til God giue the the light of his Spirit, and that this light shineth to none but to those that are in his Church.
c Meaning, ye Iudea shulde be as the morning starre & ye the Gẽtiles shulde receiue light of her.
d An infinite nomber from all contreis, as Chap. 49, 18.
e For ioye, as ye heart is drawen in for sorowe.
f Meaning, ye euery one shal honour ye Lord with that, wherewith he is able: signifyig that it is no true seruĩg of God, except we offer our selues to serue his glorie, & all that we haue.
g That is, the Arabians, ye haue great abundance of cattel.
h Because the altar was a figure of Christ, Ebr. 13, 10: he sheweth that nothing can be acceptable to him, which is not offred to him by this altar, who was bothe the offring and the altar it self.

house of my glorie.
8 Who are these i that flee like a cloude, &
as the doues to their windowes?
9 Surely the yles shal waite for me, and the
shippes k of Tarshish, as at the beginning
ye thei may bring thy sonnes from farre, &
their siluer, and their golde with thẽ, vnto
the Name of the Lord thy God, & to the
holy one of Israél, because he hathe glorified thee.
10 And the sonnes of strangers shal buylde
vp thy walles, and their l Kings shal minister vnto thee: for in my wrath I smote
thee, but in my mercie I had compassion
on thee.
11 Therefore thy gates shal be open continually: nether day nor night shal they be
shut that men may bring vnto thee the riches of the Gentiles, and that their Kings
may be broght.
12 For the nacion and the m kingdome, that
wil not serue thee, shal perish: & those nacions shalbe vtterly destroyed.
13 The n glorie of Lebanón shal come vnto
thee, ye fyrre tre, the elme & ye boxe tre together, to beautifie ye place of my Sanctuarie: for I wil glorifie the place of my o fete.
14 The sonnes also of them that afflicted
thee, shal come and bowe vnto thee: and
all thei that despised thee, shal fall p downe
at the soles of thy fete: and they shal call
thee, The citie of the Lord, Zión of the
holy one of Israél.
15 Where as thou hast bene forsaken & hated: so that no man went *by thee*, I wil make thee an eternal glorie, and a ioye from
generacion to generacion.
16 Thou shalt also sucke the milke of the
Gentiles, and shalt sucke the q breasts of
Kings: and yu shalt knowe, that I the Lord
am thy Sauiour, & thy Redemer, ye mightie
one of Iaakób.
17 For brasse wil I bring golde, & for yron
wil I bring siluer, & for wood brasse, & for
stones yrõ. I wil also make thy gouernemẽt
r peace, & thine exactours righteousnes.
18 Violence shal no more be heard of in
thy land, nether desolacion, nor destruction within thy borders: but thou shalt call
ſ saluacion, thy walles, and praise, thy gates.
19 Thou shalt haue no more sunne to shine
by day, nether shal the brightnes of the
t moone shine vnto thee: for the Lord shalbe thine euerlasting light, and thy God,
thy glorie.
20 Thy sunne shal neuer go downe, nether
shal thy moone be hid: for the Lord shal be
thine euerlasting light, & the daies of thy
sorowe shalbe ended.
21 Thy people also shalbe all righteous: thei
shal possesse the land for euer, the u graffe
of my planting shalbe the worke of mine
hands,

i Shewing what great nõber shal come to the Church & with what great diligence and zeale.
k The Gẽtiles that are now enemies, shal become friẽds & fetters forthe of the Church.
l Meaning, Cyrus and his successors: but chiefly this is accomplished in them that serue Christ beĩg conuerted by his Gospel.
m He sheweth ye God hathe giuẽ all power & autoritie here in earth for the vse of his Church: and that they which wil not serue and profit ye same, shal be destroied.
n There is nothing so excellent which shal not serue the necessitie of ye Church.
o Signifying, that Gods maiestie is not included in ye temple, w is but the place for his fete, ye we may learne to rise vp to ye heauens.
p To worship their head Christ by obeyig his doctrine.
q Bothe hie and lowe shal be readie to helpe and succour thee.
r Thy gouernours shal loue thee and seke thy wealth and prosperitie.
ſ Meaning, not a temporal felicitie, but a spiritual, w is fulfilled in Christs kingdome.
t Signifying that all worldlie meanes shal cease, & that Christ shalbe all in all, as Reuel. 21, 22. & 22, 5.
u The children of the Church.

hands, that I maie be glorified.
22 A litle one shal become as a [x] thousand, &
a smale one as a strong nation: I the Lord
wil hasten it in due time.

CHAP. LXI.

1 He prophecyeth that Christ shalbe anointed and sent to preache. 10 The ioye of the faithful.

1 THe *Spirit of the Lord God *is* [a] vpon
me, therefore hathe the Lord anointed me: he hathe sent me to preache good
tidings vnto the poore, to binde vp the
[b] broken hearted, to preache libertie to the
[c] captiues, and to them that are bounde, the
opening of the prison,
2 To preache the [d] acceptable yere of the
Lord, and the daie of [e] vengeance of our
God, to comfort all that mourne,
3 To appoint vnto thē that mourne in Zión, & to giue vnto thē beautie for [f] ashes,
the oyle of ioye for mourning, the garmēt
of gladnes for the spirit of heauines, that
thei might be called [g] trees of righteousnes, the planting of ẏ Lord, that he might
be glorified.
4 And thei shal buylde the olde waste places, & raise vp the former desolations, &
thei shal repaire the cities ẏ were desolate
and waste through manie [h] generations.
5 And the strangers shal [i] stande and fede
your shepe, & the sonnes of the strangers
shalbe your plowe men & dressers of your
vines.
6 But ye shalbe named [k] the Priests of the
Lord, & men shal saie vnto you, The ministers of our God, Ye shal eat the [l] riches
of the Gentiles, and shalbe exalted with
their glorie.
7 For your shame *you shal receiue* [m] double,
and for confusion [n] they shal reioyce in
[o] their porcion: for in their land thei shal
possesse the [p] double: euerlasting ioye shalbe vnto them.
8 For I the Lord loue iudgement & hate
[q] robberie for burnt offring, and I wil direct their worke in trueth, and wil make an
euerlasting couenant with them.
9 And [r] their sede shal be knowen among ẏ
Gentiles, & their buddes among the people. All that se thē, shal knowe them, ẏ thei
are the sede which the Lord hathe blessed.
10 [f] I wil greatly reioyce in the Lord, *and*
my soule shalbe ioyful in my God: for he
hathe clothed me with the garments of
saluacion, and couered me with the robe
of righteousnes: he hathe decked me like a
bridegrome, and as a bride tireth her self
with her iewels.
11 For as the earth bringeth forthe her budde, & as the garden causeth to growe that
which is sowen in it: so the Lord God wil
cause righteousnes to growe & praise before all the heathen.

CHAP. LXII.

1 The great desire that the Prophetes haue had for Christs comming. 6 The diligence of the Pastors to preache.

1 FOr Zions sake I wil not [a] holde my
tongue, and for Ierusalems sake I wil
not rest, vntil the righteousnes thereof
breake forthe as the [b] light, and saluacion
thereof as a burning lampe.
2 And the Gentiles shal se thy righteousnes, and all Kings thy glorie: and thou
shalt be called by [c] a newe name, which ẏ
mouth of the Lord shal Name.
3 Thou shalt also be a [d] crowne of glorie
in the hand of the Lord, & a royal diademe in the hand of thy God.
4 It shal no more be said vnto thee, [e] Forsaken, nether shal it be said any more to thy
lād, Desolate, but ẏ shalt be called ‖ Hephzi-báh, and thy land ‖ Beuláh: for the Lord
deliteth in thee, and thy land shal haue an
[f] housband.
5 For *as* a yong man marieth a virgine, *so*
shal thy sonnes [g] mary thee: and *as* a bridegrome is glad of the bride, *so* shal thy God
reioyce ouer thee.
6 I haue set [h] watche men vpō thy walles, ô
Ierusalém, which all the daie and all the
night continually shal not cease: [i] ye that
are mindeful of the Lord, kepe not silence,
7 And giue him no rest, til he repaire and
vntil he set vp Ierusalém the [k] praise of
the worlde.
8 The Lord hathe sworne by his right hād
& by his strōg arme, Surely I wil no more
giue thy corne to be meat for thine enemies, & surely the sonnes of the strangers
shal not drinke thy wine, for the which
thou hast labored.
9 But thei that haue gathered it, shal eat it,
& praise the Lord, & the gatherers thereof shal drinke it in the courts of my Sanctuarie.
10 [l] Go through, go through the gates: prepare you the waie for the people: cast vp,
cast vp the waie, and gather out the stones
& set vp a standart for the people.
11 Beholde, the Lord hathe proclaimed vn
to the ends of the worlde: [m] tel the daughter Zión, Beholde, thy Sauiour commeth:
beholde, his wages [n] *is* with him, and his
worke *is* before him.
12 And thei shal call thē, The holie people,
the redemed of the Lord, and thou shalt be
named, A [o] citie soght out & not forsaken.

x Meaning, ẏ ẏ Church shulde be miraculously multiplied.

Luk. 4,18.

a This apperteineth to all the Prophetes and ministers of God, but chiefly to Christ, of whose abundāt graces euerie one receiueth according as it pleaseth him to distribute.
b To them that are liuely touched with the feeling of their sinnes.
c Which are in the bondage of sinne.
d The time when it pleased God to shewe his good fauour to man, which S. Paul calleth the fulnes of time, Gal. 4,4.
e For when God deliuereth his Church, he punisheth his enemies.
f Which was the signe of mourning.
g Trees that bring forthe good frutes, as Mat. 3,8.
h That is, for a long time.
i Thei shalbe readie to serue you in all your necessities.
k This is accōplished in the time of Christ, by whome all ẏ faithful are made Priests and Kings, 1. Pet. 2,9, reuel. 1,6, & 5,10.
l Read Chap. 60,16, & chap. 60,11.
m Abundāt recompence, as this worde is vsed, Chap. 40,2.
n That is, the Iewes.
o To wit, of the Gentiles.
p Where as the Gentiles had dominion ouer ẏ Iewes in times past, now they shal haue double autoritie ouer them and possesse twise so muche.
q I wil not receiue their offring, which are extorsioners, deceiuers, hypocrites, or that depriue me of my glorie.
r That is, of the Church.
f He sheweth what shalbe the affection, when they fele this their deliuerance.

a The Prophet saith that he wil neuer cease to declare vnto the people ẏ good tydings of their deliuerance.
b Til they haue ful deliuerance: and this the Prophet speaketh to incourage all other ministers to the setting forth of Gods mercies toward his Church.
c Thou shalt haue a more excellent fame then thou hast had hetherto.
d He shal esteme thee as dere & p̄cious as a King doeth his crowne.
e Thou shalt nomore be cōtemned as a woman forsaken of her housband.
‖ Or, my delite in her.
‖ Or, maried.
f That it may be replenished with children.
g For asmuche as thei confesse one faith & religion with thee, thei are in the same bond of mariage with thee: and thei are called the children of the Church, in asmuch as Christ maketh her plentiful to bring forthe children vnto him.
h Prophets, pastors, and ministers.
i He exhorteth the ministers neuer to cease to call vpon God by praier for the deliuerance of his Church and to teache others to do ẏ same.
k For the restauratiō whereof all the worlde shal praise him.
l Signifying ẏ great nomber ẏ shulde come to the Church, & what meanes he wolde prepare for ẏ restitution of ẏ same, as Chap. 57,14.
m Ye Prophets and ministers shew ẏ people of this their deliuerance: ẏ was chiefly ment of our saluaciō by Christ, Zach 9,9. mat. 21,5.
n He shal haue all power to bring his purpose to passe, as Chap. 40,10.
o That is, one ouer whome God hathe had a singular care to recouer her whē she was lost.

CHAP. LXIII.

1 God shal destroy his enemies for his Churches sake. 7 Gods benefites towards his Church.

a This prophecie is against ŷ Idumeans, and enemies which persecuted ŷ Church, on whome God wil take vengeance, and is here set forthe all bloody after that he hathe destroyed them in Bozráh, the chief citie of the Idumeans: for these were their greatest enemies, and vnder the title of circumcisiõ, and the kinred of Abrahám claimed to thẽ selues ŷ chief religion, and hated ŷ true worshippers, Psal.137,7.
b God answereth them that asked this question, Who is this? &c. and saith, Ye se now pformed in dede the vengeance, ŵ my Prophetes threatned.
c Another question, to the which ŷ Lord answereth.
d Shewing, ŷ when God punisheth his enemies, it is for the profite and deliuerance of his Church.
e God sheweth that he hathe no nede of mans helpe for the deliuerance of his, and thogh men refuse to do their duetie through negligence, & ingratitude, yet he him self wil deliuer his Church, and punish the enemies, read cha. 59,16.
f I wil so astonie them, and make thẽ so giddy, that they shal not knowe, which way to go.
g The Prophet speaketh this to moue the people to remember Gods benefites in times past, that they may be confirmed in their troubles
h For I did chuse them to be mine, that they shulde be holy, & not deceiue mine expectation.

1 WHo is this that commeth [a] from
Edóm, with red garments from
Bozráh? he is glorious in his apparel and
walketh in his great strength: [b] I speake in
righteousnes, & am mightie to saue.
2 [c] Wherefore is thine apparel red, and
thy garments like him that treadeth in the
wine presse?
3 I haue troden the wine presse alone, and
of all people there *was* none with me: for
I wil tread them in mine angre, & tread
them vnder fote in my wrath, and their
blood shalbe sprincled vpon my garmentes, and I wil staine all my raiment.
4 For the daie of vengeance *is* in mine
heart, & the [d] yere of my redemed is come.
5 And I loked, & there was none to helpe,
& I wondered that there was none to vpholde: therefore mine owne [e] arme helped
me, and my wrath it self susteined me.
6 Therefore I wil treade downe the people
in my wrath, and make them drunken [f] in
mine indignatiõ, & wil bring downe their
strength to the earth.
7 I wil [g] remembre the mercies of ŷ Lord
& the praises of the Lord according vnto
all that the Lord hathe giuen vs, and for
the great goodnes towarde the house of
Isráél, which he hathe giuen them according to his tendre loue, and according to
his great mercies.
8 For he said, Surely thei are my [h] people,
children that wil not lie: so he was their sa
uiour.
9 In all their troubles he was [i] troubled,
& the Angel [k] of his presence saued them:
in his loue and in his mercie he redemed
them, and he bare them and caried them all
waies continually.
10 But thei rebelled and vexed his holie
Spirit: therefore was he turned to be their
enemie & he foght against them.
11 Then he [l] remembred the olde time of
Mosés and his people, saying, Where is he
that broght them vp out of the Sea with
the [m] shepherd of his shepe? where is he ŷ
put his holie Spirit within [n] him?
12 He led *them* by the right hand of Mosés
with his owne glorious arme, deuiding
the water before them, to make him self
an euerlasting Name.
13 He led thẽ through the depe, as an [o] horse in the wildernes, that thei shulde not
stomble,
14 As the beast goeth downe into ŷ valley,
the Spirit of the Lord gaue them rest: so
didest thou lead thy people, to make thy
self a glorious Name.

i He bare their afflictiõs and griefs as thogh they had bene his owne. k Which was a witnes of Gods presence: and this may be referred to Christ, to whome belongeth the office of saluation. l That is, the people of Isráél being afflicted, called to remembrance Gods benefites, which he had bestowed vpon their fathers in times past. m Meaning, Mosés. n That is, in Mosés that he might wel gouerne the people: some referre this giuing of the Spirit to the people. o Peaceably and gently, as an horse is led to his pasture.

15 [p] Loke downe from heauẽ, and beholde
frõ the dwelling place of thine holines, &
of thy glorie. Where is thy [q] zeale and thy
strength, the multitude of thy mercies, &
of thy compassions? they are restrained
from [r] me.
16 Doutles ŷ art our Father: thogh [s] Abrahám be ignorant of vs, and Isráél knowe
vs not, *yet* thou, ô Lord, art our Father, *and*
our redemer: thy Name *is* for euer.
17 O Lord, why hast [t] thou made vs to erre
from thy wayes? *and* hardened our heart
from thy feare? Returne for thy [u] seruants sake, *and* for the tribes of thine inheritance.
18 The people of thine holines haue possessed it, but a litle [x] while: for our aduersaries haue troden downe thy Sanctuarie.
19 We haue bene *as they*, ouer whome ŷ neuer barest rule, and vpon whome thy Name was not called.

p Hauing declared Gods benefites shewed to their forefathers, he turneth him self to God by prayer, desiring hĩ to continue the same graces toward them.
q Thy great affectiõ which thou barest towards vs.
r Meanĩg frõ ŷ whole bodie of the Church.
s Thogh Abrahám wolde refuse vs to be his childrẽ, yet ŷ wilt not refuse to be our father.
t By taking away thy holie Spirit from vs, by whome we were gouerned, and so for our ingratitude, didest deliuer vs vp to our owne cõcupiscence, & didest punish sinne by sinne according to thy iuste iudgemẽt. u Meaning, for the couenants sake made to Abrahám, Izhák & Iaakób his seruants. x That is, in respect of the promes, which is perpetual: albeit thei had now possessed the land of Canáã, a thousand, & foure hundreth yere: and thus they lament, to moue God rather to remember his couenant then to punish their sinnes.

CHAP. LXIIII.

1 The Prophet prayeth for the sinnes of the people. 6 Mãs righteousnes is like a filthy cloth.

1 OH, that thou woldest [a] breake the
heauens, & come downe, *and* that ŷ
mountaines might melt at thy presence!
2 As ŷ melting fyre burned, *as* the fyre caused [b] the waters to boile, (that thou mightest declare thy Name to thy aduersaries)
the people did tremble at thy presence.
3 When thou didest terrible things, which
we looked not for, thou camest downe, &
the mountaines melted at thy presence.
4 For since the beginning of the worlde
they haue not [c] heard nor vnderstand with
the eare, nether hathe the eye sene *another*
God beside thee, which doeth so to him
that waiteth for him.
5 Thou didest mete him, [d] that reioyced
in thee, and did iustely: they remẽbred thee
in thy [e] wayes: beholde, thou art angrie,
for we haue sinned: *yet* in [f] them *is* continuance, and we [g] shal be saued.
6 But we haue all bene as an vncleane thĩg
& all our [h] righteousnes *is* as filthy cloutes,
and we all do fade like a leafe, and our iniquities like the winde haue taken vs away.
7 And there *is* none that calleth vpon thy
Name, nether that stirreth vp him self to
take holde of thee: for thou hast hid thy
face from vs, and hast consumed vs because of our iniquities.
8 But now, ô Lord, thou art our Father: we
are the [i] claye, and thou art our potter, &

a The Prophet continueth his prayer, desiring God to declare his loue toward his Church by miracles, and mightie power as he did in mount Sinái.
b Meaning, ŷ raine, haile, fyre, thũder, & lightenings.
c S. Paul vseth the same kinde of admiration, 1 Cor. 2, 9, marueling at Gods great benefite shewed to his Church by the preaching of the Gospel.
d Thou shewedst fauour toward our fathers, when thei trusted in thee, and walked after thy commandements.
e Thei cõsidered thy great mercies.
f That is, in thy mercies, ŵ he calleth the waies of the Lord.
g Thou wilt haue pitie vpõ vs.
h We are iustely punished & broght into captiuitie, because we haue prouoked thee to angre, and thogh we wolde excuse our selues, yet our righteousnes, & best vertues are before thee as vile cloutes, or, (as some read) like the menstruous clothes of a woman. i Albeit, ô Lord, by thy iuste iudgement thou maiest vtterly destroye vs, as the potter may his pot, yet we appeale to thy mercies, whereby it hathe pleased thee to adopt vs to be thy children.

we

we all are the worke of thine hands.
9 Be not angrie, ô Lord, [k] aboue measure, ne
ther remẽber iniquitie for euer: lo, we beseche thee beholde, we are all thy people.
10 [l] Thine holie cities lye waste: Zión is a
wildernes, & Ierusalém a desert.
11 The House of our Sanctuarie & of our
glorie, [m] where our fathers praised thee, is
burnt vp with fyre, and all our pleasant
things are wasted.
12 Wilt thou holde thy self stil [n] at these
things, ô Lord? wilt thou holde thy peace
and afflict vs aboue measure?

k For so ẏ flesh iudgeth when God doeth not immediatly send succor.
l Which were dedicat to thy seruice and to call vpon thy Name.
m Wherein we reioyced and worshiped thee
n That is, at the contempt of thine owne glorie? thogh our sinnes haue deserued this, yet thou wilt not suffer thy glorie thus to be diminished.

CHAP. LXV.

1 The Vocation of the Gentiles and the reiection of the Iewes. 13 The ioy of the elect and the punishment of the wicked.

1 I Haue bene soght of them that [a] asked
not: I was founde of them that soght
me not: I said, Beholde me, beholde me,
vnto a nation that called not vpon my
Name.
2 I haue [b] spred out mine hands all the
day vnto a rebellious people, which walked in a way that was not good, *euen* after
their owne [c] imaginacions:
3 A people that prouoked me euer vnto my
face: that sacrificeth in [d] gardens, and burneth incense vpon [e] brickes.
4 Which remaine among the [f] graues, and
lodge in the deserts, which eat [g] swines
flesh, and the broth of things polluted
are in their vessels.
5 Which say, [h] Stand aparte, come not nere
to me: for I am holier then thou: these are
a smoke in my wrath & a fyre that [i] burneth all the day.
6 Beholde, it is [k] writen before me: I wil
not kepe silence, but wil rendre it and recompense it into their bosome.
7 Your iniquities & the iniquities of your
fathers *shalbe* [l] together (saith the Lord)
which haue burnt incense vpon the mõutaines, and blasphemed me vpon the hilles: therefore wil I measure their olde wor
ke into their bosome.
8 Thus saith the Lord, As the wine is foũde in the cluster, and one saith, Destroy it
not, for a [m] blessing *is* in it, so wil I do for
my seruants sakes, that I may not destroy
them whole.
9 But I wil bring a sede out of Iaakób, &
out of Iudáh, that shal enherit my mountaine: and mine elect shal inherit it, & my
seruants shal dwell there.
10 And Sharón [n] shalbe a shepe folde,
and the valley of Achór shalbe a resting
place for the cattel of my people, that haue soght me.
11 But ye are thei that haue forsaken the
Lord and forgotten mine holie Mountaine, & haue prepared a table for the [o] multitude, & furnish the drinke offrings vnto
the nomber.
12 Therefore wil I [p] nomber you to the
sworde, and all you shal bowe downe to ẏ
slaughter, because I called, and ye did not
answer: I [q] spake, & ye heard not, but did
euil in my sight and did chuse that thing
which I wolde not.
13 Therefore thus saith the Lord God, Beholde, my seruants shal [r] eat, & ye shal be
hungrie: beholde, my seruants shal drinke,
and ye shal be thirstie: beholde, my seruãtes shal reioyce, and ye shalbe ashamed.
14 Beholde, my seruants shal sing for ioye
of heart, and ye shal crye for sorowe of
heart, & shal howle for vexation of minde.
15 And ye shal leaue your name as a curse
vnto my [s] chosen: for the Lord God shal
slaie you and call his seruants by [t] another
name.
16 He that shal blesse in the [u] earth, shal
blesse him self in the true God, and he that
sweareth in the earth, shal sweare by the
true God: for the former [x] troubles are
forgotten, and shal surely hide them selues
from mine eyes.
17 For lo, I wil creat [y] newe heauens and a
newe earth: and the former shal not be remembred nor come into minde.
18 But be you glad & reioyce for euer in ẏ
things that I shal creat: for beholde, I wil
creat Ierusalém *as* a reioycing & her people *as* a ioye,
19 And I wil reioyce in Ierusalém, & ioye
in my people, and the voice of weping
shalbe no more heard in her, nor the voice
of crying.
20 There shalbe no more there a childe of
yeres, nor an olde man that hathe [z] not fil
led his daies: for he that shalbe an hũdreth
yeres olde, shal dye *as* a yong man: but the
sinner being [a] an hũdreth yeres olde shalbe
accursed.
21 And thei shal [b] buylde houses and inhabit them, and thei shal plant vineyardes,
and eat the frute of them.
22 Thei shal not buylde, and another inhabit: thei shal not plant, and another eat:
for as the daies of the tre are the daies of
my people, and mine elect shal inioye in
olde age the worke of their hands.
23 Thei shal not labour in vaine, nor bring
forthe in feare: for thei are the sede of the
blessed of ẏ Lord, & their buddes with thẽ.
24 Yea, before thei call, I wil answer, & whiles thei speake, I wil heare.
25 The [c] wolfe & the lambe shal fede together, and the lion shal eat strawe like the

a Meaning, the Gentiles which knew not God, shulde seke after him when he had moued their hearts with his holy Spirit, Rom. 10,20.
b He sheweth the cause of the reiection of the Iewes, because they wolde not obey him for anie admonitiõ of his Prophetes, by whome he called them continually & stretched out his hand to drawe them.
c He sheweth that to delite in our owne fantasies is the declining from God & the beginning of all superstition & idolatrie.
d Which were dedicat to idoles.
e Meanig their altars, ẇ he thus nameth by contempt.
f To consult ẇ spirits & to coniure deuils ẇ was forbiddẽ, Deut. 18,11.
g Which was contrarie to Gods commandement, Leu. 11,7. deut. 14,8.
h He sheweth that hypocrisie is euer ioyned with pride & contempt of others.
i Their punishement shal neuer haue end.
k So that ẏ remẽbrance thereof can not be forgotten.
l Shalbe bothe punished together: and this declareth how the children are punished for their fathers fautes: to wit, when the same fautes or like are founde in them.
m That is, it is profitable: meaning, that God wil not destroy the faithful branches of his vineyard when he destroieth the roten stockes, that is the hypocrites.
n Which was a plentiful place in Iudea to fede shepe, as Achór was for cattel.

o By the multitude & nomber he meaneth their innumerable idoles, of whome they thoght they colde neuer haue ynough.
p Seing you cã not nomber your gods, I wil nomber you with the sworde.
q By my Prophetes, whome ye wolde not obey.
r By these wordes, Eat & drinke, he meaneth the blessed life of the faithful, ẇ haue alwaies consolacion, & ful contentement of all things in their God, thogh some times they lacke these corporal things.
s Meaning, ẏ he wolde call the Gentiles, who shulde abhorre, euen the very name of the Iewes for their infidelities sake.
t Then by the name of the Iewes.
u By blessing, & by swearig, is ment the praising of God for his benefites, and the true worshipig of him, which shal not be onely in Iudea, but through all the worlde.
x I wil no more suffer my Church to be desolate as in times past.
y I wil so alter and change the state of my Church, that it shal seme to dwel in a newe worlde.
z Meaning, in this wonderful restauraciõ of the Church there shulde be no weakenes of youth, nor infirmities of age, but all shulde be fresh, and florishing: & this is accoplished in the heauenlie Ierusalém, when all finnes shal cease and teares shalbe wiped away.

a Whereby he sheweth that the infideles and vnrepentant sinners haue no parte of this benedictiõ b He proposeth to the faithful the blessings which are conteined in the Law, and so vnder temporal things comprehendeth the spiritual promises. c Read Chap 11,6.

bullocke: and to the serpent dust *shalbe* his
meat. Thei shal no more hurt nor destroy
in all mine holie Mountaine, saith ẏ Lord.

CHAP. LXVI.

1 God dwelleth not in temples made with hands. 3 He despiseth sacrifices done without mercie and faith. 5 God comforteth them that are troubled for his sake. 19 The vocation of the Gentiles. 23 The perpetual Sabbath. 24 The punishment of the wicked is euerlasting.

1 Thus saith the Lord, *The [a] heauen *is*
my throne, and the earth *is* my footestole: where is ẏ house that ye wil buylde
vnto me? & where is that place of my rest?
2 For all these things hathe mine hād made,[b] & all these things haue bene, saith the
Lord: & to him wil I loke, euen to him,
that is poore, and of [c] a contrite spirit and
trembleth at my wordes.
3 He that killeth a bullocke, *is as* if he [d] slew
a man: he that sacrificeth a shepe, *as* if he
cutte of a dogges necke: he that offreth an
oblation, *as* if he offred swines blood: he ẏ
remēbreth incense, *as* if he blessed an idole: yea, thei haue chose their owne waies, &
their soule deliteth in their abominaciōs.
4 Therefore wil I [e] chuse out their delusiōs,
& I wil bring their feare vpon thē, because
I called, & none wolde answer: I spake and
they wolde not heare: but they did euil in
my sight, & chose ẏ things ẇ I wolde not.
5 Heare the worde of the Lord, all ye that
tremble at his [f] worde, Your brethren that
hated you, & cast you out for my Names
sake, said, Let the Lord be glorified: but
he shal appeare to your ioye, and thei shal
be ashamed.
6 [g] A voyce soundeth from the citie, *euen* a
voyce from the Temple, the voyce of the
Lord, that recōpenceth his enemies fully.
7 Before [h] she trauailed, she broght forthe:
and before her peine came, she was deliuered of a man childe.
8 Who hathe heard such a thing? who hathe
sene suche things? shal the earth be broght
forthe in one [i] day? or shal a nation be borne at once? for assone as Zión trauailed,
she broght forthe her children.
9 Shal I [k] cause to trauaile, and not bring
forthe? shal I cause to brīg forthe & shalbe
baren, saith thy God?
10 Reioyce ye with Ierusalém, and be glad
with her, all ye that loue her: reioyce for
ioye with her, all ye that mourne for her,
11 That ye may sucke [l] & be satisfied with
the breasts of her cōsolation: that ye may
milke out & be delited with the brightnes
of her glorie.
12 For thus saith the Lord, Beholde, I wil

Act. 7,48.

a My maiestie is so great ẏ it filleth bothe heauē & earth, & therefore cā not be included in a temple like an idole: cōdemning hereby their vaine confidence, ẇ trusted in the Temple & sacrifices.

b Seing that bothe the Tēple & ẏ things therein ẇ the sacrifices were made & done by his appointment, he sheweth that he hathe no nede thereof, & that he can be without the Psal. 50, 10.

c To him that is humble and pure in heart, which receiueth my doctrine with reuerence & feare.

d Because the Iewes thoght thē selues holy by offring of their sacrifices, and in the meane season had nether faith nor repētance, God sheweth that he doeth no lesse detest these ceremonies, then he doeth the sacrifices of the heathen who offred mē, doggs & swine to their idoles which things were expressely forbidden in the Law.

e I wil discouer their wickednes & hypocrisie, wherewith thei thinke to blinde mine eies, to all the worlde

f He incourageth ẏ faithful by promising to destroy their enemies which pretended to be as brethren, but were hypocrites and hated them that feared God

g The enemies shal shortely heare a more terrible voyce, euen fyre and slaughter, seing thei wolde not heare the gentle voyce of the Prophets which called them to repentance.

h Meaning, that the restauration of the Church shulde be so suddē & contrarie to all mens opinion: as when a woman is deliuered before she loke for it, and that without peine in trauail.

i This shal passe the capacitie of man to se suche a multitude that shal come vp at once, meaning vnder the preaching of the Gospel, whereof thei that came vp out of Babylon, were a figure.

k Declaring hereby, that as by his power, & prouidence woman trauaileth & is deliuered: so hathe he power to bring forth his Church at his time appointed

l That ye may reioyse for all ẏ benefites that God bestoweth vpon his Church.

extend [m] peace ouer her like a flood & the
glorie of ẏ [n] Gentiles like a flowing streame: then shal ye sucke, ye shal be [o] borne
vpō *her* sides, and be ioyful vpō *her* knees.
13 As one whome his mother comforteth,
so wil I comforte you, and ye shalbe comforted in Ierusalém.
14 And when ye se this, your heart shal reioyce, and your [p] bones shal florish like an
herbe: and the hand of the Lord shal be
knowen among his seruants, and *his* indignacion against his enemies.
15 For beholde, ẏ Lord wil come with fyre,
& his charets like a whirlewinde, that he
may [q] recōpence his angre with wrath, &
his indignacion with the flame of fyre.
16 For the Lord wil iudge with fyre, and ẇ
his sworde all flesh, & the slaine of ẏ Lord
shalbe manie.
17 They that sanctifie [r] thē selues, & purifie
them selues in the gardens behinde one *tre*
in ẏ middes eating [s] swines flesh, & suche
abominacion, euen the mouse, shalbe con
sumed together, saith the Lord.
18 For I *wil visit* their workes, and their ima
ginations: *for* it shal come that I wil gather
all nations, and tongues, and thei shal come, and se my [t] glorie.
19 And I wil set a [u] signe amōg thē, & wil
send those that [x] escape of them, vnto the
nacions of [y] Tarshísh, [z] Pul, and [a] Lud, *&*
to them that drawe the [b] bowe, to [c] Tubál
and [d] Iauán, yles a farre of, that haue not
heard my fame, nether haue sene my glorie, & [e] thei shal declare my glorie among
the Gentiles.
20 And they shal bring all your [f] brethren
for an offring vnto the Lord out of all nations, vpon [g] horses, and in charets, and in
horse litters, & vpō mules, & swift beasts,
to Ierusalē mine holie Moūtaine, saith the
Lord, as the children of Israél, offer in a
cleane vessel in the House of the Lord.
21 And I wil take of them for [h] Priests, *and*
for Leuites, saith the Lord.
22 For as ẏ newe [i] heauēs, & the newe earth
which I wil make, shal remaine before me,
saith the Lord, so shal your sede and your
name continue.
23 And from moneth to moneth, and from
Sabbath to Sabbath shal all flesh come to
worship before me, saith the Lord.
24 And they shal go forthe, and loke vpon
the [k] carkeises of the men that haue transgressed against me: for their [l] worme shal
not dye, nether shal their fyre be quēched,
& thei shalbe an abhorrīg [m] vnto all flesh.

m I wil giue her felicitie, & prosperitie in great abūdāce.

n Read Chap. 60, 16

o Ye shalbe cherished, as her derelie beloued children.

p Ye shal haue newe strength and newe beautie.

q This vēgeāce God began to execute at ẏ destruction of Babylon, and hathe euer cōtinued it agaīst the enemies of his Church; & wil do til the last day, which shalbe the acōplishement thereof.

r Meaning, the hypocrites.

s Whereby are ment them that did maliciously transgresse ẏ Law, by eatīg beasts forbidden, euē to the mouse which abhorreth nature.

t The Gētiles shalbe partakers of that glorie, which before I shewed to the Iewes.

u I wil marke these ẏ I chuse that they perish not with the rest of the infideles: whereby he alludeth to ẏ marking of the posts of his people, whome he preserued, Exod 12, 7.

x I wil scatter the rest of the Iewes, which escape destruction, into diuers nations.

y That is, Cilicia

z Meaning, Affrica.

a To wit, Lidia, of Asia minor.

b Signifying, the Parthians.

c Italie.

d Grecia.

e Meaning, ẏ Apostles, disciples, & others which he did first chuse of ẏ Iewes to preache vnto the Gentiles.

f That is, the Gentiles, ẇ by faith shalbe made the children of Abrahám as you are.

g Whereby he meaneth ẏ no necessarie meanes shal want whē God shal call ẏ Gentiles to ẏ knowledge of the Gospel.

h To wit, of ẏ Gētiles, as he did Luke, Timothie & Tite first, & others after to preache his worde.

i Hereby he signifieth ẏ kigdome of Christ wherein his Church shal be renued, & where as before there were appointed seasons to sacrifice: in this there shalbe one continual Sabbath so ẏ all times and seasons shalbe mete.

k As he hathe declared ẏ felicitie that shalbe within ẏ Church for ẏ cōfort of the godlie, so doeth he shewe what horrible calamitie shal come to the wicked, ẏ are out of the Church.

l Meaning, a cōtinual tormēt of consciēce, ẇ shal euer gnawe them & neuer suffer them to be at rest, Mark. 9, 44.

m This is the iuste recompence for the wicked, which contemning God and his worde, shalbe by Gods iuste iudgemēt abhorred of all his creatures.

IEREMIAH.

THE ARGUMENT.

THe Prophet Ieremiáh borne in the citie of Anathóth in the countrey of Beniamín, was the sonne of Hilkiáh, whome some thinke to be he that founde out the boke of the Lawe, and gaue it to Iosiáh. This Prophet had excellent giftes of God, and moste euident reuelations of prophecie, so that by the commandement of the Lord he began very yong to prophecie, that is, in the thirtenth yere of Iosiáh, and continued eightene yere vnder the said King, and thre moneths vnder Iehoaház, and vnder Iehoiakím eleuen yeres, and thre moneths vnder Iehoiachín, and vnder Zedekiáh eleuen yeres: vnto the time that they were caryed away into Babylon. So that this time amounteth to aboue fourty yere, besides the time that he prophecied after the captiuitie. In this boke he declareth with teares, and lamentation the destruction of Ierusalém, and the captiuitie of the people, for their idolatrie, couetousnes, subtiltie, crueltie, excesse, rebellion, and contempt of Gods worde, and for the consolacion of the Church, reueileth the iuste time of their deliuerance. And here chiefly are to be considered thre things. First the rebellion of the wicked, which waxe more stubberne and obstinate, when the Prophetes do admonish them moste plainely of their destruction. Next how the Prophetes and ministers of God oght not to be discouraged in their vocatió, thogh they be persecuted & rigorously handeled of the wicked for Gods cause. And thirdely, thogh God shewe his iuste iudgemét against the wicked, yet wil he euer shewe him self a preseruer of his Church, and when all meanes seme to mans iudgement to be abolished, thé wil he declare him self victorious in preseruing his.

CHAP. I.

1 In what time Ieremiáh prophecied. 6 He acknowledgeth his imperfection, and is strengthened of the Lord. 11 The Lord sheweth him the destruction of Ierusalém. 17 He commandeth him to preache his worde without feare.

1 THE [a] wordes of Ieremiáh
the sonne of [b] Hilkiáh one
of the Priests that were at
[c] Anathóth in the land of
Beniamín.
2 To whome the [d] worde of
the Lord came in the daies
of Iosiáh the sonne of Amón King of Iudáh in the thirtenth yere of his reigne:
3 And also in the daies of Iehoiakím the
[e] sonne of Iosiáh King of Iudáh vnto the
end of the eleuenth yere of Zedekiáh the
sonne of Iosiáh King of Iudah, *euen* vnto
the carying awaie of Ierusalém captiue in
the fift [f] moneth.
4 Then the worde of the Lord came vnto
me, saying,
5 Before I [g] formed thee in the wombe, I
knewe thee, and before thou camest out of
the wombe, I sanctified thee, & ordeined
thee to be a Prophet vnto the [h] nations.
6 Then said I, [i] Oh, Lord God, beholde, I
can not speake, for I am a childe.
7 But the Lord said vnto me, Saie not, I
am a childe: for thou shalt go to all that
I shal send thee, and whatsoeuer I commande thee, shalt thou speake.
8 Be not afraid of their faces: for I am with
thee to deliuer thee, saith the Lord.
9 Then the Lord stretched out his hand &
[k] touched my mouth, and the Lord said vnto me, Beholde, I haue put my wordes in
thy mouth.
10 Beholde, this daie haue I set thee ouer ŷ
[l] natiós and ouer the kingdomes to plucke
vp, and to roote out, and to destroy and
throwe downe, to buylde, and to plant.
11 After this ŷ worde of the Lord came vnto me, saying, Ieremiáh, what seest thou?
And I said, I se a [m] rod of an almonde tre.
12 Then said the Lord vnto me, Thou hast
sene aright: for I wil hasten my worde to
performe it.
13 Againe the worde of the Lord came vnto me the seconde time, saying, What seest
thou? And I said, I se a seething [n] pot lokīg
out of the North.
14 Then said the Lord vnto me, Out of the
[o] North shal a plague be spred vpon all
the inhabitans of the land.
15 For lo, I wil call all the families of the
kingdomes of the North, saith the Lord,
and thei shal come, and euerie one shal set
his throne in the entring of the gates of
Ierusalém, and on all the walles thereof
rounde about, and in all ŷ cities of Iudáh.
16 And I wil declare vnto them my [p] iudgements touching all the wickednes of them
that haue forsaken me, and haue burnt incense vnto other gods, and worshiped the
workes of their owne hands.
17 Thou therefore trusse vp thy loynes, &
arise & speake vnto them all that I commande thee: be not afrayed of their faces,
lest I [q] destroye thee before them.
18 For I, beholde, I this day haue made thee a

a That is, the sermons and prophecies.
b Which is thoght to be he ŷ founde ŷ booke of the Law vnder King Iosiáh, 2.King 22,8.
c This was a citie about thre miles distát fró Ierusalém, and belonged to ŷ Priests ŷ sonnes of Aarón, Iosh.21,18.
d This is spoken to cófirme his vocation & office: forasmuche as he did not presume of him self to preache, & prophecie, but was called thereunto by God.
e Meaning, ŷ nephewe of Iosiáh: for Iehoaház was his father, who reigned but thre moneths and therefore is not mencioned, no more is Ioachín that reigned no longer.
f Of the eleuenth yere of Zedekiáh, who was also called Mattaniáh, and at this time the Iewes were caried away into Babylon by Nebuchadnezzár.
g The Scripture vseth this maner of speache to declare, that God hathe appointed his ministers to their offices before thei were borne, as Isa.49,1 gal.1,15.
h For Ieremiáh did not onely prophecie against the Iewes, but also against the Egyptians, Babylonians, Moabites, and other nations.
i Considering the great iudgements of God, which according to his threatenings shulde come vpon the worlde, he was moued with a certeine compassion on the one side to pitie them that shulde thus perish, & on the other side by ŷ infirmitie of mās nature knowing how hard a thing it was to enterprise suche a charge, as Isa.6,11. exod 3,11. & 4,1.

k Which declareth, ŷ God maketh them mete, & assureth thé, whome he calleth to set forthe his glorie: giuing them all meanes necessarie for the same, Exod.4,12. Isa 6,7.
l He sheweth, what is ŷ autoritie of Gods true ministers, ŵ by his worde haue power to beat downe whatsoeuer lifteth it self vp against God: & to plant & assure the humble, & suche as giue them selues to the obedie̅ce of Gods worde, 2.Cor. 10,4. ebr.4,12. and these are ŷ keyes which Christ hathe left to loose, & binde, Mat. 18,18.
m He ioyneth ŷ signe with ŷ worde for a more ample confirmation: signifying by the rod of the almond tre, ŵ first buddeth, ŷ hastie cóming of the Babylonians against the Iewes.
n Signifying, that the Caldeans, & Assyriās shuld be as a pot to seethe ŷ Iewes, which boyled in their pleasures, and lustes.
o Syria & Assyria were Northward in respect of Ierusalém, which were the Caldeans dominion.
p I wil giue them charge and power to execute my vengeance against the idolaters, ŵ haue forsaken me for their idoles.
q Which declareth ŷ Gods vengeāce is prepared against them, ŵ dare not execute their duetie faithfully, ether for feare of mā, or for anie other cause, 1.Cor.9,16.

r Signifying on ye one parte, that the more that Satan, and the worlde rage against Gods ministers, the more present wil he be to help thẽ, Iosh. 1,5. ebr. 13,5. & on the other parte, that thei are vtterly vnmete to serue God, and his Church, which are afraide, and do not resist wickednes, whatsoeuer danger depende thereon, Isa. 50,7, ezek. 3,8.

defenced citie, and an [r] yron piller & walles of brasse against the whole lãd, against
the Kings of Iudáh, & against the princes
thereof, against the Priests thereof and a-
gainst the people of the land.
19 For they shal fight against thee, but thei
shal not preuaile against thee: for I am wt
thee to deliuer thee, saith the Lord.

CHAP. II.

2 God rehearseth his benefites done vnto the Iewes. 8 Against the Priests and false prophetes. 12 The Iewes are destroyed, because they forsake God.

1 MOreouer, the worde of the Lord came vnto me, saying,
2 Go, and cry in the eares of Ierusalém,
saying, Thus saith the Lord, I remember
thee, with the [a] kindenes of thy youth *and*
ye loue of thy mariage, when thou wentest
after me in the wildernes [b] in a land that
was not sowen.
3 Israél *was as* a thing [c] halowed vnto the
Lord, & his first frutes: all they [d] that eat
it, shal offend: euil shal come vpon them,
saith the Lord.
4 Heare ye the worde of the Lord, ô house
of Iaakób, and all the families of the house of Israél.
5 Thus saith the Lord, What iniquitie haue your fathers founde in me, that they
are gone [e] farre from me, and haue walked
after vanitie, and are become [f] vaine?
6 For they said not, Where is ye Lord that
broght vs vp out of the land of Egypt?
that led vs through ye wildernes, through
a desert, and waste land, through a drye
land, and [g] by the shadowe of death, by
a land that no man passed through, and
where no man dwelt?
7 And I broght you into a plentiful countrey, to eat the frute thereof, and the commodities of the same: but when ye entred,
ye defiled [h] my land, and made mine heritage an abominacion.
8 The Priests said not, [i] Where is the
Lord? and they that shulde minister the
[k] Law, knewe me not: ye [l] pastours also offended against me, and the prophetes prophecied in [m] Báal, and went after *things*
that did not profite.
9 Wherefore I wil yet [n] plead with you,
saith the Lord, and I wil plead with your
childrens children.
10 For go ye to the yles of [o] Chittím, & beholde, and send vnto [p] Kedár, and take diligent hede, and se whether there be suche
things.
11 Hathe *anie* nation changed their gods,

a According to that grace, and fauour, wc I shewed thee from the beginning, when I did first chuse thee to be my people, and maried thee to my self, Ezek. 16,3.
b When I had deliuered thee out of Egypt.
c Chosen aboue all other to serue the Lord onely, & the first offred to the Lord of all other natiõs
d Whosoeuer did chaleng this people, or els did annoy them, was punished.
e That is, fallen to moste vile idolatrie.
f Altogether giuen to vanitie, and are become blinde and insensible as the idoles, that thei serue.
g Where for lacke of all things necessarie for life, ye colde loke for nothing euerie houre but present death.
h By your idolatrie, & wicked maners, Psal. 78,58, and 106,38.
i Thei taught not the people to seke after God.
k As the Scribes, wc shulde haue expounded the Law to the people.
l Meaning, the princes and ministers: signifying that all estates were corrupt.
m That is, spake vaine things, and broght the people from the true worship of God to serue idoles: for by Báal, which was the chief idole of the Moabites, are ment all idoles.
n Signifying, that he wolde not as he might, streight way condemne them, but sheweth them by euident examples their great ingratitude, that they might be ashamed, and repent.
o Meaning, the Grecians & Italians.
p Vnto Arabia.

which yet are no gods? but my people haue
chãged their [q] glorie, for that which doeth
not [r] profite.
12 O ye [s] heauens, be astonied at this: be
afrayed and vtterly cõfounded, saith the
Lord.
13 For my people haue cõmitted two euils:
they haue forsakẽ me [t] the fountaine of liuing waters, to digge thẽ pittes, *euen* broken pittes, that can holde no water.
14 Is Israél a [u] seruant, or is he borne in the
house? why *then* is he spoiled?
15 The [x] lyons roared vpon him & yelled,
and they haue made his land waste: his cities are burnt without [y] an inhabitant.
16 Also the children of [z] Noph and Taha-
panés haue [a] broken thine head.
17 Hast not thou procured this vnto thy
self, because thou hast forsaken the Lord
thy God, when he [b] led thee by the way?
18 And what hast thou now to do in the
way of [c] Egypt? to drinke the water of
Nilus? or what makest thou in the way of
Asshúr? to drinke the water of the [d] Riuer?
19 Thine owne wickednes shal [e] correct
thee, and thy turnings backe shal reproue
thee: knowe therefore and beholde, that it
is an euil thing, and bitter, that thou hast
forsaken the Lord thy God, and that my
feare *is* not in thee, saith the Lord God of
hostes.
20 For of olde time I haue brokẽ thy yoke,
& burst thy bõds, and thou saidest, [f] I wil
no more trãsgresse, but *like* an harlot thou
runnest about vpon all hie hilles, and vnder all grene trees.
21 Yet I had plãted thee, a noble vine, whose " plants were all natural: how then art
thou turned vnto me into the plants of a
strange vine?
22 Thogh thou wash thee with [g] nitre, &
take thee muche sope, *yet* thine iniquitie is
marked before me, saith the Lord God.
23 How canst thou say, I am not polluted,
nether haue I [h] followed Baalím? beholde
thy wayes in the valley, and knowe, what
thou hast done: *thou art like* a swift [i] drome-
darie, that runneth by his wayes.
24 *And as* a wilde [k] asse, vsed to the wildernes, that snoffeth vp the winde by occasiõ
at her pleasure: who cã turne her backe? all
thei that seke her, wil not weary them selues, *but* wil finde her in her [l] moneth.

q That is, God which is their glorie, & who maketh them glorious aboue all other people: reprouing the Iewes, that they were lesse diligẽt to serue ye true God, then were the idolaters to honour their vanities.
r Meaning, the idoles, which were their destruction, Psal. 106,36.
s He sheweth, that the insensible creatures abhorre this vile ingratitude, and as it were, tremble for feare of Gods great iudgements against the same.
t Signifying, yt when men forsake Gods worde, which is the fountaine of life, they reiect God him self, and so fall to their owne inuencions, & vaine confidẽce, and procure to thẽ selues destructiõ. Iona 2,8. zach. 10,2.
u Haue I ordered them like seruants, & not like dere-lie beloued children? Exo. 4,22. therefore it is their faut onely, if the enemie spoile them.
x The Babylonians, Chaldeans & Assyrians.
y Not one shal be left to dwell there.
z That is, the Egyptians: for these were two great cities in Egypt
a Haue grieuously vexed thee at sondrie times.
b Shewing, yt God wolde haue stil led them aright, if thei wolde haue followed hĩ.
c To seke helpe of man, as thogh God were not able ynough to defende thee, which is to drinke of the puddels, and to leaue the fountaine, read Isa. 31,1.
d To wit, Euphrates.
e Meaning, that the wicked are insensible til the punishment for their sinne waken them, as verse 26. Isa. 3,9.
f When I deliuered thee out of Egypt, Deu. 27,12. iosh. 24,16. ezrá. 10, 12. nehem. 8,7. "Ebr. *sede was all true.*
g Thogh thou vse all ye purifications and ceremonies of the Law, thou canst not escape punishment, except thou turne to me by faith, and repentance
h Meaning, that hypocrites denie yt thei worship the idoles, but that they honour God in them, and therefore they call their doings Gods seruice.
i He compareth the idoles to these beastes, because they neuer cease running to and fro: for bothe valleis, and hils are ful of their idolatrie.
k He compareth the idolaters to a wilde asse: for she cã neuer be tamed, nor yet wearied: for as she rũneth, she can take her winde at euerie occasion
l That is, whẽ she is wt fole, & therefore the hũters waite their time: so thogh thou canst not be turned backe now from thine idolatrie, yet when thine iniquitie shalbe at the ful, God wil mete with thee.

25 Kepe thou thy fete from [m] barenes, and
thy throte from thirſt:but thou ſaidſt deſ-
peratly,No,for I haue loued ſtrangers,&
them wil I followe.
26 As the [n] theſe is aſhamed, when he is
founde, ſo is the houſe of Iſraél aſhamed,
they,their Kings, their princes and their
Prieſts,and their Prophetes,
27 Saying to a tre, Thou art my [o] father,&
to a ſtone, Thou haſt begotten me: for
they haue turned their backe vnto me,and
not their face: but in ỹ time of their trouble they wil ſay, Ariſe,and helpe vs.
28 But where are thy gods, that thou haſt
made thee?let them ariſe, if thei can helpe
thee in the time of thy trouble:for according [p] to the nomber of thy cities, are thy
gods,ô Iudáh.
29 Wherefore wil [q] ye pleade with me? ye
all haue rebelled againſt me, ſaieth the
Lord.
30 I haue ſmitten your children in vaine,
they receiued no correction: your [r] owne
ſworde hathe deuoured your Prophetes
like a deſtroying lyon.
31 O generacion, take hede to the worde of
the Lord:haue I bene *as* a [ſ] wildernes vnto
Iſraél? or a land of darkenes? Wherefore
ſaith my people *then*, We are [t] lords, we
wil come no more vnto thee?
32 Can a maide forget her ornament, or a
bride her attire? yet my people haue forgotten me,daies without nomber.
33 Why doeſt thou prepare thy way,to [u] ſeke amitie?euen therefore wil I teache *thee*,
that thy waies *are* wickednes.
34 Alſo in thy [x] wings is founde the blood
of the ſoules of the poore innocents:I haue not founde it in holes,but vpon all theſe *places*.
35 Yet thou ſaiſt, Becauſe I am giltles, ſurely his wrath ſhal turne frõ me:beholde,
I wil entre with thee into iudgement, becauſe thou ſaieſt, I haue not ſinned.
36 Why runneſt thou about ſo muche to
change thy waies? for thou ſhalt be confounded of Egypt, [y] as thou art confounded of Aſſhúr.
37 For thou ſhalt go forthe from thence, &
thine hands vpon [z] thine head,becauſe the
Lord hathe reiected thy confidence, and
thou ſhalt not proſper thereby.

m Hereby he warneth them that thei ſhulde not go into ſtrange countreis to ſeke helpe: for thei ſhuld but ſpẽd their labour,& hurt them ſelues, which is here ment by the bare fote and thirſt, Iſa.57,10.
n As a theſe wil not acknowledge his faute,til he be taken with the dede, & ready to be puniſhed, ſo they wil not confeſſe their idolatrie,til the plagues due to ỹ ſame light vpon them.
o Meaning, ỹ idolaters ſpoyle God of his honour:& whereas he hathe taught to call him the father of all fleſh, they attribute this title to their idoles.
p Thou thoghteſt that thy gods of blockes and ſtones colde haue holpẽ thee,becauſe they were many in nomber & preſent in euery place: but now let vs ſe whether ether the multitude, or their preſence can deliuer thee from my plague,Chap 11,13
q As thogh I did you iniurie in puniſhĩg you,ſeing that your fautes are ſo euident.
r That is, you haue killed your Prophetes,that exhorted you to repentance,as Zechariáh,Iſaiáh,&c.
ſ Haue I not giuen them abundance of all things?
t But wil truſt in our owne power & policie.
u With ſtrangers.
x The Prophetes and the faithful are ſlayne in euery corner of your countrey.
y For the Aſſyrians had taken away the ten tribes out of Iſraél,and deſtroyed Iudá, euen vnto Ieruſalém:and the Egyptians ſlewe Ioſiáh, and vexed the Iewes in ſondry ſortes.
z In ſigne of lamentacion,as 2 Sam.13,19.

CHAP. III.

God calleth his people vnto repentance. 14 He promiſeth the reſtitucion of his Church. 20 He reproueth Iudáh & Iſraél,comparing them to a woman diſobedient to her houſband.

1 THey [a] ſay,If a mã put away his wife,
and ſhe go from him,and become another mans, ſhal he returne againe vnto
her? ſhal not this land [b] be polluted? but ỹ
haſt plaied the harlot with manie [c] louers:
yet [d] turne againe to me, ſaith the Lord.
2 Lift vp thine eies vnto the high places,&
beholde, where thou haſt not plaied the
harlot:thou haſt ſit *waiting* for them in the
waies,as the [e] Arabian in the wildernes: &
ỹ haſt polluted the land with thy whoredomes,and with thy malice.
3 Therefore the ſhowres haue bene reſtrai-
ned, and the [f] latter raine came not, and
thou haddeſt a [g] whores forheade: thou
woldeſt not be aſhamed.
4 Dideſt thou not ſtil crye [h] vnto me, Thou
art my father, & the guide of my youth?
5 Wil he kepe *his angre* for euer? wil he reſerue it to the end? thus haſt thou ſpoken,
but thou doeſt euil, euen more and more.
6 The Lord ſaid alſo vnto me,in the daies
of Ioſiáh the King, Haſt thou ſene what
this rebel [i] Iſraél hathe done?*for* ſhe hathe
gone vp vpon euery high mountaine, and
vnder euery grene tre, & there plaied the
harlot.
7 And I ſaid, when ſhe had done all this,
Turne thou vnto me:but ſhe returned not,
as her rebellious ſiſter Iudáh ſawe.
8 When I ſawe, how that by all occaſions
rebellious Iſraél had plaied the harlot, I
caſt [k] her away, and gaue her a byl of de-
uorcement: yet her rebellious ſiſter Iudáh
was not afrayed,but ſhe went alſo,& plaied the harlot.
9 So that for the [l] lightnes of her whoredome ſhe hathe euen defiled the land: for
ſhe hathe committed fornicaciõ with ſtones and ſtockes.
10 Neuertheles for all this,her rebellious
ſiſter Iudáh hathe not returned vnto me
with [m] her whole heart,but fainedly, ſaith
the Lord.
11 And the Lord ſaid vnto me, The rebellious Iſraél hathe [n] iuſtified her ſelf more
then the rebellious Iudáh.
12 Go and crye theſe wordes towarde [o] the
North and ſaie, Thou diſobedient Iſraél,
returne,ſaith the Lord,& I wil not let my
wrath fall vpon you: for I am merciful,
ſaith the Lord,& I wil not alway kepe *mine angre*.
13 But knowe thine iniquitie:for thou haſt
rebelled againſt the Lord thy God & haſt
[p] ſcatered thy waies to the ſtrange *gods* vnder euerie grene tre, but ye wolde not o-
beye my voyce,ſaith the Lord.
14 O ye diſobedient childrẽ, turne againe,
ſaith the Lord, for I am your Lord,and I
wil take you one of a citie, and two of a
tribe and wil bring you to Zión,
15 And I wil giue you paſtours according

a According as it is writẽ, Deut.24,4.
b If he take ſuche one to wife againe.
c That is,with idoles,& with them, whome thou haſt put thy confidence in.
d And I wil not caſt thee of,but receiue thee,accordĩg to my mercie.
e Which dwelleth in tents & waiteth for thẽ that paſſe by to ſpoyle them
f As God threatned by his Law, Deut.28,24
g Thou woldeſt neuer be aſhamed of thine actes & repent: & this impudencie is cõmune to idolaters, ỽ wil not giue of,thogh they be neuer ſo manifeſtly cõuicted
h He ſheweth that ỹ wicked in their miſeries wil crye vnto God and vſe outward praier as the godlie do,but becauſe they turne not frõ their euil, they are not heard, Iſa.18,41.
i Meaning, ỹ ten tribes.
k And gaue her vnto the hands of the Aſſyrians.
l The Ebrew worde may ether ſignifie lightnes& wãtõnes,or noiſe and brute.
m Iudáh fayned for a time as that ſhe did returne, as vnder Ioſiáh and other good Kings, but ſhe was neuer truely touched, or wholy reformed,as appeared when occaſion was offred by any wicked price.
n Iſraél hathe not declared her ſelf ſo wicked,as Iudáh, which yet hathe had more admonicions and examples to call her to repentance
o Where as ỹ Iſraelites were now kept in captiuitie by the Aſſyrians,to whome he promiſeth mercie,if they wil repent.
p There was no way,which thou dideſt not hante to ſeke after the idoles,and to trot a pilgrimage.

to mine heart, which shal fede you with
knowledge and vnderstanding.
16 Moreouer, when ye be increased & multiplied in the land, in those daies, saith the
Lord, thei shal say no more, The [q] Arke of
the couenant of the Lord: for it shal come
no more to minde, nether shal they remẽber it, nether shal they visit it, for that
shalbe no more done.
17 At that time they shal call Ierusalém,
[r] The throne of the Lord, & all the nacions shalbe gathered vnto it, *euen* to ŷ Name of the Lord in Ierusalém: and thence
forthe they shal followe no more the hardenes of their wicked heart.
18 In those daies the house of Iudáh shal
walke with the house of Israél, & thei shal
come together out of ŷ land of ŷ [s] North,
into the land, that I haue giuen for an inheritance vnto your fathers.
19 But I said, How did I take thee for children & giue thee a pleasant land, *euen* the
glorious heritage of the armies of the
heathen, and said, Thou shalt call me, *saying*, My father, and shalt not turne frõ me?
20 But *as* a woman rebelleth against her
[t] housbãd: so haue ye rebelled against me,
ô house of Israél, saith the Lord.
21 [u] A voyce was heard vpon the high places, weping and supplicacions of the childrẽ of Israél: for thei haue peruerted their
way, & forgotten the Lord their God.
22 O ye disobedient children, returne *and*
I wil heale your rebellions. [x] Beholde, we
come vnto thee, for thou art the Lord our
God.
23 Truely *the hope* of the hilles *is* but vaine,
nor the multitude of mountaines: but in
the Lord our God is the health of Israél.
24 For confusion hathe deuoured our [y] fathers labour, from our youth their shepe &
their bullockes, their sonnes and their
daughters.
25 We lie downe in our confusion, and our
shame couereth vs: [z] for we haue sinned
against the Lord our God, we and our fathers from our youth: euen vnto this day,
& haue not obeied the voyce of the Lord
our God.

q This is to be vnderstand of the comming of Chirst: for then they shal not seke the Lord by ceremonies, & all figures shal cease.
r Meaning the Church, where the Lord wil be presẽt to the worldes end, Mat. 28,20.
s Where they are now in captiuitie.
t The Ebrewe worde signifieth a friẽd or companiõ, & here may be taken for a housbãd, as it is vsed also Hoseáh 3,1.
u Signifying, ŷ God, whome they had forsaken, wolde brĩg their enemies vpon thẽ, who shulde lead thẽ captiue and make them to crye and lament.
x This is spoken in the persone of Israél to the shame of Iudáh, which staied so long to turne vnto God.
y For their idolatrie Gods vengeance hathe light vpon thẽ & theirs.
z They iustifie not thẽ selues, or say ŷ they wolde follow their fathers, but condemne their wicked doings and desire forgiuenes of the same, 1. Ezra 9 7. as psal. 106,6. isa. 64,6.

CHAP. IIII.

1 True repentance. 4 He exhorteth to the circumcision of the heart. 5 The destruction of Iudáh is prophecied, for the malice of their hearts. 19 The Prophet lamẽteth it.

1 O Israél, if thou returne, [a] returne vnto me, saith the Lord: & if thou put
away thine abominaciõs out of my sight,
then shalt thou not remoue.
2 And thou shalt [b] sweare, The Lord liueth
in trueth, in iudgement, and in righteousnes, and the nacions shalbe blessed in him,
and shal glorie in him.
3 For thus saith the Lord to the men of Iudáh, and to Ierusalém,
4 Breake vp [c] your fallow grounde, & sowe
not among the thornes: be circumcised to
the Lord, and take away the foreskinnes
of your hearts, ye men of Iudáh, and inhabitants of Ierusalém, lest my wrath come forthe like fyre, and burne, that none
can quench it, because of the wickednes
of your inuentions.
5 [d] Declare in Iudáh, and shewe forthe in
Ierusalém, and say, Blowe the trumpet in
the land: crye, and gather together, & say,
Assemble your selues, and let vs go into
strong cities.
6 Set vp the standart in Zión: [e] prepare
to flee, & stay not: for I wil bring a plague
from the North, and a great destruction.
7 The [f] lyon is come vp from his denne,
and the destroyer of the Gentiles is departed, & gone forthe of his place to lay
thy land waste, *and* thy cities shalbe destroyed without an inhabitant.
8 Wherefore girde you with sackecloth:
lament, and howle, for the fierce wrath of
the Lord is not turned backe from vs.
9 And in that day, saith the Lord, the heart
of the King shal perish, and the heart of
the princes and the Priests shalbe astonished, and the [g] Prophetes shal wonder.
10 Then said I, Ah, Lord God, surely thou
hast [h] deceiued this people & Ierusalém,
saying, Ye shal haue peace, and the sworde
perceth vnto the heart.
11 At that time shal it be said to this people and to Ierusalém, A drye [i] winde in
the hie places of the wildernes *cometh* toward the daughter of my people, *but* nether
[k] to fan, nor to clense.
12 A mightie winde shal come vnto me frõ
those *places, and* now wil I also giue sentence vpon them.
13 Beholde, he shal come vp as the [l] cloudes,
and his charets *shalbe* as a tempest: his horses are lighter then egles. [m] Wo vnto vs,
for we are destroied.
14 O Ierusalém, wash thine heart from
wickednes, that thou maiest be saued: how
long shal thy wicked thoghts remaine
within thee?
15 For a voyce declareth from [n] Dan, and
publisheth affliction frõ mout [o] Ephráim.
16 Make ye mentiõ of the heathẽ, *and* publish in Ierusalém, Beholde, the skoutes
come from a farre countrey, and crye out
against the cities of Iudáh.
17 They haue compassed her about as the
watchemen of the [p] field, because it hathe
prouoked me to wrath, saith the Lord.
18 Thy waies & thine inuentions haue pro-

Chap. IIII.
a That is, wholy, & without hypocrisie, Ioel. 2,12, not dissembling to turne & serue God as they do which serue him by halues, as Hos. 7, 16.
b Thou shalt detest the name of idoles, Psal 16,4. & shalt with reuerence sweare by the lyuing God, when thine othe may aduance Gods glorie, & profite others, & here, by swearing he meaneth the true religion of God.

c He willeth them to plucke vp the impietie and wicked affection and worldelie respectes out of their heart that the true sede of Gods worde may be sowen therein, Hos. 10, 12. and this is the true circumcisiõ of ŷ heart, Deut. 10,16. rom. 2,29. col. 2,11.
d He warneth them of the great dangers ŷ shal come vpon them by the Caldeans, except they repent, and turne to ŷ Lord.
e He speaketh this to admonish them of ŷ great danger when euery mã shal prepare to saue him self, but it shal be to late 2. King 25,4.
f Meanĩg Nebuchadnezzár King of Babylõ 2 King 24,1.
g That is, the false prophetes which stil prophecied peace and securitie.
h By the false prophetes, ŵ promised peace and tranquillitie: and thus thou hast punished their rebellious stubbernes by causing them to hearken vnto lies which wolde not beleue thy trueth 2. King 22,23. ezek. 14,9. 2. thess 2,11.
i The North winde whereby he meaneth Nebuchadnezzár.
k But to cary away bothe corne and chaffe.
l Meaning ŷ Nebuchadnezzár shulde come as suddenly, as a cloude that is caryed with ŷ winde.
m This is spoken in the persone of all the people who in their affliction shulde crye thus.
n Which was a citie in the vtmost border of Israél Northward toward Babylon.
o Which was in the midway betwene Dan and Ierusalém.
p Which kepe the frutes so streitly, that nothing can come in nor out: so shulde the Babylonians compasse Iudáh.

cured

cured thee these things, suche is thy wickednes: therefore it shalbe bitter, therefore it shal perce vnto thine heart.
19 My bely, q my bely, I am peined, euen
at the very heart: mine heart is troubled
within me: I can not be styl: for my soule
hathe heard the sounde of the trumpet, &
the alarme of the battel.
20 Destruction vpon destruction is cryed,
for the whole land is wasted: suddenly a-
re my r tentes destroyed, *and* my curteines
in a moment.
21 How long shal I se the standart, & heare the sounde of the trumpet?
22 For my people is foolish, thei haue not
knowen me: thei are foolish childrē, & haue none vnderstanding: s thei are wise to
do euil, but to do wel thei haue no knowe-
ledge.
23 I haue loked vpon the earth, and lo, it
was without forme and t voide: and to the
heauens, and thei had no light.
24 I beheld the moūtaines: & lo, they trem
bled and all the hilles shooke.
25 I beheld, and lo, there was no man, and
all the birdes of the heauen were departed.
26 I beheld, and lo, the fruteful place *was* a
wildernes, and all their cities thereof were
brokē downe at the presence of the Lord,
and by his fierce wrath.
27 For thus hathe ẏ Lord said, The whole
land shalbe desolate: yet wil I u not make
a ful end.
28 Therefore shal the earth mourne, and
the heauens aboue shalbe darkened, because I haue pronounced it: I haue thoght
it, and wil not repent, nether wil I turne
backe from it.
29 The whole citie shal flee, for the noise
of the horsmen and bowe mē: thei shal go
into thickets, and clime vp vpon the rockes: euerie citie shalbe forsaken, and not a
man dwell therein.
30 And when thou shalt be destroyed, what
wilt thou do? Thogh thou x clothest thy
self with skarlet, thogh thou deckest thee
with ornamēts of golde, thogh thou pain-
test thy face with colours, yet shalt thou
trimme thy self in vaine: *for* thy louers wil
abhorre thee & seke thy life.
31 For I haue heard a noise as of a woman trauailing, or as one laboring of her
first childe, *euen* the voice of the daughter
Ziōn that sigheth and stretcheth out her
hands: y wo is me now: for my soule fainteth because of the murtherers.

q He sheweth that the true ministers are liuely touched with the calamities of the Church, so that all the partes of their bodie fele the grief of their heart, albeit with zeale to Gods glorie thei pronounce his iudgements against the people.

r Meaning the cities, which were as easely cast downe as a tent.

s Their wisdome and policie tende to their owne destruction, and pulleth them from God.

t By these maner of speaches he sheweth the horrible destruction that shulde come vpon the land, and also condemneth the obstinacie of the people, who repent not at the feare of these terrible tydings, seing that ẏ insensible creatures are moued therewith, as if the order of nature shulde be chāged, Isa. 13, 10 and 24, 23 ezek. 32, 7. ioel. 2, 31. & 3, 15.

u But for his mercie sake he wil reserue him selfe a residue to be his Church, and to praise him in earth, Isa 2, 9.

x Nether thy ceremonies nor riche gyftes shal deliuer thee.

y As the Prophetes were moued to pitie the destructiō of their people, so thei declared it to the people to moue them to repentance, Isa. 22, 4 chap. 9.

CHAP. V.

1 In Iudáh no righteous man found nether among the people nor the rulers. 15 Wherefore Iudáh is destroied of the Caldeans.

1 RVnne to & fro by the stretes of Ierusalém, and beholde now, & knowe, &
inquire in the open places thereof, if ye
can finde a man, *or* if there be any that executeth iudgement, and seketh the trueth,
and I wil spare a it.
2 For thogh thei say, The b Lord liueth,
yet do thei sweare falsely.
3 O Lord, are not thine eies vpon ẏ c trueth?
thou hast d striken them, but thei haue not
sorowed: thou hast cōsumed them, *but* thei
haue refused to receiue correction: thei
haue made their faces harder then a stone, *and* haue refused to returne.
4 Therefore I said, Surely thei are poore,
they are foolish, for thei knowe not the way
of the Lord, *nor* ẏ iudgement of their God.
5 I wil get me vnto the e great men, and wil
speake vnto them: for thei haue knowen ẏ
way of the Lord, *and* the iudgement of
their God: but these haue altogether broken the yoke, *and* burst the bondes.
6 Wherefore f a lion out of the forest shal
slay them, and a wolfe of the wildernes
shal destroye them: a leoparde shal watche
ouer their cities: euerie one that goeth out
thence, shalbe torne ī pieces, because their
trespaces are many, *and* their rebellions a-
re encreased.
7 How shulde I spare thee for this? thy chil
dren haue forsakē me, & g sworne by them
ẏ are no gods: thogh I fed them to ẏ ful,
yet thei committed adulterie, and assembled them selues by companies in the har
lottes houses.
8 They rose vp in ẏ morning *like* fed horses:
for euerie man neyed after his neighbours Ezek. 22, 11.
wife.
9 Shal I not visit for these things, saith the
Lord? Shal not my soule be auenged on
suche a nation, as this?
10 h Clime vp vpon their walles, and destroy
them, but make not a ful end: i take away
their batilmēts, for thei are not the Lords.
11 For the house of Israél, and the house of
Iudáh haue grieuously trespaced against
me, saith the Lord.
12 Thei haue k denied the Lord, & said, It
is not he, nether shal ẏ plague come vpon
vs, nether shal we se sworde nor famine.
13 And the Prophetes shalbe *as* l winde, and
the worde is m not in them: thus shal it
come vnto them.
14 Wherefore thus saith the Lord God
of hostes, Because ye speake suche wordes, beholde, I wil put my wordes n into
thy mouth, like a fyre, and this people shal
be *as* wodde, and it shal deuoure them.
15 Lo, I wil bring a nation vpon you o from
far, ô house of Israél, saith the Lord, which
is a mightie nacion, & an ancient nacion, a
nacion whose language ẏ knowest not, nether vnderstandest what thei say.
16 Whose quiuer is as an p open sepulchre:
thei are all very strong.

a That is, the citie.

b Thogh they pretend religion and holines, yet all is but hypocrisie for vnder this kinde of swearing is conteined the true religion.

c Doest not ẏ loue vprightnes and faithful dealing?

d Thou hast oft times punished them, but all is in vayne, Isa. 9, 13

e He speaketh this to the reproche of thē, which shulde gouerne and teache others, & yet are farther out of ẏ way then the simple people.

f Meaning, Nebuchadnezzár and his armie.

g He sheweth that to sweare by any thing then by God, is to forsake him.

h He cōmandeth the Babylonians and enemies to destroye them.

i Read Chap. 4, 27.

k Because thei gaue no credit to the wordes of his Prophetes, as Isa. 28, 15.

l Their wordes shalbe of none effect, but vaine.

m Thei are not sent of ẏ Lord, & therefore that ẇ thei threaten to vs, shal come vpō them.

n Meaning Ieremiáh.

o To wit, the Babylonians & Caldeans.

p Who shal kil many with their arrowes.

17 And thei ſhal eat thine harueſt and thy
bread: thei ſhal deuoure thy ſonnes & thy
daughters: thei ſhal eat vp thy ſhepe and
thy bullocks: thei ſhal eat thy vines & thy
figtrees: thei ſhal deſtroie with yͤ ſworde
thy fenſed cities, wherein yͧ dideſt truſt.
18 Neuertheles at thoſe daies, ſaith the
Lord, I wil not make a ful end of [q] you.
19 And when *ye ſhal ſaie, Wherefore doeth
yͤ Lord our God do theſe things vnto vs?
then ſhalt [r] thou anſwer them, Like as ye
haue forſaken me and ſerued ſtrange gods
in your land, ſo ſhal ye ſerue ſtrangers in
a land that is not yours.
20 Declare this in the houſe of Iaakób &
publiſh it in Iudáh, ſaying,
21 Heare now this, ô fooliſh people, and
"without vnderſtãding, which haue *eyes
and ſe not, which haue eares & heare not.
22 Feare ye not me, ſaith the Lord? or wil ye
not be afraid at my preſence, which haue
placed the ſande for the bondes of the ſea
by the perpetual decre that it can not paſſe
it, and thogh the waues thereof rage, yet
can thei not preuaile, thogh thei roare, *yet*
can thei not paſſe ouer it?
23 But this people hathe an vnfaithful and
rebellious heart: thei are departed & gone.
24 For they ſay not in their heart, Let vs
now feare the Lord our God, that giueth
raine bothe early & late in due ſeaſon: he
reſerueth vnto vs the appointed wekes of
the harueſt.
25 *Yet* your [ſ] iniquities haue turned awaie
theſe things, and your ſinnes haue hindred
good things from you.
26 For among my people are founde wicked
perſones, that laie waite as he that ſetteth
ſnares: thei haue made a pit to catche mẽ.
27 As a cage is ful of birdes, ſo are their
houſes ful of deceit: thereby thei are become great and waxen riche.
28 Thei are waxen fat *&* ſhining: thei do
ouerpaſſe the dedes of yͤ wicked: *thei execute no iudgement, no not the iudgemẽt
of the fatherles: yet thei [t] proſper, thogh
thei execute no iudgement for the poore.
29 Shal I not viſite for theſe things, ſaith
the Lord? or ſhal not my ſoule be auenged
on ſuche a nation as this?
30 An horrible and filthie thing is committed in the land.
31 The [u] Prophetes Prophecie lies, and the
Prieſtes * receiue *giftes* in their hãdes, and
my people delite therein. What wil ye
then do in the end thereof?

CHAP. VI.

1 The comming of the Aſſyrians and Caldeans. 16 He exhorteth the Iewes to repentance.

1 O Ye children of [a] Beniamín, prepare
to flee out of the middes of Ieruſalém and blow the trumpet in [b] Tekoá: ſet
vp a ſtandart vpon [c] Beth-haccérem: for
a plague appeareth out of the North and
great deſtruction.
2 I haue compared the daughter of Zión
to [d] a beautiful and deintie woman.
3 The paſtors with their flockes [e] ſhal come
vnto her: thei ſhal pitch *their* tents round
about by her, *&* euerie one ſhal fede in his
place.
4 [f] Prepare warre againſt her: ariſe, and let
vs go vp toward the South: wo vnto vs: for
the day declineth, and the ſhadowes of the
euening are ſtretched out.
5 Ariſe, and let vs go vp by night, and deſtroy her palaces.
6 For thus hathe the Lord of hoſtes ſaid,
Hewe downe wood, and caſt a mount a-
gainſt Ieruſalém: this citie muſt be viſited: all oppreſsion is in the middes of it.
7 As yͤ fountaine caſteth out her waters, ſo
ſhe caſteth out her malice: [g] crueltie and
ſpoile is continually heard in her before
me *with* ſorow and ſtrokes.
8 Be thou inſtructed, ô [h] Ieruſalém, leſt my
ſoule departe from thee, leſt I make thee
deſolate *as* a land, that none inhabiteth.
9 Thus ſaith the Lord of hoſtes, Thei ſhal
gather as a vine, the reſidue of Iſraél: turne [i] backe thine hand as the grape gatherer into the baſkets.
10 Vnto whome ſhal I ſpeake, & admoniſh
that thei may heare? beholde, their eares *a-*
re [k] vncircumciſed, and thei can not hearken: beholde, the worde of yͤ Lord is vnto them as a reproche: thei haue no delite in it.
11 Therefore I am ful of the wrath of the
Lord: I am wearie with holding it: [l] I wil
powre it out vpon the [m] childrẽ in yͤ ſtrete, & likewiſe vpõ yͤ aſſemblie of the yong
men: for the houſband ſhal euen be taken
with the wife, *&* the aged with him that is
ful of daies.
12 And their houſes *with* their lands, and
wiues alſo ſhalbe turned vnto ſtrangers:
for I wil ſtretch out mine hand vpon the
inhabitants of the land, ſaith the Lord.
13 For frõ the leaſt of them, euen vnto the
greateſt of them, euerie one is giuen vnto
couetouſnes, and from the Prophet euen
vnto the Prieſt, thei all deale falſely.
14 Thei haue healed alſo the hurt of the
daughter of my people with ſwete wordes, ſaying, [n] Peace, peace, when there is no
peace.
15 Were thei aſhamed when they had com
mitted abominacion? nay, thei were not
aſhamed, no nether colde they haue anie
ſhame: therefore thei ſhal fall among the
"ſlaine: when I ſhal viſit them, they ſhalbe
caſt downe, ſaith the Lord.
16 Thus ſaith the Lord, Stand in the waies
and beholde, and aſke for the [o] olde waie,
which is the good waye & walke therein,

q Here yͤ Lord declareth his vnſpeakeable fauour toward his Church, as Chap. 4,27.

Chap. 16,10.

r Meaning the Prophet Ieremiáh.

"*Ebr. without heart.*

Iſa. 6,9. mat. 13,14. act. 28,40. rom. 11,8.

Iob. 26,10.

ſ If there be anie ſtay, that we receiue not gods bleſsings in abundance, we muſt conſider that it is for our owne iniquities, Iſa. 59,1.

Iſa. 3,23. Zechar. 7,10.

t Thei fele not the plague of God for it.

u Meaning, that there colde be nothing but diſorder where yͤ miniſters were wicked perſones & corrupt.

**Or, beare rule.*

Chap. VI.

a He ſpeaketh to thẽ chiefly becauſe thei ſhuld take hede by yͤ example of their brethren, yͤ other halfe of their tribe, wͨ were now caried away priſoners.

b Which was a citie in Iudáh six miles from Bethléhem, 2. Chro. 11,6.

c Read Nehe. 3,14.

d I haue intreated her gẽtely & giuen her abundance of all things.

e She ſhalbe ſo deſtroied, yͭ yͤ ſhepe may be fed in her.

f He ſpeaketh this in yͤ perſone of yͤ Babylonians, wͨ complaine that the time faileth them before thei haue broght their enterpriſes to paſſe.

g He ſheweth yͤ cauſe why it ſhulde be deſtroyed & how it cometh of them ſelues.

h He warneth thẽ to amẽd by his correctiõs, & to turne to him by repentance.

i He exhorteth yͤ Babyloniãs to be diligent to ſearche out all & to leaue none.

k Thei delite to heare vayne thĩgs & to ſhut vp their eares to true doctrine.

l As the Lord had giuen him his worde to be as a fyre of his indignatiõ to burne yͤ wicked, Chap. 5,14 ſo he kĩdeleth it now whẽ he ſeeth yͭ all remedies are paſt.

m None ſhalbe ſpared.

n When yͤ people bagan to feare Gods iudgements, yͤ falſe Prophets cõforted them by flatterings, ſhewing yͭ God wolde ſend peace and not warre.

"*Ebr. them that fall.*

o Wherein the patriarkes and Prophets walked, directed by yͤ worde of God: ſignifyĩg yͭ there is no true way, but that wͨ God preſcribeth.

and ye shal finde rest for your soules: but
thei said, We wil not walke *therein*.
17 Also I set p watchemen ouer you, *which*
said, Take hede to ỹ sound of the trumpet:
but thei said, We wil not take hede.
18 Heare therefore, ye q Gentiles, and thou
Congregacion knowe, what is among
them.
19 Heare, ô earth, beholde, I wil cause a plague to come vpon this people, *euen* the
frute of their owne imaginacions: because thei haue not taken hede vnto my wordes, nor to my Law, but cast it of.
20 To what purpose bringest thou me r incense from Shebá, and swete calamus frõ
a farre countrey? Your burnt offrings a-
re not pleasant, nor your sacrifices swete
vnto me.
21 Therefore thus saith the Lord, Beholde, I wil lay stumbling blockes before this
people, and the fathers and the sonnes together shal fall vpon them: the neighbour
and his friend shal perish.
22 Thus saith the Lord, Beholde, a people
cometh from the s North countrey, and a
great nation shal arise from the sides of
the earth.
23 With bowe and shield shal they be weaponed: thei are cruel and wil haue no com
passion: their voyce roareth like the sea,
and they ride vpon horses, wel appointed,
like men of warre against thee, ô daughter
Zión.
24 We haue heard their fame, & our hands
waxe t feble: sorowe is come vpon vs, as
the sorowe of a woman in trauail.
25 Go not forthe into the field, nor walke
by the way: for the sworde of the enemie
& feare *is* on euerie side.
26 O daughter of my people, gird thee with
sackecloth, and wallowe thy self in the a-
shes: make lamentation, and bitter mourning *as* for thine onely sonne: for the destroier shal suddenly come vpon vs.
27 I haue set u thee for a defence & fortresse among my people, that thou maiest
knowe and trye their waies.
28 Thei are all rebellious traitors, walking
craftely: *they are* brasse, & yron, thei all are
destroyers.
29 The x bellowes are burnt: the leade is
cõsumed in the fyre: the founder melteth
in vaine: for the wicked are not taken a-
way.
30 Thei shal call them reprobate siluer, because the Lord hathe reiected them.

p Prophetes ŵ shulde warne you of the dangers that were at hand.
q God taketh all ỹ worlde to witnes and the insensible creatures of ỹ ingratitude of the Iewes.
r Read Isa.1,11. & Amos.5,21.
s From Babylon by Dan, ŵ was North frõ Ierusalém.
t For feare of the enemie, he speaketh this in the persone of the Iewes.
u Meaning, Ieremiáh, whom God had appointed to trie out the godlie from ỹ wicked as a founder doeth ỹ pure mettal from ỹ drosse.
x All the paine & labour ỹ hathe bene takẽ with them, is lost.

CHAP. VII.

2 Ieremiáh is commanded to shewe vnto the people the worde of God, which trusteth in the outward seruice of the Temple. 13 The euils that shal come to the Iewes for the despising of their Prophetes. 21 Sacrifices doeth not the Lord chiefly require of the Iewes, but that they shulde obeye his worde.

1 THe wordes that came to Ieremiáh
from the Lord, saying,
2 Stand in the gate of the Lords House &
crye this worde there, and saie, Heare the
worde of the Lord, all ye of Iudáh that entre in at these gates to worship the Lord.
3 Thus saith the Lord of hostes, the God
of Israél, * Amẽd your waies & your workes, and I wil let you dwell in this place.
4 Trust not in a lying wordes, saying, The
Temple of the Lord, the Temple of the
Lord: this is the Temple of the Lord.
5 For if you amend & redresse your waies
and your workes: if you execute iudgemẽt
betwene a man and his neighbour,
6 *And* oppresse not the stranger, the fatherles and the widdowe & shed no innocent
blood in this place, nether walke after o-
ther gods to your destruction,
7 Then b wil I let you dwell in this place
in the land that I gaue vnto your fathers,
for euer and euer.
8 Beholde, you truste in lying wordes, that
can not profite.
9 Wil you steale, murder, and commit adul
terie and sweare falsely and burne incense
vnto Báal, & walke after other gods whome ye knowe not?
10 And come and stand before me in this
House, whereupon my Name is called, &
saie, We are deliuered, thogh we haue
done all these abominations?
11 Is this House become c a dẽne of theues,
whereupõ my Name is called before your
eies? beholde, euen I see it, saith the Lord.
12 But go ye now vnto my place which was
in Shiló, d where I set my Name at the
beginning, and beholde, what I did to it
for the wickednes of my people Israél.
13 Therefore now because ye haue done
all these workes, saith the Lord, (& I e rose
vp earely and spake vnto you: but when I
spake, ye wolde not heare me, nether whẽ
I called, wolde f ye answer)
14 Therefore wil I do vnto this House,
whereupõ my Name is called, wherein al
so ye trust, euen vnto the place that I gaue
to you and to your fathers, as I haue done
vnto Shiló.
15 And I wil cast g you out of my sight, as I
haue cast out all your brethren, *euen* the
whole sede of Ephráim.
16 Therefore thou shalt not h praie for this
people, nether lift vp crie or praier for thẽ
nether intreat me, for I wil not heare thee.
17 Seest thou not what thei do in the cities
of Iudáh and in the stretes of Ierusalém?
18 The children gather wood, and the fathers kindle ỹ fyre, and the women knede
the dough to make cakes to i the Queen

Chap.26,13.
a Beleue not ỹ false Prophetes ŵ say that for ỹ Tẽples sake, & the sacrifices there, ỹ Lord wil preserue you, & so nourish you in your sinne, & vaine cõfidẽce
b God sheweth on what cõdition he made his promes to this Temple: ỹ they shulde be an holie people vnto him, as he wolde be a faithful God to them
c As theues hid in holes, and dennes thinke thẽ selues safe, so whẽ you are in my Tẽple. you thinke to be coue-red ŵ ỹ holines thereof, & that I can not se your wickednes, Mat. 21,12.
d Because thei depended so muche on the Temple, ŵ was for his ꝑmes, that he wolde be present, and defend them where ỹ Arke was: he sendeth them to Gods iudgements against Shiló, where ỹ Arke had remained about 300 yeres. and after was takẽ, the Priests slaine, & ỹ people miserably disconfited, 1. Sam 4.11, Cha. 26,6.
e That is, I neuer ceased to warne you, as Isa. 65,2 prouer.1,23.
f He sheweth what is ỹ onelie remedie to redresse our fautes; to suffer God to lead vs into ỹ way, & to obey his calling, Isa. 66,4.
g I wil send you into captiuitie as I haue done Ephráim, that is, the ten tribes.
h To assure thẽ ỹ God had determined ŵ him self to punish their wickednes, he sheweth that ỹ prayer of the godlie can nothing auaile them, whiles they remaine in their obstinacie against God, & wil not vse ỹ meanes ỹ he vseth to call thẽ to repentãce, Chap.11,14 & 14,11.
i That is, thei sacrifice to ỹ sunne, mone & starres, which thei called the Quene of heauen, Chap 44,17. 2 king.23,5.

of heauen & to powre out drinke offrings
vnto other gods, that thei maie prouoke
me vnto angre.
19 Do thei prouoke me to angre, saith the
Lord, and not them selues to the confusion of their owne faces?
20 Therefore thus saith the Lord God, Beholde, mine angre and my wrath shalbe
powred vpon this place, vpon man & vpon beast, and vpon the tre of the field
and vpon the frute of the grounde, and it
shal burne and not be quenched.
21 Thus saith the Lord of hostes, the God
of Israél, Put your burnt offrings vnto
your sacrifices, and eat the flesh.
22 For [k] I spake not vnto your fathers, nor
commanded them, when I broght them
out of the land of Egypt, cōcerning burnt
offrings and sacrifices.
23 But this thing commanded I them, saying, Obey my voice, & I wil be your God,
and ye shal be my people: and walke ye in
all the waies which I haue commanded
you, that it maie be wel vnto you.
24 But thei wolde not obey, nor incline their
eare, but went after the counsels *and* the
stubbernes of their wicked heart, & went
backewarde and not forwarde.
25 Since the daie that your fathers came
vp out of the Land of Egypt, vnto [l] this
day, I haue euen sent vnto you all my seruants the Prophetes, [m] rising vp early euerie daie, and sending them.
26 Yet wolde thei not heare me nor incline
their eare, but hardened their necke *and*
did worse then their fathers.
27 Therefore shalt þu speake all these wordes vnto thē, but thei [n] wil not heare thee:
thou shalt also crye vnto thē, but thei wil
not answer thee.
28 But thou shalt saie vnto them, This is a
nation þt heareth not the voice of þe Lord
their God, nor receiueth discipline: trueth
is perished, and is cleane gone out of their
mouth.
29 Cut of thine [o] heere, ô Ierusalém, & cast
it awaie, and take vp a complaint on the
hie places: for the Lord hathe reiected &
forsaken the generation of his [p] wrath.
30 For the children of Iudáh haue done e-
uil in my sight, saith the Lord: thei haue set
their abominations in the House, whereupon my Name is called, to pollute it.
31 And thei haue buylt the hie place of [q] Tópheth, which is in the vallei of Ben-Hinnóm to burne their sonnes & their daughters in the fyre, which I [r] commanded thē
not, nether came it in mine heart.
32 Therefore beholde, þe daies come, saith
the Lord, that it shal no more be called
Tópheth, nor the vallei of Ben-Hinnóm,
but the valley of slaughter: for thei shal
burye in Tópheth til there be no place.

k Shewing that it was not his chief purpose and intēt that thei shulde offer sacrifices: but that thei shuld regarde, wherefore thei were ordeined: to wit, to be ioyned to the worde as seales and confirmations of remission of sins in Christ: for without þe worde thei were vaine & vnprofitable.

l Which was about foretene hundreth yeres.

m Read vers. 13

n Whereby he sheweth that the pastours oght not to leaue their flockes in their obstinacie: for þe Lord wil vse the meanes of his seruants to make the wicked more fautie and to proue his.

o In signe of mourning, as Iob 1,20. mich. 1,16.

p Against whome he had iuste occasion to powre out his wrath.

q Of Topheth read 2. King 23, 10.

r But commanded the contrarie, as Le 18,21 & 20,3 deu. 18,10.

33 And the carkeises of this people shalbe
meat for the foules of the heauen & for the
beastes of the earth, and none shal fray
them awaie.
34 *Thē I wil cause to cease from the cities of Iudáh and from the stretes of Ierusalém the voyce of mirth and the voice of
gladnes, the voyce of the bridegrome and
the voyce of the bride: for the land shalbe
desolate.

Ezek. 26,13.

CHAP. VIII.

1 The destruction of the Iewes. 4 The Lord moueth the people to amendement. 10 He reprehendeth the lying doctrine & the couetousnes of the Prophetes & Priests.

1 AT that time, saith the Lord, thei shal
bring out the bones of the Kings of
Iudáh, and the bones of their princes, and
the bones of the Priestes and the bones of
the Prophetes, and the bones of the inhabitans of Ierusalém out of their [a] graues.
2 And thei shal spread thē before the sunne
& the moone, and all the hoste of heauen,
whome they haue loued, and whome thei
haue serued, & whome thei haue followed, & whome thei haue soght, and whome
thei haue worshiped: thei shal not be gathered nor be buryed, *but* shal be as dung
vpon the earth.
3 And death shalbe desired [b] rather then
life of all þe residue that remaineth of this
wicked familie, which remaine in all the
places where I haue scatred them, saith þe
Lord of hostes.
4 Thou shalt saie vnto them also, Thus
saith the Lord, Shal thei [c] fall & not arise?
shal he turne awaie and not turne againe?
5 Wherefore is this people of Ierusalém tur
ned backe by a perpetual rebellion? thei ga
ue thē selues to deceit, & wolde not returne
6 I hearkened and heard, *but* none spake a-
right: no man repented him of his wickednes, saying, What haue I done? euerie [d] one
turned to their race, as the horse rusheth
into the battel.
7 Euen the storcke in the aire knoweth her
appointed times, & the turtle and the cra
ne and the swallowe obserue the time of
their coming, but my people knoweth not
the [e] iudgement of the Lord.
8 How do ye saie, We are wise, & the Lawe
[f] of þe Lord *is* with vs? Lo, certeinly in vaine
made he it, þe pen of the scribes is in vaine.
9 The [g] wise men are ashamed: thei are a-
fraid and taken. lo, thei haue reiected the
worde of the Lord, and what wisdome is
in them?
10 Therefore wil I giue their wiues vnto
others, & their fields to thē that shal possesse thē: *for euerie one from the least euē
vnto the greatest is giuen to couetousnes
& from the Prophet euē vnto the Priest,
euerie one dealeth falsely.
11 For thei haue healed þe hurt of þe daughter
of

a The enemie for gaines of gaine shal rifle your graues, and laye you before those idoles, which in your life you worshiped; to se if they can helpe you.

b Because of the afflictions that thei shal fele through Gods iudgements.

c Is there no hope, that thei wil returne?

d They are ful of hypocrisie, and euerie one followeth his owne fantasie without any consideracion.

e He accuseth them in that þe they are more ignorant of Gods iudgements then these birdes are of their appointed seasons to discerne the colde, and heat, as Isa. 1,3.

f The Lawe doeth not profite you, nether ned it to haue bene writen for oght that you haue learned by it.

g They that seme wise, may be ashamed of their ignorance: for all wisdome cōsisteth in Gods worde.

Isa. 56,11. chap. 5,31. & 6,13.

of my people with swete wordes, saying,
[h] Peace, peace, when there is no peace.
12 Were thei ashamed whẽ they had cõmit
ted abominatiõ? nay, thei were not ashamed, nether colde they haue anie shame:
therefore shal they fall among the slaine:
when I shal visit them, they shalbe cast
downe, saith the Lord.
13 I wil surely cõsume them, saith ỹ Lord:
there shal be no grapes on the vine, nor
figs on the figtre, and the leaf shal fade, &
the things that I haue giuen them, shal
departe from them.
14 Why do we stay? [i] assemble your selues,
& let vs entre into the strong cities, & let
vs be quiet there: for the Lord our God
hathe put vs to silence and giuen vs water
with [k] gall to drinke, because we haue sinned against the Lord.
15 *We loked for peace, but no good *came*, &
for a time of health, & beholde troubles.
16 The neying of his horses was heard frõ
[l] Dan, the whole land trembled at the noise of the neying of his strõg *horses*: for thei
are come, and haue deuoured the lãd with
all that is in it, the citie, and those that
dwell therein.
17 For beholde, I wil [m] send serpents, & coc
katrices among you, which wil not be char
med, & they shal sting you, saith ỹ Lord.
18 I wolde haue [n] cõforted my self against
sorowe, *but* mine heart is heauie in me.
19 Beholde, the voyce of the crye of ỹ daughter of my people *for feare of thẽ* of a farre countrey, Is not ỹ Lord in Ziõn? is not
her King in her? Why [o] haue they prouoked me to angre with their grauẽ images,
and with the vanities of a strange *god*?
20 The [p] haruest is past, the somer is ended
and we are not holpen.
21 I am [q] sore vexed for ỹ hurt of ỹ daughter of my people: I am heauy, & astonishment hathe taken me.
22 Is there no balme [r] at Gileád? is there
no Phisiciõ there? Why thẽ is not ỹ health
of the daughter of my people recouered?

CHAP. IX.

1 *The complaint of the Prophet for the malice of the people. 24 In the knowledge of God oght we onely to reioyce. 26 The Vncircumcision of the heart.*

1 OH, that mine head were *ful* of [a] water
and mine eyes a fountaine of tea-
res, that I might wepe day and night for
the slaine of the daughter of my people.
2 Oh, that I had in the wildernes a [b] cottage of way faring men, that I might leaue my people, & go from them: for thei be
all [c] adulterers & an assemblie of rebels,
3 And they bend their tongues *like* their bowes for [d] lies: but they haue no courage
for the trueth vpon ỹ earth: for thei procede from euil to worse, and they haue not
knowen me, saith the Lord.
4 Let euerie one take hede of his neigh
bour, & trust you not in anie [e] brother: for
euerie brother wil vse deceit, and euerie
friend wil deale deceitfully,
5 And euerie one wil deceiue his friend, &
wil not speake the trueth: *for* they [f] haue
taught their tongues to speake lies, and take great paines to do wickedly.
6 Thine habitation is in the middes of deceiuers: [g] because of *their* deceit they refuse to knowe me, saith the Lord.
7 Therefore thus saith the Lord of hostes,
Beholde, I wil [h] melt them, & trye thẽ: for
what shulde I *els* do for the daughter of
my people?
8 Their tongue* *is* as an arrowe shot out, &
speaketh deceit: one speaketh peaceably
to his neighbour with his mouth, but in
his heart he layeth waite for him.
9 Shal I not visit thẽ for these things, saith
the Lord? or shal not my soule be auenged on suche a nation as this?
10 Vpon the [i] mountaines wil I take vp a
weping and a lamentacion, and vpon the
faire places of the wildernes a mourning,
because they are burnt vp: so that none cã
passe through them, nether can men heare
the voyce of the flocke: bothe the foule of
ỹ aire, & the beast are fled away & gone.
11 And I wil make Ierusalém an heape, & a
den of dragons, & I wil make the cities of
Iudáh waste, without an inhabitant.
12 Who is [k] wise, to vnderstand this, and to
whome ỹ mouth of the Lord hathe spokẽ,
euẽ he shal declare it. Why doeth ỹ land
perish, & is burnt vp like a wildernes, that
none passeth through?
13 And the Lord saith, Because they haue
forsaken my Law, which I set before them,
& haue not obeied my voice, nether walked there after,
14 But haue walked after the stubbernes of
their owne heart, and after Baalims, which
[l] their fathers taught them,
15 Therefore thus saith the Lord of hostes,
the God of Israél, Beholde, I wil fede this
people with wormewodde, and giue them
waters of gall [m] to drinke:
16 I wil scatre them also among the heathẽ,
whome nether they nor their fathers haue
knowen, and I wil send a sworde after thẽ,
til I haue consumed them.
17 Thus saith the Lord of hostes, Take hede, & call for [n] the mourning women, ỹ thei
may come, & send for skilful womẽ that
thei may come,
18 And let thẽ make haste, & let thẽ take vp a
lamẽtation for vs, ỹ our eyes may cast out
teares & our eye liddes gush out of water.
19 For a lamentable noyse is heard out
of Ziõn, How are we destroyed, *and*

h Read Chap. 6,14

i He speaketh in the persone of the people, who when the enemie cometh, wil runne about to hide them selues, & acknowledge that it is Gods hand.

k That is, hathe broght vs into extreme affliction, and thus they shal not attribute this plague to fortune, but to Gods iust iudgement, Chap. 9,15 & 23,15.

Chap. 14,19.

l Read Chap. 4,15.

m God threateneth to send ỹ Babylonians among them, who shal vtterly destroye them in suche sorte as by no meanes they shal escape.

n Read Chap. 4,19.

o Thus the Lord speaketh.

p The people wonder that they haue so long time loked for succour in vaine.

q The Prophet speaketh this.

r Meaning, ỹ no mans helpe or meanes cold saue thẽ: for in Gileád was precious balme, Chap. 46,11. or els deriding the vaine confidẽce of the people who loked for helpe at their Priests, who shulde haue bene the phisitions of their soules, & dwelt at Gileád, Hose. 6,8.

a The Prophet sheweth the great cõpassiõ that he had toward this people, seing, that he colde neuer sufficiently lament the destruction that he saw to hãg ouer them. Which is a special note to discerne the true pastours from the hirelings, read chap. 4,19

b He sheweth that this were more quietnes, & greater safety for him to dwell among the wilde beastes then among this wicked people, saue that God hathe inioyned him this charge.

c Vtterly turned from God.

d To belye, and sclander their neighbours.

e Meaning, ỹ all were corrupt and none colde finde an honest man.

f They haue so practised deceit ỹ thei can not forsake it.

g They had rather forsake God, then leaue their wicked trade.

h With the fyre of affliction.

Psal. 28,3. & 120,4.

i Signifying that all ỹ places about Ierusalém shulde be destroyed.

k Meaning, ỹ they are all without sense, and vnderstãding, and that God hathe taken his Spirit from them.

l He sheweth that the children can not excuse them selues by their fathers: for bo the father, & childe if they be wicked, shal perish.

m Read Chap. 8,14.

n Seing you cã not lament your owne sinnes, call for those foolish women, whome of a superstition you haue to lament for the dead, ỹ they by their fained teares may prouoke you to some sorow.

vtterly confounded,for we haue forsaken
the land,and our dwellings [o] haue cast vs
out.
20 Therefore heare the worde of ẏ Lord,
ô ye womẽ,and let your eares regarde the
wordes of his mouth, and [p] teache your
daughters to mourne,and euerie one her
neighbour to lament.
21 For death is come vp into our [q] wĩdowes,
& is entred into our palaces,to destroye ẏ
children without,and the yong men in the
stretes.
22 Speake,thus saith the Lord,The carkeises of men shal lie, euen as the dung vpon
the field,& as the hãdful after the mower,
and none shal gather *them*.
23 Thus saith the Lord, Let not the [r] wise
man glorie in his wisdome,nor the strong
man glorie in his strength, nether the riche man glorie in his riches.
24 But let him that glorieth, glorie in this,
that he vnderstandeth, and knoweth me:
for I am the Lord, which [s] shewe mercie,
iudgement,and righteousnes in the earth:
for in these things I delite,saith the Lord.
25 Beholde,the dayes come,saith the Lord,
that I wil visit all them, which are [t] circũcised with the vncircumcised:
26 Egypt and Iudáh, and Edóm,and the
children of Ammón, and Moáb, & all the
vtmost corners of them that dwell in the
wilderners: for all *these* nations *are* vncircumcised, & all the house of Israél *are* vncircumcised in the heart.

o As thogh thei were wearie of vs, because of our iniquities,Leu. 18,28,& 20,22.
p He derideth the superstitiõ of the women, which made an arte of mourning,& taught to wepe with fained teares.
q Signifying, that there is no meanes to deliuer ẏ wicked frõ Gods iudgemẽts;but whẽ thei thinke to be moste sure,and moste farre of, then are they sonest taken.
r Forasmuche as none cã saue him self by his owne labour or anie worldlie meanes,he sheweth ẏ it is in vaine to put our trust therein, but ẏ we trust in the Lord,& reioyce in him,who onely can deliuer vs,1.Cor. 1,31. 2.cor.10, 17.
s These thre pointes are neceßarie to knowe aright: his mercie wherein consisteth our saluation:his iudgement, ẇ he executeth cõtinually against the wiked,and his iustice,whereby he defendeth, and mainteineth the faithful.
t Meaning,bothe Iewes and Gentiles, as in the next verse he sheweth the cause, read Chap.4,4.

CHAP. X.

2 The constellacions of the starres are not to be feared. 5 The weaknes of idoles,& of the power of God. 21 Their pastours are become brute beasts.

1 HEare ye the worde of the Lord that
he speaketh vnto you, ô house of Israél.
2 Thus saith the Lord,Learne not the way
of the heathen, and be not afraide for the
[a] signes of heauen, thogh the heathen be
afraide of suche.
3 For the [b] customes of the people are vai-
ne:for one cutteth a tre out of the forest
(which is the worke of the hãds of the carpenter)with the axe,
4 And *another* decketh it [c] with siluer, and
with golde: they fasten it with nailes, and
hammers,that it fall not.
5 The *idoles* stand vp as the palme tre, but
speake not:they are borne because they cã
not go:feare them not,for they can not do
euil,nether can they do good.

a God forbiddeth his people to giue credit or feare the constellations & coniunctiõs of starres, and planets,which haue no power of thẽ selues, but are gouerned by him, & their secret motions & influẽces are not knowẽ to mã, and therefore there can be no certaine iudgemẽt thereof,Deut.18,9.
b Meaning not onely in the obseruation of the starres, but their laws and ceremonies whereby they confirme their idolatrie, which is forbidden,Deu.12,30.
c The Prophetes vse thus plainely & simply to set forthe the vile absurditie of the idolaters, that men might learne to be ashamed of ẏ,whereunto their corrupt nature is moste subiect,read Isa.44,12.

6 There is none like vnto thee, ô Lord:
[d] thou art great, and thy Name *is* great in
power.
7 Who wolde not feare thee, ô King of
nations?for to thee apperteineth *the domi-*
nion:for amõg all the wise men of the Gẽtiles, and in all their kingdomes there is
none like thee.
8 But altogether thei dote, and are foolish: *for* the stocke is a [e] doctrine of vanitie.
9 Siluer plates are broght from Tarshísh,
and golde [f] from Vpház, *for* the worke of
the workeman, and the hands of the foun-
der:the blewe silke, and the purple *is* their
clothing:all these things are made by cunning men.
10 But the Lord *is* the God of trueth: he is
the liuing God, and an euerlasting King:
at his angre the earth shal tremble,& the
nations can not abide his wrath.
11 (Thus shal you say vnto them,The gods
[g] that haue not made the heauens and the
earth,shal perish from the earth,and from
vnder these heauens)
12 He hathe made the earth by his power,
and established the worlde by his wisdome,and hathe stretched out the heauen by
his discretion.
13 He giueth by *his* voyce the multitude of
waters in the heauen,and he causeth the
cloudes to ascend from the ends of the
earth: he turneth lightnings to raine, and
bringeth forthe the winde out of his treasures.
14 Euerie man is a [h] beast by *his owne* know-
ledge:euerie fouder is cõfounded by the
grauen image: for his melting is but falsehode,and there is no breth therein.
15 They are vanitie,& ẏ worke of errours:
in the time of their visitation they shal
perish.
16 The [i] portion of Iaakób *is* not like thẽ:
for he is the maker of all things, & Israél
is the rod of his inheritante: the Lord of
hostes *is* his Name.
17 ¶ [k] Gather vp thy wares out of the lãd,
ô thou that dwellest in the strong place.
18 For thus saith the Lord, Beholde,at this
time I wil throwe as with a sling the inhabitans of the land, and wil trouble them,
and they shal finde it *so*.
19 Wo is me for my destruction, & my
grieuous plague: but I thoght, Yet it [l] is
my sorowe,and I wil beare it.
20 [m] My tabernacle is destroyed,and all my

d He teacheth ẏ people to lift vp their eyes to God, who hathe all power, and therefore oght onely to be feared: and hererein he sheweth them not onely the euil that they oght to eschew but the good, which they oght to follow Reuel.15.4.
e Because the people thoght that to haue images was a meane to serue God and to bring them to ẏ knowledge of him, he sheweth that nothing more displeaseth God,nor brĩgeth man into greater errors & ignorãce of God: & therefore he calleth them the doctrine of vanitie,ẏ worke of errors, ver.15, & Habak 2,18. calleth them ẏ teachers of lies: contrarie to that wicked opinion,ẏ thei are the bokes of the laye people.
f Where as they founde ẏ best golde: shewing,ẏ thei thoght nothĩg to deare for their idoles: some read Ophír,as 1 Kin. 9,28
g This declareth that all,ẏ hathe bene in this Chapter spoken of idoles, was to arme the Iewes whẽ they shulde be in Caldea among ẏ idolaters, and now ẇ one sẽtence he instructeth thẽ bothe how to protect their owne religion against ẏ idolaters, & how to answer thẽ to their shame which shulde exhorte thẽ to idolatrie, and therefore he writeth this sentence in the Caldeans tongue for a memorial, where as all the rest of his writing is Ebrewe.
h The more that man thinketh to do anie thing wel by his owne wisdome, and not as God instructeth him, the more doeth he proue him self to be a vile beast.
i By these wordes,Portion and rod,he signifieth their inheritance: meaning,that God shulde be all sufficient for them,and that their felicitie consisted in him alone, & therefore thei oght to renonce all other helpes, & succours as of idoles,&c. Deut. 32,9. psal.16,5.
k The Prophet willeth the Iewes to prepare thẽ selues to this captiuitie, shewing that it was now at hand, that they shulde fele the things,whereof he had tolde thẽ.
l It is my iuste plague & therefore I wil take it paciently: whereby he teacheth the people how to behaue thẽ selues toward God.
m He sheweth how Ierusalém shal lament.

coards are broken: my children are gone
from me, & are not: there is none to ſpread
out my tent any more, and to ſet vp my
courtaines.
21 For the paſtors [n] are become beaſtes, and
haue not ſoght ẏ Lord: therefore haue they
none vnderſtanding: and all the *flockes* of
their paſtures are ſcatered.
22 Beholde, the noiſe of the brute is come,
and a great commotion out of the [o] North
countrey to make the cities of Iudáh deſolate,
and a denne of dragons.
23 O Lord, I knowe, that [p] the way of man
is not in him ſelf, nether *is it* in man to walke and to direct his ſteps.
24 O Lord, correct me, but with [q] iudgement,
not in thine angre, leſt thou bring
me to nothing.
25 Powre out [r] thy wrath vpon the heathen,
that knowe thee not, & vpon the families
that call not on thy Name: for they haue
eaten vp Iaakób & deuoured him & conſumed him, and haue made his habitacion
deſolate.

n The gouernours and miniſters.
o Read Chap. 4,15.
p He ſpeaketh this, becauſe ẏ Nebuchadnezzár purpoſed to haue made warre againſt ẏ Moabites and Ammonites, but hearing of Zedechiahs rebelliō, he turned his power to go againſt Ieruſalém, Ezek. 21,21. therefore ẏ Prophet ſaith, ẏ this was the Lords direction.
q Conſidering that God had reueiled vnto him the certitude of their captiuitie, Chap 7,16, he onely prayeth, that he wolde puniſh them with mercie, which Iſaiáh calleth, in meaſure, Chap. 27,8. meaſuring his roddes by their infirmitie, 1. Cor 10,13. for here by iudgement is ment not onely the puniſhment, but alſo the merciful moderacion of the ſame, as Chap 30,11.
r For aſmuche as God can not onely be knowen and glorified by his mercie, that he vſeth toward his Church, but alſo by his iuſtice in puniſhing his enemies, he praieth that his glorie may fully appeare bothe in the one and the other, Pſal. 79,6.

CHAP. XI.

3 A curſe of them that obey not the worde of Gods couenant. 10 The people of Iudáh, following the ſteppes of their fathers, worſhippe ſtrange gods. 15 The Lord forbiddeth Ieremiáh to praie for them.

1 The worde that came to Ieremiáh frō
the Lord, ſaying,
2 Heare ye the wordes of this couenant, &
ſpeake vnto the men of Iudáh, and to the
inhabitants of Ieruſalém,
3 And ſay thou vnto them, Thus ſaith the
Lord God of Iſraél, [a] Curſed be the man
that obeieth not the wordes of this couenant,
4 Which I commanded vnto your fathers,
when I broght them out of the land of E-
gypt, from the yron fornace, ſaying, Obey
my voyce, and do according to all theſe
things, which I commande you: ſo ſhal ye
be my people, and I wil be your God,
5 That I may confirme the othe, that I haue
ſworne vnto your fathers, to giue them a
land, which floweth with milke and hony,
as *appeareth* this day. Then anſwered [b] I &
ſaid, So be it, ô Lord.
6 Then the Lord ſaid vnto me, Crye all
theſe wordes in the cities of Iudáh, and in
the ſtretes of Ieruſalém, ſaying, Heare ye
the wordes of this couenant, and do thē.
7 For I haue proteſted vnto your fathers,
when I broght them vp out of the land of
Egypt vnto this day, [c] riſing earely & pro-
teſting, ſaying, Obey my voyce.

a He calleth ẏ Iewes to the conſideracion of Gods mercies, who frely choſe thē, made a couenant of eternal felicitie with them, & how he euer performed it on his behalf, & how they euer ſhewed them ſelues rebellious & ingrate toward him & brake it on their parte, & ſo are ſubiect to the curſe of the Law, Deut. 27,26.
b Thus he ſpea keth in ẏ perſone of the people, which agreed to the couenant.
c Read Chap. 7,13.

8 Neuertheles they wolde not obey, nor
encline their eare: but euery one walked in
the ſtubbernes of his wicked [d] heart: therefore I wil bring vpon them all the [e] wordes of this couenant, which I commanded
them to do, but thei did it not.
9 And the Lord ſaid vnto me, A [f] conſpiracie is founde among the men of Iudáh, &
among the inhabitants of Ieruſalém.
10 They are turned backe to the iniquities
of their forefathers, which refuſed to heare my wordes: and they went after other
gods to ſerue them: *thus* the houſe of Iſraél, and the houſe of Iudáh haue broken
my couenant, which I made with their fathers.
11 Therefore thus ſaith the Lord, Beholde,
I wil bring a plague vpon them, which
they ſhal not be able to eſcape, and thogh
they crye vnto me, [g] I wil not heare them.
12 Then ſhal the cities of Iudáh, and the
inhabitants of Ieruſalém go, and crye vnto the gods vnto whome thei offer incenſe,
but they ſhal not be able to helpe them in
time of their trouble.
13 [h] For according to the nomber of thy
cities were thy gods, ô Iudáh, and *according*
to the nomber of the ſtretes of Ieruſalém
haue ye ſet vp altars of confuſion, *euen* altars to burne incenſe vnto Báal.
14 Therefore thou ſhalt not pray [i] for this
people, nether lift vp a crye, or prayer for
them: for when thei crye vnto me in their
trouble, I wil not heare them.
15 What ſhulde my [k] beloued *tary* in mine
houſe, ſeing they haue committed abominacion with many? and the holy fleſh
[l] goeth away frō thee: yet when thou doeſt
euil, thou reioyceſt.
16 The Lord called thy name, A grene oliue tre, faire, *and* of goodlie frute: *but* with
[m] noiſe and great tumult he hathe ſet fyre
vpon it, and the branches of it are broken.
17 For the Lord of hoſtes that planted thee,
hathe pronounced a plague againſt thee,
(for the wickednes of the houſe of Iſraél,
and of the houſe of Iudáh) which thei haue done againſt them ſelues to prouoke
me to angre in offring incenſe vnto Báal.
18 And the Lord hathe taught me, and I
knowe it, *euen* then ẏ ſhewedſt me [n] their
practiſes.
19 But I was like a lambe, *or* a bullocke, that
is broght to the ſlaughter, and I knewe not
ẏ thei had deuiſed thus againſt me, *ſaying*,
Let vs [o] deſtroye the tre with the frute
thereof, and cut him out of the land of the
liuing, that his name may be no more in
memorie.
20 But ô Lord of hoſtes, that iudgeſt righteouſly, and tryeſt the reines & the heart,
let me ſe thy [p] vengeance on them: for vnto thee haue I opened my cauſe.

d According to his owne fātaſie, and not as my worde appoīted him.
e Meaning, the menaces and curſes conteined in ẏ Law, Leu. 26,14. deut. 28,16.
f That is, a general conſent to rebelle againſt me.
g Becauſe they wil not pray with true faith & repentance, but for the ſmart & grief, which thei fele, Prou. 1,28.
h Read Chap. 2,28.
i Read Chap. 7,16. & 14,11.
k My people of Iſraél whome I haue hetherto ſo greatly loued.
l Meanīg, that they offer not in the Temple to God, but vpon the altars of Báal & the idoles, and ſo reioyced in their wickednes.
m Of the Babylonians and Caldeans.
n Which wēt about priuely to cōſpire my death
o Let vs deſtroy ẏ Prophet & his doctrine. Some read, let vs corrupt his meat with wood, meanīg, poyſon.
p Thus he ſpake not for hatred, but being moued with the Spirit of God, he deſireth the aduācemēt of Gods glorie and the verifying of his worde, ẇ is by the deſtructiō of his enemies.

21 The Lord therefore ſpeaketh thus of the
men of [q] Anathóth, (that ſeke thy life, &
ſay, [r] Prophecie not in the Name of the
Lord, that thou dye not by our hands)
22 Thus therefore ſaith the Lord of hoſtes,
Beholde, I wil viſit them: the yong men
ſhal dye by ẏ ſworde: their ſonnes & their
daughters ſhal dye by famine,
23 And none of them ſhal remaine: for I wil
bring a plague vpõ the men of Anathóth,
euen the yere of their viſitacion.

q To wit, bothe the prieſts and the reſte of the people: for this towne was the prieſts, & they dwelt in it, read Chap. 1,1.
r Not ẏ they colde not abide to heare God named: (for here͂ thei wolde ſhewe them ſelues moſt holy) but becauſe they colde not abide to be ſharpeſy reproued and therefore deſired to be flattered, Iſa. 30,10, and to be mainteined in their pleaſures, Mich. 2,11, and not to heare vice cõdẽned, Amos. 7,12.

CHAP. XII.

1 The Prophet marueleth at the proſperitie of the wicked, althogh he confeſſe God to be righteous. 7 The Iewes are forſakẽ of the Lord. 10 He ſpeaketh againſt paſtors and preachers, that ſeduce the people. 14 The Lord threatneth deſtruction vnto the nacions, that troubled Iudáh.

1 O Lord, if I diſpute with thee, thou
art [a] righteous: yet let me talke with
thee of *thy* iudgements: wherefore doeth
the waye of the wicked [b] proſper? *why* are
all they in welth that rebelliouſly tranſgreſſe?
2 Thou haſt planted them, and they haue
taken roote: thei growe, and bring forthe
frute: thou art nere in their mouth, and
farre from their [c] reines.
3 But thou, Lord, knoweſt me: thou haſt ſene me, and tryed mine heart toward thee:
pul them out like ſhepe for the ſlaughter,
and [d] prepare them for the day of ſlaughter.
4 How long ſhal the land mourne, and the
herbes of euery field wither, for the wickednes of them that dwell therein? the
beaſts are cõſumed and the byrdes, becauſe they ſaid, [e] He wil not ſe our laſt end.
5 If thou haſt runne with the [f] fotemen, and
they haue wearied thee, then how canſt
thou matche thy ſelf with horſes? & if thou
thoghteſt thy ſelf ſafe in a peaceable lãd,
what wilt thou do in the ſwelling of Iordén?
6 For euen thy brethren, and the houſe of
thy father, euen thei haue delt vnfaithfully with thee, and they haue cryed out altogether vpon thee: *but* beleue them not,
thogh they ſpeake faire to thee.
7 I haue forſaken [g] mine houſe: I haue left
mine heritage: I haue giuen the derelie
beloued of my ſoule into the hands of her
enemies.
8 Mine heritage is vnto me, as a [h] lyon in
the foreſt: it cryeth out againſt me, therefore haue I hated it.

Chap. XII.
a The prophet cõfeſseth God to be iuste in all his doings, althogh man be not able to giue a reaſon of all his actes.
b This queſtiõ hathe bene alway a great tentation to ẏ godlie, to ſe ẏ wicked enemies of God in proſperitie, and his dere children in aduerſitie, as Iob 21,7. pſal. 37,1. 73,1 Haba 1,3.
c They profeſſe God in mouthe, but denie him in heart, which is here ment by the reines, Iſa. 29,13. mat. 15,8.
d The Ebrewe worde is, Sanctifie them, meaning, that God wolde be ſanctified in ẏ deſtruction of the wicked, to whome God for a while giueth proſperitie, that afterwarde they ſhulde ẏ more fele his heauy iudgemẽt whẽ they lacke their riches, ẇ were a ſigne of his mercie.
e Abuſing Gods lenitie & his promiſes, they flattered thẽ ſelues as thogh God wolde euer be merciful, and not vtterly deſtroy thẽ: therfore they hardened them ſelues in ſinne, til at length the beaſtes and inſenſible creatures felt the puniſhment of their ſtubberne rebellion againſt God. f Some thinke that God reproueth Ieremiáh in that, that he wolde reaſon with him, ſaying, that if he were not able to matche with men, that he were farre vnable to diſpute with God. Others, by the fote men, meane them of Anathóth, & by ẏ horſe men them of Ieruſalém, which ſhulde trouble the Prophet worſe then his owne countrey men did. g God willeth the Prophet to denounce his iudgements againſt Ieruſalém, notwithſtanding that they ſhal bothe by threatnings and flatteries labour to put him to ſilence. h Euer ramping and raging againſt me and my Prophets.

9 Shal mine heritage be vnto me, as a birde
[i] of diuerſe colours? are not ẏ birdes about
her, *ſaying*, Come, aſſemble all the beaſts
of the field, come to eat her?
10 Many paſtors haue deſtroyed my [k] vineyarde, and troden my porcion vnder fote: of my pleaſant porcion they haue made
a deſolate wildernes.
11 They haue laid it waſte, and it, being
waſte, mourneth vnto me: *and* the whole
land lyeth waſte, becauſe no mã ſetteth *his*
minde on [l] it.
12 The deſtroyers are come vpon all the
high places in the wildernes: for ẏ ſworde
of the Lord ſhal deuoure from the one
end of the land, euen to the *other* end of the
land: no fleſh ſhal haue peace.
13 [m] They haue ſowen wheat, and reaped
thornes: they were [n] ſicke, *and* had no profite: and they were aſhamed of [o] your frutes, becauſe of the fierce wrath of ẏ Lord.
14 Thus ſaith the Lord againſt all mine e-
uil [p] neighbours, that touche the inheritãce, which I haue cauſed my people Iſraél
to inherite, Beholde, I wil plucke them out
of their land, and plucke out the houſe of
Iudáh from among them.
15 And after that I haue plucked them out,
I [q] wil returne, and haue compaſsion on
them, and wil bring againe euery man to
his heritage, and euery man to his land.
16 And if they wil learne the [r] wayes of
my people, to ſweare by my Name, ([ſ] The
Lord liueth, as they taught my people to
ſweare by Báal) then ſhal they be buylt [t] in
the middes of my people.
17 But if they wil not obey, then wil I vtterly plucke vp, and deſtroye that nacion,
ſaith the Lord.

i In ſtead of bearing my liuerey & wearing onely my colours, they haue change and diuerſitie of colours of their idoles & ſuperſtitions. therfore their enemies, as thicke as the foules of the ayre, ſhal come about thẽ to deſtroy them.
k He propheciẹth of the deſtruction of Ieruſalém by the captaines of Nebuchadnezzár, whome he calleth paſtors.
l Becauſe no man regardeth my worde, or the plagues ẏ I haue ſent vpon the land.
m To wit, the Prophetes.
n They lamented the ſinnes of the people.
o For in ſtead of amendemẽt you grewe worſe & worſe as Gods plagues teſtified.
p Meanig, the wicked enemies of his Church ẇ blaſphemed his name, & whome he wolde puniſh after that he hathe deliuered his people.
q After that I haue puniſhed ẏ Gẽtiles, I wil haue mercie vpon them.
r The true doctrine and maner to ſerue God. ſ Read Chap. 4,2. t They ſhalbe of the nomber of the faithful; and haue a place in my Church.

CHAP. XIII.

The deſtruction of the Iewes is prefigured. 11 Why Iſraél was receiued to be the people of God, and why they were forſaken. 15 He exhorteth them to repentance.

1 THus ſaith the Lord vnto me, Go, and
bye thee a linen girdle, and put it
vpon thy loynes, and put it not in water.
2 So I boght the girdle according to the
commandement of the Lord, and put it
vpon my loynes.
3 And the worde of the Lord came vnto
me the ſeconde time, ſaying,
4 Take the girdle that thou haſt boght,
which is vpon thy loynes, and ariſe, go
toward [a] Peráth, and hide it there in the
cleft of the rocke.
5 So I went, & hid it by Peráth, as the Lord
had commanded me.
6 And after many daies, the Lord ſaid vnto
me, Ariſe, go toward Peráth, and take the
girdle from thence, which I commanded
thee

a Becauſe this riuer Peráth or Euphrates was farre frõ Ieruſalém, it is euidẽt, that this was a viſion, whereby was ſignified that the Iewes ſhulde paſſe ouer Euphrates to be captiues in Babylon & there for length of time ſhulde ſeme tobe rottẽ: althogh they were ioyned to the Lord before as a girdle about a man.

thee to hide there.
7 Then wẽt I to Peráth, and digged, & toke the girdle from the place where I had
hid it, & beholde, the girdle was corrupt,
and was profitable for nothing.
8 Then the worde of the Lord came vnto
me, saying,
9 Thus saith the Lord, After this maner wil
I destroye the pride of Iudáh, & the great
pride of Ierusalém.
10 This wicked people haue refused to heare my worde, & walke after the stubbernes
of their owne heart, and walke after other
gods to serue them, and to worship them:
therefore they shalbe as this girdle, which
is profitable to nothing.
11 For as the girdle cleaueth to the loines
of a man, so haue I tyed to me the whole
house of Israél, and the whole house of Iudáh, saith the Lord, that thei might be my
people: that they might haue a name
and praise, and glorie, but thei wolde not
heare!
12 Therefore thou shalt saie vnto them this
worde, Thus saith ẏ Lord God of Israél,
Euerie [b] bottel shalbe filled with wine, and
thei shal saie vnto thee, Do we not knowe
that euerie bottle shalbe filled with wine?
13 Then shalt thou saie vnto them, Thus
saith the Lord, Beholde, I wil fil all the inhabitants of this land, euen the Kings that
sit vpon the throne of Dauid, and the
Priests and the Prophetes and all the inhabitants of Ierusalém with drunkẽnes.
14 And I [c] wil dash them one against another, euen the fathers and the sonnes together, saith the Lord: I wil not spare, I wil
not pitie nor haue compassiõ, but destroie
them.
15 Heare and giue eare, be not proude: for
the Lord hathe spoken it.
16 Giue glorie to ẏ Lord your God before he bring [d] darkenes, and or euer your
fete stumble in the darke mountaines, and
whiles you loke for [e] light, he turne it into the shadowe of death *and* make it as
darkenes.
17 But if ye wil not heare this, my soule shal
[f] wepe in secret for *your* pride, & mine eye
shal wepe and drop downe teares, because
the Lords flocke is caried awaie captiue.
18 Saie vnto the [g] King and to the Queene, Humble your selues, sit downe, for the
crowne of your glorie shal come downe
from your heads.
19 The cities of [h] the South shalbe shut vp,
and no man shal open them: all Iudáh shal
be caried awaie captiue: it shalbe wholy
caried awaie captiue.
20 Lift vp your eyes and beholde them ẏ
come from the North, where is ẏ [i] flocke
ẏ was giuẽ thee, *euen* thy beautiful flocke.
21 What wilt thou saie, when he shal visit
thee? (for thou hast [k] taught thẽ to be captaines & as chief ouer thee) shal not sorow
take thee as a woman in trauail?
22 And if thou saie in thine heart, Wherefore come these things vpon me? For the
multitude of thine iniquities are thy skirts
[l] discouered & thy heles made bare.
23 Can the blacke More change his skin? or
the leopard his spottes? *then* maie ye also
do good, that are accustomed to do euil.
24 Therefore wil I scatre thẽ, as the stubble
that is taken awaie with the South winde.
25 This is thy portion, *and* the parte of thy
measures from me, saith the Lord, because
thou hast forgoten me and trusted in lies.
26 Therefore I haue also discouered thy
skirts vpon thy face, [m] that thy shame may
appeare.
27 I haue sene thine adulteries, & thy [n] neyings, ẏ filthines of thy whoredome on the
hilles in [o] the fields, *and* thine abominatiõs. Wo vnto thee, ô Ierusalém: wilt thou
not be made cleane? when shal it once be?

CHAP. XIIII.

1 Of the dearth that shulde come. 7 The prayer of the people asking mercie of the Lord. 10 The vnfaithful people are not heard. 12 Of prayer, fasting, and of false prophetes that seduce the people.

1 THe worde of the Lord that came vnto
Ieremiáh, concerning the [a] * dearth.
2 Iudáh hathe mourned, and the gates thereof are desolate, they haue bene [b] broght
to heauines vnto the grounde, and the crye
of Ierusalém goeth vp,
3 And their nobles haue sent their inferiours to the water, who came to the welles,
and founde no water: they returned with
their vessels emptie: they were ashamed
& confounded, and [c] couered their heads.
4 For the grounde was destroyed, because
there was no raine in the earth: the plowmen were ashamed, *and* couered their
heades.
5 Yea, the hinde also calued in the field,
and forsoke [d] it, because there was no
grasse.
6 And the wilde asses did stãd in the high
places, and drewe in their winde like [e] dragons: their eyes did faile, because there
was no grasse.
7 [f] O Lord, thogh our iniquities testifie against vs, deale *with vs* according to thy
Name: for our rebellions are manie, we
sinned against thee.
8 O the hope of Israél, the sauiour thereof in the time of trouble, why art thou
as a stranger in the lãd, as one that passeth
by to tarie for a night?
9 Why art thou as a man astonied, and
as [h] a strong man that can not helpe? yet
thou, ô Lord, art in the middes of vs,
and thy Name is called vpon vs: forsake
vs not.

b Euerie one of you shalbe filled with spiritual drunkẽnes, and be without all knowledge to seke how to helpe your selues.

c It shalbe as easie for me to destroye ẏ greatest, and ẏ strongest, as it is for a man to breake earthẽ bottels.

d That is, afflictiõ & miserie by the Babyloniãs, Isa. 8, 22

e Meaning, for helpe and support of the Egyptians.

f You shal surely be led away captiue & I, according to mine affection toward you, shal wepe, and lamẽt for your stubbernes.

g For Iehoiachin, & his mother rendred them selues by Ieremiahs counsel to the King of Babylon, 2 King. 24, 12.

h That is, of Iudáh ẇ lieth Southward frõ Babylon

i He asketh ẏ King, where his people is become.

k By seking to strãgers for helpe thou hast made thẽ skilful to fight against thee.

l Thy cloke of hypocrisie shal be pulled of and thy shame sene.

m As thine iniquities haue bene manifest to all the worlde: so shal thy shame, & punishment.

n He compareth idolaters to horses inflamed after mares.

o There is no place so hie nor lo, where as the markes and signes of thine idolatrie appeare not.

a Which came for lacke of raine, as ver. 4.

* Or, restraint

b The worde signifieth to be made blacke, and so is here taken for extreme sorowe.

c To wit, with ashes in token of sorowe.

d Meaning, ẏ brute beasts for drought were compelled to forsake their yong, cõtrarie to nature, & to go seke water, which they colde not finde.

e Which are so hote of nature, that thei can not be cooled with drinking of water, but stil gape for the aire to refresh them.

f He sheweth the onely way to remedie Gods plagues, which is by vnfained confession of our sinnes, and returning to him by repentãce.

g That taketh no care for vs.

h As one that hathe strength to helpe, & yet is afraid to put to his hande

10 Thus saith the Lord vnto this people,
Thus haue they delited to wādre: they haue not refrained their fete , therefore the
Lord hathe no delite in thē: *but* he wil now
remember their iniquitie , and visit their
sinnes.

i Read Chap. 7,16 & 11,14.

11 Then said the Lord vnto me, [i] Thou
shalt not praye to do this people good.
12 Whē thei fast, I wil not heare their crye,
and when they offer burnt offring, and an
oblation , I wil not accept them: but I wil
consume them by the sworde , and by the
famine and by the pestilence.
13 Then answered I, Ah Lord God, beholde, the [k] Prophetes say vnto them, Ye shal
not se the sworde, nether shal famine come vpon you, but I wil giue you assured
peace in this place.

k He pitieth the people, & accuseth the false prophetes, which deceiued them: but the Lord answered, that bothe yͤ Prophetes, which deceiued, and the people, wͨ suffred thē selues to be seduced, shal perish, Chap. 23,15. & 27,21, & 29,8.

Chap.23,21. & 27,21. & 29,8.

14 Then the Lord said vnto me, The Prophetes prophecie lies in my Name:* I haue not sent them , nether did I commande
them, nether spake I vnto them , *but* they
prophecie vnto you a false vision, and diuination, and vanitie, and deceitfulnes of
their owne heart.
15 Therefore thus saith the Lord, Concerning the Prophetes that prophecie in my
Name, whome I haue not sent, yet they
say, Sworde and famine shal not be in this
land, by sworde & famine shal those Prophetes be consumed.
16 And the people to whome these Prophetes do prophecie, shalbe cast out in the stre
tes of Ierusalém, because of the famine , &
the sworde , & there shalbe none to burye
them, *bothe* they, and their wiues, and their
sonnes, & their daughters: for I wil powre
their wickednes vpon them.

l The false prophets promised peace, & assurāce, but Ieremiáh calleth to teares, and repentance for their affliction, wͨ is at hand, as Chap. 9,1. lament.1, 16. & 2,18.

17 Therefore thou shalt say this worde vnto them, Let mine eyes drop downe [l] teares night and day without ceasing: for yͤ
virgine daughter of my people is destroyed with a great destruction , *and* with a
sore grieuous plague.
18 For if I go into the field, beholde the slaine with the sworde: and if I entre into the
citie, beholde thē that are sicke for hunger
also: moreouer the Prophet also and the
Priest go a wandring [m] into a land that
they know not.

m Bothe hie, & lowe shalbe led captiues into Babylon.

n Thogh the Prophet knew that God had cast of yͤ multitude, which were hypocrites, and bastard children , yet he was assured that for his promes sake he wolde haue stil a Church, for the which he prayeth.

19 Hast thou vtterly reiected [n] Iudáh , or
hathe thy soule abhorred Zión? Why hast
thou smitten vs, that we can not be healed?
We loked for peace, & there is no good, &
for the time of health, & beholde trouble.
20 We [o] acknowledge, ô Lord, our wickednes
& the iniquitie of our fathers: for we haue sinned against thee.
21 Do not abhorre *vs*: for thy Names sake
cast not downe the throne of thy glorie :
remember *and* breake not thy couenant
with vs.
22 Are there anie among yͤ [p] vanities of the
Gentiles, that can giue raine? or can the
heauēs giue showers? is it not thou, ô Lord
our God? therefore we wil waite vpō thee:
for thou hast made all these things.

o He teacheth the Church a forme of prayer, to humble the selues to God by true repentance, wͨ is the onelie meane to auoide this famine, wͨ was the beginning of Gods plagues.

p Meaning, their idoles, read Chap. 10,15.

CHAP. XV.

1 The Lord wolde heare no prayer for the Iewes, 3 But threatneth to destroye them with foure plagues.

1 THē said the Lord vnto me, [a] Thogh
Mosés and Samuél stode before me,
yet mine affectiō colde not be toward this
people : cast *them* out of my sight, and let
thém departe.

a Meaning, that if there were anie man liuing moued with so great zeale toward yͤ people, as were these two, yet that he wolde not grante this request, forasmuche as he had determined the contrarie, Ezek. 14,14.

Zach.11,9.

2 And if they say vnto thee, Whether shal
we departe? then tel them , Thus saith
the Lord,* Suche as are *appointed* to death,
vnto death: & suche as are for the sworde,
to the sworde, & suche as are for the famine to the famine , and suche as are for the
captiuitie, to the captiuitie.
3 And I wil appointe ouer them foure kindes, saith the Lord, the sworde to slay, and
the [b] doggs to teare in pieces, & the foules of the heauen, & the beastes of the earth
to deuoure, and to destroye.

b The dogs, birdes & beastes shulde deuoure them, yͭ were slaine.

c The worde signifieth to rūne to & fro for feare, and vnquietnes of cōscience, as did Kain.

4 I wil [c] scater them also in all kingdomes
of the earth, [d] because of Manasséh the
sōne of Hezekiáh King of Iudáh, for that
which he did in Ierusalém.

d Not that yͤ people was punished for the Kings sinne onely, but for their owne sinnes also, because they cōsented to his wickednes, 2. King,21,9.

5 Who shal then haue pitie vpō thee, ô Ierusalém? or who shalbe sorie for thee? or
who shal go to pray for thy peace?
6 Thou hast forsaken me, saith the Lord, &
gone backwarde : therefore wil I stretch
out mine hand against thee, and destroye
thee: *for* I [e] am wearie with repenting.

e That is, I wil not call backe my plagues, or spare thee anie more.

7 And I wil scatre thē with the fanne [f] in yͤ
gates of the earth : I haue wasted , & destroyed my people, *yet* they wolde not returne from their wayes.

f Meaning, the cities.

8 Their widdowes [g] are increased by me
aboue the sand of the sea: I haue broght
vpon thē, & against the ‖ assemblie of the
yong men a destroyer at none day: I haue
caused *him* to fall vpon them , & the citie
suddenly, and ‖ spedely.

g Because I had slaine their housbands.

‖ *Or, mother.*

‖ *Or, fearefully.*

9 She that hathe borne [h] seuen, hathe bene
made weake: her heart hathe failed: the sun
ne hathe failed [i] her, whiles it was day: she
hathe bene confounded , & ashamed, and
the residue of them wil I deliuer vnto the
sworde before their enemies, saith yͤ Lord.

h She that had manie, lost all her children.

i She was destroyed in the middes of her prosperitie.

10 ¶ [k] Wo is me, my mother, that thou hast
borne me, a contentious man, & a mā that
striueth with yͤ whole earth: I haue nether
[l] lent on vsurie, nor mē haue lent vnto me
on vsurie: *yet* euerie one doeth cursse me.

k These are yͤ Prophets wordes, cōplainīg of yͤ obstinacie of yͤ people, & that he was reserued to so wicked a time wherē also he sheweth what is the cōdition of Gods ministers: to wit, to haue all the worlde against thē, thogh thei giue none occasion.

l Which is an occasion of cōtention and hatred.

11 The Lord said, [m] Surely thy remnāt shal
haue welth : surely I wil cause thine enemie to intreat thee in the time of trouble,
and in the time of affliction.

m In this perplexitie the Lord cōforted me, & said yͭ my last dayes shulde be quiet: & by yͤ enemie he meaneth here, Nebuzardán the captaine of Nebuchadnezzár, who gaue Ieremiáh yͤ choise ether ro remaine in his countrey, or to go whether he wolde; or by the enemie he meaneth the Iewes, wͨ shulde afterward knowe Ieremiahs fidelitie, and therefore fauour him.

12 Shal the [n] yron breake the yron, and the
braſſe *that commeth* from the North?
13 Thy ſubſtance & thy treaſures wil I giue to be ſpoiled without [*] gaine, and that
for all thy ſinnes euen in all thy borders.
14 And I wil make thee to go with thine
enemies into a lãd that thou knoweſt not:
for a fyre is kindled in mine angre, *which*
ſhal burne you.
15 O Lord, thou knoweſt, remembre me, &
viſit me, and reuenge me of my [o] perſecuters: take me not awaie in the continuance
of thine angre: knowe that for thy ſake I
haue ſuffred rebuke.
16 Thy wordes were founde *by me*, and I
did [p] eat them, and thy worde was vnto
me the ioye and reioycing of mine heart:
for thy Name is called vpon me, ô Lord
God of hoſtes.
17 I ſate not in the aſſemblie of the mockers, nether did I reioyce, but ſate alone
[q] becauſe of thy plague: for thou haſt filled
me with indignation.
18 Why is mine heauines continual? & my
plague deſperate *&* can not be healed? *why*
art thou vnto me [r] as a lyer, *and as* waters
that faile.
19 Therefore thus ſaith the Lord, If thou
[ſ] returne, then wil I bring thee againe,
& thou ſhalt ſtand before me: and if thou
take awaie the [t] precious from the vile,
thou ſhalt be [u] according to my worde: let
them returne [x] vnto thee, but returne not
thou vnto them.
20 And I wil make thee vnto this people
a ſtrong braſen wall, and thei ſhal fight a-
gainſt thee, but thei ſhal not [y] preuaile a-
gainſt thee: for I am with thee to ſaue thee
& to deliuer thee, ſaith the Lord.
21 And I wil deliuer thee out of the hand
of the wicked, and I wil redeme thee out
of the hand of the tyrants.

n As for the people thogh they ſemed ſtrong as yron, yet ſhulde thei not be able to reſiſt ŷ hard yron of Babylon, but ſhuld be led captiues.
*Or, ranſome.
o He ſpeaketh not this for deſire of reuẽgeãce, but wiſhĩg ŷ God wolde deliuer his Church of thẽ whome he knewe to be hardened, and incorrigible.
p I receiued thẽ wͭ as great ioye as he ŷ is affamiſhed eateth meat.
q I had nothĩg ado with the wicked cõtemners of thy worde, but lamented bitterly for thy plagues: ſhewing what the faithful ſhulde do whẽ thei ſe tokens of Gods angre.
r And haſt not aſſiſted me according to thy promes? wherein appeareth, ŷ in the Saints of God is imperfectiõ of faith, wͭ through impaciẽcie is oft times aſſailed, as Chap 20,7
ſ If thou forget theſe carnal conſideratiõs, & faithfully execute thy charge.
t That is, ſeke to winne the good from the bad
u To wit, as my mouth hathe pronoũced Chap 1, 18, & as here followeth verſ 20
x Cõforme not thy ſelf to their wickednes, but let them followe thy godlie example.
y I wil arme thee wͭ an inuĩcible ſtrẽgth & cõſtancie, ſo that all the powers of the worlde ſhal not ouercome thee

CHAP. XVI.

2 *The Lord forbidding Ieremiáh to marie, ſheweth him what ſhulde be the afflictiõs vpõ Iudah. 13 The captiuitie of Babylon. 15 Their deliuerance. 19 The calling of the Gentiles.*

1 The worde of the Lord came alſo vnto me, ſaying,
2 Thou ſhalt not take [a] thee a wife, nor haue
ſonnes nor daughters in this place.
3 For thus ſaith the Lord concerning the
ſonnes, and cõcerning the daughters that
are borne in this place, and concerning
their mothers that beare them, & concerning their fathers, that beget them in this
land.
4 Thei ſhal dye of deaths *&* diſeaſes: thei
ſhal not be lamented, nether ſhal thei be
buryed, *but* thei ſhalbe as dongue vpon the
earth, and thei ſhalbe conſumed by the
ſworde, and by famine, and their carkeiſes
ſhalbe meat for the foules of the heauen,
and for the beaſtes of the earth.

Chap XVI.
a Meaning, ŷ the affliction ſhulde be ſo horrible in Ieruſalém, that wife, and childrẽ ſhulde but increaſe his ſorowe.

5 For thus ſaith the Lord, [b] Entre not into
the houſe of mournĩg, nether go to lamẽt,
nor be moued for them: for I haue taken
my peace frõ this people, ſaith the Lord,
euen mercie and compaſsion.
6 Bothe ŷ great, & the ſmale ſhal dye in this
land: thei ſhal not be buryed, nether ſhal
men lamẽt for them [c] nor cut them ſelues,
nor make them ſelues bald for them.
7 Thei ſhal not ſtretche out *the hands* for
them in the mourning to cõfort them for
the dead, nether ſhal thei giue them the
[d] cup of conſolation to drinke for their father or for their mother.
8 Thou ſhalt not alſo go into the houſe of
feaſting to ſit with thẽ to eat & to drinke.
9 For thus ſaith the Lord of hoſtes, the
God of Iſraél, Beholde, I wil cauſe to
ceaſe out of this place in your eyes, euen in
your daies the voice of mirth, & the voice
of gladnes, the voice of the bride grome
and the voice of the bride.
10 And when thou ſhalt ſhewe this people
all theſe wordes, & thei ſhal ſaie vnto thee,
*Wherefore hathe the Lord pronounced
all this great plague againſt vs? or what is
[e] our iniquitie? and what is our ſinne that
we haue cõmitted agaĩſt ŷ Lord our God?
11 Then ſhalt thou ſaie vnto them, Becauſe
your fathers haue forſaken me, ſaith the
Lord, and haue walked after other gods,
and haue ſerued them, & worſhiped thẽ, &
haue forſakẽ me, & haue not kept my Law,
12 (*And ye haue done worſe then your fathers: for beholde, you walke euerie one af
ter the ſtubbernes of his wicked heart, and
wil not heare me)
13 Therefore wil I driue you out of this
land into a land that ye knowe not, *nether*
you, nor your fathers, and there ſhal ye
ſerue other gods daie and night: for I wil
ſhewe you no grace.
14 *Beholde, therefore, ſaith the Lord, the
daies come that it ſhal no more be ſaid,
The Lord liueth, which broght vp ŷ children of Iſraél out of the land of Egypt,
15 But the Lord liueth, that broght vp the
children of Iſraél [f] from the land of the
North, and from all the lands where he
had ſcatered them, and I wil bring them
againe into their land that I gaue vnto
their fathers.
16 Beholde, ſaith the Lord, I wil ſend out
many [g] fiſhers, and thei ſhal fiſh them, and
after, wil I ſend out many hunters, & thei
ſhal hunt them from euerie mountaine
and from euerie hill, and out of the caues
of the rockes.
17 For mine eyes *are* vpon all their waies:
thei are not hid from my face, nether
is their iniquitie hid from mine eyes.
18 And firſt I wil recompence their iniquitie and their ſinne double, becauſe they

b Signifying that ŷ afflictiõ ſhulde be ſo great ŷ one ſhulde not haue leaſure to comfort another.
c That is, ſhulde not rent their clothes in ſigne of mourning.
d For in theſe great extremities all conſolation & comfort ſhalbe in vaine.
Chap. 5, 19
e Becauſe the wicked are alwaies rebellious and diſſemble their owne ſinnes, & murmur agaĩſt Gods iudgemẽts as thogh he had no iuſt cauſe to puniſh thẽ, he ſheweth him what to anſwer.
Chap. 7, 25
Chap. 23, 7
f Signifying ŷ beneſite of their deliuerance out of Babylon ſhulde be ſo great, that it ſhulde aboliſh the remembrance of their deliuerance frõ Egypt: but he hathe here chiefly reſpect to the ſpiritual deliuerance vnder Chriſt.
g By ŷ fiſhers and hunters, are ment ŷ Babylonians and Caldeans who ſhulde deſtroy them in ſuch ſort that if they eſcaped the one, ŷ other ſhulde take them.

haue defiled my land, *and* haue filled mine inheritance with their filthie [h] carions
and their abominations.
19 O Lord, *thou art* my [i] force, & my strẽgth
& my refuge in the day of affliction: the
Gentiles shal come vnto thee frõ the ends
of the worlde, and shal say, Surely our fathers haue inherited [k] lies, & vanitie, wherein there was no profite.
20 Shal a man make gods vnto him self, &
they are no gods?
21 Beholde, therfore I wil this once [l] teache
thẽ: I wil shew thẽ mine hãd & my power,
& thei shal know ẏ my Name is the Lord.

h That is, their sonnes & daughters, ẇ they offred to Molech.
i He wondereth at ẏ great mercie of God in this deliuerance, ẇ shal not onely extend to the Iewes, but also the Gentiles.
k Our fathers were most vile idolaters: therefore it cometh onely of Gods mercie, that he performeth his promes, & hathe not vtterly cast vs of.
l They shal once againe fele my power, & mercie for their deliuerãce, that thei may learne to worship me.

CHAP. XVII.

1 The frowardnes of the Iewes. 5 Cursed be those that put their confidence in man. 9 Mans heart is wicked. 10 God is the searcher of the heart. 13 The liuing waters are forsaken. 21 The right keping of the Sabbath commanded.

1 THe sinne of Iudáh is [a] writen with a
penne of yron, & with the point of a
diamõde, & graué vpõ the [b] table of their
heart, & vpon the hornes of your [c] altars.
2 [d] They remẽber their altars as their children, with their groues by the grene trees
vpon the hie hilles.
3 [e] O my mountaine in the field, I wil giue
thy substance, & all thy treasures to be
spoiled, for the sinne of thy high places
through out all thy borders.
4 And thou shalt rest, [f] and in thee *shalbe
arest* frõ thine heritage that I gaue thee, &
I wil cause thee to serue thine enemies in
the lãd, which thou knowest not: for ye haue kindeled a fyre in mine angre, *which*
shal burne for euer.
5 ¶ Thus saith the Lord, [g] Cursed *be* the
mã that trusteth in mã, & maketh flesh his
arme, & withdraweth his heart frõ ẏ Lord.
6 For he shalbe like the heath in the wildernes, and shal not se when *anie* good cometh, but shal inhabit the partched places in the wildernes, in a salt land, and not
inhabited.
7 Blessed *be* the man, that trusteth in the
Lord, and whose hope the Lord is.
8 *For he shalbe as a tre that is planted by
the water, which spreadeth out her rootes
by the riuer, and shal not fele when the
heat cometh, but her leaf shalbe grene, and
shal not care for the yere of drought, nether shal cease from yelding frute.
9 [i] The heart is deceitful and wicked aboue
all things, who can knowe it?

a The remẽbrãce of their cõtẽpt of God can not passe, albeit for a time he deferre the punishmẽt. for it shalbe manifest to mẽ & Angels.
b In stead of ẏ Law of God, thei haue writen idolatrie & all abominations in their heart.
c Your sinnes appeare in all the altars that you haue erected to idoles.
d Some read, So that their children remẽber their altars that is follow their fathers wickednes.
e Zión ẏ was my moũtaine, shal now be left as a waste field.
f Because thou woldest not giue the lãd rest at such times, dayes, & yeres as I appoited, thou shalt here after be caried away, & it shal rest for lacke of laborers.
g The Iewes were giuen to worldelie policies, & thoght to make them selues strong by the friendship of the Egyptians, Isa. 31,3 and strangers, & in the meane season did not depẽd on God, & therefore he denounceth Gods plagues against them, shewing that they preferre corruptible man to God, which is immortal, Isa 2,22. chap. 48,6
h Read Psal. 1,3.
i Because the wicked haue euer some excuse to defend their doings, he sheweth, that their owne lewde imaginations deceiue them, & bring thẽ to these incõueniences: but God wil examine their dedes by the malice of their hearts, 1. Sam. 16,7 1. chro. 28,9. psal. 7,10. chap. 11,20, & 20,12. reuel. 2,23.

10 I the Lord searche the heart, & trye the
reines, euen to giue euerie man according
to his wayes, *and* according to the frute of
his workes.
11 [k] *As* the partryche gathereth *the yong,*
which she hathe not broght forthe: *so* he
that getteth riches, and not by right, shal
leaue them in the middes of his dayes, and
at his end shalbe a foole.
12 *As* a glorious throne [l] exalted from the
beginning, *so is* the place of our Sãctuarie.
13 O Lord, the hope of Israél, all that forsake thee, shalbe confounded: the i that departe from thee, shalbe written [m] in the
earth, because they haue forsakẽ the Lord,
the fountaine of liuing waters.
14 Heale me, ô Lord, and I shalbe whole:
[n] saue me, and I shal be saued: for thou art
my praise.
15 Beholde, [o] they say vnto me, Where is
the worde of the Lord? let it come now.
16 But [p] I haue not thrust in my self for a
pastor after thee, nether haue I desired the
daye of miserie, thou knowest: that which
came out of my lippes, was *right* before
thee.
17 Be not [q] terrible vnto me: thou art mine
hope in the day of aduersitie.
18 Let them be confounded, that persecute me, but let not me be confounded: let
them be afraid, but let not me be afraid:
bring vpon them the day of aduersitie, [r] &
destroy them with double destruction.
19 Thus hathe the Lord said vnto me, Go
and stand in the [s] gate of the children of
the people, whereby ẏ Kings of Iudáh come in, and by the which thei go out, and in
all the gates of Ierusalém,
20 And say vnto them, Heare the worde of
the Lord, ye Kings of Iudáh, and all Iudáh, and all the inhabitants of Ierusalém,
that entre in by these gates.
21 Thus saith the Lord, Take hede to your
soules, and beare no burden in the [t] Sabbath day, nor bring it in by the gates of
Ierusalém.
22 Nether carye forthe burdẽs out of your
houses in the Sabbath day: nether do ye
anie worke, but sanctifie the Sabbath, as I
commanded your fathers.
23 But they obeyed not, nether inclined
their eares, but made their neckes stiffe &
wolde not heare, nor receiue correction.
24 Neuertheles if ye wil heare me, saith
the Lord, & beare no burden through the
gates of the citie in the Sabbath day, but
sanctifie the Sabbath day, so that ye do no
worke therein,
25 Then shal the Kings and the princes entre in at the gates of this citie, and shal
sit * vpon the throne of Dauid, and shal
ride vpon charets, and vpon horses, *bothe*
thei and their princes, the men of Iudáh,
and

k As the partriche by calling gathereth others, which forsake her, when they se that she is not their dam: so the couetous man is forsaken of his riches, because he cometh by them falsely.
l Shewing that ẏ godlie oght to glorie in nothing, but in God: who doeth exalt his, and hathe left a signe of his fauour in his Temple.
m Their names shal not be registred in the boke of life.
n He desireth God to preserue him that he fall not into tentation considering the great cõtempt of Gods worde, & the multitude that fall from God.
o The wicked say ẏ my prophecie shal not come to passe because thou deferrest the time of thy vẽgeance.
p I am assured of my vocatiõ, and therefore knowe that ẏ thing which thou speakest by me, shal come to passe, & that I speake not of any worldelie affection.
q How soeuer ẏ wicked deale rigorously with me, yet let me finde cõfort in thee.
r Read Chap. 11,20.
s Where as thy doctrine may be best vnderstãd both of hie & lowe.
t By naming the Sabbath day, he cõprehendeth the thing, that is thereby signified: for if they trãsgressed in the ceremonie, they must nedes be culpable of ẏ rest, read Exo. 20,8. and by ẏ breaking of this one commandement, he maketh them transgressors of the whole Lawe, for as muche as the first and seconde table are conteined herein.
Chap. 22,4.

and the inhabitants of Ierusalém: and this
citie shal remaine for euer.
26 And thei shal come from the cities of Iu
dáh, and from about Ierusalém, and from
the land of Beniamin, and from the plaine, and from the mountaines, and from ẏ
South, which shal bring burnt offrings, &
sacrifices, and meat offrings, and incense,
& shal bring sacrifice of praise into the
House of the Lord.
27 But if ye wil not heare me to sanctifie ẏ
Sabbath daie, and not to beare a burden
nor to go through the gates of Ierusalém
in ẏ Sabbath daie, then wil I kindle a fyre
in the gates thereof, and it shal deuoure
the palaces of Ierusalém, and it shal not be
quenched.

CHAP. XVIII.

2 God sheweth by the example of a potter, that it is in his power to destroie the dispicers of his worde. 18 The conspiracie of the Iewes against Ieremiáh. 19 His praier against his aduersaries.

1 THe worde which came to Ieremiáh
from the Lord, saying,
2 Arise, & go downe into the potters house, and there shal I shewe thee my wordes.
3 Then I went downe to the potters house,
and beholde, he wroght a worke on the
wheles.
4 And the vessel that he made of [a] claie,
was broken in the hand of the potter: so he
returned, & made it another vessel, as semed good to the potter to make it.
5 Then the worde of the Lord came vnto
me, saying,
6 O house of Israél, can not I do with you
as this potter, saith the Lord? beholde, as ẏ
claie *is* in the potters hand, so are you in
mine hand, ô house of Israél.
7 I wil speake suddenly against a nation or a
against a kingdome to plucke it vp, & to
roote it out and to destroie it.
8 But if this nation, against whome I haue
pronounced, turne frō their wickednes, I
wil [b] repent of ẏ plague that I thoght to
bring vpon them.
9 And I wil speake suddenly concerning a
nacion, and concerning a kingdome to
buylde it and to plant it.
10 But if it do euil in my sight and heare
not my voice, I wil repēt of the good that
I thoght to do for them.
11 Speake ẏ now therefore vnto the men of
Iudáh, and to the inhabitāts of Ierusalém,
saying, Thus saith ẏ Lord, Beholde, I prepare a plague for you, and purpose a thing
against you: returne you therefore euerie
one from his euil waie, and make your
waies and your workes good.
12 But thei said [c] desperatly, Surely we wil
walke after our owne imaginacions & do
euerie man *after* the stubbernes of his wicked heart.

a As the potter hathe power ouer the clay to make what pot he wil, or to breake thē, when he hathe made them: so hane I power ouer you to do with you as semeth good to me, Isa 45,9. wisd.15,7 rom. 9,20.

b When ẏ Scripture attributeth repentance vnto God, it is not that he doeth contrary to that which he hathe ordeined in his secret counsel: but whē he threateneth, it is a calling to repentance, and when he giueth man grace to repent, ẏ threatening (which euercōteineth a condition in it) taketh no place: and this the Scripture calleth repentance in God, because it so appeareth to mans iudgement.

c As men that had no remorce, but were altogether bent to rebellion and to their owne self wil.

13 Therefore thus saith the Lord, Aske now
among the heathen, who hath heard suche
things? the virgine of Israél hathe done ve
rie filthily.
14 Wil a man forsake the snowe of Lebanón, *which cometh* from ẏ rocke of the field?
[d] or shal the colde flowing waters, that
come from another place, be forsaken?
15 Because my people hathe forgotten me,
& haue burnt incense to vanitie, and *their*
Prophetes haue caused them to stumble
in their waies *from* the [e] ancient waies to
walke in the paths *and* waie that is not troden,
16 To make their land desolate & a perpetual derision, *so that* euerie one that passeth
thereby, shalbe astonished and wagge his
head,
17 I wil scattre them with an East winde
before the enemie: I wil shewe them the
backe, and [f] not the face in the day of their
destruction.
18 Then said they, Come, and let vs imagine some deuise against Ieremiáh: for
the Law [g] shal not perish from the Priest,
nor counsel from the wise, nor the worde
from the Prophet: come, and let vs smite
him with the [h] tongue, and let vs not
giue hede to any of his wordes.
19 Hearken vnto me, ô Lord, and heare the
voyce of them that contend with me.
20 Shal euil be recompenced for good? for
they haue digged a pit for my soule: remembre that I stode before thee, to speake good for them, *and* to turne away thy
wrath from them.
21 Therefore, [i] deliuer vp their children
to famine, and let them drop away by
the force of the sworde, and let their wiues be robbed of their children, and be
widdowes: and let their housbands be put
to death, *and* let their yong men be slayne by the sworde in the battel.
22 Let the crye be heard from their houses, when thou shalt bring an hoste suddenly vpon them: for they haue digged
a pit to take me, and hid snares for my
fete.
23 Yet Lord thou knowest all their counsel
against me *tendeth* to death: forgiue not
their iniquitie, nether put out their sinne
from thy sight, but let them be ouerthrowen before thee: deale *thus* with them in
the time of thine angre.

CHAP. XIX.

He prophecieth the destruction of Ierusalém for the contempt and despisyng of the worde of God.

1 THus said the Lord, Go, and bye an
earthen bottel of a potter, and *take*
of the ancients of the people, and of the
ancients of the Priests,
2 And go forthe vnto ẏ vallei of Ben-hin-

d As no man ẏ hathe thirst, refuseth fresh cōduit waters which he hathe at home, to go and seke waters abroad to quench his thirst: so they oght not to seke for helpe & succour at strāgers and leaue God, which was present with them.

e That is, the way of trueth, which God had taught by his Law, read chap.6,16

f I wil shewe mine angre & not my fauour toward them.

g This argument ẏ wicked haue euer vsed against the seruants of God, The Church can not erre: we are the Church, and therefore who soeuer speaketh agaist vs, they oght to dye, 1.King.22, 24, cha.7,4.& 20,2.mala.2,4. and thus the false Church persecuteth ẏ true Church, which stādeth not inoutward pompe, and in multitude, but is knowen by the graces of the holie Gost.

h Let vs sclander him, and accuse him: for we shalbe beleued.

i Seing the obstinate malice of the aduersaries, which grewe daicly more & more, the Prophet being moued with Gods Spirit, without any carnal affection praieth for their destruction, because he knew that it shulde tend to Gods glorie, & profite of his Church.

°Or, gate of the sunne.

nóm, which is by the entrie of the °East ga
te: & thou shalt preache there the wordes,
that I shal tel thee,
3 And shalt say, Heare ye the worde of the
Lord, ô [a] Kings of Iudáh, and inhabitãts
of Ierusalém, Thus saith the Lord of hostes, ỹ God of Israél, Beholde, I wil bring
a plague vpon this place, the which whosoeuer heareth, his eares shal [b] tingle.
4 Because they haue forsaken me, and prophaned this place, and haue burnt incense in it vnto other gods, whome *nether*
they, nor their fathers haue knowen, nor
the Kings of Iudáh(they haue filled this
place also with the blood of innocents,
5 And they haue buylt the hie places of
Báal, to burne their sonnes with fyre for
burnt offrings vnto Báal, which I [c] commãded not, nor spake it, nether came it into my minde)
6 Therefore beholde, the dayes come, saith
the Lord, that this place shal nomore be
called [d] Tópheth, nor the vallei of Ben-
hinnóm, but the vallei of slaughter.
7 And I wil bring the counsel of Iudáh &
Ierusalém to noght in this place, and I
wil cause thẽ to fall by the sworde before
their enemies, & by the hand of them that
seke their liues: & their carkeises wil I giue to be meat for the foules of ỹ heauen,
and to the beastes of the field.
8 *And I wil make this citie desolate & an
hissing, *so that* euerie one ỹ passeth thereby, shalbe astonished & hisse because of all
the plagues thereof.
9 *And I wil fede thẽ with ỹ flesh of their
sonnes and with the flesh of their daughters, and euerie one shal eat the flesh of
his friend in the siege and streitnes, wherewith their enemies that seke their liues,
shal holde them streit.
10 Then shalt thou breake the bottle in the
sight of the men that go with thee,
11 And shalt saie vnto them, Thus saith the
Lord of hostes, Euen so wil I breake this
people & this citie, as one breaketh a [e] potters vessel, that can not be made whole a-
gaine, & thei shal burye *them* in Tópheth
til there be no place to burye.
12 Thus wil I do vnto this place, saith the
Lord, and to the inhabitans thereof, and I
wil make this citie like Tópheth.
13 For the houses of Ierusalém, and the
houses of the Kings of Iudáh shalbe defiled as the place of Tópheth, because of all
the [f] houses vpon whose [g] roses thei haue
burnt incense vnto all the hoste of heauen, and haue powred out drinke offrings
vnto other gods.
14 Then came Ieremiáh from Tópheth,
where the Lord had sent him to prophecie, and he stode in the court of the Lords
house, and said to all the people,

a By Kings here and in other places are ment counsellours & gouernours of ỹ people: which he called the Ancients, ver. 1.
b Read of this phrase, 1. Sam. 3,11.
c Whereby is declared that what so euer is not cõmanded by Gods word touchĩg his seruice, is against his worde.
d Read Chap. 7,31 & 2. king. 23,10. isa. 30,33.
Chap. 18,16. & 49,30. & 50,13.
Deut. 28,53 lament. 4,10
e This visible signe was to confirme them touching ỹ assurãce of this plague, which ỹ Lord threatened by his Prophet.
f He noteth the great rage of the idolaters, which left no place fre frõ their abominations, insomuche as they polluted their owne houses therewith, as we se yet among the papistes.
g Read Deut. 22,8.

15 Thus saith the Lord of hostes, the God
of Israél, Beholde, I wil bring vpon this
citie, and vpon all her townes, all the plagues ỹ I haue pronounced against it, because they haue hardened their neckes, and
wolde not heare my wordes.

CHAP. XX.

2 Ieremiáh is smitten and cast into prison for preaching of the worde of God. 3 He prophecieth the captiuitie of Babylon. 7 He complaineth that he is a mocking stocke for the worde of God. 9 He is compelled by the Spirit to preache the worde.

1 WHen Pashúr, the sonne of Immér,
the Priest, which was appointed
gouernour in ỹ House of the Lord, heard
that Ieremiáh prophecied these things,
2 Then Pashúr smote Ieremiáh the Prophet, and put him in the [a] stockes that were in the hie gate of Beniamín which was
by the House of the Lord.
3 And on the morning, Pashúr broght Ieremiáh out of the stockes. Then said Ieremiáh vnto him, The Lord hathe not cal
led thy name Pashúr, but °Magór-missa-
bíb.
4 For thus saith the Lord, Beholde, I wil
make thee to be a terrour to thy self, & to
all thy friends, and thei shal fall by the
sworde of their enemies, & thine eyes shal
beholde it, and I wil giue all Iudáh into
the hand of the King of Babél, and he shal
carie them captiue into Babél, and shal
slaie them with the sworde.
5 Moreouer I wil deliuer all the substance
of this citie, and all the labours thereof
& all the precious things thereof, and all ỹ
treasures of the Kings of Iudáh wil I giue
into the hand of their enemies, which shal
spoyle them, and take them awaie and carie them to Babél.
6 And thou Pashúr, & all that dwell in thine house, shal go into captiuitie, and thou
shalt come to Babél, and there thou shalt
dye, and shalt be buryed there, thou & all
thy [b] friends, to whome thou hast prophecied lies.
7 O Lord, thou hast deceiued me, and I am
[c] deceiued: thou art stronger then I, and
hast [d] preuailed: I am in derision daiely:
euerie one mocketh me.
8 For since I spake, I cryed out of wrong,
and proclaimed [e] desolation: therefore
the worde of the Lord was made a reproche vnto me, and in derision daiely.
9 Then I said, I wil not make mencion of
him, nor speake any more in his Name.
But *his worde* was in mine heart as a burning fyre shut vp in my bones, and I was
wearie with forbearing, & I colde not *stay*.
10 For I had heard the railing of many, &
feare on euerie side. [f] Declare, *said thei*, & we
wil declare it: all my familiars watched for
mine

a Thus we se that the thing which nether the King, nor the princes nor the people durst entreprise agaĩst ỹ Prophet of God, this priest as a chief instrumẽt of Satan first attẽpted, read Chap 18,18.
°Or, feare round aboute.
b Which haue suffred thẽ selues to be abused by thy false prophecies.
c Herein appeareth ỹ impaciencie, ỽ oftentimes ouercometh the seruants of God, whẽ thei se not their labours to profite, and also fele their owne weaknes, read cha. 15,18.
d Thou didest thrust me forth to this worke agaĩst my wil.
e He sheweth that he did his office in that he reproued ỹ people of their vices & threatened them ỽ Gods iudgements: but because he was derided and persecuted for this, he was discouraged & thoght to haue ceased to preache, saue that Gods Spirit did force him thereunto.
f Thus the enemies conferred together to knowe what they had heard him say ỹ they might accuse him thereof, read Isa. 29,21.

mine halting, *saying*, It may be that he is
deceiued: so we shal preuaile against him,
and we shal execute our vengeance vpon
him.

g Here he sheweth how his faith did striue against tentation and foght to the Lord for strength.

11 g But the Lord is with me like a mightie
gyant: therefore my persecuters shalbe o-
uerthrowen, and shal not preuaile, & shal
be greatly confoúded: for they haue done
vnwisely, *and their* euerlasting shame shal
neuer be forgotten.

1.Sam.16,7. 1.chro.28,9. psal.7,10. chap.11,20. & 17,10.

12 * But, ô Lord of hostes, that tryest the
righteous, & seest the reines & the heart,
let me se thy vengeance on them: for vnto
thee haue I opened my cause.
13 Sing vnto the Lord, praise ye the Lord:
for he hathe deliuered the soule of the
poore from the hand of the wicked.

h How the children of God are ouercome in this battel of the flesh and the Spirit, and into what incôueniences thei fall til God raise them vp againe, read Iob 3, 1, and chap.15,10.

14 ¶ h Cursed *be* the day wherein I was borne: & let not the day wherein my mother
bare me, be blessed.
15 Cursed *be* the man, that shewed my father, saying, A man childe is borne vnto
thee, and comforted him.

i Alluding to the destructiô of Sodóm and Gomoráh, Ge. 19,25.

16 And let that man be as the i cities, which
the Lord hathe ouer turned and repented
not: & let him heare the crye in the morning, and the showting at noone tide,
17 Because he hathe not slayne me, *euen* frô
the wombe, or that my mother might haue bene my graue, or her wombe a perpetual k conception.

k Meanig, that the frute thereof might neuer come to profite.

18 How is it, *that* I came forthe of the wombe, to se labour and sorowe, that my daies
shulde be consumed with shame?

CHAP. XXI.

He prophecieth that Zedekiáh shalbe taken, and the citie burned.

1 THe worde which came vnto Ieremiáh from the Lord, when King Zedekiáh sent vnto him Pashúr, the sonne of
Malchiáh, & Zephaniáh, the sonne of Maaseiáh the Priest, saying,

a Not that the King was touched with repentãce of his sinnes and so soght to God, as did Hezekiáh when he sent to Isaiáh, 2.King.19,1. isa.37,2, but because the Prophet might pray vnto God to take this present plague away, as Pharaóh soght vnto Moses, Exod 9,28

b To wit, from your enemies to destroye your selues.

2 a Inquire, I pray thee, of the Lord for
vs (for Nebuchad-nezzár King of Babél
maketh warre against vs) if so be that the
Lord wil deale with vs according to all
his wonderous workes, that he may returne vp from vs.
3 Then said Ieremiáh, Thus shal you say to
Zedekiáh,
4 Thus saith the Lord God of Israél, Beholde, I wil b turne backe the weapons of
warre that are in your hands, wherewith
ye fight against the King of Babél, and a-
gainst the Caldeans, which besiege you
without the walles, & I wil assemble them
into the middes of this citie.
5 And I my self wil fight against you with
an outstretched hand, and with a mightie
arme, euen in angre and in wrath, and in
great indignacion.
6 And I wil smite the inhabitants of this
citie, bothe man, and beast: thei shal dye of
a great pestilence.
7 And after this, saith the Lord, I wil deliuer Zedekiáh the King of Iudáh, and his
seruants, and the people, and suche as are
left in this citie, from the pestilence, from
the sworde and from the famine into the
hád of Nebuchad-nezzár King of Babél,
and into the hand of their enemies, and
into the hand of those that seke their liues, and he shal smite them with the edge
of the sworde: he shal not spare them, nether haue pitie nor compassion.
8 ¶ And vnto this people thou shalt say,
Thus saith the Lord, Beholde, I set before
you the c way of life, & the way of d death.
9 *He that abideth in this citie, shal dye by
the sworde and by the famine, and by the
pestilence: but he that goeth out, and falleth to the Caldeans, that besiege you, he
shal liue, and his life shalbe vnto him for a
e pray.

c By yeldíng your selues to Nebuchadnezzár.
d By resisting him.
Chap.38,2.

e As a thing recouered frô extreme danger, Chap 37,2 & 39,18, & 45,5.

10 For I haue set my face against this citie,
for euil and not for good, saith the Lord:
it shal be giuen into the hand of the King
of Babél, and he shal burne it with fyre.
11 ¶ And *say* vnto the house of the King
of Iudáh, Heare ye the worde of ye Lord.
12 O house of Dauid, thus saith the Lord,
*Execute iudgement f in the morning, and
deliuer the oppressed out of the hand of
the oppressor, lest my wrath go out like
fyre and burne, that none can quenche it,
because of the wickednes of your workes.

Chap.22,3.
f Be diligent to do iustice.

13 Beholde, I *come* against thee, g ô inhabitant of the valley, & rocke of the plaine,
saith the Lord, which say, Who shal come
downe against vs? or who shal enter into
our habitacions?

g Meaning, Ierusalém, which was buylded parte on the hill and parte in ye valley, & was côpassed about with mountaines.

14 But I wil visite you according to ye frute
of your workes, saith the Lord, and I wil
kindle a fyre h in the forest thereof, and it
shal deuoure rounde about it.

h That is, in ye houses therof, which stode as thicke as trees in the forest.

CHAP. XXII.

2 He exhorteth the King to iudgement and righteousnes. 9 Why Ierusalém is broght into captiuitie. 11 The death of Shallúm the sonne of Iosiáh is prophecied.

1 THus said the Lord, Go downe to the
house of the King of Iudáh, and speake there this thing,
2 And say, Heare the worde of the Lord, ô
King of Iudáh, that sittest vpon the throne of Dauid, thou and thy seruants, and
thy people that enter in by these gates.
3 Thus saith the Lord, *Execute ye iudgement and a righteousnes, and deliuer the
oppressed from the hand of the oppressor,
and vexe not the stranger, the fatherles,
nor the widdowe: do no violence, nor shede innocent blood in this place.

Chap.21,12.
a This was his ordinarie maner of preaching before ye Kings from Iosiah vnto Zedekiáh, which was about fourtie yeres.

4 For if ye do this thing, then shal the
Kings sitting vpon the throne of Dauid
enter in by the gates of this house, * and
ride vpon charets, and vpon horses, *bothe* he

Chap.17,25.

and his seruants and his people.
5 But if ye wil not heare these wordes, I
[b] sweare by my self, saith ŷ Lord, that this
House shalbe waste.
6 For thus hathe the Lord spoken vpon the
Kings house of Iudáh, Thou art [c] Gileád
vnto me, *and* the head of Lebanón, *yet* surely I wil make thee a wildernes *&* *as* cities not inhabited,
7 And I wil [d] prepare destroyers against
thee, euery one with his weapons, and thei
shal cut downe thy chief [e] cedre trees, and
cast them in the fyre.
8 [f] And many nacions shal passe by this citie, & thei shal say euery man to his neighbour, Wherefore hathe ŷ Lord done thus
vnto this great citie?
9 Then shal they answer, Because they haue forsaken the couenant of ŷ Lord their
God, and worshiped other gods & serued
them.
10 ¶ Wepe not for the dead, & be not moued for them, *but* wepe for him [g] that goeth out: for he shal returne no more, nor se
his natiue countrey.
11 For thus saith the Lord, As touching
[h] Shallúm the sonne of Iosiáh King of Iudáh, which reigned for Iosiáh his father,
which wét out of this place, he shal not returne thether,
12 But he shal dye in ŷ place, whether they
haue led him captiue, and shal se this land
no more.
13 ¶ Wo vnto him ŷ buyldeth his house by
[i] vnrighteousnes, & his chambers without
equitie: he vseth his neighbour without
wages and giueth him not for his worke.
14 He saith, I wil buylde me a wide house
and large chambers: so he wil make him
self large windowes, and siling with cedre
and painte them with vermelon.
15 Shalt thou reigne, because thou closest
thy self in cedre? did not thy [k] father eat
and drinke and prosper, when he executed
iudgement and iustice?
16 When he iudged the cause of ŷ afflicted
& the poore, he prospered: was not this because he knewe me, saith the Lord?
17 But thine eies and thine heart are but o-
nely for thy couetousnes, and for to shed
innocent blood, & for oppresion, and for
destruction, *euen* to do this.
18 Therefore thus saith the Lord against
Iehoiakím, the sonne of Iosiáh Kĩg of Iudáh, Thei shal [l] not lamẽt him, *saying*, Ah,
my brother, or ah, sister: nether shal they
mourne for him, *saying*, Ah, lord, or ah, his
glorie.
19 He shalbe buryed as an asse [m] is buryed,
euẽ drawen and cast forthe without the gates of Ierusalém.
20 ¶ Go vp to [n] Lebanón, & crye: showte in
[o] Basħán & crye by the passages: for all thy
louers are destroyed.
21 I spake vnto thee whẽ thou wast in prosperitie: *but* thou saidst, I wil not heare: this
hathe bene thy maner from thy youth that
thou woldest not obey my voyce.
22 The winde shal fede all thy pastors, [p] &
thy louers shal go into captiuitie: and then
shalt thou be ashamed and confounded of
all thy wickednes.
23 Thou that dwellest in Lebanón, *and* makest thy nest in the [q] cedres, how beautiful
shalt thou be when sorowes come vpon
thee, as the sorow of a woman in trauail?
24 As I liue, saith the Lord, thogh [r] Coniáh the sonne of Iehoiakím King of Iudáh, were the signet of my right hand, yet
wolde I plucke thee thence.
25 And I wil giue thee into the hand of thẽ
that seke thy life, and into the hand of
them, whose face thou fearest, euẽ into the
hand of Nebuchad-nezzár King of Babél, and into the hand of the Caldeans.
26 And I wil cause them to cary thee away,
and thy mother that bare thee, into another countrey, where ye were not borne, &
there shal ye dye.
27 But to the land, whereunto they desire
to returne, they shal not returne thether.
28 Is not this man Coniáh *as* a despised *and*
broken idole? or *as* a vessel, wherein is no
pleasure? Wherefore are thei caryed away,
he and his sede, & cast out into a land that
they knowe not?
26 O [s] earth, earth, earth, heare the worde
of the Lord.
30 Thus saith the Lord, Write this [t] man
destitute of *children*, a man that shal not
prosper in his dayes: for there shalbe no
man of his sede that shal prosper and sit
vpõ the throne of Dauid, or beare rule any
more in Iudáh.

CHAP. XXIII.

Against false Pastors. 5 A prophecie of the great Pastor Iesus Christ.

1 WO *be* vnto [a] the Pastors that destroie and scatter [b] the shepe of
my pasture, saith the Lord.
2 Therefore thus saith the Lord God of
Isráel vnto the Pastors that [c] fede my people, Ye haue scattred my flocke and thrust
them out, & haue not visited thẽ: beholde,
I wil visite you for the wickednes of your
workes, saith the Lord.
3 And I wil gather the [d] rẽnant of my shepe out of all countreys, whether I had driuen them, and wil bring them againe to
their foldes, and they shal growe and encrease.
4 And I wil set vp shepherdes ouer them,
which shal fede them: and they shal dread
no more nor be afraid, nether shal any of
them be lacking, saith the Lord.

b Shewing ŷ there his none greater then he is, Ebr. 6, 13, and that he wil moste certeinly performe his othe.
c He compareth Ierusalém to Gileád, ŵ was beyonde Iordén, and ŷ beautie of Iudeáh to Lebanón.
d The Ebrewe worde signifieth to sanctifie, because ŷ Lord doeth dedicate to his vse & purpose suche as he prepareth to execute his worke, Isa. 13, 3 chap. 6, 4. and 12, 3.
e Thy buyldings made of cedre trees.
f As they that wonder at a thing which they thoght wolde neuer haue come so to passe, Deut. 29, 24. 1. king. 9, 8.
g Signifying ŷ they shulde lose their Kĩg: for Iehoiachĩ went forth to mete Nebuchad-nezzár & yelded hĩ self and was caryed into Babylon, 2. King. 24 12.
h Whome some thinke to be Iehoiachín & ŷ Iosiáh was his grand father: but as semeth, this was Iehoiakím, as vers. 18.
i By bribes & extorsion.
k Meaning, Iosiáh, who was not giuen to ambition and superfluitie, but was cõtent with mediocritie and did onely delite in setting forthe Gods glorie & to do iustice to all.
l For euery one shal haue ynough to lament for him self.
m Not honorably amongs his fathers, but as carions are cast in a hole because their stinke shulde not infect, read 2. King 24, 9. Iosephus Antiq. 10, 8. writeth that the enemie slewe him in the citie & commanded him to be cast before the walles vnburyed.
n To call to the Assyrians for helpe.
o For this was the way out of Iudeáh to Assyria: whereby is mẽt that all helpes shulde faile: for the Caldeans haue subdued bothe them and the Egyptians.
p Bothe thy gouernours & they ŷ shulde helpe thee, shal vanish away as wind.
q Thou that art buylt of ŷ faire cedre trees of Lebanón.
r Who was called Iehoiachin or Ieconiáh, whome he calleth here Coniáh in cõtempt, who thoght his kingdome colde neuer departe frõ him, because he came of ŷ stocke of Dauid, and therefore for ŷ promes sake colde not be taken from his house: but he abused Gods promes, and therefore was iustely depriued of the kingdome.
s He sheweth that all posteritie shalbe witnesses of this iuste plague as thogh it were registred for perpetual memorie.
t Not that he had no children (for after he begate Salathiél in the captiuitie, Ma. 1, 12) but that none shulde reigne after him as King.

Chap. XXIII
a Meanĩg, the princes, gouernours & false prophetes, as Ezek. 34, 2.
b For the which I haue especial care and haue prepared good pastures for them.
c Whose charge is to fede the flocke, but they eat the frute thereof, Ezek. 34, 3.
d Thus the Prophets euer vse to mixt the promises with ŷ threatnings, lest the godlie shulde be to muche beaten downe, and therefore he sheweth how God wil gather his Church after this dispersion.

5 Beholde, The daies come, saith the
Lord, that I wil raise vnto Dauid a righteous [e] branche, & a King shal reigne, and
prosper, and shal execute iudgement, and
iustice in the earth.
6 In his daies * Iudáh shalbe saued, and Israél shal dwell safely, and this is the name
whereby thei shal call him, * The Lord
our righteousnes.
7 Therefore beholde, the daies come,
saith the Lord, that thei shal no more say,
The [f] Lord liueth, which broght vp the
children of Israél out of ӯ land of Egypt,
8 But the Lord liueth, which broght vp and
led the sede of the house of Israél out of
the North countrey & from all contreys
where I had scattered them, and thei shal
dwell in their owne land.
9 Mine heart breaketh within me, because of
the [g] Prophetes, all my bones shake: I am
like a drunken man (& like a man whome
wine hathe "overcome) for the presence
of the Lord and for his holie wordes.
10 For the land is ful of adulterers, *and* because of othes ӯ land mourneth, the pleasant places of the wildernes are dryed vp,
and their [h] course is euil, and their force is
not right.
11 For bothe the Prophet and the Priest
"do wickedly: and their wickednes haue I
founde in mine [i] House, saith the Lord.
12 Wherefore their waie shalbe vnto them
as sliperie *waies* in the darkenes: thei shal
be driuen forthe and fall therein: for I wil
bring a plague vpon them, *euen* the yere
of their visitacion, saith the Lord.
13 And I haue sene foolishnes in the Prophetes of Samaria, ӯ prophecied in Báal
and caused my people Israél to erre.
14 I haue sene also in the Prophetes of Ieru
salém [k] filthines: thei commit adulterie &
walke in lies: thei strengthen also the hãds
of the wicked that none can returne from
his wickednes: thei are all vnto [l] me as Sodóm, and the inhabitants thereof as Gomoráh.
15 Therefore thus saith the Lord of hostes
concerning the Prophetes, Beholde, I wil
fede them with [m] wormewood, and make
them drinke the water of gall: for from ӯ
Prophetes of Ierusalém is "wickednes gone
forthe into all the land.
16 Thus saith the Lord of hostes, Heare
not the wordes of the Prophetes that prophecie vnto you, and teache you vanitie:
thei speake the visiõ of their owne [n] heart
& not out of the mouth of the Lord.
17 Thei saie stil vnto them that despise me,
The Lord hath said, Ye [o] shal haue peace:
& thei saie vnto euerie one that walketh
after the stubbernes of his owne heart,
No euil shal come vpon you.
18 For [p] who hathe stand in the counsel of

e This prophecie is of the restitution of the Church in the time of Iesus Christ, who is ӯ true branche, read Isa. 11, 1. & 45, 8. chap. 33, 15. dani. 9, 24.

Deut. 33, 28.

chap. 33, 16.

f Read Chap. 16, 13.

g Meaning, the false prophets which deceiue ӯ people: wherein appeareth his great loue toward his naciõ, read Chap. 14, 13.

"*Ebr. passed ouer or troubled.*

h They runne head long to wickednes, and seke vaine helpe.

"*Or, are hypocrites.*

i My Temple is ful of their idolatrie and superstitions.

k They which shulde haue profited by my roddes against Samaria, are become worse then they

l Thogh to ӯ worlde they seme holy fathers, yet I detest them as I did these abominable cities.

m Read Chap. 8, 14.

"*Or, hypocrisie.*

n Which thei haue inuented of their owne braine.

o Read Chap. 6, 14, & 8, 11

p Thus thei did deride Ieremiáh as thogh the worde of God were not reueiled vnto him: so also spake Zedekiáh to Micháh, 1. King. 22, 24.

the Lord that he hathe perceiued & heard [q]
his worde? Who hathe marked his worde
and heard it?
19 Beholde, the tempest of the Lord goeth
forthe in *his* wrath, & a violent whirlwinde shal fall downe vpon the head of the
wicked.
20 The angre of the Lord shal not returne
vntil he haue executed, and til he haue
performed the thoghts of his heart: in the
latter daies ye [q] shal vnderstand it plainely.
21 * I haue not sent these Prophetes, saith
the Lord, yet thei ranne: I haue not spokẽ
to them, and yet thei prophecied.
22 But if thei had stand in my counsel, and
[r] had declared my wordes to my people, [x]
then they shulde haue turned them from
their euil waie, and from the wickednes
of their inuentions.
23 Am I a God *at hand*, saith the Lord, and
not a God [s] farre of?
24 Can anie hide him self in secret places,
that I shal not se him, saith the Lord?
Do not I fil heauen and earth, saith the
Lord?
25 I haue heard what the Prophetes said,
that prophecie lies in my Name, saying, I
[t] haue dreamed, I haue dreamed.
26 How long? "Do the Prophetes delite
to prophecie lies, euen prophecying the
deceit of their owne heart?
27 Thinke thei to cause [u] my people to
forget my Name by their dreames, which
thei tel euerie man to his neighbour, as
their forefathers haue forgottẽ my Name
for Báal?
28 The Prophet that hathe a dreame, let
him [x] tel a dreame, and he that hathe my
worde, let him speake my worde faithfully: [y] what is ӯ chaffe to the wheat, saith
the Lord?
29 Is not my worde euen like a fyre, saith
the Lord? and like an hammer, that breaketh the stone?
30 Therefore beholde, I *wil come* against the
Prophetes, saith the Lord, that [z] steale my
worde euerie one from his neighbour.
31 Beholde, I *wil come* against the Prophetes, saith the Lord, which haue swete tongues, and saye, [a] He saith.
32 Beholde, *I wil come* against them that
prophecie false dreames, saith the Lord, &
do tel them, and cause my people to erre
by their lies, and by their flatteries, and I
send them not, nor cõmanded them: therefore thei bring no profite vnto this people, saith the Lord.
33 And when this people, or the Prophet, or
a Priest shal aske thee, saying, What is the
[b] burden of the Lord? thou shalt then say
vnto them, What burden? I wil euen forsake you, saith the Lord.

q Bothe that God hathe sent me, and that my wordes shal be true.

Chap. 14, 13. & 27, 21. & 29, 8.

r He sheweth the difference betwene the true Prophetes and the false, betwene the hireling and the true minister.

s Do not I se your falsehode, howsoeuer you cloke it, and wheresoeuer you commit it?

t I haue a prophecie reueiled vnto me, as Nombr 12, 6.

"*Ebr. Is it in the heart of the prophetes?*

u He sheweth that Satan raiseth vp false prophetes to bring the people from God.

x Let the false prophet declare that it is his owne fantasie, & not sclãder my worde as thogh it were a cloke to couer his lyes.

y Meaning, ӯ it is not sufficient for Gods ministers to abstaine from lies, & to speake the worde of God: but that there be iudgement in alledging it, & that it may appeare to be applied to the same purpose ӯ it was spoken, Ezek. 3, 17. 1. cor 2, 17. & 4, 2. 2. tim. 2, 15. 1. pet. 4, 11.

z Which set forthe in my Name ӯ which I haue not cõmanded

a To wit, the Lord.

b The Prophetes called their threatenings Gods burden, which the sinners were not able to susteine: therefore ӯ wicked in deriding the worde, wolde aske of the Prophetes, what was the burden, as thogh thei wolde say, You seke nothing els, but to lay burdens on our shulders: and thus thei reiected the worde of God, as a grieuous burden.

34 And the Prophet, or the Prieſt, or the
people that ſhal ſay, The [c] burden of the
Lord, I wil euen viſit euerie ſuche one, &
his houſe.
35 Thus ſhal ye ſay euerie one to his neighbour, and euerie one to his brother, What
hathe the Lord anſwered? and what hathe
the Lord ſpoken?
36 And ẏ burden of the Lord ſhal ye mencion no more: for euerie mans [d] worde ſhal
be his burden: for ye haue peruerted the
wordes of the liuing God, the Lord of
hoſtes our God.
37 Thus ſhalt thou ſay to ẏ Prophet, What
hathe the Lord anſwered thee? and what
hathe the Lord ſpoken?
38 And if you ſay, The burden of the Lord,
Then thus ſaith the Lord, Becauſe ye ſay
this worde, The burden of the Lord, and I
haue ſent vnto you, ſaying, Ye ſhal not ſay,
The burden of the Lord,
39 Therefore beholde I, euen I, wil vtterly
'forget you, and I wil forſake you, & the ci
tie that I gaue you & your fathers, *and caſt you* out of my preſence,
40 And wil bring * an euerlaſting repro-
che vpõ you, & a perpetual ſhame which
ſhal neuer be forgotten.

c Becauſe this worde was broght to contempt & deriſion, he wil teache them another maner of ſpeache, and wil cauſe this worde Burden to ceaſe, and teache them to aſke with reuerẽce, What ſaith ẏ Lord?

d The thing which they mocke & contemne, ſhal come vpon them.

Or, take you away.

Chap. 20, 11.

CHAP. XXIIII.

1 The viſion of the baſkets of figges 5 Signifieth that parte of the people ſhulde be broght againe from captiuitie. 8 And that Zedekiáh and the reſt of the people ſhulde be caryed away.

1 THe Lord ſhewed me, & beholde, two
[a] baſkets of figges were ſet before ẏ
Tẽple of the Lord, after that Nebuchad-
nezzár Kĩg of Babél had caried away captiue Ieconiáh ẏ ſonne of Iehoiakím King
of Iudáh, and the princes of Iudáh with
the workemen, and cunning men of Ieruſalém, and had broght them to Babél.
2 One baſket *had* verie good figgs, *euen* like the figges that are firſt ripe: & the other
baſket *had* verie noghtie figges which colde not be eaten, thei were ſo euil.
3 Then ſaid the Lord vnto me, What ſeeſt
thou, Ieremiáh? And I ſaid, Figges: the
good figgs verie good, & the noghtie verie noghtie, which can not be eaten, thei
are ſo euil.
4 Againe the worde of the Lord came vnto me, ſaying,
5 Thus ſaith the Lord, the God of Iſraél,
Like theſe good figges, ſo wil I knowe
them that are caried away captiue of Iudáh to be good, whome I haue ſent out of
this [b] place, into the land of the Caldeans.
6 For I wil ſet mine eyes vpon them for
good, and I wil bring them againe to this
land, and I wil buylde them, and not deſtroy them, and I wil plant them, and not
roote them out,
7 And I wil giue them [c] an heart to knowe
me, that I am the Lord, and they ſhalbe
my* people, and I wil be their God: for
they ſhal returne vnto me with their
whole heart.
8 *And as the noghtie figges which can
not be eaten, they are ſo euil (ſurely thus
ſaith the Lord) ſo wil I giue Zedekiáh
the King of Iudáh, and his princes, and
the reſidue of Ieruſalém, that remaine in
this land, & them that dwell [d] in the land
of Egypt:
9 I wil euen giue them for a terrible plague to all the kingdomes of the earth, *and*
for a reproche, and for a prouerbe, for a
commune talke, and for a curſſe, in all places, where I ſhal caſt them.
10 And I wil ſend the ſworde, the famine,
and the peſtilence among them, til they
be conſumed out of the land, that I gaue
vnto them and to their fathers.

a The good figgs ſignified thẽ that were gone into captiuitie, and ſo ſaued their life, as chap. 21, 8. and the noghty figgs them ẏ remained, which were yet ſubiect to the ſworde, famine and peſtilence.

b Whereby he approueth the yelding of Ieconiáh, & his companie, becauſe thei obeied the Prophet, who exhorted them thereunto.

c Which declareth that man of him ſelfe can knowe nothing, til God giue the heart and vnderſtanding.

Chap. 31, 33. ebr. 8, 10.

Chap. 29, 17.

d Which fled thether for ſuccour.

CHAP. XXV.

1 He prophecieth that thei ſhalbe in captiuitie ſeuentie yeres. 12 And that after the ſeuentie yeres the Babylonians ſhulde be deſtroyed. 14 The deſtruction of all nations is prophecied.

1 THe worde that came to Ieremiáh,
concerning all the people of Iudáh
in the [a] fourth yere of Iehoiakím the ſonne of Ioſiáh King of Iudáh that was in
the firſt yere of Nebuchad-nezzár King
of Babél:
2 The which Ieremiáh the Prophet ſpake
vnto all the people of Iudáh, & to all the
inhabitants of Ieruſalém, ſaying,
3 From the thirtẽth yere of Ioſiáh the ſonne of Ammón King of Iudáh, euen vnto
[b] this daye (that is the thre and twentieth
yere) the worde of the Lord hathe come
vnto me, & I haue ſpoken vnto you [c] riſing early and ſpeaking, but ye wolde not
heare.
4 And the Lord hathe ſent vnto you all
his ſeruants the Prophetes, riſing early and
ſending *them*, but ye wolde not heare, nor
encline your eares to obeie.
5 Thei [d] ſaid, Turne againe now euerie one
from his euil waie, and from the wickednes of your inuencions, & ye ſhal dwell in
the land that the Lord hathe giuen vnto
you, and to your fathers for euer and euer.
6 And go not after other gods to ſerue thẽ
& to worſhip them, and prouoke me not to
angre with the workes of your hands, & I
wil not puniſh you.
7 Neuertheles ye wolde not heare me, ſaith
the Lord, but haue prouoked me to angre
with the workes of your hands to your
owne hurt.
8 Therefore thus ſaith the Lord of hoſtes,
Becauſe ye haue not heard my wordes,
9 Beholde, I wil ſend and take *to me* all the

[e] fami-

a That is, in ẏ third yere accompliſhed, & in the beginning of the fourth: for thogh Nebuchad-nezzár began to reigne in the end of the thirde yere of Iehoiakĩs reigne, yet that yere is not here counted, becauſe it was almoſt expired, Dan. 1, 1.

b Which was the fift yere & the ninth moneth of Iehoiakims reigne.

c That is, I haue ſpared no diligence or labour, Chap. 7, 13.

d He ſheweth that the Prophets wholly with one conſent did labour to pul ẏ people from thoſe vices, ẇ then reigned: to wit, frõ idolatrie, and the vaine confidence of men: for vnder theſe two all other were conteined. 2 King 17, 13. cha 18, 11 & 35, 15. Ionáh. 3, 8

e families of the North, saith the Lord, &
Nebuchad-nezzár the King of Babél my
f seruant, and wil bring them against this
land, and against the inhabitants thereof,
& against all these nations g rounde about,
and wil destroye them, and make them an
astonishment and an hissing, and a continual desolation.
10 * Moreouer * I wil take from them the
voice of mirth and the voice of gladnes,
the voice of the bridegrome and the voice of the bride, the noise of the h mille-
stones, and the light of the candle.
11 And this whole land shal be desolate,
and an astonishment, & these nacions shal
serue the King of Babél seuenty yeres.
12 And when the i seuentie yeres are accom
plished, I wil visite k the King of Babél
and that nacion, saith the Lord, for their
iniquities, euen the land of the Caldeans,
and wil make it a perpetual desolation,
13 And I wil bring vpon that land all my
wordes which I haue pronounced against
it, *euen* all ý is writen in this boke, which
Ieremiáh hathe prophecied against all
nations.
14 For many nacions, and great Kings shal
euen l serue them selues of them: thus
wil I recompēce them according to their
dedes, and according to the workes of
their owne hands.
15 For thus hathe the Lord God of Israél
spoken vnto me, m Take the cup of wine
of this *mine* indignacion at mine hand,
and cause all the nacions, to whome I send
thee, to drinke it.
16 And they shal drinke, and be moued
& be madde, because of the sworde, that I
wil send among them.
17 Then toke I the cuppe at ý Lords hand,
and made all people to drinke, vnto whome the Lord had sent me:
18 *Euen* Ierusalém, and the cities of Iudáh,
and the Kings thereof, and the princes
thereof, to make them desolate, an astonishment, an hissing, and a cursse, n as *appeareth* this day:
19 Pharaóh *also*, King of Egypt, and his seruantes, and his princes, and all his people:
20 And all sortes of people, and all the
Kings of the land o of Vz: and all the
Kings of the land of the Philistims, & p A-
shkelón, and Azzáh, & Ekrón, and ý remnant of Ashdód:
21 q Edóm, and Moáb, and the Ammonites,
22 And all the Kings of Tyrus, and all the
Kings of Zidón, & the Kings of ý r Yles,
that are beyonde the sea,
23 And Dedán, and s Temá, & Buz, and all
that dwell in the vttermost corners,

e The Caldeans, & all their power.
f So the wicked and Satan him selfe are Gods seruants, because he maketh them to serue him by constreint and turneth that which thei do of malice, to his honour & glorie.
g As the Philistims, Ammonites, Egyptiās and others.
Chap.16,9.
Or, destroy.
h Meaning, ý bread and all things that shulde serue vnto their feastes, shulde be taken away.
i This reuelacion was for the confirmacion of his prophecie, because he tolde thē of ý time, that thei shuld entre & remaine in captiuitie, 2.Chro.36, 22, ezra. 1, 1. chap 29,10 dani.9,2.
k For seing the iudgement began at his owne house, the enemies must nedes be punished most grieuously, Ezek 9,6 1. pet.4,17.
l That is, of the Babylonians, as Chap. 27,7.
m Signifying the extreme afflictions that God had appointed for euerie one, as Psal. 75,8. isa. 51,17 and this cup, which the wicked drinke is more bitter thē that which he giueth to his children, for he measureth ý one by mercie, and the other by iustice.
n For now it beginneth and shal so continue til it be accomplished.
o Read Iob 1, 1.
p Which were cities of the Philistims.
q Edóm is here taken for the whole countrey, and Vz for a part thereof.
r As Grecia, Italie, and the rest of those countreis.
s These were people of Arabia, which came of Dedan the sonne of Abrahám and Keturáh.

24 And all the Kings of Arabia, and all the
Kings of Arabia, that dwell in the t desert,
25 And all the Kings of Zimrí, and all the
Kings of * Elám, and all the Kings of the
Medes.
26 And all ý Kings of the North farre, and
nere one to another, and all the kingdomes
of the worlde, which are vpon the earth,
& the King of u Sheshách shal drinke after them.
27 Therefore say thou vnto them, Thus
saith the Lord of hostes, the God of Israél, Drinke and be drunken, and spewe and
fall, and rise no more, because of the
sworde, which I wil send among you.
28 ¶ But if thei refuse to take ý cup at thine
hand to drinke, then tel them, Thus saith
ý Lord of hostes, ye shal certeinly drinke.
29 For lo, x I beginne to plague the citie,
where my Name is called vpon, & shulde
you go fre? Ye shal not go quite: for I wil
call for a sworde vpon all the inhabitants
of the earth, saith the Lord of hostes.
30 Therefore prophecie thou against them
all these wordes, and saie vnto them, * The
Lord shal roare from aboue, and thrust out
his voice from his holie habitacion: he shal
roare vpon his habitacion, & crye aloude,
as thei that presse the grapes against all ý
inhabitants of the earth,
31 The sounde shal come to the ends of the
earth: for the Lord hathe a controuersie ẘ
the natiōs, and wil entre into iudgement
with all flesh, & he wil giue them that a-
re wicked, to the sworde, saith the Lord.
32 ¶ Thus saith the Lord of hostes, Beholde, a plague shal go forthe from nation to
nation, and a * great whirlewinde shalbe
raised vp from the coastes of the earth,
33 And y the slaine of the Lord shalbe at ý
daie, from *one* end of the earth, euen vnto
the *other* end of the earth: thei shal not
be mourned, nether gathered nor buryed,
but shalbe as the dōgue vpon the grounde.
34 Howle, z ye shepherds, and crye, and wallowe your selues in the ashes, ye principal
of the flocke: for your daies of slaughter
are accomplished, and of your dispersion,
and ye shal fall like a precious vessels.
35 And the b flight shal faile from the shepherds, and the escaping from the principal
of the flocke.
36 A voice of the crye of the shepherds,
and an howling of the principal of the
flocke *shalbe heard*: for the Lord hathe destroyed their pasture.
37 And the * best pastures are destroyed because of the wrath and indignation of the
Lord.
38 He hathe forsaken his couert, as the lion:
for their land is waste, because of ý wrath
of the oppressor, and because of the wrath
of his indignation.

t For there were two coūtreis so named the one called plentiful, and the other baren, or desert.
Or, Persia.
u That is, of Babylon, as Chap.51,41.
x That is, Ierusalém, read vers.12.
Ioel.3,16. amos 1,2.
Chap.30,23.
y Thei which are slaine at ý Lords appointement.
z Ye that are chief rulers, & gouernours.
a Which are moste easily broken.
b It shal not helpe them to seke to flee.
Ebr. peaceable.

CHAP. XXVI.

2 Ieremiáh mouth the people to repentance. 7 He is taken of the false Prophetes and Priestes and broght to iudgement. 23 Vriiáh the Prophet is killed of Iehoiakim cõtrarie to the wil of God.

1 IN the beginning of the reigne of Iehoiakím the sonne of Iosiáh King of
Iudáh, came this worde from the Lord,
saying,
2 Thus saith the Lord, Stand in the [a] court
of the Lords House, and speake vnto all
the cities of Iudáh, which come to worship in the Lords House, all the wordes ỹ
I cõmãd thee to speake: kepe not [b] a worde backe,
3 If so be they wil hearken, and turne euerie man from his euil way, that I may [c] repent me of the plague, which I haue determined to bring vpon them, because of
the wickednes of their workes.
4 And ỹ shalt say vnto thẽ, Thus saith the
Lord, If ye wil not heare me to walke in
my Lawes, which I haue set before you,
5 And to heare the wordes of my seruants
the Prophetes, whome I sent vnto you, bothe rising vp early, and sending *them*, and
wil not obeie *them*,
6 Then wil I make this House like [d] Shilóh, and wil make this citie [e] a cursse to
all the nacions of the earth.
7 So the Priestes, and the Prophetes, and all
the people heard Ieremiáh speaking these
wordes in the House of the Lord.
8 Now when Ieremiáh had made an end of
speaking all that the Lord had commanded *him* to speake vnto all the people, thẽ
the Priestes, and the Prophetes, and all the
people toke him, and said, Thou shalt dye
the death.
9 Why hast thou prophecied in the Name
of ỹ Lord, saying, This [f] House shalbe like
Shilóh, & this citie shalbe desolate without an inhabitãt? & all the people were ga
thered against Ieremiáh in the House of
the Lord.
10 And when the princes of Iudáh heard of
these things, thei came vp from ỹ Kings
house into the House of the Lord, & sate
downe in the entrie of the [g] newe gate of
the Lords *House*.
11 Then spake the Priestes, and the Prophetes vnto the princes, & to all ỹ people,
saying, " This man is worthie to dye: for
he hathe prophecied against this citie, as
ye haue heard with your eares.
12 Then spake Ieremiáh vnto all the princes, & to all the people, saying, The Lord
hathe [h] sent me to prophecie against this
House and against this citie all the things
that ye haue heard.
13 Therefore now amẽd your waies & your
workes, & heare the voice of ỹ Lord your
God, ỹ the Lord may repent him of ỹ plague, ỹ he hathe pronounced against you.

a That is, in that place of the Temple whereunto the people resort out of all Iudáh to sacrifice.
b To the intent that they shulde pretend no ignorance, as Act 20,27.
c Read Chap. 18,8.
d Read Chap. 7,12.
e So ỹ when they wolde cursse any, thei shal say, God do to thee as to Ierusalém.
f Because of Gods promes to the Temple, Psal. 132, 14. ỹ he wolde for euer remaine there, ỹ hypocrites thoght this Temple colde neuer perish, and therefore thoght it blasphemie to speake against it, Mat. 26, 61. act. 6, 13, not cõsidering ỹ this was ment of ỹ Church, where God wil remaine foreuer.
g So called, because it was repaired by Ioathám, 2. Kings 15,35.
" Ebr. iudgement of death belongeth to this man.
h He bothe sheweth the cause of his doings plainely, and also threateneth them ỹ they shulde nothĩg auaile, thogh they shulde put him to death, but heape greater vengeance vpon their heads.

14 As for me, beholde, I am in your hands:
do with me as ye thinke good and right.
15 But knowe ye for certeine, ỹ if ye put me
to death, ye shal surely bring innocent
blood vpon your selues, and vpon this citie, and vpon the inhabitants thereof: for
of a trueth ỹ Lord hath sent me vnto you,
to speake all these wordes in your eares.
16 Then said the princes and all the people
vnto the Priests & to the Prophetes, This
man is not worthie to dye: for he hathe
spoken vnto vs in the Name of the Lord
our God.
17 ¶ Then rose vp certeine of the Elders of
the land, and spake to all the assemblie of
the people, saying,
18 Micháh the Morashite *prophecied in ỹ
dayes of Hezekiáh King of Iudáh, and
spake to all the people of Iudáh, saying,
Thus saith ỹ Lord of hostes, Zión shalbe
plowed *like* a field, and Ierusalém shalbe
an heape, & the mountaine of the [i] House *shalbe* as the high places of the forest.
19 Did Hezekiáh King of Iudáh, and all
Iudáh put him to death? did he not feare
the Lord, and prayed before the Lord, and
the Lord repented him of the [k] plague,
that he had pronoũced against them? thus
might we procure great euil against our
soules.
20 And there was also a man that prophecí-
ed in ỹ Name of the Lord, *one* Vriiáh the
sonne of Shemaiáh, of Kiriáth-iarem, who
prophecied against this citie, and against
this land, according to all the wordes of
Ieremiáh.
21 Now when Iehoiakím the King with all
his men of power, & all the princes heard
his wordes, the King soght to slaie him.
But when Vriiáh heard it, he was afraied
and fled, and went into Egypt.
22 Thẽ Iehoiakím the King [l] sent men into
Egypt, *euen* Elnathán the sonne of Achbór,
and certeine with him into Egypt.
23 And thei fet Vriiáh out of Egypt, and
broght him vnto Iehoiakím the King,
who slewe him with the sworde, and [m] cast
his dead bodie into the graues of the children of the people.
24 But the hand of Ahikám [n] the sonne of
Shaphán was with Ieremiáh ỹ thei shulde
not giue him into the hand of the people
to put him to death.

* Micháh 1,1. & 3,12.
i That is, of the House of ỹ Lord: to wit, Zión, and these examples the goulie alledged to deliuer Ieremiáh out of the Priests hands whose rage els wold not haue bene satisfied, but by his death.
k So that the citie was not destroyed, but by miracle was deliuered out of the hands of Saneheríb.
l Here is declared the furie of tyrants, who can not abide to heare Gods worde declared, but persecute the ministers thereof, and yet in the end they preuaile nothing, but prouoke Gods iudgements so muche ỹ more.
m As in the first Hezekiahs example is to be followed, so in this other Iehoiakims act is to be abhorred: for Gods plague did light on him, and his housholde
n Which declareth that nothing colde haue appeased their furie, if God had not moued this noble man to stãd valiantly in his defence.

CHAP. XXVII.

1 Ieremiáh at the commandement of the Lord sendeth bondes to the King of Iudáh and to the other Kings that were nere, whereby thei are monished to be subiectes vnto Nebuchad-nezzár 9 He warneth the people & the Kings & rulers that thei beleue not false Prophetes.

1 IN the beginning of the reigne of [a] Iehoiakím ỹ sonne of Iosiáh King of Iu
dáh

a As touching the dispositiō of these prophecies, they that gathered them into a booke, did not altogether obserue the order of times, but did set some afore, which shulde be after, and contrarie wise: which if the reader marke wel, it shal auoide many doutes, & make the reading muche more easy.

dáh came this worde vnto Ieremiáh from
the Lord, saying,
2 Thus saith the Lord to me, Make thee
[b] bondes, and yokes, and put them vpon
thy necke,
3 And send them to the King of Edóm, &
to the King of Moáb, and to the King of
the Ammonites, and to the King of Tyrus, and to the King of Zidón, by the hād
of the messengers which come to Ierusalém vnto Zedekiáh the King of Iudáh,
4. And commande them to say vnto their
masters, Thus saith the Lord of hostes
the God of Isráel, Thus shal ye say vnto
your masters,
5 I haue made the earth, the man, and the
beast that are vpō the groūde, by my great
power, & by my outstretched arme, & haue
giuen it vnto whome it pleased me.
6 But now I haue giuen all these lands into the hād of Nebuchad-nezzár the King
of Babél my [c] seruant, and the beastes of
the field haue I also giuē him to serue him.
7 And all nations shal serue him, and his
[d] sonne, and his sonnes sonne vntil the verie time of his land come also: then manie
nations and great Kings shal [e] serue them
selues of him.
8 And the nation & kingdome which wil
not serue ẙ same Nebuchad-nezzár King
of Babél, and that wil not put their necke
vnder the yoke of the King of Babél, the
same nation wil I visite, saith the Lord,
with the sworde, and with the famine, and
with the pestilence, vntil I haue wholy *giuen* them into his hands.
9 Therefore heare not your Prophetes nor
your southsaiers, nor your dreamers, nor
your inchanters, nor your sorcerers, which
saie vnto you thus, Ye shal not serue the
King of Babél.
10 For thei prophecie a lie vnto you to cau
se you to go farre from your land, and
that I shulde cast you out, and you shulde
perish.
11 But the nation that put their neckes vnder the yoke of the King of Babél, & serue
him, those wil I let remaine stil in their
owne land, saith the Lord, and thei shal
occupie it and dwell therein.
12 ¶ I spake also to Zedekiáh King of Iudáh according to all these wordes, saying,
Put your neckes vnder the yoke of the
King of Babél, and serue him and his people, that ye may liue.
13 Why wil ye dye, thou, & thy people by
the sworde, by the famine, and by the pesti
lēce, as the Lord hathe spokē against ẙ nation, that wil not serue ẙ King of Babél?
14 Therefore heare not the wordes of the
Prophetes, that speake vnto you, saying, Ye
shal not serue the King of Babél: for they
prophecie a lie vnto you.

b By suche signes ẙ Prophetes vsed some times to confirme their prophecies, ẇ notwithstanding they colde not do of them selues, but inasmuche as they had a reuelation for the same, Isa. 20,2. and therefore the false prophetes to get more credit did vse also suche visible signes, but they had no reuelation, 1.King. 22,11.

c Read Chap. 25,9.

d Meaning, Emilmerodách, and his sonne Belshazár.

e They shal bring him, and his kingdome in subiection, as Chap. 25,14.

15 For I haue not * sent thē, saith the Lord,
yet they prophecie a lie in my Name, that
I might cast you out, and that ye might pe
rish, *bothe* you, & the Prophetes that prophecie vnto you.
16 ¶ Also I spake to ẙ Priestes, & to all this
people, saying, Thus saith the Lord, Heare not the wordes of your Prophetes that
prophecie vnto you, saying, Beholde, * the
vessels of the House of the Lord shal now
shortely be [f] broght againe from Babél,
for they prophecie a lie vnto you.
17 Heare thē not, *but* serue the King of Babél, that ye may liue: wherefore shulde
this citie be desolate?
18 But if they be Prophetes, and if the worde of the Lord be with thē, let them [g] intreat the Lord of hostes, that the vessels,
which are left in the House of the Lord, &
in the house of the King of Iudáh, & at Ie
rusalém, go not to Babél.
19 For thus saith the Lord of hostes, concerning the * pillers, and concerning the
sea, and concerning the bases, and concerning the residue of the vessels that remaine in this citie,
20 Which Nebuchad-nezzár King of Babél toke not, when he caryed * away captiue Ieconiáh the sonne of Iehoiakím King
of Iudáh from Ierusalém to Babél, with all
the nobles of Iudáh and Ierusalém.
21 For thus saith the Lord of hostes ẙ God
of Isráel, cōcerning the vessels ẙ remaine
in the House of the Lord, & in ẙ house of
the King of Iudáh, and at Ierusalém,
22 They shalbe broght to Babél, and there
thei shalbe vntil the day that I visite [h] thē,
saith the Lord: then wil I bring them vp,
and restore them vnto this place.

Chap. 14,15. & 23,21. & 29,8.

Chap. 28,3.

f Which were taken whē Ieconiáh was led captiue into Babél.

g For it was not onely the Prophetes office to shewe the worde of God, but also to pray for the sinnes of the people, Gen. 20,7. Which these colde not do because they had no expresse worde: for God had pronounced ẙ contrarie.

2.King. 25,13

2.King. 24,12

h That is, for the space of seuentie yeres, til I haue caused the Medes and Persiās to ouercome the Caldeans.

CHAP. XXVIII.

1 The false prophecie of Hananiáh. 12 Ieremiáh reproueth Hananiáh, and prophecieth.

1 AND that same yere in the beginning
of the [a] reigne of Zedekiáh King of
Iudáh in the [b] fourth yere, *and* in the fift
moneth Hananiáh the sonne of Azúr the
Prophet, ẇ was of [c] Gibeón, spake to me in
the House of the Lord in the presence of
the Priests, and of all the people, and said,
2 Thus speaketh the Lord of hostes, the
God of Isráel, saying, I haue broken the
yoke of the King of Babél.
3 " Within two yeres space I wil bring
into this place all the vessels of the Lords
House, ẙ Nebuchad-nezzár King of Babél toke away from this place, and caried
them into Babél.
4 And I wil bring againe to this place Ieconiáh the sonne of Iehoiakím King of
Iudáh, with all thē that were caryed away
captiue of Iudáh, and wēt into Babél, saith
the Lord: for I wil breake the yoke of the
King of Babél.

a When Ieremiáh began to beare these bondes and yokes.

b After that the land had rested, as Leu. 25,1. deu. 15,1.

c This was a citie in Beniamín belonging to the sonnes of Aarón, Iosh. 21,17.

" Ebr. two yeres of dayes.

5 Then the Prophet Ieremiáh said vnto the
[d] Prophet Hananiáh in the presence of the
Priests,& in the presence of all the people
that stode in the House of the Lord.
6 Euẽ the Prophet Ieremiáh said, So be it:
the [e] Lord so do, the Lord confirme thy
wordes which thou hast prophecied to restore the vessels of the Lords House,and
all that is caried captiue from Babél into
this place.
7 But heare thou now this worde that I wil
speake in thine eares and in the eares of all
the people.
8 The Prophetes that haue bene before me
and before thee in time past, [f] prophecied
against manie countreis,and against great
kingdomes, of warre,& of plagues,and of
pestilence.
9 *And* the Prophet which prophecieth of
peace,when the worde of the Prophet shal
come to passe, *then* shal the Prophet be
knowen that the Lord hathe truely sent
him.
10 Then Hananiáh the Prophet toke the
yoke from the Prophet Ieremiahs necke,
and [g] brake it.
11 And Hananiáh spake in the presence of
all the people, saying, Thus saith ỹ Lord,
Euen so wil I breake the yoke of Nebuchad-nezzár King of Babél,frõ the necke
of all nations within the space of two yeres : and the Prophet Ieremiáh went his
way.
12 ¶ Then the worde of the Lord came vnto Ieremiáh the Prophet,(after that Hananiáh the Prophet had broken the yoke
from the necke of the Prophet Ieremiáh)
saying,
13 Go,& tel Hananiáh,saying, Thus saith
the Lord,Thou hast broken the yokes of
wood:but thou shalt make for them yokes
of yron.
14 For thus saith the Lord of hostes the
God of Israél,I haue put a [h] yoke of yron
vpon ỹ necke of all these natiõs,that they
may serue Nebuchad-nezzár King of Ba
bél:for thei shal serue him, and I haue giuen him the [i] beasts of the field also.
15 Thẽ said the Prophet Ieremiáh vnto the
Prophet Hananiáh , Heare now Hananiáh,the Lord hathe not sent thee,but thou
makest this people to trust in a lye.
16 Therefore thus saith the Lord,Beholde,
I wil cast thee from of the earth: this yere
thou shalt dye, because thou hast spoken
rebelliously against the Lord.
17 So Hananiáh the Prophet [k] dyed the same yere in the seuenth moneth.

d He was so estemed,thogh he was a false Prophet.

e That is, I wolde with ỹ same for Gods honour,& welthe of my people,but he hathe appointed the contrarie.

f Meaning,that the Prophetes that did ether denounce warre or peace, were tryed ether true or false by the successe of their prophecies. Albeit God maketh to come to passe sometime that which the false prophet speaketh, to trye the faith of his, Deut. 13,3.

g This declareth the impudencie of the wicked hirelings, which haue no zeale to the trueth, but are led ẘ ambition to get the fauour of mẽ,& therefore can not abide any,that might discredit them, but burst forthe into rages,and contrarie to their owne cõscience, passe not what lies they report,or how wickedly they do, so ỹ thei may maintein their estimation.

h That is, a hard,and cruel seruitude.

i Signifying, that all shulde be his,as Dan. 2,38.

k Seing this thing was euident in the eyes of ỹ people, and yet they returned not to ỹ Lord, it is manifest, that miracles can not moue vs,nether the worde it self, except God touche the heart.

CHAP. XXIX.

1 Ieremiáh writeth vnto them that were in captiuitie in Babylon. 10 He prophecieth their returne after seuentie yeres. 16 He prophecieth the destruction of the King and of the people that remaine in Ierusalém. 21 He threateneth the prophetes that seduce the people. 25 The death of Semeiah is prophecied.

1 Now these are ỹ wordes of the [*] boke
that Ieremiáh the Prophet sent frõ
Ierusalém vnto [a] the residue of the Elders
which were caryed away captiues , and to
the Priests,and to the Prophetes,and to all
the people whome Nebuchad-nezzár had
caryed away captiue from Ierusalém to
Babél.
2 (After that Ieconiáh the King, and the
[b] Quene , and the eunuches, the [*] princes
of Iudáh,and of Ierusalém, and the worke
men,and cũning men were departed from
Ierusalém)
3 By the hand of Elasáh the sonne of Shaphán and Gemariáh the sonne of Hilkiáh
(whome Zedekiáh King of Iudáh [c] sent
vnto Babél to Nebuchad-nezzár King of
Babél) saying,
4 Thus hathe the Lord of hostes the God
of Israél spoken vnto all that are caryed
away captiues, whome I haue [d] caused to
be caried away captiues from Ierusalém
vnto Babél
5 Buylde you houses to dwell in, and plant
you gardens,and eat the frutes of them.
6 Take you wiues , and beget sonnes, and
daughters,and take wiues for your sonnes,
and giue your daughters to housbands,
that they may beare sonnes & daughters,
that ye may be increased there, and not
diminished.
7 And seke the prosperitie of the citie,whe-
ther I haue caused you to be caryed away
captiues,and [e] pray vnto the Lord for it:
for in the peace thereof shal you haue
peace.
8 ¶ For thus saith ỹ Lord of hostes the God
of Israél, Let not your prophetes, & your
sothesayers that be amõg you,deceiue you,
nether giue eare to your dreames , which
you dreame.
9 For they prophecie you a lye in my Name: I haue not sent them,saith the Lord.
10 But thus saith the Lord , That after seuentie yeres be accomplished at Babél, I
wil visit you,and performe my good promes toward you, and cause you to returne to this place.
11 For I knowe ỹ thoghts,that I haue thoght
towardes you, saith the Lord , *euen* the
thoghts of peace,and not of trouble,to giue you an end,and *your* hope.
12 Then shal you crye vnto me,and ye shal
go and pray vnto me, and I wil heare you,
13 And ye shal seke me and finde *me*, because ye shal seke me with all [f] your heart.
14 And I wil be founde of you,saith ỹ Lord,
and I wil turne away your captiuitie, and
I wil gather you from all the nations and
from all the places , whether I haue cast
you, saith the Lord , and wil bring you
againe

* Or,lettre.

a For some dyed in the way.

b Meaning,Iec oniahs mother.

* Chap.24,1.

c To intreat of some equal cõditions.

d To wit,the Lord, whose worke this was.

e The Prophet speaketh not this for the affection that he bare to the tyrant, but that they shulde pray for the commune rest, and quietnes, ỹ their troubles might not be increased, and that they might ẘ more pacience and lesse grief waite for the time of their deliuerance, which God had appointed moste certeine: for els not onely the Israelites, but all the worlde, yea,& the insensible creatures shulde reioyce when these tyrants shulde be destroyed,as Isa. 14,4.

f When your oppression shalbe great,& your afflictiõs cause you to repent your disobedience, & also whẽ ỹ seuentie yeres of your captiuitie shalbe expired,2.Chro 36,22.ezra.1,1. chap.25,12. dan.9,2.

againe vnto the place, whence I caused
you to be caryed away captiue.
15 ¶ Because ye haue said, The Lord hathe
raised vs vp [g] Prophetes in Babél,
16 Therefore thus saieth the Lord of the
King, that sitteth vpon the throne of Dauid, & of all the people, that dwell in this
citie, your brethren that are not gone forthe with you into captiuitie:
17 *Euen* thus saith the Lord of hostes, Beholde, I wil send vpon them the [h] sworde,
the famine, and the pestilence, & wil make
them like vile [i] figges, that can not be eatẽ,
they are so noghtie.
18 And I wil persecute them with the sworde, with the famine, & with the pestilẽce: &
I wil make them a terror to all kingdomes
of the earth, & [k] a cursse, and astonishmẽt
and an hissing, and a reproche among all
the nations whether I haue cast them,
19 Because thei haue not heard my wordes,
saith the Lord, which I sent vnto them by
my seruãts the Prophetes, [l] rising vp care-
ly, & sending *them*, but ye wolde not heare,
saith the Lord.
20 ¶ Heare ye therefore the worde of the
Lord all ye of the captiuitie, whome I haue sent from Ierusalém to Babél.
21 Thus saith the Lord of hostes, the God
of Israél, of Aháb the sonne of Kolaiáh, &
of Zedekiáh the sonne of Maaseiáh, which
prophecie lies vnto you in my Name, Beholde, I wil deliuer them into the hand of
Nebuchad-nezzár Kĩg of Babél & he shal
slaye them before your eyes.
22 And all they of the captiuitie of Iudáh,
that are in Babél, shal take vp this cursse
against them, & say, The Lord make thee
like Zedekiáh and like Aháb, whome the
King of Babél burnt [m] in the fyre,
23 Because they haue cõmitted [n] vilenie in
Israél, and haue committed adulterie with
their neighbours wiues, and haue spoken
lying wordes in my Name, which I haue
not commanded them, euen I knowe it, &
testifie it, saith the Lord.
24 ¶ Thou shalt also speake to Shemaiáh
the [*] Nehelamite, saying,
25 Thus speaketh ẏ Lord of hostes, the God
of Israél, saying, Because thou hast sẽt letters in thy name vnto all the people, that
are at Ierusalém, & to Zephaniáh the sonne of Maaseiáh the Priest, and to all the
Priests, saying,
26 The Lord hathe made thee Priest, for
[o] Iehoiadá the Priest, that ye shulde be officers in the House of ẏ Lord, for euery mã
that raueth & maketh him self a Prophet,
to put him in prison and in the stockes.
27 Now therefore why hast not thou reproued Ieremiáh of Anathóth, which prophecieth vnto you?
28 For, for this cause he sent vnto vs in Ba-

g As Aháb, Zedekiáh, and Shemaiáh.

h Whereby he assureth them, ẏ there shalbe no hope of returning before the time appointed.

i According to ẏ comparison, Chap. 24, 1.

k Read Chap. 26, 6.

l Read Chap. 7, 13 & 25, 3 & 26, 5.

m Because thei gaue the people hope of spedy returning.

n Which was adulterie, and falsifying the worde of God.

* Or, dreamer.

o Shemaiáh ẏ false prophet flattereth Zephaniáh the chief Priest, as thogh God had giuen him the spirit and zeale of Iehoiadá to punish whosoeuer trespaced against the worde of God, of the ẇ he wolde haue made Ieremiáh one, calling him a rauer & a false pphet.

bél, saying, This *captiuitie* is long: buylde
houses to dwell in, and plant gardens, and
eat the frutes of them.
29 And Zephaniáh the Priest red this lettre in the eares of Ieremiáh the Prophet.
30 Then came the worde of the Lord vnto
Ieremiáh, saying,
31 Send to all thẽ of the captiuitie, saying,
Thus saith the Lord of Shemaiáh the Nehelamite, Because that Shemaiáh hathe pro
phecied vnto you, & I sent him not, & he
caused you to trust in a lye,
32 Therefore thus saith the Lord, Beholde,
I wil visite Shemaiáh the Nehelamite, and
his sede: he shal not haue a man [p] to dwell
among this people, nether shal he beholde the good, that I wil do for my people,
saith ẏ Lord, because he hathe spoken rebelliously against the Lord.

p He & his sede shalbe destroied, so that none of thẽ shulde se the benefite of this deliuerance.

CHAP. XXX.

1 *The returne of the people from Babylon.* 16 *He me-*
naceth the enemies, 18 *And comforteth the Church.*

1 THe worde, that came to Ieremiáh frõ
the Lord, saying,
2 Thus speaketh the Lord God of Israél,
saying, Write thee all the wordes, that I
haue spoken vnto thee in [a] a boke.
3 For lo, the daies come, saith the Lord, that
I wil bring againe ẏ captiuitie of my people Israél and Iudah, saith the Lord: for
I wil restore them vnto the land, that I gaue to their fathers, & they shal possesse it.
4 Againe, these are the wordes ẏ the Lord
spake concerning Israél, and concernig
Iudáh.
5 For thus saith the Lord, We haue heard
a [b] terrible voyce, of feare & not of peace.
6 Demande now & beholde, if man trauail
with childe? wherefore do I beholde euery
man with his hands on his loines as a woman in trauail, & all faces are turned into
a palenes?
7 Alas, for this [c] day is great: none *hathe bene*
like it: it is euen the time of Iaakobs trouble, yet shal he be deliuered from it.
8 For in that [d] day, saith the Lord of hostes,
I wil breake [e] his yoke from of thy necke,
and breake thy bondes, and strangers shal
no more serue them selues [f] of him.
9 But they shal serue the Lord their God,
& [g] Dauid their King, whome I wil raise
vp vnto them.
10 Therefore feare not, ô my seruãt Iaakób,
saith the Lord, nether be afraied, ô Israél:
for lo, I wil deliuer thee from a farre *coun-*
trey, and thy sede from the land of their
captiuitie, & Iaakób shal turne againe, &
shalbe in rest and prosperitie & none shal
make him afraid.
11 For I am with thee, saith the Lord, to saue thee, thogh I vtterly destroy all the nacions where I haue scattered thee: yet wil I
not vtterly destroy thee, but I wil correct

a Because thei shulde be assured and their posteritie confirmed in the hope of this deliuerance promised.

b He sheweth that before ẏ this deliuerãce shal come, the Caldeans shulde be extremely afflicted by their enemies, and ẏ they shulde be in suche perplexitie & sorow as a woman in her trauail, as Isa. 13, 8.

c Meaning, ẏ the time of their captiuitie shulde be grieuous.

d When I shal visit Babylon.

e Of the King of Babylon.

f To wit, of Iaakób.

g That is, Messiáh, ẇ shulde come of ẏ stocke of Dauid, according to the flesh and shulde be the true pastor, as Ezek. 34, 23. who is set forth and his kingdome that shulde be euerlasting in the persone of Dauid, Hos. 3, 5.

thee by iudgement, and not [h] vtterly cut
thee of.
12 For thus saith the Lord, Thy bruising is
incurable, *and* [i] thy wounde is dolorous.
13 There is none to iudge thy cause, *or to lay*
a plaister: there are no medecines, nor helpe for thee.
14 All thy [k] louers haue forgotten thee: thei
seke thee not: for I haue striken thee with
the wounde of an enemie, & with a sharpe
chastisemẽt for the multitude of thine iniquities, *because* thy sinnes were increased.
15 Why cryest thou for thine affliction? thy
sorowe is incurable, for the multitude of
thine iniquities: *because* thy sinnes were increased, I haue done these thĩgs vnto thee.
16 [l] Therefore all they that deuoure thee,
shal be deuoured, and all thine enemies e-
uery one shal go into captiuitie: and they
that spoyle thee, shalbe spoyled, & all thei
that robbe thee, wil I giue to be robbed.
17 For I wil restore helth vnto thee, & I wil
heale thee of thy woundes, saith the Lord,
because they called thee, The cast away,
saying, This is Zión, whome no man seketh
after.
18 Thus saith the Lord, Beholde, I wil brĩg
againe the captiuitie of Iaakobs tentes,
and haue compassion on his dwelling places: and the citie shalbe buylded vpon her
owne heape, [m] and the palace shal remaine after the maner thereof.
19 And out of them shal procede [n] thankesgiuing, and the voyce of them that are
ioyous, and I wil multiplie them, and thei
shal not be fewe: I wil also glorifie them,
and they shal not be diminished.
20 Their childrẽ also shalbe as afore time,
and their congregacion shalbe establisshed
before me: & I wil visite all that vexe thẽ.
21 And their [o] noble *ruler* shalbe of them
selues, and their gouernour shal procede
from the middes of them, and I wil cause
him to drawe nere, and approche vnto me:
for who is this that directeth his [p] heart to
come vnto me, saith the Lord?
22 And ye shalbe my people, and I wil be
your God.
23 Beholde, [q] the tẽpest of the Lord goeth
forthe with wrath: the whirlwinde ŷ hangeth ouer, shal light vpon the head of the
wicked.
24 The fierce wrath of the Lord shal not
returne, vntil he haue done, and vntil he
haue performed the intents of his heart: in
the [r] latter daies ye shal vnderstand it.

h Read Chap. 10,24.
i Meaning, that no man is able to finde out a meane to deliuer them, but ŷ it must be the worke of God.
k The Asyrians & Egyptians whome thou didest enterteine with giftes, who left thee in thine affliction.
l Herein is commended Gods great mercie toward his, who doeth not destroye them for their sinnes, but correct and chastise them, til he haue purged & pardoned them, & so burneth the roddes by the which he did punish them, Isa.33,1.
m Meaning, ŷ the citie and the Temple shulde be restored to their former state.
n He sheweth how the people shal with praise and thãkesgiuing acknowledge this benefite.
o Meaning, Zerubbabél, who was the figure of Christ, in whome this was accomplished.
p Signifying, ŷ Christ doeth willingly submit him self to the obedience of God his Father.
q Lest the wicked hypocrites shulde flatter thẽ selues with these promises, the Prophet sheweth what shalbe their portion.
r When this Messiáh and deliuerer is sent.

CHAP. XXXI.

1 He rehearseth Gods benefites after their returne from Babylon. 23 And the spiritual ioye of the faithful in the Church.

1 AT the [a] same time, saith the Lord,
wil I be the God of all the families
of Israél, and they shalbe my people.

a When this noble gouernour shal come: meaning Christ, not onely Iudáh & Israél, but the rest of ŷ worlde shalbe called.

2 Thus saith the Lord, The people which
[b] escaped the sworde, founde grace in the
wildernes: [c] he walked *before* Israél to cause
him to rest.
3 The Lord hathe appeared vnto me [d] of
olde, *say they*: [e] Yea, I haue loued thee with
an euerlasting loue, therefore with mercie
I haue drawen thee.
4 Againe I wil buylde thee, and thou shalt
be buylded, ô virgine Israél: thou shalt stil
[f] be adorned with thy tymbrels, and shalt
go forthe in the dãce of thẽ that be ioyful.
5 Thou shalt yet plãt vines vpon the moũtaines of [g] Samaria, and the planters that
plant them, [h] shal make them commune.
6 For the daies shal come that the [i] watchemen vpon the moũt of Ephráim shal crye,
Arise, and let vs go vp vnto [k] Zión to the
Lord our God.
7 For thus saith the Lord, Reioyce with
gladnes for Iaakób, and shoute for ioye a-
mong the chief of the [l] Gentiles: publish
praise, and say, O Lord, saue thy people,
the remnant of Israél.
8 Beholde, I wil bring thẽ from the North
countrey, and gather them from the coastes of the worlde, *with* the blinde & the
lame among them, *with* the woman with
childe, & her that is deliuered also: a great
companie shal returne hether.
9 They shal come [m] weping, and with mercie wil I bring them againe: I wil leade
them by the riuers of [n] water in a straight
way, wherein they shal not stumble: for I
am a Father to Israél, and Ephráim is [o] my
first borne.
10 ¶ Heare the worde of the Lord, ô ye Gẽtiles, and declare in the yles a farre of, &
say, He ŷ scattered Israél, wil gather him
and wil kepe him, as a shepherd *doeth* his
flocke.
11 For the Lord hathe redemed Iaakób, &
rãsomed him from the hand [p] of him, that
was stronger then he.
12 Therefore they shal come, and reioyce
in the light of Zión, and shal runne to the
boũtifulnes of the Lord, *euen* for ŷ [q] wheat
and for the wine, and for the oyle, and for
the increase of shepe, and bullockes: and
their soule shalbe as a watered garden, and
thei shal haue no more sorow.
13 Thẽ shal the virgine reioyce in the [r] dãce, and the yong men, & the olde men together: for I wil turne their mourning into
ioye, and wil comforte them, & giue them
ioye for their sorowes.
14 And I wil replenish the soule of the
Priests with [s] fatnes, and my people shalbe
satisfied with my goodnes, saith the Lord.

b Which were deliuered frõ the crueltie of Pharaóh.
c To wit, God.
d The people thus reason as thogh he were not so benefical to them now, as he had bene of olde.
e Thus the Lord answereth that his loue is not changeable.
f Thou shalt haue stil occasiõ to reioyce: which is mẽt by tabrets and dancing, as their custome was after notable victories. Exod. 15, 20. iudg. 5,2. and chap. 11,34.
g Because the Israelites, ŷ were the ten tribes, neuer returned to Samaria, therefore this must be spiritually vnderstand vnder ŷ kingdome of Christ, which was ŷ restauracion of the true Israél.
h That is, shal eat the frute therof, as Leu. 19,23. dan 20,6
i The ministers of the worde.
k They shal exhorte all to the imbracĩg of the Gospel, as Isa. 2,3.
l He sheweth what shal be the concorde and loue of all vnder the Gospel, where none shalbe refused for their infirmities: & euery one shal exhort one another to imbrace it.
m That is, lamenting their sinnes, which had not giuen eare to the Prophetes, & therefore it followeth ŷ God receiued thẽ to mercie. Chap. 50, 4. Some take it ŷ they shulde wepe for ioy.
n Where they founde no impedimẽts, but abundance of all things.
o That is, my derely beloued, as ŷ first childe is to the father.
p That is, from the Babylonians, and other enemies.
q By these temporal benefites he meaneth the spiritual graces, which are in the Church, and whereof there shulde be euer plentie, Isa.58,21.
r In the companie of the faithful, which euer praise God for his benefites.
s Meaning the Spirit of wisdome, knowledge and zeale.

15 Thus saith the Lord, A voice was heard
on hie, a mourning *and* bitter weping. [t] Rahél weping for her children, refused to be
comforted for her children, because thei
were not.
16 Thus saith the Lord, Refraine thy voice from weping, and thine eyes from teares: for thy worke shalbe rewarded, saith ẏ
Lord, and thei shal come againe from the
land of the enemie:
17 And there is hope in thine end, saith the
Lord, that *thy* children shal come againe
to their owne borders.
18 I haue heard [u] Ephráim lamenting *thus*,
Thou hast corrected me, and I was chastised as an [x] vntamed calfe: [y] conuert thou
me, and I shalbe conuerted: for thou art ẏ
Lord my God.
19 Surely after that I conuerted, I repented:
& after that I was instructed, I smote vpon *my* [z] thigh: I was ashamed, yea, euen
confounded, because I did beare the repro
che of my youth.
20 Is Ephráim [a] my dere sonne or pleasant
childe? yet since I spake vnto him, I stil
[b] remembred him: therefore my bowelles
are troubled for him: I wil surely haue cōpassion vpon him, saith the Lord.
21 Set thee vp [c] signes: make thee heapes:
set thine heart towarde the path and waie,
that thou hast walked: turne againe, ô virgine of Israél: turne againe to these thy
cities.
22 How long wilt thou go astraie, ô thou re
bellious daughter? for the Lord hathe created [d] a newe thing in the earth: A WOMAN
shal compasse a man.
23 Thus saith the Lord of hostes, the God
of Israél, Yet shal thei saie this thing in
the land of Iudáh, and in the cities thereof, when I shal bring againe their captiuitie, The Lord blesse thee, ô habitation of
iustice *&* holie mountaine.
24 And Iudáh shal dwell in it, & all the cities thereof together, the housbandmen
and thei that go forthe with the flocke.
25 For I haue satiat the weary soule, and I
haue replenished euerie sorowful soule.
26 Therefore I awaked and behelde, and
my slepe [e] was swete vnto me.
27 Beholde, the daies come, saith the Lord,
that I wil sowe the house of Israél, and
the house of Iudáh [f] with the sede of man
and with the sede of beast.
28 And like as I haue watched vpon them,
to plucke vp and to roote out, & to throwe downe, and to destroye, and to plague
them, so wil I watche ouer them, to buylde
and to plant *them*, saith the Lord.

t To declare the greatnes of Gods mercie in deliuering the Iewes he sheweth them that thei were like to the Beniamites, or Israelites: that is, vtterly destroyed, and caryed away in so muche that if Rahél the mother of Beniamin colde haue risen againe to seke for her childrē she shulde haue founde none remaining.

u That is, the people that were led captiue.

x Which was wanton and colde not be subiect to the yoke.

y He sheweth how ẏ faithfulvse to pray: that is, desire God to turne them, for as muche as they can not turne of them selues.

z In signe of repentance, & detestation of my sinne.

a As thogh he wolde say, No: for by his iniquitie he did what laye in him to cast me of.

b To wit, in pitying him for my promes sake.

c Marke by what way thou didest go into captiuitie, and thou shalt turne againe by the same.

d Because their deliuerance from Babylón was a figure of their deliuerance from sinne, he sheweth how this shulde be procured, to wit by IesusChrist whome a woman shulde conceiue, & beare in her wōbe. Which is a strange thing in earth, because he shulde be borne of a virgine with out man: or, he meaneth, that Ierusalém which was like a barē woman in her captiuitie shulde be fruteful as she, that is ioyned in mariage, and whome God blesseth with children.

e Hauing vnderstand this visiō of the Messiah to come in whome the two houses of Israél, and Iudáh shulde be ioyned, I reioyced.

f I wil multiplie, and enriche them with people and cattel.

29 In those dayes shal they say no more,
The fathers haue [g] eaten a sowre grape, &
the childrens teeth are set on edge.
30 But euerie one shal dye for his owne iniquitie: euerie man that eateth the sowre
grape, his teeth shalbe set on edge.
31 ¶ Beholde, the daies come, saith ẏ Lord,
that I wil mak a [h] newe couenant with
the house of Israél, and with the house of
Iudáh,
32 Not according to the couenant that I
made with their fathers, when I toke them
by the hand to bring them out of the land
of Egypt, the which my couenant they
[i] brake, althogh I was [*] an housband vnto
them, saith the Lord.
33 But this shalbe the couenant that I wil
make with the house of Israél, After [k] those daies, saith the Lord, I wil put my Law
in their inwarde partes, & write it in their
hearts, & wil be their God, and thei shalbe
my people.
34 And thei shal [l] teache nomore euerie mā
his neighbour and euerie man his brother,
saying, Knowe the Lord: for they shal all
knowe me from the least of them vnto the
greatest of them, saith the Lord: for I wil
forgiue their iniquitie, and wil remember their sinnes no more.
35 Thus saith the Lord, which giueth
[m] the sunne for a light to the day, *and* the
courses of ẏ moone and of the starres for
a light to the night, which breaketh the
sea, whē the waues thereof roare: his Name *is* the Lord of hostes.
36 If these ordinances departe out of my
sight, saith the Lord, then shal the sede
of Israél cease from being a nation before me, for euer.
37 Thus saith the Lord, If the heauens can
be measured, [n] or the fundacions of the
earth be searched out beneth, then wil I
cast of all the sede of Israél, for all that
they haue done, saith the Lord.
38 Beholde, the dayes come, saith the Lord,
that the [o] citie shalbe buylt to the Lord
frō the tower of Hananeél, vnto the gate
of the corner.
39 And the line of the measure shal go forthe in his presence vpon the hil Garéb, &
shal compasse about to Goáth.
40 And the whole valley of the dead bodies, and of the asshes, and all the fields
vnto the broke of Kidrón, *and* vnto the
corner of the horsegate towarde the East,
shalbe holie vnto the Lord, nether shal it
be plucked vp nor destroyed anie more
for euer.

g The wicked vsed this prouerbe, when they did murmure against Gods iudgements pronoūced by the Prophetes, saying, That their fathers had committed the faute, and that the children were punished, Eze. 18,3.

h Thogh the couenant of redemptiō made to the fathers, & this which was giuen after, seme diuers, yet thei are all one, & grounded on Iesus Christ, saue that this is called newe because of the manifestation of Christ, and the abundant graces of the holie Gost giuen to his Church vnder the Gospel.

i And so were the occasion of their owne diuorcement through their infidelitie, Isa. 50,1.

* Or, master.

k In the time of Christ my Law shal in stead of tables of stone be writen in their heartes by mine holie Spirit, Ebr. 8,8.

l Vnder the kingdome of Christ there shalbe none blinded with ignorance, but I wil giue the faith, & knowledge of God for remission of their sinnes, and daily increase the same: so that it shal not seme to come so muche by the preaching of my ministers, as by the instruction of mine holie Spirit, Isa. 54,13. but the ful accomplishing hereof is referred to the kingdome of Christ, when we shalbe ioyned with our head.

m If the sunne, moone, and starres can not but giue light according to mine ordinance, so long as this worlde lasteth, so shal my Church neuer faile, nether shal anie thing hinder it: and as sure as I wil haue a people, so certeine is it, that I wil leaue them my worde for euer to gouerne them with.

n The one and the other is impossible.

o As it was performed, Nehemiáh 3,1. By this description he sheweth that the citie shulde be as ample, and beautiful as euer it was: but he alludeth to the spiritual Ierusalém, whose beautie shulde be incomparable.

CHAP. XXXII.

Ieremiáh is caſt into priſon becauſe he prophecied that the citie ſhulde be takẽ of the King of Babylon. 7. He ſheweth, that the people ſhulde come againe to their owne poſſeſsion. 38 The people of God are his ſeruants, and he is their Lord.

1 THe worde that came vnto Ieremiáh
from the Lord, in the [a] tenth yere of
Zedekiáh King of Iudáh, which was the
eightenth yere of Nebuchad-nezzár.
2 For then the King of Babels hoſte beſieged Ieruſalém: and Ieremiáh the Prophet
was ſhut vp in the court of the priſon, ẘ
was in the King of Iudahs houſe.
3 For Zedekiáh Kĩg of Iudáh had ſhut him
vp, ſaying, Wherefore doeſt thou prophecie, & ſay, Thus ſaith the Lord, *Beholde, I wil giue this citie into the hands of
the King of Babél, and he ſhal take it?
4 And Zedekiáh the King of Iudáh ſhal
not eſcape out of the hand of ẏ Caldeans,
but ſhal ſurely be deliuered into the hãds
of the King of Babél, and ſhal ſpeake with
him mouthe to mouthe, and his eyes ſhal
beholde his face,
5 And he ſhal lead Zedekiáh to Babél, and
there ſhal he be, vntil [b] I viſite him, ſaith
the Lord: thogh ye fight with the Caldeans, ye ſhal not proſper.
6 ¶ And Ieremiáh ſaid, The worde of the
Lord came vnto me, ſaying,
7 Beholde, Hanameél, the ſonne of Shallúm thine vncle, ſhal come vnto thee and
ſaie, [c] Bye vnto thee my field, that is in A-
nathóth: for the ″title by kinred *apperteineth* vnto thee [d] to bye it.
8 So Hanameél, mine vncles ſonne, came
to me in the court of the priſon, according to the worde of the Lord, and ſaid
vnto me, Bye my [e] field, I praie thee, that is
in Anathóth, which is in the countrei of
Beniamín: for the right of the poſſeſsion
is thine, and the purchaſe *belongeth* vnto
thee: bye it for thee. Then I knewe that
this was the worde of the Lord.
9 And I boght the field of Hanameél, mine vncles ſonne, that was in Anathóth and
weighed him ẏ ſiluer, *euen* ſeuen [f] ſhekels,
and ten *pieces* of ſiluer.
10 And I writ it in the boke and ſigned it,
& toke witneſſes, and weighed him the ſil
uer in the balances.
11 So I toke the boke of the poſſeſsion, being
ſealed [g] *according* to the Law, and cuſtome,
with the boke that was open,
12 And I gaue the boke of the poſſeſsion
vnto Barúch the ſonne of Neriáh, the ſon
ne of Maaſeiáh, in the ſight of Hanameél
mine vncles *ſonne*, and in ẏ preſence of the
witneſſes, writen in the boke of the poſſeſ-
ſion, before all the Iewes that ſate in the
court of the priſon.
13 And I charged Barúch before them, ſaying,

a So that Ieremiáh had now prophecied frõ the thirtenth yere of Ioſiáh vnto the laſt yere ſaue one of Zedekiahs reigne, which was almoſt fourtie yeres.

Chap. 29, 16. & 34, 2.

b Til I take Zedekiáh awaie by death: for he ſhal not dye by the ſworde, as Chap. 34, 4.

c Whereby was ment that the people ſhulde returne againe out of captiuitie and enioye their poſſeſsions & vineyardes, as ver. 15, & 44.

″*Or, right to redeme it.*

d Becauſe he was next of ẏ kinred, as Ruth 4.4

e Of the poſſeſsion of the Lenites read Leu. 25, 32.

f Which mouñteth to of our money, about ten ſhilings ſix pence, if this ſhekel were ẏ commune ſhekel, read Gen. 23, 15. for the ſhekel of the Temple was of double value & tẽ pieces of ſiluer were halfe a ſhekel: for twentie made the ſhekel.

g According to the cuſtome the inſtrumẽt or euidẽce was ſealed vp with ẏ cõmune ſeale, and a copie thereof remained, which cõteined the ſame in effect, but was not ſo authentical as the other, but was left open to be ſene if any thĩg ſhulde be called into dout.

14 Thus ſaith the Lord of hoſtes, the God
of Iſraél, Take the writings, *euen* this boke
of the poſſeſsion, bothe that is ſealed, and
this boke that is open, and put them in an
earthen [h] veſſel, that thei maie continue a
long time.
15 For the Lord of hoſtes, the God of Iſraél
ſaith thus, Houſes and fields, and vineyardes ſhalbe poſſeſſed againe in this land.
16 ¶ Now when I had deliuered the boke of
the poſſeſsion vnto Barúch, the ſonne of
Neriáh, I prayed vnto the Lord, ſaying,
17 Ah Lord God, beholde, thou haſt made
the heauẽ and the earth by thy great power, and by thy ſtretched out arme, and there is nothing ″hard vnto thee.
18 *Thou ſheweſt mercie vnto thouſands,
and recompenceſt the iniquitie of the fathers into ẏ boſome of their [i] childrẽ after
them: ô God the great and mightie, whoſe
Name *is* the Lord of hoſtes,
19 Great in counſel, and mightie in worke,
(for thine eyes are opẽ vpon all the waies
of the ſonnes of men, to giue to euerie one
according to his waies, and according to
the frute of his workes)
20 Which haſt ſet ſignes and wonders in the
land of Egypt vnto this [k] day, & in Iſraél,
and among *all* men, and haſt made thee a
Name, as *appeareth* this daie,
21 And haſt broght thy people Iſraél out
of the lãd of Egypt with ſignes, and with
wonders, and with a ſtrong hand, with
a ſtretched out arme, and with great
terror,
22 And haſt giuen them this land, which
thou dideſt ſweare to their fathers to giue them, *euen* a land, that floweth with
milke and honie,
23 And they came in, and poſſeſſed it, but
they obeyed not thy voyce, nether walked
in thy Law: all that thou commandedſt
them to do, they haue not done: therefore thou haſt cauſed this whole plague to
come vpon them.
24 Beholde, the [l] mounts, they are come
into the citie to take it, and the citie is giuen into the hand of the Caldeans, that
fight againſt it by meanes of the ſworde,
and of the famine, and of the peſtilence,
and what thou haſt ſpoken, is come to
paſſe, and beholde, thou ſeeſt it.
25 And thou haſt ſaid vnto me, ô Lord God,
Bye vnto thee the field for ſiluer, and take
witneſſes: for the citie ſhalbe giuen into
the hand of the Caldeans.
26 ¶ Thẽ came the worde of the Lord vnto
Ieremiáh, ſaying,
27 Beholde, I am the Lord God of all
[m] fleſh: is there anie thing to hard for me?
28 Therefore thus ſaith the Lord, Beholde,
I wil giue this citie into the hand of the
Caldeans, and into the hand of Nebuchad-nezzár

h And ſo to hide them in the grounde, ẏ thei might be preſerued as a token of their deliuerance.

″*Or, hid.*

Exod. 34, 7. deut. 5, 9.

i Becauſe the wicked are ſubiect to the curſe of God, he ſheweth, ẏ their poſteritie, which by nature are vnder this malediction, ſhalbe puniſhed bothe for their owne wickednes & that the iniquitie of their fathers, ẘ is likewiſe in thẽ, ſhal be alſo reuenged on their head.

k Meaning, ẏ his miracles in deliuering his people, ſhulde neuer be forgotten.

l The worde ſignifieth anie thing that is caſt vp, as a mount or rampart, and is alſo vſed for ingines of warre, which were layed on an hie place to ſhoot into a citie, before that gonnes were in vſe.

m That is, of euerie creature: who as thei are his workes, ſo doeth he gouerne and guide them as pleaſeth him, whereby he ſheweth ẏ, as he is the autor of this their captiuitie for their ſinnes, ſo wil he for his mercies be their redemer to reſtore thẽ againe to libertie.

chad-nezzár, King of Babél, and he shal
take it.
29 And the Caldeans shal come and fight
against this citie, and set fyre on this citie
and burne it, with the houses, vpon whose
roofes they haue offred incense vnto
Báal, and powred drinke offrings vnto
other gods, to prouoke me vnto angre.
30 For the children of Israél, and the children
of Iudáh haue surely done euil before
me from their [n] youth: for the children
of Israél haue surely prouoked me to angre
with the workes of their hands, saith
the Lord.

n From the time, ẏ I broght them out of Egypt, & made them my people, & called them my first borne.

31 Therefore this citie hathe bene vnto me
as a prouocation of mine angre, and of my
wrath, from the daye, that they buylt it, euen
vnto this daye, that I shulde remoue it
out of my sight,
32 Because of all the euil of the children of
Israél, and of the children of Iudáh, which
they haue done to prouoke me to angre,
euen they, their Kings, their princes, their
Priests, and their Prophetes, and the mē
of Iudáh, and the inhabitāts of Ierusalém.
33 And they haue turned vnto me the backe
& not the face: thogh I taught them, [o] rising
vp early, and instructing them, yet
they were not obediēt to receiue doctrine,

o Read Prou. 1,25. Isa 65,2. chap 7,13. and 19,7. & 25,3 & 26,5. & 29,19.

34 But they set their abominations in the
house (whereupon my Name was called)
to defile it,
35 And they buylt the hye [p] places of Báal,
which are in the valley of [q] Ben-hinnóm,
to cause their sonnes, and their daughters
to [r] passe through *the fyre* vnto Moléch, ẇ I
cōmāded them not, nether came it into
my minde, that they shulde do suche abomination,
to cause Iudáh to sinne.

p That is, the altars, which were made to offer sacrifice vpon to their idoles.
q Read Chap. 7,30 2. King. 21,4.
r Read 2 King. 16,3.

36 And now [s] therefore, thus hathe the
Lord God of Israél spoken, concerning
this citie, whereof ye say, It shalbe deliuered
into the hand of the King of Babél by
the sworde, and by the famine, and by the
pestilence,

s Read Chap. 30,16.

37 *Beholde, I wil gather thē out of all countreis,
wherein I haue scatred them in
mine angre, & in my wrath, and in great
indignation, and I wil bring them againe
vnto this place, and I wil cause them to
dwell safely.

Deut. 30,3.

38 And they shal be * my people, and I wil
be their God.

Chap. 30,22.

39 And I wil giue thē [t] one heart & one way
ẏ thei may feare me for euer for the welth
of them, & of their children after them.

t One consent and one religion, as Ezek. 11,19, & 39,27.

40 And I wil make an [u] euerlasting couenāt
ẇ thē, that I wil neuer turne away frō thē
to do thē good, but I wil put mẏ feare in
their hearts, ẏ thei shal not departe frō me.

u Read Chap. 31,31.

41 Yea, I wil delite in thē to do thē good,
& I wil plant them in this land assuredly
with my whole heart, & with all my soule.
42 For thus saith the Lord, Like as I haue
broght all this great plague vpon this people,
so wil I bring vpon them all the good
that I haue promised them.
43 And the fields shal be possessed in this
land, whereof ye say, It is desolate without
man or beast, and shalbe giuen into the
hand of the Caldeans.
44 Mē shal bye [x] fields for siluer, and make
writings, and seale them, and take witnesses
in the land of Beniamín, and round
about Ierusalém, & in the cities of Iudáh,
and in the cities of the mountaines, and in
the cities of the plaine, and in the cities of
the South: for I wil cause their captiuitie
to returne, saith the Lord.

x This is the declaration of that, which was spoken, ver. 8.

CHAP. XXXIII.

1 The Prophet is monished of the Lord to pray for the deliuerance of the people, which the Lord promised. 8 God forgiueth sinnes, for his owne glorie. 15 Of the birth of Christ. 20 The kingdome of Christ in the Church shal neuer be ended.

1 Moreouer, the worde of the Lord
came vnto Ieremiáh the seconde time
(while he was yet shut vp in the [a] court
of the prison) saying,
2 Thus saith the Lord, the maker [b] thereof,
the Lord that formed it, and established
it, the Lord is his Name.

a Which was in the Kings house at Ierusalém, as Chap 32,1.
b To wit, of Ierusalém, who as he made it, so wil he preserue it, read Isa. 37,26.

3 Call vnto me, and I wil answer thee, and
shewe thee great & mightie things, which
thou knowest not.
4 For thus saith the Lord God of Israél,
concerning the houses of this citie, and
concerning the houses of the Kings of Iudáh,
which are destroied by the [c] mountes,
and by the sworde,
5 Thei come to [d] fight with the Caldeans,
but it *is* to fil thē selues with the dead bodies
of men, whome I haue slaine in mine
angre and in my wrath: for I haue hid
my [e] face from this citie, because of all
their wickednes.

c Read Chap. 32,24.
d The Iewes thinke to ouercome the Caldeans, but thei seke their owne destruction.
e He sheweth ẏ Gods fauour is cause of all prosperitie, as his angre is of all aduersitie.

6 ¶Beholde, [f] I wil giue it helth & amendement:
for I wil cure them, and wil reueile
vnto them the abundance of peace,
and trueth.
7 And I wil cause the captiuitie of Iudáh,
and the captiuitie of Israél to returne, &
wil buylde them as at the first.

f In the middes of his threatnings God remembreth his and comforteth them.

8 And I wil [g] cleanse them from all their
iniquitie, whereby they haue sinned agaīst
me: yea, I wil pardone all their iniquities,
whereby thei haue sinned against me, and
whereby thei haue rebelled against me.
9 And it shalbe to me a name, a [h] ioy, a praise,
and an honour before all the nacions of
the earth, which shal heare all the good
that I do vnto them: and thei shal feare,
& tremble for all the goodnes, and for all
the welth, that I shewe vnto this *citie*.
10 Thus saith the Lord, Againe there shalbe
heard in this place (which ye say shalbe

g Declaring ẏ there is no deliuerance nor ioye, but where as we fele remissiō of sinnes.
h Whereby he sheweth that the Church, wherein is remission of sinnes, is Gods honour & glorie, so ẏ whosoeuer is enemie to it, laboreth to dishonour God.

desolote, without man, and without beast,
euen in the cities of Iudáh, & in the stretes
of Ierusalém, that are desolate without
man, and without inhabitant, and without
beast)
11 The voyce of ioye & the voyce of gladnes, the voice of the bridegrome, and the
voyce of the bride, the voyce of them that
shal say, [i] Praise the Lord of hostes, because the Lord is good: for his mercie *endureth* for euer, *&* of them that offre *the sacrifice* of praise in ye House of the Lord, for
I wil cause to returne the captiuitie of the
land, as at the first, saith the Lord.

i Which was a song appointed for the Leuites to praise God by, 1 Chro. 16,8 psal. 105,1. isa. 12,4.

12 Thus saith the Lord of hostes, Againe in
this place, which is desolate, without man,
and without beast, and in all the cities hereof there shalbe dwelling for shepherdes to rest their flockes.
13 In the cities of the [k] mountaines, in the
cities in the plaine, and in the cities of the
South, and in the land of Beniamín, and
about Ierusalém, and in the cities of Iudáh
shal the shepe passe againe, vnder the hand
of him that telleth them, saith the Lord.

k Meaning, yt all the coūtrei of Iudáh shal-be inhabited a gaine.

14 Beholde, the dayes come, saith the Lord,
that I wil performe ye good thing, which
I haue promised vnto the house of Israél,
and to the house of Iudáh.
15 In those daies and at that time, wil I cause [l] the brāche of righteousnes to growe
vp vnto Dauid, & he shal execute iudgement, and righteousnes in the land.
16 In those dayes shal Iudáh be saued, and
Ierusalém shal dwell safely, & he that shal
call [m] her, is the Lord our [n] righteousnes.
17 For thus saith the Lord, Dauid shal neuer want a man to sit vpō the throne of the
house of Israél.
18 Nether shal the Priests and Leuites wāt
a man before me to offer [o] burnt offrings,
and to offer meat offrings, and to do sacrifice continually.
19 ¶ And the worde of the Lord came vnto
Ieremiáh, saying,
20 Thus saith the Lord, If you can breake
my couenāt of the [p] day, and my couenāt
of the night, that there shulde not be day,
and night in their season,
21 Then may my couenant be broken with
Dauid my seruant, that he shulde not haue a sonne to reigne vpon his throne, and
with the Leuites, *&* Priests my ministers.
22 As ye armie of heauen can not be nōbred,
nether the sand of the sea measured: so wil
I multiplie the sede of Dauid my seruant,
and the Leuites, that minister vnto me.
23 ¶ Moreouer, the worde of the Lord came
to Ieremiáh, saying,
24 Considerest thou not what [q] this people
haue spoken, saying, The two families,
which the Lord hathe chosen, he hathe
euen cast them of? thus they haue despised
my people, that they shulde be no more a
nacion before them.
25 Thus saith the Lord, If my couenant be
not with day and night, *and if* I haue not
appointed the ordre of heauen and earth,
26 Then wil I cast away the sede of Iaakób
and Dauid my seruāt, & not take of his sede to be rulers ouer the sede of Abrahám,
Izhák, and Iaakób: for I wil cause their
captiuitie to returne, and haue compassion on them.

l That is, I wil sende the Messiáh, which shal come of ye house of Dauid, of whome this prophecie is ment, as testifie all the Iewes, and that which is writen Chap. 23,5.

m To wit, Christ that shal call his Church.

n That is, Christ is our Lord God, our righteousnes, sanctification, & redemptiō, 1 Cor 1,30.

o This is chiefly ment of the spiritual sacrifice of thankesgiuing, which is left to the Church in the time of Christ, who was the euerlasting Priest and the euerlasting sacrifice figured by the sacrifices of ye Law.

p Read Chap. 31,35.

q Meaning, the Caldeans and other infidels which thoght God had vtterly cast of Iudáh and Israél or Beniamín, because he did correct them for a time for their amendement.

CHAP. XXXIIII.

2 He threatneth that the citie, and the King Zedekiáh shalbe giuen into the hands of the King of Babylon.
11 He rebuketh their crueltie towarde their seruants.

1 The worde wc came vnto Ieremiáh
frō the Lord (when [a] Nebuchad-nezzár King of Babél, and all his hoste, & all
the kingdomes of the earth, *that were* vnder the power of his hand, and all people
foght against Ierusalém, and against all
the cities thereof) saying,

a Who commonly of Ieremiáh was called Ne bu-had-rezzár and of others Nebuchad-nezzár.

2 Thus saith the Lord God of Israél, Go,
and speake to Zedekiáh King of Iudáh,
& tel him, Thus saith the Lord, Behold,
*I wil giue this citie into the hand of the
King of Babél, and he shal burne it wt fyre,
3 And thou shalt not escape out of his hād,
but shalt surely be taken, and deliuered
into his hand, and thine eies shal beholde
the face of the King of Babél, and he shal
speake with thee mouthe to mouthe, and
thou shalt go to Babél.

2 Chr. 36,19. chap. 29,16. & 23,3.

4 Yet heare the worde of the Lord, ô Zede
kiáh, King of Iudáh: thus saith the Lord
of thee, Thou shalt not dye by ye sworde,
5 *But* thou shalt dye in [b] peace: & according
to the burning for thy fathers the former
Kings which were before thee, so shal thei
burne *odours* for thee, and thei shal lament
thee, *saying*, Oh [c] lord: for I haue pronounced the worde, saith the Lord.

b Not of any violent death.

c The Iewes shal lamēt for thee their lord & King.

6 Then Ieremiáh ye Prophet spake all these wordes vnto Zedekiáh King of Iudáh
in Ierusalém,
7 (When the King of Babels hoste foght a-
gainst Ierusalém, and against all the cities
of Iudáh, that were left, *euen* against Lachísh, & against Azekáh: for these strong
cities remained of the cities of Iudáh)
8 This *is* the worde that came vnto Ierе-
miáh from the Lord, after that the King
Zedekiáh had made a couenant with all ye
people, which were at Ierusalém, [d] to proclaime libertie vnto them,
9 That euerie man shulde let his [e] seruant
go fre, & euerie man his handmaide, which
was an Ebrue or an Ebruesse, & that none
shulde serue him selue of them, *to wit*, of a
Iewe his brother.
10 Now when all the princes, & all the peo
ple which had agreed to ye couenant, heard
that euerie one shulde let his seruāt go fre,
&

d When the enemie was at hand, and thei sawe them selues in danger, thei wolde seme holy, & so began some kinde of reformation: but sone after they vttered their hypocrisie.

e According to ye Lawe, Exod. 21,2. deut. 15,12.

and euerie one his handmaide, and that
none shulde serue them selues of them any
more, thei obeied and let them go.

*Ebr. returned.

11 But afterwarde thei *repented and caused the seruants & the handmaids, whome
thei had let go fre to returne & helde thē
in subiection as seruants and handmaides.
12 Therefore the worde of the Lord came
vnto Ieremiáh from the Lord, saying,
13 Thus saith ye Lord God of Israél, I made a couenant with your fathers, when I
broght them out of the land of Egypt, out
of the house of *seruants, saying,

*Or, bondage.

Deut.15,1.

14 *At the terme of seuen yeres let ye go, e-
uerie mā his brother an Ebrewe which hathe bene solde vnto thee: & when he hathe
serued thee six yeres, thou shalt let him
go fre from thee: but your fathers obeied
me not, nether inclined their eares.
15 And ye were now turned, and had done right in my sight in proclaiming libertie, euerie man to his neighbour, and ye
had made a couenant before me in [f] the
House, whereupon my Name is called.

f Meaning, in the Temple, to declare that it was a most solemne & streit couenant, made in the Name of ye Lord.

16 But ye repented, and polluted my Name: for ye haue caused euerie man his seruant, & euerie man his handmaide, whome
ye had set at libertie at their pleasure, to re
turne, and holde them in subiection to be
vnto you as seruants and as handmaides.
17 Therefore thus saith the Lord, Ye haue
not obeied me, in proclaiming fredome e-
uerie man to his brother, and euerie man
to his neighbour: beholde, I proclaime a
libertie for you, saith ye Lord, to [g] the sworde,
to the pestilence, and to the famine, &
I wil make you a terrour to all the kingdomes of the earth.

g That is, I giue the sworde libertie to destroy you.

18 And I wil giue those men that haue broken my couenant, and haue not kept the
wordes of the couenant, which thei had
made before me, when thei [h] cut the calfe
in twaine, and passed betwene the partes
thereof.

h As touching this maner of solemne couenant which the Ancient vsed by passing betwene the two partes of a beast, to signifie that ye transgressor of the same couenant shulde be so diuided in pieces, read Gene.15,10.

19 The princes of Iudáh, and the princes of
Ierusalém, the Eunuches, and the Priestes,
and all the people of the land, which passed betwene the partes of the calfe,
20 I wil euen giue them into the hand of
their enemies, and into the hands of thē
that seke their life: and their dead bodies
shalbe for meat vnto the foules of the hea
uen, and to the beastes of the earth.
21 And Zedekiáh King of Iudáh, and his
princes wil I giue into the hand of their
enemies, and into the hand of thē that seke their life, & into the hand of the King
of Babels hoste, wc [i] are gone vp from you.

i To fight against ye Egyptians, as Chap. 37,11.

22 Beholde, I wil cōmande, saith the Lord,
and cause them to returne to this citie, and
thei shal fight against it, and take it, and
burne it with fyre: and I wil make ye cities
of Iudáh desolate without an inhabitant.

CHAP. XXXV.

He proposeth the obedience of the Rechabites, & thereby confoundeth the pride of the Iewes.

1 THe worde which came vnto Ieremiáh from the Lord, in the daies [a] of
Iehoiakím the sonne of Iosiáh King of Iudáh, saying,

a For the disposition and order of these prophecies, read, Chap.27,1

2 Go vnto the house of the [b] Rechabites, &
speake vnto them, & bring them into the
House of ye Lord into one of the chābers,
and giue them wine to drinke.

b Thei came of Hobáb Moses father in law, who was no Israelite, but after ioyned with them in the seruice of God.

3 Then toke I Iaazaniáh, the sonne of Ieremiáh the sonne of Habazziniáh, and his
brethren, and all his sonnes, and the whole
house of the Rechabites,
4 And I broght them into ye House of the
Lord, into the chamber of the sonnes of
Hanán, the sonne of Igdaliáh a man [c] of
God, which was by the chamber of the
princes, which was aboue the chamber of
Maaseiáh the sonne of Shallúm, the keper
of the *treasure.

c That is, a Prophete.

*Or, dore.

5 And I set before the sonnes of the house
of the Rechabites, pottes ful of wine, and
cuppes, and [d] said vnto them, Drinke wine.

d The Prophet saith not, The Lord saith thus: for then thei oght to haue obeyed: but he tendeth to another end: yt is, to declare their obedience to man, seing the Iewes wolde not obey God him selfe.

6 But thei said, We wil drinke no wine: for
[e] Ionadáb the sonne of Recháb our father
commanded vs, saying, [f] Ye shal drinke
no wine, *nether* you nor your sonnes for
euer.

e Whome Iehu the King of Israel fauored for his zeale, 2. King 10,15.

7 Nether shal ye buylde house, nor sowe
sede, nor plant vineyarde, nor haue any,
but all your daies ye shal dwell in tentes,
that ye may liue a long time in the land
where ye be strangers.

f Teaching them hereby to flee all occasiō of intemperancie, ambicion and auarice, and that thei might knowe that thei were strangers in ye earth, and be ready to depart at all occasions.

8 Thus haue we obeied ye voice of Ionadáb
the sonne of Recháb our father, in all that
he hathe charged vs, and we drinke no
wine all our daies, *nether* we, our wiues, our
sonnes, nor our daughters.
9 Nether buylde we houses for vs to dwell
in, nether haue we vineyarde, nor field, nor
sede,
10 But we haue remained in tētes, and haue
obeied, & done according to [g] all that Ionadáb our father commanded vs.

g Which was now for the space of thre hundreth yeres from Iehu to Iehoiakim.

11 But when Nebuchad-nezzár King of
Babél came vp into the land, we said, Come, and let vs go to Ierusalém, from the
hoste of the Caldeans, and from the hoste
of Arám: so we [h] dwell at Ierusalém.

h Which declareth that thei were not so bound to their vowe, that it colde not be broke for any necessitie: for where thei were cōmanded to dwel in tētes, thei dwel now at Ierusalēm for feare of ye warres.

12 Then came the worde of the Lord vnto
Ieremiáh, saying,
13 Thus saith the Lord of hostes, the God
of Israél, Go, and tel the men of Iudáh,
and the inhabitans of Ierusalém, Wil ye
[i] not receiue doctrine to obey my wordes,
saith the Lord?

i Whome I haue chosen to be my childrē, seing these were the children of an heathen man, obeied the commandement of their father.

14 The cōmandement of Ionadáb the sonne of Recháb that he cōmanded his sonnes, that thei shulde drīke no wine, is surely kept: for vnto this day thei drīke none,
but obey their fathers commandement:

notwithstanding I haue spoken vnto you,
[k] rising early, and speaking, but ye wolde
not obeie me.
15 I haue sent also vnto you all my seruantes the Prophetes, rising vp early, and sending *them*, saying, *Returne now euerie mã
from his euil waie, and amende your workes, and go not after other gods to serue
them, & ye shal dwell in the land which I
haue giuen vnto you, and to your fathers,
but ye wolde not incline your eare, nor o-
beie me.
16 Surely the sonnes of Ionadáb the sonne
of Recháb, haue kept ẏ cõmandement of
their father, which he gaue them, but this
people hathe not obeied me.
17 Therefore thus saith the Lord of hostes,
ẏ God of Israél, Beholde, I wil bring vpon Iudáh, and vpon all the inhabitants of
Ierusalém, all ẏ euil that I haue pronounced against them, because I haue [l] spoken
vnto them, but thei wolde not heare, and
I haue called vnto them, but thei wolde
not answer.
18 And Ieremiáh said to the house of the
Rechabites, Thus saith ẏ Lord of hostes
the God of Israél, Because ye haue obeied
the commandement of Ionadáb your father, and kept all his precepts, and done ac
cording vnto all that he hathe commanded you,
19 Therefore thus saith the Lord of hostes,
the God of Israél, Ionadáb the sonne of
Recháb shal [m] not want a man, to stãd before me for euer.

k I haue most diligently exhorted & warned you bothe by my selfe & my Prophetes. *Chap.18,11. & 25,5.*

l That is by his Prophets & ministers: which sheweth that it is as muche as thogh he shulde speake to vs him selfe, when he sendeth his ministers to speake in his Name.

m His posteritie shal continue and be in my fauour for euer.

CHAP. XXXVI.

1 Barúch writeth, as Ieremiáh enditeth, the boke of the curses against Iudáh and Israél. 9 He is sent with the boke vnto the people and readeth it before them all. 14 He is called before the rulers and readeth it before thẽ alsõ. 23 The King casteth it in the fyre. 28 There is another writen at the commandement of the Lord.

1 AND in the fourth [a] yere of Iehoiakím the sonne of Iosiáh King of
Iudáh, came this worde vnto Ieremiáh
from the Lord, saying,
2 Take thee a roole *or* boke, and write therein all the wordes that I haue spoken to
thee against Israél, & against Iudáh, and a-
gainst all the nacions, from the daie that I
spake vnto thee, *euen* [b] from the daies of
Iosiáh vnto this daie.
3 It maie be that thẽ house of Iudáh wil
heare of all the euil, which I determined to do vnto them that thei may returne
euerie man from his euil waie, that I maie
forgiue their iniquitie and their sinnes.
4 Then Ieremiáh called Barúch the sonne
of Neriáh, and Barúch wrote [c] at ẏ mouth
of Ieremiáh all the wordes of the Lord,
which he had spoken vnto him, vpõ a roole *or* boke.
5 And Ieremiáh cõmanded Barúch, saying,

a Read Chap. 25,1.

b Which were twenty and thre yere, as Cha 25,3. counting from the thirteenth yere of Iosiahs reigne.

c As he did indite.

I am shut vp, [d] & can not go into ẏ House of the Lord.
6 Therefore go thou, and read the roole
wherein thou hast writen at my mouth the
wordes of the Lord in the audience of the
people in the Lords House vpon the [e] fasting day: also thou shalt read them in the
hearing of all Iudáh, ẏ come out of their
cities.
7 It may be that thei wil [f] pray before the
Lord, and euerie one returne from his e-
uil way, for the angre & the wrath, that
the Lord hathe declared against this people.
8 So Barúch the sonne of Neriáh did according vnto all, that Ieremiáh ẏ Prophet
commanded him, reading in the boke the
wordes of the Lord in the Lords House.
9 ¶ And in the fift [g] yere of Iehoiakím the
sonne of Iosiáh King of Iudáh, in the
ninth moneth, they proclaimed a fast before the Lord to all the people in Ierusalém, and to all the people that came from
the cities of Iudáh vnto Ierusalém.
10 Then red Barúch in the boke the wordes of Ieremiáh in the House of the Lord,
in the chambre of Gemariáh the sonne of
Shaphán the secretarie, in the hier court at
the entrie of the [h] newe gate of the Lords
House, in the hearing of all the people.
11 When Michaiáh the sonne of Gemariáh, the sonne of Shaphán had heard out
of the boke all the wordes of the Lord,
12 Then he went downe to the Kings house into the Chancellours chamber, and lo,
all ẏ princes sate there, *euen* Elishamá the
Chancellour, & Delaiáh the sonne of Shemaiáh, and Elnathán ẏ sonne of Achbór,
and Gemariáh the sonne of Shaphán, and
Zedekiáh the sonne of Hananiáh, and all
the princes.
13 Then Michaiáh declared vnto them all
the wordes that he had heard whẽ Barúch
red in the boke in the audience of the people.
14 Therefore all the princes sent Iehudí the
sonne of Nethaniáh, the sonne of Shelemiáh, the sonne of Chushí, vnto Barúch,
saying, Take in thine hand the roole, wherein thou hast red in the audience of the
people, and come. So Barúch the sonne of
Neriáh, toke the roole in his hand, and came vnto them.
15 And thei said vnto him, Sit downe now,
and read it, that we may heare. So Barúch
red it in their audience.
16 Now when thei had heard all the wordes, they where [i] afraied bothe one and
other, and said vnto Barúch, We wil certifie the King of all these wordes.
17 And thei examined Barúch, saying, Tel
vs now, how didest ẏ write all these wordes at his mouth.

d Meaning, in prisõ, through the malice of the Priestes.

e Which was proclaimed for feare of the Babylonians, as their custome was when thei feared warre or any great plague of God

f He sheweth that fasting without praier and repentãce auaileth nothing, but is mere hypocrisie.

g The fast was then proclaimed, and Barúch red this roole, which was a litle before that Ierusalém was first taken, and then Iehoiakím and Daniel, and his cõpanions were led away captiues.

h Which is ẏ East gate of the Temple.

i The godlie were afraid, seing God so offended, & the wicked were astonied for ẏ horror of the punishement.

18 Then

18 Then Barúch answered them,He pronounced all these wordes vnto me with his
mouth, and I wrote *them* with yncke in the
boke.
19 Then said the princes vnto Barúch, Go,
[k] hide thee, thou and Ieremiáh, and let no
man knowe where ye be.
20 ¶And thei wẽt in to the Kĩg to ẏ court,
but thei laied vp ẏ roole in the chãbre of
Elishamá the Chancellour & tolde ẏ King
all the wordes,that he might heare.
21 So the King sent Iehudí to fet ẏ roole,&
he toke it out of Elishamá the Chancellors
chambre,and Iehudí red it in the audience
of the King,and in the audience of all the
princes,which stode beside the King.
22 Now the King sate in the winter house,
in the [l] ninth moneth,and there was a fyre
burning before him.
23 And when Iehudí had red thre, or foure
sides, he cut it with the penknife and cast
it into the fyre,that was on the herth vntil
all the roole was cõsumed in the fyre, that
was on the herth.
24 Yet thei were not afraid,nor rent [m] their
garments , *nether* the King,nor any of his
seruants,that heard all these wordes.
25 Neuertheles,Elnathán,and Delaiáh,and
Gemariáh had besoght the King , that he
wolde not burne the roole : but he wolde
not heare them.
26 But the King commanded Ierahmeél
the sonne of Hammélech , & Seraiáh the
sonne of Azriél,& Shelemiáh the sonne of
Abdiél, to take Barúch the scribe, and Ieremiáh the Prophet, but the Lord [n] hid
them.
27 ¶Then the worde of the Lord came to
Ieremiáh (after that the King had burnt
the roole and the wordes ẇ Barúch wrote
at the mouth of Ieremiáh) saying,
28 Take thee againe [o] another roole and
write in it all ẏ former wordes that were
in the first roole which Iehoiakím ẏ King
of Iudáh hathe burnt,
29 And ẏ shalt say to Iehoiakím Kĩg of Iudáh , Thus saith ẏ Lord, Thou hast burnt
this roole,saying,[p] Why hast thou writen
therein,sayĩg,that the King of Babél shal
certeinly come and destroye this land,and
shal take thence *bothe* man and beast?
30 Therefore thus saith the Lord of Iehoiakím King of Iudáh,He shal haue [q] none
to sit vpon the throne of Dauid, and his
[r] dead bodie shalbe cast out in the day to
the heate,and in the night to the frost.
31 And I wil visite him and his sede,and his
seruãtes for their iniquitie, & I wil bring
vpon them,and vpon the inhabitans of Ierusalém , & vpon the men of Iudáh all the
euil that I haue pronoũced against them:
but they wolde not heare.
32 Then toke Ieremiáh another roole, and

k Thei ẏ were godlie among the princes, gaue this counsel, by whose meanes it is like that Ieremiáh was deliuered : for thei knewe the rage of ẏ King and of ẏ wicked to be suche that they colde not escape without dãger of their liues.

l Which conteined parte of Nouember & parte of Decẽber.

m Shewing,ẏ the wicked in stead of repenting,when thei heare Gods judgements, grow into farther malice against him and his worde.

n Thus we se the continual care,that God hathe euer ouer his to preserue them frõ the rage of the wicked.

o Thogh the wicked thinke to haue abolished the worde of God, when they haue burnt the boke thereof: yet this declareth that God wil not onely raise it vp againe,but also increase it in greater abundance to their condemnation, as vers. 32.

p These are Iehoiakims wordes.

q Thogh Iehoiachin his sone succeded hĩ, yet because he reigned but thre moneths, it was estemed as no reigne.

r Read Chap. 22,19.

gaue it Barúch the scribe ẏ sonne of Neriáh, which wrote therein at the mouth of
Ieremiáh all the wordes of the boke which
Iehoiakím Kĩg of Iudáh had burnt in the
fyre, and there were added besides them
many like wordes.

CHAP. XXXVII.

Zedekiáh succeded Ieconiáh. 3 He sendeth vnto Ieremiáh to praye for him. 12 Ieremiáh, going into the land of Beniamin,is taken. 15 He is beaten and put in prison.

1 AND*Kĩg Zedekiáh the sonne of Iosiáh reigned for [a] Coniáh the sonne
of Iehoiakím,whome Nebuchad-nezzár
King of Babél [b] made King in the land
of Iudáh.
2 But nether he, nor his seruants, nor the
people of the land wolde obey the wordes
of the Lord,which he spake by the "ministerie of the Prophet Ieremiáh.
3 And Zedekiáh the King [c] sent Iehucál
the sonne of Shelemiáh ,and Zephaniáh
the sonne of Maaseiáh the Priest to the
Prophet Ieremiáh,saying,Pray now vnto
the Lord our God for vs.
4 (Now Ieremiáh [d] went in and out among
the people : for they had not put him into
the prison.
5 Thẽ Pharaohs hoste was [e] come out of E-
gypt:and whẽ the Caldeans that besieged
Ierusalém,heard tidings of them,thei "departed from Ierusalém)
6 Then came the worde of the Lord vnto
the Prophet Ieremiáh,saying,
7 Thus saith the Lord God of Israél, Thus
shal ye say to the King of Iudáh,ẏ sent you
vnto me to inquire of me, Beholde , Pharaohs hoste , which is come forthe to helpe you, shal returne to Egypt into their
owne land.
8 And the Caldeans shal come againe, and
fight against this citie, and take it & burne
it with fyre.
9 Thus saith the Lord, 'Deceiue not your
selues, saying , The Caldeans shal surely
departe from vs:for thei shal not departe.
10 For thogh ye had smiten the whole hoste
of the Caldeans that fight against you , &
there remained *but* wounded men among
them,*yet* shulde euery man rise vp in his
tent,and burne this citie with fyre.
11 ¶When the hoste of the Caldeans was
broken vp from Ierusalém,because of Pharaohs armie,
12 Then Ieremiáh went out of Ierusalém
to go into the [f] land of Beniamín, separating him self thence from among the
people.
13 And when he was in the [g] gate of Beniamín,there was a chief officer, whose name
was Iriiáh , the sonne of Shelemiáh, the
sonne of Hananiáh. and he toke Ieremiáh
the Prophet, saying, Thou "fleest to the
Caldeans.

* 2.King. 24,17. 2.chro.36,10.chap.52,1.

a Who was called Iehoiachin or Ieconiáh.

b And called him Zedekiáh where as before his name was Mattaniáh 2 King 24,17.

" Ebr.hand

c Because he was afraid of the Caldeans that came against him.

d That is,was out of prison and at libertie.

e To helpe the Iewes.

" Ebr. went vp.

' Or, lift not vp your mindes.

f As some thinke,to go to Anathoth his owne towne.

g By ẏ which men went into the countrey of Beniamin.

" Ebr. fallest.

14 Then said Ieremiáh, That is false, I flee
not to the Caldeās: but he wolde not heare
him: so Iriiáh toke Ieremiáh, and broght
him to the princes.
15 Wherefore the princes were angry with
Ieremiáh, and smote him, and laid him in
prison in the house of Iehonathán the scribe: for they had made that the [h] prison.

h Because it was a vile and streite prison.

16 When Ieremiáh was entred into the dō-
geon, and into the prisons, and had remained there a long time,
17 Then Zedekiáh the King sent, and toke
him out, and the King asked him secretly
in his house, and said, Is there any worde
from the Lord? And Ieremiáh said, Yea:
for, said he, thou shalt be deliuered into
the hand of the King of Babél.
18 Moreouer, Ieremiáh said vnto King Zedekiáh, What haue I offended agaīst thee,
or against thy seruants, or against this people, that ye haue put me in prison?
19 *Where are now your Prophetes, which
prophecied vnto you, saying, The King
of Babél shal not come against you, nor a-
gainst this land?

Chap. 28,4.

20 Therefore heare now, I pray thee, ô my
lord the King: let my prayer "be accepted before thee, that thou cause me not to
returne to the house of Iehonathán the
scribe, lest I dye there.

" Ebr. fall.

21 Then Zedekiáh the King commanded,
that they shulde put Ieremiáh in the court
of the prison, and that they shulde giue
him daiely a piece of bread out of the bakers strete vntil all the [i] bread in the citie
were eaten vp. Thus Ieremiáh remained
in the court of the prison.

i That is, so long as there was any bread in the citie: thus God prouideth for his ye he wil cause their enemies to preserue them to ye end whereunto he hathe apointed them.

CHAP. XXXVIII.

1 By the mocion of the rulers Ieremiáh is put into a dongeon. 14 At the request of Ebed-mélech the King commandeth Ieremiáh to be broght forthe of the dongeon. 17 Ieremiáh sheweth the King how he might escape death.

1 THen Shephatiáh the sonne of Mattán, and Gedaliáh the sonne of Pashhúr, and Iucál the sonne of Shelemiáh,
& Pashhúr the sonne of [a] Malchiáh, heard
the wordes that Ieremiáh had spoken vnto all the people, saying,
2 Thus saith the Lord, He that remaineth
in this citie, shal dye by the sworde, by the
famine and by the pestilence: but he that
goeth forthe to the Caldeans, shal liue: for
he shal haue his life for [b] a pray, and shal
liue.

a For Zedekiáh had sent these to Ieremiáh to inquire at the Lord for the state of the coūtrey now whē Nebuchad-nezzár came, as Chap. 21,1.

b Read Chap. 21,9.

3 Thus saith the Lord, This citie shal surely be giuen into the hand of the King
of Babels armie, which shal take it.
4 Therefore the princes said vnto ye King,
We beseche you, let this man be put to
death: for thus he" weakeneth the hands of
the men of warre [c] that remaine in this
citie, and the hands of all the people, in
speaking suche wordes vnto them: for this
man seketh not the wealth of this people,
but the hurt.

" Or, discourageth.

c Thus we se how the wicked whē they can not abide to heare ye trueth of Gods worde, seke to put the ministers to death as transgressors of policies.

5 Then Zedekiáh the King said, Beholde,
he is in your hands, for the King can *denie*
[d] you nothing.

d Wherein he grieuously offended in that that not onely he wolde not heare the trueth spoken by ye the Prophet, but also gaue him to ye lusts of the wicked to be cruelly intreated.

6 Then toke they Ieremiáh, and cast him
into the dongeon of Malchiáh the sonne
of Hammélech, that was in the court of
the prison: and they let downe Ieremiáh
with coards: and in the dongeon there was
no water but myre: so Ieremiáh stacke fast
in the myre.
7 Now when Ebed-mélech the " blacke
More one of the Eunuches, which was in
the Kings house, heard that they had put
Ieremiáh in the dongeon (then the King
sate in the [e] gate of Beniamín)

" Ebr. Cushite, or Ethiopian.

e To heare matters & giue sentence.

8 And Ebed-mélech wēt out of the Kings
house, and spake to the King, saying,
9 My lord the King, [f] these men haue done
euil in all ye they haue done to Ieremiáh
the Prophet, whome they haue cast into ye
dongeon, and he dyeth for hunger in the
place where he is: for there is no more bread in the citie.

f Hereby is declared that the Prophet founde more fauour at this strāgers hands then he did by all them of his coūtrey which was to their great condemnatiō.

10 Then the King commanded Ebed-mélech ye blacke More, saying, Take frō hence thirtie men" with thee, and take Ieremiáh the Prophet out of the dongeon before he dye.

" Ebr. vnder thine hand.

11 So Ebed-mélech toke the men with him
and went to the house of the King vnder
the treasurie, and toke there olde rotten
ragges, and olde worne *cloutes*, and let them
downe by coardes into the dongeon to Ieremiáh.
12 And Ebed-mélech the blacke More said
vnto Ieremiáh, Put now these olde rotten *ragges* and worne vnder thine arme
holes, betwene the coardes. And Ieremiáh
did so.
13 So they drewe vp Ieremiáh with coardes
and toke him vp out of the dongeon, and
Ieremiáh remained in [g] the court of the
prison.

g Where the King had set him before to be at more libertie, as Chap. 37,21.

14 ¶ Then Zedekiáh the King sent, and toke Ieremiáh the Prophet vnto him, into
the third entrie that is in the House of the
Lord, & the Kīg said vnto Ieremiáh, I wil
aske thee a thing: hide nothing from me.
15 Then Ieremiáh said to Zedekiáh, If I declare it vnto thee, wilt not thou slaye me?
and if I giue thee counsel, thou wilt not
heare me.
16 So the King sware secretly vnto Ieremiáh, saying, As the Lord liueth, that
made vs these soules, I wil not slaie thee,
nor giue thee into the hands of those men
that seke thy life.
17 Then said Ieremiáh vnto Zedekiáh,
Thus saith the Lord God of hostes, ye God
of Israél, If thou wilt go forthe vnto the
King

King of Babels [h] princes, then thy soule
shal liue, and this citie shal not be burnt
vp with fyre, and thou shalt liue, and thine
house.

h And yelde thy self vnto them.

18 But if thou wilt not go forthe to ẏ King
of Babels princes, then shal this citie be
giuen into the hand of the Caldeans, and
thei shal burne it with fyre, and thou shalt
not escape out of their hands.
19 And Zedekiáh the King said vnto Ieremiáh, I am careful for the Iewes that are
fled vnto the Caldeans, lest thei deliuer
me into their hands, and thei [i] mocke me.
20 But Ieremiáh said, Thei shal not deliuer *thee*: hearken vnto the voice of the
Lord, I beseche thee, which I speake vnto thee: so shal it be wel vnto thee, and
thy soule shal liue.

i Which declareth that he more feared the reproche of men, then ẏ threatenings of God.

21 But if thou wilt refuse to go forthe, this
is the worde ẏ the Lord hathe shewed me.
22 And beholde, all the women that are
[k] left in the King of Iudahs house, shalbe
broght forthe to ẏ King of Babels princes: and those *women* shal say, Thy friendes haue persuaded thee, and haue preuailed against thee: thy fete are fastned in the
myre, *and* thei are turned backe.
23 So thei shal bring out all thy wiues, and
thy children to the Caldeans, and thou
shalt not escape out of their hands, but
shalt be taken by the hand of the King of
Babél: and this citie shalt thou cause to be
burnt with fyre.

k When Ieconiáh and his mother with others were caryed away, the fewe women of the Kings house were left: ẇ shalbe taken, saith the Prophet, and tel ẏ King of Babél how Zedekiáh hathe bene seduced by his familiar friēds and false Prophetes, which haue left him in the myre.

24 Then said Zedekiáh vnto Ieremiáh, Let
no man knowe of these wordes, and thou
shalt not dye.
25 But if the princes vnderstand that I haue talked with thee, and thei come vnto
thee, and say vnto thee, Declare vnto vs
now, what thou hast said vnto the King,
hide it not from vs, and we wil not slay
thee: also what the King said vnto thee,
26 Then shalt thou say vnto them, I humbly [l] besoght the King that he wolde not
cause me to returne to Iehonathans house,
to dye there.
27 Thē came all the princes vnto Ieremiáh
and asked him. And he tolde them according to all these wordes that ẏ King had
commanded: so thei left of speaking with
him, for the matter was not perceiued.

l Herein appeareth the infirmitie of the Prophet, who did dissemble to saue his life albeit it was not to the denial of his doctrine, or to ẏ hurte of any.

28 So Ieremiáh abode stil in ẏ court of the
prison, vntil the day that Ierusalém was
taken: and he was *there*, when Ierusalém
was taken.

CHAP. XXXIX.

1 Nebuchad-nezzár besiegeth Ierusalém, 4 Zedekiáh fleing is taken of the Caldeans. 6 His sonnes are slaine. 7 His eyes are thrust out 11 Ieremiah is prouided for. 15 Ebed-mélech is deliuered from captiuitie.

2. King. 25, 1. chap. 52, 4.

1 IN [*] the ninth yere of Zedekiáh King
of Iudáh in ẏ tenth moneth, came Nebuchad-nezzár King of Babél and all his
hoste against Ierusalém, and thei besieged it.
2 *And* in the eleuenth yere of Zedekiáh in
the fourth moneth, the ninth *daie* of the
moneth, the citie was broken [a] vp.
3 And all the princes of the King of Babél came in, and sate in the middle gate,
euen Neregál, Sharézer, Samgar-nébo,
Sarsechím, Rab-sarís, Neregál, Sharézer,
Rab-mag with all the residue of the princes of the King of Babél.

a The gates & wales were broken downe.

4 And when Zedekiáh the King of Iudáh
sawe them, and all the men of warre, then
thei fled, & went out of the citie by night,
through the Kings garden, & by the [b] gate betwene the two walles, and he went
toward the wildernes.

b Which was a posterne dore, read 2. Kīg. 25, 4.

5 But the Caldeans hoste pursued after
them, and ouertoke Zedekiáh in the desert of Ierichó: and when thei had taken
him, thei broght him to Nebuchad-nezzár King of Babél vnto [c] Ribláh in the
land of Hamáth, where he gaue iudgemēt
vpon him.

c Which is called Antiochia in Syria.

6 Then the King of Babél slewe the sonnes
of Zedekiáh in Ribláh before his eyes:
also the King of Babél slewe all the nobles of Iudáh.
7 Moreouer he put out Zedekiahs eyes,
and bounde him in chaines, to carye him
to Babél.
8 And the Caldeans burnt the Kings house, and the houses of the people with fyre,
and brake downe the walles of Ierusalém.
9 Then Nebuzar adán the ″chief steward
caryed away captiue into Babél the remnāt of the people, that remained in the citie, and those that were fled and fallen vnto him, with the rest of the people that remained.

″Or, captaine of the garde.

10 But Nebuzar-adán ẏ chief steward left
the [d] poore that had nothing in the land
of Iudáh, and gaue them vineyardes and
fields at the same time.
11 Now Nebuchad-nezzár King of Babél gaue charge concerning Ieremiáh ″vn
to Nebuzar-adán ẏ chief steward, saying,
12 Take him, and ″ loke wel to him, and do
him no harme, but do vnto him [e] euen as
he shal say vnto thee.
13 So Nebuzar-adán the chief steward sent
and Nebushazbán, Rabsaris, & Neregál,
Sharézer, Rab mag, and all the King of
Babels princes:

d For ẏ riche & the mightie ẇ put their trust in their shiftes & meanes, were by Gods iust iudgements moste rigorously handeled.

″Ebr. by the hand of

″Ebr. set thine eyes vpon him.

e Thus God preserued his Prophet by his meanes, whome he made ẏ scourge to punish the King, and them that were his enemies.

14 Euen thei sent, and toke Ieremiáh out of
the court of the prison, and cōmitted him
vnto [f] Gedaliáh the sonne of Ahikám the
sonne of Shaphán, that he shulde carie him
home: so he dwelt among the people.
15 Now ẏ worde of the Lord came vnto Ieremiáh, while he was shut vp in ẏ court of

f Whome the King of Babél had now appoīted gouernour ouer the rest of the Iewes that he left behinde.

the prison, saying,
16 Go & speake to Ebed-mélech the blacke
More, saying, Thus saith the Lord of hos
tes the God of Israél, Beholde, I wil bring
my wordes vpon this citie for euil, and
not for good, and thei shalbe *accomplished*
in that daie before thee.
17 But I wil deliuer thee in that daie, saith
the Lord, and thou shalt not be giuen into the hand of the men whome thou fearest.
18 For I wil surely deliuer thee, and thou
shalt not fall by the sworde, but thy life
shalbe for a pray vnto thee, because thou
[g] hast put thy trust in me, saith the Lord.

[g] Thus God recompensed his zeale and fauour, which he shewed to his Prophet in his troubles.

CHAP. XL.

1 *Ieremiáh hathe licence to go whether he wil. 6 He dwelleth with the people that remaine with Gedaliáh.*

1 THe worde which came to Ieremiáh
from the Lord after that Nebuzar-
adán the chief steward had let him go frõ
Ramáth, when he had taken him being
bounde in chaines among all that were
caryed awaie captiue of Ierusalém and
Iudáh, which were caryed awaie captiue
vnto Babél.
2 [a] And the chief steward toke Ieremiáh,
and said vnto him, The Lord thy God
hathe pronounced this plague vpon this
place.
3 Now the Lord hathe broght it, & done
according as he hathe said: because ye
haue [b] sinned against the Lord, and haue
not obeied his voice, therefore this thing
is come vpon you.
4 And now beholde, I lose thee this daie
from the chaines which were on thine
handes, if it please thee to come with me
into Babél, come, and I wil loke wel vnto thee: but if it please thee not to come
with me into Babél, '' tary stil: beholde,
all the land *is* '' before thee: whether it semeth good, and conuenient for thee to
go, thether go.
5 For yet he was not returned: therefore *he*
said, Returne to Gedaliáh the sonne of A-
hikám, the sonne of Shaphán, whome the
King of Babél hathe made gouernour o-
uer all the cities of Iudáh, and dwell with
him among the people, or go wheresoeuer it pleaseth thee to go. So the chief
steward gaue him vitailes and a rewarde,
and let him go.
6 Then went Ieremiáh vnto Gedaliáh the
sonne of Ahikám, [c] to Mizpáh, and dwelt
there with him among the people that were left in the land.
7 Now when all the captaines of the hoste,
[d] which were in the fields, *euen* thei and
their men heard, that the King of Babél
had made Gedaliáh the sonne of Ahikám

[a] From this secõde vers. vnto chap. 42,7 it semeth to be as a parenthesis, and separated matter: & there this storie beginneth agaiae, & this visiõ is declared what it was.
[b] God moued this infidele to speake this, to declare the great blindnes and obstinacie of the Iewes, which colde not fele that which this heathen man confessed.
'' *Ebr. cease.*
'' *Or, as thy commandement.*
[c] Which was a citie of Iudáh.
[d] Which were scattered abroad for feare of the Caldeans.

gouernour in the land, and that he had
committed vnto him, men, and women,
and children, and of the poore of the land,
that were not caryed away captiue to Babél,
8 Then they came to Gedaliáh to Mizpáh, *euen* [e] Ishmaél the sonne of Nethaniáh, and Iohanán, and Ionathán the sonnes of Karéah, and Seraiáh the sonne of
Tanehuméth, and the sonnes of Ephái,
the Netophathite, and Iezaniáh the sonne of Maachathí, thei and their men.
9 And Gedaliáh the sonne of Ahikám,
the sonne of Shaphán * sware vnto them,
and to their men, saying, Feare not to
serue the Caldeans: dwell in the land, and
serue the King of Babél, and it shalbe wel
with you.
10 As for me, beholde, I wil dwell at Mizpáh to '' serue the Caldeans, which wil
come vnto vs: but you, gather you wine, and sommer frutes, and oyle, and
put them in your vessels, & dwell in your
cities, that ye haue '' taken.
11 Likewise when all the Iewes that were
in [f] Moáb, and among the Ammonites, and in Edóm, and that were in all the
countreis, heard that the King of Babél
had left a remnant of Iudáh, and that he
had set ouer them Gedaliáh the sonne of
Ahikám the sonne of Shaphán,
12 Euen all the Iewes returned out of all
places where thei were driuen, and came
to the land of Iudáh to Gedaliáh vnto
Mizpáh, and gathered wine and sommer
frutes, very muche.
13 Moreouer Iohanán the sonne of Karéah, and all the captaines of the hoste,
that were in the fields, came to Gedaliáh
to Mizpáh,
14 And said vnto him, Knowest thou not
that [g] Baalis the King of the Ammonites
hathe sent Ishmaél the sonne of Nethaniáh to slay thee? But Gedaliáh the sonne
of Ahikám beleued them not.
15 Then Iohanán the sonne of Karéah spake to Gedaliáh in Mizpáh secretly, saying, Let me go, I pray thee, and I wil slay
Ishmaél the sonne of Nethaniáh, and no
man shal knowe it. Wherefore shulde he
kyl thee, that all the Iewes, which are gathered vnto thee, shulde be scattered, and
the remnant in Iudáh perish?
16 But Gedaliáh the sonne of Ahikám said
vnto Iohanán the sonne of Karéah, Thou
shalt [h] not do this thing: for thou speakest
falsely of Ishmaél.

[e] Who was of ỹ Kings blood and after slew him, Cha. 41,2.
* 2. King. 25,24.
'' *Or, to receiue them, or to intreat them for you.*
'' *Or, chosen to dwel in.*
[f] Which were fled also for feare of the Caldeans.
[g] For vnder ỹ colour of interteinĩg of Ishmaél he soght onely to make thẽ to destroy one another.
[h] Thus the godlie, which thinke no harme to others, are sonest deceiued & neuer lacke such as conspire their destruction.

CHAP. XLI.

1 *Ishmaél killeth Gedaliáh guilefully, and many other with him. 11 Iohanán followeth after Ishmaél.*

1 BVt in the [a] seuenth moneth came Ishmaél the sonne of Nethaniáh, the

Chap XLI. [a] The citie was destroied in the fourth moneth and in the seuẽth moneth, which cõteined part of September, & part of October, was the gouernour Gedaliáh slaine.

b Meaning, Zedekiáh.

c Thei did eat together as familiar friends.

sonne of Elishamá of the sede royal,and
the princes of the [b] King, & ten men with
him, vnto Gedaliáh the sonne of Ahikám
to Mizpáh, and there thei did [c] eate bread
together in Mizpáh.
2 Then arose Ishmaél the sonne of Nethaniáh with these ten men that were with
him, and smote Gedaliáh the sonne of
Ahikám the sonne of Shaphán with the
sworde, and slewe him, whome the King
of Babél had made gouernour ouer the
land.
3 Ishmaél also slewe all the Iewes that were
with Gedaliáh at Mizpáh, & all the Caldeans that were founde there, & the men
of warre.
4 Now the seconde daie that he had slaine
Gedaliáh, and no man knewe it,
5 There came men from Shechém,frõ Shilóh,& from Samaria,*euen* foure scoremen,
hauing their beardes shauen, and their
clothes rent and cut, with [d] offrings and
incense in their hands to offre in the House of the Lord.
6 And Ishmaél the sonne of Nethaniáh
went forthe from Mizpáh to mete them,
weping as he went:& when he met them,
he said vnto them, Come [e] to Gedaliáh
the sonne of Ahikám.
7 And when thei came into the middes of
the citie, Ishmaél the sonne of Nethaniáh slewe thẽ, *and cast them* into the middes of the pit, he and the men that were
with him.
8 But ten men were founde among them,
that said vnto Ishmaél,Slay vs not:for we
haue treasures in the field, of wheat, and
of barley, and of oyle, and of honie: so he
staied, and slewe them not among their
brethren.
9 Now the pit wherein Ishmaél had cast
the dead bodies of the men(whome he
had slaine because of Gedaliáh) is it,
which Asá the King had [f] made because
of Bashá King of Israél, *and* Ishmaél the
sonne of Nethaniáh filled it with them
that were slaine.
10 Then Ishmaél caryed away captiue all
the residue of the people that were in Mizpáh,*euen* the Kings daughters, and all the
people that remained in Mizpáh, whome
Nebuzar-adán the chief steward had cõmitted to Gedaliáh the sonne of Ahikám, and Ishmaél the sonne of Nethaniáh
caryed them away captiue, and departed
to go ouer to the Ammonites.
11 But when Iohanán the sonne of Karéah,
& all the [g] captaines of the hoste that were with him,heard of all the euil that Ishmaél the sonne of Nethaniáh had done,
12 Then they all toke *their* men, and went to
fight with Ishmaél ÿ sonne of Nethaniáh,

d For they thoght that ÿ Temple had not bene destroied, & therefore came vp to the feast of Tabernacles, but hearing of the burning thereof in the way, they shewed these signes of sorowe.

e For his death was kept secret,& he fained that he lamented for the destructiõ of Ierusalém & the Temple: but after slewe thẽ when thei semed to fauour Gedaliáh

f Asá fortified Mizpáh for feare of the enemie, and cast dyches & trenches, 1. King. 15,22.

g Which had bene captaines vnder Zedekiáh.

and founde him by the great waters that
are in Gibeón.
13 Now when all the people whome Ishmaél caryed away captiue, sawe Iohanán the
sonne of Karéah, and all the captaines of
the hoste, that were with him, they were
glad.
14 So all the people, that Ishmaél had caryed away captiue from Mizpáh,returned
and came againe, and went vnto Iohanán
the sonne of Karéah.
15 But Ishmaél the sonne of Nethaniáh,escaped from Iohanán with eight men, and
went to the [h] Ammonites.
16 Thẽ toke Iohanán the sonne of Karéah,
& all the captaines of the hoste, that were
with him all the remnant of the people,
whome Ishmaél the sonne of Nethaniáh,
had caryed away captiue from Mizpáh,
(after that he had slaine Gedaliáh the sonne of Ahikám) *euen* the strong men of
warre,and the women,and the children,&
the eunuches,whome he had broght againe from Gibeón:
17 And thei departed and dwelt in Gerúth
[i] Chimham,which is by Beth-léhem,to go
& to entre into Egypt,
18 Because of the Caldeans:for they feared
them, because Ishmaél the sonne of Nethaniáh had slaine Gedaliáh the sonne of
Ahikám, whome the King of Babél made gouernour in the land.

h For Baalis ÿ King of the Ammonites was the cause of this murther.

i Which place Dauid of olde had giuen to Chimhám the sonne of Barzilai the Gileadite,2.Sam. 19,38.

CHAP. XLII.

1 The captaines aske counsel of Ieremiáh what they oght to do. 7 He admonisheth the remnant of the people not to go into Egypt.

1 THen all the captaines of the hoste,
and Iohanán the sonne of Karéah, &
Iezaniáh the sonne of Hoshaaiáh, and all
the people from the least vnto the moste,
came,
2 And said vnto Ieremiáh ÿ Prophet,"Heare our prayer,we beseche thee, & pray for
vs vnto the Lord thy God,euẽ for all this
remnant(for we are left, *but* a fewe of manie,as thine eyes do beholde)
3 That the Lord thy God may shewe vs the
way wherein we may walke, and the thing
that we may [a] do.
4 Then Ieremiáh the Prophet said vnto
them,I haue heard *you*:beholde, I wil pray
vnto the Lord your God according to
your wordes, and whatsoeuer thing the
Lord shal answer you, I wil declare it vnto you:I wil kepe nothing backe frõ you.
5 Then they said to Ieremiáh, [b] The Lord
be a witnes of trueth, and faith betwene
vs, if we do not, euen according to all
things for the which the Lord thy God
shal send thee to vs.
6 Whether it be good or euil, we wil obey
the voyce of the Lord God, to whome we

"Ebr. let our prayer fall before thee, as Chap.36,7.

a This declareth the nature of hypocrites, which wolde knowe of Gods worde what they shulde do, but wil not follow it, but in asmuche as it agreeth with ÿ thing which they haue purposed to do.

b There are none more readv to abuse ÿ Name of God and take it in vaine, thẽ the hypocrites, ÿ to colour their falsehode vse it without all reuerence,and make it a meanes for them to deceiue the simple,and the godlie.

send thee that it may be wel with vs, when
we obey the voyce of the Lord our God.
7 ¶ [c] And so after ten dayes came ẏ worde
of the Lord vnto Ieremiáh.
8 Then called he Iohanán the sonne of Ka
réah, and all the captaines of the hoste,
which were with him, and all the people
from the least to the moste,
9 And said vnto thē, Thus saith the Lord
God of Israél, vnto whome ye sent me to
present your prayers before him,
10 If ye wil dwell in this land, then I wil
buyld you, and not destroye *you*, and I wil
plant you, and not roote *you* out: for I [d] repent me of the euil that I haue done vnto
you.
11 Feare not for the King of Babél, of
whome ye are afraid: be not afraid of him,
saith the Lord: for I am with you, to saue
you, and to deliuer you [e] from his hand,
12 And I wil grant you mercie that he may
haue compassion vpon you, and he shal
cause you *to dwell in your owne land.
13 But if ye say, We wil not dwell in this
land, nether heare the voyce of the Lord
your God,
14 Saying, Nay, but we wil go into the lād
of Egypt, where we shal se no warre, nor
heare the sounde of the trumpet, nor haue
hungre of bread, and there wil we dwell,
15 (And now therefore heare the worde of
the Lord, ye remnant of Iudáh: thus saith
the Lord of hostes the God of Israél, If ye
set your faces to entre into Egypt, and go
to dwell there)
16 Then the sworde that ye feared, [f] shal
take you there in the land of Egypt, and
the famine, for ẏ which ye care, shal there
hāg vpō you in Egypt, & there shal ye dye.
17 And all the men that set their faces to
entre into Egypt to dwell there, shal dye
by the sworde, by the famine & by ẏ pestilence, & none of them shal remaine nor escape frō the plague, that I wil bring vpon
them.
18 For thus saith the Lord of hostes ẏ God
of Israél, As mine angre and my wrath
hathe bene powred forthe vpon the inhabitants of Ierusalém: so shal my wrath be
powred forthe vpō you, when ye shal entre into Egypt, & ye shalbe a detestation,
& an astonishmēt, and a [g] cursse, and a reproche, and ye shal se this place no more.
19 O ye remnant of Iudáh, the Lord hathe
said concerning you, Go not into Egypt:
knowe certeinly that I haue admonished
you this day.
20 Surely ye [h] dissembled in your hearts
when ye sent me vnto the Lord your God,
saying, Pray for vs vnto ẏ Lord our God
and declare vnto vs euen according vnto
all that the Lord our God shal say, and
we wil do it.

c Here is declared the vision & the occasiō thereof, whereof mencion was made, Chap. 40,1.

d Read Chap. 18,8.

e Because all Kings hearts and waies are in his hands, he can turne them & dispose them as it pleaseth him, and therefore they nede not to feare man, but onely obey God, Prou. 21,1

*Or, returne.

f Thus God turneth ẏ policie of the wicked to their owne destructiō: for thei thoght thēselues sure in Egypt, and there Nebuchad-nezzár destroyed them, and the Egyptians, Chap. 46,25.

g Read Chap. 26,6. & 24, 22. shewing that this shulde come vpon them for their infidelitie & stubbornes.

h For you were fully minded to go into Egypt, whatsoeuer God spake to the contrarie.

21 Therefore I haue this day declared it
you, but you haue not obeyed the voyce
of the Lord your God, nor anie thing for
the which he hathe sent me vnto you.
22 Now therefore, knowe certeinely that
ye shal dye by the sworde, by the famine,
and by the pestilence, [i] in the place whether ye desire to go and dwell.

i To wit, In Egypt.

CHAP. XLIII.

Iohanán caryeth the remnant of the people into Egypt contrarie to the minde of Ieremiáh. 8 Ieremiáh prophecieth the destruction of Egypt.

1 NOw whē Ieremiáh had made an end
of speaking vnto the whole people
all the wordes of the Lord their God, for
the which ẏ Lord their God had sent him
to them, *euen* all these wordes,
2 Then [a] spake Azariáh the sonne of Hoshaiáh, and Iohanán the sonne of Karéah
and all the [b] proude men, saying vnto Ieremiáh, [c] Thou speakest falsly: the Lord
our God hathe [d] not sent thee to say, Go
not into Egypt to dwell there,
3 But Barúch the sonne of Neriáh [e] prouoketh thee against vs, for to deliuer vs
into the hand of the Caldeans, that they
might slaye vs, and carie vs away captiues
into Babél.
4 So Iohanán the sonne of Karéah, and all
the captaines of the hoste, and all the people obeyed not the voyce of the Lord, to
dwell in the land of Iudáh.
5 But Iohanán the sonne of Karéah, and all
the captaines of the hoste toke all ẏ remnant of Iudáh, that were returned from
all [f] nacions, whether thei had bene driuē,
to dwell in the land of Iudáh:
6 *Euen* men and women, and children, and
the Kings daughters, and euerie persone,
that Nebuzar-adán the chief steward had
left with Gedaliáh the sonne of Ahikám,
the sonne of Shaphán, and Ieremiáh [g] the
Prophet, & Barúch the sonne of Neriáh.
7 So they came into the land of Egypt: for
they obeyed not the voyce of the Lord:
thus came they [h] to Tahpanhes.
8 ¶ Thē came the worde of the Lord vnto
Ieremiáh in Tahpanhes, saying,
9 Take great stones in thine hand, and [i] hide them in the clay in the bricke kil, which
is at the entrie of Pharaohs house in Tah
panhes in the sight of the men of Iudáh,
10 And say vnto them, Thus saith the Lord
of hostes the God of Israél, Beholde, I wil
send and bring Nebuchad-nezzár the
King of Babél [k] my seruant, and wil set
his throne vpō these stones ẏ I haue hid,
and he shal spreade his pauillion ouer thē.
11 And when he shal come, he shal smite the
land of Egypt: [l] suche as are *appointed* for
death, to death, & such as are for captiuitie, to captiuitie, and suche as are for the
sworde, to the sworde.

12 And

a Who was also called Iezaniáh, Chap. 42,1.

b This declareth that pride is the cause of rebellion, & contempt of Gods ministers

c When the hypocrisie of the wicked is discouered thei brast forthe into open rage: for they cā abide nothing but flatteries, read Isa. 30,10.

d He sheweth what is the nature of the hypocrites: to wit, to faine that they wolde obey God and imbrace his worde, if thei were assured that his messengers spake the trueth: thogh in dede they be moste farre from all obedience.

e Thus the wicked do not onely contemne, & hurt the messengers of God, but sclander, and speake wickedly of all thē that support or fauour the godlie.

f As from the Moabites, Ammonites, and Edomites, Chap 40,11.

g Whome these wicked led away by force.

h A citie in Egypt nere to Nilus.

i Which signified that Nebuchad-nezzár shuld come euē to the gates of Pharaoh, where were his bricke killes for his buyldings.

k Read Chap. 25,9

l Euerie one shal be slaine by that meanes ẏ God hathe appointed, Chap. 15,2.

12 And I wil kindle a fyre in the houses of
the gods of Egypt, and he shal burne them
and carye them awaie captiues, and he shal
araye him self with the land of Egypt, as a
[m] shepherd putteth on his garment, and
shal departe from thence in peace.
13 He shal breake also the images of "Beth-
shémesh, that is in the land of Egypt, and
the houses of the gods of the Egyptians
shal he burne with fyre.

m Meaning, moste easily, & suddenly shal he cary the Egyptiãs away.
"Or, the house of the sunne.

CHAP. XLIIII.

He reproueth the people for their idolatrie. 15 Thei that set light by the threatening of the Lord, are chastened. 26 The destruction of Egypt and of the Iewes therein, is prophecied.

1 THe worde that came to Ieremiáh con
cerning all the Iewes, which dwell in
the land of Egypt, and remained at Migdól and at [a] Tahpanhes, and at Noph, and
in the countrey of Pathrós, saying,
2 Thus saith the Lord of hostes the God of
Israél, Ye haue sene all the euil that I haue broght vpon Ierusalém, and vpon all
ỹ cities of Iudáh: & beholde, this day thei
are desolate, & no man dwelleth therein,
3 Because of their wickednes which thei
haue committed, to prouoke me to angre
in that thei went to burne incense, & to
serue other gods, whome thei knewe not,
nether thei *nor* you nor your fathers.
4 Howbeit I sent vnto you all my seruants
the Prophetes [b] rising early, and sending
them, saying, Oh do not this abominable
thing that I hate.
5 But thei wolde not heare nor incline their
eare to turne from their wickednes, and
to burne no more incẽse vnto other gods.
6 Wherefore [c] my wrath, and mine angre was powred forthe and was kindled in
the cities of Iudáh, and in the stretes of Ie
rusalém, and thei are desolate, & wasted, as
appeareth this daye.
7 Therefore now thus saith ỹ Lord of hostes
the God of Israél, Wherefore commit ye
this great euil against your soules, to cut
of from you man and woman, childe &
suckeling out of Iudáh, and leaue you none to remaine?
8 In that ye prouoke me vnto wrath with
the workes of your hands, burning incen
se vnto other gods in the land of Egypt
whether ye be gone to dwell: ỹ ye might
bring destruction vnto your selues, and
that ye might be a cursse and a reproche
among all nations of the earth.
9 Haue ye forgotten the wickednes of your
fathers, and the wickednes of the [d] Kings
of Iudáh and the wickednes of their wiues and your owne wickednes and the wic
kednes of your wiues, which thei haue
committed in the land of Iudáh and in ỹ
stretes of Ierusalém?
10 Thei are not " humbled vnto this daie,

a These were all famous and strong cities in Egypt, where ỹ Iewes, ỹ were fled, dwelt for their safety: but the Prophet declareth that there is no holde so strong, that can preserue them from Gods vẽgeance.

b Read Chap. 7,25. & 25,3. & 26,5. & 29,19. & 32,33.

c He setteth before their eyes Gods iudgements agaĩst Iudáh & Ierusalém for their idolatrie, that they might beware by their example, and not with the like wickednes prouoke the Lord: for then they shulde be double punished.
d He sheweth that we oght to kepe in memorie Gods plagues from the beginning that considering them, we might liue in his feare, and knowe if he haue not spared our fathers yea, Kĩgs, princes, and rulers, and also whole countreis, and nations for their sinnes, ỹ we vile wormes can not loke to escape punishmẽt for ours.
"Or, beaten downe.

nether haue thei feared nor walked in my
Lawe nor in my statutes, that I set before
you and before your fathers.
11 Therefore thus saith ỹ Lord of hostes ỹ
God of Israél, Beholde, I wil set my face
agaĩst you *to euil & to destroy all Iudáh,
12 And I wil take the remnant of Iudáh,
that [e] haue set their faces to go into the
land of Egypt there to dwell, and thei shal
all be consumed & fall in the land of E-
gypt: they shal *euen* be consumed by the
sworde & by ỹ famine: thei shal dye from
the least vnto the moste, by the sworde, &
by the famine, & thei shalbe a detestation
and an astonishment and a [f] cursse and a
reproche.
13 For I wil visit them that dwell in the lãd
of Egypt, as I haue visited Ierusalém, by ỹ
sworde, by the famine, & by the pestilence,
14 So that none of the remnant of Iudáh,
which are gone into the land of Egypt to
dwell there, shal escape or remaine, that
thei shuld returne into the lãd of Iudáh to
the which thei "haue a desire to returne to
dwell there: for none shal returne, but
[g] suche as shal escape.
15 Then all the men which knewe that their
wiues had burnt incense vnto other gods
and all the women that stode by, a great
multitude, euen all the people that dwelt
in the land of Egypt in Pathrós, answered
Ieremiáh, saying,
16 The worde that thou hast spoken vnto
vs in the Name of the Lord, we wil [h] not
heare it of thee,
17 But we wil do whatsoeuer thing goeth
out of our owne mouth, *as* to burne incense vnto [i] the Quene of heauẽ, & to powre
out drinke offrings vnto her, as we haue
done, *bothe* we and our fathers, our Kings
and our princes in the citie of Iudáh, and
in the stretes of Ierusalém: for *then* " had
we [k] plentie of vitailes and were wel and
"felt none euil.
18 But since we left of to burne incense to
the Quene of heauen, and to powre out
drinke offrings vnto her, we haue had "scarcenes of all things, and haue bene consumed by the sworde and by the famine.
19 And when we burnt incense to the Que
ne of heauen & powred out drinke offrings
vnto her, did we make her cakes to " make
her glad, and powre out drinke offrings
vnto her without [l] our housbandes?
20 Then said Ieremiáh vnto all the people,
to the men, and to the women, and to all
ỹ people ẘ had giuẽ him ỹ answer, saying,
21 Did not ỹ Lord remẽber the incẽse, that
ye burnt in ỹ cities of Iudáh, & in the stretes of Ierusalém, *bothe* you, & your fathers,
your Kings, and your princes, and the peo
ple of ỹ lãd, & " hathe he not cõsidered it?

Amos 9, 4.
e Which haue fully set their mindes, & are gone thether on purpose. Whereby he excepteth the innocentes as Ieremiáh and Barúch ỹ were forced: therefore the Lord sheweth, ỹ he wil set his face against thẽ: that is, purposely destroye them
f Read Chap. 26,6.
"Ebr lift vp their soules.
g Meaning, but a fewe.
h This declareth how dangerous a thing it is to decline once from God, & to folowe our owne fantasies: for Satan euer soliciteth suche and doeth not leaue thẽ til he haue broght them to extreme impudẽcie & madnes, euẽ to iustifie their wickednes against God, & his prophetes.
i Read Chap. 7.17. It semeth that the Papistes gathered of this place their *Salue Regina*, and *Regina celi, letare*, calling ỹ virgine Marie Quene of heauẽ, & so of the blessed virgine, & mother of our Sauiour Christ made an idole: for here the Prophet condemneth their idolatrie.
"Ebr. we were saciat with bread
k This is stil ỹ argument of idolaters, ẘ esteme religion by the bellie, & in stead of acknowledging Gods workes, who sendeth bothe plentie & dearth, healti, & sickenes, they attribute it to their idoles, and so dishonour God
"Or, sawe.
"Or, want.
"Or, to appease her.
l This teacheth vs how great dãger it is for the housbandes to permit their wiues anie thing whereof they be not assured by Gods worde: for thereby thei take an occasion to iustifie their doings, & their housbãds shal giue an accompt thereof before God, read Isa. 3,25.
"Ebr. is it not come vp into his heart?

22 So that the Lord colde no longer forbeare, becauſe of the wickednes of your
inuencions, & becauſe of the abominations, which ye haue cõmitted: therefore is
your land deſolate and an aſtoniſhment, &
a curſſe & without inhabitant, as *appeareth* this daie.
23 Becauſe ye haue burnt incẽſe and becauſe ye haue ſinned agaĩſt the Lord, & haue
not obeied the voice of the Lord, nor walked in his Law nor in his ſtatutes, nor in
his teſtimonies, therefore this plague is
come vpon you, as *appeareth* this day.
24 Moreouer Ieremiáh ſaid vnto all the
people and to all the women, Heare the
worde of the Lord, all Iudáh that are in
the land of Egypt.
25 ¶ Thus ſpeaketh ẏ Lord of hoſtes, ẏ God
of Iſraél, ſaying, Ye and your wiues haue
bothe ſpoken with your mouthes, and fulfilled with your [m] hand, ſaying, We wil
performe our vowes ẏ we haue vowed to
burne incenſe to ẏ Queene of heauen, and
to powre out drinke offrings to her: ye wil
performe your vowes and do the things
that ye haue vowed.
26 Therefore heare the worde of the Lord,
all Iudáh that dwell in the land of Egypt.
Beholde, I haue ſworne by my great Name, ſaith the Lord, that my Name [n] ſhal no
more be called vpon by the mouth of any
man of Iudáh, in all the land of Egypt,
ſaying, The Lord God liueth.
27 Beholde, I wil watche ouer them for e-
uil and not for good, and all men of Iudáh
that are in the land of Egypt, ſhal be conſumed by the ſworde, and by the famine,
vntil thei be vtterly deſtroyed.
28 Yet a ſmale nombre that eſcape the
ſworde, [o] ſhal returne out of the land of
Egypt into the land of Iudáh: and all the
remnant of Iudáh that are gone into the
land of Egypt to dwell there, ſhal knowe
whoſe wordes ſhal ſtand, mine or theirs.
29 And this ſhalbe a ſigne vnto you, ſaith
the Lord, when I viſite you in this place,
that ye maie knowe that my wordes ſhal
ſurely ſtand againſt you for euil.
30 Thus ſaith the Lord, Beholde, I wil [p] giue Pharaóh Hophrá King of Egypt into
the hand of his enemies, and into the hand
of them that ſeke his life: as I gaue Zedekiáh King of Iudáh into the hand of Nebuchad-nezzár King of Babél his enemie,
who alſo ſoght his life.

m You haue cõmitted double euil in making wicked vowes, and in performing ẏ ſame.
n This declareth an horrible plague toward idolaters, ſeing that God wil not vouchesafe to haue his Name mencioned by ſuche as haue polluted it.
o We ſe therefore, that God hathe a perpetual care ouer his, whereſoeuer they are ſcattred: for thogh they be but, two or thre, yet he wil deliuer them when he deſtroyeth his enemies.
p He ſheweth the meanes whereby they ſhulde be deſtroyed to aſſure them of ẏ certeintie of ẏ plague, and yet they remaine ſtil in their obſtinacie til they periſh: for Ioſephus lib. 10 de Antiq cap 11. writeth that fiue yere after the taking of Ieruſalém, Nebuchad-nezzár the yonger, hauing ouercome the Moabites and the Ammonites, wẽt againſt Egypt, & ſlew the King, & ſo broght theſe Iewes, and other into Babylon.

CHAP. XLV.

1 Ieremiáh cõforteth Barúch, aſſuring him that he ſhulde not periſh in the deſtruction of Ieruſalém.

1 THe worde that Ieremiáh the Prophet
ſpake vnto [a] Barúch the ſonne of
Neriáh, when he had writen theſe [b] wordes in a boke at the mouth of Ieremiáh, in
the fourth yere of Iehoiakím the ſonne of
Ioſiáh King of Iudáh, ſaying,
2 Thus ſaith the Lord God of Iſraél vnto
thee, ô Barúch,
3 Thou dideſt ſay, Wo is me now: for the
Lord hathe layed ſorowe vnto my ſorow:
I [c] fainted in my mourning, and I can
finde no reſt.
4 Thus ſhalt thou ſay vnto him, The Lord
ſaith thus, Beholde, that which I haue
buylt, wil I [d] deſtroye, & that which I haue planted, wil I plucke vp, euen this whole land.
5 And ſekeſt [e] thou great things for thy
ſelf? ſeke them not: for beholde, I wil bring
a plague vpon all fleſh, ſaith the Lord: but
thy life wil I giue thee for [f] a pray in all
places, whether thou goeſt.

a Which was Ieremiahs diſciple, & wrote his prophecies vnder him.
b Whereof read Chap. 36,9.
c Barúch moued with an inconſiderat zeale of Ieremiahs impriſonment, but chiefly for the deſtruction of the people, and the Temple, maketh this lamentation, as Pſal 6,6.
d Meaning, ẏ God might deſtroye this people becauſe he had planted them.
e Thinkeſt ẏ to haue honour and credit? wherein he ſheweth his infirmitie.
f Read Chap. 21,9.

CHAP. XLVI.

1 He prophecieth the deſtruction of Egypt. 27 Deliuerance is promiſed to Iſraél.

1 THe wordes of the Lord, which came
to Ieremiáh the Prophet againſt the
[a] Gentiles,
2 *As* againſt Egypt, againſt the armie of
[b] Pharaóh Nechó King of Egypt, which
was by the riuer Peráth in Carchemíſh,
which Nebuchad-nezzár King of Babél
ſmote in the fourth yere of Iehoiakím the
ſonne of Ioſiáh King of Iudáh.
3 [c] Make readie buckeler and ſhield, and go
fourth to battel.
4 Make readie the horſes, and let the horſemen get vp, & ſtand vp wᵗ *your* ſallets, four-
biſh the ſpeares, and put on the brigandines.
5 [d] Wherefore haue I ſene them afraide,
& driuen backe? for their mightie men are
ſmitten, and are fled away, and loke not
backe: *for* feare *was* round about, ſaith the
Lord.
6 The ſwift ſhal not flee away, nor the
ſtrong man eſcape: they ſhal ſtomble, and
fall towarde the [e] Northe by the riuer
Peráth.
7 Who is this, that cometh vp, as [f] a
flood, whoſe waters are moued like the
riuers?
8 Egypt riſeth vp like the flood, and *his*
waters are moued like the riuers, and he
ſaith, I wil go vp, & wil couer the earth:
I wil deſtroye the citie with them that
dwell therein.
9 Come vp, ye horſes, and rage ye charets,
and let the valiant men come forthe,
[g] the blacke Mores, and the Lybians that
beare the ſhield, and the Lydians that
handle & bend the bowe.
10 For this is the day of the Lord God of
hoſtes, & a day of vengeance, that he may
aduẽge him of his enemies: for the ſworde
ſhal deuoure, and it ſhalbe ſatiat, and made drunke with their blood: for the Lord
God of hoſtes hathe [h] a ſacrifice in the
North

a That is, nine nations, ẇ are rounde about the land of Egypt.
b Read 2 Kin. 23,29. & 24,7. & 2 chro. 35, 20.
c He warneth the Egyptians to prepare thẽ ſelues to warre.
d The Prophet had this viſion of the Egyptians ẇ ſhulde be put to flight by the Babylonians at Carcheміſh.
e The Babylonians ſhal diſcomfit them at the riuer Euphrates.
f He derideth ẏ boaſtings of the Egyptians who thoght by their riches, & power to haue ouercome all the worlde, alluding to the riuer Nilus, ẇ at certeine times ouerfloweth the countrey of Egypt.
g For theſe nations toke parte with the Egyptians.
h He calleth the ſlaughter of Gods enemies a ſacrifice, becauſe it is a thing that doeth pleaſe him, Iſa. 34,6.

North countrey [i] by the riuer Peráth.
11 Go vp vnto Gilead, [k] and take balme, ô
virgine, [l] the daughter of Egypt: in vaine
shalt thou vse many [m] medicines: *for* thou
shalt haue no health.
12 The nations haue heard of thy shame, &
thy crye hathe filled the land: for ẏ strong
hathe stombled against the strong *&* they
are fallen bothe together.
13 ¶ The worde that the Lord spake to Ieremiáh the Prophet, how Nebuchad-nezzár King of Babél shulde come and smite
the land of Egypt.
14 Publish in Egypt & declare in Migdól,
and proclaime in Noph, & in Tahpanhés,
& say, Stand stil, and prepare thee: for the
sworde shal deuoure rounde about thee.
15 Why are thy valiant men put backe? thei
colde not stand, because the Lord did driue them.
16 He made many to fall, and one fel vpon
another: and they said, Arise, let vs go a-
gaine to our [n] owne people, & to the land
of our natiuitie from the sworde of the
violent.
17 They did crye there, Pharaóh King of
Egypt, *and* of a great multitude [o] hathe
passed the time appointed.
18 As I liue, saith the King, whose Name is
the Lord of hostes, surely as Tabór *is* in
the mountaines, & as Carmél *is* in the sea:
so shal [p] it come.
19 O thou daughter dwellĩg in Egypt, make thee geare to go into captiuitie: for
Noph shalbe waste and desolate, without
an inhabitant.
20 Egypt *is like* a [q] faire calfe, *but* destruction cometh: out of the North it cometh.
21 Also her hired men [r] *are* in the middes of
her like fat calues: thei are also turned backe and fled away together: they colde not
stand, because the day of their destruction
was come vpon them, *&* the time of their
visitacion.
22 The voyce thereof shal go forthe like a
[s] serpent: for they shal marche with an armie, and come against [t] her with axes, as
hewers of wood.
23 They shal cut downe [u] her forest, saith ẏ
Lord: for they can not be counted, because
they are more then the [x] greshoppers, and
are innumerable.
24 The daughter of Egypt shalbe confounded: she shalbe deliuered into the hands of
the people of the North.
25 ¶ Thus saith the Lord of hostes, ẏ God
of Israél, Beholde, I wil visite the [y] cõmune people of No & Pharaóh, and Egypt,
with their gods & their Kings, euen Pharaóh, and all them that trust in him,
26 And I wil deliuer them into the hands
of those, that seke their liues, and into the
hãd of Nebuchad-nezzár King of Babél,
and into the hands of his seruantes, and
afterward she shal dwell as [z] in the olde time, saith the Lord.
27 ¶ [a] But feare not ẏ, ô my seruant Iaakób,
& be not thou afraied, ô Israél: for beholde, I wil deliuer thee from a farre *cõtrey*, &
thy sede from the land of their captiuitie,
and Iaakób shal returne and be in rest, and
prosperitie, & none shal make him afraid.
28 Feare thou not, ô Iaakób my seruãt, saith
the Lord: for I am with thee, and I wil vtterly destroy all the natiõs, whether I haue
driuen thee: but I wil not vtterly destroy
thee, but correct [b] thee by iudgement, and
not vtterly cut thee of.

i That is, at Charchemish.
k For at Gileád did grow moste soueraine balme for woundes.
l So called because Egypt had not yet bene ouercome by the enemie.
m He sheweth that no salue or medicine can preuaile where as God giueth the wounde.
n As they that shulde repent ẏ they helped the Egyptiãs.
o He derideth them ẇ shal impute their ouerthrowe to lacke of counsel & policie, or to fortune: and not obseruing of time, not considerĩg that it is Gods iust iudgement.
p To wit, that the Egyptians shalbe destroyed.
q They haue abundance of all things, and therefore are disobedient & proude.
r As vers. 9.
s They shalbe scarse able to speake for feare of the Caldeans.
t Meaning, Egypt.
u That is, they shal slay the great & mightie men of power.
x To wit, Nebuchad-nezzars armie.
y Some take the Ebrewe worde Amõn for the Kings name of No, that is of Alexandria.
z Meanĩg, that after ẏ space of fourty yeres Egypt shulde be restored Isa. 19,23. ezek 29,13.
a God comforteth all his ẏ were in captiuitie, but specially ẏ smale Church of the Iewes, whereof were Ieremiáh and Barúch, which remained amõg the Egyptiãs: for the Lord neuer forsaketh his, Isa. 44,1. chap. 30, 10.
b Read Chap. 10,24.

CHAP. XLVII.

The worde of the Lord against the Philistims.

1 The wordes of the Lord that came to
Ieremiáh the Prophet, against ẏ Philistims, before that Pharaóh smote [a] Azzáh.
2 Thus saith the Lord, Beholde, waters rise
vp out of the [b] North, & shalbe as a swelling flood, and shal ouerflowe the land, &
all that is therein, and the cities with them
that dwell therein: then the men shal crye,
& all the inhabitans of ẏ land shal howle,
3 At the noyce *&* stamping of the hoofes of
his strõg *horses*, at the noyce of his charets,
and at the rumbling of his wheles: the fathers shal not [c] loke backe to *their* children,
for feblenes of [d] hands,
4 Because of the daye that cometh to destroye all the Philistims, and to destroye
Tyrus, and Zidón, *&* all the rest, that take
their parte: for the Lord wil destroye the
Philistims, ẏ remnant of the yle of [e] Caphtór.
5 [f] Baldenes is come vpõ Azzáh: Ashkelón
is cut vp *with* the rest of their valleis. How
long wilt [g] thou cut thy self?
6 O thou sworde of the Lord, how long
wil it be or thou cease! turne againe into
thy scaberde, rest and be stil.
7 How can it [h] cease, seing the Lord hathe giuen it a charge against Ashkelón, &
against the sea bancke? euen there hathe he
appointed it.

a Which was also called Gazá a citie of ẏ Philistims
b He meaneth the armie of the Caldeans, Isa. 8,8.
c The great feare shal take away their natural affection.
d Their heart shal so faile them.
e For ẏ Caphtorims, which are also called Cappadociãs, had destroied in olde time the Philistims and dwelt in their land euẽ to Gazá, Deu. 2,23.
f They haue pulled of their heere for sorowe & heauines.
g As the heathen vsed in their mourniĩg which ẏ Lord forbade his people to do, Deut. 14,1.
h Meaning, ẏ it is not possible that the wicked shulde by any meanes escape or stay the Lord, whẽ he wil take vengeance.

CHAP. XLVIII.

The worde of the Lord against the Moabites. 26 Because of their pride and crueltie.

1 Concerning Moáb, thus saith ẏ Lord
of hostes, the God of Israél, Wo
vnto [a] Nebó: for it is wasted: Kiriatháim
is confounded *&* taken: Misgáb is confoũ
ded and afraied.
2 Moáb shal boast no more of Heshbón: *for*
thei haue deuised euil against it. [b] Come,
and let vs destroye it, that it be no more a
nacion: also thou shalt be destroyed, [c] ô
Madmén, *and* the sworde shal pursue thee.
3 A voice of crying *shalbe* from Horonáim
with desolacion & great destruction.

a These were cities of the Moabites, ẇ Nebuchad-nezzár toke before he wẽt to fight against Nechó Kĩg of Egypt.
b Thus shal the Babylonians incourage one another.
c Read Isa. 15,10.

4 Moáb is destroyed: her litle ones haue
caused their crye to be heard.
5 For at the going vp of [d] Luhith, the mourner
ner shal go vp with weping: for in ye going
downe of Horonáim, the enemies haue
heard a crye of destruction,
6 Flee and saue your liues, and be like vnto
the [e] heath in the wildernes.
7 For because thou hast trusted in thy [f] workes and in thy treasures, thou shalt also be
taken, and [g] Chemósh shal go forth into
captiuitie with his Priests and his princes
together.
8 And ye destroier shal come vpon all cities,
& no citie shal escape: the valley also shal
perish and the plaine shalbe destroied as
the Lord hathe spoken.
9 Giue wings vnto Moáb, that it may flee
and get away: for the cities thereof shalbe
desolate, without any to dwell therein.
10 [h] Cursed *be he* that doeth the worke of
ye Lord [*] negligently, and cursed *be he* that
kepeth backe his sworde from blood.
11 Moáb hathe bene at rest from his youth,
and he hathe setled on his lees, & hathe not
bene [i] powred from vessel to vessel, nether
hathe he gone into captiuitie: therefore his
taste remained in him and his sent is not
changed.
12 ¶ Therefore beholde, ye daies come, saith
the Lord, that I wil send vnto him suche as
shal cary him away, and shal emptie his
vessels, and breake their bottels.
13 And Moáb shal be ashamed of Chemósh
as the house of Israél was ashamed of
[k] Beth-él their confidence.
14 How thinke you *thus*, We are mightie &
strong men of warre?
15 Moáb is destroyed, and his cities [*] burnt
vp, & his chosen yong mé are gone downe
to slaughter, saith the King, whose name
is, The Lord of hostes.
16 The destruction of Moáb is readie to
come, and his plague hasteth fast.
17 All ye ye are about him, mourne for him,
& all ye that knowe his name, say, [l] How is
the strong staffe broken, *&* the beautiful
rod!
18 Thou daughter that doest inhabite Dibón, come downe from *thy* glorie, & sit in
thirst: for the destroyer of Moáb shal come vp vpon thee, *and* he shal destroy thy
strong holdes.
19 Thou that dwellest in Aroér, stád by the
way, and beholde: aske him that fleeth and
that escapeth, *&* say, What is done?
20 [m] Moáb is confounded: for it is destroyed: howle, and crye, tel ye it in Arnón, that
Moáb is made waste,
21 And iudgement is come vpon the plaine
countrey, vpon Holón & vpon Iahazáh,
and vpon Mephâath,
22 And vpon Dibón, and vpon Nebó, and

d Horonáim & Luhith were two places whereby the Moabites shulde flee, Isa. 15,5

e Hide your selues in baren places, where the enemie wil not pursue after you, Chap. 17, 6.

f That is, the idoles which are the workes of thine hãds. Some read in thy possessions, for so ye worde may signifie, as 1. Sam. 25,2.

g Bothe thy great idole & his mainteiners shalbe led away captiues, so that they shal then knowe that it is in vaine to loke for helpe at idoles, Isa. 15,2.

h He sheweth that God wolde punish the Caldeans, if they did not destroy the Egyptians and that with a courage, and calleth this executing of his vengeance against his enemies his worke: thogh the Caldeãs soght another end, Isa. 10,12.

* Or, deceitfully

i Hathe not bene remoued as the Iewes haue, but hath liued at ease and as a wine ye fedeth him self on his lees

k As the calfe of Beth-él was not able to deliuer the Israelites: no more shal Chemósh deliuer the Moabites.

* Ebr. gone vp, or destroyed.

l How are thei destroied that put their trust in their strength and riches!

m Thus they that flee, shal answer.

vpon the house of Diblatháim,
23 And vpon Kiriatháim, and vpon Beth-
gamúl, and vpon Beth-meón,
24 And vpon Kerióth, and vpon Bozráh, &
vpon all the cities of the land of Moáb
farre or nere.
25 The [n] horne of Moáb is cut of, and his
arme is broken, saith the Lord.
26 Make ye him [o] drunken: for he magnified
him self against the Lord: Moáb shal [*] wal-
low in his vomite, and he also shal be in
derision.
27 For didest not ye deride Israél, as thogh
he had bene founde among theues? for
when thou speakest of him, thou art [p] moued.
28 O ye that dwell in Moáb, leaue the cities, and dwell in the rockes, and be like the
doue, that maketh her neste in the sides of
the holes mouth.
29 * We haue heard the pride of Moáb (*he is*
exceding proude) his stoutnes, and his arrogancie, and his pride, and the hautenes
of his heart.
30 I knowe his wrath, saith the Lord, [q] but
it shal not *be so*: *&* his dissimulacions, *for*
thei do not right.
31 [r] Therefore wil I howle for Moáb, and I
wil crye out for all Moáb: *mine heart* shal
mourne for the men of Kir-héres.
32 O vine of Sibmáh, I wil wepe for thee, as
I wept for Iazér: thy plantes are gone ouer
the sea, thei are come to the sea [s] of Iazér:
the destroyer is fallen vpon thy sommer
frutes, and vpon thy vintage,
33 And ioye, and gladnes is taken from the
plentiful field & from the land of Moáb:
and I haue caused wine to faile from the
wine presse: none shal tread with showtĩg:
their showting *shalbe* no showting.
34 Frõ the crye of Heshbón vnto Elaléh *&*
vnto Iaház haue thei made their noyse
from Zóar vnto Horonáim, the [t] heiffer of
thre yere olde *shal go lowing*: for the waters
also of Nimrím shalbe wasted.
35 Moreouer, I wil cause to cease in Moáb,
saith the Lord, him that offred in the high
places, and him that burneth incense to his
gods.
36 Therefore mine heart shal soũd for Moáb like a [u] shaume & mine heart shal soũde
like a shaume for the men of Kir-héres, because the riches that he hathe gottẽ, is perished.
37 * For euery head shalbe [*] balde, and euery
bearde plucked: vpon all the handes shalbe cuttings, and vpon the loynes sackeclothe.
38 *And* mourning shalbe vpon all the house toppes of Moáb and in all the stretes
thereof: for I haue brokẽ Moáb like a vessel wherein is no pleasure, saith the Lord.
39 Thei shal howle, *saying*, How is he destroied

n That is, his power and strength.

o He willed ye Caldeans to lay afflictions ynough vpon them, til they be like drũken men that fall downe to their shame and are derided of all

* Or, shal be ful or clappe his hands.

p Thou reioycest to heare of his miserie.

Isa. 16,6.

q He shal not execute his malice against his neighbours

r Read Isa. 16, 1.

s Which citie was in the vtmoste border of Moáb: and hereby he signifieth that the whole land shulde be destroied & the peole caried away.

t Read Isa. 15,5

u Their custome was to play on flutes or instruments, heauie & graue tunes at buryales and in the time of mourning, as Mat. 9,23.

Isa. 15,3. ezek. 7,18.

* Or, shauen.

troyed? how hathe Moáb turned the backe
with ſhame? ſo ſhal Moáb be a deriſion, &
a feare to all them about him.
40 For thus ſaith the Lord, Beholde, [x] he
ſhal flee as an egle, & ſhal ſpread his wings
ouer Moáb.
41 The cities are taken and the ſtrong holdes are wonne, & the mightie mens hearts
in Moáb at that day ſhalbe as the heart
of a woman in trauail.
42 And Moáb ſhalbe deſtroyed from being
a people, becauſe he hathe ſet vp him ſelf
againſt the Lord.
43 [y] Feare, and pit and ſnare *ſhalbe* vpõ thee,
ô inhabitant of Moáb, ſaith the Lord.
44 He that eſcapeth from the feare, ſhal fall
in the pit, & he that getteth vp out of the
pit, ſhalbe takẽ in the ſnare: for I wil bring
vpon it, *euen* vpon Moáb, the yere of their
viſitation, ſaith the Lord.
45 They that fled, ſtode vnder ỹ ſhadowe
[z] of Heſhbón, becauſe of the force: for [a] ỹ
fyre came out of Heſhbón, & a flame frõ
Sihón, and deuoured the corner of Moáb,
and the top of the ſeditious children.
46 Wo *be* vnto thee, ô Moáb: the people of
[b] Chemóſh periſheth: for thy ſonnes are
taken captiues, and thy daughters *led* into
captiuitie.
47 Yet wil I bring againe the captiuitie of
Moáb in the [c] later daies, ſaith the Lord.
Thus farre of the iudgement of Moáb.

x That is, Nebuchad-nezzár as Chap. 49, 22.
y He that eſcapeth one dãger, ſhalbe taken of another Iſa. 24, 17.
z Thei fled thether thinking to haue ſuccour of the Amorites.
a The Amorites had deſtroied the Moabites in times paſt, and now becauſe of their power, ỹ Moabites ſhal ſeke to them for helpe.
b Which vanted thẽſelues of their idole as thogh he colde haue defended them.
c That is, thei ſhalbe reſtored by the Meſsiáh.

CHAP. XLIX.

1 The worde of the Lord againſt the Ammonites, 7 Idumea, 23 Damaſcus, 28 Kedar, 34 & Elám.

1 VNto the children of [a] Ammón thus
ſaith the Lord, Hathe Iſraél no ſonnes? or hathe he none heire? Why *then* hathe their [b] King poſſeſſed Gad? and his
people dwell in [c] his cities?
2 Therefore beholde, the dayes come,
ſaith the Lord, that I wil cauſe a noyſe of
warre to be heard in [d] Rabbáh of the Ammonites, and it ſhalbe a deſolate heape, &
her daughters ſhalbe burnt with fyre: then
ſhal Iſraél poſſeſſe thoſe that poſſeſſed
him, ſaith the Lord.
3 Howle, ô Heſhbón, for Ai is waſted: crye
ye daughters of Rabbáh: girde you with
ſackeclothe: mourne & runne to & fro by
ỹ hedges: for their King ſhal go into captiuitie, & his Prieſts, and his princes likewiſe.
4 Wherefore glorieſt thou in the [e] valleis?
thy valley floweth away, ô rebellious daughter: ſhe truſted in her treaſures, *ſaying*,
Who ſhal come vnto me?
5 Beholde, I wil bring [f] a feare vpon thee,
ſaith the Lord God of hoſtes, of all thoſe
that be about thee, and ye ſhalbe ſcatred
euerie man [g] right forthe, & none ſhal ga
ther him that fleeth.
6 And [h] afterward I wil bring againe the
captiuitie of the children of Ammón.
7 ¶ To Edóm thus ſaith the Lord of hoſtes,
Is wiſdome no more in [i] Temán? is cõuſel
periſhed from *their* children? is their wiſdome vaniſhed?
8 Flee, ye inhabitants of Dedán ([k] they a-
re turned backe, and haue conſulted to
dwell) for I haue broght the deſtruction of
Eſáu vpon him, *and* the time of his viſitation.
9 If the [l] grape gatherers come to thee,
wolde they not leaue *ſome* grapes? if theues
come by night, they wil deſtroye til they
haue ynough.
10 For I haue diſcouered Eſáu: I haue vncouered his ſecrets, and he ſhal not be a-
ble to hide him ſelf: his ſede is waſted, and
his brethrẽ and his neighbours, and there
ſhalbe none *to ſay*,
11 Leaue thy [m] fatherles children, & I wil
preſerue them aliue, and let thy widowes
truſt in me.
12 For thus ſaith the Lord, [n] Beholde, thei
whoſe iudgement was not to drinke of the
cuppe, haue aſſuredly drunkẽ, and art thou
he that ſhal eſcape fre? thou ſhalt not go
fre, but thou ſhalt ſurely drinke of it.
13 For I haue ſworne by my ſelf, ſaith the
Lord, that [o] Bozráh ſhal be waſte, and for
a reproche, and a deſolation, and a curſe,
and all the cities thereof ſhalbe perpetual
deſolations.
14 I haue heard a rumour from the Lord, &
an embaſſadour is ſent vnto the heathen,
ſaying, Gather you together, and come a-
gainſt [p] her, and riſe vp to the battel.
15 For lo, I wil make thee but ſmale among
the heathen, and deſpiſed among men.
16 Thy [*] feare, *and* the pride of thine heart hathe deceiued thee, thou that dwelleſt in the clefts of the rocke, and kepeſt
the height of the hil: thogh thou ſhulde
make thy neſt as hie as the egle, I wil bring
thee downe from thence, ſaith the Lord.
17 ¶ Alſo Edóm ſhalbe deſolate: euerie one
that goeth by it, ſhalbe aſtoniſhed, & ſhal
hiſſe at all the plagues thereof,
18 As in the ouerthrowe of Sodóm, and of
Gomoráh, and the places thereof nere a-
bout, ſaith the Lord: no man ſhal dwell
there, nether ſhal the ſonnes of men remaine in it.
19 Beholde, [q] he ſhal come vp like a lyon
from the ſwelling of Iordén vnto the
ſtrong dwelling place: for I wil make *Iſraél* to reſt, *euen* I wil make [r] him to haſte
away from her, & who is a choſen mã that
I may appoint againſt her? for who is like
me? & who wil appoint me ỹ time? & who
is the [ſ] ſhepherd that wil ſtand before me?
20 Therefore heare the cõuſel of the Lord
that he hathe deuiſed againſt Edóm, & his
purpoſe ỹ he hathe cõceiued againſt ỹ in-

a They were ſeparated frõ the Moabites by the riuer Arnón, & after that the ten tribes were caryed away into captiuitie, they inuaded ỹ countrey of Gad.
b To wit, of ỹ Ammonites.
c Meaning, of the Iſraelites.
d Which was one of ỹ chief cities of the Ammonites, as were Heſhbón and Ai: there was alſo a citie called Heſhbón amõg ỹ Moabites
e In thy plentiful countrei.
f Signifying ỹ power and riches can not preuaile when as God wil execute his iudgements.
g That is, without loking backe and as euerie one can finde away to eſcape.
h In the time of Chriſt whẽ ỹ Gentiles ſhal be called.
i Which was a citie of Edóm called by the name of Temã Eliphaz ſonne who came of Eſáu.
k The enemies that ſhal diſſẽble as thogh thei fled away, ſhal turne backe, & inuade your land, and poſſeſſe it.
l Meaning that God wolde vtterly deſtroy them, and not ſpare one, thogh the grape gatherers leaue ſome grapes, & theues ſeke but til they haue ynough, Obad. 1, 5.
m The deſtruction ſhalbe ſo great, that there ſhalbe none left to take care ouer ỹ widdowes, & fatherles.
n I haue not ſpared mine owne people, & how ſhulde I pitie thee?
o Which was a chief citie of Edóm.
p That is, Bozráh.
* Or, idole.
q To wit, Nebuchad-nezzár after he hathe ouercome Iudáh, & is ment by the ſwelling of Iordén, ſhal come againſt mount Seir & Edóm.
r That is, the Iſraelites, whome the Edomites kept as priſoners to haſte away from thence.
ſ The captaine and gouernour of the armie, meaning, Nebuchad-nezzár.

t They shal not be able to resist his petit captaines.
u To wit, the enemie.

habitans of Temán: surely the least [t] of the
flocke shal drawe them out: surely [u] he shal
make their habitations desolate with thē.
21 The earth is moued at the noyce of their
fall: the crye of their voyce is heard in the
red Sea.
22 Beholde, he shal come vp, and flie as the
egle, [x] and spread his wings ouer Bozráh,
and at that day shal the heart of the strōg
men of Edóm be as the heart of a woman
in trauail.

x As Chap 48, 40. was said of Moáb.

y Which was the chief citie of Syria, whereby he meaneth the whole countrey.

23 ¶ Vnto [y] Damascus *he saith*, Hamáth is
confoūded and Arpád, for thei haue heard
euil tidings, and they are faint hearted *as*
one on the feareful sea that can not rest.
24 Damascus is discouraged, *and* turneth
her self to flight [z] and feare hathe seased
her: anguish & sorowes haue taken her as
a woman in trauail.

z When she heard the sudden coming of the enemie.

a He speaketh this in the persone of ye King and of them of the countrey who shal wonder to se Damascus ye chief citie destroyed.

25 How is the glorious [a] citie not reserued,
the citie?
26 Therefore her yong mē shal fall in her
stretes, and all her men of warre shalbe
cut of in that day, saith the Lord of hostes.
27 And I wil kindle a fyre in the walle of
Damascus, which shal cōsume the palaces
of [b] Ben-hadád.

b Who was King of Syria, 1. King. 20, 26, and had buylt these palaces, which were stil called the palaces of Ben-hadád.

c Meaning the Arabians, and theirborderers

28 ¶ Vnto [c] Kedár, and to the kingdomes
of Hazór, which Nebuchad-nezzár King
of Babél shal smite, thus saith the Lord,
Arise, & go vp vnto Kedár, and destroye
the men of the East.
29 Their tentes and their flockes shal they
take away: yea, they shal take to thē selues
their [d] curtaines, and all their vessels, and
their camels & they shal crye vnto them,
Feare is on euerie side.

d Because thei vsed to dwell in tentes, he nameth ye things that perteine thereunto.

e The enemies wil dwell in your places.

30 Flee, get you farre of (e thei haue consulted to dwell) ô ye inhabitants of Hazór,
saith ye Lord: for Nebuchad-nezzár King
of Babél hathe taken counsel against you,
and hathe deuised a purpose against you.
31 [f] Arise, & get you vp vnto the welthie
nation that dwelleth without care, saith
the Lord, which haue nether gates nor
barres, *but* dwell alone.

f He sheweth that they of Hazór wil flee to the Arabiās for succour, but that shal not auaile thē.

32 And their camels shalbe a boutie, and the
multitude of their cattel a spoile, and I
wil scatter thē into all windes, and to the
vtmost corners, and I wil bring their destruction from all the sides thereof, saith
the Lord.
33 And Hazór shalbe a dwelling for dragons, & desolation for euer: there shal no
man dwell there, nor the sonnes of men remaine in it.
34 ¶ The wordes of the Lord that came to
Ieremiáh the Prophet, cōcerning [g] Elám,
in the beginning of the reigne of Zedekiáh King of Iudáh, saying,
35 Thus saith the Lord of hostes, Beholde,
I wil breake the [h] bowe of Elám, *euen* the
chief of their strength.

g That is, Persia, so called of Elám the sonne of Shem.
h Because the Persians were good archers, he sheweth ye the thing wherein they put their trust, shul de not profite them.

36 And vpon Elám I wil bring the foure
winds frō the foure quarters of heauen, &
wil scattre thē towardes all these windes,
and there shalbe no nation, whether the
fugitiues of Elám shal not come.
37 For I wil cause Elám to be afraied before their enemies, and before them that seke their liues, and wil bring vpon them a
plague, *euen* the indignation of my wrath,
saith the Lord, and I wil send the sworde
after them til I haue consumed them.
38 And I wil set my [i] throne in Elám, and I
wil destroye *bothe* the King and the princes from thēce, saith the Lord: but [k] in the
latter dayes I wil bring againe the captiuitie of Elám, saith the Lord.

i I wil place Nebuchad-nezzár there, and in these propheceis Ieremiáh speaketh of those countreies, which shulde be subdued vnder the first of those foure monarchies whereof Daniel maketh mencion.
k This may be referred to the empire of the Persians, and Medes after ye Caldeans, or vnto the time of Christ, as Chap. 48, 47.

CHAP. L.

He prophecieth the destruction of Babylon, and the deliuerance of Israél, which was in captiuitie.

1 THe worde that the Lord spake, concerning Babél, & cōcerning the land
of the Caldeans by the [*] ministerie of Ieremiáh the Prophet.

* Ebr. hand.

2 Declare among the nations, and publish
it, and set vp a standart, proclaime it & cō
ceile it not: say, [a] Babél is taken, Bel is con
foūded, [b] Merodách is broken downe: her
idoles are confoūded, *and* their images are
burst in pieces.
3 For out of the North there [c] cometh vp
a nation against her, which shal make her
land waste, and none shal dwell therein:
they shal flee, *and* departe, bothe man and
beast.
4 In those dayes, and at that time, saith the
Lord, the children of Israél shal [d] come,
they, and the children of Iudáh together,
going, and [e] weping shal they go, and seke
the Lord their God.
5 They shal aske the waye to Zión, with
their faces thetherward, *saying*, Come, and
let vs cleaue to the Lord in a perpetual
couenant that shal not be forgotten.

a After that God hathe vsed the Babylonians seruice to punish other nations, he sheweth that their turne shal come to be punished.
b These were two of their chief idoles.
c To wit, the Medes, and the Persians.
d When Cyrus shal take Babél.
e Read Chap. 31, 9.

6 ¶ My people hathe bene *as* lost shepe: their
[f] shepherdes haue caused them to go a-
stray, and haue turned them away to the
mountaines: they haue gone from [g] mou-
taine to hil, & forgottē their resting place.
7 All that found them, haue deuoured thē,
and their enemies said, We offend not because they haue sinned against the Lord,
[h] the habitation of iustice, euen the Lord
the hope of their fathers.
8 [i] Flee from the middes of Babél, and departe out of the land of the Caldeans, and
be ye as the he goates [k] before the flocke.
9 For lo, I wil raise, and cause to come vp
against Babél a multitude of mightie nations from the North countrey, and thei
shal set them selues in aray against her,
whereby she shalbe taken: their arrowes
shalbe as of a strong man, which is expert
for none shal returne in vaine.

f Their gouernours & ministers by their examples haue prouoked them to idolatrie.
g They haue commit idolatrie in euerie place.
h For the Lord dwelt among them in his Téple, and wolde haue mainteined thē by his iustice against their enemies.
i When God shal deliuer you by Cyrus.
k That is, moste forward and without feare.

10 And Caldea shalbe a spoile:all that spoile her, [l] shalbe satisfied,saith the Lord.

l Shalbe made riche thereby.

11 Because ye were glad and reioyced in destroying mine heritage, & because ye are
growen fat,as the calues in the grasse,[m] &
neyed like strong *horses*,

m For ioye of the victorie,ŷ ye had against my people.

12 *Therefore* your mothers shalbe sore confoūded,and she that bare you,shalbe ashamed : beholde, the vttermost of the nations *shalbe* a desert, a drye land, & a wildernes.
13 Because of the wrath of the Lord it shal
not be inhabited, but shalbe wholy deso-
late:euerie one that goeth by Babél,shal
be astonished, [n] & hisse at all her plagues.
14 [o] Put your selues in araye against Babél
round about : all ye that bend the bowe,
shoote at her,spare no arrowes:for she hathe [p] sinned against the Lord.

n In signe of contempt, and disdaine.
o He speaketh to the enemies the Medes and Persians.
p Thogh the Lord called ŷ Babyloniās his seruants , and their worke his worke in punishing his people,yet because they did it not to glorifie God , but for their owne malice , & to profite them selues,it is here called sinne.

15 Crye against her round about: she hathe
"giuen her hand:her foundacions are fallē,
& her walles are destroyed:for it is ŷ ven
geance of the Lord: take vengeance vpon
her: as she hathe done,do vnto her.

"Or,yelded or made peace.

16 Destroye the [q] sower from Babél, and
him that handleth the sieth in the time of
haruest:because of the sworde of the oppressour they shal turne euerie one to his
people,and they shal flee euerie one to his
owne land.

q Destroye her so that none be left to labour the groūde or to take ŷ frute thereof.

17 Israél *is like* scattered shepe:the lyons haue dispersed them : first the King [r] of Asshúr hathe deuoured him,& last this Nebuchad-nezzár King of Babél hathe brokē
[s] his bones.

r Meaning, Tiglath-Pelezár who caryed away the ten tribes.
s He caryed away the rest, to wit, Iudáh, & Beniamin.

18 Therefore thus saith the Lord of hostes
the God of Israél,Beholde,I wil visite the
King of Babél,and his land,as I haue visited the King of Asshúr.
19 And I wil bring Israél againe to his ha-
bitation:he shal fede on Carmél and Bashán, and his soule shalbe satisfied vpon
the mount Ephráim and Gileád.
20 In those dayes, and at that time, saith
the Lord, the iniquitie of Israél shalbe
soght for,and there shal be none: and the
sinnes of Iudáh, & they shal not be found:
for I wil be merciful vnto them, whome I
reserue.
21 Go vp against the land of the [t] rebelles,
euen against it,and against the inhabitants
* of " Pekód : destroye, and lay it waste
after them, saith the Lord, and do according to all that I haue commanded thee.

t That is, Babylon:thus the Lord raiseth vp Cyrus.
Eze.23,23.
"Or,of thē that shulde be visited.

22 A crye of battel *is* in the land,& of great
destruction.
23 How is the [u] hāmer of the whole worlde
destroyed,and broken! how is Babél become desolate among the nations!

u Nebuchad-nezzár, who had smitten downe all the princes , and people of the worlde.

24 I haue snared thee, and thou art taken,
ô Babél , and thou wast not aware : thou
art founde, and also caught,because thou
hast striuen against the Lord.
25 The Lord hathe opened his treasure,and
hathe broght forthe the weapons of his
wrath : for this is the worke of the Lord
God of hostes in ŷ land of the Caldeans.
26 Come against her " frō the vtmost bor-
der:open her store houses: tread on her as
on sheaues,and destroie her vtterly:let nothing of her be left.

"Ebr.from the end.

27 Destroie all her [x] bullockes: let them go
downe to the slaughter. Wo vnto them,
for their day is come,*and* the time of their
visitation.

x Her princes and mightie men.

28 The voice of them that [y] flee,and escape out of the land of Babél to declare in
Zión ŷ vengeance of the Lord our God,
and the vengeance of his Temple.

y Of ŷ Iewes which shulde be deliuered by Cyrus.

29 Call vp the archers against Babél:all ye
that bend ŷ bowe, besiege it rounde about:
let none thereof escape:*recompence her
according to her worke, *and* according to
all that she hathe done,do vnto her:for she
hathe bene proude against the Lord , *euen*
against the holy one of Israél.

Reuel.18,6.

30 Therefore shal her yong men fall in the
stretes,and all her men of warre shalbe destroied in that day,saith the Lord.
31 Beholde, I *come* vnto thee,ô proude *man*,
saith the Lord God of hostes : for thy day
is come,*euē* the time that I wil visite thee.
32 And the proude shal stomble and fall, &
none shal raise him vp : and I wil kindle
a fyre in his cities , and it shal deuoure all
rounde about him.
33 Thus saith the Lord of hostes,The children of Israél , and the children of Iudáh
were oppressed together:and all that toke
them captiues,helde them , *and* wolde not
let them go.
34 *But* their strong redemer,whose Name *is*
the Lord of hostes,he shal mainteine their
cause,that he may giue rest to the land, [z]&
disquiet the inhabitants of Babél.

z He sheweth ŷ when God executeth his iudgements against his enemies, that his Church shal then haue rest.

35 A sworde *is* vpon the Caldeans, saith
the Lord,and vpon the inhabitants of Babél , and vpon her princes , and vpon her
wise men.
36 A sworde *is* vpon the " sothesayers,and
thei shal dote:a sworde *is* vpon her strong
men,and thei shal be afraied.

"Ebr. Lyers.

37 A sworde *is* vpon their horses and vpon
their charets, and vpon all the multitude
that are in the middes of her,and thei shal
be like women:a sworde *is* vpon her treasures,and thei shal be spoiled.
38 A [a] drought *is* vpon her waters,and thei
shal be dryed vp:for it is the lād of grauē
images,and thei dote vpon their idoles.

a For Cyrus did cut the riuer Euphrates and deuided ŷ course thereof into many streames,so ŷ it might be passed ouer as thogh there had bene no water : which thing he did by the counsel of two of Belshazzars captaines , who cōspired agaīst their King, because he had gelded the one of them in despite, and slaine the sonne of the other.

39 Therefore ŷ [b] Ziims with the Iims shal
dwell *there*,&"the ostriches shal dwell the-
rein:for it shal be no more inhabited, nether shal it be inhabited from generacion
vnto generacion.

b Read Isa.13,21
"Ebr. sonnes of the ostriches , or yong.

40 As God destroied* Sodóm and Gomo-

Gen.19,24. Isa.13,19.

ráh with the places thereof nere about,
saith the Lord: *so* shal no man dwell there,
nether shal ẏ sonne of mã remaine therein.
41 ¶ Beholde, a people shal come from the
North, and a great natiõ, & manie Kings
shal be raised vp from [c] the coastes of the
earth.

c Meaning, ẏ the Persians shulde gather their armie of manie nations.

42 Thei shal holde ẏ bowe & the buckeler:
they are cruel & vnmerciful: their voyce
shal roare like the sea, and they shal ride
vpon horses, & be put in aray like men to
ẏ battel against thee, ô daughter of Babél.
43 The King of Babél hathe heard the report of them, and his hands [d] waxed feble:
sorowe came vpon him, *euen* sorowe as of
a woman in trauail.

d Which is ment of Belshazzár, Dan. 5,6.

44 Beholde, he *shal come vp like a lyon
frõ the swelling of Iordén vnto the strõg
habitation: for I wil make *Israél* to rest, &
I wil make them to haste away from her:
and who is a chosen man that I may appoint against her? for who is like me, &
who wil appoint me the time? and who is
the [e] shepherd that wil stand before me?

Chap. 49,19.

e Read Chap. 49,19.

45 Therefore heare the cõsel of the Lord
that he hathe deuised against Babél, and
his purpose ẏ he hathe conceiued against
the land of the Caldeans: surely the least
of the flocke shal drawe them out: surely
he shal make *their* habitatiõ desolate w̄ thẽ.
46 At the noyse of the winning of Babél
the earth is moued, and the crye is heard
among the nations.

CHAP. LI.

5 Why Babylon is destroyed. 41 The vaine confidence of the Babylonians. 43 The vanitie of idolaters. 59 Ieremiáh giueth his boke to Seraiáh.

1 THus saith the Lord, Beholde, I wil rai
se vp against Babél, and against the
inhabitants" that lift vp *their* heart against
me, a destroying [a] winde,
2 And wil send vnto Babél fanners that
shal fanne her, and shal emptie her land:
for in ẏ day of trouble thei shalbe against
her on euerie side.

"Or, of the land that riseth vp.

a The Medes, and Persians, ẏ shal destroye them as the winde doeth ẏ chaffe.

3 Also to the bender that bendeth his bowe,
and to him that lifteth him self vp in his
brigandine, *wil I say*, Spare not her yong
men, but destroye all her hoste.
4 Thus the slaine shal fall in the lãd of the
Caldeans, and they that are thrust through
in her stretes.
5 For Israél hathe bene no [b] widow, nor Iudáh from his God, from the Lord of hostes, thogh their lãd was filled with sinne
against the holy one of Israél.
6 ¶ [c] Flee out of the middes of Babél, & deliuer euerie mã his soule: be not destroyed
in her iniquitie: for this is the time of the
Lords vengeance: he wil rendre vnto her
a recompence.
7 Babél *hathe bene as* a golden cuppe in the
[d] Lords hand, that made all the earth drun-

b Thogh they were forsaken for a time, yet they were not vtterly cast of as thogh their housband were dead.

c He sheweth that there remaineth nothing for them that abide in Babylon, but destruction, Chap. 17,6. & 48,6.

d By whome ẏ Lord powred out the drinke of his vengeãce, to whome it pleased him.

ken: the nacions haue drunken of her wine, therefore do the nacions [e] rage.
8 *Babél is suddẽly fallen, & destroied: howle for her, bring balme for her sore, if she
may be healed.

e For ẏ great afflictions that thei haue felt by the Babylonians.

Isa. 21,9. reuel. 14,8.

9 We wolde haue cured Babél, but she colde not be healed: forsake her, and let [f] vs
go euerie one into his owne countreie: for
her iudgement is come vp vnto heauen, &
is lifted vp to the cloudes.

f Thus ẏ people of God exhort one another to go to Zión and praise God.

10 The Lord hathe broght forthe our
[g] righteousnes: come and let vs declare
in Zión the worke of the Lord our God.
11 Make bright the arrowes: " gather ẏ shil-
des: the Lord hathe raised vp the spirit
of the King of the Medes: for his purpose is against Babél to destroie it, because
it is the [h] vengeance of the Lord, *and* the
vengeance of his Temple.

g In approuing our cause and punishing our enemies.

"Or, fil, or multiplie.

h For the wrong done to his people and to his Temple Chap. 50,28.

12 Set vp the standart vpon the walles of
Babél, make the watche strong: set vp
the watchmen: prepare the skoutes: for the
Lord hathe bothe deuised, and done that
which he spake against the inhabitants of
Babél.
13 O thou that dwellest vpõ many [i] waters,
abundant in treasures, thine end is come,
euen the " end of thy couetousnes.
14 The Lord of hostes hathe sworne by
" him * selfe, *saying*, Surely I wil fil thee
with men, as with caterpillers, and thei
shal crye and shoute against thee.

i For ẏ land of Caldea was ful of riuers w̄ ran into Euphrates.

"Or, measure.

"Ebr. his soule.

Amos 6,8.

15 *He hathe made the earth by his power,
and established the worlde by his wisdome, and hathe stretched out the heauen
by his discretion.

Chap. 10,12.

16 He giueth by *his* voice the multitude of
waters in the heauen, and he causeth the
cloudes to ascend frõ the ends of ẏ earth:
he turneth lightnings to raine, and bringeth forthe the winde out of his treasures.
17 Euerie man is a beast by *his owne* [k] knowledge: euerie founder is cõfounded by the
grauen image: for his melting is but fal-
sehod and there is no breth therein.

k Read Chap. 10,14.

18 Thei are vanitie, & the worke of errors:
in the time of their [l] visitacion they shal
perish.
19 The [m] porcion of Iaakób *is* not like
them: for he is the maker of all things,
and *Israél is* the rod of his inheritance:
the Lord of hostes *is* his Name.
20 Thou art mine [n] hammer, *and* weapons
of warre: for with thee wil I breake the
nations, and with thee wil I destroie
kingdomes,
21 And by thee wil I breake horse and horseman, and by thee wil I breake the char-
ret and him that rideth therein.
22 By thee also wil I breake man & womã,
and by thee wil I breake olde and yong,
and by thee wil I breake the yong man &

l When God shal execute his vengeance.

m That is, the true God of Israél is not like to these idoles: for he can helpe when all things are desperate.

n He meaneth the Medes and Persians, as he did before call the Babylonians his hammer, Chap. 50, 23.

the maid.
23 I wil also breake by thee the shepherd &
his flocke, & by thee wil I breake the hous
bandman and his yoke of oxen, & by thee
wil I breake the dukes and princes.
24 And I wil rẽdre vnto Babél, & to all the
inhabitans of the Caldeans all their euil,
that thei haue done in Zión, *euen* in your
sight, saith the Lord.
25 Beholde, I *come* vnto thee, ô destroying
[o] mountaine, saith the Lord, which de-
stroiest all the earth: and I wil stretch out
mine hand vpon thee, and roll thee downe
from the [p] rockes, & wil make thee a burnt
mountaine.
26 Thei shal not take of thee a stone for a
corner, nor a stone for fundaciõs, but thou
shalt be destroied for euer, saith the Lord.
27 Set vp a standart in the land: blowe the
trumpets among the nacions: prepare the
naciõs against her: call vp the kingdomes
[q] of Ararát, Minní, and Aschenáz against
her: appoint the prince against her: cause horses to come vp as the rough caterpillers.
28 Prepare against her the nacions with the
Kings of the Medes, the dukes thereof, &
the princes thereof, and all the land of his
dominion.
29 And the land shal tremble & sorowe: for
the deuise of the Lord shal be performed
against Babél, to make the land of Babél
waste without an inhabitant.
30 The strõg men of Babél haue ceased to
fight: thei haue remained in their holdes:
their strength hathe failed, *and* thei were
like women: thei haue burnt her dwelling
places, *and* her barres are broken.
31 A post shal runne to mete the post, and a
messenger to mete the messenger, to shewe
the King of Babél, that his citie is taken
on a [r] side thereof,
32 And that the passages are stopped, and ye
redes burnt with fyre, and the mẽ of warre troubled.
33 For thus saith ye Lord of hostes the God
of Israél, The daughter of Babél *is* like a
thresshing floore: the time of her thresshing *is come*: yet a litle while, and the time
of her haruest [s] shal come.
34 Nebuchad-nezzár ye King of Babél hathe [t] deuoured me, & destroied me: he hathe made me an emptie vessel: he swalowed me vp like a dragon, and filled his belie
with my delicates, & hathe cast me out.
35 The spoile of me, & that which was left
of me, *is broght* vnto Babél, shal the inhabitant of Zión say: and my blood vnto
the inhabitants of Caldea, shal Ierusalém say.
36 Therefore thus saith the Lord, Beholde, I wil mainteine thy [u] cause, and take
vengeance for thee, and I wil drye vp the

o Not that Babylon stode on a mountaine, but because it was strong and semed inuincible

p From thy strong holdes and fortresses

q By these thre nations he meaneth Armenia the hier, and Armenia the lower, and Sythia: for Cyrus had gathered an armie of diuers nacions.

r By turning the course of the riuer one side was made open, and the redes that did growe in the water, were destroied which Cyrus did by the counsel of Gobria & Gabatha Belshazzars captaines.

s When she shalbe cut vp and threshed.

t This is spoken in the persone of the Iewes, bewayling their state and the crueltie of the Babylonians.

u Thus the Lord esteemeth the iniurie done to his Church as done to him self, because their cause is his.

sea, and drye vp her springs.
27 And Babél shal be *as* heapes, a dwelling
place for dragons, an astonishment, and
an hissing, without an inhabitant.
38 Thei shal roare together like lions, and
yell as the lions whelpes.
39 In their [x] heat I wil make them feastes,
and I wil make them drunken, that they
may reioice, and slepe a perpetual slepe,
and not wake, saith the Lord.
40 I wil bring them downe like lambes to
the slaughter, & like rams and goates.
41 How is [y] Sheshách taken! and how is the
glorie of the whole earth taken! how is Ba
bél become an astonishement among the
nacions!
42 The [z] sea is come vp vpon Babél: she is
couered with the multitude of the waues
thereof.
43 Her cities are desolate: the land is drye
& a wildernes, a land wherein no mã dwel
leth, nether doeth the sonne of man passe
thereby.
44 I wil also visite Bel in Babél, and I wil
bring out of his mouth, that which [a] he
hathe swallowed vp, and the nacions shal
runne no more vnto him, and the wall of
Babél shal fall.
45 My people, go out of the middes of her,
& deliuer ye euerie man his soule frõ the
fierce wrath of the Lord,
46 Lest your heart euen faint, and ye feare
the rumour, that shalbe heard in the land:
the rumour shal come *this* yere, and after
that in the *other* [b] yere *shal come* a rumour,
and crueltie in the land, and ruler against
ruler.
47 Therefore beholde, the dayes come, that
I wil visite the images of Babél, and the
whole land shal be confounded, & all her
slaine shal fall in the middes of her.
48 Then the heauen and [c] the earth, and all
that is therein, shal reioice for Babél: for
the destroyers shal come vnto her frõ the
North, saith the Lord.
49 As Babél caused the [d] slaine of Israél to
fall, so by Babél the slaine of all the earth
did fall.
50 Ye that [e] haue escaped the sworde, go
away, stande not stil: remembre the Lord
afarre of, & let Ierusalém come into your
minde.
51 We are [f] confounded because we haue
heard reproche: shame hathe couered our
faces, for strangers are come into the san-
ctuaries of the Lords House.
52 Wherefore beholde, the daies come,
saith the Lord, that I wil visite her grauen images, and through all her land the
wounded shal grone.
53 Thogh Babél shulde mounte vp to [g] heauẽ, & thogh she shulde defend her strẽgth
on hie, *yet* from me shal her destroiers co-

x When thei are inflamed with surfeting and drinking, I wil feast with them, alluding to Belshazzars bãket, Dan. 5, 2.

y Meaning Babél, as Chap. 25, 26.

z The great armie of the Medes and Persians.

a That is, his giftes & presents which he had receiued as part of the spoile of other nations, and wc the idolaters broght vnto him from all countreys.

b Meaning, yt Babylon shuld not be destroied all at once, but by litle & litle shulde be broght to nothing: for the first yere came the tydings, yc next yere the siege, and in the thirde yere it was taken: yet this is not that horrible destruction wc the Prophetes threatned ĩ manie places: for that was after this, whẽ they rebelled and Darius ouercame thẽ by the policie of Zopirus and hanged thre thousand gentlemen besides the cõmune people.

c All creatures in heauẽ & earth shal reioice and praise God for the destruction of Babylon the great enemie of his Churche.

d Babylon did not onely destroy Israél, but many other nacions.

e Ye that are now captiues in Babylon

f He sheweth how they shulde remember Ierusalém by lamenting the miserable affliction thereof.

g For the walles were two hundreth foote hie.

me, saith the Lord.
54 A sounde of a crye *cometh* frō Babél, and
great destruction from the land of the
Caldeans.
55 Because the Lord hathe laid Babél waste
and destroied, from her the great voyce, &
her waues shal roare like great waters, *and*
a sounde was made by their noice.
56 Because the destroier is come vpon her,
euen vpon Babél, and her strong men are
taken, their bowes are broken: for the
Lord God that recompenceth, shal surely
recompence.
57 And I wil [h] make drunke her princes, and
her wise men, her dukes, and her nobles, &
her strong men: & thei shal slepe a perpetual slepe, and not wake, saith the King,
whose Name *is* the Lord of hostes.

h I wil so astonish thē by afflictions that thei shal not know ŵ waye to turne them.

58 Thus saith ŷ Lord of hostes, The [i] thicke
wall of Babél shalbe broken, and her hye
gates shalbe burnt with fyre, and the people shal labour in vaine, and the folke in
the fyre, for thei shalbe weary.

i The thicknes of the walle was fiftie foo-se thicke.

59 The worde which Ieremiáh the Prophet
commanded Sheraiáh the sonne of Ne-
riiáh, the sonne of Maaseiáh, when he went
with Zedekiáh the King of Iudáh into Ba
bél, in the [k] fourth yere of his reigne: and
this Sheraiáh was a peaceable prince.

k This was not in the time of his captiuitie, but seuen yeres before, when he went ether to gratulat Nebuchad-nezzár or to intreat of some matters.

60 So Ieremiáh wrote in a boke all the euil
that shulde come vpon Babél: *euen* all these things, that are writen against Babél.
61 And Ieremiáh said to Sheraiáh, When
thou comest vnto Babél, and shalt se, and
shalt read all these wordes,
62 Then shalt thou say, O Lord, thou hast
spokē against this place, to destroie it, that
none shulde remaine in it, nether man nor
beast, but ŷ it shulde be desolate for euer.
63 And when thou hast made an end of reading this boke, thou shalt binde a [l] stone to it, and cast it in the middes of Euphrates,
64 And shalt say, Thus shal Babél be drowned, and shal not rise from the euil, that I
wil bring vpō her: and thei shal [m] be wearie. Thus farre *are* ŷ wordes of Ieremiáh.

l S. Iohn in his reuelation alludeth to this place when he saith that the Angel toke a millestone and cast into the sea: signifying thereby the destruction of Babylon, Reuel. 18,21.

m Thei shal not be able to resist, but shal labour invaine

CHAP. LII.

4 *Ierusalém is taken.* 10 *Zedekiahs sonnes are killed before his face, and his eyes put out.* 13 *The citie is burned.* 31 *Iehoiachin is broght forthe of prison, and fed like a King.*

Chap. LII. 2. *King* 24,18 2. *chr*. 36,11.

1 ZEdekiáh* *was* one & twentie yere olde when he began to reigne, and he
reigned eleuen yeres in Ierusalém, and his
mothers name *was* Hamutál, the daughter
of Ieremiáh of Libnáh.
2 And he did euil in the eyes of the Lord,
acccording to all that Iehoiakím had done.
3 [a] Doutles because the wrath of the Lord
was against Ierusalém and Iudáh, til he
had cast them out from his presence, therefore Zedekiáh rebelled against ŷ King
of Babél.

a So the Lord punished sinne by sinne & gaue him vp to his rebellious heart, til he had broght the enemie vpon him to lead him away and his people.

4 *But in the ninth yere of his reigne, in the
tēth moneth ŷ tēth *day* of ŷ moneth came
Nebuchad-nezzár Kig of Babél, he & all
his hoste against Ierusalém, & pitched a-
gainst it, & buylt fortes against it rounde
about.

2. *King*. 25,1. & *chap*. 39,1.

5 So the citie was besieged vnto ŷ eleuenth
yere of the King Zedekiáh.
6 Now in the fourth moneth, the ninth *day*
of the moneth, the famine was sore in the
citie, so that there was no more bread for
the people of the land.
7 Then the citie was broken vp and all the
men of warre fled, and went out of the
citie by night, by the [b] way of the gate betwene the two walles, which was by the
Kings garden: (now the Caldeans *were*
by the citie rounde about) and thei went
by the way of the wildernes.

b Read Chap. 39,4.

8 But the armie of the Caldeans pursued
after the King, and toke Zedekiáh in the
desert of Ierichó, & all his hoste was scattered from him.
9 Then thei toke the King and caryed him
vp vnto the King of Babél to Ribláh in
the land of Hamáth, [c] where he gaue iudgement vpon him.

c Read 2. King. 25,6, and chap 39,5.

10 And ŷ King of Babél slewe the sonnes of
Zedekiáh, before his eyes: he slewe also all
the princes of Iudáh in Ribláh.
11 Then he put out the eyes of Zedekiáh, &
the King of Babél bounde him in chaines, and caryed him to Babél, and put him
in prison til the day of his death.
12 Now in the fift moneth in the [d] tēth *day*
of the moneth (which was the nintenth yere of the King Nebuchad-nezzár King
of Babél) came Nebuzar-adán chief steward *which* [e] stode before the King of Babél in Ierusalém,

d In the 2. King 25, 8 it is called the seuenth day, because the fyre began then, & so continued to the tenth.

e That is, ŵ was his seruāt, as 2. King, 25,8

13 And burnt the House of the Lord, and
the Kings house, and all the houses of Ierusalém, and all the great houses burnt he
with fyre.
14 And all the armie of the Caldeans ŷ were with the chief steward, brake downe all
the walles of Ierusalém rounde about.
15 Then Nebuzar-adán the chief steward
caryed away captiue *certeine* of the poore
of the people, & the residue of the people
that remained in ŷ citie, & those that were fled, & fallen to the King of Babél, with
the rest of the multitude.
16 But Nebuzar-adán ŷ chief steward left
certeine of the poore of the land, to dresse
the vines, and to til the land.
17 Also the [f] pillers of brasse that were in
the House of the Lord, & the bases, & the
brasen Sea, that was in the House of the
Lord, the Caldeans brake, and caryed all
the brasse of them to Babél.

f Of these pillers read 1 King. 7.

18 The

g Which were also made of brasse

18 The pottes also and the g besomes, and
the instruments of musike, and the basins,
and the incense dishes, and all the vessels
of brasse wherewith they ministred, toke
they away.
19 And the bowles, and the ashpannes, & the
basins, & the pottes, and the candlesticks,
& the incense dishes, and the cuppes, *& all*
that was of golde, and that was of siluer,
toke the chief steward away,
20 With the two pillers, one Sea, & twelue
brasen bulles, that were vnder the bases,
which King Salamón had made in ý House
of the Lord: the brasse of all these vessels
was without h weight.

h It was so muche in quãtitie.

21 And concerning the pillers, the height of
one piller *was* eightene cubites, & a threde
of twelue cubites did compasse it, and the
thickenes thereof *was* foure fingers: *it was*
holow.
22 And a chapiter of brasse *was* vpon it, and
the height of one chapiter was fiue cubites
with networke, & pomegranates vpon the
chapiters roũde about, all of brasse: the seconde piller also, and the pomegranates
were like vnto these.
23 And there were ninetie & six pomegranates on a side: *and* all the pomegranates
vpon the net worke *were* an i hundreth
rounde about.

i But because of the roundenes no more colde be sene but nintye and six.

24 And the chief steward toke Sheraiáh the
chief Priest, and Zephaniáh k the seconde
Priest, and the thre kepers of the dore.

k Which serued in the hie Priests stead, if he had any necessarie impediment.

25 He toke also out of the citie an Eunuche,
which had the ouersight of the men of
warre, and l seuen men that were in the
Kings presence, which were founde in the
citie, and Sophér captaine of the hoste
who mustred the people of the land, and
thre score men of the people of the land,
ý were founde in the middes of the citie.

l In the 2. King. 25,19 is red but of fiue: those were the most excellẽt and the other two, which were not so noble, are not there mẽtioned with them.

26 Nebuzar-adán the chief steward toke
them, and broght them to the King of Babél to Ribláh.
27 And the King of Babél smote them, and
slewe them in Ribláh, in the land of Hamáth: thus Iudáh was caryed away captiue out of his owne land.
28 ¶ This is the people, whome Nebuchad-
nezzár caryed away captiue, in the m seuenth yere, *euen* thre thousand Iewes, and
thre and twentie.

m Which was the latter end of the seuenth yere of his reigne & the beginning of the eight.

29 In the n eightenth yere of Nebuchad-
nezzár he caryed away captiue from Ierusalém eight hundreth thirtie & two " persones.

n In the latter end also of ý yere, and the beginning of the nineteenth.
" *Ebr. soules.*

30 In the thre and twentieth yere of Nebuchad-nezzár, Nebuzar-adán the chief
steward caryed away captiue of the Iewes
seuen hundreth fourtie and fiue persones:
all the persones *were* foure thousand and
six hundreth.
31 And in the seuen and thirtieth yere of
the captiuitie of Iehoiachín King of Iudáh, in the twelfth moneth, in the fiue and
twentieth *day* of the moneth, Euil-merodách King of Babél, in the *first* yere of his
reigne, o lifted vp the head of Iehoiachín
King of Iudáh, and broght him out of prison,

o That is, restored him to libertie and honour.

32 And spake kindely vnto him, and set his
throne aboue the throne of the Kings,
that were with him in Babél,
33 And changed his prison p garments, and
he did continually eat bread before him
all the dayes of his life.

p And gaue him princely apparel.

34 His porcion *was* a q continual porcion
giuẽ him of the King of Babél, euery day
a certeine, all the dayes of his life vntil he
dyed.

q That is, he had allowance in the court, & thus at length he had rest & quietnes because he obeyed Ieremiáh the Prophet, where as the other were cruelly ordered, that wolde not obey him.

LAMENTACIONS.

CHAP. I.

1 The Prophet bewaileth the miserable estate of Ierusalém, 5 And sheweth that they are plagued because of their sinnes. The first and seconde chapter beginne euery Verse according to the letters of the Ebrewe Alphabet. The third hathe thre Verses for euery letter, & the fourth is as the first.

a The Prophet wondereth at the great iudgemẽt of God seing Ierusalém, which was so strõg & so ful of people, to be now destroyed and desolate.
b Which had chief rule ouer many prouinces and countreys.
c So that she taketh no rest.
d Meaning, the Egyptians and Assyrians, ý promised helpe.

HOw doeth a the citie remai
ne solitarie that was ful of
people? she is as a widdow:
she that was great among
the nacions *and* b princesse
amõg the prouinces, is made tributarie.
2 She wepeth continually in the c night, &
her teares *runne downe* by her chekes: amõg
all her d louers, she hathe none to comfort
her: all her friends haue delt vnfaithfully
with her, *&* are her enemies.
3 Iudáh is caryed away captiue, because e of
affliction, and because of great seruitude:
she dwelleth among the heathẽ, *&* findeth
no rest: all her persecuters toke her in the
streites.

e For her cruel tie toward the poore and oppression of seruants, Ierem. 34,11.

4 The wayes of Zión lament, because no
man cometh f to the solemne feasts: all her
gates are desolate: her Priests sigh: her virgines are discomfited, and she is in " heauines.

f As they vsed to come vp, ẘ myrth & ioye, Psal. 42,4.
" *Ebr. bitternes.*

5 Her aduersaries g are the chief, *and* her e-
nemies prosper: for the Lord hathe afflicted her, for the multitude of her transgressions, *&* her children are gone into captiuitie before the enemie.

g That is, haue rule ouer her, Deu. 28,44.

6 And from the daughter of Zión all her
beautie is departed: her prĩces are become

h As men pined away wͭ sorow & that haue no courage.

h like harts that finde no pasture, & thei are
gone without strength before the pursuer.
7 Ierusalém remembred the daies of her affliction, and of her rebellion, *and* all her
pleasant things, that she had in times past,
when her people [i] fell into the hand of the
enemie, & none did helpe her: ye aduersaries sawe her, & did mocke at her [k] Sabbaths.
8 Ierusalém hathe grieuously sinned, therefore she is * in derision: all yͭ honoured her,
despise her, because thei haue sene her filthines: yea, she sigheth and turneth backeward.
9 [l] Her filthines *is* in her skirtes: she remembred not her last end, therefore she came
downe wonderfully: she had no cōforter:
ô Lord, beholde mine affliction: for the e-
nemie " is proude.
10 The enemie hathe stretched out his hād
vpon all her pleasant things: for she hathe
sene the heathen entre into her Sanctuarie,
whome [m] thou didest cōmande, that *hey
shulde not entre into thy Church.
11 All her people sigh and seke *their* bread:
they haue giuen their pleasant things for
meat to refresh the soule: se, ô Lord, & consider: for I am become vile.
12 Haue ye no regarde, all ye that passe by
this way? beholde, & se, if there be any [n] sorowe like vnto my sorowe, which is done
vnto me, wherewith the Lord hathe afflicted *me* in the day of his fierce wrath.
13 From aboue hathe [o] he sent fyre into my
bones, which preuaile against them: he hathe spred a net for my fete, & turned me
backe: he hathe made me desolate, & daily
in heauines.
14 The [p] yoke of my trāsgresions is bounde vpon his hand: they are wrapped, and
come vp vpō my necke: he hathe made my
strēgth to fall: yͤ Lord hathe deliuered me
into *their* hāds, nether am I able to rise vp.
15 The Lord hathe troden vnder fote all
my valiant mē in the middes of me: he hathe called an assemblie against me to destroy my yong men: the Lord hathe troden
[q] the wine presse vpon the virgine the
daughter of Iudáh.
16 * For these things I wepe: mine eye, *euen*
mine eye casteth out water, because the
comforter that shulde refresh my soule, is
farre from me: my children are desolate,
because the enemie preuailed.
17 Zión stretcheth out her hands, and there
is none to comfort her: the Lord hathe
appointed the enemies of Iaakób rounde
about him: Ierusalém is [r] as a menstruous
woman in the middes of them.
18 The Lord is righteous: for I haue rebelled against his " commandement: heare,
I pray you, all people & beholde my sorow:
my virgines and my yong men are gone
into captiuitie.

i In her miserie she considered yͤ great benefites and cōmodities yͭ she had lost.
k At her religion and seruing of God, which was yͤ greatest grief to the godlie.
*Or, driuē away
l She is not ashamed of her sinne, althogh it be manifest.
"Ebr. hathe magnified him self.
m God forbiddeth that the Ammonites & Moabites shulde enter into the Congregation of the Lord, and vnder thē he cōprehendeth all enemies, Deu. 23,3.
n Thus Ierusalém lamenteth, mouing others to pitie her and to learne by her example.
o This declareth that we shuld acknowledge God to be the autor of all our afflictions, to the intēt that we might seke vnto him for remedie.
p Mine heauy sinnes are continually before his eies, as he that tyeth a thing to his hand for a remembrance.
q He hathe troden them vnder fote as they yͭ tread grapes in the wyne presse.
Iere. 14,17. chap. 2,18.
r Which because of her pollution was separate from her housbād, Leu. 15,19. and was abhorred for the time.
"Ebr. mouth.

19 I called for my louers, *but* they deceiued
me: my Priests and mine Elders perished
in the citie while they [f] soght their meat to
refresh their soules.
20 Beholde, ô Lord, how I am troubled: my
bowels swell: mine heart is turned within
me, for I am full of heauines: the sworde
spoyleth abroad, as death *doeth* at home.
21 They haue heard that I mourne, *but* there
is none to comfort me: all mine enemies
haue heard of my trouble, & are glad, that
thou hast done it: thou wilt bring the day,
that thou hast pronounced, and they shalbe like vnto me.
22 [t] Let all their wickednes come before thee:
*do vnto them, as thou hast done vnto me,
for all my transgresions: for my sighs a-
re many, and mine heart is heauie.

CHAP. II.

1 HOw hathe the Lord [a] darkened the
daughter of Zión in his wrath! *and*
hathe cast downe from [b] heauen vnto the
earth the beautie of Israél, & remembred
not his [c] fote stole in the day of his wrath!
2 The Lord hathe destroyed all the habitacions of Iaakób, and not spared: he hathe
throwen downe in his wrath the strong
holdes of the daughter of Iudáh: he hathe
cast them downe to the grounde: he hathe
polluted the kingdome and the princes
thereof.
3 He hathe cut of in his fierce wrath all
the [d] horne of Israél: he hathe drawē backe
his [e] right hand from before the enemie,
and there was kindled in Iaakób like a flame of fyre, which deuoured rounde about.
4 He [f] hathe bēt his bowe like an enemie: his
right hand was stretched vp as an aduersarie, and slewe all that was pleasant to the
eye in the tabernacle of the daughter of
Zión: he powred out his wrath like fyre.
5 The Lord was as an enemie: he hathe deuoured Israél, & consumed all his palaces:
he hathe destroyed his strong holdes, and
hathe increased in the daughter of Iudáh
lamentacion and mourning.
6 For he hathe destroyed his tabernacle, as
a garden, he hathe destroyed his cōgregacion: yͤ Lord hathe caused the feasts & Sabbaths to be forgottē in Zión, & hathe despised in the indignacion of his wrath the
King and the Priest.
7 The Lord hathe forsaken his altar: he hathe abhorred his Sanctuarie: he hathe giuē
into the hand of the enemie the walles of
her palaces: thei haue made a [g] noyse in the
House of yͤ Lord, as in the day of solénitie.
8 The Lord hathe determined to destroye
the wall of the daughter of Zión: he stretched out a line: he hathe not withdrawen
his hād from destroying: therefore he made the rampart [h] and the wall to lament:
they were destroyed together.

f That is, they dyed for hungre.
t Of desiring vengeance against the enemie, read Iere. 11,20. & 18,21.
*Or, gather thē like grapes.
a That is, broght her frō prosperitie to aduersitie.
b Hathe giuen her a most sore fall.
c Alluding to the Temple or to the Arke of the couenant, which was called the fotestole of yͤ Lord because they shulde not set their mindes so lowe, but lift vp their hearts toward the heauens.
d Meaning, the glorie and strength, as 1. Sam 2,1.
e That is, his succour which he was wonte to sēd vs, whē our enemies oppressed vs.
f Shewing, yͭ there is no remedie but destructiō, where God is the enemie.
g As the people were accustomed to praise God in the solēne feastes with a lowde voice, so now the enemies blaspheme hī with showting & crying.
h This is a figuratiue speache, as yͭ was, when he said, the wayes did lament, Chap. 1, 4: meaning, yͭ this sorowe was so great that the insensible thīgs had their parte thereof.

9 Her gates are sonke to the grounde:he hathe destroied and broken her barres: her
King and her princes *are* among the Gentiles : the Lawe *is* no more, nether can her
Prophetes "receiue *any* vision frō the Lord.
10 The Elders of the daughter of Ziōn sit
vpō the grounde, and kepe silence: thei haue cast vp dust vpon their heades: thei haue girded thē selues with sackecloth : the
virgines of Ierusalém hang downe their
heades to the ground.
11 Mine eyes do faile wᵗ teares : my bowels
swell: my lieuer is powred vpon the earth,
for the destruction of the daughter of my
people, because the children and sucklings
"swoune in the stretes of the citie.
12 Thei haue said to their mothers, Where
is "bread and drinke? when thei swouned
as the wounded in the stretes of the citie,
& whē thei "gaue vp the gost in their mothers bosome.
13 [i] What thig shal I take to witnes for thee?
what thing shal I cōpare to thee, ô daughter Ierusalém? what shal I likē to thee, that
I may comfort thee, ô virgine daughter
Ziōn? for thy breache *is* great like the sea:
who can heale thee?
14 Thy Prophetes haue [k] loked out vaine,
and foolish things for thee, and thei haue not discouered thine iniquitie, to turne
away thy captiuitie, but haue loked out
for thee false "prophecies, and causes of
banishement.
15 All that passe by the way, clappe their
handes at thee: thei hisse and wagge their
head vpon the daughter Ierusalém, *saying*,
Is this the citie that men call, The perfection of beautie, *and* the ioye of the
whole earth?
16 All thine enemies haue opened their mou
the against thee : thei hisse and gnash the
teeth, saying, Let vs deuoure it : certeinly
this is the day that we loked for : we haue
founde *and* sene it.
17 *The Lord hathe done that which he had
purposed: he hathe fulfilled his worde that
he had determined of olde time : he hathe throwen done, and not spared: he hathe
caused thine enemie to reioice ouer thee,
and set vp the horne of thine aduersaries.
18 Their heart * cryed vnto ẏ Lord, O wall
of ẏ daughter Ziōn, let teares runne dowe-
ne like a riuer, day and night: take thee no
rest, nether let the apple of thine eye cease.
19 Arise, crye in the night: in ẏ beginning
of the watches powre out thine heart like
water before the face of the Lord : lift vp
thine hands toward him for ẏ life of thy
yong childrē, that faint for hungre in the
corners of all the stretes.
20 Beholde, ô Lord, and considre to whome
thou hast done thus? shal the women eat
their frute, *and* children of a "spanne long?
shal the Priest and the Prophet be slaine
in the Sanctuarie of the Lord?
21 The yong and the olde lye on the grounde in the stretes: my virgines and my yong
mē are fallen by the sworde: ẏᵘ haste slaine
them in the day of thy wrath : thou haste
killed and not spared.
22 Thou hast called as in a solemne day my
"terrours rounde about, so ẏ in the day of
the Lords wrath none escaped nor remained: those that I haue nourished & broght
vp, hathe mine enemie consumed.

CHAP. III.

1 I Am the man, that hathe sene [a] affliciō
in the rod of his indignation.
2 He hathe led me, and broght me into
darcknes, but not to light.
3 Surely he is turned against me: he turneth
his hand *against me* all the day.
4 My flesh and my skinne hathe he caused
to waxe olde, & he hathe brokē my bones.
5 He hathe [b] buylded against me, & cōpassed *me* with gall, and labour.
6 He hathe set me in darke places, as thei
that be dead for euer.
7 He hathe hedged about me, that I can not
get out: he hathe made my chaines heauie.
8 Also when I crye and shoute, he shutteth
out my [c] prayer.
9 He hathe [d] stopped vp my waies with hewen stone, *and* turned away my paths.
10 [e] He was vnto me *as* a beare lyig in waite, & *as* a lion in secret places.
11 He hathe stopped my waies, & pulled me
in pieces: he hathe made me desolate.
12 He hathe bent his bow and made me a
marke for the arrowe.
13 He caused "the arrowes of his quiuer to
entre into my reines.
14 I was a derision to all my people, *and*
their song all the daye.
15 He hathe filled me with bitternes, & made me drunken with [f] worme wood.
16 He hathe also broken my teeth with stones, *and* hathe couered me with asshes.
17 Thus my soule, was farre of frō peace : I
forgat prosperitie,
18 And I said, My stregth & mine hope [g] is
perished from the Lord,
19 Remēbring mine affliction, & my mourning, the wormewood and the gall.
20 My soule hathe them in remembrance,
and is humbled [h] in me.
21 I consider this in mine heart : therefore
haue I hope.
22 It is the Lords [i] mercies that we are not
cōsumed, because his cōpassions faile not.
23 *Thei are* renued [k] euerie morning: great
is thy faithfulnes.
24 The Lord *is* my [l] porcion, saith my soule: therefore wil I hope in him.
25 The Lord is good vnto them, that trust
in him, & to the soule that seketh him.

Or, fynde.

Or, feint.

" *Ebr. wheat & wyne.*

" *Ebr. powred out the soule.*

i Meaning, ẏ her calamitie was so euidēt that it nede no witnesses.

k Because the false Prophetes called thē selues seers, as the otherwere called, therefore he sheweth that they saw amisse, because thei did not reproue the peoples fautes, but flattered them in their sinnes, which was the cause of their destruction.

" *Or, burdens.*

Leu. 26, 14. deu. 28, 35.

Iere 14, 17. chap. 1, 16.

" *Or, broght vp in their owne hands.*

" *Or, enemies, whome I feared*

Chap. III.

a The Prophet complaineth of the punishments and afflictions that he endured by the false Prophetes & hypocrites, when he declared the destruction of Ierusalém, as Ierem. 20, 2.

b He speaketh this as one ẏ felt Gods heauie iudgemēts, wᶜ he greatly feared, & therefore setteth them out with this diuersitie of wordes.

c This is a great tentacion to the godlie, when thei se not the frute of their praiers, and causeth them to thinke that thei are not heard, which thing God vseth to do, that thei might praie more earnestly and the oftener.

d And kepeth me in holde, as a prisoner.

e He hathe no pitie on me.

" *Ebr. sonnes.*

f With great angnish & sorowe he hathe made me to lose my sense.

g Thus with paine he was driuen to and fro betwene hope and dispaire, as ẏ godlie oft times are, yet in the end the Spirit getteth the victorie.

h He sheweth that God thus vseth to exercise his to the intent that hereby thei maie knowe them selues and fele his mercies.

i Considering the wickednes of man, it is maruel that anie remaineth aliue: but only that God for his owne mercies sake and for his promes wil euer haue his Church to remaine thogh thei be neuer so fewe in nōber, Isa. 1, 9.

k We felē thy benefites daily

l The godlie put their whole cōfidence in God, & therefore loke for none other inheritance, as psal. 16, 5.

26 It is good bothe to trust, and to waite
for the saluation of the Lord.
27 It is good for a man that he beare the
yoke in his [m] youth.
28 He sitteth alone, [n] and kepeth silence, because he hathe borne it vpon him.
29 He putteth his [o] mouth in the dust, if
there maie be hope.
30 He giueth his cheke to him that smiteth him: he is filled ful with reproches.
31 For the Lord wil not forsake for euer.
32 But thogh he send affliction, yet wil he
haue compassion according to the multitude of his mercies.
33 For he doeth not [p] punish "willingly,
nor afflict the children of men,
34 In stamping vnder his fete all the pri-
sonners of the earth,
35 In ouerthrowing the right of a man before the face of the most high,
36 In subuerting a man in his cause: the
Lord [q] seeth it not.
37 Who is he then that saith, and it cometh to passe, & the Lord [r] commandeth
it not?
38 Out of the mouth of the most high proceadeth not [f] euil and good?
39 Wherefore *then* is the liuing [t] man sorowful? man *suffreth* for his sinne.
40 Let vs serche and trye our waies, & turne
againe to the Lord.
41 Let vs lift vp [u] our hearts with our handes vnto God in the heauens.
42 We haue sinned, and haue rebelled, *therefore* thou hast not spared.
43 Thou hast couered *vs* with wrath, and
persecuted vs: thou hast slaine & not spared.
44 Thou hast couered thy self wt a cloude,
that *our* praier shulde not passe through.
45 Thou hast made vs *as* the * offscouring
and refuse in the middes of the people.
46 All our enemies haue opened their mouthe against vs.
47 Feare, and a snare is come vpon vs *with*
desolation and destruction.
48 Mine eye casteth out riuers of water, for
ye destruction of ye daughter of my people.
49 Mine eye droppeth without staie and
ceaseth not,
50 Til the Lord loke downe, and beholde
from heauen.
51 Mine eye [x] breaketh mine heart because
of all the daughters of my citie.
52 Mine enemies chased me sore like a
birde, without cause.
53 They haue shut vp my life [y] in the
dungeon, and cast a stone vpon me.
54 Waters flowed ouer mine head, *then*
thoght I, I am destroied.
55 I called vpon thy Name, ô Lord, out of
the lowe dungeon.
56 Thou hast heard my voice: stoppe not

m He sheweth that we can neuer begin to timely to be exercised vnder the crosse, that when the afflictiōs grow greater, our pacience also by experiēce may be stronger.
n He murmureth not agaīst God, but is pacient.
o He hūbleth him selfe as thei that falle downe wt their face to the grounde, & so with pacience waiteth for succour.
p He taketh no pleasure in it, but doeth it of necessitie for our amendement, when he suffreth the wicked to oppresse the poore.
" *Ebr. with his heart.*
q He doeth not delite therein.
r He sheweth that nothing is done without Gods prouidēce.
f That is, aduersitie, and prosperitie, Amos 3,6.
t When God afflicteth him.
u That is, both heartes & handes: for els to lift vp ye handes is but hypocrisie.
1.Cor.4,13.
x I am ouercome with sore weping for all my people.
y Read Ierem. 37, 16, how he was in the myrie dungeon.

thine eare frō my sigh & from my crye.
57 Thou drewest nere in the daye that I
called vpon thee: thou saidest, Feare not.
58 O Lord, thou hast mainteined the cause
of my [z] soule, & hast redemed my life.
59 O Lord, thou hast sene my wrong, iudge
thou my cause.
60 Thou hast sene all their vengeance, &
all their deuises against me,
61 Thou hast heard their reproche, ô Lord,
& all their imaginations against me:
62 The lippes *also* of those that rose against
me, and their whispering against me continually.
63 Beholde, their sitting downe & their rising vp, *how* I am their song.
64 * Giue them a recompence, ô Lord, according to the worke of their hands.
65 Giue them" sorowe of heart, *euen* thy
cursse to them.
66 Persecute with wrath and destroie thē
from vnder the heauen, ô Lord.

CHAP. IIII.

1 HOw is the [a] golde become so " dimme? the moste fyne golde is chāged,
& the stones of the Sanctuarie are scattered in the corner of euerie strete.
2 The noble " men of Ziōn comparable to
fyne golde, how are thei estemed as earthē
[b] pitchers, *euen* the worke of the hands of
the potter!
3 Euen the dragons [c] drawe out the breasts,
& giue sucke to their yong, *but* the daughter of my people *is become* cruel like ye [d] ostriches in the wildernes.
4 The tongue of the sucking childe cleaueth to the roofe of his mouth for thirst:
the yong children aske bread, *but* no man
breaketh it vnto them.
5 Thei that did fede delicately, perish in
the stretes: they that were broght vp in
skarlet, embrase the dongue.
6 For the iniquitie of the daughter of my
people is become greater then * the sinne
of Sodōm, that was destroied as in a moment, and " none pitched campes against
her.
7 Her Nazarites were purer then ye snowe,
and whiter then the milke: thei were more ruddie in body, then the red precious
stones: thei were *like* polished saphir.
8 Now their [e] visage is blacker then a cole:
they can not knowe them in the stretes:
their skinne cleaueth to their bones: it is
withered, like a stocke.
9 Thei that be slaine with the sworde are
better, then thei that are killed with hungre: for thei fade awaie *as* thei were striken through for the [f] frutes of the field.
10 The handes of the pitiful women haue
sodden their owne children, *which* were
their meat in the destruction of ye daughter of my people.

z Meaning, the cause wherefore his life was in danger.
Psal.28,4.
" *Or, an obstinate heart.*
a By the golde he meaneth the Princes, as by the stones he vnderstandeth the Priestes.
" *Or, hid.*
" *Or, sonnes.*
b Which are of smale estimation & haue none honour.
c Thogh the dragons be cruel, yet thei pitie their yong and nourish them, wc thing Ierusalém doeth not.
d The women forsake their childrē as the ostriche doeth her eggs, Iob. 39,17.
Gene.19,25.
" *Or, no strength was against her.*
e They that were before moste in Gods fauour, are now in greatest abomination vnto him, Nomb. 6,2.
f For lacke of fode they pyne away, and consume.

11 The Lord hathe accomplished his indignacion: he hathe powred out his fierce
wrath, he hathe kindled a fyre in Zión,
which hathe deuoured the fundaciós thereof.
12 The Kings of the earth, and all the inhabitans of the worlde wolde not haue be
leued that the aduersarie and the enemie
shulde haue entred into the gates of Ierusalém:
13 For the sinnes of her Prophetes, *and* the
iniquities of her Priestes, that haue shed
the blood of the iust in the middes of
g her.
14 Thei haue wandered *as* blinde men h in
the stretes, and they were polluted with
blood, so ỹ i thei wolde not touche their
garments.
15 *But* thei cryed vnto them, Departe, ye
polluted, departe, departe, touche not: therefore they fled away, and wandered: thei
haue said among the heathen, They shal
no more dwell there.
16 The ʺ angre of the Lord hathe scattered
them, he wil no more regarde them: k thei
reuerenced not the face of the Priests, nor
had compassion of the Elders.
17 Whiles we waited for our vaine helpe,
our eyes failed: for in our waiting we loked for l a nation that colde not saue vs.
18 They hunte our steppes that we can not
go in our stretes: our end is nere, our daies
are fulfilled, for our end is come.
19 Our persecuters are swifter then the e-
gles of the heauen: thei pursued vs vpon
the mountaines, and laied wait for vs in
the wildernes.
20 The m breth of our nostrels, the Anointed of the Lord was taken in their nets, of
whome we said, Vnder his shadowe we
shalbe preserued aliue among the heathen.
21 Reioyce & be glad, n ô daughter Edóm,
that dwellest in the land of Vz, the cup also shal passe through vnto thee: thou shalt
be drunken ʺ and vomite.
22 Thy punishment is accomplished, ô
daughter Zión: he o wil nomore carie thee
awaie into captiuitie, *but* he wil visit thine iniquitie, ô daughter Edóm, he wil
discouer thy sinnes.

g He meaneth that these things are come to passe therefore, contrary to all mens expectation.
h Some referre this to ỹ blinde men, which as they went, stombled on the blood, whereof the citie was ful.
i Meaning, the heathen which came to destroy thẽ, colde not abyde them.
ʺOr, face.
k That is, the enemies.
l He sheweth two principal causes of their destructiõ: their crueltie, & their vaine confidence in man: for they trusted in the helpe of the Egyptians.
m Our King Iosiáh, in whome stode our hope of Gods fauour, and on whome depended our state & life, was slayne whome he calleth anointed, because he was a figure of Christ.
n This is spoken by derisiõ.
ʺOr, shew thy nakednes.
o He comforteth the Churche by ỹ after seuentie yeres their sorowes shal haue an end, where as the wicked shulde be tormented for euer.

CHAP. V.

The prayer of Ieremiáh.

1 REmembre, ô Lord, what is come
vpon vs: a consider, and beholde our
reproche.
2 Our inheritance is turned to the strangers, our houses to the aliantes.
3 We are fatherles, euen without father, &
our mothers are as widowes.
4 We haue dronke our b water for money,
& our wood is solde *vnto vs*.
5 Our neckes are vnder persecution: we are
weary, and haue no rest.
6 We haue giuen our c hands to the Egyptians, & to Asshúr, to be satisfied with
bread.
7 Our fathers haue sinned, and are not, and
we haue borne their d iniquities.
8 Seruants haue ruled ouer vs, none wolde
deliuer vs out of their hands.
9 We gate our bread with the *peril* of our
liues, because of the sworde e of the wildernes.
10 Our skin was blacke like as an ouen because of the terrible famine.
11 They defiled the women in Zión, & the
maides in the cities of Iudáh.
12 The princes are hanged vp by f their
hand: the faces of the Elders were not had
in honour.
13 They toke the yong men to grinde, and
the children fell vnder g the wood.
14 The Elders haue ceased from the h gate
& the yong men from their songs.
15 The ioye of our heart is gone, our dance
is turned into mourning.
16 The crowne of our head is fallen: wo
now vnto vs, that we haue sinned.
17 Therefore our heart is heauy for these
things, our i eyes are dimme,
18 Because of the moũtaine of Zión which
is desolate: the foxes runne vpon it.
19 *But* thou, ô Lord, remainest for k euer:
thy throne is frõ generacion to generaciõ.
20 Wherefore doest thou forget vs for e-
uer, & forsake vs so long time?
21 l Turne thou vs vnto thee, ô Lord, and
we shalbe turned: renue our dayes as of
olde.
22 But thou hast vtterly reiected vs: thou
art excedingly angrie against vs.

a This prayer as is thoght, was made whẽ some of the people were caryed away captiue, others as the poorest remained, and some went into Egypt & other places for socour: albeit it semeth that ỹ Prophet foreseing their miseries to come, thus prayed.
b Meaning, their extreme seruitude and bondage.
c We are ioyned in league and amitie ŵ them, or haue submitted our selues vnto them.
d As our fathers haue bene punished for their sinnes, so we that are culpable of ỹ same sinnes, are punished.
e Because of ỹ enemie that came from the wildernes, and wolde not suffer vs to go, & seke our necessarie fode.
f That is, by ỹ enemies hand.
g Their sclauerie was so great, that thei were not able to abide it.
h There were no more laws nor forme of cõmune welth
i With wepĩg.
k And therefore thy couenant, and mercies can neuer faile.
l Whereby is declared that it is not in mãs power to turne to God, but is onely his worke to conuerte vs: and thus God worketh in vs before we can turne to him, Ierem. 31,18.

EZEKIEL.

THE ARGVMENT.

AFter that Iehoiachin by the counsel of Ieremiáh & Ezekiél had yelded him self to Nebuchadnezzár, and so went into captiuitie with his mother & diuers of his princes & of the people, certeine begã to repent and murmur that thei had obeid the Prophets counsel, as thogh the thing which thei had prophecied, shulde not come to passe, & therfore their estate shulde be stil miserable vnder the Caldeans. By reason whereof he confirmeth his former prophecies, declaring by new visions & reuelations shewed vnto him that the citie shulde moste certeinly be destroied, & the people grieuously tormēted by Gods plagues, insomuche that thei that remained, shulde be broght into cruel bondage. And lest the godlie shulde dispaire in these great troubles, he assureth them that God wil deliuer his Church at his time appointed, and also destroie their enemies which ether afflicted them or reioyced in their miseries. The effect of the one and the other shulde chiefly be performed vnder Christ, of whome in this boke are many notable promises, and in whome the glorie of the new Temple shulde perfectly be restored. He prophecied these things in Caldea at the same time that Ieremiáh prophecied in Iudáh, and there began in the fift yere of Iehoiachins captiuitie.

a After that ye boke of the Law was founde, which was the eightenth yere of the reigne of Iosiáh, so that fiue & twentie yeres after this boke was founde, Ieconiáh was led awaie captiue with Ezekiél & manie of ye people who the first yere after sawe these visions.
b Which was a part of Euphrates, so called.
c That is, notable, and excellent visions, so that it might be knowen, it was no natural dreame but came of God.

CHAP. I.

1 The time wherein Ezekiél prophecied and in what place. 3 His kinred. 15 The vision of the foure beastes. 26 The vision of the throne.

IT came to passe in the
a thirtieth yere in the
fourth *moneth*, *and* in the
fift *day* of the moneth
(as I was amōg the captiues
by the riuer b Chebár) that ye heauens were
opened and I sawe visions of c God.
2 In the fift *daye* of the moneth (which was
the fift yere of King Ioiachins captiuitie)
3 The worde of the Lord came vnto Ezekiél
the Priest, the sonne of Buzí, in the
land of the Caldeans, by ye riuer Chebár,
where the d hād of the Lord was vpō him.
4 And I loked, & beholde, e a whirlewinde
came out of the North, a great cloude &
a fyre wrapped about it, and a brightnes
was about it, and in the middes thereof, *to
wit*, in the middes of the fyre *came out* as the
likenes of ° ambre.

d That is, the Spirit of prophecie, as chap 3,22 and 37,1.
e By this diuersitie of wordes he signifieth ye feareful iudgement of God, and the great afflictions, that shulde come vpon Ierusalém.
° Or, pale yellow.

THE VISION OF EZEKIEL.

A. The whirlwinde that came out of the North, or Aquilon.
B. The great cloude.
C. The fyre wrapped about it.
D The brightnes about it.
E. The likenes of amber, or the pale colour.
F. The forme of the foure beastes.
G. Their fete like calues fete.
H. Hands comming out from vnder their wings.
I. K. L. M. The facion of the foure faces of euerie beast.
N Their wings ioyned one to another.
O. Their two wings, which couered their bodies.
P. Fyre running among the beastes.
Q. Wheles hauing euerie one foure faces.
R. The rings of the wheles which were ful of eyes.
S. The firmament like vnto chrystal.
T. The throne, which was set vpon the firmament,
V. Where sate like the appearance of a man.
X. The appearance of amber aboue, and benethe the man.
Y. The fyre about him.
Z. The brightnes of fyre like the raine bowe.

Midi, or the South.

f Which were ye foure Cherubims ye represented ye glorie of God, as Chap. 3,23.

5 Also out of the middes thereof *came* the
likenes of foure beasts, f and this was their
forme: they had the appearance of a man,
6 And euerie one had foure faces, and euerie
one had foure wings.
7 And their fete *were* streight fete, and the
sole-

sole of their fete *was* like the sole of a calues fote, and they sparkled like the appearance of bright brasse.
8 And the hands of a mã *came out* frõ vnder
their wings in the foure partes of thẽ, and
thei foure had their faces, & their wings.
9 They were [g] ioyned by their wings one
to another, & when thei went forthe, thei
returned not, *but* euerie one went streight
forwarde.
10 And the similitude of their faces *was as*
[h] the face of man: and they foure had the
face of a lyon on the right side, and they
foure had the face of a bullocke on the
left side: they foure also had the face of
an egle.
11 Thus were their faces: but their wings
were spred out aboue: two *wings* of euerie
one were ioyned one to another, and two
couered their bodies.
12 And euerie one went streight forwarde:
they went whether their "spirit led them,
& thei returned not whẽ thei wẽt forthe.
13 The similitude also of the beastes, *and*
their appearance *was* like burning coles of
fyre, *and* like the appearance of lampes:
for the fyre ran among the beastes, & the fyre gaue a glister, and out of the fyre there
went lightening.
14 And the beastes ran, and [i] returned like
vnto lightening.
15 ¶ Now as I behelde the beastes, beholde, a whele *appeared* vpon the earth by the
beastes, hauing foure faces.
16 The faciõ of the wheles and their worke
was like vnto a [k] chrysolite: & they foure
had one forme, and their facion, and their
worke *was* as one whele in *another* whele.
17 Whẽ thei wẽt, thei wẽt vpõ their foure
sides, & they returned not when thei wẽt.
18 They had also "rings, and height, & were
feareful to beholde, and their rings were
ful of eyes, round about them foure.
19 And when the beastes went, the wheles
wẽt with them: and when the beastes were
lift vp frõ the earth, ẏ wheles were lift vp.
20 Whether their spirit led thẽ, they wẽt,
and thether did the spirit of the wheles
lead them, and the wheles were lifted vp
besides them: for the Spirit of the beastes
was in the wheles.
21 When the *beastes* went, they went, and
when they stode, they stode, & when they
were lifted vp from the earth, the wheles
were lifted vp besides them: for the spirit
of the beastes *was* in the wheles.
22 And the similitude of the firmament vpõ
the heads of the beastes *was* wonderful, like
vnto chrystal, spred ouer their heads aboue
23 And vnder the firmament *were* their
wings streight, the one towarde the other:
euerie one had two, which couered thẽ, &
eueri one had two, ẇ couered their bodies.
24 And when they went forthe, I heard the
noise of their [l] wings, like ẏ noise of great
waters, *and* as the voice of the Almightie,
euen the voyce of speache, as the noise of
an hoste: *and* when they stode, they [m] let
downe their wings.
25 And there was a voyce from the firmament, that was ouer their heades, whẽ they
stode, *and* had let downe their wings.
26 And aboue the firmament that was ouer
their heades, *was* the facion of a throne like vnto a saphir stone, and vpon the similitude of the throne *was* by appearance, as
the similitude of a man aboue vpon it.
27 And I sawe as the appearance of ambre,
and as the similitude of fyre [n] rõude about
within it to loke to, euen from his loynes
vpwarde, and to loke to, euẽ from his loynes downewarde: I saw as a likenes of fyre,
and brightnes rounde about it.
28 As the likenes of the bowe, that is in the
cloude in the day of raine, so *was* the appearance of the light rounde about.
29 This was the appearance of the similitude of the glorie of the Lord: and when
I sawe it, I fel [o] vpon my face, and I heard
a voyce of one that spake.

g The wing of the one touched ẏ wing of the other.

h Euerie Cherubim had foure faces, the face of a man, & of a lyon on ẏ right side, and the face of a bullocke, and of an egle on the left side.

" Ebr. whether their spirit, or wil was to go.

i That is, when they had executed Gods wil: for afore they returned not, til God had changed the state of things.

k The Ebrewe worde is tarshish: meaning, that the coulour was like the Cilician sea, or a precious stone so called.

" Or, the treat.

l Which declared the swiftnes, & the fearefulnes of Gods iudgements

m Which signified, that they had no power of them selues but onely waited to execute Gods commãdement.

n Whereby was signified a terrible iudgement toward the earth.

o Considering the maiestie of God, and the weakenes of flesh.

CHAP. II.

The Prophet is sent to call the people from their errour.

1 AND [a] he said vnto me, [b] Sonne of
man, stand vp vpon thy fete, & I wil
speake vnto thee.
2 [c] And the Spirit entred into me, when he
had spoken vnto me, and set me vpon my
fete, so ẏ I heard him that spake vnto me.
3 And he said vnto me, Sonne of mã, I send
thee to the childrẽ of Israél, to a rebellious
nation, that hathe rebelled against me: *for*
they & their fathers haue rebelled against
me, euen vnto this very day.
4 For *thei are* "impudent children, and stiffe
hearted: I do send thee vnto them, & thou
shalt say vnto thẽ, Thus saith ẏ Lord God.
5 But surely they wil not heare, nether in
dede wil they cease: for they are a rebellious house: yet shal they knowe that [d] there
hathe bene a Prophet among them.
6 And thou sonne of man, [e] feare them not,
nether be afrayed of their wordes, althogh
rebelles, and thornes *be* with thee, & thou
remainest with scorpions: feare not their
wordes, nor be afraide at their lokes, for
they are a rebellious house.
7 Therefore thou shalt speake my wordes
vnto them: *but* surely they wil not heare,
nether wil they in dede cease: for thei are
rebellious.
8 But thou sonne of man, heare what I say
vnto thee: be not thou rebellious, like *this*
rebellious house: opẽ thy mouth, and [f] eat
that I giue thee.
9 And whẽ I loked vp, behold, an hãd was set
vnto me, & lo, a rolle of a boke *was* therein.

Chap. II.
a That is, the Lord.

b Meaning mã, which is but earth, & ashes, which was to humble him, & cause him to consider his owne state, & Gods grace.

c So that he colde not abide Gods presence til Gods Spirit did enter into him.

" Ebr. hard of face.

d This declareth on ẏ one parte Gods great affection toward his people, that notwithstanding their rebelliõ, yet he wil sẽd his Prophetes amõg them, & admonisheth his ministers on the other parte that thei cease not to do their duetie, thogh the people be neuer so obstinat: for ẏ worde of God shal be ether to their saluation or greater condẽnation.

e Read Iere. 1, 17: he sheweth ẏ for none afflictiõs thei shuld cease to do their dueties.

f He doeth not onely exhorte him to his duetie, but also giueth him the meanes where with he may be able to execute it.

10 And he spred it before me, and it was
written within and without, and there was
written therein, g Lamentacions, & mourning, and wo.

g He sheweth what were the contentes of this boke: to wit, Gods iudgements agaīst the wicked.

CHAP. III.

1 The Prophet being fed with the worde of God and with the constant boldnes of the Spirit, is sent vnto the people that were in captiuitie. 17 The office of true ministers.

1 MOreouer he said vnto me, Sonne of
mā, eat that thou findest: a eat this
rolle, and go, *and* speake vnto the house of
Israél.
2 So I opened my mouth, and he gaue me
this rolle to eat.
3 And he said vnto me, Sonne of man, cause
thy belly to eat, and fil thy bowels with
this rolle that I giue thee. Thē did I eat it,
and it was in my mouth as swete as honie.
4 And he said vnto me, Sonne of man, go,
& entre into the house of Israél, and declare them my wordes.
5 For thou art not sent to a people of an
vnknowen" tongue, or of an hard language, *but* to the house of Israél,
6 Not to manie people of an vnknowen tōgue, or of an hard language, whose wordes
thou canst not vnderstand: yet if I shulde
send thee to them, they wolde obey thee.
7 But the house of Israél wil not obey thee:
for they wil not obey me: yea, all the house
of Israél are impudent and stif hearted.
8 Beholde, I haue made thy face b strong
against their faces, and thy forehead hard
against their foreheads.
9 I haue made thy forehead as the adamāt,
& harder then the flint: feare them not
therefore, nether be afraid at their lokes:
for they are a rebellious house.
10 He said moreouer vnto me, Sonne of
man, c receiue in thine heart all my wordes that I speake vnto thee, and heare *them*
with thine eares,
11 And go & entre to them that are led a-
way captiues vnto the children of thy people, and speake vnto them, and tel them,
Thus saith the Lord God: *but* surely they
wil not heare, nether wil thei in dede cease.
12 Then the Spirit toke me vp, and I heard
behinde me a noyse of a great russhing,
saying, d Blessed *be* the glorie of the Lord
out of his place.
13 *I heard* also the noyse of the wings of the
beasts, that touched one another, and the
ratling of the wheles that were by them,
euen a noyse of a great russhing.
14 So the Spirit lift me vp, & toke me away
and I e went in bitternes, & indignation
of my spirit, but the hād of the Lord was
strong vpon me.
15 Thē I came to them that were led away
captiues to f Tel-ábib, that dwelt by the
riuer Chebár, and I sate where they sate,
and remained there astonished amōg thē
g seuen dayes.
16 And at the end of seuen dayes, the worde of the Lord came againe vnto me,
saying,
17 Sonne of man, I haue made thee a h watchman vnto the house of Israél: therefore
heare the worde at my mouth, and giue thē
warning from me.
18 When I shal say vnto the wicked, Thou
shalt surely dye, and thou giuest not him
warnīg, nor speakest to admonish the wicked of his wicked way, that he may liue, the
same wicked man shal dye in his iniquitie:
but his blood wil I require at thine hand.
19 Yet if thou warne the wicked, & he turne not from his wickednes, nor from his
wicked way, he shal dye in his iniquitie,
but thou hast deliuered thy soule.
20 Likewise if a i righteous man turne frō
his righteousnes, and commit iniquitie, I
wil lay a k stumbling blocke before him,
and he shal dye, because thou hast not giuen him warning: he shal dye in his sinne,
and his l righteous dedes, which he hathe
done, shal not be remēbred: but his blood
wil I require at thine hand.
21 Neuertheles, if thou admonish that righteous man, that the righteous sinne not,
and that he doeth not sinne, he shal liue because he is admonished: also thou hast deliuered thy soule.
22 And the m hand of the Lord was there
vpon me, and he said vnto me, Arise, & go
into the "field, and I wil there talke with
thee.
23 So when I had risen vp, and gone forthe
into the field, beholde, the n glorie of the
Lord stode there, as ȳ glorie which I sawe
by the riuer Chebár, and I fel downe vpon
my face.
24 Then the Spirit entred into me, which
o set me vp vpon my fete, and spake vnto
me, and said to me, Come, & p shut thy
self within thine house.
25 But thou, ô sonne of man, beholde, they
shal put bandes vpon thee, and shal binde
thee with them, and thou shalt not go out
among them.
26 And I wil make thy tongue q cleaue to
the roofe of thy mouth, that thou shalt be
dumme, and shalt not be to them as a man
that rebuketh: for they are a rebellious
house.
27 But when I shal haue spoken vnto thee,
I wil open thy mouth, and thou shalt say
vnto them, Thus saith the Lord God, He
that heareth, let him heare, and he that
leaueth of, * let him leaue: for they are a
rebellious house.

a Whereby is ment, that none is mete to be Gods messenger before he haue receiued the worde of God in his heart, as vers. 10, and haue a zeale thereunto, and delite therein, as Ierem. 15,16, reuel. 10,10.

" Ebr. depe lippes.

b God promiseth his assistance to his ministers, and that he wil giue them boldenes & cōstācie in their vocation, Isa. 50,7. ier. 1,18, mich. 3,8.

c He sheweth what is ment by the eating of the boke, which is, that the ministers of God may speake nothing as of thē selues, but that onely, which they haue receiued of the Lord.

d Whereby he signifieth, that Gods glorie shulde not be diminished, although he departed out of his Temple: for this declared, that ȳ citie, & Temple shulde be destroyed.

e This sheweth that there is euer an infirmitie of the flesh which can neuer be ready to render ful obedience to God, and also Gods grace who euer assisteth his, and ouercommeth their rebellious affections.

f Which was a place by Euphrates where the Iewes were prisoners.

g Declaring hereby, that Gods ministers must with aduisement, and deliberation vtter his iudgements.

h Of this read Chap. 33,2.

i If he that hathe bene instructed in the right way turne backe:

k I wil giue him vp into a reprobat minde, Rom. 1,28.

l Which semed to haue bene done in faith, and were not.

m That is, the Spirit of prophecie.

" Or, valley.

n Meaning, the vision of the Cherubims, & the wheles.

o Read Chap. 2,2.

p Signifying, that not onely he shulde not profit, but they shuld grieuously trouble, & afflict him.

q Which declareth the terrible plague of the Lord whē God stoppeth the mouthes of his ministers, & that all suche are the rods of his vēgeance that do it.

* Reuel. 22,11.

CHAP. IIII.

1 The besieging of the citie of Ierusalém is signified. 9 The long continuance of the captiuitie of Israél. 16 An hungre is prophecied to come.

1 THou also sonne of man, take thee a
bricke, and lay it before thee, & pour-
tray vpon it the citie, *euen* Ierusalém,
2 And lay siege against it, and buylde a fort
against it, and cast a mount against it: set
the campe also against it, and lay engins of
warre against it rounde about.
3 Moreouer, take an [a] yron panne, and set it
for a wall of yron betwene thee and the citie, and direct thy face toward it, & it shal
be besieged, and thou shalt lay siege agaist
it: this shalbe a signe vnto the house of Israél.
4 Slepe thou also vpon thy left side, & lay
the iniquitie of the [b] house of Israél vpon
it: *according* to the nōbre of the daies, that
thou shalt slepe vpon it, thou shalt beare
their iniquitie.
5 For I haue laied vpon thee the yeres of
their iniquitie, according to the nomber
of the daies, *euen* thre hundreth and nin-
ty daies: so shalt thou beare the iniquitie
of the house of Israél.
6 And when thou hast accomplished them,
slepe againe vpon thy [c] right side, and thou
shalt beare the iniquitie of the house of
Iudáh fourtie daies: I haue appointed thee
a day for a yere, *euen* a day for a yere.
7 Therefore ye shalt direct thy face toward
the siege of Ierusalém, & thine [d] arme *shalbe* vncouered, and thou shalt prophecie a-
gainst it.
8 And beholde, I wil lay [e] bands vpon thee,
and thou shalt not turne thee from one side to another, til thou hast ended the daies
of thy siege.
9 Thou shalt take also vnto thee wheat, &
barly, and beanes, and lentiles, and millet,
[f] and fitches, and put them in one vessel, &
make thee bread thereof *according* to the
nomber of the daies, that thou shalt slepe
vpon thy side: *euen* [g] thre hundreth & nin-
tie daies shalt thou eat thereof.
10 And the meat, whereof thou shalt eat,
shalbe by weight, *euē* [h] twētie shekels a day:
and from time to time shalt thou eat thereof.
11 Thou shalt drinke also water by measure,
euen the sixt parte of [i] an Hin: from time to
time shalt thou drinke.
12 And thou shalt eat it *as* barly cakes, and
thou shalt bake it [k] in the dongue that cometh out of man, in their sight.
13 And the Lord said, So shal the children
of Israél eat their defiled bread amōg the
Gentiles, whether I wil cast them.
14 Then said I, Ah, Lord God, beholde, my
soule hathe not bene polluted: for frō my
youth vp, euen vnto this houre, I haue not
eaten of a thing dead, or torne in pieces,
nether came there any [l] vncleane flesh in
my mouth.
15 Then he said vnto me, Lo, I haue giuen
thee bullockes [m] dōgue for mans dongue,
& thou shalt prepare thy bread therewith.
16 Moreouer he said vnto me, Sonne of mā,
beholde, I wil breake [n] the staffe of bread
in Ierusalém, and they shal eat bread by
weight, and with care, and they shal drinke
water by measure, and with astonishment.
17 Because that bread and water shal faile,
they shalbe astonied one with another, &
shal consume away for their iniquitie.

a Which signified the stubbernes & hardnes of their heart.
b Hereby he represented the idolatrie and sinne of the tē tribes (for Samaria was on his left hand from Babylō) and how they had remained therein, thre hundreth and ninetie yeres.
c Which declared Iudáh, who had now from the time of Iosiáh slept in their sinnes fourty yeres.
d In token of a spedie vengeance.
e The people shulde so streitely be besieged, that they shulde not be able to turne them.
f Meanīg, that the famine shulde be so great, ye they shulde be glad to eat whatsoeuer they colde get.
g Which were fourtene monethes that the citie was besieged, & this was as many daies as Israél sinned yeres.
h Which make a pounde.
i Read. Exod. 29,40.
k Signifying hereby ye great scarsetie of fuel, and matter to burne.
l Muche lesse suche vile corruption.
m To be as fyre to bake thy bread with.
n That is, the force & strēgth wherewith it shulde nourish, Isa. 3, 1. chap. 5,17. & 14,13.

CHAP. V.

The signe of the heeres, whereby is signified the destruction of the people.

1 ANd thou sonne of man, take thee a
sharpe knife, *or* take thee a barbours
rasor & cause it [a] to passe vpō thine head,
and vpon thy beard: then take thee balances to weigh, and deuide the *heere*.
2 Thou shalt burne with fyre the third part
in the middes of [b] the citie, whē the dayes
of the siege are fulfilled, & thou shalt take
the *other* third parte, & smite about it with
a knife, and the *last* third parte thou shalt
scatter in the winde, and I wil drawe out a
sworde after them.
3 Thou shalt also take thereof a fewe in
nomber, and binde them in thy [c] lappe.
4 Then take of them againe and cast them
into the middes of the fyre, & burne them
in the fyre: [d] *for* thereof shal a fyre come
forthe into all the house of Israél.
5 Thus saith the Lord God, This is Ierusalém: I haue set it in the middes of the nacions and countreys, *that* are rounde about
her.
6 And she hathe changed my [e] iudgements
into wickednes more then the nacions, &
my statutes more then the countreys, that
are rounde about her: for thei haue refused
my iudgements and my statutes, *and* they
haue not walked in them.
7 Therefore thus saith the Lord God, Because your [f] multitude is greater then the
nacions that are rounde about you, and ye
haue not walked in my statutes, nether haue ye kept my iudgements: no, ye haue not
done according to the iudgements of the
nacions, that are rounde about you,
8 Therefore thus saith the Lord God, Beholde, I, euen I *come* against thee, and wil
execute iudgement in the middes of thee,
euen in the sight of the nacions.
9 And I wil do in thee, that I neuer did *before*, nether wil do anie more the like, because of all thine abominacions.
10 For in the middes of thee, the fathers
*shal eat their sonnes, and the sonnes shal
eat their fathers, and I wil execute iudgement in thee, and the whole rēnant of thee
wil I scatter into all the windes.
11 Wherefore, as I liue, saith the Lord God,
Surely because thou hast defiled my Sanctuarie with all thy filthines, & wt all thine

a To shaue thine head & thy beard.
b To wit, of that citie which he had pourtraied vpon ye bricke, Chap. 4,1. By the fyre and pestilence he meaneth the famine, wherewith one part perished, during ye siege of Nebuchad-nezzár. By the sworde those that were slayne whē Zedekiáh fled and those that were caried away captiue. And by the scattering into the wind those that fled into Egypt and into other partes after the citie was takē.
c Meaning, that a very fewe shulde be left, which ye Lord wolde preserue among all these stormes, but not without troubles and tryal.
d Out of that fyre which ye kindelest, shal a fyre come, which shal signific the destruction of Israél.
e My worde and lawe into idolatrie and superstitions.
f Because your idoles are in greater nōber and your superstitions mo then among the professed idolaters, read Isa 65, 11: or he condēneth their ingratitude in respect of his benefites.
Leu. 26,29 deu. 28,53. 2. king. 6,29. lament. 4,10. baruch. 2,3.

abominacions,therefore wil I also destroy
thee, nether shal mine eye spare *thee*, nether wil I haue anie pitie.
12 The third parte of thee shal dye with
the pestilence, and with famine shal they
be consumed in the middes of thee: and
another third parte shal fall by the sworde
rounde about thee: and I wil scatter the
last third parte into all windes, and I wil
drawe out a sworde after them.
13 Thus shal mine angre be accomplished,
& I wil cause my wrath to cease in thē,& I
wil be [g] comforted:& thei shal knowe,that
I ẏ Lord haue spoken it in my zeale,when
I haue accomplished my wrath in them.

g That is, I wil not be pacified til I be reuenged, Isa. 1,24.

14 Moreouer,I wil make thee waste,and abhorred among the nacions,that are rounde
about thee,& in the sight of all that passe
by.
15 So thou shalt be a reproche and shame, a
chastisement and an astonishmēt vnto the
nacions,that are rounde about thee, when
I shal execute iudgements in thee,in angre
and in wrath, and in sharpe rebukes: I the
Lord haue spoken it.
16 When I shal send vpon thē the °euil [h] arrowes of famine,which shalbe for *their* destruction, *and* which I wil send to destroye
you: and I wil encrease the famine vpon
you,and wil breake your staffe of bread.
17 *So wil I send vpon you famine,and euil
beasts,and they shal spoyle thee, and pestilence and blood shal passe through thee,
& I wil bring the sworde vpon thee: I the
Lord haue spoken it.

°Or, dangerous.

h Which were ẏ grashoppers, mildewe, and whatsoeuer were occasions of famine.

Chap. 5,17. & 4,13.

CHAP. VI.

He sheweth that Ierusalém shalbe destroyed for their idolatrie. 8 He prophecieth the repentance of the remnant of the people,and their deliuerance.

1 AGaine the worde of the Lord came
vnto me,saying,
2 Sonne of man, Set thy face towards the
*mountaines of Israél, and prophecie a-
gainst them,
3 And say, Ye mountaines of Israél, heare
the worde of the Lord God:thus saith the
Lord God to the [a] mountaines and to the
hilles, to the riuers and to the valleis, Beholde, I, *euen* I,wil bring a sworde vpon
you, and I wil destroye your hie places:
4 And your altars shalbe desolate,and your
images of the [b] sunne shalbe broken: and I
wil cast downe your slayne men before
your idoles.
5 And I wil lay the dead carkeises of the
children of Israél before their idoles,and
I wil scatter your bones roūde about [c] your
altars.
6 In all your dwelling places the cities shal
be desolate,and the hie places shalbe laied
waste, so ẏ your altars shalbe made waste
and desolate,& your idoles shalbe broken,
and cease, and your images of the sunne

Chap. 36,1.

a He speaketh to all the places where the Israelites accustomed to commit their idolatries threatening them destruction.

b Read 2 Kig. 23,11.

c In contempt of their power and force, ẇ shal nether be able to deliuer you nor them selues, 2. King. 23,20.

shalbe cut in pieces, and your workes shalbe abolished.
7 And the slayne shal fall in the middes of
you,and ye shal knowe that I am ẏ Lord.
8 Yet wil I leaue a remnant, [d] that you may
haue *some* that shal escape the sworde a-
mong the nacions, when you shalbe scattred through the countreis.
9 And they that escape of you,shal remember me among the nacions, where they
shalbe in captiuitie, because I am grieued
for their whorish hearts, which haue departed from me,and for their eyes, which
haue gone awhoring after their idoles,and
they [e] shalbe displeased in them selues for
the euils, which they haue committed in
all their abominacions.
10 And thei shal knowe that I am the Lord,
and that I haue not said in vaine, that I
wolde do this euil vnto them.
13 Thus saith the Lord God, [f] Smite with
thine hand, and stretche forthe with thy
fote, and say, Alas, for all the wicked abominacions of the house of Israél: for they
shal fall by the sworde,by the famine, and
by the pestilence.
12 He that is farre of, shal dye of the pestilence, and he that is nere, shal fall by the
sworde, and he that remaineth and is besieged, shal dye by the famine: thus wil I
accomplish my wrath vpon them.
13 Then [g] ye shal knowe,that I am ẏ Lord,
when their slayne men shalbe among their
idoles rounde about their altars, vpon e-
uery hie hill in all the toppes of the mountaines, and vnder euery grenē tre, and
vnder euery thicke oke, *which is* the place
where they did offer swete sauour to all
their idoles.
14 So wil I *stretch mine hand vpon them,
& make the land waste, and desolate [h] frō
the wildernes vnto Dibláth in all their
habitacions,and they shal knowe, that I am
the Lord.

d He sheweth that in all dangers God wil preserue a few which shalbe as the sede of his Church & call vpon his Name.

e They shalbe ashamed to se that their hope in idoles was but vaine, and so shal repent.

f By these signes he wolde that the Prophet shulde signifie the great destruction to come.

g That is, all nacions, when you shal se my iudgements.

Chap. 5,14.

h Some read, more desolate then the wildernes of Dibláth, which was in Syria, and bordered vpon Israél,or from the wildernes, which was South vnto Dibláth, ẇ was North: meaning, the whole coūtrey

CHAP. VII.

The end of all the land of Israél shal suddenly come.

1 MOreouer the worde of the Lord came vnto me,saying,
2 Also thou sonne of man, thus saith the
Lord God,An end *is* come vnto the lād of
Israél:the end is come vpon the foure corners of the land.
3 Now *is* the end *come* vpon thee, and I wil
send my wrath vpon thee, and wil iudge
thee according to thy waies, and wil laye
vpon thee all [a] thine abominacions.
4 Nether shal mine eye spare thee, nether
wil I haue pitie: but I wil laie thy waies
vpon thee: and thine abominacion shalbe
in the middes of thee,and ye shal knowe
that I am the Lord.
5 Thus saith the Lord God, °Beholde, one
euil,*euen one* euil is come.

a I wil punish thee as thou hast deserued for thine idolatrie.

°Or, beholde, euil cometh after euil.

6 An

6 An end is come, the end is come, it [b] watched for thee: beholde, it is come.
7 The [c] morning is come vnto thee, that
dwellest in the land: the time is come, the
day of trouble is nere, and not the [d] sounding againe of the mountaines.
8 Now I wil shortely powre out my wrath
vpon thee, and fulfil mine angre vpō thee:
I wil iudge thee according to thy wayes,
and wil lay vpon thee all thine abominacions.
9 Nether shal mine eye spare *thee*, nether wil
I haue pitie, *but* I wil lay vpon thee according to thy wayes, and thine abominacions shal be in the middes of thee, & ye
shal know that I am the Lord that smiteth.
10 Beholde, the day, beholde, it is come: the
morning is gone forthe, the [e] rod florisheth: [f] pride hathe budded.
11 [g] Crueltie is risen vp into a rod of wicked
nes: none of them *shal remaine*, nor of their
riches, nor of anie of theirs, nether shal
there be [h] lamentation for them.
12 The time is come, the day draweth nere:
let not the byer [i] reioyce, nor let him that
selleth, [k] mourne: for the wrath is vpō all
the multitude thereof.
13 For he that selleth, shal not [l] returne to
that, which is solde, althogh they were yet
aliue: for the [m] visiō was vnto all the multitude thereof, *and* they returned not,
[n] nether doeth anie encourage him self in
the punishment of his life.
14 [o] They haue blowen the trumpet, and
prepared all, but none goeth to the battel:
for my wrath is vpon all the multitude
threof.
15 The sworde *is* without, and the pestilence, and the famine within: he that is in the
field, shal dye with ẏ sworde, & he that is
in the citie, famine and pestilence shal deuoure him.
16 But they that flee away from them, shal
escape, and shalbe in the mountaines, like
ẏ doues of the valleis: all thei shal mourne, euerie one for his iniquitie.
17 *All hands shal be weake, and all knees
shal fall away *as* water.
18 *They shal also gird them selues with
sackecloth, and feare shal couer them, and
shame *shalbe* vpon all faces, and baldenes
vpon their heads.
19 They shal cast their siluer in the stretes,
and their golde shalbe *cast* far of: their *siluer and their golde can not deliuer them
in the day of the wrath of the Lord: they
shal not satisfie their soules, nether fil their
bowels: for *this* ruine is for their iniquitie.
20 He had also set the beautie of his [p] ornament in maiestie: but they made images
of their abominations, *and* of their idoles therein: therefore haue I set it farre
from them.
21 And I wil giue it into the hands of the
[q] strangers to be spoiled, and to the wicked of the earth to be robbed, & they shal
pollute it.
22 My face wil I turne also from them, and
they shal pollute my [r] secret place: for the
destroyers shal entre into it, and defile it.
23 ¶ Make a [s] chaine: for the land is ful of
the [t] iudgement of blood, and the citie is
ful of crueltie.
24 Wherefore I wil bring the moste wicked of the heathen, and they shal possesse
their houses: I wil also make the pompe of
the mightie to cease, and their [u] holie places shalbe defiled.
25 When destruction cometh, they shal seke peace, and shal not *haue* it.
26 Calamitie shal come vpon calamitie,
and rumour shalbe vpon rumour: thē shal
they seke a vision of the Prophet: but the
Law shal perish from the Priest, & counsel
from the Ancient.
27 The King shal mourne, and the prince shalbe clothed with desolation, and
the hands of the people in the land shal
be troubled: I wil do vnto them according to their wayes, and according to
their iudgements wil I iudge them, and
they shal knowe that I am the Lord.

CHAP. VIII.

1 An appearance of the similitude of God. 3 Ezekiél is broght to Ierusalém in the spirit. 6 The Lord sheweth the Prophet the idolatries of the house of Israél.

1 AND in the [a] sixt yere, in the [b] sixt
moneth, *and* in the fift *day* of the moneth, as I sate in mine house, and the Elders of Iudáh sate before me, the hand of
the Lord God fel there vpon me.
2 Then I behelde, and lo, *there was* a likenes, as the appearance of [c] fyre, to loke to,
from his loynes downewarde, and from
his loynes vpwarde, as the appearance of
brightnes, and like vnto ambre.
3 And he stretched out the likenes of an
hand, and toke me by an heerie locke of
mine head, and the Spirit lift me vp betwene the earth, and the heauē, and broght
me "by a Diuine [d] vision to Ierusalém,
into the entrie of the inner [e] gate that lieth
toward the North, where remained the
idole of [f] indignation, which prouoked
indignation.
4 And beholde, the glorie of the God of
Israél *was* there according to the vision,
that I saw [g] in the field.
5 Then said he vnto me, Sonne of man,
lift vp thine eyes now towarde ẏ North.
So I lift vp mine eyes towarde the North,
and beholde, Northwarde, at the gate of

b He sheweth ẏ the iudgemēts of God euer watch to destroye the sinners, which not withstanding he delayeth til there be no more hope of repentance.
c The beginning of his punishments is already come.
d Which was a voyce of ioye, and mirth.
e The scourge is in a readines
f That is, the proude tyrant Nebuchad-nezzár hathe gathered his force & is ready.
g This cruel enemie shalbe a sharpe scourge for their wickednes.
h Their owne affliction shalbe so great, that they shal haue no regarde to lament for others.
i For the present profite.
k For he shal lose nothing.
l In the yere of the Iubile, meaning, that none shulde enioye the priuiledge of the Law, Leui. 25,13. for they shuld all be caryed away captiues.
m This vision signified, that all shulde be caryed away, and none shulde returne for the Iubile.
n No man for all this, indeuoreth him self or taketh heart to repent for his euil life. Some read, for none shalbe strengthened in his iniquitie of his life: meaning, that thei shulde gaine nothing by flattering them selues in euil.
o The Israelites made a brag, but their hearts failed them.
Isa. 13,7. iere. 6,24.
Isa. 15,3. iere. 48,37.
Prou. 11,4. zephan. 1,18 eccle. 5,10.
p Meaning, the Sanctuarie.
q That is, of ẏ Babyloniās.
r Which signifieth ẏ Most holie place, whereinto none might enter but the hie Priest.
s Signifying, ẏ they shulde be bounde, & led away captiues
t That is, of sinnes that deserue death.
u Which was the Temple, ẏ was diuided into thre partes, Psal. 68,35.
a Of the captiuitie of Ieconiáh.
b Which conteined parte of August, & parte of September.
c As Chap. 1,27.
" Ebr. in the visions of God.
d Meaning, ẏ he was thus caryed in spirit, and not in bodie.
e Which was the porche or the court where the people assembled.
f So called because it prouoked Gods indignation, which was the idole of Báal.
g Read Chap. 3,22.

the [h] altar, this idole of indignation *was*
in the entrie.
6 He said furthermore vnto me, Sonne of
man, seest thou not what thei do? *euen* the
great abominations that the house of Israél committeth here to cause *me* to departe from [i] my Sanctuarie? but yet turne thee & thou shalt se greater abominations.
7 And he caused me to entre at the gate of
the court: and when I loked, beholde, an
hole *was* in the wall.
8 Then said he vnto me, Sonne of man, digge now in the wall. And when I had digged in the wall, beholde, *there was* a dore.
9 And he said vnto me, Go in, and beholde
the wicked abominations that they do
here.
10 So I went in, and sawe, and beholde, *there*
was euerie similitude of creping things
and [k] abominable beastes and all the idoles of the house of Israél painted vpon
the wall rounde about.
11 And there stode before them seuentie
[l] men of the Ancients of the house of Israél, and in the middes of them stode Iaazaniáh, the sonne of Shaphán, with euerie man his censour in his hand, and the
vapour of the incense went vp *like* [m] a
cloud.
12 Then said he vnto me, Sonne of man,
hast thou sene what the Ancients of the
house of Israél [n] do in the darke, euerie one
in the chambre of his imagerie? for thei
saie, The Lord seeth vs not, the Lord
hathe forsaken the earth.
13 Againe he said also vnto me, Turne thee
againe, & thou shalt se greater abominacions that thei do.
14 And he caused me to entre into the entrie of the gate of the Lords house, which
was towarde the North: and beholde there
sate women mourning for [o] Tammúz.
15 Then said he vnto me, Hast thou sene
this, ô sonne of man? Turne thee againe, &
thou shalt se greater abominacions then
these.
16 And he caused me to entre into the inner court of the Lords house, and beholde,
at the dore of the Temple of the Lord,
betwene the porche and the altar *were* a-
bout fiue and twentie men with their backes towarde the Temple of the Lord, and
their faces towarde the East, and thei worshiped the sunne, toward the East.
17 Then he said vnto me, Hast thou sene
this, ô sonne of man? Is it a smale thing to
the house of Iudáh to commit these abominaciōs wͨ thei do here? for thei haue filled the land with crueltie, and haue returned to prouoke me: and lo, thei haue cast
out [p] stinke before their noses.
18 Therefore wil I also execute *my* wrath:

h That is, in ye court where ye people had made an altar to Báal.

i For God wil not be where idoles are.

k Which were forbidden in ye Law, Leuit. 11.

l Thus they that shulde haue kept all the rest in the feare, & true seruice of God, were the ring leaders to all abominatiō, & by their example pulled others frō God.

m It was in suche abundāce.

n For besides their commune idolatrie, they had particular seruice, which they had in secretchambers.

o The Iewes write that this was a Prophet of the idoles, who after his death was once a yere mourned for in the night.

p Declaring that the censings, and seruice of the idolaters are but infection and vilenie before God.

mine eye shal not spare *them*, nether wil I
haue pitie, and * thogh thei crye in mine
eares with a loude voyce, *yet* wil I not
heare them.

CHAP. IX.

1 The destruction of the citie. 4 They that shalbe saued,
are marked. 8 A complaint of the prophet for the
destruction of the people.

1 HE cryed also with a loude voice in
mine eares, saying, The visita-
cions of [a] the citie drawe nere, and euerie
man hathe a weapon in his hand to destroye it.
2 And beholde, six [b] men came by the way
of the hie gate, which lieth toward the
[c] North, and euerie man a weapon in his
hand to destroye it: and one man among
them was clothed with linnen, with a writers [d] ynkhorne by his side, & thei went in
and stode beside the brasen altar.
3 And the glorie of the God of Israél was
[e] gone vp from the Cherúb, whereupon he
was *and stode* on the ' dore of the house &
he called to the man clothed with linnen,
which had the writers ynkhorne by his
side.
4 And ye Lord said vnto him, Go through
the middes of the citie, *euen* through the
middes of Ierusalém, and set ' a marke
vpon the foreheads of them that [f] mourne, and crye for all the abominacions that
be done in the middes thereof.
5 And to the other he said, that I might
heare, Go ye after him through the citie,
and smite: let your eye spare none, nether
haue pitie.
6 Destroye vtterly the olde, & the yong,
and the maids, and the children, and the
women, but touche no man, vpon whome
is the [g] marke, and begin at my Sanctuarie.
Then they began at the [h] Ancient men,
which were before the house.
7 And he said vnto thē, Defile the House,
and fil the courtes with the slaine, *then* go
forthe: and they went out, and slewe *them*
in the citie.
8 Now when they had slaine them, and I
had escaped, I fel downe vpō my face, and
cryed, saying, [i] Ah Lord God, wilt thou destroye all the residue of Israél, in powring
out thy wrath vpon Ierusalém?
9 Then said he vnto me, The iniquitie of
the house of Israél, and Iudáh *is* exceding
great, so that the land is ful [k] of blood, &
the citie ful of corrupt iudgement: for thei
say, The Lord hathe forsaken the earth,
and the Lord seeth *vs* not.
10 As touching me also, mine eye shal not
spare *them*, nether wil I haue pitie, *but*
wil recompence their wayes vpon their
heads.
11 And beholde, the mā clothed with linen
which had the ynkhorne by his side, made
report

* Prou. 21, 19. isa. 46, 7. ierem. 11, 11. mich. 3, 4.

a The time to take vengeance.

b Which were Angels in the similitude of men.

c Signifying that the Babylonians shulde come from the North to destroye the citie and the Tēple.

d To marke them that shulde be saued.

e Which declared, that he was not bound thereunto, nether wolde remaine anie lōger, thē there was hope that they wolde returne frō their wickednes, & worship him aright.

' Or, threshólde.

' Or, marke with Thau.

f He sheweth what is the maner of Gods children, whome he marketh to saluation: to wit, to mourne, and crye out against ye wickednes, which they se cōmitted against Gods glorie.

g Thus in all his plagues ye Lord preserueth his smale nombre, which he marketh as Exod. 12, 22. reuel 7, 3. but the chief marke is the Spirit of adoption, wherewith ye heart is sealed vp to life euerlasting.

h Which were the chief occasiō of all these euils, as Chap. 8, 11.

i This declareth, that the seruantes of God haue a cōpassion, when they se his iudgements executed.

k That is, with all kinde of wickednes, read Isa. 1, 15.

report, and said, *Lord* I haue done as thou
hast commanded me.

CHAP. X.

1 Of the man that toke hote burning coles out of the middle of the wheles of the Cherubims. 8 A rehearsal of the vision of the wheles, of the beastes, and of the Cherubims.

Chap. 1, 22.

a Which in the first chap. ver. 5. he called the foure beastes.

1 AND as I loked, beholde, in the * firmament that was aboue the head of
the [a] Cherubims there appeared vpon thẽ
like vnto the similitude of a throne, as *it*
were a saphir stone.
2 And he spake vnto the man clothed with
linen, and said, Go in betwene the wheles,
euen vnder the Cherúb, and fil thine hands
with coles of fyre from betwene the Cherubims, and scatter them ouer [b] the citie.
And he went in in my sight.

b This signified, that the citie shulde be burnt.

3 Now the Cherubims stode vpõ the right
side of the house when the man went in, &
the cloude filled the inner court.
4 Then the glorie of the Lord [c] went vp
frõ the Cherúb, *and stode* ouer the dore of
the house, and the house was filled with
the cloude, and ẏ court was filled with the
brightnes of the Lords glorie.

c Meaning, that the glorie of God shulde departe from the Temple.

5 And the [d] soũde of the Cherubims wings
was heard into the vtter court, as the
voyce of the Almightie God, when he
speaketh.

d Read Chap. 1, 24.

6 And when he had cõmanded the man clothed with linnen, saying, Take fyre from
betwene the wheles, *&* from betwene the
Cherubims, then he went in and stode
beside the whele.
7 And one Cherúb stretched forthe his hãd
from betwene the Cherubims vnto the
fyre, that was betwene the Cherubims, &
toke *thereof*, and put it into the hands of
him that was clothed with linen: who toke
it and went out.
8 And there appeared in the Cherubims,
ẏ likenes of a mãs hãd vnder their wings.
9 And whẽ I loked vp, beholde foure wheles *were* beside the Cherubims, one whele
by one Cherúb, and another whele by ano
ther Cherúb, and the appearance of the
wheles *was* as the colour of a [e] chrysolite
stone.

e Read Chap. 1, 16.

10 And their appearance (*for* they were *all*
foure of one facion) was as if one whele
had bene in *another* whele.
11 When they went forthe, they went vpon
their foure sides, and they returned not as
they went: but to the place whether the
first went, they went after it, *&* they [f] turned not as they went.

f Vntil thei had executed Gods iudgements.

Or, strakes.

12 And their whole body, and their 'rings,
& their hãds, and their wings, & the wheles were ful of eyes round about, *euen* in the
same foure wheles.
13 And *the Cherúb* cryed to these wheles in
mine hearing, *saying*, O whele.
14 And euery *beast* had foure faces: ẏ first face
was the face of a Cherúb, and the seconde
face *was* the face of a man, and the third
the face of a lion, and the fourth the face
of an egle.
15 And the Cherubims were lifted vp: * this
is the beast that I sawe at the riuer Chebár.

Chap. 1, 5.

16 And whẽ the Cherubims went, the wheles went by them: and when the Cherubims lift vp their wings to mount vp from
the earth, the same wheles also turned not
from beside them.
17 When the *Cherubims* stode, thei stode: and
when thei were lifted vp, thei lifted them
selues vp *also*: for the [g] spirit of the beast
was in them.

g There was one consent betwene the Cherubims & the wheles.

18 [h] Then the glorie of the Lord departed
from aboue the dore of the House, & stode vpon the Cherubims.

h Read Chap. 9, 3.

19 And the Cherubims lift vp their wings,
and mounted vp frõ the earth in my sight:
whẽ thei went out, the wheles also *were* besides them: & *euerie one* stode at the entrie
of ẏ gate of the Lords House at the East
side, & the glorie of the God of Israél *was*
vpon them on hie.
20 * This is the [i] beast that I saw vnder the
God of Israél by the riuer Chebár, and I
knewe that thei were the Cherubims.

Chap. 14, 1.

i That is, the whole body of the foure beasts or Cherubims.

21 Euerie one had foure faces, and euerie
one foure wings, and the likenes of mans
hands *was* vnder their wings.
22 And the likenes of their faces *was* the selfe same faces, which I sawe by the riuer
Chebár, *and* the appearance of the *Cheru-*
bims was the selfe same, *and* thei went euerie one straight forwarde.

CHAP. XI.

1 Who thei were that seduced the people of Israél. 5 Against these he prophecieth, shewing them how thei shal be dispersed abroade. 19 The renuing of the heart commeth of God. 21 He threatneth them that leane vnto their owne counsels.

1 MOreouer, the Spirit lift me vp, and
broght me vnto the East gate of the
Lords House, which lieth Eastward, and
beholde, at the entrie of the gate *were* fiue,
and twentie mẽ: amõg whome I sawe Iaazaniáh the sonne of Azúr, & Pelatiáh the
sonne of Benaiáh, the princes of ẏ people.
2 Then said he vnto me, Sonne of man,
these are the men that imagine mischief,
and deuise wicked counsel in this citie.
3 *For* thei say, [a] It is not nere, let vs buylde houses: this *citie* is the [b] caldron, and
we be the flesh.

a Thus the wicked derided the Prophetes, as thogh they preached but errors, & therfore gaue thẽ selues stil to their pleasures.

b We shal not be pulled out of Ierusalém, til the houre of our death come as ẏ flesh is not takẽ out of the caldrõ til it be sod.

4 Therefore prophecie against them, sonne of man, prophecie.
5 And ẏ Spirit of the Lord fel vpon me, &
said vnto me, Speake, Thus saith ẏ Lord,
O ye house of Israél, this haue ye said, &
I know that ẇ riseth vp of your mindes.

6 Manie haue ye murthered in this citie,
and ye haue filled the stretes thereof with
the slaine.
7 Therefore thus saith the Lord God,
Thei that ye haue slaine, and haue layed
in the middes of it, thei are [c] the flesh, and
this *citie* is the caldrō, but I wil bring you
forthe of the middes of it.
8 Ye haue feared the sworde, and I wil
bring a sworde vpon you, saith the Lord
God.
9 And I wil bring you out of the middes
thereof, and deliuer you into [d] the hands
of strangers, and wil execute iudgements
among you.
10 Ye shal fall by ẏ sworde, & I wil iudge
you in the border of [e] Israél, and ye shal
knowe that I am the Lord.
11 This *citie* shal not be your caldron, nether shal ye be the flesh in the middes
thereof, *but* I wil iudge you in the border
of Israél.
12 And ye shal knowe that I am the Lord:
for ye haue not walked in my statutes, nether executed my iudgements, but haue
done after the maners of the heathen, that
are rounde about you.
13 ¶ And when I prophecied, Pelatiáh the
sonne of [f] Benaiáh dyed: then fel I downe
vpon my face & cryed with a loude voice, and said, Ah Lord God, wilt thou then
vtterly destroie all the remnant of Israél?
14 Againe the worde of the Lord came vn
to me, saying,
15 Sonne of man, thy [g] brethren, *euen* thy
brethren, the men of thy kindred, and all
the house of Israél, wholly *are thei* vnto
whome the inhabitants of Ierusalém haue
said, Departe ye farre from the Lord: *for*
the land is giuen vs in possession.
16 Therefore say, Thus saith the Lord
God, Althogh I haue cast them farre of a-
mong the heathen, and althogh I haue scat
tered them among the countreis, yet wil
I be to them as a litle [h] Sanctuarie in the
countreis where they shal come.
17 Therefore saie, Thus saith ẏ Lord God,
I wil gather you againe from the people,
& assemble you out of the countreis where ye haue bene scattered, and I wil giue
you the land of Israél.
18 And thei shal come thether, and thei shal
take awaie all the idoles there of, and all ẏ
abominations thereof from thence.
19 * And I wil giue them one heart, and I
wil put a newe spirit within their bowels:
and I wil take the [i] stonie heart out of their
bodies, & wil giue them an heart of flesh,
20 That thei maie walke in my statutes, &
kepe my iudgements, and execute them:
and thei shalbe my people, and I wil be
their God.
21 But vpō thē, whose heart is toward their

c Cōtrarie to their vaine cōfidence he sheweth in what sense this citie is the caldrō: that is, because of the dead bodies that haue bene murthered therein, and so lie as flesh in the caldron.
d That is, of ẏ Caldeans.
e That is, in Ribláh, read 2 King. 25,7
f It semeth ẏ this noble mā dyed of some terrible death & therefore ẏ Prophet feared some strange iudgement of God toward the rest of ẏ people.
g Thei that remained stil at Ierusalém thus reproched thē that were gone into captiuitie, as thogh thei were cast of and forsaken of God.
h Thei shalbe yet a litle Church, shewing that the Lord wil euer haue some to call vpon his Name, whome he wil preserue and restore, thogh thei be for a time afflicted.
Ierem. 32,39. chap. 36,27.
i Meaning, the heart whereunto nothing can enter, and regenerat them a newe, so that their heart may be soft, & ready to receiue my graces.

idoles, & whose affection goeth after their
abominations, I wil laie their waie vpon
their owne heades, saith the Lord God.
22 ¶ Then did the Cherubims lift vp their
wings, and the wheles besides them, and
the glorie of the God of Israél *was* vpon
them on hie.
23 And the glorie of the Lord went vp frō
the middes of the citie, and stode vpon ẏ
mountaine which is toward the East side
of the citie.
24 Afterwarde the Spirit toke me vp and
broght me in a vision by the Spirit of God
into Caldea to them ẏ were led awaie captiues: so the vision that I had sene, went vp
from me.
25 Thē I declared vnto thē that were [k] led
awaie captiues, all the things that ẏ Lord
had shewed me.

CHAP. XII.

1 The parable of the captiuitie. 18 Another parable whereby the distres of hunger and thirst is signified.

1 THe worde of ẏ Lord also came vnto
me, saying,
2 Sonne of man, thou dwellest in the middes of a rebellious house, which haue eyes
to se, and se [a] not: thei haue eares to heare,
& heare not: for thei are a rebellious house.
3 Therefore thou sonne of man, " prepare
thy stuffe to go into captiuitie & go forthe
by daie in their sight: and thou shalt passe
from thy place to another place in their
sight, if it be possible that thei maie consider it: for thei are a rebellious house.
4 Then shalt thou bring forthe thy stuffe
by daie in their sight as the stuffe of him ẏ
goeth into captiuitie: & ẏ shalt go forthe
at euen in their sight, as thei that go forthe
into captiuitie.
5 Dig thou through the wall in their sight,
and carie out thereby.
6 In their sight shalt thou beare it vpon *thy*
shulders, & carie it forthe in the darke:
thou shalt couer thy face that thou se not
the earth: for I haue set thee *as* a [b] signe vnto the house of Israél.
7 And as I was cōmanded, so I broght forthe my stuffe by day, as ẏ stuffe of one that
goeth into captiuitie: and by night I digged through the wall with mine hand, and
broght it forthe in the darke, *and* I bare it
vpon *my* shulder in their sight.
8 And in the morning came the worde of ẏ
Lord vnto me, saying,
9 Sonne of man, hathe not the house of Israél, the rebellious house, said vnto thee,
What [c] doest thou?
10 *But* saie thou vnto them, Thus saith the
Lord God, This " burden *concerneth* the
chief in Ierusalém, and all the house of Israél that are among them.
11 Saie, I am your signe: like as I haue done,
so shal it be done vnto them: thei shal go

k When Ieconiáh was led awaie captiue.
a That is, thei receiue not ẏ frute of that which thei se and heare.
" *Ebr. make thee vessels to go into captiuitie.*
b That as ẏ doest, so shal thei do, and therefore in thee thei shal se their owne plague and punishment.
c Do not thei deride thy doings?
" *Or, prophecie.*

into bondage & captiuitie.
12 And the chiefest that is amõg them, shal
beare vpon his shulder in the darke and
shal go forthe: thei shal digge through the
wall, to carie out thereby: he shal couer his
face ỹ he se not the grounde with *his* eyes.
13 My net also wil I spread vpon [d] him, and
he shalbe taken in my net, and I wil bring
him to Babél to ỹ land of the Caldeás, yet
shal he not se it, thogh he shal dye there.

d When the Kig shal thinke to escape by fleing, I wil take him in my net, as Chap 17,10. & 32,3.

14 And I wil scatter towarde euerie winde
all that are about him to helpe him, and
all his garisons, and I wil drawe out the
sworde after them.
15 And thei shal knowe that I am the Lord,
when I shal scatter thẽ amõg the nacions,
and disperse them in the countreis.
16 But I wil leaue a [e] litle nombre of them
from the sworde, from the famine, and frõ
the pestilence, that thei may declare all
these abominations among the heathen,
where thei come, and thei shal knowe, that
I am the Lord.

e Which shulde beare his Name & shuld be his Churche, read Chap 11,16.

17 ¶ Moreouer, the worde of the Lord came
vnto me, saying,
18 Sonne of man, eat thy bread with trembling, and drinke thy water with trouble,
& with carefulnes,
19 And say vnto the people of the land,
Thus saith the Lord God of the inhabitants of Ierusalém, *and* of the land of Israél, Thei shal eat their bread with careful
nes, & drinke their water with desolatiõ:
for the land shalbe desolate frõ her abundance because of the crueltie of them that
dwell therein.
20 And the cities that are inhabited, shal be
left voide, & the land shalbe desolate, and
ye shal knowe that I am the Lord.
21 ¶ And the worde of the Lord came vnto
me, saying,
22 Sonne of man, what is that prouerbe that
you haue in the land of Israél, saying, The
dayes [f] are prolonged and all visions [*] faile?
23 Tel them therefore, Thus saith the Lord
God, I wil make this prouerbe to cease,
& thei shal no more vse it as a prouerbe in
Israél: but say vnto them, The dayes are at
hand and the effect of euerie vision.
24 For no vision shalbe any more in vaine,
nether *shal there be* anie flatering diuinaciõ
within the house of Israél.

f Because thei did not immediately se the prophecies accomplished, thei contemned them as thogh thei shulde neuer be fulfilled.

* Or, take none effect.

25 For I am the Lord: I wil speake, *and* that
thing that I shal speake, shal come to passe: it shalbe no more prolonged: for in
your daies, ô rebellious house, wil I say the
thing, & wil perfome it, saith ỹ Lord God.
26 Againe the worde of the Lord came vnto me, saying,
27 Sonne of man, beholde, thei of the house
of Israél say, The vision that he seeth, is
for [g] many daies *to come*, & he prophecieth
of the times that are far of.

g That is, it shal not come to passe in our daies, and therefore we care not for it: thus ỹ wicked euer abuse Gods pacience and benignitie.

28 Therefore say vnto thẽ, Thus saith the
Lord God, All my wordes shal no longer
be delayed, but ỹ thing which I haue spoken, shalbe done, saith the Lord God.

CHAP. XIII.

2 The worde of the Lord against false prophetes, which teache the people the counsels of their owne hearts.

1 And the worde of the Lord came vnto me, saying,
2 Sonne of man, prophecie against the Prophetes of * Israél, that prophecie, and say
thou vnto thẽ, that prophecie out of their
[a] owne hearts, Heare the worde of ỹ Lord.
3 Thus saith the Lord God, Wo vnto the
foolish prophetes that followe their owne
spirit, and haue sene nothing.
4 O Israél, thy Prophetes are like the foxes
[b] in the waste places.
5 [c] Ye haue not risen vp in ỹ gappes, nether
made vp the hedge for the house of Israél,
to stand in ỹ battel in the day of the Lord.
6 Thei haue sene vanitie, & lying diuina-
tiõ, saying, The Lord saith it, & the Lord
hathe not sent thẽ: & thei haue made *others*
to hope that thei wolde confirme ỹ worde
of their prophecie.

* Chap. 14,9.

a After their owne fantasie, and not as hauing ỹ reuelatiõ of ỹ Lord, Iere. 23,16.

b Watching to destroie the vineyarde.

c He speaketh to the gouernours and true ministers that shulde haue resisted them.

7 Haue ye not sene a vaine vision? & haue
ye not spoken a lying diuination? [d] ye say,
The Lord saith it, albeit I haue not spokẽ.
8 Therefore thus saith the Lord God, Because ye haue spoken vanitie & haue sene
lies, therefore beholde, I am against you,
saith the Lord God,

d Ye promised peace to this people & now ye se their destruction, so that it is manifest, that ye are false prophetes.

9 And mine hand shal be vpõ the Prophetes ỹ se vanitie, & deuine lies: thei shal not
be in the assemblie of my people, nether
shal thei be writtẽ in the [e] writing of the
house of Israél, nether shal thei entre into
the land of Israél: and ye shal knowe that
I am the Lord God.

e That is, in the boke of life, wherein the true Israelites are writen.

10 And therefore, because thei haue deceiued my people, saying, [f] Peace, & there was
no peace: & one buyld vp a [g] wall, & beholde, ỹ others daubed it ẘ vntẽpered *morter*,
11 Say vnto thẽ which dawbe it ẘ vntempe
red *morter*, that it shal fall: *for* there shal co
me a great showre, & I wil send haile stones, *which* shal cause it to fall, and a stormie
winde shal breake it.
12 Lo, when the wall is fallen, shal it not be
said vnto you, Where is ỹ dawbing wherewith ye haue dawbed it?
13 Therefore thus saith ỹ Lord God, I wil
cause a stormie winde to breake forthe in
my wrath, & a great showre shalbe in mine
angre, & haile stones in *mine* indignation
to consume it.
14 So I wil destroy the wall ỹ ye haue dawbed with vntẽpered *morter*, & bring it downe to ỹ grounde, so ỹ the fundaciõ thereof
shal be discouered, & it shal fall, & ye shal
be consumed in the middes thereof, & ye
shal knowe, that I am the Lord.

f Read Ierem. 6,14.

g Where as ỹ true Prophetes prophecied the destruction of the citie to bring ỹ people to repentance, the false Prophetes spake the cõtrarie & flatered them in their vanities, so ỹ what one false prophet said, (which is here called ỹ buylding of ỹ wall) an other false Prophet wold affirme, though he had nether occasiõ nor good groũde to beare him.

15 Thus wil I accomplish my wrath vpon the wall, and vpon thē that haue dawbed it with [h] vntempered *morter*, & wil say
vnto you, The wall is no more, nether the
dawbers thereof.
16 *To wit*, the Prophetes of Israél, which
prophecie vpon Ierusalém, and se visions
of peace for it, and there is no peace, saith
the Lord God.
17 Likewise thou sonne of man, set thy face
against ỹ daughters of thy people, which
prophecie out of their owne heart: and
prophecie thou against them, and say,
18 Thus saith the Lord God, Wo vnto the
women that sowe [i] pillowes vnder all arme
holes, and make vailes vpon the head of
euerie one that stādeth vp, to hunt soules:
wil ye hunt the soules of my people, and
wil ye giue life to the soules that come
vnto you?
19 And wil ye pollute me among my people for handfuls of [k] barlie, & for pieces of
bread to slay the soules of them that shulde not dye, and [l] to giue life to the soules
that shulde not liue in lying to my people,
that heare *your* lies?
20 Wherefore thus saith the Lord God,
Behold, I wil *haue to do* with your pillowes,
wherewith ye hunt ỹ [m] soules to make thē
to flie, and I wil teare them from your armes, and wil let the soules go, *euen* the soules, that ye hunt to make them to flie.
21 Your vailes also wil I teare, and deliuer
my people out of your hand, and thei shal
be no more in your handes to be hunted, &
ye shal knowe that I am the Lord.
22 Because with *your* lyes ye haue made the
heart of the [n] righteous sad, whome I haue not made sad, and strengthened the
hands of the wicked, that he shulde not returne from his wicked way, by promising
him life,
23 Therefore ye shal se no more vanitie, nor
diuine diuinations: for I wil deliuer my
people out of your hand, & ye shal knowe
that I am the Lord.

CHAP. XIIII.

4 *The Lord sendeth false prophetes for the ingratitude of the people. 22 He reserueth a smale portion for his Church.*

1 THen came certeine of the Elders of
Israél vnto me, and [a] sate before me.
2 And the worde of the Lord came vnto
me, saying,
3 Sonne of man, these men haue set vp their
idoles in their [b] heart, & put the stumbling
blocke of their iniquitie before their face:
shulde I, being required, answer them?
4 Therefore speake vnto them, and say vnto them, Thus saith the Lord God, Euerie
man of the house of Israél that setteth vp
his idoles in his heart, & putteth ỹ stumbling blocke of his iniquitie before his fa-

h Whereby is ment what soeuer man of him selfe setteth forthe vnder the autoritie of Gods worde.

i These superstitious women for lucre wolde prophecie & tel euerie man his fortune, giuīg thē pillowes to leane vpō & kerchefes to couer their heades, to the intēt they might the more allure them and bewitch them

k Wil ye make my worde to serue your bellies?

l These forcerers made the people beleue that they colde preserue life or destroy it, and that it shulde come to euerie one according as thei prophecied.

m That is, to cause them to perish, & that thei shulde departe from the body.

n By threatening thē that were godly, & vpholding the wicked.

Chap XIIII.

a He sheweth the hypocrisie of the idolaters, who wil dissemble to heare the Prophetes of God thogh in their heart thei follownothīg lesse, then their admonitions, and also how by one meanes, or other God doeth discouer thē.

b Thei are not only idolaters in heart, but also worship their filthie idoles opēly, which lead thē in blindnes, and cause them to stumble, and cast them out of Gods fauour, so that he wil not heare thē, whē thei call vnto him, read Ierem. 10,15.

ce, and cometh to the [c] Prophet, I the
Lord wil answer him, that cometh according to the multitude [d] of his idoles:
5 That [e] I may take the house of Israél in
their owne heart, because thei are all departed from me through their idoles.
6 Therefore say vnto the house of Israél,
Thus saith the Lord God, Returne, and
withdrawe your selues, and turne your faces from your idoles, and turne your faces
from all your abominacions.
7 For euerie one of the house of Israél, or
of the stranger that soiourneth in Israél,
which departeth frō me, and setteth vp his
idoles in his heart, and putteth the stumbling blocke of his iniquitie before his face, and cometh to a Prophete, for to inquire of him for me, I the Lord wil answer
him [*] for my selfe,
8 And I wil set my face against that man,
and wil make him an example and prouerbe, and I wil cut him of from the middes
of my people, and ye shal knowe that I am
the Lord.
9 And if the Prophet be [f] deceiued, when
he hathe spoken a thing, I the Lord haue
deceiued that Prophet, and I wil stretche
out mine hand vpō him, and wil destroy
him frō the middes of my people of Israél.
10 And thei shal beare their punishement:
the punishement of ỹ Prophet shalbe euen
as the punishement of him that asketh,
11 That the house of [g] Israél may go no
more astray from me, nether be polluted
any more with all their transgressions, but
that thei may be my people, and I may be
their God, saith the Lord God.
12 ¶ The worde of the Lord came againe
vnto me, saying,
13 Sonne of man, when the land sinneth a-
gainst me by committing a trespas, then
wil I stretche out mine hand vpon it, [h] and
wil breake the staffe of the bread thereof,
and wil send famine vpon it, and I wil destroy man and beast forthe of it.
14 Thogh these thre men [i] Noáh, Daniél,
and Iob were among them, thei shulde deliuer *but* their owne soules by their [k] righteousnes, saith the Lord God.
15 If I bring noisome beasts into the land
and thei spoile it, so that it be desolate,
that no man may passe through, because
of beastes,
16 *Thogh* these thre men were in the middes
thereof, As I liue, saith the Lord God, thei
shal saue nether sonnes nor daughters:
thei onely shalbe deliuered, but the land
shalbe waste.
17 Or *if* I bring a sworde vpon this land,
& say, Sworde, go through ỹ land, so that
I destroy man and beast out of it,
18 Thogh these thre men were in the middes
thereof, As I liue, saith the Lord God, thei
shal

c To inquire of thigs which ỹ Lord hathe appointed to come to passe.

d As his abominatiō hathe deserued: ỹ is, he shal be led with lies according as he delited therein 2. Thess 2,10.

e That is, conuince thē by their owne cōscience.

* Or, by my self.

f The Prophet declareth that God for mans ingratitude raiseth vp false Prophetes to seduce thē that delite in lies rather thē in the trueth of God, & thus he punisheth sinne by sinne, 1. King. 22,20. and destroieth aswel those Prophetes as th..t people.

g Thus Gods iudgements against ỹ wicked are admonicions to the godlie to cleaue vnto the Lord, and not to defile them selues with like abominations.

h Read Chap. 4,16. & 5, 17. Isa. 3,1.

i Thogh Noáh and Iob were now aliue, which in their time were moste godlie men (for at this time Daniél was in captiuitie with Ezekiél) and so these thre together shulde pray for this wicked people, yet wolde I not heare thē, read Iere. 15,1.

k Meaning, ỹ a very fewe (which he calleth the remnant, ver. 22.) shulde escape these plagues whome God hathe sanctified and made righteous, so ỹ this righteousnes is a signe that thei are ỹ Church of God, whōme he wolde preserue for his owne sake.

shal deliuer nether sonnes nor daughters,
but they onely shalbe deliuered them selues.
19 Or if I send a pestilence into this land, &
powre out my wrath vpon it in blood, to
destroye out of it man and beast,
20 And *thogh* Nóah, Daniél and Iob *were in*
the middes of it, As I liue, saith the Lord
God, they shal deliuer nether sonne nor
daughter: they shal *but* deliuer their owne
soules by their righteousnes.
21 For thus saith the Lord God, How muche
more when I send my *foure sore iudgements
vpon Ierusalém, *euen* the sworde,
and famine, and the noisome beast and pestilence,
to destroy man & beast out of it?
22 Yet beholde, therein shalbe left a [l] rénant
of them ỳ shalbe caryed away *bothe* sonnes
& daughters: beholde, thei shal come forthe
vnto you, & ye shal se their way, & their
enterprises: and ye shalbe comforted, concerning
the euil that I haue broght vpon
Ierusalém, *euen* concerning all that I haue
broght vpon it.
23 And they shal comforte you, when ye se
their way and their enterprises: and ye shal
knowe, that I haue not done without cause
all that I haue done in it, saith the Lord
God.

Chap. 5,17.

l Read Chap. 6,8.

CHAP. XV.

As the vnprofitable wood of the vine tre is cast into the fyre, so Ierusalém shalbe burnt.

1 AND the worde of the Lord came vnto me, saying,
2 Sonne of man, what cometh of the vine
tre aboue all *other* trees? and of the vine
branche, which is among [a] the trees of the
forest?
3 Shal wood be takẽ thereof to do any worke?
or wil men take a pyn of it to hang any
vessel thereon?
4 Beholde, it is cast in the fyre to be consumed:
the fyre consumeth bothe the ends
of it, and the middes of it is burnt. Is it
mete for *any* worke?
5 Beholde, when it was whole, it was mete
for no worke: how muche lesse shal it be
mete for any worke, when the fyre hathe
consumed it, and it is burnt?
6 Therefore thus saith the Lord God, As
the vine tre, *that is* among the trees of the
forest, which I haue giuen to the fyre to be
consumed, so wil I giue the inhabitants of
Ierusalém.
7 And I wil set my face against them: they
shal go out from *one* [b] fyre, & *another* fyre
shal consume them: & ye shal knowe, that
I am the Lord, when I set my face against
them,
8 And *when* I make the land waste, because
they haue greatly offended, saith the Lord
God.

a Which brigeth forthe no frute, no more then the other trees of the forest do: meaning, that if Ierusalém, which bare the name of his Church, did not bring forthe frute, it shulde be vtterly destroied.

b Thogh they escape one dager, yet another shal take them.

CHAP. XVI.

The Prophet declareth the benefites of God toward Ierusalém. 15 Their vnkindnes. 46 He iustifieth the wickednes of other people in comparison of the synnes of Ierusalém. 49 The cause of the abominacions, into which the Sodomites fel. 60 Mercie is promised to the repentant.

1 AGaine, the worde of the Lord came
vnto me, saying,
2 Sonne of man, cause Ierusalém to knowe
her abominacions,
3 And say, Thus saith the Lord God vnto
Ierusalém, Thine habitacion & thy kinred
is of the land [a] of Canáan: thy father was
an Amorite, and thy mother an Hittite.
4 And in thy natiuitie whẽ thou wast [b] borne,
thy nauel was not cut: thou wast not
washed in water to soften *thee*: thou wast
not salted with salt, nor swadeled in cloutes.
5 None eye pitied thee to do any of these
vnto thee, for to haue compassion vpon
thee, but thou wast cast out in the opẽ field
to the contempt of thy persone in the day
that thou wast borne.
6 And when I passed by thee, I sawe thee
polluted in thine [c] owne blood, and I said
vnto thee, when thou wast in thy blood,
Thou shalt liue: euen when ỳ wast in thy
blood, I said vnto thee, Thou shalt liue.
7 I haue caused thee to multiplie, as ỳ bud
of the field, and thou hast increased, and
waxen great, and thou hast gotten excellent
ornamẽts: *thy* brests are facioned, thine
heere is growen, where as thou wast naked
and bare.
8 Now when I passed by thee, and loked
vpon thee, beholde, thy time *was as* the time
of loue, & I spred my skirtes ouer thee,
and couered [d] thy filthines: yea, I sware vnto
thee, and entred into a couenant with
[e] thee, saith the Lord God, and thou becamest
mine.
9 Then washed I thee with [f] water: yea, I
washed away thy blood from thee, and I
[g] anointed thee with oyle.
10 I clothed thee also with broydred worke,
and shod thee with badgers skinne: and I
girded thee about with fine linen, & I couered
thee with silke.
11 I decked thee also with ornaments, and I
put brasselets vpon thine hands, & a chaine
on thy necke.
12 And I put a frontelet vpon thy face, and
earīgs in thine eares, & a beautiful [h] crowne
vpon thine head.
13 Thus wast thou deckt with golde and siluer,
and thy raiment was of fine linen, and
silke, & broydered worke: thou didest eat
fine floure, and hony and oyle, & thou wast
very beautiful, and thou didest growe vp
into a kingdome.
14 And thy name was spred among the heathen
for thy beautie: for it was perfite
through my [i] beautie which I had set vpon
thee, saith the Lord God.

a Thou boastest to be of ỳ sede of Abrahám, but thou art degenerate and followest the abominacions of the wicked Canaanites, as children do the maners of their fathers, Isa 1 4. & 57,3.

b When I first broght thee out of Egypt, & plãted thee in this land to be my Church.

c Being thus in thy filthines and forsaken of all mẽ, I toke thee & gaue thee life: whereby is meat that before God wash his Church, & giue life, there is nothing, but filthines and death.

d These wordes, as blood, pollucion, nakednes & filthines are oft times repeted, to beate downe their pride, and to cause them to consider what thei were before God receiued them to mercie, fauoured them & couered their shame.

e That thou shuldest be a chaste wife vnto me, and that I shulde mainteine thee & endue thee ẘ all graces.

f I washed away thy sinnes.

g I sanctified thee with mine holy Spirit.

h Hereby he sheweth how he saued his Church, enriched it & gaue it power and dominion to reigne.

i He declareth wherein the dignitie of Ierusalém stode: to wit, in that the Lord gaue them of his beautie and excellencie.

15 Now thou didest [k] trust in thine owne
beautie, and plaied the harlot, because of
thy renome, and hast powred out [l] thy fornicacions on euery one that passed by, *thy
desire* was to him.
16 And thou didest take thy garments, and
deckt thine hie places with diuers colours,
[m] and plaied the harlot thereupon: the like
things shal not come, nether hathe anie
done so.
17 Thou hast also takẽ thy faire iewels *made* of my golde & of my siluer, which I had
giuen thee, & [n] madest to thy self images
of men, and didest commit whoredome
with them,
18 And toke thy broidered garments, & couered them: and thou hast set mine oyle &
my perfume before them.
19 My meat also, which I gaue thee, *as* fine
floure, oyle, & hony, *where with* I fed thee,
thou hast euen set it before thẽ for a swete sauour: thus it was, saith the Lord God.
20 Moreouer thou hast taken thy sonnes &
thy daughters, whome ẏ hast borne vnto
me, & these hast thou sacrificed vnto them,
to [o] be deuoured: is *this* thy whoredome a
smale matter?
21 That thou hast slayne my children, and
deliuered them to cause thẽ to passe *through
fyre* for them?
22 And in all thine abominacions & whoredomes thou hast not remẽbred the daies
of thy youth, when thou wast naked and
bare, & wast polluted in thy blood.
23 And beside all thy wickednes (wo, wo vnto thee, saith the Lord God)
24 Thou hast also buylt vnto thee an hie
place, and hast made thee an hie place in e-
uery strete.
25 Thou hast buylt thine hie place at euery
*corner of ẏ way, & hast made thy beautie
to be abhorred: thou hast opened thy fete
to euery one that passed by, & multiplied
thy whoredome.
26 Thou hast also cõmitted fornicacion wᵗ
the [p] Egyptians thy neighbours, which haue great members, and hast encreased thy
whoredome, to prouoke me.
27 Beholde, therefore I did stretch out mine hand ouer thee, and wil diminish thine
ordinarie, and deliuer thee vnto the wil
of them that hate thee, *euen* to the *daughters of the Philistims, which are ashamed
of thy wicked way.
28 Thou hast played the whore also with
the Assyriãs, because thou wast insatiable:
yea, thou hast played the harlot with them,
and yet coldest not be satisfied.
29 Thou hast moreouer multiplied thy fornicacion frõ the land of Canáã vnto Caldea, & yet thou wast not satisfied herewith.
30 How weake is thine heart, saith ẏ Lord
God, seing thou doest all these things, *euẽ*
ẏ worke of a *presũpteous whorish womã?
31 In that thou buyldest thine hie place in
the corner of euery way, and makest thine
hie place in euery strete, & hast not bene as
an harlot [q] that despiseth a rewarde,
32 But *as* a wife that plaieth the harlot, *and*
taketh others for her housband:
33 Thei giue giftes to all *other* whores, but ẏ
giuest giftes vnto all thy louers, & rewardest them, that they may come vnto thee
on euery side for thy fornicacion.
34 And the contrary is in thee frõ *other* women in thy fornicacions, nether *the like* fornicacion *shalbe* after thee: for in that thou
giuest a reward, & no reward is giuen vnto
thee, therefore thou art contrary.
35 Wherefore, ô harlot, heare the worde of
the Lord.
36 Thus saith the Lord God, Because thy
*shame was powred out, and thy filthines
discouered through thy fornicaciõs with
thy louers, and with all the idoles of thine
abominacions & by the blood of thy children, which thou didest offre vnto them,
37 Beholde, therefore I wil gather all [r] thy
louers, with whome thou hast takẽ pleasure, and all them that thou hast loued, with
all them that thou hast hated: I wil euen
gather them rounde about against thee, &
wil discouer thy filthines vnto them that
thei may se all thy filthines.
38 And I wil iudge thee *after* the maner of
them that are [s] harlots, and of them that
shead blood, & I wil giue thee the blood of
wrath and ielousie.
39 I wil also giue thee into their hands, and
they shal destroy thine hie place, and shal
breake downe thine hie places: they shal
strippe thee also out of thy clothes, & shal
take thy faire iewels, and leaue thee naked
and bare.
40 They shal also bring vp a companie a-
gainst thee, and they shal stone thee wᵗ stones, & thrust thee through wᵗ their swordes.
41 And thei * shal burne vp thine houses wᵗ
fyre, & execute iudgements vpon thee in
the sight of many women: and I wil cause
thee to cease from playing the harlot, and
thou shalt giue no reward any more.
42 So wil I make my wrath toward thee to
rest, & my [t] ielousie shal departe frõ thee,
and I wil cease and be no more angrie.
43 Because ẏ hast not remẽbred the daies of
thy youth, but hast prouoked me with all
these things, beholde, therefore I also haue [u] broght thy way vpon thine head, saith
the Lord God: yet hast not thou had consideracion of all thine abominacions.
44 Beholde, all that vse prouerbes, shal vse
this prouerbe against thee, saying, As *is* the
mother, [x] *so is* her daughter.
45 Thou art thy mothers daughter, ẏ hathe
cast of her housband & her children, and
thou

k In abusing my giftes and in putting thy confidence in thine owne wisdome and dignitie, which were the occasions of thine idolatrie.

l There was none idolatrie so vile wherewith thou didest not pollute thy self.

m This declareth how the idolaters put their chief delite in those things, which please ẏ eies, and outwarde senses.

n Thou hast conuerted my vessels & instruments, ẏ I gaue thee to serue me with, to the vse of thine idoles.

o Meaning, by fyre, read Leu. 18,21. 2. king. 23,10.

*Or, head.

p He noteth ẏ great impietie of this people who first falling frõ God to seke helpe at strange nacions, did also at length imbrace their idolatrie, thinking thereby to make their amitie more strong.

*Or, cities.

*Or, that wil beare rule.

q Meaning, ẏ some harlots contẽne smale rewardes, but no louers gaue a rewarde to Israél, but thei gaue to all others: signifying that the idolaters bestowe all their substance, ẏ thei receiue of God for his glorie, to serue their vile abominations.

*Or, nether partes.

r Egyptians, Assyrians and Caldeãs, whome thou tokest to be thy louers, shal come and destroy thee, Chap. 23,9.

s I wil iudge thee to death, as the adulterers and murtherers.

* 2. King. 25,9.

t I wil vtterly destroy thee & so my ielousy shal cease.

u I haue punished thy fautes, but ẏ woldest not repent.

x As were the Canaanites & the Hittites & others your predecessors, so are you their successors.

thou art ẏ sister of thy [y] sisters, which forsoke their housbands and their children:
your mother is an Hittite, and your father
an Amorite.
46 And thine elder sister is Samaria, & her
[z] daughters, that dwell at thy left hand,
and " thy yong sister, that dwelleth at
thy right hand, *is* Sodóm, and her daughters.
47 Yet hast thou [a] not walked after their
waies, nor done after their abominations:
but as it *had bene* a very litle *thing*, thou
wast corrupted more then thei in all thy
waies.
48 As I liue, saith the Lord God, Sodóm
thy sister hathe not done, *nether* she nor her
daughters, as thou hast done & thy daughters.
49 Beholde, this was the iniquitie of thy
sister Sodóm, [b] Pride, fulnes of bread, and
abundance of idlenes was in her, and in
her daughters: nether did she strengthen
the hand of the poore and nedie.
50 But thei were hautie, and cōmitted abo
minacion before me: therefore I toke thē
away, as pleased me.
51 Nether [c] hathe Samaria committed halfe of thy sinnes, but thou hast exceded thē
in thine abominacions, and hast [d] iustified thy sisters in all thine abominacions,
which thou hast done.
52 Therefore thou which hast iustified thy
sisters, beare thine owne shame for thy
sinnes, that thou hast cōmitted more abominable thē thei *which* are more righteous
then thou art: be thou therefore confounded also, and beare thy shame, seing that
thou hast iustified thy sisters.
53 Therefore I wil brīg againe [e] their captiuitie with the captiuitie of Sodóm, and
her daughters, and with the captiuitie of
Samaria, and her daughters: euen the captiuitie of thy captiues in the middes of
them,
54 That thou maist beare thine owne shame, and maist be confounded in all that
thou hast done, in that thou hast [f] comforted them.
55 And thy sister Sodóm and her daughters shal returne to their former state: Samaria also & her daughters shal returne to
their former state, ẇhē thou & thy daugh
ters shal returne to your former state.
56 For thy sister Sodóm " was not heard of
[h] by thy report in the day of thy pride.
57 Before thy wickednes was [i] discouered,
as in that same time of the reproche of the
daughters of Arám, and of all the daughters of the Philistims round about [k] her
which despise thee on all sides.
58 Thou hast borne *therefore* thy wickednes
and thine abominacion, saith the Lord.
59 For thus saith the Lord God, I might

y That is, of Samaria and Sodóm.
z That is, her cities.
" *Ebr. thy sister yonger thē thou.*
a But done farre worse.
b He alledgeth these foure vices, pride, excesse, idlenes & contempt of the poore, as foure principal causes of suche abomination, wherefore they were so horribly punished, Ge. 19, 24.
c Which worshipped ẏ calues in Bethel and Dan.
d Thou art so wicked, that in respect of thee Sodóm & Samaria were iuste.
e This he speaketh in comparison, saying, that he wolde restore Ierusalém when Sodóm shulde be restored, ẏ is, neuer: and this is mēt of the greatest parte of the Iewes.
f In that thou hast shewed thy self worse then they, and yet thoght test to escape punishement.
g Meaning, ẏ it shulde neuer come to passe.
" *Ebr. was not a rumour in thy mouth.*
h Thou woldest not call her punishement to mynde when thou wast aloft, to learne by her exāple to feare my iudgements.
i That is, til ẏ wast broght vnder by the Syriās & Philistims, 2. Chro. 28, 19.
k Which ioyned with the Syrians, or compassed about Ierusalém.

euen deale with thee, as ẏ hast done: when
thou didest despise the [l] othe, in breaking
the couenant.
60 Neuertheles, I wil [m] remember my couenant *made* with thee in the daies of thy
youth, and I wil confirme vnto thee an e-
uerlasting couenant.
61 Then thou shalt remembre thy waies, &
be ashamed, when thou shalt receiue [n] thy
sisters, *bothe* thy elder and thy yonger, and
I wil giue them vnto thee for daughters,
but not [o] by thy couenant.
62 And I wil establish my couenant with
thee, and thou shalt knowe that I am the
Lord,
63 That thou maist remembre, and be [p] a-
shamed, and neuer open thy mouthe any
more: because of thy shame when I am pacified toward thee, for all that thou hast
done, saith the Lord God.

l When thou brakest the couenant, which was made betwene thee & me, as vers. 8.
m That is, of mercie and loue I wil pitie thee, and so stand to my couenāt, thogh thou hast deserued the contrary.
n Whereby he sheweth ẏ among the moste wicked he had euer some sede of his Church which he wolde cause to fructifie in due tyme: & here he declareth how he wil call ẏ Gentiles.
o But of my fre mercie.
p This declareth what frutes Gods mercies worke in his, to wit, sorow, and repentance for their former life.

CHAP. XVII.

The parable of the two egles.

1 AND the worde of the Lord came vn
to me, saying,
2 Sonne of man, put forthe a parable and
speake a prouerbe vnto the house of Israél,
3 And say, Thus saith the Lord God, The
great [a] egle with great wings, *and* long
wings, *and* ful of fethers, which had diuers colours, came vnto Lebanón, and toke the hiest branche of the cedre,
4 And brake of the toppe of his twigge, &
caried it into the land [b] of marchants, *and*
set it in a citie of marchants.
5 He toke also of the [c] sede of the land, and
planted it in a fruteful grounde: he placed
it by great waters, and set it *as* a willow
tre.
6 And it budded vp, and was [d] like a spreading vine of [e] lowe stature, whose branches turned toward it, and the rootes thereof were vnder it: so it became a vine, &
it broght forthe branches, and shot forthe
buds.
7 There was also [f] another great egle with
great wings and many fethers, & beholde,
this vine did turne her rootes toward it, &
spred forthe her branches toward it that
she might water it by the trenches of her
plantacion.
8 It was planted in a good soile by great
[g] waters, that it shulde bring forthe branches, and beare frute, and be an excellent
vine.
9 Say thou, Thus saith the Lord God,
Shal it prosper? shal [h] he not pul vp the
rootes thereof, and destroy the frute thereof, and cause them to drye? all the leaues of her bud shal wither without great
power, or many people, to plucke it vp by
the rootes thereof.

Chap. XVII.
a That is, Nebuchadnezzár, who hathe great power, riches and many cōtreys vnder him, shal come to Ierusalém and take away Ieconiáh the King, as ver. 12.
b Meaning, to Babylon.
c That is, Zedekiáh, who was of the Kings blood, and was left at Ierusalém, & made King in stead of Ieconiáh, 2. King. 24, 17. Ier. 37, 1.
d This was Zedekiahs kingdome.
e That it might not haue power to rebell against Babylon, as ver. 14.
f Meaning, the King of Egypt of whome Zedekiáh soght succour agaīst Nebuchadnezzár.
g Thei thoght to be moistned by the waters of Nilus.
h Shal not Nebuchad-nezzár destroy it?

10 Beholde,it was planted:but shal it prosper? shal it not be dryed vp, and wither?
i when the East winde shal touche it, it
shal wither in the tréches, where it grewe.
11 Moreouer, the worde of the Lord came
vnto me,saying,
12 Say now to this rebellious house,Knowe
ye not,what these things *meane*? tel them,
Beholde,the King of Babél is come to Ierusalém, and hathe taken k the King thereof,and the princes thereof, and led them
with him to Babél,
13 And hathe taken *one* of the Kings sede,
and made a couenant with him, and hathe
taken l an othe of him: he hathe also taken
the princes of the land,
14 That the kingdome might be in subiection, and not lift it self vp, *but* kepe their
couenant,and stand to it.
15 But he rebelled against him, and sent his
ambassadours into Egypt, that thei might
giue him horses, & muche people: shal he
prosper? shal he escape, that doeth suche
things? or shal he breake the couenant, &
be deliuered?
16 As I liue, saith the Lord God, he shal
dye in the middes of Babél,in the place of
the King,that had made him King,whose
othe he despised, and whose couenant *made* with him,he brake.
17 Nether shal Pharaóh with *his* mightie
hoste,& great multitude of people, mainteine him in the warre,when thei haue cast
vp mounts, and buylded ramparts to destroy many persones.
18 For he hathe despised the othe, and broken the couenant (yet lo, he had giuen
m his hand) because he hathe done all these
things,he shal not escape.
19 Therefore,thus saith the Lord God, As
I liue,I wil surely bring mine othe that he
hathe despised, and my couenant that he
hathe broken, vpon his owne head.
20 *And I wil spread my net vpõ him,& he
shalbe taken in my net, & I wil bring him
to Babél, and wil entre into iudgement
with him there for his trespas that he hathe committed against me.
21 And all that fle from him with all his
hoste,shal fall by the sworde,and thei that
remaine,shal be scatered toward all ỹ windes:and ye shal knowe that I the Lord haue spoken it.
22 Thus saith the Lord God, I wil also take of the toppe n of this hie cedre,and wil
set it,and cut of the o toppe of the tendre
plante thereof, and I wil plante it vpon
an hie mountaine and great.
23 *Euen* in the hye mountaine of Israél wil
I plant it:and it shal bring forthe boughs
and beare frute, and be an excellent cedre, and vnder it shal remaine all birdes,
and euerie p foule shal dwell in the shadowe of the branches thereof.
24 And all ỹ q trees of the field shal knowe
that I the Lord haue broght downe ỹ hye
tre, and exalted the lowe tre, that I haue
dryed vp the grene tre, and made the drye
tre to florish:I the Lord haue spoken it, &
haue done it.

i By this drye wynde, he meaneth the Babylonians.

k That is, Ieconiáh,2.king 24,15.

l For his subiection and obedience.

m Because he toke the Name of God in vaine & brake his othe ẇ he had cõfirmed by giuing his hand,therefore ỹ Prophet declareth ỹ God wolde not suffer suche periurie and infidelitie to escape punishement.

Chap.12,13. & 32,3.

n This promes is made to the Church ẇ shal be as a smale remnãt & as the top of a tre.

o I wil trymme it and dresse it.

p Bothe the Iewes & Gentils shalbe gathered into it.

q All ỹ worlde shal know that I haue pluct downe ỹ proude enemies and set vp my Church which was lowe and contemned.

CHAP. XVIII.

2 He sheweth that euerie man shal beare his owne synne. 21 To him that amendeth,is saluacion promised. 24 Death is prophecied to the righteous, which turneth backe from the right waye.

1 THe worde of the Lord came vnto me
againe,saying,
2 What meane ye that ye speake this prouerbe,concerning ỹ land of Israél,saying,
a The fathers haue eaten soure grapes, &
the childrens teeth are set on edge?
3 As I liue,saith the Lord God, ye shal vse
this prouerbe no more in Israél.
4 Beholde, all soules are mine, bothe the
soule of the father, and also the soule of
the sonne are mine:the soule that sinneth,
it shal dye.
5 But if a man be iust, and do that which is
lawful,and right,
6 *And* hathe not eaten b vpõ the mountaines,nether hathe lift vp his eyes to the idoles of the house of Israél, nether hathe
defiled his neighbours wife, nether hathe
"lien wih a * menstruous woman,
7 Nether hathe oppressed any, *but* hathe
restored the pledge to his dettour: he
that hathe spoiled none by violence, * *but*
hathe giuen his bread to the hungrie, and
hathe couered the naked with a garment,
8 And hathe not giuen forthe vpon * vsurie, nether hathe taken any increase, *but*
hathe withdrawen his hand from iniquitie, and hathe executed true iudgement
betwene man and man,
9 And hathe walked in my statutes,and hathe kept my iudgements to deale truely,
he is iuste,he shal surely liue,saith ỹ Lord
God.
10 ¶ If he beget a sonne,that is "a thief,*or* a
sheader of blood,if he do any one of these
things,
11 Thogh he do not all these things, but ether hathe eaten vpon the mountaines, or
defiled his neighbours wife,
12 *Or* hathe oppressed the poore and nedy,
or hathe spoiled by violence, *or* hathe not
restored the pledge, or hathe lift vp his
eyes vnto the idoles, *or* hathe committed
abomination,
13 *Or* hathe giuen forthe vpon vsurie, or
hathe taken increase, shal he liue? he shal
not liue:seing he hathe done all these abominacions, c he shal dye the death,*and* his
blood shalbe vpon him.
14 ¶ But if he beget a sonne, that seeth all
his fathers sinnes, which he hathe done,
and

a The people murmured at ỹ chastisings of the Lord & therefore vsed this prouerbe, meaning that their fathers had synned & their children were punished for their transgresions,read Ier 31,29.

b If he hathe not eaten of ỹ flesh ỹ hathe bene offred vp to idoles, to honour them thereby.

"*Ebr. come nere.*

Leu.20,18.

Isa.58,7. matt.25,35.

Exo.22,25. leu.25,37. deu.23,19. psal.15,5.

"*Or,a cruel mã*

c He sheweth how the sonne is punished for his fathers faute: ỹ is, if he be wicked as his father was,and doeth not repent, he shalbe punished as his father was,or els not.

and feareth, nether doeth ſuche like,
15 That hathe not eaten vpon the mountai
nes, nether hathe lift vp his eyes to the i-
doles of the houſe of Iſraél, nor hathe defiled his neighbours wife,
16 Nether hathe oppreſſed anie, nor hathe
withholden the pledge, nether hathe ſpoiled by violence, *but* hathe giuē his bread to
the hungrie, and hathe couered the naked
with a garment,
17 *Nether* hathe withdrawen his hand frō
the afflicted, nor receiued vſurie nor increaſe, *but* hathe executed my iudgements,
& hathe walked in my ſtatutes, he ſhal
not dye in the iniquitie of his father, *but* he
ſhal ſurely liue.
18 His father, becauſe he cruelly oppreſſed
and ſpoiled his brother by violence, and
hathe not done good among his people,
lo, euen he dyeth in his iniquitie.
19 Yet ſaie ye, Wherefore ſhal not the ſonne beare the iniquitie of the father? becau
ſe the ſonne hathe executed iudgement &
iuſtice, & hathe kept all my ſtatutes, and
done them, he ſhal ſurely liue.
20 * The ſame ſoule that ſinneth, ſhal dye:
the ſonne ſhal not beare the iniquitie of
the father, nether ſhal the father beare the
iniquitie of the ſonne, *but* the righteouſnes
of the righteous ſhalbe vpon him, and the
wickednes of the wicked ſhalbe vpon him
ſelf.
21 But if the wicked wil returne from all
his ſinnes that he hathe committed, and
kepe all my [d] ſtatutes, and do that which is
lawful and right, he ſhal ſurely liue, & ſhal
not dye.
22 All his tranſgreſsions that he hathe com
mitted, thei ſhal not be ‖ mencioned vnto
him, *but* in his [e] righteouſnes that he hathe
done, he ſhal liue.
23 [f] Haue I anie deſire that the wicked ſhul
de dye, ſaith the Lord God? ‖ or ſhal he
not liue, if he returne from his waies?
24 But if the righteous turne awaie from
his righteouſnes, and commit iniquitie, &
do according to all the abominaciōs, that
the wicked man doeth, ſhal he liue? all his
[g] righteouſnes that he hathe done, ſhal not
be mencioned: *but* in his tranſgreſsion that
he hathe committed, and in his ſinne that
he hathe ſinned, in them ſhal he dye.
25 Yet ye ſaie, The waie of the Lord is not
[h] equal: heare now, ô houſe of Iſraél. Is not
my waie equal? *or* are not your waies vnequal?
26 *For* when a righteous man turneth awaie
from his righteouſnes, and cōmitteth iniquitie, he ſhal euen dye for the ſame, he
ſhal *euen* dye for his iniquitie, that he hathe done.
27 Againe when the wicked turneth a way
from his wickednes that he hathe committed, and doeth that which is lawful and
right, he ſhal ſaue his ſoule aliue.
28 Becauſe he conſidereth, & turneth awaie
from all his tranſgreſsions that he hathe
committed, he ſhal ſurely liue & ſhal not
dye.
29 Yet ſaith the houſe of Iſraél, The waie
of the Lord is not equal. O houſe of Iſraél, are not my waies equal? *or* are not your
waies vnequal?
30 Therefore I wil iudge you, ô houſe of
Iſraél, euerie one according to his waies,
ſaith the Lord God: returne *therefore* and
cauſe *others* to turne awaie from all your
trāſgreſsions: ſo iniquitie ſhal not be your
deſtruction.
31 Caſt away from you all your tranſgreſ-
ſions, whereby ye haue tranſgreſſed & ma
ke [i] you a new heart and a new ſpirit: for
why wil ye dye, ô houſe of Iſraél?
32 For I deſire not the death of him that
dyeth, ſaith the Lord God: cauſe therefore
one another to returne, and liue ye.

CHAP. XIX.

1 The captiuitie of the Kings of Iudáh ſignified by the lions whelpes, and by the lion. 10 The proſperitie of the citie of Ieruſalém that is paſt, and the miſerie thereof that is preſent.

1 THou alſo, take vp a lamentacion for
the [a] princes of Iſraél,
2 And ſaie, Wherefore laie thy [b] mother *as*
a lioneſſe among the lions? ſhe nouriſhed
her yong ones among the lyons whelpes,
3 And ſhe broght vp one of her whelpes &
it became a lion, and it learned to catch ŷ
praie, & it deuoured men.
4 The [c] nations alſo heard of him, *and* he
was taken in their nettes, and thei broght
him in chaines vnto the land of Egypt.
5 Now when ſhe ſawe, that ſhe had waited
and her hope waſt loſt, ſhe toke another of
her [d] whelpes, and made him a lion.
6 Which went among the lions, & became
a lion, and learned to catche the praie, *and*
he deuoured [e] men.
7 And he knewe their widowes, and he deſtroied their cities, and the land was waſted, and all that was therein by the noiſe
of his roaring.
8 Then the [f] nations ſet againſt him on e-
uerie ſide of the coūtreis & laid their nettes for him: ſo he was taken in their pit.
9 And thei put him in priſon & in chaines
and broght him to the King of Babél, &
thei put him in holdes, that his voice ſhulde no more be heard vpon the mountaines
of Iſraél.
10 Thy [g] mother *is* like a vine in thy blood,
planted by ŷ waters: ſhe broght forth e frute and branches by the abundant waters,
11 And ſhe had ſtrong rods for the ſcepters
of them that beare rule, and her ſtature
was exalted among the branches, and ſhe

Deu.24,16. 2.king.4,6. 2.chro.25,4.

d He ioyneth the obſeruation of the cōmandements with repentance: for none cā repent in dede except he labour to kepe the Law.

‖ *Or, not laied to his charge.*

e That is, in ŷ frutes of his faith, which declare that God doeth accept him.

f He ſpeaketh this to cōmēd Gods mercie to poore ſinners, who rather is ready to pardon, thē to puniſh, as his long ſuffering declareth Chap 33,11. Albeit God in his eternal counſel appointed the death and damnation of the reprobat, yet the end of his counſel was not their death only, but chiefly his owne glorie. And alſo becauſe he doeth not approue ſinne, therfore it is here ſaid that he wolde haue them to turne awaie from it ŷ thei might liue.

‖ *Or, rather that he maie returne frō his waies and liue.*

g That is, ŷ falſe opinion that the hypocrites haue of their righteouſnes.

h In puniſhing the father ŵ the children.

i He ſheweth that man can not forſake his wickednes til his heart be changed, ŵ is onely the worke of God

a That is, Iehoház and Iehoiakím Ioſiahs ſonnes, who for their pride and crueltie are compared vnto lyons.

b To wit, Iehoház mother, or Ieruſalém.

c By Pharaóh Nechó King of Egypt. 2. King.23,33.

d Which was Iehoiakím.

e He ſlewe of ŷ Prophets & thē, ŷ feared God, and rauiſhed their wiues.

f Nebuchadnezzár with his great armie which was gathered of diuers nations.

g He ſpeaketh this in the reproche of this wicked King, in whoſe blood, that is, in the race of his predeceſſors Ieruſalém ſhulde haue bene bleſſed, according to Gods promes, and floriſhed as a fruteful vine.

appeared in her height with ẏ multitude
of her branches.
12 But she was plucked vp in wrath: she was
cast downe to the grounde, and the [h] East
winde dryed vp her frute: *her branches* were
broken, and withered: *as for* the rod of her
strength, the fyre consumed it.
13 And now she is planted in the wildernes
in a drye and thirstie grounde.
14 And fyre is gone out [i] of a rod of her
branches, which hathe deuoured her frute,
so that she hathe no strong rod *to be* a scepter to rule: this is a lamentacion and shalbe for a lamentacion.

h Meaning, ẏ the Caldeans shulde destroy them as the East winde doeth the frute of the vine.

i Destruction is come by Zedekiáh who was the occasion of this rebellion.

CHAP. XX.

3 The Lord denieth that he wil answere them when thei praie because of their vnkindenes. 33 He promiseth that his people shal returne from captiuitie. 46 By the forest that shulde be burnt, is signified the burning of Ierusalém.

1 AND in the [a] seuenth yere in the fift
moneth, ẏ tenth *day* of ẏ moneth, came certaine of the Elders of Israél to enquire of the Lord, and sate before me.
2 Then came the worde of the Lord vnto
me, saying,
3 Sonne of man, speake vnto the Elders of
Israél, and saie vnto them, Thus saith
the Lord God, Are ye come to inquire
of me? as I liue, saith the Lord God, when
I am asked, I wil not answer you.
4 Wilt thou iudge them, sonne of mā? wilt
thou iudge *them*? cause [b] them to vnderstand the abominations of their fathers,
5 And saie vnto them, Thus saith ẏ Lord
God, In the daie when I chose Israél, and
[c] lift vp mine hand vnto the sede of the
house of Iaakób, and made my self knowē
vnto them in the land of Egypt, when I
lift vp mine hand vnto them, and said, I
am the Lord your God,
6 In the daie that I lift vp mine hand vnto
them to bring them forthe of the land of
Egypt, into a land that I had prouided for
them, flowing with milke & honie which
is pleasant among all lands,
7 Then said I vnto them, Let euerie man
cast awaie thē abominacions of his eyes,
[d] and defile not your selues with ẏ idoles
of Egypt: *for* I am the Lord your God.
8 But thei rebelled against me, and wolde
not heare me: *for* none cast awaie the abominacions of [e] their eyes, nether did thei
forsake ẏ idoles of Egypt: then I thoght
to powre out mine indignacion vpon thē,
& to accomplish my wrath against them
in the middes of the land of Egypt.
9 But I had respect to my [f] Name, that it
shulde not be polluted before the heathen,
among whome thei were, & in whose sight
I made my self knowē vnto thē in bringing them forthe of the land of Egypt.
10 Now I caried them out of the land of E-

a Of the captiuitie of Ieconiáh.

b This declareth the great lenitie and pacience of God which calleth sinners to repentance before he condemne them.

c I sware ẏ I wolde be their God. which maner of othe was obserued from all antiquitie, where thei vsed to lift vp their hands toward the heauen, ackrowledging God to be autor of trueth, and the defender thereof, & also ẏ iudge of the heart, wishing that he shulde take vengeance, if thei conceiled anie thing which thei knewe to be trueth.

d God had forbidden them to make mencion of the idoles, Exo. 23, 13, psal. 16, 4.

e Which thing declareth the wickednes of mans heart which iudge Gods seruice by their eyes and outwarde senses.

f God had euer this respect to his glorie, that he wolde not haue his Name euil spoken of among the Gētiles for ẏ punishment ẏ his people deserued, incōfidēce whereof the godlie euer praied, as Exod. 32, 12. nom. 14, 13.

gypt & broght them into the wildernes.
11 And I gaue them my statutes, and declared my iudgements vnto them, * which if
a man do, he shal liue in them.
12 Moreouer I gaue thē also my * Sabbaths
to be a signe betwene me and thē, that thei
might knowe that I am ẏ Lord, that sanctifie them.
13 But the house of Israél rebelled against
me in the wildernes: thei walked not in
my statutes, and thei cast awaie my iudgements, which if a man do, he shal liue in
them, and my Sabbaths haue thei greatly
polluted: then I thoght to powre out mine
indignation vpon them * in the wildernes
to consume them,
14 But I had respect to [g] my Name, that it
shulde not be polluted before the heathen
in whose sight I broght them out.
15 Yet neuertheles, I lift vp mine hand
vnto them in the wildernes that I wolde
not bring them into the land, which I had
giuen them, flowing with milke & hony,
which was pleasant aboue all lands,
16 Because thei cast awaie my iudgements,
and walked not in my statutes, but haue
polluted my [h] Sabbaths: for their heart
went after their idoles.
17 Neuertheles, mine eye spared thē, that
I wolde not destroye them, nether wolde I
consume them in the wildernes.
18 But I said vnto their children in the wildernes, Walke ye not in the ordinances of
your [i] fathers, nether obserue their maners,
nor defile your selues with their idoles.
19 I am the Lord your God: walke in my sta
tutes, and kepe my iudgements & do thē,
20 And sanctifie my Sabbaths, & thei shalbe a signe betwene me & you, that ye maie
knowe that I am the Lord your God.
21 Notwithstanding the children rebelled
against me: thei walked not in my statutes,
nor kept my iudgements to do thē, which
if a man do, he shal liue in them, *but* thei
polluted my Sabbaths: then I thoght to
powre out mine indignation vpon them,
& to accomplish my wrath against them
in the wildernes.
22 Neuertheles I withdrewe mine hand &
had respect to my Name that it shulde
not be polluted before the heathen, in
whose sight I broght them forthe.
23 Yet I lift vp mine hand vnto them in the
wildernes, that I wolde scatter them a-
mong the heathen, and disperce them
through the countreis.
24 Because thei had not executed my iudgements, but had cast awaie my statutes &
had polluted my Sabbaths, and their eyes
were after [k] their fathers idoles.
25 Wherefore I [l] gaue them also statutes
that were not good, & iudgemēts, wherein
they shulde not liue.

Leu. 18, 5. rom. 10, 5. gal. 3, 12.

Exod. 20, 8. & 31, 13. deut. 5, 12.

Nom. 14, 28. & 26, 65.

g Who might thereby take an occasion to blaspheme my Name & to accuse me of lacke of abilitie, or els that I had soght a meanes to destroy them more commodiously.

h That is, my true religion, which I had commanded them and gaue them selues to serue me according to their owne fantasies.

i Whereby the holy Gost cōfuteth them that saie that thei wil follow, the religion and example of their fathers, and not measure their doigs by Gods worde, whether thei be approuable thereby or no.

k Meaning ẏ thei set their delite vpon them.

l Because thei wolde not obei my Lawes, I gaue them vp to them selues that thei shulde obey their owne fantasies, as ver 39 rom. 1, 21.

26 And

26 And I polluted thē in their owne m giftes in that they caused to passe *by the fyre*
all that *first* openeth the wōbe, that I might
destroye them, to the end that they might
knowe that I am the Lord.
27 Therefore, sonne of man, speake vnto
the house of Israél, & say vnto thē, Thus
saith the Lord God, yet in this your fathers haue blasphemed me, thogh thei had
before grieuously transgressed against me.
28 n For when I had broght them into the
land, for the which I lifted vp mine hand
to giue it, then they sawe euerie hie hil, &
all the thicke trees, and they offred there
their sacrifices, and there they presented
their offring of prouocation: there also
they made their swete sauour, and powred
out there their drinke offrings.
29 Then I said vnto them, What is the hie
place whereunto ye go? And the name thereof was called o Bamáh vnto this day.
30 Wherefore, say vnto the house of Israél,
Thus saith the Lord God, Are ye not pol
luted" after the maner of your fathers? &
commit ye not whoredome after their abominations?
31 For when you offer your giftes, and make
your sonnes to passe through the fyre, you
pollute your selues with all your idoles
vnto this day: shal I answer you whē I am
asked, ô house of Israél? As I liue, saith the
Lord God, p I wil not answer you when
I am asked.
32 Nether shal that be done that cometh
into your minde: for ye say, We wil be as
the heathen, and as the families of the countreis, and serue wood, and q stone.
33 As I liue, saith the Lord God, I wil surely rule you with a mightie hand, and with
a stretched out arme, & in *my* wrath powred out,
34 And wil bring you from the people, and
wil gather you out of the countreis, wherein ye are scatred, with a mightie hand, &
with a stretched out arme and in *my* wrath
powred out.
35 And I wil bring you into the r wildernes of the people, & there wil I plead with
you face to face.
36 Like as I pleaded with your fathers in the
wildernes of the lād of Egypt, so wil I plea
de with you, saith the Lord God.
37 And I wil cause you to passe vnder the
rod, and wil bring you into the bonde of
the couenant.
38 And I wil s chuse out from amōg you the
rebelles, and them that transgresse against
me: I wil bring them out of the lād where
thei dwell, & they shal not entre into ŷ lād
of Israél, & you shal knowe ŷ I am ŷ Lord.
39 As for you, ô house of Israél, thus saith
the Lord God, t Go you, and serue euerie
one his idole, seing that ye wil not obey

m I condēned those things, & counted them as abominable which they thoght had bene excellent, & to haue declared moste zeale, Luk. 16,15. for that which God required as moste excellent, that gaue they to their idoles.

n Not onely in the wildernes, when I broght thē out of Egypt, but since I placed them in this lād: which declareth how prompt mans heart is to idolatrie, seing ŷ by no admonitiōs he can be drawen backe.

o Which signifieth, an hie place, declarig that they vanted thē selues of their idolatrie, and were not ashamed thereof, thogh God had commanded them expressely, that they shulde haue no altar lifted vp on hie by staires, Exod 20,26.

" Ebr. in the way

p He sheweth, that the ingratitude of the people deserueth, that God shulde cut thē of & that they shulde not haue the comfort of his worde.

q He declareth that mā of nature is wholy enemie vnto God & to his owne saluatiō, and therefore God calleth him to ŷ right way, partely by chastising, but chiefly by his mercie in forgiuing his rebellion, and wickednes

r I wil bring you amōg strāge nations as into a wildernes, and there wil visit you, & so call you to repentāce & thē bring the godlie home againe, Isa 65,9.

s Signifying, ŷ he wil not burne the corne with ŷ chaffe, but chuse out the wicked to punish thē whē he wil spare his.

t This is spoken to the hypocrites.

me, and pollute mine holie Name no more with your giftes and with your idoles.
40 For in mine holie mountaine *euen* in the
hie mouūtaine of Israél, saith ŷ Lord God,
there shal all the house of Israél, and all in
the land, serue me: there wil I accept thē,
and there wil I require your offrings and
the first frutes of your oblations, with all
your holy things.
41 I wil accept your swete sauour, when I
bring you from the people, & gather you
out of the countreis, wherein ye haue bene
scattered, that I may be sanctified in you
before the heathen.
42 And ye shal knowe, that I am the Lord,
when I shal bring you into the land of Israél, into the lād, for the which I lifted vp
mine hand to giue it to your fathers.
43 And there shal ye remēber your wayes,
and all your workes, wherein ye haue bene
defiled, and ye u shal judge your selues
worthy to be cut of, for all your euils, that
ye haue committed.
44 And ye shal knowe, that I am the Lord,
when I haue respect vnto you for my Names sake, *and* not after your wicked waies,
nor according to your corrupt workes,
ô ye house of Israél, saith the Lord God.
45 ¶ Moreouer, the worde of the Lord came vnto me, saying,
46 Sonne of man, set thy face toward the
way of Temán, and droppe *thy worde* towarde x the South, and prophecie towarde
the forest of the field of the South,
47 And say to the forest of the South, Heare the worde of the Lord: thus saith the
Lord God, Beholde, I wil kindle a fyre in
thee, and it shal deuoure all the y grene
wood in thee, and all the dry wood: the cōtinual flame shal not be quenched, & euerie face from the South to the North shalbe burnt therein.
48 And all flesh shal se, that I ŷ Lord haue
kindled it, & it shal not be quēched. Thē
said I, Ah Lord God, thei say of me, Doeth
not he speake z parables?

u Your owne cōsciences shal conuict you after that you haue felt my mercies.

x For Iudáh stode South from Babylon.

y Bothe strōg and weake in Ierusalém.

z The people said, that the Prophet spake darkely: therefore he desireth the Lord to giue them a plaine declaration hereof.

CHAP. XXI.

3 He threateneth the sworde, and destruction to Ierusalém. 25 He sheweth the fall of King Zedekiáh. 28 He is comanded to prophecie the destruction of the children of Ammon. 30 The Lord threatneth to destroye Nebuchad-nezzár.

1 The worde of the Lord came to me
againe, saying,
2 Sonne of man, set thy face towarde Ierusalém, a & droppe *thy worde* toward ŷ holy
places, & prophecie agaīst ŷ lād of Israél,
3 And say to the lād of Israél, Thus saith ŷ
Lord, Beholde, I *come* against thee, and wil
drawe my sworde out of his sheath, & cut
of from thee *bothe* the b righteous and the
wicked.
4 Sing thē that I wil cut of frō thee *bothe*
the righteous and wicked, therefore shal

a Speake sensibly, that all may vnderstād.

b That is, suche which seme to haue an outward shew of righteousnes, by obseruation of the ceremonies of the Law.

my ſworde go out of his ſheath againſt all
fleſh from the South to the c North,
5 That all fleſh may knowe that I the Lord
haue drawen my ſworde out of his ſheath,
& it ſhal not returne anie more.
6 Mourne therefore, thou ſonne of man, *as*
in the paine of *thy* d reines, & mourne bitterly before them.
7 And if they ſay vnto thee, Wherefore
mourneſt thou? then anſwer, Becauſe e of
the brute: for it cometh, and euerie heart
ſhal melt, and all hands ſhalbe weake, and
all mindes ſhal faint, and all knees ſhal fall
away *as* water: beholde, it cometh, and ſhal
be done, ſaith the Lord God.
8 ¶ Againe, the worde of the Lord came vnto me, ſaying,
9 Sonne of man, prophecie, and ſay, Thus
ſaith the Lord God, ſay, A ſworde, a ſworde bothe ſharpe, and fourbiſhed.
10 It is ſharpened to make a ſore ſlaughter,
& it is fourbiſhed that it may f glitter:
how ſhal we reioyce? *for* it contemneth the
g rod of my ſonne, *as* h all *other* trees.
11 And he hathe giuen it to be fourbiſhed,
that he may handle it: this ſworde is ſharpe, and is fourbiſhed, that he may giue it
into the hand of the i ſlayer.
12 Crye, and houle, ſonne of man: for this
ſhal come to my people, *and* it ſhal come
vnto all the princes of Iſraél: the terrours
of the ſworde ſhalbe vpon my people:
k ſmite therefore vpon thy thigh.
13 For *it is a* tryal, l and what ſhal this be, if
the ſworde contemne euen the rod? It ſhal
be *no more*, ſaith the Lord God.
14 Thou therefore, ſonne of man, prophecie, and ſmite m hand to hand, and let the
ſworde be doubled: let the ſworde that hathe killed, *returne* the thirde time: it is the
ſworde of the great ſlaughter entring into
their priuie chambers.
15 I haue broght the feare of the ſworde
into all their gates to make *their* heart to
faint, and to multiplie *their* ruines. Ah it is
made bright, & it is dreſſed for the ſlaughter.
16 Get thee n alone: go to the right hand, *or*
get thy ſelf to the left hād, whether ſoeuer
thy face turneth.
17 I wil alſo ſmite mine hands together, &
wil cauſe my wrath to ceaſe. I the Lord
haue ſaid it.
18 ¶ The worde of the Lord came vnto me
againe, ſaying,
19 Alſo thou ſonne of man, appoint thee
o two wayes, that the ſworde of the King
of Babél may come: bothe twaine ſhal come out of one land, and chuſe a place, and
chuſe it in the corner of the way of ye citie.
20 Appoint a way, that the ſworde may come to Rabbáth of the Ammonites, and
p to Iudáh in Ieruſalém the ſtrong *citie*.
21 And ye King of Babél ſtode at the q par-
ting of the way, at the head of the two
wayes, conſulting by diuinatiō, *and* made
his arrowes bright: he conſulted with idoles, *and* loked in r the liuer.
22 At his right hand was the diuination for
Ieruſalém to appoint captaines, to open
their mouthe in the ſlaughter, and to lift
vp *their* voyce with ſhouting, to lay engines of warre againſt the gates, to caſt a
mount, *and* to buyld a fortres.
23 And it ſhalbe vnto them f as a falſe diuination in their ſight for the othes made
vnto them: t but he wil call to remēbrance *their* iniquitie, to the intent they ſhulde
be taken.
24 Therefore thus ſaith the Lord God, Becauſe ye haue made your iniquitie to be remembred, in diſcouering your rebellion, ye
in all your workes your ſinnes might appeare: becauſe, *I ſay*, that ye are come to remembrāce, ye ſhalbe taken with the hand.
25 And thou u prince of Iſraél polluted, &
wicked, whoſe day is come, when iniquitie
ſhal haue an end,
26 Thus ſaith the Lord God, I wil take a-
way the x diademe, & take of the crowne:
this ſhalbe no more the ſame: I wil exalt
the humble, and wil abaſe him that is hie.
27 I wil ouerturne, ouerturne, ouerturne it,
and it ſhalbe no more vntil he y come,
whoſe right it is, and I wil giue it him.
28 ¶ And thou, ſonne of man, prophecie, and
ſay, Thus ſaith the Lord God to the children of Ammón, and to their blaſphemie:
ſay thou, I ſay, The ſworde, the ſworde is
drawē forthe, & fourbiſhed to the ſlaughter, to conſume, becauſe of the glittering.
29 Whiles they ſe z vanitie vnto thee, and
prophecied a lye vnto thee to bring thee
vpon the neckes of the wicked that are
ſlaine, whoſe day is come when their iniquitie *ſhal haue* an end.
30 Shal I cauſe it to returne into his ſhea-
the? I wil iudge thee in the place where
thou waſt created, *euen* in the land of thine habitation.
31 And I wil powre out mine indignacion
vpō thee, & wil blowe againſt thee in the
fyre of my wrath, & deliuer thee into the
hand of beaſtlie mē, & ſkilful to deſtroy.
32 Thou ſhalt be in ye fyre to be deuoured:
thy blood ſhalbe in the middes of the lād
and thou ſhalt be no more remembred: for
I the Lord haue ſpoken it.

CHAP. XXII.

1 Ieruſalém is reproued for crueltie. 25 Of the wicked doctrine of the falſe prophets and prieſts, and of their vnſaciable couetouſnes. 27 The tyrannie of rulers. 29 The wickednes of the people.

1 MOreouer, the worde of the Lord came vnto me, ſaying,
2 Now thou ſonne of mā, wilt thou a iudge,
wilt

c Meaning, through all the land.

d As thogh ye were in extreme anguiſh.

e Becauſe of the great noiſe of the armie of the Caldeans.

f And ſo cauſe a feare.

g Meaning, the ſceptre: ſhewing, that it wil not ſpare the King who ſhulde be as the ſonne of God, and in his place.

h That is, the reſt of the people.

i To wit, vnto the armie of ye Caldeans.

k Read Iere. 31,19.

l Ezekiél moued with compaſsion, thus complaineth fearing the deſtruction of the kingdome, wc God had confirmed to Dauid, and his poſteritie by promes: wc promes God performed, althogh here it ſemeth to mans eye yt it ſhulde vtterly periſh.

m That is, incourage the ſworde.

n Prouide for thy ſelf: for yu ſhalt ſe Gods plague of all partes on this countrey.

o This was ſpoken, becauſe that when Nebuchad-nezzár came againſt Iudáh, his purpoſe was alſo to go againſt ye Ammonites: but douting in the way, which enterpriſe to vndertake firſt, he conſulted with his ſothſaiers, and ſo went againſt Iudáh.

p That is, to ye tribe of Iudáh that kept thē ſelues in Ieruſalém.

q To knowe whether he ſhulde go againſt the Ammonites or thē of Ieruſalém.

r He vſed coniuring & ſorcerie.

ſ Becauſe there was a league betwene ye Iewes, and the Babylonians, they of Ieruſalē ſhal thinke nothīg leſſe then that this thing ſhulde come to paſſe.

t That is, Nebuchad-nezzár wil remember the rebellion of Zedekiáh, and ſo come vpon them.

u Meaning, Zedekiáh, who practiſed with the Egyptians to make him ſelf hie, and able to reſiſt the Babylonians.

x Some refer this to the Prieſts attire: for Iehozadék the Prieſt wēt into captiuitie with the King.

y That is, vnto the cōming of Meſsiáh: for thogh ye Iewes had ſome ſigne of gouernemēt afterward vnder the Perſians, Grekes, and Romains, yet this reſtitution was not til Chriſts coming, and at length ſhulde be accompliſhed, as was promiſed, Gen. 49,10.

z Thogh the Iewes and Ammonites wolde not beleue, yu thou, to wit, the ſworde, ſhuldeſt come vpō them, and ſaid that the Prophets, which threatned, ſpake lies, yet yu ſhalt as ſurely come as thogh thou wereſt already vpon their neckes.

a Art yu ready to execute thy charge, which I cōmit vnto thee againſt Ieruſalém, that murthereth ye Prophets, and them that are godlie?

wilt ẏ iudge this bloody citie? wilt thou
ſhewe her all her abominacions?
3 Then ſay, Thus ſaith the Lord God, The
citie ſheddeth blood in the middes of it,
that her [b] time may come, and maketh i-
doles [c] againſt her ſelf to pollute her ſelf.
4 Thou haſt offended in thy blood, that
thou haſt ſhed, and haſt polluted thy ſelf
in thine idoles, which thou haſt made, and
thou haſt cauſed thy dayes to drawe nere,
& art come vnto thy terme: therefore haue I made thee a reproche to the heathē, &
a mocking to all countreys.
5 Thoſe that be nere, and thoſe that be farre
from thee, ſhal mocke thee, *which art* vile in
[d] name *&* ſore in affliction.
6 Beholde, the princes of Iſraél euery one
in thee *was ready* to his power, to ſhed
blood.
7 In thee haue thei deſpiſed father & mother: in the middes of thee [e] haue they oppreſſed the ſtranger: in thee haue thei vexed the fatherles and the widowe.
8 Thou haſt deſpiſed mine holy things, &
haſt polluted my Sabbaths.
9 In thee are men that cary tales to ſhed
blood: in thee *are they* that eat vpon the
mountaines: in the middes of thee they
commit abominacion.
10 *In thee haue thei diſcouered their fathers ſhame: in thee haue they vexed her
that was polluted in *her* floures.
11 And euery one * hathe committed abominacion with his neighbours wife, and e-
uery one hath wickedly defiled his daughter in law, & in thee hathe euery man forced his owne ſiſter, *euen* his fathers daughter.
12 In thee haue they taken giftes to ſhed
blood: thou haſt taken vſurie and the encreaſe, and thou haſt defrauded thy neighbours by extorcion, and haſt forgotten me,
ſaith the Lord God.
13 Beholde, therefore I haue [f] ſmitten mine
hands vpō thy couetouſnes, that thou haſt
vſed, and vpon the blood, which hathe bene in the middes of thee.
14 Can thine heart endure, or can thine
hands [g] be ſtrong, in the daies that I ſhal
haue to do with thee? I the Lord haue ſpoken it, and wil do it.
15 And I wil ſcatter thee amōg the heathē,
and diſperſe thee in the countreis, and wil
cauſe thy [h] filthines to ceaſe from thee.
16 And thou ſhalt take thine [i] inheritance in
thy ſelf in the ſight of the heathen, and
thou ſhalt knowe, that I am the Lord.
17 ¶ And the worde of the Lord came vnto me, ſaying,
18 Sonne of man, the houſe of Iſraél is vnto
me as [k] droſſe: all they are braſſe, & tynne,
and yron, and lead in the middes of the
fournace: thei are *euen* the droſſe of ſiluer.

b That is, the time of her deſtruction.
c To her owne vndoing.
d Whoſe very name all men hate.
e He meaneth hereby that there was no kinde of wickednes, which was not committed in Ieruſalém, & therefore the plagues of God ſhulde ſpedely come vpon her.
Leui.20,11.
Iere.5,8.
f In token of my wrath and vengeance.
g That is, able to defend thy ſelf.
h I wil thus take away ẏ occaſiō of thy wickednes.
i Thou ſhalt be no more ẏ inheritance of the Lord, but forſaken.
k Which before was moſte precious.

19 Therefore, thus ſaith the Lord God, Becauſe ye are all as droſſe, beholde, therefore
I wil gather you in the middes of Ieruſalém.
20 As they gather ſiluer and braſſe, & yron,
and lead, & tynne into the middes of the
fornace, to blowe the fyre vpon it to melt
it, ſo wil I gather you in mine angre and
in my wrath, and wil put you *there* [l] & melt
you.
21 I wil gather you, I ſay, and blowe the fyre of my wrath vpon you, and you ſhal be
melted in the middes thereof.
22 As ſiluer is melted in the middes of the
fournace, ſo ſhal ye be melted in the middes thereof, and ye ſhal knowe, that I the
Lord haue powred out my wrath vpō you.
23 And the worde of the Lord came vnto
me, ſaying,
24 Sonne of man, ſay vnto her, Thou art the
land, that is vncleane, [m] *&* not rained vpon in the day of wrath.
25 *There is* a conſpiracie [n] of her Prophetes
in the middes thereof like a roaring lyon,
rauening the pray: thei haue deuoured ſoules: they haue taken the riches & precious
thīgs: thei haue made her many widdowes
in the middes thereof.
26 Her Prieſts haue broken my Law, & haue
defiled mine holy things: they haue put no
difference betwene the holy & prophane,
nether diſcerned betwene the vncleane,
and the cleane, and haue hid their [o] eyes
from my Sabbaths, and I am prophaned
among them.
27 Her princes in * the middes thereof *are*
like wolues, rauening ẏ pray to ſhed blood,
and to deſtroye ſoules for their owne couetous lucre.
28 And her [p] Prophetes haue dawbed them
with vntempered *morter*, ſeing vanities, &
diuinīg lies vnto them, ſaying, Thus ſaith
the Lord God, when the Lord had not
ſpoken.
29 The people of the land haue violently
oppreſſed by ſpoyling and robbing, & haue vexed the poore & the neady: yea, they
haue oppreſſed the ſtranger againſt right.
30 And I ſoght for a man among them, that
ſhulde [q] make vp the hedge, & ſtand in the
gap before me for the land, that I ſhulde
not deſtroy it, but I founde none.
31 Therefore haue I powred out mine indignacion vpon them, & conſumed them
with the fyre of my wrath: their owne waies haue I rendred vpon their heads, ſaith
the Lord God.

l Meaning hereby, that the godlie ſhuld be tryed and the wicked deſtroyed.
m Thou art like a baren lād which ẏ Lord plagueth with drought.
n The falſe prophetes haue conſpired together to make their doctrine more probable.
o They haue neglected my ſeruice.
Mich 3,11.
Zephan.3,3.
p They which ſhulde haue reproued thē, flattered thē in their vices and couered their doings w lies, Chap. 13, 10.
q Which wolde ſhewe him ſelf zealous in my cauſe by reſiſting vice, Iſa.59,16 & 63 5, & alſo pray vnto me to withholde my plagues, Pſal. 106,23.

CHAP. XXIII.

Of the idolatrie of Samaria and Ieruſalém, vnder the names of Aholáh and Oholibáh.

1 THe worde of the Lord came againe
vnto me, ſaying,
2 Sonne of man, there were two women,

a Meaning, Iſraél & Iudáh, which came bothe out of one familie.
b Thei became idolaters after the maner of the Egyptiās.
c Aholáh ſignifieth a manſiō or dwelling in her ſelf, meaning Samaria which was the royal citie of Iſraél: and Aholibáh, ſignifieth my manſion in her, whereby is mēt Ieruſalém where Gods Temple was.
" Ebr. vnder me
d When the Iſraelites were named the people of God, they became idolaters and forſoke God, and put their truſt in the Aſſyrians.

the daughters of one [a] mother.
3 And they committed fornicacion [b] in E-
gypt, they committed fornicacion in their
youth: there were their breaſts preſſed, &
there thei bruiſed the teates of their virginitie.
4 And the names of [c] them *were* Aholáh, the
elder, and Aholibáh her ſiſter: & thei were
mine, and thei bare ſonnes and daughters:
thus *were* their names. Samaria *is* Aholáh,
and Ieruſalém Aholibáh.
5 And Aholáh plaied the harlot " whē [d] ſhe
was mine, and ſhe was ſet on fyre with her
louers, *to wit*, with the Aſſyrians *her* neighbours,
6 Which were clothed with blewe ſilke, *bothe* captaines & princes: thei were all pleaſant yong men, & horſemen riding vpon
horſes.
7 Thus ſhe cōmitted her whoredome with
them, *euen* with all them that were the choſen men of Aſſhúr, and with all on whome
ſhe doted, & defiled her ſelf with all their
idoles.
8 Nether left ſhe her fornicaciōs, *learned* of
the Egyptians: for in her youth thei [e] laye
with her, & thei bruiſed the breaſts of her
virginitie, and powred their whoredome
vpon her.
9 Wherefore I deliuered her into the hands
of her louers, *euen* into the hands of the
Aſſyrians, vpon whome ſhe doted.
10 Theſe diſcouered her ſhame: thei toke a-
way her ſonnes & her daughters, & ſlewe
her with the ſworde, & ſhe had an *euil* name among women: for [f] thei had executed
iudgement vpon her.
11 And when her ſiſter Aholibáh ſawe this,
ſhe marred her ſelf with inordinate loue,
more then ſhe, and with her fornicacions
more then her ſiſter with *her* fornicaciōs.
12 She doted vpon the Aſſyrians *her* neighbours, *bothe* captaines and princes clothed
with diuers ſutes, horſemen riding vpon
horſes: thei were all pleaſant yong men.
13 Then I ſawe, that ſhe was defiled, *and*
that they were bothe after one ſorte,
14 And that ſhe encreaſed her fornicacions:
for when ſhe ſawe men [g] painted vpon the
wall, the images of the Caldeans painted
with vermelon,
15 And girded with girdles vpon their loynes, and with dyed attyre vpon their heads
(loking all like princes after the maner of
the Babylonians in Caldéa, ỳ land of their
natiuitie)
16 Aſſone, I ſay, as ſhe ſawe them, ſhe doted
vpon them, & ſent meſſengers vnto them
into Caldea.
17 Now when the Babylonians came to her
into the bed of loue, they defiled her with
their fornicacion, & ſhe was polluted with
them, and her luſt departed from them.

e The holy Goſt vſeth theſe termes ỳ ſeme ſtrange to chaſte eares to cauſe this wicked vice of idolatrie ſo to be abhorred ỳ vnneth any ſhulde abyde to heare ỳ name thereof mencioned.
f Meaning, the Aſſyrians.
g This declareth ỳ no wordes are able ſufficiently to expreſſe the rage of idolaters, & therefore the holy Goſt here compareth them to thoſe which in their raging loue & filthy luſtes dote vpon the images & paintings of thē after whome they luſt.

18 So ſhe diſcouered her fornicacion, & diſ
cloſed her ſhame: then mine heart forſoke
her, like as mine heart had forſakē her ſiſter
19 Yet ſhe encreaſed her whoredome more,
& called to remembrance the dayes of her
youth, wherein ſhe had plaied the harlot
in the land of Egypt.
20 For ſhe doted vpō their ſeruants whoſe
membres are *as* the membres of aſſes, and
whoſe yſſue is *like* the yſſue of horſes.
21 Thou calledſt to remembrance the wickednes of thy youth, when thy teates were
bruiſed by the Egyptians: therefore ỳ pappes of thy youth *are thus*.
22 Therefore, ô Aholibáh, thus ſaith the
Lord God, Beholde, I wil raiſe vp thy louers againſt thee, from whome thine heart
is departed, and I wil bring them againſt
thee on euery ſide,
23 *To wit*, the Babylonians, and all the Caldeans, [h] Peked, and Shoáh, and Kóa, & all
the Aſſyrians with thē: they were all pleaſant yong men, captaines and princes: all
thei were valiant & renoumed, riding vpon horſes.
24 Euen theſe ſhal come againſt thee with
charettes, waggens, and wheles, and with a
multitude of people, *which* ſhal ſet againſt
thee, buckler & ſhield, and helmet rounde
aboute: and " I wil leaue the puniſhement
vnto them, & they ſhal iudge thee according to their " iudgements.
25 And I wil lay mine indignation vpon
thee, and thei ſhal deale cruelly with thee:
they ſhal cut of thy [i] noſe and thine eares,
and thy remnant ſhal fall by the ſworde:
they ſhal cary away thy ſonnes and thy daughters, and thy reſidue ſhalbe deuoured
by the fyre.
26 They ſhal alſo ſtrippe thee out of thy
clothes, and take away thy faire iewels.
27 Thus wil I make thy wickednes to ceaſe
from thee and thy fornicacion out of the
land of Egypt: ſo that thou ſhalt not lift
vp thine eyes vnto them, nor remember E-
gypt any more.
28 For thus ſaith the Lord God, Beholde, I
wil deliuer thee into the hand of them,
whome thou hateſt: *euen* into the hands of
them frō whome thine heart is departed.
29 And they ſhal handle thee diſpitefully,
and ſhal take away all thy [k] labour, & ſhal
leaue thee naked and bare, and the ſhame
of thy fornicaciōs [l] ſhalbe diſcouered, bothe thy wickednes, and thy whoredome.
30 I wil do theſe things vnto thee, becauſe
thou haſt gone a whoring after the heathē,
& becauſe ỳ art polluted with their idoles.
31 Thou haſt walked in ỳ way of thy ſiſter:
therfore wil I giue her [m] cup into thine hād
32 Thus ſaith the Lord God, Thou ſhalt
drinke of thy ſiſters cup, depe and large:
thou ſhalt be laughed to ſcorne & had in
deriſion,

h These were the names of certeine princes & captaines vnder Nebuchad-nezzár.
" I wil giue iudgement before them.
" Or, lawes.
i They ſhal deſtroy thy princes and Prieſts with the reſt of thy people.
k All thy treaſures & riches which thou haſt gotten by labour.
l All the worlde ſhal ſe thy ſhameful forſakig of God to ſerue idoles.
m I wil execute the ſame iudgements & vengeance againſt thee, & ỳ with greater ſeueritie.

derision, because it conteineth muche.
33 Thou shalt be filled with [n] drunkénes &
sorowe, *euen* with the cup of destruction,
and desolation, with the cup of thy sister
Samaria.
34 Thou shalt euen drinke it, and wring it
out *to the dregges*, & thou shalt breake the
sherdes thereof, & teare thine owne breastes: for I haue spoké it, saith ẏ Lord God.
35 Therefore thus saith the Lord God, Because thou hast forgotten me, and cast me
behind thy backe, therefore thou shalt also
beare thy wickednes & thy whoredome.
36 ¶ The Lord said moreouer vnto me,
Sonne of man, wilt thou iudge Aholáh &
Aholibáh? and wilt thou declare to them
their abominacions?
37 For they haue played the whores, and
blood *is* in their hands, and with their idoles haue they committed adulterie, and haue also caused their sonnes, whome they
bare vnto me, to passe *by the fyre* to be their
[o] meat.
38 Moreouer thus haue they done vnto me:
they haue defiled my Sanctuarie in the same day, & haue prophaned my Sabbaths.
39 For when they had slaine their children
to their idoles, they came the same day
into my Sanctuarie to defile it: and lo, thus
haue thei done in ẏ middes of mine house.
40 And how muche more *is it* that they sent
for men to come from [p] farre vnto whome a messenger was sent, & lo, they came?
for whome thou didest wash thy self, and
painted thine eyes, & deckedst thee with
ornaments,
41 And satest [q] vpon a costlie bed, and a
table prepared before it, whereupon thou
hast set mine incense and mine oyle.
42 And a voyce of a multitude being at ease, *was* with her: and with the men to make
the companie great were broght men of
[r] Sabá from the wildernes, which put bracelets vpon their hands, and beautiful
crownes vpon their heads.
43 Then I said vnto her, that was olde in
adulteries, Now shal she and her fornicacions come to an end.
44 And they went in vnto her as they go
to a cómune harlot: so wét thei to Aholáh
and Aholibáh the wicked women.
45 And the righteous men they shal iudge
them, after the maner of [s] harlotes, and after the maner of murtherers: for they are
harlotes, and blood *is* in their hands.
46 Wherefore thus saith the Lord God, I
wil bring a multitude vpon them, and wil
giue them vnto the tumulte, and to the
spoyle,
47 And the multitude shal stone them with
stones, and cut them with their swordes:
they shal slay their sonnes, and their daughters, & burne vp their houses with fyre.
48 Thus wil I cause wickednes to cease out
of the lád, that all [t] women may be taught
not to do after your wickednes.
49 And they shal lay your wickednes vpó
you, and ye shal beare the sinnes of your
idoles, and ye shal knowe that I am the
Lord God.

n Meaning, ẏ the afflictions shulde be so great that thei shulde cause them to lose their senses, & reason.

o That is, to be sacrificesto their idoles, read Chap. 16,20.

p They sent into other countreis to haue suche as shulde reache the seruice of their idoles.

q He meaneth the altar, that was prepared for the idoles.

r Which shulde teache the maner of worshiping their gods.

s That is, worthy death, read Chap. 16,38.

t Meaning, all other cities, & countreis.

CHAP. XXIIII.

1 He sheweth the destruction of Ierusalém by a parable of a seething pot. 16 The parable of Ezekiels wife being dead.

1 AGaine in the [a] ninth yere, in the téth
moneth, in the tenth *day* of the [b] mo
neth came the worde of the Lord vnto me,
saying,
2 Sonne of man, write thee the name of the
day, *euen* of this same day: *for* the King of
Babél set him self against Ierusalém this
same day.
3 Therefore speake a parable vnto ẏ rebellious house, and say vnto them, Thus saith
the Lord God, Prepare a [c] pot, prepare it,
and also power water into it.
4 Gather the [d] pieces thereof into it, *euen*
euerie good piece, *as* the thigh and the
shuldre, *&* fil it with the chief bones.
5 Take one of the best shepe, and "burne
also the [e] bones vnder it, *&* make it boyle wel, and sethe the bones of it therein,
6 Because the Lord God saith thus, Wo
to the bloodie citie, *euen* to the pot, [f] whose
skome is therein, and whose skome is not
gone out of it: bring it out [g] piece by piece: let no [h] lot fall vpon it.
7 For her blood is in the middes of her: she
set it vpon an high [i] rocke, *and* powred it
not vpon the grounde to couer it ẇ dust,
8 That it might cause wrath to arise, & take
vengeance: *euen* I haue set her blood vpon
an high rocke ẏ it shulde not be couered.
9 Therefore thus saith the Lord God, *Wo
to the bloodie citie, for I wil make "the bur
ning great.
10 Heape on muche wood: [k] kindle the fyre, consume the flesh, and cast in spice, and
let the bones be burnt.
11 Then set it emptie vpon the coles thereof, that "the brasse of it may be hot, and
may burne, and that the filthines of it may
be molten in it, *and* that the skome of it
may be consumed.
12 [l] She hathe wearied her self with lies, &
her great skome went not out of her: *therefore* her skome *shalbe consumed* with fyre.
13 *Thou remainest* in thy filthines *&* wickednes: because I wolde [m] haue purged thee,
and thou wast not purged, thou shalt not
be purged fró thy filthines, til I haue caused my wrath to light vpon thee.
14 I the Lord haue spoken it: it shal come
to passe, and I wil do it: I wil not go backe, nether wil I spare, nether wil I repent:

a Of Ieconiahs captiuitie, and of the reigne of Zedekiáh, 2.King 25,1.

b Called Tebeth, which cóteineth parte of December and parte of Ianuarie: in ẏ which moneth and day Nebuchad-nezzár besieged Ierusalém.

c Whereby was ment Ierusalém.

d That is, the citizens, & the chief men thereof.

"Or, heape.

e Meaning, of the innocents, whome they had slaine, who were the cause of the kindeling of Gods wrath against them.

f Whose iniquities, & wicked citizens there yet remaine

g Signifying, that thei shulde not be destroyed all at once, but by litle & litle.

h Spare none estate or condition.

i The citie shewed her crueltie to all the worlde, & was not ashamed thereof, nether yet hid it.

Nah.3,1. habak.2,12.

"Or, an heape of wood.

k Meaning, ẏ the citie shulde be vtterly destroyed, and that he wolde giue the enemies an appetite thereunto.

"Or, botome.

l The citie hathe flattered her self in vaine.

m I labored by sending my Prophetes to call thee to repentance, but thou woldest not,

according to thy wayes, and according to
thy workes shal [n] they iudge thee, saith
the Lord God.
15 ¶ Also the worde of the Lord came vnto
me, saying,
16 Sonne of man, beholde, I take away frõ
thee the [o] pleasure of thine eyes with a plague: yet shalt thou nether mourne nor
wepe, nether shal thy teares runne downe.
17 Cease from sighing: make no mourning
for the dead, & binde the tyre of thine
head vpon thee, [p] and put on thy shoes
vpon thy fete, & couer not thy lippes, and
eat [q] not the bread of men.
18 So I spake vnto the people in the morning, and at euen my wife dyed: and I did
in [r] the morning, as I was commanded.
19 And the people said vnto me, Wilt thou
not tel vs what these thigs meane toward
vs, that thou doest so?
20 Then I answered them, The worde of
the Lord came vnto me, saying,
21 Speake vnto the house of Israél, Thus
saith ẏ Lord God, Beholde, I wil [s] pollute my Sanctuarie, *euen* the [t] pride of your
power, the pleasure of your eyes, and your
hearts desire, & your sonnes, & your daughters whome ye haue left, shal fall by the
sworde.
22 And ye shal do as I haue done: ye shal
not couer your lippes, nether shal ye eat
the bread of men.
23 And your tyre *shalbe* vpon your heads, &
your shoes vpon your fete: ye shal not
mourne nor wepe, but ye shal pine away
for your iniquities, & mourne one toward
another.
24 Thus Ezekiél is vnto you a signe: according to all that he hathe done, ye shal do:
and when this cometh, ye shal knowe that
I am the Lord God.
25 Also, thou sonne of man, shal it not be in
the day when I take from thẽ their power,
the ioye of their honour, the pleasure of
their eyes, and the [*] desire of their heart,
their sonnes and their daughters?
26 That he that escapeth in that day, shal
come vnto thee *to tel thee* that which he hathe heard with *his* eares?
27 In that day shal thy mouth be opened
to him which is escaped, and thou shalt
speake, and be no more domme, and thou
shalt be a signe vnto them, and they shal
knowe that I am the Lord.

n That is, the Babylonians.

o Meaning, his wife in whome he delited, as ver. 18.

p For in mourning they went bare headed and bare foted, and also couered their lippes.

q That is, ẇ the neighbour sent to them ẏ mourned.

r Meaning, the morning following.

s By sending ẏ Caldeans to destroie it, as Chap. 7, 22.

t Wherein you boast and delite.

* Ebr. lifting vp of their soules.

CHAP. XXV.

1 *The worde of the Lord against Ammon, which reioyced at the fall of Ierusalém. 8 Against Moab and Seir, Idumea and the Philistims.*

1 THe worde of the Lord came againe
vnto me, saying,
2 Sonne of man, set thy face against ẏ Ammonites, and prophecie against them,
3 And say vnto the Ammonites, Heare the
worde of the Lord God, Thus saith the
Lord God, Because thou saydest, [a] Ha,
ha, against my Sanctuarie, when it was pol
luted, and against the land of Israél, when
it was desolate, and against the house of
Iudáh, when they went into captiuitie,
4 Beholde, therefore I wil deliuer thee to ẏ
[b] mẽ of the East for a possession, and they
shal set their [c] palaces in thee, and make
their dwellings in thee: they shal eat thy
frute, and they shal drinke thy milke.
5 And I wil make [d] Rabbáh a dwelling place
for camels, and the Ammonites a shepecote, & ye shal knowe that I am the Lord.
6 For thus saith the Lord God, Because
thou hast clapped the hands, and stamped
with the fete, and reioyced in heart with
all thy despite against the land of Israél,
7 Beholde, therefore I wil stretche out mine hand vpon thee, and wil deliuer thee
to be spoiled of the heathen, & I wil roote
thee out from the people, and I wil cause
thee to be destroyed out of the countreis
& I wil destroye thee, & thou shalt knowe
that I am the Lord.
8 Thus saith the Lord God, Because that
Moáb and Seír do say, Beholde, the house of Iudáh is like vnto all the heathen,
9 Therefore, beholde, I wil open the side
of Moáb, *euen* of the cities [e] of his cities, *I
say*, in his frontiers with the pleasant countrey, Beth-ieshimóth, Báal-meon, and Ka-
riatháim.
10 *I wil call* the men of the East against the
Ammonites, and wil giue them in possession, so that the Ammonites shal no more
be remembred among the nations,
11 And I wil execute iudgements vpon
Moáb, & thei shal knowe ẏ I am the Lord.
12 ¶ Thus saith the Lord God, Because
that Edóm hathe done *euil* by taking vengeance vpõ the house of Iudáh, and hathe
cõmitted great offence, and reuenged him
self vpon them,
13 Therefore thus saith the Lord God, I
wil also stretche out mine hand vpon E-
dóm, and destroye man, and beast out of
it, and I wil make it desolate frõ Temán,
and they of Dedán shal fall by ẏ sworde.
14 And I wil execute my vengeance vpon
Edóm by the hand of my people Israél, &
they shal do in Edóm according to mine
angre, and according to mine indignatiõ,
and they shal knowe my vengeance, saith
the Lord God.
15 Thus saith the Lord God, Because the
Philistims haue executed vengeance, and
reuẽged thẽ selues with a despiteful heart,
to destroye it for the olde hatred,
16 Therefore thus saith ẏ Lord God, Beholde, I wil stretche out mine hãd vpon ẏ Phi
listims, & I wil cut of the [f] Cherethims, &
destroye the remnant of the sea coast.

a Because ye reioyced whẽ the enemie destroied my citie and Tẽple.

b That is, to ẏ Babylonians.

c Thei shal chase thee awaie and take thy gorgeous houses to dwell in.

d Called also Philadelphia, which was ẏ chief citie of ẏ Ammonites and ful of conduites, 2. Sam. 12, 27.

e So that no power or stregth shulde be able to resist the Babylonians.

f Which were certeine garisons of Philistims, whereby thei oft times molested the Iewes. of ẏ Cherethims Dauid also had a garde, 2. Sam 8, 8.

17 And I wil execute great vengeáce vpon
thé with rebukes of mine indignation, &
thei ſhal knowe that I am the Lord, when
I ſhal laie my vengeance vpon them.

CHAP. XXVI.

1 *He prophecieth that Tyrus ſhalbe ouerthrowen becau ſe it reioyced at the deſtruction of Ieruſalém. 15 The wondring and aſtoniſhment of the marchantes for the deſtruction of Tyrus.*

1 And in the [a] eleuenth yere, in the
firſt *daie* of the moneth, the worde
of the Lord came vnto me, ſaying,
2 Sonne of man, becauſe that Tyrus hathe
ſaid againſt Ieruſalém, A ha, the [b] gate of
the people is broken: it is turned vnto me:
for ſeing ſhe is deſolate, I ſhalbe [c] repleniſhed,
3 Therefore thus ſaith the Lord God, Beholde, I come againſt thee, ô Tyrus, and I
wil bring vp manie nations againſt thee,
as the ſea mounteth vp with his waues.
4 And thei ſhal deſtroie the walles of Tyrus & breake downe her towers: I wil alſo
ſcrape her duſt from her, and make her like the toppe of a rocke.
5 Thou ſhalt be for the ſpreading of nettes
in the middes of the ſea: for I haue ſpoken
it, ſaith the Lord God, and it ſhalbe a
ſpoyle to the nations.
6 And her [d] daughters which are in the fielde, ſhalbe ſlaine by the ſworde, and thei
ſhal knowe that I am the Lord.
7 For thus ſaith the Lord God, beholde, I
wil bring vpon Tyrus Nebuchad-nezzár
King of Babél, a King of Kings from the
North, with horſes and with charets, and
with horſemen, with a multitude and muche people.
8 He ſhal ſlaie with the ſworde thy daughters in the field, and he ſhal make a forte a-
gainſt thee, and caſt a mount againſt thee,
and lift vp the buckler againſt thee.
9 He ſhal ſet engines of warre before him
againſt thy walles, and with his weapons
breake downe thy towres.
10 The duſt of his horſes ſhal couer thee,
for their multitude: thy walles ſhal ſhake
at the noiſe of the horſemen, and of the
wheles, & of the charets, whé he ſhal entre
into thy gates as into the entrie of a citie
that is broken downe.
11 With ẏ houes of his horſes ſhal he tread
downe all thy ſtretes: he ſhal ſlaie thy peo
ple by the ſworde, and the [e] pillers of thy
ſtrength ſhal fall downe to the grounde.
12 And thei ſhal robbe thy riches and ſpoile thy marchandiſe, and thei ſhal breake
downe thy walles, and deſtroie thy pleaſant houſes, and thei ſhal caſt thy ſtones
and thy timbre and thy duſt into the middes of the water.
13 *Thus wil I cauſe ẏ ſounde of thy ſongs
to ceaſe, and the ſounde of thine harpes
ſhalbe no more heard.
14 I wil laie thee like the toppe of a rocke:
[f] thou ſhalt be for a ſpreading of nettes:
thou ſhalt be buylt no more: for I the
Lord haue ſpoken it, ſaith the Lord God.
15 Thus ſaith the Lord God to Tyrus, Shal
not the yles tremble at the ſounde of thy
fall? and at the crye of the wounded, when
thei ſhalbe ſlaine and murthered in the
middes of thee?
16 Then all ẏ princes of the [g] ſea ſhal come
downe from their thrones: thei ſhal laie a-
waie their robes, & put of their broydred
garments, and ſhal clothe them ſelues
with aſtoniſhment: thei ſhal ſit vpon the
grounde, and be aſtoniſhed at *euerie* moment, and be amaſed at thee.
17 And thei ſhal take vp a lamentacion for
thee, and ſaie to thee, How art thou deſtroyed, that waſt inhabited [h] of ẏ ſea *men*,
the renoumed citie which was ſtrōg in the
ſea, *bothe* ſhe & her inhabitants, which cauſe their feare to be on all ẏ haunt therein!
18 Now ſhal the yles be aſtoniſhed in the
daie of thy fall: yea, the yles that are in
the ſea, ſhalbe troubled at thy departure.
19 For thus ſaith the Lord God, Whé I ſhal
make thee a deſolate citie, like the cities
that are not inhabited, & whé I ſhal bring
the deape vpon thee, and great waters ſhal
couer thee,
20 When I ſhal caſt thee downe with them
that deſcende into the pit, with the people
[i] of olde time, and ſhal ſet thee in the lowe
partes of the earth, like the olde ruines, ẇ
them, *I ſay*, which go downe to the pit, ſo
that thou ſhalt not be inhabited, and I ſhal
ſhewe my glorie in the lād of the [k] liuing,
21 I wil bring thee to nothing, and thou
ſhalt be no *more*: thogh thou be ſoght for,
yet ſhalt thou neuer be founde againe,
ſaith the Lord God.

a Ether of the captiuitie of Ieconiáh, or of the reigne of Zedekiáh.

b That is, the famous citie Ieruſalém, whereunto all people reſorted.

c My riches & fame ſhal increaſe: thus ẏ wicked reioyce at their fail by whome thei maie haue any profite or aduantage.

d The townes that belonged vnto her.

e For Tyrus was muche buylt by art, and by labour of men was wōne out of ẏ ſea. Some refer re this vnto ẏ images of the noble men ẇ thei had erected vp for their glorie and renoume.

Iere.7.34.

f I wil make thee ſo bare ẏ thou ſhalt haue nothing to couer thee.

g The gouernours and rulers of other countreyes ẏ dwell by the ſea: whereby he ſignifieth ẏ her deſtruction ſhulde be ſo horrible, ẏ all ẏ worlde ſhulde heare thereof and be afraied.

h Meaning, marchantes ẇ by their traffique did enriche her wonderfully and increaſe her power.

i Which are dead lōg ago.

k Meaning, in Iudea, when it ſhal be reſtored.

CHAP. XXVII.

The Prophet bewaileth the deſolatiō of Tyrus, ſhewing what were the riches, power and autoritie thereof in time paſt.

1 The worde of the Lord came againe
vnto me, ſaying,
2 Sonne of man, take vp a lamentation for
Tyrus,
3 And ſay vnto Tyrus, ẏ is ſituat at the entrie of the ſea, which is the marte [a] of the
people for manie yles, Thus ſaith ẏ Lord
God, O Tyrus, thou haſt ſaid, I am of perfite beautie.
4 Thy borders are in the ** middes of ẏ ſea,
& thy buylders haue made thee of perfite
beautie.
5 Thei haue made all thy *ſhip* bordes of fyrre trees of [b] Shenir: they haue broght cedres frō Lebanón, to make maſts for thee.
6 Of ẏ okes of Baſhán haue they made thine ores: the companie of the Aſſyrians

a Which ſerueſt all the worlde ẇ thy marchandiſe.

** Ebr. heart.

b This mountaine was called Hermon, but the Amorites called it Shenir, Deu.3, 9.

haue made thy bankes of yuorie, *broght*
out of the yles of [c] Chittim.
c Which is taken for Grecia and Italie.
7 Fine linen with broydred worke, *broght*
from Egypt, was spred ouer thee to be thy
saile, blewe silke & purple, *broght* from the
yles of Elisháh, was thy couering.
8 The inhabitants of Zidón, and Aruád
were thy mariners, ô Tyrus: thy wise men
that were in thee, thei were thy " pilotes.
"Or, shipmasters.
9 The ancients of Gebál, and the wise mẽ
thereof were in thee thy [d] calkers, all the
ships of the sea with their mariners were
in thee to occupie thy marchandise.
d Meaning, ȳ thei buylt the walles of the citie, which is here ment by the ship: and of these were ȳ buylders of Salomõs Temple, 1. Kin. 5, 18.
10 Thei of Persia, and of Lud and of Phut
were in thine armie: thy men of warre thei
hanged ȳ shield & helmet in thee: thei set
forthe thy beautie.
11 The mẽ of Aruád with thine armie *were* vpon thy walles rounde about, and the
[e] Gammadims were in thy towers: thei hãged their shields vpon thy walles rounde
about: thei haue made thy beautie perfite.
e That is, thei of Cappadocia or Pigmes and dwarfs which were so called because that out of the hie towres thei semed litle.
12 They of Tarshish *were* thy marchants
for the multitude of all riches, for siluer, yron, tynne, and lead, *which* thei broght to
thy faires.
13 Thei of [f] Iauán, Tubál and Meshéch were thy marchants, [g] concerning the liues
of men, and thei broght vessels of brasse
for thy marchandise.
f Of Grecia, Italie and Cappadocia.
g By selling sclaues.
14 Thei of ȳ house of [h] Togarmáh broght
to thy faires horses, & horsmen, & mules.
h Which are takẽ for a people of Asia minor.
15 The men of Dedán *were* thy marchants:
and the marchandise of manie yles *were*
in thine hands: thei broght thee for a present [i] hornes, bones, teeth, and peacockes.
i Meaning, vnicornes hornes, and eliphants teeth
16 Thei of Arám *were* thy marchants for
the multitude of thy " wares: thei occupied in thy faires with " emeraudes, purple,
and broydred worke, and " fine linin, and
coral, and perle.
"Or, workes.
"Or, carbuncle.
"Or, silke.
17 They of Iudáh and of the land of Israél were thy marchants: thei broght for
thy marchandise wheat of [k] Minnith, and
Pannág, and hony and oyle, and " balme.
k Where ȳ best wheat growed
"Or, turpentine, or, triacle.
18 Thei of Damascus *were* thy marchants
in ȳ multitude of thy wares, for the multitude of all riches, *as* in the wine of Helbon and white wolle.
19 Thei of Dan also and of Iauán, going
to and fro, occupied in thy faires: yron
worke, cassia and calamus were amõg thy
marchandise.
20 Thei of Dedán *were* thy marchants in
precious clothes for the charets.
21 Thei of Arabia, & all the princes of Kedár " occupied with thee, in lambes, & rams
& goats: in these were thei thy marchãts.
"Or, were marchants whose marchandise passed through thine hands.
22 The marchants of Shebá, and Raamáh
were thy marchants: thei occupied in thy
faires with the chief of all spices, and with
all precious stones and golde.
23 Thei of Harám and Cannéh and Edén,
the marchants of Shebá, Asshúr & Chilmád were thy marchants.
24 These were thy marchants in all sortes
of things, in raiment of blewe silke, and of
broydred worke, and in coffers for the riche apparel, which were bounde wt cordes:
chaines also *were* among thy marchãdise.
25 The shippes of Tarshish " were thy chief
in thy marchãdise, and thou wast replenished and made very glorious in the middes of the sea.
"Or, came in companie towarde thee.
26 Thy " robbers haue broght thee into great
waters: the [l] East winde hathe broken thee
in the middes of the sea.
"Or, rowers.
l That is, Nebuchad-nezzár.
27 Thy riches and thy faires, thy marchandise, thy mariners and pilotes, thy calkers,
and the occupiers of thy marchandise and
all thy men of warre that are in thee, & all
thy multitude which is in the middes of
thee, shal fall in the middes of the sea in
the daie of thy ruine.
28 The [m] suburbes shal shake at the sounde
of the crye of the pilotes.
m That is, the cities nere about thee, as was Zidón, Aruád and others.
29 And all that handle the ore, the mariners & all the pilotes of the sea shal come
downe from their ships, & shal stand vpon the land,
30 And shal cause their voice to be heard against thee, and shal crye bitterly, and shal
cast dust vpon their heads, and wallowe
them selues in the asshes.
31 Thei shal plucke of their heere for thee
and gyrd them with a sackecloth, and thei
shal wepe for thee with sorowe of heart &
bitter mourning.
32 And in their mourning thei shal take vp a
lamẽtaciõ for thee, *saying*, What *citie* is like
Tyrus, so destroied in ȳ middes of ȳ sea!
33 Whẽ thy wares went forthe of the seas,
thou filledst manie people & ȳ didest enriche the Kings of the earth with the multitude of thy riches & of thy marchãdise.
34 When thou shalt be broken by the seas in
the depths of the waters, thy marchandise
and all thy multitude, which was in the
middes of thee, shal fall.
35 All the inhabitãts of the yles shalbe astonished at thee, & all their Kĩgs shal be sore
afraied & troubled in their countenance.
36 The marchants among the people shal
hisse at thee: thou shalt be a terrour, and ne
uer shalt be [n] anie more.
n Whereby is ment a long time: for it was prophecied to be destroyed but seuenty yeres, as Isa. 23, 15.

CHAP. XXVIII.

The worde of God against the King of Tyrus for his pride. 21 The worde of the Lord against Zidón. 25 The Lord promiseth that he wil gather together the children of Israél.

1 THe worde of the Lord came againe
vnto me, saying,
2 Sõne of mã, say vnto ȳ prince of Tyrus,
Thus saith the Lord God, Because thine
heart is exalted, and thou hast said, [a] I am
a god, I sit in the seat of God in the middes of the sea, yet thou art but a man and
not God, & " thogh thou didest thinke in
thine
a I am safe ȳ none cancome to hurt me, as God is in the heauen.
"Thogh thou set thine heart as the heart of God.

thine heart, ỹ thou wast equal with God,
3 Beholde, thou art wiser thẽ [b] Daniél: there
is no secret, that thei can hide from thee.
4 With thy wisdome and thine vnderstanding thou hast gotten thee riches, and hast
gotten gold and siluer into thy treasures.
5 By thy great wisdome *and* by thine occupying hast ỹ increased thy riches, and thine heart is lifted vp because of thy riches.
6 Therefore thus saith the Lord God, Because thou didest thĩke in thine heart, that
thou wast equal with God,
7 Beholde, therefore I wil bring strangers
vpon thee, *euen* the terrible nacions: and
thei shal drawe their swordes against the
beautie of thy wisdome, and thei shal defile thy brightnes.
8 Thei shal cast thee downe to the pit, and
thou shalt dye the death of them, that are
slaine in the middes of the sea.
9 Wilt thou say *then* before him, ỹ slaieth
thee, I am a god? but thou shalt be a man,
and no God, in the hands of him that
slaieth thee.
10 Thou shalt dye the death of the [c] vncircumcised by the hands of strangers: for I
haue spoken it, saith the Lord God.
11 ¶ Moreouer the worde of the Lord came
vnto me, saying,
12 Sonne of man, take vp a lamentacion vpon the King of Tyrus, and say vnto him,
Thus saith the Lord God, Thou sealest
vp the summe, & art ful of [d] wisdome and
perfite in beautie.
13 Thou hast bene in Eden ỹ gardẽ of God:
euerie precious stone *was* in thy garment, ỹ
rubie, ỹ topaze & the "diamód, ỹ chrysolite, ỹ onix, & the iasper, ỹ saphir, "emeraud,
& the carbũcle & golde: ỹ worke manship
of thy timbrels, & of thy pipes was prepared in thee in the day that ỹ wast created.
14 Thou art [e] the anointed Cherúb, that co
uereth, and I haue set thee [f] *in honour*: thou
wast vpõ ỹ holy mountaine of God: ỹ hast
walked in ỹ middes of the [g] stones of fyre.
15 Thou wast perfite in thy waies from the
day that thou wast [h] created, til iniquitie
was founde in thee.
16 By the multitude of thy marchandise,
thei haue filled the middes of thee with
crueltie, and thou hast sinned: therefore I
wil cast thee as prophane out of ỹ [i] mountaine of God: & I wil destroy thee, ô couering Cherúb from the middes of the stones of fyre.
17 Thine heart was lifted vp because of thy
beautie, & thou hast corrupted thy wisdo
me by reason of thy brightnes: I wil cast
thee to the grounde: I wil lay thee before
Kings that thei may beholde thee.
18 Thou hast defiled thy [k] sanctification by
ỹ multitude of thine iniquities, & by the
iniquitie of thy marchãdise: therefore wil
I bring forthe a fyre frõ ỹ middes of thee,
which shal deuoure thee: & I wil brĩg thee
to asshes vpon the earth, in the sight of all
them that beholde thee.
19 All thei ỹ knowe thee among the people,
shalbe astonished at thee: thou shalt be a
terrour, & neuer shalt thou be any more.
20 ¶ Againe, the worde of the Lord came
vnto me, saying,
21 Sonne of man, set thy face against Zidón, and prophecie against it,
22 And say, Thus saith ỹ Lord God, Behol
de, I *come* against thee, ô Zidón, & I wil be
[l] glorified in ỹ middes of thee: & thei shal
knowe that I am the Lord, when I shal haue executed iudgements in her, and shalbe sanctified in her.
23 For I wil send into her pestilẽce & blood
into her stretes, and the slaine shal fall in ỹ
middes of her: [m] *the enemie shal come* agaĩst
her with the sworde on euerie side, & thei
shal knowe that I am the Lord.
24 And thei shalbe no more a pricking thorne vnto ỹ house of Israél, nor *any* grieuous
thorne of all that are rounde about them,
and despised thẽ, and thei shal knowe that
I am the Lord God.
25 Thus saith ỹ Lord God, Whẽ I shal haue gathered ỹ house of Israél frõ ỹ people
where thei are scattred, & shal be [n] sanctified in thẽ in the sight of the heathen, then
shal thei dwell in the land, that I haue giuen to my seruant Iaakób.
26 And thei shal dwell safely therein, & shal
buyld houses, & plant vineyardes: yea, thei
shal dwell safely, whẽ I haue executed iudgemẽts vpõ all rounde about thẽ ỹ despise
thẽ, & thei shal knowe ỹ I am ỹ Lord their
God.

CHAP. XXIX.

He prophecieth against Pharaóh and Egypt. 13 The Lord promiseth that he wil restore Egypt after fourtie yeres. 18 Egypt is the rewarde of King Nebuchadnezzár for the labour, which he toke against Tyrus.

1 IN the [a] tẽth yere, & in ỹ tenth moneth
in the twelfth *day* of the moneth, the
worde of the Lord came vnto me, saying,
2 Sõne of mã, set thy face against Pharaóh
the King of Egypt, and prophecie against
him, and against all Egypt.
3 Speake, & say, Thus saith the Lord God,
Beholde, I *come* agaĩst thee, Pharaóh King
of Egypt, ỹ great [b] dragõ, that lieth in the
middes of his riuers, ẇ hathe said, The riuer is mine, & I haue made it for my self.
4 But I wil put [c] hokes in thy chawes, & I wil
cause ỹ fish of thy riuers to sticke vnto thy
scales, & I wil drawe thee out of the mid
des of thy riuers, & all the fish of thy riuers
shal sticke vnto thy scales.
5 And I wil leaue thee in ỹ wildernes, *bothe*
thee & all the fish of thy riuers: ỹ shalt fall
vpon the open field: ỹ shalt not be broght
together, nor gathered: *for* I haue giuen
thee for meat to ỹ beastes of the field, and
to the foules of the heauen.

b Thus he speaketh by derision: for Daniél had declared notable signes of his wisdome in Babylon, when Ezekiél wrote this.

c Like ỹ rest of ỹ heathen and infideles, ẇ are Gods enemies.

d He derideth the vaine opinion and confidence that ỹ Tyrians had in their riches strength and pleasures.

"Or, iasper.

"Or, carbuncle.

e He meaneth ỹ royal state of Tyrus, ẇ for the excellencie and glorie thereof he compareth to ỹ Cherubims ẇ couered ỹ Arke: and by this worde *anointed* he signifieth the same

f I did thee this honour to make thee one of the buylders of my Tẽple, which was when Hirám sent vnto Salomon things necessarie for the worke.

g To wit, among my people Israél, ẇ shined as precious stones.

h Which was when I first called thee to this dignitie.

i Thou shalt haue no parte amõg my people.

k That is, the honour, whereunto I called them.

l By executing my iudgemẽts against thy wickednes.

m That is, Nebuchadnezzár

n He sheweth for what cause God wil assemble his Church, and preserue it stil thogh he destroy his enemies: to wit, ỹ they shulde praise him, & giue thankes for his great mercies.

a To wit, of ỹ captiuitie of Iecontáh or of the reigne of Zedekiah. Of the order of these prophecies and how the forther some time standeth after the latter, read Iere. 27,1.

b He compareth Pharaóh to a dragon ẇ hideth him self in the riuer Nilus, as Isa 51,9

c I wil send enemies agaĩst thee, ẇ shal plucke thee & thy people ẇ trust in thee out of thy sure places.

6 And all ẏ inhabitāts of Egypt shal knowe
that I am the Lord,because thei haue bene a staffe of [d] reed to the house of Israél.
7 When thei toke holde of thee with their
hand,thou didest breake,and rent all their
shulder : and when thei leaned vpon thee,
thou brakest and madest all their loines to
″stand [e] vpright.
8 Therefore thus saith the Lord God, Beholde,I wil bring a sworde vpon thee,and
destroy man and beast out of thee,
9 And the land of Egypt shalbe desolate,&
waste, and thei shal knowe that I am the
Lord:because he hathe said,[f] The riuer is
mine,and I haue made it,
10 Beholde,therefore I *come* vpon thee,and
vpon thy riuers, and I wil make the land
of Egypt vtterly waste and desolate from
the towre of Seuenéh, euen vnto the borders of the ″blacke Mores.
11 No foote of mā shal passe by it,nor foote of beast shal passe by it,nether shal it be
inhabited fourtie yeres.
12 And I wil make the land of Egypt desolate in the middes of the countreis, that a-
re desolate, and her cities shalbe desolate
amōg the cities that are desolate,for fourtie yeres : and I wil scattre the Egyptians
among the nacions,and wil disperse them
through the countreis.
13 Yet thus saith ẏ Lord God, * At the end
of fourtie yeres wil I gather the Egyptiās
frō the people, where thei were scattred,
14 And I wil bring againe the captiuitie of
Egypt,and wil cause them to returne into
the land of Pathrós,into the land of their
habitation,and thei shal be there a [g] small
kingdome.
15 It shalbe the smallest of the kingdomes,
nether shal it exalt it self any more aboue
the nacions:for I wil diminish them, that
thei shal no more rule the nacions.
16 And it shal be no more the confidence of
the house of Israél,to bring *their* [h] iniquitie to remembrance by loking after them,
so shal thei knowe, that I am ẏ Lord God.
17 ¶ In the [i] seuen and twentieth yere also in
the first *moneth*, & in ẏ first *day* of the moneth came the worde of the Lord vnto
me,saying,
18 Sonne of man, Nebuchad-nezzár King
of Babél caused his armie to serue a great
[k] seruice agaīst Tyrus:euerie head was ma
de balde, and euerie shulder was made bare : yet had he no wages, [l] nor his armie
for Tyrus, for the seruice that he serued
against it.
19 Therefore thus saith the Lord God, Beholde, I wil giue the land of Egypt vnto
Nebuchad-nezzár the King of Babél,and
he shal take her multitude, and spoile her
spoile,and take her pray,and it shal be the
wages for his armie.

[d] Read.2. King 18,21.isa 36,6.

″Or, shake.

[e] When thei felt their hurt, thei wolde stay no more vpon thee,but stode vpon their fete and put their trust in others.

[f] Thus God can not suffer that man shulde arrogat any thing to him self, or put his trust in any thing saue in him alone.

″Ebr. Cush, or Ethiopia.

Ierem.46,26.

[g] Meaning, ẏ thei shuld not haue ful dominion,but be vnder the Persiās, Grecians and Romains, and the cause is,that the Israelites shulde no more put their trust in them, but learne to depend on God.

[h] Lest I shulde by this meanes punish their sinnes.

[i] Counting frō the captiuitie of Ieconiáh.

[k] He toke great paines at the siege of Tyrus and his armie was sore handled.

[l] Signifying ẏ Nebuchadnezzár had more paines then profite, by the taking of Tyrus.

20 I haue giuen him the land of Egypt for
his labour,that he serued against it,becau-
se thei wroght for me.
21 In that day wil I cause the horne of the
house of Israél to growe, and I wil giue
thee an open mouth in the middes of thē,
and thei shal knowe that I am the Lord.

CHAP. XXX.

The destruction of Egypt & the cities thereof.

1 THe worde of the Lord came againe
vnto me,saying,
2 Sonne of man, prophecie, and say, Thus
saith the Lord God,Houle *& crye*, Wo *be*
vnto this day.
3 For the day is nere,and the day of ẏ Lord
is at hand,a cloudie day, *and* it shalbe the
time of the heathen.
4 And the sworde shal come vpon Egypt,
and feare shalbe in Ethiopia,whē the slaine shal fall in Egypt, when thei shal take
away her multitude, and *when* her fundacions shalbe broken downe.
5 [a] Ethiopia, and Phut, & Lud, and all the
commune people,and Cub, and the mē of
the land, that is in league, shal fall with
them by the sworde.
6 Thus saith ẏ Lord, Thei also that mainteine Egypt,shal fall,and the pride of her
power shal come downe from the towre of
[b] Seuenéh shal thei fall by ẏ sworde, saith
the Lord God.
7 And thei shalbe desolate in the middes
of the countreis that are desolate, and her
cities shalbe in ẏ middes of the cities that
are wasted.
8 And thei shal knowe that I am the Lord,
when I haue set a fyre in Egypt, *and when*
all her helpers shalbe destroied.
9 In that day shal their messengers go forthe from me in shippes, to make the careles Mores afraied,and feare shal come vpō
them,as in the day of Egypt : for lo, it cometh.
10 Thus saith the Lord God,I wil also make the multitude of Egypt to cease by the
hād of Nebuchad-nezzár King of Babél.
11 For he and his people with him, *euen* the
terrible nacions shal be broght to destroy
the land:and thei shal drawe their swordes
against Egypt, & fil the land with ẏ slaine.
12 And I wil make the riuers drye, and sel
the land into the hands of the wicked, and
I wil make the land waste,and all that therein is by the hands of strangers : I the
Lord haue spoken it.
13 Thus saith the Lord God, I wil also destroy the idoles, and I wil cause their idoles to cease out of ″Noph, and there shal
be no more a prince of the land of Egypt,
& I wil send a feare in the land of Egypt.
14 And I wil make Pathrós desolate, & wil
set fyre in ″Zóan,and I wil execute iudgement in No.

[a] By Phut and Lud are ment Aphrica and Libya.

[b] Which was a strong citie of Egypt,cha.29,10.

″Or, Memphis, or Alkaira.

″Or, Tanes.

15 And I wil powre my wrath vpon "Sin,
which is the strength of Egypt: and I wil
destroy the multitude of "No.
16 And I wil set fyre in Egypt: Sin shal haue great sorow, and No shalbe destroyed,
and Noph shal haue sorowes daiely.
17 The yong men of "Auen, and of "Phibé-
seth shal fall by the sworde: and these *cities*
shal go into captiuitie.
18 At Tehaphnehes the day [c] shal restreine
his light, when I shal breake there the [d] barres of Egypt: and when the pompe of her
power shal cease in her, the cloude shal couer her, & her daughters shal go into captiuitie.
19 Thus wil I execute iudgemẽts in Egypt,
and they shal knowe, that I am the Lord.
20 ¶ And in the [e] eleuenth yere, in the first
moneth, & in the seuẽth *day* of the moneth,
the worde of the Lord came vnto me, saying,
21 Sonne of man, [f] I haue broken the arme
of Pharaóh King of Egypt: and lo, it shal
not be bounde vp to be healed, nether shal
they put a roole to binde it, and *so* make it
strong, to holde the sworde.
22 Therefore thus saith the Lord God, Beholde, I *come* against Pharaóh King of E-
gypt, and wil breake [g] his arme, that was
strong, but is broken, and I wil cause the
sworde to fall out of his hand.
23 And I wil scatter the Egyptians among
the nacions, and wil disperse thẽ through
the countreis.
24 And I wil strengthen the arme of the
King of Babél, and put my sworde in his
hand, but I wil breake Pharaohs armes, &
he shal cast out sighings as the sighings of
him, that is wounded before him.
25 But I wil strengthen the armes of the
King of Babél, and the armes of Pharaóh
shal fall downe, and they shal knowe, that I
am the Lord, [h] when I shal put my sworde
into the hand of the King of Babél, & he
shal stretch it out vpon the land of Egypt.
26 And I wil scatter the Egyptians among
the nacions, and disperse them among the
countreys, and they shal knowe, that I am
the Lord.

"Or, Pelusium.
"Or, Alexãdria
"Or, Heliopolis.
"Or, Pubastum.
c Meaning, that there shal be great sorowe and affliction.
d That is, the strength and force.
e Of the captiuitie of Ieremiáh, or of Zedekiahs reigne.
f For Nebuchad-nezzár destroyed Pharaóh Nechó at Carchemish, Ier. 46, 26.
g His force & power.
h Whereby we se that tyrants haue no power of them selues, nether can do any more harme the God appointeth, & when he wil, thei must cease.

CHAP. XXXI.

2 A comparison of the prosperitie of Pharaóh with the prosperitie of the Assyrians. 10 He prophecieth a like destruction to them bothe.

1 AND in the [a] eleuenth yere, in ye third
moneth, & in the first *day* of the moneth the worde of the Lord came vnto me,
saying,
2 Sonne of man, speake vnto Pharaóh Kĩg
of Egypt, and to his multitude, Whome
art thou [b] like in thy greatnes?
3 Beholde, Asshúr *was like* a cedre in Lebanón with faire branches, and with thicke
shadowing boughes, and shot vp verie hie,
and his top was amõg the thicke boughes.
4 The waters nourished him, and the depe
exalted him on hie with her riuers rũning
rounde about his plants, and sent out her
[c] litle riuers vnto all the trees of the "field.
5 Therefore his height was exalted aboue
all the trees of the field, & his boughes were multiplied, and his branches were long,
because of the multitude of the waters,
which *the depe* sent out.
6 All the foules of the heauen made their
nests in his boughes, and vnder his branches did all the beasts of the field bring
forthe their yong, and vnder his shadow
dwelt all mightie nacions.
7 Thus was he faire in his greatnes, *and* in
the length of his branches: for his roote
was nere great waters.
8 The cedres in the garden [d] of God colde
not hide him: no firre tre was like his branches, and the chessenut trees were not like
his boughes: all the trees in the garden of
God were not like vnto him in his beautie.
9 I made him faire by the multitude of his
branches: so that all the trees of Eden, that
were in the garden of God, enuied him.
10 Therefore thus saith the Lord God, Because" he is lift vp on high, and hathe shot
vp his toppe among the thicke boughes, &
his heart is lift vp in his height,
11 I haue therefore deliuered him into the
hands of the [e] mightiest among the heathen: he shal handle him, *for* I haue cast him
away for his wickednes.
12 And the strangers haue destroyed him,
euen the terrible nacions, and thei haue left
him vpon the mountaines, and in the valleis his branches are fallen, & his boughes
are [f] broken by all the riuers of the land:
and all the people of the earth are departed from his shaddowe, and haue forsaken
him.
13 Vpon his ruine shal all the foules of the
heauen remaine, and all the beasts of the
field shalbe vpon his branches,
14 So that none of all the trees by the waters shal be exalted by their height, nether
shal shoote vp their toppe amõg the thicke
boughes, nether shal their leaues stand vp
in their height, which drinke so muche
water: for thei are all deliuered vnto death
in the nether partes of the earth in the
middes of the children of men among thẽ
that go downe to the pit.
15 Thus saith the Lord God, In the daye
when he went downe to hel, I caused them
to mourne, & I [g] couered ye depe for him,
and I did restreine the floods thereof, and
the great waters were staied: I caused Lebanón to mourne for him, and all the trees
of the field fainted.
16 I made the naciõs to shake at the sounde
of his fall, when I cast him downe to hell,

a Of Zedekiahs reigne or of Ieconiahs captiuitie.
b Meaning, that he was not like in strength to the King of the Assyrians, whome the Babyloniãs ouercame.
c Many other nations were vnder their dominion.
"Or, countrey.
d Signifying, that there was no greater power in the worlde then his was.
"Or, thou wast lift vp.
e That is, of Nebuchad-nezzár, who afterward was the monarche and onelie ruler of the worlde.
f Hereby is signified the destruction of ye power of the Assyrians by the Babylonians.
g The depe waters ye caused hĩ to mourne so hie (meaning his great abundance & pompe) shal now lament as thogh they were couered w sackecloth.

with them that descend into the pit, & all
the excellent trees of Eden, and the best of
Lebanón: *euen* all that are nourished with
waters, shal [h] be comforted in the nether
partes of the earth.
17 They also went downe to hel with him
vnto them that be slaine with the sworde,
and his arme, & they that dwelt vnder his
shaddowe in the middes of the heathen.
18 To whome [i] art thou thus like in glorie
& in greatnes amõg the trees of Eden? yet
thou shalt be cast downe with the trees of
Eden vnto the nether partes of the earth:
thou shalt slepe in ẏ middes of the [k] vncircumcised, with them that be slaine by the
sworde: this is Pharaóh & all his multitude, saith the Lord God.

h To cause this destructiõ of the King of Assyria to seme more horrible, he setteth forthe other Kings and princes which are dead, as thogh thei reioyced at the fall of suche a tyrant.
i Meaning, that Pharaohs power was nothing so great as his was.
k Read Chap. 28,10.

CHAP. XXXII.

2 *The Prophet is commanded to bewaile Pharaóh King*
of Egypt. 12 He prophecieth that destruction shal co-
me vnto Egypt through the King of Babylon.

1 AND in ẏ [a] twelfth yere in the twelfth
moneth, & in the first *day* of the moneth, the worde of the Lord came vnto me,
saying,
2 Sonne of man, take vp a lamentacion for
Pharaóh King of Egypt, & say vnto him,
Thou art like a [b] lyon of the nations & art
as a [*] dragon in the sea: thou castest out thy
riuers [c] and troublest the waters with thy
fete, and stampest in their riuers.
3 Thus saith the Lord God, *I wil therefore
spread my net ouer thee with a great multitude of people, & thei shal make thee come vp into my net.
4 Then wil I leaue thee vpon the land, & I
wil cast thee vpon the open field, & I wil
cause all the foules of the heauẽ to remaine vpon thee, and I wil fil all the beasts of
the field with thee.
5 And I wil laye thy flesh vpon the mountaines, & fil the valleis [d] with thine height.
6 I wil also water with thy blood the land
wherein thou [e] swimmest, *euen* to the mouñtaines, and the riuers shalbe full of thee.
7 And when I shal [f] put thee out, I wil couer the heauen, and make the starres thereof darke: * I wil couer the sunne with a
cloude, and the moone shal not giue her
light.
8 All the lights of heauen wil I make darke for thee, and bring [g] darkenes vpon thy
land, saith the Lord God.
9 I wil also trouble the hearts of many people, when I shal bring thy destruction a-
mong the nacions, *and* vpon the countreis
which thou hast not knowen.
10 Yea, I wil make many people amased at
thee, & their Kings shalbe astonished with
feare for thee, when I shal make my sworde to glitter against their faces, & thei shal
be afraied at euery moment: euery man for
his owne life in the day of thy fall.

a Which was the first yere of the general captiuitie vnder Zedekiáh.
b Thus the scriptures cõpare tyrants to cruel and huge beastes ẇ deuoure all that be weaker then they, and suche as they may ouercome.
*Or, whale.
c Thou preparedst great armies.
Chap. 12,13. & 17,20.
d With heapes of the carkeisses of thine armie.
e As Nilus ouerfloweth Egypt, so wil I make ẏ blood of thine hoste to ouerflowe it.
f The worde signifieth to be put out as a candel is put out.
Isa. 13,10. ioel 2,31. & 3,15. matt. 24,29.
g By this maner of speache is ment the great sorowe ẏ shalbe for the slaughter of the King & his people.

11 For thus saith the Lord God, The sworde
of the King of Babél shal come vpõ thee.
12 By the swordes of the mightie wil I cause thy multitude to fall: they all shalbe terrible nacions, and they shal destroye the
[h] pompe of Egypt, and all the multitude
thereof shalbe consumed.
13 I wil destroye also all the beasts thereof
from the great watersides, nether shal the
fote of man trouble them any more, nor
the houes of beast trouble them.
14 Then wil I make [i] their waters depe, and
cause their riuers to runne like oyle, saith
the Lord God.
15 When I shal make the land of Egypt desolate, and the countrey with all that is
therein, shalbe laied wast: when I shal smite all them, which dwell therein, then shal
thei knowe, that I am the Lord.
16 This is the mourning wherewith they
shal lament her: the daughters of the nacions shal lament her: thei shal lament for
Egypt, and for all her multitude, saith the
Lord God.
17 ¶ In the twelfth yere also in the fifteenth
day of the moneth, came the worde of the
Lord vnto me, saying,
18 Sonne of man, lament for the multitude
of Egypt, and [k] cast them downe, *euen* thẽ
and the daughters of the mightie nations
vnto the nether partes of the earth, with
them that go downe into the pit.
19 Whome doest thou passe [l] in beautie? go
downe and slepe with the vncircumcised.
20 Thei shal fall in the middes of them that
are slayne by ẏ sworde: [m] she is deliuered
to the sworde: drawe her downe, & all her
multitude.
21 The moste [n] mighty & strõg shal speake
to her out of the middes of hel with them
ẏ helpe her: they are gone downe *and* slepe
with the vncircumcised that be slaine by ẏ
sworde.
22 Asshúr is there & all his companie: their
graues are about him: all they are slayne
and fallen by the sworde.
23 Whose graues are made in the side of the
pit, & his multitude are rounde about his
graue: all they are slaine *and* fallen by the
sworde, which caused feare *to be* in the land
of the liuing.
24 There *is* [o] Elám and all his multitude
rounde about his graue: all they are slaine
and fallen by the sworde ẇ are gone downe with the vncircumcised into the nether
partes of the earth, which caused thẽ selues to be feared in the land of the [p] liuing,
yet haue they borne their shame with thẽ
that are gone downe to the pit.
25 Thei haue made his bed in the middes
of the slaine with all his multitude: their
graues *are* rounde about him: all these vncircũcised are slaine by the sworde: thogh
thei

h This came to passe in lesse then foure yeres after this prophecie.
i To wit, of ẏ Caldeans thine enemies, which shal quietly enioy all thy cõmodities.
k That is, prophecie, that they shal be cast downe: thus the Lord giueth his Prophetes power bothe to plant and to destroy by his worde, read Iere 1,10
l Haue not other kigdoms, more beautiful then thou, perished?
m That is, Egypt.
n To make the matter more sensible, he bringeth in Pharaóh, whome the dead shal mete & marueile at him, read Isa 14,9.
o Meaning, ẏ Persians.
p Whome in this life all ẏ worlde feared

thei haue caused their feare in the land of
the liuing, yet haue thei borne their shame with them that go downe to the pit:
thei are laide in the middes of them, that
be slaine.
26 There *is* [q] Méshech, Tubál, & all their
multitude: their graues *are* rounde about
them: all these vncircumcised were slaine by the sworde, thogh thei caused their
feare *to be* in the land of the liuing.
27 And thei shal not lye with the valiant
[r] of the vncircumcised, that are fallen,
which are gone downe to the graue, with
their weapons of warre, and haue layed
their swordes vnder their heads, but their
iniquitie shalbe vpō their bones: because
thei were ẏ feare of the mightie in the lād
of the liuing.
28 Yea, thou shalt be broken in the middes
of the vncircumcised, and lye with them
that are slaine by the sworde.
29 There *is* Edóm, his Kings, and all his
princes, which with their strength are
laied by them that were slaine by the
sworde: they shal slepe with the vncircumcised, and with them that go downe
to the pit.
30 There *be* all the princes of the [ſ] North,
with all the Zidonians, which are gone
downe with the slaine, with their feare:
thei are ashamed of their strength, and
the vncircumcised slepe with them that
be slaine by the sworde, and beare their
shame with them that go downe to the
pit.
31 Pharaóh shal se thē, and he shalbe [t] comforted ouer all his multitude: Pharaóh, &
all his armie *shalbe* slaine by the sworde,
saith the Lord God.
32 For I haue caused my [u] feare *to be* in the
land of the liuing: and he shalbe laid in
the middes of the vncircumcised with
them, that are slaine by the sworde, *euen*
Pharaóh and all his multitude, saith the
Lord God.

q That is, the Cappadocians & Italians, or Spanyardes, as Iosephus writeth.

r Which dyed not by cruel death, but by the course of nature and are honorably buryed with their cote armour and signes of honour.

ſ The Kings of Babylon.

t As the wicked reioyce when they se others partakers of their miseries.

u I wil make the Egyptians afraid of me, as thei caused others to feare them.

CHAP. XXXIII.

3 *The office of the gouernours and ministers. 14 He strengtheneth them that dispaire, and boldeneth them with the promes of mercie. 30 The worde of the Lord against the mockers of the Prophet.*

1 AGaine, the worde of the Lord came
vnto me, saying,
2 Sonne of man, speake to the children of
thy people, and say vnto them, When I
bring the sworde vpon a land, if the people of the land take a man ″ from among
them, and make him their [a] watcheman,
3 If when he seeth the sworde come vpon
the land, he blowe the trumpet and warne the people,
4 Then he that heareth the sounde of the
trumpet, and wil not be warned, if the
sworde come, & take him away, his blood
shalbe vpon his owne head.
5 For he heard the sounde of the trumpet,
and wolde not be admonished: *therefore* his
blood shalbe vpon him: but he that receiueth warning, shal saue his life.
6 But if the watchman se the sworde come, and blowe not the trumpet, and the
people be not warned: if the sworde come, and take any persone from among
them, he is taken away for his [b] iniquitie,
but his blood wil I require at the watch-
mans hand.
7 * So thou, ô sonne of man, I haue made
thee a watchman vnto the house of Israél:
therefore thou shalt heare the worde at
my [c] mouth, and admonishe them from
me.
8 When I shal say vnto the wicked, O wicked man, thou shalt dye the death, if thou
doest not speake, and admonish the wicked of his way, that wicked man shal dye
for his iniquitie, but his blood wil I [d] require at thine hand.
9 Neuertheles, if thou warne the wicked
of his way, to turne from it, if he do
not turne from his way, he shal dye for
his iniquitie, but thou hast deliuered thy
soule.
10 Therefore, ô thou sonne of man, speake vnto the house of Israél, Thus ye speake and say, If our transgresions and our
sinnes *be* vpon vs, and we are consumed
because of them, [e] how shulde we then
liue?
11 Say vnto them, as I liue, saith the Lord
God, [f] I desire not the death of the wicked, but that the wicked turne from his
way and liue: turne you, turne you from
your euil wayes, for why wil ye dye, ô ye
house of Israél?
12 Therefore thou sonne of man, say vnto the children of thy people, The [g] righteousnes of the righteous shal not deliuer
him in the day of his transgresion, nor
the wickednes of the wicked *shal cause*
him to fall therein, in the day that he
returneth from his wickednes, nether shal
the righteous liue for *his righteousnes* in the
day that he sinneth.
13 When I shal say vnto the righteous, that
he shal surely liue, if he trust to his owne righteousnes, and commit iniquitie,
all his righteousnes shalbe no more remembred, but for his iniquitie that he
hathe cōmitted, he shal dye for the same.
14 Againe when I shal say vnto the wicked, Thou shalt dye the death, if he turne from his sinne, & do that which is lawful and [h] right,
15 *To wit*, if the wicked restore the pledge,
and giue againe that he had robbed, *and*
walke in the statutes of life, without committing iniquitie, he shal surely liue, *and*

″ Or, of their coastes.

a He sheweth that ẏ people oght to haue continually gouernours & teachers ẇ may haue a care ouer them, and to warne them euer of the dangers which are at hand.

b Signifying ẏ the wicked shal not escape punishment thogh ẏ watchman be negligent, but if the watchman blowe ẏ trumpet, and then he wil not obey, he shal deserue double punishment.

Chap. 3,17.

c Which teacheth that he ẏ receiueth not his charge at ẏ Lords mouth, is a spie, and not a true watchman.

d The watchman must answer for the blood of all ẏ perish through his negligēce.

e Thus ẏ wicked whē they heare Gods iudgements for their sinnes, despaire of his mercies and murmur.

f Read Chap. 18,23.

g Read of this righteousnes Chap. 18,23.

h Hereby he condemneth all them of hypocrisie, ẇ pretēde to forsake wickednes, & yet declare not thē selues suche by their fruites, that is, in obeying Gods commandements and by godlie life.

not dye.
16 None of his sinnes that he hathe committed, shal be mencioned vnto him: *because* he hathe done that, which is lawful, &
right, he shal surely liue.
17 Yet the children of thy people say,
*The way of the Lord is not equal: but
their owne way is vnequal.

Chap.18,25.

18 When the righteous turneth from his
righteousnes, and committeth iniquitie,
he shal euen dye thereby.
19 But if the wicked returne from his wickednes, and do that which is lawful, and
right, he shal liue thereby.
20 Yet ye say, The way of the Lord is not
equal. O ye house of Israél, I wil iudge
you euerie one after his wayes.
21 Also in the twelfth yere of [i] our captiuitie, in the tenth *moneth*, *and* in the fift *day*
of the moneth, one that had escaped out
of Ierusalém, came vnto me, and said, The
citie is smitten.

i When ỳ Prophet was led away captiue with Ieconiáh

22 Now the [k] hand of the Lord had bene
vpon me in the euening afore he that had
escaped, came, and had opened my mouth,
vntil he came to me in the morning: and
when he had opened my [l] mouth, I was
no more domme.

k I was indued with the Spirit of prophecie, Chap. 8,2.

l Whereby is signified that the ministers of God cã not speake til God giue them courage and open their mouths, Chap.24,27,& 29,21 ephe.6.19.

23 Againe the worde of the Lord came vnto me, and said,
24 Sonne of man, these that dwell in the
desolate places of the land of Israél, talke
and say, [m] Abrahám was but one, and he
possessed ỳ land: but we are many, *therfore*
the land shalbe giuen vs in possession.

m Thus ỳ wicked thinke thẽ selues more worthie to enioye Gods promes then ỳ Saĩts of God, to whome they were made: and wolde binde God to be subiect to them, though they wolde not be bounde to him.

25 Wherefore say vnto them, Thus saith
the Lord God, Ye eat with the [n] blood, and
lift vp your eyes towarde your idoles, and
sheade blood: shulde ye then possesse the
land?

n Contrary to the Law, Leui. 17,14.

26 Ye leane vpon your [o] swordes: ye worke abominacion, and ye defile euerie o-
ne his neighbours wife: shulde ye then pos
sesse the land?

o As thei that are ready stil to shed blood.

27 Say thus vnto them, Thus saith ỳ Lord
God, As I liue, so surely thei that are in
the desolate places, shal fall by the sworde:
and him that is in the open field, wil I giue vnto the beastes to be deuoured: and
thei that be in the fortes and in the caues,
shal dye of the pestilence.
28 For I wil lay the land desolate and waste, and the* pompe of her strength shal
cease: and the mountaines of Israél shalbe desolate, and none shal passe through.

Chap.7,24. & 24,21. & 30,6.

29 Then shal thei knowe that I am ỳ Lord,
when I haue laide the land desolate and
waste, because of all their abominacions,
that thei haue committed.
30 Also thou sonne of man, the children of
thy people that [p] talke of thee by the walles and in the dores of houses, and speake one to another, euerie one to his brother, saying, Come, I pray you, and heare
what is the worde that commeth from the
Lord.

p In derision.

31 For thei come vnto thee, as the people
vseth to come: and my people sit before
thee, and heare thy wordes, but thei wil
not do them: for with their mouthes thei
make [q] iestes, *and* their heart goeth after
their couetousnes.
32 And lo, thou art vnto them, as a* iesting
song of one that hathe a pleasant voice,
and can sing wel: for thei heare thy wordes, but thei do them not.
33 And when this commeth to passe (*for* lo,
it wil come) then shal thei knowe, that a
Prophet hathe bene among them.

q This declareth that we oght to heare Gods worde with suche zeale and affection that we shulde in all points obey it, els we abuse the worde to our owne condemnation, and make of his ministers as thogh they were iestes to serue mens foolish fantasies.

Or, pleasant, & loue songs.

CHAP. XXXIIII.

2 *Against the shepherdes that despised the flocke of Christ, & seke their owne gain. 7 The Lord saith that he wil visite his dispersed flocke, and gather them together. 23 He promiseth the true shepherd Christ, and with him peace.*

1 AND the worde of the Lord came vn
to me, saying,
2 Sonne of man, prophecie against the
shepherdes of Israél, prophecie and say
vnto them, Thus saith the Lord God vnto the shepherdes, * Wo *be* vnto the
[a] shepherdes of Israél, that fede them selues: shulde not the shepherdes fede the
flockes?

Ierem.23,1.

a By the shepherds he meaneth the King, the magistrates, Priests, & Prophetes.

3 Ye eat the [b] fat, and ye clothe you with
the woll: ye kil them that are fed, but ye
fede not the shepe.

b Ye seke to inriche your selues by their comodities, & so spoile their riches & substance.

4 The [c] weake haue ye not strengthened:
the sicke haue ye not healed, nether haue
ye bounde vp the broken, nor broght againe that which was driuẽ away, nether haue
ye soght that which was lost, but with
crueltie, & with rigour haue ye ruled thẽ.

c He describeth the office and duetie of a good pastor, who oght to loue and sucor his flocke and not to be cruel toward them.

5 And they were scattred without a shepherde: and when thei were dispersed, thei
were [d] deuoured of all the beasts of the
field.

d For lacke of good gouernement & doctrine they perished.

6 My shepe wãdred through all the mountaines, and vpon euerie hye hil: yea, my
flocke was scattred through all the earth,
and none did seke or serche *after them*.
7 Therefore ye shepherdes, heare the worde of the Lord.
8 As I liue, saith the Lord God, surely because my flocke was spoiled, and my shepe
were deuoured of all ỳ beastes of the field,
hauing no shepherd, nether did my shepherdes seke my shepe, but the shepherdes
fed them selues, and fed not my shepe,
9 Therefore, heare ye the worde of ỳ Lord,
ô ye shepherdes.
10 Thus saith the Lord God, Beholde, I
come against the shepherdes, and wil require my shepe at their hands, and cause them to cease from feding the shepe:
nether shal the shepherds fede them selues

any more: for I wil deliuer my shepe from
e their mouthes, and thei shal nomore deuoure them.
11 For thus saith the Lord God, Beholde, I
wil serche my shepe, and seke them out.
12 As a shepherd sercheth out his flocke,
when he hathe bene among his shepe that
are scattered, so wil I seke out my shepe &
wil deliuer them out of all places, where
thei haue bene scattered in f the cloudie &
darke daie,
13 And I wil bring them out from the people, and gather them from the countreis,
and wil bring them to their owne land,
and fede them vpon the mountaines of
Israél, by the riuers, and in all the inhabit-
ted places of the countrey.
14 I wil fede thē in a good pasture, and vpon the hie mountaines of Israél shal their
folde be: there shal thei lie in a good folde
and in fat pasture shal thei fede vpon the
mountaines of Israél.
15 I wil fede my shepe, and bring them to
their rest, saith the Lord God.
16 I wil seke that which was lost, and bring
againe that which was driuen awaie, and
wil binde vp that which was broken, and
wil strengthen the weake, but I wil destroy the fat and the g strong, & I wil fede
them with h iudgement.
17 Also you my shepe, thus saith the Lord
God, Beholde, I iudge betwene shepe, and
shepe, *betwene* the rams & the goates.
18 Semeth it a smale thing vnto you to haue eaten vp the good i pasture, but ye must
tread downe with your fete the residue of
your pasture? & to haue dronke of the depe waters, but ye must trouble the residue
with your fete?
19 And my shepe eat that which ye haue
troden with your fete, and drinke that ẇ
ye haue troubled with your fete.
20 Therefore thus saith the Lord God vnto them, Beholde, I, *euen* I wil iudge betwene the fat shepe and the leane shepe.
21 Because ye haue thrust with side & with
shulder, and pusht all the weake with your
hornes, til ye haue scattred them abroade,
22 Therefore wil I helpe my shepe, and
thei shal nomore be spoiled, and I wil iudge betwene shepe and shepe.
23 And I wil set vp a shepherd ouer them,
and he shal fede them, *euen* my seruant
k Dauid, he shal fede them, and he shalbe
their shepherde.
24 And I the Lord wil be their God, and
my seruant Dauid *shalbe* the prince amōg
them. I the Lord haue spoken it.
25 And I wil make with them a couenant
of peace, and wil cause the euil beastes to
cease out of the land: and thei shal l dwell
safely in the wildernes, and slepe in the
woods.

e By destroying the couetous hirelings and restoring true shepherdes. whereof we haue a signe so oft as God sendeth true preachers who bothe by doctrine and life labour to fede his shepe in the pleasant pastures of his worde.
f In the daie of their affliction and miserie: and this promes is to comfort the Church in all dangers.
g Meaning such as lift vp them selues aboue their brethren, & think thei haue no nede to be gouerned by me.
h That is, by putting difference betwene the good and the bad, and so giue to ether as thei deserue
i By good pasture and depe waters is mēt the pure word of God and ẏ administraciō of iustice, ẇ thei did not distribute to ẏ poore til thei had corrupt it.
k Meaning, Christ, of whome Dauid was a figure, Iere. 30,9. hosea 3,5.
l This declareth, that vnder Christ the flocke shulde be truely deliuered frō sinne, and hel, and so be safely preserued in the Church where thei shulde neuer perish.

26 And I wil seke them, *as* a blessing, euen
rounde about my mountaine: & I wil cause raine to come downe in due season, and
there shalbe raine of blessing.
27 And the m tre of the field shal yelde
her frute, & the earth shal giue her frute,
and thei shalbe safe in their land, and shal
knowe that I am the Lord, when I haue
broken the cordes of their yoke, and deliuered them out of the hands of those that
serued them selues of them.
28 And thei shal nomore be spoiled of the
heathen, nether shal the beasts of the land
deuoure them, but thei shal dwell safely
and none shal make them afraied.
29 And I wil raise vp for them a n plant of
renoume, and they shalbe no more consumed with hungre in the land, nether
beare the reproche of the heathen anie
more.
30 Thus shal thei vnderstand, that I the
Lord their God am with them, and that
thei, *euē* the house of Israél, are my people,
saith the Lord God.
31 And ye my shepe, the shepe of my pasture
are men, & I am your God, saith ẏ Lord
God.

m The frutes of Gods graces shal appeare in great abundance in his Church.
n That is, the rod that shal come out of ẏ roote of Ishai. Isa. 11,1.

CHAP. XXXV.

a *The destruction that shal come on mount Seír, because thei troubled the people of the Lord.*

1 MOreouer the worde of the Lord came vnto me, saying,
2 Sonne of man, set thy face against mount
a Seír, and prophecie against it,
3 And saie vnto it, Thus saith the Lord
God, Beholde, ô mount Seír, I *come* a-
gainst thee, and I wil stretche out mine
hand against thee, and I wil make thee desolate and waste.
4 I wil laie thy cities waste, and thou shalt
be desolate, and thou shalt knowe that I
am the Lord.
5 Because thou hast had a perpetual hatred
& hast put the children of Israél to flight
by the force of the sworde in the time of
their calamitie, when *their* b iniquitie had
an end,
6 Therefore as I liue, saith the Lord God,
I wil prepare thee vnto blood, and blood
shal pursue thee: except thou c hate blood,
euen blood shal pursue thee.
7 Thus wil I make mount Seír desolate
and waste, and cut of from it him that passeth out and him that returneth.
8 And I wil fil his mountaines with his
slaine mē: in thine hils, and in thy valleis
and in all thy riuers shal thei fall, that are
slaine with the sworde.
9 I wil make thee perpetual desolatiōs, and
thy cities shal not d returne, and ye shal
knowe that I am the Lord.
10 Because thou hast said, e These two na-

a Where the Idumeans dwelt.
b When by their punishment I called them frō their iniquitie.
c Except thou repent thy former crueltie.
d To wit, to their former estate.
e Meaning, Israél & Iudah.

cions,and these two countreis shalbe mine,and we wil possesse them (seing the
Lord was [f] there)
11 Therefore as I liue,saith the Lord God,
I wil euen do according to thy [g] wrath, &
according to thine indignatiō which thou
hast vsed in thine hatred against them: &
I wil make my self knowen among [h] them
when I haue iudged thee.
12 And thou shalt knowe, that I the Lord
haue heard all thy blasphemies which
thou hast spoken against the mountaines
of Israél, saying, Thei lye waste, thei are
giuen vs to be deuoured.
13 Thus with your mouthes ye haue boasted
against me, and haue multiplied your
wordes against me: I haue heard *them*.
14 Thus saith the Lord God, So shal all the
worlde reioyce *when* I shal make thee desolate.
15 As thou didest reioyce at the inheritance
of the house of Israél, because it was desolate, so wil I do vnto thee: thou shalt be desolate, ô mount Seír, & all Idumea wholly,
and thei shal knowe, that I am the Lord.

f And so by fighting against Gods people, thei shulde go about to put him out of his owne possession.
g As thou hast done cruelly, so shalt thou be cruelly handled.
h Shewing, ỳ when God punisheth the enemies, the godlie oght to consider that he hathe a care ouer them and so praise his Name: and also that the wicked rage as thogh there were no God, til thei felé his hand to their destruction.

CHAP. XXXVI.

8 He promiseth to deliuer Israél from the Gentiles.
22 The benefites done unto the Iewes, are to be ascribed to the mercie of God, and not vnto their deseruings.
26 God renueth our hearts, that we maie walke in his commandements.

1 ALso thou sonne of man, prophecie
vnto the *mountaines of Israél, and
saie, Ye mountaines of Israél, heare ỳ worde of the Lord.
2 Thus saith the Lord God, Because the
[a] enemie hathe said against you, Aha, euen
the [b] hie places of the worlde are ours in
possession,
3 Therefore prophecie, and saie, Thus
saith the Lord God, Because that they
haue made you desolate, and swallowed
you vp on euerie syde, that ye might be a
possession vnto the residue of the heathen,
and ye are come vnto the lippes & [c] tongues *of men*, and vnto the reproche of the
people,
4 Therefore ye mountaines of Israél, heare
the worde of the Lord God, Thus saith ỳ
Lord God to the mountaines and to the
hilles, to the riuers, and to the valleis, and
to the waste, & desolate places, and to the
cities that are forsaken: which are spoiled
and had in derision of the residue of the
heathen that are rounde about.
5 Therefore thus saith the Lord God, Surely in the fyre of mine indignation haue
I spoken against the residue of the heathē,
and against all Idumea, which [d] haue taken my land for their possession, with the
ioye of all *their* heart, & with despiteful
mindes to cast it out for a praie.
6 Prophecie therefore vpon the land of

*Chap 6,2.
a That is, the Idumean.
b That is, Ierusalém, which for Gods promises was ỳ chiefest of all the worlde.
c Ye are made a matter of talke and derision to all the worlde.
d Thei appointed with them selues to haue it, and therefore came w̄ Nebuchad-nezzár against Ierusalém for this purpose.

Israél, and saie vnto the mountaines, and
to the hilles, to the riuers, and to the valleis, Thus saith the Lord God, Beholde, I
haue spoken in mine indignation, and in
my wrath, because ye haue suffered the
[e] shame of the heathen,
7 Therefore thus saith the Lord God, I
haue [f] lifted vp mine hand, surely the heathen that are about you, shal beare their
shame.
8 But you, ô mountaines of Israél, ye shal
[g] shoote forthe your branches, and bring
forthe your frute to my people of Israél:
for thei are ready to come.
9 For beholde, I *come* vnto you, and I wil
turne vnto you, and ye shal be tilled and
sowen.
10 And I wil multiplie the men vpon you,
euen all the house of Israél wholly, & the
cities shalbe inhabited, & the desolate places shalbe buylded.
11 And I wil multiplie vpon you man and
beast, and thei shal encrease, and bring
frute, and I wil cause you to dwell after
your olde estate, & I wil bestowe benefites
vpon you more then [h] at the first, and ye
shal knowe that I am the Lord.
12 Yea, I wil cause men to walke vpon you,
[i] euē my people Israél, & thei shal possesse
* you, and ye shal be their inheritance, and
ye shal nomore hence forthe depriue thē
of men.
13 Thus saith the Lord God, Because thei
saie vnto you, Thou [k] *land* deuourest vp
men, and hast bene a waster of thy people,
14 Therefore thou shalt deuoure men nomore, nether waste thy people hēce forthe,
saith the Lord God,
15 Nether wil I cause men to heare in thee
the shame of the heathen any more, nether shalt thou beare the reproche of the
people any more, nether shalt cause thy
folke to fall any more, saith ỳ Lord God.
16 ¶ Moreouer the worde of the Lord came
vnto me, saying,
17 Sonne of man, when the house of Israél
dwelt in their owne land, thei defiled it by
their owne waies, & by their dedes: their
waie was before me as the filthines of the
menstruous.
18 Wherefore I powred my wrath vpon
them, for the blood that thei had shed in
the land, and for their idoles, *where with*
thei had polluted it.
19 And I scattred them among the heathen,
and thei were dispersed through the countreis: *for* according to their waies, and according to their dedes, I iudged them.
20 *And when thei entred vnto the heathē,
whether thei wēt, thei polluted mine holy
Name, when they said of them, These
are the people of the Lord, and are gone
out of his land.

e Because you haue bene a laughīg stocke vnto them.
f By making a solemne othe, read chap.20,5
g God declareth his mercies and goodnes toward his Church who stil preserueth his, euen when he destroieth his enemies.
h Which was accomplished vnder Christ, to whome all these temporal deliuerāces did direct thē.
i That is, vpon the mountaines of Ierusalém.
*Or, thee.
k Thus the enemies imputed as the reproche of the land which God did for ỳ sinnes of the people according to his iuste iudgements.
*Isa.52,5. rom.2,14.

21 But

21 But I fauoured mine holy [l] Name which
the house of Israél had polluted amõg the
heathen, whether they went.
22 Therefore say vnto the house of Israél,
Thus saith ŷ Lord God, I do not this for
your sakes, ô house of Israél, but for mine
[m] holie Names sake, which ye polluted a-
mong the heathen whether ye went.
23 And I wil sanctifie my great Name, ŵ
was polluted among the heathen, among
whome you haue polluted it, & the heathẽ
shal knowe that I am the Lord, saith the
Lord God, when I shalbe sanctified in you
before [*] their eyes.
24 For I wil take you from among the heathen, and gather you out of all countreis,
and wil bring you into your owne land.
25 Then wil I powre cleane [n] water vpon
you, and ye shalbe cleane: *yea*, frõ all your
filthines, and frõ all your idoles wil I clẽse you.
26 *A new heart also wil I giue you, and a
new spirit wil I put within you, and I
wil take away the stonie heart out of your
bodye, & I wil giue you an heart of flesh.
27 And I wil put my Spirit within you,
& cause you to walke in my statutes, & ye
shal kepe my iudgements and do them.
28 And ye shal dwell in the lãd, that I gaue
to your fathers, and ye shal be my people
and I wil be your God.
29 I wil also deliuer you from all your filthines, and I wil call for [o] corne, and wil
increase it, and lay no famine vpon you.
30 For I wil multiplie the frute of the
trees, and the encrease of the field, that yé
shal beare no more the reproche of famine among the heathen.
31 Thẽ shal ye remẽber your owne wicked
wayes, & your dedes that were not good,
& shal iudge your selues worthie to haue
bene [p] destroyed for your iniquities, and
for your abominacions.
32 Be it knowen vnto you that I do not
this for your sakes, saith the Lord God:
therefore, ô ye house of Israél, be ashamed,
and confounded for your owne wayes.
33 Thus saith the Lord God, What time
as I shal haue clensed you from all your
iniquities, I wil cause *you* to dwell in the
cities, and the desolate places shal be
buylded.
34 And the desolate lãd shalbe tilled, where as it lay waste in the sight of all that passed by.
35 For they said, This waste lãd was like the
garden of Eden, and these waste and deso
late and ruinous cities were strong, *and*
were inhabited.
36 Then the residue of the heathen that are
left round about you, shal [q] knowe that I
the Lord buylde the ruinous places, *and*
plant the desolate places: I the Lord haue
spoken it, and wil do it.
37 Thus saith the Lord God, I wil yet for
this be soght of the house of Israél, to performe it vnto them: I wil encrease them
with men like a flocke.
38 As the holie flocke, as the flocke of Ierusalém in their solemne feastes, so shal the
desolate cities be filled with flockes of
men, and they shal knowe, that I am the
Lord.

l And therefore wolde not suffre my Name to be had in contempt, as the heathen wolde haue reproched me, if I had suffred my Church to perish.
m This excludeth from mã all dignitie, & meane to deserue anie thing by, seing that God referreth the whole to him self, and that onely for the glorie of his holy Name.
*Or, your.
n That is, his Spirit whereby he reformeth the hearte and regenerateth his, Isa. 44,3.
Ierem. 32,39. chap. 11,19.
o Vnder the abundance of temporal benefites he concludeth the spiritual graces.
p Ye shal come to true repentance, and thinke your selues vnworthie to be of ŷ nõber of Gods creatures for your ingratitude against him.
q He declareth ŷ it oght not to be referred to the soyle or plentifulnes of the earth that anie countrey is riche, and abundant, but onely to Gods mercies, as his plagues, and curses declare when he maketh it barre.

CHAP. XXXVII.

1 He prophecieth the bringing againe of the people, being in captiuitie. 16 He sheweth the vnion of the ten tribes with the two.

1 THe hand of the Lord was vpon me,
& caryed me out in the Spirit of the
Lord, and set me downe in the middes of
the [*] field, which was ful of [a] bones.
2 And he led me round about by them, and
beholde, there *were* very manie in the opẽ
field, and lo, *they were* verie drye.
3 And he said vnto me, Sonne of man, can
these bones liue? And I answered, ô Lord
God, thou knowest.
4 Againe he said vnto me, Prophecie vpon
these bones and say vnto them, O ye drye
bones, heare the worde of the Lord.
5 Thus saith the Lord God vnto these bones, Beholde, I wil cause breath to entre into you, and ye shal liue.
6 And I wil lay sinewes vpõ you, and make
flesh growe vpon you, and couer you with
skin, and put breath in you, that ye may
liue, and ye shal knowe that I am the
Lord.
7 So I prophecied, as I was commanded:
and as I prophecied, there was a noise,
and beholde, *there was* a shaking, and the
bones came together, bone to his bone.
8 And when I behelde, lo, the sinewes, and
the flesh grewe vpon them, and aboue, the
skin couered thẽ, but there was no breath
in them.
9 Then said he vnto me, Prophecie vnto the winde: prophecie, sonne of man,
and say to the winde, Thus saith the Lord
God, Come from the foure [b] windes, ô
breath, and breathe vpon these slaine,
that they may liue.
10 So I prophecied as he had commanded
me: and the breath came into them, and
they liued, and stode vp vpon their fete,
an exceding great armie.
11 Then he said vnto me, Sonne of man,
these bones are the whole house of Is
raél. Beholde, they say, Our bones are
dryed, and our hope is gone, & we are clea
ne cut of.
12 Therefore prophecie, and say vnto thẽ,
thus saith the Lord God, Beholde, my peo
ple, I wil open your graues, and cause you
to come vp out of your sepulchres, and
bring you into the land of Israél,

*Or, valley.
a He sheweth by a greater miracle, that God hathe power, and also wil deliuer his people frõ their captiuitie in asmuche as he is able to giue life to ŷ dead bones, & bodyes, & raise them vp againe.
b Signifying, all partes where as the Israelites were scattered: that is, the faithful shal be broght to the same vnitie of Spirit, and doctrine, wheresoeuer they are scattered through the worlde.

13 And ye shal knowe that I am the Lord,
c when I haue opened your graues, ô my
people, and broght you vp out of your
sepulchres,

c That is, whē I haue broght you out of those places, and townes where you are captiues.

14 And shal put my Spirit in you, and ye
shal liue, & I shal place you in your owne
land: then ye shal knowe that I the Lord
haue spoken it, and performed it, saith
the Lord.
15 ¶ The worde of the Lord came againe
vnto me, saying,
16 Moreouer thou sonne of man, take thee a
piece of wood, and write vpon it, Vnto Iudáh, and to the children of Israél his companions: then take d another *piece* of wood
and write vpon it, Vnto Ioséph the tre of
Ephráim, and to all the house of Israél his
companions.

d Which signifieth the ioyning together of the two houses of Israél, and Iudáh.

17 And thou shalt ioyne them one to another into one tre, and they shalbe as one
in thine hand.
18 And whē the children of thy people shal
speake vnto thee, saying, Wilt thou not
shewe vs what thou meanest by these?
19 Thou shalt answer them, Thus saith the
Lord God, Beholde, I wil take the tre e of
Ioséph, which is in the hand of Ephráim,
and the tribes of Israél his fellowes, and
wil put them with him, *euen* with the tre
of Iudáh, and make them one tre, and they
shalbe one in mine hand.

e That is, the house of Israél

20 And the *pieces* of wood, whereon thou
writest, shal be in thine hand, in their
sight.
21 And say vnto them, Thus saith the Lord
God, Beholde, I wil take the children of
Israél from among the heathen, whether
they be gone, and wil gather them on euerie side, and bring them into their owne
land.
22 And I wil make them one people in the
land, vpon the mountaines of Israél, *and
one King shalbe King to them all: & they
shalbe no more two peoples, nether be deuided anie more hence forthe into two
kingdomes.

Ioh.10,16.

23 Nether shal they be polluted anie more
with their idoles, nor with their abominacions, nor with anie of their trāsgressiōs:
but I wil saue them out of all their dwelling places, wherein they haue sinned, and
wil clense them: so shal they be my people, and I wilbe their God.
24 And Dauid my *seruāt *shalbe* King ouer
them, and they all shal haue one shepherd:
they shal also walke in my iudgements,
and obserue my statutes, and do them.

Isa.40,11. ier.23,5. chap.34,23. dan.9,24.

25 And they shal dwell in the f land, that I
haue giuen vnto Iaakób my seruāt, where
your fathers haue dwelt, & they shal dwell
therein, *euen* they, and their sonnes, & their
sonnes sonnes for euer, and my seruāt Dauid *shalbe* their prince for euer.

f Meaning, ȳ the elect by Christ shal dwell in the heauenlie Ierusalém, which is ment by the land of Canaan.

26 Moreouer, I wil make *a couenant of pea
ce with them: it shal be an euerlasting couenant with them, and I wil place them, &
multiplie them, and wil set my Sanctuarie
among them for euer more.

Psal.109,4. & 116,2.

27 My tabernacle also shalbe with thē: yea,
I wil be their God, and they shalbe my
people.
28 Thus the heathen shal knowe, that I the
Lord do sanctifie Israél, when my Sā ctuarie shalbe among them for euer more.

CHAP. XXXVIII.

2 He prophecieth that Gog and Magog shal fight with great power against the people of God. 21 Their destruction.

1 AND the worde of ȳ Lord came vnto
me, saying,
2 Sonne of man, set thy face against a Gog
and against the land of Magóg, the chief
prince of Méshech and Tubál, & prophecie against him,
3 And say, Thus saith the Lord God, Beholde, I *come* against thee, ô Gog the chief
prince of Méshech and Tubál.
4 And I wil destroye thee, and put hokes
in thy chawes, and I wil bring thee forthe,
and all thine hoste *bothe* horses, and horsemen, all clothed with all sortes of *armour*,
euen a great multitude with bucklers, and
shields, all b handling swordes.

a Which was a people that came of Magog the sonne of Iaphet, Gen.10,2 Magog also here signifieth a certeine countrey, so that by these two countreis, ẇ had the gouernement of Grecia & Italie, he meaneth the principal enemies of the Church, Reuel.20,8.

b He sheweth that the enemies shulde bend them selues against the Church, but it shulde be to their owne destruction.

5 They of c Parás, of Cush, and Phut with
them, *euen* all they *that beare* shield and
helmet.
6 d Gomér and all his bandes, *and* the house of Togarmáh of the North quarters,
and all his bandes, *and* muche people with
thee.

c The Persiās, Ethiopiās and men of Aphrica.

d Gomér was Iaphets sonne, and Togarmáh the sonne of Gomér, and are thoght to be they that inhabite Asia minor.

7 Prepare thy self, and e make thee ready,
bothe thou, and all thy multitude, that are
assembled vnto thee, and be thou their
sauegarde.

e Signifying, ȳ all the people of the worlde shulde assemble them selues against the Churche and Christ their head.

8 After manie dayes thou shalt be visited:
for in the latter yeres thou shalt come into
the land, that hathe bene destroyed with
the sworde, and is gathered out of manie
people vpon the mōutaines of Israél, which
haue long lien waste: yet ‖ they haue bene
broght out of the people, and they shal
dwell all safe.

‖ *Or, it: meaning, the land of Israél.*

9 Thou shalt ascend and come vp like a tēpest, & shalt be like a cloude to couer the
land, *bothe* thou, and all thy bandes, & manie people with thee.
10 Thus saith the Lord God, Euen at the
same time shal *manie* things come into
thy minde, and thou shalt thinke f euil
thoghts.

f That is, to molest, and destroye the Church.

11 And thou shalt say, I wil go vp to the lād
that hathe no walled towres: g I wil go to
them that are at rest, and dwell in safetie,
which dwell all without walles, and haue
nether barres nor gates,

g Meaning, Israél which had now bene destroyed, & was not yet buylt againe: declaring hereby ȳ simplicitie of the godlie, who seke not so muche to fortifie them selues by outward force, as to depende on the prouidēce & goodnes of God.

12 *Thinking* to spoile the pray, and to take a
bootie,

bootie, to turne thine hand vpon the desolate places that are *now* inhabited, and
vpon the people, that are gathered out of
the nations which haue gotten cattel and
goods & dwell in the middes of the land.
13 Shebá and Dedán, and the marchantes
of Tarshish with all the lions thereof shal
say vnto thee,[h] Art thou come to spoile ye
pray? hast thou gathered thy multitude to
take a bootie? to cary away siluer and golde, to take away cattel & goods, & to spoile a great pray?
14 Therefore, sonne of man, prophecie, and
say vnto Gog, Thus saith the Lord God,
In ye day when my people of Israél[i] dwelleth safe, shalt thou not knowe it?
15 And come from thy place out of the
North partes, thou & muche people with
thee? all *shal* ride vpon horses, *euen* a great
multitude and a mightie armie.
16 And thou shalt come vp against my peo
ple of Israél, as a cloude to couer the land:
thou shalt be in the [k] latter daies, and I wil
bring thee vpon my land that the heathen
may knowe me, when I [l] shalbe sanctified
in thee, ô Gog, before their eyes.
17 Thus saith the Lord God, Art not thou
he, of whome I haue spoken in olde time
[m] by the hand of my seruants the Prophetes of Israél which prophecied in those
dayes *and* yeres, that I wolde bring thee
vpon them?
18 At the same time also whē Gog shal come against the land of Israél, saith ye Lord
God, my wrath shal arise in mine angre.
19 For in mine indignation & in the fyre of
my wrath haue I spokē it: surely at that time there shalbe a great shaking in the lād
of Israél.
20 So that the fishes of the sea, & the foules
of the heauen, and the beastes of the field
and all that moue & crepe vpon the earth,
and all the men that are vpon the earth,
shal tremble at my presence, & the mountaines shalbe ouerthrowen, & the [n] staires
shal fall, and euery wall shal fall to the
grounde.
21 For I wil call for a sworde against him
[o] through out all my mountaines, saith the
Lord God: euery mans sworde shal be a-
gainst his brother.
22 And I wil pleade against him with pestilence, and with blood, and I wil cause to
raine vpon him and vpon his bandes, and
vpon the great people, that are with him, a
sore raine, and haile stones, fyre, & brimstone.
23 Thus wil I be [x] magnified, and sanctified,
and knowen in the eyes of many nacions,
and thei shal knowe, that I am the Lord.

h One enemie shal enuie another because euery one shal thīke to haue the spoile of the Church.

i Shalt not ye spie thine occasions to come against my Church, when they suspect nothing?

k Meaning, in the last age, and from the comming of Christ vnto ye end of the worlde.

l Signifying ye God wilbe sanctified by mainteinīg his Church, and destroyīg his enemies, as Chap. 36,23 & 37,28.

m Hereby he declareth that none affliction can come to ye Church, whereof they haue not bene aduertised afore time, to teache thē to indure all things with more pacience when they knowe ye God hathe so ordeined.

n All meanes whereby man shulde thinke to saue him self shal faile, the affliction in those daies shalbe so great & the enemies destructiō shal be so terrible.

o Against the people of Gog and Magóg.

x Chap. 36,23. & 37,28.

CHAP. XXXIX.

1 He sheweth the destruction of Gog and Magog. 11 The graues of Gog and his hoste. 17 Thei shalbe deuoured of birdes and beasts. 23 Wherefore the house of Israél is captiue. 24 Their bringing againe from captiuitie is promised.

1 THerefore, thou sonne of man, prophecie against Gog, & say, Thus saith the
Lord God, Beholde, I *come* against thee,
ô Gog, the chief prince of Meshech and
Tubál.
2 And I wil destroy thee [a] & leaue but the
sixt part of thee, & wil cause thee to come
vp from the North partes and wil bring
thee vpon the mountaines of Israél:
3 And I wil smite thy bowe out of thy left
hand, and I wil cause thine arrowes to fall
out of thy right hand.
4 Thou [b] shalt fall vpon the mountaines
of Israél, and all thy bāds and the people,
that is with thee: *for* I wil giue thee vnto
the birdes *and* to euery feathered foule &
beast of the field to be deuoured.
5 Thou shalt fall vpon the open field: for I
haue spoken it, saith the Lord God.
6 And I wil send a fyre on Magóg, and
among them that dwell safely in the [c] yles,
and thei shal knowe, that I am the Lord.
7 So wil I make mine holy Name knowē in
the middes of my people Israél, and I wil
not suffer them to pollute mine holy Name anie more, and the heathen shal knowe
that I am the Lord, the holie one of Israél.
8 Beholde, [d] it is come, and it is done, saith
the Lord God: this is the day whereof I
haue spoken.
9 And thei that dwell in the cities of Israél, shal [e] go forthe, and shal burne and set
fyre vpon the weapons, and on the shields,
and bucklers, vpon the bowes, and vpon the
arrowes, and vpon the staues *in their* hands,
and vpon the speares, and thei shal burne
them with fyre seuen yeres.
10 So that they shal bring no wood out of
the field, nether cut downe *any* out of the
forests: for they shal burne the weapons
with fyre, and they shal robbe those, that
robbed them, and spoyle those that spoyled them, saith the Lord God.
11 And at ye same time wil I giue vnto Gog
[f] a place there for buryal in Israél, *euen* the
valley whereby men go toward ye East part
of the Sea: and it shal cause thē that passe
by, to stop their [g] noses, and there shal they
burye Gog with all his multitude: & they
shal call it the valley of [*] Hamón-Gog.
12 [h] And seuen moneths long shal the house
of Israél be burying of thē, that they may
clense the land.
13 Yea, all the people of the land shal bury
them, and they shal haue a name when I
shalbe glorified, saith the Lord God.
14 And they shal chuse out men to go continually through the [i] land with them that
trauail, to burye those that remaine vp-

a Or, destroy thee with six plagues, as Chap. 38,22.

b Meaning, ye by the vertue of Gods worde the enemie shalbe destroied where so euer he assaileth his Church.

c That is, among all nations where ye enemies of my people dwell, seme they neuer so farre separate.

d That is, this plague is fully determined in my counsel & can not be changed.

e After this destruction ye Church shal haue great peace and trāquillitie, and burne all their weapons because they shal no more feare the enemie: and this is chiefly mēt of the accomplishment of Christs kingdome, when by their head Christ all enemies shalbe ouercome.

f Which declareth that the enemies shal haue an horrible fall.

g For the stike of ye carkeises

* *Or, of the multitude of Gog.*

h Meaning, a long time.

i Partely that the holy lād shulde not be polluted, and partely for the compassion ye the children of God haue euen on their enemies.

on the grounde, and clense it: they shal
searche to the end of seuen moneths.
15 And the trauailers that passe through
the land, if *any* se a mans bone, then shal
he set vp a signe by it, til the buryers haue
buryed it, in the valley of Hamón-Gog.
16 And also the name of the citie *shal be*
'Hamonáh: thus shal they clense the land.

' *Or, multitude.*

17 And thou sonne of man, thus saith the
Lord God, Speake vnto euerie feathered
foule, and to all the beastes of the field,
Assemble your selues, and come: [k] gather your selues on euerie side to my sacrifice: for I do sacrifice a great sacrifice for
you vpon the mountaines of Israél, that
ye may eat flesh, and drinke blood.

k Whereby he signifieth the horrible destruction that shulde come vpon the enemies of his Church.

18 Ye shal eat the flesh of the valiant, and
drinke the blood of the princes of the
earth, of the weathers, of the lambes, and
of the goates, *and* of bullockes, *euen* of all
fat beasts of Bashán.
19 And ye shal eat fat til you be full, and
drinke blood, til ye be drunken of my sacrifice, which I haue sacrificed for you.
20 Thus you shal be filled at my table with
horses and chariots, with valiant men, and
with all men of warre, saith the Lord
God.
21 And I wil set my glorie among the heathen, and all the heathen shal se my iudgement, that I haue executed, and mine
hand, which I haue layed vpon them.
22 So the house of Israél shal knowe, that I
am the Lord their God from that day and
so forthe.
23 And the heathen shal knowe, that the
house of Israél went into captiuitie for
[l] their iniquitie, because they trespaced
against me: therefore hid I my face from
them, and gaue them into the hand of
their enemies: so fel they all by the
sworde.

l The heathen shal knowe ȳ they ouercame not my people by their strength, nether yet by ȳ weaknes of mine arme, but ȳ this was for my peoples sinnes.

24 According to their vnclennes, and according to their transgressions haue I
done vnto them, and hid my face from
them.
25 Therefore thus saith the Lord God,
Now wil I bring againe the captiuitie of
Iaakób, and haue compassion vpon the
whole house of Israél, and wil be ielous
for mine holy Name,
26 After that they haue borne their shame,
and all their transgression, whereby they
haue transgressed against me, when they
dwelt safely in their land, and without
feare of any.
27 When I haue broght them againe from
the people, and gathered them out of their
enemies lands, and am * sanctified in them
in the sight of manie nacions,

Chap. 36,23.

28 Then shal they knowe, that I am the
Lord their God, which caused them to be
led into captiuitie among the heathen: but
I haue gathered them vnto their owne
land, and haue left none of them any more there,
29 Nether wil I hide my face anie more
from them: for I haue powred out my Spirit vpon the house of Israél, saith the Lord
God.

CHAP. XL.

The restoring of the citie and the Temple.

1 IN the fiue and twentieth yere of our
being in captiuitie in the [a] beginning
of the yere, in the tenth *day* of the moneth, in the fourteth yere after that the citie was smitten, in the self same day, the
hand of the Lord was vpon me, & broght
me thether.

a The Iewes coũted the beginning of the yere after two sorts: for their feastes they began to counte in March, and for their other affaires in Septẽbre: so that this is to be vnderstand of September.

2 Into the land of Israél broght he me by
' a diuine vision, and set me vpon a verie
hie mountaine, whereupõ *was* as the buylding of a citie, toward the South.

' *Or, visions of God.*

3 And he broght me thether, and beholde, there *was* a [b] man, whose similitude was to loke to, like brasse, with a linen
threde in his hand, and a rede to measure
with: and he stode at the gate.

b Which was an Angel in forme of a mã, that came to measure out this buylding.

4 And the man said vnto me, Sonne of
man, beholde with thine eyes, and heare
with thine eares, and set thine heart vpon
all that I shal shew thee: for to the intent,
that they might be shewed thee, art thou
broght hether: declare all that thou seest,
vnto the house of Israél.
5 And beholde, *I sawe* a wall on the outside of the house rounde about: and in the
mans hand *was* a rede to measure with, of
six cubites long, by the cubite, and an hand
breadth: so he measured the breadth of the
buylding with one rede, and the height
with one rede.
6 Then came he vnto the gate, which loketh toward the East, and went vp the staires thereof, and measured the ' poste of
the gate, *which was* one rede broad, and
' the other poste of the gate, *which was* one
rede broad.

' *Or, threshold.*
' *Or, vpper poste.*

7 And *euerie* chamber was one rede long, &
one rede broad, and betwene the chambers
were fiue cubites: and the poste of the gate
by the porche of the gate within *was* one
rede.
8 He measured also the porche of the gate
within with one rede.
9 Then measured he the porche of the gate of eight cubites, and the ' postes thereof, of two cubites, and the porche of the
gate *was* inwarde.

' *Or, pentises.*

10 And the chãbers of the gate Eastwarde,
were thre on this side, & thre on that side:
they thre *were* of one measure, and the postes had one measure on this side and one
on that side.
11 And he measured the breadth of the entrie

THE DESCRIPTION OF THE FIGVRE which beginneth, vers. 5.

Vers.5 The wall that cōpasseth about the Temple & the courtes, as appeareth in the secōd and in the great figure.

A B The thickenes of the wall, was six cubites: for so lōg the rede was.

A C The height of the wall, wͨ was also six cubites: this wall cōteined two thousand cubits, that is, on the East side 500 C H & on the North side 500 H I as much on ẏ South side. C K. & 500 on the West side I K This wall did separate the Temple from the citie, Chap. 42,20.

Vers.6. This gate in the great figure is marked with D. vnto the which apperteine seuen steppes E. Thēce they go into the porche where are six chambers F. Which porche was closed wͭ a wall G.

Vers.7 E F G. The lēgth. The breadth E O G The space of fyue cubites betwene the chambers, and so muche space was on this side, and beyōde the chambers G. Frō the thresholde inward to the porche was six cubites A B. B C The porche.

Vers.9. C D. The vpper postes. H I. The breadth of the alley of the porche B C The length of the porche, wͨ was inwarde.

Vers.11. L M The breadth of ẏ gate, & the height A N

Vers.12. The space before ẏ chābers as a litle galerie O

Vers.13. The breadth of the whole porche from ẏ vtmost chamber to the gate 25. cubites P Q.

In the 14 *ver.* he speaketh of the vpper postes, or pētises wͨ in all were 60 cubites: for euerie chāber had six, & ẏ thresholde, & lintel of the dore, ether 12. K figures.

*Vers.*15 A D. The fiftie cubites.

*Vers.*17. The outward court R. so called, because it was the outwarde court in respect of the Temple as appeareth in the great figure N. but it is the inner court in respect of the porche, which hathe bene described.
S. The thirtie chambers, fyftene on a side. The two litle gates 6. which are by ẏ great gate T.

Vers. 19. The lower gate A. which had seuen steppes, & the gate within eight T. betwene A T were 100 cubites, & had as muche from South to North V X.

trie of the gate ten cubites, & the height
of the gate thirtene cubites.
12 The space also before the chambers *was*
one cubite *on this side*, & the space *was* one
cubite on that side, and the chambers *were*
six cubits on this side & six cubits on that
side.
13 He measured then the gate frō the rouse
of a chamber to the top of the *gate*: the breadth *was* fyue and twentie cubites, dore a-
gainst dore.
14 He made also postes of threscore cubites, and the postes of the court, & of the ga
te *had one measure* round about.
15 And vpon the forefront of the entrie
of the gate vnto the fore front of the porche of the gate within *were* fiftie cubites.
16 And *there were* narrow windowes in the
chambers, and in their postes within the
gate round about, and likewise to the arches: and the windowes *went* round about
within: and vpon the postes *were* palme
trees.
17 ¶Then broght he me into the outward
court, and lo, *there were* chambers, and a
pauement made for the court round about
and thirtie chambers *were* vpon the pauement.
18 And the pauemēt *was* by the side of the
gates ouer against the length of the gates,
& the pauement *was* benethe.
19 Then he measured the breadth from the
forefront of the lower gate without, vnto the forefront of the court within, an hū
dreth cubites Eastward and Northward.
20 And the gate of the outwarde court, that
loked toward the North, measured he after the length and breadth thereof.
21 And the chābers thereof *were*, thre on this
side, & thre on ẏ side, & the postes thereof
& the arches thereof were after the measure of the first gate: the length thereof
was fyftie cubites, & the breadth fyue and
twentie cubites.
22 And their windowes, & their arches with
their palme trees, *were* after the measure
of ẏ gate that loketh toward the East, and
the going vp vnto it *had* seuen steppes, &
the arches thereof *were* before them.
23 And the gate of the inner court *stode* ouer
against the gate toward the North, & toward the East, and he measured from gate to gate an hundreth cubites.
24 After ẏ, he broght me toward the South,
& lo, *there was* a gate toward the South, &
he measured the postes thereof, and the arches thereof according to those measures.
25 And *there were* windowes in it, and in the
arches thereof round about, like those win
dowes: the height *was* fiftie cubites, and
the breadth fyue and twentie cubites.
26 And there were seuen to go vp to it, and
the arches thereof *were* before them: & it
had palme trees, one on this side, and another on that side vpon the poste thereof.
27 ¶And *there was* a gate in the inner court
toward the South, & he measured frō gate
to gate toward ẏ South an hūdreth cubits.
28 And he broght me into ẏ inner court by ẏ
South gate, & he measured the South gate

*Le parvis de dedans. *Or, the inner court.

Vers.20. This must be considered in the great figure. The outwarde court in respect of ẏ Temple M R The North side. The porche S. The court without T. The length of the porche wͭ the chambers, as in the East side V X. The breadth 25 cubites Y Z.

Vers 23. The gate of the inner court B. ouer against ẏ gate of ẏ outward court R. and toward ẏ East c. An hūdreth cubites R b.

Vers.24. The South gate in the great figure d. The outward court e.

Vers.27. The inner court gate f. An hūdreth cubites. d f which was the lēgth of a court, and his chambers.

Vers.28 The inner court g. The eight steppes are hid wͭ the buylding, but they are like them of ẏ East gate Q. for all ẏ courtes were of one measure, quantitie and facion.

according to those measures.
29 And the chãbers thereof, & ye postes thereof, & ye arches therof according to these
measures, & *there were* windowes in it, & in
the arches therof roũde about, *it was* fiftie
cubits long & fiue & twẽtie cubits broad.
30 And the arches round about *were* fiue &
twentie cubites long, & fiue cubites broad.
31 And the arches thereof *were* toward the
vtter court, and palme trees *were* vpon the
postes thereof, and the going vp to it *had*
eight steppes.
32 ¶ Againe he broght me into the inner
court towarde the East, & he measured the
gate according to those measures.
33 And the chambers thereof, and the postes
thereof, and the arches thereof were accor
ding to these measures, and *there were* windowes therein, and in the arches thereof
round about, *it was* fiftie cubites long, and
fyue and twentie cubites broad.
34 And the arches thereof *were* towarde y^e
vtter court, and palme trees *were* vpõ the
postes thereof, on this side & on that side,
and the going vp to it *had* eight steps.
35 ¶ After he broght me to the North gate,
& measured it, accordĩg to these measures.
36 The chambers thereof, the postes thereof,
and the arches thereof, and *there were* windowes therein round about: the height
was fiftie cubites, and the breadth fyue and
twentie cubites.
37 And the postes thereof *were* towarde the
vtter courte, and palme trees *were* vpon
the postes thereof on this side, and on that
side, & the going vp to it *had* eight steps.
38 And *euerie* chamber, & the entrie thereof
was vnder ye postes of the gates: there they
washed the burnt offring.
39 And in the porche of the gate *stode* two
tables on this side, and two tables on that
side, vpon the which they slewe the burnt
offring, and the sinne offring, and the trespas offring.
40 And at the side beyond the steps, at the
entrie of the North gate *stode* two tables,
and on the other side, which was at ye porche of the gate *were* two tables.
41 Foure tables *were* on this side, and foure
tables on ye side by the side of ye gate, *euen*
eight tables wherupõ thei slue *their sacrifice*.
42 And the foure tables *were* of hewen stone for the burnt offring, of a cubite and an
halfe long, and a cubite and an halfe broade, and one cubite hie: whereupõ also they
layed the instrumẽts wherewith they slewe
the burnt offring and the sacrifice.
43 And within *were* borders an hand broade, fastened round about, and vpon the tables *laye* the flesh of the offring.
44 And without the inner gate *were* the chã
bers of the singers in the inwarde courte,
which was at the side of the North gate:
and their prospect *was* towarde the South,
& one *was* at the side of the East gate, hauing the prospect towarde the North.
45 And he said vnto me, This chãber whose
prospect is towarde the South, *is* for the
Priests, that haue charge to kepe ye house.
46 And the chamber whose prospect is towarde ye North, *is* for the Priests that haue
the charge to kepe the altar: these are the
sonnes of Zadók amõg the sonnes of Leuí
which may come nere to the Lord to mi-

Vers. 32. The inner court on ye East side N. And so in all he maketh six courtes, two on the East side, two on the North, & two on the South side. Loke in ye great figure.

Vers. 38. He speaketh of six chambers, w^c were in ye porche of the inner courte on the North side i The entrie of the chãbers, that is, the dores, were vnder the vpper postes or pentises which hanged ouer the chãbers, as also did ouer the gate. Loke in ye great figure.

Vers. 39 In the porche of the inner courte were foure tables. K. & as manie in the outward court S. a cubite, & an halfe long & as broade, & one cubite high.

Vers. 44. The chambers in ye inner porche on the North side for ye singers L. but the pspectiue hindereth ye sight, therefore beholde them, w^c are in ye East court, for thei are all alike: likewise on the South side. The Prophet was now in ye East courte, where he saw the altar measured, & describeth one rowe of chãbers, w^c was for the Priests.

Vers. 45. He speaketh of ye two rowes of chambers, w^c were in ye inner court N. whereof they on ye North side were for the Priests, that sacrificed O. and they on the South side for them that kept the Tẽple N. Which chambers were East and by South, as the other O. were East and by North. These must be sene in y^e great figure.

THE FIGVRE OF THE TEMPLE.

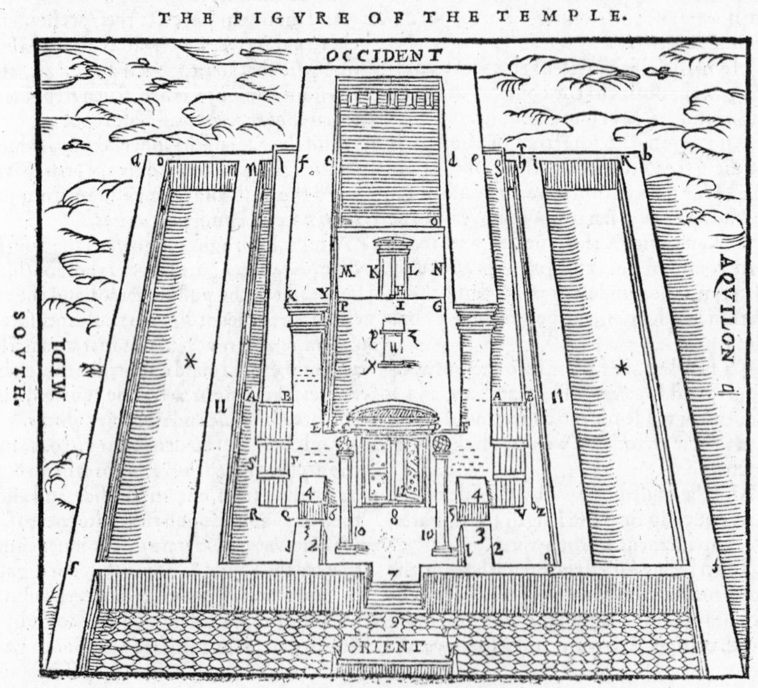

nister vnto him.
47 So he measured the court, an hundreth
cubites long, & an hundreth cubites broad
euen four square: likewise the altar *that was*
before the House.
48 And he broght me to the porche of the
house, and measured the postes of the porche, fiue cubites on this side, and fiue cubites on that side: and the breadth of the gate *was* thre cubites on this side, and thre
cubites on that side.
49 The length of the porche *was* twentie
cubites, and the breadth eleuen cubites &
he broght me by ỹ steppes whereby thei wẽt
vp to it, & *there were* pillers by the postes,
one on this side, and another on that side.

CHAP. XLI.

1 *The disposicion and order of the buylding of the Temple and the other things thereto belonging.*

1 AFterwarde, he broght me to the Tẽple, and measured the postes, six
cubites broad on the one side and six cubites broad on the other side, *which was* the
breadth of the tabernacle.
2 And the breadth of the entrie *was* ten cubits, & the sides of the entrie *were* fiue cubits on ỹ one side, & fiue cubits on ỹ other
side, & he measured the lẽgth thereof fortie cubites, & the breadth twentie cubites.
3 Thẽ went he in, and measured the postes
of the entrie two cubites, and the entrie
six cubites, and the breadth of the entrie se
uen cubites.
4 So he measured the length thereof twentie cubites & the breadth twentie cubites
before the Temple. And he said vnto me,
This is the moste holie place.
5 After, he measured the wall of the house,
six cubites, and the breadth of *euerie* cham
bre foure cubites rounde about the house,
on euerie side.
6 And the chambres *were* chambre vpon
chãbre, thre and thirtie fote *high*, & they
entred into the wall made for the chambres which was rounde about the house ỹ
the postes might be fastened *therein*, and not
be fastened in the wall of the house.
7 And it was large and went round mounting vpwarde to the chambres: for the
staire of the house *was* mounting vpward,
rounde about the house: therefore ỹ house was larger vpwarde: so thei went vp frõ
the lowest *chãbre* to ỹ hiest by the middes.
8 I sawe also the house hie rounde about: ỹ
fundacions of the chambres *were* a ful rede of six great cubites.
9 The thickenes of the wall which was for
the chamber without, *was* fiue cubites, and
that which remained, *was* the place of the

*Vers.*47. The altar. P. *Vers.*48. He entred by the gate. Q to come into the porche of the temple. R The ỹ Tẽple is here described more at large, because the thĩgs here mẽcioned might ỹ better be vnderstand. *Vers.*48. By ỹ postes of the porche he meaneth the wall which was fiue cubites thicke on ether side of the alley or porche 1.2 The two litle gates in the side of the porche 3.4 which were to go to ỹ Priests chambers that were by the Temple. A B. *Vers.*49 The lẽgth of ỹ porche 20. cubites 5.6. And ỹ breadth eleuẽ. 7.8 The steppes whereby the Prophet came into ỹ porche of the Temple 9.7. The two pillers 10.

Chap. XLI. *Vers.*1. The vpper postes or pentises, meanĩg the toppes of the chambers on the sides of ỹ Tẽple A B. The secõd chambre G goeth out more thẽ the first R. and the thirde A more then the second. *Vers.* 2. The breadth of the entrie or gate ten cubites. C D. Fiue cubites from the Temple wall to the gate on ether side E C D F. the lẽgth of fourtie cubites frõ ỹ Tẽple gate to ỹ moste holy place 8 1. The breadth of the Tẽple 20. cubites. E F. or G P He speaketh not here of the height: therefore it is made of 30 cubites according to Salomons. *Vers.*3. The Angel went into the moste holy place The poste of ỹ entrie, that is, ỹ threshold or thickenes of ỹ wall. H I. The gate 6, cubites, K L The breadth on ether side the gate. 7. cubites M K & L N which make in all 20 cubites *Vers* 4. The length 20 cubites, G O, so it was square. *Vers.*5. The first chambre was, 4 cubites. Q R The second fiue, S. T, and the third six A B. There were thre heights or stages of chambers. R S A. The turning stayre can not be shewed in the figure, but maie easely be cõceiued. *Vers* 8. The fundacions of six cubites, meaning the hie chamber was so, and the nether from thence semed so likewise bỹ a perpendicular line or plumet, B Z. *Vers* 9. The chãbre without was the hie chãbre, and frõ ỹ chãbre ỹ wall was but fiue cubites thicke B X Y: for downewarde it was six. Q 6.

chambres that were within.
10 And betwene the chambres was the wy-
denes of twentie cubites rounde about the
House on euerie side.
11 And the dores of the chãbres *were* towarde the place that remained, one dore
towarde the North, & another dore towarde the South, and the breadth of the
place that remained, *was* fiue cubites roun
de about.
12 Now the buylding that was before the
seperate place towarde the West corner,
was seuentie cubites broad, and the wall
of the buylding was fiue cubites thicke,
rounde about, & the lẽgth ninetie cubites.
13 So he measured the house an hundreth
cubites long, & the separate place and the
buylding with the walles thereof *were* an
hundreth cubites long.
14 Also the breadth of the forefront of the
house and of the separate place toward the
East, *was* an hundreth cubites.
15 And he measured the length of the buyl
ding ouer against ỹ separate place, which
was behinde it, and the chambers on the
one side and on the other side an hundreth
cubites with the Temple within, and the
arches of the court.
16 The postes and the narowe windowes, &
the chambers rounde about, on thre sides
ouer against the postes, siled with *ceder*
wood roũde about and frõ ỹ ground vp to
ỹ windowes, and the windowes were siled.
17 And from aboue the dore vnto the inner house and without, and by all the wall
rounde about within and without it was
syled according to the measure.
18 And it was made with Cherubims and
palme trees, so that a palme tree *was* betwene a Cherúb and a Cherúb: and *euerie*
Cherúb had two faces.
19 So that the face of a man *was* towarde
the palme tree on the one side, & the face
of a lion towarde the palme tree on the
other side: *thus* was it made through all the
house rounde about.
20 From the grounde vnto aboue the dore
were Cherubims and palme trees made as
in the wall of the Temple.
21 The postes of the Tẽple were squared,
& thus to loke vnto *was* the similitude &
forme of the Sanctuarie.
22 The altar of wood *was* thre cubites hie,
& the length thereof two cubites, and the
corners thereof and the length thereof &
the sides thereof *were* of wood. And he
said vnto me, This is the table that shalbe
before the Lord.
23 And the Temple & the Sanctuarie had
two dores.
24 And the dores had two wickets, *euen*
two turning wickets, two wickets for one
dore, and two wickets for another dore.

*Ver.*10 The chãbers on the one side were distant from them on the other side 20 cubites which was the breadth of the Temple. *Vers* 11 The dores of the chãbers on the North side opened toward the North V. & thei on the South side towarde ỹ South R for there was an alley of fiue cubites rounde about ỹ Temple V Z. and was so closed ẘ a wall. 11. *Vers.* 12 The buylding, or ỹ great place cõpassed with a wall of fiue cubites thicke, and was farther of the Temple then ỹ alley, or separate place*, & this is more plainly set for the in ỹ great figure. *Ver.*16 He declareth that whatsoeuer was of stone worke from ỹ bottome to ỹ toppe was couered with wood on the East, South & North side. *Vers.*22 The altar V, which was thre cubites high Y X & two cubites long Y Z.

25 And vpon the dores of the Tēple there
were made Cherubims & palme trees, like
as was made vpon the walles, & *there were*
thicke plankes vpon the forefront of the
porche without.
26 And *there were* narowe windowes & palme trees on the one side, and on the other
side, by the sides of the porche, and *vpon* ỹ
sides of the house, and thicke plankes.

CHAP. XLII.

Of the chambers of the Temple for the Priests, and the holie things.

Vers. 1 Hauīg described the length and breadth of the Tēple, he cometh to the outwarde court on ỹ North side. T. This appeareth in ỹ great figure. He broght me into the chambre: that is, the rowe of chambres, which were towarde the separate place Westwarde. t.
Vers. 2 He meaneth that the North was an hundreth cubites long x y and in breadth fiftie. b X.
Vers. 4 This gallerie appeareth in ỹ great figure by this nombre. 12.
Vers. 5 These chambres were contrary facioned to thē of the Temple
Vers. 8 So that the wall for ỹ chambres of the outwarde court and the wall of the inner, was ether fiftie cubites, and the whole court an hundreth.
Vers 9 Vnder these chambers were entries, or dores to passe from one place to another, ẘ are noted euer by z in the great figure.
Vers 10 11. The chambres, p, of the East court M. were like to ỹ chābers of the North court.
Vers 13 Which chambers wese in the East gate toward the North and South 3. and towarde the separate place or backe buylding. 4 which chambers are called holie, because thei were by the Temple.

1 THen broght he me into ỹ vtter court
by the waie towarde the North, and
he broght me into the chamber that was
ouer against the separate place, & which
was before ỹ buylding towarde ỹ North.
2 Before ỹ length of an hūdreth cubites *was*
ỹ North dore, & *it was* fiftie cubits broad.
3 Ouer against ỹ twentie *cubites* which were
for the inner court, & ouer against the pauement, which was for the vtter court, was
chambre against chambre in thre rowes.
4 And before ỹ chābres *was* a galerie of ten
cubites wide, & within *was* a waie of one
cubite, and their dores towarde ỹ North.
5 Now the chambres aboue were narower:
for those chambres *semed* to eat vp these, *to
wit*, the lower, and those that were in the
middes of the buylding.
6 For thei were in thre rowes, but had not
pillers as the pillers of the court: therefore there was a difference frō thē beneth &
frō the middlemost, *euen* frō the ground.
7 And the wall ỹ was without ouer against
ỹ chābres, towarde ỹ vtter court on ỹ fore
front of ỹ chābers, *was* fiftie cubites long.
8 For the length of the chambres that were
in the vtter court, *was* fiftie cubites: & lo,
before ỹ Tēple *were* an hundreth cubites.
9 And vnder these chambres *was* the entrie,
on the East side, as one goeth into thē frō
the outwarde court.
10 The chambres *were* in the thickenes of
the wall of the court towarde ỹ East, ouer
against the separate place, & ouer against
the buylding.
11 And the waye before them *was* after
the maner of the chambres, which were toward ỹ North as long as thei, & as broad
as thei: & all their entries were like, bothe
according to their facions, and according
to their dores.
12 And according to the dores of ỹ chambres that were towarde ỹ South, *was* a dore
in the corner of the waie, *euen* the waie directly before the wall towarde the East, as
one entreth.
13 Then said he vnto me, The North cham
bres & the South chambres which are before the separate place, thei be holy chambers, wherein the Priests that approche
vnto the Lord, shal eat the moste holie
things: there shal thei laie the moste holy things, and the meat offring, and the
sinoffring, and the trespasse offring: for
the place *is* holy.
14 When the Priests entre therein, thei shal
not go out of the holie place into the vtter
court, but there thei shal laie their garmēts
wherein thei minister: for thei are holie, &
shal put on other garmēts, & so shal appro
che to those things, ẘ are for the people.
15 Now when he had made an end of measuring ỹ inner house, he broght me forthe
towarde ỹ gate whose prospect is towarde
the East, and measured it rounde about.
16 He measured the East side with the measuring rod, fiue hundreth redes, *euen* with
the measuring rede rounde about.
17 He measured *also* ỹ North side, fiue hundreth redes, *euen* with the measuring rede
rounde about.
18 And he measured the South [f] side fiue hū- [f] *Or, winde.*
dreth redes with the measuring rede.
19 He turned about *also* to the West side, &
measured fiue hundreth redes with the
measuring rede.
20 He measured it by the foure sides: it had
a wall rounde about, fiue hundreth *redes*
long, and fiue hundreth broad to make a
separation betwene the Sanctuarie, and ỹ
prophane place.

CHAP. XLIII.

2 He seeth the glorie of God going into the Temple, from whence it had before departed. 7 He mencioneth the idolatrie of the childrē of Israél for the which thei were consumed and broght to noght. 9 He is commanded to call them againe to repentance.

1 AFterwarde he broght me to the gate,
euen the gate that turneth towarde ỹ
East.
2 And beholde, the glorie of ỹ God of Israél came frō out of the East, whose voice
was like a noise of great waters, and the
earth was made light with his glorie.
3 And the vision which I sawe *was* * like the *Chap. 9, 3.*
vision, *euen* as the vision that I sawe [a] when [a] When I propheciéd the destruction of the citie by ỹ Caldeans.
I came to destroie the citie: and the visi-
ons *were* like the vision that I sawe by the
riuer Chebár: & I fel vpon my face.
4 And the [b] glorie of the Lord came into [b] Which was departed afore, Chap. 10, 4. & 11, 22.
the house by the waie of the gate, whose
prospect is towarde the East.
5 So the Spirit toke me vp and broght me
into the inner court, and beholde, the glo
rie of the Lord filled the house.
6 And I heard one speaking vnto me out of
the house: and there stode a man by me,
7 Which said vnto me, Sonne of man, *this* [c] By their idolatries.
place is my throne, & the place of the sou-
les of my fete, where as I wil dwell among
the children of Israél for euer, and ỹ house of Israél shal no more [c] defile mine holie
Name, nether thei, nor their Kīgs by their
fornicatiōs, nor by the carkeises of [d] their [d] He alludeth to Ammon & Manasséh, who were buryed in their gardens nere the Temple & there had erected vp monumentes to their idoles.
Kings *in* their high places.

8 Albeit they ſet their thresholdes by my
thresholdes, and their poſtes by my poſtes (for there *was but* a wall betwene me &
thẽ) yet haue thei defiled mine holy Name with their abominacions, that thei haue committed: wherefore I haue cõſumed
them in my wrath.
9 Now *therefore* let thẽ put away their fornicacion, and the carkeiſes of their Kings
farre frõ me, and I wil dwell among them
for euer.
10 ¶ Thou ſonne of mã, ſhewe this Houſe to
the houſe of Iſraél, that thei may be aſhamed of their wickednes, and let them meaſure the paterne.
11 And if thei be aſhamed of all that thei
haue done, ſhewe thẽ the forme of ỷ houſe, & the paterne thereof, & the going out
thereof, & the cõming in thereof, and the
whole facion thereof, & all the ordinances
thereof, & all the figures thereof, & all the
lawes thereof: & write it in their ſight, that
thei may kepe ỷ whole facion thereof, & all
the ordinances thereof, and do them.
12 This is the " deſcription of the houſe, *It*
ſhalbe vpõ the top of the mount: all ỷ limites thereof round about ſhalbe moſte holy.
Beholde, this is ỷ deſcription of the houſe.
13 And theſe are ỷ meaſures of the Altar, after the cubites, the cubite *is* a cubite, & an
hand breadth, euen ỷ bottome *ſhalbe* a cubi
te, and the breadth a cubite, & the bordre
thereof by ỷ edge thereof roũd about *ſhal-*
be a ſpãne: & this *ſhalbe* ỷ height of ỷ altar.

" Ebr. Law.

Ver. 13 The middes or bottome A. ŵ was a cubite hie B C, & a cubite broad B D.

THE FIGVRE OF THE ALTAR.

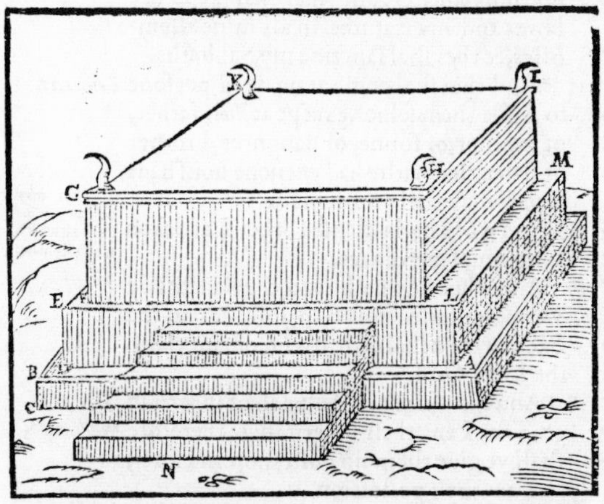

14 And from the bottome *which toucheth* the
ground to the lower piece *ſhalbe* two cubites: & the breadth one cubite, & from the
litle piece to ỷ great piece *ſhalbe* foure cubites, and the breadth one cubite.
15 So the altar *ſhalbe* foure cubites, & from
the altar vpward e *ſhalbe* foure hornes.
16 And the altar *ſhalbe* twelue *cubites* long,
and twelue broade, *and* foreſquare in the
foure corners thereof.
17 And ỷ frame *ſhalbe* fourtene *cubites* long,
& fourtene broade in the foureſquare corners thereof, and the border about it *ſhalbe*
halfe a cubite, & the bottome thereof *ſhal-*
be a cubite about, and the ſteppes thereof
ſhalbe turned towarde the Eaſt.
18 ¶ And he ſaid vnto me, Sõne of man, thus
ſaith the Lord God, Theſe are the ordinãces of the altar in the day when thei ſhal
make it to offer the burnt offring thereon,
and to ſprinkle blood thereon.
19 And thou ſhalt giue to the Prieſts, & to
the Leuites, that be of the ſede of Zadók,
which approche vnto me, to miniſter vnto
me, ſaith the Lord God, a yong bullocke
for a ſinne offring.
20 And thou ſhalt take of the blood thereof,
and put it on the foure hornes of it, & on
the foure corners of the frame, & vpon the
bordre round about: thus ſhalt thou clenſe it, and reconcile it.
21 Thou ſhalt take the bullocke alſo of the
ſinne offring, & burne it in the appointed
place of the houſe without the Sanctuarie.
22 But the ſeconde day thou ſhalt offre an
he goat without blemiſh for a ſin offring,
and thei ſhal clenſe the altar, as thei did
clenſe it with the bullocke.
23 Whẽ thou haſt made an end of clenſing
it, thou ſhalt offer a yong bullocke without blemiſh, and a ram out of the flocke
without blemiſh.
24 And ỷ ſhalt offre thẽ before the Lord, &
ỷ Prieſts ſhal caſt ſalt vpon thẽ, & thei ſhal
offre thẽ for a burnt offring vnto ỷ Lord.
25 Seuẽ daies ſhalt thou prepare euerie day
an he goat for a ſin offring: thei ſhal alſo
prepare a yong bullocke and a ram out of
the flocke, without blemiſh.
26 Thus ſhal thei ſeuen daies purifie the altar, and clenſe it, and " conſecrate it.
27 And when theſe daies are expired, vpon
the eight day and ſo forthe, the Prieſts ſhal
make your burnt offrings vpon the altar,
and your peace offrings, and I wil accept
you, ſaith the Lord God.

Verſ. 14 The lower piece which ſtandeth on ỷ bottome & is the middlemoſt piece and vnder ỷ hieſt, is two cubites D E. The breadth one cubite E F. From the litle piece, ŵ was ỷ ſeconde, to the hieſt foure cubites F G. Verſ. 15. Foure cubites, meaning, the hier parte of the altar F G. Verſ. 16. Length and breadth G H I K, Which note alſo the foure hornes of the altar.

Ver. 17. The frame whereupon the hieſt piece ſtode, is fourtene cubites: for on euery ſide it is longer by a cubite then the vppermoſte E L, L M.

" Ebr. fil his hand.

CHAP. XLIIII.

He reproueth the people for their offence. 7 The vncircumciſed in heart, & in the fleſh. 9 Who are to be admitted to the ſeruice of the Tẽple, & who to be refuſed.

1 THen he broght me toward the gate
of the outwarde Sanctuarie, which
turneth toward the Eaſt, and it was ſhut.
2 Then ſaid the Lord vnto me, This gate
ſhalbe a ſhut, & ſhal not be opened, and no
man ſhal entre by it, becauſe the Lord
God of Iſraél hathe entred by it, and it
ſhal be ſhut.
3 *It apperteineth* to ỷ Prince: the Prince him
ſelf ſhal ſit in it to eat bread before the
Lord: he ſhal entre by the way of the por-

Verſ. 1. The Eaſt gate D in the great figure.

a Meaning, frõ ỷ cõmune people, but not from the Prieſtes, nor the prince, read Chap. 46, 9.

che of that gate, and shal go out by the
way of the same.
4 ¶ Then broght he me toward the North
gate before the House: and when I loked,
beholde, the glorie of the Lord filled the
house of the Lord, and I fel vpon my face.
5 And the Lord said vnto me, Sonne of mã,
"marke wel, and beholde with thine eyes,
& heare with thine eares, all that I say vnto thee, concerning all the ordinances of
ỷ House of the Lord, & all the lawes thereof, and marke wel the entring in of the
house with euerie going forthe of the San
ctuarie.
6 And thou shalt say to the rebellious, *euen*
to the house of Israél, Thus saith the Lord
God, O house of Israél, ye haue ynough
of all your abominacions,
7 Seing, that ye haue broght into my Sanctuarie [b] strãgers, vncircũcised in heart, &
vncircũcised in flesh, to be in my Sanctuarie, to pollute mine house, whẽ ye offre my
bread, *euen* fat, and blood: and thei haue
broken my couenant, because of all your
abominacions.
8 For ye haue not kept the [c] ordinances of
mine holie thĩgs: but you your selues haue
set *other* to take ỷ charge of my Sãctuarie.
9 Thus saith the Lord God, No stranger
vncircumcised in heart, nor vncircumcised in flesh shal entre into my Sanctuarie,
of any stranger that is amõg the children
of Israél,
10 Nether yet the [d] Leuites that are gone
backe frõ me, whẽ Israél wẽt astray, which
went astray frõ me after their idoles, but
thei shal beare their iniquitie.
11 And thei shal serue in my Sanctuarie, &
kepe the gates of the House, and minister
in the House: thei shal slaye the burnt offring and the sacrifice for the people: and
thei shal stande before them to serue them.
12 Because thei serued before their idoles,
and caused the house of Israél to fall into
iniquitie, therefore haue I lift vp mine
hand against them, saith the Lord God, &
thei shal beare their iniquitie,
13 And thei shal not come nere vnto me to
do the office of the Priest vnto me, nether
shal thei come nere vnto any of mine holy
things in the moste holy place, but they
shal beare their shame and their abominacions, which thei haue committed.
14 And I wil make thẽ kepers of the watche
of the House, for all the seruice thereof, &
for all that shalbe done therein.
15 But the Priests of the Leuites, the sonnes of Zadók, that [e] kept the charge of my
Sanctuarie, when the children of Israél
went astray from me, thei shal come nere
to me to serue me, and thei shal stand before me to offre me the fat and the blood,
saith the Lord God.
16 Thei shal entre into my Sanctuarie, and
shal come nere to my table, to serue me,
and thei shal kepe my charge.
17 And when thei shal entre in at the gates
of the inner court, thei shalbe clothed
with linen garments, and no woll shal come vpon them while thei serue in the gates of the inner court, and within.
18 Thei shal haue linen bonettes vpon
their heades, and shal haue linen breches
vpon their loynes: thei shal not gyrd thẽ
selues in the sweating *places*.
19 But when they go forthe into the vtter
court, *euen* to the vtter court to the people, thei shal put of their garments, wherein thei ministred, and laye them in the
holy chambers, and thei shal put on other
garments: for thei shal not sanctifie the
people with their garments.
20 Thei shal not also [f] shaue their heades,
nor suffre their lockes to growe long, *but*
round their heades.
21 *Nether shal any Priest drinke wine whẽ Leu.21,13.
thei enter into the inner court.
22 Nether shal thei take for their wiues a
widowe, or her that is diuorced: but thei
shal take maidens of the sede of the house
of Israél, or a widow that hathe bene the
widow of a Priest.
23 And thei shal teache my people *the difference* betwene the holy and prophane, and
cause thẽ to discerne betwene the vncleane and the cleane.
24 And in controuersie thei shal stand to
iudge, and thei shal iudge it according to
my iudgements: and thei shal kepe my
lawes and my statutes in all mine assemblies, & thei shal sanctifie my Sabbaths.
25 *And thei shal come at no dead persone Leu.21,22.
to defile them selues, except at *their* father,
or mother, or sonne, or daughter, brother
or sister, that hathe had yet none housbãd:
in these may thei [g] be defiled.
26 And when he is clensed, thei shal rekon
vnto him seuen dayes.
27 And when he goeth into the Sanctuarie
vnto the inner court to minister in the
Sãctuarie, he shal offre his sin offring, saith
the Lord God.
28 *And the *Priesthode* shalbe their inheritan Deu.18,1.
ce, *yea*, I am their inheritance: therefore nomb.18,20.
shall ye giue them no possession in Israél,
for I am their possession.
29 Thei shal eat the meat offring, and the
sin offring, & the trespace offring, & euerie dedicate thing in Israél shalbe theirs.
30 *And all the first of all the first borne, & Exod.13,2.
euerie oblation, *euen* all of euerie sort of & 22,29.
your oblations shalbe the Priests. Ye shal & 34,19.
also giue vnto the Priest the first of your nomb.3,13.
dough that he may cause the blessing to
rest in thine house.
31 The Priests shal not eat of any thing,

that

" Ebr. set thine heart.

b For they had broght idolaters ỷ were of other countreis, to teache them their idolatrie Chap.23,40.

c Ye haue not offred vnto me according to my Law.

d The Leuites ỷ had cõmitted idolatrie, were put from their dignitie and colde not be receyued into ỷ Priests office, althogh they had bene of ỷ house of Aarõn, but must serue in ỷ inferior offices as to watche and to kepe ỷ dores, read 2. King. 23,9.

e Which obserued the Lawe of God, and fel not to idolatrie.

f As did the infideles and heathen.

g Thei may be at their buryal, which was a defiling

Exod.22,31. leui.22,8.

that is * dead, or torne, whether it be foule or beast.

CHAP. XLV.

1 Out of the land of promes are there separate foure porcions, of which the first is giuen to the Priests and to the Temple, the second to the Leuites, the third to the citie, the fourth to the prince. 9 An exhortacion vnto the heads of Israél. 10 Of iust weights and measures. 13 Of the first frutes, &c.

1 MOreouer when ye shal deuide the
land for inheritance, ye shal offre an
oblacion vnto the Lord an [a] holy porcion
of the land, fiue & twentie thousand redes
long, and ten thousand broad: this shalbe
holy in all the borders thereof rounde a-
bout.
2 Of this there shalbe for the Sanctuarie
fiue hundreth *in length* with fiue hundreth
in breadth, all square roúde about, and fiftie
cubites rounde about for the suburbes thereof.
3 And of this measure shalt thou measure
the length of fiue and twentie thousand, &
the breadth of ten thousand: & in it shal
be the Sanctuarie, *&* the moste holy place.
4 The holy porcion of the land shalbe the
Priests, which minister in the Sanctuarie,
which came nere to serue the Lord: and it
shalbe a place for their houses, and an holy
place for the Sanctuarie.
5 And *in* the fiue and twentie thousand of
length, and the ten thousand of breadth
shal ẏ Leuites that minister in the house,
haue their possession for twétie chambers.
6 Also ye shal appoint the possession of the
citie, fiue thousand broad, and fiue & twentie thousand long ouer against the oblacion of the holy porcion: it shalbe for the
whole house of Israél.
7 And *a porcion shalbe* for the prince on the
one side, and on that side of the oblacion of
the holy porcion, and of the possession of
the citie, *euen* before the oblacion of the
holy porcion, and before the possession of
the citie frō the West corner Westwarde,
and from the East corner Eastwarde, & the
length *shalbe* by one of the porcions from
the West border vnto the East border.
8 In this land shalbe his possessiō in Israél:
and my princes shal no more oppresse my
people, and *the rest* of the lād shal thei giue
to the house of Israél, according to their
tribes.
9 Thus saith the Lord God, Let it [b] suffice
you, ô princes of Israél: leaue of crueltie &
oppression, & execute iudgement & iustice:
take away your exactions from my peo
ple, saith the Lord God.
10 Ye shal haue iuste balances, & a true [c] E-
pháh, and a true Bath.
11 The Epháh and the Bath shal be equal: a
Bath shal conteine the tenth parte of an
Homér, & an Epháh the tenth parte of an
Homér: the equalitie thereof shalbe after
the Homér.

a Of all the land of Israél the Lord onely requireth this porcion for the Temple & for the Priests, for ẏ citie and for the prince.

b The Prophet sheweth that the heads must be first reformed afore any good ordre cā be established among ẏ people

c Epháh and Bath were bothe of one quantitie, saue that Epháh conteined in drye things, ẏ which Bath did in licour, Leui.5,11. 1. king 5,11.

12 * And the shekel *shalbe* twentie gerahs, *&*
twentie shekels, and [d] fiue and twentie shekels & fiftene shekels shalbe your Manéh.
13 ¶ This is the oblacion that ye shal offre,
the sixt parte of an Epháh of an Homér
of wheat, and ye shal giue the sixt parte of
an Epháh of an Homér of barley.
14 Concerning the ordinance of the oyle,
euen of the Bath of oyle, *ye shal offer* ẏ tenth
parte of a Bath out of ẏ Cor (ten Baths *are*
an Homér: for ten Baths *fil* an Homér)
15 And one lambe of two hundreth shepe
out of the fat pastures of Israél for a meat
offring, & for a burnt offring and for peace
offrings, to make reconciliacion for them,
saith the Lord God.
16 All the people of the land shal *giue* this
oblacion for the prince in Israél.
17 And it shal be the princes parte to giue
burnt offrings, and meat offrings, & drinke
offrings in the solemne feasts and in the
new moones, & in the Sabbaths, *&* in all ẏ
hie feastes of the house of Israél: he shal
prepare the sinne offring, and the meat offring, and the burnt offring, and the peace
offrings to make reconciliacio͂ for the house of Israél.
18 ¶ Thus saith the Lord God, In the first
moneth, in the first *day* of [e] the moneth, thou
shalt take a yōg bullocke without blemish
and clense the Sanctuarie.
19 And the Priest shal take of the blood of
the sinne offring, and put it vpon the postes of the house, and vpon the foure * corners of the frame of the altar, and vpon
the postes of the gate of the inner court.
20 And so shalt thou do the seuenth *day* of
the moneth, for euery one that hathe erred
and for him that is disceaued: so shal you
reconcile the house.
21 * In the first *moneth* in the fourtenth day
of the moneth, ye shal haue the Passeouer
a feast of seuen daies, *&* ye shal eat vnleauened bread.
22 And vpon that day, shal the prince pre-
pare for him self, and for all the people of
the land, a bullocke for a sinne offring.
23 And in the seuen dayes of the feast he
shal make a burnt offring to the Lord, *euen*
of seuen bullockes, & seuen rams without
blemish daiely for seuen dayes, and an he
goat daiely for a sinne offring.
24 And he shal prepare a meat offring of
an Epháh for a bullocke, an Epháh for a
ram, and an [f] Hin of oyle for an Epháh.
25 In the seuenth *moneth*, in the fiftenth day
of the moneth, shal he do the like in the
feast for seuen daies, according to the sinne offring, according to the burnt offring,
and according to the meat offring, and according to the oyle.

Exod.30,13. leui 27,25. nomb.3,47.

d That is, thre score shekels make a weight called Mina: for he ioyneth these thre par tes to a Mina.

e Which was Nisán, conteining parte of Marche and parte of April

*Or, court.

Exod.12,18. leui.23,5.

f Read Exod. 29,40.

CHAP. XLVI.

1 The sacrifices of the Sabbáth and of the newe moones.

8 Thorowe which dores they must go in, or come out of the Temple, &c.

Vers. 1. The inner court gate Q wherunto they went vp by eight steps, as appeareth in ẏ great figure.

1 THus saith the Lord God, The gate
of the inner court, that turneth towarde the East, shalbe shut the six working
daies: but on the Sabbáth it shalbe opened,
and in the daye of the new moone it shal
be opened.
2 And the prince shal entre by the waye of
the porche of that gate without, and shal
stand by the poste of the gate, & ẏ Priests
shal make his burnt offring, and his peace
offrings, & he shal worship at the thresholde of the gate: after, he shal go forthe, but
the gate shal not be shut til the euening.
3 Likewise the people of the land shal worship at the entrie of this gate before the
Lord on the Sabbaths, and in the new moones.
4 And the burnt offring that the prĩce shal
offre vnto the Lord on the Sabbáth daye,
shalbe six lambs without blemish, & a ram
without blemish.
5 And the meat offring *shalbe* an Epháh for
a ram: and the meat offring for the lambes
a gift of his hand, and an Hin of oyle
to an Epháh.

a That is, as muche as he wil.

6 And in the daye of the new moone *it shal*
be a yong bullocke without blemish, and
six lambs and a ram: they shalbe without
blemish.
7 And he shal prepare a meat offring, *euen*
an Epháh for a bullocke, and an Epháh for
a ram, and for the lambes [b] according as
his hand shal bring, and an Hin of oyle to
an Epháh.

b Meaning, as he shal thinke good.

8 And when the prince shal entre, he shal
go in by the way of the porche of that gate, & he shal go forthe by the way thereof.
9 But when the people of the land shal come before the Lord in the solemne feasts,
he that entreth in by the way of ẏ North
gate to worship, shal go out by the way of
the South gate: and he that entreth by the
way of the South gate, shal go forthe by
the way of the North gate: he shal not returne by the way of the gate whereby he
came in, but they shal go forthe ouer a-
gainst it.

Vers 9 He that entreth in by the North gate R, shal go out by ẏ South gate d & contrary, and in goĩg forward they worshipped in ẏ middes M.

10 And the prince shalbe in the middes of
them: he shal go in when they go in, & whẽ
thei go forthe, they shal go forthe *together*.
11 And in the feasts, and in the solemnities
the meat offring shalbe an Epháh to a bullocke, and an Epháh to a ram, and to the
lambs, the gift of his hand, and an Hin of
oyle to an Epháh.
12 Now when the prince shal make a fre
burnt offring or peace offrings frely vnto the Lord, one shal then open him the
gate, ẏ turneth toward the East, and he shal
make his burnt offring and his peace offrings, as he did on the Sabbáth day: after,
he shal go forthe, and when he is gone forthe, one shal shut the gate.
13 Thou shalt daiely make a burnt offring
vnto the Lord of a lãbe of one yere without blemish: thou shalt do it euery morning.
14 And thou shalt prepare a meat offring
for it euery morning, the sixt parte of an
Epháh, and the third parte of an Hin of
oyle, to mingle with the fine floure: *this* meat offring shalbe continually by a perpetual ordinance vnto the Lord.
15 Thus shal they prepare the lambe, and
the meat offring and the oyle euery morning, for a continual burnt offring.
16 ¶ Thus saith the Lord God, If the prince giue a gift of his inheritance vnto any
of his sonnes, it shalbe his sonnes, & it shal
be their possession by inheritance.
17 But if he giue a gift of his inheritance
to one of his seruants, then it shalbe his to
the [c] yere of libertie: after, it shal returne
to the prince, but his inheritance shal remaine to his sonnes for them.
18 Moreouer the prince shal not [d] take of
the peoples inheritance, nor thrust them
out of their possession: *but* he shal cause
his sonnes to inherit of his owne possession, that my people be not scattered euery
man from his possession.

c Which was at the Iubile, Leui. 25, 9.

d But be content with that porcion that God hathe assigned him, as Chap. 45, 8.

Vers 19. He describeth the Priests chambers, which were at the side of the Temple toward ẏ North: and so cometh to the place, which was on ẏ West side. S which vers 21 is called the vtter court, in respect of the inner court, as also where ẏ people were, was the vtter court in respect of this inner.

19 ¶ After, he broght me through the entrie,
which was at the side of the gate, into the
holy chambers of the Priests, which stode
toward the North: and beholde, there was
a place at the West side of them.
20 Then said he vnto me, This is the place
where the Priests shal seeth the trespasse
offring and the sinne offring, where they
shal bake the meat offring, that thei shulde not beare them into the vtter court, [e] to
sanctifie the people.

e That the people shulde not haue to do ẘ those thĩgs which apperteine to the Lord, & thinke it lawful for thẽ to eat them.

Vers. 21. The litle court in euery corner, was fortie cubits long. 7, 8 & thirty broad 8, 9 & 7, 9.

21 Then he broght me forthe into the vtter
court, and caused me to go by the foure
corners of the court: and beholde, in euery
corner of the court, there *was* a court.
22 In the foure corners of the court there
were courtes ioyned of fortie *cubites* long,
and thirtie broad: these foure corners were
of one measure.
23 And there *went* a wall about them, *euen*
about those foure, and kitchins were made
vnder the walles rounde about.
24 Then said he vnto me, This is the kitchin
where the ministers of the house shal seeth
the sacrifice of the people.

Vers 23 About the walles of these litle courts, ẘ were as kitchins, were litle chãbers for the cookes 10.

CHAP. XLVII.

1 The vision of the waters that came out of the Temple.
13 The coasts of the land of promes, & the deuision thereof by tribes.

Chap. XLVII. *Vers.* 1. The dore of the Temple r and from vnder ẏ thresholde yssued out waters, ẘ came out of the South side, and ran towarde ẏ East. Loke in the great figure. 11.

1 AFterward he broght me vnto the dore of the house: and beholde, [a] waters
yssued out from vnder the thresholde of
the house Eastwarde: for the forefronte
of

a Whereby are ment the spiritual graces that shulde be giuen to the Church vnder ẏ kĩgdome of Christ.

of the house *stode* towarde the East,and the
waters ran downe from vnder the right side of the House, at the South side of the
altar.
2 Then broght he me out toward ÿ North
gate, and led me about by the way without vnto the vtter gate, by the way that
turneth Eastwarde: and beholde, there came forthe waters on the right side.
3 And when the man that had the line in his
hãd,went forthe Eastwarde, he measured a
thousand cubites,& he broght me through
the waters:the waters *were* to the ancles.
4 Againe he measured a thousãd,& broght
me through th waters: the waters *were* to
the knees: againe he measured a thousand,
and broght me through: the waters *were*
to the loines.
5 Afterward he measured a thousand, *and*
it was a [b] riuer, that I colde not passe ouer:
for the waters were risen, & the waters
did flowe, *as* a riuer that colde not be passed ouer.
6 And he said vnto me, Sonne of man, hast
thou sene this? Then he broght me, & caused me to returne to ÿ brinke of the riuer.
7 Now whẽ I returned, beholde, at ÿ brinke
of the riuer *were* very many [c] trees on the
one side, and on the other.
8 Thẽ said he vnto me, These waters yssue
out towarde the East countrey, and runne
downe into ÿ plaine, and shal go into *one*
[d] sea: thei shal runne into *another* sea, and
the [e] waters shalbe holsome.
9 And euerie thing that liueth, which moueth, wheresoeuer ÿ riuers shal come, shal
liue, and there shalbe a very great multitude of fish, because these waters shal come thether: for thei shalbe holsome, & euerie thing shal liue whether ÿ riuer cometh.
10 And then the [f] fishers shal stand vpon it,
and from En-gédi euen vnto [g] En-egláim,
thei shal spreade out their nettes: *for* their
fish shalbe according to their kindes, as
the fish of [h] ÿ maine sea, exceading many.
11 But [i] the myrie places thereof, & the ma-
rises thereof shal not be holsome: thei shal
be made salt pittes.
12 And by this riuer vpon the brinke thereof, on this side, & on that side shal growe
all ″ fruteful trees, whose leafe shal not
fade, nether shal the frute thereof faile: it
shal bring forthe new frute according to
his moneths, because their waters rũne out
of the Sanctuarie: and the frute thereof
shalbe meat, & the leaf thereof shalbe for
″ medicine.
13 ¶ Thus saith ÿ Lord God, This shal be
the border, whereby ye shal inherit the
land according to ÿ twelue tribes* of Israél: Ioséph shal haue *two* porcions.
14 And ye shal inherit it, one aswel as another: *concerning the which I lift vp mi-

b Signifying that ÿ graces of God shulde neuer decrease but euer abounde in his Church.
c Meaning ÿ multitude of them ÿ shulde be refreshed by the spiritual waters.
d Shewing ÿ the abundance of these graces shulde be so great, ÿ all the worlde shulde be ful thereof, which is here ment by ÿ Persian sea or Genezareth, & the sea called Mediterraneũ, Za 14,8.
e The waters which of nature are salt & vnholsome, shalbe made swete & comfortable.
f Signifying ÿ when God bestoweth his mercies in suche abundãce, the ministers shal by their preachĩg winne many
g Which were cities at ÿ corners of the salt or dead sea.
h Thei shalbe here of all sortes, and in as great abundance as in the great Ocean where they are bred
i That is, the wicked and reprobate.
″Or, tre for meat
″Or, for bruses and sores.
Gen. 48,22.
Gen. 12,7. & 13,5. & 15,18. & 26,4.
Ach. 34,4.

ne hand to giue it vnto your fathers, and
this lãd shal fall vnto you for inheritãce.
15 And this shalbe the border [k] of the land
toward the North side, frõ the maine sea
toward Hethlón as men go to Zedádah:
16 Hamáth, Berotháh, Sibráim, which is
betwene the border of Damascus, and the
border of Hamáth, *and* Hazár, Hatticón,
which is by the coast of Haurán.
17 And the border from the sea shalbe Hazár, Enán, & the border of Damascus, and
the residue of the North, Northwarde, &
the border of Hamáth: so *shalbe* the North
parte.
18 But the East side shal ye measure from
Haurán, and from Damascus, and from
Gileád, and from the land of Israél by Ior
dén, & from the border vnto the East sea:
and so *shalbe* the East parte.
19 And the Southside *shalbe* toward Temán from Tamár to the waters of ″Mri-
bóth *in* Kadésh, & the riuer to the maine
sea: so *shalbe* ÿ South parte toward Temán.
20 The West parte also *shalbe* the great sea
frõ the border, til a mã come ouer against
Hamáth: this shalbe the West parte.
21 So shal ye deuide this land vnto you, according to the tribes of Israél.
22 And you shal deuide it by lot for an inheritãce vnto you, & to the strangers that
dwell among you, which shal beget children among you, & thei shalbe vnto you,
as borne in the countrei amõg the childrẽ
of Israél, [l] thei shal parte inheritance with
you in the middes of the tribes of Israél.
23 And in what tribe the stranger dwelleth,
there shal ye giue him his inheritance,
saith the Lord God.

CHAP. XLVIII.

The lottes of the tribes. 9 The partes of the possession of the Priestes, of the Temple, of the Leuites, of the citie and of the prince are rehearsed.

1 NOw these are the names of the [a] tribes. Frõ the North side, to the coa-
ste toward Hethlón, as one goeth to Hamáth, Hazár, Enán, & the border of Damascus Northward the coast of Hamáth,
euẽ *from* the East side to the West shalbe a
porcion for Dan.
2 And by the border of Dan from the East
side vnto the West side, a *porciõ* for Ashér.
3 And by the border of Ashér frõ the East
parte euẽ vnto the West parte a *porcion* for
Naphtalí.
4 And by the border of Naphtalí from
the East quarter vnto the West side, a *por-*
cion for Manasséh.
5 And by the border of Manasséh from the
East side vnto the West side a *porcion* for
Ephráim.
6 And by the border of Ephráim, from the
East parte euen vnto the West parte, a *por-*
cion for Reubén.

k By the land of promes he signifieth the spiritual land whereof this was a figure.
″Or, strife.
l Meaning, ÿ in this spiritual kingdome there shulde be no difference betwene Iewe nor Gentil, but that all shulde be partakers of this inheritance in their head Christ.
a The tribes after ÿ they entred into ÿ land vnder Iosua, deuided the land somwhat otherwise then is here setforthe by this vision.

7 And by the border of Reubén, from the
East quarter vnto the West quarter, *a porcion* for Iudáh.
8 And by the border of Iudáh frõ the East
parte vnto the West parte [b] shalbe the offring which thei shal offre of fiue & twentie thousand *redes* broade, and of length as
one of the *other* partes, from the East side
vnto the West side, and the Sanctuarie
shal be in the middes of it.

b That is, the portion of the grounde, wͭ they shal separat & appoint to the Lord, which shalbe deuided in to thre partes for the Priests, for the prince & for the citie.

9 The oblacion that ye shal offre vnto the
Lord, *shalbe* of fiue and twentie thousand
long, and of ten thousand the breadth.
10 And for them, *euen* for the Priests shal be
this holy oblacion, toward the North fiue
and twentie thousand *long*, and towarde
the West, ten thousand broade, & toward
the East ten thousand broade, and towarde the South fiue and twentie thousand
long, and the Sanctuarie of the Lord shal
be in the middes thereof.
11 *It shalbe* for the Priests that are sanctified
of the sonnes of * Zadók, which haue kept
my charge, which went not astray whẽ the
children of Isráel went astray, as the Leuites went astraye.

Chap. 44,15.

12 Therefore *this* oblacion of the land that
is offred, shalbe theirs, *as* a thĩg moste holie by the border of the Leuites.
13 And ouer against ẏ border of the Priests
the Leuites *shal haue* fiue and twẽtie thousand long, & ten thousand broade: all the
length *shalbe* fiue and twẽtie thousand, and
the breadth ten thousand.
14 And thei shal not sel of it, nether change it, nor abalienate the first frutes of the
land: for it is holy vnto the Lord.
15 And the fiue thousand that are left in ẏ
breadth ouer against the fiue and twentie
thousand, shalbe a prophane place for the
citie, for housing, & for suburbes, and the
citie shalbe in the middes thereof.
16 And these shalbe the measures thereof, ẏ
North parte fiue hũdreth and foure thousand, and the South parte [c] fiue hũdreth &
foure thousand, and of the East parte fiue
hundreth and foure thousand, & the West
parte fiue hundreth, and foure thousand.

c Meaning, ẏ it shulde be square.

17 And the suburbes of the citie shalbe towarde the North two hundreth and fiftie &
towarde the South two hundreth & fiftie,
and towarde the East two hundreth & fiftie, and towarde the West two hundreth
and fiftie.
18 And ẏ residue in length ouer against ẏ
oblaciõ of the holy porcion *shalbe* ten thou
sand East warde, and ten thousand West
warde: and it shalbe ouer against the obla
cion of the holy porcion, & the encrease
thereof shal be for fode vnto them that ser
ue in the citie.
19 And thei that serue in the citie, *shalbe* of
all ẏ tribes of Isráel that shal serue therein.
20 All the oblacion *shalbe* fiue and twenty
thousand wͭ [d] fiue & twentie thousand: you
shal offre this oblacion foure square for the
Sanctuarie, & for the possession of ẏ citie.

d Euerie way it shalbe fyue & twẽty thousand.

21 And the residue *shalbe* for the prince on
the one side & on the other of the oblacion
of the Sanctuarie, and of the possession of
the citie, ouer against the fiue and twentie
thousand of the oblacion towarde the East
border, & Westward ouer against the fiue
& twẽtie thousand toward the West border, ouer against *shalbe* for the porcion of
the prince: this shalbe the holie oblacion,
& the house of the Sanctuarie *shalbe* in the
middes thereof.
22 Moreouer, from the possession of the Le
uites, & from ẏ possession of the citie, that
which is in ẏ middes shalbe ẏ princes: betwene the border [e] of Iudáh, & betwene the
border of Beniamín shalbe the princes.

e So that Iudáh was on ẏ North side of the Princes & Leuites portions, and Beniamín on the Southside.

23 And the rest of the tribes *shalbe thus*: frõ
the East parte vnto the West parte Beniamín *shalbe a porcion*.
24 And by the border of Beniamín, from
the East side vnto the West side Simeón *a
porcion*.
25 And by the border of Simeón frõ the East
parte vnto ẏ West parte Isshakár *a porcion*.
26 And by ẏ border of Isshakár frõ the East
side vnto the West, Zebulún *a porcion*.
27 And by the border of Zebulún from the
East part vnto ẏ West parte, Gad a *porciõ*.
28 And by the border of Gad at the South
side, toward [f] Temáth, the border shalbe
euen frõ [g] Tamár *vnto* the waters of Me-
ribáth *in* Kadésh, *&* to the [h] riuer, *that runneth* into the mayne sea.

f Which is here taken for Idumea.
g Which was Ierichó the citie of palme trees.
h Meaning Nilus ẏ runneth into ẏ sea called mediterraneum.

29 This is the land, which ye shal distribute vnto the tribes of Isráel for inheritance, and these are their porcions, saith the
Lord God.
30 And these are ẏ boundes of the citie, on
the North side fiue hundreth, & foure thou
sand measures.
31 And the gates of the citie *shalbe* after ẏ
names of the tribes of Isráel, the gates
Northward, one gate of Reubén, one gate
of Iudáh, *&* one gate of Leuí.
32 And at the East side fiue hundreth and
foure thousand, and thre gates, & one gate
of Ioséph, one gate of Beniamín, *and* one
gate of Dan.
33 And at the South side, fiue hundreth and
foure thousand measures, and thre portes,
one gate of Simeón, one gate of Isshakár,
and one gate of Zebulún.
34 At the West side, fiue hundreth & foure
thousand, *with* their thre gates, one gate of
Gad, one gate of Ashér, *and* one gate of
Naphtalí.
35 *It was* rounde about eightene thousand
measures, and the name of the citie frõ that
day *shalbe*, * The Lord is there.

* *Ebr. Iehouah shammah.*

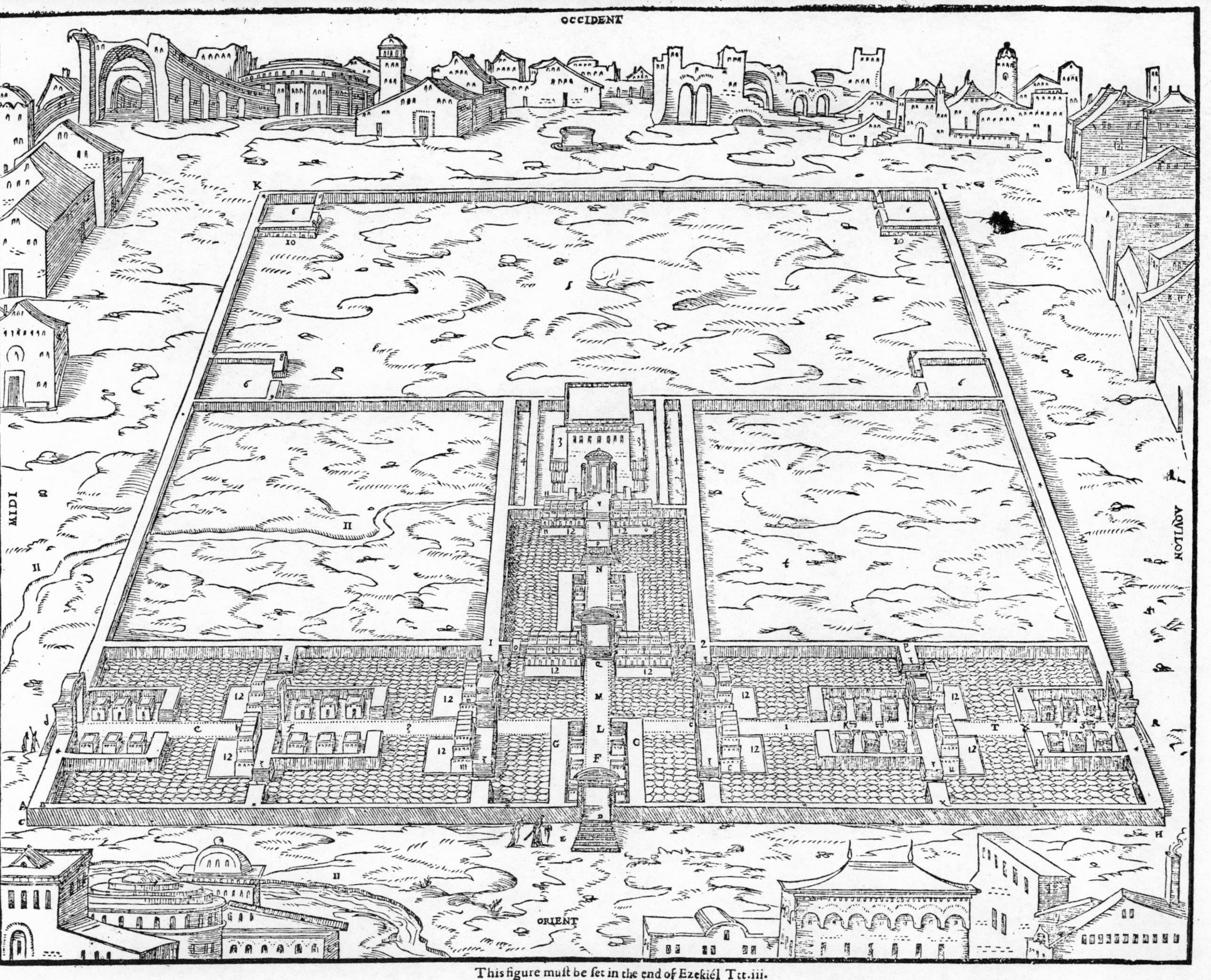

This figure must be set in the end of Ezekiél Ttt.iii.

DANIEL.

THE ARGVMENT.

The great prouidence of God, and his singular mercie toward his Church are moste liuely here set forthe, who neuer leaueth his destitute, but now in their greatest miseries and afflictions giueth them Prophetes, as Ezekiél, & Daniél, whome he adorned with suche graces of his holie spirit, that Daniél aboue all other had moste special reuelations of suche things as shulde come to the Church, euen from the time that thei were in captiuitie, to the last end of the worlde, and to the general resurrection, as of the foure Monarches and empires of all the worlde, to wit, of the Babylonians, Persians, Grecians, & Romaines. Also of the certeine nombre of the times euen vnto Christ, when all ceremonies and sacrifices shulde cease, because he shulde be the accomplishement thereof: moreouer he sheweth Christes office and the caus of his death which was by his sacrifice to take awaye sinnes, and to bring euerlasting life. And as from the beginning God euer exercised his people vnder the crosse, so he teacheth here, that after that Christ is offred, he wil stil leaue this exercise to his Church vntil the dead rise againe, and Christ gather his into his kingdome in the heauens.

CHAP. I.

1 The captiuitie of Iehoiakím King of Iudáh. 4 The King chuseth certeine yong men of the Iewes to learne his lawe. 5 Thei haue the Kings ordinarie appointed, 8 But thei abstaine from it.

IN the [a] thirde yere of the
reigne of Iehoiakím Kĩg
of Iudáh, came Nebu-
chad-nezzár, King of Ba-
bél vnto Ierusalém, & be-
seiged it.
2 And the Lord gaue Ie
hoiakím King of Iudáh into his hand, wt
parte of the vessels of the house of God,
which he caried into the land of [b] Shinár,
to the house of his god, and he broght the
vessels into his gods treasurie.
3 And the King spake vnto [c] Ashpenáz the
master of his [d] Eunuches, that he shulde
bring *certeine* of the children of Israél, of
the [e] Kings sede, and of the princes:
4 Children in whome was no blemish, but
wel [f] fauoured, & instruct in all wisdome,
and wel sene in knowledge, and able to vt
ter knowledge, and suche as were able to
stand in the Kings palace, and whome
thei might teache the [g] learning, and the
tongue of the Caldeans.
5 And the King appointed them prouision
euerie daie of a [h] portion of the Kings
meat, and of the wine, which he dranke, so
nourishing thẽ [i] thre yere, that at the end
thereof, thei might stand [k] before the
King.
6 Now among these were *certeine* of the
children of Iudáh, Daniél, Hananiáh, Mishaél and Azariáh.
7 Vnto whome the chief of the Eunuches
[l] gaue *other* names: for he called Daniél,
Belteshazár, & Hananiáh, Shadrách, & Mishaél, Meshách, and Azariáh, Abednegó.
8 ¶ But Daniél had determined in his heart,
that he wolde not [m] defile him self with the
porcion of the Kings meat, nor with the
wine which he dranke: therefore he required ye chief of the Eunuches that he might
not defile him self.
9 (Now God had broght Daniél into fauour, and tender loue with the chief of the
Eunuches)
10 And the chief of the Eunuches said vnto
Daniél, [n] I feare my lord the King, who
hathe appointed your meat and your drinke: therefore if he se your faces worse ly-
king then the *other* children, which are of
your sorte, thẽ shal you make me lose mine head vnto the King.
11 Then said Daniél to Melzár, whome
the chief of the Eunuches had set ouer Da
niél, Hananiáh, Mishaél, and Azariáh,
12 Proue thy seruants, I beseche thee, [o] ten
daies, and let them giue vs [p] pulse to eat,
and water to drinke.
13 Then let our countenãces be loked vpon
before thee, and the countenances of the
children that eat of the porcion of the
Kings meat: and as thou seest, deale with
thy seruants.
14 So he consented to them in this matter,
and proued them ten daies.
15 And at the end of ten daies, their [q] coũ-
tenãces appeared fairer, and in "better ly-
king then all the childrens, which did eat
the porcion of the Kings meat.
16 Thus Melzár toke awaie the porcion of
their meat, and the wine that thei shulde
drinke, and gaue them pulse.

a Read 2. King. 24,1. and iere. 25,1.
b Which was a plaine by Babylón where was the Temple of their great god, and is here taken for Babylón.
c Who was as master of the wardes.
d He calleth the Eunuches whome the Kĩg nourished and broght vp to be rulers of other countries afterward.
e His purpose was to kepe them as hostages, and that he might shewe him self victorious, and also by their good intreatie and learning of his religion, thei might fauour rather hĩ then the Iewes and so to be able to serue him as gouerners in their land: moreouer by this meanes ye Iewes might be better kept in subiection, fearing otherwise to procure hurt to these noble men.
f The King required thre things, that thei shulde be of noble byrth, that thei shulde be witty & learned, and yt thei shulde be of a strõg & comelie nature that thei might do him better seruice: this he did for his owne commoditie therefore it is not to praise his liberalitie: yet in this he is worthy praise, that he estemed learning, and knewe that it was a necessarie meane to gouerne by.
g That thei might forget their owne religion, and countrei facions, to serue him the better to his purpose: yet it is not to be thoght that Daniél did learne anie knowledge that was not godlie: in all pointes he refused the abuse of things and superstición, in so muche yt he wolde not eat the meat which the King appointed him, but was content to learne ye knowledge of natural things.
h That by their good interteinement thei might learne to forget the mediocritie of their owne people.
i To the intent that in this time thei might bothe learne the maners of the Caldeans and also their tongue.
k Aswel to serue at the table, as in other offices.
l That thei might altogether forget their religion: for the Iewes gaue their children names, which might euer put them in remembrance of some point of religion: therefore this was a great tentacion & a signe of seruitude which thei were not able to resist.
m Not that he thoght anie religion to be in the meat or drinke (for afterwarde he did eat) but because the Kĩg shulde not intise hĩ by this swete poyson to forget his religion & accustomed sobrietie, and yt in his meat & drinke he might daylie remembre of what people he was: and Daniél bringeth this in to shewe how God from the beginning assisted him with his Spirit, and at length called him to be a Prophet.
n He supposed thei did this for their religion, which was contrarie to the Babylonians, and therefore herein he representeth them, wc are of no religion: for nether he wolde condẽne theirs nor mainteine his owne.
o Meaning, that within this space he might haue the tryal, and that noman shulde be able to discerne it: & thus he spake, being moued by the Spirit of God.
p Not that it was a thing abominable to eat dentie meates and to drinke wine, as bothe before and after thei did, but if thei shulde haue hereby bene wonne to the King and haue refused their owne religion, that meat and drinke had bene accursed.
q This bare feding and that also of Moses when he fled from the court of Egypt, declareth that we must liue in suche sobrietie as God doeth call vs vnto, seing he wil make it more profitable vnto vs, then all denteis: for his blessing onely sufficeth.
" Ebr. fatter in flesh.

r Meaning, in the liberal sciences, and natural knowledge, and not in ẏ magical artes which are forbiddẽ, Deu. 18,11.
ſ So that he onely was a Prophet and none of the other: for by dreames & visions God appeared to his Prophetes, Nomb. 12,6.
t Of the thre yeres aboue mẽcioned ver. 5.
u That is, he was estemed in Babylon as a Prophet so lõg as ẏ commune wealth stode.

17 As for these foure childrẽ, God gaue thẽ
knowledge, and vnderstanding in all learning r and wisdome: also he gaue Daniél
vnderstanding of all ſ visions & dreames.
18 Now when the time was t expired, that
the King had appointed to bring thẽ in,
the chief of the Eunuches broght thẽ before Nebuchad-nezzár.
19 And the King cõmuned with them: and
among them all was founde none like Daniél, Hananiáh, Mishaél, and Azariáh:
therefore stode thei before the King.
20 And in all matters of wisdome, & vnder
standing that the King enquired of them,
he founde them ten times better then all
the inchanters & astrologians, that were
in all his realme.
21 And Daniél was vnto u the first yere of
King Cyrus.

CHAP. II.

1 The dreame of Nebuchad-nezzár. 13 The King commandeth all the wise men of Babylón to be slaine because thei colde not interprete his dreame. 16 Daniél requireth time to solute the question. 24 Daniél is broght vnto the King and sheweth him his dreame & the interpretacion thereof. 44 Of the euerlasting kingdome of Christ.

a The father and the sonne were bothe called by this name, so that this is ment of ẏ sonne, when he reigned alone: for he reigned also after a sort ẇ his father.
b Not that he had many dreames, but because many matters were conteined in this dreame.
c Because it was so rare and strange a dreame that he had not had the like.
d He was so heauy with slepe that he began to slepe agayne. Some read, and his slepe was broken from him
e For all these astrologers & sorcerers called them selues by this name of honour as thogh all the wisdome and knowledge of the countrey depẽded vpon thẽ, and that all other cõutreies were voide of the same.
f That is, in ẏ Syrian tongue which differed not muche from the Caldeans, saue it semed to be more eloquent, & therefore the learned vsed to speake it: as the Iewish writers do to this day. g This is a iuste rewarde of their arrogancie (which vanted of thẽ selues that they had the knowledge of all thing) ẏ thei shulde be prouen fooles & ẏ to their perpetual shame and confusion. h Herein appeared their ignorance that notwithstanding their brags, yet were thei not able to tel the dreame, except he entred them into the matter, & therefore thei wolde pretende knowledge where was but mere ignorance and so as deluders of the people, thei were worthy to dye. "*Ebr. redeme the time.*

1 And in ẏ a second yere of ẏ reigne of
Nebuchad-nezzár, Nebuchad-nez-
zár dreamed b dreames wherwith his spirit
was c troubled, & his d slepe was vpon him.
2 Then the King commanded to call ẏ inchanters, and the astrologians and the sorcerers, and the e Caldeans for to shew the
King his dreames: so thei came and stode
before the King.
3 And the King said vnto them, I haue
dreamed a dreame, & my spirit was troubled to knowe the dreame.
4 Then spake the Caldeans to the King in
the f Aramites language, O King, liue for
euer: shewe thy seruants thy dreame, and
we shal shewe the interpretacion.
5 *And* the King answered and said to the
Caldeans, The thing is gone from me. If
ye wil not make me vnderstand the dreame with the interpretacion thereof, ye
g shalbe drawen in pieces, and your houses
shalbe made a iakes.
6 But if ye declare the dreame and the interpretacion thereof, ye shal receiue of me
gifts and rewardes, and great honour: therefore shewe me the dreame and the interpretacion of it.
7 Thei answered againe, and said, Let the
King shewe h his seruants the dreame, and
we wil declare the interpretacion thereof.
8 *Then* the King answered, and said, I knowe certeinly that ye " wolde gaine the time, because ye se the thing is gone frõ me.
9 But if ye wil not declare me the dreame,
there is but one iudgement for you: for ye
haue prepared lying and corrupt wordes,
to speake before me til ẏ time be changed:
therefore tel me the dreame, that I maie
knowe, if ye can declare me the interpreta
cion thereof.
10 *Then* the Caldeans answered before the
King, and said, There is no man vpon
earth that can declare ẏ Kings matter: yea,
there is nether King nor prince nor Lord
that asked suche things at an inchanter or
astrologian or Caldean.
11 For it is a rare thing that the King requireth, & there is none other that can declare it before the King, except the gods
whose dwelling is not with flesh.
12 For this cause the King was angrie and
in great furie, and commanded to destroie
all the wise men of Babél.
13 ¶ And when sentence was giuen, the wise
men were slaine: and thei i soght Daniél &
his felowes to be put to death.
14 Then Daniél answered with counsel &
wisdome to Arióch the Kings " chief steward, which was gone forthe to put to death
the wise men of Babél.
15 *Yea*, he answered and said vnto Arióch
the Kings captaine, Why is the sentẽce so
hastie from the King? Then Arióch declared the thing to Daniél.
16 So Daniél went and desired the King ẏ
he wolde giue him leasure & that he wolde
shewe the King ẏ interpretacion thereof.
17 ¶ Then Daniél went to his house and
shewed the matter to Hananiáh, Mishaél,
and Azariáh his companions,
18 That thei shulde beseche the God of hea
uen for grace in this secret, that Daniél &
his felowes shulde not perish with the rest
of the wise men of Babél.
19 Then was the secret reueiled vnto Daniél in a vision by night: therefore Daniél
praised the God of heauen.
20 And Daniél answered & said, *The Na
me of God be praised for euer and euer:
for wisdome and strength are his,
21 And he changeth the times and seasons:
he taketh awaie Kings: he setteth vp Kĩgs:
he giueth wisdome vnto the wise, & vnderstanding to those that vnderstand.
22 He discouereth the depe & secret thĩgs:
he knoweth what is in the darkenes, and
the k light dwelleth with him.
23 I thanke thee & praise thee, ô thou God
of my l fathers, that thou hast giuen me
wisdome and m strength, and hast shewed
me now the thing that we desired of thee:
for thou hast declared vnto vs the Kings
matter.
24 ¶ Therefore Daniél went vnto Arióch,
whome the King had ordeined to destroie the wise men of Babél: he went and
said

i Which declareth, ẏ God wolde not haue his seruant ioyned in ẏ cõpanie of these sorcerers, and astrologers, whose artes were wicked, and therefore iustly oght to dye, thogh ẏ King did it vpõ a rage, and no zeale.
"*Or, the captaine of the garde.*
**Psal. 113,2. & 115,18.*
k He sheweth that mã hathe nether wisdome nor knowledge but very darke blindenes, and ignorance of him self: for it cometh onely of God, that mã vnderstandeth anie thing.
l To whome ẏ madest thy promes, and who liued in thy feare: whereby he excludeth all other gods.
m Meaning, power to interprete it.

said thus vnto him, Destroye not [n] the
wise men of Babél, *but* bring me before the
King, and I wil declare vnto the King the
interpretacion.
25 Then Arióch broght Daniél before the
King in all haste, and said thus vnto him,
I haue found a man of the children of Iudáh that were broght captiues, that wil
declare vnto the King the interpretacion.
26 Then answered the King, and said vnto
Daniél, whose name was Belteshazzár,
Art thou able to shewe me the dreame, ẇ I
haue sene, and the interpretacion thereof?
27 Daniél answered in the presence of the
King, & said, The secret which the King
hathe demanded, can nether the wise, the
astrologians, the inchanters, *nor* the southe-
saiers declare vnto the King.
28 But there is a God in [o] heauen that reueileth secrets, and sheweth the King
Nebuchad-nezzár what shalbe in the latter dayes. Thy dreame, and the things, ẇ
thou hast sene in thine head vpon thy bed,
is this.
29 O King, when ỹ wast in thy bed, thoghts
came into thy *minde*, what shulde come to
passe hereafter, and he that reueileth secrets, telleth thee, what shal come.
30 As [p] for me, this secret is not shewed
me for anie wisdome that I haue, more
then anie other liuing, but onely to shewe
the King the interpretació, and that thou
mightest knowe ỹ thoghts of thine heart.
31 O King, thou sawest, and beholde, there
was a great image: this great image whose
glorie was so excellent, stode before thee,
and the forme thereof *was* terrible.
32 This images head was of fine [q] golde,
his breast and his armes of siluer, his bellie
and his thighs of brasse,
33 His legges of yron, & his fete *were* parte
of yron, and parte of clay.
34 Thou beheldest it til a stone was cut
without hands, which smote the image
vpon his fete, that were of yron and clay,
and brake them to pieces.
35 Then was the yron, the clay, the brasse,
the siluer & the golde broken all together,
and became like the chaffe of the sommer
floores, and the winde caryed them away,
that no place was founde for them: and
the stone that smote the image, became a
great mountaine, and filled the whole
earth.
36 This is the dreame, and we wil declare
before the King ỹ interpretació thereof.
37 ¶ O King, thou art a King of Kings: for
the God of heauen hathe giuen thee a
kingdome, power, and strength, & glorie.
38 And in all *places* where the children of
men dwell, the beasts of the field, and the
foules of the heauen hathe he giuen into
thine hand, and hathe made thee ruler ouer

n Whereby appeareth that manie were slaine, as vers. 13, and the rest at Daniels offer were preserued on conditió: not that Daniél fauoured their wicked professió, but that he had respect to equitie because the King proceded according to his wicked affection, & not considering, if their science was lawful or no.

o He affirmeth that man by reason, & arte is not able to atteine to the cause of Gods secrets, but the vnderstanding onely thereof must come of God: whereby he smiteth ỹ King with a certeine feare and reuerence of God that he might be the more apt to receiue ỹ hye mysteries, that shulde be reueiled.

p Because he had said ỹ God onely must reueile the signification of this dreame, ỹ King might haue asked, why Daniél did enterprise to interpret it, & therefore he sheweth, that he was, but Gods minister, and had no giftes, but suche as God had giuē him to set forthe his glorie.

q By golde, siluer, brasse, and yron are ment the Caldean, Persian, Macedonian, & Romaine kingdome, which shulde successiuely rule all the worlde til Christ (which is here called the stone) come him selfe, and destroye the last: & this was to assure the Iewes, ỹ their afflictiōs shulde not end with the empire of the Caldeans, but that they shulde paciently abyde ỹ cōming of Messiah, ẇ shulde be at ỹ end of this fourth monarchie.

them all: thou art [r] this head of golde.
39 And after thee shal rise another kingdome, [s] inferiour to thee, *of siluer*, and another
[t] third kingdome *shalbe* of brasse, which
shal beare rule ouer all the earth.
40 And the fourth kingdome shalbe strōg
as yron: for as yron breaketh in pieces, &
subdueth all things, and as yron bruseth
all these things, *so* shal it breake in [u] pieces and bruse *all*.
41 Where as thou sawest the fete and toes,
parte of potters clay, and parte of yron:
the kingdome shalbe [x] deuided, but there
shalbe in it of the strength of the yron, as
thou sawest the yron mixt with the claye,
and earth.
42 And *as* the toes of the fete *were* parte of
yron, and parte of clay, *so* shal the kingdome be partely strong, and partely broken.
43 And where as thou sawest yrō mixt with
clay & earth, they shal mingle them selues with [y] the sede of men: but they shal
not ioyne one with another, as yron cā not
be mixed with clay.
44 And in the dayes of these Kings, shal
the God of heauē set vp a kingdome, which
[z] shal neuer be destroyed: and this kingdome shal not be giuen to another people,
but it shal breake, and destroye all these
kingdomes, and it shal stand for euer.
45 Where as ỹ sawest, that the [a] stone was
cut of the mountaine without hands, and
that it brake in pieces the yron, the brasse,
the clay, the siluer and the golde: *so* the
great God hathe shewed the King, what
shal come to passe hereafter, and the drea
me *is* true, and the interpretacion thereof
is sure.
46 ¶ Then the King Nebuchad nezzár fel
vpon his face, and [b] bowed him self vnto
Daniél, and commanded that thei shulde
offer meat offrings, & swete odoures vnto
him.
47 *Also* the King answered vnto Daniél, &
said, *I knowe* of a trueth that your [c] God is
a God of gods, & the Lord of Kings, and
the reueiler of secrets, sēing thou coldest
open this secret.
48 So the King made Daniél a great man,
and gaue him manie and great [d] giftes.
He made him gouernour ouer the whole
prouince of Babél, and chief of the rulers,
& aboue all the wise men of Babél.

r Daniél leaueth out the kingdome of the Assyrians, which was before the Babylonian, bothe because it was not a monarchie & general empire, & also because he wolde declare the things, ỹ were to come, to the comig of Christ for the cōfort of the elect among these wonderful alterations: & he calleth the Babyloniā kingdome the golden head, because in respect of the other thre, it was the best, and yet was of it self wicked and cruel.

s Meaning, the Persiās, which were not inferiour in dignitie, power, and riches, but were worse touching ambitiō, crueltie, & all kinde of vice: shewing, that ỹ worlde shulde growe worse, and worse, til it was restored by Christ.

t That is, of ỹ Macedonians shalbe of brasse, not alluding to the hardenes therof, but to the vilenes in respect of siluer.

u That is, the Romain empire shal subdue all these other afore named, ẇ after Alexāder were deuided into ỹ Macedonians, Grecians, Syriās & Egyptians.

x They shal haue ciuil warres and continual discordes among them selues.

y Thei shal by mariages, and affinities thinke to make thē selues strong: yet shal they neuer be ioyned in hearts.

z His purpose is to shewe, that all the kingdomes of ỹ worlde are transitorie, & ỹ the kingdome of Christ shal onely remaine for euer. a Meaning Christ who was sent of God, and not set vp by man, whose kingdome at the beginning shulde be smale, & without beautie to mans iudgemēt, but shulde at length growe & fil the whole earth, ẇ he calleth a great moūtaine, as vers. 35. And this kingdome, which is not onely referred to the persone of Christ, but also to the whole bodie of his Church, and to euerie member thereof, shalbe eternal: for the Spirit that is in them, is life eternal, Rom. 8, 10. b Thogh this hūbling of ỹ King semed to deserue cōmendation, yet because he ioyned Gods honour with the Prophets, it is to be reproued, & Daniél herein erred if he suffred it: but it is credible that Daniél admonished him of his faute and did not suffre it.
c This cōfession was but a sudden motiō, as it was also in Pharaoh, Exo. 9, 28. but his heart was not touched, as appeared sone afterward. d Not that the Prophet was desirous of gifts or honour, but because by this meanes he might relieue his poore breathren ẇ were grieuously oppressed in this their captiuitie, & also he receiued thē, lest he shulde offend this cruel King, ẇ willingly gaue them.

49 Then Daniél [e] made requeſt to the
King, and he ſet Shadrách, Meſhách, and
Abednegó ouer the charge of the prouince of Babél: but Daniél *ſate* in the [f] gate
of the King.

e He did not this for their priuate profit, but that the whole Church which was thẽ there in affli-ctiõ, might haue ſome releaſe and eaſe, by this benefite. f Meaning, that ether he was a iudge, or that he had the whole authoritie, ſo that none colde de admitted to the Kings preſence, but by him.

CHAP. III.

1 The King ſetteth vp a golden image. 8 Certeine are accuſed becauſe thei deſpiſed the Kings commãdemẽt, and are put into a burning ouen. 25 By beleſe in God they are deliuered from the fyre. 26 Nebuchad-nezzar confeſſeth the power of God after the ſight of the miracle.

1 NEbuchad-nezzár the King made
[a] an image of golde, whoſe height
was threſcore cubites, *&* the breadth thereof ſix cubites: he ſet it vp in the plaine of
Durá, in the prouince of Babél.
2 Then Nebuchad-nezzár the King ſent
forthe to gather together the nobles, the
princes & the dukes, the iudges, the receiuers, the counſellers, the officers, & all the
gouerners of the prouinces, that they ſhulde come to the [b] dedication of the image,
which Nebuchad-nezzár the [c] King had
ſet vp.
3 So the nobles, princes, and dukes, the iudges, the receiuers, the counſellers, the officers, and all the gouerners of the prouinces were aſſembled vnto the dedicating
of the image, that Nebuchad-nezzár the
King had ſet vp: and they ſtode before
the image, which Nebuchad-nezzár had
ſet vp.
4 Then an herald cryed aloud, Be it knowẽ
to you, ô people, [d] nations, and langages,
5 That when ye heare the ſoũd of the cornet, trũpet, harpe, ſackebut, pſalteries, dulci
mer, and all inſtruments of muſicke, ye fall
downe and worſhip the goldẽ image, that
Nebuchad-nezzár the King hathe ſet vp.
6 And whoſoeuer falleth not downe and
worſhippeth, ſhal the ſame houre be
caſt into the middes of an hote fyrie fornace.
7 Therefore aſſone as all the people heard
ẏ ſound of the cornet, trũpet, harpe, ſackebut, pſalterie, & all inſtrumẽts of muſicke,
all ẏ people, nations, & langages fel downe, and worſhiped the golden image, that
Nebuchad-nezzár the King had ſet vp.
8 ¶ By reaſon whereof at that ſame time
came men of the Caldeãs, and grieuouſly
accuſed the Iewes.
9 *For* they ſpake and ſaid to the King Nebuchad-nezzár, O King, liue for euer.
10 Thou, ô King, haſt made a decre, that
euerie man that ſhal heare the ſound of
the cornet, trumpet, harpes, ſackebut,
pſalterie, and dulcimer, and all inſtrumẽts
of muſicke, ſhal fall downe & worſhip the
golden image,
11 And whoſoeuer falleth not downe, and
worſhippeth, that he ſhulde be caſt into
the middes of an hote fyrie fornace.
12 There are certeine Iewes whome thou
haſt ſet ouer the charge of the prouince of
Babél, [e] Shadrách, Meſhách, and Abednegó: theſe men, ô King, haue not regarded thy commandement, nether wil they
ſerue thy gods, nor worſhip the golden
image, that thou haſt ſet vp.
13 ¶ Then Nebuchad-nezzár in *his* angre
and wrath commanded that they ſhulde
bring Shadrách, Meſhách, and Abednegó: ſo theſe men were broght before the
King.
14 *And* Nebuchad-nezzár ſpake, and ſaid
vnto thẽ, What diſordre? wil not you, Sha
drách, Meſhách, and Abednegó ſerue my
god, nor worſhip the goldẽ image, that I
haue ſet vp?
15 [f] Now therefore are ye ready whẽ ye heare the ſound of the cornet, trumpet, harpe,
ſackebut, pſalterie, and dulcimer, and all
inſtruments of muſicke, to fall downe, &
worſhip the image, which I haue made? for
if ye worſhip it not, ye ſhalbe caſt immediatly into the middes of an hote firie fornace: for who is that God, that can deliuer
you out of mine hands?
16 Shadrách, Meſhách, and Abednegó anſwered & ſaid to the King, O Nebuchad-
nezzár, we [g] are not careful to anſwer thee
in this matter.
17 Beholde, our God whome we ſerue, is
[h] able to deliuer vs frõ the hote fyrie for
nace, and he wil deliuer vs out of thine
hand, ô King.
18 But if not, be it knowen to thee, ô King,
ẏ we wil not ſerue thy gods, nor worſhip
the golden image, which thou haſt ſet vp.
19 ¶ Then was Nebuchad-nezzár ful of rage, and the forme of his viſage was changed againſt Shadrách, Meſhách, & Abednegó: *therefore* he charged and commanded that they ſhulde heate the fornace at
once ſeuen [i] times more then it was wonte to be heat.
20 And he charged the moſte valiant men
of warre ẏ were in his armie, to binde Shadrách, Meſhách, and Abednegó, *&* to caſt
them into the hote fyrie fornace.
21 So theſe men were bounde in their coates, their hoſen, & their clokes, with their
other garments, and caſt into the middes of
the hote fyrie fornace.
22 Therefore, becauſe the Kings commandement was ſtraite, that the fornace ſhuldẽ be exceading hote, the flame of ẏ fyre
ſlew thoſe men ẏ broght forthe Shadrách,
Meſhách,

a Vnder pretence of religion, and holines in makĩg an image to his idole Bel, he ſoght his owne ambition and vaine glorie: and this declareth, that he was not touched with the true feare of God before, but ẏ he cõfeſſed him on a ſudden motion as the wicked, when thei are ouercome with the greatnes of his workes. The Greke interpreters write, that this was done 18 yeres after the dreame, and as may appeare ẏ King feared leſt the Iewes by their religion ſhulde haue altered the ſtate of his cõmune wealth, and therefore he mẽt to brĩg all to one kinde of religion, and ſo rather ſoght his owne quietnes, then Gods glorie.

b Shewing, ẏ the idole is not knowen for an idole ſo lõg as he is with the workman: but when the ceremonies and cuſtomes are recited, & vſed and the conſent of the people is there, thẽ of a blocke they thinke they haue made a god.

c This was ſufficient with ẏ wicked at all times to approue their religion, if the Kings autoritie were alledged for ẏ eſtabliſhmẽt thereof, not conſidering in the meane ſeaſon what Gods worde did permit.

d Theſe are ẏ two dãgerous weapons wherewith Satã vſeth to fight againſt ẏ childrẽ of God, ẏ cõſent of the multitude & ẏ crueltie of ẏ puniſhment: for thogh ſome feared God, yet ẏ multitude, ẘ conſented to the wickednes, aſtonied thẽ: & here ẏ King required not an inward cõſent, but an outward geſture, that ẏ Iewes might by litle & litle learne to forget their true religion.

e It ſemeth, ẏ thei named not Daniél becauſe he was greatly in the Kings fauour, thinking if theſe thre had bene deſtroyed, they might haue had better occaſion to accuſe Daniél: and this declareth that this policie of erecting this image was inuented by ẏ malicious flatterers, ẘ ſoght nothing, but ẏ deſtruction of ẏ Iewes, whome they accuſed of rebelliõ & ingratitude.

f Signifying, ẏ he wolde receiue them to grace, if they wolde now at the lẽgth obey his decre.

g For they ſhulde haue done iniurie to God, if they ſhulde haue douted in this holie cauſe, & therefore they ſay, that they are reſolued to dye for Gods cauſe.

h They groũde on two pointes, firſt in the power, & prouidẽce of God ouer them, and ſecondly on their cauſe, ẘ was Gods glorie, and ẏ teſtifying of his true religiõ, ẘ their blood & ſo make open confeſſion, that they wil not ſo muche as outwardly conſent to idolatrie.

i This declareth that the more, that tyrants rage, & the more witty they ſhewe them ſelues in inuenting ſtrãge, and cruel puniſhements, the more is God glorified by his ſeruãts to whome he giueth paciẽce and conſtãcie to abide ẏ crueltie of their puniſhement: for ether he deliuereth them frõ death or els for this life giueth thẽ a better.

Meshách and Abednegó.
23 And these thre men Shadrách, Meshách
and Abednegó fel downe bounde into the
middes of the hote fyrie fornace.
24 ¶ Thē Nebuchad-nezzár the King was
astonied and rose vp in haste, & spake, and
said vnto his counsellers, Did not we cast
thre men bounde into the middes of the
fyre? Who answered and said vnto the
King, It is true, ô King.
25 *And* he answered, and said, Lo, I se foure
men loose, walking in the middes of the
fyre, and they haue no hurt, and the forme
of the fourth is like the [k] sonne of God.
26 Then the King Nebuchad-nezzár came
nere to the mouth of the hote fyrie fornace, & spake and said, Shadrách, Meshách
and Abednegó, the seruants of the hie
God, go forthe & come *hether*: so Shadrách,
Meshách and Abednegó [l] came forthe of
the middes of the fyre.
27 Then the nobles, princes and dukes, and
the Kings counsellers came together to se
these men, because the fyre had no power
ouer their bodies: for not an heere of their
head was burnt, nether was their coats
changed, nor any smel of fyre came vpon
them.
28 *Wherefore* Nebuchad-nezzár spake and
said, [m] Blessed *be* the God of Shadrách,
Meshách and Abednegó, who hathe sent
his Angel, and deliuered his seruants, that
put their trust in him, and haue changed
the Kings commandement, & yelded their
bodies rather thē thei wolde serue or worship anie god, saue their owne God.
29 Therefore I make a decre, that euery
people, nacion, and langage, which speake
any [n] blasphemie against the God of Shadrách, Meshách and Abednegó, shal be
drawen in pieces, and their houses shal be
made a iakes, because there is no god that
can deliuer after this sorte.
30 Then the King promoted Shadrách,
Meshách and Abednegó in the prouince
of Babél.
31 Nebuchad-nezzár King vnto all people, nacions and langages, that dwell in all
the [o] worlde, Peace be multiplied vnto
you:
32 I thoght it good to declare the signes and
wonders, that the hie God hathe wroght
towarde me.
33 How great are his signes, and how mightie are his wonders! [p] his kingdome *is* an e-
uerlasting kingdome, and his dominion *is*
from generacion to generacion.

k For the Angels were called the sonnes of God, because of their excellencie: therefore the Kīg called this Angel, whome God sent to comfort his in these great torments, the sonne of God.

l This cōmendeth their obediēce vnto God that they wolde not for any feare departe out of this fornace til the time was appoited, as Noah remained in ẏ Arke til the Lord called him forthe.

m He was moued by ẏ greatnes of the miracle to praise God, but his heart was not touched. And here we se that miracles are not sufficient to conuert men to God, but ẏ doctrine must chiefly be adioyned, without the which there can be no faith.

n If this heathen King moued by Gods Spirit, wolde not se blasphemie vnpunished, but made a Law and set a punishement to suche transgressers, muche more oght all they that professe religion, take order that suche impietie reigne not, lest acordig as their knowledge & charge is greater, so they suffer double punishement.

o Meaning, so farre as his dominion extended.

p Read Chap. 2,44.

CHAP. IIII.

2 Another dreame of Nebuchad-nezzár, which Daniél declareth. 29 The Prophet declareth how of a proude King he shulde become as a beast. 31 After he confesseth the power of God and is restored to his former dignitie.

1 I Nebuchad-nezzár being at [a] rest in
mine house, and flourishing in my palace,
2 Sawe a [b] dreame, which made me afraied,
and the thoghtes vpon my bed, and the
visions of mine head troubled me.
3 Therefore made I a decre, that thei shulde
bring all the wise men of Babél before
me, that they might declare vnto me the
interpretacion of the dreame.
4 So came the enchanters, the astrologians,
the Caldeans and the southsayers, to whome I tolde the dreame, but [c] they colde
not shewe me the interpretacion thereof,
5 Til at the last Daniél came before me,
(whose name *was* [d] Belteshazzár, accordig
to the name of my god, which hathe the
spirit of the holy gods in him) and before
him I tolde the dreame, *saying*,
6 O Belteshazzár, [e] chief of the enchanters,
because I knowe, that the spirit of the
holy gods is in thee, & no secret troubleth
thee, tel me the visions of my dreame,
that I haue sene and the interpretacion
thereof.
7 Thus *were* the visions of mine head in
my bed. And beholde, I sawe a [f] tre in the
middes of the earth and the height thereof *was* great:
8 A great tre & strong, and the height thereof reached vnto heauen, & the sight thereof to the ends of all the earth.
9 The boughes thereof *were* faire and the
frute thereof muche, and in it was meat
for all: it made a shadowe vnder it for the
beastes of the field, and the foules of the
heauen dwelt in the boughs thereof, and
all flesh fed of it.
10 I sawe in the visions of mine head vpon
my bed, and beholde, a [g] watcheman & an
holy one came downe from heauen,
11 And cryed aloude, and said thus, Hewe
downe the tre, and breake of his branches:
shake of his leaues, and scattre his frute,
that the beasts may flee from vnder it, &
the foules from his branches.
12 Neuertheles leaue the stumpe of his
rootes in the earth, and with a band of y-
ron and brasse *binde it* among the grasse of
the field, and let it be wet with the dewe of
heauen, and let his porcion *be* with the
beastes among the grasse of the field.
13 [h] Let his heart be changed from mans
nature, & let a beastes heart be giuen vnto
him, and let seuen times be passed ouer
him.
14 [i] The sentence *is* according to the decre of the watchemen, and according to
the worde of the holy ones: the demande

a There was no trouble that might cause me to dreame, and therefore it came onely of God.

b This was another dreame besides that which he sawe of the foure empires: for Daniél bothe declared what that dreame was, and what it ment: and here he onely expoundeth the dreame.

c In that that he sent abroad to others whose ignorance in times past he had experimented, and left Daniél ẘ was euer readie at hand, it declareth the nature of the vngodlie, ẘ neuer seke to the seruantes of God, but for very necessitie, and then they spare no flaterings.

d This no doute was a great grief to Daniél not onely to haue his name changed, but to be called by ẏ name of a vile idole, which thing Nebuchad-nezzár did to make him forget the true religion of God.

e Which also was a great grief to the Prophet to be nōbred among the sorcerers & men whose practises were wicked and contrary to Gods worde.

f By the tre, is signified the dignitie of a King, whome God ordeineth to be a defence for all kinde of men, & whose state is profitable for mākinde.

g Meaning, the Angel of God, which nether eateth not slepeth, but is euer ready to do Gods wil & is not infect ẘ mās corruptiō but is euer holy: and in that that he cōmandeth to cut downe this tre, he knewe ẏ it shulde not be cut downe by mā but by God.

h Hereby he meaneth ẏ Nebuchad-nezzár shulde not onely for a time loose his kingdome, but be like a beast.

i God hathe decreed this iudgement and the whole armie of heauen haue as it were subscribed vnto it, like as also thei desire the execution of his decre against all them that lift vp them selues against God.

was answered, to the intent that liuing mẽ
may knowe, that ẏ moste high hathe power ouer the kingdome of men, and giueth
it to whomesoeuer he wil, and appointeth
ouer it the moste abiect among men.
15 This is the dreame, *that* I King Nebuchad-nezzár haue sene: therefore thou, ô
Belteshazzár, declare the interpretacion
thereof: for all the wise men of my kingdome are not able to shewe me the interpretacion: but thou art able, for the spirit
of the holy gods *is* in thee.
16 ¶ Then Daniél (whose name *was* Belteshazzár) held his [k] peace by the space of
one houre, and his thoghts troubled him,
& the King spake and said, Belteshazzár,
let nether the dreame, nor the interpretacion thereof trouble thee. Belteshazzár
answered and said, My lord, the dreame *be*
to them that hate thee, and the interpretacion thereof to thine enemies.
17 The tre ẏ thou sawest, which was great
and mightie, whose height reached vnto
the heauen, and the sight thereof through
all the worlde,
18 Whose leaues *were* faire & the frute thereof muche, and in it was meat for all, vnder the which the beasts of the field dwelt,
and vpon whose branches the foules of the
heauen did sit,
19 It is thou, ô King, ẏ art great & mightie: for thy greatnes is growen, & reacheth
vnto heauen, & thy dominion to the ends
of the earth.
20 Where as the King sawe a watcheman,
& an holy one, that came downe from heauen, and said, Hewe downe the tre & destroy it, yet leaue the stumpe of the rootes
thereof in the earth, and with a bande of
yron and brasse *binde it* among the grasse
of the field, & let it be wet with the dewe
of heauen, and let his porcion be with the
beasts of the field, [l] til seuen times passe
ouer him,
21 This *is* the interpretacion, ô King, and it
is the decre of the moste high, which is
come vpon my lord the King,
22 That they shal driue thee from men, &
thy dwelling shalbe with the beasts of the
field: they shal make thee to eat grasse as ẏ
[m] oxen, & thei shal wet thee with the dewe
of heauen: and seuen times shal passe ouer
thee, til thou knowe, that [n] the moste high
beareth rule ouer the kingdome of men,
and giueth it to whome soeuer he wil.
23 Where as they said, that one shulde leaue the stũpe of the tre rootes, thy kingdome shal remaine vnto thee: after that, thou
shalt knowe, that the heauens haue the
rule.
24 Wherefore, ô King, let my counsel be
acceptable vnto thee, and [o] breake of thy
sinnes by righteousnes, & thine iniquities

k He was troubled for the great iudgemẽt of God which he sawe ordeined against ẏ King: and so the Prophetes vsed on the one parte to denounce Gods iudgemẽts for the zeale they bare to his glorie, and on the other parte to haue cõpassion vpon man, and also to consider that they shulde be subiect to Gods iudgements, if he did not regarde them ẇ pitie.

l Whereby he meaneth a lõg space, as seuẽ yeres. Some interprete seuen moneths, and others seuen wekes: but it semeth he mẽt of yeres.

m Not ẏ his shape or forme was chãged into a beast, but that he was ether striken mad, & so auoided mans companie, or was cast out for his tyrannie and so wandered among the beasts, and ate herbes & grasse.

n Daniél sheweth the cause, why God thus punished him.

o Cease from prouokĩg God to angre any longer by thy sinnes, that he may mitigate his punishmẽt, if ẏ shewe by thine vpright life that thou hast true faith & repentance.

by mercie toward the poore: lo, let there be
an [p] healing of thine errour.
25 All these things shal come vpon ẏ King
Nebuchad-nezzár.
26 ¶ At the end of twelue [q] moneths, he walked in the royal palace of Babél.
27 *And* the King spake and said, Is not this
great Babél, that I haue buylt for the house of the kingdome by the might of my
power, and for the honour of my maiestie?
28 While ẏ worde *was* in the Kings mouth,
a voyce came downe from heauen, *saying*,
O King Nebuchad-nezzár, to thee be it
spoken, Thy kingdome is departed from
thee,
29 And they shal driue thee from men, and
thy dwelling *shalbe* with the beasts of the
field: they shal make thee to eat grasse, as
the oxen, and seuen times shal passe ouer
thee, vntil thou knowest, that ẏ most high
beareth rule ouer the kingdome of men, &
giueth it vnto whome soeuer he wil.
30 The very same houre was this thing fulfilled vpon Nebuchad-nezzár, and he was
driuen from men, and did eat grasse as the
oxen, and his bodie was wet with the dewe
of heauen, til his heeres were growen as
egles *feathers* and his nailes like birds
clawes.
31 And at the end of *these* [r] dayes I Nebuchad-nezzár lift vp mine eies vnto heauẽ,
and mine vnderstanding was restored vnto me, and I gaue thankes vnto the moste
high, and I praised and honored him that
liueth for euer, * whose power *is* an euerlasting power, and his kingdome *is* from generacion to generacion.
32 And all the inhabitants of the earth are
reputed as nothing: and according to his
[s] wil he worketh in the armie of heauen, &
in the inhabitants of the earth: and none
can stay his hand, nor say vnto him, What
doest thou?
33 At the same time was mine vnderstanding restored vnto me, and *I returned* to
the honour of my kingdome: my glorie
and my beautie was restored vnto me, and
my counsellours [t] and my princes soght
vnto me, & I was established in my king
dome, and my glorie was augmented toward me.
34 Now *therefore* I Nebuchad-nezzár [u] prai
se, and extoll & magnifie the King of heauen, whose workes are all trueth, and his
wayes iudgement, and those that walke in
pride, he is able to abase.

p Suffre the errours of thy former life to be redressed.

q After that Daniél had declared this vision: & this his pride declareth that it is not in man to cõuert to God except his Spirit moue him, seing ẏ these terrible threatnings colde not moue him to repent.

r Whẽ the terme of these seuen yeres was accomplished

Chap. 7,14. mich. 4,11. luk. 1,33.

s He confesseth Gods wil to be the rule of all iustice & a moste perfite Law whereby he gouerneth bothe man and Angels and deuiles, so ẏ none oght to murmure, or aske a reason of his doĩgs, but onely to stand content therewith and giue him ẏ glorie.

t By whome it semeth that he had bene put from his kingdome before.

u He doeth not onely praise God for his deliuerãce, but also cõfesseth his faute that God may onely haue the glorie & man the shame, & that he may be exalted & mã cast downe.

CHAP. V.

5 Belshazzár King of Babylon seeth an hand writing on the wall. 8 The sothsayers called of the King, can not expounde the writing. 25 Daniél readeth it, and interpreteth it also. 30 The King is slayne. 31 Darius enioyeth the kingdome.

1 King

1 King [a] Belshazzár made a great feast
to a thousand of his princes, and
dranke wine [b] before the thousand.
2 *And* Belshazzár [*] whiles he tasted the wine, commanded to bring him the golden
and siluer vessels, which his [c] father Nebuchad-nezzár had broght from the Tem
ple in Ierusalém, that the King and his
princes, his wife, and his concubines might
drinke therein.
3 Then were broght the goldé vessels, that
were také out of the Temple of the Lords
house at Ierusalém, and the King and his
princes, his wiues, and his concubines drá-
ke in them.
4 They drõke wine and praised the [d] gods
of golde, and of siluer, of brasse, of yron, of
wood and of stone.
5 At the same houre appeared fingers of a
mans hand, which wrote ouer [e] against the
candlesticke vpon the plaister of the wall
of the Kings palace, & the King sawe the
palme of the hand that wrote.
6 Then the Kings countenance was changed, and his thoghts troubled him, so that
the ioyntes of his loines were loosed, and
his [f] knees smote one against the other.
7 *Wherefore* the King cryed loud, that they
shulde bring [g] the astrologians, the Caldeans and the sothsaiers. And the King
spake, and said to the wise men of Babél,
Whosoeuer can read this writing, and
declare me the interpretació thereof, shalbe clothed with purple, & *shal haue* a chaine of golde about his necke, and shalbe the
third ruler in the kingdome.
8 Then came all the Kings wise men, but
they colde nether read the writing, nor
shewe the King the interpretacion.
9 Then was King Belshazzár greatly trou
bled, and his coũtenance was changed in
him, and his princes were astonied.
10 *Now* the [h] Queene by reason of the talke of the King, and his princes came into
the banket house, *and* the Queene spake,
and said, O King, liue for euer: let not thy
thoghts trouble thee, nor let thy countenance be changed.
11 There is a mã in thy kingdome, in whome is the spirit of the holie gods, and in
the dayes of thy father light and vnderstanding & wisdome like the wisdome of
the gods, was found in him: whome the
King Nebuchad-nezzár thy father the
King, *I say*, thy father, made chief of the
[i] enchanters, astrologians, Caldeans, *and*
sothsaiers,
12 Because a more excellent spirit, and
knowledge, and vnderstanding (*for* he
did expounde dreames, and declare hard
sentences, and dissolued doutes) were founde in him, *euen* in Daniél, whome the
King named Belteshazzár: now let Daniél be called, and he wil declare the interpretacion.
13 ¶ Then was Daniél broght before the
King, *and* the King spake and said vnto
Daniél, Art thou that Daniél, which art
of the children of the captiuitie of Iudáh,
whome my father the King broght out of
Iewrie?
14 Now I haue heard of thee, that [k] the spirit of the holie gods *is* in thee, & that light
and vnderstanding and excellẽt wisdome
is found in thee.
15 Now therefore wisemen, & astrologians
haue bene broght before me, that they
shulde read this writing, and shewe me
the interpretacion thereof: but they colde not declare the interpretacion of the
thing.
16 Then heard I of thee, that thou coldest
shewe interpretacions, and dissolue doutes: now if thou canst read the writing, &
shewe me the interpretacion thereof, thou
shalt be clothed with purple, & *shalt haue* a
chaine of golde about thy necke, and shalt
be the third ruler in the kingdome.
17 Then Daniél answered, and said before
the King, Kepe thy rewardes to thy self, &
giue thy giftes to another: yet I wil read
the writing vnto the King and shewe him
the interpretacion.
18 O King, *heare* thou, The moste high
God gaue vnto [l] Nebuchad-nezzár thy
father a kingdome, and maiestie and honour and glorie.
19 And for the maiestie that he gaue him, all
people, nations, and langages trembled, &
feared before him: he put to death whome
he wolde: he smote whome he wolde: whome he wolde he set vp, & whome he wolde
he put downe.
20 But when his heart was puft vp, and his
minde hardened in pride, he was deposed
from his kinglie throne, and they toke his
honour from him.
21 And he was driuen from the sonnes of
men, & his heart was made like the beasts,
and his dwelling was with the wilde asses:
they fed him with grasse like oxen, and
his bodie was wet with the dewe of the
heauen, til he knewe, that the moste high
God bare rule ouer the kingdome of mẽ,
and that he appointeth ouer it, whome soeuer he pleaseth.
22 And thou his sonne, ô Belshazzár, hast
not hũbled thine heart, thogh thou knewest all these things,
23 But hast lift thy self vp against the Lord
of heauen, and they haue broght the vessels
of his House before thee, & thou and thy
princes, thy wiues and thy concubines

a Daniél reciteth this historie of King Belshazzár Euilmerodachs sonne, to shewe Gods iudgements against the wicked, for the deliuerance of his Church, and how the prophecie of Ieremiáh was true, that they shulde be deliuered after seuentie yeres.

b The Kings of the East partes then vsed to sit alone cõmunely, & disdained ẏ anie shulde sit in their cõpanie: and now to shewe his power, & how litle he set by his enemie, ẇ then besieged Babylon, he made a solemne banket, & vsed excesse in their cõpanie which is mẽt here by drinking wine: thus the wicked are moste dissolute, and negligent whẽ their destructiõ is at hãd.

* Or, ouercome with wine.

c Meaning his grand father.

d In contempt of the true God they praised their idoles, not ẏ they thoght, that ẏ golde or siluer were gods, but that there was a certeine vertue, and power in them to do them good, ẇ is also the opinion of all idolaters.

e That it might the better be sene.

f So he that before contẽned God, was moued by this sight to tremble for feare of Gods iudgements.

g Thus the wicked in their troubles seke manie meanes, who drawe them frõ God, because they seke not to him who is the onelie comfort in all afflictiõs.

h To wit, his grand mother Nebuchad-nezzars wife, which for her age was not before at the feast, but came thether when she heard of these strãge newes.

i Read Chap. 4. 6. and this declareth, that bothe this name was odious vnto him, and also that he did not vse these vile practises, because he was not among them when all were called.

k For the idolaters thoght, that ẏ Angels had power as God, and therefore had thẽ in like estimation, as they had God, thinking that the spirit of prophecie, & vnderstanding came of them.

l Before he red the writing, he declareth to ẏ King his great ingratitude toward God, who colde not be moued to giue hĩ the glorie, considering his wonderful worke toward his grand father, & so sheweth, that he doeth not sinne of ignorance, but of malice.

haue drunke wine in them , and thou hast
praised the gods of siluer and golde, of
brasse,yron, wood and stone,which nether
se, nether heare , nor vnderstand:and the
God in whose hand thy breath is and all
thy wayes , him hast thou not glorified.
24 [m] Then was the palme of the hand sent
from him,and hathe writen this writing.
25 And this is the writing that he hathe
writen,[n] MENE, MENE, TEKEL
VPHARSIN.
26 This is the interpretacion of the thing,
MENE,God hathe nôbred thy kingdome,
and hathe finished it:
27 TEKEL, thou art wayed in the balance,and art founde″ to light.
28 PERES,thy kingdome is diuided , and
giuen to the Medes and Persians.
29 Then at the commandement of Belshazzár they clothed Daniél with purple,
and *put* a chaine of golde about his necke,
and made a proclamacion cócerning him
that he shulde be the thirde ruler in the
kingdome.
30 The same night was Belshazzár ẏ King
of the Caldeans slaine.
31 And Darius [o] of the Medes toke ẏ kingdome,being threscore and two yere olde.

m After that God had so long time deferred his angre,& paciētly waited for thine amendemēt.
n This worde is twise writē for the certeintie of ẏ thing: shewing, that God had moste surely coúted: signifying also that God hathe appointed a terme for all kingdomes, & ẏ a miserable end shal come on all that raise them selues against him.
″Or, wanting.
o Cyrus his sonne in lawe gaue him this title of honour althogh Cyrus in effect had ẏ dominion.

CHAP. VI.

1 Daniél is made ruler ouer the gouerners. 5 An acte against Daniél. 16 He is put into a denne of lyons by the commandement of the King. 23 He is deliuered by faith in God. 24 Daniels accusers are put vnto the lyons. 25 Darius by a decre magnifieth the God of Daniél.

1 IT pleased Darius to set ouer the kingdome [a] an hundreth and twentie gouer
nours,which shulde be ouer ẏ whole kingdome.
2 And ouer these,thre rulers(of whome Da
niél was one) that the gouernours might
giue accompts vnto them, and the King
shulde″ haue no domage.
3 Now this Daniél [b] was preferred aboue
the rulers and gouernours,because the spirit was excellent in him , and the King
thoght to set him ouer the whole realme.
4 ¶Wherefore the rulers and gouernours
[c] soght an occasion against Daniél concer
ning the kingdome : but they colde finde
none occasiô nor faute:for he was so faithful that there was no blame nor faute founde in him.
5 Then said these mē,We shal not finde an
occasion against this Daniél,except we
finde it against him concerning the Law
of his God.
6 Therefore the rulers and these gouernours went together to the King,and said
thus vnto him,King Darius,liue for euer.
7 All the rulers of thy kingdome the officers and gouernours , the counsellers, and
dukes haue consulted together to make
a decre for the King and to establish a statute, that whosoeuer shal aske a peticion
of anie god or man for thirtie dayes saue
of thee,ô King,he shalbe cast into the denne of lyons.
8 Now,ô King,cófirme the decre, and seale the writing, that it be not changed according to the law of the Medes and Persians,which altereth not.
9 Wherefore King Darius [d] sealed the
writing and the decre.
10 ¶Now when Daniél vnderstode that he
had sealed the writing , he went into his
house,and his [e] windowe being open in his
chamber toward Ierusalém , he kneeled
vpon his knees thre times a day,& prayed
and praised his God,as he did afore time.
11 Then these men assembled, and founde
Daniél praying,and making supplicacion
vnto his God.
12 So they came, and spake vnto the King
concerning the Kings decre, Hast thou
not sealed the decre, that euerie man that
shal make request to anie god or mā within thirtie dayes, saue to thee, ô King,
shalbe cast into the denne of lyons? The
King answered ,and said, The thing is
true, according to the law of the Medes
and Persians,which altereth not.
13 Then answered they , and said vnto the
King, This Daniél which is of the children of the captiuitie of Iudáh, regardeth
not thee,ô King, nor the decre, that thou
hast sealed, but maketh his peticion thre
times a day.
14 When the King heard these wordes,he
was sore displeased with him self, and set
his heart on Daniél, to deliuer him : and
he laboured til the sunne went downe, to
deliuer him.
15 Then these men assembled vnto the
King , and said vnto the King , Vnderstand,ô King, that the law of the Medes
and Persians *is*, that no decre nor statute,
which the King confirmeth, may be [f] altered.
16 ¶Then the King commanded, and they
broght Daniél, and cast him into the denne of lyons: *now* the King spake, and said
vnto Daniél, Thy God, whome thou alway seruest, *euen* he wil deliuer thee.
17 And a stone was broght,and layed vpon
the mouthe of the denne , and the King
sealed it with his owne signet, & with the
signet of his princes, that the purpose
might not be changed,cócerning Daniél.
18 Then the King went vnto his palace,
and remained fasting, nether were the instruments of musicke broght before him,
and his slepe went from him.
19 ¶Then the King arose early in the morning , and went in all haste vnto the denne
of lyons.

a Read Estér Chap.1,1.
″Or, not be troubled.
b This heathē King preferred Daniél a stranger to all his nobles & familiars , because the graces of God were more excellent in him then in others.
c Thus the wicked cā not abide the graces of God in others, but seke by all occasions to deface them: therefore against suche assaltes there is no better remedie then to walke vprightly in ẏ feare of God, and to haue a good conscience.
d Herein is cōdemned the wickednes of the King, who wolde be set vp as a god,& passed not what wicked lawes he approued for the maintenāce of the same.
e Because he wolde not by his silēce shew that he consented to this wicked decre , he set open his windowes towarde Ierusalém, when he prayed: bothe to stirre vp hī self with the remembrance of Gods promises to his people when they shulde pray towarde that Temple,& also ẏ others might se that he wolde nether consent in heart nor dede for these fewe dayes to anie thing that was contrarie to Gods glorie.
f Thus the wicked mainteine euil laws by constancie, and autoritie, which is oft times ether lightenes , or stubbernes when as the innocents thereby perish: & therefore gouernours nether oght to feare nor be ashamed to breake suche.

20 And when he came to the denne, he cryed with a lamentable voyce vnto Daniél:
& the King spake, and said to Daniél, O
Daniél, the seruant of the liuing God, is
not thy God (whome thou alwaie seruest)
[g] able to deliuer thee from the lions?
21 Then said Daniél vnto ẏ King, O King,
liue for euer.
22 My God hathe sent his Angel and hathe
shut the lions mouthes, that thei haue not
hurt me: for [h] my iustice was found out be
fore him: & vnto thee, ô King, I haue done
[i] no hurte.
23 Then was the King exceading glad for
him, and cōmāded that thei shulde take
Daniél out of the denne: so Daniél was
broght out of the denne, and no maner of
hurte was founde vpon him, because he
[k] beleued in his God.
24 And by the commandement of the Kĩg
these men which had accused Daniél, were
broght, & were [l] cast into ẏ denne of lions,
euen thei, their children, and their wiues:
and the lions had the mastrie of them, and
brake all their bones a pieces, or euer thei
came at the grounde of the denne.
25 ¶ Afterwarde King Darius wrote, Vnto
all people, nations & langages, that dwell
in all the worlde: Peace be multiplied vnto you.
26 I make a decre that in all the dominion
of my kingdome, men tremble and feare
[m] before the God of Daniél: for he is the
[n] liuing God, and remaineth for euer: and
his kingdome shal not perish, and his dominion *shalbe* euerlasting.
27 He rescueth and deliuereth, & he worketh signes and wonders in heauen & in
earth: who hathe deliuered Daniél from
the power of the lyons.
28 So this Daniél prospered in ẏ reigne of
Darius & in ẏ reigne of Cyrus of Persia.

g This declareth that Darius was not touched with ẏ true knowledge of God, because he douted of his power.
h My iuste cause, and vprightnes in this thing, wherein I was charged, is approued of God
i For he did disobey the Kings wicked commandemēt to obey God, and so did no iniurie to the King who oght to commande nothing, whereby God shulde be dishonored.
k Because he cōmitted him self wholy vnto God whose cause he did defend, he was assured, ẏ nothĩg but good colde come vnto him: wherein we se the power of faith, as Ebr. 11, 33.
l This is a terrible example against all the wicked, which do agaĩst their conscience make cruel lawes to destroye the childrē of God & also admonisheth princes how to punish such, whē their wickednes is come to light: though not in euerie point or with like circumstāces, yet to execute true iustice vpon them.

m This proueth not that Darius did worship God aright, or els was conuerted: for then he wolde haue destroyed all superstition and idolatrie, & not onely giuen God the chief place, but onely haue set him vp, and caused him to be honored according to his worde: but this was a certeine cōfession of Gods power, whereunto he was compelled by this wonderful miracle n Which hathe not onely life in him self, but is the onelie fountaine of life, & quickeneth all things, so that without him there is no life.

CHAP. VII.

3 *A vision of foure beastes is shewed vnto Daniél·*
8 *The ten hornes of the fourth beast.* 27 *Of the euerla-*
sting kingdome of Christ.

1 IN the first yere of Belshazzár King of
Babél, Daniél sawe a dreame, and there
were visions in his head, vpon his bed:
[a] then he wrote the dreame, & declared ẏ
summe of the matter.
2 Daniél spake and said, I sawe in my vision
by night, and beholde, the foure windes of
the heauen stroue vpon [b] the great sea:
3 And foure great beastes came vp from
the sea one diuers from another.
4 The first *was* as a [c] lion, and had egles
wings: I behelde, til the wings thereof
were plukte of, and it was lifted vp from
the earth, and set vpon *his* fete as a man,
and a mans heart was giuen him.
5 And beholde, another beast *which was* the
seconde, was like a [d] beare and stode vpon
the [e] one side: and he had thre ribbes in his
[f] mouth betwene his teeth, [g] and thei said
thus vnto him, Arise & deuoure muche
flesh.
6 After this I behelde, and lo, there *was* an
other like a [h] leopard, which had vpon his
backe [i] foure wings of a foule: the beast
had also foure heads, and [k] dominion was
giuen him.
7 After this I sawe in the visions by night,
& beholde, the [l] fourth beast *was* fearful
and terrible and verie strong. It had great
[m] yrō teeth: it deuoured & brake in pieces
and stamped [n] the residue vnder his fete: &
it was vnlike to the beastes that were before it: for it had [o] ten hornes.
8 As I considered the hornes, beholde,
there came vp among them another litle
[p] horne, before whome there were [q] thre
of the first hornes plukt awaie: & beholde,
in this horne *were* [r] eyes like the eyes of
man, and a mouthe speaking presumptious
things.
9 I behelde, til the [s] thrones were set vp,
and the [t] Ancient of daies did sit, whose
garment was white as snowe, and the heere

a Where as the people of Israél loked for a continual quietnes after these seuentie yeres, as Ieremiáh had declared, he sheweth that this rest shal not be a deliuerance from all troubles, but a beginning, & therefore incouraged thē to loke for a continual affliction til the Messiáh be vttered and reuciled, by whome they shulde haue a spiritual deliuerance, and all the promises fulfilled: whereof they shulde haue a certeine token in the destruction of the Babylonical kingdome.

b Which signified ẏ there shulde be horrible troubles and afflictions in the worlde in all corners of the worlde and at sondrie times
c Meaning the Assyrian and Caldean empire, ẇ was moste strong & fierce in power, and moste sone come to their autoritie as thogh thei had had wĩgs to flye: yet their wings were pulled by the Persians, & thei wēt on their feet, and were made like other men which is here ment by mans heart.
d Meaning the Persians, which were barbarous and cruel.
e Thei were smale in ẏ beginning and were shut vp in their mountaines and had no brute.
f That is, destroyed many kingdomes, & was insaciable.
g To wit, the Angels by Gods commãdement, who by this meanes punished ẏ ingratitude of the worlde.

h Meaning, Alexander the King of Macedonie. i That is, his foure chief captaines, which had the empire among them after his death. Seleucus had Asia the great, Antigonus the lesse, Cassander, and after him Antipater was King of Macedonie, and Ptolomeus had Egypt. k It was not of him self nor of his owne power that he gate all these countreis: for his armie conteined, but thirtie thousand men, and he ouercame in one battel Darius, which had ten hundreth thousand, when he was so heauie with slepe that his eyes were scarse open, as the stories reporte: therefore this power was giuen him of God. l That is, the Romain empire which was as a monster & colde not be cōpared to anie beast, because the nature of none was able to expresse it m Signifying the tyrannie and griedines of the Romains. n That which the Romains colde not quietly enioie in other countreis, thei wolde giue it to other Kings and rulers that at all times when thei wolde, thei might take it againe: which liberalitie is here called the stamping of the rest vnder the fete. o That is, sondrie and diuers prouinces which were gouerned by the deputies and proconsuls, whereof euerie one might be compared to a King. p Which is ment of Iulius Cesar, Augustus, Tiberius, Caligula, Claudius, and Nero &c. who were as Kings in effect, but because thei colde not rule, but by the consent of the Senat, their power is compared to a litle horne. For Mahomet came not of the Romaine empire, and the Pope hathe no vocacion of gouernement: therefore this can not be applied vnto them. and also in this prophecie the Prophets purpose is chiefly to comfort the Iewes vnto the reuelation of Christ. Some take it for the whole bodie of Antichrist q Meaning, a certeine portion of the ten hornes: that is, a parte from the whole estate was pluckt awaie For Augustus toke from the Senat the libertie of chosing the deputes to send into the prouinces, and toke the gouernement of certeine countreis to him self. r These Romaine Emperours at the first vsed a certeine humanitie and gentlenes, and were content that others as the Consuls and Senat shulde beare the name of dignitie, so that thei might haue the profite, and therefore in elections and counsels wolde behaue them selues according as did other Senatours: yet against their enemies and those that wolde resist them, thei were fierce and cruel, which is here ment by the proud mouth. s Meaning the places where God and his Angels shulde come to iudge these monarchies, which iudgement shulde beginne at the first comming of Christ. t That is, God which was before all times, and is here described as mans nature is able to comprehend some portion of his glorie.

of his head like the pure woll: his throne
was like the fyrie flame, *&* his wheles *as*
burning fyre.
10 A fyrie streame yssued, and came forthe
from before him: thousand thousands ministred vnto him, and ten thousand [u]thou-
sands stode before him: the iudgement
was set, and the [x] bokes opened.
11 Then I behelde, [y] because of the voyce
of the presumpteous wordes, which the
horne spake: I behelde, euen til the beast
was slaine, and his bodie destroyed, and
giuen to the burning fyre.
12 As [z] concerning the other beastes, thei
had taken awaie their dominion: yet their
liues were prolonged for a certeine time
and season.
13 ¶ As I behelde in visions by night, beholde, [a] one like the Sonne of man came in
the cloudes of heauen, and [b] approched
vnto the Ancient of daies, & thei broght
him before him.
14 And he gaue him [c] dominion, & honour,
and a kingdome, that all people, nations
and langages shulde serue him: his dominion *is* an euerlasting dominion, which
shal neuer be taken awaie: and his kingdome shal neuer be destroied.
15 ¶ I Daniél was [d] troubled in my spirit,
in the middes of my bodie, and the visions of mine head made me afraied.
16 Therefore I came vnto [e] one of them
that stode by, and asked him the trueth of
all this: so he tolde me, and shewed me the
interpretacion of these things.
17 These great beastes which are foure, *are*
foure Kings, which shal arise out of the
earth,
18 And thei shal take the [f] kingdome of the
Sainctes of the [g] moste high, and possesse
the kingdome for euer, euen for euer and
euer.
19 ¶ After this, I wolde *knowe* the trueth of
the fourth beast, wͨ was so [h] vnlike to all
the others, very feareful, whose teeth were
of yron, and his nailes of brasse: *which* deuoured, brake in pieces, and stamped the
[i] residue vnder his fete.
20 Also *to knowe* of the ten hornes that were in his head, & of the other which came
vp, before whome thre fell, and of the horne that had eyes, and of the mouth that
spake presumpteous things, whose [k] loke
was more stoute then his felowes.
21 I behelde, & the same [l] horne made battel against the Sainctes, yea, and preuailed
against them,
22 Vntil [m] the Ancient of daies came, and
iudgement was giuen to the Sainctes of
the moste high: and the time approched,
that the Sainctes possessed the kingdome.
23 Thẽ he said, The fourth beast shalbe the
fourth kingdome in the earth, which shal
be vnlike to all the kingdomes, and shal
deuoure the whole earth, and shal treade
it downe and breake it in pieces.
24 And the ten hornes out of this kingdome *are* ten Kings that shal rise: & another
shal rise after thẽ, and he shalbe vnlike to
the first, and he shal subdue [n] thre Kings,
25 And shal speake wordes against [o] the
moste high, & shal cõsume the Sainctes of
the moste high, & thinke yͭ he maie [p] change times and lawes, and thei shalbe giuen
into his hand, vntil a [q] time, and times &
the deuiding of time.
26 But the [r] iudgement shal sit, & thei shal
take awaie his dominion, to consume and
destroie it vnto the end.
27 And the [s] kingdome, and dominion, and
the greatnes of the kingdome vnder yͤ who
le heauen shalbe giuen to the holie people
of the moste high, whose kingdome *is* an
euerlasting kingdome & all [t] powers shal
serue and obeie him.
28 Euen this is the end of the matter, I Daniél had manie [u] cogitacions *which* troubled me, and my countenance changed in
me: but I kept the matter in mine heart.

u That is, an infinit nomber of Angels, wͨ were ready to execute his commandement.
x This is ment of the first cõming of Christ when as yͤ wil of God was plainely reueiled by his Gospel.
y Meaning, yͭ he was astonied, when he sawe these Emperours in suche dignitie, & pride, & so suddely destroyed at the cõming of Christ whẽ this fourth monarchie was subiect to men of other nacions.
z As the thre former monarchies had an end at the time that God appointed, althogh thei flourished for a time, so shal this fourth haue & they that paciently abide Gods appoitement, shal inioye the promises.
a Which is ment of Christ who had not yet taken vpon him mãs nature, nether was the sonne of Dauid according to yͤ flesh, as he was afterwarde: but appeared then in a figure, and that in yͤ cloudes: that is, being separate from the commune sorte of men by manifeste signes of his diuinitie.
b To wit, whẽ he ascended into the heauens, and his diuine maiestie appeared, and all power was giuẽ vnto him in respect of that that he was our Mediator.
c This is ment of the beginning of Christs kingdome when God the Father gaue vnto him all dominion, as to the Mediator, to the intent that he shulde gouerne here his Church in earth continually til the time that he broght thẽ to eternal life.
d Through the strãgenes of the vision.
e Meaning, of the Angels, as ver. 10.
f Because Abrahám was appointed heire of all yͤ worlde Ro. 4, 13 & in him all the faithful, therefore yͤ kingdome thereof is theirs by right, which these foure beastes or tyrants shulde inuade, and vsurpe vntil the worlde were restored by Christ: and this was to confirme them that were in troubles, that their afflictiõs shulde haue an end at lẽgth.
g That is, of the moste hie things, because God hathe chosen them out of this worlde, yͭ they shulde loke vp to the heauens, whereon all their hope dependeth.
h For the other thre monarchies were gouerned by a King, and the Romain empire by Consuls: the Romains changed their gouernours yerely, & the other monarchies reteined them for terme of life: also the Romains were the strongest of all the other, and were neuer quiet amõg them selues.
i Read vers. 7.

k This is mẽt of the fourthe beast, which was more terrible then the other.
l Meaning the Romaine Emperours who were moste cruel against the Church of God bothe of the Iewes and of yͤ Gentiles.
m Til God shewed his power in the persone of Christ, and by the preaching of the Gospel gaue vnto his some rest & so obteined a famous name in the worlde, and were called yͤ Church of God, or the kingdome of God.
n Read the exposition hereof, ver. 8.
o That is, shal make wicked decrees & proclamations against Gods worde and sende through out all their dominiõ to destroy all that did professe it.
p These Emperours shal not consider yͭ thei haue their power of God but thinke it is in their owne power to change Gods lawes and mans, and as it were yͤ order of nature, as appeareth by Octauius, Tyberius Caligula, Nero, Domitianus &c.
q God shal suffre them thus to rage against his Saincts for a long time, which is ment by the time and times but at lẽgth he wil aswage these troubles and shorten the times for his elects sake, Mat. 24, 22 which is here ment by the diuiding of time.
r God by his power shal restore things that were out of order, and so destroie this litle horne, that it shal neuer rise vp againe.
s He sheweth wherefore the beast shulde be destroied, to wit, that his Church might haue rest and quietnes, which thogh thei do not fully inioye here, yet thei haue it in hope and by the preaching of the Gospel enioye the beginning thereof, which is mẽt by these wordes *vnder the heauen*: & therefore he here speaketh of yͤ beginnĩg of Christs kingdome in this worlde, which kingdome yͤ faithful haue by the participation that thei haue with Christ their head.
t That is, some of euerie sorte that beare rule.
u Thogh he had manie motions in his heart yͭ moued him to and fro to seke out this matter curiously: yet he was content with that which God reueiled, and kept it in memorie and wrote it for the vse of the Church.

CHAP. VIII.

A vision of a battel betwene a ramme and a goat.
20 The vnderstanding of the vision.

1 IN the thirde yere of the reigne of
King Belshazzár, a vision appeared
vnto me, *euen* vnto me Daniél, [a] after that
which appeared vnto me at the first.
2 And I sawe in a vision, & when I sawe it,
I was in the palace of Shushán, which is in
the prouince [b] of Elám, & in a vision me-

a After the general vision, he cometh to certeine particular visions: as touching yͤ destruction of the monarchie of the Persians, and Macedonians: for the ruine of the Babylonians was at hand, and also he had sufficiently spoken thereof.
b That is, of Persia.

thoght I was by the riuer of Vlái.
3 Then I loked vp and sawe, and beholde,
there stode before the riuer a [c] râme, which
had two hornes: and these two hornes *we-*
re hie: but one was [d] hier then another, &
the hiest came vp last.
4 I sawe the ram pusshing against ỹ West
and against the North, and against the
South: so that no [e] beastes might stande
before him, nor colde deliuer out of his
hand, but he did what he listed, and became great.
5 And as I considered, beholde, [f] a goat came from the West ouer the whole earth, &
touched not the grounde: & this goat *had*
an [g] horne that appeared betwene his eyes.
6 And he came vnto the ram that had the
two hornes, whome I had sene standing by
the riuer, and ranne vnto him in his fierce
rage.
7 And I sawe him come vnto the ramme, &
being moued against him, he [h] smote the
ramme, and brak his two hornes: & there
was no power in the râme to stand against
him, but he cast him downe to the groúde,
and stamped vpon him, & there was none
that colde deliuer the ramme out of his
power.
8 Therefore ỹ goat waxed exceadĩg great,
and when he was at the strongest, his great
[i] horne was broken: and for it came vp foure that [k] appeared towarde the foure windes of the heauen.
9 And out of one of them came forthe [l] a
litle horne, which waxed very great towarde the [m] South, and towarde the [n] East,
and towarde the [o] pleasant *land*.
10 Yea, it grewe vp vnto the [p] hoste of heauen, and it cast downe *some* of the hoste, &
of the starres to the grounde, and trode
vpon them,
11 And extolled him self against the [q] prince of the hoste from whome the [r] dailie *sa-*
crifice was taken away, and the place of his
Sanctuarie was cast downe.
12 And [s] a time shalbe giuẽ *him* ouer the dai
lie *sacrifice* for the iniquitie: & it shal [t] cast
downe the trueth to the grounde, & thus
shal it do, and prosper.
13 Then I heard one of the [u] Sainctes speaking, & one of ỹ Sainctes spake vnto a cer

c Which represented the kingdome of the Persians, and Medes, which were ioyned together.
d Meaning Cyrus, which after grewe greater ĩ power then Darius his vncle and father in lawe.
e That is, no Kings or nations.
f Meaning, Alexander that came frõ Grecia with great spede and expedition.
g Thogh he came in the name of all Grecia, yet he bare the title & dignitie of the general captaine, so that the strength was attributed to him, which is ment by this horne.
h Alexander ouercame Darius in two sondry battels, and so had ỹ two kingdomes of the Medes and Persians
i Alexanders great power was broken: for when he had ouercome all ỹ East, he thoght to returne towarde Grecia to subdue them that there had rebelled, and so dyed by the way
k That is, ŵ were famous: for almoste in the space of fiftene yere there were fiftene diuers successours before this monarchie was deuided to these foure, whereof Cassander had Macedonia, Seleucus, Syria, Antigonus Asia the lesse, and Ptolomeus Egypt
l Which was Antiochus Epiphanes, who was of a seruile and flattering nature, and also there were other betwene him & the kingdome, and therefore is here called the litle horne, because nether princelie conditions, nor any other thing was in him, why he shulde obteine this kingdome.
m That is, toward Egypt.
n Whereby he meaneth Ptolomais.
o That is, Iudea.
p Antiochus raged against the elect of God, and trod his precious starres vnder fete which are so called, because they are separated from the worlde
q That is, God, who gouerneth and mainteineth his Church.
r He labored to abolish all religion, & therefore cast Gods seruice out of his Temple, which God had chosen as a litle corner from all the rest of ỹ worlde to haue his Name there truely called vpon
s He sheweth that their sinnes are the cause of these horrible afflictions; and yet comforteth them, in that he appointeth this tyrant a time, whome he wolde not suffer vtterly to abolish his religion.
t This horne shal abolish for a time ỹ true doctrine & so corrupt Gods seruice.
u Meaning, ỹ he heard one of the Angels asking this question of Christ, whome he calleth a certeine one or a secret one, or a marueilous one.

teine one, saying, How long *shal endure* the
vision of the daiely *sacrifice*, and the iniqui
tie of the [x] desolation to tread bothe the
Sanctuarie and the [y] armie vnder fote?
14 And [z] he answered me, Vnto the [a] euening *and* the morning, two thousand and
thre hundreth: then shal the Sanctuarie be
clensed.
15 ¶ Now when I Daniél had sene the vision, and soght for the meaning, beholde,
there stode before me [b] like the similitude
of a man.
16 And I heard a mans voyce betwene *the*
bankes of Vlái, which called and said, Gabriél, [c] make this man to vnderstand the
vision.
17 So he came where I stode: and when he
came, I was afraied, and fel vpon my face:
but he said vnto me, Vnderstand, ô sonne
of man: for [d] in the last time *shalbe* the
vision.
18 Now as he was speaking vnto me, I
being a slepe *fel* on my face to the grounde: but he touched me, and set me vp in
my place.
19 And he said, Beholde, I wil shewe thee
what shal be in the last [e] wrath: for in the
end of the time appointed *it shal come*.
20 The ramme which thou sawest hauing
two hornes, *are* the Kings of the Medes &
Persians.
21 And the goat *is* the King of Grecia, &
the great horne that is betwene his eies, is
the first King.
22 And that that is broken, and foure stode vp for it, *are* foure kingdomes, which
shal stand vp [f] of that nacion, but not [g] in
his strength.
23 And in the end of their kingdome, when
the rebellious shalbe consumed, a King of
[h] fierce countenance, and vnderstanding
darke sentences, shal stand vp.
24 And his power shalbe mightie, but not
[i] in his strength: and he shal destroie won
derfully, & shal prosper, and practise, and
shal destroie the [k] mightie, and the holy
people.
25 And through his [l] policie also, he shal
cause craft to prosper in his hand, and he
shal extoll him self in his heart, and by
[m] peace shal destroy many: he shal also
stand vp against the [n] prince of princes,
but he shal be broken downe [o] without
hand.
26 And the vision of the [p] euening and the
morning, which is declared, is true: therefore seale thou vp the vision, for it *shalbe*
after many daies.
27 And I Daniél was striken & sicke [q] *cer-*
teine daies: but when I rose vp, I did the
Kings busines, and I was astonished at the
vision, but none vnderstode it.

x That is, the Iewes sinnes, which were cause of this destruction.
y That is, ŵ suppresseth Gods religiõ, & his people.
z Christ answered me for the comforte of ỹ Church.
a That is, vnto so many natural daies be past, which make six yeres thre moneths & an half: for so long vnder Antiochus was the Temple prophaned.
b Which was Christ, who in this maner declared him selfe to the olde fathers how he wolde be God manifested in flesh.
c This power to commande the Angel, declared that he was God.
d The effect of this vision shal not yet appeare, but a long time after.
e Meaning ỹ great rage ŵ Antiochus shulde shewe against the Church.
f That is, out of Grecia.
g They shal not haue like power as had Alexander.
h Noting that this Antiochus was impudent and cruel, and also craftie that he colde not be deceiued.
i That is, not like Alexãders strength.
k Bothe ỹ Gẽtils that dwel about him, & also ỹ Iewes.
l What soeuer he goeth about by his craft, he shal bring it to passe
m That is, vnder pretence of peace or as if were in sporte.
n Meaning, against God.
o For God wolde destroy him with a notable plague, & so comforte his Church, 2. Mac. 9, 9.
p Read vers. 14
q For feare & astonishmẽt.

CHAP. IX.

3 Daniél desireth to haue that performed of God, which he had promised concerning the returne of the people from their banishment in Babylon. 5 A true confession. 20 Daniels prayer is heard. 21 Gabriél the Angel expoundeth vnto him the vision of the seuentie weekes. 24 The anointing of Christ. 25 The buylding againe of Ierusalém. 26 The death of Christ.

1 IN the first yere of Darius the sonne of
[a] Ahashuerósh, of ỹ sede of the Medes,
which was made King ouer the [b] realme
of the Caldeans,
2 *Euen* in the first yere of his reigne, I Daniél vnderstode by [c] bokes the nombre of
the yeres, whereof the Lord had spoken
vnto Ieremiáh the Prophet, that he wolde accomplish seuentie yeres in the desolation of Ierusalém.
3 And I turned my face vnto the Lord
God, and [d] soght by praier and supplicacions with fasting & sackecloth & ashes.
4 And I praied vnto the Lord my God, &
made my confession, saying, Oh Lord
God, *which art* [e] great and feareful, and kepest couenant and mercie toward them
which loue " thee, & toward them ỹ kepe
thy commandements,
5 We haue sinned, & haue cōmitted iniquitie & haue done wickedly, yea, we haue rebelled, and haue departed frō thy precep-
tes, and from thy iudgements.
6 For we wolde not obei thy seruants the
Prophetes, which spake in thy Name to
our Kings, to our princes, & to our fathers,
and to all the people of the land.
7 O Lord, [f] righteousnes belōgeth vnto thee,
and vnto vs " open shame, as *appeareth* this
day vnto euerie man of Iudáh, and to the
inhabitants of Ierusalém: yea, vnto all Israél, *bothe* nere and farre of, through all the
countreis, whether thou hast driuen them,
because of their offenses, that thei haue
committed against thee.
8 O Lord, vnto vs *apperteineth* open shame,
to our [g] Kings, to our princes, and to our
fathers, because we haue sinned against
thee.
9 *Yet* compassion and forgiuenes *is* in the
Lord our God, albeit we haue rebelled a-
gainst him.
10 For we haue not obeied ỹ [h] voice of the
Lord our God, to walke in his lawes, which
he had laid before vs by the ministerie of
his seruants the Prophetes.
11 Yea, all Israél haue transgressed thy
Lawe, and are turned backe, and haue not
heard thy voice: therefore the [i] cursse is
powred vpon vs, & the othe that is writen
in the lawe of Mosés the seruant of God,
because we haue sinned against him.
12 And he hathe cōfirmed his wordes, which
he spake against vs, and against our iudges that " iudged vs, by bringing vpon vs
a great plague: for vnder the whole heauen hathe not bene the like, as hathe bene
broght vpon Ierusalém.
13 All this plague is come vpon vs, as it is
writen in the Lawe of Mosés: yet made
we not our prayer before the Lord our
God, that we might turne from our iniqui
ties and vnderstand thy trueth.
14 Therefore hathe the Lord " made readie
the plague, and broght it vpon vs: for the
Lord our God is righteous in all his workes which he doeth: for we wolde not heare his voice.
15 * And now, ô Lord our God, that hast
broght thy people out of ỹ land of Egypt
with a mightie hand, and hast gotten thee
renoume, as *appeareth* this day, we haue sinned, we haue done wickedly.
16 O Lord, according to all thy [k] righteousnes, I beseche thee, let thine angre and
thy wrath be turned away from thy citie
Ierusalém thine holy Moūtaine: for becau
se of our sinnes, & for the iniquities of our
fathers, Ierusalém and thy people *are* a reproche to all *that are* about vs.
17 Now therefore, ô our God, heare the
prayer of thy seruant, and his supplicacions, and cause thy face to [l] shine vpon
thy Sanctuarie, that lyeth waste for the
[m] Lords sake.
18 O my God, encline thine eare and heare: open thine eies, and beholde our desolations, and the citie whereupon thy Name is called: for we do not present our
supplicacions before thee for our owne-
[n] righteousnes, but for thy great tendre
mercies.
19 O Lord, heare, ô Lord forgiue, ô Lord
[o] consider, and do it: differre not, for thine
owne sake, ô my God: for thy Name is
called vpon thy citie, and vpon thy people.
20 ¶ And whiles I was speaking & praying,
and confessing my sinne, and the sinne of
my people Israél, and did present my
supplicacion before the Lord my God,
for the holy Mountaine of my God,
21 Yea, while I was speaking in praier, euen
the man * Gabriél, whome I had sene before in the vision, came flying, and touched me about the time of the euening
oblacion.
22 And he informed *me*, and talked with
me, and said, O Daniél, I am now come forthe to giue thee knowledge & vnderstanding.
23 At the beginning of thy supplicacions
the commādement came forthe, and I am
come to shewe *thee*, for thou art greatly
beloued: therefore vnderstand the matter
and consider the vision.

24 Seuentie

a Who was also called Astyages.
b For Cyrus led with ambitiō, wēt about warres in other coūtreis, and therefore Darius had ỹ title of ỹ kingdome, thogh Cyrus was King in effect.
c For thogh he was an excellēt Prophet, yet he daily increased ī knowledge by reading of ỹ Scriptures.
d He speaketh not of that ordinarie praier, which he vsed in his house thrise a day, but of a rare and vehement prayer, lest their sinnes shulde cause God to delay the time of their deliuerāce prophecied by Ieremiáh.
e That is, hast all power in thy selfe to execute thy terrible iudgemētes against obstinat sinners, as ỹ art riche in mercie to cōfort thē, which obey thy worde & loue thee.
" *Ebr. him.*
f He sheweth that whensoeuer God punisheth, he doeth it for iuste cause: and thus ỹ godlie neuer accuse him of rigour as the wicked do, but acknowledge ỹ in them selues there is iuste cause, why he shulde so intreat them.
" *Ebr. confusion of face.*
g He doeth not excuse ỹ Kīgs because of their autoritie, but praieth chiefly for thē as ỹ chief occasions of these great plagues.
h He sheweth that they rebell against God, which serue him not according to his cōmandemēt & worde.
i As Deu. 27, 15. or the cursse confirmed by an othe.
" *Or, gouerned vs.*
" *Ebr. watched vpon the euil.*
Exod. 14, 28. baru. 2, 11.
k That is, according to all thy merciful promises and the performance thereof.
l Shewe thy selfe fauorable.
m That is, for thy Christs sake in whome ỹ wilt accept all our praiers
n Declaring, ỹ the godlie flee onely vnto Gods mercies and renounce their owne workes when they seke for remission of their sinnes.
o Thus he colde not content him selfe ẃ any vehemencie of wordes: for he was so led with a feruent zeale considering Gods promes, made to the citie in respect of his Church & for ỹ aduancemēt of Gods glorie
Cha. 8, 16.

24 Seventie [p] wekes are determined vpon
[q] thy people and vpon thine holie citie, to
finish the wickednes, and to seale vp the
[r] sinnes, and to reconcile the iniquitie, and
to bring in euerlasting righteousnes, and
to seale vp the vision and prophecie, and
to anoint the moste Holie.
25 Knowe therefore and vnderstand, that
from [ſ] the going forthe of the commandement to bring againe *the people*, and to
builde Ierusalē, vnto Messiah the prince,
shalbe seuen [t] wekes, and thre sore and two
wekes, & the strete shalbe built againe, &
the wall euen in a ″ troublous time.
26 And after thre score & two [u] wekes, shal
Messiah be slayne, and shal [x] haue nothīg,
& the people of [y] the prince that shal come, shal destroye the citie and the Sanctuarie, and the end thereof *shalbe* with a
flood: and vnto the end of the battel it
shalbe destroyed by desolacions.
27 And he [z] shal confirme the couenāt with
manie for one weke: and in the middes of
the weke he shal cause the sacrifice and
the oblaciō to [a] cease, [b] and for the ouer-
spreading of the abominacions, he shal
make it desolate, euen vntil the cōsumma-
cion determined shalbe powred vpon the
desolate.

p He alludeth to Ieremiahs ꝓphecie, who prophecied ẏ their captiuitie shulde be seuentie yeres: but now Gods mercie shulde seuenfolde excede his iudgement, ẇ shulde be foure hundreth & ninetie yeres, euen to the comming of Christ, & so then it shulde continue for euer.
q Meaning Daniels nacion, ouer whome he was careful
r To shewe mercie and to put sinne out of remembrance.
ſ From the time ẏ Cyrus gaue them leaue to departe: and these wekes make 49 yere, whereof 46 are referred to the time of the building of the Temple, & 3 to the laying of ẏ fundacion.
t Coūting frō the sixt yere of Darius who gaue ẏ secōde commandemēt for the building of the Temple, are 62 weekes, which make 439 yeres, which comprehend the time from this building of the Temple vnto the Baptisme of Christ. ″ *Ebr. in streightes of time.* u In this last weeke of the seuentie shal Christ come and preache and suffer death. x He shal seme to haue no beautie, nor to be of anie estimacion, as Isa 53,2. y Meaning, Titus Vespasiās sonne, who shulde come and destroy bothe the Temple and the people without all hope of recouerie z By the preaching of the Gospel he confirmed his promes, first, to the Iewes, and after to the Gentiles.
a Christ accomplished this by his death and resurrection. b Meaning that Ierusalem and the Sanctuarie shulde be vtterly destroyed for their rebellion against God and their idolatrie: or some read that the plagues shalbe so great, that they shal all be astonied at them.

CHAP. X.

There appeareth vnto Daniel a man clothed in linen, 11 Which sheweth him wherefore he is sent.

1 IN the [a] third yere of Cyrus King of
Persia, a thing was reueiled vnto Daniél (whose name was called Belteshazzár)
and the worde *was* true, but the time appointed *was* [b] long, and he vnderstode the
thing, & had vnderstanding of the vision.
2 At the same time, I Daniél was in heauines for thre weekes of daies.
3 I ate no pleasant bread, nether came
flesh, nor wine in my mouth, nether did I
anoint my self at all, til thre weekes of daies were fulfilled.
4 And in the foure & twentieth day of the
[c] first moneth, as I [d] was by the side of that
great riuer, euen Hiddékel,
5 And I lift vp mine eyes, and loked, and
beholde, there *was* a man [e] clothed in linen, whose loynes were girded with fine
golde of * Vphaz.
6 His bodie also *was* like the Chrysolite,
and his face (to loke vpon) like the lightening, and his eyes as lampes of fyre, and
his armes and his fete *were* like in colour
to polished brasse, and the voyce of his
wordes *was* like the voyce of a multitude.
7 And I Daniél alone sawe the visiō: for the
mē that were with me, sawe not the visiō:
but a great feare fell vpon them, so that
they fled away and hid them selues.
8 Therefore I was left alone, and sawe this
great vision, & there remained no strēgth
in me: for [f] my strength was turned in me
into corruption, and I reteined no power.
9 Yet heard I the voyce of his wordes: and
when I heard the voyce of his wordes, I
slept on my face: and my face *was* towarde
the grounde.
10 And beholde, an hand [g] touched me,
which set me vp vpon my knees and vpon
the palmes of mine hands,
11 And he said vnto me, O Daniél, a man
greatly beloued, vnderstand the wordes
that I speake vnto thee, and stand in thy
place: [g] for vnto thee am I now sent. And
when he had said this worde vnto me, I
stode trembling.
12 Then said he vnto me, Feare not, Daniél: for from the first daye that thou didest
set thine heart to vnderstand, and to humble thy self before thy God, thy wordes
were heard, and I am come for thy wordes.
13 But the [h] prince of the kingdome of Persia withstode me one and twentie dayes:
but lo, [i] Michaél one of the chief princes,
came to helpe me, & I remained there by
the Kings of Persia.
14 Now I am come to shewe thee what
shal come to thy people in the latter dayes: for yet the [k] vision *is* for *manie* daies.
15 And when he spake these wordes vnto
me, I set my face towarde the grounde, &
helde my tongue.
16 And beholde, [l] one like the similitude
of the sonnes of man touched my lippes:
then I opened my mouth, and spake, and
said vnto him that stode before me, O my
Lord, [m] by the vision my sorowes are returned vpon me, and I haue reteined no
strength.
17 For how can the seruāt of this my Lord
talke with my Lord *being* suche one? for as
for me, straight way there remained no
strength in me, nether is there breth left
in me.
18 Then there came againe, and touched
me one like the appearance of a man, and
he strengthened me,
19 And said, O man, greatly beloued, feare
not: [n] peace *be* vnto thee: be strong and of

a He noteth this third yere, because at this time ẏ building of the Temple begā to be hindered by Cambyses Cyrus sonne, whē the father made warre in Asia minor against the Scythians, ẇ was a discouraging to the godlie, and a great feare to Daniél.
b Which is to declare that ẏ godlie shulde not hasten to muche, but paciently to abide the yssue of Gods promes.
c Called Abib, which conteineth parte of Marche & parte of April.
d Being caryed by the spirit of prophecie to haue the sight of this riuer Tygris.
e This was the Angel of God, which was sent to assure Daniel in this prophecie that followeth. * *Ierem.10,9.*

f The worde also signifieth comelines, or beautie, so ẏ for feare he was like a dead man for deformitie.
g Which declareth that whē we are strickē downe with the maiestie of God, we can not rise except he also lift vs vp ẇ his hand, ẇ is his power.
h Meaning, Cābyses who reigned in his fathers absence, & did not onely for this space hinder the buildīg of the Temple, but wolde haue farther raged, if God had not sent me to resist him, & therefore haue I staied for the profite of the Church
i Thogh God colde by one Angel destroy all the worlde, yet to assure his childrē of his loue, he sēdeth forthe double power euen Michaél, that is Christ Iesus ẏ head of Angels.
k For thogh the Prophet Daniel shulde end and cease, yet his doctrine shulde continue til the comming of Christ for the comfort of his Church.
l This was the same Angel that spake with him before in the similitude of a man. m I was ouercome with feare and sorowe, when I sawe the vision. n He declareth hereby that God wolde be merciful vnto the people of Israel.

good courage. And when he had spokẽ vnto me, I [o] was strengthened, and said, Let
my Lord speake: for thou hast strengthened me.
20 Then said he, Knowest thou wherefore
I am come vnto thee? but now wil I returne to fight with the prince of Persia: and
when I am gone forthe, lo, the [p] prince of
Grecia shal come.
21 But I wil shewe thee that which is decreed in the Scripture of trueth: [q] and
there is none that holdeth with me in these things, but Michaél your Prince.

o Which declareth that whẽ God smiteth downe his children, he doeth not immediatly lift them vp at once (for now ẏ Angel had touched him twise) but by litle and litle.
p Meaning ẏ he wolde not onely him self bridle the rage of Cambyses, but also ẏ other Kings of Persia by Alexander the King of Macedonia. q For this Angel was appointed for the defense of the Church vnder Christ, who is the head thereof.

CHAP. XI.

A prophecie of the kingdomes, which shulde be enemies to the Church of God, as of Persia, 3 Of Grece, 5 Of Egypt, 28 Of Syria, 36 And of the Romaines.

1 ALso I, in the first yere of Darius of
the Medes, *euen* I [a] stode to incourage and to strengthen him.
2 And now wil I shewe thee the trueth. Beholde, there shal stand vp yet [b] thre Kigs
in Persia, and the fourth shalbe farre richer then they all: and by his strength, &
by his riches he shal stirre vp [c] all against
the realme of Grecia.
3 But a [d] mightie King shal stand vp, that
shal rule with great dominion, and do according to his pleasure.
4 And when he shal stand vp, [e] his kingdome shalbe broken, [f] and shalbe deuided
towarde the [g] foure windes of heauen: &
not to his [h] posteritie, nor according to
[i] his dominion, which he ruled: for his
kingdome shalbe pluckt vp, euen *to be* for
others besides [k] those.
5 And the [l] King of the South shalbe migh
tie, and *one* of [m] his princes, and shal preuaile against him, and beare rule: his dominion *shalbe* a great dominion.
6 And in the end of yeres they shalbe ioyned together: for the Kings [n] daughter of
the South shal come to the King of the
North to make an agrement, but she shal
not reteine the power of the [o] arme, nether shal [p] he continue, nor his [q] arme: but
she shalbe deliuered *to death*, and thei that
broght her, and he [r] that begate her, & he
that comforted her in these times.
7 But out of the budde of her [s] rootes shal
one stand vp in his stead, [t] which shal come with an armie, and shal entre into the
forteresse of the King of the North, and
do with them *as he list*, and shal preuaile,
8 And shal also carye captiues into Egypt
their gods with their molten images, *and*
with their precious vessels of siluer and of
golde, and he shal continue [u] mo yeres
then the King of the North.
9 So the King of the South shal come into
his kingdome, & shal returne into his owne
land.
10 Wherefore his [x] sonnes shalbe stirred
vp, and shal assemble a mightie great armie: and *one* [y] shal come, and ouerflowe, &
passe through: then shal he [z] returne, and
be stirred vp at his forteresse.
11 And the King of the South shalbe angrie, and shal come forthe, and fight with
him, *euen* with the King of the North: for
he shal set forthe a great [a] multitude,
and the multitude shalbe giuen into his
hand.
12 Then the multitude shalbe proude, and
their heart shalbe lifted vp: for he shal cast
downe thousands: but he shal not *stil* preuaile.
13 For the King of the North [b] shal returne, and shal set forthe a greater multitude
then afore, and shal come forthe (after cer
teine yeres) with a mightie armie, & great
riches.
14 And at the same time there shal [c] manie
stand vp against the King of the South:
also the rebellious children of thy [d] people shal exalte them selues to establish the
vision, but they shal fall.
15 So the King of the North shal come, and
cast vp a mounte, & take the strong citie:
and the armes of the South shal [e] not resist, nether his chosen people, nether *shal*
there *be* anie strength to withstand.
16 But he that shal come, shal do vnto him
as he list, and none shal stand against him:
& he shal stãd in the [f] pleasant land, which
by his hand shalbe consumed.
17 Againe he shal [g] set his face to enter
with the power of his whole kingdome, &
his cõfederates with him: thus shal he do,
and he shal giue him the [h] daughter of
women, to destroye [i] her: but [k] she shal not
stande *on his side*, nether be for him.

a The Angel assureth Daniél that God hathe giuen him power to performe these things, seing he appointed him to assist Darius, whẽ he ouercame the Caldeans.
b Whereof Cãbyses ẏ now reigned, was ẏ first, the seconde Smerdes, ẏ third, Darius the sonne of Hystaspis, and the fourth Zerxes, which all were enemies to the people of God & stode against thẽ.
c For he raised vp all the East countreis to fight agaĩst the Grecians: and albeit he had in his armie nine hundreth thousãd men, yet in foure battels he was discomfited and fled away with shame.
d That is, Alexander the Great.
e For whẽ his estate was moste florishing, he ouercame him self with drinke, and so fell into a disease: or as some write, was poysoned by Cassander f For his twelue chief princes first deuided his kingdome among them selues. g After this his monarchie was deuided into foure: for Seleucus had Syria, Antigonus Asia minor, Cassander the kingdome of Macedonia, and Ptolemeus Egypt. h Thus God reuenged Alexanders ambicion & crueltie in causing his posteritie to be murthered, partely of the fathers chief friends, & partely one of another. i None of these foure shalbe able to be compared to the power of Alexãder. k That is, his posteritie hauing no parte thereof. l To wit, Ptolemeus King of Egypt m That is, Antiochus the sonne of Seleucus, and one of Alexãders princes shalbe more mightie: for he shulde haue bothe Asia & Syria. n That is, Berenice the daughter of Ptolemeus Philadelphus shalbe giuen in mariage to Antiochus Theos, thinking by this affinitie that Syria and Egypt shulde haue a continual peace together.
o That force & strength shal not continue: for sone after Berenice & her yong sonne after her housbands death, was slayne of her stepsonne Seleucus Calinicus the sonne of Laodice, the lawful wife of Antiochus, but put away for this womans sake. p Nether Ptolemeus, nor Antiochus. q Some read, seed, meaning the childe begotten of Berenice.

r Some read, she that begate her, & thereby vnderstãd her nurce, ẇ broght her vp: so that all thei that were occasion of this mariage, were destroyed.
s Meaning that Ptolemeus Euergetes after the death of his father Philadelphus shulde succede in the kingdome being of ẏ same stocke that Berenice was.
t To reuenge his sisters death against Antiochus Calinicus King of Syria.
u For this Ptolemeus reigned six & fortie yeres.
x Meaning Seleucus and Antiochus ẏ great, the sonnes of Calinicus shal make warre against Ptolemeus Philopater the sonne of Philadelphus.
y For his elder brother Seleucus dyed, or was slayne whiles the warres were preparing.
z That is, Philopater when he shal se Antiochus to take great dominions frõ him in Syria, & also readie to inuade Egypt.
a For Antiochus had six thousand horsemen & thresscore thousand fotemen.
b After the death of Ptolemeus Philopater, who left Ptolemeus Epiphanes his heire.
c For not onely Antiochus came against him, but also Philippe King of Macedonia, and these two broght great power with them.
d For vnder Onias which falsely alledged that place of Isa 19,19. certeine of the Iewes retyred with him into Egypt to fulfil this prophecie: also the Angel sheweth that all these troubles which are in the Church, are by the prouidence & counsel of God. e The Egyptians were not able to resist Stopas Antiochus captaine. f He sheweth that he shal not onely afflict the Egyptians, but also the Iewes, and shal enter into their countrey, whereof he admonisheth thẽ before that they may knowe that all these things come by Gods prouidence. g This was the seconde battel that Antiochus foght against Ptolemeus Epiphanes. h To wit, a beautiful woman, ẇ was Cleopatra Antiochus daughter. i For he regarded not the life of his daughter in respect of the kingdome of Egypt. k She shal not agre to his wicked counsel, but shal loue her housbãd, as her duetie requireth, and not seke his destruction.

18 After this ſhal he turne his face vnto the
[l] yles,& ſhal take many,but a prince[m] ſhal
cauſe his ſhame to light vpon him, beſide
that he ſhal cauſe his owne ſhame to turne
vpon [n] him ſelf.
19 For he ſhal turne his face towarde the
fortes of [o] his owne land: but he ſhalbe o-
uerthrowen & fall,& be no more [p] foũde.
20 ¶ Then ſhal ſtand vp in his place in ÿ glo
rie of the kingdome, one that ſhal raiſe
taxes: but after fewe dayes he ſhalbe deſtroyed,nether in [r] wrath,nor in battel.
21 And in his place ſhal ſtãd vp a [ſ] vile perſo
ne, to whome they ſhal not giue ÿ honour
of ÿ kingdome: but he ſhal come in peacea
bly, & obteine the kingdome by flateries.
22 And the [t] armes ſhalbe ouerthrowẽ with
a flood before him, & ſhalbe broken: and
alſo the prince of the [u] couenant.
23 And after [x] the league *made* with him, he
ſhal worke diſceitfully: for he ſhal come
vp,and ouercome with a [y] ſmale people.
24 He ſhal entre into the quiet and plentiful prouince,and he ſhal do that which his
fathers [z] haue not done, nor his fathers fathers: he ſhal deuide amõg them the pray
and the ſpoile,and the ſubſtance,yea,& he
ſhal forecaſt his deuiſes againſt the ſtrõg
holdes,euen for a [a] time.
25 Alſo he ſhal ſtirre vp his power and his
courage againſt the King of the South ẘ
a great armie, and the King of the South
ſhalbe ſtirred vp to battel ẘ a very great
and mightie armie: but he ſhal not [b] ſtãd:
for thei ſhal forecaſt & practiſe agaĩſt hĩ.
26 Yea,they that fede of the portiõ of [c] his
meat,ſhal deſtroy him: & his armie [d] ſhal
ouerflowe: & many ſhal fall,& be ſlaine.
27 And bothe theſe Kings hearts *ſhalbe* to
do [e] miſchief,& they ſhal talke of diſceite
at one table: but it ſhal not auaile: for [f] yet
the end *ſhalbe* at the time appointed.
28 Then ſhal he returne into his land with
great [g] ſubſtãce: for his heart ſhalbe agaĩſt
the holie couenant: ſo ſhal he do and retur
ne to his owne land.
29 At the time appointed he ſhal returne,
and come towarde the South: but the laſt
ſhal not be as the firſt.
30 For the ſhippes [h] of Chittím ſhal come
againſt him: therefore he ſhalbe ſorie and
returne, and freat againſt the holie couenant: ſo ſhal he do, he ſhal euen returne [i] &
haue intelligence with them that forſake
the holie couenant.
31 And armes [k] ſhal ſtand on his parte, and
thei ſhal pollute the Sãctuarie [l] of ſtrẽgth,
& ſhal take away the dailie *ſacrifice*,& they
ſhal ſet vp the abominable deſolation.
32 And ſuche as wickedly [m] breake the coue
nant,ſhal he cauſe to ſinne by flatterie: but
the people that do knowe their God, ſhal
preuaile and proſper.
33 And they that vnderſtand among [n] the
people, ſhal inſtruct many: [o] yet they ſhal
fall by ſworde,and by flame, by captiuitie
and by ſpoile many dayes.
34 Now whẽ they ſhal fall,they ſhal be hol
pen with a [p] litle helpe: but many ſhal clea
ue vnto them [q] fainedly.
35 And ſome of thẽ [r] of vnderſtanding ſhal
fall to trye them,and to purge, & to make
them white,til the time be out: for there *is*
a time appointed.
36 And the [ſ] King ſhal do what him liſt: he
ſhal exalte him ſelf, & magnifie him ſelf
againſt all,*that is* God,& ſhal ſpeake marueilous things againſt ÿ God of gods, &
ſhal proſper, til ÿ wrath [t] be accõpliſhed:
for the determination is made.
37 Nether ſhal he regarde the [u] God of his
fathers,nor the deſires [x] of women,nor care for any God: for he ſhal magnifie him
ſelf aboue all.
38 But in his place ſhal he honour the [y] god
Mauzzím, & the god whome his fathers
knewe not,ſhal he honour with [z] golde and
with ſiluer, and with precious ſtones, and
pleaſant things.
39 Thus ſhal he do in [a] the holdes of Mauzzím with a ſtrange god whome he ſhal acknowledge: he ſhal increaſe *his* glorie,and
ſhal cauſe them to rule ouer many, & ſhal
diuide the land for gaine.
40 And at the end of time ſhal the King
of the [b] South puſh at him, and the King
of the North ſhal come againſt him like a
whirle winde with charets, & with horſemen, and with many ſhippes, and he ſhal
entre into the countreis,& ſhal ouerflowe
and paſſe through.

l That is, towarde Aſia, Grecia & thoſe yles which are in the ſea called Mediterraneũ: for the Iewes called all coũtreis ÿ les which were deuided frõ them by ſea. m For where as Antiochus was wont to cõtemne the Romaines, & put their ambaſſadours to ſhame ĩ all places, Atilius ÿ Conſul, or Lucius Scipio put him to flight and cauſed his ſhame to turne on his owne head n By his wicked life and obeying of fooliſh counſel. o For feare of the Romaines he ſhal flee to his holdes. p For when as vnder the pretence of pouertie he wolde haue robbed the temple of Iupiter Dodoneus, the coũtreimẽ ſlue hĩ. q That is, Seleucus ſhal ſuccede his father Antiochus. r Not by foraine enemies or battel, but by treaſon. ſ Which was Antiochus Epiphanes, who as is thoght, was the occaſiõ of Seleucus his brothers death and was of a vile, cruel & flatering nature, and defrauded his brothers ſonne of ÿ kigdome, & vſurped ÿ kingdome without ÿ conſent of the people. t He ſheweth ÿ great foraine powers ſhal come to helpe the yong ſone of Seleucus againſt his vncle Antiochus, & yet ſhalbe ouerthrowen. u Meaning Ptolomeus Philometor Philopaters ſonne, who was this childes couſin germaine, & is here called ÿ prince of the couenãt, becauſe he was the chief, & all other followed his cõduite x For after ÿ battel Philometor & his vncle Antiochus made a league. y For he came vpõ him at vnwares, & when he ſuſpected his vncle Antiochus nothing z Meanig in Egypt. a He wil cõtent him ſelf with the ſmale holdes for a time, but euer labor by crafte to atteine to the chiefeſt. b He ſhalbe ouercome with treaſon. c Signifying his princes and ÿ chief about him d Declaring ÿ his ſoldiers ſhal braſt out & vẽture their life to ſlay & to be ſlaine for the ſauegarde of their prince e The vncle & the nephewe ſhal take truce, & banket together, yet in their hearts thei ſhal imagine miſchief one againſt another. f Signifying that it ſtandeth not in the counſel of men to bring things to paſſe, but in the prouidence of God who ruleth ÿ Kings by a ſecret bridel ÿ they cã not do what thei liſt thẽ ſelues g Which he ſhal take of ÿ Iewes in ſpoiling Ieruſalem & the Tẽple, & this is tolde thẽ before to moue thẽ to paciẽce, knowing all things are done by Gods prouidẽce. h That is, ÿ Romaine power ſhal come againſt him: for P Popilius the ambaſſador appointed him to depart in the Romaines name, to which thing he obeid, although with grief, and to reuenge his rage he came againſt the people of God the ſeconde time.

i With the Iewes which ſhal forſake the couenant of the Lord: for firſt he was called againſt ÿ Iewes by Iaſon the hie Prieſt, and this ſeconde time by Menelaus. k A great faction of ÿ wicked Iewes ſhal holde with Antiochus. l So called, becauſe ÿ power of God was nothing diminiſhed, althogh this tyrant ſet vp in the Temple ÿ image of Iupiter Olympius, and ſo began to corrupt the pure ſeruice of God. m Meaning ſuche as bare the name of Iewes but in dede were nothing leſſe: for they ſolde their ſoules, and betrayed their brethren for gaine. n They that remaine conſtant among the people, ſhal teache others by their example and edifie many in ÿ true religiõ. o Whereby he exhorteth the godlie to conſtãcie althogh they ſhulde periſh a thouſand times, and though their miſeries indure neuer ſo long. p As God wil not leaue his Church deſtitute, yet wil he not deliuer it all at once, but ſo helpe, as they may ſtil ſeme to fight vnder the croſſe, as he did in the time of the Maccabees whereof he here propheciezh q That is, there ſhalbe euen of this ſmale nomber many hypocrites. r To wit, of thẽ that feare God & wil loſe their life for the defenſe of true religion, ſignifying alſo that the Church muſt cõtinually betryed and purged & oght to loke for one perſecution after another: for God hathe appointed the time: therefore we muſt obey. ſ Becauſe ÿ Angels purpoſe is to ſhewe the whole courſe of the perſecutiõs of ÿ Iewes vnto the comming of Chriſt, he now ſpeaketh of the monarchie of the Romaines ẘ he noteth by the name of a King, who were without all religion & contemned the true God t So long the tyrants ſhal preuaile as God hathe appointed to puniſh his people: but he ſheweth that it is but for a time. u The Romaines ſhal obſerue no certeine forme of religion as other nations, but ſhal change their gods at their pleaſures, yea, cõtemne them & preferre them ſelues to their gods. x Signifying that they ſhulde be without all humanitie: for the loue of women is taken for ſingular or great loue, as 2 Sam 1,26.
y That is, the god of power and riches: they ſhal eſteme their owne power aboue all their gods & worſhip it. z Vnder pretence of worſhipping ÿ gods, they ſhal enriche their citie with the moſt precious iewels of all the worlde, becauſe that hereby all men ſhulde haue thẽ in admiration for their power & riches. a Althogh in their hearts thei had no religiõ, yet they did acknowledge the gods and worſhipped them in their temples, leſt they ſhulde haue bene deſpiſed as atheiſtes: but this was to increaſe their fame and riches: and whẽ they gate any countrey, they ſo made others the rulers thereof, ÿ the profite euer came to ÿ Romaines. b That is, bothe the Egyptians & the Syrians ſhal at length fight againſt the Romaines, but they ſhalbe ouercome.

41 He shal entre also into the [c] pleasant lãd,
& many *countreis* shalbe ouerthrowen: but
these shal escape out of his hãd, *euẽ* Edõ &
Moáb, & the chief of ỹ childrẽ of Ammõ.
42 He shal stretch forthe his hãds also vpõ
the countreis, and the land of Egypt shal
not escape.
43 But he shal haue power ouer ỹ treasures
of gold & of siluer, & ouer all ỹ precious
things of Egypt, & of the Lybians, and
of the blacke Mores where he shal passe.
44 But the tidings out of the East and the
North shal [d] trouble hĩ: therefore he shal
go forthe [e] with great wrath to destroy &
roote out many.
45 And he shal plant ỹ tabernacles [f] of his
palace betwene ỹ seas in the glorious *and*
holie mountaine, yet he shal come to his
end, & none shal helpe him.

c The Angel forewarneth ỹ Iewes ỹ when they shulde se the Romaines inuade them, and that the wicked shulde escape their hands, ỹ then they shulde not thinke but that all this was done by Gods prouidẽce, for asmuche as he warned them of it so long a fore, and therefore he wolde stil preserue him.

d Hearing ỹ Crassus was slaine & Antonius discõfited.

e For Augustus ouercame the Parthians, and recouered that which Antonius had lost.

f The Romaines after this reigned quietly through all coũtreis & frõ sea to sea, and in Iudea: but at length for their crueltie God shal destroy them.

CHAP. XII.

1 Of the deliuerance of the Church by Christ.

1 And at that [a] time shal Michaél stãd
vp, the great prince, which standeth
for the children of thy people, and there
shalbe a time of trouble, suche as neuer
was since there began to be a nation vnto
that same time: & at that time thy people
shalbe deliuered, euerie one that shal be
founde writen in the boke.
2 And many [b] of thẽ that slepe in the dust
of ỹ earth, shal awake, some to euerlasting
life, & some to shame & perpetual cõtẽpt.
3 And thei that be [c] wise, shal shine, as the
brightnes of the firmament: & they that
[d] turne many to righteousnes, *shal shine*
as the starres, for euer and euer.
4 But thou, ô Daniel, [e] shut vp the wordes, and seale the boke [f] til the end of the
time: many shal runne to and fro, & knowledge shalbe increased.
5 ¶ Then I Daniél loked, and beholde, there stode other two, the one on this side of
the brinke of the [g] riuer, and the other on
that side of the brinke of the riuer.
6 And *one* said vnto the mã clothed in linnen, which was vpon the waters of the riuer, When *shalbe* the end of these wõders?
7 And I heard the man clothed in linnen
which was vpon the waters of the riuer,
when he held vp his [h] right hand, & his left
hand vnto heauen, and sware by him that
liueth for euer, that *it shal tarie* for [i] a time,
two times & an halfe: and when he shal ha
ue accomplished [k] to scatter the power of
the holie people, all these things shalbe finished.
8 Then I heard it, but I vnderstode it not:
then said I, O my Lord, what shal be the
end of these things?
9 And he said, Go thy way, Daniél: for the
wordes are closed vp, and sealed, til the
end of the time.
10 Many shalbe purified, made white, and
tried: but the wicked shal do wickedly, &
none of the wicked shal haue vnderstanding: but the wise shal vnderstand.
11 And from the time that the [l] dailie *sacrifice* shalbe taken away, and the abominable
desolation set vp, there [m] *shalbe* a thousand,
two hundreth and ninetie dayes.
12 Blessed *is he* that waiteth and commeth
to the thousand, thre hundreth and [n] fiue
and thirtie dayes.
13 But go [o] thou thy way til the end *be*: for
thou shalt rest and stand vp in thy lot, at
the end of the dayes.

Chap. XII. a The Angel here noteth two thĩgs: first ỹ the Church shalbe in great afflictiõ & trouble at Christs comming, and next that God wil send his Angel to deliuer it, whome here he calleth Michaél, meaning Christ, ẇ is published by ỹ preaching of ỹ Gospel. b Meaning all shal rise at ỹ general resurrection, ẇ thing he here nameth, because ỹ faithful shulde haue euer their respect to ỹ: for in ỹ earth there shalbe no sure comfort. c Who haue kept the true feare of God & his religion. d He chiefly meaneth the ministers of Gods worde, & next, all the faithful which instruct ỹ ignorant, and bring them to the true knowledge of God. e Thogh the moste parte despise this prophecie, yet kepe thou it sure and esteme it as a treasure. f Til the time that God hathe appointed for the ful reuelation of these things: and then many shal runne to and fro to searche the knowledge of these mysteries, which things they obteine now by the light of the Gospel.

g Which was Tygris.

h Which was as it were a double othe & did ỹ more cõfirme the thĩg.

i Meaning, a lõg time, a longer time, & at length a short time: signifyĩg that their troubles shulde haue an end.

k When the Church shalbe scattered & diminished in suche sorte as it shal seme to haue no power.

l Frõ the time that Christ by his sacrifice shal take away ỹ sacrifice & ceremonies of ỹ Law.

m Signifying that the time shalbe long of Christs secõde coming, and yet the children of God oght not to be discouraged, thogh it be differred.

n In this nomber he addeth a moneth and an halfe to the former nõber, signifying ỹ it is not in mã to appoint the time of Christs comming, but ỹ they are blessed that paciently abide his appearing.

o The Angel warneth the Prophet paciently to abide, til the time appointed come, signifying that he shulde departe this life, and rise againe with the elect, when God had sufficiently humbled & purged his Church.

HOSEA.

HOSEA.

THE ARGUMENT.

After that the ten tribes had fallen away from God by the wicked and subtil counsel of Ieroboam the sonne of Nebat, and in stede of his true seruice commanded by his worde worshipped him according to their owne fantasies and traditions of men, giuing them selues to moste vile idolatrie and superstition, the Lord from time to time sent them Prophetes to call them to repentance: but they grewe euer worse and worse, and stil abused Gods benefites. Therefore now when their prosperitie was at the highest vnder Ieroboam the sonne of Ioash, God sent Hosea and Amos to the Israelites (as he did at the same time Isaiah and Micah to them of Iudah) to cōdemne them of their ingratitude: and where as they thoght them selues to be greatly in the fauour of God, and to be his people, the Prophet calleth them bastards and children borne in adulterie: and therefore sheweth them that God wolde take away their kingdome, and giue them to the Assyrians to be led away captiues. Thus Hosea faithfully executed his office for the space of seuentie yeres, thogh they remained stil in their vices & wickednes, & derided the Prophetes, & contemned Gods iudgements. And because they shulde nether be discoraged with threatnings onely, nor yet flatter them selues by the swetenes of Gods promises, he setteth before them the two principal partes of the Law, which are the promes of saluation, and the doctrine of life: for the first parte he directeth the faithful to Messiah, by whome onely they shulde haue true deliuerance: and for the seconde, he vseth threatnings and menaces to bring them from their wicked maners and vices, & this is the chief scope of all the Prophetes, ether by Gods promises to allure them to be godlie, els by threatnings of his iudgements to feare them frō vice: & albeit that the whole Law conteine these two pointes, yet the Prophetes moreouer note peculiarly bothe the time of Gods iudgements and the maner.

CHAP. I.

1 The time wherein Hosea prophecied. 2 The idolatrie of the people. 10 The calling of the Gētiles. 11 Christ is the head of all people.

1 The worde of the Lord
that came vnto Hoséa
the sonne of Beerí, in
the dayes [a] of Vzziáh,
Iotham, Aház, & Heze-
kiáh [b] Kings of Iudáh, &
in ẏ dayes of Ieroboám
the sonne of Ioásh King of Israél.
2 At the beginning the Lord spake by Hoséa, and the Lord said vnto Hoséa, Go,
[c] take vnto thee a wife of fornications, and
children of fornicatiōs: for the land hathe
committed great whoredome, *departing* frō
the Lord.
3 So he went, and toke [d] Gómer, the daughter of Dibláim, which conceiued and bare
him a sonne.
4 And the Lord said vnto him, Call his name [e] Izreél: for yet a litle, and I wil visite
the blood of Izreél vpon the house [f] of Iehú, and wil cause to cease the kingdome
of the house of Israél.
5 And at that [g] day wil I also breake ẏ bow
of Israél in the valley of Izreél.
6 She cōceiued yet againe, & bare a daughter, and *God* said vnto him, Call her name
[h] Lo-ruhámah: for I wil no more haue pitie vpon the house of Israél: but I wil vtter
ly [i] take them away.
7 Yet I wil haue mercie vpon the house of
Iudáh, and wil [k] saue them by the Lord
their God, and wil not saue thē by bowe,
nor by sworde nor by battel, by horses, nor
by horsemen.
8 Now when she had wained Lo-ruhámah,
she conceiued, and bare a sonne.
9 Then said *God*, Call his name [l] Lo-ammí:
for ye are not my people: therefore wil I
not be yours.
10 Yet the nomber of the [m] children of Israél shalbe as the sand of the sea, which cā
not be measured nor tolde: and in the place where it was said vnto them, Ye are not
my people, it shal be said vnto them, *Ye are*
the sonnes of the liuing God.
11 Then shal the children of Iudáh, and the
children of Israél be [n] gathered together,
and appoint them selues one head, & they
shal come vp out of the land: for great *is*
the [o] day of Izreél.

a Called also Azariáh, who being a lepre was deposed from his kingdome.
b So ẏ it may be gathered by the reigne of these foure Kings, that he preached aboue threscore yere.
c That is, one that of long time hathe accustomed to play the harlot: not that ẏ Prophet did this thing in effect, but he sawe this in a vision, or els was commanded by God to set forthe vnder this parable or figure ẏ idolatrie of ẏ Synagogue, & of the people her children.
d Gómer signifieth a consumption or corruption, & Diblaim clusters of figges, declaring, that they were all corrupt like rotten figges.
e Meaning, ẏ they shulde be no more called Israelites, of the which name they boasted, because Israel did preuaile with God: but that they were as bastards, & therefore shulde be called Izreelites, that is, scattered people, alluding to Izreel, which was ẏ chief citie of ẏ ten tribes vnder Ahab where Iehu shed so muche blood, 2 King. 10, 8.
f I wil be reuēged vpon Iehu for the blood that he shed in Izreél: for albeit God stirred him vp to execute his iudgements, yet he did them for his owne ambitiō, & not for the glorie of God, as the end declared: for he buylt vp that idolatrie, which he had destroyed.
g When the measure of their iniquitie is ful, and I shal take vengeance and destroye all their policie and force.
h That is, not obteining mercie: whereby he signifieth, that Gods fauour was departed from them.
i For the Israelites neuer returned, after ẏ they were taken captiues by the Assyrians.
k For after their captiuitie he restored thē miraculously by ẏ meanes of Cyrus, Ezr. 1, 1.
l That is, not my people.
m Because thei thoght that God colde not haue bene true in his promes except he had preserued thē, he declareth, ẏ thogh they were destroied yet the true Israelites, ẇ are the sonnes of the promes, shulde be without nomber, ẇ stand bothe of the Iewes, and the Gentiles, Rom. 9, 26.
n To wit, after the captiuitie of Babylon when the Iewes were restored: but chiefly this is referred to the time of Christ, who shulde be the head bothe of the Iewes and Gentiles.
o The calamitie and destruction of Izreel shalbe so great, that to restore them shalbe as a miracle.

CHAP. II.

1 The people is called to repentance. 5 He sheweth their idolatrie and threateneth them except they repent.

1 Say vnto your [a] brethren, Ammi, and to
your sisters, Ruhámah,
2 Plead with your [b] mother: plead *with her*:
for she is not my wife, nether am I her
housband: but let her take away her forni
cations out of her sight, and her adulteries
[c] from betwene her breastes.

a Seing, that I haue promised you deliuerance, it remaineth that you incourage one another to imbrace the same, considerīg that ye are my people on whome I wil haue mercie.
b God sheweth that the faute was not in him but in their synagogue, and their idolatries, that he forsoke them, Isa 50, 1.
c Meaning, that their idolatrie was so great, that they were not ashamed, but boasted of it, Ezek. 16, 25.

3 [d]Lest I strippe her naked, & set her as in ẏ
day that she was borne, [e] and make her as
a wildernes, & leaue her like a drye land,
and slaye her for thirst.
4 And I wil haue no pitie vpon her children: for they be the [f] children of fornications.
5 For their mother hathe played the harlot: she that conceiued them, hathe done
shamefully: for she said, I wil go after my
[g] louers that giue me my bread & my water, my woll and my flaxe, mine oile and
my drinke.
6 Therefore beholde, I wil stoppe [h] thy way
with thornes, & make an hedge, ẏ she shal
not finde her paths.
7 Thogh she followe after her louers, yet
shal she not come at them: thogh she seke
them, yet shal she not finde *them*: then shal
she say, [i]I wil go & returne to my first hous
band: for at ẏ time was I better then now.
8 Now she did not know that I [k] gaue her
corne, and wine, and oile, and multiplied
her siluer and golde, *which* they bestowed
vpon Báal.
9 Therefore wil I returne, and take away
[l]my corne in the time thereof, and my wine in the ceason thereof, and wil recouer
my woll and my flaxe *lent*, to couer her
shame.
10 And now wil I discouer her [m] lewdnes
in the sight of her louers, and no man shal
deliuer her out of mine hand.
11 I wil also cause all her myrth to cease, her
feast dayes, her newe moones, & her Sabbaths, and all her solemne feasts.
12 And I wil destroy her vines and her figtrees, whereof she hathe said, These are my
rewardes that my louers haue giuē me: &
I wil make them as a forest, and the wilde
beasts shal eat them.
13 And I wil visit vpon her the dayes [n] of
Baalím, wherein she burnt incense to thē:
and she decked her self with her [o] earings
and her iewels, & she followed her louers,
and forgate me, saith the Lord.
14 Therefore beholde, I wil [p] allure her, &
bring her into the wildernes, and speake
friendly vnto her.
15 And I wil giue her her vineyardes from
thence, and the valley [q] of Achór for the
dore of hope, and she shal [r] sing there as
in the dayes of her youth, & as in the day
when she came vp out of the land of E-
gypt.
16 And at that day, saith the Lord, thou
shalt call me [s] Ishí, and shalt call me nomore [t] Baalí.

d For thogh this people were as an harlot for their idolatries, yet he had left them with their apparel and dowrie and certeine signes of his fauour, but if they cōtinued stil, he wolde vtterly destroy them.
e When I broght her out of Egypt, Ezek 16,4.
f That is, bastardes and begotten in adulterie.
g Meaning the idoles which they serued & by whome thei thoght they had welth and abundance.
h I wil punish thee that thou ẏ maiest trye whether thine idoles can helpe thee, & brīg thee into suche streitnes, that thou shalt haue no lust to play the wanton.
i This he speaketh of ẏ faithful, which are truely conuerted, and also sheweth the vse and profite of Gods rods.
k This declareth ẏ idolaters defraude God of his honour whē thei attribute his benefites to their idoles.
l Signifying ẏ God wil take away his benefites whē man by his ingratitude doeth abuse them.
m That is, all her séruice, ceremonies and inuētions whereby she worshipped her idoles.
n I wil punish her for her idolatrie.
o By shewing how harlotes trimme them selues to please others, he declareth how the superstitious idolaters set a great parte of their religiō in decking them selues on their holie dayes.
p By my benefites in offring her grace and mercie, euen in ẏ place where she shal thinke her self destitute of all helpe and comfort. q Which was a plentiful valley, and wherein they had great comfort when they came out of the wildernes, as Iosh 7,18 and is called the dore of hope, because it was a departing from death, and an entrie into life. r She shal then praise God as she did when she was deliuered out of Egypt. s That is, mine housband, knowing that I am ioyned to thee by an inuiolable couenant. t That is, my master: which name was applied to their idoles.

17 For I wil take away the names of Baalím
out of her mouth, and they shal be no more remembred by their [u] names.
18 And in that day wil I make a couenant
for them, with the [x] wilde beasts, and with
the foule of the heauen, and with that that
crepeth vpon the earth: and I wil breake
the bowe, and the sworde and the battel
out of the earth, & wil make them to slepe
safely.
19 And I wil marie thee vnto me for euer:
yea, I wil marie thee vnto me in righteous
nes, and in iudgement, and in mercie and
in compassion.
20 I wil euen marie thee vnto me in [y] faithfulnes, and thou shalt know the Lord.
21 And in that day I wil heare, saith the
Lord, I wil *euen* heare [z] the heauens, and
they shal heare the earth,
22 And the earth shal heare the corne, and
the wine, and the oyle, and they shal heare
Izreél.
23 And I wil sowe her vnto me in the earth,
and I wil haue mercie vpon her, that was
not pitied, & I wil say to thē which were
not my people, *Thou art my people. And
they shal say, *Thou art* my God.

u No idolatrie shal once come īto their mouthe, but they shal serue me purely according to my worde.
x Meaning, ẏ he wil so blesse them that all creatures shal fauour them.
y With a couenāt that neuer shalbe broken.
z Then shal the heauen desire raine for ẏ earth which shal bring forthe for the vse of man.

Rom.9,25. 1.pet.2,10.

CHAP. III.

1 The Iewes shalbe cast of for their idolatrie. 5 Afterwarde they shal returne to the Lord.

1 THen said the Lord to me, [a] Go yet,
and loue a woman (beloued of *her*
housband, and was an harlot) according
to the loue of the Lord toward the childrē
of Israél: yet they loked to other gods, &
[b]loued the wine bottels.
2 So [c] I boght her to me for fiftene *pieces* of
siluer, and for an homer of barlie and an
halfe *homer* of barlie.
3 And I said vnto her, Thou shalt abide
with [d] me manie dayes: thou shalt not play
the harlot, and thou shalt be to none *other*
man, and I wil be so vnto thee.
4 For the children of Israél shal [e] remaine
manie dayes without a King and without
a [f]prince, and without an offring, & without an image, & without an Ephod and
without Teraphím.
5 Afterwarde shal the children of Israél
conuert, and seke the Lord their God, and
[g] Dauid their King, & shal feare the Lord,
and his goodnes in the latter dayes.

a Herein the Prophet representeth ẏ persone of God, which loued his Church before he called her, & did not withdrawe the same when she gaue her selfe to idoles.
b That is, gaue them selues wholly to pleasures, and colde not take vp, as they ẏ are giuen to drunkennes.
c Yet I loued her & payed a smale portion for her, lest she perceiuing the greatnes of my loue, shulde haue abused me and not bene vnder duetie: for fiftene pieces of siluer were but half the price of a sclaue, Exod. 21,32.

d I wil trie thee a long time as in thy widowehode whether thou wilt be mine or no. e Meaning, not onely all the time of their captiuitie, but also vnto Christ. f That is, they shulde nether haue pollicie nor religion, and their idoles also wherein they put their confidence, shulde be destroyed. g This is ment of Christs kingdome, which was promised vnto Dauid to be eternal, Psal. 72,38.

CHAP. IIII.

A complaint against the people, and the Priests of Israél.

1 Heare

1 HEare the worde of the Lord, ye chil
dren of Iſraél: for the Lord [a] hathe
a cõtrouerſie with ỹ inhabitants of the lãd
becauſe there *is* no trueth, nor mercie nor
knowledge of God in the land.
2 By ſwearing, and lying, and killing, and
ſtealing, and whoring they breake out, and
[b] blood toucheth blood.
3 Therefore ſhal the land mourne, and euerie one that dwelleth therein, ſhal be cut
of, with the beaſts in the field, and with
the foules of the heauẽ, and alſo the fiſhes
of the ſea ſhalbe taken away.
4 Yet [c] let none rebuke, nor reproue another:
for thy people *are* as they that rebuke the
Prieſt.
5 Therefore ſhalt thou fall in the [d] day, and
the Prophet ſhal fall with thee in ỹ night,
and I wil deſtroye thy [e] mother.
6 My people are deſtroyed for lacke of
knowledge: becauſe [f] thou haſt refuſed
knowledge, I wil alſo refuſe thee, that thou
ſhalt be no Prieſt to me: and ſeing [g] thou
haſt forgotten the Law of thy God, I wil
alſo forget thy children.
7 As they were [h] increaſed, ſo they ſinned
againſt me: *therefore* wil I change their glorie into ſhame.
8 [i] They eat vp the ſinnes of my people, &
lift vp their mindes in their iniquitie.
9 And there ſhalbe like people, like [k] Prieſt:
for I wil viſit their wayes vpon them, &
rewarde them their dedes.
10 For they ſhal eat, and not haue ynough:
they ſhal [l] commit adulterie, and ſhal not
increaſe, becauſe they haue left of to take
hede to the Lord.
11 [m] Whoredome, and wine, and newe wine
take away *their* heart.
12 My [n] people aſke coũſel at their ſtockes,
and their ſtaffe teacheth them: for the [o] ſpi
rit of fornications hathe cauſed *them* to
erre, and they haue gone a whoring from
vnder their God.
13 They ſacrifice vpon the toppes of the
mountaines, and burne incenſe vpon the
hilles vnder the okes, and the poplar tre,
and the elme, becauſe the ſhadowe thereof
is good: therefore your daughters ſhalbe [p] harlottes, and your ſpouſes ſhalbe
whores.
14 I wil not [q] viſite your daughters when
they are harlots, nor your ſpouſes when
they are whores: for thei them ſelues are ſeparated with harlots, and ſacrifice with
whores: therefore the people that doeth
not vnderſtand, ſhal fall.
15 Thogh thou, Iſraél, playe the harlot, *yet*
[r] let not Iudáh ſinne: come not ye vnto
[ſ] Gilgál, nether go ye vp to [t] Beth-áuen,
nor ſweare, The Lord liueth.
16 For Iſraél is rebellious as an vnrulie heif
fer. Now the Lord wil fede them as a
[u] lambe in a large place.
17 Ephráim *is* ioyned to idoles: let him
alone.
18 Their drunkennes ſtinketh: they haue
committed whoredome: their rulers loue
to ſay with ſhame, [x] Bring ye.
19 The winde hathe [y] bounde thẽ vp in her
wings, and they ſhalbe aſhamed of their
ſacrifices.

a Becauſe the people wolde not obey the admonitiõs of the Prophet, he citeth thẽ before the iudgement ſeat of God, againſt whome they chiefly offended, Iſa. 7,12. zecha. 12,10.
b In euerie place appeareth a libertie to moſte heinous vices, ſo ỹ one followeth in ỹ necke of another.
c As thogh he wolde ſay, ỹ it were in vaine to rebuke thẽ: for no mã can abide it: yea, they wil ſpeake againſt the Prophetes and Prieſts whoſe office it is chiefly to rebuke them.
d Ye ſhal periſh all together: ỹ one, becauſe he wolde not obeie, & the other becauſe he wolde not admoniſh.
e That is, the Synagogue wherein thou boaſteſt.
f That is, the Prieſts ſhalbe caſt of becauſe, ỹ for lacke of knowledge, they are not able to execute their charge, and inſtruct others, Deu 33, 3. malach. 2,7.
g Meaning, ỹ whole bodie of the people, which were wearie with hearing the worde of God.
h The more I was beneficial vnto thẽ.
i To wit, the Prieſts ſeke to eat ỹ peoples offrĩgs & flatter them in their ſinnes.
k Signifying, that as they haue ſinned together, ſo ſhal they be puniſhed together.
l Shewing, that their wickednes ſhalbe puniſhed on all ſortes: for thogh they thinke by the multitude of wiues to haue many childrẽ, yet they ſhalbe deceiued of their hope.
m In giuing them ſelues to pleaſures, thei become like brute beaſts. n Thus he ſpeaketh by deriſion in calling them his people, which now for their ſinnes they were not: for they ſoght helpe of ſtockes and ſtickes. o They are caried away with a rage. p Becauſe they take away Gods honour, and giue it to idoles, therefore he wil giue them vp to their luſtes, that they ſhal diſhonour their owne bodies, Rom 1.28. q I wil not correct your ſhame to bring you to amendement, but let you runne headlong to your owne damnation.

r God cõplaineth that Iudáh is infected, and willeth them to learne by their example to returne in time.
ſ For albeit the Lord had honored this place in time paſt by his preſence, yet becauſe it was abuſed by their idolatrie, he wolde not that his people ſhulde reſort thether.
t He calleth Beth-él, that is, the houſe of God, Beth-áuen, that is, the houſe of iniquitie, becauſe of their abominations ſet vp there, ſignifying that no place is holie where God is not purely worſhipped. u God wil ſo diſperſe them that they ſhal not remaine in anie certeine place. x They are ſo impudent in receiuing bribes, that they wil commande men to bring them vnto them. y To carie them ſuddenly away.

CHAP. V

1 Againſt the Prieſts and rulers of Iſraél. 13 The helpe of man is in vaine.

1 O Ye Prieſts, heare this, and hearken
ye, ô houſe of Iſraél, & giue ye eare,
ô houſe of the King: for iudgement *is* toward you, becauſe you haue bene a [a] ſnare
on Mizpáh, & a net ſpred vpon Tabór.
2 Yet they were profounde, to decline to
[b] ſlaughter, thogh I haue bene a [c] rebuker
of them all.
3 I knowe [d] Ephráim, and Iſraél is not hid
from me: for now, ô Ephráim thou art become an harlot, *&* Iſraél is defiled.
4 Thei wil not giue their mindes to turne
vnto their God: for ỹ ſpirit of fornication
is in the middes of them, & they haue not
knowen the Lord.
5 And the [e] pride of Iſraél doeth teſtifie to
his face: therefore ſhal Iſraél and Ephráim
fall in their iniquitie: Iudáh alſo ſhal fall
with them.
6 They ſhal go with their ſhepe, and with
their bullockes to ſeke the Lord: but they
ſhal not finde him: *for* he hathe withdrawẽ
him ſelf from them.
7 They haue trãſgreſſed againſt the Lord:
for they haue begotten [f] ſtrange children:
now ſhal [g] a moneth deuoure them ẘ their
porcions.
8 Blowe ye the trumpet in Gibeáh, *&* the
ſhaume in Ramáh: crye out at Beth-áuen,
after thee, ô [h] Beniamín.
9 Ephráim ſhalbe deſolate in ỹ day of rebuke: among the tribes of Iſraél haue I
cauſed to [i] knowe the trueth.
10 The princes of Iudáh were like thẽ that
[k] remoue the bondes: *therefore* wil I powre
out my wrath vpon them like water.
11 Ephráim is oppreſſed, *&* broken in iudgement, becauſe he willingly walked after the [l] commandement.

a The Prieſts & princes catched the poore people in their ſnares as the foulers did the birds, in theſe two high mountaines.
b Notwithſtanding they ſemed to be giuen altogether to holines, & to ſacrifices, ẘ here he calleth ſlaughter in cõtempt.
c Thogh I admoniſhed them continually by my Prophetes.
d They boaſted them ſelues not onely to be Iſraelites, but alſo Ephraimites, becauſe their King Ierobõa came of that tribe.
e Meaning, their contemning of all admonitions.
f That is their children are degenerat, ſo ỹ there is no hope in them.
g Their deſtructiõ is not farre of.
h That is, all Iſrael cõprehẽded vnder this parte, ſignifying ỹ the Lords plagues ſhulde purſue thẽ frõ place to place til they were deſtroyed.
i By the ſucceſſe thei ſhal knowe that I haue ſurely determined this. k Thei haue turned vp ſide downe all political order, and all maner of religion.
l To wit, after King Ieroboams cõmandemẽt & did not rather follow God.

12 Therefore wil I be vnto Ephráim as a
moth, and to the house of Iudáh as a rottennes.
13 Whē Ephráim sawe his sickenes, and Iudáh his wounde, then went Ephráim vnto
[m] Asshúr, & sent vnto King [n] Iaréb: yet col
de he not heale you, nor cure you of your
wounde.
14 For I wil be vnto Ephráim as a lion, and
as a lions whelpe to the house of Iudáh:
I, *euen* I wil spoyle, and go away: I wil take
away, and none shal rescue it.
15 I wil go, & returne to my place, til they
acknowledge their faute, and seke me: in
their afflictiō they wil seke me diligently.

m In stead of sekīg for remedie at Gods hand.
n Who was King of ẏ Asſyrians.

CHAP. VI.

1 Affliction causeth a man to turne to God. 9 The wickednes of the Priests.

1 COme, & let vs [a] returne to the Lord:
for he hathe spoiled, and he wil heale vs: he hathe wounded vs, and he wil binde vs vp.
2 After two dayes wil [b] he reuiue vs, & in
the thirde day he wil raise vs vp, and we
shal liue in his sight.
3 Then shal we haue knowledge, and ende-
uor our selues to knowe the Lord: his going forthe is prepared as the morning, and
he shal come vnto vs as the raine, & as the
latter raine vnto the earth.
4 O Ephráim, what shal I do vnto thee! ô
Iudáh, how shal I entreat thee! for [c] your
goodnes *is* as a morning cloude, and as the
morning dewe it goeth away.
5 Therefore haue I [d] cut downe by ẏ Prophetes: I haue slaine them by the wordes
of my mouth, and [e] thy iudgements *were*
as the light that goeth forthe.
6 For I desired [f] mercie, & not sacrifice, &
the knowledge of God more then burnt
offrings.
7 But thei like [g] men haue transgressed ẏ couenant: there haue they trespaced against
me.
8 [h] Gileád *is* a citie of them that worke iniquitie, & *is* polluted with blood.
9 And as theues waite for a mā, *so* the com
panie of Priests murther in the way by cōsent: for they worke meschief.
10 I haue sene vilenie in the house of Israél:
there *is* the whoredome of Ephráim: Israél
is defiled.
11 Yea, Iudáh hathe set a [i] plant for thee,
whiles I wolde returne the captiuitie of
my people.

a He sheweth the people howe they oght to turne to the Lord, that he might call backe his plagues
b Thogh he correct vs frō time to time, yet his helpe wil not be far of, if we returne to him.
c You seme to haue a certeine holines, & repentāce, but it is vpon the sudden, and as a morning cloude.
d I haue stil laboured by my Prophets, & as it were framed you to bring you to amendement, but all was in vaine: for my worde was not meat to fede them, but a sworde to slay them.
e My doctrine ẇ I taught thee, was moste euident.
f He sheweth to what scope his doctrine tēded ẏ they shulde ioyne ẏ obedience of God, & ẏ loue of their neighbour with outwarde sacrifice
g That is, like light & weake persones.
h Which was ẏ place where the Priests dwelt, and ẇ shulde haue bene best instructed in my worde.
i That is, doeth imitate thine idolatrie, and hathe taken graffes of thy trees.

CHAP. VII.

1 Of the vices & wantonnes of the people. 12 Of their punishment.

1 WHen I wolde haue healed Israél,
thē the iniquitie of Ephráim was
discouered, & the wickednes of Samaria:
for they haue delt falsely: and [a] the thefe
cometh in, & the robber spoyleth without.
2 And they consider not in their hearts, *that*
I remēber all their wickednes: now their
owne inuencions haue beset thē about:
they are in my sight.
3 They make ẏ [b] King glad with their wickednes, and the princes with their lies.
4 Thei are all adulterers, & as a verie [c] ouē
heated by the baker, which ceaseth frō rai
sing vp, & from kneding the dowe vntil
it be leauened.
5 *This is* the day [d] of our King: the princes haue made him sicke with flagons of wine: he
stretcheth out his hand to scorners.
6 For thei haue made readie their heart like
an ouen whiles they lie in waite: their baker slepeth all the night: in the morning it
burneth as a flame of fyre.
7 They are all hote as an ouen, and haue
[e] deuoured their Iudges: all their Kīgs are
fallen: there is none among them that calleth vnto me.
8 Ephráim hathe [f] mixt him self amōg the
people. Ephráim is as a cake on the herth
not turned.
9 Strangers haue deuoured his strength, &
he knoweth it not: yea, [g] graye heeres are
here and there vpon him, yet he knoweth
not.
10 And the pride of Israél testifieth to his
face, and they do not returne to the Lord
their God, nor seke him for all this.
11 Ephráim also is like a doue deceiued,
without [h] heart: they call to Egypt: they go
to Asshúr.
12 *But* whē they shal go, I wil spred my net
vpon them, & drawe them downe as the
foules of the heauen: I wil chastise thē as
their [i] congregation hathe heard.
13 Wo vnto them: for they haue fled away
from me: destruction *shalbe* vnto them, because they haue transgressed against me:
thogh I haue [k] redemed them, yet they haue spoken lies against me.
14 And they haue not cryed vnto me with
their hearts, [l] when they houled vpō their
beds: [m] they assemble them selues for
corne, & wine, *and* thei rebell against me.
15 Thogh I haue bounde, *and* strengthened
their arme, yet do they imagine mischief
against me.
16 Thei returne, *but* not to ẏ most high: thei
are like a deceitful bowe: their prīces shal
fall by the sworde, for the rage [n] of their
tongues: this shalbe their derision in the
land of Egypt.

a Meaning, ẏ there was no one kinde of vice among them, but that they were subiect to all wickednes, bothe secret & opē.
b Thei esteme their wicked King Ieroboā aboue God, & seke but how to flatter, and please him.
c He compareth the rage of the people to a burning ouen which ẏ baker heateth stil til his dowe be leauened, and raised.
d They vsed all riot & excesse in their feasts & solemnities, whereby their King was ouercome with surfet, & broght into diseases, and delited in flatteries.
e By their occasion God hathe depriued them of all good rulers.
f That is, he conterfaiteth the religion of the Gentiles, yet is but as a cake baked on ẏ one side, & rawe on ẏ other, that is, nether through hote nor through cold, but partely a Iewe, and partely a Gentil.
g Which are a token of his maniefolde afflictions.
h That is, without all iudgement, as they that can not tel whether it is better to cleaue onely to God, or to seke the helpe of man.
i According to my curses made to the whole congregation of Israél.
k That is, diuers times redemed them, and deliuered them from death.
l When they were in affliction, & cryed out for paine, they soght not vnto me for helpe.
m They onely seke their owne comoditie and welth, and passe not for me their God.
n Because they boast of their owne strength, and passe not what they speake against me and my seruants, Psal. 73,9.

CHAP. VIII.

1 The destruction of Iudáh and Israél, because of their idolatrie.

1 Set

1 SEt the trumpet to thy [a] mouth: *he shal come* as an egle against the House of the
Lord, because they haue transgressed my
couenant, & trespaced against my Law.
2 Israél shal [b] crye vnto me, My God, we
knowe thee.
3 Israél hathe cast of the thĩg that is good:
the enemie shal pursue him.
4 They haue set vp a [c] King, but not by
me: they haue made princes, and I knewe
it not: of their siluer and their golde haue
they made them idoles: therefore shal thei
be destroyed.
5 Thy calfe, ô Samaria, hathe cast thee of:
mine anger is kindeled against them: how
long wil they be without [d] innocencie!
6 [e] For it came euen from Israél: the workeman made it, therefore it is not God: but
the calfe of Samaria shalbe *broken* in pieces.
7 For they haue [f] sowen the winde, & they
shal reape the whirlwinde: it hathe no stalke: the budde shal bring forthe no meale: if
so be it bring forthe, the strangers shal deuoure it.
8 Israél is deuoured, now shal they be amõg
the Gentiles as a vessel wherein *is* no pleasure.
9 For they are gone vp to Asshúr: *they are
as* a [g] wilde asse alone by him self: Ephráim hathe hired louers.
10 Yet thogh they haue hired amõg the nacions, now wil I gather them, and thei shal
sorowe a litle, for the [h] burdẽ of the King,
& the princes.
11 Because Ephráim hathe made many altars to sinne, his altars *shalbe* to sinne.
12 I haue writen to them the great things
of my Law: *but* they were counted as a
[i] strange thing.
13 They sacrifice flesh for the sacrifices of
mine offrings, and eat it: *but* the [k] Lord accepteth them not: now wil he remember
their iniquitie, and visite their sinnes: they
shal returne to Egypt.
14 For Israél hathe forgotten his maker, &
buyldeth temples, and Iudáh hathe encrea
sed strong cities. but I wil send a fyre vpon his cities, and it shal deuoure the palaces thereof.

CHAP. IX.

Of the hunger and captiuitie of Israél.

1 REioyce not, ô Israél for ioye [a] as *other*
people: for thou hast gone a whoring
from thy God: thou hast loued [b] a rewarde vpon euery corne floore.
2 [c] The floore, and the wine presse shal not
fede them, and the new wine shal faile in
her.
3 They wil not dwell in the Lords land, but
Ephráim wil returne to Egypt, & they wil
eat vncleane things in Asshúr.

a God incourageth the Prophet to signifie the spedie coming of the enemie against Israél, which was once the people of God.
b They shal crye like hypocrites, but not from the heart, as their dedes declare.
c That is, Ieroboám, by whome they soght their owne libertie, and not to obey my wil.
d That is vpright iudgement and godlie life.
e Meaning, the calfe was inuented by thẽ selues, and of their fathers in the wildernes.
f Shewing that their religion hathe but a shewe, and in it self is but vanitie.
g They neuer cease but runne to and fro to seke helpe.
h That is, for the tribute wͨ the King and the princes shal lay vpon them: which meanes the Lord vseth to bring them to repentance.
i Thus the idolaters counte the worde of God as strãge in respect of their owne inuentions.
k Saying that they offer it to the Lord, but he accepteth no seruice, wͨ he him self hathe not appointed.

Chap IX.
a For thogh all other people shulde escape, yet thou shalt be punished.
b Thou hast cõmitted idolatrie in hope of rewarde, & to haue thy barnes filled, Iere. 44,17. as an harlot that had rather liue by playĩg yͤ whore then to be interteined of her owne housband.
c These outward things yͭ thou sekest, shalbe taken from thee.

4 They shal not offer [d] wine to the Lord,
nether shal their sacrifices be pleasant vnto him: *but thei shalbe* vnto thẽ as the bread
of mourners: all that eat thereof, shal be
polluted: for their bread [e] for their soules
shal not come into the House of the Lord.
5 What wil ye do [f] then in the solẽne day,
and in the day of the feast of the Lord?
6 For lo, they are gone from [g] destruction:
but Egypt shal gather them vp, and Memphis shal burye them: the nettles shal possesse the pleasant *places* of their siluer, &
the thorne *shalbe* in their tabernacles.
7 The daies of visitacion are come: the
dayes of recompense are come: Israél shal
knowe it: [h] the Prophet *is* a foole: the spiritual man *is* mad, for the multitude of
thine iniquitie: therefore the hatred is
great.
8 The watchemã of Ephráim [i] *shulde be* with
my God: *but* the Prophet *is* the snare of a
fouler in all his waies, & hatred in yͤ House of his God.
9 They [k] are depely set: they are corrupt
as in the daies of Gibeáh: *therefore* he wil
remẽber their iniquitie, he wil visite their
sinnes.
10 I founde Israél like [l] grapes in the wildernes: I sawe your fathers as the first ripe
in the fig tre at her first time: *but* they went
to Baal-Peór, and separated them selues
vnto that shame, and *their* abominacions
were according to [m] their louers.
11 Ephráim their glorie shal flee away like
a birde: frõ the birth [n] and from the wombe, and from the conception.
12 Thogh they bring vp their children, yet
I wil depriue them from being men: yea,
wo to them, when I departe from them.
13 Ephráim, as I sawe, *is as a tre* [o] in Tyrus
planted in a cottage: but Ephráim shal
bring forthe his children to the murtherer.
14 O Lord, giue them: what wilt thou giue
them? giue them a [p] baren wombe & drye
breasts.
15 All their wickednes *is* in [q] Gilgál: for
there do I hate them: for the wickednes of
their inuencions, I wil cast them out of
mine House: I wil loue them no more: all
their princes are rebelles.
16 Ephráim is smitten, their roote is dryed
vp: they can bring no frute: yea, thogh thei
bring forthe, yet wil I slaie euen the dearest of their bodie.
17 My God wil cast thẽ away, because they
did not obey him: and they shal wander a-
mong the nacions.

d All their doings bothe touching policie and religiõ shalbe reiected as things polluted.
e The meat offring which thei offred for them selues.
f When yͤ Lord shal take away all yͤ occasions of seruing him, which shalbe the moste grieuous point of your captiuitie, when you shal se your selues cut of frõ God.
g Thogh they thinke to escape by fleing yͤ destructiõ that is at hand, yet shal they be destroyed in yͤ place whether they flee for soccour.
h Then they shal knowe yͭ they were deluded by them who chalẽged to them selues to be their Prophetes & spiritual men.
i The Prophetes duetie is to bring men to God and not to be a snare to pul them from God
k This people is so rooted in their wickednes, yͭ Gibeáh which was like to Sodóm, was neuer more corrupt, Iud. 19,22.
l Meaning, yͭ he so estemed thẽ and delited in them.
m They were as abominable vnto me, as their louers yͤ idoles.
n Signifying yͭ God wold destroy their childrẽ by these sundry meanes, and so cõsume them by litle and litle.
o As they kept tender plantes in their houses in Tyrus to preserue them frõ the colde ayre of yͤ sea, so was Ephráim at the first vnto me, but now I wil giue him to the slaughter.
p The Prophet seing the great plagues of God toward Ephráim, praieth to God to make them baren, rather then that this great slaughter shulde come vpon their children.
q The chief cause of their destruction is that they commit idolatrie and corrupt my religion in Gilgál.

CHAP. X.

Against Israél and his idoles. 14 His destruction for the same.

1 ISraél *is* a [a] emptie vine, *yet* hathe it
broght forthe frute vnto it self, & according to the multitude of the frute thereof he hathe increased the altars: according to the [b] goodnes of their land they
haue made faire images.
2 Their heart is [c] deuided: now shal they
be founde fautie: he shal breake downe
their altars: he shal destroye their images.
3 For now they shal say, We haue no [d] Kĩg
because we feared not the Lord: and what
shulde a King do to vs?
4 They haue spoken wordes, swearing falsely in making [e] a couenant: thus [f] iudgement groweth as wormewood in the furrowes of the field.
5 The inhabitants of Samaria shal [g] feare
because of the calfe of Beth-áuen: for the
people thereof shal mourne ouer it, & the
[h] Chemarims thereof, that reioyced on it
for the glorie thereof, because it is departed from it.
6 It shalbe also broght to Asshúr, for a present vnto King Iareb: Ephráim shal receiue shame, & Israél shalbe ashamed of his
owne counsel.
7 Of Samaria, the King thereof is destroied, as the fome vpon the water.
8 The hie places also of [i] Auen shalbe destroied, *euen* the sinne of Israél: the thorne
and the thistle shal growe vpõ their altars,
and they shal say to the mountaines, *Couer vs, and to the hilles, Fall vpon vs.
9 O Israél, thou hast [k] sinned from the daies
of Gibeáh: there they [l] stode: the battel in
Gibeáh against the children of iniquitie
did not [m] touche them.
10 It is my desire [n] that I shulde chastise
them, & the people shalbe gathered agaĩst
them, when they shal gather them selues in
their two [o] furrowes.
11 And Ephráim *is as* an heiffer vsed to delite [p] in threshing: but I wil passe by her
[q] faire necke: I wil make Ephráim to ride:
Iudáh shal plowe, *and* Iaakób shal breake
his cloddes.
12 Sowe to your selues in righteousnes: reape after the measure of mercie: [r] breake vp
your fallowe grounde: for *it is* time to seke
the Lord, til he come & raine righteousnes vpon you.
13 *But* you haue plowed wickednes: ye haue
reaped iniquitie: you haue eatẽ the frute of
lies: because ŷ didest trust in thine owne
waies, & in the multitude of thy strong
men,
14 Therefore shal a tumult arise amõg thy
people & all thy munitions shalbe destroied, as [s] Shalmán destroyed Beth-arbél in
the day of battel: the mother with the children was dashed in pieces.
15 So shal Beth-él do vnto you, because of
your malicious wickednes: in a morning
shal the King of Israél be destroyed.

CHAP. XI.

*The benefites of the Lord toward Israél. 5 Their ingra-
titude against him.*

1 WHen Israél [a] *was* a childe, then I
loued him, and called my sonne
out of Egypt.
2 They called them, *but* they [b] went thus frõ
them: thei sacrificed vnto Baalím, & burnt
incense to images.
3 I led Ephráim also, *as one* shulde beare
them in his armes: but thei knewe not that
I healed them.
4 I led them with cordes [c] of a man, *euen*
with bandes of loue, and I was to them, as
he that taketh of the yoke from their iawes, and I laied the meat vnto them.
5 He shal no more returne into the land of
Egypt: but Asshúr shalbe his [d] King, because thei refused to conuert.
6 And the sworde shal fall on his cities, &
shal consume his barres, and deuoure thẽ,
because of their owne counsels.
7 And my people are bent to rebellion a-
gainst me: thogh [e] they called them to the
most hie, *yet* none at all wolde exalt *him*.
8 [f] How shal I giue thee vp, Ephráim? *how*
shal I deliuer thee, Israél? how shal I make
thee, as [g] Admáh? *how* shal I set thee, as Zeboím? mine heart is turned within me: [h] my
repentings are rouled together.
9 I wil not execute the fiercenes of my
wrath: I wil not returne to destroy Ephráim: for I am God, and not man, the holy o-
ne in the middes of thee, & I wil not [i] entre into the citie.
10 They shal walke after the Lord: he shal
roare like a lyon: when he shal roare, then
the children of the West shal feare.
11 [k] Thei shal feare as a sparowe out of E-
gypt, and as a doue out of the land of Asshúr, and I wil place them in their houses,
saith the Lord.
12 Ephráim cõpasseth me about with lies,
and the house of Israél with deceit: but
Iudáh yet ruleth [l] with God, and is faithful with the Sainctes.

CHAP. XII.

*He admonisheth by Iaakobs example to trust in God, and
not in man.*

1 EPhráim is fed [a] with the winde, & followeth after the Eastwinde: he encreaseth daiely lies and destruction, and they
do make a couenant with Asshúr, & [b] oyle
is caryed into Egypt.
2 The Lord hathe also a controuersie with
[c] Iudáh, & wil visite Iaakób, according to
his waies: according to his workes, wil he
recompense him.
3 He toke his brother [d] by the hele in the
wombe

a Whereof thogh the grapes were gathered, yet euer as it gathered new strength, it increased new wickednes, so that ŷ correction which shulde haue broght thẽ to obedience, did but vtter their stubbernes.
b As thei were riche and had abundãce.
c To wit, from God.
d The day shal come ŷ God shal take awai their King, & then they shal fele the frute of their sinnes, and how they trusted in him in vaine, 2. Kĩg 17,6.
e In promising to be faithful toward God.
f Thus their integritie and fidelitie which they pretẽded, was nothing but bitternes and grief.
g When ŷ calfe shalbe caried away.
h Chemarims were certeine idolatrous priestes, ŵ did weare blacke apparel in their sacrifices and cryed with a loude voice: which superstition Eliáh derided, 1. King 18,27. read. 2. king 23,5.
i This he speaketh in contẽpt of Bethél, read Chap. 4, 15.
*Isa. 2,19. luk. 23,30. reuel. 6,16. & 9,6.
k In those daies wast thou as wicked as the Gibeonites, as God there partely declared: for thy zeale colde not be good in executing Gods iudgements, seing thine owne dedes were as wicked as theirs.
l To wit, to fight, or the Israelites remained in that stubbernes frõ that time.
m The Israelites were not moued by their example to cease from their sinnes.
n Because they are so desperate, I wil delite to destroy them.
o That is, when they haue gathered all their strength together.
p Wherein is pleasure, as in plowing is labour and peine.
q I wil lay my yoke vpon her fat necke.
r Read Ierem 4,4.
s That is, Shalmanazzár in the destruction of that citie spared nether kinde nor age.

a Whiles ŷ Israelites were in Egypt and did not prouoke my wrath by their malice and ingratitude.
b They rebelled and went a cõtrary way when the Prophetes called them to repentance.
c That is, friẽdly and not as beasts or sclaues.
d Seing they contemne all this kindenes, they shalbe led captiue into Assyria.
e To wit, the Prophetes
f God considereth with him selfe and that with a certeine grief how to punish them
g Which were two of the cities that were destroied with Sodóm, Deu. 29,23
h Meanĩg, that his loue where with he first loued thẽ, made him betwene doute and assurance what to do: and herein appeareth his fatherlie affection, that his mercie toward his shal ouercome his iudgements, as he declareth in ŷ next vers.
i To consume thee, but wil cause thee to yelde and so receiue thee to mercie: & this is ment of the smale nomber who shal walke after the Lord.
k The Egyptians and Assyrians, shal be afraid whẽ the Lord maĩteineth his people.
l Gouerneth their state acordĩg to Gods worde, & doeth not degenerate.
Chap XII.
a That is, flattereth him self with vaine cõfidence.
b Meaning, presentes to get friendship.
c Which in these pointes was like to Ephráim, but not in idolatries.

wombe, & by his ſtrength he had [d] power
with God,
4 And had [e] power ouer the Angel, & preuailed: he wept and prayed vnto him: [f] he
founde him in Beth-él, and there he ſpake
with vs.
5 Yea, the Lord God of hoſtes, the Lord *is*
him ſelf his memorial.
6 Therefore turne thou to thy God: kepe
mercie and iudgement, and hope ſtil in
thy God.
7 *He is* [g] Canáan: the balances of deceit *are*
in his hand: he loueth to oppreſſe.
8 And Ephráim ſaid, Notwithſtãding I am
riche, I haue foũde me out riches in all my
labours: they ſhal finde none iniquitie in
me, [h] that were wickednes.
9 Thogh I am the Lord thy God, from the
land of Egypt, yet wil I make thee to
dwell in the tabernacles, as in [i] the dayes
of the ſolemne feaſt.
10 I haue alſo ſpoken by the Prophetes, & I
haue multiplied viſiõs, & vſed ſimilitudes
by the miniſterie of the Prophetes.
11 Is there [k] iniquitie in Gileád? ſurely thei
are vanitie: they ſacrifice bullockes in Gil
gál, and their altars *are* as heapes in the
furrowes of the field.
12 [l] And Iaakób fled into the countrey of
Arám, and Iſraél ſerued for a wife, and for
a wife he kept *ſhepe*.
13 And by a [m] Prophet the Lord broght Iſ
raél out of Egypt, and by a Prophet was
he reſerued.
14 *But* Ephráim prouoked him with hie pla
ces: therefore ſhal his blood be powred
vpõ him, and his reproche ſhal his Lord
rewarde him.

d Seing that God did thus preferre Iaakób, their father, Iudahs ingratitude was the more to be abhorred.
e Read Geneſ. 32,31.
f God founde Iaakób as he lay ſleping in Beth él, Gene. 28, 12, and ſo ſpake with hĩ there, that the frute of that ſpeache apperteined to the whole body of the people, whereof we are.
g As for Ephráim he is more like the wicked Canaanites thẽ godlie Abrahám or Iaakób.
h Thus ȳ wicked meaſure Gods fauour by outward proſperitie, & like hypocrites can not abide that anie ſhulde reproue their doĩgs.
i Seing thou wilt not acknowledge my benefites, I wil bring thee againe to dwell in tentes as in the feaſt of the Tabernacles, which thou doeſt now contemne.
k The people thoght ȳ no mã durſt haue ſpoken againſt Gileád, ȳ holie place, and yet the Prophet ſaith, that all their religion was but vanitie.
l If you boaſt of your riches and nobilitie, ye ſeme to reproche your father who was a poore fugitiue and ſeruant.
m Meaning, Moſés. Whereby appeareth, that whatſoeuer they haue, it cometh of Gods fre goodnes.

CHAP. XIII.

1 *The abomination of Iſraél.* 9 *And cauſe of their*
deſtruction.

1 WHen Ephráim ſpake, there *was*
[a] trembling: he [b] exalted him ſelf
in Iſraél, but he hathe ſinned in Báal, [c] and
is dead.
2 And now they ſinne more and more, and
haue made them molten images of their
ſiluer, & idoles accordĩg to their owne vn
derſtanding: they were all the worke of ȳ
craftesmẽ: they ſay one to another whiles
thei ſacrifice a [d] mã, Let thẽ kiſſe ȳ calues.
3 Therefore they ſhalbe as the morning
cloude, & as the morning dewe ȳ paſſeth
away, as ȳ chaffe that is driuẽ with a whirle winde out of the floore, & as the ſmoke
that goeth out of the chimney.
4 Yet I am the Lord thy God [e] frõ the lãd
of Egypt, & thou ſhalt know no God but
me: for there *is* no Sauiour beſide me.
5 I did knowe thee in the wildernes, in the
land of drought.
6 As in their paſtures, ſo were thei filled:
they were filled, and their heart was exalted: therefore haue they forgotten me.
7 And I wil be vnto them as a verie lyon,
& as a leoparde in the waye of Aſſhúr.
8 I wil mete thẽ, as a beare that is robbed
of her whelpes, and I wil breake the cal-
le of their heart, and there wil I deuoure
them like a lyon: the wilde beaſt ſhal teare them.
9 O Iſraél, [f] one hathe deſtroyed thee, but
in me *is* thine helpe.
10 [g] I am: where is thy King, that ſhulde
helpe thee in all thy cities? & thy iudges,
of whome thou ſaideſt, Giue me a King
and princes?
11 I gaue thee a King in mine angre, and I
toke him away in my wrath.
12 The iniquitie of Ephráim *is* [h] bounde
vp: his ſinne *is* hid.
13 The ſorowes of a trauailing woman ſhal
come vpon him: he is an vnwiſe ſonne, els
wolde he not ſtand ſtil at the time, *euen* at
the [i] breaking forthe of the children.
14 I wil redeme them from the power of
the graue: I wil deliuer them frõ death: ô
[k] death, I wil be thy death: ô graue, I wil be
thy deſtruction: [l] repentance is hid from
mine eyes.
15 Thogh he grewe vp among *his* brethren,
an Eaſt winde ſhal come, *euen* the winde of
the Lord ſhal come vp from the wildernes, and drye vp his veine, and his foũtaine ſhalbe dryed vp: he ſhal ſpoyle the trea
ſure of all pleaſant veſſels.
16 Samaria ſhalbe deſolate: for ſhe hathe
rebelled againſt her God: they ſhal fall by
the ſworde: their infants ſhalbe daſhed
in pieces, and their women with childe
ſhalbe ript.

a He ſheweth the excellencie & autoritie that this tribe had aboue all the reſt.
b He made a King of his tribe.
c The Ephraimites are not farre from deſtruction, and haue loſt their autoritie.
d The falſe prophetes perſuaded the idolaters to offer their children after ȳ exãple of Abrahám, & he ſheweth how they wolde exhorte one another to ȳ ſame & to kiſſe, and worſhip theſe calues ŵ were their idoles.
e He calleth them to repentance & reproueth their ingratitude.
f Thy deſtruction is certeine, & my benefites towarde thee declare that it cometh not of me: therefore thine owne malice, idolatrie and vaine confidẽce in men muſt nedes be ȳ cauſe thereof.
g I am allone, Iam. 1,17.
h It is ſurely laid vp to be puniſhed, as Ierem. 17,1.
i But wolde come out of the wombe, ȳ is, out of this dãger wherein he is, and not tarie to be ſtifeled.
k Meaning, ȳ no power ſhal reſiſt God whẽ he wil deliuer his, but euen in death wil he giue thẽ life.
l Becauſe thei wil not turne to me, I wil not chãge my purpoſe.

CHAP. XIIII.

1 *The deſtruction of Samaria.* 3 *He exhorteth Iſraél to*
turne to God, who requireth praiſe and thankes.

1 O Iſraél, [a] returne vnto the Lord thy
God: for thou haſt fallen by thine
iniquitie.
2 Take vnto you wordes, and turne to the
Lord, and ſay vnto him, [b] Take away all
iniquitie, and receiue *vs* graciouſly: ſo wil
we render the calues of [c] our lippes.
3 Aſſhúr ſhal [d] not ſaue vs, nether wil we ride vpõ horſes, nether wil we ſay anie more
to the worke of our hands, *Ye are* our gods:
for in thee the fatherles findeth mercie.
4 [e] I wil heale their rebelliõ: I wil loue thẽ
frely: for mine anger is turned away frõ hĩ.
5 I wil be as the dewe vnto Iſraél: he ſhal
growe as the lilie and faſten his rootes as
the trees of Lebanón.
6 His branches ſhal ſpreade, and his beautie ſhalbe as the oliue tre, and his ſmel as
Lebanón.

a He exhorteth them to repentance, to auoide all theſe plagues, willing them to declare by wordes their obedience and repentance.
b He ſheweth them how thei oght to confeſſe their ſinnes.
c Declaring, ȳ this is the true ſacrifices, that the faithful cã offer, euen thãkes & praiſe, Ebr 13,15.
d We wil leaue of all vaine confidence and pride.
e He declareth how ready God is to receiue them that do repent.

f Whosoeuer ioyne thē selues to this peo ple, shalbe blessed.

7 They that dwell vnder his [f] shadowe, shal
returne: they shal reuiue *as* the corne, and
florish as the vine: the sent thereof *shalbe*
as the wine of Lebanón.

g God sheweth how prōpt he is to heare his, when they repent, and to offer him self, as a protectiō, & sauegard vnto them, as a moste sufficiēt frute & profite.

8 Ephráim *shal say*, What haue I to do anie
more with idoles? I [g] haue heard him, &
loked vpō him: I am like a grene fyrre tre:
vpon me is thy frute found.
9 Who is [h] wise, and he shal vnderstand
these things? *and* prudent, & he shal knowe
them? for the wayes of the Lord *are* righteous, and the iuste shal walke in them: but
the wicked shal fall therein.

h Signifying, that the true wisdome and knowledge cōsisteth in this, euen to reste vpon God.

IOEL.

THE ARGVMENT.

The Prophet Ioél first rebuketh them of Iudáh, that being now punished with a great plague of famine, remaine stil obstinat. Secondly he threateneth greater plagues, because they grewe daily to a more hardenes of heart, & rebellion against God notwithstanding his punishments. Thirdly he exhorteth them to repentance, shewing that it muste be earnest, and procede from the heart because they had grieuously offended God. And so doing, he promiseth, that God wil be merciful, & not forget his couenant that he made with their fathers: but wil send his Christ who shal gather the scattered shepe, and restore them to life, and libertie, thogh they semed to be dead.

CHAP. I.

1 A prophecie against the Iewes. 2 He exhorteth the people to prayer, and fasting for the miserie that was at hand.

1 THE worde of the Lord
that came to Ioél the son
ne of Pethuél.
2 Heare ye this, ô [a] Elders,
and hearken ye all inha-
bitants of the land, whe-
ther [b] suche a thing hathe
bene in your dayes, or yet in the dayes of
your fathers.
3 Tell you your children of it, and let your
children *shewe* to their children, and their
children to another generacion.
4 That which is left of the palmer worme, hathe the grashopper eaten, and the
residue of the grashopper hathe the canker worme eaten, and the residue of the
canker worme hathe ye caterpiller eaten.
5 Awake ye [c] drunkardes, and wepe, and
houle all ye drinkers of wine, because of ye
new wine: for it shalbe pulled from your
mouth.
6 Yea, [d] a nation cometh vpon my land,
mightie, and without nomber, whose teeth
are like the teeth of a lyon, and he hathe the
iawes of a great lyon.
7 He maketh my vine waste, and pilleth of
the barke of my figtre: he maketh it bare,
and casteth it downe: the branches thereof
are made white.
8 Mourne like a virgine girded with sackecloth for the housband of [e] her youth.
9 The meat offring, and the drinke offring
is [f] cut of from the House of the Lord:
the Priests the Lords ministers mourne.
10 The field is wasted: the land mourneth:
for the corne is destroyed: [g] the new wine
is dryed vp, *and* the oyle is decayed.
11 Be ye ashamed, ô housbande men: houle,
ô ye vine dressers for the wheat, and for
the barly, because the haruest of the field
is perished.
12 The vine is dryed vp, and the figtre is
decayed: the pomegranate tre and the palme tre, and the apple tre, *euen* all the trees
of the field are withered: surely the ioy is
withered away from the sonnes of men.
13 [h] Girde your selues & lament, ye Priests:
houle ye ministers of the altar: come, *and*
lye all night in sackecloth, ye ministers of
my God: for the meat offring, and the
drinke offring is taken away from the
House of your God.
14 Sanctifie you a fast: call a solemne assemblie: gather the Elders, *and* all the inhabitants of the land into the House of
the Lord your God, and crye vnto the
Lord,
15 Alas: for the day, for the [i] day of the
Lord is at hand, and it cometh as a destru
ction from the Almightie.
16 Is not the meat cut of before our eyes?
and ioye, and gladnes from the House of
our God?
17 The sede is rotten vnder their cloddes:
the garners are destroyed: the barnes are
broken downe, for the corne is withered.
18 How did the beastes mourne? the herdes
of cattel pine away, because they haue
no pasture, and the flockes of shepe are
destroyed.
19 O Lord, to thee wil I crye: for the fyre
hathe deuoured the pastures of the wildernes, and the flame hathe burnt vp all
the trees of the field.
20 The beastes of the field crye also vnto
thee: for the riuers of waters are dryed vp,
and

a Signifying, the Princes, the Priests, and the gouerners.

b He calleth the Iewes to the consideration of Gods iudgements, who had now plagued the frutes of the grounde for the space of foure yere, which was for their sinnes, & to call them to repentance.

c Meaning, that the occasion of their excesse and drunkennes was taken away.

d This was another plague wherewith God had punished thē, when he stirred vp the Assyrians against them.

e Mourne grieuously as a woman, which hathe lost her housband, to whome she hathe bene maried in her youth.

f The tokens of Gods wrath did appeare in his Temple in so muche, as Gods seruice was left of.

g All comfort and substance for nourishment is taken away.

h He sheweth ye the only meanes to auoide Gods wrath, & to haue all things restored is vnfained repentance.

i We se by these great plagues that vtter destruction is at hand.

and the [k]fyre hathe deuoured the pastures
of the wildernes.

CHAP. II.

*He prophecieth of the comming and crueltie of their e-
nemies. 13 An exhortacion to moue them to conuert.
18 The loue of God towarde his people.*

1 BLowe [a] the trumpet in Zión, & shout
in mine holie Moũtaine: let all the in
habitants of the land tremble: for ỹ daie
of the Lord is come: for it *is* at hand.
2 A [b] daie of darkenes, & of blackenes, a
daye of cloudes, and obscuritie, as the
morning spreade vpon the mountaines,
so is there a [c] great people, and a mightie:
there was none like it from the beginning,
nether shal be anie more after it, vnto the
yeres of manie generacions.
3 A fyre deuoureth before him, & behinde
him a flame burneth vp: the land *is* as the
garden of [d] Eden before him, and behinde him a desolate wildernes, so that nothing shal escape him.
4 The beholding of him *is* like the sight
of horses, and like the horse men, so shal
thei runne.
5 Like the noyce of charets in the toppes
of the mountaines shal thei leape, like the
noyce of a flame of fyre that deuoureth
the stubble, *and* as a mightie people prepared to the battel.
6 Before his face shal the people tremble:
all faces [e] shal gather blackenes.
7 They shal runne like strong men, and go
vp to the wall like men of warre, and euerie man shal go forwarde in his waies, &
thei shal not staie in their paths.
8 Nether shal one [f] thrust another, *but* eue
rie one shal walke in his path: & when thei
fall vpon the sworde, they shal not be wounded.
9 Thei shal runne to and fro in the citie:
they shal runne vpon the wall: they shal
clime vp vpõ the houses, & enter in at the
windowes like the thief.
10 The earth shal tremble before him, the
heauens shal shake, the [g] sunne & the moo
ne shalbe darke, and the starres shal withdrawe their shining,
11 And the Lord shal [h] vtter his voyce before his hoste: for his hoste is verie great:
for *he is* strong that doeth his worke: * for
the daie of the Lord is great and very terrible, and who can abyde it!
12 Therefore also now the Lord saith,
Turne you vnto me with all your heart, &
with fasting, and with weping, and with
mourning,
13 And [i] rent your heart, and not your clothes: and turne vnto the Lord your God,
for he is gracious, and merciful, slowe to
angre, and of great kindenes, and repenteth him of the euil.
14 Who knoweth, *if* he wil [k]returne and repent and leaue a blessing behinde him, *euẽ*
a meat offring, and a drinke offring vnto
the Lord your God?
15 Blowe the trumpet in Zión, sanctifie a
fast, call a solemne assemblie.
16 Gather the people: sanctifie the congregacion, gather the Elders: assemble the
[l] children, and those that sucke the breasts:
let the bridegrome go forthe of his chambre, and the bride out of her bride chambre.
17 Let the Priests, the ministers of the
Lord wepe betwene ỹ porche & the altar,
and let thẽ say, Spare thy people, ô Lord,
and giue not thine heritage into reproche
that the heathen shulde rule ouer them.
* Wherefore shulde thei saie among the
people, Where is their God?
18 Then wil the Lord be [m] ielouse ouer his
land and spare his people.
19 Yea, the Lord wil answer and saie vnto
his people, Beholde, I wil send you corne,
and wine, and oyle, & you shalbe satisfied
therewith: and I wil nomore make you a
reproche among the heathen,
20 But I wil remoue farreof from you the
[n] Northren *armie*, and I wil driue him into a land, barен and desolate with his face towarde the [o] East sea, and his end to ỹ
vtmost sea, and his stinke shal come vp, &
his corruption shal ascend, because he hathe exalted him self to do *this*.
21 Feare not, ô land, *but* be glad and reioyce: for the Lord wil do great things.
22 Be not afraied, ye beastes of the field:
for ỹ pastures of the wildernes are grene:
for the tre beareth her frute: the figtre
and the vine do giue their force.
23 Be glad thẽ, ye children of Zión, and reioyce in the Lord your God: for he hathe
giuen you the rayne of [p]righteousnes, *and
he wil cause to come downe for you the
raine, *euen* the *first* raine, and the later raine in the first *moneth*.
24 And the barnes shalbe ful of wheat, and
the presses shal abounde with wine and
oyle.
25 And I wil render you the yeres that
the grashopper hathe eaten, the canker
worme and the caterpiller and the palmer
worme, my great hoste which I sent a-
mong you.
26 So you shal eat and be satisfied & praise the Name of the Lord your God, that
hathe delt marueilously with you: and my
people shal neuer be ashamed.
27 Ye shal also knowe, that I am in the mid
des of Israél, and that I am the Lord your
God and none other, and my people shal
neuer be ashamed.
28 And afterwarde wil I power [q] out my
Spirit vpon all flesh: and your sonnes and
your daughters shal prophecie: your olde

k That is, drought.

a He sheweth the great iudgemẽts of God which are at hand except thei repent.

b Of affliction and trouble.

c Meaning the Assyrians.

d The enemie destroieth our plentiful cõutrei wheresoeuer he cometh.

e Thei shalbe pale and blacke for feare, as Nahum. 2,10.

f For none shal be able to resist them.

g Read Isa. 13, 10. ezek 32, 7. chap. 3, 1 & 3, 15. math. 24, 29.

h The Lord shal stirre vp the Assyrians to execute his iudgements.

Ierem. 30, 7. amos. 5, 18. seph. 1, 15.

i Mortifie your affections and serue God wᵗ purenes of heart and not wᵗ ceremonies.

k He speaketh this to stirre vp their slothfulnes, and not that he douted of Gods mercies, if thei did repent. How God repenteth read Iere. 18, 8.

l That as all haue sinned, so all maie shewe forthe the signes of their repentance, that men seing the children, which are not fre from Gods wrath, might be the more liuely touched with the consideration of their owne sinnes.

Psal. 79, 10.

m If thei repent, he sheweth that God wil preserue & defende them with a moste ardent affection.

n That is, the Assyriãs your enemies.

o Called the salt sea, or Persian sea: meaning ỹ thogh his armie were so great, ỹ it filled all frõ this sea to the sea called mediterraneum, yet he wolde scatter them.

p That is, suche as shulde come by iuste measure & as was wont to be sent whẽ God was recõciled with thẽ.

Leu. 26, 4. deut. 11, 14.

q That is, in greater abundance and more generally then in time past: and this was fulfilled vnder Christ, when as Gods graces, and his Spirit vnder the Gospel was abundantly giuen to ỹ Church, Isa. 44, 3 act 2, 17. ioh. 7, 38.

men shal dreame [r] dreames, & your yong
men shal se visions,
29 And also vpon the seruants, and vpon
the maides in those daies wil I powre my
Spirit.
30 And I wil shewe [s] wonders in the heauẽs
and in the earth : blood and fyre, and pillers of smoke.
31 The [t] sunne shalbe turned into darkenes,
& the moone into blood, before the great
and terrible daie of the Lord come.
32 But whosoeuer shal call [u] on the Name
of the Lord, shal be saued : for in mount
Zión, and in Ierusalém shal be deliuerance, as the Lord hathe said, and in the [x] rem
nant, whome the Lord shal call.

r As they had visions, and dreames in old time, so shal they now haue clearer reuelations.
s He warneth ẏ faithful what terrible things shulde come, to the intent that thei shulde not loke for cõtinual quietnes in this worlde, & yet in all these troubles he wolde preserue them.
t The order of nature shal seme to be chãged for ẏ horrible afflictiõs that shal be in the worlde, Isa.13,10. ezek 32,7. chap.3, 15 mat.24,29. u Gods judgements are for the destruction of the infideles, and to moue the godlie to call vpon the Name of God, who wil giue them saluation. x Meaning hereby the Gentiles, Rom.10,13.

CHAP. III.

Of the iudgement of God against the enemies of his people.

1 FOr beholde, in [a] those daies and in ẏ
time, whẽ I shal bring againe the cap
tiuitie of Iudáh and Ierusalém,
2 I wil also gather all natiõs, and wil bring
them downe into the [b] vallei of Iehoshaphát, and wil plead with thẽ there for my
people, and for mine heritage Israél, whome thei haue scattered amõg the nations,
and parted my land.
3 And thei haue cast lottes for my people,
& haue giuen the childe [c] for the harlot, &
solde the girle for wine, that they might
drinke.
4 Yea, & what [d] haue you to do with me, ô
Tyrus & Zidón and all the coastes of Palestina? wil ye render me [e] a recompense?
and if ye recompense me, swiftely & spedely, wil I render your recompense vpon
your head:
5 For ye haue taken my siluer and my gold,
and haue caryed into your temples my
goodlie & pleasant things.
6 The children also of Iudáh and the children of Ierusalém haue you solde vnto ẏ
Grecians, that ye might send them farre
from their border.
7 Beholde, I wil raise them out of the place where ye haue solde them, and wil render your rewarde vpon your owne head,
8 And I wil sell your sonnes and your
daughters into the hand of the children
of Iudáh, and thei [f] shal sell them to the Sabeans, to a people farre of: for the Lord him
self hathe spoken it.
9 Publish this among the Gentiles: prepare warre, wake vp the mightie men: let all
the men of warre drawe nere & come vp.
10 [g] Breake your plowe shares into swordes,
and your sieths into speares: let the weake
saie, I am strong.
11 Assemble your selues, and come all ye
heathen and gather your selues together
rounde about: there shal ẏ Lord cast downe thy mightie men.
12 Let the heathen be wakened, and come
vp to the vallei of Iehoshaphát : for there
wil I sit to iudge all the heathen rounde
about.
13 Put in your [h] sieths, for the haruest is ripe: come, get you downe, for ẏ winepresse
is ful: yea, the winepresses runne ouer, for
their wickednes is great.
14 O multitude, ô multitude, *come* into the
vallei of threshing: for the daie of the
Lord *is* nere in the vallei of threshing.
15 The sunne and moone shalbe darkened,
and the starres shal withdrawe their light.
16 The Lord also shal roare out of Zión,
and vtter his voice from Ierusalém, & the
heauens, and the earth shal shake, but the
Lord wilbe the hope [i] of his people, and ẏ
strength of the children of Israél.
17 So shal ye knowe that I am ẏ Lord your
God dwelling in Zión, mine holie Mountaine: then shal Ierusalém be holy, & there shal no strangers go [k] thorowe her anie
more.
18 And in that daie shal the mountaines
[l] droppe downe newe wine, and the hilles
shal flowe with milke, and all the riuers of
Iudáh shal runne with waters, and a fountaine shal come forthe of the House of
the Lord, and shal watter the valley of
Shittim.
19 [m] Egypt shalbe waste, and Edóm shalbe
a desolate wildernes, for the iniuries of
the children of Iudáh, because thei haue
shed innocent blood in their land.
20 But Iudáh shal dwell for euer, and Ierusalém from generacion to generacion.
21 For I wil [n] clense their blood, that I haue
not clensed, and the Lord wil dwell in
Zión.

a When I shal deliuer my Church, ẘ standeth of the Iewes, and of the Gentiles.
b It appeareth that he alludeth to that great victorie of Iehoshaphát, when as God without mans helpe destroyed the enemies, 2. Kin. 20,26 also he hath respect to this worde, Iehoshaphát, ẘ signifieth pleading or iudgement, because God wolde iudge the enemies of his Church as he did there.
c That which the enemie gaue for the sale of my people, he bestowed it vpon harlotes and drinke.
d He taketh ẏ cause of his Church in hãd against ẏ enemie, as thogh the iniurie were done to him self.
e Haue I done you wrõg, that ye wil render me the like?

f For afterwarde God solde thẽ by Nebuchad-nezzár, and Alexãder the great, for the loue he bare to his people, and thereby they were comforted as thogh ẏ price had bene theirs.
g Whẽ I shal execute my iudgemẽts against mine enemies, I wil cause euerie one to be ready, and to prepare their weapons to destroy one another, for my Church sake.
h Thus he shal incourage the enemies ẘ when their wickednes is ful ripe to destroy one another, which he calleth the vallei of Gods iudgement.
i God assureth his against all troubles, that when he destroyeth his enemies, his children shalbe deliuered.
k The strangers shal nomore destroy his Church: ẘ if thei do, it is the people ẘ by their sinnes make the breache for the enemie.
l He promiseth to his Church abundance of graces, read Ezek 47, 1. which shulde watter and comfort ẏ moste baren places, Amós. 9,13
m The malicious enemies shal haue no parte of this grace.
n He had suffered his Church hitherto to lye in their filthines, but now he promiseth to clense them and to make them pure vnto him.

AMOS.

THE ARGVMENT.

AMong many other Prophetes that God raiſed vp to admoniſh the Iſraelites of his plagues for their wickednes and idolatrie, he ſtirred vp Amós, who was an herdman or ſhepherd of a poore towne, and gaue him bothe knowledge and conſtancie to reproue all eſtates and degrees, and to denounce Gods horrible iudgements againſt them, except thei did in time repent: ſhewing them, that if God ſpare not the other nacions about them, who had liued as it were in ignorance of God in reſpect of them, but for their ſinnes wil puniſh them, that thei colde loke for nothing, but an horrible deſtructiõ, except thei turned to the Lord by vnfained repentance. And finally, he comforteth the godlie with hope of the comming of the Meſsiáh, by whome thei ſhulde haue perfite deliuerance and ſaluacion.

CHAP. I.

1 The time of the prophecie of Amós. 3 The worde of the Lord againſt Damaſcus. 6 The Philiſtims, Tyrus, Idumea and Ammon.

1 THe wordes of Amós,
who was amõg the herdmen [a] at Tecóa, which he
ſawe vpon Iſraél, in the
daies of Vzziáh King
of Iudáh, and in the
daies of [b] Ieroboám the
ſonne of Ioáſh King of Iſraél, two yere
before the [c] earth quake.
2 And he ſaid, The Lord ſhal roare from
Zión, and vtter his voyce from Ieruſalém,
and the dwelling places of the ſhepherds
ſhal periſh, and the top of [d] Carmél ſhal
wither.
3 Thus ſaith the Lord, For [e] thre tranſgreſ-
ſions of Damaſcus, and for foure I wil
not turne to it, becauſe thei haue [f] threſhed
Gileád with threſhing inſtrumẽts of yrõ.
4 Therefore wil I ſend a fyre into the houſe of Hazaél, and it ſhal deuoure the [g] palaces of Ben-hadád.
5 I wil breake alſo the barres of Damaſcus,
and cut of the inhabitant of Bikeath á-
uen: and him that holdeth the ſcepter out
of Beth-éden, & the people of Arám ſhal
go into captiuitie vnto [h] Kir, ſaith ẏ Lord.
6 Thus ſaith the Lord, For thre tranſgreſ-
ſions of Azzáh, and for foure, I wil not tur
ne to it, becauſe thei [i] caried away priſoners the whole captiuitie to ſhut them vp
in Edóm.
7 Therefore wil I ſend a fyre vpon the
walles of Azzáh, and it ſhal deuoure the
palaces thereof.
8 And I wil cut of the inhabitant from
Aſhdód, and him that holdeth the ſcepter
from Aſhkelón, and turne mine hand to
Ekrón, and the remnant of the Philiſtims
ſhal periſh, ſaith the Lord God.
9 ¶ Thus ſaith the Lord, For thre trãſgreſ-
ſions of Tyrus, and for foure, I wil not
turne to it, becauſe thei ſhut the whole
captiuitie in Edóm, and haue not remembred the [k] brotherlie couenant.
10 Therefore wil I ſend a fyre vpon the
walles of Tyrus, and it ſhal deuoure the pa
laces thereof.
11 ¶ Thus ſaith the Lord, For thre trãſgreſ
ſions of Edóm, and for foure I wil not turne to it, becauſe he did purſue his brother
with the ſworde, and did " caſt of all pitie,
and his anger ſpoiled him euermore, and
his wrath watched him [l] alway.
12 Therefore wil I ſend a fyre vpõ Temán,
and it ſhal deuoure the palaces of Bozráh.
13 ¶ Thus ſaith the Lord, For thre trãſgreſ
ſions of the children of Ammón, and for
foure, I wil not turne to it, becauſe thei
[m] haue ript vp the women with childe of
Gileád, ẏ thei might enlarge their border.
14 Therefore wil I kindle a fyre in the wall
of Rabbáh, and it ſhal deuoure the palaces thereof, with ſhouting in the daie of
battel, & with a tempeſt in the day of the
whirlewinde.
15 And their King ſhal go into captiuitie,
he and his princes together, ſaith ẏ Lord.

CHAP. II.

Againſt Moáb, Iudáh, and Iſraél.

1 THus ſaith the Lord, For thre trãſgreſ
ſions of Moáb, and for foure, I wil
not turne to it, becauſe it burnt the [a] bones of the King of Edóm into lime.
2 Therefore wil I ſend a fyre vpon Moáb,
and it ſhal deuoure the palaces of Kerióth,
& Moáb ſhal dye with tumult, with ſhouting, & with the ſounde of a trumpet.
3 And I wil cut of the Iudge out of the mid
des thereof, & wil ſlaie all the princes thereof with him, ſaith the Lord.
4 ¶ Thus ſaith the Lord, For thre trãſgreſ-
ſions of Iudáh, & for foure, [b] I wil not turne to it, becauſe thei haue caſt away ẏ Law
of the Lord, & haue not kept his cõmandements, & their lies cauſed thẽ to erre after
the which their fathers haue walked.
5 Therefore wil I ſend a fyre vpõ Iudáh, &
it ſhal deuoure the palaces of Ieruſalém.
6 ¶ Thus ſaith ẏ Lord, For thre tranſgreſ-
ſions of [c] Iſraél, & for foure, I wil not turne to it, becauſe thei ſolde ẏ righteous for

a Which was a towne ſix miles from Ieruſalém in Iudea, but he prophecied in Iſraél.

b In his daies the kingdome of Iſraél did moſte floriſh.

c Which, as Ioſephus writeth, was whẽ Vzziah wolde haue vſurped the Priests office, and therefore was ſmiten with the leproſie.

d Whatſoeuer is frutful and pleaſant in Iſraél, ſhal ſhortely periſh.

e He ſheweth firſt that all ẏ people rounde about ſhulde be deſtroyed for their manifolde ſinnes: ẇ are ment by thre and foure which make ſeuen, becauſe the Iſraelites ſhulde the more depely conſider Gods iudgements toward them.

f If ẏ Syrians ſhal not be ſpared for cõmitting this crueltie againſt one citie, it is not poſſible ẏ Iſraél ſhulde eſcape puniſhment which hathe cõmitted ſo many & grieuous ſinnes againſt God & man.

g The antiquitie of their buyldĩgs ſhal not auoide my iudgements, read Ier. 49, 27.

h Tiglath Pileſár led the Syrians captiue, and broght thẽ to Cyrene, which he calleth here Kir.

i Thei ioyned them ſelues with the Edomites their enemies, which caryed them away captiues.

k For Eſau (of whome came the Edomites) and Iaakób were brethrẽ: therefore thei oght to haue admoniſhed them of their brotherlie friendſhip, & not to haue prouoked them to hatred.

" Ebr. corrupt his compaßions.

l He was a cõtinual enemie vnto him.

m He noteth ẏ great crueltie of the Ammonites that ſpared not ẏ women, but moſte tyrannouſly tormẽted them, and yet ẏ Ammonites came of Lot who was of ẏ houſhold of Abrahám.

a For ẏ Moabites were ſo cruel againſt ẏ King of Edóm ẏ they burnt his bones after that he was dead: ẇ declared their barbarous rage, ſeing they wolde reuenge them ſelues of the dead.

b Seing the Gentiles that had not ſo farre knowledge were thus puniſhed, Iudáh which was ſo fully inſtructed of the Lordes wil, might not thinke to eſcape.

c If he ſpare not Iudáh vnto whome his promiſes were made, much more he wil not ſpare this degenerate kingdome.

d They esteemed moste vile bribes more then mens liues.
e Whẽ thei haue spoiled him & throwẽ him to ỹ grounde, they gape for his life.
f Thinking by these ceremonies, that is, by sacrificing, and being nere mine altar, they may excuse all their other wickednes.
g They spoile others and offer thereof vnto God, thinking that he wil dispense with them, when he is made partaker of their iniquitie.
h The destruction of their enemies & his mercie toward them shulde haue caused their heartes to melt for loue toward him.
i Ye contemned my benefites & abused my graces & craftely went about to stop ỹ mouthes of my Prophetes.
k You haue wearyed me with your sinnes, Isa.1,14.
l None shalbe deliuered by any meanes.
Chap. III.
a I haue onely chosen you to be mine amõg all other people, & yet you haue forsaken me.
b Hereby the Prophet signifieth ỹ he speaketh not of him selfe, but as God guideth and moueth him, ẘ is called ỹ agrement betwene God and his Prophetes.
c Wil God threaten by his Prophetes, except there be some great occasiõ?
d Can any thing come without Gods prouidence?
e Shal his threatnings be in vayne?
f Shal the Prophets threatẽ Gods iudgements and the people not be afrayed?
g Doeth anie aduersitie come without Gods appointement? Isa.45.7.

siluer and the poore for [d] shoes.
7 Thei gape ouer the head of the poore, in
the [e] dust of the earth, and peruert ỹ waies
of the meke: and a man and his father wil
go in to a maid to dishonour mine holie
Name.
8 And thei lie downe vpon clothes laid to
pledge [f] by euerie altar: and thei [g] drinke
the wine of the condemned in the House
of their God.
9 Yet destroied I the [h] Amorite before thẽ,
whose height was like the height of the
cedres, and he was strong as the okes: notwithstanding
I destroied his frute from
aboue, and his roote from beneth.
10 Also I broght you vp frõ the land of Egypt,
and led you fourtie yeres thorow the
wildernes, to possesse the land of the Amorite.
11 And I raised vp of your sonnes for Prophetes,
and [i] of your yong men for Nazarites.
Is it not euen thus, ô ye childrẽ of
Israél, saith the Lord?
12 But ye gaue the Nazarites wine to drinke,
and commãded the Prophetes, saying,
Prophecie not.
13 Beholde, I [k] am pressed vnder you as a
cart is pressed that is ful of sheaues.
14 Therefore the flight shal perish frõ the
[l] swift, and the strong shal not strengthen
his force, nether shal the mightie saue his
life.
15 Nor he that handleth the bowe, shal
stand, and he that is swift of fote, shal not
escape, nether shal he that rideth the horse,
saue his life.
16 And he that is of mightie courage amõg
the strõg men, shal flee away naked in that
day, saith the Lord.

CHAP. III.

He reproueth the house of Israél of ingratitude. 11 For the which God wil punish them.

1 Heare this worde that the Lord pronounceth
against you, ô children of
Israél, *eue* against the whole familie which
I broght vp frõ the land of Egypt, saying,
2 You [a] onely haue I knowen of all the families
of the earth: therefore I wil visite
you for all your iniquities.
3 Can two walke together except thei be
[b] agreed?
4 Wil a [c] lion roare in the forest, when he
hathe no pray? or wil a lions whelpe crye
out of his denne, if he haue taken nothing?
5 [d] Can a birde fall in a snare vpon ỹ earth,
where no fouler is? or wil he take vp the
[e] snare from the earth, and haue taken nothing
at all?
6 Or [f] shal a trumpet be blowen in the citie,
and the people be not afraied? or shal
there [g] be euil in a citie, and the Lord hathe
not done it?
7 Surely the Lord God wil do nothing,
but he [h] reueileth his secret vnto his seruãts
the Prophetes.
8 The lion hathe roared: who wil not be
afrayed? the Lord God hathe spoken: who
can but [i] prophecie?
9 Proclame in the palaces at Ashdód, & in
the palaces in the land of Egypt, and say,
Assemble your selues vpõ the mountaines
of Samaria: so beholde the great tumultes
in the middes thereof, and the oppressed in
the middes thereof.
10 For thei knowe not to do right, saith the
Lord: thei store vp violence, and robberie
[l] in their palaces.
11 Therefore thus saith the Lord God, An
aduersarie *shal come* euen rounde about the
countrei, and shal bring downe thy stregth
from thee, and thy palaces shalbe spoiled.
12 Thus saith the Lord, As the shepherd taketh
[m] out of the mouth of the lion two
legges, or a piece of an eare: so shal the
children of Israél be taken out that dwell
in Samaria in the corner of a bed, and in
[n] Damascus, *as in* a couche.
13 Heare, and testifie in the house of Iaakób,
saith the Lord God, the God of hostes.
14 Surely in the day that I shal visite the
transgressions of Israél vpon him, I wil
also visit the altars of Beth-él, & the hornes
of the altar shal be broken of, and fall
to the grounde.
15 And I wil smite the winter house with
the sommer house, and the houses of yuorie
shal perish, and the great houses shal be
consumed, saith the Lord.

CHAP. IIII.

Against the gouernours of Samaria.

1 Heare this worde, ye [a] kine of Bashán
that are in the moũtaine of Samaria:
which oppresse the poore, *and* destroy the
nedie, & thei say to their masters, [b] Bring,
and let vs drinke.
2 The Lord God hathe sworne by his holines,
that lo, the daies shal come vpõ you,
that he wil take you away with [c] thornes, &
your posteritie with fish hokes.
3 And ye shal go out at the breaches euerie
kowe forwarde: and ye shal cast your selues
out of the palace, saith the Lord.
4 Come to [d] Beth-él, and trãsgresse: to Gilgál,
and multiplie transgression, & bring
your sacrifices in the morning, & your tithes
after thre [e] yeres.
5 And after a thãkes giuing [f] of leauẽ, publish
and proclame the fre offrings: for
this [g] liketh you, ô ye children of Israél,
saith the Lord God.
6 Therefore haue I giuen you [h] clennes
of teeth in all your cities, and scarcenes of

h God dealeth not with the Israelites as he doeth with other people: for he euer warneth them before of his plagues by his Prophetes.
i Because the people euer murmured against the Prophetes, he sheweth that Gods Spirit moued thẽ so to speake as thei did.
k He calleth the strangers, as the Philistims & Egyptians to witnesses of Gods iudgements against the Israelites for their crueltie & oppression.
l The frute of their crueltie and theft appeareth by their great riches which they haue in their houses.
m When the lion hathe saciate his hungre, ỹ shepherd findeth a legge or a tip of an eare to shewe that the shepe hathe bene woried.
n Where they thoght to haue had a sure holde, and to haue bene in safetie.
a Thus he calleth the princes and gouerners, ẘ being ouerwhelmed with the great abundance of Gods benefites, forgate God, & therefore he calleth them by the name of beastes & not of men.
b They incourage suche as haue autoritie ouer ỹ people, to powle them, so that they may haue profite by it.
c He alludeth to fishers which catche fish by hokes and thornes.
d He speaketh this in contempt of thẽ which resorted to these places, thiking ỹ their great deuociõ and good intẽtion had bene sufficient to haue bounde God vnto thẽ.
e Read Deut 14,28. f As Leu.7,13. g You onely delite in these outwarde ceremonies & haue none other respect. h That is, lacke of bread and meat.

bread in all your places,yet haue ye not returned vnto me,saith the Lord.
7 And also I haue withholden the raine frō
you,when there *were* yet thre [i] moneths to
the haruest, and I caused it to raine vpon
one citie, and haue not caused it to raine
vpon another citie : one piece was rained
vpon, and the piece whereupon it rained
not,withered.
8 So two *or* thre cities wandered vnto one
citie to drinke water,but thei were [k] not satisfied : yet haue ye not returned vnto me,
saith the Lord.
9 I haue smitten you with blasting , & mil-
dewe:your great gardens & your vineyardes , & your fig trees, and your oliue trees
did the palmer worme deuoure: yet haue
ye not returned vnto me,saith the Lord.
10 Pestilence haue I sent among you , after
the maner of [l] Egypt:your yong men haue
I slayne with the sworde, and haue taken
away your horses : and I haue made the
stinke of your tents to come vp euen into
your nostrels : yet haue ye not returned
vnto me,saith the Lord.
11 I haue ouerthrowen you , as God ouerthrewe Sodóm and Gomoráh : & ye were
as a fyre [m] brande pluct out of the burnīg:
yet haue ye not returned vnto me , saith
the Lord.
12 Therefore,thus wil I do vnto thee, ô Israél : and because I wil do this vnto thee,
prepare to [n] mete thy God,ô Israél.
13 For lo, he that formeth the moūtaines,&
createth the winde,and declareth vnto mā
what is his thoght:which maketh the mor
ning darkenes , and walketh vpon the hie
places of the earth, the Lord God of hostes *is* his Name.

i I staied the raine til the frutes of the earth were destroyed with drought,& yet you wolde not consider it to returne to me by repentāce.

k Thei colde not finde water ynough where they had heard say it had rained.

l As I plagued the Egyptiās, Exod.9,10.

m You were almost all consumed,and a fewe of you wonderfully preserued, 2. King 14,26.

n Turne to him by repentance.

CHAP. V.

A lamentacion for the captiuitie of Israél.

1 Heare ye this worde, which I lift vp
vpon you , *euen* a lamentacion of the
house of Israél.
2 The [a] virgine Israél is fallen,*and* shal no
more rise: she is left vpon her land , *&* there *is* none to raise her vp.
3 For thus saith the Lord God, The citie
which went out by a thousand, shal leaue an [b] hundreth:and that which went forthe by an hundreth,shal leaue ten to the
house of Israél.
4 For thus saith the Lord vnto the house
of Israél,Seke ye me,and ye shal liue.
5 But seke not Beth-él,nor enter into [c] Gilgál,and go not to Beer-shéba : for Gilgál
shal go into captiuitie, and Beth-él shal
come to naught.
6 Seke the Lord , and ye shal liue , lest he
breake out like fyre in the house of Ioséph
and deuoure it,& there *be* none to quenche
it in Beth-él.
7 They turne [d] iudgemēt to wormewood,

a He so calleth them because they so boasted of thē selues,or because thei were giuen to wantonnes & deintines.
b Meaning, ŷ the tenth parte shulde scarsely be saued.
c In these places thei worshipped new idoles, which afore time serued for ŷ true honour of God: therefore he saith ŷ these shal not saue them.
d In stead of iudgement & equitie they execute crueltie & oppression.

and leaue of righteousnes in the earth.
8 He [e] maketh Pleiades,and Orion, and he
turneth the shadowe of death into the
morning , and he maketh the day darcke as
night:he calleth the waters of the sea, and
powreth them out vpon the opē earth:the
Lord *is* his Name.
9 He strēgtheneth the destroyer against the
mightie : and the destroyer shal come a-
gainst the fortresse.
10 They haue hated him, [f] that rebuked in
the gate : and they abhorre him that speaketh vprightly.
11 For asmuch then as your treading *is* vpō
the poore,and [g] ye take from him burdens
of wheat, ye haue buylt houses of hewen
stone,but ye shal not dwell in them:ye haue planted pleasant vineyardes,but ye shal
not drinke wine of them.
12 For I knowe your manifolde transgressions , and your mightie sinnes : they afflict
the iust,thei take rewardes,& thei oppresse
the poore in the gate.
13 Therefore [h] the prudent shal kepe silence
in that time,for it is an euil time.
14 Seke good and not euil,that ye may liue:
and the Lord God of hostes shalbe with
you,as you haue spoken.
15 Hate the euil , and loue the good , and e-
stablish iudgement in the gate : it may be
that the Lord God of hostes wil be merciful vnto the remnant of Ioséph.
16 Therefore the Lord God of hostes, the
Lord saith thus,Mournīg *shalbe* in all stretes: and they shal say in all the hie waies,
Alas,alas:and thei shal call the [i] housbād-
man to lamentacion,& suche as can mourne,to mourning.
17 And in all the vines *shalbe* lamentacion:
for I wil passe through thee, saith ŷ Lord.
18 Wo vnto you, that [k] desire the day of
the Lord : what haue you to do with it ?
the day of the Lord *is* darkenes and not
light.
19 As if a man did flee from a lyon , and a
beare met him,or went into the house,and
leaned his hand on the wall, and a serpent
bit him.
20 Shal not the day of the Lord be darkenes, and not light ? euen darkenes and no
light in it?
21 I hate *&* abhorre your feast daies,and I
wil not smel in your solemne assemblies.
22 Thogh ye offer me burnt offrings and
meat offrings, [l] I wil not accept them: nether wil I regarde the peace offring of
your fat beasts.
23 Take thou away from me the multitude
of thy songs (for I wil not heare the melodie of thy violes)
24 And let iudgemēt runne downe as [m] waters,and righteousnes as a mightie riuer.
25 Haue ye offred vnto me sacrifices & of-

e He describeth ŷ power of God,Iob. 9,9.

f Thei hate ŷ Prophetes, ŷ reproue them in the open assemblies.

g Ye take bothe his money & also his fode wherewith he shulde liue

h God wil so plague them, that thei shal not suffer the godlie once to open their mouthes to admonish them of their fautes

i So that all degrees shal haue matter of lamentaciō for the great plagues.

k Thus he speaketh because the wicked & hypocrites said thei were cōtent to abide Gods iudgements, where as the godlie tremble & feare, Iere. 30,7 ioél.2,11. zeph.1,15.

l Because ye haue corrupt my true seruice & remaine obstinate in your vices, Isa. 1,11. iere. 6,10.
m Do your duetie to God & to your neighbour, & so ye shal fele his grace plentifully,if you shewe your abundāt affections according to Gods worde.

frings in the wildernes fortie yeres, ô house of Israél?
26 But you haue borne [n] Siccúth your King
and Chiun your images, *and* the starre of
your gods, which ye made to your selues.
27 Therefore wil I cause you to go into
captiuitie beyonde Damascus, saith the
Lord, whose Name *is* the God of hostes.

n That idole which you estemed as your King, & caryed about, as you did Chiun, in the which images you thoght ỹ there was a certeine diuinitie.

CHAP. VI.

Against the princes of Israél liuing in pleasures.

1 WO to [a] them that are at ease in Zión and trust in the mountaine of
Samaria, [b] which were famous at the beginning of the nacions: and the house of
Israél came to them.
2 Go you vnto Calnéh, & se: & from thence
go you to Hamáth the great: thẽ go downe to Gath of the Philistims: be [c] thei better then these kingdomes? or the border of
their land greater then your border,
3 Ye that put farre away the [d] euil day, and
approche to the seat of iniquitie?
4 Thei lie vpõ beddes of yuorie, & stretch
them selues vpon their beddes, and eat the
lambes of the flocke, and the calues out of
the stall.
5 They sing to the sounde of the viole: thei
inuent to them selues instruments of musicke like [e] Dauid.
6 They drinke wine in bowls, and anoint
them selues with the chief ointments, but
no man is [f] sory for the affliction of Ioséph.
7 Therefore now shal thei go captiue with
the first that go captiue, and [g] the sorowe of
them that stretched them selues, is at hãd.
8 [h] The Lord God hathe sworne by him
self, saith the Lord God of hostes, I abhorre [i] the excellencie of Iaakób, and hate his
palaces: therefore wil I deliuer vp the citie
with all that is therein.
9 And if there remaine ten men in one house, thei shal dye.
10 And his vncle [k] shal take him vp & burne him to cary out the bones out of the
house, and shal say vnto him, that is by
[l] ỹ sides of the house, Is there yet any with
thee? And he shal say, None. Then shal he
say, [m] Holde thy tongue: for we may not
remembre the Name of the Lord.
11 For beholde, the Lord commandeth, and
he wil smite ỹ great house with breaches,
and the litle houses with clefts.
12 Shal horses [n] runne vpon the rocke? or
wil one plowe *there* with oxen? for ye haue
turned iudgement into gall, and the frute
of righteousnes into [o] wormewood.
13 Ye reioyce in a thing of noght: ye say,
Haue not we gottẽ vs [p] hornes by our owne strength?
14 But beholde, I wil raise vp against you
a nacion, ô house of Israél, saith the Lord
God of hostes: and thei shal afflict you, frõ
the entring in of [q] Hamáth vnto the riuer
of the wildernes.

Chap. VI.

a The Prophet threatneth the wealthy, ỹ regarded not Gods plagues nor menaces by his Prophetes.

b These two cities were famous by their first inhabitants the Canaanites: & seing before time they did nothing auaile them that were there borne, why shulde you loke ỹ thei shulde saue you, which were broght in to dwell in other mens possessions?

c If God haue destroied these excellent cities in thre diuers kingdomes, as in Babylon, Syria, & of the Philistims, & hath broght their wide borders into a greater streitenes, thẽ yours yet are, thinke you to be better or to escape?

d Ye that continue stil in your wickednes & thinke, that Gods plagues are not at hand, but giue your selues to all idlenes, wãtonnes and riote.

e As he caused diuers kindes of instruments to be made to serue Gods glorie, so these did contend to inuent as manie to serue their wanton affections and lustes.

f Thei pitied not their brethren, whereof now manie were slayne and caryed away captiue.
g Some read, the ioye of them that stretche them selues, shal departe.
h Read Ierem. 51, 14.
i That is, the riches and pompe.
k The destruction shalbe so great that none shal almost be left to burie the dead: and therefore they shal burne them at home, to carye out the burnt ashes with more ease.
l That is, to some neighbour, that dwelleth rounde about.
m They shalbe so astonished at this destruction, that they shal boast no more of the Name of God, and that they are his people: but they shalbe dumme when they heare Gods Name and abhorre it, as they that are desperate or reprobate.
n He compareth them to baren rockes whereupõ it is in vaine to bestowe labour: shewing that Gods benefites can haue no place among them.

o Read Chap. 5, 7.

p That is, power & glorie.

q From one corner of the countrey to another.

CHAP. VII.

God sheweth certeine visions, whereby he signifieth the destruction of the people of Israél. 10 The false accusacion of Amaziáh. 12 His crafty counsel.

1 THus hathe ỹ Lord God shewed vnto
me, and beholde, he formed [a] greshoppers in the beginning of the shutting vp
of the latter groeth: and lo, *it was* in the
latter groeth [b] after the Kings mowing.
2 And whẽ they had made an end of eating
the grasse of the land, then I said, O Lord
God, spare, I beseche thee: who shal raise
vp Iaakób? for he is smale.
3 *So* the Lord [c] repented for this. It shal
not be, saith the Lord.
4 ¶ Thus *also* hathe the Lord God shewed
vnto me, and beholde, the Lord God called to iudgement by fyre, [d] and it deuoured the great depe, and did eat vp a parte.
5 Then said I, O Lord God, cease, I beseche
thee: who shal raise vp Iaakób? for he is
smale.
6 *So* the Lord repented for this. This also
shal not be, saith the Lord God.
7 ¶ Thus *againe* he shewed me, and beholde, the Lord stode vpon a wall made by line [e] with a line in his hand.
8 And the Lord said vnto me, Amós, what
seest thou? And I said, A line. Then said
the Lord, Beholde, I wil set a line in the
middes of my people Israél, and wil passe
by them no more.
9 And the hie places of Isháк shalbe desolate, and the temples of Israél shalbe destroyed: and I wil rise against the house of
Ieroboám with the sworde.
10 ¶ [f] Then Amaziáh the Priest of Beth-él
sent to Ieroboám King of Israél, saying,
Amós hathe conspired against thee in the
middes of the house of Israél: the land is
not able to beare all his wordes.
11 For thus Amós saith, Ieroboám shal dye
by the sworde, and Israél shalbe led away
captiue out of their owne land.
12 Also [g] Amaziáh said vnto Amós, O thou
the Seer, go, flee thou away into the land
of Iudáh, and there eat *thy* bread and prophecie there.
13 But prophecie no more at Beth-él: for it
is the Kings chappel, and it is the Kings
court.

a To deuoure the land: and he alludeth to the inuading of the enemies.

b After the publicke commandemẽt for mowing was giuen: or as some read, when ỹ Kings shepe were shorne.

c That is, staied this plague at my prayer.

d Meaning, ỹ Gods indignation was inflamed against ỹ stubbernes of this people.

e Signifying ỹ this shulde be the last measuring of the people, and ỹ he wolde deferre his iudgement no lõger.

f That is, whẽ Amós had prophecied that ỹ King shulde be destroyed: for this wicked Priest more for hatred he bare to the Prophet then for loue toward the King, thoght this accusation sufficient to condẽne hĩ, whereas none other colde take place.

g When this instrument of Satan was not able to cõpasse his purpose by the King, he assayed by another practise: that was, to feare the Prophet, that he might departe, and not reproue their idolatrie there openly, and so hinder his profite.

14 Then anſwered Amós, and ſaid to Amaziáh, I was no [h] Prophet, nether was I a
Prophetes ſonne, but I was an herdman,
and a gatherer of wilde figges.

h Thus he ſheweth by his extraordinarie vocation, ỷ God had giuẽ him a charge which he muſt nedes execute.

15 And the Lord toke me as I followed the
flocke, and the Lord ſaid vnto me, Go, pro
phecie vnto my people Iſraél.
16 Now therefore heare thou the worde of
the Lord. Thou ſaiſt, Prophecie not a-
gainſt Iſraél, and ſpeake nothing againſt
the houſe of Iſhák.
17 Therefore thus ſaith the Lord, [i] Thy
wife ſhal be an harlot in the citie, and thy
ſonnes and thy daughters ſhal fall by the
ſworde, and thy land ſhal be deuided by
line: and thou ſhalt dye in a polluted land,
and Iſraél ſhal ſurely go into captiuitie
forthe of his land.

i Thus God vſed to approue the autoritie of his Prophetes by his plagues & iudgemẽts againſt them, ẇ were malicious enemies, Ier. 28,12 & 29,21. & 25. as this day he doeth againſt them ỷ perſecute the miniſters of his Goſpel.

CHAP. VIII.

1 Againſt the rulers of Iſraél. 7 The Lord ſweareth.
11 The famine of the worde of God.

1 THus hathe the Lord God ſhewed vnto me, & beholde, a baſket of ſomer
frute.
2 And he ſaid, Amós, what ſeeſt thou? And
I ſaid, A baſket of ſomer [a] frute. Then
ſaid the Lord vnto me, The end is come
vpon my people of Iſraél, I wil paſſe by
them no more.

a Which signified the ripenes of their ſinnes and the readines of Gods iudgements.

3 And the ſongs of the Temple ſhal be
houlings in that day, ſaith the Lord God:
many dead bodies *ſhalbe* in euerie place:
thei ſhal caſt them forthe with [b] ſilence.
4 Heare this, ô ye that [c] ſwallow vp the
poore, that ye may make the nedie of the
land to faile,
5 Saying, When wil the [d] new moneth be
gone, that we may ſell corne? & the Sabbath, that we may ſet forthe wheat, & make [e] the Epháh ſmale, and the ſhekel great,
and falſefie the weights by deceit?
6 That we may bye the poore for ſiluer,
and the nedie for ſhoes: yea, and ſell the
refuſe of thẽ wheat.
7 The Lord hathe ſworne by the excellencie of Iaakób, Surely I wil neuer forget
any of their workes.
8 Shal not the land tremble for this, and
euerie one mourne, that dwelleth therein?
and it ſhal riſe vp wholy as a flood, and it
ſhalbe caſt out, & [f] drowned as by ỷ flood
of Egypt.
9 And in that day, ſaith the Lord God, I
wil euen cauſe the [g] ſunne to go downe
at noone: and I wil darken the earth in the
cleare day.
10 And I wil turne your feaſtes into mourning, and all your ſongs into lamentacion:
and I wil bring ſackecloth vpõ all loines,
and baldnes vpon euerie head: and I wil
make it as the mourning of an onelie ſonne, and the end thereof as a bitter day.

b There ſhalbe none left to mourne for them.
c By ſtaying the ſale of fode and neceſſarie things ẇ you haue gotten into your owne hands, & ſo cauſe the poore to ſpẽd quickely that litle that they haue, and at length for neceſſitie to become your ſclaues.
d When the dearth was once come, thei were ſo griedy of gaine, that thei thoght ỷ holy day to be an hinderance vnto them.
e That is, the meaſure ſmale & the price great.
f That is, the inhabitants of the land ſhal be drowned, as Nilus drowneth many when it ouerfloweth.
g In the middes of their proſperitie I wil ſend great affliction.

11 Beholde, the daies come, ſaith the Lord
God, that I wil ſend a famine in the land,
not a famine of bread, nor a thirſt for water, but of hearing the worde of the Lord.
12 And they ſhal wander from ſea to ſea,
and from the North euen vnto the Eaſt
ſhal thei runne to & fro to ſeke the [h] worde
of the Lord, and ſhal not finde it.
13 In that day ſhal the fayre virgines and
the yong men periſh for thirſt.
14 They that ſweare by the ſinne [i] of Samaria, and that ſay, Thy God, ô Dan, liueth, & [k] the maner of Beer-ſhéba liueth,
euen thei ſhal fall, and neuer riſe vp a-
gaine.

h Whereby he ſheweth ỷ they ſhal not onely periſh in bodie, but alſo in ſoule for lacke of Gods worde, ẇ is ỷ fode thereof.
i For the idolaters did vſe to ſweare by their idoles: which here he calleth their ſinne, as the papiſtes yet do by theirs. k That is, the cõmune maner of worſhiping and the ſeruice or religion there vſed.

CHAP. IX.

Threatnings againſt the Tẽple. 2 And againſt Iſraél.
11 The reſtoring of the Church.

1 I Sawe the Lord ſtanding vpon the [a] altar, and he ſaid, Smite the lintel of the
dore, that the poſtes may ſhake: and cut
thẽ in pieces, *euen* the [b] heads of them all,
& I wil ſlay the laſt of thẽ with the ſworde: he ỷ fleeth of them, ſhal not flee away:
& he that eſcapeth of them, ſhal not be deliuered.

a Which was at Ieruſalém: for he appeared not in the idolatrous places of Iſraél.
b Bothe the chief of them & alſo the cõmune people.

2 Thogh thei digge into the hel, thence
ſhal mine hand take thẽ: thogh thei clime
vp to heauen, thence wil I bring them
downe.
3 And thogh thei hide them ſelues in the
toppe of Carmél, I wil ſearche and take
them out thence: and thogh thei be hid
from my ſight in the bottome of the ſea,
thence wil I commande the [c] ſerpent, and
he ſhal byte them.
4 And thogh thei go into captiuitie before their enemies, thence wil I commande
the ſworde, and it ſhal ſlaye them: and I
wil ſet mine eies vpon them for euil, and
not for good.
5 And the Lord God of hoſtes ſhal touche the land, and it ſhal melt away, and
all that dwell therein, ſhal mourne, and
it ſhal riſe vp wholy like a flood, and ſhalbe drowned as by the flood of Egypt.
6 He buyldeth his [d] ſpheres in the heauen,
and hathe laid the fundacion of his glo-
be of elements in the earth: he calleth the
waters of the ſea, & powreth them out vpõ
the open earth: the Lord *is* his Name.
7 Are ye not as the Ethiopians [e] vnto me, ô
children of Iſraél, ſaith the Lord? haue not
I broght vp Iſraél out of the lãd of Egypt?
and the Philiſtims from [f] Caphtór, and
Arám from Kir?
8 Beholde, the eyes of the Lord God *are*
vpon the ſinful kingdome, and I wil deſtroy it cleane out of the earth. Neuertheles I wil not vtterly [g] deſtroy the houſe of
Iaakób, ſaith the Lord.

c He ſheweth that God wil declare him ſelfe enemie vnto them in all places, and that his elementes and all creatures ſhalbe enemies to deſtroy them.
d He declareth by ỷ wõderful power of God, by the making of the heauens and ỷ elements that it is not poſsible for man to eſcape his iudgements when he puniſheth.
e Am I more bounde to you then to the Ethiopians or blackemores? yet haue I beſtowed vpon you greater benefites.
f Read Ierem. 47,4.
g Thogh he deſtroye the rebellious multitude, yet he wil euer reſerue the remnãt his Church to call vpon his Name.

9 For lo, I wil commande and I wil sifte the
house of Israél among all nacions, like as
corne is sifted in a siue: yet shal not ỹ [h] least
stone fall vpon the earth.
10 *But* all the sinners of my people shal dye
by ỹ sworde, which say, The euil shal not
come, nor hasten for vs.
11 In that day wil I raise vp the [i] tabernacle of Dauid, that is fallen downe, and close vp the breaches thereof, and I wil raise vp his ruines, and I wil buyld it, as in
the daies of olde,
12 That thei may possesse the remnant of
[k] Edóm, and of all the heathē, because my
Name is called vpon them, saith ỹ Lord,
that doeth this.

h Meaning, ỹ none of his shulde perish in his wrath.

i I wil send ỹ Mesiáh promised and restore by him the spiritual Israél, Act. 15, 16.

k Meaning ỹ the very enemies, as were the Edomites & others, shul de be ioyned wt the Iewes in one societie and body, whereof Christ shulde be the head.

13 Beholde, the daies come, saith the Lord,
that the plowman shal [l] touche the mower,
& the treader of grapes him that soweth
sede: and the mountaines shal [m] droppe
swete wine, and all the hilles shal melt.
14 [n] And I wil bring againe the captiuitie
of my people of Israél: and thei shal buylde the waste cities, and inhabite them, and
thei shal plant vineyardes, and drinke the
wine thereof: thei shal also make gardēs, &
eat the frutes of them.
15 And I wil plant them vpon their land,
and thei shal no more be pulled vp againe out of their land, which I haue giuen
them, saith the Lord thy God.

l Signifying that there shal be great plenty of all thigs so that when one kinde of frute is ripe, another shulde followe & euerie one in course, Leu. 26 5.

m Read Ioél, 3.18.

n The accomplishement hereof is vnder Christ, when they are planted in his Church, out of ỹ which they can neuer be pulled, after they are once graffed therein

OBADIAH.

THE ARGVMENT.

THe Idumeans, which came of Esáu, were mortal enemies alway to the Israelites, which came of Iaakób, & therefore did not onely vexe them continually with sondry kindes of crueltie, but also stirred vp others to fight against them. Therefore when thei were now in their greatest prosperitie, and did moste triumphe against Israél, which was in great affliction and miserie, God raised vp his Prophet to comfort the Israelites, for asmuche as God had now determined to destroy their aduersaries, which did so sore vexe them, and to send them suche as shulde deliuer them, and set vp the kingdome of Mesiáh, which he had promised.

1 THe vision of Obadiáh.
Thus saith ỹ Lord God
against Edóm, [a] We
haue heard a rumor frō
the Lord, and an ambas-
sadour is sent amōg the
heathen: arise, and [b] let
vs rise vp against her to battel.
2 Beholde, I haue made thee smale a-
mong the heathen: thou art vtterly despised.
3 The [c] pride of thine heart hathe deceiued thee: thou that dwellest in the cleftes
of the rockes, whose habitacion *is* hie, that
saith in his heart, Who shal bring me downe to the grounde?
4 Yea thogh thou exalt thy self as the egle,
& make thy nest among the starres, thence
wil I bring thee downe, saith the Lord.
5 [d] Came theues to thee or robbers by night?
how wast thou broght to silēce? wolde thei
not haue stollen, til they had ynough? if
the grapegatherers came to thee, wolde
thei not leaue *some* grapes?
6 How are the things of Esáu soght vp, &
his treasures searched?
7 All the men of thy confederacie [e] haue
driuen thee to the borders: the men that
were at peace with thee, haue deceiued
thee, *and* preuailed against thee: *thei that eat*

a God hathe certeinly reueiled to his Prophetes ỹ he wil raise vp the heathē to destroy the Edomites, whereof ỹ rumour is now published, Ierem. 49, 14.

b Thus ỹ hea thē incourage them selues to rise against Edóm.

c Which despiseſt all others in respect of thy self & yet art but an handful in comparison of others, and art shut vp amōg the hilles as separate from the rest of the worlde.

d God wil so destroy them ỹ he wil leaue none, thogh theues when they come, take but til thei haue ynough, and they that gather grapes, euer leaue some behinde them, Ierem. 49, 9.

e They in whome thou didest trust, for to haue helpe and friendship of them shal be thine enemies and destroy thee.

thy [f] bread, haue laid a woūde vnder thee:
there is none vnderstanding in him.
8 Shal not I in that day, saith the Lord, euē
destroy the wise men out of Edóm, and
vnderstanding from the mount of Esáu.
9 And thy strong men, ô Temán, shalbe a-
fraied, because euerie one of the mount
of Esáu shalbe cut of by slaughter.
10 For thy crueltie against thy [g] brother
Iaakób, shame shal couer thee, and thou
shalt be cut of for euer.
11 When thou stodest [h] on the other side,
in the day ỹ the strangers caryed away his
substance, and strāgers entred into his gates, and cast lottes vpon Ierusalém, euen
thou wast as one of them.
12 But thou shuldest not haue beholden the
day of thy brother, in the day that he was
made [i] a stranger, nether shuldest thou haue reioyced ouer the children of Iudáh,
in the day of their destruction: thou shuldest not haue spokē proudely in the day of
affliction.
13 Thou shuldest not haue entred into the
gate of my people in the day of their destruction, nether shuldest thou haue once
loked on their affliction in the day of their
destruction, nor haue laid hands on their
substance in the day of their destruction.
14 Nether shuldest thou haue stand in the
crosse waies to cut of them, that shulde
escape, nether shuldest thou haue shut vp

f That is, thy familiar frīds and ghestes haue by secret practises destroyed thee.

g He sheweth the cause why the Edomites were so sharpely punished: to wit, because they were enemies to his Church, whome now he cōforteth by punishing their enemies.

h Whē Nebuchad-nezzár came against Ierusalém, ỹ ioynedst with him & hadest part of ỹ spoile, & so didest reioyce when my people, ỹ is, thy brother were afflicted, where as thou shuldest haue pitied & holpē thy brother.

i When the Lord depriued them of their former dignitie and gaue them to be caryed into captiuitie.

the remnant thereof in the daie of affliction.
15 For the daie [k] of the Lord *is* nere, vpon
all the heathen: as thou hast done, it shal
be done to thee: thy rewarde shal returne
vpon thine head.
16 For as ye haue [l] drunke vpon mine holy
Mountaine, *so* shal all the heathen drinke
continually: yea, thei shal drinke and swalowe vp, and thei shal be [m] as thogh thei
had not bene.
17 But vpon mount Zión shal be deliuerãce, and it shalbe holy, & the house of Iaakób shal possesse their possessions,
18 And the house of Iaakób shalbe [n] a fyre,
and the house of Ioséph a flame, and the
house of Esáu as stubble, & thei shal kindle
in them and deuoure them: and there shal
be no remnant of the house of Esáu: for
the Lord hathe spoken it.
19 And thei shal possesse the South side of
the [o] mount of Esáu: and the plaine of the
Philistims, and thei shal possesse the fieldes of Ephráim, & the fields of Samaria,
and Beniamín *shal haue* Gileád.
20 And the captiuitie of this hoste of the
children of Israél, which were among the
[p] Canaanites *shal possesse* vnto Zarepháth,
and the captiuitie of Ierusalém, which is
in Sepharád, shal possesse the cities of the
South.
21 And thei [q] that shal saue, shal come vp to
Mount Zión to iudge the mount of Esáu,
and the kingdome shalbe the Lords.

k Whẽ he wil sommon all ỹ heathen, and send them to destroy thee.
l That is, reioiced & triũphed.
m The Edomites shalbe vtterly destroyed, & yet in despite of all ỹ enemies I wil reserue my Church & restore it.
n God attributeth this power to consume his enemies to his Church which power is only is proper to hĩself, as Isa 10, 17 deu 4, 24. chr. 12, 29.
o He describeth how the Church shalbe inlarged & haue great possessions, but this chiefly is accomplished vnder Christ when as the faithful are made heires and lords of all things by him which is their head.
p By the Canaanites the Iewes meane the Dutche men, and by Zarepháth, France, and by Sepharád, Spaine.
q Meaning ỹ God wil raise vp in his Church suche as shal rule & gouerne for ỹ defence of ỹ same, and destruction of his enemies vnder Mesiáh, whome the Prophet calleth here the Lord & head of this kingdome.

IONAH.

THE ARGUMENT.

WHen Ionáh had long prophecied in Israél and had litle profited, God gaue him expresse charge to go, and denounce his iudgements against Niniueh the chief citie of the Assyrians, because he had appointed, that thei which were of the heathen shulde conuert by the mightie power of his worde, and that within thre daies preaching, that Israél might se how horribly thei had prouoked Gods wrath, which for the space of so many yeres, had not conuerted to the Lord for so many Prophetes and so diligent preaching. He prophecied vnder Ioásh, and Ierobóim, as 2 King. 14, 25.

CHAP. I.

3 Ionáh fled when he was sent to preache. 4 A tempest ariseth, and he is cast into the sea for his disobedience.

1 THe worde of the Lord
came [a] also vnto Ionáh
the sonne of Amittái,
saying,
2 Arise, *and* go to [b] Niniuéh, that [c] great citie,
and crye against it: for
their wickednes is come vp before me.
3 But Ionáh rose vp to [d] flee into Tarshísh
from the presence of the Lord, and went
downe to [e] Iaphó: & he founde a ship going to Tarshísh: so he paied the fare therof, and went downe into it, that he might
go with them vnto Tarshísh, from the
[f] presence of the Lord.
4 But the Lord sent out a great winde into
the sea, and there was a mightie tempest
in the sea, so that the ship was like to be
broken.
5 Then the mariners were afraied, and cry
ed euerie man vnto his god, and cast the
wares that were in the ship, into the sea
to lighten it of them: but Ionáh was gone
downe [g] into the sides of the ship, and he
laie downe, and was fast a slepe.
6 So the shipmaster came to him, and said
vnto him, What meanest thou, ô sleper!
Arise, call vpon thy [h] God, if so be ỹ God
wil thinke vpon vs, that we perish not.
7 And thei said euerie one to his felowe,
Come, and let vs cast [i] lottes, that we maie
knowe, for whose cause this euil *is* vpon vs.
So thei cast lots, & the lot fel vpon Ionáh.
8 Then said thei vnto him, Tel vs for whose
cause this euil *is* vpon vs? what is thine
occupacion? and whence comest thou?
which is thy countrei? and of what people
art thou?
9 And he answered them, I am an Ebrew, &
I feare the Lord God of heauen, which
hathe made the sea, and the drye land.
10 Then were the men excedingly afraid,
and said vnto him, Why hast thou done
this? (for the men knewe, that he fled from
the presence of the Lord, because he had
tolde them)
11 Then said thei vnto him, What shal we
do vnto thee, that the sea maie be calme
vnto vs? (for the sea wroght and was troublous)
12 And he said vnto them, Take me, and
cast me into the sea: so shal the sea be calme vnto you: for I knowe that for my sake
this great tempest *is* vpon you.
13 Neuertheles, the men rowed to bring it
to the land, but thei colde not: for the sea
wroght, and was troublous against them.

a After that he had preached along time in Israél: and so Ezekiél, after that for a time he had prophecied in Iuda, he had visions in Babylon, Ezek. 1, 1.
b For seing ỹ great obstination of ỹ Israelites, he sent his Prophet to the Gentiles ỹ they might prouoke thẽ to repentance or at least make thẽ inexcusable: for Niniuéh was the chief citie of the Assyrians.
c For as autors write, it cõteined in circuit about eight & fortie mile & had a thousand and fyue hũdreth towres, and at this time there were an hundreth & twẽtie thousand childrẽ therein, Chap. 4. 11.
d Whereby he declared his weakenes, that wolde not promptely follow the Lords calling, but gaue place to his owne reason, which persuaded him that he shulde nothing at all profite there, seing he had done so smale good amõg his owne people. Chap. 4, 2
e Which was the hauen, and porte to take shiping thither, called also Ioppe.
f From that vocation whereunto God had called him, and wherein he wolde haue assisted him.
g As one ỹ wolde haue cast of this care, and solicitude by seking rest and quietnes.
h As they had called on their idoles, which declareth that idolaters haue nostay nor certeintie, but in their troubles seke, thei can not tel to whome.
i Which declared that ỹ matter was in great extremitie, and doute, which thing was Gods motion in them for the trial of the cause: and this may not be done but in matters of great importance.

14 Wherefore thei cryed vnto the Lord, &
said, [k]We beseche thee, ô Lord, we beseche
thee, let vs not perish for this man's life,
and laie not vpon vs innocent blood:
for thou, ô Lord, hast done, as it pleased
thee.
15 So thei toke vp Ionáh, and cast him into
the sea, & the sea ceased from her raging.
16 Then the men [l] feared the Lord excedingly, & offred a sacrifice vnto ỳ Lord,
and made vowes.
17 Now the Lord had prepared a great fish
to swalowe vp Ionáh: and Ionáh was in the
[m] belly of the fish thre daies, and thre
nights.

k This declareth that the very wicked in their necessities flee vnto God for succour, and also that they are touched with a certein feare to shead mans blood, where as they knowe no manifest signe of wickednes.
l They were touched with a certeine repentance of their life past, and began to worship the true God, by whome they sawe them selues so wonderfully deliuered: but this was done for feare and not of a pure heart and affection, nether according to Gods worde.
m Thus the Lord wolde chastise his Prophet with a moste terible spectacle of death, & hereby also confirmed him of his fauour and support in this his charge which was inioined him.

CHAP. II.

Ionáh is in the fish bely. 3 His prayer. 11 He is deliuered.

1 THen Ionáh praied vnto the Lord
his God [a] out of the fishes belly,
2 And said, I cryed in mine affliction vnto
the Lord, & he hearde me: out of the belly [b] of hel cryed I, *and* thou heardest my
voice.
3 For thou haddest cast me into ỳ bottome
in the middes of the sea, and the floods
compassed me about: all thy surges, and
all thy waues passed ouer me.
4 Then I said, I am [c] cast awaie out of thy
sight: yet wil I loke againe towarde thine
holy Temple.
5 The waters compassed me about vnto the
soule: the depth closed me rounde about,
& the wedes were wrapt about mine head.
6 I went downe to the bottome of the moũtaines: the earth with her barres was about
me for euer, yet hast thou broght vp my
[d] life from the pit, ô Lord my God.
7 When my soule fainted within me, I remembred the Lord: and my praier came
vnto thee, into thine holy Temple.
8 Thei that waite vpon lying [e] vanities,
forsake their owne [f] mercie.
9 But I wil sacrifice vnto thee with the voice of thankesgiuing, and wil paie that
that I haue vowed: saluacion *is* of ỳ Lord.
10 And the Lord spake vnto the fish, and
it cast out Ionáh vpon the drye land.

a Being now swallowed vp of death, and seing no remedy to escape, his faith brast out vnto the Lord knowing ỳ out of the very hel he was able to deliuer him.
b For he was now in the fishes belly as in a graue or place of darkenes.
c This declared what his prayer was, & how he laboured betwene hope and despayre, considering the neglect of his vocation & Gods iudgements for the same: but yet in the end faith gate the victorie.
d Thou hast deliuered me from the belly of the fishe & all these dangers, as it were raising me from death to life.
e They that depend vpon any thing saue on God alone.
f Thei refuse their owne felicitie & that goodnes ẇ they shulde els receiue of God.

CHAP. III.

Ionáh is sent againe to Nineuéh. 5 The repentance of the King of Nineuéh.

1 ANd the worde of the Lord came vn
to [a] Ionáh the seconde time, saying,
2 Arise, go vnto Nineuéh that great citie,
and preache vnto it the preaching, which
I bid thee.
3 So Ionáh arose and went to Nineuéh according to the worde of the Lord: now
Nineuéh was a [b] great and excellent citie
of thre daies iourney.
4 And Ionáh began to entre into the citie
a daies [c] iourney, and he cryed, and said,
Yet fortie daies, & Nineuéh shalbe ouerthrowen.
5 So the people of Nineuéh [d] beleued God
and proclaimed a fast, & put on sackecloth
from the greatest of them euẽ to the least
of them.
6 For worde came vnto the King of Nineuéh, and he rose from his throne, and he
laied his robe from him, and couered him
with sackecloth, and sate in asshes.
7 And he proclaimed and said through Nineuéh, (by the counsel of the King and his
nobles) saying, Let nether mã, nor [e] beast,
bullocke nor shepe tast any thing, nether
fede nor drinke water.
8 But let man and beast put on sackecloth,
and [f] crye mightely vnto God: yea, let e-
uerie man turne from his euil waie, and
from the wickednes that is in their hands.
9 [g] Who can tel *if* God wil turne, and repẽt
and turne awaie from his fierce wrath, ỳ
we perish not?
10 And God sawe their [h] workes that thei
turned from their euil wayes: & [i] God repented of the euil that he had said that he
wolde do vnto them, and he did it not.

a This is a great declaration of Gods mercie ỳ he receiueth him againe & sendeth hi forth as his Prophet which had before shewed so great infirmitie.
b Read Chap. 1,1.
c He went forward one daie in the citie, & preached, & so he continued til ỳ citie was conuerted.
d For he declared that he was a Prophet sent to them frõ God to denoũce his iudgemẽts against them.
e Not that ỳ dumme beastes had sinned or colde repent, but ỳ by their example man might be astonished, considering ỳ for his sinne ỳ angre of God hanged ouer all creatures.
f He willed, that the men shulde earnestly call vnto God for mercie.
g For partely by the threatening of ỳ Prophet, & partely by the motion of his owne conscience he douted whether God wolde shewe them mercie.
h That is, the frutes of their repentance, ẇ did procede of faith ẇ God had planted by the ministerie of his Prophet.
i Read Ierem 18,8.

CHAP. IIII.

The great goodnes of God toward his creatures.

1 THerefore it displeased [a] Ionáh excedingly, and he was angrie.
2 And he praid vnto the Lord, and said, I
praie thee, ô Lord, was not this my sayig,
when I was yet in my countrey? therefore
I preuẽted it to flee vnto [b] Tarshish: for I
knew that thou art a gracious God, and
merciful, slowe to angre and of great kindenes, and repentest thee of the euil.
3 Therefore now ô Lord, take, I beseche
thee, my life [c] from me: for it is better for
me to dye then to liue.
4 Thẽ said the Lord, Doest thou wel to be
[d] angrie?
5 So Ionáh went out of the citie and sate on
the East side of the citie, and there made
him a boothe, and sate vnder it in the shadowe [e] til he might se what shulde be done in the citie.
6 And the Lord God prepared a [f] gourde,
& made it to come vp ouer Ionáh, that it
might be a shadowe ouer his head and de
liuer him from his grief. So Ionáh was
exceding glad of the gourde.
7 But God prepared a worme when the
morning rose the next daie, and it smote

a Because hereby he shulde be taken as a false prophet, & so the Name of God, which he preached, shulde be blasphemed.
b Read Chap. 1,3.
c Thus he praied of grief fearing lest Gods Name by this forgiuenes might be blasphemed as thogh he sent his Prophetes forthe to denoũce his iudgements in vaine.
d Wilt thou be iudge when I do things for my glorie, and when I do not?
e For he douted as yet whe ther God wolde shewe thẽ mercie or no: and therefore after fourtie dayes he departed out of the citie, loking what yssue God wolde send.
f Which was a further meanes to couer him from the heat of the sunne, as he remained in his boothe.

the

the gourde, that it withered.
8 And when the sunne did arise, God prepared also a feruent East winde: and the
sunne bet vpon the head of Ionáh, that
he fainted, and wished in his heart to dye,
and said, It is better for me to dye, then to
liue.
9 And God said vnto Ionáh, Doest thou
wel to be angrie for the gourde? And he
said, I do wel to be [g] angry vnto ÿ death.
10 Then said the Lord, Thou hast had pitie on the gourde for the which thou hast
not laboured, nether madest it growe,
which came vp in a night, and perished in
a night,
11 And shulde [h] not I spare Nineuéh
that great citie, wherein are [i] six score
thousand persones, that can not discerne
betwene their right hand, & their left hãd,
and *also* muche cattel?

g This declareth the great incõueniences wherinto Gods seruãts do fall when they giue place to their owne affections, & do not in all things willingly submit thẽ selues to God.

h Thus God mercifully reproueth him, which wolde pitie him self & this gourde, and yet wolde restraine God to shewe his compassion to so manie thousand people.

i Meaning, ÿ they were children, & infants.

MICAH.

THE ARGVMENT.

Micáh the Prophet of the tribe of Iudáh serued in the worke of the Lord, concerning Iudáh and Israél, at the least thirtie yeres: at what time Isaiáh prophecied. He declareth the destruction, first of the one kingdome, and then of the other, because of their manifolde wickednes, but chiefly for their idolatrie. And to this end he noteth the wickednes of the people, the crueltie of the princes and gouernours, and the permission of the false prophetes, and the deliting in them. Then he setteth forthe the cõming of Christ, his kingdome, & the felicitie thereof. This Prophet was not that Micáh which resisted Ahab, & all his false prophetes, as 1. King. 22, 8, but another of the same name.

CHAP. I.

1 The destruction of Iudáh & Israél because of their idolatrie.

1 The worde of the Lord,
that came vnto Micáh
the [a] Morashite in the
dayes of Iothám, Aház,
and Hezekiáh Kings of
Iudáh, which he sawe cõ-
cerning Samaria and Ie-
rusalém.
2 Heare, [b] all ye people: hearken thou, ô
earth, and all that therein is, and let the
Lord God be witnes against you, *euen* the
Lord from his holie Temple.
3 For beholde, the Lord cometh out of his
place, and wil come [c] downe, & tread vpõ
the hie places of the earth.
4 And the moũtaines shal melt vnder him
(so shal the valleis cleaue) as waxe before the fyre, & as the waters that are powred
downeward.
5 For the wickednes of Iaakób *is* all this, &
for the sinnes of the house of Israél: what
is the wickednes of Iaakób? Is not [d] Samaria? & which are the hie [e] places of Iudáh?
Is not Ierusalém?
6 Therefore I wil make Samaria as an heape of the field, & for the planting of a vineyarde, and I wil cause the stones thereof
to tumble downe into the valley, & I wil
discouer the fundacions thereof.
7 And all the grauen images thereof shalbe
broken, and all [f] the gifts thereof shalbe
burnt with the fyre, and all the idoles thereof wil I destroye: for she gathered it of
the hyre of an harlot, and they shal returne [g] to the wages of an harlot.
8 Therefore I wil mourne & houle: I wil
go without clothes, and naked: I wil make lamentacion like the dragons, & mourning as the ostriches.
9 For her plagues are grieuous: for it is come into Iudáh: *the enemie* is come vnto the
gate of my people, vnto Ierusalém.
10 Declare ye it not at [h] Gath, nether wepe
ye: for the house of [i] Aphráh roule thy self
in the dust.
11 Thou that dwellest at [k] Shaphír, go together naked with shame: she that dwelleth
at Zaanán, shal not come forthe in ÿ mour
ning of Beth-ézel: *the enemie* shal [l] receiue
of you for his standing.
12 For the inhabitant of Maróth waited for
good, but euil came from the Lord vnto
the [m] gate of Ierusalém.
13 O thou inhabitant of Lachísh, binde the
charet to the *beastes* [n] of price: she [o] is the
beginning of the sinne to the daughter of
Zión: for the transgressions of Israél were
founde in thee.
14 Therefore shalt thou giue presents to
Morésheth [p] Gath: the houses of Achzíb
shalbe as a lie to the Kings of Israél.
15 Yet wil I bring an [q] heire vnto thee, ô inhabitant of Maresháh, he shal come vnto
Adullám, [r] the glorie of Israél.
16 Make thee balde: and shaue thee for thy
delicate children: enlarge thy baldenes as
the egle, for they are gone into captiuitie
from thee.

a Borne in Mareshah a citie of Iudáh.

b Because of the malice, & obstinacie of ÿ people whome he had so oft exhorted to repentance, he sõmoneth thẽ to Gods iudgements taking all creatures, & God him self to witnes, that the preaching of his Prophetes, ŵ they haue abused, shal be reuenged.

c Meaning hereby that God wil come to iudgement against ÿ strõg cities & holdes d Samaria, ŵ shulde haue bene an exãple to all Israél of true religiõ, & iustice, was ÿ puddle, and stewes of all idolatrie, and corruption, & boasted them selues of their father Iaakób.

e That is, the idolatrie and infection.

f Which they gathered by euil practises, & thoght that their idoles had inriched them therewith for their seruice vnto them.

g The gaine ÿ came by their idoles, shalbe consumed as a thĩg of noght: for as ÿ wages or riches of harlottes are wickedly gotten, so are they vilely and spedely spent.

h Lest the Philistims our enemies reioyce at our destruction.

i Which was a citie nere to Ierusalẽ, Iosh. 18, 23, & signifieth dust: therefore he willeth them to mourne, & roule thẽ selues in ÿ dust, for their dustie citie.

k These were cities whereby ÿ enemie shulde passe as he came to Iudáh.

l He shal not departe before he hathe ouercome you, and so you shal pay for his tarying.

m For Rabshakéh had shut vp Ierusalém, ÿ thei colde not send to succour them.

n To flee away: for Saneheríb laid siege first to ÿ citie, & remained there in whẽ he sent his captaines, & armie against Ierusalém.

o Thou first receiuedst ÿ idolatrie of Ieroboám, & so didest infect Ierusalém. p Thou shalt bribe ÿ Philistims thy neighbours, but they shal deceiue thee, as wel as thei of Ierusalém. q He prophecieth against his owne citie, & because it signified an heritage, he saith ÿ God wolde send an heire to possesse it. r For so they thoght them selues for the strength of their citie.

CHAP. II.

1 Threatnings against the wanton & deintie people.
6 They wolde teache the Prophetes to preache.

1 WO vnto thẽ,that imagine iniquitie, and worke wickednes vpon
their beddes: [a]whẽ ẏ morning is light thei
practise it because their hãd"hathe power.
2 And they couet fields, and take them by
violence,and houses,and take them away:
so they oppresse a man and his house, *euen*
man and his heritage.
3 Therefore thus saith the Lord, Beholde,
against this familie haue I deuised a plague, whereout ye shal not plucke your nec
kes,and ye shal not go so proudly,for this
time is euil.
4 In that day shal they take vp a parable
against you, and lament with a dolful la-
mẽtacion,& say, [b] We be vtterly wasted:
he hathe changed the porcion of my people: how hathe he taken it away to restore
it vnto me?he hathe diuided our fields.
5 Therefore thou shalt haue none that shal
cast a coard by lot in [c] the Congregacion
of the Lord.
6 [d] They that prophecied, Prophecie ye
not.[e] Thei shal not prophecie to them,ne-
ther shal they take shame.
7 O thou that art named the house of Iaakób, is the Spirit of the Lord shortened?
[f] are these his workes? are not my wordes
good vnto him [g] that walketh vprightly?
8 But he that was [h] yester day my people,
is risen vp on the other side,*as* against an
enemie:they spoyle the [i] beautiful garmẽt
from thẽ that passe by peaceably,as thogh
they returned from the warre.
9 The women of my people haue ye cast
out from their pleasant houses, & from
their children haue ye taken away [k] my
glorie continually.
10 Arise and departe, for this is not *your*
[l]rest:because it is polluted,it shal destroye
you,euen with a sore destruction.
11 [m]If a mã walke in the Spirit,& wolde lie
falsely, *saying*, [n] I wil prophecie vnto thee
of wine, and of strong drinke, he shal euẽ
be the Prophet of this people.
12 I wil surely gather [o] thee wholy, ô Iaakób: I wil surely gather the remnant of Ifraél: I wil put them together as the shepe
of Bozráh,*euen* as the flocke in the middes
of their folde: *the cities* shalbe ful of brute
of the men.
13 The [p] breaker vp shal come vp before
them: they shal breake out, and passe by
the gate, and go out by it,and their King
shal go before them,and the Lord *shalbe*
[q] vpon their heads.

a Assone as they rise,they execute their wicked deuises of ẏ night, and according to their power hurt others. "*Ebr.it is power.*

b Thus the Iewes lament and say that there is no hope of restitutiõ seing their possessions are diuided among the enemies.

c Ye shal haue no more lands to diuide,as you had in times past, and as you vsed to measure them in the Iubile.

d Thus the people warne the Prophetes that they speake to them no more:for they can not abide their threatenings.

e God saith, that they shal not prophecie, nor receiue no more of their rebukes nor tantes.

f Are these your workes according to his Law?

g Do not the godlie finde my wordes comfortable?

h That is, afore time.

i The poore can haue no cõmoditie by them,but they spoyle them, as thogh they were enemies.

k That is,their substance, and liuing, which is Gods blessing,and as it were, parte of his glorie.

l Ierusalém shal not be your sauegarde:but, the cause of your destruction.

m That is,shewe him self to be a Prophet. n He sheweth what Prophetes they delite in:that is,in flatterers,which tel them pleasant tales,& speake of their commodities. o To destroye thee. p The enemie shal breake their gates,and walles,and lead them in to Caldea. q To driue them forwarde,and to helpe their enemies.

CHAP. III.

1 *Against the tyrannie of princes and false prophetes.*

1 ANd I said, Heare, I pray you, ô
heads of Iaakób, and ye princes of
the house of Israél: shulde not ye knowe
[a] iudgement?
2 *But* they hate the good, & loue the euil:
thei plucke of their skinnes from them, &
their flesh from their bones.
3 And they eat also the [b] flesh of my people,and flay of their skinne from them, &
they breake their bones,& chop them in
pieces,as for the pot, & as flesh within the
caldron.
4 Then [c] shal they crye vnto the Lord,but
he wil not heare them:he wil euẽ hide his
face from them at that time, because they
haue done wickedly in their workes.
5 Thus saith the Lord,Cõcerning the prophetes that disceiue my people,and [d] bite
them with their teeth, and crye peace,but
if a man put not into their mouthes, they
prepare warre against him,
6 Therefore [e] night shalbe vnto you for a
vision,and darkenes *shalbe* vnto you for a
diuination,and the sunne shal go downe
ouer the Prophetes, and the day shalbe
darke ouer them.
7 Then shal the Seers be ashamed, and the
sothesaiers confounded: yea, they shal all
couer [f] their lippes,for they haue none answer of God.
8 Yet notwithstanding I am ful [g] of power
by the Spirit of the Lord, and of iudgement and of strength to declare vnto Iaakób his transgression, and to Israél his
sinne.
9 Heare this, I pray you, ye heads of the
house of Iaakób,and princes of the house
of Israél:they abhorre iudgemẽt,and peruert all equitie.
10 They buyld vp Zión with [h] blood, and
Ierusalém with iniquitie.
11 The heads thereof iudge for rewardes,
and the Priests thereof teache for hyre, &
the Prophetes thereof prophecie for mo-
ney:yet wil they [i] leane vpon the Lord,&
say, Is not the Lord among vs? no euil can
come vpon vs.
12 Therefore shal Zión for your sake be
[k] plowed *as* a field, & Ierusalém shal be an
heape,and the mountaine of the house, as
the hie places of the forest.

a That thing which is iuste & lawful, bothe to gouerne my people aright,& also to discharge your owne consciẽce?

b The Prophet condemneth the wicked gouerners not onely of couetousnes, theft, and murther, but compareth them to wolues, lyons, & moste cruel beasts.

c That is,whẽ I shal visite their wickednes: for thogh I heare ẏ godlie before they crie,Isa 65,24, yet I wil not heare these thogh they crye, Isa. 1,15. iam.2,13.1.pet. 3,11.

d They deuoure all their substance, & then flatter them, promising that all shal go wel: but if one restraine from their bellies, then they inuent all wayes to mischief.

e As you haue loued to walke in darkenes, and to prophecie lies so God shal rewarde you with grosse blindenes, and ignorance,so ẏ whẽ all others shal se the bright beames of Gods graces,ye shal as blinde men grope as in ẏ night.

f When God shal discouer them to the worlde, they shal be afraid to speake:for all shal knowe ẏ they were but false prophetes,and did belye the worde of God.

g The Prophet being assured of his vocatiõ by the Spirit of God, setteth him self alone against all the wicked,shewing how God bothe gaue him giftes, habilitie, and knowledge, to discerne betwene good & euil, and also constancie to reproue the sinnes of the people,and not to flatter them. h They buylde them houses by briberie,which he calleth blood and iniquitie. i They wil say, that they are the people of God,and abuse his Name as a pretence to cloke their hypocrisie. k Read Ieremiáh,26,18.

CHAP. IIII.

1 *Of the kingdome of Christ,and felicitie of his Church.*

1 BVt in the [a] last dayes it shal come to
passe,that the mountaine of the House of the Lord shal be prepared in the top
of the mountaines, and it shalbe exalted
aboue the [b] hilles, and people shal flowe
vnto it.

a When Christ shal come,and the Temple shalbe destroyed.

b Read Isa 2,2

2 Yea,

2 Yea, many nacions shal come and say, Come, and let vs go vp to the Mountaine of
the Lord, and to the House of the God of
Iaakób, and he wil [c] teache vs his waies, &
we wil walke in his paths: for the Law shal
go forthe of Zión, and the worde of the
Lord from Ierusalém.
3 And he shal iudge among many people, &
[d] rebuke mightie nacions a farre of, & thei
shal breake their swordes into mattockes,
and their speares into [e] sieths: nacion shal
not lift vp a sworde against nacion, nether
shal they [f] learne to fight any more.
4 But thei shal sit euery mã vnder his vine,
and vnder his fig tre, and none shal make
them afraied: for the mouth of the Lord
of hostes hathe spoken it.
5 For all people wil walke [g] euery one in the
name of his god, and we wil walke in the
Name of the Lord our God, for euer and
euer.
6 At the same day, saith the Lord, wil I gather her that halteth, and I wil gather her
that is cast out, & her that I haue afflicted.
7 And I wil make her that halted, [h] a remnant, & her that was cast farre of, a mightie nacion: and the Lord shal reigne ouer
them in Mount Zión, from hence forthe e-
uen for euer.
8 And thou, ô [i] towre of the flocke, ỹ strong
holde of the daughter Zión, vnto thee shal
it come, euen [k] the first dominion, & kingdome shal come to the daughter Ierusalém.
9 Now why doest thou crye out with lamẽ-
tacion? *is* [l] there no King in thee? is thy
counseller perished? for sorow hathe taken
thee, as a woman in trauail.
10 Sorow and mourne, ô daughter Zión, like
a woman in trauail: for now shalt thou go
forthe of the citie, and dwell in the field,
& shalt go into Babél, *but* there shalt thou
be deliuered: there the Lord shal redeme
thee from the hand of thine enemies.
11 Now also many nacions are gathered a-
gainst thee, saying, Zión shalbe cõdemned
and our eye shal loke vpon Zión.
12 But they [m] knowe not the thoghts of the
Lord: they vnderstand not his counsel, for
he shal gather them as the sheaues in the
barne.
13 Arise, and thresh, [n] ô daughter Zión: for I
wil make thine horne yron, and I wil make
thine hooues brasse, & thou shalt breake in
pieces many people: and I wil consecrate
their riches vnto the Lord, and their substance vnto the ruler of the whole worlde.

c He sheweth that there is no true Church but where as the people are taught by Gods pure worde.
d By his corrections and threatnings he wil bring the people into subiection which are in the vtmost corners of the worlde.
e They shal absteine from all euil doing, and exercise them selues in godlines & in wel doing to others.
f Read Isa. 2,4
g He sheweth that the people of God oght to remaine constant in their religion, albeit all the worlde shulde giue them selues to their supersticion & idolatrie.
h I wil cause that Israél, ỽ is now as one lame & haltĩg, and so almost destroied, shal liue againe & growe into a great people.
i Meaning Ierusalém where the Lords flocke was gathered.
k The florishing state of the kĩgdome, as it was vnder Dauid & Salomón, ỽ thing was accomplished to the Church by the cõming of Christ.
l In the meane seasõ he sheweth that they shulde indure great troubles and tentations when they sawe thẽ selues nether to haue King nor counsel.
m He sheweth that ỹ faithful oght not to measure Gods iudgements by the bragges and threatnings of ỹ wicked, but thereby are admonished to lifte vp their heartes to God to call for deliuerance.
n God giueth his Church this victorie so oft as he ouercometh their enemies: but the accomplishment hereof shalbe at the last comming of Christ.

CHAP. V.

1 *The destruction of Ierusalém.* 2 *The excellencie of Beth-léem.*

1 NOw assemble thy garisons, ô daughter [a] of garisons: he hathe laied siege
against vs: they shal smite the iudge of Israél with a rodde vpon the cheke.
2 And thou Beth-léem Ephráthah art [b] litle to be amõg the thousands of Iudáh, *yet*
out of thee shal he come forthe vnto me,
that shal be the ruler in Israél: whose [c] goings forthe *haue bene* from the beginning
& from euerlasting.
3 Therefore wil he giue them vp, vntil the
time that [d] she which shal beare, shal trauail: then the remnant of their brethren
shal returne vnto the children of Israél.
4 And he shal [e] stand, and fede in ỹ strength
of the Lord, & in the maiestie of the Name of the Lord his God, & they shal dwell
stil: for now shal he be magnified vnto the
ends of the worlde.
5 And he [f] shal be *our* peace whẽ Asshúr shal
come into our land: when he shal tread in
our palaces, then shal we raise against him
seuen shepherds, and eight principal men.
6 And they shal destroie [g] Asshúr with the
sworde, & the land of Nimród with their
swordes: thus shal he [h] deliuer *vs* from
Asshúr, when he cometh into our land, &
when he shal tread within our borders.
7 And the [i] remnãt of Iaakób shalbe amõg
many people, as a dewe from the Lord, *and*
as the showres vpon the grasse, that waiteth not for man, nor hopeth in the sonnes
of Adám.
8 And the remnant of Iaakób shal be amõg
the Gentiles in the middes of many people, as the lyon among the beasts of the forest, *and* as the lyons whelpe among the
flockes of shepe, who when he goeth thorow, treadeth downe and teareth in pieces,
and none can deliuer.
9 Thine hand shal be lift vp vpon thine aduersaries, & all thine enemies shalbe cut of.
10 And it shal come to passe in that day,
saith ỹ Lord, that I wil cut of thine [k] horses out of the middes of thee, and I wil
destroie thy charets.
11 And I wil cut of the cities of thy land,
and ouerthrowe all thy strong holdes.
12 And I wil cut of thine inchanters out of
thine hand: and thou shalt haue no more
sothsayers.
13 Thine idoles also wil I cut of, & thine i-
mages out of the middes of thee: and thou
shalt no more worship the worke of thine
hands.
14 And I wil plucke vp thy groues out of
the middes of thee: so wil I destroy thine
enemies.
15 And I wil execute a vengeance in *my*

a He forewarneth them of the dangers ỹ shal come, before thei enioy these comfortes, shewing ỹ forasmuche as Ierusalém was accustomed ỽ her garisons to trouble others the Lord wolde now cause other garisons to vexe her, and that her Rulers shulde be smitten on the face moste contempteously.
b For so the Iewes deuided their coũtrey, that for euery thousand there was a chief captaine: and because Beth-léhem was not able to make a thousand, he calleth it litle, but yet God wil raise vp his captaine and gouernour therin: & thus it is not the least by reasõ of this benefit, as mat. 2,6.
c He sheweth that the comming of Christ & all his waies were apoĩted of God frõ all eternitie
d He compareth the Iewes to women ỽ childe, who for a time shulde haue great sorowes, but at length they shulde haue a comfortable deliuerãce, Ioh 16,21.
e That is, Christes kingdome shalbe stable and euerlasting, and his people, aswel the Gẽtiles as the Iewes shal dwel in safetie
f This Messiáh shalbe a sufficient sauegarde for vs, and thogh the enemie inuade vs for a time, yet shal God stirre vp many ỽ shal be able to deliuer vs.
g These whome God shal raise vp for ỹ desliuerance of his Church, shal destroy all the enemies thereof, which are ment here by ỹ Assyriãs and Babylonians which were the chief at that time. h By these gouernours wil God deliuer vs when the enemie cometh into our land. i This Remnãt or Church which God shal deliuer, shal onely depend on Gods power and defense, as doeth the grasse of the field, and not on the hope of man. k I wil destroy all things wherein thou puttest thy confidence, as thy vaine confidẽce and idolatrie, and so wil helpe thee.

wrath and indignacion vpon the heathen,
[l] which they haue not heard.

CHAP. VI.

An exhortacion to the dumme creatures to heare the iudgement against Israél being vnkinde. 6 What maner of sacrifices do please God.

1 HEarken ye now what the Lord saith,
Arise thou, *and* contend *before* the
[a] mountaines, and let the hilles heare thy
voyce.
2 Heare ye, ô moutaines, the Lords quarel,
and ye mightie fundacions of the earth:
for the Lord hathe a quarel against his
people, and he wil pleade with Israél.
3 O my people, what haue I done vnto thee?
or wherein haue I grieued thee? testifie a-
gainst me.
4 Surely I [b] broght thee vp out of the land
of Egypt, & redemed thee out of the house of seruants, and I haue sent before thee,
Mosés, Aarón, and Miriám.
5 O my people, remember now what Balák King of Moáb had diuised, and what
Balaám the sonne of Beór answered him,
from [c] Shittím vnto Gilgál, that ye may
knowe the [d] righteousnes of the Lord.
6 Wherewith [e] shal I come before ẏ Lord,
& bowe my self before the hie God? Shal
I come before him with burnt offrings, &
with calues of a yere olde?
7 Wil the Lord be pleased with thousands
of rams, or wt ten thousand riuers of oyle?
Shal I giue my [f] firstborne for my trãsgression, *euen* the frute of my bodie for the sinne of my soule?
8 He hathe shewed thee, ô mã, what is good,
and what the Lord requireth of thee: [g] surely to do iustely, and to loue mercie, and
to humble thy self, to walke with thy
God.
9 The Lords voyce cryeth vnto the [h] citie,
and the man of wisdome shal se thy name:
Heare the rod, and who hathe appointed it.
10 Are yet the treasures of wickednes in the
house of the wicked, and the scant measure, that is abominable?
11 Shal I iustifie the wicked balances, and
the bag of deceitful weights?
12 For the riche men [i] thereof are ful of crueltie, & the inhabitants thereof haue spoken lies, & their tongue *is* deceitful in their
mouth.
13 Therefore also wil I make thee sicke in
smiting thee, & in making *thee* desolate
because of thy sinnes.
14 Thou shalt eat and not be satisfied, &
[k] thy casting downe *shalbe* in the middes of
thee, and thou [l] shalt take holde, but shalt
not deliuer: & that which thou deliuerest,
wil I giue vp to the sworde.

l Meaning, that the citie shulde go about to saue her men, as they that lay holde on that which they wolde preserue.

l It shal be so terrible that ẏ like hathe not bene heard of

Chap. VI.

a He taketh ẏ hie moũtaines and hard rockes to witnes against the obstinacie of his people.

b I haue not hurt thee, but bestowed infinite benefites vpon thee.

c That is, remember my benefites from ẏ beginnĩg how I deliuered you from Balaams curse, and also spared you frõ Shittím, which was in ẏ plaine of Moáb, til I broght you into the land promised.

d That is, the trueth of his promes & his manifolde benefites towarde you.

e Thus the people by hypocrisie ask how to please God, and are contẽt to offer sacrifices, but wil not chãge their liues.

f There is nothing so deare to man, but the hypocrites wil offer it vnto God, if they thĩke thereby to auoide his anger: but they wil neuer be broght to mortifie their owne affections & to giue them selues willingly to serue God as he cõmandeth.

g The Prophet in few wordes calleth thẽ to the obseruacion of the secondetable, to knowe if they wil obey God aright or no, saying ẏ God hathe prescribed them to do this.

h Meaning, ẏ when God speaketh to any citie or natiõ, the godlie wil acknowledge his maiestie and consider not the mortal mã that bringeth the threatening, but God that sendeth it.

i That is, of Ierusalém.

k Thou shalt be consumed with inwarde grief and euils.

15 Thou shalt sowe, but not reape: thou shalt
treade the oliues, but thou shalt not anoint
thee with oyle, and *make* swete wine, but
shalt not drinke wine.
16 For the [m] statutes of Omrí are kept, and
all the maner of the house of Aháb, and
ye walke in their counsels, that I shulde
make thee waste, and the inhabitants thereof an hissing: therefore ye shal beare the
reproche of my people.

m You haue receiued all the corruptiõ and idolatrie, wherewith the tẽ tribes were infected vnder Omrí and Aháb his sonne: and to excuse your doings, you alledge the Kings autoritie by his statutes, and also wisdome & policie in so doing, but you shal not escape punishement, but as I haue shewed you great fauour, and taken you for my people, so shal your plagues be accordingly, Luk. 12, 47.

CHAP. VII.

1 A complaint for the smale nomber of the righteous. 4 The wickednes of those times. 14 The prosperitie of the Church.

1 WO is me, for I am as [a] the somer
gatherings, & as the grapes of the
vintage: there *is* no cluster to eat: my soule
desired the first ripe frutes.
2 The good man is perished out of the
earth, and there *is* none righteous among
men: [b] thei all lie in waite for blood: euery
man hunteth his brother with a net.
3 To make good for the euil of *their* hands,
the prince asked, and the iudge *iudgeth* for
a rewarde: therefore the [c] great man he
speaketh out the corruption of his soule:
so [d] they wrap it vp.
4 The best of them *is* as [e] a brier, and the
most righteous of them *is sharper* then a
thorne hedge: the day of [f] thy watchmen
& the visitacion cometh: then shalbe their
confusion.
5 Trust ye not in a friend, nether put ye cõfidence in a counseller: kepe the dores of
thy mouth from her that lieth in thy bosome.
6 For the sonne reuileth the father: the
daughter riseth vp against her mother: the
daughter in law against her mother in law,
and a mans enemies *are* ẏ men of his owne
house.
7 Therefore [g] I wil loke vnto the Lord: I
wil waite for God my Sauiour: my God
wil heare me.
8 Reioyce not against me, [h] ô mine enemie:
thogh I fall, I shal arise: when I shal sit
in darkenes, the Lord *shal be* a light vnto
me.
9 I wil beare the wrath of the Lord because
I haue sinned against him, vntil he pleade
my cause, and execute iudgement for me:
then wil he bring me forthe to the light, &
I shal se his righteousnes.
10 Then she that is mine enemie, shal loke
vpon it, and shame shal couer her, which
said vnto me, Where is the Lord thy God?
Mine eies shal beholde her: now shal she be
troden downe as the myre of the stretes.

a The Prophet taketh vpon him the persone of ẏ earth, which complaineth that all her frutes are gone, so ẏ none is left: ẏ is, that there is no godlie mã remaining: for all are giuen to crueltie & deceit, so that none spareth his owne brother.

b He sheweth that ẏ prince, the iudge and the riche man are linked together, all to do euil and to cloke the doings one of another.

c That is, the riche man that is able to giue money, absteineth from no wickednes nor iniurie.

d These mẽ agre among thẽ selues & conspire with one consent to do euil.

e They that are of moste estimation and are cõnted moste honest among thẽ, are but thornes & briers to pricke.

f Meaning of the Prophetes & gouernours.

g The Prophet sheweth that the onelie remedy for the godlie in desperat euils is to flee vnto God for succour.

h This is spoken in the persone of the Church which calleth the malignant Church her enemie.

11 *This is* [i] the day, that thy walles shal be
buylt: this day shal driue farre away [k] the
decre.
12 In this day also they shal come vnto
thee from [l] Asshúr, and *from* the strong cities, and from the strong holdes euen vnto
the riuer, and from sea to sea, & *from* moūtaine to mountaine.
13 Notwithstanding, the land shalbe desolate because of thē that dwell therein, *and*
for the frutes of [m] their inuentions.
14 [n] Fede thy people with thy rod, the flocke
of thine heritage (which dwell solitarie in
the wood) *as* in the middes of Carmél: let
them fede in Bashán and Gileád, as in olde time.
15 [o] According to the dayes of thy comming out of the land of Egypt, wil I shewe
vnto thee marueilous things.
16 The nacions shal se, and be confounded
for all their power: they shal [p] laye their
hand vpon their mouth: [q] their eares shal
be deafe.
17 They shal [r] licke the dust licke a serpēt:
thei shal moue out of their holes like wormes: they shal be afraide of the Lord our
God, and shal feare because of thee.
18 Who is a God like vnto thee, that taketh
away iniquitie, & [s] passeth by the trāsgres-
sion of the remnant of his heritage! He reteineth not his wrath for euer, because
mercie pleaseth him.
19 He wil turne againe, *and* haue compassiō
vpon vs: he wil subdue our iniquities, &
cast all [t] their sinnes into the bottome of
the sea.
20 Thou wilt performe *thy* [u] trueth to Iaakób, & mercie to Abrahám, as thou hast
sworne vnto our fathers in olde time.

i To wit, whē God shal shew him self a deliuerer of his Church, and a destroyer of his enemies.
k Meaning, the cruel empire of the Babylonians.
l When the Church shalbe restored, they that were enemies afore, shal come out of all the corners of the worlde vnto her, so that nether holdes, riuers, seas nor mountaines shalbe able to let them.
m Afore this grace appeare, he sheweth how grieuously the hypocrites them selues shal be punished, seing that the earth it self, which can not sinne, shal be made waste because of their wickednes.
n The Prophet prayeth to God to be merciful vnto his Church, when they shulde be scattered abroad as in solitarie places in Babylon and to be beneficial vnto them as in time past.
o God promiseth to be fauorable to his people as he had bene afore time.
p They shalbe as dumme men & dare bragge no more.
q They shalbe astonished, and afraid to heare men speake, lest they shulde heare of their destruction.
r They shal fall flat on the grounde for feare.
s As thogh he wolde not se it, but winke at it.
t Meaning, of his elect.
u The Church is assured, that God wil declare in effect the trueth of his merciful promes, which he had made of olde to Abrahám, and to all that shulde apprehende the promes by faith.

NAHVM.

THE ARGVMENT.

AS they of Nineueh shewed them selues prompt and ready to receiue the worde of God at Ionahs preaching, and so turned to the Lord by repentance: so after a certeine time rather giuing thē selues to worldelie meanes to increase their dominion, then seking to continue in the feare of God, and trade wherein they had begōne, they cast of the care of religion, and so returned to their vomite, and prouoked Gods iuste iudgement against them, in afflicting his people. Therefore their citie Nineueh was destroyed, and Meróch-baladan King of Babél (or as some thinke Nebuchad-nezzár) enioyed the empire of the Assyrians. But because God hathe a continual care of his Church, he stirreth vp his Prophet to comfort the godlie, shewing that the destruction of their enemies shulde be for their consolation. And as it semeth, he prophecied about the time of Hezekiáh, and not in the time of Manasséh his sonne, as the Iewes write.

CHAP. I.

Of the destruction of the Assyrians, and of the deliuerance of Israél.

1 THe [a] burdē of Nineuéh.
[b] The boke of the vision
of Nahúm ye [c] Elkeshite.
2 God *is* [d] ielous, and the
Lord reuengeth: ye Lord
reuengeth: euē the Lord
[e] of angre, the Lord wil
take vengeance on his aduersaries, and he
reserueth *wrath* for his enemies.
3 The [f] Lord *is* slowe to angre, but *he is*
great in power, and wil not surely cleare
the wicked: the Lord *hathe* his way in the
whirle winde, and in the storme, and the
cloudes *are* the dust of his fete.
4 He rebuketh the sea, and dryeth it, and
he dryeth vp all the riuers: Bashán is wasted and Carmél, and the floure of Lebanón is wasted.
5 The mountaines tremble for him, & the
hilles melt, & ye earth is burnt at his sight,
yea, the worlde, and all that dwell therein.
6 [g] Who can stand before his wrath? or
who cā abide in the fiercenes of his wrath?
his wrath is powred out like fyre, and the
rockes are broken by him,
7 The Lord is good [h] *and* as a strong holde in the day of trouble, and he knoweth
them that trust in him.
8 But pasing ouer *as* with a flood, he wil
vtterly destroye the [i] place thereof, and
darkenes shal pursue his enemies.
9 What do ye [k] imagine against the Lord?
he wil make an vtter destruction: afflictiō
shal not rise vp the seconde time.
10 For *he shal come as* vnto [l] thornes folden
one in another, and as vnto drunkardes in
their drunkennes: thei shalbe deuoured as
stubble fully dryed.

a Read Isa 13,1.
b The vision or reuelation, which God cōmāded Nahúm to write concerning ye Nineuites.
c That is, borne of a poore village in the tribe of Simeón.
d Meaning, of his glorie.
e With his he is but angrie for a time, but his angre neuer aswageth toward the reprobat, thogh for a time he deferre it.
f Thus ye wicked wolde make Gods mercie an occasiō to sinne, but ye Prophet willeth them to consider his force and iustice.
g If all creatures be at Gods cōmandement & none is able to resist his wrath, shal mā flatter him self and thinke by anie meanes to escape whē he prouoketh his God to angre?
h Lest ye faithful shulde be discouraged by hearing the power of God, he sheweth thē that his mercies apperteine vnto them, & that he hathe the care ouer them.
i Signifying, ye God wil suddenly destroye Nineuéh, and ye Assyrians in suche sort as thei shal lie in perpetual darkenes, & neuer recouer their strength againe.
k He sheweth that the enterprises of the Assyrians against Iudáh and the Church, were against God, & therefore he wolde so destroye thē at once, ye he shulde not nede to returne ye seconde time.
l Thogh ye Assyriās thinke thē selues like thornes ye pricke on all sides, yet ye Lord wil set fyre on thē, & as drunkē mē are not able to stād agaīst anie force, so thei shalbe nothīg able to resist hī.

11 There [m] cometh one out of thee that
imagineth euil againſt the Lord, *euen* a
wicked counſelour.
12 Thus ſaith the Lord, Thogh they be
[n] quiet, & alſo manie, yet thus ſhal they be
cut of when he ſhal paſſe by: thogh I haue
afflicted thee, I wil afflict thee no more.
13 For now I wil breake his yoke from thee,
and wil burſt thy bondes in ſondre.
14 And the Lord hathe giuen a commandement concerning thee, that no more of
thy name be [o] ſowe: out of the houſe of thy
gods wil I cut of the grauen, and the molten image: I wil make it thy graue for
thee, for thou art vile.
15 *Beholde vpon the mountaines the fete
of him that declareth, & publiſheth [p] peace: ô Iudáh, kepe thy ſolẽne feaſtes, performe thy vowes: for the wicked ſhal no more paſſe through thee: he is vtterly cut of.

m Which may be vnderſtand ether of Saneherib, or of ye whole body of the people of Nineuéh.
n Thogh they thinke thẽ ſelues in moſte ſafetie, and of greateſt ſtrẽgth yet when God ſhal paſſe by, he wil deſtroye them: notwithſtanding he cõforteth his Church and promiſeth to make an end of puniſhing them by the Aſſyrians.
Iſa.52,7. rom.10,15.
o Meaning Sancherib, who ſhulde haue no more childrẽ, but be ſlaine in the houſe of his gods, 2.King.19,35.
p Which peace the Iewes ſhulde enioy by the death of Sanecherib.

CHAP. II.

He deſcribeth the victories of the Caldeans againſt the Aſſyrians.

1 THe [a] deſtroyer is come before thy face: kepe thy munitiõ, loke to the way:
make *thy* loynes ſtrong: increaſe *thy* ſtrẽgth
mightely.
2 For the Lord hathe [b] turned away the
glorie of Iaakób, as the glorie of Iſraél:
for the emptiers haue emptied them out, &
[c] marred their vine branches.
3 The ſhield of his mightie men is made
red: [d] the valiant men are in ſkarlet: the
charrets *ſhalbe as* in the fyre & flames in
the day of his preparation, and [e] the firre
trees ſhal tremble.
4 The charrets ſhal rage in the ſtretes: thei
ſhal runne to and fro in the hie wayes: thei
ſhal ſeme like lampes: they ſhal ſhote like
the lightning.
5 [f] He ſhal remember his ſtrõg men: they
ſhal ſtumble as they go: they ſhal make
haſte to the walles thereof, and the defenſe ſhalbe prepared.
6 The gates of the riuers ſhalbe opened,
and the palace ſhal melt.
7 And Huzzáb *the Queene* ſhalbe led away
captiue, and her maides ſhal leade *her* as
with the voyce of doues, ſmiting vpon
their breaſts.
8 But Nineuéh is [g] of olde like a poole of
water: yet they ſhal flee away. Stand, ſtãd,
ſhal they crye: but none ſhal loke backe.
9 [h] Spoyle ye the ſiluer, ſpoyle the golde:
for there is none end of the ſtore, & glorie of all the pleaſant veſſels.
10 [i] She is emptie and voyde and waſte, &
the heart melteth, and the knees ſmite together, and ſorow is in all loines, and the
faces [k] of them all gather blackenes.

a That is, Nebuchad-nezzár is in a redines to deſtroye the Aſſyrians: & the Prophet derideth the enterpriſes of ye Aſſyriãs which prepared to reſiſt him.
b Seing God hathe puniſhed his owne people Iudáh and Iſraél, he wil now puniſh ye enemies by whome he ſcourged thẽ, read Iſa.10,12.
c Signifying, that the Iſraelites were vtterly deſtroyed.
d Bothe to feare the enemie, and alſo that they them ſelues ſhulde not ſo ſone eſpie blood one of another to diſcourage them.
e Meaning, their ſpeares ſhulde ſhake and craſhe together.
f Thẽ the Aſſyrians ſhal ſeke by all meanes to gather their power, but all things ſhal faile them.
g The Aſſyriãs wil flatter thẽ ſelues & ſay, that Nineuéh is ſo anciẽt that it can neuer periſh, & is as a fiſhpoole, whoſe waters they that walke on the bãckes cã not touche, but they ſhalbe ſcattered, & ſhal not loke backe thogh mẽ wolde call them.
h God cõmandeth the enemies to ſpoile Nineuéh, & promiſeth thẽ infinite riches, & treaſures.
i That is, Nineuéh, & the mẽ thereof ſhalbe after this ſorte.
k Read Ioél 2,6.

11 Where is the [l] dwelling of the lyons, &
the paſture of the lyõs whelpes? where the
lyon, & the lyoneſſe walked, *and* the lyons
whelpe, and none made them afraied.
12 The lyon did teare in pieces ynough for
his whelpes, and woryed for his lyoneſſe,
and filled his holes with praye, & his dennes with ſpoyle.
13 Beholde, I *come* vnto thee, ſaith the Lord
of hoſtes, & I wil burne her charrets in the
[m] ſmoke, and the ſworde ſhal deuoure thy
yong lyons, & I wil cut of thy ſpoile from
the earth, & the voice of thy [n] meſſengers
ſhal no more be heard.

l Meaning, Nineuéh, whoſe inhabitãs were cruel like the lyons & giuen to all oppreſſion & ſpared no violence or tyrannie to prouide for their wiues & children.
m That is, aſſone as my wrath beginneth to kindle.
n Signifying ye heraldes, which were accuſtomed to proclame warre. Some read of thy gumme tethe wherewith Nineuéh was wont to bruſe the bones of the poore.

CHAP. III.

1 Of the fall of Nineuéh. 8 No power can eſcape the hand of God.

1 O Bloodie citie, it is all ful of lies, *and*
robberie: [a] the pray departeth not:
2 The noyce of a whippe, [b] & the noyce of
the mouing of the wheles, and the beating of the horſes, and the leaping of the
charrets.
3 The horſeman lifteth vp bothe the bright
ſworde, and the glitering ſpeare, and a mul
titude *is* ſlaine, and the dead bodies *are*
manie: there *is* none end of their corpſes:
they ſtumble vpon their corpſes.
4 Becauſe of the multitude of the fornications of the [c] harlot that is beautiful, and
is a maſtreſſe of witchcraft, and ſelleth the
people thorowe her whoredome, and the
nations thorowe her witchcraftes.
5 Beholde, I *come* vpon thee, ſaith the Lord
of hoſtes, and wil diſcouer thy ſkirtes vpõ
thy face, and wil ſhewe the nations thy
filthines, and the kingdomes thy ſhame.
6 And I wil caſt filth vpon thee, and make
thee vile, and wil ſet thee as a gaſing
ſtocke.
7 And it ſhal come to paſſe that all they
that loke vpõ thee, ſhal flee from thee, and
ſay, Nineuéh is deſtroyed, who wil haue
pitie vpon her? where ſhal I ſeke comforters for thee?
8 Art thou better then [d] No, *which was* ful
of people? that laye in the riuers, and *had*
the waters round about it? whoſe ditche
was the ſea, & her wall *was* from the ſea?
9 Ethiopia and Egypt *were* her ſtrength &
there *was* none end: Put and Lubim were
"her helpers.
10 Yet was ſhe caryed away, & went into
captiuitie: her yong children alſo were daſhed in pieces at the head of all the ſtretes: & thei caſt lottes for her noble mẽ, &
all her mightie mẽ were bound in chaines.
11 Alſo thou ſhalt be drunken: thou ſhalt
hide thy ſelf, and ſhalt ſeke helpe becauſe
of the enemie.
12 All thy ſtrong cities *ſhalbe like* figtrees which
the firſt ripe figs: for if thei be ſhaken, thei
fall into the mouth of the eater.

Chap. III.
a It neuer ceaſeth to ſpoile and robbe.
b He ſheweth how the Caldeans ſhal haſte, and how couragious their horſes ſhalbe in beating the groũde when they come againſt the Aſſyrians.
c He compareth Nineuéh to an harlot, which by her beautie and ſubtiltie entiſeth yong men, & bringeth them to deſtruction.
d Meaning, Alexandria, which was in league with ſo manie nacions, and yet was now deſtroyed.
"*Or, thiae.*

13 Beholde,

13 Beholde, thy people withĩ thee *are* womẽ:
the gates of thy land ſhalbe opened vnto
thine enemies, & the fyre ſhal deuoure thy
barres.
14 Drawe thee waters for the ſiege: fortifie
thy ſtrong holdes: go into the claye, and
temper the morter: make ſtrong bricke.
15 There ſhal ẏ fyre deuoure thee: the ſwor
de ſhal cut thee of: it ſhal eat thee vp like ẏ
[e]locuſtes, *thogh* thou be multiplied like ẏ
locuſtes, & multiplied like ẏ graſhopper.
16 Thou haſt multiplied thy marchantes a-
boue the ſtarres of heauen: the locuſt ſpoi-
leth and flieth awaie.

e Signifying, ẏ Gods iudgements ſhulde ſuddenly deſtroye the Aſſyrians, as theſe vermine are with raine or change of wether.

17 Thy princes *are* as the graſhoppers, and
thy captaines as the great graſhoppers ẇ
remaine in the hedges in the colde daye:
but when the ſunne ariſeth, they flee awaie
& their place is not knowẽ where thei are.
18 Thy [f]ſhepherdes do ſlepe, ô King of
Aſſhúr: thy ſtrong mẽ lie downe: thy people is ſcattered vpon the mountaines, and
no man gathereth *them*.
19 There is no healing of thy wounde: thy
plague is grieuous: all that heare ẏ brute
of thee, ſhal clappe the hands ouer thee:
for vpon [g] whome hathe not thy malice
paſſed continually?

f Thy princes and cõſelors.

g Meaning, ẏ there was no people, to whome ẏ Aſſyrians had not done hurt.

HABAKKVK

THE ARGVMENT.

THe Prophet complaineth vnto God, conſidering the great felicitie of the wicked, and the miſerable oppreſſion of the godlie, which indure all kinde of affliction & crueltie, and yet can ſe none end. Therefore he had this reuelation ſhewed him of God, that the Caldeans ſhulde come and take them awaie captiues, ſo that they colde loke for none end of their troubles as yet, becauſe of their ſtubbernes and rebellion against the Lord. And leſt the godlie ſhulde deſpaire, ſeing this horrible confuſion, he comforteth them by this that God wil puniſh the Caldeans their enemies, when their pride and crueltie ſhalbe at height: wherefore he exhorteth the faithful to pacience by his owne example, and ſheweth them a forme of prayer, wherewith they ſhulde comfort them ſelues.

CHAP. I.

2 *A cõplaint againſt the wicked that perſecute the iuſt.*

1 THe burden, which Ha-
bakkúk ẏ Prophet did ſe.
2 O Lord, how long ſhal
I crye, and thou wilt not
heare! *euen* crye out vnto
thee [a] for violence, and
thou wilt not helpe!
3 Why doeſt thou ſhewe me iniquitie, and
cauſe me to beholde ſorowe? for ſpoyling,
and violence *are* before me: and there are
that raiſe vp ſtrife and contention.
4 Therefore the Law is diſſolued, and iudgement doeth neuer go forthe: for the wic
ked doeth [b]compaſſe about the righteous:
therefore [c] wrong iudgement procedeth.
5 Beholde among the heathen, and regarde, & wonder, & marueil: for I wil worke
a worke in your daies: [d]ye wil not beleue it,
thogh it be tolde you.
6 For lo, I raiſe vp the Caldeans, that bitter
and furious nacion, which ſhal go vpõ the
breadth of the land to poſſeſſe the dwelling places, *that are* not theirs.
7 Thei are terrible & fearful: [e] their iudgement and their dignitie ſhal procede of
them ſelues.
8 Their horſes alſo are ſwifter thẽ the leo-
pards, and are more fierce then the wolues in the * euening: & their horſemen are
many: & their horſemen ſhal come frõ far
re: thei ſhal flie as ẏ egle haſting to meat.

a The Prophet complaineth vnto God and bewaileth that amõg ẏ Iewes is left none equitie nor brotherlie loue: but in ſtead hereof reigneth crueltie, theft, contention & ſtrife.

b To ſuppreſſe him if any ſhulde ſhewe him ſelf zealous of Gods cauſe.

c Becauſe the iudges which ſhulde redreſſe this exceſſe are as euil as the reſt.

d As in times paſt you wolde not beleue Gods worde, ſo ſhal ye not now beleue the ſtrãge plagues which are at hand.

e They them ſelues ſhal be your iudges in this cauſe, and none ſhal haue autoritie ouer thẽ to cõtrolle them.

Zeph.3,3.

9 They come all to ſpoyle: before their faces *ſhalbe* an [f] Eaſtwinde, and they ſhal gather the captiuitie, [g] as the ſand.
10 And thei ſhal mocke the Kings, and the
princes *ſhalbe* a ſkorne vnto them: thei ſhal
deride euery ſtrong holde: for they ſhal
gather [h] duſt, and take it.
11 Then ſhal thei [i] take a courage, & tranſgreſſe & do wickedly, *imputing* this their
power vnto their god.
12 Art not thou of olde, ô Lord my God
mine holy one? we ſhal [k] not dye: O Lord,
ẏ haſt ordeined them for iudgemẽt, and ô
God, thou haſt eſtabliſhed them for correction.
13 *Thou art* of pure eyes, and canſt not ſe e-
uil: ẏ canſt not beholde wickednes: wherefore doeſt thou loke vpon the trãſgreſ-
ſors, & holdeſt thy tongue when the wicked deuoureth the man, that is more righteous then he?
14 And makeſt men as the [l] fiſh of the ſea,
& as the creping things, that haue no ruler ouer them.
15 Thei take vp all with the angle: thei catche it in their net, and gather it in their
yarne, whereof they reioyce & are glad.
16 Therefore thei ſacrifice vnto their [m]net
and burne incenſe vnto their yarne, becauſe by them their porcion *is* fat & their
meat plenteous.
17 Shal thei therefore ſtretch out their net
& not ſpare cõtinually to ſlaye [n] ẏ naciõs?

f For ẏ Iewes moſte feared this winde, becauſe it deſtroyed their frutes.

g They ſhalbe ſo many in nõber.

h They ſhal caſt vp mountes againſt it.

i The Prophet cõforteth the faithful that God wil alſo deſtroy the Babylonians, becauſe they ſhal abuſe this victorie and become proude and inſolẽt, attributing the praiſe hereof to their idoles

k He aſſureth the godlie of Gods protection, ſhewing that the enemie can do no more then God hathe appointed, and alſo that their ſinnes required ſuche a ſharpe rod.

l So that the great deuoureth the ſmalle and the Caldeans deſtroy all the worlde

m Meaning, ẏ the enemies flatter thẽ ſelues and glorie in their owne force, power, wit.

n Meaning, ẏ they ſhulde not.

CHAP. II.

2 A viſion. 5 Againſt pride, couetouſnes, drunkennes and idolatrie.

1 I Wil ſtand vpon my [a] watche, and ſet
me vpon the towre, and wil loke & ſe
what he wolde ſay vnto me, & what I ſhal
anſwer to him that rebuketh me.
2 And the Lord anſwered me, & ſaid, Write the viſion, and make it plaine vpon tables, that he may runne [b] that readeth it.
3 For the viſiō *is* yet for an appointed time,
but at ẏ laſt it ſhal ſpeake, & not lie: thogh
it tary, waite: for it ſhal ſurely [c] come, &
ſhal not ſtay.
4 Beholde, [d] he that lifteth vp him ſelf, his
minde is not vpright in him, but the iuſte
ſhal liue by his faith.
5 Yea, in dede the proude man *is as* he that
tranſgreſſeth by wine: [e] therefore ſhal he
not endure, becauſe he hathe enlarged his
deſire as the hel, and is as death, and can
not be ſatiſfied, but gathereth vnto him
all nacions, and heapeth vnto him all
people.
6 Shal not all theſe take vp a parable agaīſt
him, and a tanting prouerbe againſt him,
and ſay, Ho, he that increaſeth *that which is*
not his? [f] how long? and he that ladeth
him ſelf with thicke claye?
7 Shal [g] they not riſe vp ſuddenly, that
ſhal bite thee? and awake, that ſhal ſtirre
thee? and thou ſhalt be their pray?
8 Becauſe thou haſt ſpoiled manie nations,
all the remnant of the people ſhal ſpoile
thee, becauſe of mens blood, and for the
wrong *done* in the land, in the citie, & vnto
all that dwell therein.
9 Ho, he that coueteth an euil couetouſnes
to his houſe, that he may ſet his neſt on
hie, to eſcape from the power of euil.
10 Thou [h] haſt conſulted ſhame to thine
owne houſe, by deſtroying manie people,
and haſt ſinned againſt thine owne ſoule.
11 For the [i] ſtone ſhal crye out of the wall,
and the beame out of the timber ſhal anſwer it.
12 Wo vnto him that buyldeth a towne
with blood, and erecteth a citie by iniquitie.
13 Beholde, is it not of the [k] Lord of hoſtes that the people ſhal labour in the very
fyre? the people ſhal euen weary them ſelues for very vanitie.
14 For the earth ſhal [l] be filled with the
knowledge of the glorie of the Lord, as
the waters couer the ſea.
15 Wo vnto him that giueth his neigboure
[m] drinke: thou ioyneſt thine heate, & makeſt *him* drunken alſo, that thou maiſt ſe
their priuities.
16 Thou art filled with ſhame [n] for glorie:
drinke thou alſo, and be made naked: the
cuppe of the Lords right hand ſhal be tur
ned vnto thee, and ſhameful ſpuing *ſhalbe* for thy glorie.
17 For the [o] crueltie of Lebanón ſhal couer
thee: ſo ſhal the ſpoile of the beaſtes, which
made them afraide, becauſe of mēs blood,
and for the wrong *done* in the land, in the
citie, and vnto all that dwell therein.
18 What profiteth the [p] image? for the maker thereof hathe made it an image, and a
teacher of lies, thogh he that made it, truſt
therein, when he maketh dumme idoles.
19 Wo vnto him that ſaith to the wood, A-
wake, *and* to the dumme ſtone, Riſe vp, it
ſhal teache thee: [q] beholde, it is laide o-
uer with golde and ſiluer, and there *is* no
breath in it.
20 But the Lord *is* in his holie Temple:
let all the earth kepe ſilence before him.

a I wil renoūce mine owne iudgement, and onely depend on God to be inſtructed what I ſhal anſwer them that abuſe my preaching, and to be armed againſt all tentations.
b Write it in great letters, that he that runneth, may read it.
c Which conteined the deſtruction of the enemie, & the comfort of the Church: which thing thogh God execute not according to mans haſtie affections, yet the yſſue of bothe is certeine at his time appointed.
d To truſt in him ſelf or in anie worldlie thing, is neuer to be quiet: for the onelie reſt is to ſtay vpon God by faith, Rom. 1, 17. galat. 3, 11. ebr. 10, 38.
e He compareth the proude, and couetous man to a drunkard that is without reaſon and ſenſe, whome God wil puniſh, & make him a laughing ſtocke to all the worlde: & this he ſpeaketh for the comfort of the godlie, and againſt the Caldeans.
f Signifying, that all the worlde ſhal wiſh the deſtruction of tyrants, and that by their oppreſsion, & couetouſnes thei heape but vpon them ſelues more heauie burdens: for the more they get, the more are they troubled.
g That is, the Medes and Perſians, that ſhuld deſtroye ẏ Babyloniās?
h Signifying, that the couetous man is the ruine of his owne houſe, when as he thinketh to enriche it by crueltie and oppreſsion.
i The ſtones of the houſe ſhal crye, and ſay that they are buylt of blood, and the wood ſhal anſwer and ſay the ſame of it ſelf.
k Meaning, that God wil not deferre his vengeance long, but wil come, and deſtroye all their labours, as thogh thei were conſumed with fyre.
l In the deſtruction of the Babylonians his glorie ſhal appeare through all the worlde.
m He reprocheth thus the King of Babylon, who as he was drunken with couetouſnes and crueltie, ſo he prouoked others to the ſame & inflamed them by his rage, & ſo in the end broght them to ſhame.
n Where as ẏ thoghteſt to haue glorie of theſe thy doings, they ſhal turne to thy ſhame: for ẏ ſhalt drinke of the ſame cup ẇ others in thy turne.
o Becauſe the Babylonians were cruel not only againſt other nacions, but alſo agaīſt the people of God, which is ment by Lebanón, and the beaſtes therein, he ſheweth that the like crueltie ſhalbe executed againſt them.
p He ſheweth that the Babylonians gods colde nothing auaile them: for they were but blockes or ſtones, read Ierem. 10, 8.
q If thou wilt conſider what it is, and how that it hathe nether breath nor life, but is a dead thing.

CHAP. III.

2 A praier for the faithful.

1 A Praier of Habakkúk the Prophet for
the [a] ignorances.
2 [b] O Lord, I haue heard thy voyce, *and*
was afraide: ô Lord, reuiue thy [c] worke in
the middes of the people, in the middes
of the yeres make it knowen: in wrath remember mercie.
3 God commeth from [d] Temán, and the
holie one from mounte Parán, Sélah. His
glorie couereth the heauens, & the earth
is ful of his praiſe,
4 And *his* brightnes was as the light: [e] he
had hornes *coming* out of his hands, and
there was the hiding of his power.
5 Before him went the peſtilence, and burning coles went forthe before his fete.
6 He ſtode and meaſured the earth: he
behelde and diſſolued the nacions and the
euerlaſting mōutaines were broken, & the
ancient hilles did bowe: his [f] waies *are* e-
uerlaſting.
7 [g] For *his* iniquitie I ſawe the tentes of Cu-
ſhán, *and* the curtaines of the land of Midián did tremble.

a The Prophet inſtructeth his people to pray vnto God not onely for their great ſinnes, but alſo for ſuche as they had committed of ignorance.
b Thus the people were afraied when they heard Gods threatenings, and praied.
c That is, the ſtate of thy Church which is now ready to periſh before it come to half a perfect age which ſhulde be vnder Chriſt.
d Temán and Parán were nere Sinái where the Law was giuen: whereby is ſignified that his deliuerāce was as preſent now as it was then.
e Whereby is ment a power, that was ioyned with his brightnes, which was hid to the reſt of the worlde, but was reueiled in Mount Sinái to his people, Pſal. 31, 19.
f Signifying that God hathe wonderful meanes, and euer had a marueilous power when he wolde deliuer his Church.
g The iniquitie of this King of Syria in vexing thy people was made manifeſt by thy iudgement, to the comfort of thy Church, Iudg. 3, 10. and alſo of the Midianites, which deſtroied them ſelues, Iudg. 7, 22.

8 Was the Lord angrie against the h riuers?
or was thine angre against the floods? or
was thy wrath against the sea, that thou
didest ride i vpon thine horses? thy charettes broght saluation.
9 Thy k bowe was manifestely reueiled, &
the l othes of the tribes *were* a sure worde, Sélah. y̆ m didest cleaue the earth with
riuers.
10 The mountaines sawe thee, and they
trembled: the streame of the water n passed by: the depe made a noise, and lift vp
his hand on hie.
11 The o sunne *and* moone stood stil in *their*
habitacion: p at the light of thine arrowes
thei went, *and* at the bright shining of thy
speares.
12 Thou trodest downe the land in angre,
and didest thresh the heathen in displeasure.
13 Thou wentest forthe for the saluation of
thy people, *euen* for saluation with thine
q Anointed: thou hast wounded the head
of the house of the wicked, and discoue-
redst the fundations vnto the r necke,
Sélah.
14 Thou didest s strike thorowe with his
owne staues the heades of his villages:
they came out as a whirlewinde to scatter
me: their reioycing *was* as to deuoure the
poore secretly.
15 Thou didest walke in the sea with thine
horses vpon the heape of great waters.
16 When I t heard, my belie trembled: my
lippes shoke at the voyce: rottenes entred
into my bones, and I trembled in my selfe, that I might rest in u the day of trouble: *for* when he cometh vp x vnto the peo
ple, he shal destroy them.
17 For the figtre shal not florish, nether
shal frute *be* in the vines: the labour of the
oliue shal faile, and the fieldes shal yelde
no meat: the shepe shalbe cut of from the
folde, and there shalbe no bullocke in the
stalles.
18 But I wil reioyce in the Lord: I wil ioy
y in the God of my saluation.
19 The Lord God *is* my strength: he wil
make my fete like hindes *fete*, & he wil make me to walke vpon mine hie places. z To
the chief singer on Neginothái.

h Meaning, y̆ God was not angrie with y̆ waters, but y̆ by this meanes he wolde destroy his enemies and deliuer his Church.
i And so didest vse all y̆ elements as instrumēts for the destructiō of thine enemies.
k That is, thy power.
l For he had not only made a couenant w̆ Abrahám, but renued it with his posteritie.
m Read Nom. 20,11.
n He alludeth to y̆ red sea & Iordén, which gaue passage to Gods people, & shewed signes of their obedience, as it were by liftīg vp of their hands.
o As appeareth Iosh. 10, 12.
p According to thy cōmandement the sunne was directed by the weapons of thy people, that foght in thy cause, as thogh it durst not go forwarde.
q Signifying that there is no saluation, but by Christ.
r From the top to the toe thou hast destroyed the enemies.
s God destroyed his enemies bothe great and smale with their owne weapōs, thogh they were neuer so fierce against his Church.
t He returneth to that which he spake in y̆ 2, ver. and sheweth how he was afraide of Gods iudgements.
u He sheweth that y̆ faithful cā neuer haue true rest, except they fele before y̆ weight of Gods iudgements.
x That is, the enemie: but y̆ godlie shalbe quiet, knowīg that all things shal turne to good vnto thē.
y He declareth wherein standeth the comfort & ioy of the faithful, thogh theise neuer so great afflictions prepared.
z The chief singer vpon the instrumentes of musicke shal haue occasion to praise God for h is great deliuerance of his Church.

ZEPHANIAH.

THE ARGUMENT.

SEing the great rebellion of the people, and that there was now no hope of amendement, he denounceth the great iudgement of God, which was at hand, shewing that their countrei shulde be vtterly destroied, and they caried away captiues by the Babylonians. Yet for the comfort of the faithful he prophecied of Gods vengeance against their enemies, as the Philistims, Moabites, Asyrians and others, to asure them that God had a continual care ouer them. And as the wicked shulde be punished for their sinnes and transgreßions: so he exhorteth the godlie to pacience, and to trust to finde mercie by reason of the fre promes of God made vnto Abrahám: and therefore quietly to abyde til God shewe them the effect of that grace, whereby in the end they shulde be gathered vnto him, and counted as his people and children.

CHAP. I.

4 Threatnings against Iudáh and Ierusalém, because of their idolatrie.

1 THe worde of the Lord,
which came vnto Zepha
niáh the sonne of Cu-
shí, the sonne of Geda-
liáh, the sonne of Ama-
riáh, the sonne of Hiz-
kiáh, in the daies of * Io-
siáh, the sonne of * Amón King of Iudáh.
2 I wil surely destroy all things frō of the
land, saith the Lord.
3 I wil destroy man and beast: I wil destroy
the a foules of the heauen, & the fish of the
sea, & ruines *shalbe* to the wicked, & I wil
cut of man from of the land, saith y̆ Lord.
4 I wil also stretche out mine hand vpō Iudáh, and vpon all the inhabitāts of Ierusalém, & I wil cut of the remnāt of Báal frō
this place, and the names of the b Chema
rims with the Priestes,
5 And them that worship the hoste of heauen vpon the house toppes, and them that
worship and sweare by the Lord, and by
c Malchám,
6 And them that are turned backe frō the
Lord, and those that haue not soght the
Lord, nor inquired for him.
7 Be stil at the presence of the Lord God:
for the day of the Lord is at hand: for the
Lord hathe prepared a sacrifice, & hathe
sanctified his ghestes.

2.King. 22, 1.
2.King. 21, 19
a Not y̆ God was angrie w̆ these dumme creatures, but because man was so wicked for whose cause they were created, God maketh them to take parte of the punishmēt with him.
b Which were an order of superstitious men appointed to minister in the seruice of Báal, and were as his peculiar chapelens, read 2. King 23, 5: hosea. 10, 5.
c He alludeth to their idole Molech, which was forbidden Leu. 20, 2, yet they called him their king and made him as a god: therefore he here noteth them that wil bothe saye they worship God, & yet wil sweare by idoles and serue them: which halting is here cōdemned, as Ezek 20, 39. 2 king. 17, 33.

8 And it shalbe in the day of the Lords sacrifice, that I wil visite the princes & the
Kings children, and all suche as are clothed with [d] strange apparel.
9 In the same day also wil I visit all those
that [e] dance vpō the thresholde so proudly, which fil their masters houses by crueltie and deceit.
10 And in that day, saith ẏ Lord, there *shalbe* a noyce, *and* crye from the [f] fish gate, &
an howling frō the seconde *gate*, & a great
destruction from the hilles.
11 Howle ye inhabitants of [g] the lowe place: for the cōpanie of the marchants is destroied: all thei that bare siluer, are cut of.
12 And at that time wil I searche Ierusalém with [h] lightes, and visite the men that
are frosen [i] in their dregges, & say in their
hearts, The Lord wil nether do good nor
do euil.
13 Therefore their goods shalbe spoiled,
& their houses waste: * thei shal also buylde houses, but not inhabit *them*, and thei
shal plant vineyardes, but not drinke the
wine thereof.
14 The great day of the Lord *is* nere: it *is*
nere, and hasteth greatly, *euen* the voyce of
the day of the Lord: [k] the strong man shal
crye there bitterly.
15 *That day *is* a day of wrath, a day of trou
ble and heauines, a day of destruction and
desolation, a day of obscuritie and darkenes, a day of cloudes & blackenes,
16 A day of the trūpet and alarme against
the strong cities, & against the hie towres.
17 And I wil bring distres vpon men, that
thei shal walke like blinde men, because
thei haue sinned against the Lord, and
their blood shalbe powred out as dust, and
their flesh as the dongue.
18 *Nether their siluer nor their golde shal
be able to deliuer them in the day of the
Lords wrath, but the * whole land shal be
deuoured by the fyre of his ielousie: for he
shal make euen a spedie riddance of all thē
that dwell in the land.

d Meaning the courtears ẇ did imitate ẏ strāge apparel of other nacions to winne their fauour thereby, & to appeare glorious in ẏ eyes of all other, read Eze. 23,14.
e He meaneth the seruantes of the rulers which inuade other mens houses and reioyce and leape for ioy whē they can get any pray to please their master withall.
f Signifying ẏ all ẏ corners of the citie of Ierusalém shulde be ful of trouble.
g This is mēt of the strete of the marchātes which was lower then ẏ rest of the place about it.
h So that nothing shal escape me.
i By their prosperitie they are hardened in their wickednes.
Deut. 28, 30. amós 5,11.
k They that trusted in their owne strength and contemned the Prophets of God.
Ier 30,7. ioél 2,11. amós 5,18.
Ezek. 7,19.
Chap. 3,8.

CHAP. II.

He moueth to returne to God. 5 Prophecying destruction against the Philistims, Moabites & others.

1 GAther [a] your selues, euen gather you,
ô nacion not worthy to be loued,
2 Before the decre come forthe, *and ye be* as
chaffe that passeth in a day, & before the
fierce wrath of the Lord come vpon you,
& before the day of the Lords angre come vpon you.
3 Seke ye the Lord all the meke of ẏ earth,
which [b] haue wroght his iudgement: seke
righteousnes, seke lowlines, if so be that ye
may be hid in the day of the Lords wrath.
4 For [c] Azzáh shal be forsaken, and Ashkelón desolate: thei shal driue out Ashdód at
the none day, & Ekrón shal be rooted vp.
5 Wo vnto ẏ inhabitants of the sea [d] coast:
the nacion of the Cherethims, the worde
of the Lord *is* against you: ô Canáan, the
land of the Philistims, I wil euen destroy
thee without an inhabitant.
6 And the sea coast shalbe dwellings & co-
tages for shepherdes and shepefoldes.
7 And *that* coast shal be for the [e] remnant of
the house of Iudáh, to fede thereupon: in
the houses of Ashkelón shal thei lodge
towarde night: for ẏ Lord their God shal
visite them, & turne away their captiuitie.
8 I haue heard the reproche of Moáb, and
the rebukes of the children of Ammón,
whereby they vpbraided my people, and
[f] magnified thē selues against their borders.
9 Therefore, as I liue, saith the Lord of hostes, the God of Israél, surely Moáb shal
be as Sodóm, and the children of Ammón
as Gomoráh, *euen* the breeding of nettels
and salt pittes, and a perpetual desolation:
the residue of my folke shal spoile them, &
the remnant of my people shal possesse
them.
10 This shal thei haue for their pride, becau
se thei haue reproched and magnified thē
selues against the Lord of hostes people.
11 The Lord *wil be* terrible vnto thē: [g] for
he wil consume all the gods of the earth,
and euerie man shal worship him frō his
place, *euen* all the yles of the heathen.
12 Ye Moriás also shalbe slaine by my sworde with them.
13 And he wil stretche out his hand against
the North, and destroy Asshúr, and wil
make Nineuéh desolate, *and* waste like a
wildernes.
14 And flockes shal lie in the middes of her,
and all the beastes of the nacions, and the
[h] pellicane, & the *owle shal abide in the vp
per postes of it: the voyce *of birdes* shal sing
in the windowes, *and* desolations *shalbe*
vpon the postes: for the cedres are vncou-
uered.
15 This is [i] the reioycing citie that dwelt
carelesse, that said in her heart, I am, and
there *is* none besides me: how is she made
waste, and the lodging of the beastes! euerie one that passeth by her, shal hisse and
wagge his hand.

a He exhorteth them to repentance & willeth them to descēd into them selues & gather them selues together, lest they be scattered like chaffe.
b That is, ẇ haue liued vprightly & godly according as he prescribeth by his worde.
c He comforteth the faithful in that, ẏ God wolde change his punishmēts from them vnto the Philistims their enemies and other nacions.
d That is, Galilea: by these nacions he meaneth the people that dwelt there to the Iewes and in stead of friendship were their enemies: therfore he calleth them Canaanites whome the Lord appointed to be slaine.
e He sheweth why God wolde destroy their enemies, because their contrei might be a resting place for his Church.
f These nacions presumed to take from ẏ Iewes that countrey ẇ the Lord had giuen them.
g When he shal deliuer his people and destroy their enemies and idoles, his glorie shal shine through out all the worlde.
h Read Isa. 34,11.
*Or, hedgehogge
i Meaning, Nineuéh, which reioycing so muche of her strength and prosperitie, shulde be thus made waste & Gods people deliuered.

CHAP. III.

4 Against the gouerners of Ierusalém. 8 Of the calling of all the Gentiles. 13 A comfort to the residue of Israél.

1 WO to her that is filthy and polluted, to the robbing [a] citie.
2 She heard not the voyce: she receiued not
correctiō: she trusted not in the Lord: she
drue not nere to her God.
3 Her princes within her *are* as roaring * liōs:
her iudges *are* as * wolues in the euening,
which

a That is, Ierusalém.
Ezek. 22, 27. mic. 3,11. Habak. 1,8.

which,[b] leaue not the bones til the morowe.
4 Her prophetes are light, & wicked persones: her priests haue polluted the Sanctuarie: they haue wrested the Law.
5 The [c] iust Lord *is* in the middes thereof:
he wil do none iniquitie: euery morning
doeth he bring his iudgement to light, he
faileth not: but the wicked wil not learne
to be ashamed.
6 I haue [d] cut of the natiōs: their towres a-
re desolate: I haue made their streates waste, that none shal passe by: their cities are
destroyed without man *and* without inhabitant.
7 I said, Surely thou wilt feare me: ỳ wilt
receiue instruction: so their dwelling shulde not be destroied how soeuer I visited
thē, but [e] they rose early & corrupted all
their workes.
8 Therefore [f] waite ye vpon me, saith the
Lord, vntil the daye that I rise vp to the
pray: for I am determined to gather the
nacions, and that I wil assemble the kingdomes to powre vpon them mine indignacion, *euen* all my fierce wrath: for all the
earth shalbe deuoured with the fyre of my
ielousie.
9 Surely [g] then wil I turne to the people a
pure langage, that they may all call vpon
the Name of the Lord, to serue him" with
one consent.
10 From beyonde the riuers of Ethiopia,
the [h] daughter of my dispersed, praying
vnto me, shal bring me an offring.
11 In that daye shalt thou not be ashamed
for [i] all thy workes, wherein thou hast trāsgressed against me: for then I wil take
away out of the middes of thee them that
reioyce of thy pride, & thou shalt no more be proude of mine holie Mountaine.
12 Then wil I leaue in the middes of thee
an humble and poore people: and thei shal
trust in the Name of the Lord.
13 The remnant of Israél shal do none iniquitie, nor speake lies: nether shal a deceitful tongue be founde in their mouth: for
they shalbe fed, and lie downe, and none
shal make them afraid.
14 Reioyce, ô daughter Zión: be ye ioyful,
ô Israél: be glad and reioyce with all *thine*
heart, ô daughter Ierusalém.
15 The Lord hathe taken away thy [k] iudgements: he hathe cast out thine [l] enemie:
the King of Israél, *euen* the Lord *is* in the
middes of [m] thee: thou shalt se no more
euil.
16 In that day it shalbe said to Ierusalém,
Feare thou not, ô Zión: let not thine hāds
be faint.
17 The Lord thy God in ỳ middes of thee
is mightie: he wil saue, he wil reioyce ouer
thee with ioye: he wil quiet him self in
[n] his loue: he wil reioyce ouer thee with
ioye.
18 After a certeine time wil I gather the afflicted that were of thee, & them that bare the reproche for [o] it.
19 Beholde, at that time I wil bruise all that
afflict thee, & I wil [p] saue her that halteth,
and gather her that was cast out, and I wil
get them praise and fame in all the [q] lands
of their shame.
20 At that time wil I bring you againe, &
then wil I gather you: for I wil giue you a
name and a praise amōg all people of the
earth, when I turne backe your captiuitie
before your eyes, saith the Lord.

b They are so griedy ỳ they eat vp bones and all.
c The wicked thus boasted that God was euer among them, but the Prophet āswereth that that can not excuse their wickednes: for God wil not beare with their sinnes: yet that he did paciently abide and sent his Prophetes continually to call them to repētāce, but he profited nothing.
d By the destruction of other nations he sheweth that the Iewes shulde haue learned to feare God.
e They were moste earnest & ready to do wickedly.
f Seing ye wil not repēt, you shal loke for my vengeance aswel as other nations.
g Lest any shulde thinke thē that Gods glorie shulde haue perished whē Iudáh was destroyed, he sheweth that he wil publish his grace through all ỳ worlde.
" Ebr. with one shulder, as Hos. 6,9
h That is, the Iewes shal come aswel as ỳ Gētiles: which is to be vnderstand vnder the time of the Gospel.
i For they shal haue ful remission of their sinnes: and the hypocrites which boasted of the Temple, which was also thy pride in time past, shal be taken from thee.
k That is, ỳ punishment for thy sinne.
l As the Assyrians, Caldeās, Egyptians, and other nations.
m To defende thee as by thy sinnes thou hast put him away and left thy selfe naked, as Exod. 32,25.
n Signifying, ỳ God deliteth to shewe his loue and great affectiō toward his Church.
o That is, them that were had in hatred and reuiled for ỳ Church and because of their religion.
p I wil deliuer the Church ŵ now is afflicted, as Micáh 4,6.
q As among the Assyrians and Caldeans ŵ did mocke them and put thē to shame.

HAGGAI.

THE ARGVMENT.

WHen the time of the seuentie yeres captiuitie prophecied by Ieremiáh, was expired, God raised vp Haggái, Zechariáh and Malachí to comforte the Iewes and to exhorte them to the buylding of the Temple, which was a figure of the spiritual Temple and Church of God, whose perfection and excellencie stode in Christ. And because that all were giuen to their owne pleasures & commodities, he declareth that that plague of famine, which God sent then among them, was a iuste rewarde of their ingratitude, in that they contemned Gods honour, who had deliuered them. Yet he comforteth them, if they wil returne to the Lord, with the promes of greater felicitie, forasmuche as the Lord wil finish the worke that he hathe begonne, and send Christ whome he had promised, and by whome they shulde atteine to persite ioy and glorie.

a Who was ỹ ſonne of Hyſtaſpis, and the third King of the Perſiâs, as ſome thinke.
b Becauſe the buylding of ỹ Tẽple begã to ceaſe by reaſon that the people were diſcouraged by their enemies: & if theſe two notable men had nede to be ſtirred vp and admoniſhed of their dueties, what ſhal we thinke of other gouernours whoſe doings are ether against God, or very colde in his cauſe?
c Not ỹ they condemned ỹ buildĩg thereof, but thei preferred policie, & priuate profite to religiõ, being content with ſmale beginnings.
d Shewing ỹ they ſoght not onely their neceſsities, but their very pleaſures before Gods honour?
e Conſider ỹ plagues of God vpon you for preferring your policies to his religiõ, and becauſe ye ſeke not hĩ firſt of all.
f Meaning, that they ſhulde leaue of their owne cõmodities, and go forwarde in the buyldĩg of Gods Temple and in the ſetting forthe of his religion.
g That is, I wil heare your praiers accordĩg to my promes, 1. King. 8,21.
h That is, my glorie ſhal be ſet forthe by you.
i And ſo bring it to nothing.
k This declared that God was the autor of the doctrine, and that he was but the miniſter, as Exod. 14,31. iudg. 7,20. act. 15,28.
l Which declareth that men are vnapt and dul to ſerue ỹ Lord, nether can thei obey his worde or his meſſengers before God reforme their hearts & giue them new ſpirits, Ioh. 6,44.

CHAP. I.

1 *The time of the prophecie of Haggái. 8 An exhortaciõ to buylde the Temple againe.*

1 IN the secõde yere of
King [a] Darius, in the
ſixt moneth, the firſt
day of the moneth,
came the worde of the
Lord (by the mini-
ſterie of the Prophet
Haggái) vnto [b] Zerub
babél the ſonne of Shealtiél, a prince of
Iudáh, and to Iehoſhúa the ſonne of Iehozadák the hie Prieſt, ſaying,
2 Thus ſpeaketh ỹ Lord of hoſtes, ſaying,
This people ſay, The time is not yet come, [c] that the Lords Houſe ſhulde be
buylded.
3 Then came the worde of the Lord by the
miniſterie of ỹ Prophet Haggái, ſaying,
4 Is it time for your ſelues to dwell in
your [d] ſiled houſes, & this Houſe lie waſte?
5 Now therefore thus ſaith the Lord of
hoſtes, Conſider your owne waies in your
hearts.
6 [e] Ye haue ſowen muche, & bring in litle:
ye eat, but ye haue not ynough: ye drinke,
but ye are not filled: ye clothe you, but ye
be not warme: and he that earneth wages,
putteth the wages into a broken bagge.
7 Thus ſaith the Lord of hoſtes, Conſider
your owne waies in your hearts.
8 Go [f] vp to the mountaine, & bring wood,
& buylde this Houſe, & [g] I wil be fauorable in it, and I wil [h] be glorified, ſaith
the Lord.
9 Ye loked for muche, and lo, *it came* to litle: and when ye broght it home, I did
blowe [i] vpon it. And why, ſaith the Lord
of hoſtes? Becauſe of mine Houſe that is
waſte, and ye runne euery man vnto his
owne houſe.
10 Therefore the heauen ouer you ſtaied
it ſelf from dewe, and the earth ſtaied her
frute.
11 And I called for a drought vpon the lãd,
and vpon the mountaines, and vpon the
corne, and vpon the wine, and vpon the
oyle, vpon *all* that the grounde bringeth
forthe: bothe vpon men and vpon cattel,
and vpon all the labour of the hands.
12 When Zerubbabél the ſonne of Shealtiél,
and Iehoſhúa the ſonne of Iehozadák the
hie Prieſt with all the remnãt of the people, heard the [k] voyce of the Lord their
God, & the wordes of the Prophet Haggái (as the Lord their God had ſent him)
then the people did feare before ỹ Lord.
13 Then ſpake Haggái the Lords meſſenger in the Lords meſſage vnto the people, ſaying, I am with you, ſaith the Lord.
14 And the Lord ſtirred vp [l] the ſpirit of
Zerubbabél, the ſonne of Shealtiél a prince of Iudáh, and the ſpirit of Iehoſhúa
the ſonne of Iehozadák the hie Prieſt, and
the ſpirit of all the remnant of the people,
and they came, and did the worke in the
Houſe of the Lord of hoſtes their God.

CHAP. II.

He ſheweth that the glorie of the ſeconde Temple ſhal exceade the firſt.

1 IN the foure and twentieth daye of the
ſixt moneth, in the ſeconde yere of
King Darius,
2 In the ſeuenth *moneth*, in the one & twentieth *day* of the moneth, came the worde
of the Lord by the miniſterie of the Prophet Haggái, ſaying,
3 Speake now to Zerubbabél the ſonne of
Shealtiél prince of Iudáh, & to Iehoſhúa
the ſonne of Iehozadák the hie Prieſt, &
to the reſidue of the people, ſaying,
4 Who is left among you, that ſawe this
[a] Houſe in her firſt glorie, & how do you
ſe it now? Is it not in your eyes, in compa-
riſon of it as nothing?
5 Yet now be of good courage, ô Zerubbabél, ſaith the Lord, and be of good comfort, ô Iehoſhúa, ſonne of Iehozadák the
hie Prieſt: and be ſtrong, all ye people of
the land, ſaith the Lord, and [b] do it: for I
am with you, ſaith the Lord of hoſtes,
6 *According* to the worde that I couenan-
ted with you, when ye came out of Egypt:
ſo my Spirit ſhal remaine among you,
feare ye not.
7 For thus ſaith the Lord of hoſtes, [c] Yet
a litle while, and I wil ſhake the heauens
and the earth, and the ſea, and the drye
land:
8 And I wil moue all nacions, and [d] the deſire of all nacions ſhal come, and I wil fil
this Houſe with glorie, ſaith the Lord of
hoſtes.
9 The [e] ſiluer *is* mine, and the golde *is* mine,
ſaith the Lord of hoſtes.
10 The glorie of this laſt Houſe ſhalbe greater then the firſt, ſaith the Lord of hoſtes:
and in this place wil I giue [f] peace, ſaith
the Lord of hoſtes.
11 ¶ In the foure and twentieth *day* of the
ninth moneth, in the ſeconde yere of Darius, came the worde of the Lord vnto ỹ
Prophet Haggái, ſaying,
12 Thus ſaith the Lord of hoſtes, Aſke now
the Prieſts *concerning* the Law, and ſay,
13 If one beare [g] holy fleſh in the ſkirt of
his garment, and with his ſkirt do touche
the bread, or the potage, or the wine, or
oyle, or any meat, ſhal it be holy? And the
Prieſts anſwered and ſaid, No.
14 Thẽ ſaid Haggái, If a polluted perſone
touche any of theſe, ſhal it be vncleane?
And the Prieſts anſwered, & ſaid, It ſhal
be vncleane.
15 Then anſwered Haggái, and ſaid, So

a For the people according as Iſa. 32,11, & ezek. 41,1, had prophecied, thoght this Tẽple ſhulde haue bene more excellent then Salomõs Tẽple, which was deſtroied by the Babylonians, but ỹ Prophets mẽt the ſpiritual Temple, the Church of Chriſt.
b That is, go forwarde in buylding the Temple.
c He exhorteth them to paciẽce thogh they ſe not as yet this Temple ſo glorious as the Prophets had declared: for this ſhulde be accompliſhed in Chriſt by whome all things ſhulde be renued.
d Meaning, Chriſt whome all oght to loke for and deſire: or by deſire, he may ſignifie all precious things, as riches and ſuche like.
e Therefore when his time cometh, he can make all the treaſures of ỹ worlde to ſerue his purpoſe: but the glorie of this ſecõde Temple doeth not ſtand in material thĩgs nether can be buylt.
f Meaning, all ſpiritual bleſſings and felicitie purchaſed by Chriſt, Phil 4,7.
g That is, the fleſh of the ſacrifices: whereby he ſignifieth that that thĩg, ỽ of it ſelf is good, can not make another thing ſo: and therefore they oght not to iuſtifie thẽ ſelues by their ſacrifices and ceremonies: but cõtrary he that is vncleane and not pure of heart, doeth corrupt thoſe things & make them deteſtable vnto God which els are good and godlie.

is this people, and so is this nacion before
me, saith the Lord: and so *are* all the workes of their hands, and that which they offre here, is vncleane.
16 And now, I pray you, consider in your
minds: from this [h] day, and afore, *euen* a-
fore a stone was laid vpon a stone in the
Temple of the Lord:
17 Before these things were, [i] when one came to an heape of twentie *measures*, there
were but ten: when one came to the wine
presse for to drawe out fiftie *vessels* out of
the presse, there were but twentie.
18 I smote you with blasting, and with mildewe, and with haile, in all the labours of
your hands: yet you *turned* not to me, saith
the Lord.
19 Consider, I pray you, in your mindes
from [k] this day, and afore from the foure
and twétieth day of the ninth *moneth*, *euen*
from the day that the fundacion of the
Lords Temple was laid: consider it in
your mindes.

h Consider how God did plague you with famine afore you began to buylde the Temple.
i That is, before the buildĩg was begõne.
k From the time they begã to buylde the Temple, he promiseth ỷ God wolde blesse them: & albeit as yet the frute was not come forthe, yet in the gathering they shulde haue plentie.

20 Is the [l] seed yet in the barne? as yet the
vines, and the figtre, & the pome granate, and the oliue tre hathe not broght forthe: from this day wil I blesse *you*.
21 And againe the worde of the Lord came vnto Haggái in the foure & twentieth
day of the moneth, saying,
22 Speake to Zerubbabél the prince of Iudáh, and say, I [m] wil shake the heauens and
the earth,
23 And I wil ouerthrowe the throne of
kingdomes, and I wil destroy the strength
of the [n] kingdomes of the heathen, & I wil
ouerthrowe the charets, & those that ride
in them, and the horse and the riders shal
come downe, euerie one by the sworde of
his brother.
24 In that day, saith the Lord of hostes, wil
I take thee, ô Zerubbabél my seruant, the
sonne of Shealtiél, saith the Lord, & wil
make thee as a [o] signet: for I haue chosen
thee, saith the Lord of hostes.

l He exhorteth them to pacience and to abide til ỷ haruest came, and then they shulde se Gods blessings.
m I wil make a change and renue all thigs in Christ, of whome Zerubbabél here is a figure.
n Hereby he sheweth that there shalbe no let or hinderance when God wil make this wõderful restitution of his Church.
o Signifying that his dignitie shulde be most excellẽt, which thing was accomplished in Christ.

ZECHARIAH.

THE ARGVMENT.

Two moneths after that Haggái had begonne to prophecie, Zechariáh was also sent of the Lord to helpe him in the labour, and to cõfirme the same doctrine. First therefore he putteh them in remembrance, for what cause God had so sore punished their fathers: and yet comforteth thẽ, if they wil repent vnfainedly, & not abuse this great benefite of God in their deliuerance, which was a figure of that true deliuerance, that all the faithful shulde haue from death and sinne by Christ. But because they stil remained in their wickednes and coldenes to set forthe Gods glorie, & were not yet made better by their long banishemẽt, he rebuketh thẽ moste sharpely: yet for the comfort of the repentant, he euer mixeth the promes of grace, that they might by this meanes be prepared to receiue Christ, in whome all shulde be sanctified to the Lord.

CHAP. I.

2 He exhorteth the people to returne to the Lord, & to eschewe the wickednes of their fathers. 16 He signifieth the restitution of Ierusalém and the Temple.

1 IN the eight moneth of ỷ
seconde yere of [a] Darius,
came the worde of the
Lord vnto [b] Zechariáh ỷ
sonne of Berechiáh, the
sonne of Iddo, the Pro-
phet, saying,
2 The Lord hathe bene [c] sore displeased
with your fathers.
3 Therefore say thou vnto thẽ, Thus saith
the Lord of hostes, [d] Turne ye vnto me,
saith the Lord of hostes, & I wil turne vnto you, saith the Lord of hostes.
4 Be ye not as your fathers, vnto whome ỷ
former *Prophets haue cryed, sayĩg, Thus
saith the Lord of hostes, Turne you now
from your euil wayes, & from your wicked
workes: but they wolde not heare, nor hear
ken vnto me, saith the Lord.
5 Your fathers, where [e] are they? and do the
Prophetes liue for euer?
6 But did not my wordes and my statutes,
which I commanded by my seruants the
Prophetes, take holde of [f] your fathers? &
[g] they returned, & said, As the Lord of hostes hathe determined to do vnto vs, according to our owne wayes, & according
to our workes, so hathe he delt with vs.
7 Vpon the foure and twentieth day of the
eleuẽth moneth, which is the moneth [h] She
bat, in the seconde yere of Darius, came
the worde of the Lord vnto Zechariáh ỷ
sonne of Berechiáh, the sonne of Iddo the
Prophet, saying,
8 I [i] sawe by night, and beholde [k] a man ri-

a Who was the sonne of Hystaspis.
b This was not ỷ Zechariáh, whereof is mencion 2. Chro. 24, 20, but had the same name, & is called ỷ sonne of Berechiáh, as he was, because he came of those progenitors, as of Ioiada or Berechiáh and Iddo.
c He speaketh this to feare thẽ with Gods iudgements ỷ they shulde not prouoke him as their fathers had done, whome he so grieuously punished.
d Let your frutes declare, ỷ you are Gods people & that he hathe wroght in you by his Spirit & mortified you: for els mã hathe no power to returne to God, but God must conuert him, as Ier. 31, 18. lam 5, 21. *Isa.* 21, 8, & 31, 6. & 45, 21. *iere*, 3, 12 *ezek*. 18, 30. *hos*. 14, 2. *ioel* 2, 12.

e Thogh your fathers be dead, yet Gods iudgements in punishing thẽ oght stil to be before your eyes: & thogh the Prophetes be dead, yet their doctrine remaineth for euer, 2. Pet. 1, 15.
f Seing ye saw the force of my doctrine in punishĩg your fathers, why do not ye feare ỷ threatnings conteined in the same and declared by my Prophetes?
g As men astonished with my iudgements, and not that they were touched with true repentance.
h Which conteineth parte of Ianuarie and parte of Februarie.
i This vision signifieth the restauration of the Church, but as yet it shulde not appeare to mans eyes, which is here ment by the night, by the bottome & by ỷ mirre trees, which are blacke and giue a darke shadowe: yet he compareth God to a King, who hathe his postes and messengers abroad, by whome he stil worketh his purpose and bringeth his matters to passe.
k Who was the chief among the rest of the horse men.

ding vpon a red horse, and he stode amõg
the mirre trees, that were in a bottome, &
behinde him were there [l] red horses spec-
keled and white.
9 Then said I, O my Lord, what are these?
And the Angel that talked with me, said
vnto me, I wil shewe thee what these be.
10 And the man that stode among the mirre trees, answered and said, These are they
whome the Lord hathe sent to go through
the worlde.
11 And they answered the Angel of the
Lord, that stode among the mirre trees, &
said, We haue gone thorowe the worlde:
and beholde, all the worlde sitteth stil, and
is at rest.
12 Then the [m] Angel of the Lord answered
and said, O Lord of hostes, how long wilt
thou be vnmerciful to Ierusalém, and to
the cities of Iudáh, with whome thou hast
bene displeased now these thre score and
ten yeres?
13 And the Lord answered the Angel that
talked with me, with good wordes *and* cõfortable wordes.
14 So the Angel that communed with me,
said vnto me, Crye thou, and speake, Thus
saith the Lord of hostes, I am [n] ielouse
ouer Ierusalém and Zión wͭ a great zeale,
15 And am greatly angrie against the careles heathen: for I was angrie but [o] a litle, & they helped forwarde the afflictiõ.
16 Therefore thus saith the Lord, I wil returne vnto Ierusalém with tender mercie:
mine house shal be buylded in it, saith the
Lord of hostes, & a line [p] shal be stretched
vpon Ierusalém.
17 Crye yet, and speake, Thus saith ŷ Lord
of hostes, My cities shal yet [q] be broken
with plentie: the Lord shal yet comforte
Zión, and shal yet chuse Ierusalém.
18 Then lift I vp mine eyes and sawe, and
beholde, [r] foure hornes.
19 And I said vnto the Angel that talked
with me, What be these? And he answered
me, These are the hornes which haue scattered Iudáh, Israél, and Ierusalém.
20 And the Lord shewed me foure [ſ] carpenters.
21 Thẽ said I, What come these to do? And
he answered, and said, These are the hornes, which haue scattered Iudáh, so that a
man durst not lift vp his head: but these
are come to fraye them, and to cast out the
hornes of the Gentiles, which lift vp
their horne ouer the land of Iudáh, to
scattre it.

l These signified ŷ diuers offices of Gods Angels by whome God somtime punisheth and somtime comforteth & brĩgeth forthe his workes in diuers sortes.

m That is, Christ the Mediator praied for the saluation of his Church, wͨ was now troubled when all the countreys about them were at rest.

n Thogh for a time God differre his helpe & comfort frõ his Church, yet this declareth that he loueth them stil moste derely, as a moste merciful father his childrẽ, or an housband his wife, and when it is expedient for them, his helpe is euer ready.

o In destroyĩg the reprobat I shewed my self, but a litle angrie toward my Church, but ŷ enemie wolde haue destroied them also, and considered not the end of my chastisements.

p To measure out the buyldings.

q The abundance shalbe so great that the places of store shal not be able to conteine these blessings that God wil send, but shal euen breake for fulnes.

r Which signified all the enemies of the Church, East, West, North, South. ſ These carpenters or smithes are Gods instruments, which with their mallets and hammers breake these hard and strong hornes, which wolde ouerthrowe the Church, and declare that none enemies horne is so strong, but God hathe an hammer to breake it in pieces.

CHAP. II.

The restoring of Ierusalém and Iudáh.

1 I Lift vp mine eyes againe and loked,
and beholde, a [a] man with a measuring
line in his hand.
2 Then said I, Whither goest thou? And
he said vnto me, To measure Ierusalém,
that I may se what is the breadth thereof,
and what is the length thereof.
3 And beholde, the Angel that talked with
me, went forthe: and another Angel went
out to mete him,
4 And said vnto him, Runne, speake to this
[b] yong man, and say, [c] Ierusalém shal be
inhabited without walles, for the multitude of men and cattel therein.
5 For I, saith the Lord, wil be vnto her a
wall of [d] fyre rounde about, and wil [e] be
the glorie in the middes of her.
6 Ho, ho, *come* [f] *forthe*, and flee from the land
of the North, saith the Lord: for I haue
scattered you into ŷ foure [g] windes of the
heauen, saith the Lord.
7 [h] Saue thy self, ô Zión, that dwellest with
the daughter of Babél.
8 For thus saith the Lord of hostes, After
this [i] glorie hathe he sent me vnto the nacions, which spoiled you: for he that toucheth you, toucheth the [k] apple of his eye.
9 For beholde, I wil lift vp mine hand
[l] vpon them: and [m] they shal be a spoile
to those that serued them, and ye shal
knowe, that the Lord of hostes hathe [n] sent
me.
10 Reioyce, and be glad, ô daughter Zión:
for lo, I come and wil dwell in the middes of thee, saith the Lord.
11 And many nacions shalbe ioyned to the
Lord in that day, and shal be my people:
and I wil dwell in the middes of thee, and
thou shalt knowe that the Lord of hostes
hathe sent me vnto thee.
12 And the Lord shal inherit Iudáh his portion in the holy land, and shal chuse Ierusalém againe.
13 Let all flesh be stil before the Lord: for
he is raised vp out of his holy place.

a That is, the Angel who was Christ: for in respect of his office he is oft times called an Angel, but in respect of his eternal essence, is God and so called.

b Meaning him self Zecharíah.

c Signifying ŷ spiritual Ierusalém and Church vnder Christ, which shulde be extẽded by ŷ Gospel through all the worlde and shulde nede no material walles, nor trust in any worldelie strength, but shulde be safely preserued, and dwell in peace among all their enemies.

d To defende my Church, to feare the enemies, and to destroy them if they approche nere.

e In me they shal haue their ful felicitie & glorie.

f He calleth to thẽ, which partely for feare and partely for their owne ease remained stil in captiuitie, and so preferred their owne priuate commodities to the benefites of God promised in his Church.

g As it was I that scattered you, so haue I power to restore you.

h By fleing from Babylon and coming to the Church. i Seing that God hathe begonne to shewe his grace among you by deliuering you, he continueth the same stil towarde you, and therefore sendeth me his Angel, and his Christ to defend you from your enemies, that they shal not hurt you, nether by the way nor at home. k Ye are so deare vnto God, that he can no more suffer your enemies to hurt you, then a man can abide to be thrust in the eye, Psal. 17,8 l Vpon the heathen your enemies. m They shalbe your seruantes as you haue bene theirs. n This must necessarely be vnderstand of Christ, who being God equal with his Father, was sent as he was Mediator to dwell in his Church, and to gouerne them.

CHAP. III.

A prophecie of Christ and of his kingdome.

1 ANd he shewed me Iehoshúa the hie
Priest, [a] stãding before the Angel of
the Lord, and [b] Satan stode at his right
hand to resist him.

a He praied to Christ the Mediator for the state of the Church.

b Which declareth that the faithful haue not onely warre with flesh and blood, but with Satan him self and the spiritual wickednes, Eph. 6,12.

e That is, Christ speaketh to God as the Mediator of his Church that he wolde rebuke Satan: and here he sheweth him self to be the continual preseruer of his Church.

d Meaning ŷ Iehoshúa was wonderfully preserued in the captiuitie, and now Satã soght to afflict & trouble him when he was doig his office

e In respect of ŷ glorious garments, and precious stones that the Priestes did weare before the captiuitie: and by this contemptible state the Prophet signifieth that these smale beginnings shulde be made excellent when Christ shal make the ful restitution of his Church.

f He sheweth of what apparel he speaketh, ŵ is whẽ our filthy sinnes are taken away and we are clad with Gods mercies, which is ment of the spiritualr stitutiõ.

g The Prophet praieth that besides the raiment the

2 And the [c] Lord said vnto Satã, The Lord
reproue thee, ô Satan: euen the Lord that
hathe chosen Ierusalém, reproue thee. Is
not this a [d] brande taken out of the fyre?
3 Now Iehoshúa was clothed with filthy
garments, and stode before the Angel.
4 And he answered and spake vnto those
that stode before him, saying, Take away
the [e] filthy garments from him. And vnto
him he said, Beholde, I haue [f] caused thine iniquitie to departe from thee, & I wil
clothe thee with change of raiment.
5 And I said, Let them [g] set a faire diademe
vpon his head. So they set a faire diademe vpon his head, and clothed him with
garments, & the Angel of ŷ Lord stode by.
6 And the Angel of the Lord testified vnto Iehoshúa, saying,
7 Thus saith the Lord of hostes, If thou
wilt walke in my waies, and kepe my watche, thou shalt also [h] iudge mine House, &
shalt also kepe my [i] courtes, and I wil giue thee place among [k] these that stand by.
8 Heare now, ô Iehoshúa ŷ hie Priest, thou
and thy fellowes that sit before thee: for
they [l] are monstruous persones: but beholde, I wil bring forthe the [m] Branche my
seruant.
9 For lo the [n] stone that I haue laid before
Iehoshúa: vpon one stone shalbe seuen
eyes: beholde, I wil [o] cut out the grauing
thereof, saith ŷ Lord of hostes, & I wil take [p] away ŷ iniquitie of this lãd in one day.
10 In that day, saith the Lord of hostes, shal
ye call euerie mã his neighbour vnder the
[q] vine, and vnder the fig tree.

Priest might also haue tyre for his head accordingly, that is, that the dignitie of the Priesthode might be perfect: and this was fulfilled in Christ, who was bothe Priest and King: and here all suche are condemned that can content them selues with any meane reformation in religion, seing the Prophet desireth the perfection, and obteineth it. h That is, haue rule and gouernement in my Church as thy predecessours haue had. i Whereby he meaneth to haue the whole charge and ministerie of the Church. k That is, the Angels who represented the whole nomber of the faithful: signifying that all the godlie shulde willingly receiue him. l Because they followe my worde, thei are contemned in the worlde, and estemed as monsters, Isa. 8,18. m That is, Christ, who did so humble him self, that not onely he became the seruant of God, but also the seruant of men: and therefore in him they shulde haue comfort, althogh in the worlde they were contemned, Isa. 11,1 iere. 23,5 & 33,14 n He sheweth that the ministers can not buylde, before God lay ŷ first stone, which is Christ, who is ful of eyes, bothe because he giueth light vnto all others, & that all oght to seke light at him, Chap. 4,10. o That is, I wil make it perfite in all pointes, as a thing wroght by the hand of God p Thogh I haue punished this land for a time, yet I wil euen now be pacified, & visit their sinnes no more. q Ye shal then liue in peace & quietnes, that is, in the kingdome of Christ, Isa. 2,2. micáh 4,4.

CHAP. IIII.

The vision of the golden candelsticke, and the exposition thereof.

1 AND the Angel that talked with me,
came againe & waked me, as a man
that is raised out of his slepe,
2 And said vnto me, What seest thou? And
I said, I haue loked, & behold, a [a] cãdelsticke all of gold with a bowle vpõ the top of
it, & his seuẽ lampes therein, & seué pipes
to ŷ [b] lampes, ŵ were vpõ the top thereof.

a Which was euer in the middes of the Temple, signifying ŷ ŷ graces of Gods Spirit shulde shine there in moste abundance, and in all perfection. b Which conueied the oyle that dropped frõ the trees into the lampes, so that the light neuer failed: & this visiõ was to cõfirme the faithful that God had sufficient power in him selfe to cõtinue his graces, & to bring his pures to passe, thogh he had no help of mã.

3 And two oliue trees ouer it, one vpõ the
right side of the bowle, & the other vpon
the left side thereof.
4 So I answered, & spake to the Angel that
talked with me, saying, What are these,
my Lord?
5 Thẽ the Angel that talked ŵ me, answered
and said vnto me, Knowest thou not what
these be? And I said, No, my Lord.
6 Then he answered and spake vnto me,
saying, This is the worde of the Lord vnto [c] Zerubbabél, saying, Nether by [d] an armie nor strength, but by my Spirit, saith
the Lord of hostes.
7 Who art thou, ô [e] great mountaine, before Zerubbabél? *thou shalt be* a plaine, & [f] he
shal bring forthe the head stone thereof,
ŵ showtings, *crying*, Grace, grace vnto it.
8 Moreouer, the worde of the Lord came
vnto me, saying,
9 The hands of Zerubbabél haue laid the
fundaciõ of this house: his hands shal also
finish it, and [g] thou shalt knowe that the
Lord of hostes hathe sent me vnto you.
10 For who hathe despised the day of the
[h] smale things? but they shal reioyce, and
shal se the stone of [i] tinne in the hand of
Zerubbabél: [k] these seuen are the eies of ŷ
Lord, which go thorowe ŷ whole worlde.
11 Then answered I, and said vnto him,
What are these two oliue trees vpon the
right and vpon the left side thereof?
12 And I spake moreouer, and said vnto
him, What be these two oliue branches,
which thorowe the two goldẽ pipes emptie them selues into the golde?
13 And he answered me and said, Knowest
thou not what these be? And I said, No, my
Lord.
14 Then said he, These are the two [l] oliue
branches, that stande with the ruler of the
whole earth.

c Who was a figure of Christ and therefore this doctrine was directed to all ŷ Church who are his bodie & mẽbers.

d He sheweth ŷ Gods power onely is sufficient to preserue his Church, thogh he vse not mãs helpe thereunto.

e He compareth the power of the aduersaries to a great moũtaine, who thoght the Iewes nothĩg in respect of them, and wolde haue hindred Zerubbabél who represẽted Christ whome ŷ enemies daily labour to let in the buylding of his spiritual Temple, but all in vaine.

f Thogh ŷ enemies thinke to stay this buyldĩg, yet Zerubbabél shal lay the hiest stone thereof, and bring it to perfection, so that all the godlie shal reioyce, & pray vnto God that he wolde cõtinue his grace, and fauour toward ŷ Tẽple

g Meaning, ŷ Prophet, that I am Christ sent of my Father for the buylding, & preseruation of my spiritual Tẽple. h Signifying ŷ all were discouraged at ŷ smale & poure beginnings of the Tẽple i Whereby he signifieth ŷ plũmet & line, that is, ŷ Zerubbabél which represented Christ, shulde go forward with his buylding to ŷ ioye & cõfort of ŷ godlie, thogh the worlde be against him, & thogh his for a while be discouraged, because thei se not things pleasant to ŷ eye k That is, God hathe seuen eyes: meaning, a cõtinual prouidẽce, so that nether Satan nor anie power in the worlde can go about or bring anie thing to passe to hinder his worke, Chap 3,9 l Which were euer grene & ful of oyle, so that stil they powred forthe oyle into the lampes: signifying, that God wil continually mainteine and preserue his Church, and indue it stil with abundance and perfection of graces.

CHAP. V.

1 The vision of the flying booke, signifying the curse of theues, and suche as abuse the Name of God. 6 By the vision of the measure is signified the bringing of Iudahs afflictions into Babylon.

1 THEN I turned me, & lift vp mine eyes
and loked, & beholde, a flying booke.
2 And he said vnto me, What seest ŷ? And
I answered, I se a flying [a] booke: the lẽgth
thereof *is* twentie cubites, & the breadth
thereof ten cubites.
3 Then said he vnto me, This is the curse

a Because the Iewes had prouoked Gods plagues by cõtemning his worde, and casting of all iudgement & equitie, he sheweth that Gods curses writen in this booke had iustely light bothe on them, & their fathers: but now if they wolde repẽt, God wolde send the same among the Caldeans their former enemies.

that goeth forthe ouer the whole earth: for
euerie one that [b] ſtealeth, ſhalbe cut of
aſwel on this [c] ſide, as on that: & euerie one
that [d] ſweareth, ſhal be cut of *aſwel* on this
ſide, as on that.
4 I wil bring it forthe, ſaith the Lord of ho
ſtes, and it ſhal enter into the houſe of the
thief, & into ye houſe of him, ye falſely ſweareth by my Name: & it ſhal remaine in the
middes of his houſe, and ſhal conſume it,
with the timbre thereof, & ſtones thereof.
5 Then the Angel that talked with me, wẽt
forthe, & ſaid vnto me, Lift vp now thine
eyes, and ſe what is this that goeth forthe.
6 And I ſaid, What is it? And he ſaid, This
is an [e] Epháh yt goeth forthe. He ſaid moreouer, This is the [f] ſight of them, through
all the earth.
7 And beholde, there was lift vp a [g] talent
of lead: & this is a [h] woman that ſitteth in
the middes of the Epháh.
8 And he ſaid, This is [i] wickednes, & he caſt
it into the middes of the Epháh, & he caſt
the weight of lead vpõ the mouth thereof.
9 Then lift I vp mine eyes, and loked: and
beholde, there came out two [k] women, &
the winde *was* in their wings (for thei had
wings like the wings of a ſtorke) & they
lift vp the Epháh betwene the earth and
the heauen.
10 Then ſaid I to ye Angel that talked with
me, Whither do theſe beare the Epháh?
11 And he ſaid vnto me, [l] To buyld it an
houſe in ye land of Shinár, & it ſhalbe eſtabliſhed and ſet there vpon her owne place.

b That is, vſeth any iniurie towarde his neighbour. c Meaning, whereſoeuer he be in the worlde. d He that trãſgreſſeth the firſt table, and ſerueth not God aright, but abuſeth Gods Name. e Which was a meaſure in dry things cõteining about ten pottels. f That is, all the wickednes of the vngodlie is in Gods ſight, wc he kepeth in a meaſure and can ſhut it or open it at his pleaſure. g To couer ye meaſure. h Which repreſenteth iniquitie, as in ye next verſe. i Signifying yt Satan ſhulde not haue ſuche power againſt the Iewes to tempt them, as he had in time paſt, but yt God wolde ſhut vp iniquitie in a meaſure as in a priſon. k Which declared yt God wolde execute his iudgementes by the meanes of weake and infirme meanes. l To remoue the iniquitie and afflictions that came for the ſame from Iudáh, to place it for euer in Babylon.

CHAP. VI.

By the foure charettes he deſcribeth the foure monarchies.

1 AGaine, I turned and lift mine eyes,
and loked: and beholde, there came
foure [a] charettes out from betwene [b] two
mountaines, and the mountaines were
mountaines of braſſe.
2 In the firſt charet *were* [c] red horſes, and in
the ſeconde charet [d] blacke horſes,
3 And in the thirde charet [e] white horſes, &
in the fourte charet, horſes of [f] diuers colours, and reddiſh.
4 Then I anſwered, and ſaid vnto the Angel that talked with me, What are theſe,
my Lord?
5 And the Angel anſwered, and ſaid vnto
me, Theſe are the [g] foure ſpirits of ye heauen, which go forthe from ſtanding with
the Lord of all the earth.

a By charets here, as by horſes afore, he meaneth ye ſwift meſſengers of God to execute & declare his wil. b By the braſen mouñtaines he meaneth ye eternal coũſel & prouidence of God, whereby he hathe from before all eternitie decreed what ſhal come to paſſe, & that wc nether Satan nor all the worlde can alter. c Which ſignified the great crueltie and perſecutions that the Church had indured vnder diuers enemies. d Signifying that they had indured great afflictions vnder the Babylonians. e Theſe repreſented their ſtate vnder the Perſians which reſtored them to libertie. f Which ſignified that God wolde ſomtime giue his Church reſt, and powre his plagues vpon their enemies, as he did in deſtroying Nineueh and Babylon, and other their enemies. g Meaning, all the actions and motions of Gods Spirit, which according to his inchangeable counſel he cauſeth to appeare through all the worlde.

6 That with the blacke horſe wẽt forthe into the land of the North, and the white
went out after them, & they of diuers colours went forthe towarde the [h] South
countrey.
7 And the [i] reddiſh went out, & required
to go, and paſſe through the worlde, and
he ſaid, Go paſſe through the worlde. So
they went thorowout the worlde.
8 Then cryed he vpon me, and ſpake vnto
me, ſaying, Beholde, theſe that go towarde
the North countrey, haue pacified my
[k] ſpirit in the North countrey.
9 And the worde of the Lord came vnto
me, ſaying,
10 Take of them of the captiuitie, *euen* of
Heldái, & of Tobiiáh, and Iedaiáh, which
are come from Babél, and come thou the
ſame day, and go vnto the houſe [l] of Ioſhiáh, the ſonne of Zephaniáh.
11 Take euen ſiluer, and golde, and make
crownes, and ſet *them* vpon the [m] head of
Iehoſhúa, the ſonn of Iehozadák the hie
Prieſt,
12 And ſpeake vnto him, ſaying, Thus
ſpeaketh the Lord of hoſtes, and ſaith,
Beholde the mã whoſe name is the [n] Branche, and he ſhal growe [o] vp out of his place, and he ſhal [p] buylde the Temple of the
Lord.
13 Euen he ſhal buylde the Temple of the
Lord, and he ſhal beare the [q] glorie, and
ſhal ſit and rule vpon his throne, and he
ſhalbe a Prieſt vpon his throne, & the coũ
ſel of peace ſhalbe betwene [r] thẽ bothe.
14 And the crownes ſhalbe to [ſ] Helém, and
to Tobiiáh and to Iedaiáh, and to [t] Hen
the ſonne of Zephaniáh, for a [u] memorial
in the Temple of the Lord.
15 And thei that are [x] farre of, ſhal come &
buyld in the Temple of the Lord, and ye
ſhal know, that the Lord of hoſtes hathe
ſent me vnto you. And this ſhal come to
paſſe, if ye wil [y] obey the voyce of the
Lord your God.

h That is, toward Egypt, and other coũtreies there about. i That is, they of diuers colours, wc aſke leaue, to ſignifie yt Satan hathe no power to hurt or afflict til God giue it him, Iob.1,12. k By puniſhing the Caldeãs mine angér ceaſed, and you were deliuered. l To receiue of him and the other thre, money to make ye two crowns: wc were men of great autoritie among ye Iews, and douted of the reſtitution of ye kingdome & of ye Prieſthode, and hurt others by their example. m Becauſe this colde not be attribute to anie one accor ding to ye Law, therefore it followeth that Iehoſhúa muſt repreſente the Meſſiáh who was bothe Prieſt & King. n Meaning Chriſt, of whome Iehoſhuã was ye figure: for in Greke they were bothe called Ieſus. o That is, of him ſelf without the helpe of man. p Which declareth yt none colde buylde this Temple, whereof Haggái ſpeaketh, but only Chriſt: and therefore it was ſpiritual, & not material, Hag 2,10 q Whereof Iehoſhúa had but a ſhadowe. r The two offices of the kingdome, & prieſthode ſhalbe ſo ioyned together, yt they ſhalbe no more diſſeuered. ſ Who was alſo called Heldái. t He alſo was called Ioſhiáh. u That they maie acknowledge their infirmitie, which loked that all things ſhulde haue bene reſtored incontinently: & of this their infidelitie theſe two crownes ſhal remaine as tokens, Act.1,6. x That is, the Gentiles by the preaching of the Goſpel ſhal helpe towarde the buylding of this ſpiritual Temple. y If ye wil beleue & remaine in the obedience of faith.

CHAP. VII.

5 The true faſting. 11 The rebellion of the people is the cauſe of their affliction.

1 ANd in the fourth yere of King Darius, the worde of ye Lord came vnto
Zechariáh in the fourth *day* of the ninth
moneth, euen in [a] Chiſleu.
2 For [b] thei had ſent vnto ye Houſe of God
Sharézer, and Regem mélech and their
men to praye before the Lord,

a Which cõteined parte of Nouember and parte of December. b That is, the reſt of ye people yt remained yet in Caldea, ſẽt to ye Church at Ieruſalẽ for the reſolution of theſe queſtions, becauſe theſe feaſts were cõſented vpon by the agrement of the whole Church, the one in the moneth, that the Temple was deſtroyed, and the other when Gedaliáh was ſlaine, Iere.41,2.

c By weping, and mourning appeare what exercises thei vsed in their fasting.
d That is, prepare my self with all deuocion to this fast.
e Which was now since the time the Temple was destroyed.
f For there were bothe of the people, and of the Priests, which douted as touching this controuersie, besides thē which as yet remained in Caldea, & reasoned of it as of one of the chief poits of their religion.
g For they thoght they had deserued toward God because of this fast, which they inuented of them selues: and thogh fasting of it self be good, yet because they thoght it a seruice towarde God, and trusted therein, it is here reproued.
h Did ye not eat, and drinke for your owne commoditie, & necessitie? and so likewise ye did absteine according to your owne fantasies, and not after the prescript of my Law?
i Hereby he condemneth their hypocrisie, ẘ thoght by their fasting to please God, and by suche things as they inuented, and in the meane season wolde not serue him as he had commanded.

3 *And* to speake vnto ỹ Priests, which were
in the House of the Lord of hostes, and to
the Prophetes, saying, Shulde I [c] wepe in
the fifte moneth, and [d] separate my self
as I haue done these so manie [e] yeres?
4 Then came the worde of the Lord of hostes vnto me, saying,
5 Speake vnto all the people of the land, &
to the [f] Priests, and say, When ye fasted,
and mourned in the fifte and seuenth moneth, euen these seuentie yeres, did ye fast
vnto me? [g] do I *approue it*?
6 And when ye did eat, and when ye did
drinke, did ye not eat [h] for your selues, &
drinke for your selues?
7 Shulde ye not *heare* the wordes, which ỹ
Lord [i] hathe cryed by the ministerie of
the former Prophetes whē Ierusalém was
inhabited, and in prosperitie, and the cities
thereof rounde about her, when the South
and the plaine was inhabited?
8 And the worde of the Lord came vnto
Zechariáh, saying,
9 Thus speaketh ỹ Lord of hostes, saying,
[k] Execute true iudgement, and shewe mer
cie and compassion, euerie man to his
brother,
10 And oppresse not the widowe, nor the fa
therles, the stranger nor the poore, and let
none of you imaginē euil against his brother in your heart.
11 But they refused to hearken, & [l] pulled
away the shulder, and stopped their eares,
that they shulde not heare.
12 Yea, thei made their hearts as an adamāt
stone, lest they shulde heare the Lawe and
the wordes which the Lord of hostes sent
in his [m] Spirit by the ministerie of the former Prophetes: therefore came a great
wrath from the Lord of hostes.
13 Therefore it is come to passe, that as he
cryed, and they wolde not heare, so they
cryed, & I wolde not heare, saith the Lord
of hostes.
14 But I scattred them amōg all the natiōs,
whome they knewe not: thus the land was
desolate [n] after them, that no man passed
through nor returned: for they laid the
pleasant land [o] waste.

k He sheweth, that thei did not fast with a syncere heart, but for an hypocrisie, & that it was not done of a pure religion, because that they lacked these offices of charitie, ẘ shulde haue declared that thei were godlie, Mat 23,23.
l And wolde not cary the Lords burden, which was swete and easy, but wolde beare their owne, which was heauie & grieuous to the flesh, thinking to merit thereby: ẘ similitude is taken of oxen, ẘ shrinke at the yoke, Nehem. 9,29. m Which declareth, that they rebelled not onely against ỹ Prophetes but against ỹ Spirit of God that spake in them. n That is, after they were caryed captiue. o By their sinnes whereby they prouoked Gods angre.

CHAP. VIII.

2 *Of the returne of the people unto Ierusalém, and of the*
mercie of God towarde them. 16 *Of goed workes.*
20 *The calling of the Gentiles.*

1 AGaine the worde of the Lord of
hostes came *to me*, saying,
2 Thus saith ỹ Lord of hostes, I was [a] ielous
for Zión with great ielousie, & I was ielous for her with great wrath.
3 Thus saith the Lord, I wil returne vnto
Zión, and wil dwell in thē middes of Ierusalém, & Ierusalém shalbe called a [b] citie of trueth, and the Mountaine of the
Lord of hostes, the holie Mountaine.
4 Thus saith ỹ Lord of hostes, There shal
yet olde [c] men and olde women dwell in
the stretes of Ierusalém, and euerie man
with his staffe in his hand for very age.
5 And the stretes of the citie shalbe ful of
boyes and girles, playing in the stretes
thereof.
6 Thus saith the Lord of hostes, Thogh it
be [d] vnpossible in the eyes of the remnant
of this people in these dayes, shulde it
therefore be vnpossible in my sight, saith
the Lord of hostes?
7 Thus saith the Lord of hostes, Beholde,
I wil deliuer my people from the East coū
trey, and from the West countrey.
8 And I wil bring them, & they shal [e] dwell
in the middes of Ierusalém, and they shal
be my people, and I wil be their God in
trueth and in righteousnes.
9 Thus saith the Lord of hostes, Let your
[f] hands be strong, ye that heare in these
dayes these wordes by the mouth of the
Prophetes, which were in the day, that the
fundacion of the House of the Lord of
hostes was laide, that the Temple might
be buylded.
10 For before these dayes there was no hier
for [g] man nor anie hier for beast, nether
was there anie peace to him that went out
or came in because of the affliction: for I
set all men, euerie one against his neighbour.
11 But now, I wil not *intreate* the residue of
this people as afore time, saith the Lord
of hostes.
12 For the sede *shalbe* prosperous: the vine
shal giue her frute, and the grounde shal
giue her increase & the heauens shal giue
their dewe, & I wil cause the remnant of
this people to possesse all these things.
13 And it shal come to passe, that as ye were
a curse amōg the heathē, ô house of Iudáh,
and house of Israél, so wil I deliuer you, &
ye shalbe a blessing: feare not, *but* let your
hands be strong.
14 For thus saith the Lord of hostes, As I
thoght to punish [h] you: when your fathers
prouoked me vnto wrath, saith the Lord
of hostes, and repented not,
15 So againe haue I determined in these
dayes [i] to do wel vnto Ierusalém, and to
the house of Iudáh: feare ye not.
16 These are the things that ye shal do.
Speake ye euerie man the trueth vnto his
neighbour: execute iudgement truely and
vprightly in your gates,

a I loued my citie ẘ a singular loue, so that I colde not abide that anie shulde do her anie iniurie.
b Because she shalbe faithful, and loyal towarde me her housband.
c Thogh their enemies did greatly molest and trouble them, yet God wolde come, and dwell amōg them, & so preserue them so lōg as nature wolde suffer them to liue, and increase their children in great abundance.
d He sheweth wherein our faith standeth, that is, to beleue that God cā performe that ẘ he hathe promised thogh it seme neuer so vnpossible to man, Rom. 4,20.
e So that their returne shal not be in vaine: for God wil accōplish his promes, & their prosperitie shalbe sure and stable.
f Let nether respect of your priuate cōmodities, nether counsel of others, nor feare of enemies discourage you in the going forwarde with ỹ buylding of ỹ Temple, but be constāt & obei the Prophetes, ẘ incourage you thereūto.
g For God cursed your worke, so that nether man nor beast had profite of their labours.
h Read Ezek. 18,20.
i Which declareth, that man can not turne to God til he change mans heart by his Spirit, and so beginne to do well, which is to pardon his sinnes and to giue him his graces.

17 And let none of you imagine euil in
your hearts against his neighbour,& loue
no false othe: for all these are the things
that I hate,saith the Lord.
18 And the worde of the Lord of hostes came vnto me,saying,
19 Thus saith the Lord of hostes, The fast
of the fourthe *moneth*, and the fast of the
fifte, and the fast of the seuenth, and the
fast of the [k] tenth, shal be to the house of
Iudáh ioye and gladnes, and prosperous
hie feastes: therefore loue the trueth and
peace.
20 Thus saith the Lord of hostes,That there shal yet come [l] people, and the inhabitants of great cities.
21 And they that dwell in one *citie*, shal go
to another,saying,*Vp,let vs go and pray
before the Lord, and seke the Lord of ho-
stes:I wil go also.
22 Yea, great people and mightie nations shal come to seke the Lord of hostes in Ierusalém,and to pray before the
Lord.
23 Thus saith the Lord of hostes, In those
dayes shal ten men take holde out of all
langages of the nacions, *euen* take holde
of the skirt of him that is a Iewe, & say,
We wil go with you: for we haue heard,
that God is with you.

k Which fast was appointed when the citie was besieged, & was the first fast of these foure: & here the Prophet sheweth, that if ẏ Iewes wil repent,and turne wholy to God,they shal haue no more occasiō to fast, or to shewe signes of heauines: for God wil send them ioy & gladnes.
l He declareth the great zeale that God shuld giue the Gentiles to come to his Church & to ioyne ẇ the Iewes in his true religion, ẇ shulde be in the kingdome of Christ.
Isa.2,2. mic.4,1.

CHAP. IX.

1 The threatening of the Gentiles. 9 The comming of Christ.

1 THe burden of the worde of the Lord
in the land of [a]Hadrách:and Damas-
cus *shalbe* his [b] rest.whē the [c] eyes of man,
euen of all the tribes of Israél *shalbe* toward
the Lord.
2 And Hamáth also shal border [d]thereby:
Tyrus *also* and Zidón, thogh *they be* [e] verie wise.
3 For Tyrus did buylde her self a strong
holde, and heaped vp siluer as the dust, &
golde as the myre of the streates.
4 Beholde, the Lord wil spoile her,and he
wil smite her [f] power in the sea,& she shal
be deuoured with fyre.
5 Ashkelón shal se it,and feare,and Azzáh
also shalbe verie sorowful,and Ekrón: for
her countenance shalbe ashamed, and the
King shal perish from Azzáh, and Ashkelón shal not be inhabited.
6 And the [g] stranger shal dwell in Ashdód,
and I wil cut of the pride of ẏ Philistims.
7 And I wil take away his blood out of his
mouth,and his abominacions from betwene his [h] teeth:but he that remaineth,euē he
shalbe for our God,& he shalbe as a prince in Iudáh,but [i]Ekrón *shalbe* as a Iebusite.

a Whereby he meaneth Syria.
b Gods angre shal abide vpō their chief citie,and not spare so muche as that.
c When the Iewes shal cōuert and repēt, then God wil destroye their enemies.
d That is, by Damascus: meaning that Hamáth or Antiochia shulde be vnder ẏ same rod and plague.
e He secretly sheweth ẏ cause of their destructiō,because they deceiued all other by their craft, and subtiltie, which they cloked with this name of wisdome.
f Thogh they of Tyrus thinke them selues inuincible by reason of the sea, that compasseth them round about, yet they shal not escape Gods iudgements. g Meaning,that all shulde be destroyed saue a verie fewe,that shulde remaine as strangers. h He promiseth to deliuer the Iewes when he shal take vengeance on their enemies for their crueltie,and wrongs done to them i As the Iebusites had bene destroyed,so shulde Ekrón and all the Philistims.

8 And I wil campe about [k] mine House a-
gainst the armie,against him that passeth
by,and against him that returneth,and no
oppressour shal come vpon them anie mo-
re:for now [l] haue I sene with mine eyes.
9 Reioyce greatly,ô daughter Zión:shoute
for ioye, ô daughter Ierusalém: beholde,
thy King cometh vnto thee:[m] he is iuste &
saued, poore and riding vpon an [n] asse,and
vpon a colte the fole of an asse.
10 And I wil cut of the [o] charrets from E-
phráim,and the horse from Ierusalém:the
bowe of the battel shalbe broken,and he
shal speake peace vnto the heathen, & his
dominion *shalbe* from [p] sea vnto sea, and
from the [q] riuer to the end of the land.
11 [r] Thou also *shalt be saued* through ẏ blood
of thy couenant. I haue losed thy [s] prisoners out of the pit wherein *is* no water.
12 Turne you to the [t] strong holde,ye [u] pri
soners of hope: euen to day do I declare,
that I wil render the [x] double vnto thee.
13 For Iudáh haue I [y] bent as a bowe for me:
Ephráims hand haue I filled, and I haue
raised vp thy sonnes, ô Zión, against thy
sonnes,ô Grecia,and haue made thee as a
gyants sworde.
14 And the Lord shalbe sene ouer them, &
his arrowe shal go forthe as ẏ lightning:
and the Lord God shal blowe the trumpet,and shal come forthe with the whirle-
windes of the South.
15 The Lord of hostes shal defend them,&
they shal deuoure them, [z]and subdue them
with sling stones, and they shal drinke, &
make a noyse as thorowe wine, and they
shalbe filled like bowles, & as the hornes
of the altar.
16 And the Lord their God shal deliuer
them in that day as the flocke of his peo-
ple:for *they shalbe as* the [a] stones of ẏ crowne lifted vp vpon his land.
17 For how great is his goodnes! and how
great is his beautie! corne shal make the
yong men chereful,& new wine ẏ maides.

k He sheweth ẏ Gods power onely shalbe sufficient to defend his Church agaīst all aduersaries b thei neuer so cruel or assemble their power neuer so often.
l That is,God hathe now sene the great iniuries and afflictions wherewith they haue bene afflicted by their enemies.
m That is, he he hathe righteousnes, and saluatiō in him self for the vse & cōmoditie of his Church.
n Which declareth ẏ thei shulde not loke for suche a King as shulde be glorious in the eyes of mā but shulde be poore,and yet in him self haue all power to deliuer his: & this is mēt of Christ, as Mat.21,5.
o No power of man or creature shalbe able to let this kingdome of Christ,and he shal peaceably gouerne thē by his worde.
p That is, frō the red sea,to the sea called Syriacum: and by these places which ẏ Iewes knewe,he mēt an infinite space & compasse ouer the whole worlde.
q That is, frō Euphrátes.
r Meaning,Ierusalém or the Church,which is saued by ẏ blood of Christ whereof the blood of the sacrifices was a figure,and is here called the couenant of the Church because God made it with his Church, and left it with them for the loue that he bare vnto them. s God sheweth that he wil deliuer his Church out of all dangers,seme they neuer so great. t That is,into the holie land where the citie and the Temple are,where God wil defend you. u Meaning the faithful,which semed to be in danger of their enemies on euerie side,and yet liued in hope that God wolde restore them to libertie. x That is, double benefites,and prosperitie in respect of that which your fathers enioyed from Dauids time to the captiuitie. y I wil make Iudáh and Ephráim,that is, my whole Church,victorious against all enemies, which he here meaneth by the Grecians. z He promiseth that the Iewes shal destroye their enemies and haue abundance,and excesse of all things,as there is abundance on the altar whē the sacrifice is offred. Which things are not to moue them to intemperancie,but to sobrietie,and a thankful remembrance of Gods great liberalitie. a The faithful shal be preserued,and reuerenced of all,that the verie enemies shalbe compelled to esteme them:for Gods glorie shal shine in them, as Iosephus declareth of Alexander the great when he met Iadi the hie Priest.

CHAP. X.

1 The vanitie of idolatrie. 3 The Lord promiseth to visite & comforte the house of Israél.

1 ASke you of the [a] Lord raine in the
time of the latter raine:*so* shal ẏ Lord

a The Prophet reproueth the Iewes because by their owne infidelitie thei put backe Gods graces promised,& so famine came by Gods iuste iudgemēt:therefore to auoide this plague he willeth thē to turne to God, & to pray in faith to him,and so he wil giue them abundance.

make

make white cloudes,and giue you showres
of raine,& to euerie one grasse in ẏ field.
2 Surely [b] the idoles haue spoken vanitie,
and the sothsayers haue sene a lie,and the
dreamers haue tolde a vaine thing : they
cõfort in vaine:therefore [c] thei went away
as shepe:thei were troubled, because there
was no shepherd.
3 My wrath was kindled against the shepherds,and I did visite the [d] goates: but the
Lord of hostes wil visite his flocke the
house of Iudáh,& wil make them as [e] his
beautiful horse in the battel.
4 Out [f] of him shal the corner come forthe:
out of him the naile, out of him the bowe
of battel,& out of him euery [g] appointer
of tribute also.
5 And they shalbe as ẏ mightie men,which
treade downe *their enemies* in the myre of
the stretes in the battel , & thei shal fight,
because the Lord *is* with them , and the riders on horses shalbe confounded.
6 And I wil strengthen the house of Iudáh,
and I wil preserue the house [h] of Iosépli,
and I wil bring them againe , for I pitie
them: and they shalbe as thogh I had not
cast them of:for I am the Lord their God,
and wil heare them.
7 And they of Ephráim shalbe as a gyant,
& their heart shal reioyce as thorowe wi-
ne:yea,their children shal se it,& be glad:
& their heart shal reioyce in the Lord.
8 I wil [i] hisse for them,and gather them:for
I haue redemed them: & they shal encrease,as they haue encreased.
9 And I wil [k] sowe them among the people,
and they shal remember me in farre coun-
treis:and thei shal liue with their children
and [l] turne againe.
10 I wil bring them againe also out of the
land of Egypt,& gather them out of Asshúr : and I wil bring them into the land
of Gileád,and Lebanón, & *place* shal not
be founde for them.
11 And he [m] shal go into the sea with affliction , and shal smite the waues in the sea,
and all the depthes of the riuer shal drye
vp:and the pride of Asshúr shalbe cast
downe , and the sceptre of Egypt shal departe away.
12 And I wil strengthen them in the Lord,
and they shal walke in his Name,saith the
Lord.

b He calleth to remẽbrance Gods punishments in times past because they trusted not in him,but in their idoles and sorcerers who euer deceiued them.
c That is , the Iewes went into captiuitie.
d Meaning,the cruel gouernours which did oppresse ẏ poore shepe, Ezek.34,17.
e He wil be merciful to his Church and cherish them as a King or Prince doeth his best horse which shalbe for his owne vse in the warre.
f Out of Iudáh shal the chief gouernour procede,who shal be as a corner to vpholde the buylding and as a naile to fasten it together.
g Ouer their enemies.
h That is, the ten tribes, ẇ shulde be gathered vnder Christ to the rest of ẏ Churche.
i Whereby he declareth the power of Gód who nedeth no great preparation when he wil deliuer his:for with a becke or hisse he can call them from all places suddély
k Thogh they shal yet be scattered & seme to be lost, yet it shalbe profitable vnto them: for there thei shal come to the knowledge of my Name , ẇ was accomplished vnder the Gospel, amõg whome it was first preached.
l Not ẏ they shulde returne into their cõutrey , but be gathered and ioyned in one faith by the doctrine of the Gospel.
m He alludeth to the deliuerance of the people out of Egypt where as the Angel smote the floods and riuers.

CHAP. XI.

1 The destruction of the Temple. 4 The care of the faithful is committed to Christ. 7 A grieuous vision against Ierusalém and Iudáh.

1 OPen thy dores,ô [a] Lebanón, and the
fyre shal deuoure thy cedres.
2 Houl, [b] fyrre trees:for the cedre is fallẽ,
because all ẏ mightie are destroyed: houle ye,ô okes of Bashán, for the [c] defensed
forest is cut downe.
3 There *is* the voyce of the houling of the
shepherds:for their [d] glorie is destroyed:
ẏ voyce of the roaring of lyons whelpes:
for the pride of Iordén is destroyed.
4 Thus saith the Lord my God , Fede the
shepe of the [e] slaughter.
5 They that possesse them,slaye them [f] and
sinne not:and thei that sell thẽ,say, [g] Blessed *be* the Lord : for I am riche , and their
owne shepherds spare them not.
6 Surely I wil no more spare those ẏ dwell
in the land, saith the Lord : but lo, [h] I wil
deliuer the men euerie one into his neighbours hand , and into the hand of his
[i] King : and they shal smite the land , and
out of their hands I wil not deliuer *them*.
7 For I fed the shepe of slaughter,euen the
[k] poore of the flocke, and I toke vnto me
[l] two staues:the one I called, Beautie, and
the other I called , Bandes, and I fed the
shepe.
8 [m] Thre shepherdes also I cut of in one
moneth, & my soule lothed [n] thẽ,& their
soule abhorred me.
9 Then said I,I wil not fede you : that that
dyeth, let it dye : and that that perissheth,
let it perish:& let the remnant eat, euerie
one the flesh of his neighbour.
10 And I toke my staffe, *euen* Beautie,and
brake it,that I might disanul my couenãt,
which I had made with all people.
11 And it was broken in that day:and so the
[o] poore of the shepe that waited vpon me,
knewe that it was the worde of the Lord.
12 And I said vnto them , If ye thinke it
good,giue *me* [p] my wages:and if no,leaue
of : so they weighed for my wages thirtie
pieces of siluer.
13 And the Lord said vnto me,Cast it vnto
the [q] potter:a goodlie price,that I was valued at of them. And I toke the thirtie *pie-*
ces of siluer , and cast them to the potter
in the House of the Lord.
14 Then brake I mine other staffe, *euen* the
Bandes,that I might dissolue the brotherhode betwene Iudáh and Israél.
15 And ẏ Lord said vnto me , Take to thee
yet [r] ẏ instruments of a foolish shepherd.
16 For lo, I wil raise vp a shepherd in the
lãd,which shal not loke for the thing,that
is lost,nor seke the tender lambes,nor heale that that is hurt, nor fede ẏ that [s] stan-

a Because the Iewes thoght them selues, so strong by reason of this mõtaine,that no enemie colde come to hurt them, the Prophet sheweth that when God sendeth the enemies,it shal shewe it self ready to receiue them.
b Shewing ẏ if the strong men were destroied,ẏ weaker were not able to resist.
c Seing that Lebanón was destroied,ẇ was the strõgest municion, ẏ weaker places colde not thinke to holde out.
d That is,the renoume of Iudáh & Israél shulde perish.
e Which being now destinate to be slayne, were deliuered as out of the liõs mouthe.
f Their gouernours destroie them without any remorce of conscience, or yet thinkĩg that they do euil.
g He noteth ẏ hypocrites, ẇ euer haue the Name of God in their mouthes, thogh in their life and doings thei denie God,attributing their gaine to Gods blessing , ẇ cometh of the spoile of their brethren.
h I wil cause one to destroy another
i Their gouernours shal execute crueltie ouer them.
k That is, the smale remnãt, whome he thoght worthie to shewe mercie vnto.
l God sheweth his great benefites towarde his people to cõuince them of greater ingratitude, ẇ wolde nether be ruled by his moste beautiful order of gouernement , nether continue in ẏ bandes of brotherlie vnitie, and therefore he breaketh bothe the one and the other. Some read,for Bãdes,Destroiers, but in the 14 vers.ẏ first reading is confirmed.
m Whereby he sheweth his care and diligence that he wolde suffer them to haue no euil rulers,because they shulde consider his great loue,
n Meaning the people, because they wolde not acknowledge these great benefites of God.
o He sheweth that the least parte euer profit by Gods iudgements.
p Besides their ingratitude God accuseth them of malice & wickednes,which did not onely forget his benefites , but estemed them as things of noght.
q Shewing that it was to litle to pay his wages,which colde scarse suffice to make a fewe tiles for to couer the Tẽple.
r Signifying,that thei shulde haue a certeine kinde of regiment,& outwarde shewe of gouernement:but in effect it shulde be nothing:for they shulde be wolues,and deuouring beasts in stead of shepherds.
s And is in health and sounde.

deth vp : but he shal eat the flesh of the
fat, and teare their clawes in pieces.
17 O idole shepherd that leaueth the flocke: the sworde *shall* e vpon his [t] arme, and
vpon his right eye. His arme shalbe cleane dryed vp, and his right eye shal be vtterly darkened.

t By the arme he signifieth strength, as he doeth wisdome and iudgement by the eye: that is, ŷ plague of God shal take away both thy strength and iudgement.

CHAP. XII.

Of the destruction and buylding againe of Ierusalém.

1 THe burden of the worde of the Lord
vpon [a] Israél, saith the Lord, which
spred the heauens, and layed the fundaciõ
of the earth, and formed the spirit of man
within him.
2 Beholde, I wil make Ierusalém a [b] cuppe
of poyson vnto all the people rounde a-
bout: and also with Iudáh wil he be, in the
siege against Ierusalém.
3 And in that day wil I make Ierusalém
an heauie stone for all people : all that lift
it vp, shalbe torne, thogh all the people of
the earth be gathered together against it.
4 In that day, saith the Lord, I wil smite e-
uery horse with stonishment, & his rider
with madnes, and I wil open mine eyes
vpon the house of Iudáh, and wil smite e-
uery horse of the people with blindenes.
5 And the princes of Iudáh shal say in their
hearts, The [c] inhabitants of Ierusalém *shal*
be my strength in the Lord of hostes their
God.
6 In that day wil I make the princes of Iudáh like coles of fyre among the wood, &
like a fyre brande in the sheafe, and they
shal deuoure all the people rounde about
on the right hand, and on the left: and Ierusalém shalbe inhabited againe in her
owne place, *euen* in Ierusalém.
7 The Lord also shal preserue the [d] tentes
of Iudáh, *as* afore time: therefore the glorie of the house of Dauid shal not boast,
nor the glorie of the inhabitants of Ierusalém against Iudáh.
8 In that day shal the Lord defende the
inhabitants of Ierusalém, and he that is
feble among them, in that daye shalbe as
Dauid: and the house of Dauid *shalbe* as
gods *house*, *&* as the Angel of the Lord
before them.
9 And in that day wil I seke to destroye all
the nacions that come against Ierusalém.
10 And I wil powre vpon the house of Dauid, & vpon the inhabitants of Ierusalém
the Spirit of [e] grace and of compassion,
and they shal loke vpon me, whome they
haue [f] perced, and they shal lament for
[g] him, as one mourneth for *his* onelie *sonne*,
and be sorie for him as one is sorie for *his*
first borne.
11 In that day shal there be a great mourning in Ierusalém : as the [h] mourning of
[i] Hadadrimmón in ŷ valley of Megiddón.
12 And the [k] lãd shal bewaile euerie familie
a [l] parte, the familie of the [m] house of Dauid a parte, and their wiues a parte: the familie of the house of Nathan a parte, and
their wiues a parte:
13 The familie of the house of Leuí a parte, and their wiues a parte : the familie of
[n] Shemeí a parte, and their wiues a parte:
14 All the families that [o] remaine, euery familie a parte, and their wiues a parte.

Chap. XII. a That is, the ten tribes, ŵ neglected Gods benefite in deliuering their brethrẽ, and had rather remaine in captiuitie, then to returne home, when God called them.

b Ierusalém shalbe defended against all her enemies: so shal God defend all Iudáh also, and shal destroye the enemies.

c Euerie captaine, that had many vnder him afore, shal now thinke ŷ ŷ smale power of Ierusalém, shalbe sufficient to defend them against all enemies, because the Lord is among them.

d The people ŵ are now as it were dispersed by the fields, and lie open to their enemies, shalbe no lesse preserued by my power, then if they were vnder their Kĩgs (which is mẽt by the house of Dauid) or in their defensed cities.

e They shal haue ŷ feelĩg of my grace by faith, and knowe that I haue compassion on them.

f That is, whome they haue cõtinually vexed with their obstinacie, and grieued my Spirit, Iohn. 19,38. where it is referred to Christs bodie, which here is referred to ŷ Spirit of God.

g They shal turne to God by true repentance, whome before they had so grieuously offended by their ingratitude.

h They shal lament and repent excedingly for their offences against God.

i Which was the name of a towne & place nere to Megiddó where Iosiáh was slayne, 2. Chro. 35, 22.

k That is, in all places where the Iewes shal remaine.

l Signifying ŷ this mourning or repentance shulde not be a vaine ceremonie: but euery one touched with his owne grief shal lament.

m Vnder these certeine families he conteineth all the tribes, and sheweth that bothe the Kings and the Priests had by their sinnes perced Christ

n Called also Simeón.

o To wit, which were elect by grace, and preserued from the commune destruction.

CHAP. XIII.

1 *Of the fountaine of grace.* 2 *Of the cleane riddance of idolatrie.* 3 *The zeale of the godlie against false prophetes.*

1 IN that day there [a] shalbe a fountaine
opened to the house of Dauid, and to
the inhabitants of Ierusalém, for sinne &
for vnclennes.
2 And in that day, saith the Lord of hostes,
I wil cut of the [b] names of the idoles out
of the land : and they shal no more be remembred: and I wil cause the [c] prophetes,
and the vncleane spirit to departe out of
the land.
3 And when anie shal yet [d] prophecie, his
father & his mother that begate him, shal
say vnto him, Thou shalt not liue : for
thou speakest lies in the Name of ŷ Lord:
and his father and his mother that begate
him, [e] shal thrust him through, when he
prophecieth.
4 And in that daye shal the Prophetes [f] be
ashamed euerie one of his vision, when
he hathe prophecied: nether shal thei weare a rough garment to deceiue.
5 But he shal say, I am no [g] Prophet : I am
an housband man: for man taught me to
be an herdman from my youth vp.
6 And one shal say vnto him, What are these [h] woundes in thine hands? Then he shal
answere, Thus was I woũded in the house
of my friends.
7 ¶ Arise, ô sworde, vpon my [i] shepherd,
and vpon the man, *that is* my fellow, saith
the Lord of hostes: smite the shepherd, &
the shepe shalbe scattred : and I wil turne
mine hand vpon the litle ones.
8 And in all the land, saith the Lord, [k] two
partes therein shalbe cut of, *&* dye: but the
third shalbe left therein.
9 And I wil bring that third parte thorow
the fyre, and wil fine them as the siluer is
fined, and wil trye them as golde is tryed:

a He sheweth what shal be the frute of their repentãce, to wit, remissiõ of sinnes by ŷ blood of Christ, ŵ shalbe a continual rũning fountaine, and purge thẽ frõ all vnclennes.

b He promiseth that God wil also purge them from all superstition & that their religion shalbe pure.

c Meaning, ŷ false prophets and teachers, who are the corrupters of all religion, whome the Prophet here calleth vncleane spirits.

d That is, whẽ they shal prophecie lies & make God, who is the autor of trueth, a cloke thereunto.

e He sheweth what zeale the godlie shal haue vnder the kingdome of Christ Deu 13,6

f God shal make them ashamed of their errors and lies and brĩg them to repentance, and they shal no more weare Prophetes apparel to make their doctrine seme more holy.

g They shal confesse their former ignorance, & be cõtent to labour for their liuĩg.

h Hereby he sheweth that thogh their parents and friends delt more gently with them, and put them not to death, yet they wolde so punish their children, that became false prophetes that the markes & signes shulde remaine for euer

i The Prophet warneth the Iewes, ŷ before this great comfort shulde come vnder Christ, there shulde be an horrible dissipacion among the people: for their gouernours and pastors shulde be destroyed, and the people shulde be as scattered shepe: and the Euangelist applieth this to Christ, because he was the head of all Pastours, Matt 26,31.

k The greatest parte shal haue no porcion of these blessings, and yet they that shal enioye them, shalbe tryed with great afflictions, so that it shalbe knowen that onely Gods power and his mercies do preserue them.

they ſhal call on my Name, & I wil heare
them: I wil ſay, It is my people, and they
ſhal ſay, The Lord *is* my God.

CHAP. XIIII.

Of the doctrine that ſhal procede out of the Church, & of the reſtauration thereof.

1 Beholde, the day of the Lord cometh,
and thy ſpoyle ſhal be [a] diuided in
the middes of thee.
2 For I wil gather all natiõs againſt Ieruſalém to battel, and the citie ſhalbe taken, &
the houſes ſpoyled, and the women defiled, & half of the citie ſhal go into captiuitie, & the reſidue of the people ſhal not
be cut of from the citie.
3 Then ſhal the Lord go forthe, and fight
againſt thoſe nacions, as when [b] he foght
in the day of battel.
4 And his fete ſhal ſtand in that day vpon
the [c] mount of oliues, which is before Ieruſalém on the Eaſt ſide, and the mount
of oliues ſhal cleaue in the middes thereof: toward the Eaſt & towarde the Weſt
there *ſhalbe* a very great [d] valley, & halfe
of the moũtaine ſhal remoue towarde the
North, and halfe of the mountaine towarde the South.
5 And ye ſhal flee vnto the [e] valley of the
moũtaines: for the valley of the mountaines ſhal reache vnto Azál: yea, ye ſhal flee
like as ye fled from the [f] earthquake in the
dayes of Vzziáh King of Iudáh: and the
Lord [g] my God ſhal come & all the Saintes with thee.
6 And in that day ſhal there be no cleare
light, but darke.
7 And there ſhalbe a day (it is knowen to
ỹ Lord) [h] nether day nor night, but about
the euening time it ſhalbe light.
8 And in that day ſhal there [i] waters of life
go out from Ieruſalém, halfe of thẽ towarde the Eaſt ſea, & halfe of them towarde
the vttermoſt ſea, *&* ſhalbe, bothe in ſomer and winter.
9 And the Lord ſhalbe King ouer all the
earth: in that day ſhal there be one [k] Lord,
and his Name ſhalbe one.
10 All the land ſhalbe turned [l] as a plaine
frõ Géba to Rimmón, towarde the South
of Ieruſalém, and it ſhalbe lifted vp, & inhabited in her place: from Beniamins gate vnto the place of the firſt gate, vnto
the corner gate, and from the towre of Ha
naniél, vnto the Kings wine preſſes.
11 And men ſhal dwell in it, and there ſhalbe no more deſtruction, but Ieruſalém
ſhalbe ſafely inhabited.
12 And this ſhalbe the plague, wherewith
the Lord wil ſmite all people, that haue
foght againſt Ieruſalém: their fleſh ſhal
conſume away, thogh thei ſtand vpõ their
fete, and their eyes ſhal conſume in their
holes, & their tõgue ſhal conſume in their
mouth.
13 But in that day [m] a great tumult of the
Lord ſhalbe among them, and euerie one
ſhal take [n] the hand of his neighbour, and
his hand ſhal riſe vp againſt the hand of
his neighbour.
14 And Iudáh ſhal fight alſo againſt Ieruſalém, and the arme of all the heathen
ſhalbe gathered round about, with [o] golde and ſiluer, and great abundance of apparel.
15 Yet this ſhal be the plague of the horſe, of the mule, of the camel and of the aſſe
and of all the beaſts that be in theſe tentes
as this [p] plague.
16 But it ſhal come to paſſe that euerie one
that is left of all the nations, which came
againſt Ieruſalém, ſhal go vp from yere
to yere to worſhip the King the Lord of
hoſtes, and to kepe the feaſt of Tabernacles.
17 And who ſo wil not come vp of *all* the
families of the earth vnto Ieruſalém to
worſhip the King the Lord of hoſtes, euen
vpon them ſhal come no raine.
18 And if the familie of [q] Egypt go not vp,
and come not, it ſhal not *raine* vpon them.
This ſhal be the plague wherewith ỹ Lord
wil ſmite all the heathen, that come not
vp to kepe the feaſt of Tabernacles.
19 This ſhal be the puniſhement of Egypt,
& the puniſhement of all the nations that
come not vp to kepe the feaſt of Tabernacles.
20 In that day ſhal there be *writen* vpon the
[r] bridels of ỹ horſes, The holines vnto the
Lord, and the [ſ] pottes in the Lords Houſe
ſhal be like the bowles before the altar.
21 Yea, euerie pot in Ieruſalém and Iudáh
ſhalbe holie vnto the Lord of hoſtes, and
all they that ſacrifice, ſhal come and take
of them and ſeeth therein: and in that day
there ſhal be no more the [t] Canaanite in
the Houſe of the Lord of hoſtes.

a He armeth the godlie againſt the great tentaciõs, that ſhulde come, before they enioyed this proſperous eſtate promiſed vnder Chriſt, that when theſe dangers ſhulde come, they might knowe that they were warned of them afore.
b As your fathers, and you haue had experience bothe at the red Sea and at all other times.
c By this maner of ſpeache the Prophet ſheweth Gods power, and care ouer his Church, and how he wil as it were by miracle ſaue it.
d So that out of all the partes of ỹ worlde they ſhal ſe Ieruſalẽ, ẇ was before hid ẇ this mountaine: and this he meaneth of the ſpiritual Ieruſalém ỹ Church.
e He ſpeaketh of the hypocrites, which colde not abide Gods preſence, but ſhulde flee into all places where they might hide them amõg the mountaines.
f Read Amos, 1,1.
g Becauſe thei did not credit the Prophetes wordes, he turneth to God, and cõforteth him ſelf in ỹ that he knewe ỹ theſe things ſhulde come, & ſaith, Thou, ô God, with thine Angels wilt come to performe this great thing.
h Signifying, that there ſhulde be great troubles in the Church, and that the time hereof is in the Lords hands, yet at length (which is here ment by the euening) God wolde ſend cõfort.
i That is, the ſpiritual graces of God, which ſhulde euer continue in moſte abundance.
k All idolatrie and ſuperſtition ſhalbe aboliſhed, and there ſhalbe one God, one faith, and one religion.
l This newe Ieruſalém ſhalbe ſene through all the worlde & ſhal excell the firſt in excellencie, welth and greatnes.

m God wil not onely raiſe vp warre without but ſedition at home to trye them.
n To hurt, and oppreſſe him.
o The enemies are riche, and therefore ſhal not come for a pray, but to deſtroy & ſheade blood.
p As the men ſhulde be deſtroyed, ver. 12.
q By ỹ Egyptians, which were greateſt enemies to true religion, he meaneth all the Gentiles.
r Signifying, that to what ſeruice they were put now (whether to labour, or to ſerue in warre) thei were now holie, becauſe the Lord had ſanctified thẽ.
ſ As precious the one as the other, becauſe they ſhalbe ſanctified.
t But all ſhalbe pure, and cleane & there ſhal nether be hypocrite, or anie that ſhal corrupt ỹ true ſeruice of God.

MALACHI.

THE ARGUMENT.

THis Prophet was one of the thre, which God raised vp for the comfort of his Church after the captiuitie, and after him there was no more vntil Iohn Baptist was sent, which was ether a token of Gods wrath, or an admonition that they shulde with more feruent desires loke for the comming of Messiah. He confirmeth the same doctrine, that the two former do, but chiefly he reproueth the Priests for their couetousnes, and for that they serued God after their owne fantasies, and not according to the prescript of his worde. He also noteth certein peculiar sinnes, which were then among them, as marying of idolatrous and manie wiues, murmurings against God, impaciencie, and suche like. Notwithstanding for the comfort of the godlie he declareth that God wolde not forget his promes made vnto their fathers, but wolde send Christ his messenger, in whome the couenant shulde be accomplished, whose comming shulde be terrible to the wicked, and bring all consolation and ioye vnto the godlie.

CHAP. I.

A complaint against Israél and chiefly the Priests.

1 THE [a] burdē of the worde of ẏ Lord to Israél by
ẏ ministerie of Malachí.
2 I haue loued you, saith
the Lord: yet ye say,
[b] Wherein hast thou
loued vs? Was not Esáu
Iaakobs brother, saith ẏ Lord? yet I loued
Iaakób,
3 And I [c] hated Esáu, and made his mountaines
waste, and his heritage a wildernes
for dragons.
4 Thogh Edóm say, We are impouerished,
but we wil returne and buyld the desolate
places, yet saith the Lord of hostes, they
shal buylde, but I wil destroye it, and they
shal call them, The border of wickednes,
and the people, with whome the Lord is
angrie for euer.
5 And your eyes shal se it, and ye shal say,
The Lord wil be magnified vpon the border
of Israél.
6 A sonne honoreth *his* father, and a seruant
his master. If then I be a father, where
is mine honour? & if I be a master, where
is my feare, saith the Lord of hostes vnto
you, [d] ô Priests, that despise my Name?
and ye say, [e] Wherein haue we despised
thy Name?
7 Ye offer [f] vncleane bread vpon mine altar,
& you say, Wherein haue we polluted
thee? In that ye say the table of the Lord is
not [g] to be regarded.
8 And if ye offer the blinde for sacrifice, it
is [h] not euil: and if ye offer the lame and
sicke, it is not euil: offer it now vnto thy
prince: wil he be content wͭ thee, or accept
thy persone, saith the Lord of hostes?
9 And now, I pray you, [i] pray before God,
that he may haue mercie vpō vs: this hathe
bene by your meanes: wil he regarde [k] your
persones, saith the Lord of hostes?
10 Who is there euen among you, [l] that
wolde shut the dores? and kindle not *fyre*
on mine altar in vaine, I haue no pleasure
in you, saith the Lord of hostes, nether wil
I accept an offring at your hand.
11 For from the rising of the sunne vnto
the going downe of the same, my Name
is [m] great among the Gentiles, and in
euerie place incense shalbe offred vnto
my Name, and a pure offring: for my Name
is great among the heathen, saith the
Lord of hostes.
12 But ye haue polluted it, in that ye say,
The table of the Lord is [n] polluted, and
the frute thereof, *euen* his meat is not to be
regarded.
13 Ye said also, Beholde, *it is* a [o] wearines,
and ye haue snuffed at it, saith the Lord of
hostes, and ye offred that which was torne
& the lame and the sicke: thus ye offred an
offring: shulde I accept this of your hand,
saith the Lord?
14 But cursed be the deceiuer, which hathe
in his flocke [p] a male, and voweth, and sacrificeth
vnto ẏ Lord a corrupt thing: for
I am a great King, saith the Lord of hostes,
and my Name is terrible among the
heathen.

a Read Isa 13,1.

b Which declareth their great ingratitude that did not acknowledge this loue, which was so euident, in that he chose Abrahám from out of all ẏ worlde, and next chose Iaakób the yonger brother of whome they came, and left Esáu the elder.

c For besides that the signes of mine hatred appeared euen when he was made seruant vnto his yōger brother, being yet in his mothers belly, and also afterward in ẏ he was put frō his birthright, yet euen now before your eyes the signes hereof are euident, in that ẏ his countrey lieth waste, & he shal neuer returne to inhabit it, where as ye my people whome ẏ enemie hated more then thē are by my grace and loue towarde you deliuered, read Rom. 9,13.

d Besides the rest of the people he condēneth ẏ Priests chiefly because they shulde haue reproued others for theit hypocrisie, & obstinacie against God, & not haue hardened them by their example to greater euils. e He noteth their grosse hypocrisie, wͨ wolde not se their fautes, but moste impudently couered them, & so were blinde guides. f Ye receaue all maner offrings for your owne griedines, and do not examine whether they be according to my Law or no. g Not that they said thus, but by their doings they declared no lesse. h You make it no faute: whereby he cōdēneth thē, ẏ thinke it sufficiēt to serue God partely, as he hathe cōmanded, & partely after mās fantasie, and so come not to that purenes of religion, which he requireth, & therefore in reproche he sheweth thē ẏ a mortal man wolde not be content to be so serued.

i He derideth ẏ Priests who bare ẏ people in hād, ẏ they praied for thē, & sheweth ẏ they were the occasion, that these euils came vpon the people.

k Wil God cōsider your office and state, seing you are so couetous, & wicked?

l Because the Leuites who kept ẏ dores, did not trye whether ẏ sacrifices that came in, were according to the Law, God sheweth, that thei wolde rather shut the dores then to receiue suche as were not perfite.

m God sheweth, ẏ their ingratitude, and neglect of his true seruice shalbe ẏ cause of the calling of the Gētiles: & here ẏ Prophet that was vnder the Law framed his wordes to the capacitie of ẏ people, and by the altar, and sacrifice he meaneth the spiritual seruice of God, which shulde be vnder the Gospel, when an end shulde be made to all these legal ceremonies by Christs onely sacrifice. n Bothe ẏ Priests and ẏ people were infected wͭ this error, ẏ they passed not what was offred: for they thoght ẏ God was aswel content wͭ the leane as with the fat: but in the meane season they shewed not that obedience to God, which he required, & so cōmitted bothe impietie, and also shewed their contempt of God & couetousnes. o The Priests & people were bothe weary with seruing God, & passed not what maner of sacrifice & seruice they gaue to God, for that wͨ was least profitable, was thoght good ynough for the Lord. p That is, bathe habilitie to serue the Lord according to his worde, and yet wil serue him according to his couetous minde.

CHAP. II.

Threatenings against the Priests being seducers of the people.

1 ANd now, ô ye [a] Priests, this commādement is for you.

a He speaketh vnto thē chiefly, but vnder them he conteineth the people also.

2 If ye wil not heare it, nor consider it in
your heart to giue glorie [b] vnto my Name, saith ẏ Lord of hostes, I wil euē send
a curse vpon you, and wil curse your [c] blessings: yea, I haue cursed them already because ye do not consider it in *your* heart.
3 Beholde, I wil corrupt [d] your seed, & cast
dōgue vpon your faces, *euen* the [e] dongue
of your solemne feasts, and you shalbe like
vnto it.
4 And ye shal knowe, that I haue [f] sent this
commandement vnto you, that my couenant, which I made with Leuí, might stād,
saith the Lord of hostes.
5 My [g] couenant was with him of life and
peace, and I [h] gaue him feare, & he feared
me, and was afraide before [i] my Name.
6 The law of [k] trueth was in his mouth, &
there was no iniquitie foūde in his lippes:
he walked with me in peace and equitie,
and did turne manie away from iniquitie.
7 For the Priests [l] lippes shulde preserue
knowledge, and they shulde seke the lawe
at his mouth: for he is the [m] messenger of
the Lord of hostes.
8 But ye are gone out of the way: ye haue
caused manie to fall by the Law: ye haue
brokē the couenāt of Leuí, saith the Lord
of hostes.
9 Therefore haue I also made you to be
despised, and vile before all the people, because ye kept not my wayes, but haue bene parcial in the Law.
10 Haue we not all [n] one father? hathe not
one God made vs? why do we transgresse
euerie one against his brother, and breake
the couenant of [o] our fathers?
11 Iudáh hathe transgressed, and an abominacion is committed in Israél and in Ieru
salém: for Iudáh hathe defiled the holines
of the Lord, which he loued, and hathe ma
ried the [p] daughter of a strange god.
12 The Lord wil cut of the man that doeth
this: *bothe* the master and the seruāt out of
the tabernacle of Iaakób, and him that
[q] offereth an offring vnto the Lord of
hostes.
13 And this haue ye done againe, and [r] couered the altar of ẏ Lord with teares, with
weping and with mourning: because the
offring is no more regarded, nether receiued acceptably at your hands.
14 Yet ye say, [s] Wherein? Because the Lord
hathe bene witnes betwene thee and thy
wife of thy youth, against whome thou
hast trāsgressed: yet is she thy [t] cōpanion,
and the wife of thy [u] couenant.
15 And did not [x] he make one? yet had he
ẏ abundance of spirit: and wherefore one?
because he soght a godlie [z] seed: therefore
kepe your selues in your [a] spirit, and let
none trespasse against the wife of his
youth.
16 If thou hatest *her*, [b] put her away, saith
the Lord God of Israél, yet he coureth
[c] the iniurie vnder his garment, saith the
Lord of hostes: therefore kepe your selues in your spirit, and transgresse not.
17 Ye haue wearied the [d] Lord with your
wordes: yet ye say, Wherein haue we wearied him? Whē ye say, Euerie one ẏ[e] doeth
euil, is good in the sight of the Lord, and
he deliteth in them. Or where is the God
of [f] iudgement?

b To serue me according to my worde.
c That is, the abundance of Gods benefites.
d Your seed sowen shal come to no profite.
e You boast of your holines, sacrifices and feastes, but they shal turne to your shame, and be as vile as dongue.
f The Priests obiected against the Prophet that he colde not reproue thē, but he must speake against ẏ priesthode, and the office established of God by promes, but he sheweth, that the office is nothing sclādered, when these vilenes, & dongue are called by their owne names.
g He sheweth what were the two conditiōs of the couenāt made with the tribe of Leuí, on Gods parte, that he wolde giue thē long life & felicitie, and on their parte, ẏ they shulde faithfully serue him according to his worde.
h I prescribed Leuí a certeine Law to serue me.
i He serued me & set forthe my glorie with all humilitie and submission.
k He sheweth that the Priest oght to haue knowledge to instruct other in the worde of the Lord.
l He is as the treasure house of Gods worde and oght to giue to euerie one according to their necessitie, and not to reserue it for him self.
m Shewing, that whosoeuer doeth not declare Gods wil, is not his messenger, and Priest. n The Prophet accuseth the ingratitude of the Iewes toward God and man: for seing they were all borne of one father Abrahám, and God had elected them to be his holie people, they oght nether to offend God nor their brethren. o Whereby they had bounde them selues to God to be an holie people. p Thei haue ioyned them selues in mariage with them that are of another religion. q That is, the Priests.
r Ye cause the people to lament, because that God doeth not regarde their sacrifices, so that they seme to sacrifice in vaine. s This is another faute, whereof he accuseth them, that is, that they brake the lawes of mariage.

t As the one halfe of thy selfe.
u She that was ioyned to thee by a solemne couenant, and by the inuocation of Gods Name.
x Did not God make man and woman as one flesh and not many?
y By his power & vertue he colde haue made many women for one man.
z Suche as shulde be borne in lawful and moderat mariage wherein is no excesse of lustes.
a Conteine your selues within your boundes, and be sober in minde, and bridle your affections. b Not that he doeth allowe diuorcement, but of the two fautes he sheweth, which is the lesse. c He thinketh it sufficient to kepe his wife stil, albeit he take others, and so as it were coureth his faute. d Ye murmured against God, because he heard not you assone as you called. e In thinking that God fauored the wicked, and hathe no respect to them that serue him. f Thus they blasphemed God in condemning his power and iustice, because he iudged not according to their fantasies.

CHAP. III.

1 *Of the messenger of the Lord, Iohn Baptist, and of Christs office.*

1 Beholde, I wil send my [a] messenger, &
he shal prepare the way before me: &
the [b] Lord whome ye seke, shal spedely come to his Temple: euen the [c] messenger of
the couenant whome ye desire: beholde, he
shal come, saith the Lord of hostes.
2 But who [d] may abide the day of his comming? and who shal endure, when he appeareth? for he is like a purging fyre, and
like fullers sope.
3 And he shal sit downe to trye and fine the
siluer: he shal euen fine the sonnes of [e] Leuí, and purifie them as gold & siluer, that
they may bring offrings vnto the Lord in
righteousnes.
4 Then shal the offrings of Iudáh and Ierusalém be acceptable vnto the Lord, as
in olde time and in the yeres afore.
5 And I wil come nere to you to iudgemēt,
and I wil be a swifte witnes against the sothesayers, and against the adulterers, and
against false swearers, and against those
that wrongfully kepe backe the hirelings
wages, *and vexe* the widdowe, and the fatherles, and oppresse the stranger, & feare
not me, saith the Lord of hostes.
6 For I am the Lord: I change not, and ye
sonnes of Iaakób [f] are not consumed.
7 From the daies of your fathers, ye are
gone away from mine ordinances, and haue not kept *them*: [g] returne vnto me, and I

a This is mēt of Iohn Baptist, as Christ expoundeth it, Luk.7,27.
b Meaning, Messiáh, as psal.140,1. dan.9,17.
c That is, Christ by whome the couenant was made and ratified, who is called the Angel or messenger of the couenant, because he reconcileth vs to his father: & is Lord or King, because he hath the gouernement of his Church
d He sheweth that the hypocrites which wish so much for the Lords comming, wil not abide whē he draweth nere: for he wil cōsume them, and purge his & make them cleane.
e He beginneth at ẏ Priestes that they might be lightes and shine vnto others.
f They murmured against God, because they sawe not his helpe euer present to defend them: & therefore he accuseth them of ingratitude, and sheweth that in that they are not daily consumed, it is a token, that he doeth stil defend them: and so his mercie toward them neuer changeth. g Read Zechar.1,3.

wil returne vnto you, saith the Lord of
hostes: but ye said, Wherein shal we returne?
8 Wil a [h] man spoyle *his* gods? yet haue ye
spoyled me: but ye say, Wherein haue we
spoyled thee? In [i] tythes and offrings.
9 Ye are cursed with a cursse: for ye haue
spoyled me, euen this whole nacion.
10 Bring ye all the tythes into ỳ storehouse
that there may be meat in mine House, &
proue me now herewith, saith the Lord of
hostes, if I wil not open ỳ windowes of hea
uen vnto you, & powre you out a blessing
[k] without measure.
11 And I wil rebuke the [l] deuourer for your
sakes, and he shal not destroye the frute of
your grounde, nether shal your vine be
baren in the field, saith the Lord of hostes.
12 And all nacions shal call you blessed: for
ye shalbe a pleasant land, saith the Lord
of hostes.
13 Your wordes haue bene stoute [m] against
me, saith the Lord: yet ye say, What haue
we spoken against thee?
14 Ye haue said, *It is* in vaine to serue God:
& what profite is it that we haue kept his
commandemēt, and that we walked humbly before the Lord of hostes?
15 Therefore we coūte the proude blessed:
euen they that worke wickednes, are set
vp, and they that tempte God, yea, thei are
[n] deliuered.
16 [o] Then spake they that feared the Lord,
euerie one to his neighbour, and the Lord
hearkened & heard it, and a [p] boke of remēbrance was writen before him for thē
that feared the Lord, & that thoght vpon
his Name.
17 And they shalbe to me, saith the Lord
of hostes, in that day [q] that I shal do *this*, for
a flocke, and I wil [r] spare them, as a man
spareth his owne sonne that serueth him.
18 Then shal you returne, and discerne betwene the righteous and wicked, betwene
him that serueth God, and him that serueth him not.

h There are none of ỳ heathen so barbarous, that wil defraude their gods of their honour, or deale deceitfully with them.

i Whereby the seruice of God shulde haue bene mainteined, and the Priests, & the poore relieued

k Not hauing respect how much ye nede, but I wil giue you in all abūdance: so that ye shal lacke place to put my blessings in.

l Meaning, the caterpiller, & whatsoeuer destroieth corne and frutes.

m The Prophet condemneth them of double blasphemie against God: first in ỳ they said that God had no respect to thē ỳ serued him, and next that ỳ wicked were more in his fauour then the godlie.

n They are not onely preferred to honour, but also deliuered from dāgers.

o After these admonitions of the Prophet some were liuely touched, and incouraged others to feare God.

p Bothe because the thing was strange, that some turned to God in that great and vniuersal corruption, and also that this might be an example of Gods mercies to all penitent sinners. q When I shal restore my Church according to my promes, they shalbe as mine owne propre goods. r That is, forgiue their sinnes, and gouerne them with my Spirit.

CHAP. IIII.

The day of the Lord, before the which Eliáh shulde come.

1 FOr beholde, the day cometh that shal
[a] burne as an ouen, and all the proude, yea, and all that do wickedly, shal be
stubble, & the day that cometh, shal burne them vp, saith the Lord of hostes,
and shal leaue them, nether roote nor
branche.
2 But vnto you that feare my Name, shal
the [b] Sunne of righteousnes arise, and health *shalbe* vnder his wings, and ye shal
[c] go forthe, and growe vp as fat calues.
3 And ye shal treade downe the wicked: for
they shalbe dust vnder the soles of your
fete in the day that I shal do *this*, saith the
Lord of hostes.
4 [d] Remember the Lawe of Moses my seruant, which I commanded vnto him in
Horéb for all Israél with the statutes and
iudgements.
5 Beholde, I wil send you [e] Eliáh the Prophet before the cōming of the great and
[f] feareful day of the Lord.
6 And he shal [g] turne the heart of the fathers to the children, and the heart of the
children to their fathers, lest I come [h] and
smite the earth with cursing.

a He propheciedh of Gods iudgements against the wicked, who wolde not receiue Christ, when as God shulde send him for the restauration of his Church.

b Meaning, Christ, who with his wings or beames of his grace shulde lighten, & comfort his Church, Ephe. 5,14, and he is called the sunne of righteousnes, because in him self he hathe all perfection, and also the iustice of the father dwelleth in hī: whereby he regenerateth vs into righteousnes, clenseth vs from the filth of this worlde, and reformeth vs to the image of God.

c Ye shalbe set at libertie and increase in the ioye of the Spirit, 2. Cor 3,17. d Because the time was come that the Iewes shulde be destitute of Prophetes vntil the time of Christ, because they shulde with more feruent mindes desire his coming, the Prophet exhorteth them to exercise them selues diligently in studying the Lawe of Moses in ỳ meane season, whereby they might cōtinue in the true religion and also be armed against all tentations. e This Christ expoundeth of Iohn Baptist, Mat. 11, 13, who bothe for his zeale, & restoring of religion is aptly cōpared to Eliáh. f Which as it is true for the wicked, so doeth it waken the godlie and call them to repentance. g He sheweth wherein Iohns office shulde stand: in the turning of men to God and ioyning the father & children in one vnitie of faith: so that ỳ father shal turne to that religion of his sonne which is conuerted to Christ, and the sonne shal imbrace the faith of the true fathers, Abrahám, Izhák and Iaakób. h The seconde point of his office was to denounce Gods iudgements against them that wolde not receiue Christ.

APOCRYPHA.

THE ARGUMENT.

These bokes that follow in order after the Prophetes vnto the Newe testament, are called Apocrypha, that is bokes, which were not receiued by a cōmune consent to be red and expounded publikely in the Church, nether yet serued to proue any point of Christian religion, saue in asmuche as they had the consent of the other Scriptures called Canonical to confirme the same, or rather whereon they were grounded: but as bokes proceding from godlie men, were receiued to be red for the aduancement and furtherance of the knowledge of the historie, & for the instruction of godlie maners: which bokes declare that at all times God had an especial care of his Church and left them not vtterly destitute of teachers and meanes to confirme them in the hope of the promised Messiah, and also witnesse that those calamities that God sent to his Church, were according to his prouidence, who had bothe so threatened by his Prophetes, and so broght it to passe for the destruction of their enemies, and for the tryal of his children.

I. Esdras.

CHAP. I.

1 Iosias appointeth Priestes, and kepeth the Passeouer. 7 Offrings for the Priests and the people. 11 The order of the Leuites 23 The vpright life of Iosias. 25 His death and the occasion thereof, and the lamentation for him. 34 Ioachaz appointed King. 53 The destruction of Ierusalem.

2.King 23,21 2.chro.35,1.
1 AND Iosias kept the Passeouer to his Lord in Ie
rusalem, and offred the
Passeouer, in the four-
tenth day of the first
moneth,
2 And appointed ẏ Priests
in order according to their dailie courses,
being clothed with long garments in the
Temple of the Lord.
3 And he spake to the Leuites the holy ministers of Israel, that they shulde sanctifie
them selues to the Lord, to set the holy
Arke of the Lord in the House, which
Salomon the sonne of King Dauid had
buylt,
4 And said, Ye shal no more beare the Arke vpon your shulders: now therefore serue the Lord your God, and take the charge of his people of Israel, and prepare according to your families and tribes,
5 After the writing of Dauid King of Israel, and according to the maiestie of Salomon his sonne, and stand in the Temple (according to the ordre of the dignitie of your fathers the Leuites) which were *appointed* before your brethren the children of Israel.
6 Offer in ordre the Passeouer, and make
readie the sacrifices for your brethrē, and
kepe the Passeouer after the Lords commandement giuen to Moyses.
7 And Iosias gaue to the people that was
present, thirtie thousand lambes and kiddes with thre thousand calues.
8 These were giuen of the Kings possessions according to the promes, to the people, and to the Priests, and to the Leuites. Then gaue Helkias and Zacharias and
‖ Syelus the gouernours of the Temple, to ‖Or, Iehiel.
the Priests for the Passeouer two thou-
sand shepe, and thre hundreth calues.
9 Furthermore, Iechonias, and Samaias,
and Nathanael his brother, and ‖ Sabias, ‖Or, Hasabias.
and ‖ Chielus, and ‖ Ioram captaines gaue ‖Or, Iehiel. ‖Or, Chorabā.
to the Leuites for the Passeouer fiue thou-
sand shepe and seuen hundreth calues.
10 And when these things were done, the
Priests and the Leuites stode in ordre,
hauing vnleauened bread according to ẏ
tribes,
11 And after the ordre of the dignitie of
their fathers, before the people to offre to
the Lord, as it is writen in the bokes of
Moyses: and thus *they did* in the morning.
12 And they rosted the Passeouer with fyre
as * apperteined, & they sod their offrings Exod.12,8.
with perfumes in caldrons and pottes,
13 And set it before all them that were of
the people, and afterward they prepared
for them selues, and for the Priests their
brethren the sonnes of Aaron.
14 For the Priests offred the fatte vnto the
euening, and the Leuites did make ready
for them selues, and for the Priests their
brethren the sonnes of Aaron.
15 And the holy singers, the sonnes of A-
saph, were in their orders, accordig to the
appointed ordinances of Dauid, *to wit*, A-
saph, and Azarias, and ‖ Eddimus, which ‖Or, Ieduthun.
was of the Kings appointement.
16 And the porters were at euerie gate, *so that*
it was not lawful, ẏ anie shulde passe his
ordinarie watche: for their brethrē the Le
uites made readie for them.
17 And in that day those things which apperteined to the sacrifice of the Lord, were
accomplished, that they might offre the

Passeouer,
18 And offre sacrifices vpon the altar of the
Lord, according to the commandement
of King Iosias.
19 So the children of Israel, which were
present at that time, kept the Passeouer
and the feast of vnleauened bread seuen
daies.
20 And there was not suche a Passeouer kept
in Israel since the time of Samuel the Prophet.
21 And all the Kings of Israel did not offre
suche a Passeouer, as did Iosias, and the
Priestes, and the Leuites, and the Iewes,
and all Israel, which were founde to remaine in Ierusalem.
22 In the eghtenth yere of the reigne of Iosias was this Passeouer kept.
23 The workes of Iosias were vpright before his Lord with a heart ful of godlines.
24 And concerning ẏ things which came to
passe in his time, they are writen before, *to
wit*, of those that sinned & did wickedly
against the Lord aboue euerie nacion and
kingdome, and grieued him with "sensible
things, so that the wordes of the Lord stode vp against Israel.

"Or, by worshiping sensible creatures.

2.Chro.35,20.
25 ¶ *Now after all these actes of Iosias it
came to passe that when Pharao King of
Egypt came to moue warre at Carchamis
vpon Euphrates, Iosias went out against
him.
26 But ẏ King of Egypt sent to him, saying,
What haue I to do with thee, ô King of
Iudea?
27 I am not sent of the Lord God against
thee: but my warre is vpon Euphrates, and
now the Lord is with me, and the Lord
hasteneth me forwarde: departe from me,
and be not against the Lord.
28 But Iosias wolde not turne backe his cha
riot frō him, but prepared him self to fight
with him, not regarding the wordes of Ieremias the Prophet by the mouth of the
Lord.
29 But he set him self in battel aray against
him in the field of Megeddo, & the princes came downe to King Iosias.
30 And the King said to his seruants, Conuaye me out of the battel, for I am very
weake. And by and by his seruants broght
him out of the battel.
31 So he gate vp on his seconde chariot, and
being come againe to Ierusalem he changed his life, and was buryed in his fathers
graue.
32 And in all Iudea was Iosias bewailed,
yea, Ieremias the Prophet did lament for
Iosias, and the gouernours and their wiues
did lament him vnto this day: & this was
ordeined in all the kinred of Israel to be
done continually.
33 But these things are written in the boke
of the stories of the Kings of Iudea, and
euerie one of the actes ẏ Iosias did, & his
glorie, and his knowledge in the lawe of
the Lord, and the things which he did before, and the things now *rehersed* are registred in the boke of the Kings of Israel
and Iudea.
34 Then they of the nacion toke * Ioachaz 2.King.23,31
the sonne of Iosias, and made him King 2.chro.36,1.
in steade of his father Iosias, when he was
thre and twentie yere olde.
35 And he reigned in Iudea and in Ierusalem thre moneths: for the King of Egypt
deposed him from reigning in Ierusalem.
36 He taxed also the people of an hundreth
talents of siluer, & one talent of gold.
37 And the King of Egypt made Ioacim
his brother King of Iudea & Ierusalem.
38 And he bounde Ioachaz and his gouernours: but when he had taken Zaraces his
brother, he led him away into Egypt.
39 Twentie and fiue yere olde was Ioacim,
when he reigned in Iudea and Ierusalem,
and he did euil in the sigt of the Lord.
40 Wherefore against him came vp Nabuchodonosor King of Babylon, who whē
he had boūde him with a chaine of brasse,
led him away into Babylon.
41 Then Nabuchodonosor toke of the holie vessels of the Lord, & caryed thē away,
and set them in his temple at Babylon.
42 But all his actes, and his prophanation,
and his reproche are written in the Chronicles of the Kings.
43 And Ioacim his sonne reigned for him:
and when he was made King, he was eightene yere olde.
44 And he reigned thre moneths and ten
dayes in Ierusalem, aud he did euil in the
sight of the Lord.
45 ¶ So a yere after Nabuchodonosor sent
and broght him to Babylon with the holy
vessels of the Lord.
46 And he made Sedecias King of Iudea
and Ierusalem when he was one and twen
tie yere olde, & he reigned eleuen yeres.
47 And he did euil in ẏ sight of the Lord,
nether did he feare the wordes spoken* by Ier.38,21.
Ieremias the Prophet from the mouth of
the Lord.
48 For after that he was sworne to King
Nabuchodonosor, he forsware him self by
the Name of the Lord and fel away, and
hardened his necke and his heart, and
transgressed the Lawes of the Lord God
of Israel.
49 Also the gouerners of the people, and
the Priests cōmitted many things against
the lawes and passed all the pollucions of
all nacions, and polluted the Temple of
the Lord, which was sanctified in Ierusalém.
50 Neuertheles the God of their Fathers
sent

sent his messenger to call them backe, because he spared them and his owne Taber
nacle.
51 But thei derided his messengers, and in
the day, that the Lord spake *vnto them*, thei
mocked his Prophetes,
52 So that he, being moued to angre against
his people for their great wickednes, commanded the Kings of the Chaldeās to inuade them.
53 These killed their yong men with the
sworde roūde about their holie Temple,
nether did they spare yong man, nor maiden, nether olde man, nor childe among
them.
54 But he deliuered thē all into their hāds,
and all the holy vessels of the Lord, bothe
great & smale with the vessels of the Arke of God: and they toke, & caryed away
the Kings treasures into Babylon.
55 And thei set fyre in the House of ẏ Lord
and brake downe the walles of Ierusalem
and burnt their towres with fyre.
56 They consumed also all the precious
things thereof, & broght them to noght,
and those that were left by the sworde, he
caryed away into Babylon.
57 And they were seruants to him, & to his
children til the Persians reigned, to fulfil
the worde of the Lord by the mouth of
*Ieremias, Ierem.25,11. & 29,10.
58 And that the lād might enioye her Sabbaths all the time, that it was desolate, til
seuentie yeres were accomplished.

CHAP. II.

1 Cyrus gaue leaue to the Iewes to returne. 10 He sent the holy vessels. 13 The names of them that returned. 16 Their aduersaries did let their buylding, and the Kings letters for the same.

1 IN *the first yere of the reigne of Cy- 2.Chro.36,22 ezra.1,1.
rus King of the Persians, to fulfil the
worde of the Lord by the mouth of Ieremias,
2 The Lord raised vp the spirit of Cyrus
King of the Persians, and he made proclamacion through out all his kingdome, e-
uen by expresse lettres,
3 Saying, Thus saith Cyrus King of the
Persians, The Lord of Israel, euen the
moste high Lord, hathe made me King o-
uer the whole worlde,
4 And he hathe commanded me to buylde
him an House in Ierusalem, which is in
Iudea.
5 If there be anie therefore of you of his
people, let the Lord, euē his Lord be with
him, & let him go vp to Ierusalem, which
is in Iudea & buylde the House of ẏ Lord
of Israel: he is the Lord which dwelleth
in Ierusalem.
6 All they then that dwell in the places
rounde about, those, *I say*, that are in his
place, let them helpe him with golde and
siluer,
7 With giftes, with horses and cattel, and
other things, which shalbe broght, according to the vowes into the Temple of the
Lord, which is in Ierusalem.
8 ¶ Then arose the chief of the families of
Iudea, and of the tribe of Beniamin, and
the Priests & Leuites, & all whose minde
the Lord had moued to go vp, and buylde
an House to the Lord in Ierusalem.
9 And those that were about them, helped
them in all things with siluer and golde,
horses, and cattel, and with diuers vowes
of many whose mindes were stirred vp.
10 Also King Cyrus broght out the holy
vessels of the Lord, which Nabuchodonosor had caryed out of Ierusalem, and
had consecrated them in the Temple of
his idoles.
11 Now when Cyrus King of the Persians
had broght them out, he deliuered thē to
Mithridates his treasurer,
12 By whome they were giuen to *Abassar Or, Shashbazar, or Sanabassar.
the gouernour of Iudea.
13 Whereof this was the nomber: a thousand golden cuppes, and a thousand siluer
cuppes, basens of siluer for the sacrifices,
nine and twentie violes, of golde thirtie,
and of siluer two thousand, foure hūdreth
and ten, and a thousand other vessels.
14 So all the vessels of golde and siluer,
which thei caried away, were fiue thousād,
foure hundreth, thre score and nine.
15 They were broght by Sanabassar with
them of the captiuitie of Babylon to Ierusalem.
16 ¶ But* in the time of Artaxerxes King Ezra.4,6.
of the Persians *Belemus, & Mithridates, Or, Bischlemus.
and Tabellius, and Rathumus, and Beel-
tethmus, & *Semellius the secretarie, & o- Or, Shimshi.
thers which were ioyned to these, dwellig
in Samaria and in other places, wrote vnto him this epistle here following against
thē, that dwelt in Iudea & Ierusalem, TO
THE KING ARTAXERXES OVR
LORD,
17 Thy seruants, Rathumus the writer of
things that come to passe, and Semellius
the secretarie, and the rest of their counsel, & the iudges which are in Coelosyria
and Phenice.
18 Be it now therefore knowen to our lord
the King, that the Iewes which came vp
from you, are come to vs into Ierusalem,
that rebellious and wicked citie, & buylde
the marked places, and make vp the walles
thereof, and laye the fundacions of the
Temple.
19 Therefore if this citie be buylt, and the
walles be finished, they wil not onely not
indure to paye tribute, but wil also resist
Kings.
20 And because the things, perteining to
the Temple, go forwarde, we thoght it not

mete to passe ouer suche a thing,
21 But to declare it to our lord the King,
that if it be thy pleasure, it may be soght
out in the bokes of thy fathers,
22 And thou shalt finde in the Chronicles
the writings concerning these things, and
shalt knowe that this citie did alwaies rebel, & did trouble bothe Kings and cities,
23 And that the Iewes are rebellious, raising
alwaies warres therein: for the which cause also this citie was made desolate.
24 Now therefore, ô lord the King, we declare it, that if this citie be buylt and the
walles thereof repared, you shal haue no
more passage into Coelosyria, nor Phenice.
25 ¶ Then the King wrote againe to Rathumus, that wrote the things that came
to passe, and to Beeltethmus, and to Sa-
mellius the secretarie, and to the rest of
those that were ioyned with them, and to
the dwellers of Samaria, Syria and Phenice, these things that followe.
26 I haue red the epistle, which ye sent to
me: therefore I commanded, that it
shulde be soght out, and it was founde,
that this citie hathe alwaies practised a-
gainst Kings,
27 And that the men thereof were giuen
to rebellion and warres, and how that
mightie Kings and fierce haue reigned in
Ierusalem, which toke tribute of Coelosyria and Phenice.
28 Now therefore I haue commanded to
forbid these men to buylde vp the citie,
and that it be taken hede that no more
be done,
29 And that those wicked things, which shulde
molest the King, go not forwarde.
30 Then when Rathumus, & Semellius the
secretarie and the rest, which were ioyned
with them, had red the things, which Kīg
Artaxerxes had writen, they moued their
tents with spede to Ierusalem with horses
and men in araye,
31 And began to let them which buylt, so
that the buylding of the Temple in Ierusalem ceased vnto the seconde yere of the
reigne of Darius King of the Persians.

CHAP. III.

1 The feast of Darius. 16 The thre wise sentences.

1 NOw when Darius reigned, he made
a great feast to all his subiects & to
all those of his owne house, and to all the
princes of Media and Persia,
2 And to all the gouernours & captaines,
and lieutenants that were with him, from
India vnto Ethiopia of an hundreth and
seuen and twentie prouinces.
3 And when they had eaten and drunke, &
were satisfied, they departed, and King
Darius went into his chamber, and slept,
til he wakened againe.
4 ¶ In the meane time thre yong men of
the garde, kepers of the Kings bodie, said
one to another.
5 Let euerie one of vs speake a sentence, &
he that shal ouercome, and whose sentence shal appeare wiser then the others, Darius the King shal giue him great gifts,
and great things in token of victorie,
6 As to weare purple & to drinke in golde,
and to slepe in golde, and a chariot with
bridles of golde, an head tyre of fine linē,
and a chaine about his necke.
7 And he shal sit next to Darius for his
wisdome, and shalbe called Darius cousin.
8 Then euerie man wrote his sentence and
sealed it, and put it vnder the pillowe of
King Darius,
9 And said, when the King rose, thei wolde giue him the writing, and whose sentēce the King and the thre princes of Persia
shulde iudge to be wisest, to him shulde
the victorie be giuen, as it was appointed.
10 One wrote, The wine is strongest.
11 The other wrote, The King is strongest.
12 The other wrote, women are strongest,
but trueth ouercometh all things.
13 ¶ And when the King rose, they toke the
writings and gaue them to him, and he
red them,
14 And sent and called all the noble men of
Persia and of Media, and the gouernours
& the captaines, and lieutenants, and the
consuls,
15 And sate him downe in the counsel, and
the writing was red before them.
16 Then he said, Call the yong men, that
they may declare their owne sentences. So
they called them, and they came in.
17 Then he said vnto them, Declare vnto
vs the writings. So the first began, which
had spoken of the strength of wine,
18 And said on this maner, O ye men, how
strong is wine! it deceiueth all men that
drinke it.
19 It maketh the minde of the King and
of the fatherles bothe one, of the bonde
man and of the fre man, of the poore man
and of the riche man.
20 It turneth also euerie thoght into ioye
and gladnes, so that one remembreth no
maner of sorow, nor det.
21 It maketh euerie heart riche, so that one
remembreth nether King nor gouernour,
& causeth to speake all things by ″talents. ″Or, poundes.
22 When men haue drunke, they haue no
minde to loue ether friends or brethren,
and a litle after they drawe out swordes.
23 But when they are from the wine, they
do not remember what they haue done.
24 O ye men, is not wine strōgest, which cōpelleth

pelleth to do ſuche things! & he helde his
peace when he had thus ſpoken.

CHAP. IIII.

Of the ſtrength of a King. 13 Of the ſtrength of women. 24 Of the ſtrength of trueth, which ſentēce is approued, 47 And his petition granted.

1 THen the ſeconde which had ſpokē of
the ſtrēgth of the King, began to ſay,
2 O ye men, are not men ſtrongeſt, which
beare rule by land and by ſea, and ouer all
things which are in them!
3 But the King is yet greater: for he ruleth
all things, & is lord of them, ſo that they
do all things which he cōmādeth them.
4 If he bid thē make warre one againſt ano
ther, they do it: if he ſend them out againſt
the enemies, they go and breake downe
mountaines and walles and towres.
5 They kil & are killed, & do not paſſe the
cōmandement of the King: if they ouercome, they bring all to the King, alwel the
ſpoyles as all other things;
6 And thoſe alſo which go not to warre &
battel, but til the earth: *for* when they haue
ſowen it againe, thei reape it, & bring it to
the King, and cōpell one another to paye
tribute to the King.
7 Yet he is *but* one man: if he bid, Kil, they
kil: if he ſai, Spare, they ſpare.
8 *If* he bid, Smite, they ſmite: *if* he bid thē,
Make deſolate, they make deſolate: *if* he
bid, Buyld, they buyld.
9 *If* he bid, Cut of, they cut of: *if* he bid,
Plante, they plante.
10 So all his people & all his armies obey
one mā: in the meane while he ſitteth downe, he eateth, and drinketh and ſlepeth.
11 For theſe kepe him rounde about: nether
can any one go & do his owne buſines, nether are they diſobedient vnto him.
12 O ye men, how ſhulde not the King be
ſtrongeſt, ſeing he is thus obeied! So he hel
de his tongue.
13 ¶ Then the thirde which had ſpoken of
women & of the trueth (this was Zorobabel) began to ſpeake,
14 O ye men, nether the mightie King, nor
many men nor wine is ſtrongeſt: who then
ruleth them or hathe dominion ouer thē!
are they not women!
15 Women haue borne the King & all the
people which beare rule by ſea & by land.
16 Euen of them were they borne, and they
nouriſhed them, which planted the vines,
of which the wine is made.
17 They alſo make mens garments & make
men honorable, nether can men be without women.
18 And if thei haue gathered together gold
& ſiluer, or any goodlie thing, do they not
loue a faire and beautiful woman!
19 Do they not leaue all thoſe things & giue thē ſelues wholy vnto her, & gape, and
gaze vpon her, & all men deſire her more
then gold, or ſiluer, or any precious thing!
20 A man leaueth his owne father which ha
the nouriſhed him, & his owne countrei,
and is ioyned with his wife.
21 And for ẏ woman he ieopardeth his life,
and nether remembreth father nor mother
nor countrey.
22 Therefore by this ye may knowe that ẏ
women beare rule ouer you: do ye not labour and trauail, and giue and bring all to
the women?
23 Yea, a man taketh his ſworde and goeth
forthe to kil & to ſteale, and to saile vpon
the ſea, and vpon riuers,
24 And he ſeeth a lion & goeth in darkenes,
& when he hathe ſtollen, rauiſhed & ſpoiled, he bringeth it to his loue.
25 Wherefore a man loueth his owne wife
more then father or mother.
26 Yea, many haue runne mad for women,
and haue bene ſeruants for them.
27 Many alſo haue periſhed & haue erred
and ſinned for women.
28 Now therefore do you not beleue me? is
not the King great in his power? do not
all regions feare to touche him?
29 *Yet* I ſawe him & Apame, the Kings concubine, the daughter of the famous Barta-
cus, ſitting on the right hand of the King.
30 And ſhe toke the crowne of the Kings
head, & put it vpon her owne, and ſtroke
the King with her left hand.
31 Yet in the meane ſeaſon the King gaped
and gazed on her: & if ſhe laughed at him,
he laughed: & if ſhe were angrie with him,
he did flatter her that he might be reconciled with her.
32 How then, ô ye men, are not women more ſtrong, ſeing they do thus?
33 ¶ Then the King and the princes loked
one vpon another, and he began to ſpeake
of the trueth.
34 O ye men, are not women ſtronger? great
is the earth, & the heauen is hie, and the
ſonne is ſwift in his courſe: for he turneth
rounde about heauē in one day, & runneth
againe into his owne place.
35 Is not he great that maketh theſe things?
therefore the trueth is greater and ſtrōger
then all.
36 All the earth calleth for trueth, and the
heauen bleſſeth it: and all things are ſhaken and tremble, nether is there any vniuſt
thing with it.
37 The wine *is* wicked, the King *is* wicked,
women *are* wicked, & all the children of
men are wicked, and all their wicked workes are ſuche, and there is no trueth in thē,
and they periſh in their iniquitie.
38 But trueth doeth abide, and is ſtrong for
euer, and liueth and reigneth for euer and
euer.

39 With her there is no receiuing of persons
nor differēce: but she doeth ŷ things which
are iuste, & absteineth from vniust & wicked things, and all men fauour her workes.
40 Nether is there any vniust thing in her
iudgement, and she is the strength and the
kingdome and the power, and maiestie of
all ages. Blessed be the God of trueth.
41 So he ceased to speake, and then all the
people cryed & said then, Trueth is great
and strongest.
42 Thē the King said vnto him, Aske what
thou wilt besides ŷ which is appointed, &
we wil giue it thee, because thou art founde the wisest, and thou shalt haue libertie
to sit by me, and shalt be called my cousin.
43 ¶ Then he said to the King, Remembre
the vowe that thou hast vowed to buylde
Ierusalem, in the day that thou tokest the
kingdome,
44 And to send againe all the vessels ŷ were
taken out of Ierusalem, which Cyrus set a
parte when he made a vowe to cut of Babylon, & vowed to send them thither.
45 Thou also hast vowed to buylde the Tēple, which the Idumeans burnt whē Iudea
was destroied by the Chaldeans.
46 And now, ô Lord the King, this is that
which I desire & require of thee, & this is
the magnificence, which *I require* of thee:
I require therefore that thou woldest accomplish the vowe which thou hast vowed
with thine owne mouth to do to the King
of heauen.
47 Then King Darius rising vp, kissed
him, & wrote him letters to all the stewar-
des and lieutenants, and captaines, and gouernours, that thei shulde bring on ŷ waye
bothe him, & all that were with him, which
went vp to buylde Ierusalem.
48 And he wrote letters to all the lieutenāts
in Coelosyria and Phenice, & to thē that
were in Libanus, that they shulde bring ce
dre wood from Libanus to Ierusalem, and
buylde the citie wih him.
49 And he wrote for all ŷ Iewes, which wēt
vp out of his kingdome vnto Iudea, cōcerning their libertie, that no prīce, nor lieutenant, nor gouernour, nor steward shulde
enter into their dores,
50 And that all the region which they kept,
shulde paye no tribute, and that the Idumeans shulde let go the villages of the
Iewes which they helde,
51 And that euerie yere there shulde be giuen for the buylding of the Temple twentie talents vntil it were buylt,
52 And to mainteine ŷ burnt offrings vpon
the altar euerie day (as they had a commandement to offer seuentene) other ten
talents euerie yere.
53 And that all they which went from Baby
lon to buylde ŷ citie, shulde haue libertie,
aswel they as their posteritie, and all the
Priests that went away.
54 He wrote also touching the charges and
the Priests garment, wherein they shulde
minister.
55 And he wrote that they shulde giue the
Leuites their charges vntil the House were finished, and Ierusalem buylt.
56 Also he wrote that they shulde giue pen-
sions & wages to them that kept the citie.
57 And he sent away all the vessels which
Cyrus had set aparte out of Babylon, and
whatsoeuer Cyrus had commanded to do,
he also commanded to do it, and to send to
Ierusalem.
58 And when the °yong man was gone for- °or, Zorobabel.
the, he lift vp his face to heauen towardes
Ierusalem, and gaue thankes to the King
of heauen,
59 Saying, Of thee is the victorie, & of thee
is wisdome, & of thee is glorie, and I *am*
thy seruant.
60 Blessed be thou which hast giuē me wisdome: for vnto thee I acknowledge it, ô
Lord of *our* fathers.
61 ¶ So he toke ŷ letters & went out & came
to Babylon & telled all his brethren.
62 And thei blessed ŷ God of their fathers, be
cause he had giuē thē fredome & libertie
63 To go vp & to buylde Ierusalem, & the
Temple, where his Name is renoumed, &
they reioyced with instruments of musicke and ioye, seuen daies.

CHAP. V.

1 The nomber of them that returne from the captiuitie. 42 Their vowes & sacrifices. 54 The Tēple is begonne to be buylt. 66 Their enemies wolde craftely ioyne with them.

1 AFter * these things, the chief of the *Ezr.2,1.
houses of their fathers were chosen
after their tribes, & their wiues, and their
sonnes, & their daughters, & their seruantes, & their maides, and their cattel.
2 And Darius sent with thē a thousand horsemen, til they were restored to Ierusalem
in safetie, & with musical *instruments*, with
tabrets and flutes.
3 And all their brethren plaied: thus he cau
sed them to go vp together with them.
4 ¶ And these are ŷ names of the men that
went vp after their families, by their tribes, *and* after the order of their dignitie.
5 The Priests. The sonnes of Phinees, the
sonne of Aarō, Iesus *sonne* of Iosedec, *sonne*
of Saraias, & Ioacim the *sonne* of Zorobabel, the *sonne* of Salathiel of the house of
Dauid, of the kinred of Phares, of the tribe of Iuda.
6 °Who spake wise wordes to Darius the °or, Zorobabel.
King of the Persians in the secōde yere of
his reigne, in the moneth Nisan, which is
the first moneth.
7 ¶ And these are thei of Iudea, which came
out of ŷ captiuitie, where thei dwelt, whome

me Nabuchodonosor King of Babylon
had caryed away into Babylon,
8 And returned vnto Ierusalem and to the
rest of Iudea, euerie one into his owne ci-
tie:which came with Zorobabel, & Iesus,
Nehemias, "Zacharias, Reesaias, Enenius,
Mardocheus, Beelsarus, Aspharasus, Ree-
lius, Roimus & Baana their guides.
9 The nōber of them of the nacion & their
gouernours: ẏ sonnes of Phares two thousand an hūdreth seuētie & two, the sonnes
of Saphat foure hundreth, seuentie & two.
10 The sonnes of "Ares seuen hūdreth, fiftie
and six.
11 The sonnes of Phaath Moab, two thousand, eight hundreth and twelue.
12 The sonnes of Elam, a thousand, two hūdreth, fiftie & foure: the sonnes of Zathui
nine hundreth fortie & fiue: the sonnes of
Corbe seuen hūdreth & fiue: the sonnes of
Bani six hundreth, fortie and eight.
13 The sonnes of "Bibe six hūdreth, twentie
and thre: the sonnes of "Sadas thre thousand, two hundreth, twentie and two.
14 The sonnes of Adonikan, six hundreth,
sixtie & seuen: the sonnes of Bagoi, two
thousand, sixtie & six: ẏ sonnes of Adinu,
foure hundreth, fiftie and foure.
15 The sonnes of "Aterisias, ninetie & two:
the sonnes of Ceilan & Azotus, sixtie &
seuē: the sonnes of Azucan foure hūdreth,
thirtie and two.
16 "The sonnes of Ananias, an hundreth &
one: the sonnes of Arom, and the sonnes of
Bassa, thre hundreth, twentie and thre: the
sonnes of Arsiphurith, an hundreth & two.
17 The sonnes of Meterus, thre thousand &
fiue: the sonnes of "Bethlomon, an hūdreth,
twentie and thre.
18 They of "Netophas, fiftie & fiue: they of
"Anaboth, an hundreth, fiftie & eight: they
of Bethsamos, fortie and two.
19 They of "Cariathiarius, twentie & fiue:
thei of Caphiras & Beroth, seuen hūdreth,
fortie & thre: they of "Piras, seuē hūdreth,
20 They of Chadias and Ammidioi, fiue
hundreth, twentie & two: they of "Cirama
& Gabdes, six hundreth, twentie and one.
21 They of "Macalon, an hundreth twentie
and two: they of "Betolius, fiftie & two: the
sonnes of "Nephis, an hundreth, fiftie & six.
22 The sonnes of Calamolalus & Orius seuen hundreth, twentie and fiue: the sonnes
of Ierechus, thre hundreth, fortie & fiue.
23 The sonnes of "Annaas, thre thousand,
thre hundreth and thirtie.
24 The Priests, the sonnes of Ieddu, ẏ sonne of Iesus, *which are counted* among the
sonnes of Sanasib, nine hundreth, seuētie
and two: the sonnes of Meruth, a thousand
fiftie and two.
25 The sōnes of "Phassaron, a thousand, fortie and seuen: the sonnes of "Carme, a thou

"or, Saraia. *"or, Areh.* *"or, Bibai.* *"or, Azgad.* *"or, Aterhezecia.* *"or, The sonnes of Anania an hundreth, the sonnes of Arom one, the sonnes of Besai thre hundreth, twēty and thre.* *"or, Bethlehem.* *"or, Netophah.* *"or, Anathoth.* *"or, Kariath-iarim.* *"or, Pirah.* *"or, Aramah.* *"or, Macamor.* *"or, Bethel.* *"or, Nebus.* *"or, Sanaah.* *"or, Phashur.* *"or, Charim.*

sand and seuentene.
26 ¶ The Leuites. The sōnes of Iessue, Cadmiel, Bannu and Suiu, seuentie and foure.
27 ¶ The sonnes *which were* holie singers.
The sonnes of Asaph, an hundreth, fortie
and eight.
28 ¶ The porters. The sonnes of Salum, the
sonnes of Iatal, the sonnes of "Tolman, the
sonnes of Dacobi, the sonnes of Teta, the
sonnes of Sami: all *were* an hundreth, thirtie and nine.
29 The ministers of the Temple. The sonnes of Esau, the sonnes of Asipha, the sonnes of Tabaoth, the sonnes of "Ceras, the
sonnes of "Sud, the sonnes of Phaleu, ẏ sonnes of Labana, the sonnes of "Agraba,
30 The sonnes of "Acraa, ẏ sonnes of "Outa,
the sonnes of Cetab, the sonnes of "Agaba,
ẏ sonnes of "Subai, the sonnes of Anan, the
sonnes of Cathua, the sonnes of "Geddur.
31 The sonnes of "Airus, the sonnes of Dai-
san, the sonnes of "Noeba, the sonnes of
Chaseba, the sonnes of "Gazera, the sonnes
of Azias, the sonnes of Phinees, the sonnes
of Asara, the sonnes of "Basthai, the sonnes
of Asana, ẏ sonnes of "Meani, the sonnes of
"Naphisi, the sonnes of "Acub, the sonnes
of "Acipha, the sonnes of "Asur, the sonnes
of Pharacim, the sonnes of "Basaloth.
32 The sonnes of "Meeda, ẏ sonnes of Cou-
tha, the sonnes of "Corea, the sonnes of
"Charcus, the sonnes of Aserar, the sonnes
of "Thomoi, the sonnes of "Nasith, the son
nes of Atipha.
33 The sonnes of the seruants of Salomon.
The sonnes of "Asaphion, the sonnes of
"Pharira, the sonnes of "Ieeli, the sonnes of
Lozon, the sonnes of Isdael, the sonnes of
"Sapheth.
34 The sonnes of Agia, ẏ sonnes of "Phach-
threth, the sonnes of "Sabie, the sonnes of
"Sarothie, the sonnes of Masias, the sonnes
of Gar, the sonnes of "Addus, the sonnes
of "Subas, the sonnes of Apherra, the sonnes of Barodis, the sonnes of Sabat, the son
nes of Allom.
35 All the ministers of the Temple, and the
sonnes of the seruāts of Salomon *were* thre
hundreth, seuentie and two.
36 These came vp from "Thermeleth and
Thelersas: Caraathalat and Aalar leading
them.
37 Nether colde they shewe their families
nor their stocke how they were of Israel,
the sonnes of "Ladan the sonne of "Ban, the
sonnes of "Necodan, six hundreth fiftie
and two.
38 And of the Priests those which exercised the office of Priests, & were not fōūde,
ẏ sonnes of "Obdia, the sonnes of "Accos,
the sonnes of Addus, *which had taken for
wife Augia, *one* of the daughters of "Ber-
zelaius.

"or, Talmon. *"or, Ceros.* *"or, Suia.* *"or, Hagaba.* *"or, Acub.* *"or, Vta.* *"or, Agab.* *"or, Sibe.* *"or, Cedur.* *"or, Raia.* *"or, Nerida.* *"or, Gazema.* *"or, Baste.* *"or, Meunim.* *"or, Naphison.* *"or, Bacubab.* *"or, Acupha.* *"or, Asur.* *"or, Baraloth.* *"or, Mehida.* *"or, Charescha.* *"or, Bareus.* *"or, Thomath.* *"or, Nasib.* *"or, Hazophoreth.* *"or, Pharuda.* *"or, Ieelah.* *"or, Staphelia.* *"or, Phacareth.* *"or, Sabia.* *"or, Spartia.* *"or, Addu.* *"or, Subah.* *"or, Thelmelah & Thelharsa. Carathalar & Alar.* *"or, Dalaias.* *"or, Tubia.* *"or, Necoda.* *"or, Hobia.* *"or, Haccoz.* *Ezra 2,61.* *"or, Barzeleus.*

39 And was called after his name,and when
the deſcription of the kinred of theſe men
had bene ſoght in the regiſtre, and colde
not be founde, they were ſet a parte from
the office of Prieſts.

ᵒor, Nehemias & Atharias.

40 For "Neemias and Attharias ſaid to thẽ
that they ſhulde not be partakers of the
holie thĩgs,til there aroſe an hie Prieſt clothed with doctrine and trueth.

41 So all they of Iſrael from them of twel-

ᵒor, fortie and two thouſand, thre hundreth & ſixty.

ue yere olde and litle children,were "fortie
thouſand beſides men ſeruants and women ſeruants, two thouſand,thre hũdreth
and ſixtie.

42 Their ſeruants and handmaides *were*
ſeuen thouſand, thre hundreth, fortie and
ſeuen: the ſinging men and women, two
hundreth,fortie and fiue:

43 Camelles, foure hundreth, thirtie and
fiue:and horſes,ſeuen hundreth,thirtie and
ſix: mules, two hundreth,fortie and fiue:

ᵒor, aſſes.

"beaſtes that bare ẏ yocke,fiue thouſand,
fiue hundreth,twentie and fiue.

44 And *there were* of the gouernours after
their families, *which* when they were come to the Temple in Ieruſalem, vowed to
buyld the Houſe in his owne place according to their power,

45 And to giue to the treaſure of the wor-

ᵒor, of gold twelue thouſand pounde, & of ſiluer fiue, &c.

kes, "a thouſand pound in golde, and fiue
thouſand pound in ſiluer,and an hundreth
prieſtlie garments.

46 And the Prieſts and the Leuites and the
people dwelt in Ieruſalem and in the coun
trei, & the holie ſingers & the porters and
all Iſrael in their "villages.

ᵒor, quarters.

Ezra.3,1.

47 ¶ But* when the ſeuenth moneth was
nere, and when the children of Iſrael were
euerie one at home, they were all gathered together with one accorde into the o-
pen place of the firſt gate, which is towarde the Eaſt.

48 Then Ieſus the ſonne of Ioſedec and his
brethren the Prieſts with Zorobabel the
ſonne of Salathiel & his brethrẽ,riſing vp,
made ready ẏ altar of the God of Iſrael,

49 To offre burnt offrings vpon it according as it is writen in the boke of Moyſes
the man of God.

50 Whither alſo there were gathered agaĩſt
them of all nacions of the land: but they
dreſſed the altar in his owne place,althogh
all the nacions of the land were their enemies and vexed them, and they offred ſacrifices according to the ſeaſon, and burnt
offrings to the Lord, morning & euening.

51 They kept alſo the feaſt of tabernacles,

Leui.23,34.

as it is *ordeined in the Law,& *offred* ſacri
fices euerie day,as was requiſite,

52 And afterwarde,the continual oblations
and offrings of the Sabbaths & of the new
moneths & of all holy feaſts.

Ezra 3,8.

53 ¶ And all*thei which had made any vowe
to God, began to offre ſacrifice vnto God
in the firſt day of ẏ ſeuẽth moneth,althogh
the Temple of God was not yet buylt.

54 They gaue alſo money to the maſons &
to the workemen, and meat and drinke
with gladnes,

55 And charrets to the Sidonians and to
thoſe of Tyrus to bring ceder wood out
of Libanus, which ſhulde be broght by
flots to the hauen of Ioppe according to
the commandement giuen vnto them by
Cyrus King of Perſia.

56 And in the ſecond yere and ſecond moneth came into the Temple of God in Ieruſalem,Zorobabel the ſonne of Salathiel,
and Ieſus the ſonne of Ioſedec, and their
brethrẽ,and the Prieſts & Leuites,and all
they that came out of captiuitie into Ieruſalem,

57 And *layed the fundacion of the Hou- *Eccles.49,13.*
ſe of God in the firſt day of the ſecond
moneth of the ſecond yere after their returne into Iudea and Ieruſalem.

58 And they appointed ẏ Leuites frõ twẽtie
yere olde ouer the workes of the Lord,and
Ieſus & his ſonne,& his brethrẽ,& his bro
ther Cadmiel, & the ſonnes of Madiabon
with the ſonnes of Ioda, the ſonne of He-
liadun, with their ſonnes, & brethren,*euen*
all the Leuites with one accorde did followe after the worke,calling vpõ the workes in the Houſe of God: thus the workemen buytl the Temple of the Lord.

59 And the Prieſts ſtode clothed with their
long garments with muſical *inſtruments* &
trumpets, and the Leuites the ſonnes of
Aſaph with cymbales,

60 Singing & bleſsing ẏ Lord,according to
the ordinãce of Dauid King of Iſrael.

61 And they ſung with loud voice ſongs to
the praiſe of the Lord,becauſe his mercie
and glorie *is* for euer in all Iſrael.

62 Then all the people blewe trumpets,and
cryed with loud voice,praiſing ẏ Lord for
the raiſing vp of the Houſe of the Lord.

63 Alſo ſome of the Prieſts & Leuites, and
chief men,*to wit*,the Ancients, which had
ſene the former Houſe,

64 Came *to ſe* the buyldĩg of this with weping and great crying, & manie with trũpets and ioye *cryed* with loude voice,

65 So that the people colde not heare the
trũpets,becauſe of the weping of the people: yet there was a great multitude that
blew trũpets ſo that thei were heard far of.

66 ¶ Wherefore when the enemies of the
tribes of Iuda & Beniamin heard it, they
came to know what noiſe of trũpets it was,

67 And they knewe that they of the captiuitie buylt the Temple to the Lord God
of Iſrael.

68 Wherefore they coming to Zorobabel,&
Ieſus, and the chief of the families, ſaid
vnto

vnto them, Let vs buyld also with you.
69 For we obey your Lord, as you do, and
sacrifice vnto him since the dayes of "As-
basareth King of the Assyrians, which
broght vs hether.

"or, Asezarets, or, Asarhadon.

70 Then Zorobabel, and Iesus, & the chief
of the families of Israel said to them, It
doeth not apperteine to vs, and to you to
buyld an House to the Lord our God.
71 For we alone wil buylde it to the Lord
God of Israel, as it becometh vs, & as *Cy
rus the King of the Persians bad vs.

Ezra.4,4.

72 Howbeit the people of the land made
them sluggish that were in Iudea, and letted them to buyld the worke, and by their
ambushments and seditions & conspiracies hindred the finishing of the buyldīg,
73 All the time of King Cyrus life: so that
they were let from the buylding two yere,
vntil the reigne of Darius.

CHAP. VI.

1 Of Aggeus and Zacharias. 2 The buylding of the Temple. 3 Sisinnes wolde let them. 7 His epistle to Darius. 23 The Kings answer to the contrarie.

Ezra.5,1. neh,1.

1 BVt *in the second yere of the reigne
of Darius, Aggeus & Zacharias the
sonne of Addo ẏ Prophetes prophecied to
the Iewes, euen vnto them that were in Iu
dea and Ierusalem, in the Name of the
Lord God of Israel, which they *called* "vpon.

"Gre. vpō them.

2 Then Zorobabel sonne of Salathiel, and
Iesus the sonne of Iosedec stode vp, and
began to buylde the House of the Lord, ẇ
is in Ierusalem, the Prophetes of the Lord
being with them, & helping them.
3 ¶ In that time Sisinnes the gouernour of
Syria, and Phenice, and Sathrabouzanes
with his companions came vnto them,
4 And said vnto them, By whose commandement buyld you this House, & this buylding, and enterprise all these other things?
and who are the buylders that enterprise
suche things?
5 But the Ancients of the Iewes had grace
of the Lord after that he had visited the
captiuitie,
6 That they were not letted to buyld, vntil
it was signified vnto Darius of these matters, and an answer was receiued.
7 ¶ The copie of the epistle, which he did
write and send to Darius, SISINNES go
uernour of Syria and of Phenice, and Sathrabouzanes, and their companiōs, presi-
dents in Syria and Phenice, salute King
Darius.
8 It may please the King our master plainely to vnderstand, that when we came to
the countrey of Iudea, and entred into the
citie of Ierusalem, we found in the citie
of Ierusalem the Ancients of the Iewes
that were of the captiuitie,
9 Buylding an House to the Lord, great &
newe, of hewen stones, and of great price,
and the timber all ready laid vpon the
walles.
10 And these workes are done with great
spede, yea, and the worke hathe good successe in their hands, so that it wil be finished with all glorie & diligence.
11 Then we asked their Ancients, saying,
By whose commandement buyld you this
House & lay ẏ fundacion of these workes?
12 We asked them these things to the intēt
to notifie them to thee, and to write to
thee the men that gouerned it: therefore
we demāded the names of the gouernours
in writing.
13 But they answered, saying, We are the
seruants of the Lord, which hathe created
the heauen and the earth.
14 And* this House was buylt vp manie yeres ago by a King of Israel great & strōg,
and was finished.

1.King.6,2.

15 But when our fathers, prouoking *God* to
wrath, sinned against the Lord of Israel,
which is in heauē, * he deliuered them into
the hands of Nabuchodonosor King of
Babylon of the Chaldeans,

2.King.24,1.

16 *Who* brake downe the House & burnt it,
& caryed the people captiue to Babylon.
17 But in the first yere of the reigne of Cyrus ouer the countrey of Babylon, King
Cyrus wrote that this House shulde be
buylt vp.
18 And ẏ holie vessels of golde & of siluer,
which Nabuchodonosor had caryed out
of the House at Ierusalem, & had dedicated them in his owne Temple, Cyrus the
King toke out of the Tēple at Babylon, &
they were giuen to Zorobabel, and to "Sanabassarus ruler.

"or, Shashbazar.

19 And a cōmandement was giuē vnto him,
ẏ he shulde cary away those vessels, & put
thē in ẏ Tēple at Ierusalē, & that this Tēple of ẏ Lord shulde be buylt in this place.
20 Thē the same Sanabassarus, being come
hether, layed the fundations of the House of the Lord at Ierusalem, and since that
time til now, it is in buylding, & is not
finished.
21 Now therefore if it please the King, let
it be soght vp in the Kings libraries concerning Cyrus.
22 And if it be found that the buylding of ẏ
House of the Lord at Ierusalem hathe bene done by the cōsent of King Cyrus, & if
it seme good to the lord our King, let him
make vs answer cōcerning these things.
23 Then King Darius commanded to searche in the Kings libraries, that were in Ba
bylon, and there was founde in Ecbatane,
which is a towre in the region of Media, a
place where suche things were layed vp
for memorie.

24 In the first yere of the reigne of Cyrus,
King Cyrus commãded the House of the
Lord at Ierusalem to be buylded, where
thei did sacrifice with the continual fyre.
25 Of the wc the height *shulde be* of threscore cubites, the breadth of threscore cubites with thre rowes of hewen stones, &
one rowe of newe wood of that countrey,
and that the costs shulde be payed out of
the house of King Cyrus.
26 And that the holie vessels of the House
of the Lord, aswel those of golde as of siluer, which Nabuchodonosor had caryed
out of the house in Ierusalem, and broght
into Babylon, shulde be restored to the
House, which is in Ierusalem, & set in the
place where they were *afore*.
27 Also he commanded that Sisinnes, gouernour of Syria and Phenice, and Sa-
thabouzanes, and their companions, and
those which were constitute captaines in
Syria and Phenice, shulde take hede to
refraine from that place, and to suffer Zorobabel the seruant of the Lord, and gouernour of Iudea, and the Elders of the
Iewes to buyld that House of the Lord in
that place.
28 And I also haue commanded to buyld
it cleane vp againe, and that they be diligent to helpe them of the captiuitie
of the Iewes, til the House of the Lord be
finished,
29 And that some parte of the tribute of
Coelosyria and Phenice shulde be diligently giuen to these men for sacrifice vn
to the Lord, and to Zorobabel the gouernour, for bulles, rams and lambes:
30 Also corne, & salte, and wine, and oile
continually euerie yere without faile, as
the Priests, which are in Ierusalem shal testifie to be spent euerie day,
31 That offrings may be made to the high
God for the King, and his children, & that
they may pray for their liues.
32 Furthermore he commanded that whosoeuer shulde transgresse anie thing afore
spoken or writen, or derogate anie thing
thereof, that a tre shulde be taken out of
his possession, and he be hanged thereon,
and that his goods shulde be the Kings.
33 And therefore let the Lord whose Name is there called vpon, destroye euerie
King and nation, which stretcheth out
his hãd to hinder or do euil to that House of the Lord which is in Ierusalem.
Ezra.6,15. 34 *I Darius the King haue ordeined that
it shulde be diligẽtly executed according
to these things.

CHAP. VII.

*1 Sisinnes and his companions fellow the Kings comman-
dement and helpe the Iewes to buyld the Tẽple. 5 The
time that it was buylt. 10 Thei kepe the Passeouer.*

1 THen Sisinnes the gouernour of Coelosyria and Phoenice, and Sathrabou
zanes, & their companiõs, obeying King
Darius commandements,
2 Assisted diligently the holie workes, working with the Ancients and gouernours
of the Sanctuarie.
3 And the holie workes prospered by Aggeus and Zacharias the Prophetes which
prophecied.
4 So they finished all things by the commãdement of the Lord God of Israel, and
with the consent of Cyrus and Darius, and
Artaxerxes Kings of the Persians.
5 Thus the holie House was finished in the
thre and twentieth day of the moneth A-
dar in the sixt yere of Darius King of the
Persians.
6 ¶ And the childrẽ of Israel, and ye Priests
and the Leuites, and the rest, which were
of the captiuitie, & had anie charge, did
according to the things *writen* in the boke
of Moses.
7 And they offred for the dedication of the
Temple of the Lord, an hundreth bulles,
two hundreth rams, foure hũdreth lambes,
8 *And* twelue goates for the sinne of all Israel, according to the nomber of the chief
of the tribes of Israel.
9 And the Priests, and the Leuites stode
according to their kinreds clothed with
long robes in the workes of the Lord God
of Israel, according to the boke of Moses,
and also the porters in euerie gate.
10 And the children of Israel offred the
Passeouer together with them of the captiuitie, in the fourtẽth *day* of the first moneth, after that the Priests and Leuites
were sanctified.
11 But all the children of the captiuitie were not sanctified together, but all the Leuites were sanctified together.
12 And they offred the Passeouer, for all
the children of the captiuitie, and for their
brethren the Priests, and for them selues.
13 Then all the children of Israel which
were of the captiuitie did eat, *euen* all they
that had separated them selues from the
abominations of the people of the land,
and soght the Lord.
14 And they kept the feast of vnleauened
bread seuen dayes, reioycing before the
Lord,
15 Because he had turned the counsel of the
King of the Assyrians towardes them to
strengthen their hands in the workes of
the Lord God of Israel.

CHAP. VIII.

*1 Esdras cometh from Babylon to Ierusalem. 10 The
copie of the commission giuen by Artaxerxes. 29 Esdras giueth thankes to the Lord. 32 The nomber of
the heads of the people that came with him. 76 His
prayer and confession.*

1 And

1 AND after these things when Artaxerxes King of the Persians reigned,
Esdras *the sonne* of "Saraias, *the sonne* of "or, Azarias.
Ezerias, *the sonne* of Helcias, *the sonne* of
Salum,
2 *The sonne* of Sadoc, *the sonne* of Achitob,
the sonne of Amarias, *the sonne* of "Ezias, *the* "or, Azarias.
sonne of "Memeroth, *the sonne* of "Zaraias, "or, Meraioth. "or, Sama.
the sonne of "Sauias, *the sonne* of Boccas, "or, Azi.
the sonne of Abisum, *the sonne* of Phinees,
the sonne of Eleazar, *the sonne* of Aaron was
the hie Priest.
3 This Esdras went out of Babylon, & was
a scribe wel taught in the Law of Moyses,
giuen by the Lord God of Israel.
4 Also the King gaue him *great* honour, &
he founde grace in his sight in all his requestes.
5 With him also there departed some of
the children of Israel, and of the Priests
and Leuites, and of the holy singers, and
of the porters, and of the ministers of the
Temple vnto Ierusalem,
6 In the seueth yere of the reigne of Artax
erxes, & in the fift moneth: this was the seueth yere of the King (for thei went out of
Babylō in the first day of the first moneth,
7 And came to Ierusalem according as the
Lord gaue them speed in their iournay)
8 For Esdras had gotten great knowledge,
so that he wolde let nothig passe that was
in the Law of the Lord, and in the cōmandements, and he taught all Israel all the
ordinances and iudgements.
9 So the commission writen by King Artaxerxes was giuen Esdras the Priest and
reader of the Law of the Lord: the copie
thereof followeth.
10 King Artaxerxes to Esdras the Priest, &
reader of the Law of the Lord, Salutaciō.
11 Forasmuche as I consider things with
pitie, I haue commanded that they that
wil and desire of the nacion of the Iewes,
and of the Priests and Leuites, which are
in our kingdome, shulde go with thee vnto Israel.
12 Therefore as many as be willing, let
them departe together, as it hathe semed
good to me and my seuen friends the counsellers,
13 That they may visite the things that are
in Iudea and Ierusalem diligently, as it is
conteined in the Law of the Lord,
14 And cary the gifts to the Lord of Israel in Ierusalem, which I and my friends
haue vowed: also all the golde and siluer,
which shal be founde in the countrey of
Babylon *apperteining* to the Lord in Ierusalem,
15 With that which is giuen of the people
to the Temple of the Lord their God,
that it might be broght to Ierusalem, aswel siluer as golde, for bulles, and rams, &
lambes, and things thereunto perteining,
16 That they may offer sacrifices to the
Lord vpon the altar of the Lord their
God, which is in Ierusalem.
17 And whatsoeuer thou and thy brethren
wil do with the golde or siluer, accōplish
it according to the wil of thy God.
18 And the holy vessels of the Lord, which
are giuen thee for the vse of the Temple
of thy God, which is in Ierusalem, thou
shalt set before thy God in Ierusalem.
19 And what other things soeuer thou shalt
remember for the vse of the Temple of
thy God, thou shalt giue it out of ẏ Kings
treasure.
20 And I also King Artaxerxes haue commanded the treasurers of Syria and Phenice, that whatsoeuer Esdras, the Priest &
reader of the Law of the hiest God, shal
send for, they shulde giue it him with all
speede, euen to *the some of* an hundreth talents of siluer,
21 And likewise vnto an hundreth cores of
corne, and an hundreth pieces of wine and
other things in abundance.
22 Let all things be done to the hiest God
according to the Law of God with diligence, that wrath come not vpō the kingdome of the King and of his sonnes.
23 Also to you it is commanded, that of none of ẏ Priests or Leuites, or holy singers,
or porters or ministers of the Temple, or
of the workemen of this Temple, no tribute nor taxe be taken, nor that any haue
power to taxe them in any thing.
24 Thou also, Esdras, according to the wisdome of God, ordeine iudges and gouernours, that they may iudge in all Syria &
Phenice all those which are wel instructed
in the Law of thy God, and teache those,
which are not instructed.
25 And let all those which shal transgresse
the Law of God & the King, be diligently punished, ether with death, or other punishment, ether with penaltie of money,
or banishment.
26 ¶ Thē Esdras the scribe said, Blessed be
the onelie Lord God of my fathers, which
hathe put this in the heart of the King to
glorifie his House which is in Ierusalem,
27 And hathe honoured me before ẏ King,
and the counsellers, and all his friends and
gouernours.
28 ¶ *Therefore I was incouraged by the Esr. 8,1.
helpe of the Lord my God, and gathered
men of Israel to go vp with me.
29 These are the guides after their families
and order of dignities, which came vp
with me out of Babylon in the reigne of
Artaxerxes the King.
30 Of the sonnes of Phinees, Gersom, of
the sonnes of Ithamar, Gamael, of the sonnes of Dauid "Lettus. "or, Hattus.

31 Of ẏ sonnes of Sechenias, of the sonnes
of Phares, Zacharias, and with him were
counted an hundreth and fiftie men.
"or, Pahath, Moab, Eliœnai.
32 Of the sonnes of " Salomõ, Abeliacnias
the sonne of Zacharias, and with him two
hundreth men.
33 Of the sonnes of Zathoe, Sechenias *the*
"or, Iexiel.
sonne of " Iezolus, & with him thre hũdreth
"or, Obed.
men: of the sonnes of Adin, " Obeth *sonne*
of Ionathas, and with him two hundreth
and fiftie men.
"or, Iesaias.
34 Of the sonnes of Elam " Iesias, *sonne* of
Gotholias, and with him seuentie men.
35 Of the sonnes of Saphatias, Zarias *sonne*
"or, Michael.
of " Machael, and with him seuentie men.
"or, Obadiah, sonne of Iechiel.
36 Of the sonnes of Ioab " Badias *sonne* of
Iezelus, and with him two hundreth and
twelue men.
"or, Baniah Esolomith.
37 Of the sonnes of " Banid, Assalimoth
sonne of Iosaphias, and with him an hundreth and threscore men.
38 Of the sonnes of Babi, Zacharias *sonne*
of Bebai, and ẇ him twentie & eight mẽ.
"or, Asgad Iohanan sonne of Eccethan.
39 Of the sonnes of " Astath, Iohannes *sonne*
of Acatan, & with him an hundreth & tẽ.
40 Of the sonnes of Adonicam the last: &
these are the names of them, Eliphalat,
"or, Iehel.
" Ieouel and " Maias, and with them seuen-
"or, Semaias.
tie men: of the sonnes of " Bagouthi *sonne*
"or, Bagoi, Vti, sonne of Istacurí.
of Iscacourus, & with him seuentie men.
41 ¶ And I gathered them together to the
Ezr. 8, 15.
flood called * Theras, & pitched our tents
there thre daies, and nombred them.
42 But when I had founde there none of the
Priests nor Leuites,
43 I sent to Eleazar, and beholde, there came
"or, Masma, Alnathan
" Maasman, and Alnathan, & Samaian, and
"or, Iorib, Elnathan, Zacharie & Mosollam.
" Ioribon, & Nathan, Ennatan, Zacharian,
& Mosollamon the chief, & best learned.
44 And I bad them to go to Daddeus the
captaine, which was in the place of the
treasurie,
45 With charge to bidde Daddeus and his
brethren, & the treasurers that were there,
to send to vs them, which shulde offer sacrifice in the House of our Lord.
46 And they broght vnto vs by the mightie hand of our Lord learned men of the
sonnes of Moli, *the sonne* of Leui, *the sonne*
"or, Seredia.
of Israel, *to wit*, " Cisebebran & his sonnes,
and his brethren being eightene.
"or, Anom, Iesaas.
47 And Asebia, and " Annon, & Osaian his
"or, Canaanien.
brethrẽ of the sonnes of " Canaineus with
their sonnes, twentie persones.
48 And of the ministers of the Temple, ẇ
Dauid gaue, & those which were rulers o-
uer the worke of the Leuites, *to wit*, ministers of the Temple, two hundreth & twẽtie, of whome all the names were registred.
Ezr. 8, 21.
49 ¶ And * there I proclaimed a fast for the
yong men before the Lord to aske of him
a good iourney bothe for vs, and for them
that were with vs, for our children, & for
our cattel.
50 For I was ashamed to aske the King fotemen, or horsemen, or conduict for sauegarde against our enemies,
51 Because we had said to the King, that
the power of our Lord shulde be with thẽ
that soght him to direct them in all thĩgs.
52 Wherefore we praied our Lord againe,
according to these things, whome we founde fauorable.
53 Then I chose from among the chief of ẏ
tribes & of the Priests, twelue men, *to wit*,
" Esebrias and Assanias, and with them ten "or, Serebias.
of their brethren.
54 And I weighed them the siluer and the
golde, & the holy vessels of the House of
our Lord, which the King and his counsellers, & *his* princes, & all Israel had giuẽ.
55 And I weighed thẽ, six hundreth & fifty
talents of siluer, & siluer vessels of an hundreth talẽts, & an hũdreth talẽts of golde,
56 And twentie golden basens, & twelue ves
sels of brasse, of fine brasse shining like
golde.
57 And I said to them, You are also holy to
the Lord, and the vessels are holy, and the
golde, and the siluer is a vowe to the Lord
of our fathers.
58 Watch and kepe *them*, til that you giue
thẽ to the heads of the families of the
Priests, and Leuites, and captaines of the
families of Israel in Ierusalem in the chãbers of the House of our God.
59 So the Priests & Leuites toke the siluer
and the golde, & the vessels, & caryed thẽ
to Ierusalem to the Temple of the Lord.
60 And we departed frõ the flood Thera,
in the twelueth *day* of the first moneth, &
came to Ierusalem, according to ẏ mightie power of our Lord with vs: and the
Lord deliuered vs from the beginning of
our iourney from all enemies. So we came
to Ierusalem.
61 And thre daies being past there, in the
fourth day, the siluer that was weighed, &
the golde was deliuered in the House of
our Lord to " Marmoth the Priest the son- "or, Marimoth the sonne of Iori of Vrie.
ne of Iouri,
62 And with him to Eleazar ẏ *sonne* of Phinees: & there were with them, Iosabad *the*
sonne of Iesus, & " Moeth *sonne* of Sabbanus, "or, Noedia, sonnes sonne of Bannus.
Leuites: all *was deliuered them* by nomber
and weight.
63 And all the weight of them was writen
that same houre.
64 Afterwards those that were come out of
the captiuitie, offred sacrifices to the Lord
God of Israel, *euen* twelue bulles for all
Israel, rams foure score and sixtene,
65 Lãbs thre score & twelue, twelue goates
for saluacion, all in sacrifice to the Lord.
66 And they presented the commandemẽts
of the King to the Kings stewards, & to ẏ
gouernours

gouernours of Coelosyria &Phenice who
honored the people, and the Temple of
God.
67 ¶ *When these things were done, the Ezra.9.1.
gouernours came to me, saying, The people of Israel, the princes and the Priests, &
the Leuites haue not separated *from them*
the strange people of the land,
68 Nor the pollutions of the Gentiles, *to*
wit, of the Cananites, and Chetites, and
Pheresites, and Iebusites, and Moabites,
and Egyptians, and Idumeans.
69 For they haue dwelt with their daughters, bothe they and their sonnes, and the
holie sede is mixed with the strange people of the lãd, & the gouernours & rulers
haue bene partakers of this wickednes frõ
the beginning of the thing.
70 And assone as I had heard these things, I
rent my clothes, and the holie garment, &
I pulled the heere of mine head, and of my
bearde, and sate me downe sorowful, and
verie sad.
71 Thẽ also all they that were moued with
the worde of the Lord God of Israel, came
to me whiles I wepte for the iniquitie, but
I sate verie sad til the euening sacrifice.
72 Then I rose from the fast with my clothes torne, and the holie garment, and
bowed my knees and stretched forthe *mine*
hands to the Lord,
73 And said, *O Lord, I am ashamed, & cõ- Ezra.9.6.
founded before thy face.
74 For our sinnes are increased aboue our
heades, & our ignorances are lifted vp to
heauen.
75 Yea, euen from the time of our fathers
we are in great sinne vnto this day.
76 For our sinnes therefore, and our fathers
we with our brethren, with our Kings and
Priests haue bene giuen vp to the Kings
of the earth, to the sworde and to captiuitie, and for a pray with all shame vnto
this day.
77 And now how great hathe thy mercie
bene, ô Lord, that *there* shulde be left vs a
roote, and name in the place of thine holines!
78 And that thou shuldest reueale to vs a
light in the House of the Lord our God,
and giue vs meat in the time of our seruitude!
79 For when we were in bondage, we were
not left of our God, but he gaue vs fauour
before the Kings of the Persians, that thei
shulde giue vs meat,
80 And that they shulde honour the Temple of our Lord, and raise vp Sion that is
desolate, and giue vs assurance in Iudea &
Ierusalem.
81 And now, ô Lord, what shal we say, hauing these things? for we haue transgressed thy commandements, which thou hast
giuen by the hands of thy seruants the Prophetes, saying,
82 *Because the land, which ye go to inhe- Deut.7.3.
rite, is a land polluted by the pollucions
of the strangers of the land, which haue
filled it with their filthines,
83 Therefore now ye shal not ioyne *their*
daughters with your sonnes, nether giue
your daughters to their sonnes,
84 Nether shal you desire to haue peace
with them for euer, that ye may be made
strong, and eat the good things of the lãd,
and leaue it for an inheritance to your
children for euer.
85 Therefore all that is come to passe, was
done for our wicked workes, and for our
great sinnes: yet, Lord, thou hast forborne
our sinnes,
86 And hast giuen vs suche a roote: *but* we a-
gaine haue turned backe to trãsgresse thy
Law, & to mixe *vs* with the vnclennes of
the people of the land.
87 Mightest thou not be angrie with vs to
destroye vs, so that thou shuldest nether
leaue vs roote nor sede nor name?
88 *But*, ô Lord of Israel, thou art true:
for there is a roote left, *euen* vnto this
day.
89 Beholde, we are now before thee with
our iniquities, nether can we indure before thee for these things.
90 ¶ And * as Esdras prayed and confessed Ezra.10.1.
and wept, and laye vpon the grounde before the Temple, a verie great multitude
was gathered vnto him out of Ierusalem
of men and women, and yong children: for
there was great lamentation among the
multitude.
91 Then Iechonias ye sonne of "Ieel of the "Or, Ieiel.
sõnes of Israel, crying out said, O Esdras,
we haue sinned against the Lord God: we
haue taken in mariage strange women of
the nacions of the land.
92 And now all Israel is douteful: therefore let vs make an othe concerning this to
the Lord to put away all our wiues, which
are strangers, with their children.
93 If it seme good to thee, and to all them
that obey the Law of the Lord, rise vp *and*
put it in execution.
94 For to thee doeth it apperteine, & we are
with thee to make thee strong.
95 Then Esdras arose, & made all the chief
of the families of the Priests and Leuites
of all Israel to sweare, that they wolde do
thus: and they sware.

CHAP. IX.

7 After Esdras had red the law for the strange wiues,
10 Thei promise to put them away.

1 THen *Esdras rose from the court of Ezra.10.6.
the Temple, & went to the chamber
of Ioannan *the sonne* of Eliasib,
2 And being lodged there, he did eat no

bread nor dranke water, but mourned for the great iniquities of the multitude.

3 And there was a proclamation in all Iudea and Ierusalem to all them, that were of the captiuitie, that they shulde be gathered to Ierusalem,

4 And that all they which shulde not mete there within two or thre dayes, according to the ordinãce of the Elders, which bare rule, shulde haue their cattel confiscate to the Temple, and he cast out from among them of the captiuitie.

5 Then all they which were of the tribe of Iuda and Beniamin, came together within thre dayes into Ierusalem: this was the ninth moneth and twentieth *day* of the moneth.

6 And all the multitude sate in the broad place of the Temple shaking, because of the extreme winter.

7 Then Esdras arose and said to them, Ye haue sinned: for ye haue maried strange wiues, so that ye haue augmented the sinnes of Israel.

8 Now therefore confesse and glorifie the Lord God of our fathers,

9 And do his wil, and separate your selues from the people of the land, and from the strange wiues.

10 Then all the multitude cryed out and said with a loude voyce, We wil do so as thou hast said.

11 But because the multitude *is* great, and the time is winter, so that we can not stãd without, and the worke is not of one day nor of two, seing that manie of vs haue sinned in this matter,

12 Let the chief men of the multitude and all they which haue strange wiues of our families, tarie:

13 And let the Priests and iudges come out of all places at the day appointed, til thei haue appeased the wrath of ye Lord against vs for this matter.

14 Then Ionathas Asaels *sonne*, and "Ezecias *sonne* of "Thecan were appointed concerning these things, and Mosollam and Sabbateus did helpe them.

" or, Iahazias. *" or, Thecua.*

15 And they which were of the captiuitie, did after all these things.

16 Esdras the Priest also chose him certeine men, chief of their families, all by name: & thei sate together in the first day of the tenth moneth to examine this matter.

17 And they made and end of the things perteining to them that had maried strange wiues in the first day of ye first moneth.

18 And there were founde of the Priests, which had maried strange wiues,

19 Of the sonnes of Iesus, the *sonne* of Iosedec, & of *his* brethren "Mathelas, & Eleazar, and Ioribus, and "Ionadan.

" or, Maasias. *" or, Iedaliah.*

20 Who also gaue their hands to cast out their wiues, and offred a ram for *their* reconciliation in their purgation.

21 And of the sonnes of Emmer "Ananias, and Zabdeus, and Canes, and Sameius, and Hiereel, and Azarias.

" or, Anani, & Zabiah.

22 And of the sonnes of "Phaisu, Ellionas, Massias, Esmaelus, and Nathanael, and "Ocidelus, and Talsas.

" or, Phashur, Elionai Maasias, Iesmael. *" or, Olridel, and Alasa.*

23 And of the Leuites "Iorabadus, and Semis, and Colius, who was called "Calitas, and Patheus, and Oudas, and Ionas.

" or, Iosabad, Semei. *" or, Galias, Pathias, Iobudas.*

24 Of the holie singers, "Eliazurus, Bacchurus.

" or, Eliasib, and Bacur.

25 Of the porters, "Sallumus, & Tolbanes.

" or, Salluno.

26 Of them of Israel, of the sonnes of Phorus, "Hiermas, and Eddias, & Melchias, & Maelus, & Eleazar, & Asibias, & "Banaias.

" or, Remias. *" or, Banadias.*

27 Of the sonnes of "Ela, Matthanias, Zacharias, and "Hierielas, and "Hieremoth, and Aedias.

" or, Elam. *" or, Iehiel.* *" or, Ieremoth, & Helias*

28 And of the sonnes of "Zamoth, Eliadas, Elisimus, Othonias, Iarimoth, and "Sabatus, and Sardeus.

" or, Zathone, Eliadas, Elisib. *" or, Sabad, and Sardai.*

29 Of the sonnes of "Bebai, Ioannes, and Ananias, and "Iosabad, and Ematheas.

" or, Bebe. *" or, Iosabat, and Emah.*

30 Of the sonnes of "Mani, Olamus, Mamuchus, Iedaias, Iasubus, Iasael, and Ieremoth.

" or, Bani, Olam, Malluch, Iedaia, Iasub.

31 And of the sonnes of "Addi, Naathus, Moosias, Laccunus, and Naidus, and Mathanias, and "Seschel, and Balnuus, and Manasseas.

" or, Addin, Naatus, Laccun. Banaias. *" or, Bezelel, Balnus, Manasses.*

32 And of the sonnes of Annas, Elionas, & Aseas, and Melchias, and Sabbeus, and Simon a Chosamite.

33 And of the sonnes of "Asom, Altaneus, & "Matthias, and Bannaias, Eliphalat, & Manasses, and Semei.

" or, Hasam. *" or, Mathmas, Matathias.*

34 And of the sonnes of "Maani, Ieremias, Momdis, Omairus, Inel, Mamai, and Paclias, and Amos, Carabasion and Euasibus, and Mamnimatanaius, Elisiasis, Vamus, Eliali, Samis, Selemias, Nathanias, & of the sonnes of Ozoras, Sesis, Esril, Azailus, Samatas, Sambis, Iosiphus.

" or, Ban, Ieremias, Moadi, Eniram.

35 And of the sonnes of Ethna, Mazitias, Zabadias, Ethes, Inel, Banaias.

36 All these maryed strange wiues, and put them away with their children.

37 And the Priests & the Leuites dwelt in Ierusalem, & in the countrey, the first day of the seuenth moneth, and the childrẽ of Israel in their owne houses.

38 ¶ * Then all the multitude assembled together with one consent into the broad place before the gate of the Temple toward the East,

Nehe. 8.

39 And spake to Esdras the Priest, and reader, that he shulde bring the Law of Moyses, which had bene giuẽ by the Lord God of Israel.

40 Then broght Esdras the chief Priest the Law to all the multitude, bothe man and woman,

woman, and to all the Priests, that they
might heare the Law the first day of the
seuenth moneth.
41 And he red in the first broad place of
the gate of the Temple, from morning to
midday, before the men and the women,
and all the multitude hearkened to ỹ Law.
42 So Esdras the Priest and reader of the
Law, stode vpō a pulpet of wood that was
prepared.
Or, Matthithias. 43 And there stode by him "Matgathias, Sā-
mus, Ananias, Azarias, Ourias, Ezecias,
Balasamus at his right hand,
Or, Pedaias. 44 And at his left hand "Phaldaius, and
Sail, Melchias, Aothasaphus, Nabarias.
45 Then Esdras toke ỹ boke of the Law before the multitude (for he sate honorably before them all)
46 And they all stode vpright when he expounded the Law, and Esdras blessed the
Lord the moste hie God, the moste mightie God of hostes.
47 And the whole multitude cryed, Amen.
Or, Bani. 48 Then Iesus and "Anus, and Sarabias, and
Adimus, & Iacobus, Sabataias, Autanias,
Maianias and Calitas, Azarias, & Ioazab-
dus, and Ananias, & Biatas the Leuites
lift vp their hands, and fell downe on the
grounde, and worshiped the Lord,
49 And taught the Law of the Lord, and
stode also earnestly vpon the reading.
50 Then said "Aththarates to Esdras the Or, Nehemias.
chief Priest and reader, & to the Leuites,
that taught the multitude in all things,
This day is holie vnto the Lord, and all
haue wept in hearing of the Law.
51 Go therefore and eat the fat meates, &
drinke the swete drinkes, and send presents
to them that haue not.
52 For this day is holie to the Lord, and be
not sorie: for the Lord God wil glorifie
you.
53 So the Leuites commanded all these
things to the people, saying, This day is
holie to the Lord: be not sad.
54 Then they departed all to eat, and drinke, and to reioyce, and to giue presents to
thē that had not, and to make good chere.
55 For they were yet filled with the wordes
wherewith they were instructed, whē they
were assembled together.

II. Esdras.

CHAP. I.

8 The people is reproued for their vnfaithfulnes.
30 God wil haue another people, if these wil not be re-
formed.

Esra.7,1. 1 He second boke of the
Prophet *Esdras, the
sonne of Saraias, ỹ son-
ne of Azarias, the sonne
of Helcias, the sonne of
Sadanias, the sonne of
Sadoc, the sonne of A-
chitob,
2 The sonne of Achias, ỹ sonne of Phinees,
the sonne of Heli, the sonne of Amerias,
the sonne of Asie, the sonne of Marimoth,
the sonne of Arua, the sonne of Ozias, the
sonne of Borith, the sonne of Abisei, the
sonne of Phinees, the sonne of Eleazar,
3 The sonne of Aaron (of the tribe of Leui) which Esdras was prisoner in the lād of
Medes, in the reigne of Artaxerxes King
of Persia.
Isa 38,1. 4 *And the worde of the Lord came vnto
me, saying,
5 Go, and shewe my people their sinnes, &
their children their wickednes, which thei
haue cōmitted against me, that they may
tel their childrens children.
6 For the sinnes of their fathers are increased in them, because they haue forgotten
me, and haue offred vnto strange gods.
7 Haue not I broght them out of the land
of Egypt from the house of bondage? but
they haue prouoked me vnto wrath, and
despised my counsels.
8 Pull thou of then the heere of thine head,
and cast all euil vpon them: for they haue
not bene obedient vnto my Law, but they
are a rebellious people.
9 How long shal I forbeare thē, vnto whome
I haue done somuche good?
10 *Many Kings haue I destroied for their Exod.14,28.
sakes: Pharao with his seruants and all his
armie haue I smitten downe.
11 All the nacions haue I destroied before Nomb.21,24
them: *I haue destroied the East, the peo- Ioshu.8,12.
ple of the two countreis Tyrus and Sidō,
and haue slaine all their enemies.
12 Speake thou therefore vnto thē, saying,
Thus saith the Lord,
13 *I haue led you thorow the Sea, and haue Exod.14,29.
giuen you a sure "way, since the begin- Or, strete.
ning: *I gaue you Moyses for a guide, and Exod.3,10.
Aaron for a Priest. & 4,14.
14 *I gaue you light in a piller of fyre, and Exo.13,21.
great wonders haue I done amōg you: yet
haue ye forgotten me, saith the Lord.
15 Thus saith ỹ Almightie Lord, The quai
les *were a tokē vnto you: I gaue you ten- Exod.16,13. Psal.104,40.
tes for sauegarde, wherein ye murmured:
16 And ye triumphed not in my Name for
the destruction of your enemies, but ye
yet murmure stil.
17 Where are the benefites, that I haue done for you? when ye were hungrie in the
wildernes, *did ye not crye vnto me? Nom.14,8.
18 Saying, Why hast thou broght vs into

this wildernes to kill vs? It had bene better for vs to haue serued the Egyptians,
then to dye in this wildernes.
19 I had pitie vpon your mournings, and
Wis.16.20. gaue you Manna to eat:* so ye did eat Angels fode.
Nom 20,11. wisd.11,4. 20 *When ye were thirstie, did not I cleaue
the stone, & waters did flowe out to satis-
fie you? from the heat I couered you with
the leaues of the trees,
21 And I gaue you fat countreis: I cast out
the Cananites, ŷ Pheresites, & Philistims
Isa.5,4. before you:* what shal I do more for you,
saith the Lord?
Exod.15,25. 22 Thus saith the almightie Lord,* When
ye were in the wildernes at the bitter waters, being a thirst, and blaspheming my
Name,
23 I gaue you not fyre for the blasphemies,
but cast a tre into the water, and made the
riuer swete.
24 What shal I do vnto thee, ô Iacob? thou
Exod.32,8. *Iuda woldest not obey: I wil turne me to
other nations, and vnto those wil I giue
my Name, that they may kepe my lawes.
25 Seing ye haue forsaken me, I wil also forsake you: when ye aske mercie of me, I wil
not haue pitie vpon you.
Isa.1,15. 26 * When ye call vpon me, I wil not heare
you: for ye haue defiled your hands with
blood, and your fete are swift to commit
murther,
27 Althogh ye haue not forsaken me, but
your owne selues, saith the Lord.
28 Thus saith the almightie Lord, Haue I
not prayed you, as a father his sonnes, and
as a mother her daughters, and as a nurse
her yong babes,
29 That ye wolde be my people, as I am
your God, and that ye wolde be my children, as I am your father?
Mat.23,37. 30 *I gathered you together as an henne ga
thereth her chikens vnder her wings: but
now what shal I do vnto you? I wil cast
you out from my sight.
Isa.1,13. 31 *Whē you bring gifts vnto me, I wil turne my face from you for your solēne feast
dayes: your new moones, & your circum-
cisions haue I forsaken.
32 I sent vnto you my seruants the Prophetes, whome ye haue taken and slaine, and
torne their bodies in pieces, whose blood I
wil reuenge, saith the Lord.
33 Thus saith ŷ almightie Lord, Your house shalbe desolate: I wil cast you out as the
winde doeth the stubble.
34 Your children shal not haue generaciō:
for thei haue despised my commandemēt,
& done the thing that I hate before me.
35 Your houses wil I giue vnto a people to
come, who shal beleue me thogh they heare me not, and they, vnto whome I neuer
shewed miracle, shal do the things that
I command them.
36 Thogh they se no Prophetes, yet shal
they hate their iniquities.
37 ¶I wil declare the grace that I wil do for
the people to come, whose children reioyce in gladnes, and thogh they haue not sene me with bodelie eyes, yet in heart they
beleue the things that I say.
38 Now therefore brother, beholde what
great glorie, and se the people that come
from the East.
39 Vnto whome I wil giue for leaders Abra
ham, Isahac, Iacob, Oseas, Amos, Micheas,
Ioel, Abdias, Ionas,
40 Naum, Habacuc, Sophonias, Aggeus,
Zacharias, and Malachias (which is called also the *messenger of the Lord) Malach. 3,1.

CHAP. II.

The Synagogue findeth faute with her owne children.
18 The Gentiles are called.

1 THus saith the Lord, I broght this
people out of bondage: I gaue them
also my commandements by my seruants
ŷ Prophetes, whome they wolde not heare, but despised my counsels.
2 The mother that bare them, saith vnto
them, Go you away, ô children: for I am a
widdowe and forsaken.
3 I broght you vp with gladnes, but with
sorowe and heauines haue I lost you: for
ye haue sinned against ŷ Lord your God,
and done the thing that displeaseth him.
4 But what shal I now do vnto you? I am
a widdowe and forsaken: go ye, ô my children, and aske mercie of the Lord.
5 And thee, ô father, I call for a witnes for
the mother of these children, which wolde not kepe my couenant,
6 That thou bring them to confusion, and
their mother to a spoile, that their kinred
be not continued.
7 Let their names be scatred amōg the hea
then: let them be put out of the earth, for
they haue despised my couenant.
8 Wo vnto thee, Assur: for thou hidest the
vnrighteous in thee: ô wicked people, remember * what I did vnto Sodom and Gen.19,24.
Gomorrha,
9 Whose lād is mixt with cloudes of pitch
and heapes of ashes: so wil I do vnto thē,
that heare me not, saith the almightie
Lord.
10 ¶Thus saith the Lord vnto Esdras, Tel
my people, that I wil giue them the kingdome of Ierusalem, which I wolde haue
giuen vnto Israel.
11 And I wil get me glorie by them, and
giue thē the euerlasting tabernacles, which
I had prepared for those.
12 They shal haue at wil the tre of life,
smelling of ointement: they shal nether
labour nor be weary.
13 Go ye, & ye shal receaue it: pray that the
time,

time,which is long,may be shortened: the
kingdome is already prepared for you:
watche.
14 Take heauen and earth to witnes: for I
haue abolished the euil, and created the
good:for I liue,saith the Lord.
15 Mother,embrace thy children,and bring
them vp with gladnes: make their fete as
fast as a piller:for I haue chosen thee,saith
the Lord.
16 And those that be dead, wil I raise vp
from their places, and bring them out of
the graues: for I haue knowen my Name
in Israel.
17 Feare not,thou mother of the children:
for I haue chosen thee,saith the Lord.
18 I wil send thee my seruants Esaie and
Ieremie to helpe thee,by whose counsel I
haue sanctified & prepared for thee twelue trees laden with diuers frutes,
19 And as many fountaines, flowing with
milke and hony,and seuen mightie mountaines, whereupon there growe roses and
lilies, whereby I wil fil thy children with
ioye.
20 Execute iustice for the widdowe: iudge
the cause of the fatherles: giue to the poo-
re:defende the fatherles:clothe the naked.
21 Heale the wounded,and sicke: laugh not
a lame man to scorne: defend the crepel,
and let the blinde come into the light of
my clerenes.
22 Kepe the olde & the yong that are within thy walles.
23 *Wheresoeuer thou findest the dead,take
them and burye them, and I wil giue thee
the first place in my resurrection.
24 Abide stil,ô my people,and rest: for thy
quietnes shal come.
25 Nourish thy childrẽ, ô thou good nur-
se:stablish their fete.
26 None of the seruants that I haue giuen
thee,shal perish: for I wil seke them from
among thy nomber.
27 Be not weary:for when the day of trouble and heauines commeth, other shal wepe and be soroweful, but thou shalt be mery and haue abundance.
28 The heathen shal enuie thee, and shal
do nothing against thee,saith the Lord.
29 Mine hands shal couer thee, so that thy
children shal not se hell.
30 Be ioyful,ô thou mother, with thy children: for I wil deliuer thee, saith the
Lord.
31 Remember thy children that slepe:for I
wil bring thẽ out of the sides of the earth,
and wil shewe mercie vnto them: for I am
merciful,saith the Lord almightie.
32 Embrace thy children, vntil I come and
shewe mercie vnto thẽ: for my fountaines
runne ouer,and my grace shal not faile.
33 I Esdras receiued a charge of the Lord
vpon the mount Horeb, that I shulde go
vnto them of Israel, but when I came to
them,thei cast me of,and despised the cõmandement of the Lord.
34 And therefore I say vnto you, ô ye heathen,that heare and vnderstand, Wait for
your shepherd, who shal giue you euerlasting rest: for he is nere at hand, that shal
come in the end of the worlde.
35 Be ready to the rewarde of the kingdo-
me:for the euerlasting light shal shine vpõ
you for euermore.
36 Flee the shadowe of this worlde: receiue
ẏ ioye of your glorie:I testifie my Sauiour
openly.
37 Receiue the gift that is giuen you, and
be glad,giuing thankes vnto him, that hathe called you to the heauenlie kingdome.
38 Arise,and stand vp, and beholde the nõber of those that are sealed for the feast of
the Lord,
39 Which are departed from the shadowe
of the worlde, and haue receiued glorious
garments of the Lord.
40 Take thy nomber, ô Sion, and shut vp
them that are clothed in white,which haue fulfilled the Law of the Lord.
41 The nõber of thy children whome thou
longest for,is fulfilled:beseche ẏ power of
the Lord,that thy people which haue bene
called frõ the begining,may be sanctified.
42 *I Esdras sawe vpõ mount Sion a great
people whome I colde not nomber, and
they all praised the Lord with songs.
43 And in the middes of them there was a
yong man hier in stature then them all, &
vpõ eueric one of their heads he set crownes,and was hier then the others, which I
muche marueiled at.
44 So I asked the Angel,and said, Who are
these, my lord?
45 Who answered,and said vnto me, These
be they, that haue put of the mortal clothing, and haue put on the immortal, and
haue cõfessed the Name of God: now are
they crowned,and receiue the palmes.
46 Then said I vnto ẏ Angel, What yong
man is it,that setteth crownes on them, &
giueth them the palmes in their hands.
47 And he answered, & said vnto me, It is
the sonne of God, whome they haue confessed in the worlde. Then began I greatly to commende them, that had stand so
strongly for the Name of the Lord.
48 Then the Angel said vnto me, Go thy
way, and tel my people, what, and how
great wonders of the Lord God thou hast
sene.

Tob.1,20.

Reuel.7,9.

CHAP. III.

4 The wonderous workes, which God did for the people, are recited. 31 Esdras marueileth that God suffreth the Babylonians to haue rule ouer his people, which yet are synners also.

1 IN the thirtieth yere after the fall of
the citie, as I was at Babylon, I lay trou
bled vpon my bed, and my thoghts came
vp to mine heart,
2 Because I sawe the desolacion of Sion, &
the wealth of them that dwelt at Babylon.
3 So my spirit was sore moued, so that I beganne to speake fearful wordes to the most
High, and said,
4 O Lord, Lord, thou spakest at the beginning when thou alone plantedst the earth,
and gauest cōmandemēt vnto the people,
Gen.2,7. 5 *And a bodie vnto Adam, without soule,
who was also the workemanship of thine
hands, and hast breathed in him the breth
of life, so that he liued before thee,
6 And leddest him into Paradise, which
thy right hand had planted, or euer the
Or, went forward. earth "broght forthe.
7 Euen then thou gauest him commandement to loue thy way: but he transgressed
it, and immediatly thou appointedst death
to him and his generacion, of whome came nacions, tribes, people and kinreds out
of nomber.
Gen.6,12. 8 *And euerie people walked after their
owne wil, and did wonderful things before thee, and despised thy commandements.
Gen.7,10. 9 *But at ý time appointed thou broghtest
the flood vpon those ý dwelt in the worlde and destroiedst them,
10 So that by the flood, that came to euerie
one of them, which came by death vnto
Adam,
1.Pet.3,20. 11 Yet thou leftest one, *euen* *Noe, with his
housholde, of whome came all righteous
men.
12 And when they that dwelt vpon ý earth,
began to multiplie, and the nomber of
the children, people and many nacions
were increased, they began to be more
vngodlie then the first.
Gen.12,1. 13 Now when they liued wickedly before
Gen.17,5. thee, *thou didest chose thee a man from
among them, whose name was *Abraham.
14 Whome thou louedst, and vnto whome
onely thou shewedst thy wil,
15 And madest an euerlasting couenāt with
him, promising him that thou woldest neuer forsake his sede.
Gen.21,2. 16 *And vnto him thou gauest Isahac, *vn-
Gen.25,25. to Isahac also thou gauest Iacob and Esau,
Malac.1,2. rom.9,13. *and didest chose Iacob, and cast of Esau,
and so Iacob became a great multitude.
17 And whē thou leddest his sede out of E-
Exod.19,1. gypt, *ý broghtest thē vp to mount Sina,
deu.4,10. 18 And enclinedst the heauens and bowedst
downe the earth, and didest moue the grounde, and cause the depths to shake, and
didest astonish the worlde.
19 And thy glorie went thorowe foure gates of fyre, with earthquakes, winde and
colde, that thou mightest giue the Lawe
vnto the sede of Iacob, and that which the
generacion of Israel shulde diligently
obserue.
20 Yet tokest thou not away from them the
wicked heart, that thy Law might bring
forthe frute in them.
21 For *Adam first hauing a wicked heart, Gen.3,6.
was ouercome and vainquished, & all they
that are borne of him.
22 Thus remained weakenes ioyned with
the lawe in the hearts of the people, with
the wickednes of the roote: so that the
good departed away, & the euil abode stil.
23 So the times passed away, and the yeres
were broght to an end, *til thou didest rai 1 Sam.16,13.
se thee vp a seruant called Dauid,
24 *Whome thou commandedst to buyld a 2.Sam.5,8.
citie vnto thy Name, to call vpon thee
therein with incense and sacrifice.
25 Whē this was done many yeres, the inhabitants forsoke thee,
26 Following the waies of Adam and all his
generacion: for they also had a wicked
heart.
27 Therefore thou gauest thy citie ouer into the hands of thine enemies.
28 But do they that dwell at Babylon, any
better, that they shulde haue the dominiō
of Sion?
29 For when I came thether, and sawe their
wicked dedes without nomber (for this is
the thirtieth yere that I se many trespacing) I was discouraged.
30 For I sawe, how thou sufferedst them
that sinne, and sparedst the wicked doers,
where as thou hast destroied thine owne
people, and preserued thine enemies, and
thou hast not shewed it.
31 I can not perceiue how this commeth to
passe. Are the dedes of Babylon better then
they of Sion?
32 Or is there any other people ý knoweth
thee besides Israel? or what generacion
hathe so beleued thy Testimonies, as Iacob?
33 And yet their rewarde appeareth not, and
their labour hathe no frute: for I haue
gone here & there thorow out the heathē,
and I se them florish, and thinke not vpon
thy commandements.
34 Weigh ý therefore our wickednes now
in the balance, and theirs also that dwell
in the worlde, and no mention of thee shal
be founde but in Israel.
35 Or when is it that they that dwell on
the earth, haue not sinned in thy sight? or
what people hathe so kept thy commandements?
36 Thou shalt surely finde that Israel by
name hathe kept thy precepts, but not the
heathen.

CHAP.

CHAP. IIII.

2 The Angel reproueth Esdras, because he semed to entre into the profounde iudgements of God.

1 AND the Angel that was sent vnto
me, whose name was Vriel, answered,
2 And said, Thine heart hathe taken to
muche vpon it in this worlde, and thou
thinkest to comprehende the waies of the
Hiest.
3 Thē said I, Yea, my lord. And he answered me, and said, I am sent to shewe thee
thre waies, and to set forthe thre similitudes before thee,
4 Whereof if thou canst declare me one,
I wil shewe thee also the way, that thou
desirest to se, and I wil shewe thee from
whence the wicked heart cometh.
5 And I said, Tell on, my lord. Then said
he vnto me, Go thy way: weigh me the
weight of the fyre, or measure me ẏ blast
of the winde, or call me againe the daye
that is past.
6 Then answered I, and said, What man is
borne, that can do that, which thou requirest me, concerning these things?
7 And he said vnto me, If I shulde aske
thee how depe dwellings are in the middes of the sea, or how great springs are in
the beginning of the depth, or how great
springs are in the stretching out of the
heauen, or which are the borders of Paradise,
8 Peraduenture thou woldest say vnto me,
I neuer went downe to the depe, nor yet
to the hell, nether did I euer clime vp to
heauen.
9 But now haue I asked thee but of fyre &
winde, and of the day, whereby thou hast
passed, and from the which things thou
canst not be separated, and yet canst thou
giue me none answer of them.
10 He said moreouer vnto me, Thine owne
things, and suche as are growen vp with
thee, canst thou not knowe:
11 How shulde thy vessel then be able to
comprehend the wayes of the Hiest, and
now outwardly in the corrupt worlde, to
vnderstand the corruption, that is euident
in my sight?
12 Then said I vnto him, It were better
that we were not at all, thē that we shulde
liue in wickednes, and to suffer, and not to
knowe wherefore.
13 And he answered me, & said, * I came to *Iudg. 9. 8. 2. chro. 25, 18.*
a forest in the plaine where the trees helde
a counsel,
14 And said, Come, let vs go fight against
the sea, that it may giue place to vs, and
that we may make vs more woods.
15 Likewise the floods of the sea toke cōūsel and said, Come, let vs go vp and fight
agaīst the trees of the wood, that we may
get another countrey for vs.
16 But the purpose of the wood was vaine:
for the fyre came and consumed it.
17 Likewise also the purpose of the floods
of the sea: for the sand stode vp and stopped them.
18 If thou were iudge betwene these two,
whome woldest thou iustifie, or whome
woldest thou condemne?
19 I answered and said, Verely it is a foolish purpose, that thei bothe haue deuised:
for the grounde is appointed for ẏ wood,
and the sea hathe his place to beare his
floods.
20 Then answered he me, and said, Thou
hast giuen a right iudgemēt: but why iudgest thou not thy self also?
21 For like as the grounde is appointed for
the wood, and the sea for his floods, so
* they that dwell vpon earth, can vnder- *Isa. 55, 8.*
stād nothing, but that which is vpō earth: *iohn 3, 32.*
& they that are in the heauens, the things *1. cor. 2, 13.*
that are aboue the height of the heauens.
22 Then answered I, & said, I beseche thee,
ô Lord, let vnderstanding be giuen me.
23 For I did not purpose to inquire of thine
hie things, but of suche as we daiely medle with all, *namely* wherfore Israel is made a reproche to the heathen, and for what
cause the people, whome thou hast loued,
is giuen ouer to wicked nacions, and why
the Law of our fathers is abolished, and
the writen ceremonies are come to none
effect,
24 Why we are tossed to and fro through
the worlde as the greshoppers, and our life
is a very feare, and we are not thoght worthie to obteine mercie.
25 But what wil he do to his Name, which
is called vpon ouer vs? Of these things
haue I asked the question.
26 Then answered he me, and said, The
more thou searchest, the more thou shalt
maruel: for the worlde hasteth fast to passe
away,
27 And can not cōprehend the things, that
are promised to the righteous in time to
come: for this worlde is ful of vnrighteousnes and weakenes.
28 But to declare thee the things whereof
thou askest, the euil is sowen, but the destruction thereof is not yet come.
29 If the euil now that is sowē, be not turned vp side downe, and if the place where
the euil is sowen, passe not away, then can
not the thing come, that is sowen ẇ good.
30 For the corne of euil sede hathe bene
sowen in the heart of Adam from the beginning, & how muche vngodlines hathe
he broght vp vnto this time? & how much
shal he bring forthe vntil the haruest come?
31 Pondre with thy self, how muche frute

of wickednes.the corne of euil sede bringeth forthe,
32 And when the stalkes shalbe cut downe,
which are without nomber, how great an
haruest must be prepared.
33 Then I answered, and said, How, & when
shal these things come to passe? wherefore are our yeres fewe and euil?
34 And he answered me, saying, Haste not
to be aboue ẏ moste High: for thou laborest in vaine to be aboue him, thogh thou
indeuer neuer so muche.
35 Did not the soules also of the righteous
aske question of these things in their chãbers, saying, How long shal I thus hope? &
when cometh the frute of my barne and
our wages?
36 And vpon this Ieremiel the Archangel
answered, and said, When the nomber of
ẏ sedes is filled in you: for he hathe weighed the worlde in the balance.
37 The measure of the times is measured:
the ages are counted by nomber, and they
shal not be moued or shaken, til the measure thereof be fulfilled.
38 Then answered I, & said, O lord, lord,
we are all euen full of sinne,
39 And for our sake paraduenture the haruest of ẏ righteous is not fulfilled, because
of the sinne of them that dwell vpõ earth.
40 So he answered me, and said, Go, & aske
a woman with childe, when she hathe fulfilled her nine moneths, if her wombe may
kepe the birth anie longer within her.
41 Then said I, No, lord, she can not. And
he said vnto me, In the graue the places of
soules are like the wombe.
42 For as she that is with childe, hasteth
to escape the necessitie of the trauail, so
do these places hast to deliuer those thĩgs
that are committed vnto them.
43 That which thou desirest to se, shalbe
shewed thee from the beginning.
44 Then answered I, and said, If I haue
founde grace in thy sight, and if it be possible, and if I be mete therefore,
45 Shewe me whether there be more to come then is past, or more things past, then
are to come.
46 What is past, I knowe, but what is to come, I knowe not.
47 And he said vnto me, Stand on the right
side, and I wil expounde thee this by example.
48 So I stode, and beholde, a whote burning ouen passed before me: and when
the flame was gone by, I loked, & beholde,
the smoke had the vpper hand.
49 After this there passed before me a wa-
terie cloude, and sent downe muche raine
with a storme: and when the stormie raine
was past, the droppes came after.
50 Then said he vnto me, Cõsider with thy
self, as the raine is more thẽ the droppes,
and as fyre exceadeth the smoke, so the
porcion that is past, hathe the vpper hãd,
& the droppes and the smoke were muche.
51 Then I praied, & said, Maie I liue, thinkest thou vntil that time? or what shal come to passe in those daies?
52 He answered me, and said, Of the tokens
whereof thou askest me, I can tell thee a
parte: but I am not sent to shewe thee of
thy life: for I do not knowe it.

CHAP. V.

1 In the latter times trueth shalbe hid. 6 Vnrighteousnes & all wickednes shal reigne in the worlde. 23 Israel is reiected, and God deliuereth thẽ. 35 God doeth all thing in season.

1 NEuertheles concerning the tokens,
beholde, the times shal come, that
thei which dwell vpon earth, shalbe taken
in a great nõber, & the way of the trueth
shalbe hid & ẏ land shalbe baren frõ faith,
2 And *iniquitie shalbe increased more thẽ Matt.24,12.
thou hast sene now, or hast heard in time
past.
3 And it shal come to passe, that one shal
set in fote, and thou shalt se the land desolate, which now reigneth.
4 Yea, if God grãte thee to liue, thou shalt
se after the third trumpet, that the sunne
shal suddenly shine againe in the night, &
the moone thre times a day.
5 Blood shal drop out of the wood, and the
stone shal giue his voyce, and the people
shalbe moued.
6 And he shal rule, of whome they hope
not that dwell vpon earth, and the foules
shal change place.
7 And the sea of Sodom shal cast out fish,
and make a noyse in the night, which many shal not knowe, but they shal all heare
the voyce thereof.
8 There shalbe a confusion in many places,
and the fyre shal oft breake forthe, & the
wilde beasts shal change their places, and
menstruous women shal beare monstres,
9 And salt waters shalbe founde in the swete, & all friẽds shal fight one against another: then shal wit hide it self, and vnderstanding departe into his secret chamber.
10 It shalbe soght of many, and yet not be
founde: then shal vnrighteousnes and vo-
luptuousnes haue ẏ vpper hand vpõ earth.
11 One land also shal aske another, & say,
Is righteous iustice gone thorowe thee?
And it shal say, No.
12 At the same time shal men hope, but not
obteine: they shal labour, but their enterprises shal not prosper.
13 To shewe thee suche tokẽs I haue leaue,
and if thou wilt praie againe and wepe as
now, and fast seuen daies, thou shalt heare
yet greater things then these.
14 ¶ Then I awaked, and a fearefulnes went
thorow

thorow all my bodie, and my minde was
feble and fainted.
15 But the Angel that was come to talke
with me, helde me, comforted me, and set
me vp vpon my fete.
16 And in the seconde night, Salathiel the
captaine of the people came vnto me, saying, Where hast thou bene? and why is thy
countenance so heauie?
17 Knowest thou not that Israel is committed vnto thee in the land of their captiuitie?
18 Vp then and eat, & forsake vs not, as the
shepherd that leaueth his flocke in ŷ hands
of the cruel wolues.
19 Then said I vnto him, Go thy waies frō
me, and come not nere me: and when he
heard it, he went from me.
20 And I fasted seuen daies, mourning and
weping, as Vriel the Angel had commanded me.
21 And after seuen daies the thoghts of
mine heart were very grieuous vnto me a-
gaine.
22 And I had a desire to reason againe, and
I beganne to talke with the moste High
againe,
23 And said, O Lord, Lord: of euerie forest
of the earth, and of all the trees thereof
thou hast chosen thee one onely vineyarde.
24 And of all lands of the worlde thou
hast chosen thee one pit, & of all the flours
of the *grounde* thou hast chosen thee one
lilie.
25 And of all ŷ depths of the sea thou hast
filled thee one riuer, and of all buylded cities thou hast sanctified Sion vnto thy self.
26 And of all the foules that are created,
thou hast named thee one doue, and of all
the cattel that are made, thou hast appointed thee one shepe.
27 And among all the multitude of people
thou hast gotten thee one people, and vnto this people whome thou louedst, thou
gauest a Law, that is proued of all.
28 And now, ô Lord, why hast thou giuen
this one *people* ouer vnto many? and vpon
one roote thou hast set others, & hast scatred thine onelie *people* among many.
29 They treade them downe, which haue
withstand thy promises, and beleue not
thy testimonies.
30 And if thou didest somuche hate thy peo
ple, they shulde haue bene punished with
thine owne hands.
31 ¶ Now when I had spoken these wordes,
ŷ Angel that came to me the night afore,
was sent vnto me,
32 And said vnto me, Heare me, and I wil
teache thee, & hearkē that I may instruct
thee further.
33 And I said, Speake on, my lord. Then
said he vnto me, Thou art sore vexed and
troubled for Israels sake. Louest thou thē
better, then he doeth that made them?
34 And I said, No, lord: but of very sorow
haue I spokē: for my raines paine me euerie houre, while I labour to comprehend
the way of the moste High, & to seke out
parte of his iudgement.
35 And he said vnto me, Thou canst not.
And I said, Wherefore, lord, wherefore
was I borne? or why was not my mothers
wombe then my graue? so had I not sene
the trouble of Iacob, and the grief of the
stocke of Israel.
36 And he said vnto me, Nomber vnto me
the things that are not yet come, or gather me the droppes, that are scatred, or
make me the withered floures grene a-
gaine.
37 Open me the places that are closed, and
bring me forthe the windes, that are shut
vp therein: shewe me the image of a voyce, and then wil I declare thee the thing,
that thou askest and laborest to knowe.
38 And I said, O Lord, Lord, who cā knowe
these things, but he that hathe not his dwel
ling with men?
39 But I that am ignorant, how can I speake of these things, whereof thou askest
me?
40 Then said he vnto me, Like as thou canst
do none of these things, that I haue spoken of, so canst thou not finde out my iudgement, nor the least benefite, that I haue
promised vnto my people.
41 Then I said, Beholde, ô Lord, the last
things are present vnto thee, and what
shal they do that haue bene before me, or
we that be now, or they that shal come after vs?
42 And he said vnto me, I wil compare my
iudgemēt vnto a ring: as there is no slack-
nes of the last, so is there no swiftnes of
the first.
43 Then I answered, and said, Coldest thou
not make at once those ŷ haue bene, those
that are now, & those that shal come, that
thou mightest shewe thy iudgement the
soner?
44 Thē answered he me, The creature, said
he, can not preuent the Creator, nether
can the worlde holde them at once, that
shalbe created therein.
45 And I said, As thou hast taught thy seruant, that thou, which giuest strength *to all*,
hast giuen life at once to all the worke
created by thee, and hast susteined it, so
might it now also conteine all men at
once.
46 And he said vnto me, Aske the wombe
of a woman, and say vnto her, Why must
thou haue time before thou bringest forthe? require her to bring forthe ten at once.

47 And I said,Surely she can not,but by distance of time.
48 Then said he vnto me,So haue I deuided
the nomber of the earth by times when sede is sowen vpon it.
49 For as a yong child begetteth not that
that belongeth to the aged, so haue I ordeined the time which I haue created.
50 ¶I asked againe, and said, Seing thou
hast now shewed me ẏ way, I wil procede
to speake before thee:for our mother,who-
me thou hast tolde me is yong, draweth
she nere vnto age?
51 He answered me,and said,Aske a woman
that traueileth,and she wil tell thee.
52 Say vnto her, Wherefore are not they
(whome thou hast now broght forthe) like those that were before thee, but lesse of
stature?
53 And she shal answer thee,Some were borne in ẏ floure of youth, others were borne
in the time of age, when the wombe
failed.
54 Consider now thy self, how that ye are
lesse of stature, then those that were before you,
55 And so are they that come after you,les-
se then ye,as the creatures which now beginne to be olde, and haue passed ouer the
strength of youth.
56 Then said I, Lord, I beseche thee, if I
haue founde fauour in thy sight,shewe thy
seruant,by whome doest thou gouerne thy
workemanship?

CHAP. VI.

God hathe foresene all things in his secret counsel, and is autor thereof, and hathe created them for his childrẽ. 25 The felicitie of the age to come.

1 AND he said vnto me, In the beginning when the rounde worlde was
made, and before the borders of the worlde were set, and before the windes blewe
one against another:
2 Before the noyce of thundres sounded,
before the bright lighteniġ did shine forthe, before the fundacions of Paradise
were laide:
3 Before the faire floures did appeare,befo-
re the moueable powers were stablished,
before the innumerable armies of Angels
were gathered:
4 Before the heights of the aire were lifted
vp,before ẏ measures of the heauens were
named, before the chimneis in Sion were
hote:
5 Before the present yeres were soght out,
and before the affectiōs of them that now
sinne, were turned away, and they that haue laid vp the treasure of faith, were sealed,
6 Then did I purpose these things, & they
were made by me alone, and by none o-
ther: by me also they shalbe ended,and by
none other.
7 Then answered I, and said, What shalbe
the diuision of times? or when shalbe the
end of the first, and the beginning of it
that followeth?
8 And he said vnto me, From Abraham vnto Isaac, when Iacob and Esau were bor-
ne of him, *Iacobs hand helde first the *Gen.25,26.*
hele of Esau.
9 For Esau is the end of this worlde,and Iacob is the beginning of it that followeth.
10 The hand of man is betwixt the hele
and the hand. Other thing, Esdras, aske
thou not.
11 ¶I answered thẽ,& said,O Lord,Lord,
if I haue founde fauour in thy sight,
12 I beseche thee, make an end to shewe
thy seruāt thy tokens, whereof thou shewedst me parte the last night.
13 So he answered me, and said, Stand vp
vpon thy fete, and heare a mightie sounding voyce.
14 There shal come as an earthquake, but
the place where thou standest,shal not be
moued.
15 And therefore when he speaketh, be not
afraied: for of the end shal be the worde,
& of the fundacion of the earth shal it be
vnderstand.
16 Therefore while one speaketh of thẽ, it
trembleth and is moued: for it knoweth,
that it must be changed at the end.
17 And when I had heard it, I stode vp vpō
my fete,and hearkened,and beholde,there
was a voye that spake,and the sounde of it
was like the sounde of many waters:
18 And it said,Beholde,the daies come,that
I wil come & inquire of them that dwell
vpon the earth,
19 And when I beginne to inquire of them,
who by their vnrighteousnes haue hurt
others,and when the affliction of Sion shal
be fulfilled,
20 And the worlde, that shal vanish away,
shalbe sealed, thẽ wil I shewe these signes:
the bokes shalbe opened before the heauen,and they shal se all it together.
21 And the children of a yere olde shal
speake with their voyces:the womẽ with-
child shal bring forthe vntimelie childrẽ
of thre or foure moneths olde, and they
shal liue that are raised vp.
22 Then suddēly shal the sowen places appeare as the vnsowne, & the ful store houses shal suddenly be founde emptie.
23 And the trūpet shal sounde, and all they
that heare it,shalbe suddenly afraied.
24 At that time shal friends fight with
friends, as with enemies, and the earth
shal feare with them: the springs of the
welles shal stand stil,& in thre houres they
shal not renne.
25 Whosoeuer remaineth from all these
things

things that I haue tolde thee, shal be saued & se my saluacion, & the end of your worlde.
26 And the men that are receiued, shal se it: they that haue not tasted death from their birth, and the heart of the inhabitants shal be changed, and turned to another meaning.
27 For euil shal be put out, and disceate shal be quenched,
28 But faith shal flourish: corruption shalbe ouercome, and the trueth which hathe bene so long without frute, shal come forthe.
29 ¶ And when he talked with me, beholde, I loked a litle vpon him before whome I stode.
30 And these wordes said he vnto me, I am come to shewe thee the time of the night to come.
31 If thou wilt pray againe, and fast seuen daies more, I wil tel thee more things, & greater then these, which I haue heard in the day.
32 For thy voyce is heard before ỹ Highest: surely ỹ mightie hathe sene thy righteous dealing: he hathe sene also thy chastitie, which thou hast kept since thy youth.
33 Therefore hathe he sent me to shewe thee all these things, and to say vnto thee, Be of good comfort, and feare not,
34 And haste not in the vaine consideratiō of the first times, nor make haste to the latter times.
35 And after this I wepte againe and fasted seuē daies in like maner, that I might fulfil the thre wekes, which he had appointed me.
36 And in the eight night was mine heart vexed within me againe, and I began to speake before the moste High.
37 For my spirit was greatly set on fyer, & my soule was in distresse,
38 And I said, ô Lord, thou spakest expresly in the first creation (euen the first day)
and cōmandedst* that the heauen and the Gen.1,1.
earth shulde be made, and the worke followed thy worde.
39 And then was there the spirit, and the darknes was on euerie side with silence: there was no mans voyce as yet created of thee.
40 Then commandedst thou a bright light to come forthe out of thy treasures, that it might giue light to thy worke.
41 Vpon the second day thou createdst the heauenlie ayre, and commandedst it, that, going betwene, it shulde make a diuision betwene the waters, that the one parte might remaine aboue, and the other beneth.
42 Vpon the third day thou commandedst, that ỹ waters shulde be gathered together in the seuēth parte of ỹ earth: six partes didest thou drye, & kept them to the intent that of these there shulde be that shulde serue thee, being sowen of God and tilled.
43 Assone as thy worde went forthe, the worke was incontinently made.
44 For immediatly great and innumerable frute did spring vp, and manie diuerse pleasures for the taste, and floures of vnchangeable colour, and odours of a moste wonderful smel & these things were created the third day.
45 *Vpō the fourth day thou createdst the Gen.1,14.
light of the sunne, and of the moone, and the order of the starres,
46 And gauest them a charge, to do *seruice Gen.1,14. & 15
euen vnto man that was for to be made. deu.4.19.
47 And vpon the fift day thou saidest vnto
the seuenth parte* where the waters were Gen.1,20.
gathered, that it shulde brig forthe beasts, *as* foules and fishes: and it was so.
48 For the dōme waters, and without life broght forthe liuing things at the commādement of God that the nations might praise thy wonderous workes.
49 Then didest thou prepare two liuing
things: the one thou calledst *Behemoth, & *Or, Enoch.
the other thou calledst Leuiathan,
50 And didest separate the one from the other: for the seuēth parte, where the water was gathered, colde not holde them.
51 Vnto Behemoth thou gauest one parte, which was dryed vp the third day, that he shulde dwell in the same parte, wherein are a thousand hilles.
52 But vnto Leuiathan thou gauest ỹ seuēth parte, that is wett, and hast prepared him to deuoure what thou wilt, and when thou wilt.
53 Vpon the sixt day thou gauest commandement vnto the earth, that before thee it shulde bring forthe beasts, catel and creping things.
54 And besides this Adam, whome thou madest lord ouer all the workes which ỹ hast created, of him come we all, and the people also, whome thou hast chosen.
55 All this haue I spokē before thee, ô Lord, because thou hast created the worlde for our sakes.
56 As for the other people, which also come of Adam, thou hast declared them that they are nothing before thee, but be like vnto spitle, and hast compared their riches vnto a drop that falleth from a vessel.
57 And now, ô Lord, beholde these heathen which haue bene reputed as nothing, haue begonne to be lords ouer vs, and to deuoure vs.
58 And we thy people (whome thou hast called the first borne, the onely begotten, and thy feruent louer) are giuen into their hands.
59 If the worlde then be created for our

sakes,why haue we not the inheritãce thereof in possession?or how long shal we suffer these things?

CHAP. VII.

5 Without tribulation none can come to felicitie. 12 God aduertiseth all in time. 28 The coming and death of Christ. 32 The resurrection and last iudgemēt. 43 After the which all corruption shal cease. 48 All fell in Adam. 59 The true life. 62 The mercies and goodnes of God.

1 AND when I had made an end of these wordes,there was sent vnto me an Angel, which had bene sent downe to me the nights afore.
2 And he said vnto me, Vp, Esdras, and heare the wordes that I am come to tell thee.
3 And I said,Speake on,my God.Then said he vnto me, The sea is set in a wyde place,that it might be deepe and great,
4 But presuppose that the entrance thereof were narow,and like the riuers,
5 Who colde go into the sea to loke vpon it, and to rule it? If he went not thorowe the narowe, how colde he come into the broade?
6 There is also another thing: a citie is buylded and set vpon a broade field, and is ful of all good things:
7 The entrance thereof is narrowe and in a dangerous place to fall, that there is fyre at the right hand,and a deepe water at the lefte,
8 And there is but one path betwixt them, euen betwene the fyre and the water, so that there colde but one man go there.
9 If this citie were giuen vnto a man for an inheritance, if he neuer went thorowe the peril before it, how colde he receaue his inheritance?
10 And I said, It is so, Lord. Then said he, So is the portion of Israel.
11 Surely for their sakes haue I made the worlde: and when Adam transgressed my statutes,then came this thing to passe.
12 Then were the entrances of the worlde made narowe, full of sorowe and trauail: they are but fewe and euil, and full of perils,and very peineful.
13 For the entrances of the fore worlde were wyde and sure, and broght immortal frute.
14 If then they that are liuing, labour not to enter by these strait and brittel things, they can not atteine to those things that are hid.
15 Why then disquietest thou thy self,seing thou art corruptible? and why art thou moued,seing thou art mortal?
16 And why hast thou not considered in thy minde the things to come, rather then them that are present?
Deut.8,1. 17 Then said I,O Lord,Lord,* seing thou hast ordeined in thy Law, that the righteous shulde inherite these things, and that the vngodlie shulde perish,
18 Shulde the righteous suffer straitnes in hoping for large things?yet thei that haue liued vngodly and suffered straitnes,shal not se the large things.
19 Then he said vnto me, There is no iudge more iuste then God,and there is none more wise then the moste High.
20 For manie perish in this life, because they despise the Law of God that is appointed.
21 For God hathe diligently admonished suche as came, so oft as they came, what they shulde do to haue life, and what they shulde obserue, to auoid punishment.
22 Neuertheles, they were not obedient vnto him,but spake against him, and imagined vaine things,
23 And deceiued them selues by their wicked dedes, & denied the power of the moste High,and regarded not his waies.
24 But they despised his Law, and refused his promises:they haue vnfaithfully broken his ordinances, and haue not performed his workes.
25 And therefore, Esdras, vnto the emptie are emptie things,& to the ful ful things.
26 Beholde, the time shal come,that these tokens which I haue tolde thee, shal come to passe, and the bride shal appeare, and she shal come forthe,and be sene that now is vnder the earth.
27 And whosoeuer shal escape these euils, he shal se my wonders.
28 For my sonne Iesus shal appeare with those that be with him, and they that remaine, shal reioyce within foure hũdreth yeres.
29 After these same yeres shal my sonne Christ dye,and all men that haue life.
30 And the worlde shalbe turned into the olde silence for seuen dayes,as in the fore iudgements,so that no man shal remaine.
31 But after seuen dayes,the worlde that is yet a slepe, shalbe raised vp: and that shal dye,that is corrupt.
32 Then the earth shal restore those,that haue slept in her,and so shal the dust those that dwell therein in silence,and the secret places shal deliuer the soules that were committed vnto them.
33 And the most High shal appeare vpon the seate of iudgement, and miseries shal vanish away, and long suffring shal haue an end.
34 Iustice onely shal continue: the trueth shal remaine,and faith shal be strong.
35 The worke shal followe, and the rewarde shalbe shewed:the good dedes shalbe of force, and vnrighteousnes shal beare no more rule.

Then

Gen.18,23. exod.32,3. 36 Then said I,* Abraham prayed first for
the Sodomites,and Moyses for the fathers
that sinned in the wildernes,
37 And they that came after him, for Israel
in the time of Achaz,and Samuel,
2.Sam.24,17. 2.Chro.6,14. 38 And * Dauid for the destruction,* and
Salomon for them that came into the
Sanctuarie,
1.King.17,21. & 18,25. 2.king.19,15. 39 *And Elias for those that receiued raine,
and for the dead that he might liue,
40 And Ezechias for the people in the time of Sennacherib, and diuerse others for
manie.
41 Euen so now, seing vice is increased, &
wickednes abundeth, and the righteous
haue prayed for the vngodlie, wherefore shal not the same effect followe also
now?
42 Then he answered me,& said, This pre
sent life is not the end:oft times honour is
reteined in it:therefore haue they prayed
for the weake.
43 But the day of iudgement shal be the
end of this worlde, and the beginning of
the immortalitie to come,wherein all corruption shal cease.
44 Intemperancie shal passe away:infideli-
tie shalbe cut of:righteousnes shal growe
vp,and the veritie shal spring vp.
45 Thẽ shal no mã be able to saue him that
is destroyed, nor oppresse him that hathe
gotten the victorie.
46 I answered then, and said, This is my
first and last saying, that it had bene better not to haue giuen the earth vnto Adã,
or when it was giuen him, to haue kept
him that he shulde not haue sinned.
47 For what profit is it for men in this present life to be in heauines, and after death
to feare punishment?
Rom.5,18. 48 O Adam,what hast thou done?* for in
that that thou hast sinned,thou art not fallen alone, but the fall also redundeth vnto
vs that come of thee.
49 For what profit is it vnto vs, if there be
promised an immortal life, when we do
the workes that bring death?
50 And that an euerlasting hope shulde be
promised vs, seing that we bitide our selues to deadlie vanitie?
51 And that there shulde be appointed vs
dwellings of health and safetie,if we haue
liued wickedly?
52 And that the glorie of the moste High
shulde be kept to defende thẽ which haue
led a pacient life,if we haue walked in the
wicked wayes?
53 And that an eternal Paradise shulde be
shewed, whose frute remaineth incorruptible, wherein is safetie and health,if we
wil not enter into it?
54 (For we haue bene conuersant in vnplea
sant places)
55 And that the faces of them, which haue
absteined, shulde shine more then starres,
if our faces be blacker then darckenes?
56 For while we liued, we did not remẽber
whẽ we did vnrighteously, that we shulde
suffer after death.
57 Then answered he me, and said, This is
the maner of the battel, which man, that
is borne in the earth, shal fight,
58 That if he be ouercome, he shulde suffer
as thou hast said: but if he get the victorie, he shulde receaue the thing that I
said.
59 For this is the life, whereof Moyses spake vnto the people,while he liued,saying,
*Chuse thee life that thou maist liue. Deu.30,19.
60 Neuertheles, they beleued him not,
nether the Prophetes after him, nor me
also which haue said vnto them,
61 That heauines shulde not so be to their
destruction, as ioye shulde come vnto thẽ,
to whome saluacion is persuaded.
62 I answered then and said, I know, Lord,
that the moste High is called merciful, in
that he hathe mercie vpõ them, which are
not yet come to that worlde,
63 And ẏ he hathe pitie on those that walke
in his Law,
64 And that* he is pacient: for he long suf Rom 2,4.
freth those ẏ haue sinned as his creatures,
65 And that he is liberall: for he wil giue as
muche as nedeth,
66 And that he is of great mercie: for he
ouercometh in mercie those that are present,and that are past,and them which are
to come.
67 For if he were not abundant in his mercies,the worlde colde not continue,nor thei
that haue the possession thereof.
68 He pardoneth also: for if he gaue not of
his goodnes that they, which haue done
euil,might be relieued from their wickednes, the ten thousand parte of men shulde
not remaine aliue.
69 And if he,being iudge, forgaue not those that be healed with his worde, and toke
away the multitude of sinnes,
70 There shulde peraduẽture be verie fewe
left in an vnnumerable multitude.

CHAP. VIII.

1 The nomber of the godlie is smale 6 The workes of God are excellent. 20 Esdras prayer for him and for his people. 39 The promes of saluation to the iuste. 55 The destruction of the vniust.

1 AND he answered me, saying, The
most High made this worlde for ma
nie,but the worlde to come for fewe.
2 I wil tel thee a similitude,ô Esdras. As whẽ
thou askest the earth,it shal say vnto thee,
that it giueth muche earthlie matter to
make pottes, but litle dust that golde cometh of, so is it with the worke of this
worlde.

Mat.20,16. 3 *There be manie created, but fewe shalbe
saued.
4 Then answered I, and said, Thē swalowe
vp the wit, ô my soule, and deuoure vnderstanding.
5 For thou hast promised to heare, and thou
wilt prophecie: for thou hast no longer
space, but the life giuen thee.
6 O Lord, if thou suffer not thy seruant,
that we may intreat thee, that thou maist
giue sede vnto our heart, and prepare our
vnderstanding, that there may come frute
of it, whereby euerie one which is corrupt, may liue, who cā set him self for mā?
7 For thou art alone, and we all are one wor
kemanship of thine hands, as thou hast
said.
8 For when the bodie is facioned now in
the wombe, & thou hast giuē it members,
thy creature is preserued by fyre & water,
and the worke, created by thee, doeth suffer nine moneths the creature, which is
facioned in it.
9 But the thing that conteineth, and that
which is cōteined, shal bothe be preserued,
and when time is come, the wombe, being
preserued, deliuereth ȳ things that grewe
in it.
10 For thou hast cōmāded the members,
euē the breasts, to giue milke vnto ȳ frute
appointed to the breasts,
11 That the thing, which is created, may be
nourished for a time, til thou disposest it
to thy mercie.
12 Thou bringest it vp with thy righteousnes, nurturest it in thy Law, & reformest
it with thy iudgement.
13 Thou slayest it as thy creature, & giuest
it life as thy worke.
14 Seing then that thou destroyest him,
which with so great labours is facioned,
it is an easie thing to appoint by thy cōmā
demēt, that the thing also which is made,
might be preserued.
15 Now therefore, ô Lord, I wil speake (as
touching men in general thou shalt rather
prouide) but concerning thy people, for
whose sake I am sorie,
16 And for thine inheritāce for whose cause I mourne: for Israel, for whome I am
woful, and for Iacob, for whose sake I am
grieued.
17 For them wil I pray before thee, aswel
for my self, as for them: for I se our fautes
that dwelt in the land.
18 ¶ But I haue heard the sudden comming
of the iudge, which is to come.
19 Therefore heare my voyce, and vnderstand my wordes, which I wil speake before thee. The beginning of ȳ wordes of
Esdras, before he was taken vp.
20 O Lord, that liuest for euer, which beholdest from aboue that which is aboue,
and in the ayre,
21 Whose throne is inestimable, & his glorie incomprehensible, before whome the
hoste of the Angels stand with trembling,
22 Whose keping is turned in winde and
fyre, whose worde is true, and sayings sted
fast, whose commandement is strong, and
gouernement terrible,
23 Whose loke dryeth vp the depths, and
wrath maketh ȳ mountaines to melt away
as the thing beareth witnes.
24 Heare the prayer of thy seruant, and receiue into thine eares the peticion of thy
creature.
25 For while I liue, I wil speake, and so long
as I haue vnderstanding, I wil answer.
26 Lkoe not vpon the sinnes of thy people,
rather then thy faithful seruants.
27 Haue not respect vnto the wicked dedes
of men, rather then to them that haue thy
testimonies in afflictions.
28 Thinke not vpon those that haue walked fainedly before thee, but remember
them that reuerence thy wil.
29 Let it not be thy wil to destroye them,
which haue liued like beasts, but loke
vpon them that haue clearly taught thy
Law.
30 Take not displeasure with them, which
appeare worse then beasts, but loue them,
that alway put their trust in thy righteousnes and glorie.
31 For we and our fathers haue all the same
sicknes: but because of vs that are sinners,
thou shalt be called merciful.
32 If therefore thou wilt haue mercie vpon
vs, thou shalt be called merciful towardes
vs which haue no workes of righteousnes.
33 For the righteous, which haue laid vp ma
nie good workes, let them receiue the rewarde of their owne dedes.
34 But what is man, that thou shuldest take
displeasure at him? or what is this mortal generacion, that thou shuldest be so
grieued towards it?
35 *For verely there is no man among them 1.King.8.46.
that be borne, but he hathe done wickedly, 2.chro.6,36.
nor anie that doeth confesse thee, which
hathe not done amisse.
36 For in this, ô Lord, thy righteousnes and
thy goodnes shalbe praised, if thou be mer
ciful vnto them, which haue not the substance of good workes.
37 ¶ Then answered he me, and said, Some
things hast thou spoken aright, and according vnto thy wordes it shalbe.
38 For I wil not verely consider the workes of them, before the death, before the
iudgement, before destruction:
39 But *I wil reioyce in the wayes of the Gen.4.14.
righteous, and I wil remember the pilgrimage, the saluation and the rewarde that
they shal haue.

40 Like

40 Like as I haue spoken now, so shal it come to passe.
41 For as the housbād man soweth muche
sede vpon the grounde, & planteth many
trees, & yet alway the thing that is sowen,
cometh not vp in time, nether yet doeth
all that is plāted, take roote: so nether shal
thei all that are broght into the worlde, be
saued.
42 I answered then & said, If I haue founde
grace, let me speake.
43 Like as the housband mans sede perisheth, if it come not vp, and receiue not
raine in due season, or if it be destroyed
with to muche raine,
44 So perisheth man, which is created with
thine hands, & thou art called his patern,
because he is created to thine image, for
whose sake thou hast made all things, and
lickened him vnto the housbandmans
sede.
45 Be not wroth with vs, ô Lord, but spare
thy people & haue mercie vpō thine inheritāce: for thou wilt be merciful vnto thy
creature.
46 Then answered he me, and said, The
things present are for the present, and the
things to come for suche as be to come.
47 For thou art farre of that thou shuldest
loue my creature aboue me: but I haue oft
times drawen nere vnto thee and vnto it,
but neuer to the vnrighteous.
48 In this also thou art maruelous before
the Highest,
49 In that thou hast humbled thy self, as it
becometh thee, and hast not iudged thy
self worthie to boast thy self greatly amōg
the righteous.
50 For many miseries & calamities remaine for them that shal liue in the latter time, because thei shal walke in great pride.
51 But learne thou for thy self, and seke out
the glorie for suche as be like thee.
52 For vnto you is paradise opened: the tre
of life is planted: the time to come is prepared, plenteousnes made ready: the citie
is buylded, and rest is prepared, perfite
goodnes and absolute wisdome.
53 The roote of euil is sealed vp from you:
the weakenes and moth is destroyed from
you, and into hell fleeth corruption to be
forgotten.
54 Sorowes are vanished away, and in the
end is shewed ẏ treasure of immortalitie.
55 Therefore aske thou no more questions
concerning the multitude of them that
perish.
56 For when thei had libertie, thei despised
the most High: they contemned his Law
& forsoke his wayes.
57 Moreouer, they haue troden downe his
righteous,
58 *Saying in their heart, that there was no
God, thogh they knewe that they shulde
dye.
59 For as the thing that I haue spoken of, is
made readie for you: so is thirst and peine
prepared for them: for God wolde not that
man shulde perish:
60 But they, after that they were created,
haue defiled the Name of him that made
them, & are vnthankeful vnto him, which
prepared life for them.
61 Therefore my iudgement is now at hād.
62 These things haue I not shewed vnto
all men, but vnto thee, and to a fewe like
thee: then I answered, and said,
63 Beholde now, ô Lord: thou hast shewed
me the many wonders, which thou art determined to do in ẏ last time, but in what
time, thou hast not shewed me.

*Psal.14,1. & 53,1.

CHAP. IX.

1 All things in this worlde haue a beginning and an end. 10 Torments for the wicked after this life. 15 The nomber of the wicked is more then of the good. 29 The Iewes ingratitude: 36 Therefore they perish. 38 The vision of a woman lamenting.

1 HE answered me then, & said, Measure the time with it self, & when thou
seest that one parte of the tokens come to
passe, which I haue tolde thee before,
2 Then shalt thou vnderstand, that it is the
time wherein the moste High wil begin to
visite the worlde which he made.
3 Therefore whē there shalbe sene an*erth- *Matt.24,7.*
quake in the worlde, and an vproare of the
people,
4 Thē shalt thou vnderstād that the moste
High spake of those things, frō the daies
that were before thee, euen from the beginning.
5 For as all that is made in the worlde, hathe a beginning and an end, and the end
is manifest,
6 So the times also of the most High haue
plaine beginnings in wonders and signes,
and end in effect and miracles.
7 And euerie one that shal escape safe, &
shalbe deliuered by his workes, and by
the faith wherein ye haue beleued,
8 Shalbe preserued from the said perils and
shal se my saluacion in my land, and within my borders: for I haue kept me holy frō
the worlde.
9 Then shal they haue pitie of them selues,
which now haue abused my waies: & thei
that haue cast them out dispitefully, shal
dwell in peines.
10 For suche as in their life haue receiued
benefites, and haue not knowen me,
11 But haue abhorred my Law, while they
were yet in libertie, and when they had
yet leasure of amendement, and wolde not
vnderstand but despised it,
12 They must be taught it after death by
peine.

13 And therefore be thou no more careful,
to knowe how the vngodlie shalbe punished, but inquire how the righteous shalbe saued, and whose the worlde is, and for
whome it is, and when.
14 Then answered I, and said,
15 I haue afore said that which I say now &
wil speake it hereafter, that there be many
mo of them which perish, then of thē that
shalbe * saued, Chap. 8, 3. mat. 20, 16.
16 As the flood is greater then a drop.
17 And he answered me, saying, As the field
is, so is also the sede: as the floures be, so
are the colours also: suche as the workemā
is, suche is the worke: and as the housbād-
man is, so is his housbādrie: for it was the
time of the worlde.
18 Surely whē I prepared the worlde, which
was not yet made for thē to dwell in that
now liue, no man spake against me.
19 For then euerie one obeyed, but now the
maners of them that are created in this
worlde, that is made, are corrupted by a
perpetual sede, & by a Law, whereout thei
can not rid them selues.
20 So I considered the worlde, & beholde,
there was peril, because of the deuises, that
were sprung vp into it.
21 Yet when I sawe it, I spared it greatly,
and haue kept me one grape of the cluster,
and a plant out of a great people.
22 Let therefore ẏ multitude perish, which
are borne in vaine: and let my grape be
kept, and my plant, which I haue dressed
with great labour.
23 ¶ Neuertheles, if thou wilt cease seuen
daies mo (but thou shalt not fast in them,
24 But shalt go into a faire field, where no
house is buylded, & shalt eat onely of the
floures of the field, and eat no flesh, nor
drinke wine, but the floures onely,
25 And pray vnto ẏ moste High continually) then wil I come, and talke with thee.
26 So I went my waye, as he had commanded me, into the field, which is called Ar-
dath, & there I sate among the floures, &
did eat of the herbes of the field, and the
meat of the same satisfied me.
27 And after seuen dayes, as I sate vpō the
grasse, and mine heart was vexed within
me, as afore,
28 I opened my mouth, and began to talke
before the moste High, and to say,
29 O Lord, when thou woldest shewe thy
self vnto vs, * thou declaredst thy self vn- Exod. 19, 9. & 24, 3. deut. 4, 12.
to our fathers in the wildernes, in a place
where no man dwelleth, in a baren place,
when they came out of Egypt,
30 And expressely spakest vnto thē, saying,
Heare me, ô Israel, and marke my wordes,
thou sede of Iacob.
31 For beholde, I sawe my Law in you, that
it may bring forthe frute in you, and that
ye may be honored by it for euer.
32 But our fathers, which receiued the Law,
kept it not, nether obserued thine ordinances, nether did the frute of the Law appeare, nether colde it, for it was thine.
33 * For they that receiued it, perished be- Exod. 32, 28.
cause they kept not the thing ẏ was sowen
in them.
34 And lo, it is a custome when the grounde
receiueth sede, or the sea a ship, or a vessel
meat and drinke, if that perish wherein a
thing is sowē, or wherein any thing is put,
35 Likewise the thing that is sowen, or is
put therein, and the things that are receiued, must perish: so the things that are receiued, do not remaine with vs: but in vs it
cometh not so to passe.
36 For we that haue receiued the Law, perish in sinne, and our heart also which receiued it.
37 But the Law perisheth not, but remaineth
in his force.
38 ¶ And when I spake these things in mine
heart, I loked about me, & vpon the right
side * I sawe a woman, which mourned so- Chap. 10, 44.
re, and lamented with a loude voyce, and
was grieued in heart, and rent her clothes,
and she had ashes vpon her head.
39 Then I left my thoghts, wherein I was
occupied, and turned me vnto her,
40 And said vnto her, wherefore wepest
thou? why art thou so sory in minde?
41 And she said vnto me, Syr, let me alone,
that I may bewaile my self, and increase
sorowe: for I am sore vexed in my minde,
and broght verie lowe.
42 Then I said vnto her, What aileth thee?
tel me.
43 And she said vnto me, I thy seruant haue
bene baren, & haue had no childe, hauing
an housband thirtie yeres.
44 And euery houre, & euery day these thirtie yeres I pray to the moste High day &
night.
45 And after thirtie yeres God heard me
thine handmaid, & loked vpō my miserie,
cōsidered my trouble, & gaue me a sonne,
& I was glad of him: so was mine housbād
also, and all they of my countrey, and we
gaue great honour vnto the Almightie.
46 And I nourished him with great trauail.
47 So when he grewe vp, and came to take
a wife, I made a feast.

CHAP. X

Esdras and the woman that appeareth vnto him, commune together.

1 BVt when my sonne went into his
chamber, he fell downe, and dyed.
2 Then we all ouerthrewe the lights, & all
my neighbours rose vp to comfort me: so
I rested vntil the seconde day at night.
3 And when thei had all left of to comfort
me, that I shulde be quiet, thē I rose vp by
night,

night,&fled,and am come into this field as
thou seest,
4 And am not purposed to returne into the
citie,but to remaine here,and nether to eat
nor drinke, but continually to mourne &
fast,vntil I dye.
5 Then left I my purpose wherein I was,
and spake to her angerly,and said,
6 Thou foolish womā aboue all other,seest
thou not our heauines, and what cometh
vnto vs?
7 For Sion our mother is all woful and is
sore afflicted, and mourneth extremely.
8 Seing we be all now in heauines, and
make our mone(for we be all sorowful) art
thou sorie for one sonne?
9 Demande the earth,and she shal tell thee
that it is she which oght to mourne for
the fall of so manie that growe vpon her.
10 For frō the beginning all men are borne
of her,and other shal come,and beholde,
they walke almoste all into destruction, &
the multitude of them shalbe destroyed.
11 Who shulde then rather mourne,she
that hathe lost so great a multitude, or
thou which art sorie but for one?
12 But if thou woldest say vnto me, My
mourning is not like the mourning of the
earth(for I haue lost the frute of my wōbe,which I broght forthe with heauines,&
bare with sorowes,
13 But the earth is according to the maner
of the earth,and the present multitude returneth into her as it came)
14 Then say I vnto thee, As thou hast borne with trauail, so the earth also from the
beginning giueth her frute vnto man,euen
to him that labored her.
15 Now therefore withholde thy sorow in
thy self, and beare constantly that which
cometh vnto thee.
16 For if thou allowest Gods purpose, and
receiuest his counsel in time, thou shalt be
commended therein.
17 Go thy way then into the citie to thine
housband.
18 ¶Then she said vnto me,I wil not,I wil
not go into the citie,but here wil I dye.
19 So I continued to speake more with her,
and said,
20 Do not so, but be coūseled: for how manie falles hathe Sion? Be of good comfort
because of the sorowe of Ierusalem.
21 For thou seest ỹ our Sanctuarie is layed
waste: our altar is broken downe: our Tēple is destroyed.
22 Our psalterion fainteth, and the song
ceaseth, and our mirth is vanished away,
and the light of our candelsticke is quenched,and the Arke of our coucnant is takē
away,and our holie things are defiled,and
the Name that is called vpō ouer vs,is almoste dishonored, and our children are
put to shame,and our Priests are burnt,&
our Leuites are caryed into captiuitie,and
our virgines are defiled,and our wiues rauished,and our righteous men spoyled, &
our children destroyed,and our yong men
are broght in bondage,and our strong mē
are become weake,
23 And,which is the greatest of all,Sion the
seale hathe lost her worship: for she is deliuered into the hands of them that hate vs.
24 And therefore shake of thy great heauines, and put away the multitude of sorowes,that the Almightie may be merciful
vnto thee, and that the moste High may
giue thee rest and ease from thy labour.
25 And when I was talking with her,her face and beautie shined suddenly, and her
countenance was bright, so that I was a-
frayed of her & mused what it might be.
26 And beholde,immediatly she cast out a
great voyce, very fearful, so ỹ the earth
shoke at the noyce of the woman.
27 And I loked, and beholde,the woman
appeared vnto me nomore: but there was a
citie buylded, and a place was shewed frō
the grounde and fundacion. Then was
I afrayed,and cryed with a loude voyce,
and said,
28 Where is Vriel the Angel * which came Chap.4.1.
to me at the first? for he hathe caused me
to come into manie and depe considera-
ciōs,and mine end is turned into corruption,and my prayer to rebuke.
29 And as I was speaking these wordes, beholde, he came vnto me, and loked vpon
me.
30 And lo,I laye as one dead, and mine vnderstanding was altered,and he toke me
by the right hand and comforted me, and
set me vpon my feete, and said vnto me,
31 What aileth thee? and why is thine vnderstanding vexed? and the vnderstanding of thine heart? & wherefore art thou
sorie?
32 And I said, Because thou hast forsaken
me,and I haue done* according vnto thy Chap.5.20.
wordes: I went into the field,and there haue I sene things, & se that I am not able
to expresse.
33 Then said he vnto me, Stand vp manly,
and I wil giue thee exhortacion.
34 Then said I, Speake vnto me, my lord,
and forsake me not, lest I dye through
rashnes.
35 For I haue sene that I knewe not, and
heare that I do not knowe.
36 Or is mine vnderstanding disceiued, or
doeth my minde,being hautie,erre?
37 Now therefore I beseche thee that thou
wilt shewe thy seruant of this wondre.
38 Thē he answered me,and said,Heare me,
and I wil informe thee, & tel thee where-

fore thou art afrayed: for the moste High
hathe reueiled manie secret things vnto
thee.
39 He hath sene thy good purpose, that thou
art sorie continually for thy people, and
makest great lamentacion for Sion.
40 This therefore is the vnderstanding of
the visiõ, which appeared vnto thee a litle
while ago.
41 Thou sawest a womã mourning, & thou
beganest to comfort her:
42 But now seest thou the lickenes of the
woman no more, but there appeared vnto
thee a citie buylded.
43 And where as she tolde thee of the death
of her sonne, this is the solution,
44 This woman, which thou sawest, she is
Sion: and where as she tolde thee (euen she
which thou seest now as a citie buylded)
45 And as touching that she said vnto thee,
that she was baren thirtie yeres, this was
concerning that, there was euen thirtie
yeres wherein there was no offring offred
in her.
46 But after thirtie yeres, Salomon buylt
the citie, and offred offrings: then bare the
baren a sonne.
47 And where as she tolde thee, that she
nourished him with labour, that was the
inhabiting of Ierusalem.
48 But where as she tolde thee that her sonne, as his chance was, dyed when she came
into her chamber, that is the fall that is come to Ierusalem.
49 And when thou sawest her like one that
mourned for her sonne, thou begãnest to
cõfort her: of these things which haue chã
ced these are to be opened vnto thee.
50 For now the moste High seeth, that thou
art sorie in thy mind, & because thou suffrest with all thine heart for her, he shewed
thee the clerenes of her glorie, and the fai-
renes of her beautie.
51 And therefore I bad thee remaine in the
field where no house was buylt.
52 For I knewe that the moste High wolde
shewe these things vnto thee.
53 Therefore I commãded thee to go into
ӯ field, where no fundaciõ nor buylding is.
54 For the worke of mans buylding can not
stand in that place where the citie of the
moste High shulde be shewed.
55 And therefore feare not, nether let thine
heart be afrayed, but go in, and se the beau
tie & greatnes of the buylding as muche
as thou art able to se with thine eyes.
56 And after this shalt thou heare, as muche
as thine eares may comprehende.
57 For thou art blessed aboue manie, & art
called with ӯ moste High among the few.
58 But to morow at night thou shalt remaine here,
59 And the moste High shal shewe thee vi-
siõs of high things, which the moste High
wil do vnto them that dwell vpõ earth, in
the last dayes. So I slept the same night &
another, as he had commanded me.

CHAP. XI.

1 The vision of an egle coming forthe of the sea, and of her feathers. 37 Of a lyon coming out of the forest.

1 THen saw I a dreame, & beholde, there
came vp from the sea an egle, which
had twelue feathered wings & thre heads.
2 And I sawe and beholde, she spred her
wings ouer all the earth, & all the windes
of the ayre blewe on her, and gathered
them selues.
3 And I beholde, & out of her feathers grew
out other contrarie feathers, and they became litle feathers and smale.
4 But her heads remained stil, & the head
in the middes was greater then the other
heads, yet rested it with them.
5 Moreouer, I sawe that the egle flewe with
his feathers and reigned vpõ earth & ouer
them that dwelt therein.
6 And I sawe that all things vnder heauen
were subiect vnto her, and no man spake
against her, no not one creature vpõ earth.
7 I sawe also that the egle stode vp vpon
her clawes, & spake to her feathers, saying,
8 Watch not all together: slepe euerie one
in his owne place, and watch by course.
9 But let the heads be preserued for the last.
10 Neuertheles, I sawe that ӯ voice went
not out of her heads, but from the middes
of her bodie.
11 Then I nombred her contrarie feathers,
and beholde, there were eight of them.
12 And I loked, and beholde vpon the right
side there arose one feather, and reigned
ouer all the earth.
13 And when it had reigned, the end of it
came, and the place thereof appeared no
more. So the next stode vp, and reigned: it
continued a long time.
14 And when it had reigned, the end of it
came also, and as the first, so it appeared
no more.
15 Then there came a voyce vnto it, and
said,
16 Heare thou that hast kept the earth so
long: this I say vnto thee, before thou be-
ginnest to appeare no more,
17 There shal none after thee atteine vnto
thy time, nether to the halfe thereof.
18 Then arose the third and reigned as the
other afore, and it appeared no more also.
19 So came it to all ӯ others one after another, so that euerie one reigned, and then
appeared no more.
20 Then I loked, and beholde in processe of
time ӯ feathers that followed, stode vp on
the right side, that they might rule also, &
some of thẽ ruled, but within a while they
appeared no more.

21 For

21 For some of thẽ were set vp, but ruled not.
22 After this I loked & beholde, ẏ twelue fea
thers appeared nomore, nor ẏ two wings.
23 And there was no more vpon the egles
bodie, but two heads that rested and six
wings.
24 Then sawe I also that two wings deuided them selues from the six, and remained vnder the head, that was vpõ the right
side: for the foure cõtinued in their place.
25 So I loked, & beholde, the vnderwings
thoght to set vp them selues, and to haue
the rule.
26 Then was there one set vp, but shortly
it appeared no more.
27 And the second were soner gone then
the first.
28 Thẽ I behelde, & lo, the two that remained, thoght also in them selues to reigne.
29 And whẽ they so thoght, beholde, there
awaked one of the heads that were at rest,
which was in the middes: for that was grea
ter then the two.
30 And then I sawe, that the two heads were
ioyned therewith.
31 And beholde, the head was turned with
them, that were with it, and did eat vp the
two vnderwings that wolde haue reigned.
32 But this head put the whole earth in feare and bare rule in it, ouer all those that
dwelt vpon earth with muche labour, & it
had the gouernãce of the worlde, more thẽ
all the wings that had bene.
33 After this I loked, and beholde, the head
that was in the middes, suddenly appeared
no more, as did the wings.
34 But the two heads remained, which also ruled likewise vpõ earth, and ouer those
that dwelt therein.
35 And I behelde, and lo the head vpon the
right side deuoured that was vpon the
left side.
36 ¶ Then I heard a voyce which said vnto
me, Loke before thee, and consider ẏ thing
that thou seest.
37 So I sawe, and beholde as it were a lyon
that roareth, renning hastely out of the
wood: and I sawe that he sent out a mans
voyce vnto the egle, and spake, and said,
38 Heare thou, I wil talke with thee, & the
moste High shal say vnto thee,
39 Art not thou that that of the foure beasts
remainest, whome I made to reigne in my
worlde, that by them the end of times
might come,
40 And the fourth is come, and hathe ouercome all the beasts that were past, & hathe
power ouer the worlde with great fearful
nes, and ouer the whole compasse of the
earth with moste wicked oppresion, and
that dwelleth so long time in all ẏ worlde
with disceite?
41 For ẏͧ hast not iudged the earth ẇ trueth.
42 Seing thou hast troubled the meke, thou
hast hurte the peaceable, and thou hast loued lyers, and destroied the dwellings of
them that broght forthe frute, & hast cast
downe the walles of suche as did thee no
harme,
43 Therefore is thy wrongful dealing come vp vnto the moste High, and thy pride vnto the Mightie.
44 The moste High also hathe loked vpon
the proude times, & beholde, they are ended, and their abominacions are fulfilled.
45 Therefore appeare no more, thou egle,
nor thine horrible wings, nor thy wicked
feathers, nor thy malicious heads, and thy
wicked clawes, nor all thy vaine bodie,
46 That all the earth may be refreshed, &
come againe, as one deliuered from thy
violence, & that she may hope for the iudgement and mercie of him that made her.

CHAP. XII.

The declaration of the former visions.

1 AND when the lion spake these wordes to the egle, I sawe,
2 And beholde, the head that had the vpper hand, appeared no more, nether did
the foure wings appeare any more, that
came to it, and set vp them selues to reigne, whose kingdome was smale and ful of
vproares.
3 And I sawe, and beholde, they appeared
no more, and the whole bodie of the egle
was burnt, so that the earth was in great
feare. Then I awaked out of the trouble
and trance of my minde, and frõ the great
feare, and said vnto my spirit,
4 Lo, this hast thou done vnto me in that
thou searchest out the waies of the moste
High.
5 Lo, yet am I wearie in my minde, and very weake in my spirit, and litle strength
is there in me, for the great feare that I receiued this night.
6 Therefore now I wil beseche the moste
High that he wil cõfort me vnto the end.
7 And I said, O Lord, Lord, if I haue foũde
grace before thy sight, & if I am iustified
with thee before many other, and if my
praier in dede be come vp before thy face,
8 Comfort me, and shewe me thy seruant
the interpretacion and difference of this
horrible sight, that thou maist perfectly
comforte my soule,
9 Seing thou hast iudged me worthie to
shewe me the last times.
10 ¶ Then he said vnto me, This is the interpretacion of this vision,
11 The egle, whome thou sawest come vp
from the sea, is the * kingdome which was
sene in the vision of thy brother Daniel. Dan. 7, 7.
12 But it was not expounded vnto him: therefore now I declare it vnto thee.
13 Beholde, the daies come, that there shal

rise vp a kingdome vpon the earth, and it
shalbe feared aboue all kingdomes that
were before it.
14 In it shal twelue Kings reigne one after
another,
15 Whereof the seconde shal beginne to
reigne and shal haue more time then the
twelue.
16 And this do the twelue wings signifie,
which thou sawest.
17 As for the voice that thou heardest speake,
and that thou sawest not go out from
the heads, but from the middes of the bodie
thereof, this is the interpretacion,
18 That after the time of that kingdome
there shal arise great strife, & it shalbe in
danger to fall, but it shal not then fall, but
shalbe restored againe to his beginning.
19 Cõcerning the eight vnderwings, which
thou sawest hang vnto her wings, this is
the interpretacion,
20 In him shal arise eight Kings, whose time
shal be but smale, and their yeres swift,
and two of them shal perish.
21 But when the midde time cometh, there
shalbe foure kept a time, whiles his time
beginneth to come, that it maye be ended,
but two shalbe kept vnto the end.
22 And where as thou sawest thre heads resting,
this is the interpretacion,
23 In his last dayes shal ẏ moste High raise
vp thre kingdomes, and shal call againe
manie things into thẽ, and they shal haue
the dominion of the earth,
24 And of those that dwell therein, with
muche grief aboue all those that were before
them: therefore are they called the
heads of the egle.
25 For they shal accomplish his wickednes,
and shal finish his last end.
26 And where as thou sawest that the great
head appeared no more, it signifieth that
one of them shal dye vpon his bed, and yet
with peine.
27 For the two that remaine, the sworde shal
deuoure them.
28 For the sworde of the one shal deuoure
the other: but at the last, shal he fall by the
sworde him self.
29 And where as ẏ sawest two vnderwings,
that went of towarde the head, which was
on the right side, this is the interpretaciõ,
30 These are thei whome ẏ moste High hathe
preserued for their end, whose kingdome
is litle, and ful of trouble as thou sawest.
31 And the lyon whome thou sawest rising
vp out of the wood and roaring, and speaking
vnto the egle, and rebuking her for
her vnrighteousnes with all the wordes
that thou hast heard,
32 This is the winde which the moste High
hathe kept for them, and for their wickednes
vnto the end, & he shal reproue them,
and cast before them their spoiles.
33 For he shal set them aliue in the iudgement,
and shal rebuke them and correct
them.
34 For he wil deliuer the residue of my people
by affliction, which are preserued vpon
my borders, and he shal make them ioyful,
vntil the comming of the day of iudgement,
whereof I haue spoken vnto thee
from the beginning.
35 This is the dreame that thou sawest, and
these are the interpretacions.
36 Thou onely hast bene mete to know this
secret of the moste High.
37 Therefore write all these things that
thou hast sene, in a boke and hide them,
38 And teache them the wise of the people,
whose hearts thou knowest may comprehende
and kepe these secrets.
39 But waite thou here yet seuen daies mo,
that it may be shewed thee whatsoeuer it
pleaseth the moste High to declare vnto
thee: and with that he went his way.
40 And when all the people perceiued, that
the seuen daies were past, and I not come
againe into the citie, they gathered them
all together, from the least vnto the moste,
and came vnto me, and spake vnto me,
saying,
41 What haue we offended thee? or what
euil haue we done against thee, that thou
forsakest vs, and sittest in this place?
42 For of all the people thou onely art left
vs as a grape of the vine, and as a candle in
a darke place, & as an hauen or shippe preserued
from the tempest.
43 Are not the euils which are come vnto
vs, sufficient?
44 If thou then forsake vs, how muche better
had it bene for vs, that we had bene
burnt also as Sion was burnt?
45 For we are no better then they that dyed
there: and they wept with a loude voyce.
Then answered I them, and said,
46 Be of good comfort, ô Israel, and be not
heauie, thou house of Iacob.
47 For the moste High hathe you in remẽbrãce,
& the Almightie hathe not forgotten
you in temptacion.
48 As for me I haue not forsakẽ you, nether
am I departed from you, but am come into
this place to praye for the desolation of
Sion, that I might seke mercie for the low
estate of your Sanctuarie.
49 And now go your way home euerie mã,
and after these daies wil I come vnto you.
50 So the people went their way into the
citie, as I commanded them:
51 But I remained stil in the field seuen
daies, as he had commanded me, and did
eat onely of the floures of the field, & had
my meat of the herbes in those daies.

CHAP.

CHAP. XIII.

The vision of a winde coming forthe of the sea. 3 Which became a man. 5 His propertie & power against his enemies. 21 The declaration of this vision.

1 AND after the seuen daies I dreamed
a dreame by night.
2 And beholde, there arose a winde frō the
sea, and it moued all the waues thereof.
3 And I loked, & beholde, there was a mightie man with the thousands of heauen: and
when he turned his countenāce to loke, all
the things trembled that were sene vnder
him.
4 And whē the voyce wēt out of his mouth,
all they burned that heard his voyce, as the
earth faileth when it feeleth the fyre.
5 After these things I sawe, and beholde,
there was gathered together a multitude
of men out of nōber, frō the foure windes
of the heauē, to fight against the man that
came out from the sea.
6 And I loked, and beholde, he graued him
self a great mountaine, and flewe vp vpon it.
7 But I wolde haue sene the countrei or
place whereout the hil was grauen, and I
colde not.
8 I sawe after these things, and beholde, all
they which came to fight against him, were
sore afraied, and yet they durst fight.
9 Neuertheles, when he sawe the fiercenes
of the multitude that came, he lifted not
vp his hand: for he helde no sworde nor a-
ny instrument of warre,
10 But onely, as I sawe, he sent out of his
mouth, as it had bene a blaste of fyre, and
out of his lippes the winde of the flame,
and out of his tongue he cast out sparkes
and stormes.
11 And they were all mixt together, *euen*
this blast of fyre, the winde of the flame,
and the great storme, and fell with violēce vpon the multitude, which was prepared to fight, and burnt them vp all, so that
of the innumerable multitude there was
nothing sene, but onely dust, and smel of
smoke. When I sawe this, I was afraied.
12 ¶ Afterwarde sawe I the same man come
downe from the mountaine, and calling
vnto him another peaceable multitude.
13 And there came many vnto him, some
with ioyful countenāce, & some with sad:
some of thē were bound, and some broght
of them that were offred: and I was sicke thorow great feare, and awaked, and
said,
14 Thou hast shewed thy seruāt these wonders from the beginning, and hast counted me worthie to receiue my praier.
15 Shewe me now therefore the interpretacion of this dreame.
16 For thus I consider in mine vnderstanding, wo vnto them ẏ shalbe left in those
daies, and muche more wo vnto them that
are not left behinde.
17 For they that were not left, were in heauines.
18 Now vnderstand I the things that are
laid vp in the latter daies, which shal come bothe vnto them, and to those that are
left behinde.
19 Therefore are they come into great perils and many necessities, as these dreames
declare.
20 Yet is it easier, that he that is in danger,
shulde fall into these, & forese the things
to come hereafter, then to passe away as a
cloude out of the worlde.
21 ¶ Then answered he me, & said, The interpretaciō of the vision wil I shewe thee,
and I wil open to thee the thing that thou
hast required.
22 Where as thou hast spoken of them that
are left behinde, this is the interpretacion,
23 He that shal beare the danger in that
time, he shal kepe him self. They that
be fallen into danger, are suche as haue
workes and faith towarde the moste
Mightie.
24 Knowe therefore, that they which be
left behinde, are more blessed thē thei that
be dead.
25 These are the meanings of the vision,
Where as thou sawest a man comming
vp from the middes of the sea,
26 The same is he whome the moste High
hathe kept a great season, who by his owne
self shal deliuer his creature, & he shal order them that are left behinde.
27 ¶ And where as thou sawest, that out of
his mouth there came as a blast with fyre
and storme,
28 And ẏ he nether helde sworde nor weapon, but that by his fiercenes he destroied
the whole multitude, that came to fight a-
gainst him, this is the interpretacion,
29 Beholde, the daies come that the moste
High wil beginne to deliuer thē that are
vpon the earth:
30 And he shal astonish the hearts of them
that dwell vpon the earth:
31 And one shal prepare to fight against a-
nother, citie against citie, & place against
place, *and nation against nation, & real- *Mat. 24,7.*
me against realme.
32 When this commeth to passe, then shal
the tokens come, that I shewed thee before, & then shal my Sonne be reueiled, whome thou sawest go vp as a man.
33 And when all the people heare his voyce, euerie mā shal in their owne land leaue
the battel that they haue one against a-
nother.
34 And an innumerable multitude shalbe
gathered as one, as they that be willing to
come, and to fight against him.

35 But he shal stand vpō the toppe of mount
Sion.
36 And Sion shal come, and shalbe shewed
to all, being prepared and buylded, as thou
sawest the hil grauen forthe without any
hands.
37 And this my Sonne shal rebuke the wicked inuentions of those nacions, which
for their wicked life are fallen into the
tempest,
38 And into torments like to flame, whereby they shalbe tormented: and without a-
ny labour wil he destroy them, euen by the
Law, which is compared vnto the fyre.
39 And where as thou sawest that he gathered another peaceable people vnto him,
40 Those are the ten tribes which were caryed away captiues out of their owne lād,
* in the time of Oseas the King, whome 2.King.17.3.
Salmanasar the King of the Assyrians toke captiue, and caryed them beyonde the
riuer: so were they broght into another
land.
41 But they toke this counsel to thē selues,
that they wolde leaue the multitude of the
heathen, and go forthe into a further coun
trey, where neuer mankinde dwelt,
42 That they might there kepe their statutes, which they neuer kept in their owne
land.
43 And they entred in at the narowe passages of the riuer Euphrates.
44 For the moste High then shewed thē sig-
nes, * and stayed the springs of the flood Exod.14,28. iof.3,15.
til they were passed ouer.
45 For thorow ẏ countrey there was a great
iourney, euen of a yere and an halfe, and
the same region is called 'Arsareth. 'Or, Ararath.
46 Then dwelt they there vntil the latter
time: and when they come forthe againe,
47 The moste High shal holde stil the
springs of the riuer againe, that they may
go thorow: therefore sawest thou the multitude peaceable.
48 But thei that be left behinde of thy people, are those that be founde within my
borders.
49 Now when he destroieth the multitude
of the nacions that are gathered together,
he shal defende the people that remaine,
50 And then shal he shewe great wonders
vnto them.
51 Then said I, O Lord, Lord, shewe mé
this, wherefore haue I sene the man comming vp from the middes of the sea?
52 And he said vnto me, As thou canst nether seke out, nor knowe these things, that
are in the deepe of the sea, so can no man
vpon earth se my Sonne, or those that be
with him, but in the time of that day.
53 This is the interpretation of the dreame which thou sawest, and whereby thou
onely art lightened.
54 For thou hast forsaken thine owne Law,
and applied thy diligence vnto mine, and
soght it.
55 Thy life hast thou ordered in wisdome,
& hast called vnderstanding thy mother.
56 Therefore haue I shewed thee ẏ rewardes with the moste High: and after thre
other daies I wil speake other things vnto
thee, and wil declare the great and wonderous things.
57 Then went I forthe vnto the field, glorifying and praising the moste High for
the wonders which he did in time,
58 Which he gouerneth, and suche things
as come in their seasons: and there I sate
thre dayes.

CHAP. XIIII.

3 How God appeared to Moses in the bush. 10 All things decline to age. 15 The latter times worse then the former. 29 The ingratitude of Israel. 35 The resurrection and iudgement.

1 VPon the thirde day I sate vnder an
oke, and beholde, there came forthe
a voyce vnto me out of the bush, & said,
Esdras, Esdras?
2 And I said, Here am I, Lord, & stode vp
vpon my fete.
3 Then said he vnto me, * In the bush I re Exo.3,8.
ueiled my self, and spake vnto Moyses, whē
my people serued in Egypt:
4 And I sent him, and led my people out of
Egypt, and broght him vpon the mount
Sinai, & I helde him with me a lōg season,
5 And I tolde him many wōders, & shewed
him the secrets of the times and the end,
and commanded him, saying,
6 These wordes shalt thou declare, & these shalt thou hide.
7 And now I say vnto thee, that thou lay
vp in thine heart the signes that I haue
shewed, and the dreames that thou hast sene, & the interpretacions which thou hast
heard.
8 For thou shalt be taken away from all, and
thou shalt remaine hence forthe with my
counsel, & with suche as be like thee, vntil
the times be ended.
9 For the worlde hathe lost his youth, & the
times beginne to waxe olde.
10 For the worlde is deuided into twelue
partes, & ten partes of it are gone alreadie
and halfe of the tenth parte.
11 And there remaineth that which is after
the halfe of the tenth parte.
12 Therefore set thine house in order, and
reforme thy people, and comfort suche of
them as be in trouble, and now renounce
the corruption.
13 Let go from thee mortal thoghts: cast a-
way from thee the burdens of men, & put
of now the weake nature,
14 And set aside thy moste grieuous thoghts,
and haste thee to departe from these times.

15 For

15 For greater euils then those, which thou
hast sene now, shal thei commit.
16 For the weaker that the worlde is by reason of age, the more shal the euils be increased vpon them that dwell therein.
17 For the trueth is fled farre away, & lies
are at hand: for now hasteth the vision to
come, that thou hast sene.
18 ¶ Then answered I, and said before thee,
19 Beholde, ô Lord, I wil go as thou hast
commanded me, and reforme the people,
which are present: but they that shal be
borne afterwarde, who shal admonish thẽ?
20 Thus the worlde is set in darkenes, and
they that dwell therein, are without light.
21 For thy Law is burnt, therefore no man
knoweth the things that are done of thee,
or the workes that shalbe done.
22 But if I haue founde grace before thee,
send the holie Gost into me, & I wil write
all that hathe bene done in the worlde since the beginning, which was writen in thy
Law, that men may finde the path, & that
thei which wil liue in the latter daies, may
liue.
23 And he answered me, saying, Go, and gather the people, and say vnto them, that
thei seke thee not for fortie daies,
24 But prepare thee many boxe tables, and
take with thee these fiue, Sarea, Dabria, Se
lemia, Ecanus, and Asiel, which are readie
to write swiftly,
25 And come hether, & I wil light a candle
of vnderstãding in thine heart, which shal
not be put out til the things be performed
which thou shalt beginne to write.
26 And thẽ shalt thou declare some things
openly vnto the perfite men, and some
things shalt thou shewe secretly vnto the
wise: to morowe this houre shalt thou beginne to write.
27 Then went I forthe, as he commanded
me, and gathered all the people together,
and said,
28 Heare these wordes, ô Israel,
Gen 47.4. 29 *Our fathers at ỳ beginning were strangers in Egypt, from whence they were deliuered,
Act.7.53. 30 And receiued the Law of life, *which
they kept not, which ye also haue trãsgressed after them.
31 Then was the land, euen the lãd of Sion
parted amõg you by lot: but your fathers
and ye also haue done vnrighteously, and
haue not kept the wayes, which the moste
High commanded you.
32 And for so muche as he is a righteous
Iudge, he toke from you in time the thing
that he had giuen you.
33 And now are ye here, and your brethren
among you.
34 Therefore if so be that ye wil subdue
your owne vnderstanding, and reforme
your heart, ye shalbe kept aliue, and after
death shal ye obteine mercie.
35 For after death shal the iudgemẽt come,
when we shal liue againe: & then shal the
names of the righteous be manifest, and
the workes of the vngodlie shalbe declared.
36 Let no man therefore come now vnto
me, nor seke me these fortie daies.
37 So I toke the fiue men, as he commanded me, and we went into the field, and remained there.
38 The next daye beholde, a voyce called
me, saying, Esdras, * open thy mouth, and Ezech.3.2.
drinke that I giue thee to drinke.
39 Then opened I my mouth, and beholde,
he reached me a full cuppe, which was full
as it were with water: but the colour of it
was like fyre.
40 And I toke it and dranke, and when I
had dronke it, mine heart had vnderstanding and wisdome grewe in my brest: for
my spirit was strẽgthened in memorie.
41 And my mouth was opened, and shut no
more.
42 The moste High gaue vnderstanding
vnto the fiue men, that they wrote the hie
things of the night, which they vnderstode not.
43 But in the night they did eat bread, but
I spake by day, & helde not my tongue by
night.
44 In fortie daies, they wrote two hundreth and foure bokes.
45 And when the fortie dayes were fulfilled, the moste High spake, saying, The
first that thou hast writen, publish openly,
ỳ the worthie and vnworthie may read it.
46 But kepe the seuentie last, that thou
maiest giue them to the wise among thy
people.
47 For in them is the veine of vnderstanding, and the fountaine of wisdome, and
the riuer of knowledge: and I did so.

CHAP. XV.

1 The prophecie of Esdras is certeine. 5 The euils that shal come on the worlde. 9 The Lord wil aduenge the innocent blood. 12 Egypt shal lament. 16 Sedicion. 20 And punishment vpon the Kings of the earth. 24 Cursed are they that sinne. 29 Troubles & warres vpon the whole earth. 53 God is the reuenger of his elect.

1 Beholde, speake thou in the eares of
my people the wordes of prophecie,
which I wil put in thy mouth, saith the
Lord:
2 And cause them to be writen in a lettre:
for they are faithful and true.
3 Feare not the imaginacions against thee:
let not the vnfaithfulnes of the speakers
trouble thee, that spake against thee.
4 For euery vnfaithful shal dye in his vnfaithfulnes.
5 Beholde, saith the Lord, I wil bring pla-

gues vpō all the worlde, the sworde, famine, death and destruction:
6 Because that iniquitie hathe fully polluted all the earth, and their wicked workes are fulfilled.
7 Therefore, saith the Lord, I wil holde my tongue no more for their wickednes, (they do vngodlie) nether wil I suffer thē in the things, that they do wickedly.
Reuel.6,10. & 19,2. 8 Beholde, *the innocent and righteous blood cryeth vnto me, and the soules of the iust crye continually.
9 I wil surely auenge them, saith the Lord, and receiue vnto me all ẏ innocent blood from among them.
10 Beholde, my people is led as a flocke to the slaughter: I wil not suffer them now to dwell in the land of Egypt,
11 But I wil bring them out with a mightie hand, and a stretched out arme, & smite it with plagues as afore, & wil destroie all the land thereof.
12 Egypt shal mourne, and the fundacions thereof shalbe smitten with the plague and punishment, that God shal bring vpon it.
13 The plowemē that till the grounde, shal mourne: for their sedes shal faile thorowe the blasting and haile, and by an horrible starre.
14 Wo to the worlde, & to them that dwell therein.
15 For the sworde and their destruction draweth nere, and one people shal stand vp to fight against another with swordes in their hands.
16 For there shalbe sedicion among men, & one shal inuade another: they shal not regarde their King, & the princes shal measure their doings by their power.
17 A man shal desire to go into a citie, and shal not be able.
18 Because of their pride the cities shalbe troubled, the houses shalbe afraied, & men shal feare.
19 A man shal haue no pitie vpon his neighbour, but shal destroye their houses with the sworde, & their goods shalbe spoyled for lacke of bread, and because of great trouble.
20 Beholde, saith God, I call together all the Kings of the earth to reuerence me,
"Or, West. which are from the "East, and from the South, from the East, and from Libanus, to turne vpon thē, & to repay the things, that they haue done to them.
21 As they do yet this day vnto my chosen, so wil I do also, and recompense them in their bosome: thus saith the Lord God,
22 My right hād shal not spare the sinners, nether shal the sworde cease from them, that shed innocent blood vpon earth.
23 The fyre is gone out from his wrath, and hathe consumed the fundacions of the earth, and the sinners like the strawe, that is kindled.
24 Wo to them that sinne, and kepe not my commandements, saith the Lord.
25 I wil not spare them: departe, ô childrē, from the power: defile not my Sanctuarie.
26 For the Lord knoweth all them that sinne against him, and therefore deliuereth he them vnto death and destruction.
27 For now are the plagues come vpon the worlde, and ye shal remaine in them: for God wil not deliuer you, because ye haue sinned against him.
28 Beholde, an horrible vision cometh from the East,
29 Where generacions of dragons of Arabia shal come out with manie charets, and the multitude of them shalbe caryed as the winde vpon the earth, that all they which heare them, may feare and tremble.
30 Euen the Carmanians raging in wrath, shal go forthe as the bores of the forest, and shal come with great power, and stād against them in battel, and shal destroye a porcion of the land of the Assyrians.
31 But after this shal the dragons haue the vpper hand, and remember their nature, and shal turne about, and conspire to consume them with a great power.
32 Then these shalbe troubled, and kepe silence by their power, and shal flee.
33 From the land of the Assyrians shal the enemie besiege them, and consume some of them, and in their hoste shalbe feare & dread, and strife among their Kings.
34 Beholde cloudes from the East, & from the North vnto the South, and they are verie horrible to loke vpon, ful of wrath and storme.
35 They shal smite one vpon another: and they shal smite downe a great multitude of starres vpon the earth, euen their owne starre, & the blood shalbe from the sworde vnto the bellie,
36 And the dongue of mā vnto the Camels litter.
37 And there shalbe great fearefulnes, and trembling vpon earth, and thei that se the wrath, shalbe afraied, and a trembling shal come vpon them.
38 And then there shal come great stormes from the South, and from the North, and parte from the West.
39 And from the East shal windes arise and shal open it with the cloude, which he raised vp in wrath, & ẏ starre, raised to feare the East & West winde, shalbe destroyed.
40 And the great, and mightie cloudes shal be lift vp, ful of wrath, and the starre, that they may make all the earth afraied, and
them

them that dwell therein, & that they may
powre out ouer euerie hie place, and lifted
vp, an horrible constellation,
41 As fyre and hayle, and flying swordes, &
many waters, that all fields may be full, &
all riuers w^t the abundãce of great waters.
42 And they shal breake downe the cities
and walles, and mountaines, and hilles, and
the trees of the wood, and the grasse of
the medowes, and their corne.
43 And they shal go with a streight course
vnto Babylon, and make it afraied.
44 They shal come to her, and besiege her,
and shal powre forthe the constellation, &
all the wrath against her: then shal the dust
and smoke go vp vnto the heauen, and all
they that be about her, shal bewaile her.
45 And thei that remaine vnder her, shal do
seruice vnto them, ẏ haue put her in feare.
46 ¶ And thou Asia, that art partaker of the
hope of Babylon, and the glorie of her
persone,
47 Wo vnto thee, ô wretch, because thou
hast made thy self like vnto her, and hast
deckt thy daughters in whoredome, ẏ they
might please & glorie in thy louers, which
haue alway desired to cõmit whoredome
with thee.
48 Thou hast followed her that is hated in
all her workes, and in her inuencions: therefore saith God,
49 I wil send plagues vpõ thee, wedowhed,
pouertie, and famine, & the sworde, and pe
stilẽce, to waste thine houses with destruction and death.
50 And ẏ glorie of thy power shalbe dryed
vp, as a floure when the heat riseth, that is
sent vpon thee.
51 Thou shalt be sicke as a poore wife ẏ is
plagued and beaten of women, so that the
mightie and the louers shal not be able to
receiue thee.
52 Wolde I thus hate thee, saith ẏ Lord,
53 If thou hadest not alway slaine my chosen, exalting the stroke of thine hands, and
said ouer their death, when ẏ wast drõken,
54 Set forthe ẏ beautie of thy countenãce?
55 The rewarde of thy whoredome *shalbe*
in thy bosome: therefore shalt thou receiue a rewarde.
56 As thou hast done vnto my chosen, saith
the Lord, so wil God do vnto thee, & wil
deliuer thee vnto the plague.
57 And thy children shal dye of hunger, &
thou shalt fall by the sworde, & thy cities
shalbe broken downe, and all thy men shal
fall by the sworde in the field.
58 And they that be in the mountaines shal
dye of hunger, and eat their owne flesh, &
drinke their owne blood for wãt of bread
and thirst of water.
59 And thou, as vnhappie, shalt come thorowe the sea, and receiue plagues againe.
60 In the passage they shal cast downe the
slaine citie, and shal roote out one parte of
thy land, & consume ẏ porcion of thy glo
rie, & shal returne to her ẏ was destroied.
61 When thou shalt be cast downe, thou
shalt be to them as stubble, and they shalbe
to thee as fyre.
62 And they shal destroy thee, & thy cities,
thy land, & thy mountaines: all thy woods
and all thy fruteful trees shal they burne
with fyre.
63 Thy childrẽ shal they carye away captiue, and shal spoile thy substance, & marre
the beautie of thy face.

CHAP. XVI.

*1 Against Babylon, Asia, & Egypt and Syria. 18, 38 Of
the euils that shal come vpon the worlde, with admonition how to gouerne them selues in afflictions. 54 To
acknowledge their sinnes, & to cõmit them selues to the
Lord. 55 Whose mightie prouidence and iustice is to
be reuerenced.*

1 WO to thee, Babylon & Asia: wo to
thee, Egypt and Syria.
2 Gird your selues with sacke & heereclothe, and mourne your children, & be sorie:
for your destruction is at hand.
3 A sworde is sent vnto you, and who wil
turne it backe? a fyre is sent among you, &
who wil quenche it?
4 Plagues are sent vnto you, and who can
driue them away?
5 May any mã driue away an hungrie lion
in the wood? or quenche the fyre in stubble
whẽ it hathe once begonne to burne? may
one turne againe the arowe, that is shot of
a strong archer?
6 The mightie Lord sendeth the plagues,
and who can driue them away? the fyre is
gone forthe in his wrath, and who can
quench it?
7 He shal cast lightenings, & who shal not
feare? he shal thunder, and who shal not be
afraied?
8 The Lord shal threaten, & who shal not
vtterly be broken in pieces at his presence? the earth quaketh & the fundaciõ thereof: the sea ariseth vp with waues frõ the
depe, & the waues thereof are troubled, &
the fishes thereof, before the Lord and the
glorie of his power.
9 For strõg is his right hand, ẏ bendeth the
bowe: his arrowes ẏ he shooteth, are sharpe, & shal not misse, when they beginne to
be shot into the ends of the worlde.
10 Beholde, the plagues are sent, & shal not
turne againe, til they come vpon earth.
11 The fyre is kindled, & shal not be put out,
til it cõsume the fundacions of the earth.
12 As an arow w^c is shot of a mightie archer,
returneth not backward, so ẏ plagues that
shalbe sẽt vpõ earth, shal not turne againe.
13 Wo is me, wo is me: who wil deliuer me
in those daies?
14 The beginning of sorowes and great

mourning: the beginning of famine, and
great death: the beginning of warres, and
the powers shal feare: the beginning of e-
uils, and all shal tremble. What shal I do
in these things, when the plagues come?
15 Beholde, famine and plague, and trouble,
and anguish are sent as scourges for amẽdement.
16 But for all these things they wil not turne frõ their wickednes, nor be alway mindeful of the scourges.
17 Beholde, vitailes shalbe so good cheape
vpon earth, that they shal thinke them selues to be in good case: but then shal the e-
uils bud forthe vpon earth, euen the sworde, the famine and great confusion.
18 For many of them that dwell vpon earth,
shal perish with famine, and the other that
escape ŷ famine, shal the sworde destroy.
19 And the dead shalbe cast out as dongue,
and there shalbe no man to comforte thẽ:
for the earth shalbe wasted, and the cities
shalbe cast downe.
20 There shalbe no mã left to till the earth,
and to sowe it: the trees shal giue frute,
but who shal gather them?
21 The grapes shalbe ripe, but who shal
treade them? for all places shalbe desolate, so that one mã shal desire to se another,
or to heare his voyce.
22 For of one citie there shalbe ten left, and
two of the field, which shal hide them selues in the thicke woods, and in the cleftes
of rockes.
23 As when there remaine thre or foure o-
liues in the place where oliues growe, or
among other trees,
24 Or as whẽ a vineyarde is gathered, there are left some grapes of them that diligently soght thorowe the vineyarde:
25 So in those daies there shalbe thre or foure left by them that searche their houses ŵ
the sworde.
26 And the earth shalbe left waste, and the
fields thereof shal waxe olde, & her waies
and all her paths shal growe full of thornes, because no man shal trauail there-
through.
27 The virgines shal mourne, hauing no
bridegromes: the women shal make lamentacion, hauing no housbands: their
daughters shal mourne hauing no helpers.
28 In the warres shal their bridegromes be
destroied, and their housbands shal perish
with famine.
29 But, ye seruants of the Lord, heare these
things, and marke them.
30 Beholde the worde of the Lord, receaue
it: beleue not the gods of whome ŷ Lord
speaketh: beholde the plagues drawe nere,
and are not slacke.
31 As a trauailing womã which in the ninthe moneth bringeth forthe her sonne,
when the houre of birth is come, two or
thre houres afore the peines come vpon
her bodie, and when the childe cometh to
the birth, they tarie not a whit,
32 So shal not the plagues be slacke to come
vpõ the earth, & the worlde shal mourne, &
sorowes shal come vpon it on euerie side.
33 O my people, heare my worde: make you
ready to the battel, and in the troubles be
euen as strangers vpon earth.
34 He that selleth, let him be as he ŷ fleeth
his way: & he that byeth, as one ŷ wil lose.
35 Who so occupieth marchãdise, as he that
winneth not: and he that buyldeth, as he
that shal not dwell therein:
36 He ŷ soweth, as one that shal not reape:
he that cutteth the vine, as he that shal not
gather the grapes:
37 They that mary, as they that shal get
no children: and they that mary not, so as
the widdowes.
38 Therefore they that labour, labour in
vaine.
39 For strangers shal reape their frutes, and
spoile their goods, and ouerthrowe their
houses, and take their children captiue: for
in captiuitie & famine shal they get their
children.
40 And they that occupie their marchãdise with couetousnes, the more they decke
their cities, their houses, their possessions,
and their owne persones,
41 So muche more wil I be angrie against
them for their sinnes, saith the Lord.
42 As a whore enuieth an honest and vertuous woman,
43 So shal righteousnes hate iniquitie, whẽ
she decketh her self, & shal accuse her opẽly, when he shal come that shal bridle the
autor of all sinne vpon earth.
44 And therefore be ye not like thereunto,
nor to the workes thereof: for or euer it be
long, iniquitie shalbe taken away out of
the earth, and righteousnes shal reigne a-
mong you.
45 Let not the sinner say, that he hathe not
sinned: for coles of fyre shal burne vpon
his head, which saith, I haue not sinned before the Lord God and his glorie.
46 Beholde, the Lord *knoweth all the wor- *Luk.16,15.*
kes of men, their imaginaciõs, their thoghtes and their hearts.
47 *For assone as he said, Let the earth be *Gen.1,1.*
made, it was made: let the heauen be made,
and it was created.
48 By his worde were the starres established, and he * knoweth the nomber of *Psal.147,4.*
them.
49 He searcheth the depth, and the treasures thereof: he hathe measured the sea,
and what it conteineth.
50 He hathe shut the sea in the middes of
the waters, and with his worde hathe he
hanged

hanged the earth vpon the waters.
51 He ſpreadeth out the heauē like a vawte:
vpon the waters hathe he founde it.
52 In the deſert hathe he made ſprings of
water, and poles vpon the toppe of the
mountaines, to powre out floods from the
hie rockes to water the earth.
53 He made man, and put his heart in the
middes of the bodie, and gaue him breth,
life and vnderſtanding.
54 And the Spirit of the almightie God,
which made all things, & hathe ſearched
all the hid things in the ſecrets of ẏ earth,
55 He knoweth your inuencions, and what
ye imagine in your heart when ye ſinne &
wolde hide your ſinnes.
56 Therefore hathe the Lord ſearched and
ſoght out all your workes, and wil put you
all to ſhame.
57 And when your ſinnes are broght forthe
before men, ye ſhalbe confounded, and
your owne ſinnes ſhal ſtand as your accuſers in that day.
58 What wil ye do, or how wil ye hide
your ſinnes before God and his Angels?
59 Beholde, God him ſelfe is the iudge: feare him: ceaſe from your ſinnes, and forget
your iniquities, and medle no more from
hence forthe with them: ſo ſhal God lead
you forthe, and deliuer you from all
trouble.
60 For beholde, the heate of a great multitude is kindled againſt you, and they ſhal
take away certeine of you, and ſhal ſlaye
you for meat to the idoles.
61 And they that conſent vnto them, ſhalbe
had in deriſion and in reproche, and troden vnder foote.
62 For in euerie place and cities that are
nere, there ſhalbe great inſurrectiō againſt
thoſe that feare the Lord.
63 They ſhalbe like mad men: they ſhal ſpare none: they ſhal ſpoyle, & waſte ſuche as
yet feare the Lord.
64 For they then ſhal waſte and ſpoile their
goods, and caſt them out of their houſes.
65 Thē ſhal the tryal of my choſen appeare, as the golde is tryed by the fyre.
66 Heare, ô ye my beloued, ſaith the Lord:
beholde, the daies of trouble are at hand,
but I wil deliuer you from them: be not
ye afraied: doute not, for God is your captaine.
67 Who ſo kepeth my commādements and
precepts, ſaith ẏ Lord God, let not your
ſinnes weigh you downe, and let not your
iniquities lift them ſelues vp.
68 Wo vnto thē that are bounde with their
ſinnes, and couered with their iniquities,
as a field is hedged in with buſhes, and the
path thereof couered with thornes, wherby no man may trauail: it is ſhut vp, and is
appointed to be deuoured with fyre.

TOBIT.

CHAP. I.

1 Tobits parentage. 3 His godlines. 6 His equitie. 8 His charitie and proſperitie. 23 He fleeth, and his goods are confiſcate, 25 And after, reſtored.

Tobias, being captiue amōgeſt the Aſſyrians, did not leaue the way of trueth.

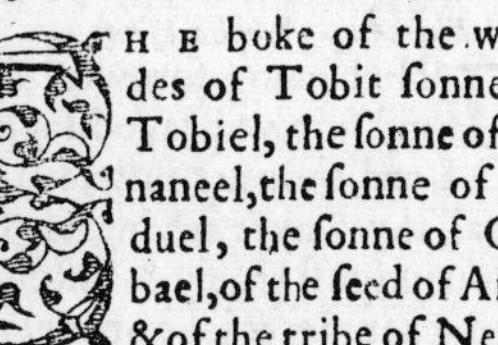

1 THE boke of the wor-
des of Tobit ſonne of
Tobiel, the ſonne of A-
naneel, the ſonne of A-
duel, the ſonne of Ga-
bael, of the ſeed of Aſael
& of the tribe of Neph-
thalim,
2 Who in the time of "Enemeſſar King of
the Aſſyriās was * ledde away captiue out
of Thiſbe, which is at the right hand of
that citie, ẇ is called properly Nephthalim, in Galilee aboue Aſer.

"Or, Salmanaſar.
2.King. 17,3.

3 I Tobit haue walked all my liue long in
the way of trueth and iuſtice, and I did
manie things liberally to the brethren, ẇ
were of my nation, and came with me to
Niniue into the land of the Aſſyrians.

Tobias was merciful.

4 And when I was in mine owne countrei
in the land of Iſrael, being but yong, all
the tribe of Nephthalim my father fell
from the houſe of Ieruſalem, which was
choſen out of all the tribes of Iſrael, that
all the tribes ſhulde ſacrifice there, where
the Tēple of the tabernacle of the moſte
High was conſecrated, and buylt vp for
all ages.
5 * Now all the tribes, which fell from God, 1.King. 12,30
yea, and my father Nephthalims houſe of-
fred to the heifar called Baal.
6 But I (as it was ordeined to all Iſrael by
an euerlaſting decre) went alone often to
Ieruſalem, * bringing the firſt frutes, and
the tenth of beaſts, with that which was
firſt ſhorne, and offred them at the altar to
the Prieſts the children of Aaron.

He fledde frō idoles.
Exod. 22,29.
deu. 12,6.

7 The firſt tenth parte I gaue to ẏ Prieſts
the ſonnes of Aaron, which miniſtred in
Ieruſalē: the other tēth parte I ſolde, & ca
me & beſtowed it euerie yere at Ieruſalē.
8 The thirde *tenth parte* I gaue vnto them
to whome it was mete, as Debora my fathers mother had commanded me: for my
father left me as a pupil.
9 ¶ Furthermore when I was come to the
age of a mā, I maried Anna of * mine owne
kinred, and of her I begate Tobias.

He maryeth to wiſe Anna, ẇ beareth him Tobiah.
Nomb. 36,7.

10 ¶ But whē I was ledde captiue to Niniue, all my brethren, & thoſe ẇ were of my
kinred did eate of the * bread of ẏ Gētiles. Gen. 43,32.

11 But I kept my self from eating,
12 Because I remembred God with all mine heart.

He found grace in the sight of Salmanasar

13 Therefore the most High gaue me grace and fauour before Enemessar, so that I
was his puruoyer.
14 ¶And I went into Media, and I deliuered ten talēts of siluer to Gabael the "brother of Gabrias "in the land of Media.

"Or, sonne.
"Or, in Rages a citie of Media.

15 But when Enemessar was dead, Sennacherib his sonne reigned in his stead: whose
state because it was troubled, I colde not
go into Media.

"Or, Salmanasar
The charitie of Tobias.

16 ¶But in the time of "Enemessar, I gaue
many almes to my brethren, and gaue my
bread to them which were hungrie,
17 And my clothes to the naked: and if I
sawe any of my kinred dead, or cast about
the walles of Nineue, I buryed him.
18 And if the King Sennacherib had slaine
any, when he* was come and fled from Iudea, I buryed thē priuely (for in his wrath
he killed many) but the bodies were not
foūde whē they were soght for of ẏ King.

2.King.19,35 isa.37,36. eccles.48,14. 1.mac.7,41. 2.mac.8,19.

19 Therefore whē a certeine Nineuite had
accused me to the King, because I did bury them, I hid my self: and because I knewe
that I was soght to be slaine, I withdrewe
my self for feare.

Tobit fleeth from the face of Sennacherib.

20 Then all my goods were spoyled, nether
was there any thing left me besides my
wife Anna and my sonne Tobias.
21 Neuertheles *within fiue and fiftie daies
two of his sonnes killed him, and they fled
into the mountaines of Arrarath, & Sarchedonus his sonne reigned in his stead,
who appointed ouer his fathers accōptes
and ouer all his domestical affaires Achiacharus my brother Anaels sonne.

2.King.19,37 2.chr.32,21.

22 And when Achiacharus had made a request for me, I came againe to Nineue:
now Achiacharus was cupbearer & keper
of ẏ signet, & steward, & ouersawe the ac-
comptes: so Sarchedonus appointed him
next vnto him, & he was my brothers sonne.

Tobit returneth.

CHAP. II.

1 Tobit calleth the faithful to his table. 3 He leaueth the feast to bury the dead. 10 How he became blinde. 13 His wife laboreth for her liuing. 16 She reprocheth him bitterly.

1 NOw when I was come home againe,
& my wife Anna was restored vnto
me with my sonne Tobias, in the feast of
Pentecoste, which is the holy *feast* of the
seuen wekes, there was a great dinner prepared me, in the which I sate downe to eat.

Tobit doeth bid to diner those which feare God.

2 And when I sawe abundāce of meat, I said
to my sonne, Go, & bring what poore man
soeuer ẏ shalt finde of our brethrē which
doth remēber God, & lo I wil tary for thee.
3 But he came againe, and said, Father, one
of our nation is strangled, and is cast out
in the market place.

Tobit, leauing his gestes, taketh vp the dead bodie into his house to burye it.

4 Thē before I had tasted anie meat, I start
vp, and broght him into mine house vntil
the going downe of the sunne.
5 Then I returned and washed, and ate my
meat in heauines,
6 Remembring that prophecie of* Amos,
ẘ had said, your solēne feasts shalbe turned
into mourning, & your ioyes into wailing.

Amos 8,10. 1.mac.1,41.

7 Therefore I wept, & after ẏ going downe
of ẏ sūne I wēt & made a graue & buried hī.
8 But my neighbours mocked me, and said,
Doeth he not feare, to dye for this cause,
who *fled away, and yet, lo, he buryeth the
dead againe.

Tobit is rebuked of his neighbours.
Chap.1,22.

9 The same night also when I returned frō
the buryal, & slept at ẏ wall of mine house
because I was polluted, & hauing my face
vncouered,
10 And I knewe not ẏ sparowes were in the
wall, & as mine eyes were open, the sparowes cast downe warme dōgue into mine eyes, & a whitenes came in mine eies, &
I went to the phisiciās who helped me not.
Moreouer, Achiacharus did nourish me,
vntil I went into Elimais.

He is made blinde for an example of patiencie to his posteritie.

11 And my wife Anna did take womens
workes to do.
12 And whē she had sent them home to the
owners, thei paied the wages, & gaue a kid.

The wife of Tobit laboreth for her liuing.

13 Which whē it was at mine house, and began to bleat, I said vnto her, From whēce
is this kid? is it not stollen? render it to the
owners: *for it is not lawful to eat anie
thing that is stollen.

The innocencie of Tobit.
Deu.22,1.

14 But she said, It was giuē for a gifte more
thē ẏ wages: but I did not beleue, & bade
her to rēder it to ẏ owners, & I did blush,
because of her. Furthermore she said, *Whe
re are thine almes, & thy righteousnes? beholde, they all now appeare in thee.

Iob.2,9.

CHAP. III.

3 The prayer of Tobit. 7 Sarra Raguels daughter, & the things that came vnto her. 12 Her prayer heard. 19 The Angel Raphael sent.

1 THē I, being sorowful, did wepe, & in
my sorowe prayed, saying,
2 O Lord, thou art iuste, & all thy workes,
& all thy wayes are mercie & trueth, and
thou iudgest truely & iustely for euer.
3 Remēber me & loke on me, nether punish
me accordīg to my sins or mine ignorāces
or my fathers, ẘ haue sinned before thee.
4 For thei haue not obeied thy cōmandemēts: wherefore ẏ hast deliuered vs *for a
spoile, & vnto captiuitie, and to death, and
for a prouerbe of a reproche to all them a-
mong whome we are dispersed, and now
"thou hast manie and iuste causes,

Deu.28,15.
"Or, thy iudgements are manie and true.

5 To do ẘ me accordīg to my sinnes, & my
fathers, because we haue not kept thy cōmandemēts, nether haue walked in trueth
before thee.
6 Now therefore deale with me as semeth
best vnto thee, & cōmande my spirit to be
takē frō me, ẏ I may be dissolued, & become earth: for it is better for me to dye thē to
liue, because I haue heard false reproches,

& am verie sorowful: cōmande therefore
that I may be dissolued out of this distresse, *and* go into the euerlasting place: turne
not thy face away from me.
7 ¶ It came to passe the same day that in
Ecbatane a citie of Media Sarra the daughter of Raguel was also reproched by
her fathers maides,

Sarra is checked of her fathers maides.

8 Because she had bene maryed to seuē hous
bands, whome Asmodeus the euil spirit
had killed, before that they had lien with
her. Doest thou not knowe, said they, that
thou hast strangled thine housbands? thou
hast had now seuen housbāds, nether wast
thou named after anie of them.
9 Wherefore doest thou "beat vs for them?
if they be dead, go thy wayes hence to thē,
that we may neuer se of thee ether sonne
or daughter.

"Or, *when she bette them for their fautes, thei said.*

10 When she heard these things, she was
verie sorowful, so that she thoght to haue
strangled her self. And she said, I am the
onely daughter of my father, & if I do this
I shal sclander him, and shal bring his age
to the graue with sorowe.
11 Then she prayed towarde the windowe
& said, Blessed art thou, ô Lord my God,
and thine holie & glorious Name is blessed, and honorable for euer: let all thy wor
kes praise thee for euer.

Sarra prayeth, & fasteth that she may be deliuered from shame.

12 And now, ô Lord, I set mine eyes, & my
face toward thee,
13 And say, Take me out of the earth, that I
may heare no more anie reproche.
14 Thou knowest, ô Lord, that I am pure
from all sinne with man,

The innocēcie of Sarra.

15 And that I haue neuer polluted my name, nor the name of my father in the land
of my captiuitie: I am the onely daughter
of my father, nether hathe he anie mā child
to be his heire, nether anie " nere kinsman
or childe borne of him, to whome I may
kepe my self for a wife: my seuen *housbands*
are now dead, & why shulde I liue? But if
it please not thee that I shulde dye, cōmāde to loke on me, and to pitie me that I do
no more heare reproche.

Her chastitie.

"Gre. *nere brother.*

16 So the prayers of them bothe were heard
before the maiestie of the great God.
17 And Raphael was sent to heale them bothe, *that is*, to take away ẏ whitenes of Tobits eyes, & to giue Sarra the daughter of
Raguel for a wife to Tobias the sonne of
Tobit, & to binde Asmodeus ẏ euil spirit
because she belonged to Tobias by right.
The self same time came Tobit home, and
entred into his house, and Sarra the daughter of Raguel came downe frō her chāber.

The prayers of Tobit, and Sarra areheard bothe at a time.

CHAP. IIII.

Precepts and exhortacions of Tobit to his sonne.

1 IN that day Tobit remēbred *ẏ siluer,
which he had deliuered to Gabael in
Rages *a citie* of Media,
2 And said with him self, I haue wished for
death: wherefore do I not call for my sonne Tobias that I may admonish him before I dye?

Chap.1,14.

3 And when he had called him, he said, My
sonne, after that I am dead, bury me, & despise not thy mother, but honour her all
the dayes of thy life, & do that which shal
please her, and anger her not.

Tobits exhortation to his sonne, whē he thoght he shul de dye.

The mother is to be reuerenced.

4 Remēber, my sonne, how manie dangers
she susteined when thou wast in her wōbe,
and whē she dyeth, burye her by me in the
same graue.

Exod.20,12. eccles.7,19.

6 My sonne, set our Lord God alwayes before thine eyes, & let not thy wil be set to
sinne or to transgresse the cōmandements
of God. Do vprightly all thy life long, and
followe not the wayes of vnrighteousnes:
for if yͧ deale truely, thy doings shal prosperously succede to thee, & to all thē which
liue iustely.

God must be in our hearts.

7 Giue *almes of thy substance: and when
thou giuest almes, let not thine eye be enuious, nether turne thy face frō anie poore, lest that God turne his face from thee.
8 * Giue almes according to thy substance:
if thou haue but a litle, be not afraide to
giue a litle almes.
9 For thou laiest vp a good store for thy
self against the day of necessitie,
10 * Because that almes doeth deliuer from
death, & suffreth not to come into darknes.
11 For almes is a good gift before the moste High to all them which vse it.

Almes. *Prou.3,9. eccles 4,1. & 14,13. luk.14,13.*

Eccles.35,4.

Eccles.29,15.

12 Beware of all *whoredome, my sonne, &
chiefly take a wife of ẏ sede of thy fathers,
& take not a strange womā to wife which
is not of thy fathers stocke: for we are the
childrē of the Prophetes. Noe, Abraham,
Isaac and Iacob are our fathers from the
beginning. Remember my sonne that thei
maryed wiues of their owne kinred, and
were blessed in their children and their
sede shal inherite the land.

Aduoutrie. *1.Thes.4,3.*

13 Now therefore, my sonne, loue thy brethren, & despise not in thine heart ẏ sonnes
& daughters of thy people in not taking a
wife of thē: for in pride is destruction, and
muche trouble, & in fiercenes is scarcetie,
& great pouertie: for " fiercenes is the mother of famine.

Pride.

"Or, *vnprofitablenes.*

14 Let not the *wages of anie man, ẇ hathe
wroght for thee, tarie with thee, but giue
him it out of hād: for if thou serue God, he
wil also paye thee: be circumspect, my sonne, in all things that thou doest, and be wel
instructed in all thy conuersation.

Wages of an hired seruant. *Leu.19,13. deu.24,14.*

15 *Do that to no mā ẇ thou hatest: drinke
not wine to make thee dronken, nether let
dronkennes go with thee in thy iournay.

Mat.7,12. luk.6,31.

16 *Giue of thy bread to ẏ hūgry, & of thy
garmēts to thē ẏ are naked, &* of all thine
abundance giue almes, & let not thine eye
be enuious, when thou giuest almes.

Luk.14,13. The hungry. *Mat.6,1.*

Or, be liberal to the iuste, euen to their death.

Counsel.

God is to be blessed.

17 "Powre out thy bread on ẏ buryal of the
iuste, but giue nothing to the wicked.
18 Aske counsel alway of the wise, and despise not anie counsel that is profitable.
19 Blesse thy Lord God alway, and desire
of him ẏ thy wayes may be made streight
and that all thy purposes, and counsels
may prosper: for euerie nation hathe not
counsel: but the Lord giueth all good
things, and he humbleth whome he wil, as
he wil: now therefore, my sonne, remember my commandements, nether let them
at anie time be put out of thy minde.

Chap. 1, 14.

20 *Furthermore I signifie this to thee, that
I deliuered ten talents to Gabael the sonne of Gabrias at Rages in Media.

Pouertie with the feare of God.

21 And feare not, my sonne, for asmuche as
we are made poore: for thou hast manie
things, if ẏ feare God, & flee frõ sinne, &
do ẏ thing which is acceptable vnto him.

CHAP. V.

1 Tobias sent to Rages, 5 He meteth with the Angel Raphael, which did conduct him.

1 Tobias then answered & said, Father,
I wil do all things which thou hast
commanded me.
2 But how can I receiue the siluer, seing I
knowe him not?
3 Then he gaue him the hand writing, and
said vnto him, Seke thee a man, which may
go with thee, whiles I yet liue, and I wil giue him wages, and go and receiue the
money.

Tobias, sent by his father to Rages, seketh a companion, & meteth with Raphael, whome he bringeth to his father.

4 Therefore when he was gone to seke a
man, he founde Raphael the Angel.
5 But he knewe not, & said vnto him, May
I go with thee into the land of Media? and
knowest thou those places wel?
6 To whome the Angel said, I wil go with
thee: for I haue remained with our brother Gabael.
7 Then Tobias said to him, Tarie for me,
til I tell my father.
8 Then he said vnto him, Go, and tary not:
so he went in & said to his father, Beholde,
I haue founde one, which wil go with me.
Then he said, Call him vnto me, that I
may know of what tribe he is, and whether
he be faithful to go with thee.
9 So he called him, and he came in, & they
saluted one another.
10 Thẽ Tobit said vnto hĩ, Brother, shewe
me of what tribe and familie thou art.
11 To whome he said, Doest ẏ seke a stocke or familie, or an hired man to go with
thy sonne? Then Tobit said vnto him, I
wolde knowe thy kinred and thy name.
12 Then he said, I am of the kinred of Azarias & Ananias ẏ great, & of thy brethrẽ.

Or, thou commest happely.

13 Then Tobit said, "Thou art welcome: be
not now angrie with me, because I haue
enquired to knowe thy kinred, and thy familie: for thou art my brother of an honest
and good stocke: for I knewe Ananias and
Ionathas, sonnes of that great Samaias: for
we went together to Ierusalem to worship, and offred the first borne, & the tẽths
of the frutes, and they were not deceiued
with ẏ errour of our brethren: my brother,
thou art of a great stocke.
14 But tel me, what wages shal I giue thee?
wilt thou a grote a day & things necessarie,
as to mine owne sonne?
15 Yea, moreouer if ye returne safe, I wil
adde some thing to the wages.
16 So thei agreed. Then said he to Tobias,
Prepare thy self for the iourney, and go
you on Gods Name. And whẽ his sonne
had prepared all things for the iourney,
his father said, Go thou with this man, &
God which dwelleth in heauen, prosper
your iourney, and the Angel of God kepe
you companie. So they went forthe bothe
and departed, and the dogge of the yong
man with them.

Tobias goeth forthe, ẏ Angel keping him cõpanie.

His mother wepeth.

Chap. 10, 4.

17 But * Anna his mother wept, and said to
Tobit, Why hast thou sent away our sonne? is he not the staffe of our hand to minister vnto vs?
18 Wolde to God we had not laid money
vpõ money, but that it had bene cast away
in respect of our sonne.
19 For that which God hathe giuen vs to
liue with, doeth suffice vs.
20 Then said Tobit, Be not careful, my sister: he shal returne in safetie, & thine eyes
shal se him.
21 For the good Angel doeth kepe him cõpanie, and his iourney shal be prosperous,
and he shal returne safe.
22 Then she made an end of weping.

CHAP. VI.

2 Tobias deliuered from the fish. 8 Raphael sheweth him certeine medecines. 10 He conducteth him toward Sarra.

1 And as they went on their iourney,
they came at night to the flood Tygris, and there abode.
2 And when the yong man went to wash
him self, a fish leaped out of the riuer, and
wolde haue deuoured him.

Tobias, inuaded of a fish, is deliuered by the Angel.

3 Then the Angel said vnto him, Take the
fish. And the yong man toke the fish, and
drewe it to land.
4 To whome the Angel said, Cut the fish,
and take the heart, and the liuer, and the
gall, and put them vp surely.
5 So the yong man did as the Angel commanded him: & when they had rosted the
fish, they ate it: then they bothe went on
their way, til they came to Ecbatane.
6 ¶ Then the yong man said to the Angel,
Brother Azarias, what auaileth the heart,
and the liuer, and the gall of the fish?
7 And he said vnto him, Touching ẏ heart
and the liuer, if a deuil or an euil spirit
trouble

trouble any, we must make a perfume of
this before the man or the woman, and he
shalbe no more vexed.
8 As for the gall, anoint a man that hathe
whitenes in his eyes, and he shalbe healed.
9 ¶ And when they were come nere to Rages,
10 The Angel said to the yong man, Brother, to day we shal lodge w Raguel, who
is thy cousin: he also hath one onelie daughter named Sarra: I wil speake for her
that she may be giuen thee for a wife.
11 For to thee doeth * the right of her perteine, seing thou alone art remnant of
his kinred,

Nomb.27,8. & 36,8.

12 And the maid is faire and wise: now therefore heare me, and I wil speake to her
father, that we may make the mariage
when we are returned from Rages: for I
knowe that Raguel cã not marie her to another according to the Law of Moyses: els
he shulde deserue death, because the right
doeth rather apperteine to thee then to a-
nie other man.
13 Then the yong man answered the Angel,
I haue heard, brother Azarias, that this
maid hathe bene giuen to seuen men, who
all dyed in the mariage chamber:
14 And I am the onely begotten sonne of
my father, and I am afraied, lest I go into
her, and dye as the other: for a wicked spirit loueth her, which hurteth no bodie, but
those which come into her: wherefore I
also feare lest I dye, and bring my fathers
and my mothers life because of me to the
graue with sorrowe: for thei haue no other
sonne to burye them.
15 Then the Angel said vnto him, Doest
thou not remẽber the precepts which thy
father gaue thee, that thou shuldest marie
a wife of thine owne kinred? wherefore
heare me, ô my brother: for she shalbe thy
wife, nether be ÿ careful of the euil spirit:
for this same night shal she be giuen thee
in mariage.
16 And when thou shalt go into thy bed,
thou shalt take of the hote coles for perfumes, and make a perfume of the heart,
and of the liuer of the fish,
17 Which if the spirit do smell, he wil flee
away, and neuer come againe anie more:
but when thou shalt come to her, rise vp
bothe of you, and praye to God which is
merciful, who wil haue pitie on you, and
saue you: feare not, for she is appointed vn
to thee from the beginning, & thou shalt
kepe her, & she shal go with thee: moreouer I suppose that she shal beare thee children: now when Tobias had heard these
things, he loued her, and his heart was effectually ioyned to her.

CHAP. VII.

Tobias maryeth Sarra Raguels daughter.

1 And when they were come to Ecbatane, they came to the house of Raguel: and Sarra met them, and after they
had saluted one another, she broght them
into the house.

Raphael & Tobias come to Raguel.

2 Then said Raguel to Edna his wife, How
like is this yong man to Tobit my cousin?
3 And Raguel asked, Whence are you, my
brethrẽ? To whome thei said, that thei were of the tribe of Nephthalim, and of the
captiues that dwelt at Nineue.
4 Thẽ he said to them, Do ye knowe Tobit our kinsman? And they said, We
knowe him. Then said he, Is he in good
health?
5 And they said, He is bothe aliue, and in
good health: and Tobias said, He is my
father.
6 Then Raguel leaped, and kissed him, and
wept,
7 And blessed him, & said vnto him, Thou
art the sonne of a good and honest man:
but when he had heard that Tobit was
blinde, he was sorowful and wept.
8 And likewise Edna his wife, and Sarra
his daughter wept. Moreouer they receiued them with a readie minde, and after
that they had killed a ram of the flocke,
thei set muche meat on the table. Thẽ said
Tobias to Raphael, Brother Azarias, put
forthe those things whereof thou spakest
in the waye, that this busines may be dis-
patched.

Tobias asketh Raguels daughter to wife

9 So he communicated the matter with
Raguel, and Raguel said to Tobias, Eat,
and drinke and make merry.
10 For it is mete that thou shuldest marie
my daughter: neuertheles, I wil declare vn
to thee the trueth.
11 I haue giuen my daughter in mariage to
seuen men, who dyed that night which
thei came in vnto her: neuertheles, be thou
of a good courage and merry. But Tobias said, I wil eat nothing here, vntil ye
bring her hether, and betrothe her to
me.
12 Raguel said then, Marie her then according to the custome: for thou art her cousin, and she is thine. God which is merciful, make this prosperous to you in all
good things.
13 Then he called his daughter Sarra, & she
came to her father, and he toke her by the
hand, & gaue her for wife to Tobias, saying, Beholde, take her after the * Law of
Moyses, and lead her away to thy father:
and he blessed them,

Raguel giueth his daughter Sarra to Tobias.

Nomb.36,6.

14 And called his wife Edna, and he toke a
boke and wrote a contract, and sealed it.
15 Then they began to eate.
16 After, Raguel called his wife Edna, and
said vnto her, Sister, prepare another chã-

her,and bring her inthether.
17 Which when she had done, as he had
bidden her, she broght her thether: then
Sarra wept and her mother wiped away
her daughters teares,
18 And said vnto her, Be of good comfort,
my daughter:the Lord of heauen & earth
giue thee ioye for this thy sorrow:be of
good comfort,my daughter.

CHAP. VIII.

Tobias driueth away the euil spirit. 4 He prayeth to God with his wife. 11 Raguel prepareth a graue for his sonne in law. 16 Raguel blesseth the Lord.

1 AND when they had supped, they
broght Tobias in vnto her.
2 And as he went,he remembred the wordes of Raphael,& toke coles for perfumes,
and put the heart and liuer of the fish thereupon,and made a perfume.

Tobias followeth Raphaels counsel, as Chap 6,7.

3 The which smel when the euil spirit had
smelled,he fled into the" vtmost partes of
Egypt,whome the Angel bounde.

"Or,vpmoste.

4 And after that they were bothe shut in,
Tobias rose out of the bed, and said, Sister,arise and let vs pray, that God wolde
haue pitie on vs.

Tobias praier

5 Then began Tobias to say, Blessed art
thou, ô God of our fathers,and blessed is
thine holie and glorious Name for euer:
let the heauens blesse thee, and all thy
creatures.

Gen.2,7.

6 Thou madest Adam,and gauest him *E-
ua his wife for an helpe,and stay:of them
came mankinde: thou hast said, It is not
good, that a man shulde be alone: let
vs make vnto him an aide like vnto him
self.
7 And now,ô Lord,I take not this my sister
for fornicacion,but vprightly: therefore
grante me mercie,that we may become a-
ged together.
8 And she said with him,Amen.

Raguel, thinking Tobias was dead,made a graue for him.

9 So they slept bothe that night, and Raguel arose,and went and made a graue,
10 Saying,Is not he dead also?
11 But when Raguel was come into his
house,
12 He said to his wife Edna, Send one of
the maides, and let them se whether he be
aliue:if not,that I may burye him,& none
knowe it.
13 So the maid opened the dore, and went
in,and founde them bothe a slepe,
14 And came forthe,and tolde them that he
was a liue.

Raguel praiseth God for Tobias.

15 Thē Raguel praised God,& said,O God,
thou art worthie to be praised with all pure, & holie praise: therefore let thy Saintes praise thee with all thy creatures,and
let all thine Angels and thine elect praise
thee for euer.
16 Thou art to be praised,ô Lord: for thou
hast made me ioyful,and that is not come
to me which I suspected:but thou hast delt
with vs according to great mercie.
17 Thou art to be praised because thou hast
had mercie of two that were the onely begotten children of their fathers: grante
them mercie,ô Lord, & finish their life in
health with ioye and mercie.
18 Then Raguel bade his seruants to fil the
graue.
19 And he kept the wedding feast fourtene
daies.
20 For Raguel had said vnto him by an o-
the,that he shulde not departē before that
the fourtene daies of the mariage were
expired,
21 And then he shulde take the halfe of his
goods and returne in safetie to his father,
and *shulde haue* the rest, when he and his
wife were dead.

Raguel giueth halfe of his goods toward the mariage of his daughter to Tobias.

CHAP. IX.

Raphael leadeth Gabael to Tobias mariage.

1 THen Tobias called Raphael, & said
vnto him,
2 Brother Azarias, take with thee a seruant and two camels, and go to Rages of
the Medes to Gabael, and bring me the
money and bring him to the wedding.
3 For Raguel hathe sworne that I shal not
departe.
4 But my father counteth the daies: and if
I tary long,he wil be verie sory.

Tobits care for his sonne.

5 So Raphael went out and came to Gabael, and gaue him the hand writing, who
broght forthe bagges which were sealed
vp,and gaue them to him.

The Angel goeth on Tobias message.

6 And in the morning they went forthe,
bothe together,and came to the wedding.
And Tobias begate his wife with childe.

CHAP. X.

1 Tobit and his wife thinke long for their sonne. 10 Raguel sendeth away Tobias and Sarra.

1 NOw Tobit his father counted euery
day, & when the daies of the iournay were expired,and they came not,
2 Tobit said, Are they not mocked? or is
not Gabael dead, and there is no man to
giue him the money?

The father & mother are in heauines for Tobias taryīg

3 Therefore he was verie sory.
4 Then his wife said to him, My sonne is
dead, seing he tarieth: and she began to
bewaile him,and said,
5 Now * I care for nothing, my sonne,
since I haue lost thee the light of mine
eyes.

Chap.5,23.

6 To whome Tobit said, Holde thy peace: be not careful, for he is safe.
7 But she said,Holde thy peace,and deceiue me not:my sonne is dead:and she went
out euerie day by the waye, which they
went, nether did she eat meat on the daye
time,& did consume whole nights in bewailing her sonne Tobias vntil the fourtene

tene daies of the wedding were expired,
ẇ Raguel had ſworne, that he ſhulde tarie
there. Then Tobias ſaid to Raguel, Let
me go:for my father and my mother loke
no more to ſe me.
8 But his father in law ſaid vnto him, Tarie with me, and I wil ſend to thy father,
and they ſhal declare him thine affaires.
9 But Tobias ſaid,No,but let me go to my
father.

Raguel giueth Tobias, & his wife leaue to departe.

10 Then Raguel aroſe,and gaue him Sarra
his wife,and halfe his goods, as ſeruants,
and cattel,and money,
11 And he bleſſed them, & ſent them away,
ſaying,The God of heauen make you,my
children,to proſper before I dye.

Sarra is inſtructed by her parents.

12 And he ſaid to his daughter, Honour
thy father,& thy mother in law which are
now thy parents, that I may heare good
reporte of thee: and he kiſſed them. Edna
alſo ſaid to Tobias, The Lord of heauen
reſtore thee, my dere brother, and grante
that I may ſe thy children of my daughter
Sarra,that I may reioyce before the Lord.
Beholde now, I committe to thee my
daughter as a pledge: do not intreat her
euil.

CHAP. XI.

1 The returne of Tobias to his father. 9 How he was receiued. 10 His father hathe his ſight reſtored and praiſeth the Lord.

1 After theſe things Tobias went his
way,praiſing God that he had giuen
him a proſperous iournay, and bleſſed Ra
guel and Edna his wife, and went on his
way til he drewe nere to Nineue.
2 Then Raphael ſaid to Tobias, Thou
knoweſt,brother,how thou dideſt leaue thy
father.

The Angels counſel to Tobias.

3 Let vs haſte before thy wife,and prepare
the houſe,
4 And take in thine hãd the gall of the fiſh.
So they went their way, & the dogge followed them.
5 Now Anna ſate in the way loking for her
ſonne,
6 Whome when ſhe ſawe coming, ſhe ſaid
to his father,beholde,thy ſonne cometh,&
the man that went with him.
7 Then ſaid Raphael,I knowe,Tobias,that
thy father ſhal receiue his ſight.
8 Therefore anoint his eyes with the gall,
and being pricked therewith, he ſhal rubbe and make the whitenes to fall away,and
ſhal ſe thee.
9 ¶ Then Anna rãne forthe, and fel on the
necke of her ſonne, and ſaid vnto him, Seing I haue ſene thee,my ſonne,from hence
forthe I am content to dye,and they wepte bothe.
10 Tobit alſo went forthe towarde the dore, and ſtombled, but his ſonne ranne vnto him,
11 And toke holde of his father & ſprinkled
of the gall on his fathers eyes, ſaying, Be
of good hope,my father.
12 And when his eyes began to pricke, he
rubbed them.
13 And the whitenes pilled away from the
corners of his eyes, and when he ſawe his
ſonne,he fel vpon his necke,
14 And he wept and ſaid, Bleſſed art thou,
ô Lord, & bleſſed be thy Name for euer,
and bleſſed be all thine holie Angels.
15 For thou haſt ſcourged me, and haſt had
pitie on me:*for* beholde, I ſe my ſonne To
bias:and his ſonne, being glad went in, &
tolde his father the great things that had
come to paſſe in Media.
16 Then Tobit went out to mete his daughter in lawe,reioycing and praiſing God
to the gate of Nineue: and they which
ſawe him go, marueiled, becauſe he had
receiued his ſight.
17 But Tobit teſtified before them all that
God had had pitie on him. And when he
came nere to Sarra his daughter in law,he
bleſſed her, ſaying, Thou art welcome,
daughter: God be bleſſed, which hathe
broght thee vnto vs,&*bleſſed be* thy father:
and there was great ioye among all his
brethren which were at Nineue.
18 And Achiacharus & Naſbas his brothers
ſonne came.
19 And Tobias mariage was kept ſeuen
dayes with great ioye.

CHAP. XII.

2 Tobias declareth to his father the pleaſures that Raphael had done him. 5 The which he wolde recompenſe. 11.15. Raphael declareth that he is an Angel ſent of God.

1 Then Tobit called his ſonne Tobias,and ſaid vnto him, Prouide, my
ſonne,wages for the man, which wẽt with
thee,and thou muſt giue him more.
2 And he ſaid vnto him,O father,it ſhal not
grieue me to giue him halfe of thoſe thĩgs
which I haue broght.
3 For he hathe broght me againe to thee
in ſafetie,and hathe made whole my wife,
and hathe broght me the money, & hathe
likewiſe healed thee.
4 Then the olde man ſaid, It is due vnto
him.
5 So he called the Angel,& ſaid vnto him,
Take halfe of all that ye haue broght,and
go away in ſafetie.
6 But he toke them bothe a parte, and ſaid
vnto them,Praiſe God,and confeſſe him,
and giue him the glorie, and praiſe him
for the things which he hathe done vnto
you before all them that liue. It is good
to praiſe God, and to exalte his Name,
and to ſhewe forthe his euident workes
with honour: therefore be not wearie to
confeſſe him.

7 It is good to kepe close the secrets of a
King, but it is honorable to reueile the
workes of God: do that which is good, &
no euil shal touche you.
8 Prayer is good with fasting, and almes, &
righteousnes. A litle with righteousnes is
better then muche with vnrighteousnes:
it is better to giue almes then to laye vp
golde.
9 For almes doeth deliuer from death, and
doeth purge all sinne. Those which exercise almes and righteousnes, shalbe filled
with life.
10 But they that sinne, are enemies to their
owne life.
11 Surely I wil kepe close nothing frō you:
neuertheles, I said it was good to kepe
close the secret of a King, but that it was
honorable to reueile the workes of God.
12 Now therefore whē thou didest pray, &
Sara thy daughter in lawe, I did bring to
memorie your prayer before yͤ holie one:
& when thou didest burye the dead, I was
with thee likewise.
13 And when thou wast not grieued to rise
vp, and leaue thy diner to burye the dead,
thy good dede was not hid from me: but
I was with thee.

He that wilbe acceptable to God, must be proued with tentacion.

14 And now God hathe sent me to heale
thee, and Sarra thy daughter in law.
15 I am Raphael one of the seuē holie Angels, which present yͤ prayers of the Saintes, and which go forthe before his holie
maiestie.
16 Then they were bothe troubled, and fell
vpon their face: for they feared.
17 But he said vnto them, Feare not, for it
shal go wel with you: praise God therefore.
18 For I came not of mine owne pleasure,
but by the good wil of your God: wherefore praise him in all ages.
19 *All these dayes I did appeare vnto you,
but I did nether eat nor drinke, but you
sawe it in vision.

Gen 18,8. & 19,3. iudg. 13,16.

20 Now therefore giue God thankes: for I
go vp to him that sent me: but write all
things which are done, in a boke.
21 And when they rose, they sawe him no
more.
22 Then they confessed the great & wonderful workes of God, and how the Angel
of the Lord had appeared to them.

CHAP. XIII.

A thankes giuing of Tobit, who exhorteth all to praise the Lord.

1 THen Tobit wrote a prayer of reioycing, and said, Blessed be God that
liueth for euer, & *blessed be* his kingdome.
2 *For he doeth scourge, and hathe pitie: he
leadeth to hel, and bringeth vp, nether is
there anie that can auoide his hand.

Deu. 32,39. 1 sam 2,6. wisd. 16,13.

3 Confesse him before the Gētiles, ye children of Israel: for he hathe scattred you a-
mong them.
4 There declare his greatnes, and extoll
him before all the liuing: for he is our
Lord and our God & our father for euer.
5 He hathe scourged vs for our iniquities,
and wil haue mercie againe, & wil gather
vs out of all naciōs, among whome we are
scattred.
6 If you turne to him with your whole
heart, and with your whole minde, and
deale vprightly before him, then wil he
turne vnto you, and wil not hide his face
frō you, but ye shal se what he wil do with
you: therefore confesse him with your
whole mouth, and praise the Lord of righ
teousnes, and extoll the euerlasting King.
I wil confesse him in the land of my captiuitie, and wil declare his power, & greatnes to a sinful naciō. O ye sinners, turne &
do iustice before him: who can tel if he wil
receiue you to mercie, and haue pitie on
you?
7 I wil extoll my God, and my soule *shal*
praise the King of heauen, and shal reioyce in his greatnes.
8 Let all men speake, and let all praise him
for his righteousnes.
9 O Ierusalem the holie citie, he wil scour
ge thee for thy childrens workes, but he
wil haue pitie againe on the sōnes of righteous men.
10 Giue praise to the Lord duely, & praise
the euerlasting King, that his tabernacle
may be buylded in thee againe with ioye:
and let him make ioyful there in thee those that are captiues, and loue in thee for
euer those that be miserable.
11 Manie nacions shal come frō farre to the
Name of the Lord God, with giftes in
their hands, *euen* giftes to the King of heauen: all generacions shal praise thee, & giue signes of ioye.
12 Cursed are all they, which hate thee: but
blessed are they for euer which loue thee.
13 Reioyce, and be glad for the children of
the iuste: for thei shalbe gathered, and shal
blesse the Lord of the iuste.
14 Blessed are they which loue thee: for thei
shal reioyce in thy peace. Blessed are they
which haue bene sorowful for all thy scour
ges: for they shal reioyce for thee, when
they shal se all thy glorie, and shal reioyce
for euer.
15 Let my soule blesse God the great King.
16 For Ierusalem shalbe buylt vp with Sap-
phires, and emerodes, and thy walles with
pretious stones, and thy towres, and thy
bulwarkes with pure golde.
17 And the streetes of Ierusalem shalbe pa
ued with beral, and carbuncle, and stones
of "Ophir.
18 And all her streetes shal say, "Halleluiah,
and

"*Or, Sophir.*

"*Or, praise ye the Lord.*

*That is, Ierusalem.

and they shal praise *him*, saying, Blessed be
God which hathe extolled "it for euer.

CHAP. XIIII.

4 *Lessons of Tobit to his sonne. 5 He prophecieth the destruction of Nineue. 7 And the restoring of Ierusalem and the Temple. 13 The death of Tobit, and his wife. 16 Tobias age and death.*

1 SO Tobit made an end of praising
God.
2 And he was eight and fiftie yere olde,
when he lost his sight, which was restored
to him after eight yere, and he gaue almes,
and he continued to feare the Lord
God, and to praise him.
3 And when he was verie aged, he called
his sonne, and six of his sonnes sonnes, and
said to him, My sonne, take thy children
(for beholde, I am aged, and am ready
to departe out of this life)
4 Go into Media, my sonne: for I beleue
that those things which Ionas the Prophet
spake of Nineue, that it shal be destroied,
& for a time peace shal rather be in Media,
and that our brethren shal be scattred in
the earth from that good land, & Ierusalē
shal be desolate, and the House of God in
in it shal be burned, and shal be desolate
for a time.
5 Yet againe God *wil haue pitie on them
and bring them againe into the lād where
they shal buylde a Temple, but not like to
the first, vntil the times of that age be fulfilled,
ẘ being finished, they shal returne
frō euerie place out of captiuitie, & buylde
vp Ierusalem gloriously, and the House
of God shal be buylt in it for euer with a
glorious buylding, as the Prophetes haue
spoken thereof.
6 And all nations shal turne, and feare the
Lord God truely, & shal burye their idoles.
7 So shal all nations praise the Lord, & his
people shal confesse God, and the Lord
shal exalte his people, and all those which
loue the Lord in trueth and iustice, shal
reioyce, & those also which shewe mercie
to our brethren.

*Ezra. 3, 8. & 6, 14.

8 And now, my sonne, departe out of Nineue,
because that those things which the
Prophet Ionas spake, shal surely come to
passe.
9 But kepe thou the Law, & the commandements,
& shewe thy self merciful & iust
that it may go wel with thee.
10 And burye me honestly, and thy mother
with me: but tarie no lōger at Nineue. Remember,
my sonne, how a man handled
Achiacharus that broght him vp, how out
of light he broght him into darkenes, and
how he rewarded him againe: yet Achiacharus
was saued, but the other had his rewarde:
for he went downe into darkenes.
Manasses gaue almes, & escaped the snare
of death, which they had set for him, but
Aman fell into the snare and perished.
11 Wherefore now, my sonne, cōsider what
almes doeth, and how righteousnes doeth
deliuer. Whē he had said these things, "he
gaue vp the gost in the bed, being an hundreth
and eight and fiftie yere olde, and
he buryed him honorably.
12 And when Anna was dead, he buryed her
with his father: but Tobias went with his
wife and children to Ecbatane to Raguel
his father in lawe.
13 Where he became olde with honour, and
he buryed his father and mother in lawe
honorably, & he inherited their substance
and Tobits his father.
14 And he dyed at Ecbatane in Media, being
an hundreth and seuē & twentie yere olde.
15 But before he dyed, he heard of the destruction
of Nineue, which was taken by
Nabuchodonosor and Assuerus, and before
his death, he reioyced for Nineue.

"Or, his soule failed him in the bed.

IVDETH.

CHAP. I.

1 *The buylding of Ecbatane. 5 Nabuchodonosor made warre against Arphaxad and ouercame him. 12 He threateneth them that wolde not helpe him.*

1 IN the twelfth yere of
the reigne of Nabucho
donosor, who reigned
in Nineue the great citie
(in the daies of Arphaxad,
which reigned
ouer the Medes in Ecbatane,
2 And buylt in Ecbatane the walles rounde
about, of hewen stone, thre cubites broad,
and six cubites long, and made the height
of the wall seuētie cubites, & the breadth
thereof fiftie cubites,
3 And made the towres thereof in the gates
of it of an hūdreth cubites, & the breadth
thereof in the fundaciō threscore cubites,
4 And made the gates thereof, euen gates
that were lifted vp on hie, seuentie cubites,
& the breadth of them fortie cubites,
for ẙ going forthe of his mightie armies,
and for the setting in aray of his fotemen)
5 Euen in those daies, King Nabuchodono
sor made warre with Kīg Arphaxad in the
great field, which is the field in the coastes
of Ragau.
6 Then came vnto him all they that dwelt
in the mountaines, & all that dwelt by Euphrates,
and Tygris and Hydaspes, & the

countrey of Arioch the King of the Ely-
means, and verie manie nations assembled
them selues to the battel of the sonnes of
Chelod.
7 And Nabuchodonosor King of the Assy
rians sent vnto all that dwelt in Persia, &
to all that dwelt in the West, & to those
that dwelt in Cilicia, and Damascus, and
Libanus and Antilibanus, and to all that
dwelt vpon the sea coast,
8 And to the people, that are in Carmel, &
Galaad, and the hier Galile, and the great
field of Esdrelam,
9 And to all that were in Samaria, & the ci
ties thereof, & beyonde Iorden vnto Ieru
salē, & Betane, & Chellus, & Cades, & the
riuer of Egypt, and Taphnes, and Ramesse
and all the land of Gesem,
10 Vnto one come to Tanis, & Memphis, &
to all the inhabitants of Egypt, & to one
come to the mountaines of Ethiopia.
11 But all the inhabitants of this countrey
did not passe for the commandement of
Nabuchodonosor King of the Assyrians,
nether wolde they come with him to the
battel: for they did not feare him: yea, he
was before them as one mā: therefore they
sent away his ambassadours from them
without effect, and with dishonour.
12 Therefore Nabuchodonosor was very
angrie with all this countrey, and sware
by his throne and kingdome that he wolde surely be auenged vpon all those coastes of Cilicia and Damascus, and Syria,
and that he wolde slay with the sworde all
the inhabitants of the land of Moab, and
the children of Ammon, and all Iudea, and
all that were in Egypt, til one come to the
borders of the two seas.
13 Then he marched in battel aray with his
power against King Arphaxad in the seuententh yere, aud he preuailed in his bat
tel: for he ouerthrewe all the power of Ar
phaxad, and all his horse men, and all his
chariots.
14 And he wanne his cities, and came vnto
Ecbatane, and toke the towres, and spoiled
the stretes thereof, and turned the beautie
thereof into shame.
15 He toke also Arphaxad in the mountaines of Ragau, & smote him through with
his dartes and destroyed him vtterly that
daye.
16 So he returned afterwarde to Nineue,
bothe he and all his companie with a verie great multitude of men of warre, and
there he passed the time, and banketed,
bothe he, and his armie an hundreth and
twentie dayes.

CHAP. II.

*3 Nabuchodonosor cōmanded presumpteously that all peo
ple shulde be broght in subiection. 6 And to destroy
those that disobeyed him. 15 The preparation of O-
lophernes armie. 23 The conquest of his enemies.*

1 AND in the eightenth yere, the two
and twentieth *day* of the first moneth, there was talke in the house of Nabu
chodonosor King of the Assyrians, that he
shulde aduenge him selfe on all the earth,
as he had spoken.
2 So he called vnto him all his officers and
all his nobles, and cōmunicated with thē
his secret counsel, and set before them with
his owne mouth all the malice of the earth.
3 Then they decreed to destroie all flesh,
that had not obeied the commandement
of his mouth.
4 And when he had ended his counsel, Nabuchodonosor King of ẏ Assyrians called
Olofernes his chief captaine, and which
was next vnto him, and said vnto him,
5 Thus saith the great King, the lord of the
whole earth, Beholde, thou shalt go forthe
from my presence, and take with thee men
that trust in their owne strength, of fotemen, an hundreth and twentie thousand,
& the nomber of horses with their riders,
twelue thousand,
6 And thou shalt go against all the West
countrey, because they desobeied my com
mandement.
7 And thou shalt declare vnto them, that
they prepare for me the land and the water: for I wil go forthe in my wrath against
them, and wil couer the whole face of the
earth with the fete of mine armie, and I
wil giue them as a spoyle vnto them,
8 So that their wounded shal fil their valleis, & their riuers, & the flood shal ouerflowe, being filled with their dead.
9 And I wil bring their captiuitie to the
vtmost partes of all the earth.
10 Thou therefore shalt departe hence, and
take vp for me all their countrey: and if
they yelde vnto thee, thou shalt reserue
thē for me vntil the day that I rebuke thē.
11 But concerning them that rebell, let not
thine eye spare thē, but put thē to death, &
spoyle them wheresoeuer thou goest.
12 For as I liue, and the power of my kingdome, whatsoeuer I haue spoken, that wil I
do by mine hand.
13 And take thou hede that thou transgresse
not any of the cōmandemēts of thy Lord,
but accōplish them fully, as I haue cōman
ded thee, and differre not to do them.
14 ¶ Then Olofernes went forthe from the
presence of his lord, and called all the gouernours, and captaines, and officers of the
armie of Assur,
15 And he mustred the chosen men for the
battel, as his lord had commanded him,
vnto an hundreth & twentie thousand, and
twelue thousand archers on horsbacke.
16 And he set them in aray according to the
maner of setting a great armie in aray.
17 And he toke camels & asses for their burdens,

deus, a very great nomber, and shepe, and
oxen, & goates without nomber for their
prouision,
18 And vitaile for euerie man of the armie,
and very muche golde & siluer out of the
Kings house.
19 Then he went forthe and all his power,
to go before in the viage of King Nabuchodonosor,& to couer all the face of the
earth Westwarde,with their charets, and
horsemen,and chosen fotemen.
20 A great multitude also of sundrie sortes
came with them like grashoppers,and like
the grauel of the earth: for the multitude
was without nomber.
21 And they went forthe of Nineue thre
daies iornay towarde the countrey of Bectileth, and pitched from Bectileth nere the mountaine which is at the left hand
of the vpper Cilicia.
22 Then he toke all his armie, his fotemen
and horsemen,and charets, and went from
thence into the mountaines,
23 And he destroied Phud and Lud, and
spoyled all the children of Rasses, and the
children of Ismael, which were towarde
the wildernes at the South of the Che-
lians.
24 Then he went ouer Euphrates,and went
through Mesopotamia,& destroied all the
hie cities that were vpō the riuer of Arbo-
nai,vntil one come to the sea.
25 And he toke the borders of Cilicia, and
destroied all that resisted him,and came to
ẏ borders of Iapheth,which were towarde
the South and ouer against Arabia.
26 He cōpassed also all the children of Ma
dian, and burnt vp their tabernacles, and
spoyled their lodges.
27 Then he went downe into the countrey
of Damascus, in the time of wheat haruest
and burnt vp all their fields,and destroied
their flockes and the herds:he robbed their
cities, and spoyled their countrey, and
smote all their yong men with the edge of
the sworde.
28 Therefore feare and trembling fel vpon
all the inhabitants of the sea coast, which
were in Sidon and Tyrus, and them that
dwelt in Sur & Ocina, & all that dwelt in
Iemnaan: & they that dwelt in Azotus, &
Ascalon feared him greatly.

CHAP. III.

The people subiect to Olofernes. 8 He destroied their gods that Nabuchodonosor might onely be worshipped.

1 SO they sent ambassadours to him with
messages of peace,saying,
2 Beholde,we are the seruātes of Nabuchodonosor the great King: we lie downe
before thee: vse vs as shalbe good in thy
sight.
3 Beholde, our houses and all our places,
and all our fields of wheat, and our flockes,and our herdes, and all our lodges and
tabernacles lie before thy face: vse them
as it pleaseth thee.
4 Beholde,euen our cities and the inhabitants thereof are thy seruants:come, and
take them,as semeth good to thee.
5 ¶ So the men came to Olofernes,and declared vnto them after this maner.
6 Then came he downe towarde the sea
coast, bothe he and his armie, and set garisons in the hie cities,and toke out of thē
chosen men for the warre.
7 So they and all the countrey rounde a-
bout receiued thē,with crownes,with dan
ces,and with timbrels.
8 Yet he brake downe all their borders,and
cut downe their woods: for it was inioyned him to destroy all the gods of the lād,
that all nacions shulde worshippe Nabuchodonosor onely, and that all tongues and tribes shulde call vpon him as
God.
9 Also he came against Esdraelon, nere vnto Iudea, ouer against the great strait of
Iudea,
10 And he pitched betwene Geba, and a citie of the Scythians, and there he taried a
moneth,that he might assemble all ẏ baggage of his armie.

CHAP. IIII.

The Israelites were afraied and defended their countrey. 6 Ioacim the Priest writeth to Bethulia, that they shulde fortifie them selues. 9 They cryed to the Lord, and humbled them selues before him.

1 NOw the childrē of Israel that dwelt
in Iudea, heard all that Olofernes
the chief captaine of Nabuchodonosor
King of the Assyrians had done to the nacions,and how he had spoiled all their tem
ples,and broght them to noght.
2 Therefore they feared greatly his presence, and were troubled for Ierusalem,and
for the Temple of the Lord their God.
3 For they were newly returned from the
captiuitie, and of late all the people was
assembled in Iudea, and the vessels and the
altar of the House had bene sanctified because of the pollution.
4 Therefore they sent into all the coastes
of Samaria, and the villages, and to Be-
thoro, and Belmen, and Iericho, and to
Choba, and Esora, and to the valley of
Salem,
5 And toke all the toppes of the hie mountaines, and walled the villages that were
in them, and put in vitailes for the prouision of warre: for their fields were of late
reaped.
6 Also Ioacim the hie Priest which was in
those daies in Ierusalem,wrote to thē that
dwelt in Bethulia & Betomestham, which
is ouer against Esdraelon towarde the opē
countrey nere to Dothaim,

7 Exhorting them to kepe the passages of
the mountaines: for by them there was an
entrie into Iudea, & it was easie to let thẽ
that wolde come vp, because the passage
was streit for two men at the moste.
8 And the children of Israel did as Ioacim
the hie Priest had commanded them with
the Ancients of all the people of Israel,
which dwelt at Ierusalem.
9 Then cryed euerie man of Israel to God
with great feruencie, and their soules with
great affection.
10 Bothe they, and their wiues, & their chil
dren, and their cattel, and euerie stranger,
and hireling, and their boght seruants put
sackecloth vpon their loynes.
11 Thus euerie man & woman, and the chil
dren, and the inhabitãts of Ierusalem fell
before the Temple, & sprinkled ashes vpon their heades, and spred out their sackecloth before the face of the Lord: also
they put sackecloth about the altar,
12 And cryed to the God of Israel, all with
one consent moste earnestly, that he wolde not giue their children for a pray, and
their wiues for a spoyle, and the cities of
their inheritance to destruction, & the San
ctuarie to pollution and reproche, and vnto derision to the heathen.
13 So God heard their prayers, and loked
vpon their affliction: for the people fasted
many daies in all Iudea and Ierusalem before the Sãctuarie of the Lord almightie.
14 And Ioacim the hie Priest, and all the
Priests that stode before the Lord, & ministred vnto ẏ Lord, had their loynes girt
with sackecloth, and offred the continual
burnt offring, with praiers and the fre giftes of the people,
15 And had ashes on their mytres, & cryed
vnto ẏ Lord with all their power for grace, and that he wolde loke vpõ all the house of Israel.

CHAP. V.

Achior the Ammonite doeth declare to Olofernes of the maner of the Israelites.

1 THen was it declared to Olofernes
the chief captaine of the armie of As
sur, that the children of Israel had prepared for warre, and had shut the passages of
the mountaines, and had walled all the top
pes of the hie hilles, and had laied impediments in the champion countrey.
2 Wherewith he was very angrie, and called all the princes of Moab, and the captaines of Ammon, and all the gouernours
of the sea coast.
3 And he said vnto thẽ, Shewe me, ô ye sonnes of Chanaã, who is this people ẏ dwelleth in the mountaines? and what are the
cities that they inhabite? and what is the
multitude of their armie? and wherein is
their strength and their power? and what
King or captaine is raised among them
ouer their armie?
4 And why haue they determined not to
come to mete me, more then all the inhabitants of the West?
5 ¶ Then * said Achior the captaine of all *Chap.11,7.*
the sonnes of Ammon, Let my lord heare
the worde of the mouth of his seruant, and
I wil declare vnto thee the trueth concerning this people, that dwell in these moũtaines, nere where thou remainest: & there shal no lie come out of the mouth of thy
seruant.
6 This people come of the stocke of the
Chaldeans.
7 And * they dwelt before in Mesopotamia, *Gen.11,3.*
because they wolde not follow the gods
of their fathers, which were in the land of
Chaldea.
8 But they went out of the way of their ancestres and worshipped the God of heauẽ,
the God whome they knewe: so they cast
them out from the face of their gods, and
they fled into Mesopotamia, & soiourned
there many daies.
9 Then * their God cõmanded them to de- *Gen.12,1.*
parte frõ the place where they soiourned,
and to go into the land of Chanaan, where
they dwelt, and were increased with golde
and siluer, and with very muche cattel.
10 But when a famine couered all the land
of Chanaan, they went downe into Egypt,
and dwelt there til they returned, and became there a great multitude, so that one
colde not nomber their linage.
11 * Therefore the King of Egypt rose vp a- *Exo.1,8.*
gainst them, and vsed deceit against them,
and broght them lowe with laboring in
bricke, and made them sclaues.
12 Then they cryed vnto their God, and he
smote all the lãd of Egypt with incurable
plagues: so the * Egyptians cast them out *Exod.12,3.*
of their sight.
13 And * God dryed the red Sea in their pre *Exod.14,21.*
sence,
14 And * broght them into mount Sina and *Exo.19,1.*
Cades barne, and cast forthe all that dwelt
in the wildernes.
15 So they dwelt in the land of the Amorites, and they destroied by their strength
all them of Esebon, and passing ouer Iordan, they inherited all the mountaines.
16 And they * cast forthe before them the *Iosh.12,21.*
Chanaanites & the Pheresites, and the Iebusites, and them of Sichem, and all the
Gergesites, and they dwelt in that countrey many daies.
17 And whiles they sinned not before their
God, they prospered, because the God that
hated iniquitie, was with them.
18 But * when they departed from the way *Iudg.2,11. & 3,8.*
which he appointed them, they were de-
stroied in many battels after a wonderful
sorte,

2.King.25,1. sorte,* & were led captiues into a lãd that
was not theirs: & the Tẽple of their God
was cast to the grounde & their cities were
taken by the enemies.
Ezr.2,1. 19 But * now they are turned to their God,
& are come vp frõ the scattering wherein
thei were scattered, and haue possessed Ierusalem, where their Temple is, and dwell
in the mountaines which were desolate.
20 Now therefore, my lord & gouernour,
if there be anie faute in this people, so
that they haue sinned against their God,
let vs consider that this shalbe their ruine,
and let vs go vp, and we shal ouercome
them.
21 But if there be none iniquitie in this peo
ple, let my lord passe by, lest their Lord
defend them, and their God be for them,
and we become a reproche before all the
worlde.
22 ¶And when Achior had finished these
sayings, all the people, standing rounde a-
bout the tent, murmured: & the chief men
of Olofernes, and all that dwelt by the
sea side and in Moab, spake that he shulde
kill him.
23 For, *say they*, we feare not to mete ỹ children of Israel: for lo, it is a people that haue no strength nor power against a mightie armie.
24 Let vs therefore go vp, ô lord Olofernes, and they shal be meat for thy whole
armie.

CHAP. VI.

Olofernes blasphemeth God whome Achior confessed. 14 Achior is deliuered into the hands of them of Bethulia. 18 The Bethulians crye vnto the Lord.

1 AND when the tumulte of the men
that were about the counsel, was cea
sed, Olofernes, the chief captaine of the
armie of Assur, said vnto Achior before
all the people of the strangers, and before
all the children of Moab, & of them that
were hired of Ephraim,
2 Because thou hast prophecied among vs
to day, and hast said that the people of Ierusalem is able to fight, * because their
Chap.5,5. God wil defend them: and who is god but
Nabuchodonosor?
3 He wil send his power, and wil destroye
them from the face of the earth, and their
God shal not deliuer them: but we his seruants wil destroye them as one man: for
they are not able to susteine the power of
our horses.
4 For we wil tread them vnder fete with
them, and their mountaines shalbe drunken with their blood, and their fields shal
be filled with their dead bodies, and their
fotesteppes shal not be able to stand before vs: but they shal vtterly perish.
5 The King Nabuchodonosor, lord of all
the earth, hathe said, euen he hathe said,
None of my wordes shalbe in vaine.
6 And thou Achior an hireling of Ammon,
because thou hast spoken these wordes in
the day of thine iniquitie, thou shalt se
my face no more from this day vntil I take vengeance of that people that is come
out of Egypt.
7 And then shal the yron of mine armie,
and the multitude of them that serue me,
passe through thy sides, and thou shalt fall
among their slayne, when I shal put them
to flight.
8 And my seruants shal cary thee into the
mountaines, and they shal leaue thee at o-
ne of the hie cities: but thou shalt not perish, til thou be destroyed with them.
9 And if thou persuade thy self in thy
minde, that they shal not be taken, let not
thy countenance fall: I haue spoken it, and
none of my wordes shalbe in vaine.
10 Then commanded Olofernes them cõcerning Achior, that they shulde bring
him to Bethulia, and deliuer him into the
hands of the children of Israel.
11 So his seruants toke him, and broght him
out of the campe into the plaine: and thei
went out from the middes of the plaine
into the mountaines, and came vnto the
fountaines that were vnder Bethulia.
12 And when the men of the citie sawe thẽ
from the toppe of the mountaine, they toke their armour, and went forthe of the
citie vnto the toppe of the mountaine, e-
uen all the throwers with slings, and kept
them from comming vp, by casting stones
against them.
13 But they went priuely vnder the hill, &
bounde Achior, and left him lying at the
fote of the hill, & returned to their lord.
14 Then the Israelites came downe from
their citie, and stode about him, and losed
him & broght him into Bethulia, & presen
ted him to the gouernours of their citie,
15 Which were in those daies, Ozias the
sonne of Micha, of the tribe of Simeon,
and Chabris the sonne of Gothoniel, &
Charmis the sonne of Melchiel.
16 And they called together all the Ancients of the citie, and all their youth ranne
together, and their women to the assemblie: and they set Achior in the middes of
all their people. Then Ozias asked him
of that which was done.
17 And he answered & declared vnto them
the wordes of the counsel of Olofernes,
and all the wordes that he had spoken in
the middes of the princes of Assur, and
whatsoeuer Olofernes had spoken proudely against the house of Israel.
18 Then the people fel downe and worshipped God, and cryed vnto God, saying,
19 O Lord God of heauen, beholde their
pride, and haue mercie on the basenes of

our people, and beholde this day the face
of those that are sanctified vnto thee.
20 Then they comforted Achior, & praised him greatly.
21 And Ozias toke out of the assemblie into his house, & made a feast to the Elders,
and they called on the God of Israel all
that night for helpe.

CHAP. VII.

1 Olofernes doeth besiege Bethulia. 8 The counsel of the Idumeans and other against the Israelites. 23 The Bethulians murmure against their gouernours for lacke of water.

1 THe next day, Olofernes commanded
all his armie and all his people, which
were come to take his parte, that thei shulde remoue their campes against Bethulia,
and that they shulde take all the streites
of the hill, and to make warre against the
children of Israel.
2 Then their strong men remoued their
camps in that daye, and the armie of the
men of warre was an hundreth thousand
and seuentie fotemen, & twelue thousand
horsemē, beside the baggage & other men
that were afote among them, a very great
multitude.
3 And they camped in the plaine nere vnto
Bethulia, by the fountaine, and thei spred
abroad toward Dothaim vnto Belbaim,
and in length from Bethulia vnto Ciamō,
which is ouer against Esdraelom.
4 Now the children of Israel, when they
sawe ỷ multitude, were greatly troubled,
& said euerie one to his neighbour, Now
wil they shut vp all the whole earth: for
nether the hie mountaines nor the valleis,
nor ỷ hilles are able to abide their burden.
5 Then euerie one toke his weapōs of warre, and burning fyres in their towres, they
remained and watched all that night.
6 But in the secōde day, Olofernes broght
forthe all his horsemen in the sight of the
childrē of Israel, which were in Bethulia,
7 And vewed the passages vp to their citie,
and came to the fōutaines of their waters,
& toke thē & set garisons of men of warre
ouer thē, and remoued toward his people.
8 Then came vnto him all the chief of the
children of Esau, and all the gouernours
of the people of Moab, & all the captaines of the sea coast, and said,
9 Let our captaine now heare a worde, lest
an inconuenience come in thine armie.
10 For this people of the children of Israel do not trust in their speares, but in the
height of the mountaines, wherein they
dwell, because it is not easy to come vp to
the toppes of their mountaines.
11 Now therefore, my lord, fight not a-
gainst them in battel aray, and there shal
not so muche as one man of thy people
perish.
12 Remaine in thy campe, and kepe all the
men of thine armie, and let thy men kepe
stil the water of the countrey, that cometh
forthe at the fote of the mountaine.
13 For all the inhabitants of Bethulia haue
their water thereof: so shal thirst kill thē,
and they shal giue vp their citie: and we
and our people wil go vp to the toppes of
the mountaines that are nere, & wil campe vpon them, & watche that none go out
of the citie.
14 So thei & their wiues, & their children
shalbe consumed with famine, & before
the sworde come against thē, thei shalbe
ouerthrowen in ỷ stretes where thei dwel.
15 Thus shalt thou rēder them an euil reward, because thei rebelled & obeied not
thy persone peaceably.
16 And these wordes pleased Olofernes &
all his soldiers, and he appointed to do as
they had spoken.
17 So the campe of the children of Ammon departed, & with them fiue thousand
of the Assyrians, and they pitched in the
valley, & toke the waters, and the fountaines of the waters of the childrē of Israel.
18 Then the children of Esau went vp with
the children of Ammon, & camped in the
mountaines ouer against Dothaim, & thei
sent some of thē selues towarde the South,
and towarde the East, ouer against Rebel,
which is nere vnto Chusi, that is vpon the
riuer Mochmur: and the rest of the armie
of the Assyrians camped in the field, and
couered the whole land: for their tents &
their baggage were pitched in a wonderful great place.
19 Then the children of Israel cryed vnto
the Lord their God, because their heart
failed: for all their enemies had cōpassed
them about, and there was no way to escape out from among them.
20 Thus all the companie of Assur remained about them, bothe their fotemen, chariots and horsemen, foure and thirtie dayes: so that euē all the places of their waters
failed all the inhabitants of Bethulia.
21 And the cisternes were emptie, and they
had not water ynough to drinke for one
day: for they gaue them to drinke by measure.
22 Therefore their children swoned, and
their wiues & yong men failed for thirst,
and fel downe in the stretes of the citie, &
by the passages of the gates, and there was
no strength in them.
23 Then all the people assembled to Ozias,
and to the chief of the citie, bothe yong
men and women, and children, and cryed
with a loude voyce, and said before all the
Elders,
24 The *Lord iudge betwene vs & you: for *Exod 5,21.*
you haue done vs great iniurie, in that ye
haue

haue not required peace of the children
of Assur.
25 For now we haue no helper: but God hathe solde vs into their hands, that we shulde be throwen downe before them with
thirst and great destruction.
26 Now therefore call them together, & deliuer the whole citie for a spoile to ŷ people of Olofernes, and to all his armie.
27 For it is better for vs to be made a spoile
vnto thē, then to dye for thirst: for we wil
be his seruants that we may liue, & not se
ŷ death of our infants before our eyes, nor
our wiues, nor our children to dye.
28 We take to witnes against you the heauē
and the earth, & our God and Lord of our
fathers, which punisheth vs, according to
our sinnes & the sinnes of our fathers, that
he lay not these things to our charge.
29 Then there was a great crye of all ŵ one
cōsent in ŷ middes of the assemblie, & thei
cryed vnto ŷ Lord God ŵ a loude voyce.
30 Then said Ozias to thē, Brethren, be of
good courage: let vs waite yet fiue daies,
in the which space the Lord our God may
turne his mercie toward vs: for he wil not
forsake vs in the end.
31 And if these daies passe, and there come
not helpe vnto vs, I wil do according to
your worde.
32 So he separated the people, euerie one vn
to their charge, & thei wēt vnto the walles
and towres of their citie, & sent their wiues & their children into their houses, and
they were very lowe broght in the citie.

CHAP. VIII.

The parentage, life & conuersation of Iudeth. 11 She rebuketh the faintenes of the gouernours. 12 She sheweth that they shulde not tempt God, but wait vpon him for succour. 33 Her enterprise against the enemies.

1 NOw at that time, Iudeth heard thereof, which was the daughter of Me
rari the sonne of Ox, the sonne of Ioseph,
the sonne of Oziel, the sonne of Elcia, the
sonne of Ananias, the sonne of Gedeō, the
sonne of Raphaim, the sonne of Acito, the
sonne of Eliu, the sonne of Eliab, the sōne
of Nathanael, the sonne of Samael, ŷ sonne of Salasadai, the sonne of Israel.
2 And Manasses was her housband, of her
stocke and kinred, who dyed in the barely
haruest.
3 For as he was diligēt ouer thē that boūde
sheaues in ŷ field, the heat came vpon his
head, & he fel vpon his bed, & dyed in the
citie of Bethulia, & thei buryed him with
his fathers in the field betwene Dothaim
and Balamo.
4 So Iudeth was in her house a widowe thre
yeres and foure moneths.
5 And she made her a tente vpon her house,
and put on sackecloth on her loynes, and
ware her widowes apparel.
6 And she fasted all ŷ daies of her widowhode, saue the day before the Sabbath and
the Sabbaths, and the day before the newe
moones, & in the feastes & solemne daies
of the house of Israel.
7 She was also of a goodlie countenance &
very beautiful to beholde: & her housband
Manasses had left her golde & siluer, and
men seruants, and maide seruants, and cattel, and possessions, where she remained.
8 And there was none ŷ colde bring an euil
reporte of her: for she feared God greatly.
9 Now when she heard ŷ euil wordes of the
people against the gouernour, because thei
fainted for lacke of waters (for Iudeth had
heard all the wordes ŷ Ozias had spoken
vnto them, and that he had * sworne vnto *Chap. 7, 35.*
thē to deliuer the citie vnto the Assyrians
within fiue daies)
10 Then she sent her maide ŷ had the gouer
nement of all things that she had, to call
Ozias and Chabris and Charmis the Ancients of the Citie.
11 And they came vnto her, and she said vnto them, Heare me, ô ye gouernours of the
inhabitants of Bethulia: for your wordes ŷ
ye haue spokē before the people this day,
are not right, touching this othe which ye
made & pronounced betwene God & you,
& haue promised to deliuer ŷ citie to the
enemies, vnles within these daies the Lord
turne to helpe you.
12 And now who are you that haue tempted
God this day, & set your selues in the place
of God among the children of men?
13 So now you seke the Lord almightie, but
you shal neuer knowe any thing.
14 For you can not finde out ŷ depth of the
heart of mā, nether cā ye perceiue ŷ things
ŷ he thinketh: thē how can you search out
God, that hathe made all these things, and
knowe his minde, or comprehend his purpose? Nay my brethren, prouoke not the
Lord our God to anger.
15 For if he wil not helpe vs within these
fiue daies, he hathe power to defend vs
when he wil, euen euerie day, or to destroy
vs before our enemies.
16 Do not you therefore binde ŷ counsels of
the Lord our God: for God is not as man
that he may be threatned, nether as ŷ sonne of man to be broght to iudgement.
17 Therefore let vs waite for saluacion of
him & call vpon him to helpe vs, & he wil
heare our voyce if it please him.
18 For there appeareth none in our age, nether is there any now in these daies, nether
tribe, nor familie, nor people, nor citie a-
mōg vs, which worship ŷ gods made with
hands, as hathe bene afore time.
19 For * ŷ which cause our fathers were giuē *Iud. 2, 11. &*
to the sworde, & for a spoile, & had a great *4, 1. & 6, 1.*
fall before our enemies.
20 But we knowe none other God: there fo-

re we trust that he wil not despise vs, nor
any of our linage.
21 Nether when we shalbe taken, shal Iudea
be so famous: for our Sanctuarie shalbe
spoiled, and he wil require the prophana-
cion thereof at our mouth,
22 And the feare of our brethren, and the
captiuitie of the countrey, & the desolatiō
of our inheritance wil he turne vpon our
heads amōg the Gentiles, where soeuer we
shalbe in bondage, & we shalbe an offence & a reproche to all thē that possesse vs.
23 For our seruitude shal not be directed by
fauour, but the Lord our God shal turne
it to dishonour.
24 Now therefore, ô brethren, let vs shewe
an example to our brethren, because their
hearts depend vpō vs, & the Sanctuarie, &
the House, and the altar rest vpon vs.
25 Moreouer, let vs giue thākes to the Lord
our God, which tryeth vs euen as he did
our fathers.
Gen.22,1. 26 Remember what things he did to *Abraham, and how he tryed Isaac, and all that
Gen.28,7. he did to *Iacob in Mesopotamia of Syria
when he kept the shepe of Laban his mothers brother.
27 For he hathe not tryed vs as he did them
to the examination of their hearts, nether
doeth he take vengeance on vs, but the
Lord punisheth for instruction them that
come nere to him.
28 ¶ Then said Ozias to her, All that thou
hast spoken, hast thou spoken with a good
heart, and there is none that is able to resist thy wordes.
29 For it is not to day that thy wisdome
is knowen, but from the beginning of thy
life all the people haue knowen thy wisdome: for the deuice of thine heart is good.
30 But the people were very thirstie, and
compelled vs to do vnto them, as we haue
spoken, & haue broght vs to an othe which
we may not transgresse.
31 Therefore now pray for vs, because thou
art an holy womā, that the Lord may send
vs rayne to fill our cisternes, and that we
may faint no more.
32 Then said Iudeth vnto them, Heare me,
and I wil do a thing, which shalbe declared in all generations, to the children of
our nacion.
33 You shal stand this night in the gate, and
I wil go forthe with mine handmaid: and
within the daies that ye haue promised to
deliuer the citie to our enemies, the Lord
wil visit Israel by mine hand.
34 But inquire not you of mine acte: for I
wil not declare it vnto you, til the things
be finished that I do.
35 Then said Ozias & the princes vnto her,
Go in peace, and the Lord God be before
thee, to take vengeance on our enemies.
36 So they returned from the tent, and went
to their wardes.

CHAP. IX.

1 Iudeth humbleth her self before the Lord, and maketh her prayers for the deliuerance of her people. 7 Against the pride of the Assyrians. 11 God is the helpe of the humble.

1 THen Iudeth fel vpon her face, and
put ashes vpon her head, and put of
the sackecloth wherewith she was clothed.
And about the time that the incense of
that euening was offred in Ierusalē in the
House of the Lord, Iudeth cryed with a
loude voyce, and said,
2 O Lord God of my father * Simeon, to Gen 34,25.
whome thou gauest a sworde to take vengeance of the strangers which opened the
wombe of the maide, and defiled her, and
discouered the thigh with shame, and polluted the wombe to reproche (for thou hadest commanded that it shulde not so be,
3 Yet thei did things for the which thou ga
uest their princes to the slaughter, for they
were deceiued & washed their beds with
blood) and hast striken the seruants with
the gouernours, and the gouernours vpon
their thrones,
4 And hast giuen their wiues for a pray and
their daughters to be captiues, & all their
spoiles for a bootie to ẏ children that thou
louedst: which were moued with thy zeale, and abhorred the pollution of their
blood, & called vpō thee for aide, ô God,
ô my God, heare me also a widdowe.
5 For thou hast wroght the things afore, &
these, and the things that shalbe after, and
thou cōsiderest the things that are present,
and the things that are to come.
6 For the things which ẏ doest purpose, are
present, & say, Beholde, we are here: for all
thy waies are ready, & thy iudgements are
foreknowen.
7 Beholde, the Assyrians are multiplied by
their power: they haue exalted thē selues
with horses & horsemen: they glorie in the
strength of their fotemen: they trust in
shield, speare and bowe, and sling, and do
not knowe that thou art ẏ Lord that breakest the battels: the Lord is thy Name.
8 Breake thou their strength by thy power,
and breake their force by thy wrath: for
they haue purposed to defile thy Sanctuarie, & to pollute the tabernacle where thy
glorious Name resteth, and to cast downe
with weapons the hornes of the altar.
9 Beholde their pride, and send thy wrath
vpō their heads: giue into mine hād which
am a widow, ẏ strength ẏ I haue cōceiued.
10 Smite by the deceit of my lippes the ser- Iud.4,21. & 5,26.
uant with the prince, and the prince with
the seruant: abbate their height by the hād
of a woman. Iud.7,2.
11 *For thy power standeth not in the multi 2.chr.14,11. & 6,8.
tude, nor thy might in strōg men: but thou, & 20,6.

ô Lord, art the helpe of the humble and
litle ones, the defender of the weake, & the
protector of them that are forsaken, & the
Sauiour of them that are without hope.
12 Surely, surely *thou art* the God of my father,
& the God of ŷ inheritance of Israel,
the Lord of heauen and earth, the creator
of the waters, the King of all creatures:
heare thou my prayer,
13 And grant me wordes & craft, & a wounde,
and a stroke against thē that entreprise
cruel things against thy couenant, and against
thine holy House, & against the toppe
of Sion, and against the house of the
possession of thy children.
14 Shewe euidently among all thy people,
& all the tribes, that they may knowe that
thou art the God of all power & strength,
& that there is none other that defendeth
the people of Israel, but thou.

CHAP. X.

1 Iudeth decketh her self & goeth forthe of the citie. 11 She is taken of the watch of the Assyrians and broght to Olofernes.

1 NOw after she had ceased to crye vnto
the God of Israel, and had made
an end of all these wordes,
2 She rose where she had fallen downe, and
called her maide, & went downe into the
house, in the which she abode in the Sabbath
daies and in the feast daies,
3 And putting away the sackecloth wherewith
she was clad, & putting of the garments
of her widowhode, she washed her
body with water, & anoĩted it with muche
ointemēt, & dressed the heere of her head,
and put attire vpon it, and put on her garments
of gladnes, wherewith she was clad
during the life of Manasses her housbād.
4 And she put slippers on her fete, & put on
bracelets, & sleues, and rings, & earings, &
all her ornaments, and she decked her selfe
brauely to allure the eyes of all men that
shulde se her.
5 Then she gaue her maide a bottel of wine,
and a pot of oyle, and filled a scrippe
with floure, & with drye figges, & with fine
bread: so she lapped vp all these things together
and laid them vpon her.
6 Thus they went forthe to the gate of the
citie of Bethulia, and found standing there
Ozias, and the ancients of the citie, Chabris
and Charmis.
7 And whē they sawe her that her face was
changed, & that her garment was chāged,
they marueiled greatly at her wonderful
beautie, and said vnto her,
8 The God, ŷ God of our fathers giue thee
fauour, and accomplish thine enterprises
to the glorie of the children of Israel, and
to the exaltation of Ierusalem. Then they
worshipped God.
9 And she said vnto them, Cōmande the gates
of the citie to be opened vnto me, that
I may go forthe to accomplish the things
which you haue spoken to me. So they cōmanded
the yong men to open vnto her,
as she had spoken.
10 And when they had done so, Iudeth wēt
out, she and her maide with her, and the
men of the citie loked after her, vntil she
was gone downe the mountaine, and til
she had passed the valley, and colde se her
no more.
11 Thus they went streight forthe in the
valley, and the first watche of the Assyriās
met her,
12 And toke her, & asked her, Of what people
art thou? and whēce comest thou? and
whether goest thou? And she said, I am a
womā of the Hebrewes, and am fled from
them: for they shalbe giuen you to be consumed.
13 And I come before Olofernes, the chief
captaine of your armie, to declare him
true things, and I wil shewe before him
the way whereby he shal go and winne all
the mountaines, without losing the bodie
or life of anie of his men.
14 Now when the men heard her wordes, &
behelde her countenance, they wondered
greatly at her beautie, and said vnto her,
15 Thou hast saued thy life, in that thou
hast hasted to come downe to the presence
of our lord: now therefore come to
his tente, and some of vs shal cōduct thee
vntil thei haue deliured thee into his hāds.
16 And when ŷ standest before him, be not
afraid in thine heart, but shewe vnto him
according as thou hast to say, and he wil
intreat thee wel.
17 Then they chose out of thē an hundreth
men, and prepared a charet for her and
her maide, and broght her to the tent of
Olofernes.
18 Then there was a running to and fro,
throughout the campe: for her comming
was bruted among the tentes: & thei came
and stode rounde about her: for she stode
without the tent of Olofernes vntil they
had declared vnto him concerning her.
19 And they marueiled at her beautie, and
wondered at the children of Israel because
of her, & euerie one said vnto his neighbour,
Who wolde despise this people, that
haue among thē suche women? surely it is
not good that one mā of them be left: for
if thei shulde remaine, they might deceiue
the whole earth.
20 Then Olofernes garde went out, and all
his seruantes, and they broght her into the
tente.
21 Now Olofernes rested vpon his bed vnder
a canopie, which was wouen with purple
and golde and emeraudes, and precious
stones.

22 So they shewed him of her, and he came
forthe vnto the entrie of his tent,and they
caried lampes of siluer before him.
23 And when Iudeth was come before him
and his seruants, they all marueiled at the
beautie of her countenance, and she fel
downe vpon her face,& did reuerence vnto him,& his seruants toke her vp.

CHAP. XI.

2 Olofernes comforteth Iudeth, 3 And asketh the cause of her comming. 5 She deceiueth him by her faire wordes.

1 THen said Olofernes vnto her, Womã,
be of good comfort:feare not in thine heart: for I neuer hurt any that wolde
serue Nabuchodonosor ẏ King of all the
earth.
2 Now therefore if thy people that dwelleth in the mountaines, had not despised
me, I wolde not haue lifted vp my speare
against them:but they haue procured these things to them selues.
3 But now tel me wherefore thou art fled
from them,and art come vnto vs: for thou
art come for safegard: be of good cõfort,
thou shalt liue frõ this night,& hereafter.
4 For none shal hurt thee, but intreat thee
wel, as they do the seruants of King Nabuchodonosor my lord.
5 Then Iudeth said vnto him, Receiue the
wordes of thy seruãt, & suffer thine handmaide to speake in thy presence, and I wil
declare no lie to my lord this night.
6 And if thou wilt follow the wordes of thine handmaide, God wil bring the thing
perfectly to passe by thee, & my lord shal
not faile of his purpose.
7 As Nabuchodonosor King of all ẏ earth
liueth, and as his power is of force, who
hathe sent thee to reforme all persones,not
onely men shal be made subiect to him by
thee,but also the beastes of the fields,& the
cattel, & the foules of the heauen shal liue
by thy power vnder Nabuchodonosor &
all his house.
8 For we haue heard of thy wisdome and of
thy prudẽt spirit, & it is declared through
the whole earth, that thou onely art excellent in all the kingdome, and of a wonderful knowledge, and in feates of warre
marueilous.
9 Now *as concerning the matter which A- Chap.5.5.
chior did speake in thy counsel,we haue
heard his wordes:for the men of Bethulia
did take him, & he declared vnto them all
that he had spoken vnto thee.
10 Therefore, ô lord & gouernour, reiect
not his worde,but set it in thine heart,for it
is true: for there is no punishment against
our people, nether can the sworde preuaile against them, except they sinne against
their God.
11 Now therefore lest my lord shulde be
frustrate,and voide of his purpose, & that
death may fall vpon them, and that they
may be taken in their sinne whiles they
prouoke their God to angre, *which is* so oft
times as they do that which is not be-
seming,
12 (For because their vittailes faile,and all
their water is wasted, thei haue determined to take their cattel,and haue purposed
to consume all things that God had forbidden them to eat by his Lawes:
13 Yea,they haue purposed to consume the
first frutes of the wheat, and the tithes of
the wine, and of the oile which they had
reserued and sanctified for the Priests that
serue in Ierusalem before the face of our
God:the which things it is not lawful for
anie of the people to touche ẇ their hãds.
14 Moreouer they haue sent to Ierusalem,
because they also that dwel there,haue done the like, suche as shulde bring them licence from the Senate)
15 Now when they shal bring them worde,
they wil do it,and they shalbe giuen thee
to be destroyed the same day.
16 Wherefore I thine handmaid, knowing
all this, am fled from their presence, and
God hathe sent me to worke a thing with
thee, whereof all the earth shal wonder,&
whosoeuer shal heare it.
17 For thy seruant feareth God, and worshipeth the God of heauẽ day and night,
and now let me remaine with thee, my
lord, and let thy seruant go out in the
night into the valley,and I wil pray vnto
God, that he may reueile vnto me when
they shal commit their sinnes,
18 And I wil come and shewe it vnto thee:
then thou shalt go forthe with all thine ar
mie,& there shalbe none of them that shal
resist thee.
19 And I wil lead thee through the middes
of Iudea, vntil thou come before Ierusalem,and I wil set thy throne in the middes
thereof,and thou shalt driue them as shepe
that haue no shepherd, and a dogge shal
not barcke with his mouthe against thee:
for these things haue bene spokẽ vnto me,
& declared vnto me accordĩg to my foreknowledge,and I am sent to shewe thee.
20 ¶Then her wordes pleased Olofernes,
and all his seruants, and they marueiled at
her wisdome,and said,
21 There is not suche a woman in all the
worlde,bothe for beautie of face,and wisdome of wordes.
22 Likewise Olofernes said vnto her, God
"hathe done this,to send thee before ẏ peo- "Or, hathe done wel.
ple,that strẽgth might be in our hãds, and
destruction vpõ thẽ that despise my lord.
23 And now thou art bothe beautiful in thy
coũtenãce,& wittie in thy wordes:surely if
thou do as ẏ hast spoken, thy God shalbe
my

my God, and thou shalt dwell in the house
of Nabuchodonosor, & shalt be renomed
throughout the whole earth.

CHAP. XII.

1 Iudeth wolde not pollute her self with the meat of the Gentiles. 5 She maketh her request that she might go out by night to pray. 11 Olofernes causeth her to come to the banket.

1 THen he commanded to bring her in
where his treasures were layed, and
bade that they shulde prepare for her of
his owne meates, and that she shulde drinke of his owne wine.

Gen.43,32. dan.1,8. tob.1,12.

2 But Iudeth said, *I may not eat of them,
lest there shulde be an offence, but I can
suffice my selfe with the things that I haue broght.
3 Then Olofernes said vnto her, If the
things that thou hast, shulde faile, how shul
de we giue thee the like? for there is none
with vs of thy nation.
4 Then said Iudeth vnto him, As thy soule liueth, my lord, thine handmaide shal
not spend those things that I haue, before
the Lord worke by mine hand the things
that he hathe determined.
5 Then the seruants of Olofernes broght
her into the tent, and she slept vntil midnight, and rose at the morning watche,
6 And sent to Olofernes, saying, Let my
lord commãde that thine hãdmaide may
go forthe vnto prayer.
7 Then Olofernes commanded his garde
that thei shuld not stay her: thus she abode
in the campe thre dayes, and went out in
the night into the valley of Bethulia, and
washed her self in a fountaine, euen in the
water by the campe.
8 And when she came out, she prayed vnto
the Lord God of Israel, that he wolde direct her way to the exaltation of the children of her people.
9 So she returned, & remained pure in the
tent, vntil she ate her meat at euening.
10 ¶ And in the fourthe day, Olofernes ma
de a feast to his owne seruants onely, and
called none of them to the bãket, that had
the affaires in hand.
11 Thẽ said he to Bagoas the eunuche who
had charge ouer all that he had, Go and
persuade this Hebrewe woman, which is
with thee, that she come vnto vs and eat, &
drinke with vs.
12 For it were a shame for vs, if we shulde
let suche a womã alone, & not talke ẇ her,
& if we do not allure her, she wil mocke vs
13 Then wẽt Bagoas frõ the presence of O-
lofernes, & came to her, & said, Let not this
faire maide make difficultie to go into my
lord, & to be honored in his presence, and
to drinke wine with vs ioyfully, & to be intreated as one of the daughters of the children of Assur, which remaine in the house
of Nabuchodonosor.
14 Then said Iudeth vnto him, Who am I
now, that I shulde gainesay my lord? Surely what soeuer pleaseth him, I wil do spedely, and it shalbe my ioye vnto the day
of my death.
15 So she arose & trimmed her ẇ garments,
and with all ẏ ornaments of women, & her
maide wẽt, & spred for her skinnes on the
groũde ouer against Olofernes, which she
had receiued of Bagoas for her daily vse,
that she might sit and eat vpon them.
16 Now when Iudeth came & sate downe,
Olofernes heart was rauished with her,
and his spirit was moued, and he desired
greatly her companie: for he had waited
for the time to deceiue her from the day
that he had sene her.
17 Then said Olofernes vnto her, Drinke
now, and be mery with vs.
18 So Iudeth said, I drinke now, my lord,
because my state is exalted this day more
then euer it was since I was borne.
19 Thẽ she toke, & ate & drãke before him
the things, that her maide had prepared.
20 And Olofernes reioyced because of her
& drãke muche more wine thẽ he had drũkẽ
at anie time in one day since he was borne.

CHAP. XIII.

1 Iudeth praieth for strẽgth. 8 She smiteth of Olofernes necke. 10 She returneth to Bethulia & reioyceth her people.

1 NOw whẽ the euening was come, his
seruants made haste to departe, and
Bagoas shut his tent without, & dimissed
those that were present, from the presence
of his lord, & they went to their beddes:
*for they were all wearie, because the feast Eccl.31,12.
had bene long.
2 And Iudeth was left alone in the tent, &
Olofernes was stretched along vpon his
bed: for he was filled with wine.
3 ¶ Now Iudeth had cõmanded her maide
to stãd without her chãber, & to waite for
her cõming forthe as she did daily: for she
said, she wolde go forthe to her prayers, &
she spake to Bagoas according to the same purpose.
4 So all went forthe of her presence, & none was left in the chãber, nether litle nor
great: thẽ Iudeth standing by his bed, said
in her heart, O Lord God of all power, beholde at this present the workes of mine
hands for the exaltation of Ierusalem.
5 For now is ẏ time to helpe thine inheritãce, & to execute mine enterprises, to ẏ destructiõ of ẏ enemies ẇ are risen agaĩst vs.
6 Then she came to the post of ẏ bed which
was at Olofernes head, & toke downe his
fauchin from thence,
7 And approched to the bed, & toke holde
of the heere of his head, and said, Strengthen me, ô Lord God of Israel this day.
8 And she smote twise vpon his necke with

all her might, and she toke away his head
from him,
9 And roled his bodie downe from the bed,
and pulled downe the canopie from the
pillers, and anone after she went forthe, &
gaue Olofernes head to her maid,
10 And she put it in her scrippe of meat: so
they twaine went together according to
their custome vnto prayer, and pressing
through the tentes, went about by that
valley, and went vp the mountaine of Bethulia, and came to the gates thereof.
11 ¶ Thẽ said Iudeth afarre of to the watche men at the gates, Open now the gate: God, euen our God is with vs to shewe
his power yet in Ierusalem, and his force
against his enemies, as he hathe euen done
this day.
12 Now whẽ the men of her citie heard her
voyce, thei made haste to go downe to the
gate of their citie, and they called the Elders of the citie.
13 And thei ranne all together bothe smale
and great: for it was aboue their expectation, that she shulde come. So they opened
the gate & receiued her, & made a fyre for
a light, & stode rounde about thẽ twaine.
14 Then she said to thẽ with a loude voyce, Praise God, praise God: for he hathe
not taken away his mercie from the house
of Israel, but hathe destroyed our enemies
by mine hands this night.
15 So she toke the head out of the scrippe &
shewed it, and said vnto them, Beholde the
head of Olofernes, the chief captaine of ỳ
armie of Assur, and beholde the canopie,
wherein he did lie in his drunkẽnes, & the
Lord hathe smitten him by the hand of a
woman.
16 As the Lord liueth, who hathe kept me
in my way that I went, my countenance
hathe deceiued him to his destructiõ, & he
hathe not cõmitted sinne with me by anie
pollution or vilenie.
17 Then all the people were wonderfully
astonished, and bowed them selues, and
worshiped God, and said with one accorde, Blessed be thou, ô our God, which hast
this day broght to noght the enemies of
thy people.
18 Then said Ozias vnto her, O daughter,
blessed art thou of the moste hie God a-
boue all the women of the earth, and blessed be the Lord God, which hathe created
the heauens and the earth, which hathe directed thee to the cutting of of the head
of the chief of our enemies.
19 Surely this thine hope shal neuer departe out of the heartes of men: for they shal
remember the power of God for euer.
20 And God turne these things to thee for
a perpetual praise, and visite thee with
good things, because thou hast not spared
thy life, because of the affliction of our na
cion, but thou hast holpen our ruine, walking a streight way before our God. And
all the people said, So be it, so be it.

CHAP. XIIII.

1 Iudeth causeth to hang vp the head of Olofernes.
10 Achior ioyneth him selfe to the people of God.
11 The Israelites go out against the Assyrians.

1 THen said Iudeth vnto them, Heare
me also, my brethren, and * take this 2.Mac.15,35
head, and hang it vpon the hiest place of
your walles.
2 And so sone as the morning shal appeare
and the sonne shal come forthe vpon the
earth, take you euerie one his weapons, and
go forthe euerie valiant man out of the
citie, and set you a captaine ouer them, as
thogh you wolde go downe into the field,
towarde the watche of the Assyrians, but
go not downe.
3 Then they shal take their armour, & shal
go into their campe, and raise vp the captaines of the armie of Assur, and they shal
runne to the tent of Olofernes, but shal not
finde him: then feare shal fall vpon thẽ,
and they shal flee before your face.
4 So you and all that inhabite the coastes
of Israel, shal pursue them, & ouerthrowe
them as they go.
5 But before you do these things, call me
Achior the Ammonite, that he may se, and
knowe him that despised the house of Israel, and that sent him to vs as to death.
6 Then they called Achior out of the house
of Ozias, and when he was come and sawe
the head of Olofernes in a certeine mans
hand in the assemblie of the people, he fel
downe on his face, and his spirit failed.
7 But when they had taken him vp, he fel
at Iudeths fete, & reuerenced her, and said,
Blessed art thou in all the tabernacle of Iu
da, and in all nacions, which, hearing thy
name, shalbe astonished.
8 Now therefore tel me all the things, that
thou hast done in these dayes. Thẽ Iudeth
declared vnto him in the middes of the
people all that she had done from the day
that she went forthe, vntil that houre she
spake vnto them.
9 And whẽ she had left of speaking, the people reioyced with a great voyce, and made
a noyce of gladnes through their citie.
10 And Achior, seing all things that God
had done for Israel, beleued in God vnfainedly, and circumcised the foreskine of
his flesh, and was ioyned vnto the house of
Israel vnto this day.
11 ¶ Assone as the morning arose, thei hãged the head of Olofernes out at the wall,
& euerie man toke his weapons, and they
went forthe by bandes vnto the straites of
the mountaine.
12 But when the Assyrians sawe them, they
sent

ſent to their captaines, which went to the
gouernours and chief captaines, and to
all their rulers.
13 So they came to Olofernes tent and ſaid
to him ẏ had the charge of all his things,
Wakē our lord: for the ſclaues haue bene
bolde to come downe againſt vs to battel,
that they may be deſtroyed for euer.
14 Then went in Bagoas, & knocked at the
dore of the tent: for he thoght that he had
ſlept with Iudeth.
15 But becauſe none anſwered, he opened
it, and went into the chamber, and founde
him caſt vpon the floore, and his head was
taken from him.
16 Therefore he cryed with a loude voyce,
with weping and mourning, & a mightie
crye, and rent his garments.
17 After, he went into the tent of Iudeth
where ſhe vſed to remaine, and founde her
not: then he leaped out to the people and
cryed,
18 Theſe ſclaues haue committed wickednes: one woman of the Hebrewes hathe
broght ſhame vpon the houſe of King
Nabuchodonoſor: for beholde, Olofernes
lieth vpon the grounde without an head.
19 When the captaines of the Aſſyrians
armie heard theſe wordes, they rent their
coates, and their heart was wonderfully
troubled, and there was a crye and a verie
great noyce throughout the campe.

CHAP. XV.

1 The Aſſyrians are afraied and flee. 3 The Iſraelites purſue them. 8 Ioacim the hie Prieſt cometh to Bethulia to ſe Iudeth and to praiſe God for her.

1 AND whē thei that were in the tents,
heard, they were aſtoniſhed at the
thing that was done.
2 And feare and trembling fel vpon them,
ſo that there was no man that durſt abide
in the ſight of his neighbour: but altogether amaſed, thei fled by euerie way of the
plaine and of the mountaines.
3 They alſo that had camped in the mountaines rounde about Bethulia, were put to
flight: thē the children of Iſrael, eueryone
that was a warriour among them, ruſſhed
out vpon them.
4 Then ſent Ozias to Bethomaſthem, and
to Bebai, and Chobai, and Chola and to
all the coaſtes of Iſrael, ſuche as ſhulde
declare vnto them the things that were
done, and that all ſhulde ruſhe forthe vpon their enemies to deſtroy them.
5 Now when the children of Iſrael heard
it, they all fell vpon them together vnto
Choba: likewiſe alſo thei that came from
Ieruſalem & from all the mountaines: for
men had tolde thē what things were done
in the campe of their enemies, and they
that were in Galaad and in Galile chaſed
them with a great ſlaughter vntil they
came to Damaſcus and to the coaſtes thereof.
6 And the reſidue that dwelt at Bethulia,
fel vpon the campe of Aſſur and ſpoiled
them, and were greatly enriched.
7 And the children of Iſrael that returned
from the ſlaughter, had the reſt: & the villages & the cities that were in the mountaines & in the plaine, had a great bootie:
for the abundance was verie great.
8 Then Ioacim the hie Prieſt, and the Ancients of the children of Iſrael that dwelt
in Ieruſalem, came to confirme the benefites that God had ſhewed to Iſrael, and
to ſe Iudeth, and to ſalute her.
9 And when they came vnto her, thei bleſſed her with one accorde, & ſaid vnto her,
Thou art the exaltacion of Ieruſalem:
thou art the great glorie of Iſrael: thou
art the great reioycing of our nacion.
10 Thou haſt done all theſe things by thine hand: thou haſt done muche good to Iſrael, & God is pleaſed therewith: bleſſed
be thou of the almightie Lord for euermore: and all the people ſaid, So be it.
11 And the people ſpoyled the campe the
ſpace of thirtie daies, and thei gaue vnto
Iudeth Olofernes tent, and all his ſiluer &
beddes, and baſins, and all his ſtuffe, & ſhe
toke it and laied it on her mules, & made
readie her charets, & laied them thereon.
12 Then all the women of Iſrael came together to ſe her, and bleſſed her, and made
a dance among them for her, and ſhe toke
branches in her hand, and gaue alſo to the
women that were with her.
13 They alſo crowned her with oliues, and
her that was with her, and ſhe went before
the people in the dance, leading all the
women: and all the men of Iſrael followed
in their armour, with crownes and with
ſongs in their mouthes.

CHAP. XVI.

Iudeth praiſeth God with a ſong. 19 She offreth to the Lord Olofernes ſtuffe. 23 Her continence, life and death. 25 All Iſrael lamenteth her.

1 THen Iudeth began this confeſsion in
all Iſrael, and all the people ſang this
ſong with a loude voyce.
2 And Iudeth ſaid, Beginne vnto my God
with tymbrels: ſing to my Lord with cymbales: tune vnto him a pſalme: exalt his
praiſe, and call vpon his Name.
3 For God breaketh the battels, and *pitched*
his campe in the middes of the people, &
deliuered me out of the hand of the perſecuters.
4 Aſſur came from the mountaines forthe
of the North: he came with thouſands in
his armie, * whoſe multitude hathe ſhut Chap. 2, 11.
vp the riuers and their horſemen haue co-

uered the valleis.
5 He said that he wolde burne vp my borders & kill my yong men with the sworde,
and dash the sucking children against the
grounde, & make mine infants as a pray,
and my virgines a spoile.
6 But the almightie Lord hathe broght
them to naught by the hand of a woman.
7 For the mightie did not fall by the yong
men,nether did the sonnes of Titan smite him, nor the hie gyants inuade him,but
Iudeth the daughter of Merari did dis-
comfite him by the beautie of her countenance.
8 For she put of the garment of her wid-
dowhode,for the exaltacion of those that
were oppressed in Israel,and anointed her
face with ointment, and bounde vp her
heere in a coife, and toke a linen garment
to deceiue him.
9 Her slippers rauished his eyes: her beautie toke his minde prisoner, and the fauchin passed through his necke.
10 The Persiãs were astonished at her boldenes, and the Medes were troubled with
her hardines.
11 But mine afflicted reioyced, & my feble
ones showted: then they feared, they lifted vp their voyce and turned backe.
12 The children of maides perced them,
and wounded them as they fled away like
children:they perished by the battel of the
Lord.
13 I wil sing vnto the Lord a song and
praise, O Lord, thou art great and glorious, maruelous and inuincible in power.
14 Let all thy creatures serue thee: * for
thou hast spoken and they were made:thou
hast sent thy Spirit,and he made them vp:
& there is none that can resist thy voyce.
15 For the mountaines leape vp from their
fundacions with the waters: the rockes
melt at thy presence like waxe: yet thou
art merciful to them that feare thee.
16 For all sacrifice is to litle for a swete sauour,and all the fat is to litle for thy burnt
offring: but he that feareth the Lord, is
great at all times.
17 Wo to the nacions that rise vp against
my kinred: the Lord almightie wil take
vengeance of them in the day of iudgement, in sending fyre and wormes vpon
their flesh, and they shal fele them & wepe for euer.
18 ¶ After, when they went vnto Ierusalem,
they worshiped the Lord, and assone as
the people were purified,they offred their
burnt offrings, and their fre offrings, and
their giftes.
19 Iudeth also offred all the stuffe of Olofernes, which the people had giuen her,
and gaue the canopie which she had taken
of his bed,for an oblacion to the Lord.
20 So the people reioyced in Ierusalem by
the Sanctuarie, for the space of thre moneths, and Iudeth remained with them.
21 After this time, euerie one returned to
his owne inheritance, and Iudeth went to
Bethulia, and remained in her owne possession, and was for her time honorable in
all the countrey.
22 And manie desired her, but none had
her companie all the dayes of her life after
that Manasses her housband was dead, &
was gathered to " his people.
23 But she increased more and more in honour, and waxed olde in her housbands
house, being an hundreth and fiue yere
olde, & made her maid fre: so she dyed in
Bethulia, and they buryed her in the graue of her housband Manasses.
24 And * the house of Israel lamented her
seuen daies, & before she dyed, she did distribute her goods to all them that were
nerest of kinred to Manasses her housband, and to them that were the nerest of
her kinred.
25 And there was none that made the children of Israel anie more afraied in the
daies of Iudeth, nor a long time after her
death.

Gen. 1,24. Psal. 33,9.

" Or, her people.

Gen. 50,10.

Esther.

ESTHER.

Certeine porcions of the storie of Esther, which are founde in some Greke and Latin translations.

Which follow the tenth chapter.

4 THEN Mardocheus said,
God hathe done these
things.
5 For I remember a dreame,
which I sawe concer-
ning these matters, and
there was nothing there-
of omitted.
6 A litle fountaine which became a flood,
and was a light, and as the sunne, & as muche water, this flood was Esther whome the
King maried, and made Quene.
7 And the two dragons are I and Aman.
8 And the people are they that are assembled to destroye the name of the Iewes.
9 And my people is Israel, which cryed to
God, and are saued: for the Lord hathe saued his people, and the Lord hathe deliuered vs from all these euils, and God hathe
wroght signes, and great wonders, which
haue not bene done among the Gentiles.
10 Therefore hathe he made two lottes, one
for the people of God, and another for all
the Gentiles.
11 And these two lottes came before God
for all nations, at the houre and time appointed, and in the day of iudgement.
12 So God remembred his owne people, &
iustified his inheritance.
13 Therefore those dayes shalbe vnto thē
in the moneth Adar ẏ fourtenth and fiftēth
day of the same moneth, with an assemblie
and ioye, and with gladnes before God,
according to the generations for euer a-
mong his people.

CHAP. XI.

1 IN the fourth yere of the reigne of Ptolomeus and Cleopatra Dositheus, who
said he was a Priest and Leuite, and Ptolomeus his sonne, that broght the former
letters of " Phrurai, which thei said Lysi- "Or, lottes.
machus the sonne of Ptolomeus, which
was at Ierusalem, interpreted,
2 In the second yere of the reigne of great
Artaxerxes in the first day of the moneth
Nisan Mardocheus the sonne of Iarus, the
sonne of Semei the sonne of Cis of the
tribe of Beniamin had a dreame,
3 A Iewe dwelling in the citie of Susis, a no
ble man, that bare office in ẏ Kings court.
4 He was also one of the captiuitie which
Nabuchodonosor the King of Babylon
broght from Ierusalem with Iechonias.
5 And this was his dreame, Beholde a noice
of a tempest with thunders, and earth qua-
kes, and vproare in the land.
6 Beholde two great dragons came forthe
ready to fight one against another.
7 Their crye was great, whereby all the
heathen were ready to fight against the
righteous people.
8 And the same day was ful of darkenes &
obscuritie, & trouble, & anguish: yea, aduer
sitie, and great afflictiō was vpon ẏ earth.
9 For then the righteous fearing their afflictions, were amased, and being ready to
dye, cryed vnto God.
10 And while they were crying, the litle wel
grewe into a great riuer, and flowed ouer
with great waters.
11 The light & the sunne rose vp, & ẏ lowlie were exalted, & deuoured the glorious.
12 Now when Mardocheus had sene this
dreame, he awoke and rose vp and thoght
in his heart vntil ẏ night, what God wolde
do, & so he desired to know all the matter.

CHAP. XII.

1 AT the same time dwelt Mardocheus
in the Kings court with Bagathas,
and Thara, the Kings eunuches & kepers
of the palace.
2 *But when he heard their purpose, and *Esther. 2, 21. & 6, 2.
their imaginaciōs, he perceiued that they
went about to lay their hands vpon the
King Artaxerxes, and so he certified the
King thereof.
3 Then caused the King to examine ẏ two
eunuches with torments, and when they
had confessed it, they were put to death.
4 This the King caused to be put in the
Chronicles. Mardocheus also wrote the
same thing.
5 So the King cōmāded that Mardocheus
shulde remaine in the court, and for the
aduertisement, he gaue him a rewarde.
6 But Amā the sonne of Amadathus ẏ Agagite, ẇ was in great honour and reputaciō
with the King, went about to hurt Mardocheus & his people, because of the two
eunuches of ẏ King ẏ were put to death.

CHAP. XIII.

1 The copie of the letters of Artaxerxes against the Iewes, 8 The prayer of Mardocheus.

1 THe copie of the letters was this, The Ioseph Antiq. li. 11. chap. 6.
great King Artaxerxes writeth these
things to ẏ princes & gouernours ẏ are vnder him from India vnto Ethiopia in an
hundreth and seuen and twētie prouinces.

2 When I was made lord ouer manie people, & had subdued the whole earth vnto
my dominion, I wolde not exalte my self
by the reason of my power, but purposed
with equitie alway and gẽtelnes to gouerne my subiects, and wholy to set them in
a peaceable life, and thereby to bring my
kingdome vnto trãquilitie, that mẽ might
safely go thorow on euerie side, and to re-
new peace againe, which all men desire.
3 Now when I asked my counselers how
these things might be broght to passe, one
that was conuersant with vs, of excellent
wisdome, and constant in good wil, and
shewed him self to be of sure fidelitie,
which had the seconde place in the kingdome, euen Aman,
4 Declared vnto vs, that in all naciõs there
was scatered abroade a rebellious people,
that had Lawes contrarie to all people,
and haue alway dispised the commandements of Kings, and so that this general
empire, that we haue begonne, can not be
gouerned without offence.
5 Seing now we perceiue, that this people
alone are altogether contrarie vnto euerie man, vsing strange and other maner of
lawes, and hauing an euil opinion of our
doings, and go about to stablishe wicked
matters, that our kingdome shulde not
come to good estate,
6 Therefore haue we commanded, that all
they that are appointed in writing vnto
you by Aman (which is ordeined ouer the
affaires, & is as our seconde father) shal all
with their wiues and childrẽ be destroyed
and rooted out with the sworde of their
enemies without all mercie, and that none
be spared the fortenth day of the twelfth
moneth Adar of this yere,
7 That they which of olde, and now also
haue euer benẽ rebellious, may in one day
with violence be thruste downe into the
hell, to the intente that after this time our
affaires may be without troubles, and wel
gouerned in all pointes.
8 Then Mardocheus thoght vpon all the
workes and of the Lord, and made his
prayer vnto him,
9 Saying, O Lord, Lord, the King almightie (for all things are in thy power) and
if thou hast appointed to saue Israel, there is no man that can withstande thee.
10 For thou hast made heauen and earth,
and all the wonderous things vnder the
heauen.
11 Thou art Lord of all things, and there is
no man that can resist thee, which art the
Lord.
12 Thou knowest all things, & thou knowest, Lord, that it was nether of malice, nor
presumption, nor for anie desire of glorie,
that I did this, and not bowe downe to
proude Aman.
13 For I wolde haue bene cõtent with good
wil for the saluation of Israel, to haue kist
the sole of his fete.
14 But I did it, because I wolde not preferre the honour of a man aboue the glorie
of God, and wolde not worship anie but
onely thee, my Lord, and this haue I not
done of pride.
15 And therefore, ô Lord God and King,
haue mercie vpon thy people: for they i-
magine how thei may bring vs to naught,
yea, they wolde destroye the inheritance,
that hathe bene thine frõ the beginning.
16 Dispise not the porcion, which thou
hast deliuered out of Egypt for thine
owne self.
17 Heare my prayer, and be merciful vnto
thy portion: turne our sorowe into ioye,
that we may liue, ô Lord, and praise thy
Name: shut not the mouthes of them that
praise thee.
18 All Israel in like maner cryed moste earnestly vnto the Lord, because that death
was before their eyes.

CHAP. XIIII.

The prayer of Esther for the deliuerance of her, and her people.

1 Quene Esther also, being in danger
of death, resorted vnto the Lord,
2 And laid away her glorious ap
parel, and put on the garments of sighing,
and mourning. In the stead of precious
ointement, she scatered ashes, and dongue
vpon her head: and she humbled her bodie
greatly with fasting, and all the places
of her ioye filled she with the heere that
she plucte of.
3 And she prayed vnto the Lord God of
Israel, saying, O my Lord, thou onely art
our King: helpe me desolate womã, which
haue no helper but thee.
4 For my danger is at hand.
5 Frõ my youth vp I haue heard in the kinred of my father, that thou, ô Lord, tokest
Israel from among all people, and our fathers from their predecessours for a perpetual inheritance, and thou hast performed that which thou didest promise
them.
6 Now Lord, we haue sinned before thee:
therefore hast thou giuen vs into the hãds
of our enemies.
7 Because we worshipped their gods, ô
Lord, thou art righteous.
8 Neuertheles, it satisfieth them not, that
we are in bitter captiuitie, but they haue
stroken hands with their idoles,
9 That thei wil abolish the thing that thou
with thy mouth hast ordeined, & destroye
thine inheritance, to shut vp the mouthe
of them that praise thee, and to quence
the glorie of thy tẽple, and of thine altar,

10 And to open the mouthes of the heathen, that they may praise the power of the
idoles, and to magnifie a fleshlie King for
euer.
11 O Lord, giue not thy scepter vnto them
that be nothing, lest thei laugh vs to scorne
ne in our miserie: but turne their deuise
vpon them selues, and make him an example, that hathe begonne the same a-
gainst vs.
12 Thinke vpon vs, ô Lord, and shewe
thy self vnto vs in the time of our distresse, and strengthen me, ô King of gods, and
Lord of all power.
13 Giue me an eloquét speache in my mouth
before the Lion: turne his heart to hate
our enemie, to destroye him, and all suche
as consent vnto him.
14 But deliuer vs with thine hand, and helpe me that am solitarie, which haue no defence but onely thee.
15 Thou knowest all things, ô Lord: thou
knowest, that I hate the glorie of the vnrighteous, & that I abhorre the bed of the
vncircumcised, and of all the heathen.
16 Thou knowest my necessitie: for I hate
this token of my preeminence, which I
beare vpō mine head, what time as I must
shewe my self, & that I abhorre it as a mē-
struous cloth, & that I weare it not when
I am alone by my self,
17 And that I thine hand maide haue not
eaten at Amans table, and that I haue had
no pleasure in the Kings feast, nor drunke the wine of the drinke offrings,
18 And that I thine hand maide haue no
ioye sence the day that I was broght hether, vntil this day, but in thee, ô Lord
God of Abraham.
19 O thou mightie God aboue all, heare
the voyce of them, that haue none other
hope, and deliuer vs out of the hand of
the wicked, and deliuer me out of my
feare.

CHAP. XV.

1 Mardocheus moueth Esther to go in to the King and make intercession for her people. 9 And she performeth his request.

1 MArdocheus also bade Esther to go
in vnto the King, and pray for her
people, and for her countrey.
2 Remember, saith he, the daies of thy lowe
estate, how thou wast nourished vnder mine hand: for Aman which is next vnto
the King, hathe giuen sentence of death a-
gainst vs.
3 Call thou therefore vpon the Lord, and
speake for vs vnto the King, and deliuer vs
from death.
4 And vpon the thirde day when she had
ended her prayer, she laid away the mourning garments, and put on her glorious
apparel,
5 And decte her self goodly, after that she
had called vpon God, which is the beholder and sauiour of all things, & toke two
handmaides with her.
6 Vpon the one she leaned her self, as one
that was tender.
7 And the other followed her, and bare the
traine of her vesture.
8 The shine of her beautie made her face
rose coloured: and her face was chearful
& amiable, but her heart was sorowful for
great feare.
9 Then she went in thorow all the dores,
and stode before the King, and the King
sate vpon his royal throne, & was clothed
in his goodlie araye, all glittering with
golde and precious stones, and he was very terrible.
10 Then he lift vp his face, that shone with
maiestie, and loked fiercely vpon her: therefore the Quene fel downe, and was pale
and faint and leaned her self vpō the head
of the maide, that went with her.
11 Neuertheles, God turned the Kings min
de ẏ he was gentle, who being careful, leaped out of his throne, and toke her in his
armes, til she came to her self againe: and
comforted her with louing wordes, and
said,
12 Esther, what is the matter? I am thy brother, be of good cheare,
13 Thou shalt not dye: for our commandement toucheth the cōmons, and not thee.
Come nere.
14 And so he helde vp his golden sceptre, &
laid it vpon her necke,
15 And kissed her, and said, Talke with me.
16 Then said she, I sawe thee, ô lord, as an
Angel of God, & mine heart was troubled
for feare of thy maiestie.
17 For wonderful art thou, ô lord, and thy
face is ful of grace.
18 And as she was thus speaking vnto him,
she fel downe againe for faintnes.
19 Then the King was troubled, and all his
seruants comforted her.

CHAP. XVI.

The copie of the letters of Artaxerxes, whereby he reuoketh those which he first sent forthe.

1 THe great King Artaxerxes, which *Ioseph Anti. 11. chap. 6.*
reigneth from India vnto Ethiopia,
ouer an hundreth and seuen and twentie
prouinces, sendeth vnto the princes and
rulers that haue the charge of our affaires,
Salutation.
2 There be many that through the goodnes
of Princes and honour giuen vnto them,
become very proude,
3 And indeuoure not onelye to hurt our
subiects, but not content to liue in wealth,
do also imagine destruction against those
that do them good,
4 And take not onely all thākefulnes away

from men, but in pride & presumption, as
they that be vnmindeful of benefites, thei
thinke to escape the vengeance of God,
that seeth all things, & is cōtrarie to euil.
5 And oft times manie, which be set in office, and vnto whome their friends causes are committed, by vaine intisemēts do
wrappe them in calamities, that can not be
remedied: for thei make them partakers of
innocent blood,
6 And disceitfully abuse the simplicitie, &
gentlenes of princes with lying tales.
7 This may be proued not onely by olde
histories, but also by those things that are
before our eyes, and are wickedly commit
ted of suche pestilences as are not worthie
to beare rule.
8 Therefore we must take hede hereafter,
that we may make ỹ kingdome peaceable
for all mē, what chāge so euer shal come,
9 And discerne the things that are before
our eyes, to withstand thē with gentlenes.
10 For Aman, a Macedonian, the sonne of
Amadathus, being in dede a strāger from
the Persians blood, and farre from our
goodnes, was receiued of vs,
11 And hathe proued the friendship that
we beare towarde all nations, so that he
was called our father, and was honored of
euerie man, as the next persone vnto
the King.
12 But he colde not vse him self soberly
in this great dignitie, but wēt about to depriue vs of the kingdome, & of our life.
13 With manifolde disceite also hathe he
desired to destroye Mardocheus our preser
uer, which hath done vs good in all thīgs,
and innocent Esther the partaker of our
kingdome, with all her nation.
14 For his minde was (when he had taken
them out of the way) to lay waite for vs,
and by this meanes to translate the kingdome of the Persians vnto them of Macedonia.
15 But we finde that the Iewes (which were
accused of this moste wicked mā that thei
might be destroyed) are no euil doers, but
vse moste iust Lawes,
16 And that they be ỹ children of the moste
high and almightie and euer liuing God,
by whome the kingdome hathe bene preserued vnto vs, and our progenitours in
verie good ordre.
17 Wherefore ye shal do wel, if ye do not
put in execution those letters, that Aman
the sonne of Amadathus did write vnto
you.
18 For he that inuented them, hāgeth at Susis before the gates with all his familie, &
God (which hathe all things in his power)
hathe spedely rewarded him after his deseruing.
19 Therefore ye shal publishe the copie of
this letter in all places, that the Iewes may
frely liue after their owne Lawes.
20 And ye shal aide them, that vpon the thir
tenth day of the twelfth moneth Adar thei
may be aduenged of them, which in the
time of their trouble wolde haue oppressed them.
21 For almightie God hathe turned to ioye
the day, wherein the chosen people shulde
haue perished.
22 Moreouer, among other solemne daies
ye shal kepe this day with all gladnes,
23 That bothe now & in time to come this
day may be a remēbrance of deliuerāce for
vs and all suche as loue the prosperitie of
the Persians, but a remēbrance of destruction to those that be sedicious vnto vs.
24 Therefore all cities and countreis that
do not this, shal horribly be destroyed
with sworde and fyre, and shal not onely
not be inhabited of men, but be abhorred
also of the wilde beastes and foules for
euer.

THE WISDOME of Salomon.

CHAP. I.

1 How we oght to searche and enquire after God. 2 Who be those that finde him. 5 The holy Gost. 8.11 We oght to flee from backbyting and murmuring. 12 Whereof death cometh. 15 Righteousnes & vnrighteousnes.

1.King.3.3. isa.36,1.
1 
Oue * righteousnes, ye
that be Iudges of the
earth: thinke reuerently
of the Lord, & seke him
in simplicitie of heart.
Deu.4,29. 2.chro.15,4.
2 * For he wil be founde
of them that tempte him not, & appeareth
vnto suche as be not vnfaithful vnto him.
3 For wicked thoghts seperate from God:
and *his* power when it is tryed, reproueth
the vnwise,
4 Because wisdome can not enter into a wicked heart, nor dwell in the body that is sub
iect vnto sinne.
5 For the holy * Spirit of discipline fleeth Ier.4,22.
from disceit, & withdraweth him self from
the thoghts ỹ are without vnderstanding,
and is rebuked when wickednes cometh.
6 For the Spirit of wisdome * is louing, and Gal.5,22.

wil not absolue him, ẏ blasphemeth with
his lippes: for God is a witnes of his reines, and a true beholder of his heart, and an
hearer of the tongue.
7 For the Spirit of the Lord filleth all the
worlde: and the same that mainteineth all
things, hathe knowledge of the voyce.
8 Therefore he that speaketh vnrighteous
things, can not be hid: nether shal the iudgement of reproche let him escape.
9 For inquisitiō shalbe made for the thoghtes of the vngodlie, and the sounde of his
wordes shal come vnto God for the correction of his iniquities.
10 For ẏ eare of ielousie heareth all things,
and the noyce of the grudgings shal not
be hid.
11 Therefore beware of murmuring, which
profiteth nothing, & refraine your tongue
from slander: for there is no worde so secret, that shal go for noght, & the mouth
that speaketh lies, slaieth the soule.
12 Seke not death in the errour of your life:
*destroye not your selues thorow the wor-
kes of your owne hands. Deu.4,23.
13 *For God hathe not made death, nether
hathe he pleasure in the destruction of the
liuing. Ezek.18,23. & 33,11.
14 For he created all things, that thei might
haue their being: and the generacions of
the worlde are preserued, and there is no
poyson of destruction in them, & the kingdome of hell is not vpon earth.
15 For righteousnes is immortal, but vnrighteousnes bringeth death.
16 And the vngodlie call it vnto them bothe with hands and wordes: and while they
thinke to haue a friend of it, they come to
naught: for they are confederate with it:
therefore are they worthie to be partakers
thereof.

CHAP. II.

The imaginacions and desires of the wicked, & their coun sel against the faithful.

1 FOr *the vngodlie* say, as they falsely
imagine with them selues, * Our life
is shorte and tedious: and in the death of a
man there is no recouerie, nether was any
knowen that hathe returned from the
graue. Iob.7,1. mat.22,23. 1.cor.15,32.
2 For we are borne at all aduenture, and we
shalbe hereafter as thogh we had neuer
bene: for the breth is a smoke in our nostrels, and the wordes as a sparke raised out
of our heart.
3 Which being extinguished, the body is
turned into ashes, and the spirit vanisheth
as the soft aire.
4 Our life shal passe away as the trace of a
cloude, & come to naught as the mist that
is driuen away with ẏ beaumes of the sunne, and cast downe with the heat thereof.
Our name also shalbe forgotten in time,
and no man shal haue our workes in remembrance.
5 *For our time is as a shadowe that passeth 2.Chro.29,15. chap.5,9.
away, and after our end there is no retur-
ning: for it is fast sealed, so that no man
cometh againe.
6 *Come therefore, and let vs enioye the Isa.22,13. & 56,12.
pleasures, that are present, & let vs chere- 1.cor.15,32.
fully vse the creatures as in youth.
7 Let vs fill our selues with costlie wine
and ointements, and let not the floure of
life passe by vs.
8 Let vs crowne our selues with rose buddes afore they be withered.
9 Let vs all be partakers of our wantonnes: let vs leaue some token of our pleasure in euerie place: for that is our porciō,
and this is our lotte.
10 Let vs oppresse the poore, that is righteous: let vs not spare the widdowe, nor reuerence the white heeres of the aged, that
haue liued many yeres.
11 Let our strength be the lawe of vnrighteousnes: for the thing that is feble, is reproued as vnprofitable.
12 Therefore let vs defraude the righteous:
for he is not for our profite, & he is cōtrarie to our doings: he checketh vs for offen
ding against the Lawe, and blameth vs as
transgressours of discipline.
13 He maketh his boaste to haue the knowledge of God: and he calleth him self the
sonne of the Lord.
14 He is made *to reproue our thoghts. Ioh.7,7.
15 It grieueth vs also to loke *vpon him: for ephes.5,13.
his life is not like other mens: his waies a- Isa.53,3.
re of another facion.
16 He counteth vs as bastardes, and he withdraweth him self from our waies as from
filthines: he commendeth greatly the latter end of the iust, and boasteth that God
is his father.
17 Let vs se *then* if his wordes be true: let vs
proue what end he shal haue.
18 For if the righteous mā be the* sonne of Psal.22,9.
God, he wil helpe him, & deliuer him frō mat.27,43.
the hands of his enemies.
19 Let vs * examine him with rebukes and Iere.11,19.
tormēts, that we may knowe his mekenes,
and proue his pacience.
20 Let vs condemne him vnto a shameful
death: for he shal be preserued as he him
self saith.
21 Suche things do they imagine, and go
astraye: for their owne wickednes hathe
blinded them.
22 And they do not vnderstād the mysteries
of God, nether hope for the rewa de of
righteousnes, nor can discerne the honour
of the soules that are fauteles.
23 For God created man without corrup- Gen.1,27.
tion, and made him after the* image of & 2,7.
his owne likenes. & 5,1. eccles.17,2.

Gen.3,2. 24 *Neuertheles, thorow enuy of the deuil
came death into the worlde: and they that
holde of his side, proue it.

CHAP. III.

1 The conuersacion and assurance of the righteous. 7 The rewarde of the faithful. 11 Who are miserable.

Deut.33,3. 1 BVt the *soules of the righteous are
in the hand of God, and no torment
shal touche them.

Chap.5,4. 2 *In the sight of the vnwise thei appeared
to dye, and their end was thoght grieuous,
3 And their departing from vs, destruction,
but they are in peace.
4 And thogh they suffer paine before men,
Rom.8,24. yet is *their hope ful of immortalitie.
2 cor.5,1. 5 They are punished, but in fewe things,
1.pet.1,13. yet in many things shal they be wel re-
Exod.16,2. warded: *for God proueth them, & findeth
deut.8,2. them mete for him self.
6 He tryeth them as the golde in the forna
ce, and receiueth them as a perfect frute
offring.
Mat.13,43. 7 *And in the time of their vision they shal
shine, and runne through as the sparkes a-
mong the stubble.
Mat.19,28. 8 They *shal iudge the nacions, and haue
1.cor.6,2. dominion ouer the people, and their Lord
shal reigne for euer.
9 They that trust in him, shal vnderstand
the trueth, and the faithful shal remaine
with him in loue: for grace and mercie is
among his Saintes, and he regardeth his
elect.
Mat.25,41. 10 *But the vngodlie shalbe punished according to their imaginacions: for they
haue despised the righteous, and forsaken
the Lord.
11 Who so despiseth wisdome and discipline, is miserable, and their hope is vaine, &
their labours are foolish, and their workes
vnprofitable.
12 Their wiues are vndiscrete, & their children wicked: their offring is cursed.
13 Therefore the barren is blessed which is
vndefiled, and knoweth not the sinful bed:
Isa.56,5. *she shal haue frute in the visitation of the
soules,
14 And the eunuche, which with his hands
hathe not wroght iniquitie, nor imagined
wicked things against God: for vnto him
shal be giuen the special gift of faith, and
an acceptable porcion in the Temple of
the Lord.
15 For glorious is ẏ frute of good labours,
and the roote of wisdome shal neuer fade
away.
16 But the children of adulterers shal not
be partakers of the holy things, and the
seed of the wicked bed shalbe rooted out.
17 And thogh they liue lōg, yet shal they be
nothing regarded, and their last age shalbe without honour.
18 If they dye hastely, they haue no hope,
nether comfort in the day of tryal.
19 For horrible is the end of the wicked generacion.

CHAP. IIII.

Of vertue and the commoditie thereof. 10 The death of the righteous, and the condemnation of the vnfaithful.

1 BEtter is barennes with vertue: for the
memorial thereof is immortal: for it
is knowen with God and with men.
2 When it is present, mē take example thereat, and if it go away, yet they desire it: it
is alway crowned and triumpheth, and
winneth the battel and the vndefiled rewardes.
3 But the multitude of the vngodlie which
abunde in children, is vnprofitable: & the
bastard plātes shal take no depe roote, nor
laye any fast fundacion.
4 For thogh they budde forthe in the branches for a time, * yet they shal be shaken Mat.7,19.
with the winde: for they stand not fast, and
thorowe the vehemēcie of the winde they
shalbe rooted out.
5 For the vnperfect branches shalbe brokē,
& their frute shalbe vnprofitable & sower
to eat, and mete for nothing.
6 For all the children that are borne of the
wicked bed, shalbe witnes of the wickednes against their parents when they be
asked.
7 But thogh the righteous be preuented
with death, yet shal he be in rest.
8 For the honorable age is not that which
is of long time, nether that which is measu
red by the nomber of yeres.
9 But wisdome is the graye heere, and an
vndefiled life is the olde age.
10 *He pleased God, & was beloued of him, Gen.5,24.
so that where as he liued amōg sinners, he Ebr.11,5.
translated him.
11 He was takē away, lest wickednes shulde
alter his vnderstanding, or deceit beguile
his minde.
12 For wickednes by bewitching obscureth
the things that are good, & the vnstedfast-
nes of concupiscēce peruerteth the simple
minde.
13 Thogh he was sone dead, yet fulfilled he
muche time.
14 For his soule pleased God: therefore hasted he to take him away from wickednes.
15 Yet the people se & vnderstand it not, &
cōsider no suche things in their hearts, how
that grace and mercie is vpon his Saintes,
and his prouidence ouer the elect.
16 Thus the righteous that is dead, cōdemneth the vngodlie which are liuing: & the
youth that is sone broght to an end, the
long life of the vnrighteous.
17 For they se the end of the wise, but they
vnderstand not what *God* hathe deuised for
him, and wherefore the Lord hathe preserued

serued him in safetie.
18 They se him and despise him, but the
Lord wil laugh them to scorne,
19 So that they shal fall hereafter without
honour, and shal haue a shame among the
dead for euermore: for without anie voyce shal he burste them and cast them downe, and shake them from the fundacions, so
that they shalbe vtterly wasted, and they
shalbe in sorowe, and their memorial shal
perish.
20 So they being afraied, shal remember
their sinnes, & their owne wickednes shal
come before them to conuince them.

CHAP. V.

1 The constantnes of the righteous before their persecuters. 14 The hope of the vnfaithful is vaine. 15 The blessednes of the saintes and godlie.

1 THen shal the righteous stãd in great
boldenes before the face of suche as
haue tormented him, and taken away his
labours.
2 When thei se him, thei shalbe vexed with
horrible feare, and shalbe amased for his
wonderful deliuerance,
3 And shal change their mindes, and sigh
for grief of minde, and say within them
selues, This is he whome we sometime
had in derision, and in a parable of reproche.
Chap.3,2. 4 *We fooles thoght his life madnes, and
his end without honour.
5 How is he counted among the children
of God, and his porcion is among the
Saintes!
6 Therefore we haue erred from the waye
of trueth, and the light of righteousnes
hathe not shined vnto vs, and the sunne of
vnderstanding rose not vpon vs.
7 We haue wearied our selues in the waye
of wickednes and destruction, and we haue
gone through dãgerous waies: but we haue not knowen the way of the Lord.
8 What hathe pride profited vs? or what
profite hathe the pompe of riches broght
vs?
1.Chro.29,15 chap.2,5. 9 All those things are *passed away like a
shadow, and as a poste that passeth by:
10 As a shippe that passeth ouer the waues
of the water, which when it is gone by, the
trace thereof can not be founde, nether
the path of it in the floods:
Prou.30.19. 11 Or as * a birde that fleeth thorowe in
the aire, and no man can se anie token of
her passage, but onely heare the noise of
her wings, beating the light winde, par-
ting the aire thorow the vehemencie of
her going, & fleeth on shaking her wings,
where as afterwarde no token of her way
can be founde:
12 Or as when an arrowe is shot at a marke,
it parteth the aire, which immediatly cometh together againe, so that a man cannot knowe where it went thorowe.
13 Euen so we, assone as we were borne, we
beganne to drawe to our end, and haue
shewed no token of vertue, but are consumed in our owne wickednes.
14 For*the hope of the vngodlie is like the *Iob.8,9. psal.*
dust that is blowne away with the winde, *1,4.& 143,4.*
and like a thinne fome that is scattered a- *prou.10,25.*
broad with the storme, and as the smoke, *iam.1,10.*
which is dispersed with the winde, and as
the remembrance of him passeth, that tarieth but for a day.
15 But the righteous shal liue for euer: their
rewarde also is with the Lord, & ỹ moste
High hathe care of them.
16 Therefore shal they receiue a glorious
kingdome, and a beautiful crowne of the
Lords hand: for with his right hand shal
he couer them, and with his arme shal he
defende them.
17 He shal take his ielousie for armour, &
shal arme the creatures to be reuenged of
the enemies.
18 He shal put on righteousnes for a brestplate, and take true iudgement in stead of
an helmet.
19 He wil take holines for an inuincible
shield.
20 He wil sharpẽ his fierce wrath for a sworde, and the worlde shal fight with him a-
gainst the vnwise.
21 Then shal the thunder boltes go streight
out of the lightnings, and shal flee to the
marke as out of the bent bowe of ỹ clouds,
and out of his angre that throweth stones,
shal thicke haile be cast; and the water of
the sea shalbe wrothe against them, & the
floods shal mightely ouerflowe.
22 And a mightie winde shal stand vp a-
gainst them, and like a storme shal scatter
them abroad. Thus iniquitie shal bring
all the earth to a wildernes, and wickednes
shal ouerthrowe the thrones of the mightie.

CHAP. VI.

The calling of Kings, princes and iudges, which are also exhorted to searche wisdome.

1 HEare therefore, ô ye Kings, and vnderstand: learne, ye that be iudges of
the ends of the earth.
2 Giue eare, ye that rule the multitudes &
glorie in the multitude of people.
3 For the rule * is giuen you of the Lord, *Rom.13,2.*
and power by the moste High, which wil
trye your workes, and searche out your i-
maginacions.
4 Because that ye being officers of his kingdome haue not iudged aright, nor kept
the Law, nor walked after the wil of God,
5 Horribly and sodenly wil he appeare vnto you: for an hard iudgement shal they
haue that beare rule.
6 For he that is moste lowe, is worthie mer-

cie, but the mightie shalbe mightely tormented.
7 For he that is Lord ouer all, wil spare no
Deut.10,17. * persone, nether shal he feare anie great-
2.chro,19.7. nes: for he hathe made the small and great,
iob.34,19. and careth for all a like,
eccles 35,16. 8 But for the mightie abideth ȳ sorer tryal.
act.10,34. 9 Vnto you therefore, ô tyrants, do I spea-
rom.2,11,gal 2,6.eph.6,9. ke, that ye may learne wisdome, and not
col.3,25. 1. go amisse.
pet,1,17. 10 For they that kepe holines holily, shalbe
holie, and they that are learned there, shal
finde a defence.
11 Wherefore set your delite vpō my wordes & desire them, & ye shalbe instructed.
12 Wisdome shineth & neuer fadeth away,
and is easely sene of them that loue her, &
founde of suche as seke her,
13 She preuenteth them that desire her, that
she may first shewe her self vnto them.
14 Whoso awaketh vnto her betimes, shal
haue no great trauail: for he shal finde her
sitting at his dores.
15 To thinke vpon her then is perfite vnderstanding: and who so watcheth for her,
shalbe sone without care.
16 For she goeth about, seking suche as are
mete for her, and sheweth her self cherefully vnto them in the wayes, and meteth
them in euerie thoght.
17 For the moste true desire of discipline
is her beginning: and the care of discipline is loue:
18 And loue is the keping of her lawes: and
the keping of the lawes is the assurance of
immortalitie:
19 And immortalitie maketh vs nere vnto
God.
20 Therefore the desire of wisdome leadeth to the kingdome.
21 If your delite be then in thrones, & scepters, ô Kings of the people, honour wisdome, that ye may reigne for euer.
22 Now I wil tell you what wisdome is, &
whence it cometh, & wil not hide the mysteries from you, but wil seke her out from
the beginning of her natiuitie, and bring
the knowledge of her into light, and wil
not kepe backe the trueth.
23 Nether wil I haue to do with consuming
enuie: for suche a man shal not be partaker of wisdome.
24 But the multitude of the wise is the preseruacion of the worlde, and a wise King
is the staye of the people.
25 Be therefore instructed by my wordes, &
ye shal haue profite.

CHAP. VII.

Wisdome oght to be preferred aboue all things.

1 I My self am also mortal and a man like all other, and am come of him that
was first made of the earth.
2 And in my mothers wōbe was I facioned
to be flesh in ten moneths: I was * broght Iob.10,10.
together into blood of the sede of man,
and by the pleasure that cometh with
slepe.
3 And when I was borne, I receiued the cōmune aire, and fel vpon the earth, which is
of like nature, crying & weping at the first
as all other do.
4 I was nourished in swadling clothes, and
with cares.
5 For there is no King that had anie other
beginning of birth.
6 All * men then haue one entrance vnto li- Iob.1,21.
fe, and a like going out. 1.tim.6,7.
7 Wherefore I praied, and vnderstanding
was giuen me: I called & the Spirit of wisdome came vnto me.
8 I preferred her to scepters and thrones, &
counted riches nothing in comparison of
her.
9 * Nether did I compare precious stones Iob.28,15.
vnto her: for all golde is but a litle grauel
in respect of her, and siluer shalbe counted
but clay before her.
10 I loued her aboue health and beautie, &
purposed to take her for my light: for her
light can not be quenched.
11 All * good things therefore came to me 1.King.3,13.
together with her, and innumerable riches matt.6,33.
thorow her hands.
12 So I was glad in all: for wisdome was the
autor thereof, & I knewe not that she was
the mother of these things.
13 And I learned vnfainedly, & communicated without enuie, and I do not hide her
riches.
14 For she is an infinite treasure vnto men,
which whoso vse, become partakers of the
loue of God, & are accepted for the gifts
of knowledge.
15 God hathe granted me to speake according to my minde, and to iudge worthely
of the things, that are giuen me: for he is
the leader vnto wisdome, and the direc-
ter of the wise.
16 For in his hand are bothe we and our
wordes, and all wisdome, & the knowledge
of the workes.
17 For he hathe giuē me the true knowledge of the things that are, so that I knowe
how the worlde was made, and the powers
of the elements,
18 The beginning and the end, & the middes of the times: how the times alter, and
the change of the seasons,
19 The course of the yere, the situacion of
the starres,
20 The nature of liuing things, and the fu-
riousnes of beasts, the power of ȳ windes,
and the imaginacions of men, the diuersities of plants, and the vertues of rootes.
21 And all things bothe secret and knowen
do I knowe: for wisdome the worker of
all

all things, hathe taught me it.
22 For in her is the spirit of vnderstanding,
which is holie, the onely begotten, manifolde, subtil, moueable, cleare, vndefiled, e-
uident, not hurtful, louing the good, sharpe, which can not be letted, doing good,
23 Courteous, stable, sure, without care, hauing all power, circumspect in all things,
and passing through all, intellectual, pure
and subtil spirits.
24 For wisdome is nimbler then all nim-
ble things: she goeth thorow and atteineth
to all things, because of her purenes.
25 For she is ẏ breth of the power of God,
and a pure influence that floweth from the
glorie of the Almightie: therefore can no
defiled thing come vnto her.
26 For * she is the brightnes of the euer- Ebr.1,3.
lasting light, the vndefiled mirroure of
the maiestie of God, and the image of his
goodnes.
27 And being one, she can do all things, and
remaining in her self, renueth all, and according to the ages she entreth into the
holie soules, and maketh them the friends
of God and Prophetes.
28 For God loueth none, if he dwell not
with wisdome.
29 For she is more beautiful then the sunne,
and is aboue all the order of the starres,
and the light is not to be compared vnto her.
30 For night cometh vpō it, but wickednes
can not ouercome wisdome.

CHAP. VIII.

The effects of wisdome.

1 SHe also reacheth from one end to another mightely, and comely doeth she
order all things.
2 I haue loued her, and soght her from my
youth: I desired to marye her, suche loue
had I vnto her beautie.
3 In that she is conuersant with God, it
commendeth her nobilitie: yea, the Lord
of all things loueth her.
4 For she is the scholemastres of the knowledge of God, and the choser out of his
workes.
5 If riches be a possesion to be desired in
this life, what is richer then wisdome, that
worketh all things?
6 For if prudencie worketh, what is it a-
mong all things, that worketh better then
she?
7 If a man loue righteousnes, her labours
are vertuous: for she teacheth sobernes &
prudēcie, righteousnes and strēgth, which
are the moste profitable things that men
can haue in this life.
8 If a man desire great experience, she can
tell the things that are past, and discerne
things to come: she knoweth the subtilties
of wordes, and the solutions of darke sentences: she foreseeth the signes and wonders, or euer they come to passe, and the
succes of seasons and times.
9 Therefore I purposed to take her vnto my
companie, knowing that she wolde counsel me good things, and comfort me in cares and griefs.
10 For her sake shal I haue glorie among
the multitude and honour among the Elders thogh I be yong.
11 I shal be founde of sharpe iudgement,
so that I shal be marueilous in the sight of
great men.
12 When I holde my tongue, they shal
abide my leasure: when I speake, they shal
heare diligently, & if I talke muche, they
shal laye their hands vpon their mouth.
13 *Moreouer*, by her I shal obteine immortalitie, and leaue an euerlasting memorial
among them that come after me.
14 I shal gouerne the people, and the nacions shalbe subdued vnto me.
15 Horrible tyrants shalbe afraied when
they heare me: among the multitude I
shalbe counted good, and mightie in
battel.
16 When I come home, I shal rest with her:
for her companie hathe no bitternes, and
her felowshippe hathe no tediousnes, but
mirthe and ioye.
17 *Now* when I considered these things by
my self, and pondered them in mine heart,
how that to be ioyned vnto wisdome is
immortalitie,
18 And great pleasure is in her friendshippe, and that in the workes of her hands
are infinite riches, and that in the exercise of talking with her is prudencie, and
glorie by communing with her, I went a-
bout, seking how I might take her vnto
me.
19 For I was a wittie childe, and was of a
good spirit.
20 Yea, rather being good, I came to an
vndefiled bodie.
21 Neuertheles, when I perceiued that I
colde not enioye her, except God gaue
her (and that was a pointe of wisdome
also, to knowe whose gifte it was) I went
vnto the Lord, and besoght him, and with
my whole heart I said,

CHAP. IX.

A praier of Salomon to obteine wisdome.

1 O God of fathers, and Lord of mercie,
which hast made all things with thy
worde,
2 And ordeined man thorow thy wisdome,
that he shulde haue * dominion ouer the Gen.1,1,28.
creatures which thou hast made,
3 And gouerne the worlde according to e-

quitie and righteousnes, & execute iudgement with an vpright heart.
1.King.3,9. 4 Giue *me that wisdome, which sitteth by thy throne, and put me not out frō among thy children.
Psal.116,16. 5 For I thy *seruant, & sonne of thine handmaide am a feble persone, & of a shorte time, and yet lesse in the vnderstanding of iudgement and the lawes.
6 And thogh a man be neuer so perfite among the children of men, yet if thy wisdome be not with him, he shalbe nothing regarded.
1.Chr.28,5. 2 chr.1,9. 7 *Thou hast chosen me to be a King of thy people, and the iudge of thy sonnes & daughters.
8 Thou hast cōmanded me to buyld a temple vpon thine holy Mount, & an altar in the citie, wherein thou dwellest, a likenes of thine holie Tabernacle, which thou hast prepared from the beginning,
Prouer.8,12. ioh.1,9. 9 And thy *wisdome w̄ thee, which knoweth thy workes, which also was when thou madest the worlde, and which knewe what was acceptable in thy sight, and right in thy commandements.
10 Send her out of thine holy heauēs, & send her from the throne of thy maiestie that she may be with me, & labour, that I may know what is acceptable in thy sight.
11 For she knoweth and vnderstandeth all things, and she shal lead me soberly in my workes, & preserue me by her glorie.
12 So shal my workes be acceptable, & then shal I gouerne thy people righteously, & be mete for my fathers throne.
Isa.40,13. rom.11,34. 1.cor.2,16. 13 For * what man is he that can knowe the counsel of God? or who can thinke what the wil of God is?
14 For the thoghts of mortal men are fearefull, and our forecastes are vncerteine,
15 Because a corruptible bodie is heauie vnto the soule, & the earthlie māsion kepeth downe the minde that is ful of cares.
16 And hardly can we discerne the things that are vpon earth, and with great labour finde we out the things which are before vs: who can then seke out the things that are in heauen?
17 Who can know thy counsel, except thou giue him wisdome, and send thine holy Spirit from aboue?
18 For so the waies of them which are vpon earth, are reformed, & men are taught the things that are pleasant vnto thee, and are preserued thorow wisdome.

CHAP. X.

The deliuerance of the righteous and destruction of the enemies cometh thorowe wisdome.

1 SHe preserued the first father of the worlde, that was formed, and kept him whē he was created alone, and broght him out of his offence,
2 And * gaue him power to rule all things, Gen.2,20.
3 *But the vnrighteous in his wrath departed from her, and perished by killing his brother in his furie. Gen.4,8.
4 For whose cause the * earth was ouerflowen, but wisdome preserued it againe, gouerning the iust man by a litle wood. Gen.7,12.
5 Moreouer, * when the nacions were ioyned in their malicious confederacies, she knewe the righteous, and preserued him fauteles vnto God, and "kept him sure, because she loued him tenderly as a sonne. Gen.11,1. "Or, kept him strong in his tender loue toward his sonne.
6 She preserued the righteous, * when the vngodlie perished, when he fled from the fyre that fel downe vpon the fiue cities. Gen.20,17.
7 Of whose wickednes the waste land that smoketh, yet giueth testimonie, and the trees that beare frute that neuer cometh to ripenes: and for a remembrance of the vnfaithful soule, there standeth a piller of salte.
8 For all suche as regarded not wisdome, had not onely this hurt, that they knewe not the things which were good, but also left behinde them vnto men a memorial of their foolishnes, so that in the things wherein they sinned, they can not lie hid.
9 But wisdome deliuered them, that serued her.
10 *When the righteous fled because of his brothers wrath, she led him the right way, shewed him the kingdome of God, gaue him knowledge of holie things, made him riche in his labours, and made his peines profitable. Gen.28,5.
11 Against the couetousnes of suche as defrauded him, she stode by him and made him riche.
12 She saued him from the enemies, and defended him from them, that lay in waite, and she gaue him the price in a mightie battel, that he might knowe that the feare of God is stronger then all things.
13 *When the righteous was solde, she forsoke him not, but deliuered him from sinne: she went downe with him into the dongeon, Gen.37,28. & 39,7. act.7,10.
14 And failed him not in the bandes, til she had broght him the scepter of the realme, and power against those that oppressed him, and them that had accused him, she declared to be liers, and gaue him perpetual glorie.
15 *She deliuered the righteous people and fautles sede from the nacions that oppressed them. Exod.1,10.
16 She entred into the soule of the seruant of the Lord, and stode * by him in wonders and signes against the terrible Kings. Exod.5,1.
17 She gaue the Saintes the rewarde of their labours, and led them forthe a marueilous way: on the day time she was a shadow

vnto

vnto them, and a light of starres in the
night.
Exod.14,21. psal.78,13. 18 *She broght thẽ thorow the red sea, and
caryed them through the great water,
19 But she drowned their enemies, and
broght thẽ out of the botome of the depe.
20 So the righteous toke the spoiles of the
Exod 15,1. vngodlie, *& praised thine holy Name, ô
Lord, and magnified thy victorious hand
with one accorde.
21 For wisdome openeth the mouth of the
domme, and maketh the tongues of babes
eloquent.

CHAP. XI.

1 The miracles done for Israel. 13 The vengeance of sinners. 28 The great power and mercie of God.

1 SHe prospered their workes in the hãds
of thine holy Prophet.
Exod.16,1. 2 *They went through the wildernes that
was not inhabited, and pitched their tentes in places where there lay no way.
Exod.17,10. 3 *They stode against their enemies, & were auenged of their aduersaries.
Nom.20,11. 4 *When they were thirsty, they called vpõ
thee, and water was giuen them out of the
hie rocke, and their thirst was quenched
out of the hard stone.
5 For by the things whereby their enemies were punished, by the same were the
Israelites helped in their nede.
6 For in steade of a fountaine of running
water, the *enemies* were troubled at the
corrupt blood, which was to rebuke the
commandement of the killing of the childrẽ, *but* thou gauest vnto thine owne abun
dance of water vnloked for,
Exod.7,20. 7 Declaring by the thirst that was at that
time * how thou hadest punished thine
aduersaries.
8 For when they were tryed and chastised
with mercie, they knewe how the vngodlie were iudged and punished in
wrath.
9 For these hast thou exhorted as a father,
and proued them: but thou hast condemned ẏ other as a righteous King, whẽ thou
didest examine them.
10 Whether they were absent or present,
their punishment was alike: for their
grief was double with mourning, and the
remembrance of things past.
11 For when they perceiued that through
their torments good came vnto them, they
felt the Lord.
12 And seing the things that came to passe,
at the last they wondered at him, whome
afore they had cast out, denied and derided: for they had another thirst then the
iuste.
13 Because of the foolish deuises of their
wickednes wherewith they were deceiued,
Chap.12,24. rom.1,23. and worshiped *serpents, that had not the
vse of reason, & vile beastes, thou sendidst
a multitude of vnreasonable beastes vpon
them for a vengeance, that they might
knowe, that wherewith a man sinneth, by
the same also shal he be punished.
14 *For vnto thine almightie hand, ẏ made Leu.16,20. ier.8,22.
the worlde of naught, it was not vnposi- chap.16,1.
ble to send among them a multitude of
beares, or fierce lyons,
15 Or furious beastsnewly created, and vnknowen, which shulde breathe out blastes
of fyre, and cast out smoke as a tempest, or
shoote horrible sparkes like lightnings out
of their eyes.
16 Which might not onely destroye them
with hurting, but also to kill them with
their horrible sight.
17 Yea, without these might they haue bene
cast downe with one winde, being persecu
ted by thy vengeãce, and scattered abroade thorow the power of thy Spirit: but
thou hast ordered all things in measure,
nomber & weight.
18 For thou hast euer had great strength &
might, and who can withstand the power
of thine arme!
19 For as the small thing that the balance
weigheth, so is the worlde before thee, & as
a droppe of the morning dewe, that falleth
downe vpon the earth.
20 But thou hast mercie vpon all: for thou
hast power of all things, and makest as
thogh thou sawest not the sinnes of men,
because they shulde amende.
21 For thou louest all the things that are, &
hatest none of them whome thou hast made: for thou woldest haue created nothing
that thou hadest hated.
22 And how might anie thing endure, if it
were not thy wil? or how colde anie
thing be preserued, except it were called
of thee?
23 But thou sparest all: for they are thine, ô
Lord, which art the louer of soules.

CHAP. XII.

1 The mercie of God toward sinners. 14 The workes of God are vnreprouable. 19 God giueth leasure to repent.

1 FOr thine incorruptible spirit is in all
things.
2 Therefore thou chastnest thẽ measurably
that go wrong, and warnest thẽ by putting
them in remembrance of the things wherein they haue offended, that leauing wickednes they may beleue in thee, ô Lord.
3 *As for those olde inhabitãts of the holy Deut.9,3.
land, thou didest hate them. 12,20 & 18,9.
4 For they committed abominable workes, as sorceries and wicked sacrifices,
5 And slaying of their owne children without mercie, and eating of the bowels of
mans flesh in banketing, where the raging

Priests *shed* abominable blood.
6 And the fathers were the chief murtherers of the soules, destitute of all helpe,
whome thou woldest destroy by the hands
of our fathers,
7 That the land which thou louest aboue
all other, might be a mete dwelling for the
children of God.
Exod.33,2. deut.7,22. 8 *Neuertheles, thou sparedst them also, as
men, and sendedst the forerunners of thine
hoste, euen hornettes to destroie them by
litle and litle,
9 Not that thou wast vnable to subdue the
vngodlie vnto the righteous in battel, or
with cruel beastes, or with one rough worde to destroie them togethcr.
10 But in punishing them by litle and litle,
thou gauest thē space to repent, knowing
wel, that it was an vnrighteous nacion &
wicked of nature, & that their thoght colde neuer be altered.
11 For it was a cursed sede from the beginning: yet hast thou not spared them when
they sinned, because thou feared any man.
Rom.9,20. 12 For who dare say, *What hast thou done?
or who dare stand against thy iudgement?
or who dare accuse thee for the nacions
that perish, whome thou hast made? or
who dare stand against thee to reuenge the
wicked men?
1.Pet.5,7. 13 For there is none other God but thou,
*that carest for all things, that ẏ maist de-
clare how ẏ thy iudgement is not vnright.
14 There dare nether King nor tyrant in
thy sight require accountes of them whome thou hast punished.
15 For so muche then as thou art righteous
thy self, thou ordrest all thīgs righteously,
Iob.10,3. *thinking it not agreable to thy power to
condemne him, that hathe not deserued to
be punished.
16 For thy power is the beginning of righteousnes, and because thou art Lord of all
things, it causeth thee to spare all things.
17 Whē men thinke thee not to be of a perfite power, thou declarest thy power, and
reprouest the boldenes of the wise.
18 But thou ruling the power, iudgest with
equitie, & gouernest vs with great fauour:
for thou maist shew thy power when thou
wilt.
19 By suche workes now hast thou taught
thy people, that a man shulde be iust and
louing, and hast made thy children to be
of a good hope: for thou giuest repentance to sinners.
20 For if thou hast punished the enemies of
thy children that had deserued death with
so great consideration, and requesting *vnto them*, giuing them time & place that they
might change from their wickednes,
21 With how great circumspection wilt
thou punish thine owne childrē, vnto whose
fathers thou hast sworne and made couenants of good promises?
22 So when thou doest chasten vs, thou punishest our enemies a thousād times more,
to the intent that when we iudge, we shulde diligently consider thy goodnes, and
when we are iudged, we shulde hope for
mercie.
23 Wherefore thou hast tormented the wic
ked that haue liued a dissolute life by their
owne imaginations.
24 * For they went astray verie farre in the Chap.11,16.
waies of errour, and estemed the beasts, rom.1,23.
which their enemies dispised, for gods, being abused after the maner of childrē, that
haue none vnderstanding.
25 Therefore hast thou sent this punishmēt
that they shulde be in derision as children
without reason.
26 But they that wil not be reformed by
those scorneful rebukes, shal fele the worthie punishment of God.
27 For in those things when they suffred,
they disdeined: but in these whome they
counted godlie when they sawe thē selues
punished by them, they all acknowledged
ẏ true God whome afore they had denied
to knowe: therefore came extreme damnation vpon them.

CHAP. XIII.

1 *All things be vaine, except the knowledge of God.*
10 *Idolaters and idoles are mocked.*

1 SVrely all men are vaine by nature,
and are ignorant of God, *and colde Rom.1,19.
not knowe him that is, by the good things
that are sene, nether consider by the workes the worke master.
2 *But thei thoght the fyre, or the winde or Deu.4,19. & 17,3.
the swift aire, or the course of the starres,
or the raging water, or the lights of heauen to be gouernours of the worlde, and
gods.
3 Thogh they had suche pleasure in their
beautie that they thoght them gods, yet
shulde they haue knowen, how muche more excellent he is that made them: for the
first autor of beautie hathe created these
things.
4 Or if they marueiled at the power, and
operation of them, yet shulde they haue
perceiued thereby, how muche he that
made these things, is mightier.
5 For by the greatnes of their beautie, and
of the creatures, the Creator being compa
red with them, may be considered.
6 But yet the blame is lesse in these, that
seke God and wolde finde him, & yet peraduenture do erre.
7 For* they go about by his workes to seke Rom.1,20.
him, and are persuaded by the sight, because the things are beautiful that are sene.
8 Howbeit they are not to be excused.
9 For if they can knowe so muche, that they
can

can discerne the worlde, why do they not
rather finde out the Lord thereof?
10 But miserable are they, and among the
dead is their hope, that call them gods
which are the workes of mens hands, golde,
and siluer, and the thing that is inuented
by arte, and the similitude of beasts, or
anie vaine stone that hathe bene made by
the hand of antiquitie.
11 *Or as when a carpenter cutteth downe a tre mete for the worke, and pareth of all (Isa.44,13. iere.10,3.)
the barke thereof cunningly, and by arte
maketh a vessel profitable for the vse of
life.
12 And the things that are cut of from his
worke, he bestoweth to dresse his meat to
fil him self,
13 And that which is left of these things,
which is profitable for nothing (*for* it is a
croked piece of wood and ful of knobbes)
he carueth it diligently at his leasure, and
according as he is expert in cunning, he
giueth it a proporcion, and facioneth it
after the similitude of a man,
14 Or maketh it like some vile beast, and
straketh it ouer with red, and painteth it,
and couereth euerie spotte that is in it.
15 And when he hathe made a conuenient
tabernacle for it, he setteth it in a wall, and
maketh it fast with yron,
16 Prouiding so for it, lest it fall: for he
knoweth ẏ it can not helpe it self, because
it is an image, ẇ hathe nede of helpe.
17 Then he prayeth for his goods, and for
his mariage and for children: he is not ashamed
to speake vnto it, that hath no life.
18 He calleth on him that is weake for health:
he prayeth vnto him that is dead for
life: he requireth him of helpe that hathe
no experience at all.
19 And for his iourney, him that is not able
to go, and for gaine, and worke, and successe
of his affaires he requireth furtherãce
of him, that hathe no maner of power.

CHAP. XIIII.

1 The detestacion and abominacion of images, 8 A curse of them, and of him that maketh them. 14 Whereof idolatrie proceded. 23 What euils come of idolatrie.

1 AGaine, another man purposing to
saile, and intẽding to passe thorowe
the raging waues, calleth vpon a stocke
more rotten then the shippe that carieth
him.
2 For as for "it, couetousnes of money hathe (*Or, the shippe.*)
founde it out, and the craftesman made it
by cunning.
3 But thy prouidence, ô father, gouerneth
it: *for thou hast made away, euen in the (Exod.14,22.)
sea, and a sure path among the waues,
4 Declaring thereby, that thou hast power
to helpe in all things, yea, thogh a man wẽt
to the sea without meanes.
5 Neuertheles thou woldest not, that the
workes of thy wisdome shulde be vaine,
and therefore do men commit their liues
to a smale piece of wood, and passe ouer
the stormie sea in a shippe, and are saued.
6 *For in the olde time also whẽ the proude (Gen.6,4. & 7,10.)
gyants perished, the hope of the worlde
went into a shippe which was gouerned by
thine hand, and so left sede of generacion
vnto the worlde.
7 For blessed is the tre whereby righteousnes
commeth.
8 But that is cursed that is made with hãds,
*bothe it, & he that made it: he because he (Psal.115,8. baruc.6,3)
made it, and it being a corruptible thing,
because it was called god.
9 *For the vngodlie, and his vngodlines are (Psal.7,5.)
bothe like hated of God: so truely the
worke & he that made it, shalbe punished
together.
10 Therefore shal there be a visitation for
the idoles of the nations: for of the creatures
of God they are become abominacion,
* and stumbling blockes vnto the (Iere.10,8. habak.2,18.)
soules of men, & a snare for the fete of the
vnwise.
11 For the inuenting of idoles was the beginning
of whoredome, and the finding of
them is the corruption of life.
12 For they were not from the beginning,
nether shal they continue for euer.
13 The vaine glorie of men broght them
into the worlde: therefore shal they come
shortly to an end.
14 When a father mourned grieuously for
his sonne that was taken away suddenly, he
made an image for him ẏ was once dead,
whome now he worshipeth as a god, & ordeined
to his seruants ceremonies and sacrifices.
15 Thus by proces of time this wicked custome
preuailed, and was kept as a law, and
idoles were worshiped by the commandement
of tyrants.
16 As for those that were so farre of that
men might not worship them presently,
they did counterfet the visage that was farre
of, and made a gorgeous image of a
King, whome they wolde honour, that thei
might by all meanes flatter him that was
absent, as thogh he had bene present.
17 Againe the ambition of the craftesman
thrust forwarde the ignorãt to increase the
superstition.
18 For he peraduenture willing to please a
noble man, labored with all his cunning
to make the image of the best facion.
19 And so thorowe the beautie of the worke
the multitude was allured, and so toke
him now for a god, which a litle afore was
but honored as a man.
20 And this was the deceiuing of mãs life,
when men, being in seruitude, through ca-

lamitie and tyrannie ascribed vnto stones
and stockes the name, which oght not to
be communicate vnto anie.
21 Moreouer, this was not ynough for them
that they erred in the knowledge of God:
but where as they liued in great warres of
ignorance, those so great plagues called
they peace.
Deu.18,10. iere.7,9. & 19,4. 22 For ether *they slewe their owne childrẽ
in sacrifice, or vsed secret ceremonies, or
raging dissolutenes by strange rites,
23 And so kept nether life nor mariage cleane: but ether one slewe another by treason,
or els vexed him by adulterie.
24 So were all mixt together, blood and
slaughter, thefte & deceit, corruption, vnfaithfulnes, tumultes, periurie,
25 Disquieting of good men, vnthankeful-
nes, defiling of soules, changing of birth,
disordre in mariage, adulterie & vnclẽnes.
26 For the worshiping of idoles that oght
not to be named, is the beginning and the
cause and the end of all euil.
27 For either they be mad when they be
merie, or prophecie lies, or liue vngodlie,
or els lightly forsweare them selues.
28 For in so muche as their trust is in the
idoles, which haue no life, thogh thei sweare falsely, yet they thinke to haue no hurt.
29 Therefore for two causes shal they iustely be punished, because they haue an
euil opinion of God, addicting them selues vnto idoles, and because they sweare
vniustly to deceiue, and despise holines.
30 For it is not the power of them by whome they sweare, but the vengeance of them
that sinne, which punisheth alwayes the
offence of the vngodlie.

CHAP. XV.

The voyce of the faithful, praising the mercie of God by whose grace they serue not idoles.

1 BVt thou, ô our God, art gracious and
true, long suffring, and gouernest all
things by mercie.
2 Thogh we sinne, yet are we thine: for we
knowe thy power: but we sinne not, knowing that we are counted thine.
3 For to knowe thee, is perfite righteousnes,
and to knowe thy power is the roote of im
mortalitie.
4 For nether hathe the wicked inuention
of men disceiued vs, nor the vnprofitable
labour of the painters, nor an image spotted with diuers colours.
5 Whose sight stirreth vp the desire of
the ignorant: so that he coueteth the forme
that hathe no life, of a dead image.
6 They that loue suche wicked things, are
worthie to haue suche things to trust to,
and they that make them, and they that desire them, and they that worship them.
Rom.9,20. 7 The *potter also tempereth soft earth, &
facioneth euerie vessel with labour to our
vse: but of the same clay he maketh bothe
the vessels, that serue to cleane vses, and
the contrarie likewise: but whereto euerie vessel serueth, the potter is the iudge.
8 So by his wicked labour he maketh a vaine god of the same claye: euen he, which a
litle afore was made of earth him self, and
within a litle while after goeth thither a-
gaine whence he was taken, *when he shal Luk.12,20.
make accounte for the lone of his life.
9 Notwithstanding he careth not for the
labour he taketh, nor that his life is shorte, but he striueth with the goldesmithes,
and siluersmithes, and counterfaiteth the
copersmithes, and taketh it for an honour
to make deceiuable things.
10 His heart is ashes, and his hope is more vile then earth, and his life is lesse worthie of honour then claye.
11 For he knoweth not his owne maker, that
gaue him his soule, that had power & brea
thed in him the breth of life.
12 But they counte our life to be but a pastime, and our conuersacion as a market,
where there is gaine: for they say we oght
to be getting on euerie side, thogh it be by
euil meanes.
13 Now he that of earth maketh fraile vessels and images, knoweth him self to offend aboue all other.
14 All the enemies of thy people, that holde them in subiection, are moste vnwise,
& more miserable then the verie fooles.
15 For they iudge all the idoles of the nacions to be gods, which nether haue eye
sight to se, nor noses to smel, nor eares to
heare, nor fingers of hãds to grope, & their
fete are slowe to go.
16 For man made them, and he that hathe
but a borowed spirit, facioned them: but
no man can make a god like vnto him
self.
17 For seing he is but mortal him self, it is
but mortal that he maketh with vnrighteous hands: he him self is better thẽ thei
whome he worshippeth: for he liued, but
they neuer liued.
18 Yea, they worshipped beasts also, which
are their moste enemies, & which are the
worste, if thei be cõpared vnto others, because they haue none vnderstanding.
19 Nether haue they anie beautie to be desired in respect of other beasts: for they
are destitute of Gods praise, and of his
blessing.

CHAP. XVI.

The punishment of idolaters. 20 The benefites done vnto the faithful.

1 THerefore by suche things they are Chap.11,18. nomb.11,33.
worthely punished &* tormented by
the multitude of beastes.
2 In steade of the which punishment thou
hast bene fauorable to thy people, & to sa-

tisfie their appetite,hast prepared a meat of
a strange taste,euen quailes,
3 To the intent that thei that desired meat,
by the things which were shewed and sent
among them,might turne awaye their necessarie desire, & that thei,which had suffred penurie for a space, shulde also fele a
newe taste.
4 For it was requisite, that they which vsed
tyrannie, shulde fall into extreme pouertie, and that to these onelie it shulde be
shewed,how their enemies were tormẽted.
Nomb.21,6. 1.cor.10,6. 5 *For when the cruel fiercenes of ẏ beasts
came vpon them,and they were hurt with
the stings of cruel serpents,
6 Thy wrath endured not perpetually, but
they were troubled for a litle season, that
they might be reformed, hauing a "signe
of saluacion, to remember the commandement of thy Law.
"The signe of the brasen serpent.
7 For he that turned toward it,was not healed by the thing that he sawe, but by thee,
ô Sauiour of all.
8 So in this thou shewedst our enemies,
that it is thou, which deliuerest from all
euil.
Exod.8,24. & 10,4.reuel 9,7. 9 *For the biting of greshopers and flyes
killed them,and there was no remedie fo-
unde for their life: for they were worthie
to be punished by suche.
10 But the teeth of the venemous dragons
colde not ouercome thy children :for thy
mercie came to helpe them, & healed thẽ.
11 For they were pricked,because thei shulde remember thy wordes, and were spedely healed,lest they shulde fall into so depe
forgetfulnes,that thei colde not be called
backe by thy benefite.
12 For nether herbe nor plaster healed them,
but thy worde, ô Lord, which healeth all
things.
13 For thou hast the power of life & death,
*and leadest downe vnto the gates of hel,
and bringest vp againe.
Deut.32,39. 1.sam.2,6. tob.13,2.
14 A man in dede by his wickednes may
slaie *another*: but when the Spirit is gone
forthe,it turneth not againe,nether can he
call againe the soule that is taken away.
15 But it is not posible to escape thine
hand.
Exod.9,23. 16 *For the vngodlie that wolde not knowe
thee, were punished by the strength of
thine arme, with strange raine and with
haile, and were pursued with tempest,that
they colde not auoide, & were consumed
with fyre.
17 For it was a wonderous thing that fyre
might do more then water, which quencheth all things: but the worlde is the aduenger of the righteous.
18 For some time was the fyre so tame, that
the beasts,which were sent against the vngodlie, burnt not: and that, because they
shulde se and knowe, that they were persecuted with the punishment of God.
19 And some time burnt the fyre in ẏ middes of the water aboue the power of fyre, that it might destroye the generacion
of the vniust land.
20 *In the stead whereof thou hast fed thine Exod.16,14.
owne people with Angels fode, and sent nomb.11,7.
them bread readie from heauen without psal 78,25.
their labour, which had abundance of all ioh.6,31.
pleasures in it & was mete for all tastes.
21 For thy sustinance declared thy swetnes
vnto thy children,which serued to the appetite of him, that toke it, & was mete to
that that euerie man wolde.
22 Moreouer the *snowe and yce abode the Exod.9,23.
fyre & melted not,that thei might knowe,
that the fyre burning in the hayle,& spar-
keling in the raine, destroyed the frute of
the enemies.
23 Againe it forgate his owne strength,that
the righteous might be nourished.
24 For the creature that serueth thee which
art the maker, is fierce in punishing the
vnrighteous : but it is easie to do good
vnto suche as put their trust in thee.
25 Therefore was it changed at the same
time vnto all facions to serue thy grace,
which nourisheth all things,according to
the desire of them that had nede thereof,
26 That thy children whome thou louest,ô
Lord,might knowe, *that it is not the in- Deut.8,3
crease of frutes that fedeth men, but that mat.4,4.
it is thy worde, which preserueth thẽ that
trust in thee.
27 For that which colde not be destroyed
with the fyre, being onely warmed a litle
with the sunne beames,melted,
28 That it might be knowen that we oght
to preuente the sunne rising to giue thankes vnto thee, and to salute thee before
the daye spring.
29 For the hope of the vnthankeful shal
melt as the winter yce,and flowe away as
vnprofitable waters.

CHAP. XVII.

The iudgements of God against the wicked.

1 FOr thy iudgements are great, and
can not be expressed: therefore men
do erre,that wil not be reformed.
2 For when the vnrighteous thoght to
haue thine holie people in subiection,thei
were bounde with the bands of darkenes,
and long night, and being shut vp vnder
the rofe, did lie there to escape the euerlasting prouidence.
3 And while they thoght to be hid in their
darke sinnes,thei were scattered abroad in
the darke couering of forgetfulnes,fearīg
horribly and troubled with visions.
4 For the denne that hid them,kept them
not from feare:but the soundes that were
about them, troubled them, and terrible

visions and sorowful sights did appeare.
5 No power of the fyre might giue light,
nether might the clere flames of the starres lighten the horrible night.
6 For there appeared vnto them onely a
sudden fyre, verie dredful: so that being
afraied of this vision, "which they colde
not se, they thoght the things, which they
sawe, to be worse.
7 *And ẏ illusions of the magical artes were broght downe, and it was a moste shameful reproche for the boasting of their
knowledge.
8 For they that promised to driue away fea
re and trouble from the sicke persone, were
sicke for feare, & worthie to be laughed at.
9 And thogh no feareful thing did feare
them, yet were they afraied at the beastes
which passed by them, and at the hyssing
of the serpents: so that thei dyed for feare,
and said they sawe not the ayre, which by
no meanes can be auoided.
10 For it is a feareful thing, when malice is
condemned by her owne testimonie: and a
cõscience that is touched, doeth euer fore-
cast cruel things.
11 For feare is nothing els, but a betraying
of the succours, which reason offreth.
12 And the lesse that the hope is within, the
more doeth he esteme the ignorance of
the thing, that tormenteth him, great.
13 But they that did endure the night that
was intollerable, and that came out of the
dungeon of hell, which is insupportable,
slept the same slepe,
14 And sometimes were troubled with mõ-
struous visions, and sometime they sow-
ned, as thogh their owne soule shulde betray them: for a sudden feare not loked
for, came vpon them.
15 And thus, whosoeuer fel downe, he was
kept and shut in prison, but without chaines.
16 For whether he was an housband man,
or a shepherd, or one that was set to worke
alone, if he were taken, he must suffer this
necessitie, that he colde not auoide:
17 (For with one chaine of darkenes were
they all bõude) whether it were an hyssing
winde, or a swete song of the birds among
the thicke branches of the trees, or the vehemencie of hastie running water,
18 Or a great noyce of the falling downe
of stones, or the running of skipping beastes, that colde not be sene, or the noyce
of cruel beastes that roared, or the "sounde
that answereth againe in the holow mountaines: these feareful things made them
to swone.
19 For all the worlde shined with clere
light, and no man was hindred in his labour.
20 Onely vpon them there fel an heauie
night, an image of that darkenes that was
to come vpon them: yea, they were vnto
them selues more grieuous then darkenes.

"That is, the mightie visiõ.

Exod.7,12. & 8,7.

"Or, Echo.

CHAP. XVIII.

3 The fyrie piller that the Israelites had in Egypt. 8 The deliuerance of the faithful. 10 The Lord smote the Egyptians. 20 The sinne of the people in the wildernes. 21 Aaron stode betwene the liuing and the dead with his censure.

1 BVt thy Saĩts had a very great *light,
whose voyce because "they heard, and
sawe not the figure of them, they thoght
them blessed, because thei also had not suf
fred the like.
2 And because they did not hurt thẽ, which
did hurt them afore, they thanked them,
and asked pardon for their enimitie.
3 *Therefore thou gauest them a burning
piller of fyre to lead them in the vnknow-
en way, & madest the sunne that it hurted
not them in their honorable iourney.
4 But they were worthie to be depriued
of the light, and to be kept in darkenes,
which had kept thy children shut vp, by
whome the vncorrupt light of the Law
shulde be giuen to the worlde.
5 *Where as they thoght to slay the babes
of the Saintes, by one childe that was cast
out, and preserued to reproue them, thou
hast taken awaye the multitude of their
children and destroyed them all together
in the mightie water.
6 Of that night were our fathers certified
afore, that they knowing vnto what othes
they had giuen credit, might be of good
chere.
7 Thus thy *people receiued the health of
the righteous, but the enemies were destroyed.
8 For as thou hast punished the enemies,
so hast thou glorified vs whome thou hast
called.
9 For the righteous children of the good
men offred secretly, and made a law of
righteousnes by one consent, that ẏ Saints
shulde receiue good and euil in like maner, and that the fathers shulde first sing
praises.
10 But a disagreing price was heard of the
enemies, and there was a lamentable noice for the children that were bewailed.
11 For the *master and the seruant were
punished with like punishment, & the cõmune people suffred alike with the King.
12 So they altogether had innumerable
that dyed with one kinde of death: nether
were the liuing sufficient to burye them:
for in the twinckling of an eye the noblest
offspring of them was destroied.
13 So they that colde beleue nothing, because of the inchantments, confessed this
people to be the children of God, in the
destruction of the first borne

Exod.10,23. "Or, the Egyptians.

Exod 13,21. & 14,24. psal.78,14. & 105,39.

Exod.1,16.

Exod.14,24.

Exod.12,27.

14 For while all things were in quiet silẽce,
& the night was in the middes of her swift
course,
15 Thine almightie worde leapt downe frõ
heauen out of thy royal throne, as a fierce
man of warre in the middes of the lãd that
was destroyed,
16 And broght thine vnfained commandement as a sharpe sworde, and stode vp, and
filled all things with death, & being come
downe to the earth, it reached vnto the
heauens.
17 Then the sight of the feareful dreames
vexed them suddenly, and fearefulnes came vpon them vnawares.
18 Then laye there one here, another there
halfe dead, & shewed ỳ cause of his death.
19 For the visions that vexed them, shewed
them these things afore: so that they were
not ignorant, wherefore they perished.
20 Now tentacion of death touched the
righteous also, and *among the multitude Nom.16,46
in the wildernes there was a plague, but
the wrath indured not long.
21 For the blameles man made haste, & defended them, and toke the weapons of his
ministraciõ, euen prayer, & the reconciliation by the perfume, & set him self against
the wrath, and so broght the miserie to an
end, declaring that he was thy seruant.
22 For he ouercame not the multitude with
bodelie power, nor with force of weapõs,
but with the worde he subdued him that
punished, alledging the othes and couenãt
made vnto the fathers.
23 For when the dead were fallen downe by
heapes one vpon another, he stode in the
middes, and cut of the wrath, and parted
it from comming to the liuing.
24 *For in the long garment was all the or- Exod.28,11.
nament, and in the foure rowes of the stones was the glorie of the fathers grauen
with thy maiestie in the diademe of his
head.
25 Vnto these the destroyer gaue place, and
was afraid of them: for it was sufficient,
that they had tasted the wrath.

CHAP. XIX.

1 The death of the Egyptians, and the great ioye of the Hebrewes. 11 The meat that was giuen at the desire of the people. 17 All the elements serue to the wil of God.

1 AS for the vngodlie, the wrath came
vpon them without mercie vnto the
end: for he knewe what shulde come vnto
them,
2 That they (when they had consented to
let them go, and had sent them out with
diligence) wolde repent, and pursue them.
3 For while yet sorow was before them, and
they lamented by the graues of the dead,
thei deuised another foolishenes, so ỳ they
persecuted thẽ in their fleing, whome they
had cast out afore with prayer.
4 For the destinie, whereof they were worthie, broght them to this end, and caused them to forget the things that had come to passe, that they might accomplish
the punishment, which remained by torments,
5 Bothe ỳ thy people might trye a marueilous passage, and that these might finde a
strange death.
6 For euerie creature in his kinde was facioned of newe, and serued in their owne offices inioyned thẽ, that thy children might
be kept without hurt.
7 For the cloude ouershadowed their tentes, and the drye earth appeared, where a-
fore was water: so that in the red Sea there
was a way without impediment, and the
great depe became a grene field.
8 Through the which all the people went
that were defended with thine hand, seing
thy wonderous marueiles.
9 For they "neyed like horses, and leaped "Or, were fedde.
like lambes, praising thee, ô Lord, which
hadest deliuered them.
10 For thei were yet mindeful of those thĩgs
which were done in the land where they
dwelt, how the groũde broght forthe flies
in steade of cattel, & how the riuer scrau-
led with the multitude of frogges in steade of fishes.
11 *But at the last they sawe a new genera- Exod.16,13.
tion of birdes, when thei were intised with nom.11,32.
lust, and desired delicate meates.
12 *For the quailes came forthe of the sea Chap 16,1.
vnto them for comfort, but punishments
came vpon the "sinners not without signes "Or, Egyptians.
that were giuen by great thundrings: for
they suffred worthely according to their
wickednes, because they shewed a cruel
hatred towarde strangers.
13 For the one sorte wolde not receiue thẽ
whẽ thei were present, because they knewe
them not: the other sorte broght the strangers into bondage ỳ had done thẽ good.
14 Beside all these things some *wolde not suffer*, that anie regarde shulde be had of
them: for thei handeled the strangers dispitefully.
15 Others that had receiued thẽ with great
banketing, and admitted them to be partakers of the same lawes, did afflict them
with great labours.
16 Therefore thei were strikẽ with blindenes, as in olde time certeine were at the
dores of the *righteous, so that euerie one Gen.19,11.
being compassed with darknes, soght the
entrance of his dore.
17 Thus the elements agreed among them
selues in this change, as when one tune is
changed vpon an instrument of musike,
and the melodie stil remaineth, which may
easely be perceiued by the sight of the

things that are come to passe.
18 For the things of the earth were chãged
into things of the water, & the thing that
did swimme,went vpon the grounde.
19 The fyre had power in the water,contra-
rie vnto his owne vertue, & the water forgate his owne kinde to quench.
20 Againe, ỹ flames did not hurte the flesh
of the corruptible beasts that walked therein,nether melted they that which semed
to be yce, and was of a nature that wolde
melt, and yet was an immortal meat.
21 For in all things,ô Lord, thou hast magnified and glorified thy people , and hast
not despised to assist them in euerie time
and place.

THE WISDOME OF Iesus the sonne of Sirach, called Ecclesiasticus.

This argument was founde in a certeine Greke copie.

THis Iesus was the sonne of Sirach, and Sirachs father was also called Iesus, and he liued in the latter times, after the people had bene led away captiue, and broght home againe, and almoste after all the Prophetes. Now his grandfather, as he him self witnesseth, was a man of great diligence, and wisdome among the Hebrewes, who did not onely gather the graue sentences of wise men, that had bene before him, but he him self also spake manie ful of great knowledge and wisdome. So this first Iesus dyed, and left this which he had gathered, and Sirach afterwarde left it to Iesus his sonne, who toke it and put it in order in a boke, and called it WISDOME, intituling it bothe by his owne name, his fathers name, and his grandfathers: thinking by this title of Wisdome to allure the reader to read this boke with more great desire, and to consider it more diligently. Therefore this boke conteineth wise sayings, and darke sentences, and similitudes with certeine diuine histories which are notable and ancient, euen of men that were approued of God, and certeine prayers, and songs of the autor him self: moreouer, what benefites the Lord had bestowed vpon his people, and what plagues he had heaped vpon their enemies. This Iesus did imitate Salomon, and was no lesse famous in wisdome and doctrine, who was therefore called a man of great knowledge, as he was in dede.

The prologue of the Wisdome of Iesus the sonne of Sirach.

WHere as manie, and great things haue bene giuen vs by the Law, and the Prophetes, and by others that haue followed them, (for the which things Israel oght to be cõmended by the reason of doctrine and wisdome, whereby the readers oght not onely to become learned them selues, but also may be able by the diligent studie thereof to be profitable vnto strãgers bothe by speaking & writing) after that my grand father Iesus had giuen him self to the reading of the Law, and the Prophetes, & other bokes of our fathers, and had gotten therein sufficient iudgement, he purposed also to write some thing perteining to learning and wisdome, to the intent that they which were desirous to learne, & wolde giue them selues to these things, might profite muche more in liuing according to the Law. Wherefore, I exhorte you to receiue it louingly, and to read it with diligence, and to take it in good worthe, thogh we seme to some in some things not able to atteine to the interpretation of suche wordes as are hard to be expressed: for the things that are spoken in the Hebrewe tongue, haue another force in them selues then whẽ they are translated into another tõgue, and not onely these things, but other things also, as the Law it self, & the Prophetes, & other bokes haue no smale difference when they are spoken in their owne lãguage. Therefore in the eight and thirtieth yere, when I came into Egypt vnder King Euergetes, and continued there, I founde a copie ful of great learning, and I thoght it necessarie, to bestowe my diligence, and trauaile to interpret this boke. So for a certeine time with great watching and studie I gaue my self to the finishing of this boke, that it might be published, that they which remaine in banishement, and are desirous to learne, might applie them selues vnto good maners, and liue according to the Law.

CHAP. I.

1 Wisdome cometh of God. 11 A praise of the feare of God. 29 The meanes to come by wisdome.

1 ALL wisdome *cometh of
the Lord, [and hathe be-
ne euer with him] and is
with him for euer.
2 Who can nõber the sand
of the sea, and the drop-
pes of the raine, and the
dayes of the worlde? [who can measure]
the height of heauen, the bredth of the
earth,

1.King 3,9. & 4,29.

That which is marked with these two markes [ ] is red in the Latin copies, & not in the Greke.

earth, and the depth?
3 Who can finde the wisdome [of God
which hathe bene afore all things?]
4 Wisdome hathe bene created before all
things, and the vnderstanding of prudence from euerlasting.
5 [The worde of God moste high is the
fountaine of wisdome, and the euerlasting
commandements are the entrance vnto
her]
Rom.11,34. 6 *Vnto whome hathe the roote of wisdome bene declared? or who hathe knowẽ
her wise counsels?
7 [Vnto whome hathe the doctrine of wisdome bene discouered & shewed? and who
hathe vnderstand the manifolde entrance
vnto her?]
8 There is one wise, [euen the moste high
Creator of all things, the almightie, the
King of power] and verie terrible, which
sitteth vpon his throne.
9 He is the Lord, that hathe created her
[thorow ẏ holie Gost:] he hathe sene her,
nombred her, [and measured her.]
10 He hathe powred her out vpon all his
workes, and vpon all flesh, according to
his gift, and giueth her abundantly vnto
them that loue him.
11 The feare of the Lord is glorie, & gladnes, and reioycing, and a ioyful crowne.
12 The feare of the Lord maketh a mery
heart, and giueth gladnes, and ioye and
long life.
13 Whoso feareth the Lord, it shal go wel
with him at the last, and he shal finde fauour in the day of his death.
14 [The loue of God is honorable wisdome, and vnto whome it appeareth in a vision, they loue it for the vision, and for the
knowledge of the great workes thereof]
Psal.111,10. prou.9,10. iob.28,28. 15 *The feare of the Lord is the beginning
of wisdome, and was made with the faith-
ful in the wõbe: [she goeth with the chosen women, and is knowen with the righteous and faithful.
16 The feare of the Lord is an holie knowledge.
17 Holines shal preserue, & iustifie ẏ heart,
and giueth mirth and gladnes.
18 Who so feareth the Lord, shal prosper,
& in the day of his end, he shalbe blessed]
19 She hathe buylt her euerlasting fundacions with men, and is giuen to be with
their sede.
20 To feare God is the fulnes of wisdome,
and filleth men with her frutes.
21 She filleth their whole house with [all]
things desireable, and the garners with the
things, that she bringeth forthe, and bothe twaine are giftes of God.
22 The feare of the Lord is the crowne of
wisdome, & giueth peace & perfite health:
he hathe sene her and nombred her.
23 "She raineth downe knowledge, and vn- "Or wisdom.
derstãding of wisdome, and hathe broght
vnto honour, them that possessed her.
24 The feare of the Lord is the roote of
wisdome, and her branches are long life.
25 [In the treasures of wisdome is vnderstanding, and holie knowledge, but wisdome is abhorred of sinners.]
26 The feare of the Lord driueth out sinne: and when she is present, she driueth a-
way anger.
27 ¶For wicked angre can not be iustified:
for his rashnes in his angre shalbe his destruction.
28 A pacient man wil suffer for a time, and
then shal he haue the rewarde of ioye.
29 He wil hide his wordes for a time, and
manie mens lippes shal speake of his wisdome.
30 In the treasures of wisdome are the secrets of knowledge, but ẏ sinner abhorreth
the worship of God.
31 If thou desire wisdome, kepe the cõmandements, and the Lord shal giue her vnto
thee, [and wil fil her treasures.]
32 For the feare of the Lord is wisdome and
discipline: he hathe pleasure in faith and
mekenes.
33 Be not disobedient to the feare of the
Lord, and come not vnto him with a double heart.
34 ¶Be not an hypocrite that men shulde
speake of thee, but take hede what thou
speakest.
35 Exalte not thy self, lest thou fall & bring
thy soule to dishonour, and so God discouer thy secretes, & cast thee downe in the
middes of the cõgregacion, because thou
woldest not receiue the true feare of God,
and thine heart is ful of disceite.

CHAP. II.

1 He exhorteth the seruants of God to righteousnes, loue, vnderstanding, and pacience. 11 To trust in the Lord. 13 A cursse vpon them that are fainte hearted and impacient.

1 MY sonne, if thou wilt come into the
seruice of God, [stand fast in righteousnes and feare, and] prepare thy soule
to tentacion.
2 Settle thine heart, and be pacient: [bow
downe thine eare, and receiue the wordes
of vnderstanding] and shrinke not awaie,
whẽ thou art assailed, [but waite vpõ God
paciently.]
3 Ioyne thy self vnto him, and departe not
away, that thou maist be increased at thy
last end.
4 Whatsoeuer cometh vnto thee, receiue
it paciently, and be pacient in the change
of thine affliction.
5 *For as golde [& siluer are] tryed in the Wisdo.3,6.
fyre, euen so are men acceptable in the prou.17,3.
fornace of aduersitie.

6 Beleue in God and he wil helpe thee: order thy waye aright, & trust in him: [holde fast his feare, and growe olde therein.]
7 Ye that feare the Lord, waite for his mercie: shrinke not awaye from him that ye fall not.
8 Ye that feare the Lord, beleue him and your rewarde shal not faile.
9 O ye that feare the Lord, trust in good things, & in the euerlasting ioy & mercie.
10 [Ye that feare ẏ Lord, loue him, & your hearts shalbe lightened.]
11 Consider the olde generacions [of men, ye children,] and marke them wel: * was there euer anie confounded, that put his trust in the Lord? or who hathe continued in his feare, and was forsaken? or whome did he euer dispise, that called vpon him?

Psal. 38, 25.

12 For God is gracious and merciful, and forgiueth sinnes and saueth in the time of trouble, [& is a defender for all thē that seke him in the trueth.]
13 Wo vnto them, that haue a "feareful heart, [and to the wicked lippes] and to the faint hands, and to the sinner that goeth two * maner of wayes.

"Or, double.

1. King. 18, 21.

14 Wo vnto him that is faint hearted, for he beleueth not: therefore shal he not be defended.
15 Wo vnto you that haue lost pacience, [& haue forsaken the right wayes, and are turned backe into frowarde wayes:] for what wil ye do when the Lord shal visit you?
16 They that feare the Lord, wil not disobey his worde: and they that * loue him, wil kepe his wayes.

Ioh. 14, 24.

17 They that feare the Lord, wil seke out the things that are pleasant vnto him: and they that loue him, shalbe fulfilled with his Law.
18 They that feare the Lord, wil prepare their hearts, and humble their soules in his sight.
19 [Thei that feare the Lord, kepe his commandements, and wil be pacient til he se them,
20 Saying, If we do not repent] we shal fall into the hāds of the Lord, and not into the hands of men.
21 Yet as his greatnes is, so is his mercie.

CHAP. III.

2 To our father and mother oght we to giue double honor. 10 Of the blessing and curse of the father and mother. 22 No man oght ouer curiously to searche out the secrets of God.

1 T[He children of wisdome are the Church of the righteous, & their ofspring is obedience and loue.]
2 Heare your fathers iudgement, ô childrē, and do thereafter, that ye may be safe.
3 For the Lord wil haue the father honored of he children, and hathe confirmed the autoritie of the mother ouer the children.
4 Who so honoreth his father, his sinnes shalbe forgiuen him, [and he shal absteine from them, & shal haue his daily desires.]
5 And he that honoreth his mother, is like one that gathereth treasure.
6 Who so honoreth his father, shal haue ioye of his owne children, & when he maketh his prayer, he shalbe heard.
7 He that honoreth his father, shal haue a long life, and he that is obedient vnto the Lord, shal comfort his mother.
8 He that feareth the Lord, honoreth his parents, and doeth seruice vnto his parēts, as vnto lords.
9 *Honour thy father and mother in dede and in worde [& in all paciēce,] that thou maist haue "Gods blessing, [& that his blessing may abide with thee in the end.]

Exod. 20, 12. deut. 5, 16. mat. 15, 4. ephes. 6, 2.
"Or, the blessing of men.

10 For ẏ blessing of the father establisheth the houses of the children, & the mothers curse rotteth out the fundacions.
11 Reioyce not at the dishonour of thy father: for it is not honour vnto thee, but shame.
12 Seing that mās glorie cometh by his fathers honour, & the reproche of ẏ mother is dishonour to the children,
13 My sonne, helpe thy father in his age, and greue him not as long as he liueth.
14 And if his vnderstanding faile, haue pacience with him, & despise him not when thou art in thy ful strength.
15 For the good intreatie of thy father shal not be forgottē, but it shalbe a forteres for thee against sinnes, [and for thy mothers offence thou shalt be recompensed with good, and it shalbe founded for thee in righteousnes.]
16 And in the day of trouble thou shalt be remembred: thy sinnes also shal melt away as the yce in the faire wether.
17 He that forsaketh his father, shal come to shame, and he that angreth his mother, is cursed of God.
18 ¶ My sonne, performe thy doings with mekenes, so shalt thou be beloued of them that are approued.
19 The * greater thou art, the more humble thy self [in all things,] & thou shalt finde fauour before the Lord.

Philip. 2, 3.

20 Many are excellent & of renoume: but the secrets are reueiled vnto the meke.
21 For the power of the Lord is great, & he is honored of the lowlie.
22 *Seke not out the things that are to hard for thee, nether searche the things rashly which are to mightie for thee.

Prou. 25, 27. rom. 12, 3.

23 [But] what [God] hathe cōmanded thee, thinke vpon that with reuerence, [and be not curious in many of his workes:] for it is not

is not nedeful for thee to se with thine eyes
the things that are secret.
24 Be not curious in superfluous things: for
many things are shewed vnto thee aboue
the capacitie of men.
25 The medling with suche hathe beguiled
many, and an euil opinion hathe deceiued
their iudgement.
26 Thou canst not se without eyes: professe
not the knowledge therefore that thou
hast not.
27 A stubberne heart shal fare euil at the
last: and he that loueth danger, shal perish
therein.
28 An heart that goeth two waies, shal not
prosper: and he that is frowarde of heart,
shal stumble therein.
29 An obstinate heart shalbe ladē with sorowes: and the wicked man shal heape sinne vpon sinne.
30 The persuasion of the proude is without
remedie, & his steppes shalbe plucked vp:
for the plant of sinne hathe taken roote in
him, [and he shal not be estemed.]
31 The heart of him that hathe vnderstanding, shal perceiue secret things, and an attentiue eare is the desire of a wise man.
32 [An heart that is wise & vnderstanding,
wil absteine from sinne, and shal prosper
in the workes of righteousnes.]
Dan. 4, 24. 33 Water quencheth burning fyre, *and almes taketh away sinnes.
34 And he that rewardeth good dedes, wil
remēber it afterward, & in the time of the
fall, he shal finde a staye.

CHAP. IIII.

1 Almes must be done with gentlenes. 12 The studie of wisdome and her frute. 20 An exhortation to eschewe euil, and to do good.

1 MY sonne, defraude not the poore of
his liuing, and make not the nedie
eyes to waite long.
2 Make not an hungrie soule sorowful, nether vexe a man in his necessitie.
3 Trouble not the heart that is grieued, &
differre not the gift of the nedie.
4 Refuse not the prayer of one that is in
trouble: turne not away thy face from the
poore.
5 Turne not thine eyes a side [in angre]
from the poore, and giue him none occasion to speake euil of thee.
6 For if he cursse thee in the bitternes of
his soule, his prayer shalbe heard of him
that made him.
7 Be courteous vnto the cōpanie [of poore,
and humble thy soule vnto the Elder,] and
bowe downe thine head to a man of worship.
8 Let it not greue thee to bowe downe thine eare vnto the poore, [but pay thy dette,] and giue him a friendlie answer.
9 ¶Deliuer him that suffreth wrong, from
the hand of the oppressour, & be not faint
hearted "when thou iudgest. "Or, to defende him.
10 Be as a father vnto the fatherles, and as
an housband vnto their mother: so shalt
thou be as the sonne of the moste High:
and he shal loue thee more then thy mother doeth.
11 Wisdome exalteth her children, and receiueth them that seke her, [& wil go before them in the way of righteousnes.]
12 He that loueth her, loueth life, and they
that seke life in the morning, shal haue
great ioye.
13 He that kepeth her, shal inherit glorie:
for vnto whome she entreth, him the Lord
wil blesse.
14 They that honour her, shalbe the seruants of the holie one, and them that loue
her, the Lord doeth loue.
15 Who so giueth eare vnto her, shal iudge
the nacions, and he that goeth vnto her,
shal dwell safely.
16 He that is faithful vnto her, shal haue
her in possession, and his generacion shal
possesse her.
17 For first she wil walke with him by croked waies, and bring him vnto feare, and
drede, and torment him with her disciplī-
ne vntil she haue tryed his soule, and haue
proued him by her iudgements.
18 Then wil she returne the straight way
vnto him, and comfort him, and shew him
her secrets, [and heape vpon him the treasures of knowledge, and vnderstanding of
righteousnes.]
19 But if he go wrong, she wil forsake him,
and giue him ouer into the hands of his
destruction.
20 [¶My sonne,] *Make muche of time, Rom. 12, 11.
and eschewe the thing that is euil,
21 And be not ashamed [to say the trueth]
for thy life: for there is a shame that brīgeth sinne, and a shame that bringeth worship and fauour.
22 Accept no persone against thine owne
conscience, that thou be not confounded
to thine owne decaye, [and forbeare not
thy neighbour in his faute.]
23 And kepe not backe counsel when it may
do good, nether hide thy wisdome when
it may be famous.
24 For by the talke is wisdome knowen, and
learning by the wordes of the tongue, [&
counsel, wisdome and learning by the talking of the wise, & stedfastnes in the workes of righteousnes.]
25 In no wise speake against the worde of
trueth, but be ashamed of the lies of thine
owne ignorance.
26 Be not ashamed to confesse thy sinnes, &
resist not the course of the riuer.
27 Submit not thy self vnto a foolish man,
nether accept the persone of the mightie.

28 Striue for the trueth vnto death, [and
defend iustice for thy life,] and the Lord
God shal fight for thee [against thine e-
nemies.]
29 Be not hastie in thy tongue, nether slacke and negligent in thy workes.
30 Be not as a lion in thine owne house, nether beat thy seruãts for thy fantasie, [nor
oppresse them that are vnder thee.]
31 * Let not thine hand be stretched out
to receiue, and shut whẽ thou shuldest
giue.

Act.20,35.

CHAP. V.

1 In riches may we not put any confidence. 7 The vengeance of God oght to be feared, and repentance may not be differred.

1 TRust not vnto thy riches, and say not,
I haue ynough for my life: [for it
shal not helpe in ỹ time of vengeance and
indignation.]
2 Followe not thine owne minde and thy
strength to walke in the wayes of thine
heart:
3 Nether say ỹ, [How haue I had strength?]
or who wil bring me vnder for my workes? for God the aduenger wil reuenge the
wrong done by thee.
4 And say not, I haue sinned, and what e-
uil hathe come vnto me? for the Almightie
is a pacient rewarder, but he wil not leaue
thee vnpunished.
5 Because thy sinne is forgiuen, be not without feare, to heape sinne vpon sinne.
6 And say not, The mercie of God is great:
he wil forgiue my manifolde sinnes: for
mercie & wrath come from him, & his indignacion cometh downe vpon sinners.
7 Make no tarying to turne vnto the Lord,
and put not of from day to day: for suddenly shal the wrath of the Lord breake
forthe, & in thy securitie thou shalt be destroied, and thou shalt perish in time of
vengeance.
8 Trust not in wicked riches: for they shal
not helpe thee in the day of punishment
[and vengeance.]
9 Be not caryed about with euerie winde,
and go not into euerie way: for so doeth
the sinner that hathe a double tongue.
10 Stand fast in thy sure vnderstanding [&
in the way and knowledge of the Lord] &
haue but one maner of worde, [& followe
the worde of peace and righteousnes.
11 Be humble to heare the worde of God,
that thou maist vnderstand it, and make a
true answere with wisdome.]
12 Be swift to heare good things, and let
thy life be pure, & giue a pacient answer.
13 If thou hast vnderstanding, answer thy
neighbour: if not, laye thine hand vpõ thy
mouth, [lest thou be trapped in an vndiscrete worde, and so be blamed.]
14 Honour and shame is in the talke, & the
tongue of a man causeth him to fall.
15 Be not counted a talebearer, & lie not in
waite with thy tongue: for shame [and re-
pentance] followe the thief, and an euil
condemnacion is ouer him that is double
tõgued: [but he that is a backebiter, shalbe
hated, enuied and confounded.]
16 Do not rashly, nether in small things nor
in great.

CHAP. VI.

1 It is the propertie of a sinner to be euil tongued. 6 Of friendship. 33 Desire to be taught.

1 BE not of a friend [thy neighbours]
enemie: for suche shal haue an euil
name, shame and reproche, and he shal be
in infamie as the wicked that hathe a double tongue.
2 Be not proude in the deuice of thine owne minde, lest thy soule rent thee as a bull,
3 And eat vp thy leaues, and destroie thy
frute, and so thou be lefte as a drye tree [in
the wildernes.]
4 For a wicked soule destroieth him that
hathe it, and maketh him to be laughed to
scorne of his enemies, [and bringeth him
to the porcion of the vngodlie.]
5 A swete talke multiplieth the friends [&
pacifieth them that be at variance,] and a
swete tõgue increaseth muche good talke.
6 Holde friendship with manie, neuertheles haue but one counseler of a thousand.
7 If thou gettest a friẽd, proue him first, &
be not hastie to credit him.
8 For some man is a friend for his owne
occasion, and wil not abide in the day of
thy trouble.
9 And there is some friend that turneth to
enimitie, and taketh parte against thee, &
in contention he wil declare thy shame.
10 Againe some friend is but a companion
at the table, and in the day of thine affliction he continueth not.
11 But in thy prosperitie he wil be as thou
thy self, and wil vse libertie ouer thy seruants.
12 If thou be broght low, he wil be against
thee, and wil hide him self from thy face.
13 Departe from thine enemies, and beware
of thy friends.
14 A faithful friend is a strong defence, and
he that findeth suche one, findeth a treasure.
15 A faithful friend oght not to be changed
for any thing, and the weight [of golde &
siluer] is not to be compared to the goodnes [of his faith.]
16 A faithful friend is the medicine of life
[and immortalitie,] & thei that feare the
Lord, shal finde him.
17 Who so feareth the Lord, shal direct his
friendship a right, and as his owne self, so
shal his friend be.

18 ¶My

18 ¶My sonne, receiue doctrine from thy
youth vp: so shalt thou finde wisdome
[which shal indure] til thine olde age.
19 Go to her as one that ploweth, and soweth, and waite for her good frutes: for thou
shalt haue but litle labour in her worke:
but ẏ shalt eat of her frutes right sone.
20 How exceading sharpe is she to the vnlearned? he that is without iudgement, wil
not remaine with her.
21 Vnto suche one she is as a fine touchestone, and he casteth her from him without
delay.
22 For thei haue the name of wisdome, but
there be but fewe that haue the knowledge
of her.
23 [For with them that knowe her, she abideth vnto the appearing of God.]
24 Giue eare, my sonne: receiue my doctrine, and refuse not my counsel,
25 And put thy fete into her linkes, and thy
necke into her chaine.
26 Bowe downe thy shulder vnto her, and
beare her, and be not wearie of her bands.
27 Come vnto her with thy whole heart, &
kepe her waies with all thy power.
28 Seke after her, and searche her, & she shal
be shewed thee: and when thou hast gotten
her, forsake her not.
29 For at the last thou shalt finde rest in her,
and that shalbe turned to thy ioye.
30 Then shal her fetters be a strong defence for thee, [and a sure fundacion] & her
chaines a glorious raiment.
31 For there is a golden ornament in her, &
her bands are the laces of purple colour.
32 Thou shalt put her on as a robe of honour, & shalt put her vpon thee, as a crowne of ioye.
33 My sonne, if thou wilt, thou shalt be taught, and if thou wilt applie thy minde,
thou shalt be wittie.
34 If thou loue to heare, thou shalt receiue
[doctrine,] and if thou delite in hearing,
thou shalt be wise.
35 Stand with the multitude of the Elders,
which are wise, and ioyne with him that
is wise.
36 *Desire to heare all godlie talke, and let (Chap.8,9.)
not the graue sentences of knowledge escape thee.
37 And if thou seest a man of vnderstanding, get thee sone vnto him, and let thy
foote weare the steppes of his dores.
38 Let thy minde be vpon the ordinances
of the Lord, and be "continually occupied in his cōmandements: so shal he stablish thine heart, and giue thee wisdome
at thine owne desire. ("Or, earnestly.)

CHAP. VII.

2 We must forsake euil, and yet not iustifie our selues. 23 The behauiour of the wise towarde his wife, his friend, his children, his seruants, his father and mother.

1 Do no euil: so shal no harme come
vnto thee.
2 Departe from the thing that is wicked,
and sinne shal turne away from thee.
3 My sonne, sowe not vpon the forowes of
vnrighteousnes, lest that thou reape them
seuen folde.
4 Aske not of the Lord preeminence, nether of the King the seate of honour.
5 *Iustifie not thy self before the Lord: [for (Iob.9,2.)
he knoweth thine heart,] & boast not thy (psal.143,2.)
wisdome in the presence of the King. (eccl.7,17.)
6 Seke not to be made a iudge, lest thou be (luk.18,11.)
not able to take away iniquitie, and lest
thou, fearing the persone of the mightie,
shuldest commit an offence against thine
vprightnes.
7 Offend not against the multitude of a
citie, and cast not thy self amōg the people.
8 *Binde not two sinnes together: for in o- (Chap.12,5.)
ne sinne shalt thou not be vnpunished.
9 Say not, God wil loke vpon the multitude of mine oblacions, and when I offer to
the moste high God, he wil accept it.
10 Be not faint hearted, when thou makest
thy praier, nether slacke in giuing of almes.
11 Laugh no mā to scorne in the heauines
of his soule: for [God which seeth all
things] is he *that can bring downe, & set (1.Sam.2,7.)
vp againe.
12 Sow not a lie against thy brother, nether
do the same against thy friend.
13 Vse not to make anie maner of lie: for
the custome thereof is not good.
14 Make not manie wordes when thou art
among the Elders, nether repeate a thing
in thy prayer.
15 Hate not laborious worke, nether the
housbandrie, which the moste High hathe created.
16 Nomber not thy self in the multitude
of the wicked, but remember that vengeance wil not slacke.
17 Humble thy minde greatly: for the
vengeance of the wicked is fyre and wormes.
18 Giue not ouer thy friend for anie good,
nor thy true brother for ẏ golde of Ophir.
19 Departe not from a wise and good womā, [that is fallen vnto thee for thy porciō in the feare of the Lord:] for her grace is aboue golde.
20 ¶*Where as thy seruāt worketh truely, (Leui.19,13.)
intreate him not euil, nor ẏ hireling that (chap.33,30.)
bestoweth him self wholie for thee. (& 34,7.)
21 Let thy soule loue a good seruant, and
defraude him not of libertie, [nether leaue him a poore man.]
22 *If thou haue cattel, loke wel to them, (Deut.25,4.)
and if thei be for thy profite, kepe them
with thee.

23 If thou haue sonnes,instruct them, and
holde their necke from their youth.
24 If thou haue daughters, kepe their bodie, and shewe not thy face chereful towarde them.
25 Marie thy daughter,&so shalt thou performe a weightie matter: but giue her to
a man of vnderstanding.
26 If thou haue a wife after thy minde,for-
sake her not, but commit not thy self to
the hateful.
Chap.3,9. 27 *Honour thy father frõ thy whole heart,
tob.4,3. & forget not the sorowes of thy mother.
28 Remember that thou wast borne of thẽ,
and how canst thou recompense them the
things that they haue done for thee?
29 ¶Feare the Lord with all thy soule, and
honor his ministers.
30 Loue him that made thee, with all thy
Deut.12,18. strength,*and forsake not his seruants.
31 Feare the Lord with all thy soule, and
Leui.2,3. honor the Priests, *and giue them their
nomb.18,15. porcion,as it is commanded thee,the first
frutes, [and purificacions] and sacrifices
for sinne, & the offrings of the shoulders,
and the sacrifices of sanctificacion, and
the first frutes of the holie things.
32 Stretche thine hand vnto the poore that
"Or,liberalitie. thy "blessing, [and reconciliacion] may
be accomplished.
33 Liberalitie pleaseth all men liuing,and
Tob.2,21. *from the dead restraine it not.
Rom.12,15. 34 *Let not them that wepe, be without
[cõfort:] but mourne wͭ suche as mourne.
Mat.25,36. 35 *Be not slowe to visit the sicke: for that
shal make thee to be beloued.
36 Whatsoeuer thou takest in hand,remem-
ber the end,& thou shalt neuer do amisse.

CHAP. VIII.

We must take hede with whome we haue to do.

1 STriue not with a mightie mã,lest thou
fall into his hands.
Mat.5,25. 2 *Make not variance with a riche mã, lest
he on ŷ other side weigh downe thy weight:
Chap.31,6. *for golde [and siluer] hathe destroyed
manie & hathe subuerted ŷ hearts of Kĩgs.
3 Striue not with a man that is ful of wordes,and laie no stickes vpon his fyre.
4 Playe not with a man that is vntaught,
lest thy kinred be dishonored.
Galat.6,1. 5 *Despise not a man that turneth him self
away from sinne, nor cast him not in the
teeth with all,but remẽber that we are all
worthie blame.
Leui.19,32. 6 *Dishonour not a man in his olde age:
for they were as we which are not olde.
7 Be not glad of the death of thine enemie, but remember that we must dye all,
[and so enter into ioy.]
Chap.6,35. 8 *Despise not the exhortacion of the [El-
ders] ŷ be wise, but acquaint thy self with
their wise sentences: for of thẽ thou shalt
learne wisdome, [and the doctrine of vnderstanding,] and how to serue great men
[without complaint.]
9 Go not from the doctrine of the Elders:
for they haue learned it of their fathers,&
of them thou shalt learne vnderstanding,
and to make answer in the time of nede.
10 Kindle not the coles of sinners, [when
thou rebukest them,] lest thou be burnt in
the fyrie flames [of their sinnes.]
11 Rise not vp against him that doeth wrõg,
ŷ he lay not waite as a spie for thy mouth.
12 *Lend not vnto him that is mightier Chap.29,4.
then thy self: for if thou lendest him,coũt
it but lost.
13 Be not suretie aboue thy power: for if
thou be suretie,thinke to paie it.
14 Go not to law with ŷ iudge:for thei wil
giue sentẽce accordĩg to his owne honour.
15 *Trauaile not by the way with him that Gen.17,8.
is rash, lest he do thee iniurie: for he followeth his owne wilfulnes, & so shalt thou
perish thorowe his folie.
16 *Striue not with him that is angrie,& go Prou.22,24.
not with him into the wildernes: for blood
is as nothing in his sight, and where there
is no helpe,he wil ouerthrowe thee.
17 Take no counsel at a foole: for he can
not kepe a thing close.
18 Do no secret thing before a stranger: for
thou canst not tell what he goeth about.
19 Open not thine heart vnto euerie man,
lest he be vnthankeful to thee, [and put
thee to reprofe.]

CHAP. IX.

Of ielousie. 12 An olde friend is to be preferred before a newe. 18 Righteous men shulde be bidden to thy table.

1 BE not ielous ouer thy wife of thy
bosome, nether teache her by thy
meanes an euil lesson.
2 Giue not thy life vnto a woman, lest she
ouercome thy strength, [and so thou be
confounded.]
3 Mete not an harlot, lest thou fall into her
snares.
4 Vse not the companie of a woman that
is a singer, [& a dancer, nether heare her,]
lest thou be taken by her craftines.
5 Gaze not on a* maide, that thou fall not Gen 6,2.
by that that is precious in her.
6 *Cast not thy minde vpon harlots [in ã- Prou.5,2.
nie maner of thing,] lest thou destroye
[bothe thy self and] thine heritage.
7 Go not about gazĩg in the streates of the
citie, nether wander thou in the secret places thereof.
8 *Turne awaye thine eye from a beautiful Mat 5,28.
woman, and loke not vpon others beautie:
for manie* haue perished by the beautie Gen.34,1.
of women: for thorow it loue is kindled as 2 Sam 11,2.
a fyre. iudeth.10,17.
9 [Euerie woman that is an harlot, shalbe
troden vnder fote as dõgue, of euerie one
that goeth by the waye.

10 Manie

10 Many wondering at ẏ beautie of a strange womã, haue bene cast out: for her wordes burne as a fyre.]
11 Sit not at all with another mãs wife, [nether lie with her vpon the bed,] nor banket with her, lest thine heart incline vnto her, and so through thy desire fall into destruction.
12 ¶ Forsake not an olde friend: for the new shal not be like him: a newe friend is as newe wine: when it is olde, thou shalt drinke it with pleasure.
Iudg.9,3. 2.sam.15,12.
13 *Desire not ẏ honour [& riches] of a sinner: for ẏ knowest not what shalbe his end.
14 Delite not in the thing that the vngodlie haue pleasure in, but remẽber that they shal not be founde iust vnto their graue.
15 Kepe thee frõ the man that hathe power to slaye: so shalt thou not doute the feare of death: and if thou come vnto him, make no faute, lest he take away thy life: remember that thou goest in the middes of snares, and that thou walkest vpon the towres of the citie.
16 Trye thy neighbour as nere as thou cãst, *and aske counsel of the wise.
Chap.7,8.
17 Let thy talke be with the wise, & all thy cõmunicatiõ in the Law of ẏ moste High.
18 Let iust men eat and drinke with thee, and let thy reioycing be in the feare of the Lord.
19 In *the hands of the craftesmen shal the workes be commended, and the wise prince of the people by his worde, [& the worde by the wisdome of the Elders.]
*Or, the workeman is praised according to the workes.
20 A man ful of wordes is dangerous in his citie, and he that is rash in his talking, shalbe hated.

CHAP. X.

1 Of Kings and iudges. 7 Pride and couetousnes are to be abhorred. 28 Labour is praised.

1 A Wise iudge wil instruct his people with discretion: the gouernance of a prudent man is wel ordered.
2 As the iudge of the people is him self, so are his officers, and what maner of man the ruler of the citie is, suche are all they that dwell therein.
1 King.12,1.
3 *An vnwise King destroieth his people, but where they that be in autoritie, are men of vnderstãding, there the citie prospereth.
4 The gouernement of the earth is in the hand of the Lord, [and all iniquitie of the nacions is to be abhorred,] and when time is, he wil set vp a profitable ruler ouer it.
5 In the hand of God is the prosperitie of man, and vpon the scribes wil he laye his honour.
Leu.19,17.
6 *Be not angrie for any wrong, with thy neighbour, and do nothing by iniurious practises.
7 Pride is hateful before God and man, & by bothe doeth one commit iniquitie.
8 * Because of vnrighteous dealing and wrongs and riches gotten by deceit, the kingdome is translated from one people to another. Ier.27,6. dan.4,14.
9 There is nothing worse then a couetous man: [why art thou proude, ô earth and ashes? there is not a more wicked thing, then to loue money:] for suche one wolde euen sel his soule, & for his life euerie one is compelled to pul out his owne bowels.
10 [All tyrannie is of smale indurance, and the disease that is hard to heale, is grieuous to the physicion.]
11 The physiciõ cutteth of ẏ sore disease, & he that is to day a King, to morow is dead.
12 Why is earth & ashes proude, seing that when a man dyeth, he is the heire of serpents, beastes and wormes?
13 The beginning of mans pride, is to fall away from God, & to turne away his heart from his maker.
14 For pride is the original of sinne, and he that hathe it, shal powre out abominacion, til at last he be ouerthrowen: therefore the Lord bringeth the persuasious [of the wicked] to dishonour, and destroieth them in the end.
15 The Lord hathe cast downe the thrones of the [proude] princes, & set vp the meke in their steade.
16 The Lord plucketh vp the rootes of the [proude] nacions, and planteth the lowlie with glorie among them.
17 The Lord ouerthroweth the lands of the heathen, and destroieth thẽ vnto ẏ fundacions of ẏ earth: he causeth thẽ to wither away, & destroieth them, and maketh their memorial to cease out of the earth.
18 [God destroieth the memorial of the proude, & leaueth the remembrance of the humble.]
19 Pride was not created in mẽ, nether wrath in the generacion of women.
20 There is a sede of mã, which is an honorable sede: the honorable sede are they ẏ feare ẏ Lord: there is a sede of mã, which is without honour: ẏ sede without honour, are they that trãsgresse the cõmandemẽts of the Lord: it is a sede that remaineth ẇ feareth the Lord, & a faire plant, that loue him: but they are a sede without honour, that despise the Law, & a deceiueable sede that breake the commandements.
21 He ẏ is the chief amõg brethrẽ, is honorable: so are they ẏ feare ẏ Lord in his sight.
22 The feare of the Lord causeth that the kingdome faileth not, but the kingdome is lost by crueltie and pride.
23 The feare of the Lord is ẏ glorie aswel of the riche & the noble, as of the poore.
24 It is not mete to despise the poore man

that hathe vnderstanding, nether is it conuenient to magnifie the riche that is a wicked man.
25 The great man and the iudge & the man of autoritie, are honorable, yet is there none of them greater, then he that feareth the Lord.
Prou 17,2. 26 *Vnto the seruant that is wise, shal they that are free, do seruice:*he ẏ hathe knowledge, wil not grudge whẽ he is reformed, [& the ignorant shal not come to honor.] 2.Sam.12,13.
27 Seke not excuses when thou shuldest do thy worke, nether be ashamed thereof through pride in the time of aduersitie.
Prou.12,9. 28 *Better is he that laboreth & hathe plenteousnes of all things, then he that is gorgeous, and wanteth bread.
29 My sonne, get thy self praise by mekenes, and esteme thy self as thou deseruest.
30 Who wil counte him iust that sinneth against him self? or honour him, that dishonoreth his owne soule?
31 The poore is honored for his knowledge [and his feare,] but the riche is had in reputacion because of his goods.
32 He that is honorable in pouertie, how muche more shal he be when he is riche? & he that is vnhonest beĩg riche, how muche more *wil he be so* when he is in pouertie?

CHAP. XI.

1 The praise of humilitie. 2 After the outward appearance oght we not to iudge. 7 Of rash iudgement. 14 All things come of God. 29 All men are not to be broght into thine house.

Gen.41,40. dan.6,3. 1 WIsdome *lifteth vp ẏ head of him that is lowe, and maketh him to sit among great men.
2 Commend not a man for his beautie, nether despise a man in his vtter appearance.
3 The bee is but smal among the foules, yet doeth her frute passe in swetenes.
Act.12,2. 4 Be not proude of clothing & raimẽt,*& exalte not thy self in the day of honour: for the workes of the Lord are wõderful, [and glorious,] secret, [and vnknowen] are his workes among men.
5 Many tyrãts haue sit downe vpon ẏ earth, * & the vnlikelie hathe worne the crowne. 1.Sam 15,28.
esther.6,10. 6 Many mightie men haue bene broght to dishonour, & the honorable haue bene deliuered into other mens hands.
Deu.13,14. & 17,6. iosh.7,22. 7 ¶*Blame [no mã] before thou haue inquired the matter: vnderstand first, and then reforme [righteously.]
Pro.18,13. 8 *Giue no sentence, before thou hast heard the cause, nether interrupt men in the middes of their tales.
9 Striue not for a matter that thou hast not to do with, and sit not in the iudgement of sinners.
10 My sonne, medle not with many matters:
Mat.19,22. 1.tim.6,9. *for if thou gaine muche, thou shalt not be blameles, and if thou follow after it, yet shalt thou not atteine it, nether shalt thou escape, thogh thou flee from it.
11 *There is some man that laboreth and Pro.10,3.
taketh peine, and the more he hasteth, the more he wanteth.
12 Againe there is some that is slouthful, &
*hathe nede of helpe: for he wãteth stregth, Iob.42,10.
and hathe great pouertie, yet the eye of the Lord loketh vpõ him to good, and setteth him vp from his lowe estate,
13 And he lifteth vp his head: so that manie men marueil at him, [& giue honour vnto God.]
14 *Prosperitie & aduersitie, life & death, Iob.14,12.
pouertie and riches come of the Lord. eze.28,4.
15 Wisdome & knowledge, and vnderstanding of the Lawe are of the Lord: loue & good workes come of him.
16 Errour and darckenes are appointed for sinners, and they that exalte them selues in euil, waxe olde in euil.
17 The gift of the Lord remaineth for the godlie, & his good wil giueth prosperitie for euer.
18 ¶Some man is riche by his care and nigardship, & this is ẏ porcion of his wages,
19 In that he saith, *I haue gotten rest, and Luk.12,19.
now wil I eat continually of my goods, yet he considereth not, ẏ the time draweth nere, that he must leaue all these things vnto other men, and dye him self.
20 Stand thou in thy state, and exercise thy self therein, and remaine in thy worke vnto thine age.
21 Marueil not at the workes of sinners, but trust in the Lord, and abide in thy labour: for it is an easie thing in the sight of the Lord suddenly to make a poore man riche.
22 The blessing of the Lord is in the wages of the godlie, and he maketh his prosperitie sone to florish.
23 ¶Say not, What profite and pleasure shal I haue? and what good things shal I haue hereafter?
24 Againe say not, I haue ynough, & possesse many things, * & what euil can come to Chap.18,25.
me hereafter?
25 In thy good state remẽber aduersitie, & in aduersitie forget not prosperitie.
26 For it is an easie thing vnto the Lord in the day of death to rewarde a man according to his waies.
27 The aduersitie of an houre maketh one to forget pleasure: and in a mans end, his workes are discouered.
28 Iudge none blessed before his death: for a man shalbe knowen by his children.
29 Bring not euerie man into thine house: for the disceitful haue many traines, [and are like stomackes that belche stinkingly.]
30 As a partriche is takẽ vnder a basket, [& the hinde is taken in the snare,] so is the heart of the proude man, which like a spie watcheth

watcheth for thy fall.
31 For he lieth in waite & turneth good vnto euil, and in things worthie praise he wil
finde some faute.
32 Of one litle sparke is made a great fyre,
[& of one disceitful man is blood increased:] for a sinful mã laieth waite for blood.
33 Beware of a wicked man: for he imagineth wicked things to bring thee into a
perpetual shame.
34 Lodge a strãger, and he wil destroie thee
with vnquietnes, & driue thee from thine
owne.

CHAP. XII.

1 Vnto whome we oght to do good. 10 Enemies oght not to be trusted.

1 WHen thou wilt do good, knowe
to whome thou doest it, so shalt
thou be thanked for thy benefites.
2 Do good vnto the righteous, & thou shalt
finde [great] rewarde, thogh not of him,
yet of the moste High.
3 He can not haue good that continueth in
euil, and giueth no almes: [for the moste
High hateth the sinners, and hathe mercie
vpon them that repent.]
4 Giue vnto suche as feare God, and receiue not a sinner.
5 Do wel vnto him that is lowlie, but giue
not to ye vngodlie: holde backe thy bread,
and giue it not vnto him, lest he ouercome
thee thereby: els thou shalt receiue twise
as muche euil for all the good that thou
doest vnto him.
6 For the moste High hateth the wicked, &
wil repay vengeance vnto the vngodlie, &
kepeth them against the day of horrible
vengeance.
7 Giue vnto the good, and receiue not the
sinner.
8 A friend can not be knowen in prosperitie, nether can an enemie be vnknowen in
aduersitie.
9 When a man is in wealth, it grieueth his
enemies, but in heauines & trouble a mans
very friend wil departe from him.
10 Trust neuer thine enemie: for like as an
yron rusteth, so doeth his wickednes.
11 And thogh he make muche crouching &
kneeling, yet aduise thy self, & beware of
him, & thou shalt be to him, as he that wipeth a glasse, and thou shalt knowe that all
his rust hathe not bene wel wiped away.
12 Set him not by thee, lest he destroy thee, &
stand in thy place.
13 Nether set him at thy right hand, lest he
seke thy roume, & thou at the last remẽber
my wordes, & be pricked with my sayings.
14 Binde not two sinnes together: for there
shal not one be vnpunished.
15 Who wil haue pitie of ye charmer, that is
stinged of the serpẽt? or of all suche as come nere the beastes? so is it wt him that kepeth companie with a wicked man, & wrap
peth him self in his sinnes.
16 For a season wil he bide with thee: but
if thou stomble, he taryeth not.
17 *An enemie is swete in his lippes: he can Iere. 41,6.
make manie good wordes, and speake ma
nie good things: yea, he can weepe with
his eyes, but in his heart he imagineth
how to throwe thee into the pit: and if
he may finde opportunitie, he wil not be
satisfied with blood.
18 If aduersitie come vpon thee, thou shalt
finde him there first, and thogh he pretẽd
to helpe thee, yet shal he vndermine thee:
he wil shake his head, and clappe his hãds,
and wil make manie wordes, and disguise his countenance.

CHAP. XIII.

1 The companies of the proude & of the riche are to be eschewed. 15 The loue of God. 17 Like do companie with their like.

1 HE *that toucheth pitch, shalbe defi- Deu. 7,2.
led with it: and he that is familiar
with the proude, shal be like vnto him.
2 Burthen not thy self aboue thy power,
whiles thou liuest, and companie not
with one that is mightier, and richer then
thy self: for how agre the kettel and the
earthen pot together? for if the one be
smitten against the other, it shalbe brokẽ.
3 The riche dealeth vnrighteously, and
threatneth with all: but the poore being
oppressed must intreat: if the riche haue
done wrong, he must yet be intreated: but
if the poore haue done it, he shal straight
waise be threatned.
4 If thou be for his profite, he vseth thee:
but if yu haue nothing, he wil forsake thee.
5 If thou haue anie thing, he wil liue with
thee: yea, he wil make thee a bare man, and
wil not care for it.
6 If he haue nede of thee, he wil defraude
thee, and wil laugh at thee, and put thee
in hope, and giue thee all good wordes, &
say, What wantest thou?
7 Thus wil he shame thee in his meat, vntil
he haue supt thee cleane vp twise or thrise, and at the last he wil laugh thee to scorne: afterwarde, when he seeth thee, he wil
forsake thee, and shake his head at thee.
8 [Submit thy self vnto God, & waite vpõ
his hand.]
9 Beware that yu be not disceiued in thine
owne conceit & broght downe by thy sim
plenes: [be not to hũble in thy wisdome.]
10 ¶If thou be called of a mightie man,
absent thy self: so shal he call thee the
more oft.
11 Prease not thou vnto him, that thou be
not shut out, but go not thou farre of, lest
he forget thee.
12 Withdrawe not thy self frõ his speache,
but beleue not his manie wordes: for with
muche communicatiõ wil he tempt thee,

and laughingly wil he grope thee.
13 He is vnmerciful, & kepeth not promes: he wil not spare to do thee hurt, and to put thee in prison.
14 Beware, & take good hede: for thou walkest in peril of thine ouerthrowing: when thou hearest this, awake in thy slepe.
15 Loue the Lord all thy life, and call vpon him for thy saluacion.
16 ¶Euerie beast loueth his like, and euerie man loueth his neighbour.
17 All flesh wil resorte to their like, & euerie man wil kepe companie with suche as he is him self.
18 How can the wolfe agre with the lambe? nomore cā the vngodlie with ẏ righteous.
19 What felowship hathe "hyena with a dogge? and what peace is betwene the riche and the poore?
20 *As* the wilde asse is the lions praye in the wildernes, so are poore men the meat of the riche.
21 As the proude hate humilitie, so do the riche abhorre the poore.
22 If a riche mā fall, his frieds set him vp againe: but whē the poore falleth, his frieds driue him away.
23 If a riche man offend, he hathe many helpers: he speaketh proude wordes, and yet men iustifie him: but if a poore man faile, they rebuke him, & thogh he speake wisely, yet can it haue no place.
24 Whē the riche man speaketh, euerie mā holdeth his tongue: and loke what he saith, they praise it vnto the cloudes: but if the poore mā speake, they say, What felow is this? and if he do amisse, they wil destroie him.
25 Riches are good vnto him that hathe no sinne [in his conscience,] and pouertie is euil in the mouth of the vngodlie.
26 The heart of a man chāgeth his countenance, whether it be in good or euil.
27 A chearful countenance is a token of a good heart: for it is an hard thīg to knowe the secrets of the thoght.

*Which is a wilde beast ẏ counterfaiteth the voyce of men, and so entiseth thē out of their houses and deuoureth them.

CHAP. XIIII.

3 The offence of the tongue. 17 Man is but a vaine thing. 21 Happie is he that continueth in wisdome.

1 BLessed is the man *that hathe not fallen by [the worde of] his mouth, & is not tormented with the sorow of sinne.
2 Blessed is he that is not condemned in his conscience, and is not fallen from his hope in the Lord.
3 Riches are comelie for a nigarde, and what shulde an enuious man do with money?
4 He that gathereth together from his owne soule, heapeth together for others, that wil make good cheare with his goods.
5 He that is wicked vnto him self, to whome wil he be good? for suche one can haue no pleasure of his goods.

Chap 19,7. iam. 3,2.

6 There is nothing worse, then when one enuieth him self: and this is a rewarde of his wickednes.
7 And if he do anie good, he doeth it, not knowing thereof, and against his wil, and at the last he declareth his wickednes.
8 The enuious man hathe a wicked loke: he turneth away his face, and dispiseth men.
9 A couetous mans eye hathe neuer ynough of a porciō, and his wicked malice withereth his owne soule.
10 A *wicked eye enuieth the bread, & there is scarcenes vpon his table. *Prou. 17,20.*
11 My sonne, do good to thy self of that thou hast, and giue the Lord his due offrings.
12 Remēber that death tarieth not, & that the couenant of the graue is not shewed vnto thee.
13 *Do good vnto thy fried before thou dye, & according to thine habilitie stretch out thine hand, and giue him. *Chap. 4,8. tob. 4,7. luk. 14,13.*
14 Defraude not thy self of the good day, and let not the porcion of the good desires ouerpasse thee.
15 Shalt thou not leaue thy trauails vnto another, and thy labours for the deuiding of the heritage?
16 Giue and take and sanctifie thy soule: [worke thou righteousnes before thy death:] for in the hell there is no meat to finde.
17 ¶*All flesh waxeth olde, as a garment, & this is the condition of all times, Thou shalt dye the death. *Isa. 40,6. 1 pet. 1,24. iam. 1,10.*
18 As the grene leaues on a thicke tree, some fall, and some growe, so is the generacion of flesh and blood: one cometh to an end, and another is borne.
19 All corruptible things shal faile, and the worker thereof shal go withal.
20 [Euerie excellēt worke shalbe iustified, and he that worketh it, shal haue honour thereby.]
21 *Blessed is the man that doeth meditate honest things by wisdome, [& exerciseth him self in iustice,] and he that reasoneth of holie things by his vnderstanding, *Psal. 1,2.*
22 Which cōsidereth in his heart her wayes, and vnderstandeth her secrets.
23 Go thou after her as one that seketh her out, and lie in waite in her wayes.
24 He shal loke in at her windowes, & hearken at her dores.
25 He shal abide beside her house, and fasten a stake in her walles: he shal pitche his tent besides her.
26 And he shal remaine in the lodging of good men, & shal set his childrē vnder her couering, and shal dwell vnder her branches.

27 By

27 By her he ſhalbe couered from the heat,
and in her glorie ſhal he dwell.

CHAP. XV.

1 The goodnes that followeth him which feareth God. 8 God reiecteth and caſteth of the ſinner. 11 God is not the author of euil.

1 HE that feareth the Lord, wil do good:
and he that hathe the knowledge of
the Law, wil kepe it ſure.
2 As an [honorable] mother ſhal ſhe mete
him, and ſhe, as his wife maried of a virgine, wil receiue him.
3 With the bread [of life] and vnderſtanding ſhal ſhe fede him, & giue him the wa
ter of [wholſome] wiſdome to drinke.
4 He ſhal aſſure him ſelf in her, and ſhal not
be moued, and ſhal holde him ſelf faſt by
her, and ſhal not be confounded.
5 She ſhal exalt him aboue his neighbou-
res, and in the middes of the congregació
ſhal ſhe open his mouth: [with the ſpirit of wiſdome, and vnderſtanding ſhal ſhe
fil him, and clothe him with the garment
of glorie.]
6 She ſhal cauſe him to inherit ioye, & the
crowne of gladnes, & an euerlaſting name.
7 But fooliſh men wil not take holde vpó
her: [but ſuche as haue vnderſtanding, wil
mete her:] the ſinners ſhal not ſe her.
8 For ſhe is farre fró pride [and diſceite,]
& men that lie, cã not remember her: [but
men of trueth ſhal haunt her, & ſhal proſper euen vnto the beholding of God.]
9 Praiſe is not ſemelie in the mouth of the
ſinner: for that is not ſent of the Lord.
10 But if praiſe come of wiſdome, [and be
pléteous in a faithful mouth] thé the Lord
wil proſper it.
11 Say not thou, It is through the Lord that
I turne backe: for thou oghteſt not to do
the things that he hateth.
12 Say not thou, He hathe cauſed me to erre: for he hathe no nede of the ſinful man.
13 The Lord hateth all abominacion [of
errour:] and they that feare God, wil loue it.
Gen.1,27. 14 *He made man from the beginning, and
left him in the hand of his counſel, [and
gaue him his commandements and precepts.]
15 If thou wilt, thou ſhalt obſerue the commandements, and teſtifie thy good wil.
16 He hathe ſet water and fyre before thee:
ſtretche out thine hand vnto which thou
wilt.
Iere 21,8. 17 *Before man is life and death, [good &
euil:] what him liketh, ſhalbe giuen him.
18 For the wiſdome of the Lord is great, &
he is mightie in power, and beholdeth all
things [continually.]
Pſal.34,16. 19 *And the eyes [of the Lord] are vpon
them that feare him, and he knoweth all
the workes of man.
20 He hathe commanded no man to do vngodlie, nether hathe he giuen anie man
licéce to ſinne: [for he deſireth not a multitude of infidels, & vnprofitable childré.]

CHAP. XVI.

1 Of vnhappie, and wicked children. 17 No man can hide him ſelf from God. 24 An exhortacion to the receiuing of instruction.

1 DEſire not the multitude of vnprofitable children, nether delite in vngodlie childré: thogh thei be manie, reioy
ce not in thé, except the feare of the Lord
be with them.
2 Truſt not thou to their life, nether reſt
vpon their multitude.
3 For one that is iuſte, is better then a thouſand ſuche, and better it is to dye without
children, then to leaue behinde him vngodlie children.
4 For by one that hathe vnderſtãding, ſhal
the citie be inhabited: but the ſtocke of the
wicked ſhal be waſted incontinently.
5 Manie ſuche things haue I ſene with mine eyes, and mine eare hathe heard greater
things then theſe.
6 *In the congregació of the vngodlie ſhal Chap.21,10.
a fyre be kindeled, and among vnfaithful
people ſhal the wrath be ſet on fyre.
7 *He ſpared not the olde gyants, ẘ were Gen.6,4.
rebellious, truſting to their owne ſtrẽgth,
8 *Nether ſpared he where as Lot dwelt, Gen.19,21.
thoſe whome he abhorred for their pride.
9 He had no pitie vpon the people that
were deſtroyed, & puffed vp in their ſins.
10 *And ſo he preſerued the ſix hundreth Nom.14,15.
thouſand fotemen, that were gathered in & 26,46.
the hardnes of their heart, in afflicting thé
& pitying them, in ſmiting them & healing thé, with mercie, & with chaſtiſemét.
11 Therefore if there be one ſtiffe necked
among the people, it is marueil if he ſcape
vnpuniſhed: for mercie and wrath are with
him: he is mightie to forgiue, & to powre
out diſpleaſure.
12 *As his mercie is great, ſo is his puniſh- Chap.5,16.
ment alſo: he iudgeth a man according to
his workes.
13 The vngodlie ſhal not eſcape with his
ſpoile, and the pacience of the godlie ſhal
not be delayed.
14 He wil giue place to all good dedes, &
euerie one ſhal finde according to his wor
kes, [and after the vnderſtanding of his
pilgrimage.]
15 The Lord hardened Pharao, that he ſhulde not knowe him, and that his workes
ſhulde be knowen vpon the earth vnder
the heauen.
16 His mercie is knowen to all creatures:
he hathe ſeparate his light from the darknes with an adamant.
17 Say not thou, I wil hide my ſelf from the
Lord: for who wil thĩke vpó me fró aboue?

I shal not be knowen in so great an heape
of people: for what is my soule among suche an infinite nomber of creatures?
2.Pet.3,10. 18 Beholde, the heauen, and the *heauen of
heauens, which are for God, the depth,
and the earth, and all that therein is, shalbe moued when he shal visite.
19 All the worlde which is created and made by his wil, the mountaines also, and the
fundacions of the earth shal shake for
feare, when the Lord loketh vpon them.
20 These things doeth no heart vnderstãd
worthely, [but he vnderstandeth euerie
heart.]
21 And who vnderstandeth his wayes? and
the storme that no man can se? for the moste parte of his workes are hid.
22 Who can declare ẏ workes of his righteousnes? or who can abide them? for his
ordinance is farre of, and the trying out
of all things faileth.
23 He that is humble of heart, wil consider
these things: but an vnwise and erronious
mã casteth his minde vpõ foolish things.
24 My sonne, hearken vnto me, and learne
knowledge, and marke my wordes with
thine heart.
25 I wil declare thee weightie doctrine, & I
wil instruct thee exactly in knowledge.
26 The Lord hathe set his workes in good
order frõ the beginning, & parte of them
hathe he sundred from the other when he
first made them.
27 He hathe garnished his workes for euer,
and their beginnings so long as they shal
indure, they are not hungrie nor wearied
in their labours, nor cease from their
offices.
28 None of them hindreth another, nether
was anie of them disobedient vnto his
wordes.
29 After this the Lord loked vpõ the earth
and filled it with his goods things.
30 With all maner of liuing beasts hathe he
couered the face thereof, and they returne into it againe.

CHAP. XVII.

1 The creacion of man, and the goodnes that God hathe done vnto him. 20 Of almes, 26 And repentance.

Gen.1,27. & 5,1. wisd.2,23. & 9,6. 1.cor.11,7. col.3,10.
1 THe *Lord hathe created man of the
earth, and turned him vnto it againe.
2 He gaue him the nomber of dayes & cer
teine times, and gaue him power of the
things, that are vpon earth.
3 He clothed them with strength, as they
had nede, and made them according to
his image.
4 He made all flesh to feare him, so that he
had the dominion ouer the beasts, and
foules.
Gen.2,22. 5 [*He created out of him an helper like
vnto him self,] and gaue them discrecion
and tongue, and eyes, eares, and an heart
to vnderstand, and sixtly he gaue them a
spirit, and seuently he gaue them speache
to declare his workes.
6 And he filled them with knowledge of
vnderstanding, and shewed them good
and euil.
7 He set his eye vpon their hearts, declaring
vnto them his noble workes,
8 And gaue thẽ occasion to reioyce perpetually in his miracles, that they shulde pru
dently declare his workes, & that the elect
shulde praise his holie Name together.
9 Beside this, he gaue them knowledge, and
gaue thẽ the Law of life for an heritage,
that thei might now knowe that thei were
mortal.
10 He made an euerlasting couenant with
them, and shewed them his iudgements.
11 Their eyes sawe the maiestie of his glorie, and their eares heard his glorious
voyce.
12 And he said vnto them, Beware of all vnrighteous things. *He gaue euerie man al- Exod.20,23. & 22,23.
so a cõmandement concerning his neigh-
bour.
13 Their wayes are euer before him, and are
not hid from his eyes.
14 Euerie man frõ his youth is giuẽ to euil,
and their stonie hearts can not become
flesh.
15 He appointed a ruler vpõ euerie people,
when he deuided the nacions of the whole
earth.
16 *And he did chuse Israel, as a peculiar Deu.4,20. & 10,15.
people to him self, whome he nourisheth
with discipline as his first borne, and giueth him moste louing light, and doeth
not forsake him.
17 All their workes are as the sunne before
him, and his eyes are continually vpon
their wayes.
18 None of their vnrighteousnes is hid frõ
him, but all their sinnes are before ẏ Lord.
19 And as he is merciful, and knoweth his
worke, he doeth not leaue them nor forsake
them, but spareth them.
20 *The almes of a man, is as a thing Chap.29,16.
sealed vp before him, and he kepeth the
good dedes of man as the apple of the eye,
and giueth repentance to their sonnes, and
daughters.
21 *At the last shal he arise, & rewarde thẽ, Mat.25,35.
and shal repay their rewarde vpon their
heads.
22 *But vnto them that wil repẽt, he giueth Act 3,19.
them grace to returne, and exhorteth su-
che as faile, with pacience, [and sendeth
them the porcion of the veritie.]
23 *Returne thẽ vnto the Lord, and forsake Ierem.3.12.
thy sinnes: make thy prayer before his face
and take away the offence.
24 Turne againe vnto ẏ most High: for he
wil bring thee from darkenes to wholsome
light:

light: forsake thine vnrighteousnes, and
hate greatly all abominacion.
25 [Knowe the righteousnes & iudgemẽts
of God: stand in the porcion that is set
forthe for thee, and in the prayer of the
most high God, & go in the partes of the
holie worlde with suche as be liuing and
confesse God.]
Psal.6,6. Isa.38,9. 26 *Who can praise the moste High in the
hell, as do all they that liue and confesse
him?
27 [Abide not thou in the errour of the
vngodlie, but praise ẏ Lord before death]
28 Thankefulnes perissheth from the dead,
as thogh he were not: but the liuing, and
he that is sounde of heart, praiseth the
Lord, [and reioyceth in his mercie.]
29 How great is the louing kindenes of the
Lord our God, and his compassion vnto
suche as turne vnto him in holines!
30 For all things can not be in men, because the sonne of man is not immortal, [and
they take pleasure in the vanitie of wickednes.]
31 What is more cleare then the sunne? yet
shal it faile.
32 So flesh and blood that thinketh euil,
[shalbe reproued.]
33 He seeth the power of the high heauen,
and all men are but earth and ashes.

CHAP. XVIII.

1 The maruelous workes of God. 6.7 The miserie & wretchednes of man. 9 Against God oght we not to complaine. 21 The performing of vowes.

Gen.1,1. 1 HE ẏ liueth for euer,* made all things
together: ẏ Lord who onelie is iust,
and there is none other but he, [and he remaineth a victorious King for euer.]
2 He ordereth the worlde with the power
of his hand, and all things obey his wil:
for he gouerneth all things by his power,
and deuideth the holie things from the
prophane.
3 To whome hathe he giuen power to expresse his workes? who wil seke out the
grounde of his noble actes?
4 Who shal declare the power of his greatnes? or who wil take vpõ him to tell out
his mercie?
5 As for the wonderous workes of ẏ Lord,
there may nothing be taken from them,
nether can anie thing be put vnto them,
nether may the grounde of them be founde out.
6 But when a man hathe done his best, he
must beginne againe, and when he thinketh to come to an end, he must go againe
to his labour.
7 ¶What is man? whereto serueth he? what
good or euil can he do?
Psal.19,10. 8 *If the nomber of a mans daies be an hũdreth yere, it is muche: and no man hathe
certeine knowledge of his death.
9 As droppes of raine are vnto the sea, and
as a grauel stone is in comparison of the
sand, so are a thousand yeres to the dayes
euerlasting.
10 Therefore is [God] pacient with them,
and powreth out his mercie vpon them.
11 He sawe & perceiued, that [the arrogancie of their heart, and their ruine was euil:
therefore heaped he vp his mercie vpon
them, and shewed them the way of righteousnes.]
12 The mercie that a man hathe, reacheth
to his neighbour: but the mercie of the
Lord is vpon all flesh: he chasteneth, and
nurtureth, & teacheth, & bringeth backe,
as a shepherd his flocke.
13 He hathe mercie of them that receiue
discipline, and that diligently seke after
his iudgements.
14 ¶My sonne, when thou doest good, reproue not: and whatsoeuer thou giuest, vse
no discomfortable wordes.
15 Shal not the dewe aswage the heat? so is
a worde better then a gift.
16 Lo, is not a worde better then a good
gift? but a gracious man giueth them
bothe.
17 A foole wil reproche churlishly, and a
gift of the enuious putteth out the eyes.
18 [Get thee righteousnes before thou come to iudgemẽt:] learne before thou speа-
ke, and vse physike or euer thou be sicke.
19 *Examine thy self, before ẏ be iudged, 1.Cor.11,31.
& in the day of the visitacion thou shalt
finde mercie.
20 Humble thy self before thou be sicke, &
whiles thou maiest yet sinne, shewe thy
conuersion.
21 Let nothing let thee to pay thy vowe in
time, and differre not vnto death to be reformed: [for the rewarde of God endureth for euer.]
22 Before thou praiest, prepare thy self, and
be not as one that tempteth the Lord.
23 Thinke vpon the* wrath, that shalbe at Chap.7,18.
the end, and the houre of vẽgeance, when
he shal turne away his face.
24 *When thou hast ynough, remẽber the Chap.11,27.
time of hunger: and when thou art riche,
thinke vpon pouertie and nede.
25 From the morning vntil the euening the
time is changed, and all suche things are
sone done before the Lord.
26 A wise man feareth in all things, and in
the daies of transgression he kepeth him
self from sinne: but the foole doeth not
obserue the time.
27 ¶Euerie wise man knoweth wisdome, &
knowledge, and praiseth him that findeth
her.
28 They that haue vnderstanding, deale
wisely in wordes: [they vnderstand the
trueth and righteousnes,] and powre out

with modestie graue sentẽces for mãs life.
29 The chief autoritie of speaking is of the
Lord alone : for a mortal man hathe but a
dead heart.
Rom.6,6. & 13,14. 30 ¶ *Followe not thy lustes, but turne thee
from thine owne appetites.
31 For if thou giuest thy soule her desires,
it shal make thine enemies that enuie thee,
to laugh thee to scorne.
32 Take not thy pleasure in great volup-
teousnes, and intangle not thy self with
suche companie.
33 Become not a begger by making bankets of that that thou hast borowed, and so
leaue nothing in thy purse : els ỹ shuldest
sclanderously lie in waite for thine owne
life.

CHAP. XIX.

2 Wine & whoredome bring men to pouertie. 6 In thy wordes vse discretion. 22 The difference of the wisdome of God and man. 27 Whereby thou maist knowe what is in man.

1 A Laboring man that is giuen to drũ-
kennes, shal not be riche: & he that
cõtemneth smale things, shal fall by litle
and litle.
Gen.19,33. 1 king.11,1. 2 *Wine and women leade wise men out of
the way, [and put men of vnderstanding
to reprofe.]
3 And he that companieth adulterers, shal
become impudent: rottennes and wormes
shal haue him to heritage, and he that is
to bolde, shalbe taken away, and be made a
publicke example.
Iosh.22,18. 4 *He that is hastie to giue credit, is light
minded, and he that erreth, sinneth against
his owne soule.
5 Whoso reioyceth in wickednes, shal be
punished: [he that hateth to be reformed,
his life shalbe shortened, and he that abhorreth babling of wordes, quencheth
wickednes :] but he that resisteth pleasures, crowneth his owne soule.
6 He that refraineth his tongue, may liue
with a troublesome man, and he that hateth babling, shal haue lesse euil.
7 Rehearse not to an other, that which is
tolde vnto thee: so ỹ shalt not be hindred.
8 Declare not other mens maners, nether
to friend nor foe : and if the sinne apperteine not vnto thee, reueile it not.
9 For he wil hearken vnto thee, and marke
thee, and when he findeth opportunitie, he
wil hate thee.
Chap.22,18. & 27,17. 10 *If thou hast heard a worde [against thy
neighbour,] let it dye with thee, & be su-
re, it wil not burst thee.
11 A foole trauaileth when he hathe heard
a thing, as a woman that is about to bring
forthe a childe.
12 As an arrowe that sticketh in ones thigh,
so is a worde in a fooles heart.
Leui.19,17. mat.18,15. 13 * Reproue a friend lest he do *euil*, and if
he haue done it, that he do it no more.
14 Reproue a friend that he may kepe his
tongue: and if he haue spoken, that he say
it no more.
15 Tell thy friend his faute: for oft times a
sclander is raised, and giue no credence to
euerie worde.
16 A man falleth with his tongue, but not
with his wil: *and who is he, that hathe not Iam.3,2.
offended in his tongue?
17 Reproue thy neighbour before thou
threaten him, & being without anger, giue
place vnto the Law of the moste High.
18 The feare of the Lord is the first degre
to be receiued of him, and wisdome obteineth his loue.
19 The knowledge of the commandemẽts
of the Lord is the doctrine of life, & they
that obey him, shal receiue the frute of im
mortalitie.
20 The feare of the Lord is all wisdome,
and the performing of the Law is perfite
wisdome, & the knowledge of his almightie power.
21 If a seruant say vnto his master, I wil not
do as it pleaseth thee, thogh afterward he
do it, he shal displease him that nourisheth
him.
22 The knowledge of wickednes is not wisdome, nether is there prudencie where as
the counsel of sinners is: but it is euen execrable malice : and the foole is voide of
wisdome.
23 He that hathe smale vnderstanding, and
feareth *God*, is better then one that hathe
muche wisdome, & transgresseth the Law
of the moste High.
24 There is a certeine subtiltie that is fine,
but it is vnrighteous: & there is that wras-
teth the open and manifest Law : yet there is that is wise and iudgeth righteously.
25 There is some that being about wicked
purposes, do bowe downe them selues, and
are sad, whose inward partes burne altogether with deceit: he loketh downe with
his face, and faineth him self deafe: yet before thou perceiue, he wil be vpon thee to
hurt thee.
26 And thogh he be so weake that he can
do thee no arme, yet when he may finde
opportunitie, he wil do euil.
27 ¶ A man may be knowen by his loke, and
one that hathe vnderstanding, may be perceiued by the marking of his countenãce.
28 * A mans garment, and his excesiue Chap.21,23.
laughter, and going declare what persone
he is.

CHAP. XX.

Of correction & repentance. 6 To speake & kepe silence in time. 17 The fall of the wicked 23 Of lying. 24 The thief & the murtherer. 28 Giftes blinde the eyes of the wise.

1 There is some rebuke that is not comelie: againe, some man holdeth his
tongue, and he is wise.
2 It is muche better to reproue, then to
beare

beare euil wil: and he that acknowledgeth
his faute, shalbe preserued from hurt.
Chap 30,22. 3 As*whē a gelded mā thorowe lust wolde
defile a maide, so is he that vseth violence
in iudgement.
4 How good a thing is it, when thou art
reproued, to shewe repentance! for so shalt
thou escape wilful sinne.
5 Some man kepeth silence, and is founde
wise, and some by muche babling becometh
hateful.
6 Some man holdeth his tongue, because
he hathe not to answere: and some kepeth
silence, waiting a conuenient time.
Chap 32,6. 7 *A wise man wil holde his tongue til he
se opportunitie: but a trifler & a foole wil
regarde no time.
8 He that vseth manie wordes, shal be abhorred,
and he that taketh autoritie to him
self, shalbe hated.
9 Some man hathe oft times prosperitie in
wicked things, and *some time* a thing that is
founde, bringeth losse.
10 There is some gift that is not profitable
for thee, and there is some gift, whose rewarde
is double.
11 Some man humbleth him self for glories
sake, and some by humblenes lifteth
vp the head.
12 Some man byeth muche for a litle price:
for the which he payeth seuen times more.
Chap.6,5. 13 * A wise man with his wordes maketh
him self to be loued, but the mery tales of
fooles shal be powred out.
14 The gift receiued of a foole, shal do
thee no good, nether yet of the enuious for
his importunitie: for he loketh to receiue
manie things for one: he giueth litle, & he
vpbraideth muche: he openeth his mouthe
like a towne crier: to day he lendeth,
to morowe asketh he againe, and suche
one is to be hated of God and man.
15 The foole saith, I haue no friend: I haue
no thanke for all my good dedes: and they
that eat my bread, speake euil of me.
16 How oft, and of how manie shal he
be laughed to scorne? for he comprehendeth
not by right iudgemēt that which he
hath: & it is all one as thogh he had it not.
17 The fall on a pauement is verie sudden:
so shal ẏ fall of the wicked come hastely.
18 A man without grace is as a foolish tall
which is oft tolde by the mouthe of the
ignorant.
19 A wise sentence loseth grace when it cometh
out of a fooles mouthe: for he speaketh
not in due season.
20 Some man sinneth not because of pouertie,
and yet is not grieued when he is
alone.
21 Some man there is that destroyeth his
owne soule, because he is ashamed, and for
the regarde of persones loseth it.
22 Some man promiseth vnto his friend
for shame, and getteth an enemie of him
for naught.
23 *A lie is a wicked shame in a mā: yet is it Chap.25,4.
oft in the mouth of the vnwise.
24 A thief is better, then a man that is accustomed
to lye: but they bothe shal haue
destruction to heritage.
25 The condicions of liers are vnhonest,
and their shame is euer with them.
26 A wise man shal bring him self to honor
with his wordes, and he that hathe vnderstanding,
shal please great men.
27 *He that tilleth his land, shal increase Prou.12,11. & 28,19.
his heape: [he that worketh righteousnes,
shalbe exalted,] and he that pleaseth
great mē, shal haue pardō of his iniquitie.
28 *Rewardes and giftes blinde the eyes of Exod 23,8. deu.16,19.
the wise, and make them dōme, that they
can not reproue fautes.
29 Wisdome that is hid, and treasure that
is horded vp, what profite is in thē bothe?
30 Better is he that kepeth his ignorance
secret, then a man that hideth his wisdome.
31 The necessarie pacience of him, that followeth
the Lord, is better then he that gouerneth
his life without the Lord.

CHAP. XXI.

*1 Not to continue in sinne. 5 The prayer of the afflicted.
6 To hate to be reproued. 17 The mouthe of the wise
man. 26 The thoght of the foole.*

1 MY sonne, hast thou sinned? do so no
more, *but pray for the fore sinnes Chap 5,5. psal 41,5. luk.15,21.
[that they may be forgiuen thee.]
2 Flee from sinne, as from a serpent: for if
thou comest to nere it, it wil bite thee: the
teeth thereof are as the teeth of a lyon, to
slaye the soules of men.
3 All iniquitie is as a two edged sworde, the
woundes whereof can not be healed.
4 Strife & iniuries waste riches: so the house
of the proude shalbe desolate.
5 *The prayer of the poore going out of the Exod.3,9 and 22,23.
mouth, cometh vnto the eares *of the Lord*,
and iustice is done him incontinently.
6 Who so hateth to be reformed, is in the
way of sinners: but he that feareth the
Lord, conuerteth in heart.
7 An eloquent talker is knowen afarre of:
but he that is wise, perceiueth when he
falleth.
8 Who so buyldeth his house with other
mēs money, is like one that gathereth stones
to make his graue.
9 *The congregacion of the wicked is like Chap.16,7.
towe wrapped together: their end is a flame
of fyre to destroye them.
10 The waye of sinners is made plaine with
stones, but at the end thereof is hel, [darkenes
and paines.]
11 He that kepeth the Law of the Lord,
"ruleth his owne affections thereby: and *Or, kepeth the vnderstanding thereof.*

the increase of wisdome is the end of the
feare of God.
12 He that is not wise,wil not suffer him self
to be taught:but there is some wit that increaseth bitternes.
13 The knowledge of the wise shal abounde
like water that runneth ouer,and his counsel is like a pure fountaine of life.
Chap.23,1. 14 *The inner partes of a foole are like a
broken vessel : he can kepe no knowledge
whiles he liueth.
15 When a man of vnderstanding heareth a
wise worde,he wil cōmend it,and increase
it:but if an ignorant man heare it, he wil
disalowe it,and cast it behinde his backe.
16 The talking of a foole is like a burden in
the way,but there is comelines in the talke of a wise man.
17 Thei inquire at the mouthe of the wise
man in the congregacion, and they shal
ponder his wordes in their heart.
18 As is an house that is destroyed,so is wisdome vnto a foole, and the knowlege of
the vnwise is as wordes without order.
19 Doctrine vnto fooles is as fetters on the
fete, and like manicles vpō the right hād.
Chap.19,27. 20 *A foole lifteth vp his voyce with
laughter, but a wise mā doeth scarse smile
secretly.
21 Learning is vnto a wise man a iewel of
golde, and like a bracelet vpon his right
arme.
22 A foolish mans fote is sone in [his
neighboures] house: but a man of experience is ashamed to loke in.
23 A foole wil pepe in at the dore into the
house: but he that is wel nurtered, wil
stand without.
24 It is the point of a foolish mā to hearkē
at the dore:for he that is wise, wil be grieued with suche dishonour.
25 The lippes of talkers wil be telling suche
things as perteine not vnto thē,but ẏ wordes of suche as haue vnderstanding, are
weighed in the balance.
26 The heart of fooles is in their mouth:
but the mouth of the wise is in their heart.
27 When the vngodlie curseth Satan, he
curseth his owne soule.
Chap.28,19. 28 *A backebiter defileh his owne soule, &
is hated wheresoeuer he is: [but he that kepeth his tongue, and is discrete, shal come
to honour.]

CHAP. XXII.

1 Of the sluggard. 12 Not to speake muche to a foole.
16 A good conscience feareth not.

1 A Slothful man is like a filthie stone,
which euerie man mocketh at for
his shame.
2 A slothful man is to be compared to the
dongue of oxē,& euerie one that taketh it
vp,wil shake it out of his hand.
3 An euil nurtered sonne is the dishonour
of the father: & the daughter is least to be
estemed.
4 A wise daughter is an heritage vnto her
housband:but she that liueth dishonestly,
is her fathers heauines.
5 She that is bolde, dishonoreth bothe her
father and her housband, [and is not inferior to the vngodlie,] but they bothe shal
dispise her.
6 A tale out of time is as musicke in mour-
ning:but wisdome knoweth the seasons of
correction and doctrine.
7 Who so teacheth a foole, is as one that
gleweth a potcherde together, and as he
that waketh one that slepeth,from a sounde slepe.
8 If children liue honestly, & haue wherewith,they shal put away the shame of their
parents.
9 But if children be proude, with hautines
and foolishnes they defile the nobilitie of
their kinred.
10 Who so telleth a foole of wisdome,is as
a man, which speaketh to one ẏ is a slepe:
whē he hathe tolde his tale,he saith,What
is the matter?
11 *Wepe for the dead,for he hathe lost the *Chap.38,16.*
light:so wepe for the foole,for he wanteth
vnderstanding : make smale weping for
the dead,for he is at rest:but the life of the
foole is worse then the death.
12 Seuē dayes do men mourne for him that
is dead:but the lamentacion for the foole,
& vngodlie [shulde endure] all the dayes
of their life.
13 Talke not muche with a foole, & go not
to him that hathe no vnderstanding: *be- *Chap.12,12.*
ware of him, lest it turne thee to paine,
and lest thou be defiled when he shaketh
him self. Departe from him, & thou shalt
finde rest,and shalt not receiue sorowe by
his foolishnes.
14 What is heauier then lead?and what o-
ther name shulde a foole haue?
15 *Sād and salt,and a lumpe of yron is ea- *Prou.27,3.*
sier to beare, then an vnwise, [foolish and
vngodlie man.]
16 As a frame of wood ioyned together
in a buylding can not be losed with shaking, so the heart that is stablished by aduised counsel,shal feare at no time.
17 The heart that is confirmed by discrete
wisdome,is as a faire plaistering on a plaine wall.
18 As reedes that are set vp on hie,can not
abide the winde,so the fearful heart with
foolish imaginacion can indure no feare.
19 He that hurteth the eye,bringeth forthe
teares,& he that hurteth ẏ heart, bringeth
forthe the affection.
20 Who so casteth a stone at ẏ birdes,frai-
eth them away: & he that vpbraideth his
friend,breaketh friendship.

21 Thogh thou drewest a sworde at thy
friend, yet dispaire not: for there may be a
returning to fauour.
22 If thou haue opened thy mouth against
thy friend, feare not: for there may be a
reconcilation, so that vpbraiding or pride or disclosing of secrets or a traiterous
woũde do not let: for by these things euerie friend wil departe.
23 Be faithful vnto thy friend in his pouertie, that thou maist reioyce in his prosperitie. Abide stedfast vnto him in the time of his trouble, that thou maist be heire
with him in his heritage: for pouertie is
not alwayes to be contemned, nor the riche that is foolish, to be had in admiration.
24 As the vapour, and smoke of the chim-
nay goeth before the fyre, so euil wordes,
[rebukes & threatenings] go before blo-
odsheding.
25 I wil not be ashamed to defende a frie͂d:
nether wil I hide my self from him, thogh
he shulde do me harme: whosoeuer heareth "it, shal beware of him.
26 Who shal set a watch before my mouth,
and a seale of wisdome vpon my lippes,
that I fall not suddenly by them, and that
my tongue destroye me not?

CHAP. XXIII.

1 A prayer of the autor. 13 Of othes, blasphemie, and vnwise communication. 16 Of thre kindes of sinnes. 23 Manie sinnes procede of adulterie. 27 Of the feare of God.

1 O Lord, father & gouernour of all my
whole life, leaue me not to their cou͂-
sel, and let me not fall by "them.
2 Who wil correct my thoght, and put the
doctrine of wisdome in mine heart, that
they may not spare me in mine ignora͂ce,
nether let ‖their fautes passe?
3 Lest mine ignorances increase, and my
sinnes abounde to my destruction, and
lest I fall before mine aduersarie, and mine enemies reioyce ouer me, whose hope
is farre from thy mercie.
4 O Lord, father & God of my life, [leaue
me not in their imaginacion] nether giue
me a proude looke, but turne away from
thy seruants a stoute minde.
5 Take from me vaine hope, and concupiscence, and reteine him in obedience, that
desireth continually to serue thee.
6 Let not ẏ griedines of the bellie, nor lust
of the flesh holde me, and giue not me thy
seruant ouer into an impudent minde.
7 ¶ Heare, ô ye children, the instruction of
a mouth that shal speake trueth: who so
kepeth it, shal not perishe thorow his
lippes, [nor be hurte by wicked workes.]
8 The sinner shalbe taken by his owne
lippes: for the euil speaker and the proude
do offende by them.

"Or, my lippes.

‖That is of ẏ tongue and lippes.

9 *Accustome not thy mouth to swearing:
[for in it there are many falles,] nether ta
ke vp for a custome the naming of the Ho
ly one: [for thou shalt not be vnpunished
for suche things.]
10 For as a seruant which is oft punished,
can not be without some skarre, so he that
sweareth and nameth God co͂tinually, shal
not be fauteles.
11 A man that vseth muche swearing, shalbe filled with wickednes, and the plague
shal neuer go from his house: when he shal
offend, his faute shalbe vpo͂ him, and if he
knowledge not his sinne, he maketh a double offence: and if he sweare in vaine, he
shal not be innocent, but his house shalbe
ful of plagues.
12 There is a worde which is clothed with
death: God grante that it be not founde in
the heritage of Iacob: but they that feare
God, eschewe all suche, & are not wrapped
in sinne.
13 Vse not thy mouth to "ignorant rashnes:
for therein is the occasion of sinne.
14 ¶ Remember thy father and thy mother
when thou art set among great men, lest
thou be forgotten in their sight, and so
through thy custome become a foole, and
wish that thou hadest not bene borne, and
curse the day of thy natiuitie.
15 *The man that is accustomed to oppro-
brious wordes, wil neuer be reformed all
the daies of his life.
16 There are two sortes [of me͂] that abou͂-
de in sinne, and the third bringeth wrath
[and destruction:] a minde hote as fyre,
that can not be quenched til it be consumed: an adulterous man that giueth his
bodie no rest, til he haue kindled a fyre.
17 (All bread is swete to a whoremonger: he
wil not leaue of til he perish.)
18 A man that breaketh wedlocke, & thinketh thus in his heart, * Who seeth me? I
am co͂passed about with darkenes: the walles couer me: no bodie seeth me: whome ne
de I to feare? the moste High wil not remember my sinnes.
19 Suche a man onely feareth the eyes of
men, & knoweth not that the eyes of the
Lord are ten thousand times brighter the͂
the sunne, beholding all the waies of me͂,
[and the ground of the deepe,] and considereth the moste secret partes.
20 He knewe all things or euer they were
made, and after they be broght to passe also he loketh vpon them all.
21 *The same man shalbe punished in the
streates of the citie, [& shalbe chased like
a yong horsefoale,] and when he thinketh
not vpon it, he shalbe taken: [thus shal he
be put to shame of euerie man, because he
wolde not vnderstand the feare of the
Lord.]

Exod.20,7. chap.27,15. mat.5,33.

"Or, inordinate swearing.

2.Sam.16,7.

Isa.29,15.

Leu.20,10. deut.22,22.

22 And thus shal it go also with euerie wife,
that leaueth her housband, and getteth
inheritance by another.
Exod 20,14. 23 *For first she hathe disobeid the Law of
the moste High, and secondly, she hathe
trespaced against her owne housband, &
thirdly, she hathe plaide the whore in adul
terie, and gotten her children by another
man.
24 She shalbe broght out into the congregacion, and examinacion shalbe made of
her children.
25 Her children shal not take roote, and her
branches shal bring forthe no frute.
26 A shameful reporte shal she leaue, and
her reproche shal not be put out.
27 And they that remaine, shal knowe that
there is nothing better then the feare of
the Lord, and that there is nothing swete
then to take hede vnto the commandements of the Lord.
28 It is great glorie to followe the Lord,
and to be receiued of him is long life.

CHAP. XXIIII.

1 A praise of wisdome proceding forthe of the mouth of God. 6 Of her workes and place where she resteth. 20 She is giuen to the children of God.

1 WIsdome shal praise her self, [and
be honored in God,] and reioyce in the middes of her people.
2 In the congregacion of the moste High
shal she open her mouth, and triumph before his power.
3 [In the middes of her people shal she be
exalted, and wondred at in the holy assemblie.
4 In the multitude of the chosen she shalbe
commended, and among suche as be blessed, she shalbe praised, and shal say,]
5 I am come out of the mouth of the moste
High, [first borne before all creatures.
6 I caused ẏ light that faileth not, to arise
in the heauen,] and couered the earth as a
cloude.
7 My dwelling is aboue in the height, and
my throne is in the piller of the cloude.
8 I alone haue gone round about the compasse of heauen and haue walked in the bo-
tom of the depth.
9 I possessed the waues of the sea, and all
the earth, and all people, and nacion, [and
with my power haue I troden downe the
hearts of all, bothe High and low.]
10 In all these things I soght rest, & a dwelling in some inheritance.
11 So the creator of all things gaue me a cō
mandement, and he that made me, appoin
ted me a tabernacle, and said, Let thy dwel
ling be in Iacob, and take thine inheritance in Israel, and roote thy selfe among
my chosen.
Prou. 8,23. Exod. 31,3. 12 *He created me frō the beginning, & be
fore the worlde, & I shal neuer faile: *In
the holie habitacion haue I serued before
him, and so was I stablished in Sion.
13 *In the welbeloued citie gaue he me rest, Psa. 132,8.
and in Ierusalem was my power.
14 I toke roote in an honorable people, euē
in the porcion of the Lords inheritance.
15 I am set vp on hie like a ceder in Libanus, and as a cipers tre vpon the mountaines of Hermon.
16 I am exalted like a palme tre "about the "Or, in Cades.
bankes, and as a rose plante in Iericho, as
a faire oliue tre in a pleasant field, and am
exalted as a plane tre by the water.
17 I smelled as the cinnamom, & as a bagge
of spices: I gaue a swete odour as the best
myrrhe, as galbanum, and onix, and swete
storax, & perfume of incense in an house.
18 As the terebinth, haue I stretched out my
branches, and my branches are the brāches
of honour and grace.
19 *As the vine haue I broght forthe [fru- Iohn. 15,5.
te] of swete sauour, and my floures are the
frute of honour and riches.
20 I am the mother of beautiful loue,
and of feare, and of knowledge, and of ho
ly hope: I giue eternal thīgs to all my chil
dren to whome God hathe commanded.
21 [In me is all grace of life and trueth: in
me is all hope of life and vertue.]
22 Come vnto me all ye that be desirous of
me, and fill your selues with my frutes.
23 *For the remembrance of me is sweter Psal. 19,10
then honie, and mine enheritance [sweter]
then the honie combe: [the remembrance
of me endureth for euer more.]
24 They that eat me, shal haue ẏ more hunger, and they that drinke me, shal thirst
the more.
25 Who so hearkeneth vnto me, shal not come to confusion, & they that worke by me,
shal not offende: [they that make me to be
knowen, shal haue euerlasting life.]
26 All these things are the boke [of life,] &
the couenant of the moste high God, [&
the knowledge of the trueth,] *& the Law Exod. 20,1. & 24,1.
that Moyses [in the precepts of righteous deu. 4,1. & 29,9.
nes] commanded for an heritage vnto the
house of Iacob, [and the promises perteining vnto Israel.]
27 Be not weary to behaue your selues va-
liātly with the Lord, that he may also con
firme you: cleaue vnto him: for the Lord
almightie is but one God, & besides him
there is none other Sauiour.
28 [Out of Dauid his seruant he ordeined
to raise vp a moste mightie King ẏ shulde sit in the throne of honour for euer
more.]
29 He filleth all things with his wisdome, as
*Physon, & as Tygris, in the time of the Gen. 2,11.
newe frutes.
30 He maketh the vnderstanding to a-
boūde like *Euphrates, & as Iorden in the Ios. 3,15.
time

time of the haruest.
31 He maketh the doctrine of knowledge
to appeare as the light, and ouerfloweth as
Geon in the time of the vintage.
32 The first man hathe not knowen her perfitely: no more shal the last seke her out.
33 For her consideratious are more abundant then the sea, and her counsel is pro-
founder then the great depe.
34 I wisdome [haue cast out floods:] I am
as an arme of the riuer: I runne into Paradise as a watercondite.
35 I said, I wil watter my faire garden, and
wil watter my pleasant grounde: and lo,
my ditche became a flood, and my flood
became a sea.
36 For I make doctrine to shine as the light
of the morning, and I lighten it for euer.
37 [I wil pearce thorow all the lower partes of the earth: I wil loke vpō all suche as
be a slepe, & lighten all them that trust in
the Lord.]
38 I wil yet powre out doctrine, as prophecie, and leaue it vnto all ages for euer.
39 *Beholde that I haue not labored for my
self onely, but for all them that seke wisdome.

Chap.33,18.

CHAP. XXV.

1 Of thre things which please God, and of thre which he hateth. 7 Of nine things that be not to be suspect. 15 Of the malice of a woman.

1 THre things reioyce me, and by them
am I beautified before God & men:
*the vnitie of brethren, the loue of neigh-
bours, a man and wife that agre together.

Gen.13,2. rom.12,10.

2 ¶Thre sortes of men my soule hateth, &
I vtterly abhorre the life of them: a poore man that is proude: a riche man that is a
lier, and an olde adulterer that doteth.
3 ¶If thou hast gathered nothing in thy
youth, what canst thou finde in thine age?
4 ¶Oh, how pleasant a thing is it whē graie
headed men minister iudgement, & when
the elders can giue good counsel!
5 Oh, how comelie a thīg is wisdome vnto
aged men, and vnderstanding and prudencie to men of honour!
6 The crowne of olde mē is to haue muche
experience, and the feare of God is their
glorie.
7 ¶There be nine thīgs, which I haue iudged in mine heart to be happie, and the
tenth wil I pronounce with my tongue:
a man that while he liueth, hathe ioye of
his children, and seeth the fall of his enemies.
8 ¶Wel is him that dwelleth with a wise
of vnderstanding, *and that hathe not
fallen with his tongue, and that hathe
not serued suche as are vnworthie of
him.

Chap.14,1. & 19.16. iam.3,2.

9 Wel is him that findeth prudencie, and
he that can not speake in the eares of them
that wil heare.
10 ¶Oh, how great is he that findeth wisdome! yet is there none aboue him, that feareth the Lord.
11 The feare of the Lord passeth all things
in clerenes.
12 [Blessed is the man, vnto whome it is
granted to haue the feare of God.] Vnto
whome shal he be likened that hathe atteined it?
13 The feare of the Lord is the beginning
of his loue, and faith is the beginning to
be ioyned vnto him.
14 [¶The greatest heauines is the heauines of the heart, and the greatest malice is
the malice of a woman.]
15 Giue me any plague, saue onely the plague of the heart, and any malice, saue the
malice of a woman:
16 Or any assalt, saue the assalt of them
that hate, or any vengeance, saue the vengeance of the enemie.
17 There is not a more wicked head then
the head of the serpent, and there is no
wrath aboue the wrath of an "enemie.

"Or, woman.

18 *I had rather dwell with a lion and dragon, then to kepe house with a wicked
wife.

Prou.21,19.

19 The wickednes of a woman chāgeth her
face, and maketh her countenance blacke
as "a sacke.

"Or, a beare.

20 Her housband is sitting among his
neighbours: because of her he sigheth sore
or he beware.
21 All wickednes is but litle to the wickednes of a woman: let the porcion of the sinner fall vpon her.
22 As the climing vp of a sandie way is to
the fete of the aged, so is a wife ful of wordes to a quiet man.
23 *Stumble not at the beautie of a woman, and desire her not for thy plea
sure.

Chap.42,12. 2.sam.13,2.

24 If a woman nourish her housband, she
is angrie and impudent and ful of reproche.
25 A wicked wife maketh a sorie heart, an
heauie countenance, and a wounded minde, weake hands and feble knees, and can not
comfort her housband in heauines.
26 Of the *woman came the beginning of
sinne, and thorow her we all dye.

Gen.3,6. 1.tim.2,14.

27 Giue the water no passage, [no not a
litle,] nether giue a wicked woman libertie to go out.
28 If she walke not in thine obedience, [she
shal confound thee in the sight of thine
enemies.] Cut her of then from thy flesh:
a Giue her, and forsake her.

a To wit, the bill of diuorcement.

CHAP. XXVI.

1 The praise of a good woman. 5 Of the feare of thre things, and of the fourth. 6 Of the ielous and drunken woman. 28 Of two things that cause sorow, and of the thirde which moueth wrath.

1 BLessed is the man that hathe a verteous wife: for the nomber of his yeres shalbe double.
2 An honest womã reioyceth her housbãd,
and she shal fill the yeres of his life with
peace.
3 A verteous womã is a good portiõ which
shalbe giuen for a gift vnto suche as feare
the Lord.
4 Whether a man be riche or poore, he hathe a good heart toward the Lord, & they
shal at all times haue a chereful countenance.
5 ¶There be thre things that mine heart
feareth, & my face is afraied of the fourth:
treason in a citie: the assemblie of the people, and false accusation: all these are heauier then death.
6 ¶But the sorow and grief of the heart is
a woman that is ielous ouer another: and
she that communeth with all, is a scourge
of the tongue.
7 An euil wife is as a yoke of oxen ỹ drawe
diuerse waies: he that hathe her, is as thogh
he helde a scorpion.
8 A drunken woman and suche as can not be
tamed, is a great plague: for she can not co
uer her owne shame.
9 The whordome of a womã may be knowẽ
in the pride of her eyes, and eyeliddes.
Chap.42,11. 10 ¶*If thy daughter be not shamefast, holde her straitly, lest she abuse her self thorowe ouer muche libertie.
11 Take hede of her that hathe an vnshamefast eye: & marueile not if she trespace
against thee.
12 As one that goeth by the way, and is
thirstie, so shal she open her mouth, and
drinke of euerie next water: by euerie hedge shal she sitte downe, & open her quiuer
against euerie arowe.
13 The grace of a wife reioyceth her housband, and fedeth his bones with her vnderstanding.
14 A peaceable woman and of a good heart
is a gift of the Lord, and there is nothing
so muche worthe as a womã wel instructed.
15 A shamefast & faithful woman is a double grace, and there is no weight to be cõpared vnto her continent minde.
16 As the sunne when it ariseth in the high
places of the Lord, so is the beautie of a
good wife the ornament of her house.
17 As the clere light is vpon the holie candlesticke, so is the beautie of the face in a
ripe age.
18 As the golden pillers are vpon the soc-
kettes of siluer: so are faire fete with a con
stant minde.
19 [Perpetual are the fundaciõs that be laide vpon a strong rocke; so are the cõmandements of God in the heart of an holie
woman.]
20 My sonne, kepe the strength of thine age
stable, and giue not thy strength to strangers.
21 When thou hast gotten a fruteful posses
siõ through all the fields, sowe it with thine owne sede, trusting in thy nobilitie.
22 So thy stocke that shal liue after thee,
shal growe, trusting in the great liberalitie
of their nobilitie.
23 An harlot is compared to a sowe: but the
wife that is maried, is counted as a towre
against death to her housband.
24 A wicked womã is giuen as a rewarde to
a wicked man: but a godlie woman is giuẽ
to him that feareth the Lord.
25 A shameles woman contemneth shame:
but a shame fast woman wil reuerence her
housband.
26 A shameles woman is cõpared to a dogge: but she that is shamefast, reuerẽceth the
Lord.
27 A woman that honoreth her housband,
shalbe iudged wise of all: but she that despi
seth him, shalbe blased for her pride.
28 A lowde crying woman and a babler let
her be soght out to driue away ỹ enemies:
the minde of euerie man that liueth with
suche, shalbe conuersant among the troubles of warre.
29 There be two things that grieue mine
heart, and the thirde maketh me angrie: a
mã of warre that suffreth pouertie: and mẽ
of vnderstãding that are not set by: & whẽ
one departeth from righteousnes vnto sinne: the Lord appointeth suche to ỹ sworde.
30 [There be two things, which me thinke
to be hard and perilous.] A marchant can
not lightly kepe him from wrong, and a
vitailer is not without sinne.

CHAP. XXVII.

3 Of the poore that wolde be riche. 5 The probacion of the man that feareth God. 13 The vnconstantnes of a foole. 16 The secrets of friends are not to be vttered. 26 The wicked imagineth euil which turneth vpon him self.

1 BEcause of pouertie haue manie sinned: and* he that seketh to be riche, 1.Tim.6,9.
turneth his eyes aside. prou.23,4.
2 As a naile in the wall sticketh fast betwene the ioyntes of the stones, so doeth sinne
sticke betwene the selling and the bying.
3 If he holde him not diligently in the feare of the Lord, his house shal sone be ouerthrowen.
4 As when one sifteth, the filthines remaineth in the siue, so the filth of man remaineth in his thoght.
5 The fornace proueth the potters vessel:
*so

Prou.27,21. *so doeth [tentacion] trye mens thoghts.
6 The frute declareth if the tre haue bene
trimmed: so the worde [declareth] what
man hathe in his heart.
7 Praise no man except thou haue heard
his talke: for this is the tryal of men.
8 ¶If thou followest righteousnes, thou
shalt get her, & put her on as a faire garment,
[and shalt dwell with her, and she
shal defend thee for euer: and in the daye
of knowledge thou shalt finde stedfastnes.]
9 The birdes resorte vnto their like: so doeth
the trueth turne vnto them, that are
practised in her.
10 As the lyon waiteth for the beast, so
doeth sinne vpon them that do euil.
11 The talking of him that feareth God,
is all wisdome: as for a foole, he changeth
as the moone.
12 If thou be among the vndiscrete, obserue
the time, but haunte stil the assemblie
of them that are wise.
13 The talking of fooles is grieuous, and
their sporte is in the plaiser of sinne.
Chap.23,10. 14 *The talke of him that sweareth muche,
maketh the heere to stand vp: & to striue
with suche, stoppeth the eares.
15 The strife of the proude is blood shedding,
and their skouldings are grieuous
to heare.
Chap.19,10. & 22,28. 16 *Who so discouereth secrets, leseth his
credit, & findeth no friend after his wil.
17 Loue thy fried, & be faithful vnto him:
but if thou bewrayest his secrets, thou
shalt not get him againe.
18 For as a man destroyeth his enemie, so
doest thou destroye the friendship of thy
neighbour.
19 As one that letteth a birde go out of his
hand, so if thou giue ouer thy fried, thou
canst not gette him againe.
20 Followe after him no more, for he is to
farre of: he is as a roe escaped out of the
snare: [for his soule is wounded.]
21 As for woundes, they may be bounde vp
againe, and an euil worde may be reconciled:
but whoso bewrayeth the secrets of
a friend, hathe lost all his credit.
Prou.10,10. 22 *He that winketh with the eyes, imagineth
euil: and he that knoweth him, wil let
him alone.
23 When thou art present, he wil speake
swetely, and praise thy wordes: but at the
last he wil turne his tale, and sclander thy
saying.
24 Manie things haue I hated, but nothing
so euil as suche one: for the Lord also hateth
him.
25 Who so casteth a stone on hie, casteth it
vpon his owne head: and he that smiteth
with guile, maketh a great wounde.
Prou.26,27. eccles.10,8. 26 Who so* diggeth a pit, shal fall therein,
[and he that laieth a stone in his neighbours
way, shal stomble thereon,] and he
that laieth a snare for another, shalbe take
in it him self.
27 He that worketh euil, shalbe wrapped
in euil, and shal not knowe from whence
they come vnto him.
28 Mockerie & reproche followe the proude,
and vengeance lurketh for them as a
lyon.
29 They that reioyce at the fall of ye righteous,
shalbe taken in the snare, & anguish
shal consume them before they dye.
30 Dispite & angre are abominable thigs,
and the sinful man is subiect to thē bothe.

CHAP. XXVIII.

1 We oght not to desire vengeance, but to forgiue the offence. 13 Of the vices of the tongue, and of the dangers thereof.

1 HE* that seketh vengeance, shal finde
vengeance of the Lord, and he wil
surely kepe his sinnes. Deut 32,35. rom.12,19.
2 ‖Forgiue thy neighbour the hurt that he
hathe done to thee, so shal thy sinnes be
forgiuen thee also, when thou praiest. ‖Man oght not to take vengeance.
3 Shulde a man beare hatred against man,
and * desire forgiuenes of the Lord? Matt.6,14.
4 He wil shewe no mercie to a man, which
is like him self: and wil he aske forgiuenes
of his owne sinnes?
5 If he that is but flesh, nourishe hatred,
[and aske pardone of God,] who wil intreate
for his sinnes?
6 Remembre the end, & let enimitie passe:
imagine not death and destruction to another
through angre, but perseuere in the
commandements.
7 Remember the commādements: so shalt
thou not be rigorous against thy neighbour:
[consider diligently] the couenant
of the moste High, and forgiue his ignorance.
8 * Beware of strife, & thou shalt make thy
sinnes fewer: for an angrie man kindleth
strife. Chap.8,1.
9 And the sinful man disquieteth friends,
and bringeth in false accusations among
them that be at peace.
10 *As the matter of the fyre is, so it burneth,
and mans angre is according to his
power: and according to his riches his angre
increaseth, and the more vehement
the angre is, the more is he inflamed. Prou.16,28.
11 An hastie brauling kindleth a fyre, and
an hastie fighting shedeth blood: [a tōgue
that beareth false witnes, bringeth death.]
12 If thou blowe the sparke, it shal burne: if
thou spit vpon it, it shal be quenched, and
bothe these come out of the mouth.
13 ‖*Abhorre the sclāderer and double tongued:
for suche haue destroyed many that
were at peace. ‖The tongue Chap.21,30.
14 The double tongue hathe disquieted

manie, and driuen them from nacion to
nacion: strong cities hathe it broken downe, and ouerthrowen the houses of great
men: [the strength of the people hathe it
broght downe, & bene the decaye of migh
tie nacions.]
15 The double tongue hathe cast out manie vertuous women, and robbed them of
their labours.
16 Whoso hearkeneth vnto it, shal neuer
finde rest, and neuer dwell quietly.
17 The stroke of the rodde maketh markes
in the flesh, but the stroke of the tongue
breaketh the bones.
18 There be manie that haue perished by
the edge of the sworde, but not so manie
as haue fallen by the tongue.
19 Wel is him that is kept frõ an euil tongue, and cometh not in the angre thereof,
which hathe not drawen in that yoke, nether hathe bene bounde in the bandes thereof.
20 For the yoke thereof is a yoke of yron,
and the bands of it are bandes of brasse.
21 The death thereof is an euil death: hell
were better then suche one.
22 It shal not haue rule ouer them that feare God, nether shal they be burnt with
the flame thereof.
23 Suche as forsake the Lord, shal fall therein: and it shal burne them, and no man
shalbe able to quenche it: it shal fall vpon them as a lyon, and deuoure them as a
leopard.
24 Hedge thy possession with thornes, and
make dores and barres for thy mouth.
25 Binde vp thy siluer and golde, & weigh
thy wordes in a balance, and make a dore
and a barre, [and a sure bridle] for thy
mouth.
26 Beware that thou slide not by it, and so
fall before him that lieth in waite, [and
thy fall be incurable, euen vnto death.]

CHAP. XXIX.

1 To lend money, and do almes. 15 Of a faithful man answering for his friend. 24 The poore mans life.

‖Of weldoing. 1 HE that wil shewe mercie, ‖lendeth to
his neighbour: and he that hathe
power ouer him self, kepeth the commandements.
2 Lend to thy neighbour in time of his nede, and pay thou thy neighbour againe in
due season.
3 Kepe thy worde and deale faithfully with
him, and thou shalt alwaye finde the thing
that is necessarie for thee.
4 Manie when a thing was lent them, rekened it to be founde, & grieued them that
had helped them.
5 Til they receiue, they kisse his hands, and
for their neighbours good they humble
their voyce: but when they shulde paie a-
gaine, they prolong the terme, and giue a
careles answer, and make excuses by reason of the time.
6 And thogh he be able, yet giueth he scarse the halfe againe, and rekeneth the other
as a thing founde: els he deceiueth him of
his money, & maketh him an enemie without a cause: he paieth him with cursing &
rebuke, & giueth him euil wordes for his
good dede.
7 There be manie which refuse to lend because of this inconuenience, fearing to be
defrauded without cause.
8 Yet haue thou pacience with him that hũbleth him self, & differre not mercie from
him.
9 Helpe the poore for the commandemẽts
sake, and turne him not away, because of
his pouertie.
10 Lese thy money for thy brothers and
neighbours sake, and let it not rust vnder
a stone to thy destruction.
11 *Bestowe the treasure after the commã- *Dan.4,24. luk.11,41. act.10,4.*
dement of the moste High, & it shal bring
thee more profite then golde.
12 "Lay vp thine almes in thy secret cham- *"Or, giue thine almes secretly.*
bers, & it shal kepe thee from all afflictiõ.
13 [A mans almes is as a purse with him,
and shal kepe a mans fauour as the apple
of the eye, and afterwarde shal it arise,
and paye euerie man his rewarde vpon his
head.]
14 It shal fight for thee against thine enemies, better then the shield of a strong
man, or speare of the mightie.
15 An honest man is ‖suretie for his neigh- ‖Of suretiship.
bour: but he that is impudent, forsaketh
him.
16 Forget not the friendship of thy suretie: for he hathe laied his life for thee.
17 The wicked despiseth the good dede of
his suretie.
18 The wicked wil not become suretie: and
he that is of an vnthankeful minde, forsaketh him that deliuered him.
19 [Some man promiseth for his neighbour: and when he hathe lost his honestie,
he wil forsake him.]
20 Suretieshippe hathe destroyed manie a
riche man, & remoued them as the waues
of the sea: mightie men hathe it driuen a-
way from their houses, and caused them
to wander among strange nacions.
21 A wicked man, transgresing the commandements of the Lord, shal fall into
suretieshippe: and he that medleth muche
with other mens busines, is intangled in
controuersies.
22 ¶ Helpe thy neighbour according to
thy power, and beware that thou thy self
fall not.
23 * The chief thing of life is water, and *Chap.39,31.*
bread, and clothing, and lodging to co-
uer thy shame.

24 ‖The

Sober liuing. 24 ‖The poore mans life in his owne lodge
is better then delicate fare in another
mans.
25 Be it litle or muche, holde thee contented,that the house speake not euil of thee.
26 For it is a miserable life to go from house to house: for where thou art a stranger,
thou darest not open thy mouth.
27 Thou shalt lodge and fede vnthankeful
men, & after shalt haue bitter wordes for
the same,*saying*,
28 Come,thou stranger,and prepare the table,and fede me of that thou hast readie.
29 Giue place,thou stranger,to an honorable man: my brother cometh to be lodged,
and I haue nede of mine house.
30 These things are heauie to a mã that hathe vnderstanding, the vpbraiding of the
house,and the reproche of the lender.

CHAP. XXX.

1 Of the correction of children. 14 Of the commoditie of health. 17 Death is better then a sorowful life. 22 Of the ioye and sorow of the heart.

Prou.13,24. & 13,13. 1 HE that loueth his sonne,* causeth
him oft to fele the rodde, that he
may haue ioye of him in the end.
2 He that chastiseth his sõne, shal haue ioy
in him, and shal reioyce of him amõg his
acquaintance.
Deu.6,7. 3 He that* teacheth his sonne, grieueth the
enemie, and before his friends he shal reioyce of him.
4 Thogh his father dye,yet is he as thogh
he were not dead:for he hathe left one behinde him that is like him.
5 In his life he sawe him, and had ioye in
him, and was not sorie in his death, [ne-
ther was he ashamed before his enemies.]
6 He left behinde him an aduenger against
his enemies, and one that shulde shewe fauour vnto his friends.
7 He that flattereth his sonne, bindeth vp
his woundes, and his heart is grieued at e-
uerie crye.
8 An vntamed horse wil be stubburne, and
a wanton childe wil be wilful.
9 If thou bring vp thy sonne delicately, he
shal make thee afraide: and if thou playe
with him,he shal bring thee to heauines.
10 Laugh not with him, lest thou be sorie
with him, and lest thou gnash thy teeth
in the end.
Chap.7,25. 11 *Giue him no libertie in his youth, and
winke not at his folie.
12 Bowe downe his necke while he is yong,
and beat him on the sides, while he is a
childe,lest he waxe stubburne, and be disobedient vnto thee,and so bring sorow to
thine heart.
13 Chastise thy childe,and be diligent therein,lest his shame grieue thee.
¶The praise of health. 14 ¶ ‖Better is the poore,being whole and
strong, then a riche man that is afflicted
in his bodie.
15 Health and strength is aboue all golde,
and a whole bodie aboue infinite treasure.
16 There is no riches aboue a sounde bodie, and no ioye aboue the ioye of the
heart.
17 Death is better then a bitter life, [and
long rest,] then continual sickenes.
18 The good things that are powred on a
mouth shut vp, are as messes of meat set
vpon a graue.
19 What good doeth the offring vnto an
idole?for he can nether eat,nor smell: so is
he that is persecuted of the Lord, [& beareth the rewarde of iniquitie.]
20 He seeth with his eyes, and groneth like* a gelded man, that lieth with a virgin Chap.20,3.
and sigheth.
21 *Giue not ouer thy minde to heauines, Prou.12,25.
and vexe not thy self in thine owne coun- & 15,13.
sel. & 17,20.
22 The ioye of the heart is the life of mã,
and a mans gladnes is the prolonging of
his daies.
23 Loue thine owne soule, and comforte
thine heart: driue sorow farre from thee:
for sorow hathe slaine many, and there is
no profite therein.
24 Enuie and wrath shorten the life,and carefulnes bringeth age before the time.
25 A noble and good heart wil haue consideration of his meat and diet.

CHAP. XXXI.

Of couetousnes. 2 Of them that take paine to gather riches. 8 The praise of a riche man without a faute. 12 We oght to flee drunkennes and folowe sobernes.

1 WAking ‖ after riches pineth away ‖Couetousnes.
the bodie, and the care thereof
driueth away slepe.
2 This waking care breaketh the slepe, as a
great sickenes breaketh the slepe.
3 The riche hathe great labour in gatherĩg
riches together, and in his rest he is filled
with pleasures.
4 The pore laboreth in liuing poorely, and
when he leaueth of, he is stil poore.
5 He that loueth golde, shal not be iustified,
and he that followeth corruption, shal haue ynough thereof.
6 *Many are destroied by the reason of gol Chap.8,3.
de, and haue founde their destruction before them.
7 It is as a stumbling blocke vnto thẽ that
sacrifice vnto it, and euerie foole is taken
therewith.
8 Blessed is the *riche which is foũde with- Luk.6,24.
out blemish, and hathe not gone after gol-
de, [nor hoped in money and treasures.]
9 Who is he, and we wil commende him?
for wonderful things hathe he downe a-
mong his people.
10 Who hathe bene tryed thereby, & foun-

de perfite? let him be an exãple of glorie,
who might offende, and hathe not offended, or do euil, and hathe not done it.
11 Therefore shal his goods be stablished,
and the congregacion shal declare his
almes.
‖Temperancie 12 If thou sit at a costlie table, ‖ open not
thy mouth wide vpon it, & say not, Behol-
de muche meat.
13 Remembre that an euil eye is a shrewe: &
what thing created is worse then a wicked
eye? for it wepeth for euerie cause.
14 Stretch not thine hand wheresoeuer it
loketh, and thrust it not with it into the
dish.
15 Consider by thy self him that is by thee,
and marke euerie thing.
16 Eat modestly that which is set before
thee, and deuoure not, lest thou be hated.
17 Leaue thou of first for nourtours sake, &
be not insaciable, lest thou offend.
18 When thou sittest among many, reache
not thine hand out first of all.
Chap. 37.32. 19 *How litle is sufficient for a man wel
taught? and thereby he belcheth not in his
chamber, [nor feleth any paine.]
20 A wholsome slepe cometh of a temperat
bellie: he riseth vp in the morning, and is
wel at ease in him self: but paine in watching and cholericke diseases, and pangs
of the bellie are with an vnsaciable man.
21 If thou hast bene forced to eat, arise, go
forthe, vomit, and then take thy rest: [so
thou shalt bring no sickenes vnto thy
bodie.]
22 My sonne, heare me, and dispise me not,
and at the last thou shalt finde as I haue
tolde thee: in all thy workes be quicke, so
shal there no sicknes come vnto thee.
Prou. 22.9. ‖Liberalitie. 23 *Who so is ‖ liberal in his meat, men shal
blesse him: and the testimonie of his ho-
nestie shal be beleued.
24 But against him that is a nigard of his
meat, the whole citie shal murmure: the testimonies of his nigardnes shalbe sure.
25 Shewe not thy valiantnes in wine: for
Iudeth. 13.8. *wine hathe destroied manie.
26 The fornace proueth the edge in the
tẽpering: so doeth wine the hearts of the
proude by drunkennes.
Psal. 104.15. prou. 31.4. 27 *Wine soberly dronken, is profitable for
the life of mã: what is his life that is ouer-
come with wine?
28 Wine was made [from the beginning]
to make men glad, [and not for drunkennes.] Wine mesurably dronken and in
time, bringeth gladnes and cherefulnes of
the minde.
29 But wine dronken with excesse, maketh
bitternes of minde with braulings and
skouldings.
30 Drunkennes increaseth the courage of a
foole, til he offẽd: it diminisheth his strẽgth
and maketh woundes.
31 *Rebuke not thy neighbour at the wine, Chap. 20.1.
and dispise him not in his mirth: giue
him no dispiteful wordes, and presse not
vpon him with contrarie wordes.

CHAP. XXXII.

1 An exhortation to modestie. 3 Let the ancient speake. 14 To giue thankes after the repast. 15 Of the feare, faith and confidence in God.

1 IF thou be made ẏ master *of the feast*, ‖ lift ‖Humblenes.
not thy self vp, but be among them, as
one of the rest: take diligent care for thẽ,
and so sit downe.
2 And when thou hast done all thy duetie,
sit downe, that ẏ maist be merie with them,
and receiue a crowne for thy good behauiour.
3 Speake thou that art the elder: for it becometh thee, but with sounde iudgement,
and hinder not musicke.
4 Powre not out wordes, where there is
no audience, *and shewe not forthe wisdo- Chap. 3.7. & 20.7.
me out of time.
5 The consent of musicians at a banket is as
a signet of carbuncle set in golde.
6 And as the signet of an emeraude wel
trimmed with golde, so is the melodie of
musicke in a pleasant banket.
7 [Giue eare, and be stil, and for thy good
behauiour thou shalt be loued.]
8 Thou that art yong, speake if nede be,
and yet scarsely when thou art twise asked.
9 Comprehende muche in fewe wordes:
[in manie things be as one that is ignorant.] be as one that vnderstãdeth, and yet
holde thy tongue.
10 If thou be among great men, compare
not thy self vnto them: and when an elder
speaketh, bable not muche.
11 Before the * thonder goeth lightning, Iob. 32.6.
and before a shamefast man goeth fa-
uour.
12 Stand vp betimes, and be not the last:
but get thee home without delay,
13 And there take thy pastime, and do what
thou wilt, so that thou do none euil, or vse
proude wordes.
14 But aboue all things, giue thankes vnto
him that hathe made thee, and replenished
thee with his goods.
15 ¶ Who so feareth the Lord, wil receiue
his doctrine, and they that rise early, shal
finde fauour.
16 He that seketh the Law, shalbe filled therewith: but the hypocrite wil be offended
thereat.
17 They that feare the Lord, shal finde
that which is righteous, and shal kindle
iustice as a light.
18 An vngodlie man wil not be reformed,
but findeth out excuses according to his
wil.
19 A man of vnderstanding dispiseth not
counsel:

counsel:but a lewde and proude mā is not
touched with feare, euē when he hathe done rashly.
20 [My sonne,] do nothing without aduisement: so shal it not repent thee after the
dede.
21 Go not in the way where thou maist fall,
nor where thou maist stumble among the
stones, nether trust thou in the way that is
plaine.
22 And beware of thine owne children,
[and take hede of them that be thine owne
housholde.]
23 In euerie good worke be of a faithful
heart: for this is the keping of the commandements.
|Or, the Lawe. 24 Who so beleueth in |the Lord, kepeth
the commandements: and he that trusteth
in the Lord, shal take no hurt.

CHAP. XXXIII.

1 The deliuerance of him that feareth God. 4 The answere of the wise. 12 Man is in the hand of God, as the clay is in the hand of the potter. 25 Of euil seruants.

1 THere shal no euil come vnto him
||The feare of God. that ||feareth the Lord: but when he
is in tentation, he wil deliuer him a-
gaine.
2 A wise man hateth not the Law: but he
that is an hypocrite therein, is as a shippe
in a storme.
3 A man of vnderstanding walketh faithfully in the Law, and the Law is faithful
vnto him.
4 As the question is made, prepare the answer, and so shalt thou be heard: be sure of
the matter, and so answer.
Chap. 21, 17. 5 The heart of the *foolish is like a carte-
whele: and his thoghts are like a rolling
axeltre.
6 As a wilde horse neieth vnder euerie one
that sitteth vpon him, so is a scorneful
friend.
7 Why doeth one day excell another, seing
that the light of the daies of the yere come of the sunne?
8 The knowledge of the Lord hathe parted
them a sondre, and he hathe by them dispo
sed the times and solemne feastes.
9 Some of them hathe he chosen and sanctified, & some of them hathe he put among
the daies to nomber.
Gen 1, 27. & 2, 7. 10 And all men are of the *grounde, and
Adam was created out of the earth: but the
Lord hathe deuided them by great knowledge, and made their waies diuers.
11 Some of them hathe he blessed and exalted, and some of them hathe he sanctified,
and appropriate to him self: but some of
thē hathe he cursed, and broght thē lowe,
and put them out of their estate.
Isa 45, 9. rom. 9, 20. 12 *As the claye is in the potters hand, to
order it at his pleasure, so are men also in
the hand of their creator, so that he may
rewarde them as liketh him best.
13 Against euil is good, and against death
is life: so is the godlie against the sinner,
and the vngodlie against the faithful.
14 So in all the workes of the moste High
thou maist se that there are euer two, one
against another.
15 ¶I am awaked vp last of all, as one that
gathereth after them in the vintage. In the
blessing of the Lord I am increased, and
haue filled my wine presse, like a grape gatherer.
16 *Beholde, how I haue not labored one- Chap. 24, 28.
ly for my self, but for all them that seke
knowledge.
17 Heare me, ô ye great men of the people,
& hearken with your eares, ye rulers of the
congregacion.
18 Giue not thy sonne and wife, thy brother and friēd, power ouer thee while thou
liuest, and giue not away thy substance to
another, lest it repent thee, and thou in-
traat for the same againe.
19 As long as thou liuest, and hast breth,
giue not thy self ouer to anie persone.
20 For better it is that thy children shulde
pray vnto thee, then that thou shuldest loke vp to the hands of thy children.
21 In all thy workes be excellent, that thine honour be neuer stained.
22 At the time when thou shalt end thy
dayes, and finish thy life, distribute thine
inheritance.
23 ¶The fodder, the whippe and the burden
belong vnto the asse: and meat, correctiō
and worke vnto thy seruant.
24 If thou set thy seruant to labour, thou
shalt finde rest: but if thou let him go idle,
he shal seke libertie.
25 The yoke & the whippe bow downe the
hard necke: so tame thine euil seruāt with
the whippes and correction.
26 Send him to labour, that he go not idle:
for idlenes bringeth muche euil.
27 Set him to worke, for that belongeth
vnto him: if he be not obedient, ||put on ||How sclaues were ordered in olde time.
more heauie fetters.
28 But be not excessiue towarde anie, and
without discrecion do nothing.
29 *If thou haue *a faithful* seruant, let him be Chap. 7, 20.
vnto thee as thine owne soule: for in blood
hast thou goten him. If thou haue a seruant, intreat him as thy brother: for thou
hast nede of him, as of thy self. If thou intreat him euil, and he runne away, wilt
thou seke him?

CHAP. XXXIIII.

Of dreames. 13 The praise of them that feare God. 18 The offrings of the wicked. 22 The bread of the nedie. 27 God doeth not alowe the workes of an vnfaithful man.

Dreames.
1 THe hope of a foolish man is vaine &
false, ‖& dreames make fooles to haue wings.
2 Who so regardeth dreames, is like him
that wil take holde of a shadowe, and followe after the winde.
3 Euen so is it with the appearings of dreames, as the likenes of a face is before another face.
4 Who can be clensed by the vncleane? or
what trueth can be spoken of a lier?
5 Sothsayings, witchcraft, and dreaming is
but vanitie, and a minde that is occupied
with fantasies, is as a woman that trauaileth.
6 Where as suche visiōs come not of ẏ moste High to trye thee, set not thine heart
vpon them.
7 For dreames haue disceiued many, and
thei haue failed that put their trust therein.
8 The Law shalbe fulfilled without lies, &
wisdome is sufficient to a faithful mouth:
[what knowledge hathe he that is not
tryed?]
9 A man that is instructed, vnderstandeth
muche, and he that hathe good experiēce,
can talke of wisdome.
10 He that hathe no experience, knoweth
litle, and he that erreth, is ful of crafte.
11 Whē I wandred to and fro, I sawe many
things, and mine vnderstanding is greater
then I can expresse.
12 I was oft times in danger of death, yet I
was deliuered by these things.
13 ¶The spirit of those that feare the Lord,
shal liue: for their hope is in him that can
helpe them.
The feare of the Lord.
14 Who so ‖ feareth the Lord, feareth no
man, nether is afraied: for he is his hope.
15 Blessed is the soule of him that feareth
ẏ Lord: in whome putteth he his trust? who
is his strength?
Psal. 33, 18. Psal. 91, 1.
16 *For the eyes of the Lord haue respect
vnto them, that loue him: he is their* mightie protection, and strong grounde, a defense from the heat, and a shadowe for the
noone day, a succour frō stombling, & an
helpe from falling.
17 He setteth vp the soule, & lighteneth the
eyes: he giueth health, life and blessing.
Prou. 21, 17.
18 ¶He that* giueth an offring of vnrighteous goods, offreth a mocking sacrifice, &
the giftes of the vnrighteous, please not
him.
19 [But ẏ Lord is theirs onely, that paciētly abide him in the way of trueth & righteousnes.]
The offrings of the wicked & their prayer. Prou. 15, 8.
20 The moste High doeth not alowe the ‖of
frings of the wicked,* nether is he pacified
for sinne by the multitude of sacrifice.
21 Who so bringeth an offring of the goods
of ẏ poore, doeth as one that sacrifiseth ẏ
sonne before the fathers eyes.
22 The bread of the nedeful is the life of
the poore: he that defraudeth him thereof, is a murtherer.
23 He ẏ taketh away his neighbours liuing,
slayeth him, * and he that defraudeth the
labourer of his hyre, is a bloodshedder. Deu 24, 14. chap. 7, 22.
24 ¶When one buyldeth, and another brea-
keth downe, what profite haue they then
but labour?
25 When one prayeth and another curseth,
whose voyce wil the Lord heare?
26 *He that washeth him self because of a
dead bodie, and toucheth it againe, what
auaileth his washing? Nomb. 19, 11.
27 *So is it with a man that fasteth for his
sinnes, and committeth them againe: who
wil heare his prayer? or what doeth his fasting helpe him? 2. Pet. 2, 22.

CHAP. XXXV.

1 Of true sacrifices. 14 The prayer of the fatherles, and of the widdowe, and him that humbleth him self.

1 WHoso kepeth the Law,* bringeth
offrings ynough: he that holdeth
fast the commandements, ‖offreth an of-
fring of saluacion. 2. Sam. 15, 22. iere. 7, 3. True sacrifices.
2 He that is thākeful to them that haue wel
deserued, offreth fine floure: *and he that
giueth almes, sacrifiseth praise. Philip. 4, 18.
3 To departe from euil is a thākeful thing
to the Lord, and to forsake vnrighteousnes, is a reconciling vnto him.
4 *Thou shalt not appeare emptie before
the Lord. Exod. 23, 15. & 34, 23. deu. 6, 16.
5 For all these things are done because of
the commandement.
6 *The offring of the righteous maketh the
altar fat, and the smel thereof is swete before the most High. Gen. 4, 4.
7 The sacrifice of the righteous is acceptable, and the remembrance thereof shal neuer be forgoten.
8 Giue the Lord his honour with a good
and liberal eye, and diminish not the first
frutes of thine hands.
9 *In all thy giftes shewe a ioyeful countenance, and dedicate thy tithes with
gladnes. 2. Cor. 9, 7.
10 Giue vnto the moste High according as
he hathe enriched thee,* and loke what thine hand is able, giue with a cheareful
eye. Tob. 4, 8.
11 For the Lord recompenseth, and wil giue thee seuen times as muche.
12 *Diminish nothing of thine offring: for
he wil not receiue it, and absteine from
wrōgful sacrifices: for the Lord is the iud-
ge, and regardeth no* mans persone. Leu. 22, 21. deu 15, 20. Deu 10, 17. 2. chro. 19, 7. iob 34, 19.
13 He accepteth not the persone of the poo-
re, but he heareth the prayer of the oppressed. wisdom. 6, 8. act. 10, 34. rom 2, 11.
14 He despiseth not the desire of the fatherles, nor the widdow, when she powreth out
her prayer. gal 2, 6. ephe. 6, 9. col. 3, 25. 1. pet. 1, 17.

15 Doeth

15 Doeth not the teares runne downe the
widdowes chekes? and her crye is against
him that caused them: [for from her chekes do they go vp vnto heauen, and the
Lord which heareth them, doeth accept
them.]
16 He that serueth ẏ Lord, shalbe accepted
with fauour, and his prayer shal reache
vnto the cloudes.
17 The prayer of him that humbleth him
self, goeth thorowe the cloudes, and ceaseth not til it come nere, and wil not departe til the moste High haue respect thereunto to iudge righteously, and to execute iudgement.
18 And the Lord wil not be slacke, nor the
Almightie wil tarie long from thẽ, til he
hathe smitten in sunder the loynes of the
vnmerciful, and aduenged him self of the
heathen, til he haue taken away the multitude of the cruel, and broken the scepter
of the vnrighteous, til he giue euerie man
after his workes, and rewarde them after
their deuises, til he haue iudged the cause
of his people, and comforted them with
his mercie.
19 Oh, how faire a thing is mercie in the time of anguish and trouble! It is like a
cloude of raine, that cometh in the time of
a drought.

CHAP. XXXVI.

1 A prayer to God in the persone of all faithful men, against those that persecute his Church. 22 The praise of a good woman.

1 HAue mercie vpon vs, ô Lord God
of all things, and beholde vs, & [she-
we vs the light of thy mercies,]
2 And send thy feare ‖among the nacions, ‖Against the wicked.
which seke not after thee, [that they may
know that there is no God but thou, and
ẏ they may shewe thy wõderous workes.]
3 Lift vp thine *hand vpon the strange na- *Iere.10,25.*
cions, that they may se thy power.
4 As thou art sanctified in vs before them,
so be thou magnified among them before vs,
5 That they may knowe thee, as we knowe
thee: for there is none other God but onely thou, ô Lord.
6 Renue the signes, & change the wonders:
shewe the glorie of thine hand, and thy
right arme, that they may shewe forthe thy
wonderous actes.
7 Raise vp thine indignacion, & powre out
wrath: take away the aduersarie, and smite
the enemie.
8 Make the time shorte: remember thine
othe, that thy wonderous workes may be
praised.
9 Let the wrath of the fyre consume them
that escape, and let them perish that oppresse the people.
10 Smite in sonder the heades of the princes
that be our enemies, and say, There is none other but we.
11 ‖Gather all the tribes of Iacob together, ‖A prayer for the godlie.
[that they may knowe that there is none
other God but onely thou, and ẏ thei may
shew thy wonderous workes,] and inherit
thou them as from the beginning.
12 O Lord, haue mercie vpon the people,
that is called by thy Name, & vpon Isra-
el, *whome thou hast likened to a first bor- *Exod.4,22.*
ne sonne.
13 Oh, be merciful vnto Ierusalem the citie
of thy Sanctuarie, the citie of thy rest.
14 Fill Sion, that it may magnifie thine oracles, and *fill* thy people with thy glorie.
15 Giue witnes vnto those that thou hast
possessed from the beginning, and raise vp
the prophecies that haue bene shewed in
thy Name.
16 Rewarde them that waite for thee, that
thy Prophetes may be founde faithful.
17 O Lord, heare the prayer of thy seruãts
according to the *blessing of Aaron ouer *Nomb.6,24.*
thy people, [& guide thou vs in the way
of righteousnes] that all they which dwell
vpon the earth, may knowe that thou art
the Lord the eternal God.
18 ¶ The belie deuoureth all meates, yet is
one meat better then another.
19 As the throte tasteth venisone, so doeth
a wise minde *discerne* false wordes.
20 A frowarde heart bringeth grief, but a
man of experience wil resist it.
21 A woman is apt to receiue euerie man;
yet is one daughter better then another.
22 The beautie of a womã chereth the face,
and a man loueth nothing better.
23 If there be in her tongue gentlenes, mekenes, and wholesome talke, then is not
her housband like other men.
24 He that hathe ‖gotten a [vertuous] wo- ‖The praise of a good woman.
man, hathe begone to get a possession: she
is an helpe like vnto him self, and a piller
to rest vpon.
25 Where no hedge is, there the possession
is spoiled: and he that hathe no wife, wandereth to and fro, mourning.
26 Who wil trust a thief that is alway readie
and wandereth from towne to towne? and
likewise him, that hathe no rest, and lodgeth, wheresoeuer the night taketh him?

CHAP. XXXVII.

1 How a man shulde knowe friends & counselers. 12 To kepe his companie that feareth God.

1 EVerie friend saith, ‖I am a friend vnto ‖Of friendship.
him also: but there is some friend,
which is onely a friend in name.
2 Remaineth there not heauines vnto death, when a companion and friend is turned to an enemie?
3 O wicked presumption, from whence art
thou sprong vp to couer the earth with
disceite?

Chap 6,10.
4 *There is some companiō which in prosperitie reioyceth with his friēd: but in the
time of trouble he is against him.
5 There is some companion that helpeth
his friend for the bellie sake, & taketh vp
the buckeler against the enemie.
6 Forget not thy friend in thy minde, and
thinke vpon him in thy riches.
‖Of whome we shulde take counsel.
7 Seke ‖no counsel at him of whome thou
art suspected, and disclose not thy counsel vnto suche as hate thee.
Chap. 8,21. & 9,21.
8 *Euerie counseler praiseth his owne coūsel: but there is some that counseleth for
him self.
9 Beware of the counseler, and be aduised
"Or, what nede he hathe.
afore"whereto thou wilt vse him: for he
wil coūsel for him self, lest he cast the lot
vpon thee,
10 And say vnto thee, Thy way is good, &
afterwarde he stand against thee, and loke
what shal become of thee.
11 [Aske no counsel for religion of him,
that is without religion, nor of iustice, of
him that hathe no iustice,] nor of a womā
touching her of whome she is ielous, nor
of a cowarde in matters of warre, nor of
a marchant concerning exchange, nor of
a bier for the sale, nor of an enuious man
touching thankefulnes, nor of the vnmerciful touching kindenes, [nor of an
vnhonest man of honestie,] nor of the
slothful for anie labour, nor of an hireling for the finishing of a worke, nor of
an idle seruant for muche busines: hearken not vnto these in anie matter of counsel.
12 But be cōtinual with a godlie man whome thou knowest to kepe the commandements of the Lord, whose minde is accor
ding to thy minde, & is sorie for thee whē
thou stumblest.
13 Take counsel of thine owne heart: for
there is no man more faithful vnto thee,
then it.
14 For a mans minde is sometime more accustomed to shewe more thē seuen watchmen that sit aboue in an high tower.
15 And aboue all this pray to ẏ most High,
that he wil direct thy waye in trueth.
16 Let reason go before euerie enterprise, &
counsel before euerie action.
17 ¶ The [changing] of the countenance is
a signe of the changing of the heart: foure
things appeare good and euil, life and death, but the tongue hathe euer more the
gouernement ouer them.
18 ¶ Some mā is wittie, & hathe instructed
manie, and yet is vnprofitable vnto him
self.
19 Some man wil be wise in wordes, and is
"Or, wisdome.
hated, yea, he is destitute of all"foode,
20 Because grace is not giuen him of the
Lord: for he is destitute of all wisdome.

21 Another is wise for him self, and the frutes of vnderstanding are faithful in his
mouth.
22 A wise man instructeth his people, and
the frutes of his wisdome faile not.
23 A wise mā shalbe plēteously blessed, and
all they ẏ se him, shal thinke him blessed.
24 The life of man standeth in the nomber
of dayes: but the dayes of Israel are innumerable.
25 A wise man shal obteine credit among
his people, and his name shalbe perpetual.
26 My sonne, proue thy soule in thy life, &
se what is euil for it, and permit it not to
do it.
27 For all things are not profitable for all
men, nether hathe euerie soule pleasure in
euerie thing.
28 Be not ‖ griedie in all delites, and be not ‖Of tēperācie.
to hastie vpon all meates.
29 *For excesse of meates bringeth sickenes, Chap. 31,22.
and glotonie cometh into choliricke dis-
eases.
30 By surfet haue manie perished: but he
that"dieteth him self, prolongeth his life. "Or, taketh hede.

CHAP. XXXVIII.

1 A physicion is commendable. 16 To burye the dead. 24 The wisdome of him that is learned.

1 HOnor ẏ ‖physicion with that honor ‖Of physiciōs & phisicke.
that is due vnto him, because of ne-
cessitie: for the Lord hathe created him.
2 For of the moste High cometh healing,
and he shal receiue giftes of the King.
3 The knowledge of the physicion lifteth
vp his head, and in the sight of great men
he shalbe in admiration.
4 The Lord hathe created medecines of
the earth, and he that is wise, wil not abhorre it.
5 *Was not ẏ water made swete with wood, Exod. 15,25.
that men might know the vertue thereof? iudeth. 5,15.
6 So he hathe giuen men knowledge, that
he might be glorified in his wonderous
workes.
7 With suche doeth he heale men, and taketh away their paines.
8 Of suche doeth the apothecarie make a
confection, and yet he can not finish his
owne workes: for of ẏ Lord cometh prosperitie and welth ouer all the earth.
9 My sonne, faile not in thy sickenes, but
*praye vnto the Lord, & he wil make thee Isa. 38,2.
whole.
10 Leaue of from sinne, and order thine
hands a right, and clense thine heart from
all wickednes.
11 Offer swete incense, and fine floure for a
remembrāce: make the offring fat, for thou
art not the ‖first giuer.
12 Then giue place to the physicion: for the
Lord hathe created him: let him not go
from thee, for thou hast nede of him.
13 The houre may come, that their enter-
‖God bestoweth first his benefites, and we must render a porciō thereof to suche vses as he appointeth.
prises

prises may haue good successe.
14 For they also shal praye vnto the Lord,
that he wolde prosper that, which is giuen
for ease, & their physicke for the prolonging
of life.
15 He that sinneth before his maker, let him
fall into the hands of the physicion.
Chap.22,10. 16 My sonne, *powre forthe teares ouer the
‖Of mourning dead, ‖ and beginne to mourne, as if thou
hadest suffred great harme thy self, & then
"Or, the custome. couer his bodie according to "his appointement, and neglect not his buryal.
17 Make a grieuous lamentacion, and be
earnest in mourning, & vse lamentacion
as he is worthie, & that, a daye or two, lest
thou be euil spoken of, and then comforte
thy self for thine heauines.
Prou.15,13 18 *For of heauines cometh death, and the
& 17,22. heauines of the heart breaketh ŷ strength.
19 Of the affection of the heart cometh sorow,
and the life of him that is afflicted, is
according to his heart.
20 Take no heauines to heart: driue it away
and remember the last end.
21 Forget it not: for there is no turning againe:
thou shalt do him no good, but
hurte thy self.
22 Remember his iudgement: thine also
shalbe likewise, vnto me yester daye, and
vnto thee to day.
2.Sam.12,20. 23 *Seing the dead is at rest, let his remembrãce
rest, & comforte thy self againe for
him, when his spirit is departed from
him.
24 ¶ The wisdome of a learned mã cometh
by vsing wel his vacant time: and he that
ceaseth from his owne matters and labour,
may come by wisdome.
25 How can he get wisdome that holdeth
the plough, and he that hathe pleasure in
the gode, and in driuing oxen, and is occupied
in their labours, and talketh but of
the brede of bullockes?
26 He giueth his minde to make forowes,
and is diligent to giue the kine fodder.
27 So is it of euerie carpenter, and workemaster
that laboreth night and daye: and
they that cut, and graue seales, and make
sondrie diuersities, and giue them selues
to contrefait imagerie, and watch to performe
the worke.
28 The smithe in like maner abideth by
his anuil, and doeth his diligẽce to labour
the yron: the vapour of the fyre dryeth
his flesh, and he muste fight with the heat
of the fornace: the noyce of the hammer
is euer in his eares, and his eyes loke stil
vpon the thing that he maketh: he setteth
his minde to make vp his workes: therefore
he watcheth to polish it perfitely.
29 So doeth the potter sit by his worke: he
turneth the whele about with his fete: he is
careful alwaye at his worke, and maketh
his worke by nomber.
30 He facioneth the claye with his arme, &
with his fete he tempereth the hardnes
thereof: his heart imagineth how to couer
it with lead, and his diligence is to clense
the ouen.
31 All these hope in their hands, and euerie
one bestoweth his wisdome in his worke.
32 Without these can not ŷ cities be mainteined,
nor inhabited, nor occupied.
33 And yet they are not asked their iudgement
in the counsel of the people, nether
are thei hie in the congregacion, nether
sit they vpon the iudgement seates,
nor vnderstand the order of iustice: they
can not declare matters according to the
forme of the Law, and they are not mete
for hard matters.
34 But thei mainteine the state of the worlde,
and their desire is concerning their
worke and occupacion.

CHAP. XXXIX.

1 A wise man. 16 The workes of God. 24 Vnto the good, good things profite, but vnto the euil, euen good things are euil.

1 HE onelie that applieth his minde to
the Law of the moste High, and is
occupied in the meditacion thereof, seketh
out the ‖wisdome of all the ancient, & ex- ‖Of true wisdome.
erciseth him self in the prophecies.
2 He kepeth the sayings of famous men, &
entreth in also to the secrets of darke sentences.
3 He seketh out the mysterie of graue sentences,
and exerciseth him self in darke
parables.
4 He shal serue among great men and appeare
before the prince: he shal traueil
through strange countreis: for he hathe
tryed the good and the euil among men.
5 He wil giue his heart to resorte early
vnto the Lord that made him, & to praye
before the moste High, and wil open his
mouth in prayer, and praie for his sinnes.
6 When the great Lord wil, he shalbe filled
with the Spirit of vnderstanding, that
he may powre out wise sentences, & giue
thankes vnto the Lord in his praier.
7 "He shal direct his counsel, & knowledge: "Or, the Lord.
so shal he meditate in his secrets.
8 He shal shewe forthe his sciẽce and learning,
and reioyce in the Law & couenant
of the Lord.
9 Manie shal commend his vnderstanding,
and his memorie shal neuer be put out, nor
departe away: but his name shal continue
from generacion to generacion.
10 *The congregacion shal declare his wis Chap.44,14.
dome, and shewe it.
11 Thogh he be dead, he shal leaue a greater
fame then a thousand: and if he liue
stil, he shal get the same.
12 Yet wil I speake of mo things: for I am

ful as the moone.
13 Hearken vnto me,ye holy children, and
bring forthe frute,as the rose that is planted by the brokes of the field,
14 And giue ye a swete smel as ″ incense, ″Or, Libanus.
and bring forthe flowres as the lilie: giue
a smel and sing a song of praise:blesse the
Lord in all his workes.
15 Giue honour vnto his Name,and shewe
forthe his praise with the songs of your
lippes,and with harpes,and ye shal say after this maner,
16 * All the workes of the Lord are excea- Gen.1,31.
ding good , and all his commandements mar.7,37.
are done in due season.
17 And none may say, What is this? wherefore is that? for at time conuenient they
shal all be soght out:at his commandemēt
the water stode as an heape,&at the worde
of his mouth the waters gathered them
selues.
18 His whole fauour *appeared* by his commandement, and none can diminish that
which he wil saue.
19 The workes of all flesh are before him,
and nothing can be hid from his eyes.
20 He seeth from euerlasting to euerlasting , & there is nothing wonderful vnto
him.
21 A man nede not to say , What is this?
wherefore is that? for he hathe made all
things for their owne vse.
22 His blessing shal renne ouer as the streame,and moisture the earth like a flood.
23 As he hathe turned the waters into salt-
nes,so shal the heathen fele his wrath.
24 As his waies are plaine and right vnto
the iust, so are they stumbling blockes to
the wicked.
25 ¶For the good,are good things created
from the beginning , and euil things for
the sinners.
26 * The principal things for the whole vse Chap.39,38.
of mans life is water, fyre , and yron,and
salt,and meale,wheate and hony,& milke,
the blood of the grape,and oyle, and clothing.
27 All these things are for good to ye godlie:
but to ye sinners they are turned vnto euil.
28 There be spretes that are created for vē
geance, which in their rigour laye on sure
strokes: in the time of destruction they
shewe forthe their power,and accomplish
the wrath of him that made them.
29 Fyre , and haile, and famine, and death:
all these are created for vengeance.
30 The teeth of wilde beasts, and the scorpions,and the serpents,and the sworde execute vengeance for the destructiō of the
wicked.
31 They shalbe glad to do his commandements: & when nede is,they shalbe readie
vpon earth:and whē their houre is come,
they shal not ouerpasse the commandement.
32 Therefore haue I taken a good courage
vnto me from the beginning , and haue
thoght on these things,and haue put them
in writing.
33 *All the workes of the Lord are good,& Gen.1,31.
he giueth euerie one in due season,&when
nede is:
34 So that a man nede not to say , This is
worse then that: for in due season they are
all worthie praise.
35 And therefore praise ye Lord with whole
heart and mouth , and blesse the Name of
the Lord.

CHAP. XL.

1 Many miseries in mans life . 14 Of the blessing of the righteous and prerogatiue of the feare of God.

1 GReat ‖ trauail is created for all men, ‖The miseries of mans life.
and an heauie yoke vpon the sonnes
of Adam from the day that they go out of
their mothers wombe,til the day that thei
returne to the mother of all things,
2 *Namely* their thoghts , and feare of the
heart , & their imaginacion of the things
they waite for,and the daye of death,
3 From him that sitteth vpon the glorious
throne,vnto him that is beneth in ye earth
and ashes:
4 From him that is clothed in blewe silke,
and weareth a crowne, euen vnto him that
is clothed in simple linen.
5 Wrath & enuie,trouble,and vnquietnes,
and feare of death, & rigour,and strife,&
in the time of rest the slepe in the night
vpon his bed,change his knowledge.
6 A litle or nothing is his rest, and afterwarde in sleping he is as in a watche-
towre in the daye:he is troubled with the
visions of his heart , as one that renneth
out of a battel.
7 And when all is safe, he awaketh, & marueileth that the feare was nothing.
8 Suche things come vnto all flesh , bothe
man and beast , but seuen folde to the vngodlie:
9 Moreouer,* death & blood,and strife,& Chap.39.38.
sworde, oppression, famine , destruction,
and punishment.
10 These things are all created for the wicked , and for their sakes came the * flood Gen.7,11.
also.
11 *All things that are of the earth , shal Gen.3,19.
turne to earth againe : and they that are chap.41,13.
of the * waters, shal returne into the sea. Eccles.1,7.
12 ¶ All bribes and vnrighteousnes shalbe
put awaye : but ‖ faithfulnes shal endure ‖ Faithfulnes.
for euer.
13 The substance of the vngodlie shalbe
dryed vp like a riuer, and they shal make a sounde like a great thonder in the
raine.
14 When he openeth his hād, he reioyceth:
but

but all the transgressours shal come to
naught.
15 The children of the vngodlie shal not
obteine manie branches: for the vncleane
rootes are as vpon the high rockes.
16 Their tender stalke by what water soeuer it be or water banke, it shalbe pulled
vp before all other herbes.
17 ¶ Friendlines is as a moste plentiful gar
dẽ of pleasure, & mercie endureth for euer.
18 *To labour and to be content with that
a man hathe, is a swete life: but he that findeth a treasure, is aboue them bothe.
19 Children, and the buylding of the citie
maketh a perpetual name: but an honest
woman is counted aboue them bothe.
20 Wine & musicke reioyce the heart: but
the loue of wisdome is aboue them bothe.
21 The pipe and the psalterion make a swete noyce: but a pleasant tongue is aboue
them bothe.
22 Thine eye desireth fauor & beautie: but
a grene sede time, rather then them bothe.
23 A friend, and companion come together
at opportunitie: but aboue them bothe is a
wife with her housband.
24 Friends and helpe *are good* in the time of
trouble, but almes shal deliuer more then
them bothe.
25 Golde and siluer fasten the fete: but counsel is estemed aboue them bothe.
26 Riches and strength lift vp the minde:
but the feare of the Lord is aboue them
bothe: there is no want in the feare of the
Lord, and it nedeth no helpe.
27 The feare of the Lord is a pleasant gar
den of blessing, and there is nothing so
beautiful as it is.
28 ¶ My sonne, lead not a beggers life: for
better it were to dye then to begge.
29 The life of him that dependeth on another mans table, is not to be counted for
a life: for he tormẽteth him self after other
mens meat: but a wise man and wel nour-
tred, wil beware thereof.
30 Begging is swete in the mouth of the
vnshamefast, and in his bellie there burneth a fyer.

Philip.4,12. 1.tim 6,6.

CHAP. XLI.

1 Of the remembrance of death. 3 Death is not to be feared 8 A curse vpon them that forsake the Law of God 12 Good name & fame. 14 An exhortacion to giue hede vnto wisdome. 17 Of what things a man oght to be ashamed.

‖Of death.

1 O ‖Death, how bitter is the remembrãce of thee to a man that liueth at rest
in his possessions, vnto the man that hathe
nothing to vexe him, and that hathe prosperitie in all things: yea, vnto him that
yet is able to receiue meat!
2 O death, how acceptable is thy iudgemẽt vnto the nedeful, and vnto him whose
strength faileth, and that is now in the last
age, & is vexed with all things, and to him
that dispaireth, and hathe lost pacience!
3 Feare not the iudgement of death: remẽber them that haue bene before thee, and
that come after: this is the ordinãce of the
Lord ouer all flesh.
4 And why woldest thou be against ẏ pleasure of the moste High? whether it be ten
or an hundreth, or a thousand yeres, there is no defense for life against the graue.
5 ¶ The children of the vngodlie are abominable children, and so are they that kepe companie with the vngodlie.
6 The inheritance of vngodlie children
shal perish, and their posteritie shal haue a
perpetual shame.
7 The children complaine of an vngodlie
father, because they are reproched for
his sake.
8 Wo be vnto you, ô ye vngodlie, which
haue forsaken the Law of the moste high
God: for thogh you increase, yet shal you
perish.
9 If ye be borne, ye shalbe borne to cursing:
if ye dye, the curse shalbe your porcion.
10 All that is of ẏ earth, shal turne to earth
againe: so the vngodlie *go* from the curse to destruction.
11 Thogh men mourne for their bodie, yet
the wicked name of the vngodlie shalbe
put out.
12 Haue regarde to thy name: for that shal
continue with thee aboue a thousand trea
sures of golde.
13 A good life hathe the dayes nombred:
but ‖ a good name endureth euer. ‖A good name
14 *My children, kepe wisdome in peace: *Chap.20,33.*
for wisdome that is hid, and a treasure ẏ
is not sene, what profite is in them bothe?
15 A man that hideth his foolishnes, is better then a man that hideth his wisdome.
16 Therefore beare reuerence vnto my
wordes: for it is not good in all things to
be ‖ ashamed: nether are all things alowed ‖Of shame-fastnes.
as faithful in all men.
17 Be ashamed of whordome before father
and mother: be ashamed of lies before the
prince and men of autoritie:
18 Of sinne before the iudge and ruler: of
offence before the congregacion and people: of vnrighteousnes before a companiõ
and friend,
19 And of theft before ẏ place where thou
dwellest, & before the trueth of God & his
couenant, and to leane with thine elbowes
vpon the "bread, or to be reproued for gi- *"Or, table.*
uing or taking.
20 And of silence vnto them that salute
thee, and to loke vpon an harlot,
21 And to turne away thy face from thy
kinsman: or to take away a portiõ or a gift,
or to be euil minded toward another mãs
wife,

22 Or to sollicite anie mans maide, or to
stand by her bed, or to reproche thy frieds
with wordes,
23 Or to vpbraide when thou giuest anie
thing, or to reporte a matter that thou hast
heard, or to reueile secret wordes.
24 Thus maiest thou wel be shamefast, and
shalt finde fauour with all men.

CHAP. XLII.

*1 The Law of God must be taught. 9 A daughter.
14 A woman. 18 God knoweth all things, yea, euen
the secrets of thine heart.*

‖In what thigs we oght not to be ashamed.

1 OF these things be not thou‖ashamed,
nether haue regarde to offed for anie
persone,
2 Of the Law of the most High & his couenant, & of iudgemēt to iustifie the godlie:
3 Of the cause of thy companion, and of
strangers, or of distributing the heritage
among friends:
4 To be diligent to kepe true balance, and
weight, whether thou haue muche or litle:
5 To sel marchandise at an indifferent price, and to correct thy children diligently,
and to beat an euil seruant to the blood:
6 To set a good locke where an euil wife is,
and to locke where manie hands are:
7 If thou giue anie thing by nomber, and
weight, to put all in writing, bothe that ẏ
is giuen out, and that that is receiued
againe:
8 To teache the vnlearned, & the vnwise,
& the aged, that contend against ẏ yong:
thus shalt thou be wel instructed, and approued of all men liuing.
9 ¶ The daughter "maketh the father to
watche secretly, and the carefulnes that
he hathe for her, taketh away his slepe in
the youth, lest she shulde passe ẏ floure of
her age: and when she hathe an housband,
lest she shulde be hated:
10 In her virginitie, lest she shulde be defiled, or gotten with childe in her fathers
house, and, when she is with her housbād,
lest she misbehaue her self: and when she
is maried, lest she continue vnfruteful.
11 *If thy daughter be vnshamefast, kepe her
straitly, lest she cause thine enemies to
laugh thee to scorne, and make thee a cōmune talke in the citie, and diffame thee
among the people, and bring thee to publicke shame.
12 *Beholde not euerie bodies beautie, and
companie not among women.
13 For as the moth cometh out of garmēts:
*so doeth wickednes of the woman.
14 The wickednes of a man is better then
the good intreatie of a woman, to wit, of a
woman that is in shame, and reproche.
15 ¶ I wil remember the workes of the
Lord, and declare the thing that I haue
sene: by the worde of the Lord are his
workes.

"Or, is a secret watche to the father.

Chap. 26, 10.

Chap. 25, 28.

Gen. 3, 6.

16 The sunne that shineth, loketh vpon all
things, and all the worke thereof is ful of
the glorie of the Lord.
17 Hathe not the Lord appointed that his
Saincts shulde declare all his wonderous
workes, which the almightie Lord hathe
stablished to confirme all things by in his
maiestie?
18 He seketh out the depth, and the heart,
and he knoweth their practises: for ẏ Lord
knoweth all science, and he beholdeth the
signes of the worlde.
19 He declareth the things that are past,
and for to come, and discloseth the paths
of things that are secret.
20 *No thoght may escape him, nether may
anie worde be hid from him.
21 He hathe garnished the excellent workes
of his wisdome, and he is from euerlasting
to euerlasting, and for euer: vnto him may
nothing be added, nether can he be mini-
shed: he hathe no nede of anie counseler.
22 Oh, how delectable are all his workes, &
to be cōsidered euē vnto ẏ sparkes of fyre!
23 They liue all, and endure for euer: and
when soeuer nede is, they are all obedient.
24 Thei are all double, one agāst another:
he hathe made nothing ẏ hathe anie faute.
25 The one "commendeth the goodnes of
the other, & who can be satisfied with beholding Gods glorie?

Iob. 41, 4. Isa. 29, 15.

"Or, stablisheth.

CHAP. XLIII.

The summe of the creacion of the workes of God.

1 THis high ornament‖the cleare firmament, the beautie of the heauē so glorious to beholde,
2 The sunne also, a marueilous instrument
when it appeareth, declareth, at his going
out, the worke of the moste High.
3 At noone it burneth the countrey, & who
may abide for the heat thereof?
4 The sunne burneth the mountaines thre
times more then he that kepeth a fornace
with cōtinual heat: it casteth out the fyrie
vapours, & with the shining beames blindeth the eyes.
5 Great is the Lord that made it, and by
his commandement he causeth it to runne
hastely.
6 *The moone also hathe he made to appeare according to her season, that it shul-
be be a declaration of the time, and a signe
for the worlde.
7 *The feasts are appointed by the moone:
the light thereof diminisheth vnto ẏ end.
8 The moneth is called after ẏ name thereof, & groweth wōdrously in her chāging.
9 It is a campe pitched on high, shining in
the firmament of heauen: the beautie of
heauē are the glorious starres, and the ornament that shineth in the high places of
the Lord.
10 By the commandement of the holie one
they

‖The wonderful workes of God.

Gen. 1, 16.

Exod. 12, 2.

they continue in their order, and faile not
in their watche.
Gen.9.14. 11 ¶*Loke vpon the raine bowe, and praise him that made it: verie beautiful is it in
the brightnes thereof.
Isa.40,12. 12 *It compasseth the heauen about with a
glorious circle, and the hands of the moste High haue bended it.
13 ¶Thorowe his cõmandement he maketh
the snowe to haste, and sendeth swiftly the
lightning of his iudgement.
14 Therefore he openeth his treasures, and
the cloudes flie forthe as the foules.
15 In his power hathe he strengthened the
cloudes, and broken the haile stones.
16 The mountaines leape at the sight of
him: the South winde bloweth according
to his wil.
17 The sounde of his thonder beateth the
earth: so doeth the storme of the North: ẏ
whirlewinde also, as birdes that flie, scattereth the snowe, and the falling downe
thereof is as ẏ gresshoppers ẏ light downe.
18 The eye marueileth at the beautie of the
whitenes thereof, & the heart is astonished
at the raine of it.
19 He also powreth out the frost vpon the
earth like salt, and when it is frosen, it sticketh on the toppes of pales.
20 When the colde North winde bloweth,
an yce is frosen of the water, it abideth
vpon all the gatherings together of water,
and clotheth the waters as ẘ a brest plate.
21 It deuoureth the mountaines, & burneth
the wildernes, and destroyeth that that is
grene, like fyre.
22 The remedie of all these is when a cloude cometh hastely, & when a dewe cometh
vpon the heat, it refresheth it.
23 [By his worde he stilleth the winde:] by
his counsel he appeaseth the depe, and plãteth ylands therein.
24 They that saile ouer the sea, tel of the pe
rils thereof, and when we heare it with
our eares, we marueile thereat.
25 For there be strange, & wonderous workes, diuers maner of beasts, and the creation of whales.
26 Thorowe him are all things directed to
a good end, & are stablished by his worde.
27 And whẽ we haue spoken muche, we can
not atteine vnto them: but this is ẏ summe
of all, that he is all.
28 What power haue we to praise him: for
he is aboue all his workes?
Psal.96,4. 29 The Lord is terrible, and verie great, *&
marueilous is his power.
30 Praise ẏ Lord, & magnifie him as muche
as ye can, yet doeth he farre excede: exalt
him with all your power, & be not wearie,
yet can ye not atteine vnto it.
Psal.106,2. 31 *Who hathe sene him, that he might
tel vs? and who can magnifie him as he is?
32 For there are hid yet greater things thẽ
these be, & we haue sene but a fewe of his
workes.
33 For the Lord hathe made all things, and
giuen wisdome to suche as feare God.

CHAP. XLIIII.

The praise of certein holie men, Enoch, Noe, Abraham, Isaac and Iacob.

1 LEt vs now cõmende the famous men,
and our fathers, of whome we are begotten.
2 The Lord hathe gotten great glorie by
them, and that through his great power
from the beginning.
3 Thei haue borne rule in their kingdomes,
and were renoumed for their power, and
were wise in counsel, and declared prophecies.
4 *They gouerned the people by counsel & Exod.18,22.
by the knowledge of learning mete for the
people, in whose doctrine were wise sentences.
5 They inuented the melodie of musicke,
and expounded the verses that were writen.
6 They were riche and mightie in power,
and liued quietly at home.
7 All these were honorable men in their ge
neracions, & were wel reported of in their
times.
8 There are of them that haue left a name
behinde them, so that their praise shal be
spoken of.
9 There are some also which haue no memorial, *and are perished, as thogh they Gen.7,22.
had neuer bene, and are become as thogh
they had neuer bene borne, and their children after them.
10 But the former were merciful men, whose righteousnes hathe not bene forgottẽ.
11 For whose posteritie a good inheritance
is reserued, and their sede is conteined in
the couenant.
12 Their stocke is conteined in the couenant, and their posteritie after them.
13 Their sede shal remaine for euer, & their
praise shal neuer be taken away.
14 Their bodies are buryed in peace, but
their name liueth for euermore.
15 *The people speake of their wisdome, & Chap.39,14.
the congregacion talke of their praise.
16 ‖*Enoch pleased the Lord God: therefo ‖Enoch. Gen.5,14.
re was he translated for an example of re- ebr.11,5.
pentance to the generacions.
17 ‖*Noe was founde perfite, and in the ti- ‖Noe. Gen.6,9.
me of wrath he had a rewarde: therefore and 7,1.
was he left as a remnant vnto the earth, ebr.11,7
when the flood came.
18 An euerlasting couenant was made with
him, that all flesh shulde* perish no more Gen 9,11.
by the flood. ‖Abraham.
19 ‖Abrahã was a*great father of manie peo Gen.12,3. & 15,5.
ple: in glorie was there none like vnto him. & 17,4.

20 He kept the Law of the moste High, &
was in couenant with him, and he set the
couenant* in his flesh, and in tentation he *Gen 21,4.*
was founde faithful.
21 Therefore he assured him by an *othe, ẏ *Gen 22,16. gal.3,8.*
he wolde blesse the nacions in his sede, &
that he wolde multiplie him as the dust of
the earth, and exalte his sede as the starres, and cause them to inherite from sea to
sea, and from the Riuer vnto the end of
the worlde.
22 *With ‖ Isaac did he confirme likewise *Gen.26,2.* ‖Isaac.
for Abraham his fathers sake, the blessing
of all men, and the couenant,
23 And caused it to rest vpon the head of
‖Iacob, and "made him self knowen by *his ‖Iacob. *"Or, knewe him.*
blessings, and gaue him an heritage and *Gen.27,28. & 28,1.*
deuided his porcions, * and parted them *Gen 28,1.*
among the twelue tribes. *Ios.18,19 4*
24 And he broght out of him a ‖merciful ‖Ioseph.
man, which founde fauour in the sight of
all flesh.

CHAP. XLV.

The praise of Moyses, Aaron, and Phinees.

1 AND ‖Moyses, the *beloued of God & ‖Moyses. *Exod.11,3. act 7,22.*
men, *broght he forthe*, whose remēbran-
ce is blessed.
2 He made him like to the glorious Saints,
and magnified him by the feare of his e-
nemies.
3 By his wordes he caused the wonders
to cease, and he made him * glorious in *Exod.6,7,8,9*
the sight of Kings, and gaue him commãdements for his people, and shewed him
his glorie.
4 *He sanctified him with faithfulnes, and *Nomb.12,3.*
mekenes, and chose him out of all men.
5 He caused him to heare his voyce, and
broght him into the darke cloude, * and *Exod.19,7.*
there he gaue him the commandements
before his face, euen the Law of life and
knowledge, that he might teache Iacob ẏ
couenant, and Israel his iudgements.
6 He exalted ‖Aaron an holie man like vn- ‖Aaron.
to him, euē his *brother of ẏ tribe of Leui. *Exod.4,28.*
7 An euerlasting couenant made he with
him, and gaue him the priesthode among
the people, and made him blessed through
his comelie ornament, & clothed him with
the garment of honour.
8 He put perfite ioye vpō him, and girded
him with ornaments of strength, as with
breches, and a tunicle, and an ephod.
9 He compassed him about with belles of
golde, & with manie belles round about,
*that when he went in, the sound might be *Exod.28,35.*
heard, and might make a noyce in the San
ctuarie, for a remembrance to the childrē
of Israel his people,
10 And with an holie garment, with golde
also, and blewe silke, and purple, & diuers
kindes of workes, and with a brestlappe
of iudgemēt, & with the ‖signes of trueth, ‖Vrim and Thummim.
11 And with worke of skarlet conningly
wroght, and with precious stones grauen
like seales, & set in golde by goldesmithes
worke for a memorial with a writing grauen after the nomber of the tribes of Israel.
12 And with a crowne of golde vpon the
mitre, bearing the forme and marke of holines, an ornamēt of honour, a noble worke garnished, and pleasant to loke vpon.
13 Before him were there no suche faire ornaments: there might no strāger put them
on, but onely his children, and his childrēs
children perpetually.
14 Their sacrifices were wholy consumed
euerie day twise continually.
15 *Moyses filled his hands, and anointed *Leu.8,12.*
him with holie oyle: this was appointed
vnto him by an euerlasting couenant, & to
his sede, so long as the heauens shulde remaine, that he shulde minister before him,
& also to execute the office of the priesthode, and blesse his people in his name.
16 Before all men liuing the Lord chose
him that he shulde present offrings before
him, and a swete sauour for a remembrance to make reconciliation for his people.
17 *He gaue him also his commandements *Deu.17,10. & 21,5.*
and autoritie according to the Lawes ap-
pointed, that he shulde teache Iacob the
testimonies, and giue light vnto Israel by
his Law.
18 *Strangers stode vp against him, & en- *Nom.16,1.*
uied him in the wildernes, euen the men
that toke Dathans and Abirams parte, &
the companie of Core in furie and rage.
19 This the Lord sawe, and it displeased
him, and in his wrathful indignacion were they consumed: he did wonders vpon
them, and consumed them with the fyrie
flame.
20 *But he made Aaron more honorable, *Nom.17,8.*
and gaue him an heritage, and parted the
first frutes of the first borne vnto him:
vnto him specially he appointed bread in
abundance.
21 For the *Priests* did eat of the sacrifices of
the Lord, which he gaue vnto him and to
his sede.
22 *Els had he none heritage in the land of *Deu.12,12. & 18,1.*
his people, nether had he any porcion a-
mōg the people: for *the Lord* is the porcion
of his inheritance.
23 The third in glorie is ‖*Phinees the son- ‖Phinees. *Nom.25,13. 1.mac.2,54.*
ne of Eleazar, because he had zeale in the
feare of the Lord, & stode vp with good
courage of heart, when the people were
turned backe, and made reconciliation
for Israel.
24 Therefore was there a couenant of peace made with him, that he shulde be the
chief of the Sanctuarie and of his people, and that he and his posteritie shulde
haue

haue the dignitie of the priesthode for
euer,
25 And according to the couenant made
with Dauid, that the inheritance of the
kingdome shulde remaine to his sonne of
the tribe of Iuda: so the heritage of Aarõ
shulde be to the onelie sonne of his sonne,
and to his sede. God giue vs wisdome in
our heart to iudge his people in righteousnes, that the good things that they haue,
be not abolished, and that their glorie may
endure for their posteritie.

CHAP. XLVI.

The praise of Iosue, Caleb, and Samuel.

‖Iosue. Nom. 27,18. deu. 34,9. iosu.1,2. & 11,7. 1 IEsus ‖*the sonne of Naue was valiãt in
the warres, & was ẏ successour of Moy-
ses in prophecies, who according vnto his
name, was a great sauiour of the elect of
God, to take vengeance of ẏ enemies that
rose vp against them, and to set Israel in
their inheritance.
Iosu.8,2. 2 *What glorie gate he, when he lift vp his
hand, and drewe out his sworde against
the cities?
3 Who was there before him, like to him?
for he foght the battels of the Lord.
Iosu.10,12. 4 *Stode not the sunne stil by his meanes, &
one day was as long as two?
5 He called vnto ẏ moste high Gouernour
when the enemies preased vpon him on e-
uerie side, & the mightie Lord heard him
with the haile stones, and with mightie
power.
6 He rushed in vpõ the nacions in battel, &
Iosu.10,11. in the*going downe *of Bethorõ* he destroied
the aduersaries, that they might knowe his
°Or, that the Lord fauored his battel. weapons, and that he foght "in the sight
°Or, pursued the mightie men. of the Lord: for he "followed the Almightie.
Nom.14,6. 1.mac.2,5. ‖Caleb. 7 *In ẏ time of Moyses also he did a good
worke: he and ‖Caleb the sonne of Iephune
stode against the enemie, and withhelde
the people from sinne, & appeased the wic
ked murmuring.
Nom.26,65. deu.1,35. 8 *And of six hundreth thousand people of
fote, they two were preserued to bring thẽ
into the heritage, euen into the land that
floweth with milke and honey.
Iosu.14.11. 9 *The Lord gaue strẽgth also vnto Caleb,
which remained with him vnto his olde
age, so that he went vp into the high places of the land and his sede obteined it for
an heritage,
10 That all the children of Israel might se,
that it is good to follow the Lord.
‖Iudges. 11 Concerning the ‖Iudges, euerie one by
name, whose heart went not a whoring,
nor departed from the Lord, their memorie be blessed.
Chap.49,12. 12 Let*their bones florish out of their place, and their names by succession remai-
ne to them that are moste famous of their
children.
13 ¶‖Samuel the Prophet of the Lord, be- ‖Samuel.
loued of his Lord, * ordeined Kings, and 1.Sam.10,1.
anointed the princes ouer his people. & 16,13.
14 By the Lawe of the Lord he iudged the
congregacion, and the Lord had respect
vnto Iacob.
15 This Prophete was approued for his
faithfulnes, and he was knowen faithful in
his wordes and visions.
16 *He called vpon the Lord almightie, 1.Sam.7,11.
when his enemies preased vpon him on
euerie side, when he offred the sucking
lambe.
17 And the Lord thondred from heauen,
& made his voyce to be heard with a great
noyce.
18 So he discomfited the princes of ẏ Tyrians, and all the rulers of the Philistims.
19 *And before his long slepe he made pro- 1.Sam.12,3.
testacion in the sight of the Lord, and his
anointed, that he toke no substance of a-
ny man, no, not so muche as a shooe, and
no man colde accuse him.
20 *After his slepe also he tolde of ẏ Kings 1.Sam.28,18.
death, & from the earth lift he vp his voy-
ce, and prophecied that the wickednes of
the people shulde perish.

CHAP. XLVII.

The praise of Nathan, Dauid and Salomon.

1 AFter him rose vp ‖ *Nathã to prophe ‖Nathan.
cie in the time of Dauid. 2.Sam.12,1.
2 For as the fat is taken away from the peace offring, so was ‖Dauid chosen out of the ‖Dauid.
children of Israel.
3 *He plaied with the lions, as with kiddes, 1.Sam.17.34.
and with beares, as with lambes.
4 *Slewe he not a gyante when he was yet 1.Sam.17.49.
but yong, and toke away the rebuke from
the people, when he lift vp his hand with
the stone in the sling, to beat downe the
pride of Goliah?
5 For he called vpon the moste high Lord,
which gaue him strength in his right hãd,
to slay that mightie warriour, and that he
might set vp the horne of his people a-
gaine.
6 *So "he gaue him ẏ praise of ten thousand 1.Sam.18,7.
and honored him with "great praises, and °Or, the people.
gaue him a crowne of glorie. °Or, with blessings of the Lord
7 *For he destroied the enemies on euerie 2.Sam.5,7.
side, and rooted out the Philistims his aduersaries, and brake their horne in sunder
vnto this day.
8 In all his workes he praised the Holy o-
ne, and the moste High with honorable
wordes, and with his whole heart he sung
songs, and loued him that made him.
9 *He set singers also before the altar, and 1.Chr.16,4.
according to their tune he made swete
songs, that they might praise *God* daily
with their songs.

10 He ordeined to kepe the feast daies comely, and appointed the times perfitely,
that they might praise the holy Name of
God, and make the Temple to sounde in
the morning.
2.Sam. 12,13. 11 *The Lord toke away his sinnes, and exalted his horne for euer: he gaue him ẏ couenant of the kingdome, and the throne of
glorie in Israel.
12 After him rose vp a wise sonne, who by
him dwelt in a large possession.
‖Salomon. 13 ‖*Salomon reigned in a peaceable time,
1.King.4,21. and was glorious: for God made all quiet
roũde about, that he might buyld an hou-
se in his Name, and prepare the Sanctuarie for euer.
1.King.4,29 14 *How wise wast ẏ in thy youth, and wast
filled with vnderstãding, as with a flood!
15 Thy minde couered the whole earth, and
hathe filled it with graue and darke sentences.
16 Thy Name went abroade in the yles, &
for thy peace thou wast beloued.
1.King.4,31. 17 *The coũtreis marueiled at thee for thy
songs, and prouerbes, and similitudes, and
interpretations.
18 By the Name of the Lord God, which is
1.King.10,27 called the God of Israel, thou hast*gathered golde as tinne, and hast had as muche
siluer as lead.
1.King.11,1. 19 *Thou didest bowe thy loines to womẽ,
and wast ouercome by thy bodie.
20 Thou didest staine thine honour, and
hast defiled thy posteritie, and hast broght
wrath vpon thy children, and hast felt sorowe for thy folie.
1.King.12,17. 21 *So the kingdome was deuided, and E-
phraim begã to be a rebellious kingdome.
2.King.7,15. 22 *Neuertheles the Lord left not of his
mercie, nether was he destroied for his
workes, nether did he abolish the posteritie of his elect, nor toke away the sede of
him that loued him, but he left a remnant
vnto Iacob, & a roote of him vnto Dauid.
23 Thus rested Salomon with his fathers, &
‖Roboam. of his sede he left behinde him ‖ Roboam,
*Or, a moste eui-dent foole. euen*the foolishnes of the people, and one
1.King.12,10. that had no vnderstanding, *who turned a-
‖Ieroboam. way the people thorow his counsel, & ‖ Ie-
1.King.12,28. roboam the sonne of Nabat, * which caused Israel to sinne, & shewed Ephraim the
way of sinne,
24 So that their sinnes were so muche increased, that they were driuen out of the
land.
25 For they soght out all wickednes, til the
vengeance came vpon them.

CHAP. XLVIII.

The praise of Elias, Eliseus, Ezekias and Isaias.

‖Elias. 1 THen stode vp ‖* Elias the Prophete
1.King.17,1. as a fyre, and his worde burnt like a
lampe.
2 He broght a famine vpon thẽ, and by his
zeale he diminished thẽ: [for they might
not away with the commandements of
the Lord.]
3 By the worde of the Lord he shut the hea
uen, * and thre times broght he the fyre 1.King.18,38.
from heauen. and.2.king.
4 O Elias, how honorable art thou by thy 1,10.
wonderous dedes! who may make his boast
to be like thee!
5 * Which hast raised vp the dead from 1.King.17,21
death, & by the worde of the moste High
out of the graue:
6 Which hast broght Kings vnto destruction, and the honorable from their seate:
7 Which heardest the rebuke of the Lord
in Sina, * and in Horeb the iudgement of 1.Kin.19,15.
the vengeance:
8 *Which didest anoint Kings that they 1.Kin.19,17.
might ‖recompense, and Prophetes to be ‖The wicked-nes of Achab and Iezabel.
thy successours:
9 * Which wast taken vp in a whirle win- 2.King.2,11.
de of fyre, and in a charet of fyrie horses:
10 Which wast appointed*to reproue in due Mala.4,5.
season, & to pacifie the wrath of the Lords
iudgemẽt before it kindled, & to turne the
hearts of the fathers vnto the childrẽ, and
to set vp the tribes of Iacob.
11 Blessed were they that sawe thee, & slept
in loue: for [a] we shal liue. a That is, they that are suche
12 *When Elias was couered with the stor- 2.King.2,11.
me, ‖Eliseus was filled with his spirit: whi- ‖Eliseus.
le he liued, he was not moued for any prince, nether colde any bring him into subiection.
13 Nothing colde ouercome him, * and af- 2.King.13,21
ter his death his bodie prophecied.
14 He did wonders in his life, and in death
were his workes marueilous.
15 For all this the people repented not, nether departed they from their sinnes: * til 2.King.18,11
they were caryed away prisoners out of
their land, and were scatered through all
the earth, so that there remained but a very few people with the prince vnto the
house of Dauid.
16 Howbeit some of them did right, and
some heaped vp sinnes.
17 ‖*Ezekias made his citie strong, & con- ‖Ezekias.
ueied water into the middes thereof: he 2.King.18,2.
digged thorow the rocke with yron, and
made fountaines for waters.
18 *In his time came Sennacherib vp, and 2.King.18,13.
sent Rabsaces, and lift vp his hand against
Sion, and boasted proudely.
19 Then trembled their hearts and hands,
so ẏ they sorowed like a woman in trauel.
20 But they called vpon the Lord, which is
merciful, and lift vp their hands vnto him,
and immediatly the holy one heard them
out of heauen.
21 [He thoght no more vpon their sinnes,
nor gaue them ouer to their enemies,] but
deliuered

deliuered them by the hand of Esai.
2.King.19,35 isa 37,36.
22 *He smote the hoste of the Assyrians,
and his Angel destroyed them.
Iob.1,21. 1.mac.7,41. 2 mac.8,19. ‖Isaias.
23 For Ezekias had done ye thing that pleased the Lord, and remained stedfastly in
the wayes of Dauid his father, as ‖Esai the
great Prophet, and faithful in his vision
had commanded him.
2 King.20,10 isa.38,8.
24 *In his time the sonne went backwarde,
and he lengthened the Kings life.
25 He sawe by an excellēt Spirit what shulde come to passe at the last, and he comforted them that were sorowful in Sion.
26 He shewed what shulde come to passe
for euer, and secret things, or euer thei came to passe.

CHAP. XLIX.

Of Iosias, Hezekiah, Dauid, Ieremi, Ezechiel, Zorobabel, Iesus, Nehemias, Enoch, Ioseph, Sem & Seth.

‖Iosias. 2.King.22,1. & 23,2. 2.chro.34,3.
1 THe remembrance of ‖* Iosias is like
the composition of the perfume that
is made by the arte of the apothecarie:
it is swete as honie in all mouthes, and as
musicke at a banket of wine.
2 He behaued him self vprightly in the reformacion of the people, and toke away
all abominacions of iniquitie.
2.King.23,4
3 He * directed his heart vnto the Lord, &
in the time of ye vngodlie he established
religion.
4 All, except Dauid and Ezekias, and Iosias, committed wickednes: for euen the
Kings of Iuda forsoke the Law of the
moste High, and failed.
°Or, power.
5 Therefore he gaue their "horne vnto o-
ther, and their honor to a strange naciō.
6 He burnt the elect citie of the Sanctuarie, * and destroied the stretes thereof ac-
2.King.25,9. °Or, hand ‖Ieremias
cording to the "prophecie of ‖Ieremias.
Ierem.38,6. Ierem.1,5.
7 For thei * intreated him euil, which neuertheles was a Prophete, *sanctified frō
his mothers wombe, that he might roote
out, and afflict, and destroye, and that he
might also buyld vp, and plant.
‖Ezechiel. Ezech.1,2.
8 ‖*Ezechiel sawe the glorious visiō, which
was shewed him vpon the charet of the
Cherubims.
Ezech.13, & 38.
9 *For he made menciō of the enemies vnder *the figure* of the raine, and directed thē
that went right,
Chap.46,14.
10 *¶ And let the bones of the twelue Prophetes florish out of their place, and let
their memorie be blessed: for they comforted Iacob, and deliuered them by assured hope.
Hag.2,24. ezr.3,2. ‖Zorobabel.
11 ¶*How shal we praise ‖Zorobabel, which
was as a ring on the right hand!
‖Iesus. Zechar 3,1. ezr.13,2. hag.1,12,& 2,3
12 So was ‖*Iesus also the sonne of Iosedec:
these men in their time buylded the house, and set vp the Sanctuarie of the Lord
againe, which was prepared for an euerlasting worship.
Nehe.7,1. ‖Neemias.
13 ¶ * And among the elect was ‖Neemias
whose renoume is great, which set vp for
vs the walles that were fallen, and set vp
the gates and the barres, and laied the fundacions of our houses.
14 ¶ But vpon the earth was no man created like ‖*Enoch: for he was takē vp from
‖Enoch. Gen.5,24. ebr.11,5.
the earth.
chap.44,16. ‖Ioseph. Gen 41,44. & 42,6. & 45,8.
15 Nether was there a like man vnto ‖*Ioseph the gouernour of his brethren, & the
vpholder of his people, whose bones were
kept.
‖Sem. Gen.5,3. ‖Seth. ‖Adam.
16 ‖ * Sem and ‖Seth were in great honour
among men: and so was ‖ Adam aboue e-
uerie liuing thing in the creacion.

CHAP. L.

Of Simon the sonne of Onias. 22 An exhortacion to praise the Lord. 27 The autor of this boke.

‖Simon. 2.Mac.3,4.
1 ‖SImon * the sonne of Onias the hie
Priest, which in his life set vp the
house againe, and in his dayes established
°Or, people.
the "Temple,
2 Vnder him was the fundaciō of the double height laied, and the hie walles that
compasseth the Temple.
3 In his daies the places, to receiue water
that were decaied, *were restored* & the bras-
a Which Salomon made, 1. King.7,23.
se was about in measure as the a sea.
4 He toke care for his people, that they
shulde not fall, & fortified the citie against
the siege.
5 How honorable was his conuersation a-
mong the people, and when he came out
of the house couered with the vaile!
6 He was as the morning starre in the middes of a cloude, and as the moone when it
is ful,
7 And as the sunne shining vpon the Tem
ple of the moste High, and as the rainebowe that is bright in the faire cloudes,
8 And as the floure of the roses in ye spring
of the yere, and as lilies by the springs of
waters, and as the branches of the frankē-
cense tre in the time of somer,
9 As a fyre & incense in the censer, and as
a vessel of massie golde, set with all maner of precious stones,
10 And as a faire oliue tre that is fruteful,
and as a cypresse tre, which groweth vp to
the cloudes.
11 When he put on the garment of honour
and was clothed with all beautie, he went
vp to the holy altar, and made the garmēt
of holines honorable.
12 When he toke the porcions out of the
Priests hands, he him self stoode by the
herth of the altar, compassed with his brethrē rounde about, as the branches do the
cedre tre in Libanus, & thei cōpassed him
as the branches of the palme trees.
13 So were all the sonnes of Aaron in their
glorie, and the oblacions of the Lord in
their hands before all the cōgregacion of
Israel.

14 And that he might accomplish his ministerie vpon the altar, and garnish the
offring of the moste High, and almightie,
15 He stretched out his hand to the drinke
offring, and powred of the blood of the
grape, and he powred at the fote of the altar a perfume of good sauour vnto the
moste high King of all.
16 Then showted the sonnes of Aaron, and
blowed with brasen trumpets, and made a
great noyce to be heard, for a remēbrance
before the moste High.
17 Then all the people together hasted, &
fell downe to the earth vpō their faces to
worship their Lord God almightie, and
moste high.
18 The singers also sang with their voyces,
so that the sounde was great, and the melodie swete.
19 And the people prayed vnto the Lord
moste high with prayer before him that
is merciful, til the honour of the Lord were performed, and they had accomplished
his seruice.
20 Then went he downe, and stretched out
his hands ouer the whole congregacion of
the children of Israel, that they shulde giue praise with their lippes vnto the Lord,
and reioyce in his Name.
21 He began againe to worship, ŷ he might
receiue the blessing of the moste High.
22 Now therefore giue praise all ye vnto
God, that worketh great thīgs euerie where, which hathe increased our dayes from
the wombe, and delte with vs according
to his mercie,
23 That he wolde giue vs ioyfulnes of heart,
& peace in our dayes in Israel, as in olde
time,
24 That he wolde cōfirme his mercie with
vs, and deliuer vs at his time.
25 ¶ There be two maner of people, ŷ mine
heart abhorreth, & the third is no people:
26 They that sit vpon the mountaine of
Samaria, the Philistims, and the foolish
people that dwell in ″ Sicinus. ″Or, Sitchem.
27 ¶ Iesus the sonne of Sirach, *the sonne* of
Eleazarus, of Ierusalem, hathe writen the
doctrine of vnderstanding and knowledge in this boke, and hathe powred out the
wisdome of his heart.
28 Blessed is he that exerciseth him self
therein: and he that layeth vp these in his
heart, shalbe wise.
29 For if he do these things, he shalbe strōg
in all things: for he setteth his steppes in
the light of the Lord, which giueth wisdome to the godlie. The Lord be praised for
euer more: so be it, so be it.

CHAP. LI.

A prayer of Iesus the sonne of Sirach.

1 I Wil confesse thee, ô Lord and King,
and praise thee, ô God, my Sauiour: I
giue thankes vnto thy Name.
2 For thou art my defender and helper, and
hast preserued my bodie from destruction, and from the snare of the sclanderous tongue, and from the lippes that are
occupied with lies: thou hast holpen me
against mine aduersaries,
3 And hast deliuered me according to the
multitude of thy mercie, and for thy Names sake, from the roaring of them that
were readie to deuoure me, and out of the
hands of suche as soght after my life, and
from the manifolde afflictions, which I
had,
4 And from the fyre that choked me rounde about, and from the middes of the fyre
that I burned not,
5 And from the botome of the belie of hel,
from an vncleane tōgue, from lying wordes, from false accusation to the King, &
frō the sclander of an vnrighteous tōgue.
6 [My soule shal praise the Lord vnto death:] for my soule drewe nere vnto death:
my life was nere to the hel beneth.
7 They cōpassed me on euerie side, & there was no man to helpe me: I loked for the
succour of men, but there was none.
8 Then thoght I vpon thy mercie, ô Lord,
and vpon thine actes of olde, how thou
deliuerest suche as waite for thee, and sa-
uest them out of the hands of the ″enemies. ″Or, nacions.
9 Then lift I vp my prayer from the earth,
and praied for deliuerance from death.
10 I called vpon the Lord the father of my
Lord, that he wolde not leaue me in the
daye of my trouble, and in the time of the
proude without helpe.
11 I wil praise thy Name continually, and
wil sing praise with thankesgiuing: & my
prayer was heard.
12 Thou sauedst me from destruction, and
deliueredst me from the euil time: therefore wil I giue thankes and praise thee, &
blesse the Name of the Lord.
13 Whē I was yet yong, or euer I wēt abroad, I desired wisdome opēly in my praier.
14 I praied for her before the Temple, and
soght after her vnto farre countreis, and
she was as a grape that waxeth ripe out of
the floure.
15 Mine heart reioyced in her: my foote
walked in the right way, & from my youth
vp soght I after her.
16 I bowed somewhat downe mine eare, &
receiued her, & gate me muche wisdome:
17 And I profited by her: therefore wil I
ascribe the glorie vnto him, that giueth me
wisdome.
18 For I am aduised to do thereafter: I wil
be ielous of that that is good: so shal I
not be confounded.
19 My soule hathe wresteled with her, and
I haue examined my workes: I lifted vp
mine

mine hands on hye, and considered the
ignorances thereof.
20 I directed my soule vnto her, and I founde her in purenes: I haue had mine heart
ioyned with her from the beginning: therefore shal I not be forsaken.
21 My bowels are troubled in seking her:
therefore haue I gotten a good possessiō.
22 The Lord hathe giuē me a tōgue for my
rewarde, wherewith I wil praise him.
23 Drawe nere vnto me, ye vnlearned, and
dwell in the house of learning.
24 Wherefore are ye slowe? and what say
you of these things, seing your soules are
very thirstie?
25 I opened my mouth, and said, *Bye her Isa.55,1.
for you without money.
26 Bowe downe your necke vnder the yoke,
& your soule shal receiue instruction: she
is ready that ye may finde her.
27 Beholde with your eyes, *how that I haue had but litle labour, & haue gotten vnto me muche rest. Chap.6,28.
28 Get learning with a great some of money: for by her ye shal possesse muche
golde.
29 Let your soule reioyce in the mercie *of
the Lord*, and be not ashamed of his praise.
30 Do your duetie betimes, and he wil giue you a rewarde at his time.

BARUCH.

CHAP. I.

1 Baruch wrote a boke during the captiuitie of Babylon, which he red before Iechoniah and all the people. 10 The Iewes sent the boke with money vnto Ierusalem to their other brethren, to the intēt that they shulde pray for them.

1 And these are the wordes of the boke, which
Baruch ẏ sonne of Nerias, the sonne of Maasias, the sonne of Sedecias, the sonne of *Asadias, the sonne of Helcias wrote in at Babylon, *Or, Sedeias.
2 In the fift yere, and in the seuenth *day* of
the moneth, what time as the Chaldeans
toke Ierusalem, and burnt it with fyre.
3 And Baruch did read the wordes of this
boke, that Iechonias the sonne of Ioacim
King of Iuda might heare, & all the people that were come to heare the boke,
4 And in the audience of the gouernour, &
of the Kings sonnes, & before the Elders,
& before the whole people, frō the lowest
vnto the hiest, before all them that dwelt
at Babylon by the riuer *Sud. *Or, Sodi.
5 Which *when they heard it*, wept, fasted and
made praiers before the Lord.
6 They made a collection also of money,
according to euerie mans power,
7 And sent it to Ierusalem vnto Ioacim the
sonne of Helcias the sōne of Salom Priest,
and vnto the other Priests, and to all the
people, which were with him at Ierusalē,
8 When he had receiued the vessels of the
Temple of the Lord, that were taken away out of the Temple, to bring thē againe into the land of Iuda, the tenth day of
the moneth Siuan, *to wit*, siluer vessels, which *Or, Sibon.
Sedecias the sonne of Iosias King of Iuda had made,
9 After that Nabuchodonosor King of Babylon had led away Iechonias from Ierusalem, and his princes, & his nobles, prisoners, and the people, and caryed them to
Babylon.
10 And they said, Beholde, we haue sent you
money, wherewith ye shal bye burnt offrīgs
for sinne, and incense, and prepare a *meat
offring, & offre vpon the altar of the Lord
our God, *Or, manna for minhah which was the euening and morning sacrifice.
11 And pray for the life of Nabuchodonosor King of Babylon, and for the life of
Baltasar his sonne, that their daies may be
vpon earth, as the daies of heauen,
12 And that God wolde giue vs strength &
lighten our eyes, that we may liue vnder
the shadowe of Nabuchodonosor King of
Babylon, and vnder the shadowe of Baltasar his sonne, that we may long do the seruice, and finde fauour in their sight.
13 Pray for vs also vnto the Lord our God
(for we haue sinned against the Lord our
God, and vnto this day the furie of the
Lord and his wrath is not turned from vs)
14 And rede this boke (which we haue sent
to you to be rehearsed in the Tēple of the
Lord) vpon the feast daies, and at time
conuenient.
15 Thus shal ye say, *To the Lord our God Chap 2,6.
belongeth righteousnes, but vnto vs ẏ confusion of our faces, as it is come to passe
this day vnto them of Iuda, and to the inhabitants of Ierusalem,
16 And to our Kings, and to our princes, &
to our Priests, and to our Prophetes, and
to our fathers,
17 Because we haue *sinned before the Lord Dan 9,5.
our God,
18 And haue not obeied him, nether hearkened vnto the voyce of the Lord our God,
to walke in the commandements that he
gaue vs openly.
19 From the day that the Lord broght our
fathers out of the land of Egypt, euen vnto this day, we haue bene disobedient vn-

to the Lord our God, and we haue bene
negligent to heare his voyce.

Deu.28.15.
20 *Wherefore these plagues are come vpō
vs, and the curse which the Lord appointed by Moyses his seruant at the time that
he broght our fathers out of the land of
Egypt, to giue vs a land that floweth with
milke and honie, as *appeareth* this day.
21 Neuertheles, we haue not hearkened vnto the voyce of the Lord our God, according to all the wordes of the Prophetes,
whome he sent vnto vs.
22 But euerie one of vs followed the wicked imaginacion of his owne heart, to serue strange gods, and to do euil in the sight
of the Lord our God.

CHAP. II.

*1 The Iewes confesse that they suffer iustely for their sin-
nes. The true confession of the Christiās 11 The Iewes desire to haue the wrath of God turned from them 32 He
promiseth that he wil call againe the people from captiuitie, and giue them a newe and euerlasting testament.*

1 THerefore the Lord our God hathe
performed his worde, which he pronounced against vs, & against our iudges
that gouerned Israel, and against our
Kings, and against our princes, & against
the men of Israel and Iuda,
2 To bring vpon vs great plagues, suche as
neuer came to passe vnder ẏ whole heauē,
as they that were done in Ierusalē, *according to things, that were written in the
Lawe of Moyses,

Deu.28.53.

3 That some among vs shulde eat the flesh
of his owne sonne, & some the flesh of his
owne daughter.
4 Moreouer, he hathe deliuered them to be
in subiection to all the kingdomes, that are
rounde about vs, to be as a reproche and
desolation among all the people rounde about where the Lord hathe scattred
them.
5 Thus they are broght beneth and not
aboue, because we haue sinned against
the Lord our God, and haue not heard his
voyce.

Chap.1.15.
6 *To the Lord our God *apperteineth* righteousnes, but vnto vs & to our fathers open
shame, as *appeareth* this day.
7 *For* all these plagues are come vpon vs,
which the Lord hathe pronounced a-
gainst vs.
8 Yet haue we not prayed before the Lord,
that we might turne euerie one from the
imaginacions of his owne wicked heart.
9 So the Lord hathe watched ouer the plagues, and the Lord hathe broght them
vpon vs: for the Lord is righteous in all
his workes, which he hathe commanded
vs.
10 Yet we haue not hearkened vnto his voyce, to walke in the commandements of the
Lord that he hathe giuen vnto vs.
11 *And now, ô Lord God of Israel, that Dan 9,15.
hast broght thy people out of the land of
Egypt with a mightie hand, and an hie arme, and with signes, and with wonders, and
with great power, and hast gotten thy self
a Name, as *appeareth* this day,
12 O Lord our God, we haue sinned: we haue done wickedly: we haue offended in all
thine ordinances.
13 Let thy wrath turne from vs: for we are
but a fewe left among the heathen, where
thou hast scattred vs.
14 Heare our praiers, ô Lord, and our peticions, and deliuer vs for thine owne sake, and giue vs fauour in the sight of thē,
which haue led vs away,
15 That all the earth may know that thou
art the Lord our God, and that thy Name
is called vpon Israel and vpon their posteritie.
16 Therefore loke downe from thine holy
Temple, and thinke vpon vs: encline thine
eare, ô Lord, and heare vs.
17 *Open thine eyes, and beholde: for the Deu.26.15. isa.63.15.
dead that are in the graues, and whose sou-
les are out of their bodies, *giue vnto the Psal.6.6. & 115.17. isa.38.18.
Lord, nether "praise, nor righteousnes. "Or, glorie, nor praise of righteousnes.
18 But the soule that is vexed for the great-
nes *of sinne*, and he that goeth crokedly,
and weake, and the eyes that faile, and the
hungrie soule wil giue thee praise & righteousnes, ô Lord.
19 For we do not require mercie in thy
sight, ô Lord our God, for the righteousnes of our fathers, or of our Kings,
20 But because thou hast sent out thy wrath
and indignacion vpon vs, as thou hast
spoken by "thy seruants the Prophetes, "Or by the hand of thy seruants.
saying,
21 *Thus saith the Lord, Bowe downe your Iere.27.7.
shulders, and serue the King of Babylon:
so shal ye remaine in the land, that I gaue
vnto your fathers.
22 But if ye wil not heare the voyce of the
Lord, to serue the King of Babylon,
23 I wil cause to cease in the cities of Iuda,
and in Ierusalem, I wil cause to cease the
voyce of mirthe, and the voyce of ioye, &
the voyce of the bridegrome, and the voyce of the bride, & the land shalbe desolate
of inhabitants.
24 But we wolde no hearken vnto thy voyce, to serue the King of Babylon: therefore hast thou performed the wordes that
thou spakest by thy seruāts the Prophetes:
namely, that the bones of our Kings, and
the bones of our fathers shulde be caryed
out of their places.
25 And lo, they are cast out to the heat of
the day, and to the colde of the night, and
are dead in great miserie with famine, &
with

with the sworde, and in banishment.
26 And the Temple wherein thy Name
was called vpon, thou hast broght to the
state, as *appeareth* this day, for the wickednes of the house of Israel, and the house of
Iuda.
27 O Lord our God, thou hast intreated vs
according to equitie, and according to
all thy great mercie.
28 As thou spakest by thy seruant Moyses,
in the day when thou didest cōmand him
to write thy Lawe before the childrē of Israel, saying,
Leu.26.14. deu.18.15. 29 *If ye wil not obey my voyce, then shal
this great swarme and multitude be tur-
ned into a verie fewe among the nacions
where I wil scater them.
30 For I knowe that they wil not heare me:
for it is a stifnecked people: but in the
land of their captiuitie they shal remember them selues,
31 And knowe that I am ẏ Lord their God:
then wil I giue them an heart *to vnderstand*,
and eares.
32 And they shal heare, and praise me in
the land of their captiuitie, & thinke vpon
my Name.
33 Then shal they turne them from their
harde backes, and from their euil workes:
for they shal remember the way of their
fathers, which sinned before the Lord.
34 And I wil bring them againe into the
land, which I promised with an othe vnto
their fathers, Abraham, Isaac and Iacob,
and they shal be lords of it: and I wil increase them, aud they shal not be diminished.
35 And I wil make an euerlasting couenant
with them, that I wil be their God, & they
shalbe my people: and I wil no more driue my people of Israel out of the land
that I haue giuen them.

CHAP. III.

*1 The people continueth in their praier begon for their de-
liuerance. 9 He praiseth wisdome vnto the people,
shewing that so great aduersities came vnto them for
the despising thereof 36 Onely God was the finder of
wisdome. 37 Of the incarnacion of Christ.*

1 O Lord almightie, ô God of Israel, the
soule that is in trouble, and the spirit
that is vexed, cryeth vnto thee.
2 Heare, ô Lord, and haue mercie: for thou
art merciful, and haue pitie vpon vs, because we haue sinned before thee.
3 For thou endurest for euer, and we vtterly perish.
4 O Lord almightie, the God of Israel,
heare now the praier of the dead Israelites, and of their children, which haue sinned before thee, and not hearkened vnto
the voyce of thee their God, wherefore
these plagues hang vpon vs.
5 Remember not the wickednes of our fathers, but thinke vpon thy power, and thy
Name at this time.
6 For thou art the Lord our God, & thee, ô
Lord, wil we praise.
7 And for this cause hast thou put thy feare in our hearts, that we shulde call vpon
thy Name, and praise thee in our captiuitie: for we haue considered in our mindes all the wickednes of our fathers, that
sinned before thee.
8 Beholde, we are yet this day in our captiuitie, where thou hast scatered vs, to be a
reproche, and a curse, and subiect to pay-
ments, according to all the iniquities of
our fathers, which are departed from the
Lord their God.
9 O Israel, heare the commandements of
life: hearken vnto them, that thou maiest
learne wisdome.
10 What is the cause, ô Israel, that thou art
in thine enemies land, and art waxen olde
in a strange countrey?
11 And art defiled with the dead? and art
counted with them, that go downe to the
graues?
12 Thou hast forsaken the fountaine of wis
dome.
13 *For* if thou hadest walked in the way of
God, thou shuldest haue remained safe
for euer.
14 Learne where is wisdome, where is
strength, where is vnderstādīg, that thou
maist knowe also from whence cometh
long continuance, and life, and where the
light of the eyes, and peace is.
15 Who hathe found out her place? or who
hathe come into her treasures?
16 Where are the princes of the heathen, &
suche as ruled the beasts vpon the earth?
17 They that had their pastime with the
foules of the heauen, that hoorded vp siluer, and golde, wherein men trust, & made none end of their gathering?
18 For they that coyned siluer, and were so
careful of their worke, and whose inuention had none end,
19 Are come to naught, and gone downe to
hel, and other men are come vp in their
steades.
20 Whē thei were yong, they sawe ẏ light,
and dwelt vpon the earth: but they vnderstode not the way of knowledge,
21 Nether perceiued the paths thereof,
nether haue their children receiued it: but
they were farre of from that way.
22 It hathe not bene heard of in the land of
Chanaan, nether hathe it bene sene in
Theman,
23 Nor the Agarines that soght after wisdome vpon the earth, nor the marchants
of Nerran, and of Theman, nor the ex-
pounders of fables, nor the searchers out
of wisdome haue knowen the way of wis-

dome, nether do they thinke vpon the pathes thereof.

24 O Israel, how great is the House of God! and how large is the place of his possession!

25 It is great, and hathe none end: it is hie, and vnmeasurable.

26 There were the gyants, famous from the beginning, that were of so great stature, and so expert in warre.

27 Those did not the Lord chose, nether gaue he the way of knowledge vnto them.

28 But thei were destroied, because thei had no wisdome, and perished through their owne foolishnes.

29 Who hathe gone vp into heauen, to take her, and broght her downe frō the cloudes?

30 Who hathe gone ouer the sea, to finde her, and hathe broght her, rather then fine golde?

31 No man knoweth her waies, nether considereth her paths.

32 But he that knoweth all things, knoweth her, and he hathe founde her out with his vnderstanding: this same is he which hathe prepared the earth for euermore, and hathe filled it with foure footed beastes.

33 When he sendeth out the light, it goeth: and when he calleth it againe, it obeieth him with feare.

34 And the starres shine in their watch, and reioyce. When he calleth them, they say, Here we be: and so with cherefulnes they shewe light vnto him that made them.

35 This is our God, and there shal none other be compared vnto him.

36 He hathe founde out all ẏ way of knowledge, and hathe giuen it vnto Iacob his seruant, and to Israel his beloued.

37 Afterwarde he was sene vpon earth, and dwelt among men.

CHAP. IIII.

The reward of them that kepe the Law, and the punishment of them that despise it. 12 A comforting of the people being in captiuitie. 19 A complaint of Ierusalem & vnder the figure thereof the Church. 25 A consolacion and comforting of the same.

1 THis is the boke of the cōmandements of God, and the Law that endureth for euer: all they that kepe it, shal come to life: but suche as forsake it, shal dye.

2 Turne thee, ô Iacob, and take holde of it: walke by this brightnes before the light thereof.

3 Giue not thine honour to another, nor the thīgs that are profitable vnto thee, to a strange nacion.

4 O Israel, we are blessed: for the thīgs that are acceptable vnto God, are declared vnto vs.

5 Be of good comfort, ô my people, which art the memorial of Israel.

6 Ye are solde to the nacions, not for your destruction: but because ye prouoked God to wrath, ye were deliuered vnto the enemies.

7 For ye haue displeased him that made you, offring vnto deuils and not to God.

8 Ye haue forgotten him that created you, euen the euerlasting God, & ye haue greiued Ierusalem, that nourished you.

9 When she sawe the wrath comming vpō you from God, she said, Hearken, ye that dwell about Sion: for God hathe broght me into great heauines.

10 I se the captiuitie of my sonnes and daughters, which ẏ Euerlasting wil bring vpon them.

11 With ioye did I nourish thē, but I must leaue them with weping and mourning.

12 Let no man reioyce ouer me a widdowe, and forsakan of manie, which for the sinnes of my children am desolate, because they departed from the Law of God.

13 They wolde not knowe his righteousnes, nor walke in the wayes of his commādements: nether did they enter into the paths of discipline, through his righteousnes.

14 Come, ye that dwell about Sion, and call to remembrance the captiuitie of my sonnes and daughters, which the Euerlasting hathe broght vpon them.

15 For he hathe broght vpon them a nation from farre, an impudent nacion, and of a strange langage,

16 Which nether reuerence the aged, nor pitie the yong: these haue caried away the dere beloued of the widdowes, leauing me alone, and destitute of my daughters.

17 But what can I helpe you?

18 Surely he that hathe broght these plagues vpon you, can deliuer you from the hands of your enemies.

19 Go your way, ô children, go your way: for I am left desolate.

20 I haue put of the clothing of peace, and put vpon me the sackecloth of prayer, and so long as I liue, I wil call vpon the Euerlasting.

21 Be of good comfort, ô children: crye vnto God, and he wil deliuer you from the power, and hand of the enemies.

22 For I haue hope of your saluatiō through the Euerlasting, and ioye is come vpon me frō the Holy one, because of the mercie, which shal quickely come vnto you frō our euerlasting Sauiour.

23 For I sent you away with weping, and mourning: but with ioye and perpetual gladnes wil God bring you againe vnto me.

24 Like as now the neighbours of Sion saw your captiuitie, so shal they also se shortly your saluaciō from God, which shal come vnto you with great glorie, and brightnes from

from the Euerlasting.
25 My children, suffer paciently the wrath
that is come vpon you from God: for thine enemie hathe persecuted thee, but shor
tely thou shalt se his destruction, and shalt
treade vpon his necke.
26 My darlings haue gone by rough wayes,
and were led away as a flocke that is scatered by the enemies.
27 Be of good comfort, my children, and
crye vnto God: for he that led you away,
hathe you in remembrance.
28 And as it came into your minde to go a-
stray from your God, so endeuoure your
selues ten times more, to turne againe and
to seke him.
29 For he that hathe broght these plagues
vpon you, wil bring you euerlasting ioye
againe, with your saluation.
30 Take a good heart, ô Ierusalem: for he
which gaue thee that name, wil comfort
thee.
31 They are miserable that afflict thee, and
suche as reioyce at thy fall.
32 The cities are miserable whome thy chil
dren serue: miserable is she that hathe takē
thy sonnes.
33 For as she reioyced at thy decay, and was
glad of thy fall, so shal she be sorie for her
owne desolation.
34 For I wil take away the reioycing of her
great multitude, and her ioye shalbe turned into mourning.
35 For a fyre shal come vpon her from the
Euerlasting, long to endure, & she shalbe
inhabited of deuils for a great season.
36 O Ierusalem, loke towarde the East, and
beholde the ioye that cometh vnto thee
from thy God.
37 Lo, thy sonnes (whome thou hast let go)
come gathered together from the East vnto the West, reioycing in the worde of the
Holy one vnto the honour of God.

CHAP. V.

1 Ierusalem is moued vnto gladnes for the returne of her people, and vnder the figure thereof the Church.

1 PVt of thy mourning clothes, ô Ierusalem and thine affliction, and decke
thee with the worshippe and honour, that
cometh vnto thee from God, for euermore.
2 Put on the garment of righteousnes, that
cometh from God, and set a crowne vpon
thine head of the glorie of the Euerlastig.
3 For God wil declare thy brightnes to
euerie countrey vnder the heauen.
4 And God wil name thee by this name
for euer, The Peace of righteousnes, and
the glorie of the worship of God.
5 Arise, ô Ierusalem, & stand vpon hie, and
loke about thee towarde the East, and beholde thy children gathered from the East
vnto the West by the worde of the Holie
one, reioycing in the remembrance of
God.
6 For thei departed from thee on foote, and
were led away of their enemies: but God
wil bring thē againe vnto thee, exalted in
glorie, as children of the kingdome.
7 For God hathe determined to bring downe euerie high mountaine, and the long
enduring rockes, and to fil the valleys,
to make the grounde plaine, that Israel
may walke safely vnto the honour of
God.
8 The woods and all swete smelling trees
shal ouershadowe Israel at the commandement of God.
9 For God shal bring Israel with ioye in
the light of his maiestie, with the mercie
and righteousnes that cometh of him.

CHAP. VI.

A COPIE OF THE PISTLE, that Ieremias sent vnto them that were led away captiues into Babylon by the King of the Babylonians, to certifie thē of the thing that was commanded him of God.

1 BEcause of the sinnes, that ye haue com
mitted against God, ye shalbe led a-
way captiues vnto Babylon, by Nabuchodonosor, King of the Babylonians.
2 So when ye be come into Babylon, ye shal
remaine there manie yeres, and a long season, euen seuen generacions, and after that
wil I bring you away peaceably frō thēce.
3 Now shal ye se in Babylon gods of siluer,
and of golde, and of wood, borne vpon
mēs shulders, to cause the people to feare.
4 *Beware therefore that ye in no wise be
like the strangers, nether be ye afraide of
them, when ye se the multitude before thē
and behinde them worshipping them,
5 But say ye in your hearts, O Lord, we must
worshippe thee.
6 For mine Angel shalbe with you, & shal
care for your soules.
7 As for their tongue, it is polished by the
carpenter, and they them selues are gilted,
and laied ouer with siluer: yet are they but
lyes, and can not speake.
8 And as they take golde for a maide that
loueth to be deckt,
9 So make they crownes for the heads of
their gods: some times also the Priests
them selues conuey away the golde, and
siluer from their gods, and bestow it vpon
them selues.
10 Yea, they giue of the same vnto the
harlots, that are in their house: againe,
they decke these gods of siluer, and gods
of golde, and of wood with garments like
men,
11 Yet can not they be preserued from rust
and wormes,

Isa.44,10. psal.115,9. wis.13,14.

12 Thogh they haue couered thē with clothing of purple, and wipe their faces because of the dust of the Temple, whereof
there is muche vpon them.
13 One holdeth a scepter, as thogh he were
a certeine iudge of the coūtrey: yet can he
not slay suche as offende him.
14 Another hathe a dagger or an axe in his
right hand: yet is he not able to defende
him self from battel, nor from theues: so
then it is euident, that they be no gods.
15 Therefore feare them not: for as a vessel
that a man vseth, is nothing worthe when
it is broken,
16 Suche are their gods: when they be set vp
in their temples, their eyes be ful of dust
by reason of the fete of those ẏ come in:
Or, courtes. 17 And as the "gates are shut in round about
vpon him that hathe offended the King:
or as one that shulde be led to be put to
death, so the Priests kepe their tēples with
doores, and with lockes, & with barres, lest
their *gods* shulde be spoyled by robbers.
18 They light vp candels before them: yea,
more thē for them selues whereof they cā
not se one: for they are but as one of the
postes of the temple.
19 They confesse, that euen their hearts are
gnawen vpon: but when the things, that
crepe out of the earth, eat them and their
clothes, they feele it not.
20 Their faces are blacke thorow the smoke that is in the temple.
21 The owles, swalowes and birdes flie vpō
their bodies, and vpon their heads, yea, &
the cattes also.
22 By this ye may be sure, that they are not
gods: therefore feare them not.
23 Notwithstādìng the golde, that is about
them to make them beautiful, except one
wipe of the rust, they can not shine: nether
when they were molten, did they fele it.
24 The things wherein is no breth, are
boght for a moste high price.
Isa.46,7. 25 *They are borne vpon mens shulders,
because they haue no feete, whereby they
declare vnto men, that they be nothing
worthe: yea, & they that worship them, are
ashamed.
26 For if they fall to the grounde at anie
time, they can not rise vp againe of them
selues, nether if one set them vp right, can
they moue of them selues, nether if they be
bowed downe, can they make them selues
streight: but they set giftes before them, as
vnto dead men.
27 As for the things ẏ are offred vnto them,
their Priests sell them, and abuse them: likewise also the women lay vp of the same:
but vnto the poore and sicke they giue
nothing.
28 The menstruous women, and they that
are in childebed, touche their sacrifices:
by these things ye may knowe that they
are no gods: feare them not.
29 From whence cometh it then, that they
are called gods? because the women bring
giftes to the gods of siluer, and golde, and
wood.
30 And the Priests sit in their temples, hauing their clothes rent, whose heades and
beardes are shauen, & being bare headed,
31 Thei roare, & crye before their gods, as
men do at the feast of one that is dead.
32 The Priests also take away of their garments, and clothe their wiues and childrē.
33 Whether it be euil that one doeth vnto thē, or good, they are not able to recom
pense it: they can nether set vp a King
nor put him downe.
34 In like maner they cā nether giue riches,
nor money: thogh a man make a vowe
vnto them and kepe it not, they wil no require it.
35 They can saue no mā from death, nether
deliuer the weake from the mightie.
36 They can not restore a blinde man to
his sight, nor helpe anie man at his nede.
37 They can shewe no mercie to the widdowe, nor do good to the fatherles.
38 Their gods of wood, golde and siluer,
are as stones, that be hewen out of the
mountaine, and they that worship them,
shalbe confounded.
39 How shulde a man thē thinke or say that
they are gods?
40 Moreouer the Chaldeās them selues dishonor them: for when thei se a dōme man,
that cā not speake, thei present him to Bel,
41 And desire that he wolde make him to
speake, as thogh he had anie felig: yet thei
that vnderstand these things, can not leaue them: for they also haue no sense.
42 Furthermore the women, girded with
coards, sit in the stretes, and burne "strawe. Or, branne.
43 And if one of them be drawen away, and
lie with anie suche as come by, she casteth
her neighbour in the teeth, because she was
not so worthely reputed, nor her coard
broken.
44 Whatsoeuer is done amōg them, is lies:
how may it then be thoght or said, that
they are gods?
45 Carpenters and goldesmithes make thē,
nether be they anie other thing, but euen
what the workeman wil make them.
46 Yea, they that make them, are of no lōg
continuance: how shulde then the things
that are made of them, be gods?
47 Therefore they leaue lies, and shame
for their posteritie.
48 For when there cometh anie warre or
plague vpō thē, the Priests imagine with
them selues, where they may hide thē selues with them.
49 How then can men not perceiue, that
they

they be no gods,which can nether defend
them selues from warre,nor from plagues?
Psal.115,3. wisd.13,10. 50 For *seing they be but of wood, and of
siluer,and of golde,men shal knowe here-
after that they are but lies, and it shalbe
manifest to all nacions & Kings,that they
be no gods,but the workes of mens hands,
and that there is no worke of God in thẽ.
51 Whereby it maye be knowen, that they
are no gods.
52 They can set vp no King in the lãd, nor
giue raine vnto men.
53 They can giue no sentence of a matter,
nether preserue from iniurie:they haue no
power,but are as crowes betwene the heauen and the earth.
54 When there falleth a fyre vpõ the house of those gods of wood, and of siuer,&
of golde, the Priests wil escape & saue thẽ
selues, but thei burne as ye balkes therein.
55 Thei can not withstand anie King or e-
nemies: how can it then be thoght or said
that they be gods?
56 Moreouer these gods of wood, of golde, and of siluer can nether defend them
selues from theues nor robbers.
57 For they that are strongest, take awaye
their golde and siluer,and apparel,where-
with they be clothed: and when they haue
it,they get them awaye: yet can they not
helpe them selues.
58 Therefore it is better to be a King,& so
to shewe his power,or els a profitable vessel in an house,whereby he that oweth it,
might haue profite,then suche false gods:
or to be a dore in an house,to kepe suche
things safe as be therein, then suche false
gods:or a piller of wood in a palace, then
suche false gods.
59 For the sunne, and the moone, and the
starres that shine,when thei are sent downe for necessarie vses,obey.
60 Likewise also the lightning when it shineth,it is euident: and the winde bloweth
in euerie countrey.
61 And when God cõmandeth the cloudes
to go about the whole worlde, they do as
thei are bidden.
62 Whẽ the fyre is sent downe from aboue
to destroye hilles and woods,it doeth that
which is commanded: but these are not
like anie of these things, nether in forme,
nor power.
63 Wherefore men shulde not thinke, nor
say that they be gods, seing thei can nether giue sentence in iudgement, nor do
men good.
64 For so muche now as ye are sure, that
they be no gods,feare them not.
65 For they can nether curse, nor blesse
Kings:
66 Nether can thei shewe signes in the heauen among the heathẽ,nether shine as the
moone.
67 The beastes are better thẽ they:for thei
can get them vnder a couert,and do them
selues good.
68 So ye may be certified that by no maner
of meanes,they are gods: therefore feare
them not.
69 For as a skarcrowe in a garden of cucumbers kepeth nothing,so are their gods
of wood,and of siluer,and of golde:
70 And likewise their gods of wood, and
golde and siluer are like to a white thorne
in an orcharde, that euerie birde sitteth
vpon, and as a dead bodie that is cast in
the darke.
71 By the purple also and brightnes,which
fadeth vpon them,ye may vnderstãd,that
they be no gods:yea,they them selues shal
be consumed at the last, and they shalbe
a shame to the countrey.
72 Better therefore is the iuste man, that
hathe none idoles: for he shalbe farre frõ
reprofe.

THE SONG OF THE thre holie children, which followeth in the third chapter of Daniel after this place, Thei fell downe bound into the middes of the hote fyrie fornace.

CHAP. I.

25 The praier of Azarias. 46 The crueltie of the King. 48 The flame deuoureth the Chaldeans. 49 The Angel of the Lord was in the fornace. 51 The thre children praise the Lord and prouoke all creatures to the same.

24 AND they walked in the
middes of the flame,
praising God, & mag-
nified the Lord.
25 Then Azarias stode
vp, and praied on this
maner,and opening his-
mouth in the middes of the fyre,said,
26 Blessed be thou, ô Lord God of our fa-
thers:thy Name is worthie to be praised
and honored for euermore.
27 For thou art righteous in all the things,
that thou hast done vnto vs, and all thy
workes are true,and thy waies are right,&
all thy iudgements certeine.
28 In all the things that thou hast broght
vpon vs,& vpon Ierusalem,the holie citie
of our fathers, thou hast executed true

iudgements: for by right and equitie hast
thou broght all these things vpon vs, because of our sinnes.
29 For we haue sinned and done wickedly,
departing from thee: in all things haue we
trespased,
30 And not obeied thy commandements,
nor kept them, nether done as thou hadest
commanded vs, that we might prosper.
31 Wherefore in all that thou hast broght
vpon vs, & in euerie thing that thou hast
done to vs, thou hast done them in true
iudgement:
32 As in deliuering vs into the hands of
our wicked enemies, & moste hateful traitors, and to an vnrighteous King, and the
moste wicked in all the worlde.
33 And now we may not open our mouthes:
we are become a shame and reprofe vnto
thy seruants, and to them that worshippe
thee.
34 Yet for thy Names sake, we beseche thee,
giue vs not vp for euer, nether breake thy
couenant,
35 Nether take awaye thy mercie from vs,
for thy beloued Abrahams sake, and for
thy seruant Isaaks sake, & for thine holy
Israels sake,
36 To whome thou hast spoken and promised, that thou woldest multiplie their sede
as the starres of heauen, and as the sand,
that is vpon the seashore.
37 For we, ô Lord, are become lesse then a-
nie nacion, and be kept vnder this daye in
all the worlde, because of our sinnes:
38 So that now we haue nether prince, nor
Prophet, nor gouernour, nor burnt offrīg,
nor sacrifice, nor oblacion, nor incense,
nor place to offer ẏ first frutes before thee,
that we might finde mercie.
39 Neuertheles in a contrite heart, and an
humble spirit, let vs be receiued.
40 As in the burnt offring of rams and bullockes, & as in ten thousand of fat lambs,
so let our offring be in thy sight this day,
that it may please thee: for there is no confusion vnto thē that put their trust in thee.
41 And now we followe thee with all our
heart, and feare thee, and seke thy face.
42 Put vs not to shame, but deale with vs
after thy louing kindenes, and according
to the multitude of thy mercies.
43 Deliuer vs also by thy miracles, & giue
thy Name the glorie, ô Lord,
44 That all they which do thy seruants e-
uil, may be confounded: euen let them be
confounded by thy great force and power,
and let their strength be broken,
45 That they maye knowe, that thou onelie art the Lord God, and glorious ouer
the whole worlde.
46 ¶ Now the Kings seruants that had cast
them in, ceased not to make the ouen hote
with [a] naphtha, and with pitche, and with
towe, and with fagotes,
47 So that the flame went out of the fornace fortie and nine cubites.
48 And it brake forthe, & burnt those Chaldeans, that it founde by the fornace.
49 But the Angel of the Lord went downe
into the fornace with thē that were with
Azarias, and smote the flame of the fyre
out of the fornace,
50 And made in the middes of the fornace
like a moyste hissing winde, so that the fyre touched thē not at all, nether grieued,
nor troubled them.
51 Then these thre (as out of one mouth)
praised, and glorified, and blessed God in
the fornace, saying,
52 Blessed be thou, ô Lord God of our fathers, and praised, and exalted aboue all
things for euer, & blessed be thy glorious
& holie Name, & praised aboue all thīgs,
and magnified for euer.
53 Blessed be thou in the Temple of thine
holy glorie, and praised aboue all things,
and exalted for euer.
54 Blessed be thou that beholdest ẏ depths,
& sittest vpon the Cherubims, & praised
aboue all things, and exalted for euer.
55 Blessed be thou in the glorious Throne
of thy kingdome, and praised aboue all
things, and exalted for euer.
56 Blessed be thou in the firmament of heauen, and praised aboue all things, & glorified for euer.
57 All ye workes of the Lord, blesse ye the
Lord: praise him, and exalte him aboue
all things for euer.
58 O *heauens, blesse ye the Lord: praise *Psal.148.4.
him, and exalte him aboue all things for
euer.
59 O Angels of the Lord, blesse ye ẏ Lord:
praise him, & exalte him aboue all things
for euer.
60 All ye waters that be aboue the heauen,
blesse ye the Lord: praise him, and exalte
him aboue all things for euer.
61 All ye powers of the Lord, blesse ye the
Lord: praise him, and exalte him aboue all
things for euer.
62 O sunne and moone, blesse ye the Lord:
praise him, & exalte him aboue all things
for euer.
63 O starres of heauē, blesse ye ẏ Lord: praise
him, & exalte him aboue all thīgs for euer.
64 Euerie shower, & dewe, blesse ye ẏ Lord:
praise him, & exalte him aboue all things
for euer.
65 All ye windes, blesse ye the Lord: praise him, and exalte him aboue all things
for euer.
66 O fyre & heat, blesse ye the Lord: praise
him, & exalte hī aboue all things for euer.
67 O "winter and sommer, blesse ye the
Lord:

[a] Which is a certeine kinde of fat & chalkie claye, as Plinius writeth, 2. boke chap. 105.

" Or, colde.

Lord:praiſe him,and exalte him aboue all
things for euer.
68 O dewes and *ſtormes of ſnowe, bleſſe
ye the Lord:praiſe him,and exalte him a-
boue all things for euer.
69 O froſt and colde, bleſſe ye the Lord:
praiſe him,& exalte him aboue all things
for euer.
70 O yce, and ſnowe, bleſſe ye the Lord:
praiſe him,& exalte him aboue all things
for euer.
71 O nightes & dayes, bleſſe ye the Lord:
praiſe him,& exalte him aboue all things
for euer.
72 O light and darkenes, bleſſe ye ẏ Lord:
praiſe him,& exalte him aboue all things
for euer.
73 O lightenings and cloudes,bleſſe ye the
Lord:praiſe him,and exalte him aboue all
things for euer.
74 Let the earth bleſſe the Lord:let it prai
ſe him, and exalte him aboue all things
for euer.
75 O mountaines, and hilles, bleſſe ye the
Lord:praiſe him,and exalte him aboue all
things for euer.
76 All things that growe on the earth,bleſ-
ſe ye the Lord:praiſe him,and exalte him
aboue all things for euer.
77 O fountaines,bleſſe ye the Lord:praiſe
him,& exalte hĩ aboue all things for euer.
78 O Sea, and floods, bleſſe ye the Lord:
praiſe him, & exalte him aboue all things
for euer.
79 O whales, and all that moue in the waters,bleſſe ye the Lord:praiſe him,and exalte him aboue all things for euer.
80 All ye foules of heauẽ,bleſſe ye ẏ Lord:
praiſe him,& exalte him aboue all things
for euer.
81 All ye beaſts and cattel, bleſſe ye the
Lord:praiſe him,and exalte him aboue all
things for euer.
82 O children of men, bleſſe ye the Lord:
praiſe him, & exalte him aboue all things
for euer.
83 Let Iſrael bleſſe the Lord, praiſe him
and exalte him aboue all things for euer.
84 O Prieſts of the Lord,bleſſe ye ẏ Lord:
praiſe him,& exalte him aboue all things
for euer.
85 O ſeruãts of the Lord,bleſſe ye the Lord:
praiſe him,& exalte him aboue all things
for euer.
86 O ſpirits and ſoules of the righteous,
bleſſe ye the Lord: praiſe him,and exalte
him aboue all things for euer.
87 O Saints and humble of heart,bleſſe ye
the Lord:praiſe him, & exalte him aboue
all things for euer.
88 O Ananias,Azarias,and Miſael,bleſſe ye
the Lord:praiſe him,& exalte him aboue
all things for euer:for he hathe deliuered
vs from the hel, and ſaued vs from the
hand of death,and deliuered vs out of the
middes of the fornace, & burning flame:
euen out of the middes of the fyre hathe
he deliuered vs.
89 Confeſſe vnto the Lord,that he is gra-
cious:for his mercie endureth for euer.
90 All ye that worſhippe the Lord, bleſſe
the God of gods:praiſe him,and acknowledge him:for his mercie *endureth* worlde
without end.

*Or, froſtes.

THE HISTORIE OF *Suſanna, which ſome ioyne to the end of Daniel, and make it the 13. chap.

*Or, Soſanna.

8 The two gouerners are taken with the loue of Suſanna. 19 They take her alone in the garden. 20 They ſolicite her to wickednes. 23 She choſeth rather to obey God, thogh it be to the danger of her life. 34 She is accuſed. 45 Daniel doeth deliuer her. 62 The gouerners are put to death.

1 THERE dwelt a mã in Ba-
bylon called Ioacim,
2 And he toke a wife, whoſe name was Suſanna,the
daughter of Helcias, a
verie faire woman, and
one that feared God.
3 Her father and her mother alſo were godlie people,& taught their daughter according to the Law of Moſes.
4 Now Ioacim was a great riche man,and
had a faire garden ioyning vnto his houſe,and to him reſorted the Iewes,becauſe
he was more honorable then all others.
5 The ſame yere were appointed two of
the anciẽts of the people to be iudges,ſu-
che as the Lord ſpeaketh of, that the iniquitie came from Babylon, & frõ the anciẽt iudges, which ſemed to rule ẏ people.
6 Theſe hanted Ioacims houſe, & all ſuche
as had anie thing to do in the Law, came
thither vnto them.
7 Now when the people departed away at
noone, Suſanna went into her houſbands
garden to walke.
8 And the two Elders ſawe her that ſhe wẽt
in daily and walked, ſo that their luſt was
inflamed towarde her.
9 Therefore thei turned away their [a] mĩde,
& caſt downe their eyes, ẏ thei ſhulde not
ſe heauen, nor remẽbre iuſte iudgements.

a To wit, from God.

10 And albeit thei bothe were woũded with
her loue, yet durst not one shewe another
his grief.
11 For they were ashamed to declare their
lust, that they desired to haue to do w̃ her.
12 Yet they watched diligently from day to
day to se her.
13 And the one said to the other, Let vs go
now home, for it is diner time.
14 So they went their way, and departed,
one from another: yet they returned a-
gaine, and came into the same place, and
after that they had asked one another the
cause, thei acknowledged their lust: thẽ ap
pointed they a time bothe together whẽ
they might finde her alone.
15 Now when they had spied out a conuenient time, that she went in, as her maner
was, with two maides onely, and thoght
to wash her self in the garden (for it was an
hote season)
16 And there was no bodie there, saue the
two Elders that had hid them selues, and
watched for her:
17 She said to her maides, Bring me oyle &
sope, and shut the gardẽ dores, that I may
wash me.
18 And they did as she bade them, and shut
the garden dores, and went out them selues at a backe dore, to fet the thing that
she had commanded them: but they sawe
not the Elders, because they were hid.
19 Now whẽ the maides were gone forthe,
the two Elders rose vp & ranne vnto her,
saying,
20 Beholde, the garden dores are shut, that
no man can se vs, & we burne in loue with
thee: therefore consent vnto vs, and lye
with vs.
21 If thou wilt not, we wil beare witnes a-
gainst thee, that a yong mã was with thee,
and therefore thou didest send away thy
maides from thee.
22 Then Susanna sighed, and said, I am in
trouble on euerie side: for if I do this thĩg,
it is death vnto me: & if I do it not, I can
not escape your hands.
23 It is better for me to fall into your hãds,
and not do it, then to sinne in the sight of
the Lord.
24 With that Susanna cryed with a loude
voyce, and the two Elders cryed out a-
gainst her.
25 Then ranne the one, and opened the gar
den dore.
26 ¶ So whẽ the seruants of the house heard
the crye in the garden, they rushed in at
ẏ backe dore, to se what was done vnto her.
27 But when the Elders had declared their
matter, the seruants were greatly ashamed:
for there was neuer suche a reporte made
of Susanna.
28 On the morow after, came the people to
Ioacim her housband, & the two Elders
came also, ful of mischieuous imaginaciõ
against Susanna, to put her to death,
29 And said before the people, Send for Susanna the daughter of Helcias Ioacims
wife. And immediatly they sent.
30 So she came with her father & mother,
her children and all her kinred.
31 Now Susanna was very tender, and faire
of face.
32 And these wicked mẽ cõmanded to vncouer her *face* (for she was couered) that thei
might so be satisfied with her beautie.
33 Therefore they that were about her, and
all they that knewe her, wept.
34 Thẽ the two Elders stode vp in the middes of the people, and layed their hands
vpon her head,
35 Which wept and loked vp towarde heauen: for her heart trusted in the Lord.
36 And the Elders said, As we walked in the
garden alone, she came in with two maides, whome she sent away from her, and
shut the garden dores.
37 Then a yong man, which there was hid,
came vnto her, and lay with her.
38 Then we which stode in a corner of the
gardẽ, seing this wickednes, rãne vnto thẽ,
and we sawe them as they were together,
39 But we colde not holde him: for he was
stronger then we, and opened the dore, and
leaped out.
40 Now when we had taken this woman,
we asked her what yong man this was, but
she wolde not tel vs: of these things are
we witnesses.
41 Then the assemblie beleued them, as
those that were the Elders and iudges of
the people: so thei condẽned her to death.
42 Then Susanna cryed out with a loude
voyce, and said, O euerlasting God, that
knowest the secrets, and knowest all things
afore they come to passe,
43 Thou knowest, that they haue borne
false witnes against me, and beholde, I
must dye, where as I neuer did suche thĩgs
as these men haue maliciously inuented
against me.
44 And the Lord heard her voyce.
45 ¶ Therefore when she was led to be put
to death, the Lord raised vp ẏ holie spirit
of a yong childe, whose name was Daniel.
46 Who cryed with a loude voyce, I am
cleane from the blood of this woman.
47 Thẽ all the people turned them toward
him, and said, What meane these wordes,
that thou hast spoken?
48 Thẽ Daniel stode in the middes of thẽ,
and said, Are ye suche fooles, ô Israelites,
that without examination, or knowledge
of the trueth, ye haue condemned a daughter of Israel?
49 Returne againe to iudgement: for they
haue

haue borne false witnes against her.
50 Wherefore the people turned againe in
all haste, & the Elders said vnto him, Come,sit downe among vs,& shew it vs,seing
God hathe giuen thee ŷ office of an Elder.
51 Then said Daniel vnto them, Put these
two aside,one farre from another,and I wil
examine them.
52 So when they were put a sonder, one frō
another,he called one of them & said vnto
him,O thou that art olde in a wicked life,
now thy sinnes which thou hast committed afore time,are come to light.
53 For thou hast pronounced false iudgements,and hast condemned the innocent,
and hast let the giltie go fre, albeit the
Lord saith, * The innocent and righteous (Exod.23,7.)
shalt thou not slay.
54 Now then,if thou hast sene her, tel me,
vnder what tre sawest thou them compa-
nying together? Who answered,Vnder a
lentiske tre.
55 Thē said Daniel, Verely thou hast lyed
against thine owne "head: for lo,the Angel (Or,life.)
of God hathe receiued the sentence of
God,to cut thee in two.
56 So put he him aside, & commanded to
bring the other, & said vnto him, O thou
sede of Chanaan,and not of Iuda, beautie
hathe disceiued thee,and lust hathe subuer
ted thine heart.
57 Thus haue ye dealt with the daughters
of Israel,and they for feare cōpanied with
you:but the daughter of Iuda wolde not
abide your wickednes.
58 Now therefore tel me vnder what tre didest thou take them cōpanying together?
Who answered, Vnder a "prime tree. (Or,mirtle tre.)
59 Then said Daniel vnto him,Verely thou
hast also lyed against thine head : for the
Angel of God waiteth with the sworde to
cut thee in two,& so to destroie you bothe.
60 ¶With that all ŷ whole assemblie cryed
with a loude voyce , and praised God,
which saueth them that trust in him.
61 And they arose against the two Elders,
(for Daniel had conuict them of false witnes by their owne mouth)
62 *And according to the Law of Moyses (Deu.19.19. prou.19.5.)
they delt with them,as they delt wicked-
ly against their neighbour , and put them
to death . Thus the innocent blood was
saued the same day.
63 Therefore Helcias, and his wife praised
God for their daughter Susanna,with Ioacim her housband, and all the kinred,
that there was no dishonestie foūde in her.
64 From that day forthe was Daniel had in
great reputacion in the sight of the people.
65 And King Astyages was laide with his
fathers,and Cyrus of Persia reigned in his
steade.

THE HISTORIE OF Bel and of the dragon , which is the fourtenth chapter of Daniel after the Laten.

1 NOw when King Astya-
ges was laide with his
fathers,Cyrus ŷ Persian
receiued his kingdome.
2 And Daniel did eat at
the Kings table , & was
honored aboue all his
friends.
3 Now the Babylonians had an idole , called Bel, and there were spent vpon him e-
uerie day , twelue [a] great measures of fine
floure,and fortie shepe,and six great [b] pottes of wine.
4 And the King worshipped it, and went
daily to honour it : but Daniel worshipped his owne God. And the King said vnto him, Why doest not thou worship Bel?
5 Who answered,and said , Because I may
not worship idoles made with hands , but
the liuing God , which hathe created the
heauen & the earth, and hathe power vpō
all flesh.
6 Then said the King vnto him , Thinkest
thou not that Bel is a liuīg God? seest thou
not how muche he eateth and drinketh e-
uerie day?
7 Then Daniel smiled and said , O King,
be not deceiued: for this is but claye within,and brasse without,and did neuer eat a-
ny thing.
8 So the King was wroth, and called for his
Priests , and said vnto them, If ye tell me
not,who this is that eateth vp these expen
ses,ye shal dye:
9 But if ye can certifie me that Bel eateth
them , then Daniel shal dye : for he hathe
spokē blasphemie against Bel. And Daniel
said vnto the King , Let it be according
to thy worde.
10 (Now the Priests of Bel were thre score and ten beside their wiues and childrē:)
and the King went with Daniel into the
temple of Bel.
11 So Bels Priests said , Beholde ,we wil go
out , and set thou the meat there , ô King,
& let the wine be filled: then shut the dore

a Called Artaba, whereof euerie one conteined somewhat more thē nine galons, which make in all an hundreth & eight galons at the least.
b Called Metreta, and euerie one of these measures cōteined about ten galons, which in all make thre score.

fast,and seale it with thine owne signet.
12 And to morowe when thou commest in,
if thou findest not that Bel hathe eaten vp
all, we wil suffer death, or els Daniel that
hathe lyed vpon vs.
13 Now thei thoght thẽ selues sure ynough:
for vnder the table thei had made a priuie
entrance, and there went they in euer,
and toke away the things.
14 So whẽ they were gone forthe, the King
set meates before Bel. Now Daniel had
commanded his seruants to bring ashes,
and these they strowed thorowout all the
temple,in the presence of the King alone:
then went they out, and shut the dore, &
sealed it with the Kings signet, and so departed.
15 Now in the night came the Priests, with
their wiues and children,(as they were
wonte to do)and did eat and drinke vp all.
16 In the morning betimes, the King arose
and Daniel with him.
17 And the King said,Daniel,are the seales
whole? Who answered,Yea, ô King,thei
be whole.
18 And assone as he had opened the dore,
the King loked vpon the table, and cryed
with a loude voyce, Great art thou,ô Bel,
and with thee is no disceite.
19 Then laughed Daniel, and helde the
King that he shulde not go in, & said, Beholde now the pauement, and marke wel
whose footesteppes are these.
20 And the King said, I se the footesteppes of men,women,and children:therefo-
re the King was angrie,
21 And toke the Priests, with their wiues,
and children,and they shewed him the pri
uie dores, where they came in, and consumed suche things as were vpon the table.
22 Therefore the King slewe them, and deliuered Bel into Daniels power,who destroyed him and his temple.
23 ¶Moreouer in that same place there was
a great dragon,which the Babyloniãs wor
shipped.
24 And the King said vnto Daniel, Sayest
thou,that this is of brasse also?lo,he liueth
and eateth and drinketh,so that thou cãst
not say,that he is no liuing god: therefore worshippe him.
25 Then said Daniel vnto the King, I wil
worshippe the Lord my God:for he is the
liuing God.
26 But giue me leaue,ô King,and I wil slay
this dragon without sworde or staffe. And
the King said,I giue thee leaue.
27 Then Daniel toke pitche, and fatte, &
heere, and did seeth them together,& made lompes thereof: this he put in the dragons mouthe, and so the dragon burst in
sunder. And Daniel said,Beholde,whome
ye worshippe.
28 When the Babylonians heard it, they
were wonderful wroth,and gathered them
together against the King, saying, The
King is become a Iewe: for he hathe destroyed Bel, and hathe slaine the dragon,
and put the Priests to death.
29 So they came to the King, and said,De-
liuer vs Daniel, or els we wil destroy thee
and thine house.
30 Now whẽ the King sawe,that thei preased sore vpon him,and that necessitie con
streined him, he deliuered Daniel vnto
them:
31 Who cast him into the lions denne,whe-
re he was six daies.
32 In the denne there were seuen lions, and
they had giuẽ them euerie day two bodies
and two shepe,which then were not giuen
them, to the intent that they might deuour Daniel.
33 ¶Now there was in Iewrie a Prophet cal
led Abbacuc,which had made potage,and
broken bread into a bowle, and was going
into the field for to bring it to the reapers.
34 But ẏ Angel of the Lord said vnto Abbacuc,Go,carye the meat ẏ thou hast,into
Babylon vnto Daniel,which is in the liõs
denne.
35 And Abbacuc said, Lord, I neuer sawe
Babylõ,nether do I knowe where the denne is.
36 Then the Angel toke him by the crowne
of the head, and bare him by the heere of
the head, and through a mightie winde set
him in Babylon vpon the denne.
37 And Abbacuc cryed, saying, O Daniel,
Daniel, take the dinner that God hathe
sent thee.
38 Then said Daniel, O God, thou hast
thoght vpon me,and thou neuer failest thẽ
that seke thee and loue thee.
39 So Daniel arose,and did eat,and the Angel of the Lord set Abbacuc in his owne
place againe immediatly.
40 Vpon the seuenth day, the King went to
bewaile Daniel: and when he came to the
denne,he loked in, and beholde,Daniel sate *in the middes of the lions.*
41 Then cryed the King with a loude voyce,saying, Great art thou, ô Lord God of
Daniel, and there is none other besides
thee.
42 And he drewe him out of the denne, and
cast thẽ that were the cause of his destruction into the denne, & they were deuoured
in a momente before his face.

THE FIRST BOKE OF the Maccabees.

CHAP. I.

1 The death of Alxāder the King of Macedonia. 11 Antiochus taketh the kingdome. 12 Many of the children of Israel make couenant with the Gentiles. 21 Antiochus subdueth Egypt and Ierusalem vnto his dominion. 50 Antiochus setteth vp idoles.

1 After that Alexander the
Macedonian, ẏ sonne of
Philippe, went forthe of
the land of Chettiim, &
slewe Darius King of
the Persiās and Medes,
and reigned for him,
as he had before in Grecia,
2 He toke great warres in hand, and wan
strong holdes, and slewe the Kings of the
earth.
3 So went he thorow to ẏ ends of the worlde,
and toke spoiles of many nacions, in so
muche that ẏ worlde stode in awe of him:
therefore his heart was puffed vp and was
hawtie.
4 Now when he had gathered a mightie
strong hoste,
5 And had reigned ouer regions, nacions
and kingdomes, they became tributaries
vnto him.
6 After these things he fel sicke, and knewe
that he shulde dye.
7 Then he called for the chief of his seruātes,
which had bene broght vp with him of
children, and parted his kingdome among
them, while he was yet aliue.
8 So Alexander had reigned twelue yeres
when he dyed.
9 And his seruants reigned euerie one in
his roume.
10 And they all caused thē selues to be crowned
after his death, and so did their children
after thē many yeres, and muche wickednes
increased in the worlde.
11 For out of these came the wicked roote,
euen Antiochus [o] Epiphanes the sonne of
King Antiochus, which had bene an hostage
at Rome, and he reigned in the hundreth
and seuen and thirtieth yere of the
kingdome of the Grekes.
12 In those daies wēt there out of Israel wic
ked men, which entyced many, saying, Let
vs go, and make a couenant with the heathen,
that are rounde about vs: for since
we departed frō them, we haue had muche
sorowe.
13 So this deuice pleased them wel.
14 And certeine of the people were readie,
& went to ẏ King which gaue thē licence
to do after the ordinances of the heathen.
15 Thē set thei vp a place of exercise at Ierusalē,
according to the faciōs of ẏ heathē,
16 And made them [a] selues vncircūcised, &
forsoke the holy couenant, & ioyned them
selues to the heathen, and were solde to do
mischief.
17 So whē Antiochus kingdome was set in
order, he wēt about to reigne ouer Egypt,
that he might haue the dominion of two
realmes.
18 Therefore he entred into Egypt with a
mightie cōpanie, with charets, & elephantes,
& with horsemē, & with a great nauie,
19 And moued warre against Ptolemeus
King of Egypt: but Ptolemeus was afraid
of him, and fled, and manie were wounded
to death.
20 Thus *Antiochus* wanne many strong cities
in the land of Egypt, and toke away
the spoiles of the land of Egypt.
21 And after that Antiochus had smitten
Egypt, he turned againe in the hundreth,
fortie and thre yere,
22 And went vp towarde Israel and Ierusalē
with a mightie people.
23 And entred proudly into the Sanctuarie,
and toke away the golden altar, and the
candlesticke for the light, & all the instruments
thereof, & the table of ẏ shewbread,
and the powring vessels, and the bowles, &
the golden basins, and the vaile, and the
crownes, & the golden apparel, which was
before the Temple, and brake all in pieces.
24 He toke also the siluer and golde, & the
precious iewels, & he toke the secret treasures
that he founde, & when he had taken
away all, he departed into his owne land,
25 After he had murthered many men, and
spoken verie proudely.
26 Therefore there was a great lamētacion
in euerie place of Israel.
27 For the princes & the Elders mourned:
the yong women, and the yong men were
made feble, & the beautie of the women
was changed.
28 Euerie bridegrome toke him to mourning,
and she that sate in the mariage chāber,
was in heauines.
29 The land also was moued for the inhabi
tāts thereof: for all the house of Iacob was
couered with confusion.
30 After two yeres the King sent his chief
taxe master into ẏ cities of Iuda, which came
to Ierusalem with a great multitude.
31 Who spake peaceable wordes vnto them
in disceite, & they gaue credit vnto him.
32 Then he fell suddenly vpon the citie, &
smote it with a great plague, & destroied
muche people of Israel.

[o] Or, noble.

Ioseph Antiq 12, chap. 6.

[a] By drawing ẏ skinne ouer the parte that was circumcised, as Cels. 7. chap 25 Epiph. lib de pōderib & mensur.

33 And when he had spoiled the citie, he set
fyre on it, casting downe the houses thereof, and walles thereof on euerie side.
34 The womē and their children toke they
captiue, and led away the cattel.
35 Then fortified they the citie of Dauid
with a great & thicke wall, & with mightie towres, and made it a strong holde for
them.
36 Moreouer they set wicked people there,
and vngodlie persones, and fortified them
selues therein.
37 And they stored it with weapons and vitailes, and gathered the spoile of Ierusalē,
and laied it vp there.
38 Thus became they a sore snare & were
in ambushment for ẏ Sanctuarie, and were
wicked enemies euermore vnto Israel.
39 For thei shed innocēt blood on euerie side
of the Sanctuarie & defiled the Sãctuarie,
40 In so muche that the citizens of Ierusalem fled away because of them, and it became an habitacion of strãgers, being desolate of them whome she had borne: for
her owne children did leaue her.
41 Her Sãctuarie was left waste as a wildernes: her holie daies were turned into mour
ning, her Sabbaths into reproche, and her
honour broght to naught.
42 As her glorie had bene great, so was
her dishonour, and her excellencie was tur
ned into sorowe.
43 Also the King wrote vnto all his kingdome, that all the people shulde be as one,
and that euerie mã shulde leaue his lawes.

Ioseph. Anti. 12.cha.6.& 7

44 And all the heathen agreed to the commandement of the King.
45 Yea, many of the Israelites consented to
his religion, offring vnto idoles, & defiling
the Sabbath.
46 So the King sent letters by the messengers vnto Ierusalem, and to the cities of
Iuda, that they shulde followe the strange
lawes of the countrey,
47 And that they shulde forbid the burnt
offrings and sacrifices, and the " offrings in
the Sanctuarie,

" Or, drinke offrings.

48 And that they shulde defile the Sabbaths
and the feasts,
49 And pollute the Sanctuarie and the holie men,
50 And to set vp altars, & groues, & chap-
pels of idoles, & offer vp swines flesh, and
vncleane beasts,
51 And that they shulde leaue their childrẽ
vncircumcised, & defile their soules with
vnclennes, and pollute them selues, that
they might forget the Law, & change all
the ordinances,
52 And that whosoeuer wolde not do according to the commandement of the King,
shulde suffer death.
53 In like maner wrote he thorow out all his
kingdomes, and set ouerseers ouer all the
people, *for to compell them to do these things.*
54 And he commanded the cities of Iuda
to do sacrifice, citie by citie.
55 Then went many of the people vnto thẽ
by heapes, euery one that forsoke ẏ Law,
and so they committed euil in the land.
56 And they droue the Israelites into secret places, euen wheresoeuer they colde
flee for succour.
57 The fifteenth day of Casleu, in the hundreth and fiue and fortieth yere, they set
vp the abominacion of desolacion vpon
the altar, & thei buylded altars thorow out
the cities of Iuda on euerie side.
58 And before the dores of the houses, and
in the stretes they burnt incense.
59 And the bokes of the Law, which they
founde, they burnt in the fyre, and cutte in
pieces.
60 Whosoeuer had a boke of the Testament founde by him, or whosoeuer consented vnto the Law, the Kings commandement was, that they shulde put him to
death by their autoritie,
61 And they executed these things euerie
moneth vpon the people of Israel that were founde in the cities.
62 And in the fiue and twentieth day of the
moneth, they did sacrifice vpon the altar,
which was in the stead of the altar of sacrifices.
63 And according to the commandement,
they put certeine women to death, which
had caused their children to be circumcised,
64 And they hãged vp the children at their
neckes, and they spoiled their houses, and
slewe the circumcisers of them.
65 Yet were there many in Israel, which
were of courage, and determined in them
selues, that they wolde not eat vncleane
things,
66 But chose rather to suffer death, then to
be defiled with those meats: so because thei
wolde not breake the holie couenant, they
were put to death.
67 And this " tyrannie was verie sore vpon
the people of Israel.

" Or, rage.

CHAP. II.

*1 The mourning of Mattathias and his sonnes for the de-
structiō of the holy citie. 19 They refuse to do sacrifice
vnto idoles. 24 The zeale of Mattathias for the Law
of God. 33 They are slaine and wil not fight againe
because of the Sabbath day. 49 Mattathias dying
commandeth his sonnes to sticke by the worde of God,
after the example of the fathers.*

1 IN those dayes stode vp Mattathias the
Priest, *the sonne* of Ioannes, *the sonne* of
Simeon, of the sonnes of Ioarib of Ierusa-
lem, and dwelt in Modin.

Iosep. Antiq. 12.chap.7.

2 And he had fiue sonnes, Ioanan called
Gaddis,

3 Simon

3 Simon called Thaſsi,
4 Iudas which was called Maccabeus,
5 Eleazar called "Abaron, & Ionathã, whoſe
name was Apphus.
Or, Auaran.
6 Now he ſawe the blaſphemies, which
were committed in Iuda and Ieruſalem:
7 And he ſaid, Wo is me: wherefore was
I borne, to ſe this deſtruction of my people, and the deſtruction of the holy citie,
and thus to ſit ſtil? it is deliuered into the
hands of the enemies,
8 And the Sanctuarie *is* in the hands of
ſtrangers: her Temple is, as a man that
hathe no renoume.
9 Her glorious veſſels are caryed away into captiuitie: her infants are ſlayne in the
ſtretes, and her yong men are fallen by
the ſworde of the enemies.
10 What people is it, that hathe not ſome
poſſeſsion in *her* kingdome, or hathe not
gotten of her ſpoyles?
11 All her glorie is taken away: of a fre woman, ſhe is become an handmaid.
12 Beholde, our Sanctuarie & our beautie,
and honor is deſolate, and the Gentiles
haue defiled it.
13 What helpeth it vs then to liue anie longer?
14 And Mattathias rent his clothes, he, and
his ſonnes, and put ſackecloth vpon them,
and mourned verie ſore.
15 ¶ Then came men from the King to the
citie of Modin to compell them to forſake God, and to ſacrifice.
16 So manie of the Iſraelites conſented
vnto them: but Mattathias and his ſonnes
aſſembled together.
17 Then ſpake the commiſsioners of the
King, and ſaid vnto Mattathias, Thou art
the chief and an honorable man, & great
in this citie, and haſt many children and
brethren.
18 Come thou therefore firſt, and fulfil the
Kings commandement, as all the heathen
haue done, and alſo the men of Iuda, and
ſuche as remaine at Ieruſalẽ: ſo ſhalt thou
and thy familie be in the Kings fauour &
thou and thy children ſhalbe enriched
with ſiluer & golde, & w̃ manie rewards.
19 Then Mattathias anſwered & ſaid with
a loude voyce, Thogh all nacions that are
vnder the Kings dominion, obey him, and
fall away euerie man from the religion of
their fathers, and conſent to his commandements,
20 Yet wil I and my ſonnes, and my brethren, walke in yͤ couenant of our fathers.
21 God be merciful vnto vs, that we forſake
not the Law and the ordinances.
22 We wil not hearken vnto the Kings
wordes to tranſgreſſe our religion, nether
on the right ſide, nor on the left.
23 And when he had left of ſpeaking theſe
wordes, there came one of the Iewes, in
the ſight of all to ſacrifice vpon the altar
which was at Modin, according to the
Kings commandement.
24 Now when Mattathias ſawe it, he was ſo
inflamed with zeale, that his raines ſhoke,
and his wrath was kindled according to
the ordinance *of the Law*: therefore he ran
vnto him, and killed him by the altar:
25 And at the ſame time he ſlewe yͤ Kings
commiſsioner, that compelled him to do
ſacrifice, and deſtroied the altar.
26 Thus bare he a zeale to yͤ Law of God,
* *doing*, as Phinees did vnto Zambri the *Nomb.25,7.*
ſonne of Salom.
27 ¶ Then cryed Mattathias with a loude
voyce in the citie, *ſaying*, Whoſoeuer is
zealous of the Law, and wil ſtand by the
couenant, let him come forthe after me.
28 So he, and his ſonnes fled into the mountaines, & left all that thei had in the citie.
29 Then manie that " ſoght after iuſtice &
iudgement,
Or, that liued iuſtly and vprightly.
30 Went downe into yͤ wildernes to dwell
there, bothe they, and their children, and
their wiues, and their cattel: for the afflictions increaſed ſore vpon them.
31 ¶ Now whẽ it was tolde vnto the Kings
ſeruants, and to the gariſons, which were
in Ieruſalem in the citie of Dauid, that
men had broken the Kings commandement, & were gone downe into the ſecret
places in the wildernes,
32 Then many purſued after them: and hauing ouertaken them, thei camped againſt
them, and ſet the battel in array againſt
them on the Sabbath day,
33 And ſaid vnto them, Let this now be ſufficiẽt: come forthe & do according to the
commandement of the King, and ye ſhal
liue.
34 But they anſwered, We wil not go forthe, nether wil we do the Kings commandement, to defile the Sabbath day.
35 Then they gaue them the battel.
36 But the other anſwered them nothing,
nether caſt anie one ſtone at thẽ, nor ſtopped the priuie places,
37 But ſaid, We wil dye all in our innocencie: the heauen and earth ſhal teſtifie for
vs, that ye deſtroy vs wrongfully.
38 Thus thei gaue them the battel vpon the
Sabbath, and ſlewe bothe men and cattel,
their wiues and their children to the nomber of a thouſand people.
39 ¶ When Mattathias & his friends vnderſtode this, thei mourned for them greatly,
40 And ſaid one to another, If we all do as
our brethren haue done, and fight not a-
gainſt the heathen for our liues, & for our
Lawes, then ſhal thei incõtinently deſtroy
vs out of the earth.
41 Therefore they concluded at the ſame

time, sayĩg, Whosoeuer shal come to make battel with vs vpon the Sabbath daye,
we wil fight against him, that we dye not
all, as our brethren that were murthered
in the secret places.
42 Then came vnto them the assemblie of
the Asideans, which were of the strongest
men of Israel, all suche as were wel minded toward the Law.
43 And all they that were fled for persecucion, ioyned them selues vnto them, and
were an helpe vnto them.
44 So they gathered a power, and smote
the wicked men in their wrath, & the vngodlie in their angre: but the rest fled vnto the heathen, and escaped.
45 Then Mattathias and his friends went
about, and destroyed the altars,
46 And circumcised the children by force
that were vncircumcised, as manie as they
founde within the coasts of Israel,
47 And they pursued after the proude mẽ:
and this acte prospered in their hands.
48 So they recouered the Law out of the
hand of the Gentiles, & out of the hand
of Kings, and gaue not place to ẏ wicked.
49 Now when the time drewe nere, that
Mattathias shulde dye, he said vnto his
sonnes, Now is pride and persecucion increased, and the time of destruction, and
the wrath of indignacion.
50 Now therefore, my sonnes, be ye zealous of the Law, & giue your liues for the
couenant of our fathers.
51 Call to remembrance what actes our fathers did in their time: so shal ye receiue
great honour and an euerlasting name.
52 *Was not Abraham founde faithful in
tentacion, and it was imputed vnto him
for righteousnes?
53 *Ioseph in the time of his trouble kept
the commandement, & was made the lord
of Egypt.
54 *Phinees our father, because he was zealous and feruent, obteined the couenant of
the euerlasting priesthode.
55 *Iesus for fulfilling the worde, was made
the gouernour of Israel.
56 *Caleb, because he bare witnes before
the congregacion, receiued the heritage
of the land.
57 *Dauid, because of his mercie obteined
the throne of ẏ kingdome for euermore.
58 *Elias, because he was zealous and feruẽt
in ẏ Law, was taken vp euen vnto heauen.
59 *Ananias, Azarias and Misael by their
faith were deliuered out of the flame.
60 *Daniel, because of his innocencie, was
deliuered from the mouth of the lyons.
61 And thus ye may consider thorowe out
all ages, that whosoeuer put their trust in
him, shal not want strength.
62 Feare not ye then the wordes of a sinful

Gen.22,9. *Gen.41,40.* *Nomb.25,13 eccles 45,28.* *Iosh.1,2.* *Nomb.14,6. iosh.14,13.* *2.Sam.2,4.* *2.King.2,11.* *Dan.3,16.* *Dan.6,22.*

mã: for his glorie is but dongue and wormes.
63 To day is he set vp, & to morowe he shal
not be foũde: for he is turned into his dust,
and his purpose perisheth.
64 Wherefore, my sõnes, take good hearts,
and shewe your selues men for the Law:
for by it shal you obteine glorie.
65 And beholde, I knowe that your brother
Simon is a man of counsel: giue eare vnto him alway: he shalbe a father vnto you.
66 And Iudas Maccabeus hathe bene mightie and strong, euen from his youth vp: let
him be your captaine and fight you the
battel for the people.
67 Thus shal ye bring vnto you all those
that obserue the Law, & shal aduenge the
iniuries of your people.
68 Recompense fully the heathen, and giue
your selues to the commandement of the
Law.
69 So he blessed them, and was laied with
his fathers,
70 And dyed in the hundreth, fortie & six
yere, and his sonnes buryed him in his fathers sepulchre at Modin, & all Israel made great lamentacion for him.

CHAP. III.

1 Iudas is made ruler ouer the Iewes. 11 He killeth Apollonius & Seron the princes of Syria. 44 The confidence of Iudas towarde God. 55 Iudas determineth to fight against Lysias, whome Antiochus had made captaine ouer his hoste.

1 THen Iudas his sonne, called Maccabeus, rose vp in his place.
2 And all his brethren helped him, and all
they that helde with his father, and foght
with courage the battel of Israel.
3 So he gate his people great honour: he put
on a brestplate as a gyant, and armed him
self, and set the battel in array, and defended the campe with the sworde.
4 In his actes he was like a lyon, and as a
lyons whelpe roaring after the pray.
5 For he pursued the wicked, & soght them
out, & burnt vp those that vexed his people,
6 So that the wicked fled for feare of him,
and all the workers of iniquitie were put
to trouble: and saluacion prospered in his
hand.
7 And he grieued diuers Kings, but Iacob
reioyced by his actes, and his memorial is
blessed for euer.
8 He went also thorowe the cities of Iuda, and destroyed the wicked out of them,
and turned away the wrath from Israel.
9 So was he renoumed vnto the ends of the
earth, and he assembled together those
that were readie to perish.
10 ¶But [a] Apollonius gathered the Gentiles, and a great hoste out of Samaria, to
fight against Israel.

a Who was gouernour of Syria. Ioseph Antiq.12. chap.9.

11 Which

11 Which when Iudas perceiued, he went
forthe to mete him, and smote him, & slue
him, so that many fel downe slaine, & the
rest fled.
12 So Iudas toke their spoiles, and toke also
Apollonius sworde, and soght with it all
his life long.
13 ¶ Now whē Seron a prince of ỹ armie of
Syria, heard that Iudas had gathered vnto
him the congregacion, and Church of the
faithful, and went forthe to the warre,
14 He said, I wil get me a name, and wil be
glorious in the realme: for I wil go fight
with Iudas, & thē that are with him, which
haue despised the Kings commandement.
15 So he made him readie to go vp, and there went with him a mightie hoste of the
vngodlie to helpe him, & to be auenged
of the children of Israel.
16 And when he came nere to the going vp
of Bethhoron, Iudas went forthe to mete
him with a smale companie.
17 But when they sawe the armie coming a-
gainst them, they said to Iudas, How are
we able, being so fewe, to fight against so
great a multitude, & so strong, seing we be
so wearie, and haue fasted all this day?
18 Then said Iudas, It is an easie thing for
many to be shut vp in the hands of fewe,
and there is no difference before *the God* of
heauen, to deliuer by a great multitude, or
by a smale companie.
19 For the victorie of the battel stādeth not
in the multitude of ỹ hoste, but the strēgth
cometh from heauen.
20 They come against vs with a cruel and
proude multitude, to destroy vs, and our
wiues, and our children, and to robbe vs.
21 But we do fight for our liues, and for our
Lawes,
22 And God him self wil destroie thē befo-
fore our face: therefore be not ye afraied
of them.
23 And whē he had left of speaking, he lept
suddenly vpon them: so was Seron and
his hoste destroied before him.
24 And they pursued them from the going
downe of Bethhorō vnto the plaine: where there were slaine eight hundreth men of
them, and the residue fled into the land of
the Philistims.
25 Then the feare & terrour of Iudas & his
brethrē fel vpon the naciōs rounde about,
26 So that his fame came vnto the King:
for all the Gentiles colde tell of the warres of Iudas.
27 ¶ But when King Antiochus heard these
tidings, he was angrie in his minde: wherefore he sent forthe, & gathered all ỹ power
of his realme a very strong armie,
28 And opened his treasurie, and gaue his
hoste a yeres wages in hand, commanding
thē to be readie for a yere for all occasiōs.
29 Neuertheles, when he sawe that the money of his treasures failed, & that the tribu
tes in the countrey were smale, because of
the dissencion, & plagues ỹ he had broght
vpon the land, in taking away the lawes
which had bene of olde time,
30 He feared lest he shulde not haue now
at the seconde time, as at the first, for the
charges & giftes that he had giuē with a li
beral hand afore: for in liberalitie he farre
passed the other Kings ỹ were before him.
31 Wherefore he was heauie in his minde,
and thoght to go into Persia, for to take
tributes of the countreis, and to gather
muche money.
32 So he left Lysias a noble man and of the
Kings blood to ouerse the Kings busines,
from the riuer of Euphrates vnto the borders of Egypt,
33 And to bring vp his sonne Antiochus, til
he came againe.
34 Moreouer, he gaue him halfe of his hoste
and elephantes, & gaue him the charge of
all things that he wolde haue done,
35 And concerning those which dwelt in Iu
da and Ierusalem, that he shulde send an
armie against them, to destroy and roote
out the power of Israel & the remnant of
Ierusalem, and to put out their memorial
from that place,
36 And to set strangers for to inhabite all
their quarters, & parte their lād amōg thē.
37 And the King toke the halfe of the hoste that remained, & departed from Antio
chia his royal citie, in the yere an hūdreth
fortie and seuen, and passed the riuer Euphrates, & went thorow the hie countreis.
38 Then Lysias chose Ptolemeus the sonne
of Doriminus, & Nicanor, and Gorgias,
mightie men, and the Kings friends,
39 And sent with them fortie thousand fote
men, & seuen thousand horsemen, to go into the land of Iuda, & to destroie it, as the
King commanded.
40 So they wēt forthe with all their power
and came and pitched by ‖ Emmaus in the ‖ Emmaus.
plaine countrey.
41 Now when the marchants of the countrey heard the rumour of them, they toke
very muche siluer & golde, & seruants, &
came into the campe to bye the childrē of
Israel for sclaues, & the strength of Syria
& of strange nacions ioyned with them.
42 ¶ Now when Iudas & his brethren sawe
that trouble increased, and that the hoste
drewe nere vnto their borders, cōsidering
the Kings wordes, whereby he had commanded to destroy the people, and vtterly abolish them,
43 They said one to another, Let vs redresse the decay of our people, and let vs fight
for our people, and for our Sanctuarie.
44 Then the cōgregaciō were sone readie

gathered to fight, and to praye, and to desire mercie and compassion.

45 As for Ierusalem, it was not inhabited, but was as a wildernes. There went none that was borne in it, in or out at it, and the Sanctuarie was troden downe, and the strangers kept the fortresse, and it was the habitacion of the heathen: & the mirth of Iacob was taken away: the pipe and the harpe ceased.

46 So they gathered them selues together, and came to Maspha before Ierusalem: for in Maspha was ŷ place where they praied afore time in Israel.

47 And they fasted that day, and put sackecloth vpon them, and cast ashes vpon their heads, and rent their clothes,

48 And opened the boke of the Law, wherein the heathẽ soght to paint the lickenes of their idoles,

49 And broght the Priests garments, and the first frutes, and the tithes, and set there the Nazarites, which accomplished their daies.

50 And they cryed with a loude voyce, towarde heauen, saying, What shal we do with these? and whether shal we carye them away?

51 For thy Sanctuarie is troden downe and defiled, and thy Priests are in heauines, & broght downe.

52 And beholde, the heathẽ are come against vs to destroie vs: thou knowest what thĩgs they imagine against vs.

53 How can we stand before them, except thou helpe vs?

54 Then they blewe the trumpets, & cryed with a loude voyce.

55 And after this Iudas ordeined captaines ouer the people, euen captaines ouer thousands, and captaines ouer hundreths, and captaines ouer fifties, and captaines ouer ten.

56 And they cõmanded them that buylded houses, or maried wiues, or planted vineyardes, or were fearful, that thei shulde returne euerie one to his owne house, according* to the Law. *Deut.20,5. iud.7,3.*

57 So the hoste remoued, and pitched vpon the Southside of Emmaus.

58 And Iudas said, Arme your selues, and be valiant men, & be readie against the morning to fight with these naciõs, which are gathered together against vs, to destroie vs and our Sanctuarie.

59 For it is better for vs to dye in battel, then to se the calamities of our people & of our Sanctuarie.

60 Neuertheles as the wil of *God* is in heauen, so be it.

CHAP. IIII.

1 Iudas goeth against Gorgias which lieth in wait. 14 He putteth Gorgias and his hoste to flight 28 Lysias inuadeth Iudea, 29 But Iudas driueth him out. 43 Iudas purifieth the Temple and dedicateth the altar.

1 THen toke Gorgias fiue thousand fote men, and a thousand of the best horsemen, and departed out of the campe by night, *Ioseph lib.12. chap.10.*

2 To inuade the campe of the Iewes, and to slaye thẽ suddenly: and the men of the fortresse were his guides.

3 Now when Iudas heard it, he remoued, & they that were valiant men to smite the Kings armie which was at Emmaus,

4 Whiles yet the armie was dispersed frõ the campe.

5 In the meane season came Gorgias by night into Iudas campe: & when he founde no man there, he soght thẽ in the mountaines: for said he, They flee from vs.

6 But assone as it was day, Iudas shewed him self in the field with thre thousand mẽ, which had nether harnes nor swordes to their mindes.

7 And thei sawe that the armies of the heathen were strong and wel armed, and their horsemen about them, and that these were experte men of warre.

8 Then said Iudas to the mẽ that were with him, Feare ye not their multitude, nether be afraied of their assalt.

9 Remember, how our fathers were deliuered* in the red Sea, when Pharao pursued them with an armie. *Exod.14,9.*

10 Therefore now let vs crye vnto heauen, and the Lord wil haue mercie vpon vs, & remember the couenant of our fathers, & wil destroie this hoste before our face this day:

11 So shal all the heathen knowe, that there is one, which deliuereth and saueth Israel.

12 Then the strangers lift vp their eyes, & sawe them coming against them,

13 And they went out of their tẽtes into the battel, and they that were with Iudas, blew the trumpets.

14 So they ioyned together, and the heathẽ were discomfited and fled by the plaine.

15 But the hinmoste of thẽ fel by the sworde, and they pursued them vnto " Gazerõ, and into the plaines of Idumea, and of Azotus, and of Iamnia, so that there were slaine of them about thre thousand men. *"Or, Assaremoth*

16 So Iudas turned againe with his hoste frõ pursuing them,

17 And said vnto the people, Be not griedie of the spoiles: for there is a battel before vs.

18 And Gorgias and the armie is here by vs in the mountaine: but stand ye now fast against your enemies, and ouercome them: then may ye safely take the spoiles.

19 As Iudas was speaking these wordes, there appeared one parte which loked from the

the mountaines.
20 But when *Gorgias* sawe that his were fled,
and that Iudas soldiers burnt the tentes:
(for the smoke that was sene,declared what
was done.)
21 When they sawe these things,they were
sore afraied, and when they sawe also that
Iudas and his hoste were in the field readie
to set them selues in array,
22 They fled euerie one into the land of
strangers.
23 So Iudas turned againe to spoile the tentes,where he gate muche golde and siluer,
and precious stones,and purple of the sea,
and great riches.
24 Thus they went home, and sang psalmes, and praised towarde the heauen : for
he is gracious, and his mercie endureth
for euer.
25 And so Israel had a great victorie in that
day.
26 ¶ Now all the strangers that escaped,ca-
me,& tolde Lysias all the things that were done.
27 Who when he heard these things,was sore afraied,and discouraged, because suche
things came not vpon Israel as he wolde,
nether suche things as the King had commanded him,came to passe.
28 Therefore the next yere following, gathered Lysias thre score thousande chosen
fote men, and fiue thousande horsemen to
fight against Ierusalem.
29 So they came into ᵃIdumea,and pitched
their tentes at ᵇBeth-sura, where Iudas came against them with ten thousand men.
30 And whē he sawe that mightie armie,he
praied and said,Blessed be thou,ô Sauiour
of Israel,*which didest destroie the assalte
of ẏ mightie man by the hād of thy seruāt
Dauid, *& gauest the hoste of the strāgers
into the hād of Ionathan,ẏ sonne of Saul,
and of his armour bearer:
31 Shut vp this armie in ẏ hand of thy people of Israel,& let thē be confounded with
their power,and with their horsemen.
32 Make them afraied, and consume their
boldenes & strength,that thei may be astonished at their destruction.
33 Cast them downe by the sworde of them
that loue thee:thē shal all thei that knowe
thy Name,praise thee with songs.
34 So they ioyned together,and there were
slaine of Lysias hoste, fiue thousand men,
and they fell before them.
35 Thē Lysias,seing his armie put to flight
and the manlines of Iudas soldiers, and
that they were readie,either to liue or dye
valiantly,he went into Antiochia,and gathered strangers, and when he had furnished his armie, he thoght againe (being
prepared)to come against Iudea.
36 Then said Iudas & his brethrē,Beholde,
our enemies are discomfited: let vs now
go vp to clense, and to repaire the Sanctuarie.
37 So all the hoste gathered them together,
and went vp into the mountaine of Sion.
38 Now whē they sawe the Sanctuarie layed waste,and the altar defiled,and the dores burnt vp,and the shrubbes growing in
the courtes, as in a forest,or as on one of
the mountaines, and that the Priests chābers were broken downe,
39 They rent their clothes, and made great
lamentation, and cast ashes vpon their
heads,
40 And fel downe to the grounde on their
faces,and blewe an alarme with the trumpets,and cryed towarde heauen.
41 Then Iudas commanded certeine of the
men to fight against those which were in ẏ
castel,til he had clensed the Sanctuarie.
42 So he chose Priests that were vndefiled,
suche as delited in the Law,
43 And they clensed the Sāctuarie, and bare out the defiled stones into an vncleane
place,
44 And consulted what to do with the altar of burnt offrings, which was polluted.
45 So they thoght it was best to destroie it,
lest it shulde be a reproche vnto them,be-
cause the heathen had defiled it : therefore they destroyed the altar,
46 And layed vp the stones vpon the moūtaine of the Temple in a conuenient place, til there shulde come a Prophet, to
shewe what shulde be done with them.
47 So they toke whole stones according
to the Law, and buylded a new altar accor
ding to the former,
48 And made vp the Sanctuarie, and the
things that were within the Temple, and
the courts,and all things.
49 They made also new holie vessels, and
broght into the Temple the candelsticke,
and the altar of burnt offrings, and of incense and the table.
50 And they burnt incense vpō the altar,&
lighted the lampes which were vpon the
candelsticke, that they might burne in the
Temple.
51 Thei set also the shewbread vpon the table,and hanged vp the vailes,and finished
all the workes that they had begon to
make.
52 And vpon the fiue and twentieth day of
the ninth moneth, which is called the moneth of Chaslu, in the hundreth and eight
and fortieth yere they rose vp betimes in
the morning,
53 And offred sacrifice according to the
Law, vpō the new altar of burnt offrings,
that they had made.
54 According to the time,and according to
the day,that the heathen had defiled it, in

ᵃ Or, Iudea.
ᵇ Or, Bethhoron.
1 Sam.17,50.
1 Sam.14,13.

the same day was it made new with songs, and harpes, and lutes, and cymbales.
55 And all the people fel vpon their faces, worshipping & praising towarde the heauen him that had giuen thẽ good successe.
56 So they kept the dedicacion of the altar eight daies, offring burnt offrings with gladnes, & offred sacrifices of deliuerance and praise,
57 And decte the forefronte of the Temple with crownes of golde and shields, & dedicated the gates and chambers, & hanged dores vpon them.
58 Thus there was very great gladnes amõg the people, and the reproche of the heathen was put away.
59 So Iudas and his brethren with the whole cõgregacion of Israel ordeined that the daies of dedicacion of the altar shulde be kept in their season from yere to yere, by the space of eight daies, from the fiue and twentie day of the moneth Chasleu, with mirth and gladnes.
60 And at the same time buylded they vp mount Sion with hie walles and strong towers rounde about, lest the Gentiles shulde come, and treade it downe, as they had done afore.
61 Therefore they set a garison there to kepe it, & fortified Beth-sura to kepe it, that the people might haue a defense against Idumea.

CHAP. V.

3 Iudas vanquished the heathen that go about to destroie Israel, & is holpen of his brethren Simon and Ionathan 50 He ouerthroweth the citie of Ephron, because they denyed him passage thorowe it.

1 NOw when the nacions rounde about heard, that the altar was buylded, & the Sanctuarie renued, as afore, they were sore grieued.
2 Therefore they thoght to destroie the generacion of Iacob that was among them, and begãne to slaye and destroy the people.
3 Then Iudas foght against the children of Esau in Idumea at "Arrabathene, because they besieged the Israelites, and he smote them with a great plague, and droue them to straites, and toke their spoiles.

"Or, Arrabathane.

4 He thoght also vpõ the malice of the children of Bean, which had bene a snare and an hinderance vnto the people, when they laye in waite for them in the hie way.
5 Wherefore he shut them vp in towers, and besieged them, and destroied them vtterly, and burnt their towers with fyre, with all that were in them.
6 Afterward, went he against the children of Ammon, where he founde a mightie power, and a great multitude with Timotheus their captaine.
7 So he had manie battels with them, but they were destroyed before him, and so he discomfited them,
8 And toke Gazer with the townes thereof, and so turned againe into Iudea.
9 ¶ Then the heathen that were in Galaad, gathered them together against the Israelites that were in their quarters, to slay them: but they fled to the castel of Datheman,
10 And sent letters to Iudas, and to his brethren, saying, The heathen that are about vs, are gathered against vs, to destroye vs,
11 And they make them readie for to come, and to take the fortresse, whereunto we are fled, and Timotheus is captaine of their hoste.
12 Come now therefore, and deliuer vs out of their hands: for manie of vs are slaine:
13 And all our brethrẽ that were at Tubin, are slaine, and they haue taken away their wiues, and their children, and their goods, and destroyed there almoste a thousand men.
14 While these letters were yet a reading, beholde, there came other messengers frõ Galile with their clothes rẽt, which tolde the same tidings,
15 And said, that they of Ptolemais, and of Tyrus, and of Sidon, and of all Galile of the Gentiles were gathered against them to destroye them.
16 When Iudas, and the people heard these wordes, a great Congregacion came together, to cõsulte what they might do for their brethrẽ, that were in trouble, & whome they besieged.
17 Then said Iudas to Simon his brother, Chuse thee out men, and go & deliuer thy brethren in Galile, and I and my brother Ionathan, wil go into the countrey of Galaad.
18 ¶ So he left Iosephus the sonne of Zacharias, and Azarias to be captaines of the people, and to kepe the remnant of the hoste in Iudea,
19 And commanded them, saying, Take the ouersight of this people, and make no warre against the heathen, vntil we come againe.
20 And vnto Simon were giuen thre thousand men to go into Galile, and to Iudas eight thousand men for the countrey of Galaad.
21 Then went Simon into Galile, and gaue diuers battels to the heathen, and the heathen were discomfited by him.
22 And he pursued them vnto the gates of Ptolemais: & there were slaine of the heathen almoste thre thousand men: so he toke their spoiles.
23 Thus they rescued them that were in Galile

lile and in Arbattis with their wiues, and
their children, and all that they had, and
broght them into Iudea with great ioye.
24 ¶Iudas Maccabeus also, and his brother
Ionathan went ouer Iorden, and trauailed
thre dayes iourney in the wildernes,
25 Where they met with the Nabathites,
who receiued them louingly, & tolde thẽ
euerie thing that was done vnto their bre
thren in the countrey of Galaad,
26 And how that manie of them were besieged in Bosorra, & Bosor, in Alemis, 'Chas-
bon, Maged and Carnaim (all these cities
are strong, and great)

Or, Chasphor.

27 And that they were kept in other cities
of Galaad, and to morow they are appoin
ted to bring their hoste vnto these fortes,
and to take them, and to destroye them all
in one day.
28 So Iudas & his hoste turned in all haste
by the way of the wildernes towarde Bosorra, and wan the citie, and slewe all the
males with the edge of the sworde, and toke all their spoile, and set fyre vpõ *the citie*.
29 And in the night he remoued from thence, and went towarde the fortresse.
30 And betimes in the morning when thei
loked vp, beholde, there was an innumerable people bearing ladders, and instruments of warre, to take the forte, and had
assalted them.
31 When Iudas sawe that the battel was
begon, and that the crye of the citie went
vp to heauen with trumpets, and a great
sounde,
32 Then he said vnto the armie, Fight this
day for your brethren.
33 So he wẽt forthe behinde them with thre
companies, and they blew the trumpets, &
cryed with prayer.
34 Then the hoste of Timotheus knewe,
that it was Maccabeus, and they fled from
him, & he smote them with a great slaughter, so that there was killed of them the same day, almoste eight thousand men.
35 ¶Then departed Iudas vnto Maspha, &
laid siege vnto it, and wanne it, and slewe
all the males thereof, and spoiled it, and
set fyre vpon it.
36 From thence went he and toke Chasbõ,
Maged, and Bosor, and the other cities in
Galaad.
37 After these things gathered Timotheus
another hoste, and he camped before Ra-
phon beyonde the flood.
38 Now Iudas had sent to espie the hoste,
& they broght him worde againe, saying,
All the heathen that be rounde about vs,
are gathered vnto him, and the hoste is ve
rie great,
39 And he hathe hyred the Arabians to hel
pe them, and they haue pitched their tentes beionde the flood, & are readie to come
and fight against thee. So Iudas went to
mete them.
40 Then Timotheus said vnto the captaines of his hoste, When Iudas and his hoste come nere the flood, if he passe ouer
first vnto vs, we shal not be able to withstand him: for he wil be to strong for vs.
41 But if he be afraid, and campe beyonde
the flood, we wil go ouer vnto him, and
shal preuaile against him.
42 Now whẽ Iudas came nere to the flood,
he caused the gouernours of the people to
remaine by the flood, and commãded thẽ,
saying, Suffer none to pitche a tent, but let
euerie man come to the battel.
43 So he went first ouer towarde them, and
all people after him: and all the heathen
were discomfited before him, & cast away
their weapons, and fled into the temple
that was at Carnaim.
44 Which citie Iudas wanne, and burnt the
temple with all that were in it: so was Car
naim subdued, and might not withstand
Iudas.
45 ¶Then Iudas gathered all the Israelites
that were in the countrey of Galaad, from
the least vnto the moste, with their wiues and their children, and their baggage,
a verie great hoste, to come into the lãd
of Iuda.
46 So they came vnto Ephron, which was a
great citie by the way, and strongly defensed: they colde not passe, nether at the
right hand nor at the left, but must go
thorowe it.
47 But they that were in the citie, shut thẽ
selues in, and stopped vp the gates with
stones: and Iudas sent vnto them with pea
ceable wordes, saying,
48 Let vs passe thorowe your land, that we
may go into our owne countrey, and none
shal hurt you: we wil but onely go thorowe on fote: but they wolde not open
vnto him.
49 Wherefore Iudas commanded a procla
macion to be made thorowe out the hoste, that euerie man shulde assalt it according to his standing.
50 So the valiant men set vpon it, and assalted the citie all that day, and all that
night, and the citie was giuen ouer into
his hands:
51 Who slewe all the males with the edge
of the sworde, and destroyed it, and toke
the spoile thereof, and went thorowe the
citie ouer them that were slaine.
52 Then went they ouer Iorden into the
great plaine before Bethsan.
53 And Iudas gathered together those that
were behinde, and gaue the people good
exhortation all the way thorowe, til they
were come into the land of Iuda.
54 Thus they went vp with ioye, and glad-

nes vnto mount Sion, where they offred
burnt offrings, because there were none of
them slaine, but came home againe in
safetie.
55 ¶Now whiles Iudas and Ionathan were
in the land of Galaad, and Simon their
brother in Galile before Ptolemais,
56 Ioseph the sonne of Zacharias, and Aza
rias the captaines, hearing of the valiant
actes, and battels which they had achi-
ued, said,
57 Let vs get vs a name also, and go fight
against the heathen that are round a-
bout vs.
58 So they gaue their hoste a commandement
ment and went towarde Iamnia.
59 But Gorgias and his men came out of
the citie to fight against them.
60 And Ioseph and Azarias were put to
flight and pursued vnto the borders of Iu
dea: and there were slaine that day of the
people of Israel about two thousand men:
so ỳ there was a great ouerthrowe among
the people of Israel,
61 Because they were not obedient vnto Iu
das, and his brethrẽ, but thoght to do some
valiant thing.
62 Also they came not of the stocke of these men, by whose hands deliuerãce was giuen to Israel.
63 But the man Iudas, and his brethren
were greatly commended in the sight of
all Israel, and of all the heathen, wheresoeuer their name was heard of.
64 And the people came vnto them, bidding them welcome.
65 Afterwarde went Iudas forthe with his
brethren, and foght against the children
of Esau in the lãd toward the South, where
he wanne Hebron, and the townes thereof,
& he destroyed the castel thereof, & burnt
the towres thereof round about.
66 Then remoued he to go into the land of
the "strangers, and went thorow Samaria.
67 At the same time were the Priests of the
cities slaine in ỳ battel, which wolde shewe
their valiantnes, and went forthe to battel
without counsel: and when Iudas came to
Azotus in the strangers lãd, he brake downe their altars, and burnt with fyre the ima
ges of their gods, and toke away the spoiles of the cities, and came againe into the
land of Iuda.

Ioseph Antiq. 12. chap. 11 & 12.

"Or, Philistims.

CHAP. VI.

3 Antiochus, willing to take the citie of Elimais, is driuen away of the citizens. 8 He falleth into sickenes, and dyeth. 17 His sonne Antiochus is made King. 34 The maner to prouoke elephantes to fight. 43 Eleazarus valiant acte. 49 The siege of Sion.

Ioseph Anti. 12. chap. 13.

1 NOw when King Antiochus trauailed thorow the high countreis, he
heard that Elimais in the countrey of Persia was a citie greatly renoumed for riches,
siluer and golde,
2 And that there was in it a verie riche tẽple, where as were couerings of golde, cote
armoures, and harnes, which Alexandre
Kĩg of Macedonia the sonne of Philippe
(ỳ reigned first in Grecia) had left there.
3 Wherefore he went about to take the citie, and to spoile it, but he was not able:
for ỳ citizens were warned of the matter,
4 And rose vp against him in battel, & he
fled and departed thence with great heauines, and came againe into Babylon.
5 Moreouer, there came one which broght
him tidings in the coũtrey of Persia, that
the armies that went against the land of
Iuda, were driuen away,
6 And that Lysias, which went forthe first
with a great power, was driuen away of the
Iewes, and that they were made strong by
the armour, and power, and diuers spoyles
which they had gotten of the armies whome they had destroyed,
7 And that they had pulled downe the abominacion, which he had set vp vpon the
altar at Ierusalem, and fensed the Sãctuarie with high walles, as it was afore, and
Beth-sura his citie.
8 So when the King had heard these wordes, he was astonished, and sore moued:
therefore he laid him downe vpõ his bed,
& fel sicke for verie sorowe, because it was
not come to passe, as he had thoght.
9 And there continued he manie dayes: for
his grief was euer more & more, so that he
sawe he must nedes dye.
10 Therefore he sent for all his friends, &
said vnto them, The slepe is gone from
mine eyes, and mine heart faileth for verie care.
11 And I thinke with my self, Into what
aduersitie am I come? & into what floods
of miserie am I fallen now, where as afore
time I was in prosperitie, and greatly set
by, by reason of my power?
12 And now do I remember the euils that
I haue done at Ierusalem: for I toke all
the vessels of golde & of siluer that were
in it, and sent to destroye the inhabitants
of Iuda without cause.
13 I knowe that these troubles are come vpon me for the same cause, and beholde,
I must dye with great sorowe in a strange land.
14 Then called he for Philippe, one of his
friends, whome he made ruler of all his
realme,
15 And gaue him the crowne, and his robe,
and the ring, that he shulde instruct his
sonne Antiochus, and bring him vp, til he
might reigne him self.
16 So King Antiochus dyed there in the
hundreth, and fortie and ninth yere.
17 ¶When Lysias knewe, that the King
was

Ioseph Antiq.12.chap.14.

was dead, he ordeined Antiochus his sonne (whome he had broght vp) to reigne in
his fathers stead, and called him Eupator.
18 Now they that were in the castle *at Ierusalem*, kept in the Israelites rounde about
the Sanctuarie, and soght alwaies their
hurt, and the strengthening of ye heathen.
19 Therefore Iudas thoght to destroy thẽ,
& called all the people together to besiege them.
20 So they came together, and besieged thẽ
in the hundreth and fiftie yere, and made
instruments to shoote and other engins of
warre.
21 But certeine of them that were besieged,
gate forthe, (vnto whome some vngodlie
men of Israel ioyned them selues.)
22 And they went vnto the King, saying,
How long wilt thou cease from executing
iudgement, and auenge our brethren?
23 We haue bene readie to serue thy father,
& to go forwarde in those things, that he
appointed, & to obey his commandemẽts.
24 Therefore they of our nacions fel from
vs for this cause, and wheresoeuer they
founde anie of vs, they slewe them, and
spoyled our inheritance.
25 And thei haue not onely laied hand vpon vs, but vpon all about their borders.
26 And beholde, this day are they besiegig
the castle at Ierusalem to take it, and haue
fortified the Sanctuarie, and Beth-sura.
27 And if thou doest not preuent thẽ quickely, thei wil do greater things then these,
and thou shalt not be able to ouercome
them.
28 When the King heard this, he was verie angrie, and called all his friends, the
captaines of his armie, and his horsemen,
29 And bandes that were hired, came vnto
him frõ the Kings, that were confederate,
and from the yles of the sea.
30 So the nomber of his armie was an hundreth thousand fote men, & twentie thousand horsemen, and two and thirtie elephantes exercised in battel.
31 These came through Idumea and drewe
nere to Beth-sura, and besieged it a long
season, and made engins of warre: but thei
came out, and burnt them with fyre, and
foght valiantly.
32 Then departed Iudas from the castle, &
remoued the hoste towarde Beth-zacarias
ouer against the Kings campe.
33 So the King arose verie earely, & broght
the armie and his power towarde the way
of Beth-zacarias, where the armies set thẽ
selues in array to the battel, and blewe the
trumpets.
34 And to prouoke the elephantes for to
fight, thei shewed thẽ the blood of grapes
and mulberies,
35 And they set the beasts according to the
ranges: so that by euerie elephant there
stode a thousand men armed with coates
of maile and helmets of brasse vpõ their
heads, and vnto euerie beast were ordeined fiue hundreth horsemen of the best,
36 Which were readie at all times wheresoeuer the beast was: and whethersoeuer
the beast went, they went also, and departed not from him.
37 And vpon them were strong towres of
wood that couered euerie beast, which
were fastened thereon with instruments, &
vpon euerie one was two and thirtie men,
that foght in them, and the Indian that
ruled him.
38 They set also the remnant of the horsemen vpon bothe the sides in two wings of
the hoste to stirre them vp, and to kepe
them in the valleis.
39 And when the sunne shone vpon the
golden shields, the mountaines glistered
therewith, and gaue light as lãpes of fyre.
40 Thus parte of the Kings armie was
spred vpon the hie mountaines, and parte
beneth: so they marched forwarde warely
and in order.
41 And all they that heard the noyce of
their multitude, and the marching of the
companie, and the ratteling of the harnes,
were astonished: for the armie was verie
great and mightie.
42 Then Iudas and his hoste entred into
the battel, & thei slewe six hundreth men
of the Kings armie.
43 ¶ Now when Eleazar, *the sonne* of "Abaron, sawe one of the elephãtes armed with Or, Saura.
royal harnes, and was more excellent then
all ye other beasts, he thoght that the King
shulde be vpon him.
44 Wherefore he ieoparded him self to deliuer his people, and to get him a perpetual name,
45 And ranne boldely vnto him through
the middes of the hoste, slaying on the
right hand, and on the left, so that thei departed away on bothe sides.
46 So went he to the elephantes fete, and
gate him vnder him, and slewe him: then
fel the elephant downe vpon him, & there
he dyed.
47 But *the other*, seing the power of ye King
and the fiercenes of his armie, departed
from them.
48 ¶ And the Kings armie went vp to mete
them towarde Ierusalem, and the King
pitched his tents in Iudea towarde mount
Sion.
49 Moreouer, the King toke truce with thẽ
that were in Beth-sura: but when they came out of the citie, because they had no
vitailes there, and were shut vp therein, &
the land had rested,
50 The King toke Beth-sura, and set there

a garison to kepe it,
51 And besieged the Sanctuarie many dayes,& made instruments to shoote,& other
engins of warre, and instruments to cast
fyre and stones, and pieces to cast dartes
and slings.
52 "Thei also made engins against their engins,and foght a long season.
53 But in the garners there were no vitailes:
for it was the seuenth yere, and then they
that were in Iudea, & were deliuered from
the Gentiles, had eaten vp the residue of
the store,
54 So that in the Sanctuarie were fewe men
left: for the famine came so vpon thẽ,that
they were scattered euerie mã to his owne
place.
55 ¶ Now when Lysias heard that Philippe
(whome Antiochus the King, whiles he
liued, had ordeined to bring vp Antiochus his sonne,that he might be King)
56 Was come againe out of Persia,& Media, and the Kings hoste with him, and
thoght to take vnto him the rule of thĩgs,
57 He *and his* hasted, and were stirred forwarde by them in the castel to go and tell
the King, and the captaines of the hoste,
and to others, *saying*, We decrease dayly,
& our vitailes are but smale:and the place
that we laye siege vnto,is strong, and the
affaires of the realme depende vpon vs.
58 Now therefore let vs "agre with these
men, & take truce with them, and with all
their nacion,
59 And grãte them to liue after their Law,
as they did afore:for they be grieued,and
do all these things,because we haue broken
their Lawes.
60 So the King and the princes were content,and sent vnto them to make peace,&
they receiued it.
61 When the King & the princes had made an othe vnto them, they came vpõ this
out of the fortresse.
62 And the King went vp to mount Sion:
but when he sawe that the place was wel
defensed, he brake his othe that he had
made, and commanded to breake downe
the wall rounde about.
63 Then departed he in all haste, and returned vnto Antiochia where he founde
Philippe hauing dominion of the citie: so
he foght against him, and toke the citie
by force.

"Or, the Iewes.

"Or, giue hands.

CHAP. VII.

1 Demetrius reigned, after he had killed Antiochus and Lysias. 5 He troubleth the children of Israel thorowe the counsel of certeine wicked persones. 37 The praier of the Priests against Nicanor. 41 Iudas killeth Nicanor, after he had made his praier.

1 IN the hundreth and one and fiftieth
yere, departed Demetrius the sonne of
Seleucus from Rome, and came vp with a
fewe men vnto a citie of the sea coast,and
reigned there.
2 And when he came into the possession of
his fathers kĩgdome, his soldiers toke Antiochus and Lysias,and broght them vnto
him.
3 But when it was tolde him,he said, Shewe
me not their faces.
4 So thei put thẽ to death. Now when Demetrius was set vpon the throne of his
kingdome,
5 There came vnto him all the wicked and
vngodlie men of Israel, whose captaine
was Alcimus,that wolde haue bene the hie
Priest.
6 These men accused the people vnto the
King,saying,Iudas and his brethren haue
slayne all thy friends, and driuen vs out
of our owne land.
7 Wherefore send now some man,whome
thou trustest, that he maye go and se all
the destruction,which he hathe done vnto
vs,and to the Kings land,and let him punish them with all their partakers.
8 Then the King chose Bacchides a friẽd
of his,which was a great man in the realme,and ruled beyonde the flood, and was
faithful vnto the King,and sent him,
9 And that wicked Alcimus,whome he made hie Priest, and commanded him to be
auenged of the children of Israel.
10 So they departed,and came with a great
hoste into the land of Iuda, and sent messengers to Iudas and his brethren, deceitfully with peaceable wordes.
11 But they beleued not their saying: for
thei sawe that they were come with a great
hoste.
12 Then a companie of the gouernours assembled vnto Alcimus and Bacchides to
intreat of reasonable points.
13 And the "Asideans were the first that
required peace among the children of Israel.
14 For said they, He that is a Priest of the
sede of Aarõ,is come with this armie:therefore he wil not hurt vs.
15 Then he spake vnto them peaceably,and
swore vnto them,and said,We wil do you
no harme,nether your friends:
16 And they beleued him: but he toke of thẽ
thre score men,and slewe them in one day
according to the wordes that were writen.
17 *Thei haue *cast* ỹ bodies of thy Saintes,
and their blood rounde about Ierusalem, and there was no man that wolde burye them.
18 So there came a feare and trembling among all the people: for they said, There
is nether trueth nor righteousnes in them:
for they haue broken the appointment &
othe that they made.
19 Thẽ Bacchides remoued frõ Ierusalem,
and

Ioseph Antiq.12.chap.5

"Or, Hasidims.

*Psal 79,2.

"Or, Bethseth, or, Bezeth.

& pitched his tente at" Beth-zecha, where
he sent forthe & toke manie of the mē that
had forsaken him, & certeine of the people
whome he slewe & *cast* into the great pit.
20 Then committed he the countrey vnto
Alcimus, & left men of warre with him to
helpe him: so Bacchides wēt vnto ẏ King.
21 Thus Alcimus stroue for ẏ priesthode.
22 And all suche as troubled the people
resorted vnto him: in somuche, that they
obteined the land of Iuda, and did muche
hurt in Israel.
23 Now when Iudas sawe all the mischief,
that Alcimus and his companie had dene
amōg the Israelites more then the heathē,
24 He went forthe rounde about all the
borders of Iudea, and punished those, that
were fallen away, so that they came no
more abroade in the countrey.
25 But when Alcimus sawe that Iudas & his
people had goten the vpper hād, & knewe
that he was not able to abide them, he
went againe to the King, and accused thē
of wicked things.
26 Then the King sent Nicanor one of his
chief princes, which hated Israel deadly, &
commanded him, that he shulde destroye
the people.

Ioseph Anti. 12. chap. 16.

27 ¶ So Nicanor came to Ierusalem with
a great hoste, and sent vnto Iudas, and
his brethren deceitfully with friendlie
wordes, saying,
28 Let there be no warre betwene me, and
you: I wil come with fewe men, to se how
ye do, friendly.
29 So he came vnto Iudas, and they saluted
one another peaceably: but the enemies
were prepared to take away Iudas.
30 Neuertheles, it was tolde Iudas, that he
came vnto him vnder disceit: therefore
he feared him, and wolde not se his face
no more.
31 When Nicanor perceiued that his counsel was bewrayed, he went out to fight
against Iudas, beside" Carphasalama.
32 Where there were slaine of Nicanors ho
ste about fiue thousand men: so they fled
vnto the citie of Dauid.
33 After this came Nicanor vp vnto mōut
Sion, and some of the Priests with the Elders of the people went forthe of the Sanctuarie to salute him peaceably, & to shew
him the burnt offring that was offered for
the King.
34 But he laughed at them, and mocked thē
and counted them prophane, and spake
proudly,
35 And swore in his wrath, saying, If Iudas
and his hoste be not deliuered now into
mine hands, if euer I come againe in safetie, I wil burnt vp this house. With that,
went he out in a great anger.
36 Then the Priests came in, and stode be-

"Or, Capharsalama.

fore the altar in the Temple, weping, and
saying,
37 For so muche as thou, *o Lord*, hast chosen
this House, that thy Name might be called vpon therein, and that it shulde be
an house of prayer, and peticion for thy
people,
38 Be auenged of this man and his hoste,
and let them be slaine by the sworde: remember their blasphemies, & suffre them
not to continue.
39 ¶ When Nicanor was gone from Ierusalem, he pitched his tent at Beth-horon, &
there an hoste met him out of Syria.
40 And Iudas pitched in "Adasa with thre
thousand mē where Iudas prayed, saying,
41 *O Lord*, * because the messengers of King
Sēnacherib blasphemed thee, thine Angel
went forthe, and slewe an hundreth, foure
score, and fiue thousand of them.
42 So destroye thou this hoste before vs to
day, that all other may knowe that he hathe spokē wickedly against thy Sāctuarie,
& punish him according to his malice.
43 So the armies ioyned together in battel,
the thirtenth day of the moneth Adar: but
Nicanors hoste was discomfited, and he
him self was first slaine in the battel.
44 Now when his armie sawe that Nicanor was slaine, they cast away their weapons and fled.
45 But they pursued after thē a dayes iourney from Adasa vnto Gasera, blowing
an alarme with the trumpets after them.
46 So they came forthe of all the townes
of Iudea rounde about, and russhed vpon
them, and threwe them from one to another, so that they all fel by the sworde, &
there was not one of them lefte.
47 Then they toke the spoyles, and the pray
and smote of Nicanors head, and his right
hand, which he helde vp so proudly, and
broght it with them, and hanged them vp
afore Ierusalem.
48 So the people reioyced greatly, and kept
that day as a day of great gladnes.
49 And they ordeined, to kepe yerely that
day on the thirtenth day of the moneth
Adar.
50 Thus the land of Iuda was in rest a litle while.

"Or, Adarsa.

2. King. 19, 35. tob. 1, 21. eccles. 48, 24. isa. 37, 36. 2. mac. 8, 19.

CHAP. VIII.

1 Iudas, considering the power and policie of the Romains, maketh peace with them. 22 The conditions of mutual friendship sent to the Iewes.

1 IVdas heard also the fame of the Romains, that thei were mightie, and valiant, and agreable to all things that were
required of them, and made peace with all
that came vnto them,
2 And that they were men of great power,
and they tolde him of their battels, and
their worthie actes, which they did amōg

Ioseph Anti. 12. chap. 18.

the "Galatiãs whome they had conquered, and made to paye tribute, *Or, frenchmen.
3 And what they had done in the countrey
of Spaine: how that they had wonne there
the mines of siluer and golde,
4 And that by their counsel, and gentle behauiour they were rulers in euerie place,
thogh the place was farre from them, and
that they had discomfited, and giuen great
ouerthrowes to ẏ Kings that came against
them, from the vttermost parte of ẏ earth,
and that others gaue them tribute euerie
yere,
5 How they had also discomfited by bat-
tel Philippe and Perses Kings of the "Ma- *Or, Citims.
cedoniãs, and others, that rose against thẽ,
and how they ouercame them,
6 And how great Antiochus King of Asia
that came against thẽ in battel, hauing an
hundreth and twentie elephãts, with horsemen, & charrets, and a verie great armie,
was discomfited by them,
7 And how they toke him aliue, and ordeined him, with suche as shulde reigne
after him, to paye a great tribute, & to giue hostages, and a separate porcion,
8 Euen the countrey of India, and Media,
and Lydia, and of his best coũtreys, which
they toke of him and gaue them to King
Eumenes.
9 Againe when it was tolde them that the
Greciãs were comming to destroye them,
10 They sent against thẽ a captaine, which
gaue them battel, & slewe manie of thẽ, &
toke manie prisoners with their wiues, and
children, and spoyled them, and conquered their land, and destroyed their strong
holdes, and subdued them to be their bõd-
men, vnto this day:
11 Moreouer, how they destroyed, & broght
into subiection other kingdomes & yles,
whosoeuer had withstand them:
12 But that thei kept amitie with their owne
friends, and those that stayed vpon them:
finally, that conquered kingdomes, bothe
farre and nere, in so muche that whosoeuer
heard of their renoume, was afrayed of
them.
13 For whome they wolde helpe to their
kingdomes, those reigned, and whome
they wolde, they put downe: thus were thei
in moste high autoritie.
14 Yet for all this that none of them ware
a crowne, nether was clothed in purple, to
be magnified thereby,
15 But that thei had ordeined them selues a
counsel, wherein thre hundreth and twẽtie
men consulted daiely, and prouided for
the commune affaires, to gouerne them
wel,
16 And that they committed their gouernement to one man euerie yere, who did rule
ouer all their countrey, to whome euerie
man was obedient: and there was nether
hatred nor enuie among them.
17 ¶ Then Iudas chose Eupolemus the sonne of Iohn, *the sonne* of Accus, and Iason,
the sonne of Eleazar, and sent them vnto
Rome to make friẽdship, & mutual felowship with them,
18 That they might take from them the
yoke (for they sawe that the kingdome of
the Grecians wolde kepe Israel in bondage)
19 So they went vnto Rome, which was a
verie great iourney, and came into the
"Senat where they spake and said, *Or, counsel.
20 Iudas Maccabeus with his brethren, and
the people of the Iewes hathe sent vs vnto
you, to make a bonde of friendship, and
peace with you, and ye to register vs as
your partakers and friends.
21 And the matter pleased them.
22 And this is the copie of the epistle that
they wrote in tables of brasse and sent to
Ierusalem, that they might haue by them
a memorial of the peace, and mutual felowship.
23 Good successe be to the Romaines, and
to the people of the Iewes, by sea, and by
land for euer, and the sworde, and enemie
be from them.
24 If there come first anie warre vpon the
Romaines, or anie of their friẽds throughout all their dominion,
25 The people of the Iewes shal helpe thẽ,
as the time shalbe appointed, with all their
heart,
26 Also "they shal giue nothing to thẽ that *Or, the Romains.
come to fight for thẽ, nor serue them with
wheat nor weapõs, nor monei, nor shippes
as it pleaseth the Romaines, but "they shal *Or, the Iewes.
kepe their couenantes without taking a-
nie thing of them.
27 Likewise also if warre come first against
the nacion of the Iewes, the Romains shal
helpe them with a good wil, according as
the time shalbe appointed them.
28 Nether shal wheat be giuen vnto them,
that take their parte, nor weapons, nor money, nor shippes, as it pleaseth ẏ Romains,
who wil kepe these couenants without
deceite.
29 According to these articles ẏ Romains
made the bonde with the people of the
Iewes.
30 If after these pointes the one partie, or
the other wil adde or diminish, they may
do it, at their pleasures, & whatsoeuer they
shal adde, or take away, shal be ratified.
31 And as touching the euil that Demetrius
hathe done vnto the Iewes, we haue written vnto him, saying, Wherefore layest
thou thine heauie yoke vpon our friends,
and confederates the Iewes?
32 If therefore they complaine anie more
against

against thee, we wil do them iustice, and
fight with thee by sea and by land.

CHAP. IX.

1 *After the death of Nicanor Demetrius sendeth his armie against Iudas. 18 Iudas is slaine. 31 Ionathan is put in the stead of his brother. 47 The battel betwene Ionathan, and Bacchides. 55 Alcimus is smitten with the palsie, and dyeth. 68 He cometh vpon Ionathan by the counsel of certeine wicked persones, and is ouercome. 70 The truce of Ionathā with Bacchides.*

Ioseph. Anti. 12. chap. 18.

1 IN the meane season when Demetrius
had heard how Nicanor, and his hoste
had giuen the battel, he sent Bacchides,
and Alcimus againe into Iudea, and his
"chief strength with them.

"Or, the right horne.

2 So they went forthe by the way that is towarde Galgala, and pitched their tentes
before Mesaloth which is in Arbelis, and
wanne it and slewe muche people.
3 And in the first moneth of the hundreth,
fiftie and two yere, they layed their siege
against Ierusalem.
4 But they raised their campe, and came to
Berea, with twentie thousand fote men &
two thousand horsemen.

"Or, Laisa.

5 Now Iudas had pitched his tent at "Elea-
sa, & thre thousand chosen men with him.
6 And when they sawe, that the multitude
of the armie was great, they were sore a-
fraide, and manie conueied them selues
out of the hoste, so that there abode no
mo of them, but eight hundreth men.
7 When Iudas sawe that his hoste failed
him, and that he must nedes fight, he was
sore troubled in minde that he had no time to gather them together, and was discouraged.
8 Neuertheles, he said vnto them that remained, Let vs rise, and go vp against our
enemies, if peraduenture we may be able
to fight with them.
9 But they wolde haue staied him, saying,
We are not able: but let vs rather saue our
liues: turne backe now, seing our brethren
are departed: for shal we fight against thē,
that are so fewe?
10 Then Iudas said, God forbid, that we
shulde do this thing, to fle from them: if
our time be come, let vs dye manfully for
our brethren, and let vs not staine our
honour.
11 Then the hoste remoued out of the tentes, and stode against them, who had deuided their horsemen into two troupes, and
they that threwe with slings, and the archers marched in the forewarde, and they
that foght in the forewarde, were all valiant men.
12 And Bacchides was in the right wing.
So the armie drewe nere on bothe sides, &
blewe the trumpets.
13 They of Iudas side blew the trumpets also, & the earth shoke at the noyce of the armies, and the battel continued from morning to night.
14 And when Iudas sawe that Bacchides
and the strength of his armie was on the
right side, he toke with him all the hardie
men,
15 And brake the right wing, and followed
vpon them vnto mount Azotus.
16 Now when they which were of the left
wing, sawe that the right wing was discom
fited, they followed Iudas behinde, and thē
that were with him hard at the heles.
17 Then was there a sore battel: for many
were slaine of bothe the parties.
18 Iudas also him self was killed, and the
remnant fled.
19 So Ionathan and Simon toke Iudas their
brother, and buryed him in his fathers sepulchre in the citie of Modin.
20 And all the Israelites wept for him, and
mourned greatly for him, and lamēted ma
ny daies, saying,
21 How is the valiant man fallen which deliuered Israel!
22 Concerning the other things of Iudas,
bothe the battels and the valiant actes that
he did, & of his worthines, they are not wri
ten: for they were very many.
23 ¶ Now after the death of Iudas, wicked *Ioseph Anti.*
men came vp in all the coastes of Israel, & *13. cha. 1. & 8*
there arose all suche as gaue them selues
to iniquitie.
24 In those daies was there a very great famine in the land, and all the countrey gaue
ouer them selues with them.
25 And Bacchides did chuse wicked men,
and made them lords in the land.
26 These soght out, and made searche for
Iudas friends, and broght them vnto Bacchides, which auēged him self vpon thē,
and mocked them.
27 And there came so great trouble in Israel, as was not since the time that no Prophet was sene among them.
28 Then came all Iudas friends together, &
said vnto Ionathan,
29 Seing thy brother Iudas is dead, & there
is none like him to go forthe against our
enemies, euen against Bacchides, and " a-
gainst thē of our nacion that are enemies
vnto vs,

"Or, against the enemies of our nacion.

30 Therefore, this day we chuse thee that
thou maist be our prince and captaine in
his place to order our battel.
31 So Ionathan toke the gouernance vpon
him at the same time, and ruled in stead of
his brother Iudas.
32 But when Bacchides knewe it, he soght
for to slay him.
33 Then Ionathan and Simon his brother,
perceiuing that, fled into the wildernes of
Thecua with all their companie, and pitched their tentes by the water poole of
Asphar.

34 Which when Bacchides vnderstode, he
came ouer Iorden with all his hoste vpon
the Sabbath day.
35 (Now had Ionathan sent his brother
Iohn,a captaine of the people,to pray his
friends the Nabathites, that they wolde
kepe their baggage which was muche.
36 But the children of "Ambri came out of *Or, Iambri.
Medaba,& toke Iohn, and all that he had,
& when they had taken it,went their way.
37 After this came worde vnto Ionathan,
and to Simon his brother,that the children
of Ambri made a great mariage,& broght
the bride from "Medaba with great pom- *Or, Nadabath.
pe:for she was daughter to one of the noblest princes of Canaan.
38 Therefore they remembred Iohn their
brother, and went vp, and hid them selues
vnder the couert of the mountaine.
39 So they lift vp their eyes,and loked,and
beholde,there was a great noyce,&muche
preparation: then the bridegrome came
forthe, and his friends and his brethren
met them with tymbrels, and instruments
of musike,and manie weapons.
40 Then Ionathans men that lay in ambushe,rose vp against thē,& slewe manie of
them,and the remnant fled into the moūtaines,so that they toke all their spoiles.
41 Thus the mariage was turned to mourning,and the noyce of their melodie into
lamentacion.
42 And so when they had aduenged the
blood of their brother, they turned againe vnto Iorden.
43 When Bacchides heard this, he came
vnto the border of Iorden with a great
power vpon the Sabbath day.)
44 Then Ionathan said vnto his cōpanie,
Let vs rise now, & fight against our ene-
mies:for it is not to day as in time past.
45 Beholde,ẏ battel is before vs,and behinde vs,and the water of Iorden on this side
and that side, and the marise, and forest,
so ẏ there is no place for vs to turne aside.
46 Wherefore crye now vnto heauen,that
ye may be deliuered from the power of
your enemies:so they ioyned battel.
47 Then Ionathan stretched out his hand
to smite Bacchides:but he turned aside frō
him and reculed.
48 Then Ionathan,and they that were with
him,leapt into Iorden,and swimmed ouer
vnto the further bāke:but the other wolde
not passe through Iorden after them.
49 So in that day were slaine of Bacchides
side about a thousand men.
50 Then he turned againe to Ierusalem, &
buylt vp the strong cities in Iuda, as the
castel of Iericho, and Emmaus,and Beth-
horon, and Bethel, and Thamnatha,Pha-
rathoni,& Tepho, with high walles, with
gates,and with barres,

51 And set garisons in thē, that they might
vse their malice vpon Israel.
52 He fortified also the citie Beth-sura,and
Gazara, and the castel, & set a garison in
them with prouision of vitailes.
53 He toke also the chiefest mens sonnes in
the countrey for hostages,and put them in
the castel at Ierusalem to be kept.
54 ¶ Afterwarde in the hundreth,fiftie and
thre yere,in the seconde moneth, Alcimus
commanded, that the walles of the inner
court of the Sāctuarie shulde be destroied,
and he pulled downe the monumentes of
the Prophetes,and began to destroy them.
55 But at the same time Alcimus was plagued, and his enterprises were hindred, &
his mouth was stopped:for he was smitten
with a palsie, & colde no more speake, nor
giue order concerning his house.
56 Thus dyed Alcimus with great torment
at the same time.
57 And when Bacchides sawe,that Alcimus
was dead,he turned againe to the King, &
so the land of Iuda was in rest two yeres.
58 Then all the vngodlie men helde a counsel,saying, Beholde, Ionathan and his companie dwell at ease,&without care:where-
fore let vs bring Bacchides hither, and he
wil take them all in one night.
59 So they went and consulted with him.
60 Who arose and came with a great hoste,and sent letters priuely to his adheren-
tes,which were in Iudea, to take Ionathan
and those that were with him:but they col
de not, for their counsel was knowen vnto them.
61 And "they toke fiftie men of the coun- *Or, Ionathan.
trey, which were the chief workers of this
wickednes,and slewe them.
62 ¶ Then Ionathan and Simon with their
cōpanie departed vnto "Beth-basin which *Or, Beth-bessen.
is in the wildernes,and repaired the decay
thereof,and made it strong.
63 Whē Bacchides knewe this,he gathered
all his hoste, and sent worde to them that
were of Iudea.
64 Then came he & laid siege to Beth-basin, and foght against it a long season, and
made instruments of warre.
65 But Ionathan had left his brother Simō
in the citie, & went forthe into the countrey,and came with a certeine nomber,
66 And slewe "Odomeras and his brethren *Or, Odares.
and the children of Phasiron in their tentes: so he began to slaye, and increased in
power.
67 Simon also and his companie went out
of the citie, and burnt vp the instruments
of warre,
68 And foght against Bacchides,and discōfited him, and vexed him sore, so that his
counsel and iorney was in vaine.
69 Wherefore he was very wroth at ẏ wicked

ked men, that gaue him counsel to come
into the countrey, & slewe many of them,
and purposed to returne into his owne
countrey.
70 Whereof when Ionathan had knowledge, he sent ambassadours vnto him, to intreat of peace with him, & that the prisoners shulde be deliuered.
71 Which thing he accepted, and did according to his desire, and made an othe, that he wolde neuer do him harme all the daies of his life.
72 So he restored vnto him the prisoners that he had taken afore time out of the lād of Iuda, and so returned and went into his owne land, nether did he come any more into their borders.
73 Thus the sworde ceased from Israel, and Ionathan dwelt at Machmas, and began there to gouerne the people, and destroied the vngodlie men out of Israel.

CHAP. X.

4 Demetrius desireth to haue peace with Ionathan. 18 Alexander also desireth peace with the Iewes 48 Alexander maketh warre against Demetrius. 50 Demetrius is slayne. 51 The friendship of Ptolemeus & Alexander.

Iosep. Antiq. 13. chap. 2, 3.

1 IN the hundreth and thre score yere came Alexander the sonne of Antiochus Epiphanes, and toke Ptolemais, and they receiued him, and there he reigned.
2 Now when Demetrius the King heard it, he gathered an exceading great hoste, and went forthe against him to fight.
3 Also Demetrius sent letters vnto Ionathā, with louīg wordes, as thogh he wolde preferre him.
4 For he said, We wil first make peace with him, before he ioyne with Alexander against vs.
5 Els he wil remember all the euil that we haue done against him, & against his brethren and his nacion.
6 And so he gaue Ionathan leaue to gather an hoste, and to prepare weapons, and to be confederate with him, and commanded the hostages that were in the castel, to be deliuered vnto him.
7 ¶ Then came Ionathan to Ierusalem, and red the letters in the audience of all the people, & of them that were in the castel.
8 Therefore they were sore afraied, because they heard that the King had giuē him licence to gather an armie.
9 So they that were of the castel, deliuered the hostages vnto Ionathan, who restored them to their parents.
10 Ionathan also dwelt at Ierusalem, & began to buyld, and repaire the citie.
11 And he commanded the workemen to buylde the walles, & the mount Sion rounde about with hewen stone, to fortifie it: & so they did.
12 Then the strangers that were in the castels which Bacchides had made, fled,
13 So that euerie man left his place, & went into his owne countrey.
14 Onely at Beth-sura remained certeine which had forsaken the Law and the commandements: for it was their refuge.
15 ¶ Now when King Alexander had heard of the promises that Demetrius had made vnto Ionathan: and when it was tolde him of the battels and noble actes, which he and his brethren had done, and of the paines that they had indured,
16 He said, Might we finde suche a mā? now therefore we wil make him our friend and confederate.
17 Vpon this he wrote a letter, and sent it vnto him, with these wordes, saying,
18 KING ALEXANDER to his brother Ionathan sendeth salutation.
19 We haue heard of thee, that thou art a very valiant man, and worthie to be our friend.
20 Wherefore this day we ordeine thee to be the hie Priest of thy nacion, and to be called the Kings friend: and he sent him a purple robe, and a *crowne of golde, that thou maist *consider what is for our profite, and kepe friendship towarde vs.

**Or, mitre.*
**Or, take our parte.*

21 So in the seuēth moneth of the hundreth and thre score yere, vpon the feast daye of the tabernacles, Ionathan put on the holie garment, & gathered an hoste, & prepared many weapons.
22 ¶ Which when Demetrius heard, he was marueilous sory, and said,

Ioseph. Antiq 13 chap 3.

23 What haue we done, that Alexander hathe preuented vs in getting the friendship of the Iewes for his strength?
24 Yet wil I write and exhorte them, and promes them dignities and rewardes, that they may helpe me.
25 Whereupon he wrote vnto them these wordes, KING DEMETRIVS vnto the nacions of the Iewes sendeth greting.
26 We haue heard that ye haue kept your couenant towarde vs, and continued in our friendship, and haue not ioyned with our enemies, whereof we are glad.
27 Now therefore remaine stil, and kepe fidelitie towarde vs, and we wil recompense you for the good things that ye haue done for vs,
28 And wil release you of many charges, & giue you rewardes.
29 And now I discharge for your sake all ȳ Iewes from tributes, & fre you from the customes of salte, and the crowne taxes, and from the thirde parte of the sede.
30 And frō the halfe of the frute of ȳ trees which is mine owne duetie, I so release thē

that frō this day forthe, none shal take any
thing of the land of Iuda, or of the thre
gouernements which are added thereunto
as of Samaria and of Galile, [a] from this
dayc forthe for euermore.

a And of the cōutrey beyon de Iorden, as Iosephus writeth.

31 Ierusalem also with all things belonging
thereto, shalbe holie and fre from the tenthes and tributes.
32 Also I release the power of the castel
which is at Ierusalem, and giue it vnto the
hie Priest, ẏ he may set in it suche men, as
he shal chuse to kepe it.
33 Moreouer I frely deliuer euerie one of
the Iewes that were taken away prisoners
out of the land of Iuda through out all my
realme, and euerie one of them shalbe free
from tributes, yea, euen their catel,
34 And all the feastes, and Sabbaths, & new
moones, and the daies appointed and the
thre daies before the feast, & the thre daies
after the feast, shalbe daies of fredome &
libertie for all the Iewes in my realme,
35 So that *in them* no man shal haue power
to do any thing, or to vexe any of them in
any maner of cause.
36 Also thirtie thousand of the Iewes shalbe
writen vp in the Kings hoste, and haue
their wages paied them as apperteineth to
all them that are of the Kings armie: and
of thē shalbe ordeined certeine to kepe ẏ
Kings strong holdes.
37 And some of them shalbe set ouer the
Kings moste secret affaires, and their gouernours
and their princes shalbe of them
selues, and they shal liue after their owne
lawes, as the King hathe cōmanded in the
land of Iuda.
38 And the thre gouernements that are added
vnto Iudea from the countrey of Samaria,
shalbe ioyned vnto Iudea, and they
shalbe as vnder one, and obey none other
power, but the hie Priest.
39 And I giue Ptolemais & the borders thereof
vnto the Sanctuarie at Ierusalem, for
the necessarie expēses of the holie things.
40 Moreouer, I wil giue euerie yere fiftene
thousand sicles of siluer of the Kings reuenues
out of the places apperteining vnto me.
41 And all the ouerplus which they haue
not paied for the things due, as they did in
the former yeres, from hence forthe they
shal giue it towarde the workes of the
Temple.
42 And besides this, the fiue thousand sicles
of siluer which they receiued yerely of the
accounte appointed for the interteinemēt
of the Sanctuarie, these yeres passed, euen
these things shalbe released because they
apperteine to the Priests that minister.
43 Item, whosoeuer they be that flee vnto
the Temple at Ierusalem, or within the liberties
thereof, and are indetted to ẏ King
for any maner of thing, they shalbe pardoned,
and all that they haue in my realme.
44 For the buylding also and repairing of
the workes of the Sāctuarie, expenses shal
be giuen of the Kings reuenues.
45 And for the making of the walles of Ierusalem,
and fortifying it rounde about
that the holdes in Iudea may be buylt vp,
shal also the costes be giuen out of the
Kings reuenues.
46 ¶ But when Ionathan & the people heard
these wordes, thei gaue no credit vnto thē,
nether receiued them: for thei remembred
the great wickednes that he had done in
Israel, and how sore he had vexed them.
47 Wherefore they agreed vnto Alexander:
for he was the first that had intreated
of true peace with them, and so were confederat
with him alway.
48 Then gathered King Alexander a great
hoste, & camped ouer against Demetrius.
49 So the two Kings ioyned battel, but Demetrius
hoste fled, and Alexander pursued
him, and preuailed against them.
50 So that sore battel continued til the sunne
went downe, and Demetrius was slaine
the same day.
51 ¶ Then Alexander sent ambassadours *Ioseph. Antiq*
vnto Ptolemeus the King of Egypt with *13. chap. 5.*
these wordes, saying,
52 For so muche as I am come againe to my
realme, and am set in the throne of my fathers,
and haue gotten the dominion, and
haue destroied Demetrius, and enioye my
countrey,
53 Seing that I haue euen giuen him the battel,
and he and his armie is discomfited by
me, & I sit in the throne of his kingdome,
54 Let vs now make friēdship together, and
giue me now thy daughter to wife: so shal
I be thy sonne in law, and giue thee rewardes,
and vnto her things according to thy
dignitie.
55 Then Ptolemeus the King gaue answer,
saying, Happie be the day, wherein thou
art come againe vnto the lande of thy fathers,
and sittest in the throne of their
kingdome.
56 Now therefore wil I fulfil thy writing:
but mete me at Ptolemais that we may se
one another, and that I may make thee my
sonne in law, according to thy desire.
57 So Ptolemeus wēt out of Egypt with his
daughter Cleopatra, & came vnto Ptolemais
in the hūdreth threscore & two yere,
58 Where King Alexander met him, and he
gaue vnto him his daughter Cleopatra,
and maried them at Ptolemais with great
glorie, as the maner of Kings is.
59 ¶ Then wrote King Alexander vnto Ionathan,
that he shulde come and mete him.
60 So he went honorably vnto Ptolemais,
and there he met the two Kings, and gaue
them

them great presents of siluer and golde,
and to their friends, and founde fauour in
their sight.
61 And there assembled certeine pestilent
felowes of Israel, & wicked men to accuse
him: but the King wolde not heare them.
62 And the King commanded that they
shulde take of the garments of Ionathan,
& clothe him in purple: and so they did:
& the King appointed him to sit by him,
63 And said vnto his princes, Go with him
into the middes of the citie, and make a
proclamacion, that no man complaine a-
gainst him of anie matter, & that no man
trouble him for anie maner of cause.
64 So when his accusers sawe his honour ac
cording as it was proclaimed, and that he
was clothed in purple, they fled all away.
65 And the King preferred him to honour,
and wrote him among his chief friends,
and made him a duke, and partaker of his
dominion.
66 Thus Ionathan returned to Ierusalem
with peace and gladnes.
67 ¶ In the hundreth, thre score & fiue yere
came Demetrius the sonne of Demetrius
from Creta into his fathers land.
68 Whereof whẽ King Alexander heard,
he was verie sorie, and returned vnto Antiochia.
69 Then Demetrius appointed Apollonius
ẏ gouernour of Celosyria, who gathered
a great hoste, and camped in Iamnia, and
sent vnto Ionathan the hie Priest, saying,
70 Darest thou, being but alone, lift vp thy
self against vs? and I am laughed at, and
reproched, because of thee: now therefore why doest thou vant thy self against vs
in the mountaines?
71 Now then if thou trust in thine owne
strength, come downe to vs into the plaine field & there let vs trye the matter together: for I haue the strength of cities.
72 Aske and learne who I am, and thei shal
take my parte: and they shal tell thee that
your fote is not able to stand before our
face: for thy fathers haue bene twise chased in their owne land.
73 And now how wilt thou be able to abide
so great an hoste of horsemen and fotemẽ
in the plaine, where is nether stone, nor
rocke, nor place to flee vnto?
74 When Ionathan heard the wordes of A-
pollonius, he was moued in his mĩde: wherefore he chose ten thousand men, and
went out of Ierusalem, & Simon his brother met him for to helpe him.
75 And he pitched his tents at Ioppe: but
they shut him out of the citie: for Apollonius garison was in Ioppe.
76 Then they foght against it, and they
that were in the citie, for verie feare let
him in: so Ionathan wan Ioppe.
77 Apollonius hearing of this, toke thre
thousand horsemẽ with a great hoste *of fote*
men & went towarde Azotus, as thogh he
wolde go forwarde, & came immediatly
into ẏ plaine field, because he had so manie horsemen, and put his trust in them.
78 So Ionathan followed vpon him to A-
zotus, and the armie skirmished with his
arriere bande.
79 For Apollonius had left a thousand horsemen behinde them in ambush.
80 And Ionathan knewe that there was an
ambushment behinde him, and thogh they
had compassed in his hoste, & shot dartes
at the people from the morning to the e-
uening,
81 Yet the people stode stil, as Ionathan had
commanded them, til their horses were
wearie.
82 Then broght Simon forthe his hoste, &
set them against the bande: but the horses
were wearie, and he discomfited them, &
thei fled: so the horsemen were scattered
in the field,
83 And they fled to Azotus, and came into
the temple of Dagon their idole, that thei
might there saue them selues.
84 But Ionathan set fyre vpon Azotus and
all the cities rounde about it, & toke their
spoiles, and burnt with fyre the temple of
Dagon with all thẽ that were fled into it.
85 Thus were slayne and burnt about eight
thousand men.
86 So Ionathan remoued the hoste from
thence, and camped by Ascalon, where the
men of the citie came forthe, & met him
with great honour.
87 After this went Ionathan and his hoste
againe to Ierusalem with great spoiles.
88 And when King Alexander heard these
things, he begã to do Ionathan more honour,
89 And sent him a colar of golde, as the v-
se is to be giuen vnto suche as are of the
Kings blood: he gaue him also Accaron,
with the borders thereof in possession.

CHAP. XI.

3 The dissension betwene Ptolemeus and Alexander his sonne in law. 17 The death of Alexander. 19 Demetrius reigneth after the death of Ptolemeus. 22 Sion is besieged of Ionathan. 42 Demetrius seing that no man resisted him, sendeth his armie againe. 54 Tryphon moueth Antiochus against Demetrius.

1 AND the King of Egypt gathered a *Ioseph Antiq.13.chap.7*
great hoste, like the sand that lyeth
vpon the sea shore, and manie ships, and
went about through deceit to obteine the
kingdome of Alexander, and to ioyne it
vnto his owne realme.
2 Vpon this he went into Syria with friendlie wordes, and was let into the cities, and
men came forthe to mete him: for King
Alexander had commanded them to mete
him, because he was his father in Law.

3 Now when he entred into the citie of
Ptolemais, he lefte bands and garisons in
euerie citie.
4 And when he came nere to Azotus,they
shewed him the temple of Dagō that was
burnt, and Azotus, and the suburbes thereof that were destroyed, and the bodies
cast abroad,and them that he had burnt in
the battel: for they had made heapes of
them by the way where he shulde passe.
5 And thei tolde the King what Ionathan
had done,to the intēt thei might get him
euil wil:but the King helde his peace.
6 And Ionathan met the King with great
honour at Ioppe; where they saluted one
another,and laye there.
7 So when Ionathan had gone with ẏ King
vnto the water that was called Eleutherus,
he turned againe to Ierusalem.
8 So King Ptolemeus gate the dominion
of the cities by the sea vnto Seleucia vpō
the sea coast, imagining wicked counsels
against Alexander,
9 ¶ And sent ambassadours vnto King Demetrius,sayig,Come,let vs make a league
betwene vs,and I wil giue thee my daughter,which Alexander hathe,and thou shalt
reigne in thy fathers kingdome.
10 For I repent that I gaue Alexander my
daughter:for he goeth about to slaye me.
11 Thus he sclandered Alexander, as one
that shulde desire his realme.
12 And he toke his daughter from him,and
gaue her vnto Demetrius,and forsoke A-
lexander, so that their hatred was openly
knowen.
13 Then Ptolemeus came to Antiochia,
where he set two crownes vpon his owne
head,of Asia and of Egypt.
14 In the meane season was King Alexander in Cilicia: for they that dwelt in those
places,had rebelled against him:
15 But when Alexander heard it,he came to
warre against him,and Ptolemeus broght
forthe his hoste,and met him with a migh
tie power,and put him to flight.
16 Then fled Alexander into Arabia, there
to be defended: so Ptolemeus was exalted.
17 And Zabdiel the Arabian smote of A-
lexanders head,& sent it vnto Ptolemeus.
18 But the third day after,King Ptolemeus
dyed: and thei that were in the holdes,we-
re slayne one of another.
19 And Demetrius reigned in the hūdreth,
thre score and seuenth yere.
20 ¶ At the same time gathered Ionathan
them that were in Iudea,to laye siege vnto the castle, which was at Ierusalem, and
they made manie instruments of warre
against it.
21 Then went there certeine vngodlie per-
sones(which hated their owne people) vnto King *Demetrius*,and tolde him that Ionathan besieged the castle.
22 So when he heard it, he was angrie, and
immediatly came vnto Ptolemais,& wrote vnto Ionathan, that he shulde laye no
more siege vnto it,but that he shulde mete
him and speake with him at Ptolemais in
all haste.
23 Neuertheles when Ionathan heard this,
he commanded to besiege it: he chose also
certeine of the Elders of Israel, and the
Priests,and put him self in danger,
24 And toke with him siluer and golde,and
apparel,and diuerse presents, and went to
Ptolemais vnto the King, and founde fauour in his sight.
25 And thogh certeine vngodlie men of
his owne nacion had made complaintes
vpon him,
26 Yet the King intreated him as his predecessers had done, and promoted him in
the sight of all his friends,
27 And confirmed him in the hie priesthode with all the honorable things, that
he had afore,& made him his chief friēd.
28 Ionathan also desired the King, that he
wolde make Iudea fre with the thre gouer-
nemēts,& the countrey of Samaria,& *Ionathan* promised him thre hūdreth talents.
29 Whereunto the King consented,& gaue
Ionathan writing of the same, conteining
these wordes,
30 KING DEMETRIVS vnto his brother Ionathan, and to the nacion of the
Iewes sendeth greting.
31 We send you here a copie of the letter,
which we did write vnto our cousin Lasthenes concerning you,that ye shulde se it.
32 King Demetrius vnto Lasthenes his father sendeth greting.
33 For the faithfulnes that our friends the
nacion of the Iewes kepe vnto vs, and for
their good wil towardes vs we are determined to do them good.
34 Wherefore we assigne to thē the coasts
of Iudea with the thre gouernements A-
pherema,and Lydda,and Ramathe(which
are added vnto Iudea from the countrey
of Samaria) and all that apperteineth to
all them that sacrifice in Ierusalem: bothe
concerning the paiments which the King
toke yerely aforetime,bothe for the frutes
of the earth,& for the frutes of the trees.
35 As for the other things apperteining vnto vs of the tenths & tributes, which were
due vnto vs,and the customes of salte, &
crowne taxes, which were payed vnto vs,
we discharge thē of all frō hence forthe.
36 And nothing hereof shalbe reuoked frō
this time forthe and for euer.
37 Therefore se that ye make a copie of
these things, and deliuer it vnto Ionathā,
that it may be set vp vpon the holy mount
in an open place.

38 After

38 After this when Demetrius the King
sawe that his land was in rest, and that no
resistance was made against him, he sent
away all his hoste, euerie man to his owne
place, except certeine bandes of strangers,
whome he broght from the yles of the hea
then: wherefore all his fathers hoste hated
him.
39 Now was there one Tryphon, that had
bene of Alexanders parte afore, which whē
he sawe that all ẏ hoste murmured against
Demetrius, he went to "Simalcue the Arabian, that broght vp Antiochus the sonne
of Alexander,
40 And lay sore vpon him, to deliuer him
this yong Antiochus, that he might reigne in his fathers stead: he tolde him also
what great euil Demetrius had done, and
how his men of warre hated him, and he
remained there a long season.
41 Also Ionathan sent vnto King Demetrius to driue them out which were in the
castel at Ierusalem, and those that were in
the forteresses: for they foght against Israel.
42 So Demetrius sent vnto Ionathā, saying,
I wil not onely do these things for thee &
thy nacion, but if opportunitie serue, I wil
honour thee and thy nacion.
43 Now therefore thou shalt do me a pleasure, if thou wilt send me mē to helpe me:
for all mine armie is gone from me.
44 So Ionathā sent him thre thousand strōg
men vnto Antiochia, and they came vnto
the King: wherefore the King was verie
glad at their comming.
45 ¶But they that were of the citie, euen an
hundreth, and twentie thousand men, gathered them together in the middes of the
citie, & wolde haue slaine the King.
46 But the King fled into the palace, & the
citizens kept the stretes of the citie, and
beganne to fight.
47 Then the King called to the Iewes for
helpe, which came to him altogether, and
went abroade through the citie,
48 And slewe the same day an hūdreth thou
sand, and set fyre vpon the citie, and toke
many spoiles in that day, & deliuered the
King.
49 So when the citizens sawe that the Iewes
had gotten th vpper hand of the citie, and
that they them selues were disappointed
of their purpose, they made their supplica
tion vnto the King, saying,
50 "Grant vs peace, and let the Iewes cease
from vexing vs and the citie.
51 So they cast away their weapons, & made peace, and the Iewes were greatly honored before the King, and before all
that were in his realme, and they came a-
gaine to Ierusalem with great pray.
52 Then King Demetrius sate in the throne of his kingdome, and had peace in his
land.
53 Neuertheles he dissembled in all that e-
uer he spake, and withdrewe him self from
Ionathan, nether did he rewarde him according to the benefites which he had done for him, but troubled him verie sore.
54 ¶After this returned Tryphon with the
yong childe Antiochus, which reigned, &
was crowned.
55 Then there gathered vnto him all the mē
of warre, whome Demetrius had scatered,
and they foght against him, who fled and
turned his backe.
56 So Tryphon toke the "beastes, and wan
Antiochia.
57 And yong Antiochus wrote vnto Ionathan, saying, I appoint thee to be the chief
Priest, and make thee ruler ouer the foure
gouernements, that thou maist be a friend
of the Kings.
58 Vpon this he sent him golden vessels to
be serued in, and gaue him leaue to drinke in golde, and to weare purple, & to haue a colar of golde.
59 He made his brother Simon also captaine frō the coastes of Tyrus vnto the borders of Egypt.
60 Then Ionathan went forthe and passed
through the cities beyonde the flood, and
all the men of warre of Syria gathered vn
to him for to helpe him: so he came vnto
Ascalon, & they of the citie receiued him
honorably.
61 And from thence went he vnto Gaza:
but they of Gaza shut him out: wherefore he laid siege vnto it, and burned the
suburbes thereof with fyre, and spoiled
them.
62 Then they of Gaza made supplication
vnto Ionathan, and he made peace with
them, and toke of the sonnes of the chief
men for hostages, and sent them to Ierusalem, and went through the countrey vnto
Damascus.
63 And when Ionathan heard that Demetrius prīces were come into Cades, which
is in Galile, with a great hoste, purposing
to driue him out of the countrey,
64 He came against them, & left Simon his
brother in the countrey.
65 And Simon besieged Beth-sura, and
foght against it a long season, and shut
it vp.
66 So they desired to haue peace with him,
which he granted them, and afterwarde
put them out from thence, and toke the citie, and set a garison in it.
67 Then Ionathan with his hoste came to
the water of Genesar, and betimes in the
morning came to the plaine of Azor.
68 And beholde the hostes of the "strangers
met him in the plaine, and had layed am-

"Or, Emalcuel.

"Or, giue vs the right hand.

"Or, elephantes.

"Or, heathen.

bushments for him in the mountaines.
69 So that when they came against them, the
ambushments rose out of their places and
skirmished.
70 So that all that were of Ionathans side,
fled: and there was not one of them left,
except Mattathias the sonne of "Absalo-
mus, and Iudas the sonne of Calphi the
captaines of the hoste.
71 Then Ionathan rent his clothes, and cast
earth vpon his head, and prayed,
72 And turned againe to them to fight, and
put them to flight, so that they fled away.
73 Now when his owne men that were fled,
sawe this, they turned againe vnto him, &
helped him to followe after all vnto their
tentes at Cades, and there they camped.
74 So there were slaine of the strangers the
same day about thre thousand men, & Ionathan turned againe to Ierusalem.

*Or, Abessalomus.

CHAP. XII.

1 Ionathan sendeth ambassadours to Rome, 2 And to the people of Sparta, to renewe their couenãt of friendship. 20 Ionathan putteth to flight the princes of Demetrius. 40 Tryphon taketh Ionathan by disceite.

Ioseph. Anti. 13. chap 8.

1 IOnathan now seing that the time was
mete for him, chose certeine men, and
sent them vnto Rome, to establish and re-
new the friendship with them.
2 He sent letters also vnto "the Spartians
and to other places, for the same purpose.
3 So they went vnto Rome, and entred into the Senate, and said, Ionathan the hie
Priest and the nacion of the Iewes sent vs
vnto you, for to renewe friendship with
you, and the bonde of loue, as in times
past.
4 So the *Romaines* gaue them fre pasports,
that men shulde lead them home into the
land of Iuda peaceably.
5 ¶ AND THIS is the copie of
the letters that Ionathan wrote vnto the
Spartians,
6 Ionathan the hie Priest with the Elders
of the nacion, and the Priests, and the rest
of the people of the Iewes, send greting
vnto the Spartians their brethren.
7 Heretofore were letters sent vnto Onias
the hie Priest, from "Arius, which then reigned among you, that ye wolde be our
brethren, as the copie here vnder writen
specifieth.
8 And Onias intreated the ambassadour ho
norably, and receiued the letters: wherein
there was mencion made of the bonde of
loue and friendship.
9 But as for vs, we nede no suche writings:
for we haue the holy bokes in our hands
for comfort.
10 Neuertheles we thoght it good to send
vnto you, for the renewing of the brotherhode and friendship, lest we shulde be

*Or, Lacedemonians.

Ioseph. Anti. 12. chap. 5.
*Or, Darius.

strange vnto you: for it is long since the
time that ye sent vnto vs.
11 Wherefore we remember you at all seasons continually, and in the feastes and o-
ther daies appointed when we offre sacrifices and prayers, as it is mete and conuenient to thinke vpon our brethren.
12 And we reioyce at your prosperous estate.
13 And thogh we haue bene enuironed with
great troubles & warres, so that the Kings
rounde about vs haue foght against vs,
14 Yet wolde we not be grieuous vnto you,
nor to other of our cõfederates & friends
in these warres.
15 For we haue had helpe from heauen, that
hathe soccoured vs, and we are deliuered
from our enemies, and our enemies are
subdued.
16 Yet haue we chosen Numenius *the sonne*
of Antiochus, and Antipater *the sonne* of
Iason, and sent them vnto the Romaines,
for to renewe the former friendship with
them, and league.
17 We commanded them also to go vnto
you, and to salute you, and to deliuer you
our letters, cõcerning the renewing of our
brotherhode.
18 And now ye shal do vs a pleasure to giue
vs an answer of these things.
19 ¶ And this was the copie of the letters,
which Arius the King of Sparta sent vnto Onias.
20 THE KING of the Spartians
vnto Onias the hie Priest sendeth greting.
21 It is founde in writing, that the Spartiãs
and Iewes are brethren, and come out of
the generacion of Abraham.
22 And now for somuche as this is come to
our knowledge, ye shal do wel, to write vnto vs of your prosperitie.
23 As for vs, we haue writen vnto you, that
your cattel and goods are ours, and ours
are yours: these things haue we commanded to be shewed vnto you.
24 ¶ Now when Ionathan heard, that Demetrius princes were come to fight agaĩst
him, with a greater hoste then afore,
25 He went from Ierusalem, and met them
in the land of Hamath: for he gaue thẽ not
space to come into his owne countrey.
26 And he sent spies vnto their tẽtes, which
came againe, and tolde him, that they
were appointed to come vpon him in the
night.
27 Wherefore, whẽ the sunne was gone downe, Ionathan commanded his men to watche, and to be in armes ready to fight all
the night, & sent watchmen rounde about
the hoste.
28 But when the aduersaries heard that Ionathan was ready with his men to the battel, they feared, and trembled in their
hearts,

hearts, and kindled fyres in their tentes,
and fled away.
29 Neuertheles Ionathan and his companie
knewe it not til the morning: for thei sawe
the fyres burning.
30 Then Ionathan followed vpon them, but
he colde not ouertake them: for they were
gone ouer the flood Eleutherus.
31 So Ionathã turned to the Arabiãs, which
were called Zabedei, and slewe them, and
toke their spoile.
32 He proceded further also, and came vnto Damascus, and went through all the
countrey.
33 But Simon his brother went forthe, and
came to Ascalon and to the next holdes,
departing vnto Ioppe, and wanne it.
34 For he heard that they wolde deliuer the
holde to them that toke Demetrius parte:
wherefore he set a garison there to kepe it.
35 ¶After this came Ionathan home, and
called the Elders of the people together,
and deuised with them for to buyld vp the
strong holdes in Iudea,
36 And to make the walles of Ierusalem
hier, and to make a great mount betwixt
the castel and the citie, for to separate it
from the citie, that it might be alone, and
that men shulde nether bye, nor sel in it.
37 So they came together to buylde vp the
citie: for parte of the wall vpon the broke
of the East side was fallen downe, and they
repaired it, and called it Caphenatha.
38 Simon also set vp Adida in Sephela, &
made it strong with gates and barres.
39 ¶In the meane time Tryphon purposed
to reigne in Asia, and to be crowned when
he had slaine the King Antiochus.

Ioseph. Anti. 13. chap. 9.

40 But he was afraied that Ionathan wolde not suffer him, but fight against him:
wherefore he went about to take Ionathan,
and to kil him: so he departed, and came
vnto Bethsan.
41 Then went Ionathã forthe against him
to the battel with fortie thousand chosen
men, and came vnto Bethsan.
42 But when Tryphon sawe that Ionathan
came with so great an hoste, he durst not
lay hand vpon him,
43 But receiued him honorably, and commended him vnto all his friends, and gaue him rewardes, and cõmanded his men
of warre to be as obedient vnto him as to
him self,
44 And said vnto Ionathan, Why hast
thou caused this people to take suche
trauail, seing there is no warre betwene vs?
45 Therefore send them now home againe,
and chuse certeine men to wait vpon thee,
and come thou with me to Ptolemais: for I
wil giue it thee, with the other strong holdes, and the other garisons, and all them
that haue the charge of the cõmune affaires: so wil I returne, & departe: for this is
the cause of my comming.
46 Ionathan beleued him, & did as he said,
and sent away his hoste, which went into
the land of Iuda,
47 And reteined but thre thousand with
him, whereof he sent two thousãd into Ga
lile, & one thousand went with him self.
48 Now assone as Ionathã entred into Ptolemais, they of Ptolemais shut the gates,
and toke him, and slewe all them with the
sworde, that came in with him.
49 Then sent Tryphon an hoste of fotemen, & horsemen into Galile, & into the
great plaine, to destroye all Ionathãs com
panie.
50 But when they knewe that Ionathã was
taken, and slaine, and those that were with
him, they incouraged one another, and
came forthe against them readie to the
battel.
51 But when thei which followed vpon thẽ,
sawe that it was a matter of life, they turned backe againe.
52 By this meanes all they came into the
land of Iuda peaceably, and bewailed Ionathan, and them that were with him, and
feared greatly, and all Israel made great
lamentacion.
53 For all the heathẽ that were round about
them, soght to destroye them.
54 For they said, Nowe haue they no captaine, nor anie man to helpe them: therefore let vs now fight against them, and
roote out their memorie from amõg men.

CHAP. XIII.

1 After Ionathan was taken, Simon is chosen captaine. 17 Tryphon, taking his children, and money for the redemption of Ionathan, killeth him and his children. 31 Tryphon killeth Antiochus, and possesseth the realme. 36 Demetrius taketh truce with Simon. 43 Simon winneth Gaza. 50 He possesseth the tower of Sion. 53 He maketh his sonne Iohn captaine.

1 NOw when Simõ heard that Tryphõ *Ioseph. Anti 13. chap. 9.*
gathered a great hoste to come into
the land of Iuda, and to destroye it,
2 And sawe that the people was in great
trembling and feare, he came vp to Ierusa
lem, and gathered the people together,
3 And gaue them exhortacion, saying, Ye
knowe what great things I, & my brethrẽ,
& my fathers house haue done for ye Law,
and the Sanctuarie, and the battels, & trou
bles that we haue sene.
4 By reason whereof all my brethren are
slaine for Israels sake, and I am left alone.
5 Now therefore God forbide, that I
shulde spare mine owne life in anie time
of trouble: for I am not better then my
brethren.
6 But I wil auenge my nacion, and the
Sanctuarie, and our wiues, and our children: for all the heathen are gathered to-

gether to destroy vs of very malice.
7 In hearing these wordes the hearts of the
people were kindled,
8 So that they cryed with a loude voyce,
sayig, Thou shalt be our captaine in stead
of Iudas and Ionathan thy brethren.
9 Fight thou our battels, and whatsoeuer
thou commandest vs, we wil do it.
10 ¶So he gathered all the men of warre,
making haste to finish the walles of Ierusa
lem, and fortified it rounde about.
11 Then sent he Ionathan the sonne of Ab-
salomus with a great hoste vnto Ioppe,
which droue them out that were therein, &
remained there him self.
12 Tryphon also remoued from Ptolemais
with a great armie, to come into the lād of
Iuda, & Ionathā was with him as prisoner.
13 And Simon pitched his tentes at "Addi-
dis vpon the open plaine.

*Or, Addus.

14 But when Tryphon knewe that Simon
stode vp in stead of his brother Ionathan,
& that he wolde fight against him, he sent
messengers vnto him, saying,
15 Where as we haue kept Ionathā thy brother, it is for money that he is owing in the
Kings account cōcerning the busines that
he had in hand.
16 Wherefore send now an hūdreth talents
of siluer, & his two sonnes for hostages, ŷ
when he is letten forthe, he wil not turne
from vs, and we wil send him againe.
17 Neuertheles Simō knewe that he dissem
bled in his wordes, yet commanded he the
money and children to be deliuered vnto
him, lest he shulde be in greater hatred of
the people of Israel.
18 Who might haue said, Because he sent
him not the money and the children, therefore is Ionathan dead.
19 So he sent the children and an hundreth
talents: but he dissembled, and wolde not
let Ionathan go.
20 ¶Afterwarde came Tryphon into the
land to destroye it, & went rounde about
by the way, that leadeth vnto Adora: but
wheresoeuer thei went, thether went Simō
and his hoste.
21 Now they that were in the castel, sent
messengers vnto Tryphon, that he shulde
make haste to come by the wildernes, & to
send them vitailes.
22 So Tryphon made readie all his horsemen: but the same night fell a very great
snowe, so that he came not, because of the
snowe: but he remoued and went into the
countrey of Galaad.
23 And when he came nere to Bascama, he
slewe Ionathan and he was buryed there.
24 So Tryphon returned, & went into his
owne land.
25 ¶Then sent Simon to take the bones of
Ionathan his brother, & they buryed him
in Modin his fathers cities.
26 And all Israel bewailed him with great
lamētacion, & mourned for him verie lōg.
27 And Simon made vpon the sepulchre of
his father & his brethren, a buylding high
to loke vnto, of hewen stone behinde and
before,
28 And set vp seuen pillers vpon it, one a-
gainst another, for his father, his mother,
and foure brethren,
29 And set great pillers round about them,
and set armes vpon the pillers for a perpetual memorie, and carued shippes beside the armes, that they might be sene of
men sailing in the sea.
30 This sepulchre which he made at Modin, standeth yet vnto this day.
31 ¶Now as Tryphon wēt forthe with the
yong King Antiochus, he slewe him traiterously,

Ioseph Anti. 13. chap. 10.

32 And reigned in his stead, and crowned
him self King of Asia, and broght a great
plague vpon the land.
33 Simon also buylte vp the castels of Iudea, and compassed them about with high
towers, & great walles, euen with towers,
and gates and barres, and laid vp vitailes
in the strong holdes.
34 Moreouer Simon chose certeine men
and sent them to King Demetrius, that he
wolde discharge the lād: for all Tryphons
doings were robberies.
35 Whereupon Demetrius the King answered him, and wrote vnto him after this
maner,
36 DEMETRIUS the King vnto Simon the high Priest, and the friend of
Kings, and to the Elders and to the nation
of the Iewes sendeth greting.
37 The golden crowne, and "precious stone
that ye sent vnto vs, haue we receiued, and
are readie to make a stedfast peace with
you, and to write vnto the officers, to release you of the things wherein we made
you fre.

Or, Celar, or, bandricke: in Greke Baïnen, or bahen.

38 So the things that we haue granted you,
shalbe stable: the strong holdes which ye
haue buylded, shalbe your owne.
39 Also we forgiue the ouersights, and fautes cōmitted vnto this day, and the crowne taxe that ye oght vs: and where as was
anie other tribute in Ierusalem, it shalbe
now no tribute.
40 And they that are mete among you to
be writen with our men, let them be writē
vp, that there may be peace betwene vs.
41 Thus the yoke of the heathē was takē frō
Israel in the hundreth, & seuentie yere.
42 And the people of Israel began to write
in their letters, & publike instruments, IN
THE FIRST yere of Simō, the high
and chief Priest, gouernour, and prince
of the Iewes.

43 In

43 In thoſe dayes Simon camped againſt
Gaza,and beſieged it rounde about,where
he ſet vp an engine of warre, and approched nere the citie, and bet a towre, and
toke it.
44 So thei that were in the engine,leapt into the citie, and there was great trouble in
the citie,
45 In ſo muche that the people of the citie
rent their clothes,and climed vp vpon the
walles with their wiues,and children, and
cryed with a loude voyce, beſeching Simon to grant them peace,ſaying,
46 Deale not with vs according to our wic
kednes,but according to thy mercie.
47 Then Simon pitied them, and wolde
fight no more againſt them, but put them
out of the citie, and clenſed the houſes,
wherein the idoles were,and ſo entred thereunto with pſalmes and thankeſgiuing.
48 So when he had caſt all the filthines out,
he ſet ſuche men in it as kept the Law,and
fortified it, and buylded there a dwelling
place for him ſelf.
49 Now, when they in the caſtel at Ieruſalem were kept, that they colde not come
forthe nor go into the coũtrey, nether bye
nor ſel, they were very hungrie, and manie of them were famiſhed to death,
50 In ſo muche that they beſoght Simon to
make peace with them: which he granted
them,and put them out from thence, and
clenſed the caſtel from filthines.
51 And vpon the thre, and twentie day of
the ſeconde moneth in the hũdreth,ſeuẽtie
and one yere,they entred into it with thã-
keſgiuing, and branches of palme trees,
and with harpes,and with cymbales, and
with violes, and with pſalmes, and ſongs,
becauſe the great enemie of Iſrael was o-
uercome.
52 And he ordeined that the ſame day ſhulde be kept euerie yere with gladnes.
53 And he fortified the mount of the Tẽple
that was beſide the caſtel where he dwelt
him ſelf with his companie.
54 Simon alſo ſeing that Iohn his ſonne was
now a mã,he made him captaine of all the
hoſtes, & cauſed him to dwell in Gazaris.

CHAP. XIIII.

1 Demetrius is ouercome of Arſaces. 11 Simon being captaine,there is great quietnes in Iſrael. 18 The couenant of friendſhip with the Romains, and with the people of Sparta is renewed.

1 IN the hundreth,ſeuentie and two yere
gathered King Demetrius his hoſte, &
departed vnto Media,to get him helpe for
to fight againſt Tryphon.
2 But when Arſaces the King of Perſia and
Media heard, that Demetrius was entred
within his borders,he ſent one of his princes to take him aliue.
3 So he went, and ouercame the armie of
Demetrius, and toke him,and broght him
to Arſaces,which kept him in warde.
4 Thus all the land *of Iuda* was in reſt,
ſo long as Simon liued: for he ſoght the
welth of his nacion : therefore were they
glad to haue him for their ruler,and to do
him worſhip alway.
5 Simon alſo wanne the citie of Ioppe to
his great honour to be an hauen towne,
and made it an entrance vnto the yles of
the ſea.
6 He enlarged alſo the borders of his people,and conquered the countreis.
7 He gathered vp manie of their people
that were priſoners, and he had the dominion of Gazaris, and Beth-ſura, and the
caſtel, which he clenſed from filthines, &
there was no man that reſiſted him,
8 So that euerie man tilled his grounde in
peace,and the land gaue her frutes, & the
trees gaue their frute.
9 The Elders ſate in the opẽ places, & conſulted altogether for the commune welth,
and the yong mẽ were honorably clothed
and armed.
10 He prouided vitailes for the cities, and
all kinde of munition,ſo that his glorious
fame was renoumed vnto the end of the
worlde.
11 He made peace thorow out the land,and
Iſrael had perfite mirth and ioye.
12 For euerie mã ſate vnder his vine, & the
fig trees,& there was no man to fray them.
13 There was none in the land to fight a-
gainſt them: for then the Kings were o-
uercome.
14 He helped all thoſe that were in aduerſitie among his people: he was diligent to
ſe the Law kept, and he toke away the vngodlie,and wicked.
15 He beautified the Sãctuarie, and encreaſed the veſſels of the Temple.
16 Whẽ the Romains heard, and the Spartians had knowledge, that Ionathan was
dead,they were very ſorie.
17 But whẽ they heard,that Simon his brother was made high Prieſt in his ſteade,&
how he had wonne the land againe with
the cities in it,
18 They wrote vnto him in tables of braſſe,
to renewe the friendſhip,and bonde of loue,which they had made with Iudas & Ionathan his brethren.
19 Which writings were red before the
congregacion at Ieruſalem,and this is the
copie of the letters that the Spartiãs ſent,
20 THE SENATORS and citie of
Sparta vnto Simon the great Prieſt, and
to the Elders,and to the Prieſts,and to the
reſidue of the people of the Iewes their
brethren ſend greting.
21 When your ambaſſadours that were ſent
vnto our people,certified vs of your glorie

& honour,we were glad of their cõming,
22 And haue registred their ambassage in ÿ
publike recordes in this maner, Numenius
the sonne of Antiochus, and Antipater *the*
sonne of Iason the Iewes ambassadours came vnto vs,to renewe amitie with vs.
23 And it pleased the people, that the men
shulde be honorably intreated, and that
the copie of their ambassage shulde be registred in the publike recordes, that it
might be for a memorial vnto the people
of Sparta:and a copie of the same was sent
to Simon the chief Priest.
24 After this Simon sent Numenius to Ro
me,with a great shield of golde of a thousand pounde weight, to cõfirme the friẽdship with them.
25 Which when the people vnderstode,thei
said, What thankes shal we recompense
againe vnto Simon and his children?
26 For he and his brethren, and the house
of his father haue stablished Israel, and
ouercome their enemies, and haue confirmed the libertie thereof: therefore they
wrote this in tables of brasse,and set it vpõ
pillers in mount Sion.
27 The copie of the writing is this, In the
eight and twentie day of the moneth *Elul
in the hundreth, seuentie and two yere, in
the thirde yere of Simon the high Priest.
28 In "Saramel in the great cõgregacion of
the Priests, and of the people, and of the
gouernours of the nacion,and of the Elders of the countrei, we wolde signifie vnto you,ÿ manie battels haue bene foghten
in our countrey.
29 Wherein Simon the sonne of Mattathias (come of the children of Iareb) and
his brethren put them selues in dãger,and
resisted the enemies of their nacion, that
their Sanctuarie,and Law might be mainteined,& did their nacion great honour.
30 For Ionathan gathered his nacion together,and became their high Priest, and is
laid with his people.
31 After that wolde their enemies haue inuaded their countrey,and destroyed their
land, and lay their hands on their Sanctuarie.
32 Then Simõ resisted them,& foght for his
nacion, and spent muche of his owne substance, and armed the valiant men of his
nacion,and gaue them wages.
33 He fortified also the cities of Iudea, and
Beth-sura that lyeth vpon the borders of
Iudea (where the ordinance of their enemies lay sometime) and set there a garison
of the Iewes.
34 And he fortified Ioppe,which lyeth vpõ
the sea, and Gazara that bordreth vpon
Azotus (where the enemies dwelt afore)
and there he placed Iewes, and furnished
them with thĩgs necessarie for the reparation thereof.
35 Now when the people sawe the faithfulnes of Simon,and to what glorie he thoght
to bring his nacion vnto,they made him
their gouernour,and the chief Priest, because he had done all these things, and for
the vprightnes, and fidelitie that he had
kept to his nacion, and that soght by all
meanes to exalte his people.
36 For in his time they prospered wel by
him,so that the heathen were taken out of
their countrey, and they also which were
in the citie of Dauid at Ierusalem,where
they had made them a castel, out of the
which they wẽt,and defiled all things that
were about the Sanctuarie, and did great
hurt vnto religion.
37 And he set Iewes in it, and fortified it,
for the assurance of the land, and citie,
and raised vp the walles of Ierusalem.
38 And King Demetrius confirmed him in
his high priesthode for these causes,
39 And made him one of his friẽds, and gaue him great honour.
40 For it was reported that the Romains
called the Iewes their friends, and confederates, & that they honorably receiued
Simons ambassadours,
41 And that the Iewes,& Priests cõsented,
that Simon shulde be their prince, & high
Priest perpetually, til God raised vp the
true Prophet,
42 And that he shulde be their captaine,
and haue the charge of the Sanctuarie,and
so set men ouer the workes, and ouer the
countrey,and ouer the weapons, and ouer
the fortresses, and that shulde make prouision for the holie things,
43 And that he shulde be obeyed of euery
man,and that all the writings in the coun
trey shulde be made in his name, and that
he shulde be clothed in purple,and weare
golde,
44 And that it shulde not be lawful for anie
of the people or Priests to breake anie of
these things,or to withstand his wordes,or
to call anie congregacion in the countrey
without him, or be clothed in purple, or
weare a colar of gold:
45 And if anie did contrarie to these things
or brake anie of them, he shulde be punished.
46 So it pleased all the people to agre that
it shulde be done to Simon according vnto these wordes.
47 Simon also accepted it,and was content
to be the high Priest, and the captaine, &
the prince of the Iewes,and of the Priests,
and to be the chief of all.
48 And they commanded to set vp this writing in tables of brasse, and to fasten it to
the wall that compassed the Sanctuarie in
an open place,

Auguste.

"Or, Ierusalem.

49 And that a copie of the same shulde be
laied vp in the treasurie, that Simon and
his sonnes might haue it.

CHAP. XV.

1 Antiochus maketh a couenant of friendship with Simō 11 Tryphon is pursued. 15 The Romains write lettres vnto Kings and nacions in the defence of the Iewes. 27 Antiochus refusing the helpe that Simon sent him, breaketh his couenant.

1 MOreouer King Antiochus the sonne of Demetrius sent lettres from
the yles of the sea vnto Simon the Priest,
and prince of the Iewes, and to all the nacion,
2 Cōteining these wordes, ANTIOCHVS
the King vnto Simon the great Priest, &
to the nacion of the Iewes sendeth gretīg.
3 For so muche as certeine pestilent men
haue vsurped ẏ kingdome of our fathers,
I am purposed to chalenge the realme a-
gaine, and to restore it to the olde estate:
wherefore I haue gathered a great hoste,
and prepared shippes of warre,
4 That I may go thorowe the countrey, &
be aduenged of them, which haue destroied our countrey, and wasted manie cities
in the realme.
5 Now therefore I do confirme vnto thee
all the liberties, whereof all the Kings
my progenitours haue discharged thee,
and all the paiments, whereof they haue
released thee.
6 And I giue thee leaue to coyne money of
thine owne stampe within thy countrey,
7 And that Ierusalem, and the Sanctuarie
be fre, and that all the weapons, that thou
hast prepared, and the fortresses, which
thou hast buylded, & kepest in thine hāds,
shalbe thine.
8 And all that is due vnto the King, and all
that shalbe due vnto ẏ King, I forgiue it
thee, from this time forthe for euermore.
9 And when we haue obteined our kingdome, we wil giue thee, & thy nacion & the
Temple great honour, so that your honor
shalbe knowen thorowe out the worlde.
10 ¶ In the hūdreth, seuentie & foure yere, *Ioseph Antiq.13, chap. 11.*
went Antiochus into his fathers land, and
all the bandes came together vnto him, so
that fewe were left with Tryphon.
11 So the King Antiochus pursued him, but
he fled and came to Dora, which lyeth by
the sea side.
12 For he sawe that troubles were towarde
him, and that the armie had forsaken him.
13 Then camped Antiochus against Dora
with an hundreth and twentie thousand
fighting men, and eight thousand horsemen.
14 So he compassed the citie about, and the
shippes came by the sea. Thus they pressed the citie by land, & by sea, in so muche
that thei suffered no man to go in nor out.
15 In the meane season came Numenius,
and his companie from Rome, hauing lettres writen vnto the Kings and countreis,
wherein were conteined these wordes,
16 LVCIVS THE Consul of Rome vnto King Ptolemeus sendeth greting.
17 The ambassadours of ẏ Iewes are come
vnto vs as our friends and confederates
from Simon the hie Priest, and from the
people of the Iewes to renue friendship,
and the bonde of loue,
18 Who haue broght a shield of golde wey-
ing a thousand pounde.
19 Wherefore we thoght it good to write
vnto the Kings and countreis, that they
shulde not go about to hurt them, nor to
fight against them, nor their cities, nor
their countreie, nether to mainteine their
enemies against them.
20 And we were content to receiue of them
the shield.
21 If therefore there be anie pestilēt felowes
fled from their countrey vnto you, deliuer them vnto Simon the hie Priest, that
he maye punish them according to their
owne Law.
22 The same things were writen to Demetrius the King, and to Attalus, and to A-
rathes and to Arsaces,
23 And to all countreis, as "Sampsames, and *"Or, Sampsacen*
to them of Sparta, and to Delus, and to
Mindus and to Sicion, and to Caria, and
to Samos, and to Pamphylia, and to Lycia, and to Halicarnassus, and to Rho-
dus, and to Phaselis, and to Cos, and to Si-
den, and to Cortyna, and to Gnidon, and
to Cyprus, and to Cyrene.
24 And they sent a copie of them to Simon
the hie Priest.
25 ¶ So Antiochus the King cāped against
Dora the seconde time euer readie to take
it, and made diuers engins of warre, and
kept Tryphon in, that he colde nether go
in nor out.
26 Thē Simon sent him two thousand chosen men to helpe him with siluer & golde,
and muche furniture.
27 Neuertheles, he wolde not receiue thē,
but brake all the couenant, which he had
made with him afore, and withdrewe him
self from him,
28 And sent vnto him Athenobius one of
his friends to commune with him, saying,
Ye withholde Ioppe, and Gazara with the
castle that is at Ierusalem, the citie of my
realme,
29 Whose borders ye haue destroyed and
done great hurt in the land, and haue the
gouernement of manie places of my kīgdome.
30 Wherefore now deliuer the cities, which
ye haue taken, with the tributes of the
places, that ye haue rule ouer without the

borders of Iudea,
31 Or els giue me for them fiue hundreth
talents of siluer, and for the harme that ye
haue done, and for the tributes of the places other fiue hundreth talents: if not, we
wil come, and fight against you.
32 So Athenobius the Kings friend came
to Ierusalem, & when he sawe the honour
of Simon, and the cubbert of golde and
siluer plate, and so great preparacion, he
was astonished, and tolde him the Kings
message.
33 Then answered Simon, and said vnto
him, We haue nether taken other mens
lãds, nor withholden that which apperteineth to others: but our fathers heritage,
which our enemies had vnrighteously in
possession a certeine time.
34 But when we had occasion, we recouered
the inheritance of our fathers.
35 And whereas thou *requirest Ioppe and
Gazara, they did great harme to our people, and through our countrey, yet wil we
giue an hundreth talents for them. But A-
thenobius answered him not one worde,
36 But turned againe angrie vnto the King,
and tolde him all these wordes, and the
dignitie of Simon, with all that he had
sene: and the King was verie angrie.
37 ¶ In the meane time fled Tryphon by
shippe vnto Orthosias.
38 Then the King made Cendebeus captaine of the sea coast, and gaue him bãdes
of fotemen and horsemen,
39 And cõmanded him to remoue ỹ hoste
towarde Iudea, and to buylde vp Cedron,
& to fortifie the gates, & to warre against
the people: but ỹ King pursued Tryphon.
40 So Cendebeus came vnto Iamnia, and
began to vexe the people, and to inuade
Iudea, and to take the people prisoners, &
to slay them.
41 And he buylte vp Cedron, where he set
horsemen and garisons, that they might
make outrodes by the waies of Iudea, as
the King had commanded him.

*Or, complainest concerning.

CHAP. XVI.

8 Cendebeus the captaine of Antiochus hoste is put to flight by the sonnes of Simon. 11 Ptolemeus the sonne of Abobus killeth Simon and his two sonnes at a banket. 23 Iohn killeth them that lye in waite for his life.

Ioseph Antiq. 13. chap. 12.

1 THen came Iohn vp from Gazara, &
tolde Simon his father, what Cendebeus had done.
2 So Simon called two of his eldest sonnes,
Iudas and Iohn, and said vnto them, I, and
my brethren, and my fathers house, haue
euer from our youth vnto this day foghtẽ
against ỹ enemies of Israel, & the matters
haue had good successe vnder our hands, &
we haue deliuered Israel often times.
3 But I am now olde, & ye by *Gods* mercie are
of a sufficient age: be ye therefore in stead
of me, & my brother, & go forthe & fight
for our nacion, & the helpe of heauen be
with you.
4 So he chose twentie thousand fighting
men of the countrey with the horsemen,
which went forthe against Cendebeus, &
rested at Modin.
5 In the morning thei arose, and went into
the plaine field: & beholde, a mightie great
hoste came against them bothe of fotemẽ,
& horsemẽ: but there was a riuer betwixt
them.
6 And Iohn ranged his armie ouer against
him, and when he sawe that the people was
afrayed to go ouer the riuer, he went ouer
first him self, and the men seing him, passed through after him.
7 Then he deuided his men, & set the horsemen in the middes of the fotemen.
8 For their enemies horsemen were verie
manie: but when thei blewe the trumpets,
Cẽdebeus fled with his hoste, whereof manie were slayne, & the remnant gate them
to the fortresse.
9 Then was Iudas Iohns brother wounded:
but Iohn followed after them, til he came
to Cedron, which *Cendebeus* had buylt.
10 Also thei fled vnto the towres, that were
in the fields of Azotus, and those did *Iohn*
burne with fyre: thus were there slaine two
thousand mẽ of them: so he returned peaceably into the land of Iuda.
11 ¶ Now in the field of Iericho was Ptolomeus the sonne of Abubus made captaine,
and he had abundance of siluer and golde.
12 (For he had maried the daughter of the
hie Priest.)
13 Therefore he waxed proude in his minde, and thoght to rule the land, & thoght
to slay Simon and his sonnes by deceit.
14 Now as Simon went about thorowe the
cities of the countrey, & studied carefully
for them, he came downe to Iericho with
Mattathias, and Iudas his sonnes in the
hundreth, seuentie & seuen yere, in the eleuenth moneth, which is the moneth Sabat.
15 Thẽ *the sonne* of Abubus receiued them
by treason into a litle holde, called Do-
chus, which he had buylte, where he made them a great banket, and had hid men
there.
16 So when Simon and his sonnes had made
good chere, Ptolemeus stode vp with his
men, and toke their weapons, and entred
in to Simon in the banket house, and slewe
him with his two sonnes, and certeine of
his seruants.
17 Whereby he committed a great vilenie,
and recompensed euil for good.
18 Then wrote Ptolemeus these things and
sent to the King, that he might send him
an hoste to helpe him, & so wolde deliuer
him the countrey with the cities.

19 He

19 He sent other men also vnto Gazara, to
take Iohn, and sent letters vnto the captaines
to come to him, and he wolde giue thē
siluer, and golde and rewardes.
20 And to Ierusalem he sent other to take
it, and the mountaine of the Temple.
21 But one ranne before, and tolde Iohn in
Gazara, that his father, and his brethren
were slaine, and that *Ptolemeus* had sent to
slay him.
22 When he heard this, he was sore astonished,
& laid hands of them that were come
to slay him, and slewe them: for he
knewe that they went about to kill him.
23 Cōcerning other things of Iohn, bothe
of his warres, and of his noble actes (wherein
he behaued him self manfully) of the
buylding of walles which he made, and
other of his dedes,
24 Beholde, they are writen in the chronicles
of his priesthode, frō the time, that
he was made high Priest after his father.

THE SECONDE BOKE OF THE MACCABEES.

CHAP. I.

1 An epistle of the Iewes that dwelt at Ierusalem, sent vnto them that dwelt in Egypt, wherein they exhorte them to giue thankes for the death of Antiochus. 19 Of the fyre that was hid in the pitte. 24 The prayer of Neemias.

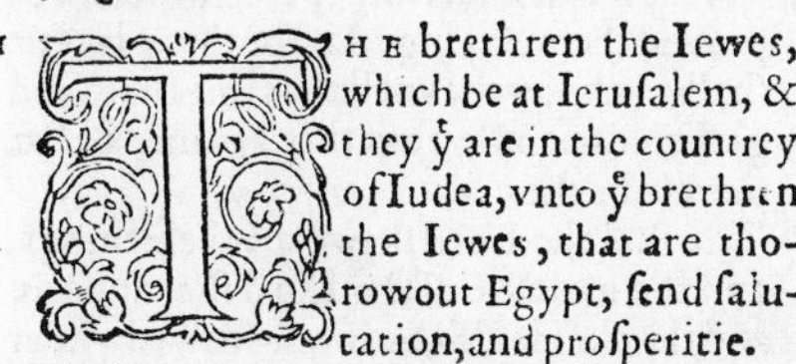

1 The brethren the Iewes,
which be at Ierusalem, &
they ẏ are in the countrey
of Iudea, vnto ẏ brethren
the Iewes, that are thorowout
Egypt, send salutation,
and prosperitie.
2 God be gracious vnto you and remember
his couenant made with Abraham, and Isaac,
and Iacob his faithful seruants,
3 And giue you all an heart, to worship
him, and to do his wil with a whole heart
and with a willing minde,
4 And open your hearts in his Law, and
commandements, and send you peace,
5 And heare your prayers, and be reconciled
with you, and neuer forsake you in time
of trouble.
6 Thus now we praye here for you.
7 When Demetrius reigned, in the hundreth,
threscore and nine yere, we Iewes
wrote vnto you in the trouble, and violence
that came vnto vs in those yeres, after
that Iason, and his companie departed out
of the holie land and kingdome,
8 And burnt the porche, and shed innocent
blood. Then we praid vnto the Lord, and
were heard: we offred sacrifices and fine
floure, and lighted the lampes, and set forthe
the bread.
9 Now therefore kepe ye the dayes of the
feast of the Tabernacles in the moneth
Chasleu.
10 ¶In the hundreth, fourescore and eight
yere, the people that was at Ierusalem, and
in Iudea, ānd the counsel and Iudas, vnto
Aristobulus King Ptolemeus master,
which is of the stocke of the annointed
Priests, & to the Iewes that are in Egypt,
sendeth greting and helth.
11 In so muche as God hathe deliuered vs
from great perils, we thāke him highly, as
thogh we had ouercome the King.
12 For he broght them into Persia by heapes,
that foght against the holie citie.
13 For albeit the captaine, and the armie,
that was with him, semed inuincible, yet
they were slaine in the temple of Nanea,
by the disceit of Naneas Priests.
14 For Antiochus, as thogh he wolde dwell
with her, came thether, he, and his friends
with him, to receiue money vnder the title
of a dowrie.
15 But when the Priests of Nanea had laid
it forthe, and he was entred with a smale
companie within the Temple, they shut
the Temple, when Antiochus was come
in.
16 And by opening a priuie dore of the
vaute, they cast stones, as it were thunder,
vpon the captaine *& his*, and hauing bruised
them in pieces, they cut of their heads
& threwe thē to those that were without.
17 God be blessed in all things, which hathe
deliuered vp the wicked.
18 Whereas we are now purposed to kepe ẏ
purification of the Tēple vpon the fiue &
twētie day of ẏ moneth Chasleu, we thoght
it necessarie to certifie you thereof, ẏ ye also
might kepe the feast of ẏ Tabernacles,
& of the fyre *which was giuen vs* when Neemias
offred sacrifice, after ẏ he had buylt
the Temple, and the altar.
19 For whē as our fathers were led away vnto
Persia, ẏ Priests, which soght the honor
of God, toke the*fyre of the altar priuely, *Leuit.6,13. & 10,2. & 16,3*
and hid it in an hollow pit, which was drie
in ẏ bottom, & therein they kept it, so that
the place was vnknowen vnto euerie mā.
20 Now after manie yeres when it pleased
God that Neemias shulde be sent from
the King of Persia, he sent of ẏ posteritie of

those Priests, which had hid it to fetche
the fyre, and as they tolde vs, they founde
no fyre, but thicke water.
21 Then commanded he them to drawe it
vp, and to bring it: and when the things
apperteinĩg to the sacrifices were broght,
Neemias commanded the Priests to sprin
kle the wood, and the things laid thereupõ
with water.
22 When this was done, and the time came
that the sunne shone, which afore was hid
in the cloude, there was a great fyre kindled, so that euerie man marueiled.
23 Now the Priests, and all prayed, while
the sacrifice was consuming: Ionathan began, and the other answered thereunto.
24 And the prayer of Neemias was after
this maner, O Lord, Lord God maker of
all things, which art feareful, and strong,
& righteous, and merciful, and the onelie
and gracious King,
25 Onely liberal, onely iuste and almightie
and euerlasting, thou that deliuerest Israel from all trouble, and hast chosen the fathers, and sanctified them,
26 Receiue the sacrifice for thy whole people of Israel, and preserue thine owne porcion, and sanctifie it.
27 Gather those together, that are scatered from vs: deliuer them that serue amõg
the heathen: loke vpon them which are
despised, and abhorred, that the heathen
may knowe that thou art our God.
28 Punish them that oppresse vs, and with
pride do vs wrong.
29 Plant thy people againe in thine holie
Deut. 30,5. place *as Moyses hathe spoken.
30 And the Priests sang psalmes thereunto.
31 Now when the sacrifice was consumed,
Neemias commanded the great stones to
be sprinkled with the residue of the water.
32 Which whẽ it was done, there was kindled a flame, which was consumed by the
light, that shined from the altar.
33 ¶ So when this matter was knowen, it was
tolde the King of Persia, that in the place
where the Priests, which were led away,
had hid fyre, there appeared water, wherewith Neemias and his companie had purified the sacrifices.
34 The King tryed out the thing, and closed the place about, and made it holie.
35 And to them that the King fauoured, he
gaue and bestowed manie giftes.
36 And Neemias called the same place
Ephthar, which is to say, purification: but
Or, Nephi. manie men call it "Nephthar.

CHAP. II.

4 How Ieremie hid the tabernacle, the Arke, and the altar in the hil. 23 Of the fiue bokes of Iason conteined in one.

1 IT is founde also in the writings of Ieremias the Prophet, that he commanded them, which were caried away, to take
fyre, as was declared, & as the Prophet cõ
manded thẽ that were led into captiuitie,
2 *Giuing them a Law that they shulde *Baruc.6.*
not forget the commandemẽts of ẏ Lord,
& that they shulde not erre in their mindes, when they sawe images of golde and
siluer, with their ornaments.
3 These and suche other things commanded he them, and exhorted them that they
shuld not let ẏ Law go out of their hearts.
4 It is writen also, how the Prophet, by an
oracle that he had, charged them to take
the tabernacle and the arke, and follow
him: & when he came vp into ẏ mountaine
where Moyses went vp, *and sawe the he- *Deu. 34,1.*
ritage of God,
5 Ieremias went forthe, and founde an hol-
lowe caue, wherein he laid the Tabernacle, and the Arke, and the altar of incense,
and so stopped the dore.
6 And there came certeine of those that
followed him, to marke the place: but they
colde not finde it.
7 Which when Ieremias perceiued, he reproued them, saying, As for that place, it
shalbe vnknowen, vntil the time that God
gather his people together againe, & that
mercie be shewed.
8 Thẽ shal the Lord shewe thẽ these things,
and the maiestie of the Lord shal appeare
and the cloude also, as it was shewed vnder
Moyses, and as *when Salomõ desired, that *1.King.8,68.*
the place might be honorably sanctified. *2.chro.6,21.*
9 For it is manifest that he, being a wise
man, offred the sacrifice of dedication, and
consecracion of the Temple.
10 *And as when Moyses prayed vnto the *Leu. 9.24. & 10,16.*
Lord, the fyre came downe from heauẽ, &
consumed the sacrifice: so, when Salomon
prayed, *the fyre came downe frõ heauen, *2.Chro.7,1.*
and consumed the burnt offring.
11 And Moyses said, Because the sinoffring
was not eaten, therefore is it consumed.
12 So Salomon kept those eight dayes.
13 These thĩgs also are declared in the writings, and registers of Neemias, and how
he made a librarie, and how he gathered
the actes of the Kings, & of the Prophets,
and the actes of Dauid, and the epistles of
the Kings concerning the holie giftes.
14 Euen so Iudas also gathered all things
that came to passe by the warres that were
among vs, which things we haue.
15 Wherefore if ye haue nede thereof, send
some to fetche them vnto you.
16 Where as we then are about to celebrate the purification, we haue writen vnto
you, and ye shal do wel, if ye kepe the same dayes.
17 We hope also that the God, which deliuered all his people, and gaue an heritage
to them all & the kingdome, & the priesthode,

hode, and the Sanctuarie,

Deu.30,5. 18 *As he promised in the Law, wil shortly
haue mercy vpō vs, & gather vs together
from vnder the heauen into his holie place:
for he hathe saued vs from great perils,
and hathe clensed the place.

19 As concerning Iudas Maccabeus, & his
brethren, the purification of the great Tēple,
and the dedicacion of the altar,

20 And the warres against Antiochus Epiphanes,
and Eupator his sonne,

21 And the manifest signes, that came frō
heauen vnto those, which manfully stode
for the Iewes religiō: (for thogh they were
but fewe, yet they rāne through whole coūtreis,
and pursued the barbarous armies,

22 And repaired the Tēple that was renoumed
thorow out all the worlde, and deliuered
the citie, and established the Lawes,
that were like to be abolished, because the
Lord was merciful vnto thē w̄ all lenitie)

23 We wil assay to abbridge in one volume
those things, that Iason the Cyrenean hathe
declared in fiue bokes.

24 For considering the wonderful nomber,
& the difficultie that thei haue that wolde
be occupied in the rehearsal of stories, because
of the diuersitie of the matters,

25 We haue indeuored, that they that wolde
read, might haue pleasure, and that thei
which are studious, might easily kepe
them in memorie, & that whosoeuer read
them, might haue profite.

26 Therefore to vs that haue taken in hand
this great labour, it was no easie thing to
make this abbridgement, but required bothe
sweat, and watching.

27 Like as he that maketh a feast, & seketh
other mens commoditie, hathe no smale
labour: so we also for manie mens sakes are
verie wel content to vndertake this great
labour.

28 Leauing to the autor the exact diligence
of euerie particular, we will labour to go
forwarde according to the prescript order
of an abbridgement.

29 For as he that wil buylde a newe house,
must prouide for the whole buylding, but
he that setteth out ŷ plat or goeth about
to painte it, seketh but onely what is comlie
for the decking thereof:

30 Euen so I thinke for vs, that it apperteineth
to the first writer of a storie to enter
depely into it, and to make mencion of all
things, and to be curious in euerie parte.

31 But it is permitted to him that wil shorten
it, to vse fewe wordes, and to auoyde
those things that are curious therein.

32 Here then wil we beginne the storie,
adding thus muche to our former wordes,
that it is but a foolish thing to abonde in
wordes before the storie, and to be shorte
in the storie.

CHAP. III.

2 Of the honour done vnto the Temple by the Kings of the Gentiles. 6 Simon vttereth what treasure is in the Temple. 7 Heliodorus is sente to take them away. 26 He is striken of God and healed at the prayer of Onias.

1 WHat time as the holy citie was inhabited
with all peace, and when
the Lawes were very wel kept, because of
the godlines of Onias the hie Priest, and
hatred of wickednes,

2 It came to passe that euen the Kings did
honour the place, and garnished the Temple
with great giftes.

3 In so muche that Seleuchus King of Asia
of his owne rentes, bare all the costes belonging
to the seruice of the sacrifices.

4 But one Simon of the tribe of Beniamin
being appointed ruler of the Temple, contended
with the hie Priest concerning "the *"Or, the stat & prouision.*
iniquitie committed in the citie.

5 And whē he colde not ouercome Onias,
he gate him to Apollonius the sonne of
Thraseas, which then was gouernour of
Coelosyria and Phenice,

6 And tolde him that the treasurie in Ierusalē
was ful of innumerable money, which
did not belong to the prouision of the sacrifices,
and that it were possible that these
things might come into ŷ Kings hands.

7 Now whē Apollonius came to the King,
and had shewed him of the money, as it
was tolde him, the King chose out Heliodorus
his treasurer, and sent him with a
commandement, to bring him the foresaid
money.

8 Immediatly Heliodorus toke his iourney
as thogh he wolde visite the cities of Coelosyria
& Phenice, but in effect to fulfil the
Kings purpose.

9 So when he came to Ierusalem, and was
courteously receiued of the hie Priest into
the citie, he declared what was determined
concerning the money, & shewed the
cause of his coming, and asked if these
things were so in dede.

10 Then the hie Priest tolde him that there
were suche things laide vp by ŷ widdowes
and fatherles,

11 And that a certeine of it belonged vnto
Hircanus *the sonne* of Tobias a noble mā,
and not as that wicked Simon had reported,
and that in all there were but foure
hundreth talents of siluer, and two hundreth
of golde,

12 And that it were altogether vnpossible
to do this wrong to them that had committed
it of trust to the holines of the place
and Temple, which is honored thorowe
the whole worlde for holines & integritie.

13 But Heliodorus because of the Kings cōmandemēt
giuen him, said that in any wise
it must be broght into ŷ Kings treasurie.

14 So he appointed a day, and went in to
take order for theſe things: then there was
no ſmale grief thorowout the whole citie.
15 For ẏ Prieſts fell downe before the altar
in the Prieſts garments, and called vnto
heauen vpon him which had made a Law
concerning things giuen to be kept, that
they ſhulde be ſafely preſerued for ſuche
as had committed them to be kept.
16 Then thei that loked the high Prieſt in
the face, were wounded in their heart: for
his countenance, and the changing of his
colour declared the ſorowe of his minde.
17 The man was ſo wrapped in feare & trẽ-
bling of the bodie, that it was manifeſt to
thẽ that loked vpon him, what ſorowe he
had in his heart.
18 Others alſo came out of their houſes by
heapes vnto the cõmune prayer, becauſe ẏ
place was like to come vnto contempt.
19 And the women, girt with ſakecloth vnder their breaſtes, filled the ſtretes, and the
virgines that were kept in, ranne ſome to
the gates and ſome to the walles, & others
loked out of the windowes.
20 And all helde vp their hands toward
heauen, and made prayer.
21 It was a lamentable thing to ſe the multitude that fell downe of all ſortes, and the
expectation of the high Prieſt being in
ſuche anguiſh.
22 Therefore thei called vpõ the almightie Lord that he wolde kepe ſafe and ſure
the things, which were layed vp for thoſe
that had deliuered them.
23 Neuertheles, the thing ẏ Heliodorus was
determined to do, that did he performe.
24 And as he & his ſouldiers were now there preſent by the treaſurie, he that is the
Lord of the ſpirits, & of all power, ſhewed
a great viſion, ſo that all thei which preſu-
med to come with him, were aſtoniſhed
at the power of God, and fell into feare,
and trembling.
25 For there appeared vnto them an horſe
with a terrible mã ſitting vpon him, moſte
richely barbed, and he ranne fiercely, and
ſmote at Heliodorus with his fore fete, &
it ſemed that he that ſate vpon the horſe,
had harnes of golde.
26 Moreouer, there appeared two yong mẽ,
notable in ſtrength, excellent in beautie,
and comelie in apparel, which ſtode by
him on ether ſide, and ſcoureged him continually, and gaue him manie ſore ſtripes.
27 And Heliodorus fel ſuddenly vnto the
grounde, and was couered with great darkenes: but they that were with him, toke
him vp, and put him in a litter.
28 Thus he that came with ſo great cõpanie, & manie ſouldiers into ẏ ſaid treaſurie, was borne out: for he colde not helpe
him ſelf with his weapons.
29 So they did knowe the power of God ma
nifeſtly, but he was domme by the power
of God, and lay deſtitute of all hope and
helth.
30 And they praiſed the Lord that had honored his owne place: for the Tẽple which
a litle afore was ful of feare and trouble,
when the almightie Lord appeared, was fil
led with ioye and gladnes.
31 Then ſtreight wayes certeine of Heliodorus friends prayed Onias, that he wolde
call vpõ the moſte High to grant him his
life, which lay readie to giue vp the goſte.
32 So the hie Prieſt, conſidering that the
King might ſuſpect that the Iewes had do
ne Heliodorus ſome euil, he offered a ſacri
fice for the helth of the man.
33 Now when the hie Prieſt had made his
prayer, the ſame yong men in the ſame clo
thing appeared, and ſtode beſide Heliodorus, ſaying, Giue Onias ẏ hie Prieſt great
thankes: for his ſake hathe the Lord granted thee thy life.
34 And ſeing that thou haſt bene ſcourged
frõ heauen, declare vnto all mẽ the mightie power of God: & when they had ſpokẽ
theſe wordes, they appeared no more.
35 So Heliodorus offred vnto the Lord ſacrifice, and made great vowes vnto him,
which had granted him his life, and thanked Onias, & went againe with his hoſte to
the King.
36 Then teſtified he vnto euerie man of the
great workes of God that he had ſene with
his eyes.
37 And when the King aſked Heliodorus,
who were mete to be ſent yet once againe
to Ieruſalem, he ſaid,
38 If thou haſt anie enemie or traitor, ſend
him thether, & thou ſhalt receiue him wel
ſcourged, if he eſcape with his life: for in
that place, no doubte, there is a ſpecial power of God.
39 For he that dwelleth in heauen, hathe his
eye on ẏ place, and defendeth it, & he beateth & deſtroieth thẽ that come to hurt it.
40 This came to paſſe concerning Heliodorus, and the keping of the treaſurie.

CHAP. IIII.

1 Simon reporteth euil of Onias. 7 Iaſon obteineth the office of the hie Prieſt by corrupting the King, 27 And was by Menelaus defrauded by like bribing. 34 Onias is ſlayne traiterouſly by Andronicus.

1 THis Simon now, of whome we ſpake
afore, being a bewraier of the money
and of his owne natural countrey, report-
ted euil of Onias, as thogh he had moued
Heliodorus vnto this, and had bene the inuenter of the euil.
2 Thus was he bolde to call him a traitour
that was ſo beneficial to the citie, and a defender of his nacion, and ſo zealous of
the Lawes.

3 But

3 But when his malice increased so farre,
that thorow one that belonged to Simon,
murthers were committed,
4 Onias considering the danger of this con
tention,& that Apollonius as he that was
the gouernour of Coelosyria and Phenice, did rage, and increased Simons malice,
5 He went to the King not as an accuser of
the citizens, but as one that intended the
commune welth bothe priuatly and publikely.
6 For he sawe it was not possible except the
King toke order to quiet the matters, and
that Simon wolde not leaue of his folie.
7 But after the death of Seleucus, when Antiochus, called Epiphanes, toke the kingdome, Iason the brother of Onias labored by vnlawful meanes to be hie Priest.
8 For he came vnto the King, and promised
him thre hundreth and thre score talents
of siluer, and of another rente, fourescо-
re talents.
9 Besides this he promised him an hundreth and fiftie, if he might haue licence
to set vp a place for exercise, and a place
for the youth, and that they wolde * name
them of Ierusalem Antiochians.
10 The which thing when the King had
granted,& he had gotten the superioritie,
he began immediatly to drawe his kinsmē
to the customes of the Gentiles,
11 And abolished ỷ friendlie priuiledges of
the Kings, that the Iewes had set vp by
Iohn, the father of Eupolemus, which was
sent ambassadour vnto Rome, to become
friends and confederates: he put downe
their lawes & policies, & broght vp newe
statutes, and contrarie to the Lawe.
12 For he presumed to buylde a place of exercise vnder the castel, & broght the chief
yong men vnder his subiection, and made
them weare * hattes.
13 So there began a great desire to follow
the maners of the Gentiles, and they toke
vp the facions of strange nacions by the
exceading wickednes of Iason, not the hie
Priest, but the vngodlie persone,
14 So that the Priestes were now no more
diligent about the seruice of the altar, but
despised the Temple, and regarded not the
sacrifices, but made haste to be partakers
of the wicked expenses at the playe a after
the casting of the stone.
15 For they did not set by the honour of
their fathers, but liked the glorie of the
Gentiles best of all.
16 By reason whereof great calamitie came
vpon them: for they had them to be their
enemies and punishers, whose custome
they followed so earnestly, and desired to
be like them in all things.
17 For it is not a light thing to transgresse

* Or, that he wolde write the Antiochians that were at Ierusalem, among them

* Or, buskius in token of wantones as the Gentiles did.

a This game was to trye stregth by casting a stone ỷ had an hole in the middes, or a piece of metal.

against the Lawes of God, but the time
following shal declare these things.
18 ¶ Now when the games that were vsed
euerie fiue yere, were plaide at Tyrus, the
King being present,
19 This wicked Iason sent from Ierusalem
men to loke vpon them, as thogh they had
bene Antiochians, ẇ broght thre hundreth
drachmes of siluer for a sacrifice to Hercules: albeit they that caryed them, desired they might not be bestowed on the sacrifice (because it was not comelie) but to
be bestowed for other expenses.
20 So he that sent them, sent them for the
sacrifice of Hercules: but because of those that broght them, they were giuen to
the making of galleis.
21 ¶ Now Apollonius the sonne of Me-
nestheus was sent into Egypt because of
the coronation of King Ptolemeus Philometor: but when Antiochus perceiued
that he was euil affectioned towarde his
affaires, he soght his owne assurance, and
departed from thence to Ioppe, and so came to Ierusalem,
22 Where he was honorably receiued of Ia
son, and of the citie, & was broght in with
torche light, & with great showtings, and
so he went with his hoste vnto Phenice.
23 Thre yere afterwarde Iason sent Menelaus, the foresaid Simons brother, to beare
the money vnto the King, and to bring to
passe certeine necessarie affaires, whereof
he had giuen him a memorial.
24 But he, being commended to the King,
magnified him for the appearance of his
power, & turned the priesthode vnto him
self: for he gaue thre hundreth talents of
siluer more then Iason.
25 So he gate the Kings * letters patentes, albeit he had nothing in him self worthie of
the hie priesthode, but bare the stomacke
of a cruel tyrant, and the wrath of a wilde beast.
26 Thē Iason, which had disceiued his owne brother, being deceiued by another, was
compelled to flee into the countrey of the
Ammonites.
27 So Menelaus gate the dominion: but as
for the money that he had promised vnto
the King, he toke none order for it, albeit
Sostratus ỷ ruler of the castel required it.
28 For vnto him apperteined the gathering
of ỷ customes: wherefore they were bothe
called before the King.
29 Now Menelaus left his brother Lysimachus in his stead in the priesthode, and Sostratus *left* Crates which was gouernour
of the Cyprians.
30 ¶ Whiles these things were in doing, the
Tharsians and they of Mallot made insur-
rectiō, because they were giuē to the Kings
concubine called Antiochis.

* Or, commandements.

31 Then came the King in all haste, to ap-
peasc the busines, leauing Andronicus a
man of autoritie to be his lieutenant.
32 Now Menelaus, supposing that he had
gotten a cōuenient time, stole certeine vessels of golde out of the Temple, and gaue
certeine of them to Andronicus: and some
he solde at Tyrus & in the cities thereby.
33 Which when Onias knewe of a suretie,
he reproued him, and withdrewe him self
into a Sāctuarie at Daphne by Antiochia.
34 Wherefore Menelaus, takīg Andronicus
a parte, prayed him to slay Onias: so whē
he came to Onias, he coūseled him craftely, giuing him his right hand with an othe:
(howbeit he suspect him, & persuaded him
to come out of the Sanctuarie) so he slewe
him incontinently without any regarde of
righteousnes.
35 For the which cause not onely the Iewes,
but many other nacions also were grieued,
and toke it heauily for the vnrighteous
death of this man.
36 ¶ And when the King was come againe
from the places about Cilicia, the Iewes
that were in the citie, and certeine of the
Grekes that abhorred the fact also, complained because Onias was slaine without
cause.
37 Therefore Antiochus was sorie in his
minde, and he had compassion, and wept
because of the modestie and great discretion of him that was dead.
38 Wherefore being kindled with angre,
he toke away Andronicus garment of purple, and rent his clothes, and commanded
him to be led through out the citie, and in
the same place where he had cōmitted the
wickednes against Onias, he was slaine as
a murtherer. Thus the Lord rewarded him
his punishment, as he had deserued.
39 ¶ Now when Lysimachus had done many wicked dedes in the citie through the
counsel of Menelaus, and the brute was
spred abroad, ẏ multitude gathered them
together against Lysimachus: for he had
caryed out now muche vessel of golde.
40 And when the people arose, & were ful
of angre, Lysimachus armed about thre
thousand, & began to vse vnlauful power,
a certeine tyrant being their captaine, who
was no lesse decayed in wit then in age.
41 But whē they vnderstode the purpose of
Lysimachus, some gate stones, some great
clubbes, and some cast handfuls of dust,
which lay by, vpon Lysimachus men, and
those that inuaded them.
42 Whereby manie of them were wounded,
some were slaine, and all the other chased
away: but the wicked Churchrobber him
self they killed besides the treasurie.
43 For these causes an accusation was laide
against Menelaus.
44 And when the King came to Tyrus, thre
men sent from the Senat pleaded the cause
before him.
45 But Menelaus, being now cōuinced, promised to Ptolemeus *the sonne* of Dorimenes muche money, if he wolde persuade
the King.
46 So Ptolemeus went to the King into a
courte, where as he was to coule him self, &
turned the Kings minde.
47 In so muche that he discharged Menelaus from the accusacions (notwithstanding he was the cause of all mischief) and
condēned those poore men to death, which
if they had tolde their cause, yea, before
the Scythians, thei shulde haue bene heard
as innocent.
48 Thus were they sone punished vniustly, which followed vpō the matter for the
citie, and for the people, and for the holie
vessels.
49 Wherefore they of Tyrus hated that
wickednes, and ministred all things liberally for their buryal.
50 And so through the couetousnes of thē
that were in power, Menelaus remained in
authoritie, increasing in malice, and declared him selfe a great traitor to the citizēs.

CHAP. V.

2 Of the signes and tokens sene in Ierusalem. 6 Of the end and wickednes of Iason. 11 The pursute of Antiochus against the Iewes. 15 The spoiling of the Temple 27 Maccabeus fleeth into the wildernes.

1 ABout the same time Antiochus vndertoke his seconde voyage into Egypt:
2 And then were there sene through out all
the citie of *Ierusalem*, fortie dayes long,
horsemen running in the aire, with robes
of golde, and as bandes of speare men,
3 And as troupes of horsemen set in array,
incountering & coursing one against another with shaking of shields and multitude of dartes and drawing of swordes, and
shoting of arrowes, and the glittering of
the golden armour sene, and harnes of all
sortes.
4 Therefore euerie man prayed, that those
tokens might turne to good.
5 Now when there was gone forthe a false
rumour, as thogh Antiochus had bene
dead, Iason toke at ẏ least a thousand mē,
and came suddenly vpon the citie, & they
that were vpon the walles, being put backe
and the citie at length taken,
6 Menelaus fled into the castel, but Iason
slewe his owne citizēs without mercie, not
considering that to haue the aduantage against his kinsmē is greatest disaduātage,
but thoght that he had gotten the victorie
of his enemies, & not of his owne nacion.
7 Yet he gate not the superioritie, but at the
last receiued shame for the rewarde of his
traison,

traison, and went againe like a vagabound
into the countrey of the Ammonites.
8 Finally he had this end of his wicked cō-
uersation, ŷ he" was accused before Areta, ||Or, shut vp.
the King of the Arabians, and fled from
citie to citie, being pursued of euerie mā,
and hated as a forsaker of the Lawes, and
was in abominacion, as an enemie of his
countrey and citizens, and was driuen into Egypt.
9 Thus he that had chased manie out of
their owne countrey, perished as a banished man, after that he was gone to the
Lacedemonians, thinking there to haue
gotten succour by reason of kinred.
10 And he that had cast manie out vnburyed, was throwen out him self, no man
mourning for him, nor putting him in his
graue: nether was he partaker of his fathers sepulchre.
11 ¶ Now when these things that were done, were declared to the King, he thoght
that Iudea wolde haue fallen from him:
wherefore he came with a furious minde
out of Egypt, & toke the citie by violēce.
12 He commanded his men of warre also,
that they shulde kill, and not spare suche
as they met, and to slay suche as went into
their houses.
13 Thus was there a slaughter of yong mē,
and olde men, and a destruction of men &
women & children, and virgines, and infants were murthered:
14 So that within thre dayes were slayne
foure score thousand, and fortie thousand
taken prisoners, and there were as manie
solde as were slayne.
15 Yet was he not content with this, but
durst go into the moste holy Temple of
all the worlde, hauing Menelaus that traitour to the Lawes, and to his owne countrey, to be his guide,
16 And with his wicked hāds toke the holie
vessels, which other Kings had giuen for ŷ
garnishing, glorie and honour of that place, & handled them with his wicked hāds.
17 So hautie in his minde was Antiochus,
that he considered not, that God was not
a litle wrothe for the sinnes of them that
dwelt in the citie, for the which suche cōtempt came vpon that place.
18 For if they had not bene wrapped in manie sinnes, he, assone as he had come, had
suddēly bene punished, & put backe from
his presumption, as Heliodorus was, whome Seleucus the King sent to vewe the
treasurie.
19 But God hathe not chosen the nacion
for the places sake, but the place for the
nacion sake.
20 And therefore is the place become partaker of the peoples trouble, but afterwarde shal it be partaker of the benefites of
the Lord, and as it is now forsaken in the
wrath of the Almightie, so when the great
Lord shalbe reconciled, it shalbe set vp in
great worship againe.
21 ¶ So when Antiochus had taken eighten
hundreth talents out of the Temple, he
gate him to Antiochia in all haste, thinking in his pride to make men sayle vpon
the drye land, and to walke vpon the sea:
suche an hie minde had he.
22 But he left deputes to vexe the people:
at Ierusalem Philippe a Phrygiā by birth,
in maners more cruel then he that set him
there:
23 And at Garizin Andronicus, & with thē
Menelaus, which was more grieuous to
the citizens then the other, and was despiteful against the Iewes his citizens.
24 He sent also Apollonius a cruel prince,
with an armie of two & twentie thousand,
whome he commanded to slaye those that
were towarde mans age, and to sell the women, and the yonger sorte.
25 So when he came to Ierusalem, he fained
peace, and kept him stil vntil the holy day
of Sabbath: and then finding the Iewes
keping the feast, he commanded his men
to take their weapons.
26 And so he slewe all them that were gone
forthe to the shewe, and running through
the citie with his men armed, he murthered a great nomber.
27 But Iudas Maccabeus, being as it were
the tenth, fled into the wildernes, & liued
there in the mountaines with his companie among the beastes, and dwelling there,
and eating grasse, lest they shulde be partakers of the filthines.

CHAP. VI.

1 The Iewes are compelled to leaue the Law of God. 4 The Temple is defiled 10 The women cruelly punished. 28 The grieuous paine of Eleazarus.

1 NOt long after this, sent the King
an olde man of" Athens, for to com ||Or, Antiochia.
pell the Iewes, to transgresse the Lawes of
the fathers, and not to be gouerned by the
Law of God,
2 And to defile the Temple that was at Ierusalem, and to call it the temple of Iupiter Olympius, and that of Garizin, accor
ding as they did that dwelt at that place,
Iupiter, that kepeth hospitalitie.
3 This wicked gouernement was sore and
grieuous vnto the people.
4 For the Temple was ful of dissolucion,
and glottonie of the Gentiles, which dal-
lied with harlots, & had to do with women
within the circuit of the holie places, and
broght in suche things as were not lawful.
5 The altar also was ful of suche things, as
were abominable & forbiden by the Law.
6 Nether was it lawful to kepe ŷ Sabbaths,
nor to obserue their anciēt feasts, nor plai-

nely to confesse him self to be a Iewe.
7 In the day of the Kings birth they were
grieuously compelled parforce euerie mo
neth to banket,and when the feast of Bacchus was kept,they were constrained to go
in the procesion of Bacchus with garlandes of yuie.
8 Moreouer through the counsel of Ptolemeus,there went out a commandemẽt vnto the next cities of the heathen against
the Iewes,that the like custome,and "banketting shulde be kept.

*Or, eating of the flesh that was sacrificed.

9 And who so wolde not conforme them
selues to the maners of the Gentiles, shulde be put to death: then might a man haue
sene the present miserie.
10 For there were two women broght forthe, that had circumcised their sonnes,
whome when they had led rounde about
ẏ citie(the babes hanging at their breasts)
they cast them downe headlong ouer the
walles.
11 Some that were runne together into dennes to kepe the Sabboth day secretly,were
discouered vnto Philippe, and were burnt
together,because that for the reuerence of
the honorable day they were afraied to
helpe them selues.
12 ¶Now I beseche those which reade this
boke,that thei be not discouraged for these calamities,but that thei iudge these afflictions,not to be for destruction, but for
a chastening of our nacion.
13 For it is a token of his great goodnes not
to suffer sinners long to continue, but
straight waies to punish them.
14 For the Lord doeth not lõg waite for vs,
as for other nacions,whome he punisheth
whẽ thei are come to ẏ fulnes of their sins.
15 But thus he dealeth with vs, that our sinnes shulde not be heaped vp to the ful, so
that afterwarde he shulde punish vs.
16 And therefore he neuer withdraweth his
mercie from vs: & thogh he punish with
aduersitie, yet doeth he neuer forsake his
people.
17 But let this be spoken now for a warnĩg
vnto vs: & now wil we come to the declaring of the matter in fewe wordes.
18 ¶Eleazar then one of the principal scribes,an aged man,& of a wel fauoured countenance, was constrained to open his
mouth,and to eat swines flesh.
19 But he desiring rather to dye gloriously
thẽ to liue with hatred,offred him self willingly to the torment,and spit it out.
20 As thei oght to go *to death* which suffer
punishment for suche things, as it is not
lawful to taste of for the desire to liue.
21 But thei that had the charge of this wicked banket,for that olde friẽdship of the-
mã, toke him aside priuely,& prayed him,
that he wolde take suche flesh, as was lauful for him to vse, & as he wolde prepare
for him self, & dissemble as thogh he had
eaten of the things appointed by ẏ King,
euen the flesh of the sacrifice,
22 That in so doing he might be deliuered
from death,and that for the olde friẽdship
that was among them, he wolde receiue
this fauour.
23 But he began to consider discretely,& as
became his age,and the excellencie of his
ancient yeres,and the honour of his gray
heeres, whereunto he was come,&his moste honest conuersation from his childehode,but chiefly the holie Law made and
giuen by God: therefore he answered con-
sequently, and willed them straight waies
to send him to the graue.
24 For it becometh not our age, *said he*, to
dissemble,whereby manie yong persones
might thinke, that Eleazar being foure
score yere olde and ten were now gone to
"another religion,

*Or, to another maner of life.

25 And so through mine hypocrisie(for a
litle time of a transitorie life) they might
be deceiued by me, and I shulde procure
maledictiõ,& reproche to mine olde age.
26 For thogh I were now deliuered frõ the
torments of mẽ,yet colde I not escape the
hand of the Almightie, nether aliue nor
dead.
27 Wherefore I wil now change this life
manfully, and wil shewe my self suche as
mine age requireth,
28 And so wil leaue a notable exãple for suche as be yong,to dye willingly & courageously for the honorable & holie Lawes.
And whẽ he had said these wordes,imme-
diatly he went to torment.
29 Now they that led him, changed ẏ loue
which they bare him before, into hatred,
because of the wordes that he had spoken:
for they thoght it had bene a rage.
30 And as he was readie to giue the gost
because of the strokes,he sighed and said,
The Lord that hathe the holy knowledge,
knoweth manifestly, that whereas I might
haue bene deliuered frõ death,I am scourged and suffer these sore paines of my bodie: but in my minde I suffer them gladly
for his religion.
31 Euẽ now after this maner ẽded he his life,
leauing his death for an exãple of a noble
courage,and a memorial of vertue, not o-
nely vnto yong mẽ,but vnto all his naciõ.

CHAP. VII.

The punishment of the seuen brethren & of their mother.

1 IT came to passe also that seuen brethren, with their mother, were taken
to be compelled by the King against the
Law, to taste swines flesh, and were tormented with scourges and whippes.
2 But one of them, which spake first, said
thus, What sekest thou?and what woldest ẏ
knowe

knowe of vs? we are readie to dye, rather
thẽ to trãsgresse the Lawes of our fathers.
3 Then was the King angrie, and commanded to heat pannes and cauldrons, which
were incontinently made hote.
4 And he cõmanded the tõgue of him that
spake first, to be cut out, and to flay him &
to cut of the vtmost partes of his bodie in
ẏ sight of his other brethren & his mother.
5 Now when he was thus mangled in all his
membres, he cõmanded him to be broght
aliue to the fyre & to frye him in the panne: & while the smoke for a long time smo
ked out of the pãne, the *other brethren* with
their mother, exhorted one another to dye
courageously, saying in this maner,
6 The Lord God doeth regarde vs, & in dede taketh pleasure in vs, as Moyses* declared in the song wherein he testified openly, saying,
That *God* wil take pleasure in his seruãts.

Deut. 32, 36.

7 ¶ So when the first was dead after this ma
ner, they broght the seconde to make him
a mocking stocke: and when they had pulled the skinne with ẏ heere ouer his head,
they asked him, if he wolde eat, or he were
punished in all the members of the bodie.
8 But he answered in his owne langage, &
said, No. Wherefore he was tormented
forthewith like the first.
9 And when he was at ẏ last breth, he said,
Thou murtherer takest this present life
from vs, but the King of the worlde wil
raise vs vp, which dye for his Lawes, in
the resurrection of euerlasting life.
10 ¶ After him was the thirde had in derision, and when they demanded his tongue,
he put it out incõtinently, & stretched forthe his hands boldely,
11 And spake manfully, These haue I had
from the heauen, but now for the Law of
God, I despise them, and trust that I shal
receiue them of him againe.
12 In so muche that the King & they which
were with him, marueiled at the yong mãs
courage, as at one that nothing regarded ẏ
paines.
13 ¶ Now when he was dead also, they vexed
and tormented the fourth in like maner.
14 And when he was now readie to dye, he
said thus, It is better that we shulde chãge
this which we might hope for of men, &
wait for our hope from God, that we may
be raised vp againe by him: as for thee,
thou shalt haue no resurrection to life.
15 ¶ Afterwarde they broght the fift also &
tormented him,
16 Who loked vpon the King, & said, Thou
hast power among men, and thogh thou be
a mortal man, thou doest what thou wilt:
but thinke not, that God hathe forsaken
our nacion.
17 But abide a while, and thou shalt se his
great power, how he wil torment thee and
thy sede.
18 After him also they broght the sixt, who
being at the point of death, said, Deceiue
not thy self foolishly: for we suffer these
things, which are worthie to be wõdred at
for our owne sakes, because we haue offended our God.
19 But thinke not thou, which vndertakest
to fight against God, that thou shalt be
vnpunished.
20 But the mother was marueilous aboue
all other, & worthie of honorable memorie: for when she sawe her seuẽ sonnes slaine within ẏ space of one day, she suffred it
with a good wil, because of the hope that
she had in the Lord.
21 Yea, she exhorted euerie one of them in
her owne langage, and being ful of courage and wisdome, stirred vp her womanlie
affections with a mãlie stomacke, and said
vnto them,
22 I can not tel how ye came into my wombe: for I nether gaue you breth nor life: it
is not I that set in order the members of
your bodie,
23 But douteles the Creator of the worlde,
which formed the birth of man, & founde
out the beginning of all things, wil also of
his owne mercie giue you breth and life a-
gaine, as ye now regarde not your owne
selues, for his Lawes sake.
24 Now Antiochus thinking him self despised, & considering the iniurious wordes,
while the yongest was yet aliue, he did exhorte him not onely with wordes, but swore also vnto him by an othe ẏ he wolde ma
ke him riche and welthie, if he wolde forsake ẏ Lawes of his fathers, & that he wolde take him as a friẽd, & giue him offices.
25 But when the yong mã wolde in no case
hearken vnto him, the King called his mo
ther, and exhorted that she wolde counsel
the yong man to saue his life.
26 And when he had exhorted her with
manie wordes, she promised him that she
wolde counsel her sonne.
27 So she turned her vnto him, laughing the
cruel tyrant to scorne, & spake in her owne
langage, O my sonne, haue pitie vpon me,
that bare thee nine moneths in my wombe,
& gaue thee sucke thre yeres, & nourished
thee, and toke care for thee vnto this age,
and broght thee vp.
28 I beseche thee, my sonne, loke vpon the
heauen & the earth, and all that is therein,
& consider that God made thẽ of things ẏ
were not, & so was mãkinde made likewise.
29 Feare not this hangman, but shewe thy
self worthie suche brethren by suffering
death, that I may receiue thee in mercie
with thy brethren.
30 While she was yet speaking these wor-

des, the yong man said, Whome wait ye
for? I wil not obey the Kings commandement: but I wil obey the commandement
of the Lawe that was giuen vnto our fathers by Moyses.
31 And thou that imaginest all mischief a-
gainst the Hebrewes, shalt not escape the
hand of God.
32 For we suffer these things, because of our
sinnes,
33 But thogh the liuing Lord be angrie with
vs a litle while for our chastening and cor
rection, yet wil he be reconciled with his
owne seruants.
34 But thou, ô man without religion & moste wicked of all men, lift not thy self vp
in vaine, which art puffed vp with vncerteine hope, and liftest thine hands against
the seruants of God.
35 For thou hast not yet escaped the iudgement of almightie God, which seeth all
things.
36 My brethrẽ that haue suffered a litle paine, are now vnder the diuine couenant of
euerlasting life: but thou through the iudgemẽt of God, shalt suffer iust punishmẽts
for thy pride.
37 Therefore I, as my brethren haue done,
offer my bodie and life for the Lawes of
our fathers, beseching God, that he wil sone be merciful vnto our nacion, and that
thou by torment and punishment mayest
confesse, that he is the onelie God,
38 And that in me and my brethren ỹ wrath
of the Almightie, which is righteously fal
len vpon all our nation, may cease.
39 Then the King being kindled with anger, raged more cruelly against him then
the others, and toke it grieuously, that he
was mocked.
40 So he also dyed holely, and put his whole trust in the Lord.
41 Last of all after the sonnes, was the mother put to death.
42 Let this now be ynough spoken concerning the bankets, and extreme cruelties.

CHAP. VIII.

1 Iudas gathereth together his hoste. 9 Nicanor is sent against Iudas. 16 Iudas exhorteth his souldiers to constancie. 20 Nicanor is ouercome. 27 The Iewes giue thankes, after they haue put their enemies to flight, diuiding parte of the spoiles vnto the fatherles and vnto the widdowes. 30 Timotheus and Bacchides are discomfited. 35 Nicanor fleeth vnto Antiochus.

1 THen Iudas Maccabeus, and they that
were with him, went priuely into the
townes, & called their kinsfolkes & frieds
together, & toke vnto thẽ all suche as continued in the Iewes religiõ, and assembled
six thousand men.
2 So they called vpõ the Lord, that he wolde haue an eye vnto his people, which was
vexed of euerie mã, & haue pitie vpõ the
Temple that was defiled by wicked men,
3 And that he wolde haue compassion vpon
the citie ỹ was destroyed, & almost broght
to the grounde, & that he wolde heare the
voyce of the blood that cryed vnto him,
4 And that he wolde remember the wicked
slaughter of the innocent children, & the
blasphemies cõmitted against his Name,
& that he wolde shewe this hatred against
the wicked.
5 Now when Maccabeus had gathered this
multitude, he colde not be withstand by
the heathen: for the wrath of the Lord was
turned into mercie.
6 Therefore he came at vnwares, & burnt
vp the townes and cities: yet he toke the
moste commodious places, and slewe many of the enemies.
7 But specially he vsed the nightes to make
suche assalts, in so muche that the brute of
his manlines was spred euerie where.
8 ¶ So when Philippe sawe that this mã increased by litle and litle, and that things
prospered with him for the moste parte, he
wrote vnto Ptolemeus the gouernour of
Coelosyria and Phenice, to helpe him in
the Kings busines.
9 Then sent he spedely Nicanor *the sonne*
of Patroclus, a special friend of his, & gaue him of all nacions of the heathẽ no lesse then twentie thousand men, to rote out
the whole generacion of the Iewes, & ioyned with him Gorgias a captaine, which
in matters of warre had great experience.
10 Nicanor ordeined also a tribute for the
King of two thousand talents, which the
Romaines shulde haue, to be taken of the
Iewes that were taken prisoners.
11 Therefore immediatly he sent to the cities on the seacoast, prouoking them to bye
Iewes to be their seruants, promising to sel
foure score & ten for one talent: but he cõsidered not the vengeance of almightie
God, that shulde come vpon him.
12 When Iudas then knewe of Nicanors co
ming, he tolde thẽ that were with him, of
the coming of the armie.
13 Now were there some of them fearful,
which trusted not vnto ỹ righteousnes of
God, but fled away, & abode not in ỹ place.
14 But the other solde all that they had left,
and besoght the Lord together, to deliuer
them frõ that wicked Nicanor, which had
solde them, or euer he came nere them.
15 And thogh he wolde not do it for their
sakes, yet for the couenant made with their
fathers, and because they called vpon his
holie and glorious Name.
16 And so Maccabeus called his men together, about six thousand, exhorting thẽ not
to be afraied of their enemies, nether to
feare the great multitude of the Gentiles,
which came against them vnrighteously,
but to fight manly,

17 Setting

17 Setting before their eyes the iniurie that
they had vniustly done to the holy place,
and the crueltie done to the citie by derision, and the destruction of the orders esta
blished by their fathers.
18 For they, said he, trust in their weapons &
boldenes: but our confidence is in the almightie God, which at a becke can bothe
destroy them that come against vs, and all
the worlde.
19 Moreouer he admonished them of the
helpe that *God* shewed vnto their fathers,
as when there perished an hundreth and
foure score, and fiue thousand vnder *Sennacherib,

2.King.19,35. isa.37,36. tob.1,21. eccles.48,24. 1.mac.7,41.

20 And of the battel that they had in Babylon against the Galacians, how they came
in all to ỳ battel eight thousand, with foure thousand Macedonians: and when the
Macedonians were astonished, the eight
thousand slewe an hũdreth & twentie thou
sand through the helpe that was giuen thẽ
from heauen, whereby they had receiued
many benefites.
21 Thus when he had made thẽ bolde with
these wordes, & readie to dye for ỳ Lawes
and the countrey, he deuided his armie into foure partes,
22 And made his owne brethren captaines
ouer ỳ armie, *to wit*, Simõ, & Ioseph & Iona
than, giuing eche one fiftene hũdreth men.
23 And when Eleazarus had red the holie
boke, & giuen them a token of the helpe of
God, *Iudas* which led the forewarde, ioyned with Nicanor,
24 And because the Almightie helped thẽ,
they slewe aboue nine thousand men, and
wounded and maimed the moste parte of
Nicanors hoste, and so put all to flight,
25 And toke the money frõ those that came
to bye them, and pursued them farre: but
lacking time they returned.
26 For it was the day before the Sabbath, &
therefore they wolde no longer pursue thẽ.
27 So they toke their weapõs, & spoiled the
enemies, & kept the Sabbath, giuing thãkes
and praising the Lord wonderfully, which
had deliuered them that day, and powred
vpon them the beginning of his mercie.
28 And after the Sabbath, *they distributed
the spoiles to the sicke, & to the fatherles,
& to the widdowes, & deuided the residue
among them selues and their children.

Nomb.31,27. 1.sam.30,24.

29 When this was done, & they all had made a general prayer, they besoght the merciful Lord to be reconciled at the length
with his seruants.
30 Afterwarde with one cõsent they fel vpõ
Timotheus and Bacchides, & slewe aboue
twẽtie thousand, & wanne hie & strong hol
des, & deuided great spoiles, & gaue an e-
qual porciõ vnto ỳ sicke, & to ỳ fatherles,
& to ỳ widdowes, & to aged persones also.
31 Moreouer they gathered their weapons
together, and layed them vp diligently in
conuenient places, and broght the remnãt
of the spoyles to Ierusalem.
32 They slewe also Philarches a moste wicked persone, which was with Timotheus,
and had vexed the Iewes manie wayes.
33 And when they kept the feast of victorie
in their countrey, they burnt Callisthenes
that had set fyre vpon the holie gates,
which was fled into a litle house: so he receiued a rewarde mete for his wickednes.
34 And that moste wicked Nicanor, which
had broght a thousand marchants to bye
the Iewes,
35 He was through the helpe of the Lord
broght downe of them whome he thoght
as nothing, in so muche that he put of his
glorious raiment, and fled ouerthwart the
countrey like a fugitiue seruant, and came
alone to Antiochia, with great dishonour
through the destruction of his hoste.
36 Thus he that promised to pay tribute to
the Romaines, by meanes of the prisoners
of Ierusalem, broght newes, that the Iewes
had a "defender, and for this cause none
colde hurt ỳ Iewes, because they followed
the Lawes appointed by him.

"Or, God their defender.

CHAP. IX.

1 Antiochus willing to spoyle Persepolis, is put to flight. 5 As he persecuteth the Iewes, he is striken of the Lord. 13 The fained repentance of Antiochus. 28 He dyeth miserably.

1 AT the same time, came Antiochus
againe with dishonour out of the
countrey of Persia.
2 For when he came to Persepolis, & went
about to robbe the Temple, and to subdue the citie, the people ranne in a rage to
defended them selues with their weapons,
and put them to flight, and Antiochus was
put to flight by the inhabitants, and returned with shame.
3 Now when he came to Ecbatana, he vnderstode the things that had come vnto
Nicanor, and Timotheus.
4 And then being chafed in his fume, he
thoght to impute to ỳ Iewes their faute, ẇ
had put him to flight, and therefore commanded his charet man to driue cõtinually, and to dispatche the iourney: for Gods
iudgement compelled him: for he had said
thus in his pride, I wil make Ierusalem a
cõmune burying place of the Iewes, whẽ
I come thether.
5 But the Lord almightie & God of Israel
smote him with an incurable and inuisible
plague: for assone as he had spoken these
wordes, a paine of the bowels, that was re-
mediles, came vpon him, & sore tormẽts
of the inner partes,
6 And that moste iustely: for he had tormẽted other mens bowels with diuerse, and

strange torments.
7 Howbeit he wolde in no wise cease from
his arrogancie, but swelled the more with
pride, breathing out fyre in his rage a-
gainst the Iewes, and commanded to haste
the iornay: but it came to passe that he fel
downe from the charet that rãne swiftely,
so that all the membres of his bodie were
bruised with the great fall.
8 And thus he that a litle afore thoght he
might commande the floods of the sea (so
proude was he beyonde the condicion of
man) & to weigh the hie mountaines in ȳ
balance, was now cast on the ground, and
caried in an horselitter, declaring vnto all
the manifest power of God,
Act.12,23. 9 *So that the wormes came out of the bodie of this wicked man in abundance: and
whiles he was aliue, his flesh fel of for paine and torment, and all his armie was grie-
*Or, stench. ued at his" smel.
10 Thus no man colde beare because of his
stinke, him ȳ a litle afore thoght he might
reach to the starres of heauen.
11 Then he began to leaue of his great pride, & self wil, when he was plagued & came to the knowledge of him self by the
scourge of God, & by his paine which increased euerie moment.
12 And when he him self might not abide
his owne stinke, he said these wordes, It is
mete to be subiect vnto God, & that a man
which is mortal, shulde not thinke him self
equal vnto God through pride.
13 This wicked persone prayed also vnto ȳ
Lord, who wolde now haue no mercie on
him,
14 And said thus ȳ he wolde set at libertie ȳ
holie citie vnto ȳ which he made haste to
destroy it, & to make it a burying place.
15 And as touching the Iewes, whome he had
iudged not worthie to be buryed, but wolde haue cast them out with their children
to be deuoured of the foules & wilde beastes, he wolde make thẽ all like the citizens
of Athenes.
16 And whereas he had spoiled ȳ holie Tẽple afore, he wolde garnish it with great
giftes, and encrease the holie vessels, and of
his owne rentes beare the charges belonging to the sacrifices.
17 Yea, & that he wolde also become a Iewe
him self, & go through all the worlde that
was inhabited, & preache ȳ power of God.
18 But for all this his paines wolde not cease: for the iust iudgemẽt of God was come
vpõ him: therefore despairing of his helth,
he wrote vnto the Iewes this letter vnder
writen, cõteining ȳ forme of a supplicatiõ.
19 ¶ THE KING & prince Antiochus vnto the Iewes his louing citizens wisheth
muche ioye and helth and prosperitie.
20 If ye and your children fare wel, & if all
things go after your minde, I giue great
thãkes vnto God hauing hope in ȳ heauẽ.
21 Thogh I lie sicke, yet I am mindeful of
your honour, & good wil for ȳ loue I beare you: therefore when I returned frõ the
countrey of Persia, and fel into a sore disease, I thoght it necessarie to care for the
commune safetie of all,
22 Not distrusting mine helth, but hauing
great hope to escape this sickenes.
23 Therefore considering that when my father led an hoste against ȳ high cõutreys,
he appointed who shulde succede him:
24 That if anie controuersie happened cõtrary to his expectation, or if that anie
tidings were broght that were grieuous,
they in the lãd might knowe to whome ȳ
affaires were committed, that they shulde
not be troubled.
25 Againe, when I ponder how that the gouernours, ȳ are borderers, and neighbours
vnto my kingdome, waite for all occasiõs,
& loke but for opportunitie, I haue ordeined that my sõne Antiochus shal be King
whome I oft cõmẽded & cõmitted to many
of you, whẽ I went into ȳ hie prouinces, &
haue writẽ vnto hĩ as followeth hereafter.
26 Therefore, I pray you & require you, to
remẽber the benefites ȳ I haue done vnto
you generally, & particularly, and ȳ euerie
mã wil be faithful to me and to my sonne.
27 For I trust that he wil be gentle, & louing
vnto you according to my minde.
28 ¶ Thus ȳ murtherer & blasphemer suffered moste grieuously, & as he had intreated
other mẽ, so he dyed a miserable death in a
strange countrey among the mountaines.
29 And Philippe that was broght vp with
him, carryed away his bodie, who fearing
the sonne of Antiochus, went into Egypt
to Ptolemeus Philometor.

CHAP. X.

1 Iudas Maccabeus taketh the citie and the Temple. 10 The actes of Eupator. 16 The Iewes fight against the Idumeans. 24 Timotheus inuadeth Iudea, with whome Iudas ioyneth battel. 29 Fiue men appeare in the aire to the helpe of the Iewes. 37 Timotheus is slaine

1 MAccabeus now and his companie,
through the helpe of the Lord, wan
the Temple and the citie againe,
2 And destroyed the altars, and chapels that
the heathẽ had buylded in the open places,
3 And clensed the Tẽple, & made another
altar, & burned stones, & toke fyre of thẽ,
and offred sacrifices, & incense two yeres,
and six monethes after, and set forthe the
lampes, and the shewebread.
4 When that was done, they fel downe flat
vpon the grounde, and besoght the Lord,
that they might come no more into suche
troubles: but if they sinned anie more a-
gainst him, that he him self wolde chastẽ
them with mercie, & that they might not
be

be deliuered to the blasphemous, and barbarous nacions.
5 Now vpō the same day, that the strāgers
polluted the Tēple, on the verie same day
it was clēsed againe euen ẏ fiue & twētieth
day of the same moneth, which is Chasleu.
6 They kept eight dayes with gladnes as in
the feast of the Tabernacles, remēbring,
that not long afore they held the feast of
the Tabernacles when they liued in the
mountaines and dennes like beastes.
7 And for the same cause they bare grene
bowes, and faire branches and palmes, and
sang psalmes vnto him that had giuen thē
good successe in clensing his place.
8 They ordeined also by a commune statute, and decre that euerie yere those dayes
shulde be kept of ẏ whole naciō of ẏ Iewes.
9 And this was the end of Antiochus called
Epiphanes.
10 ¶ Now wil we declare the actes of Antiochus Eupator, which was the sonne of
this wicked man gathering briefly the calamities of the warres, that followed.
11 For when he had taken the kingdome,
he made one Lysias, which had bene captaine of the hoste in Phenice, & Celosyria, ruler ouer the affaires of the realme.
12 For Ptolemeus that was called Macron,
purposed to do iustice vnto the Iewes for
ẏ wrōg, ẏ had bene done vnto thē, & went
about to behaue him self peaceably ẇ thē.
13 For the which cause he was accused of his
friends before Eupator, & was called oft times traitour, because he had left Cyprus
that Philometor had cōmitted vnto him,
and came to Antiochus Epiphanes: therefore seing that he was no more in estimation, he was discouraged, and poysonned
him self, and dyed.
14 ¶ But when Gorgias was gouernour of
the same places, he interteined strangers, &
made warre oft times against the Iewes.
15 Moreouer the Idumeans that helde the
strōg holds, which were mete for their purpose, troubled the Iewes, and by receiuing
them that were driuen frō Ierusalem, toke
in hand to continue warre.
16 Then thei that were with Maccabeus made prayers, & besoght God that he wolde
be their helper, and so they fel vpon the
strong holdes of the Idumeans,
17 And assalted them sore, that they wanne
the places, & slewe all that foght against
them on the wall, and killed all ẏ they met
with, & slewe no lesse thē twētie thousand.
18 And because certeine (which were no
lesse then nine thousand) were fled into
two strong castels, hauing all maner of
things conuenient to susteine the siege,
19 Maccabeus left Simō, & Ioseph, & Zaccheus also, & those that were with thē, ẇ
were ynowe to besiege them, and departed
to those places ẇ were more necessarie.
20 Now thei that were with Simon, being
led with couetousnes, were intreated for
monei, (thorowe certeine of those that
were in ẏ castel,) & toke seuentie thousand
drachmes, and let some of them escape.
21 But when it was tolde Maccabeus what
was done, he called the gouernours of the
people together, & accused those mē, that
they had solde their brethren for money,
and let their enemies go.
22 So he slewe thē when they were cōuict of
treason, & immediatly wan ẏ two castels:
23 And hauing good successe, as in all the
warres that he toke in hand, he slew in the
two castels mo then twentie thousand.
24 Now Timotheus whome the Iewes had
ouercome afore, gathered an armie of strāgers of all sortes, and broght a great troupe of horsemen out of Asia to winne Iewrie by strength.
25 But when he drewe nere, Maccabeus, and
thei ẏ were with him, turned to praye vnto
God, & sprinkled earth vpō their heads, &
girded their reines with sackecloth,
26 And fel downe at the fote of the altar, &
besoght *the Lord* to be merciful to them, &
to be an enemie to their enemies, and to
be an aduersarie to their aduersaries, * as
the Law declareth. *Exod.23.22. deu.20.4.*
27 So after the prayer, they toke their weapons, & went on further from the citie, &
when they came nere to the enemies, they
toke hede to them selues.
28 And whē ẏ morning appeared, they bothe ioyned together: the one parte had ẏ
Lord for their refuge, & pledge of prosperitie, & noble victorie, and the other toke
courage as a guide of the warre.
29 But when ẏ battel waxed strong, there appeared vnto the enemies frō heauen fiue
comelie men vpon horses with bridles of
golde, and two of them led the Iewes,
30 And toke Maccabeus betwixt them, & couered him on euerie side with their weapons, & kept him safe, but shot dartes, &
lightenings against the enemies, so ẏ thei
were cōfounded with blindenes, and beaten downe and ful of trouble.
31 There were slaine of *fotemen* twētie thousand & fiue hūdreth & six hūdreth horsmē.
32 As for Timotheus him self, he fled vnto
Gazara, ẇ was called a very strōg holde,
wherein Chereas was captaine.
33 But Maccabeus & his cōpanie laid siege agaīst ẏ fortresses ẇ courage for foure daies.
34 And thei that were within, trusting to the
height of the place, blasphemed excedingly, and spake horrible wordes.
35 Neuertheles vpō the *fifth day in ẏ morning twentie yōg men of Maccabeus cōpanie, whose hearts were inflamed, because of
ẏ blasphemies, came vnto ẏ wall, & ẇ bolde **Or, the fiue, & twentieth day.*

stomackes smote downe those ŷ they met.
36 Others also that climed vp vpon the engines of warre against thē that were within, set fyre vpon the towers, & burnt those blasphemers quicke with the fyres that
they had made, & others brake vp the gates, and receiued the rest of the armie, and
toke the citie.
37 And hauing found Timotheus, that was
crept into a caue, they killed him, & Chereas his brother with Apollophanes.
38 When this was done, they praised ŷ Lord
with psalmes, and thankesgiuing, which
had done so great things for Israel, & giuen them the victorie.

CHAP. XI.

1 Lysias goeth about to ouercome the Iewes. 8 Succour is sent from heauen vnto the Iewes. 16 The letter of Lysias vnto the Iewes. 20 The letter of King Antiochus vnto Lysias. 27 A letter of the same vnto the Iewes. 34 A letter of the Romains to the Iewes.

1 VErie shortely after this, Lysias the
Kings stewarde, and a kinsmā of his,
which had the gouernance of the affaires,
toke sore displeasure for the things that
were done.
2 And when he had gathered about fourescore thousand, with all the horsmen he ca
me against the Iewes, thinking to make
the citie an habitacion of the Gentiles.
3 And the Temple wolde he haue to get
money by, like the other temples of the
heathen: for he wolde sel the Priests office
euerie yere.
4 And thus being puffed vp in his minde,
because of the great nomber of fotemen, &
thousands of horsmen, & in his foure score elephants,
5 He came into Iudea, and drewe nere to
Beth-sura, which was a castel of defence,
fiue [a]furlōgs from Ierusalem, and laid sore
siege vnto it.

a Whereof eight make a mile.

6 But when Maccabeus, and his companie
knewe that he besieged the holdes, they, &
all the people made prayers with weping,
and teares before the Lord, that he wolde
send a good Angel to deliuer Israel.
7 And Maccabeus him self first of all toke
weapons, exhorting the other that they
wolde ieoparde them selues together with
him to helpe their brethren: so they went
forthe together ŵ a courageous minde.
8 And as thei were there besides Ierusalem,
there appeared before them vpon horsebacke a man in white clothing, shaking his
harnes of golde.
9 Then they praised the merciful God all
together, and toke heart, in so muche that
they were ready, not onely to fight ŵ mē,
but with the moste cruel beasts, & to breake downe walles of yron.
10 Thus they marched forwarde in array,
hauing an helper from heauen: for the
Lord was merciful vnto them.
11 And rūning vpō their enemies like liōs,
they slewe eleuen thousand *fotemen*, and
sixten hundreth horsemen, & put all the
other to flight.
12 Manie of them also being wounded, esca
ped naked, and Lysias him self fled away
shamefully, and so escaped,
13 Who as he was a man of vnderstanding
cōsidering what losse he had had, & knowing, that the Hebrewes colde not be ouercome because the almightie God helped
them, sent vnto them,
14 And promised, that he wolde consent to
all things which were reasonable, and persuade the King to be their friend.
15 Maccabeus agreed to Lysias requestes,
hauing respect in all things to ŷ commune
welth, and whatsoeuer Maccabeus wrote
vnto Lysias concerning the Iewes, the
King granted it.
16 For there were letters writen vnto the
Iewes frō Lysias cōteining these wordes,
LYSIAS vnto the people of the Iewes
sendeth greting.
17 Iohn & Abessalom, which were sent frō
you, deliuered me the things that you demande by writing, and required me to fulfil the things that they had declared.
18 Therefore what things soeuer were mete
to be reported to the King him self, I haue
declared them, and he granted that that
was possible.
19 Therefore if ye behaue your selues as
friēds toward his affaires, hereafter also
I wil indeuour my self to do you good.
20 As concerning these things, I haue giuē
commandement to these men, and to those
whome I sent vnto you, to commune with
you of the same particularly.
21 Fare ye wel, the hundreth and eight and
fortie yere, the foure and twētieth day of
the moneth Dioscorinthius.
22 ¶ Now the Kings letter conteined these
wordes, KING ANTIOCHVS vnto
his brother Lysias sendeth greting.
23 Since our father is translated vnto the
gods, our wil is, that they which are in our
realme, liue quietly, that euerie man may
applie his owne affaires.
24 We vnderstand also that the Iewes wolde not consent to our father, for to be
broght vnto the custome of the Gentiles,
but wolde kepe their owne maner of liuing: for the which cause they require of
vs, that we wolde suffer them to liue after
their owne Lawes.
25 Wherefore our minde is that this naciō
shalbe in rest, and haue determined to restore them their Temple, that thei may be
gouerned according to the custome of
their fathers.
26 Thou shalt do wel therefore to send vnto
them

them, and grante them peace, that when
they are certified of our minde, they maie
be of good comfort, and cheresfully go a-
bout their owne affaires.
27 And this was the Kings letter vnto the
nacion, KING ANTIOCHVS vnto
the Elders of the Iewes, and to the rest of
the Iewes sendeth greting.
28 If ye fare wel, we haue our desire: we are
also in good helth.
29 Menelaus declared vnto vs that your desire was to returne home, & to applie your
owne busines.
30 Wherefore, those that wil departe, we
giue them fre libertie, vnto the thirtie
daye of the moneth of "Panthicus, "Or, April.
31 That the Iewes may vse their owne maner of liuing and Lawes, like as afore, and
none of them by anie maner of waies to
haue harme for things done by ignorance.
32 I haue sent also Menelaus to comfort
you.
33 Fare ye wel: the hũdreth and eight & fortie yere, the fiftenth day of the moneth of
Panthicus.
34 ¶ The Romains also sent a letter conteining these wordes, QVINTVS MEM-
MIVS and Titus "Manilius embassadours "Or, Manlius.
of the Romains, vnto the people of the
Iewes send greting.
35 The things that Lysias the Kings kinsman hathe granted you, we grant the same
also.
36 But concerning that which he shal report
vnto the King, send hether some with spede, when ye haue considered the matter
diligently, that we may consult thereupõ
as shalbe best for you: for we must go vnto Antiochia.
37 And therefore make haste and send some
men, that we may knowe your minde.
38 Fare wel: this hundreth and eight, and
fortie yere, the fiftenth day of the moneth
of Panthicus.

CHAP. XII.

2 Timotheus troubleth the Iewes. 3 The wicked dede of thẽ of Ioppe against the Iewes. 6 Iudas is aduenged of thẽ 9 He setteth fyre in the hauẽ of Iamnia. 20 The pursute of the Iewes against Timotheus. 24 Timotheus is taken and let go vnhurt. 32 Iudas pursueth Gorgias.

1 WHen these couenãts were made,
Lysias went vnto the King, and
the Iewes tilled their grounde.
2 But the gouernours of the places, *as* Timotheus & Apollonius the sonne of Gen-
neus, and Ieronimus, & also Demophon,
and besides them Nicanor the gouernour
of Cyprus, wolde not let them liue in rest
and peace.
3 ¶ They of Ioppe also did suche a vile act:
they prayed the Iewes that dwelt among
them, to go with their wiues and children
into the shippes, which they had prepared
as thogh they had oght them nõne euil
wil.
4 And so by the commune aduise of the
citie, they obeyed them, and suspect nothing: but when they were gone forthe into the depe, they drowned no lesse then
two hundreth of them.
5 Now when Iudas knewe of this crueltie
shewed against his nacion, he cõmãded
those men that were with him, to make
them readie.
6 And hauing called vpon God the righteous Iudge, he went forthe against the
murtherers of his brethren, and set fyre
in the hauen by night, & burnt the ships,
and those that fled thence, he slewe.
7 And when the citie was shut vp, he departed as thogh he wolde come againe, and
roote out all them of the citie of Ioppe.
8 ¶ But when he perceiued that the Iãnites
were minded to do in like maner vnto the
Iewes, which dwelt among them,
9 He came vpon the Iamnites by night, &
set fyre in the hauẽ with the nauie, so that
the light of the fyre was sene at Ierusalẽ,
vpon a two hundreth and fortie furlongs.
10 Now when they were gone from thence nine furlongs, in their iourney towarde
Timotheus, about fiue thousand mẽ *of fote*
and fiue hundreth horsemen of the Arabians set vpon him.
11 So the battel was sharpe, but it prospered
with Iudas thorowe the helpe of God: the
a Nomades of Arabia, being ouercome, be- a So called because they were shepherds.
soght Iudas to make peace with them, and
promised to giue him certeine cattel, and
to helpe him in other things.
12 And Iudas thinking that they shulde in
dede be profitable cõcerning manie thĩgs,
granted them peace: whereupõ thei shoke
hands, and so they departed to their tents.
13 ¶ Iudas also assalted a citie called Cas-
pis, which was strong by reason of a brid-
ge, and fenced rounde about with walles,
and had diuers kindes of people dwelling
therein.
14 So thei ỹ were within it, put suche trust in
the strength of the walles, and in store of
vitailes, that they were the slacker in their
doings, reuiling thẽ that were with Iudas,
and reproching thẽ: yea, they blasphemed
& spake suche wordes as were not lawful.
15 But Maccabeus souldiers, calling vpon
the great Prince of ỹ worlde (which with-
out anie "instruments, or engins of warre, "Or, battel rammes.
did *cast downe the walles of Iericho, in *Iosh. 6, 20.
the time of Iesus) gaue a fierce assalt a-
gainst the walles,
16 And toke the citie by the wil of God,
and made an exceding great slaughter, in
so muche that a lake of two furlongs broad, which laye thereby, semed to flowe
with blood.

17 ¶Then departed thei from thence, seuen
hundreth and fiftie furlongs, and came to
Characa vnto the Iewes, that are called
Tubieni.
18 But they founde not Timotheus there:
for he was departed from thence, and had
done nothing, and had left a garison in a
verie strong holde.
19 But Dositheus, & Sosipater, which were
captaines with Maccabeus, went forthe, &
slewe those that Timotheus had left in
the fortresse more thē ten thousand men.
20 And Maccabeus prepared, & ranged his
armie by bandes, & went courageously a-
gainst Timotheus, which had with him an
hundreth and twentie thousand men of
fote, and two thousand and fiue hundreth
horsemen.
21 Whē Timotheus had knowledge of Iudas comming, he sent the women, & children, and the other baggage afore vnto a
fortresse called Carnion (for it was hard
to besiege, & vneasie to come vnto because of the straites on all sides.)
22 But when Iudas first bāde came in sight,
the enemies were smiten with feare, and a
trembling was among them thorow the
presence of him that seeth all things, in so
muche that thei fleing one here, another
there, were oft times hurt by their owne
people, and wounded with the pointes of
their owne swordes.
23 But Iudas was verie earnest in pursuing,
and slewe those wicked men: yea, he slewe
thirtie thousand men of them.
24 Timotheus also him self fell into the
hands of Dositheus, & Sosipater, whome
he besoght with muche crafte to let him
go with his life, because he had manie of
the Iewes parents & the brethren of some
of them, which if they put him to death,
shulde be despised.
25 So when he had assured thē with manie
wordes, & promised that he wolde restore
them without hurt, thei let him go for the
helth of their brethren.
26 ¶Then went Maccabeus towarde Car-
mon, and Atargation, and slewe fiue and
twentie thousand persones.
27 And after that he had chased away and
slayne thē, Iudas remoued the hoste towarde Ephron a strong citie, wherein was
Lysias & a great multitude of all naciōs,
& the strōg yong men kept the walles de-
fendīg thē mightely: there was also great
preparacion of engins of warre, & dartes.
28 But when they had called vpō the Lord,
which with his power breaketh the strēgth
of the enemies, they wan the citie, & slewe
fiue and twentie thousand of them that
were within.
29 ¶Frō thence went thei to Scythopolis, wͨ
lieth six hundreth furlongs frō Ierusalē.
30 But when the Iewes which dwelt there,
testified, that the Scythopolitans delt louingly with them, & intreated them kindely in the time of their aduersitie,
31 They gaue them thankes, desiring them
to be friendlie stil vnto them, and so thei
came to Ierusalem, as the feast of the wekes approched.
32 ¶And after ẏ feast called Penticost thei
went forthe against Gorgias the gouernour of Idumea.
33 Who came out with thre thousand men
of fote and foure hundreth horsemen.
34 And when they ioyned together, a fewe
of the Iewes were slayne,
35 And Dositheus one of the Baccenors,
which was on horsebacke and a mightie
man, toke Gorgias, and laied holde of his
garment, and drewe him by force, because he wolde haue taken the wicked man a-
liue: but an horseman of Thracia fell vpon him, and smote of his shulder, so that
Gorgias fled into Marisa.
36 And when they that were "with Esrin, "Or, with Gorgias.
had foghten long, and were wearie, Iudas
called vpō the Lord, that he wolde shewe
him self to be their helper, and captaine
of the field.
37 And then he began in his owne langage,
and sung psalmes with a loude voyce, in
so muche that straight wayes he made
thē that were about Gorgias, to take their
flight.
38 ¶So Iudas gathered his hoste, and came
into the citie of Odolla. And when the
seuenth day came, they clensed them selues (as the custome was) and kept the Sabbath in the same place.
39 And vpon the daye following, as necessitie required, Iudas and his companie came to take vp the bodies of them that
were slayne, and to burye them with their
kinsemen in their fathers graues.
40 Now vnder the coates of euerie one,
that was slayne, they founde iewels that
had bene consecrate to the idoles of the
*Iamnites, which thing is forbidden the Deut.7.25. iosh.7.26.
Iewes by the Law. Thē euerie man sawe,
that this was the cause wherefore thei were slayne.
41 And so euerie man gaue thankes vnto
the Lord, the righteous Iudge, which had
opened the things that were hid.
42 And they gaue them selues to prayer, &
besoght him, that they shulde not vtterly
be destroied for the faute committed. Besides that, noble Iudas exhorted the people to kepe them selues from sinne, for so
muche as they sawe before their eyes the
things which came to passe by the sinne
of these that were slayne,
43 And hauing made a gathering through
the companie, sent to Ierusalē about two
thousand

thousand drachmes of siluer, to offer a sin-
neoffring, doing very wel, and honestly
that he thoght of the resurrection.
44 For if he had not hoped, that thei which
were slaine, shulde rise againe, it had bene superfluous, and vaine, to [a] pray for the
dead.
45 And therefore he perceiued, that there
was great fauour laid vp for those ẏ dyed
godly. (It was an holie, & a good thoght)
So he made a reconciliation for the dead
that they might be deliuered from sinne.

a Frõ this verse to the end of this chapter the Greke text is corrupt, so that no good sense, muche lesse certeine doctrine can be gathered thereby: also it is euident that this place was not writen by the holie Gost, bothe because it dissenteth frõ the rest of the holie Scriptures, and also ẏ autor of this boke acknowledgĩg his owne infirmitie, desireth pardõ, if he haue not atteined to ẏ he shulde. And it semeth, that this Iason the Cyrenean, out of whome he toke this abbridgement, is Ioseph Ben Gorion, who hathe writen in Ebrewe fiue bookes of these matters, and intreating this place, maketh no mencion of this prayer for the dead, lib. 3 chap. 19. for it is cõtrarie to the custome of the Iewes, euen to this day, to pray for the dead. And thogh Iudas had so done, yet this particular example is not sufficiẽt to establish a doctrine no more then Ziporahs was to proue that women might minister the sacraments, Exo. 4,25, or the example of Razis that one might kil him self, whome this autor so muche cõmendeth, 2. Macc. 14,41.

CHAP. XIII.

1 The comming of Eupator into Iudea. 4 The death of Menelaus. 10 Maccabeus going to fight against Eupator, moueth his souldiers vnto prayer. 15 He killeth fouretene thousand men in the tentes of Antiochus. 21 Rhodocus the betrayer of the Iewes is taken.

1 IN the hundreth, fortie and nine yere it
was tolde Iudas, that Antiochus Eupator was comming with a great power into Iudea,
2 And Lysias the stewarde and ruler of his
affaires with him. hauing bothe in their ar
mie an hundreth and ten thousand men
of fote of the Grecians, and fiue thousand horsemen, and two and twentie elephants, and thre hũdreth charets set with
hookes.
3 Menelaus also ioyned him self with them
and with great disceit incouraged Antiochus, not for the safegard of the countrei,
but because he thoght to haue bene made
the gouernour.
4 But the King of Kings moued Antiochus minde against this wicked man, and
Lysias informed the King that this man
was the cause of all mischief, so that the
King commanded to bring him to Berea
to put him vnto death as the maner was in
that place.
5 Now there was in that place a tower of
fiftie cubites high, ful of ashes, and it had
an instrument that turned rounde, and
on euerie side it rouled downe into the
ashes.
6 And there whosoeuer was condemned
of sacrilege, or of anie other grieuous crime, was cast of all men to the death.
7 And so it came to passe that this wicked
man shulde dye suche a death, and it was
a moste iuste thing that Menelaus shulde
want buryal,
8 For because he had committed manie sinnes by the altar, whose fyre and ashes
were holie: he him self also dyed in the
ashes.
9 ¶ Now the King raged in his minde, and
came to shewe him self more cruel vnto
the Iewes then his father.
10 Which things when Iudas perceiued, he
commanded the people to call vpon the
Lord night and day, that if euer he had
holpen them, he wolde now helpe them,
when they shulde be put from their Law,
from their countrey and from the holie
Temple:
11 And that he wolde not suffer the people, which a litle afore began to recouer,
to be subdued vnto the blasphemous nacions.
12 So when they had done this all together,
and besoght the Lord for mercie with
weping, and fasting, and falling downe
thre daies together, Iudas exhorted them
to make them selues readie.
13 And he being aparte with the Elders,
toke counsel to go forthe, afore the King
broght his hoste into Iudea, & shulde take
the citie, & commit the matter to the helpe
of the Lord.
14 So committing the charge to the Lord
of the worlde, he exhorted his souldiers
to fight manfully, euen vnto death for the
Lawes, the Temple, the citie, their countrey, and the commune wealth, and camped by Modin.
15 And so giuing his souldiers for a watche
worde, The victorie of God, he piked out
the manliest yong men, and went by night
into the Kings campe, and slewe of the
hoste fourtene thousand men, & the greatest elephant with all that sate vpon him.
16 Thus when they had broght a great feare, and trouble in the campe, & all things
went prosperously with them, they departed.
17 This was done in the breake of the day,
because the protection of the Lord did
helpe them.
18 ¶ Now when the King had tasted the
manlines of the Iewes, he went about to
take the holdes by policie,
19 And marched towarde Beth-sura, which
was a strõg holde of the Iewes: but he was
chased away, hurt and lost of his men.
20 For Iudas had sent vnto them that were
in it, suche things as were necessarie.
21 But Rhodocus which was in the Iewes
hoste, disclosed the secretes to ẏ enemies:
therefore he was soght out, and when they
had gotten him, they put him in prison.
22 After this did the King commune with
them that were in Beth-sura, and "toke truce with them, departed, and ioyned battel
with Iudas, who ouercame him.

" Or, gaue and toke the right hand.

23 But when he vnderstode, that Philippe (whome he had left to be ouerseer of
his busines at Antiochia) did rebell a-
gainst him, he was astonished, so that he
yelded him self to the Iewes, and made
them an othe to do all things that were
right, and was appeased towarde them, &
offred sacrifice and adorned the Temple, and shewed great gentlenes to the
place,

24 And embraced Maccabeus, and made
him captaine and gouernour from Ptolemais vnto the Gerreneans.
25 Neuertheles, whē he came to Ptolemais,
the people of the citie were not content
wit this agrement: and because they were
grieued, they wolde that he shulde breake
the couenants.
26 Then went Lysias vp into the iudgemēt
seat, and excused the fact as wel as he colde, & persuaded them, and pacified them,
and made them wel affectioned, and came
againe vnto Antiochia. This is the matter
concerning the Kings iournay, and his
returne.

CHAP. XIIII.

1 Demetrius moued by Alcimus sendeth Nicanor to kil the Iewes. 18 Nicanor maketh a compacte with the Iewes. 29 Which he yet breaketh through the mocion of the King. 37 Nicanor commandeth Razis to be taken, who slayeth him self.

1 After thre yeres was Iudas enformed
that Demetrius the sonne of Seleucus was come vp with a great power and
name by the hauen of Tripolis,
2 When he had wonne the countrey, and
slaine Antiochus and his lieutenāt Lysias.
3 Now Alcimus, which had bene the high
Priest, and wilfully defiled him self in the
time that all things were cōfounded, seing
that by no meanes he colde saue him self,
nor haue anie more entrance to the holie altar,
4 He came to King Demetrius in the hundreth, fiftie and one yere, presenting vnto
him a crowne of golde, and a palme, & of
the boughes, which were vsed solemnely in the Temple, and that day he helde
his tongue.
5 But when he had gotten opportunitie, &
occasion for his rage, Demetrius called
him to counsel, and asked him what deuises or counsels the Iewes leaned vnto.
6 To the which he answered, the Iewes that
be called Asideans whose captaine is Iudas
Maccabeus, mainteine warres, and make
insurrections, and wil not let the realme
be in peace.
7 Therefore I, being depriued of my fathers honour (I meane the high priesthode) am now come hether,
8 Partely because I was wel affectioned vnto the Kings affaires, and secondly because I soght ẏ profite of mine owne citizēs:
for all our people, thorowe their rashnes,
are not a litle troubled.
9 Wherefore, ô King, seing thou knowest
all these things, make prouision for the
countrey, and our nacion which is abused,
according to thine owne humanitie, that
is readie to helpe all men.
10 For as long as Iudas liueth, it is not possible that the matter shulde be wel.
11 When he had spoken these wordes, other
friends also hauing euil wil at Iudas, set
Demetrius on fyre.
12 Who immediatly called for Nicanor,
the ruler of the elephantes, and made him
captaine ouer Iudea,
13 And sent him forthe, commanding him
to slay Iudas, and to scatter thē that were
with him, & to make Alcimus high Priest
of the great Temple.
14 Then the heathen which fled out of Iudea from Iudas, came to Nicanor by flockes, thinking the harme and calamities of
the Iewes to be their welfare.
15 Now whē the Iewes heard of Nicanors
comming, and the gathering together of
the heathen, they sprinkled them selues
with earth, & prayed vnto him which had
appointed him self a people foreuer, and
did alwais defende his owne porcion with
euident tokens.
16 So at the commandement of the captaine, they remoued straight wayes from
thence, and came to the towne of Dessan,
17 Where Simō Iudas brother had ioyned
battel with Nicanor, and was somewhat
astonished thorowe the sudden silence of
the enemies.
18 Neuertheles Nicanor hearing the manlines of them that were with Iudas, & the
bolde stomackes that they had for their
countrey, durst not proue the matter with
blood shedding.
19 Wherefore, he sent Posidonius, "Theodo- *"Or, Theodotus.*
cius, and "Matthias before, to make peace. *"Or, Mattathias*
20 So when they had taken long aduisemēt
thereupō, and the captaine shewed it vnto
the multitude, they were agreed in one
minde, and consented to the couenants.
21 And they appointed a day when they
shulde particularly come together: so whē
the day was come, they set for euerie man
his stoole.
22 Neuertheles Iudas commanded certeine men of armes to waite in conuenient
places, lest there shulde suddenly arise
anie euil thorowe the enemies: and so they
communed together of the things whereupon they had agreed.
23 Nicanor, while he abode at Ierusalem,
did none hurt, but sent away the people
that were gathered together.
24 He" loued Iudas, and fauoured him in *"Or, had Iudas before his eyes.*
his heart.
25 He praid him also to take a wife, and to
beget children: sō he maried, & they liued
together.
26 But Alcimus perceiuing the loue that
was betwene them, and vnderstanding the
couenantes that were made, came to Demetrius, and tolde him that Nicanor had
taken strange matters in hand, and ordeined Iudas a traitour to the realme, to be
his

his successour.
27 Then the King was displeased, and by
the reportes of this wicked man, he wrote
to Nicanor, saying, that he was very angrie for the couenants, commanding him
that he shulde send Maccabeus in all haste
prisoner vnto Antiochia.
28 When these things came to Nicanor, he
was astonished & sore grieued, ẏ he shulde breake the things wherein they had a-
greed, seing that that man had committed
no wickednes.
29 But because it was not cōmodious to him
to withstand the King, he soght craftely
to accomplish it.
30 Notwithstanding when Maccabeus perceiued that Nicanor beganne to be rough
vnto him, and that he intreated him more
rudely thē he was wonte, he perceiued that
suche rigour came not of good, and therefore he gathered a fewe of his men, and
withdrewe him self from Nicanor.
31 But the other perceiuing that he was pre
uented by *Maccabeus* worthie policie, came
into the great & holie Temple, and commanded the Priests, which were offring
their vsual sacrifices, to deliuer him the
man.
32 And when they sware that they colde
not tell where the man was, whome he
soght,
33 He stretched out his right hand towarde
the Temple, and made an othe in this maner, If ye wil not deliuer me Iudas as a pri
soner, I wil make this Temple of God a
plaine field, and wil breake downe the altar, and wil erect a notable Temple vnto Bacchus.
34 After these wordes he departed: then the
Priests lift vp their hands towarde heauē,
and besoght him that was euer the defender of their nacion, saying in this maner,
35 Thou, ô Lord of all things, which hast
nede of nothing, woldest that the Temple
of thine habitacion shulde be among vs.
36 Therefore now, ô moste holie Lord, kepe
this house euer vndefiled, which lately was
clensed, and stoppe all the mouths of the
vnrighteous.
37 Now was there accused vnto Nicanor,
Razis one of the Elders of Ierusalem, a louer of the citie, and a man of very good reporte, which for his loue was called a father of the Iewes.
38 For this man afore times when the Iewes
were minded to kepe them selues vndefiled and pure, being accused to be of the re
ligion of the Iewes, did offer to spend his
bodie and life with all constancie for the
religion of the Iewes.
39 So Nicanor willing to declare the hatred
that he bare to the Iewes, sent about fiue
hundreth men of warre to take him.
40 For he thoght by taking him to do the
Iewes muche hurte.
41 But when this companie wolde haue taken his castel, and wolde haue broken the
gates by violence, and cōmanded to bring
fyre to burne the gates, so that he was readie to be taken on euerie side, he [a] fel on
his sworde,
42 Willing rather to dye manfully, thē to
giue him self into the hāds of wicked men,
and to suffer reproche vnworthie for his
noble stocke.
43 Notwithstanding what time as he missed of his stroke for haste, and the multitude russhed in violently between the dores, he ran boldely to the wall, and cast him
self downe manfully amōg the multitude.
44 Which conueyed them selues lightly
away, and gaue place, so that he fell vpon
his bellie.
45 Neuertheles while there was yet breth
in him, being kindled in his minde, he rose
vp, and thogh his blood gushed out like a
fountaine, and he was verie sore wounded,
yet he ran thorow the middes of the people,
46 And gate him to ẏ toppe of an hie rocke: so when his blood was vtterly gone, he
toke out his owne bowels with bothe his
hands, and threwe them vpon the people,
calling vpon the Lord of life and spirit,
that he wolde restore them againe vnto
him, and thus he dyed.

a As this priuate example oght not to be followed of ẏ godlie, because it is cōtrary to ẏ worde of God, althogh the autor seme here to approue it: so that place as touching prayer chap. 12, 44. thogh Iudas had appointed it, yet were it not sufficient to proue a doctrine, because it is onely a particular example.

CHAP. XV.

2 Nicanor goeth about to come vpon Iudas on the Sabbath day. 5 The blasphemie of Nicanor. 14 Maccabeus expounding vnto the Iewes the vision, incourageth them. 21 The prayer of Maccabeus. 30 Maccabeus commandeth Nicanors head and hands to be cut of, and his tongue to be giuen vnto the foules. 39 The autor excuseth him self.

1 NOw when Nicanor knewe that Iudas and his companie were in the
countrey of Samaria, he thoght with all as
surance to come vpon them, vpon the Sabbath day.
2 Neuertheles the Iewes that were compel
led to go with him, said, O kill not so cruel
ly and barbarously, but honour and sanctifie the day, that is appointed by him that
seeth all things.
3 But this moste wicked persone demāded,
Is there a Lord in heauen, that commanded the Sabbath day to be kept?
4 And whē theis said, There is a liuīg Lord,
which ruleth in the heauen, who comman
ded the seuenth day to be kept,
5 Thē he said, And I am mightie vpō earth
to commande them for to arme them selues, and to performe the Kings busines.
Notwithstanding, he colde not accomplish his wicked enterprise.
6 For Nicanor lifted vp with great pride,

purposed to set vp a memorial of the victorie obteined of all them that were with
Iudas.
7 But Maccabeus had euer sure confidence and a perfite hope that the Lord wolde
helpe him,
8 And exhorted his people not to be afraid
at the coming of the heathen, but alway to
remember the helpe that had bene shewed
vnto them from heauen, and to trust now
also, that they shulde haue the victorie by
the Almightie.
9 Thus he incouraged them by the Law &
Prophetes, putting them in remembrance
of the battels that they had wõne afore, &
so made them more willing,
10 And stirred vp their hearts, and shewed
them also the disceitfulnes of the heathẽ,
and how they had broken their othes.
11 Thus he armed euerie one of them, not
with the assurance of shields and speares,
but with wholsome wordes and exhortacions, and shewed them a dreame worthie
to be beleued, and reioyced them greatly.
12 And this was his vision, He thoght that
he sawe Onias (which had bene the high
Priest, a vertuous & a good man, reuerent
in behauiour, and of sober conuersation,
wel spoken, and one that had bene exercised in all pointes of godlines from a childe) holding vp his hands towarde heauen,
and praying for the whole people of the
Iewes.
13 ¶After this there appeared vnto him
another man which was aged, honorable,
and of a wonderful dignitie, and excellen
cie aboue him.
14 And Onias spake, & said, This is a louer
of the brethren, who prayeth muche for
the people, and for the holie citie, *to wit*, Ieremias the Prophet of God.
15 He *thoght also* that Ieremias helde out his
right hand, and gaue vnto Iudas a sworde
of golde: & as he gaue it, he spake thus,
16 Take this holie sworde a gifte frõ God,
wherewith thou shalt wounde the aduersaries.
17 And so being comforted by the wordes
of Iudas, which were very swete and able
to stirre them vp to valiantnes and to incourage the heartes of the yong men, they
determined to pitch no campe, but courageously to set vpon them, and mãfully to
assaile them, and to trye the matter hand
to hand, because the citie and the Sanctuarie, and the Temple were in danger.
18 As for their wiues, and children, and brethren and kinsfolkes, they set lesse by their
danger: but their greatest and principal
feare was for the holie Temple.
19 Againe they that were in the citie, were
careful for the armie that was abroad.
20 Now whiles thei all waited for the tryal
of the matter, and the enemies now met
with them, and the hoste was set in araye,
and the *beastes were separated into con- *Or, elephants.
uenient places, and the horsemen were pla
ced in the wings,
21 Maccabeus considering the coming of
the multitude and the diuers preparations
of weapons, and the fiercenes of the beastes, helde vp his hands towarde heauen,
calling vpõ the Lord that doeth wonders,
and that loked vpon thẽ, knowing that the
victorie cometh not by the weapons, but
that he giueth the victorie to them that a-
re worthie, as semeth good vnto him.
22 Therefore in his prayer he said after this
maner, O Lord, * thou that didest send 2.King.19,35
thine Angel in the time of Ezecias King isa.37,36.
of Iudea, who in the hoste of Sennacherib tob.1,21.
slewe an hundreth, forescore & fiue thou- eccles.48,24.
sand,
23 Send now also thy good Angel before vs,
ô Lord of heauens, for a feare and dreade
vnto them,
24 And let thẽ be discõfited by the strength
of thine arme, which come against thine
holie people to blaspheme. Thus with these wordes he made an end.
25 Then Nicanor and they that were with
him, drewe nere with trumpets and shou-
tings for ioye.
26 But Iudas and his companie praying and
calling vpon God, incountered with the
enemies,
27 So that with their hands they foght, but
with their hearts they prayed vnto God,
and slewe no lesse then fiue & thirtie thousand mẽ: for thorowe the presence of God
they were wonderously comforted.
28 Now when they left of, & were turning
againe with ioye, they vnderstode that
Nicanor him self was slaine for all his
armour.
29 Then they made a great shoute and a
crye, praising the Almightie in their owne langage.
30 Therefore *Iudas*, which was euer ye chief
defender of his citizens bothe in bodie &
minde, and which bare euer good affectiõ
towardes them of his nacion, commanded
to smite of Nicanors head, with his hand
and shulder, and to bring it to Ierusalem.
31 And when he came there, he called all thẽ
of his nacion, and set the Priests by the altar, and sent for them of the castel,
32 And shewed thẽ wicked Nicanors head,
& the hand of that blasphemour which he
had holden vp against the holie Temple
of the Almightie with proude bragges.
33 He caused the tongue also of wicked Ni
canor to be cut in litle pieces, & to be cast
vnto the foules, and that the rewardes of
his madnes shulde be hanged vp before
the Temple.

34 So euerie man praised towarde the heauen the glorious Lord, saying, Blessed be
he, that hathe kept his place vndefiled.
35 He hanged also Nicanors head vpon the
hie castel, for an euident and plaine token
vnto all of the helpe of God.
36 And so they established all together by
a cōmune decre that they wolde in no case suffer this day without keping it holie:
37 And that the feast shulde be the thirtenth day of the twelfth moneth, which is
called Adar in the Syriās langage, the day
before Mardocheus day.
38 Thus farre as concerning Nicanors mat
ters, and from that time the Hebrewes had
the citie in possession. And here wil I also
make an end.
39 If I haue done wel, and as the storie required, it is the thing that I desired: but if
I haue spoken slenderly & barely, it is that
I colde.
40 For as it is hurtful to drinke wine alone,
and then againe water: and as wine tempered with water is pleasant and deliteth the
taste, so the setting out of the matter deliteth the eares of them that read the storie.
And here shalbe the end.

THE
NEWE TESTAMENT
OF OVR LORD
IESVS CHRIST,

Conferred diligently with the Greke, and best approued translacions in diuers languages.

EXOD. XIIII, VER. XIII.

FEARE YE NOT, STAND STIL, AND BEholde the saluacion of the Lord, which he wil shewe to you this day.

Great are the troubles of the righteous: but the Lord deliuereth them out of all, Psal.34.19.

THE LORD SHAL FIGHT FOR YOU: therefore holde you your peace, Exod.14, vers.14.

AT GENEVA.

PRINTED BY ROVLAND HALL.

M. D. LX.

THE DESCRIPTION OF THE HOlie land, conteining the places mencioned in the foure Euangelistes, with other places about the sea coasts, wherein may be sene the wayes and iourneis of Christ and his Apostles in Iudea, Samaria, and Galile: for into these thre partes this land is diuided.

THE PLACES SPECIFIED IN this mappe with their situation by the obseruation of the degrees concerning their length and breadth.

Ascalon	65,24: 31, 32.
Azot	65, 35: 32.
Bethlehem	65, 55:31, 51.
Bethphage	68, 31, 58.
Bethsaida	66, 51: 32, 29.
Bethabara	66, 34: 32, 1.
Bethania	66, 31, 58.
Cana of Galile	66, 52: 32, 48.
Capernaum	66, 53: 32, 29.
Carmel mount	66, 31: 32, 50.
Cesarea Stratonis	66, 16: 32, 25.
Cesarea Philippi	67, 39: 33, 5.
Corasim	66, 53: 32, 29.
Dan one of the founteins whence Iordan springeth	67, 25: 33, 8.
Ennon	66, 40: 32,18.
Emaus	65, 54: 31,59.
Ephen	66, 8, 32.
Gadara or Garaza	66, 48: 32,29.
Gaza	65, 10: 31,40.
Iericho	66, 10: 32, 1.
Ierusalem	66, 31, 55.
Ioppe	65, 40: 32, 5.
Ior the other founteine whence Iordan springeth	67, 31: 33, 7.
Magdalon called also Dalmanutha	66, 48: 32,28.
Naim	66, 35: 32, 33.
Nazareth	66,56: 32,42.
Ptolemais	66, 50: 32,58.
Samaria the citie	66, 22: 32, 19.
Sidon	67, 15: 33, 30.
Silo	66, 27: 32, 19.
Tyrus	67, 33, 20.
Tyberias	66, 44: 32, 26.

The description of the holie land and of the places mencioned in the foure Euangelistes.

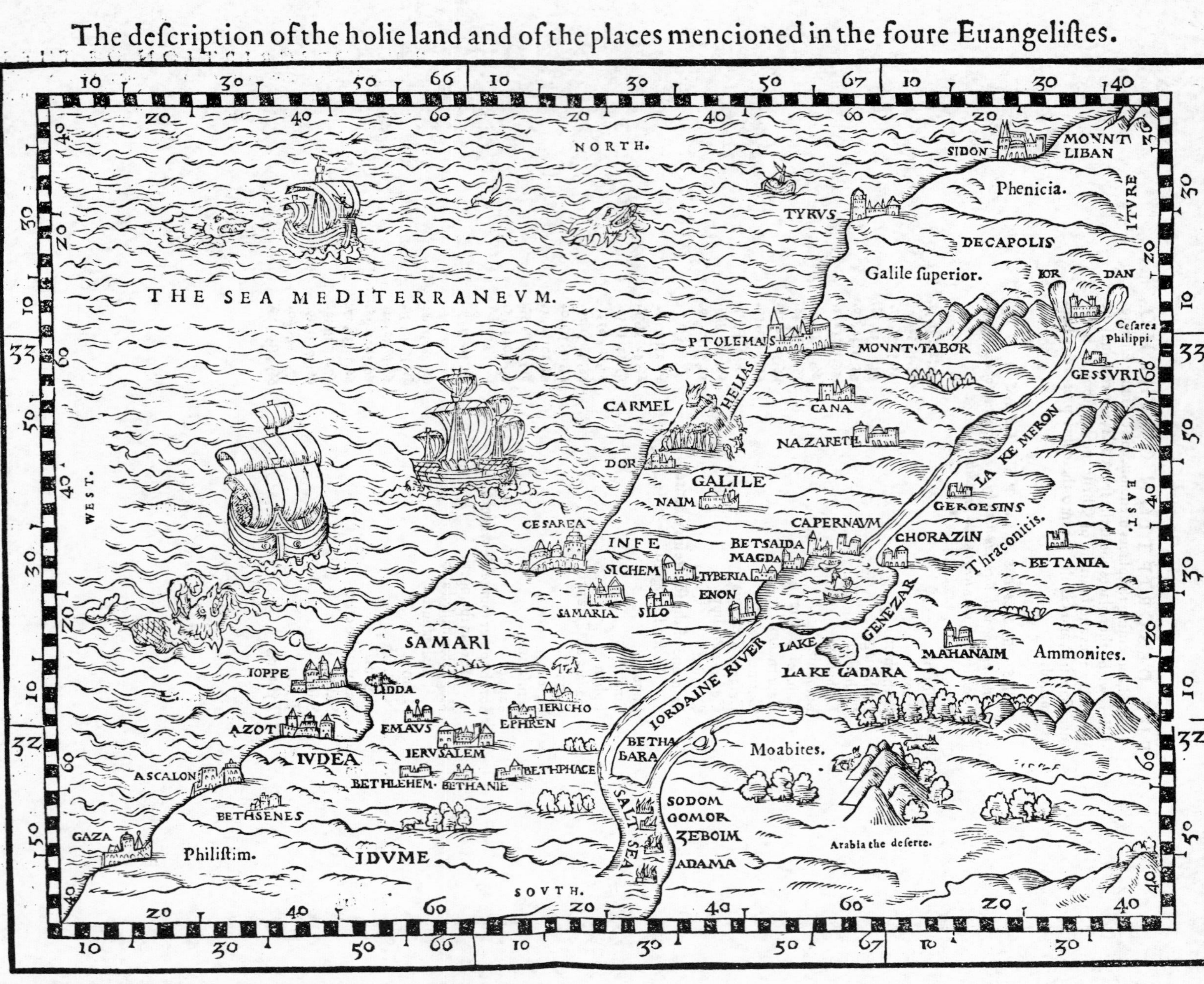

THE HOLY [a] GOSPEL of Iesus Christ, [b] according to Matthewe.

a This worde signifieth good tidinges, and is taken here for the storie which conteineth the ioyful message of the comming of the Sonne of God promised from the beginning.
b That is, writen and taught by Matthewe.

THE ARGUMENT.

IN this historie written by Matthewe, Marke, Luke, and Iohn, the Spirit of God so gouerned their hearts, that althogh they were foure in nōber, yet in effect and purpose they so consent, as thogh the whole had bene composed by any one of them. And albeit in stile and maner of writing they be diuers, and sometime one writeth more largely that which the other doeth abbridge: neuertheles in matter and argument they all tende to one end: which is, to publish to the worlde the fauour of God towarde mankinde through Christ Iesus, whome the Father hathe giuen as a pledge of his mercie & loue. And for this cause they intitle their storie, Gospel, which signifieth good tidings, for asmuche as God hathe performed in dede that which the fathers hoped for. So that hereby we are admonished to forsake the worlde, and the vanities thereof, and with moste affectioned hearts embrace this incomparable treasure frely offred vnto vs: for there is no ioye nor consolacion, no peace nor quietnes, no felicitie nor saluacion, but in Iesus Christ, who is the very substance of this Gospel, and in whome all the promises are yea, and amen. And therefore vnder this worde is conteined the whole Newe testament: but communely we vse this name for the historie, which the foure Euangelists write, conteining Christs coming in the flesh, his death and resurrection, which is the perfite summe of our saluation. Matthewe, Marke, and Luke are more copious in describing his life and death: but Iohn more laboureth to set forthe his doctrine, wherein bothe Christs office, and also the vertue of his death and resurrection more fully appeare: for without this, to knowe that Christ was borne, dead & risen againe, shulde nothing profite vs. The which thing notwithstanding that the thre first touche partely, as he also sometime intermedleth the historical narration, yet Iohn chiefly is occupied herein. And therefore as a moste learned interpreter writeth, they describe, as it were, the bodie, and Iohn setteth before our eyes the soule. Wherefore the same aptely termeth the Gospel writ by Iohn, the keye which openeth the dore to the vnderstanding of the others: for whosoeuer doeth knowe the office, vertue and power of Christ, shal reade that which is written of the Sonne of God come to be the redemer of the worlde, with moste proffit. Now as concerning the writers of this historie, it is euident that Matthewe was a Publicane or custome gatherer, and was thence chosen of Christ to be an Apostle. Marke is thoght to haue bene Peters disciple, and to haue planted the first Church at Alexandria, where he dyed the eight yere of the reigne of Nero. Luke was a phisition of Antiochia and became Pauls disciple, and fellowe in all his traueils: he liued foure score and foure yeres, and was buryed at Constantinople. Iohn was that Apostle whome the Lord loued, the sonne of Zebedeus, and brother of Iames: he dyed thre score yeres after Christ, and was buryed nere to the Citie of Ephesus.

CHAP. I.

1 The genealogie of Christ, that is, the Messias promised to the fathers. 18 Who was conceiued by the holy Gost, and borne of the virgine Marie, when she was betroushed vnto Ioseph. 20 The Angel satisfieth Iosephes minde. 21 Why he is called Iesus, and wherefore Emmanuel.

Luk. 3,23.

1 THe [c] boke of the generaciō of IESVS CHRIST
the [d] sonne of [e] Dauid, the
sonne of Abraham.
2 *Abrahā begate Isaac.
*And Isaac begate Ia-
cob. And *Iacob bega-
te Iudas and his brethren.
3 *And Iudas begate Phares, and Zara [f] of
Thamar. And *Phares begate Esrom. And
Esrom begate Aram.
4 And Aram begate Aminadab. And Aminadab begate Naasson. And Naasson begate Salmon.
5 And Salmon begate Booz of [g] Rachab.
And * Booz begate Obed of Ruth. And
Obed begate Iesse.
6 And *Iesse begate Dauid the King. And
*Dauid the King begate Solomon of her
that was *the wife* of Vrias.
7 And *Solomon begate Roboam. And Ro
boam begate Abia. And Abia begate Asa.
8 And Asa begate Iosaphat. And Iosaphat
begate Ioram. And Ioram begate Ozias.
9 And Ozias begate [h] Ioatham. And Ioatham begate Achaz. And Achaz begate
Ezecias.
10 And *Ezecias begate Manasses. And
Manasses begate Amon. And Amon begate Iosias.
11 And *Iosias begate Iacim. And Iacim be
gate Iechonias & his brethren about the
time they were caryed away to Babylon.
12 And after they were caryed away into
Babylon, *Iechonias begate [i] Salathiel.
*And Salathiel begate Zorobabel.

c This is the rehearsal of the progenie, whereof Iesus Christ is sprōg according to the flesh.
d So called, for that he came of the stocke of Dauid.
e These two are first rehearsed, because Christ was especially promised to come of them and their sede, and therefore Christ communely was called the sonne of Dauid, because the promes was more euidently confirmed vnto him. *Gen. 21,2. *Gen. 25,24. *Gen. 29,35. *Gen. 38,27.
f By incestuous adulterie, the which shame setteth forthe his great humilitie, who made him self of no reputation, but became a seruant for our sakes: yea, a worme and no man, the reproche of men, and contempt of the people, and at length suffred the accursed death of the crosse. *2. Chron. 2,5. Ruth 4,18.

g Rachab and Ruth, being Gentiles, signifie that Christ came not onely of ỹ Iewes, and for them, but also of ỹ Gentiles, and for their saluation.
Ruth 4,18.
1. Sam. 16,1. & 17,12.
2. Sam. 12,24.
1. King. 11,43
1. chro. 3,10.
h He hathe omitted thre Kings, Ioas, Amasia, Azaria, abbridgig the nomber to make the times fourtene generations.
2. King. 20,21 & 21,18.
1. chro. 3,13.
2. King. 23. 34. & 24,1.
1. chro. 36,4.
2. King. 24,6.
2. chro. 36,9.
i After the captiuitie, the title royal was appointed vnto him: so that notwithstanding that they were as sclaues for the space of seuentie yeres, yet by the prouidence of God the gouernemēt remained in the familie of Dauid, where it continued til the coming of Christ. *1. Chro 3,17. ezra. 3,2. & 5,2.

13 And Zorobabel begate Abiud. And A-
biud begate Eliacim. And Eliacim begate
Azor.
14 And Azor begate Sadoc. And Sadoc begate Achim. And Achim begate Eliud.
15 And Eliud begate Eleazar. And Eleazar
begate Matthan. And Matthan begate Iacob.
16 And Iacob begate Ioseph, the housband
of Marie, [k] of whome was borne IESVS,
that is called [l] Christ.
17 So all the generaciōs from Abraham to
Dauid, *are* fourtene generacions. And
from Dauid vntil they were caryed away
into Babylon, fourtene generacions: and
after they were caryed away into Babylon vntil Christ, fourtene generacions.
18 ¶ Now the byrth of IESVS Christ was
thus, When as his mother Marie was * betrowthed to Ioseph, [m] before they came
together, she was founde [n] with childe of
the holie Gost.
19 Then Ioseph her housband being a
[o] iust man, and not willing to * make her a
publike example, was minded to put her
away secretly.
20 But whiles he thoght these things, beholde, the Angel of the Lord appeared
vnto him in a [p] dreame, saying, Ioseph the
[q] sonne of Dauid, feare not to take Marie
for thy wife: for that which is conceiued
in her, is of the holie Gost.
21 And she shal bring forthe a sonne, and
thou shalt * call his name [r] IESVS: for he
shal * saue his people from their sinnes.
22 And all this was done that it might be
fulfilled, which was spoken of the Lord by
the Prophet, saying,
23 * Beholde, a virgine shalbe with childe,
and shal beare a sonne, and "they shal call
his name Emmanuel, which is by interpretacion, [s] God with vs.
24 ¶ Then Ioseph, being raised from slepe,
did as the Angel of the Lord had inioyned him, and toke his wife.
25 But he knewe her not, til she had broght
forthe her [t] first borne sonne, and he called
his name IESVS.

k Albeit the Iewes nomber their kinred by the male-kind: yet this linage of Marie is cōprehended vnder the same, because she was maried to a man of her owne stocke & tribe.
l Who is the true King, Priest, and Prophet annointed of God to accomplish ẏ office of ẏ redemer.
Luk.1,27.
m Before he toke her home to him.
n As the Angel afterwarde declared to Ioseph.
o Vpright and fearing God, & therefore suspecting ẏ she had cōmitted fornicatiō, before she was betrowthed, wolde nether receiue her, w͏ͨ by the Law shulde be maried to another nether by accusing her put her to shame for her fact.
Deut 24,1.
p This dreame is witnessed by the holie Gost, and is a kinde of reuelation, Nom.12,6.
q This name putteth him in remembrance of Gods promes to Dauid.
Luk.1,38.
r That is, a Sauiour.
Act.4,12.
phil.2,10.
Isa.7,14.
"Or, thou.

s God is ioyned with vs by the meanes of Iesus Christ, who is bothe God and man. t Christ is here called the first borne, because she had neuer none before, and not in respect of any she had after. Nether yet doeth this worde (til) import alwayes a time following: wherein the contrarie may be affirmed, as our Sauiour, saying, that he wil be present with his disciples, til the end of the worlde, meaneth not, that after this worlde he wil not be with them.

CHAP. II.

1 *The time and place of Christs birth. 11 The Wisemen offer their presents. 14 Christ fleeth into Egypt. 16 The yong children are slaine. 23 Ioseph turneth into Galile.*

1 WHen * IESVS then was borne at
Beth-lehē in [a] Iudea, in the dayes
of Herode the King, beholde, there came
[b] Wisemen from the East to Ierusalem,
2 Saying, Where is the King of the Iewes
that is borne? for we haue sene his [c] starre
in the East, and are come [d] to worship him.
3 When King Herode heard *this*, he was
troubled, and all Ierusalem with him.
4 And gathering together all the chief
Priests & Scribes of the people, he asked
of them, where Christ shulde be borne.
5 [e] And they said vnto him, At Beth-lehem
in Iudea: for so it is written by the Prophet,
6 * And thou Beth-lehem in the land of Iuda, art not the least among the Princes of
Iuda: for out of thee shal come the gouernour that shal fede my people Israel.
7 Then Herode [f] priuely called the Wisemen, *and* diligently inquired of them the
time of the starre that appeared,
8 And sent them to Beth-lehem, saying,
Go, and searche diligently for the babe:
and when ye haue founde him, bring me
worde againe, that I may come also, and
worship him.
9 ¶ So when they had heard the King, they
departed: and lo, the [g] starre which they
had sene in the East, went before them, til
it came, and stode ouer *the place* where the
babe was.
10 And when they sawe the starre, they reioyced with an exceading great ioye,
11 And went into the house, and "founde
the babe with Marie his mother, and fel
downe, and worshipped him, and opened
their treasures, and presented vnto him
giftes, [h] *euen* golde, and incense, and myrrhe.
12 And after they were warned of God in
a dreame, that they shulde [i] not go againe
to Herode, they returned into their countrey another way.
13 ¶ After their departure, beholde the Angel of the Lord appeareth to Ioseph in a
dreame, saying, Arise, & take the babe and
his mother, and flee into Egypt, and be
there til I bring thee worde: for Herode
wil seke the babe, to destroye him.
14 So he arose and toke the babe and his
mother by night, and departed into E-
gypt,
15 And was there vnto the death of Herode, [k] that it might be fulfilled, which was
spoken of the Lord by the * Prophet,
saying, Out of Egypt haue I called my
Sonne.
16 ¶ [l] Thē Herode, seing that he was mocked of ẏ Wisemen, was exceading wroth,
and sent forthe, & slewe all the male children that were in Beth-lehem, and in all
the coastes thereof, from two yere olde &
vnder, according to the time which he had
diligently searched out of the Wisemen.

Luk.2,6.
a For there is another Beth-lehem in the tribe of Zebulun.

b Wisemen, or Magi, in the Persians and Chaldeans tongue signifie Philosophers, Priests, or astronomers, & are here the first frutes of the Gentiles that came to worship Christ.
c An extraordinarie signe to set forth ẏ Kings honour, whome ẏ worlde did not esteme.
d Which was a declaration of that reuerēce, which the Gentiles shulde beare vnto Christ.
e They colde wel tell of Christ in general: but when they shulde professe his name, and giue him his due honor, thei waxe colde, and shrinke backe
Micah 5,2.
iohn 7,42.
f An euil conscience is a burning fyre.
g The starre vanished away before, to ẏ intēt thei shulde tary at Ierusalem, and there inquire of the thing, to the confusion of the Iewes.
"Or, sawe.
h The Persiās maner was not to salute Kīgs without a present, and therefore they broght of that which was most precious in their contrei, whereof euery one of them offred.
i Promes oght not to be kept, where Gods honour and preaching of his trueth is hindered: or els it oght not to be broken.
k That which was prefigured by the deliuerance of the Israelites out of Egypt, w͏ͨ were Christs Church and his bodie, is now verified, and accomplished in the head Christ.
Hose 11,1.
l Within a certeine time after.

17 So

17 Then was that fulfilled which was spokẽ
by the Prophet Ieremias,saying,
18 *In [m] Rama was a voyce heard, mourning,and weping and great lamentation:
Rachel weping for her children, and wolde not be comforted, because they [n] were
not.
19 And when Herode was dead,beholde,an
Angel of the Lord appeareth in a dreame
to Ioseph in Egypt,
20 Saying,Arise,and take the babe and his
mother, and go into the land of Israel:
for they are [o] dead which soght the babes
life.
21 Then he arose vp,and toke the babe and
his mother, and came into the land of Israel.
22 But when he heard that Archelaus did
reigne in Iudea in steade of his father He
rode,he was afrayed to go thether: "yet after he was warned of God in a dreame, he
turned aside into the parties of Galile,
23 And went and dwelt in a citie called Na
zaret, that it might be fulfilled which was
spoken by the Prophetes, *which was*, That
he shulde be called" a [p] Nazarite.

Iere.31,15.
m Herode renewed the sorowe which ẏ Beniamites had suffred long before: yet for all his crueltie he colde not bring to passe, that Christ shulde not reigne.
n That is,they were killed & dead.
o Thus the faithful may se how God hathe infinite meanes to preserue them frõ the rage of tyrants.
"Or,therefore.
"Or, of Nazaret.
p Which is holie and consecrated to God: alluding vnto those that were Nazarites in the olde Law, which were a figure of that holines which shulde be manifested in Christ,as was Sãson, Ioseph, &c.

CHAP. III.

1 The office,doctrine,& life of Iohn. 7 The Pharises are reproued. 8 The frutes of repentance 13 Christ is baptized in Iordan, 17 And autorised by God his Father.

1 A*Nd in [a] those dayes, Iohn the Baptiste came and preached in the [b] wildernes of Iudea,
2 And said,"Repent: for the [c] kingdome of
heauen is at hand.
3 For this is he of whome it is spoken by the
Prophet Esaias, saying,* The voyce of
him that cryeth in the wildernes, *is*,Prepa-
re ye the way of the Lord:make his paths
straight.
4 *And this Iohn had his [d] garment of camels heere, and a girdle of a skin about
his loynes: his meat was also [e] "locustes &
wilde honie.
5 *Then went out to him Ierusalem and all
Iudea, and all the region rounde about
Iordan.
6 And they were baptized of him in Iordan, [f] confessing their sinnes.
7 Now when he sawe many of the Pharises
and of the Sadduces come to his baptisme, he said vnto them, * O "generacions
of vipers, who hathe forewarned you to
flee from the angre to come?
8 Bring forthe therefore [g] frutes worthie
amendement of life,
9 And thinke not to say with your selues,

Mar.1,4. luk.3,3.
a In ẏ first yere of ẏ reigne of Tiberius, after Christ had long time remained in Nazaret, and was now about 30 yere olde.
b So called in respect of the playne countrey and fertile valleis: and not because it was not inhabited.
"Or,be sorie for your fautes past, and amend.
c Which is,ẏ God wil reigne ouer vs, gather vs vnto him, pardon our sinnes,and adopte vs by the preaching of the Gospel
Isa.40,3. mar.1,3. luk.3,4. ioh.1,23.
Mar.1,6.
d Wouen with heere,as grosse heereclothe.
e Suche meates as nature broght forthe without mans labour or diligence: reade Leuit. 11, 22.
"Or,grashoppers. *Mar.1,5. luk.3,7.* f Acknowledging their fautes:for there is no repentance without confession. *Chap.13,34* *"Or,broodes* g He menaceth those venemous and malicious Pharises with the iudgement of God, except they shewe before men suche workes as are agreable to the profession of the godlie, whome Isai calleth the trees of righteousnes,chap.61,3.

*We haue Abraham to *our* father:for I say
vnto you,that God is able of these stones
to raise vp children vnto Abraham.
10 And now also is the [h] axe put to the roote of the trees:*therefore euerie tre,which
bringeth not forthe good frute, is hewen
downe,and cast into the fyre.
11 *In dede I baptize you ẇ water to amendemẽt of life,but he that cometh after me,
is mightier then I, whose shoes I am not
worthie to beare: he wil baptize you with
the holie Gost,and with [i] fyre.
12 Which hathe his [k] fanne in his hand, &
wil make cleane his floore, and gather his
wheat into his garner,but wil burne vp the
chaffe with vnquencheable fyre.
13 ¶*Thẽ came Iesus frõ Galile to Iordan
vnto Iohn,to be baptized of him.
14 But Iohn put him backe, saying,I haue
nede to be baptized of thee,and commest
thou to me?
15 Then Iesus answering, said to him, Let
be now: for thus it becometh vs to [l] fulfil
all righteousnes. So he suffred him.
16 And Iesus when he was baptized,came
straight out of the water.And lo,the heauens were opened vnto him, & *Iohn* sawe
ẏ Spirit of God descending like a [m] doue,
and lighting vpon him.
17 And lo,a voyce *came* from heauen, saying,* [n] This is my *beloued Sõne,in whome I am wel pleased.

Iohn.8,39. act.13,26.
h The iudgement of God is at hand to destroye suche as are not mete to be of his Church.
Chap.7,19.
Marc.1,8. luk.3,19. ioh.1,26. act.1,5. & 2,1.& 8,5 &19,4.
i When God baptizeth inwardely with the vertue of his Spirit, he burneth, & cõsumeth the vices and inflameth the heartes with loue towarde him.
k Which is ẏ preaching of the Gospel, whereby he gathereth the faithful as good corne, & scatereth the infideles as chaffe.
Mar.1,9. luk.3,22.
l We must rẽder perfit obedience to God in all things, which he hathe ordeined.
m To shewe the state of his kingdome,which is in all mekenes & lowlines. *Chap.17,5.2.pet.1,17.* n The fauour of God resteth on Iesus Christ,that frõ him it might be powred on vs,which deserue of our selues his wrath, and indignation. **Coloss* 1,13.*

CHAP. IIII.

1 Christ fasteth & is tempted. 11 The Angels minister vnto him. 17 He beginneth to preache. 18 He calleth Peter,Andrew,Iames and Iohn,and healeth all the sicke.

1 THen *was Iesus led aside [a] of the Spirit into the wildernes,to be [b] tẽpted
of the deuil.
2 And when he had fasted fortie dayes,and
fortie nights,he was afterwarde hungrie.
3 Then came to him the tempter,and said,
If thou be the Sonne of God, [c] commande that these stones be made bread.
4 But he answering, said,It is writtẽ,*Man
shal not liue by bread onely, but by euerie
[d] worde that proceadeth out of the mouth
of God.
5 Then ẏ deuil toke him vp into the [e] holie
Citie,& set him on a"pinacle of the tẽple,
6 And said vnto him, If thou be the Sonne
of God,cast thy self downe: for it is written,* ẏ he wil giue his Angels charge ouer
thee,and with their hands they shal [f] lifte
thee vp, lest at anie time ẏͧ shuldest dash
thy fote against a stone.
7 Iesus said vnto him,It is written againe,
*Thou shalt not [g] tẽpt the Lord thy God.

Marc.1,12. luk.4,1.
a By the holie Gost.
b To ẏ end ẏ he ouercomĩg these tentatiõs might get the victorie for vs
c Satan wolde haue Christ to distrust God, and his worde and followe other strange and vnlawful meanes.
Deu.8,3.
d He meaneth the ordre that God hathe ordeined to mainteine his creatures by.
e To wit, Ierusalem.
"Or, vane which shewed where the windestode.
Psal.92,11.
f He alledgeth but halfe the sentẽce to deceiue thereby the rather,and cloke his craftie purpose. *Deut.6,16.* g We must not leaue suche lawful meanes as God hathe appointed,to seke others after our owne fantasie.

8 Againe the deuil toke him vp vnto an exceading hie mountaine, and [h] shewed him
all the kingdomes of the worlde, and the
glorie of them,
9 And said to him, All these wil I giue
thee, if thou wilt fall downe, and worship
me.
10 Then said Iesus vnto him, Auoide Satã:
for it is written, *Thou shalt worship the
Lord thy God, and him onely shalt thou
serue.
11 Then the deuil [i] left him: and beholde,
the Angels [k] came, and ministred vnto
him.
12 ¶ *And when Iesus had heard ỷ Iohn was
[l] deliuered vp, he returned into Galile,
13 And leauing Nazaret, went and dwelt
in Capernaum, which is nere the [m] sea in
the borders of Zabulon & Nephthalim,
14 That it might be fulfilled which was spo
ken by Esaias the Prophet, saying,
15 *The land of Zabulon, and the land of
Nephthalim *by* the way of the sea, beyond
Iordan, [n] Galile of the Gentiles:
16 The people which sate in [o] darkenes, sawe
great light: and to them which sate in the
region and shadowe of death, light is risen vp.
17 *From that time Iesus began to preache,
and to say, Amend your liues: for ỷ kingdome of heauen is at hand.
18 ¶ *And Iesus walking by the sea of Galile, sawe two brethren, Simõ, which was cal
led Peter, and Andrew his brother, casting a net into the sea (for they were
[p] fishers.)
19 And he said vnto them, Followe me, and
I wil make you fishers [q] of men.
20 And they straight way leauing the nets,
followed him.
21 And when he was gone forthe from thence, he sawe other two brethren, Iames *the*
sonne of Zebedeus, and Iohn his brother in
a ship with Zebedeus their father, mẽding
their nets, and he called them.
22 And they [r] without tarying, leauing the
ship and their father, followed him.
23 So Iesus went about all Galile, teaching
in their Synagogues, and preaching the
Gospel of the [s] kingdome, and healing e-
uerie sickenes and euerie disease among
the people.
24 And his fame spred abroad through all
Syria: and they broght vnto him all sicke
people, that were taken with diuers diseases and gripings, and them that were
possessed with [t] deuils, & those which were [u] lunatike, and those that had the palsey:
and he healed them.
25 And there followed him great multitudes out of Galile, and [x] Decapolis, and Ierusalem, and Iudea, and from beyonde
Iordan.

h In a vision.
Deut.6,13. & 10,20.
i The worde of God is the sworde of the spirit, wherewith Satan is ouercome.
k To comfort him.
Mar.1,14. luk.4,14. ioh.4,43.
l And cast in prison by Herode.
m For so they called ỷ lake of Genesareth.
Isa.9,1.
n Christ had preached now almost a yere in Iudea, and Samaria, and after went to preache in the vppermost Galile, which was out of the borders of Palestina.
o Which was without comfort, hathe receiued consolation.
Mar.1,15.
Mar.1,16.
p God hathe chosen ỷ weake things of the worlde to confounde the mightie, 1.Corin.1,27.
q To drawe them out of the sea of this worlde, wherein they are drowned.
r We oght to be moste ready to followe Christ, when he calleth, leauing all worldelie respects aparte.
s That is, the blessed tidings of forgiuenes of sinnes & reconciliation with God.
t So that by healing incurable diseases Christs diuinitie appeared.
u They that were mad or sicke at a certeine time of the moone.
x It was a coutrey wherein was tẽ cities, as ỷ worde signifieth.

CHAP. V.

3 Christ teacheth who are blessed. 13 The salt of the earth & light of the worlde. 16 Good workes 17 Christ came to fulfil the Law. 21 What is ment by killing. 23 Reconciliation. 27 Adulterie. 29 Offences. 31 Diuorcement. 33 Not to sweare. 39 To suffer wrong. 43 To loue our enemies. 48 Perfection.

1 AND when he sawe the multitude,
he went vp into a mountaine: and
whẽ he was set, his disciples came to him.
2 And he opened his mouthe and taught
them, saying,
3 *Blessed *are* the [a] poore in spirit, for theirs
is the kingdome of heauen.
4 *Blessed *are* they that [b] mourne: for they
shalbe comforted.
5 *Blessed *are* the [c] meke: for they shal inhe
rite the earth.
6 Blessed *are* they which [d] honger & thirst
for righteousnes: for they shal be filled.
7 Blessed *are* the merciful: for thei shal obteine mercie.
8 Blessed *are* the *pure in heart: for they shal
se God.
9 Blessed *are* the peace makers: for they
shalbe called the [e] children of God.
10 Blessed *are* they *which suffer persecutiõ for righteousnes sake: for theirs is the
kingdome of heauen.
11 *Blessed are ye when men reuile you, and
persecute *you*, and say all maner of euil a-
gainst you for my sake, falsely.
12 Reioyce and be glad, for great is your
rewarde in heauen: for so persecuted they
the Prophets which were before you.
13 *Ye are the [f] salte of the earth: but if the
salte haue lost his sauour, wherewith shal
it be salted? It is thenceforthe good for
nothing, but to be cast out, & to be troden
vnder fote of men.
14 Ye are the light of the worlde. A citie
that is set on an hill, can not be hid.
15 *Nether do men light a candel, and put
it vnder a bushel, but on a candelsticke, &
it giueth light vnto all that are in the
house.
16 *Let [g] your light so shine before men,
that they may se your good workes, & glo
rifie your Father which is in heauen.
17 Thinke not that I am come to destroye
the Law, or the Prophetes. [h] I am not come to destroye them, but to fulfil them.
18 *For truely I say vnto you, Til heauen,
and earth perish, one iote, or one title of
the Law shal not scape, til [i] all things be
fulfilled.
19 *Whosoeuer therefore shal breake one
of [k] these least commandements, & teache
men so, he shalbe called the least in the
kingdome of heauen: but whosoeuer shal
obserue and teache *them*, the same shal be
called great in the kingdome of heauen.
20 For I say vnto you, except your righteousnes *excede the *righteousnes* of ỷ [l] Scribes
and

Luk.6,20.
a That feele them selues voide of all righteousnes that thei may onely seeke it in Christ.
Isa.61,2. luk.6,21.
b Which feele their owne miserie, & seke their comfort in God.
Psal.73,11.
c Who rather wolde suffer all iniuries, then they wolde reuenge thẽ selues.
Psal.24,4.
d Being in necessitie, desire nothing but ỷ w is vpright & godlie.
e For he is called ỷ God of peace, 1.Cor.14,33.
1.Pet.3,14.
1.Pet.4,14. act.5,41.
Mar.9,50. luk.14,34.
f Your office is to season men with the salt of ỷ heauẽlie doctrine.
Mar.4,21. luk.8,16. & 11,33.
g Because you are sene farre of, giue good example of life.
h The Gospel is the stablishing, & accõplishing of ỷ Law.
1.Pet.2,12.
i The doctrine of the Law conteineth nothing vnprofitable or superfluous.
Luk.16,17.
Iam.2,10.
k Whosoeuer shal transgresse the least of the ten cõmandements in worde and exãple, he shal be cast out of the kingdome of God, except it be pardoned him in Christ.
Luk.11,39.
l Which nether expound the Law truely, nor obserue it wel.

& Pharises, ye shal not enter into the kingdome of heauen.
21 m Ye haue heard that it was said vnto
thẽ of the olde time, *Thou shalt not kil:
for whosoeuer killeth, shal be "culpable of
iudgement.
22 But I say vnto you, whosoeuer is angrie
with his brother " n vnaduisedly, shal be
culpable of iudgement. And whosoeuer
saieth vnto his brother, o Raca, shalbe
worthie to be punished by the p Counsel.
And whosoeuer shal say, Foole, shalbe
worthie to be punished with hel fyre.
23 If thẽ thou bring thy gift to the altar, &
there remembrest that thy brother hathe
oght against thee,
24 Leaue there thine offring before the altar, and go thy way: first be q reconciled to
thy brother, & then come & offer thy gift.
25 * Agre with thine aduersarie quickely,
whiles thou art in the way with him, lest
thine aduersarie deliuer thee to the iudge,
and the iudge deliuer thee to the sergeãt,
and thou be cast into prison.
26 Verely I say vnto thee, thou shalt not co
me out thence, til thou hast payed the vtmost farthing.
27 ¶ Ye haue heard that it was said to them
of olde time, * Thou shalt not commit adulterie.
28 But I say vnto you, ỷ whosoeuer loketh
on a womã to lust after her, hathe cõmitted r adulterie wher already in his heart.
29 *Wherefore if thy right s eye cause thee
to offend, plucke it out, and cast it frõ thee:
for better it is for thee, that one of thy mẽ
bers perish, "thẽ that thy whole bodie shul
de be cast into hel.
30 Also if thy right hand make thee to offend, cut it of, and cast it frõ thee: for better it is for thee that one of thy members
perish, thẽ that thy whole bodie shulde be
cast into hel.
31 It hathe bene said also, *Whosoeuer shal
put away his wife, let him giue her a testimonial of diuorcement.
32 But I say vnto you, whosoeuer shal put
away his wife (except it be for fornicatiõ)
t causeth her to commit adulterie: and
whosoeuer shal marie her that is diuorced, committeth adulterie.
33 Againe, ye haue heard that it was said to
them of olde time, * Thou shalt not forsweare thy self, but shalt performe thine
othes to the Lord.
34 But I say vnto you, u Sweare not at all,
nether by heauẽ, for it is ỷ throne of God:
35 Nor yet by the earth: for it is his fote sto
le: nether by Ierusalem: for it is the citie
of the great King.
36 Nether shalt thou sweare by thine head,
because thou canst not make one heere
white or blacke.

m He sheweth how these worthie docters haue falsely glosed this cõmandement.
Exod 20,13. deu 5,17.
"Or, subiect to punishment.
"Or, without cause.
n For God knowing his secret malice wil punish hĩ.
o Which signifieth in the Syrians tõgue an idle braine, & is spoken in contempt.
p Like iudgement almoste the Romains obserued: for Triumuiri had the examination of smale matters, ỷ coũsel of xxiii of greater causes & finally great matters of importance were decided by the senate of lxxi iudges which here is compared to the iudgement of God, or to be punished ỷ hel fyre.
Luk 12,58.
q For that thou hast offended him, or he hathe offẽded thee: for God preferreth brotherlie reconciliation to sacrifice.
Exod. 20,14. rom. 13,9.
r Chastitie is required bothe in bodie & in minde.
Chap. 18,8. mar. 9,47.
s Nothing is so precious ỷ oght not to be reiected in respect of the glorie of God.
"Or, & not that.
Chap. 19,7. deu. 24,1. mar. 10,4. luk. 16,18. 1. cor. 7,10.
t In that he giueth her leaue to mary another by ỷ testimonial.
Exod. 20,7. leu. 19,12. deut. 5,11.
u All superfluous othes are vtterly debarred, whether the Name of God be therein mencioned, or otherwise.

37 *But let your communication be, x Yea,
yea: Nay, nay. For whatsoeuer is more thẽ
these, commeth of ỷ euil.
38 ¶ Ye haue heard that it hathe bene said,
An*z eye for an eye, & a tooth for a tooth.
39 But I say vnto you, * Resist not "euil: but
whosoeuer a shal smite thee on thy right
cheke, turne to him the other also.
40 And if anie man wil sue thee at the law,
and take away thy coate, let him haue thy
cloke also.
41 And whosoeuer wil compell thee *to go* a
mile, go with him twaine.
42 *Giue to him that asketh, and from him
ỷ wolde borow of thee, turne not away.
43 Ye haue heard that it hathe bene said,
*Thou shalt loue thy neighbour, and b ha-
te thine enemie.
44 But I say vnto you, * Loue your enemies:
blesse them that curse you: do good to thẽ
that hate you, *and praye for them which
"hurt you, and persecute you,
45 *That ye may be the childrẽ of your Father that is in heauen: for he maketh his
sunne to arise on the euil, and the good,
and sendeth raine on the iuste, & vniuste.
46 For if ye loue them, which loue you,
what rewarde shal you haue? Do not the
c Publicanes euen the same?
47 And if ye " be friendlie to your brethrẽ
onely, what singular thing do ye? do not
euen the Publicanes likewise?
48 Ye shal therefore be d perfite, as your Father which is in heauen, is perfite.

CHAP. VI.

1 Of almes, 5 Prayer, 14 Forgiuing one another, 16 Fasting. 19 He forbiddeth the careful seeking of worldlie things, & willeth men to put their whole trust in him.

1 TAke hede that ye giue not your almes before men, to be sene of them,
or els ye shal haue no rewarde of your
Father which is in heauen.
2 * Therefore when thou giuest thine almes, thou shalt not make a trumpet to be
blowen before thee, as the a hypocrites do
in the Synagogues and in the stretes, to be
praised of men. Verely I say vnto you,
they haue their b rewarde.
3 But when thou doest thine almes, let
not thy c left hand knowe what thy right
hand doeth,
4 That thine almes may be in secret, & thy
Father that seeth in secret, he wil rewarde
thee d openly.
5 And when thou prayest, be not as the hypocrites: for they loue to stand, and pray
in the Synagogues, & in the corners of the
stretes, because they wolde be sene of mẽ.
Verely I say vnto you, they haue their
rewarde.
6 But when thou prayest, e enter into thy
chamber: & when thou hast shut thy dore,

Iam. 5,12.
x Let simplicitie, & trueth be in your wordes, and then ye shal not be so light, and ready to sweare.
y When a mã speaketh otherwise then he thĩketh in heart, it cometh of an euil cõscience, and of the deuil.
Exod. 21,24. deu. 19,21. leui. 24,20.
z Albeit this was spokẽ for the iudges, yet euerie mã applied it to reuenge his priuate quarel.
Luk. 6,29. rom. 12,17. 1. cor. 6,7.
"Or, iniurie.
a Rather receiue double wrong, then reuenge thine owne griefs.
Deut. 15,8. Leuit. 19,18.
b This was added by the false expositers ỷ Pharises
Luk. 6,27. Luk. 23,34. act. 7,60. 2. cor. 4,13.
"Or, rush in vpõ you.
Luk. 6,32.
"Or, imbrace.
c These did take to farme ỷ taxes, towls, & other payements, & therefore were greatly in disdaine with all men.
d We must labour to atteine vnto ỷ perfectiõ of God, who of his free liberalitie, doeth good to them that are vnworthie.

VI.

Rom. 12,8.
a Whose workes procede not of a right faith, but are done for vaine glorie.
b In that thei are praised & commended of men.
c It is sufficient that God approue our workes.
d In that day when all thĩgs shalbe reueiled.
e Withdrawe thy self rather aparte.

pray vnto thy Father which is in secret, &
thy Father which seeth in secret, shal rewarde
thee openly.
7 Also when ye pray," f vse no vaine repetitions
as the heathen: for they thinke to
be heard for their muche babling.
8 Be ye not like them therefore: for your
g Father knoweth whereof ye haue nede,
before ye aske of him.
9 After this h maner therefore pray ye,
*Our father which art in heauen, halowed
be thy i Name.
10 Thy k kingdome come. Thy wil be done
euen in earth, as *it is* in heauen.
11 Giue vs this day our daily bread.
12 And forgiue vs our dettes, as we also
forgiue our detters.
13 And lead vs not into l tentation, but deliuer
vs * frō euil: for m thine is the kingdome,
and the power, and the glorie for
euer, Amen.
14 * For if ye do forgiue men their trespaces,
your heauenlie Father wil also forgiue
you.
15 But if ye do not forgiue men their trespaces,
no more wil your Father forgiue *you*
your trespaces.
16 Moreouer, when ye fast, loke not sowre
as the hypocrites: for they n disfigure their
faces, that they might seme vnto men to
fast. Verely I say vnto you, that they haue
their rewarde.
17 But when thou fastest, o anoint thine
head, and wash thy face,
18 That thou seme not vnto men to fast,
but vnto thy Father which is in secret: &
thy Father which seeth in secret, wil rewarde
thee openly.
19 ¶ Lay not vp treasures for your selues
vpon the earth, where the mothe & canker
corrupt, & where theues digge through,
and steale.
20 * But lay vp treasures for your selues in
heauen, where nether the mothe nor canker
corrupteth, and where theues nether
digge through, nor steale.
21 For where your treasure is, there wil
your heart be also.
22 ¶ * The light of the bodie is the eye: if thē
thine eye be p single, thy whole bodie shal
be light.
23 But if thine eye be q wicked, then all
thy bodie shalbe darke. Wherefore if the
r light ẏ is in thee, be darkenes, how great
is that darkenes!
24 *No man can serue two masters: for either
he shal hate the one, and loue the other,
or els he shal leane to the one, and
despise the other. Ye can not serue God
and riches.
25 * Therefore I say vnto you, be not s carefull
for your life, what ye shal eat, or what
ye shal drīke: nor yet for your bodie, what

" *Or, bable not muche.*
f He commandeth vs to beware of muche babling & superfluous repetes.
g Who is not persuaded by eloquent speache, and long talke, as men are.
h Christ bindeth them not to the wordes, but to the sense, and forme of prayer.
Luk.11,2.
i We must seeke Gods glorie first, and aboue all thīgs.
k Reigne thou ouer all, and let vs render vnto thee perfit obedience, as thine Angels do.
l To be ouercome thereby.
Chap.13,19.
m This conclusion excludeth mans merites, and teacheth vs to grounde our prayers onely on God.
Mar.11,25.
eccles.28,2.
n Make their faces to seme of another sorte thē they were wōte to do.
o Whereby is commanded to auoyde all vaine ostentation.
Luk.12,33.
1.tim.6,19.
Luk.11,34.
p If thine eye be disposed to liberalitie, prouer. 22. 9.
q If thine affection be corrupt & giuen to couetousnes, deu. 15,9.
r If the cōcupiscēce, & wicked affections ouercome reason, we must not marueil thogh men be blīded, & be like vnto beastes
Luk.16,13.
Psal.55,22.
luk.12,22.
philip.4,6.
1.timo.6,8.
1.pet.5,7.
s Mans trauel nothing auaileth where God giueth not increase.

ye shal put on. Is not the life more worth
then meat? and the bodie then raiment?
26 Beholde the foules of the heauen: for
they sowe not, neither reape, nor carie into
the barnes: yet your heauenlie Father
feedeth them. Are ye not muche better
then they?
27 Which of you by taking care, is able to
adde one cubit vnto his stature?
28 And why care ye for raiment? Learne,
how the lilies of t the field do growe:
they u labour not, nether spinne:
29 Yet I say vnto you, that euen Solomon
in all his glorie was not arayed like one of
these.
30 Wherefore if God so clothe the grasse
of the field which is to day, and to morowe
is cast into the ouen, shal he not *do*
muche more vnto you, ô ye of litle faith?
31 Therefore take no thoght, saying, What
shal we eat? or what shal we drinke? or wherewith
shal we be clothed?
32 (For after all these things x seke the Gētiles)
for your heauenlie Father knoweth,
that ye haue nede of all these things.
33 But seke ye first the kingdome of God,
and his y righteousnes, & all these things
shalbe ministred vnto you.
34 Care not then for the morowe: for the
morowe shal care for " it z self: the day
hathe ynough with his owne grief.

t The goodnes of God euen towards ẏ herbes of ẏ field, farre passeth all things that man can compasse by his power and labour.
u The worde signifieth, they weary not thē selues.
x With care and distrust.
y That is, to be regenerate, and amende your liues.
" *Or, his owne things.*
z God wil prouide for euerie day ẏ that shalbe necessarie, thogh we do not increase the present griefe by the carefulnes how to liue in time to come.

CHAP. VII.

1 Christ forbiddeth rash iudgement. 6 Not to cast holie things to doggs. 7 To aske, seke, or knocke. 12 The scope of the Scripture. 13 The streict and wide gate. 15 Of false Prophetes. 16 The good tre and euil. 22 False miracles. 24 The house on the rocke or vpon the sand.

1 I a Vdge not, that ye be not iudged.
2 For with what * iudgement ye iudge, ye
shal be iudged, and with what * measure ye
mette, it shal be measured to you againe.
3 And why seest thou the mote, that is in
thy brothers eye, and perceiuest not the
beame that is in thine owne eye?
4 *Or how saist thou to thy brother, Suffer
me to cast out the mote out of thine
eye, and beholde a beame is in thine owne
eye?
5 Hypocrite, first cast out the beame out
of thine owne eye, and then shalt thou se
clearely to cast out the mote out of thy
brothers eye.
6 ¶ b Giue ye not that which is holie, to dogges,
nether cast ye your pearles before
swine, lest they treade them vnder their fete,
and turning againe, all to rent you.
7 ¶ * Aske, and it shalbe giuen you: seke, &
ye shal finde: knocke, & it shalbe opened
vnto you.
8 For whosoeuer asketh, receiueth: and he,
that seeketh, findeth: and to him that knocketh,
it shalbe opened.
9 For what man is there among you, which
if his

a He commandeth, not to be curious or malicious to trye out, and condemne our neighbours fautes: for hypocrites hide their owne fautes, and seke not to amēde them, but are curious to reproue other mens.
Luk.6,37.
rom.2,1.
1.cor.4,3.
Mar.4,24.
luk.6,38.
Luk.6,38.
and 43.
b Declare not the Gospel to the wicked cōtēners of God whome thou seest left to them selues & forsaken.
Chap.21,22.
mar.11,24.
luk.11,9.
ioh.14,13.
& 16,14.
iam.1,6.

if his sonne aske him bread, wolde giue
him a stone?
10 Or if he aske fish, wil he giue him a serpent?
11 If ye then, which are euil, can giue to
your childrẽ good gifts, how muche more shal your Father which is in heauen,
giue good things to them that aske him?
12 *Therefore whatsoeuer ye wolde that
men shulde do to you, euen so do ye to
them: for this is the c Law and the Prophetes.

Luk.6,31.
tob.4,16.
c The whole Law and the Scriptures set forthe vnto vs, & commende charitie.

13 ¶* d Enter in at the streicte gate: for it is
the wide gate, and broad e waye that leadeth to destruction: and manie there be
which go in thereat,
14 Because the gate is streicte, and the way
narowe that leadeth vnto life, and fewe
there be that finde it.

Luk.13,24.
d We must ouercome and mortifie our affections, if we wil be true disciples of Christ.
e For the most parte of men seke their owne libertie, and runne headlõg to euil.

15 ¶ Beware of false prophetes, which come to you in shepes clothing, but inwardely they are rauening wolues.
16 Ye shal knowe thẽ by their frutes. * Do
men gather grapes of thornes? or figges
of thystels?
17 So euerie good tre brĩgeth forthe good
frute, and a "corrupt tre bringeth forthe
euil frute.
18 A good tre can not bring forthe euil
frute: nether can a corrupt tre bring forthe good frute.
19 * Euerie tre ỹ bringeth not forthe good
frute, is hewen downe, and cast into the
fyre.
20 Therefore by their frutes ye shal knowe
them.

Luk.6,43.
"*Or, a rotten.*
Chap.3,10.

21 ¶ Not euerie one that saieth vnto me,
f Lord, Lord, shal enter into the kingdome of heauen, *but he that doeth my Fathers wil which is in heauen.
22 *Manie wil say to me in that day, Lord,
Lord, haue we not g by thy Name prophecied? and by thy Name cast out deuils?
and by thy Name done manie "great
workes?
23 And then wil I professe to them, h * I
neuer knewe you: * departe from me, ye
that worke iniquitie.
24 Whosoeuer then heareth of me these
wordes, * and doeth the same, I wil liken
him to a wise man, which hathe buylded
his house on a rocke:

f He meaneth hirelĩgs & hypocrites, who rather serue God ẇ their lippes then ẇ their heart.
Rom.2,13.
Iam.1,22
g By thy vertue, autoritie and power.
"*Or, miracles.*
h I neuer accepted you to be my true ministers and disciples.
Luk.13,76.
Psal.6,9.
Luk.6,47.

25 And the raine fell, and the floods came,
and the windes blewe, and beat vpon that
house, and it fell not: for it was grounded
on a rocke.
26 But whosoeuer heareth these my wordes, and doeth them not, shalbe lickened
vnto a foolish man, which hathe buylded
his house vpon the sand:
27 And the raine fell, and the floods came,
and the windes blewe, and beat vpon that
house, and it fell, and the fall thereof was
great.
28 ¶*And it came to passe, when Iesus had
ended these wordes, the people were astonied at his doctrine.
29 For he taught them as one hauing i autoritie, and not as the Scribes.

Mar.1,12.
luk.4,32.
i The mightie power of Gods Spirit appeared in him, whereby he declared him self to be God and caused others to beleue in him.

CHAP. VIII.

2 Christ healeth the leper. 5 The captaines faith. 11 The vocacion of the Gentiles. 14 Peters mother in law. 19 The Scribe that wolde followe Christ. 21 Christs pouertie. 24 He stilleth the sea and the winde. 28 And driueth the deuils out of the possessed into the swine.

1 NOw when he was come downe from
the mountaine, great multitudes
followed him.
2 *And lo, there came a leper and worshipped him, saying, Master, if thou wilt, thou
canst make me cleane.
3 And Iesus putting forthe his hand, touched him, saying, I wil, be thou cleane: and
immediatly his a leprosie was clensed.
4 Then Iesus said vnto him, Se thou tell
b no mã, but go, & shewe thy self vnto the
c Priest, and offer the gift that *Moyses cõmanded, for d a witnes to them.

Mar.1,40.
luk.5,12.
a It was not like that leprosie that is now, but was a kinde thereof, ẇ was incurable.
Leui.14,4.

5 ¶*Whẽ Iesus was entred into Capernaũ,
there came vnto him a "Centurion, beseching him,
6 And said, Master, my "seruant lieth sicke
at home of the palsie, and is grieuously
pained.
7 And Iesus said vnto him, I wil come and
heale him.
8 But the Centuriõ answered, saying, Master, I am not worthie that thou shuldest
come vnder my rofe: but speake the worde onely, and my seruant shalbe healed.
9 For I am a man also vnder the autoritie
of another, and haue souldiers vnder me: &
I say to one, Go: and he goeth, and to another, Come: and he cometh, & to my seruant, Do this: and he doeth it.

Luk.7,1.
b He wolde not yet be throughly knowen, but had his time & houre appointed.
c Our Sauiour wolde not cõtemne ỹ which was ordeined by the Law, seing as yet ỹ ceremonies thereof were not abolished.
d To condemne them of ingratitude, whẽ they shal se thee whole.
"*Or, a captaine ouer an hundreth.*
"*Or, sonne.*

10 When Iesus heard *that*, he marueiled, &
said to them that followed *him*, Verely, I
say vnto you, I haue not founde so great
faith, euen in Israel.
11 But I say vnto you, that e manie shal come from the East and West, and shal sit
downe with Abraham, and Isaac, and Iacob in the kingdome of heauen.
12 And the children of the kingdome shal
be cast out into f vtter * darkenes: there
shalbe weping and gnashing of teeth.
13 Then Iesus said vnto the Cẽturion, Go
thy way, and as thou hast beleued, so be it
vnto thee. And his seruant was healed the
same houre.

e Which are strange people & the Gẽtiles, to whome the couenant of God did not properly aperteine.
Chap.22,13.
f For there is nothing but mere darkenes out of ỹ kingdome of heauen.

14 ¶*And whẽ Iesus came to Peters house,
he sawe his wiues mother laied downe, &
sicke of a feuer.
15 And he touched her hand, and the feuer
left her: so she arose, and ministred vnto
them.

Mar.2,29.
luk.4,38.

16 *When the euen was come, they broght
vnto him manie that were possessed with
deuils : and he cast out the spirits with
his worde, and healed all that were sicke,
17 That it might be fulfilled, which was
spoken by *Esaias the Prophet, saying,
[g] He toke our infirmities, and bare *our* sic-
kenesses.
18 ¶ * And when Iesus sawe great multitudes of people about him, he commanded
them to go ouer *the water*.
19 Then came there a certeine Scribe, and
said vnto him, Master, [h] I wil followe thee
whethersoeuer thou goest.
20 But Iesus said vnto him, The foxes haue holes, and the birdes of the heauen haue nestes, but the Sonne of man hathe
not whereon to rest his head.
21 ¶ And [i] another of his disciples said vnto him, Master, suffer me first to go, and
[k] burye my father.
22 But Iesus said vnto him, Followe me, &
let the [l] dead burye their dead.
23 ¶ * And whē he was entred into the ship,
his disciples followed him.
24 And beholde, there arose a great tempest
in the sea, so ỷ the ship was couered with
waues: but he was a slepe.
25 Then his disciples came, & awoke him,
saying, Master, saue vs: we perish.
26 And he said vnto thē, Why are ye feareful, ô ye of litle faith? Then he arose, and
rebuked the windes and the sea: and *so* there was a great calme.
27 And the men marueiled, saying, What
man is this, that bothe the windes and the
sea obey him!
28. ¶ * And when he was come to the other
side, into the countrey of the Gergesenes,
there met him two possessed with deuils,
which came out of the graues verie fierce, so that no man might go by that
waye.
29 And beholde, they cryed out, saying, Iesus the Sonne of God, what haue we to do
with thee? Art thou come hether to torment vs [m] before the time?
30 Now there was afarre of from them, a
great herd of swine feeding.
31 And the deuils besoght him, saying, If
thou cast vs out, [n] suffer vs to go into the
herd of swine.
32 And he said vnto them, Go. So thei went
out, and departed into the herd of swine:
& beholde, the whole herd of swine was
caryed with violence from a stiepe downe place into the [o] sea, and dyed in the
water.
33 Then the herdmen fled: and when thei
were come into the citie, they tolde all
things, and what was become of them that
were possessed with the deuils.
34 And beholde all the citie came out, to

Mar.1,32. luk.4.40.

Isa.53.4. 1.pet.2,24. Luk.9,17.

g The Prophete speaketh chiefly of the feblenes & disease of our soules, ŵ Iesus Christ hathe borne: therefore he setteth his great mercie and power before our eyes by healing the bodie.

h He thoght by this meanes to courrie fauour with the worlde: but Iesus sheweth him that he is farre wide frō that he loketh for: for in stead of worldelie welth, there is but pouertie in Christ.

Mar.4,35. luk.8,22.

i Luke maketh mencion of thre, which were hindred by worldelie respects from comming to Christ.

k To succour & helpe him in his olde age til he dye, and then I wil followe thee wholy.

l No duetie or loue is to be preferred to Gods calling: therefore Iesus calleth them dead, ŵ are hindered by any worldlie thing to followe Christ.

Mar.5,8. luk.8,26.

m The wicked wolde euer differre their punishment, thinking all correction to come to sone.

n The deuil desireth euer to do harme, but he can do no more, then God doeth appoint.

o Meaning the lake of Genesareth.

mete Iesus: and when thei sawe him, [p] thei
besoght hī to departe out of their coasts.

CHAP. IX.

2 He healeth the palsie. 3 And forgiueth sinnes. 9 He calleth and visiteth Matthewe. 13 Mercie. 15 He answereth the Pharises and Iohns disciples. 16 Of the rawe cloth and new wine. 22 He healeth the woman of the bloodie yssue. 25 He raiseth Iairus daughter. 29 Giueth two blinde men their sight. 33 Maketh a domme man to speake. 35 Preacheth and healeth in diuerse places. 38 And exhorteth to prayers for the aduancement of the Gospel.

1 THen he entred into a ship, & passed
ouer, and came into his owne citie.
2 And * lo, they broght to him a man sicke
of ỷ palsie, lying on a bed. And Iesus seig
their [a] faith, said to the sicke of the palsie,
Sonne, be of good comfort: thy [b] sinnes a-
re forgiuen thee.
3 And beholde, certeine of the Scribes said
with them selues, This man blasphemeth.
4 But when Iesus sawe their thoghts, he
said, Wherefore thinke ye euil things [c] in
your hearts?
5 For whether is it [d] easier to say, Thy sinnes are forgiuen thee, or to say, Arise, and
walke?
6 And that ye may knowe that the Sonne
of man hathe autoritie in earth to forgiue sinnes, (then said he vnto the sicke of
the palsie,) Arise, take vp thy bed, and go
to thine house.
7 And he arose, and departed to his owne
house.
8 So when the multitude sawe it, they marueiled, and glorified God, which had giuē
suche autoritie to men.
9 ¶ * And as Iesus passed forthe from thence, he sawe a man sitting at the receite of
custome named Matthewe, & said to him,
Followe me. And he arose, and followed
him.
10 And it came to passe, as Iesus sate at meat in *his* house, beholde, manie Publicanes
and sinners, that came *thether*, sate downe
at the table with Iesus and his disciples.
11 And when the Pharises sawe that, they
said to his disciples, Why eateth your
master with Publicanes and sinners?
12 Now when Iesus heard it, he said vnto
them, The [e] whole nede not a physicion,
but thei that are sicke.
13 But go [f] ye and learne what this is, * I
[g] wil haue mercie, and not sacrifice : for I
am not come to call the righteous, but the
*sinners to repentance.
14 ¶ * Then came the disciples of Iohn to
him, saying, Why do we and the Pharises
fast oft, and thy disciples fast not?
15 And Iesus said vnto them, Cā the [h] children of the mariage chamber mourne as
lōg as the bridegrome is with them? But ỷ
daies wil come when ỷ bridegrome shalbe
taken

p These Gergesenes estemed more their hogges then Iesus Christ.

Mar.2,3. luk.5,24.

a And also his faith that had the palsie: for except we haue faith, our sinnes can not be forgiuen.

b Iesus toucheth the principal cause of all our miseries, ŵ is sinne.

c Because thei did maliciously refuse Christ, who offred him self vnto them.

d Christ speaketh accordig to their capacitie: for they more estemed outwarde miracles, thē the vertue & power of Iesus Christ, whereby their sinnes might be forgiuen.

Mar.2,14. luk.5,27.

e He reproueth the vaine persuasion of thē, which thoght thē selues whole, & contēned the poore sicke sinners, ŵ soght Iesus Christ to be their physiciō.

f Which are puffed vp with vaine confidence of your owne righteousnes.

Hose.6,7. chap.12,7.

g God requireth not ceremonies, but brotherlieloue of one towardes another.

1 Tim.1,5. Mar.2,18. luk.5,33.

h Christ wolde spare his disciples a while, not burdening them to muche, lest he shulde discourage them.

taken from them, and then shal they fast.
16 Moreouer no man pieceth an i olde garment with a piece of "newe cloth: for that
that shulde fil it vp, taketh away from the
garment, and the breache is worse.
17 Nether do they put newe wine into
k olde "vessels: for then the vessels wolde
breake, and the wine wolde be spilt, and
the vessels shulde perishe: but they put
newe wine into new vessels, and *so* are bothe preserued.
18 ¶ *While he thus spake vnto them, beholde there came a certeine ruler, & worshipped him, saying, My daughter is now
deceased, but come and lay thine hand on
her, and she shal liue.
19 And Iesus arose and followed him with
his disciples.
20 (And beholde a woman which was diseased with an yssue of blood twelue yeres,
came behinde him, and touched the hēme
of his garment.
21 For she said in her self, If I may touche but his garmēt onely, I shalbe whole.
22 Then Iesus turned him about, and seing
her, did say, Daughter, be of good comfort: thy faith hathe made thee whole.
And the woman was made whole at that
houre.)
23 Now when Iesus came into the rulers
house, and saw the l minstrels and the mul
titude making noise,
24 He said vnto them, Get you hense: for
the maide is not dead, but slepeth. And
they laughed him to skorne.
25 And whē the multitude were put forthe,
he went in and toke her by the hand, and
the maide arose.
26 And this bruite went through out all
that land.
27 And as Iesus departed thence, two
blinde men followed him, crying, and saying, O sonne of Dauid, haue mercie vpon vs.
28 And when he was come into the house,
the blinde came to him, and Iesus said vnto them, m Beleue ye that I am able to do
this? And they said vnto him, Yea, Lord.
29 Then touched he their eyes, saying, According to your faith be it vnto you.
30 And their eyes were opened, and Iesus
charged them, saying, Se that no man
knowe it.
31 But when they were departed, they
spred abroad his fame throughout all
that land.
32 ¶ *And as they went out, beholde, they
broght to him a domme man possessed wt
a deuil.
33 And when the deuil was cast out, the
domme spake: then the multitude marueiled, saying, The like was neuer sene in
Israel.

i Christ compareth his disciples for their infirmitie, to olde garmentes, and olde vessels, which are not able as yet to beare ye perfection of his doctrine, which he meaneth by new cloth, and new wine.
"Or, rawe and vndressed.
Mar. 5,22. luk. 8,41.
k The minde which is infected with the dregges of superstitious ceremonies, is not mete to receiue the pleasant wine of the Gospel.
"Bottels or bagges of ledder or skinne, wherein wine was caried on asses or camels.
l Players vpō flutes or pipes or other instruments, which in those dayes they vsed at buryales.
m He wolde proue whether they bare him that reuerence which was due to Messias.
Luk. 11,14.

34 But the Pharises said, *He n casteth out
deuils, through the prince of deuils.
35 ¶ And *Iesus wēt about all cities & townes, teaching in their Synagogues, & preaching the Gospel of the o kingdome, &
healing euerie sicknes and euerie disease
among the people.
36 But *when he sawe the multitude, he had
compassion vpon them, because they were dispersed, and scatered abroad, as shepe
hauing no shepherde.
37 Then said he to his disciples, *Surely ye
p haruest *is* great, but ye laborers *are* fewe.
38 Wherefore pray the Lord of the haruest
that he wolde "send forthe laborers into
his haruest.

Chap. 12,24. mar. 3,22. luk. 11,17.
n This blasphemie proceded of extreme impietie, seing all the people confessed the contrarie.
Mar. 6,6. luk. 13,22.
o Whereby God gathereth his people together, that he may reigne ouer them.
Mar. 6,34. Luk. 10,2. Iohn 4,36.
p He meaneth the people are ripe, and ready to receiue ye Gospel, comparing the nomber of the elect to a plentiful haruest.
"Or, thrust forthe.

CHAP. X.

1 Christ sendeth out his Apostles to preache in Iudea. 7 He giueth them charge, teacheth them, and comforteth them against persecution. 20 The holie Gost speaketh by his ministers. 26 Whome we oght to feare. 30 Our heeres are counted. 32 To confesse Christ. 37 Not to loue our parents more then Christ. 38 To take vp our crosse 39 To saue or lose the life. 40 To receiue the preachers.

1 AND *he called his twelue disciples
vnto him, and gaue them power a-
gainst vncleane spirits, to cast them out,
and to heale euerie sickenes, & euerie disease.
2 Now the names of the twelue Apostles
are these. The first *is* Simon, called Peter,
and Andrewe his brother: Iames *the sonne*
of Zebedeus, and Iohn his brother.
3 Philippe and Bartlemewe: Thomas, and
Matthewe the Publicane: Iames *the sonne*
of Alpheus, and Lebbeus whose surname
was Thaddeus:
4 Simon "the Cananite, and Iudas Iscariot,
who also betrayed him.
5 These twelue did Iesus send forthe, and
commanded them, saying, Go not into the
way of the Gentiles, and into the cities of
the Samaritans enter ye not:
6 But go rather *to the a lost shepe of the
house of Israel.
7 *And as ye go, preach, saying, The kingdome of heauen is at hand.
8 Heale the sicke: clense the lepers: raise vp
the dead: cast out the deuils. Frely ye haue receiued, b frely giue.
9 *"Possesse not c golde, nor siluer, nor mo
ney in your "girdels,
10 Nor a scrippe for the iorney, nether two
coates, nether shoes, nor a staffe: *for the
workeman is worthie of his meat.
11 And into *whatsoeuer citie or towne ye
shal come, enquire who is worthie in it, &
there abide til ye go thence.
12 And when ye come into an house, salute
the same.
13 And if the house be worthie, let your
peace come vpō it: but if it be not worthie,

Mar. 3,13. luk. 9,1.
"Or, the zealous
a For the kingdome of God must first be preached vnto them, because Christ was especially promised vnto them.
Act. 13,46. Luk. 10,59.
b He commandeth them to offer them selues frely to ye Lords worke, without respect of gaine or lucre.
Mar. 6,8. luk. 9,3. & 22,35.
"Or, prouide not for
c Because he sendeth them not for a long time, but onely for one iourney, he defendeth ye things that might let them: nether is this a perpetual commandement.
"Or, purses.
1. Tim. 5,18. luk. 10,7. Luk. 10,8.

let your peace returne to you.
14 *And whosoeuer shal not receiue you,
nor heare your wordes, when ye departe
out of that house,or that citie,* d shake of
the dust of your fete.
15 Truely I say vnto you, it shalbe easier
for them of the land of e Sodom and Gomorrha in the day of iudgement, then for
that citie.
16 ¶ * Beholde, I send you as shepe in the
middes of wolues: be ye therefore wise as
serpentes,and " f innocent as doues.
17 But beware of men, for they wil deliuer
you vp to the Councils, and wil scourge
you in their Synagogues.
18 And ye shal be broght to the gouernours
and Kings for my sake,in g witnes to thē,
and to the Gentiles.
19 *But when they deliuer you vp, take no
thoght how or what ye shal speake : for it
sha be giuen you in that houre, what ye
shal say.
20 For it is not ye that speake,but the spirit
of your Father which speaketh in you.
21 And the*brother shal betray the brother
to death, and the father the sonne,and the
children shal rise against *their* parents,and
shal cause them to dye.
22 And ye shalbe hated of all men for my
Name: *but he that endureth to the end,
he shalbe saued.
23 And when they persecute you in this citie,flee h into another:for verely I say vnto you,ye shal not finish *all* the cities of Israel,til the i Sonne of man be come.
24 *The disciple is not aboue his master,
nor the seruant aboue his lord.
25 It is ynough for the disciple to be as his
master *is*, and the seruant as his lord . *If
they haue called the master of the house
k Beelzebub, how muche more them of
his housholde?
26 Feare them not therefore : *for there
is nothing couered , that shal not be disclosed, nor hid, that shal not be knowen.
27 What I tel you in darkenes, that speake
ye in light : and what ye heare in the eare,
that preache ye on the l houses.
28 And feare ye not them which kil the bodie,but are not able to kil the soule:but rather feare him, which is able to destroye
bothe soule and bodie in hel.
29 Are not two sparrowes solde for a farthing,and one of them shal not fall on the
ground without your Father?
30 * Yea, and all the heeres of your heade
are nombred.
31 Feare ye not therefore,ye are of more value then manie sparrowes.
32 *Whosoeuer therefore shal m confesse me
before men,him wil I confesse also before
my Father,which is in heauen.
33 But whosoeuer shal denie me before mē,
him wil I also denie before my Father,
which is in heauen.
34 * Thinke not that I am come to send
n peace into the earth: I came not to send
peace,but the sworde.
35 For I am come to set a man at o variance against his father, and the daughter a-
gainst her mother, & the daughter in law
against her mother in law.
36 * And a mans enemies *shalbe* they of his
owne housholde.
37 *He that loueth father or mother more
then me,is not worthie of me. And he that
loueth sonne, or daughter more then me,
is not worthie of me.
38 *And he that taketh not his crosse,& p followeth after me,is not worthie of me.
39 *He that wil saue his q life, shal lose it,
and he that loseth his life for my sake,shal
saue it.
40 He that receiueth you, receiueth me:
and he that receiueth me, receiueth him
that hathe sent me.
41 * He that receiueth a r Prophet in the
name of a Prophet, shal receiue a Prophe
tes rewarde:and he that receiueth a righteous mā in the name of a righteous man,
shal receiue the rewarde of a righteous
man.
42 * And whosoeuer shal giue vnto one of
these litle ones to drinke a cup of colde
water onely , in the name of a Disciple,
verely I say vnto you, he shal not lose his
rewarde.

CHAP. XI.

1 Christ preacheth 2 Iohn Baptist sendeth his disciples vnto him. 7 Christs testimonie concerning Iohn. 18 The opiniō of the people cōcerning Christ and Iohn. 20 Christ vpbreadeth the vnthankful cities. 25 The Gospel is reueiled to the simple. 28 They that labour,and are laden . 29 Christs yoke.

1 AND it came to passe that when Iesus
had made an end of commāding his
twelue disciples , he departed thence to
teach and to preach in their cities.
2 ¶ *And whē Iohn heard in the prison the
workes of Christ,he a sent two of his disciples,and said vnto him,
3 Art thou he that shulde come,or shal we
loke for another?
4 And Iesus answering , said vnto them,
Go, and shewe Iohn,what things ye haue
heard and sene.
5 The blinde receiue sight,& the halt go:
the lepers are clensed,and the deaf heare:
the dead are raised vp,*and the " poore receiue the Gospel.
6 And blessed is he that shal not b be offended in me.
7 And as they departed, Iesus begā to speake vnto the multitude,of Iohn, What wēt
ye out into the wildernes to se? A c reed sha
ken with the winde?
8 But what went ye out to se? A mā clothed
in soft

Mar.6,11. luk.9,8. Act.13,51. and 18,6.
d To signifie that their lād is polluted, & that you consent not to their wickednes.
Luk.10,3.
e Who were not so liuely taught, and aduertised.
" *Or,simple.*
f Not reuenging wrong, muche lesse doing wrong.
g To take frō them all pretence of ignorance, and to make them inexcusable.
Mar.13,11. luk.12,11.
Luk.21,16.
Mar.13,13. luk.21,19.
h To profite & do good, & not to be idle.
i And wil cōfort you & giue manifest euidence of his presence: and he speaketh not of their first sending, but of ye whole time of their Apostleship.
Luk.6,40. iohn.13,16. and 15,20. Chap.12,24.
k It was the name of an idole which signified the god of flyes,& in dispite thereof was attributed to the deuil. read 2.Kig.1,2. and ye wicked called Christ by this name.
Mar.4,22. luk.8,17. and 12,2.
l Which in those coūtreis are so made yt men may walke vpō them.
2.Sam.14,11. act.27,34.
Mar.8,38. luk.9,26. and 12,8. 2.tim.2,12.
m And acknowledge me his onelie Sauiour

Luk.12,51.
n He giueth vs inwarde peace in our cōsciēces, but outwardly we must haue warre with wicked worldelings.
o Which thīg cometh not of the propertie of Christ, but procedeth of the malice of men, wc loue not the light, but darkenes, and are offended with the worde of saluation.
Micah.7,6.
Luk.14,26.
Chap.16,24. Mar.8,34. luk.9,23. and 14,27.
p Also they yt inuent anie other way to honour God, then that he hathe prescribed by his worde,follow not Christ,but go before him.
q He that dothe preferre his life before my glorie.
Luk.10,16. ioh.3,20.
r We must reuerēce Christ in his seruāts, & receiue thē, as sēt frō him, & honour thē for their office sake.
Mar.9,41.
Luk.7,18.
a Not because Iohn was ignorant of Christ : but yt he might teach his disciples yt his office was to lead them to Christ.
Isa.61,1. luk.4,18.
" *Or,the Gospel is preached to the poore.*
b That take no occasiō by Christ to be hindered from the Gospel
c A man inconstant?

in soft raiment? Beholde,they that weare
soft clothing,are in Kings houses.
9 But what went ye out to se? A Prophet?
Yea, I say vnto you, and [d] more then a
Prophet.
10 For this is he of whome it is written,
* Beholde,I send my messenger before thy
face, which shal prepare thy way before
thee.
11 Verely I say vnto you,among thẽ which
are [e] begotten of women, arose there not
a greater then Iohn Baptist: notwithstanding,he that is the [f] least in the kingdome of heauen,is greater then he.
12 And from * the time of Iohn Baptist hitherto, the kingdome of heauen [g] suffreth violence, and the violent take it by
force.
13 For all the Prophetes & the Law [h] prophecied vnto Iohn.
14 And if ye wil receiue [i] it, this is * Elias,
which was to come.
15 ¶He that hathe eares to heare, let him
heare.
16 * But whereunto shal I liken this generation?It is like vnto litle children which
sit in the markets, and call vnto their felowes,
17 And say,We haue piped vnto you,& ye
haue not danced, we haue " mourned vnto
you,and ye haue not lamented.
18 For Iohn came nether eating nor drinking,and they say,He hathe a deuil.
19 The Sonne of man came eating & drinking,and they say, Beholde a glotton & a
drinker of wine,a friend vnto Publicanes
& sinners:but [k] wisdome is iustified of her
children.
20 ¶*Then begã he to vpbraide the cities,
wherein moste of his great workes were
done,because they repented not.
21 Wo *be* to thee,Chorazin: Wo *be* to thee,
Bethsaida: for if the great workes, which
were done in you,had bene done in [l] Tyrus
& Sidon, they had repẽted long agone in
sackecloth and ashes.
22 " But I say to you, It shalbe easier for
Tyrus and Sidon at the day of iudgemẽt,
then for you.
23 And thou,Capernaum, which art lifted vp vnto heauen, shalt be broght downe to hel:for if ỹ great workes, which haue bene done in thee, had bene done a-
mong them of Sodom, they had remained to this day.
24 But I say vnto you,that it shalbe easier
for them of the land of Sodom in the day
of iudgement,then for thee.
25 *At that time Iesus answered,and said, I
giue thee thãkes, ô Father, Lord of heauẽ
& earth,because thou hast hid these things
from the wise and men of vnderstanding,
and hast opened them vnto babes.
26 It is so,ô Father,because thy good [m] plea
sure was suche.
27 *All things are giuen vnto me of my Father: and *no man knoweth the Sonne,but
the Father: nether knoweth any man the
Father,but the Sonne, & he to whome the
Sonne wil reueile *him*.
28 Come vnto me,all ye that [n] are wearie &
laden,and I wil ease you.
29 Take my [o] yoke on you, and learne of
me,that I am meke and lowlie in heart: &
ye shal finde * rest vnto your soules.
30 *For my yoke is easie, and my burden
light.

CHAP. XII.

3 Christ excuseth his disciples which plucke the eares of corne. 10 He healeth the dryed hand, 22 Helpeth the possessed that was blinde and domme. 31 Blasphemie. 34 The generacion of vipers. 35 Of good wordes. 36 Of idle wordes. 38 He rebuketh the vnfaithful that wolde nedes haue tokens. 49 And sheweth who is his brother, sister and mother.

1 AT *that time Iesus wẽt on a Sabbath
day through the corne,and his disciples were an hungred, & began to plucke
the eares of corne and to eat.
2 And when the Pharises sawe it, they said
vnto him, Beholde, thy disciples do that
which is not lawful to do vpõ the Sabbath.
3 But he said vnto them, * [a] Haue ye not
red what Dauid did when he was an hungred,and they that were with him?
4 How he entred into the House of God,
& ate the shewe bread, which was not law
ful for him to eat, nether for them which
were with him,but onely for the*Priests?
5 Or haue ye not red in the Law how that
on the Sabbath dayes the Priests in the
Temple * [b] breake the Sabbath, and are
blameles?
6 But I say vnto you,that here is one greater then the Temple.
7 Wherefore if ye knewe what this is, * I
wil haue mercie and not sacrifice,ye wolde
not haue condemned the innocents.
8 For the sonne of man is [c] Lord,*euen* of the
Sabbath.
9 *And he departed thence, and went into
their Synagogue:
10 And beholde,there was a mã which had
his hand dryed vp. And they asked him,
saying, Is it lawful to heale vpõ a Sabbath
day?that they might accuse him.
11 And he said vnto them, What man shal
there be amõg you, that shal haue a shepe,
and if it fall on a Sabbath day into a pit,
wil not he take it and lift it out?
12 How muche more then is a man better
thẽ a shepe?therefore,it is lawful to do wel
on a Sabbath day.
13 Then said he to the man, Stretch forthe
thine hãd. And he stretched it forthe, and
it was made whole as the other.

d For ỹ Prophetes declared Christ lõg before he came, but Iohn as it were poisted him with his finger.

Malach.3,1.

e Which were begotten and borne by the meanes of mã, and after the cõmune course of nature: for Christ was conceiued by the holie Gost.

f The least of them that shal preache ỹ Gospel in the new estat of Christs Church, shal haue more cleare knoledge then Iohn, and their message shal be more excellẽt.

Luk.16,16.

g Mens zeales are inflamed with desire to receiue Gods mercies offered, and are moste greadie to heare the worde.

h They prophecied things to come, ỹ now we se present and more cleare.

i Meaning his testimonie cõcerning Iohn.

Malach.4,5.

Luk.7,32.

" *Or, sung mornningly.*

k They that are wise in dede, acknowledge the wisdome of God in him, whome ỹ Pharises contemne, read Luk 7.29.

Luk.10,13.

l Cities of great marchãdise ful of dissolution and wantonnes.

" *Or, therfore.*

Luk.10,21.

m Faith cometh not of mans wil or power, but by the secret illumination of God, which is the declaration of his eternal counsel

Iohn 3,36.

Ioh.6,46.

n Which fele the waight,& grief of your sinnes and miseries.

o To be gouerned by my Spirit, and to mortifie your affections.

Ier.6,16.

1.Iohn.5,3.

Mar.2,23.

luk.6,1.

deu.23,25.

1.Sam.21,6.

a Necessitie maketh that lawful, which is prohibited for a certeine respect, in things perteining to ceremonies.

Exod.29,33.

leu.8,31.

& 24,9.

Nomb.28,9.

b Not that the Priests brake the Sabbath in doing that, which was cõmanded by the Law, but he speaketh thus to cõfute ỹ error of the people, who thoght the Sabbath broken, if any necessarie worke was done that day.

Hose 6,7.

chap.9,13.

c Christ hathe power to exempt his frõ keping of the Sabbath, seing the seruice required in the Temple, was able to excuse thẽ that labored in the same.

Mar.3,1.

luk.6,6.

14 Then the Phariſes went out, and conſulted againſt him, how they might deſtroye
him.
15 But whē Ieſus knewe it, he departed thēce, and great multitudes followed him, &
he healed them all,
16 And charged them that they ſhulde not
make him knowen,
17 That it might be fulfilled, which was ſpo
ken by Eſaias the Prophet, ſaying,
18 *Beholde my ſeruant whome I haue cho
ſen, my beloued in whome my ſoule deliteth: I wil put my Spirit on him, & he ſhal
ſhewe [d] iudgement to the Gentiles.
19 He ſhal not [e] ſtriue, nor crye, nether ſhal
anie man heare his voyce in the ſtretes.
20 A [f] bruiſed rede ſhal he not breake, and
ſmoking flaxe ſhal he not quenſhe, til he
bring forthe iudgements vnto victorie.
21 And in his Name ſhal the Gētiles truſt.
22 ¶ *Then was broght to him one, poſſeſſed with a deuil, *bothe* blinde, and domme,
and he healed him, ſo that he *which was*
blinde and domme, bothe ſpake and ſawe.
23 And all the people were amaſed, & ſaid,
Is not this the ſonne of Dauid?
24 But whē the Phariſes heard it, they ſaid,
*This mā caſteth the deuils no otherwi-
ſe out, but through Beelzebub the prince
of deuils.
25 But Ieſus knewe their thoghtes, and
ſaid to them, Euerie kingdome deuided
againſt it ſelf, ſhalbe "broght to naught: &
euerie citie or houſe, deuided againſt it
ſelf, ſhal not ſtand.
26 So if Satan caſt out Satan, he is deuided
againſt him ſelf: how ſhal then his kingdome endure?
27 Alſo if I through Beelzebub caſt out
deuils, by whome do your [h] children caſt
them out? Therefore they ſhalbe your
iudges.
28 But if I caſt out deuils by the Spirit of
God, then is the kingdome of God come
vnto you.
29 Els how can a man enter into a ſtrong
mans houſe and ſpoile his goods, except
he firſt binde the ſtrong man, and then
ſpoile his houſe.
30 He [i] that is not with me, is againſt me:
& he ẏ gathereth not with me, ſcattereth.
31 *Wherefore I ſay vnto you, euerie ſinne
and blaſphemie ſhalbe forgiuen vnto men:
but the blaſphemie *againſt* the holie Goſt
ſhal not be forgiuen vnto men.
32 And whoſoeuer ſhal ſpeake a worde a-
gainſt the Sōne of man, it ſhalbe forgiuen
him: but whoſoeuer ſhal ſpeake againſt ẏ
[k] holie Goſt, it ſhal not be forgiuē him, nether in this world nor in ẏ worlde to come.
33 Ether make the tre good, and his frute
good: or els make the tre "euil, & his frute
euil: for the tre is knowen by the frute.

Iſa.42,1.
d The right trade of gouernemēt, not onely to the Iewes, but alſo to ſtrange nacions.
e He ſhal not make great noiſe, nor ſeke outwarde pōpe and glorie.
f He wil beare with them that be infirme & weake.
Luk.11,14.
g Chriſt ſhal ouercome all lettes, ẇ hinder the courſe of the Goſpel, and then ſhal giue ſentence as a conquerer againſt all his enemies.
Chap.9,34. mar.3,22. luk.11,17.
"Or, deſolate.
h Which coniured deuils by the vertue of Gods name, al beit it was expreſly againſt the Law of God.
i He declareth to the Phariſes, that they were in two ſortes his enemies, not onely becauſe thei did forſake him, but alſo make opē warre againſt him.
Mar.3,28. luk.12,10. 1.ioh.5,13.
k That is, he that ſtriueth againſt the trueth which he knoweth, and againſt his owne conſciēce, can not returne to repētance: for he ſinneth againſt the holie Goſt.
"Or, corrupt.

34 O "generacions of vipers, how can you
ſpeake good things, when ye are euil? For
of the * abundance of the heart the mouth
ſpeaketh.
35 A good man out of the good treaſure of
his heart bringeth forthe good things: &
an euil man out of an euil treaſure, bringeth forthe euil things.
36 But I ſay vnto you, that of euerie [l] idle
worde that men ſhal ſpeake, they ſhal giue
acounte thereof at the day of iudgement.
37 For by thy wordes thou ſhalt be [m] iuſtified, and by thy wordes thou ſhalt be condemned.
38 ¶ *Then anſwered certeine of the Scribes & of the Phariſes, ſaying, Maſter, [n] we
wolde ſe a ſigne of thee.
39 But he anſwered, and ſaid to them, An e-
uil and [o] adulterous generacion ſeketh a
ſigne, but no ſigne ſhalbe giuen vnto it,
ſaue the ſigne of the Prophet Ionas.
40 * For as Ionas was thre dayes, and thre
nights in the whales bellie: ſo ſhal the Son
ne of man be thre [p] dayes and thre nights
in the heart of the earth.
41 The men of Nineue ſhal riſe in iudgement with this generacion, and condemne it: for they * repented at the preaching
of [q] Ionas: and beholde, a greater then Ionas is here.
42 * The Quene of the South ſhal riſe in
iudgement with this generacion, and ſhal
[r] condemne it: for ſhe came from the vtmoſt parties of the earth to heare the wiſdome of Solomon: and beholde a greater
then Solomon *is* here.
43 ¶ *Now whē the vncleane ſpirit is gone
out of a man, he walketh throughout "drye
places, ſeking reſt, and findeth none.
44 Then he ſaith, I wil returne into mine
houſe, frō whence I came: & when he is come, he findeth it emptie, ſwept & garniſhed.
45 ¶ Then he goeth, & taketh vnto him [ſ] ſeuen other [t] ſpirits worſe then him ſelf, and
they entre in, and dwell there: * and the
end of that man is worſe then the beginning. Euen ſo ſhal it be with this wicked
generacion.
46 ¶ *While he yet ſpake to the multitude,
beholde, his mother, & his [u] brethren ſtode
without, deſiring to ſpeake with him.
47 Thē one ſaid vnto him, Beholde, thy mo
ther and thy brethren ſtand without, deſiring to ſpeake with thee.
48 But he anſwered, and ſaid to him that
tolde him, Who is my mother? and who a-
re my brethren?
49 And he ſtretched forthe his hand towarde his diſciples, & ſaid, Beholde my [x] mother and my brethren.
50 For whoſoeuer ſhal do my Fathers wil
which is in heauen, the ſame is my brother
and ſiſter and mother.

"Or, broodes.
Luk.6,45.
l Muche more they ſhal giue a counte of their blaſphemies.
m Their wicked wordes ſhal be a ſuffiſcient proffe to condemne the vngodlie, if there were no other thing.
Chap.16,2. luk.11,29. 1.cor.1,22.
n This was to finde ſome newe ſhift or pretext to reſiſt his doctrine.
Iona.2,8.
o They were become baſtardes and degenerate from their holie anceſters.
Iona.3,1.
p He taketh parte of the day for the whole day.
1.King.10,2. 2.chro.9,1.
q Who was a poore ſtrāger, and yet theſe knowe not the Meſsias which was promiſed to be their King.
Luk.11,24.
r It is ment as touching her fact in cōming to ẏe Solomon, and not her perſone: for ſhe was not inſtructed in the Lawe of God.
"Or, wildernes.
2.Pet.2,20. ebr.6,4. & 10,26.
Mar.3,31. luk.8,20.
ſ Meaning an infinite nomber.
t If Satan be caſt out, we muſt watche ſtil, ẏ he enter not againe: for ſince he was once mās olde geſt, he knoweth euerie hole and corner of our houſe.
u This worde in the Scriptures ſignifieth oft times euerie kinſman.
x Chriſt preferreth the ſpiritual kinred to the carnal.

CHAP.

CHAP. XIII.

3 The state of the kingdome of God set forthe by the parable of the sede. 24 Of the tares. 31 Of the mustarde sede. 33 Of the leauē. 44 Of the treasure hid in the field. 45 Of the perles. 47 And of the nette. 57 The Prophet is contemned in his owne countrey.

Mar.4,1. luk.8,5.

1 THe * same day went Iesus out of the
house, and sate by the sea side.

a All desired to heare his doctrine, but there was not like affection in all.

2 And [a] great multitudes resorted vnto hī,
so that he went into a ship, and sate downe: and the whole multitude stode on the
shore.
3 Then he spake many things to them in
parables, saying, Beholde, a sower went
forthe to sowe.
4 And as he sowed, some fel by the wayes
side, and the foules came and deuoured
them vp.
5 And some fel vpon stonie grounde, where
they had not muche earth, and anone they
sprong vp, because they had no depth of
earth.
6 And when the sunne rose vp, they were
parched, and for lacke of rooting, withred
away.
7 And some fel among thornes, & the thornes sprong vp, and choked them.
8 Some againe fel in good grounde, and
broght forthe frute, one *corne* an hundreth folde, some sixtie folde, and another
thirtie folde.

b He sheweth that all men can not vnderstād these mysteries, and also maketh his disciples more atentiue.

9 He that [b] hathe eares to heare, let him
heare.
10 ¶ Then the disciples came, and said
to him, Why speakest thou to them in parables?
11 And he answered and said vnto them, Because it is giuen vnto you, to knowe the
secrets of the kingdome of heauen, but to
them it is not [c] giuen.

c The Gospel is hid to them that perish.

Chap.25,29.

d Christ increaseth in his children his graces.

e Euen that which he semeth to haue.

12 * [d] For whosoeuer hathe, to him shalbe giuen, and he shal haue abundance: but whosoeuer hathe not, from him shalbe taken
away, euen [e] that he hathe.
13 Therefore speake I to them in parables,
because they seing, do not se: and hearing,
they heare not, nether vnderstand.

Isa.6,9. mar.4,12. luk.8,10. iohn.12,40. act.18,26. rom.11,8.

14 So in them is fulfilled the prophecie of
Esaias, which *prophecie* saith, * By hearing,
ye shal heare, and shal not vnderstand, and
seing ye shal se, and shal not perceiue.

f That which the Prophet referreth to the secret counsel of God, is here attributed to the hard stubbernes of the people: for the one can not be separated frō the other.

15 [f] For this peoples heart is waxed fatte,
and their eares are dul of hearing, and
with their eyes they haue winked, lest
they shulde se with their eyes, and heare
with their eares, and shulde vnderstand
with their hearts, and shulde returne, that
I might heale them.

g To wit, the glorie of the Sonne of God, to acknowledge him their Sauiour.

16 But blessed *are* your eyes, for they [g] se: &
your eares, for they heare.

Luk.10,24.

17 *For verely I say vnto you, that many
Prophetes, & righteous men haue desired
to se those things which ye se, & haue not
sene *them*, and to heare those things which
ye heare, & haue not heard *them*.
18 ¶ * Heare ye therefore the parable of the *Mar.4,15. luk.8,11.*
sower.
19 Whensoeuer a man heareth the worde
of the kingdome, and vnderstandeth it
not, the euil one cometh, and catcheth away that which was sowen in his heart: &
this is he which [*] hathe receiued the sede *Or, was sowen.*
by the way side.
20 And he that receiued sede in the stonie
grounde, is he which heareth the worde, &
incontinently with ioye receiueth it.
21 Yet hathe he no roote in him self, & dureth but a season: for assone as tribulation
or persecution cometh because of the worde, by and by he is offended.
22 And he that receiueth the sede among
thornes, is he that heareth the worde: but
the care of this worlde, and the deceitfulnes of riches choke the worde, and he is
made vnfruteful.
23 But he that receiueth the sede in the good
grounde, is he that heareth the worde, and
vnderstādeth it, which also beareth frute,
& bringeth forthe, some an hūdreth folde,
some sixtie folde, & some thirtie folde.
24 ¶ Another parable put he forthe vnto
them, saying, The kingdome of heauen
is like vnto a man which sowed good seed
in his field.
25 [h] But while men slept, there came his enemie, and sowed tares among the wheat, &
went his way.

h He teacheth that the good and the bad shal be mixte together in the Church to the end that the faithful may arme thē selues with patience and cōstancie.

26 And when the blade was sprong vp, and
broght forthe frute, then appeared the tares also.
27 Then came the seruants of the householder, and said vnto him, Master, sowedst
not thou good sede in thy field? frō whence then hathe it tares?
28 And he said to them, The enuious man
hathe done this. Then the seruāts said vnto him, Wilt thou then that we go and gather them vp?
29 But he said, Nay, lest while ye go about
to gather the tares, ye plucke vp also with
them the wheat.
30 [i] Let bothe growe together vntil the haruest, and in time of haruest I wil say to the
reapers, Gather ye first the tares, and binde
them in sheaues to burne them: but gather
the wheat into my barne.

i Christ meaneth onely ỳ the Church shal neuer be without some wicked men: although they be neuer so sharpely punished by suche meanes as he hathe left to purge his Church.

Mar.4,30. luk.13,18.

31 ¶ * Another parable he put forthe vnto
them, saying, The kingdome of heauen is
like vnto a graine of mustard sede, which
a man taketh and soweth in his field:
32 Which in dede is the [k] least of all sedes:
but when it is growen, it is the greatest among herbes, and it is a tre, so that the
birdes of heauen come and buylde in the
branches thereof.

k This teacheth vs not to be astonished at the smale beginnings of the Gospel.

Luk.13,21.

33 ¶ * Another parable spake he to thē, The

kingdome of heauen is like vnto leauen,
which a woman taketh and hideth in thre
peckes of meale, [l] til all be leauened.

l By this he admonissheth them to waite til the frute of the Gospel appeare.

34 ¶*All these things spake Iesus vnto the
multitude in parables, and without parables spake he not to them,

Mar.4,33.

35 That it might be fulfilled, which was spo
ken by the Prophet, saying, *I wil open my
mouth in [m] parables, & wil vtter the things
which haue bene kept secret from the fundacion of the worlde.

Psal.78,2.
m This worde signifieth graue and sentencious prouerbes, to the end that the doctrine might haue the more maiestie, and the wicked might thereby be cōfounded.

36 Then sent Iesus the multitude away, and
went into the house. And his disciples came vnto him, saying, Declare vnto vs the
parable of the tares of the field.
37 Then answered he, and said to them, He
that soweth the good sede, is the Sonne of
man,
38 And the field is the worlde, & the good
sede, they are the children of the kingdome, and the tares are the children of the
wicked,
39 And the enemie that soweth them, is the
deuil, * and the haruest is the end of the
worlde, and the reapers be the Angels.

Ioel.3,13.
reuel.14,15.

40 As then the tares are gathered and burned in the fyre, so shal it be in the end of
this worlde.
41 The Sonne of man shal send forthe his
Angels, and they shal gather out of his
kingdome all things that [n] offend, & them
which do iniquitie,

n The wicked which hurt others by their euil example.

42 And shal cast thē into a furnais of fyre.
There shalbe wailing and gnasshing of
teeth.
43 *Then shal the iust men shine as the sunne in the kingdome of their Father. He
that hathe eares to heare, let him heare.

Dan.12,3.
wis.3,7.

44 ¶Againe the kingdome of heauē is like
vnto a treasure hid in ẏ field, which whē a
man hathe founde, he hideth it, & for ioye
thereof departeth and selleth all that he
hathe, and byeth that field.
45 ¶Againe the kingdome of heauē is like
to a marchāt man, that seketh good perles,
46 Who hauing founde a perle of great
price, went and solde all that he had, and
boght it.
47 ¶Againe the kingdome of heauen is like [o] vnto a drawe net cast into the sea, that
gathereth of all kindes *of things*.
48 Which, whē it is ful, men drawe to land,
and sit and gather the good into vessels,
and cast the [p] bad away.

o It is a kinde of nette that gathereth in all things that come in the waye.
p The Greke worde signifieth rotten things.

49 So shal it be at the end of the worlde.
The Angels shal go forthe, and seuer the
bad from among the iust,
50 And shal cast them into a furnais of fyre: there shal be wailing, and gnasshing of
teeth.
51 ¶Iesus said vnto them, Vnderstand ye
all these things? They said vnto him, Yea,
Lord.
52 Then said he vnto thē, Therefore euerie
[q] Scribe which is taught vnto the kingdome of heauen, is like vnto an housshol-
der, which bringeth forthe out of his [r] trea
sure things bothe new and olde.

q Because the Scribes office was to expound ẏ Scriptures, he meaneth him that doeth interpret them aright, and according to the Spirit.
r The preachers of Gods worde must haue store of sondrie and ample instructions.

53 ¶And it came to passe, that when Iesus
had ended these parables, he departed
thence,
54 *And came into his owne countrey, and
taught them in their Synagogue, so that
they were astonied, and said, Whence cometh this wisdome and great workes vnto this man?

Mar.6,1.
luk.4,16.

55 Is not this the carpenters sonne? Is not
his mother called Marie, *& his " brethren
Iames and Ioses, and Simon and Iudas?

Iohn.6,42.
" or Cousins.

56 And are not his sisters all with vs? Whēce
then hathe he all these things?
57 And they were offended with him. Then
Iesus said to thē, *A Prophet is not without honour, [s] saue in his owne countrey, &
in his owne house.
58 And he did not many great workes there, for their vnbeliefes sake.

Mar.6,4.
luk.4,24.
iohn 4,44.
s Mē comunely neglect thē, whome they haue knowen of children: also thei do enuie them of the same countrei: and suche is their ingratitude that they take light occasion to contemne the graces of God in others.

CHAP. XIIII.

2 Herodes opinion concerning Christ. 10 Iohn is beheaded. 19 Christ fedeth fiue thousand men with fiue loaues and two fishes. 23 He prayeth in the mountaine. 25 He appeareth by night vnto his disciples vpon the sea, 31 And saueth Peter. 33 They confesse him to be the sonne of God. 36 He healeth all that touched the hemme of his garment.

1 AT *that time Herode the Tetrarche
heard of the fame of Iesus,

Chap.XIIII.
Mar.6,14.
luk.9,7.

2 And said vnto his seruants, This is Iohn
Baptist. [a] He is risen againe from the dead,
and therefore great [b] workes are wroght
by him.

a He spake after the commune errour: for they thoght that the soules of them that were departed, entred into another bodie.

3 *For Herode had takē Iohn, and bounde
him, and put him in prison for Herodias
sake, his brother Philips wife.
4 For Iohn said vnto him, It is not * [c] lawful
for thee to haue her.

Mar.6,17.
luk.3,14.

5 And whē he wolde haue put him to death,
he feared the multitude, because thei coun
ted him as a * Prophet.

Leui.18,16.& 20,21.
b To approue his resurrection, and to get him greater autoritie.

6 But when Herodes birthday was kept, the
daughter of Herodias danced before thē,
and pleased Herode.

c Aswel because nature abhorreth suche horrible incest, as also that he had taken her by force from his brother.

7 Wherefore he [d] promised with an othe,
that he wolde giue her whatsoeuer she wol
de aske.
8 And she being before instructed of her
mother, said, Giue me here Iohn Baptist
head in a platter.

Chap.21,26.
d The promes was wicked: but yet it was more vile to be obstinate in the same, that he might seme constant.

9 And the King was sorie: neuertheles because of the othe, and them that sate with
him at the table, he commanded it to be giuen *her*,
10 And sent, and beheaded Iohn in the
prison.
11 And his head was broght in a platter, and
giuen to the maide, and she broght it vnto
her mother.

12 And

12 And his disciples came, and toke vp his
"bodie, and buryed it, and went, and tolde
Iesus.

*Or, karkeis.

13 *And when Iesus heard it, he departed
thence by ship into a [e] desert place aparte. And when the multitude had heard it,
thei followed him a fote out of the cities.

Mar.6,38. luk.9,10.

e To the intent that his disciples now after their ambassage might some what rest thé, orels that he might instruct them to greater entreprises

14 And Iesus went forthe and sawe a great
multitude, and was moued with compassion towarde them, and he healed their
sicke.

15 ¶ And when euen was come, *his disciples came to him, saying, This is a desert
place, and the houre is alreadie paste: let
the multitude departe, that they may go
into the townes, and bye them vitailes.

Mar.6,35. luk.9,12. iohn 6,5.

16 But Iesus said to them, They haue no
[f] nede to go away: giue ye them to eat.

f Christ leaueth them not destitute of bodelie nourishment, which seke the fode of the soule.

17 Then said they vnto him, We haue
here but fiue loaues, and two fishes.
18 And he said, Bring them hether to me.
19 And he commanded the multitude to
sit downe on the grasse, and toke the fiue
loaues and the two fishes, and loked vp to
heauen and "blessed, and brake, and gaue
the loaues to his disciples, & the disciples
to the multitude.

*Or, praied and gaue thankes to God.

20 And they did all eat, and were sufficed,
and they toke vp of the fragments that
remained, twelue baskets ful.
21 And thei that had eaten, were about fiue
thousand men, beside women & litle children.
22 ¶ And straight waye Iesus [g] cõpelled his
disciples to enter into a ship, and to go o-
uer before him, while he sent the multitude away.

g The disciples were lothe to departe from Christ: but yet they shewed their obedience.

23 And assone as he had sent the multitude away, he went vp into a mountaine a-
lone to pray: *and when the euening was
come, he was there alone.

Mar.6,46. iohn 6,16.

24 And the ship was now in the middes of
the sea, and was tossed with waues: for it
was a contrarie winde.
25 And in the [h] fourth watche of the night,
Iesus went vnto them, walking on the sea.
26 And when his disciples sawe him walkĩg
on the sea, they were troubled, saying, It
is a spirit, and cryed out for feare.

h The night was deuided into foure watches, whereof euerie one cõteined thre houres.

27 But straight way Iesus spake vnto them,
saying, [i] Be of good comfort. It is I: be
not afraied.

i The presence of Christ maketh his bolde.

28 Then Peter answered him, & said, Master, if it be thou, [k] byd me come vnto thee
on the water.

k His zeale was great, but he had not sufficiently considered ẙ measure of his faith.

29 And he said, Come. And when Peter was
come downe out of the ship, he walked on
the water, to go to Iesus.
30 But when he sawe a mightie winde, he
was afraied: and as he [l] beganne to sinke,
he cryed, saying, Master, saue me.

l His enterprise was to great, & therefore he must nedes fall in danger, when his faith failed.

31 So immediatly Iesus stretched forthe his
hand, and caught him, and said to him,
[m] O thou of litle faith, wherefore didest
thou dout?

m Christ correcteth his faute, and also giueth remedie bothe at once.

32 And assone as they were come into the
ship, the winde ceased.
33 Then they that were in the ship, came
and worshipped him, saying, Of a trueth
thou art the sonne of God.
34 ¶ *And when they were come ouer, thei
came into the land of Gennesaret.

Mar.6,54.

35 And when the men of that place knewe
him, they sent out into all that countrey
rounde about, and broght vnto him all
that were sicke,
36 And besoght him, that they might touche the hemme of his [n] garment onely: &
as manie as touched it, were made whole.

n It semeth they were led with a certeine superstitiõ, notwithstanding our Sauiour wolde not quenche the smoking flaxe, and therefore did beare with these smale beginnings.

CHAP. XV.

3 Christ excuseth his disciples, and rebuketh the Scribes, & Pharises, for transgreßing Gods commandement by their owne tradicions. 13 The plant that shalbe rooted out. 18 What things defile a mã. 22 He deliuereth the woman of Cananees daughter. 26 The bread of the children. 30 He healeth the sicke, 36 And fedeth foure thousand men, beside women and children.

1 THen came to Iesus the Scribes and
Pharises, which were of Ierusalem,
saying,
2 *Why do thy disciples transgresse the
tradicion of the Elders? for they [a] wash
not their hands when they eat "bread.

Mar.7,1.

a Mẽ are more rigorous to obserue their owne traditions then Gods cõmandement.

*Or, meat.

3 But he answered & said vnto them, Why
do ye also transgresse the commandemẽt
of God by your tradicion?
4 *For God hathe commanded, saying,
Honour thy father and mother: *and he
that curseth father or mother, let him dye
the death.

Exod.20,12. deut.5,16. ephes.6,2. exod.21,17. leuit.20,9. prou.20.20.

5 But ye say, Whosoeuer shal say to father
or mother, [b] By the gift that is *offred* by
me, thou maiest haue profite,
6 Thogh he honour not his father, or his
mother, *shalbe fre*: thus haue ye made the
commandement of God of no autoritie
by your tradicion.

b The Scribes dispensed with them that did not their dueties to their owne parents, so ẙ thei wold recompense ẙ same to their profite by their offrings.

7 O hypocrites, Esaias prophecied wel of
you, saying,
8 *This people draweth nere vnto me
with their mouth, and honoureth me with
the lippes, but their heart is farre of from
me.

Isai.29,13.

9 But [c] in vaine they worship me, teachĩg
for doctrines, mens precepts.

c God wil not be honoured according to mans fantasie, but detesteth all good intentions, which are not grounded on his worde.

10 *Then he called the multitude vnto
him, and said to them, Heare and vnderstand.

Mar.7,17.

11 That which goeth into the mouth, defileth not the man, but that which cometh
out of the mouth, that defileth the man.
12 ¶ Then came his disciples, and said vnto him, Perceiuest thou not, that the Pharises are offended in hearing *this* saying?
13 But he answered & said, *[d] Euerie plant
which mine heauenlie Father hathe not
planted, shalbe rooted vp.

Iohn 15,2.

d All thei ẙ are not grafted in Iesus Christ by free adoption, and euerie doctrine, that is not established by Gods worde.

e They are not worthie to be cared for.
Luk.6,39.

14 e Let them alone: they be the *blinde
leaders of the blinde: & if the blinde leade
the blinde, bothe shal fall into the ditche.

Mar.7,17.

15 ¶ *Then answered Peter, and said to
him, Declare vnto vs this parable.
16 Then said Iesus, Are ye yet without vnderstanding!
17 Perceiue ye not yet, that whatsoeuer entreth into ẏ mouth, goeth into the bellie,
and is cast out into the draught?
18 But those things which procede out of
the mouth, come from the heart, and they
defile the man.

Gen.6,5.& 8,21.
f All vices procede of the corrupt affection of the heart.

19 For out of ẏ heart *come euil f thoghts,
murders, adulteries, fornicacions, thefts,
false testimonies, sclanders.
20 These are the things, which defile the
man: but to eat with vnwashen hands, defileth not the man.

Mar.7,24.

21 *And Iesus went thence, and departed
into the coasts of Tyrus and Sidon.
22 And beholde, a woman a Cananite came
out of the same coasts, and cryed, saying
vnto him, Haue mercie on me, ô Lord, the
sonne of Dauid: my daughter is miserably vexed with a deuil.
23 But he answered her not a worde. Then
came to him his disciples, and besoght
him, saying, g Send her away, for she cryeth after vs.

g The disciples were offēded at her importunitie.
Chap.10,6.

24 But he answered, and said, I am not sent,
but vnto the *lost shepe of the house of Israel.
25 Yet she came & worshipped him, sayĩg,
Lord, helpe me.
26 And he answered, & said, It is not good
to take the childrens bread, and to cast it
to h whelpes.

h Christ calleth thē dogs, or whelpes ẏ are strangers from the house of God.

27 But she said, Trueth, Lord: yet in dede
the whelpes eat of the crommes, which fall
from their masters table.
28 Then Iesus answered, and said vnto her,
O womã, great is thy i faith: be it to thee,
as thou desirest. And her daughter was
made whole at that houre.

i Christ granted her petition, for her faiths sake, and not at the request of his disciples.
Mar.7,31.

29 ¶ So Iesus *went away from thence, and
came nere vnto the sea of Galile, & went
vp into a mountaine and sate downe
there.
30 And great multitudes came vnto him,
*hauing with them, halt, blinde, domme,
maymed and manie other, and cast them
downe at Iesus fete, and he healed them,

Isa.35,5.

31 In so muche that the multitude wondered, to se the domme speake, the maymed
whole, the halt to go, and the blinde to se:
and they glorified the God of Israel.
32 *Then Iesus called his disciples vnto
him, and said, I k haue compassion on this
multitude, because they haue continued
with me alreadie thre daies, and haue nothing to eat: and I wil not let thē departe
fasting, lest they fainte in the way.

Mar.8,1.
k Christ can not forget those that followe him.

33 And his disciples said vnto him, Whence shulde we get so muche bread in the
wildernes, as shulde suffice so great a multitude!
34 And Iesus said vnto them, How manie
loaues haue ye? And they said, Seuen, and
a fewe litle fishes.
35 Then he commanded the multitude to
sit downe on the grounde,
36 And toke the seuen loaues, and the fishes,
and gaue thankes, & brake *them*, and gaue
to his disciples, and the disciples to the
multitude.
37 And they did all eat, and were sufficed:
& thei toke vp of the fragments that remained, seuen baskets ful.
38 And they that had eaten, were foure
thousand men, beside women, and litle
children.
39 Then *Iesus* sent away the multitude, and
toke shippe, and came into the partes of
°Magdala.

°or, Magadan.

CHAP. XVI.

1 The Pharises require a token. 6 Iesus warneth his disciples of the Pharises doctrine. 16 The confession of Peter. 19 The keyes of heauen. 24 The faithful must beare the crosse. 25 To winne or lose the life. 27 Christs comming.

Chap.12,38. mar.8,11. luk.12,54.
a Althogh they did not agre in doctrine, yet thei ioyned together to fight against ẏ trueth.
b Men tempt God ether by their incredulitie, or curiositie.

1 THen *came the a Pharises and Sadduces, and did b tempt *him*, desiring
him to shewe them a signe from heauen.
2 But he answered, and said vnto them,
When it is euening, ye say, Fayre wether:
for the skie is red.
3 And in the morning *ye say*, To day *shal
be* a tempeste: for the skie is red and low-
ring. O hypocrites, ye can discerne the face of the skie, and can ye not *discerne* the
c signes of the times?

c Which apperteine to the heauenlie and spiritual life.
Chap.12,34.
d Christ shal be to them as a Ionas raised vp from death.
Ionas.2,1.

4 *The wicked generacion, and adulterous seketh a signe, and there shal no signe
be giuen it, but the d signe of the Prophet
*Ionas: so he left them, and departed.
5 ¶ And when his disciples were come to
the other side, they had *forgotten to take bread *with them*.

Mar.8,14. luk.12,1.

6 Then Iesus said vnto them, Take hede
and beware of the leauen of the Pharises
and Sadduces.
7 And they °thoght in them selues, saying,
It is because we haue broght no bread.

°or, reasoned with thē selues.

8 But Iesus e knowing it, said vnto them, O
ye of litle faith, why thinke you *thus* in
your selues, because ye haue broght no
bread?

e A token of Christs diuinitie, to knowe mens thoghts.

9 Do ye not yet perceiue, nether remember the fiue loaues, when there were *fiue
thousand *men*, and how manie baskets toke ye vp?

Chap.14,17. iohn 6,9.

10 Nether the seuen loaues when there were *foure thousand *men*, and how manie
baskets toke ye vp?

Chap.15,34.

11 Why perceiue ye not that I said not
vnto

vnto you concerning bread, that ye ſhulde beware of the leauen of the Phariſes &
Sadduces?
12 Then vnderſtode they that he had not
ſaid that they ſhulde beware of the leauen
of bread, but of the f doctrine of the Phariſes, and Sadduces.
13 ¶ *Now when Ieſus came into the coaſtes
of Ceſarea Philippi, he aſked his diſciples,
ſaying, Whome do men ſay that I, the Son
ne of man am?
14 And thei ſaid, Some ſay, Iohn Baptiſt:
and ſome, Elias: & others, Ieremias, or one
of the Prophetes.
15 He ſaid vnto them, But whome ſay ye
that I am?
16 Then Simon Peter anſwered, and ſaid,
*Thou art the Chriſt the Sonne of the li-
uing God.
17 And Ieſus anſwered, & ſaid to him, Bleſ
ſed art thou, Simon, the ſonne of Ionas: for
g fleſh & blood hathe not reueiled it vnto
thee, but my Father which is in heauen.
18 And I ſay alſo vnto thee, that thou art
*Peter, and vpon h this rocke I wil buylde
my Church: and the i gates of hel ſhal not
ouercome it.
19 k And I *wil giue vnto thee the keyes of
the kingdome of heauen, and whatſoeuer
thou ſhalt l binde vpō earth, ſhalbe bound
in heauen: and whatſoeuer thou ſhalt "loſe
on earth, ſhalbe loſed in heauen.
20 Then he charged his diſciples, that they
ſhulde m tell no man that he was Ieſus the
Chriſt.
21 ¶ n From that time forthe Ieſus began to
ſhewe vnto his diſciples, that he muſt go
vnto Ieruſalem, and ſuffer manie things
of the Elders, and of the hie Prieſts, and
Scribes, and be ſlaine, and riſe againe the
thirde day.
22 Then Peter toke him aſide, and began
to rebuke him, ſaying, Maſter, pitie thy
ſelf: this ſhal not be vnto thee.
23 Then he turned backe, and ſaid vnto Peter, Get thee behinde me, o Satan: thou art
an offence vnto me, becauſe thou vnder-
ſtādeſt not the things that are of God, but
the things that are of men.
24 Ieſus then ſaid to his diſciples, *If any
man wil followe me, let him forſake him
ſelf, & take vp his croſſe, and followe me.
25 For *whoſoeuer wil p ſaue his life, ſhal
loſe it: and whoſoeuer ſhal loſe his life for
my ſake, ſhal finde it.
26 *For what ſhal it profite a man thogh he
ſhulde winne the whole worlde, if he loſe
his owne ſoule? or what ſhal a man giue
for recompenſe of his ſoule?
27 For the Sonne of man ſhal come in the
glorie of his Father with his Angels, and

f We may boldely by Chriſts admonition reiect and cōtemne all erronious doctrine and mans inuentions, and oght onely to cleaue to the worde of God

Mar 8,27. luk 9,28.

Ioh.6,69.

g He meaneth any thing that is in man.

Iohn 1,42.

h Vpon that faith whereby thou haſt confeſſed and acknoledged me: for it is grounded vpon an infallible trueth.

Iohn 20,21.

i The power of Satā which ſtandeth in craft and violence.

k The preachers of the Goſpel open the gates of heauen with the worde of God, which is ŷ right keye: ſo that where this worde is not purely taught, there is nether key, nor autoritie.

l Condēne by Gods worde.

"Or, abſolue.

m Becauſe he wolde yet inſtruct them, & not preuēt his time.

n He wolde plucke out of their hearts that falſe opinion, which they had of his temporal kingdome.

Chap. 10,38. mar. 8,34. luk. 9,23. & 14,27.

Chap. 10,39. mar. 8,34. luk. 9,24. & 17,33.

Mar. 8,36. luk. 9,25. iohn 12,25.

o Which worde ſignifieth an aduerſarie, who reſiſteth the wil of God, either of malice, as did Iudas, or of raſhenes and arrogancie, as Peter did. p That is, whoſoeuer thinketh to ſaue him ſelf by forſaking Ieſus Chriſt.

*then ſhal he giue to euerie mā according
to his dedes.
28 *Verely I ſay vnto you, there be ſome
of them that ſtād here, which ſhal not taſte
of death, q til they haue ſene the Sonne of
man come in his kingdome.

CHAP. XVII.

2 The transfiguration of Chriſt vpon the mountaine of Thabor. 5 Chriſt oght to be heard. 11.13 Of Elias and Iohn Baptiſte. 15 He healeth the lunatike. 20 The power of faith. 21 Prayer & faſting. 22 Chriſt telleth thē before of his paſsion. 27 He payeth tribute.

1 ANd *"after ſix dayes, Ieſus toke Peter, and Iames, and Iohn his brother,
and broght them vp into an hie mountaine aparte,
2 And was a transfigured before them: and
his face did ſhine as the ſunne, and his clothes were as white as the light.
3 And beholde, there appeared b vnto them
Moſes, and Elias, talking with him.
4 Then anſwered Peter, and ſaid to Ieſus,
Maſter, it is c good for vs to be here: if
thou wilt, let vs make here thre tabernacles, one for thee, and one for Moſes, and
one for Elias.
5 While he yet ſpake, beholde, a bright clou
de ſhadowed them: and beholde, there came a voyce out of ŷ cloude, ſaying, *This
is my beloued Sonne, d in whome I am wel
pleaſed: e heare him.
6 And when the diſciples heard that, they
f fel on their faces and were ſore afrayed.
7 Then Ieſus came and touched them, and
ſaid, Ariſe, and be not afraid.
8 And when they lifted vp their eyes, they
ſawe no man, ſaue Ieſus onely.
9 ¶ And as they came downe frō the moun
taine, Ieſus charged them, ſaying, Shewe
the viſion to no man, g vntil the Sonne of
man riſe againe from the dead.
10 *And his diſciples aſked him, ſaying,
Why then ſay the Scribes that *Elias muſt
firſt come?
11 And Ieſus anſwered, and ſaid vnto them,
Certeinely Elias muſt firſt come, & reſtore
all things.
12 But I ſay vnto you, that Elias is come
already, and they knewe him not, but haue
done vnto him whatſoeuer they wolde:
likewiſe ſhal alſo the Sonne of man ſuffer
of them.
13 Then the diſciples perceiued that he ſpake vnto them of Iohn Baptiſt.
14 ¶ *And when they were come to the multitude, there came to him a certeine man,
and kneled downe to him,
15 And ſaid, Maſter, haue pitie on my ſonne:
for he is lunatike, and is ſore vexed: for
oft times he falleth into the fyre, and oft
times into the water.
16 And I broght him to thy diſciples, and
they colde not heale him.

Pſal.62,12. rom 2.6.

Mar.9,1. luk 9,17.

q This was fulfilled in his reſurrection ŵ was as an ētrie into his kingdome, and was alſo confirmed by ſending the holie Goſt, whereby he wroght ſo great and ſondrie miracles.

Chap. XVII. Mar.9,2. luk.9,28.

"Or, the ſixt day after.

a Chriſt ſhewed them his glorie, that they might not thinke ŷ he ſuffred through infirmitie, but that he offered vp him ſelf willingly to dye.

b By theſe two witneſſes are repreſented the Lawe and the Prophetes, which lead vs to Chriſt.

Chap.3,17. 2.peter 2, 17.

c After Moſes & Elias departure Peter fearing he ſhulde loſe that ioyful ſight, ſpeaketh as a man diſtract & wolde haue lodged them in earthlie houſes, ŵ were receiued in glorie.

d We are reconciled to God by Chriſt onely.

Mar.9,11.

e Chriſt is our chief and onelie ſcholemaſter.

Chap.11, 14. mal 4,5.

f And ſo worſhipped Chriſt

g For men wolde not haue belieued them, before that Chriſt had made his glorie more manifeſt by his reſurrection.

Mar.9,14. luk.9,37.

17 Then Ieſus anſwered,and ſaid,[h]O gene
racion,faithles,and croked,how long now
ſhal I be with you!how lōg now ſhal I ſuf
fer you!bring him hither to me.
18 And Ieſus rebuked the deuil, & he went
out of him : and the childe was healed at
that houre.
19 Thē came the diſciples to Ieſus a parte,
and ſaid, Why colde not we caſt him out?
20 And Ieſus ſaid vnto them, Becauſe of
your vnbeliefe : for * verely I ſay vnto
you,if ye haue faith *as muche* as *is* a graine
of muſtard ſede,ye ſhal ſay vnto this moūtaine,[i] Remoue hence to yonder place, &
it ſhal remoue:and nothing ſhalbe vnpoſ-
ſible vnto you.
21 How be it this kinde goeth not out, but
by [k] prayer and faſting.
22 ¶And as"thei*abode in Galile,Ieſus ſaid
vnto them, The Sonne of man ſhal be deliuered into the hands of men,
23 And they ſhal kil him,but the thirde day
ſhal he riſe againe : and they were very
ſorie.
24 ¶And when they were come to Capernaum , they that receiued [l] polle money,
came to Peter, and ſaid, Doeth not your
Maſter pay tribute?
25 He ſaid, Yes. And when he was come
into ỹ houſe,Ieſus preuented him,ſaying,
What thinkeſt thou Simō? Of whome do
the Kings of the earth take tribute, or pol
le money?of their children,or of ſtrāgers?
26 Peter ſaid vnto him,Of ſtrangers. Then
ſaid Ieſus vnto him, Then are the children fre.
27 Neuertheles, leſt we ſhulde [m] offende
them,go to the ſea, and caſt in an angle, &
take the firſt fiſhe that cometh vp, & when
thou haſt opened his mouth , thou ſhalt
finde a [n] piece of twentie pence:that take,
and giue it vnto them for me and thee.

h He ſpeaketh chiefly to the Scribes, who began to bragge, as if they had now gotten the victorie ouer Chriſt becauſe his diſciples were not able to do this miracle.

Luk.17,6.

i By this maner of ſpeache is ſignified,ỹ they ſhulde do things by their faith ỹ ſhulde ſeme impoſsible.

Chap.20,17. mar.9,31. luk.9,44. & 24,7.

k The beſt remedie to ſtrēgthen the weake faith is prayer, which hathe faſting added to it,as an helpe to the ſame.

"*Or,were conuerſant, or returned into Galile.*

l The Greke worde is (didrachma) ỹ was of value about 10 pence of olde ſterling monie , & the Iſraelites payed it once by the Lawe, Exo.30,13, and at this time they payed it to the Romāis

m Or giue occaſion to forſake ỹ trueth.

n The worde is (Statera) ỹ cōteineth two didrachmas,& is valued about 5.grotes of olde ſterling.

CHAP. XVIII.

1 The greateſt in the kingdome of heauen. 3 He teacheth his diſciples to be humble and harmeles, 6 To auoide occaſions of euil, 10 Not to contemne the litle-ones. 11 Why Chriſt came. 15 Of brotherlie correction. 17 Of the autoritie of the Church. 19 The commendacion of prayer and godlie aſſemblies. 21 Of brotherlie forgiuenes.

1 THe *ſame time the diſciples came vn
to Ieſus,ſaying,[a]Who is the greateſt
in the kingdome of heauen?
2 And Ieſus called a litle childe vnto him,
and ſet him in the middes of them,
3 And ſaid, Verely I ſay vnto you, except
ye be *conuerted,& become as litle [b] children,ye ſhal not enter into the kingdome
of heauen.
4 Whoſoeuer therefore ſhal humble him
ſelf as this litle childe, the ſame is ỹ greateſt in the kingdome of heauen.
5 [c]And whoſoeuer ſhal receiue ſuche a litle
childe in my Name,receiueth me.
6 *But whoſoeuer ſhal offende one of theſe
litleones which beleue in me, it were better for him,that a [d] mylſtone were hanged
about his necke,and that he were drowned
in the depth of the ſea.
7 [e]Wo *be* vnto the worlde becauſe of offen
ces:for it muſt nedes be that offences ſhal
come,but wo *be* to that mā,by whome the
offence cometh.
8 *Wherefore , if thine hand or thy fote
cauſe thee to offende,cut thē of,& caſt *thē*
from thee:it is better for thee to enter into life,halt, or maimed , then hauing two
hands or two fete , to be caſt into euerlaſting fyre.
9 And if thine eye cauſe thee to offend,
plucke it out,& caſt it from thee : it is better for thee to enter into life with one eye,
then hauing two eyes , to be caſt into hel
fyre.
10 [f]Se that ye deſpice not one of theſe litle-
ones : for I ſay vnto you , that in heauen
their *[g] Angels alwayes beholde the face
of my Father which is in heauen.
11 For * the Sonne of man is come to [h] ſaue
that which was loſt.
12 How thinke ye? * If a man haue an hundreth ſhepe, & one of thē be gone aſtray,
doeth he not leaue ninetie & nine, and go
into the mountaines, and ſeke that which
is gone aſtray?
13 And if ſo be that he finde it, verely I ſay
vnto you,he reioyceth more of that ſhepe,
then of the ninetie and nine which went
not aſtray.
14 So is it not the wil of your Father which
is in heauen, that one of theſe litleones
ſhulde periſh.
15 ¶*Moreouer, if thy brother treſpace a-
gainſt [i]thee,go,and "tell him his faute betwene thee & him alone:if he heare thee,
thou haſt wonne thy brother.
16 But if he heare thee not, take yet with
thee one or two,that by ỹ * mouth of two
or thre witneſſes euerie worde may be cōfirmed.
17 And if he wil not vouchesaue to heare
thē,tel it vnto the [k] Church : & if he refuſe
to heare the Church alſo , let him be vnto
thee as an heathen man , and a Publicane.
18 Verely I ſay vnto you, * Whatſoeuer ye
[l]binde on earth, ſhalbe bounde in heauen:
and * whatſoeuer ye loſe on earth , ſhal
be loſed in heauen.
19 Againe,verely I ſay vnto you,that if two
of you ſhal agre in earth vpon any thing,
whatſoeuer they ſhal deſire,it ſhal be"giuē

Mar.9,33. luk.9,46.

a They ſtriue for the rewarde before they haue taken any payne : and where as they ſhulde haue holpen & reuerēced one another, they were ambitious and deſpicers of their brethren.

Chap.19,24. 1.cor.14,20.

b Not in lacke of diſcretion , but that they be not vayne glorious, ſeking to aduance them ſelues to worldelie honours.

c He calleth them litle children now,ỹ humble them ſelues with all humilitie and ſubiection.

Mar.9,42. luk.17,1.

d The worde ſignifieth a great milſtone ỹ an aſſe tourneth, and it is ſpoken in reſpect of that which is tourned with mans hand , which is leſſe.

Chap.5,30. mar.9,45.

e Chriſt warneth his to take heed that they ſhrinke not backe frō him for any euil example or offence that man can giue.

f Chriſt toucheth the cauſe of this offence , which is pride and diſdeyne of our inferiours.

Pſal.34,7. Luk.19,10. Luk.15,4.

g Seing God hathe comāded his Angels to take ỹ charge of his children, the wicked may be aſſured that if they deſpice them, God wil reuenge their cauſe.

h We may not loſe by our offence that which God hathe ſo derely boght.

Leu.19,17. eccle.19,13. luk.17,3. iam.5,18.

i Wherewith thou maiſt be offended: he ſpeaketh of ſecret or particular ſinnes, & not of open or knowen to others.

"*Or, reproue him*

Deu.19,15. iohn 8,17. ebr.10,28. 2.cor.13,1. 1.Cor.5,9. 2.theſ.3,14. Iohn.20,23.

k He meaneth according to the order that was amongs the Iewes,who had their coūcel of ancient and expert mē to reforme maners , and execute diſcipline . This aſſemblie repreſented the Church, which had appointed them to this charge.

l In the 16. chap. 19. he ment this of doctrine, and here of eccleſiaſtical diſcipline, which dependeth of the doctrine.

"*Or, done to.*

them

them of my Father which is in heauen.
20 For where two or thre are gathered together in my Name, there am I in the middes of them.
21 Then came Peter to him, & said, Master,
how oft shal my brother sinne against me,
& I shal forgiue him? *vnto seuen times?

Luk.17,4.

22 Iesus said vnto him, I say not to thee, vnto seuen times, but vnto [m] seuentie times
seuen times.

m We muste be cotinually ready to forgiue and be forgiuen.

23 Therefore is the kingdome of heauen likened vnto a certeine King, which wolde
take a countes of his seruants.
24 And when he had begonne to recken, one
was broght vnto him, which oght him ten
thousand [n] talents.

n A commune talent was valued at thre score pounde: some also were greater and some lesse.

25 And because he had nothing to paye, his
master commanded him to be solde, & his
wife, & *his* children, and all that he had, and
the dette to be payed.
26 The seruant therefore fel downe, and besoght him, saying, Master, appease thine an
gre towarde me, and I wil pay thee all.
27 Then that seruants master had compassion, and losed him, and forgaue him the
dette.
28 But when the seruant was departed, he
founde one of his felowes, which oght him
an hundreth [o] pence, & he layed hands on
him, and toke him by the throte, saying,
Pay me that thou owest.

o Which amounteth of our money to the summe of 25. shillings, or verie nere, and was nothing in respect of ye former which his master forgaue him.

29 Then his felow fel downe at his fete, and
besoght him, saying, Appease thine angre
towards me, and I wil pay thee all.
30 Yet he wolde not, but went and cast him
into prison, til he shulde pay the dette.
31 And whẽ his *other* felowes sawe what was
done, they were very sorie, and came, and
declared vnto their master all yt was done.
32 Then his master called him, and said to
him, O euil seruant, I forgaue thee all that
dette, because thou prayedst me.
33 Oghtest not thou also to haue had pitie
on thy felow, euen as I had pitie on thee?
34 So his master was wroth, and deliuered
him to the iaylers, til he shulde pay all that
was due to him.
35 So likewise shal mine heauẽlie Father do
vnto you, except ye forgiue [p] from your
hearts, eche one to his brother their trespaces.

p God esteemeth onely the heart and affection.

CHAP. XIX.

2 Christ sheweth for what cause a woman may be diuorced. 11 Continence is a gift of God. 14 He receiueth litle babes. 16 To obteine life euerlasting. 24 That riche men can scarsely be saued. 28 He promiseth them which haue left all to followe him life euerlasting.

Mar.10,1.

1 AND *it came to passe, that whẽ Iesus
had finished those sayings, he departed from Galile, and came into the coastes
of Iudea beyonde Iordan.
2 And great multitudes followed him, and
he healed them there.
3 ¶ Then came vnto him the Pharises tẽp-
ting him, and saying to him, Is it lawful
for a man to put away his wife for euerie
"faute?

"Or, cause.

4 And he answered and said vnto them,
Haue ye not red, *that he which made
them at the beginning, made them male
and female,

Gen.1,27.

5 And said, *For this cause, shal a man leaue father and mother, and cleaue vnto his
wife, and they [a] twaine shalbe one "flesh?

Gene.2,24. 1.cor.6,16. ephe.5,31.
a They that afore were as two, shalbe now as one persone.
"Or, persone.

6 Wherefore they are no more twaine, but
one flesh. Let not man therefore put a sundre that, which God hathe coupled toge
ther.
7 They said to him, Why did then* Moses commãde to giue a bil of diuorcemẽt,
and to put her away?

Deu.24,1.

8 He said vnto them, Moses, because of the
[b] hardnes of your heart, suffred you to put
away your wiues: but [c] from the beginning
it was not so.

Chap.5,32. mar.10,11. luk.16,18. 1.cor.7,11.

9 I say therefore vnto you, *that whosoeuer shal put away his wife, except *it be* for
whoredome, and marie another, [d] committeth adulterie: and whosoeuer marieth
her which is diuorced, doeth commit adulterie.

b It was to auoide the crueltie, that men wolde haue vsed towards their wiues, if they had bene forced to reteine them in their displeasure, furie and malice.
c That is, at ye beginning, and by Gods ordinance.
d For this bãde can not be broken at mãs pleasure.

10 *Then* said his disciples to him, If the mat
ter be so betwene man and wife, it is not
good to marie.
11 But he said vnto them, All men can not
receiue this thing, saue they to whome it
is giuen.
12 For there are [e] some [f] chaste, which were
so borne of *their* mothers bellie: and there
be some chaste, which be made chaste by
men: & there be some chaste, [g] which haue made them selues chaste for the kingdome of heauen. He [h] that is able to receiue *this*, let him receiue it.

e Some by nature are vnable to marie, and some by arte.
f The worde signifieth (gelded:) and they were so made because they shulde kepe the chambers of noble women: for they were iudged chaste.
g Which haue the gift of cõtinence, & vse it to serue God with more free libertie.
h This gift is not commune for all mẽ, but is verie rare, and giuen to fewe: therefore mẽ may not rashly absteine from mariage.

13 ¶ *Thẽ were broght to him litle childrẽ,
that he shulde put *his* hands on them, and
pray: and the disciples rebuked them.
14 But Iesus said, Suffer the litle children,
and forbid them not to come to me: for of
suche is the kingdome of heauen.
15 And whẽ he had put his hands on them,
he departed thence.

Chap.18,3. mar.10,13. luk.18,15.

16 ¶ *And beholde one came, and said vnto
him, Good Master, what good thing shal
I do, that I may haue eternal life?

Mar.10,17. luk.18,18.

17 And he said vnto him, [i] Why callest
thou me good? there is none good but one,
euen God: but if thou wilt entre into life,
[k] kepe the commandements.
18 He said to him, Which? And Iesus said,
*These, Thou shalt not kil: Thou shalt
not cõmit adulterie: Thou shalt not steale:
Thou shalt not beare false witnes.
19 Honour thy father and mother: and thou

i Because this yong mã knewe nothing in Iesus Christ but his manhode, he leadeth him to higher things, to the intent, that his doctrine might better take place. k He spake this that he might learne to knowe him self. *Exod 20,13. de[illegible] 5,16 rom.13,9.

ſhalt loue thy neighbour as thy ſelf.
20 The yong man ſaid vnto him, I haue
[l] obſerued all theſe things from my youth:
what lacke I yet?
21 Ieſus ſaid vnto him, If thou wilt be perfite, go, [m] ſel that thou haſt, & giue it to the
poore, and thou ſhalt haue treaſure in heauen, and come and followe me.
22 And when the yong man heard that ſaying, he went away ſorowful: for he had
great [n] poſſeſsions.
23 Then Ieſus ſaid vnto his diſciples, Verely I ſay vnto you, that a riche man ſhal
hardely enter into the kingdome of heauen.
24 And againe I ſay vnto you, It is eaſier
for a " camel to go through the eye of a
nedle, then for a riche man to enter into
the kingdome of God.
25 And when his diſciples heard it, thei were excedingly amaſed, ſaying, Who then
can be ſaued?
26 And Ieſus behelde them, and ſaid vnto
thẽ, With men this is vnpoſsible, but with
God [o] all things are poſsible.
27 ¶ *Then anſwered Peter, & ſaid to him,
Beholde, we haue forſaken all, & followed
thee: what ſhal we haue?
28 And Ieſus ſaid vnto them, Verely I ſay to
you, that when the Sonne of man ſhal ſit in
the throne of his maieſtie, ye which followed me [p] in the regeneracion, * ſhal ſit
alſo vpon twelue thrones, and iudge the
twelue tribes of Iſrael.
29 And whoſoeuer ſhal forſake houſes, or
brethren, or ſiſters, or father, or mother, or
wife, or children, or lands, for my Names
ſake, he ſhal receiue an [q] hundreth folde
more, & ſhal inherite euerlaſting life.
30 *But manie that are firſt, ſhalbe laſt, and
the laſt *ſhalbe* firſt.

CHAP. XX.

1 Chriſt teacheth by a ſimilitude, that God is detter vnto no man, and how he alway calleth men to his labour. 18 He admoniſheth them of his paſsion. 20 He teacheth his to flee ambition. 28 Chriſt payeth our ranſome. 30 He giueth two blinde men their ſight.

1 FOr the kingdome of heauen is like vn
to a certeine houſe holder, which wẽt
out at the dawning of the day to hier laborers into his vineyarde.
2 And he agreed with ẏ laborers for a [a] penie
a day, and ſent them into his vineyarde.
3 And he went out about the [b] thirde houre,
and ſawe other ſtanding ydle in the market place,
4 And ſaid vnto them, Go ye alſo into *my*
vineyarde, & whatſoeuer is right, I wil giue you: and they went their way.
5 Againe he went out about the ſixt and
ninth houre, and did likewiſe.
6 And he went about the eleuenth houre,
and founde other ſtanding ydle, and ſaid
vnto them, Why ſtand ye here all the day
ydle?
7 They ſaid vnto him, Becauſe no man hathe hired vs. He ſaid to them, Go ye alſo
into *my* vineyarde, & whatſoeuer is right,
that ſhal ye receiue.
8 ¶ And when euen was come, the maſter of
the vineyard ſaid vnto his ſteward, Call ẏ
laborers, and giue them their hier, beginning at the laſt, til *thou come* to the firſt.
9 And they *which were hired* about the eleuenth houre, came and receiued euerie
man a penie.
10 Now when the firſt came, they ſuppoſed
that they ſhulde receiue more, but they likewiſe receiued euerie man a penie.
11 And when they had receiued it, they mur
mured againſt the maſter of the houſe,
12 Saying, Theſe laſt haue wroght but o-
ne houre, and thou haſt made them equal
vnto vs, which haue borne the burden, &
heat of the day.
13 And he anſwered one of them, ſaying,
"Friend, I do thee no wrong: dideſt thou
not agre with me for a penie?
14 Take that which is thine owne, and go
thy way: I wil giue vnto this laſt, as muche
as to thee.
15 Is it not lawful for me to do as I wil with
mine owne? Is thine eye [c] euil becauſe I
am good?
16 * So [d] the laſt ſhalbe firſt, and the firſt laſt:
*for manie are called, but fewe choſen.
17 * And Ieſus went vp to Ieruſalem, and
toke the twelue diſciples aparte in the
way, and ſaid vnto them,
18 Beholde, we go vp to Ieruſalem, and the
Sonne of man ſhalbe deliuered vnto the
chief Prieſts, and vnto the Scribes, & they
ſhal condemne him to death,
19 And * ſhal deliuer him to the Gentiles,
to mocke, and to ſcourge, and to crucifie
him: but the thirde day he ſhal riſe againe.
20 * Then came to him the mother of Zebedeus children with her ſonnes, worſhipping *him*, & deſiring a certeine thing
of him.
21 And he ſaid vnto her, What woldeſt
thou? She ſaid to him, Grante that theſe
my two ſonnes may ſit, the one at thy right
hand, and the other at thy left hand in thy
kingdome.
22 And Ieſus anſwered and ſaid, Ye knowe
not what ye aſke. Are ye able to drinke
of the [e] cup that I ſhal drinke of, and to
be baptized with the baptiſme that I ſhalbe baptized with? They ſaid to him, We
are able.
23 And he ſaid vnto them, Ye ſhal drinke
in dede of my cup, and ſhalbe baptized
with ẏ baptiſme, that I am baptized with,
but to ſit at my right hand, and at my left
hand,

l He boaſteth muche becauſe as yet he knewe not him ſelf.
m Chriſt hereby diſcouered his hyprocriſie, and cauſed him to feele his owne weakenes, not generally commanding all to do the like.
n What hinderance men haue by riches.
"Or, cable rope.
o Who can frame mens heartes, ſo that they ſhal not ſet their mindes on their riches.
Mar.10,28.
luk.18,28.
p In this worke whereby the worlde is changed, renued and regenerate: or to ioyne this worde with the ſentence following and ſo take regeneration for the day of iudgement, when the elect ſhal in ſoule and bodie enioye their inheritãce, to the end ẏ they might knowe that it is not ſufficiẽt to haue begõne once.
Luk.22,30.
Chap.20,16.
mar.10,31.
luk.13,30.
q The ioye of conſcience ẇ Gods children feele euen in their afflictiõs is a 1000 folde more worthe then all worldelie treaſures

a Which was called denarius, & was of value about foure pence halfe penie of olde money, and was communely a workemans hier.
b They deuided the day into twelue houres, so that the third was the fourth part of the day, ſix of ẏ clocke was none, nine was thre of the clocke after dynner, & the eleuenth houre was an houre before the ſunne ſete.

"Or, felowe.
c Or enuious, becauſe of my liberalitie, deut 15,19.
Chap.19,30.
mar.10,31.
luk.13,30.
Chap.22,14.
Mar.10,32.
luk.18,31.
d Therefore euerie man in his vocation, as he is called firſt, oght to go forwarde, & encourage others, ſeing the hyer is indifferent for all.
Ioh.18,32.
Mar.10,35.
e He ſetteth ẏ croſſe before their eyes to drawe thẽ frõ ambition, calling it a cup, to ſignifie the meaſure of the afflictions, ẇ God hathe ordeined for euerie man: the which thing alſo he calleth baptiſme

hand,is [f] not mine to giue: but *it shalbe giuen* to them for whome it is prepared of
my Father.

f God my Father hathe not giuen me charge to bestowe offices of honour here: but to be an exãple of humilitie vnto all.

24 *And when the *other* ten heard this, they
disdained at the two brethren.
25 Therefore Iesus called them vnto him,
and said, Ye knowe that the lords of the
Gentiles haue domination ouer them,and
they that are great,exercise autoritie ouer
them.

Mar.10,41. luk.22,25.

26 But it shal not be so amõg you: but whosoeuer wil be great among you, let him be
your seruant,
27 And whosoeuer wil be chief amõg you,
let him be your seruant,
28 *Euen as the Sonne of man came not to
be serued,but to serue,and to giue his life
for the ransome of manie.

Philip.2,7.

29 ¶*And as they departed from Iericho,
a great multitude followed him.

Mar.10,46. luk.18,35.

30 And beholde,two blinde men,sitting by
the way side, when they heard that Iesus
passed by,cryed saying, O Lord,the sonne
of Dauid,haue mercie on vs.
31 And the multitude rebuked them,becau-
se they shulde holde their peace: but they
cryed the more,saying,O Lord, the sonne
of Dauid,haue mercie on vs.
32 Then Iesus stode stil,and called them,&
said, What wil ye that I shulde do to you?
33 They said to him, Lord, that our eyes
may be opened.
34 And Iesus moued with compassion touched their eyes, & immediatly their eyes
receiued sight,and they followed him.

CHAP. XXI.

7 Christ rideth into Ierusalem on an asse. 12 The byers and sellers are chased out of the Temple. 15 The children wish prosperitie vnto Christ. 19 The figtre withereth. 22 Faith requisit in prayer. 25 Iohns baptisme. 28 The two sonnes. 33 The parable of the housband men. 42 The corner stone reiected. 43 The Iewes reiected & the Gentiles receiued.

1 AND * when they drew nere to Ierusalem,and were come to Bethphage,
vnto the mount of the oliues, then sent
Iesus two disciples,

Mar.11,1. luk.19,29.

2 Saying to them, Go into the towne that
is ouer against you,and anone ye shal finde an [a] asse bounde, and a colte with her:
lose them,and bring them vnto me.

a By this entrie Christ wolde shewe the state and condition of his kingdome, which is farre contrarie to the põpe and glorie of the worlde.

3 And if anie man say oght vnto you, say
ye,that the Lord hathe nede of them, and
straight way he wil let them go.
4 All this was done that it might be fulfilled which was spoken by the Prophet,saying,

Isa.62,11. zach.9,9. iohn.12,15.

5 ¶*Tel ye the [b] daughter of Siõ,Beholde,
thy King cometh vnto thee, meke and sitting vpon an asse,and a [c] colte, the fole of
an asse vsed to the yoke.

b That is, the citie Sion, or Ierusalem.

c It is a maner of speache called synechdoche, whereby two are taken for one.

6 So the disciples wẽt,and did as Iesus had
commanded them,
7 And broght the asse & the colte,& put on
[d] them their clothes,and set him thereon.

d He ridde on the fole & the dãme wẽt by.

8 And a great multitude spred their garments in the way: and other cutte downe
brãches from the trees, and strawed them
in the way.
9 Moreouer, the people that went before, and they also that followed, cryed,
saying, [e] Hosanna the sonne of Dauid:
blessed *be* he that cometh in the Name of
the Lord, Hosanna *thou which art* in the
[f] hiest *heauens*.

e Which is to say, Saue I pray thee, desiring God to prosper & sende good successe to the Messias.

f For God which is in heauen, must onely saue.

10 *And when he was come into Ierusalem,
all the citie was moued,saying,Who is this?
11 And the people said, This is Iesus the
Prophet of Nazaret in Galile.

Mar.11,11. luk.19,45. ioh.2,13.

12 ¶And Iesus wẽt into the Tẽple of God,
and cast out all them that solde & boght
in the [g] Temple,and ouerthrew the tables
of the money changers,and the seates of
them that solde doues,

g In the porche or entrie into the Tẽple.

13 And said to thẽ,It is writtẽ,*Mine house shalbe called the house of prayer: [h] but
* ye haue made it a denne of thieues.

Isa.56,7. Iere.7,11. Mar.11,17. luk.19,46.

h Vnder the pretence of religion hypocrites seke their owne gaine,and spoyle God of his true worship.

14 Then *the blinde, and the halt came to
him in the Temple,and he healed them.
15 But when the chief Priests and Scribes
sawe the marueils that he did, & the children crying in the Tẽple,& saying, Hosanna the sonne of Dauid, they disdained,
16 And said vnto him, Hearest thou what
these say?And Iesus said vnto thẽ, Yea:red
ye neuer,*By the [i] mouth of babes & sucke-
lings thou hast [k] made perfite the praise?

Psal.8,2.

i If God reueile his glorie & might by babes, that cã not as yet speake, is it marueil, if they that can speake,do set forthe,and magnifie the same?

k In Ebrewe it is, hast ordeined or grounded the stregth: which is all to one purpose, because God is then moste praised when his strength is best knowen.

17 ¶So he left them,and went out of the citie vnto Bethania,and lodged there.
18 And *in the morning as he returned into the citie,he was hungrie,
19 And seing a figge tre in the way,he came
to it,and founde nothing thereon,but leaues onely,and said to it,Neuer frute grow
on thee hence forwardes. And anone the
figge tree withered.

Mar.11,13.

20 And when his disciples sawe it,they mar
ueiled, saying , How sone is the figge tre
withered!
21 And Iesus answered and said vnto them,
*Verely I say vnto you, if ye haue faith,
and dout not , ye shal not onely do that,
which I haue done to the figge tree, but also
if ye say vnto this mountaine, [l] Take thy
self away,and cast thy self into the sea,it
shalbe done.

Chap.17,20.

l Which thing semeth to be imposible.

22 *And whatsoeuer ye shal aske in prayer,
if ye beleue,ye shal receiue it.

Chap.7,7. ioh.15,7. 1ioh.3,24.

23 ¶*And when he was come into the Tẽple,
the chief Priests,and the Elders of the peo
ple came vnto him,as he was teaching,and
said, By what autoritie doest thou these
things?and who gaue thee this autoritie?

Mar.11,27. luk.20,1.

24 Then Iesus answered and said vnto thẽ,
I also wil aske of you a certeine thing, which
if ye tel me, I likewise wil tell you by
what autoritie I do these things.
25 The baptisme of Iohn whẽce was it? [*] frõ

*Or, of God.

heauen, or of men? Then they reasoned a-
mong them selues, saying, If we shal say
from heauen, he wil say vnto vs, Why did
ye not then beleue him?

m The hypocrites feare man more thē God, & malice neuer iustifieth the truth.

26 And if we say, Of men, we m feare ẏ people: *for all holde Iohn as a Prophet.

Chap.14,5. mar.6,20.

27 Then they answered Iesus, and said, We
cā not tel. And he said vnto them, Nether
tel I you by what autoritie I do these
things.
28 ¶But what thinke ye? A *certeine* man had
two sonnes, and came to the elder, & said,
Sōne, go & worke to day in my vineyard.
29 But he answered and said, I wil not: yet
afterwarde he repented him self, and wēt.
30 Then came he to the seconde, and said
likewise. And he answered, and said, I wil,
syr: yet he went not.
31 Whether of them twaine did the wil of
the father? They said vnto him, The first.
Iesus said vnto thē, Verely I say vnto you,
that the n Publicanes and the harlots shal
go before you into the kingdome of God.

n So farre it is impossible for them to repēt & be saued, ẏ stande in their owne conceite, that the greatest sinners that are, shal more sone come to repentance.

32 For Iohn came vnto you in the o way of
righteousnes, and ye beleued him not: but
the Publicanes, & the harlots beleued him,
and ye, thogh ye sawe it, were not moued
with repentāce afterwarde, that ye might
beleue him.

o God taught by Iohn the way of righteousnes, whose life was vpright and perfite.

33 ¶Heare another parable, There was a
certeine housholder, *which planted a
p vineyarde, and q hedged it round about,
and "made a winepresse therein, and buylt
a tower, and let it out to housband men,
and went into a strange countrey.

Isa.5,1. ierem.2,21. mar.12,1. luk.20,9.

p The vineyarde is the people, whome he had elected.

q Vsed all meanes to preserue it, and to make it frutefull.

" or, digged.

34 And when the time of the frute drewe
nere, he sent his seruants to r the houshād
men to receiue the frutes thereof.

r Which were the Priests & rulers.

35 And the housbandmē toke his s seruants
and beat one, and killed another, and stoned another.

s The Prophetes.

36 Againe he sent other seruāts, mo thē the
first: and they did the like vnto them.
37 But last of all he sent vnto thē his owne
t sonne, saying, They wil reuerence my
sonne.

t Iesus Christ.

38 But when the housbandmen sawe the
sonne, they said amōg them selues, *This
is the heire: come, let vs kill him, & let vs
take his inheritance.

Chap.26,3. & 27,1. ioh.11,53.

39 So they toke him, and cast him out of
the vineyarde, and slewe him.
40 When therefore the Lord of the vineyarde shal come, what wil he do to those
housbandmen?
41 They said vnto him, He wil cruelly destroye those wicked men, and wil let out
his vineyarde vnto other housbandmen,
which shal deliuer him the frutes in their
seasons.
42 Iesus said vnto them, Red ye neuer in
the Scriptures, *The stone which ẏ buylders u refused, the same is made the x head
of the corner? This was the Lords doing,
and it is marueilous in our eyes.

Psal.118,22. act.4,11. rom.9,33. 1.pet.2,7.

u As not mete or fit for their buyldīg.

x To fasten & ioyne the buylding together, & to vpholde the whole.

43 Therefore say I vnto you, the kingdome of God shalbe taken frō you, & shalbe giuen to a naciō, which shal bring forthe the frutes thereof.
44 * And whosoeuer shal fall on this stone,
he shalbe broken: but on whomesoeuer it
shal fall, it wil grinde him to powder.

Isa.8,14.

45 And when the chief Priests and Pharises had heard his parables, they perceiued
that he spake of them.
46 And they seking to lay hands on him,
feared the people, because they toke him
as a Prophet.

CHAP. XXII.

2 The parable of the mariage. 9 The vocation of the Gentiles. 11 The mariage garment. 17 Of paying of tribute. 23 Of the resurrection. 36 The Scribes question. 44 Christs diuinitie.

1 THen *Iesus answered, and spake vnto
them againe in parables, saying,

Luk.14,16. reuel.19,9.

2 The kingdome of heauen is like vnto a
certeine King which maried his sonne,
3 And a sent forthe his seruants, to call thē
that were bid to the wedding, but they
wolde not come.

a Christ reprocheth ẏ Iewes of their ingratitude & obstinate malice, in that they reiected the grace of God, ẇ was so plentifully offered vnto them.

4 Againe he sent forthe other seruants,
saying, Tel thē which are bidden, Beholde, I haue prepared my dinner: mine oxen
and my fatlings are killed, and all things
are readie: come vnto the mariage.
5 But they made light of it, and went their
wayes, one to his ferme, & another about
his marchandise.
6 And the remnant toke his seruants, & intreated them sharpely, and slewe them.
7 But when ẏ King heard it, he was wroth,
& sent forthe his warriers, & b destroyed
those murtherers, and burnt vp their citie.

b God punisheth extremely suche ingratitude.

8 Then said he to his seruants, Truely the
wedding is prepared: but they which were
bidden, were not worthie.

c The ingratitude of thē ẇ are bid, cā not cause Gods liberalitie & his holie meates to perish, ẇ he hathe prepared for his.

9 Go ye therefore out into the high wayes,
and as manie as ye finde, bid them to the
mariage.
10 So c those seruants went out into the *hie*
wayes and gathered together all that euer
they founde, bothe d good and bad: so the
wedding was furnished with ghestes.

d In ẏ Church the hypocrites are mixed ẇ the godlie.

11 Thē the King came in, to se the ghestes,
and saw there a man which had not on a
e wedding garment.

e He had not a pure affectiō & vpright cōscience, which proceded of faith.

12 And he said vnto him, Friend, how f camest thou in hither, & hast not on a wedding garment? And he was speacheles.

f Thogh God suffre for a time hypocrites in the Church, yet he knoweth how to trie thē, & fanne them out.

13 Then said the King to the seruants, Binde him hand and fote: take him away, and
cast him into vtter darkenes: * there shal
be weping and gnasshing of teeth.

Cha.8,12.& 13,42.& 25,30.

14 *For manie are g called, but fewe
chosen.

Chap.20,16.

g By the outwarde, & general calling.

15 ¶*Thē went the Pharises & toke coūsel
how

Mar.12,13. luk.20,20.

how they might tangle him in talke.
16 And they sent vnto him their disciples
with the [h] Herodians, saying, Master, we
knowe that thou art true, and teachest the
way of God truely, nether carest for anie
man: for thou considerest not the [i] persone of men.

h These were certeine flatterers of the court, which euer mainteined that religion, wͨ King Herode best approued: and thogh they were enemies to the Pharises: yet in this thing thei consented, thinkīg to intangle Christ, and so ether to accuse him of treason, or to brīg him into ẏ hatred of all his people.

17 Tell vs therefore, how thinkest thou? Is
it lawful to giue tribute vnto Cesar, or
not?
18 But Iesus perceiued their wickednes, &
said, Why tempt ye me, ye hypocrites?
19 Shewe me the " tribute money. And thei
broght him a [k] penie.
20 And he said vnto them, Whose is this
image and superscription?
21 They said vnto him, Cesars. Then said
he vnto them, *Giue therefore to Cesar,
the things which are Cesars, and giue vnto God, those which are Gods.

Rom.13,7.
i As touching the outwarde qualitie, as whether a man be riche or poore.
" *Or, the coyne of the tribute.*
k Which was of value about foure pence halfe penie.

22 And when they heard it, thei marueiled,
and left him, and went their way.
23 ¶ * The same day the Sadduces came to
him (which say that there is no resurrection) and asked him,
24 Saying, Master, * Moses said, If a man
dye, hauing no " children, let his brother
[l] marie his wife, and raise vp sede vnto
his brother.

Mar.12,10. luk.20,17. act.23,6.
Deut.25,5.
" *Or, sonnes.*
l By the title of aliance: and here by brother he meaneth the next kinsman, ẏ lawfully might marie her.

25 Now there were with vs seuen brethren,
and the first maried a wife, and deceased:
and hauing none yssue, left his wife vnto
his brother.
26 Likewise also the seconde, & the third,
vnto the seuenth.
27 And last of all the woman dyed also.
28 Therefore in the resurrection, whose
wife shal she be of the seuen? for all had
her.
29 Then Iesus answered, and said vnto thē,
Ye [m] are deceiued, not knowing the Scrip
tures, nor the power of God.
30 For in the resurrection they nether marie wiues, nor wiues are bestowed in mariage, but are as the [n] Angels of God in
heauen.

m Where Gods worde is not preached and vnderstand, there must nedes reigne blindenes and errours.
n Forasmuche as thei shalbe exempted frō the infirmities of this present life.

31 And concerning the resurrection of the
dead, haue ye not red what is spoken vnto
you of God, saying,
32 * I am the God of Abraham, & the God
of Isaac, and the God of Iacob? God is
not the God of the dead, but of the liuīg.

Exod.3,6.

33 And when the people heard it, they were
astonied at his doctrine.
34 ¶ * But when the Pharises had heard,
that he had put the Sadduces to silence,
they assembled together.

Mar.12,28.

35 And one of them, *which was* an expounder of the Law, asked him a question, tēp-
ting him, and saying,
36 Master, which is the great commandement in the Law?
37 Iesus said to him, * Thou shalt loue the

Deut.6,5. luk.10,27.

Lord thy God with all thine heart, with
all thy soule, and with all thy minde.
38 This is the first and the great commandement.
39 And the seconde is like vnto this, * Thou
shalt loue thy neighbour as thy self.
40 On these two commandements hāgeth
the whole Law, and the Prophetes.

Leui.19,18. mar.12,31. rom.13,9. gal.5,14. iam.2,8.
o Of what stocke or familie.
Mar.12,35. luk.20,41.

41 ¶ * While the Pharises were gathered
together, Iesus asked them,
42 Saying, What thinke ye of Christ? whose [o] sonne is he? They said vnto him, Dauids.
43 He said vnto them, How then doeth Da
uid in [p] spirit call him Lord, saying,
44 *The Lord said to my Lord, Sit on my
[q] right hand, til I make thine enemies thy
fote stole?
45 If then Dauid call him [r] Lord, how is he
his sonne?
46 And none colde answer him a worde,
nether durst anie from that daye forthe
aske him anie mo questions.

p By the spirit of prophecie speaking of the kingdome of Christ.
q By the right hand is signified ẏ autoritie and power, wͨ God giueth his Sonne Christ in making him his lieutenāt & gouernour ouer his Church.
Psal.110,1.
r Not that his kingdome shal then end: but ẏ office of his humanitie shal cease, and he wͭ the Father and holie Gost shal reigne for euer as one God all in all.
s Christ is Dauids sōne touching his manhode, and his Lord, concerning his Godhead.

CHAP. XXIII.

3 Christ condemneth the ambicion, couetousnes, and hypocrisie of the Scribes and Pharises. 31 Their persecutions against the seruants of God. 37 He prophecieth the destruction of Ierusalem.

1 THen spake Iesus to the multitude, &
to his disciples,
2 Saying, The * Scribes and the Pharises
[a] sit in Moses seat.
3 All therefore whatsoeuer they byd you
obserue, that [b] obserue and do: but after
their workes do not: for they say, and do
not.

Chap XXIII.
Nehe.8,4.
a And teache that which Moses saith.
b According to Moses whome they read, but not ẏ wͨ thei teache of thē selues.

4 * For they binde heauie burdens, and
grieuous to be borne, and laye them on
mens shulders, but they them selues wil
not moue them with *one* of their fingers.
5 All their workes they do for to be sene
of men: for they make their [c] phylacteries
broad, and make long the * fringes of their
garments,
6 * And loue the chief place at feasts, and
to haue the chief seates in the assemblies,
7 And gretings in the markets, and to be
called of men, " Rabbi, Rabbi.
8 *But be not ye called, [d] Rabbi: for one is
your " doctor, *to wit,* Christ, and all ye are
brethren.
9 And * call no man your father vpon the
earth: for their is but one, your Father
which is in heauen.
10 Be not called [e] doctors: for one is your
doctor, *euen* Christ.
11 But he that is [f] greatest among you, let
him be your seruant.
12 * For whosoeuer wil exalt him self, sha'-
be broght low: and whosoeuer wil humble

Luk.11,46. act.15,10.
c Thei were skroles of parchemēt wherein the commādements were written: and to this day the Iewes vse the same & close thē in a piece of lether, & so binde them to their browe & left arme, to the intent thei might haue cōtinual remembrance of the Law.
Nom.15,38. deut.22,12.
Mar.12,38. luk.11,43. & 20,46.
" *or, master.*
Iam.3,1.
" *or, teacher.*
Mal.1,6.
Luk.14,11. & 18,14.

d Christ forbiddeth not to giue iuste honour to Magistrates and Masters, but condemneth ambicion and superioritie ouer our brothers faith, which office apperteineth to Christ alone. e The Pharises were called Masters or Fathers, and the Scribes Doctors. f The highest dignitie in the Church is not lordshippe, or dominion, but ministerie and seruice.

him self, shalbe exalted.
13 ¶ Wo therefore *be* vnto you Scribes and
Pharises, hypocrites, because ye [g] shut vp
the kingdome of heauen before men: for
ye your selues go not in, nether suffer ye
them [h] that wolde enter, to come in.
14 * Wo *be* vnto you Scribes and Pharises, hypocrites: for ye deuoure widdowes
houses, euen vnder a colour of long prayers: wherefore ye shal receiue the greater
damnacion.
15 Wo *be* vnto you, Scribes and Pharises,
hypocrites: for ye compasse [i] sea and land
to make one of your profession: and when
he is made, ye make him two folde more
the childe of hel, then you your selues.
16 Wo *be* vnto you blinde guides, which
say, Whosoeuer sweareth by the Tēple, it
is nothing: but whosoeuer sweareth by the
golde of the Temple, he" offendeth.
17 Ye fooles and blinde, whether is greater,
the golde, or the Tēple that [k] sanctifieth
the golde?
18 And whosoeuer sweareth by the altar, it
is nothing: but whosoeuer sweareth by the
offring *that is* vpon it, offendeth.
19 Ye fooles and blinde, whether is greater,
the offring, or the altar which sanctifieth
the offring?
20 Whosoeuer therefore sweareth by the
altar, sweareth by it, and by all things thereon.
21 * And whosoeuer sweareth by the Temple, sweareth by it, and by him that dwelleth therein.
22 * And he that sweareth by heauen, sweareth by the throne of God, and by him
that sitteth thereon.
23 ¶ * Wo *be* to you, Scribes and Pharises,
hypocrites: for ye tythe mynt, & annyse,
& cōmyn, and leaue the weightier matters
of the Law, *as* iudgement, and mercie, &
fidelitie. These oght ye to haue done, &
not to haue left the other.
24 Ye blinde guides, which [l] straine out a
gnatte, and swallow a camel.
25 ¶ Wo *be* to you, Scribes and Pharises,
hypocrites: [m] for ye make cleane the vtter side of the cup, and of the platter: but
within thei are ful of briberie & " excesse.
26 Thou blinde Pharise, clense first the inside of the cup and platter, that the outside of them may be cleane also.
27 Wo *be* to you, Scribes and Pharises,
hypocrites: for ye are like vnto " whited
tombes, which appeare beautiful outwarde, but are within ful of dead mēs bones,
and of all filthines.
28 So are ye also: for outwarde ye appeare
righteous vnto men, but within ye are ful
of hypocrisie and iniquitie.
29 ¶ Wo *be* vnto you, Scribes and Pharises,
hypocrites: for ye buylde the tombes of
the [n] Prophetes, & garnish the sepulchres
of the righteous,
30 And say, If we had bene in the dayes of
our fathers, we wolde not haue bene parteners with them in the blood of the Prophetes.
31 So thē ye be witnesses vnto your selues,
that ye [o] are the children of them that
murthered the Prophetes.
32 Fulfil ye also ȳ measure of your fathers.
33 O serpents, the generacion of viperes,
how shulde ye escape ȳ damnacion of hel!
34 Wherefore beholde, I send vnto you
[p] Prophetes, and wise men, and Scribes, &
of them ye shal kil and crucifie: and of
thē shal ye scourge in your Synagogues,
and persecute from citie to citie,
35 That vpon [q] you may come all the righ
teous blood that was shed vpon ȳ earth,
* from the blood of Abel the righteous
vnto the blood [r] of Zacharias the sonne
of Barachias, * whome ye slewe betwene ȳ
Temple and the altar.
36 Verely I say vnto you, all these things
shal come vpon this generacion.
37 * Ierusalem, Ierusalem, which killest the
Prophetes & stonest them which are sent
to thee, how often wolde I haue gathered
thy children together, * as the henne gathereth her chickens vnder her wings, and
ye wolde not!
38 Beholde, your habitacion shalbe left
vnto you desolate.
39 For I saye vnto you, ye shal not se me
[s] hence forthe til that ye say, Blessed *is* he
that cometh in the Name of the Lord.

CHAP. XXIIII.

1 Christ sheweth his disciples the destruction of the Temple. 5. 24 The false Christs. 13 To perseuere. 14 The preaching of the Gospel. 6. 29 The signes of the end of the worlde. 42 He warneth them to wake. 44 The sudden comming of Christ.

1 AND * Iesus went out, & departed frō
the Temple, and his disciples came
to him, to shewe him the [a] buylding of the
Temple.
2 And Iesus said vnto them, Se ye not all
these things? Verely I say vnto you, * there
shal not be here left a stone vpon a stone,
that shal not be cast downe.
3 And as he sate vpon the mount of Oliues, his disciples came vnto him aparte,
saying, Tell vs when these things shalbe,
and what signe *shalbe* of thy comming,
[b] and of the end of the worlde.
4 And Iesus answered, and said vnto them,
* [c] Take hede that no man deceiue you.
5 For manie shal come in my Name, sayīg,
I am Christ, and shal deceiue manie.
6 And ye shal heare of warres, and rumors
of warres: se that ye be not troubled: for
all these things must come to passe, but
the end is not yet.

7 For

g Ye kepe backe the pure religion & knowledge of God when men are readie to embrace it.

Mar.12,40. luk.20,47.

h Which haue now their fote within the dores.

i They soght all meanes, ȳ thei colde inuent, to make of a Gentile a Iewe.

"*Or, is a detter.*

k And maketh it to be taken as an holie thing, because of the vse: and hereby Christ sheweth that mans doctrine doeth not onely obscure the worde of God, but is contrarie to it.

1.King.8,13. 2.chro.6,1.

Chap.5,34.

Luk.11,42.

l Ye staye at ȳ ẘ is nothing, & let passe that ẘ is of greater importance.

m Ye seke how to get estimacion with men and passe not whether ye haue a good conscience or no.

"*Or, intemperancie.*

"*Or, painted.*

n For a remēbrance of thē, & in the meane season they passed not for their doctrine.

o It is not now onely ȳ your nacion hathe begonne to be cruel against the seruants of God, & therefore it is no marueil thogh the children of suche murtherers handle roughly ȳ Prophetes.

p To conuince you of greater ingratitude.

Gen.4,8. ebr.11,44.

q Christ meneth that all their race shal be punished, so that the iniquitie of ȳ fathers shalbe powred into the bosome of the children, ẘ resemble their fathers.

r Read 2. Chro.24,22.

Luk.13,34. 2.Esdr.1,30.

s He wil returne no more to them, as a teacher, but as a iudge, when as they shalbe cōpelled to confesse (althogh to late) that he is the verie Sōne of God.

Chap. XXIIII.

Mar.13,1. luk.21,5.

a Whose excellencie appeareth in that that Herode for the space of 8. yeres kept 10000. men in worke, the stones were 15 cubites long, in height 12, in breadth 8, as Iosephus writeth.

Luk.19,44.

b Thei thoght ȳ worlde shulde be at an ēd, when Ierusalē were destroyed.

Ephe.5,6. coloss.2,28.

c He answereth them not according to their mindes, but admonisheth them of that which is necessarie for thē to knowe.

7 For nacion ſhal riſe againſt nacion, and
realme againſt realme, & there ſhalbe peſtilence, and famine, and earthquakes in
diuers places.
8 All theſe are but the [d] beginning of ſorowes.
9 *Then ſhal they deliuer you vp to be afflicted,and ſhal kil you,and ye ſhalbe [e] hated of all nacions for my Names ſake.
10 And then ſhal manie be offended,& ſhal
betray one another , and ſhal hate one
another.
11 And manie falſe prophetes ſhal ariſe,&
ſhal deceiue manie.
12 And becauſe [f] iniquitie ſhal be increaſed,the loue of manie ſhalbe colde.
13 *But he that endureth to the end,he ſhalbe ſaued.
14 And this Goſpel of the kingdome ſhalbe preached through the whole worlde
for a witnes vnto all nacions,and thē ſhal
the end come.
15 ¶When [g] ye*therefore ſhal ſe the [h] abomination of deſolation ſpoken of by*Daniel the Prophet,ſtāding in the holie place,(let him that readeth conſider it.)
16 Then let them which be in Iudea, flee
into the mountaines.
17 Let him wͨ is on the houſe top,not come
downe to fetch anie thing out of his houſe.
18 And he that is in the field, let not him
returne backe to fetch his clothes.
19 And wo *ſhalbe* to them that are with chil
de, and to them that giue ſucke in thoſe
dayes.
20 But pray that your flight be not in the
winter,nether on the "Sabbath *day*.
21 For then ſhalbe great tribulation, ſuche
as was not frō the beginning of the worlde to this time,nor ſhalbe.
22 And except thoſe dayes ſhulde be ſhortened, there ſhulde no "fleſh be ſaued: but
for the [i] electes ſake thoſe dayes ſhalbe
ſhortened.
23 *Then if anie ſhal ſay vnto you,Lo,here
is Chriſt,or there,beleue it not.
24 For there ſhal ariſe falſe Chriſts,& falſe prophetes, and ſhal ſhewe great ſignes
and wonders, ſo that if it were poſsible,
they ſhulde deceiue the verie elect.
25 Beholde,I haue tolde you before.
26 Wherefore if they ſhal ſay vnto you,
Beholde,he is in the [k] deſert,go not forthe:
Beholde,he is in the "ſecrete places,beleue
it not.
27 For as the lightning cometh out of the
Eaſt, and ſhineth in to the Weſt, ſo ſhal
alſo the comming of the Sonne of man be.
28 *For whereſoeuer a dead [l] carkeis is,thi-
ther wil the egles reſort.
29 *And immediatly after the [m] tribulatiōs
of thoſe dayes,ſhal the ſunne [n] be darkened,& the moone ſhal not giue her light,

d Great and cruel warres haue enſued ſince amongs the heathē for the contempt of the Goſpel and increaſe more & more.
Chap.10,17. luk.21,12. ioh.15,20. and 16,2.
e As if you were the cauſe of theſe troubles.
f Manie wil kepe backe their charitie , becauſe they are vnthankeful and euil,vpon whome they ſhulde beſtowe it.
2.Theſ.3,13. 2 tim.2,3. Mar.13,14 luk.22,20. Dan.9,27.
g When the Tēple ſhal be polluted, it ſhal be a ſigne of extreme deſolation: the ſacrifices ſhal end & neuer be reſtored.
h The horrible deſtructiō of the Temple & ẏ corruptiō of Gods pure religion.
Act.1,12. "Or, man.
i God prouideth for his childrē in the middes of troubles.
k Whither the falſe Chriſts, and deceiuers lead the people,hiding thē ſelues in holes as if they were aſhamed of their profeſsion.
Mar.13,21 luk.17,23. "Or, cloſettes.
l In deſpite of Satan ẏ faithful ſhal be gathered & ioyned wͭ Chriſt, as the egles aſſemble to a dead carkeis.
Luk.17,37. Mar.13,24. luk.21,25. iſa.13,10. eze.32,7. ioel 2,31. & 3,15.
m When God hathe made an end of ẏ troubles of his Church.
n He meaneth an horrible trēbling of ẏ worlde,& as it were, an alteration of ẏ order of nature.

and the ſtarres ſhal fall from heauen,& the
powers of heauen ſhalbe ſhaken.
30 And then ſhal appeare the ſigne of the
Sonne of man in heauen: and then ſhal all
the kinreds of the earth mourne, and they
ſhal ſe the Sonne of mā come in ẏ cloudes
of heauen with power and great glorie.
31 *And he ſhal ſend his Angels with a great
ſounde of a trumpet, and they ſhal gather
together his elect, from the foure windes
& from the one end of the heauen vnto
the other.
32 Now learne the parable of the figge tre:
whē her bough is yet tender,& it bringeth
forthe leaues, ye knowe ẏ ſommer *is* nere.
33 So likewiſe ye,whē ye ſe all theſe things,
knowe that *the kingdome of God* is nere, *euen*
at the dores.
34 Verely I ſay vnto you,this [o] generation
ſhal not paſſe,til all theſe things be done.
35 *Heauen and earth ſhal paſſe away: but
my wordes ſhal not paſſe away.
36 But of that day and houre knoweth no
man,no not the Angels of heauen, but my
Father onely.
37 But as the dayes of Noe *were*, ſo likewiſe
ſhal the comming of the Sonne of mā be.
38 *For as in the dayes *before* the flood they
did eat and drinke, mary,and giue in mariage,vnto the day that Noe entred into
the Arke,
39 And [p] knewe nothing, til the flood came
and toke them all awaye, ſo ſhal alſo the
comming of the Sonne of man be.
40 *[q] Thē two men ſhalbe in the fields, the
one ſhalbe receiued, and the other ſhalbe
refuſed.
41 Two women ſhalbe grinding at the mil:
the one ſhalbe receiued, & the other ſhalbe refuſed.
42 *Wake therefore : for ye knowe not
what houre your maſter wil come.
43 Of*this be ſure, that if the good man of
the houſe knewe at what watche the thief
wolde come , he wolde ſurely watche,
and not ſuffre his houſe to be digged
through.
44 Therefore be ye alſo readie: for in the
houre that ye thinke not, wil the Sonne of
man come.
45 *Who then is a faithful ſeruant & wiſe,
whome his maſter hathe made ruler ouer
his houſeholde,to giue thē meat in ſeaſon?
46 Bleſſed *is* that ſeruāt whome his maſter,
when he cometh,ſhal finde ſo doing.
47 Verely I ſay vnto you,he ſhal make him
ruler ouer all his goods.
48 But if that euil ſeruāt ſhal ſay in his heart,My maſter doeth deferre his cōming,
49 And begin to ſmite his felowes, and to
eat and to drinke with the drunken,
50 That ſeruants maſter wil come in a day,
when he loketh not for him, & in an houre

Reuel 1,7. 1.cor.15,52. 1 theſ.4,16.
o For within fiftie yeres after, Ieruſalem was deſtroied: ẏ godlie were perſecuted, falſe teachers ſeduced the people, religiō was polluted,ſo that ẏ worlde ſemed to be at an end.
Mar.13,32. Gene.7,5. luk.17,28. 1.pet.3,20.
p Becauſe of their incredulitie.
Luk.17,35. 1.theſ.4,17.
q This teacheth euerie man to walke warely not reſpecting his cōpaniō although he be neuer ſo dere vnto him.
Mar.13,35. Luk.12,39. 2.theſ.5,2. reuel.16,15 Luk.12,42.

that he is not ware of,
51 And wil "cut him of, and giue him his
portion with hypocrites: *there shalbe weping, and gnasshing of teeth.

"Or, separat him. Chap.13,42. & 25,30.

CHAP. XXV.

1 By the similitude of the virgines Iesus teacheth euerie man to watche. 14 And by the talents to be diligent. 31 The last iudgement. 32 The shepe and the goates. 35 The workes of the faithful.

1 Then the [a] kingdome of heauen shalbe likened vnto ten virgins, which toke their lampes, and went to [b] mete the
bridegrome.
2 And fiue of thē were wise, & fiue foolish.
3 The foolish toke their lāpes, but toke none oyle with them.
4 But ȳ wise toke oyle in their vessels with
their lampes.
5 Now while the bridegrome taryed long,
all slombred and slept.
6 And at midnight there was a crye made,
Beholde, the bridegrome cometh: go out to
mete him.
7 Then all those virgins arose, & trimmed
their lampes.
8 And the foolish said to the wise, [c] Giue vs
of your oyle, for our lampes are "out.
9 But the wise answered, saying, *We feare*
lest there wil not be ynough for vs & you:
but [d] go ye rather to them that sel, and bie
for your selues.
10 And while they went to bie, the bridegrome came: & they that were readie, wēt
in with him to the wedding, and the gate
was shut.
11 Afterwardes came also the other virgins,
saying, Lord, Lord, open to vs.
12 But he answered, and said, Verely I say
vnto you, [e] I knowe you not.
13 *Watche therefore: for ye knowe nether
the day, nor the houre, when the Sonne of
man wil come.
14 * [f] For *the kingdome of heauen is* as a man
that going into a strange countrey, called his seruants, and deliuered to them
his goods.
15 And vnto one he gaue fiue [g] talents, and
to another two, & to another one, to euerie
man after his owne habilitie, and straight
way went from home.
16 Then he that had receiued the fiue talents, went and occupied with them, and
"gained other fiue talents.
17 Likewise also, he that *receiued* two, he also gained other two.
18 But he that receiued that one, wēt & dig
ged it in ȳ earth, & hid his masters money.
19 But after a long season, ȳ master of those seruants came, and rekened with them.
20 Then came he that had receiued fiue talents, and broght other fiue talents, saying, Master, thou deliueredst vnto me fiue
talents: beholde, I haue gained with them
other fiue talents.
21 Then his master said vnto him, It is wel
done good seruāt and faithful, Thou hast
bene faithful in litle, I wil make thee ruler
ouer much: [h] entre in into thy masters ioy.
22 Also he that had receiued two talents, came & said, Master, thou deliueredst vnto
me two talents: beholde, I haue gained two
other talents with them.
23 His master said vnto him, It is wel done
good seruāt, and faithful, Thou hast bene
faithful in litle, I wil make thee ruler ouer
muche: enter in into thy masters ioye.
24 Then he which had receiued the one talent, came and said, Master, I knewe that
thou wast an hard mā, which reapest where thou sowedst not, and gatherest where
thou strawedst not:
25 I was therefore afraide, and went and
hid thy talent in the earth: beholde, thou
hast thine owne.
26 And his master answered, and said vnto
him, Thou euil seruant, & "slouthful, thou
knewest that I reap where I sowed not, and
gather where I strawed not.
27 Thou oghtest therefore to haue put my
money to the exchangers, and then at my
cōming shulde I haue receiued mine owne with vantage.
28 Take therefore the talent from him, and
giue it vnto him which hathe ten talents.
29 *For vnto euerie man that hathe, it shal
be giuen, and he shal haue abundance, and
[i] from him that hathe not, euē that he hathe, shalbe taken away.
30 *Cast therefore that vnprofitable seruant
into vtter *darkenes: there shalbe weping,
and gnasshing of teeth.
31 ¶ And when the Sonne of man cometh in
his glorie, and all the holie Angels ẇ him,
thē shal he sit vpon ȳ throne of his glorie.
32 And before him shalbe gathered all nacions, and he shal separate them one from
another, as a shepherde separateth the
shepe from the goates.
33 And he shal set the shepe on his right
hand, and the goates on the left.
34 Then shal the King say to them on his
right hand, Come ye [k] blessed of my Father: inherite ye ȳ kingdome prepared for
you frō the [l] fundations of the worlde.
35 *For [m] I was an hungred, and ye gaue me
meat: I thursted, and ye gaue me drinke: I
was a stranger, and ye lodged me:
36 *I was* naked, and ye clothed me, I was
* "sicke, and ye visited me: I was in prison,
and ye came vnto me.
37 Then shal the righteous answere him,
saying, Lord, when sawe we thee an hungred, and fed thee? or a thurst, and gaue
thee drinke?
38 And when sawe we thee a stranger, and
lodged thee? or naked, and clothed thee?

a This similitude teacheth vs, that it is not sufficient to haue once giuen our selues to follow Christ, but that we must continue.
b To do him honor, as the maner was.
c Manie seke that ẇ they haue contemned, but it is to late.
"Or, quenched.
d This was spoken in reproche, because they made not prouision in time.
e I wil not open to you because you haue failed in ȳ midde way.
Chap.24,43. mar.13,33. Luk.19,12.
f This similitude teacheth how we oght to continue in the knowledge of God, and do good with those graces ȳ God hathe giuē vs.
g Euerie talēt communely made threscore pounde, read chap.18,24.
"Or, made.
h The master receiueth him into his house to giue him parte of his goods and cōmodities.
"Or, lingerer.
Chap.13,12. luk.8,18. and 19,26. mar.4,25.
i The graces of God shalbe takē away frō hī that doeth not bestowe them to Gods glorie and his neighbours profite.
Chap.8,12. and 22,13.
k For our saluation cometh of the blessing and fauour of God.
l Hereby God declareth the certeinetie of our predestination, whereby we are saued because we were chosen in Christ before the fundacions of the worlde, Ephe.1,4.
Isa.58,7. eze.18,7. Eccl.7,39.
m Christ meaneth not that our saluation dependeth on our workes or merites, but teacheth what it is to liue iustly according to godlines, & charitie, and ȳ God recompēseth his of his fre mercie, likewise as he doeth elect them.
"Or, inferme.

39 Or when sawe we thee sicke, or in prison, and came vnto thee?
40 And the King shal answere and say vnto
them, Verely I say vnto you, in as muche
as ye haue done it vnto one of the least of
these my brethren, ye haue done it to me.
41 Then shal he say vnto them on the left
hand, * Departe from me ye cursed, into
euerlasting fyre which is prepared for the
deuil and his angels.

Psal.6,9. chap.7,23. luk 13,27.

42 For I was an hungred, & ye gaue me no
meat: I thursted, & ye gaue me no drinke:
43 I was a stranger, and ye lodged me not:
I was naked, and ye clothed me not: sicke,
and in prison, and ye visited me not.
44 Thẽ shal they also answere him, saying,
Lord, when saw we thee an hungred, or a
thurst, or a strãger, or naked, or sicke, or in
prison, and did not minister vnto thee?
45 Thẽ shal he answer them, & say, Verely
I sai vnto you, in as muche as ye did it not
to one of ye least of these, ye did it not to me
46 * And these [n] shal go into euerlasting
paine, and the righteous into life eternal.

Dan.12,2. iohn 5,29

n We muste therefore onely do that, w God requireth of vs, and not followe mens foolish fantasies.

CHAP. XXVI.

3 Conspiracie of the Priests against Christ. 10 He excuseth Magdalene. 26 The institution of the Lords supper. 31 The disciples weakenes. 48 The traison of Iudas. 62 The sworde. 64 Because Christ calleth him self the Sonne of God, he is iudged worthie to dye. 69 Peter denieth, and repenteth.

1 AND * it came to passe, whẽ Iesus had
finished all these sayings, he said vnto his disciples,

Mar.14,1. luk.22,1.

2 Ye knowe that within two dayes is the
Passeouer, and the Sonne of man shalbe
deliuered to be crucified.
3 * Then assembled together ye chief Priests
and the Scribes, and the Elders of the
people into the hall of the high Priest, called Caiaphas,

Ioh.11,47.

4 And consulted how they might take Iesus by subtiltie, and kill him.
5 But they said, Not on the feast *day*, lest
anie vprore be among the people.
6 ¶ * And when Iesus was in Bethania, in
the house of Simon the leper,
7 There came vnto him a womã, which had
a boxe of verie costelie ointemẽt, & [a] powred it on his head, as he sate at the table.
8 And whẽ his disciples sawe it, thei had [b] indignation, saying, What neded this waste?
9 For this ointment might haue bene solde
for muche, and bene giuen to the poore.
10 And Iesus knowing it, said vnto them,
Why trouble ye the woman? for she hathe
wroght a good worke vpon me.
11 * For ye haue the poore alwayes with you,
but me shal ye not [c] haue alwayes.
12 For in that she powred this ointment on
my bodie, she did it to [d] burye me.
13 Verely I say vnto you, Wheresoeuer this
Gospel shalbe preached throughout all ye
worlde, there shal also this that she hathe
done, be spoken of for a memorial of her.

Mar.14,3. iohn 11,2. and 12,3.

a He sheweth what occasion Iudas toke to commit his traison.

b This was through Iudas motiõ to whome they gaue credit.

Deu.15,11.

c This fact was extraordinarie, nether was it left as an example to be followed: also Christ is not present w vs bodelie or to be honoured with anie outwarde põpe.

d To honour my buryal with all.

14 ¶ * Then one of the twelue, called Iudas
Iscariot, went vnto the chief Priests,

Mar.14,10. luk.22,4.

15 And said, What wil ye giue me, and I wil
deliuer him vnto you? and they appointed
vnto him thirtie [e] *pieces* of siluer.

e Euery one in value was about foure pẽce halfe pennie of olde sterling.

16 And from that time, he soght opportunitie to betraye him.
17 ¶ * Now on ye first *day* of the feast of vnleauened bread ye disciples came to Iesus,
saying vnto him, Where wilt thou that we
prepare for thee to eat the Passeouer?

Mar.14,12. luk.22,7.

18 And he said, Go into the citie to suche a
man, & say to him, The master saith, [f] My
time is at hand: I wil kepe the Passeouer
at thine house with my disciples.

f He maketh haste to a more worthie sacrifice, to wit, to that which the Passeouer signified.

19 And the disciples did as Iesus had giuen
them charge, and made ready the Passeouer.
20 * So when the euen was come, he sate
downe with the twelue.
21 And as they did eat, he said, Verely I say
vnto you, that one of you shal betraye me.

Mar.14,18. luk.22,14. iohn 13,21.

22 And they were exceading sorowful, and
began euerie one of them to say vnto him,
Is it I, Master?
23 And he answered and said, He that [g] dippeth his hand with me in the dish, he shal
betraye me.
24 Surely the Sonne of man goeth his way,
[h] as it is written of him: but wo *be* to that
man, by whome the Sonne of man is betrayed: it had bene good for that mã, if he
had neuer bene borne.

g He that is accustomed to eat with me daily at the table, Psal. 41,9.

h To the intẽt his disciples might knowe that all this was appointed by the prouidence of God.

25 Then Iudas which betrayed him, answered, and said, Is it I, Master? He said vnto
him, Thou hast said it.
26 ¶ * And as they did eat, Iesus toke the
bread: and when he had giuen thankes, he
brake it, and gaue it to the disciples, and
said, Take, eat: [i] this is my bodie.
27 Also he toke ye cup, & when he had giuen
thankes, he gaue it them, saying, Drinke
ye all of it.
28 For this is my [k] blood of the Newe testament, that is shed for manie, for the remission of sinnes.
29 I say vnto you, that [l] I wil not drinke
hence forthe of this frute of the vine vntil
that day, when I shal drinke it newe with
you in my Fathers kingdome.

1.Cor.11,24.

i That is, a true signe and testimonie that my bodie is made yours, and by me your soules are nourished.

k The wine signifieth that our soules are refreshed and satiffied with the blood of Christ, spiritually receiued, so that without him we haue no nourishment.

l You shal no more enioye my bodelie presence til we mete together in heauen.

30 And when they had sung a psalme, they
went out into the mount of oliues.
31 ¶ * Then said Iesus vnto them, All ye shal
be [m] offended by me this night: for it is
written, I * wil smite the shepherd, and
the shepe of the flocke shalbe scattred.

Mar.14,27. iohn 16,32. & 18,8.

m Shal turne backe and be discouraged.

Zach 13,7.

32 But * after I am risen againe, I wil go
before you into Galile.

Mar. 14, 28. & 16,7.

33 But Peter answered, and said vnto him,
[n] Thogh that all men shulde be offended
by thee, yet wil I neuer be offended.

n This declareth what danger it is to trust to muche to our owne strength.

34 *Iesus said vnto him, Verely I say vnto
thee, that this night, before ẏ cocke crowe,
thou shalt denie me thrise.
35 Peter said vnto him, Thogh I shulde dye
with thee, yet wil I not denie thee. Likewise also said all the disciples.
36 ¶*Then wẽt Iesus with thẽ into a place
which is called Gethsemane, and said vnto his disciples, Sit ye here, while I go and
pray yonder.
37 And he toke Peter, and the two sonnes
of Zebedeus, and begã to waxe sorowful,
[o] and grieuously troubled.
38 Then said Iesus vnto them, My soul is
verie heauie *euen* vnto the [p] death: tarie ye
here, and watche with me.
39 So he went a litle further, and fel on his
face, and prayed, saying, O my Father,
if it be possible, let this [q] cup [r] passe from
me: neuertheles, not as I wil, but as thou
wilt.
40 After he came vnto the disciples, and
founde thẽ a slepe, & said to Peter, What?
colde ye not watche with me one houre?
41 Watch, and pray, that ye enter not into
tentation: the spirit in dede is readie, but
the flesh is [s] weake.
42 Againe he wẽt away the secõde time &
prayed, saying, O my Father, if this cup cã
not passe away from me, but that I must
drinke it, thy wil be done.
43 And he came, and founde them a slepe
againe: for their eyes were heauie.
44 So he left them and went away againe,
and prayed the third time, saying the same wordes.
45 Then came he to his disciples, and said
vnto them, [t] Slepe henceforthe, and take
your rest: beholde, the houre is at hand,
and the Sonne of man is giuen into the
hands of sinners.
46 [u] Rise, let vs go: beholde, he is at hand
that betrayeth me.
47 *And while he yet spake, lo, Iudas, one
of the twelue, came, and with him a great
multitude with swordes and staues, from
the high Priests and Elders of the people.
48 Now he that betrayed him, had giuen
them a token, saying, Whomesoeuer I shal
kisse, that is he, lay holde on him.
49 And forthewith he came to Iesus, and
said, "God saue thee, Master, & kissed him.
50 Then Iesus said vnto him, [x] Friend,
wherefore art thou come? Thẽ came they,
and laid hands on Iesus, and toke him.
51 And beholde, one of them which were
with Iesus, stretched out *his* hand, & drewe
his sworde, and stroke a seruant of the high
Priest, and smote of his eare.
52 Then said Iesus vnto him, Put vp thy
sworde into his "place: *for all that
[y] take the sworde, shal perishe with the
sworde.

Iohn 13,38
Mar.14,32. luk.22,39.
o He feared not death of it self, but trẽbled for feare of Gods anger towarde sinne, the burden whereof he bare for our sakes.
p For he sawe Gods angre kindled towardes vs.
q That is, the angre of God for mans sinnes.
r He knewe wel what his Father had determined, and therefore was ready to obey but he prayeth as ẏ faithful do in their troubles without respect of the eternal counsel of God.
s And therefore we must continually fight against the flesh.
t He speaketh this in a contrarie sense, meaning they shulde anone be wel wakened.
u Christ dyed willingly, and therefore presented himself to his enemies.
Mar.14,43 luk.22,47. iohn 18,3.
*Or, Haile, rabbi.
x He rebuketh his vnkindenes vnder the cloke of pretensed friendshippe.
*Or, sheathe.
Gen.9,6. reuel.13,10.
y The exercising of the sworde is forbidde to priuate persones. Also he wolde haue hindered by his indiscrete zeale the worke of God.

53 Ether thinkest thou, that I can not now
pray to my Father, and he wil giue me mo
then twelue [z] legions of Angels?
54 How then shulde the * Scriptures be fulfilled, *which say*, that it must be so?
55 The same houre said Iesus to the multitu
de, Ye be come out as *it were* against a
thief, with swordes and staues, to take me:
I sate daily teaching in the Temple amõg
you, and ye toke me not.
56 But all this was done, that the * Scriptures of ẏ Prophetes might be fulfilled. *Thẽ
all the disciples forsoke him, and fled.
57 ¶*And they toke Iesus, and led him to
Caiaphas the hie Priest, where the Scribes
and the Elders were assembled.
58 And Peter followed him a farre of vnto
the hie Priests hall, and went in, & sate with
the seruants to se the end.
59 Now *the chief Priests & the Elders, and
all the whole council [a] soght false witnes
against Iesus, to put him to death.
60 But they founde none, and thogh many
false witnesses came, yet founde they [b] none: but at the last came two false witnesses,
61 And said, This man said, *I can destroy
the Temple of God, and buylde it in thre
dayes.
62 Then the chief Priest arose, and said to
him, Answerest thou nothing? What is the
matter that these men witnes against thee?
63 But Iesus [c] helde his peace. Then the
chief Priest answered, and said to him, I
[d] charge thee by the liuing God, that thou
tell vs, if thou be the Christ the Sonne of
God.
64 *Iesus said to him, [e] Thou hast said it:
neuertheles I say vnto you, hereafter shal
ye se the Sonne of man, sitting at the right
hand of the power of *God*, and come in the
cloudes of the heauen.
65 Then the hie Priest rent his [f] clothes, saying, He hathe [g] blasphemed: what haue we
any more nede of witnesses? beholde, now
ye haue heard his blasphemie.
66 What thinke ye? They answered, & said,
He is worthie to dye.
67 *Then spat they in his face, and buffeted him: and [h] other smote him with their
roddes,
68 Saying, [i] Prophecie to vs, ô Christ, Who
is he that smote thee?
69 ¶*Peter sate without in ẏ hall: & a maide
came to him, saying, Thou also wast with
Iesus of Galile.
70 But he denied before them all, saying, I
wot not what thou saist.
71 And when he went out into the porche,
another *maide* sawe him, and said vnto
them that were there, This man was also
with Iesus of Nazaret.
72 And [k] againe he denyed with an othe,
saying, I knowe not the man.

z Euery legiõ conteined communely 6000. footemen, and 732. horsemen. whereby here he meaneth an infinit nomber
Isa.53,10.
Lamen.4,20
Chap.20,3. Mar.14,53. luk.22,54. iohn 18,14.
Mar.14,55.
a He declareth how Iesus was wrõgfully accused, to the end that we may knowe his innocencie, and not that he suffered for him self, but for vs.
b Which colde iustely witnes against him.
Iohn 2,19.
c Christ did neglect their false reportes and more ouer he was not there to defend his cause, but to suffer condemnation.
d Or adiure thee by thine allegeance towards God.
e Christ cõfesseth that he is the Sonne of God.
Chap.16,27. rom.14,10. 1.thes.4,16.
f This was one of their owne traditions, if they had heard any Israelite blaspheme.
g The ennemies of God call a true confessiõ blasphemie.
Isa.50,6.
h The officers smite Christ with their roddes or litle staues.
i They mocked him after this sorte that he might not seme to be a Prophet, and so wolde turne the peoples mindes from him.
Mar.14,66. luk.22,55. iohn 18,25.
k An example of our infirmitie that we may learne to depende vpon God and not put our trust in our selues.

73 So after a while, came vnto him thei that
stode by, and said vnto Peter, Surely thou
art also one of them: for euen thy speache
bewrayeth thee.
74 Then began he to curse *him self*, and to
sweare, saying, I knowe not the man. And
immediatly the cocke crewe.
75 Then Peter remembred the wordes of
Iesus, which had said vnto him, Before the
cocke crowe, thou shalt deny me thrise. So
he went out, and [l] wept bitterly.

[l] He was liuely touched with repentance by the motion of Gods Spirit, who neuer suffereth his to perish vtterly, thogh for a time they fall, to the intent they may fele their owne weaknes & acknolege his great mercie.

CHAP. XXVII.

2 Christ is deliuered vnto Pilate. 5 Iudas hangeth him self. 24 Christ is pronounced innocent by the iudge, and yet is condemned, and crucified among thieues. 46 He prayeth vpon the crosse. 51 The vaile is rent. 52 The dead bodies arise. 57 Ioseph buryeth Christ. 64 Watchmen kepe the graue.

Mar.15,1. luk.22,66. iohn 17,20.

1 WHen* the morning was come, all
the chief Priests, & the Elders of
the people toke counsel against Iesus, to
put him to death,
2 And led him away bounde, and [a] deliuered
him vnto Pontius Pilate the gouernour.
3 ¶ Then when Iudas which betrayed him,
sawe that he was condemned, [b] he repented
him self, and broght againe the thirtie
pieces of siluer to the chief Priests, and
Elders,
4 Saying, I haue [c] sinned betraying the
innocēt blood. But they said, What is that
to vs? [d] se thou to it.
5 And whē he had cast downe the siluer *pieces*
in the Temple, he departed, and went,
*and hanged him self.
6 And the chief Priests toke the siluer *pieces*,
and said, It is not [e] lawful for vs to put
them into the *treasure, because it is the
price of blood.
7 And they toke counsel, and boght with
them a potters field, for the buryal of
[f] strangers.
8 Wherefore that field is called, * the field
of blood, vntil this day.
9 (Then was fulfilled that which was spoken
by Ieremias the Prophet, saying, *And
they toke thirtie siluer *pieces*, the price of
him that was valued, whome *they* of the
children of Israel valued.
10 And thei gaue them for the potters field,
as the Lord appointed me.)
11 ¶ *And Iesus stode before the gouernour,
and the gouernour asked him, saying, Art
thou the King of ẏ Iewes? Iesus said vnto
him, Thou saist it.
12 And when he was accused of the chief
Priests and Elders, he answered nothing.
13 Thē said Pilate vnto him, Hearest thou
not how many things they laye against
thee?
14 But he answered him not to one worde,
in so muche that the gouernour marueiled
greatly.

[a] For they had no autoritie to condemne him or to put any to death.
[b] Ouer late repentāce bringeth despaire-tion.
[c] Althogh he abhorre his sinnes, yet is he not displeased there with, but dispaireth in Gods mercies, and seketh his owne destruction.
Act.1,18.
[d] These hypocrites laye the whole faute vpon Iudas.
[e] The hypocrites are full of conscience in a matter of nothing, but to shede innocēt blood they make nothing at it.
Or, corbana.
Act.1,19.
Zach.11,13.
[f] For ẏ Iewes thoght it a great offence to be buryed in the same place that the strangers were
Mar.15,3. luk.23,3. iohn 18,33.

15 Now at the feast, ẏ gouernour was wont
to *deliuer vnto the people a [g] prisoner,
whome they wolde.
16 And they had thē a notable prisoner, called
Barabbas.
17 *When they were then gathered together,
Pilate said vnto them, Whether wil
ye that I let loose vnto you Barabbas, or
Iesus which is called Christ?
18 (For he knewe wel, that for enuie they
had deliuered him.
19 Also whē he was set downe vpō the iudgemēt
seat, his wife sent to him, saying, [h] Haue
thou nothing to do with that iuste man:
for I haue suffered many things this day in
a dreame by reason of him.)
20 *But the chief Priests & the Elders had
persuaded the people that thei shulde aske
Barabbas, and shulde destroy Iesus.
21 Then the gouernour answered, and said
vnto them, Whether of the twaine wil ye
that I let loose vnto you? And they said,
[i] Barabbas.
22 Pilate said vnto them, What shal I do
then with Iesus which is called Christ?
Thei all said to him, Let him be crucified.
23 Then said the gouernour, But what euil
hathe he done? Then thei cryed the more,
saying, Let him be crucified.
24 When Pilate sawe that he auailed nothing,
but that more tumulte was made, he
toke water and wasshed his hands before
the multitude, saying, I am innocent of
the blood of this [k] iust man: loke you to it.
25 Then answered all the people, and said,
His [l] blood *be* on vs, and on our children.
26 Thus let he Barabbas loose vnto them,
and scourged Iesus, and deliuered him to
be crucified.
27 ¶ *Thē the souldiours of the gouernour
toke Iesus into the commune hall, and gathered
about him the whole bande.
28 And thei stripped him, & put vpon him a
[m] skarlet robe,
29 And platted a crowne of thornes, and
put it vpō his head, and a rede in his right
hand, and bowed their knees before him,
and mocked him, saying, God saue thee
King of the Iewes,
30 And spitted vpon him, and toke a rede,
and smote him on the head.
31 Thus when they had mocked him, they
toke the robe from him, and put his owne
raiment on him, and led him away to crucifie
him.
32 *And as they came out, they founde a
man of Cyrene, named Simon: him they
compelled to beare his crosse.
33 * And when they came vnto the place called
Golgotha, (that is to say, the place of
dead mens skulles.)
34 Thei gaue him [n] vineger to drinke, mingled
with gall: and when he had tasted the-

*Or, quite.
[g] It was a tradition of the Iewes to deliuer a prisoner at Easter.
[h] This was to the greater cōdemnation of Pilate, whome neither his owne knowledge colde teache, nor counsel of others, to defende Christs innocencie.
Mar.15,11. luk.23,18. ioh.18,40. act.3,14.
[i] The multitude preferre the wicked to the righteous.
[k] Pilate beareth witnes ẏ he is innocent, before he condemne him.
[l] If his death be not lawful, let the punishment fall on our heades & our childrens. and as they wished, so this curse taketh place to this day.
Mar.15,16. iohn 19,1.
[m] To deride him, because he called him self a King.
Mar.15,21. luk.23,26.
Iohn 19,16.
[n] It was a kinde of drinke to open the vaines, and so to hasten his death, which was giuen him vpon ẏ crosse.

reof,he wolde not drinke.
35 ¶And when they had crucified him,they
parted his garments,& did cast lottes,that
it might be fulfilled, which was spoken by
the Prophet,*They deuided my garmēts
among them, and vpon my vesture did
cast lottes.
36 And they sate,and watched him there.
37 ¶Thei set vp also ouer his head his cause written,[o] THIS IS IESVS THE
KING OF THE IEWES.
38 ¶And there were two thieues crucified
with him, one on the right hand, and another on the left.
39 And they that passed by, reuiled him,
wagging their heads,
40 And saying, * Thou that destroyest the
Temple,and buyldest it in thre dayes, saue thy self: if thou be the Sonne of God,
come downe from the crosse.
41 Likewise also the hie Priests mocking
him,with the Scribes,and Elders,and Pharises,said,
42 He saued others, *but* he can not saue him
self: if he be the King of Israel, let him
now come downe from the crosse, and we
wil beleue him.
43 *He[p] trusteth in God, let him deliuer
him now, if he wil haue him: for he said,I
am the Sonne of God.
44 That same also the[q] thieues which were
crucified with him,cast in his teeth.
45 Now from the [r] sixt houre was there
darkenes ouer all the [s] land, vnto the ninth
houre.
46 And about the ninth houre Iesus cryed
with a loude voyce,sayīg,*Eli,Eli,lama sa-
bacthani? that is,[t] My God,my God, why
hast thou forsaken me?
47 And some of them that stode there,whē
thei heard it,said,This man calleth[u] Elias.
48 And straight way one of them ran, and
toke* a sponge, and filled it with vineger,
and put it on a "rede, and gaue him to
drinke.
49 Other said,Let be: let vs se, if Elias wil
come and saue him.
50 Then Iesus cryed againe with a loude
voyce,and yelded vp the [x] gost.
51 And beholde ,* the [y] vaile of the Temple was rent in twayne, from the top to the
bottome,and the earth did quake,and the
stones were clouen,
52 And the graues did open them selues , &
many bodies of the Sainctes which slept,
arose,
53 And came out of the graues after his resurrection,and went into the "holie Citie,
and appeared vnto many.
54 When the Centurion , & they that were
with him watching Iesus , sawe the earth-

Psal.22,19. mar.15,24.

o The maner then was to set vp a writing to signifie wherefore a man was executed: but here God gouerned Pilates hand to write otherwise then he thoght.

Iohn 2,19.

Psal.22,9. wis.2,28.

p This was a great tētation, to go about to take from him his truste in God,and so to bring him to despaire.

q Meaning by this synechdoche the one of the theeues.

r That was frō none til thre of the clocke

s Of Iewrie and the countrey there about.

Psal.22,2.

t Notwithstanding that he feeleth him self as it were wounded with Gods wrath and forsaken for our sinnes, yet he ceaseth not to put his cōfidēce ī God and call vpon him: which is writen to teache vs in all afflictiōs to trust stil in God, be the assautes neuer so grieuous to the flesh.

u They mocked at Christs prayer, as if it had bene in vaine.

Psal.69,22.

"Or, hyssope stalke, Iohn 19,29.

x Voluntarely after he had obeyed his Father in all things. *1.Chro.3,14. y Which signified an end of all the ceremonies of the Lawe. "Or, Ierusalem.

quake,and the things that were done,they
feared greatly , saying, Truely [z] this was
the Sonne of God.
55 ¶And many women were there , beholding him a farre of, which had followed
Iesus from Galile,ministring vnto him.
56 Among whome was Marie Magdalene,
and Marie the mother of Iames & Ioses,
and the mother of Zebedeus sonnes.
57 ¶*And when the euen was come , there
came a [a] riche man of Arimathea, named
Ioseph , who had also him self bene Iesus
disciple.
58 He went to Pilate , and asked the bodie
of Iesus. Then Pilate commanded the bodie to be deliuered.
59 So Ioseph toke the bodie,and wrapped it
in a cleane linnen cloth,
60 And put it in his newe [b] tombe,which he
had hewen out in a rocke , & rolled a great
stone to the dore of the sepulchre , and departed.
61 And there was Marie Magdalene , and
the other Marie sitting ouer against the
sepulchre.
62 ¶Now the next day that followed the
[c]Preparation *of the Sabbath*,the hie Priests
and Pharises assembled to Pilate,
63 And said, Sir,we remember that that deceiuer said, while he was yet aliue , Within thre dayes I wil rise.
64 Commande therefore,that the sepulchre
be made sure vntil ÿ thirde day,lest his dis
ciples come by night , & steale him away,
and say vnto the people, He is risen from
the dead: so shal the last [d] errour be worse
then the first.
65 Then Pilate said vnto them, Ye haue [e] a
watche: go,and make it sure as ye knowe.
66 And they went , and made the sepulchre
[f] sure with the watche,and sealed the stone.

CHAP. XXVIII.

6 The resurrection of Christ. 10 The brethren of Christ. 12 The hie Priests bribe the souldiers. 17 Christ appeareth to his disciples, and sendeth thē forthe to preache,and to baptize. 20 Promising to them continual assistance.

1 NOw * in the "end of the [a] Sabbath,
whē the first *day* of the weke began
to dawne,Marie Magdalene, and the other
Marie came to se the sepulchre.
2 And beholde, there was a great earthquake : for the [b] Angel of the Lord descended
frō heauen, and came and rolled backe the
stone from the dore,and sate vpon it.
3 And his countenance was like lightning,
and his raiment white as snowe.
4 And for feare of him , the kepers were a-
stonied,and became as dead men.
5 But the Angel answered , and said to the
women, Feare ye not : for I knowe that ye
seke Iesus which was crucified:
6 He is not here, for he is risen, as he said:
come,

z This iudgemēt of an heathen man was sufficient to condemne the grosse malice of the Iewes.

Mar.15,42. luk.23,50. iohn 19,38.

a Who was so muche the more in danger by declaring him self to be Iesus disciple.

b Christs burying doeth so much more verifie his death & resurrectiō.

c Which was the day before the Sabbath

d More wil folow his doctrine then did afore he was put to death.

e That is,men appointed for the keping of the Temple.

f The more ÿ men go aboute to subdue Christs power ÿ more shewe they their owne malice,and procure to thē selues ÿ greater condemnation, for as muche as Gods glorie the more appeareth thereby.

Mar.16,1. iohn 20,11.

"Or, euening.

a Here the Euangeliste reckeneth the natural day from the sunne rising to his rising againe, & not as the Iewes did, w began to count at the first houre after the sunne set.

b There were two: but it is a maner of speache to vse the singular nōber for ÿ plural, and contrarie.

come, se the place where ẏ Lord was laid,
7 And go quickely, and tell his disciples
that he is risen from the dead: and beholde, he goeth before you into Galile:
there ye shal se him:[c] lo, I haue tolde you.
8 So they departed quickely from the sepulchre with feare and great [d] ioye, & did
runne to bring his disciples worde.
9 And as they went to tell his disciples, beholde, Iesus also met them, saying, God
saue you. And they came, and toke him by
the fete, and worshipped him.
10 Then said Iesus vnto them, Be not a-
fraied. Go, *and* tell my brethren, that thei
go into Galile, and there shal they se me.
11 ¶ Now when they were gone, beholde,
some of the watche came into the citie, &
shewed vnto the hie Priests all ẏ things
that were done.
12 And thei gathered them together with
the Elders, and toke counsel, & gaue large
money vnto the souldiers,
13 Saying, Say, His disciples came by night
and stole him away while we slept.
14 And if ẏ gouernour heare of this, we wil
persuade him, and saue you harmeles.
15 So they toke the money, & did as they
were taught: and this [e] saying is noised
among the Iewes vnto this day.
16 ¶ Then the eleuen disciples went into
Galile, into a mountaine, where Iesus had
appointed them.
17 And when they sawe him, they worshipped him: but some douted.
18 And Iesus came, and spake vnto them,
saying, * All power is giuen vnto me in
heauen, and in earth.
19 * Go therefore, and teache all nacions,
baptizing them in the Name of the Father, and the Sonne, and the holie Gost,
20 Teaching them to obserue all things,
whatsoeuer I [f] haue commanded you: &
lo, * I am with you alway, vntil the [g] end
of the worlde, Amen.

c He assureth them ẏ it is so.

d Their ioye was mixt with feare, bothe be cause of ẏ Angels presence, & also for that thei were not assured.

e An extreme vengeance of God, whereby the Iewes were ẏ more hardened, so that thei cā not fele the profite of his death & resurrection.

Ebr.1,3.
chap.11,27.
iohn 17,2.
Mar.16,15.

f Men maie not teache their owne doctrine, but whatsoeuer Christ hathe taught thē: for he reserueth this autoritie to hi self, to be ẏ onelie teacher and autor of ẏ doctrine.

Iohn 14,16.

g By power, grace and vertue of the holie Gost.

THE HOLY GOSPEL
of Iesus Christ, according to Marke.

CHAP. I.

a The office, doctrine & life of Iohn the Baptiste. 9 Christ is baptized, 13 And tempted. 14 He preacheth. 17 Calleth the fishers. 23 Christ healeth the man with the vncleane spirit. 27 New doctrine. 29 He healeth Peters mother in law. 34 The deuils knewe him. 41 He clenseth the leper, and healeth diuers others.

1 The [a] beginning of the
Gospel of Iesus Christ,
the Sonne of God:
2 As it is written in the
Prophetes, * Beholde, I
send my [b] messenger be-
fore thy face, which shal
prepare thy way before thee.
3 * The voyce of him that cryeth in ẏ wildernes *is*, [c] Prepare the way of the Lord:
make his paths straight.
4 * Iohn did baptize in the wildernes, and
[d] preache the baptisme of amendement
of life, for remission of sinnes.
5 And all the countrey of Iudea, and they
of Ierusalem went out vnto him, and were
all baptized of him in the riuer Iordan,
confessing their sinnes.
6 Now Iohn was clothed with camels heere, and with a girdle of a skinne about his
loines: and he did eat ″ * locustes & wilde
honie,
7 * And preached, saying, A stronger then
I, cometh after me, whose shoes latchet I
am not worthie to stoup downe, & vnlose.

a He sheweth ẏ Iohn Baptist was the first preacher of the Gospel.

Malac.3,1.

b In Greke, Angel, or Ambassadour.

Isa.40,3.
luk.3,4.
iohn 1,15.
Mat.3,4.

c Take awaye all lettes, ẇ might hinder Christ to come to you.

d He did bothe baptize & preache, but preached first, & after baptized, as appeareth by Mat. 3,1: so that the ordre is here inuerted, which thing is commune in the Scriptures.

″*Or, grasshoppers.*
Leui.11,22.
Mat.3,12.
luk.3,16.
iohn 1,27.

8 Trueth it is, I haue * baptized you with
[e] water: but he wil baptize you with the
holie Gost.
9 ¶ * And it came to passe in those dayes,
that Iesus came from Nazaret *a citie* of
Galile, and was baptized of Iohn in Iordan.
10 And assone as ″ he was come out of the
water, *Iohn* sawe the heauens clouen in
twaine, and the [f] holie Gost descending
vpon him like a doue.
11 Then there was a voyce from heauen,
saying, Thou art my beloued [g] Sonne, in
whome I am wel pleased.
12 * And immediatly the ″ Spirit driueth
him into the wildernes.
13 And he was there in the wildernes fortie
daies, and was [h] tempted of Satan: he was
also with the wilde beasts, and the Angels
ministred vnto him.
14 ¶ * Now after that Iohn was committed
to prison, Iesus came into Galile, preaching
[i] the Gospel of the kingdome of God,
15 And saying, The time is fulfilled, and
the kingdome of God is at hand: repent
and beleue the Gospel.
16 ¶ * And as he walked by the ″ sea of Galile, he sawe Simon, and Andrewe his brother, casting a nette into the sea, (for they
were fishers.)
17 Thē Iesus said vnto them, Followe me,

Act.1,5.& 2,4.& 11,16.& 19,4.
Mat.3,14.
luk.3,22.
iohn 1,33.

e He declareth that he is but the minister of the outwarde signe, and ẏ it is Iesus Christ that giueth the force & vertue.

″*Or, Iesus.*

f This was done for the confirmaciō of Iohn and them that stode bye.

Mat.4,1.
luk.4,1.

g The Father beareth witnes that Christ is the verie Sonne of God.

″*Or, the holie Gost.*

h Christ wolde be tempted to persuade vs, ẏ he wil helpe them that be tempted, Ebr. 2,18.

Mat.4,12.
luk.4,14.
iohn 4,43.

i By ẏ which Gospel he wil rule & reigne ouer all.

Mat.4,18.
luk.5,2.
″*Or, lake.*

and I wil make you to be [k] fishers of men.
18 And straight waye they forsoke their
nettes, and followed him.
19 And when he had gone a litle further
thence, he sawe Iames *the sonne* of Zebedeus, and Iohn is brother, as they were in
the shippe, mending their nettes.
20 And anone he called them: and they
left their father Zebedeus in the ship with
his hyred seruants, and went their way after him.
21 ¶ So *they entred into Capernaum, and
straight way on the Sabbath daye he entred into the Synagogue and taught.
22 And they were astonied at his doctrine:
* for he taught them as one that had autoritie, and [l] not as the Scribes.
23 ¶ And there was in their Synagogue a mā
which had an vncleane spirit, & he cryed,
24 Saying, Ah, what haue we to do with
thee, ô Iesus of Nazaret? Art thou come
to destroy vs? I knowe thee what thou art,
euen that holie one of God.
25 And Iesus rebuked him, saying, [m] Holde thy peace, and come out of him.
26 And the vncleane spirit tare him, and
cryed with a loude voyce, and came out
of him.
27 And they were all amased, so that they
demanded one of another, saying, What
thing is this? what [n] new doctrine is this?
for he commandeth the foule spirits with
autoritie, and they obey him.
28 And immediatly his fame spred abroad
throughout all the region bordering on
Galile.
29 ¶ *And assone as they were come out of
the Synagogue, they entred into the house of Simon and Andrewe, with Iames &
Iohn.
30 And Simons wiues mother in law laye
sicke of a feuer, and anone they tolde him
of her.
31 And he came & toke her by the hand, &
lift her vp, and the feuer forsoke her by &
by, and she ministred vnto them.
32 And when euen was come, and the sunne
was downe, they broght to him all that
were diseased, and them that were possessed with deuils.
33 And the whole citie was gathered together at the dore.
34 And he healed manie that were sicke of
diuers diseases: and he cast out manie deuils, & [o] suffred not the deuils to say that
they knewe him.
35 And in the morning verie earely, "before day *Iesus* arose and went out into a solitarie place, and there praied.
36 And Simon, and thei that were with him,
followed after him.
37 And when they had founde him, they
said vnto him, All men seke for thee.

k To drawe them from perdicion.

Mat.4,23. luk.4,31.

Mat.7,28. luk.4,32.

l Whose doctrine was dead, & nothing sauoured of the spirit.

m Christ wolde not suffer the father of lyes to beare witnes to the trueth.

n Thei referre the miracle to the kinde of doctrine, & so marueil at it, as a newe and strange thing, and do not cōsider the power of Christ, who is the autor of the one and the other.

Mat.8,14. luk.4,32.

o Christ wolde not haue suche witnesses to preache him & his Gospel. So Paule was offended that ẏ Pythonesse shulde testifie of him, Act. 16,18.

"*Or, being yet night.*

38 Then he said vnto them, Let vs go into
the next townes, that I may preache there also: for I came out for that purpose.
39 And he preached in their Synagogues,
throughout all Galile, and cast the deuils
out.
40 ¶ *And there came a leper to him, beseching him, and kneled downe vnto him, &
said to him, If thou wilt, thou canst make
me cleane.
41 And Iesus had compassion, and put forthe his hand, and touched him, and said
to him, I wil: be thou cleane.
42 And assone as he had spoken, immediatly the leprosie departed from him, and he
was made cleane.
43 And after he had giuen him a streict
[p] commandement, he sent him awaye forthewith,
44 And said vnto him, Se thou say nothing
to anie man, but get thee hence, & shewe
thy self to [q] the * Priest, and offer for thy
clensing those things, which Moses commanded, for a [r] testimonial vnto them.
45 But when he was departed, * he beganne
to tel manie things, and to publish the
matter: so that Iesus [s] colde no more o-
penly enter into the citie, but was without in desert places: and they came to
him from euerie quarter.

Mat.8,1. luk.5,12.

p Forbidding him to tell anie man, because as yet his time was not come to be knowen.

Leui.14,4.

q It belonged to the Priest to knowe if a mā were healed of the leprosie.

Luk.5,18.

r To take all maner of excuse from them, & to condēne them of ingratitude.

s The preasse was so great, that he shulde haue bene thronged.

CHAP. II.

3 He healeth the man of the palsie. 5 He forgiueth sinnes. 14 He calleth Leui the customer. 16 He eateth with sinners. 18 He excuseth his disciples, as touching fasting, and keping the Sabbath daye.

1 After * *a fewe* dayes, he entred into
Capernaum againe, and it was noy-
sed that he was in the [a] house.
2 And anone, manie gathered together, in
so muche that the places about the dore
colde not receiue anie more: and he preached the worde vnto them.
3 And there came vnto him, that broght
one sicke of the palsie, borne of foure
men.
4 And because they colde not come nere
vnto him for the multitude, they vncouered the rofe of the house where he was:
and when they had broken it open, thei let
downe the bed, wherein the sicke of the
palsie laye.
5 Now when Iesus sawe their faith, he said
to the sicke of the palsie, Sonne, thy [b] sinnes are forgiuen thee.
6 And there were certeine of the Scribes,
sitting there, and reasoning in their hearts,
7 Why doeth this man speake suche blasphemies? * who can forgiue sinnes, but
God onelie?
8 And immediatly when Iesus perceiued
in his spirit, that thus they thoght with
thē selues, he said vnto thē, Why reason
ye

Mat.9,1. luk.5,18.

a Where he was wonte to remaine.

b By these wordes Christ shewed that he was sent of his Father ẇ autoritie to take away our sinnes.

Iob.14,4. isa.43,15.

ye these things in your hearts?
9 [c]Whether is it easier to say to the sicke of
the palsie, Thy sinnes are forgiuen thee?
or to say, Arise, and take vp thy bed, and
walke?
10 And that ye may knowe, that the Sonne
of man hathe autoritie in earth to forgiue
sinnes, (he said vnto ẏ sicke of the palsie.)
11 I say vnto thee, Arise & take vp thy bed,
and get thee hence into thine owne house.
12 And by and by he arose, and toke vp his
bed, and went forthe before them all, insomuche that they were all amased, and
glorified God, saying, [d]We neuer sawe suche a thing.
13 ¶Then he went againe towarde the sea,
and all the people resorted vnto him, and
he taught them.
14 *And as Iesus passed by, he sawe Leui *the
sonne* of Alpheus sit at the receite of custome, & said vnto him, Followe me. And
he arose and followed him.
15 ¶And it came to passe, as Iesus sate at
table in his house, many Publicanes & sinners sate at table also ẇ Iesus, & his disciples: for there were many ẏ followed him.
16 And when the Scribes and Pharises sawe
him eat with ẏ Publicanes & sinners, they
said vnto his disciples, How is it, that he
eateth and drinketh with Publicanes and
sinners?
17 Now when Iesus heard it, he said vnto them, The whole haue no nede of the
physicion, but the sicke. *I came not to call
the [e]righteous, but the sinners to repentance.
18 *And the disciples of Iohn, & the Pharises did fast, and came and said vnto him,
Why do the disciples of Iohn and of the
Pharises fast, and thy disciples fast not?
19 And Iesus said vnto them, Can the [f]chil-
dren of the mariage chamber fast, whiles
the bridegrome is with them? as long as
they haue the bridegrome with them, they
can not fast.
20 But the dayes wil come, when the bridegrome shalbe taken from them, and then
shal they fast in those dayes.
21 Also no mã soweth a piece [g]of new cloth
in an olde garment: for els the new *piece*
taketh away the filling vp from the olde,
and the breache is worse.
22 Likewise, no man putteth new wine into
olde vessels: for els the new wine breaketh
the vessels, and the wine runneth out, and
the vessels are lost: but new wine must be
put into new vessels.
23 ¶*And it came to passe as he wẽt through
the corne on the Sabbath day, that his disci
ples, as they went on their way, began to
plucke the eares of corne.
24 And the Pharises said vnto him, Beholde, why do they on the Sabbath day, that
which is not lawful?
25 And he said to them, Haue ye neuer
red what *Dauid did, when he had nede,
and was an hungred, *bothe* he, and they that
were with him?
26 How he went into the house of God, in
the dayes of [h]Abiathar the hie Priest, and
did eat the shewe bread, which were not
lawful to eat, but for the *Priests, and gaue
also to them which were with him?
27 And he said to them, The Sabbath was
[i]made for man, and not man for the Sabbath.
28 Wherefore the Sonne of man is Lord,
euen of the Sabbath.

CHAP. III.

*1 He healeth the man with the dryed hand. 14 He cho-
seth his Apostles. 21 Christ is thoght of the worldelings
to be besides him self. 22 He casteth out the vncleane
spirit, which the Pharises ascribe vnto the deuil.
29 Blasphemie against the holie Gost. 35 The brother,
sister and mother of Christ.*

1 AND *he entred againe into the Synagogue, and there was a man which
had a withered hand.
2 And they watched him, whether he wolde
heale him on the Sabbath day, that they
might accuse him.
3 Then he said vnto the man which had
the withered hand, Arise: *stand forthe* in
the middes.
4 And he said to them, Is it lawful to do a
good dede on the Sabbath day, or to do
euil? to saue ẏ life, or to kil? But thei [a]helde
their peace.
5 Then he loked rounde about on them [b]an
gerly, mourning also for the hardenes of
their hearts, and said to the man, Stretch
forthe thine hãd. And he stretched it out:
and his hand was restored, as whole as the
other.
6 ¶And the Pharises departed, & straight
waye gathered a councel with the [c]Hero-
dians against him, that they might destroye him.
7 But Iesus auoyded with his disciples to
the sea: and a great multitude followed
him from Galile, and from Iudea,
8 And from Ierusalem, and from Idumea,
and beyonde Iordan: and they that dwelled about Tyrus and Sidon, when thei had
heard what great things he did, came vnto
him in great nomber.
9 And he commanded his disciples, that
a ship shulde waite for him, because of the
multitude, lest they shulde throng him.
10 For he had healed many, insomuche that
they preassed vpon him, to touche him as
many as had [*]plagues.
11 And when the vncleane spirits sawe him,
they fel downe before him, and cryed, saying, Thou art the Sonne of God.
12 And he sharpely rebuked thẽ, to the end
they shulde not vtter him.

[c] Christ speaketh according to their capacitie, who were so blinde that they wolde beleeue nothing, but that which they saw with their eyes, and therefore sheweth his autoritie ouer the soule by the power which he hathe ouer the bodie.

[d] Their owne consciences cause them to confesse the trueth.

Mat. 9, 9. luk. 5, 27.

1. Tim. 1, 13.

[e] He speaketh of suche as persuade them selues to be iuste although they be nothing lesse.

Mat. 9, 14. luk. 5, 33.

[f] Christ sheweth that he wil spare his & not burden them before it be necessarie

[g] The worde properly signifieth newe clothe which as yet hathe not passed the hãdes of the fuller.

Mat. 12, 1. luk. 6, 1.

1. Sam. 21, 6.

[h] He was also called Achimelech, as his father was, so that bothe the father and the sonne were called by bothe these names, 1. Chron. 24, 2. 2. Sam 8, 17. & 15, 29. 1. king. 2, 26.

Exod. 29, 33. leuit. 8, 31. & 24, 9.

[i] Seing ẏ Sabbath was made for mans vse, it was not mete it shulde be vsed to his hinderance, & incommoditie.

Mat. 12, 9. luk. 6, 6.

[a] They helde their tongues of malice: for they wolde nether confesse nor denie.

[b] Christ is in suche sorte angrie with man that he pitieth him & seketh to winne him.

[c] Although they hated one another deadly, yet this hindered thẽ, not to ioine their malice to resiste Christ, read Mat. 22, 16.

[*] *Or, scourges, meaning diseases.*

13 ¶*Then he went vp into a mountaine, &
called vnto him whome he wolde, & they
came vnto him.
14 And he appointed twelue that they ſhulde be with him, and that he might ſend thẽ
to preache,
15 And that they might haue power to heale ſickeneſſes, and to caſt out deuils.
16 And the firſt *was* Simon, & he named Simon, Peter.
17 Then Iames *the ſonne* of Zebedeus, and
Iohn, Iames brother (& named them Boanerges, which is the ſonnes of thunder.)
18 And Andrew, and Philippe, and Bartle-
mew, and Matthewe, & Thomas, and Iames, *the ſonne* of Alpheus, and "Thaddeus
and Simon the "Cananite.
19 And Iudas Iſcariot, who alſo betrayed
him, and they came [d] home.
20 And the multitude aſſembled againe, ſo
that they colde not ſomuche as eat bread.
21 And whẽ "his kinſfolkes heard of it, they
went out to lay [e] holde on him: for they
thoght he had bene beſide him ſelf.
22 ¶*And the Scribes which came from Ieruſalem, ſaid, He hathe Beelzebub, and
through the prince of deuils he caſteth out
deuils.
23 But he called them vnto him, and ſaid
vnto thẽ in parables, How can Satan driue out Satan?
24 For if a kingdome be deuided againſt it
ſelf, that kingdome can not ſtand.
25 Or if a houſe be deuided againſt it ſelf,
that houſe can not continue.
26 So if Satan make inſurrectiõ againſt him
ſelf, & be deuided, he can not endure, but
is at an end.
27 No mã can entre into a ſtrong mans hou
ſe, and take away his goods, except he firſt
binde that ſtrong man, and then ſpoile
his houſe.
28 ¶*Verely I ſay vnto you, all ſinnes ſhal
be forgiuen vnto the children of men, and
blaſphemies, wherewith they blaſpheme:
29 But he that [f] blaſphemeth againſt the ho
ly Goſt, ſhal neuer haue forgiuenes, but is
culpable of eternal damnation,
30 Becauſe they ſaid, He had an vncleane
ſpirit.
31 ¶*Then came his "brethren and mother,
and ſtode without, and ſent vnto him, and
called him.
32 And the people ſate about him, and they
ſaid vnto him, Beholde, thy mother, & thy
brethren ſeke for thee without.
33 But he anſwered thẽ, ſaying, Who is my
mother and my brethren?
34 And he loked rounde about on thẽ, which
ſate in compaſſe about him, and ſaid, Beholde my mother and my brethren.
35 For whoſoeuer doeth the wil of God, he
is my brother, and my ſiſter, and mother.

Chap.6,7. mat.10,1. luk.9,1.

"Or, Lebbeus, or Iudas.
"Or, zealous.

d The diſciples were now conuerſant with Chriſt bothe at home and abroad.
"Or, they that were about him.
Mat.9,34. & 12,4. luk.11,14.
e His kinſfolkes wolde haue ſhut him within dores, leſt any harme ſhulde haue come vnto them, if any tumulte had bene made: for ſome wolde haue made him a King, & the Phariſes with others ſoght his life: ſo that hereby they might haue procured ẏ hatred of Herode, and of the Phariſes and of the Romains.

Mat.12,38. luk.12,10. 1.iohn 5,16.

f Which is, when a man fighteth againſt his owne conſcience, & ſtriueth againſt the trueth which is reueiled vnto him: for ſuche one is in a reprobate ſenſe and can not come to repentance.
Mat.12,46. luk.8,19.
"Or, couſins.

CHAP. IIII.

2 By the parables of the ſede, and the muſtarde corne, Chriſt ſheweth the ſtate of the kingdome of God. 11 A ſpecial gift of God to knowe the myſteries of his kingdome. 37 He ſtilleth the tempeſte of the ſea which obeyed him.

1 AND*he begã againe to teache by the
ſea ſide, & there gathered vnto him
a great multitude, ſo that he entred into a
ſhip, and ſate in the ſea, and all the people
was by the ſea ſide on the land.
2 And he taught them many things in parables, and ſaid vnto them in [a] "his doctrine.
3 Hearken: Beholde, there went out a ſower
to ſowe.
4 And it came to paſſe as he ſowed, that ſome fel by the way ſide, & the foules of the
heauen came and deuoured it vp.
5 And ſome fel on ſtonie grounde, where it
had not muche earth, & by and by ſprang
vp, becauſe it had not depth of earth.
6 But aſſone as the ſunne was vp, it caught
heate, and becauſe it had not roote, it withered away.
7 And ſome fel among the thornes, and
the thornes grewe vp and choked it, ſo that
it gaue no frute.
8 Some againe fel in good grounde, and
did yelde frute that ſprong vp, and grew,
and it broght forthe, ſome thirtie folde,
ſome ſixtie folde, and ſome an hundreth
folde.
9 Then he ſaid vnto them, He that hathe
[b] eares to heare, let him heare.
10 And when he was alone, they that were
about him with the twelue, aſked him of
the parable.
11 And he ſaid vnto them, To [c] you it is giuen to knowe the myſterie of the kingdome of God: but vnto them that are [d] without, all things be done in parables,
12 *That they ſeing, may ſe, and not diſcerne: and they hearing, may heare, and
not vnderſtand, leſt at any time they ſhulde turne, and their ſinnes ſhulde be forgiuen them.
13 Againe he ſaid vnto them, Perceiue ye
not this parable? how thẽ ſhulde ye vnderſtand all *other* parables?
14 The ſower ſoweth the worde.
15 And theſe are they that *receiue the ſede*
by the wayes ſide, in whome the worde is
ſowen: but when they haue heard it, Satan
cometh immediatly, and taketh away the
worde that was ſowen in their hearts.
16 And likewiſe they that receiue ẏ ſede in
ſtonie grounde, are they, which when they
haue heard the worde, ſtraight wayes recei
ue it with gladnes.
17 Yet haue they no roote in them ſelues,
and endure but a time: *for* when trouble
and perſecution ariſeth for the worde, immediatly

Mat.13,1. luk.8,4.

a It is called Chriſts doctrine, either for that he was accuſtomed to ſpeake vnto them by ſimilitudes: or els becauſe it had ẏ vertue & maieſtie that men colde not denie but it came from heauen.
"Or, as he taught.

b For God doeth not opẽ all mens heartes to vnderſtand his myſteries.
c Which are led by the Spirit of God.
d And are not of the nomber of the faithful, nether atteine to the pith and ſubſtance, but onely ſtaye in the outwarde rinde and barke.
Iſa.6,9. mat.13,14. luk.8,10. iohn 12,40. act.28,26. rom.11,8.

mediatly they be offended.
18 Also they that receiue the sede among
the thornes, are suche as heare the worde:
19 But the cares of this worlde, and the
*disceifulnes of riches, and the lustes of
other things entre in, & choke the worde,
and it is vnfruteful.
20 But they that haue receiued sede in good
grounde, are they that heare the worde
and receiue it, and bring forthe frute, one
corne thirtie, another sixtie, and some an
hundreth.
21 ¶ Also he said vnto them, * Is [e] the candle" light to be put vnder a busshel, or
vnder the table, and not to be put on a
candlesticke?
22 *[f] For there is nothing hid, that shal not
be opened: nether is there a secret, but that
it shal come to light.
23 If any man haue eares to heare, let him
heare.
24 And he said vnto them, Take hede what
ye heare. * With [g] what measure ye mette,
it shalbe measured vnto you: & vnto you
that heare, shal more be giuen.
25 *For vnto him that hathe, shal it be giué,
and from him that hathe not, shalbe taken
away, [h] euen that he hathe.
26 ¶ Also he said, So is the [i] kingdome of
God, as if a man shulde [k] cast sede in the
grounde,
27 And shulde slepe, and rise vp night and
day, and the sede shulde spring and grow
vp, he not knowing how.
28 For the earth bringeth forthe frute of
her self, first the blade, then the eares, after
that ful corne in the eares.
29 And assone as the frute sheweth it self,
anone he putteth in the sickel, because the
haruest is come.
30 ¶ *He said moreouer, Whereunto shal
we liken the kingdome of God? or with
what comparison shal we compare it?
31 *It is* like a graine of mustarde sede, which
when it is sowen in the earth, is the least of
all sedes that be in the earth:
32 But after that it is sowen, it groweth vp,
and is greatest of all herbes, and beareth
great brãches, so that the foules of heauen
may buylde vnder the shadow of it.
33 And *with many suche parables he preached the worde vnto them, as they were
able to heare it.
34 And without parables spake he nothing
vnto them: but he expounded all things to
his disciples aparte.
35 ¶ *Now the same day when euen was come, he said vnto them, Let vs passe ouer
vnto the other side.
36 And they left the multitude, and [l] toke
him as he was in the ship: and there were
also with him other shippes.
37 And there arose a great storme of winde,

1.Tim.6,17.

Mat.5,15. luk.8,16. & 11,33.
e Christ setteth before their eyes the true patron of a Christiã life.
"Or, broght.
Mat.10,26. luk.8,17. & 12,2.
f We may not take occasion to do euil vnder colour to hideour doĩgs: for all shal be disclosed at the length.
Mat.7,2. luk.6,38.
g If you do your endeuour faithfully, ye shal be recompensed iustely.
Mat.13,12. & 25,29. luk.8,18. & 9,26.
h That which he thinketh him self to haue.
i These two similitudes following proue, that althogh the kingdome of God semeth to haue very litle appearance or beginning, yet God doeth increase it aboue mans reason.
Mat.13,31. luk.13,19.
k If the ministers do their duetie, God wil giue ỹ increase.
Mat.13,34.
Mat.8,23. luk.8,22.
l And set forwarde.

& the waues dashed into the ship, so that
it was now ful.
38 And he was in the sterne [m] a slepe on a
pillowe: and they awoke him, and said to
him, Master, carest thou not that we perish?
39 And he rose vp, and rebuked the winde,
and said vnto the sea, Peace, and be stil.
So the winde ceased, and it was a great
calme.
40 Then he said vnto them, Why are ye so
fearful?" how is it that ye haue no faith?
41 And they feared excedingly, & said one
to another, Who is this, that bothe the
winde and the sea obey him?

m Christ leaueth vs oftẽ times to our selues, bothe aswel that we may learne to knowe our owne weakenes, as his mightie power
"Or, haue you not yet faithe

CHAP. V.

8 Iesus casteth the deuils out of the man and suffereth them to enter into the swine. 25 He healeth a woman from the bloodie yssue. 41 And raiseth the captaines daughter.

1 AND *they came ouer to the other
side of the sea into the countrey of
the Gadarens.
2 And when he was come out of the ship,
there met him incontinently out of the gra
ues, a man which had an vncleane spirit:
3 Who had his abyding among the graues, and no man colde binde him, no not
with chaines,
4 Because that when he was often bounde
with fetters and chaines, he plucked ỹ chai
nes a sondre, and brake the fetters in pieces, nether colde anie man tame him.
5 And alwayes bothe night & day he cryed
in the mountaines, and in the graues, and
stroke him self with stones.
6 And when he saw Iesus a farre of, he ranne, and worshipped him,
7 And cryed with a loude voyce, and said,
[a] What haue I to do with thee, Iesus, the
Sonne of the moste high God? " I charge thee by [b] God, that thou torment me
not.
8 (For he said vnto him, Come out of the
man, thou vncleane spirit.)
9 And he asked him, What is thy name? &
he answered saying, My name *is* [c] Legion:
for we are manie.
10 And he prayed him instãtly, ỹ he wolde
not send them away out of the countrey.
11 Now there was there in the moũtaines a
great herd of swine, feeding.
12 And all the deuils besoght him, saying,
Send vs into the swine, that we may entre
into them.
13 And incontinently Iesus gaue them leaue. Then the vncleane spirits went out &
entred into the swine, and the herd" ran
headling from the high bãke into the sea,
(& there were about two thousand swine)
and they were drowned in the" sea.
14 And the swineherds fled and tolde it in
the citie, & in the countrey, & they came

Mat.8,28. luk.8,26.
a The deuil is coustrained to confesse Iesus Christ, and yet ceaseth not to resist him.
"Or, adiure thee to sweare by God.
b He abuseth the Name of God, to mainteine his tyrannie.
c A Legion cõteined aboue 6000 in nomber, read Mat. 26,53.
"Or, ran with violence headlong.
"Or, in the lake.

out to se what it was that was done.
15 And they came to Iesus, and sawe him
that had bene possessed with the deuil, and
had the legion, sit bothe clothed, & in his
right minde: & they were afraid.
16 And they that sawe it, tolde them, what
was done to him that was possessed with
the deuil, and concerning the swine.
17 Then [d] they began to praye him, that he
wolde [e] departe from their coastes.
18 And when he was come into the ship, he
that had bene possessed with the deuil,
prayed him that he might be with him.
19 Howbeit, Iesus wolde not suffre him, but
said vnto him, Go thy way home to thy
friends, and [f] shewe thē what great things
the Lord hathe done vnto thee, and *how* he
hathe had compassion on thee.
20 So he departed, and began to publish in
"Decapolis, what great thīgs Iesus had done vnto him: and all men did marueil.
21 ¶ And when Iesus was come ouer againe
by ship vnto the other side, a great multitude gathered to him, and he was nere vnto the sea.
22 *And beholde, there came one of the
rulers of the Synagogue, whose name was
Iairus: and when he sawe him, he fel downe
at his fete,
23 And besoght him instantly, saying, My
litle daughter lieth at point of death: *I
praye thee* that thou woldest come & laye
thine hāds on her, that she may be healed,
and liue.
24 Then he went with him, and a great mul
titude followed him, and thronged him.
25 (And there was a certeine woman, which
was diseased with an yssue of blood twelue yeres,
26 And had suffered many things of many
physicions, and had spent all that she had,
and it auailed her nothing, but she became
muche worse.
27 When she had heard of Iesus, she came
in the preasse behinde, and [g] touched his
garment.
28 For she said, If I may but touche his clothes, I shal be whole,
29 And straight way "the course of her blood
was dryed vp, & she "felt in her bodie, that
she was healed of that "plague.
30 And immediatly when Iesus did knowe
in him self the vertue that wēt out of him,
he turned him roūde about in the preasse,
and said, Who hathe touched my clothes?
31 And his disciples said vnto him, Thou
seest the multitude throng thee, & sayest
thou, Who did touche me?
32 And he loked rounde about, to se her that
had done that.
33 And the woman feared and trembled: for
she knewe what was done in her, & she came and fel downe before him, & tolde him
the whole trueth.

d Marke how loue of riches and worldelie respects hinder men to receiue Christ.
e The worldelings more esteme their swine, then they do Iesus Christ.
f We must declare vnto others the benefites which God sheweth towardes vs, that thereby they may giue him praise and glorie.
"Or, in the countrey of the ten cities.
*Mat.9,18. luk.8,41.
g Her faith broght her to Christ and moued her to approche nere vnto him, & not a superstitious opinion, to attribute any vertue to his garment.
"Or, fountaine.
"Or, knewe.
"Or, scourge.

34 And he said to her, Daughter, thy faith
hathe made thee whole: go in peace, and
be whole of thy "plague.)
35 While he yet spake, there came from the
same ruler of the Synagogues house *certeine* which said, Thy daughter is dead: why
diseasest thou the Master anie further?
36 Assone as Iesus heard that worde spoken,
he said vnto the ruler of the Synagogue,
Be not afraide: onely beleue.
37 And he suffered no man to followe him,
saue Peter and Iames, and Iohn the brother of Iames.
38 So he came vnto the house of the ruler
of the Synagogue, and sawe the tumulte, &
them that wept and wailed greatly.
39 And he went in, & said vnto them, Why
make ye this trouble, and wepe? the childe is not [h] dead, but slepeth.
40 And they [i] laught him to scorne: but he
put them all out, and toke the father, and
the mother of the childe, and [k] them that
were with him, & entred in where the chil
de laye,
41 And toke the childe by the hand, & said
vnto her, Talitha cumi, which is by interpretation, Maiden, I say vnto thee, arise.
42 And straight way the maiden arose, and
walked: for she was of the age of twelue
yeres, and they were astonied out of measure.
43 And he charged them straitely that no
man shulde knowe of it, and commanded
to giue her meat.

CHAP. VI.

4 How Christ and his are receiued in their owne countrey. 7 The Apostles commission. 15 Sondrie opinions of Christ. 25 Iohn is put to death, and buryed. 31 Christ giueth rest to his disciples. 38 The fiue loaues and two fisshes. 48 Christ walketh on the water. 55 He healeth manie.

1 AFterwarde *he departed thēce, & came into his owne countrey, and his
disciples followed him.
2 And when the Sabbath was come, he began to teache in the Synagogue, & manie
that heard him, were astonied, & said, [a] Frō
whence hathe he these things? & what wisdome is this that is giuen vnto him, that
euen "suche great workes are done by his
hands!
3 Is not this the carpenter Maries sonne,
the "brother of Iames and Ioses, and of Iuda and Simon? and are not his sisters here
with vs? And they were [b] offended in him.
4 Then Iesus said vnto them, A *Prophet
is not without honour, but in his owne coū
trey, and among his owne kinred, & in his
owne house.
5 And [c] he colde there [d] do no great workes
saue that he laid his hands vpon a fewe
sicke folke, and healed *them*.
6 *And he marueiled at their vnbeliefe,
and went about by the townes on euerie
side,

"Or, scourge.
h He ment, she was not dead to remaine so because she shulde incontinently be restored againe to life.
i For thei had no hope to se her liue againe.
k That is, his thre disciples.
*Mat.13,54. luk.4,16.
a Christ is neglected of his owne friends, and kinsfolkes.
"Or, miracles.
"Or, cousin.
b That which oght to moue thē to come to Christ, causeth thē to go backe from him, w cometh of their owne wickednes.
*Mat.13,57. luk.4,24. ioh.4,44.
c That is, he wolde not.
d Lacke of faith maketh vs vnable to receiue Gods benefites.
*Mat.4,35. luk.13,22.

side, teaching.
7 ¶ *And he called the twelue, and began to
send them two & two, and gaue thẽ power
ouer vncleane spirits,
8 And commanded them, that they shulde
take nothing for *their* iorney, saue a staffe
onely: nether [e] scrip, nether bread, nether
money in their "girdles,
9 But that thei shulde be shod w^t *[f] sandals,
& that they shulde not put on two coates.
10 And he said vnto them, Wheresoeuer
ye shal entre into an house, there abide til
ye departe [g] thence.
11 * And whosoeuer shal not receiue you,
nor heare you, whẽ ye depart thẽce, [h] *shake of ỹ dust that is vnder your feete, for a
witnes vnto thẽ. Verely I say vnto you, It
shalbe easier for Sodom, or Gomorrha at
the day of iudgement, then for that citie.
12 ¶ And they went out and preached, that
men shulde amende their liues.
13 And they cast out manie deuils: and they
*anointed manie that were sicke, with [i] oyle
and healed *them*.
14 ¶ *Then King Herode heard *of him* (for
his name was spred abroade) & said, Iohn
Baptist is risen againe frõ the dead & therefore great workes are wroght by him.
15 Other said, It is Elias: and some said, It
is a Prophet, or as one [k] of the Prophetes.
16 *So when Herode heard it, he said, It is
Iohn whome I beheaded: he is [l] risen frõ
the dead.
17 For Herode him self had sent forthe, &
had taken Iohn, and bounde him in prison
for Herodias sake, which was his brother
Philippes wife, because he had maried her.
18 For Iohn said vnto Herode, *It is not
[m] lawful for thee to haue thy brothers
wife.
19 Therefore Herodias had a quarel a-
gainst him, & wolde haue killed him, but
she colde not:
20 For Herode feared Iohn, knowing that
he *was* a iuste man, and an holie, and reuerenced him, & when he heard him, he did
manie things, and [n] heard him gladly.
21 But the time being conuenient, when
Herode on his birth day made a banket
to his princes & captaines, and chief estates of Galile:
22 And the daughter of the same Herodias
came in and [o] danced, and pleased Herode
and them that sate at table together, the
King said vnto ỹ maide, Aske of me what
thou wilt, and I wil giue it thee.
23 And he sware vnto her, Whatsoeuer
thou shalt aske of me, I wil giue it thee,
euen vnto the halfe of my kingdome.
24 *So she went forthe, and said to her mother, What shal I aske? And she said, Iohn
Baptists head.
25 Thẽ she came in straight way with haste

Mat.10,1. chap.3,14. luk.9,1.

e Christ onely forbiddeth them to carye anie thing, w^c might be burdenous, or hinder their message.

"Or, purses.

Act.12,8.

f Which were a kide of light shoes tied to the feete with strings.

Mat.10,14. luk.9,5. Act.13,51. & 18,6.

g He forbiddeth curiositie in changing their lodginges in this their speady message.

h In token of execration, & of the horrible vengeance of God which shal light vpõ them.

Iam.5,14. Mat.14,1. luk.9,7.

i The oyle was a signe of this miraculo^s working, and not a medicine to heale diseases: so that ỹ gift of miracles ceasing, the ceremonie is to no vse.

Luk.3,19.

k Meaning, of the olde Prophetes.

l They had then this cõmune error, ỹ they thoght ỹ soules being departed out of one bodie went straight into another.

Leu.18,16. and 20,21.

m The libertie that Iohn vsed to reproue vice without acception of persone, declareth how the true ministers oght to behaue them selues.

n Suche is the nature of Gods worde, ỹ it cõpelleth ỹ verie tyrants to reuerence it: as no doute the King had some good motions, but the seede fel in stonie places & so toke no roote.

o What inconuenience cometh by wanton dancing.

Mat.14,8.

vnto the King, and asked, saying, I wolde
that thou shuldest giue me euen now in a
charger the head of Iohn Baptist.
26 Then the King was verie sorye: *yet* for
his othes sake, and for their sakes which
sate at table with him, he wolde not refuse her.
27 And immediatly the King sent the hãg-
man, and gaue charge that his head shulde be broght. So he went & beheaded him
in the prison,
28 And broght his head in a charger, and
gaue it to the [p] maide, and the maide gaue
it to her mother.
29 And when his disciples heard it, they came and toke vp his " bodie, and put it in a
tombe.
30 ¶ *And the Apostles gathered them selues together to Iesus, and [q] tolde him all
things, bothe what they had done, & what
they had taught.
31 And he said vnto them, Come ye aparte
into the wildernes, [r] and reste a while: for
there were manie commers & goers, that
they had not leasure to eat.
32 *So they went by ship out of the way into a desert place.
33 But the people sawe thẽ when they departed, & manie knewe him, & ranne a foote
thither out of all cities, and came thither
before them, and assembled vnto him.
34 *Then Iesus went out, and sawe a great
multitude, and had cõpassion on them, because they were like [s] shepe which had no
shepherde: *and he began to teache them
manie things.
35 *And when the day was now farre spent,
his disciples came vnto him, saying, This
is a desert place, and now the day is farre
passed.
36 Let them departe, that they may go into
the villages and townes about, & bye thẽ
bread: for they haue nothing to eat?
37 But he answered, & said vnto them, Giue ye them to eat. And thei said vnto him,
Shal we go and bye [t] two hundreth penie
worthe of bread, and giue them to eat?
38 *Then he said vnto them, How manie
loaues haue ye? go and loke. And whẽ thei
knewe it, they said, Fiue, and two fisshes.
39 So he commanded them, to make them
all sit downe by "companies vpon the grene grasse.
40 Then they sate downe by [u] rowes, by hũdreths, and by fifties.
41 And he toke the fiue loaues, and the two
fisshes, & loked vp to heauen, & gaue thãkes & brake the loaues, & gaue them to his
disciples to set before them, and the two
fisshes he deuided among them all.
42 So they did all eat, and were satisfied.
43 And they toke vp twelue baskettes ful
of the fragments, and of the fisshes.

p Ioseph^s calleth her name Salomen, the daughter of Philippe, and Herodias.

"Or, carkeis.

Luk.9,10.

q The Apostles rendre cõute of their message, w^c is to declare their fidelitie and obedience.

r Christ beareth with the infirmitie of his seruants, & bringeth them to quietnes, ỹ he may instruct them & make them strong against troubles.

Mat.14,13. luk.9,10. Mat.9,36. & 14,14. Luk.9,11. Mat.14,15.

s This declareth ỹ there is an horrible disordre amõg ỹ people, where the true preaching of Gods worde wanteth.

t Which is about fiue poũde sterling.

Mat.14,17. luk.9,13. iohn 6,9.

"Or, by table fulls: for in euerie rãke were as manie as a table colde holde.

u The Greke worde signifieth suche beddes as are made in a gardẽ, so that the companie, w^c were there set, might seme as rowes or orders of beddes in a garden.

44 And they that had eaten, were about fiue thousand men.
45 ¶ And straight way he caused his disciples to go into the ship, and to go before
vnto the other side vnto Bethsaida, while
he sent away the people.
46 Then assone as he had sent them away,
he departed into a mountaine to pray.

Mat.14,13. ioh.6,15.

47 *And when euen was come, the ship was
in the middes of the sea, and he alone on
the land.
48 And he sawe them troubled in rowing,
(for the winde was cōtrarie vnto them) &
about the fourth [x] watche of the night, he
came vnto them, walking vpon the sea, &
wolde haue passed by them.

x Which was about two or thre houres before day.

49 And when thei sawe him walking vpon
the sea, they supposed it had bene a spirit,
and cryed out.
50 For they all sawe him, and were sore a-
fraide: but anone he talked with them, and
said vnto them, Be [y] of good comfort: it is
I, be not afraide.

y Christ assureth his & maketh the bolde, bothe by his worde, and mightie power

51 Then he went vp vnto them into the
ship, and the winde ceased, and they were
sore amased in them selues beyonde measure, and marueiled.
52 [z] For they had not considered *the matter*
of the loaues, because their hearts were
hardened.

z They had for got the miracle which was wroght wᵗ ẏ fiue loaues.

Mat.14,34.

53 ¶ *And they came ouer, and wēt into the
land of Gennesaret, and arriued.
54 So whē they were come out of the ship,
straight way they knewe him,
55 And ranne about throughout all that region round about, & began to carye hither & thither in beddes all that were sicke, where they heard that he was.
56 And whither soeuer he entred into townes, or cities, or villages, they laid their
sicke in the " stretes, and prayed him that
they might touche at the least the [a] edge
of his garment. And as manie as touched
him, were made whole.

"Or, markets.

a Not for anie suche vertue that was in his garment, but for ẏ confidence which they had in him.

CHAP. VII.

2 *The disciples eat with vnwasshen hands. 8 The commandement of God is transgressed by mans traditions. 22 What defileth man. 24 Of the woman of Syrophenissa. 32 The healing of the domme. 37 The people praise Christ.*

Mat.15,2.

1 THen * gathered vnto him the Pharises, and certeine of the Scribes which
came from Ierusalem.
2 And when they sawe some of his disciples eat meat with "cōmune [a] hands, (that
is to say vnwasshen) they complained.
3 (For the Pharises, & all the Iewes, except
they wash their hāds [b] oft, eat not, holding
the tradition of the Elders.
4 And *when they come* from the market, except they washe, they eat not: and manie
other things there be, which they haue taken vpon them to obserue, *as* the wasshing

"Or, filthie.

a The Pharises wolde not eat with vnwasshen hāds because they thoght that the commune handling of things defiled them, so that they made holines and religion to depēd in hands wasshings.

b Or contensiously, striuīg to wash best.

of cuppes, and [c] pottes, and of brasen vessels, and of tables.)
5 Then asked him the Pharises and Scribes, Why walke not thy disciples according to the tradition of the Elders, but eat
"meat with vnwasshen hands?

c Litle pottes, somewhat more in quantitie then a wine pinte.

"Or, breade.

6 Then he answered and said vnto them,
Surely * Esai hathe prophecied wel of
you, hypocrites, as it is written, This people honoreth me with their [d] lippes, but
their heart is farre away from me.

Isa.29,13.

d With an outward shew.

7 But they worship me in vaine, teaching
for doctrines the [e] cōmandements of men.
8 For ye laye the commandement of God
aparte, and obserue the tradition of men,
as the wasshing of pottes and of cuppes, &
manie other suche like things ye do.
9 And he said vnto them, Wel, ye reiect
the commandement of God that ye may
obserue your owne tradition.

e Whosoeuer teacheth anie doctrine but Gods worde, is a false worshipper, and a seducer of the people, seme his doctrine neuer so probable to the iudgement of man.

10 For Moses said, *Honour thy father, and
thy mother: &, *Whosoeuer shal curse father or mother, let him [f] dye the death.
11 But ye say, If a man say to father or mo
ther, Corban, *that is*, By the gift that is *offred* by me, thou maist haue profite, *he shalbe fre*.

Exod.20,12. deut.5,16. ephe 6,2. Exod.21,17. leu.20,9. prou.20,20.

f That is, without anie hope of pardone.

12 So ye suffre him no more to do anie thing
for his father, or his mother,
13 Making the worde of God of none autoritie, by your tradition which ye haue
ordeined: and ye do manie suche like
things.
14 *Then he called the whole multitude
vnto him, and said vnto them, Hearkē you
all vnto me, and vnderstand.

Mat.15,10.

15 There [g] is nothing without a man, that
can defile him, when it entreth into him:
but the things which procede out of him,
are they which defile the man.
16 If anie haue eares to heare, let hī heare.
17 And when he came into an house *away*
from the people, his disciples asked him
concerning the parable.
18 And he said vnto thē, What? are ye without vnderstanding also? Do ye not knowe
that whatsoeuer thing from without entreth into a man, can not defile him,
19 Because it entreth not into his heart, but
into the bellie, and goeth out into the
draught which is ẏ purging of all meates?
20 Then he said, That which cometh out
of man, that defileth man.

g There is no outwarde or corporal thīg, wᶜ entreth into man, that can defile hī: meaning chiefly of meats, which if thei be takē excessiuely, it cometh of the inordinate lust of the heart, and so the lust is euil.

21 *For frō within, *euen* out of the heart of
men, procede euil thoghts, adulteries, fornications, murthers,
22 Theftes, couetousnes, wickednes, disceite, "vnclennes, a "wicked eye, backebiting,
pride, foolishnes.
23 All these euil things come from within,
and defile a man.

Gen.6,5. & 8,21.

"Or, wantonnes "Or, ennie.

24 ¶ *And from thēce he rose, and went into the borders of Tyrus and Sidon, and
entred

Mat.15,21.

entred into an house, and wolde that no
man shulde haue knowen: but he colde not
be hid.
25 For a certeine woman, whose litle daugh
ter had an vncleane spirit, heard of him,
and came, and fel at his feete.
26 (And the woman was a Greke, a Syro-
phenisian by nacion) & she besoght him
that he wolde cast out the deuil out of
her daughter.
27 But Iesus said vnto her, Let the [h] children first be fed: for it is not good to take
the childrens bread, and to cast it vnto
[i] whelpes.
28 Then she answered, and said vnto him,
Trueth, Lord: yet in dede the whelpes eat
vnder the table of the childrens [k] crommes.
29 Then he said vnto her, For this saying
go thy way: the deuil is gone out of thy
daughter.
30 And when she was come home to her
house, she founde the deuil departed, and
her daughter lying on the bed.
31 ¶ And he departed againe from the coasts of Tyrus and Sidon, and came vnto
the sea of Galile, through the middes of
the coasts of Decapolis.
32 And they broght vnto him one that was
deafe, and stambred in his speache, and
prayed him to put his hand vpon him.
33 Then he toke him aside from the multitude, and put his fingers in his eares, and
did spit, and touched his tongue.
34 And loking vp to heauen, he [l] sighed, &
said vnto him, Ephphatha, that is, Be opened.
35 And straight way his eares were opened,
and the string of his tongue was losed,
and he spake plaine.
36 And he cōmanded them, that thei shulde tell no man: but how muche soeuer he
forbad them, the more a great deale they
published it,
37 And were beyonde measure astonied,
saying, * [m] He hathe done all things wel:
he maketh bothe the deafe to heare, and
the domme to speake.

h Meaning the Iewes, to whome the promisses were first made.

i The Iewes toke strangers no better then ẏ dogs, & therefore Christ speaketh according to their opinion.

k She asketh but the poore crōmes, & not the childrens bread, wherein she declareth her faith and humilitie.

l Declaring by this signe the compassion ẏ he hathe vpon mans miseries.

Gen. 1, 31. eccl. 39, 21.

m As if they wolde say, besides all ẏ miracles that he hathe done, euen this now declareth that whatsoeuer he doeth, is verie wel.

CHAP. VIII.

2 The miracle of the seuen loaues. 11 The Pharises aske a signe. 15 The leauen of the Pharises. 22 The blinde receiueth his sight. 29 He was knowen of his disciples. 33 He reproueth Peter. 34 And sheweth how necessarie persecucion is.

Mat. 15, 32.

1 IN *those dayes, when there was a verie
great multitude, and had nothing to
eat, Iesus called his disciples to him, and
said vnto them,
2 I haue [a] compassiō on the multitude, because they haue now continued with me
thre daies, and haue nothing to eat.
3 And if I send them away fasting to their
owne houses, they wolde faint by the way:
for some of them came from farre.
4 Then his disciples answered him, °How
can a man satisfie these [b] with bread here
in the wildernes?
5 And he asked them, How manie loaues
haue ye? And they said, Seuen.
6 Then he commanded the multitude to
sit downe on the grounde: and he toke the
seuen loaues, & gaue thankes, brake *them*,
& gaue to his disciples to set before *them*,
and they did set *them* before the people.
7 Thei had also a fewe smale fishes: & whē
he had giuen thankes, he commanded thē
also to be set before *them*.
8 So they did eat, and were suffised, and
they toke vp of the broken meat that was
left, seuen baskets ful,
9 (And thei that had eaten, were about foure thousand) so he sent them away.
10 ¶ *And anone he entred into a ship with
his disciples, and came into the parties of
[c] Dalmanutha.
11 *And the Pharises came forthe, and beganne to dispute with him, seking of him
a signe from heauen, and tempting him.
12 Then he [d] sighed diepely in his spirit, &
said, Why doeth this [e] generacion seke a
signe? Verely I say vnto you, °[f] a signe shal
not be giuen vnto this generacion.
13 ¶ So he left them, & went into the ship
againe, and departed to the other side.
14 ¶ * And thei had forgottē to take bread,
nether had thei in the ship with them, but
one loafe.
15 And he charged them, saying, Take hede, and beware of the [g] leauen of the Pharises, and of the leauen of Herode.
16 And they thoght among them selues,
saying, *It is*, because we haue no bread.
17 And when Iesus knewe it, he said vnto
them, Why reason you *thus* because ye haue no bread? perceiue ye not yet, nether
vnderstand? haue ye your hearts yet hardened?
18 Haue ye eyes and se not? and haue ye eares, and heare not? & do ye not remēber?
19 * When I brake the fiue loaues among
fiue thousand, how manie baskets ful of
broken meat toke ye vp? They said vnto
him, Twelue.
20 And when *I brake* seuen among foure
thousand, how manie baskets of the lea-
uigs of broken meat toke ye vp? And thei
said, Seuen.
21 Then he said vnto them, [h] How *is it* that
ye vnderstand not?
22 And he came to Bethsaida, & thei broght
a blinde man vnto him, and desired him
to touche him.
23 Then he toke the blinde by the hand, &
led him out of the towne, and spit in his
eyes, and put his hands vpon him, & asked
him, if he sawe oght.

a Christ prouideth for his when they seme to be destitute and forsaken.

°Or, whence.

b If bread were so hard to come by, it semed vnpossible to obteine other meat.

Mat. 15, 39.

c Which was nere to Bethsaida, betwene the lake of Genesaret & mount Thabor.

Mat. 16, 1.

d O the incōprehēsible loue of ẏ Christ! how long shal we abuse his great mercies!

e Christ goeth about by sharpenes of speache to saue thē from wilful destruction.

Mat. 16, 5.

°Or, if a signe be giuen.

f As if he wolde say, if I shewe them anie signe, let me be a lyar & deceiuer.

g He willeth them to beware contagious doctrine & suche subtile practises as ẏ aduersaries vsed to suppres his Gospel.

Iohn 6, 13.

h Christ reproueth them because their mindes are as yet vpon the material leauē notwithstanding they had prouen by diuers miracles ẏ he gaue them their daielie bread.

24 And he loked vp,and ſaid,I ſe men: for
I ſe them walking like trees.
25 After that, he put his hands againe vpon his eyes,& made him loke againe. And
he was reſtored to his ſight,& ſawe euerie
man a farre of clearely.
26 And he ſent him home to his houſe, ſaying, Nether go into the towne, nor tell it
to anie in the towne.

Mat.16,13. luk.9,19.

27 ¶* And Ieſus went out,and his diſciples
into the townes of Ceſarea Philippi.And
by the waye he aſked his diſciples, ſaying
vnto them, Whome do men ſay that I am?
28 And they anſwered, *Some ſay* Iohn Bap-
tiſt:and ſome,Elias:and ſome, one of the
Prophetes.
29 And he ſaid vnto them, But whome ſay
ye that I am? Thē Peter anſwered & ſaid
vnto him,Thou art the [i] Chriſt.
30 And he ſharpely [k] charged them that
concerning him they ſhulde tell no man.
31 Then he began to teache them that the
Sonne of man muſt ſuffer manie things,
and ſhulde be reproued of the Elders, &
of the hie Prieſts & of the Scribes, and be
ſlayne, & within thre dayes riſe againe.
32 And he ſpake that thing plainely. Then
Peter toke him aſide, and began to rebuke
him.

i He that is ẙ anointed of God & fulfilled with all grace for mās ſaluacion.
k Differring it to a more commodious time, leſt ſuddē haſte ſhulde rather hinder then further ẙ myſterie of his comming.

33 Then he turned backe, and loked on his
diſciples, and rebuked Peter, ſaying, Get
thee behinde me, [l] Satan: for thou vnderſtandeſt not the things that are of God,
but the things that are of men.
34 ¶And he called the people vnto him
with his diſciples, and ſaid vnto them,
*Whoſoeuer wil followe me, let him for-
ſake him ſelf, and take vp his croſſe, and
followe me.
35 For whoſoeuer wil *ſaue his life, ſhal
loſe it: but whoſoeuer ſhal loſe his life for
my ſake and the Goſpels, he ſhal [m] ſaue it.
36 For what ſhal it profite a man, thogh he
ſhulde winne the whole worlde, if he loſe
his ſoule?
37 Or what ſhal a man giue for recompenſe of his ſoule?
38 *For whoſoeuer ſhalbe aſhamed of me, &
of my wordes among this adulterous and
ſinful generacion, of him ſhal the Sonne
of man be aſhamed alſo, when he cometh
in the glorie of his Father with the holie
Angels.

l This worde ſignifieth, Aduerſarie, or Enemie: & he calleth him ſo, becauſe he did as muche as in him laye, to pul him from obeying God.
Mat.10,38. & 16,24.luk.9,23.& 14,27.
Mat.10,35. & 16,25 luk.9,24.& 17,33 Iohn 12,25.
m For mortalitie & corruption, he ſhal receiue immortalitie & perfection.
Mat.10,33. luk.9,26. & 12,8.

CHAP. IX.

2 The transfiguracion. 7 Chriſt is to be heard. 26 The domme ſpirit is caſt out. 29 The force of prayer and faſting. 31 Of the death and reſurrection of Chriſt. 33 The diſputacion who ſhulde be the greateſt. 38 Not to hinder the courſe of the Goſpel. 42 Offences are forbidden.

Mat.16,28. luk.9,27.
a The preaching of the Goſpel receiued & increaſed: he ſpake this to cōforte them, & ẙ they ſhulde not thinke thei trauailed invaine.

1 AND *he ſaid vnto them, Verely I ſay
vnto you, that there be ſome of thē
that ſtand here, which ſhal not taſte of
death, til they haue ſene the [a] kingdome
of God come with power.
2 *And ſix dayes after Ieſus toke Peter, and
Iames, and Iohn, & broght them vp into
an hie mountaine out of the way alone, &
he was transfigured before them.
3 And his raiment did [b] ſhine, *and was* verie white, as ſnow, ſo white as no fuller cā
make vpon the earth.
4 And there appeared vnto thē Elias with
Moſes, and they were talking with Ieſus.
5 Then Peter anſwered, and ſaid to Ieſus,
Maſter, it is good for vs to be here: let vs
make alſo thre tabernacles, one for thee,
and one for Moſes, and one for Elias.
6 [c] Yet he knewe not what he ſaid: for they
were afrayed.
7 And there was a cloude that ſhaddowed
them, & a voyce came out of the cloude,
ſaying, *This is my beloued Sonne: [d] heare him.
8 And ſuddenly they loked rounde about,
and ſawe no more anie man ſaue Ieſus o-
nely with them.
9 *And as thei came downe from the mou-
taine, he charged them that thei ſhulde
tell no man what they had ſene ſaue when
the Sonne of man were riſen from the
dead againe.
10 So they kept that matter to them ſelues,
and demanded one of another, what the
riſing frō the dead againe ſhulde meane?

Mat.17,1. luk.9,28.
b Chriſt ſheweth his maieſtie ſo farre as their infirmitie was able to cōprehend it.
c Peter meaſured this viſion according to his owne capacitie, not conſidering the end thereof.
Mat.3,17.& 17,5.luk.3,22. chap.1,11.
Mat.17,9.
d Chriſt onely muſt be ẙ chief teacher & inſtructour of all them, ẘ profes them ſelues to be his mēbers, ſeing that God the Father giueth him this autoritie & cōmādeth vs this obedience.

11 Alſo they aſked him, ſaying, Why ſay
the Scribes, that *Elias [e] muſt firſt come?
12 And he anſwered, and ſaid vnto them,
Elias verely ſhal firſt come and reſtore all
things: and *as it is written of the Sonne
of man, he muſt ſuffer manie things, and
be ſet at noght.
13 But I ſay vnto you, that [f] Elias is come,
(and they haue done vnto him whatſoeuer they wolde) as it is *written of him.
14 ¶ *And when he came to *his* [g] diſciples,
he ſawe a great multitude about them, &
the Scribes diſputing with them.
15 And ſtraight waye all the people, when
thei behelde him, were amaſed, and ranne
to him, and ſaluted him.
16 Then he aſked the Scribes, What diſpute you *among your ſelues?
17 And one of the companie anſwered, &
ſaid, Maſter, I haue broght my ſonne vnto
thee, which hathe a domme ſpirit:
18 And whereſoeuer he taketh him, he [h] teareth him, and he fometh, and gnaſſheth
his teeth, and pineth away: and I ſpake to
thy diſciples that they ſhulde caſt him
out, and they colde not.
19 Then he anſwered him, and ſaid, [i] O
faithles generacion, how long now ſhal I
be with you! how long now ſhal I ſuffer
you! Bring him vnto me.
20 So they broght him vnto him: & aſſone
as the ſpirit ſawe him, he tare him, and he
fel

Malach.4,5.
e Their falſe opinion was ẙ ether Elias ſhulde riſe againe from the dead, or that his ſoule ſhulde enter into ſome other bodie.
Iſa.53,4.
f That is, Iohn Baptiſt.
Mat.17,14. luk.9,38.
g To the nine, ẘ he left the daye before.
*Or, againſt thee.
h When ẙ ſpirit cometh vpon him, he teareth him with inward ſorow & pangs as in a colike a man feeleth ſuche grief, as if his bowels were rent a ſunder.
i It ſemeth ẙ this man deſerued not ſo ſharpe an anſwer: but Chriſt ſpeaketh in his perſone to the Phariſes, ẘ were ſtubburne & deſperate.

fel downe on the grounde, walowing and
foming.
21 Then he asked his father, How long time is it since he hathe bene thus? And he
said, Of a childe.
22 And oft times he casteth him into ẏ fyre,
and into the water to destroye him: but if
thou canst do anie thing, helpe vs, and haue compassion vpon vs.
23 And Iesus said vnto him, If [k] thou canst
beleue it, all things are [l] possible to him
that beleueth.
24 And straight way the father of the childe crying with teares, said, Lord, I beleue:
helpe my [m] vnbelief.
25 When Iesus sawe that the people came
running together, he rebuked the vncleane
spirit, saying vnto him, Thou domme &
deafe spirit, I charge thee, come out of
him, and entre no more into him.
26 Then *the spirit* cryed, and rent him sore, and came out, and [n] he was as one dead,
in so muche that manie said, He is dead.
27 But Iesus toke his hand and lift him vp
and he rose.
28 And whē he was come into the house, his
disciples asked him secretly, Why colde
not we cast him out?
29 And he said vnto them, This kinde can
by no other meanes come forthe, but by
[o] prayer, and fasting.
30 ¶ *And they departed thence, and went
through Galile, & he wolde not that anie
shulde haue knowen it.
31 For he taught his disciples, and said vnto them, The Sonne of man shalbe deliuered into the hands of men, and they shal
kil him, but after that he is killed, he shal
rise againe the third day.
32 But [p] they vnderstode not that saying,
and were afraide to aske him.
33 * After he came to Capernaum: and whē
he was in the house, he asked them, What
was it ẏ ye disputed amōg you by the way?
34 And thei held their peace: for by the way
they reasoned among them selues, who
shulde be the chiefest.
35 And he sate downe, and called the twelue, and said to them, If anie man desire to
be first, the same shalbe last of all, and seruant vnto all.
36 And he toke a litle childe and set him
in the middes of them, and toke him in
his armes, and said vnto them,
37 Whosoeuer shal receiue one of suche litle children in my Name, receiueth me:
and whosoeuer receiueth me, receiueth not
[q] me, but him that sent me.
38 ¶ *Then Iohn answered him, saying, Ma
ster, we sawe one casting out deuils by thy
Name, which followeth not vs, & we forbade him, because he followeth vs not.
39 *But Iesus said, Forbid him not: for there is no man that can do a [*] miracle by my
Name, that can lightly speake euil of me.
40 For whosoeuer is not [r] against vs, is on
our parte.
41 * And whosoeuer shal giue you a cup of
water to drinke for my Names sake, becau
se ye belong to Christ, verely I say vnto
you, he shal not lose his rewarde.
42 *And whosoeuer shal offend one of these
litle ones, that beleue in me, it were better
for him rather, that a milstone were hanged about his necke, and that he were cast
into the sea.
43 *Wherefore if thine [f] hand cause thee to
offende, cut it of: it is better for thee to entre into life, maimed, thē hauing two hāds,
to go into hel into the fyre that neuer shal
be quenched,
44 *Where their [t] worme dyeth not, & the
fyre neuer goeth out.
45 Likewise, if thy foote cause thee to offende, cut it of: it is better for thee to
go halt into life, then hauing two feete to
be cast into hel into the fyre that neuer
shalbe quenched,
46 Where their worme dyeth not, and the
fyre neuer goeth out.
47 And if thine eye cause thee to offende,
plucke it out: it is better for thee to go into the kingdome of God with one eye, thē
hauing two eyes, to be cast into hel fyre,
48 Where their worme dyeth not, and the
fyre neuer goeth out.
49 For euerie man shalbe [u] salted with fyre: and * euerie sacrifice shalbe salted
with salte.
50 *Salte is good: but if the [x] salte be vnsa-
uerie, wherewith shal it be seasoned? Haue
salte in your selues, and haue peace, one
with another.

CHAP. X.

2 Of diuorcement. 17 The riche man questioneth with Christ. 30 Their rewarde that are persecuted. 35 Of the sonnes of Zebedeus. 46 Bartimeus hathe his eyes opened.

1 AND *he arose from thence and went
into the coastes of Iudea by the farre side of Iordan, and the people resorted
vnto him againe, and as he was wont, he
taught them againe.
2 Then the Pharises came and asked him,
if it were lawful for a mā to put away *his*
wife, and tempted him.
3 And he answered, and said vnto them,
What did *Moses commande you?
4 And they said, Moses suffred to write a
bil of diuorcement, and to put her away.
5 Then Iesus answered, and said vnto thē,
For ẏ hardnes of your heart he wrote this
precept vnto you.
6 But at the [a] beginning of the creacion
*God made them male and female.
7 * For this cause shal man leaue his father

k The Lord is euer readie to helpe vs, so ẏ we put him not backe through our incredulitie.
l All things that are agreā ble to the wil of God, shalbe grāted to him that beleueth: for faith seketh nothing, that is contrarie to his wil, or that is not reueiled in his worde.
m That is, the feblenes, and imperfectiō of my faith.
n Meaning, ẏ childe.
o Meaning, ẏ prayer which is surely groūded vpō faith and hathe fasting ioyned vnto it as a profitable aide
Mat.17,22.
luk.9,22.
p Because thei imagined that Christ shulde reigne temporally, this matter of his death was so strāge, that they colde perceiue nothing.
Mat.18,1.
luk.9,45.
q To wit, onely as man, but as him in whome is all perfection & fulnes of all graces & benefites.
Luk.9,49.
1.Cor.12,3.

* Or, anie great worke.
r Althogh he shewe not him self to be myne, yet in that he beareth reuerence to my Name, it is ynough for vs
Mat.10,42.
Mat.18,6.
luk.17,1.
Mat.5,29.
& 18,8.
f It is a maner of speache, ẇ signifieth, that we shulde cut of all things, which hinder vs to serue Christ.
Isa.66,24.
t These similitudes declare the paines, & eternal tormentes of the damned.
u He teacheth ẏ it is better to be sacrificed to God by salte & fyre, ẏ is, to be purged, & sanctified, then to be sent into hel fyre.
Leu.2,23.
Mat 5,13.
luk.14,34.
x They ẇ destroye ẏ grace that thei haue receiued of God, are as salte, ẇ hathe lost it sauour and are worse thē infideles.
Matth.19,1
Deu.24,1.
a The true way to amēde abuses is to returne to the institution of thinges, and to trie them by Gods worde.
Gene.1,27.
mat.19,4
Gen.2,31.
1.cor.6,16.
ephe 5,31.

and mother, and cleaue vnto his wife.
8 And they twaine shalbe one" flesh: so
that thei are no more twaine, but one flesh.
9 *Therefore, what God hathe coupled to
gether, let not man separate.
10 And in the house his disciples asked him
againe of that matter.
11 And he said vnto thẽ, *Whosoeuer shal
put away his wife and marie another,[b] cõmitteth adulterie against her.
12 And if a womã put away her housband,
& be maried to another, she committeth
adulterie.
13 ¶*Then they broght litle childrẽ to him
that he shulde touche them: and his disciples rebuked those that broght them.
14 But when Iesus sawe it, he was displeased, and said to them, Suffre the litle childrẽ to come vnto me, & forbid them not:
for of suche is the kingdome of God.
15 Verely I say vnto you, Whosoeuer shal
not receiue the kingdome of God as [c] a
litle childe, he shal not entre therein.
16 And he toke them vp in his armes, & put
his hands vpon them, and [d] blessed them.
17 ¶And when he was gone out on the way,
there came one* running, and kneled to
him, and asked him, Good Master, what
shal I do, that I may possesse eternal life?
18 Iesus said to him, Why callest thou me
good? there is none [e] good but one, *euen*
God.
19 Thou knowest the cõmandemẽts, *Thou
shalt not commit adulterie. Thou shalt
not kil. Thou shal not steale. Thou shalt
not beare false witnes. Thou shalt hurt
no *man*. Honour thy father and mother.
20 Then he answered, and said to him, Master, all these things I haue obserued from
my youth.
21 And Iesus behelde him, and [f] loued him,
and said vnto him, One thing is lacking
vnto thee, Go & [g] sell all that thou hast,
and giue to the poore, and thou shalt haue treasure in heauen, and come, followe
me, and take vp the crosse.
22 But he was sad at that saying, and went
away sorowful: for he had great possessiós.
23 And Iesus loked rounde about, and said
vnto his disciples, How hardely do they
that haue riches, entre into the kingdome
of God!
24 And his disciples were astonied at his
wordes. But Iesus answered againe, and
said vnto them, Children, how hard is it
for them that trust in riches, to entre into
the kingdome of God!
25 It is easier for a" camel to go through the
eye of a nedle, then for a [h] riche man to
entre into the kingdome of God.
26 And they were muche more astonied,
saying with them selues, Who then can be
saued?

" Or, persone.

1. Cor. 7, 10.

Mat. 5, 32. & 19, 9. luk. 16, 18. 1. cor. 7, 10.

b For the seconde is not his wife, but his harlot.

Mat. 19, 13. luk. 18, 15.

c We must be regenerat and voide of all pride, and con cupiscence.

Mat. 19, 16. luk. 18, 18.

d It was vsual with ye Iewes that the greater shulde blesse the inferior Eb. 7, 7. therefore Christ, being head of his Church, did by a solẽne kinde of prayer offer vp and consecrat the babes to God.

Exo. 20, 13.

e Christ wolde shewe that his goodnes was farre other wayes then ye goodnes wc is atttributed to men which is ful of vanitie & hypocrisie.

f That is, he approued certeine good seed that was in him, which gaue him a litle motion.

g He toucheth his maladie, & sore, wc before he felt not.

" Or, cable rope.

h Which putteth his trust in riches.

27 But Iesus loked vpõ them, & said, With
men *it is* impossible, but not with God: for
with God [i] all things are possible.
28 ¶*Thẽ Peter began to say vnto him, Lo,
we haue forsakẽ all, & haue followed thee.
29 Iesus answered, and said, Verely I say
vnto you, there is no man that hathe forsaken house or brethren or sisters, or father
or mother, or wife, or children, or lands for
my sake and the Gospels,
30 But he shal receiue an hundreth folde
now at this present: houses, and brethren,
and sisters, and mothers, and children, and
lands with [k] persecutions, & in the worlde
to come, eternal life.
31 *But manie *that are* [l] first, shalbe last, and
the last, first.
32 ¶*And they were in the way going vp to
Ierusalem, and Iesus went before them, &
they were amased, and as they followed,
they were afraide, & Iesus toke the twelue
againe, and began to tel them what things
shulde come vnto him,
33 *Saying*, Beholde we go vp to Ierusalem,
and the Sonne of man shalbe deliuered vnto the high Priests, & to the Scribes, and
thei shal condemne him to death, and shal
deliuer him to the Gentiles.
34 And they shal mocke him, and scourge
him, and spit vpon him, and kil him: but the
thirde day he shal rise againe.
35 ¶*Thẽ Iames and Iohn the sonnes of Ze
bedeus came vnto him, saying, Master, we
wolde that thou shuldest do for vs that
that we desire.
36 And he said vnto them, What wolde ye
I shulde do for you?
37 And they said to him, Grante vnto vs,
that we may sit one at thy right hãd, & the
other at thy left hand in thy glorie.
38 But Iesus said vnto them, Ye knowe not
what ye aske. Can ye [m] drinke of the cup
that I shal drinke of, and be baptized with
the baptisme that I shalbe baptized with?
39 And thei said vnto him, We can. But Iesus said vnto them, Ye shal drinke in dede of the cup that I shal drinke of, and be
baptized with the baptisme wherewith I
shalbe baptized:
40 But to sit at my right hand & at my left,
is not [n] mine to giue, but *it shalbe giuen* to
them for whome it is prepared.
41 And when the ten heard that, they began
to disdaine at Iames and Iohn.
42 But Iesus called them vnto him, and
said to them, *Ye knowe that they which
delite to beare rule among the Gentiles,
haue domination ouer them, and they that
be great among them, exercise autoritie o-
uer them.
43 But it shal [o] not be so among you: but
whosoeuer wil be great among you, shalbe
your seruant.

i For he cã giue grace to ye riche to cause him to enioye his riches, as if he had thẽ not.

Mat. 19, 27. luk. 18, 28.

Mat. 10, 30. luk. 13, 30.

k We must not measure these promises by our owne couetous desires, but referre ye accomplishement to Gods wil, who euen in our persecutions and afflictions performeth the same so farre as they be expedient. Let vs therefore learne to haue ynough and to want, that being tryed, we may enioye our treasures in heauẽ.

Mat. 20, 17. luk. 18, 31.

l He saith this because they that are first called, shulde go stil forwarde and not disdaine others.

Mat. 20, 20.

m Can you be partakers of my crosse and afflictions?

n I haue not this commission for this time.

Luk. 22, 25.

o Christ wolde not that his disciples and ministers shulde beare rule as worldelie gouernours do.

44 And whosoeuer wil be chief of you, shal
be the seruant of all.
45 For euen the Sonne of man came not to
be serued, but to serue, and to giue his life
for the raunsome of manie.

Mat.20,29. luk.18,35.

46 ¶ *Then they came to Iericho: and as he
went out of Iericho with his disciples, and
a great multitude, [p] Bartimeus the sonne
of Timeus a blinde man, sate by the wayes
side begging.

p The other Euangelistes mencion two, but Marke nameth him that was moste knowen.

47 And when he heard that it was Iesus of
Nazaret, he began to crye and to say, Iesus
the Sonne of Dauid, haue mercie on me.
48 And manie rebuked him, because he
shulde holde his peace: but he [q] cryed muche more, O Sonne of Dauid, haue mercie
on me.

q The more that Satan resisteth vs, the more our faith oght to increase.

49 Then Iesus stode stil, and commanded
him to be called: and they called the blinde, saying vnto him, Be of good comfort:
arise, he calleth thee.
50 So he threwe away his cloke, and rose &
came to Iesus.
51 And Iesus answered, and said vnto him,
What wilt thou that I do vnto thee? And
the blinde said vnto him, Lord, that I may
receiue sight.
52 Then Iesus said vnto him, Go thy way:
thy faith hathe saued thee. And by and by,
he receiued *his* sight, and followed Iesus in
the way.

CHAP. XI.

*1 Christ rideth to Ierusalem. 13 The figge tree dryeth
vp. 15 The biers and sellers are cast out of the Temple. 24 He declareth the vertue of faith and how we
shulde pray. 27 The Pharises question with Christ.*

Mat.21,1. luk.19,29.

1 AND *when they came nere to Ierusalem, to Bethphage and Bethania vnto the mount of oliues, he sent forthe two
of his disciples,
2 And said vnto them, [a] Go your wayes into that towne that is ouer against you, and
assone as ye shal entre into it, ye shal finde
a colte bounde, whereon neuer man sate:
lose him and bring him.

a Christ sheweth by this poore entrie the state of his kingdome, and it is not like to the great magnificence of this worlde.

3 And if anie man say vnto you, Why do ye
this? Say that the Lord hathe nede of him,
and straight way he wil send him hither.
4 And they went their way and founde a
colte tied by the dore without, in a place
where two wayes met, and thei losed him.
5 Then certeine of them, that stode there,
said vnto thē, What do ye losing ẏ colte?
6 And they said vnto them, as Iesus had cō
manded them. So they let them go.

Ioh.12,14.

7 ¶ *And they broght the colte to Iesus,
and cast their garments on him, and he sate vpon him.
8 And [b] manie spred their garments in the
way: other cut downe brāches of the trees
and strawed them in the way.

b Euerie one shewed some signe of honour and reuerence.

9 And they that went before, and they that
followed, cryed, saying, "Hosanna: blessed

" Or, saue, I pray thee.

be he ẏ cometh in the Name of the Lord.
10 Blessed *be* the kingdome that cometh in
the [c] Name of the Lord of our father [d] Dauid: Hosanna, *o thou which art* in the hiest
heauens.

c Many came in their owne name, but Christ came in the Name of the Lord.

Mat.21,16. luk.19,45.

11 *So Iesus entred into Ierusalem, and into the Temple: and when he had loked a-
bout on all things, & now it was euenig, he
wēt forthe vnto Bethania with the twelue.

d Because the promes was made to him.

Mat.21,19.

12 *And on the morow when they were come out from Bethania, he [e] was hungrie.

e Christ was subiect to our infirmities.

13 And seing a figge tre a farre of, that had
leaues, he went *to se* if he might finde any
thing thereon: but whē he came vnto it, he
founde nothing but leaues: for the time of
figges was not yet.
14 Then Iesus answered, & said to it, [f] Neuer man eat frute of thee hereafter while the worlde standeth: and his disciples
heard it.

f This was to declare how muche they displease God which haue but an outwarde shewe & appearance without frute.

15 ¶ And they came to Ierusalem, and Iesus
went into the Temple, and began to cast
out them that solde & boght in the Temple, and ouerthrew the tables of the money
changers, & the seates of them that solde
doues.
16 Nether wolde he suffer that any mā shulde cary a vessel through the Temple.
17 And he taught, saying vnto them, Is it
not writtē, *Mine House shalbe called the
House of prayer vnto all nacions? *but you
haue made it a denne of theues.

Isa.56,7. Ier.7,11.

18 And the Scribes and hie Priests heard it,
and soght how to [g] destroye him: for they
feared him, because the whole multitude
was astonied at his doctrine.

g For nether colde they suffer reprehension, nor that their profite shulde be hindered.

19 But when euen was come, *Iesus* went out
of the citie.

Mat.21,19.

20 ¶ *And in the morning as they passed
by, they sawe the figge tre dryed vp from
the rootes.
21 Then Peter remembred, and said vnto
him, Master, beholde, the figge tre which
thou cursedst, is withered.
22 And Iesus answered, and said vnto them,
Haue [h] faith in God.

h Christ taketh occasion to instruct the of the vertue of faith.

23 For verely I say vnto you, that whosoeuer shal say vnto this mountaine, Take thy
self away, and cast thy self into the sea, and
shal not wauer in his heart, but shal beleue
that those things which he saith, shal come
to passe, whatsoeuer he saith, shalbe *done*
to him.

Mat.7,7. luk.11,9.

24 *Therefore I say vnto you, [i] whatsoeuer
ye desire when ye pray, beleue that ye shal
haue it, and it shalbe *done* vnto you.

i He teacheth vs not hereby to aske whatsoeuer semeth good i our fantasies: for our prayer must be grounded on faith, and our faith vpon the worde of God.

25 *But when ye shal stand, and pray, forgiue, if ye haue any thing against any man,
ẏ your Father also which is in heauen, may
forgiue you your trespaces.

Mat.6,14.

26 For if you wil not forgiue, your Father
which is in heauē, wil not pardon you your
trespaces.

Mat.21,19. luk.20,1.

27 ¶ * Then thei came againe to Ierusalem:
and as he walked in the Temple, there came to him the high Priests, and the Scribes, and the Elders,
28 And said vnto him, By what autoritie
doest thou these things? and who gaue
thee this autoritie, that thou shuldest do
these things?
29 Then Iesus answered, and said vnto thẽ,
I wil also aske of you a certeine thing, and
answer ye me, and I wil tel you by what
autoritie I do these things.
30 The [k] baptisme of Iohn, was it from heauen, or of men? answer me.
31 And they thoght with them selues, saying, If we shal say from heauen, he wil say,
Why then did ye not beleue him?
32 But if we say of men, we feare the people: for all men counted Iohn, that he had
bene a verie Prophet.
33 Then they answered, and said vnto Iesus,
We can not tel. And Iesus answered, and
said vnto them, [l] Nether wil I tel you by
what autoritie I do these things.

k He comprehendeth his whole office, and ministerie

l They came of malice, and not to learne: therefore Christ thoght them vnworthie to be taught.

CHAP. XII.

1 The vineyarde is let out. 14 Obedience and tribute due to princes. 25 The resurrection of the dead. 28 The summe of the Law. 35 Christ the sonne of Dauid. 38 Hypocrites must be eschewed. 41 The offring of the poore widowe.

1 AND he began to speake vnto them in
parables, * A *certeine* man planted a
vineyarde, and compassed it with an hedge, and digged a pit for the [a] winepresse,
and buylt a towre in it, and let it out to
housbandmen, and went into a strange
countrey.
2 And at a time, he sent to the housband
men a seruant, that he might receiue of the
housband men of the frute of ẏ vineyard.
3 But they toke him, and bet him, and sent
him away emptie.
4 And againe, he sent vnto them another
seruant, and at him they cast stones, and
brake his head, and sent him away shamefully handled.
5 And againe he sent another, & him they
slewe, and manie other, beating some, and
killing some.
6 Yet had he one sonne, his dere beloued:
him also he sent the last vnto thẽ, saying,
They wil reuerence my sonne.
7 But the housband men said among thẽ
selues, This is the heire: come, let vs kil
him, and the inheritance shalbe ours.
8 So they toke him, and killed him, and cast
him out of the vineyarde.
9 What shal then the Lord of the vineyarde do? He [b] wil come and destroye these housband men, and giue the vineyarde
to others.
10 Haue ye not red so muche as this Scripture? * The stone which ẏ buylders did re-

Isa.5,1. iere.2,21. mat.21,33. luk.20,9.

a The Greke worde signifieth the vessel or fat, ẇ standeth vnder the winepresse to receiue the ioyce or licour.

b He sheweth ẏ plague that shal befale these ambitious & couetous rulers, whose hearts are hardened against Christ.

Psal.118,22. isa.28,16. mat.22,42. act.4,11. rom.9,33. 1.pet.2,8.

fuse, is made the head of the corner.
11 This [c] was done of the Lord, & it is marueilous in our eyes.
12 Then they went about to take him, but
they feared the people: for they perceiued
that he spake that parable against them:
therefore they left him, & went their way.
13 ¶ * And they sent vnto him certeine of the
Pharises, and of the Herodians that they
might take him in *his* talke.
14 And whẽ they came, they said vnto him,
Master, we knowe that thou art true, & carest for no man: for thou considerest not
the [d] persone of mẽ, but teachest the [e] way
of God truely, Is it lawful to giue tribute
to Cesar, or not?
15 Shulde we giue it, or shulde we not giue
it? But he knewe their hypocrisie, and said
vnto them, [f] Why tempt ye me? Bring me a
penie, that I may se it.
16 So they broght it, and he said vnto thẽ,
Whose is this image and superscription?
and they said vnto him, Cesars.
17 Then Iesus answered, & said vnto them,
* Giue to Cesar the things that are Cesars,
and to God, those that are Gods: and they
marueiled at him.
18 ¶ * Then came the Sadduces vnto him,
(which say, there is no resurrection) and
they asked him, saying,
19 Master, * Moses wrote vnto vs, If any mãs
brother dye, and leaue *his* wife, and leaue
no children, that [g] his brother shulde take
his wife, and raise vp sede vnto his brother.
20 There were seuen brethren, and the
first toke a wife, and when he dyed, left
no yssue.
21 Then the seconde toke her, and he dyed,
nether did he yet leaue yssue, & the thirde
likewise.
22 So seuen had her, and left no yssue: last
of all the wife dyed also.
23 In the resurrection then, when they shal
rise againe, whose wife shal she be of them?
for seuen had her to wife?
24 Then Iesus answered, & said vnto them,
Are ye not therefore deceiued, because ye
knowe not the Scriptures, nether ẏ power
of God?
25 For when they shal rise againe from the
dead, nether men mary, nor wiues are maried, but are [h] as the Angels which are in
heauen.
26 And as touching the dead, that they shal
rise againe, haue ye not red in the boke
of Moses, how in the bush God spake
vnto him, saying, I * am the God of Abraham, and the God of Isaac, and the God of
Iacob?
27 He is not the God of the dead, but the
God of the [i] liuing. Ye are therefore greatly deceiued.

28 ¶ * Then

c It is the ordināce of God that it shulde be so, which moste communely is contrarie to mans reason: & thus that which was spoken figuratiuely of Dauid, is fulfilled in Christ, read Matth. 22,16.

Mat.22,15. luk.20,20.

d As the qualities of the minde or bodie, or of outward things.

e As godlie maners, agreable to Gods Law.

f He gaue thẽ to vnderstand that he knewe their malicious intent.

Rom.13,7.

Mat.22,25. luk.20,27.

Deu.25,5.

g This was a politike law giuen for a time for the preseruation of families, read Mat.22,24.

h Not as touching ẏ spiritual nature, but cōcerning the state of incorruption, and immortalitie, so that then there shal nede no more mariage.

Exod.3,6. mat.22,32.

i Then it followeth that they liue, although they be diceased out of this life.

28 ¶ *Thē came one of the Scribes that had
heard them disputing together, & perceiuing that he had answered them wel, he asked him, Which is the first commandement of all?
29 Iesus answered him, The first of all the
commandements *is*, *Heare, Israel, The
Lord our God is the onelie Lord.
30 Thou shalt therefore loue the Lord thy
God with all thine heart, and with all thy
soule, & with all thy "minde, & with all thy
strength: this is the first commandement.
31 And the seconde *is* [k] like, that is, *Thou
shalt loue thy neighbour as thy self. There
is none other cōmādement greater then
these.
32 Then the Scribe said vnto him, Wel Master, thou hast said the trueth, that there is
one God, and that there is none but he,
33 And to loue him with all the heart, and
with all the vnderstanding, & with all the
soule, and with all the strength, and to loue
his neighbour as him self, is more then all
burnt [l] offrings and sacrifices.
34 Then, when Iesus sawe that he answered
discretely, he said vnto hī, Thou [m] art not
farre from the kingdome of God. And no
man after that durst aske him any questiō.
35 ¶ *And Iesus answered & said teaching in
the Temple, How say the Scribes ỷ Christ
is the sonne of Dauid?
36 For Dauid him self said by ỷ [n] holie Gost,
*The Lord said to my Lord, Sit at my
right hand, til I make thine enemies thy
footestole.
37 Then Dauid him self calleth him Lord:
by what meanes is he then his sonne? and
muche people heard him gladly.
38 *Moreouer he said vnto them in " his doctrine, Beware of the Scribes which loue
to go in long [o] robes, and *loue* salutacions
in the markets,
39 And the chief seates in the Synagogues,
and the first roumes at feastes,
40 Which *deuour widowes houses, "euen
vnder a coulour of long prayers. These
shal receiue the greater damnation.
41 *And as Iesus sate ouer against the treasurie, he behelde how the people cast money into the treasurie, and many richemen
cast in muche.
42 And there came a certeine poore widowe, and she threw in two mites, which
make a [p] quadrin.
43 Then he called vnto him his disciples,
and said vnto thē, Verely I say vnto you,
that this poore widowe hathe cast [q] more
in, then all they which haue cast into the
treasurie.
44 For they all did cast in of their superfluitie: but she of her pouertie did cast in
all that she had, *euen* all her liuing.

Mat.22,35.
Exod.20,2. deut.6,4.
"Or, thoght.
Leuit.19,18. mat.22,39. rom.13,9. galat.5,14. iam.2,8.
k That is, depēdeth on the first and procedeth of the loue of God.
l He meaneth all the ceremonies of the Law, wherein the hypocrites put great holines.
m Because he shewed him self willing to be taught and wel perceiued the difference betwixt our outwarde profession, and that which God doeth prīcipally require of vs.
Mat.22,41. luk.20,41. Psal.110,1.
n Inspired by the holie Gost and by the Spirit of prophecie.
Mat.23,6. luk.11,43. & 20,45.
"Or, as he taught.
o He condemneth not their apparel, but their vaine ostentation and outwarde shewe of holines, whereby they deceiued the simple people.
Mat.23,14. luk.20,47.
Luk.21,1.
"Or, and vnder pretence praye long.
p Which is about half a farthing.
q Our Sauiour esteemeth our giftes by our affections and ready willes.

CHAP. XIII.

2 The destructiō of Ierusalem. 10 The Gospel shalbe preached to all. 9. 22 The persecutions and false Prophetes which shal be before the comming of Christ, whose houre is vncerteine. 33 He exhorteth euery one to watch.

1 AND *as he went out of the Temple,
one of his disciples said vnto him,
Master, se what stones, and what buyldings
are here.
2 *Then Iesus answered and said vnto him,
Seest thou these great buyldings? there
shal not be left one stone vpō a stone, that
shal not be throwen downe.
3 And as he sate on ỷ mount of oliues, ouer
against the Temple, Peter, and Iames, and
Iohn, and Andrew asked him secretly,
4 Tel vs, when shal these things be? & what
shalbe the signe when all these things shalbe fulfilled?
5 And Iesus answered them, and began to
say, *[a] Take hede lest any mā deceiue you.
6 For many shal come in my Name, sayīg,
I [b] am *Christ*, and shal deceiue many.
7 Furthermore when ye shal heare of warres and rumors of warres, be ye not troubled: for *suche things* must nedes be: but the
end *shal* not *be* yet.
8 For nacion shal rise against nacion, and
kingdome against kingdome, and there
shalbe earthquakes in diuers quarters, and
there shalbe famine and troubles: these *are*
the beginnings of sorowes.
9 But take ye hede to your selues: for they
shal deliuer you vp to the Councils, and
to the Synagogues: ye shalbe beaten, and
broght before rulers and Kings for my sake for a [c] testimonial vnto them.
10 And the Gospel must first be published
among all nacions.
11 *But when they lead you, and deliuer you
vp, take ye no [d] thoght afore, nether premeditate [e] what ye shal say: but whatsoeuer is giuen you at the same time, that
speake: for it is not ye that speake, but the
holie Gost.
12 Yea, and the brother shal deliuer the brother to death, and the father the sonne, and
the children shal rise against their parents,
and shal cause them to dye.
13 And ye shalbe hated of all men for my
Names sake: but whosoeuer shal endure
vnto the end, he shalbe saued.
14 *Moreouer, when ye shal se the abominacion of desolation (spoken of by *Daniel the Prophet) [f] " stādiug where it oght
not, (let him that readeth, cōsider it) *then
let thē *that be* in Iudea, flee into the [g] moutaines,
15 And let him that is vpon the house, not
come downe into the house, nether entre
therein, to fetch any thing out of his house.
16 And let him that is in the field, not turne
backe againe vnto the thīgs which he left

Mat.24,1. luk.21,5.
Luk.19,44.
Ephes.5,6. 2.thess.2,3.
a He doeth answer them of things that were more necessarie for them to know thē the things that they demanded.
b Vsurping the autoritie of Christ.
c That they may be inexcusable.
Mat.10,19. luk.12,11. & 21,14.
d He onely forbiddeth ỷ care which cometh of distrust.
e This is not to make them negligent, but to assure them that he wil assist them and instruct them sufficiently to answers, so ỷ thei may hereby perceiue that their defence standeth not in their owne wisdome, or eloquence.
Mat.24,15. Dan.9,27. Luk.21,20.
f This is ment of that time that the Romains shulde profane the Temple.
"Or, being.
g Because the destruction shal be moste extreme and cruel.

behinde him,to take his clothes.
17 Thē wo *shalbe* to thē that are with [h]chil-
de, and to them that giue sucke in those
dayes.
18 [i]Pray therefore that your flight be not in
the winter.
19 For there shalbe in those dayes suche tribulatiō, as was not from the beginning of
the creation which God created vnto this
time,nether shalbe.
20 And except that the Lord had shortened
those dayes, no "flesh shulde be saued: but
for the elects sake, which he hathe chosen,
he hathe shortened thoses dayes.
21 Then *if any man say to you,Lo,here is
Christ,or,lo,*he is* there,beleue it not.
22 For false Christs shal rise, and false Prophetes,& shal shewe signes and wonders, to
deceiue if it were [k]possible,the very elect.
23 But take ye hede:beholde,I haue shewed
you all things [l]before.
24 ¶Moreouer*in those dayes,after that tri
bulation the sunne shal waxe darke, & the
moone shal not giue her light,
25 And the [m]starres of heauen shal fall:and
the powers which are in heauen,shal shake.
26 And then shal they se the Sonne of man
coming in the cloudes, with great power
and glorie.
27 *And he shal then send his Angels, and
shal gather together his elect from the
foure windes, & from the vtmost parte of
the earth to the vtmost parte of heauen.
28 Now learne a parable of the figge tre.
When her bough is yet tender,& it bringeth forthe leaues, ye knowe that sommer *is*
nere.
29 So in like maner,when ye se these things
come to passe,knowe that *the kingdome of God*
is nere,*euen* at the dores.
30 Verely I say vnto you, that this [n]genera-
cion shal not passe, til all these things be
done.
31 Heauen and earth shal passe away, but
my wordes shal not passe away.
32 But of that [o] day and houre knoweth no
man, no, not the Angels which are in heauen, nether the [p] Sonne him self, saue the
Father.
33 *Take hede:watche,& pray:for ye knowe
not when the time is.
34 *For the Sonne of man is* as a mā going into
a strange countrey, & leaueth his house, &
giueth autoritie to his seruants,and to euerie man his worke, and commandeth the
porter to watch.
35 [q]Watch therefore, (for ye knowe not
when the Master of the house wil come, at
euen,or at midnight,at the cocke crowing,
or in the dauning)
36 Lest if he come suddenly,he shulde finde
you sleping.
37 And those things that I say vnto you, I
say vnto all men, Watch.

h For they shal not be able to flee.
i That you haue no let to hinder you when you shulde escape.
"Or,man.
Mat.24,23. luk.21,8.
k The elect may wauer & be troubled, but they can not vtterly be deceiued, and ouercome.
l Wherefore he that suffreth him self now to be seduced, hathe none excuse.
Isa.13,10. eze.32,7. ioel 2,10. & 3,15.
Mat.24,30.
m This teacheth ỹ there shalbe a change of ỹ whole ordre of nature.
n The worde signifieth the space of a 100. yeres: albeit this came to passe before fiftie yeres.
o When the destruction of Ierusalem, the persecutions and illusions shal come: but chiefly these are vnderstand of the secōde comming of Christ.
Mat.24,13.
p In that he is man and mediator.
q For of the comming we are most assured: but of the time, the yere, the day or houre, we are ignorant, and therefore must watch continually.

CHAP. XIIII.

1 The Priests conspire against Christ. 3 Marie Magdalene anointeth Christ. 12 The Passeouer is eaten. 18 He telleth afore of the treason of Iudas. 22 The Lords supper is institute. 46 Christ is taken. 67 Peter denyeth him.

1 AND* two dayes after followed *the
feast of* the Passeouer, and of vnleauened bread:and the hie Priests,and Scribes soght how they might take him by
craft,and put him to death.
2 But they said, Not in the feast *day*, lest
there be any tumult among the people.
3 *And when he was in Bethania in the house of Simon the leper, as he sate at table,
there came a womā hauing a boxe of ointment of "spikenarde, verie costlie, and she
brake the boxe,and powred it on his head.
4 Therefore [a]some disdeined among them
selues,and said, To what end is this waste
of ointment?
5 For it might haue bene solde for more thē
[b]thre hundreth pence, & bene giuen vnto
the poore, [c]& they grudged against her.
6 But Iesus said, Let her alone: why trouble ye her? she hathe wroght a good worke
on me.
7 For ye haue the poore with you alwayes,
and when ye wil ye may do them good,
but me ye shal not haue alwayes.
8 She hathe done that she colde: she came
afore hand to anoint my bodie to the burying.
9 Verely I say vnto you, wheresoeuer this
Gospel shalbe preached throughout the
whole worlde,this also that she hath done,
shalbe spoken of in remembrance of her.
10 ¶*Thē Iudas Iscariot,one of the twelue
[d]wēt away vnto the high Priests, to betray
him vnto them.
11 And when they heard it, they were glad,
& promised that they wolde giue him money: therefore he soght how he might con
ueniently betray him.
12 ¶*Now ỹ first day of vnleauened bread,
when they sacrificed the Passeouer,his disciples said vnto him, Where wilt thou
that we go & prepare, that thou maist eat
the Passeouer?
13 Then he sent forthe two of his disciples,
and said vnto them, Go ye into the citie,
and there shal a man mete you bearing a
pitcher of water: followe him.
14 And whithersoeuer he goeth in, say ye to
the good man of the house, The Master
saith, Where is ỹ lodging where I shal eat
the Passeouer with my disciples?
15 And he wil shewe you an vpper chamber *which is* large,trimmed and prepared:
there make it readie for vs.
16 So his disciples went forthe,and came to
the citie, & founde as he had said vnto thē,
and

Mat.26,1. luk.22,1.
Mat.26,6. iohn 12,1.
"Or, of pure narde and faithfully made.
a As Iudas who caused this murmuring.
b Which are in value about six pound sterling.
c To wit, Iudas: who was offēded therewith, and therefore made a busines.
Mat.26,14. luk.22,4.
d He toke occasion by this oyntment as of a thing euil done.
Mat.26,17. luk.22,8.

and made readie the Passeouer.
17 ¶ And at euen he came with the twelue.
18 *And as thei sate at table and did eat, Iesus said, Verely I say vnto you, that one
of you shal betray me, which eateth with
me.
19 Then they began to be sorowful and to
say to him one by one, Is it I? And another, Is it I?
20 And he answered and said vnto them, *It
is* one of the twelue that [e] dippeth with me
in the platter.
21 *Truely the Sonne of man goeth his
way, as it is [f] written of him: but wo *be* to
that man, by whome the Sonne of man,
is betrayed: it had bene good for that mā,
if he had neuer bene borne.
22 *And as they did eat, Iesus [g] toke the
bread, and when he had giuen thankes, he
brake it & gaue it to them, and said, *Take, eat, this is my bodie.
23 Also he toke the cup, and when he had
[h] giuen thankes, gaue it to them: and they
all dranke of it.
24 And he said vnto thē, This is my blood
of the new Testament, which is shed for
manie.
25 Verely I say vnto you, I wil drinke no
more of the frute of the vine, vntil that
day, that I drinke it new in the kingdome
of God.
26 And when they had sung a psalme, they
went out to the mount of oliues.
27 ¶ *Then Iesus said vnto them, All ye
shalbe [i] offended by me this night: for it is
written, *I wil smite the shepherd, & the
shepe shalbe scattered.
28 But after that I am risen, I wil go into
*Galile before you.
29 And Peter said vnto him, Althogh all
men shulde be offended, yet wolde not I.
30 Then Iesus said vnto him, Verely I say
vnto thee, this day, *euen* in this night, before the cocke crowe twise, thou shalt denie me thrise.
31 But he said more earnestly, If I shulde
dye with thee, I wil not denie thee: likewise also said they all.
32 ¶ *After they came into a place named
Gethsemane: then he said to his disciples,
Sit ye here, til I haue prayed.
33 And he toke with him Peter, and Iames,
and Iohn, and he began [k] to be afraied, &
in great heauines,
34 And said vnto them, My soule is verie
heauie, *euen* vnto the death: tary here and
watch.
35 So he went forwarde a litle, & fel downe on the grounde, and praied, that if it
were possible, that houre might passe frō
him.
36 And he said, [l] Abba, Father, all things
are possible vnto thee: take away this cup

Mat.26,20. luk.22,14. iohn 13,21.

e To dip the hand, is as muche to say, as he that is accustomed to eate with me.

Psal.41,10. mat.26,23. iohn 13,18. act.1,16.

f This declareth that nothing can be done without Gods prouidence.

Mat.26,26. 1.cor.11,24.

g Read Math. Chap.26,26.

h The Greke worde is to blesse, which is here taken onely to giue thankes, as S. Luk. & S. Paul interprete it, & S. Marke also speaking of the cuppe.

Iohn 16,23.

i That is, turned from me, because of the persecution.

Zac.13,7.

Chap.16,7.

Mat.26,36. luk.22,39.

k His diuinitie was as it were hid, & his humanitie shewed it self fully

l Ab in Ebrewe, & Abba in ẏ Syrian tongue signifieth Father.

from me: neuertheles not that I wil, but
that thou [m] wilt, *be done.*
37 Then he came and founde them sleping, and said to Peter, Simō, slepest thou?
coldest not thou watch one houre?
38 ¶ Watch ye, and pray, that ye entre not
into tētacion: the spirit in dede is readie,
but the flesh is weake.
39 And againe he went awaye, and prayed,
and spake the same wordes.
40 And he returned, and founde them a-
slepe againe: for their eyes were heauie:
nether knewe they what they shulde answer him.
41 And he came the thirde time, and said
vnto them, [n] Slepe hence forthe, and take
your rest: it is ynough: the houre is come:
beholde, the Sonne of man is deliuered
into the hands of sinners.
42 Rise vp: let vs go: lo, he that betrayeth
me, is at hand.
43 *And immediatly while he yet spake,
came Iudas that was one of the twelue, &
with him a great multitude with swordes
and staues from the hie Priests, and Scribes and Elders.
44 And he that betrayed him, had giuen
thē a token, saying, Whomesoeuer [o] I shal
kisse, he it is: take him & leade him awaye
safely.
45 And assone as he was come, he went
straight waye to him, and said, [p] Master,
Master, and kissed him.
46 Then they layed their hands on him, &
toke him.
47 And [q] one of them that stode by, drewe
out a sworde, and smote a [r] seruant of the
hie Priest, and cut of his eare.
48 And Iesus answered and said vnto thē,
Ye be come out as vnto a thefe with swordes and with staues to take me.
49 I was daiely with you teaching in the
Temple, & ye [s] toke me not: but *this is done*
that the Scriptures shulde be fulfilled.
50 Then they [t] all forsoke him, and fled.
51 And there followed him a certeine yong
man, clothed in linnen vpon his bare *bodie*,
and the yong men caught him.
52 But he left his linnē cloth, and fled from
them naked.
53 *So thei led Iesus away to the hie Priest,
and to him came all the [u] hie Priests, and
the Elders, and the Scribes.
54 And Peter followed him a [x] farre of, e-
uen into the hall of the hie Priest, and sate
with the seruants, and warmed *him self* at
the ⸗ fyre.
55 And the *hie Priests, and all the Council soght for witnes against Iesus, to put
him to death, but founde none.
56 For manie bare false witnes against him,
but their witnes ⸗ agreed not together.
57 Then there arose certeine, & bare false

m He standeth not so to his owne wil, but that willingly he offreth him self to obey God.

n He meaneth that the houre wil come whē they shalbe kept from sleping.

Mat.26,47. luk.22,47. ioh.18,3.

o It was the facion then to grete with kissing at their meetings, & also at their departure.

p He repeteth it twise, as if he had bene moued with a certeine pitie in taking his last leaue.

q To wit, Peter.

r Called Malchus.

s Which declareth that no man can do anie thing contrarie to Gods ordinance.

t Meaning all the disciples.

Mat.26,57. luk.22,54. iohn 18,24.

u That is, thei ẘ had chefest autoritie amōg the Priests.

x Which signified that his hot zeale begā now to be abated.

Mat.26,59.

⸗ Or, light.

⸗ Or, were not like.

witnes against him, saying,
58 We heard him say, * I [y] wil destroy this
Temple made with hands, & within thre
daies I wil buylde another, made without
hands.
59 But their witnes yet agreed not together.
60 Then the hie Priest stode vp amongs
them, and asked Iesus, saying, Answerest
thou nothing? what is the matter that these beare witnes against thee?
61 But he held his peace, and answered nothing. Againe the hie Priest asked him, &
said vnto him, Art thou Christ the Sonne
of the [z] Blessed?
62 And Iesus said, I am *he*, * and ye shal se
the [a] Sonne of man sit at the right hand
of the power of *God*, & come in the cloudes of heauen.
63 Then the hie Priest rent his clothes and
said, What haue we anie more nede of
witnesses?
64 Ye haue heard the blasphemie: what
thinke ye? And they all condemned him
to be worthie of death.
65 And some began to spit at him, and to
couer his face, and to beate him with fy-
stes, and to say vnto him, Prophecie. And
the [b] sergeants smote him with *their* rods.
66 * And as Peter was beneath in the hall,
there came one of the maides of the hie
Priest.
67 And when she sawe Peter warming *him
self*, she loked on him, and said, Thou wast
also with Iesus of Nazaret.
68 But [c] he denied it, saying, I knowe him
not, nether wot I what thou saiest. Then
he went out into the " [d] porche, & the cocke
crewe.
69 * Then a maide sawe him againe, & began to say to them that stode by, This is
one of them.
70 But he denied it againe: & anone after,
they that stode by, said againe to Peter,
Surely thou art *one* of them: for thou art
of Galile, and thy speache is like.
71 And he began to curse, & sweare, *saying*,
I knowe not this mā of whome ye speake.
72 * Then the secōde time the cocke crewe,
and Peter remembred the worde that Iesus had said vnto him, Before the cocke
crowe twise, thou shalt denie my thrise, &
"waying that with him self, he wept.

Iohn 2,19.
y These two witnesses dissēted, in that the one reported yͤ Christ said, he colde destroye the Tēple, (as Mat writeth) & yͤ other said, that he heard him saye, that he wolde do it as is here noted.

Mat.24,30.
z That is, of God, who is worthie all praise: the wͨ worde in their language the Iewes when they speake of God, vse communely in their writings euē to this day.
a Whome thei now contēned in this base estate, thei shulde se appeare at the last day with maiestie and glorie.

Mat.26,69. luk.22,55. ioh.18,25.
b This declareth the wickednes & insolencie of the gouernours, & rulers, seing their officers contrarie to all iustice, thus raged & tormēted him, that was innocent.

Mat.26,71. luk.22,51. ioh.18,25.
c We oght to consider our owne infirmitie, yͭ we may learne onely to trust ī God, and not in our owne strength.
" *Or, entrie.*
d Peter prepareth him self to flee if he were further laied vnto.

Mat.26,75. ioh.13,38.

" *Or, russhed out of the dores and wept.*

CHAP. XV.

1 Iesus is led to Pilate. 15 He is condemned, reuiled and put to death. 46 And is buryed by Ioseph.

1 AND * anone in the dawning, the hie
Priests helde [a] a coūsel with the Elders, and the Scribes, & the whole Council, and bounde Iesus, and led him away,
and deliuered him to Pilate.
2 Then Pilate asked him, Art thou the
King of the Iewes? And he answered, and
said vnto him, Thou saiest it.
3 And the hie Priests accused him of manie things.
4 * Wherefore Pilate asked him againe,
saying, Answerest thou nothing? beholde
how manie things thei witnes agaīst thee.
5 But Iesus answered [b] no more at all, so
that Pilate marueiled.
6 Now at the feast Pilate did deliuer a prisoner vnto them, whomesoeuer thei wolde desire.
7 Then there was one named Barabbas, wͨ
was boūde with his fellowes, that had made insurrection, who in the insurrection
had committed murther.
8 And the people cryed a loude, & began
to desire *that he wolde do* as he had [c] euer
done vnto them.
9 Then Pilate answered them, and said,
Wil ye that I let lose vnto you the King
of the Iewes?
10 For he knewe that the hie Priests had
deliuered him of enuie.
11 But the hie Priests had moued the people *to desire* that he wolde rather deliuer
Barabbas vnto them.
12 And Pilate answered, and said againe
vnto thē, What wil ye then that I do *with
him*, whome ye call the King of the Iewes?
13 And thei cryed againe, Crucifie him.
14 Then Pilate said vnto them, But what
euil hathe he done? And they cryed the
more feruently, Crucifie him.
15 So Pilate [d] willing to contēt the people,
losed them Barabbas, and deliuered Iesus
when he had scourged him, that he might
be crucified.
16 Then the souldiers led him awaye into
the hall, which is the " commune hall, and
called together the whole band,
17 And clad him with purple, and platted a
crowne of thornes, & put it about *his head*,
18 And began to salute him, *saying*, Haile,
King of the Iewes.
19 And they smote him on the head with a
"reede, and spat vpon him, and bowed the
knees, *&* did him reuerence.
20 And when they had mocked him, they
toke the purple of him, and put his owne
clothes on him, and led him out to crucifie him.
21 * And they [e] compelled one that passed
by, *called* Simon of Cyrene (which came
out of the countrey, and was father of A-
lexander and Rufus) to beare his crosse.
22 * And they broght him to a place named
Golgotha, which is by interpretacion, the
place of *dead mens* skulles.
23 And they gaue him to drinke wine
mingled [f] with myrrhe: but he receiued it
not.
24 And when they had crucified him, they
parted his garments, casting lottes for
them,

Mat.27,1. luk.22,66. ioh.18,20.
a For the Romains gaue thē no autoritie to put anie man to death.

Mat.27,12. luk.23,3. ioh.18,35.
b He wolde not defend his cause, but presēted him self willingly to be cōdemned.

c The people alwaies mainteine their customes, althogh thei be worthe nothing.

d When a iudge hathe respect to men, he quite forgetteth iustice.

" *Or, Pretorie.*

" *Or, stalke.*

Mat.27,31. luk.23,25.
e It was yͤ custome to make him that was condemned, to carie his crosse, but Iesus was not able for weakenes.

Mat.27,33. luk.23,33. ioh.19,16.
f Which was to hasten his death: but he wolde not drinke it, because he wolde waite for the houre yͭ his Father had appointed, that he might render vnto him perfect obedience.

g The Iewes deuided their day into 4 partes, so that by the third houre is here ment ye thirde parte of the day, which was from six a clocke to nine, at what time Mat. saith he was crucified.

them, what euerie man shulde haue.
25 And it was [g] the thirde houre, when they
crucified him.
26 And the title of his cause was writtē aboue,
THE KING OF THE IEWES.
27 Thei crucified also with him two theues,
the one on the right hand, and the other
on his left.
28 Thus the Scripture was fulfilled, which
saith, * And he was counted among the
wicked.

Isa.53,12.

29 And they that went by, railed on him,
wagging their heads, & saying, *Hey, thou
that destroyest the Temple, & buyldest it
in thre dayes,

Iohn 2,19.

30 Saue thy self, and come downe from the
crosse.
31 Likewise also euen the hie Priests mocking,
said among thē selues with the Scribes,
He saued other men, him self he can
not saue.
32 Let Christ the King of Israel now come
downe from the crosse, that we may se, and
beleue. [h] They also that were crucified
with him, reuiled him.

h Meaning the one of them that were crucified.

33 ¶ Now when ye sixt houre was come, darkenes
arose ouer [i] all the land vntil the
ninth houre.

i Because this darkenes was onely ouer the land of Chanaan, when the rest of ye worlde was light, the miracle is the greater.

34 And at the [k] ninth houre Iesus cryed with
a loude voyce, saying, * Eloi, Eloi, lamma-sabachthani?
which is by interpretacion,
My God, my God, why hast thou forsaken
me?

Psal.22,1. mat.27,46.

k Which was the third parte of the day, & about thre of the clocke after none.

35 And some of them that stode by, when
they heard it, said, [l] Beholde, he calleth
Elias.

l This was spoken mockingly.

36 And one ran, and filled a * sponge ful of
vineger, and put it on a reede, and gaue
him to drinke, saying, Let him alone: let
vs se if Elias wil come and take him
downe.

Psal 69,22.

37 And Iesus cryed with a loude voyce, and
gaue vp the gost.
38 ¶ And the vaile of the Temple was rent
in twaine, from the top to the bottome.
39 Now when the [m] Centurion, which stode
ouer against him, sawe that he thus crying
gaue vp the gost, he said, Truely this
man was the Sonne of God.

m Who had charge ouer an hundreth men.

40 ¶ There were also women, which beheld
a farreof, amōg whome was Marie Magdalene,
and Marie (the mother of Iames the
lesse, and of Ioses) and Salome,
41 Which also when he was in Galile, *followed
him and ministred vnto him, and
many other women which came vp with
him vnto Ierusalem.

Luk.8,2.

42 ¶ *And now whē night was come (because
it was the day of the preparacion that is
before the Sabbath)
43 Ioseph of Arimathea, an [n] honorable
Counsellour, which also loked for ye kingdome
of God, came, & went in [o] boldely
vnto Pilate, and asked the bodie of Iesus.

Mat.27,57. luk.23,50. iohn 19.38.

n A graue mā and of great autoritie.

o This man shewed his faith boldely when the danger semed to be moste perilous.

44 And Pilate marueiled, if he were alreadie
dead, and called vnto him the Centurion,
and asked of him whether he had
bene any while dead.
45 And whē he knewe *the trueth* of the Centurion,
he gaue the bodie to Ioseph,
46 Who boght a linnen cloth, and toke him
downe, and wrapped him in the linnen
cloth, and layd him in a tombe that was
hewen out of a rocke, & rolled a stone vnto
the dore of the sepulchre:
47 And Marie Magdalene, and Marie Ioses
mother beholde where he shulde be layd.

CHAP. XVI.

1 The women come to the graue. 9 Christ being risen againe, appeareth to Magdalene. 14 Also to the eleuen and reprouth their vnbelief. 16 He committeth the preaching of the Gospel & the ministration of baptisme vnto them.

1 And* whē the Sabbath daye was past,
Marie Magdalene, & Marie the *mother*
of Iames, & Salome, boght swete ointments
that they might come, and embaulme
him.

Luk.24,1. iohn 20,1.

2 Therefore early in the morning, the first
day of the weeke, they came vnto the sepulchre,
when the sunne was "yet rising,

"Or, not risen.

3 And they said one to another, Who shal
roll vs away the stone from the doore of
the sepulchre?
4 And when they loked, they sawe that the
stone was rolled away (for it was a very
great one.)
5 * So they went into the sepulchre, and
sawe [a] a yong man sitting at the right side,
clothed in a long white robe: and they were
afrayed.

Mat.28,1. iohn 20,12.

a The Angel of God in the likenes of a yong man.

6 But he said vnto them, Be not afrayed: ye
seke Iesus of Nazaret, which hathe bene
crucified: he is risen, he is not here: beholde
the place, where they put him.
7 But go your way, and tel his disciples, &
[b] Peter, that he wil go before you into Galile:
there shal ye se him, * as he said vnto
you.

b He especialy maketh mēcion of Peter to cōfort him, because he had fallen into greater dāger then the rest.

Mat.26,32. chap.14,28.

8 And they went out quickely and fled frō
the sepulchre: for they trembled and were
amased: nether said they any thing to any
man: for they were afrayed.
9 ¶ And when Iesus was risen againe, in the
morow (which was ye first day of the weke)
he appeared first to Marie Magdalene, *out
of whome he had cast seuen deuils.

Iohn 20,16. luk.8,2.

10 And she went and tolde them that had
bene with him, which mourned and wept.
11 And whē they heard that he was aliue, &
had appeared to her, they [c] beleued it not.

c They had sone forgotten that ye Christ had foretolde them of his resurrection.

12 ¶ *After that, he appeared vnto two of
them in another forme, as thei walked and
went into the countrey.

Luk.24,13.

13 And they went and tolde it to the remnant,
but they beleued them not.

Luk.24,36. Iohn 20,19.
d Mourning & praying.

14 ¶ *Finally, he appeared vnto the eleuen as
they [d] sate together, and reproued them of
their vnbelief & hardnes of heart, because they beleued not them which had sene
him, being risen vp againe.

Mat.28,19.
e As wel Gentile as Iewe.

15 And he said vnto them, * Go ye into all
the worlde, & preache the Gospel to [e] euerie creature.
16 He that shal beleue & be baptized, shalbe saued: *but he that wil not beleue, shalbe damned.

Iohn 12,18. Act.16,18.
f This gifte was but for a time to cause men the more willingly to receiue the Gospel which as yet was not euidently knowen.

17 And these [f] tokens shal followe thẽ that
beleue, *In my Name thei shal cast out deuils, and * shal speake with [g] newe tongues,
18 *And shal take away serpents, and if they
shal drinke any deadlie thing, it shal not
hurt them: *they shal lay their hãds on the
sicke, and they shal recouer.
19 *So after the Lord had spoken vnto thẽ,
he was receiued into heauen, & sate at the
right hand of God.
20 And they went forthe, and preached euerie where. And the * Lord wroght with
them, & confirmed the worde with [h] signes
that followed, Amen.

Act.2,4. & 10,46.
g With other and diuers, as Luke saith.
Act.28,5. Act.18,8. Luk.24,5. Eb.2,4.
h The miracles & signes followe the doctrine, as certein seales, so that if the doctrine be false, the miracles can be no better, Deute.13,3.

THE HOLY GOSPEL
of Iesus Christ, according to Luke.

CHAP. I.

5 Of Zacharias, and Elisabet. 11 The Angel sheweth him of the natiuitie of Iohn Baptist. 20 His incredulitie is punished. 28 The talke of the Angel, and Marie. 46 Her song 57 The birth, Circumcision, and graces of Iohn. 68 Zacharias giueth thankes to God, & propheceth.

a Meaning, the Apostles with whome he was conuersant.
b Or of the thing: and it may be referred ether to Christ or to the Gospel. and hereby is mẽt that they were the ministers of Christ, who is called ỹ worde: or ministers of ỹ worde ỹ is to say, of the Gospel: & this comendeth the autoritie of his doctrine, seing he receiued it of the Apostles.
c The sonne of Antipater.
d Read.1.Chr.24,10.
e By her father: for by her mothers line she was of ỹ house of Dauid.
f This perfection or iustice is iudged by the frutes and outwarde appearance, and not by the cause: which onely cometh of Gods fre mercie through Christ.
g The Greke worde signifieth, iustifications, whereby is ment the outwarde obseruation of the ceremonies commanded by God.
h That is, ỹ euening & morning sacrifice according to the Law. i The Temple was deuided into thre partes: the first was ỹ bodie of the Tẽple called Atriũ, where the people was: the second called, Sanctũ, where the Priests and Leuites were: and the third Sanctum Sanctorum, into the which the hie Priest entred once a yere to sacrifice.

1 FOr as muche as many
haue takẽ in hand to set
forthe ỹ storie of those
things, whereof we are
fully persuaded,
2 [a] As they haue deliuered them vnto vs, which
from the beginning sawe thẽ their selues,
and were ministers of the [b] worde,
3 It semed good also to me (moste noble
Theophilus) assone as I had searched out
perfitely all thĩgs frõ ỹ beginning, to write vnto thee thereof from point to point,
4 That thou mightest acknowledge the cer
teintie of those things, whereof thou hast
bene instructed.
5 IN the time of [c] Herode King of Iudea,
there *was* a certeine Priest named Zacharias, of the [d] course of Abia: & his wife
was of the [e] daughters of Aaron, and her
name *was* Elisabet.
6 Bothe were [f] iust before God, and walked
in all the commandements and [g] ordinances of the Lord, without reprofe.
7 And thei had no childe, because that Elisabet was barren: & bothe were wel strickẽ
in age.
8 And it came to passe, as he executed the
Priests office before God, as his course came in order,
9 According to the custome of the Priests
office, his lot was to [h] burne incense, when
he went into the [i] Temple of the Lord.
10 And the whole multitude of the people
were without in prayer, * while the incense was burning.
11 Then appeared vnto him an Angel of the
Lord standing at the right side of the altar of incense.
12 And when Zacharias sawe *him*, he was
troubled, and feare fel vpon him.
13 But the Angel said vnto him, Feare not,
Zacharias: for thy prayer is heard, and thy
wife Elisabet shal beare thee a sonne, and
thou shalt call his name [k] Iohn.
14 And thou shalt haue ioye and gladnes, &
many shal reioyce at his birth.
15 For he shalbe great in the sight of the
Lord, & shal nether drinke wine, nor [l] strõg
drinke: and he shalbe filled with the holie
Gost, euen from his mothers wombe.
16 *And many of the children of Israel shal
he turne to their Lord God.
17 *For he shal go [m] before him in the spi
rit & power of Elias, to turne the hearts of
the [n] fathers to ỹ children, & the disobediẽt
to the wisdome of the iust men, to make
readie a people prepared for the Lord.
18 Then Zacharias said vnto the Angel,
Whereby shal I knowe this? for I am an
olde man, and my wife is of a great age.
19 And the Angel answered, and said vnto
him, I am [o] Gabriel that stand in the presence of God, and am sent to speake vnto
thee, & to shewe thee these good tidings.
20 And beholde, thou shalt be domme, and
not be able to speake, vntil [p] the day that
these things be done, because thou bele-
uedst not my wordes, which shalbe fulfilled in their season.
21 Now the people waited for Zacharias,
and marueiled that he taried so long in
the Temple.
22 And whẽ he came out, he colde not speake vnto them: then they perceiued that he
had

Exod.30,7. leu.16,17.
k Which signifieth the grace of the Lord.
l The worde signifieth all maner of drĩke which maketh mẽ dronken
Mal.4,3. mat.11,14. Mat.3,14.
m As a King in his royaltie hathe one to go before him, who signifieth the King to be at hand.
n Whẽ Christ saieth he came to set the father against ỹ sonne &c. he meaneth the successe ỹ cometh of ỹ Gospel through the malice of men: but here he speaketh of the true end & prosperitie of the Gospel.
o Which signifieth, the strength or soueraintie of God.
p We must not measure Gods promes by our weake senses.

had sene a vision in the Temple: for he
made signes vnto them, and remained
domme.
23 And it came to passe, when the dayes of
his office were fulfilled, that he departed
q to his owne house.
24 And after those dayes, his wife Elisabet
conceiued, and hid her self fiue moneths,
saying,
25 Thus hathe the Lord dealt with me, in
the dayes wherein he loked on *me*, to take
from me r my rebuke among men.
26 ¶ And in the sixt moneth, the Angel Gabriel was sent frō God vnto a citie of Galile, named Nazaret,
27 To a virgine affianced to a man whose
name *was* Ioseph, of the house of Dauid, &
the virgins name *was* Marie.
28 And the Angel went in vnto her, & said,
"Haile thou *that art* "freely beloued: ẏ Lord
is with thee: blessed *art* thou amōg wome.
29 And when she sawe *him*, she was troubled
at his saying, & thoght what maner of salutacion that shulde be.
30 Then ẏ Angel said vnto her, Feare not,
Marie: for s thou hast founde fauour with
God.
31 *For lo, thou shalt conceiue in thy wombe, and beare a sonne, and shalt call his name IESVS.
32 He shalbe great, & shalbe called the Sonne t of the moste High, and the Lord God
shal giue vnto him the throne of his father
Dauid.
33 *And he shal reigne ouer ẏ house of Iacob
for euer, & of his kingdome shalbe nō end.
34 Then said Marie vnto the Angel, u How
shal this be, seing, I know no man?
35 And the Angel answered, and said vnto
her, The holie Gost shal come vpon thee,
& the power of the most High shal x ouershadowe thee: therefore also that y holie
thing which shalbe borne of thee, shalbe
called the Sonne of God.
36 And beholde, thy z cousin Elisabet, she hathe also conceiued a sonne in her olde age:
and this is her sixt moneth, which was called barren.
37 For with God shal nothing be vnposi-
ble.
38 Then Marie said, Beholde, the seruant of
the Lord: be it vnto me according to thy
worde. So the Angel departed from her.
39 ¶ And Marie arose in those dayes, and
went into the hill *countrey* with haste to a
a citie of Iuda,
40 And entred into the house of Zacharias,
and saluted Elisabet.
41 And it came to passe, as Elisabet heard
the salutacion of Marie, the babe b sprang

q Whiles their course endured to sacrifice, they might not lie with their wiues, nor drinke anie licour that might make one drunke
r For the barren women enioyed not the promes which God made to them that were maried, to haue yssue: but principally they were depriued of that promes which God made to Abraham, that he wolde increase his sede
"Or, gladnes be to thee.
"Or, receiued into fauour.
s Not for her merites: but onely through Gods fre mercie, who loued vs when we were sinners, that whosoeuer reioyceth, shulde reioyce in the Lord.
Isa.7,14.
mat.1,21.
chap.2,21.
t Because he is the true Sonne of God, begotten from before all beginning, and manifested in flesh at the determinat time.
Dan 7,14.
micah 4,7.
u She wolde be resolued of all doutes to the end that she might more surely embrase the promes of God
x It shalbe a secret operatiō of the holie Gost.
y He must be pure and without sinne, ẇ must take away the sinnes of the worlde.
z Notwithstāding that Elisabet was maried to one of ẏ tribe of Leui, yet she was Maries cousin which was of the stocke of Dauid. For the law which forbade mariage out of their owne tribe, was onely that ẏ tribes shulde not be mixt and confounded, which colde not bein maryig with ẏ Leuites: for they had no portiō assigned vnto thē.

in her bellie, & Elisabet was filled with the
holie Gost.
42 And she cryed with a loude voyce, and
said, Blessed art thou among women, because the c frute of thy wombe is blessed.
43 And whence *cometh* this to me, that the
mother of my Lord shulde come to me?
44 For lo, assone as the voyce of thy salu-
tatiō sōuded in mine eares, the babe sprāg
in my bellie for ioye.
45 And blessed *is* she that beleued: for those things shalbe performed, which were
tolde her d from the Lord.
46 Then Marie said, My e soule magnifieth
the Lord,
47 And my spirit reioyceth in God my
Sauiour.
48 For he hathe loked on the "poore degre
of his seruant: for beholde, from hence
forthe shal all ages call f me blessed.
49 Because, he that is mightie, hathe done
for me great things, & holie *is* his Name.
50 And his g mercie *is* from generacion to
generacion on them that feare him.
51 *He hathe shewed strength with his arme: *he hathe scattered the proude in the
h imaginacion of their hearts.
52 He hathe put downe the mightie from
their seates, and exalted thē of lowe degre.
53 *He hathe filled the hungrie with good
things, and sent away the riche emptie.
54 * He hathe vpholden Israel his seruant,
being mindeful of *his* mercie
55 (* As he hathe spoken to our fathers, *to
wit*, to Abraham and his "sede) for euer.
56 ¶ And Marie abode with her about thre
moneths: after, she returned to her owne
house.
57 ¶ Now Elisabets time was fulfilled, that
she shulde be deliuered, and she broght
forthe a sonne.
58 And her neighbours, & cousins heard tel
how the Lord had shewed his great mercie vpon her, and they reioyced with her.
59 And it was so that on the eight day they
came to circumcise the babe, & called him
Zacharias, after the Name of his father.
60 But his mother answered, and said, Not
so, but he shalbe called Iohn.
61 And they said vnto her, There is none
of thy kinred, ẏ is named with this Name.
62 Then they made signes to his father,
how he wolde haue him called.
63 So he asked for writing tables, & wrote,
saying, His name is Iohn, and they marueiled all.
64 And his mouth was opened immediatly,
and his tongue *losed*, and he i spake & praised God.
65 Then feare came on all them that dwelt
nere vnto them, and all these wordes were
noised abroade throughout all the hil *cōtrey* of Iudea.

c He sheweth the cause why Marie was blessed.
d By the message of the Angel.
e The soule, & the spirit signifie the vnderstanding & affectiō, which are the two principal partes of the soule.
"Or, lowe estate.
f This fauour that God hathe shewed me, shalbe spokē of for euer.
Isa.51,9.
Psal 33,10.
isa 29,15.
g According to the promes made to Abraham that he wolde be his God, and the God of his sede for euer.
1.Sam.2,6.
psal.34,11.
Isa 30,38.
& 41,8.
and 54,5.
iere.31,5.
Gen.17,19.
& 22,16.
psal.132,12.
h The wicked lay snares for other, wherein they them selues are taken.
"Or, posteritie.
i Not onely for his benefite in pardoning his faute, but also to shewe that he was iustly punished for his incredulitie.

a Which was also called, Kiriath-arba or Hebron, Iosh 14,15. & 21,11. b This mouing was extraordinarie and not natural, which was to commend the miracle.

66 And all they that heard them, laid *them*
vp in their hearts, saying, What maner
childe shal this be! and the [k] hand of the
Lord was with him.
67 Thē his father Zacharias was filled with
the holie Gost, and prophecied, saying,
68 Blessed *be* ẏ Lord God of Israel, because he hathe [l] visited* & redemed his people,
69 *And hathe raised vp the [m] horne of saluacion vnto vs, in the house of his seruant
Dauid,
70 *As he spake by the mouth of his holie
Prophetes, which were since the worlde
began, *saying*,
71 *That he wolde send vs* deliuerance from
our enemies, & from the hands of all that
hate vs,
72 That he wolde shewe [n] mercie towards
our fathers, and remembre his holie couenant,
73 **And* the othe which he sware to our father Abraham:
74 *Which was*, that he wolde grante vnto vs,
that we being deliuered out of the hands
of our enemies, shulde [o] serue him without feare
75 All the dayes of our life, in *holines and
righteousnes [p] before him.
76 And thou, babe, shalt be called the Prophete of the moste High: for thou shalt
go before the face of the Lord, to prepare his wayes,
77 *And* to giue knowledge of saluatiō vnto
his people, by the [q] remissiō of their sinnes,
78 Through the tender mercie of our God,
whereby * the [r] day spring from an hie hathe visited vs,
79 To giue light to them that sit in darkenes, and in the shadowe of death, & to guide our fete into the way of [s] peace.
80 And the childe grewe and waxed strong
in spirit, and was in [t] the wildernes, til the
day came, that he shulde shewe him self
vnto Israel.

CHAP. II.

7 The birth and circumcision of Christ. 22 He was receiued into the Tēple. 28 Simeon and Anna prophecie of him. 46 He was founde among the doctours. 51 His obedience to father and mother.

1 AND it came to passe in those dayes,
that there came a cōmandement frō
Augustus Cesar, that all the [a] worlde shulde be "taxed.
2 (This first [b] taxing was made when Cy-
renius was gouernour of Syria.)
3 Therefore went all to be taxed euerie mā
to his owne citie.
4 And [c] Ioseph also went vp from Galile
out of a citie called Nazaret, into Iudea,
vnto the citie of * Dauid, which is called
Beth-lehem (because he was of the house
and linage of Dauid,)
5 To be taxed with Marie that was giuen

k The mightie power of God and his graces wᶜ declared that he shulde be an excellēt persone.
Mat.1,21.
chap.2,30.
l In declaring him self mindeful of his people, & therefore is come from heauen to visit and redeme them.
Psal.132,17.
Ier.23,6.
& 30,10.
m When the promises of God semed to haue failed, & the state of Israel to haue perished, then sent he his Christ who by his inuincible strength, as with a strong horne ouerthrewe his enemies.
Gen.22,16.
iere.31,6.
ebr.6,13.
n He declareth the cause and fountaine of our redēption.
1.Pet.1,15.
o This is the end of our redemption.
p To whome no hypocrisie can be acceptable.
q He sheweth that our saluatiō cōsisteth in the remissiō of sinnes, which is the prīcipal parte of the Gospel.
Zach.3,9.
mal.4,2.
& 6,12.
r Or, branche of a tre, meaning the Messias, who is the sunne of righteousnes which shineth from heauen.
s That is, of all felicitie.
t He meaneth ẏ parte of Iudea which was least inhabited where also the grosse & rude people dwelled.
Chap. II.
a So much as was subiect to the Romains.
"Or, put in writing.
b Whereby the people were more charged and oppressed.
c He sheweth by what occasion Iesus was borne in Beth-lehem.
Iohn 7,42.

him to wife, which was with childe.
6 ¶ And so it was, that while thei were there, the daies were accomplished that she
shulde be deliuered.
7 And she broght forthe her [d] first begotten
sonne, & wrapped him in swadling clothes
and laid him in a [e] cratche, because there
was no rowme for them in the ynne.
8 ¶ And there were in the same coūtrey shep
herds, abiding in the field, and keping
watch by night because of their flocke.
9 And lo, the Angel of the Lord came vpon them, and the glorie of the Lord shone
about them, and they were sore afraide.
10 Then the Angel said vnto them, Be not
afraide: for beholde, I bring you tidings
of great ioye, that shalbe to all the people:
11 *That is*, that vnto you is borne this day in
the citie of [f] Dauid, a Sauiour, which is
Christ the Lord.
12 And [g] this *shalbe* a signe to you, Ye shal
finde ẏ childe swadled, & laid in a cratch.
13 And straight way there was with the Angel a multitude of heauenlie souldiers,
praying God, and saying,
14 Glorie *be* to God in the high *heauens*,
and peace in earth, & towards men [h] good
wil.
15 And it came to passe when the Angels
were gone away from them into heauen,
that ẏ shepherds said one to another, Let
vs go then vnto Beth-lehem, and se this
thīg that is come to passe, which the Lord
hathe shewed vnto vs.
16 So they came with haste, & founde bothe
Marie and Ioseph, and the babe laid in the
cratch.
17 And when they had sene it, they published abroade the thing, which was tolde
them of that childe.
18 And all that heard it, wōdred at ẏ things
which were tolde them of the shepherds.
19 But Marie kept all those sayings & pondered *them* in her heart.
20 And the shepherds returned, glorifying
and praising God, for all that they had
heard & sene, as it was spoken vnto them.
21 ¶ *And whē the eight daies were accomplished, that they shulde circumcise the
childe, his name was then called * IESVS,
which was named of the Angel, before he
was conceiued in the wombe.
22 *And when the dayes of "her purificatiō
after the Law of Moses were accōplished,
they broght him to Ierusalem, to present
him to the Lord.
23 (As it is writen in the Law of the Lord,
* Euerie man childe" that *first* openeth the
wombe, shalbe called holie to the Lord:)
24 And to giue an oblation, * as it is commanded in the Law of the Lord, [i] a paire
of turtle doues, or two yong pigeons.
25 And beholde, there was a mā in Ierusalē,
whose

d Read Mat. 1,25.
e Whereby apeared his pouertie, and their crueltie which wolde not pitie suche a woman in suche case.
f Which was Beth-lehem.
g Because thei shulde not be offended with Christs poore estate, the Angel preuenteth this doute, and sheweth in what sorte they shulde finde him.
h The fre mercie & good wil of God, which is the founteine of our peace and felicitie, & is chiefly declared to the elect.
Gen.17,12.
Mat.1,21.
chap.1,31.
iohn 7,22.
Leu.12,3.
"Or, their.
Exod.13,2.
nomb.8,16.
"Or, that is first borne.
Leu.12,6.
i Which offring was apointed to thē which were so poore that they were not able to offer a lambe.

whose name was Simeon: this man *was* iuste, and feared God, and waited for the
consolation of Israel, and the [k] holie Gost
was vpon him.
26 And a reuelation was giuen him of the
holie Gost, that he shulde not se death, before he had sene the Lords "Christ.
27 And he came" by *the motion* of ỳ Spirit in
to the Temple, & when the parẽts broght
in the childe Iesus, to do for him after the
custome of the Law,
28 Then he toke him in his armes, and prai
sed God, and said,
29 Lord, [l] now lettest thou thy seruant departe in peace, according to thy worde.
30 For mine eyes haue sene thy [m] saluation,
31 Which thou hast prepared before the fa
ce of all people:
32 A light to "be reueiled to the Gentiles, &
the glorie of thy people Israel.
33 And Ioseph and his mother marueiled
at those things, which were spoken touching him.
34 And Simeon [n] blessed them, and said vnto Marie his mother, Beholde, this *childe* is
appointed for the [o] * fall and rising againe of manie in Israel, & for a signe which
shalbe spoken against,
35 (Yea and a [p] sworde shal pearce through
thy soule) that the [q] thoghts of manie hearts may be opened.
36 And there was a Prophetesse, one Anna
the daughter of Phanuel, of the tribe of
Aser, which was of a great age, & had [r] liued with an housband seuen yeres frõ her
virginitie.
37 And she *was* widowe about foure score,
and foure yeres, and went [s] not out of the
Temple, but serued *God* with fastings and
prayers, night and day.
38 She thẽ coming at the same instant vpon
them, "confessed likewise the Lord, & spake of him to all that loked for redemption
in Ierusalem.
39 And when thei had performed all things
according to the Law of the Lord, they
returned into Galile to their owne citie
Nazaret.
40 And the childe grewe, and waxed strõg
in Spirit, and was filled with wisdome, and
the grace of God was with him.
41 ¶ Now his parẽts went to Ierusalẽ euerie yere, * at the feast of the Passeouer.
42 And when he was twelue yere olde, and
they were come vp to Ierusalem, after the
custome of the feast,
43 And had finished the dayes *thereof*, as
they returned, the childe Iesus remained
in Ierusalem, and Ioseph knewe not nor
his mother,
44 But they supposing, that he had bene in
the companie, went a dayes iorney, and

k The Spirit of prophecie.
"Or, Messias.
"Greke, in the Spirit.
l Simeon declareth him self to dye willingly since he hathe sene the Messias which was ꝓmised.
m The meane and substance of saluation.
"Or, for the reuelation of.
n That is, praied to God for them, and for the prosperitie of Christs kingdome.
Isa.8,14. rom.9,32. 1 pet.2,8.
o To be ỳ fall of ỳ reprobate which perishe through their owne defaut, & raising vp of the elect to whome God giueth faith
p That is, sorrowes shulde pearce her heart, as a sworde.
q This chiefly appeareth whẽ the crosse is layd vpõ vs, whereby mens hearts are tryed.
r She was seuen yeres maryed.
s She was cõtinually in the Temple.
"Or, praised.
Deut.16,1.

soght him among *their* kinsfolke, and acquaintance.
45 And whẽ they founde him not, they turned backe to Ierusalem, and soght him.
46 And it came to passe thre dayes after,
that they founde him in the Temple, sitting in the middes of the "doctours, bothe
hearing them, and asking them questions.
47 And all that heard him, were astonied at
his vnderstanding, and answers.
48 So when thei saw him, they were amased,
and his mother said vnto him, Sonne,
why hast thou thus dealt with vs? beholde, thy father and I haue soght thee with
heauie hearts.
49 Then said he vnto them, How is it that
ye soght me? [t] knewe ye not that I must
go about my fathers busines?
50 But they [u] vnderstode not the worde that
he spake to them.
51 Then he wẽt downe with them, & came
to Nazaret, and was subiect to them: & his
mother kept all these sayings in her heart.
52 And Iesus increased in wisdome, & stature, and in fauour with God and men.

"Or, learned men.
t Our duetie to God is to be preferred before father and mother.
u For his vocatiõ was not yet manifestly knowen.

CHAP. III.

3 The preaching, baptisme, and prisonment of Iohn. 15 He is thoght to be Christ. 21 Christ is baptized. 23 His age, and genealogie.

1 NOw in the fifteth yere of the reigne
of Tiberius Cesar, Pontius Pilate
being gouernour of Iudea, and [a] Herode
being tetrarch of Galile, and his brother
Philippe tetrarch of Iturea, and of the
countrey of Trachonitis, and Lysanias the
tetrarch of Abilene,
2 (*When Annas and Caiaphas were the
high [b] Priests) the worde of God came
vnto Iohn, the sonne of Zacharias in the
wildernes.
3 *And he came into all the coastes about
Iordan, preaching the baptisme of repentance for the remission of sinnes,
4 As it is written in the boke of the sayings of Esaias the Prophet, which saith,
*The voyce of him that cryeth in the wil-
dernes *is*, Prepare ye the way of the Lord:
make his paths straight.
5 Euerie [c] valley shalbe filled, and euerie
mountaine, and hil shalbe broght lowe, &
croked things shalbe made straight, & the
rough wayes *shalbe made* smothe.
6 And "all flesh shal se the [d] saluation of
God.
7 Then said he to the people that were come out to be baptized of him, "* O generations of vipers, who hathe forewarned
you to flee from the wrath to come?
8 Bring forthe therefore frutes worthie a-
mendemẽt of life, & beginne not to say ỳ
your selues, We haue Abrahã to *our* father:
for I say vnto you, ỳ God is able of these
stones to raise vp children vnto Abraham.

a This was ỳ sonne of Herode called the great.
Act.4,6.
b There colde be by Gods Law but one sacrificer at once: but because of the troubles that then reigned, the office was so mangled by reason of ambition & briberie, that bothe 'Caiaphas and Annas his father in law had it deuided betwene thẽ.
Mat.3,2. mar.1,4. Isa.40,3. ioh.1,23.
c All impediments shalbe taken away, ỳ shulde hinder ỳ way of God or of saluatiõ, so that ỳ way shalbe plaine by Christ to lead vs vnto God
"Or, euerie mã.
d That is, the Messias shalbe reueiled to ỳ worlde
Mat.3,7.
"Or, vipers brodes.

e The vengeāce of God is at hand.

9 Now also is the e axe laid vnto the roote
of the trees: therefore euerie tre which
bringeth not forthe good frute, shalbe
hewen downe and cast into the fyre.
10 ¶ Then the people asked him, saying,
What shal we do then?
11 And he answered, and said vnto them,
* He f that hathe two coates, let him parte
with him that hathe none: and he that hathe meat, let him do likewise.
12 Then came there g Publicanes also to be
baptized, and said vnto him, Master, what
shal we do?
13 And he said vnto thē, Require no more
then that which is appointed vnto you.
14 The souldiers likewise demanded of
him, saying, And what shal we do? And he
said vnto them, Do violence to no man,
nether accuse anie falsely, and be content
with your wages.
15 As the people waited, and all men mused in their hearts of Iohn, if he were not
the Christ,
16 Iohn answered, and said to them all, * In
dede I h baptize you with water, but one
stronger then I, cometh, whose shoes latchet I am not worthie to vnlose: he wil
baptize you with the holie Gost, and
i with fyre.
17 * Whose fanne *is* in his hand, and he wil
make cleane his flooer, and wil gather the
wheat into his garner, but the chaff wil
he burne vp with fyre that neuer shalbe
quenched.
18 Thus then exhorting with manie other
things, he preached vnto the people.
19 * But when k Herode the tetrarch was rebuked of him for Herodias his brother
Philippes wife, and for all the euils which
Herode had done,
20 He added yet this aboue all, that he shut
vp Iohn in prison.
21 * Now it came to passe, as all the people
were baptized, & that Iesus was baptized
& did pray, that the heauen was opened:
22 And ỳ holie Gost came downe in a bode
lie shape like a doue, vpō him, & there was
a voyce frō heauen, saying, Thou art my
beloued Sonne: in thee I am wel pleased.
23 ¶ And Iesus him self began to be about
thirtie yere of age, being as men supposed the sonne of l Ioseph, *which was the son-*
ne of Eli,
24 *The sonne* of Matthat, *the sonne* of Leui,
the sonne of Melchi, *the sonne* of Ianna, *the*
sonne of Ioseph,
25 *The sonne* of Mattathias, *the sonne* of Amos,
the sonne of Naum, *the sonne* of Esli, *the son-*
ne of Nagge,
26 *The sonne* of Maath, *the sonne* of Mattathias, *the sonne* of Semei, *the sonne* of "Ioseph,
the sonne of Iuda,

Iam. 2,15. 1 iohn. 3,17.
f He willeth that the riche helpe ỳ poore according to their necessitie.
g Whose office was to receiue the tribute and towles.
Mat. 3,11. mar. 1,8. ioh. 1,26. act. 1,5. & 8,4. & 11,16. & 19,4.
Mat. 3,12.
h The vertue and force of baptisme standeth in Iesus Christ, & Iohn was but ỳ minister thereof.
i That is, with a mightie, and vehement Spirit: whose propertie is to cōsume, and purge our filth as fyre doeth ỳ mettals.
Mat 14,3. mar. 6,17.
k Named Antipas.
Mat 3,23. mar. 1,9. ioh. 1,32.
l Luke ascendeth from the last father to ỳ first, and Matthewe descendeth from the first to ỳ last. Matthewe extēdeth not his rehearsal further then to Abrahā, w̃ is for the assurāce of ỳ promes for the Iewes. Luke referreth it euen to Adā, whereby the Gentiles also are assured of the promes, because they came of Adam, & are restored in the seconde Adam: Matthewe counteth by the legal descent, and Luke by the natural: finally bothe two speaking of the same persones applie vnto them diuers names. "Or, Iosech.

27 *The sonne* of Ioanna, *the sonne* of Rhesa,
the sonne of Zorobabel, *the sonne* of Salathiel, *the sonne* of Neri,
28 *The sonne* of Melchi, *the sonne* of Addi, *the*
sonne of Cosam, *the sonne* of Elmodam, *the*
sonne of Er,
29 ¶ *The sonne* of "Iose, *the sonne* of Eliezer, *the* "Or, Iesus.
sonne of Iorim, *the sonne* of "Matthat, *the son-* "Or, Mattha
ne of Leui,
30 *The sonne* of Simeon, *the sonne* of Iuda, *the*
sonne of Ioseph, *the sonne* of Ionan, *the son-*
ne of Eliacim,
31 *The sonne* of Melea, *the sonne* of "Mainan, "Or, Menna.
the sonne of Mattatha, *the sonne* of Nathan,
the sonne of Dauid,
32 *The sonne* of Iesse, *the sonne* of Obed, *the*
sonne of Booz, *the sonne* of Salmon, *the son-*
ne of Naasson,
33 *The sonne* of Aminadab, *the sonne* of Aram,
the sonne of Esrom, *the sonne* of Phares, *the*
sonne of Iuda,
34 *The sonne* of Iacob, *the sonne* of Isaac, *the*
sonne of Abraham, *the sonne* of Thara, *the*
sonne of Nachor,
35 *The sonne* of Saruch, *the sonne* of Ragau,
the sonne of Phalec, *the sonne* of Eber, *the son-*
ne of Sala,
36 *The sonne* of Cainā, *the sonne* of Arphaxad, *the sonne* of Sem, *the sonne* of Noe, *the*
sonne of Lamech,
37 *The sonne* of Mathusala, *the sōne* of Enoch,
the sonne of Iared, *the sonne* of Maleleel, *the*
sonne of Cainan.
38 *The sonne* of Enos, *the sonne* of Seth, *the son-*
ne of Adam, *the sonne* m of God.

m Not that Adam was ỳ sonne of God by generatiō, but by creation, in the w̃ sense God also calleth him self father, Deut. 32,6. & ver 18 & 19.

CHAP. IIII.

1 Iesus is led into the wildernes to be tempted. 13 He ouercometh the deuil. 14 He goeth into Galile, 16 Preacheth at Nazaret, and Capernaum. 22 The Iewes despise him. 38 He cometh into Peters house, and healeth his mother in law. 41 The deuils acknowledge Christ. 43 He preacheth through the cities.

1 AND Iesus ful of the holie Gost returned from Iordan, and was led by
the Spirit into the wildernes,
2 * And was *there* fourtie dayes tempted of
the deuil, and in those dayes a he did eat
nothing: but when they were ended, he afterwarde was hungrie.
3 Then the deuil said vnto him, If thou be
the Sonne of God, commande this stone
that it be made bread.
4 But Iesus answered him, saying, It is writen, * That man shal not liue by bread o-
nely, but by euerie b worde of God.
5 Then the deuil toke him vp into an high
mountaine, and shewed him all the kingdomes of the worlde, "in the twinkeling of
an eye.
6 And the deuil said vnto him, All this
power wil I c giue thee, and the glorie
of those *kingdomes*: for that is deliuered
to me: & to whomsoeuer I wil, I giue it,
7 If thou

Mat. 4,1. mar. 1,12.
a This fast was miraculous, to confirme the Gospel, and oght no more of men to be followed thē the other miracles that Christ did.
Deu. 8,3. mat. 4,4.
b That is, by the ordinance, and prouidence of God.
"Greke, In a moment of time.
c Satan promiseth that, w̃ he can not giue, thinking thereby that he might deceiue the more craftely: for he is but prince of ỳ worlde by permission, & hathe his power limited.

"Or, fall downe before me.

7 If thou therefore wilt "worship me, they
shalbe all thine.

"Greke, Go behinde me.

Deut.6,16. & 10,20.

d Christ sheweth ẏ all creatures oght onely to worship and serue God.

e This declareth how hard it is to resist ẏ tentacions of Satan: for he giueth not ouer for twise or thrise putting backe.

Psal.91,12.

Deut.6,16.

8 But Iesus answered him, and said, "Hence
from me, Satan: for it is written, * Thou
shalt worship the Lord thy d God, and
him alone thou shalt serue.
9 Then he broght him to e Ierusalem, and
set him on a pinacle of the Temple, and
said vnto him, If thou be the Sonne of
God, cast thy self downe from hence,
10 For it is written, * That he wil giue his
Angels charge ouer thee to kepe thee:
11 And with *their* hands they shal lift thee
vp, lest at anie time thou shuldest dash thy
fote against a stone.
12 And Iesus answered and said vnto him,
It is said, * Thou shalt not tẽpt the Lord
thy God.
13 And when the deuil had ended all the
tentacion, he departed from him f for a
season.

f It is not ynough, twise or thrise to resist Satã: for he neuer ceaseth to tempt: or if he relent a litle, it is to the ẽd, that he maye renewe his force & assaile vs more sharply.

14 ¶ And Iesus returned by the power of ẏ
spirit into Galile: and there went a fame
of him throughout all the region rounde
about.
15 For he taught in their Synagogues, and
was honoured of all men.

Mat.13,54. mar.6,1. iohn 4,43.

16 * And he came to Nazaret where he had
bene broght vp, and (as his custome was)
went into the Synagogue on the Sabbath
day, and stode vp to reade.
17 And there was deliuered vnto him the
boke of the Prophet Esaias: and when he
had opened the boke, he founde the place,
where it was written,

Isa.61,1.

g That is, endued with graces.

18 *The Spirit of the Lord *is* vpon me, because
he hathe g anointed me, that I shulde
preache the Gospel to the poore: he hathe
sent me, that I shulde heale the brokẽ
hearted, that I shulde preache deliuerãce
to the captiues, and recouering of sight to
the blinde, that I shulde set at libertie thẽ
that are bruised,

h He alludeth to the yere of Iubile, which is mencioned in the Law, whereby this great deliuerãce was figured

19 And that I shulde preache the h acceptable
yere of the Lord.
20 And he closed the boke, and gaue it againe
to the minister, and sate downe: and
the eyes of all that were in the Synagogue
were fastened on him.
21 Then he began to say vnto them, This
daye is this Scripture fulfilled in your
eares.

i Thei approued & commẽded what soeuer he said.

22 And all i bare him witnes, & wondered
at the gracious wordes, which proceded
out of his mouth, and said, Is not this Iosephs
sonne?

k Bestowe thy benefites vpon them, ẇ apperteine more vnto thee.

Ioh.4,44.

l Their infidelitie stayed Christ from working miracles.

23 Then he said vnto them, Ye wil surely
saye vnto me this prouerbe, Physicion,
k heale thy self: whatsoeuer we haue heard
done in Capernaum, do it here likewise
in thine owne countrey.
24 And he said, Verely I saye vnto you,
*No l Prophet is accepted in his owne countrey.

1.King.17,9. iam.5,17.

25 But I tell you of a trueth, manie widdowes
were in Israel in the dayes of * Elias,
when heauen was shut thre yeres and
six moneths, when great famine was throughout
all the land,
26 But vnto none of them was Elias sent,
saue into Sarepta, *a citie of* Sidon, vnto a
m certeine widdowe.

m He sheweth by examples ẏ God oft times preferreth the strãgers to the of the housholde.

2.King.5,14.

27 Also manie lepers were in Israel, in the
time of * Eliseus the Prophet: yet none of
them was made cleane, sauing Naaman
the Syrian.
28 Then all *that were* in the Synagogue,
whẽ thei heard it, were n filled with wrath,

n Because they perceiued that the grace of God shulde be taken frõ them & giuen to others.

29 And rose vp, and thrust him out of the
citie, and led him vnto the edge of the
hil, whereon their citie was buylt, to cast
him downe headlong.
30 But he passed o through the middes of
them, and went his way,

o And escaped miraculously out of their hands: for his houre was not yet come.

Mat.4,13. mar.1,21.

31 ¶ * And came downe into Capernaum a
citie of Galile, and there taught them on
the Sabbath dayes.

Mat.7,29. mar.1,22.

32 *And thei were astonied at his doctrine:
for his worde was with p autoritie.

p Ful of dignitie & maiestie, ẇ touched the heart of the auditours and caused them to beare reuerence to his wordes.

q That is, the mocion of the deuil, or ẏ was tormented ẇ a verie deuil.

33 And in the Synagogue there was a man
which had a q spirit of an vncleane deuil,
which cryed with a loude voyce,
34 Saying, Oh, what haue we to do with
thee, thou Iesus of Nazaret? art thou come
to destroy vs? I knowe who thou art,
euen the Holie one of God.
35 And Iesus rebuked him, saying, Holde
thy peace, and come out of him. Thẽ the
deuil throwing him in the middes *of them*,
came out of him, and hurt him not.
36 So feare came on them all, and they
spake among them selues, saying, What
thing is this? for with autoritie and power
he commandeth the foule spirits, and they
come out?
37 And the fame of him spred abroad
throughout all the places of the countrey
rounde about.

Mat.8,14. mar.1,29.

38 ¶ * And he rose vp, and came out of the
Synagogue, & entred into Simons house.
And Simons wiues mother was taken with
a great feuer, and they required him for
her.
39 Then he stode ouer her, and rebuked the
feuer, and it left her: and immediatly she
arose, and ministred vnto them.
40 Now whẽ the sunne was downe, all they
ẏ had sicke *folkes* of diuers diseases, broght
them vnto him, and he laied his hands on
euerie one of them, and healed them.

Mar.1,35.

r The deuils are cõstrained to confesse Christ to be ẏ Sonne of God, & yet it doeth nothing auaile them, because it cometh not of faith.

41 * And deuils also came out of manie,
crying, and saying, r Thou art the Christ
the Sonne of God: but he rebuked them,
& suffred them not to say that thei knewe
him to be the Christ.
42 And whẽ it was day, he departed & went

forthe into a desert place, and the people
soght him, and came to him, and kept him
that he shulde not departe from them.
43 But he said vnto them, Surely I must
also preache the kingdome of God to o-
ther cities: for therefore am I sent.
44 And he preached in the Synagogues of
Galile.

CHAP. V.

1 Christ preacheth out of the ship. 6 The great draught of fish. 10 Certeine disciples are called. 12 He clenseth the leper. 18 He healeth the man of the palsie. 27 He calleth Matthewe the customer. 30 Eateth with sinners, 34 And excuseth his, as touching fasting.

Mat.4,18. mar.1,16.

1 THen *it came to passe, as the people
preassed vpon him to heare the worde of God, that he stode by the lake of
Gennesaret,
2 And sawe two shippes stand by the lake
side, but the fisshermen were gone out of
them, and were wasshing their nettes.
3 And [a] he entred into one of the shippes,
which was Simons, and required him that
he wolde thrust of a litle from the land:
and he sate downe, and taught the people
out of the ship.

a To the intent that he might not be thronged of ẏ preasse, & also that he might the better be heard.

4 ¶ Now when he had left speaking, he
said vnto Simon, Lanche out into the depe, and let downe your nettes to make a
draught.
5 Then Simon answered, & said vnto him,
[b] Master, we haue trauailed all night, and
haue taken nothing: neuertheles at thy
[c] worde I wil let downe the net.

b The worde signifieth him that is made ruler ouer anie thing.

c He sheweth his prompt obedience to Christs commandement.

6 And when they had so done, they inclosed a great multitude of fishes, so that
their net brake.
7 And they beckened to their parteners,
which were in ẏ other ship, that thei shulde
come and helpe them, who came then, and
filled bothe the shippes, that they did
[d] sinke.

d Thei were so laden that thei almoste sunke.

8 Now when Simon Peter sawe it, he fell
downe at Iesus knees, saying, Lord, go frō
me: for I am a sinful man.
9 For he [e] was vtterly astonied, and all that
were with him, for the draught of fishes,
which they toke.

e The feeling of Gods presence maketh afrayed.

10 And so was also Iames and Iohn the sonnes of Zebedeus, which were companions
with Simon. Then Iesus said vnto Simon,
Feare not: from [f] hence forthe thou shalt
catch men.

f He appointeth him to ẏ office of an Apostle.

11 And when they had broght the shippes
to land, they forsoke all, & followed him.

Mat.8,2. mar.1,40.

12 ¶ *Now it came to passe, as he was in a
certeine citie, beholde, *there was* a man ful
of leprosie, and when he sawe Iesus, he fel
on his face, and besoght him, saying, Lord
if thou wilt, thou canst make me cleane.
13 So he stretched forthe his hand, & touched him, sayīg, I wil, be thou cleane. And
immediatly the leprosie departed from
him.
14 And he commanded him that he shulde
tell it no man: but Go, *saith he*, and shewe
thy self to the [g] Priest, and offer for thy
clensing, as *Moses hathe commanded, for
a witnes vnto them.

Leui.14,4.

g Hereby he shewed them that he wolde not transgresse the Law, and ẏ thei shulde be inexcusable, who seig ẏ miracle wroght, wolde not beleue Christ.

15 But so muche more went there a same
abroad of him, and great multitudes came together to heare, and to be healed of
him of their infirmities.
16 But he kept him self aparte in the wildernes, and praied.
17 ¶ And it came to passe, on a certeine
daye, as he was teaching, that the Pharises
& doctours of the Law sate by, which were
come out of euerie towne of Galile, and
Iudea, and Ierusalem, & the power of the
Lord was *in him* to heale them.

Mat.9,2. mar.2,3.

18 *Then beholde, men broght a man lyīg
in a bed, which was taken with a palsie, and
they soght meanes to bring him in, and to
laie him before him.
19 And when they colde not finde by what
way they might bring him in, because of
the preasse, they went vp on the house, &
let him downe through the tiling, bed &
all, in the middes before Iesus.
20 And when he sawe their faith, he said
vnto him, Man, thy [h] sinnes are forgiuen
thee.

h Christ toucheth the principal cause of all our euils.

21 Then the Scribes and the Pharises begā
to thinke, saying, Who is this that speaketh blasphemies? who can forgiue sinnes,
but God onelie?
22 But when Iesus perceiued their thoghts,
he answered, and said vnto them, What
thinke ye in your hearts?
23 Whether is easier to say, Thy [i] sinnes
are forgiuen thee, or to say, Rise and
walke?
24 But that ye may knowe that the Sonne
of man hathe autoritie to forgiue sinnes
in earth, (he said vnto the sicke of the palsie) I say to thee, Arise: take vp thy bed, &
go to thine house.

i Forasmuche as his diuinitie was sufficiently shewed by this miracle, he gaue them hereby to vnderstand ẏ he had power to forgiue sinnes.

25 And immediatly he rose vp before
them, and toke vp *his bed* whereon he laie,
and departed to his owne house, praising
God.
26 And they were all amased, and praised
God, and were filled with feare, saying,
Douteles we haue sene "strange things to
daye.

"Or, aboue our expectation.

Mat.9,9. mar.2,14.

27 ¶ *And after that, he went forthe and
sawe a Publicane named "Leui, sitting at
the receite of custome, & said vnto him,
Followe me.

"Or, Matthewe.

28 And he left all, rose vp, and followed
him.
29 Then Leui made him a great feast in
his owne house, where there was a great
companie of Publicanes, & of other, that
sate at table with them.

30 But

30 But they that were Scribes and Pharises
among them, murmured against his disci
ples, saying, Why eat ye & drinke ye with
Publicanes and sinners?
31 Then Iesus answered, and said vnto thē,
They that are whole, nede not the physicion, but they that are sicke.
32 *I came not to call the [k] righteous, but
sinners to repentance.
33 ¶*Then they said vnto him, Why do
the disciples of Iohn fast often, and "pray,
and the *disciples* of the Pharises also, but
thine eat, and drinke?
34 And he said vnto them, Can ye make the
[l] children of the wedding chamber to fast,
as long as the bridegrome is with them?
35 But the dayes wil come, euen when the
bridegrome shalbe taken away frō them:
then shal they fast in those dayes.
36 Againe he spake also vnto thē a parable,
No mā putteth a piece of a newe garmēt
into an olde vesture: for then the newe rē-
teth it, and the piece *taken* out of the new,
agreeth not with the olde.
37 [m] Also no man powreth newe wine into
olde vessels: for then the newe wine wil
breake the vessels, and it wil runne out, &
the vessels wil perish.
38 But newe wine must be powred into newe
vessels: so bothe are preserued.
39 Also no man that [n] drinketh olde wine,
straight way desireth newe: for he saith,
The olde is better.

1.Tim.1,15.
k Which seme to be righteo' and yet are but hypocrites.
Mat.9,14. mar.2,18.
"*Greke, make prayers.*
l The friends and familiars of Christ: and hereby Iesus Christ declareth that he wil not burdē his, before ẏ he hathe made them able to beare.
m Read Mat. 9,17.
n He admonisheth them not to trust to muche to their owne sense or iudgement: nor because they haue accustomed thē selues to one thing, to condēne another, which is better.

CHAP. VI.

3 Christ standeth in his disciples defence and his owne, as touching the breache of the Sabbath. 12 After watching and prayer he electeth his Apostles. 18 He healeth and teacheth the people. 20 He sheweth who are blessed. 27 To loue our ennemies. 37 Not to iudge rashly. 41 And to auoide hypocrisie.

1 AND *it came to passe on the seconde
[a] Sabbath, after the first, that he went
through the corne fields, and his disciples
plucked the eares of corne, and did eate,
and rubbe them in *their* hands.
2 And certeine of the Pharises said vnto
them, Why do ye that which is not lawful to do on the Sabbath dayes?
3 Then Iesus answered them, & said, * Haue ye not red this, that Dauid did when
he him self was an hungred, & they which
were with him,
4 How he went into the house of God, and
toke, and ate the shewe bread, & gaue also
to them which were with him, which was
not lawful to eate, but for the * Priests
onely?
5 And he said vnto them, The Sonne of mā
is [b] Lord also of the Sabbath day.
6 ¶* It came to passe also on another Sabbath, that he entred into the Synagogue &
taught, and there was a man, whose right
hand was dryed vp.
7 And the Scribes and Pharises watched
him, whether he wolde heale on the Sabbath *day*, that they might finde an accusation *against* him.
8 But he knewe their thoghts, and said to
the man which had the withered hand, A-
rise, & stand vp in the middes. And he a-
rose, and stode vp.
9 Then said Iesus vnto thē, I wil aske you
a question, Whether is it lawful on the
Sabbath dayes to do good, or to do euil? to
saue "life, or to destroye it?
10 And he beholde them all in compasse, &
said vnto the mā, Stretch forthe thine hād.
And he did so, and his hand was restored
againe, as whole as the other.
11 Then they were filled ful of madnes, &
communed one with another, what they
might do to Iesus.
12 ¶And it came to passe in those dayes, ẏ
he went into a mountaine to pray, & spent
the night in prayer to God.
13 *And whē it was day, he called his disciples, and of them he chose [c] twelue, which
also he called [d] Apostles.
14 (Simon whome he named also Peter, and
Andrewe his brother, Iames and Iohn, Phi
lippe, and Bartlemewe:
15 Matthewe, and Thomas: Iames *the sonne*
of Alpheus, and Simon called zelous,
16 Iudas Iames *brother*, and Iudas Iscariot,
which also was the traytour.)
17 Then he came downe with them, and
stode in "a plaine place, with the companie of his disciples, and a great multitu
de of people out of all Iudea, and Ierusa
lem, and from the sea coast of Tyrus & Si
don, which came to heare him, and to be
healed of their diseases:
18 And they that were vexed with foule
spirits, and they were healed.
19 And the whole multitude soght to touch
him: for there went vertue out of him, and
healed them all.
20 ¶*And he lifted vp his eyes vpō his disciples, and said, Blessed *be* ye [e] poore: for
yours is the kingdome of God.
21 *Blessed *are* ye that hunger now: for ye
shalbe satisfied: blessed *are* ye that * wepe
now: for ye shal laugh.
22 *Blessed are ye when men hate you, and
when [f] they separate you, and reuile *you*, &
put out your name as euil, for the Sonne
of mans sake.
23 Reioyce ye in that day, and be [g] glad: for
beholde, your rewarde *is* great in heauen:
for after this maner their fathers did to the
Prophetes.
24 *But wo *be* to you *that are* [h] riche: for ye
haue receiued your consolation.
25 * Wo *be* to you that are ful: for ye shal
hūger. Wo *be* to you that now [i] laugh: for
ye shal waile and wepe.

Mat.12,1. mar.2,13.
a Those feasts which conteined manie dais as the Passeouer, and the feast of Tabernacles, had two Sabbathes: the first day of the feast, & the last.
1.Sam.21,6.
Exo.19,33. leu.8,32. & 24,9.
b Hauing power to dispense with, & qualifie the keping of the Sabbath and other ceremonies.
Mat.12,5. mar.3,1.
"*Or, aprune.*
Mat.10,1. mar.3,13. & 6,7. chap.9,1.
c According to the similitude of the twelue Patriarkes, of whome the Churche of God is sprong.
d Ambassadors or messengers whome he had elected before, but now enioyneth thē their charge.
"*Or, champion.*
e They that are humble & submit thē selues willingly to obei: God.
Mat.5,2. Isa.65,13 Isa.61,3. Mat.5,3.
f He meaneth excōmunicatiō which also he calleth puttīg out their names S. Iohn calleth it: casting out of ẏ Synagogue: S. Paul, deliuering to Satan, ẇ punishemēt as it is moste terrible when it is iustly executed, so is it cōfortable to ẏ godlie whē they are cast out of wicked mēs cōpanie, as the Prophet declareth, Psal.1,1.
g The worde signifieth to leape for ioye, or to shewe mirthe by outwar de gesture.
Amos 6,4. eccle.31,8.

h That put your trust in your riches, & forget ẏ life to come. * *Isa.65,13.*
i Signifying them that liue at ease & after the pleasures of the flesh.

26 Wo be to you whẽ all [k] men speake wel of
you: for so did their fathers to the false
prophetes.
27 ¶*But I say vnto you which heare, Loue
your enemies: do wel to thẽ ẏ hate you.
28 Blesse them that curse you, and pray for
them which hurt you.
29 *And vnto him that [l] smiteth thee on the
one cheke, offer also the other:*& him that
taketh away thy cloke, forbid not *to take*
thy coate also.
30 Giue to euerie man that asketh of thee:
and of him that taketh away thy *goods*, [m] a-
ske them not againe.
31 *And as ye wolde that men shulde do to
you, so do ye to them likewise.
32 *For if ye loue them which loue you,
what thanke shal ye haue? for euen the
[n] sinners loue those that loue them.
33 And if ye do good for them which do
good for you, what thãke shal ye haue? for
euen the sinners do the same.
34 *And if ye lend to *them* of whome ye hope to receiue, what thãke shal ye haue? for
euen the sinners lend to sinners, to receiue
the like.
35 Wherefore loue ye your enemies, and
do good, and lend, [o] loking for nothing
againe, and your rewarde shalbe great,
and ye shalbe the children of * the moste
High: for he is kinde vnto the vnkinde, &
to the euil.
36 Be ye therefore merciful, as your Father
also is merciful.
37 ¶*Iudge not, and ye shal not be iudged:
condemne not, and ye shal not be condem
ned: forgiue, and ye shalbe forgiuen.
38 Giue, and it shalbe giuen vnto you: *a
good measure, pressed downe, shakẽ together and running ouer shal men giue into your bosome: for with what measure
ye mette, with the same shal men mette to
you againe.
39 And he spake a parable vnto them, *Can
the blinde lead the blinde? shal they not
bothe fall into the ditch?
40 *The disciple is not aboue his master:
but whosoeuer *wil be* a perfite disciple, shal
be as his master.
41 ¶*And why [p] seest thou a mote in thy bro
thers eye, and considerest not the beame,
that is in thine owne eye?
42 Ether how canst thou saye to thy brother, Brother, let me pul out the mote that
is in thine eye, whẽ thou seest not the beame that is in thine owne eye? Hypocrite,
cast out the beame out of thine owne eye
first, & then shalt thou se perfectly, to pul
out the mote that is in thy brothers eye.
43 ¶*For it is not a good tre that bringeth
forthe euil frute: nether an euil tre, that
bringeth forthe good frute.
44 *For euerie tre is knowen by his owne

k He reproueth ambition & vaine glorie when as men go about by all meanes to get fauour, & worldlie pope.

Mat.5,44.

Mat.5,39.

l Rather endure more iniurie then reuenge your selues.

1.Cor.6,7.

m Be not so careful for the losse of thy goods, ẏ thou shuldest be discouraged to serue God.

Mat.7,12.
tob.4,16.

Mat.5,45.

n They are communely called sinners, ẏ are of a wicked life, and without all feare of God.

Mat.5,42.
deu.15,8.

o Not onely not hoping for profite, but to lose the stocke & principal forasmuche as Christ bindeth him self to repay the whole with a moste liberal interest.

Mat.5,48.

Mat.7,1.

Mat.7,2.
mar.4,24.

Mat.15,14.

Mat.10,24
iohn 13,16.
& 15,10.

Mat.7,3.

p He reproueth the hypocrisie of suche as winke at their owne horrible fautes, & yet are to curious to spie out ẏ least faute in their brother.

Mat.7,17.

Mat.12,33.

frute: *for nether of thornes gather mẽ figges, nor of bushes gather they grapes.
45 A [q] good man out of the good treasure
of his heart bringeth forthe good, and an
euil man out of the euil treasure of his heart bringeth forthe euil: for of the abundance of the heart his mouth speaketh.
46 ¶*But why call ye me [r] Master, Master,
and do not the things that I speake?
47 Whosoeuer cometh to me, and heareth
my wordes, & doeth the same, I wil shewe
you to whome he is like.
48 He is like a man which buylt an house,
and digged depe, and laid the fundation
on a rocke: and when the waters arose, the
flood bet vpon that house, and colde not
shake it: for it was grounded vpõ a rocke.
49 But he that heareth and doeth not, is like a man that buylt an house vpon ẏ earth
without fundaciõ, against which the flood
did beat, and it fel by and by: and the fall
of that house was great.

CHAP. VII.

2 He healeth the captaines seruant. 11 He raiseth vp the widowes sonne from death to life. 19 He answereth the disciples whome Iohn Baptiste sent vnto him. 24 He commendeth Iohn, 31 And reproueth the Iewes for their vnfaithfulnes. 36 He eateth with the Pharise. 37 The woman wassheth his fete with her teares, and he forgiueth her sinnes.

1 WHẽ*he had ended all his sayings
in the audience of the people, he
entred into Capernaum.
2 And a certeine [a] Centurions seruant was
sicke and ready to dye, which was dere vnto him.
3 And when he heard of Iesus, he sent vnto
him ẏ Elders of the Iewes, beseching him
that he wolde come and heale his seruant.
4 So they came to Iesus, and besoght him
instantly, saying that he was worthie that
he shulde do this for him.
5 For he loueth, *said they*, our nacion, and he
hathe buylt vs a [b] Synagogue.
6 Then Iesus went with them: but when
he was now not farre from the house, the
Centurion sent friends to him, [c] saying
vnto him, Lord, trouble not thy self: for I
am not worthie that thou shuldest enter
vnder my roofe.
7 Wherefore I thoght not my self worthie
to come vnto thee: but [d] say the worde, &
my seruant shalbe whole.
8 For I likewise am a man set vnder autoritie, and haue vnder me souldiers, and I say
vnto one, Go, and he goeth, & to another,
Come, and he cometh, and to my seruant,
Do this, and he doeth it.
9 When Iesus heard these things, he marueiled at him, & turned him, & said to the
people, that followed him, I say vnto you,
I haue not found so [e] great faith, no not in
Israel.
10 And when they that were sent, turned
backe

Mat 7,16.

q The name and title are nothing worthe to proue ẏ a man is sent of God, except in effect he shewe the same.

Mat.7,21.
rom.2,13.
iam.1,21.

r He speaketh not onely to the false prophetes, but to all false pastours, hirelings and hypocrites.

Mat 8,5.

a It might be, that this captaine did lie with his garrison in Capernaum.

b In buylding them a Tẽple for their assemblies, he shewed his zeale towardes the true seruice of God.

c The friends speake to Iesus in the captaines name.

d Or, commãde by a worde onely that it so be.

e He commendeth this heathen captaine because he assureth him self vpon Christs worde alone.

backe to the house, they founde the seruãt
that was sicke, whole.
11 And it came to passe the day after, that
he went into a citie called [f] Nain, and ma
nie of his disciples went with him, and a
great multitude.
12 Now when he came nere to the gate of
the citie, beholde, there was a dead man ca
ryed out, *who was* the onelie begotten sonne of his mother, which was a widowe, &
muche people of the citie was with her.
13 And when the Lord sawe her, he had
compassion on her, and said vnto her,
Wepe not.
14 And he went and touched the "coffin
(and they that bare him, stode stil) and he
said, [g] Yong man, I say vnto thee, Arise.
15 And he that was dead, sate vp, & begã to
speake, & he deliuered him to his mother.
16 Thẽ there came a feare on them all, and
they glorified God, saying, A great Prophet is raised vp among vs, and God hathe [h] visited his people.
17 And this rumour of him went forthe
throughout all Iudea, and throughout all
the region rounde about.
18 ¶ And the disciples of Iohn shewed him
of all these things.
19 So Iohn called vnto him two certeine
men of his disciples, and sent them to Iesus, saying, Art thou [i] he that shulde come,
or shal we waite for another?
20 And when the mẽ were come vnto him,
they said, Iohn Baptist hathe sent vs vnto
thee, sayig, Art thou he that shulde come,
or shal we wait for another?
21 And at that time, he cured manie of
their sickenes, and plagues, and of euil spirits, and vnto manie blinde men he gaue sight.
22 And Iesus answered, and said vnto thẽ,
Go your wayes and shewe Iohn, [k] what
things ye haue sene and heard: ÿ the blinde se, the halte go, the lepers are clensed,
the deafe heare, the dead rise againe, & the
[l] "poore receiue the Gospel.
23 And blessed is he, that shal not be [m] offen
ded in me.
24 And when the messengers of Iohn were departed, he began to speake vnto the
people of Iohn, What wẽt ye out into the
wildernes to se? A [n] rede shaken with the
winde?
25 But what went ye out to se? A man clothed in soft raiment? beholde, they which
are gorgeously apparelled, and liue delicately, are in Kings courtes.
26 But what wẽt ye forthe to se? A Prophet?
yea, I say to you, & greater thẽ a Prophet.
27 This is he of whome it is writẽ, *Beholde, I send my "messenger before thy face,
which shal prepare thy way before thee.
28 For I say vnto you, there is no greater

f Which was a towne of Galile in the tribe of Issachar not farre from Tiberias.

"Or, biere.

g Christ calleth those things that are not, as if they were, & giueth life to them that be dead.

h That is, to establish, and restore them.

i To wit, the Messias, and redemer.

k He declareth by the vertues, and power ÿ were in him that he was ÿ Christ.

l Suche as fele their owne miserie, and wretchednes.

"Or, the Gospel is preached to the poore.

m That shal perseuere and not shrinke backe for anie thing that cã come vnto thẽ.

n Read Mat. 11,7.

Matth.3,1.

"Or, Angel.

Prophet then Iohn, among them that are
"begotten of women: neuertheles, he that
is the least in ÿ kingdome of God is greater then he.
29 Then all the people that heard, and the
Publicanes [o] iustified God, being baptized with the [p] baptisme of Iohn.
30 But the Pharises & the expoũders of the
Law despised the counsel of God [q] against
them selues, & *were* not baptized of him.
31 *And the Lord said, Whereunto shal I
liken the men of this generacion? & what
thing are they like vnto?
32 They are like vnto childrẽ sitting in the
market place, and crying one to another,
and saying, [r] We haue piped vnto you, &
ye haue not danced: we haue mourned to
you, and ye haue not wept.
33 For Iohn Baptist came, nether eating
bread, nor drinking wine: and ye say, He
hathe the deuil.
34 The Sonne of man is come, and [s] eateth
and drinketh: and ye say, Beholde, a man
which is a glotten, and a drinker of wine, a
friend of Publicanes and sinners.
35 But wisdome is [t] iustified of all her children.
36 ¶ *And one of the Pharises desired him
that he wolde eat with him: and he went
into the Pharises house, and sate downe at
table.
37 And beholde, a womã in the citie, which
was a sinner, when she knewe that Iesus sate at table in ÿ Pharises house, she broght
a boxe of ointement.
38 *And she stode at his fete behinde him
weping, and began to wash his fete with
teares, and did wipe them with the heeres
of her head, & kissed his fete, & anointed
them with the ointment.
39 Now when the Pharise which bade him,
sawe it, he spake within him self, saying, If
this man were a Prophet, he wolde surely
haue knowen who, and what maner of woman this is which toucheth him: for she is
a sinner.
40 And Iesus answered, and said vnto him,
Simon, I haue somewhat to say vnto thee.
And he said, Master, say on.
41 There was a certeine lender which had
two detters: the one oght fiue hundreth
pence, and the other fiftie.
42 Whẽ they had nothing to pay, he forgaue them bothe. Which of thẽ therefore,
tell *me*, wil loue him moste?
43 Simon answered, & said, I suppose that
he, to whome he forgaue moste. And he
said vnto him, Thou hast truely iudged.
44 Then he turned to the woman, and said
vnto Simõ, Seest thou this womã? I entred
into thine house, and thou gauest me no
water to my fete: but she hathe washed my
fete with teares, and wiped them with the

"Or, borne.

o They praised him as iust, faithful, good and merciful, so that ÿ frute of their baptisme appeared in them.

Mat.11,16.

p This words comprehendeth the whole doctrine ÿ Iohn taught.

q Meaning to their owne cõdemnation or as some read, with thẽ selues because they durst not openly speake against Iohns doctrine: for they feared the people, Matth.21,46.

r The songs of litle childrẽ are sufficient to condemne the Pharises and suche like

s Liueth according to the facion of other men.

t He sheweth that the wicked, althogh they turne frõ God, shal nothig hinder the elect to cõtinewe in the faith of the Gospel.

Mar.15,40. iohn 20,11.

heeres of her head.
45 Thou gauest me no kisse: but she since
the time I came in, hathe not ceased to kisse my fete.
46 Mine head with oyle thou diddest not
anoint: but she hathe anointed my feete
with ointement.
47 Wherefore I saye vnto thee, manie
sinnes are forgiuen her: for she [u] loued muche. To whome a litle is forgiuen, he doeth loue a litle.
48 And he said vnto her, Thy sinnes are
forgiuen thee.
49 And they that sate at table with him,
began to say within them selues, Who is
this that euen forgiueth sinnes?
50 And he said to the womā, Thy faith hathe saued thee: go in [x] peace.

u This great loue is a signe that she felt her self muche bounde vnto Christ, who had forgiuen her so manie sinnes.

x The peace of conscience cometh onely of faith.

CHAP. VIII.

1 Christ with his Apostles go from towne to towne and preache. 3 The women minister vnto them of their goods. 5 He sheweth the parable of the sede. 21 He telleth who is his mother and his brother. 24 He stilleth the raging of the lake. 27 He deliuereth the possessed. 33 The deuils enter into the heard of swine. 41 He healeth the sicke woman, and Iairus daughter.

1 AND it came to passe afterwarde, that
he him self went through euerie citie and towne, preaching, and publishing
the kingdome of God, & the twelue *were*
with him.
2 And certeine women, which were healed
of euil spirits, and infirmities, *as* *Marie
which was called Magdalene, out of whome went seuen deuils,
3 And Ioanna the wife of Chuza Herodes
stewarde, & Susanna, & manie other which
[a] ministred vnto "him of their substance.
4 *Now whē muche people were gathered
together, and were come to him out of all
cities, he spake by a parable,
5 A sower went out to sowe his seed, and as
he sowed, some fel by the way side, and it
was troden vnder fete, and the foules of
heauen deuoured it vp.
6 And some fel on the stones, and when it
was sprong vp, it withered away, because it
lacked moistnes.
7 And some fel among thornes, and ẏ thornes sprang vp with it, and choked it.
8 And some fel on good groūde, and sprāg
vp, and bare frute, an hundreth folde. And
as he said these things, he cryed, He that
hathe eares to [b] heare, let him heare.
9 Thē his disciples asked him, demāding,
what parable that was?
10 And he said, Vnto you it is giuen to
know the secrets of the kingdome of God,
but to other in [c] parables, that when *they
se, they shulde not se, and when they heare,
they shulde not vnderstand.
11 *The parable is this, The sede is the worde of God.
12 And thei that are beside the way, are thei

Mar.16,9.

a Whereby they acknowledged the benefite ẇ they had receiued of him, & also shewed their perseuerance, which proued their knowledge to be of God.
"Or, to them.
Mat.13,3.
mar.4,1.

b That is, to vnderstand, & beleue these things.
c Which worde is here taken for an obscure or darke saying.
Isa.6,9.
matth.13,14.
mar.4,12.
ioh.12,40.
act.28,26.
rom.11,8.
Mat.13,18.
mar.4,15.

that heare: afterwarde commeth the deuil,
and taketh away the worde out of their
hearts, lest they shulde beleue, & be saued.
13 But they that are on the stones, *are they*
which when they haue heard, receiue the
worde with ioye: but they haue no rootes,
which for a while [d] beleue, but in the time
of tentation go away.
14 And that which fel among thornes, are
they which haue heard, and [e] after their
departure are choked with cares and with
riches, and voluptuous liuing, and bring
forthe no frute.
15 But that *which fel* in good ground, are
they which with an honest & good heart
heare the worde, and kepe it, & bring forthe frute with pacience.
16 ¶*No [f] man when he lighteth a candel,
couereth it vnder a vessel, nether putteth
it vnder the "table, but setteth it on a candlesticke, that they that entre in, may se
the light.
17 *For nothing is secret, that shal not be
euidēt: nether any thing hid, that shal not
be knowen, and come to light.
18 Take hede therefore how ye heare: * for
whosoeuer hathe, to him shalbe giuen: and
whosoeuer hathe not, frō him shalbe taken
euen that, which [g] it semeth that he hathe.
19 ¶*Then came to him his mother & his
brethren, and colde not come nere to him
for the preasse.
20 And it was tolde him *by certeine* which
said, Thy mother and thy "brethren stand
without, and wolde se thee.
21 But he answered, & said vnto them, My
mother, and my brethrē are [h] these which
heare the worde of God, and do it.
22 ¶*And it came to passe on a certeine
day, that he went into a ship with his disci
ples, and he said vnto them, Let vs go ouer
vnto the other side of the lake. And they
lanched forthe.
23 And as they sailed, he fel a [i] slepe, & there came downe a storme of winde on the
lake, and they were filled with water, and
were in ieopardie.
24 Then they went to him, and awoke him,
saying, Master, master, we perish. And he
arose, and rebuked the winde, & the waues
of water: & they ceased, and it was calme.
25 Then he said vnto them, Where is your
faith! and they feared, & wondered among
them selues, saying, Who is this that com
mandeth bothe the windes and water, and
they obey him!
26 ¶*So they sailed vnto the region of the
Gadarenes, which is ouer against Galile.
27 And as he wēt out to land, there met him
a certeine man out of the citie, which had
a deuil long time, and he ware no clothes,
nether abode in house, but in the graues.
28 And when he sawe Iesus, he cryed out, &
fel

d That is, acknowledge & consent to the worde and, also reuerence it.
e When they returne home to their affaires.

Chap.12,33.
mat.5,15.
mar.4,21.
f Christ warneth his to do good with their light ẇ they haue receiude, and to set it forthe before all mēs faces.
"Or, bed.
Chap.12,2.
mat.10,26.
mar.4,22.
Mat.13,12.
& 25,29.
mar.4,25.
chap.19,26.
Mat.12,46.
mar.3,32.
g Bothe to him self, and to others.
"Or, kinsfolkes
h The spiritual kinred is to be prefered to the carnal & natural for asmuche as thereby of many we are made one, confessing together one God, one faith, & one baptisme, louing God aboue all thing, & our neighbour as our selues.
Mat.8,23.
mar.4,36.
i The worde signifieth a depe or sounde slepe.

Mat.8,28.
mar.5,1.

fel downe before him,& with a loude voy
ce said, What haue I to do with thee, Iesus the Sonne of God, the most high? I beseche thee [k] torment me not.
29 For he commanded the foule spirit to
come out of the mã: (for [*] oft times he had
caught him: therefore he was bound with
chaines, and kept in fetters: but he brake
the bandes, and was [l] caryed of the deuil
into wildernesses.)
30 Then Iesus asked him, saying, What is
thy name? And he said, [m] Legion, because
many deuils were entred into him.
31 And they besoght him, that he wolde
not commande them to go out into the
[n] diepe.
32 And there was there by, an herd of many
swine, feding on an hil, and the *deuils* besoght him, that he wolde suffre thẽ to entre into them. So he suffred them.
33 Then went the deuils out of the man, and
entred into the swine: and the herd was
caryed with violence from a stepe downe
place into the lake, and was choked.
34 When the herdmen sawe what was done, they fled: and when they were departed, they tolde it in the citie and in the
countrey.
35 Then they came out to se what was done,
and came to Iesus, & founde the man, out
of whome the deuils were departed, sitting
at the fete of Iesus, clothed, & in his right
minde: and they were afraid.
36 They also which sawe it, tolde them by
what meanes he that was possessed with
the deuil, was healed.
37 Then the whole multitude of the countrey about the Gadarenes, besoght him, ỹ
he wolde departe frõ them: for they were
taken with a great feare: and he went into
the ship, and returned.
38 Then the man, out of whome the deuils were departed, besoght him that he
might be with him: but Iesus sent him a-
way, saying,
39 [o] Returne into thine owne house, and
shewe what great things God hathe done
to thee. So he went his way, and preached
through out all ỹ [p] citie, what great things
Iesus had done vnto him.
40 ¶ And it came to passe when Iesus was
come againe, that ỹ people receiued him:
for they all waited for him.
41 ¶ *And beholde, there came a man named Iairus, and he was the ruler of the
[q] Synagogue, who fel downe at Iesus fete,
and besoght him that he wolde come into
his house.
42 For he had but a daughter onely, about
twelue yeres of age, & she laye a dying (&
as he went, the people thronged him.
43 And a woman hauing an yssue of blood,
twelue yeres long, which had spent all her
substance vpon physicions, and colde not
be healed of any:
44 Whẽ she came behĩde *him*, she touched
the [r] hem of his garment, and immediatly
her yssue of blood stanched.
45 Then Iesus said, Who is it that hathe
touched me? When euerie man denyed,
Peter said & thei that were with him, Master, the multitude thrust thee, & tread on
thee, and sayest ỹ, Who hathe touched me?
46 And Iesus said, Some one hathe touched
me: for I perceiue that vertue is gone out
of me.
47 When the woman sawe that she was
not hid, she came trembling, & fel downe
before him, & tolde him before all ỹ people, for what cause she had touched him,
and how she was healed immediatly.
48 And he said vnto her, Daughter, be of
good comfort: thy [s] faith hathe made thee
whole: go in peace.)
49 While he yet spake, there came one frõ
the ruler of the Synagogues house, which
said to him, Thy daughter is dead: disease not the Master.
50 When Iesus heard it, he answered [t] him,
saying, Feare not: beleue onely, & she shal
be made whole.
51 And when he went into the house, he suffred no man to go in with him, saue Peter,
and Iames, and Iohn, and the father & mother of the maide.
52 And all wept, and sorowed for her: but
he said, Wepe not: for she is not [u] dead, but
slepeth.
53 And they laught him to skorne, knowing
that she was dead.
54 So he [x] thrust them all out, and toke her
by the hand, and cryed, saying, Maid, arise.
55 And her spirit came againe, and she rose straight way: and he commanded to giue her meat.
56 Then her parents were astonied: but he
commanded them that they shulde tell no
man what was done.

[k] Satan is tormented where Christ is present.

[*] *Or, many a day agone.*

[l] The worde signifieth to be inforced with violence, as an horse when he is spurred.

[m] A Legion, as writeth Vegetius, conteined 6000 fotemen, & 732 horsemẽ: but here it is taken for an vncerteine and infinite nõber.

[n] That is, so to depart that they colde do no harme: and this worde chap 16, 25. is called hel, where the deuils are chained in the obscuritie of darkenes, 2. Pet 2, 4.

[o] Christ knewe that he shulde better serue him being absent then with him

[p] This was his owne citie called Gadaris, which was in the countrey of Decapolis, & therefore Luke dissenteth not from Marke who writeth ỹ he preached in Decapolis.

Mat. 9, 18. mar 5, 22.

[q] Of the Congregation of the Iewes.

[r] Being assured of the vertue and power of Iesus Christ and not attributing any vertue to the garment.

[s] Christ doeth not ĩpute vnto vs the weakenes of our faithe, but doeth accept it, as thogh it were perfite.

[t] Meaning the ruler of the Synagogue.

[u] Althogh she was verely dead: yet to Christ it was more easie to restore her to life, then it is for one man to wake another out of his slepe.

[x] He meaneth those which he founde in the house.

CHAP. IX.

1 He sendeth out the twelue Apostles to preache. 7 Herode heareth tel of him. 12 He feedeth fiue thousand men with fiue loaues, & two fishes. 19 Diuerse opiniõs of Christ. 28 He trãsfigureth him self vpon the mount. 42 He deliuereth the possessed. 47 And teacheth his disciples to be lowlie. 54 They desire vengeance, but he reproueth them.

1 THen * called he the twelue disciples
together, and gaue them power and
autoritie ouer all deuils, and to heale diseases.
2 *And he sent them to preache the kingdome of God, and to cure the sicke.
3 And he said to them, [a] Take nothing to
your iourney, nether [*] staues, nor scrip,
nether bread, nor siluer, nether haue two
coates.

Mat. 10, 1. mar. 3, 13. & 6, 7.

Mat. 10, 7. mar. 6, 8.

[a] To the end they might do their charge with greater diligence whẽ they had nothing to let them.

[*] *Or, roddes.*

4 And whatsoeuer house ye entre into, there abide, and [b] thence departe.

b He willeth them not to tary long, but to preache frō towne to towne.

5 And whosoeuer wil not receiue you, whē
ye go out of that citie, *shake of the very
[c] dust from your fete for a testimonie a-
gainst them.

Chap.10,11. act.13,51.

c Which was a signe of detestation, and of the vengeance which was prepared for such contemners of Gods benefites which are vnworthie ȳ one shulde receiue any thīg at their hāds.

6 And they went out, and went through e-
uerie towne preaching the Gospel, and
healing euerie where.
7 ¶*Now Herode the tetrarch heard of
all that was done by him: and he douted,
because that it was said of some, that Iohn
was risen againe from the dead:
8 And of some, that Elias had appeared: &
of some, that one of the olde Prophetes
was risen againe.

Mat.14,1. mar.6,14.

9 Then Herode said, Iohn haue I beheaded: who then is this of whome I heare
suche things? and he desired to se him.
10 ¶*And whē the Apostles returned, they
tolde him what great things they had done. *Then he toke them, & went aside into
a solitarie place, *nere* to the citie called
Bethsaida.

Mar.6,30. Mat.14,13. mar.6,32.

11 But when the people knewe it, they followed him: and he receiued them, & spake vnto them of the kingdome of God, &
healed them that had nede to be healed.
12 *And whē the day began to weare away,
the twelue came, and said vnto him, Send
the people away, that they may go into
the townes and villages rounde about, &
lodge, and get meat: for we are here in a
desert place.

Mat.14,15. mar.6,35. iohn 6,5.

13 But he said vnto them, [d] Giue ye them
to eat. And they said, We haue no mo but
fiue loaues & two fishes, except we shulde
go and bye meat for all this people.

d Christ forsaketh not them that followe him, but sendeth them sufficient relief.

14 For they were about fiue thousand men.
Then he said to his disciples, Cause them
to sit downe by fifties in a companie.
15 And they did so, and caused all to sit
downe.
16 Then he toke the fiue loaues, and the two
fishes, and loked vp to heauen, and [e] blessed them, and brake, and gaue to the disciples, to set before the people.

e Iohn sayeth, he gaue thankes, Ioh.6,11.

17 So they did all eat, and were satisfied: &
there was takē vp of that remained to thē,
twelue baskets ful of broken meat.
18 ¶*And it came to passe as he was alone
praying, his disciples were with him, and
he asked thē, saying, Whome say the people that I am?

Mat.16,13. mar.8,27.

19 They answered, and said, Iohn Baptist:
and others say, Elias: & some say, that one
of the olde Prophetes is risen againe.
20 And he said vnto them, But whome say
ye that I am? Peter answered, & said, The
Christ of God.
21 And he warned, and commanded them,
that they shulde tell [f] that to no man,

f For he knewe best his conuenient time which was appointed for him to be manifested in.

22 Saying, * The Sonne of man must suffre
many things, and be reproued of the Elders, & of the hie Priests and Scribes, and
be slaine, and the thirde day rise againe.

Mat.17,22. mar.8,31.

23 ¶*And he said to them all, If any man
wil come after me, let him denye him self,
and take vp his crosse [g] daily, and followe
me.

Chap.14,27. mat.10,38. & 16,24. mar.8,35.

g For as one day followeth another, so doeth one crosse followe in the necke of another.

24 For whosoeuer wil saue his life, shal lose
it: and whosoeuer shal lose his life for my
sake, the same shal saue it.
25 For what auātageth it a man, if he winne
the whole worlde, and destroye him self,
or lose him self?
26 * For whosoeuer shalbe ashamed of me,
and of my wordes, of him shal the Sonne
of man be ashamed, when he shal come in
his glorie, and *in the glorie* of the Father,
and of the holie Angels.

Chap.12,9. & 17,33. mat.10,33. mar.8,38. 2.tim.2,12.

27 *And I tell you of a suretie, there be some standing here, which shal not taste of
death, til they haue sene the [h] kingdome of
God.

Mat.16,28. mar.9,1.

h Established and enlarged by the preaching of the Gospel.

28 * And it came to passe about an eight
dayes after those wordes, that he toke Peter, & Iohn, and Iames, and went vp into a
mountaine to pray.

Mat.17,1. mar.9,2.

29 And as he prayed, the facion of his coun
tenance was changed, & his garment *was*
white and glistered.
30 And beholde, two men talked with him,
which were Moses and Elias,
31 Which appeared in glorie, and tolde of
his [i] departing, which he shulde accōplish
at Ierusalem.

i That is, what ysfuche shulde haue and how he shulde dye.

32 But Peter and they that were with him,
were heauie with slepe, and when they
awooke, they sawe his glorie, and the two
men standing with him.
33 And it came to passe, as they departed
from him, Peter said vnto Iesus, Master, it
is good for vs to be here: let vs therefore
make thre tabernacles, one for thee, and
one for Moses, and one for Elias, and wist
not what he said.
34 While he thus spake, there came a cloude & [k] ouershadowed them, & they feared
when these were entring into the cloude.

k For otherwayes they had not bene able to comprehend his great maiestie.

35 *And there came a voyce out of the
cloude, saying, This is my beloued Sōne,
heare him.

Mat.3,17. mar.1,11.

36 And when the voyce was past, Iesus was
founde alone: and they kept it close, and
tolde no man in [l] those dayes any of those
things which they had sene.

l Thei concealed it til Christs resurrection, as Marke writeth.

37 ¶And it came to passe on the next day,
as they came downe from the mountaine,
muche people met him.
38 *And beholde, a man of the companie
cryed out, saying, Master, I beseche thee,
beholde my sonne: for he is all that I haue.

Mat.17,14. mar.9,17.

39 And lo, a spirit taketh him, & suddenly
he cryeth, and he teareth him, that he fometh, and with muche paine departeth
from

from him, when he hathe bruised him.
40 Now I haue besoght thy disciples to
cast him out, but they colde not.
41 Then Iesus answered, and said, [m] O generacion faithles, and croked, how long
now shal I be with you, & suffer you? brĩg
thy sonne hither.
42 And whiles he was yet comming, the
deuil rent him, and tare him: and Iesus rebuked the vncleane spirit, and healed the
childe, and deliuered him to his father.
43 ¶ And thei were all amased at the mightie power of God: & while thei all wondred at all things, which Iesus did, he said
vnto his disciples,
44 [*] Marke these wordes diligently: for it
shal come to passe, that the Sonne of man
shalbe deliuered into the hands of men.
45 But they [n] vnderstode not that worde: for it was hid from them, *so* that they
colde not perceiue it: and they feared to
aske him of that worde.
46 ¶ * Then there arose a disputacion a-
mong them, which of them shulde be the
greatest.
47 When Iesus sawe the thoghts of their
hearts, he toke a litle childe, and set him
by him,
48 And said vnto them, Whosoeuer receiueth this litle childe in my Name, receiueth me: and whosoeuer shal receiue me,
receiueth him that sent me: for he that is
least among you all, he shalbe great.
49 ¶ * And Iohn answered, & said, Master,
we sawe one casting out deuils in thy Name, and we forbade him, because he followeth *thee* not with vs.
50 Then Iesus said vnto him, Forbid ye
him not: for he that is not against vs, [o] is
with vs.
51 ¶ And it came to passe, when the [p] dayes
were accomplished, that he shulde be receiued vp, he setteled him self fully to go
to Ierusalem,
52 And sent messengers before him: and
they went and entred into a towne of the
Samaritans, to prepare him *lodging*.
53 But they wolde not receiue him, because his [q] behauiour was, *as* thogh he wolde go to Ierusalem.
54 And when his disciples, Iames and Iohn
sawe it, they said, Lord, wilt thou that we
commande, that fyre come downe from
heauen, and consume them, euen as * E-
lias did?
55 But Iesus turned about, & rebuked thẽ,
and said, Ye knowe not of what [r] spirit
ye are.
56 * For the Sonne of man is not come to
destroye mens liues, but to saue thẽ. Then
they went to another towne.
57 ¶ And it came to passe that as they went
in the way, a certeine man said vnto him,

m Vnder the colour that his disciples colde not heale the sicke man, he reproueth them, whiche wolde haue diminished his autoritie.

* Greke, put these wordes into your eares.

n They were so blĩded with this opinion that Christ shulde haue a temporal kingdome, that they wolde not vnderstand when he spake of his death.

Mat.18,1. mar.9,33.

Mar.9,38.

o Forasmuche as he letteth vs not, & God is glorified by his occasion.

p Of his death whereby he was exalted.

q Or face, or apparel: for they knewe he was a Iewe, & as touching the Samaritans opinion of the Temple, read Iohn 4,20: also thei hated the Iewes, because they differed from them in religion.

2.King.1,10.

Mat.8,19.

r He reproueth their rashe & carnal affectiõ, which were not led with Elias spirit.

I wil [s] followe thee, Lord, whethersoeuer
thou goest.
58 And Iesus said vnto him, The [s] foxes
haue holes, and the birdes of the heauen
haue nestes, but the Sonne of man hathe
not whereon to laie his head.
59 But he said vnto another, Followe me.
And the same said, Lord, suffer me first to
go and [t] burye my father.
60 And Iesus said vnto him, [u] Let the dead
burye their dead: but go thou and preache
the kingdome of God.
61 Then another said, I wil followe thee,
Lord: but let me first go bid thẽ fare wel,
which are at mine house.
62 And Iesus said vnto him, No man that putteth his hand to the plough, and [x] loketh
backe, is apte to the kingdome of God.

CHAP. X.

*1 He sendeth the seuentie before him to preache, and gi-
ueth them a charge how to behaue them selues. 13 He
threateneth the obstinate. 21 He giueth thankes to his
heauenlie Father. 25 He answereth the Scribe that
tempted him. 33 And by the example of the Sama-
ritane sheweth who is a mans neighbour. 38 Martha
receiueth the Lord into her house. 40 Marie is feruent
in hearing his worde.*

1 AFter * these things, the Lord appointed other seuentie also, and sent thẽ,
two and two before him into euerie citie
and place, whether he him self shulde come.
2 And he said vnto them, * [a] The haruest
is great, but the [b] laborers *are* fewe: pray
therefore the Lord of the haruest to send
forthe laborers into his haruest.
3 * Go your waies: beholde, I send you forthe as lambs among [c] wolues.
4 Beare no bagge, nether scryp, nor shoes,
* and [d] salute no man by the way.
5 * And into whatsoeuer house ye enter, first
say, [e] Peace *be* to this house.
6 And if the [f] sonne of peace be there, your
peace shal rest vpon him: if not, it shal turne to you againe.
7 And in that house tarie stil eating, and
drinking suche things as by them *shalbe set
before you*: * for the laborer is worthie of
his wages. Go not from [g] house to house.
8 But into whatsoeuer citie ye shal enter, if
they receiue you, [h] eat suche things as are
set before you,
9 And heale the sicke that are there, & say
vnto them, The kingdome of God is come nere vnto you.
10 But into whatsoeuer citie ye shal enter,
if they wil not receiue you, go your waies
out into the stretes of the same, and say,
11 Euen the verie * dust, which cleaueth on
vs of your citie, we wipe of against you:
notwithstanding knowe this, that the [i] kingdome of God was come nere vnto you.
12 For I say to you, that it shalbe easier in
that daye for them of Sodom, then for

s We must not followe Christ for riches and commodities, but prepare our selues to pouertie and to the crosse by his example.

t That is, til he be dead & I haue done my duetie to him in buryĩg him.

u We may not followe what semeth best to vs, but onely Gods calling. & here by dead he meaneth those that are vnprofitable to serue God.

x To be hindered, or entangled with respect of anie worldlie cõmoditie, or staied to go forwarde for anie paine, or trouble.

Chap. X.

a Meaning a great nomber of people, which are readie to be broght vnto God.

b That is, the preachers.

Mat.10,18.

c Not that they shal hurt you, but that you shalbe preserued by my prouidence.

Mat.9,37. 2.King.4,29. Mat.10,12. mar.6,10.

d He willeth that thei shulde dispatche this iourney with diligẽce not occupying thẽ selues about other dueties.

e It was their maner of salutaciõ whereby they wisshed helth & felicitie.

Deut.24,14. mat.10,10. 1.tim.5,18.

f Which loueth the doctrine of peace & the Gospel.

g He wold not that they shulde tary lõg in one towne, nether yet to be careful to change their lodging.

h Doute not to receiue nourishemẽt of thẽ, for whome you trauail.

Chap.9,5. mat.10,14. act.13,51. & 18,6.

i God did presẽt hĩ self vnto you by his messengers and wolde haue reigned ouer you.

that citie.
13 *Wo *be* to thee, Chorazin: wo *be* to thee,
Beth-saida: for if the miracles had bene
done in Tyrus & Sidon, which haue bene
done in you, they had a great while agone
repented, sitting [k] in sacke clothe and
asshes.
14 Therefore it shalbe easier for Tyrus,
[l] & Sidon, at the iudgement, then for you.
15 And thou, Capernaum, which art exalted
to heauē, shalt be thrust downe to hel.
16 ¶ *He that heareth you, heareth me: &
he that despiseth you, despiseth me: and
he that despiseth me, despiseth him that
sent me.
17 ¶ And the seuentie turned againe with
ioye, saying, Lord, euen the deuils are sub
dued to vs through thy Name.
18 And he said vnto them, I sawe [m] Satan,
like lightening, fall downe from heauen.
19 Beholde, I giue vnto you power to treade
on serpents, and scorpions, and ouer all
the power of the enemie, & nothing shal
hurt you.
20 Neuertheles, in this reioyce not, that
ỹ spirits are subdued vnto you: but rather
reioyce, because your names are written
in heauen.
21 ¶ That same houre reioyced Iesus in
"the spirit, and said, I confesse vnto thee,
Father, Lord of heauen & earth, that thou
hast hid these things from the [n] wise and
learned, and hast reueiled them to babes:
euen so, Father, because it so pleased thee.
22 Then he turned to his disciples, and
said, All things are [o] giuen me of my Father:
and [p] no man knoweth who the Sonne
is, but the Father: nether who the Father
is, saue the [q] Sonne, and he to whome
the Sonne wil reueile him.
23 ¶ And he returned to his disciples, and
said secretly, *Blessed *are* the eyes, which
se that ye se.
24 For I tell you that manie Prophetes &
Kings haue desired to se those things,
which ye se, and haue not sene *them*: and to
heare those things, which ye heare, & haue
not heard *them*.
25 ¶ * Then beholde, a certeine expounder
of the Law stode vp, and tempted him,
saying, Master, what shal I do, to inherite
eternal life?
26 And he said vnto him, What is written
in the Law? how readest thou?
27 And he answered, and said, *Thou shalt
loue thy Lord God with all thine heart, &
with all thy soule, & with all thy strength,
& with all thy thoght, * & thy neighbour
as thy self.
28 Then he said vnto him, Thou hast answered
right: this do, & thou shalt liue.
29 But he willing to "iustifie him self, said
vnto Iesus, Who [r] is then my neighbour?

Mat.11,21.

k Which were the signes of repentance.

Mat.10,40. ioh.13,20.

l The mo benefites ỹ God bestoweth vpō anie people, ỹ more doeth their ingratitude deserue to be punished.

m The power of Satan is beaten downe by the preaching of the Gospel.

"*Or, in his minde.*

n He attributeth it to the free electiō of God, that the wise & worldligs knowe not the Gospel, & yet the poore base people vnderstand it.

o Christ is ỹ onlie meane to receiue Gods mercies by.

p Therefore we muste esteme him as the fathers voyce hathe taught vs, & not according to mans iudgement.

Mat.13,16.

q In whome we se God as in his liuelie image.

Mat.22,35. mar.12,28.

Deut.6,5.

Leu.19,18.

"*Or, to approue him self as iust.*

r For thei counted no man their neighbour, but their friend.

30 And Iesus answered, and said, A certeine
man went downe from Ierusalem to Iericho,
and fell among theues, and they
robbed him of his rayment, and wounded
him, & departed, leauing him halfe dead.
31 And by [s] chance there came downe a cer
teine [t] Priest that same way, and when he
sawe him, he passed by on the other side.
32 And likewise also a Leuite, when he was
come nere to the place, went and loked *on
him*, and passed by on the other side.
33 Then a certeine [u] Samaritan, as he iourneyed,
came nere vnto him, and when he
sawe him, he had compassion on him,
34 And went to him, & bounde vp his woũdes,
and powred in oyle and wine, and put
him on his owne beast, and broght him to
an ynne, and made prouision for him.
35 And on the morowe when he departed,
he toke out [x] two pence, and gaue them to
the hoste, and said vnto him, Take care of
him, and whatsoeuer thou spendest more,
when I come againe, I wil recompense
thee.
36 Which now of these thre, thinkest thou,
was neighbour vnto him that fell among
the theues?
37 And he said, He that shewed mercie on
him. Then said Iesus vnto him, Go, [y] and
do thou likewise.
38 ¶ Now it came to passe as they wēt, that
he entred into a certeine towne, and a certeine
woman named Martha, receiued him
into her house.
39 And she had a sister called Marie, which
also sate at Iesus fete, and heard his preaching.
40 But Martha was cōbred about muche
seruing, and came to him, & said, Master,
doest thou not care that my sister hathe
left me to serue alone? bid her therefore,
that she helpe me.
41 And Iesus answered, and said vnto her,
Martha, Martha, thou carest, & art [z] troubled
about manie things.
42 But one thing is nedeful, Marie hathe
chosen the good parte, [a] which shal not
be taken away from her.

s For so it semed to mans iudgement, althogh this was so appointed by Gods counsel and prouidence.

t He priuely noteth ỹ great crueltie, ẇ was amōg this people & chiefly ỹ gouernours.

u This nacion was odious to the Iewes.

x Which was about 9 pece of sterling money.

y Helpe him ỹ hathe nede of thee althogh ỹ knowe hi not.

z For she forgate the principal, ẇ was to heare Gods worde.

a It was not mete that she shulde haue bene drawen from so profitable a thing, whereunto she colde not alwaies haue opportunitie.

CHAP. XI.

2 He teacheth his disciples to pray. 14 He driueth out a deuil. 15 And rebuketh the blasphemous Pharises. 28 He preferreth the spiritual cousinage. 29 They require signes and tokens. 37 He eateth with the Pharise, and reproueth the hypocrisie of the Pharises, Scribes and hypocrites.

1 And so it was, that as he was praying
in a certeine place, when he ceased,
one of his disciples said vnto him, Master,
teache vs to praye, as Iohn also taught his
disciples.
2 *And he said vnto them, When ye pray,
say, Our Father, ẇ art in heauē, halowed
be thy Name: Thy kingdome come: Let
thy wil be done euē in earth, as *it is* in heauen:

Mat.6,9.

3 Our

3 Our daily bread giue vs [a] for the day:
4 And "forgiue vs our ſinnes: for euen we
forgiue euerie man that is indetted to vs:
And lead vs not into temptation: but deliuer vs from euil.
5 ¶Moreouer he ſaid vnto them, [b] Which
of you ſhal haue a friend, and ſhal go to
him at midnight,& ſay vnto him, Friend,
lend me thre loaues?
6 For a friend of mine is come" out of the
way to me, and I haue nothing to ſet before him:
7 And he within ſhulde anſwer, and ſay,
Trouble me not:the dore is now ſhut,and
my children are with me in bed: I can not
riſe and giue them to thee.
8 I ſay vnto you, thogh he wolde not ariſe
and giue him, becauſe he is his friend, yet
douteles becauſe of his " importunitie,
he wolde riſe, and giue him as many as he
neded.
9 *And I ſay vnto you, Aſke, and it ſhalbe
giuen you: ſeke,and ye ſhal finde: knocke,
and it ſhalbe opened vnto you.
10 For euerie one that aſketh, receiueth:&
he that ſeketh, findeth: and to him that
knocketh,it ſhalbe opened.
11 *If a ſonne ſhal aſke bread of any of you
that is a father,wil he giue him a ſtone? or
if *he aſke* a fiſhe,wil he for a fiſhe giue him
a ſerpent?
12 Or if he aſke an egge,wil he giue him a
ſcorpion?
13 If ye then which are euil, can giue good
giftes vnto your children,how muche mo
re ſhal your heauẽlie Father giue [c] the holie Goſt to them,that deſire him?
14 ¶Then he caſt out a deuil which was
domme:and when the deuil was gone out,
the domme ſpake, and the people wondered.
15 But ſome of them ſaid, He caſteth out
deuils through Beelzebub the chief of
the deuils.
16 And others tempted him,ſeking of him
a ſigne from heauen.
17 But he knewe their thoghtes, and ſaid
vnto them, *Euerie kingdome deuided a-
gainſt it ſelf,ſhalbe deſolate,and an houſe
deuided againſt an houſe, falleth.
18 So if Satan alſo be deuided againſt him
ſelf, how ſhal his kingdome ſtand, becauſe ye ſay that I caſt out deuils through
Beelzebub?
19 If I through Beelzebub caſt out deuils,
by whome do your [d] children caſt them
out? Therefore ſhal they be your iudges.
20 But if I by the [e] finger of God caſt out
deuils, douteles the kingdome of God is
come vnto you.
21 When a ſtrong man armed, kepeth his
[f] palace, the things that he poſſeſſeth, are
in "peace.

a Or euerie day, or aſmuche as is ſufficient for this day.
"Or, pardone.
b By this ſimilitude he teacheth vs that we oght not to be diſcouraged, if we obteine not incontinently ẏ which we demande.
"Or, in paſsing by the way.
"Or, impudencie
Mat.7,7. & 21,22. mar.11,24. iohn 14,13. & 16,12. iam.1,10.
Mat.9,32. & 12,21. mar.3,20.
c The chiefeſt thing that we can deſire of God, is his holie Spirit.
Mat.12,25. mar.3,44.
d That is to ſay, your coniurers.
e The finger of God is taken for ẏ vertue and power of God. And the vertue of the Father and the Sonne is the holie Goſt: for ſo Matthew doeth interpret this place.
f The worde ſignifieth, an entrie or porche before an houſe.
"Or, ſafetie.

22 But when a ſtronger then he, commeth
vpon him, and ouercommeth him: he taketh from him all his armour wherein he
truſted,and deuideth his ſpoiles.
23 He that is not [g] with me, is againſt me:
and he that gathereth not with me, ſcattereth.
24 *When the vncleane ſpirit is gone out
of a man,he walketh through drye places,
ſeking [h] reſt: and when he findeth none, he
ſaith,I wil returne vnto mine houſe whence I came out.
25 And when he commeth, he findeth it
ſwept and [i] garniſhed.
26 Then [k] goeth he,and taketh to him [l] ſeuen other ſpirits worſe then him ſelf: and
they entre in,and dwell there, * ſo the laſt
ſtate of that man is worſe then the firſt.
27 ¶And it came to paſſe as he ſaid theſe
things, a certeine woman of the cõpanie
lifted vp her voyce,& ſaid vnto him,Bleſ-
ſed *is* the wombe that bare thee, and the
pappes which thou haſte ſucked.
28 But he ſaid,[m] Yea,rather bleſſed *are* they
that heare the worde of God, and ke-
pe it.
29 ¶*And when the people were gathered
thicke together,he began to ſay, This is a
wicked generacion: they ſeke a ſigne, and
there ſhal no ſigne be giuen them, but the
ſigne of * Ionas the Prophet.
30 For as Ionas was a ſigne to the Nineuites,ſo ſhal alſo the Sõne of man be to this
generacion.
31 *The Quene of the South ſhal riſe in
iudgement, with the men of this generacion,and ſhal condemne them: for ſhe came from the vtmoſt partes of the earth to
heare the wiſdome of Solomon,and beholde,a greater then Solomon *is* here.
32 The men of Nineue ſhal riſe in iudgement with this generacion, and ſhal condemne it: for they* repented at the preaching of Ionas: and beholde, a greater
then Ionas *is* here.
33 ¶*No man lighteth a candel, & putteth
it in a priuie place,nether vnder a buſhel:
but on a candleſticke, that thei which come in,may ſe the light.
34 *"The light of the bodie is the [n] eye:the-
refore when thine eye is [o] ſingle, then is
thy whole bodie light: but if thine eye be
euil,then thy bodie is darke.
35 Take hede therefore, that ẏ light which
is in thee,be not darkenes.
36 If therefore thy whole bodie *ſhalbe* light,
hauing no parte darke,thẽ ſhal all be light,
euen as when a candel doeth light thee
with the brightnes.
37 ¶And as he ſpake, a certeine Phariſe
beſoght him to dyne with him:& he went
in,and ſate downe at table.
38 And when the Phariſe ſawe it, he mar-

g They that do not wholy applye them ſelues to deſtroy the kingdome of Satan,can not be counted to be on Chriſts ſide but are his aduerſaries: how muchemore is he againſt him that maketh open warre ẇ him as Satan doeth?
Mat.12,43.
h To the intẽt that he might worke according to his malicious nature
Ebr.6,4. 1.pet.2,20.
i More apt to receiue him then it was afore.
k If by infidelitie we turne backe frõ God, Satan hathe greater power ouer vs then he had before.
Ma.12,48.
l He meaneth an infinite nõber.
Ion 2,2.
m Chriſt gaue her a priuie taunt for that ſhe omitted ẏ chief praiſe ẇ was due vnto him:that was, that they are bleſſed in deed to whome he cõmunicateth hĩ ſelf by his worde.
1.King.10,1. 2.chro.9,1.
Ion.3,5.
Chap.8,16. mat.5,15. mar.4,21.
Mat.6,22.
"Or, candle.
n Becauſe it ſhulde guide and lead the bodie.
o Without ſpot or vice.

ueiled that he had not first washed before
dyner.
39 *And the Lord said to him, In dede ye
Pharises make cleane the outside of the
cup, and of the platter: but the inwarde
parte is ful of rauening and wickednes.
40 Ye fooles, did not he that made that
which is without, make that which is within also?
41 Therefore, p giue almes of " those things
which are within, and beholde, all things
shalbe cleane to you.
42 But wo *be* to you, Pharises: for ye tithe
the mynt and the rewe, and all maner herbes, and passe ouer " iudgement and the
loue of God: these oght ye to haue done,
and q not to haue left the other vndone.
43 *Wo *be* to you, Pharises: for ye loue the
vppermost seates in the Synagogues, and
gretings in the markets.
44 Wo *be* to you, Scribes and Pharises, hypocrites: for ye are as graues which r appeare not, & the men that walke ouer thẽ,
perceiue not.
45 ¶ *Then answered one of the expoun-
ders of the Lawe, and said vnto him, Master, thus saying thou puttest vs to rebuke also.
46 And he said, Wo *be* to you also, ye interpreters of the Lawe: for ye lade men
with burdens grieuous to be borne, and ye
your selues touche not the burdens with
one of your fingers.
47 Wo *be* to you: for ye s buylde the sepulchres of the Prophetes, and your fathers
killed them.
48 t Truely ye beare witnes, and allow the
dedes of your fathers: for they killed thẽ,
and ye u buylde their sepulchres.
49 Therefore said the wisdome of God, I
wil send them Prophetes and Apostles, &
of them they shal slay and " persecute,
50 That the blood of all the Prophetes,
shed frõ the fundacion of the worlde, may
be required of this generacion,
51 From the blood of *Abel vnto the blood
of *Zacharias, which was slaine betwene the altar and the Temple: verely I say
vnto you, it shalbe required of x this generacion.
52 Wo *be* to you, interpreters of the Law:
for ye haue y takẽ away the keye of knowledge: ye entred not in your selues, and thẽ
that came in, ye forbade.
53 And as he said these things vnto them,
the Scribes and Pharises began to vrge
him sore, and to prouoke him to speake of
many things,
54 Laying wait for him, and seking to catche some thing of his mouth, whereby
they might accuse him.

Mat.23,25.

p Christ here requireth two things: first ỹ we come truely by our meat and drinke: and next that we distribute parte to ỹ pore: for charitie is the perfection of the Lawe.

" *Or, of that that you haue.*

" *Or, that which is iust & right.*

Chap.20,46. mat.23,6. mar.12,38.

q He wolde not breake the very least commandement before all things were accomplished: but taught them to sticke to the chiefest & not preferre the inferior ceremonies w̃ must quickely be abolished.

r Whose stinke and infectiõ appeare not suddenly.

Act.15,10.

s Whereby you kepe in remẽbrance ỹ execrable dedes of your fathers.

t You shewe your selues as great hypocrites as were your fathers, making men beleue ye honour God whẽ you dishonour him.

u They were more curious to buylde their graues thẽ to followe their doctrine.

Gen.4,8. 2.Chro.24,22.

" *Or, cruelly expel them.*

x Because they were culpable of the same faute ỹ their ancestors were.

y They hid & toke away the pure doctrine & true vnderstanding of the Scriptures.

CHAP. XII.

1 Christ commandeth to auoide hypocrisie. 4 That we shulde not feare man but God. 5 To cõfesse his Name. 10 Blasphemie against the Spirit. 14 Not to passe our vocation. 15 Not to giue our selues to couetous care of this life. 32 But to righteousnes, almes, watching, patiente, wisdome and concorde.

1 IN*the meane time, there gathered together an innumerable multitude of
people, so that they trode one another: &
he begã to say vnto his disciples first, Take hede to your selues of the leauen of the
Pharises, which is hypocrisie.
2 *For there is nothing couered, that shal
not be reueiled: nether hid, that shal not
be knowen.
3 Wherefore whatsoeuer ye haue spoken
in darkenes, it shalbe heard in the light:
and that which ye haue spoken in the eare, in secret places, shalbe preached on
the a houses.
4 *And I say vnto you, my friends, be not
afraid of them that kil the bodie, and after that are not able to do any more.
5 But I wil forewarne you, whome ye shal
feare: feare him which after he hathe killed, hathe power to cast into hel: yea, I say
vnto you, him feare.
6 Are not fiue sparowes boght for two far-
things, & yet not one of them is forgottẽ
before God?
7 Yea, and all the heeres of your head are
nombred: feare not therefore: ye are more of value then many sparowes.
8 *Also I say vnto you, Whosoeuer shal
confesse me before men, him shal the Sonne of man confesse also before the Angels
of God.
9 But he that shal denye me before men,
shalbe denyed before the Angels of God.
10 And whosoeuer shal speake a worde a-
gainst the Sonne of man, it shalbe forgiuen him: but vnto him that b shal blaspheme the holie Gost, it shal not be forgiuen.
11 *And when they shal bring you vnto the
Synagogues, & vnto the rulers & princes,
take no c thoght how, or what thing ye shal
answer, or what ye shal speake.
12 For the holie Gost shal teache you in ỹ
same " houre, what ye oght to say.
13 And one of the companie said vnto him,
Master, bid my brother deuide the inheritance with me.
14 And he said vnto him, Man, who made
me a d iudge, or a deuider ouer you?
15 Wherefore he said vnto them, Take hede, and beware of couetousnes: e for thogh
a man haue abundance, *yet* his life stãdeth
not in his riches.
16 And he put forthe a parable vnto them,
saying, *The " grounde of a certeine riche
man broght forthe frutes plenteously.

Mat.16,5. mar.8,14.

Mat.10,26. mar.4,22.

a Openly that all men may heare.

Mat.10,28.

Chap.9,26. mat.10,32. mar.8,38. 2.tim.2,12.

b He that shal resiste against the worde of God purposely, and against his conscience.

c Be not so douteful that you shulde be discouraged or distrust.

" *Or, moment.*

Mat.10,29. mar.13,32.

d Christ chiefly came to be iudged & not to iudge, notwithstanding he willeth the Christians to be iudges and decide cõtrouersies betwixt their brethrẽ, 1 Cor.6,1.

e Christ condemneth the arrogancie of the riche worldelings, who as thogh they had God locked vp in their coffres & barnes, set their whole felicitie in their goods, not considering that God gaue thẽ life and also can take it away when he wil.

" *Or, countrey.*

Eccle.11,19.

17 Therefore he thoght with him self, saying, What shal I do, because I haue no
roume, where I may lay vp my frutes?
18 And he said, This wil I do, I wil pul
downe mẏ barnes, and buylde greater, &
therein wil I gather all my frutes, and my
goods.
19 And I wil say to my soule, Soule, thou
hast muche goods laid vp for many yeres: liue at ease, eat, drinke, and take thy
pastime.
20 But God said vnto him, O foole, this
night wil they fetche away thy soule from
thee: thẽ whose shal those things be which
thou hast prouided?
21 So *is* he that gathereth riches to him self,
and is not riche in [f] God.
22 And he spake vnto his disciples, Therefore I say vnto you, * Take no thoght for
your life, what ye shal eat: nether for your
bodie, what ye shal put on.
23 The life is more then meat: and the bodie *more* then the raiment.
24 [g] Consider the rauens: for they nether
sowe nor reape: which nether haue store
house nor barne, & *yet* God fedeth them:
how muche more are ye better thẽ foules?
25 And which of you with taking thoght,
can adde to his stature one cubit?
26 If ye then be not able to do the least
thing, why take ye thoght for the remnant?
27 [h] Cõsider the lilies how they grow: they
labour not, nether spin they: yet I say vnto
you, ẏ Solomon him self in all his royaltie
was not clothed like one of these.
28 If then God so clothe the grasse which is
to day in the field, & to morow is cast into
the ouẽ, how muche more *wil he clothe* you,
ô ye of litle faith?
29 Therefore aske not what ye shal eat, or
what ye shal drinke, nether "stand in doute.
30 For all suche things the people of the
worlde seke for: and your Father knoweth
that ye haue nede of these things.
31 But rather seke ye after the kingdome of
God, [i] & all these things shalbe ministred
vnto you.
32 Feare not, litle flocke: for it is your Fathers pleasure, to giue you the [k] kingdome.
33 ¶* Sel that ye haue, and giue almes: make you bagges, which waxe not olde, a
treasure that can neuer faile in heauen,
where no thefe commeth, nether moth
corrupteth.
34 For where your treasure is, there wil your
hearts be also.
35 ¶* Let your loines be [l] girde about, and
your lights burning,
36 And ye your selues like vnto men that
wait for their master, when he wil returne
from the wedding, that when he commeth
and knocketh, they maye open vnto him

f To depende onely on his prouidẽce knowing that he hathe ynough for all.
Mat.6,25.
1.pet.5,7
psal 55,26.

g He exhorteth vs to cast our care on God, & to submit our selues to his prouidence.

h The liberalitie of God which shineth in the herbes and floures, surmounteth all that man can do by his riches or force

" *Or, make discourses in the ayre.*

i Which are but accessaries, and are commune as wel to the wicked men as to the godlie.
Mat.6,20.
k Which is ẏ chiefest thing that can be giuen, and therefore you can not wãt those things which are of lesse importance.
1.Pet.1,13.
l Be in a readines to execute the charge which is committed vnto you.

immediatly.
37 Blessed *are* those seruants, whome the
Lord when he cometh shal finde waking:
verely I say vnto you, he wil [m] girde him
self about, and make them to sit downe at
table, and wil come forthe, & serue them.
38 And if he come in the seconde watche,
or come in the thirde watche, & shal finde them so, blessed are those seruants.
39 * Now vnderstande this, that if the good
man of ẏ house had knowen at what houre
the thefe wolde haue come, he wolde haue
watched, and wolde not haue suffered his
house to be digged through.
40 Be ye also prepared therefore: for the
Sonne of man wil come at an houre when
ye thinke not.
41 Then Peter said vnto him, Master, tellest thou this parable vnto vs, or euen
to all?
42 And the Lord said, Who is a faithful
stewarde, & wise, whome the master shal
make ruler ouer his housholde, to giue
them their [n] portion of meat in season?
43 Blessed *is* that seruant, whome his master
when he cometh, shal finde so doing.
44 Of a trueth I say vnto you, that he wil
make him ruler ouer all that he hathe.
45 But if that seruant say in his heart, My
master doeth deferre his comming, and
shal beginne to smite the seruants, and
maidens, and to eat, and drinke, and to
be drunken,
46 The master of that seruãt wil come in a
day whẽ he thinketh not, & at an houre whẽ
he is not ware of, and wil cut him of, & giue him his portion with the vnbeleuers.
47 ¶ And that seruant that knewe his masters wil, and prepared not him self, nether
did according to his wil, shalbe beatẽ with
manie *stripes*.
48 But he that knewe it not, and yet did cõmit things [o] worthie of stripes, shalbe beaten with fewe *stripes*: for vnto whome soeuer [p] muche is giuẽ, of him shalbe muche
required, and to whome men muche commit, the more of him wil they aske.
49 ¶ I am come to put [q] fyre on the earth, &
what is my desire, if it be all ready kindled?
50 Notwitstanding I must be [r] baptized wᵗ
a baptisme, and how am I grieued, til it be
ended?
51 * Thinke ye that I am come to giue peace
on earth? I tel you, nay, but rather debate.
52 For from hence forthe there shalbe fiue
in one house deuided, thre against two, &
two against thre.
53 The father shalbe deuided against the
sonne, and the sonne against the father: the
mother against ẏ daughter, & the daughter against the mother: the mother in law
against her daughter in law, & the daughter in law, against her mother in law.

m Because they did vse long garmẽts, the maner was to girde or trusse thẽ vp whẽ they wẽt about anie busines.
Mat.24,43.
reuel.16,15.

n The porciõ of seruants euerie moneth was foure peckes of corne, as Donatus writeth in Phormio.

o Therefore ignorance is inexcusable.

p To whome God hathe giuen manie graces.

q The Gospel is as a burnĩg fyre moste vehement, which maketh a chãge of things through all ẏ worlde.

Mat.10,34.

r If there be great troubles and alteratiõs vpon ẏ earth, wᶜ things come not by the proprietie of the Gospel, but through the wickednes of man.

s He compareth his death to baptisme.

Mat 16,2.

54 ¶ *Then ſaid he to the people, When ye
ſe a cloude riſe out of the Weſt, ſtraight
way ye ſay, A ſhower cõmeth: and ſo it is.
55 And when *ye ſe* the South winde blow,
ye ſay, that it wil be hote: and it commeth
to paſſe.
56 Hypocrites, ye can diſcerne the face of
the earth, and of the ſkie: but why diſcerne
ye not this time?
57 Yea, and why iudge ye not of your ſelues what is right?
58 ¶ *While thou goeſt with thine aduerſarie to the ruler, as thou art in the way, giue
diligence in the way, ŷ thou maiſt be [t] deliuered from him, leſt he bring thee to the
iudge, & the iudge deliuer thee to the iayler, and the iayler caſt thee into priſon.
59 I tell thee, thou ſhalt not departe thẽce,
til thou haſt payed the vtmoſt mite.

Mat. 5,25.

t Thogh it be to thy loſſe & hinderance.

CHAP. XIII.

1 The crueltie of Pilate. 2 We oght not to condemne all to be wicked men which ſuffre. 3 Chriſt exhorteth to repentance. 11 He healeth the croked woman. 15 Anſwereth to the maſter of the Synagogue. 18 By diuers ſimilitudes he declareth what the kingdome of God is. 23 Alſo that the nomber of them which ſhal be ſaued, is ſmale. 33 Finally he ſheweth that no worldelie policie or force can let the worke and counſel of God.

1 THere were certeine men preſent at
the ſame ſeaſon, that ſhewed him of
ŷ Galileãs, whoſe blood Pilate had [a] mingled with their owne ſacrifices.
2 And Ieſus anſwered, and ſaid vnto them,
Suppoſe ye, ŷ theſe Galileans were [b] greater ſinners then all the *other* Galileans, becauſe they haue ſuffered ſuche things?
3 I tell you, nay: but except [c] ye amende
your liues, ye ſhal all likewiſe periſh.
4 Or thinke you that thoſe eightene, vpon
whome the towre in [d] Siloam fel, & ſlewe
them, were "ſinners aboue all men that
dwell in Ieruſalem?
5 I tell you, nay: but except ye amẽde your
liues, ye all ſhal likewiſe periſh.
6 ¶ He ſpake alſo this parable, A certeine
mã had a figge tre planted in his vineyarde: and he came and ſoght frute thereon,
and founde none.
7 Then ſaid he to the dreſſer of his vineyarde, Beholde, [e] this thre yeres haue I
come and ſoght frute of this figge tre, and
finde none: [f] cut it downe: why kepeth it
[g] alſo the ground baren?
8 And he anſwered, & ſaid vnto him, Lord,
let it alone this yere alſo, til I digge round
about it, and dongue it.
9 And if it beare frute, *wel*: if not, thẽ after
thou ſhalt cut it downe.
10 ¶ And he taught in one of the Synagogues on the Sabbath day.
11 And beholde, there was a woman which
had a [h] ſpirit of infirmitie eightene yeres,

a He murthered them as they were ſacrificing: & ſo their blood was mingled with ŷ blood of the beaſtes which were ſacrificed.

b For ŷ Iewes toke occaſion hereby to condemne them as moſte wicked men.

c He warneth thẽ rather to conſider their owne eſtate, thẽ to reproue other mens.

d Which towre ſtode by the riuer Siloe or fiſhpoole in Ieruſalem.

"Or, detters.

e By this ſimilitude is declared the great patience that God vſeth toward ſinners in loking for their amendement: but this delay auaileth them nothing, when they ſtil remaine in their corruption.

f We ſe our ſtate, if we bring not forthe frute.

g For bothe it is vnfruteful it ſelf, and doeth hurt to the ground where it groweth.

h Whome Satan had ſtroken with a diſeaſe, as the ſpirit of coueтouſnes is that ſpirit, that maketh a man couetous.

& was [i] bowed together, and colde not lift
vp *her ſelf* in anie wiſe.
12 When Ieſus ſawe her, he called her to
him, and ſaid to her, Woman, thou art" loſed from thy diſeaſe.
13 And he laid his hands on her, and immediatly ſhe was made ſtraight againe, and
glorified God.
14 And the ruler of the Synagogue anſwered with indignation becauſe that Ieſus
had healed on the Sabbath *day*, & ſaid vnto the people, There are ſix dayes in which
men oght to worke: in thẽ therefore come
and be healed, and not on the Sabbath day.
15 Then anſwered him the Lord, and ſaid,
Hypocrite, doeth not eiche one of you on
the Sabbath *day* loſe his oxe or his aſſe
frõ the ſtall, & lead him away to ŷ water?
16 And oght not this daughter of Abrahã,
whome Satã had bounde, lo, eightene yeres, be loſed from this bonde on the Sabbath day?
17 And when he ſaid theſe things, all his
aduerſaries were aſhamed: but all the people reioyced at all the excellent things,
that were done by him.
18 ¶ *Then ſaid he, What is the [k] kingdome of God like? or whereto ſhal I compare it?
19 It is like a graine of muſtarde ſeed, which
a man toke and ſowed in his garden, and
it grewe, and waxed a great tre, and the
foules of the heauen made neſtes in the
branches thereof.
20 ¶ And againe he ſaid, Whereunto ſhal
I liken the kingdome of God?
21 It is like leauen, which a womã toke, and
hid in thre peckes of floure, til all was leauened.
22 ¶ *And he went through all cities and
townes, teaching, & iourneying towardes
Ieruſalem.
23 Then ſaid one vnto him, Lord, *are there*
fewe ŷ ſhalbe ſaued? And he ſaid vnto thẽ,
24 *[l] Striue to entre in at the ſtraite gate:
for manie, I ſay vnto you, wil ſeke to enter in, and ſhal not be able.
25 When the good man of the houſe is riſen vp, and hathe ſhut to the dore, and ye
beginne to ſtand without, and to knocke
at the dore, ſaying, Lord, Lord, open to vs,
and he ſhal anſwer and ſay vnto you, I
knowe you not whence ye are,
26 [m] Then ſhal ye beginne to ſay, We haue
eaten and drunke in thy preſence, & thou
haſt taught in our ſtretes.
27 *But he ſhal ſay, I tel you, I know you
not whence ye are: departe from me, all
ye workers of iniquitie.
28 There ſhalbe weping and gnaſhing of
teeth, when ye ſhal ſe Abraham and Iſaac,
and Iacob, and all the Prophetes in the
kingdome of God, and your ſelues thruſte
out

i As they are whoſe ſinewes are ſhronke.

"Or, ſet at libertie out of Satans bandes.

Mat. 13,31. mar. 4,31.

k By theſe ſimilitudes he ſheweth the increaſe, whereby God augmenteth his kingdome, cõtrarie to all mens opiniõs.

Mat. 9,35. mar. 6,6.

Mat. 7,13.

l We muſt endeuour & cut of all impediments, which may let vs.

m He warneth the Iewes, ŷ they depriue not thẽ ſelues by their own negligence of that ſaluatiõ which was offred vnto thẽ.

Mat. 7,13. & 25,41. pſal. 6,13.

cut at dores.
29 Then shal come *manie* from the [n]East, &
from the West, and from the North, and
from the South, and shal sit at table in the
kingdome of God.
30 *And beholde, [o] there are last, which
shalbe first, and there are first, which shal
be last.
31 The same day there came certeine Pharises, and said vnto him, Departe, and go
hence: for Herode wil kil thee.
32 Thē said he vnto thē, Go ye & tell that
foxe, Beholde, I [p] cast out deuils, and wil
heale stil [q] to day, and to morowe, and the
third day [r] I shalbe "perfited.
33 Neuertheles I must walke to daye, and
to morowe, and the day following: for it
can not be, that a Prophet [s] shulde perish
out of Ierusalem.
34 *O Ierusalem, Ierusalem, which killest
the Prophetes, and stonest them that are
sent to thee, how often wolde I haue gathered thy children together, as the henne
gathered her broode vnder *her* wings, &
ye wolde not!
35 Beholde, your [t] house is left vnto you
desolate: and verely I tel you, ye shal not
se me vntil *the time* come that ye shal say,
[u]Blessed *is* he that cometh in the name of
the Lord.

n The people which thē were strangers.
o Christ cutteth of the vaine confidence of the Iewes who glorified in that, that God had chosen them for his people: yet they obeied him not according to his worde.
Mat.19,30. & 20,16. mar.10,31.
p Nether the enuie of the Pharises, who wolde haue put him in feare of Herode, nor yet anie policie of man colde stay him from that office which God had enioyned him.
q Meaning a litle while.
r By Christs death we are made perfite for euer.
"*Or, make an end.*
s He noteth their malice, which by all meanes soght his death more thē did the tyrant, of whome they willed him to beware. **Mat 23,37.* t Christ forewarneth them of the destruction of the Temple, and of their whole policie.
u When your owne conscience shal reproue you and cause you to confesse that which ye nowe denie, which shalbe when you shal se me in my maiestie.

CHAP. XIIII.

1 Iesus eateth with the Pharise. 4 Healeth the dropsie vpon the Sabbath. 8 Teacheth to be lowlie & to bid the poore to our table. 15 He telleth of the great supper. 28 He warneth them that wil followe him, to lay their accountes before, what it wil cost them. 34 The salt of the earth.

1 AND it came to passe that whē he was
entred into the house of one of the
chief Pharises on the Sabbath *day*, to "eat
bread, they watched him.
2 And beholde, there was a certeine mā before him, which had the dropsie.
3 Then Iesus answering, spake vnto the ex-
pouders of the Law, and Pharises, saying,
Is it lawful to heale on the Sabbath *day*?
4 And they held their peace. Then he toke
him, and healed him, and let him go,
5 And answered them, saying, Which of
you *shal haue* an asse, or an oxe fallen into a
pit, and wil not straightway pul him out
on the Sabbath day?
6 And they colde not answer him againe
to those things.
7 ¶He spake also a parable to the ghests,
when he marked how they chose out the
chief roumes, and said vnto them,
8 [a]When thou shalt be bidden of anie mā
to a weddīg, set not thy self downe in the
chiefest place, lest a more honorable man
then thou, be bidden of him,
9 And he that bade bothe him and thee, come, and say to thee, Giue this man roume,
and thou then beginne with shame to take
the lowest roume.
10 *But whē ȳ art bidden, go & sit downe in
the lowest roume, that when he that bade
thee, cometh, he may say vnto thee, Friend,
sit vp hier: thē shalt thou haue worship in
the presence of them that sit at table with
thee.
11 *For whosoeuer exalteth him self, shalbe broght low, and he that humbleth him
self, shalbe exalted.
12 ¶Thē [b] said he also to him that had bid
den him, *When thou makest a dyner or a
supper, call not thy friends, nor thy brethren, nether thy kinsemen, nor the riche
neighbours, lest they also bid thee againe,
and a recompense be made thee.
13 But when thou makest a feast, call the
poore, the maimed, the lame, & the blind,
14 And thou shalt be blessed, because they
cā not recōpense thee: for thou shalt be re-
cōpensed at the resurrection of the iuste.
15 ¶Now whē one of them that sate at table, heard these things, he said vnto him,
Blessed *is* he that eateth bread in the kingdome of God.
16 Then said he to him, * [c] A certeine man
made a great supper, and bade manie,
17 And sent his seruant at supper time to
say to them that were bidden, Come: for
all things are now ready.
18 But they all with one *minde* begā to make excuse: The first said vnto him, I haue
boght a ferme, and I must nedes go out &
se it: I pray thee haue me excused.
19 And another said, I haue boght fiue yoke of oxen, and I go to proue them: I pray
thee, haue me excused.
20 And another said, I haue maried a wife,
and therefore I can not come.
21 So ȳ seruant returned, & shewed his master these things. Thē was the good mā of
the house angrie, & said to his seruāt, [d]Go
out quickely into ȳ places & stretes of the
citie, and bring in hither the poore, & the
maimed, and the halt, and the blinde.
22 And the seruant said, Lord, it is done as
thou hast cōmāded, & yet there is roume.
23 Then the master said to the seruant, Go
out into the [e] hie wayes, and hedges, and
[f] compel them to come in, that mine house
may be filled.
24 For I say vnto you, that none of those
men which were bidden, shal taste of my
supper.
25 Now there went great multitudes with
him, and he turned and said vnto them,
26 If anie man come to me, and [g] hate not
his father, and mother, & wife, & children,
and brethren, and sisters: yea, and his owne
life also, he can not be my disciple.

"*Or, take his refection.*
a He reproueth their ambition, which desire to sit in the hiest places.
Prou.25,7.
Chap.18,14. mat.23,2.
Prou.3,9. tob.4,7.
b Christ reprehendeth onely the blinde affectiō of mā, which regardeth nothing but a worldelie recompense.
Mat.22,2. reuel 19,9.
c He casteth the Iewes in ȳ teeth ẇ their ingratitude, ẇ wolde not eat of those holie meates of Gods worde, which was presented vnto thē, & whereunto they were bid a long time before.
d Here is signified the calling of the Gētiles.
e God wil rather receiue all the raskal people of the worlde to his banket, then them which are vnthākful.
f This cōpulsiō cometh of the feling of the power of Gods worde, after that his worde hathe bene preached.
g That is, he ȳ casteth not of all affectiōs and desires, ẇ drawe vs frō Christ.

27 *And whosoeuer beareth not his crosse,
and cometh after me, can not be my disciple.
28 For which of you minding to buylde a
towre, sitteth not downe before, and [h] cou-
teth the cost, whether he haue sufficient to
performe it,
29 Lest that after he hathe laid the fundation, and is not able to performe it, all
that beholde it, beginne to mocke him,
30 Saying, This man began to buylde, and
was not able to make an end?
31 Or what King going to make warre a-
gainst another King, sitteth not downe
first, & taketh counsel, whether he be able
with tē thousand, to mete him that cometh
against him with twentie thousand?
32 Or els while he is yet a great way of, he
sendeth an ambassage, and desireth condi
cions of peace.
33 So likewise, whosoeuer he be of you, that
[i] forsaketh not all that he hathe, he can not
be my disciple.
34 *Salt is good: [k] but if salt haue loste his
sauour, wherewith shal it be "salted?
35 It is nether mete for the land, nor yet
for the dongue hil, but men cast it out. He
that hathe eares to heare, let him heare.

Chap. 9, 23. mat. 10, 37. & 16, 24. mar. 8, 24.

h He that wil professe the Gospel, muste diligently consider what his profession requireth, & not rashely to take in hand so great an enterprise: nether yet when he hathe taken in hand, in anie case to forsake is.

i He that is not persuaded to leaue all at euerie houre to bestowe hi self frankely in Gods seruice.

Mat. 5, 13. mar. 9, 50.

k If they that shulde season others, haue lost it thē selues, wheresshulde a man recouer it?

"Or, seasoned.

CHAP. XV.

2 The Pharises murmure because Christ receiueth sinners. 4 The louing mercie of God is openly set forthe in the parable of the hundreth shepe, 7 Ioye in heauen for one sinner. 12 Of the prodigal sonne.

1 THen resorted vnto him all the Publicanes, and sinners, to heare him.
2 Therefore the Pharises and scribes murmured, saying, He receiueth sinners, & eateth with them.
3 Then spake he this parable to them,
saying,
4 *What man of you hauing an hundreth
shepe, if he loose one of them, doeth not
leaue ninetie and nine in the wildernes, &
go after that which is lost, vntil he finde it?
5 And when he hathe founde it, he laieth
it on his shulders with ioye.
6 And whē he cometh home, he calleth together his friends and neighbours, saying
vnto them, Reioyce with me: for I haue
founde my shepe, which was lost.
7 I say vnto you, that likewise ioye shalbe
in heauen for one sinner that conuerteth,
more then for ninetie and nine [a] iuste men,
which nede none amendement of life.
8 Ether what woman hauing ten [b] pieces
of siluer, if she loose one piece, doeth not
light a candel, & swepe the house, and seke
diligently til she finde it?
9 And when she hathe foūde it, she calleth
her friends, and neighbours, saying, Reioyce with me: for I haue founde the piece
which I had lost.
10 Likewise I say vnto you, there is ioye

Mat. 18, 12.

a Which iustifie thē selues, & knowe not their owne fautes.

b The worde is *drachma*, which is some what more in value then fyue pence of olde sterling money, & was equal with a Romaine penie.

in the presence of the Angels of God, for
one sinner that conuerteth.
11 ¶He said moreouer, A certeine man had
two sonnes.
12 And the yonger of thē said to his father,
Father, giue me the [c] portion of the goods
that falleth to me. So he deuided vnto
them *his* substance.
13 So not long after, when the yonger sonne had gathered all together, he toke his
iorney into a farre countrey, and there he
wasted his goods with [d] riotous liuing.
14 Now when he had spent all, there arose
a great dearth throughout that land, and
he began to be in necessitie.
15 Then he went and claue to a citizen of
that countrey, and he sent him to his farme, to feede swine.
16 And he wolde faine haue filled his bellie with ẏ huskes, that the swine ate: [e] but
no man gaue *them* him.
17 Then he came to him self, and said, How
manie hired seruants at my fathers haue
bread ynough, and I dye for hunger?
18 I wil rise and go to my father, and say
vnto him, Father, I haue sinned against
[f] heauen, and before thee,
19 And am no more worthie to be called thy
sōne: make me as one of thy hired seruāts.
20 So he arose and came to his father, and
whē he was yet a [g] great way of, his father
sawe him, and had compassion, and ran &
fel on his necke, and kissed him.
21 And the sonne said vnto him, [h] Father,
I haue sinned against heauen, and before
thee, and am no more worthie to be called
thy sonne.
22 Then the father said to his seruants,
Bring forthe the best robe, and put it on
him, and put a ring on his hand, and shoes
on his feete,
23 And bring the fat calf, and kil him, and
let vs eat, and be merie.
24 For this my sonne was dead, and is aliue
againe: and he was lost, but he is founde.
And they began to be merie.
25 Now the [i] Elder brother was in the field,
and when he came and drewe nere to the
house, he heard melodie, and dancing,
26 And called one of his seruants, & asked
what those things ment.
27 And he said vnto him, Thy brother is
come, and thy father hathe killed the fat-
ted calfe, because he hathe receiued him
safe and sounde.
28 Thē he was angrie, & wolde not go in:
therefore came his father out and entreated him.
29 But he answered & said to his father, Lo
these manie yeres haue I done thee seruice, nether brake I at anie time thy cōmādement, & yet thou neuer gauest me a kid
that I might make merie with my friēds.
30 But

c This declareth that we oght not to desire to haue our portion separate from God except we wil lose all.

d The Greke worde signifieth, so to waste all that a man reserueth nothing to him self.

e For no man had pitie vpō him.

f That is, against God.

g God preuenteth vs and heareth our gronings before we crye to him.

h He was touched with the feeling of his sinne & therefore was ashamed thereof, and heauie in heart.

i God reproueth the enuie of suche as grudge when God receiueth sinners to mercie.

30 But whẽ this thy sonne was come, which
hathe deuoured thy goods with harlots,
thou hast for his sake killed the fat calfe.
31 And he said vnto him, [k] Sonne, thou art
euer with me, and all that I haue, is thine.
32 It was mete that we shulde make mery, &
be glad: for this thy brother was dead, and
is aliue againe: and he was lost, but he is
founde.

k Thy parte, ẏ art a Iewe, is nothing diminished by that ẏ Christ was also killed for the Gentiles: for he accepteth not ẏ persone, but feedeth indifferẽtly all thẽ that beleue in him, with his bodie and blood to life euerlastig.

CHAP. XVI.

1 Christ exhorteth his to wisdome and liberalitie by the example of the steward. 13 None can serue two masters. 14 He reproueth the couetousnes and hypocrisie of the Pharises. 16 Of the end and force of the Law. 18 Of the holie state of mariage. 19 Of the riche and Lazarus.

1 AND he said also vnto his disciples,
[a] There was a certeine riche man,
which had a stewarde, and he was accused
vnto him, that he wasted his goods.
2 And he called him, and said vnto him,
How *is it* that I heare this of thee? Giue
an accounts of thy stewardship: for thou
maiest be no longer stewarde.
3 Then the stewarde said within him self,
What shal I do: for my master wil take a-
way from me the stewardeship? I can not
digge, & to begge I am ashamed.
4 I knowe what I wil do, that when I am put
out of the stewardeship they may receiue
me into their houses.
5 Then called he euerie one of his masters
detters, & said vnto the first, How muche
owest thou vnto my master?
6 And he said, An hũdreth measures of oyle. And he said to him, Take thy writing,
and sit downe quickely, and write fiftie.
7 Then said he to another, How muche
owest thou? And he said, An hũdreth mea
sures of wheat. Then he said to him, Take
thy writing, and write foure score.
8 And the Lord commended [b] the vniust
stewarde, because he had done wisely.
Wherefore the children of this worlde a-
re in their generacion wiser thẽ the children of light.
9 And I saye vnto you, Make you friends
[c] with the riches of iniquitie, that when
ye shal want, they may receiue you into e-
uerlasting habitacions.
10 He that is faithful in the least, he is also
faithful in muche: and he that is vniust in
the least, is vniust also in muche.
11 If thẽ ye haue not bene faithful in [d] the
wicked riches, who wil trust you in ẏ true
treasure?
12 And if ye haue not bene faithful in [e] another mans *goods*, who shal giue you that
which is [f] yours?
13 *No seruant can serue two masters: for
ether he shal hate the one, and loue the o-
ther: or els he shal leane to the one, & despise the other. Ye can not serue God and
riches.

a Christ teacheth hereby, ẏ likewise as he ẇ is in autoritie & hathe riches, if he get friends in his ꝓsperitie, may be relieued in his aduersitie: so our liberalitie towards õ neighbour shal stand vs in suche steade at ẏ daye of iudgement that God wil accept it as done vnto him.

b God, who doeth here represent ẏ master of the house, doeth rather commende the prodigal waste of his goods, & the liberal giuing of the same to ẏ poore, then ẏ strait keping & hardin of them.

c That is, ether wickedly gotten, or wickedly kept, or wickedly spẽt: & hereby we be warned to suspect riches which for the moste parte are an occasion to their possessours of great wickednes.

d Thei which can not wel bestowe worldelie goods, wil bestowe euil spiritual treasures: & therefore they oght not to be committed vnto them.

e As are riches and suche like things, which God hathe giuen not for your selues onely, but to bestowe vpon others.

Mat.6,24.

f Christ calleth the gifts, which he giueth vnto vs, ours.

14 All these things heard the Pharises also
which were couetous, and they [g] mocked
him.
15 Then he said vnto them, Ye are they,
which [h] iustifie your selues before men:
but God knoweth your hearts: for that
which is highly estemed amõg men, is abominacion in the sight of God.
16 *The Law and the Prophetes *endured*
vntil Iohn: and since that time the kingdome of God is preached, and euerie man
[i] preasseth into it.
17 *Now it is more easie that heauen and
earth shulde passe away, then that one title of the Law shulde fall.
18 ¶ *Whosoeuer putteth away his wife, &
marieth another, committeth adulterie: &
whosoeuer marieth her that [k] is put away
from her housband, cõmitteth adulterie.
19 ¶ There was a [l] certeine riche mã, which
was clothed in purple and fine linen, and
fared wel and delicately euerie day.
20 Also there was a certeine begger named
Lazarus, which was laied at his gate ful of
sores,
21 And desired to be refreshed with the
crommes that fell from the riche mans table: yea, and the dogs came and licked his
sores.
22 And it was so that the begger dyed, and
was caryed by the Angels into [m] Abrahams [n] bosome. The riche man also dyed
and was buryed.
23 And being in hel in torments, he lift vp
his eyes, and sawe Abraham a farre of, &
Lazarus in his bosome.
24 Then he cryed, and said, Father Abraham, haue mercie on me, and send Lazarus that he may dippe ẏ typ of his [o] finger
in water, and coole my tongue: for I am
tormented in this flame.
25 But Abraham said, [p] Sonne, remember
that thou in thy life time receiuedst thy
"pleasures, and likewise Lazarus "paines:
now therefore is he comforted, and thou
art tormented.
26 Besides all this, betwene you and vs there is a great "gulfe set, so that they which
wolde go from hence to you, can not, nether can they come from thence to vs.
27 Then he said, I pray thee therefore father, that thou woldest send him to my fathers house,
28 (For I haue fiue brethrẽ) that he may testifie vnto them, lest they also come into
this place of torment.
29 Abraham said vnto him, They haue
Moses & the [q] Prophetes: let them [r] heare them.
30 And he said, Nay, father Abraham:

g Because thei iudged no man happie, but those ẏ were riche.

h Which loue outwarde apparance, and vaine glorie.

Mat.11,12.

i Their zeale is so inflamed, ẏ thei followe the Gospel without respect of world lie things.

Mat.5,18.

Mat.5,32.19. 9.1 cor.7,11.

k That is, ẇ is not lawfully diuorced

l By this storie is declared what punishement thei shal haue, which liue deliciously & neglect the poore.

m As the fathers in the olde Law were said to be gathered into ẏ bosome of Abraham, because thei receiued the frute of the same faith ẇ him: so in the newe Testament we say ẏ the members of Christ are ioyned to their head, or gathered vnto him.

n Whereby is signified that moste blessed life, ẇ they ẏ dye in the faith that Abraham did, shal enioye after this worlde.

o Christ describeth spiritual things by suche maner of speache, as is moste propre to our vnderstãding: for our soules haue nether fingers nor eyes, nether are they thirstie or speake: but ẏ Lord as it were in a table, painteth forthe the state of the life to come, as our capacitie is able to comprehend it.

p In calling him sonne, he causeth his vaine boastig, who in his life vanted him self to be the sonne of Abraham: warning vs also hereby how litle glorious titles auaile.

"Or, good things. "Or, euil things "Or, swallowing pit.

q Which declareth that it is to late to be instructed by the dead, if in their life time thei can not profite by the liuelie worde of God.

r As faith cometh by Gods worde, so is it mainteined by the same. So that nether we oght to loke for Angels from heauen, or the dead to confirme vs therein, but onelie the worde of God is sufficient to life euerlasting.

but if one came vnto thẽ from the dead,
they wil amend their liues.
31 Then he said vnto him, If they heare
not Moses and the Prophetes, nether wil
thei be persuaded, thogh one rise from the
dead againe.

CHAP. XVII.

2 Christ teacheth his disciples to auoide occasiõs of offẽce. 3 One to forgiue another. 5 We oght to pray for the increase of faith. 6 He magnifieth the Vertue of faith. 10 And sheweth the vnhabilitie of mã. 11 Healeth ten lepers. 20 Speaketh of the latter dayes, and of the end of the worlde.

Mat.18,7. mar.9,42.

1 THen said he to the disciples, * It can
not be auoided, but that offẽces wil
come, but wo *be* to him by whome they
come.
2 It were better for him that a great milstone were hanged about his necke, and
that he were cast into the sea, then that he
shulde [a] offende one of these litle ones.

a That is, to turne him backe from ỹ knowledge of God, and his saluacion.

3 ¶ Take hede to your selues: if thy brother trespace against thee, rebuke him: &
if he repent, forgiue him.

Mat.18,21.

4 *And thogh he sinne against thee [b] seuen
times in a daye, and seuen times in a daye
turne againe to thee, saying, It repenteth
me, thou shalt forgiue him.

b That is, manie times: for by a certeine nõber he meaneth an vncerteine.

5 ¶ And the Apostles said vnto the Lord,
Increase our faith.

Mat.17,20.

6 And the Lord said, * If ye had faith *as*
muche as is [c] a graine of mustard sede, and
shulde say vnto this mulbery tre, [d] plucke
thy self vp by the rootes, and plante thy
self in the sea, it shulde euen obey you.

c That is, if thei had neuer so litle of pure and perfite faith.

d Meanĩg, thei shulde do wonderful and incrediblethĩgs.

7 ¶ Who is it also of you that hauing a ser
uant plowing or feding cattel, wolde saye
vnto him by & by, when he were come frõ
the field, Go, and sit downe at table?
8 And wolde not rather say to him, [e] Dresse wherewith I may suppe, and girde thy
self, and serue me, til I haue eaten and
dronken, and afterward eat thou, & drinke
thou?

e Hereby is declared ỹ it is not ynough to do a piece of our duetie for a time, but also we must continue to the end.

9 Doeth he thanke that seruant, because he
did that which was commãded vnto him?
I trowe not.
10 So likewise ye, when ye haue done all
those things, which are commanded you,
say, We are [f] vnprofitable seruants: we
haue done that which was our duetie
to do.

f For God receiueth nothĩg of vs, whereby he shulde stãd boũde vnto vs.

11 ¶ And so it was when he went to Ierusalem, that he passed through the middes of
Samaria and Galile.
12 And as he entred into a certeine towne,
there met him ten men that were lepers,
which stode a farre of.
13 And they lift vp their voyces and said,
Iesus, Master, haue mercie on vs.

Leui.14,2.

14 And when he sawe *them*, he said vnto
them, * Go, shewe your selues vnto the
[g] Priests. And it came to passe, that as thei
went, they were clensed.

g To whome it did apperteine to iudge of the leprosie, Leui. 14,2: and hereby also the Priests shulde haue no occasion to grudge, or murmure.

15 Then one of them, when he sawe that he
was healed, turned backe, and with a loude voyce praised God,
16 And fell downe on his face at his fete,
and gaue him thankes: and he was a Samaritan.
17 And Iesus answered, and said, Are there not ten clensed? but where *are* the
[h] nine?
18 There are none founde that returned
to giue God praise, saue this stranger.

h He noteth hereby their ingratitude, & ỹ the greatest parte neglect the benefites of God.

19 And he said vnto him, Arise, go thy way,
thy faith hathe made thee whole.
20 ¶ And when he was demanded of the
Pharises, when the kingdome of God
shulde come, he answered them, & said,
The kingdome of God cometh not [i] with
obseruacion.
21 Nether shal men say, Lo here, or lo there: for beholde the kingdome of God is
" [k] within you.

i It can not be decerned by anie outwarde shew, or maiestie, whereby it might the rather be knowẽ.

" Or, among you.

k Ether by reason of the worde of God, w is receiued by faith, or that ỹ Messias whome thei soght, as absent, is now present, eũ within their owne dores, and yet they knowe hĩ not, Iohn 1,11.

22 And he said vnto the disciples, The
dayes wil come, when ye shal desire to se
[l] one of the dayes of the Sonne of man,
and ye shal not se it.

Mat.24,23. mar.13,21.

23 * Then they shal saye to you, Beholde
here, or beholde there: *but* go not thither,
nether followe them.
24 For as the lightening that lighteneth
out of the one *parte* vnder heauen, shineth
vnto the other *parte* vnder heauen, so shal
the Sonne of man be in his [m] daye.

l He speaketh of his first cõming into the worlde.

m Meaning his seconde comming, wherein he shal appeare in glorie.

25 But first must he suffer manie things, &
be reproued of this generacion.

Gen.7,5. mat. 24,38. 1.pet.3.20.

26 * And as it was in the [n] dayes of Noe,
so shal it be in the dayes of the Sonne of
man.
27 They ate, they dranke, they maried wiues, and gaue in mariage vnto the daye
that Noe went into the Arke: & the flood
came, and destroyed them all.

n When men contemned the iudgement of God, wherewith they were before menaced.

28 * Likewise also, as it was in the dayes of
Lot: they ate, they dranke, they boght,
they solde, they planted, they buylt.

Gen.19,24.

29 But in the daye that Lot went out of Sodom, it rained fyre and brimstone from
heauen, and destroyed them all.
30 After these *ensamples* shal it be in the
daye when the Sonne of man shalbe reueiled.
31 At that daye he that is vpon the [o] house,
and his stuffe in the house, let him not come downe to take it out: and he that is in
the field likewise, let him not turne backe
to that he left behinde.

o We must forget that which we haue left behinde vs, to the end, that we may ỹ better followe ỹ heauenlie vocacion.

Gen.19,26.

32 *Remember Lots wife.

Chap.9,24. & 16,25. matth.10,39. mar.8,35. iohn 12,25.

33 * Whosoeuer wil seke to saue his soule,
shal lose it: & whosoeuer shal lose it, [p] shal
get it life.

p This corporal death shal engendre life euerlasting.

Mat.24,41.

34 * I tell you, in that night there shalbe

q He meaneth ẏ no bāde or coniunction is so strait ẏ shulde stay vs.

two in one q bed: the one shalbe receiued,
and the other shalbe left.
35 Two women shalbe grinding together:
the one shalbe taken, and the other shalbe left. ‖
36 And they answered, and said to him,
Where, Lord? And he said vnto them,
*r Wheresoeuer ẏ bodie *is*, thither wil also
the egles resorte.

Mat.24,28.
r Nothing can hinder ẏ faithful to be ioyned to their head Iesus Christ: for thei shal gather vnto him, as ẏ rauening birdes about a carian.
‖ *Two shalbe in the field: one shalbe receiued, & another shal be left.*

CHAP. XVIII.

2 *By the example of the widowe, and the Publicane Christ teacheth how to pray. 15 By the example of children he exhorteth to humilitie. 18 Of the way to be saued, and what things let. 29 The rewarde promised to his, 31 And of the crosse.*

1 AND *he spake also a parable vnto thē,
to this end, that they oght alwayes to
pray, and not to a waxe fainte,
2 Saying, There was a iudge in a certeine
citie, which feared not God, nether reuerēced man.
3 And there was a widow in ẏ citie, which
came vnto him, saying, " Do me iustice a-
gainst mine b aduersarie.
4 And he wolde not for a time: but afterwarde he said with him self, Thogh I feare not God, nor reuerence man,
5 Yet because this widowe troubleth me,
I wil do her right, lest at the last she come
and make me wearie.
6 And the Lord said, Heare what the vnrighteous iudge saith.
7 Now shal not God aduenge his elect, ẇ
crye day and night vnto him, yea, thogh
c he suffer long for them?
8 I tel you he wil aduenge thē quickely: but
when the Sonne of man cometh, shal he
finde faith on the earth?
9 ¶He spake also this parable vnto certeine which trusted in them selues that they
were iuste, and despised other,
10 Two men wēt vp into ẏ Tēple to pray:
the one a Pharise, and the other a Publicā.
11 The Pharise d stode & prayed thus with
him self, O God, I thanke thee that I am
not as other mē, extorsioners, vniust, adulterers, or euen as this Publican.
12 I fast twise in the weke: I giue tithe of all
that euer I possesse.
13 But the Publicane standing a farre of,
wolde not lift vp so muche as his e eyes to
heauē, but smote his brest, saying, O God,
be merciful to me a sinner.
14 I tel you, this man departed to his house iustified, "rather then the other: * for e-
uerie man that exalteth him self, shalbe
broght low, & he that humbleth him self,
shalbe exalted.
15 ¶* They broght vnto him also f babes,
that he shulde touche them. And when his
disciples sawe it, they rebuked them.
16 But Iesus called g them vnto him and
said, Suffre the babes to come vnto me, &

Eccle.18,22. rom.12,12. 1.thes.5,17.
a The Greke worde signifieth, not to shrinke backe as cowards do in warre, or to giue place in afflictions or dāgers.
"Or, auenge me.
b Who pleadeth against me.
c And seme slowe in reuenging their wrongs.
d Whereby he declared his proude, & disdainful heart.
e These were signes of an humble and lowlie heart.
"Or, and not the other.
Chap.14,11. matth.23,12. Mat.19,13. mar.10,13.
f The worde signifieth yong sucking babes ẇ thei caryed in their armes.
g He meaneth the nources or them that bare the babes, whome ẏ Apostles rebuked.

forbid them not: for of h suche is the kingdome of God.
17 Verely I say vnto you, whosoeuer receiueth not the kingdome of God as i a babe, he shal not enter therein.
18 *Thē a certeine ruler asked him, saying,
Good master, what oght I to do, to inherite eternal life?
19 And Iesus said vnto him, Why callest
thou me k good? none is good, saue one,
euen God.
20 Thou knowest the commandements,
*Thou shalt not commit adulterie: Thou
shalt not kil: Thou shalt not steale: Thou
shalt not beare false witnes: Honour thy
father and thy mother.
21 And he said, All these haue I kept from
my youth.
22 Now whē Iesus heard that, he said vnto
him, Yet lackest thou one thing. Sel all ẏ
euer thou hast, & distribute vnto the poore, and thou shalt haue treasure in heauen,
and come, folowe me.
23 But when he heard those things, he was
verie heauie: for he was marueilous riche.
24 And when Iesus sawe him sorowful, he
said, With what difficultie shal they that
haue riches, entre into the kingdome of
God?
25 Surely it is easier for a "camel to go
through a nedles eye, then for a riche man
to entre into the kingdome of God.
26 Then said they that heard it, And who
then can be saued?
27 And he said, The things which are vnpossible with mē, are l possible with God.
28 ¶*Then Peter said, Lo, we haue left all,
and haue followed thee.
29 And he said vnto thē, Verely I say vnto
you, there is no man that hathe left house,
or parents, or brethren, or wife, or childrē
for the kingdome of Gods sake,
30 Which shal not receiue m muche more
in this worlde, and in the worlde to come
life euerlasting.
31 ¶*Then Iesus toke vnto him the twelue,
and said vnto them, Beholde, we go vp to
Ierusalem, and all things shalbe fulfilled
to the Sonne of man, that are written by
the Prophetes.
32 For he shalbe deliuered vnto the Gētiles
and shalbe mocked, and shalbe spitefully
entreated, and shalbe spitted on.
33 And when they haue scourged him, they
wil put him to death: but the third day he
shal rise againe.
34 But thei vnderstode none of these thīgs,
and this saying was hid from them, nether
perceiued they the things, which were
spoken.
35 ¶*And it came to passe, that as he was
come nere vnto Iericho, a certeine blinde
man sate by the way side begging.

h He comprehēdeth aswel them ẏ are infants of age, as them also, ẇ are like vnto infants in simplicitie and plainenes.
Mat.19,16. mar.10,17.
i Signifying ẏ they oght to lay aside all malice and pride.
Exod 20,13.
k Because cōmunely they abused this worde, Iesus sheweth him that he colde not confesse him to be good except also he acknowledged that he was of God.
"Or, cable rope.
l For he so gouerneth the hearts of his, that their riches do not blinde them.
Mat.19,27. mar 10,28.
m The litle ẏ a mā hathe ẇ the grace of God, is an hādreth folde better thē all ẏ abundance ẏ one can haue without him: but the chief recompense is in heauen.
Mat.20,17. mar.10,32.
Mat.20,29. mar.10,46.

36 And when he heard the people passe by,
he asked what it ment.
37 And thei said vnto him, that Iesus of Na
zaret passed by.
38 Then he cryed, saying, Iesus the Sonne
of Dauid, haue mercie on me.
39 And they which wēt before, rebuked him,
that he shulde holde his peace, but he cryed muche more, O [n] Sonne of Dauid, haue
mercie on me.
40 And Iesus stode stil, and commanded
him to be broght vnto him. And when he
was come nere, he asked him,
41 Saying, What wilt thou that I do vnto
thee? And he said, Lord, that I may receiue
my sight.
42 And Iesus said vnto him, Receiue thy
sight: thy faith hathe saued thee.
43 Then immediatly he receiued his sight,
and followed him, [o] praising God: and all
the people, when they sawe *this*, gaue praise
to God.

n The people vsed to call ye Messias by this Name, because they knewe he shulde come of ye stocke of Dauid, Psal 132,11 act.2,30.

o He was mindeful of the benefite receiued & also the people were moued thereby to glorifie God.

CHAP. XIX.

2 Of Zaccheus. 12 The ten pieces of money. 28 Christ rideth to Ierusalem, & wepeth for it. 45 He chaseth out the marchāts, 47 And his enemies seke to destroy him.

1 NOw when Iesus entred and passed
through Iericho,
2 Beholde, there was a mā named Zaccheus,
which *was* the chief receiuer of the tribute, and he was riche.
3 And he soght to se Iesus, who he shulde
be, and colde not for the preasse, because
he was of a lowe stature.
4 Wherefore he ran before, and climed vp
into a wilde figge tre, that he might se
him: for he shulde come that *way*.
5 And when Iesus came to the place, he loked vp, and sawe him, and said vnto him,
Zaccheus, come downe at once: for to day
I must abide at thine house.
6 Then he came downe hastely, and receiued him ioyfully.
7 And when all they sawe it, they murmured, saying, that he was gone in to lodge
with a "sinneful man.
8 And Zaccheus stode forthe, & said vnto
the Lord, Beholde, Lord, the halfe of my
goods I giue to the poore: and if I haue ta
ken frō anie man by "forged cauillation,
I restore him foure folde.
9 Then Iesus said to him, This day is
saluation come vnto this [a] house, forasmuche as he is also become the [b] sonne of
Abraham.
10 *For the Sonne of man is come to seke,
and to saue that which was lost.
11 And whiles they heard these things, he
continued and spake a parable, because
he was nere to Ierusalem, and because also they thoght that the kingdome of God
shulde shortely appeare.

" Or, a man of a wicked life.

" Or, false accusation.

a Zaccheus adoption was a signe that ye whole familie was receiued to mercie. Notwithstanding this promes, God reserueth to him self fre libertie ether to chuse or forsake as in Abrahams house.

Mat.18,11.

b To be the sonne of Abraham, is to be chosen frely, Rom. 9,8. to walke in the steppes of the faith of Abraham, Rom.4,12: to do the workes of Abraham, Iohn 8,39. by the wc things we are moste assured of life euerlasting, Ro,8,29.

12 He said therefore, *A certeine noble
mā went into [c] a farre countrey, to receiue
for him self a kingdome, and so to come
againe.
13 And he called his ten seruants, and deliuered them ten [d] pieces of money, and said
vnto them, [e] Occupie til I come.
14 Now his citizēs hated him, and sent an
ambassage after him, saying, We wil not
haue this man to reigne ouer vs.
15 And it came to passe, when he was come
[f] againe, and had receiued his kingdome, yt
he cōmanded the seruants to be called to
him, to whome he gaue his money, that he
might knowe what euerie mā had gained.
16 Thē came the first, saying, Lord, thy piece hathe encreased ten pieces.
17 And he said vnto him, Wel, good seruāt:
because yu hast bene faithful in a verie litle thing, take thou autoritie ouer tē cities.
18 And the seconde came, saying, Lord, thy
piece hathe encreased fiue pieces.
19 And to the same he said, Be thou also *ruler* ouer fiue cities.
20 So the other came and said, Lord, beholde thy piece, which I haue laid vp in a
napkin.
21 For I feared thee, because thou art a strait
man: thou takest vp, that thou laidest not
downe, and reapest that thou diddest not
sowe.
22 Then he said vnto him, Of thine owne
[g] mouth wil I iudge thee, ô euil seruāt. Thou
knewest that I am a strait man, taking vp
that I laid not downe, and reaping that I
did not sowe.
23 Wherefore thē gauest not thou my money into the bāke, that at my comming I
might haue required it with vantage?
24 And he said to them that stode by, Take from him that piece, and giue it him
that hathe ten pieces.
25 (And they said vnto him, Lord, he hathe
ten pieces.)
26 *For I say vnto you, that vnto all them
that haue, it shalbe [h] giuen: and from him
that hathe not, euen that he hathe, shalbe
taken from him.
27 Moreouer those mine enemies, which
wolde not that I shulde reigne ouer them,
bring hither, and slay them before me.
28 ¶ And when he had thus spoken, he went
forthe [i] before, ascēding vp to Ierusalem.
29 *And it came to passe, when he was come
nere to Bethphage, and Bethania, besides
the mount which is called *the mount* of oliues, he sent two of his disciples,
30 Saying, Go ye to the towne which is before *you*, wherein, assone as ye are come, ye
shal finde a colte tied, whereon neuer man
sate: lose him, and bring him *hither*.
31 [k] And if anie man aske you, why ye lose *him*, thus shal ye say vnto him, Because
the

Mat.25,14.

c This was to declare to thē that he must yet take great paines before his kingdome shulde be established.

d This piece of money is called Mina, and the whole some mounteth about the value of 17. pounde, esteming euerie piece, about fiue nobles & seuen pence.

e God wil not that his graces remaine idle with vs.

f Whereby we learne that the seconde comming of our Sauiour Christ shalbe more glorious, and excellent, thē it doeth now appeare.

g They that suppresse the giftes of God, & liue in idlenes, are without all excuse.

Chap 8,18. matth.13,12. & 25,39. mar 4,25.

h He yt faithfully bestoweth the graces of God, shal haue them increased: but they shalbe taken away frō him that is vnprofitable, and vseth them not to Gods glorie.

Mat.21,1. mar.11,1.

i Hereby we perceiue the excellent constancie of Christ, who notwithstanding he did now fight against the terrour of death, and Gods iudgemēt: yet wēt before his feareful disciples and led the way to death.

k Christ preuenteth suche difficulties as might haue troubled his disciples.

the Lord hathe nede of him.
32 So they that were sent, went their way,
and founde it as he had said vnto them.
33 And as they were losing the colte, the
owners thereof said vnto them, Why lose ye the colte?
34 And they said, The Lord hathe nede of
him.
35 ¶*So they broght him to Iesus, and they
cast their garments on the colte, and set
Iesus thereon.
36 And as he went, they spred their clothes
in the way.
37 And when he was now come nere to the
going downe of the mount of oliues, the
whole multitude of the disciples began to
reioyce, & to praise God with a loude voi
ce, for all the great workes ŷ thei had sene,
38 Saying, Blessed *be* the King that cometh
in the Name of the Lord: [l] peace in heauen, and glorie in the hiest *places*.
39 Then some of the Pharises of the companie said vnto him, Master, rebuke thy
disciples.
40 But he answered, and said vnto them, I
tel you, that if these shulde holde their pea
ce, the stones wolde crye.
41 ¶*And whē he was come nere, he behelde the citie, and wept for it,
42 Saying, [m] O if thou haddest euen knowē
at the least in this thy day [n] those things,
which *belong* vnto thy peace: but now are
they [o] hid from thine eyes.
43 For the dayes shal come vpon thee, that
thine enemies shal cast a trēche about thee,
and compasse thee rounde, and kepe thee
in on euerie side,
44 And shal make thee euen with the grou
de, and thy children which are in thee, and
they shal not leaue in thee a stone vpon
a stone, because thou knewest not the time
of thy [p] visitation.
45 ¶*He went also into the Temple, and
began to cast out them that solde therein,
and them that boght,
46 Saying vnto them, It is written, * Mine
house is the house of prayer, * but ye haue
made it a denne of theues.
47 And he taught *daily in the Tēple. And
the high Priests & the Scribes, & the chief
of the people soght to destroye him.
48 But they colde not finde what thei might
do to him: for all the people [q] hanged vpō
him when they heard him.

Mat.21,7. iohn 12,14.

l They wish that God may be appeased, & reconciled w men: and so by this meanes be glorified.

Chap 21,6. mat.24,1. mar.13,1.

m Christ partely pitieth ŷ Citie which was so nere her destructiō, & partely vpbraideth their malice which wolde not embrace Christ their Sauiour, and therefore pronounceth greater punishment to Ierusalem then to other cities, which had not receiued like graces.

n Meaning Christ, without whome there is no saluation, & with whome is all felicitie.

o Through thine owne malice thou art blinded.

Isa.56,7. mat.21,12 mar.11,17. Iere.7,11.

p And receiuedst not the redemer, ŵ was sent thee. *Or in the day time.*

q That is, were moste attēt to heare.

CHAP. XX.

4 Christ stoppeth his aduersaries mouthes by another question. 9 Sheweth their destructiō by a parable 22 The autoritie of princes. 27 The resurrection, & his diuine power. 46 He reproueth the ambition of the Scribes.

Mat.21,23. mar.11,27.

1 AND *it came to passe that on one of
those dayes, as he taught the people
in the Temple, and preached the Gospel,
the high Priests & the Scribes came vpon
him with the Elders,
2 And spake vnto him, saying, Tell vs by
what autoritie thou doest these things, or
who is he that hathe giuen thee this autoritie?
3 And he answered and said vnto them, I
also wil aske you one thing: tell me therefore:
4 The [a] baptisme of Iohn was it from heauen, or of men?
5 And they reasoned within them selues,
saying, If we shal say from heauen, he wil
say, Why then beleued ye him not?
6 But if we shal say, Of men, all the people wil stone vs: for thei be persuaded that
Iohn was a Prophet.
7 Therefore they answered, that they colde
not tell whence it *was*.
8 Then Iesus said vnto them, [b] Nether tell
I you, by what autoritie I do these things.
9 ¶*Thē began he to speake to the people
this parable, * A certeine man planted a
[c] vineyarde, & [d] let it forthe to housbandmen: and went into a strange countrey, for
a great season.
10 And at a time he sent a [e] seruant to the
housband men, that they shulde giue him
of the frute of the vineyarde, but the hous
band men did beat him, and sent him a-
way emptie.
11 Againe he sent yet another seruant: and
they did beat him, and fowle entreated
him, and sent him away emptie.
12 Moreouer, he sent the third, and him
they wounded, and cast out.
13 Then said the Lord of the vineyarde,
What shal I do? I wil send my beloued
sonne: it may be that thei wil do reuerēce,
when they se him.
14 But when the housband men sawe him,
they reasoned with them selues, saying,
This is the heire: come, let vs kil him, that
the enheritance may be ours.
15 So they cast him out of the vineyarde, &
killed him. What shal the Lord of the vineyarde therefore do vnto them?
16 He wil come & destroy these housbandmen, and wil giue out his vineyarde to o-
thers. But when they heard it, they said,
God forbid.
17 ¶And he behelde them, and said, What
meaneth this then that is written, * The
stone that the buylders refused, that is made the head [f] of the corner?
18 [g] Whosoeuer shal fall vpon that stone,
shalbe broken: & on whomesoeuer it shal
fall, it wil grinde him to powder.
19 Then the hie Priests and the Scribes the
same houre went about to lay hands on
him: (but they feared the people) for they
perceiued that he had spoken this parable
against them.
20 *And they [h] watched *him*, & sent forthe

a By baptisme he cōprehēdeth all Iohns ministerie, who bare witnes to Christ.

b By this meanes he made them ashamed and astonished

Mat.21,33. mar.12,1. Isa.5,1. ier.2,21.

c The Iewes were as Gods plantes & his owne graftig.

d God cōmitted his people to the Gouernors & Priests

e He raised vp Prophetes.

Psal.117,22. isa.28,16. act.4,11. rom.9,33. 1.pet.2,8.

f For by it the building is ioyned together & made strong

g They that stumble & fall on Christ, thinking to oppresse him, shalbe ouerthrowen them selues & destroyed.

Mat.22,16. mar 12,13.

h They wayted for a conuenient time and place.

spies,which shulde faine them selues iuste
men,to take him in his talke, and to deliuer him vnto the power and autoritie of
the gouernour.
21 And they asked him, saying, Master, we
knowe that thou sayest,and teachest right,
nether doest thou accept mās persone, but
teachest the way of God truely.
22 Is it ilawful for vs to giue Cesar tribute
or no?
23 But he perceiued their craftines, & said
vnto them, Why tempt ye me?
24 Shewe me a penie. Whose image and superscription hathe it? They answered and
said, Cesars.
25 Then he said vnto them, *kGiue thē vnto Cesar the things which are Cesars, and
to God those which are Gods.
26 And they colde not reproue his saying
before the people: but they marueiled at
his answer, and helde their peace.
27 *Then came to him certeine of the Sad
duces (which denie that there is anie resur
rection) and they asked him,
28 Saying, Master, *Moses wrote vnto vs, If
anie mans brother dye hauing a wife, and
he dye without children, that his brother
shulde take *his* wife, and raise vp sede vnto
his brother.
29 Now there were seuen brethren, and the
first toke a wife, & he dyed without children.
30 And the seconde toke the wife, and he
dyed childeles.
31 Then the third toke her: and so likewise
the seuen dyed, and left no children.
32 And last of all, the woman dyed also.
33 Therefore at the resurrection, whose
wife of them shal she be? for seuen had her
to wife.
34 Thē Iesus answered, & said vnto them,
The lchildren of this worlde marie wiues
and are maried.
35 But they which shalbe counted worthie
to enioye that worlde, and the resurrectiō
from the dead, nether marie wiues, nether
are maried.
36 m For they can dye no more, forasmuche
as thei are equal vnto the Angels, and are
the Sonnes of God, n since they are the
children of the resurrection.
37 And that the dead shal rise againe, euen
*Moses shewed it besides the bushe, when
he said, The Lord *is* the God of Abraham,
& the God of Isaac, & the God of Iacob.
38 For he is not the God of the odead, but of
them which liue: p for all liue vnto him.
39 Then certeine of the Pharises answered
and said, Master, thou hast wel said.
40 And after that, durst they not aske him
anie thing at all.
41 ¶*Then said he vnto them, How say thei
that Christ is Dauids sonne?

i They thoght it vnlawful to pay to a prince being an infidel, that which thei were wōt to pay to God in his Tēple.

Rom.13,7.

k The duetie ẏ we owe to princes, letteth nothīg that ẏ is due vnto God.

Mat.22,23. mar.12,18.

Deu.25,5.

l In this place he calleth all them children of this worlde which remaine in the same: or els matrimonie shulde not seme to apparteine to ẏ children of God, as that wicked monstre pope Syricius taught against the manifest Scriptures.

m Since mariage is ordeined to mainteine & increase mākinde, whē we shal be immortal, it shal not be in anie vse.

n For althogh the wicked rise againe, yet that life is but death and an eternal destruction.

Exo.3,6.

o Of them ẏ are not, but of thē which are.

p The immortalitie of the soule cā not be separate from the resurrectiō of the bodie, whereof here Christ properly speaketh.

Mat.22,44. mar.12,35.

42 And Dauid him self saith in the boke of
the Psalmes, *The Lord said vnto my
Lord, sit at my right hand,
43 Til I shal make thine enemies thy fotestole.
44 Seing Dauid calleth him Lord, how is
he then his q sonne?
45 ¶Then in the audiēce of all the people
he said vnto his disciples,
46 *Beware of the Scribes, which desire to
go in long robes, and loue salutations in
the markets, and the hiest seates in the Synagogues, and the chief roumes at feasts:
47 Which deuoure widowes houses, euen
vnder a colour of long praying: these shal
receiue greater damnation.

Psal.110,1.

q For the sonne is not Lord of his father, and therefore it followeth that Christ is God

Chap.11,43. mat.23,6. mar.12,38.

CHAP. XXI.

3 Christ commendeth the poore widdowe. 6 He forewarneth of the destruction of Ierusalem. 8 Of false teachers. 9 Of the tokens and troubles to come. 27 Of the end of the worlde, 37 And of his daylie exercise.

1 AND *as he behelde, he sawe the riche
men, which cast their giftes into the
treasurie,
2 And he sawe also a certeine poore widowe, which cast in thither two mites,
3 And he said, Of a trueth I say vnto you,
that this poore widowe hathe cast in more
then they all.
4 aFor they all haue of their superfluitie
cast into the offrings of God: but she of
her penurie hathe cast in all the liuing that
she had.
5 *Now as some spake of the Temple, how
it was garnished with goodlie stones and
with "consecrat things, he said,
6 Are these the things that ye loke vpon?
the dayes wil come wherein a stone shal
not be left vpon a stone, that shal not be
throwen downe.
7 Then they asked him, saying, Master, but
when shal these things be? and what signe
shal there *be* when these things shal come to passe?
8 *And he said, b Take hede, that ye be not
deceiued: for many wil come in my Name, saying, I am *Christ*, & the time draweth
nere: followe ye not them therefore.
9 And when ye heare of warres and seditions, be not afrayed: for these things must
first come, but the end followeth not by
and by.
10 Then said he vnto them, Nacion shal
rise against nacion, and kingdome against
kingdome,
11 *And great earthquakes shalbe in diuers
places, and hunger, and pestilence, and feareful things, and great signes shal there be
from heauen.
12 But before all these, they shal lay their
hands on you, & persecute *you*, deliuering
you vp to the Synagogues, and into prisones,

Mar.12,41.

a God estemeth not the gift or almes by the quantitie or value, but by ẏ heart & affection.

Chap.19,43. mat.24,1. mar.13,1.

"Or, giftes.

b Christ then maketh answer of that, which was more necessarie for them, and not to the question they demanded.

Mat.24,8. mar.13,8.

sones, and bring you before Kings and rulers for my Names sake.

c This their suffrance shal bothe be a greater confirmation to the Gospel, and also by their constancie the tyrannie of their ennemis shal at length be manifest before God & man

13 And this shal turne to you, for a [c] testimonial.
14 *Lay it vp therefore in your hearts, that
ye premeditate not, what ye shal answer.
15 For I wil giue you a mouth and wisdome, where agaist all your aduersaries shal
not be able to speake, nor [d] resist.
16 Yea, ye shalbe betrayed also of your parents, and of your brethren, and kinsmen,
and friends, and *some* of you shal they put
to death.
17 And ye shal be hated of all men for my
Names sake.
18 *Yet there shal not one heere of your
heades perish.
19 By your pacience [e] possesse your soules.
20 ¶*And when ye se Ierusalem besieged
with souldiers, then vnderstand that the
desolation thereof is nere.
21 Then let them which are in Iudea, flee to
the mountaines: and let them which are in
the middes thereof, departe out: and let
not them that are in the countrey, enter
therein.
22 For these be the dayes of vengeance, to
fulfil all things that are written.
23 But wo *be* to them that be with childe, &
to them that giue sucke in those dayes: for
there shalbe great distresse in this land, &
[f] wrath ouer this people.
24 And they shal fall on the edge of the
sworde, and shalbe led captiue into all nacions, and Ierusalem shalbe troden vnder
fote of the Gentiles, vntil the [g] time of the
Gentiles be fulfilled.
25 *Then there shalbe signes in the sunne,
and in the moone, and in the starres, and
vpon the earth trouble among the nacions
with perplexitie: the sea and the waters
shal roare.
26 And mens hearts shal faile them for feare, and for loking after those things which
shal come on the worlde: for the powers
of heauen shal be shaken,
27 And then shal they se the Sonne of man
come in a cloude, with power and great
glorie.
28 And when these things begin to come
to passe, then loke vp, and lift vp your
heads: * for your [h] redemption draweth
nere.
29 And he spake to them a parable, Beholde, the figge tre, and all trees,
30 When they now shote forthe, ye seing
them, knowe of your owne selues, that sommer is then nere.
31 So likewise ye when ye se these things
come to passe, knowe ye that the kingdome of God is nere.
32 Verely I say vnto you, This age shal not
[i] passe, til all *these* things be done.

Chap. 12, 12. mat. 10, 19. mar. 13, 11.

d For though they were so impudent to resist, yet trueth euer gaineth ÿ victorie.

Mat. 10, 13.

e That is, liue ioyfully and blessedly, euen vnder the crosse.

Mat. 24, 15. mar. 13, 14. dan. 9, 17.

f Gods wrath agaist this people shal appeare by the calamities and plagues, wherewith he wil punish them.

g He meaneth their iniquities to receiue likewise their punishment afterwarde.

Isa. 13, 10. ezek. 32, 7. mat. 24, 29. mar. 13, 24.

Rom. 8, 23.

h The effect of that redemption which Iesus Christ hathe purchased, shal then fully appeare.

i For all these things came within 50 yeres after.

33 Heauen and earth shal passe away, but my
wordes shal not passe away.
34 Take hede to your selues, lest at any
time your hearts be oppressed with surfeting and drunkennes, and cares of this
life, and lest that day come on you at vnwares.
35 For as a [k] snare shal it come on all them
that dwell on the face of the whole earth.
36 Watche therefore, & pray continually,
°that ye may be counted worthie to escape
all these things that shal come to passe, and
that ye may stand before the Sonne of mã.
37 ¶Now in the day time he taught in the
Temple, & at night he went out, and abode in the mount that is called *the mount* of
oliues.
38 And all the people came in the morning
to him, to heare him in the Temple.

k To catch & intangle them, wheresoeuer they be in the worlde.

°Or, that ye may be made worthie

CHAP. XXII.

4 Conspiracie against Christ. 7 They eat the Passeouer. 19 The institucion of the Lords supper. 24 They striue who shalbe greatest, and he reproueth thẽ. 42 He prayeth vpon the mount. 47 Iudas treason. 54 They take him, & bring him to the hie Priests house 60 Peter denieth him thrise, and yet repenteth. 67 Christ is broght before the Council, where he maketh ample confession.

1 NOw *the [a] feast of vnleauened bread
drewe nere, which is called the Passeouer.
2 And the hie Priests & Scribes soght how
they might kill him: for they feared the
people.
3 Then entred Satan into Iudas, who was
called Iscariot, and was of the nomber of
the twelue.
4 And he went his way, and cõmuned with
the hie Priests & [b] captaines, how he might
betray him to them.
5 So they were [c] glad, and agreed to giue
him money.
6 And he consented, and soght opportunitie to betray him vnto them, when the people were away.
7 ¶*Thẽ came ÿ day of vnleauened bread
when the Passeouer [d] must be sacrificed.
8 And he sent Peter and Iohn, saying, Go,
and prepare vs the Passeouer, that we may
eat it.
9 And they said to him, Where wilt thou,
that we prepare it?
10 Then he said vnto them, Beholde, when
ye be entred into the citie, there shal a man
mete you, bearing a pitcher of water: followe him into ÿ house that he entreth in,
11 And say vnto the good man of the house, The Master saith vnto thee, Where is
the lodging where I shal eat my Passeouer with my disciples?
12 Then he shal shewe you a great hie chãber trimmed: there make it readie.
13 So they went & founde as he had said vnto them, and made readie the Passeouer.

Mat. 26, 1. mar. 14, 1.

a The feast was so called, becuse they colde eat no leauened bread for the space of seuen daies: for so long the feast of ÿ Passeouer continued.

b Suche as were appointed to kepe the Temple

c For thei were in doute what way to take before this occasion was offred.

Mat. 26, 17. mar. 14, 13.

d According to Gods commandement & was first to offer it, and after to eat it.

14 *And when the [e] houre was come, he sate
downe, and the twelue Apostles with him.
15 Then he said vnto them, I haue earnestly desired to eat this Passeouer with you
before I suffre.
16 For I say vnto you, [f] Hence forthe I wil
not eat of it any more, vntil it be fulfilled
in the kingdome of God.
17 And he toke the cup, and gaue thankes,
and said, Take this, and deuide it among
you.
18 For I say vnto you, I wil not drinke of
the frute of the vine, vntil the kingdome
of God be come.
19 *And he toke bread, and when he had giuen thankes, he brake it, and gaue to them,
saying, [g] This is my bodie, which is giuen
for you: do this in the remẽbrance of me.
20 Likewise also after supper *he toke* the
cup, saying, This cup *is* the new [h] Testament in my blood, which is shed for you.
21 *Yet beholde, the hand of him that betrayeth me, is with me at the table.
22 And truely the Sonne of man goeth as it
is * [i] appointed: but wo *be* to that man, by
whome he is betrayed.
23 Then they began to enquire among thẽ
selues which of thẽ it shulde be, that shulde do that.
24 ¶ *And there arose also a strife amõg thẽ,
which of them shulde seme to be the greatest.
25 But he said vnto them, The Kings of the
Gentiles reigne ouer them, and they that
beare rule ouer thẽ, are called [k] Gracious
lords.
26 But ye *shal* not *be* so: but let the greatest
among you be as the ° least: & the chiefest
as he that serueth.
27 For who is greater, he that sitteth at table, or he that serueth? Is not he that sitteth
at table? And I am among you as he that
serueth.
28 And ye are they which haue continued
with me in my tentations.
29 Therefore I ° appoint vnto you a kingdome, as my Father hathe appoĩted to me,
30 *That ye may [l] eat, and drinke at my table in my kingdome, and sit on seates, and
iudge the twelue tribes of Israel.
31 ¶ And the Lord said, Simon, Simon, beholde,* Satan hathe desired you, [m] to wy-
nowe you, as wheat.
32 But I haue prayed for thee, that thy faith
[n] faile not: therefore when thou art conuerted, strengthen thy brethren.
33 *And he said vnto him, Lord, I am ready
to go with thee into prison, and to death.
34 But he said, I tell thee, Peter, the cocke
shal not crowe this day, before thou hast
thrise denyed that thou knewest me.
35 ¶ And he said vnto thẽ, * Whẽ I sent you
without bagge, and scrip, and shoes, lacked

Mat.26,20. mar.14,18.
e Which was in the euening about ẏ twye light, which time was appointed to eat the Passeouer.
f He meaneth that this is the last time that he wolde be conuersant ẘ thẽ as he was before, or so eat with them
Mat.26,28. mar.14,22. 1.cor.11,24.
g The bread is a true signe, and an assured testimonie that the bodie of Iesus Christ is giuen for the nourriture of our soules: likewise the wine signifieth ẏ his blood is our drinke to refreshe and quicken vs euerlastingly.
Iohn 13,18. Psal.40,11.
h The signe of the new couenant which is established & ratified by Christs blood.
Mat.20,25. mar.10,42.
i By the secret coũsel of God, as Act 4, 28.
k Meaning ẏ thei haue vaine & flattering titles giuen them, for asmuche as they are nothing lesse then their names do signifie.
° *Or, yongest.*
° *Or, leaue by bequest.*
Mat.19,28.
l By these similitudes he declareth that they shalbe partakers of his glorie: for in heauen is nether eating nor drinking.
1.Pet.5,8.
m Satã seketh by all meanes to disquiet the Church of Christ, to disperse it, and to shake it from the true faith.
n It was sore shakẽ, but yet not ouerthrowen.
Mat.26,34. mar.14,30. iohn 13,38.
Mat.10,9.

ye any thing? And they said, Nothing.
36 Then he said to them, But now he that
hathe a bagge, let him take it, and likewise
a scrip: and he that hathe none, let him sel
his coate, and [o] bye a sworde.
37 For I say vnto you, That yet the same
which is written, must be performed in
me, * Euen with the wicked was he nombred: for douteles those things which *are*
written of me, haue an end.
38 And they said, Lord, beholde, here are
[p] two swordes. And he said vnto them, It
is ynough.
39 ¶ *And he came out, and went (as he was
wonte) to the mounte of oliues: and his
disciples also followed him.
40 *And when he came to the place, he said
to them, Pray, lest ye enter into tentation.
41 And he gate him self from them, about
a stones cast, and kneled downe, & prayed,
42 Saying, Father, if thou wilt, take away
this [q] cup from me: neuertheles, not my
wil, but thine be done.
43 And there appeared an Angel vnto him
from heauen, comforting him.
44 But being in an [r] agonie, he prayed more
earnestly: and his sweate was like droppes
of blood, trickling downe to the grounde.
45 And he rose vp from prayer, & came to
his disciples, and founde them sleping for
heauines.
46 And he said vnto them, Why slepe ye?
rise and pray, lest ye entre into tentation.
47 ¶ *And while he yet spake, beholde a cõpanie, and he that was called Iudas one of
the twelue, went before them, and came
nere vnto Iesus to kisse him.
48 And Iesus said vnto him, Iudas, betrayest
thou the Sonne of man with a kisse?
49 Now when they which were about him,
sawe what wolde followe, they said vnto
him, Lord, shal we smite with sworde?
50 And one of them smote a seruant of the
hie Priest, and strake of his right eare.
51 Then Iesus answered, and said, Suffre
them thus farre: and he touched his eare, &
healed him.
52 Then Iesus said vnto the hie Priests, &
captaines of the Temple, and the Elders
which were come to him, Be ye come out
as vnto a thefe with swordes and staues?
53 When I was daily with you in the Tẽple,
ye stretched not forthe the hands against
me: but this is your very houre, and the
[s] power of darkenes.
54 ¶ Then toke they him, and led him, and
broght him to the hie Priests house. And
Peter followed a farre of.
55 *And whẽ they had kindled a fyre in the
middes of the hall, and were set downe together, Peter also sate downe among thẽ.
56 And a certeine maide behelde him as he
sate by the fyre, and hauing wel loked on
him,

o By this he sheweth them that they must susteine great troubles and afflictions.
Isa.53,12.
p They were yet so rude ẏ they thoght to haue resisted with material weapons, whereas Christ warneth them of a spiritual fight, wherein aswel their life as faith shulde be in danger.
Mat.26,36. mar.14,32. iohn 18,1.
Mat.26,41. mar.14,38.
q Meaning, his death and passion.
r The worde signifieth that horrour that Christ had cõceiued not onely for feare of death, but of his fathers iudgmẽt & wrath against sinne.
Mat.26,47. mar.14,43. iohn 18,3.
s For now God gaue libertie to Satã whose ministers they were, to execute his rage agaĩst him: which thing we se is gouerned by the prouidence of God.
Mat.26,54. mar.14,66. iohn 18,26.

him, said, This man was also with him.
57 But he denied him, saying, Woman, I
knowe him not.
58 And after a litle while, another mã sawe
him, and said, Thou art also of them. But
Peter said, Man, I am not.
59 And about the space of an houre after a
certeine other affirmed, saying, Verely e-
uen this man was with him: for he is also a
Galilean.
60 And Peter said, Man, I knowe not what
thou saiest. And immediatly while he yet
spake, the cocke crewe.
61 Then the Lord turned backe, and loked
vpon Peter: and Peter remembred the
worde of the Lord, how he had said vnto
him, * Before the cocke crowe, thou shalt
denie me thrise.

Mat.26,34. ioh.13,38.

62 And Peter went out, & wept bitterly.
63 ¶ And the men that helde Iesus, mocked
him, and stroke him.
64 And when they had blindefolded him,
thei smote him on the face, & asked him,
saying, [t] Prophecie who it is ẏ smote thee.
65 And manie other things blasphemously
spake they against him.
66 * And assone as it was day, the Elders of
the people, and the hie Priests & the Scribes came together, and led him into their
Council,

t Thei skoffed at him, because the people thoght he was a Prophet.

Mat.27,1. mar.15,1. iohn 18,28.

67 Saying, [u] Art thou the Christ? tell vs.
And he said vnto thẽ, If I tell you, ye wil
not beleue it.
68 And if also I aske you, ye wil not answer
me, nor let me go.
69 [x] Hereafter shal the Sonne of man sit at
the [y] right hand of the power of God.
70 Then said they all, Art thou then the
Sonne of God? And he said to thẽ, Ye say
that I am.
71 Then said they, What nede we anie further witnes? for we our selues haue heard
it of his owne mouth.

u They asked not to the end that the trueth might be knowen, (for the thing was to manifest) but for malice thei bare towardes Christ.

x At his secõde coming.

y As in the seconde place of honour & dignitie.

CHAP. XXIII.

1 Iesus is broght before Pilate and Herode. 18 Of Barabbas, 26 Of Simon the Cyrenian. 27 The women make lamentacion. 33 Christ crucified. 34 He praieth for his enemies. 40 He conuerteth the thefe & manie others at his death, 53 And is buryed.

1 THen * the whole multitude of them
arose, and led him vnto [a] Pilate.
2 And they began to accuse him, saying,
We haue founde this man peruerting the
people, and forbidding to paye tribute to
Cesar, saying, That he is Christ a King.
3 * And Pilate asked him, saying, Art thou
the King of the Iewes? And he answered
him, and said, Thou saist it.
4 Then said Pilate to the hie Priests, and
to the people, I finde no faute in this
man.
5 But they were the more fierce, saying,
He moueth the people, teaching through

Mat.27,2. mar.15,1. (Mat.22,21. mar.12,17.)

a Who was the chief gouernour, and had the examinacion of matters of life & death

Mat.27,11 mar.15,2. iohn 18,33.

out all Iudea, beginning at Galile, euen
to this place.
6 Now when Pilate heard of Galile, he asked whether the man were a Galilean.
7 And when he knewe that he was of Herodes iurisdiction, he [b] sent him to Herode, which was also at Ierusalem " in those
daies.
8 And when Herode sawe Iesus, he was exceadingly glad: for he was [c] desirous to se
him of a long season, because he had heard manie things of him, and trusted to
haue sene some " signe done by him.
9 Then questioned he with him of manie
things: but he answered him [d] nothing.
10 The hie Priests also and Scribes stode
forthe and accused him vehemently.
11 And Herode with his " men of warre,
despised him, and mocked him, and array-
ed him in [e] " white, and sent him againe to
Pilate.
12 * And the same daye Pilate and Herode were made friends together: for before
they were enemies one to another.
13 ¶ Then Pilate called together the hie
Priests, and the rulers, and the people,
14 And said vnto them, Ye haue broght this
man vnto me, as one that peruerted the
people: and beholde, I haue examined him
before you, and haue founde no faute in
this man, of those things whereof ye accuse him:
15 No, nor yet Herode: for I sent you to
him: and lo, nothing worthie of death is
done " to him.
16 I wil therefore chastise him, and let him
lowse.
17 (For of [f] necessitie he must haue let one
lowse vnto them at the feast.)
18 Then all the multitude cryed at once,
saying, Away with him, and deliuer to vs
Barabbas:
19 Which for a certeine insurrection made
in the citie, & murther was cast in prison.
20 Then Pilate spake againe to them, willing to let Iesus lowse.
21 But they cryed, saying, Crucifie, crucifie
him.
22 And he said vnto them the third time,
But what euil hathe he done? I finde [g] no
cause of death in him: I wil therefore chastise him, and let him lowse.
23 But they were instant with loude voyces,
and required that he might be crucified:
and the voyces of them and of the hie
Priests preuailed.
24 So Pilate gaue sentence, that it shulde
be as they required.
25 And he let lowse vnto them him that for
insurrection and murther was cast into
prison, whome thei desired, and deliuered
Iesus to do with him what they wolde.
26 ¶ * And as they led him awaye, they

b To rid his hands, and to gratifie Herode.

" Or, at that time

c Of a certeine curiositie.

" Or, miracle.

d For Christ came not to defend him self, nether yet wold de please the vaine curiositie of this tyrant.

" Or, bande, or traine.

e Communely this was a robe of honour, or excellencie: but it was giuen to Christ in mockage.

Mat.27,23. mar.15,14. iohn 18,38. & 19,4.

" Or, in bright colour.

" Or, by him.

f For the Romains had giuen suche frãches & liberties to ẏ Iewes, which was but a tradition, & not according to the worde of God.

g The iudge giueth sentence with Christ, before he condemneth him, whereby plainely appeareth Iesus innocencie.

Mat.27,32. mar.15,21.

caught one Simon of Cyrene, comming
out of the field, and on him they laid the
crosse, to beare it after Iesus.
27 And there followed him a great multitude of people, and of women, which women bewailed and lamented him.
28 But Iesus turned backe vnto them, and
said, "Daughters of Ierusalem, wepe not
for me, but wepe for your selues, and for
your children.
29 For beholde, the daies wil come, when
men shal say, Blessed *are* the barren, & the
wombes that neuer bare, and the pappes
which neuer gaue sucke.
30 Then shal they beginne to say to the
mountaines,* Fall on vs: and to the hilles,
Couer vs.
31 * For if they do these things to a [h] grene
tre, what shalbe done to the drye?
32 * And there were two others, which were
euil doers, led with him to be slayne.
33 And when they were come to the place,
which is called "Caluerie, there thei crucified him, and the euil doers: one at the
right hand, and the other at the left.
34 Then said Iesus, Father, forgiue them:
for they knowe not what thei do. And thei
parted his rayment, and cast lots.
35 And the people stode, and behelde: and
the rulers mocked him with them, saying,
He saued others: let him saue him self, if
he be the Christ, the [i] Chosen of God.
36 The souldiers also mocked him, and came and offred him [k] vineger,
37 And said, If thou be the King of the
Iewes, saue thy self.
38 And a superscription was also written
ouer him, in [l] Greke lettres, and in Latin,
& in Hebrewe, THIS IS THE KING
OF THE IEWES.
39 ¶ And one of the euil doers, which were
hanged, railed on him, saying, If thou be
the Christ, saue thy self and vs.
40 But the other answered, and rebuked
him, saying, [m] Fearest thou not God, seig
thou art in the same condemnacion?
41 We are in dede righteously *here*: for we
receiue things worthie of that we haue
done: but this man hathe done nothing a-
misse.
42 And he said vnto Iesus, Lord, remember me, when thou comest into thy kingdome.
43 Then Iesus said vnto him, Verely I say
vnto thee, to day shalt thou be with me in
Paradise.
44 ¶ And it was about the [n] sixt houre: and
there was a darkenes ouer all the land, vntil the ninth houre.
45 And the sunne was darkened, and the
vaile of the Temple rent through the
middes.
46 And Iesus cryed with a loude voyce, and
said, * Father, into thine hands I commēd
my spirit. And when he thus had said, He
gaue vp the gost.
47 ¶ Now whē the " [o] Cēturion sawe what
was done, he glorified God, saying, Of a
suretie this man was iuste.
48 And all the people that came together
to that sight, beholding the things, which
were done, smote their brests, and returned.
49 And all his acquaintance stode a farre
of, & the women that followed him from
Galile, beholding these things.
50 ¶ * And beholde, there was a mā named
Ioseph, which was a counseller, a good mā
and a iust.
51 He did not consent to the counsel and
dede of them, *which was* of Arimathea, a
citie of ẏ Iewes: who also him self " [p] waited for the kingdome of God.
52 He went vnto Pilate, and asked the bodie of Iesus,
53 And toke it downe, and wrapped it in a
linnen cloth, & laid it in a toumbe hewen
out of a rocke, wherein was neuer man
yet laid.
54 And that day was the [q] Preparacion, &
the Sabbath [r] drewe on.
55 And the women also that followed after,
which came with him frō Galile, behelde
the sepulchre, & how his bodie was laid.
56 And thei returned and prepared odores,
and ointments, and rested the Sabbath
day according to the commandement.

CHAP. XXIIII.

*1 The women come to the graue. 13 Christ appeareth vn-
to the two disciples that go towarde Emmaus. 36 He
standeth in the middes of his disciples, and openeth their
vnderstanding in the Scriptures. 47 He giueth them
a charge. 51 He ascendeth vp to heauen. 52 His disciples worship him, 53 And of their daiely exercise.*

1 NOw the * [a] first *day* of ẏ weke early
in the morning, they came vnto the
sepulchre, and broght the odores, which
they had prepared, & certeine *women* with
them.
2 And they founde the stone rolled awaye
from the sepulchre,
3 And went in, but founde not the bodie
of the Lord Iesus.
4 And it came to passe, that as they were
amased thereat, beholde, [b] two men suddenly stode by them in shining vestures.
5 And as they were afrayed, and bowed
downe their faces to the earth, they said
to them, Why seke ye him that liueth, a-
mong the dead?
6 He is not here, but is risen: remember
*how he spake vnto you, when he was yet
in Galile,
7 Saying, that the sonne of man must be
deliuered into the hands of sinful men,
and be crucified, and the third daye rise
againe.

8 And

" Or, women of Ierusalem.
Isa.2,19. hose.10,8. reuel.6,16.
1.Pet.4,17.
Mat.27,38. mar.15,27. iohn 19,18.
h If the innocent be thus handled, what shal the wicked man be?
" Or, the place of skulles.
i Whome God hathe before all others appointed to be the Messias: otherwise the Scriptures calleth them the elect of God, whome he hathe chosen before all beginning to life euerlasting.
k Mixt with myrrhe & gall to hasten his death.
l That the thing might be knowen to all nacions, because these thre languages were moste commune.
m The condēnacion which thou now suffrest, causeth it thee not to feare God?
n Which was middaye.
Psal.30,6.
" Or, Captaine.
o The Romaine Captaine who had charge ouer an hūdreth men.
Mat.27,57. mar.15,43. iohn 19,38.
" Or, had embraced.
p He loked for the redemer, by whome all shulde be restored.
q When men prepared all things readie for the feast.
r That is, begā the same euening.
Mat.28,1. mar.16,1. iohn 20,1.
a Which was the first day after ẏ first Sabbath of the feast.
b Two Angels in forme of men.
Chap.9,22. mat.17,23. mar.1,31.

8 And they remembred his wordes,
9 And returned from the sepulchre, & tolde all these things vnto the eleuen, and to
all the remnant.
10 Now it was Marie Magdalene & Ioanna,
& Marie the *mother* of Iames, & other women with them, which tolde these things
vnto the Apostles.
11 But their wordes semed vnto them, as a
fained thing, nether beleued they them.
12 Then arose Peter, and ran vnto the sepulchre, and loked in, and sawe the linnen clothes laid by them selues, & departed wondering in him self at that which was come
to passe.
13 ¶ *And beholde, two of them went that
same day to a towne which was from Ierusalem about [c] thre score furlongs, called
Emmaus.
14 And they [d] talked together of all these
things that were done.
15 And it came to passe, as they communed
together, and reasoned, that Iesus him self
drewe nere, and went with them.
16 But their eyes [e] were holden, that they
colde not knowe him.
17 And he said vnto them, What maner
of communications are these that ye haue
one to another as ye walke, and are sad?
18 And the one (named Cleopas) answered and said vnto him, Art thou onely a
[f] stranger in Ierusalem, & hast not knowen
the things which are come to passe therein in these dayes?
19 And he said vnto them, What things?
And they said vnto him, Of Iesus of Nazaret, which was a Prophet, mightie in
dede and in worde before God, and all the
people,
20 And how the hie Priests, and our rulers
deliuered him to be condemned to death,
and haue crucified him.
21 But we [g] trusted that it had bene he that
shulde haue deliuered Israel, and as touching all these things, to day is the third
day, that they were done.
22 Yea, and certeine women among vs made vs astonied, which came early vnto the
sepulchre.
23 And whē they founde not his bodie, they
came, saying, that they had also sene a visiō
of Angels, which said that he was aliue.
24 Therefore certeine of them which were
with vs, went to the sepulchre, and founde
it euen so as the women had said, but him
they sawe not.
25 Then he said vnto them, [h] O fooles and
slowe of heart to beleue all that the Prophetes haue spoken,
26 Oght not Christ to haue suffred these
things, and to enter into his glorie?
27 And he began at [i] Moses, & at all the Prophetes, and interpreted vnto them in all
the Scriptures the things which were *written* of him.
28 And they drewe nere vnto the towne,
which they went to, but he [k] made as thogh
he wolde haue gone further.
29 But they constrained him, saying, Abide
with vs: for it is towardes night, and the
day is farre spent. So he went in to tarie
with them.
30 And it came to passe, as he sate at table
with them, he toke the bread, [l] and gaue
thankes, and brake it, and gaue it to them.
31 Thē their eyes were opened, & thei knewe
him: but he was taken out of their sight.
32 And they said betwene them selues, Did
not our hearts burne within vs, while he
talked with vs by the way, and when he opened to vs the Scriptures?
33 And they rose vp the same houre, and returned to Ierusalem, and founde the Eleuen gathered together, and them that were with them,
34 Which said, The Lord is risen in dede,
and hathe appeared to Simon.
35 Then they tolde what things *were* done
in the way, and how he was knowen of thē
in [m] breaking of bread.
36 ¶ *And as they spake these things, Iesus
him self stode in the middes of them, and
said vnto them, Peace *be* to you.
37 But they were abashed & afraid, supposing that they had sene a spirit.
38 Then he said vnto them, Why are ye
troubled? and wherefore do doutes arise in
your hearts?
39 Beholde mine hands and my fete: for it
is I my self: handle me, and se: for a spirit
hathe not flesh & bones, as ye se me haue.
40 And when he had thus spoken, he shewed
them *his* hands and fete.
41 And while they yet beleued not for ioye,
and wondered, he said vnto them, Haue ye
here any meat?
42 And they gaue him a piece of a broiled
fish, and of an honie combe,
43 And he toke it, & did eat before them.
44 And he said vnto them, These are the
wordes, which I spake vnto you while I
was yet with you, that all must be fulfilled which are written of me in the Law
of Moses, and in the Prophetes, and in the
Psalmes.
45 Then opened he their vnderstanding,
that they might vnderstād the Scriptures,
46 And said vnto them, Thus is it written,
and thus it behoued Christ to suffre, & to
rise againe from the dead the thirde day,
47 And that repentance, and remission of
sinnes shulde be preached in his Name amōg all nacions, beginning at Ierusalem.
48 Now ye are witnesses of these things.
49 And beholde, I wil send the *promes of
my Father vpō you: but tary ye in the citie

Mat.16,12.

c Which is about seuen miles & an halfe.

d Hereby appeareth ȳ they had faith, althogh it was weake.

e This declareth that we can nether se, nor vnderstand til God open our eyes.

f For the thīg was so notorious, that all men might haue knowen it.

g They vnderstode not yet what was the deliuerance ȳ Iesus Christ purchased for vs, but loked for some worldelie prosperitie.

h Infidelitie is reproued.

i Christ onely is the interpreter of ȳ Scriptures: for bothe the beginning and end thereof direct vs to him, because he is the Sauiour that is promised.

k Because Christ did bothe shut their eyes and open thē, he wolde kepe them in suspens til his time came to manifest him self vnto them

l Accordīg to the custome: ȳ which maner of praying before meales they vse to this day.

m So sone as he beganne to breake bread.

Mar.16,14. iohn 20,19.

Iohn 15,26. act.1,4.

of Ierusalem, [n] vntil ye be endued with
power from an hie.
50 Afterwarde he led them out into Bethania, and lift vp his hands, & blessed them.
51 And it came to passe, that as he blessed
them, * he departed from them, and was
caryed vp into heauen.
52 And they worshipped him, and returned
to Ierusalem with great ioye,
53 And were continually in the Temple,
praising, and lauding God, Amen.

n Which was til witsontide, when the holie Gost was sent from heauen.

Mar.16,19. act.1,9.

THE HOLY GOSPEL

of Iesus Christ, according to Iohn.

CHAP. I.

1.14.17. The diuinitie, humanitie, & office of Iesus Christ. 15 The testimonie of Iohn. 39 The calling of Andrewe, Peter, &c.

1 IN ″ the beginning was
the Worde, and the
Worde was with [a] God
and that Worde was
God.
2 The same was [b] in
the beginning w̃ God.
3 All things were made by it, & [c] without it
was made nothing that was made.
4 In it was [d] life, and the life was the [e] light
of men.
5 And the light shineth in [f] ỹ darkenes, &
the darkenes comprehended it not.
6 ¶ * There was a man sent frõ God, whose
name *was* Iohn.
7 The same came for a witnes, to beare witnes of the light, that all mẽ through him
might beleue.
8 He was not that light, but *was sent* to beare witnes of the light.
9 That was the true light, which lighteth
euerie man that ″cometh into the worlde.
10 He was in the worlde, and the worlde
was * made by him: & the worlde [g] knewe
him not.
11 He came vnto [h] his owne, and his owne
receiued him not.
12 But as many as receiued him, to them
he gaue [i] power to be the sonnes of God,
euen to them that beleue in his Name,
13 Which are borne not of blood, nor of
the wil of the flesh, nor of the wil of man,
but of God.
14 * And the Worde was made [k] flesh, and
dwelt among vs, (and we * sawe the glorie
thereof, as the glorie of the onely begotten *Sonne* ″of the Father) * ful of grace and
trueth.
15 ¶ Iohn bare witnes of him, & cryed, saying, This was he of whome I said, He
that cõmeth after me, is preferred before
me: for he was ″before me.
16 And of his fulnes haue all we receiued,
and [l] grace for grace.
17 For the Lawe was giuen by Moses, but
grace and trueth came by Iesus Christ.

″Or, before the begining.
a Christ is God before all time.
b The Sõne is of the same substance with the Father.
c No creature was made without Christ.
d Whereby all thĩgs are quickened and preserued.
e The life of man is more excellent then of any other creature, because it is ioyned with light and vnderstanding.
Mat.3,1. mar.1,4. luk.3,3.
f Mans minde is ful of darkenes because of the corruption thereof.
″*Or, are borne.*
Ebr.11,4.
g Because they did not worship him as their God, Ro.1,21. act.14,15.
h To the Israelites who were his peculiar people.
i Meaning a priuiledge, or dignitie.
Mat.1,16. luk.2,7.
Mat.17,2. 2.pet.1,17.
Colos.1,19. & 2,9.
k He was formed and made man by the operation of the holie Gost without the operation of mã.
″*Or, proceding frõ the Father.*
″*Or, more excellent then I.*
l More abundant grace thẽ by Moses.

18 * No man hathe sene God at any time:
the onely begotten Sonne, which is in the
[m] bosome of the Father, he hathe [n] declared him.
19 ¶ Then this is the recorde of Iohn, whẽ
the Iewes sent Priests and Leuites from
Ierusalem, to aske him, Who art thou?
20 And he confessed and denyed not, and
said plainely, I * am not the Christ.
21 And they asked him, What thẽ? Art thou
Elias? And he said, I am not. Art thou the
[o] Prophet? And he answered, No.
22 Then said they vnto him, Who art thou
that we may giue an answer to them that
sent vs? what saist thou of thy self?
23 He said, I * am the voyce of him that
cryeth in the wildernes, Make straight the
way of ỹ Lord, as said the Prophet Esaias.
24 Now they which were sent, were of the
Pharises.
25 And they asked him, and said vnto him,
Why baptizest thou then, if thou be not
the Christ, nether Elias, nor the Prophet?
26 Iohn answered them, saying, I baptize
with water: but there is one among you,
whome ye knowe not.
27 * He it is that commeth after me, which
is preferred before me, whose shoe latchet
I am not worthie to vnlose.
28 These things were done in Bethabara
beyonde Iordan, where Iohn did baptize.
29 ¶ The next day Iohn seeth Iesus cõming
vnto him, and saith, Beholde the lambe
of God, which taketh away the [p] sinne of
the worlde.
30 This is he of whome I said, After me cometh a mã, which is preferred before me:
for he was before me.
31 And I knewe [q] him not: but because he
shulde be declared to Israel, therefore am
I come, baptizing with water.
32 So Iohn bare recorde, saying, I sawe * the
Spirit come downe from heauen, like a doue, and it abode vpon him.
33 And I knewe him not: but he that sent me
to baptize with water, he said vnto me,
Vpõ whome thou shalt se the Spirit come
downe, & tary stil on him, that is he which
baptizeth with the [r] holie Gost.

1.Tim.6,16. 1.iohn 4,12.
m Meaning he is moste deare, and straictly ioyned to his Father, not onely in loue, but also in nature and vnion.
n And so God that before was inuisible, was made, as it were, visible in Christ.
Act.13,25.
o Whome the i loked for to be suche one as Moses was, Deut.18,15.
Isa.40,3. mat.3,3. luk.3,4.
Mat.3,11. mar.1,7. luk.3,16. act.1,5. & 11,16. & 19,4.
p Signifiĩg the original sinne, which is the foũtaine of all sinnes & there with all other sinnes.
q That is, by sight, but onely by the reuelation of God.
Mat.3,16. mar.1,10. luk.3,22.
r Who giueth the vertue and effect to baptisme, accomplishĩg that thĩg which is thereby represented.

34 And

34 And I sawe, and bare recorde that this
is the Sonne of God.
35 ¶ The next day, Iohn stode againe, and
two of his disciples:
36 And he behelde Iesus walking by, and
said, Beholde the [s] lambe of God.
37 And the two disciples heard him speake,
and followed Iesus.

s He alludeth to the Paschal lambe, which was a figure of Christ.

38 Then Iesus turned about, and sawe them
followe, & said vnto them, What seke ye?
And they said vnto him, Rabbi (which is
to say by interpretation, Master) [t] where
dwellest thou?
39 He said vnto them, Come, and se. They
came and sawe where he dwelt, and abode
with him that day: for it was about the
[u] tenth houre.

t Or where is thy lodgig? or whither goest thou? For he dwelled in Nazaret, and was there as a străger.

u That was, two houres before night.

40 Andrewe, Simō Peters brother, was one
of the two which had heard [x] it of Iohn, &
that followed him.

x How Iohn said, that Iesus was the lambe of God.

41 The same founde his brother Simon
first, and said vnto him, We haue founde
the Messias, which is by interpretation,
"the Christ.

"Or, the Anointed.

42 And he broght him to Iesus. And Iesus
behelde him, & said, Thou art Simon the
sonne of Iona: thou shalt be called Cephas,
which is by interpretation, "a stone.

"Or, Petrus.

43 ¶ The day following, Iesus wolde go into
Galile, and founde Philippe, and said
vnto him, Followe me.
44 Now Philippe was of Bethsaida, the citie
of Andrewe and Peter.
45 Philippe founde Nathanael, and said
vnto him, We haue founde him, of whome
* Moses did write in the Law, and the
*Prophetes, Iesus of Nazaret the sonne of
Ioseph.

Gen. 49,10. deut. 18,18. Isa. 42,4,10. 45,8. ier. 23,5. eze. 34,25. & 37,24. dan. 9,24.

46 Then Nathanael said vnto him, Can
there any [y] good thing come out of Nazaret?
Philippe said to him, Come, and se.

y Those thigs which are contemptible to the worlde, are estemed and preferred of God: and those things which ẏ worlde preferreth, God abhorreth.

47 Iesus sawe Nathanael coming to him, &
said of him, Beholde, in dede an Israelite,
in whome is no guile.
48 Nathanael said vnto him, Whēce knewest
thou me? Iesus answered, & said vnto
him, Before that Philippe called thee, whē
thou wast vnder the figge tre, I sawe thee.
49 Nathanael answered, & said vnto him,
Rabbi, thou art the Sonne of God: thou
art the King of Israel.
50 Iesus answered, and said vnto him, Because
I said vnto thee, I sawe thee vnder
the figge tre, "beleuest thou? thou shalt se
greater things then these.

"Or, thou beleuest.

51 And he said vnto him, Verely, verely, I
say vnto you, hereafter shal ye se heauen
[z] open, & the Angels of God * ascending,
and descending vpon the Sonne of man.

z Christ openeth the heauens, that we may haue accesse to God, and maketh vs felowes to the Angels.

Gen. 28,12.

CHAP. II.

8 Christ turneth the water into wine. 14 He driueth the byers, and sellers out of the Tēple. 19 He forewarneth his death and resurrection. 23 He conuerteth many, and distrusteth man.

1 AND the thirde day, was there a mariage
in Cana *a towne* of Galile, &
the mother of Iesus was there.
2 And Iesus was called also, and his disciples
vnto the mariage.
3 Now when the wine failed, the mother of
Iesus said vnto him, They haue no wine.
4 Iesus said vnto her, Woman, what haue
I to do with thee? mine houre is not yet
come.
5 His mother said vnto the seruants, Whatsoeuer
he saith vnto you, do it.
6 And there were set there, six waterpottes
of stone, after the maner of the [a] purifying
of the Iewes, conteining two or thre "[b] firkins
a piece.

a Who vsed cōtinual washigs to purifie them selues. Which superstition Hebion the heretike wolde haue broght into ẏ Church and now the Papistes haue receiued it.

"Or, measures.

b Whereof euerie one conteined 15 gallons.

7 And Iesus said vnto them, Fil the waterpottes
with water. Then they filled them
vp to the brim.
8 Then he said vnto them, Drawe out now
& beare vnto the "gouernour of the feast.
So they bare it.

"Or, stewarde.

9 Now whē the gouernour of the feast had
tasted the water that was made wine, (for
he knewe not whence it was: but ẏ seruāts,
which drewe the water, knewe) the gouernour
of the feast called the bridegrome,
10 And said vnto him, All men at the beginning
set forthe good wine, and when
men haue wel drunke, then that which is
worse: *but* thou hast kept backe the good
wine vntil now.
11 This beginning of "miracles did Iesus in
Cana *a towne* of Galile, and shewed forthe
his glorie: & his disciples beleued on him.

"Or, signes.

12 After ẏ he went downe into Capernaū,
he and his mother, and his "brethren, and
his disciples: but they continued not manie
dayes there.

"Or, cousins.

13 For the Iewes Passeouer was at hand.
Therefore Iesus went vp to Ierusalem.
14 * And he founde in the Temple those
that solde oxen, and shepe, and doues, and
changers of money, sitting *there*.

Mat. 21,12. mar. 11,17. luk. 19,46.

15 Thē he made a scourge of smale cordes,
& draue them all out of the Temple with
the shepe, and oxen & powred out the chāgers
money, and ouerthrewe the tables,
16 And said vnto them that solde doues,
Take these things hence: make not my Fathers
house, an house of marchandise.
17 And his disciples remembred, that it was
written, * The [c] zeale of thine house hathe
eaten me vp.

Psal. 68,10.

c This affectiō was so burnig in him, that it surmoūted and swallowed vp all the others.

18 Then answered the Iewes, and said vnto
him, What "signe shewest thou vnto vs,
that thou doest these things?

"Or, miracle.

19 Iesus answered and said vnto them, * Destroye
this temple, and in thre dayes I wil
raise it vp againe.

Mat. 26,61. & 27,40. mar. 14,58. & 15,29.

20 Then said the Iewes, Fortie and six yeres
was this Temple a buylding, and wilt
thou reare it vp in thre dayes?

21 But he ſpake of the temple of his [d] bodie.
22 Aſſone therefore as he was riſen from
the dead, his diſciples remembred that he
thus ſaid vnto them: and they beleued the
Scripture, and the worde which Ieſus had
ſaid.
23 Now when he was at Ieruſalẽ at ẏ Paſſeouer in ẏ feaſt, many beleued in his Name, when they ſawe his miracles ẇ he did.
24 But Ieſus [e] did not commit him ſelf vnto them, becauſe he knewe them all,
25 And had no nede that any ſhulde teſtifie
of man: for he knewe what was in man.

d Chriſts bodie might iuſtly be called the temple, becauſe the fulnes of the God head dwelleth in it corporally, Colo. 2,9.
e For he toke not them for true diſciples, as he knewe by their inwarde thoghtes, what religion ſoeuer they did pretende outwardely.

CHAP. III.

3 Chriſt inſtructeth Nicodemus in the regeneration. 15 Of faith. 16 Of the loue of God towards the worlde. 23 The doctrine and baptiſme of Iohn, 28 And the witnes that he beareth of Chriſt.

1 THere was now a mã of ẏ Phariſes named Nicodemus, a ruler of ẏ Iewes.
2 He came to Ieſus by night, and ſaid vnto
him, Rabbi, we knowe that thou art a teacher come from God: for no man colde
do theſe miracles that thou doeſt, except
God were with him.
3 Ieſus anſwered, and ſaid vnto him, Verely, verely I ſay vnto thee, except a man
be borne againe, he can not [a] ſe the [b] kingdome of God.
4 Nicodemus ſaid vnto him, How can a
man be borne which is olde? can he enter
into his mothers wombe againe, and be
borne?
5 Ieſus anſwered, Verely, verely I ſay vnto
thee, except that a man be borne of [c] water and of the Spirit, he can not enter into
the kingdome of God.
6 That which is borne of the fleſh, is fleſh:
& that that is borne of the Spirit, is ſpirit.
7 Marueile not that I ſaid to thee, Ye muſt
be borne againe.
8 The [d] winde bloweth where it liſteth, &
thou heareſt the ſounde thereof, but canſt
not tel whence it cometh, and whether it
goeth: ſo is euerie man that is borne of
the Spirit.
9 Nicodemus anſwered, and ſaid vnto him,
How can theſe things be?
10 Ieſus anſwered, and ſaid vnto him, Art
thou a teacher of Iſrael, and [e] knoweſt not
theſe things?
11 Verely, verely I ſay vnto thee, we ſpeake that we [f] knowe, & teſtifie, that we haue
ſene: but ye [g] receiue not our witnes.
12 If when I tel you [h] earthlie things, ye beleue not, how ſhulde ye beleue, if I ſhal
tell you of heauenlie things?
13 For no man aſcendeth vp to heauen, but
he that hathe deſcended from heauen, the
Sonne of man which is in [i] heauen.
14 *And as Moſes lift vp the ſerpent in the
wildernes, ſo muſt the Sonne of man be
[k] lift vp,

a To entre therein.
b Which thĩg is to be aſſembled and incorporate into ẏ Church of God.
c Which is the ſpiritual water where the holie Goſt doeth waſhe vs into newnes of life.
d As ẏ power of God is manifeſt by the mouing of the aire, ſo is it in changing and renuing vs, althogh the maner be hid frõ vs.
e Although he was excellently learned, yet knewe he not thoſe things which the very babes in Chriſts ſchole oght to knowe
f We may not teache our owne inuentions.
g He reproueth him, for that men do teache things which they vnderſtande not, and yet others beleue them: but Chriſt teacheth thĩgs moſte certeine & knowen, & mẽ wil not receiue his doctrine.
h Which was after a commune and groſſe maner.
i By reaſon of the vnion of his Godhead with his manhoode.
Nom. 21,9.
k His power muſt be manifeſt, which is not yet knowẽ

15 That whoſoeuer beleueth in him, ſhulde
not periſh, but haue eternal life.
16 *For God ſo loued the worlde, that he
hathe giuen his onely begotten Sõne, that
whoſoeuer beleueth in him, ſhulde not pe
riſh, but haue euerlaſting life.
17 *For God ſent not his Sonne into the
worlde, that he ſhulde [l] condemne the
worlde, but that the [m] worlde through him
might be ſaued.
18 He that beleueth in him, ſhal not be cõdemned: but he that beleueth not, is condẽ
ned already, becauſe he beleueth not in ẏ
Name of the onely begottẽ Sõne of God.
19 *And this is the [n] condemnation, that
light is come into the worlde, & mẽ loued
darkenes rather then light, becauſe their
dedes were euil.
20 For euerie man that euil doeth, hateth
the light, nether commeth to light, leſt
his dedes ſhulde be reproued.
21 But he that doeth [o] trueth, commeth to
the light, that his dedes might be made
manifeſt, that they are wroght "[p] according to God.
22 ¶After theſe things, came Ieſus and his
diſciples into the "land of Iudea, and there
taried with them, and * baptized.
23 And Iohn alſo baptized in Enon beſides
Salim, becauſe there was much water there: and they came, and were baptized.
24 For Iohn was not yet caſt into priſon.
25 Thẽ there aroſe a queſtiõ betwene Iohns
diſciples & the Iewes, about [q] purifying.
26 And they came vnto Iohn, and ſaid vnto him, Rabbi, [r] he that was with thee
beyonde Iordan, to whome * thou bareſt
witnes, beholde, he baptizeth, and all men
come to him.
27 Iohn anſwered, & ſaid, A mã can receiue
nothing, except it be giuẽ him frõ heauẽ.
28 Ye your ſelues are my witneſſes, that *I
ſaid, [ſ] I am not the Chriſt, but ẏ I am ſent
before him.
29 He that hathe the bride, is the bridegrome: but the friẽd of the bridegrome which
ſtãdeth and heareth him, reioyceth greatly, becauſe of ẏ bridegromes voice. This
my ioye therefore is fulfilled.
30 He muſt [t] increaſe, but I *muſt* decreaſe.
31 He that is come from on high, is aboue
all: he that is of the [u] earth, is of the earth,
and ſpeaketh of the earth: he that is come
from heauen, is aboue all.
32 And what he hathe ſene and heard, that
he teſtifieth: but no man receiueth his teſtimonie.
33 He that hathe receiued his teſtimonie,
hathe ſealed that * God is true.
34 For he whome God hathe ſent, ſpeaketh
the wordes of God: for God giueth *him*
not the Spirit by [x] meaſure.
35 The Father loueth the Sonne, and hathe
*giuen

1. Iohn 4,9.
Chap. 9,39. and 12,47.
l The contẽpt of Chriſt, and the ſinnes of the wicked cõdemne thẽ: yet Chriſt as a iuſte iudge giueth ſentence againſt the reprobate.
m Not onely ẏ Iewes, but whoſoeuer ſhulde beleue in him.
Chap. 1,9.
n The cauſe and matter of condemnation
o In walking roundely, and ſincerely.
" Or, in God.
p As they do which ſet God onely before their eyes, and followe the rule of his worde
" Or territorie.
Chap. 4,1.
q That is, how they might be made cleane, before God, ẇ the waſhings vnder the law did repreſent.
Chap. 1,17.
r They were led ẇ ambitiõ fearing leſt their maſter ſhulde haue loſt his fame.
Chap. 1,20.
ſ No mã oght to vſurpe anie thing further then God giueth him.
t And he be exalted, and I eſtemed as his ſeruant.
u The miniſter compared to Chriſt is but earth.
Rom. 3,4.
x For vnto Chriſt was giuen the ful abundance of all grace, that we might receiue of him as of ẏ onelie fountaine.

Mat.10,26.
Abac.2,4.
1.iohn.5,10.

*giuen all things into his hand.
36 * He that beleueth in the Sonne, hathe
euerlasting life, & he that obeieth not the
Sonne, shal not se life, but the wrath of
God abideth on him.

CHAP. IIII.

1 The communication of Christ with the woman of Samaria. 34 His zeale towarde his Father & his haruest. 39 The conuersion of the Samaritans. 45 And Galileans. 47 How he healeth the rulers sonne.

1 NOw when the Lord knewe, how the
Pharises had heard, that Iesus made
and baptized mo disciples then Iohn,
2 (Thogh Iesus him self baptized not:but
his disciples)

a To giue place to their rage.

3 He [a] left Iudea, and departed againe into
Galile.
4 And he must nedes go through Samaria.
5 Then came he to a citie of Samaria called "Sychar, nere vnto the possesion that
*Iacob gaue to his sonne Ioseph.
6 And there was Iacobs well. Iesus thẽ wea
ried in the iorney, sate [b] thus on the well: it
was about the [c] sixt houre.

"Or, Sichem. Gen.33,19. & 48,22. Iosh.24,32.
b Euen wearie as he was.
c Which was midday.

7 There came a woman of Samaria to
drawe water. Iesus said vnto her, Giue me
drinke.
8 For his disciples were gone away into the
citie, to bye meat.
9 Then said the woman of Samaria vnto
him, How is it, that thou being a Iewe, askest drinke of me, which am a woman of
[d] Samaria? For the Iewes medle not with
the Samaritans.
10 Iesus answered & said vnto her, If thou
knewest the [e] gift of God, and who it is
that saith to thee, Giue me drinke, thou
woldest haue asked of him, and he wolde
haue giuen thee [f] "water of life.
11 The woman said vnto him, Syr, thou hast
nothing to drawe with, & the well is depe: from whence then hast thou that water of life?
12 Art thou greater then our father Iacob,
which gaue vs the well, & he him self drãke thereof, & his children, and his cattel?
13 Iesus answered, and said vnto her, Whosoeuer drinketh of this water, shal thirst
againe:

d For ỹ Iewes estemed the Samaritans as wicked, and prophane.
e Meaning of him self whome his Father had sent to cõuert this woman.
f Which is ỹ loue of God in his Sõne powred into our hearts by the holie Gost vnto euerlasting life, Rom.5,5. 1 iohn 3,5.
"Or, the liuelie water.

14 But whosoeuer drinketh of the [g] water
that I shal giue him, shal neuer be more [h] a
thirst: but the water that I shal giue him,
shalbe in him a well of water, springing
vp into euerlasting life.

g "Of the spiritual grace.
h He shal neuer be dryed vp or destitute

15 The woman said vnto him, Syr, giue me
of that water, that I may not thirst, nether
come hither to drawe.
16 Iesus said vnto her, Go, call thine housband, and come hither.
17 The woman answered, and said I haue
no housband. Iesus said to her, Thou hast
wel said, I haue no housband.
18 For thou hast had fiue housbands, and he
whome thou now hast, is not thine housband: that saidest thou truely.
19 The womã said vnto him, Syr, I [i] se that
thou art a Prophet.

i Til she was liuely touched with her fautes, she mocked and wolde not heare Christ.

20 Our fathers worshiped in this mountaine, and ye say, that in *Ierusalem is the pla
ce where men oght to worship.

Deut.12,6.

21 Iesus said vnto her, Woman, beleue me,
the houre cometh, when ye shal nether in
this mountaine, nor at Ierusalem worship
the Father.
22 Ye worship that which ye *knowe not: we
worship that which we knowe: for saluation is of the Iewes.

2 Kin.17,29.

23 But the houre cometh, and now is, when
the true worshippers shal worshippe ỹ Father in spirit, & trueth: for the Father requireth euen suche to worship him.
24 *God is a [k] Spirit, and they that worship
him, must worship him in spirit & trueth.

2.Cor.3,17.
k God being of a spiritual nature, requireth a spiritual seruice, and agreable to his nature.

25 The woman said vnto him, I know wel
that Mesias shal come, which is called
Christ: when he is come, he wil tell vs all
things.
26 Iesus said vnto her, I am he, that speake
vnto thee.
27 ¶ And vpon that came his disciples, and
marueiled that he talked with a woman:
yet no man said vnto him, What askest
thou? or why talkest thou with her?
28 The woman then left her waterpot, and
wẽt her way into the citie, & said to ỹ mẽ,
29 Come, se a mã which hathe tolde me all
things that euer I did: is not he the Christ?
30 Then they went out of the citie, & came
vnto him.
31 ¶ In the meane while, ỹ disciples prayed
him, saying, Master, eat.
32 But he said vnto thẽ, I haue meat to eat,
that ye knowe not of.
33 Then said the disciples betwene thẽ selues, Hathe anie man broght him meat?
34 Iesus said vnto them, [l] My meat is that
I may do the wil of him that sent me, and
finish his worke.

l There is nothing, that I hunger for more, or wherein I take greater pleasure.

35 Say not ye, There are yet foure moneths,
& *then* cometh haruest? Beholde, I say vnto you, Lift vp your eyes, and loke on the
regions: * for they are white already vnto
haruest.

Mat.9.37.
luk.10,2.

36 And he that reapeth, receiueth wages, &
gathereth frute vnto life eternal, that bothe he that soweth, & he ỹ reapeth, might
[m] reioyce together.

m Without grudging the one at the others labour.

37 For herein is the "saying true, that one
soweth and another reapeth.

"Or, prouerbe.

38 I sent you to reape that, whereon ye bestowed no labour: [n] other men laboured, &
ye are entred into their labours.

n Meaning, ỹ Prophetes.

39 Now manie of the Saamaritans of ỹ citie
[o] beleued in him, for the saying of the womã which testified, He hathe tolde me all
things that euer I did.

o The Samaritans shewed them selues willing to receiue his doctrine, who being but strãgers and skarsely knowing Christ, are a condemnation to the Iewes, & all others, which neglect Gods worde when it is offered.

40 Then when the Samaritans were come
vnto him,they besoght him,that he wolde
tarie with them: and he abode there two
dayes.
41 And manie mo [p] beleued because of his
owne worde.

p That is,had the right and true faith.

42 And thei said vnto the woman,Now we
beleue, not because of thy saying: for we
haue heard him our selues, & knowe that
this is in dede the Christ the Sauiour of
the worlde.
43 ¶ So two dayes after he departed thence,and went into Galile.
44 For Iesus him self had * testified that a
Prophet hathe none honour in [q] his owne
countrey.

Mat.13,58. mar.6,4. luk.4,24.
q Here by his owne coūtrey he meaneth Ierusalem,& the coūtrey about.

45 Then whē he was come into Galile, the
Galileans receiued him, which had sene
all the things that he did at Ierusalem at
the feast:for they went also vnto the feast.
46 And Iesus came againe into * Cana *a
towne* of Galile,where he had made of water wine. And there was a certeine [r] ruler,
whose sonne was sicke at Capernaum.
47 Whē he heard that Iesus was come out
of Iudea into Galile, he went vnto him, &
besoght him that he wolde " go downe, &
heale his sonne: for he was euen ready
to dye.

Chap.2,1.
r The worde signifieth royal or one of ẏ Kings court: & it semeth,ẏ he was one of Herods court, who was in great estimation with Herode, whome the people called King,Mar.6,14.
" Or,come.

48 Then said Iesus vnto him, Except ye se
signes and wonders,ye wil not beleue.
49 The ruler said vnto him,Sir,go downe
before my sonne dye.
50 Iesus said vnto him, Go thy way, thy
sonne liueth:and the man beleued the wor
de that Iesus had spoken vnto him,&went
his way.
51 And as he was now " going downe,his ser
uants met him,saying, Thy sonne liueth.

" Or,returning.

52 Then enquired he of thē the houre whē
he began to amende. And they said vnto
him, Yesterday the seuenth houre the feuer left him.
53 Then the father knewe, that it was the
same houre in the which Iesus had said
vnto him,Thy sonne liueth. And he beleued,and all his houshold.
54 This seconde miracle did Iesus againe, after he was come out of Iudea into
Galile.

CHAP. V.

8 He healeth the man that was sicke eight and thirtie yeres. 10 The Iewes accuse him. 19 Christ answereth for him self,and reproueth them. 32 Shewing by the testimonie of his Father. 33 Of Iohn. 36 Of his workes. 39 And of the Scriptures who he is.

1 AFter * that, there was a feast of the
Iewes,& Iesus wēt vp to Ierusalem.
2 And there is at Ierusalem by " the place
of the shepe, a [a] poole called in Ebrewe
[b] Bethesda,hauing fiue porches:

Leu.23,2. deu.16,1.
" Or,the shepe market.
a Where the shepe were washed,that shulde be sacrificed.
b Which signifieth the house of powring out,because the water ranne out by conduits.

3 In the which lay a great multitude of sicke folke,of blinde, halte, & withered,wai-
ting for the mouing of the water.
4 For an Angel went downe at a certeine
season into the poole, and troubled the
water:whosoeuer then first,after the stirring of the water, stepped in, was made
whole of whatsoeuer disease he had.
5 And a certeine man was there,which had
bene diseased eight and thirtie yeres.
6 When Iesus sawe him lie,and knewe that
he now lōg time had bene diseased,he said
vnto him,Wilt thou be made whole?
7 The sicke man answered him,Sir, I haue
no man,when the water is troubled,to put
me into ẏ poole: but while I am cōming,
another steppeth downe before me.
8 Iesus said vnto him, Rise: [c] take vp thy
bed,and walke.
9 And immediatly the mā was made whole,and toke vp his bed,and walked: & the
same day was the Sabbath.

c This was,to the end that the miracle might be so euidēt,that no mā colde speake against it.

10 The Iewes therefore said to him that
was made whole,It is the Sabbath *day*:* it
is not lawful for thee to carie thy bed.

Ier.17,22.

11 He answered them, He that made me
whole,he said vnto me, Take vp thy bed,
and walke.
12 Then asked they him,What man is that
which said vnto thee, Take vp thy bed,&
walke?
13 And he that was healed, knewe not who
it was: for Iesus had conueyed him self
away from the multitude that was in that
place.
14 And after that, Iesus founde him in the
Temple,and said vnto him,Beholde,thou
art made whole: [d] sinne no more, lest a
worse thing come vnto thee.

d The afflictiōs that we endure,are chastisements for our sinnes.

15 ¶ The man departed, and tolde the Iewes that it was Iesus,which had made him
whole.
16 And therefore the Iewes did persecute
Iesus,& soght to slay him, because he had
done these things on the Sabbath *day*.
17 But Iesus answered thē,My Father worketh hitherto,and I worke.
18 Therefore the Iewes soght the more to
kil him:not onely because he had broken
the Sabbath: but said also that God was
[e] his [f] Father,and made him self equal with
God.
19 Then answered Iesus,& said vnto them,
Verely,verely I say vnto you, The Sonne
can do nothing of him self, saue that he
seeth ẏ Father do:for whatsoeuer things he
doeth, the same things doeth ẏ Sōne also.
20 For the Father loueth the Sōne,& [g] sheweth him all things,whatsoeuer he him self
doeth,and he wil shewe him greater workes then these,that ye shulde marueile.
21 For likewise as the Father raiseth vp
the dead,& quickeneth them,so the Sonne
quickeneth

e That is,propre & peculiar to him alone.
f It was lawful for all Israel to call God their Father, Exod. 4,22, but because Christ did attribute to hī self, ẏ he had power ouer all things, and wroght as his Father did, thei gathered ẏ Christ did not onely make him self ẏ Sonne of God, but also equal with him.
g That is, he doeth communicate wᵗ him, hauing the same power and the same wil.

quickeneth whome he wil.
22 For the Father iudgeth no man, but hathe committed all [h] iudgement vnto the
Sonne,

h In giuing him power & rule ouer all.

23 Because that all men shulde honour the
Sonne, as they honour the Father: he that
honoreth not the Sonne, the same honoreth not the Father, which hathe sent him.
24 Verely, verely, I say vnto you, he that
heareth my worde, & beleueth in him that
sent me, hathe euerlasting life, & shal not
come into condemnacion, but hathe passed from death vnto life.
25 Verely, verely, I say vnto you, the houre shal come, and now is, when the dead
shal heare the voyce of the Sõne of God:
and they that [i] heare it, shal liue.

i Thei that receiue it by faith.

26 For as the Father hathe life in [k] him self,
so likewise hathe he giuẽ to the Sonne to
haue life in him self,

k To communicate it w vs.

27 And hathe giuen him power also to execute [l] iudgement, in that he is the Sõne of
man.

l That is, to gouerne and rule all thigs.

28 Marueile not at this: for the houre shal
come in the which all that are in the graues, shal heare his voyce.
29 And they shal come forthe, * that haue
done good, vnto the resurrection of life:
but they that haue done euil, vnto the resurrection of condemnacion.

Mat. 25, 41.

30 I can do nothing of mine owne self: as
I heare, I iudge: and my iudgemẽt is iust,
because I seke not mine owne wil, but the
wil of the Father who hathe sent me.
31 If I * shulde beare witnes of my self, my
witnes were not [m] true.

Chap. 8, 14. mat. 3, 17.
m Christ had respect to their weakenes, ŷ heard him, and therefore said his owne witnes shulde not be sufficient.

32 There is another that beareth witnes of
me, and I knowe that the witnes, which he
beareth of me, is true.
33 * Ye sent vnto Iohn, and he bare witnes
vnto the trueth.

Chap. 1, 27.

34 But I receiue not the recorde of man:
neuertheles these things I say, ŷ ye might
be saued.
35 He was a burning, and a shining " cãdle:
and ye wolde for a [n] season haue reioyced
in his light.

" Or, lampe.
n But ye left him quickely & did not perseuere.

36 But I haue greater witnes then the witnes of Iohn: for the workes which the Father hathe giuen me to finish, the same
workes that I do, beare witnes of me, that
the Father sent me.
37 And the * Father him self, which hathe
sent me, [o] beareth witnes of me. Ye haue
not heard his voyce at anie time, * nether
haue ye sene his shape.

Mat. 3, 17. & 17, 5. Deut. 4, 12.
o In the Law & Prophetes.

38 And his worde haue ye not abiding in
you: for whome he hathe sent, him ye beleue not.
39 * Searche the Scriptures: for in them ye
thinke to haue eternal life, & thei are thei
which testifie of me.

Act. 17, 11.

40 But ye wil not come to me, ŷ ye might
haue life.
41 I receiue not praise of men.
42 But I knowe you, that ye haue not the
loue of God in you.
43 I am come in my Fathers Name, and ye
receiue me not: if [p] another shal come in
his owne name, him wil ye receiue.

p The people are more readie to receiue false prophetes, then Iesus Christ.

44 How can ye beleue, which [q] receiue * honour one of another, and seke not the honour that cometh of God alone!

q Vaine glorie is a great let for a man to come to God.
Chap. 12, 43.
Gen. 3, 15. & 22, 18. & 49, 10. deut. 18, 15

45 Do not thinke that I wil accuse you to
my Father: there is one that [r] accuseth
you, *euen* Moses, in whome ye trust.
46 For had ye beleued Moses, ye wolde
haue beleued me: * for he wrote of me.
47 But if ye beleue not his writings, how
shal ye beleue my wordes!

r As Moses shal accuse thẽ that trust in him: so they shal haue no greater enemies at the daye of iudgement, then the uirgine Marie & the Saintes, vpon whome now thei call: but whosoeuer doeth accuse, Christ & their owne consciẽce shal condẽne ŷ reprobat.

CHAP. VI.

10 Iesus fedeth fiue thousand men with fiue loaues & two fishes. 15 He departeth awaye, that thei shulde not make him King. 26 He reproueth the fleshlie hearers of his worde. 41 The carnal are offended at him. 63 The flesh profiteth not.

1 After these things, Iesus went his way
ouer the [a] sea of Galile, *or* of [b] Tiberias.

a Called the lake of Genesareth.
b Tiberias, Bethsaida, and Capernaũ were on this side the lake, in respect of Galile: but it is here said ŷ he went ouer, because there were diuers crikes & turnings, ouer the which mẽ feried.

2 And a great multitude followed him, because they sawe his miracles, which he
did on them that were diseased.
3 Then Iesus went vp into a mountaine,
and there he sate with his disciples.
4 Now ŷ Passeouer, a * feast of the Iewes,
was nere.

Leui. 23, 2. deut. 16, 1.

5 * Then IESUS lift vp *his* eyes, and seing
that a great multitude came vnto him, he
said vnto Philippe, Whence shal we bye
bread, that these might eat?

Mat. 14, 16. mar. 6, 38. luk. 9, 13.

6 (And this he said to proue him: for he
him self knewe what he wolde do)
7 Philippe answered him, [c] Two hundreth
penyworthe of bread is not sufficient for
them, that euerie one of them may take a
litle.

c This summe amoũteth to about fiue poũde sterling.

8 Then said vnto him one of his disciples,
Andrewe, Simon Peters brother,
9 There is a litle boye here, which hathe
fiue barlie loaues, and two fishes: but what
are they among so manie?
10 And Iesus said, Make the people sit
downe. (Now there was muche grasse in
that place) Then the men sate downe in
nomber, about fiue thousand.
11 And Iesus toke the bread, and [d] gaue
thankes, and gaue to the disciples, and the
disciples to them that were set downe: &
likewise of the fishes as muche as they
wolde.

d Praier and thankesgiuing do sanctifie our meates wherewith we are nourished.

12 And when they were satisfied, he said
vnto his disciples, Gather vp the broken
meat which remaineth, that [e] nothing be
lost.

e The abundãt store of Gods gifts oght not to make vs prodigal to waste them.

13 Then they gathered it together, and filled twelue baskets with the broken meat

of the fiue barlie loaues, which remained
vnto them that had eaten.
14 Then the men when they had sene the
miracle that Iesus did, said, This is of a
trueth the Prophet that shulde come into
the worlde.
15 When Iesus therefore perceiued that
they wolde come, and take him to make
him a [f] King, he departed againe into a
mountaine him self alone.
16 ¶ Whē euen was now come, his disciples
went downe vnto the sea,
17 * And entred into a ship, and went [g] ouer
the sea towardes Capernaum: and now it
was darke, & Iesus was not come to them.
18 And the sea arose with a great winde
that blewe.
19 And when they had rowed about fiue &
twentie, or thirtie [h] furlongs, they sawe Iesus walking on the sea, and drawing nere
vnto the ship: so they were afraied.
20 But he said vnto them, It is I: be not a-
fraied.
21 Then willingly they receiued him into
the ship, and the ship was by and by at the
land, whether they went.
22 ¶ The day following, the people which
stode on the other side of the sea, sawe that
there was none other ship there, saue that
one, whereinto his disciples were entred,
and that Iesus went not with his disciples
in the ship, but that his disciples were gone [i] alone,
23 And that there came other shippes from
Tiberias nere vnto the place where they
ate the bread, after the Lord had giuen
thankes.
24 Now when the people sawe that Iesus
was not there, nether his disciples, thei also toke shipping, & came to Capernaum,
seking for Iesus.
25 And when they had founde him on the
[k] other side of the sea, thei said vnto him,
Rabbi, when camest thou hither?
26 Iesus answered them, and said, Verely,
verely I say vnto you, ye seke me not, because ye sawe the miracles, but because ye
ate of the loaues, and were filled.
27 Laboure not for the meat which perisheth, but for the meat that [l] endureth vnto euerlasting life, which the Sonne of mā
shal giue vnto you: for him hathe * God
the Father [m] sealed.
28 Then said they vnto him, What shal we
do, that we might worke the [n] workes of
God?
29 Iesus answered, & said vnto them, * This
is ye worke of God, that ye beleue in him,
whome he hathe sent.
30 They said therefore vnto him, What
signe shewest thou then, that we maye
se it, and beleue thee? what doest thou
worke?

f Thei imagined an earthlie kīgdome without the testimonie of Gods worde, so that by this meanes his spiritual kīgdome shulde haue bene abolished.

Mat.14,25. mar.6,47.

g Ouer a corner of ye lake.

h Whereof eight make a mile.

i Wherefore it must nedes folowe yt Christ passed miraculously.

k This was not straight ouer ye lake frō side to side, but ouer a crike, or arme of ye lake, which saued muche labour to them yt shulde haue gone about by land.

l Which nourisheth & augmenteth our faith.

Chap.1,32. mat.3,17. & 17,3.

1.Iohn 3,23.

m For when he appointed him to be the Mediator, he set his marke & seale in him to be ye onelie one to reconcile God & man together.

n Suche as be acceptable vnto God.

31 * Our fathers did eat Māna in the desert,
as it is * written, He gaue them bread frō
heauen to eat.
32 Then Iesus said vnto them, Verely, verely I say vnto you, [o] Moses gaue you not
bread from heauen, but my Father giueth
you the true bread from heauen.
33 For the bread of God is he which cometh downe from heauen, and giueth life
vnto the worlde.
34 Then thei said vnto him, Lord, euermore giue vs this bread.
35 And Iesus said vnto thē, I am the bread
of life: he that cometh to me, shal not hūger, and * he that beleueth in me, shal
[p] neuer thurst.
36 But I said vnto you, that ye also haue
sene me, and beleue not.
37 All [q] that the Father giueth me, shal come to me: and him that cometh to me, I
cast not away.
38 For I came downe from heauen, not to
do mine owne wil, but his wil which hathe
sent me.
39 And this is the Fathers wil which hathe
sent me, that of all which he hathe giuen
me, I shulde lose nothing, but shulde raise it vp againe at the last day.
40 And this is the wil of him that sent me,
that euerie man which seeth the Sonne, &
beleueth in him, shulde haue euerlasting
life: and I wil raise him vp at the last day.
41 The Iewes then murmured at him, because he said, I am the bread, which is come downe from heauen.
42 And they said, * Is not this Iesus the
sonne of Ioseph, whose father & mother
we knowe? how thē saith he, I came downe from heauen?
43 Iesus then answered, & said vnto them,
Murmure not among your selues.
44 No man can [r] come to me, except the
Father, which hathe sent me, [s] drawe him:
and I wil raise him vp at the last day.
45 It is written in the * Prophetes, And
they shalbe all taught of God. Euerie
man therefore that hathe heard, & hathe
learned of the Father, cometh vnto me,
46 * Not that anie man hathe sene the Father, saue he which is of God, he hathe sene the Father.
47 Verely, verely I say vnto you, He that
beleueth in me, hathe euerlasting life.
48 I am the bread of life.
49 * Your fathers did eat Manna in the wildernes, [t] and are dead.
50 This is the bread, which cometh downe
from heauen, that he which eateth of it,
shulde not dye.
51 I am the [u] liuīg bread, which came downe from heauen: if anie man eat of this
bread, he shal liue for euer: and the bread
that I wil giue, is my flesh, which I wil
giue

Exod.16,14. nomb.11,7. Psal.77,24. wisd.16,20.

o He compareth Moses wt the Father, & manna with Christ, who fedeth vs into euerlasting life, 1.Cor.10,3.

Eccl.24,29.

p He shal neuer want spiritual nourishment.

q God doeth regenerate his elect, & causeth them to obey the Gospel.

Mat.13,55.

r That is, or beleue in me.

s By lightening his heart with his holie Spirit

Isa.54,13. ierem.31,33.

Mat.11,27.

Exod.16,15.

t Then there is no fode that can nourish ye soules, but Iesus Christ.

u Which giue life to the worlde.

giue for the life of the worlde.
52 Then the Iewes ſtroue among them ſelues, ſaying, How can this man giue vs *his*
fleſh to eat?
53 Then Ieſus ſaid vnto them, Verely, verely I ſay vnto you, Except ye eat the fleſh
of the Sõne of man, and drinke his blood,
ye haue [x] no life in you.
54 Whoſoeuer * eateth my fleſh, and drinketh my blood, hathe eternal life, and I
wil raiſe him vp at the laſt day.
55 For my fleſh is meat in dede, & my blood
is drinke in dede.
56 He [y] that eateth my fleſh, and drinketh
my blood, [z] dwelleth in me, and I in him.
57 As the liuing Father hathe ſent me, ſo liue I by the Father, and he that eateth me,
euen he ſhal liue by me.
58 This is the bread which came downe
from heauen: not as your fathers haue eaten Manna, and are dead. He that eateth
of this bread, ſhal liue for euer.
59 Theſe things ſpake he in the Synagogue
as he taught in Capernaum.
60 Manie therefore of his diſciples (when
thei heard this) ſaid, This is an hard ſaying: who can [a] heare it?
61 But Ieſus knowing in him ſelf, that his
diſciples murmured at this, ſaid vnto thẽ,
Doeth this offende you?
62 *What* then if ye ſhulde ſe the Sõne of mã
[b] aſcende vp * where he was before?
63 It is the Spirit that quickeneth: the fleſh
[c] profiteth nothing: the wordes that I ſpeake vnto you, are ſpirit and life.
64 But there are ſome of you that beleue
not: for Ieſus knewe from the beginning,
which they were that beleued not, & who
ſhulde betraye him.
65 And he ſaid, Therefore ſaid I vnto you,
that no man can come vnto me, except it
be giuen vnto him of my Father.
66 From that time, manie of his diſciples
went backe, and walked no more with
him.
67 Thẽ ſaid Ieſus to the twelue, Wil ye alſo go away?
68 Then Simon Peter anſwered him, Maſter to whome ſhal we go? Thou haſt the
wordes of [d] eternal life:
69 And we beleue and knowe that thou art
the Chriſt the Sonne of the liuing God.
70 Ieſus anſwered thẽ, Haue not I * choſen
you twelue and [e] one of you is a deuil?
71 Now he ſpake it of Iudas Iſcariot the
ſonne of Simõ: for he it was that ſhulde betraye him, thogh he was one of ẏ twelue.

x Where Chriſt is not, there death reigneth
1.Cor.11,27.
y As our bodies are ſuſteined with meat & drinke: ſo are our ſoules nouriſhed with the bodie, and blood of Ieſus Chriſt.
z To eat the fleſh of Chriſt and drinke his blood, is to dwell in Chriſt and to haue Chriſt dwelling in vs.
a That is, vnderſtand it.
Chap.3,13.
b He meaneth not that his humanitie deſcended from heauen: but he ſpeaketh touching ẏ vnion of bothe natures, attributing to the one that which apperteineth to the other.
c To wit, if it be ſeparate from ẏ Spirit, whereof it hathe the force: for it cometh of the power of the Spirit that the fleſh of Chriſt giueth vs life.
d Thẽ without Chriſt there is but death: for his worde onely leadeth vs to life
Mat.16,16.
e Althogh your number be ſmale, yet ſhal ye be diminiſhed.

CHAP. VII.

6 Ieſus reproueth the ambition of his couſins. 12 There are diuers opinions of him among the people. 17 He ſheweth how to knowe the trueth. 20 The iniurie they do vnto him. 47 The Phariſes rebuke the officers becauſe they haue not taken him. 52 And chide with Nicodemus for taking his parte.

1 After theſe things, Ieſus walked in
Galile, and wolde not walke in Iudea: for the Iewes ſoght to kil him.
2 Now the Iewes * [a] feaſt of the Tabernacles was at hand.
3 His brethren therefore ſaid vnto him,
Departe hence, and go into Iudea, that
thy diſciples may ſe thy workes that thou
doeſt.
4 For there is no mã that doeth anie thing
ſecretly, & he him ſelf ſeketh to be "famous.
If thou doeſt theſe things, ſhewe thy ſelf
to the worlde.
5 For as yet his brethrẽ beleued not in him.
6 Then Ieſus ſaid vnto thẽ, My time is not
yet come: but your time is alway readie.
7 The worlde can not hate you: but me it
hateth, [b] becauſe I teſtifie of it, that the
workes thereof are euil.
8 Go ye vp vnto this feaſt: I wil [c] not go vp
yet vnto this feaſt: for my time is not yet
fulfilled.
9 ¶ Theſe things he ſaid vnto them, and a-
bode ſtil in Galile.
10 But aſſone as his brethren were gone
vp, then wẽt he alſo vp vnto the feaſt, not
openly, but as *it were* priuely.
11 Then the Iewes ſoght him at the feaſt, &
ſaid, Where is he?
12 And muche murmuring was there of him
amõg the people. Some ſaid, He is a good
man: other ſaid, Naye: but he deceiueth
the people.
13 Howbeit no man ſpake openly of him
for feare of the [d] Iewes.
14 Now whẽ half the feaſt was done, Ieſus
went vp into the Temple and taught.
15 And the Iewes marueiled, ſaying, How
knoweth this man the " Scriptures, ſeing
that he neuer learned.
16 Ieſus anſwered them, & ſaid, My doctrine is not [e] mine, but his that ſent me.
17 If anie mã wil do his wil, he ſhal knowe
of the doctrine, whether it be of God, or
whether I ſpeake of my ſelf.
18 He [f] that ſpeaketh of him ſelf, ſeketh his
owne glorie: but he that ſeketh his glorie that ſent him, the ſame is true, and no
[g] vnrighteouſnes is in him.
19 * Did not Moſes giue you a Law, and *yet*
none of you kepeth the Law? * Why go ye
about to kil me?
20 The [h] people anſwered, and ſaid, Thou
haſt a deuil: who goeth about to kil thee?
21 Ieſus anſwered, and ſaid to them, I haue
done one worke, and ye all [i] marueile.
22 * Moſes therefore gaue vnto you circũ-
ciſion, (not becauſe it is of Moſes, but of
the * fathers) and ye on the Sabbath *day* cir
cumciſe a man.
23 If a man on the Sabbath receiue circumciſion, that the Law of Moſes ſhulde not
be broken, be ye angrie with me, becauſe I

Leui.23,34.
a At this feaſt they dwelled ſeuen dayes in the tentes, ẇ put thẽ in remembrance, ẏ they had no citie here permanent, but ẏ they muſt ſeke one to come.
" Or, manifeſt.
b Why the worlde hateth Chriſt.
c Chriſt doeth not vtterly denie that he wolde go to ẏ feaſt, but ſignifieth ẏ as yet he was not fully determined.
d Theſe were the heads of ẏ people who did enuie Chriſt.
" Or, letters.
e In that, that he is man onely.
f By this marke we may knowe whether the doctrine be of God, or of man.
g Nothing cõterfait or vntrue.
Exod.24,3.
Chap.5,18.
h Who did not know the fetche of the Scribes.
i Becauſe I did it on the Sabbath day.
Leui.12,3.
Gen.17,10.

haue made a man euerie whit whole on the
Sabbath *day*?

Deu.1,16.

24 *Iudge not according to the appearance, but iudge righteous iudgement.
25 ¶ Then said some of them of Ierusalem,
Is not this he, whome they go about to kil?

"Or, frely.

26 And beholde, he speaketh "openly, and
they say nothing to him: do ẏ rulers know
in dede that this is the verie Christ?
27 Howbeit we know this man whence he
is: but when the Christ cometh, no man
shal knowe whence he is.

k He speaketh this, as it were scornefully.

28 ¶ Then cryed Iesus in the Temple as he
taught, saying, Ye [k] bothe knowe me, and
knowe whence I am: yet am I not come of
my self, but he that sent me, is true, whome
ye knowe not.
29 But I knowe him: for I am of him, and he
hathe sent me.
30 Then they soght to take him, but no mã
laid hands on him, because his houre was
not yet come.

l They were wel minded to heare him: ẇ preparation is here called (althogh improperly) faith

31 Now manie of the people [l] beleued in
him, and said, When the Christ cometh,
wil he do mo miracles then this man hathe done?
32 The Pharises heard that the people murmured these things of him, and the Pharises, and high Priests sent officers to take him.

m He sheweth vnto thẽ that they haue no power ouer hĩ, til the time come that his Father hathe ordeined.

33 Then said Iesus vnto them, Yet am I [m] a
litle while with you, and then go I vnto
him that sent me.

Chap.13,35.
"Or, shalbe.

34 *Ye shal seke me, & shal not finde *me*, &
where I "am, can ye not come.
35 Then said the Iewes amongs them selues, Whither wil he go, that we shal not
finde him? Wil he go vnto them that are
"dispersed among the [n] Grecians, and teache the Grecians?

"Greke, dispersion.
n Among the Iewes ẇ were scatered here and there among the Gẽtiles.

36 What saying is this that he said, Ye shal
seke me, and shal not finde *me*? and where I
am, can ye not come?

Leu.23,36.

37 Now in the last & *great day of ẏ feast,
Iesus stode and cryed, saying, If anie man
thirst, let him come vnto me, and drinke.

Deu.18,15.
o The true way to come to Christ, is by faith.
p Which shal neuer drye vp.

38 He that [o] beleueth in me, * as saith the
Scripture, out of his bellie shal flowe riuers of water [p] of life.

Ioel.2,28.
act.2,17.
q These were the visible graces, which were giuen to the Apostles after his ascension.

39 (*This spake he of the Spirit which they
that beleued in him, shulde receiue: for the
[q] holie Gost was not yet *giuen* because that
Iesus was not yet glorified)

r They loked for some notable Prophet besides the Messias, chap.1,21.

40 So manie of the people, whẽ they heard
this saying, said, Of a trueth this is the
[r] Prophet.
41 Other said, This is the Christ: and some
said, But shal Christ come out of Galile?

Micah 5,2.
mat.2,5.

42 *Saith not the Scripture that the Christ
shal come of the sede of Dauid, and out of
the towne of Beth-lehẽ, where Dauid was?
43 So was there dissention amõg the people for him.
44 And some of them wolde haue taken
him, but no man laid hands on him.
45 Then came the officers to ẏ high Priests
& Pharises, & they said vnto them, Why
haue ye not broght him?

s Wherein appeareth the mightie power of Christs worde against his enemies.

46 The officers answered, [s] Neuer mã spake like this man.
47 Then answered them the Pharises, Are
ye also deceiued?

t They alledge the autoritie of man against Gods autoritie.

48 Doeth anie of the [t] rulers, or of the Pharises beleue in him?
49 But this people, which knowe not the
Law, are cursed.

Chap.3,2.

50 Nicodemus said vnto thẽ, (*he that came to Iesus by night, & was one of them.)

Deu.17,8. & 19,15.

51 Doeth our Law iudge a man before it
heare him, * & knowe what he hathe done?
52 They answered and said vnto him, Art
thou also of Galile? Search and loke: for
out of Galile ariseth no Prophet.
53 And euerie man went vnto his owne
house.

CHAP. VIII.

*11 Christ deliuereth her that was taken in adulterie.
12 He is the light of the worlde. 14 He sheweth from
whence he is come, wherefore, and whether he goeth.
33 Who are fre, & who are bounde. 34 Of fre men and
sclaues, & their rewarde. 46 He defieth his enemies.
59 And being persecuted, withdraweth him self.*

1 AND Iesus went vnto the mount of O-
liues,
2 And early in the morning came againe
into the Temple, and all the people came
vnto him, and he sate downe, and taught
them.
3 Then the Scribes, & the Pharises broght
vnto him a woman, taken in adulterie, &
set her in the middes,
4 And said vnto him, Master, this woman
was taken in adulterie, in the verie act.

Leu.20,10.

5 *Now Moses in the Law commanded vs,
that suche shulde be stoned: what saist
thou therefore?

a Ether for breaking the Law, if he did deliuer her, or of lightnes, & inconstantie, if he did condẽne her.

6 And this they said to tempt him, that thei
might haue, whereof to [a] accuse him. But
Iesus stouped downe, and with his finger
wrote on the grounde.

Deu.17,7.

7 And while they continued asking him,
he lift him self vp, & said vnto them, *Let
him that is among you without sinne, cast
the first stone at her.
8 And againe he stouped downe, and wrote
on the grounde.
9 And when they heard it, being accused
by their owne conscience, they went out
one by one, beginning at the eldest euen
to the last: so Iesus was left alone, and the
woman standing in the middes.
10 When Iesus had lift vp him self againe,
and sawe no man, but the woman, he said
vnto her, Woman, where are those thine
accusers? hathe no man condemned thee?
11 She said, No man, Lord. And Iesus said,

[b] Nether do I condemne thee: go and sinne no more.
12 Then spake Iesus againe vnto them,
saying, I*am the light of ẏ worlde: he that
followeth me, shal not walke in darkenes,
but shal haue the *light of life.
13 The Pharises therefore said vnto him,
Thou bearest recorde of thy self: thy recorde is not *true.
14 *Iesus answered, and said vnto them,
[c]Thogh I beare recorde of my self, *yet* my
recorde is true: for I knowe whence I came
& whether I go: but ye can not tel [d] whence I come, and whether I go.
15 Ye iudge after the flesh: [e] I iudge no
man.
16 And if I also iudge, my iudgemēt is true:
for I am not alone, but I and the Father,
that sent me.
17 And it is also written in your Law,*that
the testimonie of two men is true.
18 I am [f] one that beare witnes of my self,
& the Father that sent me, beareth witnes
of me.
19 Then said they vnto him, Where is thy
Father? Iesus answered, Ye nether knowe
me, nor my Father. If ye had knowen me,
ye shulde haue knowen my Father also.
20 These wordes spake Iesus in the [g] treasurie, as he taught in the Temple, and no
man laid hands on him: for his houre was
not yet come.
21 Then said Iesus againe vnto them, I go
my way, and ye shal seke me, and shal dye
in your [h] sinnes. Whether I go, can ye
not come.
22 Then said the Iewes, Wil he kil him self
because he saith, Whether I go, can ye not
come?
23 And he said vnto them, [i] Ye are frō beneth: I am frō aboue: ye are of this worlde:
I am not of this worlde.
24 I said therefore vnto you, That ye shal
dye in your sinnes: for except ye beleue,
that I am he, ye shal dye in your sinnes.
25 Then said they vnto him, Who art
thou? And Iesus said vnto them, *Euen the
same thing that I said vnto you [k] from the
beginning.
26 I haue manie things to say, and to iudge
of you: but he that sent me, is true, and
the things that I haue heard of him, those
speake I to the worlde.
27 They vnderstode not that he spake to
them of the Father.
28 Then said Iesus vnto them, Whē ye haue [l] lift vp the Sonne of man, then shal ye
[m] knowe that I am [n] he, and that I do nothing of my self, but as my Father hathe
taught me, *so* I speake these things.
29 For he that sent me, is with me: the Father hathe not left me alone, because I do
alwayes those things that please him.

b Iesus wolde not medle, but with ẏ which did apperteine to his office, to wit, to bring sinners to repentance: and therefore did not abolish the Law against adulterie.
Chap.1,5. & 9,5.
**Or, liuelie light.*
**Or, iuste.*
Chap.5,31.
c That which Christ denied chap 5,37, here he granteth, to declare vnto thē their stubbernes: and saith that being God he beareth witnes to his humanitie: likewise doeth God ẏ father witnes ẏ same which are two distīct psones, thogh but one God.
d In that he came from his father, he sheweth that he is not onely man, but God also.
Deu.17,6. & 19,15. mat.18,16. 2.cor.13,1. ebr.10,28.
e He wolde not iudge rashely, as they did.
f Which place proueth Christ to be verie God, and man.
g That is, the place where ẏ vessel and other things belonging to the Temple, were kept.
h Because of their rebelliō wherein they did perseuere.
i He sheweth the differēce betwene the Gospel, & the subtil wit of man.
**Or, from the beginning euen that I said vnto you.*
k That is, who he was, whēce he was & why he came into this worlde.
l Their endeuours & practises whereby they thinke to destroye him, shal serue to exalte, & magnifie his glorie.
m Not to beleue in him, but to be consulted.
n To wit, the Messias.

30 ¶ As he spake these things, many beleued in him.
31 Then said Iesus to the Iewes which beleued in him, If ye continue in my worde,
ye are verely my disciples,
32 And shal knowe the trueth, & the trueth
[o]shal make you fre.
33 They answered him, [p]We be Abrahams
sede, and were neuer bonde to any man:
why saist thou then, Ye shalbe made fre?
34 Iesus answered them, Verely, verely I
say vnto you, that whosoeuer committeth
sinne, is the *seruant of sinne.
35 And the seruant abideth not in the house for euer: but the Sonne abideth for euer.
36 If the Sōne therefore shal make you fre,
ye shalbe fre in dede.
37 I [q] knowe that ye are Abrahams sede, but
ye seke to kill me, because my worde hathe
no place in you.
38 I speake that which I haue sene with my
Father: and ye do that which ye haue sene
with your father.
39 They answered, and said vnto him, A-
braham is our father. Iesus said vnto thē,
If ye were Abrahams children, ye wolde
do the [r] workes of Abraham.
40 But now ye go about to kill me, a man
that haue tolde you the trueth, which I haue heard of God: this did not Abraham.
41 Ye do the workes of your father. Then
said they to him, We are not borne of fornicatiō: we haue one Father, which is God.
42 Therefore Iesus said vnto them, If God
were your Father, then wolde ye loue me:
for I proceded forthe, & came from God,
nether came I of my self, but he sent me.
43 Why do ye not vnderstand my talke? because ye can not [s] heare my worde.
44 *Ye are of your father the deuil, and the
lustes of your father ye wil do: he hathe
bene a murtherer [t] from the beginning, &
[u]abode not in the trueth, because there is
no trueth in him. When he speaketh a lie,
then speaketh he of his [x] owne: for he is a
liar, and the father thereof.
45 And because I tell you the trueth, ye beleue me not.
46 Which of you can rebuke me of sinne?
and if I say the trueth, why do ye not beleue me?
47 *He that is of God, heareth Gods wordes: ye therefore heare them not, because
ye are not of God.
48 Then answered the Iewes, and said vnto
him, Say we not wel that thou art a Samaritan, and hast a deuil?
49 Iesus answered, I haue not a deuil, but
I honour my Father, and ye haue dishonored me.
50 And I seke not mine owne praise: but
there is one that seketh it, and [y] iudgeth.
51 Verely, verely I say vnto you, If a man

o For we were sclaues to sin.
p These were not the beleuing Iewes, but the mockers that answered thus.
Rom.6,20. 2.pet.2,19.
q He granteth their sayings in suche sorte, ẏ he sheweth vnto them that their owne dedes proue thē liers.
r Which were his obedience, charitie & suche good workes which proceded of faith.
s For you are carnal and can not vnderstād spiritual thīgs
1.Iohn 3,8.
t Since the first creatiō of man.
u It followeth then that he was once in the trueth: for he was not created euil.
x Accordīg to his wont and custome.
1.Iohn 4,6.
y Who wil reuenge ẏ iniurie that you do against me, or rather against him.

z For the faithful euen in death se life.

kepe my worde, he shal neuer [z] se death.
52 Then said ye Iewes to him, Now knowe
we that thou hast a deuil. Abrahã is dead,
and the Prophetes, and thou saist, If a man
kepe my worde, he shal neuer tast of death.
53 Art thou greater then our father Abraham,
which is dead? and the Prophetes are
dead: whome makest thou thy self?
54 Iesus answered, If I honour my self, mine
honour is nothing worthe: it is my Father
that honoureth me, whome ye say, that he
is your God.
55 Yet ye haue not knowẽ him: but I knowẽ
him, and if I shulde say I knowe him not,
I shulde be a liar like vnto you: but I knowe
him, and kepe his worde.
56 Your father Abraham reioyced to se my
[a] day, and he sawe it, and was glad.
57 Then said the Iewes vnto him, Thou
art not yet fiftie yere olde, and hast thou
sene Abraham?
58 Iesus said vnto them, Verely, verely I say
vnto you, before Abraham was, [b] I am.
59 *Thẽ toke they vp stones, to cast at him,
but Iesus hid him self, and went out of the
Temple ‖.

a Which was to se ye coming of Christ in ye flesh: wc thing Abrahã sawe farre of with ye eyes of faith, Ebr. 11, 10.

Chap. 10, 31.

b Not onely God, but the Mediator betwene God, & mã, appointed from before all eternitie.

‖ *And he passed through the middes of them and so went his way.*

CHAP. IX.

1 Of him that was borne blinde. 11 The confession of him that was borne blinde. 39 To what blinde men Christ giueth sight.

1 And as Iesus passed by, he sawe a mã
which was blinde from his birth.
2 And his disciples asked him, saying, Master,
who did sinne, this man, or his parẽts,
that he was borne blinde?
3 Iesus answered, [a] Nether hathe this man
sinned, nor his parents, but that the workes
of God shulde be shewed on him.
4 I must worke the workes of him that sent
me, while it is [b] day: the night cometh whẽ
no man can worke.
5 As long as I am in the worlde, *I am the
light of the worlde.
6 Assone as he had thus spoken, [c] he spate
on the grounde, & made claye of the spettle,
and anointed the eyes of the blinde
with the clay,
7 And said vnto him, Go wash in the poole
of Siloam (which is by interpretatiõ, [d] Sẽt)
He went his way therefore, and washed, &
came againe seing.
8 Now the neighbours and they that had
sene him before, when he was blinde, said,
Is not this he that sate and begged?
9 Some said, This is he: & others said, He is
like him: but he him self said, I am he.
10 Therefore they said vnto him, How were
thine eyes opened?
11 He answered, and said, The man that is
called Iesus, made claye, and anointed mine
eyes, and said vnto me, Go to the poole
of Siloam and wash. So I went and washed
and receiued sight.
12 Then they said vnto him, Where is he?
He said, I can not tell.
13 ¶ They broght to the Pharises him that
was once blinde.
14 And it was the Sabbath *day*, when Iesus
made the claye, and opened his eyes.
15 Thẽ againe the Pharises also asked him,
how he had receiued sight. And he said vnto
them, He laid claye vpon mine eyes, &
I washed, and do se.
16 Then said some of the Pharises, This
man is not of God, because he kepeth not
the Sabbath *day*. Others said, How can a
man that is a sinner, do suche miracles? and
there was a dissension among them.
17 Then spake they vnto the blinde againe,
What saist thou of him, because he hathe
opened thine eyes? And he said, He is a
Prophet.
18 Then the Iewes did not beleue him (that
he had bene blinde, and receiued his sight)
vntil they had called the parents of him
that had receiued sight.
19 And they asked thẽ, saying, Is this your
sonne, whome ye say was borne blinde?
How doeth he now se then?
20 His parents answered them, & said, We
knowe that this is our sonne, and that he
was borne blinde:
21 But by what meanes he now seeth, we
knowe not: or who hathe opened his eyes,
[e] can we not tell: he is olde ynough: aske
him: he shal answer for him self.
22 These wordes spake his parents, because
they feared the Iewes: for the Iewes had
ordeined alreadie, that if any mã did confesse
that he was the Christ, he shulde be
excommunicate out of the Synagogue.
23 Therefore said his parents, He is olde
ynough: aske him.
24 Then againe called they the man that
had bene blinde, and said vnto him, [f] Giue
glorie vnto God: we knowe that this man
is a sinner.
25 Then he answered, and said, Whither
he be a sinner or no, [g] I can not tell: one
thing I knowe, that I was blinde, and
now I se.
26 [h] Thẽ said they to him againe, What did
he to thee? how opened he thine eyes?
27 He answered them, I haue tolde you alreadie,
and ye haue not heard it: wherefore
wolde ye heare it againe? [i] wil ye also be
his disciples?
28 Then checked they him, & said, Be thou
his disciple: we be Moses disciples.
29 We knowe that God spake with Moses:
but this man we knowe not frõ whence
he is.
30 The man answered, and said vnto them,
Doutles, this is a marueilous thing, that
ye [k] knowe not whence he is, and yet he

a God doeth not alwayes punish mẽ for their sinnes.

b Whẽ opportunitie & the season serueth

Chap. 1, 9. & 8, 12. & 12, 35.

c This was not for any vertue that was in the earth, in the spittle, or in the claye to make one se: but it onely pleased him to vse these signes & meanes.

d Hereby was prefigured the Messias, who shulde be sent vnto them.

e They durst not speake the trueth for feare they shulde be excommunicate.

f That is, Consider that nothĩg is hid frõ God: therefore tel vs ye trueth that God may be glorified thereby, Ios. 7, 29, 1. Sam. 6, 5.

g He spake this in mockery.

h They thoght ether to driue him from the trueth, or to make hĩ swerue by their oft times examining hĩ: which practise Satãs members euer do obserue in examining the Christians.

i He derideth their wilful malice and ignorance.

k They douted not of his cõtrey or parents, but of his office and autoritie.

hathe

hathe opened mine eyes.
31 Now we knowe that God heareth not
l sinners: but if any man be a worshipper of
God, and doeth his wil, him heareth he.

l Or, wicked men, contemners of God & suche as delite in sinne.

32 Since the worlde began was it not heard
that any man opened the eyes of one that
was borne blinde.
33 If this man were not of God, he colde
haue done nothing.
34 They answered, & said vnto him, Thou
art altogether borne in sinnes, and doest
thou teache vs? so they cast him out.
35 Iesus heard that they had * cast him out:
and when he had founde him, he said vnto him, Doest thou beleue in the Sonne
of God?

* Or, excommunicate him.

36 He answered, and said, Who is he, Lord,
that I might beleue in him?
37 And Iesus said vnto him, Bothe thou hast
sene him, & he it is that talketh with thee.
38 Then he said, Lord, I beleue, and m worshipped him.
39 And Iesus said, I am come vnto n iudgement into this worlde, that they which se
not, might se: & that they * which se, might
be made blinde.

m As all astonished he fel downe & worshipped him.
n Meaning, ÿ rule & autoritie, to make the poore blinde to se, and ÿ proude seers blinde.
Chap. 3, 17. & 12, 47.

40 And some of the Pharises which were
with him, heard these things, and said vnto him, Are we blinde also?
41 Iesus said vnto them, If ye were blinde,
o ye shulde not haue sinne: but now ye say,
We se: therefore your sinne remaineth.

o You shulde not be so muche in faute.

CHAP. X.

1 Christ is the true shepherd, and the dore. 19 Diuers opinions of Christ. 24 He is asked if he be Christ. 32 His workes declare that he is God. 34 The princes called gods.

1 Verely, verely I say vnto you, He that
entreth not in by the dore into the
shepefolde, but climeth vp another way,
he is a thefe and a robber.
2 But he that goeth in by the dore, is the
shepherd of the shepe.
3 To him the porter openeth, and the shepe
heare his voyce, and he a calleth his owne
shepe by name, and leadeth them out.
4 And when he hathe sent forthe his owne
shepe, he goeth before them, and the shepe
followe him: for they knowe his voyce.

a That is, there is mutual agrement & consent of faith betwene the pastour and ÿ shepe.

5 And they wil not followe a stranger, but
they flee from him: for they knowe not the
voyce of strangers.
6 This parable spake Iesus vnto them: but
they vnderstode not what things they were which he spake vnto them.
7 Then said Iesus vnto them againe, Verely, verely I say vnto you, I am the dore
of the shepe.
8 All, b that euer came before me, are theues & robbers: but the shepe did not heare them.
9 I am the dore: by me if any man enter in,
he shalbe saued, and shal c go in and go
out, and finde pasture.

b He meaneth all ÿ false prophetes, who led not men to Christ, but frō him.
c He shalbe sure of his life

10 The thefe commeth not, but for to steale, and to kill, and to destroye: I am come
that they might haue life, and haue it in
abundance.
11 *I am the good shepherd: the good shepherd giueth his life for his shepe.

Isa. 40, 11. Ezek. 34, 23.

12 But an hireling, and he which is not the
shepherd, nether the shepe are his owne,
seeth the wolfe cōming, & he leaueth the
shepe, and fleeth, and the wolfe catcheth
them, and scattereth the shepe.
13 So the hireling fleeth, because he is an hireling, and careth not for the shepe.
14 I am the good shepherd, and d knowe
mine, and am knowen of mine.
15 e As the Father f knoweth me, so knowe
I the Father: and I lay downe my life for
my shepe.
16 g Other shepe I haue also, which are
not of this folde: them also must I bring,
and they shal heare my voyce: and * there
shal be one shepefolde, & one shepherd.
17 h Therefore doeth my Father loue me,
because * I lay downe my life, ÿ I might
take it againe.

d Christ knoweth his because he loueth them, careth and prouideth for them.
e As ÿ Father can not forget him, no more can he forget vs.
f In that he loueth and aproueth me.
Eze. 37, 22.
g To wit, among the Gentiles, which then were strāgers from the Church of God.

18 No man taketh it from me, but I lay it
downe of my self: I haue power to lay it
downe, and haue power to take it againe:
this * commandement haue I receiued of
my Father.

Isa. 53, 7. Act. 2, 24.

19 ¶ Then there was a dissention againe a-
mong the Iewes for these sayings.
20 And many of them said, He hathe a deuil, and is madde: why heare ye him?
21 Others said, These are not the wordes of
him that hathe a deuil: can the deuil open
the eyes of the blinde?

h Christ euen in that that he is mā, hathe deserued his Fathers loue and euerlasting life, not to his fleshe onely, but to vs also which by his obedience and perfect iustice are imputed righteous, Ro. 5, 19. phil. 2, 7.

22 And it was at Ierusalem the i *feast of the*
*Dedication, and it was winter.
23 And Iesus walked in the Temple, in k Solomons porche.
24 Thē came the Iewes rounde about him,
and said vnto him, How long doest thou
* make vs doute? If thou be the Christ, tell
vs plainely.

1. Mac. 4, 59.
i Which was institute, that the people might giue thākes to God for their deliuerance and restoring of their religion and Temple, which Antiochus had corrupted and polluted.
k Which was builded againe after the patron of that which Solomō builded.
* Or, holdest our minde in suspense.

25 Iesus answered them, I tolde you, and ye
beleue not: the workes that I do in my Fathers Name, they beare witnes of me.
26 But ye beleue not: l for ye are not of my
shepe, as I said vnto you.
27 My shepe heare my voyce, and I knowe
them, and they followe me,
28 And I giue vnto them eternal life, and
they shal neuer perish, nether shal any
plucke them out of mine hand.
29 My Father which gaue *them* me, is m grea
ter then all, and none is able to take them
out of my Fathers hand.
30 I and my Father are one.
31 * Then the Iewes againe toke vp stones,
to stone him.
32 Iesus answered them, Many good workes

l The cause wherefore the reprobate can not beleue.
m Whereby we learne how safely we are preserued against all dangers.
Chap. 8, 59.

haue I shewed you from my Father : for
which of these workes do ye stone me?
33 The Iewes answered him, saying, For the
good worke we stone thee not, but for blasphemie, and that thou being a man, makest thy self God.
34 Iesus answered them, Is it not written in
your Law, *I said, ye are [n] gods?
35 If he called them gods, vnto whome the
worde of God was *giuen*, and the Scripture can not be broken,
36 Say ye of him, whome the Father hathe
sanctified, and sent into the worlde, Thou
blasphemest, because I said, I am the Sonne of God?
37 If I do not the workes of my Father, beleue me not.
38 But if I do, then thogh ye beleue not
me, *yet* beleue the workes, that ye may
knowe & beleue, that the Father *is* in me,
and I in him.
39 Againe they went about to take him: but
he escaped out of their hands,
40 And went againe beyonde Iordan, into
the place where Iohn first baptized, and
there abode.
41 And many resorted vnto him, and said,
Iohn did [o] no miracle : but all things that
Iohn spake of this man, were true.
42 And many beleued in him there.

*Psal.82,6.

n Meaning of Princes and rulers, who for their office sake are called gods, and are made here in earth as his Lieutenants: wherefore if this noble title be giuen to man, muche more it apperteined to him that is the Sonne of God equal with his Father.

o Whereby they gathered that Christ was more excellent then Iohn.

CHAP. XI.

1 Christ raiseth Lazarus from death. 47 The hie Priests and Pharises gather a counsel against him. 50 Caiaphas prophecieth. 54 Christ getteth him out of the way.

1 AND a certeine man was sicke, *named*
Lazarus of Bethania, the towne of
Marie, and her sister Martha.
2 (And it was that *Marie which anointed
the Lord with ointment, and wiped his fete with her heere, whose brother Lazarus
was sicke.)
3 Therefore *his* sisters sent vnto him, saying, Lord, beholde, he whome thou louest,
is sicke.
4 When Iesus heard it, he said, This sickenes is not [a] vnto death, but for the glorie
of God, that the Sonne of God might be
glorified thereby.
5 ¶ Now Iesus loued Martha and her sister
and Lazarus.
6 And after he had heard that he was sicke,
yet abode he two dayes stil in ỹ same place where he was.
7 Then after that, said he to his disciples,
Let vs go into Iudea againe.
8 The disciples said vnto him, Master, the
Iewes lately soght to * stone thee, & doest
thou go thither againe.
9 Iesus answered, Are there not [b] twelue
houres in the day? If a man walke in the
day, he stombleth not, because he seeth the
light of this worlde.

*Chap.12,3. mat.26,7.

a For althogh he dyed, yet being restored so sone to life, it was almost no death in cōparison.

*Chap.7,30. & 8,59. & 10,31.

b He that walketh in his vocation, & hathe ỹ light of God for his guyde, nédeth to feare no dāgers. The day also, bothe sōmer & winter was with the Iewes diuided into 12. houres.

10 But if a man walke in the night, he stombleth, because there is no light in him.
11 These things spake he, and after he said
vnto thē, Our friend Lazarus slepeth: but
I go to wake him vp.
12 Then said his disciples, Lord, if he slepe,
he [c] shal be safe.
13 Howbeit, Iesus spake of his death: but
they thoght that he had spoken of the "natural slepe.
14 Then said Iesus vnto them plainely, Lazarus is dead.
15 And I am glad for your sakes, that I was
not there, that ye may beleue: but let vs
go vnto him.
16 Then said Thomas (which is called
[d] Didymus) vnto his fellowe disciples, Let
vs also go, that we may dye with him.
17 ¶ Thē came Iesus, & founde that he had
line in the graue foure dayes already.
18 (Now Bethania was nere vnto Ierusalē,
about [e] fiftene furlongs of.)
19 And many of the Iewes were come to
Martha and Marie to comfort them for
their brother.
20 Then Martha, when she heard that Iesus was coming, wēt to mete him: but Marie sate stil in the house.
21 Then said Martha vnto Iesus, Lord, if
thou haddest bene here, my brother had
not bene dead.
22 But now [f] I knowe also, that whatsoeuer
thou askest of God, God wil giue it thee.
23 Iesus said vnto her, Thy brother shal rise
againe.
24 Martha said vnto him, I knowe that he
shal rise againe in the resurrection at the
last day.
25 Iesus said vnto her, [g] I am the resurrection and the life: he that beleueth in me,
thogh he were dead, *yet* shal he liue.
26 And whosoeuer liueth, and beleueth in
me, shal neuer dye. Beleuest thou this?
27 She said vnto him, Yea, Lord, I beleue
that thou art the Christ the Sōne of God,
which shulde come into the worlde.
28 ¶ And when she had so said, she went her
way, and called Marie her sister secretly,
saying, The Master is come, and calleth
for thee.
29 And when she heard it, she arose quickely, and came vnto him.
30 For Iesus was not yet come into the towne, but was in the place where Martha
met him.
31 The Iewes then which were with her in
the house, and comforted her, when they
sawe Marie, that she rose vp [h] hastely, and
went out, followed her, saying, She goeth
vnto the graue, to wepe there.
32 Then when Marie was come where Iesus was, and sawe him, she fel downe at
his fete, saying vnto him, Lord, if thou
haddest

c They labored to stay Christ from going into Iudea, as thogh there had bene no nede.

"Or, slombering slepe.

d Which signifieth in our tōgue, a twynne in birth.

e Which were almost two mile.

f She sheweth some faith, ỹ notwithstandīg was almost ouercome by her affections.

g Christ restoreth vs from death to giue vs euerlasting life.

h Wherein she declared her affection and reuerence that she bare to Christ.

haddeſt bene here, my brother had not
bene dead.
33 When Ieſus therefore ſawe her wepe, &
the Iewes *alſo* wepe which came with her,
he [i] groned in the ſpirit, & was troubled
in him ſelf,

i For compaſſion: for he felt our miſeries, as thogh he ſuffred ỹ like.

34 And ſaid, Where haue ye laid him? Thei
ſaid vnto him, Lord, come, and ſe.
35 *And* Ieſus [k] wept.

k We read not that his affections were ſo exceſsiue that he kept no meaſure, as we do in our ſorowes, ioyes & other affectiōs.

36 Then ſaid the Iewes, Beholde, how he
loued him.
37 And ſome of them ſaid, Colde not he,
which opened the eyes of the blinde, haue
made alſo, that this man ſhulde not haue
dyed?
38 Ieſus therefore againe groned in him
ſelf, and came to the graue. And it was a
caue, and a ſtone was laid vpon it.
39 Ieſus ſaid, Take ye away the ſtone. Martha
the ſiſter of him that was dead, ſaid
vnto him, Lord, he ſtinketh alreadie: for
he hathe bene *dead* foure daies.
40 Ieſus ſaid vnto her, Said I not vnto thee,
that if thou diddeſt beleue, thou ſhuldeſt
ſe the [l] glorie of God?

l That is, a miracle whereby Gods Name ſhulde be glorified.

41 Then they toke away the ſtone *from the
place* where the dead was laid. And Ieſus
lift vp his eyes, and ſaid, Father, I thanke
thee, becauſe thou haſt heard me.
42 I knowe that thou heareſt me alwayes,
but becauſe of the people that ſtand by,
I ſaid it, that they maye beleue, that thou
haſt ſent me.
43 As he had ſpoken theſe things, he cryed
wͭ a loude voyce, Lazarus, come forthe.
44 Then he that was dead, came forthe,
bounde hand and fote with bandes, & his
face was bounde with a napkin. Ieſus ſaid
vnto them, Loſe him, and let him go.
45 ¶ Then manie of the Iewes, which came
to Marie, and had ſene the things, which
Ieſus did, beleued in him.
46 But ſome of them went their way to the
Phariſes, and tolde them what things Ieſus
had done.
47 Then gathered the hie Prieſts, and the
Phariſes a council, and ſaid, What ſhal we
do? For this man doeth manie miracles.
48 If [m] we let him thus alone, all men wil
beleue in him, and the Romaines wil come
and take away bothe our place, and the
nacion.

m They reſiſt God, thinking to hinder his worke by their owne policies.

49 Then one of them *named* Caiaphas,
which was the hie Prieſt [n] that ſame yere,
ſaid vnto thē, Ye perceiue nothing at all,

n Or, for that preſent time.

50 Nor yet do you conſider that it is expedient
for vs, that one man dye for the
people, and that the whole nacion periſh
not.
51 This ſpake he not of him ſelf: but being
hie Prieſt that ſame yere, he [o] prophecied
that Ieſus ſhulde dye for the nacion:
52 And not for the nacion onely, but that
he ſhulde gather together in one ỹ children
of God, which were ſcattered.

o God made him to ſpeake, nether colde his impietie let Gods purpoſe, who cauſed this wicked man euen as he did Balaam, to be an inſtrument of ỹ holie Goſt.

53 Then from that day forthe they conſulted
together, to put him to death.
54 Ieſus therefore walked no more openly
among the Iewes, but went thence vnto
a countrey nere to the wildernes, into a
citie called Ephraim, and there cōtinued
with his diſciples.
55 ¶ And the Iewes Paſſeouer was at hand,
and manie went out of the countrey vp to
Ieruſalem before the Paſſeouer, to [p] purifie
them ſelues.

p Becauſe thei thoght hereby to make them ſelues more holie againſt thei ſhulde eat the Paſſeouer: but they were not commanded by God to vſe this ceremonie.

56 Then ſoght they for Ieſus, and ſpake among
them ſelues, as thei ſtode in the Tēple,
What thinke ye, that he cometh not
to the feaſt?
57 Now bothe the hie Prieſts and the Phariſes
had giuen a commandement, that if
anie man knewe where he were, he ſhulde
ſhewe it, that they might take him.

CHAP. XII.

7 Chriſt excuſeth Maries fact. 13 The affection of ſome towards him, and the rage of others againſt him and Lazarus. 25 The commoditie of the croſſe. 27 His praier. 28 The anſwer of the Father. 32 His death, and the frute thereof. 36 He exhorteth to faith. 40 The blindenes of ſome, and the infirmities of others.

1 THen * Ieſus ſix dayes before the Paſſeouer
came to Bethania, where Lazarus
was, which was dead, whome he had
raiſed from the dead.

Mat.26,6. mar.14,3.

2 There they made him a ſupper, & Martha
ſerued: but Lazarus was one of them
that ſate at the table with him.
3 Then toke Marie a pound of ointment
of ſpikenarde verie coſtlie, and anointed
Ieſus [a] fete, & wipte his fete with her heere,
& the houſe was filled with the ſauour
of the ointment.

a Euen frō the head to ỹ fete.

4 Then ſaid one of his diſciples, *euen* Iudas
Iſcariot Simons *ſonne*, which ſhulde
betraye him,
5 Why was not this ointment ſolde for
[b] thre hundreth pence, and giuen to the
poore?

b Read Mar. 14,15.

6 Now he ſaid this, not that he cared for
the poore, but becauſe he was a thefe, and
* had the bagge, and bare that which was
giuen.

Chap.13,29.

7 Then ſaid Ieſus, Let her alone: againſt
the day of my burying ſhe kept it.
8 For the poore alwayes ye haue with you,
but me ye ſhal not haue alwaies.
9 Then muche people of the Iewes knewe
that he was there: and they came, not for
Ieſus ſake onely, but that they might ſe
Lazarus alſo, whome he had raiſed from
the dead.
10 The hie Prieſts therefore cōſulted, that
they might put Lazarus to death alſo,
11 Becauſe that for his ſake manie of the
Iewes went away, and beleued in Ieſus.
12 ¶ * On the morowe a great multitude

Mat.21,8. mar.11,7. luk.19,35.

that were come to the feast, when they
heard that Iesus shulde come to Ierusalē,
13 Toke branches of palme trees, & went
forthe to mete him, and cryed, [c] Hosanna,
Blessed *is* the King of Israel that cometh
in the Name of the Lord.
14 And Iesus founde a [d] yong asse, and sate
thereon, as it is written,
15 * Feare not, daughter of Sion: beholde,
thy Kig cometh sitting on an asses colte.
16 But his disciples vnderstode not these
things at the first: but when Iesus was glorified,
then remembred they, that these
things were written of him, and that they
had done these things vnto him.
17 The people therefore that was with him,
bare witnes that he called Lazarus out of
the graue, and raised him from the dead.
18 Therefore met him the people also, because
thei heard that he had done this miracle.
19 And the Pharises said among them selues,
Perceiue ye how ye preuaile nothing?
Beholde, the "worlde goeth after him.
20 ¶ Now there were certeine [e] Grekes among
them that came vp to worship at
the feast.
21 And they came to Philippe, which was
of Bethsaida in Galile, and desired him,
saying, Syr, we wolde se Iesus.
22 Philippe came and tolde Andrewe: and
againe Andrewe & Philippe tolde Iesus.
23 And Iesus answered them, saying, The
houre is come, that the Sonne of mā must
be [f] glorified.
24 Verely, verely I say vnto you, Except
the wheate corne fall into the grounde &
dye, it bideth alone: but if it dye, it bringeth
forthe muche frute.
25 * He that [g] loueth his life, shal lose it, &
he that [h] hateth his life in this worlde, shal
kepe it vnto life eternal.
26 * If anie man serue me, let him followe
me: for where I am, there shal also my seruant
be: and if anie man serue me, him wil
my Father honour.
27 Now is my soule troubled: & what shal
I say? Father, saue me from this houre: but
therefore came I vnto this houre.
28 Father, glorifie thy Name. Then came
there a voyce from heauen, *saying*, I haue
bothe glorified it, and wil glorifie it againe.
29 Then said the people that stode by and
heard, that it was a thundre: others said,
An Angel spake to him.
30 Iesus answered, and said, This voyce came
not because of me, but for your sakes.
31 Now is the [i] iudgement of this worlde:
now shal the prince of this worlde be
cast out.
32 *And [k] I, if I were lift vp from the earth,
wil drawe [l] all men vnto me.

c That is, saue, I beseech thee.

d This doeth wel declare ẏ his kingdome stode not in outwarde things.

Zach. 9, 9.

"Or, the presse.

e They were of the race of the Iewes, and came out of Asia & Grecia: for els ẏ Iewes wolde not haue permitted ẏ they shulde worship with them in the Tēple.

f Which is, ẏ ẏ knowledge of him shulde be manifest through all ẏ worlde.

Mat. 10, 39. & 16, 5. mar. 8, 35. luk. 9, 24. & 17, 33.

Chap. 17, 24.

g If the loue thereof let hī from comming to Christ.

h And so loseth it for Christs sake.

i The reformacion and restoring of those things, which were out of order.

Chap. 3, 14.

k The crosse is the meane to gather the Church of God together, and to drawe mē to heauen.

l Not onely ẏ Iewes but also the Gentiles.

33 Now this said he, signifying what death
he shulde dye.
34 The people answered him, We haue
heard out of the * Law, that the Christ
bydeth for euer: and how saist thou, that
the Sonne of man must be lift vp? who is
that Sonne of man?
35 Then Iesus said vnto them, Yet a litle
while is * the light with you: walke while
ye haue light, lest the darkenes come vpon
you: for he that walketh in the darke,
knoweth not whether he goeth.
36 While ye haue light, beleue in ẏ light,
that ye may be the children of the light.
These things spake Iesus, and departed, &
hid him self from them.
37 ¶ And thogh he had done so manie miracles
before them, *yet* beleued they not
on him:
38 That the saying of Esaias the Prophet
might be fulfilled, that he said, * Lord,
who beleued our reporte? and to whome is
the [m] arme of the Lord reueiled?
39 Therefore colde thei not beleue, because
that Esaias saith againe,
40 * He hathe blinded their eyes, and hardened
their heart, that they shulde not se
with *their* eyes, nor vnderstand with *their*
heart, and shulde be conuerted, & I shulde
[n] heale them.
41 These things said Esaias when he sawe
his glorie and spake of him.
42 Neuertheles euen among the chief rulers
manie beleued in him: but because of
the Pharises, they did not confesse him,
lest they shulde "be *cast* out of the Synagogue.
43 *For they loued the [o] praise of men, more
then the praise of God.
44 And Iesus cryed, and said, He that beleueth
in me, beleueth not in me, but in
him that sent me.
45 And he that seeth me, seeth him that
sent me.
46 I * am come a light into the worlde,
that whosoeuer beleueth in me, shulde not
abide in darkenes.
47 And if anie man heare my wordes, and
beleue not, I "iudge him not: for I came
not to "iudge the worlde, but to saue the
worlde.
48 He that refuseth me, and receiueth not
my wordes, hathe one that "iudgeth him:
* the worde that I haue spokē, it shal iudge
him in the [p] last day.
49 For I haue not spoken of my self: but
the Father, which sent me, he gaue me a
commandement what I shulde say, and
what I shulde speake.
50 And I knowe that his commandement
is life euerlasting: the things therefore
that I speake, I speake *thē* so as the Father
said vnto me.

Psal. 89, 37. & 110, 4 & 117, 2. ezek. 37, 25.

Chap. 1, 9.

Isa. 53, 1. rom. 10, 16.

m That is, the Gospel, w is ẏ power of God to saluaciō to euerie one that doeth beleue.

Isa. 6, 9. mat. 13, 14. mar. 4, 12. luk. 8, 11. act. 28, 26. rom. 11, 8.

n By deliuering thē from their miseries, & giuing them true felicitie.

"Or, excommunicate.

Chap. 5, 44.

o To be esteemed of men.

Chap. 3, 19. & 9, 39.

"Or, condemne.

"Or, condemne.

"Or, condemneth.

Mar. 16, 26. chap. 3, 17.

p For that day shalbe the approbacion of the Gospel.

CHAP.

CHAP. XIII.

1 Christ washeth the disciples fete, 14 Exhorting them to humilitie & charitie. 21 Telleth them of Iudas the traitour, 34 And commandeth them earnestly to loue one another. 38 He forewarneth of Peters denial.

Mat.26,2. mar.14,1. luk.22,1.

1 NOw * before the feast of the Passeouer, when Iesus knewe that his houre was come, that he shulde departe out of
this worlde vnto the Father, for asmuche
as he loued his owne which were in the
worlde, vnto the end he [a] loued them.

a Because he sawe the danger great ẏ was towarde thē, therefore he toke ẏ greater care for them

b Which was the eating of the Passeouer.

2 And when [b] supper was done (and that the
deuil had now put in the heart of Iudas Is
cariot, Simons *sonne*, to betraye him)
3 Iesus knowing that the Father had giuen
all things into his hands, & that he was come from God, and went to God,
4 He riseth from supper, and layeth aside
his vpper garments, and toke a towel, and
girde him self.
5 After that, he powred water into a basin,
and began to wash the disciples fete, and
to wipe them with the towel, wherewith
he was girde.
6 Then came he to Simon Peter, who said
to him, Lord, doest thou wash my fete?
7 Iesus answered and said vnto him, What
I do, thou knowest not now: but thou shalt
knowe it hereafter.
8 Peter said vnto him, Thou shalt neuer
wash my fete. Iesus answered him, If I
[c] wash thee not, thou shalt haue no parte
with me.

c And make thee cleane from thy sinnes.

9 Simon Peter said vnto him, Lord, not my
fete onely, but also the hands & the head.
10 Iesus said to him, He that is washed,
nedeth not, saue to [d] wash *his* fete, but
is cleane euerie whit: and ye are * cleane,
but not all.

d That is, to be continually purged of his corrupt affections and worldlie cares ẇ remaine dayly in vs.

Chap.15,3.

11 For he knewe who shulde betraye him:
therefore said he, Ye are not all cleane.
12 ¶ So after he had washed their fete, and
had taken his garments, and was set downe
againe, he said vnto them, Knowe ye what
I haue done to you?
13 Ye call me Master, and Lord, and ye say
wel: for so am I.
14 If I then your Lord, and Master, haue
washed your fete, ye also oght to wash
[e] one anothers fete.

e To serue one another.

15 For I haue giuen you an example, that
ye shulde do, euen as I haue done to you.
16 Verely, verely I say vnto you, * The seruant is not greater then his master, nether
the ambassadour greater then he that sent
him.

Chap.15,20. mat.10,4. luk.6,40.

17 If ye knowe these things, blessed are ye,
if ye do them.
18 ¶ I speake not of you all: I knowe whome
I haue chosen: but *it is* that the Scripture
might be fulfilled, * He ẏ eateth bread with
me, hathe [f] lift vp his hele against me.

Psal.41,10.

f Vnder pretence of friendship seketh his destruction.

19 From hence forthe tell I you before it
come, ẏ when it is come to passe, ye might
beleue that I am [g] he.

g To wit, the Christ and redemer of the worlde.

20 * Verely, verely I say vnto you, If I send
anie, he that receiueth him, receiueth me,
and he that receiueth me, receiueth him
that sent me.

Mat.10,40. luk.10,16.

21 When Iesus had said these things, he was
[h] troubled in the Spirit, & [i] testified, and
said, Verely, verely I say vnto you, that
one of you shal betraye me.

h For very horror & indignation of suche an abominable acte as Iudas shulde commit

i He did openly affirme.

22 * Then the disciples loked one on another, douting of whome he spake.
23 Now there was one of his disciples, ẇ
leaned on Iesus [k] bosome, whome Iesus
loued.

Mat.26,21. mar.14,18. luk.22,21.

k Their facion was not to sit at table, but hauing their shoes of, and cusshions vnder their elbowes, leaned on their sides, as it were halfe lying.

24 To him beckened therefore Simon Peter, ẏ he shulde aske who it was of whome he spake.
25 He then, as he leaned on Iesus brest, said
vnto him, Lord, who is it?
26 Iesus answered, He it is, to whome I shal
giue a soppe, when I haue dipte it: and he
wet a soppe, and gaue it to Iudas Iscariot,
Simons *sonne*.
27 And after the soppe, [l] Satan entred into
him. Thē said Iesus vnto him, That thou
doest, do quickely.

l Satā toke ful possession of him.

28 But none of them that were at table, knewe, for what cause he spake it vnto him.
29 For some of them thoght because Iudas
had the bagge, that Iesus had said vnto hī,
Bie those things that we haue nede of a-
gainst the feast: or that he shulde giue some thing to the poore.
30 Assone then as he had receiued the soppe, he went immediatly out, and it was
night.
31 ¶ When he was gone out, Iesus said,
[m] Now is the Sonne of man glorified, and
God is glorified in him.

m Meaning, ẏ his crosse shal ingender a marueilous glorie, and that in it shal shine the infinite bountie of God.

32 If God be glorified in him, God shal also glorifie him in him self, & shal straight
way glorifie him.
33 Litle childrē, yet a litle while am I with
you: ye shal seke me, but as I said vnto the
* Iewes, Whither I go, can ye not come:
also to you say I now,

Chap.7,34.

34 * [n] A new commandement giue I vnto
you, that ye loue one another: as I haue loued you, that ye also loue one another.

Leuit.19,18. mat.22,39. chap.15,12. 1.iohn 4,21.

n Whereof we oght to haue continual remēbrance as though it were euen newly giuen.

35 By this shal all mē knowe that ye are my
disciples, if ye haue loue one to another.
36 Simō Peter said vnto him, Lord, whither
goest thou? Iesus answered him, Whither
I go, thou canst not followe me now: but
thou [o] shalt followe me afterwardes.

o When thou shalt be more strong

37 Peter said vnto him, Lord, why can I
not followe thee now? * I wil lay downe my
life for thy sake.

Mat.26,34. mar.14,30.

38 Iesus answered him, Wilt thou lay downe thy life for my sake? Verely, verely I
say vnto thee, The cocke shal not crowe,

til thou haue denyed me thrise.

CHAP. XIIII.

1 He armeth his disciples with consolation against trouble. 2 He ascendeth into heauen to prepare vs a place. 6 The way, the trueth and the life. 10 The Father and Christ one. 13 How we shulde pray. 23 The promes vnto them that kepe his worde.

1 AND he said to his disciples, Let not
your heart be troubled: ye beleue in
God, [a] beleue also in me.
2 In my Fathers house are [b] many dwelling
places: if it were not so, I wolde haue tolde you:
I go to prepare a place for you.
3 And thogh I go to prepare a place for
you, I wil [c] come againe, and receiue you
vnto my self, that where I am, there may
ye be also.
4 And whither I go, ye knowe, and the way
ye knowe.
5 Thomas said vnto him, Lord, we [d] knowe
not whither thou goest: how can we then
knowe the way?
6 Iesus said vnto him, I am the [e] Way, and
the Trueth, & the Life. No man cometh
vnto the Father, but by me.
7 If ye had knowen me, ye shulde haue
knowen my Father also: and from hence
forthe ye knowe him, and haue sene him.
8 Philippe said vnto him, Lord, shewe vs
thy Father, and it suffiseth vs.
9 Iesus said vnto him, I haue bene so long
time with you, and hast thou not knowen
me, Philippe? he that hathe sene me, hathe
sene my Father: how then saist thou, Shewe
vs *thy* Father?
10 Beleuest thou not, that I am in the Father,
and [f] the Father is in me? The wordes
that I speake vnto you, I speake not of my
[g] self: but the Father that dwelleth in me,
he [h] doeth the workes.
11 Beleue me, that I *am* in the Father, and
the Father in me: at the least, beleue me
for the very workes sake.
12 Verely, verely I say vnto you, he that
beleueth in me, the workes that I do, [i] he
shal do also, & greater then these shal he
do: for I go vnto my Father.
13 *And whatsoeuer ye aske in my Name,
that wil I do, that the Father may be glorified
in the Sonne.
14 If ye shal aske any thing in my Name, I
wil do it.
15 If ye loue me, kepe my commandements,
16 And I wil pray the Father, and he shal
giue you another [k] Comforter, that he may
abide with you for euer,
17 *Euen* the Spirit of [l] trueth, whome the
worlde can not receiue, because it seeth
him not, nether knoweth him: but ye knowe
him: for he dwelleth with you, and shalbe
in you.
18 I wil not leaue you comfortles: *but* I wil
[m] come to you.

a For in so beleuing no troubles shal ouercome them.
b So that there is not onely place for him, but for all his.
c At the latter day, Act.1,11.
d He was not altogether ignorant, but his knowledge was weake and imperfite.
e Therefore we must begin in him, continewe in him, & end in him.
f For the verie fulnes of the diuinitie remaineth in Christ.
g In that, that he is man.
h Who declareth his maiestie and vertue by his doctrine and miracles.
i This is referred to the whole bodie of the Church in whome this vertue of Christ doeth shine & remaine for euer.
Chap.16,23. mat.7,7. mar.11,24. iam.1,5.
k I haue comforted you whiles I was with you, but henseforthe ẏ holie Gost shal comfort you, and preserue you.
l So called because he worketh in vs the trueth.
m Which thing he doeth by ẏ vertue of his Spirit.

19 Yet a litle while, and the worlde shal se
me no more, but ye shal se me: because I
liue, ye shal liue also.
20 At that day shal ye knowe that I am in
my Father, and you in me, and I in you.
21 He that hathe my commandements, and
kepeth them, is he that loueth me: and he
that loueth me, [n] shalbe loued of my Father:
and I wil loue him, and wil shewe
mine owne self to him.
22 Iudas said vnto him (not [o] Iscariot) Lord,
what is the cause that thou wilt shewe thy
self vnto vs, and not vnto the worlde?
23 Iesus answered, and said vnto him, If any
man loue me, he wil [p] kepe my worde, &
my Father wil loue him, and we wil come
vnto him, and wil dwell with him.
24 He that loueth me not, kepeth not my
wordes, and the worde which ye heare, is
not [q] mine, but the Fathers which sent me.
25 These things haue I spoken vnto you,
being present with you.
26 But the Comforter, which is the holie
Gost, whome the Father wil send in my
Name, he shal teache you all things, and
bring all things to your remembrance,
which I haue tolde you.
27 [r] Peace I leaue with you: my peace I giue
vnto you: not as the worlde giueth, giue
I vnto you. Let not your heart be troubled,
nor feare.
28 Ye haue heard how I said vnto you, I go
away, and wil come vnto you. If ye loued
me, ye wolde verely reioyce, because I
said, I go vnto the Father: for my Father
is [s] greater then I.
29 And now haue I spoken vnto you, before
it come, that when it is come to passe, ye
might beleue.
30 Hereafter wil I not speake many things
vnto you: for the [t] prince of this worlde
commeth, and hathe [u] noght in me.
31 But *it is* that the worlde may knowe that
I loue *my* Father: & as the Father hathe commanded
me, so I do. Arise, let vs go hence.

CHAP. XV.

6 The swete consolation, and mutual loue betwene Christ and his membres vnder the parable of the vine. 18 Of their commune afflictions and persecutions. 26 The office of the holie Gost and the Apostles.

1 I Am the true vine, and my Father is an
housband man.
2 *Euerie branche that beareth not frute in
me, he taketh away: & euerie one that beareth
frute, he purgeth it, that it may bring
forthe more frute.
3 *Now are ye cleane through the worde,
which I haue spoken vnto you.
4 Abide in me, and I in you: as the branche
can not beare frute of it self, except it abide
in the vine, no more can ye, [a] except ye
abide in me.
5 I am the vine: ye *are* the branches: he that
abideth

n He shal sensibly feele ẏ the grace of God abideth in him.
o But the brother of Iames.
p Whereby he aduertiseth them not to haue respect to ẏ worlde, lest they shulde be drawen backe by euil example.
q That is, not his alone: for he had nothig separate from his Father.
r All comfort & prosperitie.
s In that, that Christ is become man to be Mediator betwene God & vs.
t Satan executeth his rage & tyrannie by the permission of God.
u Satan shal assaile me with all his force, but he shal not finde that in me which he loketh for: for I am that innocent lambe without spot.
Mat.15,13.
Chap.13,10.
a We can bring forthe no frute, except we be ingraffed in Christ.

abideth in me,& I in him,the same bringeth forthe muche frute: for without me cã
ye do nothing.
6 If a man abide not in me, he is cast forthe as a branche,and withereth : and men
gather them, and cast *them* into the fyre,
and they burne.
7 If ye abide in me and my [b] wordes abide
in you,aske [c] what ye wil,and it shalbe done to you.
8 Herein is my Father glorified, that ye
beare muche frute,and be made my disciples.
9 As the Father hathe loued me, so haue I
loued you: continue in [d]my loue.
10 If ye shal kepe my commandements,ye
shal abide in my loue, as I haue kept my
Fathers commandements,and abide in his
loue.
11 These things haue I spokẽ vnto you,that
my ioye might remaine in you, and that
your ioye might be [e] ful.
12 *This is my commandement,that ye loue one another,as I haue loued you.
13 Greater loue then this hathe no man,
when any man bestoweth his life for his
friends.
14 Ye are my friends, if ye do whatsoeuer
I commande you.
15 Henceforthe,call I you not seruants:for
the seruant knoweth not what his master
doeth: but I haue called you friends : for
[f]all things that I haue heard of my Father,haue I made knowen to you.
16 Ye haue not chosen me, but I haue chosen you, and ordeined you, *that ye go &
bring forthe frute, and that your frute remaine, that whatsoeuer ye shal aske of the
Father in my Name,he may giue it you.
17 These things commande I you, that ye
loue one another.
18 If the worlde hate you, ye knowe that it
hated me before you.
19 If ye were of the worlde,the worlde wolde loue his owne: but because ye are not
of the worlde, but I haue chosen you out
of the worlde, therefore the worlde hateth you.
20 Remember the worde that I said vnto
you, * The seruant is not greater then his
master.*If they haue persecuted me, they
wil persecute you also : if they haue [g] kept
my worde,they wil also kepe [h] yours.
21 But all these things wil they do vnto you
for my Names sake,because they haue not
knowen him that sent me.
22 If I had not come and spoken vnto thẽ,
they [i] shulde not haue had sinne : but now
haue they no [k] cloke for their sinne.
23 He ͤ hateth me,hateth my Father also.
24 If I had not done workes among them
which none other man did, they had not
had sinne:but now haue thei bothe sene,&

b We must be rooted in Iesus Christ by faith,which cometh of the worde of God
c So that ye folowe Gods worde, which ye comprehẽd by faith.
d Wherewith I loue you.
e Perfect and entier.
Chap.13,34. 1.thess.1,9. 1.iohn 3,11. & 4,21.
f So that there is nothing omitted that is necessarie for vs and concerning our saluation.
Mat.28,19.
g The worde also signifieth, to be diligent to espie fautes to trippe one in.
h Which is ͤ self same worde, but called theirs because they preache it.
Chap.13,16. mat.10,24.
Mat.24,9.
i But shulde haue semed to be innocent, if I had not discouered their malice.
k In that they refused Christ it taketh from them all excuse wherewith they wolde haue iustified them selues as if they had bene very holie & without all sinne.

haue hated bothe me,and my Father.
25 But *it is* that the worde might be fulfilled,that is written in their [l] Law, * They
hated me without a cause.
26 But when ͤ Comforter shal come,*whome I wil send vnto you from the Father,
euen the Spirit of trueth,which proceadeth
of the Father,he shal testifie of me.
27 And ye shal witnesse also,because ye haue bene with me from the beginning.

Psal.35,19.
l That is, in the holie Scriptures.
Chap.14,26. luk.24,49.

CHAP. XVI.

2 He putteth them in remembrance of the crosse, and of their owne infirmitie to come. 7 And therefore doeth comfort thẽ with the promes of the holie Gost. 16 Of the comming againe of Christ. 17 Of his ascension. 23 To aske in the Name of Christ. Peace in Christ,& in the worlde affliction.

1 These things haue I said vnto you,
that ye shulde not be [a] offended.
2 They shal "excommunicate you:yea,the
time shal come, that whosoeuer killeth
you,wil thinke that he doeth God seruice.
3 And these things wil they do vnto you,
because they haue not knowen the Father,
nor me.
4 But these things haue I tolde you, that
when the houre shal come,ye might remẽ
ber,that I tolde you thẽ. And these things
[b] said I not vnto you from the beginning,
because I was with you.
5 But now I go my way to him that sent me
and none of you asketh me, [c] Whither
goest thou?
6 But because I haue said these things vnto
you,your hearts are ful of sorowe.
7 Yet I tel you the trueth, It is expedient
for you that I go away: for if I go not a-
way,the Cõforter wil not come vnto you:
but if I departe, I wil send him vnto you.
8 And when he is come,he wil [d]reproue the
worlde of sinne, and of righteousnes, and
of iudgement.
9 Of [e] sinne, because they beleue not
in me:
10 Of [f] righteousnes, because I go to my
Father,and ye shal se me no more:
11 Of [g] iudgemẽt,because the prince of this
worlde is iudged.
12 I haue yet [h] manie things to say vnto
you,but ye can not beare them now.
13 Howbeit, when he is come which is the
Spirit of trueth, he wil lead you into all
trueth : for he shal not speake of him self,
but whatsoeuer he shal heare,shal he speake, and he wil shewe you the things [i] to
come.
14 He shal glorifie me : for he shal receiue
of mine,and shal shewe it vnto you.
15 All thiñgs that the Father hathe, are mi-

a And so shrinke from me.
"Greke, put you out of the Synagogues.
b He bare ͤ them because they were but weakelings.
c For if you did consider, ye wolde reioyce.
d Or, conuince. This is to be vnderstand of the cõming of the holie Gost when his vertue and strength shal shine in the Church.
e His enemies which contẽned him,& put him to death, shalbe couict by their owne conscience,for that they did not beleue in him, Act.2,37. and shal know that without Iesus Christ there is nothing but sinne.
f Wherefore ͤ wicked must nedes cõfesse ͭ he was iuste, & beloued of his Father, & not condemned by him as a blasphemer or transgressor. g When they shal knowe that I(whome they called the carpenters sonne,and willed to come downe frõ the crosse) am the verie Sõne of God which haue ouercome all the power of hel and reigne ouer all,2 Cor.10,12.ephe.1,19. h These things are conteined in the doctrine of the Apostles which onely is sufficient. i As touching the spiritual kingdome of God:for the Apostles knewe not that til after the resurrection.

ne: therefore ſaid I, that he ſhal take of
mine,and ſhewe it vnto you.
16 [k] A litle *while*,and ye ſhal not ſe me:and
againe a litle *while*, and ye ſhal ſe me: for
I [l] go to my Father.
17 Thē ſaid *ſome* of his diſciples amōg thē
ſelues, What is this that he ſaith vnto vs,
A litle *while*,and ye ſhal not ſe me,& againe,a litle *while*, and ye ſhal ſe me, and, For
I go to my Father?
18 They ſaid therefore, What is this that
he ſaith, A litle *while*? we knowe not what
he ſaith.
19 Now Ieſus knewe that they wolde aſke
him,and ſaid vnto them, Do ye enquire a-
mong your ſelues, of that I ſaid, A litle
while,and ye ſhal not ſe me: and againe, a
litle *while*,and ye ſhal ſe me?
20 Verely, verely I ſay vnto you, that ye
ſhal wepe and lament,and the worlde ſhal
reioyce:& ye ſhal ſorowe,but your ſorowe
ſhalbe turned to ioye.
21 A woman when ſhe trauaileth, hathe ſorowe,becauſe her houre is come: but aſſone as ſhe is deliuered of the childe, ſhe remembreth no more the anguiſh, for ioye
that a man is borne into the worlde.
22 And ye now therefore are in ſorowe:but
I wil ſe you [m] againe,and your hearts ſhal
reioyce, and your ioye ſhal [n] no man take
from you.
23 And in ỹ day ſhal ye aſke me [o] nothing.
*Verely, verely I ſay vnto you, whatſoe-
uer ye ſhal aſke the Father in my Name,
he wil giue it you.
24 Hitherto haue ye aſked [p] nothing in my
Name:aſke,and ye ſhal receiue, that your
ioye may be ful.
25 Theſe things haue I ſpoken vnto you in
parables: but the time wil come, when I
ſhal no more ſpeake to you in parables:
but I ſhal ſhewe you plainely of ỹ Father.
26 At that day ſhal ye aſke in my Name,&
I ſay not vnto you, that I [q] wil pray vnto
the Father for you.
27 For the Father him ſelf loueth you, becauſe ye haue loued me, * and haue beleued that I came out from God.
28 I am come out from the Father, & came
into the worlde: againe I leaue the worlde,and go to the Father.
29 His diſciples ſaid vnto him, Lo, now
ſpeakeſt thou plainely, and thou ſpeakeſt
no parable.
30 Now knowe we that thou knoweſt all
things, and nedeſt not that any mā ſhulde
aſke thee. By this we beleue, that thou art
come out from God.
31 Ieſus anſwered them, Do you beleue
now?
32 *Beholde,the houre cometh, & is alreadie come, that ye ſhalbe ſcattred euerie
mā into his owne,and ſhal leaue me alone:

k Mine abſence ſhal not be long: for I wil ſend you ỹ holie Goſt, who ſhal remaine with you for euer.
l Frō death I paſſe to glorie and ſo wil I in due you with mine heauēlie vertue.
m By ỹ power and vertue of the holie Goſt.
n For it ſhalbe grounded vpō my reſurrectiō & the grace of the holie Goſt.
Chap.14,13. mat.7,7. & 21,22. mar.11,24. luk.11,9. iam 1,5.
o For ye ſhal haue perfect knowledge, & ſhal no more doute as you were wont.
p In reſpect of that that you ſhal obteine, if you aſke in faith.
Chap.17,8.
q Chriſt denieth not that he is ỹ mediator, but ſheweth that they ſhal obteine their requeſtes without difficultie or any paine.
Mat.26,31. mar.14,27.

but I am not [r] alone: for the Father is
with me.
33 Theſe things haue I ſpoken vnto you,
ỹ [ſ] in me ye might haue peace: in the worlde ye ſhal haue affliction, but be of good
comfort: I haue ouercome the worlde.

CHAP. XVII.

1 The prayer of Chriſt vnto his Father, bothe for him ſelf and his Apoſtles, and alſo for all ſuche as receiue the trueth.

1 THeſe things ſpake Ieſus, and lift vp
his eyes to heauen, & ſaid, Father the
houre is come: glorifie thy Sonne, that thy
Sonne alſo may glorifie thee,
2 *As thou haſt giuen him [a] power *ouer* all
fleſh,that he ſhulde giue eternal life to all
[b] them that thou haſt giuen him.
3 And this is life eternal, that they knowe
thee *to be* the onely verie God,and whome
thou haſt ſent, Ieſus [c] Chriſt.
4 I haue [d] glorified thee on the earth: I haue finiſhed the worke which thou gaueſt
me to do.
5 And now glorifie me, thou Father, with
thine owne ſelf, with ỹ glorie which I had
with thee before the worlde was.
6 I haue declared thy Name vnto the men
which thou gaueſt me out of the worlde:
[e] thine they were, and thou gaueſt thē me,
and they haue kept thy worde.
7 Now they knowe that all things whatſoeuer thou haſt giuen me, are of thee.
8 For I haue giuen vnto them the wordes,
which thou gaueſt me, and they haue recei
ued *them*, *and haue knowen ſurely that I
came out from thee, and haue beleued that
thou haſt ſent me.
9 I pray for them: I pray not for [f] ỹ worlde, but for them which thou haſt giuen
me: for they are thine.
10 And all mine are thine, and thine are mine, and I am glorified in them.
11 And now am I no more in the worlde, but
theſe are in the worlde, & I come to thee.
Holie Father, kepe them in thy Name, *euen*
them whome thou haſt giuen me, that they
may be [g] one, as we *are*.
12 While I was with them in the worlde,
I kept them in thy Name: thoſe that thou
gaueſt me, haue I kept, and none of them
is loſt, but the [h] childe of perdition, that
the * Scripture might be fulfilled.
13 And now come I to thee, & theſe things
ſpeake I in ỹ worlde, that they might haue my ioye fulfilled in them ſelues.
14 I haue giuen them thy worde, and the
worlde hathe hated them, becauſe they are
[i] not of the worlde, as I am not of ỹ worlde.
15 I pray not that thou ſhuldeſt take them
out of the worlde, but that thou kepe them
from euil.
16 They are not of the worlde, as I am not
of the worlde.

r Althogh mē forſake Chriſt, yet is he no whit diminiſhed: for he & his Father are one
ſ We haue reſt & cōfort when we are truely graffed in Chriſt.
Mat.28,18.
a Chriſt hathe all rule & dominion ouer men.
b Which are the elect.
c That is, that thei acknowledge bothe ỹ Father, & the Sonne to be verie God.
d Aſwel by doctrine as miracles.
e Our electiō ſtādeth in the good pleaſure of God, which is the onlie fundation, & cauſe of our ſaluation, and is declared to vs in Chriſt, through whome we are iuſtified by faith and ſanctified, Rom.8,39. ephe.1,4.
Chap.16,27.
f That is, the reprobate.
g That they may be ioyned in vnitie of faith & ſpirit.
h He was ſo called, not onely for ỹ he periſhed, but becauſe God had appointed and ordeined him to this end, Act.1,16. & 4,27.
Pſal.109,8.
i But are ſeparate by the ſpirit of regeneration.

17 *[k] Sanctifie

17 "k Sanctifie thẽ with thy trueth: thy worde is trueth.
18 As thou diddest send me into the worlde, so haue I sent them into the worlde.
19 And for their sakes sanctifie I my self,
that they also may be l sanctified through
the trueth.
20 I pray not for these alone, but for them
also which shal beleue in me, through
their worde,
21 That they all may be one, as thou, ô Father, *art* in me, and I in thee: *euen* that they
may be also one in vs, that the m worlde
may beleue that thou hast sent me.
22 And the glorie that thou gauest me, I
n haue giuen them, that they may be one,
as we are one,
23 I in them, and thou in me, that they may
be made perfect in one, & that the worlde
may know, that thou hast sent me, & hast
loued them, as thou hast loued me.
24 *Father, I wil that they which thou hast
giuen me, be o with me euen where I am,
that they may beholde my glorie, which
thou hast giuen me: for thou louedst me
before the fundation of the worlde.
25 O righteous Father, the worlde also hathe not knowen thee, but I haue knowen
thee, and these haue knowen, that thou hast
sent me.
26 And I haue declared vnto them thy
Name, and wil declare it, that the loue
wherewith thou hast loued me, may be in
them, and I in p them.

"Or, consecrat the͂ to thy self. k Renewe the͂ w͂ thine heauenlie grace, y͑ they onely may seke thy wil. l Which thi͂g declareth that Christs holines is ours. m That the infideles may by experience be conuicted to confesse my glorie. n I haue shewed the͂ the example and patron of perfect felicitie. *Chap.12,16.* o That they maie profit, and growe vp in suche sort y͑ in y͑ end they may enioy the eternal glorie with me. p For without him we ca͂ not comprehende the loue wherewith God loueth vs.

CHAP. XVIII.

3 Christ is betrayed. 6 The wordes of his mouth smite the officers to the grounde. 10 Peter smiteth of Malchus eare. 13 Iesus is broght before Annas and Caiaphas. 25 Where Peter denieth him. 36 He telleth Pilate what his kingdome is.

1 WHen Iesus had spokẽ these things,
he went forthe with his disciples
ouer y͑ a broke *Cedrõ, where was a gardẽ,
into the which he entred, and his disciples.
2 And Iudas which betrayed him, knewe
also the place: for Iesus oft times resorted
thither with his disciples.
3 *Iudas then after he had receiued a b bãde of men and officers of the high Priests,
and of the Pharises, came thither with lan-
ternes and torches, and weapons.
4 Then Iesus, knowing all things that shul
de come vnto him, went forthe and said
vnto them, Whome seke ye?
5 They answered him, Iesus of Nazaret. Iesus said vnto thẽ, I am he. Now Iudas also
which betrayed him, stode with them.
6 Assone then as he had said vnto them, I
am he, they wẽt backewards, and fel to the
grounde.
7 Then he asked them againe, Whome seke
ye? And they said, Iesus of Nazaret.
8 Iesus answered, I said vnto you, that I
am he: therefore if ye seke me, let these go
their way,
9 *This was* that the worde might be fulfilled which he spake, * c Of thẽ which thou
gauest me, haue I lost none.
10 Then Simon Peter hauing a sworde,
drewe it, and smote the high Priests seruant, and cut of his right eare. Now the
seruants name was Malchus.
11 Then said Iesus vnto Peter, Put vp thy
sworde into the sheath: shal I not drinke
of y͑ cup which *my* Father hathe giuẽ me?
12 Then the bande and the captaine, & the
officers of the Iewes toke Iesus, and bounde him,
13 And led him away to * d Annas first (for
he was Father in law to Caiaphas, which
was the high Priest e that same yere)
14 *And Caiaphas was he, that gaue counsel to the Iewes, that it was expedient that
one man shulde dye for the people.
15 ¶ *Now Simon Peter followed Iesus, &
another disciple, and that disciple was
knowẽ of the high Priest: therefore he wẽt
in with Iesus into the hall of y͑ high Priest.
16 But Peter stode at the dore without.
Then went out the other disciple which
was knowen vnto the high Priest, and spake to her that kept the dore, and broght
in Peter.
17 Then said the maide that kept the dore,
vnto Peter, Art not thou also one of this
mans disciples? He said, I am not.
18 And the seruants and officers stode there, which had made a fyre of coles: for it
was colde, and they warmed them selues.
And Peter also stode among them & warmed him self.
19 (¶ The high Priest then asked Iesus of
his disciples, and of his doctrine.
20 Iesus answered him, I spake f openly
to the worlde: I euer taught in the Synagogue & in the Tẽple, whither the Iewes
resorte continually, and in secret haue I
said nothing.
21 Why askest thou me? aske them which
heard me what I said vnto them: beholde,
they knowe what I said.
22 When he had spoken these things, one of
the officers which stode by, smote Iesus
with *his* rod, saying, Answerest thou the
high Priest so?
23 Iesus answered him, If I haue euil spoken, beare witnes of the euil: but if I haue
wel spoken, why smitest thou me?
24 ¶ Now Annas had g sent him bounde vnto Caiaphas the high Priest)
25 * And Simon Peter stode and warmed
him self, and they said vnto him, Art not
thou also of his disciples? He denied it, &
said, I am not.
26 One of the seruants of the high Priest,
his cousin whose eare Peter smote of, said,

1.Kin.15,13. mat.26,36. mar.14,32. luk.22,39. a Which was a deepe valley through y͑ which a strea me ra͂ne after a great raine. *Mat.26,47. mar.14,43. luk.22,47.* b The which he had obteined of the gouernour of the Temple.

Chap.17,12. c He bothe spareth their bodies & also saueth their soules. *Luk.3,2.* d Who sent Christ vnto Caiaphas the high Priest bounde. *Chap.11,50.* e Although this office was for terme of life by Gods ordinance, yet the ambition, and dissension of y͑ Iewes caused the Romaines from time to time to change it either for briberie or fauour. *Mat.26,58. mar.14,54. luk.22,54.* f That is, fra͂kely, and plainely. g After that Caiaphas had first sent him to him. *Mat.26,57. mar 14,59 luk.22,54.*

Did not I se thee in the garden with him?
27 Peter then denied againe, and immediatly the cocke crewe.

Mat.27,2. mar.15,1. luk.23,1. Act.10,28. & 11,3.

28 ¶ * Then led they Iesus from Caiaphas
into the commune hall. Now it was morning & thei them selues went not into the
cōmune hall, lest they shulde be *defiled,
but that they might eat the Passeouer.
29 Pilate then went out vnto them, and
said, What accusation bring ye against
this man?
30 They answered and said vnto him, If he
were not an euil doer, we wolde not haue
deliuered him vnto thee.

h He spake this disdainfully, because they were so bent against all right and equitie.

31 Then said Pilate vnto them, Take [h] ye
him, and iudge him after your owne Law.
Then the Iewes said vnto him, It is not
[i] lawful for vs to put anie man to death.

Mat.20,19.

i As if they shulde say, Thou wilt not suffre vs to do it: for he knew that it was not permitted to them by the Romaines to punish with death.

32 *It was* that the worde of Iesus * might
be fulfilled which he spake, signifyīg what
death he shulde dye.
33 *So Pilate entred into the commune hall
againe, and called Iesus, & said vnto him,
Art thou the King of the Iewes?

Mat.27,11. mar.15,2. luk.23,31.

34 Iesus answered him, Saist thou that of
thy self, or did other tel it thee of me?
35 Pilate answered, Am I a Iewe? Thine
owne nation, and the high Priests haue
deliuered thee vnto me. What hast thou
done?
36 Iesus answered, My kingdome is not of
this [k] worlde: if my kingdome were of this
worlde, my seruants wolde surely fight,
that I shulde not be deliuered to ẏ Iewes:
but now is my kingdome not from hence.

k It standeth not in strength of men nor in worldelie defence.

37 Pilate then said vnto him, Art thou a
King thē? Iesus answered, Thou saist that
I am a King: for this cause am I borne, &
for this cause came I into the worlde, that
I shulde beare witnes vnto the trueth: euerie one that is of the trueth, heareth my
voyce.

l This was a mocking and disdeineful question.

38 Pilate said vnto him, [l] What is trueth?
And when he had said that, he went out
againe vnto the Iewes, & said vnto them,
I finde in him no cause at all.

Mat.27,15. mar.15,6. luk.23,27.

m This was one of their blinde abuses: for the Law of God gaue no libertie to quite a wicked trespaser.

39 *But you haue a [m] custome, that I shulde
deliuer you one lose at the Passeouer: wil
ye then that I lose vnto you the King of
the Iewes?

Act.3,14.

40 *Thē cryed they all againe, saying, Not
him, but Barabbas: now this Barabbas was
a murtherer.

CHAP. XIX.

1 When Pilate colde not aswage the rage of the Iewes against Christ, he deliuereth him vp with his superscription to be hanged betwixt two theeues. 23 They cast lottes for his garments. 26 He commendeth his mother vnto Iohn. 28 Calleth for drinke. 33 Dyeth, and his side is perced, and taken downe from the crosse. 38 He is buryed.

Mat.27,26. mar.15,18.

1 THen * Pilate toke Iesus & [a] scourged
him.

a He thoght to haue pacified the furie of the Iewes by some indifferent correction.

2 And the souldiers platted a crowne of
thornes, and put it on his head, and they
put on him a purple garment,
3 And said, Hail, King of the Iewes. And
they smote him with *their* roddes.
4 Then Pilate went forthe againe, and said
vnto them, Beholde, I bring him forthe to
you, that ye may knowe, ẏ I finde no faute
in him at all.
5 Thē came Iesus forthe wearing a crowne
of thornes, and a purple garment. And *Pilate* said vnto them, [b] Beholde the man.

b He spake in mockerie, because Christ called him self King.

6 Then when the high Priests and officers
sawe him, they cryed, saying, Crucifie, crucifie *him*. Pilate said vnto them, Take ye
him and crucifie *him*: for I finde no faute
in him.
7 The Iewes answered him, We haue a
Law, and by our Law he oght to dye, because he made him self the [c] Sōne of God.

c Christ was in dede the Sonne of God, and therefore might iustly call him self so without breache of ẏ Law: wherefore their colored accusation was falsely applied.

8 ¶ Whē Pilate then heard that worde, he
was the more afraide,
9 And went againe into the commune hall
and said vnto Iesus, Whēce art thou? But
Iesus gaue him none answere.
10 Thē said Pilate vnto him, Speakest thou
not vnto me? Knowest thou not that I haue
power to crucifie thee, and haue power to
lose thee?
11 Iesus answered, Thou coldest haue no
[d] power at all against me, except it were gi
uen thee from aboue: therefore he that
deliuered me vnto thee, hathe the greater
sinne.

d Hereby he sheweth him, that he oght not to abuse his office and autoritie.

12 From thence forthe Pilate soght to lose
him, but the Iewes cryed, saying, If thou
deliuer him, thou art not Cesars friend: *for*
whosoeuer maketh him self a King, speaketh against Cesar.
13 ¶ When Pilate heard that worde, he
broght Iesus forthe, and sate downe in the
iudgement seat in a place called the [e] Pauement, and in Hebrewe, Gabbatha.

e A place somewhat high & raised vp.

14 And it was the Preparation of the Passeouer, and about the [f] sixt houre: and he said
vnto the Iewes, Beholde your King.

f Which was midday.

15 But they cryed, Away with him, away
with him, crucifie him. Pilate said vnto
them, Shal I crucifie your King? The high
Priests answered, We haue no King but
Cesar.
16 Then deliuered he him vnto them, to be
crucified. * And they toke Iesus, and led
him away.

Mat.27,31. mar.15,21. luk.23,26.

17 And he bare his crosse, and came into a
place named *of dead mens* Skulles, which is
called in Ebrewe, [g] Golgotha:

g Which was the place of execution.

18 Where thei crucified him, & two other ẇ
him, on ether side one, & Iesus in ẏ middes.
19 ¶ And Pilate wrote also a title and put
it on the crosse, and it was written, IESVS
OF NAZARET THE KING OF
THE IEWES.

20 This

20 This title then red manie of the Iewes:
for the place where Iesus was crucified,
was nere to the citie: and it was written in
[h] Hebrewe, Greke and Latin.
21 Then said the hie Priests of the Iewes
to Pilate, Write not, The King of the
Iewes, but that he said, I am King of the
Iewes.
22 Pilate answered, What I haue written,
I haue written.
23 ¶ Then the * souldiers, when they had
crucified Iesus, toke his garments & made
foure partes, to euerie souldier a parte, &
his coate: and the coate was without seame,
wouen from the top throughout.
24 Therefore thei said one to another, Let
vs not deuide it, but cast lots for it, whose
it shalbe. *This was* that ẏ [i] Scripture might
be fulfilled, which saith, * They departed
my garmẽts among them, & on my coate
did cast lottes. So the souldiers did these
things in dede.
25 ¶ Then stode by the crosse of Iesus his
mother, and his mothers sister, Marie *the
wife of* ″Cleopas, and Marie Magdalene.
26 And when Iesus sawe his mother, & the
disciple standing by whome he loued, he
said vnto his mother, Womã, beholde thy
sonne.
27 Then said he to the disciple, Beholde
thy mother: and from that houre, the disciple toke her home vnto him.
28 ¶ After, when Iesus knewe that all things
were performed, that ẏ * Scripture might
be fulfilled, he said, I thirst.
29 And there was set a vessel ful of vinegre: & they filled a sponge with vinegre,
and [k] put it about [l] an hyssope *stalke*, and
put it to his mouth.
30 Now when Iesus had receiued of the vinegre, he said, [m] It is finished, and bowed
his head, and gaue vp the gost.
31 The Iewes then (because it was the Preparacion, that the bodies shulde not remaine vpõ the crosse on the Sabbath *day*:
for that Sabbath was an [n] hie day) besoght
Pilate that their legges might be broken,
and that they might be taken downe.
32 Then came the souldiers and brake the
legges of the first, and of the other, which
was crucified with *Iesus*.
33 But when they came to Iesus, and sawe
that he was dead alreadie, they brake not
his legges.
34 But one of the souldiers with a speare
[o] perced his side, & forthewith came there
out blood and water.
35 And he that sawe it, bare recorde, & his
recorde is true: and he knoweth that he
saith true, that ye might beleue it.
36 For these things were done, ẏ the * Scripture shulde be fulfilled, Not a bone of
him shalbe broken.

h Because all nacions might vnderstand it.

Mat.27,35. mar.15,24. luk.23,33.

i That which was prefigured in Dauid, was accõplished in Iesus Christ.

Psal.22,20.

″Or, Clopas.

Psal.68,22.

k Or fastened it vpon an hyssope stalke.

l It may appeare that ẏ crosse was not hie, seing a man might reache Christs mouth with an hyssope stalke, ẇ as appeareth, 1. King 4,33 was the lowest amongs herbes, as ẏ cedre was hiest amongs trees.

m Mans saluacion is perfected by the onelie sacrifice of Christ: & all ẏ ceremonies of the Law are ended.

n Because the day of the Passeouer fel on the Sabbath day.

o Which declareth that he was dead in dede as he rose againe from death to life.

Exod.12,46. nomb.9,12.

37 And againe another Scripture saith,
* Thei shal se him whome thei haue thrust
through.
38 * And after these things, Ioseph of Arimathea (who was a disciple of Iesus, but
[p] secretly for feare of the Iewes) besoght
Pilate that he might take downe the bodie of Iesus. And Pilate gaue him licẽce.
He came then and toke Iesus bodie.
39 And there came * also Nicodemus (which
first came to Iesus by night) and broght of
myrrhe & aloes mingled together about
an hundreth pounde.
40 [q] Then toke thei ẏ bodie of Iesus, and
wrapped it in linnen clothes with the o-
dours, as the maner of ẏ Iewes is to burie.
41 And in that place where Iesus was crucified, was a garden, and in the garden a
new sepulchre, wherein was neuer man yet
laid.
42 There then laid they Iesus, because of
the Iewes Preparacion *day*, for the sepulchre was nere.

Zach.12,10.

Mat.27,57. mar 15,42. luk.23,50.

p That is to say, before Christs death, but now he declareth him self manifestly

Chap.3,2.

q This honorable buryal was as a preparaciõ & entrie vnto the resurrection.

CHAP. XX.

1 Marie Magdalene cometh to the sepulchre. 3 So do Peter & Iohn. 12 The two Angels appeare. 17 Christ appeareth to Marie Magdalene, 19 And to all his disciples. 27 The incredulitie & confession of Thomas.

1 NOw * the first *day* of the weke came
Marie Magdalene, earely when it
was yet [a] darke, vnto the sepulchre, and
sawe the stone taken away from the tõbe.
2 Then she ranne, and came to Simon Peter, and to the other disciple whome Iesus
loued, and said vnto them, They haue taken away the Lord out of the sepulchre,
and we knowe not where they haue laid
him.
3 Peter therefore went forthe, & the other
disciple, & they came vnto the sepulchre.
4 So they ranne bothe together, but the o-
ther disciple did out runne Peter, and came first to the sepulchre.
5 And he stouped downe, and sawe the linnen clothes lying: yet went he not in.
6 Then came Simon Peter folowing him,
and went into the sepulchre, and sawe the
linnen clothes lye,
7 And the ″kerchefe that was vpõ his head,
not lying ẇ the linnen clothes, but wrapped together in a place by it self.
8 Then went in also the [b] other disciple,
which came first to the sepulchre, and he
sawe it, [c] and beleued.
9 For as yet they knewe not the Scripture,
That he must rise againe from the dead.
10 And the disciples went away againe vnto their ″ owne home.
11 ¶ * But Marie stode without at the sepulchre weping: & as she wept, she bowed
her self into the sepulchre,
12 And sawe two Angels in white, sitting,
the one at the head, & the other at the se-

Mar.16,1. luk.24,1.

a She departed frõ home before day, & came thether about the sunne rising, Mar 16,2.

″Or, napkin.

b That is, Iohn ẇ wrote this Gospel

c He beleued ẏ Christs bodie was taken away, according as Marie reported.

″Or, to their companie.

Mat.28,1. mar.16,5.

te,where the bodie of Iesus had laine.
13 And they said vnto her, Woman, why
wepest thou? She said vnto them, Thei haue taken away my Lord, and I knowe not
where they haue laid him.
14 When she had thus said, she turned her
self backe and sawe Iesus standing, and
knewe not that it was Iesus.
15 Iesus saith vnto her, Womã, why wepest
thou? whome sekest thou? She supposing
that he had bene the gardener, said vnto
him, Syr, if thou hast borne him hence, tell
me where thou hast laid him, and I wil take him away.
16 Iesus saith vnto her, Marie. She turned
her self, & said vnto him, Rabboni, which
is to say, Master.
17 Iesus saith vnto her, Touche me not: for
I am not yet [d] ascended to my Father, but
go to my [e] brethren, and say vnto them, I
ascend vnto my Father, & to your Father,
and to my God, and your [f] God.
18 Marie Magdalene came and tolde the
disciples that she had sene the Lord, and
that he had spoken these things vnto her.
19 ¶ * The same daye then at night, which
was the first *day* of the weeke, and when
the [g] dores were shut where the disciples
were assembled for feare of the Iewes, came Iesus and stode in the middes, & said
to them, [h] Peace *be* vnto you.
20 And when he had so said, he shewed vnto them *his* hands, and his side. Then were the disciples glad when they had sene
the Lord.
21 Then said Iesus to them againe, Peace
be vnto you: as my Father sent me, so
send I you.
22 And whẽ he had said that, he [i] breathed
on them, and said vnto them, Receiue the
holie Gost.
23 * Whosoeuers sinnes ye remit, they are
remitted vnto them: & whosoeuers sinnes
ye reteine, they are reteined.
24 ¶ But Thomas one of the twelue, called
Didymus, was not with them when Iesus
came.
25 The other disciples therefore said vnto
him, We haue sene the Lord: but he said
vnto them, Except I se in his hands the
print of the nailes, and put my finger into
the "print of the nailes, and put mine hand
into his side, I wil not beleue it.
26 ¶ And eight daies after againe his disciples were within, and Thomas with them.
Then came Iesus, whẽ the dores were shut,
and stode in the middes, and said, Peace
be vnto you.
27 After, said he to Thomas, Put thy finger
here, and se mine hands, and put forthe
thine hand, and put it into my side, and be
not faithles, but faithful.
28 Then Thomas answered, and said vnto
him, *Thou art* my Lord, and my God.
29 Iesus said vnto him, Thomas, because
thou hast sene me, thou beleuest: blessed
are they that haue [k] not sene, and haue
beleued.
30 ¶ * And manie other signes also did Iesus in the presence of his disciples, which
are not written in this boke.
31 But these things are written, y^t ye might
beleue, that Iesus is the Christ the Sonne
of God, and that in beleuing ye might
haue life through his Name.

d Because she was to muche addicted to the corporal presence, Christ teacheth her to lift vp her mĩde by faith into heauẽ where onely after his ascension he remaineth, & where we sit with him at ye right hãd of the Father.

Mar.16,14. luk.24,35. 1.cor.15,5

e That is, the disciples: for he was ye first borne amongs manie brethrẽ, Psal.22,23. rom 8,29. colos 1,18.

f He is our Father & o^r God, because Iesus Christ is our brother.

Mat.28,18.

g So that no man opened him the dores, but by his diuine power he caused them to opẽ of their owne accord, as of Peter is red, Act.5,19 & 12,10.

h Or all prosperitie: w^c maner of greting ye Iewes vsed.

i To giue thẽ greater power & vertue to execute y^r weightie charge that he wolde commit vnto them.

"Or, place.

k Which depend vpon the simplicitie of Gods worde, & grounde not thẽ selues vpõ mans sense and reason.

Chap.21,23.

CHAP. XXI.

1 Christ appeareth to his disciples againe. 15 He commãdeth Peter earnestly to fede his shepe. 18 He forewarneth him of his death, 25 And of Christs manifolde miracles.

1 After these things, Iesus shewed him
self againe to his disciples at y^e "sea
of Tiberias: and thus shewed he *him self*.
2 There were together Simon Peter, and
Thomas, which is called Didymus, & Nathanael of Cana in Galile, and the *sonnes*
of Zebedeus, & two other of his disciples.
3 Simon Peter said vnto them, I go a fish-
ing. They said vnto him, We also wil go
with thee. They went their way and entred into a ship straight way, & that night
caught they nothing.
4 But when the morning was now come,
Iesus stode on the shore: neuertheles the
disciples knewe not that it was Iesus.
5 Iesus then said vnto them, "Sirs, haue ye
anie meat? They answered him, No.
6 Then he said vnto them, Cast out the
net on the right side of the ship, & ye shal
finde. So they [a] cast out, and they were not
able at all to drawe it, for the multitude
of fishes.
7 Therefore said the disciple whome Iesus
loued, vnto Peter, It is the Lord. When
Simon Peter heard that it was the Lord,
he girde his [b] coate to him (for he was naked) and cast him self into the sea.
8 But the other disciples came by shippe
(for they were not farre from land, but a-
bout two hundreth cubites) & they drewe
the net with fishes.
9 Assone then as they were come to land,
they sawe hotte coles, and fish laid thereon, and bread.
10 Iesus said vnto thẽ, Bring of the fishes,
which ye haue now caught.
11 Simon Peter stepped forthe and drewe
the net to land, ful of great fishes, an hundreth, fiftie and thre: and albeit there were so manie, yet was not the net broken.
12 Iesus said vnto them, Come, & dyne.
And none of the disciples durst aske him,
Who art thou, seing they knewe that he
was the Lord.
13 Iesus then came & toke bread, and gaue
them, and fish likewise.

"Or, lake of Gennesareth.

"Or, Children.

a Albeit they knewe him not, yet they folowed his counsel, because thei had all night takẽ paines in vaine.

b It was some linnen garmẽt, which fishers vsed to weare, which being trussed vnto him, couered his nether partes, & also letted not his swimming.

14 This

14 This is now the third time that Ieſus
ſhewed him ſelf to his diſciples, after that
he was riſen againe from the dead.
15 ¶ So whẽ they had dined, Ieſus ſaid to Simon Peter, Simon *ſonne* of Iona, [c] loueſt
thou me more thẽ theſe: He ſaid vnto him,
Yea Lord, thou knoweſt that I loue thee.
He ſaid vnto him, Fede my lambes.
16 He ſaid to him againe the ſecõde time,
Simon *the ſonne* of Iona, loueſt thou me?
He ſaid vnto him, Yea Lord, thou knoweſt
that I loue thee. He ſaid vnto him, Fede
my ſhepe.
17 He ſaid vnto him the [d] third time, Simon *the ſonne* of Iona, loueſt thou me? Peter
was ſorie becauſe he ſaid to him the third
time, Loueſt thou me: and ſaid vnto him,
Lord, thou knoweſt all things: thou knoweſt that I loue thee. Ieſus ſaid vnto him,
Fede my ſhepe.
18 Verely, verely I ſay vnto thee, When
thou waſt yong, thou girdedſt thy ſelf, &
walkedſt whither thou woldeſt: but when
thou ſhalt be olde, thou ſhalt ſtretch forthe
thine hands, & another ſhal [e] girde thee, &
lead thee whither thou woldeſt not.
19 And this ſpake he, ſignifying by what
death he ſhulde glorifie God. And whẽ he
had ſaid this, he ſaid to him, Followe me.
20 Then Peter turned about, and ſawe the
diſciple whome IESVS loued, following,
which had alſo *leaned on his breſt at ſup- *Chap. 13, 23.*
per, and had ſaid, Lord, which is he that
betrayeth thee?
21 When Peter therefore ſawe him, he ſaid
to Ieſus, Lord, what ſhal this man *do*?
22 Ieſus ſaid vnto him, If I wil that he tarie til I come, what is it to thee? followe
thou me.
23 Then went this worde abrode among
the brethren, that this diſciple ſhulde not
dye. Yet Ieſus ſaid not to him, He ſhal not
dye: but if I wil that he tarie til I come,
what is it to thee?
24 This is that diſciple, which teſtifieth of
theſe things, & wrote theſe things, and we
knowe that his teſtimonie is true.
25 * Now there are alſo manie other things *Chap. 20, 3.*
which Ieſus did, the which if they ſhulde
be written euerie one, [f] I ſuppoſe the worl
de colde not conteine the bokes that ſhulde be written, Amen.

c The miniſter can not wel teache his cõgregacion, except he loue Chriſt effectually, ẘ loue is not in them that feed not the flocke.

d Becauſe Peter ſhulde be eſtabliſhed in his office of an Apoſtle, Chriſt cauſeth him by theſe thre times cõfeſsing, to wipe away the ſhame of his thre times denying.

e In ſteed of a girdle, ẙ ſhalt be tyed with bands & cordes: & where as now thou goeſt at libertie, then thou ſhalt be drawẽ to puniſhemẽt whẽ thy fleſh ſhal after a ſorte reſiſt.

f But God wolde not charge vs ẘ ſo great an heape: ſeing therefore that we haue ſo muche as is neceſſarie, we oght to contẽt our ſelues and praiſe his mercie.

THE ACTES OF THE holie Apoſtles written by Luke the Euangeliſte.

THE ARGVMENT.

Chriſt, after his aſcenſion, performed his promes to his Apoſtles, and ſent them the holie Goſt, declaring thereby, that he was not onely mindeful of his Church, but wolde be the head & mainteiner thereof for euer. Wherein alſo his mightie power appeareth, who notwithſtanding that Satan & the worlde reſiſted neuer ſo muche againſt this noble worke, yet by a fewe ſimple men of no reputation, repleniſhed all the worlde with the ſounde of his Goſpel. And here, in the beginning of the Church, and in the increaſe thereof, we may plainely perceiue the practiſe and malice which Satan continually vſeth to ſuppreſſe, and ouerthrowe the Goſpel: he raiſeth conſpiracies, tumultes, commotions, perſecutions, ſclanders and all kinde of crueltie. Againe we ſhal here beholde the prouidence of God, who ouerthroweth his enemies enterpriſes, deliuereth his Church from the rage of tyrants, ſtrengtheneth, and incourageth his moſt valiantly and conſtantly to followe their captaine Chriſt, leauing as it were by this hiſtorie a perpetual memorie to the Church, that the croſſe is ſo ioyned with the Goſpel, that they are fellowes inſeparable, and that the end of one affliction, is but the beginning of another. Yet neuertheles God turneth the troubles, perſecutions, impriſonings and tentations of his, to a good yſſue, giuing them as it were, in ſorrowe, ioye: in bandes, fredome: in priſon, deliuerance: in trouble, quietnes: in death, life. Finally, this boke cõteineth manie excellent ſermons of the Apoſtles & diſciples, as touching the death, reſurrection, and aſcenſion of Chriſt. The mercie of God. Of the grace, and remiſsion of ſinne through Ieſus Chriſt. Of the bleſſed immortalitie. An exhortation to the miniſters of Chriſts flocke. Of repentance, & feare of God, with other principal points of our faith: ſo that this onelie hiſtorie in a maner may be ſufficient to inſtruct a man in all true doctrine and religion.

CHAP. I.

7 The wordes of Chriſt & his Angels to the Apoſtles. 9 His aſcenſiõ. 14 Wherein the Apoſtles are occupied til the holie Goſt be ſent. 26 And of the electiõ of Matthias.

1 I HAVE made the for-
mer treatiſe, ô Theo-
philus, of all that IESVS
began to [a] do, & teach,
2 Vntil the day, that he
was taken vp, after that
he through the holie
Goſt, had giuen [b] commandements vnto
the [c] Apoſtles, whome he had choſen:
3 To whome alſo he preſẽted him ſelf aliue
after that he had ſuffred, by manie infallible tokens, being ſene of them by the *ſpace*
of fourtie dayes, & ſpeaking of thoſe things
which *apperteine* to ẙ [d] kingdome of God.
4 And whẽ he had [e] gathered *them* together,
he commanded them, that they ſhulde
not departe frõ Ieruſalem, but to wait for

a Whereby is ment Chriſts doctrine, & his miracles declared for the cõfirmation of the ſame.

b To preache the Goſpel.

c Who as thei were called by God, ſo had thei their conſciences aſſured by his holie Spirit.

d Whereby God reigneth in vs.

e Becauſe thei ſhuld be all witneſſes of his aſcenſion.

the promes of the Father, *which, *said he*,
ye haue heard of me.
5 *For Iohn in dede baptized with water,
but ye shalbe baptized with the [f] holie Gost
within these fewe dayes.
6 When they therefore were come together, they asked of him, saying, Lord, wilt
thou [g] at this time restore the kingdome
to Israel?
7 And he said vnto them, It is not for you
to knowe the [h] times, or the seasons, which
the Father hathe put in his owne power,
8 But ye shal receiue power of ẏ holie Gost,
when he shal come on you: and ye shalbe
[i] witnesses vnto me bothe in Ierusalem, &
in all Iudea, and in Samaria, and vnto the
[k] vttermost parte of the earth.
9 * And when he had spoken these things,
while they behelde, he was [l] taken vp: for
a cloude toke him vp out of their sight.
10 And while thei loked stedfastly towarde
heauen, as he went, beholde, [m] two men
stode by them in white apparel,
11 Which also said, Ye men of Galile, why
stand ye [n] gasing into heauen? This Iesus
which is taken vp from you into heauen,
shal [o] so come, as ye haue sene him go into
heauen.
12 ¶ Then returned they vnto Ierusalem
from the mount that is called *the mount* of
oliues, which is nere to Ierusalem, conteining a [p] Sabbath *dayes* iourney.
13 And when thei were come in, they wẽt vp
into an vpper chamber, where abode bothe
Peter, and Iames, and Iohn, and Andrewe,
Philippe, and Thomas, Bartlemewe, and
Matthewe, Iames *the sonne* of Alpheus, and
Simon zelotes, and Iudas Iames *brother*.
14 These all continued with one [q] accorde
in [r] prayer and supplicatiõ with the *women, and Marie the mother of Iesus, and
with his brethren.
15 ¶ And in those dayes Peter stode vp in ẏ
middes of the disciples and said (now the
nomber of *names that were in one place,
were about an hundreth and twentie)
16 Ye men & brethrẽ, this [s] Scripture must
nedes haue bene fulfilled, which the * holie
Gost by the mouth of Dauid spake before
of Iudas, which was * guide to them that
toke Iesus.
17 For he was nombred with vs, and had
obteined *felowship in this ministration.
18 He therefore hathe purchased a field
with the [t] rewarde of iniquitie: and when
he * had throwẽ downe him selfe head lõg
he brast a sondre in the middes, and all his
bowels gushed out.
19 And it is knowen vnto all the inhabitãts
of Ierusalem, in so muche, that that field

Luk.24,49. iohn 14,25. & 15,26. & 16,7.
Mat.3,11. mar.1,8. luk 3,12 ioh.1,26. chap.2,2. & 11,16. & 19.4.
f That is, with those spiritual graces ẇ Iesus onely giueth by his Spirit.
g This declareth mans impaciencie who can not abide quietly til Gods appointed time come, but wolde haue all things accomplished according to their affectiõs, read Zach. 6,14.
Luk.24,52.
h For this passeth our capacitie, and God reserueth it to him self.
i To stand in the face of ẏ whole worlde ẇ signifieth that thei must entre into heauen by afflictiõs, & therefore must fight before thei get the victorie.
k Hereby thei might learne that the Messias was not onely for the Iewes, but also for ẏ Gẽtiles.
l Whereby they knewe certeinely whether he went.
m Which were Angels in mens forme.
n And seking him with carnal eyes.
o As the true redemer to gather vs vnto him.
p Which was two mile, according to the Iewes traditiõ, albeit it was not so appointed by ẏ Scriptures.
Psal.49,9. Iohn 13,18.
q A liuelie patron to learne how to dispose our selues to receiue the giftes of the holie Gost.
Mat.27,5.
r Partely to obteine the holie Gost, & partely to be deliuered from the present dangers. *Or, witnes. *Or, men. s The offense, which might haue come by Iudas fall, is hereby taken away, because the Scripture had so forewarned. *Or, porcion. t Perpetual infamie is the rewarde of all suche as by valawfully gotten goods bye anie thing.

is called in their owne lãgage, Aceldama,
that is, The field of blood.
20 For it is written in the boke of Psalmes,
* Let his habitacion be voyde, and let no
man dwell therein: *also, Let another take his *charge.
21 Wherefore, of these men which haue cõ
panied with vs, all the time that the Lord
Iesus was *conuersant among vs,
22 Beginning from the Baptisme of Iohn,
vnto the day that he was taken vp from
vs, must one of thẽ be made a witnes with
vs of his [u] resurrection.
23 And they presented two, Ioseph called
Barsabas, whose surname was Iustus, and
Matthias.
24 And they prayed, saying, Thou Lord,
which knowest the hearts of all men, shewe
whether of these two [x] thou hast chosen,
25 That he may take the roume of this
ministration and Apostleship, from which
Iudas hathe gone astray, to go to his owne
place.
26 Then they gaue forthe their lottes: and
the lot fel on Matthias, and he was by a
commune consent counted with the Eleuẽ
Apostles.

Psal.68,26.
Psal 109,8.
*Or, ministerie.
*Greke, went in & went out.
u In that he mencioneth ẏ principal article of our faith, he comprehendeth al so the rest.
x To the intent that he shulde take in hand ẏ excellent office of an Apostle, might be chosen by the autoritie of God.

CHAP. II.

3 The Apostles hauing receiued the holie Gost, make their hearers astonished. 14 When Peter had stopped the mouthes of the mockers, he sheweth by the visible graces of the holie Spirit that Christ is come. 41 He baptizeth a great nõber that were conuerted. 42 The godlie exercise, charitie, and diuers vertues of the faithful.

1 AND when the [a] day of Pentecoste
was come, they were [b] all with one
accorde in one place.
2 And *suddenly there came a sounde from
heauen, as of a russhing *and* mightie
[c] winde, and it filled all the house where
they sate.
3 ¶ And there appeared vnto them clouen
[d] tongues, like [e] fyre, and it sate vpon eche
of them.
4 And they were all filled with the holie
Gost, and began to speake with other tongues, as the Spirit gaue them *vtterance.
5 And there were dwelling at Ierusalem
Iewes, men that feared God, of euerie nation vnder heauen.
6 Now when this was [f] noised, the multitude came together and were astonied, because that euerie man heard them speake
his owne langage.
7 And they wondred all, and marueiled,
saying amõg them selues, Beholde, are not
all these which speake, of Galile?
8 How then heare we euerie man our owne
[g] langage, wherein we were borne?
9 Parthians, and Medes, and Elamites, and
the inhabitants of Mesopotamia, and of
Iudea, & of Cappadocia, of Pontus, and
Asia,

a The holie Gost was sent when muche people was assembled in Ierusalem at the feast, Exod 23, 16. leui. 23, 16. deu. 16,9 because ẏ thing might not onely be knowẽ there, but also through the worlde.
Chap.1,5. and 11,15. & 19,6. mat.3,11. mar.1,8. luk 3,16.
b That is, the Apostles.
c Whereby is signified the holie Gost.
d This signe agreeth with ẏ thing, which is signified thereby.
e To declare the vertue, and force ẏ shulde be in them.
*Or, to speake.
f How the Apostles spake diuers langages.
g For they colde speake all langages, so that they were able to speake to euerie man in his owne langage.

10 And of Phrygia,& Pãphilia, of Egypt,
and of the parties of Lybia, which is beſide Cyrene, and ″ ſtrangers of Rome, and
h Iewes,and i proſelytes,
11 Cretes,and Arabians: we heard thẽ ſpeake in our owne tõgues the wonderful *workes* of God.
12 They were all then amaſed,and douted,
ſaying one to another,What may this be?
13 And others k mocked,and ſaid,They are
ful of ″newe wine.
14 ¶ But Peter ſtanding with the Eleuen,
lift vp his voice, and ſaid vnto them, Ye
mẽ of Iudea, *and* ye all that inhabit Ieruſalem,be this knowen vnto you, and hearken vnto my wordes.
15 For theſe are not dronken, as ye ſuppoſe, ſince it is but the thirde houre of the
day.
16 But this is that,which was ſpoken by the
l Prophet *Ioel,
17 And it ſhalbe in ẏ laſt dayes, ſaith God,
I wil powre out of my Spirit vpon all
m fleſh, and your ſonnes, and your daughters ſhal prophecie,and your yong mẽ ſhal
ſe viſions, and your n olde men ſhal dreame dreames.
18 And on my ſeruants,and on mine hande-
maides I wil o powre out of my Spirit in
thoſe dayes,and they ſhal prophecie.
19 And I wil ſhewe wõders in heauẽ aboue,
and tokens in the earth beneth,blood,and
fyre,and the vapour of ſmoke.
20 * The p ſunne ſhalbe turned into darkenes, & the moone into blood, before that
great and notable day of the Lord come.
21 And it ſhalbe, *that whoſoeuer ſhal call
on the q Name of the Lord,ſhalbe ſaued.
22 Ye mẽ of Iſrael,heare theſe wordes, IE-
SVS of Nazaret,a man approued of God
among you with great workes, and wondres, and ſignes,which God did by him
in the middes of you, as ye your ſelues alſo knowe:
23 Him,*I ſay*,haue ye taken by the hands of
r the wicked,being deliuered by the ſ determinate counſel,&″foreknowledge of God,
and haue crucified and ſlaine:
24 Whome God hathe raiſed vp, & loſed
the t ſorrowes of death,becauſe it was vnpoſsible that he ſhulde be holden of it.
25 For Dauid ſaith concerning him,* I beheld the Lord alwayes before me: for he
is at my u right hand,that I ſhulde not be
ſhaken.
26 Therefore did mine heart reioyce, and
my tongue was glad, and moreouer alſo
my fleſh ſhal reſt in x hope,
27 Becauſe thou wilt not leaue my ″ ſoule
in graue, nether wilt ſuffer thine holie one
to ″ſe corruption.

″Or, thoſe that dwelt at Rome.
h Whoſe anceſtres were not of the Iewiſh nation, but were conuerted to the Iewes religion, which their children did profeſſe.
i That is, ſuche as were conuerted to the Iewiſh religion, which were before paimms and idolaters.
k There is no worke of God ſo excellent, which the wicked ſkoffers do not deride.
″Or, ſwete.
Ioel.2,28.
iſa.44,3.
l He expoundeth Ioels minde without binding him ſelf to his wordes.
m Or mã: meaning yong and olde, man and woman.
n Meaning, ẏ God wil ſhewe him ſelf verie familiarely & plainely bothe to olde & yong.
o Euen in great abunoãce.
Ioel.2,32.
p God wil ſhewe ſuche ſignes of his wrath through all the worlde, that men ſhalbe no leſſe amazed thẽ if the whole ordre of nature were changed.
Rom.10,13.
q He teacheth this remedie to auoyde the wrath, and threatenings of God, and to obteine ſaluation.
r God cauſed their wickednes to ſet forthe his glorie contrarie to their mindes.
Pſal.15,7.
ſ As Iudas trayſon and ẏ Iewes crueltie towards Chriſt were moſte deteſtable, ſo were thei not onely knowen to the eternal wiſdome of God, but alſo directed by his immutable counſel to a moſte bleſſed end. ″Or, prouidence. t Bothe as touching the paine, & alſo the horror of Gods wrath and curſe. u To ſignifie that nothing can comfort vs in our afflictiõs except we know that God is preſent with vs. x Our hope ſtandeth in Gods defenſe. ″Or, life, or, perſone. ″Or, feele.

28 Thou haſt ſhewed me the y wayes of life,and ſhalt make me ful of ioye with thy
countenance.
29 Men & brethrẽ,I may boldely ſpeake vnto you of the Patriarke Dauid, * that he is
bothe dead and buryed, and his ſepulchre
remaineth with vs vnto this day.
30 Therefore,ſeing he was a z Prophet, and
knewe that God had * ſworne with an othe
to him, that of the frute of his loines he
wolde raiſe vp Chriſt concerning the fleſh
to ſet him vpon his throne,
31 He knowing this before,ſpake of the reſurrection of Chriſt, that *his ″ ſoule ſhulde not be left in a graue, nether his fleſh
ſhulde ″ ſe corruption.
32 This Ieſus hathe God raiſed vp,whereof
we all are witneſſes.
33 Since then that he by the b right hand of
God hathe bene exalted,and hathe c receiued of his Father the promes of the holie
Goſt, he hathe ſhed forthe this which ye
now ſe and heare.
34 For Dauid is not aſcended into heauen,
but he ſaith, * The Lord ſaid to my Lord,
d Sit at my right hand,
35 Vntil I e make thine enemies thy fote-
ſtole.
36 Therefore, let all the houſe of Iſrael
knowe for a ſuretie, that God hathe f ma
de him bothe Lord,and Chriſt,this Ieſus,
I ſay,whome ye haue crucified.
37 Now when they heard it,they were pricked in their hearts, and ſaid vnto Peter &
the other Apoſtles, Men & brethren,what
ſhal we do?
38 Then Peter ſaid vnto them, Amend your
liues, and be g baptized euerie one of you
in the Name of Ieſus Chriſt for the remiſ
ſion of ſinnes: & ye ſhal receiue the h gift
of the holie Goſt.
39 For the promes i *is made* vnto you, and
to your children, and to all that are a farreof, *euen* as many as the Lord our God
ſhal call.
40 And with many other wordes he ″ be-
ſought, & exhorted *them*,ſaying, Saue your
ſelues from this frowarde generacion.
41 Then they that gladly receiued his worde,were baptized: and the ſame day,there
were added *to the Church* about thre thouſand ″ ſoules.
42 And they continued in the Apoſtles doctrine, and k felowſhip, and l breaking of
bread,and prayers.
43 ¶ And feare came vpõ euerie ſoule: and
many wonders and ſignes were done by
the Apoſtles.
44 And all that beleued, were in one place,
and had all things * commune.
45 And thei ſolde their poſſeſsiõs & m goods

m Not ẏ their goods were mingled all together: but ſuche order was obſerued that euerie man frankely relieued anothers neceſsitie.

y In reſtoring me from death to life.
1.King.2,10.
z And ſo knewe by reuelation & ſpecial promes that ẇ els he colde not haue knowen.
Chap.13,36.
pſal.131,11.
Pſal.15,10.
chap.13,35.
″Or, perſone.
a The worde ſignifieth a place where one can ſe nothing
″Or, feele.
b By the vertue & power.
c He obteined of his father power to accõpliſh the promes which he made to his Apoſtles, as touching the holie Goſt to be ſent vnto them
Pſal.110,1.
d And therefore Chriſt doeth farre excell Dauid.
e Chriſt is the onelie redemer vnto whome all powers are ſubiect & muſt obey.
f That is, hathe appointed as King & ruler: and note, that in all this Sermon Peter ſpeaketh of Chriſts manhode, as he was dead, buryed, riſen & aſcended to heauen.
g He ſpeaketh not here of the forme of baptiſme, but teacheth that the whole effect thereof conſiſteth in Ieſus Chriſt.
h The viſible ſignes.
i Chriſt is promiſed bothe to the Iewes and Gentiles, but the Iewes haue the firſt place.
″Or, proteſted before God.
″Or, perſones.
k Which ſtandeth in brotherlie loue, & liberalitie, Rom.15,26. 2.cor.9,13. ebr.13,16.
l Which was ẏ miniſtration of the Lords ſupper.
Chap.4,32.

and parted them to all men, as euerie one
had nede.
46 And they continued daily with one accorde in the Temple,*& n breaking bread
"at home, did eat their meat together with
gladnes and singlenes of heart,
47 Praising God, and had fauour with
all the people; and the Lord added to the
Church o from day to day, suche as shulde
be saued.

Chap.20,7. n They did eat together, and at these feasts did vse to minister the Lords supper, 1 Cor 11,21. Iude 12.
"Or, from house to house.
o Whereby we se that the Apostles trauailed not in vaine.

CHAP. III.

The lame is restored to his fete. 12 Peter preacheth Christ vnto the people.

1 NOw Peter and Iohn went vp together into the Temple, at the a ninthe
houre of prayer.
2 And a certeine man which was a creple
frō his mothers wombe, was caryed, whome they laid daily at the gate of the Tem
ple called Beautiful, to aske b almes of thē
that entred into the Temple.
3 Who seing Peter and Iohn, that they
wolde entre into the Tēple, desired to receiue an almes.
4 And Peter earnestly beholding him with
Iohn, said, Loke on vs.
5 And he gaue hede vnto them, trusting to
receiue some thing of them.
6 Then said Peter, Siluer and golde haue
I none, but suche as I c haue, that giue I
thee: In the d Name of Iesus Christ of Na
zaret rise vp and walke.
7 And he toke him by the right hand, and
lift *him* vp, and immediatly his fete and
ancle bones receiued strength.
8 And he leaped vp, stode, and walked, and
entred with them into the Tēple, walking
and leaping, and praising God.
9 And all the people sawe him walke, and
praising God,
10 And thei knewe him, that it was he which
sate for the almes at the Beautiful gate of
the Temple: & they were amased, and sore astonied at that, which was come vnto
him.
11 ¶And as the creple which was healed,
helde Peter and Iohn, all the people ran
amased vnto them in the porche which is
called Solomons.
12 So whē Peter sawe it, he answered vnto
the people, Ye men of Israel, why marueile ye at this? or why loke ye so stedfastly
on vs, as thogh by our owne e power or
godlines, we had made this man go?
13 The GOD of Abraham, and Isaac, and
Iacob, the *GOD of our fathers hathe glo
rified his Sonne Iesus, whome ye betrayed,
and denied in the presence of Pilate, whē
he had iudged him to be deliuered.
14 *But ye denyed the holie one & the iust,
and desired a f murtherer to be giuen you,
15 And killed the Lord of life, whome God
hathe raised from the dead, whereof we

a Which is w vs, thre a clocke after none, w was their euening sacrifice, at which the Apostles were present to teache, y the shadowes of the Law were abolished by that lābe that toke away the sinnes of the worlde.
b Because his disease was incurable, he gaue him self to liue of almes.
c He had the gift of healing sicknesses.
d In the vertue of Iesus: for Christ was y autor of this miracle, and Peter was the minister.
e He correcteth the abuse of men who attribute that to mans holines, which onely apperteineth to God.
Chap.5,30.
Mat.27,20. mar.15,11. luk 23,18. iohn.18,40.
f To wit, Barrabbas.

are witnesses.
16 And his g Name hathe made this man
sounde, whome ye se, and knowe, through
faith in * his " Name: & the faith which is
by him, hathe giuē to him this disposition
of his whole bodie in y presēce of you all.
17 And now brethrē, I knowe that through
h ignorance ye did it, as *did* also your i gouerners.
18 But those things which God before had
shewed by the mouth of all his Prophetes, that Christ shulde suffre, he hathe thus
fulfilled.
19 Amend your liues therefore, and turne,
that your sinnes may be put away, whē the
time of refresshing k shal come from the
presence of the Lord.
20 And he shal send Iesus Christ, which before was preached vnto you.
21 Whome the heauen must l conteine vntil the time that all things m be restored,
which God had spoken by the mouth of
all his holie Prophetes since the worlde
began.
22 *For Moses said vnto the Fathers, The
Lord your God shal raise vp vnto you a
Prophet, *euen* of your n brethren like vnto
me: ye shal heare him in all things, whatsoeuer he shal say vnto you.
23 For it shalbe that euerie persone which
shal not heare that Prophet, shalbe destroyed out of the people.
24 Also all the Prophetes from Samuel, and
thence forthe as many as haue spoken, haue likewise foretolde of these dayes.
25 Ye are the o children of the Prophetes, &
of the couenant, which God hathe made
vnto our fathers, saying to Abraham, *E-
uen in thy sede shal all the p kinreds of the
earth be q blessed.
26 First vnto you hathe God raised vp his
Sonne Iesus, & him he hathe sent to blesse
you, in r turning euerie one of you from
your iniquities.

CHAP. IIII.

3 Peter and Iohn deliuered out of prison, preache the Gospel boldely. 10 Thei cōfesse plainely the Name of Christ. 16 They are commanded to preache no more in that name. 24 They pray for the good successe of the Gospel. 32 The increase, vnitie and charitie of the Church.

1 ANd as they spake vnto the people, y
Priests & the a captaine of the Tem
ple, & the Sadduces came vpon them,
2 Taking it grieuously that they taught the
people, and preached in Iesus *Name* the
b resurrection from the dead.
3 And they laid handes on them, & put thē
in holde, vntil y next day: for it was now
euen tide.
4 Howbeit, many of them which heard the
worde, beleued, and the nōbre of the men
was about c fiue thousand.
5 ¶And it came to passe on y morrow, that
their

g To wit, Gods Name whereby it appeareth that they did striue against God.
1. Peter.1, 21.
"Or, in Christ.
h He doeth not excuse their malice, but because that ignorance and a blinde zeale led many, he putteth them in hope of saluation.
i He meaneth some, & not all.
k When Iesus shal come to judge the worlde, ye shal knowe that he wilbe your redemer & not your Iudge.
l We therfore beleue constantly, y he is in none other place.
m Which is begon & continueth: but the ful accomplishement, & perfectiō is differred to the last day.
Deut.18,15. chap.7,37.
n Of the stocke of Abrahā.
o Because they came of the same nacion, and therefore were heires of the same promes w apperteined to the whole bodie of y people.
Gen.12,3. gala.3,8.
p Bothe Iew & Gentile.
q None are blessed but in Christ.
r So that our regeneration and newnes of life is inclosed vnder this blessing.
a It is to be thoght that this was the Captaine of the Romaines garison.
b The Sadduces were great enemies to this doctrine.
c The whole Church was increased to this nomber.

their rulers, and Elders, and Scribes, were
gathered together at Ierusalem,
6 And Annas the chief Priest, & Caiaphas,
and Iohn, and Alexander, and as many as
were of the kinred of the hie Priestes.
7 And when they had set thē before them,
they asked, By what power, or [d] in what
Name haue ye done this?
8 Then Peter ful of the [e] holie Gost, said
vnto them, Ye rulers of the people, & Elders of Israel,
9 For asmuche as we this day are examined of the [f] good dede *done* to the impotent man, *to wit*, by what meanes he is made whole,
10 Be it knowen vnto you all, and to all the
people of Israel, that by the Name of Iesus Christ of Nazaret, whome ye haue cru
cified, whome God raised againe frō the
dead, *euen* by him doeth this man stand
here before you, whole.
11 * This is the stone cast a side of you
[g] buylders, which is become the head of
the [h] corner.
12 Nether is there saluation in any other:
for among men there is giuen none other
name [i] vnder heauen, whereby we must be
saued.
13 Now when they sawe the boldnes of Peter and Iohn, & vnderstode that they were
vnlearned men and without knowledge,
they marueiled, & knewe them, that they
had bene with Iesus:
14 And beholding also the man which was
healed standing with them, they had nothing to say against it.
15 Then they commanded them to go a-
side out of the Council, and [k] conferred a-
mong them selues,
16 Saying, What shal we do to these men?
for surely a manifest signe is done by thē,
& it is openly knowen to all thē that dwell
in Ierusalem: and we can not denye it.
17 But that it be noised no farther among
the people, let vs threaten and charge thē,
that they speake henceforthe to no man
in this [l] Name.
18 So they called them, and commanded
them, that in [m] no wise they shulde speake
or teache in the Name of Iesus.
19 But Peter and Iohn answered vnto thē,
and said, Whether it be right in the sight
of God, to obey you rather then God,
iudge ye.
20 For we can not but speake the things
which we haue [n] sene and heard.
21 So they [o] threatened them, and let them
go, and founde nothing how to punish
them, because of the people: for all men
praised God for that which was done.
22 For the man was aboue fourtie yere olde, on whome this miracle of healing was
shewed.

d By whose autoritie or cōmandement?
e For he colde not haue so spoken of him self.
f Iudges oght not to condemne, but approue and commend ỷ which is wel done.
Psal.117,22. isa.28,16. mat.21,42. mar.12,10. luk.20,17. rom.9,33. 1 pet.2,7.
g Meaning Priests, Elders and Gouerners
h For to vphold the waight & force of the buylding.
i That is, none other cause or meane.
k The wicked stil rage agaīst Christ, though their owne cōscience do condemne them.
l They gaue commandemēt to preache Christ nomore
m They prefer their autoritie to the ordinance of God.
n To the intēt that we shulde beare witnes, & preache the
o God hathe put a ring through the wickeds noses so that he stayeth thē frō their mischiuous purposes.

23 Then assone as they were let go, they came to their [p] felowes, & shewed all that the
hie Priests & Elders had said vnto them.
24 And when they heard it, they lift vp
their voyces to God with one accorde, &
said, O Lord, thou art the God which hast
made the heauen and the earth, the sea, &
all things that are in them.
25 Which [q] by the mouth of thy seruāt Da
uid hast said, * Why did the Gētiles rage,
and the people imagine vaine things?
26 The Kings of the earth assembled, and
the rulers came together against ỷ Lord,
and against his Christ.
27 For [r] douteles, against thine holie Sonne Iesus, whome thou haddest [s] anointed,
bothe Herode & Pontius Pilate, with the
Gentiles and the people of Israel gathered them selues together,
28 To do whatsoeuer thine [t] hand, and thy
[u] cōusel had determined before to be done.
29 And now, ô Lord, beholde their [x] threatnings, & [y] grante vnto thy seruants with
all boldenes to speake thy worde,
30 So that thou stretche forthe thine hand,
that healing, and signes, and wonders may
be done by the Name of thine holie Sonne Iesus.
31 And when as they had prayed, the place
was shaken where they were assembled together, and they were all [z] filled with the
holie Gost, and they spake the worde of
God [a] boldely.
32 And the multitude of them that beleued, were of one heart, and of one [b] soule:
nether any of them said, that any thing of
that which he possessed, was his [c] owne,
but they had all things * commune.
33 And with great power gaue the Apostles
witnes of the resurrection of the Lord Ie
sus: and great grace was vpon them all.
34 Nether was there any among them,
that [d] lacked: for as many as were possessers of lands or houses, solde them, and
broght the price of the things that were solde,
35 And laid it downe at the Apostles fete,
and it was distributed vnto euerie man,
[e] according as he had nede.
36 Also Ioses which was called of the Apostles, Barnabas (that is by interpretation
the sonne of consolation) being a Leuite,
and of the countrey of Cyprus,
37 Where as he had land, solde it, & broght
the money, and laid it downe at the Apostles fete.

p To encourage one another, & to glorifie God.
q They groūde their praiers vpō Gods promes, who had assured that he wolde enlarge the kingdome of Christ.
Psal.2,1.
r This is the verifying of ỷ prophecie.
s And appointed to be King
t Power, and iustice.
u All things are done by ỷ force of Gods purpose, according to the decre of his wil, Ephe.1,11.
x Aswage their rage and malice which they enterprise against thee
y They seke not how to liue at ease, but whereby they may moste glorifie God.
z This was a signe of Gods presence and the performās of his promes
a This boldenes & constancie declared that their praier toke effect.
Chap.2,44.
b Of one minde, wil, consent and affection.
c Their hearts were so ioined in God, ỷ being all membres of one bodie, they colde not suffer their fellow membres to be destitute.
d As the Apostles suffred none to lacke, so S Paul commandeth, that no idle loyterers be mainteined, 2. Thes. 3,10.
e The goods were not alike deuided amongs all, but as euerie man had want, so was his necessitie moderatly relieued.

CHAP. V.

5 The hypocrisie of Ananias and Sapphira is punished. 12 Miracles are done by the Apostles. 17 They are taken, but the Angel of God bringeth them out of prison 29 Their bolde confession before the Council. 34 The counsel of Gamaliel. 40 The Apostles are beat, and reioyce in trouble.

1 BVt a certeine man named Ananias,
with Sapphira his wife, solde a possession,
2 And [a] kept away *parte* of the price, his
wife also being of counsel, & broght a certeine parte, and laid it downe at the Apostles fete.
3 Then said Peter, Ananias, why hathe Satan filled thine heart, that thou shuldest
lie vnto the holie [b] Gost, and kepe away
parte of the price of the possession?
4 Whiles it remained, [c] apperteined it not
vnto thee? and after it was solde, was it not
in thine owne [d] power? how is it that thou
hast conceiued this thing in thine heart?
thou hast not lied vnto mē, but vnto God.
5 Now when Ananias heard these wordes,
he fel downe, and gaue vp the gost. Then
great feare came on all them that heard
these things.
6 And the yong men rose vp, and toke him
vp, and caryed *him* out, and buryed *him*.
7 And it [e] came to passe about the space of
thre houres after, that his wife came in,
ignorant of that which was done.
8 And Peter said vnto her, Tell me, solde
ye the lād for so muche? And she said, Yea,
for so muche.
9 Then Peter said vnto her, Why haue ye
agreed together, to [f] tempt the Spirit of
the Lord? beholde, the fete of them which
haue buryed thine housbād, *are* at the dore, and shal carye thee out.
10 Then she fell downe straight way at his
fete, and yelded vp the gost: and the yong
men came in, and founde her dead, and
caryed her out, and buryed her by her
housband.
11 And great feare came on all the Church,
and on as many as heard these things.
12 Thus by the hands of the Apostles were
many signes and wonders shewed among
the people (and they were all with one accorde in [g] Solomons porche.
13 And of the other [h] durst no man ioyne
him self to them: neuertheles the people
[i] magnified them,
14 Also the nombre of them that beleued
in the Lord, bothe of men & womē, grewe
more and more)
15 In somuche that thei broght the sicke into the stretes, and laid them on beddes and
couches, that at the least way the shadowe
of Peter, whē he came by, might shadowe
some of them.
16 There came also a multitude out of the
cities rounde about vnto Ierusalē, bringing sicke folkes, & them which were vexed with vncleane spirits, who were all
healed.
17 ¶ Then the chief Priest rose vp, & all
they that were with him (which was the
secte of the [k] Sadduces) and were ful of
[l] indignation,
18 And laid hands on the Apostles, and put
them in the commune prison.
19 But the Angel of the Lord, by night opened the prison dores, & broght them forthe, and said,
20 Go your way, and stand in the Temple,
& speake to the people all the wordes [m] of
this life.
21 So when they heard it, they entred into
the Tēple early in the morning & taught.
And the chief Priest came, and they that
were with him, and called the Council together, and all the Elders of the children
of Israel, and sent to the prison, to cause
them to be broght.
22 But when the officers came, and founde
them not in the prison, they returned and
tolde it,
23 Saying, Certeinely we founde ẏ prison
shut as sure as was possible, & the kepers
[n] standing without, before the dores: but
when we had opened, we founde no man
within.
24 Then whē the *chief* Priest, and the captaine of the Temple, and the hie Priests
heard these things, they douted of them,
whereunto this wolde growe.
25 Then came one and shewed thē, saying,
Beholde, the men that ye put in prison, are
standing in the Temple, and teache the
people.
26 Then went the captaine with the officers, and broght them without violence
(for they feared the people, lest they shulde haue bene stoned)
27 And when they had broght them, they
set them before the Council, and the chief
Priest asked them,
28 Saying, Did not we straitely commande
you, that ye shulde not teache in this Name? and beholde, ye haue filled [o] Ierusalem
with your doctrine, & ye wolde bring this
mans [p] blood vpon vs.
29 Then Peter and the Apostles answered,
and said, We oght rather to obey God
then [q] men.
30 The *God of our fathers hathe raised vp
Iesus, whome ye slew, & hanged on a tre.
31 Him hathe God lift vp with his right
hand, *to be* a Prince and a [r] Sauiour, to giue
repentance to Israel, and forgiuenes of
sinnes.
32 And we are his witnesses cōcerning these things which we say: yea, and the holie
Gost, whome God hathe giuen to them
that obey [s] him.
33 Now when they heard it, they brast for
anger, and consulted to slay them.
34 Then stode there vp in the Coūcil a cer
teine Pharise named Gamaliel, a doctour
of the Law, honored of all the people,
and commāded to put the Apostles forthe
a litle

a Which signified their sacriledge, distrust, & hypocrisie.
b Who moued thine heart to sel thy possession: where as ẏ turnest parte to another vse, as if God did not se thy dissimulation.
c His sinne therefore was so muche greater in that he cōmitted it willingly.
d Then no mā was cōpelled to sel his possessions, nor to put his money to the commune vse.
e Because that God so disposed it.
f And to mocke him, as if he shulde not haue knowen your craftie fetche, which declareth that when men do any thīg of an euil cōscience, they do not onely pronoūce the sentēce of damnatiō vpō them selues, but also prouoke the wrath of God, because they do proue, as it were, purposely, whether God be righteous and almightie.
g Read the annotatiō vpō the figure. 1. King. 6. page 152.
h Because of their owne euil cōsciences which made them to tremble: for they that were not assured of Gods mercies in Christ, were astonished at these his strāge iudgements.
i That is, thei gaue them great praise.
k Which then were the chief among them.
l They were ful of blinde zeale, emulatiō and ielousie, in defence of their superstition.
m That is, of the liuelie doctrine, whereby the way to life is declared.
n So ẏ there was no fraude nor deceit, nor negligence; but it liuelie setteth forthe the power of God & his prouidēce for his.
o He accuseth them of rebellion & seditiō.
p And to make vs giltie of Christs death.
q When they commande, or forbid vs any thing contrary to the worde of God.
*Chap. 3, 13.
r Meaning that he is the mediator & onelie meane betwene God & man
s That is, Christ.

a litle space,
35 And said vnto them, Men of Israel, take
hede to your selues, what ye entend to do
touching these men.
36 For before these times, rose vp [t] Theudas boasting him self, to whome resorted
a nomber of men, about a foure hundreth,
who was slayne: and thei all which obeied
him, were scattered, & broght to noght.
37 After this man, arose vp [u] Iudas of Galile, in the daies of the tribute, and drewe a-
way muche people after him: he also perished, and all that obeied him, were scattered abroad.
38 And now I say vnto you, refraine your
selues from these men, and let them alone: for if this counsel, or this worke be of
men, it wil come to noght:
39 But if it be of [x] God, ye cã not destroie
it, lest ye be founde euen fighters against
God.
40 And to him they agreed, and called the
Apostles: and when thei had beaten them,
they commanded that they shulde not
speake in the Name of Iesus, & let thẽ go.
41 So they departed from the Council, reioycing, that they were counted worthie
to suffer rebuke for his Name.
42 And daiely in the Temple, & frõ house
to house they ceased not to teache, and
preache Iesus Christ.

CHAP. VI.

*3 Seuen Deacons are ordeined in the Church. 8 The gra-
ces and miracles of Steuen, whome they accused falsely.*

1 AND in those daies, as the nomber of
the disciples grewe, there arose a
murmuring of the [a] Grecians towardes
the Hebrewes, because their widdowes
were [b] neglected in the daielie ministring.
2 Then the twelue called the multitude of
the disciples together, and said, It is not
mete that we shulde leaue the worde of
God to serue the [c] tables.
3 Wherefore brethren, loke ye out among
you seuen men of honest reporte, and ful
of the holie Gost, and of wisdome, which
we may appoint to this busines.
4 And we wil giue our selues continually
to prayer, and to the ministracion of the
worde.
5 And the saying pleased the whole multitude: and they chose Steuen a man ful of
[d] faith & of the holie Gost, and *Philippe,
and Prochorus, and Nicanor, & Timon,
and Parmenas, and Nicolas a [e] proselyte
of Antiochia,
6 Which they set before the Apostles: and
they praied, and [f] laid their hands on thẽ.
7 And the worde of God increased, & the
nomber of the disciples was multiplied
in Ierusalem greatly, and a great cõpanie
of the Priests were obedient to ẏ [g] faith.
8 ¶ Now Steuen ful of faith and power, did

t This Theudas was aboue thirtie yeres before him, of whome Iosephus mencioneth, li. 20. de Antiq chap. 4. that was after the death of Herode ẏ Great, whẽ Archelaus his sonne was at Rome, at what time Iudea was ful of insurrections: so that it is not sure to giue credit to Eusebius in this point.

u Of hĩ maketh mencion Iosephus li. 18. where he speaketh of the taxĩg, Luk. 2, 1.

x He groũdeth vpõ good principles, but he douteth of the qualitie of the cause, nether dare affirme whether it be good or bad: wherein appeareth he was but a worldeling.

Chap. VI.

a Whose ancesters were Iewes & dwelled in Grecia: therefore these spake Greeke, and not Hebrewe.

b They were not loked vnto in the distribucion of the almes.

c That is, to make prouisiõ for the maintenance of the poore, forasmuche as they were not able to satisfie bothe ẏ offices.

d He ioyneth faith with the other gifts of ẏ holie Gost.

e Meaning one ẏ was turned to the Iewish religion.

Chap. 21, 8.

f This ceremonie ẏ Iewes obserued in solẽne sacrifices, Leui 3, 2 & also in praier & priuate blessings, Gen 48, 14: likewise in the primitiue Church it was vsed, ether whẽ they made ministers or gaue the gifts of ẏ holie Gost: ẇ gifts beĩg now takẽ away, the ceremonie must cease

g That is, to the Gospel, ẇ is receiued by faith.

great wonders and miracles among the
people.
9 Then there arose certeine of the [h] Synagogue, which are called Libertines, and
Cyrenians, and of Alexandria, and of thẽ
of Cilicia, and of Asia, and disputed with
Steuen.
10 But they were not able to resist the wisdome, & the Spirit by the which he spake.
11 Thẽ they [i] suborned mẽ, which said, We
haue heard him speake blasphemous wordes against Moses, and God.
12 Thus they moued the people & the Elders, and the Scribes: and running vpon
him, caught him, and broght him to the
Council,
13 And set forthe false witnesses, which said,
This man ceaseth not to speake blasphemous wordes against this holie place, and
the Law.
14 For we haue heard him say, that [k] this
Iesus of Nazaret shal destroye this place, and shal change the ordinances, which
Moses gaue vs.
15 And as all that sate in the Coũcil, loked
stedfastly on him, they sawe his face as *it
had bene* the [l] face of an Angel.

CHAP. VII.

*Steuen maketh answer by the Scriptures to his accusers.
51 He rebuketh the hardnecked Iewes, 57 And is stoned to death. 58 Saul kepeth the tormentours clothes.*

1 THen said the chief Priest, Are these
things so?
2 And he said, Ye [a] men, brethren and fathers, hearken. The God of [b] glorie appeared vnto our father Abraham, while
he was in [c] Mesopotamia, before he dwelt
in Charran,
3 *And said vnto him, Come out of thy
countrey, and from thy kinred, and come
into the land, which I shal shewe thee.
4 Then came he out of the land of ẏ Chaldeans, & dwelt in Charran. And after that
his father was dead, *God* broght him from
thence into this land, wherein ye now
dwell,
5 And he gaue him none inheritance in it,
no, not the breadth of a fote: yet he promi
sed that he wolde giue it to him for a possession, and to his sede after him, when as
yet he had no childe.
6 But God spake thus, that his *sede shulde
be a soiourner in a strange land, and that
thei shulde kepe it in bondage, & entreate
it euil [d] foure hundreth yeres.
7 But the nacion to whome they shalbe in
bondage, wil I [e] iudge, saith God: and after that, they shal come forthe and serue
me in this place.
8 *He gaue him also the couenant of circumcision: and so *Abraham* begate *Isaac,
and circumcised him the eight daye: and
Isaac *begate* *Iacob, and Iacob the twelue

h Or colledge: diuers nacions had colledges at Ierusalem, wherein their youth was instructed, as we se in vniuersities.

i That is, instructed & set forthe false witnesses: and thus malice seketh false shiftes when trueth faileth her

k Thei speake this in cõtẽpt.

l Not onely a certeine confidence, but also great maiestie appearing in him.

a Steuen was accused that he denied God, & therefore he is more diligẽt to purge this crime.

Gen. 12, 1.

b Hereby he is discerned from the false gods

c He speaketh here of Mesopotamia, as it conteineth Babylon & Chaldea in it.

Gen. 15, 13.

d Beginning to recken the yeres from the time that Isaac was borne.

e Take vengeance of them & deliuer my people.

Gen. 17, 9.

Gen. 21, 3.

Gen 25, 24.

*Patriarkes.
9 And the Patriarkes moued with enuie
solde *Ioseph into Egypt: but God was
[f] with him,
10 And deliuered him out of all his afflictions,and *gaue him fauour and wisdome
in the sight of Pharao King of Egypt,
who made him gouernour ouer Egypt, &
ouer his whole house.
11 ¶ Then came there a famine ouer all the
land of Egypt and Canaan, and great affliction, that our fathers founde no sustenance.
12 But when *Iacob heard that there was
corne in Egypt,he sent our fathers first.
13 *And at the seconde time, Ioseph was
knowen of his brethren, and Iosephs kinred was made knowen vnto Pharao.
14 Then sent Ioseph and caused his father
to be broght,& all his kinred, euen [g] thre
score and fiftene soules.
15 So *Iacob went downe into Egypt, and
he *dyed,and our fathers,
16 And were remoued into *Sychem, and
were put in the sepulchre,that [h] Abraham
had boght *for money of the sonnes of
Emor,*sonne* of Sychem.
17 But when the time of the promes drewe
nere,which God had sworne to Abraham,
the people*grewe & multiplied in Egypt,
18 Til another King arose, which knewe
not Ioseph.
19 The same dealt [i] subtely with our kinred, and euil intreated our fathers,& made them to cast out their yong children,
that they shulde not remaine aliue.
20 *The same time was Moses borne, and
was acceptable vnto God,which was nourished vp in his fathers house thre moneths.
21 And whẽ he was cast out,Pharaos daugh
ter toke him vp, & nourished him for her
owne sonne.
22 And Moses was learned in all the wisdome of the Egyptians,and was mightie
in wordes and in dedes.
23 Now when he was ful fortie yere olde,it
came into his heart to visit his brethren,
the children of Israel.
24 *And when he sawe one *of them* suffer
wrong,he defended him,and auenged his
quarel that had the harme done to him, &
smote the Egyptian.
25 For he supposed his brethren wolde haue vnderstand,that God by his hand shulde giue them deliuerance:but thei vnderstode it not.
26 *And the next day, he shewed him self
vnto them as they stroue,and wolde haue
set them at one againe,saying,Syrs,ye are
brethrẽ:why do ye wrong one to another?
27 But he that did his neighbour wrong,
thrust him away,saying, Who made thee

Gen.29,33. & 30,5.& 35 23.
Gen.37,28.
f That is,preserued,& broght all things to a good yssue.
Gen.41,37.
Gen.42,1.
Gen.45,4.
g After the Hebrewe, thre score & ten.
Gen.46,5.
Gen.49,33.
Gen.50,7.
Iosh.24,32.
Gen.23,16.
Exod.1,7.
h It is probable that some writer through negligence put in Abraham in this place, in stede of Iacob, who boght this field, Gen. 33,19, or, by Abrahã he meaneth the posteritie of Abraham.
Exod.2,2.
Ebr.11,23.
i He inuented craftie waies bothe to destroye the Israelites wouer muche labour, & also to get great profite by thẽ, Exod. 1,10.
°Or,that their race shulde faile.
Exod.2,11.
Exod.2,13.

a prince, and a iudge ouer vs?
28 Wilt thou kil me, as thou diddest the
Egyptian yesterday?
29 Then fled Moses at that saying, & was
a stranger in the land of Madian, where
he begate two sonnes.
30 And when fourtie yeres were expired,
there appeared to him in the *wildernes
of mount Sina,an Angel of the Lord in a
flame [k] of fyre,in a bush.
31 And when Moses sawe it,he wondred at ye
sight:&as he drewe nere to consider it,the
voyce of the Lord came vnto him,*saying*,
32 I am the [l] God of thy fathers, the God
of Abraham,and the God of Isaac,& the
God of Iacob. Then Moses trembled, &
durst not beholde it.
33 Then the Lord said to him, [m] Put of thy
shooes from thy fete: for the place where
thou standest,is holie grounde.
34 I haue sene, I haue sene the affliction of
my people, which is in Egypt, and I haue
heard their groning, and am come downe
to deliuer them:and now come, and I wil
send thee into Egypt.
35 This Moses whome thei forsoke,saying,
Who made thee a prince and a iudge?the
same God sent for a prince, and a deliuerer by the hands of the Angel, which appeared to him in the bush.
36 He *broght them out, doing wonders,
and miracles in the land of Egypt, and
in the red sea, and in the wildernes *fourtie yeres.
37 This is that Moses, which said vnto the
childrẽ of Israel,*A [n] Prophet shal ye Lord
your God raise vp vnto you,*euen* of your
brethren,like vnto me:him shal ye heare.
38 *This is he that was in the Congregacion, in the wildernes with the [o] Angel,
which spake to him in mount Sina, & with
our fathers, who receiued the [p] liuelie o-
racles to giue vnto vs.
39 To whome our fathers wolde not obey,
but refused,& in their hearts turned backe
againe into Egypt,
40 Saying vnto Aaron, *Make [q] vs gods
that may go before vs:for [r] we knowe not
what is become of this Moses that broght
vs out of the land of Egypt.
41 And they made a calfe in those daies,
and offred sacrifice vnto the idole,and reioyced in the workes of their owne hãds.
42 Then God turned himself away,&*gaue them vp to serue the [s] hoste of heauen,
as it is written in the boke of the Prophe
tes,*[t] O house of Israel,haue ye offred to
me slayne beasts & sacrifices by the space
of fourtie yeres in the wildernes?
43 And ye [u] toke vp the tabernacle of *Mo-
loch,& ye starre of your god Remphan, figures,wc ye made to worship them: therefore I wil carie you away beyõde Babylõ.

Exod.3,2.
k This fyre represented the fornace of afflictiõ wherein the people of God were.
l Seing this Angel called him self God, it declareth ye he was Christ the Mediator, who is the eternal God.
m In signe of reuerence, read Exod 3,5.
Exod.7,8,9,10 11,14.
Exod.16,1.
Deut.18,15.
chap.3,22.
n He proueth that Christ is the end of the Law and the Prophetes.
Exod.19,2.
o Moses was the Angels or Christs minister, & a guide to the fathers.
p By oracles is ment ye sayings that God spake to Moses.
Exod.32,1.
q Figures, or testimonies of the presence of God.
r Yet they knewe he was absẽt for their commoditie, & so wolde shortely returne & bring them the Law.
Rom.1,24.
s As the sunne, moone & other starres, Deut. 17,3
Amos.5,25.
t Your fathers begin in wildernes to contẽne mine ordinãces, & you now farre passe them in impietie.
Leui.20,2.
u And caryed it vpon your shulders.

44 Our

44 Our fathers had the tabernacle of [x] witnes in the wildernes, as he had appointed,
ſpeaking vnto *Moses, that he ſhulde make
it according to the facion that he had
ſene.
45 Which *tabernacle* alſo our fathers receiued, and broght in with * Ieſus into the
poſſeſsion of the Gẽtiles, which God draue out before our fathers, vnto the dayes
of Dauid:
46 *Who founde fauour before God, and
deſired that he might * finde a tabernacle
for the God of Iacob.
47 *But Solomon buylt him an houſe.
48 Howbeit the moſte High * dwelleth not
in [y] temples made with hands, as ſaith the
*Prophet,
49 Heauen *is* my throne, & earth *is* my fo-
teſtole: what [z] houſe wil ye buylde for me,
ſaith the Lord? or what place is it that I
ſhulde reſt in?
50 Hathe not mine hand made all theſe
things?
51 *Ye ſtiffenecked and of vncircumciſed
[a]hearts & eares, ye haue alwayes reſiſted ỹ
holie Goſt: as your fathers *did*, ſo *do* you.
52 Which of the Prophetes haue not your
fathers perſecuted? and they haue ſlaine
them, which ſhewed before of the coming
of that [b] Iuſt, of whome ye are now the be-
trayers and murtherers,
53 *Which haue receiued the Law by the
[c]ordinance of Angels, & haue not kept it.
54 But when they heard theſe things, their
hearts braſt for anger, and they gnaſhed
at him with *their* teeth.
55 But he being ful of the holie Goſt, loked
ſtedfaſtly into heauen, and ſawe the glorie
of God, and Ieſus ſtanding at [d] the right
hand of God,
56 And ſaid, Beholde, I ſe the heauẽs open,
and the Sonne of man ſtanding at the
right hand of God.
57 Then they gaue a ſhoute with a loude
voyce, and ſtopped their eares, and [e] ranne vpon him all at once,
58 And caſt him out of the citie, and ſtoned him: and the * witneſſes laid downe
their clothes at a yong mans fete, named
Saul.
59 And they ſtoned Steuen, who called on
God, & ſaid, Lord Ieſus, receiue my ſpirit.
60 And he kneled downe, and cryed with a
loude voyce, * Lord, lay not this ſinne to
their charge. And when he had thus ſpoken, he ſlept.

x They oght to haue bene content with this couenant onely, & not to haue gone after their lewd fantaſies.

Exo.25,40. ebr.8,5. Ioſ.3,14. 1.Sam.13,14. pſal 89,21. 2.Sam.7,2. pſal,132,5. 1.Chro.17,12. 1.king.6,1. Chap.17,24.

y He reproueth the groſſe dulnes of the people ỽ abuſed the power of God in that they wolde haue conteined it within the tẽple.

Iſa.66,1.

z God can not be conteined in any ſpace of place.

Ier.9,26. ezek 44,9.

a Which nether forſake your olde wickednes, nor ſo muche as heare when God ſpeaketh to you, but ſtil rebel.

b Which is Ieſus Chriſt who is not onely iuſt for his innocẽcie, but becauſe all true iuſtice cõmeth of him.

Exo.16,13.

c By their miniſterie or office.

d And reignig in his fleſh, wherein he had ſuffered.

e This was done of furious violence & by no forme of iuſtice.

Chap.22,20.

Mat.5,44. luk.23,34. 1.cor.4,12.

CHAP. VIII.

2 Steuen is lamented & buryed. 3 The rage of the Iewes and of Saul againſt them. 4 The faithful ſcattred, preache here & there. 9 Samaria is ſeduced by Simõ the ſorcerer, but was conuerted by Philippe, and confirmed by the Apoſtles. 18 The couetouſnes and hypocriſie of Simon. 26 And conuerſion of the Eunuche.

1 AND Saul conſented to his death, and
at that time, there was a great perſecution againſt the Church which was at Ieruſalem, & they were all ſcattred abroade
through the regions of Iudea & of Samaria, except the Apoſtles.
2 Then *certeine* men fearing God, [a]caryed
Steuen amongs thẽ, *to be buryed*, and made
great [b] lamentation for him.
3 But Saul made hauocke of the Church,
and entred into euerie houſe, and drewe
out bothe men and women, and put them
into priſon.
4 Therefore they that were ſcattred abroade, went to and fro preaching the worde.
5 ¶ Then came Philippe into the citie [c] of
Samaria, & preached Chriſt vnto them.
6 And the people gaue hede vnto thoſe
things which Philippe ſpake, with one accorde, hearing & ſeing the miracles which
he did.
7 For vncleane ſpirits crying with a loude
voyce, came out of many that were poſſeſ
ſed *of them*: and many taken with palſies, &
that halted, were healed.
8 And there was great ioye in that citie.
9 And there was before in the citie a certeine man called Simon, which vſed wit-
checraft, and bewitched the people of Samaria, ſaying, that he him ſelf was ſome
great man.
10 To whome they [d] gaue hede from the
leaſt to the greateſt, ſaying, This man is
the great [e] power of God.
11 And they gaue hede vnto him, becauſe
that of long time he had bewitched them
with ſorceries.
12 But aſſone as they beleued Philippe,
which preached the things that concerned
the kingdome of God, and in the Name
of Ieſus Chriſt, they were baptized bothe
men and women.
13 Then Simon him ſelf [f] beleued alſo and
was baptized, & continued with Philippe,
and wondred, when he ſawe the ſignes and
great miracles which were done.
14 ¶ Now whẽ the Apoſtles, which were at
Ieruſalem, heard ſay, that Samaria had receiued the worde of God, they ſent vnto
them Peter and Iohn.
15 Which when they were come downe,
prayed for them, that they might receiue
the [g] holie Goſt.
16 (For as yet, he was come downe on none
of them, but they were baptized [h] onely in
the Name of the Lord Ieſus)
17 Then laid they their hands on them, &
they receiued the holie Goſt.
18 And when Simon ſawe, that through laying on of the Apoſtles hãds the holie Goſt
was giuen, he offred them money,
19 Saying, Giue me alſo this power, that on
whome ſoeuer I lay the hands, he may receiue the holie Goſt.

a Frõ the place where he was ſtoned.

b When the Church is depriued of any worthie member, there is iuſte cauſe of ſorrowe: and note that here is no mention of any relikes or prayers for the dead, or worſhiping.

c The conuerſion of Samaria was as it were the firſt frutes of the calling of the Gentiles.

d This declareth how muche more we are inclined to follow the illuſions of Satan then the trueth of God.

e This is the craft of Satan to couer all his illuſiõs vnder the Name of God.

f The maieſtie of Gods worde forced him to confeſſe the trueth: but yet was he not regenerat therefore.

g Meaning the particular gifts of ỹ holie Spirit.

h They had onely receiued the commune grace of adoption & regeneracion which are offered to all ỹ faithful in baptiſme, & as yet had not receiued the gift to ſpeake in diuers langages, & to do miracles.

20 Then ſaid Peter vnto him, Thy money
periſh with thee, becauſe thou thinkeſt
that ẏ gift of God may be obteined with
money.
21 Thou haſt nether parte nor [i] fellowſhip
in this buſines: for thine heart is not right
in the ſight of God.
22 [k] Repent therefore of this thy wickednes, and pray God, that if it be [l] poſsible,
the thoght of thine heart may be forgiuen
thee.
23 For I ſe that thou art [m] in ẏ gall of * bitternes, and in the bonde of iniquitie.
24 Then anſwered Simon, & ſaid, Pray ye
to the Lord for me, ẏ none of theſe things
which ye haue ſpoken, come vpon me.
25 ¶ So they, when they had teſtified and
preached the worde of the Lord, returned
to Ieruſalem, and preached the Goſpel in
many townes of the Samaritans.
26 Then the Angel of the Lord ſpake vnto
Philippe, ſaying, Ariſe, and go towarde the
South vnto the way that goeth downe frõ
Ieruſalem vnto Gaza, which is [n] waſte.
27 And he aroſe and went on: and beholde,
a certeine [o] Eunuche of Ethiopia Cãdaces
the Quene of the Ethiopians chief Gouerner, who had the rule of all her treaſure, &
came to Ieruſalem to worſhip:
28 And as he returned ſitting in his charet,
he red Eſaias the Prophet.
29 Then the Spirit ſaid vnto Philippe, Go
nere & ioyne thy ſelf to yonder charet.
30 And Philippe ranne thether, and heard
him read the Prophet Eſaias, & ſaid, But
vnderſtandeſt thou what thou readeſt?
31 And he ſaid, How can I, except I had a
guide? And he deſired Philippe, that he
wolde come vp and ſit with him.
32 Now the place of the Scripture which
he red, was this, * He was led as a ſhepe to
ẏ ſlaughter: & like a lambe domme before
his ſhearer, ſo opened he not his mouth.
33 [p] In his humilitie his [q] iudgement hathe
bene exalted: but who ſhal declare his [r] generaciõ? for his life is taken frõ the [ſ] earth.
34 Then the Eunuche anſwered Philippe,
and ſaid, I pray thee of whome ſpeaketh
the Prophet this? of him ſelf, or of ſome
other man?
35 Then Philippe [t] opened his mouth, and
began at the ſame Scripture, and preached
vnto him Ieſus.
36 And as they went on their way, they came vnto a certeine water, and the Eunuche
ſaid, Se, *here is* water: what doeth let me to
be baptized?
37 And Philippe ſaid vnto him, If thou be-
leueſt with [u] all thine heart, thou maiſt.
Then he anſwered, and ſaid, I beleue that

i Thou art not worthie to be of the nomber of ẏ faithful.
k That is, turne away from thy wickednes
l Hereby he wolde make him to feele his ſinne and not ẏ he douted of Gods mercies, if he colde repent.
Deut.29,18.
m Or thine heart is ful of diſpiteful malice, & deueliſh peyſon of impietie, ſo that now Satan hathe thee tied as captiue in his bands.
n After that Alexãder had deſtroyed it, it was not much peopled, as it was afore, and therefore in reſpect was as waſte.
o Eunuche ſignifieth him that is gelded: but becauſe in the Eaſt partes great affaires were commit to ſuche, it came in vſe that noble men were called Eunuches, although they were not gelded: alſo all maner officers and ſeruants, that were put in credit or neceſſarie affaires, were called by this name, as Iſa.39,7
Iſa.53,7.
p Albeit Chriſt was in graue and in deathes bandes, feling alſo his Fathers angre againſt ſinne, yet he brake the bãdes of death and was exalted, Act.2,24.
q The puniſhmẽt which he ſuffred, was the beginning of his glorie.
r That is, how long his age ſhal endure: for being riſen frõ death, death ſhal no more reigne, nether ſhal his kingdome euer haue end: or els we may take generation, for his Church ẇ neuer ſhal haue ende: for now they ſit in the heauẽlie places with Chriſt their head, as Epheſ.2,6.
ſ And he now reigneth in heauen.
t He declared at length this matter of ſo great importance.
u With a pure and perfect heart.

Ieſus Chriſt is the Sonne of God.
38 Then he commanded the charet to ſtand
ſtil: and they went downe bothe into the
water, bothe Philippe & the Eunuche, and
he baptized him.
39 And aſſone as they were come vp out of
the water, the Spirit of the Lord caught
away Philippe, that ẏ Eunuche [x] ſawe him
no more: ſo he went on his way reioycing.
40 But Philippe * was founde at [y] Azotus, &
he walked to and fro preaching in all the
cities, til he came to Ceſarea.

x This was, to the intent that he might knowe ſo muche the better ẏ Philip was ſent to him by God.
* *Or, perceiued him ſelf to be.*
y Some thinke this citie was alſo called Aſdod, Ioſ. 15,47.

CHAP. IX.

3 The conuerſion of Saul. 15 His vocation to the Apoſtleſhip. 20 His zeale to execute the ſame. 25 How he eſcapeth the Iewes conſpiracies. 26 His acceſſe to the Apoſtles. 31 The proſperitie of the Church. 34 Peter healeth Æneas. 40 Raiſeth Tabitha. 42 He conuerteth many to Chriſt. 43 And lodgeth in a tãners houſe.

1 AND * Saul yet [a] breathing out threatnings & ſlaughter againſt the diſciples of the Lord, went vnto the hie Prieſt,
2 And deſired of him letters to Damaſcus
to the Synagogues, that if he founde any
that were of that [b] way (ether men or women) he might bring them bounde vnto
Ieruſalem.
3 Now as he iourneyed, it came to paſſe ẏ
as he was come nere to Damaſcus, * ſuddenly there ſhined rounde about hĩ a light
from heauen.
4 And he fel to the earth, and heard a voyce, ſaying to him, Saul, Saul, why perſecu-
teſt thou me?
5 And he ſaid, Who art thou, Lord? And
the Lord ſaid, I am Ieſus whome thou per-
ſecuteſt: it is hard for thee to kicke againſt
[c] prickes.
6 He *then* bothe trembling and aſtonied,
ſaid, Lord, what wilt thou that I do? And ẏ
Lord ſaid vnto him, Ariſe and go into the
citie, and it ſhalbe tolde thee what thou
ſhalt do.
7 The men alſo which iorneyed with him,
ſtode amaſed, hearing [d] *his* voyce, but [e] ſeing no man.
8 And Saul aroſe from the grounde, and
opened his eyes, *but* [f] ſawe no man. Then
led they him by the hand, and broght him
into Damaſcus,
9 Where he was thre dayes without ſight,
and nether [g] ate nor dranke.
10 And there was a certeine diſciple at Damaſcus named Ananias, & to him ſaid the
Lord in a viſion, Ananias. And he ſaid, Beholde, I am *here*, Lord.
11 Then the Lord ſaid vnto him, Ariſe, and
go into ẏ ſtrete which is called Straight,
and ſeke in the houſe of Iudas after one
called Saul of Tarſus: for beholde, he
prayeth.
12 (And he ſawe in a viſion a man named
Ananias coming in to him, & putting his
hands

Rom.9,3. gal.1,13.
a He perſecuted with a great rage, and crueltie the innocent blood which he thirſted for: ẇ declareth wherunto mã is led by his raſhe zeale, before he haue the true knowledge of God.
b That is of ẏ ſecte, or ſorte.
Chap.22,6. 1.cor.15,8.
c That is, to reſiſt God whẽ he pricketh & ſoliciteth our conſciences.
d Meaning Sauls voice, as Chap.22,9.
e For onely Saul knewe that Ieſus ſpake vnto him.
f For he was blinde.
g He was ſo rauiſhed with the viſion that he did meditate nothing, but heauẽlie thĩgs and therewith was ſatiſfied.

hands on him, that he might receiue his
sight.)
13 Then Ananias answered, Lord, I haue
heard by many of this mã, how muche euil
he hathe done to thy sainctes at Ierusalẽ.
14 Moreouer here he hathe autoritie of the
hie Priests, to binde all that call on thy
Name.
15 Then the Lord said vnto him, Go thy
way: for he is a [h] chosen vessel vnto me, to
[i] beare my Name before the Gentiles, &
Kings, and the children of Israel.
16 For I wil shewe him, how many things
he must suffre for my Names sake.
17 Then Ananias went his way, and entred
into the house, and put his hands on him,
and said, Brother Saul, the Lord hathe sent
me (*euen* Iesus ẏ appeared vnto thee in the
way as thou camest) that thou mightest
receiue thy sight, and be filled with the holie Gost.

h A worthie seruãt of God and endued with excellent graces aboue others.
i To beare me witnes, and set forthe my glorie.

18 And immediatly there fel from his eyes
as *it had bene* scales, & suddenly he receiued sight, and arose, and was baptized,
19 And receiued meat, & was strẽgthened.
So was Saul certeine dayes with the disciples which were at Damascus.
20 And straight way he preached Christ in
the Synagogues, that he was the Sonne of
God,
21 So that all that heard him, were amased,
and said, Is not this he, that destroyed thẽ
which called on this Name in Ierusalem,
& came hither for that intent, ẏ he shulde
bring them bounde vnto the hie Priests?
22 But Saul encreased the more in strẽgth,
and confounded the Iewes which dwelt at
Damascus, [k] confirming, that this was the
Christ.
23 And after [l] that many dayes were fulfilled, the Iewes toke counsel together, to
kill him.
24 But their laying await was knowen of
Saul: now they [m] watched the gates day
and night, that they might kill him.
25 Then the disciples toke him by night,
and put him through the wall, and let him
downe in a basket.

k Prouing by the conference of the Scriptures.
l That was after thre yeres, that he had remained at Damascus, and in the countrey about, Gal 1,18.
2.Cor.11,32.
m The Gouernour at their request appointed a watche as he declareth to the Corinthiãs

26 And when Saul was come to Ierusalem,
he assaide to ioyne him self with the disciples: but they were all afraid of him, and
beleued not that he was a disciple.
27 But Barnabas toke him, and broght him
to the Apostles, and declared to them, how
he had sene the Lord in the way, & that he
had spoken vnto him, & how he had spokẽ
boldely at Damascus in ẏ Name of Iesus.
28 And he " was conuersant with [n] them at
Ierusalem,
29 And spake boldely [o] in the Name of the
Lord Iesus, & spake and disputed with the
[p] Graeciãs: but they went about to slay him.
30 But when the brethren knewe it, they

" Greke, went in and out.
n With Peter and Iames, Gal.1,19.
o Making opẽ profession of the Gospel.
p Which were Iewes, but so called because they were dispersed through Grecia and other countreis.

broght him to Cesarea, & sent him forthe
to [q] Tarsus.
31 Then had the Churches rest through all
Iudea, and Galile, and Samaria, and were
edified, & walked in the feare of the Lord,
and were multiplied by the comfort of
the holie Gost.

q Because it was his owne countrey, and there he might haue some autoritie.

32 And it came to passe, as Peter walked
through out all *quarters*, he came also to
the sainctes which dwelt at Lydda.
33 And there he founde a certeine man named AEneas, which had kept his bed eight
yeres, and was sicke of the palsie.
34 Thẽ said Peter vnto him, AEneas, Iesus
Christ maketh thee whole: arise and " make
vp thy bed. And he arose immediatly.
35 And [r] all that dwelt at Lydda and [s] Sa-
ron, sawe him, and turned to the Lord.
36 There was also at Ioppa a certeine *womã*
a disciple named Tabitha (which by inter
pretation is called [t] Dorcas) she was " ful
of good workes & almes which she did.

" Or, trusse thy couche together
r Meaning, the greatest parte.
s A place so called, and not a citie.
t That is, a dere, or rebucke.
" Or, riche.

37 And it came to passe in those dayes, that
she was sicke and dyed: and when they had
[u] washed her, they laid her in an vpper
chamber.
38 Now forasmuche as Lydda was nere to
Ioppa, and the disciples had heard that
Peter was there, they sent vnto him two
men, desiring that he wolde not delaye to
come vnto them.

u To the intẽt they might burie her afterwarde: for this was their custome.

39 Then Peter arose and came with them:
and when he was come, they broght him
into the vpper chamber, where all the wid
dowes stode by him weping, and shewing
the coates and garments, which Dorcas
made, while she was with them.
40 But Peter put them all forthe, and kneled downe, and praid, and turned him to
the bodie, and said, Tabitha, arise. And she
opened her eyes, and when she sawe Peter, sate vp.
41 Then he gaue her the hand & lift her
vp, and called the [x] sainctes & widdowes,
and restored her aliue.
42 And it was knowen throughout all Ioppa, and manie beleued in the Lord.
43 And it came to passe that he taryed manie dayes in Ioppa ẘ one Simon a " tãner.

x For she was restored to life, rather that others might haue occasion to beleue, and glorifie God, then for her owne sake.
" Or, corier.

CHAP. X.

3 Cornelius admonished by the Angel. 7 He sendeth to Ioppa. 11 The visiõ that Peter sawe. 17 How he was sent to Cornelius. 19 The Gentiles also receiue the Spirit, and are baptized.

1 FVrthermore there was a certeine mã
in Cesarea called Cornelius, a captaine of the bande called the Italian *bande*,
2 A deuout mã, and [a] one that feared God
with all his housholde, which gaue muche
almes to the people, and prayed God continually.
3 He sawe in a vision euidently (about
the ninte houre of the day) an Angel of

a Who had forsaken all superstitions, & gaue him self to the true seruice of God.

God comming in to him, and saying vnto
him, Cornelius.
4 But when he loked on him, he was afraid,
and said, What is it, Lord? And he said vnto him, Thy prayers & thine almes are come [b] vp into remembrance before God.
5 Now therefore send men to Ioppa, & call
for Simon, whose surname is Peter.
6 He lodgeth with one Simon a tãner, whose house is by the sea side: ‖he shal tell thee
what thou oghtest to do.
7 And when the Angel which spake vnto
Cornelius, was departed, he called two of
his seruãts, & a souldier that feared God,
one of them that waited on him,
8 And tolde them all things, and sent them
to Ioppa.
9 On the morowe as they went on their
iorney, and drewe nere vnto the citie, Peter went vp vpon the house to pray, about
the [c] sixt houre.
10 Then waxed he an hungred, and wolde
haue eatẽ: but while they made *some thing*
readie, he fel into a trance.
11 And he sawe heauen opened, and a certeine vessel come downe vnto him, as *it
had bene* a great shete, knit at the foure cor
ners, and was let downe to the earth.
12 Wherein were [d] all maner of foure foted
beastes of the earth, and wilde beastes and
creping things, and foules of the heauen.
13 And there came a voyce to him, Arise, Pe
ter: kill, and eat.
14 But Peter said, Not so, Lord: for I haue
neuer eaten any thing that is ″ polluted, or
vncleane.
15 And the voyce *spake* vnto him againe
the seconde time, The things that God
hathe [e] purified, [f] pollute thou not.
16 This was so done thrise: and the vessel
was drawen vp againe into heauen.
17 ¶ Now while Peter douted in hĩ self what
this visiõ which he had sene, meant, beholde, the men which were sent from Cornelius, had inquired for Simons house, and
stode at the gate,
18 And called, & asked, whether Simõ, which
was surnamed Peter, were lodged there.
19 And while Peter thoght on the vision,
the Spirit said vnto him, Beholde, thre mẽ
seke thee.
20 Arise therefore, and get thee downe, &
go with them, and [g] doute nothing: for I
haue sent them.
21 ¶ Then Peter wẽt downe to ẏ men, which
were sent vnto him frõ Cornelius, & said,
Beholde, I am he whome ye seke: what is
the cause wherefore ye are come?
22 And they said, Cornelius the captaine, a
iust man, and one that feareth God, and
of good reporte among all the nacion of
the Iewes, was warned from heauen by an
holie Angel, to send for thee into his house, and to heare thy wordes.
23 Then called ″he them in, & lodged them,
and the next day, Peter went forthe with
them, and certeine brethren from Ioppa
accompanied him.
24 ¶ And the day after, thei entred into Ce
sarea. Now Cornelius waited for them, &
had called together his kinsmen, and special friends.
25 And it came to passe as Peter came in,
that Cornelius met him, and fel downe at
his fete and [h] worshipped him.
26 But Peter toke him vp, saying, Stand vp:
for euen I my self am a man.
27 And as he talked with him, he came in,
& founde manie that were come together.
28 And he said vnto them, Ye knowe that
it is an vnlawful thing for a man that is a
Iewe, to companie or come vnto one of
another nation: but God hathe shewed
me, that I shulde not call anie man ″pollu-
ted, or vncleane.
29 Therefore came I vnto you without saying naye, when I was sent for. I aske therefore, for what intent haue ye sent for me.
30 Then Cornelius said, Foure dayes ago,
about this houre, I fasted, and at the ninthe houre I praid in mine house, and beholde, a man stode before me in bright
clothing,
31 And said, Cornelius, thy prayer is heard,
and thine almes are had in remembrance
in the sight of God.
32 Send therefore to Ioppa, and call for Simon, whose surname is Peter (he is lodged
in the housẽ of Simon a tanner by the sea
side) who when he cometh, shal speake vnto thee.
33 Then sent I for thee immediatly, and
thou hast wel done to come. Now therefore are we all here present before God, to
heare all things that are commanded thee
of God.
34 Then Peter opened *his* mouth, and said,
Of a trueth I perceiue, that *God is no ac
cepter of persones.
35 But in euerie natiõ he that [i] feareth him,
and worketh [k] righteousnes, is accepted
with him.
36 Ye knowe the worde which God hathe
sent to ẏ childrẽ of Israel, preaching [l] peace by Iesus Christ, which is Lord of all.
37 *Euen* the worde which came through all
Iudea * beginning in Galile, after the baptisme which Iohn preached,
38 *To wit*, how God [m] annointed Iesus of
Nazaret with the holie Gost, and with
power: who went about doing good, and
healing all that were oppressed of the deuil: for God was with him.
39 And we are witnesses of all things which
he did bothe in the land of the Iewes, and
in Ierusalem: whome they slewe, hanging
him

b That is, God did accept thẽ: whereof it foloweth that he had faith: for els it is impossible to please God.

‖*He shal speake wordes vnto thee whereby thou shalt be saued & all thine house.*

c Which was midday.

d As camels horses, dogs, oxẽ, shepe, swine & suche like which man nourisheth for his vse.

″*Or, commune.*

e In taking away the difference betwixt vncleane beastes and cleane he sheweth there is no difference betwixt ẏ Iewes and Gentiles.

f Take it not for polluted & impure.

g The true obedience which procedeth of faith, oght to be without dout or questioning.

″*Or, Peter.*

h Shewed to muche reuerẽce, and farre passing decẽt ordre, as thogh Peter had bene God.

″*Or, commune.*

Deu.10,17. 2.chro.19,17. iob.34,19. wisd.6,8. eccles.35,16. rom.2,11. gal.2,6. ephe 6,9. col.3,25. 1.pet.1,17.

i By this speache the Ebrewes meane the whole religiõ of God, which without faith profiteth vs nothing.

Luk.4,14.

k That is, he that is vpright & doeth hurt to no man, but doeth good to all.

l Meaning the reconciliation betwene God & mã through Christ Iesus, Luk.2,14.

m That is, endued him with graces & giftes aboue all others.

him on a tre.
40 Him God raised vp the third day, and
caused that he was shewed openly:
41 Not to all the people, but vnto the witnesses chosen before of God, *euen* to vs
which did eat and drinke with him, after
he arose from the dead.
42 And he commanded vs to preache vn-
to the people, & to testifie, that it is he that
is ordeined of God a iudge of quicke and
dead.
43 To him also giue all the *Prophetes witnes, that through his Name all that beleue
in him, shal receiue remission of sinnes.
44 While Peter yet spake these wordes, the
holie Gost fel on all them which heard
the worde.
45 So they of the circumcision which beleued, were astonied, as manie as came with
Peter, because that on the Gentiles also
was powred out the gift of the holie Gost.
46 For they heard them speake with tõgues,
& magnifie God. Then answered Peter,
47 Can anie man [n] forbid water, that these shulde not be baptized, which haue receiued the holie Gost, as wel as we?
48 So he commanded them to be baptized
in the Name of the Lord‖. Then prayed
they him to tarie certeine dayes.

Iere.31,34. micah.7,11. chap.15,9.

n We oght not to debarre them of baptisme whome God testifieth to be his: for seing they haue the principal, that is lesse, oght not to be denied thẽ.

‖ *Iesus Christ.*

CHAP. XI.

4 Peter sheweth the cause wherefore he went to the Gentiles. 18 The Church approueth it. 21 The Church increaseth. 22 Barnabas and Paul preache at Antiochia. 28 Agabus prophecieth dearth to come. 29 And the remedie.

1 NOw the Apostles and the brethren
that were in Iudea, heard, that the
Gentiles had also receiued the worde of
God.
2 And when Peter was come vp to Ierusalem, they of the circumcision [a] contended
against him,
3 Saying, Thou wentest in to men vncircumcised, and hast eaten with them.
4 Then Peter began, and expounded *the
thing* in order to [b] them, saying,
5 I was in the citie of Ioppa, praying, and
in a trance I sawe *this* vision, A certeine
vessel cõming downe as *it had bene* a great
shete, let downe from heauen by the foure corners, and it came to me.
6 Toward the which when I had fastened
mine eyes, I considered, and sawe foure foted beastes of the earth, and wilde beastes,
and creping things, & foules of the heauẽ.
7 Also I heard a voyce, saying vnto me, A-
rise, Peter: slay and eat.
8 And I said, God forbid, Lord: for nothing
polluted or vncleane hathe at anie time
entred into my mouth.
9 But the voyce answered me the second ti
me from heauen, The things that God
hathe purified, pollute thou not.

a For they colde not yet comprehende this secret, w was hid from the Angels thẽ selues, euen from the creation of the worlde, Eph. 3,8. col. 1,26.

b He purgeth his fact before ẏ Church.

10 And this was done thre times, and all
were taken vp againe into heauen.
11 Then beholde, immediatly there were
thre mẽ already come vnto the house where I was, sent from Cesarea vnto me.
12 And the Spirit said vnto me, that I shulde go with them, without douting: moreouer these six brethren came with me, &
we entred into the mans house.
13 And he shewed vs, how he had sene an
Angel in his house, which stode and said
to him, Send men to Ioppa, and call for Simon whose surname is Peter.
14 He shal speake wordes vnto thee, whereby bothe thou and all thine house shalbe
saued.
15 And as I began to speake, the holie Gost
fel on them, *euen as vpon vs at the beginning.
16 Then I remembred the worde of the
Lord, how he said, *Iohn baptized with
water, but ye shalbe [c] baptized with the
holie Gost.
17 For as muche then as God gaue them a
like gift, as *he did* vnto vs, when we beleued in the Lord Iesus Christ, who was I,
that I colde let God‖?
18 When they heard these things, [d] they
helde their peace, and glorified God, saying, Then hathe God also to the Gentiles
granted [e] repentance vnto life.
19 ¶ And thei which were *scattred abroade
because of the "affliction that arose about
Steuen, walked throughout til they came
vnto Phenice and Cyprus, and Antiochia,
preaching the worde to no man, but vnto
the Iewes onely.
20 Now some of them were men of Cyprus
and of Cyrene, which when they were come into Antiochia, spake vnto the [f] Grecians, and preached the Lord Iesus.
21 And the [g] hand of the Lord was with thẽ
so that a great nomber beleued & turned
vnto the Lord.
22 Then tidings of those things came vnto
the eares of the Church, which was in Ierusalem, & they sent forthe Barnabas that
he shulde go vnto [h] Antiochia.
23 Who when he was come & had sene the
grace of God, was glad, and exhorted all,
that with purpose of heart they wolde
"cleaue vnto the Lord.
24 For he was a good man, and ful of the
holie Gost, and faith, and muche people
ioyned them selues vnto the Lord.
25 ¶ Then departed Barnabas to Tarsus to
seke Saul:
26 And when he had founde him, he broght
him vnto Antiochia, and it came to passe
that a whole yere they were conuersant
with the Church, and taught muche people, insomuche, that the disciples were
first called [i] Christians in Antiochia.

Chap.2,4. & 8,6.

Chap.1,5. & 19,4. mat.3,11. mar.1,8. luk.3,16. iohn.1,17.

c That is, indued with the graces of the holie Gost.

‖ *Not to giue them the holie Gost?*

d Their modestie declareth that they were not ashamed to vnsay that whereof they had vniustly blamed Peter.

Chap.8,1.

e This repentãce depẽdeth vpon faith.

"Or, trouble.

f He meaneth not the Iewes which being scatered abroade in diuers countreis were called by this name, but the Grecians, w were Gẽtiles.

g The power and vertue.

h This was the moste famous citie of Syria, and bordered vpon Cilicia.

"Or, continue with the Lord.

i Where as before they were called disciples, now they are named Christians.

27 In those dayes also came Prophetes frõ
Ierusalem vnto Antiochia.
28 And there stode vp one of them named
Agabus, and signified by the [k] Spirit, that
there shulde be great famine throughout
all the worlde, which also came to passe
vnder Claudius Cesar.
29 Then the disciples, euerie man according to his habilitie, [l] purposed to send
succour vnto the brethren which dwelt in
Iudea.
30 Which thing they also did, and sent it
to the Elders, by the hands of Barnabas
and Saul.

k This prophecie was an occasion to the Antiochiãs to releiue the necessitie of their brethrẽ in Ierusalem.

l To signifie that it came of a charitable minde towardes them.

CHAP. XII.

2 Herode persecuteth the Christians. 2 He killeth Iames, 4 And putteth Peter in prison. 7 Whome the Lord deliuereth by an Angel. 21 The horrible death of Herode. 24 The Gospel florisheth. 25 Barnabas & Saul returning to Antiochia take Iohn Marke with them.

1 NOw about that time, [a] Herode the
King stretched forthe *his* hands to
vexe certeine of the Church.
2 And he killed Iames the [b] brother of Iohn
with the sworde.
3 And when he sawe that it [c] pleased the Iewes, he proceded further, to take Peter also (then were ỹ daies of vnleauened bread)
4 And whẽ he had caught him, he put him
in prison, and deliuered him to [d] foure
quaternions of souldiers to be kept, inten-
ding after the Passeouer to bring him forthe to the people.
5 So Peter was kept in prison, but earnest
prayer was made of the Church vnto God
for him.
6 And when Herode wolde haue broght
him out vnto the people, the same night
slept Peter betwene two souldiers, bounde
with two chaines, and the kepers before
the dore kept the prison.
7 *And beholde, the Angel of the Lord came vpon them, and a light shined in the
house, and he smote Peter on the side, and
raised him vp, saying, Arise quickely. And
his chaines fel of from *his* hands.
8 And the Angel said vnto him, Girde thy
self, and binde on thy [e] sandales. And so he
did. Then he said vnto him, Cast thy garment about thee, and followe me.
9 So *Peter* came out and followed him, &
knewe not that it was true, which was done by the Angel, but thoght he had sene
a vision.
10 Now when they were past the first and
the secõde watche, they came vnto the yrõ
gate, that leadeth vnto the citie, which o-
pened to them by it owne accorde, and
they went out, and passed through one
strete, and by and by the Angel departed
from him.
11 ¶ And when Peter was come to him self,
he said, Now I know for a trueth, that the
Lord hathe sent his Angel, and hathe deliuered me out of the hand of Herode, and
from all the [f] waiting for of the people
of the Iewes.
12 And as he considered *the thing*, he came to
the house of Marie, the mother of Iohn,
whose surname was Marke, where manie
were gathered together and prayed.
13 And when Peter knocked at the entrie
dore, a maide came forthe to hearken, named Rhode.
14 But when she knew Peters voyce, she o-
pened not the entrie *dore* for gladnes, but
ran in, and tolde how Peter stode before
the entrie.
15 But they said vnto her, Thou art mad.
Yet she affirmed it constantly, that it was
so. Then said they, It is his [g] Angel.
16 But Peter continued knocking, and whẽ
thei had opened it, and sawe him, they were astonied.
17 And he beckened vnto them with the
hand, to holde their peace, and tolde them
how the Lord had broght him out of the
prison. And he said, Go shewe these things
vnto Iames and to the brethren: and he departed and went into [h] another place.
18 ¶ Now assone as it was day, there was no
smale trouble among the souldiers, what
was become of Peter.
19 And when Herode had soght for him, &
founde him not, he examined the kepers,
and commanded them to be led to be punished. And he went downe from Iudea
to Cesarea, and *there* abode.
20 Then Herode intended to make warre
against them of Tyrus and Sidõ, but they
came all with one accorde vnto him, and
[i] persuaded Blastus the Kings chamber-
laine, and they desired peace, because their
coũtrey was nourished by the Kings *land*.
21 And vpon a day appointed, Herode a-
rayed him self in royal apparel, and sate
on the iudgement seat, and made an ora-
tion vnto them.
22 And the people gaue a shoute, *saying*,
The voyce of God, and not of man.
23 But immediatly the Angel of the Lord
smote him, because he [k] gaue not glorie
vnto God, so that he was eatẽ [l] of wormes,
and gaue vp the gost.
24 And the worde of God [m] grewe, and
multiplied.
25 So Barnabas and Saul returned from Ierusalem, when they had fulfilled their [n] office, and toke with them Iohn, whose surname was Marke.

a Who was called Agrippa the sone of Aristobulus: he was nephewe vnto Herode ỹ Great, and brother of Herodias.

b There was another so named which was the sonne of Alpheus.

c It came thẽ of no zeale nor religion, but onely to flatter the people.

d The nõber being fixtene was deuided by foures, to kepe diuers wardes.

Chap. 5,19.

e Read Marke 6,9.

f For they thoght ỹ Herode wolde haue put him to death, as he had purposed.

g For thei did know by Gods worde that Angels were appointed to defende ỹ faithful, and also in those dayes thei were accustomed to se suche sights.

h Which was lesse suspect, by reason of the brethren.

i Bothe by flatering wordes, & also by briberie.

k Which he shulde haue done, if he had punished the flatterers, of whose vanitie he cõplained, when he was a dying, as Iosephus writeth.

l The vilenes of the punishmẽt declareth how God detesteth pride, and tyrannie: his grande father also was eaten of lise.

m The more that tyrãts go about to suppresse Gods worde, the more doeth it increase.

n Which was to distribute ỹ almes sent frõ Antiochia, Chap. 11,29.

CHAP. XIII.

2 Paul and Barnabas are called to preache among the Gentiles. 7 Of Sergius Paulus, and Elymas the sorcerer. 13 The departure of Marke 14 Paul preacheth at Antiochia. 42 The faith of the Gentiles. 46 The Iewes reiected. 48 Thei that are ordeined to life, beleue. 52 The frute of faith.

1 THere were also in the Church that
was at Antiochia, certeine Prophetes
and teachers, as Barnabas, & Simeon called Niger, and Lucius of Cyrene, & [a]Ma-
nahen (which had bene broght vp with
Herode the Tetrarch) and Saul.
2 Now as they [b] ministred to the Lord, &
fasted, the holie Gost said, Separate me
Barnabas & Saul, for the worke whereunto I haue called them.
3 Then fasted they and praied, and laid
their hands on them, and let them go.
4 And they, after they were * sent forthe of
the holie Gost, came downe vnto Seleucia, and from thence they sailed to Cyprus.
5 And whẽ thei were at Salamis, thei preached the worde of God in the Synagogues of the Iewes: and they had also Iohn
to *their* minister.
6 So when they had gone throughout the
yle vnto Paphus, they founde a certeine
sorcerer, a false prophet, being a Iewe, named Bariesus,
7 Which was with ẏ Deputie Sergius Pau
lus, a prudent man. He called vnto him
Barnabas and Saul, and desired to heare
the worde of God.
8 But Elymas, the sorcerer (for so is his name by interpretacion) withstode them, &
soght to turne away the Deputie frõ the
faith.
9 Then Saul (which also *is called* Paul) being ful of the holie Gost, set his eyes on
him,
10 And said, O ful of all subtiltie and all
mischief, the childe of the deuil, & enemie of all righteousnes, wilt ẏ not cease
to peruert the straight [c] waies of ẏ Lord?
11 Now therefore beholde, the hand of the
Lord *is* vpon thee, & thou shalt be blinde,
& not se the sunne for a season. And immediatly there fell on him a miste and a
darkenes, and he went about, seking some
to lead him by the hand.
12 Then the Deputie when he sawe what
was done, beleued, and was astonied at the
doctrine of the Lord.
13 Now when Paul and they that were with
him were departed by ship from Paphus,
they came to Perga *a citie* of Pamphylia:
then Iohn departed from them, and returned to Ierusalem.
14 But when thei departed from Perga, thei
came to [d] Antiochia *a citie* of Pisidia, and
went into the Synagogue on the Sabbath
day, and sate downe.
15 And after the lecture of the Law & Prophetes, the rulers of the Synagogue
sent vnto them, saying, Ye men and brethren, if ye haue anie worde of [e] exhortacion for the people, say on.
16 Then Paul stode vp and beckened with

a This declareth that God calleth of all sortes bothe hie & lowe.

b The worde signifieth to execute a publicke charge, as the Apostleship was: so ẏ here is shewed, that they preached, and prophecied.

Chap.14,26.

c Which are ẏ doctrine of the Apostles, ẏ onelie leadeth vs to God.

d This was another Antiochia then that which was in Syria.

e This declareth that the Scripture is giuẽ to teache & exhorte vs, & that thei refused none ẏ had giftes to set forth Gods glorie & to edifie his people.

the hand, and said, Men of Israel, and ye
that feare God, hearken.
17 The God of this people of Israel chose
our fathers, and exalted the people when
they dwelt in the land of * Egypt, & with
an * high arme broght them out thereof.
18 And about the time * of fortie yeres, suffred he their [f] maners in the wildernes.
19 And he destroyed seuen nacions in the
land of Chanaan, & * deuided their land
to them by lot.
20 Then afterwarde he gaue vnto them
* Iudges [g] about foure hundreth and fiftie
yeres, vnto the time of Samuel ẏ Prophet.
21 So after that they desired a * King, and
God gaue vnto them * Saul, the sonne of
Cis, a man of the tribe of Beniamin, *by the
space* of fortie yeres.
22 And after he had takẽ him away, he raised vp * Dauid to be their King, of whome
he witnessed, saying, I haue foũde Dauid
the sonne of Iesse, a man after mine owne
heart, which wil do all things that I wil.
23 Of this mans sede hathe God * accordĩg
to *his* promes raised vp to Israel, the Sauiour Iesus:
24 When * Iohn had first preached before
his comming the baptisme of repentance
to all the people of Israel.
25 And when Iohn had fulfilled *his* [h] course,
he said, * Whome ye thinke that I am, I
am not he: but beholde, there cometh one
after me, whose shoe of *his* fete I am not
worthie to lose.
26 Ye men and brethren, children of the
generacion of Abraham, and whosoeuer
among you feareth God, to you is the
[i] worde of this saluacion sent.
27 For the inhabitants of Ierusalem, and
their rulers, because they [k] knewe him
not, nor yet the wordes of the Prophetes,
which are [l] red euerie Sabbath *daye*, they
haue fulfilled them in condemning him.
28 And thogh thei foũde no cause of death
in him, * yet desired thei Pilate to kill him.
29 And when they had [m] fulfilled all things
that were written of him, they toke him
downe from the tre, and put him in a sepulchre.
30 But God * raised him vp from the dead.
31 And he was sene manie dayes of them,
which came vp with him from Galile to
Ierusalem, which are his witnesses vnto
the people.
32 And we declare vnto you, that touching
the promes made vnto the fathers,
33 God hathe fulfilled it vnto vs their children, in that he [n] raised vp Iesus, euen as it
is written in the seconde Psalme, * Thou
art my Sonne: this day haue I begotẽ thee.
34 Now as concerning that he raised him
vp frõ the dead, no more to returne to the
graue, he hathe said thus, * I wil giue you

Exod.1,1. *Exod.13,14.* *Exod.16,1.*

f Here is declared the great pacience & lõg suffring of God before he punisheth.

Iosh.14,1. *Iud.3,9.* *1.Sam.8,5.* *1.Sam.9,15. & 10,1.*

g For these 450 yeres were not fully accõplished, but there lacked 3. yeres counting from the birth of Isaac to the distribucion of ẏ land of Canaã.

1.Sam.16,13. *psal.89,21.* *Isa.11,1.*

Mat.3,1. mar.1,2. luk.3,2.

Mar.1,7. ioh.1,20.

h Whẽ his office drewe to an end, he sent his disciples to Christ.

i That is, this message & tidings of saluacion.

k He rebuketh them for their ignorance.

l Althogh thei red the Law, yet their hearts are couered that they can not vnderstand, 2.Cor. 3,14.

Mat.27,22. mar.15,13. luk.23,23. ioh.19,6.

Mat.28,2. mar.16,6. luk.24,7. iohn 20,19.

m In Christ all ẏ promises are Yea, & Amen, 2.Cor.1,20.

n In that he was borne and incarnate.

Psal.2,7. ebr.1,5. & 5,5.

Isa.55,3.

the [o] holie things of Dauid, which are
faithful.
35 Wherefore he saith also in another place,* Thou wilt not suffre thine Holie one
to se corruption.
36 Howbeit, Dauid after he had serued his
time by ẏ counsel of God, he* slept, & was
laid with his fathers, & sawe corruption.
37 But he whome God raised vp, sawe no
corruption.
38 Be it knowen vnto you therefore, men
and brethren, that through this man is
preached vnto you ẏ forgiuenes of sinnes.
39 And from all things, from which ye
colde not be iustified by the Law of Moses, by him euerie one that beleueth, is iustified.
40 Beware therefore, lest that come vpon
you, which is spoken of in the Prophetes,
41 * Beholde, ye [p] despisers, & wonder, and
vanish away: for I worke a [q] worke in your
daies, a worke which ye shal not beleue, if
a man wolde declare it you.
42 ¶ And when they were come out of the
Synagogue of the Iewes, the Gentiles besoght, that they wolde preache these wordes to them the next Sabbath *day*.
43 Now when the Congregacion was dissolued, manie of the Iewes, and proselytes
that feared God, folowed Paul & Barnabas, which spake to them, and exhorted
them to continue in the grace of God.
44 And the next Sabbath *day* came almost
the whole citie together, to heare ẏ worde
of God.
45 But whẽ the Iewes sawe the people, thei
were ful of [r] enuie, & spake against those things, which were spoken of Paul, con-
trarying *them*, and railing on *them*.
46 Then Paul and Barnabas spake boldely, and said, * It was necessarie that the
worde of God shulde first haue bene spoken vnto you: but seing ye put it frõ you,
and iudge your selues vnworthie of [s] e-
uerlasting life, lo, we turne to the Gẽtiles.
47 For so hathe the Lord commanded vs,
saying, * I haue made thee a light of the
Gentiles, that thou shuldest be the saluacion vnto the end of the worlde.
48 And when the Gentiles heard it, they
were glad, and glorified the worde of the
Lord: and as manie as were [t] ordeined vnto eternal life, beleued.
49 Thus the worde of the Lord was published throughout the whole countrey.
50 But ẏ Iewes stirred *certeine* [u] deuoute &
honorable womẽ, & the chief men of ẏ citie, & raised persecuciõ agaĩst Paul & Barnabas, & expelled thẽ out of their coasts.
51 But they* shouke of the dust of their fete against them, and came vnto Iconium.
52 And the disciples were filled with ioye,
and with the holie Gost.

Psal.15,10. *chap.2,31.*
o Meaning, ẏ he wolde faithfully accõplish the promises, ẏ he made of his fre mercie ẇ the forefathers: and he sheweth that as the grace, ẇ God hathe giuen to his Sõne, is permanẽt for euer, so likewise the life of ẏ Sonne is eternal.
1.King.2,10. *chap.2,29.*
Habak.1,5.
p He reproueth them sharpely because softenes wolde not preuaile.
q Which is, vẽgeance vnspeakeable, for the contempt of Gods worde.
r Thei disdained ẏ the Gentiles shulde be made equal ẇ them.
Mat.10,6.
s Which is, to knowe one onelie God, and whome he hathe sent, Iesus Christ.
Isa.49,6. *luk.2,31.*
t None cã beleue, but they whome God doeth appoint before all beginnings to be saued.
u He meaneth superstitious women, & suche, as were led ẇ a blinde zeale, albeit ẏ commune people esteemed thẽ godlie: & therefore Luke speaketh as ẏ world estemed them.
Mat.10,14. *mar.6,11.* *luk.9,5.* *chap.18,6.*

CHAP. XIIII.

3 God giueth successe to his worde. 6 Paul and Barnabas preache at Iconium and are persecuted. 13 At Lystra thei wolde do sacrifice to Barnabas & Paul, which refuse it, & exhorte the people to worship the true God. 19 Paul is stoned. 22 They confirme the disciples in faith and pacience, 23 Appointe ministers, 26 And passing through manie places, make reporte of their diligence at Antiochia.

1 AND it came to passe in Iconiũ, that
they went bothe together into the
Synagogue of the Iewes, and so spake,
that a great multitude bothe of the Iewes
and of the Grecians beleued.
2 But the [a] vnbeleuing Iewes stirred vp,
and corrupted the mindes of the Gentiles against the brethren.
3 So therefore they abode there a long time, and spake boldely in the Lord, which
gaue testimonie vnto the worde of his
grace, and caused signes and wonders to
be done by their hands.
4 But the people of the citie were diuided:
and some were with the Iewes, and some
with the Apostles.
5 And when there was an assaut made bothe of the Gentiles, and of the Iewes with
their rulers, to do them violence, and to
stone them,
6 They were ware of it, and fled vnto Lystra, and Derbe, cities of Lycaonia, & vnto the region rounde about,
7 And there were preaching the Gospel ‖.
8 ¶ *Now there sate a certeine man at Lystra, impotent in his fete, which was a creple from his mothers wombe, who had neuer walked.
9 He heard Paul speake: who beholding
him, and perceiuing that he had faith to
be healed,
10 Said with a loude voyce, ‖ Stand vpright
on thy fete. And he leaped vp, & walked.
11 Then whẽ the people sawe what Paul had
done, thei lift vp their voyces, sayĩg in the
speache of Lycaonia, Gods are come downe to vs in the likenes of men.
12 And thei called Barnabas, Iupiter, & Paul,
Mercurius, because he was ẏ chief speaker.
13 Then Iupiters priest, which was before
their citie, broght bulles with [b] garlandes
vnto the [c] gates, & wolde haue sacrificed
with the people.
14 But when the Apostles, Barnabas and
Paul heard it, thei [d] rent their clothes, &
ran in among the people, crying,
15 And saying, O men, why do ye these
things? We are euen men [e] subiect to the
like passions that ye *be*, and preache vnto
you, that ye shulde turne from these vaine
idoles vnto the liuing God, * which made
heauen and earth, and the sea, & all things
that in them are.
16 Who in times past *suffred all the Gentiles to walke in their owne [f] waies.

a Which wolde not obey ẏ doctrine, nether suffer thẽ selues to be persuaded, to beleue ẏ trueth and to embrace Christ.
‖ In so muche that all the people were moued at the doctrine. So bothe Paul & Barnabas remained at Lystra.
‖ I say to thee in the Name of the Lord Iesus Christ.
b That is, trimmed ẇ flowres & garlandes.
c He meaneth before the gates of ẏ house where ẏ Apostles lodged: for the tẽple was without the towne, & therefore ẏ Priest broght the sacrifice (as he thoght) to the gods them selues.
d In signe of detesting & abhorring it.
e That is, not without our infirmities and sinnes, & also subiect to death.
Gen.1,1. *psal.145,6.* *reuel.14,7.*
f To liue after their owne fantasies not prescribing vnto them anie religion.
Psal.81,13. *rom.1,2.*

17 Neuertheles, he left not him self without[g] witnesse, in that he did good *and* gaue vs raine from heauen, and fruteful seasons, filling our hearts with foode, and
[h] gladnes,
18 And speaking these things, scarse refrained they the people, that they had not sacrificed vnto them‖.
19 Then there came certeine Iewes frõ Antiochia and Iconium, which whẽ they had
persuaded the people, ‖ *stoned Paul, and
drewe him out of the citie, supposing he
had bene dead.
20 Howbeit, as the disciples stode rounde
about him, he arose vp, and came into the
citie, and the next day he departed with
Barnabas to Derbe.
21 And after they had preached to that citie, & had taught manie, they returned to
Lystra, and to Iconium, and to Antiochia,
22 Confirming the disciples hearts, & exhorting them to continue in the faith, *affir
ming* ỹ we must through manie afflictions
entre into the kingdome of God.
23 And when they had ordeined thẽ Elders
by [i] election in euerie Church, and praid,
and fasted, they commended them to the
Lord in whome they beleued.
24 Thus they went through out Pisidia, &
came to Pamphilia.
25 And when they had preached the worde
in Perga, they came downe to Attalia,
26 And thence sailed to Antiochia, * from
whence they had bene commended vnto
the grace of God, to the worke which they
had fulfilled.
27 And when they were come & had gathered ỹ Church together, they rehearsed all
the things that God had done [k] by them,
and how he had opened the dore of faith
vnto the Gentiles.
28 So there they abode a long time with the
disciples.

g To take frõ men all excuse.

h That being satisfied they might reioyce.

‖ *but that they shulde go euerie man home. And whiles they taried & taught, there came, &c.*

2.Cor.11,22.

‖ *And disputing boldely persuaded the people to forsake thẽ: for, said thei, they say nothing true, but lie in all things.*

i The worde signifieth to elect by putting vp ỹ hãds which declareth that ministers were not made without the consent of the people.

Chap.13,1.

k By their ministerie.

CHAP. XV.

1 Variance about circumcision. 22 The Apostles send their determination to the Churches. 35 Paul and Barnabas preache at Antiochia, 39 And separate companie because of Iohn Marke.

1 THen came downe [a] certeine from Iudea, and taught the brethren, *saying*,
*Except ye be circumcised after the maner
of Moses, ye can not be saued.
2 And when there was great dissention, and
disputation by Paul & Barnabas against
them, they ordeined that Paul and Barnabas, and certeine other of them, shulde go
vp to Ierusalem vnto the Apostles & Elders about this question.
3 Thus being sent forthe by the Church,
they passed through Phenice, and Samaria, declaring the conuersion of the Gentiles: and they broght great ioye vnto all
the brethren.

a As Cerinth° and others: so writeth Epiphanius agaĩst ỹ Cerinthians: also the fame of the place whence they came, did muche preuaile to persuade abrode.

Gal.5,1.

4 And when they were come to Ierusalem,
they were receiued of the Church, and of
the Apostles and Elders, and they declared
what things God had done by them.
5 But *said they*, certeine of the secte of the
[b] Pharises, which did beleue, rose vp, saying, that it was nedeful to circumcise thẽ,
and to commande *them* to kepe the Law
of Moses.
6 Then the Apostles & Elders came together to loke to this matter.
7 And when there had bene great disputation, Peter rose vp, & said vnto them, *Ye
mẽ & brethrẽ, ye knowe that a good while ago, among vs God chose out *me*, that
the Gentiles by my mouth shulde heare
the worde of the Gospel, and beleue.
8 And God which knoweth the hearts, bare them witnes, in giuing vnto them the
holie Gost, euen as *he did* vnto vs.
9 And he put no [c] difference betwene vs &
them, after that by faith he [d] had *purified
their hearts.
10 Now therefore, why [e] tempt ye God,
to *lay a yoke on ỹ disciples neckes, which
nether our fathers, nor we were able to
beare?
11 But we beleue, through the [f] grace of
the Lord Iesus Christ to be saued, euen as
they *do*.
12 Then all the multitude kept silence, and
heard Barnabas & Paul, which tolde what
signes and wondres God had done among
the Gentiles by them.
13 And when they helde their peace, Iames
answered, saying, Men & brethren, hearken
vnto me.
14 *Simeon hathe declared, how God first
did visite the Gẽtiles, to take *of them* a peo
ple vnto his Name.
15 And to this agre the wordes of the Prophetes, as it is written,
16 * After this I wil returne, and wil buylde
againe the [g] tabernacle of Dauid, which is
fallen downe, and the ruines thereof wil I
buylde againe, and I wil set it vp,
17 That the residue of men might seke after the Lord, and all the [h] Gentiles vpon
whome my Name is called, saith ỹ Lord
which doeth all these things.
18 From the beginning of the worlde God
knoweth all his workes.
19 Wherefore my sentence is, that we trouble not them of the Gentiles that are turned to God,
20 But that we write vnto them, that they
absteine them selues frõ [i] filthines of idoles, and [k] fornication, and that that is strã-
gled, and from blood‖.
21 For [l] Moses of olde time hathe in euerie

b Which were fa&tious, & giuen to dissension.

Chap.10,20.

c As touching adopcion, and eternal life.

1.Cor.1,2.

chap.10,43.

d By faith God purifieth the heart.

Mat.23,4.

e Thei purposely tẽpt God ẘ lay greater charges on mens consciences, then they are able to beare.

f And not by the Law: for it is a clog to ỹ consciẽce, and we can not be deliuered thereby.

2.Pet.1,1.

Amos.9,11.

g That is, the Church whereof the Tẽple was a figure.

h Which are gathered into one familie ẘ the Iewes to the intẽt thei shulde acknowledge all one God, and one Sauiour Christ Iesus.

i For some thoght it none offence to be present in the idoles tẽples, & there to bãket: ẘ S. Paul saith, is to drinke the cup of the deuils, 1. Cor. 10,21.

k The heathẽ thoght this no vice, but made it a commune custome. As touching a strangled thing & blood, they were not vnlawful of thẽ selues, & therefore were obserued but for a time. ‖ *And whatsoeuer they wolde not shulde be done to them selues, that they shulde not do it to others.*] Therefore the ceremonies cõmanded by God colde not so sone be abolished, til the libertie of the Gospel were better knowen.

citie them that preache him, seing he is
red in ẏ Synagogues euerie Sabbath *day*.
22 Then it semed good to the Apostles and
Elders with ẏ whole Church, to send chosen men of their owne cōpanie to Antiochia with Paul and Barnabas: *to wit*, Iudas
whose surname was Barsabas and Silas, ẇ
were chief men among the brethren,
23 And wrote letters by them after this maner, THE APOSTLES, AND ẏ Elders,
& the brethren, vnto the brethren which
are of the Gentiles in Antiochia, & in Syria, and in Cilicia, send greting.
24 Forasmuche as we haue heard, that certeine which departed from vs, haue troubled you with wordes, and cumbred your
mindes, saying, Ye must be circumcised &
kepe the Law: to whome we gaue no suche
commandement,
25 It semed therefore good to vs, when we
were come together with one accorde, to
send chosen men vnto you, ẇ our beloued
Barnabas and Paul,
26 Men that haue giuen vp their liues for
the Name of our Lord Iesus Christ.
27 We haue therefore sent Iudas and Silas,
which shal also tell you the same things
by mouth.
28 For it semed good to the holie Gost, and
m to vs, to lay no more burden vpon you,
then these necessarie things,
29 *That is*, that ye absteine from things offered to idoles, and blood, and that that is
strangled, and from fornication: ‖ from
which if ye kepe your selues, ye shal do
wel. Fare ye wel.
30 Now when they were departed, they came to Antiochia, & after that they had assembled the multitude, they deliuered the
epistle.
31 And when they had red it, they reioyced
for the consolation.
32 And Iudas and Silas being Prophetes,
″exhorted the brethrē with manie wordes,
and strengthened them.
33 And after they had taried there a space,
they were let go in n peace of the brethren
vnto the Apostles.
34 Notwithstanding o Silas thoght good
to abide there stil ‖.
35 Paul also and Barnabas cōtinued in Antiochia, teaching and preaching with manie other the worde of the Lord.
36 ¶ But after certeine dayes, Paul said vnto
Barnabas, Let vs returne, & visite our bre
thren in euerie citie, where we haue preached ẏ worde of ẏ Lord, *&* se how thei do.
37 And Barnabas ‖ counseled to take with
them Iohn, called Marke.
38 But Paul thoght it not mete to take him
vnto their companie, which departed frō
them from Pamphilia, and went not with
them to the worke.

m Whome the holie Gost hathe moued & directed to ordeine, & write these things, not as the autors of this doctrine, but as ẏ ministers of Gods ordinance, Exod 14, 31. iudg. 7. 20. hag 1, 12.

‖ *and whatsoeuer ye wolde not that men shulde do vn to you, do not to others.*

″ *Or, comforted.*

n Hauing desired leaue of the Church, ẏ brethrē prayed God to prosper their iorney.

‖ *and onely Iudas went.*

o Who for iuste causes, chāged his minde.

‖ *wolde take Iohn, &c.*

39 Then were they so stirred that they
p departed a sunder one from the other, so
that Barnabas toke Marke, and sailed vnto Cyprus.
40 And Paul chose Silas and departed, being commended of the brethren vnto the
grace of God.
41 And he went through Syria and Cilicia, stablishing the Churches.

CHAP. XVI.

1 When Paul had circumcised Timothie, he toke him with him. 7 The Spirit calleth them from one countrey to another. 24 Lydia is conuerted. 28 Paul and Silas imprisoned conuert the iailer. 37 And are deliuered as Romaines.

1 THen came he to Derbe & to Lystra:
and beholde, a certeine disciple was
there named * Timotheus, a womans sonne, which was a Iewesse & beleued, but his
father was a Grecian.
2 Of whome the brethren which were at
Lystra and Iconium, reported wel.
3 Therefore Paul wolde that he shulde go
forthe with him, & toke and a circumcised
him, because of the Iewes, which were in
those quarters: for they knew all, that his
father was a Grecian.
4 And as they went through the cities, they
deliuered them the decrees to kepe, ordeined of the Apostles and Elders, which were at Ierusalem.
5 And so were the Churches stablished in
the faith, and encreased in nombre daily.
6 ¶ Now when they had gone through out
Phrygia, and the region of Galacia, they
were b forbidden of the holie Gost to prea
che the worde in c Asia.
7 Then came they to Mysia, & soght to go
into Bithynia: but ẏ Spirit ‖ suffred thē not.
8 Therefore they passed through Mysia, &
came downe to d Troas,
9 Where a vision appeared to Paul in the
night. There stode a man of Macedonia, &
prayed him, saying, Come into Macedonia, and helpe vs.
10 And after he had sene the vision, immediatly we prepared to go into Macedonia,
being e assured that the Lord had called
vs to preache the Gospel vnto them.
11 Thē went we forthe from Troas, & with
a straight course came to Samothracia, &
the next day to f Neapolis,
12 ¶ And from thence to Philippi, which is
the chief citie in the partes of Macedonia,
and g whose inhabitants came from Rome
to dwell there, and we were in that citie
abiding certeine dayes.
13 And on the Sabbath day, we went out
of the citie, besides a riuer, where they were wont to h pray: and we sate downe, and
spake vnto the women, which were come
together.
14 And a certeine woman named Lydia, a
seller

p God suffreth the moste perfite to fall, and yet turneth their infirmities to the setting forthe of his glorie, as this breache of companie caused the worde to be preached in mo places.

Rom. 16, 21. phil. 2, 19. 1. thes. 3, 2.

a Lest the Iewes shulde disdaine him as one that were prophane, and without God.

b God chuseth not onely mē, but also appointeth coūtreis where his worde shalbe preached, and onely as he wil.

c Meaning, Asia the lesse.

‖ *of Iesus.*

d Called also Antigonia, & Alexandria.

e We oght not to credit visions, except we be assured thereof by ẏ Spirit of God.

f Which is in the borders of Thracia and Macedonia.

g In Greke & Latine ẏ worde is called Colonia which can not otherwise be wel expressed, but by suche circumstance of wordes

h Where the Christians accustomed to assemble their Church, whē the infideles psecuted thē.

seller of purple, of the citie of the Thya-
tirians, which worshipped God, heard *vs*:
whose heart the Lord opened, that she at-
tended vnto the things, which Paul spake.
15 And when she was baptized, and her
housholde, she besoght vs, saying, If ye haue iudged me to be faithful to the Lord,
come into mine house, and abide *there*: and
she constrained vs.
16 And it came to passe that as we went to
prayer, a certeine maide hauing *a spirit
[i] of diuination, met vs, which gate her masters muche vantage with diuining.
17 She followed Paul and vs, and cryed,
saying, These men are the seruants of the
moste high God, which shewe vnto vs the
[k] way of saluation.
18 And this did she manie dayes: but Paul
being grieued, [l] turned about, and said to
the spirit, I commande thee in the Name
of Iesus Christ, that thou come out of her.
And he came out the same houre.
19 Now whē her masters sawe that the hope of their gaine was gone, they caught
Paul & Silas, and drewe thē into the market place vnto the magistrates,
20 And broght them to the gouernours,
saying, These mē which are Iewes, trouble
our citie,
21 And preache ordinances, which are not
lawful for vs to receiue, nether to obserue,
seing we are Romaines.
22 The people also rose vp together against
them, and the gouernours rent [m] their clothes, and * commanded *them* to be beaten
with roddes.
23 And when they had beatē them sore, they
cast *them* into prison, cōmanding the iailer to kepe them surely.
24 Who hauing receiued suche commandement, cast them into the "inner prison, &
made their fete fast in the stockes.
25 Now at midnight Paul and Silas prayed, & sang a psalme vnto God: and the pri
soners heard them.
26 And suddēly there was a great earthquake, so that the fundation of the prison was
shaken: & by and by all the dores opened,
and euerie mans bandes were losed.
27 Then the keper of the prison waked out
of his slepe, and when he sawe the prison
dores open, he drewe out his sworde and
wolde haue killed him self, supposing the
prisoners had bene fled.
28 But Paul cryed wͭ a loude voyce, saying,
Do thy self no harme: for we are all here.
29 Then he called for a light and leaped in
and came trembling, and fel downe before Paul and Silas,
30 And broght thē out, and said, Syrs, what
must I do to be saued?
31 And they said, Beleue in the Lord Iesus
Christ, & ỷ shalt be saued, and thine housholde.

Leu.20,27. deu.18,7. 1 sam.28,7.

i Which colde gesse & foredeme of things past, present & to come: wͨ knowledge in manie things God permitteth to the deuil.

k Satā althogh he spake the trueth, yet was his malicious purpose to cause the Apostles to be troubled as seditious persones and teachers of strange religion.

l For Satans subtiltie increased, & also it might seme that Satan, & the Spirit of God taught bothe one doctrine, Read Mar.1,34.

m To wit, the clothes of Paul & Silas.

2.Cor.11,3. 1 thes.2,2.

"Or, in the bottome of the prison, or in a dungeon.

32 And they preached vnto him the worde
of ỷ Lord, & to all that were in his house.
33 Afterwarde he toke thē the same houre
of the night, & washed *their* "stripes, and
was baptized with all that belonged vnto
him, straight way.
34 And when he had broght them into his
house, he "set meat before them, and reioyced that he with all his housholde beleued
in God.
35 And when it was day, ‖ the gouernours
sent the sergeants, saying, Let those men
go.
36 Then the keper of the prison tolde these
wordes vnto Paul, *saying*, The gouernours
haue sent to lose you: now therefore get
you hence, and go in peace.
37 Then said Paul vnto them, After that
they haue beaten vs openly vncōdemned,
which are [n] Romaines, they haue cast vs
into prison, & now wolde they put vs out
priuely? nay verely: but let them come &
bring vs out.
38 And the sergeants tolde these wordes vnto the gouernours, who [o] feared when they
heard that they were Romaines.
39 Then came they and prayed them, and
broght them out, and desired them to departe out of the citie.
40 And they went out of the prison, and
entred into the *house of* Lydia: and when
they had sene the brethrē, they comforted
them, and departed.

"Or, woundes or hurtes.

"Greke, he set the table.

‖ The Gouernours assembled together in the market, & remēbring the earthquake that was, they feared and sent, &c.

n No man had autoritie to beat, or put to death a citizen Romaine, but the Romaines them selues by the cōsent of the People.

o For the punishment was great against them that did iniurie to a citizen Romaine.

CHAP. XVII.

1 Paul commeth to Thessalonica. 4 Where some receiue him, and others persecute him. 11 To searche the Scriptures. 17 He disputeth at Athens, and the frute of his doctrine.

1 NOw as they passed through Amphipolis, and Apollonia, they came to
Thessalonica, where was a Synagogue of
the Iewes.
2 And Paul, as his maner was, went in vnto
them, & thre Sabbath *dayes* disputed with
them by the Scriptures,
3 Opening, and alledging that Christ must
haue suffred, and risen againe from the
dead: and this is Iesus Christ, whome, *said
he*, I preache to you.
4 And some of them beleued, & ioyned in
cōmpanie with Paul and Silas: also of the
Grecians that feared God a great multitude, & of the chief women not a fewe.
5 But the Iewes which beleued not, moued
with enuie, toke vnto them certeine vaga-
bondes & wicked felowes, and when they
had assembled the multitude, they made a
tumulte in the citie, & made assaut against
the house of Iason, & soght to bring them
out to the people.
6 But when they founde them not, they
drewe Iason & certeine brethren vnto the
heades of the citie, crying, These are they

which haue ſubuerted the ſtate of the worl
de,and here they are,
7 Whome Iaſon hathe receiued, and theſe
all do againſt the decrees of Ceſar,ſaying
that there is another [a]King,one Ieſus.
8 Then they troubled the people, and the
heads of the citie, when they heard theſe
things.
9 Notwithſtanding when they had receiued "ſufficient aſſurance of Iaſon and of
the other,they let them go.
10 And the brethren immediatly ſent away
Paul & Silas by night vnto Berea , which
when they were come thither, entred into
the Synagogue of the Iewes.
11 Theſe were alſo [b] more noble men then
they which were at Theſſalonica, which
receiued the worde with all readines,and
*ſearched the Scriptures daily, [c] whether
thoſe things were ſo.
12 Therefore manie of them beleued, & of
honeſte women,which were Grecians,and
men not a fewe.
13 ¶But when the Iewes of Theſſalonica
knewe, that the worde of God was alſo
preached of Paul at Berea, they came thither alſo,and moued the people.
14 But by & by ý brethren ſent away Paul
to go as *it were* to the ſea:but Silas and Ti
motheus abode there ſtil.
15 And they that "did conduit Paul,broght
him vnto Athenes: and when they had receiued a commandement vnto Silas and
Timotheus that they ſhulde come to him
at once,they departed.
16 ¶Now while Paul waited for them at A-
thenes,his ſpirit was ſtirred in him,when
he ſawe the citie [d] ſubiect to idolatrie.
17 Therefore he diſputed in the Synagogue with the Iewes , and with them that
were religious , and in the market daily
[e] with whome ſoeuer he met.
18 Then certeine philoſophers of the [f] Epi
cures,and of the [g] Stoickes, diſputed with
him,and ſome ſaid, What wil this "babler
ſay?Others *ſaid*, He ſemeth to be a ſetter
forthe of ſtrange gods (becauſe he preached vnto them Ieſus , & the reſurrectiō.)
19 And they toke him, and broght him into
[h] Mars ſtrete, ſaying, May we not knowe,
what this new doctrine,whereof thou ſpea
keſt, is?
20 For thou bringeſt certeine ſtrāge things
vnto our eares: we wolde knowe therefore,what theſe things meane.
21 For all the Athenians , and ſtrangers
which dwelt there,"gaue them ſelues to
nothing els,but ether to tel,or to heare ſome newes.
22 Then Paul ſtode in the middes of [i] Mars
ſtrete,& ſaid,Ye mē of Athenes,I perceiue
that in all things ye are to ſuperſtitious.

a Like quarel-pikīg thei vſed againſt Chriſt: & theſe be the weapons wherewith ý worlde continually fighteth agaīſt the mēbres of Chriſt,trayſon & ſedition.
Or, a ſufficient anſwer.
b Not more excellent of birth,but more prompt,and couragious in receiuing the worde of God: for he compareth thē of Berea ŵ thē of Theſſalonica who perſecuted ý Apoſtles in Berea.
Ioh.5,39.
c This was not onely to trie if theſe things which thei had heard, were true, but alſo to confirme them ſelues in the ſame, and to increaſe their faith.
Or, had the charge to conduit him ſafely.
d That citie ŵ was the fountaine of all knowledge, was now the ſinke of moſte horrible idolatrie.
e Suche was his feruēt zeale towards Gods glorie, that he labored to amplifie the ſame bothe in ſeaſon,and out of ſeaſon , as he taught afterwarde to Timothie.
f Who helde, that pleaſure was mās whole felicitie.
g Who taught ý vertue was onely mans felicitie, which notwithſtanding they neuer atteined vnto.
Or, raſcal, or, triſter.
h Where iudgement was giuen of waightie matters, but chiefely of impietie againſt their gods, whereof Paul was accuſed: or els was led thither becauſe of ý reſorte of people whoſe eares euer tickled to heare newes. *Or, had leaſure.* i Which was alſo called Areopagus.

23 For as I paſſed by,& behelde your deuo-
cions,I founde an altar wherein was written, [k] VNTO THE VNKNOWEN
GOD. Whome ye then ignorantly worſhip,him ſhewe I vnto you.
24 God that made the worlde, & all things
that are therein , ſeing that he is Lord of
heauen & earth, * dwelleth not in temples
made with hands,
25 *Nether is worſhipped with mens hāds,
as thogh he neded any thing , ſeing he giueth to all life and breath and all things,
26 And hathe made of one blood all mankinde,to dwell on all the face of the earth,
and hathe [l] aſsigned the times which were
ordeined before, and the boundes of their
[m] habitation,
27 That they ſhulde ſeke the Lord, if ſo be
they might haue groped after him , and
founde [n] *him*,thogh douteles he be not farre from euerie one of vs.
28 For in him we liue , and moue , and haue
our being , as alſo certeine of your owne
[o] Poetes haue ſaid, For we are alſo his generacion.
29 *For aſmuche then, as we are the generacion of God, we oght not to thinke that
the Godhead is like vnto [p] gold, or ſiluer,
or ſtone grauen by arte and the inuention
of man.
30 And the time of this ignorāce God [q] re
garded not : but now he admoniſheth [r] all
men euerie where to repent,
31 Becauſe he hathe appointed a day in the
which he wil iudge the worlde in righteouſnes , by that man whome he hathe appointed , *whereof* he hathe giuen an aſſurance to all mē,in that he hathe raiſed him
from the dead.
32 Now when they heard of the reſurrectiō
from the dead,ſome mocked,& other ſaid,
We wil heare thee againe of this thing.
33 And ſo Paul departed from among them.
34 Howbeit certeine men claue vnto Paul,
and beleued: among whome was alſo De-
nis "Areopagita, and a woman named Damaris,and other with them.

k Hereby Paul taketh an occaſion to bring them to ý true God.
Chap.7,48.
Pſal.50,8.
l Before man was created, God had appointed his ſtate & condition
m This is ment as touching the ſondrie changes of the worlde, as when ſome people do parte out of a countrey, & others come to dwel therein.
n Men grope in darkenes til Chriſt the true light ſhine in their hearts.
Iſa.40,23.
o As Aratus & others.
p He condemneth the matter and the forme wherewith God is coūterfaited.
q But pardoned it,and did not puniſh it as it deſerued.
r This is ment of the vniuerſal worlde,and not of euery particular mā: for whoſoeuer ſinneth without the Lawe, ſhal die without the Lawe.
Or, a iudge of Mars ſtrete.

CHAP. XVIII.

3 Paul laboureth with his hands, and preacheth at Corinthus. 6 He is deteſted of the Iewes. 8 Yet receiued of many, 9 And cōforted of the Lord. 14 Gallio refuſeth to medle with religion. 18 Pauls vowe. 21 His faith in the prouidēce of God, 22 And care for the brethren. 24 The praiſe of Apollos.

1 AFter theſe things,Paul departed frō
Athenes,and came to Corinthus,
2 And founde a certeine Iewe, named * A-
quila, borne in Pontus , lately come from
Italie,and his wife Priſcilla (becauſe that
[a] Claudius had cōmanded all Iewes to departe frō Rome)and he came vnto them.
3 And becauſe he was of the ſame crafte,he
abode

Rom.16,3.
a This was Claudius Ceſar who then was Emperour.

b Thus he vſed where euer he came: but principally at Corinthus becauſe of ẏ falſe Apoſtles which preached without wages to winne the peoples fauour.
c Or pauilliõs which thẽ were made of ſkĩnes.
d And boyled with a certeine zeale.
Chap.13,32.
mat.16,14.
e Becauſe they haue none excuſe, he denoũceth the vengeance of God againſt them through their owne faute.
1.Cor.1,14.
f God promiſeth him a ſpecial protectiõ, whereby he wolde defende him from the violent rage of his enemies.
"Or, Grecia.
g They accuſed him becauſe he trãſgreſſed the ſeruice of God appointed by ẏ Law.
h Of whome is ſpokẽ 1.Co.1,1.
i Paul did thus beare with the Iewes infirmities which as yet were not ſufficiently inſtructed.
Nom 6,18.
chap.21,24.

abode with them and [b] wroght (for their
craftewas to make [c] tentes.)
4 And he diſputed in the Synagogue euerie Sabbath *day*, and exhorted the Iewes, &
the Grecians.
5 Now when Silas & Timotheus were come from Macedonia, Paul [d] burned in
ſpirit, teſtifying to the Iewes that Ieſus
was the Chriſt.
6 And when they reſiſted and blaſphemed,
he *ſhouke his raiment, & ſaid vnto them,
[e] Your blood *be* vpon your owne head: I
am cleane: frõ hence forthe wil I go vnto
the Gentiles.
7 So he departed thence, and entred into a
certeine mans houſe, named Iuſtus, a worſhipper of God, whoſe houſe ioyned hard
to the Synagogue,
8 And *Criſpus the chief ruler of the Synagogue, beleued in the Lord with all
his houſholde: and many of the Corinthiãs hearing it, beleued & were baptized.
9 Then ſaid the Lord to Paul in the night
by a viſion, Feare not, but ſpeake, & holde
not thy peace.
10 For [f] I am with thee, and no man ſhal lay
hands on thee to hurt thee: for I haue muche people in this citie.
11 So he continued there a yere and ſix moneths, and taught the worde of God amõg
them.
12 ¶ Now when Gallio was Deputie of "Achaia, the Iewes aroſe with one accorde
againſt Paul, and broght him to the iudgement ſeat,
13 Saying, This felow perſuadeth men to
worſhip God contrary to the [g] Law.
14 And as Paul was about to opẽ his mouth,
Gallio ſaid vnto the Iewes, If it were a
matter of wrong, or an euil dede, ô ye
Iewes, I wolde according to reaſon mainteine you.
15 But if it be a queſtion of wordes, and names, and of your Law, loke ye to it your
ſelues: for I wil be no iudge of thoſe
things.
16 And he draue them from the iudgemẽt
ſeat.
17 Then toke all the Grecians [h] Soſthenes
the chief ruler of the Synagogue, and bet
him before the iudgement ſeat: but Gallio
cared nothing for thoſe things.
18 But when Paul had taried there yet a
good while, he toke leaue of the brethren,
and ſailed into Syria (and with him Priſcilla and Aquila) after that he had [i] ſhorne his head in Cenchrea: for he had a
*vowe.
19 Then he came to Epheſus, and left them
there: but he entred into the Synagogue
and diſputed with the Iewes.
20 Who deſired him to tary a longer time
with them: but he wolde not conſent,
21 But bade them fare wel, ſaying, I muſt
nedes kepe this feaſt that commeth, in Ieruſalẽ: but I wil returne againe vnto you,
*if God wil. So he ſailed from Epheſus.
22 ¶ And whẽ he came downe to [k] Ceſarea,
he went vp *to Ieruſalem*: & when he had ſaluted the Church, he wẽt downe vnto Antiochia.
23 Now when he had taried *there* a while, he
departed, and went through the countrey
of Galacia & Phrygia by order, ſtrengthening all the diſciples.
24 And a certeine Iewe named *Apollos,
borne at Alexãdria, came to Epheſus, an eloquent mã, & "mightie in the Scriptures.
25 The ſame was [l] inſtructed in the way of
the Lord, & he ſpake feruently in the Spirit, and taught diligently the things of the
Lord, & knewe but the [m] baptiſme of Iohn
onely.
26 And he began to ſpeake boldely in the
Synagogue. Whome when Aquila & Priſcilla had heard, they toke him vnto them,
and [n] expounded vnto him the [o] way of
God more perfectly.
27 And when he was minded to go into Achaia, the brethren exhorting him, wrote
to the diſciples to receaue him: and after
he was come thither, he holpe thẽ muche
which had beleued through grace.
28 For mightely he confuted publikely the
Iewes with great vehemencie, ſhewing by
the Scriptures, that Ieſus was the Chriſt.

1.Cor.4,19.
iam.4,15.
k Called Ceſarea Stratonis.
2 Cor.1,12.
"Or, wel inſtructed.
l That is, was ſomewhat entred.
m He had but as yet ẏ firſt principles of Chriſts religiõ: and by baptiſme is here mẽt the doctrine.
n This great learned, and eloquent man diſdained not to be taught of a poore craftes man.
o The way to ſaluation.

CHAP. XIX.

6 The holie Goſt is giuen by Pauls hands. 9 The Iewes blaſpheme his doctrine, which was confirmed by miracles. 13 The raſhenes, and puniſhment of the coniurers, & the frute that came thereof. 24 Demetrius raiſeth ſedition vnder pretence of Diana. 41 Yet God deliuereth his and appeaſeth it by the towne clarke.

1 AND it came to paſſe, while Apollos
was at Corinthus, that Paul whẽ he
paſſed through the vpper coaſtes, came to
Epheſus, and founde certeine diſciples,
2 And ſaid vnto thẽ, Haue ye receiued the
[a] holie Goſt ſence ye beleued? And they
ſaid vnto him, We haue not ſo muche as
heard whether there be an holie Goſt.
3 And he ſaid vnto them, [b] Vnto what were ye then baptized? And they ſaid, Vnto
Iohns baptiſme.
4 Then ſaid Paul, *Iohn verely baptized
with the baptiſme of repentance, ſaying
vnto the people, that they ſhulde beleue
in him, which ſhulde come after him, that
is, in Chriſt Ieſus.
5 So when they heard it, they were [c] baptized in the Name of the Lord Ieſus.
6 And Paul laid his hands vpon them, and

a That is, the particular giftes of the Spirit: for as yet they knewe not the viſible gifts.
b Meaning, what doctrine they did profeſſe by their baptiſme: for to be baptized in Iohns baptiſme ſignifieth to profeſſe the doctrine which he taught, & ſealed with the ſigne of baptiſme: to be baptized in the Name of the Father, &c. is to be dedicate and conſecrate vnto him: to be baptized in the death of Chriſt, or for the dead, or into one bodie, vnto remiſsion of ſinnes, is, that ſinne by Chriſts death may be aboliſhed, and dye in vs, & that we may growe in Chriſt our head, and that our ſinnes may be waſhed away by the blood of Chriſt. * *Mat 3,11. mar.1,8. luk 3,16. iohn 1.27. chap.1,5. & 2,2. & 11,16.*
c Endewed with the viſible graces of the holie Goſt.

the holie Gost came on them, & they spake the tongues, and prophecied.
7 And all the men were about twelue.
8 ¶ Moreouer he went into the Synagogue,
& spake boldely for the space of thre moneths, disputing & exhorting to the things
that *apperteine* to the kingdome of God.
9 But when certeine were hardened, and
disobeyed, speaking euil of the way *of God*
before the multitude, he departed from
them, and separated the disciples, and disputed daily in the schole of one [d] Tyran-
nus‖.
10 And this was done by the space of two
yeres, so that all they which dwelt in Asia,
heard the worde of the Lord Iesus, bothe
Iewes and Grecians.
11 And God wroght no smale miracles by
the hands of Paul,
12 So that from his bodie were broght vnto the sicke, "kerchefs [e] or handkerchefs,
and the diseases departed from them, and
the euil spirits went out of them.
13 Then certeine of the vagabonde Iewes,
"exorcistes, toke in hand to name ouer thē
which had euil spirits, the Name of the
Lord Iesus, saying, We [f] adiure you by Iesus, whome Paul preacheth.
14 (And there were certeine sonnes of Sce-
ua a Iewe, the Priest, *about* seuen which
did this)
15 And the euil spirit answered, and said,
Iesus I acknowledge, and Paul I knowe:
but who are ye?
16 And the man in whome ẏ euil spirit was,
ran on them, & ouercame them, & preuailed against them, so that they fled out of
that house, naked, and wounded.
17 And this was knowen to all the Iewes &
Grecians also, which dwelt at Ephesus, &
feare came on them all, and the Name of
the Lord Iesus was magnified.
18 And many that beleued, came and cōfessed, and [g] shewed their workes.
19 Many also of them which vsed curious
artes, broght their bokes, and burned them
before all men, and they counted the price
of them, & founde it [h] fiftie thousand *pieces* of siluer.
20 So the worde of God grewe mightely,
and preuailed.
21 ¶ Now when these things were accomplished, Paul purposed [i] by the Spirit to
passe through Macedonia and Achaia, and
to go to Ierusalem, saying, After I haue
bene there, I must also se Rome.
22 So sent he into Macedonia two of them
that ministred vnto him, Timotheus and
Erastus, *but* he remained in Asia for a season.
23 And the same time there arose no smale
trouble about that [k] way.
24 For a certeine man named Demetrius a

d That is, of a certeine man so called.

‖ *From fiue a clocke vnto ten.*

"*Or, napkins.*

e This was to autorize the Gospel, and to cōfirme Pauls ministerie, not to cause men to worship hī or his napkins.

"*Or, coniurers.*

f They abuse Pauls autoritie, & without any vocation of God, vsurpe that which is not in mans power.

g That is, declared by confessiō of their sinnes and by their good workes ẏ they were faithful.

h This mounteth to of our money about 2000 markes.

i By the motion of the holie Gost, he vndertoke this iorney.

k That is, about the state of the Christians: for they contemned the Christians because they left the olde religion, & broght in another trade of doctrine.

siluersmith, which made siluer "temples
of Diana, [l] broght great gaines vnto the
craftes men:
25 Whome he called together, with the
workemen of like things, and said, Sirs, ye
knowe that by this crafte [m] we haue our
goods.
26 Moreouer ye se and heare, that not alone
at Ephesus, but almoste through out all A-
sia this Paul hathe persuaded, & turned a-
way muche people, saying, That they be
not gods which are made with hands,
27 So that not onely this thing is dangerous vnto vs, [n] that the state shulde be reproued, but also that the [o] temple of the
great goddesse Diana shulde be nothing
estemed, and that it wolde come to passe
that her magnificence, which all Asia and
the [p] worlde worshippeth, shulde be destroyed.
28 Now when they heard it, they were ful
of wrath, and cryed out, saying, Great *is*
Diana of the Ephesians.
29 And the whole citie was ful of cōfusion,
and they rushed into the commune place
with one assent, and caught * Gaius, and
* Aristarchus, men of Macedonia, & Pauls
companions of his iourney.
30 And whē Paul wolde haue entred in vnto the people, the disciples suffred him not.
31 Certeine also of the chief of Asia which
were his friēds, sent vnto him, desirīg him
that he wolde not present him self in the
commune place.
32 Some therefore cryed one thing, and some another: for the assemblie was out of
order, and the more parte knewe not wherefore they were come together.
33 And *some* of the companie [q] drewe forthe
Alexander, the Iewes thrusting him forwardes. Alexander then beckened with the
hand, and wolde haue excused the matter
to the people.
34 But when they knewe that he was a Iewe,
there arose a shoute almoste for the space
of two houres, of all men crying, Great *is*
Diana of the Ephesians.
35 Then the towne clarke when he had
stayed the people, said, Ye mē of Ephesus,
what man is it that knoweth not how that
the citie of the Ephesians is a worshipper
of the great goddesse Diana, and of *the
image*, which came downe from [r] Iupiter?
36 Seing then that no man can [s] speake a-
gainst these things, ye oght to be appeased, and to do nothing rashly.
37 For ye haue broght hither these men,
which haue nether commit sacrilege, nether do blaspheme your goddesse.
38 Wherefore, if Demetrius and the craftes
men which are with him, haue a matter a-
gainst any mā, the lawe is open, & there are
Deputies: let them accuse one another.

"*Or, shrines.*

l What impietie doeth not couetousnes driue a man vnto?

m He was moued with his profit: & the others for their bellies, so that they wolde rather lose bothe their liues, & religion then their filthie gaine.

n Meaning their arte and occupation.

o Religion is his seconde argument which he lesse estemeth, then his profit, and therefore putteth it last, which thing is contrary to the doīgs of the faithful: for they preferre religion aboue all.

p He groūdeth his religiō vpon the multitude & autoritie of ẏ worlde, as do the Papistes.

Rom. 16, 23.
1. cor. 1, 14.
Colos. 4, 10.

q And set him in an hie place where the people colde not come nere him but whēce thei might wel heare his voyce.

r Antiquitie & the couetousnes of the Priests broght in this superstition: for it is writen that the temple being repaired seuen times, this idole was neuer chāged, Plin. li. 16, 40. by suche delusions ẏ worlde is moste easely abused.

s He pacifieth the people by worldelie wisdome, & hathe no respect to religion.

39 But

39 But if ye inquire anie thing concerning
other matters it maye be determined in a
lawful assemblie.
40 For we are euen in ieopardie to be accused of this daies sedicion, forasmuche
as there is no cause, whereby we may giue a reason of this concourse of people.
41 And when he had thus spoken, he let the
assemblie departe.

CHAP. XX.

Paul goeth into Macedonia and into Grecia. 7 He celebrateth the Lords supper and preacheth. 9 At Troas he raiseth vp Eutychus 17 At Ephesus he calleth the Elders of the Church together, committeth the keping of Gods flocke vnto them, warneth them of false teachers, maketh his praier with them, and departeth by ship towards Ierusalem.

1 NOw after the tumulte was ceased,
Paul called the disciples vnto him,
and embrased them, and departed to go
into Macedonia.
2 And when he had gone through those
parties, and had exhorted them with manie wordes, he came into Grecia.
3 And hauing taried *there* thre moneths, because the Iewes laid waite for him, as he
was about to saile into Syria, he purposed
to returne through Macedonia.
4 And there accompanied him into Asia
Sopater of Berea, and of them of Thessalonica, Aristarchus, and Secundus, & Gaius of Derbe, and Timotheus, & of them
of Asia Tychicus, and Trophimus.
5 These wēt before, & taried vs at Troas.
6 And we sailed forthe from [a] Philippi, after the daies of vnleauened bread, & came vnto them to Troas in fiue daies, where we abode seuen daies.
7 And [b] the first day of the weke, the disciples being come together to [c] breake bread, Paul preached vnto thē, readie to departe on the morowe, and continued the
preaching vnto midnight.
8 And there were manie lightes in an vpper chamber, where" they were gathered
together.
9 And there sate in a windowe a certeine
yong "man, named Eutychus, fallen into a
depe slepe: & as Paul was lōg preaching,
he ouercome with slepe, fell downe from
the third lofte, and was taken vp dead.
10 But Paul went downe, and laid him self
vpon him, & embrased him, saying, Trouble not your selues: for his life is in him.
11 So when *Paul* was come vp againe, and
had broken bread, & eaten, he commoned
a long while til the dawning of the daye,
and so he departed.
12 And they broght the boie aliue, and thei
were not a litle comforted.
13 ¶ Then we went forthe to ship, & sailed
vnto *the citie* [d] Assos, that we might receiue Paul there: for so had he appointed,
and wolde him self go a fote.

a He remained there these daies, because he had better opportunitie to teache: also ye abolishing of the Law was not yet knowē.
b Which we call Sōday. Of this place and also of the 1. Cor.16, 2. we gather that the Christiās vsed to haue their solemne assemblies this day, laying aside ye ceremonie of the Iewish Sabbath.
c To celebrate the Lords Supper, Chap 2,46
"Or, we.
"Or, boye.
d Which was a citie of Mysia called otherwise Apollonia, Plī li.5. chap.50

14 Now when he was come vnto vs to Assos, and we had receiued him, we came to
Mitylenes.
15 And we sailed thence, and came the next
day ouer against Chios, and the next daye
we arriued at Samos, and taried at Tro-
gyllium: the next daye we came to Miletum.
16 For Paul had determined to saile by E-
phesus, because he wolde not spend the time in Asia: for he hasted to be, if he colde
possible, at Ierusalem, at the day of" Pentecoste.
17 ¶ Wherefore from Miletum he sent to
Ephesus, & called the Elders of ye Church.
18 Who when they were come to him, he
said vnto them, Ye knowe frō the first day
that I came into Asia, after what maner I
haue bene with you at all seasons,
19 [e] Seruing the Lord with all [f] modestie,
and with manie teares, and tentacions,
which came vnto me by the layings awai-
te of the Iewes,
20 And how I kept [g] backe nothing that
was profitable, but haue shewed you, and
taught you openly, & throughout euerie
house,
21 Witnessing bothe to the Iewes, & to the
Grecians the [h] repentance towarde God,
& [i] faith towarde our Lord Iesus Christ.
22 And now beholde, I go [k] bounde in the
spirit vnto Ierusalem, and knowe not what
things shal come vnto me there,
23 Saue that the holie Gost [l] witnesseth in
euerie citie, saying, that bandes and afflictions abide me‖.
24 But I passe not at all, nether is my life
deare vnto my self, so that I may fulfil my
course with ioye, and the ministracion
which I haue receiued of the Lord Iesus,
to testifie ye Gospel of the grace of God.
25 And now beholde, I knowe that hence
forthe ye all, through whome I haue gone
preaching the kingdome of God, shal se
my face no more.
26 Wherefore I take you to recorde this
day, that I am pure from the [m] blood of
all men.
27 For I haue kept nothing backe, but haue shewed you [n] all the counsel of God.
28 Take hede therefore vnto your selues,
and to all the flocke, whereof the holie
Gost hathe made you Ouerseers, to fede
the Church of God, which he hathe purchased with his [o] owne blood.
29 For I knowe this, that after my departīg
shal grieuous wolues entre in among you,
not sparing the flocke.
30 Moreouer of your owne selues shal mē
arise speaking [p] peruerse things, to drawe
disciples after them.
31 Therefore watche and remember, that
by *the space* of thre yeres I ceased not to

"Or, Witsontide
e In my vocacion & ministerie.
f This vertue is contrarie to boasting & hie minded: wc vices are detestable in the seruants of Iesus Christ.
g I nether held my tongue for feare, nor dissembled for gaine.
h Which is ye tourning to God by newnes of life.
i Which is the receiuing of ye grace, which Christ doeth offer vs.
k That is, by the impulsion & commandement of the holie Gost, who draweth me as with a band.
l By the Prophetes.
‖ *In Ierusalem.*
m I am not the occasion of anie of your destructions.
n Which cōcerneth your saluacion.
o That wc apperteineth to ye humanitie of Christ, is here attributed to his diuinitie, because of the communion of the proprieties, & vniō of the two natures in one persone.
p Through their ambitiō, wc is mother of all herefie and wickednes.

warne euerie one, bothe night and daye
with teares.

32 And now brethren, I commende you to
God, and to the worde of his grace, which
q is able to buylde further, & to giue you
an r inheritance: among all them, which a-
re sanctified.

33 I haue coueted no mans siluer, nor golde, nor apparel.

34 Yea, ye knowe, that these hands haue
ministred vnto my *necessities, & to them
that were with me.

35 I haue shewed you all things, how that
so laboring, ye oght to supporte the weake, & to remember the wordes of the Lord
Iesus, how that he said, f It is a blessed
thing to giue, rather then to receiue.

36 And when he had thus spoken, he kneled
downe, and praied with them all.

37 Then they wept all abundantly, and fel
on Pauls necke, and kissed him,

38 Being chiefly sorie for the wordes which
he spake, That they shulde se his face no
more. And thei accompanied him vnto
the ship.

q To increase you with further graces & to finish his worke in you. r He promiseth to the faithful continual increase of grace, til they enter into ẏ possession of that inheritance, ẇ is prepared for them.

1.Cor.4,12. 1.thes.2,9. 2.thes.3,8.

f Althogh this be not orderly so writ in anie one place, yet it is gathered of diuers places of ẏ Scripture in effect.

CHAP. XXI.

1 The commune prayers of the faithful. 8 Philippes foure daughters prophetesses. 23 Pauls constancie to beare the crosse, as Agabus & others forespake, althogh he was otherwise counseled by the brethren. 28 The great danger that he was in, and how he escaped.

1 And as we lau̅ched forthe, and were
departed from them, we came with
a straight course vnto Coos, and the daye
following vnto the Rhodes, & from thence vnto Patara.

2 And we founde a ship that went ouer vnto Phenice, and went aboarde, & set forthe.

3 And when we had discouered Cyprus, we
left it on the left hand, and sailed towarde
Syria, and arriued at Tyrus: for there the
ship vnladed the burden.

4 And when we had founde disciples, we
taryed there seuen dayes. And they tolde
Paul a through the b Spirit, that he shulde
not go vp to Ierusalem.

5 But whe̅ the daies were ended, we departed, and went our way, and thei all accompanied vs with *their* wiues and children,
euen out of the citie: & we kneling downe
on the shore, prayed.

6 Then when we had embraced one another, we toke ship, & thei returned home.

7 And when we had ended the course from
Tyrus, we arriued at Ptolemais, and saluted the brethren, and abode with them
one daye.

8 And the next day, Paul & thei that were
with him, departed, and came vnto Cesarea: and we entred into the house of *Philippe the Euangelist, which was one of the
c seuen *Deacons*, and abode with him.

a By the reuelacio̅ of Gods Spirit.
b The holie Spirit reueiled vnto them the persecucions ẏ Paul shulde haue made against him, and the same Spirit also strengthened Paul to susteine them.

Chap.6,5.
c This office of Deaconship was but for a time, according as the Congregacion had nede, or otherwise.

9 Now he had foure daughters virgines,
which did prophecie.

10 And as we taryed there manie dayes,
there came a certeine Prophet fro̅ Iudea,
named Agabus.

11 And when he was come vnto vs, he toke
Pauls girdle, and bounde his owne hands
and fete, and said, d Thus saith the holie
Gost, So shal the Iewes at Ierusale̅ e binde
the man that oweth this girdle, and shal
deliuer him into the hands of ẏ Gentiles.

12 And when we had heard these things,
bothe we and other of the same place besoght him that he wolde not go vp to Ierusalem.

13 Then Paul answered, and said, What do
ye weping and breaking mine heart? For I
am readie not to be bounde onely, but also to dye at Ierusalem for the Name of the
Lord Iesus.

14 So when he wolde not be persuaded, we
ceased, saying, The wil of the Lord be
done.

15 And after those dayes we trussed vp our
fardeles, and went vp to Ierusalem.

16 There went with vs also *certeine* of the
disciples of Cesarea, & broght with them
one Mnason of Cyprus, an olde disciple,
with whome we shulde lodge.

17 And when we were come to Ierusalem,
the brethren receiued vs gladly.

18 And the next daye Paul went in with vs
vnto f Iames: and all the Elders were there assembled.

19 And when he had embraced them, he
tolde by ordre all things, that God had
wroght among the Gentiles by his ministracion.

20 So when thei heard it, they glorified the
Lord, and said vnto him, Thou seest, brother, how manie thousand Iewes there are
which beleue, and they are all zealous of
the Law.

21 Now they are informed of thee, that
thou teachest all the Iewes, which are a-
mong the Gentiles, to forsake Moses, and
saist, that they oght not to circumcise
their children, nether to liue *after* the g customes.

22 What is then *to be done*? the multitude
must nedes come together: for they shal
heare that thou art come.

23 Do therefore this that we saye to thee.
We haue h foure men, which haue made
a vowe.

24 Them take, & i purifie thy self with the̅,
and contribute with them, that they maye
*shaue their heades: and all shal knowe,
that those things, whereof they haue bene
informed concerning thee, are nothing,
but that thou thy self also walkest and kepest the Law.

25 For as touching the Gentiles, which
beleue

d God wolde haue his seruants bandes knowen, to the intent that no man shulde thinke that he cast him self into wilful danger.
e This was not to make Paul afraied, but to encourage him agaist ẏ brunt.

f Who was ẏ chief, or superintendent of ẏ Church of Ierusalem.

g That is, according to the maners that ȯ fathers obserued, ẇ were co̅manded by God.
h Who as yet were not wel instructed in Christ.

Nomb.6,18. chap.18,18.

i The end of this ceremonie was thankesgiuing, & was instituted by God, and partely of ignorance and infirmitie reteined: therefore S. Paul supported therein ẏ weakenes of others & made him self all to all men, not hindering his conscience.

beleue, we haue written, and determined
*that thei obserue no suche thing, but that
they kepe them selues from things offred
to idoles, and from blood, and frõ that that
is strangled, and from fornication.

Chap. 15,20.

26 Then Paul toke the men, and the next
day was purified with them, and entred into the Temple, * declaring the accõplishment of the daies of the purification, vntil that an offering shulde be offered for e-
uerie one of them.

Nom. 6,13. chap. 24,8.

27 And when the seuen dayes were almoste
ended, the Iewes which were of Asia (whẽ
they sawe him in the Temple) moued all
the people, and [k] laid hands on him,
28 Crying, Men of Israel, helpe: this is the
man that teacheth all men euery where a-
gainst the people, and the Law, and this
place: moreouer, he hathe broght Greciãs
into the Temple, and hathe [l] polluted this
holie place.

k In thinking to appease the faithful, and to support the infirme, he falleth into the hands of his enemies.

l By bringing in suche as were not circũcised.

29 For they had sene before Trophimus an
Ephesiã with him in the citie, whome they
supposed that Paul had broght into the
Temple.
30 Then all the citie was moued, & the people ran together: and they toke Paul, and
drewe him out of the Tẽple, & forthewith
the dores were shut.
31 But as they went about to kill him, tydings came vnto the chief Captaine of
the bãde, that all Ierusalem was on an vproare.
32 Who immediatly toke souldiers and
[m] Centurions, and ran [n] downe vnto them:
and when they sawe the chief Captaine &
the souldiers, they left beating of Paul.
33 Then the chief Captaine came nere and
toke him, & commanded him to be bounde with two chaines, and demãded who he
was, and what he had done.

m Which were vndercaptains and had charge ouer an hundreth souldiers.

n A notable example of Gods prouidẽce for the defence of his.

34 And one cryed this, another that, among
the people. So when he colde not knowe
the certeinetie for the tumulte, he cõmanded him to be led into the castle.
35 And whẽ he came vnto the grieces, it was
so that he was borne of the souldiers, for ẏ
violence of the people.
36 For the multitude of ẏ people followed
after, crying, Away with him.
37 And as Paul shulde haue bene led into
the castle, he said vnto the chief Captaine,
May I speake vnto thee? Who said, Canst
thou *speake* Greke?
38 Art not thou the * [o] Egyptian, who before these dayes raised a sedition, & led out
into the wildernes foure thousand mẽ that
were murtherers?

Chap. 5,36.

o Iosephus li. Antiq 20 cha. 11. & de bello Iuda. li. 2. cha. 12.

39 Then Paul said, Douteles I am a man
which am a Iewe, & citizen of * Tarsus, a
famous citie in Cilicia, & I beseche thee,
suffre me to speake vnto the people.

Chap. 22,3.

40 And when he had giuẽ him licence, Paul
stode on the grieces, & beckened with the
hand vnto the people: and when there was
made great silence, he spake vnto them in
the Hebrue tongue, saying,

CHAP. XXII.

3 Paul rendreth an account of his life and doctrine.
25 He escapeth the whippe by reason he was a citizen of Rome.

1 YE men, brethren & fathers, heare my
"defence now towards you.
2 (And whẽ they heard that he spake in the
Hebrue tongue to them, they kept the more silence, and he said)
3 I am verely a man, *which am* a Iewe, borne
in * Tarsus in Cilicia, but broght vp in
this citie at the [a] fete of Gamaliel, and
instructed according to the perfect maner
of the Law of the Fathers, and was zealous towarde God, as ye all are this day.

" Or, raison, or excuse.

Chap. 21,39.

a Whereby he declareth his modestie, diligence & docilitie.

4 * And I persecuted this " way vnto the
death, binding and deliuering into prison
bothe men and women,

Chap. 8,3.

" Or, this profession of the Christians.

5 As also ẏ chief Priest doeth beare me witnes, & all the state of the Elders: of whome also I receiued letters vnto the [b] brethren, and went to Damascus to bring thẽ
which were there, bounde vnto Ierusalem,
that they might be punished.

b To ẏ Iewes to whome the letters were directed.

6 ¶ And so it was, as I iourneid and was come nere vnto Damascus about noone, that
suddenly there shone from heauen a great
light rounde about me.
7 So I fel vnto the earth, and heard a voyce, saying vnto me, Saul, Saul, why persecutest thou me?
8 Then I answered, Who art thou, Lord?
And he said to me, I am Iesus of Nazaret,
whome thou persecutest.
9 Moreouer they that were with me, sawe
in dede a light and were afraid: but they
heard not the voyce of him that spake vnto me.
10 Then I said, What shal I do, Lord? And
the Lord said vnto me, Arise, and go into
Damascus: and there it shalbe tolde thee
of all things, which are appointed for thee
to do.
11 So when I colde not se for the glorie
of that light, I was led by the hand of
them that were with me, and came into
Damascus.
12 And one Ananias a godlie man, as perteining to the Law, hauing good reporte of
all the Iewes which dwelt there,
13 Came vnto me, and stode, and said vnto
me, Brother Saul, receiue thy sight: & that
same houre I loked vpon him.
14 And he said, The God of our fathers hathe [c] appointed thee, that ẏ shuldest know
his wil, and shuldest se that [d] Iust one, and
shuldest heare the voyce of his mouth.
15 For thou shalt be his witnes vnto all men

c This may be referred to the eternal cõusel of God, or els to the execution & declaration of ẏ same which semeth here to be more propre.

d Which is Christ, 1. Ioh 3, 1.

of the things, which thou haſt ſene and
heard.
16 Now therefore why tarieſt thou? Ariſe,
and be baptized, and waſhe away thy ſinnes, in calling on the [e] Name of the Lord.
17 ¶ And it came to paſſe, that when I was
come againe to Ieruſalem, and prayed in
the Temple, I was in a traunce,
18 And ſawe him ſaying vnto me, Make haſte, & get thee quickely out of Ieruſalem:
for they wil not receiue thy witnes cõcerning me.
19 Then I ſaid, Lord, they knowe ẏ I * pri-
ſoned, and bet in euerie Synagogue them
that beleued in thee.
20 And when the blood of thy martyr Steuen was ſhed, I alſo * ſtode by, and conſented vnto his death, and kept the clothes
of them that ſlewe him.
21 Thẽ he ſaid vnto me, Departe: for I wil
ſend thee farre hence vnto the Gentiles.
22 ¶ And they heard vnto this worde, *but* thẽ
they lift vp their voyces, and ſaid, Away
with ſuche a felowe from the earth: for it is
not mete that he ſhulde liue.
23 And as they cryed and caſt of their clothes, and threwe duſt into the aire,
24 The chief captaine commanded him to
be led into the caſtle, & bade that he ſhulde
be ſcourged, and examined, that he might
knowe wherefore they cryed ſo on him.
25 And as they bounde him with thongs,
Paul ſaid vnto the Cẽturion that ſtode by,
Is it lawful for you to ſcourge one that is
a [f] Romaine, and not condemned?
26 Now when the Centurion heard it, he
went, and tolde the chief captaine, ſaying,
Take hede what thou doeſt: for this man is
a Romaine.
27 Then the chief captaine came, and ſaid
to him, Tell me, art thou a Romaine? And
he ſaid, Yea.
28 And the chief captaine anſwered, With
a great ſumme obteined I this burgeſſhip.
Then Paul ſaid, But I was [g] ſo borne.
29 Then ſtraight way they departed from
him, which ſhulde haue examined him: &
the chief captaine alſo was afraid, after he
knewe that he was a Romaine, and that he
had bounde him.
30 On the next day, becauſe he wolde haue
knowen the certeinetie wherefore he was
accuſed of the Iewes, he loſed him from
his bondes, & commanded the hie Prieſts
and all their Council to come *together*:
and he broght Paul, and ſet him before
them.

e He ſheweth that ſinnes cã not be waſſhed away, but by Chriſt who is the ſubſtance of Baptiſme: in whome alſo is comprehended the Father & the holie Goſt.

Chap.8,3.

Chap.7,58.

f Not becauſe he was borne at Rome, but by reaſon of his citie: for Tarſus was inhabited by the Romains, and was their Colonia, whereof read cha. 16,12.

g This priuiledge was oft times giuen in recompenſe of ſeruice to them that were farre of Rome, & to their childrẽ, thogh they were not borne in the citie.

CHAP. XXIII.

8 The anſwer of Paul being ſmit, and the ouerthrowe of his enemies. 11 The Lord encourageth him. 23 And becauſe the Iewes layed waite for him, he is ſent to Ceſarea.

1 AND Paul behelde earneſtly ẏ Coun
cil, and ſaid, Men *and* brethren, I
haue in all good conſcience ſerued God
vntil this day.
2 Then the hie Prieſt Ananias commanded thẽ that ſtode by, to ſmite him on the
mouth.
3 Then ſaid Paul to him, God [a] wil ſmite
thee, thou whited wall: for thou ſitteſt to
iudge me according to the Law, and com-
mandeſt thou me to be ſmiten contrary to
the Law?
4 And thei that ſtode by, ſaid, Reuileſt thou
Gods hie Prieſt?
5 Then ſaid Paul, I [b] knewe not, brethren,
that he was the hie Prieſt: for it is written,
* Thou ſhalt not ſpeake euil of ẏ Ruler of
thy people.
6 But whẽ Paul perceiued that the one parte were of the Sadduces, and the other of ẏ
Phariſes, he cried in the Council, Men *and*
brethren, * I am a Phariſe, the ſonne of a
Phariſe: I am accuſed of the hope and [c] reſurrection of the dead.
7 And when he had ſaid this, there was a diſ
ſenſion betwene the Phariſes and the Sadduces, ſo that the multitude was deuided.
8 * For the Sadduces ſay that there is no reſurrection, nether Angel, nor ſpirit: but ẏ
Phariſes confeſſe [d] bothe.
9 Then there was a great crye: & the Scribes of the Phariſes parte roſe vp, and ſtroue, ſaying, We finde none euil in this mã:
but if a ſpirit or an Angel hathe ſpoken to
him, let vs not fight againſt God.
10 And when there was a great diſſenſion,
the chief captaine, fearing leſt Paul ſhulde haue bene pulled in pieces of them, cõmanded the ſouldiers to go downe, and to
take him from among them, and to bring
him into the caſtel.
11 ¶ Now the night following the Lord
ſtode by him, & ſaid, Be of good courage,
Paul: for as thou haſt teſtified of me in Ieruſalem, ſo muſt thou beare witnes alſo at
Rome.
12 And when the day was come, certeine of
the Iewes made an aſſemblie, and bounde
them ſelues with an [e] othe, ſaying, that thei
wolde nether eat nor drinke, til they had
killed Paul.
13 And they were more then fourtie, which
had made this conſpiracie.
14 And they came to the chief Prieſts and
Elders, and ſaid, We haue bounde our ſelues with a ſolẽne othe, that we wil eat nothing, vntil we haue ſlaine Paul.
15 Now therefore, ye and the Council ſignifie to the chief captaine, that he bring
him forthe vnto you to morow, as thogh
ye wolde knowe ſome thing more perfitely of him, and we, or euer he come nere, wil
be readie to kil him.

a Paul doeth not curſe the hie Prieſt, but denounceth ſharpely ẏ puniſhment of God ẇ ſhulde light vpõ him, who vnder pretence of mainteinĩg ẏ Lawe doeth tranſgreſſe it.

Exod.22,18.

b He made this excuſe as it were in mockerie, as if he wolde ſay, I knowe nothĩg in this man worthie ẏ office of the hie Prieſt.

Phil.3,5.

chap.24,21.

c He denieth not but there were other points, but he expreſſeth that for the which the Sadduces that were the chief gouerners, hated hĩ moſte for.

Mat.22,23.

d Vnderſtanding both kindes, the Angels & the ſpirits, which he concludeth vnder one, & the reſurrection ẇ is the other parte.

e The worde ſignifieth curſing, as when a man either ſweareth, voweth or wiſheth him ſelf to die, or to be giuen to the deuil, except he bring his purpoſe to paſſe.

16 But

16 But when Pauls sisters [f] sonne heard of
their laying await,he went, and entred into the castle,and tolde Paul,
17 And Paul called one of ẏ Cēturions vnto him, & said, Bring this yong man vnto
the chief captaine : for he hathe a certeine
thing to shewe him.
18 So he toke him, and broght him to the
chief captaine, and said, Paul the prisoner called me vnto him, and prayed me to
bring this yong mā vnto thee,which hathe
some thing to say vnto thee.
19 Then the chief captaine toke him by the
hand, and went aparte with him alone,
and asked him, What hast thou to shewe
me?
20 And he said, The Iewes haue conspired
to desire thee,that thou woldest bring forthe Paul to morow into the Council, as
thogh they wolde inquire somewhat of
him more perfitely.
21 But let them not persuade thee : for there lie in waite for him of them, more then
fourtie men, which haue bounde them
selues with an othe, that they wil nether
eat nor drinke, til they haue killed him:
and now are they readie, and wait for thy
promes.
22 The chief captaine then let the yong
man departe,and charged him to speake it
to no man,that he had " shewed him these
things.
23 And he called vnto him two certeine
Centurions, saying, Make readie two hundreth souldiers,that they may go to Cesarea, and horsmen thre score and ten, and
two hundreth, with dartes at the thirde
houre of the night.
24 And let them make readie an horse that
Paul being set on,may be broght safe vnto
Felix the Gouernour.
25 And he wrote an [g] epistle in this maner,
26 Claudius Lysias vnto the moste noble
Gouernour Felix sendeth greting.
27 As this man was taken of the Iewes, and
shulde haue bene killed of them, I came
vpon them with the garison, and rescued
him, [h] perceiuing that he was a Romaine.
28 And when I wolde haue knowen the cause, wherefore they accused him, I broght
him forthe into their council.
29 *There* I perceiued that he was accused of
questions of their Law, but had no crime
worthie of death,or of bondes.
30 And whē it was shewed me, how that the
Iewes laid wait for the man, I sent *him*
straight way to thee, and commanded his
accusers to speake before thee the things
that they had against him. Fare wel.
31 Then the souldiers as it was commanded them, toke Paul, and broght him by
night to Antipatris.
32 And the next day, they left the horsmen
to go with him, and returned vnto the
castel.
33 Now when they came to Cesarea, they
deliuered the epistle to the Gouernour,&
presented Paul also vnto him.
34 So when the Gouernour had red it, he
asked of what [i] prouince he was: and whē
he vnderstode that he was of Cilicia,
35 I wil heare thee, said he, when thine accu
sers also are come, & commanded him to
be kept in Herodes iudgement hall.

f This declareth that God hathe so many meanes to deliuer his children out of dāger as there are creatures in the worlde, so that the aduersaries can not cōspire so craftely against them, but he hathe infinite meanes to defeat their wicked practises.

" Greke, that thou hast shewed these things to me.

g This letter was writ partely in the fauour of Paul, that his aduersaries might not oppresse him.

h The Captaine dissembleth to cōmend his owne diligence : for he did not knowe ẏ Paul was a Romaī before he had rescued him, & giuen hī to be straictly examined.

i By this name the Romaines called euerie countrey which they had subdued.

CHAP. XXIIII.

10 Paul being accused, answereth for his life and doctrine against his accusers. 25 Felix gropeth him, thinking to haue a bribe. 28 And after leaueth him in prison.

1 NOw after fiue dayes, Ananias the
high Priest came downe with the
Elders,and *with* Tertullus a certeine ora-
tour, which appeared before the Gouernour against Paul.
2 And whē he was called forthe, Tertullus
began to accuse *him*, saying, Seing that we
haue obteined great quietnes through
thee, and that manie worthie things are
done vnto this nation through thy prouidence,
3 We acknowledge it wholy,and in all places, moste [a] noble Felix,with all thankes.
4 But that I be not tedious vnto thee, I pray
thee, that ẏ woldest heare vs of thy cour-
tesie a fewe wordes.
5 Certeinely we haue founde this man a pestilent felowe, and a mouer of sedition a-
mōg all the Iewes throughout the worlde
and a chief mainteiner of the [b] secte of the
[c] Nazarites:
6 And hathe gone about to pollute the Tēple: therefore we toke him, and wolde haue iudged him according to our Law:
7 But the " chief captaine Lysias came vpō
vs, and with great violence toke him out
of our hands,
8 Cōmāding his accusers to come to thee:
of whome thou maist (if thou wilt inquire) know all these things whereof we accu
se him.
9 And the Iewes likewise affirmed, saying
that it was so.
10 Then Paul, after that the gouernour had
beckened vnto him that he shulde speake,
answered, I do the more gladly answer
for my self, for asmuche as I knowe that
thou hast bene of manie yeres a [d] iudge
vnto this [e] nation,
11 Seing that thou maist knowe, that there
are but twelue dayes since I came vp [f] to
worship in Ierusalem.
12 And thei nether founde me in the Temple disputing with anie man, nether making vproare among the people, nether in

a For Felix by his diligēce had taken Eleazarus the captaine of ẏ murtherers, & put the Egyptian to flight which raised vp tumultes in Iudea : for these the orator praiseth him: otherwise he was bothe cruel & couetous, read Ioseph li.20. Antiq. chap 11, & 12. & li.2. de bello Iudaico chap 12.

b Or herisie: for so the wicked termed ẏ true Christian religion.

c Which taught the people to mainteine their libertie against the Romaines : and thogh ẏ accusers approued bothe this secte and their doctrine, yet to get Paul punished, thei seme to condēne it.

" Or, captaine of a thousand.

d Or, gouerner: for before this he ruled Trachonites, Batanea, and Gaulanites.

e So that thou art not ignorant of their facions.

f Not that his purpose was to worship there, but the Iewes so founde him by the counsel of others for he thoght to haue wonne the simple brethren, and to stop the enemies mouthes.

the Synagogues, nor in the citie.
13 Nether can they proue the things, whereof they now accuse me.
14 But this I confesse vnto thee, that after
the way (which they call [g] heresie) so worship I the God of my fathers, beleuing
all things which are written in the Law &
the Prophetes,
15 And haue hope towards God, that the
resurrection of the dead which they them
selues loke for also, shalbe bothe of iust
and vniust.
16 And herein I endeuour my self to haue
alway a cleare conscience towarde God, &
towarde men.
17 Now after [h] many yeres, I came and
broght *almes to my nacion & offrings.
18 * At what time, certeine Iewes of Asia
founde me purified in the Temple,
19 Nether with multitude, nor with tumult.
20 Who [i] oght to haue bene present before thee, and accuse *me*, if they had oght a-
gainst me.
21 Or let these them selues say, if they haue founde any vniust thing in me, while I
stode in the Council,
22 Except *it be* for this one voyce, that I
cryed standing among them, * Of the resurrectiō of the dead am I accused of you
this day.
23 Now when Felix heard these things, he
differred them, & said, When I shal more
perfitely knowe the things which cōcerne
this "way, by the coming of Lysias ẏ chief
Captaine, I wil decise your matter.
24 Then he cōmanded a Centurion to kepe Paul, and that he shulde haue ease, and
that he shulde forbid none of his acquaintance to minister vnto him, or to come vnto him.
25 ¶ And after certeine dayes, came Felix
with his wife Drusilla, which was a [k] Iewesse, & he called forthe Paul, & heard him of
the faith in Christ.
26 And as he disputed of righteousnes, and
temperance, & of the iudgement to come,
Felix [l] trembled, & answered, Go thy way
for this time, and when I haue conuenient
time, I wil call for thee.
27 He hoped also that money shulde haue
bene giuen him of Paul, that he might lose him: wherefore he sent for him the oftener, and communed with him.
28 When two yeres were expired, Porcius
Festus came into Felix roume: and *Felix*
willing to "get fauour of the Iewes, left
Paul bounde.

[g] As the Scribes and Pharises termed the Christians doctrine.

[h] Meaning, ẏ it was a long time since he had bene at Ierusalem, ẇ was when he broght almes.

Chap.11,29. rom.15,26. 2.cor.9,2.

Chap.21,27.

[i] For his accusers spake but vpon a false reporte, which these belowes of Satan had blowen abroad, and durst not them selues appeare.

Chap.23,7.

" *Or, sect.*

[k] By whose counsel Felix called for Paul

[l] The worde of God maketh the verie wicked astonished, and therefore to them it is the fauour of death vnto death.

" *Or, to do a pleasure.*

CHAP. XXV.

3 *The Iewes accuse Paul before Festus.* 8 *He answereth for him self.* 11 *And appealeth vnto the Emperour.* 14 *His matter is rehearsed before Agrippa,* 23 *And he is broght forthe.*

1 When Festus was then come into
the prouince, after thre dayes he
went vp from Cesarea vnto Ierusalem.
2 Then the high Priest, and the chief of the
Iewes appeared before him against Paul:
and they besoght him,
3 And [a] desired fauour against him, that he
wolde send for him to Ierusalem: and they
laid wait to kil him by the way.
4 But Festus answered, that Paul shulde
be kept at Cesarea, & ẏ he him self wolde
shortly departe *thither*.
5 Let them therefore, said he, which amōg
you are [b] able, come downe with vs: and if
there be anie wickednes in the man, let
them accuse him.
6 ¶ Now when he had taried among thē no
more then ten dayes, he went downe to Ce
sarea, and the next day sate in the iudgement seat, & cōmanded Paul to be broght.
7 And when he was come, the Iewes which
were come from Ierusalē, stode about him
and laid manie and grieuous complaintes
against Paul, which they colde not proue,
8 Forasmuche as he answered, [c] that he had
nether offended anie thing against ẏ Law
of the Iewes, nether against the Temple,
nor against Cesar.
9 Yet Festus willing to "get fauour of the
Iewes, answered Paul, and said, Wilt thou
go vp to Ierusalem, and there be iudged
of these things before me?
10 Then said Paul, I stand at [d] Cesars iudgemēt seat, where I oght to be [e] iudged: to
the Iewes I haue done no wrong, as thou
verie wel knowest.
11 For if I haue done wrong, or committed
anie thing worthie of death, I refuse not
to die: but if there be none of these things
whereof they accuse me, no man can deliuer me to them: I appeale vnto Cesar.
12 Then when Festus had spoken with [f] the
Council, he answered, Hast thou appealed
vnto Cesar? vnto Cesar shalt thou go.
13 ¶ And after certeine dayes, King Agrippa and [g] Bernice came downe to Cesarea
to salute Festus.
14 And when they had remained there manie dayes, Festus proposed Pauls cause vn
to the King, saying, There is a certeine
man left in prison by Felix.
15 Of whome when I came to Ierusalem,
the high Priests & Elders of the Iewes informed me, and desired to haue iudgemēt
against him.
16 To whome I answered, that it is not the
maner of the Romaines for fauour to deliuer anie man to the death before that he
which is accused, haue the accusers before
him, and haue place to defend him self, cōcerning the crime.
17 Therefore when they were come hither,
without delay the day following I sate
on the

[a] The enuious sute of the Priests against Paul.

[b] Which may moste commodiously.

[c] Paul defendeth him self in iudgement.

" *Or, to do pleasure.*

[d] Seing him self betrayed by the ambition of the iudge, he desireth that in consideratiō of his fredome, he may be sent to Rome.

[e] It is lawful to require the defense of the Magistrate to mainteine our right.

[f] Without whose consent he colde do nothing.

[g] This was his owne sister whome he enterteined.

on the iudgement seat,and cōmanded the
man to be broght forthe.
18 Against whome when the accusers stode
vp,they broght no crime of suche things
as I supposed:
19 But had certeine questions against him
of their owne h superstition, and of one
Iesus which was dead, whome Paul affirmed to be aliue.
20 And because I douted of suche maner
of question,I asked him whether he wolde
go to Ierusalem, and there be iudged of
these things.
21 But because he appealed to be reserued
to the examination of Augustus, I commanded him to be kept, til I might send
him to Cesar.
22 Then Agrippa said vnto Festus,I wolde
also heare the man my self. To morowe,
said he,thou shalt heare him.
23 And on the morow when Agrippa was
come and Bernice with great pompe,and
were entred into the " Cōmune hall with
the chief captaines and chief men of the
citie, at Festus commandement Paul was
broght forthe.
24 And Festus said, King Agrippa,and all
men which are present with vs, ye se this
man, about whome all the multitude of
the Iewes haue called vpō me,bothe at Ierusalem,and here,crying, that he oght not
to liue anie longer.
25 Yet haue I founde nothing worthie of
death, ỷ he hathe cōmitted : neuertheles,
seing that he hathe appealed to Augustus,
I haue determined to send him.
26 Of whome I haue no certeine thing to
write vnto my i Lord: wherefore I haue
broght him forthe vnto you, & specially
vnto thee,King Agrippa,ỷ after examina-
tiō had, I might haue somewhat to write.
27 For me thinketh it vnreasonable to send
a prisoner, and not to shewe the causes
which are *layed* against him.

h This worde doeth also signifie religion: but he speaketh in contempt of the true doctrine.

" Or, auditorie.

i Flatterers first vsed to call Tyrants by this name, and after it so growed into vse,that vertuous princes refused it not, as appeareth by Plinies epistles to Traiane.

CHAP. XXVI.

1 The innocencie of Paul is approued by rehearsing his conuersation. 25 His modest answer against the iniurie of Festus.

1 THen Agrippa said vnto Paul, Thou
art permitted to speake for thy self.
So Paul stretched forthe thē hand,and answered for him self.
2 I thīke my self happie,King Agrippa,be-
cause I shal answer this daye before thee
of all the things whereof I am accused of
the Iewes:
3 Chiefly, because thou hast knowledge
of all customes, and questions which are
among ỷ Iewes:wherefore,I beseche thee,
a to heare me paciently.
4 As touching my life from *my* childehode
and what it was from the beginning a-
mong mine owne nation at Ierusalem,

a Forasmuche as he best vnderstode the religion, he oght to be more attentiue.

knowe all the Iewes,
5 Which knewe me heretofore (if they
wolde testifie) that after the moste straite b sect of our religion I liued a Pharise.
6 And now I stand and am accused for the
hope of the promes made of God vnto
our fathers.
7 Whereunto our twelue tribes instantly
seruing *God* day and night, hope to come:
for ỷ which hopes sake,ô King Agrippa,
I am accused of the Iewes.
8 Why shulde it be thoght a thing incredible vnto you, that God shulde raise a-
gaine the dead?
9 I also verely thoght in my self, that I
oght to do manie contrarie things against
the Name of Iesus of Nazaret.
10 *Which thing I also did in Ierusalem: *Chap.8.3.*
for manie of the Sainctes I shut vp in prison,hauing receiued autoritie of the high
Priests,and when they were put to death,I
c gaue *my* sentence.
11 And I punished thē throughout all ỷ Sy
nagogues,and cōpelled them to blaspheme,and being more mad against them, I
persecuted them,euen vnto strange cities.
12 At which time, euen as I went to * Da- *Chap.9.3.*
mascus with autoritie, & cōmission from
the high Priests,
13 At midday, ô King, I sawe in the way a
light from heauen, passing the brightnes
of the sunne, shine rounde about me,and
them which went with me.
14 So when we were all fallen to the earth,
I heard a voice speaking vnto me , and
saying in the Hebrewe tongue,*Saul,Saul, *Chap.9.4. & 22,7.*
why persecutest thou me ? It is hard for
thee to kicke against prickes.
15 Then I said, Who art thou, Lord? And he
said, I am Iesus whome thou persecutest.
16 But rise and stand vp on thy fete: for I
haue appeared vnto thee for this purpose,to appoint thee a minister and a witnes,
bothe of the things which thou hast sene,
& of the things in the which I wil appeare vnto thee,
17 Deliuering thee from the d people,& frō
the Gētiles, vnto whome now I send thee,
18 To e opē their eyes,that they may turne
from darkenes to light, and frō the power
of Satan vnto God,that they may receiue
forgiuenes of sinnes, and inheritāce amōg
them, which are sanctified by faith in me.
19 Wherefore,King Agrippa,I was not disobedient vnto the heauenlie vision,
20 * But shewed first vnto them of Damas- *Chap.13,14.*
cus,and at Ierusalem, and throughout all
the coastes of Iudea, and *then* to the Gentiles,that they shulde repent,and turne to
God,and do workes worthie amendemēt
of life.
21 For this cause the Iewes caught me in the
*Temple,and went about to kil me. *Chap.21,30.*

b Paul speaketh of this sect according to the peoples estimatiō who preferred it as moste holie aboue all others:fortheir doctrine was least corrupt.

c That is, I approued their crueltie which they vsed against him.

d Of the Iewes.

e Althogh this properly apperteineth vnto God, yet he applieth this vnto his ministers vnto whome he giueth his holie Spirit.

22 Neuertheles, I obteined helpe of God,
and continue vnto this day, witnesing
bothe to smal & to great, sayig none other
things, then those which the Prophetes &
Moses did say shulde come,
23 *To wit*, that Christ shulde suffer, and that
he shulde be the first that shulde rise from
the dead, and shulde shewe light vnto the
people, and to the Gentiles.
24 And as he thus answered for him self,
Festus said with a loude voyce, Paul, thou
art besides thy self: muche learning doeth
make thee mad.
25 But he said, I am not mad, ô noble Festus, but I speake the wordes of trueth and
sobernes.
26 For the King knoweth of these things,
before whome also I speake boldely: for
I am persuaded that f none of these things
are hid from him: for this thing was not
done in a corner.
27 O King Agrippa, beleuest thou the Prophetes? I know that thou beleuest.
28 Then Agrippa said vnto Paul, Almost
thou persuadest me to become a Christiã.
29 Thẽ Paul said, I wolde to God that not
onely thou, but also all that heare me to
daye, were bothe almost, & altogether suche as I am, except these bondes.
30 And when he had thus spoken, the King
rose vp, and the gouernour, and Bernice,
and they that sate with them.
31 And when they were gone aparte, they
talked betwene them selues, saying, This
man doeth nothing worthie of death, nor
of bondes.
32 Then said Agrippa vnto Festus, This mã
might haue bene losed, if he had not appealed vnto Cesar.

f He knewe ŷ the Law and the Prophetes were of God, but he did not vnderstand the true applying of the same.

CHAP. XXVII.

8 Pauls dangerous viage and his companie towarde Rome. 44 How, and where they arriue.

1 NOw when it was concluded, that
we shulde saile into Italie, they deliuered bothe Paul, & certeine other prisoners vnto a Centurion named Iulius, of
the bande of Augustus.
2 And * we entred into a ship of Adramyt-
tium purposing to saile by the costes of A-
sia, and launched forthe, and had Aristarchus of Macedonia, a Thessalonian, wͭ vs.
3 And the next day we arriued at Sidon: &
Iulius courteously entreated Paul, & gaue him libertie to go vnto his friends, that
they might refresh him.
4 And from thence we launched, and sailed harde by a Cyprus, because the windes
were contrarie.
5 Then sailed we ouer the sea by Cilicia,
and Pamphylia, and came to Myra, *a citie*
in Lycia.
6 And there the Centurion founde a ship
of Alexandria, sailing into Italie, and put

* 2.Cor.11,25.

a From Sidon to Myra they shulde haue failed north, & by west: but ŷ windes caused them to saile to Cyprus plaine North: thẽce to Cilicia North and by East, and so to Pamphylia, & Myra plaine West.

vs therein.
7 And when we had sailed slowly manie
dayes, and scarce were come against Gni-
dum, because the winde suffered vs not,
we sailed harde by ‘Candie, nere to b Sal-
mone,
8 And with muche a do sailed beyonde it,
and came vnto a certeine place called the
Faire hauens, nere vnto the which was the
citie Lasea.
9 So when muche time was spent, and sailing was now ieoperdous, because also the
c Fast was now passed, Paul exhorted *thẽ*,
10 And said vnto them, Syrs, I se that this
viage wil be with hurt & muche domage,
not of the lading & shippe onely, but also
of our liues.
11 Neuertheles ŷ Centurion beleued rather
the gouerner & the master of the ship, thẽ
those things which were spoken of Paul.
12 And because the hauen was not commodious to winter in, manie toke counsel
to departe thence, if by anie meanes they
might atteine to Phenice, *there* to winter,
which is an hauen of Candie, and lieth
towarde the Southwest and by West, and
Northwest and by West.
13 And when the southern winde blewe softely, they supposing to obteine their purpose, losed nerer, and sailed by Candie.
14 But anone after, there arose by it a stormie winde called d Euroclydon.
15 And when the ship was caught, & colde
not resist the winde, we let her go, & were
caryed away.
16 And we rã vnder a litle yle named e Clau
da, and had muche a do to get the boat.
17 Which they toke vp and vsed all helpe,
vndergirding the ship, fearing lest they
shulde haue fallen into Syrtes, and they
let downe the ‘vessel, and so were caryed.
18 The next day when we were tossed with
an exceading tempest, they ‘lightened the
shippe.
19 And the third day we cast out with our
owne hands the takling of the ship.
20 And when nether sunne nor starres in
manie dayes appeared, and no smal tẽpest
lay vpon vs, all hope that we shulde be saued, was then taken away.
21 But after long abstinence, Paul stode
forthe in the middes of thẽ, and said, Syrs,
ye shulde haue hearkened to me, and not
haue losed from Candie: so shulde ye haue f gained this hurt and losse.
22 But now I exhorte you to be of good
courage: for there shalbe no losse of anie
mans life among you, saue of the shippe
onely.
23 For there stode by me this night the Angel of g God, whose I am, & whome I serue,
24 Saying, Feare not, Paul: for thou must
be broght before Cesar: and lo, God hathe
giuen

‘ Or, Creta.

b Which was an high hil of Candie bowing to the sea warde.

c This fast the Iewes obserued about the moneth of October in the Feast of their expiatiõ, Leui. 23,37. So that Paul thoght it better to winter there, then to saile in the diepe of winter ŵ was at hand.

d That is, the Northeast winde, or euerie East winde that is furious and stormie.

e This yle was West and by South from Candie straight towarde the goulf Syrtes, which were certeine boiling sandes ŷ swallowed vp all that thei caught.

‘ Or, boat.

‘ Or, cast out the wares.

f That is, ye shulde haue saued the losse by auoiding the danger.

g They colde not the reproue him of rashenes, feing that this was the ordinance of God.

giuen vnto [h] thee all that saile with thee.
25 Wherefore, sirs, be of good courage: for
[i] I beleue God, that it shalbe so as it hathe
bene tolde me.
26 Howbeit, we must be cast into a certeine
yland.
27 And when the fourtenth night was come, as we were caryed to & fro in the [k] A-
driatical *sea* about midnight, the shipmen
demed that some coūtrey approched vnto them,
28 And sounded, and founde it twentie fathoms: & when they had gone a litle further, they sounded againe, and founde fiftene fathoms.
29 Then fearing lest they shulde haue fallen into some rough places, they cast foure ancres out of the sterne, & wished that
the day were come.
30 Now as the mariners were about to flee
out of the ship, & had let downe the boate
into the sea vnder a colour as thogh they
wolde haue cast ancres out of the foreship,
31 Paul said vnto the Centurion and the
souldiers, Except these abide in the ship,
[l] ye can not be safe.
32 Then the souldiers cut of the ropes of
the boat, and let it fall away.
33 And when it began to be daye, Paul exhorted them all to take meat, saying, This
is the fourtenth daye that ye haue taryed,
and continued [m] fasting, receiuing nothing.
34 Wherefore I exhorte you to take meat:
for this is for your sauegarde: for there
shal not [n] an heere fall from the head of
anie of you.
35 And when he had thus spoken, he toke
bread, and gaue thankes to God, in presence of them all, and brake it, and began
to eat.
36 Then were they all of good courage, &
they also toke meat.
37 Now we were in the ship in all two hun
dreth, thre score and sixtene soules.
38 And when they had eaten ynough, they
lightened the ship, and cast out the wheat
into the sea.
39 And when it was daye, they knewe not
the countrey, but they spyed a certeine
creeke with a banke, into the which they
were minded (if it were posible) to thrust
in the ship.
40 So when they had taken vp the ancres,
they committed *the ship* vnto the sea, and
losed the rudder bondes, and hoysed vp
the maine saile to the winde, & drewe to
the shore.
41 And when they fell into a place, where
two seas met, they thrust in the ship: and
the fore parte stucke fast, and colde not
be moued, but the hinder parte was brokē
with the violence of the waues.

h The graces & blessings, ẇ God giueth to his children, profite manie times the enemies, ẇ are vnworthie to receiue ẏ frute thereof.

i Faith is grounded vpon ẏ worde of God.

k This sea in Strabos time was taken for all that parte, which was about the moūtaines called Ceraunii, & so deuideth Italie frō Dalmatia, & goeth vp to Venice.

l Paul wolde vse suche meanes, as God had ordeined, lest he shulde seme to haue tēpted him.

m He meaneth an extraordinarie abstinence, ẇ came of the feare of death, & so toke away their appetite.

n By this Hebrewe phrase is ment ẏ they shulde be in all points safe and sounde, 1. Sam. 14:45 1. king. 1,52. mat. 10,30.

42 Then the souldiers counsel was [o] to kil
the prisoners, lest anie of them, when he
had swome out, shulde flee away.
43 But the Centurion willing to saue Paul,
staied them from *this* counsel, and commanded that they that colde swime, shulde cast them selues first into the sea, and
go out to land:
44 And the other, some on boardes, & some on certeine *pieces* of the ship: and so it
came to passe, ẏ thei came all safe to land.

CHAP. XXVIII.

2 Paul with his companie are gently intreated of the barbarous people. 5 The viper hurteth him not. 8 He healeth Publius father and others, and being furnished by them of things necessarie, he fared towarde Rome, 15 Where being receiued of the brethren, he declareth his busines, 30 And there preacheth two yeres.

1 AND when they were come safe, then
they knewe that the yle was called
[a] Melita.
2 And the Barbarians shewed vs no litle
kindenes: for they kindled a fyre, and receiued vs euerie one, because of the present showre, and because of the colde.
3 And when Paul had gathered a nomber
of stickes, and laid them on the "fyre, there
came a viper out of the heat, and leapt on
his hand.
4 Now when the Barbarians sawe the worme hang on his hand, they said among
them selues, This man surely is a [b] murtherer, whome, thogh he hathe escaped the
sea, yet [c] Vengeance hathe not suffred to
liue.
5 But he shoke of the worme into the fyre,
and felt no harme.
6 Howbeit thei waited when he shulde haue swolne, or fallen downe dead suddenly: but after they had loked a great while,
and sawe no inconuenience come to him,
thei changed their mindes, and said, That
he was a [d] God.
7 In the same quarters, the chief man of
the yle (whose name was Publius) had pos
sessions: the same receiued vs, and lodged
vs thre daies courteously.
8 And so it was, that the father of Publius
lay sicke of the feuer, & of a bloodie flixe:
to whome Paul entred in, & when he praied, he laid *his* hands on him, and healed
him.
9 When this then was done, other also in
the yle, which had diseases, came to him
and were healed,
10 Which also did vs great honour: and
when we departed, they laded vs ẇ things
necessarie.
11 ¶ Now after thre moneths we departed
in a ship of Alexādria, which had wintred
in the yle, whose badge was [e] Castor and
Pollux.
12 And when we arriued at Syracuse, we ta

o This declareth the great and barbarous ingratitude of the wicked, ẇ can not be wōne by no benefites.

a Now called Malta.

" Or, heape.

b Suche is the peruers iudgement of men, that they condemne suche as thei se in anie affliction.

c Whome thei made a Goddesse & called her Dice, or Nemesis.

d Beholde the extremitie of these infideles, & how muche thei are bent to superstitiō: for after one rage & errour thei fell into another.

e These ẏ Paynims fained to be Iupiters childrē, & gods of the sea.

ryed *there* thre dayes.
13 And from thence we set a compasse, and
came to Rhegium: and after one daye, the
South winde blewe, & we came the secōde daie to Putioli,
14 Where we founde brethren, and were
desired to tarie with them seuen dayes, &
so we went towarde Rome.
15 ¶ And from thence, when the brethren
heard of vs, they came to mete vs at the
Market of Appius, and at the [f] Thre [*] ta-
uernes, whome when Paul sawe, he thanked God, and waxed bolde.
16 So when we came to Rome, the Centurion deliuered the prisoners to the general Captaine: but Paul was [g] suffred to
dwel by him self with a souldier that kept
him.
17 And the third day after, Paul called the
chief of the Iewes together: & when thei
were come, he said vnto them, Men *&* brethren, thogh I haue committed nothing
agaist the people, or Lawes of the fathers,
yet was I deliuered prisoner from Ierusalē
into the hands of the Romaines.
18 Who when thei had examined me, wolde haue let me go, because there was no
cause of death in me.
19 But when the Iewes spake contrarie, I
was constrained to appeale vnto Cesar,
not because I had oght to accuse my nacion of.
20 For this cause therefore haue I called
for you, to se *you*, and to speake with *you*: for
the hope [h] of Israels sake, I am bounde
with this chaine.
21 Then they said vnto him, We nether receiued letters out of Iudea concerning
thee, nether came anie of the brethrē that
shewed or spake anie euil of thee.
22 But we wil heare of thee what thou thinkest: for as cōcerning this secte, we knowe
that euerie where it is spoken against.
23 And when they had appointed him a
daye, there came manie vnto him into *his*
lodging, to whome he expounded and testified the [i] kingdome of God, and preached vnto them concerning Iesus bothe
out of the Law of Moses and out of the
Prophetes, from morning to night.
24 And some were persuaded with the
things, which were spoken, and some beleued not.
25 Therefore when thei agreed not among
them selues, they departed, after that Paul
had spoken one worde, *to wit*, Wel spake ye
holie Gost by Esaias the Prophet vnto
our fathers,
26 Saying, * [k] Go vnto this people, and say,
By hearing ye shal heare, and shal not
vnderstand, and seing ye shal se, and not
perceiue.
27 For the heart of this people is waxed
fat, and their eares are dull of hearing,
and with their eyes haue they winked, lest
they shulde se with *their* eyes, & heare with
their eares, & vnderstand with *their* hearts,
and shulde returne that I might [l] heale
them.
28 Be it knowen therefore vnto you, that
this saluacion of God is sent to the Gentiles, and they shal heare it.
29 And when he had said these things, the
Iewes departed, and had great reasoning
among them selues.
30 And Paul remained two yeres ful in an
house hired for him self, and receiued all
that came in vnto him,
31 Preaching the kingdome of God, & teaching those things, which concerne the
Lord Iesus Christ, with all boldenes of
speache, without let.

THE

*Or, shoppes.

f These places were distant from Rome a daies iourney, or there about

g No doute the Captaine vnderstode bothe by Festus lettres, & also by the reporte of the vnder captaine yt Paul had cōmitted no faute.

h That is, for Iesus Christs cause, whome thei had long loked for as he that shulde be ye redemer of ye worlde.

i That this kingdome, wc was spoken of by the Prophetes, was offred vnto them by the cōming of Christ.

Isa.6,9. mat.13,14. mar.4,12. luk.8,10. ioh.12,40. rom.11,8.

k Hereby the hearts of the infideles oght to be molified, & ye weakelings confirmed that thei be not offended by the stubbernes of the wicked.

l The worde of God healeth when the vertue of the Spirit is ioyned wt it: & it is preached generally, yt all might be inexcusable.

THE DESCRIPTION OF THE

COVNTREIS AND PLACES MENCIONED IN THE Actes of the Apostles frõ Italie on the West parte, vnto the Medes & Persians towardes the East, conteining about 2200 mile in length. The which description serueth for the peregrination of S. Paul, & other of the Apostles, and for the vnderstanding of manie things conteined in this boke.

The names of the yles and contreis mencioned in this mappe.

Achaia.
Arabia the deserte.
Arabia the stonie.
Armenia.
Asia the lesse.
Bythinia.
Cappadocia.
Chios yle.
Cilicia.
Chaldea.
Clauda yle.
Coos yle.
Creta or Candia yle.
Cyprus.
Galatia.
Grecia.
Italie.
Illyria, or Sclauonie.
Iudea.
Lesbos yle.
Lycaonia.
Lycia.
Malta yle.
Macedonia.
Mysia.
Media.
Pamphilia.
Persia.
Pontus.
Phenicia.
Pisidia.
Phrygia.
Rhodes yle.
Samos yle.
Samothracia yle.
Sicilia yle.
Syria.

The Townes specified in this mappe and their situation with the obseruation of the legth and breadth

Amphipolis	50,0:41,30.	Lystri	64,0:39,0.
Antiochia of Syria	70,15:37,20.	Miletum	58,0:37,0.
Antiochia of Pisidia	62,30:39,0.	Myra	61,36:40,0.
Apollonia	49,30:40,30.	Mytilene	55,0:35,0.
Assos	56,0:40,15.	Neapolis	51,15:41,40.
Athenes	52,45:37,15.	Paphos in Cyprus	65,0:36,0.
Attalia	62,15:36,30.	Patara	60,30:36,0.
Babylon	79,0:35,0.	Perge	62,15:36,56.
Beroe	48,45:39,50.	Phenix an hauen	53,45:34,20.
Cenchrea hauen	51,20:37,0.	Philippi	50,45:41,46.
Cesarea Straton.	66,16:32,25.	Ptolemais	66,50:32,58.
Charram	73,55:37,10.	Puteoli	39,50:41,0.
Corinthus	51,15:36,55.	Rhegium	40,0:39,0
Damascus	68,55:33,0.	Rome	56,40:41,40.
Derbe	64,20:38,15.	Salamine yle of Cyprus	66,40:35,30.
Ephesus	57,40:37,40.	Samaria	66,20:32,19.
Fayre hauen	56,46:35,10.	Seleucia	68,35:25,40.
Gaza	65,10:31,40.	Sidon	67,15:33,30.
Gnidum	57,10:35,30.	Syracuse	39,30:37,15.
Iconium	64,30:38,45.	Tarsus	67,40:36,50.
Ierusalem	66,0:31,55.	Thessalonica.	49,50:40,30.
Ioppe	66,40 31,55.	Troas	55,0:41,0
Laodicea.	68,30:35,5.	Tyrus	67,3:33,20.

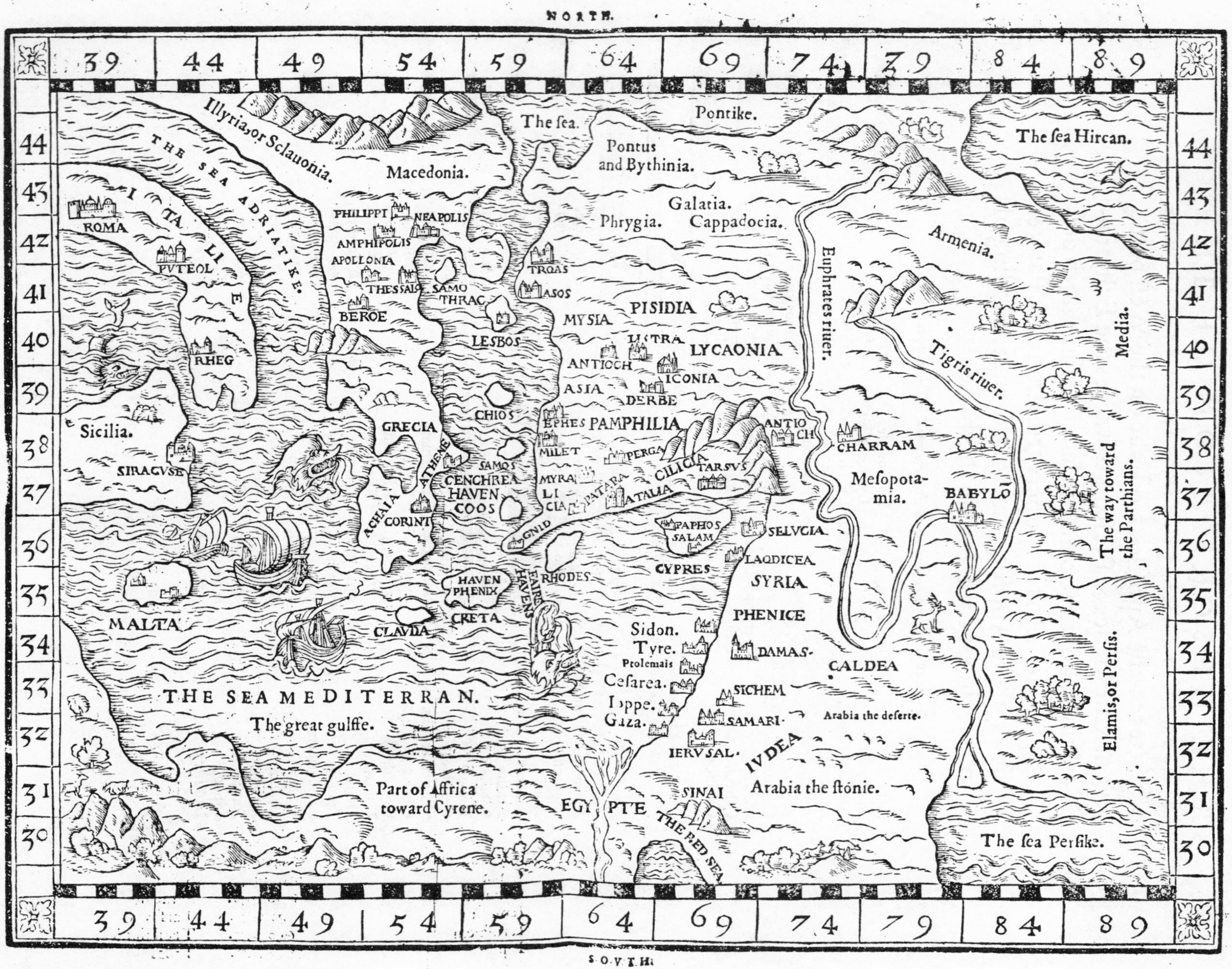

NORTH.

WEST.

EAST.

SOUTH.

Illyria, or Sclauonia.
Macedonia.
The sea.
Pontike.
The sea Hircan.
Pontus and Bythinia.
Galatia.
Phrygia.
Cappadocia.
Armenia.
Media.
Euphrates riuer.
Tigris riuer.
THE SEA ADRIATIKE.
ITALIE
ROMA
PUTEOL
RHEG
Sicilia.
SIRACUSE
MALTA
PHILIPPI
NEAPOLIS
AMPHIPOLIS
APOLLONIA
THESSAL
SAMO THRAC
BEROE
TROAS
ASOS
LESBOS
MYSIA
PISIDIA
LISTRA
LYCAONIA
ANTIOCH
ICONIA
ASIA
DERBE
CHIOS
EPHES
PAMPHILIA
MILET
GRECIA
ATHENE
SAMOS
CENCHREA
HAVEN
COOS
ACHAIA
CORINT
MYRA
LICIA
PATARA
PERGA
CILICIA
TARSUS
ATALIA
ANTIOCH
CHARRAM
Mesopotamia.
BABYLO
The way toward the Parthians.
GNID
PAPHOS
SALAM
SELUCIA
LAODICEA
CYPRES
SYRIA
RHODES
FAIRE HAVENS
HAVEN PHENIX
CRETA
CLAUDA
PHENICE
Sidon.
Tyre.
Ptolemais
Cesarea.
Ioppe.
Gaza.
DAMAS.
CALDEA
SICHEM
SAMARI.
IERUSAL.
IUDEA
Arabia the deserte.
Arabia the stonie.
Elamis, or Persis.
THE SEA MEDITERRAN.
The great gulffe.
Part of Affrica toward Cyrene.
EGYPTE
SINAI
THE RED SEA
The sea Persike.

39 44 49 54 59 64 69 74 79 84 89

44 43 42 41 40 39 38 37 36 35 34 33 32 31 30

THE EPISTLE OF the Apostle Paul to the Romaines.

THE ARGVMENT.

The great mercie of God is declared towarde man in Christ Iesus, whose righteousnes is made ours through faith. For when man by reason of his owne corruption colde not fulfil the Law, yea, committed moste abominably, bothe against the Law of God and nature, the infinite bountie of God, mindeful of his promes made to his seruant Abraham, the father of all beleuers, ordeined that mans saluation shulde onely stand in the perfect obedience of his Sonne Iesus Christ: so that not onely the circumcised Iewes, but also the vncircumcised Gentiles shulde be saued by faith in him: euen as Abraham before he was circumcised, was counted iuste onely through faith, and yet afterwarde receiued circumcision, as a seale or badge of the same righteousnes by faith. And to the intent, that none shulde thinke that the couenant which God made to him, and his posteritie, was not performed: ether because the Iewes receiued not Christ (which was the blessed sede) or els beleued not that he was the true redemer, because he did not onely, or at least more notably preserue the Iewes, the examples of Ismael and Esau declare, that all are not Abrahams posteritie, which come of Abraham according to the flesh: but also the verie strangers and Gentiles grafted in by faith, are made heires of the promes. The cause whereof is the onelie wil of God: forasmuche as of his fre mercie he electeth some to be saued, and of his iuste iudgement reiecteth others to be damned, as appeareth by the testimonies of the Scriptures. Yet to the intent that the Iewes shulde not be to muche beaten downe, nor the Gentiles to muche puffed vp, the example of Elias proueth, that God hathe yet his elect euen of the natural posteritie of Abraham, thogh it appeareth not so to mans eye: and for that preferment that the Gentiles haue, it procedeth of the liberal mercie of God, which he at length wil stretch towarde the Iewes againe, and so gather the whole Israel (which is his Church) of them bothe. Thus grounde worke of faith and doctrine layed, instructions of Christian maners followe: teaching euerie man to walke in roundenes of conscience in his vocation, with all patience and humblenes, reuerencing, and obeying the magistrate, exercising charitie, putting of the olde man, and putting on Christ, bearing with the weake, and louing one another according to Christs example. Finally S. Paul after his commendacions to the brethren exhorteth them to vnitie, and to flee false preachers and flatterers, and so concludeth with a prayer.

CHAP. I.

1 Paul sheweth by whome, and to what purpose he is called. 13 His ready wil. 16 What the Gospel is. 20 The vse of creatures and wherefore they were made. 21. 24 The ingratitude, peruersitie and punishment of all mankinde.

*Or, minister.

a Through Gods mercie, and also appointed by cōmandement to this Apostleship.

Act.13,2.

Deu.18,15. act.3,22.

b Or chosen by the eternal cōūsel of God, or by the declaration of the same counsel.

c The Scriptures onely set forthe ẏ great benefite of God promised and performed to the worlde in Iesus Christ.

d Meaning of the posteritie and of ẏ flesh of the virgine Marie.

1 PAVL a *seruāt of IESVS
CHRIST, [a] called *to be*
an Apostle, [b] *put aparte
to preache the Gospel of
God,
2 (Which he had promised afore by his *Prophe
tes in the [c] holie Scriptures)
3 Concerning his Sonne Iesus Christ our
Lord (which was made of the [d] sede of Da
uid according to the flesh,
4 And declared mightely *to be* the Sonne
of God, touching the Spirit of [e] sanctification by the resurrection frō the dead)
5 By whome we haue receiued [f] grace and
Apostleship (that obedience might be giuen vnto the faith) in his Name among all
the Gentiles,
6 Among whome ye be also the [g] called
of Iesus Christ:
7 To all *you* that be at Rome beloued of
God, called *to be* Saints: * [h] Grace *be* with
you, and peace from God our Father, and
from the Lord Iesus Christ.
8 First I thanke my God through Iesus
Christ for you all, because your faith is
published throughout [i] the whole worlde.
9 For God is my witnes (whome I serue in
my [k] spirit in ẏ [l] Gospel of his Sōne) that
without ceasing I make mēcion of you
10 Alwayes in my prayers, beseching, that
by some meanes one time or other I might
haue a prosperous iourney by the wil of
God, to come vnto you.
11 *For I long to se you, that I might bestowe among you some spiritual gifte, to
strengthen you,
12 That is, that I might be comforted together with you, through *our* mutual faith,
bothe yours and mine.
13 Now my brethren, I wolde that ye shulde not be ignorant, how that I haue often
times purposed to come vnto you (but haue bene [m] let hitherto) that I might haue
some [n] frute also among you, as *I haue* a-
mong the other Gentiles.
14 I am detter bothe to the Grecians, and
to the Barbarians, bothe to the wisemen &
vnto the vnwise.
15 Therfore, asmuche as in me is, I am ready

e By the Spirit he declareth that Christ is God whose power did so sanctifie his humanitie, that it colde not fele corruption, nor yet remaine in death. f Which was that moste liberal benefite to preache the vnsearcheable riches of Christ. g That is, by the mercie of God are adopted in Iesus Christ.

1.Cor.1,2. gal.1,3. 2.tim.1,6.

h The fre mercie of God & prosperous successe in all things.

i That is, through all Christian Churches.

k Earnestly, and from the heart.

l In preaching the Sonne of God, that is, reconciliation and peace through Christ

Chap.15,23.

m Ether by Satan 1.Thess. 2,18. or by the holie Gost, Act. 16, 6. or called to some other place to preache the Gospel, Chap. 15,20.

n Whereof is spoken Iohn. 15,16.

to preache the Goſpel to you alſo that are
at Rome.
16 For I am not o aſhamed of the Goſpel of
Chriſt: for it is the * p power of God vnto
ſaluatiō to euerie one that beleueth, to the
Iewe firſt, and alſo to the "Grecian.
17 For by it the q righteouſnes of r God is
reueiled, from faith to faith: as it is writtē,
*The iuſte ſhal liue by faith.
18 For the wrath of God is reueiled from
heauen againſt all ſ vngodlines, and vnrighteouſnes of men, which withholde the
trueth t in vnrighteouſnes,
19 Foraſmuche as ŷ, which may be knowen
of God, is manifeſt in them: for God hathe ſhewed it vnto them.
20 For the inuiſible things of him, that is,
his eternal power and Godhead, are ſene by the creation of the worlde, being cō
ſidered in *his* workes, to the intēt that they
ſhulde be without excuſe:
21 * Becauſe that when they knewe God,
they u glorified him not as God, nether
were thankeful, but became vaine in their
imaginations, and their fooliſh heart was
ful of darkenes.
22 When they profeſſed them ſelues to be
wiſe, they became fooles.
23 For thei turned the glorie of the incorrup
tible God to the ſimilitude of the image of a corruptible man, & of birdes, and
foure foted beaſtes, & of creeping things.
24 Wherefore alſo God x y gaue them vp
to their hearts luſtes, vnto vnclēnes, to defile their owne bodies betwene thē ſelues:
25 Which turned the trueth of God vnto a
lie, and worſhipped and ſerued the creature, " forſaking the Creator, which is bleſſed for euer, Amen.
26 For this cauſe God gaue them vp vnto
vile affections: for euen their women did
change the natural vſe into that which is
againſt nature.
27 And likewiſe alſo the men left the natural vſe of the woman, and burned in their
"luſte one towarde another, and man with
man wroght filthines, & receiued in them
ſelues ſuche recompenſe of their errour, as
was mete.
28 For as thei regarded not to knowe God,
euen ſo God deliuered them vp vnto a z reprobat mīde, to do thoſe things which are
not conuenient,
29 Being ful of all vnrighteouſnes, fornication, wickednes, coueteouſnes, maliciouſ-
nes, full of enuie, of murther, of debate,
of diſceite, taking all things in the euil
parte, whiſperers,
30 Backebiters, haters of God, doers of wrōg,
proude, boaſters, inuenters of euil things,
diſobedient to parents, without vnderſtanding, couenant breakers, without natural affection, ſuche as can neuer be ap-

o He paſſeth not for the mocking of ŷ wicked.
1.Cor.1,18.
p Or, effectual inſtrument.
"*Or, Gentile.*
Habak.2,4. gal.3,11. ebr.10,37.
q The perfection, & integritie ŵ whoſoeuer hathe, appeareth before God holie, blameles, & cā be accuſed of no faute: and this iuſtice is contrarie to mans iuſtice, or ŷ iuſtice of workes, & onely is apprehēded by faith which daily increaſeth, Pſal 84,7.
r Which God approueth.
Ephe.4,18.
ſ He deuided the law of nature corrupt into vngodlines, & vnrighteouſnes. Vngodlines conteineth the falſe worſhiping of God: vnrighteouſnes, breache of loue towarde man.
t In that they nether worſhip God, as nature partely teacheth thē, nor loue one another.
u They worſhiped him not as he preſcribed, but after their good intentions.
x Or deliuered them as a iuſte iudge.
y Seing men wolde not according to the knowledge ŷ God gaue thē, worſhip him aright, he ſmote their hearts with blindnes that they ſhulde not knowe them ſelues, but do iniurie one to another and commit ſuche horrible vilenie.
"*Or, aboue the Creator.*
"*Or, appetite.*
z That is, ſuche one as was deſtitute of all iudgement.

peaſed, merciles.
31 Which mē, thogh they knewe a the "Law
of God, how that they which commit ſuche things, are worthie of death, *yet* not
onely do the ſame, but alſo b fauour them
that do them.

CHAP. II.

1 He feareth the hypocrites with Gods iudgemēt. 7 And cōforteth the faithful. 12 To beat downe all vaine pretence of ignorance, holines, and of alliance with God, he proueth all men to be ſinners, 15 The Gentiles by their conſcience, 17 The Iewes by the Law written.

1 THerefore thou art inexcuſable, ô mā,
whoſoeuer thou art that " a iudgeſt:
*for in that that thou iudgeſt another, thou
cōdemneſt b thy ſelf: for thou that iudgeſt,
doeſt the ſame things.
2 But we knowe that the iudgemēt of God
is according to c trueth, againſt thē which
commit ſuche things.
3 And thinkeſt thou this, ô thou man, that
iudgeſt them which do ſuche things, and
doeſt the ſame, that thou ſhalt eſcape the
iudgement of God?
4 Or deſpiſeſt thou the riches of his bountifulnes, and *pacience, and long ſufferan-
ce, not knowing that the bountifulnes of
GOD leadeth thee to repentance?
5 But thou, after thine hardnes and heart
that can not repent, *heapeſt vnto thy ſelf
wrath againſt the day of d wrath and of
the declaration of the iuſte iudgement of
God,
6 *Who wil rewarde euerie mā according
to his e workes:
7 *That is,* to them which by continuance in
wel doing ſeke glorie, and honour, & immortalitie, eternal life:
8 But vnto them that are contentious and
diſobey the trueth, and obey vnrighteouſnes, *ſhalbe* indignation and wrath.
9 Tribulation and anguiſh *ſhalbe* vpon the
ſoule of euerie man that doeth euil: of the
Iewe firſt, and *alſo* of the f Grecian.
10 But to euerie man that doeth good, *ſhalbe* glorie, and honour, and peace, to the
Iewe firſt, and *alſo* to the Grecian.
11 For there is no * reſpect of g perſones
with God.
12 For as manie as haue ſinned without the
Law, ſhal periſh alſo h without the Law: &
as manie as haue ſinned in the Law, ſhalbe
iudged by the Law
13 (*For the hearers of the Law *are* not righ
teous before God: but ŷ doers of the Law
ſhalbe iuſtified.
14 For when the Gentiles which haue not
the Law, do by nature the things *conteined* in the Law, they hauing not the Law,
are a Law vnto them ſelues,
15 Which ſhewe ŷ effect of the Law written

a Which Law God writ in their conſciences, and ŷ Philoſophers called it the Law of nature: the lawers, ŷ law of natiōs, whereof Moſes Law is a plaine expoſition.
"*Or, righteouſnes*
b Or conſent to thē: which is the ful meaſure of all iniquitie.
"*Or, blameſt.*
a Nether thei which do approue euil doers, nor they which reproue them, are excuſable before God.
Mat.7,1. 1 cor.4,5.
b For ether thou art giltie of the ſame faute, or like.
c For he iudgeth the heart and regardeth not the outwarde perſone.
2.Pet.3,13.
Iam.5,3.
d The wicked ſhalbe condemned, and ŷ faithful deliuered.
Pſal.62,13. reuel.22,2. mat.16,27.
e The commune ſorte of mē are moſte vnable to be iuſtified by their workes, ſeing Abraham the father of beleuers hathe nothing to glorie of before God, & therefore all mens workes ſhal cōdemne them, & they onely ſhalbe ſaued, which apprehende Ieſus Chriſt by faith to be their onelie iuſtice, & ſanctification.
Deu.10,17. 2.chro.19,7. iob.37,19. act 10,34.
Mat.7,21. iam.1,22.
f By the Grecian he vnderſtandeth the Gentile, & euerie one that is not a Iewe.
g As touching anie outwarde qualitie, but as the potter before he make his veſſels, he doeth appoint ſome to glorie, and others to ignominie.
h That is, without the knowledge of the Law written, which was giuen by Moſes.

"in their

in their [i] hearts, their conscience also bearing witnes, & their thoghts accusing one
another, or excusing,)
16 At the day when God shal iudge the secretes of men by Iesus Christ, according
to my Gospel.
17 ¶ [k] Beholde, thou art called a Iewe, and
restest in the Law, and *gloriest in God,
18 And knowest *his* wil, and "alowest the
things that are excellent, in that thou art
instructed by the Law:
19 And persuadest thy self that thou art a
guide of the blinde, a light of them which
are in darkenes.
20 An instructer of them which lacke discretion, a teacher of the vnlearned, which
hast the [l] forme of knowledge, and of the
trueth in the Law.
21 Thou therefore, ẇ teachest another, teachest thou not thy self? ẏ that preachest,
A man shulde not steale, doest thou steale?
22 Thou that saist, A man shulde not commit adulterie, doest thou commit adulterie? thou that abhorrest idoles, committest
thou sacrilege?
23 Thou that gloriest in the Law, through
breaking the Law dishonorest thou God?
24 For the Name of God is blasphemed
among the Gentiles through you, *as it is
written.
25 For circumcision verely is profitable, if
thou do the Law: but if thou be a transgres
sor of the Law, thy [m] circumcision is made
vncircumcision.
26 Therefore if the vncircumcision kepe
the ordinances of the Law, shal not his
vncircumcision be counted for circumcision?
27 And shal not vncircumcision which is
by nature (if it kepe the Law) "iudge thee,
which by the [n] letter and circumcision *art*
a transgressor of the Law?
28 For he is not a Iewe, which is one outwarde: nether is that circumcision, which is
outwarde in the flesh:
29 But he is a Iewe which is one within, &
the * circumcision *is* of the heart, in the
[o] spirit, not in ẏ letter, whose praise is not
of men, but of God.

CHAP. III.

1 Hauing granted some prerogatiue to the Iewes, because of Gods fre and stable promes, 10 He proueth by the Scriptures, bothe Iewes and Gentiles to be sinners, 21. 24 And to be iustified by grace through faith, & not by workes, 31 And so the Law to be established.

1 WHat is then the preferment of
the Iewe? or what is the profite of
circumcision?
2 Muche euerie maner of way: for chiefly,
because vnto them were committed the
"oracles of God.
3 For what, thogh some did not beleue? shal
their * vnbelief make the " faith of God

i For mans cõsciẽce sheweth him when he doeth good or euil.

k He awaketh the Iewes, ẇ were a slepe through a certeine securitie & confidence in the Law.

Chap.9,4.

"Or, trist the things that dissent from it.

l The way to teache others in the knowledge of the grueth.

Isa.52,5.
eze.36,20.

m The end of circumcision was ẏ keping of the Law, & the Sacramẽt separated frõ his end is of none effect.

"Or, condemne.

n When the Law is called the letter, or that it prouoketh death in vs, or that it killeth, or is ẏ ministerie of death, or ẏ it is ẏ strẽgth of sinne, it is mẽt as we consider the Law of it selfe without Christ.

Col.2,11.

o In the inwarde man & heart.

"Or, wordes.
Isa 46,13.
chap.9,5.
2 tim.2,12.
"Or, promes.

without effect?
4 God forbid: yea, let God be *true, and *e-
uerie man a liar, as it is writtẽ, *That thou
mightest be [a] iustified in thy wordes, and
ouercome, when thou art iudged.
5 Now if [b] our vnrighteousnes commende
the righteousnes of God, what shal we say?
Is God vnrighteous which punisheth? (I
speake [c] as a man.)
6 God forbid: els how shal God iudge the
worlde?
7 For if ẏ veritie of God hathe more abũ-
ded through my lie vnto his glorie, why
am I yet condemned as a sinner?
8 And (as we are blamed, and as some affirme that we say) why do we not euil, that
good may come *thereof*? whose damnation
is iust.
9 What then? [d] are we more excellent? No,
in no wise: for we haue already proued,
that all, bothe Iewes and Gentiles are *vnder sinne.
10 As it is writtẽ, *There is none righteous,
no not one.
11 There is none that vnderstandeth: there
is none that seketh God.
12 They haue all gone out of the way: they
haue bene made altogether vnprofitable:
there is none that doeth good, no not one.
13 *Their throte is an open sepulchre: they
haue vsed their tõgues to deceit: *the poyson of aspes *is* vnder their lippes.
14 *Whose mouth is ful of cursing and bitternes.
15 *Their fete are swift to sheade blood.
16 Destruction and calamitie *are* in their
wayes,
17 And the [e] way of peace they haue not
knowen.
18 *The feare of God is not before their
eyes.
19 * Now we knowe that whatsoeuer the
[f] Law saith, it saith it to them which are vn
der the Law, that euerie mouth may be
stopped, and all the worlde be [g] culpable
before God.
20 Therefore by the workes of the [h] Law
shal no flesh be iustified in his sight: for
by the Lawe *commeth* the knowledge of
sinne.
21 But now is the * righteousnes of God made manifest without the Law, hauing witnes of the Law and of the Prophetes,
22 *To wit*, the righteousnes of God by the
faith of Iesus Christ, vnto all, and vpon all
that beleue.
23 For there is no difference: for all haue
sinned, and are [i] depriued of the glorie of
God,
24 And are iustified frely by his grace,
through the redemption that is in Christ
Iesus,
25 Whome God hathe set forthe *to be* a re-

Iohn 3,34.
Psal.116,11.
Psal.51,6.

a That thou maist be declared iuste, and thy goodnes and trueth in performĩg thy promises may appeare, when man ether of curiositie or arrogãcie wolde iudge thy workes.

b He sheweth how ẏ wicked do reason against God.

c Whose carnal wisdome wil not obey the wil of God

d Lest the Iewes shulde be puffed vp in that he preferred them to the Gẽtiles, he sheweth that this their preferment standeth onely in the mercie of God, for asmuche as bothe Iewe and Gẽtil through sinne are subiect to Gods wrath, that they might bothe be made equal in Christ.

Gal.3,21.
Psal.14,1. & 53,4.
Psal.5,10.
Psal.140,4.
Psal.10,7.
Isai.59,7.
prou.1,16.

e A peaceable & innocẽt life.

Psal. 36,1.
Gal.2,17.

f That is, the olde testament

g The Law doeth not make vs giltie, but doeth declare that we are giltie before God, & deserue condemnation.

h He meaneth the Law ether written or vnwriten which commandeth or forbiddeth any thing, whose workes can not iustifie because we can not performe them.

Chap.2,17.

i The worde signifieth them which are left behinde in the race and are not able to runne to the marke, ẏ is to euerlasting life, which here is called the glorie of God.

conciliation through faith in his blood
to declare his [k] righteousnes, by the forgiuenes of the sinnes that are passed through
the pacience of God,
26 To shewe at this time his righteousnes,
that he might be iuste, and a iustifier of
him which is of the faith of Iesus.
27 Where is then the reioycing? It is exclu
ded. By what Law? of workes? Nay: but by
the [l] Law of faith.
28 Therefore we conclude that a man is iustified by faith without the workes of the
Law.
29 *God*, is he the God of the Iewes onely, &
not of the Gentiles also? Yes, euen of the
Gentiles also.
30 For it is one God who shal iustifie circumcision [m] of faith, and vncircumcision
through faith.
31 Do we then make the Law of none effect
through faith? God forbid: yea [n] we establish the Law.

k Or fidelitie in performing his promes.

l The Law of faith is the Gospel which offreth saluation with condition (if thou beleuest) w^c^ cōdition also Christ frely giueth to vs. So the conditiō of the Law is (if thou doest all these things) the w^c^ onely Christ hathe fulfilled for vs.

m Meaning, that they are all iustified by one meanes, & if they wil haue anie difference, it onely standeth in wordes: for in effect there is none.

n The doctrine of faith is the ornament of the Law: for it embraceth Christ, who by his death hathe satisfied the Law: so that the Law which colde not bring vs to saluation by reason of our owne corruption, is now made effectual to vs by Christ Iesus.

CHAP. IIII.

1, 17 He declareth that iustification is a fre gift euen by them them selues, of whome the Iewes moste boasted as of Abraham and of Dauid. 15 And also by the office of the Law & faith.

1 WHat shal we say then, that Abraham our father hathe foūde [a] cōcerning the flesh?
2 For if Abraham were iustified by workes,
he hathe wherein to [b] reioyce, but not with
God.
3 For what saith the Scripture? *Abraham
beleued God, and it was counted to him
for righteousnes.
4 Now to him that [c] worketh, the wages is
not counted by fauour, but by dette,
5 But to him that [d] worketh not, but beleueth in him that [e] iustifieth the vngodlie,
his faith is counted for righteousnes.
6 Euen as Dauid declareth the blessednes of the mā, vnto whome God imputeth
righteousnes without workes, *saying*,
7 *Blessed *are* thei, whose iniquities are forgiuen, and whose sinnes are couered.
8 Blessed *is* the mā, to whome the Lord imputeth not sinne.
9 *Came* this blessednes then vpon the [f] circumcision *onely*, or vpon the vncircumcision also? For we say, that faith was imputed vnto Abraham for righteousnes.
10 How was it then imputed? when he was
circumcised, or vncircumcised? not when
he was circumcised, but when he was vncircumcised.
11 *After he receiued the signe of circum-
cisiō, as ẏ seale of the righteousnes of the
faith which he had, when he was vncircūcised, that he shulde be the father of all
them that beleue, not being circumcised,
that righteousnes might be imputed to
them also,
12 And the father of circumcision, not vnto them onely which are of the circumcision, but vnto them also that walke in the
[g] steppes of the faith of our father Abraham, *which he had* when he was vncircumcised.
13 For the promes that he shulde be the
heire of the worlde, was not *giuen* to Abra
ham, or to his seed, through the [h] Law, but
through the righteousnes of faith.
14 For if they which [i] are of the Law, *be*
[k] heires, faith is made voyde, & the promes
is made of none effect.
15 For the Law causeth [l] wrath: for where
no Law is, there *is* no [m] transgression.
16 Therefore *it is* by faith, that *it might come* by grace, and the promes might be sure to [n] all the sede, not to that onely which
is of the Law: but also to that which is of
the faith of Abraham, who is the father
of vs all,
17 (As it is written, *I haue made thee a father of many nacions) *euen* [o] before God
whome he beleued, who quickeneth the
[p] dead, and calleth those things which be
not, as thogh they were.
18 Which *Abraham* aboue hope, beleued
vnder hope, that he shulde be the father of
many naciōs: according to that which was
spoken *to him*, *So shal thy sede be.
19 And he [q] not weake in the faith, considered not his owne bodie, which was now
dead, being almost an hundreth yere olde,
nether [r] the deadnes of Saras wombe.
20 Nether did he doute of the promes of
God through vnbeliefe, but was strengthened in ẏ faith, & gaue [s] glorie to God,
21 Being fully assured that he which had
promised, was also able to do it.
22 And therefore it was imputed to him
for righteousnes.
23 Now it is not written for him onely, that
it was imputed to him for righteousnes,
24 But also [t] for vs, to whome it shalbe imputed *for righteousnes*, which beleue in him
that raised vp Iesus our Lord from the
dead.
25 Who was deliuered *to death* for our sinnes, & [u] is risen againe for our iustification.

a That is, by workes.

b He might pretende some merite or worke worthie to be recompensed.

Gen.15,6. gal.3,6. iam.2,23.

c Meriteth by his workes.

d That dependeth not on his workes, nether thīketh to merit by them.

e Which maketh him that is wicked in him self, iuste in Christ.

Psal.32,1.

f Vnder this excellent sacrament he comprehēdeth the whole Law.

Gen.17,11.

g This may not be vnderstande of the frutes of faith: (for thereof ẏ Apostle doeth hereafter expresly intreat) but of ẏ faith it selfe.

h In fulfilling the workes thereof.

i And thinke to performe ẏ same by workes.

k If it be requisit to fulfil the Law for him that shalbe of Abrahās inheritance, then it is in vaine to beleue ẏ promes: for it serueth to no vse.

Gen.17,4.

l Through our defaut, and not of it self.

m That is no breache of cōmandement.

n Which beleue.

o By a spiritual kinred which God chiefly accepteth.

Gen.15,5.

p Abraham begate the circūcised sede by ẏ vertue of faith and not by ẏ power of nature, which was extinguished: so the Gentils which were nothīg, are called by the power of God to be of the nōber of ẏ faithful.

q But moste strong & constant.

r In that she was past childe bearing.

s For his mercie and trueth.

t For our instruction: for we shalbe iustified by the same meanes.

u To accomplish & make perfect our iustification.

CHAP. V.

1 He declareth the frute of faith. 7 And by comparison setteth forthe the loue of God and obedience of Christ, which is the fundacion and grounde of the same.

1 THen being iustified by faith, we haue
[a] peace towarde God through our
Lord Iesus Christ,
2 *By whome also we haue accesse through

a By peace here is mēt that incredible and moste constant ioye of minde persuaded of the fauour of God: and this peace is the frute of faith.

*Ephes.2,13.

faith vnto this grace, wherein we stand, &
reioyce vnder ẙ hope of the glorie of God.
3 Nether *do we so* onely, but also we *reioyce in tribulatiõs, knowing that tribulation
bringeth forthe patience,
4 And patience experience, and experience hope,
5 And hope maketh not [b] ashamed, because
the [c] loue of God is shed abroade in our
hearts by the holie Gost, which is giuẽ vnto vs.
6 For Christ, when we were yet of no
strength, at *his* time, dyed for the * vngodlie.
7 Douteles one wil scarse dye for a [d] righteous man: but yet for a [e] good mã it may
be that one dare dye.
8 But God setteth out his loue towarde vs,
seing ẙ while we were yet sinners, Christ
dyed for vs.
9 Muche more then, being now iustified by
his blood, we shal be saued from wrath
through him.
10 For if when we were [f] enemies, we were
recõciled to God by the death of his Sonne, muche more being recõciled, we shalbe saued by his life.
11 And not onely *so*, but we also reioyce in
God through our Lord Iesus Christ, by
whome we haue now receiued ẙ atonemẽt.
12 Wherefore, as by one man sinne entred
into the worlde, and death by sinne, and so
death wẽt ouer all men: for asmuche as all
men haue sinned.
13 For vnto the [g] time of the Law was sinne in the worlde, but sinne is not imputed,
while there is no Law.
14 But death reigned from Adam to Moses
euen ouer them also that sinned not [h] after
the like maner of the transgression of [i] A-
dam, which was ẙ figure of [k] him that was
to come.
15 But yet the gift is not so, as is the offence:
for if through the offence of one, many be
dead, muche more the grace of God, and
the gift by grace, which is by one man Iesus Christ, hathe abunded vnto many.
16 Nether is the gift *so*, as *that which entred
in* by one that sinned: for the faute *came* of
one *offence* vnto condẽnacion: but the gift
is [l] of many offences to iustification.
17 For if by ẙ offence of one, death reigned
through one, muche more shal they which
receiue the abundance of grace, and of
the gift of [m] righteousnes, reigne in life
through one, *that is* Iesus Christ.
18 Likewise thẽ as by the offence of one *the
faute came* on all men to condemnation, so
by the iustifying of one *the benefite abunded*
toward [n] all men to ẙ iustification of life.
19 For as by one mans disobedience many
were made sinners, so by the obedience of
one shal many also be made righteous.

Iam.1,3.

b For it hathe euer good successe.

c He meaneth that loue wherewith God loueth vs.

Ebr.9,15.

1.pet.3,18.

d By this comparison he amplifieth the death of Christ.

e That is, for suche one of whome he hathe receiued good.

f Because of sinne: yet friendes by the grace of Christ.

g From Adam to Moses.

h He meaneth yong babes, which nether had the knowledge of the Law of nature, nor any motiõ of concupiscẽce, muche lesse cõmitted any actual sinne: & this may also comprehend ẙ Gentiles.

i Yet all mankide, as it were sinned whẽ thei were as yet inclosed in Adames loynes.

k Which was Christ.

l For by Christ we are not onely deliuered from ẙ sinnes of Adam, but also from all suche as we haue added thereunto.

m The iustice of Iesus Christ which is imputed to ẙ faithful.

n Which beleue to be saued in Iesus Christ.

20 Moreouer the [o] Law entred thereupon
that the offence shulde [p] abunde: neuertheles where sinne abunded, *there* grace
abunded muche more:
21 That as sinne had reigned vnto death, so
might grace also reigne by righteousnes
vnto eternal life, through Iesus Christ our
Lord.

CHAP. VI.

*Because no man shulde glorie in the flesh, but rather se-
ke to subdue it to the Spirit, 3 He sheweth by the vertue & end of Baptisme. 5 That regeneration is ioyned
with iustification, and therefore exhorteth to godlie life.
21 Setting before mens eyes the rewarde of sinne and
righteousnes.*

1 What shal we say then? Shal we con
tinue stil in sinne, that grace may
abunde? God forbid.
2 How shal we, that are [a] dead to sinne, liue
yet therein?
3 Knowe ye not, that * all we which haue
bene baptized into [b] Iesus Christ, haue bene baptized into his death?
4 * We are buryed then with him by baptisme into his death, that like as Christ
was raised vp from the dead by the glorie
of the Father, so we also shulde * walke in
newnes of life.
5 *For if we be [c] grafted with him [d] to the
similitude of his death, euen so shal we be
to the similitude of his resurrection,
6 Knowing this, that our olde man is crucified with him, that the [e] bodie of sinne
might be destroyed, that henceforthe we
shulde not serue sinne.
7 For he that is dead, is [f] freed from sinne.
8 Wherefore, if we be dead with Christ, we
beleue that we shal liue also with him,
9 Knowing that Christ being raised from
ẙ dead, dyeth no more: death hath no more dominion ouer him.
10 For in that he dyed, he dyed once [g] to sinne: but in that he liueth, he liueth to
[h] God.
11 Likewise thinke ye also, that ye are [i] dead
to sinne, but are aliue [k] to God in Iesus
Christ our Lord.
12 Let not sinne reigne therefore in your
mortal bodie, that ye shulde obey it in the
[l] lustes thereof.
13 Nether giue ye your membres *as* "weapons of vnrighteousnes vnto sinne: but
giue your selues vnto God, as they that a-
re aliue from the dead, and *giue* your
membres *as* weapons of righteousnes vnto God.
14 For sinne shal not haue dominion ouer
you: for ye are not vnder the [m] Law, but
vnder [n] grace.

o The Lawe of Moses.

p That it might be more manifestly knowen, & see before all mẽs eyes.

a He dyeth to sinne in whome the strẽgth of sinne is broken by ẙ vertue of Christ, and so now liueth to God.

Gal.3,27.

Col.2,12.

b Which is, that growing together with him, we might receiue vertue to kill sinne, and raise vp our new man.

Ephes.4,23.

col.3,8.

ebr.12,1.

2.pet.2,1.

1.Cor.6,14.

2.tim.2,11.

c The Greke worde meaneth, that we growe vp together with Christ, as we se mosse, yuie, misteltowe, or suche like growe vp by a tre and are nourished with the ioyse thereof.

d If we by his vertue dye to sinne.

e The flesh wherein sinne sticketh fast.

f Because that being dead we can not sinne.

" *Or, instrumẽts, or armoure.*

g That he might destroy sinne in our flesh.

h And sitteth at the right hand of the Father.

i We may gather ẙ we are dead to sinne, when sinne beginneth to dye in vs: which is by the participation of Christs death, by whome also being quickened we liue to God, that is, to righteousnes. k In that ye are led with the Spirit of God. l The minde first ministreth euil motions, whereby mans wil is entised: thence burst forthe the lustes, by ẙ bodie is prouoked, and the bodie by his actions doeth solicite the minde: therefore he commandeth, at the least that we rule our bodies. m Which is the declaration of sinne. n Indewed with the Spirit of Christ.

15 What then? shal we sinne, because we are
not vnder the Law, but vnder grace? God
forbid.
16 *Knowe ye not, that to whomesoeuer ye
giue your selues as seruãts to obey, his seruants ye are to whome ye obey, whether it
be of sinne vnto death, or of [o] obedience
vnto righteousnes?
17 But God *be* thanked, that ye haue bene
the seruants of sinne, but ye haue obeyed
from the heart vnto the forme of the doctrine, whereunto ye were [p] deliuered.
18 Being then made [q] fre from sinne, ye are
made the seruants of righteousnes.
19 I speake [r] after the maner of man, because of the infirmitie of your flesh: for as ye
haue giuen your members seruants to vnclennes and to iniquitie, to *commit* iniquitie, so now giue your mẽbers seruants vnto
righteousnes in holines.
20 For when ye were the seruants of sinne,
ye were freed from righteousnes.
21 What frute had ye then in those things,
whereof ye are now ashamed? For the [s] end
of those things *is* death.
22 But now being freed from sinne, and
made seruants vnto God, ye haue your
frute in holines, and the end, euerlasting
life.
23 For the [t] wages of sinne is death: but the
gifte of God *is* eternal life through Iesus
Christ our Lord.

Iohn 8,34. 2.pet.2,19.

o Shewĩg that none can be iust which doeth not obey God.

p To confor me your selues vnto it.

q It is a most vile thing for him that is deliuered frõ ỹ sclauerie of sinne, to returne againe to the same.

r Leauing to speake of heauenlie things, according to your capacicitie, I vse these similitudes of seruitude & fredome, that ye might the better vnderstand.

s Or, ỹ rewarde and recompense.

t Sinne is compared to a tyrant which reigneth by force, who giueth death as an allowance to them that were preferred by the Lawe.

CHAP. VII.

1.7.12 The vse of the Law, 6.24 And how Christ hathe deliuered vs from it. 16 The infirmitie of the faithful. 23 The dangerous fight betwene the flesh & the Spirit.

1 KNowe ye not, brethren, (for I speake
to them that knowe the Lawe) that
the [a] Law hathe dominion ouer a man as
long as he liueth?
2 *For the [b] woman which is in subiection
to a man, is bounde by the law to the man,
while he liueth: but if the man be dead, she
is deliuered from the law of the man.
3 So then, if while the man liueth, she take
another man, she shalbe called an *adulteresse: but if the man be dead, she is fre frõ
the Law, so that she is not an adulteresse,
thogh she take another man.
4 So ye, my brethrẽ, are dead also to ỹ Law
by the bodie of Christ, that ye shulde be
vnto another, *euen* vnto [c] him that is raised vp frõ the dead, that we shulde bring
forthe frute vnto God.
5 For when we were [d] in the flesh, the ″mo-
tions of sinnes, which were by the Law,
had force in our membres, to bring forthe
frute vnto death.
6 But now we are deliuered from the Law,
being dead [e] vnto it, wherein we were
holden, that we shulde serue in newnes of
Spirit, and not in the oldenes of the letter.

a Meaning, ỹ moral Lawe.

1.Cor.7,39.

b Bothe in this first mariage & in the seconde, the housband & the wife must be considered within our selues: the first housband was Sinne, and our flesh was the wife: their children were the frutes of the flesh, Gal 5 19. In the secõde mariage ỹ Spirit is the housband, the new creature is the wife, & their children are the frutes of the Spirit, Gal.5,22.

c Which is ỹ Spirit or the seconde housband.

d When we were destitute of the Spirit of God.

″Or, affections.

e Meaning to sinne, our first housband.

7 [f] What shal we say then? *Is* the Law sinne? God forbid. Nay, I knewe not sinne,
but by the Law: for I had not knowen
[g] lust, except the Law had said, * Thou
shalt not lust.
8 But sinne toke an occasion by the commandement, and wroght in me all maner
of cõcupiscence: for without the Law sinne *is* dead.
9 For I once [h] was a liue, without the Law:
but when the commandement came, sinne
reuiued,
10 But I dyed: and the same cõmandement
which was *ordeined* vnto life, was founde
to be vnto me vnto death.
11 For sinne toke occasion by the commandement, and disceiued me, and thereby
slew *me*.
12 Wherefore the Law *is* * holie, and the
commandement *is* holie, and iust, & good.
13 Was that thẽ which is good, made death
vnto me? God forbid: but sinne, that it
might [i] appeare sinne, wroght death in me
by that which is good, that sinne might be
out of measure sinful by the commandement.
14 For we knowe that the Lawe [k] is spiritual,
but I am carnal, solde vnder sinne.
15 For I alowe not that which I do: for
what I [l] wolde, that do I not: but what I
hate, that do I.
16 If I do then that which I wolde not, I
consent to the Law, that *it is* good.
17 Now then, it is no more I, that do [m] it,
but the sinne that dwelleth in me.
18 For I knowe, that in me, that is, in my
″flesh, dwelleth no good thing: for to wil
is present with me: but I finde no meanes
to performe that which is good.
19 For I do not the good thing, which I
wolde, [n] but the euil, which I wolde not,
that do I.
20 Now if I do that I wolde not, it is no
more I that do it, but the sinne that dwelleth in me.
21 I finde then by the Law, that when I
wolde do good, euil is present with me.
22 For I delite in the Law of God, concerning the [o] inner man:
23 But I se another ″law in my [p] membres,
rebelling against the law of my minde, &
leading me captiue vnto the law of sinne,
which is in my membres.
24 O wretched mã that I am, who shal deliuer me from the [q] bodie of this death!
25 I thanke God through Iesus Christ our
Lord. Then I my self in my [r] minde serue the Law of God, but in my [s] flesh the
law of sinne.

f There is nothĩg more enemie to sinne thẽ the Law: if so be therefore that sinne rage more by reason thereof then before, why shulde it be imputed to the Lawe ẘ discloseth the sleightes of sinne her enemie?

Exod.20,17. deut.5,21.

g Which is an inwarde vice not openly knowen.

h He thoght him self to be aliue, when he knewe not the Lawe.

1.Tim.1,8.

i Sinne being disclosed by the Lawe, is so muche more detestable, because it turneth the goodnes of ỹ Lawe to our destruction.

k So that it cã iudge the affections of the heart.

l He is not able to do that which he desireth to do, & therefore is farre from the true perfection

m He doeth not excuse hĩ self, but sheweth that he is not able to accomplish ỹ good desire ẘ is in him.

″Or, in my nature.

n The flesh stayeth euen ỹ moste perfect to runne forwarde as the spirit wisheth.

o That is, in my spirit.

″Or, commandement.

p Euen the corruption which yet remaineth.

q This fleshlie lump of sinne and death.

r In that parte which is regenerate.

s Which is the parte corrupted.

CHAP. VIII.

1 The assurance of the faithful and of the frutes of the holie Gost in them. 3 The weakenes of the Lawe & who accomplish edit. 4 And wherefore. 5 Of what

sorte

sorte the faithful oght to be. 6 The frute of the Spirit in them. 17 Of hope. 18 Of pacience vnder the crosse. 28 Of the mutual loue betwixt God and his children. 29 Of his foreknowledge.

1 NOw then there *is* no [a] cōdemnacion
to them that are in Christ Iesus,
which walke not [b] after the flesh, but after
the Spirit.
2 For the [c] Law of the Spirit of life *which*
is in [d] Christ Iesus, hathe freed me from
the law of sinne and of death.
3 For (that that was imposible to the Law,
in as muche as it was "weake, because of
the flesh) God sending his owne Sonne,
in the [e] similitude of sinful flesh, and "for
sinne, condemned sinne in the flesh,
4 That the [f] righteousnes of ỳ Law might
be fulfilled in vs, which walke not after the
flesh, but after the Spirit.
5 For they that are after the flesh, sauour
the [g] things of the flesh: but they that are
after the Spirit, the things of the Spirit.
6 For the wisdome of the flesh *is* death: but
the wisdome of the Spirit *is* life & peace,
7 Because the wisdome of the flesh *is* enimitie against God: for it is not subiect to
the Law of God, nether in dede can be.
8 So then they that are in the flesh, can not
please God.
9 Now ye are not in the flesh, but in the
Spirit, "because the Spirit of God dwelleth in you: but if anie man hathe not the
Spirit of Christ, the same is not his.
10 And if Christ be in you, the "bodie is
dead, because of sinne: but the [h] Spirit *is* life for righteousnes sake.
11 But if the Spirit of him that raised vp
Iesus from the dead, dwell in you, he that
raised vp Christ from the dead, shal also
quicken your mortal bodies, because that
his Spirit dwelleth in you.
12 Therefore brethren, we are detters not
to the flesh, to liue after the [i] flesh:
13 For if ye liue after the flesh, ye shal dye:
but if ye mortifie the dedes of the bodie
by the Spirit, ye shal liue.
14 For as manie as are led by the Spirit of
God, they are the sonnes of God.
15 For ye haue not receiued the Spirit of
bondage to feare againe: but ye haue receiued the Spirit of [k] adopcion, whereby
we crye *Abba, Father.
16 The same Spirit [l] beareth witnes with
our Spirit, that we are the childrē of God.
17 If *we be* children, *we are* also [m] heires, e-
uen the heires of God, & heires annexed
with Christ, if so be that we suffer with
him, that we maye also be glorified with
him.
18 For I counte that the afflictions of this
present time *are* not "worthie of the glorie, which shalbe shewed vnto vs.
19 For the feruent desire of the creature

a Thogh sinne be in vs, yet it is not imputed vnto vs through Christ Iesus.
b He annexeth the condicion lest we shulde abuse ỳ libertie.
c The power & autoritie of the Spirit, that is, the grace of regeneracion.
d Whose sanctificacion is made ours.
"Or, of no strēgth
"Or, by sinne.
e Christ did take flesh, ẘ of nature was subiect to sinne, ẘ notwithstādig he sanctified euen in the verie instant of his conceptiō, & so did appropriate it vnto him, that he might destroie sinne in it, 2. Cor. 5, 21.
f That which the Law requireth.
g The worde comprehēdeth all ỳ which is moste excellēt in man, as wil, vnderstanding, reasō, wit, &c.
"Or, if so be.
"Or, flesh.
h The Spirit of regeneraciō ẘ abolisheth sinne in our flesh, not all at once, but by degrees: wherfore we muste in ỳ meane time call to God through pacience.
i But to liue after the Spirit.
k So he nameth the holie Gost of the effect, ẘ he causeth in vs, when he proposeth vs saluacion by ỳ Law with an imposible cōdicion, who also doeth seale our saluacion in our hearts by Christs fre adopcion, that we cōsider not God now as a rigorous Lord, but as a moste merciful Father.
Gal. 4, 5.
l So ỳ we haue two witnesses, Gods Spirit & ours, who is certified by ỳ Spirit of God.
m Frely made partakers of the Fathers treasures.
"Or, of like value.

waiteth when the sonnes of God shalbe
reueiled.
20 Because the [n] creature is subiect to [o] vanitie, not of it owne wil, but by reason of
him, which hathe subdued it vnder hope,
21 Because the creature also shalbe deliuered from the bondage of corruption into
the glorious libertie of ỳ sonnes of God.
22 For we knowe that euerie [p] creature
groneth with vs also, and trauaileth in
paine together vnto this present.
23 And not onely *the creature*, but we also
which haue the [q] first frutes of the Spirit,
euen we do sigh in our selues, waiting for
the adopcion, *euen* the *redemption of our
[r] bodie.
24 For we are saued by hope: but [s] hope that
is sene, is not hope: for how can a man hope for that which he seeth?
25 But if we hope for that we se not, we do
with pacience abide for it.
26 Likewise the Spirit also helpeth our infirmities: for we knowe not what to praie
as we oght: but the Spirit it self maketh
request for vs with sighs, which can not
be expressed.
27 But he that searcheth ỳ hearts, knoweth
what is the meaning of the Spirit: for he
[t] maketh request for the Sainctes, according to *the wil of* God.
28 Also we knowe that all things worke together for the best vnto them that loue
God, euen to them that are called of *his*
purpose.
29 For those which he [u] knewe before, he
also predestinate to be made like to the
image of his Sonne, that he might be the
first borne among manie brethren.
30 Moreouer whome he predestinate, them
also he called, and whome he called, them
also he iustified, and whome he iustified,
them he also glorified.
31 What shal we then say to these things?
If God be on our side, who *cā be* agaīst vs?
32 Who spared not his owne Sonne, but
gaue him for vs all *to death*, how shal he
not with him giue vs all things also?
33 Who shal lay anie thing to the charge of
Gods chosen? *it is* God that *[x] iustifieth,
34 Who shal condemne? *it is* Christ, which
is dead, yea or rather, which is risen againe, who is also at the right hand of God,
and maketh request also for vs.
35 Who shal separate vs from the loue of
[y] Christ? shal tribulacion or anguish, or
persecucion, or famine, or nakednes, or
peril, or sworde?
36 As it is writtē, *For thy sake are we [z] killed all day long: we are counted as shepe
for the slaughter.
37 Neuertheles, in all these things we are
more then conquerers through him that
loued vs.

n The creatures shal not be restored before that Gods children be broght to their perfection: in the meane season thei waite.
o That is, to destruction, because of mans sinne.
p He meaneth not the Angels nether deuils nor men.
q And yet are farre from the perfection.
Luk. 21, 28.
r Which shalbe in the resurrection when we shalbe made cōformable to our head Christ.
s By hope is ment ỳ thing, which we hope for.
t In ỳ he stirreth their hearts to pray, & sheweth bothe whome to aske, and how.
u He sheweth by the ordre of our election that afflictions are meanes to make vs like the Sonne of God.
Isa. 50, 8.
x Who pronounceth his iust in his Sonne Christ.
y Wherewith he loued vs, or God in Christ: ẘ loue is grounded vpō his determinate purpose, and Christ is the pledge thereof
Psal. 44, 23.
z Which is to signifie the cōdiciō of Christes Church.

38 For I am perſuaded that nether death,
nor life, nor Angels, nor [a] principalities,
nor powers, nor things preſent, nor things
to come,
39 Nor height, nor depth, nor anie other
creature ſhalbe able to ſeparate vs from
the [b] loue of God, which is in Chriſt Ieſus our Lord.

a Paul ſetteth forthe by theſe wordes the wonderful nature of the ſpirits, aſwel the good, Eph 1,21 col.1,1. as the euil ſpirits, Epheſ.6,12. col. 2,15.
b That is, wherewith God loueth vs in his Sonne Chriſt Ieſus.

CHAP. IX.

1 Hauing teſtified his great loue towardes his nacion, & the ſignes thereof, 11 He entreateth of the election and reprobacion. 24 Of the vocacion of the Gentiles, 30 And reiection of the Iewes.

1 I Say the trueth [a] in Chriſt, I lye not,
my conſcience bearing me witnes in
the holie Goſt,
2 That I haue great heauines and continual ſorowe in mine heart.
3 * For I wolde wiſh my ſelf to be [b] ſeparate from Chriſt, for my brethrẽ that are
my kinſmen according to the fleſh,
4 Which are the Iſraelites, to whome *perteineth* the adoption, and the [c] glorie, and
the [d] * Couenantes, and the giuing of the
Law, and the ſeruice *of God*, and the promiſes.
5 Of whome *are* the fathers, and of whome
concerning the fleſh, Chriſt *came*, who is
[e] God ouer all bleſſed for euer, Amen.
6 * Notwithſtanding it can not be that the
worde of God ſhulde "take none effect:
for all they are not [f] Iſrael, which are of
Iſrael:
7 Nether *are thei* all children, becauſe thei
are the ſede of Abraham: * but, In [g] Iſaac
ſhal thy ſede be called:
8 That is, they which are the children of
the [h] fleſh, are not the children of God:
but the * children of the promes are counted for the ſede.
9 For this is a worde of promes, * In this
ſame time wil I come, and Sara ſhal haue
a ſonne.
10 Nether *he onelie felt this*, but alſo * Rebecca when ſhe had conceiued by one, *e-
uen* by our father Iſaac.
11 For yer *the children* were borne, & when
they had nether done good, nor euil (that
the purpoſe of God might remaine accor
ding to electiõ not by workes, but by him
that calleth)
12 It was ſaid vnto her, * The elder ſhal
ſerue the yonger.
13 As it is written, * I haue loued Iacob, &
haue hated Eſau.
14 What ſhal we ſay then? Is there vnrigh
teouſnes with God? God forbid.
15 For he ſaith to Moſes, * I [i] wil haue mercie on him, to whome I wil ſhewe mercie:
and wil haue compaſsion on him, on whome I wil haue compaſsion.
16 So then *it is* not in him that willeth, nor
in him that rũneth, but in God that ſheweth mercie.

a As becometh him that reuerenceth Chriſt, or whoſe tongue Chriſt ruleth & ſo taketh Chriſt for his witnes.
Act 9,2.
1.cor.15,8.
b He wolde redeme the reiection of ẏ Iewes w his owne damnacion, w declareth his zeale towarde Gods glorie, read Exod.32, 32.
Chap.2,17.
ephes 2,12.
Chap.2,28.
c The Arke of the couenant, becauſe it was a ſigne of Gods preſence, was called Gods glorie, 1.Sam. 4,21. pſal.26,8.
Gen.21,12.
ebr.11,17.
d The two tables of the couenant, Deut. 11,9.
e Chriſt is verie God.
Gal 4,28.
Gen.18,10.
"*Greke, fall away.*
f That is, of Iacob whoſe name was alſo Iſrael.
Gen.25,1.
g The Iſraelites muſt not be eſtemed by their kinred, but by the ſecret election of God, which is aboue the external vocaciõ
h As, Iſmael.
Gen.25,23.
Malac.1,2.
Exod.33,19.
i As the onelie wil & purpoſe of God is the chief cauſe of election & reprobacion: ſo his fre mercie in Chriſt is an inferior cauſe of ſaluacion, & the hardening of the heart, an inferior cauſe of damnacion.

17 For the [k] Scripture ſaith vnto Pharao,
* For this ſame purpoſe haue I ſtirred thee
vp, that I might ſhewe my power in thee,
and that my Name might be declared
through out all the earth.
18 Therefore he hathe mercie on whome
he wil, & whome he wil, he hardeneth.
19 Thou wilt ſay then vnto me, Why doeth he yet complaine? for who hathe reſiſted his wil?
20 But, ô man, who art thou which "plea-
deſt againſt God? ſhal the * thing formed
ſay to him that formed it, Why haſt thou
made me thus?
21 Hathe not the potter power of the claie
to make of the ſame lompe one veſſel to
"honour, and another vnto diſhonour?
22 *What* and if God wolde, to ſhewe his
wrath, and to make his power knowen, ſuffre with lõg pacience the veſſels of wrath,
prepared to deſtruction?
23 And that he might declare the riches of
his glorie vpon ẏ veſſels of mercie, which
he hathe prepared vnto glorie?
24 Euen vs, whome he hathe called, not of
the Iewes onely, but alſo of the Gentiles,
25 As he ſaith alſo in Oſee, * I wil call them,
My people, which were not my people: &
her, Beloued, which was not beloued.
26 And it ſhalbe in the place where it was
ſaid vnto them, * Ye are not my people,
that there they ſhalbe called, The childrẽ
of the liuing God.
27 Alſo Eſaias cryeth concerning Iſrael,
* Thogh the nomber of the children of
Iſrael were as the ſand of the ſea, *yet* ſhal
but a remnant be ſaued.
28 [l] For he wil make his account, & gather
it into a ſhort ſũme with righteouſnes: for
the Lord wil make a ſhort count in the
earth.
29 * And as Eſaias ſaid before, Except the
Lord of hoſtes had left vs a ſede, we had
bene made as [m] Sodom, and had bene like to Gomorrha.
30 What ſhal we ſay then? That the Gentiles which folowed not righteouſnes, haue
atteined vnto righteouſnes, euen the righ
teouſnes which is of faith.
31 But Iſrael which folowed the Law of
righteouſnes, colde not atteine vnto the
Law of righteouſnes.
32 Wherefore? Becauſe *they ſoght it* not by
faith, but as *it were* by the workes of the
Law: for they haue ſtombled at the ſtombling ſtone,
33 As it is written, * Beholde, I lay in Sion
a [n] ſtombling ſtone, and a rocke to make
men fall: and euerie one that beleueth in
him, ſhal not be aſhamed.

k That is, God in ẏ Scripture.
Exod.9,16.
"*Or ſpeakeſt againſt.*
Iſa.45,9.
ierem.18,6.
wiſd.15,7.
"*Or, vnto honeſt vſes.*
Hoſe.2,23.
1.pet.2,10.
Hoſe.1,10.
Iſa.10,21.
l God wil make ſuche waſte of that people that the fewe, w ſhal remaine, ſhalbe a worke of his iuſtice, & ſhal ſet forthe his glorie in his Church.
Iſa.1,9.
m That is, vtterly loſt.
Iſa.8,14. & 28,16. 1.pet.2, 6. pſal.118,22.
n Ieſus Chriſt is to the infideles deſtructiõ, & to the faithful life & reſurrection.

CHAP. X.

1 After that he had declared his zeale towardes them,

3 He

3 He sheweth the cause of the ruine of the Iewes. 4 The end of the Lawe. 5 The difference betwene the iustice of the Lawe, and of faith. 17 Whereof faith cometh, and to whome it belongeth. 19 The reiection of the Iewes, and calling of the Gentiles.

1 BRethrē, mine hearts desire & prayer
to God for Israel is, that they might
be saued.
2 For I beare them recorde, that they haue
[a]the zeale of God, but not according to
knowledge.
3 For they, being ignorāt of the righteousnes of God, & goīg about to stablish their
owne righteousnes, haue not submitted
them selues to the righteousnes of God.
4 *For Christ *is* the [b]end of the Law for
righteousnes vnto euerie one ẏ beleueth.
5 For Moses *thus* describeth the righteousnes which is of the Lawe, *That the man
which doeth these thīgs, shal liue thereby.
6 But the righteousnes which is of faith,
speaketh on this wise, [c]*Say not in thine
heart, Who shal ascende into heauē? (that
is to bring Christ from aboue)
7 Or, Who shal descende into the depe? (ẏ
is to bring Christ againe from the dead)
8 But what saith it? *The worde is nere
thee, *euen* in thy mouth, and in thine heart.
This is ẏ [d]worde of faith which we preache.
9 For if thou shalt cōfesse with thy mouth
the Lord Iesus, and shalt beleue in thine
heart, that God raised him vp from the
dead, thou shalt be saued.
10 For with the heart man beleueth vnto
righteousnes, and with [e]the mouth man
confesseth to saluation.
11 For the Scripture saith, *Whosoeuer beleueth in him, shal not be ashamed.
12 For there is no difference betwene the
Iewe & the Grecian: for he ẏ is Lord ouer
all, is riche vnto all, that call on him.
13 *For whosoeuer shal call vpō the Name
of the Lord, shalbe saued.
14 But how shal thei call on him, in whome
they haue not beleued? and how shal they
beleue in him, of whome they haue not
heard? and how shal they heare without a
preacher?
15 And how shal they preache, except they
be sent? as it is written, *How beautiful are the "[f]fete of them which bring glad tydings of peace, and bring glad tydings of
good things!
16 But they haue not all obeyed the Gospel: for Esaias saith, *Lord, who hathe beleued our [f]reporte?
17 Then faith *is* by hearing, & hearing [g]by
the worde of God.
18 But I demāde, Haue [h]thei not heard? *No
doute their [i]sounde went out through all
the earth, & their wordes into the ends of
the [k]worlde.
19 But I demande, Did not Israel knowe
God? First Moses saith, *I wil prouoke you
to enuie by a nation that is not *my* nation,
& by a foolish *nation* I wil anger you.
20 *And Esaias is bolde, and saith, I was
founde of them that soght me not, and
haue bene made manifest to them that asked not after me.
21 And vnto Israel he saith, *All the day
long haue I stretched forthe mine hand
vnto a "disobedient, and gainesaying people.

a That is a certeine affection, but not a true knowledge.
b The end of the Lawe is to iustifie thē which obserue it: therefore Christ hauing fulfilled it for vs, is made our iustice, sanctification, &c.
Gal. 3,24.
Leu. 18,5.
ezek. 20,11.
gal. 3,12.
Deut. 30,12.
Deut. 30,14.
c Because we can not performe the Law, it maketh vs to dout, who shal go to heauen & to say, Who shal go downe to the depe to deliuer vs thēce: but faith teacheth vs ẏ Christ is ascended vp to take vs with him & hathe descended into the depth of death to destroy death, & deliuer vs.
Isa. 28,16.
d That is, the promes & the Gospel which agreeth with the Lawe.
Ioel. 2,32.
act. 2,21.
e That is, the way to be saued is to beleue with heart that we are saued onely by Christ, and to confesse the same before the worlde.
Isa. 32,7.
naum 1,15.
"*Or, the coming.*
f Meaning the Gospel & the good tydings of saluation ẇ thei preached.
Isa 53,8.
iohn 12,38.
g That is, by Gods commandemēt, of whome they are sent that preache the Gospel. It may be also taken for the very preaching it self.
Psal 19,5.
h Bothe the Iewes & Gentiles. i The Hebrewe worde signifieth the line or proportion of the heauens, whose moste excellent frame, besides the rest of Gods creatures, preacheth vnto the whole worlde and setteth forthe the worthines of the Creator.
k Then seing all the worlde knewe God by his creatures, the Iewes colde not be ignorant, and so sinned of malice.
Deut 32,21.
Isa. 65,1.
Isa. 65,2.
"*Or, vnbeleuing.*

CHAP. XI.

4 God hathe his Church althogh it be not sene to mās eye. 5 The grace shewed to the elect. 7 The iudgement of the reprobate. 8 God hathe blinded the Iewes for a time, and reueiled him self to the Gentiles. 18 Wh me he warneth to humble thē selues. 29 The giftes of God without repentāce. 33 The depth of Gods iudgements.

1 I Demande then, Hathe God cast away
his people? God forbid: for I also am
an Israelite, of the sede of Abrahā, of the
tribe of Beniamin.
2 God hathe not cast away his people which
he [a]knewe before. Knowe ye not what the
Scripture saith of Elias, how he maketh request vnto God [b]against Israel, saying,
3 *Lord, they haue killed thy Prophetes, &
digged downe thine altars: and I am left
alone, and they seke my life?
4 But what saith ẏ answer of God to him?
*I haue reserued vnto my self [c]seuē thousand men, which haue not bowed the knee
to Baal.
5 Euē so then at this present time is there a
remnant through the "election of grace.
6 And if *it be* of grace, it is no more of workes: or els were grace no more grace: but
if it be of workes, it is no more grace: or
els were worke no more worke.
7 What then? Israel hathe not obteined ẏ
he soght: but the electiō hathe obteined it,
and the rest haue bene hardened,
8 According as it is written, *God hathe
giuen thē the spirit of "slomber: eyes that
they shulde not se, & eares that they shulde not heare vnto this day.
9 And Dauid saith, *Let their [d]table be made a snare, & a net, & a stombling blocke,
euen for a recompense vnto them.
10 Let their eyes be darkened that they se
not, & [e]bowe downe their backe alwayes.
11 I demande then, Haue they stombled,
that they [f]shulde fall? God forbid: but
through their fall saluation *commeth* vnto the Gentiles, to [g]prouoke them to follow them.
12 Wherefore if the fall of them *be* the riches of the worlde, & the diminishing of
thē the [h]riches of the Gētiles, how muche
more shal their abundance *be*?

a And elected before all beginning.
1. King 19,10.
b He talked with God not that he shulde punish Israel, but yet lamented their falshode & so his wordes made against them.
1. King 19,18
c Meaning an infinit nomber
"*Or, fre election*
Isa. 6,29.
& 9,10.
mat. 13,14.
iohn 12,40.
act. 28,26.
Psal. 69,22.
"*Or, pricking.*
d Christ by ẏ mouth of the Prophet wisheth that which came vpon ẏ Iewes, that is, that as birdes are taken where as they thinke to finde fode, so ẏ Law which the Iewes of a blinde zeale preferred to the Gospel thinking to haue saluation by it, shulde turne to their destruction.
e Take frō thē thy grace and strength.
f Without hope to be restored.
g The Iewes to followe the Gentiles.
h In that the Gentiles haue the knowledge of the Gospel.

13 For *in that* I speake to you Gentiles, in
asmuche as I am the Apostle of the Gentiles, I magnifie mine office,
14 *To trie* if by any meanes I might [i] prouoke them of my flesh to followe them, &
might saue some of them.
15 For if the casting away of them *be* the
recōciling of the worlde, what *shal* the receiuing *be*, but [k] life from the dead?
16 For if [l] the first frutes *be* holie, so *is* the
whole lompe: and if the [m] roote be holie, so
are the branches.
17 And thogh some of the brāches be broken of, & thou being a wilde oliue tre, wast
grafte in ‖ for them, and made partaker of
the roote, and fatnesse of the [n] oliue tre,
18 Boast not thy self against the branches:
and if thou boast thy self, thou bearest not
the roote, but the roote thee.
19 Thou wilt say then, The brāches are broken of, that I might be grafte in.
20 Wel: through vnbelefe they are broken
of, and thou standest by faith: be not hie
minded, but [o] feare.
21 For if God spared not the natural branches, *take hede*, lest he also spare not thee.
22 [p] Beholde therefore the bountifulnes, &
seueritie of God: towarde them which haue fallen, seueritie: but towarde thee, bountifulnes, if thou continue in *his* bountifulnes: or els thou shalt also be cut of.
23 And thei also, if thei abide not stil in vnbelefe, shalbe graffed in: for God is able to
graffe them in againe.
24 For if thou wast cut out of the oliue tre,
which was wilde by nature, and wast graffed contrary to nature in a right oliue tre,
how muche more shal they that are by nature, be graffed in their owne oliue tre?
25 For I wolde not, brethrē, that ye shulde
be ignorant of this secret (lest ye shulde
be arrogant in your selues) ẏ partely [q] obstinacie is come to Israel, vntil the fulnes
of the Gentiles be come in.
26 And so [r] all Israel shalbe saued, as it is
written, * The deliuerer shal come out of
Sion, and shal turne away the vngodlines
from Iacob.
27 And this is my couenāt to them, * When
I shal take away their sinnes.
28 As cōcerning the Gospel, *they are* enemies
for your sakes: but as touching the electiō,
they are beloued for the fathers sakes.
29 For the [s] giftes and calling of GOD are
without repentance.
30 For euen as ye in time past haue not beleued God, yet haue now obteined mercie
through their vnbelefe,
31 Euen so now haue they not beleued ‖ by
the mercie *shewed* vnto you, that they also
may obteine mercie.
32 For God hathe shut vp [t] all in vnbelefe,
that he might haue mercie on all.

i That they might be ielouse ouer Christ against the Gētiles, and so to be more feruēt in loue toward Christ then ẏ Gentiles.
k The Iewes now remaine, as it were, in death for lacke of the Gospel: but when bothe they & the Gentiles shal ēbrace Christ, ẏ worlde shalbe restored to a newe life.
l Abrahā was not onely sanctified, but his sede also ẇ neglected not the promes.
m Meaning Abraham.
‖ Or, in them.
n That is, the Church of the Israelites.
o Be careful: worship God, & trust in his promes.
p He speaketh of the Iewes and Gētiles in general.
q Meaning stubbernes & induration against Gods worde.
Isa. 59,20.
r He sheweth that the time shal come that the whole natiō of ẏ Iewes thogh not euery one particularly, shalbe ioyned to the Church of Christ.
Isa 27,9.
iere 22,33.
ebr. 8,8.
& 10,16.
s To whome God giueth his Spirit of adoption, and whome he calleth effectually, he can not perish: for Gods eternal counsel neuer changeth.
‖ Or, that by your mercie.
t That is, bothe Iewes and Gentiles.

33 O the depnes of the riches, bothe of the
wisdome, & knowledge of God! how vnsearcheable are his iudgemēts, & his wayes
past finding out!
34 * For [u] who hathe knowen the minde of
the Lord? or who was his counseller?
35 Or who hathe [x] giuen vnto him first, and
he shalbe recompensed?
36 For of [y] him, and through him, and for
him are all things: to him *be* glorie for
euer. Amen.

CHAP. XII.

The conuersation, loue and workes of suche as beleue in Christ. 19 Not to seke reuengeance.

1 I Beseche you therefore, brethrē, by the
mercies of God, that ye giue vp your
bodies a [a] liuing sacrifice, holie, acceptable
vnto God, *which is* your [b] reasonable seruing of God.
2 And facion not your selues like vnto this
worlde, but be ye changed by ẏ renuing of
your minde, ẏ ye may * proue what is the
[c] good wil of God, & acceptable, & perfite.
3 For I say through the grace that is giuen
vnto me, to euerie one that is amōg you, ẏ
no man presume to vnderstand aboue that
which is mete to vnderstand, but that he
[d] vnderstand according to [e] sobrietie, as
God hathe dealt to euerie man the * measure of faith.
4 For as we haue many mēbers in one bodie, and all members haue not one office,
5 So we being many are one bodie in Christ,
and euerie one, one anothers members.
6 * Seing then ẏ we haue giftes that are diuers, according to ẏ grace that is giuē vnto
vs, whether *we haue* [f] prophecie, *let vs prophecie* according to ẏ proportiō of [g] faith:
7 Or an office, *let vs waite* on the office: or
he that teacheth, on teaching:
8 Or he ẏ exhorteth, on exhortatiō: he that
[h] distributeth, *let him do it* * with simplicitie: he that ruleth, with diligence: he that
[i] sheweth mercie, with * cherefulnes.
9 *Let* loue *be* without dissimulation. * Abhorre that which is euil, and cleaue vnto
that which is good.
10 * Be affectioned to loue one another with
brotherlie loue. In giuing honor, go one
before another,
11 Not slouthful to do seruice: feruēt in spirit: seruing ‖ the Lord,
12 Reioycing in hope, paciēt in tribulatiō,
* continuing in prayer,
13 * Distributing vnto the necessities of the
Saites: * giuing your selues to hospitalitie.
14 * Blesse thē which persecute you: blesse,
I say, and curse not.
15 Reioyce with them that reioyce, & wepe
with them that wepe.

Isa. 40,13.
wisdo 9,13.
1. cor. 2,16.
u He reproueth the rashnes of men ẇ murmure agaīst the iudgemēts of God.
x That is, prouoked him by his good workes?
y All things are created and preserued of God to set forth his glorie.
a In stede of dead beasts, liuelie sacrifice: in stede of the blood of beastes which was but a shadowe & pleased not God of it self, the acceptable sacrifice of the spiritual man, framed by faith to godlines and charitie.
Ephe. 5,17.
1. thess. 3,1.
b That is, true, lawful & spiritual, 1 Pet. 2,5.
1. Cor. 12,11.
ephes. 4,7.
c Whatsoeuer is not agreable to Gods wil, is euil, displeasāt and vnperfect.
1. Pet. 4,10.
d Two things are required, if we wil iudge soberly of Gods giftes in vs: the one that we do not arrogate to our selues that ẇ we haue not: next, that we boast not of the giftes, but reuerently vse them to Gods honour.
Mat. 6,2.
2. Cor. 9,7.
Amos. 5,15.
e That is, soberly, not neglecting Gods giftes, but vsing them to his glorie.
Ephes. 4,2.
1. pet. 2,17.
ebr. 13,1.
‖ Or, the time.
Luk. 18,1.
1. Cor. 16,1.
Ebr. 13,2
1. pet. 4,18.
Mat. 5,44.
f By prophecying here he meaneth preaching and teaching, & by office or ministerie, all suche offices, as apperteine to the Church, as Elders, Deacons, &c. g By faith he meaneth the knowledge of God in Christ with the gifts of the holie Gost. h Of these officers some are Deacons, some Gouernors, some kepe the poore. i He meaneth them which were appointed to loke vnto the poore, as for the moste parte were the widowes, Act. 6,1. 1. tim 5,9.

16 Be of like affection one towards another:
*be not hie minded: but make your selues
equal to them of the lower sorte: be not
wise in [k] your selues.
17 *Recõpense to no mã euil for euil: [l] procure things honest in the sight of all men.
18 *If it be possible, asmuche as in you is, ha
ue peace with all men.
19 Dearly beloued, *auenge not your selues,
but giue place vnto wrath: for it is written,
*Vengeãce is mine: I wil repaye, saith the
Lord.
20 *Therefore, if thine enemie hunger, fede him: if he thirst, giue him drinke: for
in so doing, thou shalt heape [m] coles of fyre on his head.
21 Be not ouercome of euil, but ouercome
euil with goodnes.

CHAP. XIII.

1 The obedience to the Rulers. 4 Why they haue the sworde. 8 Charitie oght to measure all our doings. 11 An exhortation to innocencie & puritie of life.

1 LEt * euerie soule be subiect vnto the
higher powers: for there is no power
but of God: & the powers that be, are ordeined of God.
2 Whosoeuer therefore resisteth ỹ power,
resisteth the ordinance of God: and they
that resist, shal receiue to them selues [a] iudgement.
3 For princes are not to be feared *for* good
workes, but *for* euil. Wilt ỹ then be without feare of the power? do wel: so shalt
thou haue praise of the same.
4 For he is the minister of God for thy
wealth: but if thou do euil, feare: for he
beareth not the sworde for noght: for he is
the minister of God " to take vengeãce on
him that doeth euil.
5 Wherefore ye must be subiect, not becau
se of wrath onely, but also for [b] conscience sake.
6 For, for this cause ye paye also tribute: for
they are Gods ministers, applying them
selues for the same [c] thing.
7 *Giue to all men therefore their duetie:
tribute, to whome *ye owe* tribute: custome, to whome custome: feare, to whome
feare: honour, to whome *ye owe* honour.
8 Owe nothing to any man, but to loue o-
ne another: for he that loueth another, hathe fulfilled the [d] Law.
9 For this, * Thou shalt not commit adulterie, Thou shalt not kil, Thou shalt not
steale, Thou shalt not beare false witnes,
Thou shalt not couet: and if there be any
other commandement, it is briefly com
prehẽded in this saying, *euẽ* in this, *Thou
shalt loue thy neighbour as thy self.
10 Loue doeth not euil to his neighbour:
therefore is loue ỹ *fulfilling of the Law.
11 And that, cõsidering the season, that *it is*
now time that we shulde arise from slepe:

Prou.3,7. isa.5,11.
k That is, in your owne cõceit.
Prou.20,22. mat.5,39. 1.pet.3,9. 2.cor.8,11.
l Liue so honestly & godly that no mã can finde faute with you.
Ebr.12,14. Eccle 28,1. mat.5,38. Deu.32,35. ebr.10,30. Prou.25,21.
m For ether thou shalt wõne him with thy benefit, or els his consciẽce shal beare him witnes ỹ Gods burning wrath hãgeth ouer him.
Wisd.6,4. tit.3,1. 1.pet 2,13.
a Not onely the punishmẽt of the Iudges, but also the vengeance of God.
"Greke, a reuenger with wrath
b For no priuate man can contemne that gouernemẽt ẇ God hathe appointed without ỹ breache of his cõscience: and here he speaketh of ciuil magistrats: so that Antichrist and his can not wrast this place to establish their tyrannie ouer the cõscience.
Mat.22,11.
c That is, to defend ỹ good and to punish the euil.
d He meaneth onely the secõde table.
Exod.20,14. deut 5,18 Leuit.19,18. mat 22,39. gal 5,14. iam 2,8. 1 Tim.1,5.

for now is our saluation [e] nerer, then whẽ
we beleued it.
12 The night is past, & the day is at hand:
let vs therefore cast away the workes of
darkenes, and let vs put on the [f] armour
of light,
13 So that we walke honestly, as in the day:
not in* "glotonie, and dronkennes, nether
in chambering and wantonnes, nor in strife and enuying:
14 *But put ye on the Lord IESUS CHRIST,
and take no thoght for the flesh, to *fulfil* the
lustes of it.

CHAP. XIIII.

1 The weake oght not to be despised. 10 No man shulde offende anothers conscience. 15 But one to supporte another in charitie and faith.

1 HIm that is weake in the [a] faith, receiue vnto you, *but* not [b] for controuersies of disputations.
2 One beleueth ỹ he may eat of all things:
& another, which is weake, eateth herbes.
3 Let not him that eateth, despise him that
eateth not: and let not him which eateth
not, iudge him that eateth: for God hathe
receiued him.
4 *Who art thou that condemnest another
mans seruant? he standeth or falleth to his
owne [c] master: yea, he shalbe established:
for God is able to make him stande.
5 This mã estemeth one day aboue another
day, & another man counteth euerie daye
a like: let euerie man be [d] fully persuaded
in his minde.
6 He that [e] obserueth the day, obserueth it
to the [f] Lord: and he that obserueth not the
day, obserueth it not to the Lord. He that
eateth, eateth to the Lord: for he giueth
God thãkes: and he ỹ [g] eateth not, [h] eateth
not to the Lord, and giueth God thankes.
7 For none of vs liueth [i] to him self, nether
doeth anie dye to him self.
8 For whether we liue, we liue vnto the
Lord: or whether we dye, we dye vnto the
Lord: whether we liue therefore, or dye,
we are the Lords.
9 For Christ therefore dyed and rose agai
ne, and reuiued, that he might be Lord bothe of the dead and the quicke.
10 But why doest thou iudge thy brother?
or why doest thou despise thy brother?
*for we shal all appeare before the iudge-
ment seat of Christ.
11 For it is written, *I [k] liue, saith the Lord,
and euerie knee shal bowe to me, and al
tongues shal [l] confesse vnto God.
12 So then euerie one of vs shal giue accountes of him self to God.
13 Let vs not therefore iudge one another
anie more: but vse *your* iudgement rather

e Before we beleued, it had bene in vaine to tel vs these thĩgs: but now seing our saluation is nere, let vs take hede that we neglect not this occasion.
Luk.21,34.
f That is, honest maners & godlie.
"Or, riote.
Gal.5,16. 1.pet.2,11.
a That is, the doctrine of ỹ Gospel.
b Lest he shulde departe ether more ignorant then he came, or els ẇ a greater scruple of cõsciẽce.
Iam.4,12.
c It is the Lords matter & not thine.
d We must be assured in our conscience by Gods worde in all things that we do: ỹ if we be strõg, we may know what is our libertie: and if we be weake, we may learne to profit daily.
e That counteth one day more holie thẽ another
f Who iudgeth whether he doeth wel or no.
g Because he thinketh the meates vncleane by ỹ Law.
h Here we must note thre things: first, ỹ he speaketh of things which of them selues are indifferẽt, albeit in the Law thei were not: next, that he reproueth not the condẽning of the a & but of the persones: thirdly that he meaneth not the stubburne and malicious, who me he calleth dogges & concision, but the weake and infirme to whome as yet God had not reueiled the perfite libertie. i Bothe our life, and death oght to profite our brother. *2. Cor 5,10. *Isa. 45,23 phil. 2,10. k This othe particularly apperteineth to God who is the true life of him self, & giueth it to all others. l And acknowledge me for their God.

in this, that no man putte an occasion to
fall, or a stombling blocke before *his* brother.
14 [m]I knowe, & am persuaded through the
Lord Iesus, that there is nothĩg vncleane
of it self: but vnto him that iudgeth any
thing to be vncleane, to hĩ *it is* vncleane.
15 But if thy brother be grieued for the
meat, now walkest thou not charitably:
*destroy not him with thy meat, for whome
Christ dyed.
16 Cause not your [n] commoditie to be euil
spoken of.
17 For the [o] kingdome of God is not meat
nor drinke, but righteousnes, and peace, &
ioye in the holie Gost.
18 For whosoeuer [p] in these things serueth
Christ, is acceptable vnto God, and is approued of men.
19 Let vs then followe those things which
concerne peace, and wherewith one may
edifie another.
20 Destroy not ÿ worke of God for meats
sake: *all things in dede are pure: but *it
is* euil for the man which eateth with offence.
21 **It is* good nether to eat flesh, nor to
drinke wine, nor any thing, whereby thy
brother stombleth, or is offended, or made weake.
22 Hast thou [q] faith? haue it with thy self
before God: blessed is he ÿ [r] condemneth
not him self in ÿ thing which he aloweth.
23 For he that douteth, is condemned if he
eat, because *he eateth* not of faith: & whatsoeuer is not of [s] faith, is sinne.

m He preuenteth the obiection which the Christians might vse.

1.Cor.8,11.

n Which is the benefite of Christiã libertie by abusing whereof ye cause ÿ weakelĩgs to blaspheme the Gospel which might seme to them contrarie to Gods wil, and the doctrine of the Lawe.

o God wil not reigne ouer his by suche obseruations.

Tit.1,15.

p In peace & righteousnes.

1.Cor.8,13.

q Faith here is taken for a ful persuasion of the Christian libertie in things indifferent as the Apostle interpreteth it in the 14. verse.

r Which hathe none euil remorse of cõscience in his doing.

s Meaning, of a right consciẽce.

CHAP. XV.

1 *Paul exhorteth thẽ to support & loue one an other by the example of Christ, 9 And by the onelie mercie of God which is the cause of saluation bothe of the one & the other. 14 He sheweth his zeale to warde them, & the Church, 30 And requireth the same of them.*

1 WE which are strong, oght to beare
the infirmities of the weake, and
not to please our selues.
2 *Therefore* let euerie mã please his neighbour in that that is good to [a] edification.
3 For Christ also wolde not please him self,
but as it is written, *The rebukes of them
which rebuke thee, fel [b] on me.
4 For whatsoeuer things are written afore
time, are written for our learning, that we
through pacience, & cõforte of the Scriptures might haue hope.
5 Now the God of [c] pacience and consolation giue you that ye be *like minded
one towards another, according to Christ
Iesus,
6 That ye with one minde, *and* with one
mouth may praise God euẽ the Father of
our Lord Iesus Christ.
7 Wherefore receiue ye one another, as
Christ also receiued vs to the [d] glorie of
God.
8 Now I say, that Iesus Christ was a [e] minister of the circumcision, for the [f] trueth
of God, to cõfirme the promises *made* vnto the fathers.
9 And let the Gentiles praise God for *his*
mercie, as it is writtẽ, *For this cause I wil
confesse thee amõg the Gentiles, and sing
vnto thy Name.
10 And againe he saith, *Reioyce, ye Gentiles with his people.
11 And againe, *Praise the Lord, all ye Gẽtiles, & laude ye him, all people together.
12 And againe Esaias saith, *There shalbe
a roote of Iesse, and [g] he that shal rise to
reigne ouer [h] the Gentiles, in him shal the
Gentiles trust.
13 Now the God of hope fil you with all
ioye, and peace in beleuing, that ye may
abunde in hope through the power of the
holie Gost.
14 And I my self also am persuaded of you,
my brethren, that ye also are ful of goodnes, and filled with all knowledge, and are
able to admonish one another.
15 Neuertheles brethrẽ, I haue somewhat
boldly after a sort writtẽ vnto you, as one
that putteth you in remembrãce, through
the grace that is giuen me of God,
16 That I shulde be the minister of Iesus
Christ towarde the Gentiles, ministring
the Gospel of God, that the offring vp of
the Gentiles might be acceptable [i] being
sanctified by the holie Gost.
17 I haue therefore whereof I may reioyce
in Christ Iesus in those things which *perteine* to God.
18 For I dare not [k] speake of anie thing,
which Christ hathe not wroght by me, *to
make* the Gentiles obedient in worde and
dede,
19 With the power of signes and wonders,
by the power of the Spirit of God: so that
from Ierusalem, and rounde about vnto
Illyricum, I haue caused to abunde the
Gospel of Christ.
20 Yea, so I enforced my self to preache the
Gospel, not where Christ was named, lest
I shulde haue buylt on another mans fundation.
21 But as it is written, *To whome he was
not spoken of, they shal se *him*, & they that
heard not, shal vnderstand *him*.
22 Therefore also I haue bene *oft let to co
me vnto you.
23 But now seing I haue no more place in
these quarters, and also haue *bene desirous manie yeres agone to come vnto you,
24 When I shal take my iourney into Spaine, I wil come to you: for I trust to se you
in my

Psal.69,10.

a To edifie, signifieth to do all maner dueties to our neighbour, ether to bring him to Christ, or if he be wõne, that he may growe from faith to faith: for ÿ faithful are called the temple of God wherein he is resident by his holie Spirit: & these faithful are the stones of ÿ newe Ierusalẽ: that is, the vniuersal Church, Isa.54. reuel.21. of the which buylding Christ is the chief corner stone, Eph 2,20.

b I did so beare them, as if they had bene done to me and not to my Father.

c Which is ÿ autor of paciẽce.

1.Cor.1,10. philip.3,16.

d To make vs partakers of Gods glorie.

e First to gather ÿ Iewes, and then the Gentiles that bothe might be made one flocke.

f That God might be knowen true.

Psal.18,50. 2 Sam 22,50.

Deu.32,43.

Psal.117,1.

Isa.11,10.

g Which is Christ who did spring as a yong budde out of ÿ drye and dead rote.

h Then seing he toke bothe the Iewes and Gẽtiles to his Fathers glorie, they oght by his example to loue together.

i The minister offreth vp the people to God by the Gospel

k God gaue him suche ample occasions to set forthe his excellent workes ÿ he had done by him, that the Apostle nede not to seke anie other thing to boast vpon.

Isa.52,15.

Chap.1,13. 1.thes.2,17.

Chap.1,11.

in my iorney, & to be broght on my way
thitherwarde by you, after that I haue bene somewhat filled with your *companie*.
25 But now go I to Ierusalem, to [l] minister
vnto the Saintes.
26 For it hathe pleased them of Macedonia
and Achaia, to make a certeine distributiō
vnto the poore Saintes which are at Ierusalem.
27 For it hathe pleased them, and their detters are they: *for if the Gentiles be made
partakers of their spiritual things, their
duetie is also to minister vnto them in car
nal things.
28 When I haue therefore performed this,
and haue [m] sealed them this [n] frute, I wil
passe by you into Spaine.
29 *And I knowe when I come, that I shal
come to you with [o] abundance of the blessing of the Gospel of Christ.
30 Also brethrē I beseche you for our Lord
Iesus Christs sake, and for the loue of the
Spirit, that ye *wolde striue with me by
prayers to God for me.
31 That I may be deliuered frō them which
are disobediēt in Iudea, & that my seruice
which I haue to do at Ierusalem, may be
[p] accepted of the Saintes,
32 That I may come vnto you with ioy by
the wil of God, & may wt you be refreshed.
33 Thus the *God of peace *be* with you all.
Amen.

l Which was to carie the almes.
1.Cor.9,11.
m I shal faithfully leaue it with them, & as it were sealed moste surely.
Chap.1,10.
n Almes is ye frute of faith and charitie.
o His coming shalbe profitable vnto thē: for God wil giue him abundant knowledge of Diuine mysteries to cōmunicate vnto them.
2.Cor.1,11.
p He feared lest sclādrous tongues wolde haue made his message ether odious, or lesse acceptable.
Isa.9,6.

CHAP. XVI.

1 After manie recommendations, 17 He admonisheth them to beware false brethren and to be circumspect. 20 He prayeth for them, and giueth thankes to God.

1 I Commende vnto you Phebe our sister
which is a seruant of the Church of Cē
chrea,
2 That ye receiue her in the Lord, as it becometh Saintes, and that ye assist her in
whatsoeuer busines she nedeth of your
aide: for she hathe giuen hospitalitie vnto
manie, and to me also.
3 Grete *Priscilla and Aquila my fellow
helpers in Christ Iesus.
4 (Which haue for my life laid downe
their owne necke. Vnto whome not I onely giue thankes, but also all the Churches
of the Gentiles)
5 Likewise *grete* the Church that is in their
house. Salute my beloued Epenetus, which
is the [a] first frutes of ‖Achaia in Christ.
6 Grete Marie which bestowed muche labour on vs.
7 Salute Andronicus and Iunia my cousins
and fellow prisoners, which are notable
among the Apostles, and [b] were in Christ
before me.
8 Grete Amplias my beloued in the Lord.
9 Salute Vrbanus our felowe helper in
Christ, and Stachys my beloued.
10 Salute Apelles approued in Christ. Salute them which are of Aristobulus *friends*.
11 Salute Herodion my kinsman. Grete thē
which are of the *frieds* of Narcissus which
are in the Lord.
12 Salute Tryphena and Tryphosa, which
women labour in the Lord. Salute the beloued Persis, which *woman* hathe laboured
muche in the Lord.
13 Salute Rufus chosen in the Lord, & his
mother and mine.
14 Grete Asyncritus, Phlegon, Hermas, Pa-
trobas, Mercurius, and the brethrē which
are with them.
15 Salute Philologus and Iulias, Nereas, &
his sister, and Olympas, & all the Saintes
which are with them.
16 Salute one another with an *holie [c] kisse.
The Churches of Christ salute you.
17 ¶ Now I beseche you brethren, marke
them diligently which cause diuision and
offences, contrarie to the doctrine which
ye haue learned, and *auoide them.
18 For they that are suche, serue not the
Lord Iesus Christ, but their owne [d] bellies, and with [e] faire speache & flattering
deceiue the hearts of the simple.
19 For your obediēce is come abrode amōg
all: I am glad therefore of you: but yet I
wolde haue you wise, vnto that which is
good, and simple concerning euil.
20 The God of peace shal treade Satan vnder your fete shortly. The grace of our
Lord Iesus Christ *be* with you.
21 *Timotheus my companion, and Lucius
and Iason, and Sosipater my kinsmen, salute you.
22 I Tertius, which wrote out this epistle,
salute you in the Lord.
23 *Gaius mine hoste, & of ye whole Church
saluteth you. Erastus the ‖chamberlaine of
[f] the citie saluteth you, and Quartus a
brother.
24 The grace of our Lord Iesus Christ *be*
with you all. Amen.
25 *To him now that is of power to establi
she you according to my Gospel, and prea
ching of Iesus Christ, *by the reuelation
[g] of the mysterie, which was kept secret
since the worlde began:
26 (But now is opened, & published amōg
all nations by the Scriptures of the Prophetes, at the commandement of the euerlasting God for the obedience of faith)
27 To God, *I say*, onely wise, be praise
through Iesus Christ for euer. Amen.

Act.18,3.
a The first yt was cōsecrate to the Lord by embracing the Gospel ‖Or, Asia.
b They were grafted in Christ by faith afore I was called, and were wel estemed of the Apostles, and of the Churches.
1.Cor.16,20. 2.cor 13,12. 1.pet.5,14.
c This was a signe of amitie among the Iewes, which he willeth to be holie, that is, that it come from a minde ful of godlie charitie.
2.Iohn 10.
d These be markes to knowe the false Apostles by.
e The worde signifieth him that promiseth muche & performeth nothing, who semeth also to speake for thy profite, but doeth nothing lesse.
Act.16,1 phil.2,19.
1.Cor.1,14.
‖Or, receiuer.
f Corinthus.
Eph.3,19.
Ephe.3,9. col.1,26. 2.tim.1,10. tit.1,2. 1.pet.1,10
g Bothe as touching the doctrine of ye Gospel, and also the calling of the Gentiles.

Written to the Romaines from Corinthus *and sent* by Phebe, seruant of the Church, which is at Cenchrea.

THE FIRST EPISTLE
of Paul to the Corinthians.

THE ARGVMENT.

After that S. Paul had preached at Corinthus a yere and an halfe, he was compelled by the wickednes of the Iewes to saile into Syria. In whose absence false Apostles entred into the Church, who being puffed vp with vaine glorie, and affectat eloquence, soght to bring into contept the simplicitie which Paul vsed in preaching the Gospel. By whose ambition suche factions & schismes spräg vp in the Church, that frō opinions in pollicies & ceremonies they fel to false doctrine and heresies, calling into doute the resurrection frō the dead, one of the chiefest points of Christian religiō. Against these euils the Apostle procedeth, preparing the Corinthians hearts, & eares with gentle salutations: but sone after he reproueth their contentions and debates, their arrogancie & pride, and exhorteth thē to cōcorde & humilitie, setting before their eyes the spiritual vertue, & heauēlie wisdome of the Gospel, which cā not be persuaded by worldlie wit and eloquent reasons, but is reueiled by Gods Spirit, and so sealed in mens hearts. Therefore this salutation may not be attribute to the ministers, but onely to God, whose seruants they are, and haue receiued charge to edifie his Church: wherein S. Paul behaued him self skilfully, buylding according to the fundation (which is Christ) and exhorteth others to make the end proportionable to the beginning, taking diligent hede that they be not polluted with vaine doctrine, seing they are the Temple of God. And as for those which douted of his Apostleship, he sheweth them that he dependeth not on mans iudgement, albeit he had declared by manifest signes that he neuer soght his owne glorie, nether yet how he might liue, but onely the glorie of Christ: which thing at his comming he wolde declare more amply, to the shame of those vaine glorious braggers, who soght them selues onely, & therefore suffred moste horrible vices vnreproued & vnpunished, as incest, contentions, pleadings before infideles, fornication, & suche like, to the great sclander of the Gospel. This done, he answereth to certeine points of the Corinthians letter, as touching single life, duetie of mariage, of discorde & dissension among the maried, of virginitie, & seconde mariage. And because some thoght it nothing to be present at idole seruice, seing in their heart they worshiped the true God, he warneth them to haue respect to their weake brethren, whose faith by that dissembling was hindred, & their consciences wounded, which thing rather thē he wolde do, he wolde neuer vse that libertie which God had giuen him. But forasmuche as pride, & self wil was the cause of those great euils, he admonisheth them by the example of the Iewes not to glorie in these outwarde giftes, whose horrible punishment for the abuse of Gods creatures, oght to be a warning to all men to followe Christ vprightly, without all pollution and offence of others. Then he correcteth diuers abuses in their Church, as touching the behauiour of men, and women in the assemblies: of the Lords Supper, the abuse of the spiritual giftes, which God hathe giuen to mainteine loue and edifie the Church: as concerning the resurrection from the dead, without the which the Gospel serueth to no vse. Last of all he exhorteth the Corinthians to relieue the poore brethren at Ierusalem, to perseuere in the loue of Christ, and wel doing, sending his commendations, and wishing them peace.

CHAP. I.

2 He praiseth the great graces of God shewed towarde them, 10 Exhorting them to concorde and humilitie. 19 He beateth downe all pride, and wisdome which is not grounded on God, 26 Shewing whome God hathe chosen to confounde the wisdome of the worlde.

1 PAVL called *to be* an A-
postle of IESVS
CHRIST, through the
wil of God, and *our* brother Sostenes,
2 Vnto ye Church of God
which is at Corinthus,
to them that are * a sanctified in Christ
Iesus, * b Saintes by calling, * with all that
c call on the Name of our Lord Iesus
Christ in euerie place, bothe their *Lord*,
and ours:
3 Grace *be* with you, and peace from God
our Father, & *from* the Lord Iesus Christ.
4 I thanke my God alwayes on your behalfe for the d grace of God, which is giuen
you in Iesus Christ,
5 *That in all things ye are made riche e in
him, in f all kinde of speache, and in all
knowledge:
6 As the testimonie of Iesus Christ hathe
bene confirmed in you.
7 So that ye are not destitute of anie gift:
*wayting for the appearing of our Lord
Iesus Christ.
8 Who shal also confirme you vnto ye end,
that ye may be g blamelesse in the day of
our Lord Iesus Christ.
9 *God is faithful, by whome ye are called
vnto ye felowship of his Sōne Iesus Christ
our Lord.

Act.15,9. 1.thes.4,7. Rom.1,7. eph.1,1. col.1,22. 2.tim.1,9. tit.2,1. 2.Tim.2,23.

a Whome God hathe separate from the rest of the worlde, purified, and giuen to his Sonne, that he might be in them, and they in him. b Made holie by the fre mercie & calling of God. c Which is to acknowledge him to be verie God, to worship him, and seke vnto him for helpe.

d For all the benefites wc ye haue receiued by the Gospel

Colos.1,10. & 2,7. philip.3,20. tit.2,11.

e As mēbres of the same bodie which communicate with their head.

1.Thes.3,12. & 5,23.

f He commendeth those giftes in them, whose abuse after he doeth reproue, as eloquence, philosophie, and their knowledge of Gods worde. g For there is no condemnation to them that are grafted in Christ Iesus. **Psal.138,8 1 thes.5,24.*

10 Now

10 Now I beseche you, brethrẽ, by the Name of our Lord Iesus Christ, * that ye all
[h] speake one thing, and that there be no
dissentions among you: but be ye knit together in one minde, and in one iudgement.
11 For it hathe bene declared vnto me, my
brethren, of you by them that are of the
house of [i] Cloe, that there are cõtentions
among you.
12 Now this I say, that euerie one of you
saith, I am Paules, and I am * Apollos, and
I am Cephas, and I am Christs.
13 Is Christ deuided? was Paul crucified
for you? ether were ye baptized [k] into the
name of Paul?
14 I thanke God, that I baptized none of
you, but * Crispus, and [l] Gaius,
15 Lest anie shulde say, that I had baptized
into mine owne name.
16 I baptized also the housholde of Stephanas: furthermore knowe I not, whether
I baptized anie other.
17 For Christ sent me not to [m] baptize, but
to preache the Gospel, not with * [n] wisdome of wordes, [o] lest the crosse of Christ
shulde be made of none effect.
18 For the preaching of the crosse is to thẽ
that perish, foolishnes: but vnto vs, which
are saued, it is the * power of God.
19 For it is written, I * wil destroye the wisdome of the wise, and wil cast away the
vnderstanding of the prudent.
20 Where is the wise? where is the [p] Scribe?
where is the [q] disputer of this worlde? hathe not God made the wisdome of this
worlde foolishnes?
21 For seing the worlde by wisdome knewe
not God in the wisdome of God, it pleased God by the foolishnes of preaching
to saue them that beleue:
22 Seing also that the Iewes require a * signe, and the Grecians seke after wisdome.
23 But we preache Christ crucified: vnto
the Iewes, euen a stombling blocke, & vnto the Grecians, foolishnes:
24 But vnto them which are called, bothe
of the Iewes & Greciãs *we preache* Christ,
the power of GOD, and the wisdome of
God.
25 For the [r] foolishnes of God is wiser thẽ
men, and the weakenes of God is stronger
then men.
26 For brethren, you se your calling, how
that not manie wise men [s] after the flesh,
not manie mightie, not manie noble *are
called*.
27 But God hathe chosen the foolish thĩgs
of the worlde to confounde the wise, and
God hathe chosen the weake things of the
worlde, to confounde the mightie things.
28 And vile things of the worlde & things
which are despised, hathe God chosen, &

Rom.15,5. *philip.3,16.*
h Disagreing in wordes ingẽdreth dissentiõ of minde, whereof procedeth repugnancie of iudgemẽt, ẘ is the mother of schisme and heresie.
i Which was a vertuous woman & zealous of Gods glorie and soght the quietnes of the Church.
Act.18,24.
k Read the annotacion, Act. 3,16.
Act.18,8.
l This Gaius was Pauls hoste, in whose house also the Church was at Corinthus, Rom.16,23: there was yet another so called, ẘ was of Derbe, & followed Paul, Act 20,4.
Chap.2,19. *galat.5,4.* *2.pet.1,16.*
m That is, chiefly & peculiarly.
Rom.1,16. *Isa.29,14.*
n As rhetoricke, or arte oratorie.
o When men shulde attribute that vnto eloquence, ẘ onely belonged to the power of God.
p That is, the interpreter of the Law.
Mat.12,38.
q He that is so subtil in discussing questions? & herein Paul reprocheth euen the best learned, as thogh not one of them colde perceiue by his owne wisdome this mysterie of Christ reueiled in the Gospel.
r He speaketh in the persone of the wicked, who contrarie to their cõscience rather attribute these things to God, then acknowledge their owne follie & weakenes.
s According as the worlde termeth wise mẽ.

things [t] which are not, to bring to noght
things [u] that are,
29 That no [x] flesh shulde reioyce in his
presence.
30 But ye are of him in Christ Iesus, who
of God is made vnto vs * wisdome and
righteousnes, and sanctificacion, and redempcion,
31 That, according as it is written, * He that
reioyceth, [y] let him reioyce in the Lord.

CHAP. II.

*1 He putteth for example his maner of preaching, which
was according to the tenor of the Gospel. 8 Which Gos
pel was contemptible & hid to the carnal. 10 And a-
gaine honorable and manifest to the spiritual.*

1 AND I, brethren, when I came to you,
came not with * excellencie of wordes, or of wisdome, shewing vnto you the
* [a] testimonie of God.
2 For I estemed not to * knowe anie thing
among you, saue Iesus Christ, and him
crucified.
3 * And I was among you in [b] weakenes, and
in feare, & in muche trembling.
4 Nether *stode* my worde, & my preaching
in the * entising speache of mans wisdome, but in plaine euidence of [c] the Spirit
and of power,
5 That your faith shulde not be in the wisdome of men, but in the power of God.
6 And we speake wisdome among them
that are [c] perfite: not the wisdome of this
worlde, nether of the [d] princes of this
worlde, which come to noght.
7 But we speake the wisdome of God in a
mysterie, *euen* the hid *wisdome*, which God
had determined before the worlde, vnto
our glorie.
8 Which [e] none of the princes of this
worlde hathe knowen: for had thei knowẽ
it, thei wolde not haue crucified ẏ [f] Lord
of glorie.
9 But as it is written, * The things which
eye hathe not sene, nether eare hathe heard, nether [g] came into mãs heart, *are*, which
God hathe prepared for them that loue
him.
10 But God hathe reueiled *them* vnto vs by
his Spirit: for the Spirit [h] searcheth all
things, yea, the deepe things of God.
11 For what man knoweth the things of a
man, saue the spirit [i] of a man, which is in
him? euen so the things of God knoweth
no man, but the Spirit of God.
12 Now we haue [k] receiued not the Spirit
of the worlde, but the Spirit, which is of
God, that we might knowe the [l] thĩgs that
are giuen to vs of God.
13 Which things also we speake, not in the
* wordes which mans wisdome teacheth,

t Which are in mans iudgement almost nothing, but taken for abiects & castawaies.
u Estemed & in reputacion.
Ierem.23,5.
x Thus he calleth man in cõtempt & to beate downe his arrogancie.
Ierem.9,24. *2.cor.10,17.*
y That is, attribute all things to God with thankesgiuing
Chap.1,17.
Or, mysterie.
a That is, the Gospel, whereby God doeth manifest him self to ẏ worlde, or whereof God is the autor & witnes.
Or, I thoght nothing worthie to be knowen.
Act.18,1. *Chap.1,17.* *2.pet.1,16.*
b Herein appeareth his great modestie, who was not glorious, but abiect & humble, not ful of vaineboastings & arrogancie, but ẘ feare & trembling set forthe ẏ mightie power of God.
c They whose vnderstandĩgs are illuminate by faith, acknowledge this wisdome, ẘ the worlde calleth follie.
d The worde is here taken for thẽ whome ether for wisdome, riches or power men moste esteme.
Isa.64,4.
e That is, very fewe.
f He calleth Iesus ẏ mightie God, ful of true glorie & maiestie, whome Dauid also calleth ẏ King of glorie, Psal.24,7. and Steuen nameth him the God of glorie, Act 7,2: & hereby appeareth the diuinitie of Christ & cõiunctiõ of two natures in one persone.
Chap.1,17. *2.pet.1,16.*

g Man is not able to thinke Gods prouidence towards his. h For he is one God with the Father and the Sonne. i Mans minde, which vnderstandeth and iudgeth. k We are not moued with that Spirit, which teacheth things wherewith the worlde is delited, and which men vnderstand by nature. l All the benefites of God in Iesus Christ.

but which the holie Gost teacheth, comparing [m] spiritual things with spiritual
things.
14 But the [n] natural man perceiueth not
the things of the Spirit of God: for they
are foolishnes vnto him: nether can he
knowe *them*, because they are spiritually
discerned.
15 But he that is * spiritual, discerneth all
things: yet he him self is [o] iudged of no
man.
16 *For who hathe knowen the minde of the
Lord, that he might instruct him? But we
haue the [p] minde of Christ.

m As that we teache is spiritual, so ỹ kinde of teaching must be spiritual, that ỹ wordes may agre with the matter.
n Whose knowledge & iudgement is not cleared by Gods Spirit.
Prou.27,19.
Isa.40,13.
wisd.9,17.
rom.11,34.
o For the trueth of God is not subiect to the iudgement of man.
p That is, Christs Spirit, Iohn 16,13. rom 8,9.

CHAP. III.

3 Paul rebuketh the sectes and autours thereof. 7 No man oght to attribute his saluacion to the ministers, but to God. 10 That they beware erronious doctrines. 11 Christ is the fundacion of his Church. 16 The dignitie and office bothe of the ministers and also of all the faithful.

1 AND I colde not speake vnto you,
brethrē, as vnto spiritual mē, but as
vnto carnal, *euen* as vnto [a] babes in Christ.
2 I gaue you milke to drinke, & not meat:
for ye were not yet able *to beare it*, nether
yet now are ye able.
For ye are yet carnal: for where as *there is*
3 among you enuying, and strife, and diuisions, are ye not carnal, and walke as men?
4 For when one saith, I am Pauls, and another, I am Apollos, are ye not carnal?
5 Who is Paul then? and who is Apollos,
but the ministers by whome ye beleued, &
as the Lord gaue to euerie man?
6 I haue planted, Apollos watred, but God
gaue the encrease.
7 So then, nether is he that planteth, anie
thing, nether he that watreth, but God
that giueth the encrease.
8 And he that planteth, & he that watreth,
are [b] one, *and euerie man shal receiue his
wages, according to his labour.
9 For we together are Gods [c] laborers: ye
are Gods housbandrie, *and* Gods buylding.
10 According to the grace of God giuen
to me, as a skilful master buylder, I haue
laid the fundacion, and another buyldeth
thereon: but let euerie man [d] take hede
how he buyldeth vpon it.
11 For other fundacion can no man lay,
then that which is laid, which is Iesus
Christ.
12 And if anie man buylde on this fundacion, golde, siluer, precious stones, tymber,
haye, *or* stubble,
13 Euerie mans worke shalbe made manifest: for the [e] daye shal declare it, because
it shalbe reueiled by the [f] fyre: & the fyre shal trye euerie mans worke of what
sorte it is.
14 If anie mans worke, that he hathe buylt
vpon, abide, he shal receiue wages.

a Being ingrafted in Christ by faith, we begin to moue by his Spirit, & as we profite in faith, we growe vp to a ripe age. And here let him take hede that teacheth, lest for milke he giue poyson: for milke and strong meat in effect are one, but onely differ in maner & forme.
Psal.62,13.
galat.6,5.
b He chargeth them with two fautes: the one, ỹ thei attributed tomuche to ỹ ministers, & ỹ other, that thei preferred one minister to another.
c So made by his grace.
d He reproueth the ministers of Corinth, as teachers of curious doctrines & questions.
e Or the time: which is, whē the light of ỹ trueth shal expel the darkenes of ignorance, then the curious ostentacion of mans wisdome shalbe broght to noght.
f By the tryal of Gods Spirit.

15 If anie mans worke burne, he shal [g] lose,
but he [h] shalbe [i] safe him self: neuertheles
yet as it were by the fyre.
16 *Knowe ye not that ye are the Temple
of God, and that the Spirit of God dwelleth in you?
17 *If anie man destroy the Tēple of God,
him shal God destroy: for the Temple of
God is holie, which ye are.
18 Let no man deceiue him self. If anie
man among you seme to be wise in this
worlde, let him be a foole, that he may be
wise.
19 For ỹ wisdome of this worlde is foolishnes with God: for it is written, *He catcheth the wise [k] in their owne craftines.
20 *And againe, The Lord knoweth that
the thoghts of the wise be vaine.
21 Therefore let no man [l] reioyce in men:
for all things are yours.
22 Whether it be Paul, or Apollos, or Cephas, or the worlde, or life, or death:
whether they be things present, or things
to come, *euen* all are yours,
23 And ye Christs, and Christ Gods.

g Bothe his labour & rewarde.
Chap.6,19.
2 cor.6,16.
h He reproueth thē not as false apostles, but as curious teachers of humaine sciēces, as they which lothing at the simplicitie of Gods worde, preache philosophical speculacions.
i As touching his life, if he holde fast the fundacion.
Iob.5,13.
k When they them selues are entāgled in ỹ same snares, wc thei laid for others.
Psal.94,11.
l But in God who worketh by his ministers to his owne glorie & the cōfort of his Church.

CHAP. IIII.

1 After that he had described the office of a true Apostle. 3 Seing they did not acknowledge him suche one. 4 He appealeth to Gods iudgement. 7 Beating downe their glorie which hindered them to praise that, which they dispraised in him. 16 He sheweth what he requireth on their parte, & what they oght to loke for of him at his returne.

1 LET a man so thinke of vs, as of the
[a] ministers of Christ, and disposers
of the secrets of God.
2 And as for the rest, it is required of the
disposers, ỹ euerie mā be founde faithful.
3 *As touching me, I passe verie litle, to be
iudged of you, or of " mans iudgement:
no, I iudge not [b] mine owne self.
4 For I [c] knowe nothing by [d] my self, yet
am I not thereby iustified: but he that iud
geth me, is the Lord.
5 Therefore * iudge nothing before the time, vntil the Lord come, who wil lighten
things that are hid in darkenes, and make
the counsels of the hearts manifest: and
then shal euerie man haue praise of God.
6 Now these things, brethren, I haue figuratiuely applied vnto mine owne self &
Apollos, for your sakes, that ye might learne [e] by vs, that no man presume aboue
that which is written, that one swel not a-
gainst another for anie mans cause.
7 For who [f] separateth thee? and what hast
thou, that thou hast not receiued? if thou
hast receiued it, why reioycest thou, as
thogh thou hadest not receiued it?
8 Now ye are ful: now ye are made riche:
ye reigne as Kings without vs, and wolde
to God ye did reigne, that we also might
reigne with you.
9 For I thinke that God hathe set forthe

a As it is a thing intollerable to contēne ỹ true ministers of God, so it is greatly reprehensible to attribute more vnto thē then is mete.
Mat.7,1.
" *Greke, mans day.*
Mat.7,1.
rom.2,1.
b Whether I haue great gifts or litle, few or manie.
c For as I do not knowe, whereby I shulde take anie occasion of glorie: so I am certeine ỹ before God another maner of iustice is required.
d Concerning mine office.
e By our example.
f To wit, from other men and pferreth thee?

vs g the laste Apostles, as men appointed
to death: for we are made a gasing stocke
vnto the worlde, and to the Angels, and
to men.
10 We *are* h fooles for Christs sake, and ye
are wise in Christ: we *are* weake, and
ye strong: ye *are* honorable, and we *are*
despised.
11 Vnto this houre we bothe hũger, & thirst,
and are naked, and are buffeted, and haue
no certeine dwelling place,
12 *And labour, working wᵗ our owne hands:
we are reuiled, & *yet* we blesse: we are persecuted,
and suffer it.
13 *We are euil spoken of, and we "pray:
we are made as the filthe of the worlde,
the offskowring of all things, vnto this
time.
14 I write not these things to shame you,
but as my beloued childrẽ I admonish you
15 For thogh ye haue ten thousand "instru-
ctours in Christ, yet *haue ye* not manie fathers: for in Christ Iesus I haue begotten
you through the Gospel.
16 Wherefore, I pray you, be ye followers
of me.
17 For this cause haue I sent vnto you Timotheus, which is my beloued sonne, and
faithful in the Lord, wᶜ shal put you in i remembrance of my wayes in Christ as I teache euerie where in euerie Church.
18 Some are puffed vp as thogh I wolde not
come to you.
19 But I wil come to you shortely, *if the
Lord wil, and wil knowe, not the speache
of them which are puffed vp, but the
power.
20 For the k kingdome of God *is not* in
worde, but in l power.
21 What wil ye? shal I come vnto you
with a rod, or in loue, and in the spirit of
mekenes?

g To diminish his autoritie they obiected, that he was not made an Apostle by Christ, but afterwardes.
h By this bitter tanting in abiecting him self and exalting the Corinthians, he maketh them ashamed of their vaine glorie.
Act. 20,34. 1. thess. 2,9. 2. thess. 3,8.
Mat. 5,44. luk 23,34. act 7,60.
"Or, vse gentle wordes.
"Or, pedagogues & scolemasters.
i Forasmuche as they had so sone forgottẽ.
Act. 19,21. iam. 4,15.
k That is, whatsoeuer giftes we haue receiued of God to this end, ỷ he may reigne among vs.
l Of the holie Gost.

CHAP. V.

1 He reproueth sharpely their negligence in punishing him that had committed inceste, 3 Willing them to excommunicate him, 7 To embrace puritie, 9 And flee wickednes.

1 IT is heard certeinely *that there is* fornication amõg you, and suche fornicatiõ
as is not once named among the a Gentils,
*that one shulde haue his fathers wife.
2 And ye are puffed vp & haue not rather
sorowed, that he which hathe done this dede, might be put from among you.
3 *For I verely as absent in bodie, but present in spirit, haue determined already as
thogh I were present, that he that hathe
b thus done this thing,
4 When ye are gathered together, and my
c spirit, d in the Name of our Lord Iesus
Christ, that suche one, I *say*, by the power
of our Lord Iesus Christ,
5 *Be deliuered vnto e Satan, for the
f destructiõ of the flesh, that the spirit may
be saued in the day of the Lord Iesus.
6 Your reioycing is not g good: *know ye
not that a litle leauẽ, leaueneth the whole
lumpe?
7 Purge out therefore the olde leauen, that
ye may be a newe lumpe, h as ye are vnleauened: for Christ our Passeouer is sacrificed for vs.
8 Therefore let vs kepe the feast, not with
olde leauẽ, nether in the leauen of maliciousnes and wickednes: but with the vnleauened bread of sinceritie and trueth.
9 I wrote vnto you in an epistle, *that ye
shulde not cõpanie together wᵗ fornicators,
10 And i not all together with the fornicators of this worlde, or with the couetous,
or with extorcioners, or with idolaters: for
then ye muste go out of the worlde.
11 But now I haue written vnto you, that ye
companie not together: if anie that is called a brother, be a fornicator, or couetous,
or k an idolater, or a railar, or a drunkard,
or an extorcioner, with suche one eat not.
12 For what haue I to do, to iudge them also, which are l without? do ye not iudge thẽ
that are m within?
13 But God iudgeth them that are without.
Put away therefore frõ among your selues that wicked man.

a Who wolde thinke that you wolde suffer that mischief vnpunished, which ỷ moste barbarous nations abhorre to speake of.
Leu. 18,8. Col. 2,5.
b Hauing now receiued the Gospel.
c My wil and consent.
d With inuocatiõ of Gods Name, as becometh them wᶜ procure the Lords busines and not their owne.
1. Tim. 1,20.
e Which is, to be as an heathen man and publicane.
f For being wõded with shame & sorrowe, his flesh or olde man shal dye: and the spirit or newe man shal remaine aliue & enioye the victorie in ỷ day when the Lord shal iudge the quicke and dead. 2. Cor 4,18. 1 pet 4,6.
Gal. 5,9.
g Seing you suffer suche mõstrous vices among you.
Mat. 18,17. 2. thess. 3,14.
h As euerie mã particularly is pure, so ỷ whole Church in general may be pure.
i But he meãt of those that were conuersant in the Church, whome they oght by discipline to haue corrected: for as touching strãgers they oght by all meanes godly to winne thẽ to Christ.
k Who to please bothe partes wolde be present at idole seruice, & yet professe the Gospel. l Vnto whome the Ecclesiastical discipline doeth not stretch. m Which are subiect to Gods worde, & to the discipline of the Church.

CHAP. VI.

1 He rebuketh them for going to law together before the Heathen. 7 Christians oght rather to suffer. 12 He reproueth the abusing of Christian libertie. 15 And sheweth that we oght to serue God purely bothe in bodie, and in soule.

1 DAre anie of you, hauing busines against another, be iudged vnder "the
a vniust, and not vnder the Saintes?
2 *Do ye not knowe, that the Saintes shal
iudge the worlde? If the worlde then shalbe iudged by you, are ye vnworthie to iud
ge the smallest matters?
3 Knowe ye not ỷ we shal iudge the b Angels? how muche more things that perteine to this life?
4 If then ye haue iudgemẽts of things perteining to this life, c set vp them which are
d least estemed in the Church.
5 I speake it to your shame. Is it so that
there is not a wise man among you? no
not one, ỷ can iudge betwene his brethrẽ?
6 But a brother goeth to lawe with a brother, and that vnder the infideles.
7 Now therefore there is vtterly "a faute
among you, because ye go to law one with
another: *why rather suffer ye not wrong?
why rather susteine ye not harme?
8 *Nay, ye your selues e do wrong, and do
harme, and that to your brethren.

"Or, iudges & magistrates which are infideles
Wis. 3,2.
a He calleth them vniuste, whosoeuer are not sanctified in Christ.
b Who are now apostates & deuils, Mat. 25,41.
c That is, make them iudges.
d If ye so burne with desire to pleade, kepe a court amoug your selues, and make the least estemed your iudge: for it is moste easie to iudge betwene brethren.
"Or, impotencie of minde.
Mat. 5,39. luk. 6,29. rom. 12,19. 1. Thes. 4,6.
e He doeth not reproue ỷ godlie, which with a good conscience vseth ỷ magistrat to defende his right, but condemneth hatred, grudges & desires of reuengeance.

9 Knowe ye not that the vnrighteous shal
not inherite the kingdome of God? Be
not deceiued: *nether fornicatours, nor
idolaters, nor adulterers, nor wãtons, nor
bouggerers,
10 Nor theues, nor couetous, nor drunkards,
nor railers, nor extorcioners shal inherite
the kingdome of God.
11 And suche were *some of you: but ye are
washed, but ye are sanctified, but ye are iustified in the Name of the Lord Iesus, and
by the Spirit of our God.
12 ¶ *All [f] things are lawful vnto me: but
all things are not profitable. I may do all
things, but I wil not be broght vnder [g] the
power of anie thing.
13 Meates *are ordeined* for the bellie, and the
bellie for ẏ meates: but God shal destroie
bothe it, and them. Now the bodie *is* not
for [h] fornication, but for the [i] Lord, & the
Lord for the bodie.
14 And God hathe also raised vp ẏ Lord,
and *shal raise vs vp by his power.
15 Knowe ye not, that your bodies are the
members of Christ? shal I then take the
mẽbers of Christ, and make them the mẽbers of an [k] harlot? God forbid.
16 Do ye not knowe, that he which coupleth
him self with an harlot, is one bodie? *for
two, saith he, shalbe one flesh.
17 But he that is ioyned vnto the Lord, is
one spirit.
18 Flee fornication: euerie sinne that a man
doeth, is without the bodie: but he ẏ cõmit
teth fornicatiõ, sinneth against his [l] owne
bodie.
19 Know ye not, that *your bodie is ẏ tẽple
of the holie Gost, *which is* in you, whome ye
haue of God? and ye are not your owne.
20 *For ye are boght for a price: therefore
glorifie God in your bodie, and in your
spirit: for they are Gods.

Ephe.5,3. 1.tim.1,9.
Eph 2,12. tit.3,3. 1.pet.4,3.
Chap.10,23. eccle.37,31.
f Here he speaketh of things indifferent of their nature, & first as touchīg carnal libertie
g For we are subiect to those thīgs which we can not want.
h They abused meates, bothe in that they offended others thereby, & also prouoked their owne lusts to vnclennes.
Rom.6,5.
i God wil be Lord bothe of the soul and bodie.
k Whereby he signifieth, that bothe we shal se the glorie of the resurrection of the iuste, and also that dignitie, and priuiledge where by we be made the mẽbers of Christ.
Gen.2,24. mat.19,5. mar.10,7. eph 5,31.
Chap.3,17. 2.cor.6,16.
Chap.7,23. 1.pet.1,10.
l That is, he more polluteth his owne bodie, then he that committeth anie other sinne.

CHAP. VII.

1 The Apostle answereth to certeine questions, which the Corinthians desired to knowe. 2 As of single life, 3 Of the duetie of mariage, 11 Of discordes & dissension in mariage, 13 Of mariage betwene the faithful & vnfaithful. 18 Of vncircumcising the circumcised. 21 Of seruitude. 25 Of virginitie, 39 And seconde mariage.

1 NOw concerning the things whereof
ye wrote vnto me, It *were* [a] good for
a man not to touche a woman.
2 Neuertheles, to auoide fornication, let
[b] euerie man haue his wife, and let euerie
woman haue her owne housband.
3 *Let the housbãd giue vnto the wife [c] due
beneuolence, and likewise also the wife vnto the housband.
4 The wife hathe not ẏ power of her owne
bodie, but the housband: and likewise also the housband hathe not the power of
his owne bodie, but the wife.
5 Defraude not one another, except *it be* with

a Or, expediēt because mariage, through mans corruption, and not by Gods institution bringeth cares and troubles.
1.Pet.3,7.
b Speaking to all men in general.
c Which conteineth all dueties perteining to mariage.

consent for a time, that ye may giue your
selues to fasting and prayer, & againe come together that Satan tempt you not for
your incontinencie.
6 But I speake this by permission, [d] not by
commandement.
7 For I wolde that all men were euen as I
my self *am*: but euerie man hathe his proper gift of God, one after this maner, and
another after that.
8 Therefore I say vnto the vnmaried, and
vnto the widowes, it is good for them if
they abide euen as I *do*.
9 But if they can not absteine, let thẽ marie: for it is better to marie thẽ to [e] burne.
10 And vnto the maried I cõmande, not I,
but the Lord, Let not the wife * departe
from her housband.
11 But and if she [f] departe, let her remaine
vnmaried, or be recõciled vnto her housband, and let not the housband put [g] a-
way *his* wife.
12 But to the remnant I speake, & not [h] the
Lord, If anie brother haue a wife, that beleueth not, if she be content to dwell with
him, let him not forsake her.
13 And the womã which hathe an housbãd
that beleueth not, if he be content to dwel
with her, let her not forsake him.
14 For the vnbeleuing housband is [i] sanctified by the wife, & the vnbeleuing wife is
sanctified by the housband, els were your
childrẽ vncleane: but now are they [k] holie.
15 But if the vnbeleuing departe, let him
departe: a brother or a sister is not in subiection in [l] suche things: but God hathe
called vs in peace.
16 For what knowest thou, ô wife, whither
thou shalt saue thine housband? Or what
knowest thou, ô mã, whither thou shalt saue thy wife?
17 But as God hathe distribute to euerie
mã, as the Lord hathe [m] called euerie one,
so let him walke: and so ordeine I, in all
Churches.
18 Is anie man called being circumcised?
let him not [n] gather *his vncircumcision*: is anie
called vncircumcised? let him not be circumcised.
19 [o] Circumcision is nothing, & vncircumcision is nothing, but the keping of the cõmandements of God.
20 *Let euerie man abide in the same vocation wherein he was called.
21 Art thou called *being* a seruant? [p] care not for it: but if yet thou maist be fre,
vse it rather.
22 For he that is called in the [q] Lord *being* a
seruant, is the Lords freman: likewise also

d He sheweth that he commandeth not precisely all men to marie, but that God hathe granted this remedie vnto them ẇ can not liue chaste.
e With the fyre of concupiscence, that is when mans wil so giueth place to the lust that tempteth, that he can not call vpõ God with a quiet conscience.
Mat.5,32. & 19,9. mar.10,11. luk.16,18.
f For hatred, dissension, angre, &c.
g Saue for whordome, as Matth 5,32.
h In asmuche as there was nothing expresly spoken hereof in the Law, or Prophetes: or els he spake this moued by the Spirit of God as he testifieth in the 25.ver.
i Meaning, that the faith of ẏ beleuer hathe more power to sanctifie mariage then the wickednes of the other to pollute it.
k They that are borne of ether of the parents faithful, are also counted members of Christs Church, because of ẏ promes, Act.2,39.
l When suche things come to passe, that the faithful & vnfaithful be maried together, and the one forsake ẏ other without cause.
m The lawful vocation in outwarde things must not lightly be neglected.
n Which is when the surgeon by arte draweth out the skinne to couer the parte, Celsus lib. 7 ca 25 Epiphan lib de ponderib & mensur 1. Maccab 1,16
o It is all one whither thou be Iewe or Gentil. *Ephe 4,1.1 tim 6,1. p Althogh God hathe called thee to serue in this life, yet thinke not thy condition vnworthie for a Christian: but reioyce, that thou art deliuered by Christ from the miserable sclauerie of sinne and death. q Being seruant by condition is made partaker of Christ.

he that

he that is called *being* fre, is Christs seruāt.
23 *Ye are boght" with a price: be not the
seruants of men.
24 Brethren, let euerie man, wherein he was
called, therein abide [r] with God.
25 Now concerning "virgines, I haue no
[s] commandement of the Lord: but I giue
mine aduise, as one that hathe obteined
mercie of the Lord to be "faithful.
26 I suppose then [t] this to be good for the
present [u] necesitie: *I meane* that it is good
for a man so to be.
27 Art thou boūde vnto a wife? seke not to
be losed: art thou losed from a wife? seke
not a wife.
28 But if thou takest a wife, thou sinnest not:
and if a virgine marie, she sinneth not: neuertheles, suche shal haue [x] [y] trouble in the
flesh: but I [z] spare you.
29 And this I say, brethrē, because the time
is short, "here after that bothe they which
haue wiues, be as thogh they had none:
30 And they that [a] wepe, as thogh they
wept not: and they that [b] reioyce, as thogh
thei reioyced not: & thei that bie, as thogh
they possessed not:
31 And they that vse this worlde, as thogh
they vsed it not: for the [c] facion of this
worlde goeth away.
32 And I wolde haue you without care. The
vnmaried careth for the things of ẏ Lord,
how he may please the Lord.
33 But he that is maried, careth for the
things of the [d] worlde, how he maie please
his wife‖.
34 There is differēce also betwene a virgine & a wife: the vnmaried woman careth
for the things of the Lord, that she may
be [e] holie, bothe in bodie and in spirit: but
she that is maried, careth for the things of
the worlde, how she may please her housband.
35 And this I speake for your owne cōmoditie, not to [f] tangle you in a snare, but that
ye followe that, which is honest, and that
ye may cleaue fast vnto the Lord without
separation.
36 But if anie man thinke that it is vncom-
lie for his virgine, if she passe the flowre
of *her* age, & [g] nede so require, let him do
what he wil, he sinneth not: let them be
maried.
37 Neuertheles he [h] that standeth firme in
his heart, that he hathe no nede, but hathe
[i] power ouer his owne wil, & hathe so decreed in his heart, that he wil kepe his virgine, he doeth wel.
38 So then he that giueth her to mariage,
doeth wel, but he that giueth her not to
mariage, doeth [k] better.
39 The wife is bounde by the [l] law, as long
as her housband * liueth: but if her housband be dead, she is at libertie to mary ẘ
whome she wil, onely in the Lord.
40 But she is more blessed, if she so abide, in
my iudgement: *and I thinke that I haue
also the Spirit of God.

Chap.6,20.
1.pet 1,20.
**Or, dearly.*
r Syncerely: as in the presence of God.
**Or, the state of virginitie.*
s He bindeth no man to that ẘ God hathe left fre: but sheweth what is moste agreable to Gods wil, according to the circumstance of the time, place & persones.
**Or, beloued.*
t To be single.
u In these afflictions and persecutions.
x As worldlie cares of their children & familie.
y He doeth not preferre singlenes as a thing more holie then mariage, but by reason of incommodities, ẘ the one hathe more then the other.
z In wishing that you colde liue without wiues.
**Or, it remaineth that.*
a Which be in aduersitie.
b Which be in prosperitie.
c In this worlde there is nothing but mere vanitie.
d Which onely apperteine to this present life.
‖*And he is diuided*, meaning into diuers cares.
e She may atteine vnto it soner then the other, because she is without cares.
f Seing S. Paul colde binde no mās conscięce to single life, what presumption is it that anie other shulde do it.
g That is, that she shulde marie to auoide fornication.
h Meaning, he that is fully persuaded that he hathe no nede.
i For the fathers wil dependeth on his childrēs in this point: in so muche as he is boūde to haue respect to their infirmitie, nether can he iustly require of thē singlenes, if they haue not that gift of God so to liue.
k And more cōmodious for his childrē in preseruing them from cares.
l Of matrimonie.
**Rom.7,1.*
1.Thess.4,8.

CHAP. VIII.

He rebuketh thē that vse their libertie to the sclander of other, in going to the idolatrous sacrifices. 9 And sheweth how men oght to behaue them towarde suche as be weake.

1 AND as touching things sacrificed
vnto idoles, we knowe that we all ha
ue [a] knowledge: knowledge puffeth vp, but
loue edifieth.
2 Now, if any man thinke that he knoweth
any thing, he knoweth nothing yet as he
oght to knowe.
3 But if any man loue God, the same is
"knowen of him.
4 Cōcerning therefore meat sacrificed vn
to idoles, we knowe that an idol *is* [b] nothīg
in the worlde, & that there *is* none other
God but one.
5 For thogh there be that are called gods,
whether in heauē, or in earth, (as there be
many gods, and many [c] lords)
6 Yet vnto vs there *is* but one God, *which is*
the Father, of whome are all things, & we
in him: &*one Lord Iesus Christ, by whome *are* all things, and we by him.
7 But euerie man hathe not knowledge: for
some hauing [d] cōscience of the idole, vntil this houre, eat as a thīg sacrificed vnto
the idole, and so their conscience being
weake, is defiled.
8 But meat maketh not vs acceptable to
God: for nether if we eat, haue we ẏ [e] more: nether if we eat not, haue we the lesse.
9 But take hede lest by any meanes this
"power of yours be an occasion of falling
to them that are weake.
10 For if any man se thee which hast knowledge, sit at table in the idoles temple, shal
not the cōscience of him which is weake,
be " [f] boldened to eat those things which
are sacrificed to idoles?
11 And through thy knowledge shal the
* [g] weake brother perish, for whome
Christ dyed.
12 Now when ye sinne so against the brethren, and wounde their weake conscience, ye sinne against Christ.
13 *Wherefore if meat offend my brother,
I wil eat no flesh while the worlde standeth, that I may not offend my brother.

a Of the libertie that God hathe giuen vs touchīg out warde things.
**Or, taught.*
b This he speaketh in their persone which bragged so muche of their libertie, saying that an image amōgs all thīgs that are made, is of no force.
c Which being idoles, yet are estemed of mē as Lords and Seigneurs.
Iohn 13,23.
chap.12,3.
d In that they thoght ẏ meat offered vp to the image, not to be pure, and therefore colde not eat it with a good cōscience.
e This abundance and wāt is referred to spiritual thīgs Rom 14,17.
**Or, libertie in things indifferent.*
"*Greke, buylded vp.*
f By thine example without any grounde of doctrine.
Rom.14,15.
g Which eateth against his conscience, or in doute.
Rom.14,21.

CHAP. IX.

He exhorteth them by his example to vse their libertie to the edification of other. 24 To runne on forthe in the course that they haue begonne.

1 AM I not an Apostle? am I not fre?
haue I not sene Iesus Christ our
Lord? are ye not my worke in the Lord?
2 If I be not an Apostle vnto other, yet

douteles I am vnto you: for ye are the [a] seale of mine Apostleship in the Lord.
3 My defense to thē [b] ȳ examine me, is this,
4 Haue we not power to eat [c] & to drinke?
5 Or haue we not power to [d] lead about a
wife being a [e] sister, as wel as the rest of
the Apostles, and as the ″ brethren of the
Lord, and Cephas?
6 Or I onely and Barnabas, haue not we
power [f] not to worke?
7 Who goeth a warfare anie time at his
owne cost? who planteth a vineyard, and
eateth not of the frute thereof? or who fedeth a flocke, and eateth not of the milke
of the flocke?
8 Say I these things according to man?
saith not the Law the same also?
9 For it is writtē in ȳ Law of Moses, * Thou
shalt not mussel the mouth of the oxe that
treadeth out the corne: doeth God take
[g] care for oxen?
10 Ether saith he it not all together for our
sakes? For our sakes no doute it is written,
that he which eareth, shulde eare in hope:
and that he that thresheth in hope, shulde
be partaker of his hope.
11 * If we haue sowen vnto you spiritual
things, *is it* a great thing if we reape your
carnal things?
12 If others with you be partakers of *this*
[h] power, *are* not we rather? neuertheles, we
haue not vsed this power: but ″ suffre all
things, that we shulde not hinder the Gospel of Christ.
13 Do ye not knowe, that they which minister about the * holie things, eat of ȳ things
of the Temple? and they which wait at the
altar, are partakers [i] with the altar?
14 So also hathe the Lord ordeined, that
they which preache the Gospel, shulde liue of the Gospel.
15 But I haue vsed none of these things:
nether wrote I these things, that it shulde
be so done vnto me: for it were better for
me to dye, then that anie man shulde make my [k] reioycing vaine.
16 For thogh I preache the Gospel, I haue
nothing to reioyce of: for necessitie is laid
vpon me, and wo is vnto me, if I preache
not the Gospel.
17 For if I do it willingly, I haue a reward-
de: but if I do it against my wil, [l] *notwithstanding* the dispensation is committed vnto me.
18 What is my rewarde then? verely that
whē I preache the Gospel, I make the Gospel of Christ [m] fre that I abuse not mine
autoritie in the Gospel.
19 For thogh I be fre frō all men, yet haue
I made my self seruant vnto all men, that
I might winne the mo.
20 * And vnto ȳ Iewes I become as a Iewe,
that I may winne the Iewes: to them that
are vnder the Lawe, as *thogh I were* vnder
the [n] Law, that I may winne thē that are
vnder the Law:
21 To them that are without lawe, as *thogh
I were* without law (whē I am not without
Law as perteining to God, but *am* in the
Law through Christ) that I may winne
them that are without Law.
22 To the weake I become as weake, that I
may winne ȳ weake: I am made [o] all thīgs
to all men, that I might by all meanes saue some.
23 And this I do for the Gospels sake, that
I might be partaker thereof with you.
24 Knowe ye not, that they which runne in
a race, runne all, yet one receiueth the price? so runne, that ye may obteine.
25 And euerie man that proueth masteries,
[p] absteineth from all things: and they *do it*
to obteine a corruptible crowne: but we
for an vncorruptible.
26 I therefore so runne, not as vncertein-
ly: so fight I, not as one that beateth the
ayre.
27 But I beat downe my [q] bodie, & bring
it into subiection, lest by any meanes after
that I haue preached to other, I my self
shulde be [r] reproued.

a I nede no further declaratiō but the workes that I haue wroght among you.
b And call into doute mine office.
c On ȳ Church charges.
d The Apostles led their wiues about with them
e A faithful & Christiā wife.
″ Or, cousins?
f Whether thei might not as lawfully liue without labouring for their liuing ẘ their owne hāds, as other Apostles.
Deu.25,4.
1.tim.5,18.
g Had God respect properly to the oxē them selues when he made this Law, and not rather vnto men?
Rom.15,27.
h To liue on other mens charges?
″ Or, take in worthe.
Deu.18,1.
i For ȳ parte ȳ was burnt, was deuored of the altar, & the other was due vnto the Priests by the Law.
k For now you haue no iuste cause against me, seing that I preached the Gospel frely vnto you.
l Seing he is charged to preache, he must willingly and earnestly followe it: for if he do it by constrainte, he doeth not his duetie.
m That I be not chargeable to thē vnto whome I preache, seing that they thinke that I preache for gaines.
Act.16,3.
Gal.2,3.
n As touching ȳ ceremonies.
o In things indifferent, as eating of meats, obseruation of feasts & daies and suche like, he facioned him selfe to men in suche sorte as he might best gaine them to Christ.
p That is, kepeth a straict dyet & refraineth from suche things as might distēpre his bodie.
q Or, olde mā which rebelleth against the Spirit.
r Lest he shulde be reproued of men when they shulde se him do contrarie, or contemne ȳ thing which he taught others to do.

CHAP. X.

He feareth them with the examples of the Iewes, that they put not their trust carnally in the graces of God, 14 Exhorting them to flee all idolatrie. 23 And offence of their neighbour.

1 MOreouer, brethrē, I wolde not that
ye shulde be ignorāt, that all our fa
thers were vnder * the cloude, and all passed through the * sea,
2 And were all * baptized vnto [a] Moses, in
the cloude, and in the sea,
3 And did all eat ȳ same [b] [c] spiritual meat,
4 * And did all drinke the same spiritual
drinke (for they dranke of the spiritual
Rocke that followed them: and the Rocke [d] was Christ)
5 But with many of thē God was not pleased: for they were * ouerthrowen in the
wildernes.
6 Now these are ensamples to vs, to the intent ȳ we shulde not lust after euil things
* as they also lusted.
7 Nether be ye idolaters as *were* some of
them, as it is written, * The people sate
downe to [e] eat and drinke, and rose vp to
playe.
8 Nether let vs commit fornication, as some of them committed fornication, and
fel in one * [f] daye thre & twētie thousand.
9 Nether let vs tempt [g] Christ, as some of
them also tēpted *him*, & were * destroyed
of serpents.

Exod.13,21.
nomb.9,18.
Exod.14,22.
Exod.16,15.
a Moses being their guide, or minister, or as some read, the i were baptized vnto Moses Lawe, others, by Moses.
Exod.17,6.
nomb.20,10.
b That is, Manna which was the outwarde signe or Sacrament of ȳ Spiritual grace.
Nom.26,65.
Nom.11,4.
& 26,64.
psal.106,14.
c They ate ȳ samemeat that we do, because the substance of theirs and our Sacramēts is all one.
d That is, signified Christ as all Sacraments do.
Exod.32,6.
Nom.25,9.
Nom.21,6.
psal.106,14.

e Because hereby occasion was taken to forget God, & cōmit idolatrie, there
fore these indifferent things are counted idolatrie. f Moses readeth foure
and twentie thousand, which declareth an infinite nomber. g Who was
their leader and was called the Angel of God.

Nom.14,37.
h Meaning ether the good or euil Angel whose ministerie God vseth to execute his iudgement to ỹ vtter destruction of the wicked.
i How God wil plague vs if we be subiect to the like vices.
k Or, later dais of Christs comming.
l He that led you into this tentatiō which commeth vnto you ether in prosperitie or aduersitie, or for your sinnes past, wil turne it to your commoditie & deliuer you.
" Or, thankes giuing.
m Or, prepare to this holie vse with praise and thankes giuing.
n The effectual badge of our coniūction and incorporation with Christ?
o If we that are many in nōber, are but one bodie in effect, ioyned with our head Christ, as many cornes make but one loafe, let vs renounce idolatrie which doeth separate our vnitie.
p Which is gouerned according to the ceremonies of ỹ Law.
q Which is to assemble in ỹ companie where idoles are called vpon.
Chap.6,13. eccl 37,31.
r For in those days they were accustomed to sel certeine of the flesh of beastes sacrificed in ỹ shambles & turned the money to ỹ Priests profit.
Psal.24,1.
s Or, doute not

10 Nether murmure ye, as some of them
*also murmured, and were destroyed of
the [h] destroyer.
11 Now all these things came vnto them
for ensamples, and were written to admonish [i] vs, vpō whome ỹ [k] ends of the worlde are come.
12 Wherefore, let him ỹ thinketh he standeth, take hede lest he fall.
13 There hathe no tentation taken you, but
suche as apperteineth to man: and God is
faithful, which wil not suffer you to be
tempted aboue that you be able, but [l] wil
euen giue the yssue with the tētation, that
ye may be able to beare it.
14 Wherefore my beloued, flee from idolatrie.
15 I speake as vnto them which haue vnderstanding: iudge ye what I say.
16 The cuppe " of blessing which we [m] blesse, is it not the communion of the blood
of Christ? The bread which we breake, [n] is
it not the communion of the bodie of
Christ?
17 For we that are many, are [o] one bread &
one bodie, because we all are partakers of
one bread.
18 Beholde Israel *which is* after the [p] flesh:
are not they which eat of the sacrifices,
partakers of the altar?
19 What say I then? that the idole is any
thing? or that that which is sacrificed to
idoles, is any thing?
20 Nay, but that these things which the
Gentiles sacrifice, they sacrifice to deuils,
and not vnto God: and I wolde not that
ye shulde haue [q] felowshippe with the deuils.
21 Ye can not drinke the cup of the Lord,
and the cup of the deuils. Ye can not be
partakers of the Lords table and of the ta
ble of deuils.
22 Do we prouoke the Lord to anger? are
we stronger then he?
23 *All things are lawful for me, but all
things are not expedient: all things are
lawful for me, but all things edifie not.
24 Let no man seke his owne, but euerie mā
anothers wealth.
25 Whatsoeuer is solde in the [r] shambles,
eat ye, & [s] aske no question for conscience sake.
26 *For the earth *is* the Lords, and all that
therein is.
27 If any of them which beleue not, call
you *to a feast*, and if ye wil go, whatsoeuer
is set before you, eat, asking no question
for conscience sake.
28 But if any man say vnto you, This is sacrificed vnto idoles, eat it not, because of
him that shewed it, and for the conscience (for the earth *is* the Lords, and all that
therein is)

29 And the conscience I say, not thine, but
of that other: for why shulde my [t] libertie
be condēned of another mans conscience?
30 For [u] if I through *Gods* benefite be partaker, why am I euil spoken of, for that
wherefore I giue thankes?
31 *Whether therefore ye eat or drinke, or
whatsoeuer ye do, do all to the glorie of
God.
32 Giue none offence, nether to the Iewes,
nor to the Grecians, nor to the Church
of God:
33 Euen as I please [x] all men [y] in all things,
not seking mine owne profite, but *the profite* of many, that they might be saued.

CHAP. XI.

He rebuketh the abuses which were crept into their Church. 4 As touching prayer, prophecying, 18 And ministring the Lords Supper, 23 Bringing them againe to the first institution thereof.

1 BE *ye the followers of me, euen as I
am of Christ.
2 Now, brethren, I commend you, that ye
remēbre "all my things, & kepe the ordinances, as I deliuered them to you.
3 But I wil that ye knowe, that Christ is the
*head of euerie man: & the man is the wo-
mans head: and God is Christs head.
4 Euerie mā [a] praying or "prophecying hauing *any thing* on *his* head, [b] dishonoreth
his head.
5 But euerie woman that prayeth or [c] prophecieth bareheaded, dishonoreth her
head: for it is euē one very thing, as thogh
she were shauen.
6 Therefore if the woman be not couered,
let her also be shorne: and if it be shame
for a woman to be "shorne or shauen, let
her be couered.
7 For a man oght not to couer *his* head: for
asmuche as he is the *[d] image and glorie
of God: but the woman is the [e] glorie of
the man.
8 For the man is not of the woman, but the
woman of the man.
9 *For the man was not created for the womans sake: but the woman for the mans
sake.
10 Therefore oght ỹ womā to haue [f] power
on *her* head, because of the [g] Angels.
11 Neuertheles, nether is the man without
the woman, nether the woman without the
man in the [h] [i] Lord.
12 For as the woman is of the man, so is the
man also by the woman: but all things are
of God.
13 Iudge in your selues, is it comelie that a
woman praye vnto God vncouered?
14 Doeth not nature it self teache you, that
if a mā haue long [k] heere, it is a shame vnto him?

t We must take hede that through our abuse, our libertie be not condemned.
u If by the benefite of God I may eat any kinde of meat, why shulde I by my defaut cause this benefite to be euil spokē of?
Colos.3,17.
x That is, the infirme.
y Which are indifferent.
2.Thes.3,9.
"Or, in all thigs remembre me.
Ephe.5,23.
a This is referred to commune prayer and preaching: for althogh one speake, yet the action is commune, so ỹ the whole Church may be said to praye or preache.
"Or preaching.
b This tradition was obserued according to the time and place that all things might be done in comelines & to edification.
Gen.1,26. & 5,1. & 9,6. col.3,3,10.
c Read chap. 14,34.
Gen.2,22.
"Or, powlled.
d The image of Gods glorie, in whome his maiestie & power shine concerning his autoritie.
e Or receiueth her glorie, in commendation of mā, & therefore is subiect.
f Some thing to couer her head in signe of subiection.
g To whome thei also shew their dissolution, and not onely to Christ
h Who is autor & mainteiner of their mutual cōiunction.
i For as God made the womā of mā, so now is man multiplied by the woman.
k As women vse to weare.

15 But if a woman haue long heere, it is a
praise vnto her: for her heere is [l] giuẽ her
for a couering.
16 But if any man luste to be contentious,
we haue no suche custome, nether ẏ Churches of God.
17 ¶ Now in this that I declare, I praise
you not, that ye come together, not with
profit, but with hurt.
18 For first of all, when ye come together
in the Church, I heare that there are dis-
sensions among you: and I beleue it *to be*
true [m] in some parte.
19 For there must be [n] heresies euen among
you, that they which are approued amõg
you, might be knowen.
20 When ye come together therefore into
one place, *this* is not to eat the Lords Supper.
21 For euerie man when they shulde eat, taketh his owne supper afore, and one is hun
grie, and another is drunken.
22 Haue ye not houses to eat & to drinke
in? dispise ye ẏ Church of God, and shame
thẽ that haue not? what shal I say to you?
shal I praise you in this? I praise you not.
23 For I haue receiued of the [o] Lord that
which I also haue deliuered vnto you, *to*
wit, That the Lord Iesus in the night that
he was betrayed, toke bread.
24 *And when he had giuen thãkes, he brake it, and said, Take, eat: this is my bodie,
which is [p] broken for you: this do ye in remembrance of me.
25 After the same maner also *he toke* the
cup, when he had supped, saying, This cup
is the Newe testament in my blood: this
do as oft as ye drinke it, in remẽbrance of
me.
26 For as often as ye shal eat this bread, &
drinke this cup, ye shewe the Lords death
til he come.
27 Wherefore, whosoeuer shal eat this
bread, and drinke the cup of the Lord
[q] vnworthely, shalbe giltie of the bodie &
blood of the Lord.
28 *Let a man therefore examine him self,
and so let him eat of this bread, & drinke
of this cup.
29 For he that eateth and drinketh vnworthely, eateth and drinketh his owne damnation, *because* he discerneth not [r] ẏ Lords
bodie.
30 For this cause many *are* weake, and sicke
among you, and many [s] slepe.
31 For if we wolde iudge our selues, we shulde not be iudged.
32 But when we are iudged, we are chastened of the Lord, because we shulde not be
condemned with the worlde.
33 Wherefore, my brethren, when ye come
together to eat, tary one for another.
34 And if any man be hungrie, let him eat
at home, that ye come not together vnto
condemnation. Other things wil I set in
order when I come.

l For God hathe giuen to woman longer heere thẽ vnto man, to the end she shulde trusse it vp about her head, whereby she declareth that she must couer her head.

m Not that all were so, but ẏ moste parte.

n Gods Church is not onely subiect to dissension as touching ordres and maners, but also to heresies as touching doctrine

o Who oght onely to beare autoritie in ẏ Church.

Mat.26,26. *mar.14,22.* *luk.22,19.*

p Signifying ẏ maner of his death whẽ his bodie shulde, as it were, be torne and broken with most grieuous torments (albeit not as ẏ thies of the thieues were) ẏ which thing the breakĩg of ẏ bread, as a figure, doeth moste liuely represent

q By peruertĩg the true & pure vse of the same.

2.Cor.13,5.

r But as thogh these holie mysteries of the Lords bodie & blood were cõmune meats, so without reuerence he commeth vnto thẽ

s Or, dye. Let them loke to them selues which ether adde or take away frõ the Lords institution.

CHAP. XII.

The diuersitie of the giftes of the holie Gost oght to be vsed to the edifying of Christs Church. 12 As the mẽbers of mans bodie serue to the vse one of another.

1 NOw concerning spiritual *giftes*, brethren, I wolde not haue you [a] ignorant.
2 Ye knowe that ye were Gentiles, and were caryed away vnto the [b] domme idoles,
as ye were [c] led.
3 Wherefore, I declare vnto you, that no
man *speaking by the [d] Spirit of God, cal
leth Iesus *execrable: also no man can
say that Iesus is the Lord, but by the holie Gost.
4 Now there are diuersities of giftes, but
the same Spirit.
5 And there are diuersities of administra-
tions, but the same Lord.
6 And there are diuersities of operatiõs, but
God is the same, which worketh all in all.
7 But the manifestation of the Spirit is giuen to euerie man, to [e] profit withall.
8 For to one is giuen by the Spirit the worde of wisdome: and to another the worde
of [f] knowledge, by the same Spirit:
9 And to another *is giuen* [g] faith, by the same Spirit: and to another the giftes of hea
ling, by the same Spirit:
10 And to another [h] ẏ operations of great
workes: and to another, [i] prophecie: and to
another, [k] the discerning of spirits: and to
another, diuersities of tongues: & to another the interpretation of tongues.
11 *And all these things worketh euen the
self same Spirit, distributing to euerie mã
seuerally as he wil.
12 For as the bodie is one, and hathe many
membres, and all the membres of the bodie, which is one, thogh they be many, *yet*
are *but* one bodie: euen so is Christ.
13 For by one Spirit are we all baptized into [l] one bodie, whether *we be* Iewes or
Grecians, whether *we be* bonde, or fre,
and haue bene all made to drinke into o-
ne Spirit.
14 For the bodie also is not one member,
but many.
15 If the fote wolde say, Because I am not
the hand, I am not of the bodie, is it therefore not of the bodie?
16 And if the eare wolde say, Because I am
not the eye, I am not of the bodie, is it the
refore not of the bodie?
17 If the whole bodie *were* an eye, where
were the hearing? If the whole *were* hearing, where *were* the smelling?
18 But now hathe God disposed the membres euerie one of them in the bodie at
his owne pleasure.

a The Corinthians hauing notable gifts, semed to haue forgotten, of whome, & for what end they had receiued them.

Mar.9,39.

b Which colde not heare your prayers.

Iohn 13,12. *chap.8,6.* *phil.2,10.*

c By Satãs suggestion.

d As no mã ẏ hathe the Spirit of God, can blaspheme Christ, and worship idoles, so none cã acknowledge Christ for Lord and God without the same Spirit.

e To wit, the Church, which is the whole body.

f That is, the vnderstanding of the Scriptures.

g To do onely miracles by.

h To worke by miracles against Satan & hypocrites, as was done agaist Ananias, Elymas, &c.

Rom 2,3. *ephes.4,8.*

i Meaning the declaration of Gods mysteries.

k To trie bothe ẏ doctrine & ẏ persones.

l That we might be one bodie with Christ, and the whole Church one Christ: of the which coniunctiõ Baptisme, & ẏ Lords Supper are effectual signes: for by baptisme we are regenerat into one Spirit, and by the Lords Supper we are incorporat into Christs bodie to be gouerned by the same Spirit.

19 For

19 For if they were all one member, where
were the bodie?
20 But now *are* there manie membres, yet
but [m] one bodie.
21 And the eye can not say vnto the hand,
I haue no nede of thee: nor the head a-
gaine to the fete, I haue no nede of you.
22 Yea, muche rather those membres of the
bodie, which seme to be [n] more feble, are
necessarie.
23 And vpon those *membres* of the bodie,
which we thinke moste vnhonest, put we
more [o] honestie on: and our vncomelie
partes haue more comelines on.
24 For our comelie *partes* nede it not: but
God hathe tempered the bodie together,
and hathe giuen the more honour to that
parte which lacked,
25 Lest there shulde be anie diuision in the
bodie: but that the membres shulde [p] haue the same care one for another.
26 Therefore if one member suffer, all suffer with it: if one member be had in honour, all the membres reioyce with it.
27 Now ye are the bodie of Christ, & mem
bres [q] "for *your* parte.
28 *And God hathe ordeined some in the
Church: *as* first, Apostles, secondly Prophetes, thirdly teachers, then them that
do miracles: after that, the giftes of healing, [r] helpers, [s] gouernours, diuersitie of
tongues.
29 Are all Apostles? are all Prophetes? are
all teachers?
30 Are all doers of miracles? haue all the
giftes of healing? do all speake with tongues? do all interprete?
31 But "desire you the best gifts, and I wil
yet shewe you a more excellent way.

m And therefore whatsoeuer the diuersitie is, yet the profite oght to be commune and serue to the edificacion of the Church.
n Whose vse semeth to be more vile.
o We are more careful to couer them.
p Euerie one in his office for the preseruacion of the bodie.
q For all Churches dispersed throughout ỹ worlde are diuers membres of one bodie
*Or, euerie one for his parte.
Ephes. 4.11.
r As Deacons.
s As Elders.
*Or, do you then desire the best giftes.

CHAP. XIII.

Because loue is the fountaine and rule of edifying the Church, he setteth forthe the nature, office and praise thereof.

1 THogh I speake with the tongues of
men and [a] Angels, and haue not loue,
I am *as* sounding brasse, or a tinkling
cymbal.
2 And thogh I had the *gift* of prophecie,
and knewe all secretes and all knowledge,
yea, if I had [b] all faith, so that I colde remoue * mountaines and had not loue, I
were nothing.
3 And thogh I fede the poore with all my
goods, and thogh I giue my bodie, that I
be burned, and haue not loue, it profiteth
me nothing.
4 Loue suffreth long: it is bountiful: loue
enuieth not: loue doeth not boast it self: it
is not puffed vp:
5 It disdaineth not: it seketh not her owne
things: it is not prouoked to anger: it thin
keth not euil:
6 It reioyceth not in iniquitie, but reioyceth in the trueth:
7 It suffreth all things: it beleueth [c] all
things: it hopeth all things: it endureth
[d] all things.
8 Loue doeth neuer fall away, thogh that
prophecyings be abolished, or the tõgues
cease, or knowledge vanish away.
9 For [e] we knowe [f] in parte, and we "prophecie in parte.
10 But when that which is perfite, is come,
then that which is in parte, shalbe abolished.
11 When I was a childe, I spake as a childe,
I vnderstode as a childe, I thoght as a
childe: but when I became a man, I put a-
way childish things.
12 For now we se [g] through a glasse darkely: but then *shal we* se face to face. Now
I knowe in parte: but then shal I knowe e-
uen as I am "knowen.
13 And now abideth faith, hope *&* loue, *e-*
uen these thre: but the [h] chiefest of these
is loue.

Chap. XIII.
a If the Angels had tongues, & I had the vse thereof, & did not bestowe them to profite my neighbour, it were nothĩg but vaine babling.
Mat. 17, 20. luk. 17, 6.
b Faith is here taken for the gift of doing miracles, ẘ the wicked may haue, as Mat. 7 22, & also for that faith (called historical) ẘ beleueth the mightie power of Christ, but can not apprehẽd Gods mercie through him: & this deuils haue, Iam. 2, 19: & therefore is separate from charitie, but ỹ faith that iustifieth in effect cãnot, as 1 Iohn. 2, 9.
c Not ỹ it suffreth it self to be abused, but iudgeth others by all loue & humanitie.
d Which may be without offence of Gods worde.
e Knowledge it self shalbe perfited in the worlde to come, & not abolished: but the maner of knowing & teaching shal cease, whẽ we shalbe before Gods presence, where we shal nether nede scholes nor teachers.
f That is, imperfectly.
*Or, teache.
g The mysteries of God.
*Or, taught of God.
h Because it serueth bothe here & in the life to come: but faith and hope appertei-ne onely to this life.

CHAP. XIIII.

1 He exhorteth to loue, commendeth the gift of tongues, & other spiritual gifts, 5 But chiefly prophecying. 34 He cõmandeth women to kepe silence in the Church. 40 And sheweth what good ordre oght to be obserued in the Church.

1 FOllowe after loue, and couet spiritual *gifts*, and rather that ye maye [a] prophecie.
2 For he that speaketh *a strange* tongue,
speaketh not vnto men, but vnto God: for
no man [b] heareth *him*: howbeit in [c] the spirit he speaketh secret things.
3 But he that prophecieth, speaketh vnto
men to edifying, and to exhortacion, and
to comfort.
4 He that speaketh *strange* language, edifieth [d] him self: but he that prophecieth, e-
difieth the Church.
5 I wolde that ye all spake *strange* languages, but rather that ye prophecied: for
greater is he that prophecieth, thẽ he that
speaketh *diuers* tongues, except he expoũde it, that the Church may receiue edificacion.
6 And now, brethren, if I come vnto you
speaking *diuers* tongues, what shal I profite you, except I speake to you, ether by
[e] reuelacion, or by knowledge, or by prophecying, or by doctrine?
7 Moreouer things without life which giue a sounde, whether *it be* a "pipe or an
harpe, except they make a distinction in
the sounds, how shal it be knowen what is
piped or harped?
8 And also if the trumpet giue an vncerteine sounde, who shal prepare him self
to battel?
9 So likewise you, by the tongue, except ye
vtter wordes that haue signification, how

a That is, to expounde the worde of God to the edificacion of the Church.
b Vnderstandeth him.
c By the spiritual gift, which he hathe receiued.
d For he profiteth none saue him self.
e The prophecie expoũdeth that ỹ God hath reueiled: & the doctrine teacheth, that which he hath giuen vs to vnderstand.
*Or, flute.

shal it be vnderstand what is spoken? for
ye shal speake in the [f] ayre.
10 There are so manie kindes of voyces,
("as it cometh to passe) in the worlde, and
none of them [g] is domme.
11 Except I knowe then the power of the
voyce, I shalbe vnto him that speaketh, [h] a
barbarian, and he that speaketh, shalbe a
barbarian vnto me.
12 Euen so, for asmuche as ye couet spiritual *gifts*, seke that ye maye excel vnto the
edifying of the Church.
13 Wherefore, let him that speaketh a *strãge*
tongue, praie, that he may interpret.
14 For if I pray *in* a *strange* tongue, my
spirit [i] praieth: but mine vnderstãding is
without [k] frute.
15 What is it then? I wil praye with the spirit, but I wil pray with the vnderstanding
also: I wil [l] sing with the spirit, but I wil
sing with the vnderstanding also.
16 Els, when thou blessest with the spirit,
how shal he that occupieth the roume of
the vnlearned, say [m] Amen, at thy giuing
of thankes, seing he knoweth not what
thou saist?
17 For thou verely giuest thankes wel, but
the other is not edified.
18 I thanke my God, I speake languages
more then ye all.
19 Yet had I rather in the Church to speake [n] fiue wordes with mine vnderstanding
that I might also instruct others, then ten
thousand wordes in a *strange* tongue.
20 Brethren, be not* children in vnderstãding, but as concerning maliciousnes be
children, but in vnderstanding be of a ripe age.
21 In the Law it is written, * [o] By men of o-
ther tongues, & by other languages wil I
speake vnto this people: yet so shal they
not heare me, saith the Lord.
22 Wherefore *strange* tõgues are for a [p] signe, not to them that beleue, but to thẽ that
beleue not: but prophecying *serueth* not
for thẽ that beleue not, but for thẽ which
beleue.
23 If therefore, when the whole Church is
come together in one, and all speakẽ *strãge*
tongues, there come in they that are vnlearned, or they which beleue not, wil thei
not say, that ye are out of your wittes?
24 But if all prophecie, and there come in
one that beleueth not, or one vnlearned,
[q] he is rebuked of [r] all men, and is iudged
of all.
25 And so are the secretes of his heart made manifest, & so he wil fall downe on his
face and worship God, and say plainely
that God is in you in dede.
26 What is to be *done* then, brethren? when
ye come together, *according as* euerie one
of you hathe a psalme, *or* hathe doctrine,
or hathe a tongue, *or* hathe reuelacion, *or*
hathe interpretacion, let all things be done vnto edifying.
27 If anie man speake a *strange* tongue, *let it*
be by two, or at the [s] most, by thre, and that
by course, and let one interpret.
28 But if there be no interpreter, let him
kepe silence in the Church, *which speaketh*
languages, and let him speake to him self,
and to God.
29 Let the Prophetes speake two, or thre,
and let the other iudge.
30 And if anie thĩg be reueiled to another
ỹ sitteth by, let the first holde his peace.
31 For ye may all prophecie one by one, ỹ
all may learne, & all may haue comfort.
32 And the [t] spirits of the Prophetes are
[u] subiect to the Prophetes.
33 For God is not *the autor* of confusion, but
of peace, as *we se* in all the Churches of
the Saintes.
34 * Let your women kepe [x] silence in the
Churches: for it is not permitted vnto thẽ
to speake: but *they oght* to be subiect, as also
* the Law saith.
35 And if thei wil learne anie thing, let thẽ
aske their housbands at home: for it is a
shame for women to speake in ỹ Church.
36 [y] Came the worde of God out from you?
ether came it vnto you onely?
37 If anie man thinke him self to be a Prophet, or [z] spiritual, let him acknowledge,
that the things, that I write vnto you, are
the commandements of the Lord.
38 [a] And if anie man be ignorant, let him
be ignorant.
39 Wherefore, brethrẽ, couet to prophecie,
& forbid not to speake languages.
40 Let all things be done honestly and by
order.

f Your wordes shalbe loste: for ye shal nether glorifie God thereby, nor profit mã. "Or, *as the thing requireth.* g That is, they may be able to be vnderstand. h He condemneth the Corinthians of barbarousnes in ỹ thing, whereby thei thoght to haue atteined to the greatest praise of eloquence. i And doeth his parte. k Not in respect of him, ỹ praieth, but in respect of the Church, which is nothing edified thereby. l Or, giue thankes by singing m One onely made the praiers, & the rest of the people followed in heart his wordes, & when he had prayed, thei all said, Amen, signifying that they beleued assuredly that God wolde grante their requests. n That is, moste fewe. *Mat.18,3.* *Isa.28,11. deut.28,49. ierem.5,15. ezek.3,6.* o He threatneth thẽ moste sharpely, that God wil punish the contempt of his worde, & their cõtrefait ignorance, forasmuche as to speake w̃ vnknowẽ tongues is a signe of Gods curse towards the wicked. p Of Gods curse when they are not vnderstand. q By hearing his secret fautes ript vp, & his sinnes reproued by Gods worde, he is compelled by his owne conscience to praise God. r Which expounde the wordes of God.

s Paul beareth as yet w̃ their weakenes, because also these were the gifts of God: but yet he sheweth that thei shuld not passe this measure that first one, after another & at ỹ vtmost the third shulde read in a strange language, which was to declare Gods miracle in the gift of tõgues: but chiefly he cõmandeth that nothing be done without interpretacion. *1.Tim.2,11.* t Or learning, w̃ Gods Spirit moueth them to vtter. *Gen.3,16.* u To the intẽt ỹ others maye iudge of him ỹ hathe spoken, if he haue passed the cõpas of Gods worde: wherefore S Iohn commãdeth to trye ỹ spirits whether thei be of God. x Because this disordre was in the Church, that women vsurped that w̃ was peculiar to men, the Apostle here sheweth what is mete to be done, & what is not: & albeit he mencioned this abuse afore, yet he referred it to this place to be reproued, because there he broght it in for another purpose. y Are ye the first or the last Christians, that ye nether submit your selues to the Churches, of whome you haue receiued the Gospel? nor haue respect to the others to whome the Gospel doeth likewise apperteine? z To haue vnderstanding of spiritual things. a If anie man haue iudgement, let him acknowledge that I speake of the Spirit of God, and so let him obey: and if he haue no iudgemẽt, let him acknowledge his ignorance, and trouble not the Church, but credit them that are learned.

CHAP. XV.

He proueth the resurrection of the dead. 3 And first that Christ is risen: 22 Then that we shal rise. 52 And the maner how.

1 Moreouer, * brethren, I declare vnto
you the Gospel, which I preached
vnto you, which ye haue also receiued,
and wherein ye continue,
2 And whereby ye are saued, if ye kepe in
memorie, after what maner I preached it
vnto you, [a] except ye haue beleued in
vaine.
3 For first of all, I deliuered vnto you that
which I [b] receiued, how that Christ dyed
for our sinnes according to ỹ * Scriptures,
4 And that he was buryed, & that he arose
the third day accordĩg to the * Scriptures,

Gal.1,11. a If you beleue to be saued by the Gospel, ye must beleue also the resurrection of the dead, which is one of the principal points thereof, or els your belief is but vaine. *Isa.53,5. 1.pet.2,42.* b He sheweth that nothing oght to be taught, which we haue not learned by Gods worde. *Ionas.2,1.*

5 * And

5 *And that he was sene of Cephas,then of
the [c] twelue.
6 After that, he was sene of mo then fiue
hundreth brethren at once : whereof many remaine vnto this present,& some also
are a slepe.
7 After that,he was sene of Iames: then of
all the Apostles.
8 *And last of all he was sene also of me as
of one,borne out of due time.
9 For I am the least of the Apostles, which
am not mete to be called an Apostle , because I persecuted the Church of God.
10 *But by the [d] grace of God, I am that I
am: and his grace which is in me, was not
in vaine:but I laboured more abundantly
then they all : yet not I , but the grace of
God which is with me.
11 Wherefore whether it were I,or they,so
we preache,and so haue ye beleued.
12 ¶ Now if it be preached , that Christ is
risen from the dead, how say some among
you , that there is no resurrection of the
dead?
13 For if there be no resurrection of the
dead,then is Christ not risen.
14 And if Christ be not risen , then is our
preaching [e] vaine , and your [f] faith is also
vaine.
15 And we are founde also false witnesses
of God:for we haue testified of God,that
he hathe raised vp Christ : whome he hathe not raised vp, if so be the dead be not
raised.
16 For if ŷ dead be not raised, thē is Christ
not raised.
17 And if Christ be not raised,your faith is
[g] vaine:ye are yet in your [h] sinnes.
18 And so they which are a slepe in Christ,
are perished.
19 If in this life " onely we haue hope in
Christ, we are of all men the moste miserable.
20 But now is Christ risen from the dead,
and was made the * first [i] frutes of them
that slept.
21 For since by man *came* death,by man *came* also the resurrection of the dead.
22 For as in Adam all dye,euē so in [k] Christ
shal [l] all be made aliue,
23 But euerie man in his * owne order : the
first frutes *is* Christ,afterwarde, they that
are of Christ , at his comming *shal rise a-
gaine.*
24 Then *shalbe* the end, whē he hathe [m] deliuered vp the kingdome to God, euē the
Father,when he hathe put downe all rule,
and all autoritie and power.
25 For he must reigne * til he hathe put all
his enemies vnder his fete.
26 The last enemie that shalbe destroyed,

Iohn 20,19.
c Althogh Iudas wanted,yet they were so called stil.
Act.9.4. rom.6,3. ephe.3,8. Ephe.3,7.
d For he was but the instrument,and minister and giueth the whole glorie to God.
e Christs death is not effectual except he rise from death.
f For if Christ be swaloed vp of death, there remaineth no hope of life any more.
g As mortification,and remission of sinnes depend on Christs death: so our quickening and restoring to life stand in his resurrection.
h You are not forgiuen nor sanctified.
"Or, onely for this life sake.
i As by the offring of ŷ first frute the whole frute is sanctified , so by Christ which is the first ŷ is raised,all haue assurance of ŷ resurrection.
k Who rose first from the dead to take possession in our flesh for vs his members.
l To wit , the faithful.
Col.1,18. reuel.1,5. 1.The 4,15.
m Christ as he is man & head of the Church is said to be subiect to God: but in respect of the worlde, is King of heauen and earth. This kingdome standeth in gouerning the faithful:and ouercōming the aduersaries, euen death the chiefest, which done , Christ being perfited with all his membres, shal as he is man,& head of the Church , with his felowe heires deliuer his kingdome, and be subiect to God with whome and the holie Gost in Godhead he is equal.
*Psal.110,1. act.2,34. ebr.1,13. & 10,13.

is death.
27 *For he hathe put downe all things vnder his fete . (And when he saith that all
things are subdued *to him*, it is manifest ŷ
he is excepted , which did put downe all
things vnder him.)
28 And when all things shalbe subdued vnto him,then shal the Sōne also him self be
subiect vnto him,that did subdue all thīgs
vnder him,that God may be [n] all in all.
29 Els what shal they do which are baptized [o] [p] for dead? if the dead rise not at all,
why are they then baptized for dead?
30 Why are we also in ieoperdie euerie
houre?
31 [q] By our reioycīg which I haue in Christ
Iesus our Lord,I dye daily.
32 If I haue foght with beastes at Ephesus
after [r] the maner of men,what aduātageth
it me, if the dead be not raised vp ?* let vs
eat & drinke:for to morowe we shal dye.
33 Be not deceiued: *euil speakings corrupt
good maners.
34 Awake to *liue* righteously,and sinne not:
for some haue not the knowledge of God.
I speake this to your shame.
35 But some man wil say,How are the dead
raised vp? and with what bodie come they
forthe?
36 O foole , that which thou sowest, is not
quickened,except it dye.
37 And ŷ which thou sowest , thou sowest
not that bodie that shalbe,but bare corne,
as it falleth,of wheat,or of some other.
38 But God giueth it a bodie at his plesu-
re,euen to euerie sede his owne bodie.
39 All flesh *is* not the same flesh , but there is one [s] flesh of men , and another flesh
of beastes,and another of fishes, and another of birdes.
40 There *are* also heauenlie bodies, and
earthlie bodies : but the glorie of the heauenlie *is* one,and *the glorie* of the earthlie
is another.
41 There is another glorie of the [t] sunne,
and another glorie of the moone,and another glorie of ŷ starres : for one starre differeth from *another* starre in glorie.
42 So also *is* the resurrection of the dead.
The bodie is sowen in corruption,*and* is raised in incorruption.
43 It is sowen in [u] dishonour , *and* is raised
in glorie:it is sowen in weakenes,*&* is raised in power.
44 It is sowen a natural bodie,*&* is raised a
[x] spiritual bodie : there is a natural bodie,
& there is a spiritual bodie.
45 As it is also writen , The first man * A-
dam was made a liuing soule : and the last
Adam *was made* a [y] quickening Spirit.
46 Howbeit that *was* not first *made* which
is spiritual:but that *which is* natural, & afterwarde that *which is* spiritual.

Psal.8,7. ebr.2,8.
n We shalbe perfectly fulfilled with his glorie and felicitie.
o That is, as dead,& because they were but newly come to Christ, wolde be baptized before they dyed.
p Except these things be true of Christs kingdome and his subiection, what shal become of them whome the Church daily baptizeth, for to destroye death in thē ŵ is the end of baptisme , and so they to rise againe?
Isa.22,13. wisdo 2,6.
*Menander in Thaidi.
q I take to witnes all my sorrowes, wherein I may iustly reioyce in ŷ Lord,that I haue susteined them among you
r That is , hauīg regard eto this presēt life, & not to Gods glorie,& to life euerlasting.
s There is one substance as touching the flesh bothe of man and beast, but the difference is as touching the qualitie.
t Euen as the sunne and the moone beīg of one substance differ in dignitie:so in the resurrection our bodies shal haue more excellent qualities then they haue now.
u For what is more vile to loke vnto thē the dead carkeis?
Gen.2,7.
x Not changīg the substance, but made partaker of the diuine nature.
y Christ brīgeth vs from heauen the Spirit of life.

z This is attribute to Christ as concerning his diuinitie, not in respect of his humanitie whose flesh hathe this glorie by ŷ power of God who dwelleth in it.
a Bothe in substāce & forme we are earthlie.
b This natural bodie as it is now, til it be made newe by the Spirit of Christ.
c When the Lord cometh to iudgement, some of the Saintes shalbe aliue, whome he wil change euen as if they were dead, so that this change is in steade of death to thē
Mat.24,31.
1.thess.4,16.
Isa.25,8.
reuel.7,17.
‖*O death, whereis thy victorie! o graue, where is thy sting!*
Hose.13,14.
ebr.2,14.
d Sinne first broght ī death and giueth it power ouer vs, and ŷ strength of sinne is the Law, because it doeth reueile ŷ iudgemēt of God against vs: or els the chief cause of our destructiō is in our selues
1.Iohn.5,5.
e The hope of resurrection causeth the faithful to surmounte all difficulties.

47 The first mā *is* of the earth, earthlie: the
seconde man *is* the Lord [z] from heauen.
48 As *is* the earthlie, suche *are* they that a-
re earthlie: & as *is* the heauenlie, suche *are*
they also that are heauenlie.
49 And as we haue borne the [a] image of the
earthlie, so shal we beare the image of the
heauenlie.
50 This say I, brethren, ŷ [b] flesh & blood can
not inherit ŷ kingdome of God, nether
doeth corruption inherit incorruption.
51 Beholde, I shewe you a secret thing, We
shal not all slepe, but we shal all be [c] changed,
52 In a moment, in the twinkling of an eye
at the last * trumpet: for the trumpet shal
blowe, and the dead shal be raised vp incorruptible, and we shalbe changed.
53 For this corruptible must put on incorruption: and this mortal *must* put on immortalitie.
54 So when this corruptible hathe put on
incorruption, & this mortal hathe put on
immortalitie, then shal be broght to passe
the saying that is written, * Death is swalowed vp into victorie.
55 ‖*O death, where *is* thy stig! ô graue where *is* thy victorie!
56 The sting of death *is* sinne: and the
[d] strength of sinne *is* the Law.
57 *But thankes *be* vnto God which hathe
giuen vs victorie through our Lord Iesus
Christ.
58 Therefore my beloued brethren, be ye
stedfast, vnmoueable, abūdant alwayes in
the worke of the Lord, for asmuche as ye
knowe, that your labour is not in [e] vaine
in the Lord.

CHAP. XVI.

He putteth them in remembrance of the gathering for the poore brethrē at Ierusalem. 13 We must perseuere in faith, in the loue of Christ & our neighbour. 15 After his cōmendations he wisheth to thē all prosperitie.

Act.11,29. & 12,25.
rom 12,13.
a Vpon the first day of the weke which ŷ Scripture calleth the Lords day, others Sōday, they accustomed not onely in ŷ Church but at home also according to euery mās zeale, to lay vp some piece of money towarde ŷ relief of the poore brethrē
Act.18,23.

1 CONcerning* the [a] gathering for the
Saintes, as I haue ordeined in the
Churches* of Galacia, so do ye also.
2 Euerie first *day* of the weke, let euerie one
of you put aside by him self, and laye vp
as *God* hathe prospered him, that thē there be no gatherings when I come.
3 And when I am come, whosoeuer ye shal
alowe [b] by letters, thē wil I send to bring
your liberalitie vnto Ierusalem.
4 And if it be mete that I go also, they shal
go with me.
5 Now I wil come vnto you, after I haue
gone through Macedonia (for I wil passe
through Macedonia)
6 And it may be that I wil abide, yea, or
winter with you, that ye may bring me on
my way whithersoeuer I go.
7 For I wil not se you now in my passage:
but I trust to abide a while with you, if
the Lord permit.
8 And I wil tary at Ephesus vntil Pētecost.
9 For a great dore and [c] effectual is opened
vnto me: but there are many aduersaries.
10 ¶ Now if Timotheus come, se that he be
[d] without feare with you: for he worketh
the worke of the Lord, euen as I *do*.
11 Let no man therefore [e] despise him: but
conuaye him forthe [f] in peace, that he may
come vnto me: for I loke for him with the
brethren.
12 As touchīg *our* brother Apollos, I greatly desired him, to come vnto you with the
brethren: but his minde was not at all to
come at this time: howbeit he wil come
when he shal haue conuenient time.
13 ¶ [g] Watch ye: stand fast in the faith: quite
you like men, *&* be strong.
14 Let all your things be done in [h] loue.
15 Now, brethren, I beseche you (ye knowe
the house of Stephanas, that it is the [i] first
frutes of Achaia, & that they haue giuen
them selues to minister vnto the Saintes)
16 That ye be [k] obedient euen vnto such, &
to all that helpe with vs and labour.
17 I am glad of the comming of Stephanas, & Fortunatus, and Achaicus: for they
haue [l] supplied the want of you.
18 For they haue comforted my ‖ spirit and
yours: acknowledge therefore suche men.
19 The Churches of Asia salute you: Aquila and Priscilla with the Church that is in
their house, salute you greatly in the Lord.
20 All the brethren grete you. Grete ye o-
ne another with an * holie [m] kisse.
21 The salutation of *me* Paul with mine
owne hand.
22 If any mā loue not ŷ Lord Iesus Christ,
let him be had in execration, ‖ *yea excommunicate* to death.
23 The grace of our Lord Iesus Christ *be*
with you.
24 My loue *be* with you all in Christ Iesus,
Amen.

The first *Epistle* to the Corinthians, written frō [n] Philippi, *&* *sent* by Stephanas,
and Fortunatus, and Achaicus, and Timotheus.

c Because God blessed his labour.
d Willing that they shulde defende him against the aduersaries of Christ because it is ŷ Churchs duetie to be careful for the preseruatiō of their ministers
e As thogh he were to yōg to be a minister.
f That is, safe and sounde.
g Lest Satan steale vpō you at vnwares.
h For they had euery man respect to hī self contrary to loue.
i That is, the first which embraced ŷ Gospel.
k And reuerence them.
l The grief ŷ I toke for your absence, was greatly aswaged by their presence.
‖*Or, minde.*
Rom.16,16.
2.cor.13,12.
1.pet.5,19.
m In token of mutual loue, which thing was obserued in the primatiue Church when ŷ Lords Supper was ministred.
‖*Or, Maranatha.*
n Or, as is most probable, from Ephesus.

b Which ye shal send by them that cary the money.

THE

THE SECONDE EPI-
stle of Paul to the Corinthians.

THE ARGVMENT.

AS nothing can be written, either so perfitly, or with so great affection and zeale, which is not vnprofitable to many, and resisted by some: so the first epistle written by S. Paul to the Corinthians, besides the puritie and perfection of the doctrine, sheweth a loue towarde them farre passing all natural affections: which did not onely not profit all, but hardened the hearts of many to remaine in their stubbernes, and contemne the Apostles autoritie. By reason whereof S. Paul, being let with iuste occasions to come vnto them, wrote this epistle from Macedonia, minding to accomplish the worke which he had begonne among them. First therefore he wisheth them wel in the Lord, declaring that albeit certeine wicked persones abused his afflictions to condemne thereby his autoritie, yet they were necessarie schoolings, and sent to him by God for their bettering. And where as they blame his long absence, it came of no inconstancie, but to beare with their inhabilitie and imperfection, lest contrary to his fatherlie affection, he shulde haue bene compelled to vse rigour and seueritie. And as touching his sharpe writing in the former epistle, it came through their faute, as is now euident bothe in that, that he pardoneth the trespacer, seing he doeth repent: and also in that he was vnquiet in his minde, til he was certified by Titus of their estate. But forasmuche as the false Apostles went about to vndermine his autoritie, he confuteth their arrogant bragges, and commendeth his office, and the diligent executing of the same: so that Satan must haue greatly blinded their eyes, which se not the brightnes of the Gospel in his preaching the effect whereof is newnes of life, forsaking of our selues, cleauing to God, fleing from idolatrie, embracing the true doctrine, and that sorrowe which engendreth true repentance: to the which is ioyned mercie and compassion towards our brethren: also wisdome to put difference betwixt the simplicitie of the Gospel, and the arrogancie of the false preachers, who vnder pretence of preaching the trueth, soght onely to fil their bellies, where as he contrariwise, soght them, and not their goods, as those ambitious persones sclandered him: wherefore at his comming he menaceth suche as rebell against his autoritie, that he wil declare by liuelie example, that he is the faithful ambassadour of Iesus Christ.

CHAP. I.

4 He declareth the great profite that cometh to the faithful by their afflictions. 15.17 And because they shulde not impute to lightnes, that he differred his comming contrarie to his promes, he proueth his constancie, bothe by the synceritie of his preaching, and also by the immutable trueth of the Gospel. 21 Which trueth is grounded on Christ, and sealed in our hearts by the holie Gost.

1 Aul an Apostle of IESVS
CHRIST by the wil of
God, & *our* brother Timotheus,
to the Church
of God, which is at Corinthus
with all the Saintes,
which are in all
[a]Achaia:
2 Grace *be* with you, and peace from God
our Father, & *from* the Lord Iesus Christ.
3 *[b]Blessed *be* God euen the Father of our
Lord Iesus Christ, the Father of mercies,
and the God of all comforte,
4 Which comforteth vs in all our tribulation,
that we may be able to comforte thē
which are in anie affliction by the cōforte
wherewith we our selues are comforted of
God.
5 For as the [c]sufferings of Christ abunde in
vs, so our consolation abundeth through
Christ.
6 And whether we be afflicted, *it is* for your
consolation and [d]saluation, which [e]is
wroght in the induring of the same suffrings,
which we also suffer: or whether we
be comforted, *it is* for your consolation ad
saluation.
7 And our hope is stedfast cōcerning you,
in as muche as we knowe that as ye are
partakers of the suffrings, so *shal ye be* also
of the consolation.
8 For brethrē, we wolde not haue you ignorant
of our affliction, which came vnto vs
in Asia, how we were pressed [f]out of measure
passing strength, so that we all together
douted, euen of life.
9 Yea, we [g]receiued the sentēce of death in
our selues, because we shulde not trust in
our selues, but in God, ẘ raiseth the dead.
10 Who deliuered vs from so [h]great a death,
and doeth deliuer *vs*: in whome we
trust, that yet here after he wil deliuer *vs*,
11 *So that ye labour together in prayer for
vs, that for the gift *bestowed* vpon vs for
manie, thankes may be giuen by manie persones
for vs.
12 [i]For our reioycing is this, the testimonie
of our conscience, that in simplicitie
and godlie purenes, & not in fleshlie wisdome,
[k]but by the grace of God we haue
had our conuersation in the worlde, and
moste of all to you wardes.

a Meaning ẏ countrey whereof Corinthus was the chief citie.

Ephes.1,3. 1.pet.1,3.

b Or praise & glorie begiuē.

c Which I suffer for Christ, or ẘ Christ suffereth in me, Rom 7,5 & 8,5.col 1,24

d For seing hi indure so muche, they had occasion to be confirmed in the Gospel.

e As God onely worketh all things in vs: so doeth he also our saluation by his fre mercie, and by suche meanes as he hathe here left in this life for vs to be exercised in.

f Hereby he sheweth his owne infirmitie ẏ it might appeare how wonderfully Gods graces wroght in him

g I was vtterly resolued in my self to dye

h So manie dāgers of death.

Rom 15,30.

i He rendreth a reason why they oght to praye vnto God for his recouerie.

k Vsing that wisdome ẘ God gaue me from heauen.

13 For we [l] write none other things vnto
you, then ẏ ye read or els that ye acknowledge, & I trust ye shal acknowledge vnto the end.
14 Euen as ye haue acknowledged vs partely, that we are your [m] reioycing, euen as ye
are [n] ours, in the [o] day of *our* Lord Iesus.
15 And in this confidence was I minded
first to come vnto you, that ye might haue
had a double grace,
16 And to passe by you into Macedonia, &
to come againe out of Macedonia vnto
you, and to be led forthe towarde Iudea
of you.
17 When I therefore was thus minded, did
I vse lightnes? or minde I those things
which I minde, [p] according to ẏ flesh, that
ẇ me shulde be, [q] Yea, yea, and Nay, nay?
18 Yea, [r] God is faithful, that our worde
towarde you was not Yea, and Nay.
19 For the Sonne of God Iesus Christ who
was preached among you by vs, *that is* by
me, and Siluanus, and Timotheus, was not
Yea, and Nay: but in him it was [s] Yea.
20 For all the promises of God in him *are*
[t] Yea, and *are* in him Amen, vnto the glorie of God through vs.
21 And it is God which stablisheth vs with
you in Christ, and hathe anointed vs.
22 Who hathe also sealed vs, & hathe giuē
the *earnest of the Spirit in our hearts.
23 Now, I call God for a recorde vnto my
soule, that to spare you, I came not as yet
vnto Corinthus.
24 Not that we [u] haue dominion ouer your
faith, but we are helpers of your ioye: for
by [x] faith ye stande.

l Ye knowe partely my cōstancie bothe by my dwellīg with you, and also my writing vnto you: and I trust ye shal knowe me to be the same to ẏ very end.
m In that we haue taught you ẏ Gospel so syncerely.
n Because we haue wōne you to Christ.
o Which shal abolish all worldelie glorie.
p Which is rashely to promes and not to performe.
q Now to affirme one thing, and then to deny it, which is a signe of incōstancie.
r He taketh God to witnes that he preacheth ẏ trueth
s He preached nothing vnto them but onely Iesus Christ who is the moste constant and infallible trueth of the Father.
t They are made, performed & we are partakers onely by him, who is our Amen, in that he hathe fulfilled them for vs.
Ephe.4,30.
u In that I say I came not because I wolde spare you, I meane not that I haue autoritie to alter true religiō, or to binde your cōsciences: but that I am Gods minister to confirme and comfort you.
x And faith is not in subiection to man.

CHAP. II.

He sheweth his loue towardes them. 7 Requiring like wise that thei wolde be fauorable to the incestuous adulterer, seing he did repent. 14 He also reioyceth in God for the efficacie of his doctrine. 17 Confuting thereby suche qnarelpikers, as vnder pretence of speaking against his persone, soght nothing, but the ouerthrowe of his doctrine.

1 BVt I determined thus in my self, that
I wolde not come againe to you in
heauines.
2 For if I make you sorie, who is he then
that shulde make me glad, but the same
which is made [a] sorie by me?
3 And I wrote [b] this same thing vnto you,
lest when I came, I shulde take heauines of
them, of whome I oght to reioyce: this
confidence haue I in you all, that my ioye
is the *ioye* of you all.
4 For in great affliction, and anguish of
heart I wrote vnto you with many teares:
not that ye shulde be made sorie, but that
ye might perceiue the loue which I haue,
specially vnto you.
5 And if any hathe caused sorow, the same
hathe not [c] made me sorie, but partely (lest
I shulde [d] more charge *him*) you all.
6 It is sufficient vnto the same man, that he
was rebuked of manie.
7 So that now contrarie wise ye oght rather to forgiue *him*, and comforte *him* lest
the same [e] shulde be swalowed vp with
ouer muche heauines.
8 Wherefore, I praye you, that you wolde
[f] confirme your loue towards him.
9 For this cause also did I write, ẏ I might
knowe the profe of you, whether ye wolde
be obedient in all things.
10 To whome ye forgiue anie thing, I *forgiue* also: for verely if I forgaue anie thīg,
to whome I forgaue it, for your sakes *forgaue I it* in the [g] sight of Christ,
11 Lest Satan shulde [h] circumuent vs: for
we are not ignorant of his enterprises.
12 ¶ Furthermore, when I came to Troas
to preache Christs Gospel, & a dore was ope
ned vnto me of the Lord,
13 I had no rest *in my spirit, because I foūde not Titus my brother, but toke my leaue of thē, and went away into Macedonia.
14 [i] Now thankes *be* vnto God which alwayes maketh vs [k] to triumph in Christ,
and maketh manifest the sauour of his
knowledge by vs in euerie place.
15 For we are vnto God the swete sauour of
Christ, in them that are saued, and in them
which perish.
16 To the one *we are* the [l] sauour of death,
vnto death, and to the other the sauour of
life, vnto life, *and who is sufficient for
these things?
17 *For we are not as manie, [m] which make
marchandise of the worde of God: but as
of synceritie, but as of God in the sight of
God speake we in *Christ.

a Which was giuen to Satan but now doeth repent.
b Which made you & him sory in my further epistle.

c After this adulterer did repēt & amēd, Paul did so vtterly cast of all sorowe, ẏ he denieth that in maner he was anie whit sorie.
d And so shulde increase his sorowe which I wolde diminish.
e The adulterer, which interteined his mother in Law.
f That at my intercession you wolde declare by the publike consent of the Church that you embrace him againe as a brother: seing he was excommunicate by the commune consent.
g That is, truely, and from mine heart, euen as in the presence of Christ.
h By our rigorous punishīg.
*Or, in my minde.
i Frō this place vnto the 6. chap.11. he entreateth onely of ẏ ministers, saue he sometime intermedeleth that ẇ apperteineth to the whole Church, as Chap.3,17, and 18 verses, and not onely to ẏ ministers.
Rom.11,16.
Chap.4,2.
k In working mightely by vs he maketh vs partakers of his victorie and triumph.
l The preaching of the crosse bringeth death to them which onely consider Christs death as a cōmune death, & be therat offēded, or els thinke it folie: & brīgeth againe life to thē who in his death beholde their life.
m That is, ẇ preache for gaine, & corrupt it to serue mens affectiones.
*Or, through Christ, or of Christ

CHAP. III.

1 He taketh for example the faith of the Corinthians for a probation of the trueth which he preached. 6 And to exalte his Apostleship against the bragges of the false apostles. 7. 13 He maketh comparison betwixt the Law and the Gospel.

1 DO [a] we begīne to praise our selues a-
gaine? or nede we as some other, epistles of recommendation vnto you, or *letters* of recommendation from you?
2 Ye are our epistle, written in our hearts,
which is vnderstand and red of all men,
3 In that ye are manifest, to be the epistle
of Christ, [b] ministred by vs, and written,
not with yncke, but with the Spirit of the
liuing God, not in [c] tables of stone, but in
fleshlie tables of the heart.
4 And suche trust haue we through Christ
to God:

a Meaning him self, Timotheus and Siluanus.
b Who were Gods penne.
c The hardnes of mans heart before he be regenerat, is as a stonie table, Eze. 11,19, & 36, 26: but being regenerat by the Spirit of God, it is as softe as flesh, ẏ the grace of the Gospel may be written in it, as in new tables, Ier.31,33.

5 Not that we are sufficient of our selues,
to thinke anie thing, as of our selues: but
our sufficiencie *is* of God.
6 Who also hathe made vs able ministers
of the New testament, not of the [d] letter
but of the [e] Spirit: for the letter killeth, but
the [f] Spirit giueth life.
7 If then the ministration [g] of death *written*
w^t letters & ingraué in stones, was glorious
so ye the childrẽ of Israel colde not beholde
the face of Moses for the [h] glorie of his
countenance (which *glorie* is done away)
8 How shal not the ministration of the Spi
rit be more glorious?
9 For if the ministerie of [i] cõdẽnation *was*
glorious, muche more doeth the ministra
tion of [k] righteousnes excede in glorie.
10 For euen that which was glorified, was
not glorified in this point, *that is*, as touching the exceding glorie.
11 For if that which shulde be abolished,
was glorious, much more shal that which
remaineth, be glorious.
12 Seing then that we haue suche trust, we
vse [l] great boldenes of speache.
13 *And *we are* not as Moses, *which* [m] put a
vaile vpon his face, that the children of Israel shulde not looke vnto the end of that
which shulde be abolished.
14 Therefore their mindes are hardened:
for vntil this day remaineth the same couering vntaken away in the reading of
the Olde testament, which *vaile* in Christ
is put away.
15 But euen vnto this day, when Moses is
red, the vaile is layed ouer their hearts.
16 Neuertheles when their *heart* shalbe
turned to the Lord, the vaile shalbe taken
away.
17 Now the [n] Lord is the *Spirit, and where the Spirit of the Lord *is*, there *is* libertie.
18 But we all beholde as in a [o] mirrour
the glorie of the Lord with open face, and
are changed into the same image, from
glorie to glorie, as by the Spirit of the
Lord.

d Whose minister Moses was. e Which Christ gaue. f Meaning, the spiritual doctrine, w^c is in our hearts. g Thus he nameth the Law in cõparison of the Gospel. h After ye God had spoken w^t him and giuen him the Law. i For the Law declareth all men to be vnder condemnation. k Meaning, of the Gospel w^c declareth that Christ, is made our righteousnes.

l In preaching the Gospel. *Exo. 34,33.* m Moses shewed the Law as it was couered w^t shadowes, so that ye Iewes eyes were not lightened but blinded, and so colde not come to Christ who was the end thereof: againe the Gospel setteth forthe the glorie of God clearely, not couering our eyes, but driuing ye darkenes away from them. *Ioh. 4,24.* n Christ is our mediator, & autor of the New testamẽt, whose doctrine is spiritual, & giueth life to the Law. o In Christ, who is God manifested in the flesh, we se God ye Father as in a moste cleare glasse.

CHAP. IIII.

1 He declareth his diligence, and roundenes in his office. 8 And that which his enemies toke for his disaduantage, to wit, the crosse and afflictions which he endured, he turned it to his great aduantage. 11.17 Shewing what profit cometh thereby.

1 THerefore, seing that we haue this ministerie, as we haue receiued mercie,
[a] we fainte not:
2 But haue cast from vs the [b] clokes of shame & *walke not in craftines, nether handle we the worde of God disceitfully: but
in declaration of the trueth we approue
our selues to euerie mans conscience in
the sight of God.
3 If our Gospel be then hid, it is hid to thẽ,
that are lost.
4 In whome the [c] god of this worlde hathe
blinded the mindes, *that is*, of the infideles,
that the light of the glorious Gospel of
Christ, which is the [d] image of God, shulde not shine vnto them.
5 For we preache not our [e] selues, but Christ
Iesus the Lord, and our selues your seruãts
for Iesus sake.
6 For God that *commanded the light to
shine out of darkenes, *is he* which hathe
shined in [f] our hearts, to giue the [g] light
of the knowledge of the glorie of God in
the face of Iesus Christ.
7 But we haue this [h] treasure in earthẽ vessels, ye the excellencie of that power might
be of God and not of vs.
8 We are afflicted on euerie side, yet *are we*
not in distresse: in pouertie, but not ouercome of pouertie.
9 *We are* persecuted, but not forsaken: cast
downe, but we perish not.
10 Euerie where we beare about in our bodie the [i] dying of the Lord Iesus, that the
life of Iesus might also be made manifest
in our bodies.
11 For we which liue, are alwayes deliuered vnto death for Iesus sake, that the life
also of Iesus might be made manifest in
our mortal flesh.
12 So then [k] death worketh in vs, and life
in you.
13 And because we haue the same [l] Spirit
of faith, according as it is written, *I beleued, & therefore haue I spoken, we also
beleue, and therefore speake,
14 Knowing that he which hathe raised vp
the Lord Iesus, shal [m] raise vs vp also by
Iesus, and shal set vs with you.
15 For all things *are* for your sakes that
moste plenteous grace by the thankesgiuing of [n] manie may redoũde to the praise of God.
16 Therefore we faint not, but thogh our
outwarde man "perish, yet the inwarde
man is [o] renewed daily.
17 For our [p] light afflictiõ w^c is but for a mo
ment, causeth vnto vs a farre moste excellent & an eternal waight of glorie:
18 While we loke not on the things which
are sene, but on the things, which are not
sene: for the things which are sene, *are* tem
poral: but the things which are not sene,
are eternal.

a For anie troubles or afflictions. b Meaning, suche shiftes & pretences as become not them that haue suche a great office in hand. *Chap. 3,17.*

c To wit Satã, Ioh. 12,31, & 14,30. eph. 6,12. d In whome God doeth shewe him self to be sene: and here Christ is called so in respect of his office. *Gene. 1,3.* e As they, w^c preache for gaine, or els w^c rather seke to be sene and knowen, then to edifie. f Which are your seruants. g That we hauing receiued light, shuld cõmunicate the same w^t others and therefore Christ calleth thẽ the light of the world, Mat. 5,14. h Albeit the ministers of ye Gospel be cõtemptible as touching their persone, yet ye treasure which they carie, is nothing worse or inferior. i All ye faithful, & chiefly the ministers must drinke of this cup, because ye worlde hateth Christ: & also that the members shulde be conformable to Christ their head, yet by ye mightie power of Christ, who ouercame death, they are made conquerours. *Psal. 116,10.* k By our death you haue life: so that the frute of our afflictions cometh to you. l The same faith by ye inspiration of ye holie Gost. m In deliuering vs from these dangers, which is as it were a restoring frõ death to life. n That I beĩg deliuered and restored to you againe, may not onely my self giue God thankes for this infinite benefite of deliuerance, but also you all, which are bothe partakers of mine affliction and comforte, may abundantly set forthe his glorie. " Or, be corrupted. o Groweth stronger. p Which is so called in respect of the euerlasting life.

CHAP. V.

1 Paul procedeth to declare the vtilitie that cometh by the crosse. 4 How we oght to prepare our selues vnto it. 5 By whome, 9 And for what end. 14. 19 He setteth forthe the grace of Christ, 20 And the office of ministers, and all the faithful.

1 FOr we knowe that if [a] our earthlie
house of this tabernacle be destroied,
we haue a buylding *giuen* of God, *that is*, an
house not made with hands, *but* eternal in
the heauens.
2 For therefore we sigh, desiring to be clothed with our house, which is frō heauen.
3 "Because that if we be clothed, we shal
not be founde *naked.
4 For in dede we that are in this tabernacle, sigh and are burdened, "because we
wolde not be vnclothed, but wolde be clothed vpon, that mortalitie might be swalowed vp of life.
5 And he that hathe created vs for this
thing, *is* God, who also hathe giuen vnto
vs the earnest of the Spirit.
6 Therefore we are alway [b] bolde, thogh we
knowe that whiles we are "at home in the
bodie, we are absent from the Lord.
7 (For we [c] walke by faith, & not by sight)
8 Neuertheles, we are bolde, & loue rather
to remoue out of the bodie, and to dwell
with the Lord.
9 Wherefore also we couet, that bothe
dwelling [d] at home, and remouing [e] from
home, we may be acceptable to him.
10 *For we must all appeare before the iudgemēt seat of Christ, that euerie man may
receiue the things which are *done* in his bo
die, according to that he hathe done, whether *it be* [f] good or euil.
11 Knowing therefore the [g] terror of the
Lord, we [h] persuade men, & we [i] are made
manifest vnto God, & I trust also that we
are made manifest in your consciences.
12 For we praise not our selues againe vnto
you, but giue you an occasion to reioyce
of vs, that ye may haue *to answere* against
them, which reioyce in the [k] face, and not
in the heart.
13 For whether we be [l] out of our wit, *we
are it* [m] to God: or whether we be in our
right minde, *we are it* vnto you.
14 For the loue of Christ constraineth vs:
because we thus iudge, that if one be dead
for all, then were [n] all dead,
15 And he dyed for all, that they [o] which
liue, shulde not hence forthe liue vnto thē
selues, but vnto him which dyed for thē,
and rose againe.
16 Wherefore, hēce forthe know we no mā
[p] after the flesh, yea thogh we had knowen
Christ after the flesh, yet now hēce forthe
[q] know we *him* no more.
17 Therefore if anie man *be* in Christ, *let
him be* a [r] new creature. *Olde things are

a After this bodie shalbe dissolued, it shalbe made incorruptible and immortal.

"Or, if so be we shalbe founde clothed, & not naked.

Reuel.16,15.

"Or, wherein.

b Not onely quiet in mīde, but also ready to susteine all dangers: being assured of the good successe thereof.

"Or, strangers in the bodie.

c For here onely we beleue in God, & se him not.

d In this bodie.

Rom.14,10.

e Out of this bodie, to heauen.

f That is, ether glorie, or shame.

g His fearefulludgement.

h He proueth the dignitie of his ministerie by ye frute and effect thereof, which is to bring men to Christ.

i By imbracing the same faith which we preache to others.

k As they, which more estemed the outwarde shewe of wisdome and eloquence, then true godlines.

l As the aduersaries said, which colde not abide to heare them praised.

m Our folie serueth to Gods glorie.

n Therefore whosoeuer giueth place to ambition or vaine glorie, is yet dead, and liueth not in Christ.

Isa.43,19.

Reuel.21,5.

o As the onely faithful do in Christ. p According to the estimation of the worlde: but as he is guided by the Spirit of God. q We do not esteme, nor commende Christ him self now, as he was an excellent man: but as he was the Sonne of God, partaker of his glorie, and in whome God dwelled corporally: and do you thinke, that I wil flatter my self or anie man in setting forthe his giftes? Yea, when I praise my ministerie, I cōmende the power of God: when I commende our worthie factes, I praise the mightie power of God, set forthe by vs wormes and wretches. r Let him be regenerat, and renounce him self, els all the rest is nothing.

passed away: beholde, all things are become new.
18 And all things *are* of God, which hathe
recōciled vs vnto him self by Iesus Christ,
and hathe giuen vnto vs the ministerie of
reconciliation.
19 For God was [s] in Christ, and reconciled
the worlde to him self, not imputing their
sinnes vnto them, and hathe committed to
vs the worde of reconciliation.
20 Now then are we ambassadours for
Christ: as thogh God did beseche *you*
through vs, we praye you in Christs stede,
that ye be reconciled to God.
21 For he hathe made him *to be* [t] sinne for
vs, which knew no sinne, that we shulde be
[u] made the righteousnes of God in him.

CHAP. VI.

1 An exhortation to Christian life. 11 And to beare him like affection, as he doeth them. 14 Also to kepe them selues from all pollution of idolatrie bothe in bodie, and soule, and to haue none acquaintance with idolaters.

1 SO we therefore as workers together be
seche *you*, that ye receiue not the grace
of God in vaine.
2 For he saith, *I haue heard thee in a time
accepted, and in the day of saluation haue
I succered thee: beholde now the [a] accepted time, beholde now the daye of saluation.
3 We giue no occasion of offence in anie
thing, that *our* ministerie shulde not be
[b] reprehended.
4 But in all things we approue our selues
as *the ministers of God, in muche patience, in afflictions, in necessities, in
distresses,
5 In stripes, in prisones, in tumultes, in labours,
6 By [c] watchings, by fastings, by puritie, by knowledge, by long suffering, by
kindnes, by the [d] holie Gost, by [e] loue vnfained,
7 [f] By the worde of trueth, by the power of
God, by the armour of righteousnes on the
right hand and on the lefte,
8 By honour, and dishonour, by euil reporte
& good reporte, as deceiuers, and *yet* true:
9 As vnknowen, and *yet* knowen: as dying,
and beholde, we liue: as chastened, and *yet*
not killed:
10 As sorowing, & *yet* alway reioycing: as
poore, and *yet* make manie riche: as hauing
nothing, and *yet* possesing all things.
11 O Corinthians, our [g] mouth is open vnto you: our heart is made large.
12 Ye are not kept straite in vs, but ye are
kept straite in your owne [h] bowelles.
13 Now for the same recompense, I speа-
ke as to *my* children, [i] Be you also enlarged.

s Therefore without Christ we can not enioye the life euerlasting nor come to God.

t That is, a sacrifice for sinne.

u By imputation, when we shalbe clad with Christs iustice.

Isa.49,8.

a To wit, Gods fre mercie, wherein he hathe powred forthe his infinite loue.

b By the infideles, if they sawe no frute come thereof.

1.Cor.4,1.

c He declareth with what weapons he resisted his afflictions.

d Who is the efficient cause.

e Which is, the final cause

f By the Gospel, and the power of God and his owne integritie, he ouerthrew Satan, and the worlde, as with weapons on euerie side most ready.

g Signifying his moste vehement affection.

h Their iudgement was so corrupted, that they were not likewise affectioned towardes him, as he was towardes them. i Shewe like affection towardes me.

14 k Be

14 [k] Be not vnequally yoked with the infideles: for * what felowship hathe righteous
nes with vnrighteousnes? and what communion hathe light with darkenes?
15 And what concorde hathe Christ with
[u] Belial? or what parte hathe the beleuer
with the infidel?
16 And what agrement hathe the Temple of God with idoles? * for ye are the
Temple of the [l] liuing God: as God hathe said, * I wil dwell among them, and
walke there: and I wil be their God, and
they shalbe my people.
17 * Wherefore come out from among thē,
and separate your selues, saith the Lord:
and touche none vncleane thing, & I wil
receiue you.
18 * And I wil be a Father vnto you, and ye
shalbe my sonnes and daughters, saith the
Lord almightie.

Eccl.13,21.
k He semeth to allude to ẏ ẇ is written, Deut 22,10. where ẏ Lord commandeth that an oxe & an asse be not yoked together, because ẏ match is vnequal: so if the faithful marie with the infideles, or els haue to do ẇ them in anie thig vnlawful, it is here reproued.
1.Cor.3.13. & 6.19.
Leui.26,11.
Isa.52,11.
Ierem.31,1.
u Or, the deuil.
l So called because he hathe not onely life in him self, but giueth it also to all liuing creatures.

CHAP. VII.

1 He exhorteth them by the promises of God to kepe them selues pure. 3. 7 Assuring them of his loue. 8. 13 And doeth not excuse his seueritie towarde them, but reioyceth thereat, considering what profite came thereby. 10 Of two sortes of sorow.

1 SEing then we haue these promises,
dearely beloued, let vs [a] clense our selues from all filthines of the [b] flesh & spirit, and growe vp vnto ful holines in the
feare of God.
2 [c] Receiue vs: we haue done wrong to no
man: we haue consumed no man: we haue
[d] defrauded no man.
3 I speake it not to your condemnacion: for
I haue said before, that ye are in our hearts, to dye and liue together.
4 I vse great boldenes of speache towarde
you: I reioyce greatly in you: I am filled
with comfort, and am exceading ioyous
in all our tribulacion.
5 For whē we were come into Macedonia,
our flesh had no reste, but we were troubled on euerie side, fightings [e] without, &
terrours within.
6 But God, that comforteth the abiect,
comforted vs at the comming of Titus:
7 And not by his comming onely, but also
by the consolacion wherewith he was cōforted of you, whē he tolde vs your great
desire, your mourning, your feruent minde to mewarde, so that I reioyced [f] muche
more.
8 For thogh I made you sorie with a letter, I repent not, thogh I did repent: for I
perceiue that the same epistle made you
sorie, thogh *it were* but for a season.
9 I now reioyce, not that ye were sorie, but
that ye sorowed to repentance: for ye sorowed godly, so that in nothing ye were
hurt by vs.
10 * For godlie sorowe causeth repentance
vnto saluacion, not to be repented of: but
the worldlie sorowe causeth death.
11 For beholde, this thing that ye haue bene [g] godly sorie, what great care it hathe
wroght in you: yea, what [h] clearīg of your
selues: yea *what* indignacion: yea, *what* feare: yea, *how* great desire: yea, *what* a zeale:
yea, *what* [i] punishmēt: in all things ye haue
shewed your selues, that ye are pure in
this matter.
12 Wherefore, thogh I wrote vnto you, I
did not it for his cause that had done the
wrōg, nether for his cause that had the iniurie, but that our care towarde you in the
sight of God might appeare vnto you.
13 Therefore we were comforted, because
ye were comforted: but rather we reioyced muche more for the ioy of Titus, because his [*] spirit was refreshed by you all.
14 For if ẏ I haue boasted anie thig to him
of you, I haue not bene ashamed: but as I
haue spoken vnto you all things in trueth,
euen so our boastīg vnto Titus was true.
15 And [k] his inwarde affection is more a-
bundant towarde you, when he remembreth the obedience of you all, *and* how
with feare & trembling ye receiued him.
16 I reioyce *therefore* that I may [l] put my
confidence in you in all things.

a Consider this wel, ye ẏ serue idoles ẇ your bodies, & yet thinke your cō sciences pure towarde God: God wil one day smite you for your halting.
b Of bodie & soule.
c That we may teache you.
d By griedie couetousnes.
e He had nether rest in bodie, nor spirit. & it semeth ẏ he alludeth to that which is written, Deut. 32,25 for the crosse to mans eye is commune bothe to ẏ godlie & to the wicked, althogh to contrarie ends.
f This ioye ouercame all my sorowes.
2.Pet.2,19.
g Whose heart Gods Spirit doeth touche, he is sorie for his sinnes committed against so mercifull a Father: & these are the frutes of his repētance, as witnes Dauids & Peters teares: others which are sorie for their sinnes onely for feare of punishment & Gods vengeance, fall into desperaciō, as Cain, Saul, Achitophel & Iudas.
h In asking God forgiuenes.
i For in iudging & chastising your selues, you preuēted Gods angre.
* Heart.
k The Greke worde signifieth, his bowelles, whereby is ment moste great loue and tender affections.
l Bothe in thinking & reporting wel of you.

CHAP. VIII.

1 By the example of the Macedonians. 9 And Christ he exhorteth them to continue in relieuing the poore Saintes, commending their good beginning. 23 After he commendeth Titus and his felowes vnto them.

1 WE do you also to wit, brethren, of
the [a] grace of God bestowed vpon the Churches of Macedonia,
2 Because in great tryal of affliction their
ioye abunded, and their moste extreme
pouertie [b] abunded vnto their riche liberalitie.
3 For to *their* power (I beare recorde) yea, &
beyonde their power, they were willing,
4 And praied vs with great instance that
we wolde receiue the [c] grace, & felowship
* of the ministring which is towarde the
Saintes.
5 And *thus they did*, not as we loked for: but
gaue their owne selues, first to the Lord,
and *after* vnto vs by the wil of God,
6 That we shulde exhorte Titus, that as
he had begonne, so he wolde also accomplish the same grace among you also.
7 Therefore, as ye abunde in euerie thing,
in faith and worde, and knowledge, and in
all diligence, and in your loue towards vs,
euen so se that ye abūde in this grace also.
8 This say I not by commandement, but
because of the diligence of others: therefore proue I the naturalnes of your loue.
9 For ye knowe the grace of our Lord Iesus Christ, that he being riche, for your sakes became poore, that ye through his pouertie might be made riche.

a This benefite of God appeared in two things: first, ẏ the Macedonians being in so great afflictiōs were so prōpt to helpe others: & next ẏ being in great pouertie, were verie liberal towards others.
b So that a moste abundāt riuer of riches flowed out of their pouertie.
c So he calleth their liberalitie, ether because thei were the bestowers of Gods graces, or because thei receiued them of God frely, and so they desired Paul to se to ẏ distribution thereof.

10 And I shewe *my* minde herein: for this
is expedient for you, w̃ haue begonne not
to do onely, but also to [d] wil, a yere a go.
11 Now therefore performe to do it also,
that as *there was* a readines to wil, euẽ so ye
maye performe it of that which ye haue.
12 For if there be first a willing minde, it
is accepted according to that a mã hathe,
& not according to that he hathe not.
13 Nether *is it* that other men shulde be eased and you grieued.
14 But vpon like condicion, at this time
your [e] abundance *supplieth* their lacke, that
also their abundance may be for your lacke, that there may be [f] equalitie:
15 As it is written, *He that *gathered* muche,
had nothing ouer, and he that *gathered* litle, had not the lesse.
16 And thankes *be* vnto God, which hathe
put in the heart of Titus the same care
for you.
17 Because he accepted the [g] exhortacion,
yea, he was so careful that of his owne accorde he went vnto you.
18 And we haue sent also with him the brother, whose praise *is* [h] in ỹ Gospel throughout all the Churches,
19 (And not so onely, but is also chosen of
the Churches to be a felowe in our iourney concerning this grace that is ministred by vs vnto the glorie of the same
Lord, and *declaracion* of your prõpt minde)
20 Auoyding this, that no man shulde blame vs in this abundance that is ministred
by vs,
21 *Prouiding for [i] honest things, not onely
before the Lord, but also before men.
22 And we haue sent with thẽ our brother,
whome we haue oft times proued to be
diligent in manie things, but now muche
more diligent, for the great confidence,
which I *haue* in you.
23 Whether *anie do enquire* of Titus, *he is*
my felowe and helper to you warde: or of
our brethren, they are messengers of the
Churches, & the [k] glorie of Christ.
24 Wherefore shewe towarde them, & before the Churches the profe of your loue,
and of the reioycing that we haue of you.

d Euerie man may do good that hathe abilitie therevnto, but to wil, and haue a minde to do good, cometh of perfite charitie.

e That as you helpe others in their nede, so others shal releue your want.

Exod 16 18.

f That bothe you & others, as occasiõ shal serue, may relieue ỹ godlie according to their necessities.

g And willingly offred him self to gather your almes.

h In preaching the Gospel. Some vnderstand Luke, others Barnabas.

Rom.12,17.

i His weldoing is approued before God & man.

k That is, by whome Christs glorie is greatly aduanced.

CHAP. IX.

3 The cause of Titus and his companions comming to thẽ. 6 He exhorteth to giue almes cherefully. 7 Shewing what frute wil come thereof.

1 FOr as touching the ministring to the
Saintes, it is superfluous for me to
write vnto you.
2 For I knowe your readines of mĩde, whereof I boast my self of you vnto them of
Macedonia, & *say*, that Achaia was prepared a yere a go, and your zeale hathe
prouoked manie.
3 Now haue I sent the brethren, lest our reioycing ouer you shulde be in vaine in
this behalfe, that ye (as I haue said) be
readie:
4 Lest if thei of Macedonia come with me,
and finde you vnprepared, we (I nede not
to say, you) shulde be ashamed in this my
constant boasting.
5 Wherefore, I thoght it necessarie to exhorte the brethren to come before vnto
you, and to finish your beneuolence appointed afore, that it might be readie, *and
come* as of beneuolence, and not as of sparing.
6 This yet *remember*, that he which soweth sparingly, shal reape also sparingly,
and he that soweth liberally, shal reape also liberally.
7 As euerie man wisheth in his heart, *so let
him giue* not * grudgingly, or of necessitie: *for God loueth a chereful giuer.
8 And God is able to make all grace to a-
bounde towarde you, that ye alwaies hauing [a] all sufficiencie in all things, may a-
bounde in euerie [b] good worke,
9 * As it is written, [c] He hathe sparsed a-
broad and hathe giuen to the poore: his
beneuolence remaineth for euer.
10 Also he that findeth seede to the sower,
wil minister likewise bread for foode, and
multiplie your sede, and increase the frutes of your beneuolence,
11 That on all partes ye may be made riche vnto all liberalitie, w̃ causeth through
vs thankesgiuing vnto God.
12 For the ministracion of this seruice not
onely supplieth the necessities of ỹ Saintes, but also is abundant by the thankesgiuing of manie vnto God,
13 (Which by the experimente of this ministracion praise God for your voluntarie
submission to the Gospel of Christ, and
for your liberal distribution to them, and
to all men)
14 And by [d] their praier for you, " desiring
after you greatly, for the abundant grace
of God in you.
15 Thankes therefore *be* vnto God for his
vnspeakeable gift.

Prou.11,25. rom.12,8. Eccle.35,11.

a Lest thei shulde giue but litle, distrusting to impouerish thẽ selues thereby, he sheweth ỹ God wil so blesse their liberal hearts, ỹ bothe they shal haue ynough for thẽ selues & also to helpe others withall.

Psal.112,9.

b That ye may do good & helpe others at all times.

c Dauid speaketh of that man w̃ feareth God & loueth his neighbour.

d Besides that by their liberalitie God shal be praised, thei also shalbe cõmẽded to God by their prayers whome thei haue holpen, yea, & all men shal reuerence them, as being endued with an excellent gift of God.

" Or, greatly affectioned towarde you.

CHAP. X.

He toucheth the false apostles and defendeth his autoritie, exhorting them to obedience, 11 And sheweth what his power is, 13 And how he vseth it.

1 NOw I Paul my self beseche you by
the mekenes, & gentlenes of Christ,
which when I am present among you, *am*
[a] base, but am bolde towarde you being
absent:
2 And *this* I require you, that I nede not to
be bolde when I am present, with that same confidence, wherewith I thinke to be
bolde against some, w̃ esteme vs as thogh
we walked [b] according to the flesh.
3 Neuertheles, thogh we walke in the flesh,
yet we do not warre after the flesh,

a These wordes his bacbiters vsed, thinking thereby to diminish his autoritie, as verse.10.

b As thogh we boasted of our selues by a carnal affection.

4 (For

4 (For the weapons of our warrefare are
not carnal, but mightie through God, to
cast downe holdes)
5 Casting downe the imaginations, and
euerie high thing that is exalted against
the knowledge of God, and bringing into
captiuitie euerie thoght to the obedience
of Christ,
6 And hauing ready the vengeance against
all disobedience, when your obedience is
fulfilled.
7 Loke ye on things after the appearance?
If anie man trust in him self that he is
Christs, let him consider this agaïne of
him self, that as he *is* Christs, euē so *are we*
Christs.
8 For thogh I shulde boast somewhat more of our autoritie, which the Lord hathe
giuen vs for edification, and not for your
destruction, I shulde haue no shame.
9 *This I say* that I may not seme as *it were*
to feare you with letters.
10 For the letters, [c] saith he, are sore and
strong, but his bodelie presence is weake,
and his speache is of no value.
11 Let suche one thinke this, that suche as
we are in worde by letters when we are absent, suche *wil we be* also in dede, when we
are present.
12 For we dare not make our selues of the
nomber, or to compare our selues to thē,
which praise them selues: but they vnderstand not that they [d] measure them selues
with them selues, & compare them selues
with them selues.
13 But we wil not reioyce of things, which
are not within *our* measure, * but according to the [e] measure of the line, whereof
God hathe distributed vnto vs a measure
to atteine euen vnto you.
14 For we stretch not our selues beyonde
our measure, as thogh we had not atteined
vnto you: for euen to you also haue we come *in preaching* the Gospel of Christ,
15 Not boasting of thīgs which are without
our measure: *that is*, of other mens labours:
and we hope, when your faith shal increase, to be magnified by you according to
our line abundantly,
16 And to preache the Gospel in those *regions* which *are* beyōde you: not to reioyce
in [f] another mans line, *that is* in the things
that are prepared already.
17 *But let him that reioyceth, reioyce in
the Lord.
18 For he that praiseth him self, is not alowed, but he whome the Lord praiseth.

c Meaning, a certeine man among thē, ẘ thus spake of Paul.

d He ẏ measureth anie thīg, must haue some line or measure to mette by, and not to measure a thing by it self: so these boasters must measure them selues by their worthie actes: & if they wil compare with others, let thē shewe what cōtreis, what cities, & people they haue wonne to the Lord: for who wil praise ẏ souldier, ẘ onely at the table can finely talke of the warres, & whē he cometh to the brunt, is nether valiant nor expert?

Eph.4,8.

e That is, the giftes & vocation, ẘ God had giuen him to winne others by.

f God gaue ẏ whole worlde to ẏ Apostles to preache in, so that Paul here meaneth by ẏ line his porcion of the cōtreis where he preached

Ier.9,24, 1.cor.1,31.

CHAP. XI.

2 He declareth his affection towarde them. 5 The excellencie of his ministerie, 9 And his diligence in the same. 13 The fetches of the false apostles. 16 The peruerse iudgement of the Corinthians, 22 And his owne praises.

1 Wolde to God, ye colde suffer a litle my [a] foolishnes, and in deed,
[b] ye suffer me.
2 For I am ielous ouer you, with godlie ielousie: for [c] I haue prepared you for one
housband, to present you *as* a pure virgine
to Christ:
3 But I feare lest as the * serpent beguiled
Eue through his subtiltie, so your mindes
shulde be corrupte from the simplicitie
that is in Christ.
4 For if he that cometh, preacheth another
[d] Iesus then him whome we haue preached: or if ye receiue another [e] spirit then
that which ye haue receiued: ether another Gospel, then that ye haue receiued,
ye might wel haue suffered *him*.
5 Verely I [f] suppose that I was not inferior
to the verie chief Apostles.
6 And thogh *I be* [g] rude in speaking, yet *I
am* not *so* in knowledge, but amōg you we
haue bene made manifeste to the vtmost,
in all things.
7 Haue I committed an offence, because I
abased my self, that ye might be exalted, &
because I preached to you the Gospel of
God frely?
8 I [h] robbed other Churches, and toke wages *of them* to do you seruice.
9 And when I was present with you, and
had nede, I was [i] not slothful to the hinde
rance of anie man: for that which was lacking vnto me, the brethren which came
frō Macedonia, supplied, and in all things
I kept and wil kepe my self that I shulde
not * be grieuous to you.
10 [k] The trueth of Christ is in me, that this
reioycing shal not be shut vp against me
in the regions of Achaia.
11 Wherefore? because I loue you not? God
knoweth.
12 But what I do, that wil I do: that I may
cut away occasion from them which desire
[l] occasion, that they might be founde like
vnto vs in that wherein they reioyce.
13 For suche false [m] apostles are deceitful
workers, and transforme them selues into
the Apostles of Christ.
14 And no maruel: for Satan him self is
transformed into an Angel of light.
15 Therefore it is no great thing, thogh
his ministers transforme them selues, as
thogh *they were* the ministers of righteousnes, whose end shalbe according to their
workes.
16 I say againe, let no mā thinke, that I am
foolish: or els take me euē as a foole, that I
also may boast my self a litle.
17 That I speake, I speake it not after the
[n] Lord: but as *it were* foolishly, in this *my*
great boasting.

a He calleth the praising of hī self dotage to the ẘ thīg the arrogācie of the false apostles cōpelled him, who soght nothing els, but to ouerthrowe the Church by diminishing the autoritie of his ministerie.

Gene.3,4.

b To speake in mine owne cōmendation.

c The minister marieth Christ & his Church as housband and wife by ẏ preaching of the Gospel.

d That is, more perfite doctrine concerning Christ Iesus.

e More excellent giftes of the spirit by other mens preaching

f They did not preache Christ more purely then I did: for in this behalfe I was nothing inferior to the chiefest Apostles.

g That is, vse no worldelie eloquence.

h Other Churches relieued me

i He did not onely labour with his hāds for his liuing, but in his extreme pouertie preached diligently, without burdening anie mā, or els waxing slothful to do his duetie to euerie man.

Chap.12,13. act 20,34.

k Let not the trueth of Christ be thoght to be in me, if I suffer my ioye to be shut vp, ẘ I haue conceiued of Grecia.

l To sclander my ministerie, if I shulde receiue wages.

m By false apostles here is not ment suche as teache false doctrine (ẘ doutles, they wolde haue growen vnto) but suche as were vaineglorious, and did not their duetie syncerely.

n In his heart he had respect to the Lord: but this facion of boasting semed according to man, whereunto they compelled him.

18 Seing that manie reioyce [o]after the flesh,
I wil reioyce also.
19 For ye suffer fooles gladly, because that
ye are wise.
20 For ye suffre euen if a man bring you into bondage, if a man deuoure *you*, if a man
take *your goods*, if a man exalte him self, if a
man smite you on the face.
21 [p] I speake as concerning the reproche: as
thogh that we had bene [q] weake: but wherein anie man is bolde (I speake foolishly)
I am bolde also.
22 They are Ebrewes, * so am I: they are Israelites, so am I: they are the sede of Abraham, so am I:
23 They are the ministers of Christ (I [r]spea
ke as a foole) I am more: in labours more
abundant: in stripes aboue measure: in prison more plenteously: in [s] death oft.
24 Of the Iewes fiue [t]times receiued I fortie *stripes* * saue one.
25 [u] I was thrise * beaten with roddes: I was
*once stoned: I suffered thrise * shipwrac-
ke: night & day haue I bene in ẏ depe sea.
26 In iornaying *I was* often, in perils of waters, in perils of robbers, in perils of mine owne nation, in perils among the Gentiles, in perils in the citie, in perils in wildernes, in perils in ẏ sea, in perils amongs
false brethren,
27 In wearines & painefulnes, in watching
often, in honger & thirst, in fastings oftē,
in colde and in nakednes.
28 Beside the things which are outwarde,
I am combred daily, *and haue* the care of
all the Churches.
29 Who is weake, and I am not weake? who
is offended, and I burne not?
30 If I must nedes reioyce, I wil reioyce of
mine [x]infirmities.
31 The God, euen the Father of our Lord
Iesus Christ, which is blessed for euermore, knoweth that I lye not.
32 In * Damascus the gouerner of the people vnder King Aretas, laide watche in
the citie of the Damascēs, and wolde haue
caught me.
33 But at a windowe was I let downe in a ba
sket through the wall, & escaped his hāds.

o In outwarde things.

p I note this dishonour, ẇ they do vnto you.

Philip 3,5.

q That is, abiect, vile, miserable, a craftes man, an idiot, & subiect to a thousand calamities, which things the false apostles obiected against him as moste certeine testimonies of his vnworthines.

r Put case ye terme it so, yet is it true.

Deu. 25,3.

Act. 16,25.

Act 14,19.

Act. 27,14.

s In the present danger of death.

t At fiue seueral times euerie time thirtie, and nine.

u Of the Romaine magistrates.

x As imprisonements, beating, hongre, thirst, colde, nakednes and suche like: which things the aduersaries condemne as infirme in me.

Act. 9,24.

CHAP. XII.

1 He reioyceth in his preferment, 5. 7 But chiefly in his humblenes, 11 And layeth the cause of his boasting vpon the Corinthiās. 14 He sheweth what good wil he beareth them. 20 And promiseth to come vnto them.

1 IT is not expedient for me no dout to
reioyce: for I wil come to visions and
reuelations of the Lord.
2 * I knowe a man [a] in Christ aboue fourtene yeres agone, (whether *he were* in the bodie, I can not tel, or out of the bodie, I can
not tel: God knoweth) which was taken vp
into the [b] thirde heauen.
3 And I knowe suche a man (whether in the
bodie, or out of ẏ bodie, I can not tel: God
knoweth.)
4 How that he was takē vp into Paradise,
& heard [c]wordes which can not be spoken,
which are not "posible for man to vtter.
5 Of suche a man wil I reioyce: of my self
wil I not reioyce, except it be of mine infirmities.
6 For thogh I wolde reioyce, I shulde not be
a foole: for I wil say the trueth, but I refrai
ne, lest anie mā shulde thinke of me aboue
that he seeth in me, or ẏ he heareth of me.
7 And lest I shulde be exalted out of measure through the abundance of reuelatiōs,
there was giuen vnto me [d] a pricke in the
flesh, ẏ messenger of Satā to buffet me, because I shulde not be exalted out of measure.
8 For this thing I besoght the Lord [e]thrise,
that it might departe from me.
9 And he said vnto me, My grace is sufficiēt
for thee: for my power is made [f] perfite
through weakenes. Verie gladly therefore
wil I reioyce rather in mine infirmities,
that the power of Christ may dwell in me.
10 Therefore [g] I take pleasure in infirmities, in reproches, in necessities, in persecu
tions, in anguish for Christs sake: for whē
I am weake, then am I strong.
11 I was a foole to boast my self: ye haue cō
pelled me: for I oght to haue bene cōmen-
ded of you: for in nothing was I inferior
vnto the verie chief Apostles, thogh I be
nothing.
12 The signes of an Apostle were wroght
among you with all pacience, with signes,
and wonders, and great workes.
13 For what is it, wherein ye were inferiors
vnto other Churches, * except that I haue
not bene "slothful to your hinderāce? forgiue me this wrong.
14 Beholde, the [h] thirde time I am readie to
come vnto you, and yet wil I not be slothful to your hinderāce: for I seke not yours,
but [i] you: for the children oght not to laye
vp for the fathers, but the fathers for the
children.
15 And I wil moste gladly bestowe, and wil
be bestowed for your " soules: thogh the
more I loue you, the lesse I am loued.
16 But be it that I charged you not: [k] yet
forasmuche as I was craftie, I toke you
with guile.
17 Did I pill you by anie of them whome I
sent vnto you?
18 I haue desired [l] Titus, & with him I haue sent a brother: did Titus pil you of anie
thing? walked we not in the self same spirit? *walked we* not in the same steppes?
19 Againe, thinke ye that we excuse our selues vnto you? we speake before God in
Christ. But *we do* all things, dearly beloued, for your edifying.

Act. 9,8

a That is, a Christian, or, I speake it in Christ.

b That is to say, into the highest heauē.

c Mans infirmitie was not able to declare thē, nether were they shewed vnto him for that end.

"Or, *lawful.*

d The greke worde signifieth a sharpe piece of wood as a pale, or stake, and also a litle spilde or sharpe thīg ẇ pricketh one as he goeth through busshie & thicke places, and entring into the flesh, can not be taken out without cutting of the flesh: and this was the rebelling of ẏ flesh against the spirit, & warned him that Satā was at hand.

e That is to say, often times.

f Is knowen, & euidently sene.

g He doeth not onely paciently beare his afflictions, but also ioyfully, and as one that taketh pleasure therein for Christs sake.

Chap. 11,9.

"Or, *chargeable.*

h For first, he was minded to departe from Ephesus into Macedonia, & so to Corinthus, 1. Cor. 16, 5. Then when the Lord letted this purpose, he appointed to go straight from Ephesus to Corinthus, Chap 1, 15. ẏ intent being chāged, he wēt to Macedonia, from whence now he appointeth the third time to come vnto them.

i Which declareth his fatherlie affectiō.

"Or, *your cause or persones.*

k Thus said his aduersaries that thogh he toke it not by him self, yet he did it by ẏ meanes of others

l To go to you.

20 For

20 For I feare lest when I come, I shal not
finde you suche as I wolde: and that I
shalbe founde vnto you [m] suche as ye wolde
not, and lest *there be* strife, enuying,
wrath, contentions, backebitings, whisperings,
swellings & discorde.
21 *I feare* lest when I come againe, my God
[n] abase me among you, and I shal bewaile
manie of them which haue sinned already,
and haue not repented of the * vnclennes,
and fornication, and wantonnes, which
they haue committed.

m Meaning, sharpe & seuere.

n There was nothing whereat he so muche reioyced, as when his preaching profited: & therefore he calleth the Thessalonians his glorie & ioye: as also nothing did more cast downe his heart as when his labour did no good.

CHAP. XIII.

1 He threateneth the obstinate. 5 And declareth what his power is by their owne testimonie. 10 Also he sheweth what is the effect of this epistle. 11 After hauing exhorted them to their duetie, he wisheth them all prosperitie.

1 THis *is* the [a] thirde time that I come vnto
you. * In the mouth of two or thre
witnesses shal euerie worde stand.
2 [b] I tolde you before, and tel you before:
as thogh I had bene present the seconde
time, so write I now being absent to them
which heretofore haue sinned, and to all
others, that if I come againe, I wil not
spare,
3 Seing that ye seke experience of Christ,
that speaketh in me, which towarde you
is not weake, but is mightie in you.
4 For thogh he was crucified concerning
his [c] infirmitie, yet liueth he through the
power of God. And we no dout are weake
in him: [d] but we shal liue with him, through
the power of God towarde you.
5 * Proue your selues whether ye are in the
faith: examine your selues: knowe ye not
your owne selues, how that Iesus Christ is
in you, except ye be reprobates?
6 But I trust that ye shal knowe that we are
not reprobates.
7 Now I pray vnto God that ye do none euil,
not that we shulde seme approued, but that
ye shulde do that which is honest: thogh
we be as [e] reprobates.
8 For we can not *do* anie thing against the
trueth, but for the trueth.
9 For we are glad when we are weake, and
that ye are [f] strong: this also we wish for
euen your perfection.
10 Therefore write I these things being absent,
lest when I am present, I shulde vse
sharpenes, according to the power which
the Lord hathe giuen me, to [g] edification,
and not to destruction.
11 Finally brethren, fare ye wel: be perfite:
be of good comfort: be of one minde: liue
in peace, and the God of loue and peace
shalbe with you.
12 Grete one another with an * holie [h] kisse.
All the Saintes salute you.
13 The grace of our Lord Iesus Christ, and
the loue of God, and the communion of the
holie Gost be with you all, Amen.

a His first comming was his dwelling among them: his seconde was his first epistle, & now he is ready to come the third time: which thre commings he calleth his thre witnesses.

Deu. 19, 15. mat. 18, 16. iohn 8, 17. ebr. 10, 28.

b In my first epistle, Chap. 4, 20.

c In that he humbled him self and toke vpon him the forme of a seruant.

d Christ as touching the flesh in mans iudgement was vile & abiect: therefore we that are his members, can not be otherwise estemed: but being crucified, he shewed him self verie God: so thinke, that we whome ye contemne as dead men & castawayes, haue through God suche power to execute against you, that ye may fele sensibly that we liue in Christ.

1. Cor. 11, 28.

e In mans iudgement who for the most parte reiecteth the best, and approueth the worste.

f Hauing abundance of the grace of God.

g Commit not by your negligence that, that which is ordeined to saluation, turne to your destruction.

Rom. 16, 16. 1. cor. 16, 20. 1. pet 5, 14.

h Which was according to those countreis in those dayes bothe of the Iewes and of other nations.

The seconde *epistle* to the Corinthians, written from Philippi, a citie in Macedonia, & *sent* by Titus and Lucas.

THE EPISTLE OF the Apostle Paul to the Galatians.

THE ARGVMENT.

THe Galatians after they had bene instructed by S. Paul in the trueth of the Gospel, gaue place to false Apostles, who entring in, in his absence corrupted the pure doctrine of Christ, & taught that the ceremonies of the Law must be necessarily obserued, which thing the Apostle so earnestly reasoneth against, that he proueth that the granting thereof is the ouerthrowe of mans saluacion purchassed by Christ: for thereby the light of the Gospel is obscured: the conscience burdened: the testaments confounded: mans iustice established. And because the false teachers did pretend, as thogh they had bene sent of the chief Apostles, and that Paul had no autoritie, but spake of him self, he proueth bothe that he is an Apostle ordeined by God, and also that he is not inferior to the rest of the Apostles: which thing established, he procedeth to his purpose, prouing that we are frely iustified before God without any workes or ceremonies: which notwithstanding in their time had their vse and commoditie: but now they are not onely vnprofitable figures, but also pernicious, because Christ the trueth and the end thereof is come: wherefore men oght now to embrace that libertie, which Christ hathe purchassed by his blood, & not to haue their consciences snared in the grennes of mans traditions: finally he sheweth wherein this libertie standeth, and what exercises apperteine thereunto.

CHAP. I.

6 Paul rebuketh their inconstancie which suffred them selues to be seduced by the false apostles who preached that the obseruation of the ceremonies of the Law were necessarie to saluation. 8 And detesteth them that preache anie otherwise then Christ purely. 13 He sheweth his owne conuersation, magnifieth his office & Apostleship, and declareth him self to be equal with the chief Apostles.

1 PAul*an Apostle(not [a]of
men,nether by [b] mã,but
by IESVS CHRIST,
and God the Father ẇ
hathe raised him from
the dead)
2 And all the brethren ẇ
are with me, vnto ẏ Churches of Galatia:
3 Grace *be* with you and peace from God
the Father,& *from* our Lord Iesus Christ,
4 Which gaue him self for our sinnes, that
he might deliuer vs * from this [c] present
euil worlde according to the wil of God
euen our Father,
5 To whome *be* glorie for euer and euer,
Amen.
6 I marueile that ye are so sone remoued a-
way vnto another "Gospel, from him that
had called you in the [d] grace of Christ,
7 Which is not another *Gospel*, saue ẏ there
be some which trouble you,and intende to
[e] peruert the Gospel of Christ.
8 But thogh that we, or an [f] Angel from
heauen preache vnto you other wise, thẽ
that which we haue preached vnto you, let
him be "accursed.
9 As we said before,so say I now againe, If
anie man preache vnto you otherwise,thẽ
ẏ ye haue receiued,let him be accursed.
10 For [g] now preache I mans *doctrine*, or
Gods? or go I about to please men? for if
I shulde yet please men, I were not the ser
uant of Christ.
11 *Now I certifie you, brethren, that the
Gospel which was preached of me, was
not after [h] man.
12 For nether receiued I it of man, nether
was I taught it, but by the [i] reuelation of
Iesus Christ.
13 For ye haue heard of my conuersation in
time paste, in the Iewish religiõ, how that
* I persecuted the Church of God extremely, and wasted it,
14 And profited in the Iewish religiõ aboue
manie of my "companions of mine owne
nacion, and was muche more zealous of ẏ
[k] traditions of my fathers.
15 But when it [l] pleased God (which had separated me from my mothers wombe, and
called *me* by his grace)
16 To reueile his Sonne "in me, that I shulde preache him*among the Gentiles, immediatly I cõmunicated not with [m] flesh
and blood:
17 Nether came I againe to Ierusalem to
them which were Apostles before me, but
I went into Arabia, & turned againe vnto Damascus.
18 Then after thre yeres I came againe to
Ierusalem to visite Peter, and abode with
him fiftene dayes.
19 And none other of the Apostles sawe I,
saue Iames the Lords brother.
20 Now the things which I write vnto
you, beholde, *I witnesse* before God, that I
lie not.
21 After that, I went into the coastes of Syria & Cilicia: for I was vnknowen by face
vnto the Churches of Iudea, which were
in Christ.
22 But they had heard onely *some say*, He ẇ
persecuted vs in time past, now preacheth
the [n] faith, which before he destroyed.
23 And they glorified God for me.

Tit.1,3.
a For God is the autor of all ministerie.
b This prerogatiue was peculiar to the Apostles.
Luk.1,74.
c Which is, ẏ corrupt life of man without Christ.
"*Or, doctrine.*
d That is, to be partakers of the saluatiõ offred frely by Christ.
e For what is more cõtrarie to our fre iustification by faith, then the iustificatiõ by ẏ Law, or our workes? therefore to ioyne these two together, is to ioyne light ẇ darkenes, death with life, & doeth vtterly ouerthrow the Gospel.
f If it were possible, that an Angel shulde so do: wherby Paul declareth the certeinetie of his preaching.
1.Cor.15,1.
"*Or, abominable*
g Since that of a Pharise I was made an Apostle.
h That is, doctrine inuẽted by mã, nether by mãs autoritie do I preache it
Act.9,1.
i By an extraordinarie reuelation.
"*Or, age.*
k That is, of ẏ Law of God ẇ was giuen to the ancient fathers.
l He maketh thre degrees in Gods eternal predestination: first his eternal cõusel, then his appointing from the mothers wõbe, & thirdly his calling.
Ephes 3,8.
"*Or, to me.*
m That is, ẇ anie man, as thogh I had nede of his cõusel to approue my doctrine.

n That is, the Gospel which is the doctrine of faith.

CHAP. II.

Confirming his Apostleship to be of God. 3 He sheweth why Titus was not circumcised, 6 And that he is nothing inferior to other Apostles: 11 Yea, and that he hathe reproued Peter the Apostle of the Iewes. 16 After he cometh to the principal scope, which is to proue that iustification onely commeth of the grace of God by faith in Iesus Christ, and not by the workes of the Lawe.

1 THen fourtene yeres after, I went vp
againe to Ierusalem with Barnabas,
and toke with me Titus also.
2 And I went vp by reuelation, and [a] communicated with thẽ of the Gospel which
I preache among the Gentiles,*but particularly with them that were the chief, lest
by any meanes I shulde runne, or had run
ne" in vaine:
3 But nether yet Titus which was with me,
thogh he were a Grecian, was [b] compelled to be circumcised
4 For all the false brethren that crept in:
who came in priuely to spie out our liber
tie, which we haue in Christ Iesus, ẏ they
might bring vs into bondage.
5 To whome we [c] gaue not place by subiection for an houre, that the trueth of the
Gospel might continue with you.
6 And of them which semed to be great, *I
was not taught* (what they [d] were in time past
sed, it maketh no matter to me:*God accep
teth no mans persone) neuertheles, they ẏ
are the chief, [e] did communicate nothing
with me.
7 But cõtrariwise, when they sawe that the
Gospel ouer the vncircumcision was com
mitted vnto me, as *the Gospel* ouer the Cir
cumcision was vnto Peter:
8 (For he that was mightie by Peter in the
Apostleship ouer the Circumcisiõ, was also mightie by me towarde the Gentiles)
9 And when Iames, and Cephas, and Iohn
knewe of the grace that was giuen vnto
me, ẇ are counted to be pillers, thei gaue
to

a Paul nothing douted of his doctrine: but because many reported that he taught contrary doctrine to ẏ other Apostles, which rumors hindered the course of the Gospel, he endeuored to remedie it, and to proue that they consented with him.
Act.15,2.
"*Grek. without profit.*
b Which declareth that the other Apostles agreed with him.
c Lest we shulde haue betraied ẏ Christian libertie.
d Albeit they had bene conuersant with Christ afore time.
Deut.10,17.
2.chro.19,7.
iob.34,19.
wisdo.6,8.
ecclés.35,16.
act.10,34.
rom.2,11.
ephe.6,9.
coloss.3,25.
1.pet.1,17.
e But approued my doctrine perfect in all points.

to me and to Barnabas the [f] right hands of
felowship, that we *shulde preache* vnto the
Gentiles, and thei vnto the Circumcision,
10 *Warning onely that we shulde remember the poore : which thing also I was diligent to do.
11 ¶ And whẽ Peter was come to Antiochia,
I withstode him [g] to his face: for he was to
be blamed.
12 For before that certeine came from Iames, he ate with the Gentiles : but when
they were come, he withdrewe & separated him self, fearing them which were of
the Circumcision.
13 And the other Iewes dissembled likewise with him, in somuche that Barnabas
was broght into their dissimulation also.
14 But when I sawe, that they went not the
"right way to the trueth of the Gospel, I
said vnto Peter before all men, If ỹ being
a Iewe, liuest as the Gẽtiles, & not like the
Iewes, why [h] cõstrainest thou the Gentiles
to do like the Iewes?
15 We *which are* Iewes by nature, and not
[i] sinners of the Gentiles,
16 Knowe that a man is not iustified by the
workes of the Law, but by the faith of Iesus Christ : euen we, *I say*, haue beleued in
Iesus Christ, that we might be iustified by
the faith of Christ, and not by the workes
of the Law, because that by the workes of
the Law no "flesh shalbe iustified.
17 *If then while we seke to be made righteous by Christ, we our selues are founde
[k] sinners, is Christ therefore the minister
of sinne? God [l] forbid.
18 For if I buylde againe the things that I
haue destroyed, [m] I make my self a trespaser.
19 For I through the Law am dead to the
Law, & that I might liue vnto God, I am
[n] crucified with Christ.
20 Thus I liue *yet*, [o] not I now, but Christ
liueth in me: & in that that I now liue in
the [p] flesh, I liue by the faith in the Sonne
of God, who hathe loued me, & giuen him
self for me.
21 I do not abrogate the [q] grace of God: for
if righteousnes *be* by ỹ Law, then Christ
dyed "without a cause.

f In tokẽ that we all agreed in doctrine.
Act.11,30. 1.cor 9,3.
g Meaning, before all men.
"Greke, with a right fote.
h In bringing their consciences into doute by thine exãple & autoritie: and here the Apostle commeth to his chief point.
i For so ỹ Iewes called the Gentiles in reproche.
"Or, man.
k Except our frutes be agreable to õ faith, we declare ỹ we haue not Christ.
Rom 3,19. phil.3,9.
l For he caused thẽ not to sinne, but disclosed it, nether toke he away ỹ righteousnes of the Law, but shewed their hypocrisie which were not able to performe ỹ whereof they boasted.
m For my doctrine is to destroy sinne by faith in Christ and not to establish sinne.
n And fele his strength in me which killeth sinne.
o Not as I was once, but regenerat, and changed into a new creature, in qualitie, & not in substance.
p In this mortal bodie.
q As did the false Apostles which preached not the faith in Christ
"Or, for nothing.

CHAP. III.

1 He rebuketh them sharpely. 2 And proueth by diuers reasons that iustification is by faith. 6 As appeareth by the example of Abraham, 10.19.24. And by the office, & the end, bothe of the Law, 11.25. And of faith.

1 O Foolish Galatiãs, who hathe bewitched you that ye shulde not obey the
trueth, to whome Iesus Christ before [a] was
described in your sight, & among you cru
cified?
2 This onely wolde I learne of you, Receiued ye the [b] Spirit by the workes of ỹ Law,
or by the hearing of [c] faith *preached*?
3 Are ye so foolish, that after ye haue begonne in the Spirit, ye wolde now [d] be made perfite by the [e] flesh?
4 Haue ye suffred so many things in vaine?
if so be it be euen in vaine.
5 He therefore ỹ ministreth to you the Spirit, & worketh miracles among you, *doeth
he it* through the workes of the Law, or
by the hearing of faith *preached*?
6 *Yea rather* as Abraham beleued God, &
it was * imputed to him for righteousnes.
7 Knowe ye therefore, that they which a-
re of faith, the same are the children of A-
braham.
8 For the Scripture foreseing, ỹ God wolde
iustifie ỹ Gẽtiles through faith, preached
before ỹ Gospel vnto Abrahã, *saying*, *In
thee shal all the Gentiles be blessed.
9 So then they which be of faith, are blessed with faithful Abraham.
10 For as many as are of the [f] workes of the
Law, are vnder the curse : for it is written,
*Cursed is euerie man that continueth not
in all things, which are writtẽ in the boke
of the Law, to do them.
11 And that no man is iustified by the Law
in the sight of God, it is euident: * for the
iust shal liue by faith.
12 And the [g] Law is not of faith : but * the
man that shal do those things, shal liue in
them.
13 Christ hathe redemed vs from the curse of the Law, when he was made a curse
for vs (for it is written, * Cursed is euerie
one that hangeth on tre)
14 That the blessing of Abrahã might come on the Gentiles through Christ Iesus,
that we might receiue the [h] promes of the
Spirit through faith.
15 Brethren, [i] I speake as men do, * Thogh
it be but a mans couenant when it is confirmed, *yet* no man doeth abrogate it, or
[k] addeth any thing thereto.
16 Now to Abraham and his sede were the
promises made. He saith not, And to the
sedes, as *speaking* of many: but, And to thy
sede, as of one, which [l] is Christ.
17 And this I say, that the Law which was
foure hundreth and thirtie yeres after, can
not disanul the couenant that was confirmed afore of God in respect of Christ, ỹ
it shulde make the promes of none effect.
18 For if the inheritance *be* of the Law, *it
is* no more by the promes, but God gaue
it vnto Abraham by promes.
19 Wherefore then *serueth* the Law? It was
added because of the [m] trãsgressions, til ỹ
sede came vnto ỹ which the promes was

a To whome Christ was so liuely preached, as if his liuelie image were set before your eyes, or els had bene crucified among you.
b Meaning the giftes of the Spirit.
c That is, the doctrine of saluatiõ through faith in Iesus Christ, as cha. 1,22.
d The false apostles taught ỹ Christ profited nothing, except they were circũcised, and that the Lawe was the perfection, & Christs doctrine onely the rudimẽts thereunto.
e And ceremonies of the Lawe?
Gen.15,6. rom 4,3. iam.2,23. Gen.12,13. eccle.44,20. act.3,25.
f Which thinke to be iustified by them.
Deu.27,26.
Habak.2,4. rom.1,17. ebr.10,38. Leu.18,5.
g The Lawe pronoũceth not thẽ iust, which beleue, but ỹ worke, and so condẽneth all them which in all points do not fulfil it.
Deut.21,23.
h Which is ỹ Gospel.
Ebr.9,17.
i I wil vse a cõmune example ỹ you may be ashamed to attribute lesse vnto God, thẽ to suche couenants, which one man maketh to another
k No more is the promes or couenant of God abrogate by ỹ Law, nor yet is the Law added to the promes to take any thig away that was superfluous, or to supplie any thig that wanted
l Which declareth that ỹ Iewes and Gẽtiles are bothe partakers of ỹ promes, because thei are ioyned in Christ which is this blessed sede.
m That sinne might appeare and be made more abundant, and so all to be shut vp vnder sinne.

made: & it was ordeined by [n] Angels in the
hand of a Mediatour.
20 Now a Mediatour is not *a Mediatour* of
[o] one: but God is [p] one.
21 *Is* the Law then againſt the promes of
God? God forbid: for if there had bene a Law giuẽ which colde haue giuen life, ſurely righteouſnes ſhulde haue bene
by the Law.
22 But the Scripture hathe *concluded [q] all
vnder ſinne, that the promes by the faith
of Ieſus Chriſt ſhulde be giuen to them
that beleue.
23 But before [r] faith came, we were kept vnder the Law, and ſhut vp vnto the faith,
which ſhulde afterwarde be reueiled.
24 Wherefore the *Law was our ſcholemaſter *to bring vs* to Chriſt, that we might
be made righteous by faith.
25 But after that faith is come, we are no
longer vnder [ſ] a ſcholemaſter.
26 For ye are all ẏ ſonnes of God by faith,
in Chriſt Ieſus.
27 *For all ye ẏ are [t] baptized into Chriſt,
haue put on Chriſt.
28 There is nether Iewe nor Grecian: there is nether bonde nor fre: there is nether male nor female: for ye are all [u] one in
Chriſt Ieſus.
29 And if *ye be* Chriſts, then are ye Abrahams ſede, and heires by promes.

n Who as miniſters gaue it to Moſes by the autoritie of Chriſt.
o But ſerueth bothe for the Iewes & Gentiles to ioyne them to God.
p Conſtant & alwayes like him ſelf.
Rom 3.9.
q Bothe men and all their workes.
r The ful reuelation of thĩgs which were hid vnder the ſhadowes of ẏ Law.
Rom.10,4.
ſ Not that the doctrine of the Law is aboliſhed, but the condemnation thereof is taken away by faith.
Rom.6,3.
t So that Baptiſme ſucceedeth Circumciſion, and ſo through Chriſt bothe Iewe and Gentile is ſaued.
u As all one man.

CHAP. IIII.

1 He ſheweth wherefore the ceremonies were ordeined. 3 Which being ſhadowes muſt end when Chriſt the trueth commeth. 9 He moueth them by certeine exhortations, 22 And confirmeth his argument with a ſtrong example or allegorie.

1 THen I ſay, that the [a] heire as long as
he is a childe, differeth nothing from
a ſeruant, thogh he be Lord of all,
2 But is vnder [b] tuters and gouerners, vntil
the time appointed of the father.
3 Euen ſo, we when we were children, were
in bondage vnder the [c] rudiments of the
worlde.
4 But when the fulnes of time was come,
God ſent forthe his Sonne made of a woman, & made [d] vnder the Law,
5 That he might redeme them which were vnder the Law, that we *might receiue the adoption of the ſonnes.
6 And becauſe ye are ſonnes, God hathe
ſent forthe the [e] Spirit of his Sonne into
your hearts, which cryeth, [f] Abba, Father.
7 Wherefore, thou art no more [g] a ſeruant,
but a ſonne: now if *thou be* a ſonne, *thou art*
alſo the heire of God through Chriſt.
8 But euen then, when ye [h] knewe not God,
ye did ſeruice vnto them, which by [i] nature are not gods.

a The Church of Iſrael was vnder ẏ Lawe as the pupil ſubiect to his tutor, euen vnto the time of Chriſt, when ſhe waxed ſtrong, and thẽ her tutelſhip ended.
b That is, the Lawe, which before he called a ſcholemaſter, chap 3, 25.
c That is, vnder the Law, which was but an, a.b.c. in reſpect of ẏ Goſpel.
d That is, who was ſubiect vnto the Lawe.
Rom.8,15.
e For our adoption vnto Chriſt is ſealed by him.
f He inſtructeth both Iewes, & Gentiles to call God their Father in euerie lãgage, ſo that none are excepted. g Which maiſt not vſe thy libertie. h When ye receiued the Goſpel, ye were idolaters: therefore it is ſhame for you to refuſe libertie and become ſeruants, yea, and ſeing the Iewes deſire to be out of their tutelſhip. i Not in dede, but in opinion.

9 But now ſeing ye knowe God, yea, rather
are knowen of God, how turne [k] ye againe
vnto impotent and beggerlie rudiments,
whereunto *as* from the beginning ye wil
be in bondage againe?
10 Ye obſerue [l] dayes, and moneths, and times, and yeres.
11 I am in feare of you, leſt I haue beſtowed on you labour in vaine.
12 Be ye as [m] I: for I am euen as you: brethren, I beſeche you: ye haue not hurt [n] me
at all.
13 And ye knowe, how through [o] infirmitie
of the fleſh I preached the Goſpel vnto
you at the firſt.
14 [p] And the tryal of me which was in my
fleſh, ye deſpiſed not, nether abhorred:
but ye receiued me as an [q] Angel of God,
yea, as Chriſt Ieſus.
15 What was then your felicitie? for I beare you recorde, that if it had bene poſſible, ye wolde haue plucked out your owne
eyes, and haue giuen them to me.
16 Am I therefore become your enemie,
becauſe I tell you the trueth?
17 They are ielous ouer you [r] amiſſe: yea,
they wolde exclude [ſ] you, that ye ſhulde
altogether loue them.
18 But it is a good thing to loue earneſtly
alwayes in a good thing, & not onely whẽ
I am preſent with you,
19 My litle children, of whome I trauaile
in birth againe, vntil Chriſt be [t] formed
in you.
20 And I wolde I were with you now, that
I might change my voyce: for I am in
doute of you.
21 Tell me, ye that wil be vnder the Law,
do ye not heare the Law?
22 For it is written, that Abraham had two
ſonnes, *one by a ſeruant, & *one by a fre
woman.
23 But he which was of the ſeruãt, was borne after the fleſh: and he which was of the
fre woman, *was borne* by promes.
24 By the which things another thing is
ment: for theſe *mothers* [u] are the two Teſta-
ments, the one which is [x] Agar of mounte
Sina, which gendreth vnto bondage,
25 (For Agar *or* Sina is a mountaine in ẏ A-
rabia, & it anſwereth to Ieruſalem which
now is) and ſhe is in bondage with her
children.
26 But Ieruſalem, which is "aboue, is fre:
which is the mother of vs all.
27 For it is written, *Reioyce thou [z] barren
that beareſt no children: breake forthe, &
crye, thou that trauaileſt not: for the deſolate hathe many mo children, then ſhe
which hathe an houſband.
28 *Therefore, brethrẽ, we are after the ma-

k The Galatians, of Painims began to be Chriſtians, but by falſe apoſtles were turned backewarde to begine a newe the Iewiſh ceremonies, and ſo inſtede of going forward towarde Chriſt, they ran backewarde from him.
l Ye obſerue dayes, as Sabbaths, newe moones, &c: ye obſerue moneths as the firſt and ſeueth moneth: ye obſerue times, as Eaſter, witſontide, the feaſt of Tabernacles: ye obſerue yeres as the Iubile, or, yere of forgiuenes, which beggerlie ceremonies are moſte pernicious to them which haue receiued ẏ ſwete libertie of the Goſpel, and thruſt thẽ backe into ſuperſtitious ſclauerie.
m So friendful to me, as I am affectioned towarde you.
n For I pardon you, if you repent.
o Being in great dangers and afflictions, or without pope & oſtentation.
p That is, the troubles and vexacions ẇ God ſent to trie me while I was among you.
q For my miniſteries ſake.
r For they are but ambitious
ſ They wolde turne you frõ me that you might followe them.
t And imprinted ſo in your hearts ẏ you loue none other.
Gen.16,15.
Gen.21,2.
u That is, ſignifie.
x Agar, and Sina repreſente the Lawe: Sara and Ieruſalem ẏ Goſpel: Iſmael ẏ Iewiſh Synagogue, and Iſaac the Church of Chriſt.
Iſa.54,1
y That is, one of the land of promes.
Rom.9,8.

"Or, hie & heauenlie. z Meaning Sara.

ner of Isaac,children of the promes.
29 But as then he that was borne after the
flesh ,persecuted him that *was borne* after
the spirit,euen so *it is* now.
30 But what saith the Scripture? * Put out
the seruant and her sonne: for the sonne of
the seruant shal not be heire with the sonne of the fre woman.
31 Then brethren , we are not children of
the seruant,but of the [a] fre woman ‖.

CHAP. V.

2 He laboureth to drawe them away from Circumcision, 17 And sheweth them the battel betwixt the Spirit & the flesh,and the frutes of them bothe.

1 STand fast therefore in the libertie
wherewith Christ hathe made vs fre,
and be not intangled againe with the yoke of bondage.
2 * Beholde,I Paul say vnto you,that,if ye
be [a] circumcised , Christ shal profite you
nothing.
3 For I testifie againe to euerie man, which
is circumcised , that he is bounde to kepe
the whole Law.
4 Ye are * abolished from Christ: whosoeuer are iustified by the Law , ye are fallen
from grace.
5 For we through the Spirit [b] waite for the
hope of righteousnes through faith.
6 For in Iesus Christ nether Circumcision
auaileth anie thing,nether vncircũcision,
but faith which worketh by loue.
7 Ye did runne wel : who did let you , that
ye did not obeie the [c] trueth?
8 *It is* not the persuasion of him that [d] calleth you.
9 *A litle [e] leauen doeth leauen the whole
lompe.
10 I haue trust in you through the Lord,
that ye wil be none otherwise [f] minded:
but he that troubleth you , shal beare *his*
condemnacion,whosoeuer he be.
11 And brethren , if I yet preache circumcision, why do I yet suffer persecucion?
Then is the [g] sclander of the crosse abolished.
12 Wolde to God they were euen cut of,
which do disquiet you.
13 For brethren , ye haue bene called vnto
libertie:onely vse not *your* libertie as an oc
casion vnto the flesh,but by loue serue one
another.
14 For [h] all the Law is fulfilled in one worde , which is this, * Thou shalt loue thy
neighbour as thy self.
15 If ye byte & deuoure one another, take
hede lest ye be consumed one of another.
16 Then I say , * walke in the [i] Spirit , and
ye shal not fulfil the lustes of the flesh.
17 For the [k] flesh lusteth against the Spirit,
and the Spirit against the flesh:and these
are contrarie one to the other , so that ye
can not do the same things that ye wolde.
18 And if ye be led by the [l] Spirit,ye are not
vnder the Law.
19 Moreouer the workes of the flesh are
manifest,which are adulterie, fornicaciõ,
vnclennes,wantonnes,
20 Idolatrie,witchcraft,hatred,debate,emu
lacions,wrath,contentions,sedicions, heresies,
21 Enuie,murthers,dronkennes,glottonie,
and suche like, whereof I tell you before,
as I also haue tolde you before, that they
which do suche things , shal not inherite
the kingdome of God.
22 But the frute of the Spirit is loue, ioye,
peace, long suffring, gentlenes, goodnes,
faith,
23 Mekenes, temperancie : against suche
there is [m] no Law.
24 For they that are Christs , [n] haue crucified the flesh with the affections and the
lustes.
25 If we liue in the Spirit, let vs also walke
in the [o] Spirit.
26 Let vs not be desirous of vaine glorie,
prouoking one another,enuying one another.

CHAP. VI.

1 He exhorteth them to vse gentlenes towarde the weake, 2 And to shewe their brotherlie loue and modestie: 6 Also to prouide for their ministers. 9 To perseuere. 14 To reioyce in the crosse of Christ, 15 To newnes of life, 16 And last of all wisheth to them with the rest of the faithful all prosperitie.

1 BRethren, if a man be [a] fallen by occasion into anie faute , ye which are
spiritual, restore suche one with the spirit
of mekenes,considering thy self, lest thou
also be tempted.
2 Beare ye one anothers burden , and so
[b] fulfil the Law of Christ.
3 For if anie man seme to him self,that he
is some what , when he is [c] nothing,he deceiueth him self in his imaginacion.
4 But let euerie man proue his owne worke , and then shal he haue [d] reioycing in
him self onely and not in another.
5 *For euerie man shal beare his owne burden.
6 Let him that is taught in the worde,ma-
ke him that hathe taught him,partaker of
all *his* [e] * goods.
7 Be not deceiued: God is not mocked: for
whatsoeuer a man soweth, that shal he also reape.
8 For he that [f] soweth to his flesh , shal of
the flesh reape corruptiõ: but he that soweth to the spirit, shal of the spirit reape
life euerlasting.
9 * Let vs not therefore be wearie of wel
doing: for in due season we shal [g] reape,if
we faint not.
10 While we haue therefore time,let vs do
good vnto all men,but specially vnto thẽ,
which are of the housholde of faith.
11 ¶ Ye se how large a lettre I haue written

Gen.21,10.

‖ By the libertie wherewith Christ hathe made vs fre.

a For we are in ȳ Church of Christ,which is our mother, & not of the Synagogue ẇ is a seruant vnder the Law.

Act.15,1

a If you ioyne circumcisiõ to the Gospel, as a thing necessarie to saluacion.

1.Cor.1,17.

b We liue in hope through that Spirit ẇ causeth faith, & ẇ is giuen to the faithful ȳ we shulde by faith & not by the Law obteine the croune of glorie , ẇ Christ giueth frely.

1.Cor.5,6.

c Then whatsoeuer is not ȳ worde of God, ẇ here he calleth trueth,is verie lies.

d Which is God.

e A litle corruption doeth destroy ȳ whole doctrine.

f That ye wil imbrace the worde of God purely.

g That is,the doctrine of ȳ Gospel,which the worlde abhorred, as a sclanderous thing,& therewith were offended.

h Meaning the seconde table.

Leui.19,18. mat.22,39. mar.12,31. iam.2,8.

Rom. 13,14. 1.pet.2,10.

i In the man regenerat.

k That is,the natural mã striueth against ȳ Spirit of regeneracion.

l If you be guided by ȳ Spirit of adoptiõ, that which ye do,is agreable to God althogh it be not perfite.

m For thei are vnder the Spirit,or grace.

n Christ hathe not onely remitted their sinnes,but sanctified thẽ into newnes of life.

o That being dead to sinne & liuĩg to God, we may declare the same in holines & innocencie of life.

Chap.VI.

a Ether by reason of his flesh or Satan.

b Christ exhorteth in sondrie places to mutual loue, and therefore brotherlie loue is here called ȳ Law of Christ, & his commãdement, Iohn 13,34 & 15,12.

c He sheweth that mã hathe nothing of his self whereof he shulde reioyce.

d For his reioycing is a testimonie of a good conscience, 2.Cor.1,12. wherein he may reioyce before mẽ, but not before God.

e For it were a shame not to prouide for their corporal necessities, ẇ fedeour soules ẇ the heauenlie deinties.

1.Cor.3,8.

1.Cor 9,7

f He proueth ȳ the ministers must be nowrished : for if men onely prouide for worldelie things without respect of ȳ life euerlastig, thẽ they procure to them selues death,& mocke God, who hathe giuen them his ministers to teache them heauẽlie things.

2.Thes.3,13.

g The frute ẇ God hathe promised.

vnto you with mine owne hand.
12 As manie as desire to make a faire shewe
[h] in the flesh, they constraine you to be cir
cumcised, onely because they wolde not
suffer persecuciō for the [i] crosse of Christ.
13 For they them selues which are circumcised, kepe not the Law, but desire to haue you circumcised, that thei might reioyce [k] in your flesh.
14 But God forbid that I shulde reioyce,
but in ŷ crosse of our Lord Iesus Christ,
whereby the [l] worlde is crucified vnto me,
and I vnto the worlde.
15 For in Christ Iesus nether circumcision
auaileth anie thing, nor vncircumcision,
but a newe [m] creature.
16 And as manie as walke according to this
rule, peace *shal* be vpon them, & mercie,
and [n] vpon the Israel of God.
17 From hence forthe let no man [o] put me
to busines: for I beare in my bodie the
[p] markes of the Lord Iesus.
18 Brethren, the grace of our Lord Iesus
Christ *be* with your spirit, Amen.

Vnto the Galatians written from Rome.

h By the outwarde ceremonies.
i That is, for preaching Christ crucified.
k That thei haue made you Iewes.
l By ŷ worlde he meaneth all outwarde pompe, ceremonies & thigs, which please mens fantasies.
m Which is regenerate by faith.
n That is, vpō the Iewes, as Rom 2,19.
o Let no man trouble my preaching frō hence forthe: for my markes are witnesses how valiantly I haue foght.
p Which are odious to the worlde, but glorious before God.

THE EPISTLE OF Paul to the Ephesians.

THE ARGVMENT.

While Paul was prisoner at Rome, there entred in among the Ephesians false teachers, who corrupted the true doctrine which he had taught them, by reason whereof he wrote this Epistle to confirme them in that thing, which they had learned of him. And first after his salutacion, he assureth them of saluacion, because they were thereunto predestinate by the fre election of God, before they were borne, and sealed vp to this eternal life by the holie Gost, giuen vnto them by the Gospel, the knowledge of the which mysterie he prayeth God to confirme towarde them. And to the intent they shulde not glorie in them selues, he sheweth them their extreme miserie, wherein they were plonged before they knewe Christ, as people without God, Gentiles to whome the promises were not made, and yet by the fre mercie of God in Christ Iesus, they were saued, and he appointed to be their Apostle, as of all other Gentiles: therefore he desireth God to lighten the Ephesians hearts with the persite vnderstanding of his Sonne, & exhorteth them likewise to be mindeful of so great benefites, nether to be moued with the false apostles, which seke to ouerthrowe their faith, and treade vnder fote the Gospel, which was not preached to them, as by chance or fortune, but according to the eternal counsel of God: who by this meanes preserueth onely his Church. Therefore the Apostle commendeth his ministerie, forasmuche as God thereby reigneth among men, and causeth it to bring forthe moste plentiful frutes, as innocencie, holines, with all suche offices apperteining to godlines. Last of all, he declareth not onely in general what oght to be the life of the Christians, but also sheweth particularly, what things concerne euerie mans vocacion.

CHAP. I.

After his salutacion, 4 He sheweth that the chief cause of their saluacion standeth in the fre election of God through Christ. 16 He declareth his good wil towarde them, giuing thankes and praying God for their faith. 21 The maiestie of Christ.

1 Paul an Apostle of Iesus
Christ, by ŷ wil of God,
to the *Saintes, which a-
re at Ephesus, & to the
faithful in Christ Iesus:
2 Grace *be* with you, &
peace frō God our Fa-
ther, & *from* the Lord Iesus Christ.
3 *Blessed *be* God euen the Father of our
Lord Iesus Christ, which hathe blessed vs
with all [a] spiritual blessing in heauenlie
"things in Christ,
4 *As he hathe [b] chosen vs in him, before ŷ
fundacion of the worlde, ŷ we * shulde be
[c] holie, & without blame before hī in loue:
5 Who hathe predestinate vs, to be [d] adopted through Iesus Christ vnto him self, ac
cording to the good pleasure of his wil,
6 To the [e] praise of the glorie of his grace, wherewith he hathe made vs accepted
in *his* beloued,
7 By whome we haue redemption through
his blood, *euen* the forgiuenes of sinnes, according to his riche grace:
8 Whereby he hathe bene abūdant toward
vs in all wisdome & vnderstanding,
9 And hathe opened vnto vs the mysterie
of his wil according to his good pleasure,
which he had purposed [f] in him,
10 That in the dispensacion of the fulnes
of the times he might gather together in
one [g] all things, bothe which are in heauē
and which are in earth, *euen* in Christ:
11 In whome also we are chosen when we
were predestinate according to the purpose of him, which worketh all things after the counsel of his owne wil,
12 That [h] we, which first trusted in Christ,
shulde be vnto the praise of his glorie:
13 In whome also ye *haue trusted* after that
ye heard the worde of trueth, *euen* ŷ Gospel of your saluacion, wherein also after
that ye beleued, ye were sealed with the
holie

a As with the knowledge of God in Christ, ŵ faith, hope, charitie and other gifts.
" Or, places.
b This electiō to life euerlasting can neuer be chāged: but in temporal offices, ŵ God hathe appointed for a certeine space, when the terme is expired, he changeth his election, as we se in Saul and Iudas.
1.Cor.1,2.
c Whē Christs iustice is imputed ours.
2.Cor.1,3.
1.pet.1,3.
2.Tim.1,9.
d Where as we were not ŷ natural childrē he receiued vs by grace, and made vs his children.
Colos.1,22.
e The principal end of our election is to praise & glorifie the grace of God.
f That is, in Christ.
g By this he meaneth the whole bodie of the Church, ŵ he diuideth into them, ŵ are in heauen, & them which are in earth: also ŷ faithful which remaine in earth, stand of the Iewes & the Gentiles.
h To wit, the Iewes.

holie Spirit of promes,
14 Which is the ernest of our inheritance,
i vntil the redẽption of the possession pur
chassed vnto the praise of his glorie.
15 Therefore also after that I heard of the
faith, which ye haue in the Lord Iesus, &
loue towarde all the Saintes,
16 I cease not to giue thankes for you, making mention of you in my prayers,
17 That the God of our Lord Iesus Christ
the Father of glorie, might giue vnto you
the Spirit of wisdome, and reuelation
through the knowledge of [k] him,
18 That ẏ eyes of your vnderstanding may
be lightened that ye may knowe what the
hope is of his calling, and what the riches of his glorious inheritance *is* in the
Saintes,
19 And what is ẏ exceading greatnes of his
power toward vs, which beleue, *accordĩg to the working of his mightie power,
20 Which he wroght in Christ, whẽ he raised him from the dead, and [l] set him at his
right hand in the heauenlie *places*,
21 Farre aboue all principalitie, and power,
& might, & domination, & euerie Name,
that is named, not in this worlde onely,
but also in that that is to come,
22 *And hathe made all things subiect vnder his fete, & hathe appointed him ouer
all things *to be* the head to the Church,
23 Which is his bodie, *euen* the [m] fulnes of
him that filleth all in all things.

i Thogh we be redemed frõ ẏ bondage of sinne by the death of Christ, Rom 6,22, yet we hope for this secõde redemptiõ which shalbe when we shal possesse our inheritance in the heauens, whereof we haue the holie Gost for a gage, as Chap. 4,30.
k Of Christ.
l Made him Gouernour of all things bothe in heauen & in earth: so that Christs bodie is now onely there, or els it shulde not be a true bodie and his ascencion shulde be but a fantastical thing and onely imagined.
Col.2,12.
chap.3,7.
Psal.8,8.
ebr.2,8.
m This is the great loue of Christ towarde his Church that he counteth not him self perfect without vs ẇ are his members: and therefore the Church is also called Christ, as 1.Cor.12,12.

CHAP. II.

5 To magnifie the grace of Christ, which is the onelie cause of saluation. 11 He sheweth them what maner of people they were before their conuersion. 18 And what they are now in Christ.

1 AND *you *hathe he quickened*, that were
dead in trespasses and sinnes,
2 Wherein, in time past ye walked, according to the course of this worlde, *&* after
the *[a] prince that ruleth in the aire, *euen*
the spirit, that now worketh in the childrẽ
of disobedience,
3 Among whome we also had our cõuersa-
tion in time past, in the lustes of our flesh,
in fulfilling the wil of the flesh, & of the
minde, and were [b] by nature the children
of wrath, as wel as others.
4 But God which is riche ĩ mercie, through
his great loue wherewith he loued vs,
5 Euen when we were dead by sinnes, hathe
quickened vs [c] together "in Christ, *by whose* grace ye are saued,
6 And hathe [d] raised vs vp together, and
made vs sit together in the heauenlie *places* in Christ Iesus,
7 That he might shew in the ages to come
the exceding riches of his grace, through
his kindnes towarde vs in Christ Iesus.
8 For by grace are ye saued through faith,
and that not of your selues: it *is* the gifte
of God,
9 Not of workes, lest any man shulde boaste him self.
10 For we are [e] his workemanship created
in Christ Iesus vnto good workes, which
God hathe ordeined, that we shulde walke in them.
11 Wherefore [f] remember that ye being in
time past Gentiles in the flesh, *&* called
*vncircumcision of them ẏ which are cal-
led circumcision in the flesh, made with
hands,
12 That ye were, *I say*, at ẏ time without
Christ, & were aliantes from the cõmune
welth of Israel, & were *strangers frõ the
[g] couenants of promes, & had no [h] hope, &
were "without God in the worlde.
13 But now in Christ Iesus, ye which once
were farre of, are made nere by the blood
of Christ.
14 For he is our peace, which hathe made
of bothe one, & hathe broken the [i] stoppe
of the particion wall,
15 In abrogating through his [k] flesh the hatred, *that is*, the Law of commandements
which standeth in ordinances, for to make
of twaine one newe man in him self, *so* making peace,
16 And that he might reconcile bothe vnto God in one [l] bodie by *his* "crosse, & slaye
hatred thereby,
17 And came, and preached peace to you ẇ
were a farre of, & to them that were nere.
18 *For through him we bothe haue an entrance vnto the Father by one Spirit.
19 Now therefore ye are no more strangers
& foreners: but citizens with the Saintes,
and of the housholde of God,
20 And are buylt vpõ the fundacion of the
Apostles and Prophetes, Iesus Christ him
self being the chief corner stone,
21 In whome all the buylding coupled together, groweth vnto an holie Temple in
the Lord,
22 In whome ye also are buylt together to
be the habitation of God by the Spirit.

Col.2,13.
Chap.6,12.
a Meaning Satan.
b Not by creation, but by Adams transgression, and so by byrth.
c Bothe Iewe and Gentil.
"Or, with Christ
d We that are the members, are raised vp from death & reigne with our head Christ in heauen by faith.
e Here he meaneth, as concerning grace, and not by nature.
f He sheweth here that the further ẏ Gentiles were of from the grace of God, the greater detters they are now to the same.
1.Sam.17,26.
eze.44,7.
Rom.9,4.
g It was but one couenãt, but because it was diuers times confirmed & established, therefore here he calleth them Couenants.
"Or, Atheistes.
h Where no promes is, there is no hope.
i That is, the cause of the diuision that was betwene the Iewes and the Gentiles.
k For in Christ all things were accomplished, which were prefigurate in the Law.
l For of the Iewes and the Gentils he made one flocke.
"Or, death.
Rom.5,2.

CHAP. III.

1 He sheweth the cause of his imprisonment: 13 Desireth them not to faint because of his trouble. 14 And prayeth God to make them stedfast in his Spirit.

1 FOr this cause, I Paul *am* the [a] prisoner of Iesus Christ for you Gentiles,
2 If ye haue heard of the [b] dispensation of
the grace of God, which is giuen mẽ to
you warde,
3 *That is*, that God by reuelatiõ hathe shewed
this mysterie vnto me (as I wrote [c] aboue
in fewe wordes,
4 Whereby whẽ ye read, ye may know mine
vnderstanding in the mysterie of Christ)
5 Which in other ages was [d] not opened

a He reioiceth in that he suffred imprisonment for the maintenãce of Christs glorie.
b Which was his vocation to preache vnto the Gentiles
c That is, in ẏ first chap. of this Epistle, ver.9.
d Althogh the fathers, & the Prophetes had reuelations certeine, yet it was not in cõparison of that abũdance which was shewed whẽ the Gentiles were called: nether yet was the time, nor the maner knowen.

vnto the ſonnes of men, as it is now reueiled vnto his holie Apoſtles and Prophetes by the Spirit,
6 That the Gentiles ſhulde be inheriters
alſo, and of the ſame bodie, and partakers
of his promes in Chriſt by the Goſpel,
7 Whereof I am made a miniſter by the
gifte of the grace of God giuen vnto me
*through the working of his power.
8 *Euen vnto me the leaſt of all Saintes is
this grace giuen, that I ſhulde preache a-
mong the *Gentiles the vnſearcheable riches of Chriſt,
9 And to make cleare vnto all men what the
felowſhip of the *myſterie is, which from
the beginning of the worlde hathe bene
hid in God, who hathe created all things
by Ieſus Chriſt,
10 To the intent, that now vnto [e] principalities and powers in heauelie *places* might
be knowen [f] by the Church the manifolde wiſdome of God,
11 According to the eternal purpoſe, which
he wroght in Chriſt Ieſus our Lord.
12 By whome we haue boldnes & entrance
with confidence, by faith in him.
13 Wherefore I deſire that ye faint not at
my tribulations for your ſakes, which is
your glorie.
14 For this cauſe I bowe my knees vnto the
Father of our Lord Ieſus Chriſt,
15 (Of whome is named the whole [g] familie in [h] heauen and in earth)
16 That he might grante you according to
the riches of his glorie, yͤ ye may be ſtrēg-
thened by his Spirit in the inner man,
17 That Chriſt may dwell in your [i] hearts
by faith, that ye, being rooted and grounded in loue,
18 May be able to cōprehend with all Saintes, what is the [k] breadth, and length, and
depth, and height:
19 And to knowe the loue of Chriſt, which
paſſeth knowledge, that ye may be filled
with all [l] fulnes of God.
20 *Vnto him therefore that is able to do
exceading abundantly aboue all that we
aſke or thinke, according to the power yͭ
worketh in [m] vs,
21 *Be* praiſe in the Church by Chriſt Ieſus,
throughout all generatiōs for euer, Amen.

Chap.3,19. 1.Cor.15,9. Gal.1,16. Rom.16,25. col.1,26. 2.tim.1,10. tit.1,2. 2.pet.1,20.

e The Angels.

f The Church being gathered of ſo many kindes of people, is an example, or a glaſſe for the Angels to beholde the wiſdome of God in, who hathe turned their particular diſcords into an vniuerſal concorde, & of yͤ Sinagogue of bondage, hathe made the Church of fredome.

g He that is not of the bodie of Chriſt, is in death.

h The faithful which dyed before Chriſt came, were adopted by him, & make one familie with the Saincts which yet remaine aliue.

i For we confeſſe that, wͭ we beleue.

k All perfectiō on euerie ſide is in him.

Rom.16,25.

l That all the graces of God may abounde in you.

m In that we fele Chriſt in vs.

CHAP. IIII.

He exhorteth them vnto mekenes, long ſuffering, vnto loue and peace. 3 Euerie one to ſerue and edifie another with the gift that God hathe giuen him. 14 To beware of ſtrange doctrine. 22 To lay aſide the olde conuerſation of griedie luſtes, and to walke in a newe life.

1 I *Therefore, beīg priſoner in yͤ [a] Lord,
praye you that ye walke worthie of the
vocation whereunto ye are called,
2 With all humblenes of minde, and mekenes, with long ſuffring, ſupporting one

Phil.1,27. col.1,10. 1.theſſ.2,12.

a For yͤ Lords cauſe.

another through loue,
3 Endeuoring to kepe the vnitie of the Spi
rit in the bonde of peace.
4 There *is* [b] one bodie, and one [c] Spirit, e-
uen as ye are called in one hope of your
vocation.
5 *There is* one Lord, one Faith, one Baptiſme,
6 *One God & Father of all, which is [d] aboue all, and [e] through all, & in you all.
7 *But vnto euerie one of vs is giuen grace, according to the meaſure of the [f] gift
of Chriſt.
8 Wherefore he ſaith, *When he aſcended
vp on hie, he [g] led captiuitie captiue, and
gaue giftes vnto men.
9 (Now, in that he aſcended, what is it but
that he had alſo deſcended firſt into the lo
weſt partes of the earth?
10 He that deſcēded, is euen the ſame that
aſcended, farre aboue all heauens, that he
might fill [h] all things)
11 *He therefore gaue ſome *to be* Apoſtles,
and ſome Prophetes, & ſome Euāgeliſtes,
and ſome Paſtours, and Teachers,
12 For the [i] gathering together of the Saintes, for the worke of the miniſterie, [k] *and*
for the edificatiō of the bodie of Chriſt,
13 Til we all mete together (in the vnitie of
faith & knowledge of the Sonne of God)
vnto a [l] perfite man, *&* vnto the meaſure
of the age of the fulnes of Chriſt,
14 That we hence forthe be no more children, wauering & caryed about with euerie winde of doctrine, by the deceit of mē,
and with craftines, whereby they laye in
waite to deceiue.
15 But let vs followe the trueth in loue, and
in all things growe vp into him, which is
the [m] head, *that is* Chriſt,
16 By whome all the bodie being coupled
and knit together by euerie ioynt, for the
furniture *thereof* (according to the effectual power, *which is* in the meaſure of e-
uerie parte) receiueth increaſe of yͤ bodie,
vnto the edifying of it ſelf in loue.
17 This I ſay therefore and teſtifie in the
Lord, that ye henceforthe walke not as
*other Gentiles walke, in vanitie of their
[n] minde,
18 Hauing their cogitation darkened, and
being ſtrangers from the life of [o] God
through the ignorāce that is in them, becauſe of the [p] hardenes of their heart:
19 Which being "paſt *feling, haue giuen
them ſelues vnto wantonnes, to worke all
vnclennes, *euen* with griedines.
20 But ye haue not ſo learned Chriſt.
21 If ſo be ye haue heard him, and haue be
ne taught by him, as the [q] trueth is in Ieſus,
22 *That is*, *that ye caſt of, concerning the

q As they are taught which truely knowe Chriſt.

b Which by diſſentiōs you ſeparate aſonder.

c So that ye can not diſſent one from another, ſeing the Spirit, which ioyneth you in one bodie, can not diſſent frō him ſelf.

Mal.2,10.

d In power.

e By his prouidence.

Rom.12,3. 1.cor.12,11.

f Which he giueth vs.

2.Cor.10,13. pſal.68,19.

g The Meſſias came downe from heauen into the earth, to triumph ouer Satā, death and ſinne, and led thē as priſoners & ſclaues, wͭ before were conquerers, and kept all in ſubiectiō: which victorie he gate and alſo gaue it as a moſt precious gift to his Church.

1.Cor.12,27.

h With his gifts & benefites.

i To reſtore yͭ which was out of order.

k That the bodie of Chriſt might be perfect.

l That we may be of a ripe Chriſtiā age & come to yͤ ful meaſure of yͤ knowledge wͭ we ſhal haue of Chriſt.

m Chriſt being head of his Church, nouriſheth his mēbres & ioyneth them together by iointes, ſo that euerie parte hathe his iuſte proportion of fode, that at length the bodie may grow vp to perfectiō.

n Man not regenerat hathe his minde, vnderſtanding & heart corrupt.

o By yͤ which God liueth in his.

p The hardenes of heart is the founteine of ignorāce.

1.Tim.4,2.

" Or, without remorſe of conſcience.

Col.3,12.

con-

conuersation in time past, the [r] olde man,
which is corrupt through the deceiueable
lustes,
23 And be renewed in the spirit of your
minde,
24 *And put on the new man, which [ſ] after
God is created in righteousnes, and trye
holines.
25 *Wherefore cast of lying, & speake euerie man trueth vnto his neighbour: for we
are members one of another.
26 *Be [t] angry, but sinne not: let not the sunne go downe vpon your wrath,
27 *Nether giue place to the deuil.
28 Let him that stole, steale no more: but
let him rather labour and worke with his
hãds the thing which is good, that he may
haue to giue vnto him that nedeth.
29 *Let no corrupt communication procede out of your mouths: but that which is
good, to the vse of edifying, that it may
minister [u] grace vnto the hearers.
30 And [x] grieue not the holie Spirit of God
by whome ye are sealed vnto the day of
redemption.
31 Let all bitternes, and angre, and wrath,
crying, and euil speaking be put away frõ
you, with all maliciousnes.
32 *Be ye courteous one to another, & tender hearted, forgiuing one another, euen
as God for Christs sake forgaue you.

r That is, all the natural corruption that is in vs.

Rom.6,4. col.3,8. ebr.12,2. 1.pet.2,1. & 4,2. Zacha.8,16.

ſ Which is created according to ỹ image of God.

Psal.4,5. Iam.4,7.

t If so be that ye be angry, so moderat your affection, that it burst not out into any euil worke, but be sone apeased.

Chap.5,3. col.4,6.

u And cause them to profit in godlines.

x So behaue your selues ỹ the holie Gost may willingly dwel in you, & giue him no occasion to departe for sorrow by your abusing of Gods graces.

Col.3,19.

CHAP. V.

2 He exhorteth them vnto loue, 3 Warneth them to beware of vnclennes, couetousnes, foolish talking, and false doctrine, 17 To be circumspecte. 18 To auoide dronkennes. 19 To reioyce and to be thankeful towarde God, 21 To submit them selues one to another. 22 He entreateth of corporal mariage and of the spiritual betwixt Christ and his Church.

1 Be ye therefore followers of God, as
dere children,
2 *And walke in loue, euen as Christ hathe
loued vs, and hathe giuen him self for vs,
to be an offring and a sacrifice of a swete
[a] smelling sauour to God.
3 *But fornication, & all vnclennes, or couetousnes, let it not be once named amõg
you, as it becommeth Saintes,
4 Nether filthines, nether foolish talking,
nether [b] iesting, which are things not comelie, but rather giuing of thankes.
5 For this ye knowe, that no whoremõger,
nether vncleane persone, nor couetous
persone, which is [c] an idolater, hathe any
inheritance in the kingdome of Christ, &
of God.
6 *Let no [d] man deceiue you with vaine
wordes: for for suche things commeth the
wrath of God vpon the children of diso
bedience.
7 Be not therefore companions with them.
8 For ye were once darkenes, but are now
light in the Lord: walke as [e] children of
light,
9 (For the frute of the Spirit *is* in all goodnes, and righteousnes, and trueth)
10 Approuing that which is pleasing to the
Lord.
11 And haue no fellowship with ỹ vnfruteful workes of darkenes, but euen [f] reproue
them rather.
12 For it is shame euẽ to speake of ỹ things,
which are done of them in secret.
13 But all things when they are reproued of
the [g] light, are manifest: for it is light that
maketh all things manifest.
14 Wherefore he saith, [h] Awake thou that
slepest, & stãd vp from the dead, & Christ
shal giue thee light.
15 Take hede therefore that ye walke cir-
cumspectly, not as fooles, but as *wise,
16 [i] Redeming the time: for the [k] dayes are
euil.
17 *Wherefore, be ye not vnwise, but vnderstand what the wil of the Lord is.
18 And be not drunke with wine, wherein
is excesse: but be fulfilled with the Spirit,
19 Speaking vnto your selues in psalmes,
and "hymnes, and spiritual songs, singing,
and making melodie to the Lord in your
[l] hearts,
20 Giuing thãkes alwaise for all things vnto God euen the Father, in the Name of
our Lord Iesus Christ,
21 Submitting your selues one to another
in the [m] feare of God.
22 ¶ *Wiues, submit your selues vnto your
housbands, as vnto the Lord.
23 *For the housband is the wiues head, euẽ
as Christ is the head of the Church, & the
same is the sauiour of *his* [n] bodie.
24 Therefore as the Church is in subiectiõ
to Christ, euen so *let* the wiues *be* to their
housbands in euerie thing.
25 ¶ * Housbands, loue your wiues, euen as
Christ loued the Church, & gaue him self
for it,
26 That he might sanctifie it, & clẽse it by
the [o] washing of water through ỹ worde,
27 That he might make it vnto him self a
glorious Church, not hauĩg [p] spot or wrin
cle, or anie suche thing: but that it shulde
be holie and without blame.
28 So oght men to loue their wiues, as their
owne bodies: he that loueth his wife, loueth him self.
29 For no mã euer yet hated his owne flesh,
but nourisheth & cherisheth it, euẽ as the
Lord *doeth* the Church.
30 For we are mẽbers of his bodie, [q] of his
flesh, and of his bones.

Iohn 13,24. & 15,12. 1.iohn 3,23.

a Alluding to the perfumes and incẽsing in the Law.

Mar.7,21. chap 4,19. col.3,5. 2.thess.2,17.

b Which is ether vaine, or els by exãple and euil speaking may hurt your neighbour: for other wise there be diuers exãples in the Scriptures of pleasant talke, which is also godlie, as 1 King.18,27.

c Because he thinketh that his life standeth in his riches.

Mat.24,4. mar.13,5. luk.21,8. 2.thess.2,3.

d Ether in excusing sinne, or in mocking at the menaces, and iudgements of God.

e Seing God hathe adopted you for his, ỹ ye shulde be holie.

f And make them knowen by your honest and godlie life.

g The worde of God discouereth the vices which were hid before.

h God thus speaketh by his seruants to drawe the infideles frõ their blindenes.

Colos.4,5.

i Selling all worldlie pleasures to bye time.

Rom 12,2. 1.thes.4,3.

k In these perilous dayes & crafte of the aduersaries, take hede how to bye againe the occasions of godlines, ỹ the worlde hathe taken from you.

" Or, songs of praise and thãkesgiuing.

l And not onely with tongue.

Col.3,18. tit.2,5. 1.pet.3,1. 1.Cor.11,3.

m Except our friendship be ioyned, & knit in God, it is not to be estemed

n The Church: so the housband oght to nourish, gouerne and defend his wife from perils.

Col 3,19.

o Baptisme is a token that God hathe cõsecrated the Church to him self, and made it holie by his worde: that is, his promes of fre iustification, and sanctification in Christ.

p Because it is couered and cledde with Christs iustice and holines.

q This our coniunction with Christ must be considered as Christ is the housband, and we the wife, which are not onely ioyned to him by nature, but also by the cõmunion of substance, through the holie Gost and by faith: the seale and testimonie thereof is the Supper of the Lord.

Gen.2,24. mat.19.5. mar.10,7. 1.cor.6,16.

31 *For this cause shal a man leaue father &
mother, & shal cleaue to his wife, & they
twaine shalbe one flesh.
32 This is a great secret, but I speake concerning Christ, & cōcerning the Church.
33 Therefore euerie one of you, *do ye so*: let
euerie one loue his wife, euē as him self, &
let the wife *se* that she feare her housband.

CHAP. VI.

1 How children shulde behaue them selues towarde their fathers and mothers, 4 Likewise parents towarde their children, 5 Seruants towarde their masters, 9 Masters towarde their seruants. 13 An exhortation to the spiritual battel and what weapons the Christians shulde fight with all.

Colos.3,20.

1 CHildren, * obey your parents in the
Lord: for this is right.

Exo.20,12. deut.5,16. eccle.3,10. mat.15,4. mar.7,10.

a This is the first commandement of the seconde table and hathe the promes with condition.

2 *Honour thy father and mother (which is
the first commandement with [a] promes)
3 That it may be wel with thee, and that
thou maist liue long on earth.
4 And ye, fathers, prouoke not your childrē
to [b] wrath: but bring them vp in [c] instruction and information of the Lord.

b By austeritie

Col.3,22. tit.2,9. 1.pet.2,18.

c That they be not broght vp in wātōnes, but in the feare of the Lord

d Which haue dominion ouer your bodies, but not ouer ye soules.

°Or, bothe yours & their masters

e Whether he be seruant or master.

5 *Seruants, be obedient vnto them that are
your masters, [d] according to the flesh, with
feare and trembling in singlenes of your
hearts as vnto Christ,
6 Not with seruice to the eye, as men pleasers, but as the seruants of Christ, doing
the wil of God from the heart,
7 With good wil seruing the Lord, and
not men.
8 And knowe ye that whatsoeuer good
thing any man doeth, that same shal he receiue of the Lord, whether *he be* bonde
or fre.
9 And ye masters, do the same things vnto
them, putting away threatning: & knowe
that euen "your master also is in heauē, nether is there * [e] respect of persone wt him.
10 ¶ Finally, my brethren, be strong in the
Lord, and in the power of his might.
11 Put on the " whole armour of God, that
ye may be able to stand against the assauts
of the deuil.
12 For we wrestle not against [f] flesh and

Deu.10,17. 2.chro.19,7. iob.34,19. wisdo.6,8. eccle.35,16. act.10,34. rom.2,11. gal 2,6. col.3.25. 1.pet.1,17.

°Or, complet harnesse.

f The faithful haue not only to striue agaīst men and them selues, but against Satan the spiritual enemie, who is moste dangerous: for he is ouer our heades so that we can not reache him, but he must be resisted by Gods grace.

blood, but against * principalities, against
powers, *and* against the worldlie gouernours, *the princes* of the darkenes of this
worlde, agaīst spiritual wickednesses, *which*
are in the hie places.
13 For this cause take vnto you the whole
armour of God, that ye may be able to resist in the euil daye, & hauing finished all
things, stand fast.
14 Stand therefore, and your loines girde
about with veritie, & hauing on the brest
plate of [g] righteousnes,
15 And your fete shod with the [h] preparation of the Gospel of peace.
16 Aboue all, take the shield of faith, wherewith ye may quench all the fyrie dartes of the wicked,
17 *And take the helmet of [i] saluation, and
the sworde of ye Spirit, which is the worde
of God.
18 And pray alwaise with all maner prayer
and supplicatiō in the Spirit: and * watch
thereunto with all perseuerāce and suppli
cation for all Saintes,
19 *And for me, that vtterance may be giuē
vnto me, that I may open my mouth boldely to publish the secret of the Gospel,
20 Whereof I am the ambassadour in bondes, that therein I may speake boldely, as
I oght to speake.
21 ¶ But that ye may also knowe mine affaires, & what I do, Tychicus *my* deare brother and faithful minister in the Lord, shal
shewe you of all things,
22 Whome I haue sent vnto you for ye same
purpose, that ye might knowe mine affaires, & that he might comfort your hearts.
23 Peace *be* with the brethren, and loue with
faith from God the Father, and *from* the
Lord Iesus Christ.
24 Grace *be* with all them which loue our
Lord Iesus Christ, to *their* [k] immortalitie,
Amen.

Written from Rome vnto the Ephesians,
& sent by Tychicus.

Chap.2,2.

g Innocencie & godlie life.

h That ye may be ready to suffer all thīgs for the Gospel

Isa.59,17. 1 thes.5,8.

i The saluatiō purchased by Iesus Christ.

Col.4,3.

2.Thess.3,1.

k Or to be without corruptiō, that is, to haue life euerlasting, which is the end of this grace.

THE EPISTLE OF Paul to the Philippians.

THE ARGVMENT.

PAul being warned by the holie Gost to go to Macedonia, planted first a Church at Philippi a citie of the same countrey: but because his charge was to preache the Gospel vniuersally to all the Gentiles, he trauailed from place to place, til at the length he was taken prisoner at Rome, whereof the Philippians, being aduertised, sent their minister Epaphroditus with relief vnto him: who declaring him the state of the Church, caused him to write this Epistle, wherein he commendeth them that they stode manfully against the false apostles, putting them in minde of his good wil towarde them, and exhorteth them that his imprisonment make them not to shrinke: for the Gospel thereby was confirmed and not diminished: especially he desireth them to flee ambition, and to

embrace

embrace modestie, promising to send Timotheus vnto them, who shulde instruct them in matters more amply yea, and that he him self wolde also come vnto them, adding likewise the cause of their ministers so long abode. And because there were no greater enemies to the crosse then the false apostles, he cōfuteth their false doctrine, by prouing onely Christ to be the end of all true religion, with whome we haue all thing, and without whome we haue nothing, so that his death is our life, and his resurrection our iustification. After this followe certeine admonitions bothe particular and general, with testification of his affection towarde them, and thankeful accepting of their beneuolence.

CHAP. I.

1 S. Paul discouereth his heart towarde them. 3 By his thankes giuing, 4 Prayers, 8 And wishes for their faith and saluation. 7. 12. 20. He sheweth the frute of his crosse. 15. 27 And exhorteth them to vnitie, 28 And pacience.

1 PAul & Timotheus the
seruants of IESVS
CHRIST, to all the
Saintes in Christ Iesus
which are at Philippi,
with the [a] Bisshops, and
Deacons:
2 Grace *be* with you, and peace from God
our Father, & *from* the Lord Iesus Christ.
3 *I thanke my God *hauing* you in perfect
memorie,
4 (Alwaise in all my prayers for all you,
praying with gladnes)
5 Because of the [b] fellowship which ye haue in the Gospel, from the [c] first day vnto
now.
6 And I am persuaded of this same thing
that he that hathe begone *this* good worke
in you, wil performe it vntil the [d] day of
Iesus Christ,
7 As it becometh me so to iudge of you all
because I haue you in remembrāce [e] that
bothe in my bādes, and in *my* defense, and
confirmation of the Gospel you all were
partakers of my [f] grace.
8 For God is my recorde, how I long after
you all from the verie heart rote in Iesus
Christ.
9 And this I pray, that your loue may abūde, yet more and more in knowledge, and
in all iudgement,
10 That ye may discerne things that "differ *one from another*, that ye may be pure,
and [g] without offence, vntil the day of
Christ,
11 Filled with the frutes of [h] righteousnes,
which are by Iesus Christ vnto the glorie
and praise of God.
12 ¶I wolde ye vnderstode, brethren, that
the things which *haue come* vnto me, a-
re turned rather to the furthering of the
Gospel,
13 So that my bādes in [i] Christ are famous
throughout all the [k] iudgement hall, and
in all other *places*,
14 In so muche that manie of the brethren
in the Lord are boldned through my bandes, and dare more frankely speake the
[l] worde.

a By bisshops here he meaneth them that had charge of the worde & gouerning, as pastours doctors, elders: by deacons, suche as had charge of the distribution, & of the poore and sicke.
1. Thess. 1, 2.
b With other Churches.
c That ye receiued the Gospel.
d When you shal receiue the crowne of glorie.
e It was a sure token of their loue, that they did helpe him by all meanes possible, when he was absent, & in prison, euen as if they had bene prisoners with him.
f Of this peculiar benefite to suffer for Christs sake.
"Or, are excellēt
g That you so increase in godlines that not onely ye can put difference betwene good & euil: but also that ye profit more and more without slippīg backe, or standing in a staye.
h Righteousnes is the tre, good workes the frute.
i Which I susteine for Christs cause.
k That is, in the court or Palais of the Emperour Nero.
l Or, professe the Gospel, cōsidering my cōstancie.

15 Some preache Christ euē through enuie
and strife, and some also of good wil.
16 The one parte preacheth Christ of contention *&* not [m] purely, supposing to adde more affliction to my bandes.
17 But the others of loue, knowing that I
"am set for the defense of the Gospel.
18 What then? yet Christ is preached all
maner wayes, whether *it* [n] *be* vnder a pretence, or syncerely: and I therein ioye: yea,
and wil ioye.
19 For I knowe that this shal turne to my
saluation, through your prayer, & by the
helpe of the Spirit of Iesus Christ,
20 As I hartely loke for, and hope, that in
nothing I shalbe ashamed, but that with
all confidence, as all wayes, so now Christ
shal be magnified in my bodie, whether *it*
be by life or by death.
21 For Christ *is* to me bothe in life, and in
death aduantage.
22 And whether to [o] liue in the flesh *we-*
re profitable for me, and what to chose I
know not.
23 For I am greatly in doute on bothe sides, desiring to be losed and to be with
Christ, which is beste of all.
24 Neuertheles, to abide in the "flesh *is* more nedeful for you.
25 And this am I sure of, that I shal abide,
and with you all continue, for your furtherance and ioye of *your* faith,
26 That ye may more abundantly reioyce
in Iesus Christ for me, by my comming to
you againe.
27 *Onely let your cōuersation be, as it becometh ẏ Gospel of Christ, that whether
I come and se you, or els be absent, I may
heare of your matters that ye "continue in
one Spirit, *&* in one minde fighting together through the faith of the Gospel.
28 And in nothing feare your aduersaries,
which is to them a [p] token of perdition, &
to you of saluation, and [q] that of God.
29 For vnto you it is giuen "for Christ, that
not onely ye shulde beleue in him, but also suffer for his sake,
30 Hauing the same fight, which ye sawe
in me, and now heare *to be* in me.

CHAP. II.

3 He exhorteth them aboue all things to humilitie, whereby pure doctrine is chiefly mainteined. 19 Promising that he and Timotheus wil spedily come vnto them. 27 And excuseth the long tarying of Epaphroditus.

m But with a corrupt minde
"Or, lie in bādes
n Their pretēce was to preache Christ, & therefore their doctrine was true: but they were ful of ambition & enuie thinking to deface Paul & preferre them selues.
o To liue in the flesh is to liue in this brittel bodie, til we be called to liue euerlastingly: but to liue according to the flesh or to be in the flesh, signifie, to be destitute of the Spirit and to be plonged in the filthie concupiscences of the flesh.
"Or, bodie.
Ephes. 4, 1. col. 1, 10. 1. thess. 2, 12.
"Or, stand.
p The more ẏ tyrants rage against the Gospel, the more manifestly they declare that thei runne to their owne destruction: and againe constāt perseuerance for Christs sake is an euident signe of saluation.
q God sheweth by this meanes of bearing the crosse who are his, and who are not.
"Or, Christs cause.

1 IF *there be* therefore anie [a] consolation
in Christ, if anie cõfort of loue, if anie
felowship of the Spirit, if anie compassion
and mercie,
2 Fulfil my ioye, that ye be like minded, hauing the same loue, being of one accorde,
and of [b] one iudgement,
3 That nothing *be done* through contentiõ
or vaine glorie, but that in mekenes of min
de * euerie man esteme other better then
him self.
4 Loke not euerie mã on his owne things,
but euerie man also on the things of o-
ther men.
5 Let the same minde be in you that was
euen in Christ Iesus,
6 Who [c] being in the forme of God, thoght
it no [d] robbery to be equal with God:
7 *But he made him self of no reputation,
and toke on him the [e] forme of a seruant,
and was made like vnto men, and was fou-
de in [f] shape as a man.
8 *He humbled him self, and became obedient vnto the death, euen the death of
the crosse.
9 Wherefore God hathe also highly exalted him, and giuen him a Name aboue
euerie name,
10 *That at the Name of Iesus shulde euerie [g] knee bowe, *bothe* of things in heauen,
and things in earth, and things vnder the
earth,
11 *And that euerie tongue shulde confesse that Iesus Christ *is* the Lord, vnto the
glorie of God the Father.
12 Wherefore my beloued, as ye haue alwaise obeyed, not as in my presence onely,
but now muche more in mine absence, *so*
[h] make an end of your owne saluatiõ with
[i] feare and trembling.
13 For it is God which worketh in you, bothe the wil and the dede, *euen* of *his* [k] good
pleasure.
14 Do all things without *murmuring and
reasonings,
15 That ye may be blameles, and pure, *&*
the sonnes of God without rebuke in the
middes of a naughtie and croked nation,
among whome ye shine as * lights in the
worlde,
16 [l] Holding forthe the [m] worde of life, that
I may reioyce in the day of Christ, that I
haue not runne in vaine, nether haue labored in vaine.
17 Yea, and thogh I be [n] offered vp vpon
the sacrifice, and seruice [o] of your faith, I
am glad, and reioyce with you all.
18 For the same cause also be ye glad, and
reioyce with me.
19 And I trust in the Lord Iesus, to send

a If you so loue me that you desire my comforte.

b From the cõsent of wils & mindes he procedeth to the agrement in doctrine, that there might be ful and perfect concorde.

Rom.12,10.

Mat.20,28.

c If Christ being verie God equal with ỹ Father, laid aside his glorie, and being Lord, became a seruant, and willingly submitted him self to moste shameful death, shal we which are nothing but vile sclaues, through arrogancie treade downe our brethren, & preferre our selues?

Ebr.2,9.

d For he that was God, shulde haue done none iniurie to the Godhead.

Rom.14,11. Isa.45,23. Iohn 13,13. 1.cor.8,6. & 12,3.

e The poore and weake nature of man.

f He was sene and heard of men, so that his behauiour and persone declared that he was as a miserable man.

1.Pet.4,9.

g Worship, & be subiect to him.

Mat.5,19.

h Runne forwarde in that race of righteousnes, wherein God hathe frely placed you through Iesus Christ and cõducteth you his children by his Spirit to walke in good workes, and so to make your vocation sure.

i Which may make you careful & diligent. k Which is his fre grace.
l As they which in the night set forthe a candle to giue light to others.
m The Gospel. n The worde signifieth to power out as the drinke offring was powred on the sacrifice. o To confirme you in your faith.

*Timotheus shortly vnto you, that I also
may be of good comforte, when I knowe
your state.
20 For I haue no man like minded, who
wil faithfully care for your matters.
21 *For all [p] seke their owne, *&* not ỹ which
is Iesus Christs.
22 But ye knowe the profe of him, that as a
sonne with ỹ father, he hathe serued with
me in the Gospel.
23 Him therefore I hope to send assone as I
knowe how it wil go with me,
24 And trust in the Lord, that I also my self
shal come shortly.
25 But I supposed it necessarie to send *my*
brother Epaphroditus vnto you, my companion in labour, and fellowe souldier, euẽ
your messenger, and he that ministred vnto me suche things as I wanted.
26 For he longed after all you, and was ful
of heauines, because ye had heard, that he
had bene sicke.
27 And no doute he was sicke, verie nere vnto death: but God had mercie on
him, & not on him onely, but on me also,
lest I shulde haue sorowe vpon sorowe.
28 I sent him therefore the more diligẽtly,
that when ye shulde se him againe, ye
might reioyce, and I might be the lesse
sorowful.
29 Receiue him therefore in the Lord with
all gladnes, and make muche of suche:
30 Because that for [q] the worke of Christ
he [r] was nere vnto death, & regarded not
his life, to fulfil that seruice which was
lacking on your parte towarde me.

Act.16,1.

1.Cor.10,24.

p They rather soght profite by their preaching then Gods glorie.

q He calleth it here ỹ worke of Christ to visit Christ who was bõde in the persone of Paul, & was in nede of necessaries

r He approueth them ỹ hazard their life to relieue the prisoners of Christ.

CHAP. III.

2 *He warneth them to beware of false teachers. 3 Against whome he setteth Christ. 4 Likewise him self. 9 And his doctrine. 12 And reproueth mans owne righteousnes.*

1 MOreouer, my brethren, reioyce in
the Lord. It grieueth me not to wri
te [a] the same things to you, and for you it
is a sure thing.
2 Beware of [b] dogges: beware of euil workers: beware of the [c] concision.
3 For we are the circumcision, which worship God in the spirit, & reioyce in Christ
Iesus, & haue no confidence [d] in the flesh:
4 Thogh I might also haue confidence in
the flesh. If anie other man thinketh that
he hathe whereof he might trust in ỹ flesh,
muche more I:
5 Circumcised the eight day, of the kinred
of Israel, of the tribe of Beniamin, * an E-
brewe of ỹ Ebrewes, *by the law a Pharise.
6 Cõcerning zeale, I persecuted ỹ Church:
touching the righteousnes which is in the
Law, I was vnrebukeable.
7 But ỹ things that were vantage vnto me,
the same I counted losse for Christs sake.
8 Yea, doutles I thinke all things but losse
for the

a Which ye haue often heard of me.

b Which barke against the true doctrine to fil their bellies.

c The false apostles gloried in their circũcision, whereunto S. Paul here alludeth, calling them concision, ỹ is cutting of and tearing asundre of the Church.

d In outward things.

1.Cor.11,22. Act.23,6.

Or, profession.

for the excellēt knowledge sake of Christ
Iesus my Lord, for whome I haue coūted
all things losse, and do iudge *them* to be
dongue, that I might winne Christ,
9 And might be [e] founde in him, *that is*, not
hauing mine owne righteousnes, which is
of the Law, but that which is through the
faith of Christ, *euen* ỳ righteousnes which
is of God through faith,
10 That I may knowe him, and the vertue
of his resurrection, and the fellowship of
his afflictions, and be made conformable
vnto his death,
11 If by anie meanes I might atteine vnto
the [f] resurrection of the dead:
12 [g] Not as thogh I had alreadie atteined
to it, ether were alreadie perfect: but I followe, if that I may comprehende *that* for
whose sake also I am [h] comprehended of
Christ Iesus.
13 Brethren, I counte not my self, that I haue atteined *to it*, but one thing *I do*: I forget
that which is behinde, and endeuoure my
self vnto that which is before,
14 And followe hard toward the [i] marke,
for the prise of the hie calling of God in
Christ Iesus.
15 Let vs therefore as manie as [k] be [l] perfect, be thus minded: and if ye be otherwise minded, God shal reueile euē the[m] same vnto you.
16 Neuertheles, *in that* whereunto we are
come, let vs procede by one rule, * that we
may minde one thing.
17 Brethren, be folowers of me, and loke
on them, which walke so, as ye haue vs for
an ensample.
18 *For manie walke, of whome I haue tolde you often, & now tell you weping, *that
they are* the enemies of the [n] Crosse of
Christ,
19 Whose " end *is* damnacion, whose God
is their belie, and *whose* [o] glorie *is* to their
shame, which minde earthlie things.
20 But our [p] conuersacion is in heauen, frō
whence also we loke for the *Sauiour, *euen*
the Lord Iesus Christ,
21 Who shal change our vile bodie, that it
may be facioned like vnto his glorious
bodie, according to the working, whereby
he is able euen to subdue all things vnto
him self.

e As one grafted in him by faith.
f That is, to life euerlastīg.
g Or haue now taken ful possession thereof, not that he douted to atteine vnto it, but because he wolde declare the excellēcie thereof.
h We can rūne no further thē God giueth vs strength, and sheweth vs ỳ way.
i That is, to obteine the croune of glorie in the heauens
k Or, haue more profited thē others
Rom.15,5. 1.cor 1,10.
l This perfection standeth in forsaking sinne, & to be renued through faith by him which is onely perfite.
Rom 16,17.
m That is, that this is ỳ true wisdome, and straight rule of liuing
n That is, of the Gospel, ẇ is ỳ preaching of the crosse.
" *Or, rewarde.*
1.Cor.1,7. tite 2,11.
o The vaine glorie which thei seke after in this worlde, shal turne to their confusiō, and shame.
p In minde, & affection.

CHAP. IIII.

1 He exhorteth them to be of honest conuersacion, 15 And thanketh them because of the prouision that they made for him being in prison, 21 And so concludeth with salutacions.

1 THerefore, my brethren, beloued and
longed for, *my* ioy and my crowne, so
continue in the Lord, ye beloued.
2 I pray Euodias, & beseche Syntyche, that
they be of one accorde in the Lord.
3 Yea, and I beseche thee, faithful yokefe-
lowe, helpe those *women*, which laboured
with me in the Gospel, with Clemente also, and with other my felowe laborers,
whose names *are* in the * [a] boke of life.
4 Reioyce in the Lord alway, againe I say,
reioyce.
5 Let your patient minde be knowen vnto
all men. The Lord *is* [b] at hand.
6 * Be nothing careful, but in all things let
your requestes be shewed vnto God in
praier, and supplicacion with giuing of
thankes.
7 And the peace of God which passeth all
vnderstanding, shal [c] preserue your hearts
and mindes in Christ Iesus.
8 Furthermore, brethrē, whatsoeuer things
are true, whatsoeuer things *are* honest,
whatsoeuer things *are* iust, whatsoeuer
things *are* pure, whatsoeuer things perteine to loue, whatsoeuer things *are* of good
reporte, if there *be* anie vertue, or if there
be anie praise, thinke on these things,
9 Which ye haue bothe learned and receiued, and heard, and sene in me: those thīgs
do, and the God of peace shalbe with you.
10 Now I reioyce also in the Lord greatly,
that now at the last ye are [d] reuiued aga-
ne to care for me, wherein notwithstādīng
ye were careful, but ye lacked opportunitie.
11 I speake not because of [e] want: for I haue learned in whatsoeuer state I am, therewith to be content.
12 And I can be abased, and I can abunde:
euerie where in all things I am instructed
bothe to be ful, and to be hongrie, and to
abunde, and to haue want.
13 I am able to *do* all things through the
helpe of [f] Christ, which stregtheneth me.
14 Notwithstanding ye haue wel done, that
ye did communicate to mine affliction.
15 And ye Philippians knowe also that in
the [g] beginning of the Gospel, when I departed from Macedonia, no Church communicated with me cōcerning the [h] matter of giuing and receiuing, but ye onely.
16 For euen *when I was* in Thessalonica, ye
sent once, and afterwarde againe for my
necessitie,
17 Not that I desire a gift: but I desire the
frute which may " further your reckening.
18 Now I haue receiued all, and haue plentie: I was euen filled, after that I had receiued of Epaphroditus that which *came*
from you, an odour that smelleth swete, a
sacrifice acceptable and pleasant to God.
19 And my God shal fulfil all your necessities through his riches with glorie in Iesus
Christ.
20 Vnto God euen our Father *be* praise for
euermore, Amen.
21 Salute all the Saintes in Christ Iesus.
The brethren, which are ẇ me, grete you.

Psal.69,28. luk 10,20. reuel.3 5. & 20,8 & 21,27. Mat.6,25.
a This boke Ezekiel calleth the writing of the house of Israel, & ỳ secret of the Lord, Chap.13,9.
b To succour you.
c From Satan, who seketh to take from vs this peace of conscience.
d That is, beginne anew to helpe me.
e That I was not able to endure my pouertie.
f Not of his owne vertue or fre wil.
g When I first preached the Gospel vnto you.
h He had giuē of his parte in communicatīg ẇ them spiritual things, but he receiued nothing of them, ẇ oght at least to haue relieued him in his necessitie.
" *Or, abunde towarde your conte.*

22 All the Saintes salute you, and moste
of all they which are of [i] Cesars housholde.
23 The grace of our Lord Iesus Christ *be*
with you all, Amen.

i Of suche as did belong to the Emperour Nero.

Written to the Philippians from Rome, *&* *sent* by Epaphroditus.

THE EPISTLE OF Paul to the Colossians.

THE ARGUMENT.

IN this Epistle S. Paul putteth difference betwene the liuelie, effectual and true Christ, and the fained, contrefait and imagined Christ, whome the false apostles taught. And first, he confirmeth the doctrine which Epaphras had preached, wisshing them increase of faith, to esteme the excellēcie of Gods benefite towarde them, teaching them also that saluacion, and whatsoeuer good thing can be desired, standeth onely in Christ, whome onely we embrace by the Gospel. But forasmuche as the false brethrē wolde haue mixed the Law with the Gospel, he toucheth those flatterers vehemently, and exhorteth the Colossians to staye onely on Christ, without whome all things are but mere vanitie. And as for Circumcision, abstinence from meates, external holines, worshiping of Angels as meanes whereby to come to Christ, he vtterly condemneth; shewing what was the office and nature of ceremonies, which by Christ are abrogate: so that now the exercises of the Christians stande in mortificacion of the flesh, newenes of life, with other like offices apperteining bothe generally & particularly to all the faithful.

CHAP. I.

3 He giueth thankes vnto God for their faith. 7 Confirmeth the doctrine of Epaphras. 9 Praieth for the increase of their faith. 13 He sheweth vnto them the true Christ, and discouereth the contrefait Christ of the false apostles. 25 He approueth his autoritie & charge, 28 And of his faithful executing of the same.

1 PAul an Apostle of Iesus
Christ, by ẏ wil of God,
& Timotheus *our* bro-
ther,
2 To thē, which are at
[a] Colosse, Saītes & faith
ful brethren in Christ:
Grace *be* with you, & peace from God our
Father, and *from* the Lord Iesus Christ.
3 We giue thankes to God euē the Father
of our Lord Iesus Christ, alwaies praying
for you:
4 Since we heard of your faith [b] in Christ
Iesus, and of *your* loue towarde all Saintes,
5 For the hopes sake, which is layd vp for
you in heauen, whereof ye haue heard before by the worde of trueth, *which is* the
Gospel,
6 Which is come vnto you, euen as *it is* vnto all the worlde, and is fruteful, as *it is* also among you, from the day that ye heard
and truely knewe the grace of God,
7 As ye also learned of Epaphras our deare felowe seruant, which is for you a faithful minister of Christ:
8 Who hathe also declared vnto vs your
loue, *which ye haue* [c] by the Spirit.
9 For this cause we also, since the daye we
heard *of it*, cease not to pray for you, and
to desire that ye might be fulfilled with
knowledge of [d] his wil, in all wisdome, &
spiritual vnderstanding,
10 * That ye might walke worthie of the
Lord, and please *him* in all things, being
*fruteful in all good workes, and increa-
sing in the knowledge of God,
11 Strengthened with all might through
his glorious power, vnto all pacience, &
long suffring with ioyfulnes,
12 Giuing thankes vnto the Father, which
hathe made vs mete to be partakers of the
inheritance of the Saintes in light,
13 Who hathe deliuered vs from the power
of darkenes, and hathe translated vs into
the kingdome * of his deare Sonne,
14 In whome we haue redemption through
his blood, *that is*, the forgiuenes of sinnes,
15 Who is the * [e] image of the inuisible
God, the [f] first borne of euerie creature.
16 *For by him were all things created,
which are in heauen, and which are in
earth, things visible and inuisible: whether *they be* Thrones, or Dominions, or
Principalities, or Powers, all things were
created by him and for him,
17 And he is before all things, and in him
all things consist.
18 And he is the head of the bodie of the
Church: he is the beginning, * *&* [g] the first
borne of the dead, that in all things he
might haue the preeminence.
19 *For it pleased *the Father*, that in him
shulde all [h] fulnes dwell,
20 And by him to reconcile [i] all things vnto him self, and to set at peace through
the blood of his crosse bothe the things in

a Which was a citie of Phrygia.

b For without Christ there is no faith to be saued by, but onely a vaine opinion.

c Which cometh of the holie Gost.

d That is, Gods.

Ephes.4,1. philip.1,27. 1.thes.2,12. 1 Cor.1,5.

Mat.3,17. & 17,5. 2.pet.1,17.

e For God is made visible in the flesh of Christ, & the diuinitied welleth in him corporally.

Ebr.1,3.

f Borne before anie thing was created.

Iohn 1,3.

g He that rose first againe frō the dead to take possession of life euerlasting: which rising may be called a new birth.

1.Cor.15,20. reuel.1,5. Ioh.1,14. chap.2,9.

h That the Church, which is his bodie, might receiue of his abundāce.

i That is, the whole Church.

earth,and the things in heauen.
21 And you which were in times past strangers and enemies , because *your* mindes
were set in euil workes , hathe he now also
reconciled,
22 In the bodie of his flesh through death,
to make you* holie,and vnblameable and
without faute in his sight,
23 *If ye continue , grou̅ded and stablished
in the faith, and be not moued away from
the hope of the Gospel , whereof ye haue
heard, and which hathe bene preached to
euerie creature which is vnder heaue̅ whereof I Paul am a minister.
24 Now reioyce I in my suffrings for [k]you,
and fulfil [l] the rest of the afflictions of
Christ in my flesh , for his bodies sake,
which is the Church,
25 Whereof I am a minister , according to
the dispensatio̅ of God,which is giuen me
vnto youwarde , to fulfil the [m] worde of
God,
26 *Which *is* the mysterie hid since the worlde began,and from *all* ages,but now is made manifest to his [n] Saintes,
27 To whome God wolde make knowen
what is the riches of this glorious mysterie among the Gentiles, w^t^ *riches* is Christ
in you,*the hope of glorie,
28 Whome we preache,admonishing euerie man, and teaching euerie man in all
wisdome,that we may present euerie man
perfect in Christ Iesus*
29 Whereunto I also labour and striue, according to his working which worketh in
me mightely.

Luk.1,75.
1 cor.1,2.
ephe.1,4.
tit 2,11.
Ioh.15,6.

k Or your co̅moditie
l As Christ hathe once suffered in him self to redeme his Church, & to sanctifie it: so doeth he daily suffer in his members, as partaker of their infirmities , & therefore are ueger of their iniuries.
Rom.16,25.
ephes 3,9.
2.tim.1,10.
tit 1,2.
1.pet.1,20.
m Which is ye promises of Christ, and of the calling of the Gentiles.
1.Tim.1,1.
n Whome he hathe elected and consecrated to him by Christ.

CHAP. II.

1 Hauing protested his good wil towarde them, 4 He admonisheth them not to turne backe fro̅ Christ, 8 To the seruice of angels or anie other inuention, or els ceremonies of the Law, 17 Which haue finished their office,and are ended in Christ.

1 FOr I wolde ye knewe what great "figh
ting I haue for your sakes,and for the̅
of Laodicea,and for as manie as haue not
sene my [a] persone in the flesh,
2 That their hearts might be comforted &
they knit together in loue , and in all riches of the ful assurance of vnderstãding,
to knowe the mysterie of God euen the
Father,and of Christ:
In whome are hid all the treasures of wis-
3 dome and knowledge.
4 And this I say,lest anie mã shulde beguile you with entising wordes.
5 *For thogh I be absent in the [b] flesh, yet
am I with you in the [c] spirit reioycing,and
beholding your ordre, and your stedfast
faith in Christ.
6 As ye haue therefore receiued Christ Iesus the Lord,*so* walke in him,
7 Roted and buylt in him, and stablished
in the faith,as ye haue * bene taught,abu̅-

"Or, peine and care.
a Me present in bodie.
1.Cor.5,3.
b In bodie.
c In minde.
1.Cor.1,5.

ding therein with thankes giuing.
8 Beware lest there be anie man that spoile
you through [d] philosophie, and vaine deceit,through the traditions of men,accor-
ding to the rudiments of the worlde, and
not after Christ.
9 *For in him dwelleth all the fulnes of the
[e] Godhead "bodely.
10 And ye are compleate in him , which is
the head of all Principalitie and Power:
11 In whome also ye are circumcised with
* circumcision made without hãds,by putting of ye sinful bodie of the flesh, through
the circumcision [f] of Christ,
12 In that ye are*buryed with him through
baptisme, in whome ye are also raised vp
together through * the faith [g] of the operation of God which raised him from the
dead.
13 *And ye which were dead in sinnes, and
in the vncircumcisio̅ of your flesh, hathe
he quickened together with him,forgiuĩg
" you all *your* trespaces.
14 And putting out the *" [h] hand writing
of ordinances that was against vs , w^c^ was
contrarie to vs, he euen toke it out of the
way,& fastened it vpon the crosse,
15 And hathe [i] spoiled the Principalities,
and Powers , and hathe made a shewe of
them openly , and hathe triumphed ouer
them in the same *crosse*.
16 Let no man therefore condemne you in
meat and drinke,or in respect of an [k] holie day , or of the new moone , or of the
Sabbath *dayes*,
17 Which are *but* a shaddowe of things to
come:but the bodie is in Christ.
18 *Let no man [l] at his pleasure" beare rule
ouer you by humblenes of minde, & worshiping of Angels , aduancing him self in
those things which he neuer sawe, rashly
puft vp with his fleshlie minde,
19 And holdeth not the head , whereof all
the bodie furnished and knit together by
iointes and bandes,encreaseth with the increasing of God.
20 Wherefore if ye *be* dead with Christ
from the ordinances of the worlde, why,
as thogh ye liued in the worlde,are ye bur
dened with traditions?
21 *As*, Touche not, Taste not, Handel
not.
22 Which all [m] perish with the vsing , *and
are* after the commandements and doctri
nes of men.
23 Which things haue in deed a shewe of
wisdome,in [n] voluntarie religion and hum
blenes of minde,and in not sparing the bo
die:"nether haue they it in anie estimation
to satisfie the [o] flesh.

d Teaching you vaine speculations , as worshiping of Angels,of blinde ceremonies and beggerlie traditions: for now they haue none vse seing Christ is come.
Chap.1,19.
iohn 1,14.
Rom.2,19.
e In saying that the *Godhead* is really in Christ, he sheweth that he is verie God:also saying, *in him*, he declareth two distincte natures, and by this worde *dwelleth* he proueth that it is there for euer.
"*Or, essentially.*
"*Or, vs all* our.
Rom.6,4.
Ephe.1,19.
Ephe.2,1.
Ephe.2,13.
f Made by the Spirit of Christ.
g In beleuing that God by his power raised vp Christ, whereof we haue a sure token in our baptisme.
"*Or, obligation.*
h The ceremonies, and rites were as it were a publike profession, and hand writing of the miserable state of man kinde: for circumcision did declare our natural pollution: the purifyings, & washings signified the filth of sinne: the sacrifices testified that we were giltie of death , which were all taken away by Christs death.
Mat.24,4.
i As Satan & his Angels fro̅ whome he hathe taken all power.
k Or, distinction,as to make difference betwixt dayes
"*Or, defraude you of your prise.*
l Meaning, that the hypocrites led them at their pleasure into all superstitio̅ and error. m And apperteine nothing to the kingdome of God "*Or, but they are of no value saue for the filling of the flesh.* n Suche as men haue chosen according to their owne fantasie. o They pinche and defraude their bodie to shewe them selues greater hypocrites.

CHAP. III.

1 He sheweth where we shulde seke Christ. 5 He exhorteth to mortification, 10 To put of the olde man and to put on Christ. 12 To the which he addeth exhortations, bothe general and particular to charitie & humilitie.

a After that ye haue bene dead to beggerlie ceremonies.

1 IF ye then be [a] risen with Christ, seke
those things which are aboue, where
Christ sitteth at the right hand of God.
2 Set your affections on things which are
aboue, *and* not on things, which [b] are on the
earth.

b Which ether serue but for a time, or els are inuented by men.
c With Christ.

3 For ye are [c] dead, and your life is hid with
Christ in God.
4 When Christ which is our life, shal appeare,
then shal ye also appeare with him
in glorie.

Ephe.5,3.
d Extinguish all the stregth of the corrupt nature which resisteth agaist the Spirit, that ye may liue in the Spirit, and not in ẏ flesh.

5 *[d] Mortifie therefore your mẽbers which
are on the earth, fornicatiõ, vnclennes, the
inordinate affection, euil concupiscence, &
couetousnes which is idolatrie.
6 For the which things sakes the wrath of
God cometh on the children of disobedience.
7 Wherein ye also walked once, when ye
liued in them.

Rom.6,4. ephe.4,25. ebr.12,3. 1.pet.2,1. & 4,1.

8 *But now put ye away euẽ all these thĩgs,
wrath, angre, maliciousnes, cursed speaking,
filthie speaking, out of your mouth.
9 Lie not one to another, seing that ye haue
put of the olde man with his workes,
10 And haue put on the newe, which is renewed
in knowledge * after the image of
him that created him,

Gene.1,26. & 5,1.& 9.6

11 Where is nether Grecian nor Iewe, circumcision
nor vncircumcision, Barbarian,
Scythian, bonde, fre: but Christ is all and
in all things.

Ephe.6,11.
e He sheweth what frutes are in thẽ that are dead to ẏ worlde & are risen againe with Christ.
°Or, the bowels of mercies.

12 *Now therefore as the elect of God [e] holie
& beloued, put on ° tender mercie, kindnes,
humblenes of minde, mekenes, long
suffring:
13 Forbearing one another, and forgiuing
one another, if anie man haue a quarel to
another: euen as Christ forgaue you, euen
so do ye.
14 And aboue all these things *put on* loue,
which is the bonde of perfectnes.

f Let it guide all your doĩgs
°Or, gracious, or thankeful.
g The doctrine of the Gospel.
h Psalmes ꝑperly cõteine complainings to God, narrations, & expostulatiõs: hymnes, onely thãkes giuing: sõgs conteine praises, & thãkes giuing, but not so largely and amply, as hymnes do.

15 And let the peace of God [f] rule in your
hearts, to the which ye are called in one
bodie, and be ye ° amiable.
16 Let ẏ [g] worde of Christ dwell in you plẽteously
in all wisdome, teaching & admonishing
your owne selues, in [h] psalmes, and
hymnes, and spiritual songs, singing with
a * ° grace in your hearts to the Lord.
17 *And whatsoeuer ye shal do, in worde
or dede, *do* all in the Name of the Lord
Iesus, giuing thankes to God euen the Father
by him.

Ephe.4,29.
°Or, thankes giuing.
1.Cor 10,31.
Ephe.5,22. 1.Pet.3,1.

18 ¶ *Wiues, submit your selues vnto your
housbands, as it is comelie in the Lord.
19 *Housbands, loue your wiues, and be not
bitter vnto them.
20 ¶ *Children, obey your parentes in [i] all
things: for that is wel pleasing vnto the
Lord.

Ephe.6,1.
i Which are in the Lord.
k By to muche rigour.

21 Fathers, [k] prouoke not your children to
anger, lest they be discouraged.
22 ¶ *Seruants, be obedient vnto thẽ that are
your masters according to the flesh in
all things, not with eye seruice as men pleasers,
but in singlenes of heart, fearing God.
23 And whatsoeuer ye do, do it heartely, as
to the Lord, and not vnto men,
24 Knowing that of the Lord ye shal receiue
the rewarde of the inheritance: for ye
serue the Lord Christ.

Ephe.6,5. tit.2,9. 1.pet.2,18.

25 But he [l] that doeth wrong, shal receiue
for the wrong that he hathe done, & there
is no * [m] respect of persones.

l The cruel master.
Deu.10,17. wis.6,8. eccle.35,26. rom.2,11. gal.2,6. eph.6,9
m Whether he be master or seruant.

CHAP. IIII.

2 He exhorteth them to be feruent in prayer. 5 To walke wisely towarde them that are not yet come to the true knowledge of Christ. He saluteth them, and wisheth them all prosperitie.

1 YE masters, do vnto your seruãts, that
which is iuste, and equal, knowing
that ye also haue a master in heauen.
2 *Continue in prayer, and watch in the same
with thankes giuing,
3 *Praying also for vs, that God may open
vnto vs the [a] dore of vtterance, to speake
the mysterie of Christ: wherefore I am also
in bondes,
4 That I may vtter it, as it becometh me to
speake.

Luk.18,1. 1.thes.5,17. Ephe.6,18. 2.thes.3,1.
a That I may frely preache the Gospel.
Ephe.5,15.

5 ¶ *Walke [b] wisely towarde them that are
without, and [c] redeme the time.
6 *Let* your speache *be* gracious alwais, and
powdred with [d] salt, that ye may knowe
how to answer euerie man.

b To the commoditie of your neighbours.
c Bestowe the time wel, ẘ the malice of men euerie where plucketh from you and causeth you to abuse it.
d Perteining to edification and mixt with no vanitie.

7 ¶ Tychicus *our* beloued brother, and
faithful minister, and felowe seruant in
the Lord, shal declare vnto you my whole
state,
8 Whome I haue sent vnto you for the same
purpose that he might knowe your state,
and might comforte your hearts,
9 *With Onesimus a faithful & a beloued
brother, who is one of you. They shal shewe
you of all things here.

Phile.10.

10 Aristarchus my prison fellowe saluteth
you, & Marcus, Barnabas sisters sonne (touching
whome ye receiued cõmandements,
If he come vnto you, receiue him)
11 And Iesus which is called Iustus, which
are of the circumcision. These [e] onely are
my [f] workefellowes vnto the kingdome of
God, which haue bene vnto my cõsolatiõ.
12 Epaphras the seruant of Christ, which
is one of you, saluteth you, and a'wais
striueth for you in prayers, that ye may
stande perfite, and ful in all the wil of
God.
13 For I beare him recorde, that he hathe a
great zeale for you, & for thẽ of Laodicea,

e If they onely did helpe him to preache the Gospel at Rome, where was Peter? or those fiue & twentie yeres that thei faine he abode at Rome?
f In preachĩg the Gospel.

and

and them of Hierapolis.
2.Tim.4,11.
14 *Luke the beloued physitiō greteth you,
and Demas.
15 Salute the brethren which are of Laodicea, and Nymphas, and the Church which
is in his house.
16 And when this epistle is red of you, cause that it be red in the Church of the Laodiceans also, and that ye likewise read the
epistle g *written* from Laodicea.

g Ether to Paul, or els ẘ they wolde write as an answere to this epistle sēt to ẙ Colosiās

17 And say to Archippus, Take hede to the
ministerie, that thou hast receiued in the
Lord, that thou fulfil it.
18 The salutation by the hand of me Paul.
Remember my bādes. Grace *be* with you,
Amen.

Written from Rome to the Colosians *and sent* by Tychicus, and Onesimus.

THE FIRST EPISTLE of Paul to the Thessalonians.

THE ARGVMENT.

After that the Thessalonians had bene wel instructed in the faith, persecution, which perpetually followeth the preaching of the Gospel, arose, against the which althogh they did constantly stand, yet S. Paul (as moste careful for them) sent Timothie to strengthen them, who sone after admonishing him of their estate, gaue occasion to the Apostle to confirme them by diuers arguments to be cōstant in faith, & to suffer whatsoeuer God calleth them vnto for the testimonie of the Gospel, exhorting them to declare by their godlie liuing the puritie of their religion. And as the Church can neuer be so purged, that some cockle remaine not among the wheat, so there were among them wicked men, which by mouing vaine and curious questions to ouerthrowe their faith, taught falsely, as touching the point of the resurrection from the dead: whereof he briefly instructeth them what to thinke, earnestly forbidding them to seke curiously to knowe the times, willing them rather to watche lest the sudden comming of Christ come vpon them at vnwares: and so after certeine exhortations, and his commendations to the brethren, he endeth.

CHAP. I.

2 He thanketh God for them, that they are so stedfast in faith & good workes. 6 And receiue the Gospel with suche earnestnes. 7 That they are an example to all others.

1 Paul and Siluanus, and
Timotheus, vnto the
Church of the Thessa-
loniās, *which is* in a God
the Father, and in the
Lord Iesus Christ: Gra
ce *be* with you, and pea
ce from God our Father, & *from* the Lord
Iesus Christ.

a For there is no Church ẘ is not ioyned together in God.

1.Thess.1,3.
2 *We giue God thankes alwayes for you
Philip.1,3.
all, making *mētion of you in our prayers
3 Without ceasing, remēbring your b effectual faith, & c diligent loue & the pacience of *your* hope in our Lord Iesus Christ
in the sight of God euen our Father,
4 Knowing, beloued brethren, that ye are
elect of God.
5 For our d Gospel was not vnto you in worde onely, but also in power, and in the holie Gost, & in muche assurāce, as ye knowe
after what maner we were among you for
your sakes.
6 And ye became followers of vs, and of
the Lord, and receiued the worde in muche affliction, with e ioye of ẙ holie Gost,

b Which declareth it selfe by moste liuelie frutes
c Whereby you declared your selues moste readie and painful to helpe the poore
d The effectual preaching of the Gospel is an euident token of our election
e To beleue, & to be fully persuaded to haue the gifts of the holie Gost, and ioyfully to suffer for Christs sake, are most certeine signes of our election.

7 So that ye were as " ensamples to all that
beleue in Macedonia and Achaia.
" Or, patternes.
8 For from you sounded out the worde of
the Lord, not in Macedonia & in Achaia
onely: but your faith also which is towarde God, spred abroade in all quarters, that
we nede not to speake any thing.
9 For f they them selues shewe of you what
maner of entring in we had vnto you, and
how ye turned to God from idoles, to serue the g liuing and true God,
10 And to loke for his Sonne from heauen,
whome he raised from the dead, *euen* Iesus
which deliuereth vs from the h wrath to
come.

f To wit, all ẙ faithful.
g For idoles are dead thīgs and onely fained fantasies.
h Which he shal execute vpon the wicked.

CHAP. II.

1 To the intent they shulde not faint vnder the crosse, 2 He cōmendeth his diligence in preaching, 13 And theirs in obeing. 18 He excuseth his absence, that he colde not come and open his heart to them.

1 For ye your selues knowe, brethren,
that our entrance in vnto you was not
in a vaine,
2 But euen after that we had suffred before, and were shamefully entreated at *Philippi (as ye knowe) we were bolde b in our
God, to speake vnto you the Gospel of
God with muche striuing.
3 For our exhortatiō was not by deceit, nor
by vnclennes, nor by guile.
4 But as we were alowed of God, that the

a Not in outwarde shewe and in pompe, but in trauel & in the feare of God.
Act.16,22.
b By his helpe and grace.

Gospel shulde be committed *vnto vs*,so we
speake, not as they that [c] please men, but
God,which trieth our hearts.
5 Nether yet did we euer vse flattering
wordes,as ye know,nor colored couetousnes,God *is* recorde.
6 Nether soght we praise of men,nether of
you,nor of others,
7 When we might haue bene "chargeable,
as the Apostles of Christ: but we were gen
tle among you , euen as a [d] nource cherisheth her children.
8 Thus being affectioned towarde you,
our good wil was to haue dealt vnto you,
not the Gospel of God onely,but also our
owne soules,because ye were dere vnto vs.
9 For ye remember,brethren,*our labour &
trauail:for we laboured day & night, because we wolde not be chargeable vnto a-
nie of you,& preached vnto you the Gospel of God.
10 Ye *are* witnesses, and God *also* , how holily,& iustly, & vnblameably we behaued
our selues among [e] you that beleue.
11 As ye knowe how that we exhorted you,
and comforted, and besoght euerie one of
you(as a father his children)
12 That ye * wolde walke worthie of God,
who hathe called you vnto his kingdome
and glorie.
13 For this cause also thanke we God without ceasing,that whẽ ye receiued of vs the
worde of the preaching of God, ye receiued it not as the worde of men,but as it is
in dede the worde of God,which also worketh in you that beleue.
14 For brethren, ye are become followers
of the Churches of God, which in Iudea
are in [f] Christ Iesus , because ye haue also
suffred ỹ same things of your owne countrey men,euen as they *haue* of the Iewes,
15 Who bothe killed the Lord Iesus and
their owne Prophetes , & haue persecuted
vs,and God they please not , and are contrarie [g] to all men,
16 And forbid vs to preache vnto the Gentiles , that they might be saued, to [h] fulfil
their sinnes alwais : for the wrath *of God* is
[i] come on them,to the vtmoste.
17 Forasmuche brethren , as we were kept
from you for a season,cõcerning sight,but
not in the heart,we * enforced the more to
se your face with great desire.
18 Therefore we wolde haue come vnto
you(I Paul,at least once or twise)but Satã
hindered vs.
19 For what is our hope or ioye, or crowne
of reioycĩg? are [k] not euẽ you it in ỹ presen
ce of our Lord Iesus Christ at his cõmĩg?
20 Yes,ye are our glorie and ioye.

c Which declareth a naughtie conscience.

"Or, in autoritie.

d He hũbled him self to supporte all thĩgs without all respecte of lucre : euen as ỹ tender mother which nourceth her children,and thinketh no office to vile for her childrẽs sake.

Act.20,34.
1.cor.4,14.
2.thes.3,8.

e For it is not possible to auoide the reproches of ỹ wicked,which euer hate good doings.

Eph.4,1.
philip.1,27.
col.1,10.

f In his Name and vnder his protection.

g And wolde hinder all mẽ from their saluation.

h And heape vp the measure,Mat.13,32.

Rom.1,11.

i He meaneth not this of all the Iewes in general:but of certeine of thẽ particularly ỽ ceased not after they had put Christ to death,to persecute his worde and his ministers.

k Therefore I colde not forget you,except I wolde forget my self.

CHAP. III.

2 He sheweth how greatly he was affectioned towarde them bothe in that he sent Timotheus to them, 10 And also prayed for them.

1 WHerefore since we colde no longer forbeare , we thoght it good
to remaine at Athens [a] alone,
2 *And haue sent Timotheus our brother &
minister of God , and our labour felow in
the Gospel of Christ, to stablish you, and
to comfort you touching your faith,
3 That no man shulde be moued with these
afflictions : for ye your selues knowe, that
we are appointed thereunto.
4 For verely when we were with you , we
tolde you before that we shulde suffre tribulations, euen as it came to passe, and ye
knowe it.
5 Euen for this cause,when [b] I colde no lon
ger forbeare, I sent *him* ỹ I might knowe
of your faith,lest the [c] tẽpter had tempted
you in any sorte , and that our labour had
bene in vaine.
6 But now lately when Timotheus came
from you vnto vs , and broght vs good tidings of your faith & loue,and that ye haue good remẽbrance of vs alwayes , desiring to se vs,as we also *do* you,
7 Therefore, brethren, we had consolation
in you, in all our affliction and necessitie
through your faith.
8 For now are we [d] aliue , if ye [e] stand fast
in the Lord.
9 For what thãkes can we recõpense to God
againe for you for all the ioye wherewith
we reioyce for your sakes before our God,
10 Night and day * praying excedingly ỹ
we might se your face,& might [f] accõplish
that which is lacking in your faith?
11 Now God him self,euen our Father,and
our Lord Iesus Christ , guide our iorney
vnto you,
12 And the Lord increase you & make you
abunde in loue one towarde another , and
towarde all mẽ,euẽ as we *do* towarde you:
13 *To make your hearts stable and vnblameable in holines before God euen our Fa
ther , at the comming of our Lord Iesus
Christ with all his Saints.

a Rather sekĩg your commoditie, then mine owne in sendĩg of Timotheus to you.

Act.16,1.

b His great affection towarde the smale flocke.

c Meaning Satan.

d If ye remaine constant in faith and true doctrine, I shal thinke that all mine afflictiõs be so many pleasures, and shalbe restored from death to life.

Rom.1,10. & 15,23.

e If you perseuere in faith.

f We must daily growe from faith to faith.

Chap.5,23.
1.corin.1,8.

CHAP. IIII.

1 He exhorteth them to holines, 6 Innocencie, 9 Loue, 11 Labour, 13 And moderation in lamenting for the dead, 17 Describing the end of the resurrection.

1 ANd furthermore we beseche you,bre
thrẽ, & exhorte you in the Lord Iesus that [a] ye increase more and more, as ye
haue receiued of vs,how ye oght to walke,
and to please God.
2 For ye knowe what [b] commandements we
gaue you by the Lord Iesus.
3 *For this is the wil of God *euen* your sanctification, [c] *&* that ye shulde absteine frõ
fornication,
4 That euerie one of you shulde know, how
to possesse his [d] vessel in holines & honour,

a And as it were , ouer come your selues.

b The greke worde signified suche commãdements as one receiueth from some mã to giue them in his name to others.

Rom.12,2.
ephe.5,17.

c That is,that you shulde dedicate your selues wholy vnto God.

d That is , his bodie which is prophaned by suche filthines.

5 *And*

5 *And* not in the lust of cōcupiscence, euen
as the Gentiles which knowe not God:
6 *That no man oppresse or defraude his
brother in any matter: for ẏ Lord *is* a ven-
ger of all suche things, as we also haue tolde you before time and testified.
7 *For God hathe not called vs vnto vnclennes, but vnto holines.
8 He therefore that despiseth [e] *these things*,
despiseth not man, but God who hathe e-
uen giuen* you his holie Spirit.
9 But as touching brotherlie loue, ye nede
not ẏ I write vnto you: *for ye are taught
of God to loue one another.
10 Yea, & that thing verely ye do vnto all ẏ
brethren, which are throughout all Macedonia: but we beseche you, brethrē, that ye
increase more and more,
11 *And that ye studie to be quiet, and to
medle with your owne busines, & to worke with your [f] owne hands, as we commanded you,
12 That ye may behaue your selues honestly towarde them that [g] are without, & that
nothing be [h] lacking vnto you.
13 ¶ I wolde not, brethren, haue you ignorāt
concerning thē which are a slepe, that ye
[i] sorowe not euē as other ẇ haue no hope.
14 For if we beleue that Iesus is dead, and
is risen, euē so them which slepe in [k] Iesus,
wil God [l] bring with him.
15 For this say we vnto you by the [m] worde
of the Lord, *that we which liue, & are remaining in the cōming of the Lord, shal
not preuent them which slepe.
16 For the Lord him self shal descēd from
heauē with a showte, & with the voyce of
the Archāgel & *with the trūpet of God:
and the dead in Christ shal rise first.
17 Then shal [n] we which liue and remaine,
be [o] caught vp with them also in the cloudes, to mete the Lord in the ayer: & so shal
we euer be with the Lord.
18 Wherefore, comfort your selues one another with these wordes.

1.Cor.6,8.
1.Cor.1,2.
e By these precepts of godlie life it appeareth what were the commandemēts which Paul gaue vnto them.
1.Cor.7,40.
Iohn 13,34. & 15,12.
1.iohn 2,8. & 4,21.
2 Thess.3,7.
f And not be idle.
g As strangers and infideles.
h But that ye may be able by your diligence to supplie your want and necessitie.
i He doeth not condemne all kinde of sorow, but that which procedeth of infidelitie.
k Or, haue continued constātly in the faith of Christ.
l By raising their bodies out of the graue.
m Which is in the Name of the Lord, and as he shulde speake hī self.
1.Cor.15,23.
Mat.24,31.
1.cor.15,52.
n Meaning thē which shal be founde a liue.
o In this suddē taking vp there shalbe a kinde of mutatiō of the qualities of our bodies which shalbe as a kinde of death.

CHAP. V.

1 He enformeth them of the day of iudgement & comming of the Lord, 6 Exhorting thē to watch, 12 And to regard suche as preache Gods worde among them.

1 BVt of the [a] times & seasons, brethren,
ye haue no nede ẏ I write vnto you.
2 For ye your selues knowe perfitely, that
the *day of the Lord shal come, euen as a
thefe in the night.
3 For when they shal say, Peace, and safetie,
then shal come vpon them sudden destruction, as the [b] trauail vpon a woman with
childe, and they shal not escape.
4 But ye, brethren, are not in darkenes, that
that day shulde come on you, as *it were* a
thefe.
5 Ye are all the children of light, and the
childrē of the day: we are not of the night
nether of darkenes.
6 Therefore let vs not [c] slepe as do other,
but let vs [d] watch and be sober.
7 For they that slepe, slepe in the night, &
they that be dronken, are dronken in the
night.
8 But let vs which are of the [e] day, be sober,
*putting on ẏ brest plate of faith & loue,
& of the hope of saluation for an helmet.
9 For God hathe not appointed vs vnto
wrath, but to obteine saluatiō by the meanes of our Lord Iesus Christ,
10 Which dyed for vs, that whether we wake or [f] slepe, we shulde liue together with
him.
11 Wherefore exhorte one another, & edifie one another, euen as ye do.
12 Now we beseche you, brethren, that ye
knowe them, which labour among you, &
are ouer you in the Lord, and [g] admonish
you,
13 That ye haue them in singular loue for
[h] their workes sake. Be at peace amōg your
selues.
14 We desire you, brethrē, admonish them
that are vnrulie: comforte the feble minded: beare with the weake: be pacient towarde all men.
15 *Se that none recompense euil for euil
vnto any man: but euer followe that which
is good, bothe towarde your selues, and
towarde all men.
16 [i] Reioyce euermore.
17 *Pray continually.
18 In all things giue thankes: for this *is* the
wil of God in Christ Iesus towarde you.
19 Quench not the [k] Spirit.
20 Despise not [l] prophecying.
21 Trye all things, *and* kepe that which is
good.
22 Absteine from all appearance of euil.
23 Now the verie God * of peace sanctifie
you throughout: and *I pray God* that your
[m] whole spirit and soule and bodie, may be
kept blameles vnto the comming of our
Lord Iesus Christ.
24 *Faithful *is he* which calleth you, which
wil also do it.
25 Brethren, pray for vs.
26 Grete all the brethrē with an holie kisse.
27 I charge you in ẏ Lord, that this epistle
be red vnto all the brethren the Saintes.
28 The grace of our Lord Iesus Christ *be*
with you, Amen.

The first *epistle* vnto the Thessalonians written from Athens.

a So muche ẏ more we oght to beware of all dreames & fantasies of mē which wearie them selues & others in searching out curiously the time that the Lord shal appeare, alledgig for them selues a vaine prophecie, and moste falsely ascribed to Elias that 2000 yere before the Lawe, 2000 vnder the Lawe and 2000 after the Law the worlde shal endure.
*Mat.24,44. 2 peter 3,10. reuel.3,3 & 16,15.
b That is, suddenly & vnloked for.
c Here slepe is taken for cōtempt of saluation, when men continewe in sinnes and wil not awake to godlines.
d And not be ouercome with the cares of ẏ worlde.
e That is, lightned by ẏ Gospel.
Isa.59,17. ephe.6,17.
f Here it is taken onely to dye, & is ment of the faithful
g As the flocke is bounde to loue ẏ shepherde, so is it his duetie to teache thē and exhort them in true religion.
h Where this cause ceaseth, that they worke not: the honor also ceaseth, and they must be expelled as wolues out of the flocke.
Prou.17,13. & 20,22. mat.5,39. rom.12,17. 1.pet.3,9.
i Haue a quiet minde & consciēce in Christ which shal make you reioice in the middes of sorrowes, Rom 5,3. 2.cor. 6,10.
Luk 18,1. eccle.18,12. colos.4,3.
k God that hathe giuen his Spirit to his elect, wil neuer suffer it to be quenched, but hathe reueiled by what meanes it may be mainteined, ẏ is, by suche exhortations as these, & by cōtinual increase in godlines.
l The preachig of ẏ worde of God.
Chap.3,12.
1.cor.1,8.
1.Cor.1,8.
m Then is a man fully sanctified & perfect, when his minde thinketh nothig, his soule, that is, his vnderstanding and wil, couet nothig: nether his bodie doeth execute any thing contrary to the wil of God.

THE SECONDE EPI-
ſtle to the Theſſalonians.

THE ARGVMENT.

LEſt the Theſſalonians ſhulde thinke that Paul neglected them, becauſe he went to other places, rather then came to thẽ, he writeth vnto them and exhorteth thẽ to pacience and other frutes of faith, nether to be moued with that vaine opinion of ſuche as taught that the comming of Chriſt was at hand, foraſmuche as before that day there ſhulde be a falling away from true religion, euen by a great parte of the worlde, and that Antichriſt ſhulde reigne in the Temple of God: finally commending him ſelf to their prayers, & encouraging them to conſtancie, he willeth thẽ to correct ſuche ſharpely, as liue idelly of other mens labours, whome, if they do not obey his admonitions, he commandeth to excommunicate.

CHAP. I.

3 He thanketh God for their faith, loue and patience. 11 He praieth for the encreaſe of the ſame. 12 And ſheweth what frute ſhal come thereof.

1 Aul and Siluanus, and
Timotheus vnto the
Church of the Theſſa-
lonians, *which is* in God
our Father, and in the
Lord Ieſus Chriſt:
2 Grace *be* with you, and
peace from God our Father, and *from* the
Lord Ieſus Chriſt.
1.Theſſ.1,2. 3 *We oght to thãke God alwayes for you,
brethren, as it is mete, becauſe that your
faith groweth excedingly, and the loue of
euerie one of you towarde another abundeth,
4 So that we our ſelues reioyce of you in
the Churches of God, becauſe of your [a]pa-
cience and faith in all your perſecutions
and tribulations that ye ſuffre,
5 **Which is* a [b]token of the righteous iudgemẽt of God, that ye may be counted worthie of the kingdome of God, for ye which
ye alſo ſuffre.
6 For it is a righteous thing with God, to
recompenſe tribulation to them that trou
ble you,
7 And to you which are troubled, reſt with
vs * when the Lord Ieſus ſhal ſhewe him
ſelf from heauen with his [c] mightie Angels,
8 In flaming fyre, rendring vengeance vnto them, that do not knowe God, & which
obey not vnto the Goſpel of our Lord
Ieſus Chriſt,
9 Which ſhalbe puniſhed with [d] euerlaſting perdition, from the preſence of the
Lord, and from the glorie of his power,
10 When he ſhal come to be glorified in
his Saintes, and to be made marueilous in
all thẽ that beleue (becauſe our teſtimonie towarde you was beleued) in that day.
11 Wherefore, we alſo praye alwayes for
you, that our God may make you worthie
of his calling, and fulfil [e]all the good pleaſure of *his* goodnes, & the [f] worke of faith
with power,
12 That ye Name of our Lord Ieſus Chriſt
may be [g] glorified in you, & ye in him, according to the grace of our God, and of
the Lord Ieſus Chriſt.

a Which procedeth of your faith as a moſte notable frute.

Iude.6.

b The faithful by their afflictions ſe, as in a cleare glaſſe the end of Gods iuſt iudgemẽt, when as they ſhal reigne with Chriſt which haue ſuffered with him, and the wicked ſhal feele his extreme wrath and vengeance

1.Theſſ. 4,16.

c By whome he declareth his might.

d As God is euerlaſting, ſo ſhal their puniſhment be euerlaſting: and as he is moſte mightie of power, ſo ſhal their puniſhment be moſte ſore.

e The fre beneuolence of Gods goodnes, comprehẽdeth his purpoſe, his predeſtination and vocation: the worke of faith conteineth our iuſtification, to the which God addeth glorification: and all theſe he worketh of his mere grace through Chriſt. f Faith is Gods wonderful worke in vs. g As the head with the bodie.

CHAP. II.

3 He ſheweth them that the day of the Lord ſhal not come, til the departing from the faith come firſt, 9 And the kingdome of Antichriſt. 15 And therefore he exhorteth them not to be deceiued, but to ſtand ſtedfaſt in the things that he hathe taught them.

1 NOw we beſeche you, brethren, by ye
comming of our Lord Ieſus Chriſt,
and by our aſſembling vnto him,
2 That ye be not ſuddenly moued frõ *your*
minde, nor troubled nether by [a] ſpirit, nor
by [b] worde, nor by letter, as *it were* from
vs, as thogh the daye of Chriſt were at
hand.
3 *Let no man deceiue you by any meanes:
for *that day ſhal not come*, except there co
me a [c] departing firſt, and that that [d] man
of ſinne be diſcloſed, *euen* ye ſonne of [e]per-
dition,
4 Which is an aduerſarie, and exalteth him
ſelf againſt all that is called God, or that
is worſhipped: ſo that he doeth ſit as God
in the Temple of God, ſhewing him ſelf
that he is God.
5 Remẽber ye not, that whẽ I was yet with
you, I tolde you theſe things?
6 And now ye knowe what [f] withholdeth,
that he might be reueiled in his time.
7 For the myſterie of iniquitie doeth alreadie [g]worke: onely he which [h]now with-

a As falſe reuelation, or dreames.

b Which are ſpoken or written.

Ephe.5,6.

c A wonderful departing of the moſte parte from the faith.

d This wicked Antichriſt cõprehendeth the whole ſucceſſion of the perſecuters of the Church, & all that abominable kingdome of Satan, whereof ſome were beares, ſome lyons, others leopardes, as Daniel deſcribeth thẽ, and is called ye man of ſinne becauſe he ſetteth him ſelf vp agaĩſt God.

e Who as he deſtroyeth others, ſo ſhal he be deſtroyed him ſelf. f Becauſe the falſe apoſtles had perſuaded after a ſorte the Theſſalonians, that the day of the Lord was nere, and ſo the redemption of the Church, Paul teacheth them to loke for this horrible diſſipation before, and therefore rather to prepare them ſelues to patience, then to reſt and quietnes: for as yet there was a let, that is, that the Goſpel ſhulde be preached throughout all, Mat.24,14. g To wit, priuely, and is therefore called a myſterie becauſe it is ſecret. h Which ſhal ſtay for a time.

holdeth,

holdeth, *shal let* til he be taken out of the
waye.
8 And then shal the wicked man be reueiled,* whome the Lord shal consume with
the [i] Spirit of his mouth, and shal abolish
with the brightnes of his comming,
9 *Euen him* whose [k] comming is by the working of Satan, with all power and signes,
and lying wonders,
10 And in all deceiueablenes of vnrighteousnes, amõg thẽ that [l] perish, because thei
receiued not the loue of the trueth, that
they might be saued.
11 And therefore God shal send thẽ strong
delusion, that they shulde beleue lyes,
12 That all they might be damned which
beleued not the trueth, but had [m] pleasure
in vnrighteousnes.
13 But we oght to giue thankes alwaye to
God for you, brethren [n] beloued of the
Lord, because that God hathe from [o] the
begining chosen you to saluaciõ, through
sanctificacion of the Spirit, and the faith
of [p] trueth,
14 Whereunto he called you by [q] our Gospel, to obteine the glorie of our Lord Iesus Christ.
15 Therefore, brethren, stand fast and kepe
the [r] instructions, which ye haue bene taught, ether [s] by worde, or by our Epistle.
16 Now the same Iesus Christ our Lord &
our God euen the Father which hathe loued vs, and hathe giuen vs euerlasting cõsolacion and good hope through grace,
17 Comforte your hearts, and stablish you
in euerie worde and good worke.

Isa.11,4.
i That is, with his worde.
k Meaning the whole time ỳ he shal remaine.
l Satans power is limited that he cã not hurt the elect to their destruction
m Delited in false doctrine.
n The fouteine of our electiõ is the loue of God: the sanctificacion of ỳ Spirit, & beleuing the trueth are testimonies of the same election.
o Before the fundacion of the worlde.
p And Gospel.
q By our preaching.
r That is, the doctrine, 1. Thes. 2,2. chap 3,6.
s That is, by my preaching of the Gospel.

CHAP. III.

1 He desireth them to pray for him, that the Gospel may prosper, 6 And giueth them warning to reproue the ydle, 16 And so wissheth them all wealth.

1 Furthermore, brethren,* pray for vs, ỳ
the worde of the Lord may haue fre
passage, and be glorified, euen as *it is* with
you,
2 And that we may be deliuered from vnreasonable and euil men: for all men haue
not [a] faith.
3 But the Lord is faithful, which wil stablish you, and kepe you from [b] euil.
4 And we are persuaded of you through
the Lord, that ye bothe do, and wil do the
things which we [c] commande you.
5 And the Lord guide your hearts to the
loue of God, & the weating for of Christ.
6 We commande you, brethren, in the Na
me of our Lord Iesus Christ, that ye withdrawe your selues frõ euerie brother that
walketh inordinately, and not after the
[d] instruction, which he receiued of vs.
7 For ye your selues knowe * how ye oght
to folowe vs:* for we behaued not our selues inordinately among you,
8 Nether toke we bread of anie man for
noght: but we wroght with labour & trauaile night & day, because we wolde not
be chargeable to anie of you.
9 Not but that we had autoritie, * but that
we might make our selues an ensample
vnto you to folowe vs.
10 For euen when we were with you, this
we warned you of, that if there were anie,
which wolde not [e] worke, that he shulde
not eat.
11 For we heard, that there are some which
walke among you inordinately, and worke not at all, but are busie bodies.
12 Therefore them that are suche, we commande and exhorte by our Lord Iesus
Christ, that they worke with quietnes, and
eat their owne bread.
13 * And ye, brethren, be not wearie in wel
doing.
14 If anie man obey not our sayings, note
him by a lettre, * and haue no companie
with him, that he maie be ashamed.
15 Yet count him not as an [f] enemie, but
admonish him as a brother.
16 Now the Lord of peace giue you peace
alwaies by all meanes. The Lord *be* with
you all.
17 The salutacion of me Paul, with mine
owne hand, which is the [g] token in euerie
Epistle: so I write,
18 The grace of our Lord Iesus Christ *be*
with you all, Amen.

The seconde *Epistle* to the Thessalonians, written from Athens.

Ephes.6,18. colos.4,3.
a Althogh thei boast them selues thereof.
b From the slaights of Satan.
c By ỳ worde of God.
d Which is, to trauail, if he wil eat, Chap. 2,15.
1.Cor.4,12. 1.thes.4,11. Act.20,34. 1.cor.4,12. 1.thes.2,9.
1.Cor.11,1.
e Then by the worde of God none oght to liue idelly, but oght to giue him self to some vocacion, to get his liuĩg by, and to do good to others
Galat.6,9.
Mat.18,27. 1.cor.5,9.
f The end of excommunicacion is not to driue from the Church suche as haue fallen, but to winne them to the Church by amendement.
g Whether thei be mine Epistles or other mens.

THE FIRST EPIstle of Paul to Timotheus.

THE ARGUMENT.

IN writing this Epistle Paul semed not onely to haue respect to teache Timotheus, but chiefly to kepe other in awe, which wolde haue rebelled against him, because of his youth. And therfore he doeth arme him against those ambitious questionistes, which vnder pretence of zeale to the

Law, disquieted the godlie with foolish and vnprofitable questions, whereby they declared, that professing the Law they knewe not what was the chief end of the Law. And as for him self,he so confesseth his vnworthines, that he sheweth to what worthines the grace of God hathe preferred him: and therefore he willeth praiers to be made for all degrees and sortes of men, because that God by offring his Gospel and Christ his Sonne to them all, is indifferent to euerie sorte of men, as his Apostleship, which is peculiar to the Gentiles, witnesseth. And forasmuche as God hathe left ministers as ordinarie meanes in his Church to bring men to saluacion,he describeth what maner of men they oght to be, to whome the mysterie of the Sonne of God manifested in flesh is committed to be preached. After this he sheweth him what troubles the Church at all times shal susteine,but specially in the latter dayes, when as vnder pretence of religion men shal teache things contrarie to the worde of God. This done,he teacheth what widdowes shulde be receiued or refused to minister to the sicke: also what Elders oght to be chosen into office, exhorting him nether to be hastie in admitting, nor in iudging anie: also what is the duetie of seruants, the nature of false teachers, of vaine speculacions, of couetousnes, of riche men, and aboue all things he chargeth him to beware false doctrine.

CHAP. I.

3 He exhorteth Timotheus to waite vpon his office,namely to se that nothing be taught but Gods worde, &c. 5 Declaring that faith,with a good conscience,charitie & edificacion are the end thereof,20 And admonisheth of Himeneus and Alexander.

1 PAul an Apostle of Iesus
Christ,by the ″comandement of God our Sauiour, and of our Lord
Iesus Christ*our hope,
2 *Vnto Timotheus *my*
[a] natural sonne in the
faith: Grace, mercie, & peace from God
our Father, & *from* Christ Iesus our Lord.
3 As I besoght thee to abide stil in Ephesus,
when I departed into Macedonia, *so do*,
that thou maiest comande some, that thei
teache none other doctrine,
4 Nether that they giue hede to * fables
and genealogies, **which are* endles, which
brede questiones rather then godlie edifying which is by faith.
5 For * the [b] end of the ″ commandement
is loue out of a pure heart, and of a good
conscience, and of faith vnfained.
6 From the which things some haue erred,
and haue turned vnto vaine iangling.
7 They wolde be doctours of the Law, and
yet vnderstand not what they speake, nether whereof they affirme.
8 * And we knowe, that the Law is good,
if a man vse it lawfully,
9 Knowing this, that the Law is not giuen
vnto a [c] righteous man, but vnto the lawles and disobedient, to the vngodlie, and
to [d] sinners, to the vnholie, and to the prophane, to murtherers of fathers and mothers, to manslayers,
10 To whoremogers, to buggerers, to [e] mē
stealers, to liers, to the periured, & if there
be anie other thing, that is contrarie to
wholsome doctrine,
11 *Which is* according to the glorious Gospel of the * blessed God, which is comitted vnto me.
12 Therefore [f] I thanke him, which hathe
made me strong, *that is*, Christ Iesus our
Lord: for he counted me faithful, and put
me in *his* seruice:
13 When before I was a blasphemer, and a
persecuter, and an oppresser: but I was receiued to mercie: for I did it [g] ignorantly
through vnbeliefe.
14 But the grace of our Lord was exceding
abundant with [h] faith and [i] loue, which is
in Christ Iesus.
15 This *is* a ″true saying, and by all meanes
worthie to be receiued, that * Christ Iesus
came into the worlde to saue sinners, of
whome I am chief.
16 Notwithstanding, for this cause was I receiued to mercie, that Iesus Christ shulde
first shewe on me all lōg suffring vnto the
ensample of them, which shal in time to
come beleue in him vnto eternal life.
17 [k] Now vnto the King euerlasting, immortal, inuisible, vnto God onely wise, *be*
honour *and* glorie for euer, and euer, Amen.
18 This commandement commit I vnto
thee, sonne Timotheus, according to the
[l] prophecies, which went before vpō thee,
that thou by them shuldest * fight a good
fight,
19 Hauing [m] faith and a good conscience,
which some haue put away, and as concerning faith, haue made shipwracke.
20 Of whome is Himeneus, and Alexander, * whome I haue [n] deliuered vnto Satan, that thei might learne not to blaspheme.

CHAP. II.

1 He exhorteth to pray for all men. 4 Wherefore, 8 And how. 9 As touching the apparel and modestie of women.

1 I Exhorte therefore, that first of all supplicacions, praiers, intercessions & giuing of thankes be made for [a] all men,
2 For [b] Kings, and for all that are in autoritie, that we may lead a quiet and a peaceable life, in all godlines and honestie.
3 For this is good and acceptable in the
sight of God our Sauiour,
4 *Who wil that [c] all men shalbe saued, &
come

″*Or, ordinance.*
a So called because he followed the simplicitie of ye Gospel.
b Because these questionistes preferred their curious fables to all other knowledge, & beautified them wt the Law, as if thei had bene the verie Law of God, S. Paul sheweth that ye end of Gods Law is loue, wc cānot be without a good cōscience, nether a good conscience without faith, nor faith without ye worde of God: so their doctrine wc is an occasion of cōtentiō, is worth nothing.
Colos.1,8.
Act.16,1.
Chap.4,7.
tit.1,14.
Chap.6,4.
Rom.13,10.
″*Or, of the Law.*
c Whose hearts Gods Spirit doeth direct to do yt willigly wc the Law requireth: so yt their godlie affection is to them as a Law without further cōstraint.
Rom.7,12.
d Suche as onely delite in sinning.
e Which steale away childrē, or seruants.
f He declareth to Timothie the excellent force of Gods Spirit in them whome he hathe chosen to beare his worde, althogh before they were Gods vtter enemies, to encourage him in this battel that he shulde fight against all infideles & hypocrites.
Chap.6,13.

g Not knowig that I foght against God.
h Which chased away infidelitie.
i Which ouercame crueltie.
Mat.9,13.
mar.2,17.
″*Or, faithful & assured.*
k He brasteth forthe into these godlie affections, cōsidering Gods great mercie toward him.
Chap.6,12.
l It appeareth yt the vocaciō of Timothie was approued by notable prophecies, which then were reueiled in ye primatiue Church as Paul & Barnabas by the oracle were appointed to go to the Gētiles.
1.Cor.5,5.
m That is, sounde doctrine.
n Excommunicate, & cast out of the Church.
Chap. II.
a That is, of euerie degre, & of all sortes of people.
b Althogh thei persecute the Church of God, so it be of ignorance: els if thei do it maliciously, as Iulianus Apostata, they maye not be prayed for, Galat 5,12. 1 thes.2,16. 2 tim 4,14. 1 iohn 5,16.
c As Iewe & Gentile, poore and riche.
1.Pet.3,9.

come vnto the knowledge of the trueth.
5 For there is one God, and one [d] Mediator betwene God & man, *which is* the [e] man
Christ Iesus,
6 Who gaue him self a [f] raunsome for all
[g] men, *to be* a [h] testimonie in due time,
7 * Whereunto I am ordeined a preacher
& an Apostle (I speake yͤ trueth in Christ,
and lie not) *euen* a teacher of the Gentiles
in faith and veritie.
8 I wil therefore that the men pray, euerie
where lifting vp [i] pure hands without
wrath, or douting.
9 *Likewise also the women, that they a-
raye them selues in comelie apparel, with
shamefastnes & modestie, not with [k] broyded heare, or gold, or pearles, or costlie
apparel,
10 But (as becōmeth women that professe
the feare of God) with good workes.
11 Let the woman learne in silence with all
subiection.
12 I permit not a woman to [l] teache, nether
to vsurpe autoritie ouer the man, but to be
in silence.
13 For * Adam was first formed, then Eue.
14 *And Adam was [m] not deceiued, but the
woman was deceiued, & was in the [n] transgression.
15 Notwithstanding, through bearing of
children she shalbe saued if "they continue in faith, and loue, and holines with
modestie.

d Who wil reconcile of all nations, people and sortes to one God.
e Who being God was made man.
f He sheweth that there can be no Mediator, except he be also the redemer.
2.Tim 1,11.
g Which shulde beleue.
h Which the Prophetes testified, yͭ Christ shulde offre him self for the redemption of man at yͤ time that God had determined.
1.Pet.3,3.
i As testimonies of a pure heart & conscience.
k The worde signifieth to plat, to crispe, to broyde, to folde, to bush, to curle, or to lay it curiously: whereby all pompe and wantōnes is condemned which women vse in triming their heades.
Gen.1,27.
Gen.3,6.
l Read 1.cor. 14,34.
m The woman was first deceiued, & so became the instrument of Satan to deceiue the man: and thogh therefore God punisheth them with subiection and paine in their trauel, yet if they be faithful and godlie in their vocacion, they shal be saued. n That is, giltie of the transgression.
"Or, women.

7 He must also be wel reported of, euen of
them which are [h] without, lest he fall into
[i] rebuke, and the snare of the deuil.
8 Likewise *must* deacōs *be* honest, not double tongued, not giuen vnto muche wine,
nether to filthie lucre,
9 *[k] Hauing the mysterie of the faith in pure conscience.
10 And let them first be proued: then let
them minister, if they be founde blameles.
11 Likewise their [l] wiues *must be* honest, not
euil speakers, *but* sober, *and* faithful in all
things.
12 Let the deacons be the housbands of o-
ne wife, and suche as can rule their children wel, and their owne housholdes.
13 For they that haue ministred wel, get thē
selues a [m] good degre, & great [n] libertie in
the faith, which is in Christ Iesus.
14 These things write I vnto thee, trusting
to come very shortely vnto thee.
15 But if I tary long, that thou maist yet
knowe, how thou oghtest to behaue thy
self in the house of God, which is the
Church of the liuing God, the [o] pillar &
grounde of trueth.
16 And without controuersie, great is the
mysterie of godlines, *which is*, God is mani
fested in the flesh, [p] iustified in the Spirit,
[q] sene of Angels, preached vnto the Gentiles, beleued on in the worlde, *and* receiued vp in [r] glorie.

h That is, no man may haue any thing iustely to lay to his charge.
i As being defamed, shulde become impudent, & do muche harme.
Chap.1,19.
k Hauing the true doctrine of the Gospel, and the feare of God.
l Of the bishopes and Deacons.
m The good reporte of all men.
n To serue God wͭ greater assurance, because they haue alway a good conscience.
o This is spoken in respect of men, for as muche as in this worlde yͤ trueth onely remaineth in yͤ Church, by reason of Gods worde: for otherwise Christ is the fundation, and the corner stone, which bothe beareth, & mainteneth his Church.
p Approued iuste in that he was not onely a mā, but God also. q So that the Angels marueiled at his excellencie. r To the right hand of God the Father.

CHAP. III.

2 He declareth what is the office of ministers, 11 And as touching their families, 15 The dignitie of the Church, 16 And the principal point of the heauenlie doctrine.

1 THis *is* a true saying, *If any mā [a] desire the office of a [b] bishoppe, he desireth [c] a worthie worke.
2 A bishop therefore must be vnreproueа-
ble, the housband of [d] one wife, watching,
sober, modest, harberous, apt to teache,
3 Not giuen to wine, no striker, not giuen
to filthie lucre, but gentle, no fighter, not
couetous,
4 One that can rule his owne house honestly, hauing children vnder obedience with
all "honestie.
5 For if any can not rule his owne house,
how shal he [e] care for the Church of God?
6 He may not be a yong [f] scholer, lest he
being puffed vp fall into the [g] condemnation of the deuil.

Tit.2,6.
a With a feruēt zeale to profit the Church of God, wheresoeuer he shal call him.
b Whether he be Pastor or Elder.
c Bothe for yͤ difficultie of yͤ charge and also the excellencie thereof, and the necessitie of the same.
d For in those countreis at yͤ time some men had mo thē one, which was a signe of incōtinencie.
"Or, reuerence.
e If it be requisite that a man shulde take care in gouerning his owne house, how muche more are they bounde to be careful which shal gouerne the Church of God? f In the doctrine of faith. g Lest being proude of his degree he be likewise condemned as the deuil was for lifting vp him self by pride.

CHAP. IIII.

2 He teacheth him what doctrine he oght to flee, 6.8.11. And what to followe, 15 And wherein he oght to exercise him self continually.

1 NOw yͤ Spirit speaketh euidētly, that
in yͤ * latter times some shal departe
from the faith, & shal giue hede vnto [a] spirits of errour, and doctrines of deuils,
2 Which speake lyes through hypocrisie,
and haue their [b] consciences burned with
an hote yron,
3 Forbidding to marie, *and commanding* to
absteine from meats which God hathe
created to be receiued with giuing than
kes of them which beleue and knowe the
trueth.
4 For euerie creature of God *is* good, and
nothing *oght* to be refused, if it be receiued with thankesgiuing.
5 For it is [c] sanctified by the worde of God,
and prayer.
6 If thou put the brethren in remembrance of these things, thou shalt be a good
minister of Iesus Christ, which hast bene
nourished vp in the wordes of faith, and
of good doctrine, which thou hast continually followed.

2.Tim.3,1.
2.peter.3,3.
iud.18
a False teachers, which boast them selues that they haue the reuelation of the holie Gost.
b Their dull consciences first waxed harde, then after, canker and corruption bred therein, last of all it was burnt of with an hote yron, so that he meaneth suche as haue no cōscience, Eph. 4,19.
c Vnto vs, wͭ receiue it, as at Gods hands

7 *But cast away prophane, and *olde wiues
fables, & exercise thy self vnto godlines.
8 For [d] bodelie exercise profiteth litle : but
[e] godlines is profitable vnto all things, ẘ
hathe the promes of the life present, and
of that that is to come.
9 This *is* a true saying, and by all meanes
worthie to be receiued.
10 For therefore we labour & are rebuked,
because we trust in the liuing God, which
is the [f] Sauiour of all mẽ, specially of those that beleue.
11 These things commande and teache.
12 Let no man despise thy youth, but be
vnto thẽ that beleue, an ensample, in worde, in conuersation, in loue, in [g] spirit, in
faith, *&* in purenes.
13 Til I come, giue attendance to reading,
to exhortation, *&* to doctrine.
14 Despise not the gift that is in thee which
was giuen thee [h] by prophecie with the
laying on of the hands of the companie
of the [i] Eldership.
15 These things exercise, *and* giue thy self
vnto them, that *it may be sene how thou
profitest among all men.
16 Take hede vnto thy self, and vnto learning : continue therein : for in doing this
thou [k] shalt bothe saue thy self, and them
that heare thee.

Chap.1,4. & 6,20. 2.tim 2,16. & 23. tit.3,9.

d Meaning to be giuẽ to ceremonies and to suche thĩgs as delite the fantasie of mã.

e That is, he ẙ hathe faith and a good cõscience, is promised to haue all things necessarie for this life, and to enioy life euerlasting.

f The goodnes of God declareth it self towarde all mẽ, but chiefely towarde the faithful by preseruing them: and here he meaneth not of life euerlasting.

g In godlie zeale or giftes of the Spirit.

h And reuelation of the holie Gost.

i Vnder this name he conteineth ẙ whole ministerie of the Church which was at Ephesus.

**Or, that all may se how thou profitest.*

k Thou shalt faithfully do thy duetie which is an assurance of thy saluation.

CHAP. V.

1 He teacheth him how he shal behaue him self in rebuking all degrees. 3 An ordre concerning widowes. 17 The establishing of ministers. 23 The gouernãce of his bodie. 24 And the iudgement of sinnes.

1 REbuke not an elder, but exhort him
as a father, *&* the yonger men as bre
thren,
2 The elder women as mothers, the yonger
as sisters, with all purenes.
3 [a] Honour widowes, which are widdowes
in dede.
4 But if any widowe haue children or nephewes, let [b] thẽ learne first to shewe godlines towarde their owne house, and to re-
compẽse their kinred: for that is an honest
thing and acceptable before God.
5 And she ẙ is a widowe [c] in dede and left a-
lone, trusteth in God, & continueth in supplications and prayers night and day.
6 But she that liueth in pleasure, is [d] dead,
while she liueth.
7 These things therefore commande, that
they may be blameles.
8 If there be any that prouideth not for his
owne, & namely for them of his housholde, he denieth the faith, and is worse then
an infidel.
9 Let not a widowe be taken into the nõber
vnder thre score yere olde, that hathe bene the wife of [e] one housband,

a Take care for them.

b Paul willeth that the widdowes put the Church to no charge which haue ether children or kinsfolkes, that are able to relieue them, but that the children nourish their mother or kĩsfolkes according as nature bindeth them.

c Which hathe no maner of worldelie meanes to helpe her selfe ẘ.

d Because she is vtterly vnprofitable.

e He meaneth such widowes which being iustely diuorced from their first housbands maried againe to the sclander of the Church: for els he doeth not reproue the widowes that haue bene oftener maried thẽ once.

10 And wel reported of for good workes: if
she haue nourished her childrẽ, if she haue lodged the strãgers, if she haue washed
the Saintes fete, if she haue ministred vnto
them which were in aduersitie, if she were
cõtinually giuẽ vnto euerie good worke.
11 But refuse the yonger widowes : for whẽ
they haue begõne to waxe [f] wãton against
Christ, they wil marie,
12 Hauing [g] damnation, because they haue
broken the [h] first faith.
13 And likewise also being ydle they learne
to go about from house to house: yea, *they
are* not onely ydle, but also prattelers and
busibodies, speaking things which are not
comelie.
14 I wil therefore that the yonger women
marie, and beare children, & gouerne the
house, *and* giue none occasion to the aduersarie to speake euil.
15 For certeine are already turned backe
after Satan.
16 If any faithful man, or faithful woman
haue widowes, let them minister vnto
them, and let not the Church be charged,
that there may be sufficient for them that
are widowes in [i] dede.
17 ¶ The Elders that rule wel, are worthie
of * double honour, specially they which
labour in the worde and doctrine.
18 For the Scripture saith, *Thou shalt not
mousel the mouth of the oxe that treadeth
out the corne: and, *The labourer is worthie of his wages.
19 Against an Elder [k] receiue none accusation, but vnder two or thre witnesses.
20 Them that sinne, [l] rebuke openly, that
the rest also may feare.
21 ¶ *I *charge *thee* before God and the
Lord Iesus Christ, and the elect Angels,
that thou obserue these things without
*preferring one to another, & do nothing
parcially.
22 Lay hands suddenly on nõ man, [m] nether
be partaker of other mens sinnes: kepe thy
self [n] pure.
23 Drinke no longer water, but vse a litle
wine for thy stomakes sake, and thine often infirmities.
24 Some mens sinnes are open [o] before hãd,
and go before vnto iudgement : but some
mens [p] followe after.
25 Likewise also the good workes are manifest before hãd, and they that are otherwise, can not be hid.

f Forgetting their vocatiõ.

g Not onely haue sclandred the Church in leauing their charge, but haue forsaken their religion, and therefore shalbe punished with euerlasting death.

h They haue not onely done dishonor to Christ in leauing their vocatiõ, but also haue broken their faith.

i Which are without all mans helpe & succour.

Deut.15,18.

Deut.25,4. 1.cor.9,9. Mat.10,10. luk.10,7.

k Except that he ẘ doeth accuse him, haue at least two witnesses ẘ promesse with the accuser to proue that ẘ they laye to his charge.

Chap.6,13.

l Chiefly the ministers & so all others.

**Or, protest.*

**Or, without hastie iudgement.*

m In admittĩg them without sufficient trial

n Frõ iuste offence.

o As Simõ the sorcerer.

p Their sinnes followe, which for a time haue deceiued ẙ godlie, & after are detected, as Saul, Iudas, & other hypocrites.

CHAP. VI.

1 The duetie of seruantes towarde their masters. 3 Against suche as are not satisfied with the worde of God. 6 Of true godlines, and contentation of minde. 9 Against couetousnes. 11 A charge giuen to Timothie.

1 LEt as many *seruants as are vnder the
yoke, counte their masters worthie of
all

Ephe 6,5. col.3,22. 1.pet.2,18.

all honour, that the Name of God, and *his*
doctrine be not euil spoken of.
2 And thei which haue beleuing masters, let
thē not despise them, because they are brethren, but rather do seruice, because they
are faithful, and beloued, and partakers of
the [a] benefite. These things teache and
exhorte.

a That is, of ẏ grace of God, as their seruāts are, & hauing the same adoption.

3 If any man teache other wise, and con-
senteth not to the wholsome wordes of
our Lord Iesus Christ, & to the doctrine,
which is according to godlines,
4 He is pufte vp and knoweth nothing, but
doteth about * questiōs and strife of wordes, whereof cometh enuie, strife, railings,
euil surmisings,

Chap. 1, 4.

5 Vaine disputations of men of corrupt
mindes, and destitute of the trueth, which
thinke that gaine is godlines: from suche
separate thy self.
6 [b] But godlines is great gaine, if a man be
content with that he hathe.

b They ẏ measure religion by riches, are here taught, that onely religion is ẏ true riches.

7 *For we broght nothing into ẏ worlde, &
it is certeine, that we can carie nothig out.

Iob. 1, 21. prou. 27, 26. eccles. 5, 14.

8 Therefore when we haue fode & raimēt,
let vs therewith be content.
9 For they that wil be [c] riche, fall into tētation and snares, and into many foolish &
noysome lustes, which drowne men in perdition and destruction.

c That set their felicitie in riches.

10 For the desire of money is the roote of
all euil, which while some lusted after, thei
erred from the faith, & [d] perced them selues through with many sorowes.

d For they are neuer quiet nether in soule nor bodie.

11 But thou, ô [e] man of God, flee these thīgs,
and followe after righteousnes, godlines,
faith, loue, pacience, & meeknes.

e Whome Gods Spirit doeth rule.

12 Fight the good fight of faith: laye holde
of eternal life, whereunto thou art also cal
led, & hast professed a good professiō before many witnesses.
13 *I charge thee in the sight of God, who
quickneth all things, & before Iesus Christ
which vnder Pontius Pilate * witnessed a
good confession,

Chap. 5, 21. Mat. 27, 11. iohn 18, 37.

14 That thou kepe *this* commandement
without spot, and vnrebukeable, vntil the
appearing of our Lord Iesus Christ,
15 Which in due time he shal shewe, that is
*blessed and prince onely, [e] the King of
Kings, and Lord of Lords,

Chap. 1, 11. reuel. 17, 14. & 19, 16.

16 Who onely hathe immortalitie, & dwelleth in the light that none can atteine vnto, *whome neuer man sawe, nether can se,
vnto whome *be* honour and power euerlasting, Amen.

e By this mightie power of God the faithful are admonished boldly to stande in their vocation althogh the worlde, Satan and hell rage against thē.

Iohn 1, 18. 1. iohn 1, 12.

17 Charge thē that are riche [f] in this worlde, that they be not high minded, and that
they *trust not in vncerteine riches, but in
the liuing God, (which giueth vs abun
dantly all things to enioye)

Mat. 4, 19. luk. 22, 15.

f In thigs perteining to this life.

18 That they do good, & be riche in good
workes, & readie to distribute, and communicate,
19 *Laying vp in store for thē selues a good
fundation against the time to come, that
they may obteine eternal life.

Mat. 6, 20. luk. 6, 9.

20 O Timotheus, kepe [g] that which is committed vnto thee, and * auoide profane & vaine bablings, and [h] oppositions of
science falsely so called,

g The gifts of God for the vtilitie of the Church.

Chap. 1, 4. & 4, 7.

21 Which while some professe, they haue
erred concerning the faith. Grace *be* with
thee, Amen.

h As when question engendreth question.

The first *epistle* to Timotheus written from
Laodicea, which is the chiefest citie of
Phrygia Pacaciana.

THE SECONDE EPI-stle of Paul to Timotheus.

THE ARGVMENT.

THe Apostle being now ready to confirme that doctrine with his blood, which he had professed and taught, encourageth Timotheus (& in him all the faithful) in the faith of the Gospel, & in the cōstant & syncere confessiō of the same: willing him not to shrinke for feare of afflictiōs, but patiētly to attende the yssue, as do housband men, which at length receiue the frutes of their labours, & to cast of all feare & care, as souldiers do which seke onely to please their capteine: shewing him briefly the summe of the Gospel, which he preached, cōmanding him to preache the same to others, diligently taking hede of contentiōs, curious disputatiōs, & vaine questiōs, to the intent that his doctrine may all together edifie. Cōsidering that the exāples of Hymeneus & Philetus, which subuerted the true doctrine of the resurrectiō, were so horrible: & yet to the intent that no mā shulde be offended at their fall, being men of autoritie and in estimatiō, he sheweth that all that professe Christ, are not his, & that the Church is subiect to this calamitie that the euil must dwell amōg the good til Gods trial come: yet he reserueth them whome he hathe elected, euen to the end. And that Timotheus shulde not be discouraged by the wicked, he declareth what abominable men, & dāgerous times shal followe, willing him to arme him self with the hope of the good yssue that God wil giue vnto his, and to exercise him self diligently in the Scriptures, bothe against the aduersaries, and for the vtilitie of the Church, desiring him to come to him for certeine necessarie affaires, and so with his and others salutations endeth.

CHAP. I.

6 Paul exhorteth Timotheus to stedfastnes and patience in persecution, and to continue in the doctrine, that he had taught him. 12 Whereof his bonds and afflictions were a gage. 16 A commendation of Onesiphorus.

1 PAul an Apostle of Ie-
sus Christ, by the wil of
God, [a]according to the
promes of life, which is
in CHRIST IESVS,
2 To Timotheus *my*
beloued sonne: Grace,
mercie, & peace from God the Father, &
from Iesus Christ our Lord.
3 I thanke God, * whome I serue frō *mine*
[b]elders with pure conscience, that without
ceasing I haue remembrāce of thee in my
prayers night and day,
4 Desiring to se thee, mindful of thy teares, that I may be filled with ioye:
5 When I call to remembrance the vnfained faith that is in thee, which dwelt first
in thy grandmother Lois, and in thy mother Eunice, & am assured that *it dwelleth*
in thee also.
6 Wherefore, I put thee in remembrance
that thou [c] stirre vp the gifte of God
which is in thee, by the putting on of [d] mi
ne hands.
7 For God hathe not giuen to vs the Spirit
of [e] feare, but of power, and of loue, and of
a sounde minde.
8 Be not therefore ashamed of the testimo
nie of our Lord, nether of me his prisoner: but be partaker of the afflictiōs of the
Gospel, according to the power of God,
9 Who hathe saued vs, & called vs with an
*holie calling, not according to our * wor-
kes, but according to his owne purpose &
grace, which was giuen to vs through
Christ Iesus before the *worlde was,
10 But is now made manifest by the [f] appearing of our Sauiour Iesus Christ, who
hathe abolished death, and hathe broght
life and immortalitie vnto light through
the Gospel.
11 *Whereunto I am appointed a preacher,
& Apostle, & a teacher of the Gentiles.
12 For the which cause I also suffre these
things, but I am not ashamed: for I knowe
whome I haue beleued, & I am persuaded
that he is able to kepe that which I haue
[g]committed to him against that day.
13 Kepe the true paterne of the wholsome
wordes, which ŷ hast heard of me in faith
and loue which is in Christ Iesus.
14 That [h] worthie thing, which was committed to thee, kepe through the holie
Gost, which dwelleth in vs.
15 This thou knowest, that all they which
are in Asia, be turned from me: of which
sorte are Phygellus and Hermogenes.
16 The Lord giue mercie vnto the house of
Onesiphorus: for he oft refreshed me, and
was not ashamed of my chaine.
17 But when he was at Rome, he soght me
out verie diligently, and founde *me*.
18 The Lord grant vnto him, that he may
finde mercie with the Lord at that day, &
in how manie things he hathe ministred
vnto me at Ephesus, ŷ knowest verie wel.

a Being sent of God to preache that life which he had promised in Christ Iesus.

Act. 22,3.
b Following ŷ steppes of mine ancestres, as Abraham, Isaac, Iacob, & others of whome I am come and of whome I receiued the true religion by succession.

c The gift of God is a certein liuelie flame kindeled in our hearts, ŵ Satan and the flesh labour to quenche, and therefore we must nourish it, and stirre it vp.
d With ŷ rest of the Elders of Ephesus, 1. Tim. 4,14.
1. Cor. 1,2.
ephe. 1,3.
Tit. 3,5.
e As thogh God wolde destroye vs.
Rom. 16,25.
eph. 3,9.
col. 1,26.
tit. 1,2.
1. pet. 1,20.
1. Tim. 2,7.
f He speaketh here of his first comming, which thoght it semed poore & contemptible, yet was honorable and glorious: therefore our mindes oght to be lifted vp frō the consideration of worldlie things, to contemplate the maiestie thereof.
g Which is my self.
h The graces of ŷ holie Gost

CHAP. II.

2 He exhorteth him to be constant in trouble, to suffer manly, and to abyde faste in the wholsome doctrine of our Lord Iesus Christ. 11 Shewing him the fidelitie of Gods counsel touching the saluation of his. 19 And the marke thereof.

1 THou therefore, my sonne, be strong in
the grace that is in Christ Iesus.
2 And what things thou hast heard of me,
°by manie witnesses, the same deliuer to
faithful men, which shalbe able to [a] teache
other also.
3 Thou therefore suffer afflictiō as a good
souldier of Iesus Christ.
4 No man that warreth, entangleth him
self with [b] the affaires of *this* life, because
he wolde please him that hathe chosen him
to be a souldier.
5 And if anie mā also striue for a masterie,
he is not crowned, except he striue as he
oght to do.
6 The housband man [c] must labour before he receiue the frutes.
7 Consider what I say: and the Lord giue
thee vnderstanding in all things.
8 Remember that Iesus Christ *made* of the
sede of Dauid, was raised againe from the
dead according to my Gospel.
9 Wherein I suffer trouble as an euil doer,
euen vnto bondes: but the worde of God
is not [d] bounde.
10 Therefore I suffer all things, for the
* [e] elects sake, that they might also obteine the saluation which is in Christ Iesus,
with eternal glorie.
11 It *is* a true saying, For if we be *dead with
him, we also shal liue with him.
12 If we suffer, we shal also reigne with him:
* if we denie him, he also wil denie vs.
13 If * we beleue not, *yet* abideth he faithful: he can not denie him self.
14 Of these things put them in remembrāce, and protest before the Lord, that they
striue not about wordes, which is to no
profit, *but* to the peruerting of the hearers.
15 Studie to shewe thy self approued vnto
God, a workemā that nedeth not to be asha
med, [f] diuiding the worde of trueth aright.
16 *Stay prophane, and vaine bablings:
for they shal encrease vnto more vngodlines.
17 And their worde shal fret as a cancre:
of which sorte is Hymeneus and Philetus,

°*Or, in the presence of manie witnesses.*
a So that the trueth of God may remaine perfite.

b As with his housholde, & other ordinarie affaires.

c So that the paine must go before the recompense.

d Notwithstāding mine imprisonment ŷ worde of God hathe it race, & increaseth.
2. Cor. 1,4.
col. 1,24.
Rom. 6,5.
e To confirme their faith, more estemīg the edification of ŷ Church thē him self.
Mat. 10,33.
mar. 8,38.
Rom 3,3.
& 9,6.
f Giuing to euerie one his iuste portion. Wherein he alludeth to the Priests of the olde Law ŵ in their sacrifice gaue to God his parte, toke their owne parte and gaue to him ŷ broght ŷ sacrifice, his duetie.
1. Tim. 4,7.
& 6,20.
tit. 3,9.

18 Which as concerning the trueth haue
erred, saying that the resurrection is past
already, and do destroye the faith of certeine.
19 But the fundation of God remaineth
sure, and hathe this seale, [g] The Lord,
knoweth who are his, and, Let euerie one
that calleth on the Name of Christ, depar
te from iniquitie.
20 Notwithstanding in a [h] great house are
not onely vessels of golde & of siluer, but
also of wood and of earth, & some for honour, and some vnto dishonour.
21 If anie man therefore purge him self frõ
[i] these, he shalbe a vessel vnto honour, sanctified, and mete for the Lord, and prepared vnto euerie good worke.
22 Flee also from the lustes of youth, and
followe after righteousnes, faith, loue,
& peace, with them that* call on the Lord
with pure heart.
23 *And put away foolish, and [k] vnlearned
questions, knowing that they ingendre
strife.
24 But the seruant of the Lord must not
striue, but *must* be gentle towarde all men
apt to teache, [l] suffring the euil men *pa-*
tiently,
25 Instructing them with mekenes that are
contrarie [m] minded, *prouing* if God at anie
time wil giue them repentance, that they
may knowe the trueth,
26 And "that they may come to amendemẽt
out of the snare of the deuil, which are taken of him at his wil.

g He groundeth vpõ Gods election and mans faith.
h Because the wicked shulde not couer thẽ selues vnder ye name of the Church, he sheweth by this similitude, yt bothe good & bad may be therein.
i That is, bothe separate him self from the wicked, & also purge his natural corruption by Gods Spirit.
2.Cor.1,2.
1.Tim.1,4. & 4,7.
tit.3,9.
k Which do not edifie.
l Which faile of ignorance.
m He meaneth not this of Apostates, or heretikes, whom he willeth to flee: but of thẽ onely which as yet are not come to the knowledge of the trueth, & fall through ignorance.
"Or, that being deliuered out of the snare of the deuil of whome they are taken, they may come to amendement & performe his wil.

CHAP. III.

1 He prophecieth of the perilous times, 2 Setteth out hy-
pocrites in their colours. 12 Sheweth the state of the
Christians, 14 And how to auoide dangers. 16 Also
what profit cometh of the Scriptures.

1 THis knowe also, that in the*last dayes
shal come perilous times.
2 For [a] men shalbe louers of their owne selues, couetous, boasters, proude, cursed
speakers, disobedient to parents, vnthankeful, vnholie,
3 Without natural affectiõ, trucebreakers,
false accusers, intemperate, fierce, despi-
cers of them which are good,
4 Traitours, headie, high minded, louers of
pleasures more then louers of God,
5 Hauing a shewe of godlines, but haue denied the power thereof: turne away therefore from suche.
6 For of this sorte are they which [b] crepe
into houses, and lead captiue simple women laden with sinnes, and led with diuers
lustes,
7 *Which women are* euer learning, and are
neuer able to come to the knowledge of
the trueth.
8 *And as Iannes and Iambres withstode
Moses, so do these also resiste the trueth,

1 Tim.4,1. 2.pet.3,3. iude 18.
a He speaketh of them which make profession to be Christians.
b As, monkes, friers, and suche hypocrites.
Exod.7,12.

men of [c] corrupte mindes, reprobate concerning the faith.
9 But they shal preuaile no lõger: for their
madnes shalbe euident vnto all men, as
theirs also was.
10 ¶ But thou hast fully knowen my doctri
ne, maner of liuing, [d] purpose, faith, lõg suf
fering, loue, pacience,
11 Persecutions, & afflictions which came
vnto me at* Antiochia, at Iconium, and at
Lystri, which persecutions I suffered: but
from them all the Lord deliuered me.
12 Yea, & all that wil liue godly in Christ
Iesus, shal suffer persecution.
13 But the euil men and [e] deceiuers, shal waxe worsse and worsse, deceiuing, and being
deceiued.
14 But continue thou in the things which
thou hast learned, and art persuaded *the-*
reof, knowing of whome thou hast learned *them*:
15 And yt thou hast knowẽ the holie Scriptures of a childe, which are able to make
thee wise vnto saluation through the faith
which is in Christ Iesus.
16 *For the whole Scripture *is* giuen by inspiration of God, and *is* profitable to teache, to improue, to correct *and* to instructe
in righteousnes,
17 That the [f] man of God may be [g] absolute, being made perfite vnto all good
workes.

c Which can iudge nothing aright.
d Not onely what I taught and did, but also what my minde & wil was.
Act.13,14.
e The worde signifieth thẽ, that by anie craftie packing or conueiance beguile mẽ wt false colors, flatteries & illusions, & suche God setteth vp to exercise his by them: & here S. Paul admonisheth vs of them.
2.Pet.1,20.
f Which is cõtent to be gouerned by Gods worde.
g The onelie Scripture sufficeth to lead vs to perfection.

CHAP. IIII.

1 He exhorteth Timotheus to be feruent in the worde, and
to suffer aduersitie, 6 Maketh mention of his owne
death, 9 And biddeth Timothie come vnto him.

1 I "Charge *thee* therefore before God, &
before the Lord Iesus Christ, which shal
iudge the quicke and dead at his appearing, and in his kingdome,
2 Preache the worde: be instant, [a] in season
and out of season: improue, rebuke, exhorte with all long suffring and doctrine.
3 For the time wil come, when they wil not
suffer wholsome doctrine: but hauing their
eares itching, shal after their owne lustes
get them an heape of teachers,
4 And shal turne their eares frõ the trueth,
and shal be giuen vnto [b] fables.
5 But watch thou in all things: suffer aduer
sitie: do the worke of an Euangeliste: make
[c] thy ministerie fully knowen.
6 For I am now ready to be [d] offered, and
the time of my " departing is at hand.
7 I haue foght a good fight, and haue finished *my* course: I haue kept the faith.
8 *For* hence forthe is laid vp for me the
crowne of righteousnes, which the Lord
the righteous iudge shal giue me at that
day: and not to me onely, but vnto all thẽ
also that loue his appearing.
9 Make spede to come vnto me atonce.
10 For Demas hath forsakẽ me, & hathe em-

"Or, adiure.
a Leaue none occasion to preache and to profite.
b To false, & vnprofitable doctrine.
c So behaue thy self in this office, that men may be able to charge thee wt nothing, but rather approue thee in all things.
"Or, dissoluing.
d Read Phil. 2,17.

braced this preſent worlde,and is departed
vnto Theſſalonica.Creſcens *is gone* to Ga
lacia,Titus vnto Dalmacia.

Coloſ.4,19.

11 * [e] Onely Luke is with me. Take Marke
and bring him with thee: for he is profitable vnto me to miniſter.

e Hereby it is manifeſt that Peter as yet was not at Rome,and if euer he was there it is vncerteine.

12 And Tychicus haue I ſent to Epheſus.
13 The [f] cloke that I left at Troas with Car
pus,when thou comeſt, bring with thee, &
the bokes, but ſpecially the parchements.

f Some reade coffre: others, booke.

14 Alexander the copper ſmith hathe done
me muche euil: the Lord [g] rewarde him
according to his workes.

g For Paul ſawe in him manifeſt ſignes of reprobation.

15 Of whome be thou ware alſo;for he with-
ſtode our preaching ſore.
16 At my firſt anſwering [h] no man aſsiſted
me, but all forſoke me: *I praye God*, that it
may not be laid to their charge.

h If S Peter had bene there he wolde not haue forſaken him.

17 Notwithſtanding the Lord aſsiſted me,
and ſtrengthened me,that by me the preaching might be fully knowen,and that all
the Gentiles ſhulde heare, and I was deliuered out of the mouth of the [i] lion.

i Out of the great danger of Nero.

18 And the Lord wil deliuer me from euerie [k] euil worke, and wil preſerue me vnto
his heauẽlie kingdome:to whome *be* praiſe for euer and euer, Amen.

k That I commit nothing vnworthie mine office.

19 Salute Priſca,and Aquila,and the * houſholde of Oneſiphorus.

Chap.1,16.

20 Eraſtus abode at Corinthus: Trophimus
I left at Miletum ſicke.
21 Make ſpede to come before winter. Eubu
lus greteth thee,and Pudens,and Linus,&
Claudia,and all the brethren.
22 The Lord Ieſus Chriſt *be* with thy ſpirit. Grace *be* with you, Amen.

The ſeconde *Epiſtle* written from Rome vnto Timotheus the firſt biſhope elected, of the Church of Epheſus, when Paul was preſented the ſeconde time before the Emperour Nero.

THE EPISTLE OF Paul to Titus.

THE ARGVMENT.

When Titus was left in Creta to finiſh that doctrine which Paul had there begonne, Satan ſtirred vp certeine which went about not onely to ouerthrowe the gouernemẽt of the Church, but alſo to corrupt the doctrine: for ſome by ambition wolde haue thruſt in them ſelues to be paſtours: others, vnder pretext of Moſes Law broght in manie trifles. Againſt theſe two ſortes of men Paul armeth Titus: firſt teaching him what maner of miniſters he oght to choſe, chiefly requiring that they be men of ſounde doctrine to the intent they might reſiſt the aduerſaries, and amongs other things he noteth the Iewes which put a certeine holines in meates & ſuche outwarde ceremonies, teaching them which are the true exerciſes of a Chriſtian life, & what things apperteine to euerie mans vocation. Againſt the which if anie man rebelle or els doeth not obey, he willeth him to be auoyded.

CHAP. I.

3 He aduertiſeth Titus touching the gouernement of the Church. 7 The ordonance and office of miniſters. 12 The nature of the Cretans, and of them which ſowe abroade Iewiſh fables and inuentions of men.

"Or, miniſter.

1 Paul a "ſeruant of God,
and an Apoſtle of IE-
SVS CHRIST, accor-
ding to the [a] faith of
Gods elect & ỹ know-
ledge of the trueth, w^c is
according to godlines,

a That is, to preache the faith, to increaſe their knowledge, to teache them to liue godly ỹ at length they may obteine eternal life.

2 Vnder the hope of eternal life, which
God that can not lie, hathe [b] promiſed before the * worlde began:

Rom.16,25. ephe.3,9. col.1,26. 2.tim.1,10. 1.pet.1,20. Gal.1,1.

3 But hathe made his worde manifeſt in
due time through the preaching, which is
* committed vnto me, according to the cõ
mandement of God our [c] Sauiour:

b Hathe willingly, and of his mere liberalitie promiſed without fore ſeing our faith or workes as a cauſe to moue him to this fre mercie. c Who bothe giueth life, and preſerueth life.

4 To Titus *my* natural [d] ſonne according
to the commune faith, Grace, mercie *and*
peace from God the Father, and *from* the
Lord Ieſus Chriſt our Sauiour.

d In reſpect of faith which was commune to thẽ bothe, ſo that hereby they are brethrẽ: but in reſpect of the miniſterie Paul begate him as his ſonne in faith.

5 For this cauſe left I thee in Creta, that
thou ſhuldeſt cõtinue to redreſſe ỹ things
that remaine, and ſhuldeſt ordeine Elders
in euerie citie, as I appointed thee,

1.Tim.3,2.

6 * If anie [e] be vnreproueable, the houſbãd
of one wife, hauing faithful childrẽ, which
are not ſclandered of riote, nether are diſobedient.

e That is, without all infamie whereby his autoritie might be diminiſhed.

7 For a biſhop muſt be vnreproueable, as
[f] Gods ſtewarde, not "frowarde, not angrie,
not giuen to wine, no ſtriker, not giuen to
filthie lucre,

f Who hathe the diſpenſation of his gifts.

"Or ſelf willy.

8 But harberous, one that loueth "goodnes,
wiſe, [g] righteous, [h] holie, temperate,

"Or, good men.

g Towarde men.

h Towarde God.

9 Holding faſt the faithful worde according to doctrine, that he alſo may be able
to exhorte with wholſome doctrine, and
improue them that ſay againſt it.

10 For

10 For there are manie diſobedient & vaine talkers and deceiuers of mindes, chiefly they of the [i] Circumciſion,
11 Whoſe mouths muſt be ſtopped, which
ſubuert whole houſes, teaching things,
which thei oght not, for filthie lucres ſake.
12 One of them ſelues, *euen* one of their
owne [k] prophetes ſaid, The Cretians *are*
alwaies lyars, euil beaſtes, ſlowe belyes.
13 This witnes is true: wherefore rebuke thẽ
ſharpely, that they maye be ſounde in the
faith,
14 And not taking hede to * Iewiſh fables
and commandements of men, that turne
from the trueth.
15 Vnto the pure * *are* all things pure, but
vnto them that are defiled, and vnbeleuing, *is* nothing pure, but euen their mindes and conſciences are defiled.
16 Thei profeſſe that they knowe God, but
by [l] workes thei denie *him*, and are abominable and diſobedient, and vnto euerie
good worke reprobate.

i Which were not onely the Iewes, but alſo ẙ Hebionites, & Cherinthiãs heretikes, ẘ taught that ẙ Law muſt be ioyned with Chriſt.

k He calleth Epimenides ẙ Philoſopher, or Poet, whoſe verſe he here reciteth, a Prophet, becauſe the Cretiãs ſo eſtemed him: & as Laertius writeth, thei ſacrificed vnto him as to a God, forasmuche as he had a maruelous gift to vnderſtand things to come: ẘ thing Satan by the permiſsion of God hathe opened to the infideles from time to time, but it turneth to their greater condemnacion.

1.Tim.1,4.

Rom.14,20.

l Forasmuche as thei ſtay at things of nothing, & paſſe not for them, that are of importance, & ſo giue them ſelues to all wickednes.

CHAP. II.

1 He commendeth vnto him the wholſome doctrine, and telleth him how he ſhal teache all degrees to behaue thẽ ſelues, 11 Through the benefite of the grace of Chriſt.

1 BVt ſpeake thou the things which become [a] wholſome doctrine,
2 That the Elder men be ſobre, honeſt, diſcrete, ſounde in the faith, in loue, & in pacience:
3 The Elder women likewiſe, that they be
in ſuche behauiour as becometh holines,
not falſe accuſers, not giuen to muche
wine, *but* teachers of honeſt things,
4 That they may inſtruct the yong women
to be ſobre minded, that they loue their
houſbands, that they loue their children,
5 That thei be diſcrete, chaſt, [b] kepĩg at home,
good and * ſubiect vnto their houſbands,
ẙ the worde of God be not euil ſpoken of.
6 Exhorte yong men likewiſe, that thei be
ſobre minded.
7 Aboue all things ſhewe thy ſelf an enſample of good workes with vncorrupt
doctrine, with grauitie, integritie,
8 *And* with the wholſome worde, which
can not be reproued, that he which with-
ſtandeth, may be aſhamed, hauing nothĩg
concerning you to ſpeake euil of.
9 *Let ſeruants be ſubiect to their maſters,
and pleaſe *them* in all things, not anſwerĩg
againe,
10 Nether pykers, but that they ſhewe all
good faithfulnes, that thei may adorne the
doctrine of God our Sauiour in all thĩgs.
11 * For the grace of God, that bringeth
[c] ſaluacion vnto all men, hathe appeared,
12 And teacheth vs that we ſhulde denie
vngodlines, and worldlie luſtes, & that we
ſhulde liue ſobrely and righteouſly, and
godly in this preſent worlde,
13 Loking for the bleſſed hope, and appearing of the glorie of the mightie God,
and of our Sauiour Ieſus Chriſt,
14 Who gaue him ſelf for vs, that he might
redeme vs from all iniquitie, and purge
vs *to be* a [d] peculiar people vnto him ſelf,
zealous of good workes.
15 Theſe things ſpeake, and exhorte, and
rebuke with all [e] autoritie. Se that no man
deſpice thee.

Chap II.

a Wherewith our ſoules are fed & mainteined in helth.

Ephes.5,23.

b Not running to & fro without neceſſarie occaſions, ẘ is a ſigne of lighnes.

Ephes.6,5.
Coloſ.3,22.
1.pet.2,18.

1.Cor.1,2.
Coloſ.1,22.

c Of what condicion or ſtate ſoeuer thei be.

d Moſte dere and precious.

e As becometh the ambaſſadour of God.

CHAP. III.

1 Of obedience to ſuche as be in autoritie. 9 He warneth Titus to beware of fooliſh and vnprofitable queſtions, 12 Concluding with certeine priuate matters, 15 And ſalutacions.

1 PVt them in remembrance that they
* [a] be ſubiect to the Principalities &
Powers, & that they be obedient, & readie to euerie good worke,
2 That they ſpeake euil of no mã, that thei
be no fighters, *but* ſofte, ſhewing all mekenes vnto all men.
3 * [b] For we our ſelues alſo were in times
paſt vnwiſe, diſobediẽt, deceiued, ſeruing
the luſtes and diuers pleaſures, liuing in
malicious nes and enuie, hateful, & hating
one another.
4 But when the bountifulnes and loue of
God our Sauiour towarde man appeared,
5 * Not [c] by the workes of righteouſnes,
which we had done, but according to his
mercie he ſaued vs, by the [d] waſhing of
the new birth, and the renuing of the holie Goſt,
6 Which he ſhed on vs abũdantly, through
Ieſus Chriſt our Sauiour,
7 That we, beĩg iuſtified by his grace, ſhulde be made heires according to the hope
of eternal life.
8 This *is* a true ſaying, and theſe things I
wil thou ſhuldeſt affirme, that they which
haue beleued in God, might be careful to
ſhewe forthe good workes. Theſe things
are good and profitable vnto men.
9 * But ſtay fooliſh queſtions, and genealogies, and contentions, and brawlings a-
bout the Law: for thei are vnprofitable &
vaine.
10 [e] Reiect him that is an heretike, after
once or twiſe admonicion,
11 Knowing that he that is ſuche, is [f] peruerted, and [g] ſinneth being damned of his
owne ſelf.
12 When I ſhal ſend Artemas vnto thee,
or Tychicus, be diligent to come to me
vnto Nicopolis: for I haue determined
there to winter.
13 Bring Zenas [h] the expoũder of the Law,
and Apollos on their iourney diligently,
that they lacke nothing.
14 And let ours alſo learne to ſhewe forthe

Rom.13,1.
1.pet.2,13.

a Although ẙ rulers be infideles, yet we are bounde to obey them in ciuil polices, and where as thei cõmande vs nothing againſt ẙ worde of God.

1.Cor.6,11.

b For let vs conſider what we our ſelues were whẽ God ſhewed vs fauour.

2.Tim.1,9.

c God doeth not iuſtifie vs for reſpect of anie thing, ẘ he ſeeth in vs, but doeth preuent vs with his grace and frely accepteth vs.

d Baptiſme is a ſure ſigne of our regeneracion, which is wroght by the holie Goſt.

e This commãdement is giuẽ to ẙ miniſter, & ſo particularly to all men to whome the ſworde is not cõmitted: but els the magiſtrate, whoſe chief office is to mainteine Gods glorie in his Church, oght to cut of all ſuche rottẽ and infectuous members from the bodie.

1.Tim.1,4.
& 4,7.2.tim.2,23.

f So that there is no hope of amendement.

g Willingly, & wittingly.

h It is probable, ẙ he was an interpreter of the Law of Moſes, as Apollos, &c.

good workes for necessarie vses that thei
be not vnfruteful.
15 All that are with me, salute thee. Grete
them that loue vs in the faith. Grace *be*
with you all, Amen.

To Titus, elect the first bishope
of the Church of the Cretians, written
from
Nicopolis in Macedonia.

THE EPISTLE OF Paul to Philemon.

THE ARGUMENT.

Albeit the excellencie of Pauls spirit wonderfully appeareth in other his Epistles, yet this Epistle is a great witnes, and a declaracion of the same. For farre passing the basenes of his matter, he fleeth as it were vp to heauen, and speaketh with a diuine grace and maiestie. Onesimus seruant to Philemon bothe robbed his master, and fled away, whome Paul hauing wonne to Christ, sent againe to his master, earnestly begging his pardone, with moste waightie arguments prouing the duetie of one Christian to another, & so with salutacions endeth.

8 He reioyceth to heare of the faith and loue of Philemō. 9 Whome he desireth to forgiue his seruant Onesimus, and louingly to receiue him againe.

1 Paul a prisoner of Iesus
Christ, and *our* brother
Timotheus, vnto Philemon
our dere friend,
& fellow helper,
2 And to *our* dere sister
Apphia, and to Archippus
our felowe souldier, & to the Church
that is in thine house:
3 Grace *be* with you, and peace from God
our Father, & *from* the Lord Iesus Christ.
4 I *giue thankes to my God, making mencion
alwaies of thee in my praiers,
5 (When I heare of thy loue & faith, which
thou hast towarde the Lord Iesus, & towarde
all Saintes)
6 That the [a] felowship of thy faith may be
made fruteful, and that whatsoeuer good
thīg is in you [b] through Christ Iesus, may
be knowen.
7 For we haue great ioye and consolacion
in thy loue, because by thee, brother, the
Saintes [c] hearts are comforted.
8 Wherefore, thogh I be verie bolde in
Christ to commande thee that which is
conuenient,
9 *Yet* for loues sake I rather beseche thee,
thogh I be as I am, euen Paul aged, and
euen now a prisoner for Iesus Christ.
10 I beseche thee for my sonne *Onesimus,
whome I haue begotten in my bondes,
11 Which in time past was to thee vnprofitable,
but now profitable bothe to thee
and to me,
12 Whome I haue sent againe: thou therefore
receiue him, ỷ is mine owne bowels,
13 Whome I wolde haue reteined with me,
that in thy stede he might haue ministred
vnto me in the bondes of the Gospel.
14 But without thy minde wolde I do nothing,
that thy benefite shulde not be as it
were of necessitie, but willingly.
15 It may be that he therefore [d] departed
for a season, that thou shuldest receiue him
for euer,
16 [e] Not now as a seruant, but aboue a seruant,
euen as a brother beloued, specially
to me: how muche more then vnto thee,
bothe in the flesh, and in the Lord?
17 If therefore thou counte our things
[f] commune, receiue him as my self.
18 If he hathe hurt thee, or oweth thee
oght, that put on mine accountes.
19 I Paul haue written *this* with mine owne
hand: I wil recompense it, albeit I do not
say to thee, that thou owest vnto me euen
thine owne self.
20 Yea, brother, let me obteine this pleasure
of thee in the Lord: cōforte my [g] bowels
in the Lord.
21 Trusting in thine obedience, I wrote vnto
thee, knowing that thou wilt do euen
more then I say.
22 Moreouer also prepare me lodging: for
I trust through your praiers I shalbe giuen
vnto you.
23 There salute thee Epaphras my fellowe
prisoner [h] in Christ Iesus,
24 Marcus, Aristarchus, Demas & Luke,
my fellowe helpers.
25 The grace of our Lord Iesus Christ *be*
with your spirit, Amen.

Written from Rome to Philemon,
and sent by Onesimus a
seruant.

1.Thes.1,2. 2.thes.1,3.

a Thy beneuolence towarde the Saintes, ẘ procedeth of a liuelie and effectual faith.

b That experience may declare ỷ you are the mēbers of Iesus Christ.

c Meanīg their inwarde partes & affectiōs were through his charitie comforted.

Colos.4,9.

d He fled away from thee.

e For he is thy seruant by cōdicion, & also now ỷ Lords, so ỷ bothe for thine owne sake and for the Lords ỷ oghtest to loue him.

f That all thine is mine, & all mine is thine.

g Grant me this benefite, ẘ shalbe moste acceptable vnto me of all others.

h That is, for Christs cause.

THE

THE EPISTLE TO the Ebrewes.

THE ARGVMENT.

Forasmuche as diuers, bothe of the Greke writers and Latines witnesse, that the writer of this Epistle for iuste causes wolde not haue his name knowen, it were curiositie of our parte to labour muche therein. For seing the Spirit of God is the autor thereof, it diminisheth nothing the autoritie, althogh we knowe not with what penne he wrote it. Whether it were Paul (as it is not like) or Luke, or Barnabas, or Clement, or some other, his chief purpose is to persuade vnto the Ebrewes (whereby he principally meaneth them that abode at Ierusalem, and vnder them all the rest of the Iewes) that Christ Iesus was not onely the redemer, but also that at his comming all ceremonies must haue an end: forasmuche as his doctrine was the conclusion of all the prophecies, and therefore not onely Moses was inferior to him, but also the Angels: for they all were seruants, and he the Lord, but so Lord, that he hathe also taken our flesh, and is made our brother to assure vs of our saluation through him self: for he is that eternal Priest, whereof all the Leuitical Priests were but shadowes, and therefore at his comming they oght to cease, and all sacrifices for sinne to be abolished, as he proueth from the seuenth chap. verse 11. vnto the 12. chap. verse 18. Also he was that Prophet of whome all the Prophetes in time past witnessed, as is declared from the 12. chapter, verse 18. to the twentie and fiue verse of the same chapter: yea, and is the King to whome all things are subiect, as appeareth from that verse 25. to the beginning of the last chapter. Wherefore according to the examples of the olde fathers we must constantly beleue in him, that being sanctified by his iustice, taught by his wisdome, and gouerned by his power, we may stedfastly, and courageously perseuere euen to the end in hope of that ioye that is set before our eyes, occupying our selues in Christian exercises that we may bothe be thankful to God, and duetiful to our neighbour.

CHAP. I.

1 He sheweth the excellencie of Christ 4 Aboue the Angels, 7 And of their office.

1 AT sondrie times & in di
uers maners [a]God spake
in ye olde time to *our* fathers by the Prophetes:
2 In these [b] last dayes he
hathe spoken vnto vs by
his Sonne, whome he
hathe made heir of all things,[c] by whome
also he made the worldes,
3 *Who being the brightnes of the glorie,
and the [d] ingraued forme of his persone, &
bearing vp all things by his mightie worde, hathe by him self [e] purged our sinnes,
and sitteth at the right hand of the maiestie in the highest places,
4 And is made so muche more excellent
then the [f] Angels in as muche as he hathe
obteined a more excellēt name then thei.
5 For vnto which of the Angels said he at
anie time, *Thou art my Sonne, [g] this day
begate I thee? and againe, I *wil be his Fa
ther, and he shalbe my sonne?
6 And againe when he bringeth in *his*
first begotten Sonne into the worlde, he
saith, *And let all the Angels of God worship him.
7 And of the Angels he saith, *He maketh
the [h] Spirits his messengers, and his ministers a flame of fyre.
8 But vnto the Sonne *he saith*, *O God,
thy throne *is* for euer and euer: the [i] scepter of thy kingdome *is* a scepter of righteousnes.
9 Thou hast loued righteousnes and hated
iniquitie. Wherefore God, *euen* thy God,
hathe [k] anointed thee with ye oyle of gladnes aboue thy fellowes.
10 And, *Thou, Lord, in the beginning hast
established the earth, and the heauens are
the workes of thine hands.
11 They shal perish, but thou doest remaine: and they all shal waxe olde as doeth a
garment.
12 And as a vesture shalt thou folde them
vp, and they shalbe changed: but thou art
the same and thy yeres shal not faile.
13 Vnto which also of the Angels said he at
anie time, *Sit at my right hand, til I make thine enemies thy fote stole?
14 Are they not all ministring spirits, sent
forthe to minister, for their sakes which
shalbe heires of saluation?

a God, who is euer constant, and merciful to his Church, declared his wil in time past, not all at once, or after one sorte, but from time to time, and in sondrie sortes: but now last of all he hathe fully declared all trueth to vs by his Sōne.

Wis.7,26. col.1,14.

b So that now we may not credit anie new reuelatiōs after him.

Psal.2,7. chap.5,9. act.13,33.

2.Sam.7,14. 1.chro.22,10.

Psal.97,8.

c He entreateth here of Christ, bothe as touching his persone, which is verie God, & verie man, by whome all things are made, and also as touching his office, whereby he is King, Prophet & Priest. d The liuelie image and paterne, so that he that seeth him, seeth the Father, Iohn 14,9: for els the persone of the Father is not sene, but apprehended by faith. e So that our sinnes can be purged by none other meanes. f Muche more then then all other things created. g Because he was at the time appointed declared to the worlde.

Psal.104,4.

h He compareth the Angels to the windes, which are here beneth as Gods messengers.

Psal.45,7.

i The administration of thy kingdome is iuste.

k This is mēt in that that ye worde is made flesh, and that the holie Gost was powred on him without measure, yt we may all receiue of him euerie one according to his measure.

Psal.102,26.

Psal 110,1. mat.22,44. 1 cor.15,25. chap.10,12.

CHAP. II.

1 He exhorteth vs to be obedient vnto the new Law which Christ hathe giuen vs, 9 And not to be offended at the infirmitie and lowe degre of Christ, 10 Because it was necessarie that for our sakes he shulde take suche an humble state vpon him, that he might be like vnto his brethren.

1 WHerefore we oght diligētly to gi
ue hede to the things wc we haue

heard,leſt at anie [a] time we ſhulde let thē
ſlippe.
2 For if the [b] worde ſpoken by Angels was
ſtedfaſte, and euerie tranſgreſsion, and
diſobedience receiued a iuſte recompenſe
of rewarde,
3 How ſhal we eſcape, if we neglect ſo
[c] great ſaluation, which at the firſt began
to be preached by the Lord, and *afterwarde* was confirmed vnto vs by [d] them that
heard him,
4 *God bearing witnes thereto, bothe with
ſignes and wonders, & with diuers miracles, and giftes of the holie Goſt, according to his owne wil?
5 For he hathe not put in ſubiection vnto
the Angels the [e] worlde to come, whereof
we ſpeake.
6 But* one in a certeine place witneſſed,
ſaying, [f] What is man, that thou ſhuldeſt
be mindeful of him! or the ſonne of man
that thou woldeſt conſider him!
7 Thou madeſt him a litle inferior to the
Angels: thou crownedſt him with [g] glorie
and honour, and haſt ſet him aboue the
workes of thine hands.
8 *Thou haſt put all things in ſubiection
vnder his fete. And in that he hathe put
all things in ſubiection vnder him, he left
nothing that ſhulde not be ſubiect vnto
him. [h] But we yet ſe not all things ſubdued
vnto [i] him.
9 But we ſe Ieſus [k] crowned with glorie &
honour, which was made a litle inferior
to the Angels, through the ſuffering of
death, that by Gods grace he might taſte
death for all men.
10 For it became him, for whome *are* all
things, and by whome *are* all things, ſeing
that he broght manie children vnto glorie, that he ſhulde conſecrate the [l] Prince
of their ſaluation through [m] afflictions.
11 For he that ſanctifieth, & they which are
ſanctified, are all [n] of one: wherefore he is
not aſhamed to call them brethren,
12 Saying, * I wil declare thy Name vnto
my [o] brethrē: in the middes of the Church
wil I ſing praiſes to thee.
13 And againe, *I wil put my [p] truſt in him.
And againe, * [q] Beholde, here am I, and the
children which God hathe giuen me.
14 Foraſmuche then as the children were
partakers of fleſhe and bloode, he alſo
him ſelf likewiſe toke parte with them,
that he might deſtroye * through death,
him that had the power of death, that is
the deuil,
15 And that he might deliuer all thē, which
for feare of [r] death were all their life time
ſubiect to bondage.

a We muſt diligently kepe in memorie the doctrine, which we haue learned, leſt like veſſels ful of chappes we leake, and runne out on euerie parte.
b Which was the Law giuen to Moſes by the hands of the Angels, Gal.3,19. act. 7,53.
Mar.16,20.
c As the Goſpel is which onely offereth ſaluation.
d That is, the Apoſtles
e Which Eſai calleth the new heauens, and the newe earth, chap 65, 17. whereof Chriſt is the father, Iſa.9,6. that is, the head of vs his members.
Pſal 8,5.
f He ſpeaketh here chiefly of the faithful, which are made through Chriſt citizēs of ẏ worlde to come where they ſhal enioye ẇ their prince all theſe things ẇ now they haue onely but in parte.
Mat.28,18.
1.cor.15,27.
phil 2,8.
g In making him fellowe heire ẇ Chriſt
h To them ẇ obiect ẏ they ſe not theſe things accompliſhed in mā, the Apoſtle āſwereth that they are fulfilled in Chriſt our captaine who leadeth his to the ſame glorie ẇ him.
Pſal.22,25.
i To man, as he is of Chriſt.
k By his vertue which moſte manifeſtly appeareth in the Church.
Pſal 18,3.
Iſa.8,18.
Hoſe.13,14.
1.cor.15,55.
l Ieſus Chriſt by hūbling hī ſelf & taking vpon him the forme of a ſeruāt, ẇ was our fleſh, & mortalitie, giueth vs aſſurāce of our ſaluation.

m Therefore we by afflictiōs are made like to the Sōne of God. n The head & the mēbers are of one nature: ſo Chriſt ẇ ſanctifieth vs, & we ẏ are ſanctified, are all one by the vnion of our fleſh. o This proueth Chriſts humanitie. p Meaning, that Chriſt touching his humanitie put his truſt in God. q Iſai ſpeaketh this of him ſelf, & his diſciples, but properly it is applied to Chriſt ẏ head of all miniſtres. r And Gods angre.

16 For he in no ſorte toke the [s] Angels, but
he toke the ſeed of Abraham.
17 Wherefore [t] in all things it became
him to be made like vnto his brethrē, that
he might be merciful, and a faithful high
Prieſt in things concerning God, that he
might make reconciliation for the ſinnes
of the people.
18 For in that he [u] ſuffered, and was tempted, he is able to ſucker them that are
tempted.

CHAP. III.

1 He requireth them to be obedient vnto the worde of Chriſt, 3 Who is more worthie then Moſes. 12 The puniſhement of ſuche as wil harden their hearts, and not belieue, that they might haue eternal reſt.

1 Therefore, holie brethren, partakers of
the heauenlie vocatiō, [a] conſider the
Apoſtle and high Prieſt of our [b] profeſsiō
Chriſt Ieſus:
2 Who was faithful to him that hathe appointed [c] him, euen as * Moſes *was* in all
his houſe.
3 For this man is counted worthie of more
glorie then Moſes, inaſmuche as he which
hathe buylded the houſe, [d] hathe more honour then the houſe.
4 For euerie houſe is buylded of ſome man,
& he that hathe buylt all things, *is* [e] God.
5 Now Moſes verely was faithful in all his
houſe, as a ſeruant, for a witnes of ẏ things
which ſhulde be ſpoken after.
6 But Chriſt *is* as the Sonne, ouer his owne
houſe, whoſe [f] houſe we are, if we holde faſt
the confidence and the reioycing of the
hope vnto the end.
7 Wherefore, as the holie Goſt ſaith, * To
day if ye ſhal heare his voyce,
8 Harden not your hearts, as in the [g] prouocation, according to the day of the tentation in the wildernes,
9 Where your fathers tempted me, proued
me, and ſawe my workes fortie yeres long.
10 Wherefore I was grieued with that gene
ration, and ſaid, They erre euer in *their* heart, nether haue they knowen my wayes.
11 Therefore I ſware in my wrath, [h] If thei
ſhal enter into my [i] reſt.
12 Take hede, brethren, leſt at anie time
there be in anie of you an euil heart, and
vnfaithful, to departe away from the liuing God.
13 But exhorte one another daily, while it
is called [k] To day, leſt anie of you be hardened through the deceitfulnes of ſinne.
14 For we are made partakers of Chriſt, if
we kepe ſure vnto the [l] end the "beginning,
wherewith we are vpholden,
15 So long as it is ſaid, To day if ye heare
his voyce, hardē not your hearts, as in the
prouocation.
16 For ſome when they heard, prouoked
[m] him to angre: howbeit, not all that came
out

s Not the nature of Angels but of man.
t Not onely as touching nature, but alſo qualities, onely ſinne except.
u Foraſmuche as he is exerciſed in our miſeries, we may be aſſured, that at all times in our tentations he wil ſucker vs.
a Take hede to his wordes & receiue him.
b Of that doctrine ẇ we beleue, & oght to confeſſe
c To be the ambaſſadour & high Prieſt.
Nomb.12,7.
d Moſes was but parte of ẏ houſe, ẏ is, of ẏ Church wherof ẏ paſtours are the liuelie ſtones, but Chriſt buylded it, & layed the ſtones: therefore he deſerueth more praiſe.
e That is Chriſt: for Chriſt is ẏ fundation, & head of his Church: he is our brother, & Lord: he is the Sonne of God, & verie God, working all things by his owne power.
f For in obeying the Sonne we are made the houſe of God.
Pſal 95,8.
chap 4,7.
g As when ye prouoked Gods anger in Maſſa and Meriba, Exod.17,7.
h Meaning by this othe that they ſhulde not enter.
i As diſobeīg God, they in olde time were debarred frō ẏ quietnes of the land of Chanaā: ſo thei ẇ do not obey Chriſt, ſhal not enter into the heauenlie reſt.
k Which is all ẏ time wherein God doeth call vs: while he therefore ſpeaketh, let vs heare.
l Which is by faith to embrace, and holde faſt ẏ true doctrine of Ieſus Chriſt.
"*Or, fundaciō of our aſſurance.*
m To wit, the Lord.

out of Egypt by Moses.
17 But with whome was he displeased fortie yeres? Was he not displeased with thẽ
that sinned, * whose "carkeises fell in the
wildernes?
18 And to whome sware he that they shulde
not enter into his rest, but vnto them, that
obeyed not?
19 So we se that they colde not enter in because of vnbeliefe.

Nom.14,37.
"Or, bodies and members.

CHAP. IIII.

2 The worde without faith is vnprofitable. 3 The Sabbath or rest of the Christians. 6 Punishement of vnbeleuers. 12 the nature of the worde of God.

1 LEt vs feare therefore, lest at anie time
by forsaking the promes of entring
into his rest anie of you shulde seme to be
depriued.
2 For vnto vs was the Gospel preached as
also vnto them: but the worde that they
heard, profited not them, because it was not
[a] mixed with faith in those that heard it.
3 For we which haue beleued, do enter into
rest, as he said *to the other*, * As I haue sworne
in my wrath, If [b] they shal enter into my
rest: althogh [c] the workes were finished
from the fundation of the worlde.
4 For he spake in a certeine place of the
seuenth day on this wise, * And God did
rest the seuenth day from all his workes.
5 And in this place againe, If they shal enter into my rest.
6 Seing therefore it remaineth that some
must enter thereinto, and they to whome
it was first preached, entred not therein
for vnbeleses sake:
7 Againe he appointed [d] in Dauid a certeine day by To day, after so long a time,
saying, as it is said, * This day if ye heare
his voyce, harden not your hearts.
8 For [e] if Iesus had giuen them rest, then
wolde he not after this day haue spoken of
another.
9 There remaineth therefore a rest to the
people of God.
10 For he that is entred into his rest, [f] hathe
also ceased from his owne workes, as God
did from his.
11 Let vs studie therefore to entre into that
rest, lest anie man fall after the same ensample of disobedience.
12 For the worde of God *is* liuelie, & mightie in operation, and sharper then anie two
edged sworde, & [g] entreth through, euen
vnto the diuiding a sonder of the [h] soule
& the [i] spirit, and of the ioynts, & the marie, and is a discerner of the thoghtes and
the intentes of the heart.
13 Nether is there anie creature, which is
not manifest in his sight: but all things *are*
naked & [k] open vnto his eyes, "with whome
we haue [l] to do.

a He compareth the preaching of the Gospel, as it were, to wine, whereof if we wil taste, that is, heare & vnderstand with ꝓfite, we must tẽper or mixe it with faith.
Psal.95,11.
b Althogh ỹ God by his rest, after the creation of his workes, signified the spiritual rest of the faithful, yet he sware to giue rest in Chanaã which was but a figure of the heauenlie rest, and dured but for a time.
Gene.2,2. deu.5,14.
Chap.3,7.
c The perfection of Gods workes, and so his rest, signifie our heauẽlie rest.
d That is, in the psalmes.
e Meaning Iosua.
f Hathe cast of his appetites, mortified his flesh, renoũced him self, and followeth God.
g For it mortally woũdeth the rebellious, and in ỹ elect it killeth the olde man that they shulde liue vnto God.
h Where the affections are.
i Which conteineth wil & reason.
k As that thĩg which is cleaft a sunder euen through the middes of the backe, and so is made opẽ that it may be sene throughout.
"Or, concerning whome we speake.
l Therefore when we heare his worde, we must tremble, knowing thereby that God soundeth our hearts.

14 Seing thẽ that we haue a great hie Priest,
which is entred into heauen, *euen* Iesus
the Sonne of God, let vs holde fast our
profession.
15 For we haue not an hye Priest, which can
not be touched with the feling of our infirmities, but was in all things tempted in
like sorte, *yet* without sinne.
16 Let vs therefore go boldely vnto ỹ throne of grace, that we may receiue mercie,
& finde grace to helpe in time of nede.

CHAP. V.

5 He compareth Iesus Christ with the Leuitical Priests, shewing wherein they ether agre or dissent. 11 Afterwarde he reproueth the negligence of the Iewes.

1 FOr euerie hie Priest is taken from a-
mong men, and is [a] ordeined for men,
in things perteining to God, that he may
offer bothe [b] giftes & [c] sacrifices for sinnes,
2 Which is able sufficiently to haue cõpassion on them [d] that are ignorant, & that are
out of the way, because that he also is cõpassed with infirmitie,
3 And for the sames sake he is bonde to offer for sinnes, as wel for his owne parte, as
for the peoples.
4 *And no man taketh this honour vnto
him self, but he that is called of God, as
was Aaron.
5 So likewise Christ toke not to him self
this honour, to be made the hie Priest, but
he that said vnto him, * Thou art my Sonne, this day begate I thee, *gaue it him.*
6 As he also in another place speaketh,
* Thou art a Priest for euer after the [e] order of Melchi-sedec.
7 Which in the [f] dayes of his flesh did offer vp prayers and supplications, with
[g] strong crying and teares vnto him, that
was able to saue him from death, and was
also heard [h] in that which he feared.
8 And thogh he were the Sonne, yet learned he obedience, by the things which he
suffred.
9 And being consecrate was made the autor of eternal saluation vnto all them that
obey him:
10 And is called of God an hie Priest after
the order of Melchi-sedec.
11 [i] Of whome we haue many things to say,
which are hard to be vttered, because ye
are dull of hearing.
12 For when as cõcerning the time ye oght
to be teachers, yet haue ye nede againe ỹ
we teache you the first "principles of the
worde of God: and are become suche as
haue nede of [k] milke, and not of strong
meat.
13 For euerie one that vseth milke, is inex-
perte in the [l] worde of righteousnes: for
he is a babe.
14 But strong meat belongeth to them that
are of age, which through lõg custome ha-

a He sheweth ỹ man cã haue none acces to God without an hie Priest, because that of him self he is prophane & sinful.
b Which were of things with out lif.
c As, of beasts which are killed.
d That is, of sinners.
1.Chro.13,10.
Psal.2,7. chap.1,5.
Psal.110,4. chap.7,17.
e Who was bothe Priest and King.
f Whẽ he liued in this worlde.
g He meaneth that most earnest prayer ỹ Christ prayed in the garden where he swet droppes of blood.
h Being in perplexitie & fearing the horrors of death.
i He digresseth til he come to the begĩning of the 7. chap.
"Or, rudiments.
k Read.1.Cor. 3,2.
l That is, the Gospel which is ỹ true knowledge that teacheth vs where we haue our iustice.

ue their wittes exercised, to discerne bothe
good and euil.

CHAP. VI.

1 He procedeth in reprouing them, and exhorteth them not to faint, 12 But to be stedfast & patient, 18 Forasmuche as God is sure in his promes.

1 THerefore, leauing the doctrine of the
[a] beginning of Christ, let vs be led
forward vnto perfection, not laying againe ẏ fundation [b] of repentance from dead
workes, and of faith towarde God,
2 Of the doctrine of [c] baptismes, & laying
on of hands, and of the resurrection from
the dead, and of eternal iudgement.
3 And this wil we do [d] if God permit.
4 *For it is impossible that they, which were once lightened, and haue tasted of the
heauenlie gift, and were made partakers of
the holie Gost,
5 And haue tasted of the good worde of
God, and of the powers of the worlde to
come,
6 If they fall away, shulde be renued againe by repentance: seing they [e] crucifie a-
gaine to them selues the sonne of God &
make a mocke of him.
7 For the earth which drinketh in the raine that cometh ofte vpon it, and bringeth
forthe herbes mete for them by whome it
is dressed, receiueth blessing of God.
8 But that which beareth thornes & briars,
is reproued, and is nere vnto cursing, whose end *is* to be burned.
9 But beloued, we haue persuaded our selues
better things of you, and suche as accom-
panie saluation, thogh we thus speake.
10 For God *is* not vnrighteous, that he shul
de forget your worke, and labour of loue,
which ye shewed towarde his Name, in
that ye haue ministred vnto the Saintes, &
yet minister.
11 And we desire that euerie one of you shewe the same diligence, to the [f] ful assurance of hope vnto the end,
12 That ye be not slothful, but followers of
[g] them, which through faith and patience,
inherite the promises.
13 For whẽ God made the promes to Abraham, because he had no greater to sweare
by, he sware by him self,
14 Saying, *Surely I wil abundantly blesse
thee and multiplie thee marueilously.
15 And so after that he had taryed paciently, he enioyed the promes.
16 For men verely sweare by him that is
greater *then them selues*, and an othe for
confirmation is among them an end of all
strife.
17 So God willing more [h] abundantly to
shewe vnto the heires of promes the stablenes of his counsel, bound him self by
an othe,
18 That by [i] two immutable things, wherein it is vnpossible that God shulde lye,
we might haue strong consolation, which
haue our refuge to holde fast the hope that
is set before vs,
19 Which we haue, as an ancre of the soule,
bothe sure and stedfast, & it [k] entreth into
that which is within the [l] vaile,
20 Whether the forerunner is for vs entred
in, *euen* Iesus that is made an hie Priest for
euer after the order of Melchi-sedec.

a That is, the first rudiments of our Christian religion.
b He mencioneth fiue poits of the catechisme, ẇ was then in vse: ẏ confession of amẽdement of life: the sũme of the faith: a brief explication of Baptisme, and laying on of hands: ẏ article of the resurrection, & the last iudgement.
Mat.12,49. 2.pet.2,20. chap.10,26.
c Then the vse of baptisme was declared when on the solemne dayes appointed to baptize the Church came together.
d It is Gods singular gift to increase in knowledge, & to go forward in the vnderstanding of Gods worde.
e They which are apostats, & sinne against ẏ holy Gost, hate Christ, crucifie & mocke him, but to their owne destruction, & therefore fall into desperation, & cã not repẽt.
f Whereby it may appeare, that you are fully psuaded of life euerlasting.
g As the holie fathers, Prophetes & martyrs, that were before vs.
Gen.12,3. & 17,4. & 22,16.
h Because of mans wickednes, which wil not beleue God except he sweare.
i Gods worde & othe, are two things in him vnchangeable.
k He returneth to the comparison betwene Christs Priesthode & the Leuitical which he had begon in the 5. chap.
l Which is heauen whether Christ is gone before to prepare vs place.

CHAP. VII.

1 He compareth the Priesthode of Christ vnto Melchi-sedec. 11 Also Christs Priesthode with the Leuites.

1 FOr this Melchi-sehec *was Kĩg of Sa
lem, the Priest of the most hie God,
who met Abraham, as he returned frõ the
slaughter of the Kings, and blessed him:
2 To whome also Abraham gaue the tithe
of all things: who first is by interpretation
King of righteousnes: after that, *he is* also
King of Salem, that is, King of peace,
3 Without [a] father, without mother, without kinred, and hathe nether beginning of
his dayes, nether end of life: but is likened
vnto the Sonne of God, and continueth a
Priest for euer.
4 Now consider how great this man *was*,
vnto whome euen the [b] Patriarke Abrahã
gaue the tithe of the spoiles.
5 For verely they which are the children
of Leui, which receiue the office of the
Priesthode, haue a* [c] commandement to take, according to the Law, tithes of the peo
ple (that is, of their brethren) thogh they
[d] came out of the loynes of Abraham.
6 But he whose kinred is not counted amõg
them, [e] receiued tithes of Abraham, and
blessed him that had the promises.
7 And without all contradiction the lesse
is blessed of the greater.
8 And here mẽ that dye, receiue tithes: but
there he *receiueth them*, of whome it is witnessed, that he [f] liueth.
9 And to say as the thing is, Leui also which
receiueth tithes, payed tithes in Abraham.
10 For he was yet in the loines of his father
Abraham, when Melchi-sedec met him.
11 If therefore perfection hah bene by the
Priesthode of the Leuites (for vnder it
the Law was established to the people)
what neded it furthermore, that another
Priest shulde rise after the order of Melchi-sedec, & not to be called after the order of Aaron?
12 For if the Priesthode be changed, then
of necessitie must there be a change of
the [g] Law.
13 For he of whome these things are spokẽ,
perteineth vnto another tribe, whereof no
man serued at the altar.
14 For it is euident, that our Lord sprong
out of Iuda, concerning the which tribe

Gen.14,18.
a So called, because that Moses maketh no mention of his parents or kinsfolkes, but as he had bene suddenly sent of God into ẏ worlde to be a figure of Christ ỏ euerlasting Priest, & shortely taken out of the world againe, so Christ as touching his humanitie had no father, and concerning his diuinitie, no mother.
Nom.18,19. deu.18,1. ios.14,1.
b That is, the chief of fathers.
c The Leuites had commandemẽt to receiue that, which Abraham gaue frely to Melchi-sedec.
d Was begotten of Abraham.
e The Leuites receiued tithes of their brethren, but Melchi sedec of Abraham, the patriarke: therefore his priesthode is more excellẽt then the Leuitical.
f Because there is no mentiõ of his death.
g The Lawe and ẏ Priesthode are bothe of one condition: so that bo the Aarons & Moses office perteine to Christ, which is Priest & Lawmaker.

be Moses spake nothing, touching the
Priesthode.
15 And it is yet a more euident thing, because that after the similitude of Melchi-
sedec, there is risen vp another Priest,
16 Which is not made *Priest* after the Law
h of the carnal commandement, but after
the power of the endles life.
17 For he testifieth *thus*, *Thou art a Priest
for euer, after the order of Melchi-sedec.
18 For the commandement that went afore,
is disanulled, because i of ẏ weakenes thereof, and vnprofitablenes.
19 For the Law made nothing perfite, but
"the bringing in of a better hope *made per*
fite, whereby we drawe nere vnto God.
20 And forasmuche as it is not without an
othe (for these are made Priests without
an othe:
21 But this, he *is made* with an othe by him
that said vnto him, *The Lord hathe swor
ne, & wil not repent, Thou art a Priest for
euer, after the order of Melchi-sedec)
22 By so muche is Iesus made a suretie of a
better "Testament.
23 And amōg thē many were made Priests,
because they were not suffred to endure,
by the reason of death.
24 But this man, because he endureth euer,
hathe an k euerlasting Priesthode.
25 Wherefore, he is able also l perfitely to
saue them that come vnto God by him,
seing he euer liueth, to make intercession
for them.
26 For suche an hie Priest it became vs to
haue, *which is* holie, harmeles, vndefiled,
separate from sinners, and made hier then
the heauens:
27 Which neded not daily as those hie
Priests to offer vp sacrifice, * first for his
owne sinnes, and then for the peoples: for
that did he m once, when he offred vp
him self.
28 For the Law maketh men hie Priests,
which haue infirmitie: but ẏ worde of the
othe that was n since the Law, *maketh* the
Sonne, who is consecrated for euermore.

h Which stode in outwarde and corporal ceremonies.

Psal.110,4. chap.5,6.

i For ẏ Lawe hathe no vertue nor profite til a man become to Christ.

"*Or, it was an entroduction of a better hope.*

Psal.110,4.

"*Or, couenant.*

k Therefore all others are blasphemous, ẏ ether make them selues his successors, or pretende any other sacrifice.

l The frute of his Priesthode is to saue & that fully and perfectly, not by supplying that ẏ wanteth, but by taking away the Lawe which is vnperfect by reason of our infirmities

m And can not without blasphemie be said to be offered againe, or els by any creature: for none colde offre him, but him self.

Leu.16,3.

n Not that it was first made after the Lawe was giuen: but because the declaration of ẏ eternal othe was thē reueiled to the worlde.

CHAP. VIII.

6 He proueth the abolishing aswel of the Leuitical Priesthode, as of the olde Couenant by the spiritual & euerlasting Priesthode of Christ. 8 And by the new Couenant.

1 NOw of the things which we haue
spoken, *this is* the summe, that we haue suche an hie Priest, ẏ sitteth at the right
hand of the throne of the maiestie in
heauens,
2 And *is* a minister of the a Sanctuarie, and
of the true b Tabernacle which the Lord
pight, and not c man.
3 For d euerie hie Priest is ordeined to offer

a That is, heauen.

b Which is ẏ bodie of Christ

c For els it shulde be corruptible.

d He proueth that Christs bodie is the true Tabernacle, and that he muste nedes be made man, to the intent that he might haue a thing to offre, which was his bodie.

bothe giftes and sacrifices: wherefore it
was of necessitie, that this man shulde haue somewhat also to offer.
4 For he were not a Priest, if he were on the
earth, seing there are Priests that according to the Law offer giftes,
5 Who serue vnto the paterne & shadowe
of heauenlie things, as Moses was warned
by God, when he was about to finish the
Tabernacle. *Se, said he, that thou make
all things according to ẏ e paterne, shewed
to thee in the mount.
6 But now *our hie Priest* hathe obteined a
more excellent office, inasmuche as he is
the Mediatour of a better "Testament,
which is established vpō better promises.
7 For if that first *Testament* had bene fauteles, no place shulde haue bene soght for
the seconde.
8 For in rebuking them he saith, *Beholde,
the dayes wil f come, saith the Lord, when
I shal make with the house of Israel, and
with the house g of Iuda a new Testamēt:
9 Not like the Testamēt that I made with
their fathers, in the day that I toke them
by the hād, to leade them out of the land
of Egypt: for they h continued not in my
Testament, and I regarded thē not, saith
the Lord.
10 For this is the Testamēt that I wil make
with ẏ house of Israel, After those dayes,
saith the Lord, I wil put my lawes in their
minde, and in their heart I wil write them,
and I wil be their God, and they shal be
my people,
11 And they shal not i teache euerie man
his neighbour & euerie man his brother,
saying, Knowe ẏ Lord: for all shal knowe
me, from the least of thē to the greatest
of them.
12 For I wil be merciful to their vnrighteousnes, and I wil remember their sinnes
and their iniquities no more.
13 In that he saith a newe *Testament*, he hathe abrogate the olde: now that ẇ is disanulled & waxed olde, is readie to vanish
away.

Exod.25,40. act.7,44.

e Seing the offerings of the Leuites were but shadowes of heauenlie things, as appeareth by the oracle to Moses, it foloweth then ẏ Christs heauenlie Sanctuarie, his Tabernacle and office are farre more excellēt.

"*Or, couenant.*

Ier.31,31. rom.11,27. chap.10,16.

f That is, whē Christ shal remit our sinnes by the preaching of the Gospel

g Signifying ẏ there shulde be no more diuision, but all shal be made one Church.

h Man by trāsgressing the bādes of the Couenant, colde not enioye the cōmoditie thereof.

i Men shal not in the time of the Gospel be so ignorant as they were before, but shal knowe God muche more perfitely through Christ.

CHAP. IX.

1 How that the Ceremonies and sacrifices of the Lawe are abolished. 11 By the eternitie and perfection of Christs sacrifice.

1 THen the first "*Testament* had also "ordinances of religion, and a a worldlie
Sanctuarie.
2 For the first * Tabernacle was made, wherein was the candlesticke, and the table, &
the shewbread, which *Tabernacle* is called
the Holie places.
3 And after the b seconde vaile *was* the
Tabernacle, which is called the Holiest
of all,
4 Which had the golden senser, and the
Arke of the Testament ouerlaide rounde
about with gold, wherein the golden pot

"*Or, Tabernacle* "*Or, ceremonies.*

a Not heauenlie and spiritual.

Exod.26,1. & 36,1.

b That is, on the inwarde side of the vaile which was hid from the people.

which had manna,*was*,and *Aarons rodde
that had budded, and the * tables of the
Testament.
5 *And ouer the Arke were the glorious
Cherubims, shadowing the "mercie seat:
of which things we wil not now speake
particularly.
6 Now when these things were thus ordeined,the Priests went alwayes into the first
Tabernacle,& accomplished the seruice.
7 But into the second went the * hie Priest
alone,once euerie yere,not without blood
which he offered for him self, and for the
"ignorances of the people.
8 Whereby the holie Gost this signified,
that the c way into the Holiest of all was,
not yet opened, while as yet the first Tabernacle was standing,
9 Which was a figure for the time present,
wherein were offred giftes and sacrifices
that colde not make "holie, concerning
the cõscience, d him that did the seruice,
10 Which onely stode in meats and drinkes,and diuers washings,and e carnal rites,
vntil the time of f reformation.
11 But Christ being come an hie Priest of
good things to come, by a greater and a
more perfite g Tabernacle,not made with
hands,that is,not of this buylding,
12 Nether by the blood of goates and calues: but by his owne blood entred he in
once vnto the h holie place, i and obteined
eternal redemption *for vs*.
13 *For if the k blood of bulles & of goates
& the ashes of an heifer, sprinkling thẽ
that are vncleane, sanctifieth as touching
the purifying of the l flesh,
14 How muche more shal ẙ *blood of Christ
which through the eternal Spirit offred
him self without spot to God, purge your
conscience from m dead workes, to * serue
the liuing God?
15 And for this cause is he the Mediatour
of the new Testamẽt,that through *death
which was for the redẽption of the transgressions *that were* in the n former Testament,they which were called,might recei
ue the promes of eternal enheritance.
16 For where a testament *is*, there must be
the death of him that made the testamẽt.
17 *For the o testament is confirmed when
men are dead: for it is yet of no force as
long as he that made it,is a liue.
18 Wherefore nether was the first ordeined
without p blood.
19 For when Moses had spoken euerie precept to the people, according to the Law,

Nom.17,10. *1.King.8,9.* *2.chron.5,10.* *Exod.25,22.*
"Or, couer of the arke.
Exo.30,10. *leu 16,2.*
"Or, errors.
c For so long as ẙ hie Priest offered once a yere for his owne sinnes & for ẙ peoples, and also while this earthlie tabernacle stode, the way to the heauẽlie Tabernacle,which is made open by Christs blood, colde not be entred into.
"Or, perfect.
d Nether yet him for whome they were offred.
e Which ceremonies although they were ordeined of God,yet considered in them selues, or els cõpared with Christ, are but carnal, grosse, and earthlie & touche not the soule.
Leu.16,14. *nom 19,4.* *1.Pet.1,19.* *1.iohn 1,9.* *reuel.1,5.*
f Til the newe testament was appointed.
Luk.1,74.
g Which was his bodie and humane nature
Rom.5,6. *1.pet.3,18.*
h Which is heauen.
i For Christ was the sacrifice,the Tabernacle and the Priest.
Gal.3,15.
k The Leuitical Priest offered beasts blood: but Christ the true and eternal Priest offered his owne blood, which was moste holie and pure:the Leuitical Priest offred yerely, and therefore did onely represent the true holines: but Christ by one onely sacrifice hathe made holie for euer all thẽ that beleue l Outwardely in the sight of man. m Which of thẽ selues procure death & are the frutes thereof n Made betwene God and Christ, who by his death shulde make vs heires. o He proueth that Christ must dye,because the couenant or testamẽt is of none effect without the death of the testatour. p Without the death of beastes that were sacrificed & signified,that Christ wolde pacifie his Fathers wrath with his blood.

he toke the blood of calues and of goates,
with water and purple wolle and hyssope, and sprinkled bothe the boke, and all
the people,
20 *Saying, This is the blood of the Te- *Exo 24,8.*
stament, which God hathe appointed vn-
to you.
21 Moreouer, he sprinkled likewise the Tabernacle with blood also,and all the ministring vessels.
22 And almost all things are by the Law
purged with blood,and without sheading
of blood is no remission.
23 It was then necessarie,that the similitudes
of heauẽlie things shulde be purified with
suche things: but the heauenlie things thẽ
selues *are purified* with better q sacrifices
then are these.
24 For Christ is not entred into the holie
places that are made with hands, which a-
re "similitudes of the true *Sanctuarie*: but
is entred into very heauen, to appeare now
in the sight of God for vs,
25 Not that he shulde offer him self r often,
as the hie Priest entred into the Holie pla
ce euerie yere with other blood,
26 (For then must he haue often suffred since the fondacion of the worlde) but now
in the s end of the worlde hathe he appeared once to put away sinne, by the sacrifice
of him self.
27 And as it is appointed vnto men that
they shal once dye, and after that *commeth*
the iudgement,
28 So *Christ was once offred to take away
the sinnes of t many, and vnto them that
loke for him, shal he appeare the seconde
time u without sinne vnto saluation.

q Albeit there is but one sacrifice, which is Christ him selfe once offered,yet because this true & eternal sacrifice is cõpared with all those which were figuratiue, & is more sufficiẽt than all they, therefore he calleth it in the plural nõber, sacrifices.
"Or, paternes.
r Therefore to make any other offrig or sacrifice for sinne after that Christs bodie was once offred, is blasphemie.
s Which is the latter daies when Christ came.
Rom.5,8. *1.pet,3,18.*
t Of the elect.
u That is, without a sacrifice for sinne: or sin abolished.

CHAP. X.

1 *The olde lawe had no power to clense awaye sinne.*
10 But Christ did it with offering of his bodie once for all. 22 An exhortation to receiue the goodnes of God thankefully with patience and stedfast faith.

1 FOr the * Lawe hauing the a shadowe
of good things to b come,and not the
very "image of the things, can neuer with
those sacrifices, which they offer yere by
yere continually, "sanctifie the commers
thereunto.
2 For wolde they not then haue ceased to
haue bene offred, because that the offerers
once purged,shulde haue had no more cõscience of sinnes?
3 But in those *sacrifices* there *is* a remẽbrance againe of sinnes euerie yere.
4 For it is vnpossible that the blood of bulles & goates shulde *take away sinnes.
5 Wherefore when he c commeth into the
worlde,he saith, * Sacrifice & offring thou
woldest not: but a d bodie hast thou ordeined me.
6 In burnt offrings, & sinne offrings thou
hast had no pleasure.

Leu.16,14.
a Which was as it were the first draught and purtrait of the liuelie paterne to come.
b Which are eternal
"Or, substance.
"Or, make perfite
c When Christ was made mã.
Leuit.16,14. *Psal.40,7.*
d In the hebrewe it is, thou hast perced mine eares throwe, that is, hast made me prompt and ready to heare: and in ẙ greke, thou hast made me a bodie, that is, to obey thee, which bothe tende to one purpose.

7 Then

e Or rolle and folding: for in olde time they vsed to folde bokes like rolles.

7 Then I said, Lo, I come (In ye beginning
of the [c] boke it is written of me) that I
shulde do thy wil, ô God.
8 Aboue, when he said, Sacrifice & offring,
and burnt offrings, & sinne offrings thou
woldest not haue, nether hadst pleasure
therein (which are offred by the Law)
9 Then said he, Lo, I come to do thy wil, ô

f That is, sacrifices.
g Which is, ye wil of God to stand content with Christs sacrifice.

God, he taketh away [f] the first, that he may
stablish the [g] seconde.
10 By the which wil we are sanctified, *euen*
by the offring of the bodie of Iesus Christ
once *made*.
11 And euerie Priest appeareth daiely ministring, and oft times offreth one maner
of offring, which can neuer take awaye
sinnes:
12 But this man after he had offred one sacrifice for sinnes, * sitteth for euer at the

Chap.1,13.

right hand of God,
13 And from hence forthe tarieth, * til his
enemies be made his fotestole.

Psal 110,1. 1.cor.15,25. chap.1,13

14 For with one offring hathe [h] he consecrated for euer them that are sanctified.

h That is, sanctified to God and made perfect.

15 For the holie Gost also beareth vs recorde: for after that he had said before,
16 * This *is* the Testament that I wil make
vnto them after those daies, saith ye Lord,
I wil put my Lawes in their heart, and in
their mindes I wil write them.

Ierem.31,33. chap.8,8. rom.11,27.

17 And their sinnes and iniquities wil I remember no more.
18 Now where [i] remission of these things
is, there *is* no more [k] offring for sinne.
19 Seing therefore, brethren, that by the
blood of Iesus we [l] may be bolde to enter
into the Holie place
20 By the new and [m] liuing way, which he
hathe prepared for vs, through the vaile,
that is, his flesh:
21 *And seing we haue* an hie Priest, *which is*
ouer the house of God,
22 Let vs drawe nere with a true heart in
assurance of faith, [n] sprinkeled in our hearts from an euil conscience, and washed
in our bodies with pure water.
23 Let vs kepe the profession of our hope,
without wauering (for *he is* faithful that
promised)
24 And let vs consider one another, to prouoke vnto loue, and to good workes,
25 Not forsaking the felowship that we haue among our selues, as the maner of some *is*: but let vs exhorte *one another*, & that
so muche the more, because ye se that the
[o] day draweth nere.
26 * For if we sinne [p] willingly after that
we haue receiued the knowledge of the
trueth, there remaineth no more sacrifice
for sinnes,
27 But a feareful loking for of iudgement,

i Where there remaine no sinnes to be forgiuen, there is no more sacrifice: seing therefore that onely Christs death hathe washed awaye all sinnes, and doeth euer a fresh whe sinners do repet, there can be none other sacrifice but ye, & it can be no more reiterat.
k For the offring of thankesgiuing, wc is ye onelie sacrifice now of the Christians, is not for sinne: but a thankesgiuing & an offring vp of our selues & ours for the same.
l We by Christ haue ye libertie wc the ancient fathers colde not haue by ye Law.
Chap.6,14.
m The blood of Christ is alwaies fresh & liuelie, before the father to sprinkle and quicken vs.
n That is, hauing our hearts made pure. o Of Christs seconde comming. p That is, forsake Iesus Christ, as Iudas, Saul, Arrius, Iulian the apostat did.

& violét fyre, which shal deuoure the aduersaries.
28 He that despiceth Moses Law, dyeth
without mercie * vnder two, or thre witnesses.
29 Of how muche sorer punishment suppose ye shal he be worthie, which treadeth
vnder fote the Sonne of God, and counteth the blood of the Testament as an vnholie thing, wherewith he was sanctified,
and [q] doeth despite the Spirit of grace?
30 For we knowe him that hathe said, * Végeance *belongeth* vnto me: I wil recompense, saith the Lord. And againe, The Lord
shal [r] iudge his people.
31 It is a feareful thing to fall into the
hands of the liuing God.
32 Now call to remembrance the dayes
that are passed, in the which, after ye had
receiued light, ye endured a great fight in
afflictions,
33 Partely while you were made a gazing
stocke bothe by reproches and afflictions,
and partely while ye became [s] companiós
of them which were ‖ so tossed to and fro.
34 For bothe ye sorowed with me for my
bondes, and suffred with ioye the spoyling
of your goods, knowig in your selues how
that ye haue in heauen a better, and an enduring substance.
35 Cast not away therefore your confidence which hathe great recompense of rewarde.
36 For ye haue nede of pacience, that after
ye haue done the wil of God, ye might
receiue the promes.
37 * For yet a verie litle while, and he that
shal come, wil come, and wil not tarie.
38 Now the iust shal liue by faith: but if *a-*
nie withdrawe him self, my soule shal haue no pleasure in him.
39 But we are not they which withdrawe
our selues vnto perdicion, but *folowe* faith
vnto the conseruacion of the soule.

Deut.19,17. mat.18,16. iohn 8,17. 2.cor.13,1.
Deut.32,35. rom.12,19.
q Whereby it is euident that the Apostle here onely meaneth of ye sinne, wc is against the holie Gost, as also Chap.6,4.
r Defend the godlie and punish ye wicked.
s For ye which thing also S. Paul praiseth the Philippiãs & Thessalonians.
‖ Or, of that state
Habak.2,4. rom.1,17. galat.3,11.

CHAP. XI.

1 What faith is, and a cõmendacion of the same. 9 Without faith we can not please God. 16 The stedfast beleife of the fathers in olde time.

1 NOw faith is the grounde of things,
which are hoped for, and the euidence of things which are not sene.
2 For by it *our* elders were wel [a] reported of.
3 * Through faith we vnderstand that the
worlde was ordeined by ye worde of God,
so that the things which we se, are not made of things, which [b] did appeare.
4 By faith Abel * offred vnto God a greater sacrifice then Cain, [c] by * the which he
obteined witnes that he was [d] righteous,
God testifying of his gifts: by the which
faith also he being dead, yet [e] speaketh.
5 By faith was * [f] Enoch taken awaye, that
he shulde not se death: nether was he fo

Chap. XI.
a Haue bene approued, and so obteined saluacion.
b For God made all things of nothing.
c Meaning, faith.
Gen.1,3. iohn 1,10.
d Because God receiued him to mercie, therefore he imputed him righteous.
e That is, liueth.
Gen.4,4. Mat.23,35.
f For Enochs & Elias taking vp was suche a thing, as is spoken of, 1. Cor 15,51, & 1. thes.4,15
Gen.5,24. eccles.44,16. & 49,16.

unde: for God had taken him away: for
before he was taken away, he was reported
of, that he had pleased God.
6 But without faith it is vnpossible to please *him*: for he that cometh to God, must beleue that *God* is, and that he is g a rewarder
of them that seke him.
7 By faith * Noe being warned of God of
the things which were as yet not sene, moued with reuerence, prepared the Arke to
the sauing of his housholde, through the
which *Arke* he condemned the worlde, &
was made heire of the righteousnes, which
is by faith.
8 By faith * Abraham, when he was called,
obeyed *God*, to go out into a place, which
he shulde afterwarde receiue for inheritãce, and he went out, not knowing whether
he went.
9 By faith he abode in the land of promes,
as in a strange countrey, as one that dwelt
in tentes with Isaac and Iacob heires with
him of the same promes.
10 For he loked for a citie hauing a h fundacion, whose buylder and maker *is* God.
11 Through faith * Sarra also receiued
strength to conceiue sede, and was deliuered of a childe when she was past age, because she iudged him faithful which had
promised.
12 And therefore sprang there of one, euẽ
of one which was i dead, *so manie* as * the
starres of the skie in multitude, and as the
sand of ỹ sea shore which is innumerable.
13 All these dyed in faith, and k receiued
not the promises, but sawe them l a farre
of, and beleued *them*, and receiued *them*
thankefully, and confessed that they were
m strangers and pilgremes on the earth.
14 For they that say suche things, declare
plainely that they seke a countrey.
15 And if they had bene mindeful of n that
countrey, from whence they came out, they
had leasure to haue returned.
16 But now they desire a better, that is an
heauenlie: wherefore God is not ashamed
of them to be called their God: for he hathe prepared for them a citie.
17 By faith * Abraham offred vp Isaac, when
he o was tryed, & he that had receiued the
promises, offred his onely begottẽ sonne.
18 (To whome it was said, * In Isaac shal
thy sede be called)
19 For he considered that God was able to
raise *him* vp euen from the dead: from
whẽce he receiued him also after a sorte.
20 By faith * Isaac blessed Iacob and E-
sau, concerning things to come.
21 By faith * Iacob when he was a dying,
blessed bothe the sonnes of Ioseph, and
* " *leaning* on the end of his staffe, worshiped *God*.
22 By faith * Ioseph when he dyed, made

Gen.6,13.
eccles.44,15.
g First God must finde vs before we can seke him: then we must seke him with a pure heart in Christ, who is reueiled in his worde: & thereby we learne to beleue Gods fre mercie towardes vs in his Sonne, through whome we obteine the rewarde of his promes, & not of our desertes.
Gen.12,4.
h For all thĩgs in the worlde are subiect to corruption.
Gen.17,19. & 21,2.
Eccles.44,22.
i Euẽ as dead.
k Which was the enioying of the land of Canaan.
l With ỹ eyes of faith.
m And therefore put not their confidence in thĩgs of this worlde.
n That is, of Mesopotamia.
Gen.22,10.
eccles.44.20.
Gen 21,12.
rom.9,7.
o For it might seme to ỹ flesh ỹ the promes was contrarie to this cõmandemẽt, to sacrifice his sonne.
Gen.27,28.
Gen 49,15.
Gen.47,31.
" Or, worshiped towarde the end of his staffe.
Gen.50,29.

mention of the departing of ỹ childrẽ of
Israel, & gaue cõmandemẽt of his bones.
23 * By faith Moses when he was borne, was
hid thre moneths of his parentes, because they sawe he was a proper childe, nether
feared they the Kings * commandement.
24 By faith * Moses when he was come to
age, refused to be called the sonne of Pha-
raos daughter,
25 And chose rather to suffer aduersitie
with the people of God, then to enioy the
p pleasures of sinnes for a ceason,
26 Esteming the rebuke of Christ greater
riches then the treasures of Egypt: for he
had respect vnto the recompense of the
rewarde.
27 By faith he forsoke Egypt, and feared
not the fiercenes of the King: for he endured, as he that sawe him which is inuisible.
28 Through faith he ordeined the * Passeouer and the effusion of blood, lest he that
destroyed the first borne, shulde touche
them.
29 By faith they * passed through the red
sea as by drye land, which whẽ the Egyptiãs had assaied to do, thei were drowned.
30 By faith the * walles of Iericho fell downe after they were compassed about seuen
dayes.
31 By faith the harlot * Rahab perished not
with them which obeied not, whẽ she had
receiued the spies peaceably.
32 And what shal I more say? for the time
wolde be to short for me to tell of * Gedeon, of * Barac & of * Sampson, & of * Iephe-
te, also of * Dauid, and Samuel, and of the
Prophetes:
33 Which through faith subdued kingdomes, wroght righteousnes, obteined the
q promises, stopped the mouthes of lyons,
34 Quenched the violence of fyre, escaped
the edge of the sworde, of weake were made strong, waxed valiant in battel, turned
to flight the armies of the aliantes.
35 The r women receiued their dead raised to life: other also were racked, and
wolde not be deliuered, that they might
receiue a better resurrection.
36 And others haue bene tryed by mockĩgs
and scourgings, yea, moreouer by bondes
and prisonment.
37 They were stoned, they were hewen a
sunder, they were tempted, they were slayne with the sworde, they wandered vp and
downe in shepes skinnes, and in goares
skinnes, being destitute, afflicted, & tormented:
38 Whome the worlde was not worthie of:
they wandred in wildernesses and mountaines, & dennes, & caues of the earth.
39 And these all through faith obteined
good reporte, & receiued s not ỹ promes,
40 God

Exod.2,2.
act.7,21.
Exod.1,16.
Exod.2,11.
p The entisinges of the worlde, ŵ drawe vs from God, and which we can not vse without prouoking of Gods angre.
Exod.12,22.
Exod.14,22.
Iosh.6,20.
Iosh.6,23.
Iosh.2,1.
Iudg.6,11.
Iudg.4,6.
Iudg.13,24.
Iudg.11,1. & 12,7.
1.Sam.1,20. & 13,14.
q Or frute thereof.
r As Elias raised vp ỹ widdowe of Sareptas sonne, and Eliseus the Sunamites sonne.
s Thei had not suche cleare light of Christ as we: for thei loked for that ŵ we haue: therefore it were shame for vs, if at least we haue not as great constancie as thei.

40 God prouiding a better thing for vs, that they [t] without vs shulde not be made perfite.

t For we are all one bodie together.

CHAP. XII.

1 An exhortation to be patient and stedfast in trouble & aduersitie, vpō hope of euerlasting rewarde. 25 A commendation of the new Testament aboue the olde.

1 WHerefore, *let vs also, seing that we are compassed with so great a "cloude of witnesses, cast away euerie thig that [a] presseth downe, and the sinne that "hangeth so fast on: let vs runne with pacience the race that is set before vs,

2 [b] Loking vnto Iesus the autor and finisher of our faith, who for the ioye that was set before him, endured the crosse, and despised the shame, and is set at the right hand of the throne of God.

3 Consider therefore him that endured suche speakīg against of sinners, lest ye shulde be wearied and fainte in your mindes.

4 Ye haue not yet resisted vnto blood, striuing aganst [c] sinne.

5 And ye haue forgotten the consolation, which speaketh vnto you as vnto childrē, *My sonne, despise not the chastening of the Lord, nether faint when thou art rebuked of him.

6 For whome the Lord loueth, he chasteneth: and he scourgeth euerie sonne that he receiueth.

7 If ye endure chastening, God offreth him self vnto you as vnto sonnes: for what sonne is it whome the father chasteneth not?

8 If therefore ye be without correction, whereof all are partakers, then are ye bastardes, and not [d] sonnes.

9 Moreouer we haue had the fathers of our [e] bodies which corrected vs, and we gaue them reuerence: shulde we not muche rather be in subiection vnto the Father of [f] spirits, that we might liue?

10 For they verely for a fewe dayes chastened vs after their owne pleasure: but he *chasteneth vs* for our profit, that we might be partakers of his holines.

11 Now no chastising for the present semeth to be ioyous, but grieuous: but afterwarde, it bringeth the quiet frute of righteousnes, vnto them which are thereby exercised.

12 Wherefore lift vp *your* hāds which hang downe, and *your* weake knees,

13 And make straight steppes vnto your fete, lest [g] that which *is* halting, be turned out of the way, but let it rather be healed.

14 *Followe peace with all men, and holines, without the which no man shal se the Lord.

15 Take hede, that no man fall away from the grace of God: let no [h] roote of bitternes spring vp and trouble *you*, lest thereby many be defiled.

Rom.6,4. ephe.4,23. collos.3,8. 1.pet.2,1.

"Or, multitude.

a As riches, cares and suche like, and so to become Christs disciples, by denyig our selues, and takingour crosse to followe him

"Or, so easely cōpasseth vs about

b As being our marke.

c Which by reason of our concupiscence assaileth vs on all sides.

Prou.3,11. reue.3,17.

d He concludeth that they which refuse the crosse, denie to be of ẏ nōber of Gods children, but are bastardes.

e Which haue naturally begotten vs.

f As he doeth creat our spirits without any worldelie meane, so he doeth instructe and mainteine them by the wonderful vertue of his Spirit.

g Their haltīg partely declared their sloenes, & partely their inconstancie in doctrine: therefore they were in danger to be punished.

Rom.12,18.

h As heresies or apostasie.

16 Let there be no fornicator, or prophane persone as *Esau, which for a portion of meat solde his byrth right.

17 *For ye knowe how that afterwarde also when he wolde haue inherited the blessing, he was reiected: for he founde no place to [i] repentance, thogh he soght *the blessing* with teares.

18 For ye are not come vnto the *mounte that [k] might be touched, nor vnto burning fyre, nor to blackenes and darkenes, and tempest,

19 Nether vnto the sounde of a trumpet, and the voyce of wordes, which they that heard it, excused them selues, that the worde shulde not be spoken to them any more.

20 (For they were not able to abyde that ẇ was commanded, *Yea, thogh a beast touche the mountaine, it shalbe stoned, or thrust thorowe with a darte:

21 And so terrible was the sight which appeared, that Moses said, I feare & quake.)

22 But ye are come vnto the mounte [l] Siō, and to the citie of the liuing God, the [m] celestial Ierusalem, and to the companie of innumerable [n] Angels,

23 And to the cōgregacion of the first borne, which are writen in heauen, & to God the iudge of all, and to the spirits of iust and perfite men,

24 And to Iesus the Mediator of the newe Testament, & to the blood of sprinkeling that speaketh better things then that of *Abel.

25 Se that ye despise not him that speaketh: for if they escaped not which refused hī, that spake on [o] earth: muche more shal we *not escape*, if we turne away from him, that *speaketh* from heauen.

26 Whose voyce then shouke the earth, and now hathe declared, saying, *Yet once more wil I shake, not the earth onely, but also heauen.

27 And this *worde*, Yet once more, signifieth the remouing of those things, which are shaken, as of things which are made *with hands*, that the things which are not shaken, may remaine.

28 Wherefore seing we receiue a kingdome, which can not be shaken, let vs haue grace, whereby we may so serue God, that we may please him with reuerēce and feare.

29 For *euen our God *is* a [p] cōsuming fyre.

Gen.25,38.

Gen.27,38.

i He was ful of despite and disdaine, but was not touched with true repentance to be displeased for his sinnes & so seke amendement.

Exod.19,13. & 20,21

k Which might be touched and sene, for as muche as it was material, but God had cōmāded that none shulde touche it.

Exod.19,13.

l Whence the worde of God must come.

m Which shal be extended through all the worlde.

n By the Gospel we are ioyned with the Angels and Patriarkes.

Gen.4,10.

o Which spake but rudely in comparison of Christ, who preached not the Lawe but the Gospel.

Hag.2,7.

Deu.4,24.

p To destroy them that resist him.

CHAP. XIII.

1 He exhorteth vs vnto loue. 2 To hospitalitie. 3 To thinke vpon suche as be in aduersitie. 4 To mainteine wedlocke. 5 To auoide couetousnes. 7 To make muche of them that preache Gods worde. 9 To beware of strange learning. 13 To be content to suffre rebuke with Christ. 15 To be thankeful vnto God. 17 And obedient vnto our gouernours.

1 LEt * brotherlie loue continue.
2 Be not forgetful to lodge ſtrãgers:
for thereby ſome haue * receiued Angels
into their houſes vnwares.
3 Remember them that are in bondes, as
thogh ye were bonde with them: and them
that are in affliction, as if ye were alſo *afflicted* in the bodie.
4 [a] Mariage *is* honorable amõg all, and the
bed vndefiled: but whoremungers & adulterers God wil iudge.
5 Let your conuerſation be without couetouſnes, and be content with thoſe things
that ye haue: for [b] he hathe ſaid, * I wil not
faile thee, nether forſake thee:
6 So that we may boldely ſay, * The Lord
is mine helper, nether wil I feare what mã
can do vnto me.
7 Remember them which haue the ouerſight of you, which haue declared vnto
you ẏ worde of God: whoſe faith followe,
conſidering what hathe bene the end of
their conuerſation.
8 Ieſus Chriſt [c] yeſter day, and to day, the
ſame alſo *is* for euer.
9 Be not caryed about with diuers & ſtrange [d] doctrines: for it is a good thing that ẏ
heart be ſtabliſhed with grace, & not with
[e] meates, which haue not profited thẽ that
haue bene occupied therein.
10 We haue an altar whereof they haue no
autoritie to [f] eate which ſerue in the Tabernacle.
11 *For the bodies of thoſe beaſtes whoſe
blood is broght into the Holie place by
the hie Prieſt for ſinne, are [g] burnt without
the campe.
12 Therefore euen Ieſus, that he might ſanctifie the people with his owne blood, ſuffred without the gate.
13 Let vs go forthe therefore out of the cãpe, bearing his reproche.

Rom.12,10. 1.pet.4,9. Gen.18,3. & 19,3.

a As incontinencie is a diſeaſe commune to men of all ſortes and degrees, ſo mariage the remedie is offred by ẏ fre mercie of God to all maner of men without reſpect.

b The Lord.

Ioſh.1,9. Pſal.118,6.

c He was, is, & ſhalbe the fundation of the Church for euer.

d Whatſoeuer doctrine is not according to the ſimple trueth of Gods worde, is ſtrange.

e By reprouĩg them which ſuperſticiouſly put difference betwixt meats he cõdemneth all the ſeruice which ſtode in ceremonies, cõparing it with the ſpiritual worſhiping, & regeneration.

Leui.6,36. & 16,27.

f They that ſticke to ẏ ceremonies of ẏ Law, can not eate, that is, cã not be partakers of our altar, which is thankeſgiuing and liberalitie, which two ſacrifices or offrings are now onely left to ẏ Chriſtiãs.

g So that the Prieſts had no piece thereof.

14 For here haue we no continuing citie:
but we ſeke one to come.
15 Let vs therefore by him offer the ſacrifice of praiſe alwayes to God, that is, the
*frute of the lippes, which confeſſe his Hoſ.14,3.
Name.
16 [h] To do good, & to diſtribute forget not:
for with ſuche ſacrifices God is pleaſed.
17 Obey them that haue the ouerſight of
you, & ſubmit your ſelues: for they watch
for your ſoules, as they that muſt giue accountes, that they may do it with ioye,
and not with grief: for that is vnprofitable for you.
18 Pray for vs: for we are aſſured that we ha
ue a good cõſcience in all things, deſiring
to liue honeſtly.
19 And I deſire you ſomewhat the more
earneſtly, that ye ſo do, that I may be reſtored to you more quickely.
20 The God of peace that broght againe
from the dead our Lord Ieſus, the great
[i] ſhepherde of ẏ ſhepe, through the blood
of the euerlaſting Coucnat,
21 Make you perfite in all good workes,
to do his wil, working in you that which
is pleaſant in his ſight through IESVS
CHRIST, to whome *be* praiſe for euer &
euer, Amen.
22 I beſeche you alſo, brethren, ſuffre the
wordes of exhortation: for I haue writen
vnto you in fewe wordes.
23 Knowe that *our* brother Timotheus is
deliuered, with whome (if he come ſhortely) I wil ſe you.
24 Salute all them that haue the ouerſight
of you, and all the Saintes. They of Italie
ſalute you.
25 Grace *be* with you all, Amen.

Written to the Hebrewes from Italie,
and ſent by Timotheus.

h Thankeſgiuing & doing good are our onelie ſacrifices which pleaſe God.

i Read Act.20,28 and Ioh.10,11.

THE *GENERAL Epiſtle of Iames.

* That is, writ to no one mã, citie or countrey, but to all the Iewes generally, being now diſperſed

THE ARGVMENT.

IAmes the Apoſtle and ſonne of Alpheus wrote this Epiſtle to the Iewes which were conuerted to Chriſt, but diſperſed throughout diuers countreis, and therefore he exhorteth them to patience and prayer, to embrace the true worde of God, & not to be partial, nether to boaſt of an ydle faith, but to declare a true faith by liuelie frutes, to auoide ambition, to bridel the tongue, to rule the affections, to be humble & loue their neighbours, to beware of ſwearing, to vtter their fautes when they haue offended, to praye one for another, and to bring him which is out of the way, to the knowledge of Chriſt.

CHAP. I.

a He exhorteth to reioyce in trouble. 6 To be feruent in prayer with stedfast belief. 17 To loke for all good things from aboue. 21 To forsake all vice, and thankefully to receiue the worde of God. 22 Not onely hearing it, & speaking of it, but to do thereafter in dede. 27 What true religion is.

1 IAMES a seruant of
God, & of the Lord
IESVS CHRIST, to
the twelue Tribes, ẘ
are scattred abroade,
salutation.
2 My brethrẽ, counte
it exceading ioye, whẽ ye fall into diuers
"tentations,
3 * Knowing that the [a] trying of your faith
bringeth forthe pacience.
4 And let pacience haue *her* [b] perfite worke,
that ye may be perfite and entier, lacking
nothing.
5 If any of you lacke [c] wisdome, let him aske
ke of God, which giueth to all men liberally,
and reprocheth no man, and it shalbe
be giuen him.
6 *But let him aske in faith, and wauer not:
for he that wauereth, is like a waue of the
sea, tost of the winde, and caryed away.
7 Nether let that man thinke that he shal
receiue any thing of the Lord.
8 A [d] "wauering minded man *is* vnstable in
all his wayes.
9 Let the brother of lowe degree reioyce
in that he is [e] exalted:
10 Againe he that is riche, in that he is made
de [f] lowe: for as the flower of the grasse,
shal he * vanish away.
11 For *as when* the sunne riseth with heat,
then the grasse withereth, and his flower
falleth away, & the beautie of the facion
of it perisheth: euen so shal the riche man
fade away in *all* his "wayes.
12 *Blessed *is* the man, that endureth tentation:
tion: for when he is tryed, he shal receiue
the crowne of life, which the Lord hathe
promised to them that loue him.
13 Let no man say whẽ he is "[g] tẽpted, I am
tẽpted of God: for God can not be tẽpted
with euil, nether tempteth he any man.
14 But euerie man is tempted, when he is
drawne away by his owne concupiscence,
and is entised.
15 Then when lust hathe cõceiued, it bringeth
eth forthe sinne, and sinne when it is finished,
shed, bringeth forthe death.
16 Erre not, my deare brethren.
17 Euerie good [h] giuing, and euerie perfite
gift is from aboue, and cõmeth downe frõ
the Father of lights, with whome is no variablenes,
riablenes, [i] nether shadowing by turning.
18 Of his owne wil begate he vs with the
worde of trueth, that we shulde be as the
first frutes of his creatures.

"Or, afflictions.

Rom. 5, 3.

a Afflictions trye our faith & ingendre pa tience.

b Our paciencẽ oght to cõ tinue to ẏ end til by working it hathe polished vs, & made vs perfect in Christ.

c To endure paciently what soeuer God layeth vpon him.

Mat. 7, 7. mar. 11, 24. luk. 11, 9. iohn 14, 13. & 16, 23.

d Douting in doctrine, or of Gods wil.

"Or, double.

e That he is called to the companie of Christ and his Angels.

Eccles. 14, 18. isa. 40, 6. 1. pet. 1, 24.

f Or contemptible to ẏ worlde.

Iob 5, 17.

"Or, in all his thoghts and dedes.

"Or, moued to euil

g He meaneth now of the inwarde tentations as of our disordered appetites, which cause vs to sinne.

h Seing all good things come of God, we oght not to make him the autor of euil.

i He alludeth vnto the sunne which in his course and turning sometime is cleare and bright, sometime darke and cloudie: but Gods liberalitie is euer like it self, bright and continually shining.

19 Wherefore my deare brethrẽ, * let euerie
rie man be [k] swift to heare, slowe to speake,
ke, & [l] slowe to wrath.
20 For the wrath of man doeth not accomplish
plish the [m] righteousnes of God.
21 Wherefore lay aparte all filthines, & superfluitie
perfluitie of maliciousnes, & receiue with
mekenes ẏ worde that is [n] graffed in you,
which is able to saue your soules.
22 *And be ye doers of the worde, and not
hearers onely, deceiuing your owne selues.
23 For if anie heare the worde, & do it not,
he is like vnto a man, that beholdeth his
natural face in a [o] glasse.
24 For when he hathe considered him self,
he goeth his way, & forgetteth immediatly
ly what maner of one he was.
25 But who so loketh in the perfit Law of
libertie, and continueth *therein*, he not being
ing a forgetful hearer, but a doer of the
worke, shalbe blessed [p] in his dede.
26 If anie man among you semeth religious,
ous, and refraineth not his tongue, but deceiueth
ceiueth his owne heart, this mans religion
gion *is* vaine.
27 Pure religion & vndefiled before God,
euen the Father, is this, to visite the fatherles,
therles, and widdowes in their aduersitie,
tie, *and* to kepe him self vnspotted of the
worlde.

Prou. 17, 27.

k That is, prompt to learne.

l For we can not heare God except we be peaceable, & modeste.

m But hindereth Gods worke in vs.

n By hearing ẏ worde preached.

Mat. 7, 21. rom. 2, 13.

o So Gods worde is a glasse wherein we must beholde our selues, & become like vnto him.

p In so behauing him self.

CHAP. II.

1 He forbiddeth to haue anie respect of persones. 5 But to regarde the poore as wel as the riche. 8 To be louing and merciful. 14 And not to boast of faith where no dedes are. 17 For it is but a dead faith, where good workes followe not.

1 MY brethren, haue not the faith of
our glorious Lord Iesus Christ [a] in
"respect of persones.
2 For if there come into your companie a
man with a golde ring, and in goodlie apparel,
parel, and there come in also a poore man
in vile raiment,
3 And ye haue a respect to him ẏ weareth
the gaye clothing, and say vnto him, Sit
thou here in a good place, & say vnto the
poore, Stand thou there, or sit here vnder
my fotestole,
4 Are ye not partial in your selues, and are
become iudges of euil [b] thoghts?
5 Hearken my beloued brethren, hathe not
[c] God chosen the poore of this worlde,
that they shulde be riche in faith, and heires
of the kingdome which he promised to
them that loue him?
6 But ye haue despised the poore. Do not
the riche oppresse you by tyrannie, and
do not they drawe you before the iudgement
ment seates?
7 Do not they blaspheme the [d] worthie Name
me after which ye be named?
8 But if ye fulfil the [e] royal Law according

a As estemīg faith and religion by the outwarde appearance of men

"Or, acceptatiō.

b That is, are ye not euil affectioned?

c Seing God estemeth thẽ, we may not contemne thẽ.

d The Name of God and Christ, whereof you make pfession: & in that they dishonour God, it is not mete that you his children shulde honour thẽ.

e Which is here taken prouerbially, for the high or brode way, wherein there is no turnings, and euerie mā as the riche.

can go it: so euerie man is our neighbour, as wel the poore

to the Scripture, *which saith*, * Thou shalt
loue thy neighbour as thy self,ye do wel.
9 * But if ye regarde the persones, ye commit sinne, and are rebuked of the Law, as
transgressours.
10 For * whosoeuer shal kepe the whole
Law,*and* yet faileth in one *point*, he is giltie of all.
11 For he that said, * Thou shalt not commit adulterie, said also, Thou shalt not
kill. Now thogh thou doest none adulterie,yet if thou killest,thou art a transgressor of the Law.
12 So speake ye,and so do,as they that shalbe iudged by the Law of [f] libertie.
13 For there shalbe iudgement merciles to
him that sheweth no mercie,& mercie [g] re
ioyceth against iudgement.
14 What auaileth it,my brethren, thogh a
man saith he hathe [h] faith,whē he hathe no
workes? can the faith saue him?
15 For if a brother or a sister be * naked and
destitute of dailie fode,
16 And one of you say vnto them, Departe
in peace: warme your selues, and fil your
bellies,notwithstanding ye giue them not
those things which are nedeful to the bodie,what helpeth it?
17 Euen so the faith, if it haue no workes,is
dead in it self.
18 But some man might say,Thou hast [i] the
faith,& I haue workes:shewe me thy faith
out of thy " [k] workes, & I wil shewe thee
my faith by my workes.
19 Thou beleuest that there is one God:
thou doest wel:the deuils also beleue it, &
tremble.
20 But wilt thou vnderstand, ô thou vaine
man, that the faith *which is* without workes,is dead?
21 Was not Abraham our father iustified
through workes, when he offred Isaac his
sonne vpon the Altar?
22 Seest thou not that ẏ faith [l] wroght with
his workes?& through the workes was the
faith made [m] perfite.
23 And the Scripture was fulfilled which
saith, * Abraham beleued God, and it was
imputed vnto him for righteousnes: & he
was called the friend of God.
24 Ye se then how that of workes a man is
[n] iustified,and not [o] of faith onely.
25 Likewise also was not * [p] Rahab the harlot iustified through workes, whē she had
receiued the messengers, and sent thē out
another waye?
26 For as the bodie without the spirit is
dead,euen [q] so the faith without workes is
dead.

Leu.19,18. mat.22,39. mar.12,31. rom.13,9. galat.5,14.
Leu.19,15. deuter.1,17. & 16,19.
Mat.5,19.
Exod 20,14. deut.5,18.
f By the mercie of God ẘ deliuereth vs from the curse of the Lawe.
g And feareth it not.
Luk.3,11. 1.iohn 3,17.
h S.Paul to ẏ Romains and Galatians disputeth against thē, which attributed iustification to the workes: & here S.Iames reasoneth against them ẘ vtterly condēne workes: therefore Paul sheweth the causes of our iustificatiō, and Iames the effectes: there it is declared how we are iustified: here how we are knowen to be iustified: there workes are excluded as not the cause of our iustificatiō: here they are approued as effects proceding thereof: there they are denied to go before them that shalbe iustified: and here they are said to followe them that are iustified.
i In thine owne opinion.
"Or, without workes.
Gen.15,6. rom.4,5. gal.3.6.
k Here dedes are considered as ioyned with true faith.
Iosh.2,1.
l So that faith was not ydle.
m The more his faith was declared by his obedience and good workes, the more was it knowen to men to be perfite, as the goodnes of a tre is knowen by her good frute,otherwise no man can haue perfectiō in this worlde: for euerie man must pray for remission of his sinnes,& increase of faith.
n Is so knowen & declared to man.
o Of that baren and dead faith whereof ye boast.
p Meaning hereby all thē that were not Iewes and were receiued to grace.
q Wherefore we are iustified onely by that liuelie faith, which doeth apprehende the mercie of God towarde vs in Iesus Christ.

CHAP. III.

1 He forbiddeth all ambition to seke honour aboue our brethren. 3 He describeth the propertie of the tongue. 15. 16 And what difference there is betwixt the wisdome of God, and the wisdome of the worlde.

1 MY brethren,be not [a] manie masters,
knowing that we shal receiue the
greater condemnation.
2 For in manie things we " [b] sinne all. * If
anie man sinne not in [c] worde, he is a perfect man,and able to bridel all the bodie.
3 Beholde, we put bits into the horses mou
thes that they shulde obey vs, and we turne about all their bodie.
4 Beholde also the shippes, which thogh
they be so great, and are driuen of fierce
windes, yet are they turned about with a
verie smale rudder, whethersoeuer ẏ gouerner listeth.
5 Euen so the tongue is a litle member, and
boasteth of great things:beholde,how gre
at a " thing a litle fyre kindleth.
6 And the tongue is fyre, *yea*, a [d] worlde of
wickednes:so is the tongue set among our
members,that it defileth the whole bodie,
and [e] setteth on fyre the course of nature,
and it is set on fyre of hel.
7 For the whole nature of beastes, and of
birdes and of creping things, and things
of the sea is tamed and hathe bene tamed
of the nature of man.
8 But the tongue can no man tame. *It is* an
vnrulie euil,ful of deadelie poyson.
9 Therewith blesse we God euen the Father,and therewith curse we mē,which are
made after the similitude of God.
10 Out of one mouth proceadeth blessing
and cursing:my brethrē,these things oght
not so to be.
11 Doeth a foūtaine send forthe at one place swete *water* and bytter?
12 Can the figge tre, my brethren, bring
forthe oliues,other a vine figges? so cā no
fountaine make bothe salte water & swete.
13 Who is a wise man and endued with
knowledge among you? let him shewe by
good conuersation his workes in mekenes
of wisdome.
14 But if ye haue bitter enuying and strife
in your hearts,reioyce not, nether be liers
against the trueth.
15 This wisdome descendeth not frō aboue,
but *is* earthlie,sensual,and diuelish.
16 For where enuying and strife *is*, there *is*
sedition,and all maner of euil workes.
17 But the wisdome that *is* from aboue, is
first [f] pure, then peaceable, gentle, easie
to be entreated, ful of mercie and good
frutes without [g] iudging, and without hypocrisie.
18 And the [h] frute of righteousnes is sowen
in peace,of them that make peace.

a Vsurpe not through ambition autoritie ouer your brethren.
Eccle.14,1. & 19,16. & 25,11.
"Or stomble.
b He that wel considereth himself, shal not be rigorous towarde his brethren.
c He that is able to moderate his tōgue, hathe atteined to an excellēt vertue.
"Or, matter.
d An heape & ful measure of all iniquitie.
e The intemperancie of ẏ tōgue is as a flame of hel fyre.
f Without mixtion and dissimulation.
g And examining things ẘ extreme rigour as hypocrites, who onely iustifie them selues,& condemne all others.
h So that their life is according to their profession.

CHAP.

CHAP. IIII.

1 Hauing ſhewed the cauſe of all wrong, and wickedne., and alſo of all graces and goodnes, 4 He exhorteth them to loue God, 7 And ſubmit them ſelues to him, 11 Not ſpeaking euil of their neighbours, 13 But patiently to depend on Gods prouidence.

1 FRom whence *are* warres and contentions among you? are they not hence,
euen of your luſtes, that [a] fight in your
members?
2 Ye luſte, and haue not: ye enuie, and haue indignation, and can not obteine: ye
fight and warre, and get nothing, becauſe
ye aſke not.
3 Ye aſke, and receiue not becauſe ye aſke a miſſe, that ye might conſume it on
your luſtes.
4 Ye adulterers and [b] adultereſſes, knowe
ye not that the amitie of the worlde is the
enimitie of God?* Whoſoeuer therefore
wil be a friend of the worlde, maketh him
ſelf the enemie of God.
5 Do ye thinke that the Scripture ſaith in
vaine, The [c] ſpirit that dwelleth in vs, lu-
ſteth after enuie?
6 But *the Scripture* offereth more grace &
therefore ſaith, * God reſiſteth the proude, and giueth grace to the humble.
7 *Submit your ſelues to God: reſiſt the deuil, and he wil flee from you.
8 Drawe nere to God, and he wil drawe
nere to you. Clenſe your hands, ye ſinners,
& purge your hearts, ye wauering minded.
9 Suffer afflictions, and [d] ſorowe ye, and
wepe: let your laughter be turned into
mourning, and *your* ioye into heauines.
10 *Caſt downe your ſelues before ye Lord,
and he wil lift you vp.
11 Speake not euil one of another, brethren.
He that ſpeaketh euil of his brother, or
he that condemneth his brother, ſpeaketh
euil of the Law, and [e] condemneth the
Law: and if thou condemneſt the Law,
thou art not an obſeruer of the Law, but a
iudge.
12 There is one [f] Law giuer, which is able
to ſaue, & to deſtroye.* Who art thou that
iudgeſt another man?
13 Go to now ye that ſay, [g] To day or to
morowe we wil go into ſuche a citie, and
continue there a yere, and bye and ſel, and
get gaine,
14 (And yet ye can not tel what *ſhalbe* to
morowe. For what is your life? It is euen a
vapour that appeareth for a litle time, and
afterwarde vaniſheth away)
15 For that ye oght to ſay, *If the Lord wil,
and, If we liue, we wil do this or that.
16 But now ye reioyce in your boaſtīgs: all
ſuche reioycing is euil.
17 Therefore, [h] to him that knoweth how
to do wel, and doeth it not, to him it is
ſinne.

a For the Law of the mēbers continually fighteth agaīſt the Law of the minde.

b He calleth adulterers here after the maner of the Scriptures, thē which preferre the pleaſures of ye worlde to the loue of God.

Iohn 2,15.

c The imagination of mās heart is wicked, Gene. 6,5, & 8,21.

Prou. 3,34.

1 pet. 5,5.

Epheſ. 4,27.

d The Greke worde ſignifieth that heauines, which is ioyned with a certeine ſham faſtnes, as appeareth in the countenance.

1. Pet. 5,6.

e In vſurping the autoritie of iudging, wc is due to the Law.

Rom. 14,4.

f He ſheweth that this ſeuere iudging of others is to depriue God of his autoritie.

g We oght to ſubmit our ſelues to the prouidence of God.

Act. 19,21

1. cor. 4,19.

h He anſwereth to them, which ſaid they knewe what was good, but they wolde not do it.

CHAP. V.

2 He threateneth the wicked riche men, 7 Exhorteth vnto pacience, 12 To beware of ſwearing. 16 One to knowledge his fautes to another. 20 And one to labour to bring another to the treuth.

1 GO to now, ye riche men: wepe, and
[a] howle for your miſeries that ſhal
come vpon you.
2 Your riches are corrupt: & your garmēts
are motheaten.
3 Your golde and ſiluer is cankred, and the
ruſt of them ſhalbe a [b] witnes againſt you,
and ſhal eat your fleſh as *it were* fyre.* Ye
haue heaped vp treaſure for ye [c] laſt dayes.
4 Beholde, the hyre of the laborers, which
haue reaped your fields (which is of you
kept backe by fraude) cryeth, and the cryes
of thē which haue reaped, are entred into
the eares of the Lord of hoſtes.
5 Ye haue liued in pleaſure on the earth, &
in wantōnes. Ye haue nouriſhed your hearts, as in a day of [d] ſlaughter.
6 Ye haue condemned *and* haue killed the
iuſte, and he hathe not reſiſted you.
7 Be pacient therefore, brethren, vnto the
comming of the Lord. Beholde, the houſband man waiteth for the precious frute
of the earth, and hathe long pacience for
it, vntil he receiue the [e] former, and the lat
ter raine.
8 Be ye alſo pacient therefore & ſetle your
hearts: for the comming of the Lord draweth nere.
9 [f] Grudge not one againſt another, brethrē,
leſt ye be condemned: beholde, the iudge
ſtandeth before the dore.
10 Take, my brethren, the Prophetes for an
enſample of ſuffering aduerſitie, and of
long pacience, which haue ſpoken in the
Name of the Lord.
11 Beholde, we count thē bleſſed which endure. Ye haue heard of the paciēce of Iob,
and haue knowē what end the Lord *made*.
For the Lord is verie pitiful & merciful.
12 But before all things, my brethren, *ſweare not, nether by heauen, nor by earth, nor
by anie other othe: but let your [g] yea, be
yea, and *your* naye, naye, leſt ye fall into
"condemnation.
13 *Is anie amōg you afflicted? Let him pray.
Is anie merie? Let him ſing.
14 Is anie ſicke amōg you? Let him call for
the [h] Elders of the Church, and let them
praye for him, and anoint him with *[i] oyle in the [k] Name of the Lord.
15 And the prayer of faith ſhal ſaue the
ſicke, and the Lord ſhal raiſe him vp: and
if he haue committed ſinne, it ſhalbe forgiuen him.
16 Acknowledge [l] your fautes one to another, & praye one for another, that ye may
be healed: for the prayer of a righteous
man auaileth muche, if it be feruent.

a He menaceth them with the vengeance of God, which ſhal not onely make them to wepe, but to howle and deſpaire.

b And kindle the wrath of God againſt you.

Rom 2,5.

c To ſuffice til the end of the worlde.

d Which were the dayes of the ſacrifices, or feaſts when they vſed to banket & fede more abūdātly then other dayes.

e Which is when the corne is ſowen, & a litle before it is mowen.

f Be not greiued nor aſke vengeance.

g That wc muſt be affirmed, affirme it ſimply and without othe: likewiſe that wc muſt be denied: by this he taketh not from the magiſtrate his autoritie who may require an othe for ye maintenance of iuſtice, iudgement, and trueth.

Mat. 5,34.

"*Or, hypocriſie.*

h The gift of healing was then in the Church.

i Which in thoſe dayes was a ſigne of the gift of healing, but now the gift being taken away, ye ſigne is to no vſe.

Mat. 6,13.

k In calling on the Name of the Lord.

l Open that wc greueth you, yt a remedie may be founde: and this is cōmanded bothe for him yt cōplaineth, & for hī that heareth ye the one ſhulde ſhew his grief to the other.

1.King.17,1. eccle.48,3. luk.4,25.

17 *Helias was a man subiect to like pasiós
as we are, and he prayed earnestly that it
might not raine, and it rained not on the
earth for thre yeres and six moneths.
18 And he prayed againe, and the heauen
gaue raine, and the earth broght forthe
her frute.
19 Brethren, if anie of you hathe erred frō
the trueth, and some man hathe conuerted him,
20 Let him knowe that he which hathe conuerted the sinner from going astraye out
of his way, shal saue a soule from death,
and shal hide a multitude of sinnes.

THE FIRST EPI-stle general of Peter.

THE ARGVMENT.

He exhorteth the faithful to denie them selues, and to contemne the worlde, that being deliuered from all carnal affections and impediments, they may more spedely atteine to the heauenlie kingdome of Christ, whereunto we are called by the grace of God reueiled to vs in his Sonne, and haue already receiued it by faith, possessed it by hope, and are therein confirmed by holines of life. And to the intent this faith shulde not faint, seing Christ contemned and reiected almost of the whole worlde, he declareth that this is nothing els but the accomplishing of the Scriptures which testifie that he shulde be the stombling stone to the reprobate and the sure fundation of saluation to the faithful: therefore he exhorteth them courageously to go forwarde, considering what they were, and to what dignitie God hathe called them. After, he entreateth particular points, teaching subiects how to obey their gouernours, and seruants their masters, and how maried folkes oght to behaue them selues. And because it is appointed for all that are godlie, to suffre persecutions, he sheweth them what good yssue their afflictions shal haue, and contrarie wise what punishment God reserueth for the wicked. Last of all he teacheth how the ministers oght to behaue them selues, forbidding them to vsurpe autoritie ouer the Church: also that yong men oght to be modest, and apt to learne, and so endeth with an exhortation.

CHAP. I.

2 He sheweth that through the abundant mercie of God we are elect and regenerate to a liuelie hope, 7 And how faith must be tried, 10 That the saluation in Christ is no newes, but a thing prophecied of olde. 13 He exhorteth them to a godlie conuersation, forasmuche as they are now borne a newe by the worde of God.

1 PETER an Apostle of
IESVS CHRIST,
to [a] the strangers that
dwell here and there
throughout Pontus, Ga
lacia, Cappadocia, Asia
and Bithynia,
2 Elect according to the [b] foreknowledge
of God the Father vnto sanctification of
the spirit, "through [c] obedience and sprinkling of the blood of Iesus Christ: Grace
and peace be multiplied vnto you.
3 *Blessed *be* God euen the Father of our
Lord Iesus Christ, which according to his
abundant mercie hathe begoten vs againe
vnto a [d] liuelie hope by the resurrectiō of
Iesus Christ from the dead,
4 To an inheritance immortal and vndefiled, and that fadeth not away, reserued
in [e] heauen for you,
5 Which are kept by the power of God
through faith vnto saluation, which is pre
pared to be shewed in the [f] last time:

a Which were Iewes to whome he was appointed to be an Apostle.
b The free election of God is the efficient cause of our saluation, the material cause is Christs obedience, our effectual calling is the formal cause, and the final cause is our sanctification.
2.Cor.1,3. ephe.1,3.
"*Or, vnto obedience.*
c To wit, of Christ.
d For it is but dead & vaine hope which is without Christ
e Therefore they oght to loke for no earthlie kingdome of the Messias.
f At the day of iudgement

6 Wherein ye reioyce, thogh now for a cea
son (if nede [g] require) ye are in heauines,
through manifolde tentations,
7 That the trial of your faith, being muche
more precious then golde that perisheth
(thogh it be tryed with fyre) might be
foūde vnto *your* praise, & honour and glorie at the [h] appearing of Iesus Christ:
8 Whome ye haue not sene, and yet loue
him, in whome now, thogh ye se him not,
yet do you beleue, and reioyce with ioye
vnspeakeable and glorious,
9 Receiuing the "end of your faith, *euen* the
saluation of your soules.
10 Of the which saluation the Prophetes
haue inquired and searched, which prophecied of the grace that shulde come vnto you,
11 Searching when or what time the Spirit
which testified before of Christ which was
in them, shulde declare the suffrings *that*
shulde come vnto Christ, and the glorie that
shulde followe.
12 Vnto whome it was reueiled, that [i] not
vnto them selues, but vnto vs they shulde
minister the things which are now shewed
vnto you by them which * haue preached
vnto you the Gospel by the holie Gost
sent downe from heauen, the which things
the Angels desire to beholde.

g And nede doeth so require, when it pleaseth God to lay his crosse vpō his, for to drawe thē from earthlie things & make them partakers of his heauenlie graces
h At his secōde comming.
"*Or, rewarde.*
i Their ministerie was more profitable to vs then to them: for we se the things accomplished which they prophecied.

13 Wherefore

Luk.12,35.
k Prepare your selues to the Lord.
l Vntil his seconde cōming.
m When you were in ignorāce and knewe not Christ.
Luk.1,75.
Leui.11,44. & 19,2. & 20,7
Deut.10,17. rom.2,11. galat.2,6.
n According to ŷ sinceritie of the heart.
o Read Ezek. 20,18.
1.Cor.6,20. & 7,27. ebr. 9,14. 1.ioh.1,7. reuel.1,6.
Rom.16,25. ephes.3,9. colos.1,26. 2.tim.1,10. tit.1,2.
p When Christ appeared vnto the worlde,& when ŷ Gospel was preached.
Rom.12,10. ephes.4,2. chap.2,17.
q Therefore we must renoūce our former nature.
Isa.40,6. eccles.14,18. iam.1,10.

13 Wherefore, [k] girde vp the * loynes of
your minde : be sober,and trust perfectly
on the grace that is broght vnto you , by
the [l] reuelacion of Iesus Christ,
14 As obedient children,not facioning your
selues vnto the former [m] lustes of your ignorance:
15 But as he which hathe called you,is holie,
so be ye holie in * all maner of conuersacion,
16 Because it is written, * Be ye holie, for I
am holie.
17 And if ye call him Father , which without * respect of persone iudgeth accordīg
to euerie mans [n] worke , passe the time of
your dwelling here in feare,
18 Knowing that ye were not redemed with
corruptible things, *as* siluer and golde, frō
your vaine conuersacion , receiued by the
tradicions of the [o] fathers,
19 *But with the precious blood of Christ,
as of a Lambe vndefiled,& without spot.
20 Which was*ordeined before the fundacion of the worlde,but was declared in the
[p] last times for your sakes,
21 Which by his meanes do beleue in God
that raised him from the dead , and gaue
him glorie, that your faith & hope might
be in God.
22 Seing your soules are purified in obeing
the trueth through the spirit, to*loue brotherly without faining , loue one another
with a pure heart feruently,
23 Being borne a new , not of mortal sede,
but of [q] immortal,by the worde of God,
who liueth and endureth for euer.
24 For all *flesh *is* as grasse,and all the glorie of man *is* as the flower of grasse. The
grasse withereth,and the flower falleth a-
way.
25 But the worde of the Lord endureth for
euer:and this is the worde which is preached among you.

CHAP. II.

1 He exhorteth them to laye a side all vice, 4 Shewing that Christ is the fundacion whereupon they buylde. 9 The excellent estate of the Christians. 11 He praieth them to absteine from fleshlie lustes. 13 To obey the rulers, 18 How seruants shulde behaue them selues toward their masters. 20 He exhorteth to suffer after the ensample of Christ.

Rom 6,4. ephes 4,23. colos.3,8. ebr 12,2.
a In this their infancie and new cōming to Christ he willeth them to take hede lest for ŷ pure milke,which is ŷ first beginings of learning the sincere worde, they be not deceiued by thē which chop and change it,and giue poyson in stede thereof.
"Or, the milke of vnderstanding which is without deceit.

1 WHerefore,*laying aside all maliciousnes & all guile , & dissimulacion,and enuie,and all euil speaking,
2 As new borne babes desire [a] the "syncere
milke of the worde , that ye maye growe
thereby,
3 If so be that ye haue tasted how bountiful the Lord *is*.
4 To whome ye come as vnto a liuing stone disalowed of men, but chosen of God
& precious.
5 And ye as liuelie stones,be made a spiritual house, and holie * Priesthode to offer
vp spiritual sacrifices acceptable to God
by Iesus Christ.
6 Wherefore it is conteined in the Scripture,* Beholde,I put in [b] Sion a chief corner stone,elect and precious : and he that
beleueth therein,shal not be ashamed.
7 Vnto you therefore which beleue, it is
precious: but vnto them which be disobedient,the *stone which the [c] buylders disalowed , the same is made the head of the
corner,
8 And a * stone to stomble at , and a rocke
of offence , euen *to them* which stomble at
the worde being disobedient, vnto the
which thing they were euen ordeined.
9 But ye are a chosen generacion, a [d] royal
* Priesthode,an holie nacion , a "peculiar
people, that ye shulde shew forthe the vertues of him that hathe called you out of
darkenes into his marueilous light,
10 *Which in time past were not a people,
yet *are* now the people of God:which in
time past were not vnder mercie,but now
haue obteined mercie.
11 Derely beloued,I beseche you, as strangers and pilgrems, *absteine from fleshlie
lustes,which fight against the soule,
12 *And haue your conuersacion honest a-
mong the Gentiles, that they which speake euil of you as of euil doers , maye by
your * good workes which they shal se, glorifie God in the day of [e] the visitacion.
13 * Submit your selues vnto all " maner ordinance of man for the Lords sake , whether it be vnto the King, as vnto the superiour,
14 Or vnto gouernours, as vnto them ŷ are
sent of him, for the punishment of euil
doers, and for the praise of them that do
wel.
15 For so is the wil of God , that by wel
doing ye may put to silence the ignorance
of the foolish men,
16 As fre,and not as hauing the libertie for
a cloke of maliciousnes,but as the seruāts
of God.
17 Honour all men : * loue [f] brotherlie felowship: feare God: honour the King.
18 *Seruāts, be subiect to your masters with
all feare,not onely to the good and courteous,but also to the [g] frowarde.
19 * For this is thanke worthie,if a man for
[h] conscience towarde God endure grief
suffering wrongfully.
20 For what praise is it , if when ye be buffeted for your fautes,ye take it paciently?
but and if when ye do wel, ye suffer *wrong*
and take it paciently , this is acceptable
to God.
21 For hereunto ye are called : for Christ
also suffred for vs, leauīg vs an ensample

Reuel.1,6.
Isa.28,16. rom.9,33.
b Meaning, ŷ God hathe appointed Christ to be chief & head of his Church.
Psal 118,22. mat 21,42. act.4,11.
Isa.8,14. rom.9,33.
c The Priests, Doctors & Ancients of the people.
Exod.19,6. reuel 5,10.
d That is partakers of Christes Priesthode & kingdome.
"Or, gotten by purchase.
Hosea 2,23. rom.9,25.
Galat.5,17. rom.13,14.
Chap 3,16.
Mat.5,16.
Rom.13,1.
e Your good conuersacion shalbe as a preparatiue against that day that God shal shew mercie vnto them and turne them.
"Or, publike gouernement.
Chap.1,22. rom.12,10.
Ephes 6,5. col.3,22.
2.Cor.7,10.
f With them ŵ acknowledge one self Father in heauē.
g In all obedience this must be before our eyes , that we obey in the Lord: for if anie commande things against God, then let vs answer, It is better to obey God then mē.
h Knowing ŷ God laieth this charge vpon him.

that ye shulde folowe his steppes.
22 *Who did no sinne, nether was there guile founde in his mouth.
23 Who when he was reuiled, reuiled not a-
gaine: when he suffred, he threatened not,
but committed it to him that iudgeth
righteously.
24 *Who his owne self bare our sinnes in
his bodie on the tre, that we being deliuered from sinne, shulde liue in righteousnes: by whose stripes ye were healed.
25 For ye were as shepe going astraye: but
are now returned vnto the shepherd and
bishope of your soules.

CHAP. III.

1 How wiues oght to ordre them selues towarde their housbands, 3 And in their apparel. 7 The duetie of men towarde their wiues. 8 He exhorteth all men to vnitie and loue. 14 And paciently to suffre trouble by the example and benefite of Christ.

1 Likewise *let the wiues be subiect to
their housbands that euen thei which
obey not the worde, may without the worde be wonne by the conuersacion of the
wiues,
2 While they beholde your pure conuersacion, which is with feare.
3 *Whose apparelling let it not be outwarde, *as* with broyded heere, and golde
put about, or in putting on of apparel.
4 But let the hid man of the heart be vncorrupt, with a meke & quiet spirit, which
is before God a thing muche set by.
5 For euen after this maner in time past did
the holie women, which trusted in God,
tier them selues, and were subiect to their
housbands.
6 As Sarra obeied Abraham, and *called
him "Syr: whose daughters ye are, whiles
ye do wel, not being [a] afraid of anie terrour.
7 *Likewise ye housbands, dwel with thẽ
as men of [b] knowledge, [c] giuing honour
vnto the womã, as vnto the weaker vessel,
euen as they which are [d] heires together
of the grace of life, that your [e] prayers be
not interrupted.
8 Finally, be ye all of one minde: one suffre with another: loue as brethren: *be* pitiful: *be* courteous,
9 *Not rendring euil for euil, nether rebuke for rebuke: but contrarie wise blesse,
knowing that ye are thereunto called, that
ye shulde be [f] heires of blessing.
10 *For if anie man long after life, and to
se good daies, let him refraine his tongue
from euil, and his lippes that they speake
not guile.
11 *Let him eschewe euil and do good: let
him seke peace, and folow after it.
12 For the eyes of the Lord *are* ouer the
righteous, and his eares *are open* vnto their
praiers: and the face of the Lord [g] *is* vpon

Isa.53.9. 1.ioh.3,5.
Isa.53.5. mat.8,17.
Col.3,18. ephes.5,22.
1.Tim.2,9.
"Or, master.
a But willigly do your duetie: for your cõdicion is not ỹ worse for your obedience.
b By nether keping them to streite, nor in giuing them to much libertie.
c Taking care, and prouiding for her.
Gene.18,12.
1 Cor.7,1.
d Man oght to loue his wife, because they lead their life together, also for ỹ she is the weaker vessel, but chiefly because ỹ God hathe made them as it were felowe heires together of life euerlasting.
Prou.17,11. & 20,22. mat.5,39. rom.12,17. 1.thes.5,15
Psal.33,13.
e For they can not pray when they are at dissention.
Isa.1,16.
f God hathe made vs when we were his enemies, heires of his kingdome, & shal not we forgiue our brethren a smale faute?
g To take vengeãce on him.

them that do euil.
13 And who is it that wil harme you, if ye
folowe that which is good?
14 *Notwithstanding blessed *are ye*, if ye
suffre for righteousnes sake. Yea, [h] feare
not their feare, nether be troubled.
15 *But [i] sanctifie the Lord God in your hearts: and be readie alwaies to giue an answer to euerie man that asketh you a reason of the hope that is in you,
16 **And that* with mekenes and reuerence, hauing a good conscience, that when
they speake euil of you as of euildoers,
thei may be ashamed, which blame your
good conuersacion in Christ.
17 For *it is* better (if the wil of God be so)
that ye suffer for wel doing, then for euil
doing.
18 *For Christ also hathe once suffred for
sinnes, ỹ iust for the vniust, that he might
bring vs to God, and was put to death cõcerning the flesh, but was quickened in the
[k] spirit.
19 By the which [l] he also went, & preached
vnto the spirits that were in prison.
20 Which were in time passed disobediẽt,
when once the long suffring of God abode in the daies of *Noe, while the arke
was preparing, wherein fewe, that is, eight
"soules were saued in the water.
21 To the which also the figure that now
saueth vs, *euen* Baptisme *agreeth* (not the
putting awaye of the filth of the flesh,
but in "that a good conscience maketh request to God) by the resurrection of Iesus
Christ,
22 Which is *at the right hand of God,
gone into heauen, to whome the Angels,
and Powers, and might are subiect.

CHAP. IIII.

1 He exhorteth men to cease from sinne, 2 To spende no more time in vice, 7 To be sober and apt to praye, 8 To loue eche other, 12 To be pacient in trouble, 15 To beware that no man suffre as an euil doer, 16 But as a Christian man, and so not to be ashamed.

1 Forasmuche then as Christ hathe suf
fred for vs in the flesh, arme your selues likewise with the same [a] minde, *which is*
that he which hathe suffred in the flesh,
hathe ceased from sinne,
2 That he henceforwarde shulde liue (as
muche time as remaineth in the "flesh)
not after the lustes of men, but after the
wil of God.
3 *For it is sufficient for vs that we haue
spent the time past of the life, after the
lust of the Gentiles, walking in wantõnes,
lustes, dronkennes, in glottonie, drinkings
and in abominable idolatries.
4 Wherein it semeth to them strange ỹ ye
runne not with thẽ vnto the same excesse
of ryote: *therefore* speake they euil *of you*.
5 Which shal giue accountes to him, that

Mat.5,10.
h That is, whẽ thei thinke to make you afraid by their threatnings.
Isa 8,13.
i Giue him praise & depẽde on him.
Chap 2,12.
Rom.5,6. ebr.9,15.
k By the power of God.
l Christ being from ỹ beginning head and gouernour of his Church, came in ỹ daies of Noe, not in bodie, ẘ then he had not, but in Spirit, and preached by ỹ mouth of Noe for the space of 120 yeres to ỹ disobedient, ẘ wolde not repẽt, & therefore are now in prison reserued to the last iudgement.
Gen.6,14. mat.24,38. luk.17,26.
Ebr.1,3.
"Or, persones.
"Or, the taking to witnes of a good conscience.
a Our sãctificacion standeth in two points, in dying to sinne, & liuing to God.
"Or, bodie
Ephes 4,18.

is ready to iudge quicke and dead.
6 For vnto this purpose was the Gospel
preached also vnto the [b] dead, that they
might be condemned, according to men,
in the flesh, but might liue according to
God in the spirit.
7 Now the end of all things is at hand.
Be ye therefore sober, and watching in
prayer.
8 But aboue all things haue feruent loue a-
mong you: *for [c] loue couereth the multitude of sinnes.
9 Be ye *herberous one to another, without
grudging.
10 *Let euerie man as he hathe receiued
the gifte, minister the same one to another, as good disposers of the manifolde
grace of God.
11 If anie man speake, *let him talke* as ẏ wordes of God. If anie man minister, *let him do
it* as of the abilitie which God ministreth,
that God in all things may be glorified
through Iesus Christ, to whome is praise
and dominion for euer, and euer, Amen.
12 Dearly beloued, thinke it not strange
cõcerning the fyrie trial, which is among
you to proue you, as thogh some strange
thing were come vnto you:
13 But reioyce, in asmuche as ye are partakers of Christs sufferings, that when his
glorie shal appeare, ye may be glad and reioyce.
14 *If ye be railed vpon for the Name of
Christ, blessed *are ye*: for the Spirit of glorie, and of God resteth vpon you: *which* on
their [d] parte is euil spoken of: but on your
parte is glorified.
15 But let none of you suffer as a murtherer,
or *as* a thefe, or an euil doer, or as a busibo-
die in other mens matters.
16 But if *anie man suffer* as a Christian, let
him not be ashamed: but let him glorifie
God in this behalfe.
17 For the time *is come*, that "iudgement
must beginne at *the house of God. If it
first *begin* at vs, what shal the end be of thẽ
which obey not the Gospel of God?
18 *And if the righteous scarsely be[e] saued,
where shal the vngodlie and the sinner
appeare?
19 Wherefore let them that suffer according to the wil of God, commit their soules *to him* in wel doing, as vnto a faithful
Creator.

b Although the wicked thinke this Gospel newe, & vexe you that imbrace it: yet, hathe it bene preached to them of time past, which now are dead, to the intent ẏ they might haue bene cõdẽned, or dead to sinne in the flesh, & also might haue liued to God in the spirit, which two are the effect of the Gospel.

Prou.10,12. Rom.12,13. ebr.13,2. Rom.12,6. phil 2,14.

c As hatred moueth vs to reproche our brother when he offendeth vs: so loue hideth and pardoneth the fautes, which he committeth against vs, thogh they be neuer so manie.

Ma.5,110.

d That is, by the infideles.

"Or, punishemẽt. Iere.25,29. luk 23,31.

Prou.2,31.

e As concerning this life where he is punished.

CHAP. V.

*2 The duetie of Pastours is to fede the flocke of Christ,
and what rewarde they shal haue if they be diligent.
5 He exhorteth yong persones to submit them selues to
the elders, 8 To be sober, and to watche that they may
resist the enemie.*

1 THe [a] elders which are among you, I
beseche which am also an elder, and
a witnes of the suffrings of Christ, and also a partaker of the glorie that shalbe reueiled,
2 Fede the flocke of "God, which "dependeth vpon you, caring for it not by con-
straint, but willingly: not for filthie lucre,
but of a readie minde:
3 Not as thogh ye were lords ouer *Gods* heritage, but that ye may be ensamples to
the flocke.
4 And when the chief shepherd shal appeare, ye shal receiue an incorruptible crowne
of glorie.
5 Likewise ye yonger, submit your selues
vnto the elders, & submit your selues euerie mã, one to another: *decke your selues
inwardely in lowlines of minde: for God
*resisteth the proude and giueth grace to
the humble.
6 Humble *your selues therefore vnder the
mightie hand of God, that he may exalt
you in due time.
7 Cast *all your care on him: for he careth
for you.
8 Be sober and watch: for *your aduersarie
the deuil as a roaring lyon walketh about,
seking whome he may deuoure:
9 Whome resist stedfast in the faith, knowing [b] that the same afflictions are accomplished in your brethren which are in the
worlde.
10 And the God of all grace, which hathe
called vs vnto his eternal glorie by Christ
Iesus, after ẏ ye haue suffred a litel, make
you perfect, confirme, strengthen and stablish *you*.
11 To him *be* glorie and dominion for euer
and euer. Amen.
12 By Siluanus a faithful brother vnto you,
as I suppose, haue I writen briefly, exhorting and testifying how that this is the
true grace of God, wherein ye stand.
13 *The Church* ẏ is at [c] Babylõ elected together with you, saluteth you, and Marcus
my sonne.
14 Grete ye one another with the *kysse of
loue. Peace *be* with you all which are in
Christ Iesus. Amen.

a By elders he vnderstandeth all thẽ which preache, teache, or minister in the Church.

"Or, Christ. "Or, which is commit vnto you or, asmuche as in you lyeth.

Rom.12,10. Iam.4,6. Iam.4,10. Psal.54,23. wisd.12,13. mat.6,25 luk.12,22. Luk.22,31.

b Nothing cometh vnto vs, which we se not to apperteine to the rest of Christs members: and therefore we oght not to refuse that condition which is commune to all the Saintes.

c Which was a famous citie in Assyria where Peter then was the Apostle of the circumcision.

Rom.16,16. 1.cor.16,20. 2 cor.13,13

THE SECONDE EPI stle general of Peter.

THE ARGUMENT.

The effect of the Apostle here is to exhorte thẽ which haue once professed the true faith of Christ, to stande to the same euen to the last breath: also that God by his effectual grace towardes mẽ moueth them to holines of life,in punishing the hypocrites which abuse his Name,& in increasing his gifts in the godlie: wherefore by godlie life he being now almost at deaths dore,exhorteth thẽ to approue their vocation,not setting their affections on worldlie things(as he had oft writ vnto them)but lifting their eyes towarde heauen, as they be taught by the Gospel, whereof he is a cleare witnes, chiefly in that he heard with his owne eares that Christ was proclaimed from heauen to be the Sonne of God,as likewise the Prophetes testified. And lest they shulde promise to them selues quietnes by professing the Gospel,he warneth thẽ bothe of troubles which they shulde susteine by the false teachers, and also by the mockers & contemners of religion,whose maners and trade he liuely setteth forthe as in a table: aduertising the faithful not onely to waite diligently for Christ,but also to beholde presently the day of his comming,and to preserue them selues vnspotted against the same.

CHAP. I.

4 Forasmuche as the power of God hathe giuen them all things perteining vnto life , he exhorteth them to flee the corruption of worldlie lusts, 10 To make their calling sure with good workes,and frutes of faith. 14 He maketh mention of his owne death, 17 Declaring the Lord Iesus to be the true Sonne of God, as he him self had sene vpon the mounte.

1 SIMON Peter a seruant
and an Apostle of IE-
SUS CHRIST, to you
which haue obteined li-
ke precious faith with
vs by the [a] righteousnes
of our God and Sauiour
Iesus Christ:
2 Grace and peace be multiplied to you,
by the knowledge of God and of Iesus our
Lord,
3 According as his [b] godlie power hathe gi
uen vnto vs all things that *perteine* vnto
[c] life and godlines,[d] through the knowledge of him that hathe called vs "vnto glorie and vertue.
4 Whereby moste great,and precious promises are giuen vnto vs, that by them ye
shulde be partakers of the [e] godlie nature,
in that ye flee the corruption, which is in
the worlde through lust.
5 Therefore giue euen all diligence there-
unto:ioyne moreouer [f] vertue with your
faith:and with vertue,knowledge:
6 And with knowledge, temperance: and
with temperance,pacience:and with paciẽ
ce,godlines:
7 And with godlines,brotherlie kindenes:
and with brotherlie kindenes,loue.
8 For if these things be among you, and
abunde, they wil make you that ye nether shalbe ydle,nor vnfruteful in ẏ knowledge of our Lord Iesus Christ.
9 For he that hathe not these things,is blin
de,& [g] can not se farre of,& hathe forgottẽ
that he was purged from his olde sinnes.

a In that he declared him self iuste and faithful in accomplishing his promes by Christ.

b He speaketh of Christ as he is God and Sauiour.

c That is, saluation.

d The summe of our saluatiõ and religion is to be led by Christ to the Father, who calleth vs in the Sonne.

"*Or, through his glorie.*

e We are made partakers of ẏ diuine nature, in ẏ we flee ẏ corruption of the worlde:or as Paul writeth,are dead to sinne. & are not in the flesh

f Godlie maners

g The Greeke worde signifieth him,that naturally can not se, except he holdeth nere his eyes. So Peter calleth suche as can not se heauẽlie things which are farre of, purre blinde or sandblĩde.

10 Wherefore,brethren,giue rather diligẽce to make your calling & election [h] sure:
for if ye do these things,ye shal neuer [i] fall.
11 For by this meanes an entring shalbe ministred vnto you abũdantly into the euerlasting kingdome of our Lord & Sauiour
Iesus Christ.
12 Wherefore,I wil not be negligẽt to put
you alwais in remẽbrance of these things,
thogh that ye haue knowledge,and be stablished in the present trueth.
13 For I thinke it mete as lõg as I am in this
[k] tabernacle,to stirre you vp by puttĩg you
in remembrance.
14 Seing I knowe that the time is at hand
that I must lay downe this my tabernacle, euen as our Lord Iesus Christ hathe
*shewed me.
15 I wil endeuour therefore alwaise,that ye
also may be able to haue remembrance of
these things after my departing.
16 For we folowed not*"deceiueable fables
when we opened vnto you the power, and
comming of our Lord Iesus Christ, but
with our eyes we saw his maiestie:
17 For he receiued of God the Father honour and glorie, when there came suche a
voyce to him from the excellent glorie,
*This is my beloued Sonne, in whome I
am wel pleased.
18 And this voyce we heard when it came
from heauen, being with him in the [l] holie mounte.
19 We haue also a moste sure [m] worde of
the Prophetes, to ẏ which ye do wel that
ye take hede, as vnto a light that shineth
in a darke place, vntil the [n] day dawne,and
the [o] daye starre arise in your hearts.
20 *So that ye first know this,that no prophecie in the Scripture is of [p] anie priuate
"motion.
21 For the Prophecie came not in olde time
by the wil of man: but holie men of God
spake

h Albeit it be sure in it self forasmuche as God can not change:yet we must confirme it in our selues, by the frutes of the Spirit,knowing ẏ the purpose of God electeth, calleth, sanctifieth,and iustifieth vs.

i For God wil euer vpholde you.

k In this bodie, 2.Cor.5,1.

Ioh.21,19.

1.Cor.1,17. & 2,1.

"*Or, sophistical and craftie.*

Mat.17,5.

l For by Christs presẽce it was for the time holie.

m That is, the doctrine of the Prophetes.

n A perfiter knowledge then vnder the Law.

2.Tim.3,16.

o Meaning, Christ the sunne of iustice, by his Gospel.

p Cometh not of men.

"*Or, interpretation.*

ſpake as they were moued by the holie
Goſt.

CHAP. II.

He prophecieth of falſe teachers, and ſheweth their puniſhment.

1 BVt* there were falſe prophetes alſo
among the people, euẽ as there ſhalbe falſe teachers among you: which priuely ſhal bring in damnable hereſies, euen
denying the Lord, that hathe boght them,
& bring vpon them ſelues ſwift dãnation.
2 And manie ſhal followe their "damnable wayes, by whome the way of trueth
ſhalbe euil ſpoken of,
3 And through couetouſnes ſhal they with
fained wordes make [a] marchandiſe of you,
whoſe iudgement long agone is not farre
of, and their damnation ſlepeth not.
4 For if God ſpared not the* Angels, that
had ſinned, but caſte them downe into hell
and deliuered them into chaines of darkenes, to be kept vnto damnation:
5 Nether hathe ſpared the olde worlde, but
ſaued *Noe the eight *perſone* a preacher of
righteouſnes, and broght in the flood vpõ
the worlde of the vngodlie,
6 And* turned the cities of Sodome and
Gomorrhe into aſhes, condemned them
and ouerthrewe them, and made them an
enſample vnto them that after ſhulde liue
vngodlie,
7 *And deliuered iuſte Loth vexed with
the vnclenlie conuerſation of the wicked,
8 (For he being righteous, and dwelling a-
mong them, in ſeing and hearing, vexed
his righteous ſoule from day to day with
their vnlawful dedes.)
9 The Lord knoweth to deliuer the godlie out of tentation, and to reſerue the
vniuſt vnto the day of iudgement to be
puniſhed:
10 And chiefely them that walke after the
fleſh, in the luſt of vnclennes, and deſpiſe
the gouernement, *which are* preſumpteous,
and ſtand in their owne conceite, and feare not to ſpeake euil of thẽ that are in dig
nitie.
11 Where as the Angels which are greater
bothe in power and might, *giue not [b] railing iudgement againſt them before the
Lord.
12 But theſe as [c] brute beaſts, led with ſenſualitie and made to be taken, and deſtroyed, ſpeake euil of thoſe things which
they knowe not, and ſhal periſh through
their owne corruption.
13 And ſhal receiue the wages of vnrighteouſnes, as they which counte it pleaſure to
liue deliciouſly for a ſeaſon. Spottes *they
are* and blottes, [d] deliting them ſelues in
their deceiuings, in feaſting with you,

Act. 20,29. 1. tim. 4,2. iud. 11.

"Or, inſolent & wanton.

a This is euidently ſene in the Pope & his Prieſts, ŵ by lies & flatteries ſel mens ſoules, ſo that it is certeine that he is not the ſucceſſour of Simon Peter, but of Simon Magus.

Iob. 4,18. iude 6.

Gen. 7,2.

Gen. 19,24.

Gen. 19,16.

1. King. 22,22 iob. 1,12.

b Albeit the Angels condemne the vices and iniquitie of wicked magiſtrates, yet they blame not the autoritie and power which is giuen them of God.

c As beaſts without reaſon or wit followe whether nature leadeth them: ſo theſe wicked men deſtitute of ỹ Spirit of God, onely ſeke to fulfil their ſenſualitie, and as they are veſſels made to deſtructiõ, & appointed to this iudgement, ſo thei fall into the ſnares of Satan to their deſtructiõ.

d For in your holie feaſts they ſit as mẽbers of ỹ Church where as in dede they be but ſpottes, & ſo deceiue you, read Iude 12.

14 Hauing eyes ful of adulterie, and that
can not ceaſe to ſinne, beguiling vnſtable
ſoules: they haue hearts exerciſed with co
uetouſnes, curſed children,
15 Which forſaking the right waye, haue
gone aſtraye, following the way of* Balaam, *the ſonne* of Boſor, which loued the
wages of vnrighteouſnes.
16 But he was rebuked for his iniquitie:
for the domme aſſe ſpeaking with mans
voyce, forbade the fooliſhnes of the Prophet.
17 *Theſe are welles without water, *and*
[e] cloudes caryed about with a tempeſt, to
whome the blacke darkenes is reſerued for
euer.
18 For in ſpeaking ſwelling wordes of vanitie, they beguile with wantõnes through
the luſtes of the fleſh them that were cleane eſcaped from them which are wrapped
in errour,
19 Promiſing vnto them libertie, and are
them ſelues the* ſeruants of corruption:
for of whome ſoeuer a man is ouercome,
euen vnto the ſame is he in bondage.
20 *For if they, after they haue eſcaped frõ
the filthines of the worlde, through the
[f] knowledge of the Lord, & of the Sauiour
Ieſus Chriſt, are yet tãgled againe therein,
and ouercome, the latter end is worſe with
them then the beginning.
21 For it had bene better for them, not to
haue knowen the way of righteouſnes, thẽ
after they haue knowen it, to turne frõ the
holie "commandement giuen vnto them.
22 But it is come vnto them, according to
the true prouerbe, *The dogge is returned to his owne vomit: and, The ſowe
that was waſhed, to the wallowing in the
myer.

Nomb. 22,23. iude 11.

Iude 12.

e Thei haue ſome appearãce outwarde, but within they are drie and barren, or at moſte they cauſe but a tempeſt.

Iohn 8,34. rom. 6,20.

Mat. 12,45. ebr. 6,4. & 10,26.

f Which cometh by hearing the Goſpel preached.

"Or, doctrine.

Prou. 26,11.

CHAP. III.

3 He ſheweth the impitie of them which mocke at Gods promiſes. 7 After what ſorte the end of the worlde ſhalbe. 8 That they prepare them ſelues thereunto. 16 Who they are which abuſe the writings of S. Paul, and the reſt of the Scriptures. 18 Concluding with eternal thankes to Chriſt Ieſus.

1 THis ſeconde Epiſtle I now write vnto you, beloued, wherewith [a] I ſtirre
vp, and warne your pure mindes,
2 To call to remẽbrance the wordes, which
were tolde before of the holie Prophetes,
and alſo the commandement of vs the A-
poſtles of the Lord and Sauiour.
3 *This firſt vnderſtand, that there ſhal come in the laſt dayes, mockers, which wil
walke after their luſtes,
4 And ſay, Where is the promes of his cõming? for ſince the fathers dyed, all things
continue a like from the beginning of the
creation.
5 For this they [b] willingly knowe not, that
the heauens were of olde, and the earth

a For we fall quickely aſlepe and forget that which we are taught.

1. Tim. 4,1. 2. tim. 3,1. iude. 18.

b He meaneth thẽ which had once profeſſed Chriſtian religion, but became afterwarde contemners & mockers, as Epicurians & atheiſtes.

that was of the water and by the water, by
the worde of God.

e As touching ỳ beautie thereof, & things which were therein, except them w were in the arke.

6 Wherefore the e worlde that then was, pe
rished, ouerflowed with the water.
7 But the heauens & earth, which are now,
are kept by the same worde in store, and
reserued vnto fyre against the day of iudgement,
and of the destruction of vngodlie men.
8 Derely beloued, be not ignorant of this
one thing, that one day is with the Lord,
* as a thousand yeres, & a thousand yere,
as one day.

Psal. 90,4.

9 The Lord is not slacke concerning *his*
promes (as some men count slackenes) but
is pacient towarde vs, and * d wolde haue
no man to perish, but wolde all men to come to repentance.

Eze. 33,32. 1. tim. 2,4.

d He speaketh not here of the secret & eternal counsel of God, whereby he electeth whome it pleaseth him, but of the preaching of the Gospel whereby all are called and bidde to the banket.

10 *But the day of the Lord wil come as a
thief in the night, in the which the heauẽs
shal passe away with a noyce, and the elements
shal melt with heate, and the earth
with the workes, that are therein, shalbe
burnt vp.
11 Seing therefore that all these things must
be dissolued, what maner persones oght ye
to be in holie conuersation and godlines,
12 Loking for, and hasting vnto the comming
of the day of God, by the which the
heauens being on fyre, shalbe dissolued, &
the elements shal melt with heat?

Mat. 24,44. 1. thes. 5,2. reuel. 3,3. & 16,15.

13 But we loke for * new heauens, and a new
earth, according to his promes, wherein
dwelleth righteousnes.

Isa. 65,17. & 66,22. reuel. 21,1.

14 Wherefore, beloued, seing that ye loke
for suche things, be diligent that ye may
be founde of him in e peace, without spotte
and blameles.

e In quiet cõscience.

15 *And suppose that the long suffring of
our Lord is saluation, euen as our beloued
brother Paul according to the wisdome giuen
vnto him wrote to f you,

Rom. 2,4.

f Albeit his epistles were writ to peculiar Churches, yet they conteine a general doctrine apperteining to all men

16 As one, that in all *his* Epistles speaketh of
these things: amõg the which some things
are g hard to be vnderstand, which they
that are vnlearned and vnstable, *peruert,
as they *do* also other Scriptures vnto their
owne destruction.

g As no man condemneth ỳ brightnes of the sunne because his eye is not able to susteine the clearnes thereof: so the hardenes ẘ we can not sometime compas or perfectly vnderstande in the Scriptures, oght not to take away from vs the vse of ỳ Scriptures.

* Or, wraste.

17 Ye therefore beloued, seing ye knowe
these things before, beware, lest ye be also
plucked away with the errour of the wicked,
and fall from your owne stedfastnes.
18 But growe in grace, and in the knowledge
of our Lord and Sauiour Iesus Christ:
to him *be* glorie bothe now and for euer
more. Amen.

THE FIRST EPIstle general of Iohn.

THE ARGVMENT.

After that S. Iohn had sufficiently declared, how that our whole saluation doeth cõsiste onely in Christ, lest that any man shoulde thereby take a boldenes to sinne, he sheweth that no man can beleue in Christ, onles he doeth endeuour him self to kepe his commandements, which thing being done, he exhorteth them to beware of false prophetes, whome he calleth Antichrists, and to trye the spirits. Laste of all he doeth earnestly exhorte them vnto brotherlie loue, and to beware of deceiuers.

CHAP. I.

2 True witnes of the euerlasting worde of God. 7 The blood of Christ is the purgation of sinne. 10 No man is without sinne.

a That is, Christ God eternal.
b That is, Christ being man.

1 THat which was a from
the beginning, which
we haue b heard, which
we haue sene with our
eyes, which we haue loked
vpon, and our hands
haue hãdled of ỳ Worde
c of life,

c Which giueth life and had it in him self, Ioh 14.
d Before all beginning.

2 (For the life appeared, and we haue sene
it, and beare witnes, and shewe vnto you
the eternal life, which was d with the Father,
and appeared vnto vs)

e The effect of the Gospel is, ỳ we all being ioyned together in Christ by faith, shulde be the sonnes of God.

3 That, *I say*, which we haue sene & heard,
declare we vnto you, that ye may also e haue
felowship with vs, and that our felowship
also may be with the Father and with
his Sonne Iesus Christ.
4 And these things write we vnto you, that
your ioye may be ful.
5 This then is the message which we haue
heard of him, and declare vnto you, that
God * is f light, & in him is no darkenes.

Iohn 8,12.
f The frutes of our faith must declare whether we be ioyned in God or no: for God being ỳ verie puritie & light wil not haue felowship with them ẘ lie in sinne and darkenes.

6 If we say ỳ we haue felowship with him,
and walke in g darkenes, we lye, & do not
truely.

g In an euil conscience, & without the feare of God.

7 But if we walke in the light as he is in the
light, we haue felowship h one with another,
and the * blood of Iesus Christ his
Sonne clenseth vs from all sinne.

h That is, Christ with vs and we with our selues.
Ebr. 9,14. 1. pet. 1,19. reu. 1,6.

8 *If we say that we haue no sinne, we deceiue
our selues, and trueth is not in vs.

1. King. 8,46. 2. chro. 6,36. pro. 20,9. eccle. 7,20.

9 If we i acknowledge our sinnes, he is faithful
and iust, to forgiue vs our sinnes, & to
clense vs from all vnrighteousnes.

i If we be not ashamed, earnestly & openly to acknowledge our selues before God to be sinners.

10 If

10 If we say we haue not sinned, we make
him a lier, and his "worde is not in vs.

CHAP. II.

1 Christ is our Aduocate. 10 Of true loue, & how it is tried. 18 To beware of Antichrist.

1 MY babes, these things write I vnto
you, that ye sinne not: and if any mã
sinne, we haue an [a] Aduocat with the Father, Iesus Christ, the Iust.
2 And he is the reconciliation for our sinnes: and not for ours onely, but also for *the*
sinnes of [b] the whole worlde.
3 And hereby we are sure that we [c] knowe
him, if we kepe his commandements.
4 He that saith, I knowe him, and kepeth
not his commandements, is a lier, and the
trueth is not in him.
5 But he that kepeth his worde, in him is
[d] the loue of God perfite in dede: hereby
we knowe that we are in him.
6 He that saith he remaineth in him, oght
euen so to walke, as he hathe walked.
7 Brethren, I write no newe "commandement vnto you: but an olde commandement, which ye haue had from the [e] beginning: the [f] olde commandement is the
worde, which ye haue heard from the beginning.
8 Againe, a newe commandement I write
vnto you, that which is true in him, and also in you: for the darkenes is past, and the
true light now shineth.
9 He that saith that he is in the light, and
hateth his brother, is in darkenes vntil this
time.
10 *He that loueth his brother, abideth in
the light, and there is none occasion of e-
uil in him.
11 But he that hateth his brother, is in darkenes, and walketh in darkenes, & knoweth
not whither he goeth, because that darkenes hathe blinded his eyes.
12 [g] Litle children, I write vnto you, because your sinnes are forgiuen you for [h] his
Names sake.
13 I write vnto you, fathers, because ye haue knowen him that is frõ the beginning.
I write vnto you, yong men, because ye haue ouercome the "wicked.
14 I write vnto you, babes, because ye haue
knowẽ the Father. I haue writẽ vnto you,
fathers, because ye haue knowen him, that
is from the beginning. I haue writen vnto
you, yong men, because ye are strong, and
the worde of God abideth in you, and ye
haue ouercome the "wicked.
15 Loue not the [i] worlde, nether the things
that are in the worlde. If any mã loue the
*worlde, ẏ loue of the Father is not in him.
16 For all that is in the worlde (as the luste
of the [k] flesh, the [l] luste of the eyes, & the
[m] pride of life) is not of ẏ Father, but is of
the worlde.

"Or, doctrine.

a Christ is our onelie Aduocate and atonement: for the office of intercession and redemptiõ are ioyned together.
b That is, of them which haue ẽbraced the Gospel by faith in all ages, degrees, & places: for there is no saluation without Christ
c That is, by faith and so obey him: for knowledge cã not be without obedience
d Whereby he loueth God: so that to loue God is to obey his worde
"Or, doctrine.
e When the Lawe was giuen.
f Loue thy neighbour as thy self, is the olde cõmandement taught in ẏ Law: but whẽ Christ saith, So loue one another as I haue loued you, he giueth a newe commandement onely as touching the forme, but not as touchĩg the nature or substance of ẏ precept.
Chap. 3, 14.
g He nameth all the faithful, children, as he being their spiritual father, attributing to olde men knowledge of great things, to yong men strength, to children obedience & reuerẽce to their gouernours.
h For Christs sake.
"Or, the deuil.
"Or, the deuil.
i As it is aduersarie to God.
Iam. 4, 4.
k To liue in pleasure.
l Wantonnes.
m Ambition & pride.

17 And the worlde passeth awaye, and the
luste thereof: but he that fulfilleth the wil
of God, abideth euer.
18 Babes, it is the last time, and as ye haue
heard that Antichrist shal come, euẽ now
are there many Antichrists: whereby we
knowe that it is the last time.
19 [n] They went out from vs, but they were
not of vs: for if they had bene of vs, they
wolde haue continued with vs. But *this cõ-*
meth to passe, that it might appeare, that
they are not all of vs.
20 But ye haue an [o] ointement frõ him, that
is [p] Holie, & ye haue knowen all things.
21 I [q] haue not writen vnto you, because ye
knowe not ẏ trueth: but because ye knowe
it, and that no lye is of the trueth.
22 Who is a lyer, but he that denyeth that
Iesus is [r] Christ? the same is the Antichrist
that denyeth the Father and the Sonne.
23 Whosoeuer denyeth the Sonne, the same [s] hathe not the Father‖.
24 Let therefore abide in you that same
which ye haue heard from the beginning.
If that which ye haue heard from the beginning, shal remaine in you, ye also shal
continewe in the Sonne, & in the Father.
25 And this is ẏ promes that he hathe promised vs, *euen* eternal life.
26 These things haue I writen vnto you,
concerning them that deceiue you.
27 But the anointing which ye receiued of
him, dwelleth in you: and ye nede not that
any man teache you: but as the same [t] A-
nointing teacheth you of all things, & it
is true, & is not lying, & as it taught you,
ye shal abide "in him.
28 And now, [u] litle children, abide in him,
that when he shal appeare, we may be bolde, and not be ashamed before him at his
comming.
29 If ye knowe that he is righteous, knowe
ye that he which doeth righteously, is borne of him.

CHAP. III.

1 The singular loue of God towarde vs. 7 And how we againe oght to loue one another.

1 BEholde, what loue the Father hathe
shewed on vs, that we shulde be [a] called the sonnes of God: for this cause the
worlde knoweth you not, because it knoweth not him.
2 Dearly beloued, now are we the sonnes
of God, but yet it doeth not appeare what
we shalbe: and we knowe that when [b] he
shal appeare, we shalbe [c] like him: for we
shal se him as he is.
3 And euerie man that hathe this hope in
him, purgeth him self, euen as he is pure.
4 Whosoeuer [d] cõmitteth sinne, transgresseth also the Law: for sinne is the trãsgression of the Law.
5 And ye knowe that he appeared that he

n Which semed to haue bene of our nomber, because for a time they occupied a place in ẏ Church
o The grace of the holie Gost
p Which is Christ.
q In this Epistle which I now write vnto you.
r He that taketh away or diminisheth ether of the natures in Christ, or he that confoundeth or separateth them, els he that putteth not difference betwene the persone of the Sonne, & also he that beleueth not to haue remission of sinnes by his onely sacrifice, denieth Christ to be ẏ true Messias.
s Then the infideles worship not the true God.
‖ *But he that cõfesseth the Sõne, hathe also the Father.*
t Christ communicateth hĩ self vnto you and teacheth you by the holie Gost & his ministers.
"Or, in Christ.
u By this name he meaneth the whole Church of Christ in general.
a Being made the sonnes of God in Christ, he sheweth what qualities we must haue to be discerned from bastardes.
b That is, Christ.
c As the members and head are which make one perfect bodie.
d That is, in whome sinne doeth reigne, so ẏ he seketh not to be sanctified.

might *take away our sinnes,and in him is
no sinne.

Isa.53,9. *1.pet.2,22.*

6 Whosoeuer abideth in him, sinneth not:
whosoeuer sinneth,hathe not sene him,ne-
ther hathe knowen him.
7 Litle children, let no man deceiue you:
he that doeth righteousnes,is righteous,as
he is righteous.
8 He that * committeth sinne, is of the deuil: for the deuil sinneth from the [e]begin-
ning: for this purpose appeared the Sonne of God, that he might lose the workes of the deuil.

Iohn 8,44.
e As appeared by Adam.

9 Whosoeuer is borne of God,sinneth not:
for his [f]sede remaineth in him,nether can
he [g] sinne,because he is borne of God.
10 In this are the childrē of God knowen,
and the children of the deuil: whosoeuer
doeth not righteousnes,is not of God,ne-
ther he that [h] loueth not his brother.
11 For this is the message, that ye heard frō
the beginning, that * we shulde loue one
another,
12 Not as * Cain which was of the wicked,
and slewe his brother: & wherefore slewe
he him? because his owne workes were e-
uil,and his brothers good.

f Which is the holie Gost.
g He can not be vnder the power of sinne because the Spirit of God correcteth his euil and corrupt affections
h He descendeth from the first table of ẏ cōmandements to the seconde.
Iohn 13,34. & 15,12.
Gen.4,8.

13 Marueile not,my brethren,thogh ẏ worlde hate you.
14 We knowe that we are translated from
death vnto life, because we [i] loue the brethren: *he that loueth not *his* brother,abi-
deth in death.
15 Whosoeuer hateth his brother,is a manslayer:& ye knowe that no mãslayer hathe
eternal life abiding in him.
16 *Hereby haue we perceiued loue,that he
laid downe his life for vs: therefore we
oght also to lay downe *our* liues for the
brethren.
17 *And whosoeuer hathe this worldes good
and seeth his brother haue nede,and shutteth vp his cōpassion from him, how dwel
leth the loue of God in him?

i This loue is the special frute of our faith and a certeine signe of our regeneration.
Chap.2,10.
leuit.19,17.
Iohn 15,13.
ephe.5,2.
Luk.3,11.

18 My litle children,let vs not loue in worde,nether in tongue *onely*, but in [k] dede &
in trueth.
19 For thereby we knowe that we are of the
trueth & shal before him assure our hearts.
20 For if our [l] heart condemne vs, God is
greater then our heart, and knoweth all
things.
21 Beloued, if our heart condemne vs not,
then haue we boldenes towarde God.
22 *And whatsoeuer we aske, we receiue of
him, because we kepe his cōmandements,
and do those things which are pleasing in
his sight.
23 *This is then his commandement, That
we beleue in the Name of his Sonne Iesus Christ,and loue one another, as he gaue commandement.
24 *For he that kepeth his cōmādements,
dwelleth in him, and he in him: & hereby
we knowe that he abydeth in vs, *euen* by
the Spirit which he hathe giuen vs.

k Which is not the cause, wherefore we are ẏ sonnes of God,but a moste certeine signe.
l If our conscience being giltie of any thing, be able to cōdemne vs, muche more ẏ iudgement of God which knoweth our hearts better thē we our selues, is able to condemne vs.
Iohn 15,7. & 16,23.
mat.21,22.
chap.5,24.
Iohn.6,29. & 17,3.
Iohn 13,34. & 15,10.

CHAP. IIII.

1 Difference of spirits. 2 How the Spirit of God may be knowen from the spirit of errour. 7 Of the loue of God and of our neighbours.

1 Derely beloued, beleue not euerie
spirit, but trye the [a] spirits whether
they are of God: for many false Prophetes are gone out into the worlde.
2 Hereby shal ye knowe the Spirit of God,
Euerie spirit that confesseth that Iesus
[b]Christ is come in the flesh,is of God.
3 And euerie spirit which confesseth not
that Iesus Christ is come in the flesh,is not
of God:but this is the *spirit* of Antichrist,
of whome ye haue heard,how ẏ he shulde
come & [c] now already he is in the worlde.
4 Litle children, ye are of God, and haue
ouercome them: for greater is he that is in
you,then [d] he that is in the worlde.
5 They are of the worlde, therefore speake
they of the worlde, and the worlde heareth them.
6 We are of God, * he that knoweth God,
[e] heareth vs: he that is not of God, heareth vs not. Hereby knowe we the Spirit
of trueth,and the spirit of errour.

a The which boast that thei haue the Spirit to preache or prophecie.
b Who being very God came from his Father and toke vpon him our flesh. He ẏ confesseth or preacheth this truely, hathe the Spirit of God,els not.
c He began to buylde the mysterie of iniquitie.
d Satan the prince of the worlde.
Iohn 8,47.
e With pure affection & obedience.

7 Beloued,let vs loue one another:for loue
cometh of God,& euerie one that loueth,
is borne of God,and knoweth God.
8 He that loueth not, knoweth not God:
for God is loue.
9 * In [f] this appeared ẏ loue of God towarde vs, because God sent his onely begottē
Sonne into the worlde,that we might liue
through him.
10 Herein is loue, not that we loued God,
but that he loued vs, and sent his sonne *to*
be a [g]reconciliation for our sinnes.
11 Beloued,if God so loued vs,we oght also to loue one another.
12 *No man hathe sene God at any time. If
we loue one another, God dwelleth in vs,
and his loue is perfite in vs.
13 Hereby knowe we,that we dwell in him,
and he in vs: because he hathe giuen vs of
his Spirit.
14 And we haue sene, and do testifie, that
the Father sent the Sōne *to be* the Sauiour
of the worlde.
15 Whosoeuer [h] confesseth that Iesus is the
Sonne of God,in him dwelleth God, and
he in God.
16 And we haue knowen, and beleued the
loue that God hathe [°][i]in vs. God is loue,&
he that dwelleth in loue,dwelleth in God,
and God in him.
17 Herein is the loue perfite in vs, that we
shulde haue boldenes in the day of iudgement: for as he is, euen so are we in this
worlde.

Iohn 3,16.
f Trueth it is, ẏ God hathe declared his loue in many other things, but herein hathe passed all other.
g By his onelie death.
Iohn 1,18.
1.tim.6,16.
h So that his cōfession procedeth of faith
°Or, towarde vs.
i By inspiring it into vs.

18 There

k Suche as shulde trouble the consciẽce.

18 There is no [k] feare in loue, but perfect
loue casteth out feare: for feare hathe pa-
infulnes: and he that feareth, is not perfect in loue.
19 We loue him, because he loued vs first.
20 If anie man say, I loue God, and hate
his brother, he is a lyer: for [l] how can he
that loueth not his brother whome he hathe sene, loue God whome he hathe not
sene?
21 * And this commandement haue we of
him, that he which loueth God, shulde loue his brother also.

l For god presẽteth him self to vs in them, which beare his image.

Iohn 13,43. & 15,12.

CHAP. V.

1.10.13 Of the frutes of faith. 14.20 The office, autoritie, & diuinitie of Christ. 21 Against images.

1 WHosoeuer beleueth that Iesus is
the Christ, is [a] borne of God, &
euerie one that loueth him, which begate,
loueth him also which is begottẽ of him.
2 In this we knowe that we loue the children of God, when we loue [b] God, & kepe his commandements.
3 For this is the loue of God that we kepe
his commandements: and his * commandements are not [c] grieuous.
4 For all that is borne of God, ouercometh
the worlde: and this is the victorie that o-
uercometh the worlde, *euen* our faith.
5 * Who is it that ouercometh the worlde,
but he which beleueth that Iesus is the Sõne of God?
6 This is that Iesus Christ that came by
[d] water [e] & blood, not by water onely, but
by water and blood: and it is the [f] spirit,
ẏ beareth witnes: for the Spirit is [g] trueth.
7 For there are thre, which beare recorde
in heauen, the Father, the Worde, and the
holie Gost: and these thre are one.
8 And there are thre, which beare recorde
in the earth, the spirit and the water and
the blood: and these thre agre in one.
9 If we receiue the witnes of men, the witnes of God is greater: for this is the witnes of God, which he testified of his Sõne.
10 * He that beleueth in the Sõne of God,
hathe the witnes || in him self: he that bele-
ueth not God, hathe made him a lyer, because he beleued not the recorde, ẏ God
witnessed of his Sonne.
11 And this is the recorde, that God hathe
giuen vnto vs eternal life, and this life is
in his Sonne.
12 He that hathe the Sonne, hathe life: and
he that hathe not the Sonne of God, hathe
not life.
13 These things haue I written vnto you,
that beleue in the Name of the Sonne of
God, that ye may knowe that ye haue eter
nal life, and that ye may beleue in the Na
me of the Sonne of God.
14 And this is the assurance, that we haue
in him, * that if we aske anie thing according to his wil, he heareth vs.
15 And if we knowe that he heareth vs,
whatsoeuer we aske, we knowe that we haue the peticions that we haue desired of
him.
16 If anie man se his brother sinne a sinne,
that is not vnto death, let him aske, and
he shal giue him life for them that sinne
not [h] vnto death. * There is a sinne [i] vnto
death: I say not that thou shuldest praye
for it.
17 All vnrighteousnes is sinne, but there is
a sinne not vnto death.
18 We knowe that whosoeuer is borne of
God, [k] sinneth not: but he that is begotten of God, [l] kepeth him self, & the [m] wicked [n] toucheth him not.
19 We knowe that we are of God, and the
whole worlde [o] lyeth in wickednes.
20 But we knowe that the Sonne of God is
* come, & hathe giuẽ vs a minde to knowe
him, which is true: and we are in him that
is true, *that is*, in his Sonne Iesus Christ:
this same is verie [p] God, and eternal life.
21 Babes, kepe your selues frõ [q] idoles, Amẽ.

a Is regenerat by the vertue of his Spirit.

b The loue of God must go before, or els we cã not loue aright.

Mat. 11,30.

c They are easie to the sonnes of God, ẇ are led with his Spirit: for thei delite therein.

1. Cor. 15,57.

d That is, regeneracion.

e The water & blood that came out of his side, declare ẏ we haue our sinnes washed by him, & he hathe made ful satisfactiõ for the same.

f Our minde inspired by ẏ holie Gost.

g Which testifieth to our hearts, that we be ẏ children of God.

Iohn 3,36.

|| *of God.*

Mat. 7,7. & 21,22. chap. 3,22.

h Althogh euerie sinne be to death, yet God through his mercie pardoneth his in his Sonne Christ.

Mat. 12,31. mar. 3,29. luk. 12,10.

i As theirs is whome God doeth so forsake that they fall into vtter dispaire.

k Giueth not him self so ouer to sinne, ẏ he forgetteth God

l Taketh hede that he sinne not.

m That is, Satan.

n With a mortal wounde.

Luk. 24,45.

o That is, all mẽ generally, as of them selues lye as it were buryed in euil.

p Christ verie God.

q Meaning frõ euerie forme and facion of thing which is set vp for anie deuocion to worship God.

THE SECONDE Epistle of Iohn.

He writeth vnto a certeine ladie, 4 Reioycing that her children walke in the trueth, 5 And exhorteth them vnto loue, 7 Warneth them to beware of suche deceiuers as denie that Iesus Christ is come in the flesh, 8 Praieth them to continue in the doctrine of Christ, 10 And to haue nothing to do with them that bring not the true doctrine of Christ Iesus our Sauiour.

1 THe Elder to the " elect
Ladie, and her chil-
dren, whome I loue in
[a] the trueth: and not I
onely, but also all that
haue knowen ẏ trueth,
2 For the trueths sake
which dwelleth in vs, and shalbe with vs
for euer:
3 Grace be with you, mercie & peace from
God the Father, and from the Lord Iesus
Christ the Sonne of the Father, with [b] trueth and loue.
4 I reioyced greatly, that I founde of thy
children walking [c] in trueth, as we haue
receiued a commandement of the Father.
5 And now beseche I thee, Ladie, (not as
writing a new commandement vnto thee,
but that same which we had from the beginning) that we * loue one another.

" *Or, worthie & noble.*

a According to godlines & not by anie worldlie affection.

b We can not receiue ẏ grace of God, except we haue the true knowledge of him, of the which knowledge loue procedeth.

c According to Gods worde.

Iohn 15,12.

6 And this is the loue, that we shulde walke
after his "commandements. This commãdement is, that as ye haue heard from the
beginning, ye shulde walke in it.
7 For manie deceiuers are entred into the
worlde, which confesse not ŷ Iesus Christ
is come in the flesh. He that is suche one,
is a deceiuer and an Antichrist.
8 Loke to your selues, that we [d] lose not the
things, which we haue done, but that we
may receiue a ful rewarde.
9 Whosoeuer [e] transgresseth, and abideth
not in the doctrine of Christ, hathe not
God. He that continueth in the doctrine
of Christ, he hathe bothe the Father and
the Sonne.
10 If there come anie vnto you, and bring
not this doctrine, * receiue him not to hou
se, nether bid him, [f] God spede.
11 For he that biddeth him, God spede, is
partaker of his euil dedes. Althogh I had
manie things to write vnto you, yet I wolde not *write* with paper and yncke: but I
trust to come vnto you, and speake mouth
to mouth, that our ioye may be ful.
12 The sonnes of thine " elect sister grete
thee, Amen.

" Or, doctrine.

d By suffring our selues to be seduced.

e He that passeth the limites of pure doctrine.

* Rom. 16, 17.

f Haue nothig to do ŵ him, nether shewe him anie signe of familiaritie or acquaintãce

" Or, worthie.

THE THIRD EPIstle of Iohn.

3 He is glad of Gaius that he walketh in the trueth, 8 Exhorteth them to be louing vnto the poore Christen in their persecucion, 9 Sheweth the vnkinde dealing of Diotrephes, 12 And the good reporte of Demetrius.

1 THe Elder vnto the beloued Gaius, whome I
loue in the trueth.
2 Beloued, I wish chiefly ŷ thou prosperedst &
faredst wel, as thy soule prospereth.
3 For I reioyced greatly when the brethren
came, and testified of the trueth that is in
thee, how thou walkest in the trueth.
4 I haue no greater ioye then this, *that is*,
to heare that my sonnes walke in [a] veritie.
5 Beloued, thou doest faithfully whatsoeuer thou doest to the brethren, & to [b] strãgers,
6 Which bare witnes of thy loue before
the Churches. Whome if thou bringest of
their iourney as it [c] besemeth according
to God, thou shalt do wel,
7 Because that for his Names sake thei wẽt
forthe, and toke nothing of the Gentiles.
8 We therefore oght to receiue suche, that
we might be helpers to the trueth.
9 I wrote vnto the Church: but Diotrephes
which loueth to haue the preeminence among them, receiueth vs not.
10 Wherefore if I come, I wil declare his
dedes which he doeth, prateling against
vs with malicious wordes, and not therewith content, nether he him self receiueth
the brethren, but forbiddeth them ŷ wolde, and thrusteth them out of the Church.
11 Beloued, folowe not that which is euil,
but that which is good: he that doeth wel,
is of God: but he that doeth euil, hathe
not " sene God.
12 Demetrius hathe good reporte of all
men, and of the trueth it self: yea, and we
our selues beare recorde, and ye knowe
that our recorde is true.
13 I haue manie things to write: but I wil
not with yncke and pen write vnto thee.
14 For I trust I shal shortly se thee, and we
shal speake mouth to mouth. Peace *be*
with thee. The friends salute thee. Grete
the friends by name.

a That is, in godlie conuersacion, as they ŷ haue bothe the knowledge & feare of God.

b By keping hospitalitie.

c If ŷ furnishest thé with necessities towarde their iourney, knowing ŷ the Lord saith, He that receiueth you, receiueth me.

" Or, knowen.

THE GENERAL Epistle of Iude.

THE ARGVMENT.

SAint Iude admonisheth all Churches generally to take hede of deceiuers which go about to drawe awaye the hearts of the simple people from the trueth of God, and willeth them to haue no societie with suche, whome he setteth forthe in their liuelie colours, shewing by diuers exãples of the Scriptures what horrible vengeance is prepared for them: finally he comforteth the faithful and exhorteth them to perseuere in the doctrine of the Apostles of Iesus Christ.

Iude

1 Vde a seruant of IE-
SVS CHRIST, and
brother of Iames, to
them which are called
& sanctified [a] of God
the Father, and [b] reserued to Iesus Christ:
2 Mercie vnto you, and peace and loue be
multiplied.
3 Beloued, when I gaue all diligence to
write vnto you of the cómune saluation,
it was nedeful for me to write vnto you to
exhorte you, that ye shulde earnestly [c] cō-
tende for *the maintenance* of ỹ faith, which
was [d] once giuen vnto the Saintes.
4 For there are certeine mē crept in which
were before of olde [e] ordeined to this cōdemnation: vngodlie men *they are* which
turne the grace of our God into wantonnes, and * denye God the onelie Lord, and
our Lord Iesus Christ.
5 I wil therefore put you in remembrance,
forasmuche as ye once knewe this, how
that the Lord, after that he had deliuered
the people out of Egypt, * destroyed them
afterwarde which [f] beleued not.
6 The * Angels also which kept not their
first ″ estate, but left their owne habitation,
he hathe reserued in euerlasting chaines
vnder darkenes vnto ỹ [g] iudgement of the
great daye.
7 As * Sodom and Gomorrhe, and the cities about thē, which in like maner as they
did, cōmitted, and followed [h] strāge flesh,
are set forthe for an ensample, and suffre
the vengeance of eternal fyre.
8 Likewise notwithstanding these [i] dreamers also defile the flesh, and despise gouernement, and speake euil of them that
are in autoritie.
9 Yet [k] Michael the Archangel, when he
stroue against the deuil, and disputed a-
bout the bodie of Moses, durst not blame
him with cursed speaking, but saith, [l] The
Lord rebuke thee.
10 But these speake euil of those things,
which they knowe not: and whatsoeuer
things they knowe [m] naturally, as beastes,
which are without reason, in those things
they corrupt them selues.
11 Wo *be* vnto thē: for they haue followed
the way * of Cain, and are cast away by the
deceite * of Balaams wages, and perish in
the [n] gainesaying * of Core.
12 These are spottes [o] in your feasts of charitie when they feast with you, without
[p] all feare, feding them selues: cloudes *they
are* without water, caryed about of windes, corrupt trees & without frute, twise
dead, & plucked vp by the rootes.
13 *They are* the raging waues of the sea, foming out their owne shame: *they are* wandring starres, to whome is reserued the
blackenes of darkenes for euer.
14 And Enoch also the seueth from Adam,
prophecied of suche, saying, * [q] Beholde,
the Lord cometh with thousands of his
Saintes,
15 To giue iudgement against all men, and
to rebuke all ỹ vngodlie among thē of all
their wicked dedes, which they haue vngodly cōmitted, & of all their cruel speakings, which wicked sinners haue spoken
against him.
16 These are murmurers, complainers, walking after their owne lustes ‖: * whose
mouths speake proude things, hauing
mens persones in admiration, because of
a vantage.
17 But, ye beloued, remember the wordes
which were spokē before of the Apostles
of our Lord Iesus Christ,
18 How that they tolde you that there shulde be mockers * in the last time, which
shulde walke after their owne vngodlie
lustes.
19 These are makers of sectes, fleshlie, hauing [r] not the Spirit.
20 But, ye beloued, edifie your selues in
your most holie faith, praying in the holie Gost,
21 And kepe your selues in ỹ loue of God,
loking for the mercie of our Lord Iesus
Christ, vnto eternal life.
22 And haue compassion of some, [f] in putting difference:
23 And other saue with [t] feare, pulling thē
out of the fyre, and hate euen the [u] garment spotted by the flesh.
24 Now vnto him that is able to kepe you,
that ye fall not, and to present you fautles
before the presence of his glorie with
ioye,
25 *That is*, to God onely wise, our Sauiour,
be glorie, and maiestie, and dominion, and
power, bothe now and for euer, Amen.

a The faithful are sanctified of God the Father in the Sonne by the holie Gost.
b That he shulde kepe you, Iohn 17,6.
c Against the assaltes of Satan and heretikes
d That ye shulde kepe it for euer.
2.Pet.2,1.
e He confirmeth their heart against the contēners of religiō and Apostats, shewing that suche men trouble not ỹ Church at all aduentures, but are appointed thereunto by ỹ determinat counsel of God.
Nom.14,37.
2.Pet.2,4.
f Their incredulitie was the fōtaine of all their euil.
″Or, original.
Gen.19,24.
g Then shalbe their extreme punishment.
h Moste horrible pollutiōs.
i Which hewe thē selues dull and impudent.
k It is moste like that this example was writ in some of those bokes of the Scripture which are now lost, Nōb. 21,14. iosh.10,13. 2.chro 9,29.
l In Zacharie 3,2 Christ vnder the name of the Angel rebuked Satan as knowing ỹ he went about to hinder the Church: but here we are admonished not to seke to reuenge our selues by euil speaking, but to referre the thing to God.
m By their carnal iudgement.
*Gen.4,8.

Nom.22,23.
Nom.16,1.
2 pet.2,16.
n For as Core, Dathan and Abirō rose vp and spake against Moses, so do these against them ỹ are in autoritie
o These were general feastes which ỹ faithful kept, partly to protest their brotherlie loue, & partely to relieue the nedie, Tertull. in Apologet. chap.39.
Reuel.1,7.
p Ether of God, or of his Church.
q This saying of Enock might for the worthines thereof haue bene as a cōmune saying among men of all times, or els haue bene written in some of those bookes which now remaine not: yet by the prouidēce of God, so many are left as are able to instruct vs in the faith of Iesus Christ to saluation, Iohn 20,31.
Psal.16,10.
‖ In vngodlines and iniquitie.
1.Tim.4,1.
2.tim.1,1.
2.pet.3,3.
r Of regeneration.
f Some may be wōne with gētlenes, other by sharpenes.
t By sharpe reprofes to drawe thē out of danger.
u He willeth not onely to cut of the euil but to take away all occasions which are as preparatiues, & accessories to the same.

THE REVELATION
of Iohn the Diuine.

*Or, declared to Iohn.

THE ARGVMENT.

IT is manifest, that the holie Gost wolde as it were gather into this moste excellent booke a summe of those prophecies, which were writen before, but shulde be fulfilled after the cōming of Christ, adding also suche things as shulde be expedient, aswel to forewarne vs of the dangers to come, as to admonish vs to beware some, and encourage vs against others. Herein therefore is liuely set forthe the Diuinitie of Christ, & the testimonies of our redēption: what things the Spirit of God alloweth in the ministers, and what things he reproueth: the prouidence of God for his elect, and of their glorie and consolation in the day of vengeance: how that the hypocrites which sting like scorpions the members of Christ, shall e destroyed, but the Lambe Christ shal defende them, which beare witnes to the trueth, who in despite of the beast and Satan wil reigne ouer all. The liuelie description of Antichrist is set forthe, whose time and power notwithstanding is limited, and albeit that he is permitted to rage against the elect, yet his power stretcheth no farther then to the hurt of their bodies: and at length he shal be destroyed by the wrath of God, when as the elect shal giue praise to God for the victorie: neuerthles for a ceason God wil permit this Antichrist, and strompet vnder colour of faire speache and pleasant doctrine to deceiue the worlde: wherefore he aduertiseth the godlie (which are but a smale portion) to auoide this harlots flateries, and bragges, whose ruine without mercie they shal se, and with the heauenlie companies sing continual praises: for the Lambe is maried: the worde of God hathe gotten the victorie: Satā that a long time was vntied, is now cast with his ministers into the pit of fyre to be tormented for euer, where as cōtrariwise the faithful (which are the holie Citie of Ierusalem, & wife of the Lambe) shal enioye perpetual glorie. Read diligently: iudge soberly, and call earnestly to God for the true vnderstanding hereof.

CHAP. I.

1 The cause of this reuelation. 3 Of them that read it. 4 Iohn writeth to the seuen Churches. 5 The maiestie and office of the Sonne of God. 20 The vision of the candlestickes and starres.

1 He[a] reuelation of IE-
SVS CHRIST, which
[b] God gaue vnto him, to
shewe vnto his seruants
things which must shor
tely be [c] done: which he
sent, and shewed by his
Angel vnto his seruant Iohn,
2 Who bare recorde of the worde of God,
and of the testimonie of Iesus Christ, and
of all things that he sawe.
3 Blessed is he that readeth, and they that
heare the wordes of this [d] prophecie, and
kepe those things which are written therein:
for the time is [e] at hand.
4 Iohn, to the [f] seuē Churches which are in
Asia, Grace be with you & peace frō him
Which * is, & Which was, & Which is to
come, and from the [g] seuen Spirits which
are before his Throne,
5 And from Iesus Christ, which is a * faithful
witnes, & * the first begotten of ӯ dead,
and Prince of the Kings of the earth, vnto
him that loued vs, & washed vs frō our
sinnes in his * blood,
6 And made vs * Kings and Priestes vnto
God euen his Father, to him be glorie, &
dominion for euermore, Amen.
7 Beholde, he cometh with * cloudes, and
euerie eye shal se him: yea, euen they which
[h] pearced him through: and all kinreds of
the earth shal waile "before him, Euen so,
Amen.
8 I * am [i] α and ω, the beginning and the
ending, saith the Lord, Which is, and
Which was, and Which is to come, euen
the Almightie.
9 I Iohn, euen your brother, & companion
in tribulation, & in the kingdome and pacience
of Iesus Christ, was in the yle called
Patmos, for the "worde of God, and
for the "witnesing of Iesus Christ.
10 And I was rauished in spirit on [k] ӯ Lords
day, and heard behinde me a great voyce,
as it had bene of a trumpet,
11 Saying, I am [l] α and ω, the first and the
last: and that which thou seest, write in a
boke, & send it vnto the [m] seuen Churches
which are in Asia, vnto Ephesus, and vnto
Smyrna, & vnto Pergamus, & vnto Thyatira,
and vnto Sardi, and vnto Philadelphia,
and vnto Laodicea.
12 Then I turned backe to se the [n] voyce,
that spake with me: & when I was turned,
I sawe [o] seuen golden candlestickes,
13 And in the middes of the seuen candlestickes,
one like vnto the [p] Sonne of man,
clothed with a garment [q] downe to the

a Of things which were hid before.
b Christ receiued this reuelation out of his fathers bosome as his owne doctrine, but it was hid in respect of vs so that Christ as Lord and God reuciled it to Iohn his seruant by the ministerie of his Angel, to the edification of his Church
c To the good & bad.
d Which expoundeth the olde prophetes, & sheweth what shal come to passe in the newe testament.
Exo.3,14.
e And began euen then.
Psal.89.38.
1.Cor.15,21.
coloss.1,18.
Ebr.9,14.
1.pet.1,19.
1.iohn.1,9.
1.Pet.2,5.
f Meaning the Church vniuersal.
g That is, from the holie Gost: or these seuen Spirits were ministers before God the Father & Christ, whome after he calleth the hornes and eyes of the Lambe, chap.5,6 In a like phrases Paul taketh God, and Christ, and the Angels to witnes, 1.Tim.5,21.

Mat.24.30.
isa.3,14.
iude 14.
h They that contemned Christ & moste cruelly persecuted him, and put him to death, shal then acknowledge him.
Chap.21,6. & 22,13.
*Or, for him
i Alpha and Omega are the first and last letters of the a b c of the Grekes.
k Which some call sunday: S. Paul the first day of the weke, 1 Cor.16,2. act. 20,7. and it was established after that the Iewes Sabbath was abolished.
l I am he before whome nothing was, yea, by whome whatsoeuer is made, was made, and he that shal remaine when all thīgs shal perish, euen I am the eternal God.
m Of ӯ which some were fallen: others decayed: some were proude: others negligent: so that he sheweth remedie for all.
n That is, him whose voyce I heard.
o Meaning the Churches.
p Which was Christ the head of the Church.
q As the chief Priest.

feete,

feete, and girde about [r] the pappes with a
golden girdle.
14 His head, and heeres *were* [s] white as
white woll, & as snowe, and his eyes *were*
as [t] a flame of fyre.
15 And his fete like vnto *fine [u] brasse, burning as in a fornace: and his [x] voyce as the
sounde of many waters.
16 And he had in his right hand seuē [y] starres: and out of his mouth went a [z] sharpe
two edged sworde: & his face *shone* as the
sunne shineth in his strength.
17 And when I sawe him, I fell at his fete
as * dead: then he laid his right [a] hand vpō
me, saying vnto me, Feare not: I am the
*[b] first and the last,
18 And am aliue, but I was dead: & beholde, I am aliue for euermore, Amen: & I ha
ue the [c] keyes of hel and of death.
19 Write the things which thou hast sene,
and the things which are, and the things
which shal come here [d] after.
20 The mysterie of the seuen starres which
thou sawest [e] in my right hand, and the seuen golden cādlestickes, *is thus*, The seuen
starres are the [f] Angels of the seuen Churches: & the seuen cādlestickes which thou
sawest, are the seuen Churches.

r For in him was no concupiscēce, which is signified by girding the loynes.
s To signifie his wisdome, eternitie & diuinitie.
t To se the secrets of the heart.
*Or, alcumine.
u His iudgements & waies are moste perfect.
x Bothe because all nations praise hī, & also his worde is heard & preached through the worlde.
Dan. 10,9.
Isa. 41,4. & 44,6.
y Which are ẏ pastors of the Churches.
z This sworde signified his worde and the vertue thereof, as is declared, Ebr. 4,12.
a To comfort me.
b Equal God with my Father, and eternal.
c That is, power ouer them.
d In the latter dayes. e In my protection. f That is, the ministers, Mal. 2,3.

CHAP. II.

1 He exhorteth foure Churches. 5 To repentance. 10 To perseuerance, pacience and amendement. 5.14 20. 23 Aswel by threatenings. 7.10 17.26 As promises of rewarde.

1 Vnto the [a] Angel of the Church of
Ephesus write, These things saith he
that [b] holdeth the seuē starres in his [c] right
hand, and [d] walketh in the middes of the
seuen golden candlestickes.
2 I knowe thy workes, and thy labour, and
thy pacience, and how thou canst not
forbeare them which are euil, and hast
examined them which say they are Apostles, and are not, and hast founde them
lyers.
3 And thou hast suffred, and hast pacience,
and for my Names sake hast labored, and
hast not fainted.
4 Neuertheles, I haue *somewhat* against
thee, because thou hast left thy first [e] loue.
5 Remember therefore from whence thou
art fallen, and repent, and do the first workes: or els I wil come against thee shortly,
and wil remoue thy [f] candlesticke out of
his place, except thou amende.
6 But this thou hast, that thou hatest the
workes of the [g] Nicolaitans, which I also hate.
7 Let him that hathe an eare, heare, what
the Spirit saith vnto ẏ Churches, To him
that ouercometh, wil I giue to eate of the
tree of [h] life which is in the middes of the
Paradise of God.
8 ¶ And vnto the [i] Angel of the Church of
the Smyrniās write, These things saith he
that is first, and last, Which was dead and
is [k] aliue.
9 I knowe thy workes and [l] tribulation, and
pouertie (but thou art [m] riche) & *I knowe*
the blasphemie of them, which say they
are Iewes and [n] are not, but *are* the Synagogue of Satan.
10 Feare none of those things, which thou
shalt suffer: beholde, it shal come to passe,
that the [o] deuil shal cast some of you into
prison, that ye may be [p] tryed, and ye shal
haue tribulation [q] ten dayes: be thou faithful vnto the death, and I wil giue thee the
crowne of life.
11 Let him that hathe an eare, heare what
the Spirit saith to the Churches. He that o-
uercometh, shal not be hurt of the [r] secōde
death.
12 And to the Angel of ẏ Church which is
at Pergamus write, This saith he which ha
the the sharpe [s] sworde with two edges.
13 I knowe thy workes & where thou dwellest, *euen* where Satans [t] throne is, and thou
kepest my Name, and hast not denied my
faith, [u] euen in those dayes when Antipas
my faithful martyr was slaine among you,
where Satan dwelleth.
14 But I haue a fewe things against thee,
because thou hast there them that mainteine the [x] doctrine of * Balaam, ẇ taught
Balac, to put a stumbling blocke before
the children of Israel, that they shulde eat
of things sacrificed vnto idoles, and commit fornication.
15 Euen so hast thou them, that mainteine
the doctrine of the Nicolaitans, which
thing I hate.
16 Repent thy self, or els I wil come vnto
thee shortely, and wil fight against them
with the sworde of my mouth.
17 Let him that hathe an eare, heare what
the spirit saith vnto ẏ Churches, To him
that ouercometh, wil I giue to eat of the
Manna that is [y] hid, and wil giue him a
[z] white stone, and in the stone a [a] new name writen, which no man knoweth sauing
he that receiueth it.
18 ¶ And vnto ẏ Angel of ẏ Church which
is at Thyatira write, These things saith
the Sonne of God, which hathe his eyes

a To the Pastor or minister which are called by this Name, because they are Gods messengers, & haue their office commune with Iesus Christ who also is called an Angel.
b Read chap. 1,3.
c In his protection.
d Accordīg to his promes, Mat. 28,20 he wilbe with them to the end of the worlde.
e Thy first loue, that thou hadest towarde God & thy neighbour at the first preaching of the Gospel.
f The office of the Pastor is compared to a candelsticke or lampe forasmuche as he oght to shine before men.
g These were heretikes ẇ helde that wiues shulde be commune, & as some thinke were named of one called Nicolas, of whome is writ Act. 6,5 which was chosen among the Deacons.
h Meaning, ẏ life euerlastīg: thus by corporal benefites he raiseth thē vp to consider spiritual blessings.
i This is thoght to be Policarpus who was minister of Smyrna 86 yeres, as he him self confessed before Herodes when as he was led to be burned for Christs cause.
k The eternal Diuinitie of Iesus Christ is here most plainely declared with his manhode, & victorie ouer death to assure his ẏ they shal not be ouercome by death.
l This was the persecution vnder the emperour Domitian.
m In spiritual treasures.
n They are not Abrahames children according to ẏ faith.
o Here he nameth the autor of all our calamitie, incouraging vs manfully to fight against him, in promising vs the victorie.
Nom. 24,14. & 25,1.
p The end of affliction is ẏ we may be tried and not destroyed.
q Signifying manie times as Genes. 31,41. nomb. 14, 22. althogh there shalbe cōfort and release.
r The first death is the natural death of ẏ bodie, the seconde is the eternal death: frō the which all are fre that believe in Iesus Christ, Ioh. 5,24.
s The worde of God is the sworde with two edges, Ebr. 4,12.
t All townes and countreies whence Gods worde & good liuing is banished, are the throne of Satan, and also those places where the worde is not preached syncerly, nor maners a right reformed.
u In the verie heat of persecution and slaughter of the Martyrs they continued in the pure faith, and therefore are commended after a sorte.
x All suche are like counsellours to Balaam, which for lucre persuade to idolatrie, or whoredome.
y And not commune to all.
z Suche a stone was wont to be giuen to them that had gotten anie victorie or prise, in signe of honour, and therefore it signifieth here a token of Gods fauour and grace: also it was a signe that one was cleared in iudgement.
a The newe name also signifieth, renome ad honour.

like vnto a flame of fyre, and his fete like *fine brasse.

*Or, alcumine.

19 I knowe thy workes and thy loue, and
[b] seruice, and faith, and thy pacience, and
thy workes, & that *they are* mo at the last,
then at the first.

b To helpe ye Saincts.

20 Notwithstanding, I haue a fewe things
against thee, that thou suffrest the woman
*[c] Iezabel, which calleth her self a Prophe
tesse, to teache and to deceiue my seruãts
to make them [d] commit fornication, & to
eat meats sacrificed vnto idoles.

1.King.16,31.
c As that harlot Iezabel mainteined strãge religion and exercised crueltie against the seruants of God, so are there amõg them that do ye like.
d They that consent to idolatrie and false doctrine, commit spiritual whoredome, whereof foloweth corporal whoredome, Hos.4,13.

21 And I gaue her space to repent of her
fornication, and she repented not.
22 Beholde, I wil cast her into a bed, and
them that commit fornication with her,
into great affliction, except they repent
them of their workes.
23 And I wil kill her [e] children with death:
& all the Churches shal knowe that I am
he which *searche the reines and hearts:
and I wil giue vnto euerie one of you according vnto your workes.

1.Sam.16,7. psal.7,10. iere.11,20. & 17,10.
e Them that followe her wayes.

24 And vnto you I say, the rest of them of
Thyatira, As many as haue not this learning, nether haue knowen the [f] depnes
of Satan (as [g] they speake) I wil put vpon
you none other burden.
25 But that which ye haue all ready, holde
fast til I come.
26 For he that ouercometh and kepeth my
workes vnto the end, *to him wil I giue
power ouer nations,
27 And he shal rule them with a rodde of
yron: & as the vessels of a potter, shal thei
be broken.
28 Euen as I receiued of my Father, so wil
I giue him the morning starre.
29 Let him that hathe an eare, heare what
the Spirit saith to the Churches.

f The false teachers termed their doctrine by this name, as thogh it cõteined the most depe knowledge of heauẽlie thĩgs, & was in deed drawen out of the depe dongeõ of hell: by suche termes now the Anabaptists, Libertines, Papists, Arriãs, &c vse to beautifie their monstruous errors and blasphemies.
Psal.2,9.
g The childrẽ of Iezabel.

CHAP. III.

He exhorteth the Churches or ministers to the true profession of faith and to watching. 12 With promises to them that perseuere.

1 AND write vnto the Angel of the
Church wc is at Sardi, These things
saith he that hathe ye seuen Spirits of God,
and the seuen starres, I know thy workes:
for thou hast a name that thou [a] liuest, but
thou art dead.

a The minister liueth whẽ he bringeth forthe good frutes, els he is dead.

2 Be awake and stregthen the things which
remeine, that are readie to dye: for I haue not founde thy workes perfite before
God.
3 Remember therefore, how thou hast receiued and heard, and holde fast, and repent. *If therefore thou wilt not watch, I
wil come on thee as a thefe, and yu shalt not
knowe what houre I wil come vpon thee.
4 *Notwithstanding* thou hast a fewe *names
yet in Sardi, which haue not [b] defiled their
garments: and they shal walke with me in
white: for they are worthie.

Chap.16,15. 1.thess.5,2. 2.pet.3,10.
*Or, persones.
b Ether by consenting to idolaters, or als polluting their conscience with any euil.

5 He that ouercometh, shalbe clothed in
white araye, & I wil not put out his name
out of the *boke of life, but I wil confesse
his name before my Father, & before his
Angels.

Chap.20,12. & 21,27. philip.4,4.

6 Let him that hathe an eare, heare what ye
Spirit saith vnto the Churches.
7 ¶ And write vnto the Angel of ye Church
which is of Philadelphia, These things
saith he that is Holie and True, which hathe the* [c] keye of Dauid, which openeth
and no man shutteth, and shutteth and no
man openeth,
8 I knowe thy workes: beholde, I haue set
before thee an open [d] dore, and no man cã
shut it: for thou hast a litel strength and
hast kept my worde, and hast not denied
my Name.
9 Beholde, I wil make them of the synagogue of Satan, which call them selues Iewes
and are not, but do lye: beholde, *I say*, I wil
make them, that they shal come and [e] wor
ship before thy fete, and shal knowe that I
haue loued thee.

Isa.22,22. iob.22,14.
c Which signifieth ye Christ hathe all the power ouer ye house of Dauid, which is ye Church, so yt he may ether receiue or put out whome he wil.
d Which is to aduance the kingdome of God.
e I wil cause thẽ in thy sight to hũble them selues, & to giue due honour to God, and to his Sonne Christ.

10 Because thou hast kept the worde of my
pacience, therefore I wil deliuer thee frõ
the houre of tentation, which wil come
vpon all the worlde, to trye them that
dwell vpon the earth.
11 Beholde, I come shortly: holde yt which
thou hast, that no man take thy [f] crowne.
12 Him that ouercometh, wil I make a pillar in the Temple of my God, and he shal
go no more out: and I wil write vpon him
the Name of my God, & the name of the
citie of my God, *which is* the new Ierusalẽ,
which cometh downe out of heauẽ frõ my
God, & *I wil write vpon him* my new Name.
13 Let him that hathe an eare, heare what ye
Spirit saith vnto the Churches.

f Let no man plucke them away wc thou hast wonne to God: for they are thy crowne, as S. Paul writeth, sayĩg, Brethrẽ, ye are my ioye & my crowne Phil.4,1.1.thes.2,19

14 And vnto the Angel of the Church of
the Laodiceans write, These things saith
[g] Amen, the faithful and true witnes, the
[h] beginning of the creatures of God.
15 I knowe thy workes, that thou art nether
colde not hote: I wolde thou werest colde
or hote.
16 Therefore, because thou art luke warme,
and nether colde nor hote, it wil come
to passe, that I shal spewe thee out of my
mouth.
17 For thou saist, I am [i] riche & increased
with goods, & haue [k] nede of nothing, and
knowest not how thou art wretched & miserable, and poore, and blinde, and naked.
18 I cousel thee to bie of me golde tryed by
the fyre, that thou maiest be made riche, &
white raimẽt, that thou maiest be clothed
and that thy filthie nakednes do not appea
re: and [l] anoint thine eyes with eye salue,
that thou maist se.
19 As manie as I loue, I *rebuke and chastẽ:
be [m] zealous therefore and amende.

g That is, Trueth it self.
h Of whome all creatures haue their beginning.
i Persuading thy self of that which thou hast not.
k Thus the hypocrites boast of their owne power and do not vnderstand their infirmities to seke to Christ for remedie.
l Suffer ye eyes of thine vnderstanding to be opened.
Prou.3,11. ebr.12,5.
m Nothing more displeaseth God then indifferẽcie, & coldenes in religiõ, & therefore he wil spewe suche out as are not zealous and feruent.

20 Beholde,

20 Beholde, I stand at the dore, and knocke. If anie man heare my voyce & opē the
dore, I wil come in vnto him, and wil suppe with him, and he with me.
21 To him that ouercometh, wil I grante
to sit with me in my n throne, euē as I ouer
came, & sit w my Father in his throne.
22 Let him that hathe an eare, heare what
the Spirit saith vnto the Churches.

n In my seate royal, and to be partaker of mine heauenlie ioyes.

CHAP. IIII.

1 The vision of the maiestie of God. 2 He seeth the throne, and one sitting vpon it, 8 And 24. seates about it with 24 elders sitting vpon them, and foure beastes praising God day and night.

1 AFter this I loked, and beholde, a a dore was open in heauen, and the first
voyce which I heard, was as it were of a
trūpet talking with me, saying, Come vp
hither, and I wil shewe thee things which
muste be done hereafter.
2 And immediatly I was *rauished* in the
spirit, & beholde, a throne was set in heauen, and one sate vpon the throne.
3 And b he that sate, was to loke vpon, like
vnto a iasper stone, and a sardine, & there
was a raine bowe rounde about the throne
in sight like to an emeraude.
4 And rounde about the throne *were* foure
and twentie seates, and vpon the seates I
sawe c foure and twentie Elders sitting,
clothed in white raimēt, and had on their
heads crownes of golde.
5 And out of the throne d proceded e ligh-
nings, and thundrings, and voyces, & there were seuen lampes of fyre, burning before the throne, which are the seuen spirits
of God.
6 And before the throne there *was* a f sea
of glasse like vnto g cristal: and in the" mid
des of the throne, & rounde about ỹ throne *were* foure h beastes full of eyes before
and behinde.
7 And the first beast *was* like a lion, & the
seconde beast like a calfe, and the thirde
beast had a face as a man, and the fourthe
beast *was* like a flying egle.
8 And the foure beasts had eche one of thē
six wings about him, and they were ful of
eyes within, and they ceased not day nor
night, saying, i * Holie, holie, holie Lord
God, almightie, which Was, & Which is
and Which is to come.
9 And when those beasts gaue glorie, and
honour, and thankes to him that sate
on the throne, which liueth for euer and
euer,
10 The foure and twentie elders fell downe before him that sate on the throne, and
worshipped him, that liueth for euer more, k & cast their crownes before the throne, saying,
11 Thou art * worthie, ô Lord, to receiue
glorie and honour, & power: for thou hast
created all things, and for thy willes sake
they are, and haue bene created.

a Before that he make menciō of ỹ great afflictions of the Church, he setteth forthe the maiestie of God, by whose wil, wisdome and prouidēce all thigs are created, & gouerned, to teache vs pacience.
b He describeth the Diuine and incomprehēsible vertue of God the father as chap. 5,6, and ỹ Sōne who is ioyned with him.
c By these are ment all the holie cōpanie of the heauēs.
d From the throne of the Father, & the Sonne procedeth the holie Gost, who hauing all but one throne, declare the vnitie of ỹ Godhead.
e The holie Gost is as a lightening vnto vs that beleue, and as a feareful thunder to the disobedient.
f The worlde is compared to a sea because of the changes and vnstablenes.
Isa.6,3.
g It is as cleare as cristal before ỹ eyes of God, because there is nothing in it so litle that is hid from him.
"*Or, vnder the throne.*
h They are called Cherubins, Eze.10,20
i We are hereby taught to giue glorie to God in all his workes
k They wil chalēge no autoritie, honour nor power before God.
Chap.5,12.

CHAP. V.

1 He seeth the Lambe opening the boke. 8. 14 And therefore the foure beasts, the 24. elders, and the Angels praise the Lambe, & do him worship 9 For their redemption and other benefites.

1 ANd I sawe in the right hand of him
that sate vpon the throne, a a Boke
written within, and on the backeside, sealed
with b seuen seales.
2 And I sawe a strong Angel which preached with a lowde voyce, Who is worthie
to open the boke, and to lose the seales
thereof?
3 And no man in heauē, nor in earth, nether
vnder the earth, was able to open the Boke
nether to loke thereon.
4 Then I wept muche, because no mā was
founde worthie to open, and to reade the
Boke, nether to loke thereon.
5 And one of the elders said vnto me, Wepe
not: beholde, the * lion which is of the tribe of Iuda, the rote of Dauid, hathe obteined to open the Boke, and to lose the seuē
seales thereof.
6 Then I behelde, and lo, in the middes of
the throne, and of the foure beasts, & in the
middes of the elders, stode c a Lambe as
thogh he had bene killed, which had d seuē
hornes, & e seuen eyes, which are the seuen
spirits of God, sent into all the worlde.
7 And he came, and toke the Boke out of
the right hand of him that sate vpon the
throne.
8 And when he had taken the Boke, the foure beasts and the foure and twentie elders
f fell downe before the Lambe, hauing eue
rie one harpes and golden viales full of
odours, w are the g prayers of the Saintes,
9 And they sung a new song, saying, Thou
art worthie to take the Boke, and to open
the seales thereof, because thou wast killed, and hast h redemed vs to God by thy
blood out of euerie kinred, and tōgue, and
people, and nation,
10 And hast made vs vnto our God * Kīgs
and Priests, and we shal i reigne on the
earth.
11 Then I behelde, and I heard the voyce
of manie Angels rounde about the throne
and *about* the beasts and the elders, & there
were * thousand thousands,
12 Saying with a loude voyce, Worthie is
the * Lābe that was killed to receiue power
and riches, and wisdome, and strength, &
honour, and glorie, and praise.
13 And all ỹ creatures which are in heauē,
and on the earth, and vnder the earth, and
in the sea, & all that are in them, heard I,
saying, Praise & honour, and glorie, and
power *be* vnto him, that sitteth vpon the
throne, & vnto the Lambe for euermore.

a A similitude taken of earthlie princes, w iudge by bokes & writigs: & here it doeth signifie all the counsels & iudgements of God w are onely knowē to Christ the Sōne of Dauid, vers 5.
b That is, manie.
Gen.49,9.
c This vision confirmeth ỹ power of our Lord Iesus, w is the Lambe of God that taketh away the sinne of the worlde.
d That is, manifolde power.
e Signifying ỹ fulnes of the Spirit, which Christ powreth vpon all.
f The Angels honour Christ: he is therefore God.
g This declareth how the prayers of the faithful are agreable vnto God, read Act. 10,4. chap.8,3.
h Our Sauiour Iesus hathe redemed his Church by his blood shedding & gathered it of all nations.
1.Pet.2,9.
i Not corporally.
Dan.7,10.
Chap.4,11.

14 And the foure beasts said, Amen, and
the foure and twentie Elders fell downe,
and worshipped him that liueth for euer
more.

CHAP. VI.

The Lambe openeth the sixe seales, and manie things follow the opening thereof, so that this conteineth a general prophecie to the end of the worlde.

1 AFter, I behelde when ye Lambe had
opened one [a] of the seales, & I heard
one of the foure beasts say, as *it were* the
[b] noyce of thunder, Come and se.
2 Therefore I behelde, and lo, there *was* a
[c] white horse, and he that [d] sate on him,
had a bowe, and a crowne was giuen vnto
him, and he went forthe cōquering that he
might ouercome.
3 And when he had opened the seconde
seale, I heard the seconde beast say, Come
and se.
4 And there went out another horse *that*
was [e] red, & power was giuen to him that
[f] sate thereon, to take peace from the earth
and that they shulde kil one another, and
there was giuen vnto him a great sworde.
5 And whē he had opened the thirde seale,
I heard the thirde beast say, Come and se.
Then I behelde, & lo, [g] a blacke horse, &
he that sate on him, had balances in his
hand.
6 And I heard a voyce in the middes of the
foure beasts say, A [h] measure of wheat for
a [i] penie, and thre measures of barlie for a
penie, and oyle, and wine hurt thou not.
7 And when he had opened the fourth seale,
I heard the voyce of the fourth beast
say, Come and se.
8 And I loked, & beholde, a [k] pale horse, &
his name that sate on him was Death, and
"Hel followed after him, and power was
giuen vnto them ouer the fourth parte of
the earth, to kil with sworde, and with hōger,
and with death, and with the beasts of
the earth.
9 And when he had opened the [l] fift seale, I
sawe vnder the altar [m] the soules of them,
that were killed for the worde of God, &
for ye testimonie which they mainteined.
10 And they cryed with a lowde voyce,
saying, How long, Lord, holie and true!
doest not thou iudge & auenge our blood
on them that dwell on the earth?
11 And long white robes were giuen vnto
euerie one, and it was said vnto them, that
they shulde rest for a litel ceason vntil
their felowe seruants, and their brethren
that shulde be killed euen as they were,
were fulfilled.
12 And I behelde when he had opened the
sixt seale, and lo, there was a great [n] earth
quake, & the [o] sunne was as blacke as [p] sackecloth
of heere, and the [q] moone was li-

a The openīg of the seale is the declaratiō of Gods wil, and the executing of his iudgements.
b Signifying, that there was marueilous things to come
c The white horse signifieth innocēcie, victorie, & felicitie which shulde come by the preaching of the Gospel.
d He that rideth on the white horse, is Christ.
e Signifying the cruel warres that ensued when the Gospel was refused.
f Who was Satan.
g This signifieth an extreme famine, and want of all things.
h The Greke worde signifieth that measure which was ordinarily giuen to seruants for their portion or stint of meate for one day.
i Which amoūted about foure pence halfe penie.
k Whereby is ment sickenes, plagues, pestilence, & death of mā & beast.
"Or, the graue.
l The continual persecution of the Church noted by the fift seale.
m The soules of the Saintes are vnder the altar which is Christ, meanīg that they are in his safe custodie in the heauens.
n Which signifieth the chāge of the true doctrine, wc is the greatest cause of motions and troubles that come to the worlde.
o That is, the brightnes of the Gospel.
p The traditions of men.
q The Church miserably defaced with idolatrie and afflicted by tyrants.

ke blood.
13 And the [r] starres of heauen fel vnto the
earth, as a figge tre casteth her grene figges
when it is shaken of a mightie winde.
14 And [s] heauen departed away, as a scrole
when it is rolled, and euerie mountaine &
yle were moued out of their places.
15 And the Kings of the earth, & the great
men, and the riche men, and the chief captaines,
and the mightie men, and euerie
bondman, and euerie fre man, hid them
selues in dennes, and among the rockes of
the mountaines,
16 And said to [t] the moūtaines and rockes,
* [u] Fall on vs, and hide vs from the presence
of him that sitteth on the throne, & frō
the wrath of the Lambe.
17 For the great day of his wrath is come,
and who can stand?

CHAP. VII.

4. 9 He seeth the seruants of God sealed in their forheades out of all nations and people. 15 Which thogh they suffer trouble, yet the Lābe fedeth them, leadeth them to the fountaines of liuing water. 17 And God shal wipe awaye all teares from their eyes.

1 ANd after that, I sawe foure Angels
stād on ye foure corners of the earth,
holding the foure [a] windes of the [b] earth, ye
the windes shulde not blowe on the earth,
nether on the [c] sea, nether on anie [d] tre.
2 And I saw another "Angel come vp from
the East, which had the seale of the liuing
God, and he cryed with a loude voyce
to the foure Angels to whome power
was giuen to hurt the earth, and the sea,
saying, [e] Hurt ye not the earth, nether the
sea, nether the trees, til we haue [f] sealed ye
seruants of our God in their foreheades.
4 And I heard the nomber of them, which
were sealed, and there *were* sealed [g] an hūdreth
and foure and fortie thousand of all
the tribes of the children of Israel.
5 Of the tribe of Iuda were sealed twelue
thousand. Of the tribe of Ruben were sealed
twelue thousand. Of the tribe of Gad
were sealed twelue thousand.
6 Of the tribe of Aser, were sealed twelue
thousand. Of the tribe of Nephthali were
sealed twelue thousand. Of the tribe of
Manasses were sealed twelue thousand.
7 Of the tribe of Simeō were sealed twelue
thousand. Of the tribe of [h] Leui were
sealed twelue thousand. Of the tribe of
Issachar were sealed twelue thousand. Of
the tribe of Zabulon were sealed twelue
thousand.
8 Of the tribe of [i] Ioseph were sealed twel
ue thousand. Of the tribe of Beniamin

r Doctours & preachers that departe from the trueth.
s The kingdome of God is hid, and withdrawen from men, & appeareth not.
t Realmes, kingdomes & persones, that did seme to be as stable in ye faith as mountaines.
* Isa. 2, 19. ose. 10, 8. luk. 23, 30.
u Suche men afterwarde, of what estate soeuer they be, shalbe desperate, and not able to susteine the weight of Gods wrath, but shal cōtinually feare his iudgement.

a The spirit is compared to winde, and the doctrine also: and thogh there be one spirit and one doctrine, yet foure are here named in respect of the diuersitie of the foure quarters of the earth where ye Gospel is spred, and for the foure writers thereof, and ye preaches of ye same through ye whole worlde.
b Meaning, ye men of the earth.
c That is, the ylands.
"Or, Christ.
d Signifying all men in general, who can no more liue without this spiritual doctrine, then trees can blossome and beare, except the winde blowe vpon them.
e God preuenteth the dangers and euils, which otherwise wolde ouerwhelme the elect.
f Those that are sealed by the Spirit of God, and marked with the blood of the Lambe, and lightened in faith by the worde of God, so that they make open profession of the same, are exempted frō euil.
g Thogh that this blindenes be broght into the worlde by the malice of Satan, yet the mercies of God reserue to him self an infinite nomber which shalbe saued bothe of the Iewes and Gentiles through Christ.
h He omitteth Dan, & putteth Leui in, whereby he meaneth the twelue tribes.
i That is, the tribe of Ephraim, which was Iosephs sonne.

were

were sealed twelue thousand.
9 After these thigs I behelde, & lo, a great
multitude, which no mã colde nomber, of
all nacions & kinreds, and people, & tongues, stode before the throne, and before
the Lambe, clothed with long [k] white robes, and [l] palmes in their hands.
10 And they cryed with a loude voyce, saying, [m] Saluacion *cometh* of our God, that
sitteth vpon the throne, & of the Lambe.
11 And all the Angels stode rounde about
the throne, and *about* the Elders, and the
foure beastes, & they fell before the throne on their faces, and worshiped God,
12 Saying, Amen. Praise and glorie, & wisdome, and thankes, and honour, & power,
and might, *be* vnto our God for euermore, Amen.
13 And one of the Elders spake, sayig vnto
me, What are these ẘ are araied in long
white robes? and whence came they?
14 And I said vnto him, Lord, thou knowest. And he said to me, These are they,
which came out of great tribulacion, and
haue washed their long robes & haue made their long robes white in [n] the blood of
the Lambe.
15 Therefore are they in the presence of
the throne [o] of God, and serue him day &
[p] night in his Temple, and he that sitteth
on the throne, wil dwell among them.
16 * They shal [q] hunger no more, nether
thirst anie more, nether shal the sunne
[r] light on them, nether anie heate.
17 For the [f] Lambe, which is in the [t] middes of the throne, shal gouerne them, and
shal leade them vnto [u] the liuelie fountaines of waters, and * God shal wipe away
all teares from their eyes.

k In signe of puritie.
l In token of victorie & felicitie.
m All that are saued, attribute their saluacion vnto God onely & to his Christ & to none other thing.
n There is no puritie nor clenes, but by the blood of Christ onely, ẘ purgeth ỏ sinnes & so maketh vs white.
Isa.49,10.
o That is, of the maiestie of God ẏ Father, the Sonne, and ẏ holie Gost.
p Meaning continually: for els in heauẽ there is no night.
Isa.25,8.
chap.21,4.
q For all infirmitie & misene shalbe then taken away. r They shal haue no more grief and paine, but stil ioy & consolacion. f Iesus Christ the mediator & redemer. t Which is verie God. u He shal giue them life and conserue them in eternal felicitie.

CHAP. VIII.

1 The seuenth seale is opened: there is silence in heauen. 6 The foure Angels blowe their trumpettes, and great plagues followe vpon the earth.

1 AND when he had opened the [a] seueth
seal, there was [b] silence in heauen a-
bout halfe an houre.
2 And I sawe the seuen Angels, which stode
[c] before God, and to them were giuen seuen trumpettes.
3 Then another Angel came and stode before the altar hauing a golden censer, and
muche odours was giuen vnto him, that he
shulde offre with the prayers of all Saintes vpon the golden altar, which is before
the throne.
4 And the smoke of the odours with the
prayers of the Saintes, went vp before
God, out of the Angels hand.
5 And the Angel toke the censer, and filled
it with [d] fyre of the altar, and cast it into
the [e] earth, and [f] there were voyces, and
thundrings, and lightenings, and earthquake.
6 Then the seuen Angels, which had the
seuen trumpettes, prepared them selues
to blowe the trumpettes.
7 So the first Angel [g] blewe the trumpet,
and there was haile & fyre, mingled with
blood, and they were cast into the earth,
and the third parte of [h] trees was burnt, &
all grene [i] grasse was burnt.
8 And the seconde Angel blewe the trumpet, and as it *were* a great [k] mountaine,
burning with fyre, was cast into the sea, &
the third parte of the sea became blood.
9 And the third parte of the creatures,
which were in the sea, and had life, dyed,
& ẏ third parte of [l] shipes were destroied.
10 Then the third Angel blewe the trumpet, & there fell [m] a great starre from hea
uen burning like a torche, and it fell into
the third parte of the riuers, and into the
fountaines of waters.
11 And the name of the starre is called
wormewood: therefore the third parte of
the waters became wormewood, and manie men dyed of the [n] waters, because thei
were made bitter.
12 And the fourthe Angel blewe the trumpet, and the third parte of the [o] sunne was
smitten, & the third parte of the [p] moone,
and the third parte of the [q] starres, so that
the third parte of them was [r] darkened:
and the day *was smitten*, that the third parte of it colde not shine, and likewise the
night.
13 And I behelde, & heard one Angel flying through the middes of heauẽ, saying
with a lowde voyce, [f] Wo, wo, wo to the
inhabitants of the earth, because of the soundes to come of the trumpet of the thre
Angels, which were yet to blowe the trũ-
pettes.

a Vnder the sixt seale he touched in general the corruption of the doctrine: but vnder the seuenth he sheweth the great danger thereof, & what troubles, sectes & heresies hathe bene & shalbe broght into ẏ Church thereby.
b That the hearers might be more attentiue.
c He sheweth the onelie remedie in our afflictions, to wit, to appeare before the face of God by the meanes of Iesus Christ, who is the Angel, the sacrifice, and the Priest, which presenteth our prayers, which remaine yet in earth, before the altar and diuine maiestie of God.

d He meaneth by fyre ẏ grace of God whereby we are purged & made cleane, Isa. 6,6.
e He powreth the graces of the holie Gost into the hearts of ẏ faithful.
f When this grace is declared, maruelous rebellions arise against it by reason of the wicked, which can nether abide to heare their sinnes touched, nor mercie offred.
g That is, proclaimeth warre against the Church, and troubles by false doctrine, & so admonisheth thẽ to watch.
h That is, the moste parte of men were seduced.
i Euen the verie elect were sore tryed and prouen.
k Diuers sectes of heretikes were spred abroad in the worlde.
l Meaning the shipmasters, & so them that had anie gouernement.
m That is, some excellent minister of the Church, which shal corrupt the Scriptures.
n Which here signifie false & corrupt doctrine.
o That is, of Christ who is the sunne of iustice, meanig that men by boastig of their workes and merites obscure Christ and tread his death vnder fete.
p That is, of the Church q Of the ministers and teachers, which haue not taught, as they oght to do. r These are plagues for the contempt of the Gospel. f Horrible threatnings against the infideles & rebellious persones.

CHAP. IX.

1 The fift and sixt Angel blowe their trumpettes: the starre falleth from heauen. 3 The locustes come out of the smoke. 12 The first wo is paste. 14 The foure Angels that were bounde, are losed. 18 And the third parte of men is killed.

1 AND the fift Angel blewe the trũpet,
& I sawe [a] a starre fall from heauen
vnto the earth, and to him was giuen the
[b] keye of the bottomles pit.
2 And he opened the bottomles pit, and
there arose the smoke of the pit, as the
[c] smoke of a great fornace, and the sunne,

a That is, the Bishoppes and ministers, ẘ forsake ẏ worde of God, & so fall out of heauen, & become Angels of darkenes.
b This autoritie chiefly is committed to the Pope in signe whereof he beareth the keyes in his armes. c Abundance of heresies and errors, which couer with darkenes Christ and his Gospel.

and the ayre were darkened by the ſmoke
of the pit.
3 And there came out of the ſmoke [d] Locuſtes vpon the earth, and vnto them was
giuen [e] power, as the [f] ſcorpions of the
earth haue power.
4 And it was commanded them, that they
ſhulde not hurt the [g] graſſe of the earth,
nether anie grene thing, nether anie tree:
but onely thoſe [h] men which haue not the
ſeale of God in their forheades.
5 And to them was commanded that they
ſhulde not [i] kil them, but that they ſhulde
be [k] vexed fiue moneths, and that their
paine ſhulde be as the paine that cometh
of a [l] ſcorpion, when he hathe ſtung a mã.
6 *Therefore in thoſe daies ſhal men [m] ſeke death, and ſhal not finde it, and ſhal deſire to dye, and death ſhal flee from them.
7 *And the forme of the locuſtes *was* like
vnto [n] horſes prepared vnto battel, and
on their heades *were* as it *were* [o] crownes,
like vnto golde, and their faces [p] *were* like
the faces of men.
8 And they had heere as the [q] heere of women, and their [r] teeth were as the teeth of
lions.
9 And they had [ſ] habbergions, like to habbergions of yron: and the ſounde of their
[t] wings *was* like the ſounde of charets
when manie horſes runne vnto battel.
10 And they had tailes like vnto ſcorpions,
and there were [u] ſtings in their tailes, &
their power was to hurt mẽ fiue moneths.
11 And they haue a King ouer them, which
is the [x] Angel of the bottomles pit, whoſe
name in Hebrewe *is*, [y] Abaddon, and in
Greke he is named Apollyon.
12 One wo is paſt, & beholde, yet two woes
come after this.
13 ¶Then the ſixt Angel blewe the trũpet,
& I heard a [z] voyce from the foure hornes
of the golden altar, which is before God,
14 Saying to the ſixt Angel, which had
the trumpet, Loſe the foure [a] Angels, ẘ
are bounde in the great riuer Euphrates.
15 And the foure Angels were loſed, which
were prepared at an [b] houre, at a day, at a
moneth, & at a yere, to ſlay the third parte
of men.
16 And the nomber of horſemen of warre
were twẽtie thouſand times ten thouſand:
for I heard the nomber of them.
17 And thus I ſawe the horſes in a viſion,
and them that ſate on them, hauing fyrie
habbergiõs, & of Iacinth & of brimſtone,
& the heads of the horſes were as ẏ heads
of lyons: and out of their mouthes went
forthe fyre and ſmoke and brimſtone.
18 Of theſe thre was the third parte of mẽ
killed, *that is*, of the fyre and of the ſmoke,
and of the brimſtone, which came out of
their mouthes.
19 For their power is in their [c] mouthes, &
in their tailes: for their tailes were like vn
to ſerpents, and had heades, wherewith
they hurte.
20 And the remnant of the men which were not killed by theſe plagues, [d] repented
not of the workes of their hands that thei
ſhulde not worſhip deuils, and * idoles of
golde and of ſiluer, and of braſſe, and of
ſtone, and of wood, which nether can ſe,
nether heare nor go.
21 Alſo thei repented not of their murther,
and of their ſorcerie, nether of their fornicacion, nor of their thefte.

d Locuſtes are falſe teachers, heretikes, and worldlie ſutil Prelates, with Monkes, Freres, Cardinals, Patriarkes, Archebiſhops, Biſhops, Doctors, Baſchelers & maſters which forſake Chriſt to mainteine falſe doctrine.
e Falſe and deceiuable doctrine, which is pleaſant to the fleſh.
f That is, ſecretly to perſecute and to ſting with their taile as ſcorpiõs do: ſuche is the facion of the hypocrites.
Iſa.2,19. hoſe.10,8. luk.23,30. chap.6,16. Wiſd.16,9.
g For the falſe prophetes cã not deſtroie the elect, but ſuche as are ordeined to perdicion.
h That is, the infideles whome Satan blindeth with the efficacie of error, 2.Theſ.2,11
i Thogh the elect be hurt, yet they can not periſh.
k The elect for a certeine ſpace and at times are in troubles: for the greſhoppers endure but frõ April to Septẽber, which is fiue moneths.
l For at the beginning ẏ ſting of their conſcience ſemeth as nothing, but except thei ſone ſeke remedie, they periſh.
m Suche is the terrour of the vnbeleuing cõſcience, which hath no aſſurãce of mercie, but feleth the iudgement of God againſt it, when men imbrace error and refuſe the true ſimplicitie of Gods worde.
n Which ſignifieth that the Popes clergie ſhalbe proude, ambicious, bolde, ſtoute, raſh, rebellious, ſtubbern, cruel, lecherous & autors of warre & deſtruction of the ſimple children of God. o They pretend a certeine title of honour, which in dede belõgeth nothing vnto thẽ, as the Prieſts by their crownes and ſtrange apparel declare. p That is, thei pretẽd great gentlenes & loue: thei are wiſe, politicke, ſubtil, eloquent & in worldlie craftines paſſe all in all their doings. q That is, effeminate, delicate, idle, trimming thẽ ſelues to pleaſe their harlots. r Signifying their oppreſſion of the poore & crueltie againſt Gods children. ſ Which ſignifie their hardenes of heart and obſtinacion in their errors, with their aſſurance vnder the protection of worldlie princes. t For as thogh they had wings, ſo are they lifted vp aboue the cõmune ſorte of men & eſtemed moſte holie & do all things ẘ rage & fiercenes. u To infect & kil ẘ their venemous doctrine x Which is Antichriſt the Pope, king of hypocrites & Satans ambaſſadour y That is, deſtroier: for Antichriſt the ſonne of perdicion deſtroieth mens ſoules ẘ falſe doctrine, & the whole worlde ẘ fyre & ſworde. z Which was the voyce of Chriſt ſitting at the right hand of the Father. a Meaning the enemies of the Eaſt contrey, which ſhulde afflict the Church of God, as did the Arabians, Saraſines, Turkes & Tartarians.
b This ſignifieth the great readines of the enemies.

c Which ſignifieth their falſe doctrine & hypocriſie.
d And therefore were iuſtely deſtroyed.
Pſal.115,4. & 135,15.

CHAP. X.

1 The Angel hathe the boke open. 6 He ſweareth there ſhalbe no more time. 9 He giueth the boke vnto Iohn, which eateth it vp.

1 AND I ſawe another mightie [a] Angel come downe from heauen, clothed with a cloude, and the [b] raine bowe
vpon his head, & his face was as the [c] ſunne, and his [d] feete as pillers of fyre.
2 And he had in his hand a litle [e] boke o-
pen, and he put his right fote vpon the
ſea, and *his* left on the earth,
3 And cryed with a [f] lowde voyce, as when
a lyon roareth: and when he had cryed, ſeuen [g] thondres vttered their voyces.
4 And when the ſeuen thonders had vttered their voyces, I was about to write: but
I heard a voyce from heauen ſaying vnto
me, * [h] Seale vp thoſe things which the ſeuen thondres haue ſpoken, & write thẽ not.
5 And the Angel which I ſawe ſtand vpon
the ſea and vpon the earth, lift vp his hãd
to heauen,
6 And ſware [i] by him that liueth for euermore, which created heauen, & the things
that therein are, & the earth & the things
that therein are, & the ſea & the things, ẘ
therein are, that time ſhulde be no more.
7 But in the daies of the voyce of the ſeuẽth Angel, whẽ he ſhal beginne to blowe
the trumpet, euen the [k] myſterie of God
ſhalbe finiſhed, as he hathe declared to his
ſeruants the Prophetes.

a Which was Ieſus Chriſt ẏ came to cõfort his Church againſt ẏ furious aſſaltes of Satan and Antichriſt: ſo that in all their troubles, the faithful are ſure to finde conſolaciõ in him.
b Ieſus Chriſt beareth ẏ teſtimonie of Gods loue towardes vs.
c It ouercame all the darkenes of the Angel of the bottomles pit.
Dan.12,7.
d Straight, ſtrong & pure frõ all corruptions.
e Meaning the Goſpel of Chriſt, which Antichriſt can not hide, ſeing Chriſt bringeth it opẽ in his hãd.
f Which declareth that in deſpite of Antichriſt ẏ Goſpel ſhulde be preached through all the worlde: ſo that the enemies ſhalbe aſtonied. g The whole graces of Gods Spirit bent them ſelues againſt Antichriſt. h Beleue that that is written: for there is no nede to write more for the vnderſtanding of Gods children. i That is, by God with whome Chriſt by his diuinitie is equall. k The faithful ſhal vnderſtand and ſe this myſterie of the laſt iudgement, the damnacion of Antichriſt and infideles, & alſo the glorie of the iuſt at the reſurrection.

8 And

8 And the voyce which I heard from heauen, spake vnto [l] me againe and said, Go &
take ye litle boke which is open in the hand
of the [m] Angel, which stãdeth vpon the sea
& vpon the earth.
9 So I wēt vnto the Angel , & said to him,
Giue me the litle [n] boke. And he said vnto
me, *Take it, & [o] eat it vp, and it shal make thy bellie bitter , but it shalbe in thy
mouth as swete as honie.
10 Then I toke the litle boke out of the An
gels hand, and ate it vp , and it was in my
mouth as [p] swete as honie: but when I had
eaten it, my bellie was bitter.
11 And he said vnto me, Thou must prophecie [q] againe among the people and nations, and tongues, and to many Kings.

l As S. Iohn vnderstode this by reuelation, so is the same reueiied to ye true preachers to discouer the Pope, & Antichrist. m Meaning, Christ. *Eze.3,1. n That is, the holie Scriptures: wc declareth yt the minister must receiue thē at ye hand of God before he can preache thē to others. o Which signifieth that the ministers oght to receiue the worde into their hearts, & to haue graue, & depe iudgement, and diligently to studie it, & with zeale to vtter it. p Signifying yt albeit that the minister haue consolation by the worde of God, yet shal he haue sore, & grieuous enemies, which shalbe troublesome vnto him. q Not onely meaning in his life time, but that this boke after his death shulde be as a preaching vnto all nations.

CHAP. XI.

1 The tēple is measured. 3 Two witnesses raised vp by the Lord, are murthered by the beast, 11 But after receiued to glorie. 15 Christ is exalted, 16 And God praised by the 24. elders.

1 THen was giuen me a rede, like vnto a
rodde, & the Angel stode by, saying,
Rise and [a] mette the tēple of God, and the
altar, and them that worship therein.
2 But [b] the court which is without the temple cast out, and mette it not : for it is giuen vnto the Gentiles , and the holie [c] citie shal they treade vnder fote [d] two & fortie moneths.
3 But I wil giue power vnto my [e] two witnesses, & they shal prophecie a [f] thousand,
two hundreth, & threscore dayes , clothed
in [g] sacke cloth.
4 These are two [h] oliue trees, & two cādel
stickes, stãding before ye God of ye [i] earth.
5 And if anie mā wil hurte them , fyre procedeth out of their mouthes, and deuoureth their enemies : for if anie man wolde
hurt them, [k] thus muste he be killed.
6 These haue power to shut [l] heauen, that
it raine not in the dayes of their prophecying, & haue power ouer waters to turne
them into [m] blood, and to smite the earth
with all maner plagues, as oftē as thei wil.
7 And when they haue finished their testimonie, the [n] beast that cometh out of
the bottomles pit, shal make warre against them, and shal [o] ouercome them, and
kill them.

a Which declareth ye Christ Iesus wil buylde his Church and not haue it destroyed: for he measureth out his spiritual Temple. b The Iewish tēple was deuided into thre parts: the bodie of the temple which is called the court, whereinto euerie mā entred: ye holie places where ye leuits were: & the holiest of all, whereinto the high Priest once a yere entred: in respect therefore of these two later, the first is said to be cast out, because as a thīg prophane it is neglected whē the temple is measured, and yet the aduersaries of Christ boast that thei are in the Tēple, and yt none are of the Tēple, but they. c That is, the Church of God. d Meaning, a certeine time: for God hathe limited the times of Antichrists tyrānie. e By two witnesses he meaneth all the preachers yt shulde buylde vp Gods Church, alluding to Zorubbabel and Iehoshua which were chiefly appointed for this thing, and also to this saying, In the mouthe of two witnesses standeth euerie worde. f Signifying a certeine time: for whē God giueth strength to his ministers, their persecutions seme, but as it were for a day or two. g In poore and simple apparel. h Whereby are signified the excellēt graces of them which beare witnes to the Gospel. i Who hathe dominion ouer the whole earth. k By Gods worde whereby his ministers discomfit the enemies. l They denounce Gods iudgement against the wicked, that they can not enter into heauen. m Which is to declare & procure Gods vengeance n That is, the Pope which hathe his power out of hel and cometh thence o . He sheweth how the Pope gaineth the victorie, not by Gods worde, but by cruel warre.

8 And their corpses shal lie in the stretes of
the great [p] citie, which spiritually is called Sodom and Egypt, where our Lord also was crucified.
9 And they of the people and kinreds , and
tōgues, and Gentiles shal se their corpses
thre dayes and an halfe, and shal not suffer
their carkeises to be put in graues.
10 And they that dwell vpon the earth ,
shal reioyce ouer them and be glad , and
shal send giftes one to another : for these
two Prophetes [q] vexed them that dwelt
on the earth.
11 But after thre dayes and an halfe, the spi
rit of life *comming* from God, shal enter into them, & they shal [r] stand vp vpon their
fete: and great feare shal come vpon them
which sawe them.
12 And they shal heare a great voyce from
heauen, saying vnto them , [s] Come vp hither . And they shal ascende vp to heauen
in a cloude , and their enemies shal se
them.
13 And the same houre shal there be a great
earthquake , and the tenth parte of the citie [t] shal fall , and in the earthquake shalbe slaine in nomber seuen thousand : and
the remnant shalbe afraid , [u] and giue glo
rie to the God of heauen.
14 The seconde wo is past, *&* beholde the
thirde wo wil come anone.
15 And the seuenth Angel blew the trumpet, and there were great voyces in heauē,
saying, The [x] kingdomes of this worlde are
our Lords, and his Christs, and he shal reigne for euermore.
16 Then the foure & twētie Elders , which
sate before God on their seates , fell vpon
their faces, and worshipped [y] God,
17 Saying , [z] We giue thee thankes, Lord
God almightie, Which art , and Which
wast, & Which art to come: for thou hast
receiued thy great might , and hast obteined thy kingdome.
18 And the Gentiles were angrie , and thy
wrath is come, and the time of the dead,
that they shulde be iudged , and that thou
shuldest giue rewarde vnto thy seruants
the Prophetes , and to the Saintes, and to
them that feare thy Name , to smale , and
great , and shuldest destroye them, which
destroye the earth.
19 Then the Temple of God was opened
in heauen, and there was sene in his Temple the Arke of his couenāt: and there were [a] lightnings, and voyces, and thōdrings,
and earthquake, and muche haile.

p Meaning the whole iurisdiction of the Pope, which is cōpared to Sodom for their abominable sinne, and to Egypt because the true libertie to serue God is taken away from the faithful : and Christ was cōdemned by Pilate, who represented the Romaine power which shulde be enemie to the godlie. q The infidels are tormented by hearing ye trueth preached. r Which shalbe at the last resurrection s For it semed that Antichrist had chased them out of the earth. t Of the power of Antichrist. u When they shal vnderstād by Gods worde the glorie of his , and the punishment of his enemies , thei shal fall from the Pope, and glorifie God. x Albeit Satā by ye Pope, Turke and other instruments troubleth the worlde neuer so muche, yet Christ shal reigne. y Iesus Christ. z This declareth the office of the godlie, which is to giue God thākes for the deliuerance of his, and to praise his iustice for punishing of his enemies. a Which signifie the destruction of the enemies.

CHAP. XII.

1 There appeareth in heauen a woman clothed with the sunne. 7 Michael fighteth with the dragon, which persecuteth the woman. 11 The victorie is gotten to the comfort of the faithful.

1 AND there appeared a great wonder
in heauen: A [a] woman clothed with
the sunne, & the [b] moone *was* vnder her fete, and vpon her head a [c] crowne of twelue starres.
2 And she was with childe and [d] cryed trauailing in birth, and was pained readie to
be deliuered.
3 And there appeared another wonder in
heauen: for beholde, a great [e] red dragon
hauing [f] seuen heades, and ten hornes, and
seuen crownes vpon his heads:
4 And his taile drue the [g] third parte of the
starres of heauen, & cast thē to the earth.
And the dragon stode before the woman,
which was readie to be deliuered, to deuoure her childe when she had broght it
forthe.
5 [h] So she broght forthe a man childe,
which shulde rule all nations with a * rod
of yron: and her sonne was taken vp vnto
God and to this throne.
6 And the womā fled into [i] wildernes where she hathe a place prepared of God, that
they shulde fede her there a thousand, two
hundreth and threscore dayes.
7 And there was a battel in heauen. [k] Michael & his Angels foght against the dra
gon, and the dragon foght & his Angels.
8 But they preuailed not, nether was their
place founde anie more [l] in heauen.
9 And the great dragon, that olde serpent,
called the deuil and Satan, was cast out,
which deceiueth all the worlde: he was *euē*
cast into the earth, & his Angels were cast
out with him.
10 Thē I heard a loude voyce, saying, Now
is saluation in heauen, and strength & the
kingdome of our God, and the power of
his Christ: for the accuser of our brethren
is cast downe, which accused them before
our God day and night.
11 But they ouercame him by the blood of
the Lambe, and by the worde of their testimonie, and they [m] loued not their liues vn
to the death.
12 Therefore reioyce, ye heauens, & ye that
dwell in thē. Wo to the [n] inhabitāts of the
earth, and of the sea: for the deuil is come
downe vnto you which hathe great wrath,
knowing that he hathe but a short time.
13 And when the dragon sawe that he was
[o] cast vnto the earth, he persecuted ẏ womā
which had broght forthe the man *childe*.
14 But to the woman were giuen two win-
ges of a great egle, ẏ she might flie into
the wildernes, into [p] her place, where she is
nourished for a time, & times, and halfe a
time, from the presence of the serpent.
15 And ẏ [q] serpēt cast out of his mouth water after ẏ woman like a flood, ẏ he might
cause her to be caryed away of the flood.
16 But the earth holpe the woman, and the
earth opened her mouth, and swalowed vp
the flood, which the dragō had cast out of
his mouth.
17 Then the dragon was wroth with the
woman, and wēt and made warre with the
[r] remnant of her sede, which kepe the cōmandements of God, and haue the testimonie of Iesus Christ.
18 And I stode on the sea sande.

CHAP. XIII.

1. 8 The beast deceiueth the reprobate. 2. 4. 12. And is confirmed by another beast. 17 The priuiledge of the beasts marke.

1 AND I sawe a [a] beast rise out of the
sea, hauing [b] seuen heads, and [c] ten
hornes, and vpon his hornes *were* ten
crownes, and vpon his heads the name of
blasphemie.
2 And the beast which I sawe, was like a
[d] leopard, and his fete like a beares, and his
mouth as the mouth of a lion: and the [e] dra
gon gaue him his power and his throne, &
great autoritie.
3 And I sawe one of his [f] heads as it *were*
wounded to death, but his [g] deadlie woūde
was healed, and all the worlde wōdred *and*
followed the beast.
4 And they worshipped the dragon which
gaue power vnto the beast, & they [h] worshipped the beast, saying, Who is like vn
to the beast? who is able to warre with him?
5 And there was giuen vnto him a mouth,
that spake great things and blasphemies,
and power was giuen vnto him, to do [i] two
and fortie moneths.
6 And he opened his mouth vnto blasphemie against God, to blaspheme his Name
and his tabernacle, & thē ẏ dwel in heauē.
7 And it was giuē vnto him to make warre
with the Saintes, and to [k] ouercome them,
& power was giuen him ouer euerie [l] kinred and tongue, and nation.
8 Therefore all that dwell vpon the earth,
shal worship him, whose [m] names are not
* writen in the Boke of life of the Lambe,
which was slaine [n] from the beginning of
the worlde.
9 If anie man haue an eare, let him heare.
10 If anie lead into captiuitie, he shal go
[o] into captiuitie: if anie kil with a sworde,
he must be killed by a sworde: here is the
pacience, & the faith of the Saintes.
11 And I behelde another beast comming
vp out of the [p] earth, which had two [q] hor-

a In this third vision is declared how ẏ Church which is compassed about with Iesus Christ the Sonne of righteousnes, is persecuted of Antichrist.
b The Church treadeth vnder fote what soeuer is mutable, and incōstant, with all corrupt affections and suche like.
c Which signifie God and his worde.
d The Church euer with a moste feruent desire longed ẏ Christ shulde be borne, & that the faithful might be regenerate by his power.
Psal.2,9.
e The deuil, & all his power which burneth with furie and is red with ẏ blood of the faithful.
f For he is prince of this worlde & almoste hathe ẏ vniuersal gouernement.
g By his flatteries & promises he gaineth manie of ẏ excellēt ministers & honorable persones, and bringeth thē to destruction.
h Which is Iesus Christ the first borne amōg manie brethrē, who was borne of ẏ virgin Marie as of a special mēber of ẏ Churche.
i The Church was remoued frō among the Iewes to the Gētiles, which were as a barē wildernes, and so it is persecuted to & fro.
k Iesus Christ and his members, as Apostles, Martyrs, and the rest of the faithful.
l For the dragon was depriued of all his dignitie and had no more place in the Church.
m They put their liues in danger so oft as nede required.
n Meaning thē that are giuen to the worlde and fleshlie lustes.
o And was ouercome of Christ, then he foght against his members.
p Which the Lord had appointed for her.
q God giueth meanes to his Church to escape the furie of Satan making his creatures to serue to the support thereof.

r Satā was not able to destroy the head nor the bodie, and therefore sheweth his rage against the mēbers.

a Here is the description of the Romaine empire which standeth in crueltie and tyrannie.
b Meaning Rome, because it was first gouerned by seuen Kings or Emperours after Nero, and also is compassed about ẇ seuen mountaines.
c Which signifie manie prouinces.
d By these beastes are signified the Macedoniās, Persians & Chaldeans whome the Romaines ouercame.
e That is, the deuil.
f This maie be vnderstand of Nero, who moued ẏ first persecution against ẏ Churche, and after slewe him self, so ẏ the familie of the Cesars ended in him.
g For ẏ empire was established againe by Vespasian.
h By receiuīg the statutes, ordināces, decrees, ceremonies, & religion of ẏ Romaine empire.
i Antichrists time & power is limited.
k In their bodies, not in soule.
l He meaneth ẏ vniuersal departing where of S. Paul speaketh to the Thessalonians.
m Antichrist hathe not power ouer ẏ elect.
n As God ordeined frō before all begining, & all ẏ sacrifices were as signes & sacramēts of Christs death.
o Thei which led soules captiues, go them selues into captiuitie.
p As the kingdome of Christ is frō heauē, & bringeth men thither: so ẏ Popes kingdome is of ẏ earth & leadeth to perditiō, & is begōne, & established by ambitiō, couetousnes, beastelines, craft, treason & tyrānie.
q Which signifie the priesthode & the kingdome, and therefore he giueth in his armes two keis, and hathe two swordes caryed before him. So Boniface the eight which first ordeined the Iubile, shewed him self one day in apparel as a Pope, & the next day in harnes as the Emperour, and the two hornes in the bishops mitre are signes hereof.

nes like the Lambe,but he [r] spake like the
dragon.
12 And he did all that the first [s] beast colde do before him,& he caused the earth,
and them which dwel therein , to worship
the first [t] beast,whose deadlie wounde was
healed.
13 And [u] he did great wonders, so that he
made fyre to come downe from heauen
on the earth,in the sight of men,
14 And deceiued thē that dwel on the earth
by the signes , which were permitted to
him to do in the [x] sight of the beast , sayīg
to them that dwell on the earth,that they
shulde make the [y] image of the beast,
which had the wounde of a sworde, & did
liue.
15 And it was permitted to him to giue a
[z] spirit vnto the image of the beast,so that
the image of the beast shulde [a] speake, and
shulde cause that as manie as wolde not
[b] worship the image of the beast, shulde be
killed.
16 And he made all, bothe small and great,
riche and poore,fre and bonde, to receiue
a [c] marke in their right hand or in their
forheads.
17 And [d] that no man might bye or sell, saue he that had the marke , or the name of
the beast,or the nomber of his name.
18 Heare is wisdome . Let him that hathe
wit , count the nomber of the beast:for it
is the nomber [e] of a man, and his nomber
is six hundreth,threscore and six.

r He spake deuelish doctrine, accused Gods worde of imperfection, set vp mans traditions, and spake things contrarie to God and his worde.
s For the Pope in ambitiō, crueltie, idolatrie,& blasphemie did folow & imitate the anciēt Romaines.
t Broght thē to idolatrie & astonished thē with the name of that holie empire (as he termeth it)
u The man of sinne accordīg to ȳ operation of Satā shalbe wt all power, signes & miracles of lies, 2.Thes.2,10.
x Before the whole empire wc representeth the first beast, and is ȳ image thereof.
y For the first empire Romaine was as the paterne,& this secōde empire is but an image & shadowe thereof.
z For except ȳ Pope confirme the autoritie of the King of Romaines , he is not estemed worthie to be made Emperour.

a The same things wc the Pope,or false prophetes instruct him in. b Receiue the ordinances & decrees of the seat of Rome, & to kisse ȳ vilens fote,if he were put thereunto. c Whereby he renoūceth Christ:for as faith,ȳ worde & the Sacramēts are ȳ Christiās markes:so this Antichrist wil accept none but suche as wil approue his doctrine:so ȳ it is not ynough to cōfesse Christ,& to belieue ȳ Scriptures,but a man must subscribe to ȳ Popes doctrine:moreouer their chrismatories,graisings,vowes ,othes & shauings are signes of this marke in so muche as no natiō was excepted ȳ had not manie of these marked beasts. d He ȳ is not sealed wt Antichrists marke, can not be suffered to liue among men. e Suche as may be vnderstād by mans reason: for about 666 yeres after this reuelatiō ȳ Pope or Antichrist begā to be manifest in the worlde:for these characters χ ξ ϛ. signifie 666:& this nōber is gathered of ȳ smale nōber, λ α τ ε ι ν ο ς. wc in the whole make 666 & signifieth Lateinus,or Latin,which noteth the Pope or Antichrist who vseth in all things ȳ Latin tōgue,& in respect thereof he contēneth ȳ Ebrewe & Greke wherein ȳ worde of God was first & best writē:& because Italie in olde time was called Latinum,the Italians are called Latini,so that hereby he noteth of what countrey chiefly he shulde come.

CHAP. XIIII.

1 The notable cōpanie of the Lābe. 6 One Angel announceth the Gospel, 8 Another the fall of Babylon, 9 And the thirde warneth to flee frō the beast. 13 Of their blessednes which dye in the Lord. 18 Of the Lords haruest.

1 THen I loked,and lo,a [a] Lābe stode on
mount Sion, and with him an [b] hundreth, fortie & foure thousand, hauing his
Fathers [c] Name writen in their forheads.
2 And I heard a voyce from heauen, as the
sounde of manie [d] waters,& as the sounde
of a great thunder : & I heard the voyce
of harpers harping with their harpes.
3 And they sung as it *were* a newe song before the throne, & before the foure beasts,
and the Elders, and no [e] man colde learne
that song , but the hundreth , fortie and
foure thousand , which were boght from
the earth.
4 These are they , which are not [f] defiled
with womē:for they are virgins:these fol
lowe the Lābe [g] whither soeuer he goeth:
these are boght from men,being the [h] first
frutes vnto God,and to the Lambe.
5 And in their mouths was founde no guile : for they are without [i] spot before the
throne of God.
6 ¶ Then I sawe another [k] Angel flee in the
middes of Heauen, hauing an euerlasting
Gospel,to preache vnto them , that dwell
on the earth,and to euerie nation,and kinred,and tongue,and people,
7 * Sayīg with a loude voyce,[l] Feare God,
and giue glorie to him : for the houre of
his iudgement is come : and worship him
that made * heauen and earth, and the sea,
and the fountaines of waters.
8 And there followed another Angel , saying,*It is fallen,it is fallen, [m] Babylon the
great citie : for she made all nations to
drinke of the wine of the [n] wrath of her
fornication.
9 ¶ And the thirde Angel followed them,
saying with a loude voyce,If any mā wor
ship the beast and his image , and receiue
his marke in his forhead , or on his hand,
10 The same shal drinke of the wine of the
wrath of God,yea,of ȳ [o] pure wine,which
is powred into the cuppe of his wrath,and
he shalbe tormented in fyre and brimstone before the holie Angels , & before the
Lambe.
11 And the smoke of their torment shal ascende euermore: & they shal haue no rest
day nor night , which worshippe the beast
and his image , and whosoeuer receiueth
the print of his name.
12 Here is the pacience of [p] Saintes:here a-
re they that kepe the commandements of
God,and the faith of Iesus.
13 Thē I heard a voyce frō heauen,saying
vnto me , Write, [q] Blessed *are* the dead,
which hereafter dye " in the [r] Lord. Euē so
saith the Spirit: for they rest from their la
bours,and their workes followe them.
14 ¶ And I loked,& beholde,a white [s] clou
de , and vpon the cloude one sitting like
vnto the Sōne of man,hauing on his head
a golden crowne , and in his hand a sharpe sickle.
15 And another Angel came out of the
Tēple , crying with a loude voyce to him

a Iesus Christ ruleth in his Church to defend and comfort it, thogh the beast rage neuer so muche:and seing Christ is present euer with his Church, there can be no vicare: for where there is a vicare, there is no Church.

b Meaning a great and ample Church. c Which was the marke of their election,to wit,their faith d Signifying that the nomber of the Church shulde be great, and that they shulde speake boldly , and aloude, and so glorifie the Lord.

e None can praise God,but the elect whome he hathe boght.
f By whoredome : and vnder this vice he cōprehendeth all other:but this is chiefly mēt of idolatrie wc is the spiritual whoredome.
g For their whole delite is in ȳ Lābe Iesus and they loue none but him.
h Which declareth that the faithful oght to liue iustely and holely, that they may be ȳ first frutes & an excellent offring of the Lord.
Psal.145,6.
i For asmuche as their sinnes are pardoned, & thei are cled wt the iustice of Christ.
Act.14,20.
k By this Angel are ment ȳ true ministers of Christ wc preache the Gospel faithfully.
Isa.21,9.
iere.51,8.
chap.18,8.
l The Gospel teacheth vs to feare God and honour him, wc is ȳ beginning of heauenlie wisdome.
m Signifying Rome, for asmuche as the vices which were in Babylon, are founde in Rome in greater abundance,as persecution of the Church of God,oppressiō & sclauerie wt destruction of the people of God, cōfusion, superstition, idolatrie,impietie , and as Babylon the first Monarchie was destroyed , so shal this wicked kingdome of Antichrist haue a miserable ruine, thogh it be great& semeth to extend throughout all Europa.
n By ȳ which fornicatiō God is prouoked to wrath : so that he suffreth many to walke in the way of the Romish doctrine to their destruction. o That is,of his terrible iudgement. p The faithful are exhorted to pacience. q For they are deliuered from the horrible troubles which are in the Church, and rest with God. " Or,for the Lords cause. r Which are ingraffed in Christ by faith , which rest and stay onely on him and reioyce to be with him: for immediatly after their death they are receiued into ioye. s Signifying that Christ shal come to iudgement in a cloude, euen as he was sene to go vp.

that sate on the cloude, * [t] Thrust in thy
sickle & reape: for the time is come to reape: for the haruest of the earth is ripe.
16 And he that sate on the cloude, [u] thrust
in his sickle on the earth, & the earth was
reaped.
17 Then another Angel came out of the
temple, which is in heauen, hauing also a
sharpe sickle.
18 And another Angel came out from the
[x] altar, which had power ouer fyre, and
cryed with a lowde crye to him that had
the sharpe sickle, and said, Thrust in thy
sharpe sickle, & gather the clusters of the
vineyarde of the earth: for her grapes are
ripe.
19 And the Angel thrust in his sharpe sickle
on the earth, & cutte downe the vines of
the vineyarde of the earth, and cast them
into the great wine presse of the wrath of
God.
20 And the [y] wine presse was trodē without
the citie, and blood came out of the wine presse, vnto the [z] horse bridles by the
space of a thousand and six hundreth furlongs.

Ioel 3,13. mat.13,39.
t The ouerthrowe of the people is compared to an haruest, Isa.19,5: also to a vintage, Isa.6,3.
u This is spoken familiarly for our capacitie, alluding vnto an housband man who suffereth him self to be aduertised by his seruants when his haruest is ripe, and not that Christ hathe nede to be tolde when he shulde come to iudgement for the cōfort of his Church and destructiō of his enemies.
x This was Christ who is also the altar, the Priest and sacrifice.
y That is, a certeine place appointed and not in the heauen.
z By this similitude he declareth the horrible confusion of the tyrāts and infideles, which delite in nothing but warres, slaughters, persecutions and effusion of blood.

CHAP. XV.

1 Seuen Angels haue the seuen last plagues. 3 The song of them that ouercome the beast. 7 The seuen viales ful of Gods wrath.

1 AND I sawe another [a] signe in heauē
great & marueilous, [b] seuen Angels
hauing the seuen last plagues: for by them
is fulfilled the wrath of God.
2 And I sawe as *it were* a [c] glassie sea, mingled with fyre, and them that had gotten
victorie of the beast, and of his image, and
of his marke, and of the nomber of his name, stand at the glassie sea, hauing the har
pes of God,
3 And they sung the song of Moses the * ser
uant of God, and the song of the Lambe,
saying, Great & marueilous *are* thy workes, Lord God almightie: iuste and true
are thy * ° wayes, King of Saintes.
4 * Who shal not feare thee, ô Lord, and
glorifie thy Name! for thou onely *art* holie, and all nations shal come & worshippe before thee: for thy iudgements are ma
de manifest.
5 And after that I loked, and beholde, the
tēple of the tabernacle of testimonie was
open in heauen.
6 And the seuen Angels came out of the
temple, which had the seuen plagues, clothed in pure and [d] bright linnen, and hauing their [e] breastes girded with golden
girdles.

a This is the fourth vision which conteineth the doctrine of Gods iudgements for the destruction of the wicked and comfort of the godlie.
b Meaning an infinite nomber of Gods ministers, which had infinite maners of sortes and punishements.
Exod.15,1.
Psal.145,17.
Iere.20,16.
c Signifying this brittel & inconstāt worlde mixt with fyre, that is, troubles and afflictions, but the Saintes of God ouercome them all, and sing diuine songs vnto God by whose power they get the victorie.
°*Or, actes and dedes.*
d Which is to declare that Gods iudgements are cleare, iust and without spot.
e As readie to execute the vengeance of God.

7 And one of the [f] foure beastes gaue vnto the seuen Angels seuen golden viales
full of the wrath of God, which liueth for
euermore.
8 And the Temple was ful of the smoke of
the glorie of God and of his power, and
no mā was able to [g] enter into the Tēple,
til the seuen plagues of the seuen Angels
were fulfilled.

f By the foure beasts are mēt all the creatures of God ẏ willingly serue him for the punishment of the infideles.
g God giueth vs ful entrie into his Church by destroying his enemies: for the Saintes can not clearely knowe all Gods iudgements before the ful end of all things.

CHAP. XVI.

1 The Angels powre out their vials full of wrath. 6 And what plagues followe thereof. 15 Admonition to take hede and watch.

1 AND I heard a great voyce out of the
Temple, saying to the seuē Angels,
Go your wayes, and powre out the *seuen*
viales of the wrath of God vpō the earth.
2 And the first went, and powred out his
vial vpon the earth: and there fell a noysome, and a grieuous [a] sore vpon the men,
which had the marke of the beast, & vpon
them which worshipped his image.
3 And the secōd Angel powred out his vial
vpon the sea, and it became as the [b] blood
of [c] a dead man: and euerie liuing thing
dyed in the sea.
4 And the thirde Angel powred out his
vial vpon the riuers & fountaines of waters, and they became [d] blood.
5 And I heard the Angel of the [e] waters
say, Lord, thou art iust, Which art, and
Which wast, and Holie, because thou hast
iudged these things.
6 For they shed the blood of the Saintes,
and Prophets, and therefore hast thou giuen them blood to drinke: for they are
worthie.
7 And I heard another out of the Sanctuarie say, Euē so, Lord God almightie, [f] true
and righteous are thy iudgements.
8 And the fourth Angel powred out his
vial on the sunne, and it was giuen vnto
him to torment men with [g] heat of fyre,
9 And men boyled in great heat, and [h] blasphemed the Name of God, which hathe
power ouer these plagues, and they repen
ted not, to giue him glorie.
10 And the fift Angel powred out his vial
vpon the throne of the [i] beast, & his kingdome waxed darke, & they [k] gnewe their
tongues for sorowe,
11 And blasphemed the God of heauen for
their paines, and for their sores, & repen
ted not of their workes.
12 And the sixt Angel powred out his vial
vpon the great riuer [l] Euphrates, and the
water thereof dryed vp, that the way of

a This was like the sixt plague of Egypt, which was sores and boiles or pockes: and this reigneth cōmunly amōg Canons, monkes, friers, nonnes, Priests and suche filthie vermin which beare the marke of ẏ beast.
b This is like to the first plague of Egypt which signifieth all kindes of pestilences and cōtagious diseases.
c That is, corrupt & infect.
d The first plague of Egypt was like vnto this.
e He bringeth forthe these two Angels: ẏ one which is gouernour of ẏ waters, and the other from vnder the altar, as witnesses & commēders of Gods iust iudgements
f For asmuche as thou destroyest the rebelles, & preseruest thine.
g Signifying famine, drought and hote diseases which procede thereof.
h The wicked were hardhearted & stubbern when God punished them.
i This answereth to ẏ ninth plague of Egypt, which signifieth ẏ the Popes doctrine is an horrible plague of God, ẏ kepeth men stil in darke ignorance and errours.
k They shal shewe their furie, rage & blasphemie against God when the light of his Gospel shal shine.
l By Euphrates which was ẏ strength of Babylon, is ment ẏ riches, strength, pleasures and commodities of Rome the second Babylon, ẏ the faithful ẏ are the true Kings & Priests in Christ, haue taken away by disclosing their wicked deceit.

the

the Kings of the East shulde be prepared.
13 And I sawe thre [m] vncleane spirits like
frogges come out of the mouth of the dra
gon,& out of the mouth of the beast, and
out of the mouth of the false prophet.
14 For they are the spirits [n] of deuils, working miracles, to go vnto the [o] Kings of
the earth,and of the whole worlde, to gather them to the battel of that great day
of God Almightie.
15 (*Beholde, I come as a thefe. Blessed *is*
he that watcheth & kepeth his [p] garmēts,
lest he walke naked, and men se his filthines)
16 And they gathered them together into
a place called in Hebrue [q] Arma-gedon.
17 ¶ And the seuenth Angel powred out his
vial into the ayre: & there came a loude
voyce out of the Temple of heauen from
the throne, saying, [r] It is done.
18 And there were voyces, and thundrings,
and lightnings, & there was a great earthquake, suche as was not since men were
vpon the earth, euen so mightie an earthquake.
19 And the great [s] citie was diuided into
thre partes, and the [t] cities of the nacions
fell: and great Babylon came in remembrance before God, * to giue vnto her
the cup of the wine of the fiercenes of his
wrath.
20 And euerie yle fled away, & the mountaines were not founde.
21 And there fell a great haile, like talents,
out of heauen vpon the men, and men
blasphemed God, because of the plague
of the haile: for the plague thereof was
exceding great.

m That is, a strong nomber of this great deuil ẏ Popes ambassadours whiche are euer crying and croking like frogs and come out of Antichrists mouth, because they shulde speake nothig but lies and vse all maner of craftie deceit to mainteine their riche Euphrates against the true Christians.

Chap.3,7. mat.24,44. luk.12,39.

n Albeit they call them selues spiritual and holie fathers.

o For in all Kings courtes ẏ Pope hathe had his ambassadours to hinder the kingdome of Christ.

p Of righteousnes and holines, wherewith we are cled through Iesus Christ.

Ier.25,15.

q As if he wolde say, The craftines of destruction whē as Kings and princes shal warre against God, but by ẏ craft of Satan are broght to that place where they shalbe destroyed.

r This is the last iudgement when Christ shal come to destroy ẏ wicked and deliuer his Church.

s Meaning the whole nomber of them that shal call them selues Christians, whereof some are so in dede, some are Papistes and vnder pretence of Christ serue Antichrist, and some are neuters which are nether on the one side nor of the other.

t Signifying, all strange religions, as of the Iewes, Turkes & others, which then shal fall with that great whore of Rome, & be tormented in eternal paines.

CHAP. XVII.

3 The description of the great whore. 8 Her sinnes and punishment. 14 The victorie of the Lambe.

1 THen there came [a] one of the seuē Angels, which had the seuen viales, and
talked with me, saying vnto me, Come: I
wil shewe thee the dānacion of the great
[b] whore that sitteth vpon many [c] waters,
2 With whome haue committed fornication the Kings of the earth, and the inhabitans of the earth are drunken with the
wine of her fornication.
3 So he caried me away into the wildernes
in the Spirit, and I sawe a woman sit vpon
a skarlat coloured [d] beast, full of names
of [e] blasphemie, which had seuen heads, &
ten hornes.
4 And the [f] woman was araied in purple &
skarlat, & guilded with golde, & precious
stones, and pearles, and had a cup of golde
in her hand, ful of [g] abominations, and filthines of her fornication.
5 And in her forhead *was* a name written, [h] A Mysterie, great Babylon, the mother of whoredomes, and abominations of
the earth.
6 And I sawe the woman drunken with the
blood of Saintes, & with the blood of the
Martyrs of Iesus: & when I sawe her, I wōdred with great marueile.
7 Then the Angel said vnto me, Wherefore marueilest thou? I wil shewe thee the
mysterie of the woman, and of the beast,
that beareth her, which hathe seuen heads,
and ten hornes.
8 The [i] beast that thou hast sene, was, and
is not, and shal ascende out of the bottomles pit, and shal go into perdicion, and
they that dwell on the earth, shal wondre
(whose names are not writen in the Boke
of life from the fundacion of the worlde)
when they beholde the beast that was, and
is not, and yet is.
9 Here *is* the minde that hathe wisdome.
The seuen heads are [k] seuen mountaines,
whereon the woman sitteth: they are also
[l] seuen Kings.
10 Fiue are fallen, and one is, and another is
not yet come: and whē he cometh, he must
continue a short space.
11 And the beast that was, and is not, is
euen the [m] eight, and is one of the seuen, &
shal go into destruction.
12 And the ten hornes which thou sawest,
are tē Kings, which yet haue not receiued
a kīgdome, but shal receiue power, as Kīgs
at one houre with the beast.
13 [n] These haue one minde, and shal giue their power, and autoritie vnto the
beast.
14 These shal fight with the Lambe, & the
Lambe shal [o] ouercome them: * for he is
Lord of Lords, & King of Kings: & they
that are on his side, called, and chosen, and
faithful.
15 And he said vnto me, The waters which
thou sawest, where the whore sitteth, are
people, and multitudes, and nations, and
tongues.
16 And the [p] ten hornes which thou sawest
vpon the beast, are they that shal hate the
whore, and shal make her desolate and na
ked, & shal eat her flesh, & burne her with
fyre.
17 For God hathe [q] put in their hearts to ful
fil his wil, & to do with one consent for to
giue their kingdome vnto the beast, vntil
the wordes of God be fulfilled.

a Which was Christ Iesus who wil take vengeance on this Romish harlot.

b Antichrist is cōpared to an harlot because he seduceth ẏ worlde with vaine wordes, doctrines of lies, & outwarde appearāce.

c Meaning, diuers natiōs & countreis.

d The beast signifieth ẏ ancient Rome: ẏ woman that sitteth thereon, the newe Rome which is the Papistrie, whose crueltie and blood sheding is declared by skarlat.

e Ful of idolatrie, superstition and contempt of the true God.

f This woman is the Antichrist, that is, the Pope with ẏ whole bodie of his filthie creatures, as is expounded, vers.18, whose beautie onely standeth in outwarde pompe & impudencie and craft like a strumpet.

g Of false doctrines & blasphemies.

h Which none can knowe to auoide but the elect.

i This is the Romaine empire which being fallen into decay, the whore of Rome vsurped autoritie, and proceded from the deuil and thether shal returne.

k Which are about Rome.

l For after ẏ ẏ empire was decayed in Nero, Galba, Otho, Vitellius, Vespasiā & Titus dyed in lesse then fourtene yeres and reigned as Kings: Domitiā then reigned, and after him Cocceius Nerua which was the seuenth.

m He meaneth Traian the emperor who was a Spanyard & adopted by Nerua, but because he persecuted ẏ faithful, he goeth also to perditiō

n He signifieth the horrible persecutions which haue bene vnder the empire of Rome, and in all other realmes subiect to the same

1.Tim.6,15. chap.19,16.

o And breake them to shyuers as a porters pot.

p Diuers natiōs as the Gothes, Vandales, Hūnes and other nations which were once subiect to Rome, shal rise agaīst it & destroy it.

q That in stede of doing homage to Christ Iesus, they shulde be cast into a reprobate sense to serue Antichrist, & to dedicat them selues and theirs wholy vnto him.

18 And the womã which thou saweſt, is the
great citie, which reigneth ouer ẏ Kings
of the earth.

CHAP. XVIII.

3.9 The louers of the worlde are sorie for the fall of the whore of Babylon 4 An admonition to the people of God to flee out of her dominion, 20 But they that be of God, haue cause to reioyce for her destruction.

1 AND after these things, I sawe *another* Angel come downe from heauen, hauing great power, so that the earth
was lightened with his glorie.
2 And he cryed out mightely with a loude
voyce, saying, *[a] It is fallen, it is fallen, Babylon ẏ great *citie*, & is become the habita
tion of [b] deuils, and the holde of all fowle
spirits, and a cage of euerie vncleane and
hateful byrde.
3 For [c] all nations haue drõken of the wine
of the wrath of her fornication, and the
Kings of the earth haue committed fornication with her, and the marchãts of the
earth are waxed riche of the abundance of
her pleasures.
4 And I heard another voyce frõ heauen
say, [d] Go out of her, my people, that ye be
not partetakers in her sinnes, and that ye
receiue not of her plagues.
5 For her sinnes are [e] come vp vnto heauen, and God hathe remembred her iniquities.
6 [f] Rewarde her, euẽ as she hathe rewarded
you, and giue her double according to her
workes: & in the cup that she hathe filled
to you, fil her the double.
7 In asmuche as she glorified her self, and
liued in pleasure, so muche giue ye to her
torment and sorowe: for she saith in her
heart, * I sit being [g] a quene, and am no
[h] widowe, and shal se no mourning.
8 Therefore shal her plagues come at one
day, death, and sorowe, and famine, & she
shalbe burnt with fyre: for strong is the
Lord God which wil condemne her.
9 And the Kings of the earth shal bewaile
her, & lament for her, which haue cõmitted fornication, & liued in pleasure with
her, when they shal se the smoke of her
burning,
10 And shal stande a farre of for feare of
her torment, saying, Alas, alas, the great
citie Babylon, the mightie citie: for in one
houre is thy iudgement come.
11 And the [i] marchãts of the earth shal wepe and waile ouer her: for no man byeth
their ware any more.
12 The ware of golde and siluer, and of
precious stone, and of pearles, and of fine
linen, and of purple, and of silke, and of
skarlet, & of all maner of Thyne [k] wood,
and of all vessels of yuorie, and of all vessels of moste precious wood, & of brasse, and of yron, and of marble,

Isa.21,9. ierem 51,8. chap.14,8.

a This description of the ouerthrowe of ẏ great whore is like to that whereby the prophetes vse to declare the destruction of Babylon

b He describeth Rome to be ẏ sincke of all abomination and deuelishnes, and a kinde of hel.

c The greateſt parte of the worlde hathe bene abused & seduced by this spiritual whoredome.

d When God threateneth ẏ wicked, he euer cõforteth & counseleth his what they oght to do, ẏ is, that they do not cõmunicat with ẏ sinnes of the wicked.

Isa.47,8.

e The greke worde is, that her sinnes so followe one an other, and so rise one after another, that they growe to suche an heape, ẏ at length they touche ẏ verie heauen

f Blessed is he that cã repaye to the whore the like, as is writen psal. 137,9.

g The glorious boasting of the strompet

h But ful of people & mightie.

i Bothe they that temporally haue had profite by the strumpet, and also the spiritual marchãts shal for sorow & wãt of their gaine crie out and despaire.

k Which is verie odoriferous and precious.

13 And of synamon, and odours, and ointments, and franckinsence, and wine, and
oile, and fine floure, and wheat, & beastes,
and shepe, and horses, and [l] charets, & seruants, and [m] soules of men.
14 (And the [n] apples that thy soule lusted
after, are departed from thee, & all things
which were fat and excellent, are departed
from thee, and thou shalt finde them no
more)
15 The marchãnts of these things which
were waxed riche, shal stand a farre of frõ
her, for feare of her torment, weping and
wailing,
16 And saying, Alas, alas, the great citie,
that was clothed in fine linen and purple,
and skarlet, and guilded with golde, and
precious stone, and pearles.
17 For in one houre so great riches are come to desolation. And euerie shippe master, and all the people that occupie shippes, and shipmen, and whosoeuer trauail
on the sea, shal stand a farre of,
18 And crye, when they se the smoke of her
burning, saying, What *citie was* like vnto
this great citie?
19 And they shal cast [o] dust on their heads,
and crye weping, and wailing, & say, Alas,
alas, the great citie, wherein were made
riche all that had shippes on the sea by
her * costlines: for in one houre she is made desolate.
20 O heauen, reioyce of her, and ye holie
Apostles and Prophetes: for God hathe
[p] giuen your iudgement on her.
21 Then a mightie Angel toke vp a stone like a great milstone, * & cast it into the sea,
saying, With suche violẽce shal the great
citie Babylon be cast, and shalbe [q] founde
no more.
22 And the voyce of harpers, & musicians,
and of pipers, & trumpetters shalbe heard
no more in thee, and no craftes man, of
whatsoeuer crafte *he be*, shalbe founde any more in thee: and the sounde of a milstone shalbe heard no more in thee.
23 And the light of a candle shal shine no
more in thee: and the voyce of the bridegrome and of the bride shalbe heard no
more in thee: for thy [r] marchants were the
great men of the earth: and with thine inchantements were deceiued all nations.
24 And in her was founde the blood of the
Prophetes, and of the Saintes, and of all
that were slaine vpon the earth.

l Suche as the wantons vse at Rome

m This is the vileſt ware ẏ these marchãts sel, and beſt cheape, which soules notwithstanding ẏ Sonne of God redemed with his precious blood, 1. pet. 1,19.

n That is, the things which thou louedſt beſt.

o And so shewe signes of great sorowe.

* Or, noble eſtate.

p And hathe reuenged your cause in punishing her.

Ier.51,63.

q It shal not be like to other cities ẏ may be buylded againe, but it shalbe destroyed without mercie.

r The Romish prelates and marchants of soules are as Kings & princes: so that their couetousnes and pride must be punished: secondely their craftes & deceites, & and thirdly their crueltie.

CHAP. XIX.

1 Praises are giuen vnto God for iudging the whore, & for auenging the blood of his seruants. 10 The Angel wil not be worshipped. 17 The foules and birdes are called to the slaughter.

1 And

1 AND after these thigs I heard a great
voyce of a great multitude in heauen, saying, [a] Hallelu-iah, saluacion & glo
rie, and honour, and power *be* to the Lord
our God.
2 For [b] true & righteous *are* his iudgemēts:
for he hathe condemned the great whore,
which did corrupt the earth with her fornicacion, and hath aduenged the blood of
his seruants *shed* by her hand.
3 And againe they said, Hallelu-iah: & her
[c] smoke rose vp for euermore.
4 And the foure and twentie Elders, & the
foure [d] beastes fell downe, and worshiped
God that sate on the throne, saying, [e] A-
men, Hallelu-iah.
5 Then a voyce came out of the throne,
saying, Praise our God, all ye his seruants,
and ye that feare him, bothe smale and
great.
6 And I heard like a voyce of a great multitude, and as the voyce of manie waters,
and as the voyce of strong thondrings,
saying, Hallelu-iah: for our Lord God almightie hathe reigned.
7 Let vs be glad and reioyce, and giue glorie to him: for the [f] mariage of the Lābe
is come, and his wife hathe made her self
readie.
8 And to her was grāted, that she shulde be
araied with pure fyne linen and shining:
for the fine linen is the righteousnes of
Sainctes.
9 Then [g] he said vnto me, Write, * Blessed
are they which are [h] called vnto the Lambes supper. And he said vnto me, These
wordes of God are true.
10 And I fell before his feete, * to worship
him: but he said vnto me, Se thou do it
not: I am thy fellowe seruant, and one of
thy brethren, which haue the [i] testimonie
of Iesus. Worship God: for the [k] testimonie of Iesus, is the spirit of prophecie.
11 And I sawe heauen open, and beholde a
white [l] horse, and he that sate vpon him,
was called, [m] Faithful & true, & he [n] iudgeth and fighteth righteously.
12 And his eyes *were* as a flame of fyre, &
on his head *were* [o] manie crownes: and he
had a name written, that no man [p] knewe
but him self.
13 And * he was clothed with a garment
dipte in [q] blood, and his name is called,
THE [r] WORDE OF GOD.
14 And the [f] warriers which were in heauē,
folowed him vpon white horses, clothed
with fine linen white and pure.
15 And out of his mouth went out a sharpe
[t] sworde, that with it he shulde smite the
heathen: for he * shal rule thē with a rodde
of yron: for he it is that treadeth the wine
presse of the fiercenes and wrath of almightie God.
16 And he hathe vpon his garment, and vpon his [u] thigh a name written, * THE
KING OF KINGS, AND LORD
OF LORDS.
17 And I sawe an Angel stand in the [x] sunne, who cryed with a lowde voyce, saying
to all the foules that did flye by the middes of heauen, Come, and gather your selues together vnto the supper of the great
God,
18 That ye may eat the flesh of Kings, &
the flesh of hie Captaines, and the flesh
of mightie men, and the flesh of horses,
and of them that sit on them, and the flesh
of all fre mē and bondemen, and of smale
and great.
19 And I sawe the beast, and the Kings of
the earth, and their [y] warriers gathered
together to make battel against him, that
sate on the horse & against his souldiers.
20 But the beast was [z] taken, and with
him that false prophete that wroght miracles before him, whereby he deceiued
them that receiued the beastes marke, &
them that worshiped his image. These
bothe were aliue cast into a lake of fyre,
burning with brimstone.
21 And the remnant were slayne with the
sworde of him that sitteth vpon the horse,
which cometh out of his mouth, and all
the foules were filled full with their flesh.

a That is, praise ye God, because ŷ Antichrist & all wickednes is takē out of the worlde.
b So that all the Saintes are confirmed and oght nothing to doute of the saluacion of ŷ faithful.
c The wicked shalbe burned in continual fyre, ŷ neuer shalbe extinguished.
d By the foure beasts are mēt all creatures.
e Signifying ŷ his iudgemēts are true & iust, and ŷ we oght to praise him euermore for the destruction of the Pope.
f God made Christ ŷ bridegrome of his Church at the beginning, and at the last day it shalbe fully accomplished when we shal be ioyned ŵ our head.
Mat.22,2.
chap.14,13.
g That is, the Angel.
Chap.22,9.
h Whome God of fre mercie calleth to be partakers of his heauenlie graces, & deliuereth from ŷ filthie pollucions of Antichrist.
i Who am charged to testifie of Iesus, or ŵ am partaker of ŷ same Gospel & faith.
Isa.63,2.
k He sheweth that none oght to be worshiped but onely God, & that he is of their nōber whome God vseth to reueile his secrets by to the Prophetes, ŷ they may declare them to others, also that we must beleue no other spirit of prophecie, but that which doeth testifie of Iesus, and lead vs to him.
l Whereby is signified that Iesus Christ our Iudge shalbe victorious, and shal triumph ouer his enemies.
m He meaneth Christ.
n So that the wicked shal tremble before his face.
o To shewe that he was ruler of all the worlde.
p That is, none can haue so ful reuelacion how Christ is verie God, eternal, infinite and almightie, as he him self.
q Whereby is signified his victorie, and the destruction of his enemies.
r Signifying that Iesus Christ, which is the worde, is made flesh, and is our Lord, our God and the Iudge of the quicke and dead.
f This declareth that his Angels shal come with him to iudge the worlde.

t Which driueth the wicked into eternal fyre.
Psal.2,9.
2.Tim.6,15.
chap.17,14.
u Which declareth his humanitie, wherein he is Lord of all, and shal iudge ŷ world.
x This signifieth ŷ the day of iudgement shalbe cleare and euident; so that none shal be hid: for the trumpet shal blowe a lowde & all shal vnderstand it.
y For the Pope & ŷ worldlie princes shal fight against Christ, euen vntil this last day.
z The ouerthrowe of the beast and his ŵ shalbe chiefly accomplished at the seconde cōming of Christ.

CHAP. XX.

2 *Satan being bounde for a certeine time.* 7 *And after let lose, vexeth the Church grieuously.* 10. 14 *And after the worlde is iudged, he and his are cast into the lake of fyre.*

1 AND I sawe an [a] Angel come downe
from heauen, hauing the [b] keye of
the bottomles pit, and a great chaine in
his hand.
2 And he toke the dragon that olde serpēt,
which is the deuil and Satan, and he bounde him [c] a thousand yeres,
3 And cast him into the bottomles pit, and
he shut him vp, and sealed *the dore* vpon
him, that he shulde deceiue the people no
more, til ŷ [d] thousand yeres were fulfilled:
for after that he must be losed for a litle
season.
4 And I sawe [e] seates: and they sate vpon

a This Angel representeth ŷ ordre of ŷ Apostles, whose vocacion & office was from heauē: or may signifie Christ, ŵ shulde treade downe the serpents head.
b Hereby he meaneth the Gospel whereby hel is shut up to ŷ faithful, & Satan is chained that he cā not hurt them, yea & ŷ ministers hereby open it to the infideles, but through their impietie and stubbernes.
c That is, from Christs natiuitie vnto the time of Pope Syluester the seconde: so long the pure doctrine shulde after a sorte remaine.
d After this terme Satan had greater power then he had before.
e The glorie and autoritie of them that suffer for Christs sake.

them, and iudgemēt was giuen vnto them,
and *I sawe* the soules of them, that were
beheaded for the witnes of Iesus, and for
the worde of God, & which did not worship ẏ beast, nether his image, nether had
taken his marke vpon their forheads, or
on their hands: and they liued, & reigned
with Christ a [f] thousand yere.
5 But the rest of the [g] dead men shal not liue againe, vntil the thousand yeres be finished: this is the [h] first resurrection.
6 Blessed and holie is he, that hathe parte
in the first resurrection: *for* on suche the
[i] seconde death hathe no power: but they
[k] shalbe the Priests of God and of Christ,
& shal reigne with him a [l] thousand yere.
7 * And when the thousand yeres are [m] expired, Satan shalbe losed out of his prison,
8 And shal go out to deceiue the people,
which are in the foure quarters of the e-
arth: *euen* [n] Gog and Magog, to gather
them together to battel, whose nomber *is*,
as the sand of the sea.
9 And they went vp into the plaine of the
earth, ẇ compassed the tents of the Saintes about, and the beloued citie: but fyre
came downe from God out of heauen, &
deuoured them.
10 And the deuil that deceiued them, was
cast into a lake of fyre & brimstone, where
the beast and the false prophet shalbe tormented euen day and night for euermore.
11 And I sawe a great white throne, and [o] o-
ne that sate on it, from whose face fled a-
way bothe the earth and heauen, & their
place was no more founde.
12 And I sawe the dead, bothe great & smal
stand before God: and the [p] bokes were o-
pened, & * another boke was opened, which
is *the boke* of life, and the dead were iudged of those things, which were written
in the bokes, according to their workes.
13 And the sea gaue vp her dead, which were in her, and [q] death and hell deliuered
vp the dead, which were in them: & they
were iudged euerie mā according to their
workes.
14 And [r] death and hell were cast into the
lake of fyre: this is the seconde death.
15 And whosoeuer was not founde written
in the boke of life, was cast into the lake
of fyre.

f That is, whiles thei haue remained in this life.
g He meaneth thē, which are spiritually dead: for in whome Satā liueth, he is dead to God.
h Which is to receiue Iesus Christ in true faith, & to rise from sinne in newenes of life.
Ezek.39,2.
i The death of the soule, ẇ is eternal damnacion.
k Shalbe true partakers of Christ and of his dignitie.
l That is, for euer.
m After that the chaine is brokē and the true preaching of Gods worde is corrupt.
n By them are ment diuers & strāge enemies of the Church of God, as the Turke, the Sarazins and others, read Ezek 38,2, by whome the Church of God shulde be grieuously tormented.
Philip.4,4. chap.3,5. & 21,23.
o Which was Christ, prepared to iudgement ẇ glorie and maiestie.
p Euerie mans conscience is as a boke wherein his dedes are writen, ẇ shal appeare whē God openeth the boke.
q Vnderstanding all kindes of death whereby men haue bene slayne.
r Hell & death ẇ are the last enemies, shalbe destroied.

CHAP. XXI.

1.24. The blessed estate of the godlie, 8.27 And the miserable condicion of the wicked. 11 The description of the heauenlie Ierusalem, and of the wife of the Lambe.

1 AND I sawe * a new heauen, & a new
earth: [a] for * the first heauen, and the
first earth were [b] passed away, & there was
no more sea.
2 And I Iohn sawe the [c] holie citie newe
Ierusalem come [d] downe from God out
of heauen, prepared as a bride trimmed
for her housband.
3 And I heard a great voyce out of heauen,
saying, Beholde, the Tabernacle of God
is with men, and he wil dwell with them: &
they shalbe his people, and God him self
shalbe their God with them.
4 * And God shal wipe [e] away all teares frō
their eyes: & there shalbe no more death,
nether sorowe, nether crying, nether shal
there be anie more paine: for ẏ first things
are passed.
5 And he that sate vpon the throne, said,
* Beholde, I make all things new: and he
said vnto me, Write: for these wordes are
faithful and true.
6 And he said vnto me, * It is done, I am α
and ω, the beginning and the end. I wil
giue to him that is a thirst, of the [f] well of
the water of life frely.
7 He that ouercometh, shal inherit all
things, and I wil be his God, & he shalbe
my sonne.
8 But the [g] fearful and vnbeleuing, and
the [h] abominable and murderers, & whoremongers, and sorcerers, and idolaters, &
all liars shal haue their parte in the lake,
which burneth with fyre and brimstone,
which is the seconde death.
9 And there came vnto me one of the seuen Angels, which had the seuen viales ful
of the seuen last plagues, and talked with
me, saying, Come: I wil shewe thee the
[i] bride, the Lambes wife.
10 And he caryed me away in the spirit to
a great & an hie mountaine, & he shewed
me the great [k] citie, holie Ierusalē, [l] descending out of heauen from God,
11 Hauing the glorie of God: and her shining was like vnto a stone most precious,
as a [m] Iasper stone cleare as cristal,
12 And had a great [n] wall and hie, and had
twelue [o] gates, and at the gates twelue Angels, and the names written, which are the
twelue tribes of the children of Israel.
13 On the East parte *there were* thre gates,
and on the Northside thre gates, on the
Southside thre gates, *and* on the Westside
thre gates.
14 And the wall of the citie had twelue
fundacions, and in them the names of the
Lambs twelue [p] Apostles.
15 And he that talked with me, had a goldē
rede to measure the citie with all, and the
gates thereof, and the wall thereof.
16 And the citie lay foure square, and the
length is as large as the bredth of it, and
he measured the citie with the rede, twelue
thousand furlongs: and the length, and the
bredth, and the height of it are equal.

17 And

Isa.65,17. & 66,21. 2.Pet 2,13.
a All things shalbe renued and restored into a moste excellent and perfect estate, and therefore the day of the resurrection is called, The day of restauracion of all thīgs, Act 3,21.
b For all things shalbe purged from their corruption, and the faithful shal enter into heauen with their head Christ.
c The holie companie of the elect.
d Meaning, that God by his diuine maiestie wil glorifie & renewe his, & take them vnto him.
Isa.25,8. chap.7,17.
e All occasiōs of sorowes shalbe taken away: so that they shal haue perpetual ioy.
Isa.43,19. 2.cor.5,17.
Chap.1,8. & 22,13.
f I that am ẏ eternal life, wil giue vnto mine to drinke of the liuelie waters of this euerlastīg life.
g Thei which feare man more then God.
h Thei which mocke & iest at religion.
i Meaning the Church, which is maried to Christ by faith.
k By this description is declared the incomprehensible excellēcie, ẇ the heauenlie companie do enioye.
l It is said to come downe from heauen, because all the benefites that the Church hathe, they acknowledge it to come of God through Christ.
m Euer grene & florishing.
n Signifying ẏ ẏ faithful shal be surely kept in heauen.
o That is, place ynough to enter: for els we knowe there is but one way & one gate, euen Iesus Christ.
p For the Apostles were meanes whereby Iesus Christ the true fundacion was reueiled to the worlde.

17 And he measured the wall thereof, an hũdreth, fortie & foure cubites, by the measure of man, that is, of the Angel.
18 And the buylding of the wall of it was of
Iasper : and the citie was pure golde like
vnto cleare glasse.
19 And the fundacions of the wall of the
citie were garnished with all maner of
precious stones : the first fundacion *was*
Iasper: the secõd of Saphire: the third of a
Chalcedonie: the fourth of an Emeraude:
20 The fift of a Sardonyx: the sixt of a Sar
dius : the seuenth of a Chrysolite : the
eight of a Beryl: the ninth of a Topaze: yͤ
tenth of a Chrysoprasus : the eleuẽth of a
Iacinth: the twelueth an Amethist.
21 And the twelue gates *were* twelue pearles, and euerie gate *is* of one pearle, and
the strete of the citie *is* pure gold, as shining glasse.
22 And I sawe no Temple therein: for the
Lord God almightie and the [q] Lambe a-
re the Temple of it.
23 *And the citie hathe no nede of the sunne, nether of the moone to shine in it : for
yͤ glorie of God did light it: & the Lambe
is the light of it.
24 *And the people which are saued, shal
walke in the light of it: and the [r] Kings of
the earth shal bring their glorie and honour vnto it,
25 *And the gates of it shal not be shut by
day: for there shalbe no night there.
26 And the glorie, and honour of the Gentiles shalbe broght vnto it.
27 And there shal entre into it none vncleane thing, nether whatsoeuer worketh abomination or lies : but they which are writen in the Lambes * Boke of life.

[q] This declareth yͭ Christ is God inseparable with his Father.
Isa.60,13.
Isa.60,5.
[r] Here we se as in infinit other places yͤ Kings & Princes (contrarie to that wicked opinion of yͤ Anabaptists) are partakers of the heauenlie glorie, if they rule in yͤ feare of the Lord.
Isa.60,11.
Phili.4,4.
chap.3,5.
& 10,11.

CHAP. XXII.

1 The riuer of the water of life. 2 The frutefulnes & light of the citie of God. 6 The Lord giueth euer his seruants warning of things to come. 9 The Angel wil not be worshipped. 18 To the worde of God may nothing be added nor diminished there from.

1 AND he shewed me a pure [a] riuer of
water of life, cleare as crystal, proceding out of the throne of God, and of
the Lambe.
2 In the [b] middes of the strete of it, and of
ether side of the riuer, was the tre of life,
which bare twelue maner of frutes, & gaue frute euerie [c] moneth : & the leaues of
the tre *serued* to heale the [d] nations with.
3 And there shalbe no more cursse, but the
throne of God & of the Lambe shalbe in
it, and his seruants shal serue him.
4 And they shal se his face, and his Name
shalbe in their forheades.
5 *And there shalbe no [e] night there, and
they nede no candle, nether light of yͤ sun
ne : for the Lord God giueth them light,
and they shal reigne for euermore.
6 And he said vnto me, These wordes are
faithful and true : & the Lord God of the
holie Prophetes sent his Angel to shewe
vnto his seruants the things which must
shortely be fulfilled.
7 Beholde, I come shortely. Blessed *is* he yͭ
kepeth the wordes of the prophecie of
this boke.
8 And I am Iohn, which sawe and heard
these things: and when I had heard & sene, * I [f] fell downe to worship before the
fete of the Angel, which shewed me these
things.
9 But he said vnto me, Se thou *do it* not: for
I am thy felowe seruant, & of thy brethrẽ
the Prophets, and of them which kepe the
wordes of this boke: worship God.
10 And he said vnto me, [g] Seale not yͤ wordes of the prophecie of this boke : for the
time is at hand.
11 He that is vniust, let him be vniust stil:
& he which is filthie, let him be filthie stil:
and he yͭ is righteous, let him be righteous
stil: & he yͭ is holie, let him be holie stil.
12 And beholde, I come shortly, & my re
warde is with me, *to giue euerie man according as his worke shalbe.
13 I am * α and ω, the beginning & the end,
the first and the last.
14 Blessed *are* they, that do his commandements, that their right may be in the [h] tre
of life, & may entre in through the gates
into the citie.
15 For without *shalbe* dogges & enchãters,
& whoremongers, & murtherers, & idolaters, & whosoeuer loueth or maketh [i] lyes.
16 I Iesus haue sent mine Angel, to testifie
vnto you these things in the Churches : I
am the roote & the [k] generaciõ of Dauid,
and the bright morning [l] starre.
17 And the Spirit and the bride say, Come.
And let him that heareth, say, [m] Come: &
let him yͭ is a [n] thirst, come: & * let whosoe
uer [o] wil, take of the water of life frely.
18 For I protest vnto euerie man that heareth the wordes of the prophecie of this
boke, * if any man shal adde vnto these
things, God shal adde vnto him the plagues, that are writen in this boke.
19 And if any man shal diminish of yͤ wordes of yͤ boke of this prophecie, God shal
take away his parte out of the Boke of life, and out of the holie citie, and frõ those
things which are writen in this boke.
20 He which testifieth these things, saith,
[p] Surely, I come quickely. Amen. Euen so
[q] come, Lord Iesus.
21 The grace of our Lord Iesus Christ *be*
with you all, Amen.

Chap. XXII.
[a] He alludeth to the visible paradise to set forthe more sensibly the spiritual : and this agreeth wͭ that which is writen, Ezek. 47,1.
[b] Meaning yͭ Christ who is the life of his Church, is commune to all his and not peculiar for any one sorte of people.
[c] For there are all things pleasant & ful of all contentation continually.
[d] Which some time were vnpure as Gẽtiles, but now are purged & made whole by Christ.
Isa.60,15.
[e] The light shal be vnchangeable and shine for euer.

[f] Now this is the seconde time that he suffered him self to be caried away with the excellencie of yͤ persone: wͨ is to admonish vs of our infirmitie & readines to fall, except God strengthẽ vs miraculously wͭ his Spirit.
Chap 19,10.
[g] This is not then as the other Prophecies which were commanded to be hyd til the time appointed, as in Daniel 12,4, because yͭ these things shulde be quickely accomplished, & did now begin
[h] They shal liue eternally wͭ yͤ Sõne of God
[i] That mainteine false doctrine and delite therein.
[k] That is, a true and natural man and yet God equal wͭ my Father.
Rom.2,6.
Isa 41,4.
& 44,6.
chap.1,8.
& 18,6.
[l] For Christ is the light yͭ giueth light to euerie one yͭ commeth into this worlde.
[m] Let them be afraid of Gods horrible iudgements, & assone as thei heare the Lambe call, let them come.
Isa.55,1.
[n] He that feleth him self oppressed with afflictions, and desireth the heauẽlie graces and comfort.
[o] That is, whẽ God begineth to reforme ŏ wil by his Spirit.
[p] Seing the Lord is at hãd, we oght to be constant and reioyce, but we must beware we esteme not the length nor shortenes of yͤ Lords cõming by our owne imagination, 2. Pet.3,9
[q] This declareth the earnest desire that the faithful haue to be deliuered out of these miseries, and to be ioyned with their head Christ Iesus.

A BRIEF TABLE OF THE INTERPRETATION OF THE PROPRE NAMES which are chiefly founde in the olde Testamēt, wherein the first nomber signifieth the chapter: the seconde the verse.

Whereas the wickednes of time, and the blindnes of the former age hathe bene suche that all things altogether haue bene abused and corrupted, so that the very right names of diuerse of the holie men named in the Scriptures haue bene forgotten, and now seme strange vnto vs, and the names of infants that shulde euer haue some godlie aduertisments in them, and shulde be memorials and markes of the children of God receiued into his housholde, hathe bene hereby also changed and made the signes and badges of idolatrie and heathenish impietie, we haue now set forthe this table of the names that be moste vsed in the olde Testament with their interpretations, as the Ebrewe importeth, partly to call backe the godlie frō that abuse, when they shal know the true names of the godlie fathers, & what they signifie, that their children now named after them may haue testimonies by their very names, that they are within that faithful familie that in all their doings had euer God before their eyes, and that they are bounde by these their names to serue God from their infancie & haue occasion to praise him for his workes wroght in them & their fathers: but chiefly to restore the names to their integritie, whereby many places of the Scriptures and secret mysteries of the holie Gost shal better be vnderstand. We haue medled rarely with the Greke names, because their interpretation is vncerteine, & many of thē are corrupted from their original, as we may also se these Ebrewe names set in the margent of this table, which haue bene corrupted by the Grecians. Now for the other Ebrewe names that are not here interpretate, let not the diligent reader be careful: for he shal finde them in places moste cōuenient amongs the annotations: at least so many as may seme to make for any edification, and vnderstanding of the Scriptures.

A

Arón, or Aháron. a teacher Exod.4,14
Abdia. ¶Abdá, a seruãt.1.King.chap.4.ver.6.
Abdeél, a seruant of God, Ierem.36,26.
Abdai. Abdí, my seruant.1.Chron.6.7
Abdi and Audias. Abdiáh, a seruant of the Lord.1.King.18,3. & Obadiáh one of the twelue Prophetes.
Abdiél, the same.1.Chron.5,15
Abdenago. Abéd-negó, seruant of shining.Dan.1,44.
Abél, mourning, the name of a citie, but Habél, the name of a man, doeth signifie vanitie. Gen.4,2
Abagatha. Abgathá, father of the wine presse.
Abiáh, the wil of the Lord.2.Chro.29,1
Abiám, father of the sea.1.King.14,31
Abisaph. Abiasáph, a gathering father.1.Chro.6,33
Abiathár, father of the remnant, or excellent father.1.King.22,21
Abidá, father of knowledge. Gen.25,4
Abidán, father of iudgement. Nomb.1,11
Abiél, my father is God.1.King.9,1
Abiézer, the fathers helpe.Iof.17,2
Abigal. Abigáil, the fathers ioye.1.King.25,3
Abihâil, the father of strength. Nom.3,35
Abiu. Abihú, he is a father. Exod.6,23
Abiud. Abihúd, the father of praise.1.Chro.8,3
Abilene, lamentable. Luk.3,1
Abimáel, a father from God. Gen.10,25
Abimélech, the Kings father, or a father of counsel, or the chief King. Gen.20,3
Aminadab. Abinadád, a father of a vowe, or of a free minde, or prince.1.King.16,8

Abinoám, father of beautie.Iud.4,6 Abinoom
Abirám, an high father.1.King.16,34 Abirom.
Abishág, the fathers ignorance.1.King.1,3
Abishái, the fathers rewarde.1.King.26,6
Abishalóm, the father of peace, or the peace of the father.1.King.15,2 Abshalon.
Abishúa, the father of saluation.1.Chro.6.4 Abisue.
Abishúr, the father of a song, or of a wall, or of righteousnes.1, Chro.2,29
Abitál, the father of the dew.2.King.3,4
Abitób, the father of goodnes.1.Chro.8,11 Abitub.
Abnér, the fathers candel.1.Sam.14,49
Abrám, an high father. Gen.11,31
Abrahám, a father of a great multitude, as ẏ name was changed. Gen.17,5
Abshalóm, a father of peace, or the fathers peace, or rewarde.2.Sam.3,3 Abesalom. Abessalom.
¶Achan, troubling. Ioshu.7,1. who is called Achár.1.Chron.2,7
¶Adadézer, read Adarézer, beautiful helpe.
Adaiáh, the witnes of the Lord.1.Chro.6,41 Adaias.
Adaliáh, pouertie. Ester.9,8
Adam, man, earthlie, read Gen.2,15
Adiél, the witnes of God.1.Chro.4,36
Adoniáh, the Lord is the ruler.2.Sam.3,4 Adonias.
Adonibézek, the Lords thunder. Iud.1,5
Adonikám, the Lord is risen. Neh.2,13
Adoniram, the high Lord.1.King.4,6
Adonizédek, the Lords iustice.Iof.10,1
¶Agabús, a greshopper. Act.11,28
Agár, a stranger. Gen.16,1
¶Aház, taking, or possesing.2.King.16,1

Ahaſuéros,a prince or head.Dan.9,1
Ahbã,a brother of vnderſtãding.1.Chr.2,29
Ahiiáh,brother of the Lord.1.Chro.2,26
Ahimáaz,brother of councel.1.Sam.14,49
Ahimán,brother of ỳ right hand.Nom.13,23
Ahimélech,a Kings brother.1.Sam.21,1
Ahimóth,a brother of death.1.Chro.6,25
Ahinóam,the brothers beautie.1.Sam.14,49
Ahiór,the brothers light.Iud.5,5
Ahalab Ahiláb,an heartie brother.Iud.1,31
Ahara Ahráh,a ſwete ſauoring medow.1.Chro.8,1
Achiam Ahikám, a brother ariſing, or aduenging. 2.King.22,12
Ahiézer,the brothers helpe.Nomb.1,12
Aholáh,a manſion or dwelling in her ſelf.
Aholibáh,my manſion in her.Ezek.23,4
Aod Ahud,praiſing or confeſsing.Iud.3,15
Aluan ¶Alián,high.1.Chro.1,40
¶Amálek,a licking people.Gen.36,21
Amariáh,the Lord ſaid, or the Lãbe of the Lord.Zephan.1,1
Amaſá,ſparing the people.2.Sam.17,25
Amaſhái,the gift of the people.1.Chro.6,24
Amaſhſi,ỳ treading of the people. Neh.11,12
Amaſiáh,ỳ burden of the Lord.2.Chro.17,15
Amithí,true or fearing.2.King.14,25
Ammiél,a people of God,or God with me. 1.Chron.3,5
Ammiſhádai, the people of the Almightie. Nomb.1,12
Ammon Ammon,a people.Gen.19,38
Aminon Amon,faithful.2.King.21,18
Amos,a burden,one of the twelue Prophets.
Amoz,ſtrong,the father of Iſhai.Iſa.1,1
Amzí,ſtrong.1.Chron.6,46
Annas ¶Anáh,afflictĩg,anſwerĩg,or ſingĩg. Ge.36,2 & Hanna,gratious or merciful.1.Sam.1,2
Ananiáh,the cloude of the Lord.Act.5,1
Andréas,manlie.Mat.4,18
Anúb,a grape.1.Chron.4,8
Antipas,for all,or againſt all.Reuela.2,13
Aphdeno ¶Apadno,ỳ wrath of his iudgemẽt.Da.11,46
Apollos Apolló,a deſtroyer.18,24.ỳ name alſo of an idole.
Apphía,brĩgĩg forthe,or encreaſing.Phile.2
Ram ¶Arám,hight or their curſe.Gen.10,23
Aran,oren Arbel,Bel or God hathe aduẽged.Hoſ.10,15
Archeláus,a prince of the people.Mat.2,22
Arelí,the altar of God.Gen.46,16
Arétas,verteous.2.Macc.5
Artahſháſte,feruent to ſpoile.Ezra 7,21
¶Aſá,a phyſicion.1.King.15,8
Aſaél,God hathe wroght.2.Sam.2,18
Aſáph,gathering.1.Chron.6,39
Aſhriel Aſharélah,the bleſſednes of God.1.Chr.25,2
Aſhbél,an olde fyre.46,21
Aſhér,bleſſednes.Gen.30,13
Aſael Aſhiél,the worke of God.1.Chro.4,35
Aſhúr,bleſſed or trauailing.Gen.10,21
Aſmodeus,a deſtroyer.Tob 3,8
Aſtyages,gouernour of the citie.Dan.13,64
Ataria ¶Ataráh,a crowne.1.Chron.2,26.
Athaiáh,the time of the Lord.Nehe.11,4
Athaliáh,time for the Lord.2.King.8,26
¶Aza,ſtrength.Eſra 2,47
Azaniáh,hearkening the Lord.Neh.10,9 Azanias
Azaréel,the helpe of God.1.Chro.12,6
Azariáh,helpe of the Lord.4.King.14,21 Aſarias
Azarikám,helpe riſing vp.Neh.11,14
Azmáueth ſtrength of death.2.Sam.23,30 Azmoth
Azubáh,forſaken.1.King.22,43
Azúr,holpen or helper.Ierem.28,1

B

BAal,Bealim,lord,lords: the name of the idole of ỳ Sydoniãs, or a general name to all idoles,becauſe they were as ỳ lords and owners of all that worſhiped them. Beel
Baaliada,a maſter of knowledge.1. Chr.14,7 Beeliada
Báal-meón, the Lord or maſter of the manſion or the houſe, as alſo Báalzibúl, ſignifieth the ſame. Luk.11,15 Beelmeon Beelmon
Báal-zebúb,the maſter of flies.
Baanáh,in affliction.2.Sam.4,2
Babél,confuſion.Gen.10,10.& 11,9 Babylon
Bacchides,one that holdeth of Bacchus,or a dronkard.1.Macc.7,8.
Bacchenor & bacenor the ſame. 2.Mac.12,15
Badaiáh,the Lord alone.Ezr.10,31 Badaias
Baladán,ancient in iudgement.2.King.20,12
Baldád,olde loue or without loue.Iob 8,1 Bildad
Barachél,bleſsing God.Iob 32,2
Barachiáh,bleſsing the Lord.Zech.1,1
Bar-ionáh,ſonne of a doue.Mat.16,17
Barnabas,the ſonne of conſolation. Act.4,36
Barabbas,ſonne of confuſion.Mat.27,16
Barúch,bleſſed.Ier.32,10
Bathſéba, the ſeuenth daughter, or the daughter of an othe.1.Sam.11,3 Bethſabe
Bathſhúa the daughter of ſaluatiõ.1.Chr.3,5
¶Belſhatsãr,without treaſure,or ſearcher of treaſure.Dan.5,1 Baltaſar Beltesha tzar Beleſhatzar
Benaiáh,the Lords buylding.1.Chro.4,36
Beniamín,ſonne of ỳ right hãd who was firſt called Benoni the ſonne of ſorow. Ge.35,18
Beraiáh,the Lords creature.1.Chro.8,20
Berák,lightening.Iud.4,6
Béred,hail.1.Chron.7,21.
Bethiáh,the Lords daughter.1.Chr.4,18 Phathourah
Bezaleél,in the ſhadow of God.Exod 31,2 Bezeleel
¶Bileám, the ancient of ỳ people.Nom.22,5 Balaam
Bilháh,olde,or fading.Gen.29,29
¶Boas,in powre,or ſtrength.Ruth 2,2 Booz

C

CAiaphas,a ſearcher.Mat.26,57
Calcól,nouriſhing.1.King.4,31
Caléb,as a heart,Nomb.13,6.
Canáan,a merchant.Gen.9,18.
Carmí,my vine. Gen.46,9
Caſeluhím,as pardoned.Gen.10,14. Chaſelon Chaſlonim
¶Cephás,a ſtone.Ioh.1.42
Cephiráh, a lioneſſe.Ezr.2,28
¶Cherúb,as a childe.Ezr.2,57
Chileáb,the reſtraint of the father.2.Sam.3,3
Chilion perfite,or all like a doue. Ruth 1,2
¶Ciſlón,hope,or confidens.Nomb.34,21
¶Clemens,meke.Philip.4,3

Cleopatra, ẏ glorie of ẏ coũtrie.1.Mac.10,57
¶Col-hózeth, seing all. Neh.3,15
Coneniah, ẏ stabilitie of ẏ Lord.2.Chr.31.13
Cosbi, a liar. Nomb.25,18
¶Cusán, Cusí, blacke or an Ethiopiã.2.Sa.18

D

Dilaias Dalaiáh, ẏ poore of the Lord.1.Chro.3,24
Delaias Dalilán, a bucket or cõsumer. Iud.16,4
Damaris, a litle wyfe. Act.17,34
Dan, a iudgement. Gen.14,15
Daniél, iudgement of God. Dan.1,6
Dathán, statute or law. Nomb.16,1
Dauíd, beloued.1.Sam.17,12
¶Deboráh, a worde or a bee. Gen.35,8
Delphón, a droping downe. Est.9,7
Demas, fauoring the people. Col.4,14
Demophón, slaying the people.2.Mac.12,2
Duel Deu-el, knowe God. Nomb.1.14
Debelaim ¶Diblám, a cluster of figges. Hos.1,3
Didymus, a twinne. Iohn 11,16
Dina Dináh, iudgement, Gen.30,21
Diotrephés, nourished of Iupiter
Dishon Dishán, a threshing. Gen.36,21
¶Dodanáh, loue.2.Chro.20,37
Rodanim Dodanim, beloued. Gen.10,4
Doég, careful.1.Sam.21,7
Dorcas, a do. Act.9,39
Dordá, generation of knowledge.3.Kin.4,31
Dositheus, giuen to God.2.Mac.19

E

Eber, passing or passage. Gen.10,23
¶Edén, pleasure.2.King.19,12
Edér, a flocke.1.Chron.23,23
Edóm, reddie or earthie. Gen.25,30
¶Elchánan, the mercie of God. 2.Sam.23,24
Eldaáh, the knowledge of God. Gen.25,4
Eldád, the loue of God. Nomb.11,26
Elead Eleadáh, witnes of God.1.Chr.7,21
Eleasáh, the worke of God.1.Chro.2,39
Eleazarus Eleazár, the helpe of God. Exod.6,22.
Eliazar Eli Eliáb, my God the father. Nomb.16,8
Elias Eliáh, God the lord.1.Chron.8,26
Eliakím, God ariseth. Isa.22,20
Eliám, the people of God.2.Sam.23,34
Eliasáph, the Lord encreaseth. Nomb.1,14
Eliashib, the Lord returneth.1.Chr.3,24
Eliathas Eliathá, thou art my God.1.Chr.25,4
Elehoenái, to the Lord mine eyes.1.Chr.26,3
Elidád, the beloued of God. Nomb.34,21
Elihú, he is my God.1.Chro.12,10
Elmelech Elimélech, my God the King, or the counsel of God. Ruth 1,2
Elionai Elioenái, to him mine eyes.1.Chro.3,23
Eliphál, a miracle of God.1.Chr.11,36
Elipelet Eliphálet, the God of deliuerãce.2.Sam.5,16
Elishua Elisseus Elishá, my God saueth.1.King.19,16
Elisseus Elisa Elisháh, the lambe of God. Gen.10,4
Elishaphár, my God iudgeth.2.Chr.23,1
Elisabeth Elishéba, the othe of God, or the fulnes of God. Exod.6,23
Elizúr, the strength of God. Nomb.1,5
Elkanáh, the zeale of God. Exod.6,24
Elmodéd, God measureth. Gen.10,24
Elnathán, Gods gifte. Ierem.26,22
Elphaal, Gods worke.2. Chro.8,11
Eluzái, God my strength.1.Chr.12,5
Elymás, a corrupter, or sorcerer. Act.13,8
¶Enós, man or miserable. Gen.4,27
¶Epaphroditus, pleasant. Philip.2,25
Epenetus, laudable. Rom.16,5
Epháh, wearie. Gen.25,4
Epher, dust. Gen.25,4 Gephar
Ephráim, fruteful, or encreasing. Gen.41,52 Ephrem
¶Erastus, amiable. Act.19,22
¶Esau, working. Genes.25,25
Eshcól, a cluster. Gen.14,14
Eshék, violence.1.Chron.8,38
Estér, hidde. Est.2,7
¶Ethán, strength.1.Kings 4,31 Esther
¶Eubulus, wise or of good cõusel.2. Tim.4,21 hester
Eupolemus, a good warriour. 1.Macc.8,27
Eutychus, fortunate. Act.20,9
¶Ezbón, hasting to vnderstand.1.Chro.7,7 Assebon
Ezekiél, strength of the Lord. Ezek.1,3
Ezeliáh, nere the Lord.2.Chro.34,7
Ezer, an helpe.1.Chro.4,4 Azaliah
Ezrá, an helper. Ezr.1,7
Ezriél, the helpe of God. Ier.36,26
Ezrikám, an helpe arising.1.Chro.3,23

G

Gaál, an abomination. Iud.9,35
Gabriél, a man of God, or the strength of God, the name of an Angel. Dan.8,16
Gad, a band, or garrison. Gen.30,11
Galál, a rolle.1.Chron.9,15
Gamaliél, Gods rewarde. Act.5,34
Gamariá, a consuming of ẏ Lord. Ier.29,3. Gamariah
Gazabár, a treasurer. Ezr.1,8
¶Gedaliáh, the greatnes of the Lord. Ier.38,1 Godoliah
Gedeon, a breaker or destroyer. Iud.6,13
Gehazí, vallie of vision.2.King.4,12 Giezi
Gerá, a pilgrime, or stranger. Gen.46,21
¶Ginath, a garden.1.King.16,21
¶Gog, a roofe of an house. Ezek.38,2
Goliáth, a captiuitie.1.King.7,4
Gomer, a consumer. Gen.10,2
Gorgias, terrible.1.Macc.3,38

H

Habakúk, a wrasteler. Hab.1,1 Abakuk
Habazaniáh, the hiding of the Lords shilde.
Habiáh, the hiding of the Lord. Nehem.7,63
Hacaliáh, waiting of ẏ Lord.2. Nehem.10,1 Achaliah
Hadád, ioye. Gen.25,15.1. Chr.1,30 Hecheliah Hadar
Hagáb, a grashopper. Nehem.7,46
Haggiáh, the Lords feast.1.Chro.6,29 Hagaba Aggia
Há, Hamathí, indignation, or heat. Ge.10,17 Amatha
Hamdán, heat of iudgement. Gen.36,26 Abatha
Hamúl, merciful. Gen.46,12
Hanaméel, the mercie of God. Ier.32,7 Anameel
Hananéel, the grace of God. Neh.3,1 Haniel
Hanáni, gratious or merciful.1.King.16,7
Hananiáh, grace of the Lord. Iere.37,12 Ananias
Harím, dedicate to God.1.Chro.24,8
Hasadiáh, the mercie of the Lord.1.Chr.3,20 Asadiah
Hattil, an howling for sinne. Ezr.2,57
Hauáh, liuing, or giuing life. Genes.3,20 Eua

Azael Hazaél,seing God.1.King.19,17
Ozea Hazaráh,seing the Lord.Neh.11,5
Chobor ¶Heber,a companion.Gen.46,17
Helchi Helkiáh,the portion of the Lord.2.Kin.18,18
Hanoch Enoch Henóch,taught or dedicate.Gen.5,18
Hépher,a digger or deluer.1.Chr 4,6
Haphsiba. Ephiba. Hephzi-báh,my delite in her.2.King.2,1
Heth,feare or breaking.Gen.23,3
Ezron Hezrí,or Hezro, Hezron,Asari,Esrí
¶Hiél,the Lord liueth.1.King.16,34
Huram! Hirám,the hight of life.2.Sam.5,11
Ezechias Hizkiiáh,strength of the Lord.2.King.18
Obab ¶Hobab,beloued.Nomb.10,29
Hori,a prince.Genes.36,22
Hoshaiáh,saluation of the Lord.Iere.42,1
Hoshea,saluation.Hos.1,1
Hosa,trusting.1.Chron.26,10
Hothám,a seale or signet.1.Chron.7,32
Huziel Hoziél,seing God.1.Chron.23,9
¶Hul,sorow or infirmitie.Genes.10,23
Hur,libertie or prince.1.Chron.4,1
Ousa Husháh,hasting.1.Chron.4,4

I

Iakob IAakób,a supplanter.Genes.25,26
Ioakan Iaakán,destroying.1.Chron.5,13
Esiel Iaasiél,the worke of God.1.Chron.11,47
Iaazaniah,the hearkening of the Lord.2.Kings 25,23
Iobel Iabál,bringing or budding.Gen.4,20
Iabesh,drought.2.Kings 15,10
Iabez,sorowe.1.Chron.4,9
Iabin,vnderstanding.Iosh.11,1
Iachin,stabilitie.Genes.46,10
Iedaiáh Iadiáh,knowing the Lord.Nehem.2,36
Iahel Iaél,a do or ascending.Iud.4,16
Ialeleel Iahalleél,praising God.1.Chr.4,16
Iahaziél,God hasteth.Gen.46,24
Asiel Iahaziel,seing God.Ezr.8,5
Achoel,Iahiel Iahehel,hope in God or beginning in God.Genes.46,14
Iacirus Iair,lightened.Deut.3,14
Iakim,stablishing.1.Chron.8,19
Iambres Iambrí,rebellious.1.Macc.9,37
Iamráh Iamín,right hand.Gen.46,10
Iemuel Iamuél,God is his day.Genes.46,10
Ianoháh,resting.Ios.16,6
Ianúm,sleping.Ios.15,53
Iápheth,persuading or enticing.Gen.5,32
Iaphie Iaphía,lightning.2.Sam.5,16
Iarephél,helth of God.Ios.18,27
Iaríb,fighting or aduenging.Gen.46,10
Iashén,ancient.2.Sam.23,32
Iaasar Iashér,righteous.Ios.21,39
Iasub. Iashúb,a returning.1.Chron.7,1
Iathanael Iathniél,a gifte of God.1.Chron.26,2
Iether Iattír,a remnant or excellent.Iosh.15,48.
Iethrai Ithri,Ithro,Ithron the same.
Iauán,making sad.Gen.10,1
Ionia Iaziél,the strength of God.1.Chron.15,18
Iazíz,brightnes.1.Chro.27,31
¶Ibhác,chosen.2.Kings 5,15
¶Ichabód,where is glorie?1.Sam.4,21
Iaddo ¶Iddo,his confession.1.Chron.27,21

¶Iechoniáh,stabilitie of the Lord.1.Chr.3,16 Chonias
Iedaiáh,the hand of the Lord or confessing the Lord.1.Chron.4,37 Ieddia
Iedidáh,beloued.2.Sam.12,1 Ieddida
Iediel,knowledge of God.1.Chron.7,6
Ieduthun,confessing.1.Chro.9,16
Iehiáh,the Lord liueth.1.Chro.5,13
Iehiél,God liueth.1.Chr.26,21.
Iehoadán,the Lords pleasure.2.King.14,2 Ioadan
Iehoahás,the possessiō of the Lord.2.Kings 23,34 Ioahas
Iehoásh,the fyre of the Lord.2.Kings 11,21 Ioas
Iehohanán,grace or mercie of the Lord.2.Chro.26,3 Ioanā,Iohānes
Iehoiada,the knowledge of ye Lord.2.King.11,15
Iehoiakím,the rising or aduenging of the Lord.2.Kings 23,34 Ioacim
Iehoshaphát,the Lord is ye iudge.1.Chr.3,10 Iosaphat
Iehoshúa,the Lords saluation.Zach.3,1
Iehozadák,the iustice of ye Lord.1.Chr.6,14 Iosedec
Iehudáth,confession or praise.Gen.29,35 Iuda
Iekannáh,the Lord shal arise,establish,or aduenge.1.Chr.2,41 Iacenna
Iekodeám,the burnīg of the people.Ios.15,56
Iephlét,deliuered.1.Chron.7,32.
Iephunnéh,beholding.Nomb.13,7
Ierahmeél,the mercie of God.Ier.36,36
Iéred,ruling.Gen.5,15 Iared
Ieriél,the feare of God.1.Chro.7,2 Ieruel
Ierimóth,fearing death.1.Chr.7,7
Ieroboám,encreasing the people.2.Kin.14,23
Ieroham,high.1.Chro 6,27 Iehoram Ioram
Ierubbaál,let baal aduenge.Iud.6,32 Ierobaal
Ieshaiáh,saluation of the Lord.Isa.1,1. Esaiah,Isaiah
Ieshúa,a sauiour.Mat.1,16 Iesus
¶Igál,redemed.2.Chr.3,22
Igdaliáh,the greatnes of the Lord.Ier.35,4
¶Ioáb,willing or voluntarie.1.Chro.2,16
Iob,sorowful or hated.Iob 1,1 Iobab
Iobamáh,ye buylding of the Lord.1.Chr.9,8
Iochébed,glorious.Exod.6,20 Iochabed
Ioél,willing or beginning.Ioel 1,1
Iokshán,an offence.Gen.25,2 Iech san
Ioktán,a litle one.Gen.10,25 Iectan
Ionáh,a doue.2.Kings 14,25
Ionadáb,voluntarie or willing.2.King.13,5 Iehonadab
Ionathán,the gifte of the Lord.Iud.18,30 Iehonathan
Ioseph,encreasing.Gen.30,24
Ioshabéth,the fulnes of the Lord.2.Chr.22,11 Ieholhabas
Ioshiáh,the fyre of the Lord.2.King.22,3
Iothám,perfite.2.Kings 15,23
Iozabád,endwed.1.Chro.12,20
¶Iphdiáh,the redemption of the Lord.1.Chro.8,25.
Iphtáh,opening.Iud.11,1
¶Irá,a watchman.1.Chro.11,28 Iras
Irád,a wilde asse.Gen.4,18
Iriáh,the feare of the Lord.Ier.37,12
Irmeiáh,exalting the Lord.1.Chro.5,24 Ieremias
¶Ishacar,a wages.Gen.30,18
Ishái,a gifte or oblation.Rut 4,17 Iessai
Ishbósheth,a man of shame.2.Sam.2,12

Scariot. Ishcariót, an hyreling, or man of death. Mat.10,1

Ishmaél, God hath heard. Gen.16,11.

Ishtób, good man.2.Sam.10,8

Israél, a prince of God, or preuailing with God.Gen.35,10

¶Ithamár, wo to the change.Exod.6,23

Ittái, strong.2.Sam.23,29

Itti, Itai Ethai Ittiél, God with me. Nehem.11,6

¶Iubal, bringing, or fading. Gen.4,21

Iehucal Iuchal, mightie. Ierem.38,1

¶Izebel, wo to the house.1.King.16,31

Isaak Izhak, laughter.Gen.17,19

Izrahiáh, the Lord ariseth, or the clearenes of the Lord.1.Chro.7,3

Izreél, the seed of God.Iosh.15,56

K

Chaath KAháth, a congregacion. Gen.46,11

Choath Kainán, a biar, or owner. Gen.5,9

Káin, a possession. Gen.4,1

Chemuel Kamuél, God is risen. Gen.22,21

Karéah, balde.2.King.25,

¶Kedár, blackenes. Gen.25,13

Kédem, East. Ierem.49,26

Kéren-happúch, the horne of beautie.

Casaiah Kallaiáh, the voyce of the Lord. Nehem. 12,19

¶Kish, harde, or sore.1.Sam.9,1

Colia ¶Kolaiáh, the voyce of the Lord. Nehem. 11,2

Kórah, balde. Gen.36,5

Koré, crying.1.Chro.9,19

¶Kushaiá, hardenes.1.Chro.15,17

L

LAadáh, to gather, or testifie.1.Chro.4,21

Leedan Laadán, for pleasure.1.Chro.7,26

Labán, white. Gen.24,29

Laél, to God, or to the mightie. Nomb.3,24

Laad Láhad, to praise.1.Chro.4,2

Lemuél Lamuél, with whome is God? Prou.31,1

Lahabim Lehabím, enflamed. Gen.10,13

Lamech Lémech, poore, or smitten. Gen.4,18

Lappidóth lightenings. Iudg.4,4

Letushim, hammer men. Gen.25,3

Leuí, ioyned, or coupled. Gen.29,34

Leáh, painful, or wearied. Gen.29,16

¶Lobín, whitenes. Exod.6,17

Lotan Lot wrapped, or ioyned. Gen.11,27

Ludim ¶Lud, a natiuitie, or generacion. Gen.10,22

¶Lysias, dissoluing.1.Mac.3,32

Lysimachus, dissoluing battel.2.Mac.4,29

M

Maacháh MAachathí, broken.2.King.25,23

Mahazióth, seing a signe.1.Chro.25,4

Mahseiáh, the protectiõ of the Lord. Ierem. 32,12

Maalá Mahlá, weakenes, or a dance. Nomb.26,33

Maasei Maasai, my worke.1.Chro.9,12

Maasias Maaseiáh, the worke of the Lord.1. Chro. 15,18

Maasaias Maaziáh, the strength of the Lord.1.Chro. 24,18

Makáz, finishing, or watching.1.King.4,9

Macbanái, my poore sonne.1.Chro.12,13 Machabanai

Machí, poore, or a smiter. Nomb.13,16

Machír, selling, or knowing. Gen.50,23

Madái, a measure, or iudging. Gen.10,2

Madán, strife. Gen.25,2 Midián

Magdalena, magnified, or exalted. Mat.27,56

Magdiél, preaching God. Gen.36,43

Magóg, couering, or melting. Gen.10,2

Mahaláh, infirmitie, or sickenes. 2.Chro.11,18 Mahalon

Maharái, hasting.2.Chro.11,30

Mahath, wiping away, or fearing. 1.Chro.6,35

Malachí, my messenger. Malach.1,1 Malachias

Mahaleél, praising God. Gen.5,12 Malaleél

Mamzér, a bastard. Deut.23,2

Manahém, a comforter.2.King.15,14

Manoách, rest. Iudg.13,2. Manoe

Maón, a dwelling place. Iosh.15,55 Maonathi

Mordechái, bitter, contricion. Ester 2,5

Marthá, bitter, or prouoking. Luk.10,38

Mattán, a gift.2.Chro.23,17 Mattanah

Mattaní, Mattaniáh, Matthaniáh, Matthatáh his gift. Ezr.10,33 Manthanaim Mattathias

Mattithía, a gift of the Lord.1.Chro.9,31 Mathias

Malchiél, God is my King. Gen.46,17 Melchiel

Malchiáh, the Lord my King. Ierem.21,1 Melchiah

Malchi-zédek, King of righteousnes. Gen. 14,18 Melchizedek

Malchishúa, my King the sauiour.1.Sam. 14,49

¶Mehetabél, how good is God! Gen.36,39

Mehumán, troubled. Ester.1,10 Aman

Mehuiaél, teaching God. Gen.4,18

Methushaél, asking death. Gen.4,18

Methushélah, spoyling his death. Gen.5,21

Melatiáh, deliuerance of the Lord. Nehem. 3,7 Meltias

Menelaus, strength of the people. 2.Mac. 4,23.

Menashéh, forgetting. Gen.41,51 Manasse

Meraióth, bitternes.1.Chro.9,11 Merari

Méred, rebellious.1.Chro.4,17

Meshá, saluacion.1.Chro.2,42 Mousa

Meshelemiáh, the peace of ẏ Lord.1.Chro. 26,1.

Meshullám, peaceable.2.King.22,3

Mephibosheth, shame of mouth. 2.Sam.4,4

Méshech prolonging. Gen.10,2

Milcháh, a woman of counsel. Gen.11,29 Melcha

Milchóm, their King, or counseller, the idole of the Ammonites.2.King.23,13

Mizzáh, a dropping, or consuming. Gen.36,13

Micháh, poore, or smitten, or who is here? 2.Chro.34,20 Micha Micheas

Michaiáh, who is like the Lord? 2.King.22,12 Michaias

Michael, who is like God? 1.Chro.7,3

Michal, who is perfect? 1.Sam.14,49

Mishael, who demandeth? Exod.6,22

Maria Miriám, exalted, or teaching. Exod. 6,20
Mithredath, dissoluing the Law. Ezr. 1,8
¶ Moáb, of the father. Gen. 19,36
Moshéh, drawne vp. Exod. 10,2
Mozá, founde, or vnleauened. 1. Chro. 2,46
¶ Musach, anointing. 2. King. 16,18
Mushí, departing. Exod. 6,19

N

Noeman NAamáh, beautiful. Gen. 4,22
Naamán, faire, or beautiful. Gen. 46,21
Naaráh, a maide, or watching. Iosh. 16,7
Naariáh, a childe of the Lord. 1. Chro. 3,22
Nebó Nabóth Nabaióth, buddes, or prophecies. Gen. 25,13
Nabál, a foole. 1. Sam. 25,3
Nadáb, a prince, or liberal. Exod. 6,23
Naggái, clearenes, Luk. 3,25
Nahaliél, the inheritance of God. Nomb. 21,19
Nahamani Nahám, Nahúm, a comforter, or repentãt. 1. Chro. 4,19.
Nahás, a serpent. 1. Chro. 4,12
Nahór, hoarse, or angrie. Gen. 11,22
Naióth, beautie, or a dwelling place. 1. Sam. 19,18
Naphtalí, wrastling, or comparison. Genes. 30,8
Nathan, giuen. 2. Sam. 5,14
Nabuchodonosor ¶ Nebuchad-nezzár, which is written for ẏ moste parte in Ieremie, and some times in Ezekiel, Nebuchadrezzar, signifieth the mourning of the generacion.
Nepheg, weake. 2. Sam. 5,15
Nephtuim, an opening. Gen. 10,13
Ner, a light. 1. Sam. 14,51
Nethaneél the gift of God. 2. Chro. 35,9
Nethaniáh, a gift of the Lord. 2. Sam. 25,23
Nemrod ¶ Nimrod, rebellious. Gen. 10,8
¶ Noadiáh, the witnessing, or testificacion of the Lord. Ezr. 8,33
Noáh rest. Gen. 5,29
Nogah, brightnes. 1. Chro. 14,16
¶ Nun, sonne, or posteritie. Nomb. 13,9

O

Obdiah Abdias OBadiáh, seruant of the Lord. 1. Chro. 3,21
Obed, a seruant. Iudg. 9,26
Obed-edóm, the seruant of Edóm, or a seruant Edomite. 2. King. 6,10
Obíl, borne, or broght. 1. Chro. 27,30
¶ Omár, speaking, or exalting. Gen. 36,11
Omán ¶ Onám, sorow, strength. Gen. 36,23
Aunan. Onán, sorow, or iniquitie. Gen. 38,4
¶ Ophél, a towre, or darkenes. 2. Chro. 27,3
Ophráh Ophír, ashes. Gen. 10,29
¶ Ornán, reioycing. 1. Chro. 21,18
Orpáh, a necke. Ruth. 1,4
Orthosias, rectified. 1. Macc. 15,37
¶ Othní, my time. 1. Chro. 26,7
Otholiáh, time to the Lord. 1. Chro. 8,26
Othoniél, the time of God. Iosh. 15,17
Oziáh ¶ Ozaziáh, ẏ strength of the Lord. 1. Chro. 15,21
Ozziél, the helpe of God. 1. Chro. 27,19

P

PAgiél, God hathe met. Nomb. 1,13
Palál, praying or iudging. Nehem. 3,25
Paltí, deliuerance. Nomb. 13,10 Phalti
Paltiél, deliuerance of God. Nomb. 34,36
Palú, marueilous. Gen. 46,19 Phaltias.
Paróh, vengeance. Exod. 8,1
Paruáh, florishing, or fleing. 1. King. 4,17
Pashúr, encreasing libertie. Ierem. 20,3
¶ Pedahél, the redemption of God. Nomb. 34,28
Pedah-zúr, a mightie redemer. Nomb. 1,10 Phadassur
Pedaiah, the Lords redeming. 2. King. 22,1
Pekaiáh, the Lords opening. 2. King. 15,22
Pelaiáh, ẏ miracle of the Lord. 1. Chro. 3,24
Pelaiáh, a miracle of the Lord. Nehem. 8,7
Pelatiáh, deliuerance of the Lord. 1. Chro. 3,21. Phalaties Phaltias
Péleg, a diuision. Gen. 10,25
Pélet, deliuerance. 1. Chro. 2,33
Penuél, seing God. 1. Chro. 4,4 Phanuel
Péresh, a horseman. 1. Chro. 7,16
Pérez, a diuision. Gen. 38,29
Perudáh, a diuision. Ezr. 2,55
Pethaiáh, the Lord openeth. Ezr. 10,23
¶ Picól, the mouth of all. Gen. 21,22 Phicol
Pinehás, a bolde countenance. Nomb. 25,7 Phinees
¶ Puah, a mouth. Gen. 46,13

R

RAamiáh, thũdre of the Lord. Nehem. 7,7
Raddái, ruling. 1. Chro. 2,14
Rahább, proude, or strong. Iosh. 2,1
Rahám, mercie, or compassion. 1. Chro. 2,44
Rahél, a shepe. Gen. 29,9
Rám, high. 1. Chro. 2
Ramiáh, exaltacion of the Lord. Ezr. 10,25
Raphá, release, or medecine. Gen. 46,21
¶ Reaiáh, a vision of the Lord. 1. Chro. 5,5
Réba, the fourth. Iosh. 13,21
Rechab, a rider. 2. King. 10,15
Reelaiáh, a shepherd to the Lord. Ezr. 2,2
Rehabeam, dilating the people. 1. King. 11,43 Roboam
Rehúm, pitieful, or pitied. Ezr. 2,2
Remaliáh, the exaltacion of the Lord. 2. King. 15,27
Rephaél, medecine of God. 1. Chro. 26,7 Raphael
Rephaiáh, medecine of ẏ Lord. 1. Chro. 3,21
Reú, his shepherd. Gen 11,19
Reubén, the sonne of vision, so named, because the Lord did see his mothers affliction. Gen. 29,32
Reuél, a shepherd of God. Exod. 2,19 Raguel
Rezón, a secretarie, or leane. 1. King. 11,23
¶ Ribái, strife, or encreased. 2. Sam. 23,29
Ribkáh, fed. Gen. 22,23 Rebecca Rebekáh
Rinnáh, song, or reioycing. 1. Chro. 4,20
Riphath, medecine, or release. Gen. 10,3
¶ Rogel, a foteman, or an accuser. Iosh. 15,8
¶ Ruth, watered, or filled. Ruth 1,4

S

SAbtáh, a compasse, or olde age. Gen. 10,7 Sabatha.
Sabteca, the cause of smiting. Gen. 10,7

Saráh

Saráh,a ladie,or dame.Gen.17,15
Sarai,my dame,or mastres.Gen.11,29
Saba ¶Sebá,a compasse.Gen.10,7
Séled,affliction 1.Chron.2,30
Semachiáh,cleauing to the Lord.1.Chr.26,7
Sheal ¶Shaál,Shaúl,asked.Ezr.10,29.1.Sam.9,2
Saaph Sháaph,flying,or thinking.1.Chro.4,7
Shabbethái,my rest.Nehem.11,16
Shachír,wages.1.Chro.11,35
Shage,ignorant.1.Chron.11,34
Sellum Sallum Shallum,peaceable.2.King.15,10
Shalmah Shalma Shalman,peaceable.Hose.10,15
Salmon Shalmon,peaceable.Ruth 4,21
Shamgár, desolation of the stranger. Iudg. 3,31
Shamma Shammáh, desolation,destructiō.1.Sam.16,9
Shammúa,obedient.Nomb.13,5
Shaphán,a conie,or one hidde.1.Chr.5,12
Shaphát,a iudge.Nom.13,6
Sharézer,a treasurer.2.King.19,37
Salathiel Shealthiél,asked of God.Hag.1,1
Sheariáh,the gate of the Lord.1.Chro.8,38
Shaba Shebá,captiuitie.Gen.10,7
Shebarím,hope.Iosh.7,5
Sheber,hope,or wheat.1.Chro.2,48
Sechia Shecaniáh, the habitation of the Lord. 1. Chron.3,21
Shéchem,a parte,or portion.Nom.26,31
Shedeúr, a field of fyre, or the light of the almightie.Nomb.1,5
Shegúb,exalted.1.King.16,34
Shehariáh,ẏ morning of ẏ Lord.1.Chr.8,26
Seir Sheír,rough,or heerie.Gen.36,20
Sheláh,dissoluing.Gen.38,5
Sheláh,sending,or spoiling.Gen.10,24
Salmiah Shelemiáh,peace of the Lord.Ezr.10,39
Shéleph,drawing out. Gen.10,26
Shélesh,a captaine.1.Chro.7,35
Shelomíth,peaceable.Leuit.24,11
Shelomóh,peaceable.2.Sam.5,15
Shelumiél,the peace of God.Nomb.1,6
Ismaiah Shemaiáh,hearing the Lord.1.Chr.4,37
Shemariáh,the keping of ẏ Lord. Ezr.10,32
Shémed,destroying.1.Chr.8,12
Shémer,a keaper.1.King.16,24
Shemidá,a name of knowledge.Nom.26,32
Semuel Shemuél,appointed of God.Nom.3,4
Samuel Shemuél,heard of God.1.Sam.1,20
Shephatiáh,the Lord iudgeth.2.Sam.3,4
Seraiah Sheraiáh,a prince of the Lord.1.Chr.4,14
Sherúg,a bough,or plante.Gen.11,20
Seth Sheth,set,or put. Gen.4,25
Shethár,a remnant,or hid.Est.1,14.
Sheuá,vanitie.1.Chron.2,49
Sechia Shiciáh,the protection of ẏ Lord.1.Chr.8,10
Shimeah Shimeí,hearing,or obedient.Exod.6,17
Simon Shimeón hearing,or obedient.Gen.29,33
Samson Shimshon,there the secōde time,because the Angel appeared the seconde time at the prayer of his father.Iud.13,24
Shiphtán,a iudge.Nomb.34,24
Shipráh,faire.Exod.1,15
Sobab Shobáb,returned.2.Sam.5,14

Shobál,a path.Gen.36,20
Shobnáh,a buylder.2.King.8,18
Shúa,crying,or sauing.Gen.38,2 Sua
Shuáh,praying,or humiliation.Gen.25,2
Shubaél,the returning of God.1.Chr.24,20 Shebuel
Shuháh,a pitte.1.Chron.4,11
Shumathí,renoumed.1.Chro.2,53
Shuní,changed,or sleping.Gen.46,16
¶Sithrí,my secret.Exod.6,22
¶Sodí,my secret.Nomb.13,11
¶Suáh,rooting vp.1.Chron.7,36

T

TAbeél,good God.Isa.7,6
Taháshi,hasting.Gen.22,24
Taháth,feare.1.Chro 6,37
Talmái,a forow.Iosh.15,14 Tholmai
Tamár,a palmetree.Gen.38,6 Thamar
Tanhúmeth,consolation.Ier.40,8
Talmón,dew prepared.1.Chr.9,17
Tapháth,a litle one.1.King.4,11
¶Tebáh,a cooke.Gen.22,24.
Tehinnáh,merciful,or prayer.1.Chr.4,12
Térah,smelling.Gen.11,24.
¶Tiknáh,hope.2.King.22,14
Tilón,murmuring.1.Chro.4,20 Thilon
Tirás,a destroyer.Gen.10,2
Tirhanáh,a searcher of mercie.1.Chro.2,48
Tiriá,a searche.1.Chro.4,16
¶Tóah,a darte.1.Chron.6,34
Tobiáh,the Lord is good. Ezr.2,60
Togarmáh,strong,or bonie.Gen.10,3 Thogorma
Tóhu,liuing.1.King.1,1
Tolá,a worme.Gen.46,13
Tom,a twine.Mat.10,3 Thomas
¶Tubál,borne,or broght,or worldlie.Gen. 10,2
Tubál-káin,worldlie possession.Gen.4,22

V

VAniáh,nourishmēt of ẏ Lord. Ezr.10,36 Ouania
Vashni,changed.1.Chr.6,28
Vashtí,drinking.Est.1,9
¶Vopsí,a thĩg brokē,or patched. Nom.13,15
¶Vri,my light.1.Chr.2,20 Hur
Vriiáh,the light of the Lord.2.Sam.11,3 Ourias
Vriél,light or fyre of God.2.Chr.13,2
¶Vthái,mine iniquitie,or time.1.Chr.9,4
¶Vzál,wandering.Gen.10,27
Vzzáh,strength.1.Chron.6,29.2.Sam.6,3 Oza
Vzzí,my strength.1.Chr.6,5
Vzziél,the strength of God.1.Chr.7,7

Z

ZAauan,trembling.Gen.36,27
Zabád,a dowrie.1.Chr.2,36
Zabadiáh,a dowry of ẏ Lord.1.Chr.8,15
Zabdiél,a dowrie of God.1.Chr.27,2
Zaccúr,mindeful.1.Chr.4,26
Zachái,pure.Ezr.2,9 Zacheus
Zachariáh mindeful of the Lord.1.Chr.5,7
Zadok,iustified,or iuste.2.Sam.8,17
Zalmonáh,our image.Nom.33,41
Zanoáh,forgetfulnes.Nehem.11,30
¶Zebulún,a dwelling.Gen.30,20
Zeeb,a wolfe.Iudg.7,25

Zelophehád,a shadow of feare. Nom.26,33
Zemiráh,a song.1.Chron.7,8
Zephaniáh,the hiding of the Lord.2.King. 25,18
Zephí,a honie combe.Gen.36,11
Zéra, clearenes,or rising vp.Gen.36,13
Zeraiáh,the Lord arising.1.Chro.6,6
Zeresh,scattering heritage.Est.5,10
Zerubbabél,strange from confusion, or a stranger at Babel.Hag.1,1
Zethan,their oliue.1.Chro.26,22
¶Zia,swete,or swelling.1.Chron.5,13
Zidkiáh,the iustice of ẏ Lord.2.King.24,17
Zidón,a hunter.Gen.10,15
Zimrí,a song.1.Chron.2,6
Ziphoráh,a mourning.Exod.2,21.
¶Zohéth,a separation.1.Chro.4,20
¶Zuph,a watch,or a couering. 1.Chro.6,35
Zuriél,the rocke of God.Nom.3,35
Zurishadái, ẏ rocke of ẏ almightie. Nõ.1,6

A TABLE OF THE PRINCIPAL THINGS THAT ARE CONTEINED IN THE BIBLE, after the ordre of the alphabet. The first nomber noteth the chapter,and the seconde the verse.

A

Aaron and his doings. exod.4, & 10,& 28,& 29.leuit.2,10. nom. 17,3.ebr.9,7
aaron and miriam speake against moses.nom.12,1
aaron,eloquent.exod.4,14
¶Abba, father. mark.14,36.rom.8,15. gal.4,6
abdon,a iudge in israel.iud.12,13
abel, a citie where dwelt the wise. 2.sam.20,18
abiathar the sonne of ahi-melech, and his doings.1.sam.22,& 23.1.kin. 1 and 2
abigail ẏ wife of nabal. 1.sam.25,3
abihu burnt with fyre frõ the lord. leuit.10,2
abihu seeth god in sina.exod.24,10
abiiam king of iudah.1.king.15,1
abimelech king of gerar, and his doings.gen.20 & 26
abimelech the sonne of gideon murdereth his brethrẽ, and after reigneth in israel.iudg.9
abishai pursueth sheba. 2.sam.20,10
abner, his doings and his death.1. sam.17,55.vnto the 2.sam.3
the Abomination of the iewes. isa. 1,3.of ierusalem.eze.16,1
abraham & his doings, from the 12 of gen. vnto the 25.his faith. rom. 4,3.ebr.11,17
abraham a prophet.gen.20,7
absalom and his doings,from the 2. sam.13 vnto the 19
absent from god.2.cor.5,6
the Abstinence of moses and eliiah. exod.34,28.1.king.19,8
abundance cometh of god.deu.8,17
¶Accesse to god by christ.rom.5,2 ephes.2,18 & 3,12
euerie man shal giue Accountes of him self to god.rom.14,12
christ is Accursed for our sakes.gal. 3,13
achan the sonne of carmi stoned & burnt to death.iosh.7,25
achior.iud.5,5 & 14,6
achish king of gath.1.sam.21,11 &27,2
¶Adã & his creation.gen.1,27 & 2,7
adam laboreth.gen.3,23
adam the figure of christ.rom.5,14
adam ẏ first,adã the last.1.cor.15,45
adoni bezek king.iudg.1,6
adoniiah dauids sonne, and his ambition.1.king.1 & 2
adopted in christ. eph. 1,5.rom.9,4. galat.4,5
adoram stoned to death. 1.king.12,18
aduersitie and prosperitie are of god.iob 2,10.prouer.3,33
adulterie forbidden. gen.26,10.exo. 20,14.1.cor.6,9.ebr.13,4
adulterie must be auoided.exod.20, 14.prou.5,3.1.cor.10,8.1.thes.4,3
the Adulterie of dauid.2.sam.11 & 12
our Aduocate towarde god the father,iesus christ.1.iohn 2,1
¶degrees of Affinitie.leuit.18
the Affliction and crosse of dauid for his sinne.2.sam.12,10
the Afflictions of this present time are not worthie,&c.rom.8,18
affliction to them, that trust in anie other then in god.deut.31,17
affliction to thẽ that afflict the faithful.2.thess.1,6
to Afflict ẏ soule for a daye. isa.58,5
¶Agabus ẏ prophet.act.11,28 & 21,10
agag kĩg of ẏ amalekites. 1.sam.15,9
agre with thine aduersarie.mat.5,25
agrippa king.act.25,13
¶Ahab and his wicked doĩgs, from the 16 of 1.king.vnto the 22
ahaziah the sonne of ahab, and his doings.1.king.22,49.2.king.1,2
ahaziah the sonne of ioram,and his doings.2.king.8
ahaz king of iudah, an idolater.2. kings.16,11
ahiah the sonne of Ahitub.1.sam.14,3
ahimaaz.2.sam.17,17.& 18,19
ahimelech.1.sam.21,1.& 22,9
ahithophel and his doings. 2.sam.15 & 16 & 17
aholah and Aholibah.eze.23,4
aholiab, an excellent workeman. exod.31,6
¶our Aide of christ.ebr.4,14
the Aide of israel is of god. deut. 33,26
¶Alcimus a wicked man. 1.mac.7,9. & 9,54.
alexander ẏ copper smith.2.tim.4,14
alexander the sonne of antiochus epiphanes.1.mac.10,1
almes dedes are pleasant sacrifices. philip.4,18
giue not thine Almes grudgingly.2. cor.9,7
christ our Altar.ebr.13,10
the Altar and the forme thereof. exod.20,24
the Altars of the gentiles. exo.34,13
¶Amalekites.exod.17,8.nomb.14,25. deut.25,17.1.sam.15,2
ama sa the ead of absaloms armie. 2.sam.17,25.& 20,4
amaziáh king of iudah.2.king.14,1
amaziah the priest of beth-el. amos 7,10
ammonites.gen.19,38.deu.23,3. iudg. 11,4.2.sam.10
amnon defileth his sister tamar.2. sam.13
amon king of iudah,wicked. 2.king. 21,19 & 23
amorites.gen.14,7.deut.2,24.& 20,17. iudg.

iudg.1,34.1.sam.7,4
amos the prophet.amos 1,1
amram the sonne of kohath.exo.6, 18
¶ioshua killeth the Anakims.iosh. 11,21.iudg.1,20
ananias and his wife sapphiras death.act.5,10
ananias the chief priest.act.23,2
ananias yͤ disciple of christ. act.9,10
andronicus is slaine.2.mac.4,38
the seuentie Ancients of the people of israel.nomb.11,16
angels and their creation.col.1,15
the Angel denyeth to be worshiped. reuel 19,10.& 22,9
the Angel guideth the hoste of israel.exod.14,19
the Angel sheweth of christs birth. luk.2,10.
angels kepers of the litle ones.mat. 18,10.peters Angel.act.12,15
the Angels minister vnto christ. mat.4,11. thei comfort him in the garden.luk.22,43
angels the ministers of god. ebr.1,7
the thre Angels that abraham receiued into his house.gen.18,5.lot also receiueth two.19,3
to be Angrie with thy brother, is dãnable.mat.5,22
anna the mother of tobie the yõg. tob.11,9
anna the prophetesse.luk.2,36
annas father in law to caiaphas. iohn 18,13
be readie alwayes to giue an Answere of the hope that is in you. 1.pet.3,15
antichrist, who? 1.iohn 2,22. & 4,3.2. thes.2,3
the Antiochians, first that were named christians.act.11,26.
antiochus epiphanes. 1.macc. 2,10. and 9,1
antiochus eupator. 1. macc. 6, 17.2. mac.10,10.& 13,1
¶Apollonius discomfited by ionathan.1.mac 10,82
apollos a learned man.act.18,24
the Apostles afflicted for christs sake.act.4,3.5,18
the Apostles aske who is yͤ greatest in yͤ kingdome of heauẽ. mat. 18,1
the Apostles first sent to the iewes. mat.10,6
the Apostles shal iudge the twelue tribes.mat.19,28
apostles, why they were ordeined in the church.1.cor.1,28
god iudgeth not according to the Appearance.1.sam.16,7
¶Aquila and priscilla do herber the church.1.cor.16,19
the ruine of the Arabians. isa.21,14
¶king Arád slaine.nomb.21,3
the Aramites.2. sam.8.& 10.1. king. 5.& 6.& 7.& 8
araunáh selleth his threshing floore to dauid.2.sam.24,24
mamré a citie of Arbáh, called also hebrón.gen.35,27
aristarchus felowe prisoner with paul.col.4,10
the Arke of god, the forme & vse thereof.exod.25,10. deut.10,3. & 3, 26.iosh.3,3.1.sam.4. vnto yͤ 7.2.sam. 15,24
the Arke of noáh. genes. 6,14.& 7,1. 1.pet.3,20
the stretched out Arme of god. 1. king.8,42.
arpachshad, his birth and age. gen. 11,10.& 12
flee Arrogancie.rom.12,3
¶Asa king of iudáh, and his doings 1.king.15,8
asahel ioabs brother slaine.2.sam. 2,23
asaph the brother of hemán, chanter.1.chr.6,39
asher iaakobs sonne. gene.30,13.his blessing & his portion. deut.33,24. iosh.19,24
ashima the idole that the men of hamath made in samaria. 2. king. 17,30
ashtaroth, the idole that the iewes worshipped.iudg.2,13 & 3,7
paul is forbid to preache in Asia. act. 16,6. at length he preacheth there.act.19,10
Askelon taken by iuda.iudg.1,18
iesus entreth on an Asse into ierusalem.mat.21,7
Asses in vse among the israelites, gen.42,26.iudg.12,14
the Asse of balaam speaketh. nomb. 22,28
asshur went out of the land of shinor.gen.10,11
assuerus kĩg, his doings & his lawes in the boke of ester.
¶Athaliah reigneth ouer iudah. 2. king.11,3
paul reproueth the Athenians for their superstitions.act.17,22
¶Azariah reigneth in stead of his father amaziah, & is striken with a leprosie.2.king.15,1 & 5
azariah the prophet.2.chron.15,1

B.

BAal-perazim, a certeine place, 2.sam.5,20
baal peor, an idole: yͤ israelites for ioyning thẽ selues thereunto, are put to death.nom.25,3.deut.4,3
baanah & rechab kill ish-bosheth. 2.sam.4,6
baasha, king of israel, & his doings, 1.king.15,16
the destruction of Babel forespoken. isa.13.
the buylding of Babels towre. gen. 11,4
babes in christ.1.cor.3,1
against Bablers.ecclesiasti.20,5
bachides, captaine of king demetrius armie, discõfited.1.mac.9,68
backebyting forbidden. leuit. 19, 16. ecclesiast.4,4.pro.26,22 1.pet.2,2
backebyting is to be auoyded.1.pet. 2,1
bagoas, the eunuch.iud.12,11
balaam, the sonne of beor. nomb. 22 & 23 & 24.2.pet.2,15.he is slaine. iosh.13,22
balak, king of yͤ moabites.nomb.22. & 24
iust Balances.leuit.19,36
one Baptisme.ephes.4,5
iohn sent to Baptize.ioh.1,33
the disciples of christ Baptize. ioh. 24
christ is Baptized.mat.3,15
to be Baptized in the name of the father, &c. or of iesus. mat. 28,19. act.2,38
to be Baptized vnto christ, is to put on christ.rom.6,3.gal.3,27
we are Baptized vnto the death of christ.rom.6,3
christ Baptizeth with yͤ holie gost and with fyre. mat. 3,11. mark.1,8. luk.3,16.ioh.1,16
barabbas, the murtherer. luk. 23,18. iohn 18,40
barak and deborah deliuer israel. iudg.4
baruch ieremiahs scribe.ier.36,4
barzillai, & his doings. 2.sam. 19,31. 1.king 2,7
the Bastard shal not entre into the congregation of the lord. deut. 23,2
¶priests are forbid to shaue their heads or Beards.leuit.21,5
the shauen Beard was a signe of sorowe to the iewes. isa.15,2
creation of Beasts.gen.1,24
paul foght with Beasts at ephesus. 1.cor.15,32
beasts cleane & vncleane. leuit.11,2. deut.14,4
when thou goest to Bed, thinke on gods worde.deut.11,19
behemóth, and his propertie. iob 40,10
bela, a citie, called also zoar. ge.14,[illegible]

beleue in iesus christ, & thy sinnes shal be forgiuen.act.10,9
to Beleue is the gift of god. mat.13, 11 & 16,17.ioh.6,44
to him that Beleueth,all things are possible.mar.9,23
he that Beleueth in christ, shal neuer perish.ioh.3,15
belshazzár king of the babylonians dan.5
benaiáh killeth ioab.1.king.2,34
ben-hadad king of aram, & his doings.1.king.15,18.2.chro.16,2
beniamin.gene.35,18 & 43 & 44 & 45. deut.33,12
beth-el or luz.gene. 28,19.iudg. 1,23. 1.sam.10,3
beth-lehem,called also ephrath.ge. 35,19.mic.5,2.luk.2,4
bethsaida an vnfaithful citie. Mat. 11,21
beth-sheba vriahs wife lyeth with dauid.2.sam.11,4
beth-shemites are punished for loking into the arke of the lord.1. sam.6,19
bethuel the father of rebekah.gene. 22,23
bethulia is deliuered from siege. iud.7
bezaleel an excellent workeman,& his doings.exod.31,2 & 35,30
¶who Bideth in christ.1.ioh.2,6
how god Bideth in vs.1.ioh.3,24
bilhah rahels maid.genes.29,29 and 30,3
a Bil of diuorcement.deut.24,1
to Binde and lose. mat.16,19. iohn 20,23
birdes created.gen.1,20
birdes cleane & vncleane.leui.11,13
esau estemeth not his Birthright. gen.25,32
the office of a true Bishop.1.tim.3. tit.1,5.1.pet.5,2
bishops must be fautles.tit.1,7
ẏ Bishop of our soules, iesus christ. 1.pet.2,25
bitternes & fiercenes to be auoided. ephes.4,31
¶the Blasphemer oght to be stoned to death.leuit.24,15
blasphemie against the holie gost. mat.12,31.mar.3,28
the description of a Blessed man. psal.1.mat.5,3
the Blessed of god are called shepe. mat.25,33
to Blesse god, for to giue thankes vnto him.gen.24,27
blessing,for gift.gene.33,11.2.cor.9,5
the maner of Blessing the people. nomb.6,24 & gen.48,20
blessing to those that obeye & serue the lord.exod.23,25. deu.8,6.& 11,27 & 28,2
laye no stombling blocke before ẏ Blinde.leuit.19,14
the Blinde borne for the glorie of god.ioh.9,3
the blinde guide.mat.15,14
the Blinde healed by christ.mat.9,29
christ healeth the Blinde with his spitle.mar.8,23
blindnes of heart. rom.11,8.ephe.4,18
the Blood,for the mã that is slaine. iosh.20,5
by the Blood of christ we haue remission of sinnes.mat.26,28.ebr.9, 14.1.pet.1,2
¶iohn and iames called Boanerges by christ,& what that is to saye. mar.3,17
boaz & his doings.ruth 2 & 3 & 4
our Bodies are cõsecrat vnto christ 1.cor.6,15.thei are the tẽples of the holie gost.1.cor.6,19
all ẏ faithful are one Bodie.rom.12,5
to bring the Bodie in subiection. 1. cor.9,27
ẏ Bodie of christ,ẏ church. eph.1,23
our Bodies are earthen vessels. 2. cor.4,7 & 5,1
to be in the Boke of life. philip. 4, 3. and to be raised out of it. exod. 32,32
the Bokes of curious artes are burnt act.19,19
iosiah commandeth to saue the prophetes Bones.2.king.23,18
he that is Borne of god,sinneth not 1.iohn 3,9
they that are Borne of god.ioh.1,13. 1.ioh.5,1
chãge not ẏ ancient Boundes. deut. 19,14.27,17.prou.22,28.23,10
the Bowe in the cloude.gen.9,14
¶man liueth not onely by Bread. deut.8,3
we are all one Bread.1.cor.10,17
christ,the liuing Bread.ioh.6,51
the feast of vnleauened Bread.exo. 23,14 & 34,18
the breaking of Bread.act.2,46
the shew Breads.leuit.24,5
Bread comforteth the heart.gen.18, 5.iudg.19,5.psal.104,15
commune Bread, halowed Bread.1. sam.21,4
to eat Bread in ẏ sweat of ẏ browes. gen.3,19
iaakob desireth onely Bread to eat, & clothes to put on.gen.28,20
breaking of Bread.act.2,42
whome iaakob calleth his Brethrẽ. gen.29,4
christ ashameth not to call vs Brethren.ebr.2,11
the Brethren or cousins of christ beleue not in him.ioh.7,5
Brotherlie loue.rom.12,10
¶Buggerers shal not possesse ẏ kingdome of heauẽ.1.cor.6,9.1 tim.1,16
euerie one shal beare his owne Burden.gal.6,5
we must beare one anothers Burdẽ. gal.6,2
Burnt offrings.leuit.6,12
the fyrie bush.exod.3,2
the faithful are gods Buyldĩg.1.cor. 3,9
to Buylde vpon christ golde,siluer, &c.1.cor.3,12

C

Caiaphas & his doings. mat.26, 57.ioh.11,49
ten Caldrõs for the temple. 1.king. 7,38
Caleb and his doings. nomb. 13,7 & 14,6.iosh.14,6
the golden Calf.exod.32.it is groũde into powder.32,20
manie Called, & fewe chosen. mat. 20,16.rom.9,6
christ is come to Call sinners. mat. 9,13
loue them that Call vpon the lord with pure heart.2.tim.2,22
the golden Calues of ieroboam. 1. king.12,28
Canaan is accursed.gen.9,25
Canaan,a fat land,flowing ẘ milke and honie.exod.3,8
the land of Canaan is the holie habitation of god.exo.15,13.promised to abraham.gen.12,7
the sõnes of Canaan,of whome descended the canaanites.ge.10,15
the Canaanites discomfited by the tribe of Iudah.iudg.1,4
the Canaanites smote ẏ Israelites. nomb.14,45
the Canaanites,that remained, were as thornes to Israel.iudg.2,3
the Canaanitish woman.mat.15,22
the Candlesticke & facion thereof. exod.25,31 & 37,17 & 40,24
Capernaum an vnbeleuing citie. mat.11,23
the Caphtorims destroyed ẏ auims. deut.2,23
the Captiuitie of the kĩgs of iudah forespoken.2.king.20,17.ierem.16, 13 & 20,4
the Cares of this worlde do choke vp the worde.mar.4,19
Cartes of yron in vse among the canaanites.iudg.1,19 & 4,3
god Caryed the children of israel

vpon egles wings.exod.19,4
¶Cendebeus, captaine of the sea coast.1.macc.15,38
the Centurion & his faith.mat.8,5
god reiecteth ȳ iewish Ceremonies isa.1,11 & 66,3.ebr.10,5
the decre of augustus Cesar.luk.2,1
¶Chamois.deut.14,5
eliiah,the Charet of israel.2.king.2,12
to make him self Chaste for ȳ kingdome of heauen.mat.19,12
blessed is the man that god Chastiseth.iob 5,17
Chastise thy childe betime. prou.13,24 & 19,18 & 22,15
Chastitie is the gift of god. wis.8,21
Chemosh the abominatiō of moab.1.king.11,7
the Cherubims kepe the way of the tre of life.gen.3,24
offend not litle Children.mat.18,6
the rodde of correctiō for Childrē. prou.22,15.ecclesiasti.30,13
the angels of litle Children. mat.18,10
Children as concerning maliciousnes, and not in vnderstanding. 1.cor.14,20
Children broght to christ. matth.19,13
christ receiueth the Childe into his armes.mar.9,36
we are the Childrē of god by faith. gal.3,26
Childrens obedience to their parents.ephes.6,1
Chorazin, a citie that christ reproueth for her vnbelief.mat.11,21
paul,a Chosen vessel.act.9,15
Christ conceiued. luk.1,35.is borne. luk.2,7. is circumcised. luk.2,21. is baptized.mat.3,15.sent to preache libertie to ȳ captiues. isa.61,1. luk.2,31 & 4, 43 & 5, 32. he speaketh the wordes of god. ioh.3, 34. he precheth ȳ the kingdome of the Messias is at hand, & exhorteth to repentance, & to beleue the gospel. mat.4,17 & 9,35.he is hungrie.mat.4,2.he is wearie.ioh.4,6.he is pore. mat.8,20.he entreth into ierusalē riding vpon an asse.mat.21,7. he is solde by iudas.mat.26,14. he is buffeted.mat.26,67.he is deliuered to be crucified.mat.27,26. he prayeth for thē that persecute him .luk.23,34.he yeldeth vp ȳ gost.mat.27,50. his resurrectiō.mat.28. he is caryed vp into heauē.mark.16,19 luk.24,51
the coming of Christ forespoken. nomb.24,17.isa.40,10
Christ,god eternal.ioh.1.
Christ greater then dauid. matth.22,44
Christ promised to adam.gen.3,5.to abraham.gen.12,3
Christ sent of god.iohn 8,42
Christ sent to saue the iewes. mat.15,24
Christ without sinne.1.pet.2,22
false Christs and false prophetes do great miracles.mat.24,5,24
Christians so named first in Antiochia.act.11,26
Christians are fre. 1. pet. 2, 16. iohn 8,32
Christiās hated of the worlde.mat.10,22.luk.21,17
the Church is the house of god. 1. timot.3,15
the Church of god is not contentious.1.cor.11,16
¶the apostles forbid the gentiles to be Circumcised.act.15,28
Circumcise the foreskinne of the heart.deut.10,16 & 30,6. rom.2,29. colos.2,11
paul Circumciseth timothie.act.16,3
god Circumciseth our hearts, and why.deut.30,6
abraham commanded to Circumcise his familie.gen.17,9
Circumcision and vncircumcision are nothing.1.cor.7,19
Circumcision is seruitude.gal.2,4
the secōde Circumcision vnder ioshua.iosh.5,2
we haue no continuing Citie here, ebr.13,14
¶none Cleane before god. iob 25, 4
Cleopatra the daughter of Ptolomeus.1.macc.10,57
the cloude filleth the house of the lord.1.king.8,10
the renting of the Clothes a signe of great heauines. iosh.7,6. mat.26,65.2.sam.1,11
¶to heape Coles vpon the head of his enemie.rom.12,20
one oght to Cōfort another. 1.thes.4,18 & 5,14
the Comforter is promised. ioh.14,16 & 15,26 & 16,7
the ten Commandements.deut.5,7
teache thy childe the commandements of God.deut 6,7
Cōmandemēts of men, being contrarie to gods,are not to be receiued.tit.1,14
the comming of Christ in the daye of iudgement.mat.24,30.2.pet.3,10. isa.3,14 & 13,9
the Cōming of christ with his angels.mat.16,27
the comming of the lord.malac.4,1. isa.35,4 & 62,11
the Cōmune vse of goods in the primatiue church.act.2,44
the worde Cōcubine for wife.iudg.19,2
ashame not to Confesse christ. 2. timot 1,8
to Confesse god, for,to praise him, is oft times in the psalmes.
to Cōfesse that iesus is christ, is the gift of god.mat.16,17
remission to thē that Cōfesse their sinnes.1.iohn 1,9
moses Cōfesseth to god the sinne of the people.exod.32,31
Confession of sinnes commāded to the priests of the Iewes. leuit.16,21
Confession of thy sinnes to god. 1. king.8,47.psal.32,5
cursed is he that hathe his Cōfidence in man.ier.17,5
god is not the autor of Confusion, but of peace.1.cor.14,33
who oght to be excluded out of the Congregation of the lord. deut.23,1
the Conscience of the wicked is alwayes feareful.prou 28,1
christ the Consolation of israel.luk.2,25
the good Cōuersation of christiās. phil.1,27 & 3,17
the Conuersation of saincts shulde prouoke vs to followe their faith. ebr.13,7
Contemners of the worde of god shalbe punished. 1. sam. 2, 30. isa.28,14
Cornelius the captaine.act.10,1
brotherlie correction. prouer. 27,5. mat.18,15
they ȳ refuse correction,are threatned of god.leuit.26,22
the Correction of the lord.ebr.12,5
it is permitted to Correct thy brother:but to hate him, is forbiddē. leuit.19,17
circumcision the Couenant of god. gen.17,13
the Couenant of god with noah. gen.9,11
Couetousnes is idolatrie.col.3,5
Couetousnes is insatiable.pro 27,20
Couetousnes the roote of all euil. 1.tim.6,10
Couetousnes to be auoided. pro.15. 16.isa.3,12.ier.8,10.ephes.5,3
be of good Courage in affliction. iohn 16,33
the Counsels of god are vnsearcheable.rom.11,33
the israelites aske Cousel of god in their affaires. iudg.1,1 & 20,18,23.

1.sam.10,22. & herein they vse the helpe of the prophetes. 1.sam.9,9. 2.king.22,13
god breaketh the Counsels of the heathen.psal.33,10
Courteousnes required in christiãs. ephes.4,32.1.cor.13,4
zealous phinehas killeth Cozbi the midianitish harlot.nomb.25,15
¶all things Created by christ. coloss.1,16
the Creation of man.gen.1,27
god is our Creator.deut.32,18
the gospel hathe bene preached to euerie Creature.colos.1,6
euerie Creature of god is good. 1. tim.4,4
the Creature is subiect to vanitie. rom.8,20
god vseth his Creatures according to his pleasure.isa.45,9
we are new Creatures by faith in christ.2.cor.5,17.gal.6,15
they of Creta, lyers.tit.1,12
the faith of Crispus, and his whole house.act.18,8
take thy Crosse.mat.10,38 & 16,24
paul reioyced in the Crosse of iesus christ.gal.6,14
ye Crowne of rightousnes. 2. tim 4,8
the Crowne of thornes.mat.27,29
who Crucifie the flesh, and the lusts thereof.gal.5,24
¶the Cuppe and bread that we receiue in remembrance of christ. 1.cor.10,16
the Cuppe, for death & crosse. mat. 20,22
cursed is he that fulfilleth not the law.gal.3,10
cursed is he that hãgeth on the tre. deut.21,23
the Curtaines of ye tabernacle.exod. 26,5 & 36,8
olde Custome can not be forgottẽ. prou.22,6
¶Cyrus king of persia, and his doings.isa.44,28 & 45,1.ezr.1,1

D

Dagon the god of the philistims.1.sam.5,2
damaris beleueth in christ. act.17,34
the Damned are called goats. mat. 25,32
daniels doings from the first chapter of his boke to the 14
dan the sonne of iaakob. gen.30, 6 & 49,16.deut.33,22.iosh.19,40
the dedes of Darkenes.rom.13,12
darius doings.dan.5,31 & 6,14.ezr.6,1
dathan for his rebellion is consumed with fyre.nomb.16.
dauid danceth before the lord. 2. sam.6,14
dauid deceiued saul. 1.sam. 20, 5. he deceiued king achish. 1.sam. 27,10
dauid despised the commandement of the lord in committing adulterie.2.sam.12,9
dauid doeth not punish the cursed speaking of shimei.2.sam.16,10
dauid lamenteth his sonne amnon. 2.sam.13,31
dauid of necesitie eateth the shewe loaues.1.sam.21,6.mat.12,3
dauid of what stocke he came. ruth 4,17
dauids doings from the 13. of the 1. sam.to the 2.of 1.king.
dauid slewe a lion.1.sam.17,34
dauid vpright before ye lord.1.king. 14,8 & 15,3
no difference of Dayes among the faithful.rom.14,5
¶Debate and strife are workes of darkenes. rom.13,12.1.cor.1,10 and 11,16
debir, a citie.iosh.10,3 & 15,15
what is required in Deacons. 1.ti.3,8
deacons ordeined in the church by the apostles.act.6,5
we must not excede measure in lamenting the Dead.1.thes.4,13
saul seketh to the Dead.1.sam.28,11
seke not to the Dead for anie thing. deut.18,11.luk.16,29
the Dead shal heare ye voyce of the sonne of god, & shal liue. ioh.5,25
christ forespeaketh his owne Death mat.16,21
death swalowed vp into victorie.1. cor.15,54
the seconde Death.reuel.20,14
death cometh through disobedience.deut.30,17
ye day of Death vncerteine. luk. 12, 40.curse not the Deafe.leuit.19,14
christ healeth the Deafe.mar.7,32
of Deborah & of barak.iudg.5,1
deborah, rebekahs nource dyeth. gen.35,8
deborah the wife of lapidoth. iudg. 4,4
deceiue not thy brother.leuit.19,14
god wil rewarde euerie one according to his Dedes.mat.16,27
delilah betrayeth samson.iudg.16.
demetrius, seleucus sonne, and his doings. 1.macc.7,1.vnto the 14. of the 2.boke.
if we Denie christ, he wil denie vs, 2.tim.2,12
the assurance of the Desperate. ezek.33,10
dettes not demanded before the yere of fredome.deut.15,2
christ healeth two possessed of Deuils.mat.8,28 & 12,22
the Deuil cõfesseth that he knoweth christ and paul. mark. 1, 24. luk. 4. 34.act.19,15
the Deuil is a murtherer.ioh.8,44
the Deuil prince of this worlde. ephes. 2,2. ioh.12, 31. colos. 2,15. the accuser of the faithful.reuel.12,10. our aduersarie & enemie. 1. pet.5, 8.ephes.6,12
deuils driuẽ out by fasting & prayer mat.17,21
the Deuil seduceth the woman, & is therefore cursed.gen.3
the king is bounde to read the boke of Deuteronomie, & why.deu. 17,19
deuteronomie is cõmãded to be red to women and children. deut.31,12
deuteronomie is deliuered to ye leuites & elders.deut.31,9
iosiah red the boke of Deuteronomie to the people.2.king.23,2
¶the Diligence of ministers. 27,23
dinah, the daughter of iaakob, rauished.gen.34,2
dionysius an areopagite beleueth in christ.act.17,34
diotrephes reproued for his arrogãcie.3.ioh.9
seuentie Disciples sent to preache. luk.10,1
the Disciples wherein they may be knowen.ioh.8,31 & 13,35
diseases are the frutes of sinne.ioh. 5,14
in Diseases god oght to be soght vnto.2.king.1,16
disguising raiment is forbidden bothe to man & woman.deut.22,5
how god hateth Disobedience. 1. sam.15,23
the Disobedient striken with madnes, and blindnes.deut.28,28
the mã that Disobeyeth the iudge, shal dye.deut.17,12
he that Disobeyeth god, is subiect to manie curses.deut.28,15
against Diuorcement.1.cor.7,10
diuination forbidden. leuit. 20, 27. deut.18,10.isa.8,19
he or she that hathe the spirit of Diuination, oght to be stoned to death.leuit.20,27
¶sounde Doctrine.tit.2,8
no Doctrine, but christs oght to be receiued.2.ioh.10.colos.2,8
doctrines of deuils.1.tim.4,1
doeg disclosed dauid to saul. 1.sam. 22,9
giue not holie things to Dogges. mat.

mat.7,6
the Dogge is returned to his vomit. 2.pet.2,22
dommage, that one doeth to another.exod.22,4
the Domme is healed.mat.9,32
the doue sent out of the arke. gen. 8,8
¶the Dragon, ẏ olde serpent.reuel. 20,2.
by Dreames god speaketh to the prophetes.nomb.12,6
spiritual Drinke.1.cor.10,4
the Dropsie is healed.luk.14,2
the euils that come of Drunkẽnes. prou.23,29
christ was sclandered to be a Drunkarde.mat.11,19 the apostles also, act.2,13
Drunkennes to be auoyded, euen of kings.prou.31,4. luk.21,34.ephes.5, 18
¶man is Dust.gen.3,19
the Dust of the feete shaken of against whome.mat.10,14
¶manie Dwelling places in ẏ house of god.ioh.14,2
¶paul desireth to Dye.phil.1,23
christ prayeth, not to Dye. mat.26, 39
christ desireth to Dye for vs.luk.12, 50
it is ordeined for all to Dye once. ebr.9,27
christ Dyed for our sinnes. rom.4,25

E

THe Earth is cursed for adams transgression.gen.3,17
the Earth is corrupt.gen.6,11
man shal returne to the Earth. gen. 3,19
to Eat the flesh of christ.ioh.6,51,63
¶Ebed-melech the blacke more. ier.38,7
Eber & his sonnes.gen.10,25
¶esau, why he is called Edom.gen. 25,30
Edom denyeth passage to israel. nomb.20,14
Edom rebelleth from vnder iudah. 2.king.8,20
¶the Egyptians eat not with the ebrewes.gen.43,32.of them loke in exod.11,& 12.deut.23,7.ier.46,2.ezek.32,12
Egypt the yron fornace. deut.4, 20
¶Ehud a iudge in israel.iudg.3,15
¶the Ekronites and their doings.1. sam.5,10
¶what condicions the Elders oght to haue.tit.2,2
Eleazar the sonne of aaron. exod. 6,25.iosh.24,33
gods purpose is by his Electiõ.rom. 9,11
election of grace.rom.11,5
make your calling & Election sure. 2.pet.1,10
as touching the Election they are loued for the fathers sakes. rom. 11,28
the Elect haue obteined that israel obteined not.rom.11,7
we knowe that ye are Elect of god. 1.thess.1,4
election lyeth in god & not in vs. rom.9,11 & 16
the Elect are fewe in nomber. mat. 7,14
elected before the fundaciõ of the worlde.ephes.1,4
the Elect of god can not be condẽned.rom.8,34
the Elect were chosen before the fundacions of the worlde. ephes. 1,4.1.pet.1,2
Eli the priest & his doings. 1.sam.1 & 2 & 3 & 4
Eliakim, called also iehoiakim. 2. king.23,34
Elias & Eliseus.luk.4,25,27
Eliah the prophet & his doings. 1. king.17 vnto the 2.king.2
Elimelech & his wife naomi. ruth 1,2
Elisabet zacharies wife.luk.1,5
Elisha balde.2.king.2,23
Elisha doeth good for euil. 2.king. 6,22
Elisha, his life & his doings.1.king. 19 vnto the 2.king.13
Elisha is called from the plow to prophecie.1.king.19,19
Elisheba aarons wife.exod.6,23
Elon a iudge in israel.iudg.12,12
Elymas the sorcerer withstanding pauls preaching.act.13,8
¶Emmanuel.mat.1,23
¶take from among you all Enchanters.deut.18,11
Enchanters and southsayers driuen out of israel by saul.1.sam.28,3
the End of all things is at hand. 1. pet.4,7
he that Endureth to the end, shalbe saued.mat.24,13.2.thess.3,13
Eneas healed by the meanes of peter.act 9,33
loue thine Enemies.mat.5,44.prou. 25,21
christ prayeth for his Enemies.luk. 23,34
Enosh the sonne of sheth. gen.4,26
flee Enuie.gal.5,26.1.pet.2,1
enuious persones.prou.23,6
¶Ephesians worshiped diana. act. 19,35
Ephraim and his doings. gen.41,52. & 48,5,49
the Ephraimites rise vp against gideon.iudg.8,1.
the Epicures dispute with paul. act. 17,18
pauls Epistles hard to be vnderstãd 2.pet.3,16
¶the Ernest of the spirit in our hearts.2.cor.1,22 & 5,5
¶Esarhadden reigneth after saneherib.2.king.19,37
Esau and his doings. gen. 25 vnto the 36
who are to be Eschewed.2.tim.3,5
Ester and her doings. ester 2 & 4 & 5 & 7
¶hate that that is Euil.rom.12,9
recompense not Euil for euil. rom. 12,17
god turneth ẏ Euil into good. gen. 50,20.rom.8,28
do not companie with Euil men. prou.24,1
we are Euil of nature.mat.7,11.gen. 6,5
an Eunuch, candaces chief gouernour, beleueth in iesus christ.act. 8,17
Eutychus restored to life.act. 20,10.
¶he that Exalteth him self, shalbe broght lowe.luk.18,14
examine all things.1.thess.5,21
examine thy self before thou come to the supper of the lord. 1. cor.11,28
excõmunicate those that loue not iesus christ.1.cor.16,22
the Excommunicacion that paul vsed.1.cor.5,5
Exorcistes, hurt by the euil spirit. act.19,13
experience bringeth hope. rom.5,4
¶the good Eye,mat.6,22
eye for Eye.exod.21,24.mat.5,38

F

OLde wiues Fables.1.tim.4,7
euerie one oght to proue his Faith.2.cor.13,5
continuance in Faith.coloss.1,23
the shield of Faith.ephes.6,16
christ prayeth for peters Faith.luk. 22,32
the definicion of Faith.ebr.11,1
faith cometh by hearing.rom.10,17
the apostles praye to haue their Faith increased.luk.17,5
faith in god by christ. 1.pet.1,21. mat.12,21
faith ioyned with charitie.1.tim.1,5
faith is the gift of god. phil. 1,29.

2.pet.1,3
the end of Faith is the saluacion of our soules.1.pet.1,9
the Faith of abrahã.gen.15,6 & 24,7
the Faith of the fathers.ebr.11
by Faith the spirit is receiued. gal. 3,2
by Faith the hearts are purified .act. 15,9.ioh.15,3
by Faith we resist ŷ deuil. 1.pet.5,9
faith without workes is dead. iam. 2,17
the Faithful are the children of abraham.rom.9,8
the Faithful shal not come into condemnacion.ioh.5,24
to Fall into the hands of the liuing god.ebr.12,31
to Fall vpon the face.gen.17,17.ruth 2,10
a great Famine in samaria. 1.king. 18,2.2.king.6,25
the Famine of gods worde forespoken. amos 8,11
moses Fasteth fortie daies and fortie nights. exod. 34,28. christ likewise.mat.4,2
fained Fastig.isa.58,3.zech.7,5.mat. 6,16
the father of christ is our Father. ioh.20,17
he that knoweth christ, knoweth the Father.ioh.14,7
honour thy Father & mother.mat. 15,4.mar.7,10
fathers are charged to teache their childrẽ the law of god.deut.11,19
he that beateth his Father, or mother, shal dye the death. exod.21, 15.prou.20,20
god doeth right vnto the Fatherles. deut.10,18
the Fatherles.deut.14,29 & 24,19 & 26,12 & 27,19
¶ the Feareful must absent them selues from warre.deut.20,8
learne to Feare god.deut.14,23
the Feare of god is true wisdome. iob.28,28
the worthiest places at Feasts. mat. 23,6
feasts made at shepeshearings. 2. sam.13,23
¶god teacheth to Fight.2.sam.22,35
the Finger of god, for his power. exod.8,19
the First borne in the land of egypt dye.exod.11,4
of First frutes.exod.22,29
the First frutes perteined to the hie priests.nomb.5,9
fishes cleane & vncleane .leuit.11,9
¶paul neuer vsed Flatterie.1.thess. 2,5
flee in time of persecuciõ.mat.10,23
the dedes of the Flesh.gal.5,17
man is but Flesh.gen.6,3
to be in the Flesh, for, to liue according to the Flesh.rom.7,5
flesh & blood, that is, whatsoeuer is in man.mat.16,17
the wisdome of the Flesh is death. rom.7,24 & 8,6
flesh lusteth agaĩst ŷ spirit. gal.5,17
the Flesh of christ eaten by faith. ioh.6,54
the care of the Flesh oght to be reiected.rom.13,14
to eat the Flesh with the blood is forbid.gen.9,4
be careful ouer your Flockes.prou. 27,23
noahs Flood.gen.6 & 7 & 8
the cause of the vniuersal Flood. gen.6,5
an offring of Floure.leuit.2,1
¶ by the Folde is vnderstand the church.ioh.10,16
a rodde belõgeth to the Fooles backe .prou.26,3
forbeare one another.ephes.4,2
christ deliuered by the determinat cousel & Foreknowledge of god. act.2,23
we are elect according to the Foreknowledge of god.1.pet.1,2
our Forerunner, christ.ebr.6,20
how oft thou oghtest to Forgiue thy brother.mat.18,21
fornicacion oght not to be named among vs.ephes.5,3
fornicators shal not inherit ŷ kingdome of god.1.cor.6,9
forsake thy father and mother for christs sake.mat.19,29
forsake thy self.mat.16,24
fooles.prou.12,vnto 18
the Foxes of samson.iudg.15,4
¶mans Fragilitie.isa.40,6
the tre is knowen by the frute.mat. 7,16
¶wo to them that be Ful.luk.6,25
¶the piller of Fyre.exod.40,38
christ is come to put Fyre on the earth.luk.12,41
euerlasting Fyre prepared for the deuil.mat.25,41
a law touching the Fyre that consumeth the corne.exod.22,6
the Fyrie law.deut.33,2

G

GAal ebeds sonne & his doings. iudg.9,26
Gad the prophet.1.sam.22,5. 2.sam. 24,11
Gad the sonne of iaakob. gen. 30,11 & 49,19.iosh.22
the counsel of Gamaliel.act.5,35
the Garment made of linen & wollen, forbidden.deut.22,11
aarons Garments.exod.28
the strait Gate leadeth to life.mat. 7,13
iudgemẽt done in the Gates of the citie.deut.22,15
gatherings for ŷ saintes.1.cor.16,1
¶Gedaliah is slayne.2.king.25,25
the Gelded shal not entre into the congregacion of ŷ lord. deut.23,1
gentlenes is praise worthie.prou. 16,21.ephes.4,2
election of the Gentiles.psal.2,8 & 18,47
israel is forbidden to be at peace with the Gentiles.deut.7,2
the conuersion of the Gentiles.isa. 2,2.act.11,17 & 14,27
the holie gost fell vpon the Gentiles.act.10,44
the vocacion of ŷ Gentiles by preaching.isa.66,18
the cõuersacion of ŷ Gẽtiles, before thei knewe the trueth.ephes.2,1
christ calleth the Gentiles, dogges. mat.15,26
god for a time suffred ŷ Gẽtiles to walke in their owne ways.act.14,16
¶the men of Gibeah and their wickednes.iosh.19,22
Gideon & his doĩgs.iudg.6 & 7 & 8
the tryal ŷ Gideon toke of his souldiers, and how manie they were. iudg.7,5
god measureth the Gift according to the heart.mar.12,44
saluacion is ŷ Gift of god.ephes.2,8
the Gift of god is not boght with money.act.8,20
Gehazi receiued Gifts of naamã. 2 king.5,27
the Gifts of the holie gost are diuers.1.cor.12,4
to be Girded w̃ veritie.ephes.6,14
giue & it shalbe giuẽ vnto you.luk. 6,38
it is a blessed thing to Giue rather then to receiue.act.20,35
god loueth a chereful Giuer.2.cor. 9,7
¶the desire of vaine glorie.gal.5,26
man oght not to Glorie in him self 1.cor.4,7, but in the knowledge of god.ierem.9,23
glotons and drunkards are to be auoyded.prou.23,20
glottonie.rom.13,13
¶the Goat charged w̃ all the iniquities of the people.leuit.16,22
the people require new Gods.exod 32,23

God is almightie. gen.17,1 & 35,11
God is a spirit. ioh.4,24
God is euerie where and seeth all things. ier.23,23
God is immortal. 1.tim.1,17 & 6,16
God is inuisible. exod.33,20. ioh.1,18. moses sawe him, & how. exod.24, 10. so did iaakob. gen.32,30
the liuing God is the god of israel. exod.29,45. leuit.26.13. 2.cor.6,16
God is with thee, a kinde of salutation. iudg.6,12 ruth.2,4
there is but one God to the faithful. 1.cor.8,6
the Gods ẏ are made ẇ mans hand, can not saue thẽ selues. bar.6,14
Gog and his fall. ezek.38 & 39
going out of egypt. exod.12,37
Goliath slaine by dauid. 1.sam.17.
Gomorrah consumed with fyre frõ heauen. gen.19,24
followe that that is Good. rom.12,9
no Goodnes dwelleth in our flesh. rom.7,18
thou that art taught, minister to thy teacher in all Good things. gal.6, 6. 1.cor.9,14
do Good without fainting. gal.6,9. euen to thine enemies. luk.6,35
the definitiõ of the Gospel. rom.1,16
the summe of the Gospel. ephes.1,7
christ preacheth ẏ Gospel. mar.1,14
the Gospel is the worde of the eternal god. 1.pet.1,23. it is the worde of trueth. ephes.1,13
the end of them that obeye not the Gospel of god. 2.thess.2,10. 1.pet. 4,17
the Gospel of iohn why it is writẽ. iohn.20,30
the Gospel oght to be preached to all creatures. mar.16,15.
blasphemie against the holie Gost. mat.12,31
the graces and giftes of the holie Gost are diuers. 1 cor.12,4
the holie Gost is sent. act.2,2
the holie Gost promised to the apostles. luk.24,49. ioh.14,16. act.1,8
god giueth the holie Gost to them that desire him. luk.11,13
to Go vnto his fathers, for, to dye. gen.15,15
¶ through Grace we are saued. ephe. 2,5
the Graine of corne that falleth on the grounde. ioh.12,24
eat of thy neighbours Grapes, but beare none awaye. deut.23,24
the Grekes seke for wisdome. 1.cor. 1,22
grieue not the holie spirit of god. ephes.4,30
¶ Gyants. gen.6,4
gyants in ẏ land of canaã. nõb.13,34

H

Habacuc feedeth daniel, read the storie of bel.
Habel murdered by his brother. ge. 4,8. ebr.11,4. mat.23,35
Hadad salomõs enemie. 1.king.11,14
Haggai the prophet. ezr.5,1
Hagar sarais maid. gen.16 & 21
Ham mocketh his father noah. gen. 9,22
Haman is hanged. ester 7,9,10
Hannah the wife of elkanah & mother of samuel. 1.sam.1 & 2
Hananiah the false prophet. ier.28,1
commune Hands. mark.7,2
the laying on of Hands. act. 19, 6. 1. tim.4,14
christ sitteth at table with vnwashẽ Hands. luk.11,38
none can escape the Hand of god. amos 9,2. deut.32,39
christ by laying on of Hãds healeth the sicke. luk.4,40
to stretch the Hãds out towards heauen. 1.king.8,22. exod.9, 22 & 17,11
the mans Hand, that was dryed vp, is healed. mat.12,10
christ layeth his Hands vpon the infants. mat.19,15
Hãnah nourced her childe. 1.sa. 1,23
of Hanun king of the ammonites, and of the il entreatie of dauids seruants. 2.sam.10,4
Haran the sonne of terah. gen.11,27
Haraphah of the stocke of gyants. 2. sam.21,16
god whome he wil, he maketh Hard hearted. rom.9,18
nothing is Hard to god. gen.18,14
the Haruest. leuit.19,9
the Haruest of the faithful. mat.9,37. ioh.4,35
Hazael king ouer aram. 1.king.19, 15. vnto the 2.king.13
¶ the Head of the church, christ. ephes.4,15
Heare christ. deut.18,18. mat.17,5
singlenes of Heart. 2.cor.1,12. 1.pet. 1,22
vncircũcised Hearts. ier.9,26. deut. 10, 16. out of the which come euil thoghts. mat.15,19
the lord seeth the Heart of man. 1. sam.16,7. rom.8,27
the Heart of man is wicked. gen.6,5. deut.29,19
gods lawes writen in the Hearts of the faithful. ebr.8,10
ẏ good Heart speaketh good thĩgs. mat.12,35
the creation of Heauen. gen.1,6
new Heauẽs & new earth. 2.pet.3,13
the Heauen shut vp because of gods wrath. deut.11,17
Hebron, a citie. gen.35,27.
it is comelie for a woman to haue long Heere. 1.cor.11,15
not an Heere of them shal perish, that suffre for christ. luk.21,18
our Heeres be nombred. mat.10,30
christ the Heire of all thĩgs. ebr.1,2
a description of Hel. isa.30,33
Heman the singer. 1.chron.6,33
Henoch the first citie. gen.4,17
Henoch the sonne of kain. gen.4,17
Henoch taken vp. gen.5,24
herbes created. gen.1,11
there must be Heresies, and why. 1. cor.11,19
heresies are dedes of ẏ flesh. gal.5,19
heretikes must be auoided. tit.3,10
the Heritage of him that dyeth without manchilde. nom.27,8
god, the Heritage of the leuites. deut.18,2
an Heritage reserued for vs in heauen. matth.25,34. gal.3,17. tit.3,7. 1. pet.1,3
christ calleth Herode a foxe. luk.13,32
Herode killeth the infants. mat.2,16
the daye of Herodes natiuitie. mar. 6,21
Herodes opinion of christ. mat.14,2
Hezekiah king of iudah, & his doings. 2. king. 18 & 19 & 20. isa. 36. vnto the 39
¶ the riuer Hiddekel. gen.2,14
giue the workeman his Hier. leuit. 19,13. deut.24,14
Hiram ẏ king of tyre, & his doings. 2.sam.5,11. and hiram the cunning workeman. 1.king.7,13
god cõmandeth the Hittites to be destroyed vtterly. deut.20,17
¶ Honie in the liõs bodie. iudg.14,8
honour all men. 1.pet.2,17
giue Honour to thy wife, as to the weaker vessel. 1.pet.3,7
giue Honour, to whome ye owe honour. rom.13,7
we are saued by Hope. rom.8,24
hope maketh not ashamed. rom.5,5
Hophni the sonne of eli. 1. sam.2,34 & 4,4
Horeb a mountaine, called also sinai. deut.1,2
god is the Horne of our saluation. 2.sam.22,3
Horims chased out by the sonnes of esau. deut.2,12
the nombre of salomons Horses. 1. king.4,26. 2.chron.9,25
abraham & lots Hospitalitie. gen. 18,2 & 19,2

vse Hospitalitie. rom. 12,13. ebr. 13,2. 1. pet. 4,9
of Housbands. 1. cor. 7,11. ephes. 5,22
the bodie of man is called an earthlie House. 2. cor. 5,1
the House infected with the plague of leprosie. leuit. 14,14
the House of god, ÿ house of prayer. isa. 56,7. mat. 21,13
the House of god, the people of israel. nomb. 12,7
the House of god, the tēple. 2. sam. 12,20
¶Huldah the prophetesse. 2. king. 22, 14. 2. chron. 34,22
he that Humbleth him self, shalbe exalted. mat. 23,12. philip. 2,8. iam. 4,10
humilitie. prou. 16,19. mat. 11,29. luk. 14,11. ephes. 4,2
an Hundreth folde is promised to thē that shal forsake that they haue to followe christ. mat. 19,29
rulers ouer Hūdreths established by moses. exod. 18,21
blessed are they that Hungre and thirst for righteousnes. mat. 5,6
christ is an Hungred. mat. 4,2
Hushai, and his doings. 2. sam. 15,32 & 17,5
¶Hypocrisie. prou. 12,6. 30,12
hypocrisie reproued. isa. 58,2
an Hyreling. iohn 10,12

I

IAakob & esau abunde in riches. gen. 36,7
iaakob and his doings. gen. 25. vnto the 49
iaakob beloued of god. rom. 9,13
iaakob is accompanied of god, whethersoeuer he goeth. gen. 28,15
iaakob is called israel. gen. 32,28
iaakob wrestleth with god. gen. 32,24
iabin king of canaan. iudg. 4,2
iahaziel a prophet. 2. chron. 20,14
iair a iudge in israel. iudg. 10,3
iames sawe christs resurrectiō. 1. cor. 15,7
iames the brother of iohn is put to death. act. 12,2
iannes and iambres resisted moses. 2. timot. 3,8
iaphet & his sonnes. gen. 10,2
iasons assurance for receiuing of paul. act. 17,9
¶Ibzan a iudge in israel. iudg. 12,8
¶Idolaters oght to dye, & wherefore. deut. 17,2. they shal not inherit the kingdome of heauen. 1. cor. 6,9
idolaters slaine by the sonnes of leui. exod. 32,26
things consecrated to Idoles. 1. cor. 8. act. 15,20
idoles are but vanitie. 1. sam. 12,21. 1. king. 16,26. they are abomination. deut. 7,25 & 27,15
idoles forbidden. leuit. 26,1. deut. 18,9
¶Iehoahaz, the sonne of Iehu the king, & his doings. 2. king. 13,1
iehoiachin succedeth iehoiakim his father. 2. king. 24
iehoiada, the hie priest. 2. king. 11,4
iehoiakim seruant to the king of babel. 2. king. 24,1
iehonadab the sonne of rechab. 2. king. 10,15
iehoram the king of iudah, and his doings. 1. king. 22,50. 2. king. 8,16
iehoram the sonne of ahab. 2. king. 3,1
iehoshaphat king of Iudah. 1. king. 15,24. 2. king. 3,1
iehoshua the sonne of iehozadak. hag. 1,1
iehu a prophet. 1. king. 16,7
iehu king of israel, and his doings. 1. king. 19,16. vnto the 2 king. 10
god is a Ielous god. exod. 20,5. deut. 5,9
the law of Ielousie. nomb. 5.
iericho destroyed. iosh. 2 & 6. buylt vp againe by hiel. 1. king. 16,34
iericho wholy consecrated to the lord. iosh. 6,17
the hand of Ieroboam dryed vp. 1. king. 13,4
ieroboam king of israel, & his doings. 1. king. 11,26. vnto the 15
the ruine of Ierusalem. mat. 23,38
ierusalem buylt againe. nehe. 3,1
ierusalem, called also iebusi. iosh. 15, 8 & 18,28
gideon called Ierubbaal, & wherefore. iudg. 6,32
iesus the name of the messias. mat. 1,21. luk. 1,31. philip. 2,10
vaine Iesting forbid. ephes. 5,4
iethro moses father in law. exod. 3, 1 & 18,1
the Iewes baptized in moses. 1. cor. 10,2
the Iewes exercised in afflictions. deut. 8,16
the Iewes obstinacie. isa. 48, 4. act. 28,27
the remnant of the Iewes shal returne. isa. 10,21
iezebel, & her cruel doings. 1. king. 16 & 18 & 19 & 21. 2. king. 9,30
¶the Image is a curse to him that maketh it. deut. 27,15
mans Imaginations are euil. gen. 6,5
¶we oght not to cōpanie with Infideles. 2. cor. 6,4
infideles are called the drye tre. luk. 23,31
infirmities come vpon vs for our sinnes. ioh. 5,14
the leuites Inheritance. deut. 10,9
euerie one shal beare his owne Iniquitie. deut. 24,16
iniuries oght to be forgottē. leu. 19,18
innocent as concerning euil & wise vnto ÿ which is good. rom. 16,19
none is Innocēt before god. exo. 34,7
thre things are Insatiable. prou. 30,15
wicked Inuentions. deut. 28,20
christ is our Intercessour. rom. 8,34
ioab, & his doings. 2. sam. 2,13 & 11 & 14 & 19. 1. king. 21,5
ioash preserued through ÿ helpe of his aunt iehosheba. 2. king. 11,2
ioash the father of gideon. iudg. 6,29
ioash the sonne of ahaziah, and Iehoash the sonne of iehoahaz. 2. king. 11 & 14
iob an exāple of pacience. iam. 5,11
iochebed, ÿ wife of amrā. exod. 6,20
iohanan. ier. 40 & 41 & 42 & 43
iohn baptist exhorteth to repentance. mat. 3,2
iohn baptist is buryed. mat. 14,12
iohn marke the minister of paul & barnabas. act. 12,25
ionathan a gouernour of the iewes. 1. mac. 9 & 11 & 12
ionathan the sonne of saul, and his doings. 1. sa. 14 & 18 & 19 & 20 & 31
ioseph & his doings, from the 30 of gen. vnto the 50.
ioseph of arimathea. mat. 27,57
ioses called barnabas. act. 4,36
the good king Iosiah, & his doings, 1. king. 13,2. 2. king. 21,24 & 22,1
ioshua, & his doings. exod. 24,13 & 32, 17. nomb. 11,28 & 13 & 14. deut. 1,38. & throughout his whole boke.
iothā the sonne of Ierubbaal. iudg. 9,5
the iourneis of the children of Israel. nom. 33
¶Iphtah, & his doings. iudg. 11 & 12
¶Isaiah the prophet. 2. king. 19, 20 & 20. his visions. 1 & 2 & 6
ishai dauids father. ruth 4,22. 1. sam. 16,11
ish-bosheth, & his doings. 2. sam. 2 & 3 & 4
ishmael, & his life. gen. 16 & 17 & 21 & 25
why iaakob was called israel. gen. 32,28
true Israelites, who. rom. 9,6
carnal Israel described. hose. 9,7
israel sinned not of ignorāce. rom. 10,19
¶Iubal, the inuentour of the harpe. gen. 4,21
the Iubile. leuit. 25,10

the

the rest of Iudah led away to babel. 2.king.25,11
iudah leahs sonne.gen.29,35
of Iudas maccabeus read the bokes of maccabies.
iudas that betrayed christ. ioh. 18,2. his repentance.mat. 27,3. he slewe him self, and brast in the middes. act.1,18
the general Iudgement. isa.2,19 and 26,11.the signes that shal come before it.mat.24,29
iudgement,for affliction.1.pet.4,17
iudgement beginneth at the house of god.1.pet.4,17
gods Iudgemēts are a great deapth, psal.36,6
the office of a Iudge.exod.23,6
speake not euil of Iudges.exo.22,28
what maner of men oght to be Iudges.exod.18,21 & 23,2
iudge not another.mat.7,1 & 12,7
the Iudge of all the worlde.ge.18,25
a Iudge oght not to haue anie respect of persones.leuit.19,15
iudges are called gods . exod. 22,8. psal.82,6
the Iudges gaue sentēce according to moses law.deut.17,11
iustified by faith . rom. 5, 1. not by workes.gal.3,10
we are Iustified, or condemned by our wordes.mat.12,37
iustified, what it signifieth .tit. 3, 4. act.13,38
¶Izhak the sonne of abraham, and his doings.gen.21.vnto the 28

K

NAtiuitie of Kain, and his doings.gen.4,1 & 2.1.ioh.3,12
¶Keilah a citie,deliuered by dauid. 1.sam.23,1
god Kepeth his as the apple of the eye.deut.32,10
keturah the wife of abrahā.gen.25,1
the Keyes of the kingdome of heauen promised.mat.16,19. are giuen by christ to his apostles. ioh.20,23
¶man oght to kepe him frō all Kinde of euil 1.thess.5,22
the rigour of a King.1.sam.8,11
what is required in Kings.deu.17,15
what is ẏ honour of Kings.pro.25,2
the Kingdome of christ eternal.isa. 9,7.luk.1,33
the Kingdome of heauen suffreth violence.mat.11,12
the Kingdome within vs.luk.17,21
kiriath-arba a citie, called also hebron.iosh.14,15
kiriath sepher a citie,called also debir.iosh.15,15
paul Kissed of ẏ faithful.act.20,37
the holie Kisse of christians . rom. 16,16.2.cor.13,12
¶god hathe not cast away his people, ẇ he Knewe before. rom. 11,2
whome god Knewe before,them he ordeined to be like facioned vnto the image of his sonne.rom.8,29
to Knowe god and iesus christ,whome he hathe sent, is life eternal. ioh.17,3
the Knowledge of saluatiō. luk.1,77
¶Kohath and his sonnes. exod.6,18. iosh.21,5
korah for his rebellion is striken of god.nomb.16
the red Kow.nomb.19

L

LAban the brother of rebekah,& his doings.gen.24,29
the Laborers are few.mat.9,37
man appointed to labour.gen.3,19
he that doeth not Labour, oght not to eat.2.thess.3,10
we oght to liue by our Labours. prou.5,15
we oght to Labour with our hands. 1.thess.4,11
the Ladder that iaakob sawe in his dreame.gen.28,12
christ calleth to him them that are Laden.mat.11,28
the pascal Lambe.exod.12,3
iesus the Lambe of god.ioh.1,29
Lamech,and his two wiues.gene.4, 19 & 5,26
the Lame, from his mothers wombe is healed.act.3,7
the Last shal be the first.mat.19,30
wo to them that Laugh,and why. luk.6,25
theLaw,a yoke. act.15,10
the end of the Law, christ. rom.10,4
by the Law cometh knowledge of sinne.rom.3,20
the Law giuen to the lawles.1.ti.1,9
the Law is giuen vnto the people. exod.20.deut.5
the Law not giuen for the iuste. gal.5,18
the Law,our schole master to bring vs to christ.gal.3,24
before the Law sinne was not counted sinne.rom.5,13
the Law writen in the heart of the faithful.ebr.8,10
Lazarus raised vp. ioh.11 & 12
Lazarus sicke.ioh.11,4
¶Lea conceiueth.gen.29,32
the Leaper,healed by faith. mat.8,2
the ten Leapers healed.luk.17,12
the iudging of Leprosies. deut.24,8. leuit.13 & 14
the Law of Lending.exod.22,14
lend to the nedie. deut.15,8.mat.5,42
the Letter killeth, and the spirit giueth life.2.cor.3,6
purge the olde Leuaine.1.cor.5,7
leuaine for wicked doctrine. mat. 16,6
Leuites elected to the ministerie. nomb.3,45
Leui the sonne of iaakob. gen.29,34. he slayeth the sichimites. ge.34,25
¶paul vseth not his Libertie. 1. cor.9,4
libertie giueth not occasion to the flesh.gal.5,13
the Libertie of the spirit.2.cor.3,17
the breuitie of mans Life.psalm.90. iob 7
to finde his Life, and to lose it.mat. 10,39
our Life,christ.ioh.14,6.colos.3,4
the Life of mā is as the dayes of an hyreling.iob 7,2
the Life of man is but a vapour. iam.4,14
the Life of the flesh is in the blood. leuit.17,11
the creation of the Light.gen.1,3
the Lion of the tribe of iuda. reuelat.5,5
the frute of the Lippes.ebr.13,15
as thy soule Liueth, a kinde of othe. 1.sam.1,26
to Liue in ioye.ecclesiasti.8,15 & 9,7
man Liueth by the worde of god. deut.8,3
¶twentie Loaues do fil an hūdreth men.2.king.4,42
lois the grand mother of timothie. 2.tim.1,5
to Lose sinnes.mat.18,18.ioh.20,23
Lot abrahās neuew, & his doings. gen.11 & 13 & 19. deut.2,9,19
Lots wife turned into a piller of salt.gen.19,26.luk.17,32.
precepts of Loue.prou.3,28
the force & power of Loue.1.cor.13
loue coueteth the multitude of sinnes.prou.10,12.1.pet.4,8
god is Loue.1.ioh.4,16
god Loued vs first.1.ioh.4, 19
loue excelleth faith and hope.1.cor. 13,13
loue enuieth not.1.cor.13,4
they Loue god that kepe his commandements.1.iohn 2,5
loue is not prouoked to angre. 1. cor.13,5
loue is the fulfilling of the law.rom. 138
the Loue of god in our hearts.ro.5,5
in whome the Loue of god is perfite.1.iohn 2,5
loue one another.iohn 13,34

to Loue the stranger as thy self. leuit.19,34. to loue thine enemies. mat.5,44
he that Loueth another, hathe fulfilled the law.rom.13,8
he that Loueth christ, kepeth his cõmandements.ioh.14,15 & 21
god so Loueth the worlde, that he hathe giuen his sonne,&c.ioh.3,16
¶Luke a physicion.colos.4,14
the Lunatike healed.mat.17,15
lust is forbidden. deut.5,21. exod.20,17.1.cor.10,6
the people Lusteth for flesh, and is punished.nomb.11,33
¶god can not Lye.tit.1,2
he that denieth christ, is a Lyer.1.ioh.2,22
all men are Lyers.isa 9,17
the father of Lyes.ioh.8,44
ẏ Lye of ananias & his wife. act.5,3
iaakob Lyeth to his father.gen.27,19
the prophet is punished for his Lying.1.king.13,18
the Lying spirit in the mouth of the prophetes.1.king.22,23
lying to be auoyded.ephes.4,25
Lysias.1.mac.3,32

M

THe worde preached to the Macedonians.act.16,10
seke not to Magicians.leuit.19,31
magiciãs banished out of israel by saul.1.sam.28,3
obeye the Magistrates.rom.13,1
magistrates that feare god. exod.18,21.deut.1,13
the bonde Maides of the iewes.exo.21,7.leuit.19,20 & 25,44.deut.15,12
Makkedah, a citie taken by ioshua. iosh.10,28
Malchus, whose eare was smiten of. ioh.18,10
he that ceaseth not frõ Malice, shal perish.1.sam.12,25
all things subiect to Man.gen.1,26
the outwarde man.2.cor.4,16
man & wife are one flesh.gen.2,24
the olde Mã is crucified with christ rom.6,6.colos.3,9
man made according to the image of god.gen.1,26
mã naturally is the childe of wrath. ephes.2,3
the Man of god, for, the prophet. 2.king.1,9 & 8,11
man, a meat vnknowen to the children of israel.exod.16,15. deut.8,3. the people lothe to eat it.nomb.11,6. it ceaseth to fall from heauen. iosh.5,12
Manasseh ẏ kĩg of iudah.2.kĩg.21,34
Manasseh the sonne of ioseph, & his doings.gen.41,51 & 48,1. iosh.13,29 & 14,4 & 22,1
the Mandrakes of leah.gen.30,14
Maneh.ezek.45,12
the Mantle of eliiah, & of elisha.1.king.19,19.2.king.2,13
Marah, the place of bitter waters. exod.15,23
the praise of Mariage.ebr.13,4
of Mariage.1.cor.7.
they that breake the lawes of Mariage, are reproued.mal.2,14
the institution of Mariage. gen.9,1 & the cõfirmation thereof. ge.9,1
vnlawful Mariages.leuit.18,6
mariage in cana.ioh.2,1
the Mariage of rebekah. gen.24. of tobias.tob.7,13
they that forbid to Marie, are spirits of errour.1.tim.4,3
Marie magdalene and her doings. mat.27,61.ioh.20,1
Marie sitteth at christs fete.luk.10,39
Marie the sister of Martha. ioh.11,1 & 12,3.luk.10,39.mat.26,7
Marie the virgine, & mother of our sauiour iesus christ, according to the flesh.luk.1,31 & 2,7.ioh.2,3
Marke barnabas sisters sonne.colos.4,10
Martha receiueth christ into her house.luk.10,38.her faith.ioh.11,27
the Martyrdome of ẏ seuẽ brethrẽ, and of their mother.2.mac.7
christ our Master. ioh.13,13. mat.23,8
christ forbiddeth vs to be called Masters.mat.23,8.iam.3,1
the duetie of Masters towards their seruants.eph.6,9
Matthewe called of Christ.mat.9,9
Matthias elected to be an apostle. act.1,26
¶iust Measures.leuit.19,36
Medad & eldad do prophecie.nom.11,27
christ our Mediatour.1.tim.2,5
moses ẏ Mediatour of Israel.deu.5,5
meditate in the worde of god day and night.deut.11,19.iosh.1,8
Melchi-zedek.gen.14,18.ebr.7,1
mortifie your Members.col.3,5
the duetie of our mẽbers.rom.6,19
Menahem who, and his crueltie.2.king.15,14,17
men oght to loue their wiues. ephe.5,28.prou.5,18
Mephibosheth the sonne of ionathã & his doĩgs.2 sam.4,4.9,7 & 16,1
ẏ gẽtiles receiued to Mercie.ro.11,30
mercie is praised. prou.14,21 & 19,17
mercie more then sacrifice. mat.9,13
the Mercie of dauid towards saul. 1.sam.24,7
the Mercie of god throughout all ages.luk.1,50
the forme of the Mercieseat. exod.25,17 & 37,6
mercie shalbe shewed to the mercieful.mat.5,7.prou.11,25
shew Mercie ẇ chearfulnes.ro.12,8
god is merciful to those that loue him.exod.20,6 & 34,7.deut.5,10
god be Merciful vnto thee, a maner of blessing.gen.43,29
Methushael.gen.4,18
¶Michael striueth agaĩst the deuil. iude 9
Michah an ephraimite.iudg.17
Michaiah the prophet, and his doings.1.king.22,8
Michal the wife of dauid.1.sam.18,19 & 25,44.2.sam.3,13 & 6,16
Micha the sonne of mephibosheth. 2.sam.9,12
the Midianites are slaine at gods commandement.nomb.25,17
beginners must be fed with Milke. ebr.5,12
the syncere Milke of the worde.1.pet.2,2
Millo buylt by salomon.1.king.9,24
the nether and vpper Milstone.deu.24,6
ẏ wicked are deliuered into a lewde Minde.isa.57,20.rom.1,28
the Ministerie of the worde is the preaching of the same.act.20,24
christ is our Minister. matth.20,28. ebr.8,2
against false Ministers.ier.23,25
whoso murmureth against ẏ Ministers, murmureth against god.exod.16,8
the Ministers of god what maner mẽ they oght to be.leuit.21,21
ministers oght for their preaching to haue sufficient.rom.15,27
ministers that tikle the eares ẇ pleasant fables.2.tim.3,6 & 4,3.tit.1,10
christ came to Minister vnto. mat.20,28
ẏ iewes demãde Miracles. mat.12,38
the lord proueth vs by Miracles. deut.13,3
he ẏ by false Miracles deceiueth ẏ people, shal dye ẏ death. deut.13,5
christ by Miracles glorifieth his father.mat.15,31
Miriã ẏ sister of moses, & her doĩgs. exo.15,20.nomb.12 & 20,1.deu.24,9
¶Moabites.nomb.21.deut.2,9.iudg.3.1.king.11,7.2.king.23,13
Moab the sonne of lot.gen.19,37
modestie required in yong men.ecclesiasti.32,9
offre not thy childrẽ to Molech.leu.18,21 & 20,2

Molech the abominació of the ammonites.1.king.11,7
monei deliuered to bekept.exo.22,7
of Money ẏ one hathe receiued to kepe.exod.22,7.leui.6,4.deut.24,10
the worshipers of the Moone were put to death.deut.17,3
Mordecai & his doings. est.4 & 6,13
the Morias & their ruine. zeph.2,12
mortifie the members of sinne. coloss.3,5
the lord buryeth Moses.deut.34,6
Moses & the prophetes are the scripture of the olde testamẽt.luk.16,29
Moses disobeyed of the israelites. act.7,39
Moses murmureth.nomb.11,11
Moses shal accuse the iewes. iohn 5,45
ẏ Mote in thy brothers eye. mat.7,3
he that doeth not honour his Mother, is accursed.deut.27,16
the froward Mouth.prou.4,24
mouth is giuen to man of god. exo. 4,11
¶a law for Murther.nomb.35,11
the Murtherer shal dye the death. leuit.24,21.deut.19,11
he is a Murtherer that hateth his brother.1.ioh.3,15
beware that thou Murmure not against god.1.cor.10,10
murmurers consumed with the fyre of the lord.nomb.11,1
ẏ Murmuring israelits are cõsumed by the hand of god.nomb.16,41

N

NAamã the leaper washeth him self in iorden, and is healed. 2.king.5,14
Nabals vnthankefulnes.1.sam.25
Naboth stoned to death.1.kin.21,13
Nadab and abihu burnt with fyre from the lord.leuit.10,2
Nadab ẏ sõne of ieroboã.1.kin.14,20
Nahor the father of terad.gen.11,24
Nahshon the sonne of amminadab. nomb.1,7
a good Name.prou.22,1
the Name of god defiled by swearing.leuit.19,12
to take the Name of god in vaine. exod.20,7.deut.5,11
the Name of god was heard of in all places.1.king.8,42
women gaue the Names to their children. genes.29,32 & 30,6.as of samson.iudg.13,24
Naomi the wife of elimelech. ruth 1,2
Naphtali.iosh.19,32
Nathanael, a true israelite. Iohn 1,47
Nathan the prophet. 2.samu.7,2.1. king.1,22
christ nourced in Nazaret. mat.2, 23 & 13,54
Nazarites and their law.nomb.6
they of Nazaret despise christ.mat. 13,55
¶Nebat.1.king.15,1
Nebuchad-nezzar.2.king.24,1.dan.1 & 2 & 3 & 4.isa.14,14.ier.27,8
Nehemiah, & his doings, read his boke.
euerie man in his necessitie is our Neighbour.luk.10,29
a good Neighbour.prou.27,10
the birds Nest.deut.22,6
newenes of life.rom.6,4
¶Nicanor & his doings.1.mac.7,26
Nicodemus.ioh.3,1 & 19,39
Nimrod.gen.10,9
Niniueh buylt vp.gen.10,11. her destruction is forewarned. nah.3,1. she repenteth.ion.3,9
¶Noah, & his doings.ge.5 vnto ẏ 9.
Noah in his dronkennes is mocked of his sonne.gen.9,21
Noah the preacher of righteousnes.2.pet.2,5
Nob, a citie that saul destroyed.1. sam.22,19

O

OBadiah hideth the prophets of god.1.king.18,4
Obed-edom blessed of the lord, & why.2.sam.6,11
Obed the sonne of ruth.ruth 4,17
Obed the prophet, reproueth the israelites.2.chro.28 9
by christs Obedience we are made righteous.rom.5,19
obedient to father & mother.exod. 20,12.deut.5,16
christ became Obedient vnto the death.philip.2,8.ebr.5,8
to Obeye god rather then men.act. 4,19 & 5,29
to Obeye is better then sacrifice.1. sam.15,22
we must Obey the voyce of God. deut.30,20
oblation for sinne.nomb.19
diuers oblations, read the boke of leuiticus.
destruction of ẏ obstinate.ezek.6,11
¶giue no occasiõ of Offence to thy brother.rom.14,13.1.cor.10,32
the disciples offended at christ.ioh. 6,66
the pharises Offended with christ. mat.15,12
offend not.mat.18,6
to offre beasts in sacrifice.leuit.1
christ was Offred once for vs. ebr. 7,27.& 9,26 & 10,10
the pure Offring of the gentiles. mal.1,11
¶Og, the king of bashan, & his people conquered.nomb.21,33
¶the praise of Olde age.prou.16,31
the persone of the Olde man shulde be honored.leuit.19,32
the wilde Oliue.rom.11,17
Olofernes, & his doings, from the 7 of iudeth vnto the 15
¶Omri king of israel.1.king.16,16
¶Onan is slaine by the lord, and why.gen.38,9
Onesiphorus.2.tim.1,16
Onias the high priest.2.mac.3 & 4
¶they beleue that are Ordeined to eternal life.act.13,48
publicke Ordonnances.prou.16,10
vnlawful Ordonances.isa.10
Oreb is slaine.iudg.7,25
orgaines inuẽted by whome.ge.4,21
¶moses calleth Oshea, the sonne of nun, iehoshua.nomb.13,17
¶an Othe is the end of all strife. ebr.6,16
Othniel iudged israel.iud.1,13 & 3,9
¶the Oxe that goreth man or woman, is stoned to death.exod.21,28
¶the holie oynting Oyle.exod.30,31
the oynting of christ.dan.9,24
the Oynting of christ, ẏ holie gost. 1.ioh.2,27
the Oynting of kings. 1.sam. 9,16 & 10,1 & 16,13
to Oynt ẏ sicke with oyle.iam.5,14

P

PAcience necessarie.ebr.10,36.
the praise of Paciẽce.prou.16,32
the Pacience of iob.iob 1 & 2
god is Pacient.exod.34,6.rom.15,5
be Pacient.1.thess.5,14.
the sicke of the Palsie is healed. mat.9,2
the Parable of the bramble.iudg.9, 14.of trees.iudg.9,8.of children sitting in the market.mat.11,16.of the vncleane spirit that turned backe to the house.mat.12,43. of ẏ sower. mat.13,3.of the tares & of ẏ leuaine & of the mustard sede.mat.13.of ẏ hid treasure.mat.13,44. of the net cast into the sea.mat.13,47. of the publicane & the pharisie. luk.18,9. of two sonnes.mat.21,28.of the figge tree. mat. 24,32. of the thief. mat.24,43.of the talents.mat. 25,15. of the samaritane.luk.10,30. of the yong man that was so riche. luk. 12,16. of the figge tree that was fruteles.luk.13,6.of ẏ prodigal sonne.luk.15,11. of him ẏ gaue accoũtes of his stewardship.luk.16,1.of ẏ

widdowes importunitie, luk.18,2.
of the ten virgines.mat.25,1
how in olde time was executed the right of Parentage.Ruth 4,1
our Paschal lambe, christ.1.cor.5,7
the Passeouer. Exod.12,21.
the daye of the Passeouer. exod.12, 14.deut.16,1
isaiah reproueth the Pastours of his time.isa.56,10
the Patriarkes.rom.9,5
Paul the minister of the gentiles. rom.15,16.gal.1,16.1.tim.2,7.the am bassadour of iesus christ. 2.cor.5, 20. a pharise.act.23,6. an ebrewe. 2.cor.11,21.phil.3,5. an example of life and doctrine. philip. 3,17. he fleeth.act.14,6. he is stoned.act.14, 19. beaten with roddes. act.16,22. in danger to be drowned in the sea.act.27,14. he fasteth and praieth.act.14,23. he laboreth with his hands. act.18,3 & 20,34. 1.thess. 2,9. 2.thes.3,8.1. cor.4, 12. he was a tent maker.act.18,3. he speaketh wel of his sclanderers.1.cor.4,12. he was no manpleaser. 1.thes. 2, 4. satan wolde not suffer him to come to the thessalonians.1.thess. 2, 18. no man assisted him before nero. 2. tim.4,16
¶we are called to Peace.col.3,15
god is the autour of Peace.1.thes. 5,23
peace be vnto you, a salutatiõ of the iewes.gen.43,23
peace makers, the children of god. mat.5,9
sacrifices of Peaceoffrings.leu.3,1
the Peace that salomon had rounde about him.1.king.4,24
peace to the churches of iewrie, galile and samaria.act.9,31
haue Peace with all men.rom.12,18
peace with god to them that are iustified by faith.rom.5,1
be peaceable.1.thes.4,11
Peleg the sonne of eber.gen.10,25& 11,16
the lost Penie.luk.15,8
Peninnah, one of elkanahs wiues. 1. sam.1,4
the feast of Pentecost.exod.23,16
the People of god are a royal priest hode.1.pet.2,9
Perah the riuer.gen.2,14
paul exhorteth vs to Perfection. ebr.6,1
against Periurie.leuit.19,12
the Perizzites.deut. 20,17. iudg.1,4.
feare not them that Persecute.mat. 10,28
blessed are they, that suffer Persecution.mat.5,10
persecutions are sent of god. psal. 39,10
persecutions make some to be offended.mar.4,17
persecution to them that wolde liue in iesus christ.2.tim.3,12
christ exhorteth vs to Perseuere in him.iohn 15,4
Peter and iohn men vnlearned. act. 4,13
andrewe bringeth Peter to christ. iohn 1,42. he is called satan. mar. 8,33
dauid of thre plagues choseth rather the Pestilence.2.sam.24,14
¶the Pharises and sadduces, generations of vipers.mat.3,7.serpẽts. mat.23,33 theues and robbers.iohn 10,8
the Pharises deuoure widdowes houses.luk.20,47
the Pharises mocke christ. luk.16,14
Pharez birth.gen. 38,29 & 46,12
Philippe is called. iohn 1,43 & 14,8. act.8,26 & 21,8
out of whome came the Philistims. gen.10,14. of them read iudg. 3 & 10 & 13 & 14 & 15 & 16. 1.sam. 4 & 5 & 6 & 7 & 13 & 2.sam.5 & 21
beware lest thou be spoiled by Philosophie.coloss.2,8
the Phioles of the temple. 2. chro. 4,11
Phinehas the sonne of eli the priest. 1.sam.1,3 & 2,12 & 4,11
Phinehas the sonne of eleazar the priest .exod.6,25.he slayeth zimri and cozbi.nomb.25,7
¶Pilate and his doings.iohn 18,29
Pilate sinned lesse then iudas.iohn 19,11
the Piller conducteth the children of israel.exod.13,21
the Pillers of the tabernacle, and their facion.1.king.7,41
Pishon one of the riuers of paradise gen.2,11
Pithom a citie.exod.1,11
¶ieroboam buyldeth the high Places.1.king.12,31. they are throwen downe by ezekiiah.2.king.18,4
plagues sent vpon the disobedient. deut.28,15
plagues sent vpon the egyptians. exod.7 vnto the 11
plagues to the disobedient . deut. 28,22
israel Planted in the mountaine of his inheritance. exod. 15, 17. 2.sam. 7,10
paul Planted the corinthians . 1. cor.3,6
men Pleasers cannot be the seruãts of christ.gal.1,10
¶Pollutiõ that cometh in the night ceason.deut.23,10
there shalbe Poore alwaies.deut.15, 11.mat.26,11
shut not thine heart from thy Poore brother.deut.15,7.pro.28,27
he that giueth to the Poore, giueth to christ.mat.25,40
poore in spirit.mat.5,3
the Poore receiue the gospel. mat. 11,5
pouertie to the disobedient. deut. 28,22
the Poole bethesda.ioh.5,2
if it be Possible, haue peace with all men.rom.12,18
christ prayed that if it were Possible, that houre might passe from him.mar.14,35
if it were Possible, the very elect shulde be deceiued. mat. 24, 24. mar.13,22
if it had bene Possible ,you wolde haue giuen to me your eyes. galat.4,15
all things are Possible to god.mat. 19,26
ezechiel prepareth a Pot.ezek.24,3
the Potter maketh of the claye what he wil.ier.18 ,6
there is no Power but of god. rom. 13,1
man by his owne Power is not able to atteine to riches.deut.8,17. nether doeth he possesse anie thing for his righteousnes.deut.9,4
the mightie Power of god.isa.50,2
the Power of god shewed in pharaoh.exod.9,16
¶Praye alwayes. mat.7, 7. luk. 18,1. rom.12,12. ephes.6,18. coloss.4,2. 1. tim.2,8
prayer and fasting.act.13,3 & 14,23
paul desireth the faithful to Praye for him. rom.15,30. 2.cor.1, 11. ebr. 13,18
praye for kings, princes, magistrates.1 tim.2,2.
praye for them that hurt thee. mat. 5,44
praye one for another.iam.5,16
christ falling flat vpon his face maketh his Prayer.mat.26,39.ioh.17,1. luk. 22, 41. the same doeth paul. act.20,36
the Prayers of all saintes.reuel.8,3
praye with the spirit and vnderstanding.1.cor.14,15
christ Prayeth all the night long. luk.6,12
moses Prayeth fortie daies & fortie nights

nights.deut.9,25
christ Prayeth for vs.ioh.16,26 & 17, 9 & 20.he prayeth for peter. luk. 22,32
christ Prayeth to the father for vs. ebr.7,25 & 9,24
paul Prayeth without ceasing.1.thes 1,2.he prayeth in the temple. act. 22,17
none can Preache, but he ẏ is sent. rom.10,15
christ Preached alwaies opēly.ioh. 18,20
preachers are gods laborers. 1.cor. 3,9
preachers oght to beware of vsurped autoritie.1.pet.5,3
christ Preacheth in the shippe.mat. 13,2
we were Predestinate according to the purpose of god.ephes.1,11
we are Predestinate to be adopted in iesus christ.ephes.1,5
pleade not against god in his Predestinacion.rom.9,20
the Presumption of the corinthiās. 1.cor.4,6.
christ our high Priest.ebr.2,17 & 3 1 & 7,15
the office of Priests.leuit.10,6 & 16, 2.their couetousnes.isa.3,12
the high Priest wherefore he was ordeined.ebr.5,1 & 8,3
an exhortaciō to Princes.ezek.45,9
wicked Princes.iob 34,30
princes are the ministers of god. rom.13,4
god leadeth awaie Prīces as a pray. iob 12,19
against those Princes that oppresse the poore.amos 4,1 & 6,5.zeph.3,3
the remembrance of Prisoners.ebr. 13,3
christ our Prophet.deut.18,15
the childe of Promes.rom.9,8
the land of Promes.deut.8,7
the Promises of god are true.gen. 32,10
the Promes of the father, the holie gost.act.1,4
to Prophecie is better then to speake strange tongues.1.cor.14,5
prophecie is the gift of god. rom. 12,6
the Prophet reproueth ieroboam.1. king.13,2
obadiah hid an hundreth Prophetes.1.king.18,4
eliiah slayeth baals Prophetes. 1. king.18,40. iehu destroyeth them also.2.king.10,19.25
the doctrine of false Prophetes. ezek.13,2 & 22,25.ierem.23,9
450 false Prophetes against eliiah ẏ true and onelie prophet of God. 1.king.18,19
the spirits of Prophetes are in the power of ẏ prophetes. 1.cor.14,32
the false Prophet shal dye ẏ death. deut.18,20 & 13,1
baals Prophetes cut thē selues with kniues.1.king.18,28
the Prophetes example to vs of pacience.iam.5,10
the autoritie of the Prophetes of god.mic.3,8.2.king.5,8
the Prophetes did desire to se christ mat.13,17
the Prophetes in olde time were called Seers.1.sam.9,9
the sonnes of the Prophetes, poore. 2.king.6,2.they were refreshed by elisha.2.king.4,43
false Prophetes worke miracles. deut.13,1.mat.24,24
prosperitie & aduersitie are of the lord.prou.3,33
the Prosperitie of ẏ wicked.iob 21,7
god resisteth the Proude.1.pet.5,5
god Proueth abraham.gen.22,1
god Proueth his people. exod.15,25 & 16,4
gods Prouidence towardes the wicked.1.king.18,1
¶ of Publicanes.luk.3,12
the Publicanes belieued in christ. mat.21,32. they iustified god. luk. 7,29
the Publicane is iustified rather thē the pharise.luk.18,14
sharpe Punishment purgeth awaye the euil.prou.20,30
the Pure of heart are blessed. mat. 5,8
christ him self hathe Purged our sinnes.ebr.1,3
phygellus turned from paul.2.tim. 1,15
physicions created of god.ecclesiasti.38,1

Q

QVailes fall vpon the campe. exod.16,13.nomb.11,31
foolish Questiōs.2.tim.2,23
auoide foolish Questions.tit.3,9
questions & strife of wordes.1.tim. 6,4

R

RAbbah, a citie of the ammonites.2.sam.12,26
Rahab the harlot.iosh.2 & 6
Rahel iaakobs wife, & her doings. gen.29 & 30 & 31 & 35
first and latter Raine.deut.11,14
christ Raised frō death, deliuereth vs from the wrath to come.1.thes. 1,10
to be Raised vp with christ.rom.6,4
we shal be Raised through christ.2. cor.4,14
ahab & iehoshaphat go vp against Ramoth gilead.1.king.22,29
Raphael.tob.5 & 6 & 9 & 12
the Rauen sent out of the arke.gen. 8,7
Rauens sent by the prouisiō of god to feede eliiah.1.king.17,6
¶ follow not thine owne Reason. deut.12,8
the Rebelliō of the israelites.deut. 9,24 & 31,27
the Rebellion of korah.nomb.16,1
the Rebellion of the people of israel.deut.9,22
Rebekah the wife of izhak. gen. 22 vnto the 27.rom.9,10
what frute they haue that Receiue christ.ioh.1,12
Rechabites.ierem.35,2
Rechab killeth ish-bosheth. 2.sam. 4,7
recōciled vnto god by christ. rom. 5,11
reconcile thee to thy brother. mat. 5,23
the day of Recōciliacion.leui.23,27
christ, our Redemer.1.cor.1,30.mar. 10,45
redemption by grace.ephes.1,7
redemption by the blood of christ. 1.pet.1,19.ephes.1,7.ebr.9,13
a bruised Reede.isa.42,3.mat.12,20
god is our Refuge.2.sam.22,2.psal. 9,10.ierem.16,19
cities of Refuge.iosh.20,2
Rehoboam, & his doings.1.king.11, 43 & 12 & 14
wherein pure Religion standeth. iam.1,27
remission of sinnes, fre. psal.32,1. coloss.1,22
the Renuing of the holie gost. tit. 3,5
exhortacion to Repentance. act.2, 38 & 3,19 & 17,30 & 26,20
repentance & conuersion.act.3,19
repentance is ẏ gift of god. lament. 5,21
god Repenteth.1.sam.15,11
god Repenteth that he had made man.gen.6,6
of the Reprobate.mat.13,13
the Resurrection of the dead. 1. cor.15,12
rest promised to them that beare the yoke of christ.mat.11,29
rest promised to the troubled. 2. thess.1,7
a Rest remaineth for the people of

god.ebr.4,9
to Reteine sinnes.ioh.20,23
Reuben, his birth and his doings. gen.29,32 & 35,23 & 37,21 & 42,22 & 49,3
Reuel the priest of midian. exod. 2,18
god taketh no Rewarde.deut.10,17
the Rewarde blīdeth the eyes.deut. 16,19
the Rewarde is according to the worke.1.cor.3,8
the Rewarde of abraham,god.gen. 15,1
the Rewarde of sinne is death.rom. 6,23
Rezin the king of aram.2.king.16,5
¶ woman was made of the Ribbe of adam.gen.2,21
wo to the Riche,and why. luk.6,24. iam.5,1.1.tim.6,9
the couetous Riche mā.ecclesiastes 6,2
man can not serue god and Riches. luk.16,13
the disceitfulnes of Riches. mar. 4,19
¶ the church is founded vpō christ, the sure Rocke.mat.16,18
water gusheth out of the Rocke horeb.exod.17,6
a prophecie of ẏ Romaines.nomb. 24,24
christ the Roote of iesse. rom.15,12
ropes on the head was a signe of submision.1.king.20,31
auoyde Roaring & cursed speaking ephes.4,31
¶ curse not the Ruler of the people.exod.22,28
Rulers appointed ouer ten by moses.exod.18,25
what maner of Rulers god requireth.exod.18,21.deut.1,13
he that Ruleth,let him rule with diligence.rom.12,8

S

THe euerlasting Sabbath.isa.66, 23
the true obseruacion of the Sabbath.isa.56,2 & 58,13
sacrifice for sinne.ebr.5,1 & 8,3
sacrifices of iustice.deut.33,10
the Sale & the seller.leuit.25
Salomon and his doings.2.sam.12,24 vnto the 1.king.12
euerie man shalbe Salted with fyre. mat.9,49
the Salt of the earth, the apostles. mat.5,13
salute no man by the way.luk.10,4
Samaria besieged.1.king.20.2.king. 6,19
Samaria ful of idolatrie. 2.king. 17,29
Samson & his doings. iudg. 13 vnto the 16 chap.
Samuel and his doings.1.sam.1.vnto the 25 chap.
sanctifie ẏ lord god in your hearts. 1.pet.3,15
the forme of the Sanctuarie. exod. 25,8
the purging of the Sanctuarie.leui. 16,16
Sarah nourceth her sōne izhak.gen. 21,7
Sarra the daughter of raguel. tob.3 & 7 & 10
Satan the god of this worlde.2.cor. 4,4
the nombre of them that shalbe Saued,is smale.luk.13,23
Saul king of israel,& his doings.1. sam.9 vnto the 31 chap.
¶ the profite of the Scriptures. 2. tim.3,16
the vnderstādіng of the Scriptures is the gift of god.luk.24,45
¶ the scribes sit in moses Seat.mat. 23,2
christ the Sede of dauid. 2.Sam.7, 12
a Seer,that is,a prophet.1.sam.9,11
the ceremonial law forbiddeth to Seeth meat on the sabbath. exod. 16,23
to Sell his goods, & to giue them. &c.mat.19,21.luk.12,33 & 18,22
the Sepulchre of christ.mat.27,60
Sergius paulus.act.13,7
the brasen Serpent set vp.nomb.21, 9. iohn 3,14. broken in pieces. 2. king.18,4
of Seruants.exod.21,2.deut.15,12
the Seruant that knoweth the wil. &c.luk.12,47
the duetie of Seruants.ephes.6,5
serue god.exod.23,25.ebr.12,28.deut. 6,13.iosh.24,14
serue god with a good heart. deut. 28,47
the true Seruice of god.isa.1,16
the outwarde Seruice, that lacketh faith,is reiected.isa.43,22
¶ Shalmaneser the king of asshur.2. king.18,9
Shaminah alone slewe manie philistims.2.sam.23,11
Shallum killeth zechariah the sonne of ieroboam.2.king 15,10
Shebnah.2.king.18,18.isa.22,15
ẏ Shechemites are burnt.iudg.9,45
Shechem slayne.gen.34,26
Shem.gen.5,32 & 10,21
Shemaiah a prophet.1.king.12,22
Shelah the sonne of arpachshad. gen.11,12
Shelah the sonne of iudah..genes. 38,5
lost Shepe.mat.15,24
the Shepe of christ heare his voyce.iohn 10,27
the office of a Shepherd.ezek.33,2
the good Shepherd,christ.ioh.10,11. 1.pet.5,4
christ the Shepherd of the faithful. ezek.34,23
christs birth declared to the Shepherds.luk.2,9
false Shepherds. ierem.12,10 & 23,1. ezek.34,2
shepherds that admonish not.ezek. 3,18
the golden Shields of salomon. 1. king.10,17 & 14,26
Shimei & his vilenie. 2.sam.16,5 & 19,16.1.king.2,36
in Shiloh was the tabernacle of the congregacion. iosh. 18,1. 1.sam. 1,24
Shuah the father of iudahs wife. gen 38,2
¶ the Sicke oght to send for the elders of the church. iam.5,14
christs Side is perced.iohn 19,34
a Signe giuen to hezekiah. 2.king. 20,9
a Signe giuen to saul for a confirmacion.1.sam.10,2
feare not the Signes of heauen.ier. 10,2
signes which shal not come before the latter daye.luk.21,25
Sion king of heshbon giuen into the hands of israel.deut.2,24
Simeon & his doings. gen.29 & 34 & 42 & 46 & 49
Simon,iudas maccabeus brother.1. mac.13,14
Simon the pharise.luk 7,36
Simon the sorcerer.act.8,9
Sinai a mountaine.exod.19,1.galat. 4,24
dauid the swete Singer of israel. 2. sam.23,1
dauids Singers.1.chro.25,1
sing spiritual songs to the lord. ephes.5,19
to Sing with the spirit and vnderstandding.1.cor.14,15
christ hathe deliuered vs from Sinne.luk.1,74
god onelie forgiueth Sinne.nomb. 14,18
the knowledge of Sinne by the law. rom.3,20
he that committeth Sinne,is of the deuil.1.iohn 3,8

he that committeth sinne,is the seruant of sinne.ioh.8,34.
sinne against the holie gost.mar.3,29
by the Sinne of adam death entred into the worlde. rom.5,12
the lord washeth awaye our Sinnes. isa.4,4.1.cor.6,11
sinners captiues.rom.7,23
christ is come to call Sinners. mat. 9,12
the penitent Sinner shal liue. ezek. 33,11.deut.30,2
Sisera.iudg.4
¶the Skye red in the morning.mat. 16,2
¶to Sleape, for, to dye. gen. 47,30. mat 9,24
he that Slayeth a man, shal dye the death.exod.21,12.leuit.24,17
¶the Smel of noahs sacrifice. gene. 8,21
what punishment he shal haue, that Smiteth his father, or a woman with childe.exod.21,22.
¶of the Sodomites.gen.13 & 14 & 19. ezek.16,48
ioseph Solde by gods prouidence. gen.45,5
the Solemne feasts of the iewes. exod.23,14
christ prayeth in a Solitarie place. mar.1,35
the Songs of moses.deut.32,1
the Songs of salomō, a thousand & fiue.1.king.14,32
the disobedient Sonne is stoned to death.deut.21,21
Sopater.act.20,4
sorcerers oght to dye the death. leuit.20,27
sorowe not aboue measure for thē that are dead.1.thes.4,13
Sosthenes.act.18,17
the duetie of Souldiers. luk.3,14
iosiah toke away Southsayers.2.kin. 23,24
what man Soweth,that shal he reape.gal.6,7
¶gods prouidence euen vpon the Sparow.mat.10,29
euil Speakers shal not inherit the kingdome of god.1.cor.6,10
whoso speaketh, let him Speake the wordes of god.1.pet.4,11
sobrietie in Speaking.prou.17,27
the Spies of the land of promes are slaine for stirring vp the people. nomb.14,36
spies sent into iericho.iosh.2,1
sanctification of the Spirit.1.pet.1,2
the frute of the Spirit.gal.5,22
the wisdome of the Spirit. rom. 8,6
we must not beleue euerie Spirit. 1.ioh.4,1
lying Spirits.isa.19,14
the Spirit and the flesh lust one against another.gal.5,17
spirit,for winde.gen.8,1
grieue not the holie Spirit of god. ephes.4,30
the Spirit prayeth for vs. rom.8,26
spoiles deuided equally.1. sam. 30, 24.iosh.22,8
the Spouse of christ, ẏ church. psal. 45,10
¶paul baptized Stephanas and his familie.1.cor.1,16
Steuen and his death.act.6,5 & 7
christ, the corner Stone, is refused. mat.21,42.1.pet.2,7.the stone to stōble at.1.pet.2,8
it raineth Stones.iosh.10,11
god loueth the Stranger. deut.10,18
oppresse not Strangers. exod.23,9. leuit.19,33
strangers had the tithes giuen thē. deut.14,29.
strangled things forbidden.gen.9,4
god is our Strength. 2. sam.22,3. exod.15,2
the waters of Strife.nomb.20,13
striue not with anie.pro.20,3.2.tim. 2,23
¶the elders of Succoth put to death and how.iudg.8,14
¶the Sunne and moone for signes, and for ceasons.gen.1,14
the Sunne stayed at the wordes of ioshua.iosh.10,12
the Supper of our lord with his disciples.mat.26,26
the Supper of the Lord oght to be done in his remembrāce. luk.22,19
¶Sweare by the name of the liuing god.deut.6,13
sweare not at all.mat.5,34
sweare not by the name of strange gods.exod.23,13
sweare not in vaine.deut.5,11
paul Sweareth.2.cor.2,1
the autoritie of the temporal Sworde.gen.9,6.rom.13,6

T

THe forme of the Tabernacle. exod.26 & 36 & 39,32
the feast of Tabernacles.leuit.23,34
tobias biddeth the godlie to his Table.tob.2,2
the Tables of testimonie.exod.32,15
Tabitha is raised vp againe.act.9,36
against Talebearers. prou.26,22.18,8
Tamar a widow,& her doings.ge.38
Tamar the daughter of dauid. 2. sam.13,1
¶Teachers ordeined in ẏ church. 1.cor.12,28
the holie gost is the Teacher of the faithful.ioh.14,26
the Temple,for,the bodie of christ. ioh.2,21
the Tēple is buylt vp againe. hag. 1,14.ezr.4,1
the Temple of salomon. 1.king.6,1. & 8,13
the Temple of the lord is burnt. 2. king.25,9
tempt not god.deut. 6,16. mat.4,7 1.cor.10,9
Terah abrahams father.gen.11,27
Terah dyeth in haran.gen.11,32
the description of the olde Testament.iosh.24.ebr.9
the blood of the Testamēt.ebr.9,20
the newe Testament. gene.3,15.ebr. 8,10 & 10,16. for the remission of sinnes.mat.26,28
¶Thankesgiuing becometh saintes. ephes.5,4
the punishment of Theft. exod.22,1
theft forbidden.exod.20,15
the Thoghts of mās heart, wicked. gen.6,5
followe not the Thoghts of thine owne heart.nomb.15,39
Thomas an apostle.ioh.11,16& 20,24
the sede choked with Thornes.mar. 4,7
Thryphon.1.mac.13,12
¶the latter Times.1.tim.4,1
the diuersitie of Times.genes.1,14. & 8,22
times must not be obserued. gal.4,10
Timotheus.1.cor.4,17
who liue of the Tithes.deut.14,29
the Tithes of sedes are at the kings pleasure.1.sam.8,15
the Tithes of the land are the lords. leuit.27,30
¶Toi the king of hamath.2.sam.8,9
Tola a iudge in israel.iudg.10,1
the faut & vertue of the Tongue. iam.3,5.prou.12,13 & 13,2 & 14,3
refraine thy Tongue from euil. 1. pet.3,10
diuersitie of Tongues.1. cor. 12,28 & 14,2
tothe for tothe.exod.21,24
¶the good Treasure of the heart. mat.12,35
drye Tre,grene Tre.luk.23,31
the good Tree beareth good frute. mat.12,33
the Tre of life, the tre of knowledge gen.2,9
the Tre that maketh the waters swete.exod.15,25
trees created for man. gen.1,12 & 2, 9,16

fruteful Trees muſt ſtand in time of warre.deut.20,19
the fruteful Trees thre yeres vncircumciſed.leuit.19,23
trueth and her commendation. 1. eſd.4,34
trumpets of ſiluer.nomb.10,2
tribulation.rom.8,35 ebr.12,5
tribulation bringeth pacience.ro.5,3
we muſt by Tribulatiõs entre into the kingdome of heauen. act.14,22
tribulations to ẏ faithful. 1.pet.4,12
paye Tribute.rom.13,7
chriſt payeth Tribute to the magiſtrate.mat.17,27
¶Tubal-kain the firſt braſier & yrõ ſmith.gen.4,22

V

VAriance a worke of the fleſh. gal.5,20
the Vaile of the tabernacle.exo.26,31
the Vaile on moſes face.exod.34,33
¶Vengeance is forbid. prou. 20, 22. 1.ſam.11, 12.leuit.19,18.luk.9,55
vengeãce perteineth to god.deut.32, 35.rom.12,19.ebr.10,30.1.theſſ.4,6
chriſt is the Veritie.ioh.14,6
the Veſſels of the yong men, that is,their bodies.1.ſam.21,5
¶noahs Vineyarde.gen.9,20
lawes cõcerning Vineyardes. exod. 22,5.deut.20,6 & 22,9 & 23,24
virgines taken in warre.nomb.31,18
¶hearts Vncircumciſed.leuit.26,41
vnclennes oght not once to be named among chriſtians.ephe.5,3
cõpanie not w ẏ Vngodlie.1.cor.5,11
an Vnion of the iewes and gentiles in chriſt.iſa. 19,24
¶Vocation of the iewes and gentiles.rom.15,9
hearken to the Voice of the lord. exod.15,26.deut.13,4 & 30,20
vowes oght to be performed.nom. 30,3.deut.23,21
¶Vriah the houſband of beth-ſheba.2.ſam.11,3
Vriiah the prieſt.2.king.16,11
¶of Vſurie.deut.23,20
a law againſt Vſurie.deut.23,19
¶Vzziah otherwiſe called azariah, the ſonne of amaziah, king of iudah.2.king.14,21,& 2.chro.26,1
¶to Walke with god.gen.5,24
diuers cauſes of fredome frõ Warre.deut.20,5
warre is ſent for the ſinne of the peo ple.1.king.8,33.leuit.26,23
no man Warreth at his owne coſt. 1.cor.9,7
to Watch. mat.24,42 & 25,1. 1. theſſ. 5,2.coloſ.4,2
vncleane Water.liuit.11,38
water changed into wine.ioh.2,8
the Water of life.ioh.4,14 & 7,38
bitter Waters.exod.15,23
Waters flowing out of the rocke. exod.17,6
the kings Waye.nomb.21,22
to go the Waye of all the earth,for, to dye.1.king.2,2
the Waye of the lord is vncorrupt. 2.ſam.22,31
the Waye of veritie.2.pet.2,2
¶the Weake in knowledge eat herbes.rom.14,2
dauids Weapons againſt goliath. 1.ſam.17,40
the Weapons of the faithful. 2.cor. 10,4.eph.6,11
a Wedding garment.mat.22 ,12
of Weights.deut.25,13.hoſ.12,7
the feaſt of Wekes.exod.34,22
wel doing cometh of the lord. phil. 1,6.prou.16,1 & 20,24
the philiſtims fil vp abrahams Wels gen.26,14
iſrael in his Welth forſoke god.deu. 32,15
bleſſed are they that Wepe. mat. 5, 4.luk.6,21
wepe with thẽ that wepe. rom. 12,15
¶the viſion of Wheles.ezek.1,15
the viſiõ of ẏ great Whore.reuel.17
whoredome puniſhed by death.ge. 38,24.leuit.18,29
the hyre of a Whore oght not to be giuen vp for a vow.deut.23,18
auoide the companie of Whores. prou.6,24 & 23,27
¶yong Widowes.1.tim.5,11
the duetie of the Wiſe.ephe.5,22 tit.2,5
ẏ praiſe of a vertuous Wiſe.pr.18,22
the good Wiſe & the bad.prou.12,4
a prudent Wiſe is the gift of god. prou.19,14
a contentious Wiſe is to be auoyded.prou.21,9
the Wiſe not founde to be a virgine.deut.22,14
the Wiſe oght to be careful for her familie.tit.2,5
ẏ Wiſe ſuſpect of adulterie.nõb.5,12
god worketh in vs both the Wil & the dede.phil.2,13
to Wil, is preſent with vs, but to performe is not.rom.7,18
prieſts may not drĩke Wine.leu.10,8
wine maketh glad the heart of man. iudg.9,13.pſal.104,15
wiſdome and ſimplicitie required. mat.10,16
the Wiſdome of the fleſh diſobedient to the law of god. rom.8,7. 1.cor.1 & 2 & 3
chriſt is the Wiſdome of god. luk. 11,49
the Wiſdome of god hid in the goſ pel.1.cor.2,7
what the Wiſdome of this worlde is with god.1.cor.1,19 & 3,19
beare no falſe Witnes. exod.20,16 & 23,1
ẏ teſtimonie of Witneſſes.deut.17,6
what puniſhement is appointed for falſe Witneſ bearing.deut.19,16.
¶ the Woman, diſeaſed ẇ an yſſue of blood,is healed.mat.9,20
the Woman that hathe the bloodie yſſue.leuit.15,19
let euerie Woman haue her houſband.1.cor.7,2.epheſ.5,22
the Woman that turneth her houſband from the true god, ſhal dye the death.deut.13,6
he that ſtriketh a Womã with childe.exod.21,22
womans duetie.1.cor.11,6 & 14,34
paul preacheth to Women. act.16,13
the iewes might not marie ſtrange Women.exod.34,16.ezr.10,3
womẽ preſerued in taking of cities. deut.20,14
the elder Women ſhulde inſtruct ẏ yõg to loue their houſbãds.tit.2,3
againſt Womẽ that diſguiſe them ſelues in mens apparel.deut. 22,5
ẏ famine of gods Worde. amos 8,11
he that ſinneth not in Worde, is perfite.iam.3,2
chriſt is the Worde of god.ioh.1,1
put nothing to the Worde of god, nor take anie thing from it.deut. 4,2 & 12,32
to caſt awaye the Worde of ẏ lord. 1.ſam.15,23
gods Worde ſhulde be laid vp in our hearts.deu.6,6 & 11,18.we oght to follow it.deut.5,32. we oght to teache it to our children. deut.4,9 & 11,19
the Worde of god how we oght to handle it.deut.6,7
by thy Wordes thou ſhalt be iuſtified.mat.12,37
the Workeman is worthie of his meat.mat.10,10
vnfruteful Workes.epheſ.5,11
the Workes do witneſſe of faith. philem.5.ebr.6,10.2.pet.1,5
workes of mercie.mat.25,35
the workes of darkenes.tit.2,12
the Workes of gentiles we muſt auoyde.epheſ.4,17
ẏ Workes of god are perfite.deu.32,4
workers of iniquitie.mat.25,41
workes of light.epheſ.5,9
the Workes ẏ defile a mã. mar.7, 20

by our Workes we are not saued. rom.11,6.ephes.2,8.tit.3,5
the saincts shal iudge the Worlde.1.cor.6,2
christ prayeth not for the Worlde. ioh.17,9
loue not the Worlde.1.ioh.2,15
the facion of this Worlde goeth awaye.1.cor.7,31
the Worlde made by christ.ioh.1,10
true Worshippers.ioh.4,23
the Worshippers of strange gods are stoned to death. deut 17,5. are deliuered into the hands of spoilers.iudg.2,14
the Worshipers of strãge gods shal dye the death.deut.6,14
to Worship god in spirit.ioh.4,23
worship god onely.mat.4,10
the Worship of strange gods is forbidden.exod.23,13
¶the Wrath of god on the childrẽ of disobedience.coloss.3,6

Y

THe Ydle are reproued.prou.21,25 & 22,13 & 26,13
the euils that come of ydlenes. pro. 24,30
ydlenes to be auoyded.prou.20,13 & 21,25
¶the Yere of iubile.leuit.25,11
¶a Yoke of yron for the disobediẽt. deut.28,48
the duetie of Yong women.tit.2,4
the lustes of Youth are to be auoided.2.tim.2,22

Z

ZAccheus the publicane. luk. 19,2
Zachariah ẏ king of israel. 2. king. 14,29
Zalmunna and zebah slaine by gideon.iudg.8,21
Zamzummin,a people.deut.2,20
¶the Zeale of god against the man that walketh according to ẏ stubbernes of his heart.deut.29,20
the Zeale of moses. exod.32,26. of phinehas. nomb.25,7. of eliiah.1. king.18,40.of iehu.2.king.10,16
Zebulun, his genealogie and his doings. gen.30,20 & 46,14 & 49,13 deut.33,18
Zechariah ẏ sonne of iehoiada the priest.2.chron.24,20
Zechariah the sonne of berechiah. zecha.1,1 mat.23,35
Zedekiah,king.2.king.24,17 & 25,7. ier.52,1.ezek.12,13
Zeeb slaine.iudg.7,25
Zerubbabel the sonne of shealtiel. hag.1,12
¶Ziba.2.sam.9,2
Zidkiiah,a false prophet.1.kĩg.22,11
Zimri the king of israel,and his doings.1 king.16,9
Zion the citie of dauid. 2 sam. 5,9. 1.chron.11,5

The end of the table.

A PERFITE SVPPVTATION OF THE YERES AND TIMES FROM ADAM VNTO Christ, proued by the Scriptures, after the collection of diuers autors.

The summe of the yeres of the first age

FRom Adam vnto Noes flood are yeres 1656.

For when Adam was a 130 yere olde, he begate Seth.

Seth being 105 yeres, begate Enos.

Enos being 90 yeres, begate Cainan.

Cainan being 70 yeres, begate Mahalaleel.

Mahalaleel being 65 yeres, begate Iared.

Iared at the age of a 162 yeres, begate Enoch.

Enoch being 65 yeres, begate Mathuselah.

Mathuselah at the age of 187 yeres, begate Lamech.

Lamech beĩg 182 yeres, begate Noe.

Noe at the comming of the flood was 600 yeres olde, as appeareth in the seuenth of Genesis.

The whole summe of the yeres are 1656.

FRom the said flood of Noe vnto Adrahams departing from Chalde were 363 yeres, and ten dayes.

For the said flood continued one whole yere and ten dayes.

Sem (which was Noes sonne) begate Arphaxat two yeres after that.

Arphaxat begate Salah whẽ he was 35 yeres olde.

Salah being 30 yeres olde, begate Heber.

Heber at his age of 34 begate Phalech.

Phalech beĩg 30 yeres, begate Regu.

Regu being 32 yeres, begate Saruch.

Saruch being 30 yeres, begate Nahor.

Nahor beĩg 29 yeres, begate Thare.

Thare being 70 yeres, begate Abraham.

And Abrahã departed from Chalde when he was 70 yeres olde.

These said yeres accounted are 363 yeres, & ten dayes.

FRom Abrahams departing frõ Vr in Chalde vnto the departing of the children of Israel frõ Egypt are 430 yeres, gathered as followeth.

Abrahã was in Charran fiue yeres, and departed in the 75 yere.

He begate Isaac when he was 100 yeres olde, and in the 25 yere of his departing.

Isaac begate Iakob when he was 60 yeres olde.

Iakob went into Egypt with all his familie, whẽ he was 130 yere olde.

Israel was in Egypt 220 yeres, which remaine from that time.

Then rebate 80 yeres from this: for so olde was Moses when he cõducted the Israelites from Egypt.

So the reste of the yeres, that is to say 130, are deuided betwixt Amram and Chath.

Then Chath begate Amram at his age of 67 yeres.

Amram being 65 yeres, begate Moses, who in the 80 yere of his age departed with the Israelites from Egypt.

So this supputation is the 430 yeres mencioned in the 12. of Exod. & the 3. to the Galatians.

FRom the going of the Israelites from Egypt vnto the first buylding of the Temple are 480 yeres, after this supputation and accounte.

Moses remained in ẏ desert or wil-

dernes 40 yeres.
Iosue & Othoniel ruled 40 yeres.
Aioth 70 yeres.
Debora 40 yeres.
Gedeon 40 yeres.
Abimelech 3 yeres.
Thela 23 yeres.
Iair 22 yeres.
Then were they without a captaine vnto the 18 yere of Iepthe.
Iepthe 6 yeres.
Abissam 7 yeres.
Elom 10 yeres.
Abaton 8 yeres.
Sampson 20 yeres.
Heli Iudge and Priest 44 yeres.
Samuel & Saul reigned 40 yeres.
Dauid was King 40 yeres.
Salomon in the 4 yere of his reigne began the buylding of the Tẽple.

These are the 480 yeres mencioned in the first of the Kings, & the 6 chap.

FRom the first buylding of the Temple vnto the captiuitie of Babylon are 419 yeres & an halfe.
Salomon reigned yet 36 yeres.
Roboam 17 yeres.
Abia 3 yeres.
Asa 41 yeres.
Iosaphat 25 yeres.
Ioram 8 yeres.
Ochasias one yere.
Athalia the Quene 7 yeres.
Ioas 40 yeres.
Amasias 29 yeres.
Ozias 52 yeres.
Ioathan 16 yeres.
Achas 16 yeres.
Ezechias 29 yeres.
Manasses 55 yeres.
Amon 2 yeres.
Iosias 31 yeres.
Ioachas 3 moneths.
Eliacim 11 yeres.
Ioachim, Iechonias 3 moneths.
And here beginneth the captiuitie of Babylon.

The summe of these yeres are 419 yeres.

IErusalem was reedified & buylded againe after the captiuitie of Babylon 143 yeres.
The captiuitie continued 70 yeres.
The children of Israel were deliuered and restored to their fredome in the first yere of Cyrus.
The Temple was begonne to be buylded in the 2 yere of the said Cyrus, & finished in the 46 yere, which was the 6 yere of Darius.
After that Darius had reigned 20 yere, Nehemias was restored to libertie, and went to buylde the citie, which was finished in the 32 yere of the said Darius.
All the yeres from the buylding of the Temple againe are 26 yeres.

The whole summe of yeres amount to 143 yeres.

FRom the reedifying of the citie vnto the cõming of Christ, are 483 yeres, after this supputatiõ or nombring.
It is mencioned in the 9 of Daniel that Ierusalem shulde be buylt vp againe, and that from that time vnto the comming of Christ are 67 weekes, & euerie weeke is reckoned for seuen yeres. So 67 weekes amount to 483 yeres. For from the 32 yere of Darius vnto the 42 yere of Augustus, in the which yere our Sauiour Christ was borne, are iust and complet so many yeres, whereupon we recken, that from Adam vnto Christ are 3974 yeres, six moneths and ten dayes, and from the byrth of Christ vnto this present yere, is 1560.
Then the whole summe and nomber of yeres from the beginning of the worlde vnto this present yere of our Lord God 1560 are iust 5534, 6 moneths, and the said odde ten dayes.

The End.

IOSHVA CHAP. 1. VERS. 8.

Let not this boke of the Law departe out of thy mouth, but meditate therein daye and night, that thou mayest obserue and do according to all that is written therein: so shalt thou make thy way prosperous, and then shalt thou haue good successe.

The order of the yeres from Pauls conuersion shewing the time of his peregrination, & of his Epistles writen to the Churches.

The yeres of ẏ natiuitie of Iesus Christ	The yeres of the cōuersion of S.Paul.		The yeres of Tyberius ẏ Emperour.
35	1	Paul a persecuter, Act.7,8,9. was cōuerted as he went towarde Damascus, Act.9.	20
36	2	From Damascus he went into Arabia to preache the Gospel: after he returned	21
37	3	to Damascus where they wolde haue taken him, but he escaped by the meanes of the faithful, which did let him downe in a basket through the walles. Act.9. Gal.1.	22
38	4	From thence he came to Ierusalem to se Peter. Gal.1. Act.9. 2.Cor.12.	23
39	5	The Iewes wolde haue put him to death, but he was led to Cesarea, and from	of Caligu-
40	6	thence sent into Syria and to Tarsus of Cilicia. Act.9. Gal.1.	la 2
41	7		3
42	8	After he was broght to Antiochia by Barnabas, where the disciples were first	4
43	9	named Christians.	
44	10	The famine was prophecied by Agabus vnder C.Cesar. Act.11.	of Clau-
45	11	S.Iames was slaine by Herode. Act.12.	dius 2
46	12	Paul the gouernour of Cyprus was conuerted by S.Paul. Act.13.	3
47	13	Paul preached the Gospel in Antiochia of Pisidia, which is a parte of Galatia.	4
		Act.14	5
48	14	Thence he went to Iconium where he remained for a time. Act.13,14.	6
49	15	He healed a lame man at Lystri, and there was stoned. Act.14	7
50	16	When he had appointed the Elders in the Church, he visited all Pisidia and	8
51	17	Pamphilia, and returned to Antiochia.	9
52	18	At this time was the Cōcil of the Apostles holden at Ierusalem where saint	10
53	19	Paul appeared, and he returned to Antiochia, whether Peter also came, and Paul resisted him openly, Act.15. Galat.2.	11
54	20	Paul went into Syria and Cilicia with Siluanus to confirme the Churches, & afterwarde to Derbe and Lystri, where he taketh Timotheus vnto him: thēce he goeth to Macedonia, and teacheth in a citie called Philippi. Act.15,16.	12
55	21	Paul preacheth at Athenes. Act.17. & frō thence writeth to the Thessalonians.	13
56	22	He remaineth at Corinthus 18. moneths, Act.18. and from thence writeth to the Romaines.	14
57	23	He returneth to Ephesus, & from thence to Cesarea: afterwarde to Ierusalem,	of Nero
58	24	and so to Antiochia: afterwarde he visiteth the Churches of Galacia and Phrygia. Act.18.	2
59	25	He commeth to Ephesus, where he preacheth two yeres, & there leaueth Timotheus. Act.19. 1.Tim.1.	3
60	26	He writeth from Ephesus the first to the Corinthians. 1.Corinth.16.	4
61	27	After the tumult that was in Ephesus, he came to Troas, & from thence to Macedonia, and being at Philippi he wrote the seconde to the Corinthians by Titus and Luke. 2.Cor.2. & 13. Act.20.	5
62	28	Thence he came into Achaia & to Corinthus as he had promised. 1.Cor.16. & 2.Cor.12. and because certeine laid waite for him, he returned bẏ Macedonia vnto Troas towarde Aristarchus and Timotheus, which were gone before him. Act.20.	6
63	29	From Troas he came to Assos, to Mitylene called Lesbos, vnto Samos, & from	7
64	30	thence to Miletum, where he toke leaue of the Ephesians. Act.20. Thence he came to Rodes, to Patara, to Tyrus, to Ptolemais, to Cesarea, & last of all to Ierusalem, where he was taken. Act.21 & 22.	8
65	31	When he was prisoner, he was led to Cesarea before the gouernour Felix. Act. 23. where he remained two yeres. Act.24.	9
66	32	Afterwarde he was sent prisoner to Rome. Act.27.	10
67	33	And being in prison there, he wrote to the Galatians, to the Ephesians, and to the Philippians.	11
68	34	Also to the Colossians, and to Philemon.	12
69	35	The seconde to Timotheus.	13
70	36	Finally he was beheaded at the commandement of Nero.	14